# THE LONGMAN
# ENCYCLOPEDIA

# THE LONGMAN
# ENCYCLOPEDIA

*EDITOR-IN-CHIEF: ASA BRIGGS*

LONGMAN

**Longman Group UK Limited,**
*Longman House, Burnt Mill, Harlow,*
*Essex CM20 2JE, England*
*and Associated Companies throughout the world.*

© Columbia University Press 1989
Additional material © Longman Group UK Ltd
and Penguin Books Ltd 1989

First published 1989


**British Library Cataloguing in Publication Data**
The Longman encyclopedia.
1. Encyclopaedias in English
I. Briggs, Asa, 1921–
032

ISBN 0–582–91620–8

Computerized by Media Conversions Ltd, Ruislip, Middlesex.

Filmset in 9pt Weidemann by Filmtype Services Limited, Scarborough, North Yorkshire.

Printed in Great Britain by William Clowes Limited, Beccles and London

# FOREWORD

The idea of an encyclopedia has fascinated different generations since the eighteenth century, and the making of this new encyclopedia has fascinated everyone who has been involved in the lengthy process of its compilation.

We started with the Concise Columbia Encyclopedia, a great scholarly enterprise which provided us with an indispensable base, and then went on to review and update each existing article, to add thousands of new ones, and to delete some others. The selection of entries and their subsequent scrutiny was entrusted to a distinguished group of scholars, each of whom has made an independent contribution to the study of his or her particular field. This has never at any point been a routine exercise.

At each stage we have had the users of the encyclopedia in mind. We know that most people will turn to it for information, but we know, too, that it will be judged not only by the accuracy of the information it contains but by the range and mode of treatment of its content. Deciding on the best way of communicating information, including communication through pictures as well as words, has been the most challenging of all our tasks; and given the continuing sequence of change in communication technology we believe that we have provided a new base capable of necessary updating and inevitable revision. Time does not stop when an encyclopedia goes to the printer's last stage.

I have enjoyed working with my colleagues in the collective venture – some inside Longman, some outside. Some I have known for many years. We have created what is, I believe, a distinctive product. Our publishers have a great reputation for the way in which they handle dictionaries. Ours is not a dictionary, but it is a necessary complement to dictionaries. It presents a conspectus of knowledge, much of it rapidly changing knowledge, towards the end of a century when both the subject matter of different disciplines and economic, political, social, and cultural bearings have changed. So, too, have their concepts and methods. Moreover, many late twentieth-century problems demand interdisciplinary treatment, and if only for this reason ours is a team effort. We feel ourselves far better informed as we present this volume in its first edition than we we started our labours.

ASA BRIGGS

# ACKNOWLEDGMENTS

**Editor-in-Chief**
Asa Briggs

**Editorial Board**
Professor John Ashworth
Professor Diane Bell
Professor Sir Hermann Bondi
Antonia Byatt
Professor Andrew Goudie
Professor Stuart Hall
Mary Warnock

## Contributors

### ARTS
Louis Allen
V Ames
Nick Ashton
Professor John Blacking
T Richard Blurton
Joyce Crick
Dr James Davidson
Nick Day
Dr Katherine Duncan-Jones
Alethea Hayter
Caroline Karslake
Helen Langdon
Professor Annette Lavers
Jean Liddiard
John Lindon
Magnus Magnusson
Norma P Miller
Patrick Nuttgens
Margaret Oliphant
Professor Kenneth Parker
Professor Patrick Parrinder
Chris Peachment
Michael Phillips
Julia E Poole
Jane Portal
Chrissie Poulter
Dr Robert Pynsent
Jane Rapley
Mary Seton-Watson
Professor A C Spearing
David Steele
Lynda Stephens
Tony Tanner
Helen Thompson
Maurice Tomlin
Professor Roger Walker
Penelope E Wallis
Jonathan Watkins
S J Wiseman
Brian M Wood
Frances Wood

### GEOGRAPHY
Dr Morag Bell
Dr David Browning
Dr Colin Clarke
Dr B H Farmer
Professor Fay Gale
Professor Andrew Goudie
Dr Robert Headland
Alan Jenkins
Dr Nick Middleton
Professor Yasuo Miyakawa
Dr David Munro
Dr Alisdair Rogers
Dr D I Scargill
C G Smith
Dr Heather Viles

### HISTORY
Dr Robert Benewick
Dr Jeremy Black
Dr Harold Blakemore
Lord Briggs
Dr J B Bullen
Professor Rosemary Cramp
Simon Davie
Professor Norman Davies
Alan J Day
Dennis Deletant
Narguess Farzad
Professor Christopher Holdsworth
Professor Maldwyn Jones
Dr David Kiyaga-Mulindwa
Dr Peter Kornicki
Dr Stuart Macintyre
Dr P T Mgadla
Dr R K K Molefi
Brian Molyneaux
David O Morgan
Professor Roger Morgan
Dr Andrew Murray
Dr R C Ostle
Laszlo Peter
Jeff Ramsay
Dr T Raychauduri
Professor Anthony Snodgrass
Keith Sword
Trevor Thomas
Mark Wheeler
Peter Whitaker
Constantine Zelenko

### HUMANITIES
Dr Barry Alpher
Professor Aziz-Al-Azmeh
Professor Diane Bell
Rabbi Dr Jeffrey Cohen
Dr Robert Giddings
Robert M Hargrave
Rev Dr J N D Kelly
Professor Bimal Matilal
John B Thompson
Dr Carol Wallace

### LIFE SCIENCES
Professor John M Ashworth
Professor Alan Bilsborough
Jennifer Cochrane
Sharon Goodyer
Judy Sadgrove
Professor Trevor Villiers
Dr W R Wooff

### PHYSICAL SCIENCES
Dr Jean Bacon
Professor A C Bajpai
Professor Sir Hermann Bondi
Professor J N R Jeffers
Michael March
Sir Peter Masefield
Professor Sir Nevill Mott
Professor R J Blin-Stoyle
Iain Nicolson
Tom Robson
Joseph Schwartz
Professor J M Thomas
Professor John West
Dr Alan Wickens

### SOCIAL SCIENCES
Janet H Clark
Felicity Edholm
Dr Bram Gieben
Liz Heron
Ian Loader
Dr Harold Silver
Chris Sinha
Alan White

### Publisher
Peter Zombory-Moldovan

### Commissioning Editor
Anna Hodson

### Coordinating Editor
Jenny Hicks

### Copy Editors
Sue Engineer
Robin Mann
Sally Rowland
Kathy Seed

### Proofreaders
Jennifer Cochrane
Richard Earthy
Maggy Hendry
Joanna Jellinek
Sue Lloyd
Louise McConnell
Vernon Robinson
Kathy Seed

### Picture Researchers
Anne-Marie Ehrlich
Hugh Olliff

### Illustrators
Craig Austin
Bernard Thornton Artists
Keith Duran
Eugene Fleury
Tony Gibbons
Linden Artists
Carol McCleeve
David More
Colin Newman
Oxford Illustrators Ltd
Sebastian Quigley
Clive Spong
Brian Watson
Clare Williams

# HOW TO USE
# THE LONGMAN ENCYCLOPEDIA

All entries are arranged alphabetically, with entry headwords in bold. The headings of biographical entries are inverted and alphabetized by the subject's surname, e.g., the British composer Harrison Birtwistle appears as Birtwistle, Harrison. Monarchs of the same name are listed alphabetically by country and numerically within the country; thus all kings Henry of England appear before any kings Henry of France.

The method of alphabetization disregards word breaks. Capetians, for example, appears before Cape Town. The following special cases of alphabetization should also be noted: (1) Names with von, de, and similar prefixes are alphabetized using the most common form of the name: Van Gogh, Vincent, but Bismarck, Otto von. (2) Names beginning with Mc and Mac are treated as though they begin with Mac; thus McTaggart, John appears before Macy, Anne Sullivan. (3) Abbreviations in entry headings are treated as though they were spelt out: St Lucia appears before Saint Mark's Church. (4) Japanese names are listed in the traditional Japanese order, e.g., Kawabata Yasunari; Europeans or Americans of Japanese descent are listed in the Western style, e.g. Noguchi, Isamu.

**Family entries**. We have combined similarly named rulers of certain empires and nations into a single article; thus all 18 kings of France named Louis appear as easily recognizable entries under the headings 'Louis, Kings of France'. Likewise, members of the same family are sometimes grouped together: for example, the Rockefellers appear under the heading 'Rockefeller, family of American industrialists, philanthropists, and bankers'. When a family member has been particularly prominent outside the family tradition, however, he or she has a separate entry, as does former US Vice President Nelson Rockefeller.

Some related subjects have also been covered under a single entry: for example, divine right has been included in the entry for monarchy, and Mendelism can be found under the entry Mendel, Gregor Johann.

**Titles of foreign works**. The titles of works of art, music, and dance are given in English unless the work is well known under the original foreign title. As for works of literature, where possible, the original foreign title is given with a translation in brackets. The dates accompanying such works are the dates of original publication, exhibition, or performance.

**Cross-references**. To utilize space efficiently, whenever possible, information included in one article is not repeated in another. Instead, cross-references are used extensively to lead the reader to entries containing additional material relevant to the entry he or she is consulting. The entries may expand upon the subject at hand, provide background, or supply clues to other aspects of the subject and to related topics. All cross-references appear in SMALL CAPITALS.

Basically there are four types of cross-references. The first type comprises those found within the text of an entry. The second type consists of those found at the end of an entry, referring the reader to related subjects, including biographies.

Cross-references also refer the reader to tables that combine a variety of facts directly relevant to the article being consulted. The third type of cross-reference appears as a boldface entry within the alphabetical sequence. It may be an acronym, an alternate spelling or name, a real name when a person is known under a pseudonym, a topic discussed under an entry other than its own name, or it may direct the reader to a number of related articles. The fourth category of cross-reference consists of those referring to a boldface sub-entry under a main heading. Such cross-references can occur within an entry or as a separate entry; often, for clarity, the words 'see under' are used.

# ABBREVIATIONS

Å = angstrom
abbr = abbreviation
AC = alternating current
AD = *anno Domini*
Adm. = Admiral
Afrik. = Afrikaans
alt. = altitude
Apr. = April
Arab. = Arabic
AU = astronomical unit(s)
Aug. = August
AV = Authorized Version
b. = born
BC = before Christ
BP = before the present
Brig. Gen. = Brigadier General
Bulg. = Bulgarian
C = Celsius
c. = circa
cal = calorie(s)
Cant. = Canticles
Capt. = Captain
cent. = century
Chin. = Chinese
Chron. = Chronicles
cm = centimetre
Co. = Company; county
Col. = Colonel; Colossians
Coll. = Collection
Comdr = Commander
Cor. = Corinthians
Corp. = Corporation
Cpl = Corporal
Cu = Cubic
d. = died
Dan. = Danish; Daniel
DC = direct current
Dec. = December
Deut. = Deuteronomy
dist. = district
Dr = Doctor
Du. = Dutch
E = east, eastern
Eccles = Ecclesiastes
Ecclus = Ecclesiasticus
e.g. = exempli gratia
Eng. = English
Eph. = Ephesians
est. = estimated; established

eV = electron volts
Ex. = Exodus
Ezek = Ezekiel
F = Fahrenheit
Feb. = February
Finn. = Finnish
fl. = *floruit*
Fr. = French
ft = foot
g = gram
Gal. = Galatians
gal = gallon
Gall. = Gallery
Gen. = General; Genesis
Ger. = German
Gov. = Governor
Gr. = Greek
grad. = graduated
Hab. = Habakkuk
Hag. = Haggai
Heb. = Hebrew; Hebrews
HMS = Her (His) Majesty's Ship;
 Her (His) Majesty's
 Service
Hon. = the Honourable
hr = hour
Hung. = Hungarian
Hz = hertz
Icel. = Icelandic
i.e. = *id est*
in = inch
inc. = incorporated
Isa. = Isaiah
Ital. = Italian
J = joule
Jan. = January
Jap. = Japanese
Jer. = Jeremiah
K = kelvin
kg = kilogram
km = kilometre
KW = kilowatt
Lam. = Lamentations
Lat. = Latin
lat. = latitude
lb = pound
Lev. = Leviticus
Lib. = Library
lim = limit

Lith. = Lithuanian
log = logarithm
long. = longitude
Lt = Lieutenant
Ltd = Limited
m = metre
Mac. = Maccabees
Mal. = Malachi
Mar. = March
Mat. = Matthew
MeV = million electron volts
Mex. = Mexican
mg = milligram
mi = mile
min = minute
mm = millimetre
Mod. = Modern
mph = miles per hour
Msgr = Monsignor
Mt = Mount
Mt., Mts = Mountain(s)
Mus. = Museum
N = north, northern
Neh. = Nehemiah
Nor. = Norwegian
Nov. = November
NS = New Style
Num = Numbers
Obad. = Obadiah
Oct. = October
OE = Old English
ON = Old Norse
OS = Old Style
oz = ounce
Pers. = Persian
Philip. = Phillippians
pl. = plural
Pol. = Polish
pop. = population
Port. = Portuguese
Pres. = President
Prime Min. = Prime Minister
prov(s). = province(s)
pseud. = pseudonym
Pss = Psalms
pt = pint
pub. = published
qt = quart
R. = river

r. = reigned
Rep. = Representative
Rev. = Revelation; the Reverend
Rom. = Romans
rpm = revolutions per minute
RR = railway
RSV = Revised Standard Version
S = south, southern
Sam. = Samuel
sec = second
Secy = Secretary
Sen. = Senator
Sept. = September
Sgt = Sergeant
Skt = Sanskrit
Song = Song of Solomon
Span. = Spanish
sq = square
SS = steamship
SSR = Soviet Socialist Republic
St = Saint
Ste = Sainte
Swed. = Swedish
Thess = Thessalonians
Tim. = Timothy
tr. = translation
Turk. = Turkish
UK = United Kingdom
Ukr. = Ukrainian
UN = United Nations
uninc. = unincorporated
Univ. = University
US = United States
USS = United States Ship
USSR = Union of Soviet Socialist
 Republics
v. = versus
V = Volt
var. = variety
Vice Pres. = Vice President
vol = volume (cubic dimension)
vol = volume (part of book)
W = west, western; watt
wt = weight
yd = yard
Zech. = Zechariah
Zeph. = Zephaniah

# COLOUR MAP SECTION

# MONOCHROME MAPS

## KEY

■ Capital City
● Town
TIBESTI Region/Area
*ANDES MOUNTAINS* Large Mountain Range
*ENNEDI MASSIF* Small Mountain Range
△ Mountain
⋈ Tunnel/Pass
∴ Archaeological Site
⌣ Canal
~ River
↦ Dam
*Little Aföld* Special Feature
Marsh/Swamp/Salt Pan
Seasonal Watercourse

# TABLES

**Aachen** or **Aix-la-Chapelle**, city (1984 pop. 241,100), North Rhine–Westphalia, W West Germany. It is an industrial centre producing textiles, machinery, and other manufactures. Its mineral baths have been famous since Roman times. CHARLEMAGNE made it his northern capital, building a palace and cathedral there, and the city was (936–1531) the coronation place of German kings. Later it was taken by France (1801) and Prussia (1815). After WORLD WAR I Aachen was occupied by the Allies, and two thirds of it was destroyed during WORLD WAR II.

**Aalto, Alvar** (ˌahltoh), 1896–1976, Finnish architect. The greatest architect in the history of Finland, he is recognized as a national hero. His first major building was the tuberculosis sanatorium in Paimio, where he designed everything, including bathroom fittings and furniture. Subsequently his distinctive furniture of laminated wood was manufactured by his own firm *Artek* and became internationally famous. His output, both in Finland and abroad, was extensive. He used his knowledge of traditional Finnish building to give a distinctive personal and humane character to MODERN ARCHITECTURE. Among his most celebrated buildings are, in Finland, the Cellulose Factory in Sunila (1935–37) the Villa Mairea near Noormakku (1937–38), the Town Hall in Säynätsalo (1949–52), and the Vuoksenniska church in Imatra (1956–59); abroad, the Baker House in the Massachusetts Inst. of Technology (1947–48).

The tuberculosis sanatorium, Paimio (1923–33) by Alvar **Aalto**

**aardvark,** nocturnal MAMMAL (genus *Orycteropus*) found in Africa. About 180 cm (6 ft) long, it has a long snout, large, erect ears, a body almost devoid of hair, and a long tail. It claws open ant and termite nests with its forefeet and uses its long, sticky tongue to capture insects.

**Aaron,** in the BIBLE, the first high priest, the brother of MOSES, and his spokesman. Through him Jehovah performed miracles, although Aaron had made the GOLDEN CALF and allowed its worship. His descendants became temple priests.

Aardvark

**abacus,** an ancient computing device using movable beads strung on a number of parallel wires within a frame. Each wire represents a decimal place: ones, tens, hundreds, and so on. The beads are grouped to form numbers and moved in specific patterns to add, subtract, multiply, or divide.

**Abadan,** city (1976 pop. 296,081), Khuzestan prov., SW Iran, on Abadan Island, in the SHATT AL ARAB delta, at the head of the PERSIAN GULF. After the discovery (1908) of oil nearby, Abadan became the terminus of major oil pipelines and an important oil-refining and shipping centre. Its major oil refinery was heavily damaged by Iraqi forces in their invasion of Khuzestan in 1980.

**abalone** (abəˌlohnee): see EAR SHELL.

**Abbas I** (Abbas the Great), 1557–1629, shah of PERSIA (1587–1629), of the Safavid dynasty. He broke the power of the tribal chiefs, ended the threat of the Uzbeks, and extended his domain at the expense of the Turks and Portuguese.

**Abbasid** or **Abbaside**, Arabic family descended from **Abbas,** d.653, the uncle of MUHAMMAD. They rose to power by massacring the ruling Umayyad family and held the CALIPHATE from 749 to 1258. Prominent Abbasid caliphs include al-MANSUR and HARUN AR-RASHID, under whom the caliphate reached its greatest power and splendour. The long Abbasid decline culminated in their overthrow by the Mongols in the 13th cent.

**Abbey Theatre,** company founded 1902 as Irish National Theatre by YEATS, Lady Gregory, and others, to produce indigenous drama. It moved to Abbey Theatre, Dublin, in 1904. Associated dramatists included Brendan BEHAN, Padraic COLUM, and J.M. SYNGE's *Playboy of the Western World* (1907), Sean O'CASEY's *Plough and the Stars* (1926) among most famous productions. The company now performs world as well as Irish drama in its new building (1966).

**abbreviation,** in writing, arbitrary shortening of a word, usually by cutting off letters from the end, as in US and Gen. (General). Contraction serves the same purpose but is understood strictly to be the shortening of

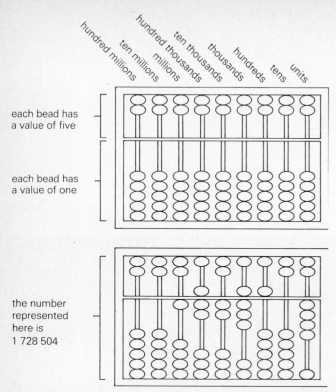

hundred millions | ten millions | hundred thousands | millions | ten thousands | thousands | hundreds | tens | units

each bead has a value of five

each bead has a value of one

the number represented here is 1 728 504

Chinese **abacus**: Numbers are represented by moving beads to the central crossbar

a word by cutting out letters in the middle, the omission sometimes being indicated by an apostrophe, as in the word *don't*. Most abbreviations are followed by a full-stop. Usage, however, differs widely, and recently omission of the full-stop has become common, as in NATO and UN. A full-stop is never used when apostrophes appear. A list of abbreviations used in this encyclopedia may be found at the front of the book.

**Abd al-Hamid,** sultans of the OTTOMAN EMPIRE (Turkey). **Abd al-Hamid I,** 1725–89 (r.1774–89), witnessed the decline of Turkey and the rise of Russia as the foremost power in the area. **Abd al-Hamid II,** 1842–1918 (r.1876–1909), suspended (1878) the constitution and ruled as an absolute monarch. The last RUSSO-TURKISH WAR was a disaster, resulting in a great loss of Turkish lands. He was eventually deposed by the Young Turks.

**Abd Al Karim, al-Kattebi,** 1882–1963, Moroccan anticolonial resistance leader. From 1920 he led opposition in the Rif mountain region against Spanish attempts to establish their authority. In 1921 the Spanish were defeated and an independent 'Republic of the Rif' was proclaimed. However in 1926 a joint Franco-Spanish force succeeded in defeating the Rifians and Al Karim was exiled. Prior to his death he refused to return to independent Morocco.

**Abd Al Qadir,** 1803–83, Algerian anticolonial resistance leader. From 1832 to his capture in 1847 he fought against French efforts to occupy his country. After a period of imprisonment he was allowed to go into exile to Syria where, prior to his death, he won additional fame by preventing a massacre of local Christians.

**Abd ar-Rahman,** Muslim rulers of Spain. **Abd ar-Rahman,** d. 732, governor of Spain (721–32), fought the Franks and was defeated by CHARLES MARTEL. **Abd ar-Rahman I,** d.788, first Umayyad emir of Córdoba (756–88), escaped after his family's massacre by the Abbasid and fled to Spain. There he defeated (756) the emir of Córdoba, established himself firmly in power, and built the Great Mosque there. **Abd ar-Rahman III** (891–961), Umayyad emir and first caliph (929–61) of Córdoba, regained lands lost by his predecessors, maintained a powerful military force, and made Córdoba one of the greatest cities in the West.

**abdication,** renunciation of sovereign power. The most controversial royal abdication in recent times was that of King EDWARD VIII on 11 Dec. 1936, following his decision to marry Wallis Simpson (see WINDSOR, WALLIS WARFIELD, DUCHESS OF), against the advice of Prime Min. Stanley BALDWIN.

**abdomen,** in vertebrates, portion of the trunk between the diaphragm and lower pelvis. In humans, the abdominal cavity is lined with a thin membrane, the peritoneum, which encloses the STOMACH, INTESTINE, LIVER, GALL BLADDER, PANCREAS, KIDNEYS, urinary bladder, and, in the female, the ovaries and uterus. In insects and some other invertebrates the term abdomen refers to the rear portion of the body.

**Abduh, Muhammad,** 1849–1905, most important Islamic reformist in the 19th cent. Initially under the influence of AFGHANI, he later became grand MUFTI of Egypt and led the modernist reforms of Muslim educational and legal institutions. Both institutionally and ideologically, the effects of Abduh's efforts are still felt today as the predominant current in the thinking of modern SUNNISM.

**Abdullah,** 1882–1951, emir of Transjordan (1921–49) and king of JORDAN (1949–51). In the first ARAB–ISRAELI WAR his forces captured substantial portions of Palestine not assigned to Israel, territory which was formally annexed in 1950. Meanwhile, he had renamed Transjordan the Hashemite Kingdom of Jordan in 1949.

**Abe Kōbō,** 1924–, Japanese novelist and dramatist. Often compared to KAFKA, he treats the contemporary human predicament in a realistic yet symbolic style. His minute descriptions of surrealistic situations often lend his works a nightmarish quality. Among Abe's novels are *Woman in the Dunes* (1962; tr. and film 1964) *The Face of Another* (1964; tr. 1966), *Secret Rendezvous* (1977; tr. 1979), *Inter Ice Age 4* (1969; tr. 1970), and his plays include *Friends* (1967; tr. 1969).

**Abel,** in the BIBLE, son of ADAM and EVE. A shepherd, he was killed by his brother CAIN. Gen. 4.1–8.

**Abel, Niels Henrik,** 1802–29, Norwegian mathematician. One of the greatest mathematicians of the 19th cent., he was a pioneer in the theory of elliptic functions, investigated generalizations of the binomial theorem, and proved the impossibility of representing a solution of a general equation of fifth or higher degree by an expression involving radicals.

**Abelard, Peter,** 1079–1142, French philosopher. Because his fame as a dialectician attracted so many students, he is usually regarded as the founder of the Univ. of Paris. His secret marriage to a pupil, Heloïse, ended when her uncle, Canon Fulbert of Notre Dame, hired ruffians to attack and emasculate him. Becoming a monk, he eventually built a hermitage and monastery, the Paraclete, which he later presented to Heloïse, who had become an abbess. Abelard's first theological work had been burned (1121) as heretical; in 1140 the mystic St BERNARD OF CLAIRVAUX secured his condemnation by the council of Sens, and he retired in submission to Cluny. Following PLATO in theology, Abelard espoused the method of ARISTOTLE's dialectic, holding that the system of LOGIC could be applied to the truths of faith. His view of universals anticipated the conceptualism of St THOMAS AQUINAS. His most influential and controversial work, *Sic et non,* collected contradictory writings of the Church fathers.

**Abell, Kjeld,** 1901–61, Danish playwright, an innovator in stage technique. His plays, concerned with justice and social protest, include *The Melody That Got Lost* (1935), *Anna Sophie Hedvig* (1939), and *The Blue Pekinese* (1954).

**Abe Masahiro,** 1819–1857, Japanese government leader and DAIMYO. As the leading administrator under the TOKUGAWA shogunate he was responsible for relaxing the traditional hostility towards the outside world. In 1854, in the teeth of conservative opposition, he concluded treaties with Britain, Russia, the Netherlands and the US. He resigned in 1855 but continued to urge reforms on Western lines.

**Abeokuta** (a'beeo,koohtə), city (1987 est. pop. 308,800), capital of Ogun state, S Nigeria, on the Ogun R. It is linked by railway to LAGOS, some 80 km (50 mi) to the south. A centre of the country's palm kernel and cocoa-producing region, it was founded in the 1820s as a refuge from slave traders. It was the chief town of the Egbas who made a treaty with the British in 1893.

**Aberdeen,** city (1985 est. pop. 212,494), Grampian region, E Scotland, on E coast, 92 km (57 mi) NE of Dundee. It is a cathedral and university city and commercial centre. Industries within the city include canning, refrigeration, engineering, and plastics. It has recently become the centre of the North Sea Oil industry. It is known as the 'Granite City', as the local granite has been used in many of the buildings. The cathedral dates partly from the 14th cent. Some 9 km (6 mi) to the NW is Aberdeen airport, which handled 1.8 million passengers in 1984.

**Aberdeen, George Hamilton-Gordon,** 4th **earl of,** 1784–1860, British statesman. He served in the cabinets of WELLINGTON and PEEL as foreign secretary (1828–30, 1841–46). In 1842 he settled the Northeast Boundary Dispute with the US by the WEBSTER–ASHBURTON TREATY. As prime minister (1852–55) he was quite successful in home affairs, but he resigned because of public anger at the mismanagement of the CRIMEAN WAR.

**Aberhart, William,** 1878–1943, premier of ALBERTA (1935–43). He helped to organize (c.1932) the SOCIAL CREDIT movement to make direct payments to all citizens and headed the first Social Credit government.

**aberration,** in optics, condition that causes a blurring and loss of clearness in the images produced by lenses or mirrors. Spherical aberration is the failure of a LENS or MIRROR of spherical section to bring parallel rays of light to a single focus; it can be prevented by using a more complex parabolic section. Chromatic aberration, the blurred colouring at the edge of an image, arises because some colours of light are bent, or refracted, more than others after passing through a lens; it can be cured by using a corrective lens.

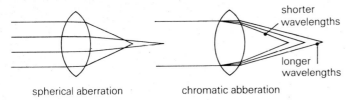

shorter wavelengths

longer wavelengths

spherical aberration          chromatic abberation

Aberration

**aberration of starlight,** dependence of the measured position of a star on the Earth's orbital velocity. As this changes during the year, the star's observed position describes a small ellipse.

**Aberystwyth,** town (1981 pop. 10,290), Dyfed, W Wales, at mouth of rivers Rheidol and Ystwyth on Cardigan Bay. A seaside resort and small port, it is also the commercial capital of mid-Wales. It is the seat of the Univ. College of Wales (founded 1872), which is a constituent part of the Univ. of Wales. The National Library of Wales was established in the town in 1911. There are the remains of a 13th-cent. castle on the seafront.

**Abidjan,** city and port (1982 est. pop. 1,850,000), capital of Côte d'Ivoire, on the northern shore of Ebrie Lagoon, which is separated from the Gulf of Guinea by a narrow strip of land. Its port is centred on an island connected with the rest of the city by two bridges. Timber, tobacco, cotton, palm oil, coffee, and cocoa are the chief exports. Its leading industries are petroleum production, motor-vehicle assembly, and the manufacture of electrical equipment, chemicals, plastics, and soap. Abidjan became the capital of French Côte d'Ivoire in 1935. The city developed in the 1950s with the building of improved port facilities at Port-Bouet and Grand-Bassam.

**ablative:** see CASE.

**ablaut** [Ger. = off-sound], in INFLECTION, a systematic change in the main vowel of a word in derivation. In English such forms as *sing, sang, sung* are examples of this process.

**ABM** (antiballistic missile): see MISSILE, GUIDED.

**abolitionists,** in US history, especially from 1830 to 1860, advocates of the compulsory emancipation of black slaves. Abolitionists are to be distinguished from free-soilers, who opposed the extension of SLAVERY. The active campaign had its mainspring in the revival (1820s) in the North of evangelical religion, with its moral urgency to end sinful practices. It reached crusading stage in the 1830s, led by Theodore D. Weld, the brothers Arthur and Lewis Tappan, and William Lloyd GARRISON. The American Anti-Slavery Society, established in 1833, flooded the country with abolitionist literature, established branches throughout the North and bombarded Congress with abolitionist petitions bearing hundreds of thousands of signatures. Writers like J.G. WHITTIER and orators such as Wendell PHILLIPS lent strength to the cause. Despite unanimity on their goal, abolitionists were divided over the method of achieving it, Garrison advocating moral suasion, others direct political action. *Uncle Tom's Cabin,* by Harriet B. STOWE, became an effective piece of abolitionist propaganda, and the KANSAS question aroused both North and South. The culminating act of abolitionism was John BROWN's raid on Harper's Ferry. Abolitionist demands for immediate freeing of the slaves after the outbreak of the CIVIL WAR contributed to Pres. Lincoln's *Emancipation Proclamation.* The abolitionist movement was one of high moral purpose and courage; its uncompromising temper hastened the demise of slavery in the US.

**Aboriginal land rights,** in Australia, a complex moral, legal, and political issue engaging Aborigines, the State, and development lobbies in prolonged and bitter campaigns. In New Zealand the British recognized Maori land laws (Treaty of Waitangi 1840), but in Australia (1788) relying on the doctrine of *terra nullius,* they deemed treaties unnecessary. Although often violated, treaties in the US, Papua New Guinea, and Canada provide a frame for negotiation. Since the 1967 constitutional referendum, the Federal government could legislate for Aborigines, but only the Aboriginal Land Rights Act (Northern Territories) 1976 has been enacted. Apart from two large settlements in South Australia (Pitjantjatjara 1981 and Maralinga 1984) and transfer of small parcels of land in Victoria and New South Wales, the states have been reluctant to exercise their powers. In Queensland and Western Australia, where the greatest number of Aborigines live, there are no special laws. Opposition from development lobbies to Aborigines' control of resources on Aboriginal land succeeded in reshaping the national land rights policy (1983–85) of the Hawke government. Through the politics of embarrassment (tent embassy 1972, bicentennial boycott 1988), international activities, direct action (Gurindji walk-off from Wave Hill 1966), and the Torres Strait Islanders' threat to secede, Aborigines keep compensation and sovereignty claims alive.

**Aboriginal languages,** group of languages spoken by ABORIGINES in Australia. They are probably all interrelated, but no relationship outside Australia has been shown. Not enough is known of Tasmanian languages to classify them. The greatest diversity is in Arnhemland and the Kimberleysi languages in the area from the Torres Straits Islands to Melbourne and Perth comprise one subfamily, Pama–Nyungan. Of perhaps 200 spoken at first British settlement, about 100 persist (whether some speech-varieties are separate languages or different dialects of the same one is an arbitrary decision). Some (e.g., Warlpiri of Central Australia and Yoingu of Arnhemland) have developed written literature and bilingual education programmes. Of current interest to linguists are case-systems, nonconfigurationality, noun-classes, the role of language and dialect in local organization, creoles, and conditions for language survival.

**Aborigines,** native inhabitants of Australia, before European colonization. Although hunter–gatherers had well-defined territories, an interlocking web of rights and obligations informed by considerations of kinship, marriage, sentiment, ceremony, resource management, and residence bound groups to the land of their forebears. In the creative era, known as the Dreamtime (see DREAMING ), the land was given form and shape, and today in religious celebration and daily practice the importance of land as an economic and spiritual resource is marked. Technological innovations include boomerang, woomera (spear thrower), eel and fish traps, and didgeridoo (musical drone pipe). The origins of and relationship between the gracile-boned people (Kow Swamp burial site, Victoria, 15,000 BP) and a more robust but later group (Lake Mungo cremation site, New South Wales, 26,000 BP) puzzle prehistorians. Recent evidence confirms Aboriginal civilization as one of the world's oldest. Probably arriving in N Australia about 53,000 years ago when the sea levels were low, Aborigines gradually colonized the drier interior, and long before the British arrived had occupied the entire continent. Estimates of the population vary from 300,000 to 2 million. Disease (smallpox, venereal diseases, influenza), massacres such as Myall Creek 1838, Coniston 1926, forceful removal of part-Aboriginal children, destruction of hunting grounds, and spirited guerrilla resistance took a great toll. In the 1930s it was believed Aborigines were a dying race but today 160,000 of 16 million Australians identify as Aboriginal. In the southern states most live in cities and on the fringes of rural towns where unemployment, ill health, and poor shelter indicate their disadvantaged position. In 1987 a nationwide enquiry into Aboriginal deaths in police custody began to hear evidence of some 100 cases. In the centre and north on cattle stations, missions, reserves, and where land rights exist, Aborigines pursue a life much in accord with that of their ancestors. The island of Tasmania, isolated for perhaps 20,000 years, developed a distinctive culture. Trucanini (1812–76) survivor of the Black Line (1830) is known as the last Tasmanian but some 3000 Tasmanians claim Aboriginal descent. The Aboriginal contribution to Australian cultural life is substantial: notable people include writers Kevin Gilbert (1933–), Kito Walker (1920–), and Jack DAVIS (1917–); artists Albert Namatjira (1902–59) painter of watercolours, Clifford Possum Tjapeitjarri (1934–) from Central Australia who paints vast acrylics, and Wandjuk Marika (1907–) from Arnhemland who paints on bark (as do many other Aboriginal artists); there is notable women's print work from Tivi (Melville and Bathurst islands) and batik silks (central Australia). In sport, many Aboriginals are prominent, including Evonne Goolagong (1951–) tennis, Lionel Rose (1948–) boxing, and the Ella brothers, football. In films are David Guipilil (1952–) and Justine Saunders. In public life are politicians Charles Perkins (1936–) and Senator Neville Bonner (1922–); lawyer Pat J'Anana (1941–); welfare worker Mum Shirl (1923–); and churchman Pastor Doug Nicholls (1906–). The WHITLAM government (1972–79), giving priority in Aborigines, set up the Woodward enquiry (reports 1973, 1974) which culminated in legislation on ABORIGINAL LAND RIGHTS. From 1977 to 1985 the Law Reform Commission investigated the recognition of customary law. Aboriginal legal aid services and land councils act as lobbies for Aboriginal interests but since the National Aboriginal Conference was dismantled, there is no national body with legislative backing. Pat Dodson (1945–), Gary Foley (1950–), and Marcia Langton (1951–) are important spokespersons. Like other indigenous peoples Aborigines are numerically weak, geographically dispersed, and their organizations vulnerable. Self-management, the official policy, is difficult without economic viability which they seek through compensation for lost lands and the right to negotiate royalties for development on their land. The civil rights movement US, other fourth-world peoples, churches, unions, students, peace, environment and anti-uranium movements have been supportive.

Members of the Wailbri tribe of **Aborigines** at Yuendumu in the Northern Territory of Australia perform a 'Murrungurru' dance

**abortion,** expulsion of the embryo or fetus before it is viable outside the uterus, i.e., before the 28th week after conception, in humans (see REPRODUCTION). Spontaneous abortion, or miscarriage, may be caused by death of the fetus due to abnormality or disease or by trauma to the expectant mother. Abortion may also be induced, the fetus removed from the uterus by such procedures as vacuum suction, dilation and curettage, intrauterine saline injection, and hysterotomy (surgical incision of the uterus). Abortion was long practised as a form of BIRTH CONTROL until pressure from the Roman Catholic Church and changing opinion led in the 19th cent. to the passage of strict antiabortion laws (e.g., in England and the US). In Britain organized agitation against these laws began with the formation of the Abortion Law Reform Association (1936) which worked towards the Abortion Act (1967). This legalized abortion under specific circumstances whose interpretation varies widely in practice according to medical opinion. It does not apply to N Ireland where abortion is still illegal, except in rare, extreme cases. By the 1980s abortion had been legalized in most European countries, the USSR, and Japan. Throughout most of Africa, and in Muslim countries, it is illegal or only available in circumstances where the woman's life is in danger. In the US a Supreme Court ruling (Roe v. Wade 1973) held that a fetus is not a 'person' under the terms of the constitution and stopped states from banning abortions in the first six months of pregnancy, though in 1977 Congress banned the use of Medicaid funds except in limited circumstances. Abortion remains a controversial issue. In Britain since 1975 the National Abortion Campaign and 'A Woman's Right to Choose Campaign' have successfully led opposition to restrictive proposed amendments to the Abortion Act, while urging changes in the law to widen the grounds on which abortion would be legal.

**Abraham** or **Abram,** progenitor of the Hebrews. He is an example of the man devoted to God, as in his willingness to sacrifice his son ISAAC. Revered by several religions, he is principally important as the founder of JUDAISM. He received the promise of CANAAN for his people, who are descended from Isaac. Gen. 11–25. Through another son, ISHMAEL, he is considered by Muslims an ancestor of the Arabs.

**Abrahams, Peter Henri,** 1919–, black South African novelist, journalist and broadcaster. He escaped to England as a seaman in 1941 and emigrated to Jamaica in 1956. He explores racism in, e.g., *Song of the City* (1945); South African history in *Wild Conquest* (1950); and the aftermath of independence in Africa in *A Wreath for Udomo* (1956) and in the Caribbean in *This Island Now* (1966), while *The View from Coyaba* (1985) explores black history from emancipation to the present. His autobiographical writings include *Return to Goli* (1953) and *Tell Freedom: Memories of Africa* (1954).

**Abram:** see ABRAHAM.

**abrasive,** material used to grind, smooth, cut, or polish another substance. Natural abrasives include SAND, PUMICE, CORUNDUM, and ground QUARTZ. Carborundum (SILICON CARBIDE) and ALUMINA (aluminium oxide) are major synthetic abrasives. The hardest abrasive is natural or synthetic DIAMOND, used in the form of dust or minuscule stones.

**Abravanel** or **Abarbanel, Judah,** c.1460–c.1523, Jewish philosopher, also known as Leone Ebreo; b. Lisbon. He was influenced by the scholars of the Platonic Academy of Florence, and by Maimonides and IBN GABIROL. His *Philosophy of Love* (pub. posthumously, 1535), a classic exposition of platonic love, had a profound effect on philosophers of the 16th and 17th cent., notably BRUNO and SPINOZA.

**Absalom,** favourite son of DAVID. He murdered his brother AMNON and fled. After being forgiven by David, Absalom stirred up a rebellion, in which he was killed. 2 Sam. 13–19.

**Abscam,** scandal resulting from an investigation begun in 1978 by the US FEDERAL BUREAU OF INVESTIGATION. The term *Abscam* is a contraction of 'Abdul scam', derived from Abdul Enterprises Ltd, a business created by the FBI as a front. FBI agents, posing as associates of an Arab sheik, met with selected public officials and offered them money or other considerations in exchange for special favours. The meetings, which were videotaped, resulted in the indictments (1980) of several officials, including one senator and six congressmen. The senator and four of the congressmen indicted were eventually found guilty on charges that included bribery and conspiracy, and one was convicted on lesser charges. The FBI's tactics in the case raised serious questions about entrapment of the defendants, and in 1982 the conviction of one of the congressmen was overturned.

**abscess,** localized accumulation of pus in tissues, usually caused by bacterial infection. Characterized by inflammation and painful swelling, it may occur in various parts of the body, e.g., skin, gum, eyelid (stye), and middle ear (mastoid infection). Many abscesses respond to treatment with ANTIBIOTIC drugs; others may require surgical incision to release the pus.

**absolute temperature:** see TEMPERATURE.

**absolute value,** magnitude of a mathematical expression, disregarding its sign; thus the absolute value is always positive. In symbols, if $|a|$ denotes the absolute value of a number $a$, then $|a| = a$ for $a > 0$ and $|a| = -a$ for $a < 0$. For a complex NUMBER, $a + ib$, the absolute value, $|a + ib|$, is the positive square root of the sum of the squares of the real and imaginary parts, i.e., $|a + ib| = \sqrt{a^2 + b^2}$.

**absolute zero:** see TEMPERATURE.

**absorption,** taking of molecules of one substance into another or the penetration of nuclei (see NUCLEUS), ELEMENTARY PARTICLES or a wave motion into a substance with resultant loss of energy. In the former case the absorption may be physical or chemical. Physical absorption depends on the solubility of the substance absorbed, and chemical absorption involves chemical reactions between the absorbed substance and the absorbing medium. Nuclei (e.g., alpha particles), elementary particles (e.g., ELECTRONS, PROTONS), and waves (e.g., X-RAYS, SOUND waves) lose energy, which is converted into other forms (e.g., HEAT, molecular excitation) as they pass through the absorbing substance and the rate of loss of energy determines the distance of penetration. The penetrating ability is specified quantitatively in terms of an absorption coefficient.

**abstract expressionism,** term used to cover the work done by artists in the New York School in the late 1940s and 1950s. It was applied to 15 artists shown at the 'New York School' exhibition at Los Angeles County Mus. (1965). However there was little stylistic unity within this group, ranging from monochromatic works of Barnett NEWMAN, to drip painting of Jackson POLLOCK and figurative works of Willem DE KOONING. Generally, abstract expressionism is marked by an attention to surface qualities, i.e., brushstroke and texture; the use of huge canvases; the exploitation of accidents that occur while painting; and an emphasis on the act of painting itself. The first important school in American painting to declare independence from European styles and to influence art abroad, abstract expressionism enormously affected the many kinds of art that followed it, especially in the use of colour and material. Other major artists in the movement include Hans HOFMANN, Robert MOTHERWELL, Franz KLINE, Mark ROTHKO and Adolph GOTTLIEB.

**Abu al-Ala al-Maarri,** 973–1057, Arabic poet. He was blind from childhood. Brilliantly original, he discarded classicism for intellectual urbanity. Later he favoured ascetic purity and wrote more stereotypical poetry.

**Abu al-Faraj Ali of Esfahan,** 897–967, Arabic scholar. He is mainly known for his poetic anthology *Kitab al-Aghani* [book of songs], an important source for information on medieval Islamic society.

**Abu Bakr,** c.573–634, first head of the Islamic community after MUHAMMAD and skilled genealogist. Accorded the title of Caliph (see CALIPHATE), he 'ruled' in a very limited fashion. During his period of office the first Arab conquests took place.

**Abu Dhabi,** city (1984 est. pop. 292,000), capital of the UNITED ARAB EMIRATES. Its international airport is an important refuelling stop.

**Abu Hanifa, al-Nu'man Ibn Thabit,** 700–67, Muslim jurist from Iraq, founder of the Hanafite school of FIQH.

**Abuja,** designated federal capital of Nigeria. Plans to move the capital from LAGOS were approved in 1976, and a 7700-km² (3000-sq mi) capital territory was created near the old town of Abuja (now renamed Sulaija). The site, near the centre of the country, has a good climate and is sparsely populated. It is still at an early stage of construction.

**Abu Nuwas,** d. c.810, Arabic poet. A favourite of the caliphs HARUN AR-RASHID and Amin, he spent much time in Baghdad. His exquisite poetry echoes the extravagance of court life.

**Abu Said ibn Abi al-Khair,** 967–1049, Persian poet, a Sufi (see SUFISM) and a DERVISH. He was the first to write rubaiyat (quatrains) in the Sufistic strain that OMAR KHAYYAM made famous.

**Abu Simbel,** site on the Nile R. in S Egypt (formerly Nubia) of two temples carved in rock cliffs in the reign of RAMSES II (c.1250 BC). The temples and their four colossi of the pharaoh (18–20 m 160–65 ft high) were sawn into blocks and moved to higher ground to avoid rising waters caused by the building of the ASWAN HIGH DAM. With UNESCO aid, the reconstruction was completed in 1968.

**Abu Tammam Habib ibn Aus,** c.805–c.845, Arabic poet, compiler of the HAMASA. Often describing historical events, his poems of valour are important as source material.

**Abyssinia:** see ETHIOPIA.

**Ac,** chemical symbol of the element ACTINIUM.

**AC:** see ELECTRICITY; GENERATOR; MOTOR, ELECTRIC.

**acacia** (ə,kaysh(y)ə), plant (genus *Acacia*) of the PULSE family, mostly tropical and subtropical thorny shrubs and trees. Some have a feathery foliage composed of leaflets; others have no leaves but have flattened leaflike stems containing chlorophyll. Various species yield lac (for shellac), catechu (a medicine and dye), gum arabic, essential oils, tannins, and hardwood timber. The acacias are the floral emblem of Australia.

The Great Temple at **Abu Simbel**

**academic freedom,** right of scholars to study, enquire, teach, and publish without control or restraint either from the institutions that employ them or from the political authorities. The concept is based on the notion that truth is best discovered through open investigation of all data. Its less clearly developed corollary is the obligation to pursue open and thorough enquiry regardless of personal considerations. Initiated during the ENLIGHTENMENT by scholars outside the university, academic freedom gained general acceptance only after university education was secularized.

**Acadia,** region and former French colony, centred on NOVA SCOTIA, but including also PRINCE EDWARD ISLAND and much of the mainland coast from Quebec to Maine. In 1605 the French founded Port Royal (now ANNAPOLIS ROYAL), the first and chief town. During the FRENCH AND INDIAN WARS, the Peace of Utrecht (1713) gave Britain possession of the Nova Scotian peninsula, and, by the Treaty of Paris (1763) (see PARIS, TREATY OF), all of Acadia fell to Britain. Doubting the loyalty of the French inhabitants (called Acadians), the British expelled many of them in 1755 and 1758. Most were scattered among the British colonies to the south, many of them later returning to the area. Other exiles found havens elsewhere, notably the Cajuns of S Louisiana, who still preserve a separate folk culture. The sufferings of the expulsion are depicted in LONGFELLOW's poem *Evangeline*.

**acanthus,** common name for the Acanthaceae, a family of chiefly perennial herbs, shrubs, and some climbers, mostly tropical. Many members have decorative spiny leaves and are cultivated as ornamentals, e.g., bear's breeches (*Acanthus mollis*), whose ornate leaves provided a motif often used in Greek and Roman art and architecture. In Christian art, the acanthus symbolizes heaven.

**Acapulco** or **Acapulco de Juárez,** city (1979 est. pop. 462,144), winter resort on the tropical Pacific coast of S Mexico, known for its fine beaches, luxury hotels and villas, and deep-sea fishing facilities. Founded on a natural harbour in 1550, it was a base for Spanish explorers and was once important in trade with the Philippines. It became a favoured haunt of wealthy holidaymakers in the 1920s.

**ACAS:** see ADVISORY, CONCILIATION AND ARBITRATION SERVICE.

**acceleration:** see MOTION.

**accelerator:** see PARTICLE ACCELERATOR.

**accent, 1** a type of pronunciation which characterizes a person or group. It may be regional or social in origin and is often linked to a specific DIALECT although it does not itself constitute one. **2** The emphasis given a certain sound within a word usually achieved by altering loudness, pitch, or length. In writing, accent may be used to show syllable stress, as in the Italian *pietá*, but often merely signals specific pronunciation.

**Acco** or **Acre**, city and small port (1986 est. pop. 37,200), W GALILEE, Israel, on the Mediterranean coast. It is an ancient town and port which declined in the 19th cent. with the growth of HAIFA, 32 km (20 mi) to the south. It has endured many sieges in its history including those by the Crusaders, Saracens, and NAPOLEON (1799). Many of the Arab population left in 1948 during the first ARAB-ISRAELI WAR. It is now a tourist centre with many buildings and archaeological sites together with churches and mosques of the Crusader and Ottoman periods. It was the last stronghold of the Crusaders in the Levant.

**accounting,** classification, analysis, and interpretation of the financial, or bookkeeping, records of an enterprise, used to evaluate the progress or failures of a business and to recognize the factors that determine its true condition. In the UK accountants who pass the required examinations qualify for membership of the Institutes of Chartered Accountants, the Chartered Association of Certified Accountants and various other bodies. An important branch of accounting is **auditing,** the examination and verification of accounts by persons who have had no part in their preparation. Annual audits are required for all publicly held businesses in the UK and many other countries.

**Accra,** city (1982 pop. 1,120,615), capital of Ghana, a port on the Gulf of Guinea. The nation's largest city and its administrative and economic centre, Accra is linked by road and rail with KUMASI, in the interior, and with the seaport of Tema. It's economy is based on cocoa, gold, timber, fruit, and livestock. The city became (1876) the capital of the British Gold Coast colony and grew economically after completion (1923) of a railway to Kumasi at the centre of cocoa-growing country. Riots in the city (1948) led to the movement for Ghana's independence. Today Accra is a sprawling, modern city with wide avenues; points of interest include a 17th-cent. Danish castle.

**acculturation,** the cultural changes caused by long contact between very different cultural groups. Usually, as in the colonial or imperialist context, the change is one way in an unequal relationship and the subordinate, relatively powerless culture has little room to resist the dominant, powerful culture that is effectively imposed upon it.

**accusative:** see CASE.

**acephalous** (ə,sefələs, ay-), [Gk., = headless], a term in anthropology referring to societies which have no centralized political authority, nor any very formalized positions of leadership.

**acetone, dimethyl ketone** or **2-propanone** (,asitohn), ($CH_3COCH_3$), colourless, flammable liquid. Acetone is widely used in industry as a solvent for many organic substances and is a component of most paint and varnish removers. It is used in making synthetic RESINS and fillers, smokeless powders (explosives that produce little smoke), and many other organic compounds.

**acetylcholine** ('asitiel,kohlin, -leen), chemical substance essential for the conduction of nerve impulses in animals. It is found in highest concentrations on neurone (nerve cell) surfaces and is liberated at nerve cell endings. There is strong evidence that acetylcholine is the neurotransmitter that conducts impulses from one cell to another in the parasympathetic NERVOUS SYSTEM, and from nerve cells to smooth muscle and skeletal muscle (see MUSCLE), and exocrine glands (see GLAND).

**acetylene** or **ethyne** (ə,setileen), ($HC \equiv CH$), colourless gas and the simplest alkyne (see HYDROCARBON). Explosive on contact with air, it is stored dissolved under pressure in ACETONE. It is used to make neoprene RUBBER, PLASTICS, and RESINS. The oxyacetylene torch mixes and burns oxygen and acetylene to produce a very hot flame as high as 3480°C (6300°F) which can cut steel and weld iron and other metals. Prior to

using ethylene (ethene), which is produced by thermally decomposing PETROLEUM, and METHANE, acetylene was the principal chemical building-block in the manufacture of plastics, synthetic fibres, and other polymers.

**Achaea** (ə,keeə), region of ancient GREECE, in the N Peloponnesus on the Gulf of Corinth. It took its name from the **Achaeans**, inhabitants of central and southern Greece in the late Bronze Age, some of whom took refuge there after 1200 BC. Before the 5th cent. BC the Achaean cities joined in the First **Achaean League**, which was dissolved after it opposed (338 BC) PHILIP II of Macedon. The Second Achaean League, formed in 280 BC, almost drove MACEDON from Achaea but was stopped by SPARTA. In 198 BC, with Roman aid, the league won power. Later, suspecting pro-Macedonian sympathies, Rome deported many Achaeans (168 BC) to Italy. In 146 BC Achaea waged a suicidal war against Rome, which easily won, dissolved the league, and ended Greek liberty.

**Achaemenids** (ə,keemənidz), dynasty of ancient PERSIA. The Achaemenid rulers (c.550–330 BC) included CYRUS THE GREAT, Cambyses, DARIUS I, XERXES I, and ARTAXERXES I. The dynasty ended with DARIUS III.

**Achebe, Chinua,** 1930–, Nigerian novelist and poet, broadcaster and university teacher. An exemplary stylist, he writes about colonialism, erosion of traditional African values, and consequences of independence in *Things Fall Apart* (1958), *No Longer At Ease* (1964), *A Man of the People* (1966), and *Anthills of the Savannah* (1987). His poetry includes *Beware, Soul Brother and Other Poems* (1972) and *Christmas in Biafra* (1973). His critical essays include *Morning Yet on Creation Day* (1975) and *Hopes and Impediments: Selected Essays 1965–87* (1988).

**Acheson, Dean Gooderham,** 1893–1971, US secretary of state (1949–53). Serving Pres. TRUMAN, he helped initiate the policy of containment of Communist expansion. He also helped to establish the NORTH ATLANTIC TREATY ORGANIZATION.

**Acheulian industry,** a stone-tool industry of the Lower PALAEOLITHIC period, named after a site in peri-glacial deposits at Saint-Acheul in the Somme valley of France. The characteristic tool, a large handaxe or chopper, is widely distributed in Europe, Africa, and Asia at sites dating before c.80,000 BP. It is known that Acheulian peoples were hunters and gatherers who exploited large mammals; at Ambrona, in Spain, the remains of more than 30 butchered elephants were discovered.

Acheulian handaxes from Hoxne and Warren Hill

**Achilles,** in Greek mythology, foremost hero of the TROJAN WAR; son of Peleus and Thetis. Thetis attempted to make him immortal by bathing him in the river STYX, but the heel she held remained vulnerable. Knowing Achilles was fated to die at Troy, Thetis disguised him as a girl and hid him at Skyros. He was found by ODYSSEUS, who persuaded him to go to war. At Troy he quarrelled with AGAMEMNON and sulked in his tent until his friend Patroclus was killed by HECTOR. Filled with grief and rage, Achilles slew Hector and dragged his body to the Greek camp. He was later killed by PARIS, who wounded his heel.

**acid rain,** form of precipitation (rain, snow, sleet, or hail) containing high levels of sulphuric or nitric acids (pH below 5.5–5.6). Produced when sulphur dioxide and various nitrogen oxides combine with atmospheric moisture, acid rain can contaminate drinking water, damage vegetation and aquatic life, and erode buildings and monuments. It has been an increasingly serious problem since the 1950s, particularly in the NE US, Canada, and W Europe, especially Scandinavia. Acid deposition (wet or dry) is thought to have damaged half of W Germany's forests by 1985 and to have killed all or most living organisms in 80,000 of Sweden's and 50,000 of Canada's lakes. Vehicle exhausts and the burning of high-sulphur industrial fuels are thought to be the main causes, but natural sources, e.g., volcanic gases and forest fires, may also be significant. The '30% Club' is a group of countries who have already reduced or are willing to commit themselves to reducing sulphur dioxide emissions by 30% on 1980 levels by 1993. See also ECOLOGY; POLLUTION; WASTE DISPOSAL.

**acid rock:** see ROCK MUSIC.

**acids and bases,** two related classes of chemicals; the members of each class have a number of common properties when dissolved in a solvent, usually water. Acids in water solutions exhibit the following common properties: they taste sour; turn LITMUS paper red; and react with certain metals, such as zinc, to yield hydrogen gas. Bases in water solutions exhibit these common properties: they taste bitter; turn litmus paper blue; and feel slippery. When a water solution of acid is mixed with a water solution of base, a SALT and water are formed; this process, called neutralization, is complete only if the resulting solution has neither acidic nor basic properties. When an acid or base dissolves in water, a certain percentage of the acid or base particles will break up, or dissociate, into oppositely charged ions. The Arrhenius theory of acids and bases defines an acid as a compound that can dissociate in water to yield hydrogen ions ($H^+$), and a base as a compound that can dissociate in water to yield hydroxyl ions ($OH^-$). The Brønsted–Lowry theory defines an acid as a proton donor and a base as a proton acceptor. The Lewis theory defines an acid as a compound that can accept a pair of electrons and a base as a compound that can donate a pair of electrons. Each of the three theories has its own advantages and disadvantages; each is useful under certain conditions. Strong acids, such as HYDROCHLORIC ACID, and strong bases, such as potassium hydroxide, have a great tendency to dissociate in water and are completely ionized in solution. Weak acids, such as acetic acid, and weak bases, such as AMMONIA, are reluctant to dissociate in water and are only partially ionized in solution. Strong acids and strong bases make very good electrolytes (see ELECTROLYSIS), i.e., their solutions readily conduct electricity. Weak acids and weak bases make poor electrolytes. See also AMPHOTERISM; BUFFER; CATALYST; INDICATORS, ACID–BASE; TITRATION; article on *p*H.

**Acmeists** (‚akmayists), school of Russian poets that arose in 1912 in reaction to the SYMBOLISTS; it emphasized concreteness of imagery and clarity of expression. The leading Acmeists were Nikolai GUMILYOV, Anna AKHMATOVA, and Osip MANDELSTAM.

**acne,** inflammatory disorder of the sebaceous glands, characterized by blackheads, cysts, and pimples. The lesions appear on the face, neck, chest, back, and upper arms, and may be mild to severe. Although most prevalent during adolescence, acne may appear in adulthood. Its cause is unknown, but contributing factors include genetic predisposition and hormonal changes during puberty. Diet, stress, and microorganisms may also be involved. Treatment includes use of cleansers, ANTIBIOTIC drugs, and ultraviolet light, surgical drainage, and, for severe cases, application of retinoic acid derivatives.

**Acoma** or **Ácoma,** pueblo in W central New Mexico, situated atop a steep-sided 357-ft (109-m) MESA. Founded c.1100–1250, it is considered the oldest continuously inhabited community in the US. The resident PUEBLO INDIANS retain aspects of their 700-year-old culture; the men are weavers, the women highly skilled and renowned potters.

**Aconcagua,** mountain 6960 m (22,835 ft) high, in the ANDES of Argentina. It is the highest peak in the Americas.

**acorn:** see OAK.

**acoustics,** the science of SOUND, including its production, propagation, and effects, and its description in terms of loudness or intensity (measured in DECIBELS), pitch or FREQUENCY, and quality of timbre. An important practical application of acoustics is in the designing of auditoriums, which requires a knowledge of the characteristics of sound WAVES. Reflection of sound can cause an ECHO, and repeated reflections in an enclosed space can cause reverberation, the persistence of sound. Some reverberation in auditoriums is desirable to avoid deadening the sound of music. Reflection can be reduced through the proper configuration and texture of walls, and by the use of sound-absorbent materials. Another acoustical problem is INTERFERENCE, which can create 'dead spots' in auditoriums for certain frequencies.

**acquired characteristics,** modifications produced in an individual plant or animal as a result of mutilation, disease, use and disuse, or any distinctly environmental influence. Belief in the inheritability of acquired characteristics was accepted by LAMARCK but ultimately rejected by modern geneticists, who have affirmed that inheritance is determined solely by reproductive cells and unaffected by somatic (body) cells.

**acquired immune deficiency syndrome:** see AIDS.

**Acre:** see ACCO.

**Acroclinum,** genus of Australian annual flowers of the COMPOSITE family, in white and shades of pink to red, used as a garden ornamental and for dried flower arrangements. Also called everlasting daisy.

**acropolis,** elevated, fortified section of ancient Greek cities. The Acropolis of Athens was adorned in the 5th cent. BC with some of the world's greatest architectural monuments. The remains of the PARTHENON, ERECHTHEUM, and Propylaea still stand.

The **Acropolis**, Athens

**Actaeon** (ak‚teeən), in Greek mythology, a hunter. Because he saw ARTEMIS bathing naked, she changed him into a stag, and he was killed by his own dogs.

**actinide series,** the radioactive metals, with atomic numbers 89 to 103, in group IIIA of the PERIODIC TABLE. They are ACTINIUM, THORIUM, PROTACTINIUM, URANIUM, NEPTUNIUM, PLUTONIUM, AMERICIUM, CURIUM, BERKELIUM, CALIFORNIUM, EINSTEINIUM, FERMIUM, MENDELEVIUM, NOBELIUM, and LAWRENCIUM. All members of the series have chemical properties similar to actinium. Those elements with atomic numbers greater than 92 are called TRANSURANIC ELEMENTS.

**actinium** (Ac), radioactive element; discovered in 1899 by André Debierne in uranium residues from pitchblende. Actinium, a silver-white metal, is the first member of the ACTINIDE SERIES. The most stable isotope has a half-life of 21.6 years. See ELEMENT (table); PERIODIC TABLE.

**action painting,** term used by the critic Harold Rosenberg in the 1950s for works that emphasized the process of their creation, as in the work of DE KOONING and POLLOCK. See also GESTURAL PAINTING.

**activation energy:** see CATALYST.

**active:** see VOICE.

**act of God,** unforeseeable event causing loss, injury or damage, e.g., earthquakes, hurricanes, and floods. In UK law, it is important in that it can provide a defence to certain TORTS (e.g., NUISANCE), if the defendant can show that the damage was caused by an act which could not have reasonably been foreseen or prevented.

**Act of Supremacy,** 1534, established the king as Head of the Church of England. It was a major legislative move in Henry VIII's break with the Papacy, and a crucial step in the creation of Anglicanism.

**Acton, John Emerich Edward Dalberg Acton,** 1st **Baron,** 1834–1902, English historian; b. Italy. A liberal and a Roman Catholic, he taught modern history at Cambridge from 1895. Acton never completed a book; his influence was felt through essays and lectures. He planned the *Cambridge Modern History.*

**Acts of the Apostles,** book of the NEW TESTAMENT. The only contemporary historical account of CHRISTIANITY's early expansion, it was written between AD 60 and 90 as a sequel to the Gospel of St LUKE, who is its traditional author. The Acts chiefly deal with the work of St PETER (1–12) and St PAUL (13–21).

**acupuncture,** system of treatment, based on traditional Chinese medicine, in which a number of very fine metal needles are inserted into the skin at any of some 800 specially designated points and stimulated by rotation, electricity, or heat. In China it has long been used for pain relief and treatment of such ailments as ARTHRITIS, HYPERTENSION, and ULCERS. More recently it has been used as an ANAESTHESIA for childbirth and some surgery. (Unlike conventional anaesthesia, it does not lower blood pressure nor depress respiration.) It has been suggested that acupuncture works by stimulating ENDORPHIN production. Western research on acupuncture has focused on its use in pain relief and anaesthesia.

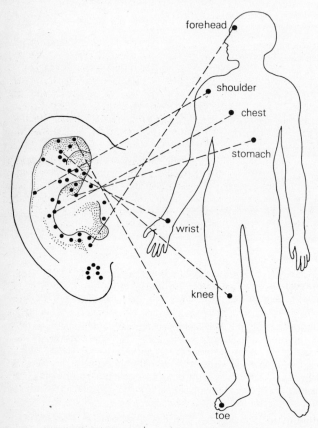

Acupuncture points in the ear for the treatment of pain

**acyclovir,** antiviral drug effective in controlling the signs of HERPES infections. Acyclovir acts by stopping the synthesis of herpes DNA and is used in the treatment of herpes simplex (cold sore, genital herpes) and herpes zoster (SHINGLES). It can also be used to prevent herpes infection in patients with suppressed immune systems (e.g., those with AIDS or patients undergoing chemotherapy).

**ADA:** see PROGRAMMING LANGUAGE.

**Adam** [Heb., = man], in the BIBLE, the first man. His story, from his creation to his expulsion (with EVE, his wife) from the Garden of EDEN, is

told in Gen. 1.26–5.5. To St PAUL, Adam was the forerunner or 'type' of Christ, the 'last Adam' (Rom. 5.12–14; 1 Cor. 15.20–22, 42–49).

**Adam, Adolphe Charles,** 1803–56, French composer. His more than 50 stage works include the ballet *Giselle* (1841). He also wrote the popular song *Cantique de Noël* (1850).

**Adam, Robert,** 1728–92, and **James Adam,** 1730–94, Scottish architects, brothers. Robert possessed the great creative talents. They designed public and private buildings in England and Scotland, and numerous interiors, pieces of furniture, and decorative objects. Robert's light, elegant style was a personal reconstitution of Palladian, Renaissance, and antique elements (including the recent discoveries at HERCULANEUM and POMPEII); his furniture, always designed as part of a unified scheme of decoration, made much use of light-coloured woods enriched with MARQUETRY of classical motifs. The Adam manner grew vastly popular and has never disappeared. Interesting examples of Adam planning and decoration are at Osterley Park (1761–80) and Syon House (1762–69), both near London.

Robert **Adam:** The entrance hall of Syon House, Isleworth, London (1762–69)

**Adams,** family of distinguished Americans from Massachusetts. **John Adams** was president of the US (see separate article). He and his wife, Abigail (Smith) Adams, were the parents of **John Quincy Adams,** who was also president of the US (see separate article). His son, **Charles Francis Adams,** 1807–86, was US minister to Great Britain (1861–68). During the Civil War he effectively upheld the Northern cause, protesting vigorously at the construction of warships for the Confederacy in British yards and countering Confederate efforts to secure British recognition. Later he represented the US in the settlement of the ALABAMA CLAIMS. His son **Charles Francis Adams,** 1835–1915, was an economist and historian. An expert on railway financing, he was president of the Union Pacific Railroad (1884–90). His works include *Three Episodes of Massachusetts History* (1892). His brother **Brooks Adams,** 1848–1927, was a historian. His belief that civilizations rose and fell according to the growth and decline of commerce was first developed in *The Law of Civilization and Decay* (1895). His ideas influenced another brother, **Henry Adams**, 1838–1915, who was also a writer and historian. In developing a philosophy of history he found a unifying principle in force, or energy, and applied it in two books, *Mont-Saint-Michel and Chartres* (1913) and *The Education of Henry Adams* (1918). He also wrote *History of the United States of America* (9 vol., 1889–91).

**Adams, Ansel,** 1902–1984, American photographer. Working against the painterly aesthetic current in the 1930s, he produced sharp, superbly detailed regional landscapes, notably of the American Southwest. He also wrote numerous technical manuals and helped to found the first museum and college photography departments.

Snake River, Wyoming, a photograph of the American West by Ansel Adams

**Adams, James Truslow,** 1878–1949, American historian. His works include *The Founding of New England* (1921) and *The Adams Family* (1930). He was editor of the *Dictionary of American History* (6 vol., 1940).

**Adams, John,** 1735–1826, 2nd president of the US (1797–1801); father of John Quincy ADAMS. He graduated from Harvard Univ. in 1755 and became a lawyer. As a moderate but forceful leader of the group who opposed British measures leading to the AMERICAN REVOLUTION, he later served in both the First and Second CONTINENTAL CONGRESS and argued eloquently for the DECLARATION OF INDEPENDENCE, which he signed. Adams served the new nation as a diplomat, negotiating the Treaty of PARIS (1783) to end the Revolution and serving (1785–88) as envoy to Great Britain. He became Pres. WASHINGTON's vice president (1789–97) and in 1797 succeeded him as president. Adams's administration as president revealed his honest and stubborn integrity. Although allied with Alexander HAMILTON and the conservative, property-respecting Federalists, he was not dominated by them in their struggle with the Jeffersonians (see JEFFERSON, THOMAS). By conciliation he prevented war with France (see XYZ AFFAIR). His wife, **Abigail (Smith) Adams,** 1744–1818, was the chief figure in the social life of her husband's administration.

**Adams, John Couch,** 1819–92, English astronomer. By mathematical calculation based on irregularities in the motion of the planet Uranus, he and U.J.J. LEVERRIER independently and accurately predicted (1845–46) the position of the then unknown planet NEPTUNE. Adams also made valuable studies of the moon's motions, of the great meteor shower of 1866, and of terrestrial magnetism.

**Adams, John Quincy,** 1767–1848, 6th president of the US (1825–29); son of John and Abigail Adams (see ADAMS, JOHN); father of Charles Francis Adams (see ADAMS, family). He gained fame as secretary of state (1817–25) under Pres. James MONROE, his greatest achievement being the MONROE DOCTRINE. Elected president (1825) by the House of

Representatives through the support of Henry CLAY, Adams had an unhappy, ineffective administration. He won new respect as a US representative from Massachusetts (1831–48), eloquently attacking all measures that would extend SLAVERY.

**Adams, Samuel,** 1722–1803, American Revolutionary patriot. His speeches and writings helped to spark the AMERICAN REVOLUTION. He signed the DECLARATION OF INDEPENDENCE, was a member (1774–81) of the CONTINENTAL CONGRESS, and was governor (1794–97) of Massachusetts.

**Adams, Will(iam),** 1564–1620, English sailor. On reaching Japan in a Dutch vessel in 1600, he became resident there and enjoyed a close relationship with TOKUGAWA IEYASU, whom he advised on commercial and other matters. With Ieyasu's approval, he invited the Dutch and English to trade with Japan.

**Adamson, Robert:** see HILL, DAVID O.

**Adana,** city (1980 pop. 574,515), capital of Adana prov., S Turkey, on the Seyhan R. Turkey's fourth largest city, it is the commercial centre of a farming region where cotton, grains, and other crops are grown. The city's manufactures include processed food and textiles. An ancient city probably founded by the HITTITES, it prospered from 66 BC as a Roman colony. It later declined but was revived (AD c.782) by HARUN AR-RASHID. In the 16th cent. it passed to the Ottoman Turks. Near Adana is a Hittite archaeological site.

**adaptation,** in biology, the adjustment of living matter to environmental conditions, including other living things. Animals and plants are adapted for securing food and surviving even in conditions of drought, great heat, or extreme cold. Adaptations are believed to arise when genetic variations that increase an organism's chances of survival are passed on to succeeding generations. See also ECOLOGY; EVOLUTION; GENETICS.

**adaptive radiation,** in biology, the evolution of an ancestral species adapted to a particular way of life into several species, each adapted to a different habitat. Illustrating the principle are the 14 species of DARWIN's finches, small land birds of the Galapagos Islands: three are ground-dwelling seed-eaters, three live on cactus plants and are seed-eaters, one is a tree-dwelling seed-eater, seven are tree-dwelling insect eaters, but all derive from a single species of ground-dwelling, seed-eating finch that probably emigrated from the South American mainland.

**Addams, Jane,** 1860–1935, American social worker. In 1889 she and Ellen Gates Starr founded Hull House, a Chicago settlement house that served the neighbourhood poor and became a centre for social reform activities. A leader of the WOMEN'S SUFFRAGE and pacifist movements, Addams shared the 1931 Nobel Peace Prize. She wrote several books on social issues and two autobiographical volumes.

**addax:** see ANTELOPE.

**adder:** see VIPER.

**Addis Ababa** or **Adis Abeba,** city (1984 est. pop. 1,412,575), capital of Ethiopia. Addis Ababa is Ethiopia's largest city, its administrative and communications centre, and the main trade centre for coffee (Ethiopia's chief export), tobacco, grains, textiles, and hides; much of its commerce is shipped by rail to the port of DJIBOUTI. Founded by Emperor Melenik II in 1887, Addis Ababa became Ethiopia's capital in 1889. In 1936 it was captured by the Italians and made the capital of ITALIAN EAST AFRICA. It was retaken by the Allies in 1941 and returned to Ethiopian rule. A modern city, it is the headquarters of the United Nations Economic Commission for Africa and of the Organization of African Unity. Notable buildings include Coptic and Roman Catholic cathedrals.

**Addison, Joseph,** 1672–1719, English essayist, poet, and statesman. His *Remarks on Italy* (1705) recorded early travels. The prominence he attained with the epic *Campaign* (1704) on MARLBOROUGH's victory at Blenheim led to political appointments, and he served in Parliament (1708–19). Addison contributed to his friend Richard STEELE's periodical the *Tatler* after 1710. There, and in the SPECTATOR and *Guardian,* he raised the English essay to an unequalled height. In prose marked by simplicity, order, and precision, Addison advocated reason and moderation in life.

**Addison's disease,** progressive disease brought about by atrophy of the outer layer (cortex) of the ADRENAL GLANDS; also called chronic adrenocortical insufficiency. The deterioration of this tissue causes a decrease in the secretion of vital STEROID hormones, producing such symptoms as ANAEMIA, weakness, dark colouring of the skin, and weight loss. The cause of the disease is unknown. First described by Thomas Addison in 1849, the disease was formerly fatal but is now treated with adrenocortical hormones that enable its victims to lead a nearly normal life.

**Adelaide,** city (1986 est. pop. 917,000), capital and chief port of South Australia, on the plains of the Torrens R., on Gulf St Vincent. It has motor vehicle, textile, and other industries, and exports grains, wool, dairy products, wine, and fruit. Founded in 1836, it was named after the consort of William IV. The biennial Adelaide Festival of Arts, begun in 1960, is held in the Adelaide Festival Centre (opened 1977). It is also known for its many parks. It has two universities, the Univ. of Adelaide and Flinders Univ. In 1985 the city hosted the First Australian International Grand Prix.

**Aden,** city (1985 est. pop. 264,300), capital and chief port of Southern Yemen (People's Democratic Republic of Yemen), on the Gulf of Aden near the southern entrance to the Red Sea. The city is built on two peninsulas, each with a high volcanic headland. Most of the population lives on Aden peninsula; on Little Aden peninsula are an oil refinery and other industries. Aden has been the chief trade and transshipment centre of S ARABIA since ancient times. It declined with the discovery (15th cent.) of an all-water route around Africa to India, but revived when the SUEZ CANAL opened in 1869. An oil refinery, completed in 1954, increased its importance as a trading and refuelling port. The town and the adjacent area of S Arabia was held by Muslim Arabs (7th–16th cent.) and by the Ottoman Turks (from 1538). The British occupied Aden in 1839 and it was governed from India until 1947. It was made a crown colony in 1935. In 1967 Aden and the adjacent Arabian protectorates became independent and, after some political confusion and fighting, were merged as Southern Yemen; Aden has been its capital since 1970.

**Aden, Gulf of,** western arm of the Arabian Sea, 885 km (550 mi) long and 300 km (180 ml) wide, between E Africa and SW Asia. It is connected with the RED SEA by the strait of BAB EL MANDEB and is an important link in the MEDITERRANEAN SEA–SUEZ CANAL–INDIAN OCEAN sea lane.

**Adenauer, Konrad,** 1876–1967, West German chancellor (1949–63). He was a member of the Catholic Centre Party until 1933, when he was stripped of his offices and imprisoned by the NAZIS. After World War II he was a founder and chairman of the Christian Democratic Union. As chancellor, he presided over the spectacular rebirth of West GERMANY's economy, and guided that nation's entry into the EUROPEAN COMMUNITY and recovery in 1955 of its full sovereignty.

**adenoids:** see under TONSILS.

**adenosine triphosphate** (ATP), compound composed of adenine (a PURINE), ribose (a SUGAR), and three phosphate units; one of the most important low-molecular-weight molecules in living matter. It is a rich source of the chemical energy necessary for a vast number of life-supporting chemical reactions in the cell. ATP also plays a role in kidney function, transmission of nerve impulses, MUSCLE contraction, active transport of materials through cell membranes, and the synthesis of NUCLEIC ACID and other large molecules.

**adhesion and cohesion,** attractive forces between material bodies. Adhesive forces act between different substances, whereas cohesive forces act within a single substance, holding its atoms, ions, or molecules together. Were it not for these forces, solids and liquids would act as gases. SURFACE TENSION in liquids results from cohesion, and CAPILLARITY results from a combination of adhesion and cohesion. FRICTION between two solid bodies depends in part on adhesion.

**adiabatic process,** a process in which change takes place within a physical system without heat being exchanged between the system and its surroundings.

**Adi Granth** [Skt., = the first book], the most sacred and highly venerated book of the Sikhs. Verses from this book are chanted in the Golden Temple of Amritsar. Regarded as the perpetual guru (spiritual guide), it is supposed to contain living voices of all prophets.

**Adirondack Mountains,** forested mountain wilderness area, NE New York, US, with many scenic gorges, waterfalls, and lakes. The Adirondacks rise to a high point of 1629 m (5344 ft) at Mt Marcy and are geologically a southern extension of the CANADIAN SHIELD. Lake Placid and Lake George are important area resorts.

**Adis Abeba:** see ADDIS ABABA.

**adjective:** see PART OF SPEECH.

**adjustment,** a state of positive psychobiological adaptation of an organism to an environment. Adjustment has frequently been seen as a goal of both individual development and PSYCHOTHERAPY. This view has however been criticized as politically reactionary, as it implies that individuals should change towards conformity with social expectations, rather than applying their energies to changing society (see ANTI-PSYCHIATRY).

**Adler, Alfred,** 1870–1937, Austrian psychoanalyst and early associate of Sigmund FREUD. Adler broke with Freud (1911), rejecting the centrality of the Oedipus COMPLEX and of sexuality as a cause of neuroses (see NEUROSIS). Adler advanced instead a social and biological theory in which bisexuality and the need of individuals for self-assertion (the 'masculine protest') play a central role. His best-known work is *The Practice and Theory of Individual Psychology* (1923).

**Adler, Felix,** 1851–1933, American educator and leader in social welfare; b. Germany. Founder of the Ethical Culture Movement (1876), he was for many years chairman of the National Child Labor Committee, and wrote *Creed and Deed* (1877) and *An Ethical Philosophy of Life* (1918), among other books.

**Adler, Guido,** 1855–1941, Austrian musicologist, specializing in music history and the analysis of style. He was Professor at Prague from 1885, the year in which he published a profoundly influential paper on the aims and scope of musicology, and then at Vienna from 1898, where he trained a whole generation of musicologists.

**Ado-Ekiti,** city (1981 pop. 291,200), Ondo state, S Nigeria.

**Adonis,** in Greek mythology, beautiful youth loved by APHRODITE and PERSEPHONE. When he was killed by a boar, both goddesses claimed him. ZEUS decreed that he spend half the year above the ground with Aphrodite, the other half in the underworld with Persephone. His death and resurrection, symbolic of the seasonal cycle, were celebrated at the festival Adonia. His love and death form the subject of SHAKESPEARE's *Venus and Adonis*, and have often been painted, e.g., by POUSSIN, TITIAN, and VERONESE.

**adoption,** act creating the legal relation of parent and child. It was known in antiquity but was not part of the English COMMON LAW; it was first recognized by a UK statute of 1926. Adoption's historical roots include the need to continue a family line where there is no natural heir; today the focus is usually the child's welfare. A hearing before a judge is generally required, as is consent of the natural parent or guardian and that of the child if it is above a certain age. The natural parents generally lose their rights and duties towards the child as the adoptive parents assume them. Unlike in SURROGACY no money is allowed to change hands between the parties involved. UK law now permits adoption by unmarried adults. Adoption by relatives is most common; in adoption by unrelated adults, the court attempts to help the child to adjust to its adoptive family by maintaining anonymity of the genetic parents; but since 1975 in the UK adopted children have had the right on reaching the age of 18 to learn the identity of their natural parents (if known). FOSTER CARE is an arrangement in which a family or institution provides a home for a child whose parent cannot care for it; unlike adoption, foster care is temporary.

**adrenal glands,** pair of small, flat, triangular endocrine glands (see ENDOCRINE SYSTEM) situated one on top of each kidney. The outer yellowish layer (cortex) secretes the CORTICOSTEROID hormones which regulate water and salt balance in the body (e.g., aldosterone), and carbohydrate metabolism (e.g., cortisol). The inner portion (medulla) of the adrenal glands secretes the emergency-response hormones ADRENALINE and NORADRENALINE.

**adrenaline,** hormone secreted by the medulla of the ADRENAL GLANDS. Strong emotions, such as fear and anger, produce an increase in heart rate, muscle strength, blood pressure, and glycogen metabolism (raising the concentration of glucose in the blood), causing adrenaline to be released into the bloodstream which reinforces and prolongs the acceleration of such bodily functions. See also CATECHOLAMINE.

**Adrian,** Roman emperor: see HADRIAN.

**Adrian I,** d. 795, pope (772–95). A Roman, he successfully urged CHARLEMAGNE to defeat the LOMBARDS and acquired from him additional lands for the PAPAL STATES. He supported the Byzantine empress Irene in her struggle against ICONOCLASM.

**Adrian IV,** c.1100-1159, pope (1154–59). The only Englishman to become pope, he was originally named Nicholas Breakspear. In 1155 Adrian defeated the opposition of Arnold of Brescia and crowned FREDERICK I emperor. He later quarrelled with both Fredcrick and William I of Sicily. His donation of Ireland as a fief to Henry II of England is disputed.

**Adrian, Edgar Douglas** (1st **Baron Adrian of Cambridge)** 1889–1977, English neurophysiologist. He was professor of physiology at Cambridge and shared with Sir Charles SHERRINGTON the 1932 Nobel Prize for physiology or medicine for their elucidation of the function of neurones.

**Adriatic Sea,** arm of the MEDITERRANEAN SEA, c.800 km (500 mi) long, between Italy (W) and Yugoslavia and Albania (E). It is 93–225 km (58–140 mi) wide, with a maximum depth of 1250 m (4100 ft). VENICE is the chief port.

**adsorption,** the preferential accumulation of molecules on the surfaces of solids, as opposed to ABSORPTION, in which the molecules actually enter the absorbing medium. Charcoal, for example, which has a great surface area because of its porous nature, can adsorb large volumes of gases, including most of the poisonous ones, and thus is used in gas masks and filters. ZEOLITES are effective adsorbents of both liquids and gases, and can possess internal areas of up to 500 $m^2/g$. Certain types of synthetic zeolites can convert alcoholic liquids into nonalcoholic ones by preferential adsorption.

**adult education** or **continuing education,** organized instruction provided to men and women beyond the age of general public education. The range of emphasis in adult education has come to include everything from the job-oriented (see VOCATIONAL EDUCATION) to the purely academic. Modern adult education probably began with European political groups and vocational classes. British adult education grew in the 19th cent. in the form of mechanics' institutes and working-class self-help movements, adult Sunday and other schools, evening classes and other movements. In the 20th cent. the Workers' Educational Association, the universities, the local authorities and others have developed the provision. In the US, some forms date from colonial times; Benjamin FRANKLIN was among those who established debating and discussion groups. In the 19th cent. the Lyceum and the Chautauqua Movement contributed to the growth of American adult education. Adult education today faces an increasing demand created by expanding leisure time, a highly competitive labour market, and greater population growth, especially among young adults and those past traditional retirement age. The field now embraces such diverse areas as work for GCSE and A-level examinations; physical and emotional development; practical arts; applied science; recreation; and academic, business, and professional subjects. Continuing education now includes in-house or in-service further education, return-to-study opportunities for married women, work for qualifications through the OPEN UNIVERSITY and other agencies, and informal activities of many kinds.

**Advent,** Christian penitential season, lasting in the West from the Sunday nearest 30 Nov. until Christmas. It is the first season of the church calendar.

**Adventists,** members of a group of religious denominations whose distinctive doctrine centres in their belief concerning the imminent second coming of Christ. Adventism is specifically applied to the teachings of William MILLER. The largest group, the Seventh-Day Adventists, were formally organized in 1863 and are fundamentally evangelical.

**adverb:** see PART OF SPEECH.

**advertising,** in general, any technique used to promote goods, services, or ideas through any medium of public communication. The main advertising media include newspapers, magazines, television, radio, cinemas (particularly in developing countries) and direct mail. The advertising agency, working on a commission basis, has been largely responsible for the development of modern commercial advertising. Defenders of advertising say that it is meant to sell products, not create values, and that it furthers product improvement through competition, while critics contend that it creates false values and impels people to buy things they neither need nor want. It is essential in a free market economy for a company's survival. Television advertising has been closely regulated in West European countries but since the mid-1980s more commercial time has been permitted. Prohibition on television advertising—such as for alcohol and tobacco—has proved effective in curbing consumption. The US is the world's largest spender in advertising with expenditure by its top 100 advertisers exceeding $26,000 million by the mid-1980s. The practice has now spread worldwide, however, and is seen as a measure of a country's affluence. The expertise of the advertising industry has also had a marked influence on politics as a public activity: politicians and policies now have to be marketed, in which process advertising now plays an important part. In the UK the industry is monitored by the Advertising Standards Authority, and exists within the context of a significant body of legislation which covers HIRE PURCHASE, COPYRIGHT, DEFAMATION, FAIR TRADING, RACE RELATIONS, trade descriptions, etc.

**Advisory, Conciliation and Arbitration Service (ACAS),** in the UK, an independent body established in 1975 to promote good industrial relations and to work for the extension of COLLECTIVE BARGAINING. It consists of a legally qualified chairperson, representatives of workers and management, and independent members. If offers a free service to both employers and TRADE UNIONS who may request it to conciliate or arbitrate, either in an industrial dispute (e.g., a STRIKE) or an individual dispute between a worker and an employer (e.g., a dismissal). In addition it offers advice on a wide range of industrial-relations matters, and holds inquiries on specific industrial-relations problems. It also issues codes of practice, which act as guides for both employers and trade unions on the conduct of good industrial relations.

**Ady, Endre,** 1877–1919, Hungarian poet. A lyric poet noted for original and creative use of language, he was influenced by the French SYMBOLISTS. Volumes of his poems include *New Poems* (1906) and *Leading the Dead* (1919).

**A.E.:** see RUSSELL, GEORGE WILLIAM.

**Aegean civilization** (i,jeeən), cultures of pre-Hellenic GREECE. Cultural continuity in the Aegean was broken with the rise of palace-building elites, first in Crete c.2000 BC (see MINOAN CIVILIZATION) and then on the southern Greek mainland some 400 years later (see MYCENAEAN CIVILIZATION). Other similar cultures appeared in Anatolia at TROY, and in the Cyclades. These early state-like societies had all collapsed by the end of the 13 cent. BC.

**Aegean Sea,** arm of the MEDITERRANEAN SEA, off SE Europe, between Greece and Turkey, centre of the classical Greek world. The island-studded sea is c.640 km (400 mi) long, 320 km (200 mi) wide, and more than 2010 m (6600 ft) deep off N CRETE at its southern limit. Major islands include ÉVVOIA, the Sporades, the CYCLADES, SÁMOS, KHÍOS, LESBOS, Thásos, and the DODECANESE. Sardines and sponges are taken from the sea, and some natural gas has been found off NE Greece.

**Aegisthus** (ee,jishəs), in Greek mythology, son of Thyestes. Aegisthus revenged his brothers' murder by killing his uncle ATREUS. He was later CLYTEMNESTRA's lover, helped her to slay AGAMEMNON, and was himself killed by ORESTES.

**Aeken, Jerom van:** see BOSCH, HIERONYMUS.

**Aeneas** (i,neeəs), in classical legend, a Trojan; son of Anchises and VENUS. After Troy's fall he escaped with his father and young son, had a love affair with DIDO at CARTHAGE, then went to Italy, where his descendants founded Rome. His deeds are celebrated in VERGIL's *Aeneid*.

**Aeolians** (ee,ohliən): see GREECE.

**aerial** or **antenna,** system of conductors used to transmit or receive electromagnetic waves such as used for broadcasting or for RADAR. A transmitting aerial is tuned to resonate electrically at the frequency of the transmitter feeding it, resulting in the propagation of electromagnetic waves through space which set up resonations in receiving aerials. The direction of the transmission depends upon the aerial design. For broadcast stations equal power in all direction is the aim but aerials can be designed to provide almost any directional pattern: radar and certain communication systems require a single narrow beam no more than one degree wide. This can be achieved by the use of parabolic dishes with the aerial element mounted at the focal point. These may be any size between about 0.5 m (1½ ft) and 90 m (300 ft) depending upon the application.

**aerobatics,** manoeuvres performed with aircraft other than those required for normal flight. The first aerobatics were inadvertent; the earliest recorded intentional instance was a loop performed in California in the summer of 1913, and aerobatics were first performed in public in Britain in Sept. 1913. The first World Aerobatic Championships were held in Paris in 1934. The championships are now based on a repertoire of 8000 different aerobatic movements, and are performed with specialist aircraft.

**aerodynamics,** study of gases in motion. Because the principal application of aerodynamics is to the design of AEROPLANES, air is the principal gas with which this science is concerned. Bernoulli's principle, which states that the pressure of a moving gas decreases as its velocity increases, has been used to explain the lift produced by a wing having a curved upper surface and a flat lower surface (see AEROFOIL). Because the flow is faster across the curved surface than across the flat one, a greater pressure is exerted in the upward direction. Aerodynamics is also concerned with the drag caused by air friction, which is reduced by making the surface area of the craft as small as possible. At speeds close to the speed of sound, or Mach 1 (see MACH NUMBER), there is also a large, sudden increase of drag, which has been called the sonic, or sound, barrier. Aerodynamics is also used in designing car bodies and trains for minimum drag and in computing wind stresses on bridges, buildings, and the like. The WIND TUNNEL is one of the basic experimental tools of the aerodynamicist. See SHOCK WAVE; SONIC BOOM.

**aerofoil,** shaped, structural surface of an aircraft's wing, control surface, or airscrew blade. It is designed to be moved through the air so as to produce an aerodynamic force (in particular, lift or thrust) at right angles to its direction of motion.

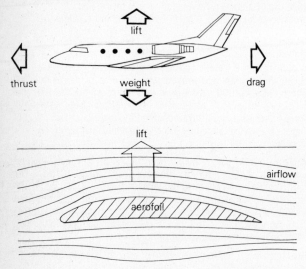

Aerofoil

**aeronautics:** see AERODYNAMICS; AEROPLANE; AVIATION.

**aeroplane,** powered, heavier-than-air craft supported in flight by fixed wings. There are many types, including landplanes, seaplanes (with floats for alighting on water), amphibians (with fixed floats and retractable wheeled undercarriage), monoplanes (with a single set of mainplanes), biplanes (two wings), and triplanes (three wings), all of which derive their lift from aerodynamic force (for other flying craft see AIRCRAFT). The first aeroplane to fly successfully was a biplane built by Orville and Wilbur WRIGHT, which on 17 Dec. 1903 made four flights (see FLIGHT, POWERED). The earliest aeroplanes were mostly biplanes of wood construction, based on bridge-building principles; as knowledge of AERODYNAMICS and of structures increased, the MONOPLANE gradually replaced the biplane, especially from the mid-1930s when stressed-skin metal construction had been successfully developed. An aeroplane has six main parts: fuselage, wings, tail plane, fin, and rudder (these last two sometimes together called the empennage), engine, and undercarriage. Aeroplanes may be classified as driven by propeller, JET PROPULSION, or ROCKET. With the use of jet engines and the resulting higher speeds, aeroplanes have become less dependent on large values of lift from the wings, and consequently wing spans have been shortened and swept-back so as to produce less drag, especially at supersonic speeds. At the trailing edge of the wings are attached movable surfaces called ailerons that are used for lateral control and to turn the aircraft. Directional stability is provided by the tail fin(s), one or more fixed vertical aerofoils at the rear of the aeroplane. The tail

plane is a fixed horizontal aerofoil at the rear, used to suppress undesired pitching motion; attached to it are the elevators, which produce control in the vertical plane. On a delta-wing aircraft (e.g., CONCORDE), the ailerons and elevators are combined into 'elevons'. The rudder, generally at the rear of the tail fin, is a movable control surface which gives the craft a yawing movement in normal flight. The undercarriage is usually retractable to reduce airborne drag. Up till the 1930s most land undercarriages comprised main wheels towards the front of the aircraft, plus tail-skids or tail-wheels; but from the early 1940s onwards landplanes were increasingly produced with tricycle undercarriages, usually with a steerable front wheel. See AIR FORCES; AIR TRANSPORT.

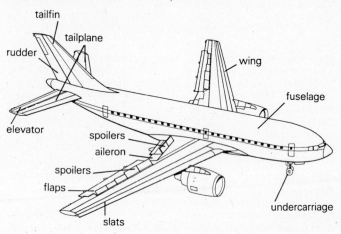

Aeroplane

**aerosol,** COLLOID in which small solid or liquid particles are suspended in a gas. Natural aerosols such as fog or smoke occur throughout the ATMOSPHERE, which is itself an aerosol. The term is also used to describe a container of paint, insecticide, or other substance held under pressure by a propellant, which releases the substance in the form of a fine spray or foam. The fluorocarbon FREON was until recently the most common aerosol propellant, but its use has diminished because it contributes to the destruction of the OZONE layer of the stratosphere.

**Aeschines,** c.390–314? BC, Athenian orator. He became politically powerful through his oratorical gifts. Opposing resistance to PHILIP II of Macedon, he was the bitter rival of DEMOSTHENES.

**Aeschylus** (ˌeskiləs), 525–456 BC, Athenian tragic poet. First of the three great Greek tragedians, he preceded SOPHOCLES and EURIPIDES. He wrote perhaps 90 plays, of which seven survive intact. Often credited with inventing TRAGEDY, he added a second actor to what had been a dialogue between actor and CHORUS, thus increasing its dramatic possibilities. His choral lyrics rank with those of PINDAR. Among his best-known plays are *The Seven against Thebes* and *Prometheus Bound (though his authorship of the latter has been challenged)*. His only extant trilogy, the *Oresteia,* a history of the house of ATREUS, is considered by many the greatest Attic tragedy.

**Aesop** (ˌeesop), semilegendary ancient Greek fabulist, supposedly a slave. The FABLES called Aesop's were preserved by various writers and include 'The Fox and the Grapes' and 'The Tortoise and the Hare'.

**aesthetics** (es; əs; eesˌthetiks), branch of philosophy dealing with the nature of art and the criteria of artistic judgment. The conception of art as imitation of nature was formulated by PLATO and developed by ARISTOTLE, both of whom held that beauty inheres in the object itself and may be judged objectively. KANT held that the subject may have universal validity, while other thinkers, e.g., HUME, identified beauty with that which pleases the observer. Modern philosophers especially concerned with aesthetic questions have included CROCE, CASSIRER, John DEWEY, and SANTAYANA.

**aestivation** ('eestiˌvaysh(ə)n), protective practice by poikilotherms (fishes, amphibians, and reptiles) of passing adversely dry conditions in a state of dormancy, as other animals spend cold winters in HIBERNATION. LUNGFISHes and TORTOISES will bury themselves in mud or tuck themselves under ledges when the water in which they live dries up in hot weather.

South African lungfish surround themselves with a cocoon of mucus that hardens as it dries, softening in rain to release the fish.

**Æthelbert** (ˌethəlbuht), d. 616, king of Kent (r.560?–616). Although he was defeated (568) by the West Saxons, he later became overlord of the South English for c.30 years, and married Bertha, daughter of the king of Paris. In 597 he was converted to Christianity by St AUGUSTINE OF CANTERBURY and became the first Christian king of Anglo-Saxon England.

**Æthelbert** (ˌethəlbuht), d. 865, king of WESSEX (r.860–65), son of ÆTHELWULF. After his father's death in 858, he ruled KENT, Surrey, SUSSEX, and ESSEX, reuniting them with Wessex when in 860 he succeeded his brother Æthelbald in that kingdom.

**Æthelflæd** or **Ethelfleda**, (ˌethəlfled), d. 918, daughter of ALFRED and wife of Æthelred, ealdorman of MERCIA. After her husband's death in 911, she ruled the semi-independent Mercia alone and was known as the Lady of the Mercians.

**Æthelred** (ˌethəlred), 965–1016, king of England (r. 978–1016), called Æthelred the Unready [Old Eng., = without counsel]. He was the son of EDGAR, and the half-brother and successor of Edward the Martyr. A weak king, he reigned at the height of Danish power. Although he began paying tribute through the DANEGELD to the Danes in 991, they returned in 997 to plunder his realm, staying until 1000. In 1002 Æthelred married Emma, sister of the duke of Normandy, possibly hoping to gain an ally. Although by 1009 a navy existed, the treason of its commanders rendered it useless. In 1013 the Danish king SWEYN returned to conquer; he was well received in the DANELAW and London capitulated. Æthelred fled to Normandy but was restored in 1014 on Sweyn's death. In 1016 Æthelred's son EDMUND IRONSIDE succeeded him, made a treaty with CANUTE, son of Sweyn, and died. Canute succeeded him and married Æthelred's widow.

**Æthelstan:** see ATHELSTAN.

**Æthelwulf** (ˌethəlwoolf), d. 858, king of WESSEX (r.839–56), son of EGBERT and father of ÆTHELBERT and ALFRED. With his son Æthelbald, he won a notable victory over the Danes at Aclea (851). He married Judith of France in 856. A man of great piety, he learned while on a pilgrimage in Rome that Æthelbald would resist his return. He left his son as king in Wessex and ruled in Kent and its dependencies.

**aether** (ˌeethə): see ETHER, in physics.

**Aetna:** see ETNA.

**Aetolia** (eeˌtohlyə), region of ancient GREECE, N of the gulfs of Corinth and Calydon, E of the Achelous R. It was the centre of the **Aetolian League**, formed in the 4th cent. BC to oppose the Achaean League (see under ACHAEA) and the Macedonians. With Rome it defeated PHILIP V of Macedon (197 BC), but then it allied itself against Rome with Antiochus III of Syria. His defeat (189 BC) marked the end of the league's power.

**affect,** a term in psychology and ethology to denote internal states, or aspects of internal states, of organisms. These may involve emotion, feeling, motivation, and mood.

**affines,** persons related through marriage. See ALLIANCE; KINSHIP; MARRIAGE.

**Afghani, Jamal al-Din,** 1839–97, islamic reformist. An Iranian by origin, this enigmatic advocate of Pan-Islamism and anti-British politics wielded an important if short-lived influence at the Ottoman and Persion courts. More durable was his influence on Islamic reform in Egypt and India, and his ideas are still influential in Islamist politics.

**Afghanistan,** officially the Republic of Afghanistan, republic (1984 est. pop. 17,150,000 of whom 3,000,000 living in Pakistan and 1,000,000 living in Iran), 647,497 km² (249,999 sq mi), S central Asia, bordered by Iran (W), Pakistan (E and S), the USSR (N), and China (NE). Principal cities include KABUL (the capital), KANDAHAR, and HERAT. Most of Afghanistan is mountainous, and the towering ranges of the HINDU KUSH reach a height of more than 7315 m (24,000 ft); fertile valleys and plains, home of most of the population, nestle in the mountains. The land is mainly dry, and the rivers (unnavigable for the most part) are used for irrigation. Agriculture is the mainstay of the economy, although less than 10% of the land is cultivated; corn, barley, rice, and fruit are grown, and sheep are raised for skins, wool, and meat. Industry and development of minerals are still in their early stages. Imports (mostly manufactured goods) greatly exceed exports (wool, hides, fruit). The population is diverse, including Afghans, Pathans, Hazararas, Tadzhiks, Uzbeks, and

nomadic Turkmen; almost all are Muslims. Afghan and Iranian are the principal languages.

*History.* Afghanistan, astride the land route to India (through the famed KHYBER PASS), has fallen to many conquerors through the ages, e.g., Darius I (c.500 BC); Alexander the Great (329–327 BC); and numerous Arab invaders (from the 7th cent. AD), who established Islam as the dominant culture. Mahmud of Ghazni, who conquered (11th cent.) an empire stretching from Iran to India, was the greatest of Afghanistan's rulers. The country was later conquered by Jenghiz Khan (c.1220) and Tamerlane (14th cent.). Afghanistan became a united state (1747) under Ahmad Shah, who founded the Durani dynasty. During the 19th cent. Britain, to protect its empire in India against Russian expansion, attempted to establish authority in neighbouring Afghanistan; the result was two British-Afghan Wars (1838–42, 1878–80). An agreement in 1907 gave Britain control over Afghanistan's foreign affairs, but in 1919 the emir Amanullah engaged Britain in a third Afghan War, which gave Afghanistan full independence. Amanullah embarked on a sweeping programme of modernization, and in 1926 proclaimed a monarchy to replace the emirate. The last king, Muhammad Zahir Shah, was overthrown in 1973 in a military coup led by Lt Gen. Muhammad Daoud Khan, who proclaimed a republic. Daoud was killed in a coup in 1978 and a Marxist regime installed, headed by the People's Democratic Party of Afghanistan (PDPA). In 1979 a Soviet-backed coup, supported by an invasion of Soviet troops, killed president Hafizulla Amin and replaced him with Babrak Karmal, leader of a rival PDPA faction. Over 4 million Afghans fled to Iran and Pakistan, but strong resistance from rebel MUJAHEDDIN forces within the country continued. Despite international pressure, an estimated 100,000 Soviet troops remained in the embattled country. In 1986, apparently at Soviet instigation, Karmal was replaced by Maj.-Gen. Mohammad Najibullah, who in early 1987 offered the insurgents a ceasefire. A partial political liberalization followed, and in 1988 an international agreement was concluded providing for the withdrawal of Soviet troops. This happened in 1989.

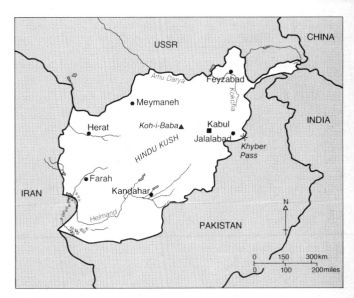

Afghanistan

**AFL-CIO:** see AMERICAN FEDERATION OF LABOR AND CONGRESS OF INDUSTRIAL ORGANIZATIONS.

**Africa,** second largest continent, c.30,244,050 km² (11,677,240 sq mi) including Madagascar and smaller offshore islands. It is connected to Asia by the narrow Isthmus of Suez. Mt Kibo (5895 m/19,340 ft), a peak of KILIMANJARO, in Tanzania, is the highest point; the lowest point, 133 m (436 ft) below sea level, is the Qattarah Depression, in Egypt. E Africa's lake-filled GREAT RIFT VALLEY is the continent's most spectacular feature. Mountain ranges include the ATLAS MOUNTAINS (N), the Ethiopian Highlands and Ruwenzori Mts (E), and the Drakensberg Mts. (S). Chief rivers are the NILE, CONGO (Zaïre), NIGER, and ZAMBEZI. Climatic conditions range from hot and rainy all year near the equator, through tropical savanna with alternating wet and dry seasons immediately north and south of the equatorial region, to hot and dry in the great SAHARA desert, in the north, and the smaller KALAHARI desert, in the south. At its north and south extremities the continent has a Mediterranean-type climate. The countries of Africa are Algeria, Angola, Benin, Botswana, Burkina Faso, Burundi, Cameroon, Cape Verde, the Central African Republic, Chad, The Comoros, the Congo Republic, Côte d'Ivoire Djibouti, Egypt, Equatorial Guinea, Ethiopia, Gabon, Gambia, Ghana, Guinea, Guinea-Bissau, Kenya, Lesotho, Liberia, Libya, Madagascar, Malawi, Mali, Mauritania, Mauritius, Morocco, Mozambique, Niger, Nigeria, Réunion, Rwanda, St Helena, São Tomé and Principe, Senegal, the Seychelles, Sierra Leone, the Somali Republic, the Republic of South Africa, Sudan, Swaziland, Tanzania, Togo, Tunisia, Uganda, Zaïre, Zambia, and Zimbabwe; other political units are Namibia and Western Sahara (see separate articles). African peoples, who make up about 10% of the world's population, are divided into more than 50 states and are further fragmented into numerous ethnic and linguistic groups (see AFRICAN LANGUAGES). See map of Africa in separate section.

**African art,** traditional art created by peoples S of the Sahara. The predominant art forms are MASKS and figures, which were generally used in religious ceremonies. The decorative arts, especially as used in TEXTILES and in the ornamentation of everyday tools, were a vital part of nearly all African cultures. Established forms evolved long before the arrival (15th cent.) of the Portuguese in Africa, but most works older than 150 years have perished. Their creators valued them for ritual use rather than aesthetic accomplishment. Wood, often embellished with clay, shells, beads, ivory, metal, feathers, and shredded raffia was the dominant material. In the Sudan and on the Guinea coast the wood-carving style was highly abstract. Distortion often emphasized features of cultic significance. The Bambara of W Mali are famous for their striking wooden headdresses in the form of antelope heads. In NW Guinea the Baga made snake carvings, drums supported by small standing figures, and spectacular masks. The southern Senufu people of the Ivory Coast made masks representing human features with geometric projections and legs jutting out of each side of the face. During the 18th and 19th cent. the ASHANTI kingdom of Ghana used a system of brass weights to weigh gold dust; these weights were small figures cast in CIRE PERDUE. From N Nigeria, the remarkable Nok terra-cotta heads are the earliest African sculpture yet found (c.500–200 BC). The art of the Yoruba of S Nigeria is often brilliantly coloured. On the banks of the Middle Cross R. are about 300 monolithic carvings, supposedly Ekoi ancestor figures from between 1600 and 1900. The small tribes of the Cameroon did wood carvings and sculptures that include large house posts and ritual objects. Among the Fang tribes of Gabon, decorative motifs on stringed musical instruments emphasized the human figure. The Bapende of W Zaïre made ivory pendants portraying human faces, while the Baluba of SE Zaïre produced bowls and stools supported by slender figures. The dynamic and expressive free-standing figures of the Badjokwe of S Zaïre and Angola are particularly outstanding. Paintings in caves and rock shelters in southern Africa are not always easy to date; some in the Cape show the arrival of white people and their domestic animals. African art came to European notice c.1905, and such artists as PICASSO and MODIGLIANI were influenced by it.

**African languages,** geographic rather than linguistic classification of languages spoken on the African continent. These languages do not belong to a single family but are divided among several distinct linguistic stocks having no common origin. The principal linguistic families of Africa are now generally said to be Hamito-Semitic; Niger-Kordofanian (including Niger-Congo); Nilo-Saharan; and Khoisan, or Click. Two other stocks, Indo-European and Malayo-Polynesian, are also represented. For a more detailed categorization of the languages of Africa, see the table accompanying this article.

**African musics.** The composers and composer–performers of sub-Saharan Africa have expressed with many different techniques, styles, and timbres the contrasting attributes of vitality and gentleness, full-bodied texture and tonal clarity, public display and individual participation. These are related to the value that was placed on developing individuality in community, whether in large kingdoms or small bands of hunter–gatherers. Common features of indigenous musical traditions are therefore call–response (solo–chorus) structures in vocal and instrumental pieces, allowing for improvization and innovation chiefly in the solo sections; polyphonic part-singing and -playing in which melodies and harmonic textures are produced from combinations of single tones or short motifs by the cooperation of different performers or the coordination of, say, left and right thumbs and forefingers on the strings of a lyre or the metal tongues of Africa's most distinctive musical instrument, the *mbira* or 'hand-piano'; balanced shifts of tonality throughout a composition and the attribution of melodic equality to each tone's 'harmonically equivalent' tone; and uneven groupings of notes in metrical patterns (e.g., short–short–long–short–long), which allow individual performers to pick out and emphasize a variety of pulses and rhythms when they are combined in a polyrhythmic texture. These features are found even in those parts of sub-Saharan Africa where Islamic influence has been strong, as well as in modern urban musical genres and in the music of the African diaspora. Also, many types of SCALE and MODE are used, with four, five, six, and seven tones to the octave and in several cases chromatic intervals. People have often forgotten or have enshrined in myth the names of the original composers of types of communal music that have become established social conventions; but the names of contemporary and recently deceased composers of particular pieces are known, whether or not they are semi-professional or professional musicians. There are some broad similarities in the styles of composers from different cultural and language zones in West, East, central, and southern Africa; but classifications of instruments, systems of music theory, aesthetics and canons of criticism vary considerably, even within contiguous regions.

African art: Benin pectoral mask

**African National Congress** (ANC), black nationalist movement, est. in 1912, seeking political rights for blacks in SOUTH AFRICA and opposing APARTHEID policies of the government. Banned in 1960 following the

## MAJOR AFRICAN LANGUAGES (*Asterisk indicates a dead language*)

### Hamito-Semitic or Afroasiatic Languages (*for Hamito-Semitic languages that were or are spoken in W Asia, see the Hamito-Semitic classification in the table "Major Languages of Europe, Asia, and Some Islands of the Pacific and Indian Oceans" accompanying the LANGUAGE article*)

SEMITIC (spoken in North Africa and Ethiopia)

| | |
|---|---|
| Arabic | Egyptian Arabic, Western Arabic |
| Ethiopic | Amharic (or Abyssinian), Geez, (Classical Ethiopic),* Tigre, Tigrinya |

HAMITIC

| | |
|---|---|
| Egyptian (was spoken in Egypt) | Ancient Egyptian,* Coptic* |
| Berber (spoken throughout North Africa except Egypt) | Kabyle, Modern Berber, Rif, Siwi, Tamachek, Tuareg, Zanaga |
| Cushitic (spoken in Ethiopia and adjoining regions) | Agau, Beja, Burji, Galla, Geleba, Gimira, Janjaro, Kaffa, Konso, Maji, Saho-Afar, Sidamo, Somali |
| CHAD (spoken near Lake Chad, central Africa, and in W Africa) | Angas, Bolewa, Gwandara, Hausa, Hiji, Kuseri, Mandara, Ngala, Ron, Shirawa, Sokoro |

### Indo-European Languages (*for a full presentation of the Indo-European language family, see table accompanying the LANGUAGE article*)

GERMANIC

| | |
|---|---|
| West Germanic *Low German* | Afrikaans (spoken in the Republic of South Africa), English (spoken in the Republic of South Africa, Zimbabwe, and a number of other African countries) |

ITALIC

| | |
|---|---|
| Romance (spoken in a number of African countries) | French, Italian, Portuguese, Spanish |

### Khoisan or Click Languages (*spoken in S and E Africa*)

| | |
|---|---|
| | Hatsa (or Hadzapi), Sandawe |
| SOUTH AFRICAN KHOISAN | Bushman, Hottentot |

### Malayo-Polynesian Languages (*spoken in Madagascar; for a full presentation of the Malayo-Polynesian language family, see table accompanying the LANGUAGE article*)

| | |
|---|---|
| WESTERN | Malagasy |

### Niger-Kordofanian Languages

NIGER-CONGO (spoken in S and central Africa and in W Africa below the Sahara)

| | |
|---|---|
| West Atlantic | Dyola, Fulani, Gola, Kissi, Temne, Wolof |
| Mande | Dyula, Malinke, Mende |
| Gur (or Voltaic) | Dagomba, Mamprusi, Mossi |
| Kwa | Akan, Ashanti, Bini, Ewe, Ibo, Ijo, Nupe, Yoruba |
| Benue-Congo *Bantu* | Bemba, Ganda, Kikuyu, Kongo, Lingala, Luba, Makua, Mbundu, Ruanda, Rundi, Shona, Sotho, Swahili, Thonga, Xhosa, Zulu |
| *Non-Bantu* | Efik, Jukun, Tiv |
| Adamawa-Eastern | Banda, Sango, Zande |

KORDOFANIAN (spoken in Sudan)

| | |
|---|---|
| Katla | Katla |
| Koalib | Koalib |
| Talodi | Talodi |
| Tegali | Tegali |
| Tumtum | Tumtum |

### Nilo-Saharan Languages

| | |
|---|---|
| SONGHAI (spoken in Mali) | Songhai |
| SAHARAN (spoken near Lake Chad and in the central Sahara) | Daza, Kanuri, Teda, Zaghawa |
| MABAN (spoken east of Lake Chad) | Maba |
| FURIAN (spoken in Sudan) | Fur |
| KOMAN (spoken in Ethiopia and Sudan) | Ganza, Gule, Gumuz, Koma, Mao, Uduk |
| CHARI-NILE (spoken in Sudan, Zaïre, Uganda, Cameroon, Chad, Central African Republic, mainland Tanzania, and Ethiopia) | |
| Eastern Sudanic *Nubian* | Birked, Midobi |
| *Nilotic* | Dinka, Masai, Nandi, Nuer, Shilluk, Suk, Turkana |
| Central Sudanic | Bongo-Bagirmi, Efe, Mangbetu Berta, Kunama |

SHARPEVILLE massacre, the ANC developed into an active guerrilla movement; it is supported by the governments of the neighbouring African states. See also MANDELA, Nelson.

**African literature.** Although ancient African Muslim books in Swahili and Arabic exist, African literature before the 19th cent. comprises almost entirely a great oral tradition. The continent's seemingly inexhaustible supply of myths, tales, legends, riddles, and proverbs continues to enrich new African writing, which appears in native, especially Bantu, languages, and in French, English, and Portuguese. The African writer best known before the 1930s was probably the South African Thomas Mofolo, whose novels (in Sesotho) included *Chaka* (tr. 1931). French-

African writers in Paris in the 1930s, led by the poet-statesman Léopold Sédar SENGHOR, espoused *négritude,* a rejection of French assimilationist policy. After World War II, writers focused on decaying colonialism and on the 'new' Africa. National literatures began to appear, notably in Nigeria with the work of Chinua ACHEBE, Wole SOYINKA, Amos TUTUOLA, and others, and in Senegal and Cameroon. Major African writers in English include Ezekiel Mphahlele and Oswald Mtshali (South Africa), Bessie Head (Botswana), Ayi Kwei Armah (Ghana), and Ngugi wa Thiong'o (Kenya) and Okot p'Bitek (Uganda). Among leading writers in French are Mongo Beti (Cameroon); Camara Laye (Guinea); Birago Diop, Sembene Ousmane, and Mariama Ba (Senegal); David Diop (born in

France), and Tchicaya U Tamsi (Congo). One of the best-known writers in Portuguese was Agostinho Neto (1922–79), president of Angola (1975–79).

**African violet**, common name for plants (mostly hybrids of *Saintpaulia ionantha*) of the GESNERIA family, grown chiefly as houseplants for their colourful flowers and ease of regeneration from leaf cuttings.

**Afrikaans** (afri̦kahnz), one of the official languages of South Africa. It is a Germanic language of the Indo-European family. See AFRICAN LANGUAGES (table).

**Afro-Americans:** see BLACK AMERICANS.

**Ag,** chemical symbol of the element SILVER.

**Agadir Crisis,** diplomatic incident in 1911–12. The crisis began when the German gunboat *Panther* was sent to the Moroccan port of Agadir to test Britain's readiness to stand by France. Anglo-French solidarity led to a German climb-down in 1912.

**Agaja,** 1673–1740, king (r.1708–40) of Dahomey (now BENIN). He expanded his small state by conquest to include the kingdoms of Alada and Whydah but in 1730 was forced to submit as a vassal to the *Oni* of Oyo.

**Aga Khan III,** 1877–1957, Muslim leader. As hereditary leader of the Muslim Isma'ili sect he was born to great power and wealth. He supported the British in India, co-founded (1906) the All-India Muslim League, and represented India in various international bodies.

**agama,** LIZARD of the family Agamidae, found throughout Africa, Asia, and Australia. The common agama (*Agama agama*) of Africa is about 30 cm (1 ft) long and has adapted to living in humans' homes and feeding on scraps. Other species include the flying lizard (*Draco*) and the frilled lizard (*Chlamydosaurus*) and the MOLOCH. Most agamas are insectivorous and can change colour. The dominant male common agama has a bright red head that fades to brown if he is frightened.

The South Indian **agama**

**Agamemnon,** in Greek mythology, leader of the Greeks in the TROJAN WAR; brother of MENELAUS; son of ATREUS. His children by CLYTEMNESTRA were IPHIGENIA, ELECTRA, and ORESTES. To obtain favourable winds for the fleet against Troy, he sacrificed Iphigenia to ARTEMIS, incurring Clytemnestra's hatred. At Troy he quarrelled with ACHILLES; that dispute forms a main theme of HOMER's *Iliad*. He withdrew from the war and returned to Mycenae, where he was murdered by Clytemnestra and her lover, AEGISTHUS. To avenge his death, Orestes and Electra killed Aegisthus and their mother. The story is told in AESCHYLUS's trilogy *The Oresteia*, and has inspired later plays, e.g., Eugene O'NEILL's *Mourning Becomes Electra* (1931).

**agar,** product obtained from some red ALGAE species (see SEAWEED). Dissolved in boiling water and cooled, agar becomes gelatinous; it is used as a culture medium in microbiology, a laxative, and a food thickener.

**Agassiz, Louis** (̦agəsee), (Jean Louis Rodolphe Agassiz) 1807–73, Swiss naturalist, geologist and teacher who had great influence on the study of natural sciences. He moved from Switzerland to the US in 1846, where he opened an experimental school of biology. His writings include *Research on Fossil Fishes* (1843), the series *Nomenclator Zoologicus*, which he started, and later works on the natural history of North America. His son, **Alexander Agassiz,** 1835–1910, was a marine zoologist and oceanographer who studied coral reefs worldwide, his expeditions including one to the Great Barrier Reef.

**agate,** extremely fine-grained variety of CHALCEDONY, banded in two or more colours. The banding occurs because agates are formed by the slow deposition of silica from solution into cavities of older rocks. Agates are found primarily in Brazil, Uruguay, India, Mexico, and the US. They are valued as semiprecious GEMS and are used in the manufacture of grinding equipment.

**agave,** common and generic name for members of the family Agavaceae, succulent plants native to tropical America. They are widely grown as greenhouse perennials and also as striking accent plants in modern garden design. They are of economic importance, providing fibre (see SISAL HEMP), soap, food, and alcoholic beverages.

**Agee, James,** 1909–55, American writer. His works include *Let Us Now Praise Famous Men* (1941), a telling commentary on Depression-era tenant farmers, and *A Death in the Family* (1957), a poetic novel. His movie criticism and scripts are collected in *Agee on Film* (2 vol., 1958–60).

**age-grade** and **age-set,** types of social groups. In some tribal societies age is a crucial factor in social organization, one which cuts across kinship and descent ties. In an *age-set* system a whole age cohort (usually only males) is grouped together into one, named, status group which has elements of a corporate group: its members are initiated together, and subsequently take on certain ceremonial or political functions, etc. Individuals remain members of the same specified group throughout their lives. In an *age-grade* system, individuals, as they age, move through a structure composed of different age-defined statuses.

**agglutination,** in linguistics: see INFLECTION.

**Agha Khan:** see ISMA' ILIS.

**Agha Muhammad Khan** or **Aga Muhammad Khan,** 1742–97, shah of PERSIA (1796–97), founder of the Kajar, or Qajar, dynasty. In 1794 he killed the last ruler of the Zand dynasty and ended his campaign for the throne with a wholesale massacre. Hated by his subjects for his brutality, he was assassinated.

**Agincourt** (̦ajin'kawt), village (1975 pop. 310), N France, where in 1415 Henry V of England defeated an army of French knights in the HUNDRED YEARS WAR. The victory of Henry's longbow men made obsolete the methods of warfare of the age of chivalry and enabled the English to conquer much of France.

**aging:** see GERIATRICS; GERONTOLOGY.

**agnates,** persons whose kinship connections are traced through the male line. See DESCENT; LINEAGE.

**Agnew, Spiro Theodore,** 1918–, 39th vice president of the US. Baltimore co. executive (1962–66) and governor of Maryland (1967–69), he was vice president (1969–73) in the Republican administration of Pres. Richard M. NIXON. An outspoken critic of liberals and VIETNAM WAR protestors, he resigned (10 Oct. 1973) after evidence was uncovered of political corruption during his years in Maryland politics. He pleaded no contest to the charge of evading income tax, was sentenced to three years' probation, and was fined $10,000. In 1981 a state court ordered Agnew to repay Maryland over $248,000, for bribes he took while in state office.

**Agnon, S(hmuel) Y(osef)** (ag̦nohn), 1888–1970, Israeli writer; b. Poland as Samuel Josef Czaczkes. Regarded as the greatest modern writer of fiction in Hebrew, he shared the 1966 Nobel Prize in literature. His novels and short stories explore many aspects of Jewish life; they include the novels *The Bridal Canopy* (1919) and *The Day Before Yesterday* (1945).

**agnosticism** (ag̦nostisizəm), form of scepticism that holds that the existence of God cannot be known. Agnosticism is not to be confused with ATHEISM, which denies the existence of God. KANT and Herbert SPENCER considered themselves agnostics.

**Agra,** former province, N central India. The presidency, or province, of Agra was created in 1833 by the British. In 1902 it became part of the United Provinces of Agra and Oudh. The city of **Agra** (1981 pop. 694,191), Uttar Pradesh state, is on the Jamuna (Jumna) R. A district administrative headquarters, it produces shoes, cotton, carpets, and other goods. AKBAR founded Agra, and it was later a MOGUL capital. The British annexed it in 1836. It is noted for its architecture, especially the TAJ MAHAL.

**agrarian laws,** in ancient Rome, the laws regulating the disposition of public lands. Wealthy patricians tended to gain and hold large areas of public land, nominally as state tenants. The poorer classes' desire to gain public land gave rise to laws, beginning in the 5th cent. BC, that included the Licinian Rogations (367 BC; see LICINIUS, fl. 375 BC), and the Sempronian Law (133 BC; revived 123 BC). They were often violated or ignored. The reform movement ended with DOMITIAN's edict (AD c.82) assigning title to public land in Italy to those who held it. This confirmed the long trend toward the dependency of the poor upon the powerful.

**agriculture,** practice of crop and livestock production, including AGRONOMY, HORTICULTURE, animal husbandry, and DAIRYING. Being concerned with the provision of food, agriculture has been basically responsible for the progress of human social evolution. Its development allowed the establishment of stable settlements, and the creation of food surpluses gave time for development of the arts and skills which are the basis of civilization. In Europe after the Renaissance, horticultural knowledge expanded rapidly and farming methods improved. The later invention of machines such as the reaper, tractor, and combine harvester, and the availability of energy from oil led to mechanized, large-scale farming. The economy of a developing country is always based on agriculture, e.g., in 1800 nearly 90% of the US population was engaged in agriculture, whereas at the present time only about 3% are directly concerned in food production, even so leaving a large surplus for export. In advanced countries government subsidies and modern techniques have caused the accumulation of huge food surpluses (the so-called 'food mountains') in spite of famine in some Third World states, and the subsidies have become a major political issue. Revival of interest in free market economies has made it necessary for farmers to consider alternative or additional ways of maintaining profits, e.g., new crops; luxury, ethnic, and health foods; craft products; game farming in association with woodland management; horse-breeding and riding stables; fish farming; added value from on-farm processing; and the use of land for building or recreational purposes.

**agronomy,** branch of AGRICULTURE concerned with land management and with the breeding, physiology, and production of major field crops. It deals mainly with large-scale crops (e.g., the cereals and forages), while HORTICULTURE concerns fruits, vegetables, and ornamentals.

**Aguascalientes,** (agwa'skal,yentez), city (1979 est. pop. 257,179), central Mexico, capital of Aguascalientes state. Founded in 1575 and situated on the main route N from Mexico City it has traditionally been an important commercial centre and more recently has attracted a range of industries. It has a university and its local hot springs are the origin of the city's name.

**Aguinaldo, Emilio** (agwee,naldoh), 1869–1964, Philippine leader. After leading (1896) a rebellion against Spanish rule, he cooperated with US forces in the SPANISH–AMERICAN WAR. He later rebelled (1899–1901) against US rule.

**Ahab,** d. c.853 BC, king of Israel (r. c.874–c.853 BC), son and successor of Omri. One of the greatest kings of the northern kingdom, he was killed in a war against Damascus. The biblical account of Ahab's reign (1 Kings 16.28–22.40) is mostly concerned with its religious aspects, especially his marriage to Jezebel, a willful woman of Tyre who was attached to foreign cults and behaviour. To the devout she represented evil, and she met her match in ELIJAH.

**AH (anno hegirae):** see HIJRA.

**Ahasuerus** (ə'hazyooh,iərəs): see ESTHER; XERXES.

**Ahaz,** d. c.727 BC, king of Judah (r. c.731–727 BC). His reign marked the end of the real independence of Judah. In the BIBLE he is opposed by ISAIAH for his alliance with Assyria against Israel and Syria, and denounced for having heathen abominations and for using the Temple gold to pay tribute to Assyria. 2 Kings 16; 2 Chron. 28; Isa. 7.

**Ahlin, Lars** (a,leen), 1915–, Swedish novelist noted for his psychological realism and concern with spiritual values. His principal works are *If* (1946) and *Bark and Leaves* (1961).

**Ahmed,** sultans of the OTTOMAN EMPIRE (Turkey). **Ahmed I,** 1590–1617 (r.1603–17), made peace (1606) with Austria, agreeing to Transylvania's independence and recognizing other European rulers as his equals for the first time. **Ahmed II,** 1642–95 (r.1691–95), saw the beginning of the Turks' forced retreat from Hungary. **Ahmed III,** 1673–1736

(r.1703–30), seized (1715) the Peloponnesus and the Ionian Isles (except Corfu) from Venice, but he lost important Balkan territories to Austria. He was overthrown by the JANISSARIES and died in prison.

**Ahmedabad** or **Ahmadabad,** city (1981 pop. 2,159,127), capital of Gujarat state, NW India, on the Sabarmati R. It is an industrial centre noted for its cotton mills. Founded in 1412, it fell to AKBAR in 1573 and prospered under the MUGHALS. It was famous for very fine muslin. The British traded there from 1619 and controlled the city by the 19th cent. It has many mosques, tombs, and temples, including the Jama Masjid, a Hindu temple converted (15th cent.) to a mosque.

**Ahura Mazdah** [Pers., = Lord of Light], name of the supreme deity in ZOROASTRIANISM. He is perfect in wisdom, purity, and goodness, and opposes the powerful force of 'Evil Spirit' Angra Mainyu.

**AID** or **artificial insemination by donor:** see ARTIFICIAL INSEMINATION.

**AIDS** or **acquired immune deficiency syndrome,** disease of viral origin in which the body's immune system (see IMMUNITY) is damaged and so may succumb to many rare infections to which the body is normally resistant. The human retrovirus which causes AIDS is now known as the human immunodeficiency VIRUS (HIV) and was identified in 1983. It is not yet known how many of the people infected (who can be identified by a test which determines the presence in the blood of antibodies to the virus) will go on to develop the disease itself. Present estimates of at least 30% are based on only a few years' study of the disease, which was first reported in the UK in 1981. The period between infection and the appearance of symptoms is often a number of years, but death from a collection of opportunistic infections (including a rare strain of pneumonia and a rare form of cancer known as Kaposi's sarcoma) follows within two or three years. These infections take advantage of the deficiency of white blood cells, which attack infection, caused by the virus. The virus appears to be passed on when blood, semen, or vaginal fluids pass directly into another person's blood stream. This can occur during acts of sexual intercourse between men and between men and women, by injection, by transfusion of infected blood products, and by transmission from infected mothers to their infants during pregnancy or at birth. ARTIFICIAL INSEMINATION of infected semen and transplantation of infected organs are other routes of infection. In the US and Europe, the number of cases of AIDS (over 25,000 and over 3500 respectively, by the end of Oct. 1986) has so far remained confined largely to groups of people considered to be at particular risk of the disease, especially homosexual men but also intravenous drug abusers and haemophiliacs and their sexual partners. In countries of central Africa, however, the disease has spread rapidly throughout the population, probably due in part to the medical use of unsterilized hypodermic needles and infected blood products. Programmes of public education have been undertaken in many countries with the aim of preventing the spread of a disease which could assume plague-like proportions.

**Aigues-Mortes** ("ayg ,mawt), town (1982 pop. 4,475) in Gard dept. of S France, close to the delta of the Rhone R. Its name, derived from Aquae Mortuae (Lat.), means 'dead waters' and describes its position, cut off from the sea by silting. Most of the town still lies within its medieval walls built between 1272 and 1300. It was the port from which St Louis (Louis IX) left for the Crusades in 1248 and 1270. He was responsible for the massive Tour de Constance which has often been used to hold prisoners.

**ailanthus** (ay,lanthəs), tree (genus *Ailanthus*) of the family Simarubaceae. Ailanthus is native to warm regions of Asia and Australia. Its wood is used in cabinetmaking and for charcoal manufacture. The bark and leaves are used medicinally, and the leaves provide food for silkworms. Females of a species called tree of heaven (*A. altissima*) are cultivated for their attractive foliage and their resistance to smoke and soot; the male plants, however, have flowers with a disagreeable odour, and are seldom seen as specimen trees.

**Ailey, Alvin,** 1931–, American dancer, teacher, and choreographer. He made his debut (1950) with the Horton Dance Theatre of which he became director, and later formed (1958) his own company, the Alvin Ailey City Centre Dance Theatre. He is noted for drama and use of African motifs.

**Aintree,** world-famous racecourse near Liverpool, N England. The GRAND NATIONAL has been run there since 1837. The course over 30 fences is 7.210 km (4 mi 850 yd), which is twice round the circuit. Flat and hurdle races are both run on the course.

**Ainu** (ˌ ienooh), aborigines of Japan, possibly of Caucasoid descent, having both European and Asian physical traits. Oriental invaders forced the Ainu north to the N Japanese island of HOKKAIDO and to Sakhalin and the Kuril Islands, in the USSR. Their animistic religion (see ANIMISM) centres on a bear cult. They live by hunting, fishing, farming, and selling crafts to tourists.

Ainu

**Air, Freedoms of the,** principles in international law. The Treaty of Versailles (1919) laid down that exclusive sovereignty was reserved to every national in the air space over its territories; this was at odds with the long-established Freedom of the Seas whereby under international law the ships of any nation were permitted to travel freely and peaceably through international waters. Ad-hoc agreements allowed the development of, e.g., the London-to-Paris air route in the 1920s and 30s, but formal agreement on international air travel was not achieved until the signature in 1946 of the Bermuda Agreement which stated that the Freedoms of the Air are (1) the right of innocent passage; (2) the right of technical stop; (3) the right to set down traffic; (4) the right to pick up traffic; and (5) the right to pick up and set down traffic between two states other than that of the airline concerned.

**air, law of the,** law connected with the use of the air (including radio and telegraph communication); more commonly, body of laws governing civil aviation. Spurred by the growth of air transport, the victorious nations of World War I, meeting in Paris in 1919, drew up the International Convention for Air Navigation, commonly called the Paris Convention; this agreement recognized national claims to air space and established rules for aircraft registration and operating safety. There are also many general conventions and bilateral agreements between nations. In 1944 a conference of 52 nations (not including the USSR) established the International Civil Aviation Organization (see UNITED NATIONS), to ensure the orderly growth of international aviation. In the UK air navigation is governed by the Civil Aviation Acts 1949–71, and is administered by the Civil Aviation Authority, established by the 1971 act.

**air conditioning,** mechanical process for controlling the temperature, humidity, cleanliness, and circulation of air in buildings and rooms. Most air conditioners operate by ducting air across the colder, heat-absorbing side of a REFRIGERATION apparatus, and directing the cooled air back into the air-conditioned space. Small window conditioners vent heat outdoors. Larger systems use circulating water to remove heat. Air conditioning provides the heat, humidity, and contamination controls essential in the manufacture of such products as chemicals and pharmaceuticals.

**aircraft,** term used to include all types of vehicle designed to fly. There are three main categories: (1) lighter-than-air, e.g., AIRSHIP, BALLOON; (2) heavier-than-air (fixed wing), e.g., AEROPLANE, GLIDER; (3) rotary-wing, e.g., GYROPLANE, HELICOPTER. See also FLIGHT, POWERED.

**aircraft carrier,** ship designed to carry aircraft and to permit takeoff and landing of planes. Its distinctive features are a flat upper deck (flight deck) that functions as a takeoff and landing field, and a main deck (hangar deck) beneath the flight deck for storing and servicing the aircraft. The latest aircraft carriers have an inclined ramp at the end of the flight deck to assist aircraft in gaining height at takeoff. The aircraft carrier remained an experimental and untested war vessel until WORLD WAR II, when the Japanese wreaked havoc on the British, Dutch, and US navies with carrier-borne aircraft. By 1942 the aircraft carrier had replaced the battleship as the major unit in a modern fleet, and during the war it was indispensable in naval operations against a sea- or shore-based enemy, with two major battles (Coral Sea and Midway, 1942) being fought entirely by aircraft, and the opposing fleets never coming within gunshot range of each other. US carriers of the *Essex* class spearheaded the island-hopping campaign in the Pacific. A new era in carrier design opened when the US launched (1960) the nuclear-powered *Enterprise,* a vessel capable of lengthy voyages without refuelling. Such military operations as the Falklands War (1982) would not be possible without aircraft carriers.

**air forces,** national military organization for air warfare. Although balloons were used by French forces in Italy in 1859 and by the Union in the American Civil War, air forces in the modern sense date from WORLD WAR I, when the offensive capabilities of the AEROPLANE were first demonstrated. Aeroplanes were first controlled by national armies and used for reconnaissance and support of ground forces, but as their effectiveness as tactical weapons increased, independent air forces were called for. Arguing that future wars would be won by strategic bombing of an enemy's industrial centres, military leaders, including Italian Gen. Giulio Douhet, US Gen. William Mitchell, and British Air Chief Marshal Sir Hugh TRENCHARD urged intensive development of air power. By WORLD WAR II, control of the air over both land and sea proved crucial in most major engagements, and the air force became a separate branch of the armed services in many countries. The first great air battle in history was the Battle of Britain (1940), in which the British ROYAL AIR FORCE defeated the German Luftwaffe over England. The effect of air power in revolutionizing naval warfare was demonstrated in the 1941 surprise attack by Japanese aircraft, launched from AIRCRAFT CARRIERS, on PEARL HARBOR. Air forces on both sides engaged in strategic and tactical bombing, attacks on naval and merchant ships, transport of personnel and cargo, mining of harbours and shipping lanes, antisubmarine patrols, and photo reconnaissance, as well as support of ground, naval, and amphibious operations. After World War II, the aeroplane was superseded by the missile as a strategic weapon, but with HELICOPTERS joining the traditional fighter planes, bombers, and cargo planes of the modern air force, air power continued to be of primary importance in tactical operations, particularly in 'limited' wars such as those in SE Asia, the Falkland Is., and the Middle East. The development of the AIRCRAFT CARRIER has been crucial, enabling small air tactical forces to be carried round the world as needed. It is argued that air forces function as deterrents to a major war by maintaining ready second-strike retaliatory capabilities.

**airline,** commercial organization for the carriage of passengers and goods by air. The first air carrier to come into operation was the German company DELAG, a subsidiary of Zeppelin, which offered pleasure flights from 1910. The world's first regular daily scheduled international air service (for both goods and passengers) began in Aug. 1919, between London and Paris. In modern times, the world's largest airline is the USSR's Aeroflot, which in 1985 employed about 500,000 people and carried 112 million passengers, 3 million on international routes. The next largest airlines are TWC (Texas International), carrying more than 90 million passengers in 1987, and US Air, 60 million. Total passenger carryings of the world's airlines have grown from 2 million per year in 1929 to 7 million in 1939 to 17 million in 1946, 77 million in 1956, 200 million in 1966, 575 million in 1976, and 926 million in 1986. Estimated traffic for 1996 is 1.5 billion passengers journeys.

**air mail,** carriage of letters and parcels by air. It began in the Franco-Prussian War (1870-71), when balloons were used to carry letters out of beseiged Paris, plus carrier pigeons for return mail. The first air mail in Britain was carried in Aug. 1910, and the first carriage of government-sponsored air mail was in India in Feb. 1911. In Sept. 1911 the first air service in Britain ran for a total of 16 flights from Hendon to Windsor (a distance of 32 km/20 mi). Mail was carried by air by military aircraft in World War I. The first international air-mail service was started in Nov. 1919, between London and Paris, and the first transatlantic service began in Aug. 1939. The use of air mail services has grown enormously since the end of World War II; by the late 1980s nearly 200 tonnes of mail per day passed through Heathrow airport.

**air plant:** see EPIPHYTE.

**air pollution:** see POLLUTION.

**airport,** substantial tract of level ground, or unobstacled stretch of water, equipped for commercial aircraft to take off and land. The first three international airports were all founded in 1919: Hounslow, London; Le Bourget, Paris; Schiphol, Amsterdam. Of London's present airports, Gatwick was first used for commercial flights in 1936, Heathrow in 1946, and Stansted in 1949. In 1987, the world's busiest airport, in terms of numbers of passengers carried, was Chicago (followed by Atlanta and Los Angeles); the busiest outside the US was Heathrow, with 32 million passengers per year, which also handled more international passengers than any other airport in the world. See AIR TRANSPORT.

**airship,** lighter-than-air AIRCRAFT propelled by one or more aero-engines. There are three main types of construction: (1) rigid, in which a number of individual gas bags are enclosed with a rigid framework covered with a fabric or metal envelope; (2) semirigid, which has a rigid keel attached to the undersurface of a gas-containing envelope; and (3) nonrigid, in which the form of the envelope is maintained by gas and air pressure, with accommodation for crew and power plant slung underneath. The first airship was a nonrigid one built in 1852 by Henri Giffard, and powered by a steam engine; it flew from Paris to Trappe, a distance of 44 km (28 mi), the first successful powered FLIGHT. The first practical rigid airship was built by Count von ZEPPELIN in 1900; subsequently, up to 1938, a total of 119 Zeppelin rigid airships were built. Zeppelin airships were used to bomb Britain in World War I, killing over 500 people, but they were not as effective as aeroplanes and were much more easily shot down. Britain built 17 rigid airships (1911–29) and the US 4 (1923–29). The safety record of rigid airships was very poor: 3 of the 4 US ships came to grief, as did 99 out of 139 German rigids and 4 of the 17 British. Nonrigids (or 'Blimps') have been more successful. During World War I, 214 British nonrigids were built, which were used for antisubmarine patrols. In recent years there has been a revival of nonrigid airships for joy-riding and advertising purposes, and it is possible that they could be useful in defence as early-warning aircraft.

*Hindenburg*, the world's largest rigid **airship**, exploded at Lakehurst, New Jersey on 6 May 1937, killing 35.

**air transport,** movement of people, goods, and mail by air for the public and private welfare. The first fare-paying passenger service was flown on 8 May 1910 by a Zeppelin AIRSHIP at Düsseldorf. Following the first AIR MAIL service (in Britain in 1910), the first commercial air cargo was flown from Shoreham to Hove (both Sussex, England) in 1911. The first regular, scheduled, international, daily, commercial passenger and goods air-transport service began in 1919 between London and Paris. The growth of international scheduled air transport is illustrated by the increase in number of passengers carried:

|      | Passengers | Passenger/kilometres |
|------|-----------|---------------------|
| 1935 | 4.6 million | 918 million |
| 1945 | 13.2 million | 8000 million |
| 1955 | 68 million | 61,000 million |
| 1965 | 177 million | 198,000 million |
| 1975 | 534 million | 697,000 million |
| 1985 | 891 million | 1,360,000 million |

During 1986, the worlds international scheduled airlines carried a total of 938 million passengers and 14.7 million tonnes of cargo on some 15 million flights (over 40,000 per day), earning revenue of about US$113 billion from the operation of some 12,000 communal transport aircraft. The social impact of this immense increase in international mobility is incalculable. Diplomacy has been transformed as leaders have been able to meet in person rather than entrusting negotiations to delegates; this has tended to produce a style of leadership marked by the individual's ability as a solo 'performer'. Business travel accounts for by far the greater part of passenger/kilometres flown, but the ease with which people of even moderate income can fly to holidays abroad has radically altered the public's perception of the world: the 'global village' is of course very dependent upon telecommunications but it would never have become a reality without air transport on its present scale.

**Aitmatov, Chingiz Torekulovich,** 1928–, Soviet writer from Kirghizia. He draws extensively on folklore, is critical of Stalinist autocracy, and in recent years has written much on nature conservation. His best-known novels are *Goodbye, Gulsary* (1966) about the post-war years in a Kirghiz village; *The Day Lasts More than a Hundred Years* (1980) set in the deserts of Kazakhstan; and *The Scaffold* (1986) which denounces the Soviet drug trade and also reveals the author's fascination with Christian legend.

**Aix-en-Provence** ('eks on pro,vons), city (1982 pop. 124,550), SE France. Originating as a Roman spa, Aix was the capital of Provence until 1789. Olive oil and sugared almonds are local specialities. Its university was founded in 1409 and it is also a legal centre; there are fine buildings dating from the 17th and 18th cent.

**Aix-la-Chapelle** (eks la sha,pel): see AACHEN, West Germany.

**Aix-la-Chapelle, Treaty of:** see AUSTRIAN SUCCESSION, WAR OF THE.

**Ajax,** in Greek mythology. 1 The Telamonian Ajax, hero of the TROJAN WAR. In the *Iliad* he is a huge man, slow of thought and speech, but very courageous. He and ODYSSEUS rescued the corpse of ACHILLES. When Odysseus was awarded Achilles' armour the disappointed Ajax went mad and committed suicide. He is the hero of SOPHOCLES's play *Ajax*. 2 The Locrian Ajax, who violated CASSANDRA in the sack of Troy. Shipwrecked by ATHENA, he was saved by POSEIDON, but struck dead by lightning for his defiance.

**Ajman,** small state on the Arabian shore of the PERSIAN GULF. See UNITED ARAB EMIRATES.

**Ajmer,** town (1981 pop. 375,493), Rajasthan state, NW India. It is a district administrative, regional communications, cultural, and marketing centre with textile and other industries, mainly small-scale. An ancient and interesting town going back at least to the 11th cent., when it was the seat of a Chauhan Rajput ruler, it played its part in the turbulent history of succeeding centuries and was for a time a provincial capital under the MOGULS: it was the home of painters and sculptors. After various vicissitudes it became the headquarters of the curious, small province of Ajmer-Merwara, an island of British territory set in a sea of Rajput princely states.

**Akbar,** 1542–1605, Mogul emperor of INDIA (r. 1556–1605). An outstanding general, Akbar added parts of AFGHANISTAN, Baluchistan, parts of central India, Gujarat, and Bengal to his domains. This reign was marked by administrative reform, religious toleration, and the flowering of art and literature. He established a new mystic cult based on religious eclecticism, formed dynastic alliances with the Rajput princes and initiated a new architectural style. His protégés included Abul Fazl who wrote a famous gazetteer of the empire, *Ain-i-Akbari*.

**akee** (a,kay), *Blighia sapida*, fruit grown in Jamaica. It is red when ripe and opens naturally exposing three large black seeds. Each seed is surrounded by a fleshy, cream-coloured part which is the section eaten, usually raw, but it can also be boiled or fried. It is poisonous when unripe.

**Akhenaton:** see IKHNATON.

**Akhmatova, Anna** pseud. of **Anna Andreyevna Gorenko** (əkh͵mahtəvə), 1889–1966, Russian poet of the ACMEIST school. Her brief, highly emotional lyrics are simply and musically written. Among her most important volumes are *The Rosary* (1914), *The Willow Tree* (1940), *Requiem* (1935–40), *Poem without a Hero* (1960), and *The Course of Time* (1966).

**Akiba ben Joseph,** AD c.50–c.135, Palestinian rabbi. He compiled a collection of Hebrew Oral Law, *Mishnah of Rabbi Akiba* (see MISHNAH). After siding with BAR KOKBA in his revolt against Rome, Akiba was imprisoned and, it is said, tortured to death by the Romans.

**Akihito** ('aki͵heetoh), 1933–, Emperor of JAPAN, son of HIROHITO. In 1952 he was officially proclaimed heir to the Japanese throne, to which he succeeded in 1989 on Hirohito's death. In 1959 he married Michiko Shoda, a commoner; their eldest child, a son, was born in 1960.

**Akkad** (͵akad), northern part of later BABYLONIA, in Mesopotamia; the southern part was SUMER. In the 4th millennium BC a Semitic city-state appeared, and under Sargon (c.2340 BC) Akkad became an imperial power. Akkad and Sumer were united as Babylonia by HAMMURABI. The name Akkad also appears as Accad.

**Akkadian** (a͵kaydeeən), language belonging to the Semitic subfamily of the Hamito-Semitic family of languages. Also called Assyro-Babylonian, Akkadian was current in ancient MESOPOTAMIA (now IRAQ) from about 3000 BC until the time of Christ. See LANGUAGE (table).

**Akola,** town (1981 pop. 225,412), Maharashtra state, C India, on a tributary of the Sonola R. It is a district administrative and commercial centre, well placed at a junction on the Bombay–Calcutta railway. It has some industry. It lies in the cotton-growing region of Berar.

**Akron,** city (1984 est. pop. 227,000), seat of Summit co., NE Ohio, US, on the Little Cuyahoga R. and the Ohio and Erie Canal; settled 1825; inc. as a city 1865. It is a port of entry and an important industrial and transport centre. From the opening of the first plant in 1870, Akron became the rubber capital of the US; corporate and research headquarters of the major producers are located there. Metalworking, aerospace industries, and polymer research are important. Akron's Art Institute is well known.

**Akte:** see ATHOS.

**Akutagawa Ryūnosuke,** 1892–1927, Japanese author. One of Japan's finest short-story writers, he derived many of his intense and often macabre tales from historical Japanese sources, but told them with modern psychological insights in a highly individualistic style. His stories 'Rashōmon' (1915) and 'In a Grove' (1921) were made into the classic 1950 film *Rashōmon*, directed by KUROSAWA AKIRA.

**al-.** For Arabic names beginning thus, see the second part of the name, e.g., SADAT, ANWAR AL-.

**Al,** chemical symbol of the element ALUMINIUM.

**Alabama,** state of the US (1984 est. pop. 3,990,000), area 133,677 km² (51,609 sq mi), situated in the SE and bordered by Tennessee (N), Georgia (E), Florida and the Gulf of Mexico (S), and Mississippi (W). The capital is MONTGOMERY; other major cities are Birmingham, Mobile, and Huntsville. The APPALACHIAN MOUNTAINS end in the NE of the state, and the rest is mostly rolling plains, including the fertile Black Belt in central Alabama. The state's industries include iron and steel, paper and wood, chemicals, processed food, and aerospace, while cattle and poultry, soya beans and peanuts have replaced cotton as the chief agricultural products. In 1980 74% of the population was white and 26% was black. The indigenous people were Creek and Cherokee Indians, defeated by Andrew JACKSON at Horseshoe Bend (1814). There followed rapid settlement and the introduction of cotton plantations using slave labour, leading to the secession from the Union in 1861. The economy recovered slowly and was forced to diversify after the boll weevil infestation of cotton fields in the first decades of the 20th cent. Alabama attained notoriety after 1954 with the segregationist politics of Gov. George Wallace and the start of the civil rights movement led by Rev. Martin Luther KING Jr. Despite recent windfall gains in revenue from oil and natural gas leases, Alabama has yet to share in the prosperity of the SUN BELT.

**Alabama claims,** claims by the US against Great Britain after the AMERICAN CIVIL WAR for damage to merchant ships caused by British-built Confederate commerce-raiders. A tribunal (1871–72) at Geneva awarded the US $15.5 million for damage caused by the Confederate ships *Alabama, Florida,* and *Shenandoah.*

**alabaster,** fine-grained, translucent variety of the mineral GYPSUM, pure white or streaked with reddish brown. Its softness makes it easily carved but also easily broken, soiled, and weathered. Quarried in England and Italy, it is used to make statuary and other decorative objects. The Oriental alabaster of ancient Egyptian and Roman tombs is actually MARBLE, a calcium carbonate, whereas gypsum is a calcium sulphate.

**Alain-Fournier** (alanh fooə͵nyay), 1886–1914, French novelist; b. Henri Alban Fournier. His single full-length work, *Le Grand Meaulnes* (1913), about a youthful search for the ideal, is a delicate blend of symbolism and realism.

**Alamo, the** [Span., = cottonwood], chapel-fort in San Antonio, Texas, built c.1744. It was held by Davy CROCKETT, Jim BOWIE, W. Travis, and about 180 other Texans against a siege by an army of several thousand Mexicans under Gen. SANTA ANNA (24 Feb.–6 Mar. 1836) during the Texas Revolution. While the defenders died, their resistance rallied others who defeated the Mexicans six weeks later, crying 'Remember the Alamo!'

**Åland Islands,** archipelago of some 7000 islands and islets in the Gulf of Bothnia midway between Finland and Sweden, under Finnish sovereignty (Finnish name: Ahvenanmaa) but inhabited by ethnic Swedes (pop. 24,000), 1,548,800 km² (597,995 sq mi). The islands were Swedish until 1809, when they came under Russian rule as part of the semi-autonomous Grand Duchy of Finland. They became part of Finland with the latter's proclamation of independence in 1917, despite the declared wish of their inhabitants for reunion with Sweden. Their status is governed by the 1921 London Convention providing that their inhabitants' language and culture should be safeguarded by the Finnish government and that they should remain demilitarized.

**Alarcón, Pedro Antonio de** (alah͵kohn), 1833–91, Spanish writer and diplomat. His novels, witty and often realistic, include *El sombrero de tres picas* (1874; tr. The Three-Cornered Hat), on which FALLA based a ballet; *El escándalo* (1875; tr. The Scandal); and *El capitán veneno* (1881; tr. Captain Venom).

**Alarcón y Mendoza, Juan Ruiz de** (alah͵kohn ee mayndohthah), 1581?–1639, Spanish dramatic poet; b. Mexico. His brilliant and lively comedies (2 vol., 1628–34) make him a major literary figure of Spain's GOLDEN AGE. The most famous, *La verdad sospechosa* (The Suspect Truth), was the model for *La menteur* (The Liar) by CORNEILLE.

**Alaric I,** c.370–410, Visigothic king. After the death of Roman Emperor THEODOSIUS I he ravaged the Balkans until stopped by STILICHO, invaded Italy, and sacked Rome (410).

**Alas, Leopoldo,** pseud. **Clarín,** 1852–1901, Spanish writer and critic. He was a professor of law at the Univ. of Oviedo. His masterpiece is the naturalistic novel *La regenta* (1885; tr. The Regent's Wife), a detailed analysis of provincial life.

**Alaska,** state of the US, least populous (1984 est. pop. 500,000) and largest in area, 1,518,000 km² (586,412 sq mi), situated in the NW of the continent and separated from conterminous US by Canada, bordered by British Columbia and Yukon Territory (E), the Pacific Ocean (S), the Bering Sea (W), and the Arctic Ocean (N). The capital city is JUNEAU; other major cities are ANCHORAGE, around which 40% of the population live, and Fairbanks. The coast is heavily indented, and peninsulas extend into the sea, one becoming the ALEUTIAN ISLANDS. The interior is dominated by mountains, including the highest point in North America, Mt MCKINLEY. Lowland regions are found in the central region and the North Slope. Alaska experiences harsh winters and short summers. The economy was transformed by the discovery of oil and natural gas in 1968 on the North Slope; coal, copper, platinum, gold, and uranium are also extracted. Alaska has the largest fishing industry in the US, but the growing season is too short for much farming. In 1980 77% of the population was white and 16% native American, mostly Inuit and Aleut. Alaska was first settled by Russian fur traders and sold to the US in 1867 for $7.2 million. Americans arrived with the gold rushes of the 1890s and 1900s, but the state was not developed until World War II when the Alaska Highway was completed. Statehood was achieved in 1959, and the discovery of off-shore oil resulted in the Trans–Alaska Pipeline System being built (1974–77), featuring many environmental safeguards. In 1980 42 million hectares (104 million acres)—49% of the land area—were designated as protected areas in some way, and subsequent negotiations have attempted to settle the native American claims to land.

The **Alaska** pipeline south of Fairbanks

**Alba, Fernando Alvarez de Toledo, 3rd duque de,** 1507–82, Spanish general who played a major role in the reign of PHILLIP II. Sent with an army to suppress the Revolt of the Netherlands in 1567, he used force and brutality to restore order, but in 1572 he was unable to cope with the invasion of the GUEUX sea beggars and he was recalled in 1573. He successfully invaded Portugal in 1580.

**Albacete** ('alba,setay), city (1981 pop. 117,126), capital of Albacete prov., SE Spain. It grew in importance when the surrounding marshes were drained for agriculture in the 19th cent. Once famed for its manufacture of daggers and clasp-knives, it still makes cutting tools.

**Albania,** Albanian *Shqipnija* or *Shqiperia,* officially People's Socialist Republic of Albania, republic (1985 est. pop. 3,050,000), 28,752 km² (11,101 sq mi), SE Europe, on the Adriatic coast of the Balkan Peninsula; bordered by Yugoslavia (N and E) and Greece (S). TIRANË is the capital. Except for the fertile ADRIATIC coast, Albania is mountainous, rising to 2763 m (9066 ft) at Mt Korab. Albania is rich in mineral resources, notably chromium, coal, copper, oil, and nickel, and mining is the largest source of income. Only one-tenth of the land is cultivated, and half of that is in vineyards and olive groves; grains, cotton, tobacco, and livestock are also important. The leading industries include food-processing, textiles, and the manufacture of petroleum products, footwear, and building materials. Industry, mines, and agriculture are nationalized. The GNP is $2501 million and the GNP per capita is $820 (1981). About 97% of the population is ethnic Albanian. Albania is officially an atheist country, but the population is predominantly Muslim, with Roman Catholic and Greek Orthodox minorities.

*History.* Albania was settled in ancient times by Illyrians and Thracians; the area then comprised parts of ILLYRIA and EPIRUS. The coast was colonized by the Greeks, and the entire region later came under Roman and Byzantine rule. SCANDERBEG (d. 1468), Albania's national hero, delayed but did not stop the OTTOMAN EMPIRE's conquest of the area, which was complete by 1478. More than four centuries of Turkish Islamic rule followed, and national aspirations were suppressed until, during the First BALKAN WAR, Albania proclaimed independence (1912). A year later an international commission assigned large areas claimed by Albania to MONTENEGRO, SERBIA, and GREECE. The scene of political chaos and a battleground for contending European and Balkan forces after WORLD WAR I, the country came (1925) under the rule of Ahmed Zogu, who proclaimed himself (1928) King ZOG. Italy invaded Albania in 1939, setting up a puppet government that fought with the Axis powers in WORLD WAR II. After 1944, power passed to antifascist guerrilla leader Enver HOXHA, a communist, who proclaimed a republic in 1946 and two years later broke with the Yugoslav Communists. Opposed to destalinization, Albania broke with the USSR in 1961 and withdrew from the WARSAW TREATY ORGANIZATION in 1968. It became a close ally of the People's Republic of CHINA, but that friendship cooled in the mid-1970s and was

formally ended in 1978. A new constitution adopted in 1976 described Albania as a socialist people's republic under the leadership of the Party of Labour of Albania (PLA). Veteran prime minister Mehmet SHEHU died in unclear circumstances in 1981 and was later denounced by Hoxha as an agent of hostile foreign powers. Hoxha himself died in 1985 and was succeeded as president and PLA leader by Ramiz ALIA.

Albania

**Albany,** US city (1980 pop. 101,727), state capital of New York State, on the Hudson R.; settled 1624, inc. 1686. A deep-water port and trading centre for a farm and resort area, it has diversified manufactures, including textiles, paper, chemicals, and motor vehicle parts. The Dutch built (1613) a fur trading post there; the English took control and named the city in 1664. State capital from 1797, it grew with the opening of the Erie and Champlain canals (1820s).

**Albany,** city (1986 pop. 16,316), Western Australia. Located 400 km (250 mi) SE of PERTH it is the oldest town in the state, established as a penal colony in 1826. The harbour, King's Sound, is an excellent sheltered, deep-water bay and was an early whaling station. Textile mills process wool from the surrounding farming district.

**Albany, Alexander Stuart or Stewart, duke of:** see STUART, ALEXANDER, DUKE OF ALBANY.

**Albany Congress,** 1754, a meeting of British colonial representatives in Albany, New York State. Because of the impending war with France, a treaty was made between seven British colonies and the Iroquois Indians. Benjamin FRANKLIN's Plan of Union for the colonies was also approved, but was later rejected by the colonial legislatures and by the crown.

**Albany Regency,** informal group of Democratic Party leaders in New York state after 1820. Developed by Martin VAN BUREN, the Regency was among the first effective political machines. It used the spoils system and maintained strict party discipline. After 1842 it split into factions (BARNBURNERS and HUNKERS) over the issues of internal improvements and slavery.

**albatross,** sea BIRD (family Diomedeidae) with tapered wings that enable it to excel at gliding and flying. Nine species are found in the Southern Hemisphere, where they nest on sub-Antarctic and oceanic islands. They use the circumpolar winds to assist their gliding flights. The wandering albatross (*Diomedea exulans*), with a wingspan of 305–366 cm (10–12 ft), was made famous by COLERIDGE's *Rime of the Ancient Mariner.* Four species of albatross live in the N Pacific.

**Albee, Edward,** 1928–, American playwright. His clever, often satiric plays include the one-act *The Zoo Story* (1959), and the full-length *Who's Afraid of Virginia Woolf?* (1962), widely regarded as his finest work; *Tiny Alice* (1965); *A Delicate Balance* (1967); and *Seascape* (1975).

**Albemarle, George Monck** or **Monk,** 1st **duke of:** see MONCK, George.

**Albéniz, Isaac,** 1860–1909, Spanish pianist and composer. Influenced by LISZT and DEBUSSY, he is best remembered for his later piano works, especially *Iberia* (1906–9), which combine Spanish folk material with brilliant pianistic idiom.

**Albers, Josef,** 1888–1976, German–American artist, designer, and teacher; b. Germany. He studied and then taught at the BAUHAUS from 1920 until its closure in 1933. Albers then emigrated to America, teaching at Harvard and then Yale (1950–58). He was one of the first teachers to introduce Bauhaus ideas to America. His main interests were the physical and psychological effects of colour and form, as written up in his book *Interaction of Colour* (1963). He is best known for a series of paintings, *Homage to the Square,* which portrays colours in quasi-concentric squares. His wife **Annie Albers,** 1899–, was head of the textile department at the Bauhaus (1922–30), and was later an influential textile designer in the US.

**Albert,** 1819–61, prince consort of VICTORIA of Great Britain; son of Ernest I, duke of Saxe-Coburg-Gotha. His devotion to the queen, his responsible concern with public affairs, particularly science, culture and diplomacy won him respect, if not affection, though at times, e.g., during the CRIMEAN WAR, he was unpopular with press and public. His hour of triumph was the GREAT EXHIBITION of 1851. His insistence on a moderate approach to the TRENT AFFAIR may have avoided war with the US. His death, from typhoid, plunged Victoria in deep gloom and was the main break in her long reign.

**Albert I,** 1875–1934, king of the Belgians (1909–34), nephew and successor of LEOPOLD II. During WORLD WAR I he led his country in resisting the German invasion (1914). He also improved social conditions in Belgium and the Belgian CONGO. His son, LEOPOLD III, succeeded him.

**Alberta,** province of Canada (1984 est. pop. 2,340,600), area 661,185 km² (255,284 sq mi), located in the W, bordered by Saskatchewan (E), Manitoba, US (S), British Columbia (W), and Northwest Territories (N). The capital, EDMONTON, and CALGARY are the principal cities, containing half the population; 77% lives in urban areas. The Rocky Mts traverse Alberta's SW corner, giving way to treeless prairies in the S and timberland in the far N. The Athabasca and Peace Rivers drain the province to the N, and the Saskatchewan and Red Deer Rivers to the E. Agriculture (notably wheat and other grain farming) was traditionally the province's main source of revenue; livestock, dairying, and timber are also important. Since the early 1960s, however, mineral exploitation has been the major industry. Alberta has some of the richest oil deposits in the world, including the tar beds of the Athabasca R., and has half of Canada's known reserves of coal and half of its natural gas. The main manufacturing industries process these raw materials. Outstanding national parks attract tourism. The region was settled by Blackfoot Indians in the S and Cree in the N, when it became part of the territory granted (1670) to the Hudson's Bay Company; the fur trade was predominant. Following the purchase of the territory by the confederation (1869), the railways and federal homesteading programmes opened up the area to ranchers and farmers. Settled by British, German, and other European immigrants, it became a province in 1905. The discovery of oil in 1947 guaranteed that Alberta's economy would be the fastest growing of any state, although in the 1980s recession has hit hard.

**Alberti, Leone Battista,** 1404–72, Italian architect, musician, painter, and humanist, sometimes thought to embody the RENAISSANCE ideal of the 'universal man'. His treatise *De re aedificatoria* (c.1450), though dependent on the Roman architect Vitruvius, was the first modern work on architecture, and influenced the development of Renaissance architectural style. Among the notable buildings erected from his designs is the Palazzo Rucellai, Florence. Alberti's treatises on painting (1436) and sculpture (c.1464) were also influential.

**Albert Memorial,** 1863–72, extravagant monument to Queen Victoria's prince consort, Albert, in Hyde Park, London. Designed by Sir George Gilbert SCOTT, it was considered by him to be the best thing he did, out of a huge output. Across the road is the **Royal Albert Hall,** an elliptical tiered concert hall used for promenade concerts and other occasions, and said to have been built with the money left over after spending as much as possible on the Memorial. It was designed by Capt. Francis Fowkes and can hold an audience of 8000.

Albert Memorial

**Albertus Magnus, Saint,** or **Saint Albert the Great,** 1206–80, scholastic philosopher, Doctor of the Church, called the Universal Doctor. A DOMINICAN, he attempted in his *Summa theologiae* to reconcile Aristotelianism with Christian thought. St THOMAS AQUINAS was his pupil. Albertus was also deeply interested in natural science; he is the patron of all students of the natural sciences. Feast: 15 Nov. See also ARISTOTLE; SCHOLASTICISM.

**Albigenses** ('albi,jenseez), religious sect of S France (12th–13th cent.) taking their name from the city of Albi, whose beliefs were similar in many ways to MANICHAEISM, sometimes known as Cathars. They were Christian heretics who believed in the coexistence of two ultimate principles, good and evil. They held that matter was evil and that Jesus only seemed to have a body. Ascetic and enthusiastic, they persisted despite papal opposition and attempts to convert them by preaching. The murder of a papal legate led INNOCENT III to declare (1209) the Albigensian Crusade, which was soon redirected toward political ends. In 1233 the INQUISITION was formed to halt Albigensianism, and slowly over 100 years the movement died.

**albino,** animal or plant lacking normal pigmentation. The albino body covering (skin, hair, and feathers) and eyes lack pigment. In humans and other animals albinism is inherited as a recessive trait. Breeding has established albino races in some domestic animals.

**Albinus:** see ALCUIN.

**Ålborg** or **Aalborg,** city (1985 pop. 154,750) and port in N Denmark. It commands the crossing of the Limfjorden, the winding sea which separates northern JUTLAND from the rest of the peninsula. Local chalk deposits are quarried for the manufacture of cement and there are drink and fertilizer industries.

**albumin,** member of a class of water-soluble, heat-coagulating PROTEINS. Albumins are widely distributed in plant and animal tissues, e.g., ovalbumin of egg, lactalbumin of milk, and leucosin of wheat. Some contain carbohydrates. Normally constituting about 55% of the proteins in blood plasma, albumins adhere chemically to various substances in the blood, e.g., amino acids or hormones, and thus play a role in their transport. Albumins and other blood proteins aid in regulating the distribution of water in the body. Albumins are also used in textile printing, the fixation of dyes, sugar refining, and other industrial processes.

**Albuquerque,** city (1980 pop. 331,767), seat of Bernalillo co., west-central New Mexico, United States, on the upper Rio Grande; inc. 1890. It is the largest city in the state, and the industrial and commercial centre of a timber and farm area. Its diverse industries include electronics, and nuclear research and weapons development conducted by federal agencies. The city's downtown section is the site of a 1980s urban renewal project. Albuquerque is also noted as a health resort and medical centre. The city was founded by the Spanish in 1706 and grew with the arrival (1880) of the railway.

**Albuquerque, Afonso de,** 1453–1515, Portuguese admiral, founder of the Portuguese empire in the East. He captured Goa (1510), Malacca (1511), and Hormuz (1515), built a series of forts in INDIA, and established shipbuilding and other industries. Control of the spice trade and of trade routes was nearly accomplished during his time.

**Albury,** city (1986 est. pop. 37,164), New South Wales, SE Australia. Situated on the MURRAY R., it was linked with Wodonga (1985 est. pop. 23,040), Victoria, as a growth centre in 1973 as part of the federal decentralization programme. Adjacent to the town is the Hume Dam (capacity 300,000 hectare-metres/2.5 million acre-feet) built to ensure adequate permanent supplies of water for irrigation downstream.

**Alcaeus** (al¸seeəs), b. c.620 BC, Greek poet, early personal LYRIC writer. Traditionally an associate of SAPPHO, he wrote both light and political verse. The Alcaic strophe was admired and adapted by HORACE.

**Alcalá Zamora, Niceto** (ahlkah¸lah thahmoh¸rah), 1877–1949, president of Spain (1931–36). He helped to lead the republican revolution of 1931 and became the first president of the second Spanish republic. He was deposed (1936) by the CORTES on a Socialist motion and went into exile.

**alcalde,** Spanish title designating a town mayor who also acts as justice of the peace. It originated in the 11th cent. to designate a judge with administrative functions. In the Spanish colonies it was used for a provincial administrator who presided over the CABILDO or municipal council.

**Alcatraz,** island in San Francisco Bay, W California, US. Discovered (1769) and fortified by the Spanish, it was (1859–1933) the site of a US military prison and then (1933–63) of a federal maximum security prison, called 'The Rock'. The island became part of the Golden Gate National Recreational Area in 1972.

**Alcestis,** in Greek mythology, the devoted wife of a Thessalian king, Admetus. She willingly died in his place, to ensure his immortality. In some myths HERCULES rescued her from the dead; in others PERSEPHONE reunited husband and wife. EURIPIDES dramatized the legend in his *Alcestis,* and she appears in CHAUCER's *Legend of Good Women.*

**alchemy,** ancient art or pseudoscience that sought to turn base metals into gold or silver through the agency of a secret substance known by various names (philosopher's stone, elixir, grand magistry). Emerging in China and Egypt by the 3rd cent. BC, alchemy was cloaked in mysticism and allegory, and in time degenerated into superstition. Revived (8th cent. AD) in Alexandria by the Arabs, who gave it its name, it reached W Europe by the Middle Ages. In the 15th–17th cent. experimentation again fell into disrepute, but the base had been laid for modern CHEMISTRY, which has in fact accomplished the transmutation of elements.

**Alcibiades** ('alsi¸bieədeez), c.450–404 BC, Athenian statesman and general. He was a pupil of SOCRATES, and features as his lover in PLATO's *Symposium.* A leader against SPARTA in the PELOPONNESIAN WAR, he proposed the alliance with Argos which was defeated at Mantinea (418 BC). He promoted the Sicilian campaign (415) but was accused (probably falsely) of sacrilege. Called home for trial, he fled to Sparta, where he aided Agis I, and then to Persia (413). Recalled to ATHENS, he won a brilliant naval victory (410) and recovered Byzantium (408). Blamed unjustly for the defeat of the Athenian fleet at Notium (c.406), he was sent into exile, and LYSANDER had him murdered.

**Alcman,** fl. late 7th cent. BC, Greek LYRIC poet, writing in SPARTA. He was famous for his love poetry, and also wrote choral lyric (the earliest that survives), and poems on the origin of the universe, and on EPIC themes.

**Alcock, Sir John,** 1892–1919, British aviator. Trained as an engineer, he became (1913) a test pilot for A.V. ROE and served in the Royal Naval Air Service in World War I. He was the first man to fly nonstop across the Atlantic (with navigator Arthur Whitten Brown), from Newfoundland to Ireland on 14–15 June 1919; the two men were knighted for the feat. Alcock was killed in a plane crash the same year.

**alcohol,** any of a class of organic compounds with the general formula R—OH, where R is an alkyl group made up of carbon and hydrogen and —OH is one or more hydroxyl groups, each made up of one atom of oxygen and one of hydrogen. Although the term *alcohol* ordinarily refers to ETHANOL, the alcohol in alcoholic drinks, the class of alcohols also includes METHANOL and the propyl, butyl, and pentyl alcohols, all with one hydroxyl group; the glycols, with two hydroxyl groups; and glycerol, with three. Many of the characteristic properties and reactions of alcohols are due to the polarity, or unequal distribution, of electric charges in the C—O—H portion of the molecule.

**Alcoholics Anonymous** (AA), worldwide organization dedicated to the curing of alcoholics; est. 1935 by two former alcoholics. The organization, which functions through local groups, is based on a philosophy of life that has enabled countless numbers of people to recover from alcoholism. In 1981 there were over 40,000 groups and 1 million members worldwide. **Al-Anon,** for spouses, relatives, and friends of alcoholics, and **Al-Ateen,** for their adolescent children, function similarly.

**alcoholism,** pathological dependence on alcohol; the habitual consumption of alcohol to a degree that interferes with physical and mental health, and with normal social behaviour. A widespread health problem, both physical and psychological addiction (see DRUG ADDICTION AND DRUG ABUSE) are involved. Alcohol is a central nervous system depressant that reduces anxiety and inhibitions; lowers alertness; impairs perception, judgment, and muscular coordination; and, in high doses, can cause unconsciousness and even death. Long-term alcoholism damages the brain, liver (see CIRRHOSIS), heart, and other organs. Symptoms of alcohol withdrawal can range from a simple hangover to severe delirium tremens (anxiety, violent trembling, sweating, and terrifying visual and sensual hallucinations). Treatment includes use of disulfiram, a drug that produces severe nausea if alcohol is consumed; drugs to reduce anxiety; psychological counselling; and support from groups such as ALCOHOLICS ANONYMOUS.

*Alcohol consumption* can be measured in standard units. Half a pint of beer, a single measure of spirits, a glass of wine or a small glass of sherry all contain 1 unit. The average weekly consumption in the UK is, in the 1980s, 20 units for men and 7 units for women. There is concern about the quantity of alcohol consumed generally and particularly by those who drive, use machinery or by those who are pregnant (even moderate drinking increases the risk of having a low-birth-weight baby). On Saturday nights in the UK two-third of drivers killed have alcohol levels above the legal limit (80 mg of alcohol per 100 ml blood). However, the government has an interest in continuing high consumption of alcohol, as there are excise duties charged on the sale of alcoholic drinks; in 1986/7 the UK government received £1966 million from the sale of beer alone.

**Alcott, (Amos) Bronson,** 1799–1888, American educational and social reformer. A leading exponent of TRANSCENDENTALISM, he was (1843) one of the founders of a cooperative vegetarian community, 'Fruitlands'; he also advocated a system of education that integrated the mental, physical and spiritual development of the child. The poverty that plagued his life was eventually alleviated by the writings of his daughter Louisa May ALCOTT.

**Alcott, Louisa May,** 1832–88, American writer, daughter of Bronson ALCOTT. Educated by her father, she was also influenced by her friends EMERSON and THOREAU. Alcott received notice for *Hospital Sketches* (1863), a collection of letters written while she was a Civil War nurse. She achieved fame with *Little Women* (1868–69), a largely autobiographical novel for young people that portrays 19th cent. American family life. Its sequels are *Little Men* (1871) and *Jo's Boys* (1886).

**Alcuin** or **Albinus,** 735?–804, English churchman and educator. Invited (781?) to CHARLEMAGNE's court at Aachen, he was the moving spirit of the CAROLINGIAN renaissance. Alcuin established the study of the seven liberal arts (grammar, rhetoric, logic—the 'trivium'; geometry, arithmetic, music, astronomy—the 'quadrivium'), which became the curriculum for medieval Europe, and encouraged the preservation of ancient texts. His letters and other writings are extant.

**Aldanov, Mark,** pseud. of **Mark Aleksandrovich Landau** (əl,dahnəf), 1886–1957, Russian writer. Aldanov emigrated to France in 1919 and to the US in 1941. His works include *The Thinker* (1923–27), a tetralogy about the era from 1793 to 1821 in France; *The Tenth Symphony* (1931), set in the Vienna of BEETHOVEN's time; and *The Fifth Seal* (1939), which portrays the decay of revolutionary idealism during the SPANISH CIVIL WAR.

**alder,** deciduous tree or shrub (genus *Alnus*) of the BIRCH family, widely distributed, especially in mountainous, moist areas of the north temperate zone. The bark of the common alder (*A. glutinosa*), once used medicinally, is still used for dyes and tanning.

**Aldermaston,** site of the UK's Atomic Weapons Research Establishment. In the late 1950s and early 1960s it was a focus for demonstrations of protest against nuclear weaponry; see CAMPAIGN FOR NUCLEAR DISARMAMENT.

**Aldershot,** town (1981 pop. 53,665), Hampshire, S England. It is a garrison town; a permanent military camp was established here in 1854. An annual international air show is held in the adjacent town of Farnborough. Both the military and civilian parts of the town have been redeveloped in the 1960s and 1970s.

**Aldington, Richard,** 1892–1962, English poet and novelist. A leading IMAGIST, he was married to Hilda DOOLITTLE. His poetry, e.g., *Images* (1915), is remarkable for verbal precision; his novels, e.g., *Death of a Hero* (1929) are bitter satires.

**Aldrich, Robert,** 1918–83, American film director. He is a director noted for films on war or grotesque relationships, usually done in a blunt, often violent style. His films include *Kiss Me Deadly* (1955), *Whatever Happened to Baby Jane* (1962), *The Dirty Dozen* (1967), and *Ulzana's Raid* (1972).

**Aldrin, Buzz** (Edwin Eugene Aldrin, Jr.), 1930–, American astronaut. During the *Apollo 11* lunar-landing mission (16–24 July 1969), Neil ARMSTRONG (the commander) and Aldrin (the lunar-module pilot) became the first and second persons, respectively, to walk on the Moon (see SPACE EXPLORATION, table). Aldrin was pilot of *Gemini 12* (11–15 Nov. 1966) and, after retiring from NASA, served (1971–72) as commandant of the Aerospace Research Pilots' School at Edwards Air Force Base, California.

**Aldus Manutius** or **Aldo Manuzio,** 1450–1515, Venetian printer. A humanist scholar, who lived for many years in the household of the outstanding Renaissance scholar Pico della Mirandola, Aldus holds a significant place in history as printer and publisher of Greek and Latin classics in editions noted for accuracy, usually in 8vo editions at popular prices which made the recently rediscovered classics widely available and thus shaped the development of the European new learning. Aldus was the first to print Greek books, and was among the very earliest printers extensively to use italics. His work was continued by his son, Paolo Manuzio, 1512–74, and *his* son, Aldus Manuzio, 1547–97. Aldo senior published influential editions of Virgil, Aristotle, Aristophanes, Thucydides, Sophocles, Herodotus, Demosthenes, Plutarch, Plato, and Quintilian as well as Dante's *Divine Comedy* and works by Erasmus and contemporary Italian authors.

**ale:** see BEER.

**Aleixandre, Vicente** (ahlay,hahndray), 1898–1984, Spanish poet. His early verse includes the surrealist *La destrucción o el amor* (1935; tr. Destruction or Love). His enormous output was last collected in *Antología total* (1975). He was awarded the 1977 Nobel Prize for literature.

**Alemán, Mateo** (alay,man), 1547–1614?, Spanish novelist. During a turbulent life he worked as an accountant and was twice jailed for debt; at 60 he settled in Mexico. His fame rests on the picaresque novel *Guzmán de Alfarache* (1599–1604).

**Alembert, Jean le Rond d',** 1717–83, French mathematician and philosopher, a leading figure of the ENLIGHTENMENT. His treatise on DYNAMICS (1743) enunciated d'Alembert's principle, which permitted the reduction of a problem in dynamics to one in STATICS. He did important work on the mechanics of rigid bodies, the motions of fluids and vibrating strings, and the three-body problem in CELESTIAL MECHANICS. DIDEROT made him coeditor of the ENCYCLOPÉDIE, for which he wrote the 'preliminary discourse' (1751) and mathematical, philosophical, and literary articles.

**Alencar, José de,** 1829–77, Brazilian writer. He was the first to treat the Amerindians as heroes in literature. His novels, e.g., *Iracema* (1865) tend to be crudely constructed but show passionate concern for the native Brazilians.

**Alepoudelis, Odysseus:** see ELYTIS, ODYSSEUS.

**Aleppo** or **Alep,** city (1981 pop. 976,727), NW Syria. Located in a semidesert region where grains, cotton, and fruit are grown, the city produces silk, cotton textiles, dried fruits, and other goods. It was settled perhaps as early as the 6th millennium BC and passed to the Assyrians, Persians, and Seleucids. By the 4th cent. AD it was a centre of Christianity in the Byzantine Empire. The Arabs, Seljuk Turks, and others later held it. It was always an important trading centre as a terminus of caravan routes across the Syrian desert. Aleppo prospered under the Ottoman Turks (from 1517) and the French (from 1918), and as part of independent Syria (from 1941). Historic structures include the Great Mosque (715) and the Byzantine and Arab citadel (12th cent.).

**Aleutian Islands,** strategically important chain of rugged, volcanic islands, W Alaska, curving westward c.1900 km (1200 mi) between the Bering Sea and the Pacific Ocean. Unalaska, the most populous island, is part of the easternmost group, the Fox Islands. Extending west to a point near the USSR are the Andreanof, Rat, Near, and Semichi island groups. The Aleutians were discovered in 1741 by Vitus BERING and bought by the US from Russia in 1867 as part of the Alaska purchase. Three western islands Attu, Agattu, and Kiska were occupied (1942–43) by Japan.

**Aleuts,** native inhabitants of the ALEUTIAN ISLANDS and W Alaska. They speak an Eskimo-Aleut language (see AMERICAN INDIAN LANGUAGES) and, like the ESKIMO, resemble Siberian peoples. Their skill in hunting sea mammals was exploited by Russian fur traders, and wars with mainland tribes contributed to reducing their numbers from the 20,000–25,000 estimated by Vitus BERING to around 1800 today.

**Alexander,** czars of Russia. **Alexander I,** 1777–1825 (r.1801–25), was the son of PAUL I. He began his reign by relaxing political repression to a degree. In 1805 he joined the coalition against NAPOLEON I, but after Russian defeats he made a tenuous alliance with France by signing the Treaty of Tilsit (1807). After the French invasion of Russia (1812) was repulsed he created the HOLY ALLIANCE, joining with METTERNICH to suppress national and liberal movements. His reactionary domestic policies led to opposition, and when his brother NICHOLAS I succeeded him in 1825 a revolt took place (see DECEMBRISTS). **Alexander II,** 1818–81 (r.1855–81), son of Nicholas I, negotiated an end to the CRIMEAN WAR (1853–56; see PARIS, TREATY OF) and adopted important reforms, principally the emancipation of the serfs (1861; see EMANCIPATION, EDICT OF) and the introduction of limited local self-government (see ZEMSTVO). His foreign policy included the suppression of the Polish uprising of 1863; the annexation of Central Asia (1865–76); and the RUSSO-TURKISH WARS (1877–78). His domestic reforms were seen as insufficient by the intelligentsia, some of whom formed populist groups. Increasing repression led to terrorism, and in 1881 Alexander was assassinated. **Alexander III,** 1845–94 (r.1881–94), was the son of Alexander II. Surrounded by reactionary advisors, he increased police power and censorship; weakened the *zemstvos;* imposed controls on the peasantry; forced Russification on national minorities; and persecuted the Jews. His foreign policy culminated in the TRIPLE ALLIANCE AND TRIPLE ENTENTE. His son NICHOLAS II succeeded him.

**Alexander,** 1893–1920, king (1917–20) of the Hellenes (Greece). He became Greek king when his father, CONSTANTINE I, was forced by the Allies to abdicate because of his pro-German sympathies. After Alexander's death, his father was restored to the throne.

**Alexander,** kings of Scotland. **Alexander I,** 1077?–1124 (r. 1107–24), was the son of MALCOLM III. He opposed English efforts to rule the church in Scotland and established abbeys at Inchcolm and Scone. **Alexander II,** 1198–1249 (r.1214–49), joined the English barons in their revolt against

King JOHN but made a tenuous peace with HENRY III. **Alexander III**, son of Alexander II, 1241–86 (r.1249–86), acquired for Scotland the HEBRIDES and also the Isle of MAN, already claimed from Norway by his father.

**Alexander,** rulers of SERBIA and YUGOSLAVIA. **Alexander** (Karadjordjević), 1806–85, prince of Serbia (r.1842–58), was the son of KARADJORDJE. Dominated by a modernizing oligarchy of notables known as the 'defenders of the [Turkish-imposed 1839] constitution', he was deposed in favour of MILOŠ Obrenović. **Alexander** (Obrenović), 1876–1903, king of Serbia (r.1889–1903) hovered between constitutional and authoritarian rule, the influence of his mother and father (ex-King Milan) and dependence on Austria and Russia until his marriage to the unpopular Draga Mašin unleashed a military conspiracy, resulting in their murders and the end of the dynasty. **Alexander** (Karadjordjević), 1888–1934), prince regent to his father, PETER I (1918–21) and king (r.1921–34), he presided over the kingdom of Serbs, Croats, and Slovenes' unsuccessful period of parliamentary government before proclaiming a personal dictatorship and renaming the state Yugoslavia (1929). He was assassinated by a gunman of the INTERNAL MACEDONIAN REVOLUTIONARY ORGANIZATION in a plot hatched by the Croat USTAŠE and backed by Italy and Hungary.

**Alexander III**, d. 1181, pope (1159–81), a Sienese born Rolando Bandinelli. His rule was contested by antipopes until 1180. He backed the LOMBARD LEAGUE in opposing Emperor FREDERICK I, who exiled him to France until 1176. A learned canon lawyer, he issued many rules for governing the church. In 1179 he convened the Third Lateran Council.

**Alexander III**, king of Macedon: see ALEXANDER THE GREAT.

**Alexander VI**, 1431?–1503, pope (1492–1503, a Catalan named Rodrigo de Borja (Ital., Borgia). An able if unscrupulous politician, denounced by Girolamo SAVONAROLA, Alexander's principal aim was the advancement of his family, including his son Cesare and his daughter Lucrezia BORGIA. As head of Christendom he fixed the line of demarcation between Spanish and Portuguese possessions in the New World (1494).

**Alexander, Harold Rupert Leofric George,** 1st 1891–1969, British field marshal. In WORLD WAR II, he commanded the retreats at Dunkirk (1940) and Burma (1942) and the triumphs in N Africa and Sicily (1943). Later he was governor general of Canada (1946–52) and minister of defence (1952–54) in Winston CHURCHILL's cabinet.

**Alexander Nevsky**, 1220–63, Russian hero. As prince of Novgorod (1236–52) he earned his surname by his victory (1240) over the Swedes on the Neva R. He later defeated the Livonian Knights, invading from Germany (1242), and the Lithuanians (1245). When the TATARS occupied Russia he was made grand duke of Vladimir-Suzdal (1252).

**Alexander the Great** or **Alexander III**, 356–323 BC, king of MACEDON. The son of PHILIP II, he was tutored by ARISTOTLE. Upon succeeding to the throne in 336 BC he won ascendancy over all of GREECE by putting down uprisings in THRACE and ILLYRIA, and by sacking THEBES. As head of an allied Greek army, viewing himself as the champion of pan-HELLENISM, he started east (334) on what was to be the greatest conquest of ancient times. He defeated the Persians at the battles of Granicus (334) and Issus (333). Tyre and Gaza fell after a year's struggle, and he entered Egypt (332), where he founded ALEXANDRIA. Moving to Mesopotamia, he overthrew the Persian Empire of DARIUS III at the battle of Gaugamela (331). Pushing on through eastern PERSIA (330–327), he invaded northern INDIA (326), but there his men would go no further. The fleet was sent back to the head of the Persian Gulf, and Alexander himself led his men through the desert, reaching Susa in 324 BC. He died of a fever a year later, at age 33. He was incontestably one of the greatest generals of all time and one of the most powerful personalities of antiquity.

**Alexandra**, 1844–1925, queen consort of EDWARD VII of Great Britain, whom she married in 1863. She was the daughter of CHRISTIAN IX of Denmark.

**Alexandra Feodorovna**, 1872–1918, czarina of Russia, consort of NICHOLAS II. A granddaughter of Queen VICTORIA and princess of Hesse, she encouraged the czar's reactionary policies under the influence of RASPUTIN. With her husband and children she was shot by the Bolsheviks (see BOLSHEVISM).

**Alexandria**, Arab. *El Iskandarîya* city (1979 est. pop. 2,500,000), N Egypt, on the Mediterranean coast, W of the Nile R. delta. The city is Egypt's leading port, a commercial and transport centre, and the heart of

a major industrial area with such industries as oil refining, motor vehicle assembly, and food processing. Founded in 332 BC by ALEXANDER THE GREAT, Alexandria was (304 BC–30 BC) the capital of the Ptolemies. The city was the greatest centre of Hellenistic and Jewish culture. It had a great university and two celebrated royal libraries, but their valuable collections have not survived. Alexandria became part of the empire of ROME in 30 BC and later of the BYZANTINE EMPIRE. The Muslim Arabs took the city in 642 AD. After Cairo became (969) Egypt's capital, Alexandria declined. It fell to NAPOLEON I in 1798 and to the British in 1801. During WORLD WAR II the city was the chief Allied naval base in the E Mediterranean. At a 1944 meeting in Alexandria, plans for the ARAB LEAGUE were drawn up. A few of Alexandria's ancient monuments are still visible. The Graeco-Roman Museum houses a vast collection of Coptic, Roman, and Greek art.

**alexandrine,** in VERSIFICATION, a line of 12 syllables (or 13 if the last is unstressed), probably named after medieval poems in this meter about ALEXANDER THE GREAT. In French, rhymed alexandrine couplets are the classic poetic form. English iambic hexameter is often called alexandrine. Alexander POPE's 'Essay on Criticism' contains what is probably the most quoted alexandrine in literature:

> A needless alexandrine ends the song
> That like a wounded snake, drags its slow length along.

**Alexius,** Byzantine emperors. **Alexius I** (Comnenus), 1048–1118 (r.1081–1118), nephew of ISAAC I, obtained the crown by overthrowing Nicephorus III. He withstood the Normans under ROBERT GUISCARD and BOHEMOND I, and defeated the Pechenegs (1091) and CUMANS (1095). During the First CRUSADE he persuaded the leaders to pledge to him their Byzantine conquests. In 1108 he forced Bohemond, who had seized Antioch, to acknowledge his suzerainty. In his last years his daughter, Anna Comnena, intrigued against his son, JOHN II. Alexius restored Byzantine power but drained the empire's resources. **Alexius II** (Comnenus), 1168–83 (r.1180–83), son of MANUEL I, ruled under the regency of his mother, Mary of Antioch. His cousin procured the deaths of Mary and Alexius and became Andronicus I. **Alexius III** (Angelus), d. after 1210 (r.1195–1203), deposed his brother ISAAC II, but the act served as pretext for the leaders of the Fourth Crusade to attack (1203) Constantinople and to restore Isaac, with his son **Alexius IV**, d. 1204, as co-emperor. **Alexius V** (Ducas Mourtzouphlos), d. 1204, son-in-law of Alexius III, overthrew Isaac and Alexius IV but was killed soon afterwards by the Crusaders, who set up the Latin empire of Constantinople.

**alfalfa** or **lucerne,** perennial plant (*Medicago sativa*) of the PULSE family, probably native to Iran and now widely cultivated. It is an important pasture and hay plant. Alfalfa is valued for its high yield of protein, its effectiveness in weed control, its role in crop rotation and nitrogen fixation, and as a source of chlorophyll and carotene.

**Al Fatah:** see ARAFAT, YASIR; PALESTINE LIBERATION ORGANIZATION.

**Alfieri, Vittorio, Count** (ahl,fyeree), 1749–1803, Italian tragedian and poet. A Piedmontese, he travelled widely and returned to Italy with a craving for freedom and heroism which he channelled into writing. His 19 tragedies, e.g., *Philip II. Saul, Myrrha*, written between 1775 and 1789, influenced BYRON and 19th-cent. liberation movements in Italy and elsewhere. He also wrote comedies, satires, lyric poetry, and a masterly autobiography. Many of these works were published posthumously by his friend the countess of Albany, former wife of the Young Pretender (see under STUART).

**Alfonsín Foulkes, Raúl** (alfon,seen ,foohks, R), 1926–, president of ARGENTINA (1983–). His election to the presidency, as candidate of the Radical Civic Union, ended seven years of rule by the military, who had been discredited by the FALKLAND ISLANDS debacle of the previous year.

**Alfonso,** kings of ARAGÓN. **Alfonso I,** d. 1134, king of Aragón and Navarre (1104–34), captured many towns from the Moors. **Alfonso II,** 1152–96, king of Aragón (1162–96), inherited Provence and conquered (1171) Teruel. **Alfonso V** (the Magnanimous), 1396–1458, king of Aragón and Sicily (r.1416–58), conquered NAPLES and was recognized by the pope as its king (r.1442–58). He maintained a splendid court there and tried to introduce Spanish institutions.

**Alfonso,** kings of Portugal. **Alfonso I,** 1109?–85, the first king (r.1139–85), extended his territories by defeating (1139) the MOORS and, with the help of allies, captured (1147) Lisbon. His grandson, **Alfonso II** (the Fat), 1185–1223 (r.1211–23), tried to confiscate Roman Catholic

Church holdings and was excommunicated (1219). His army won major victories (1212, 1217) over the Moors. His son, **Alfonso III**, 1210–79 (r.1248–79), completed (1249) the reconquest of Portugal from the Moors, instituted many reforms, and encouraged commerce and the development of towns. **Alfonso IV**, 1290–1357 (r.1325–57), warred fruitlessly against CASTILE before both kingdoms combined forces to defeat (1340) the Moors. He countenanced the murder of Inés de CASTRO. **Alfonso V**, 1432–81 (r.1438–81), put down a civil war (1449), invaded Morocco to capture Tangier (1471), and lost a war (1476–79) with Castile. **Alfonso VI**, 1643–83 (r.1656–83), ousted (1662) his mother as regent and appointed as her successor the count of Castelho Melhor, who won the war (1663–65) that secured Spain's recognition (1668) of Portugal's independence.

**Alfonso,** Spanish kings. **Alfonso I** (the Catholic), 693?–757, Spanish king of ASTURIAS (739–57), extended its territory with the help of the BERBERS' revolt (740–41) against the MOORS. His grandson, **Alfonso II** (the Chaste), 759–842, king of Asturias (791–842), established his capital at Oviedo and continued the struggle against the Moors. **Alfonso III** (the Great), 838?–911?, king of Asturias (866–911?) recovered LEÓN from the Moors, but after his forced abdication it was divided among his sons. **Alfonso V** (the Noble), 994?–1028, king of León (999–1028), chartered (1020) the city of León, but he was killed in the siege of Viseu. **Alfonso VI**, 1030–1109, king of León (1065–1109) and CASTILE (1072–1109), took Galicia (1073) and became the most powerful Christian ruler in Spain. He conquered (1085) Toledo and other cities, but was defeated twice (1086, 1108) by Muslim armies. **Alfonso VII** (the Emperor), 1105–57, king of Castile and León (1126–57), gained supremacy over other Christian states and had himself crowned emperor (1135). But his conquests of CÓRDOBA (1146) and Almería (1147) from the Moors were soon lost. **Alfonso VIII** (the Noble), 1155–1214, king of Castile (1158–1214), restored order in his kingdom and won a great victory (1212) over the Moors. **Alfonso X** (the Wise), 1221–84, king of Castile and León (1252–84), took CÁDIZ from the Moors (1262). His subjection of the nobles led to a revolt, and a civil war broke out over the succession during his last years. He was a great patron of science and the arts. The Alfonsine Tables of astronomical data were published under his aegis. **Alfonso XI**, 1311–50, king of Castile and León (1312–50), lost Gibraltar to the Moors (1333) but won the great victory of Tarifa (1340) and conquered Algeciras (1344). **Alfonso XII**, 1857–85, king of Spain (1874–85), was a popular monarch who consolidated the monarchy, suppressed republican agitation, and restored order. **Alfonso XIII**, 1886–1941, king of Spain (1886–1931), supported the military dictatorship (1923–30) of Miguel PRIMO DE RIVERA, but social unrest and a republican election victory led to his deposition and exile (1931).

**Alfred,** 848–99, king of WESSEX (r.871–99) and recognized as king of all English in his lifetime, later called Alfred the Great. The son of ÆTHELWULF, he shared his father's overseas travels when still a child. He fought alongside his elder brothers in battles against the Danes, who threatened to conquer England. When be became king in 871 he bought off the Danes, but in 878 they again attacked and Alfred took flight to the Somerset marshes. To this period is assigned the legend of the king burning the peasant woman's cakes. In May 878 the king defeated the Danes at Edington, and imposed an agreement that the Danish leaders should become Christian and that a line should be drawn between his territory and theirs (see DANELAW). Alfred then instituted law codes combining Christian doctrine with a strong centralized monarchy. His great achievements were the creation of a navy, the revival of learning among the clergy, the education of youths and nobles at court, the establishment of Old English literary prose, his own English translation of Latin works, and his influence on the extant form of the ANGLO-SAXON CHRONICLE.

**algae** (¸aljee, -gee), primitive plants that contain CHLOROPHYLL and carry on PHOTOSYNTHESIS but lack true roots, stems, and leaves. They are the chief aquatic plant life both in the sea and fresh water; all SEAWEEDS are marine algae. Algae occur as microscopic single cells (e.g., DIATOMS) and more complex forms of many cells grouped in spherical colonies (e.g., *Volvox*), in threadlike filaments (e.g., *Spirogyra*), and in giant forms (e.g., the marine kelps). The cells of colonies are generally similar, but some are specialized for reproduction and other functions. The blue-green and green algae include most of the freshwater forms, such as the green slime found in stagnant water. Brown and red algae are more complex, chiefly marine forms whose green chlorophyll is masked by the presence of other pigments. Algae are primary food producers in the food chain and also provide oxygen for aquatic life.

**Algardi, Alessandro,** 1598–1654, Bolognese sculptor. He became BERNINI's chief rival in Rome. His works, mostly in a restrained, classical style, include the relief, *The Meeting of Leo I and Attila* (1644–45; St Peter's, Rome) and several fine portrait busts.

**Algarve,** southernmost prov. of Portugal. Its name is derived from El Gharb, the Moorish term for 'western land', and there are strong N African influences in place-names and architecture. Almonds, figs, and olives are amongst the many tree crops grown and fishing is carried out from small ports such as Faro. Its scenery and its warm climate, protected from northerly winds, have made it a popular resort area. Sagres near Cape St Vincent was headquarters of Prince Henry the Navigator in the 15th cent.

**algebra,** branch of MATHEMATICS concerned with operations on sets of numbers or other elements that are often represented by symbols. In elementary algebra, letters are used to stand for numbers, e.g., in the POLYNOMIAL equation $ax^2 + bx + c = 0$, the letters $a$, $b$, and $c$ are called the coefficients of the EQUATION and stand for fixed numbers, or constants. The letter $x$ stands for an unknown number, or variable, whose value depends on the values of $a$, $b$, and $c$ and may be determined by solving the equation. Much of classical algebra is concerned with finding solutions to equations or systems of equations, i.e., finding the ROOT, or value of one or more unknowns, that upon substitution into the original equation will make the equation a numerical identity. Algebra is a generalization of arithmetic and gains much of its power from dealing symbolically with elements and operations (chiefly addition and multiplication) and relationships (such as equality) connecting the elements. Thus $a + a = 2a$ and $a + b = b + a$ no matter what numbers $a$ and $b$ represent.

**Alger, Horatio,** 1834–99, American writer of boys' stories; b. Revere, Mass. The heroes of his over 100 books, e.g., *Ragged Dick* (1867), gain success by leading exemplary lives and struggling valiantly against poverty and adversity.

**Algeria,** Arab. *Al Djazair,* Fr. *Algérie,* officially Democratic and Popular Republic of Algeria, republic (1986 est. pop. 22,500,000), 2,381,741 km² (919,590 sq mi), NW Africa, bordered by Mauritania, Morocco, and Western Sahara (W), the Mediterranean Sea (N), Tunisia and Libya (E), and Niger and Mali (S). The principal cities are ALGIERS (the capital) and ORAN. The ATLAS MOUNTAINS divide northern Algeria into a coastal lowland strip (the Tell) and a semiarid plateau (the Chotts). In the south is the much larger, but arid and sparsely populated, Saharan region; Algeria's highest point, Mt Tahat (3002 m/9850 ft) in the Ahaggar Mts, is located here. About half of Algeria's work force are farmers, producing cereals, wine, and citrus fruits, but mining and manufacturing, developed since the 1960s, contribute the bulk of the national income. Petroleum is the leading export, and much natural gas is produced, with proven reserves that are among the world's largest. The state plays a leading role in planning the economy and owns many important industrial concerns. The GNP is US$52,273 million, and the GNP per capita is US$2550 (1985). The great majority of the population are Sunni Muslim Berbers and Arabs; Europeans, who before independence accounted for 10% of the total, now are only 1% of the population. Arabic is the official language, but French is widely spoken, and a sizable minority (15%) speaks a Berber language.

*History.* The earliest known inhabitants of the region that is now Algeria were Berber-speaking nomads who were settled there by the 2nd millennium BC. As NUMIDIA, it became (9th cent. BC) a province of Carthage and then (106 BC) of Rome; during the Christian era, St AUGUSTINE (354–430) was bishop at Hippo (now Annaba). With the decline of Rome in the 5th cent. AD, Algeria was conquered by the Vandals (430–31), the Byzantine Empire (6th cent.), and finally, in the late 7th and early 8th cent., by the Arabs, whose introduction of Islam profoundly altered the character of the area. Spain captured the coastal cities in the 15th cent. but was expelled (mid-16th cent.) with the help of the Ottoman Turks, who then assumed control. During this period the Algerian coast was a stronghold of pirates and a centre of the slave trade. France invaded Algeria in 1830 and declared it a colony in 1848. Europeans began to arrive in large numbers, dominating the government and the economy, and leaving the native Muslim population with scant political or economic power. A nationalist movement began to develop after World War I, and a war for independence, led by the National Liberation Front (FLN), broke out in 1954. After more than seven years of bitter fighting, in which at least 100,000 Muslim and 10,000 French soldiers were killed, Algeria became independent on 3 July 1962. Since independence, Algeria has been one of the most prominent nonaligned states and an outspoken champion of the various movements against white minority rule in Africa. It has supported the protracted struggle of the Polisario Front for the independence of WESTERN SAHARA (formerly Spanish Sahara) from Morocco, and in 1981 it acted as intermediary between the US and Iran in negotiations for the release of American hostages seized in Iran in 1979. Following the death of Houari BOUMEDIENNE in 1978, Bendjedid CHADLI became both president and leader of the FLN, which under the 1976 constitution is the only legal party. Under Chadli Algeria has pursued more moderate external policies and 'pragmatic socialism' internally.

The old-clothes market in the Muslim quarter of **Algiers**

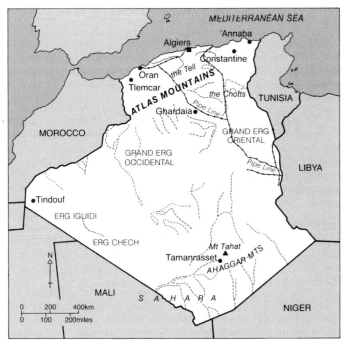

Algeria

**Algiers** or **Alger,** city (1983 pop. 1,721,607), capital of Algeria, N Algeria, on the Bay of Algiers in the Mediterranean Sea. It is a major N African port, a winter resort, and a commercial centre. Its economy is based on wine making, metallurgy, oil refining, and motor-vehicle construction. It was founded in the 10th cent. by the Berbers on the site of the Roman city of Icosium. The French captured the port in 1830. During WORLD WAR II Algiers was the Allied headquarters in N Africa. The city played an important role in the Algerian independence struggle (1954–62). Algiers is divided into the newer, French-built sector and the original Muslim quarter, with its 16th-cent. *casbah* [fortress].

**ALGOL:** see PROGRAMMING LANGUAGE.

**Alhazen:** see IBN AL-HAYTHAM.

**Ali, Muhammad,** 1942–, American boxer; b. Cassius Marcellus Clay, Jr. He changed (1964) his name on becoming a BLACK MUSLIM. After winning (1960) an Olympic gold medal, he gained the world heavyweight crown by defeating Sonny Liston in 1964, but was stripped of the title in 1967 when he refused induction into the US armed forces on religious grounds. In 1971 the US Supreme Court upheld his draft appeal. Ali regained the title in 1974 by defeating George Foreman, lost it to Leon Spinks in 1978, but won it a third time (from Spinks) later that year. Ali lost to Larry Holmes in 1980.

**Alia, Ramiz,** 1925–, communist leader in ALBANIA. A partisan during WORLD WAR II, he became president of the People's Assembly presidium (i.e., head of state) in 1982; in 1985 he succeeded Enver HOXHA as first secretary of the ruling Party of Labour of Albania.

**Alicante,** city (1981 pop. 251,387), capital of Alicante prov., Valencia, E Spain. A port on the Mediterranean coast, it handles the fruit, wine, and other agricultural products of its hinterland. There are also food-processing industries.

**Alice Springs,** town (1986 pop. 22,759), Northern Territory, central Australia. It is the centre of an area with cattle stations. Gold, copper, wolfram, and mica are mined nearby. The town was called Stuart until 1933. The town is situated on the Todd R. in the MacDonnell Ranges and renamed after Lady Alice Todd. An important tourist centre and base for AYERS ROCK, it is linked with Adelaide by the Ghan railway. A US satellite communications base at Pine Gap has significantly increased population in the area.

**alien,** in law, a resident of a state who is not a national or citizen of that state. A country may exclude individuals or groups it deems undesirable; most, for example, bar criminals, paupers, and the diseased. With some exceptions, e.g., diplomats, aliens are subject to the laws of the country in which they reside. A country may place conditions on residence, and may deport the alien to his or her country of origin. An alien may acquire citizenship by a legal procedure known as NATURALIZATION.

**Alien and Sedition Acts,** 1798, four laws passed by the Federalist-controlled US Congress in response to the threat of war with France (see XYZ AFFAIR). Designed to destroy the Jeffersonian Republicans who expressed sympathy for France, the laws lengthened the residency requirement for citizenship, empowered the president to expel 'dangerous' aliens, and proscribed spoken or written criticism of the government. The Acts provoked the KENTUCKY AND VIRGINIA RESOLUTIONS.

**alienation,** term used to describe the nature of human labour under capitalist relations of production. Under CAPITALISM the general process of the 'objectification' of labour (which occurs when human beings act on the external natural world in order to transform it) takes the particular form of alienation. MARX defined alienated labour in a number of different ways: (1), the worker is alienated from the product of his/her labour (because he/she has no control over its distribution and use); (2), the worker is alienated from his/her fellow human beings, since capitalism reduces human relations to mere economic relations; (3), work provides no intrinsic enjoyment, and is only done in order to receive a wage—the labour of the worker has become a market commodity like any other; (4), the worker is alienated from his/her 'species being'—labour under capitalism has become the same as animal activity. After its use in Marx's early works, e.g., *The Economic and Philosophical Manuscripts* (1844), the term has susequently come to acquire a broader, more subjective or psychological meaning in the social sciences; referring to the general feeling of normlessness, or isolation—a state of existence much closer to Durkheim's concept, ANOMIE.

**Aligarh,** town (1981 pop. 320,861), Uttar Pradesh state, N India. It is a district administrative, commercial, and cultural centre with textile, metal, engineering, and other industries. One of its main claims to fame lies in Aligarh Muslim Univ., founded in 1920 (its precursor, the

Anglo-Oriental College, had been founded by Sayyid Ahmad Khan in 1875). Aligarh had fallen to the British in the second Maratha War (1803–05).

**'Ali ibn Abi Talib,** c.597–660, cousin and son-in-law of MUHAMMAD, 4th caliph (656–60) and central figure in SHI'ISM. The latter believes that Muhammad designated 'Ali as his immediate successor at Ghadir Khumm. 'Ali's eventual succession resulted in a losing conflict with the governor of Syria, Mu'awiya, at the Battle of Siffin, and assassination in Kufa.

**Ali Pasha,** 1744?–1822, Turkish governor of Yannina (1787–1820), a Greek province of the OTTOMAN EMPIRE. He ruled as a quasi-independent despot over most of Albania and Epirus. He resisted (1820) Turkish military efforts to depose him, tying up troops needed against the rebels in the Greek War of Independence. He was killed after surrendering.

**alkali** (ˌalkəlie), technically, a HYDROXIDE of any of the ALKALI METALS. Alkalis are soluble in water and form strongly basic solutions. They neutralize acids, forming salts and water. Strong alkalis (e.g., those of sodium or potassium) are called caustic alkalis. In general use, the term *alkali* is applied to any water-soluble strong base, e.g., sodium or potassium carbonate or the hydroxide of one of the ALKALINE-EARTH METALS. See ACIDS AND BASES.

**alkali metals,** elements in group Ia of the PERIODIC TABLE. In order of increasing atomic number, they are LITHIUM, SODIUM, POTASSIUM, RUBIDIUM, CAESIUM, and FRANCIUM. They are softer than other metals, and have lower melting points and densities. All react violently with water, releasing hydrogen and forming hydroxides. They tarnish rapidly, even in dry air. They never occur uncombined in nature.

**alkaline-earth metals,** elements in group IIa of the PERIODIC TABLE. In order of increasing atomic number, they are BERYLLIUM, MAGNESIUM, CALCIUM, STRONTIUM, BARIUM, and RADIUM. They are softer than most other metals and react readily with water. The salts of some of these metals, particularly of beryllium and barium, are poisonous.

**alkaline earths,** oxides of the ALKALINE-EARTH METALS. They are not readily soluble in water and form solutions less basic than those of an ALKALI.

**alkaloid,** any of a class of organic compounds composed of carbon, hydrogen, nitrogen, and usually oxygen, that are often derived from plants. The name means alkali-like, but some alkaloids do not exhibit alkaline properties. Many alkaloids, though poisons, have physiological effects that render them valuable as medicines. For example, curarine, found in the deadly extract CURARE, is a powerful muscle relaxant; atropine is used to dilate the pupils of the eye; and physostigmine is used in the specific treatment of certain muscular diseases. Narcotic alkaloids used in medicine include MORPHINE and CODEINE for pain relief and COCAINE as a local anaesthetic. Mescaline, obtained from the mescal cactus, is used as a stimulant and antispasmodic, especially among Mexican Indians who also employ it as a hallucinogen and intoxicant in various ceremonies. Other common alkaloids include CAFFEINE, LSD, QUININE, SEROTONIN, STRYCHNINE, and nicotine.

**alkane, alkene,** and **alkyne:** see HYDROCARBON.

**Allah,** [Arab., = God], Supreme Being, creator of all things and sole focus of worship for Muslims. The arabic word *Allah* means literally *The God* and thus enshrines in the word itself ISLAM's fundamental principle of unassailable monotheism. Invoked as 'Merciful'and 'Compassionate' in the KORAN, he is also seen in the same work to be utterly just and severe in His dealings with wilful sinners. The question and nature of His attributes provoked much debate among medieval Muslim theologians, enshrined in works of KALAM.

**Allahabad,** city (1981 pop. 619,628), Uttar Pradesh state, N India, at the confluence of the GANGES (Ganga) and Jamuna (Jumna) Rs. It is a district administrative, cultural, commercial, and communications centre, with some industry (cotton textiles and light engineering especially). Allahabad is not surprisingly a place of pilgrimage for Hindus, given its rivers and the mythical, subterranean Saraswati, supposed to join the other two at their confluence. It is an ancient city, going back under its older name of Prayag to the 4th cent. (the Gupta period). AKBAR built a fort there in 1583, and it was a Mogul provincial capital before passing to the British. Allahabad was the home of the NEHRU family.

**allegory,** in literature, symbolic story that serves as a disguised representation for meanings other than those indicated on the surface. Its characters are often mere embodiments of moral qualities. Allegory is closely related to PARABLE and FABLE. EVERYMAN, John BUNYAN's *Pilgrim's Progress,* and Edmund SPENSER's *Faerie Queen* are notable allegories.

**Allen, Bog of,** area of peat bogs in centre of Republic of Ireland, occupying an area of some 949 km² (370 sq mi). It is drained by the Brosna, BARROW, and Boyne rivers. The peat is used for fuel, and some of the more fertile land is cultivated.

**Allen, Woody,** 1935–, American film director, writer, and actor; b. Allen Stewart Konigsberg. His film comedies, which often depict neurotic urban characters preoccupied with sex, death, and psychiatry, include *Take the Money and Run* (1969), *Play It Again, Sam* (1972), *Love and Death* (1975), *Annie Hall* (1977; Academy Award), *Manhattan* (1979), and *Hannah and her Sisters* (1986).

**Allenby, Edmund Henry Hynman Allenby,** 1st **Viscount,** 1861–1936, British field marshal. In WORLD WAR I, he invaded Palestine and ended Turkish resistance (1918). He later served as British high commissioner for Egypt and the Sudan (1919–25).

**Allende Gossens, Salvador** (ie,yenday ˌgohsayns), 1908–73, president of CHILE (1970–73). He was a founder of the Chilean Socialist Party (1933). Winning a narrow electoral victory as the leader of a left-wing coalition, he became the first elected Marxist leader in the Americas. He embarked on a sweeping socialist programme of nationalization and social reforms to benefit the lower classes. His political support proved unstable and the collapse of the economy, coupled with acute political polarization, led to military intervention under Gen. PINOCHET during which Allende died in mysterious circumstances, probably by suicide.

**allergy,** adverse physical reaction of some people to substances that are not toxic and are innocuous to other people. Allergens (allergy-producing substances) cause the release of histamine, an organic chemical compound responsible for allergic symptoms. There are various types of allergens: airborne (e.g., pollen), which may cause sneezing, as in hayfever, or ASTHMA; contact allergens (e.g., poison ivy, cosmetics, and dyes), which often cause dermatitis; food (e.g., strawberries or shell fish), which may cause a skin reaction, such as eczema or hives, a gastric reaction, or a respiratory reaction; or drugs (e.g., penicillin), which can cause a severe, sometimes fatal, reaction. Treatment includes desensitization (injections), antihistamine drugs, and avoidance of allergens (where they can be identified).

**Alleyn, Edward,** 1566–1626, English actor. The only rival of Richard BURBAGE, he played the title roles in Christopher MARLOWE's *Tamburlaine, Jew of Malta,* and *Faustus.*

**alliance,** generally used to refer to the ties established between groups by marriage. Prescriptive marriage rules—those which specify that the marriage partner comes from a particular kinship category—may ensure that some groups are permanently tied to each other as affines. An important anthropological debate exists between those who argue that the most significant organizing principle in tribal (see TRIBE) societies is DESCENT and those who, following LÉVI-STRAUSS, argue that it is alliance. The latter position stresses the central importance of exchange and RECIPROCITY in the organization of social life.

**Alliance for Progress:** see ORGANIZATION OF AMERICAN STATES.

**alligator,** aquatic REPTILE (genus *Alligator*) in the same order as the CROCODILE. A quick way to tell the difference between the two is to look at the teeth: the fourth lower tooth of an alligator fits into a pit in the upper jaw, so cannot be seen when the mouth is closed. There are two species of alligator. The larger American alligator (*Alligator missisipiensis*) is usually about 2.7m (9 ft) long, the Chinese alligator (*A. sinensis*) being about 1.2 m (4 ft). They are all CARNIVORES; the young eating INSECTS and CRUSTACEANS, the older animals taking AMPHIBIANS, SNAKES, and small MAMMALS.

**Alliluyeva, Svetlana** (alee,loohyəvə), 1926–, only daughter of Soviet leader Joseph STALIN. In 1966 she defected to the West, becoming a US citizen; in 1984, she returned to the Soviet Union with her daughter, and her Soviet citizenship was restored; however, in 1986 she again settled in the West. She has written *Twenty Letters to a Friend* (1967) and *Only One Year* (1969).

**allograft:** see under TRANSPLANTATION, MEDICAL.

**allotropy,** the occurrence of certain chemical elements in two or more forms; the forms are called allotropes. Allotropes generally differ in physical properties, such as colour and hardness; they may also differ in molecular structure or in chemical activity but are usually alike in most chemical properties. DIAMOND and GRAPHITE are two allotropes of the element CARBON

**alloy,** substance with metallic properties consisting of a METAL fused with one or more other metals or nonmetals. An alloy may be a homogeneous solid solution, a heterogeneous mixture of tiny crystals, a true chemical compound, or a mixture of these. Alloys generally have properties different from those of their constituent elements and are used more extensively than pure metals. Alloys of IRON and CARBON are among the most widely used and include CAST IRON and STEEL. BRASS and BRONZE are important alloys of COPPER. Because pure GOLD and SILVER are too soft for many uses, they are often alloyed, either with each other, forming ELECTRUM, or with other metals, e.g., copper or PLATINUM. Amalgams are alloys that contain MERCURY. Other alloys include BRITANNIA METAL, DURALUMIN, and SOLDER.

**All Saints' Day,** Christian feast observed in the West on 1 Nov., the day God is glorified for all his saints, known and unknown. In medieval England it was called All Hallows; hence the name Halloween (Hallows' eve) for the preceding day (31 Oct.).

**All Souls Day,** observed in the West on 2 Nov., the day on which Christians commemorate the souls of the faithful departed. Although officially abolished in Protestant countries at the REFORMATION, its tradition has been widely maintained, and since the 19th cent. its observance has been revived in the Catholic section of the CHURCH OF ENGLAND and the ANGLICAN COMMUNION generally.

**allspice:** see PIMENTO.

**Allston, Washington,** 1779–1843, American painter. He travelled to London, where he studied with Benjamin WEST. Many of his greatest works, marked by a controlled romanticism, were done in England (1810–18). Allston's finest paintings are lyrical landscapes, e.g., *Moonlit Landscape* (1819; Mus. Fine Arts, Boston).

**Alma-Ata,** formerly Verny, city (1985 pop. 1,068,000), capital of the KAZAKH SOVIET SOCIALIST REPUBLIC, Soviet Central Asia, in the foothills of the Tien Shan Mts. The city lies in an oasis connected with the Ili R. and is on the traditional caravan route to China and now on the road to Urumchi. The surrounding countryside supports fruit-growing and irrigated vegetables, and industries include fruit-preserving, meat-packing, and leather and wine production. Alma-Ata is a major centre for the production of metallurgical equipment and other machine building; engineering, wool, and textiles also dominate its industrial base. The city was founded (1854) as a fortress by the Russians.

**Almagest:** see PTOLEMY (Claudius Ptolemaeus).

**Almagro, Diego de,** c.1475–1538, Spanish CONQUISTADOR, partner of Francisco PIZARRO in the exploration and conquest (after 1532) of the INCA civilization in Peru. He was later (1538) executed for rebellion by order of Hernando Pizarro.

**Al Manamah,** city (1981 pop. 121,986), capital of Bahrain, on the PERSIAN GULF. It has oil refineries and light industries and is a free port. It also has an important airport.

**Al-Masjid al-Aqsa** [Arab., = the furthest sanctuary or mosque], name derived from Chap. XVIII v.1 of the KORAN which refers to the famous night journey of MUHAMMAD from MECCA to 'the furthest sanctuary'. The name has been variously held to refer to a place in Heaven or the city of Jerusalem but is now universally used to designate a particular mosque built, according to tradition, by 'Abd al-Malik on the old Temple area in Jerusalem. See also DOME OF THE ROCK.

**Almeida, Francisco de** (ahl‚maydə), c.1450–1510, Portuguese admiral, first viceroy of Portuguese India (1505–09). He developed Portugal's trade with India by making alliances with Indian rulers and other tactics. He thwarted Egypt's commercial challenge by winning a great sea battle.

**Almeida Lima, Pedro Manuel de,** 1903–83, Portuguese neurosurgeon. He worked with Egas MONIZ in the development (1927) of cerebral angiography (visualization of blood vessels by X-rays) and he carried out the first frontal LEUCOTOMY in 1935 for treatment of an organic psychosis.

**Almería,** city (1981 pop. 140,946), capital of Almería prov., SE Spain. Its port, within a sheltered bay, handles table grapes, esparto grass, salt, and metallic ores. A Roman port, it achieved greatness under the Moors from whom it was not captured until 1488. It has a Moorish castle (Alcázaba) and 16th-cent. cathedral.

**Almohads** (‚almɔhadz), Berber Muslim dynasty that ruled Morocco and Spain in the 12th and 13th cent. It had its origins in the puritanical sect founded c.1120 by ibn Tumart. By 1147 the Almohads had completely displaced the ruling ALMORAVIDS. The Almohads, in turn, were defeated in Spain by the Spanish and Portuguese in 1228, and in Morocco by the Merenid dynasty in 1269.

**almond,** name for a small tree (*Prunus amygdalus*) of the ROSE family and for the nutlike edible seed of its drupe fruit. Almonds are now cultivated principally in the Orient, Italy, Spain, and California. Almond fruit is fleshless; otherwise, the tree closely resembles the peach tree. Almond oil, pressed from the nut, is used for flavouring and in soaps and cosmetics. In cookery, almonds are used in marzipan and ratafia.

**Almoravids,** Berber Muslim dynasty that ruled Morocco and Muslim Spain in the 11th and 12th cent. They founded MARRAKESH as the capital of their powerful empire. Called on for help by the Moors in Spain, they defeated (1086) ALFONSO VI of Castile and displaced the local Moorish rulers. Never entirely stable, the dynasty was overthrown by the ALMOHADS in 1147.

**Almquist, Carl Jonas Love,** 1793–1866, Swedish writer. *The Book of the Thorn Rose* (14 vol., 1832–51) contains most of his novels, stories, plays, and poems, which range from a bizarre romanticism to realism. A clergyman, teacher, and socialist, he was accused of forgery and suspected of murder. He fled to the US and after 1865 lived in Germany under an assumed name.

**aloe,** succulent perennials (genus *Aloe*) of the LILY family, native chiefly to Africa, but cultivated elsewhere. The leaves contain aloin, a purgative. Various drug-yielding species are used medicinally, as well as for X-ray and other burn treatment, insect repellent, and transparent pigment. Biblical

*Aloe plurideus*

aloes is unrelated. American and false aloe are agaves of the AMARYLLIS family.

**Alonso, Dámaso,** 1898–, Spanish critic, poet, and philologist. He was largely responsible for the rediscovery of the poetry of Luis de GÓNGORA. Among his critical works is *Seis calas en la expresión literaria española* (1951; tr. Six Studies of Spanish Literary Expression). *Hijos de la ira* (1944; Children of Wrath) contains some of his best verse.

**alpaca,** partially domesticated South American hoofed MAMMAL. The highland tribes of Bolivia, Chile, and Peru breed the alpaca for its wool, which is shaded from black through brown to white and has been exported since 1836. Alpacas feed on grasses and require a pure water supply. Like the LLAMA, the alpaca belongs to the CAMEL family.

**Alp Arslan,** 1029–72, Seljuk sultan of PERSIA (1063–72). He won a great victory over the Byzantine Christians at Manzikert (1071), and conquered Syria. He was murdered by one of his prisoners of war.

**alphabet,** system of WRITING, theoretically having a one-for-one relation between character (or letter) and phoneme (see PHONETICS AND PHONOLOGY). Few alphabets have achieved an ideal exactness. A system of writing is called a syllabary when one character represents a syllable rather than a phoneme, e.g., the kana used in Japanese. The precursors of the alphabet were the iconographic and ideographic writing of ancient man, such as CUNEIFORM and the HIEROGLYPHIC writing of the Egyptians. The alphabet of modern Western Europe is the Roman alphabet. Russian, Serbian, Bulgarian, and many languages of the USSR are written in the Cyrillic alphabet, an augmented Greek alphabet. Greek, Hebrew, and Arabic all have their own alphabets. The most important writing of India is the Devanagari, an alphabet with syllabic features. The Roman alphabet is derived from the Greeks, who had imitated the Phoenician alphabet. The exact steps are unknown, but the Phoenician, Hebrew, Arabic, and Devanagari systems are based ultimately on signs of Egyptian hieroglyphic writing. Two European alphabets of the late Roman era were the RUNES and the ogham. An exotic modern system is the Cherokee syllabary of SEQUOYAH.

Arabic

ابتثجحخدذرزسشصضطظعغفقكلمنهوىلا

Chinese

福道用謝天婚木思討貓鼠香玩初

Cyrillic

абвгдежзийклмнопрстуфхцчшщъыьэюя
АБВГДЕЖЗИЙКЛМНОПРСТУФХЦЧ

Devanagari

किसी जाति के जीवन में उसके द्वारा प्रयुक्त शब्दों

Greek

αβγδεζηθικλμνξοπρσςτυφχψω
ΑΒΓΔΕΖΗΘΙΚΛΜΝΞΟΠΡΣΤΥΦΧΨΩ

Hebrew

אבגדהוזחטיכלמנסעפצקרשת

Japanese

と あ の め ゆ が も ど の も わ

Examples of letters in various **alphabets**

**alpha decay,** one of the three forms of natural RADIOACTIVITY in which a positively charged particle (referred to as an alpha particle) identical with the nucleus of the helium atom is emitted. See also BETA DECAY, GAMMA DECAY.

**alphanumeric** or **alphameric,** the alphabetical, numerical, and special characters such as mathematical symbols and punctuation marks used in COMPUTER input and output.

**Alps,** great mountain system of S central Europe, c.800 km (500 mi) long and c.160 km (100 mi) wide, curving in a great arc through parts of France, Italy, Switzerland, Germany, and Austria. The mountains are known for their towering, snowcapped peaks, deep U-shaped glacial valleys, major glaciers, and many fine lakes such as GENEVA, LUCERNE, Como, GARDA, and Maggiore. Famous winter sports centres in the Alps include Chamonix, SAINT MORITZ, Kitzbühel, Cortina d'Ampezzo, and INNSBRUCK. The principal peaks include MONT BLANC, 4807 m (15,771 ft), the highest; Gran Paradiso; MATTERHORN; Jungfrau; and Grossglockner. The Alps are crossed by three of the world's longest tunnels — the Simplon, St Gotthard, and Mont Cénis — and by many routes such as the BRENNER PASS and the Great and Little St Bernard passes.

**Alsace–Lorraine,** region of NE France, bounded by Belgium, Luxembourg, and West Germany (N and E). Alsace lies to the east of Lorraine. Hops are grown, and vineyards are numerous. Potassium, iron, and coal deposits are exploited, and Lorraine leads France in steel output. STRASBOURG is Alsace's leading industrial centre. Most of the population speaks French, but German is also spoken, especially around Metz. Both Alsace and Lorraine were included in the HOLY ROMAN EMPIRE. Lorraine emerged as a duchy, and Alsace was divided into many fiefs and free cities by the 13th cent. France gradually acquired both regions in the 17th and 18th cent. As a result of the FRANCO-PRUSSIAN WAR (1870–71) much of the area was annexed to Germany and formed the 'imperial land' of Alsace–Lorraine. After WORLD WAR I Alsace–Lorraine was returned to France, but it was again annexed (1940–45) to Germany during WORLD WAR II.

**Alston, Richard,** 1948–, English dancer. After studying at the London School of Contemporary Dance and Cunningham Studio, New York, he formed Strider, an independent group of choreographers and dancers. He joined Ballet Rambert (see RAMBERT, DAME MARIE) (1980) and became artistic director (1986). His works are performed by many contemporary-dance and ballet companies.

**Altaic,** subfamily of the URALIC AND ALTAIC family of languages. See LANGUAGE (table).

**Altamira,** a painted cave near Santander in the Cantabrian Mts of Spain. Lively images of bison and other animals painted with various shades of ochre and manganese pigment give the cave its present fame, but in the 19th cent. it was a focal point of the debate about the antiquity of modern human beings. The discovery of the sophisticated paintings in 1875 was greeted by many with scepticism, and it was not until the beginnning of the 20th cent. that consensus about its Upper PALAEOLITHIC origins was reached.

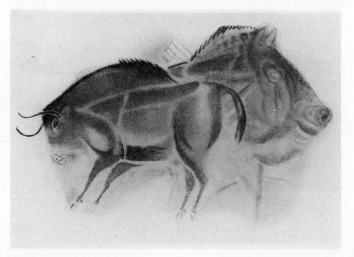

Cave paintings at **Altamira**

**Altdorfer, Albrecht,** 1480–1538, German painter and engraver. His romantic allegorical and biblical works, e.g., *Susannah at the Bath* (1526;

Albrecht **Altdorfer**, *Susannah at the Bath*, 1526. Alte Pinakothek, Munich.

Alte Pinakothek, Munich), are intensely expressive and dramatically lit. He was perhaps the first German to paint pure landscape.

**alternating current:** see ELECTRICITY; GENERATOR; MOTOR, ELECTRIC.

**alternation of generations,** reproductive cycle of plants in which a gametophyte generation reproduces sexually to produce the sporophyte generation, which in turn reproduces asexually by means of spores usually disseminated by wind. In the FERNS the visible plants are the sporophyte generation. They produce the spores which germinate to grow into a tiny free-living gametophyte (the prothallus) which bears the sex organs and is quite separate from the fern plant itself.

**alternative medicine:** see HOLISTIC MEDICINE.

**alternator:** see GENERATOR.

**Altgeld, John Peter,** 1847–1902, American politician, governor (1892–96) of Illinois; b. Germany. A Democrat and a staunch defender of human rights, he pardoned three men convicted for the HAYMARKET SQUARE RIOT of 1886, and protested against the sending of federal troops to end the Pullman strike (1894). His liberal actions, coupled with his espousal of FREE SILVER lost him reelection (1896).

**Althing,** parliament of ICELAND. The oldest assembly in Europe, first convened in 930, it voted Iceland's independence from Denmark in 1944. It comprises a lower house (two-thirds of members) and an upper house (one-third). Members are elected by a system of proportional representation.

**altimeter,** device for measuring altitude. The most common type, used in aeroplanes and balloons and by mountain climbers, consists of an aneroid BAROMETER, calibrated so that the drop in atmospheric pressure indicates the linear elevation. The radio altimeter indicates the actual altitude over the earth's surface by measuring the time it takes for a radio signal to travel to Earth and back.

**Altiplano,** densely populated upland plateau (alt. c.3600 m/12,000 ft) in the ANDES of Bolivia and Peru. It has a cool climate and bleak aspect. Potatoes and hardy grains are the chief crops; mining is the principal industry. LA PAZ and Oruro, in Bolivia, are the largest cities.

**altitude,** in astronomy: see ASTRONOMICAL COORDINATE SYSTEMS.

**Altman, Natan Isaevich,** 1889–1970, Russian painter. After studying in Paris (1910–12), he returned to Russia and exhibited in avant-garde exhibitions. After the Revolution he was active in agit-decorations, producing propagandist art celebrating the revolution in a style derived from CUBISM and FUTURISM.

**alto:** see VOICE.

**alumina** or **aluminium oxide,** chemical compound ($Al_2O_3$) that is widely distributed in nature and occurs combined with silica and other minerals in clays, feldspars, ZEOLITES, and micas, and in almost pure form in CORUNDUM. It is the major component of BAUXITE and is used in the production of ALUMINIUM metal. Alumina is also used as an ABRASIVE and as a CATALYST, in ceramics and pigments, and in the manufacture of chemicals.

**aluminium** (Al), metallic element, used in antiquity but first isolated by Friedrich WÖHLER in 1827. The silver-white metal is ductile and malleable, and conducts heat and electricity. Although very reactive chemically, aluminium resists corrosion by forming a protective oxide (alumina) coating. The most abundant metal in the earth's crust (about 8% by weight), it occurs combined with other elements in such minerals as alum, BAUXITE, CORUNDUM, CRYOLITE, FELDSPAR, MICA, and the aluminosilicates (CLAYS and ZEOLITES). Aluminium and its compounds are used in paints, foil, and jewellery, and in welding. Aluminium wire, cheaper and lighter than copper wire, is used in high-tension power transmission. The strong, hard alloy DURALUMIN is used in aircraft. See ELEMENT (table); PERIODIC TABLE.

**Alvarado, Pedro de** (ahlvah,rahdhoh), 1486–1541, Spanish CONQUISTADOR. A chief lieutenant of Hernán CORTÉS during the conquest of MEXICO, Alvarado conquered GUATEMALA in 1523 and served as governor until his death. Exercising absolute control, he founded many cities and developed the colony while searching for the fabled Seven Cities of Cibola. He was killed quelling an Indian rebellion in W Mexico.

**Alvere I,** c.1542–86, ruler (r.1567–86) of the kingdom of KONGO (now Angola and Zaire). Alvere obtained aid from the Portuguese to secure the Kongo from predatory neighbours. The Portuguese of São Tome, who regarded themselves as independent of Lisbon, subsequently usurped the authority of Alvere and the Kongo became an appendage of recently-conquered Angola.

**alyssum,** chiefly annual and perennial herb (genus *Alyssum*) of the MUSTARD family, native to the Mediterranean. Some species, with masses of yellow or white flowers, are cultivated as rock-garden and border ornamentals. The annual sweet alyssum has fragrant white or lilac blossoms. Once called madwort or healbite, alyssum was thought to cure rabies.

**Alzheimer's disease,** degenerative disease of the brain cells producing loss of memory and general intellectual impairment. It usually affects people in their 40s, 50s, and 60s, and is sometimes known as presenile dementia. As the disease progresses, a variety of symptoms may become apparent, including confusion, irritability, and restlessness, as well as disorientation and impaired judgment and concentration. The cause of the disease is unknown, and there is no known treatment, although tranquillizers are sometimes used to reduce agitation and unpredictable behaviour.

**AM:** see MODULATION.

**Am,** chemical symbol of the element AMERICIUM.

**Amadeus VIII,** 1383–1451, duke (from 1416) of Savoy and antipope (1439–49) with the name Felix V. The last of the antipopes, he was elected at the Council of BASEL, but had few supporters. He yielded his claim when Nicholas V became pope.

**Amado, Jorge,** 1912–, Brazilian novelist. His vibrant novels of the lives of ordinary Brazilians include *The Violent Land* (1942), *Gabriela, Clove and Cinnamon* (1958), and the ebullient *Doña Flor and Her Two Husbands* (1966).

**Amagasaki,** city (1986 est. pop. 501,773), S Honshu, Japan, between Kobe and Osaka. A port and industrial centre, after the Meiji Restoration it attracted many large factories producing iron, steel, and glass. In the 9th cent. it flourished as an outer port serving the old capital Kyoto and developed as a leading commercial and industrial city. In 1526, the local lord, T. Hosokawa, constructed a castle and founded the castle town. It is the site of Kosai Temple, famous for the grave of the dramatist CHIKAMATSU MONZAEMON (1653–1724).

**Amalekites** (ˌamələ'kiets), aboriginal people of CANAAN and the Sinai peninsula. They waged war against the Hebrews, until dispersed by SAUL and DAVID. Ex. 17.8–16; 1 Sam. 30.1–20.

**Amalfi**, town (1984 pop. 6419) S Italy, on Gulf of Salerno. It was a flourishing maritime republic as early as the 9th cent., but succumbed to the Normans in 1131 and thereafter was a part of the kingdom of NAPLES. The cathedral is dedicated to St Andrew the Apostle whose remains lie in the crypt.

**amalgam:** see ALLOY.

**Amalric** or **Amaury**, Latin kings of Jerusalem. **Amalric I**, c.1137–1174 (r.1162–74), lost the suzerainty of Egypt to the Turkish sultan Nur ad-Din and eventually to SALADIN. **Amalric II**, c.1155–1205 (r.1197–1205), married the daughter of Amalric I. He was also king of Cyprus (1194–1205).

**Amalthea**, in astronomy, satellite of JUPITER.

**amaranth**, common name for the family Amaranthaceae (also called the pigweed or cockscomb family), herbs, trees, and vines found mainly in warm regions of the Americas and Africa. The genus *Amaranthus* includes several species called amaranth, characterized by a red pigment in the stems and leaves which is permanent when dried, and common weeds, e.g., the green amaranth (*A. retroflexus*) introduced from America. Some species have long been used as potherbs and cereals. The globe amaranth, (genus *Gomphrenia*), and the cockscomb (genus *Celosia*) are annuals that are dried and used in everlasting bouquets.

**Amarillo**, US city (1980 pop. 149,230), N Texas; inc. 1899. A plains city, it is the commercial and industrial centre of the Texas Panhandle. Oil, gas, helium, and zinc are produced, along with various manufactures. The city handles grains and livestock grown in the area. It grew with the coming (1887) of the railway and became an industrial city after the discovery of gas (1918) and oil (1921).

**amaryllis**, common and generic name for some members of the Amaryllidaceae, a family of mostly perennial plants with flat, narrow leaves and lilylike flowers borne on separate, leafless stalks. Widely distributed, they are found especially in tropical and subtropical lowlands. Ornamentals of the family are mistaken for plants of the LILY family, which differ in the position of the ovary (see FLOWER). The family includes the showy-blossomed true amaryllis, or belladonna lily (*Amaryllis belladonna*); the daffodils and jonquils (genus NARCISSUS); and the snowdrops (genus *Galanthus*), whose small, early-blooming flowers are symbolic of consolation and promise. The genus *Agave,* the tropical American counterpart of the African genus ALOE, contains the most economically important plants in the family. Different agaves provide soap, food, beverages, and fibre (see SISAL; HEMP).

**Amateur Athletics Association**, governing body for athletics in England and Wales. Founded in Oxford on 24 Apr. 1880. The first 'Three As' championships were held in the same year and continue as the unofficial British championships.

**Amati, Andrea**, c.1520–c.1578, Italian VIOLIN maker. He experimented with the shape and size of violins and established the proportions still accepted today. Many of his instruments are still played. He passed on his craft to his sons Antonio and Girolamo, grandson Nicolo, and to the violin-making community at Cremona, e.g., GUARNIERI and STRADIVARI.

**Amaury.** For persons thus named, see AMALRIC.

**Amazon**, world's second longest river, flowing c.6300 km (3900 mi) west across N South America to enter the Atlantic Ocean through a wide delta in N Brazil. It is formed by the junction in N Peru of the Ucayili and Marañón rivers. It has more than 500 tributaries, drains c.40% of the continent, and carries more water than any other river in the world. The Amazon traverses a sparsely populated and largely undeveloped region that contains the world's largest rainforest (selva). There are no waterfalls or other obstructions along its course, and ships of 4-m (14-ft) draught can travel very nearly its full length (to Iquitos, Peru). Belém and Manaus in Brazil are other ports.

**Amazon**, in Greek mythology, one of a tribe of warlike women situated on the borders of the known world. The Amazons had a matriarchal society, in which women governed and fought while men performed the household tasks. They removed the right breasts of girls to prevent them obstructing the bow string. Several Greek heroes proved their mettle against Amazons, e.g., HERCULES and THESEUS.

**amber,** yellow to brown fossil RESIN exuded by coniferous trees of ancient forests; the best amber is transparent. Highly polished amber is used to make small decorative objects, e.g., beads and amulets. When rubbed with a cloth, amber becomes charged with static electricity. Bubbles of air, leaves, bits of wood, or insects, sometimes of extinct species, are often found trapped in amber. The chief source of the world's amber is the Baltic coast of Germany.

**ambergris,** a waxlike substance that is formed in the intestine of the sperm whale. It is found floating on tropical seas or cast up on the shore in yellow, grey, black, or variegated masses. Greatly valued from earliest times, ambergris is now used as a fixative in perfumes.

**Ambler, Eric**, 1909–86, English novelist. He is the author of popular suspense stories, usually involving international intrigue, e.g., *The Mask of Dimitrios* (1939), *To Catch a Spy* (1964), and *The Care of Time* (1981).

**Ambrose, Saint**, c.339–397, bishop of MILAN, Doctor of the Church. A popular governor in Milan, Ambrose, though still unbaptized, was made (374) bishop by popular demand. He opposed ARIANISM and was an adviser to Emperor Gratian, whom he persuaded to outlaw (379) heresy in the West. His preaching helped to convert St AUGUSTINE. Ambrose wrote many theological works and is associated with the type of PLAINSONG called Ambrosian chant. Feast: 7 Dec.

**Ameling, Elly**, 1938–, Dutch soprano. Although she has sung opera, she is noted for her sensitive interpretations of French and German art songs, particularly the LIEDER of Schubert.

**Amenemhet I** ('ahmenem,het), d. 1962 BC, king of EGYPT, founder of the XII dynasty that initiated the Middle Kingdom. He centralized the government in a virtually feudal form. The dynasty enabled the arts and science to flourish.

**Amenhotep I** or **Amenophis I** ('amen,hohtep), fl. 1570 BC, king of EGYPT of the XVIII dynasty. A great military leader, he extended Egypt's power E to the Euphrates and S to the second cataract of the NILE. THUTMOSE I succeeded him.

**American Ballet Theater:** see DANCE (table).

**American Civil War,** in US history, conflict (1861–65) between Northern states (Union) and Southern seceded states (CONFEDERACY). It is also known in the South as the War between the States, and by the official Union designation of War of the Rebellion. Many contributing causes over a number of years led to what William H. SEWARD called 'the irrepressible conflict': sectional rivalry, moral indignation aroused by the ABOLITIONISTS, the question of the extension of slavery into new territories, and a fundamental disagreement about the relative supremacy of federal control or STATES' RIGHTS. The MISSOURI COMPROMISE (1820) and the COMPROMISE OF 1850 were unsuccessful efforts towards a peaceful solution. The election of Abraham LINCOLN as president and the secession (20 Dec. 1860) of SOUTH CAROLINA, soon followed by six other Southern states, precipitated war. When Lincoln sent supplies to the federal troops at FORT SUMTER, the Confederate general P.G.T. Beauregard obeyed orders to fire on the fort (12 Apr. 1861). Four more states seceded, making an 11-state Confederacy. Early battles were Confederate victories. Beauregard defeated Irvin McDowell (21 July) at the first battle of BULL RUN. In 1862, the PENINSULAR CAMPAIGN was foiled by Confederate commander Robert E. LEE. In September, however, Lee's Antietam Campaign was checked by MCCLELLAN, and Lincoln drafted the EMANCIPATION PROCLAMATION. The year ended with a Union defeat (13 Dec.) at Fredericksburg, and spring brought a resounding Confederate victory (2–4 May 1863) at Chancellorsville, Virginia, where Lee, however, lost his ablest general, 'Stonewall' JACKSON. Confederate fortunes turned for the worse when Lee undertook the disastrous GETTYSBURG CAMPAIGN (June–July 1863). Meanwhile, the Union navy had blockaded the Southern coast, and D.G. FARRAGUT captured New Orleans (Apr. 1862). The introduction of the ironclad warship (see MONITOR AND MERRIMACK) had ended the era of the wooden battleship, but fast, unarmoured, and lightly armed Confederate commerce-raiders, built in England, were causing great losses to Northern commercial shipping. In the West, GRANT's great victory (Feb. 1862) at Fort Donelson, Tennessee, was followed by a drawn battle (6–7

April) at SHILOH. Union gunboats on the Mississippi opened the way for Grant's successful VICKSBURG CAMPAIGN. The Confederate army of Gen. Braxton Bragg was checked at the end of the Chattanooga Campaign (Aug.–Nov. 1863) and driven back to Georgia. In the WILDERNESS CAMPAIGN (May–June 1864), Grant forced Lee towards Richmond, and besieged Petersburg. Union general W.T. SHERMAN captured Atlanta, Georgia, (May–Sept. 1864) and made a destructive march through Georgia to the sea. The Confederates evacuated Richmond after P.H. SHERIDAN's victory at Five Forks (1 Apr. 1865). With his retreat blocked, Lee was forced to surrender to Grant at APPOMATTOX (9 Apr. 1865). The Union victory was saddened by the assassination of Pres. Lincoln (14 Apr.), and by the deaths of more Americans than in any other war. But the Union was saved, and slavery was abolished. The seceded states were readmitted to the Union during RECONSTRUCTION.

**American Colonization Society,** organized (Dec. 1816–Jan. 1817) to transport free blacks from the US and settle them in Africa. Land purchases (1821) in Africa by the society led to the foundation of LIBERIA, and more than 11,000 blacks were sent there before 1860. The colonization movement was attacked by ABOLITIONISTS and was unpopular with many blacks; it declined after 1840.

**American Federation of Labor and Congress of Industrial Organizations** (AFL-CIO), a federation of autonomous trade unions in the US, Canada, Mexico, Panama, and US territories. Formed in 1955 by the merger of the AFL (est. 1886) and the CIO (which had broken away from the AFL in 1938), the organization serves as the leading voice of American trade unionism, actively lobbying on the national and state levels, and supporting political candidates. Ultimate authority in the AFL-CIO is vested in a biennial convention; the executive council governs between conventions. In 1987 the AFL-C1O had 96 national affiliates and its membership totalled about 13,500,000.

**American Indian languages,** languages of the native peoples of the Americas. It is a geographical rather than linguistic classification as these languages are not easily categorized, except into groups displaying a variety of distinctive phonetics, vocabulary, and grammars. It is estimated that there were more than 380 distinct Indian languages in North America in pre-Columbian times. At present there are 200 Amerindian languages still spoken in North America, about 80 in Central America, and possibly up to 2000 in South America, although only 600 of these are actually attested, and 120 now extinct. In North America, Navajo is numerically the strongest with Aztec (also called Nahuatl) and Quiche being spoken by over two million in Central America. The South American languages of the Macro-Chibchan family are also spoken in S Central America and in certain areas of NW South America. The other two South American families of languages, Ge–Pano–Carib and Andean–Equatorial, are distributed widely over the whole of South America.

**American Indian Movement** (AIM), activist organization of the American Indian civil rights movement, est. 1968. After briefly occupying (Nov. 1972) the Bureau of INDIAN AFFAIRS to protest programmes controlling Indian development, in 1973 AIM members led 200 SIOUX in a 71-day takeover of WOUNDED KNEE, South Dakota, to demand a review of 300 treaties with the US government. AIM also sponsored talks resulting

in the 1977 International Treaty Conference with the UN in Geneva, Switzerland.

**American Indians:** see MIDDLE AMERICAN INDIANS; NORTH AMERICAN INDIANS; SOUTH AMERICAN INDIANS; and individual tribes. See also AMERICAN INDIAN LANGUAGES; AMERICAN INDIANS, PREHISTORY OF.

**American Indians, prehistory of.** It is generally agreed that the first humans to inhabit the Americas crossed the BERING STRAIT from NE Asia in migration waves beginning before 30,000 BC. By 8000 BC, Indians had spread throughout the Americas. Major Palaeolithic cultures were created c.20,000 BC by seminomadic hunters of the Great Plains of North America. Earliest evidence of human occupation in Middle and South America dates from 30,000 BC. Between 5000 BC and 1000 BC, agriculture, pottery, and complex social systems throughout the Americas marked the end of the STONE AGE and the rise of the high Indian civilizations. See MIDDLE AMERICAN INDIANS; NORTH AMERICAN INDIANS; SOUTH AMERICAN INDIANS; and articles on individual tribes.

**American Negro spiritual:** see SPIRITUAL.

**American party:** see KNOW-NOTHING MOVEMENT.

**American Revolution,** 1775–83, struggle by which the THIRTEEN COLONIES that were to become the United States won independence from Britain. By the middle of the 18th cent., differences in life, thought, and economic interests had formed between the colonies and the mother country. The British government, favouring a policy of MERCANTILISM, tried to regulate colonial commerce in the British interest, and provoked colonial opposition. The STAMP ACT passed by Parliament in 1765 roused such a violent colonial outcry as an act of taxation without representation that it was withdrawn. Two subsequent attempts at taxation, the TOWNSHEND ACT (1767) and the Tea Act (1773), led to such acts of violence as the BOSTON MASSACRE (1770), the burning of the HMS *Gaspee* (1772), and the BOSTON TEA PARTY (1773). In 1774 Britain responded with the coercive INTOLERABLE ACTS. The colonists convened the CONTINENTAL CONGRESS and petitioned the king for redress of their grievances. Fighting erupted on 19 Apr., 1775, at LEXINGTON and CONCORD, and was followed by the capture of Fort Ticonderoga from the British, the battle of BUNKER HILL, and the unsuccessful colonial assault on Quebec (1775–76). The Continental Congress appointed (1775) George WASHINGTON to command the Continental Army and, on 4 July, 1776, adopted the DECLARATION OF INDEPENDENCE. Many colonists, however, remained pro-British Loyalists. During the first phase of the war (1776–77) military operations were largely confined to the North. Washington was heavily defeated at the battles of Long Island (1776) and Brandywine Creek (1777) and Gen. William Howe's British forces captured New York and Philadelphia. The colonial victory in the SARATOGA CAMPAIGN (1777) helped forge a French-American alliance (1778), bringing vital aid to the colonists. Following the terrible ordeal of Washington's army at VALLEY FORGE, the war shifted to the South during the Carolina campaign (1780–81). The surrender (Oct. 1781) of Gen. CORNWALLIS at the close of the YORKTOWN CAMPAIGN ended the fighting, and the Treaty of Paris (1783) recognized the US as a nation.

**American Samoa,** unincorporated territory of the US (1980 pop. 32,395), 197 km² (76 sq mi), comprising the eastern half of the Samoa

---

### AMERICAN INDIAN LANGUAGE GROUPS

**Eskimo–Aleut** Five languages. The northernmost language family.

**Na–Dene** Nine languages spoken in W North America. The most important being Navajo.

**Macro–Algonquin** 21 languages, formerly spoken over the eastern two-thirds of North America. Two major families: Algonquian and Muskogean.

**Salish** Spoken in British Columbia and N California.

**Wakashan** Six languages spoken in British Columbia.

**Macro–Siouan** Approximately 18 languages and three major families: Iroquoian, Siouan, Caddoan. E and central US.

**Penutian** Approximately 58 languages spoken in North, Central, and South America. The majority are Mayan speakers in Mexico.

**Hokan** Approximately 20 languages mainly in California, NW Mexico, S Mexico, and W Arizona.

**Aztec–Tanoan** Approximately 28 languages spoken in W North America and Mexico.

**Oto–Manguean** Approximately 30 separate languages spoken exclusively in central Mexico.

**Macro–Chibchan** Southern Central America. Two major families: Chibchan and Paezan.

**Ge–Pano–Carib** Spread over the whole of South America, there are 196 languages in four major families: Macro-Carib, Macro-Ge-Bororo, Macro-Panoan, and Nambicuara.

**Andean–Equatorial** Widespread in America. Five main families: Andean, Equatorial, Arawakan, Tupi, Macro-Tucanoan.

island chain in the South Pacific. The major islands are Tutuila, the Manu'a group, Rose and Sand, and Swains. Pago Pago, the capital, is on Tutuila. The islands are mountainous and wooded; agriculture, fish canning, and some light industry are conducted. The Polynesian natives, considered US nationals, elect a governor and legislature, and send a nonvoting delegate to Congress. American Samoa, defined by treaty in 1899, was administered by the US Dept. of the Navy until 1951, when it passed to Dept. of the Interior jurisdiction.

**America's Cup,** most famous of all sailing races. In 1851 the New York Yacht Club (NYYC) sent a 170-ton schooner *America* to compete in Britain for the Hundred Guineas Cup; it won. Six years later, the NYYC made the cup a perpetual challenge trophy. Since the first challenge in 1870 there have been 16 challenges by Britain, seven by Australia, and two by Canada. The US had never lost a series before 1983, when *Australia II* won, taking the Cup from the NYYC for the first time in 132 years. The US won the Cup back in 1987 in Perth, W Australia, when Dennis Connor sailing *Stars and Stripes* defeated Iain Murray in *Kookaburra III*. Since 1964 the course has been standardized at 39.1 km (24.3 mi). After 1983, the character of the race was transformed from a relatively obscure event into a multimillion pound extravaganza in which national syndicates, often including multinational business firms, finance the competitors, some of which have also received subsidies from their home governments.

**americium** (Am), synthetic radioactive element, discovered by Glenn Seaborg and colleagues in 1944 by neutron bombardment of plutonium. The silver-white metal is in the ACTINIDE SERIES. Half-lives of the many isotopes range from 1.3 hr to over 7000 years. See ELEMENT (table); PERIODIC TABLE.

**amethyst,** most highly valued variety of QUARTZ, violet to purple in colour, used as a GEM. Amethyst is found in Brazil, Uruguay, Sri Lanka, Siberia, and North America. It has superstitious associations, being regarded as a love charm, a sleeping aid, and a guard against thieves and drunkenness.

**Amharic** (am,harik), language of ETHIOPIA. It belongs to the Ethiopic group of Hamito-Semitic languages. See AFRICAN LANGUAGES (table).

**Amherst, Jeffrey Amherst, Baron,** 1717–97, British army officer. During the last of the FRENCH AND INDIAN WARS, he commanded British forces at the capture of Louisburg, Nova Scotia (1758), Ticonderoga (1759), and Montreal (1760).

**Amiens** (,amiənz), city (1982 pop. 136,358), capital of Somme dept., N France. A textile and farm-market centre, it has been occupied by many invaders; after being devastated in both world wars the city was rebuilt. Its Cathedral of Notre Dame (begun c.1220) is France's largest Gothic cathedral.

**Amiens, Treaty of:** see FRENCH REVOLUTIONARY WARS.

**Amin, Idi,** c.1925–, president of UGANDA (1971–79). Seizing control of the government from Milton OBOTE in 1971, he instituted a harsh and brutal regime and expelled Uganda's Asian population. He was driven into exile in Saudi Arabia in 1979.

**amino acid,** any of a class of organic compounds having a carboxyl group (COOH) and an amino group ($NH_2$). Some 22 amino acids are commonly found in animals and more than 100 less common forms are found in nature, chiefly in plants. When the carboxyl carbon atom of one amino acid binds to the nitrogen of another with the release of a water molecule,

| Glycine (aminoethanoic acid) | Alanine (2-aminopropanoic acid) | Valine (2-amino-3-methylbutanoic acid) |
|---|---|---|
| H<br>\|<br>$H_2N$ — C — COOH<br>\|<br>H | H<br>\|<br>$H_2N$ — C — COOH<br>\|<br>$CH_3$ | H<br>\|<br>$H_2N$ — C — COOH<br>\|<br>CH<br>／＼<br>$CH_3$   $CH_3$ |

Structures of **amino acids**

a linkage called a peptide bond is formed. Chains of amino acids, joined head-to-tail in this manner, are synthesized by living systems and are called polypeptides (up to about 50 amino acids) and PROTEINS (over 50 amino acids). The process of digestion (see DIGESTIVE SYSTEM) releases individual amino acids from food protein by cleaving the peptide bonds.

**Amis, Kingsley,** 1922–, English novelist. He made his reputation with *Lucky Jim* (1954), a brilliant satire on academic life. Later novels include *That Uncertain Feeling* (1955), *Take a Girl Like You* (1960), *Jake's Thing* (1978) and *The Old Devils* (1986). Amis also writes poetry, literary essays, crime novels, and science fiction.

**Amman,** city (1985 est. pop. 777,500), capital of Jordan, N central Jordan, on the Jabbok R. Jordan's largest city and industrial and commercial heart, Amman is a transportation hub, especially for pilgrims en route to MECCA. It is noted for its coloured marble; textiles, cement, and other manufactures are produced. Amman is the biblical Rabbah, the Ammonite capital, and the Philadelphia of the Hellenistic period. It fell to King David, Assyria, Rome, and other conquerors. After the Arab conquest (635) it declined, reviving as the capital of Trans-Jordan after 1921 when its population was a mere 10,000. Palestinian refugees swelled the population after the Arab-Israel Wars of 1948 and 1967. The city's historic structures include a Roman amphitheatre.

**ammeter,** instrument used to measure, in AMPERES, the magnitude of an electric current. An ammeter is usually combined with a VOLTMETER and an OHMMETER in a multipurpose instrument. Although most ammeters are based on the d'Arsonval GALVANOMETER and are of the analogue type, digital ammeters are becoming increasingly common.

**ammonia,** chemical compound ($NH_3$), colourless gas with a characteristic pungent, penetrating odour. It is extremely soluble in water. Ammonia solutions are used to clean, bleach, and deodorize; to etch aluminium; to saponify oils and fats; and in chemical manufacture. Ammonia and ammonia vapours are irritating and prolonged exposure and inhalation cause serious injury and may be fatal. Water-free ammonia is used in REFRIGERATION. The major use of ammonia and its compounds is as FERTILIZERS. Ammonia is usually produced by direct combination of nitrogen with hydrogen at high temperature and pressure in the presence of an iron catalyst. More than 100 million tons of ammonia are synthesized annually from atmospheric nitrogen and hydrogen, which nowadays emanates from decomposed natural gas (METHANE). The process is essentially unchanged from that invented by Fritz HABER.

**amnesia,** condition characterized by total or partial loss of memory for long or short intervals. It may be caused by physical injury, SHOCK, drugs, or disease. In cases of psychological trauma, a painful experience and everything connected with it is unconsciously repressed (see DEFENCE MECHANISM). Attempts to cure this type of amnesia include efforts to establish associations with the past through PSYCHOTHERAPY and HYPNOSIS.

**amnesty,** in law, exemption from prosecution for some criminal action. It is distinguished from a pardon (see SENTENCE), which is an act of forgiveness following conviction. Amnesties are usually extended to groups of persons involved in disorders or insurrections. In the UK, the last general act of amnesty was granted in 1747, to those who had taken part in the second JACOBITE rising, and after the Civil War the US granted a qualified amnesty to the Confederate forces.

**Amnesty International** (AI), organization (est. 1961) that campaigns against the imprisonment of individuals solely on the grounds of their political or religious beliefs, and against other human rights violations throughout the world. It was awarded the Nobel Peace Prize in 1977 after effecting the release of more than 10,000 prisoners. In 1988 the organization included national sections in 45 countries and members or subscribers in over 150 countries.

**amniocentesis** ('amniohsen,teesis), diagnostic procedure in which a sample of the amniotic fluid surrounding the fetus is removed from the uterus with a fine needle inserted through the abdomen of the pregnant woman (see PREGNANCY). Fetal cells in the fluid are cultured in the laboratory and studied to detect the presence of certain genetic disorders (e.g., DOWN'S SYNDROME, TAY-SACHS DISEASE) or developmental abnormalities (e.g., spina bifida). Generally recommended only when there is a family history of genetic disorders or when the woman is over age 35, the procedure is usually carried out around the 14th or 15th week of pregnancy, when there is sufficient amniotic fluid and ABORTION is still an option. See also CONGENITAL ABNORMALITIES.

**Amnon,** DAVID's eldest son. He raped his half sister Tamar and was killed for it by her brother ABSALOM. 2 Sam. 13.

**amoeba,** one-celled organism (class Sarcodina) in the phylum PROTOZOA. Amoebas constantly change their body shape as they form temporary extensions called pseudopods, or false feet, used for feeding and locomotion. Most amoebas range from 5 to 20 microns in diameter. They engulf their prey (diatoms, algae, bacteria) with their pseudopods, forming vacuoles in which food is digested by ENZYMES. Reproduction is usually by binary fission (splitting) to produce two daughter amoebas, the nucleus dividing by MITOSIS; some also reproduce sexually. Amoebas live in fresh and marine waters and the upper layers of soil. Many are PARASITES of aquatic and terrestrial animals, and some cause disease, e.g., amoebic dysentery.

**Amon, Ammon** or **Amen** (ˌaymən, ˌamən, ˌahmən), ancient Egyptian deity. Originally the chief god of Thebes, Amon grew increasingly important in Egypt, and eventually, as Amon Ra, he was identified with RA as the supreme deity. He was also identified with the Greek ZEUS (the Roman JUPITER).

**Amos,** book of the OLD TESTAMENT. The shepherd–prophet of that name, preached in the northern kingdom of Israel under Jeroboam II (r. c.793–753 BC). The book falls into three parts: God's judgment on Gentile nation Israel; three sermons on the doom of Israel; five visions of destruction, the last promising restoration.

**Amoy:** see XIAMEN.

**ampere** (amp or A), basic unit of electric current and the fundamental electrical unit of the SI system of units (see METRIC SYSTEM). The ampere is officially defined as the current in a pair of equally long, parallel, straight wires 1 metre apart that produces a force of 0.0000002 newton between the wires for each metre of their length. It corresponds to a flow of electrical charge equal to 1 COULOMB per second.

**Ampère, André Marie,** 1775–1836, French physicist, mathematician, and natural philosopher. He extended the work of Hans OERSTED on the relationship of electricity and magnetism, formulated Ampère's law describing the contribution of a current-carrying part of a circuit to magnetic induction, and invented the astatic needle. The basic unit of electric-carrying part of a circuit, the AMPERE, is named after him.

**amphetamine,** any of a class of powerful drugs that act as stimulants (see DRUGS) on the central nervous system. Popularly known as 'speed' or 'uppers', amphetamines enhance mental alertness and the ability to concentrate; cause wakefulness, talkativeness, and euphoria; and temporarily reverse the effects of fatigue. They have been used to treat obesity and depression, but they are strongly addictive and easily abused; addiction can result in psychosis or death from overexhaustion or cardiac arrest. The medical use of amphetamines is restricted to a small number of patients with abnormal sleep patterns. See DRUG ADDICTION AND DRUG ABUSE.

**amphibian,** POIKILOTHERMIC (cold-blooded) animal of the class Amphibia, the most primitive of terrestrial VERTEBRATES. Unlike REPTILES, the amphibians, which include FROGS and TOADS, salamanders and NEWTS, and the limbless CAECILIANS, have moist skins without scales. Most amphibians deposit their eggs in water or a moist, protected place. The young undergo METAMORPHOSIS from aquatic, water-breathing, limbless TADPOLES to terrestrial or partly terrestrial, air-breathing, four-legged adults.

**amphibian,** AIRCRAFT designed for operation from both land and water, usually a flying boat with a retractable land undercarriage. The term is also used for a land vehicle capable of floating, e.g, the DUKW ('duck') craft used for landing troops onto a beach from a ship.

**amphibious warfare,** use of combined land and sea forces to take a military objective, typically through an air-supported assault on an enemy coastline. Although the general strategy is very ancient, e.g., the Athenian attack on Sicily in 415 BC, the term did not come into widespread use until WORLD WAR II. Early in the war, coordinated land, sea, and air attacks by the Japanese in the SW Pacific met little opposition. By contrast, Allied attacks on Europe and the Pacific islands were mounted against heavily defended coasts, requiring construction of a class of special vessels (called landing craft) that were seaworthy and yet capable of allowing TANKS and fully equipped INFANTRY to disembark in shallow water. Such landings were preceded and accompanied by continuous air and naval bombardment of coastal defences. By this method the Allies were

able to invade such Pacific strongholds as Saipan (1944), Iwo Jima (1945), and Okinawa (1945), and to launch the most spectacular amphibious invasion in history, on the coast of Normandy, France, on 6 June 1944. Amphibious landings later occurred in the KOREAN WAR and VIETNAM WAR and in the British attack (1982) on the FALKLAND ISLANDS.

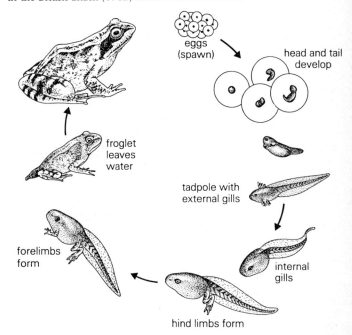

eggs (spawn)

head and tail develop

froglet leaves water

tadpole with external gills

forelimbs form

internal gills

hind limbs form

Amphibian life cycle

**amphitheatre,** open structure for the exhibition of gladiatorial contests and spectacles, built in cities throughout the Roman Empire, e.g., at Rome (see COLOSSEUM), Arles in France, and Cirencester in England. The typical amphitheatre was elliptical, with seats rising around a central arena; quarters for the gladiators and animals were under the arena. The word is now used for various quite unrelated structures. See also THEATRE.

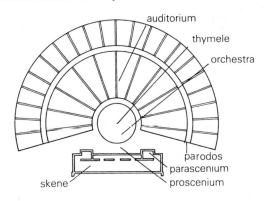

auditorium

thymele

orchestra

parodos

parascenium

proscenium

skene

Amphitheatre

**amphoterism** (amˌfotərizəm), in chemistry, the property of certain compounds of acting either as acids or as bases (see ACIDS AND BASES), depending on the reaction in which they are involved. Many hydroxide compounds and organic molecules that contain both an acidic (e.g., carboxyl) and a basic (e.g., amino) FUNCTIONAL GROUP are amphoteric.

**amplifier,** device in which a varying input signal controls a flow of energy to produce an output signal that varies in the same way but has a larger amplitude; the input signal may be a current, a voltage, a mechanical motion, or any other signal, and the output signal is usually of the same nature. The ratio of the output voltage to the input voltage is called the voltage gain. The most common types of amplifiers are electronic and have TRANSISTORS as their principal components. In most cases today, transistors are incorporated into INTEGRATED-CIRCUIT chips. Most amplifiers include more than one transistor. Transistor amplifiers are used in RADIO and TELEVISION transmitters and receivers, stereophonic RECORD PLAYERS, and intercoms.

**amplitude modulation:** see MODULATION.

**Amravati** or **Amraoti**, town (1981 pop. 261,404), Maharashtra state, C India. It is a district administrative and commercial centre, especially for cotton grown in the region known as Berar. There are cotton and oil mills. The nucleus is an old walled town.

**Amritsar**, city (1981 pop. 594,844), Punjab state, N India. It is a district administrative, route, and commercial centre which, particularly since Indian independence, has become a highly industrialized city. Its traditional craft textile industries survive, but there are now many modern establishments, large and small, making cotton, wool, and silk goods. There are also engineering, chemical, and machine-tool works. Amritsar is, however, chiefly famous for the Golden Temple, the most revered shrine of the Sikhs, the site of which was donated by AKBAR in 1577. By the Treaty of Amritsar (1809) the British confirmed Sikh rule over the Punjab west of the River Sutlej; this Treaty lasted until the second Sikh war of 1845. Amritsar became a British administrative headquarters and was the scene of the notorious Jallianwalabagh massacre of 1919.

The Golden Temple at **Amritsar**

**Amsterdam**, constitutional capital and largest city (1985 pop. 675,579, agglomeration 998, 130) of the Netherlands, on the Ij and Amstel rivers. It is a major port joined with the North Sea and the Rhine by canals. One of Europe's great commercial, intellectual, and artistic capitals, Amsterdam has a major stock exchange and is a diamond-cutting centre. It is built on piles and is cut by some 40 canals crossed by about 400 bridges. Chartered c.1300, it joined the HANSEATIC LEAGUE in 1369 and the anti-Spanish Netherland provinces in 1578. An influx of refugees contributed to its rapid growth, and the city reached its apex in the 17th cent. After French rule (1795–1814) it became the Dutch capital. Amsterdam suffered greatly under German occupation (1940–45) during WORLD WAR II. Points of interest include the city hall (16th cent.); the university (est. 1632); the Rijks Museum, with its many Rembrandts and other Dutch master paintings; and the municipal museum, with its Van Gogh collection.

**Amu Darya**, river, Soviet Central Asia, known to the ancient Greeks and Persians as the Oxus. It is c.2580 km (1600 mi) long and flows generally NW from sources in the snow-capped Pamirs through the KARA-KUM desert to a large delta on the ARAL SEA. In the early 1980s the Soviet government announced a plan to increase the flow of the river, which irrigates parts of the Turkmen and Uzbek republics, by diverting to it some of the waters of the IRTYSH R.

**Amundsen, Roald** (ˌahmoonsən), 1872–1928, Norwegian explorer. He commanded the first single ship to sail through the NORTHWEST PASSAGE (1903–06) and was the first man to reach the South Pole (1911). In 1926, with the aviator Umberto Nobile and the financier Lincoln Ellsworth, Amundsen took part in the first aeroplane flight over the North Pole.

When Nobile crashed in the Arctic in 1928, Amundsen was killed in the rescue attempt. His works, which include *The South Pole* (1913), have added much to knowledge of the polar regions.

**Amur**, river, c.2900 km (1800 mi) long, NE Asia. It flows generally SE, forming for more than 1610 km (1000 mi) the border between the Soviet Union and China, then NE through the Soviet Far East, entering the Tartar Strait opposite SAKHALIN Island. Its chief tributaries are the USSURI and SUNGARI. The river is navigable by small craft for its entire length during the ice-free season (May–Nov.).

**Amurath.** For Ottoman sultans thus named, see MURAD.

**Anabaptists**, name applied, originally in scorn, to certain Christian sects holding that infant baptism is not authorized in Scripture, but that baptism should be administered only to believers. Prominent in Europe during the 16th cent., they were persecuted everywhere. Their chief leaders were Thomas MÜNZER and JOHN OF LEIDEN. MENNONITES and Hutterites are descended from them.

**Anabasis:** see XENOPHON.

**anaconda:** see BOA.

**Anacreon**, c.570–c.485 BC, Greek LYRIC poet, celebrator of love and wine. The Anacreontics, in his style, were written from Hellenistic to late Byzantine times.

**anaemia**, a reduction in the concentration of circulating HAEMOGLOBIN due to a reduction in the number of red blood cells (erythrocytes) or their haemoglobin content. The blood's reduced capacity to carry oxygen causes symptoms of pallor, weakness, dizziness, fatigue, and breathlessness. Treatment of the condition depends on its cause, of which there are many. See SICKLE-CELL ANAEMIA.

**anaesthesia**, loss of sensation, especially that of pain, induced by drugs. General anaesthesia, first used in surgical procedures in the 1840s, induces unconsciousness; halothane and thiopentone are two widely used general anaesthetics. Local or regional anaesthesia desensitizes a particular region without loss of consciousness. Local anaesthetics include lignocaine and procaine, commonly used for dental procedures; spinal anaesthetics, primarily for lower body surgery; and epidural anaesthetics for childbirth. Various anaesthetics are often used in combination. See also ACUPUNCTURE.

**Anaheim**, US city (1984 est. pop. 234,000), S California, SE of LOS ANGELES; founded 1857, inc. 1876. A major tourist centre, Anaheim contains the amusement complex Disneyland (opened 1955); Anaheim Stadium, home of the California Angels baseball team and the Los Angeles Rams football team; and the Anaheim Convention Center. It is also the site of a large electronic equipment industry.

**analgesic**, agent which relieves pain. Analgesics include ASPIRIN and other salicylates, which also reduce fever and inflammation; NARCOTIC drugs, such as MORPHINE and CODEINE; PARACETAMOL; and synthetic narcotics.

**analogue circuit**, ELECTRIC CIRCUIT in which the output voltage and current values are considered significant over a continuum. Analogue circuits may be used for such purposes as amplifying signals corresponding to sound waves. See also DIGITAL CIRCUIT.

**analogue computer**, array of electrical elements and amplifiers connected in such a manner that the input and output signals are related mathematically in an identical or analogous manner to the phenomenon being studied. Analogue computers were much used in the 1940s and 50s as dynamic simulators in which the time-scale could be varied, i.e., made faster than the real phenomenon when this was slow and vice versa. For the skilled operator they were easy and quick to assemble for a specific problem. By their very nature they could not take advantage of the rapid advances in digital technology and the developments of the CHIP solid-state electronics. They are now largely obsolete except for special laboratory or research purposes.

**analogue-to-digital conversion**, the process of changing continuously varying data into digital quantities that represent the magnitude of the data at the moment the conversion is made. The most common use is to change analogue signals into a form that can be manipulated by a digital COMPUTER, as in data communications. See also DIGITAL-TO-ANALOGUE CONVERSION.

**analysis,** branch of MATHEMATICS that uses the concepts and methods of the CALCULUS. It includes basic calculus; advanced calculus, in which such underlying concepts as that of a LIMIT are subjected to rigorous examination; differential and integral equations, in which the unknowns are functions rather than numbers (see FUNCTION); VECTOR and tensor analysis; differential geometry; and many other fields.

**analysis of variance,** one of the principal techniques used in STATISTICS for the interpretation of numerical information by identifying the relevant sources of variability and estimating the corresponding VARIANCES. The technique is widely used in almost all of the applied sciences for the interpretation of experiments and surveys. It also greatly facilitates the DESIGN OF EXPERIMENTS or surveys, for example in cost of living surveys, the screening of new pesticides, or the determination of safe levels of drugs.

**analytical chemistry:** see CHEMISTRY.

**analytical geometry,**    branch of GEOMETRY in which points are represented with respect to a coordinate system, such as CARTESIAN COORDINATES. Analytical geometry was introduced by René DESCARTES in 1637 and was of fundamental importance in the development of the CALCULUS by Sir Isaac NEWTON and G.W. LEIBNIZ in the late 17th cent. Its most common application, the representation of an EQUATION involving two or three variables as a curve in two or three DIMENSIONS or a surface in three dimensions, allows problems in ALGEBRA to be treated geometrically and geometric problems to be treated algebraically. The methods of analytical geometry have been generalized to four or more dimensions and have been combined with other branches of geometry.

**anarchism** [Gr., = without a ruler], political philosophy and movement that seeks the abolition of government, arguing that people, although naturally good, are corrupted by artificial institutions. Anarchism dates from the ancient Greeks, but its modern form was outlined (18th and 19th cent.) by William GODWIN, P.J. PROUDHON, and others. In Russia, given a violent and collectivist tone by Mikhail BAKUNIN, it was outlawed by the Bolsheviks after the RUSSIAN REVOLUTION. Only in the Latin countries of Europe, where it was linked to SYNDICALISM, did it gain a mass following by the end of the 19th cent. After the HAYMARKET SQUARE RIOT (1886) and the assassination of Pres. MCKINLEY, fear of anarchism caused the US in 1901 to forbid anarchists from entering the country. Today anarchism remains of interest as a political theory, but is not significant as an active political movement.

**Anatolia:** see under ASIA MINOR.

**Anatolian languages,**    subfamily of the Indo-European family of languages. See LANGUAGE (table).

**anatomy,** the study of the physical structure of plants and animals. Comparative anatomy considers structural similarities and differences of various organisms, forming the basis of CLASSIFICATION. Human anatomy emphasizes individual systems composed of groups of tissues and organs (see TISSUE). See also PHYSIOLOGY.

**Anaxagoras** ('anak,sagərəs), c.500–428 BC, pre-Socratic Greek philosopher of the Milesian school, thought to have been the teacher of SOCRATES. He held that an all-pervading *nous* [world-mind] ordered the physical world by combining particles from the undifferentiated mass of the universe.

**Anaximander** (ə'naksi,mandə), c.611–c.547 BC, pre-Socratic Greek philosopher of the Milesian school. His notions of the infinite or indefinite (*apeiron*) and its processes prefigured the later concept of the indestructibility of matter, while other views anticipated the theory of evolution and certain laws of astronomy.

**Anaximenes,** d. c.528 BC, pre-Socratic Greek philosopher of the Milesian school. He held that air is the fundamental principle of the universe, everything else being produced from air by processes of condensation and rarefaction.

**ancestor,** in anthropology, deceased person of importance to the present social structure. In many tribal societies groups are recruited on the principle of shared descent from a common ancestor. Huge groups can be formed in this way tracing common descent back through tens of generations to the original founding father or mother, the apical ancestor (standing at the apex of a triangle of descendants). In most such societies power (domestic, economic, ritual, and political) is vested in the oldest men in the group, the elders. When elders die they become the subject of ancestor worship by their immediate descendants. Ancestors are in this way a projection of the authority system of the living—having considerable power, and demanding considerable attention. Ancestors can punish when rules are violated, reward when the rules are observed, and are therefore seen, particularly within the perspective of STRUCTURAL FUNCTIONALISM, as a means of reinforcing social conformity and validating the kinship system.

**Anchises** (an,kieseez), in Greek mythology, Trojan shepherd; father of AENEAS by APHRODITE.

**Anchorage,** US city (1984 est. pop. 227,000), Anchorage Borough, south-central Alaska, at the head of Cook Inlet; inc. 1920. Founded (1915) as a railway town, it has grown into the state's largest city as well as the administrative and commercial heart of south–central and W Alaska. It is one of the nation's major defence centres and a transport hub. Tourism is important, and there is a busy international airport. The city's rapid growth is due largely to its position as the focus of Alaska's expanding coal, oil, and gas industries.

**Anchouey, Laurant** (on,shway), 1897–1929, W African anti-colonial activist and journalist; b. among the Omyeme, Gabon. He founded a Gabonese branch of the French 'League des droits de l'homme' thus attracting the attention of French public opinion to colonial oppression in Gabon. He also campaigned widely in France for the removal of French colonial administration which should have led to direct cooperation between colonial peoples and France.

**anchovy,** name given to several small fishes of the family Engraulidae. Found in temperate and tropical seas, anchovies live in large shoals like their relatives, the HERRINGS, feeding on PLANKTON. The European anchovy (*Engraulis encrasicholus*) is fished for canning or for making into paste or sauce. It is 11–15 cm (4½–6 in) long. The Peruvian anchoveta (*E. ringens*) was the food of the guano-producing sea birds, the GUANO being collected and sold as fertilizer. In the 1950s the industry cut out the birds, fishing for the anchoveta themselves and grinding it into fish meal for fertilizer and animal feedstuffs. Almost 12,300,000 tonnes of fish were harvested in 1970 alone, 18% of the total world harvest of fish, most of them anchovetas, resulting in a disastrous plunge in fish stocks and the end of the industry.

**Ancona,** city (1984 pop. 105,467) and port, capital of the Marche region, E central Italy. It has naval yards and industries include oil and food-processing. Originating as a Greek (Syracusan) settlement in the 4th cent. BC, it became a medieval maritime republic. Notable historic buildings are the Byzantine–Romanesque cathedral (11th–13th cent.) and Trajan's Arch (AD 115). The city suffered extensive damage in World War II.

**Ancren Riwle** or **Ancrene Wisse** (,ahngkrən ,reeoohlə), c.1200? This anonymous devotional handbook, the most important early medieval English prose work, was written to instruct three ladies who wished to live as anchoresses.

**Andalusia,** region (87,218 km² 33,675 sq mi), on the Mediterranean Sea, the Strait of Gibraltar, and the Atlantic Ocean. Spain's largest and most populous region, it occupies all of S Spain. Grapes, olives, citrus, and other crops are grown in its subtropical climate. Mineral resources include copper, iron, and zinc. It was settled (11th cent. BC) by the Phoenicians and later ruled by Carthage (6th cent. BC), Rome (3rd cent. BC), and the Visigoths (5th cent. AD). In 711 the MOORS conquered Andalusia. Christian Spain ended the long reconquest of the region when GRANADA fell in 1492. In 1713 Spain ceded GIBRALTAR to Britain.

**Andean Group,** also known as Andean Pact, intergovernmental organization for economic cooperation between Bolivia, Colombia, Ecuador, Peru and Venezuela. It was formed in 1969 with the signature of the Cartagena Agreement creating an Andean Common Market. Chile, an original member, withdrew in 1976; Panama is an associate member and Mexico a 'working partner'.

**Andersen, Hans Christian,** 1805–75, Danish writer of fairy tales. Poverty-ridden and a failure as an actor, Andersen won the generous patronage of King Frederick VI with his poetry. Though noted for a time as a novelist, e.g., *The Improvisatore* (1835), it was his later fairy tales that established him as Denmark's greatest author and a storyteller without peer. His sense of fantasy, power of description, and acute sensitivity contributed to his mastery of the genre. Among his many widely beloved tales are 'The Little Match Girl', 'The Ugly Duckling', 'The Snow Queen', and 'The Red Shoes'.

Trajan's Arch, **Ancona**

**Andersen Nexø, Martin** (ˌandəsən ˌneksuh), 1869–1954, Danish novelist. His famous proletarian novels *Pelle the Conqueror* (1906–10) and *Ditte, Daughter of Mankind* (1917–21) focused attention on conditions of poverty in Denmark.

**Anderson, Dame Judith,** 1898–, Australian actress; b. Frances Margaret Anderson. She gave powerful performances in *Macbeth* (1937), *Medea* (1947), and the film *Rebecca* (1940).

**Anderson, Elizabeth Garrett,** 1836–1917, English physician. She was the first woman to qualify in medicine in the UK. After obtaining a private medical education under accredited physicians and in London hospitals and becoming licensed (1865) in Scotland, she was appointed (1866) physician to the Marylebone Dispensary for Women and Children, which eventually became the Elizabeth Garrett Anderson Hospital, staffed by women. Largely through her efforts, British examining boards opened their examinations to women.

**Anderson, Sherwood,** 1876–1941, American writer. He was a strongly American writer, experimental and poetic, whose greatest novel, *Winesburg, Ohio* (1919), explores the loneliness and frustration of small-town lives. His other novels include *Poor White* (1920) and *Dark Laughter* (1925). Some of his finest work is in his compassionate and penetrating short stories, e.g., the collections *The Triumph of the Egg* (1921), *Horses and Men* (1923), and *Death in the Woods* (1933).

**Andersonville,** village (1980 pop. 267), SW Georgia, US; inc. 1881. It was the site of a notorious Confederate prison, now a national historic site, where dreadful conditions led to the death of over 12,000 Union soldiers.

**Andes,** great mountain system, extending c.7200 km (4500 mi) north to south in South America, generally parallel to the Pacific coast. The mountains reach a high point of 6960 m (22,835 ft) in ACONCAGUA (highest point in the Western Hemisphere) and include many other snow-capped peaks over 6700 m (22,000 ft). The system widens in Bolivia and Peru to form multiple ranges and a high, densely populated plateau (ALTIPLANO), where the great civilization of the INCAS had its home. Copper, silver, and tin are mined, and oil has been found in the northern foothills. The Andes are geologically young and still rising. Volcanic eruptions and earthquakes are common.

**Ando Hiroshige:** see HIROSHIGE.

**Andorra,** Fr. *Andorre,* autonomous principality (1984 est. pop. 42,712), 495 km² (191 sq mi), SW Europe, between France and Spain, comprising several high valleys in the E Pyrenees. The capital is Andorra la Vella. Sheep-raising, minerals (iron, lead, marble), timber, and a growing tourist trade are the principal sources of income for the Catalan-speaking, Roman Catholic population. In 1278 Andorra was put nominally under the joint suzerainty of a French count, whose rights have subsequently passed to the president of France, and the bishop of Urgel (Spain). In effect it is independent, governed by an elected council and syndic.

**Andrade, José Oswald de Sousa** (anˌdrahday), 1890–1954, Brazilian poet and novelist. On a visit to Europe he was impressed by FUTURISM, and he became influential in Brazilian progressive literature. His deliberately anti-sentimental style is exemplified in his novel *Os Condenados* (1922).

**Andrássy, Julius, Count** (ˌondrahshee), 1823–90, Hungarian politician. A leading figure in the unsuccessful Hungarian revolution of 1848–49, he lived in exile until 1858. He later took part (1867) in the creation of the AUSTRO-HUNGARIAN MONARCHY. As premier of Hungary (1867–71) Andrássy established Magyar supremacy over the Slavs in Hungary. He was foreign minister of the Dual Monarchy (1871–79) and signed (1879) the Dual Alliance with Germany. His son **Julius, Count Andrássy,** 1860–1929, also foreign minister, tried (1918) to obtain a separate peace for Austria–Hungary in WORLD WAR I.

**André, Carl,** 1935–, American sculptor. His classic, elemental sculptures reflect the philosophy of MINIMAL ART. Andre is well known for his floor pieces, e.g., his brick sculpture *Equivalent VIII* (Tate Gall, London), which caused public outrage when purchased in 1966 due to the questioning of traditional values of creativity in sculpture.

Carl **André,** *Equivalent VIII*, 1966. Bricks, freestand sculpture, 12.7 × 68.6 × 229.2 cm. Tate Gallery, London.

**André, John,** 1751–80, British spy in the AMERICAN REVOLUTION. He was captured and hanged after negotiating with Benedict ARNOLD for the surrender of WEST POINT to the British.

**Andrea del Sarto:** see SARTO, ANDREA DEL.

**Andreas-Salomé, Lou,** 1861–1937, Austrian psychoanalyst, writer, and feminist. Well-known in Austrian–German literary circles, and one-time mistress of Nietzsche and Rilke, she was the first woman to be admitted (1910) to the Vienna psychoanalytic circle. She was a close friend and correspondent of Sigmund FREUD, and psychoanalysed Anna FREUD as a child.

**Andrew, Saint,** one of the Twelve Disciples, brother of Simon PETER. He is patron saint of Russia and Scotland.

**Andrew II**, 1175–1235, king of HUNGARY (r.1205–35). He was forced to issue (1222) the Golden Bull, the 'Magna Carta' of Hungary, which extended privileges to the lesser nobles. He took part (1217) in the Fifth CRUSADE.

**Andreyev, Leonid Nikolayevich**, 1871–1919, Russian émigré writer. His early stories, realistic studies of everyday life, were praised by GORKY, but when the Bolsheviks took power in 1917 he broke with Gorky politically and emigrated to Finland. His popularity declined when he turned to mysticism and allegory. His fiction includes *The Red Laugh* (1905), *King Hunger* (1907), and *The Seven That Were Hanged* (1908). His best-known play is the expressionistic *He Who Gets Slapped* (1916).

**Andrić, Ivo** (ˌandrich), 1892–1975, Yugoslav writer. His work includes poetry, essays, short stories, and novels, the best known being his Bosnian historical trilogy (1945) *The Bridge on the Drina, Bosnian Story,* and *Young Miss*. In 1961 he was awarded the Nobel Prize for literature.

**Andromache** (anˌdromᴈkee), in Greek mythology, wife of HECTOR of Troy; mother of Astyanax. After the TROJAN WAR, ACHILLES' son Neoptolemus abducted her; EURIPIDES and RACINE dramatized her captivity. Later she married Hector's brother Helenus.

**Andromeda**, in Greek mythology, princess of Ethiopia; daughter of Cepheus and Cassiopeia. POSEIDON, angered by her mother's claim that her beauty outshone that of the nereids, sent a sea monster that could be appeased only by her sacrifice. She was rescued by PERSEUS, who slew the monster and married her. Andromeda and her parents became constellations.

**Andromeda galaxy**, closest spiral GALAXY (2 million LIGHT-YEARS distant) to our MILKY WAY galaxy. They are similar in shape and composition. The Andromeda galaxy, visible to the naked eye as a faint patch in the constellation Andromeda, is about 120,000 light-years in diameter and contains at least 200,000 million stars.

The centre of **Andromeda galaxy**

**Andropov, Yuri Vladimirovich**, 1914–84, Soviet public official, general secretary of the Communist Party of the Soviet Union (1982–) and president (1983–84); formerly ambassador to Hungary (1954–57) and head of the KGB, the Soviet security agency (1967–82). A member of the politburo, the Communist Party's ruling body, since 1973, Andropov succeeded to the Soviet Union's most powerful office on the death of Leonid BREZHNEV. He brought with him a reputation as an ideological conservative.

**anemone**, wild or cultivated perennial herb (genus *Anemone*) of the BUTTERCUP family. Anemones, which contain a poisonous compound (anemonin), were once used to treat fevers, liver and kidney conditions, bruises, and freckles; they are often associated with evil and death. The white-blossomed wood anemone *A. sylvestris* is also called windflower.

**angel**, bodiless, immortal spirit, limited in knowledge and power, accepted in the traditional belief of Judaism, Christianity, and Islam. The three choirs of angels appear early in the Christian era; the classes are,

from the highest: seraphim, cherubim, thrones; dominations, virtues, powers; principalities, archangels, angels. Angels appear in the Bible, often in critical roles, e.g., visiting Abraham and Lot (Gen. 18; 19) and announcing the Incarnation to Mary (Luke 1). The cult of guardian angels who protect individuals or nations is especially strong in the West. The angels of HELL, or devils, led by SATAN, are viewed as initiators of evil temptations.

**Angel Falls**, waterfall, 979 m (3212 ft) high, on the Churún R., in the Guiana Highlands, SE Venezuela. It has the world's highest uninterrupted fall (807 m/2648 ft).

Angel Falls

**Angelico, Fra**, c.1400–1455, Florentine painter; b. Guido di Pietro. A Dominican monk, Fra Angelico treated only religious subjects, and his style is one of sweetness and grace. His tempera paintings, as *The Descent from the Cross* (c.1440; San Marco Mus., Florence) are distinguished by their pure and brilliant colour and by their complex treatment of space and form. His most famous work is a cycle of frescoes (after 1436) in the monastery of San Marco, Florence (now a museum of his works); these works were intended as aids to contemplation and are movingly simple.

**Angell, Sir Norman**, 1873–1967, British internationalist and economist, b. Ralph Norman Angell-Lane. In his best-known work *The Great Illusion* (1910), he argued that the common economic interests of nations make war futile. After World War I he worked for international cooperation and peace. Knighted in 1931, he was awarded the Nobel Peace Prize in 1933.

**Angelus**, family name and dynasty of Byzantine emperors (1185–1204) Isaac II, ALEXIUS III, and ALEXIUS IV.

Fra **Angelico**, *The Descent from the Cross*, c.1440. Panel, 176 × 185 cm. Museo de San Marco, Florence.

**Angers** (on,zhay), city (1982 pop. 141,143, agglomeration 195,859), capital of Maine-et-Loire dept., W France, on the Maine R. Formerly the capital of Anjou, it is a market and tourist centre with electronic industries. A massively fortified castle, built of black slate with bands of white stone, guards the bridging point. It is famous for its collection of tapestries.

The black and white castle at **Angers**

**angina** or **angina pectoris,** condition marked by sudden intense spasms of suffocating pain in the chest, brought on especially by exertion and usually relieved by rest. Angina occurs when the heart's demand for oxygen cannot be met and is usually associated with CORONARY HEART DISEASE.

**angiosperm,** plant in which the ovules, or young seeds, are enclosed within an ovary (that part of a FLOWER specialized for seed production), in contrast to the GYMNOSPERMS. Also known as the flowering plants, angiosperms have leaves (see LEAF), ROOTS, and STEMS, and VASCULAR TISSUE. They are divided into dicotyledons which have two seed leaves (cotyledons) and CAMBIUM tissue in the stems, and monocotyledons which have one seed leaf and generally lack cambium tissue. The most important

plant group economically, angiosperms include all agricultural crops and cereal GRAINS, all garden flowers, and almost all broad-leaved trees and shrubs.

**Angkor,** site of several capitals of the KHMER EMPIRE, N of Tônlé Sap, NW CAMBODIA. The ruins extend over 104 km² (40 sq mi). The first capital was established by Yasovarman I (889–900). A new temple complex, **Angkor Wat,** was built under Suryavarman II (1113–50). This impressive temple, surrounded by a vast moat, is approached by a causeway. Its extensive sculptural ornament exhibits impeccable craftsmanship. In 1177 Angkor was sacked by the Chams and fell into ruins. Jayavarman VII (1181–c.1218) established a new capital, **Angkor Thom,** which was abandoned in 1434. The ruins, overgrown by jungle, were discovered by the French in 1861.

The main temple of **Angkor Wat**

**angle,** in mathematics, figure formed by two straight lines meeting at a point; the point is known as the vertex of the angle, and the lines are its sides. Angles are commonly measured in degrees (°) or in radians. If the two sides form a single straight line but do not coincide, the angle is a *straight angle,* measuring 180° or $\pi$ radians (see PI). If the sides are perpendicular, i.e., if they form half of a straight angle, the angle is a *right angle,* measuring 90° or $\pi/2$ radians. An *acute angle* is greater than 0° but less than 90°; an *obtuse angle* is greater than 90° but less than 180°; and a *reflex angle* is greater than 180°. See also TRIGONOMETRY.

**angler fish,** number of species of FISH that have evolved a method of catching their prey, using a 'rod and line'. The rod is a modified dorsal fin spine baited with a flap of skin or a worm-like shape. Small fishes approach the lure, agitated by an otherwise motionless angler fish, to be snapped up by the angler's very large mouth. There are two groups of anglers, the deep sea anglers, found in the abyssal depths, and the batfish and frogfish group, which live in shallower waters.

**Anglican Communion,** the worldwide body of churches derived from and in communion with the Church of England (see ENGLAND, CHURCH OF). Composed of regional churches, provinces, and separate dioceses, the Communion is bound together by mutual loyalty as expressed in periodical LAMBETH CONFERENCES. Member churches include the Episcopal Church in the US (see EPISCOPAL CHURCH, PROTESTANT), the Scottish Episcopal Church, the Church in Wales, and the Anglican Church of Australia. Doctrinally all member churches are similar, having a ministry of three orders: deacons, priests, and bishops. Worship, though varied in form, is liturgical and sacramental, based ultimately on the BOOK OF COMMON PRAYER.

**angling,** art of catching fish with hook and bait or lure. It is more popular in Britain as a recreation than as a competitive sport, claiming some 3 million adherents. References exist in Homer, the Book of Isaiah, and Plutarch. Isaac Walton's treatise *The Compleat Angler* (1653) is a classic of English literature.

**Anglo-Saxon Chronicle,** collective name for English monastic chronicles in Anglo-Saxon, stemming from a compilation (c.891) of earlier sources inspired by King ALFRED. The account, from the beginning of the Christian era to 1154, draws on BEDE and adds much original material. Mostly prose, it includes such poems as *The Battle of Brunanburh*.

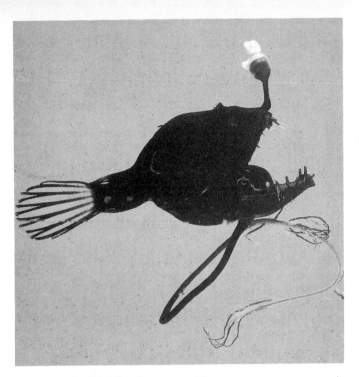

Deep sea **angler fish** (*Linophryne coronata*)

**Anglo-Saxon literature,** writings in Old English, c.650–1150. Old English poetry is heroic, drawing on Germanic myth and custom, or Christian. Nearly all of it survives in only four manuscripts, and it is the literature closest to Germanic oral sources. *Widsith* (7th cent.) is an early example. The epic *Beowulf,* based on oral sagas, survives in an 8th-cent. Christian version. The elegiac undercurrent in *Beowulf* is central to such poems as *Deor, The Wanderer,* and *The Seafarer,* which contrast a happy past with a desolate present. Heroic battles are the theme of *The Battle of Maldon* and *The Battle of Brunanburh.* Of the Christian poets, CAEDMON and CYNEWULF are known by reputation. *The Dream of the Rood* is the earliest dream vision poem in English. Old English verse is alliterative and unrhymed. Prose was written in Latin before King ALFRED, who had many works translated. The ANGLO-SAXON CHRONICLE, begun in his time, continued for three centuries. Two preeminent prose writers were Aelfric and Wulfstan, authors of homiletic sermons.

**Anglo-Saxons,** name given to the Germanic-speaking peoples who raided England during the last phases of Roman rule there and settled after the collapse of Roman authority. The Angles probably came from Schleswig late in the 5th cent. and lay the foundations of the later kingdoms of EAST ANGLIA, MERCIA, and NORTHUMBRIA. The Saxons, a Germanic tribe, settled in England at the same time; the kingdoms of SUSSEX, WESSEX, and ESSEX were outgrowths of their settlements. The Jutes, a tribe probably from the area at the mouth of the Rhine, settled in Kent and on the Isle of Wight. The term 'Anglo-Saxons', denoting non-Celtic settlers of England, dates from the 16th cent. Since the 19th cent. it has been used more loosely to denote any people (or their descendants) of the British Isles.

**Angola,** officially People's Republic of Angola, formerly Portuguese West Africa, republic (1986 est. pop. 8,800,000), 1,246,700 km² (481,351 sq mi), SW Africa, bordered by the Atlantic Ocean (W), Zaïre (N), Zambia (E), and Namibia, South West Africa (S). It includes the province of CABINDA, on the Atlantic coast, from which it is separated by a strip of land belonging to Zaïre. Major cities include LUANDA (the capital) and LOBITO. Nearly all of the land is desert or savanna, except for the densely forested valleys of the northeast and a narrow coastal strip in the west. The most prominent physical feature is the Bié Plateau (average altitude 1830 m/6000 ft), which rises abruptly from the coastal lowland and slopes eastward to the CONGO and ZAMBEZI river basins. Formerly dependent on agriculture, Angola today receives over two-thirds of its export earnings from oil production, chiefly from reserves offshore of Cabinda. Diamonds

and iron ore are also important. Principal crops include coffee (the second largest export), sugarcane, maize, and wheat. Among the leading industries are food processing (notably cereals, fish, palm oil, and meat) and the manufacture of jute, cotton textiles, and paper. The population is overwhelmingly black African, and most of the people speak a Bantu language; the Mbundu are the largest ethnic group. (The great majority of the estimated 500,000 European residents left Angola after independence was achieved.) Traditional religious beliefs prevail, but there is a large minority of Roman Catholics and other Christians.

*History.* The first Portuguese colony in Angola was established in Luanda in 1575, and, except for a short occupation (1641–48) by the Dutch, Angola remained under Portuguese control until its independence in 1975. (The Mbundu kingdom in central Angola successfully resisted the Portuguese until 1902, when it was finally subjugated.) For the Portuguese, Angola was primarily a source of slaves for their colony in Brazil. Modern industrial development began only after World War II, and Angola was upgraded from its colonial status and designated an overseas province in 1951. Repression of the African population continued, however, and in 1961 a revolt began. When this failed, guerrilla warfare was undertaken from neighbouring countries, intensifying in the early 1970s, when more than 50,000 Portuguese troops were engaged against the rebels. In 1972 Angola was made an 'autonomous state', and in 1973 elections were held for a legislative assembly. Independence was proclaimed in November 1975, touching off a struggle for power among rival nationalist groups. Civil war ensued, and by early 1976 the Popular Movement for the Liberation of Angola (MPLA), supported by the USSR and aided by Cuban troops, defeated the US-supported factions and proclaimed a people's republic aligned with the Soviet bloc. In 1977 the (Marxist-Leninist) MPLA, the sole legal party, was renamed the Popular Movement for the Liberation of Angola —Party of Labour (MPLA-PT). Openly sympathetic to black nationalist movements, since 1979 Angola has been the object of military raids by South African troops in NAMIBIA (SW Africa), ostensibly striking at bases of a guerrilla organization seeking Namibian independence. Angola's first president, Agostinho Neto, died in 1979 and was succeeded by José Eduardo dos SANTOS both as president and MPLA-PT chairman. In 1988 an international agreement was concluded providing for the withdrawal of Cuban troops from Angola, the cessation of South African military incursions, and the independence of Namibia.

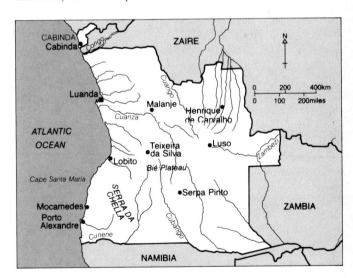

Angola

**Angostura Bridge,** a highway suspension bridge crossing the ORINOCO R. at Ciudad Guayana, Venezuela. Completed in 1967, its span of 712 m (2336 ft) is the longest in Latin America.

**Angoulême** (ongooh,lem), city (1982 pop. of agglomeration 103,552), capital of Charente dept., W France on the Charente R. It serves as market and service centre of the Angoumois region and has paper and electrical engineering industries. The distinctive roof cupolas of its 12th-cent. cathedral suggest a Byzantine influence.

Angostura Bridge

**angstrom (Å),** unit of length equal to $10^{-10}$m. It is used to measure the wavelengths of light and of other forms of electromagnetic radiation. Scientists now prefer to use the nanometer (nm); 1 nm = 10 Å.

**Ångström, Anders Jöns,** 1814–74, Swedish physicist. Noted for his study of light, especially SPECTRUM analysis, he mapped the sun's spectrum, discovered hydrogen in the solar atmosphere, and was the first to examine the spectrum of the AURORA borealis. The unit of length the ANGSTROM is named after him.

**Anguilla,** island (1984 est. pop. 6700), 91 km² (35 sq mi), West Indies, one of the Leeward Islands. Fishing, stock-raising, and salt production are the principal activities. Formerly part of the associated state of Saint Kitts-Nevis-Anguilla, the island seceded in 1967, was declared an independent republic in 1969 by local leader Ronald Webster, but returned to British dependent territory status in 1971. Elections in 1984 were won by the Anguilla National Alliance led by Emile Gumbs.

**angular momentum:** see MOMENTUM.

**angular velocity:** see MOTION.

**Anhui** or **Anhwei,** province (1985 est. pop. 51,560,000), 140,000 km² (54,054 sq mi), E central China, to the west of the coastal provinces of JIANGSU and ZHEJIANG. Major cities are Hefei, the capital, and Huainan. The Changjiang (YANGTZE) and Huaihe rivers flow W to E and divide the province into widely contrasting physical regions. The northern section is part of the N China plain, low-lying and historically threatened by floods. Hill lands separate this area from the central fertile and more humid Yangtze valley lands. To the S there are rugged mountain regions with subtropical forests. These physical contrasts are reflected in agricultural specialisms. To the N, winter wheat and maize are the principal crops; the Yangtze valley provides fertile paddy fields for rice growing, and the mountains are important for tea-growing. Anhui is not a major industrial province. Natural resources, including coal and iron, have provided the basis for industrial development. Maanshan is a steel-producing town, and recently engineering and metalworking industries have developed along principal rail routes and the S bank of the Yangtze R.

**animal,** any member of the animal kingdom (Animalia) as distinguished from the plant kingdom (Plantae). The major difference between animals and plants is their method of obtaining nourishment—animals must secure food as already organized organic substances, while plants manufacture their own food from inorganic sources (usually by PHOTOSYNTHESIS). Most animals have nervous systems, sense organs, and specialized modes of locomotion, and are adapted for securing, ingesting, and digesting food. Animals and plants are interdependent: green plants use carbon dioxide and provide oxygen (a by-product of photosynthesis) and food; animals (and plants) provide carbon dioxide (through respiration and the decomposition of their dead bodies). The scientific study of animals is called ZOOLOGY.

**animal experimentation,** formerly misleadingly known as vivisection. It is illegal in most advanced countries unless carried out by qualified research workers officially licensed by a government department. In the UK licences are issued by the Home Office only after scrutiny of the project proposed and the work may be carried out only in licensed laboratories subject to random inspection by government officials. Infringement of the regulations results in cancellation of the licence. Animals for use in experimentation may only be purchased from licensed breeders, and the vast majority used are rats, mice, hamsters, and guinea pigs. Dogs, cats, and also monkeys are used far less frequently, usually only in special circumstances. Confusion exists in the public mind about the nature of experimentation, which is defined as a procedure the outcome of which is unknown beforehand. Thus, the infection of animals such as rabbits and horses with, e.g., a micro-organism in order to obtain antibodies from their blood for medical use is not an experiment but a routine pharmaceutical procedure, because the result is known. On the other hand the use of the same animals to develop, e.g., a nutritional diet for use in animal husbandry would be classed as an experiment. The Home Office publishes reports showing the type and number of licences issued. Typically, about 55% are concerned with the selection, development, use, and safety of medical, dental, and veterinary products, 20% to study body function, 20% to meet legal requirements for the testing of non-medical products, e.g., food additives, weedkillers, pesticides, and cosmetics. Very few licences, usually about 1–2%, are concerned with cosmetics and toiletry testing. Only vertebrate animals (frogs, fish, birds, and mammals) have legal protection against their use in experimentation. Public interest is usually centred on emotionally appealing species, but the general use of animals in experimentation has come under increasing criticism in many countries, sometimes involving acts of violence by groups of protesters.

**animal transport,** the use of animals as a means of moving people or goods. The first animal used for pulling loads is believed to have been the ass, native to North Africa, and exploited as a draught animal in the Mediterranean Basin and the Middle and Far East from soon after the invention of the wheel (about 3500 BC). Pack animals, commonly used on the ancient caravan routes from Europe and North Africa to India and China, probably date back even further. Oxen, reindeer, and elephants were among the animals used for transport in earliest times, as well as camels (still widely used today). The horse, which has played such a major part in the history of animal transport, was first exploited as a draught animal in Egypt in the 17th cent. BC. More than 2000 years later, around AD 500, the harness was invented in China, but was not known to Europe till the end of the 11th cent. The introduction of the horseshoe and continued improvement in harness design enabled the development of heavier freight wagons and, around the middle of the 16th cent., the passenger coach. Coaches could weigh up to 8 tons, drawn by teams of 12 horses. They were more easily manoeuvrable than the covered wagons they replaced, and much more comfortable, especially after the introduction of spring suspension around the mid 17th cent. By the early 19th cent., Britain had around 3000 such coaches—called stagecoaches because they stopped at staging posts along the routes—operating up and down the country. The coming of the railways and, in the 20th cent., the motor car led to the eclipse of animal transport in the industrialized world but it remains important in some developing countries, especially in regions where the terrain is difficult or access by other means is impossible.

**animatism:** see ANIMISM.

**animism** and **animatism,** two different types of BELIEF SYSTEM. *Animatism* is belief in a mystical spiritual force (such as Polynesian *mana*) which manifests itself in objects or natural phenomena or gives power to human effort; *animism* is the belief that the inanimate and natural world is inhabited by and endowed with supernatural powers or spirits. Animism is widely and unspecifically used to refer to the indigenous belief systems of African tribal societies.

**anion:** see under ION.

**anise,** annual plant (*Pimpinella anisum*) of the CARROT family, native to the Mediterranean but widely cultivated for its aromatic and medicinal qualities. The seedlike fruits (aniseed) are used as flavouring and provide anise oil, which is used in medicinals, perfumes, beverages, and dentifrices. Biblical anise is DILL.

**Anjou** (ahnˌzhooh), region and former province, W France. ANGERS, the historic capital, and Saumur are the chief towns in this fertile lowland traversed by several rivers. Its vineyards produce renowned wines.

Occupied by the Andecavi, a Gallic people, Anjou was conquered by the Romans and later (5th cent.) by the FRANKS. By the 10th cent. it was held by the counts of the first Angevin dynasty; it came under English rule when its ruler became (1154) king of England as HENRY II. PHILIP II of France seized (1204) Anjou from the English, and in 1246 LOUIS IX of France gave it to his brother, later CHARLES I of Naples. In 1360 Anjou became a duchy and in 1487 it was definitively annexed to France.

**Ankara,** city (1980 pop. 1,877,755, Greater Ankara 3,196,460), capital of Turkey, W central Turkey. The second largest city in Turkey, it is an administrative, commercial, and cultural centre. Manufactures include processed food and farm equipment. Grains, vegetables, and fruits are grown nearby. A Hittite trade centre (18th cent. BC), it became (1st cent. AD) the capital of a Roman province; in the ruins of a temple in Ankara have been found tablets valuable as a record of AUGUSTUS's reign. The city fell to the Ottoman Turks in the 14th cent. It declined in the 19th and 20th cent., until Kemal ATATÜRK made it the capital of Turkey in 1923. Atatürk's massive limestone tomb can be seen from most of the city.

Atatürk's limestone tomb at **Ankara**

**ankylosing spondylitis** ('ankee,lohsing 'spondi,lietis), progressive inflammatory condition of the spine, occurring mostly in young men, which can lead to a rigid, crooked spine.

**Anna,** 1693–1740, czarina of Russia (1730–40); daughter of Ivan V and niece of PETER I. She succeeded her cousin Peter II. Allied with Holy Roman Emperor CHARLES VI, she intervened in the War of the POLISH SUCCESSION (1733–35) and attacked Turkey (1736). Her grandnephew, Ivan VI, succeeded her.

**'Annaba,** formerly Bône, city and port (1987 pop. 348,322), N Algeria, on the Mediterranean coast. A focal point of industrial development in the country, the city trades in iron ore, phosphates, cork, and wine. Nearby are the ruins of the Roman city of Hippo Regius.

**Annales,** 1929–, influential French historical periodical, founded by Marc BLOCH and Lucien FEBVRE, which has established a tradition in the study of problems rather than of events, and which has covered a wide range of topics, particularly in economic, social, and cultural history. The Annales School has an international reputation.

**Annam,** historic region, c.150,200 km² (58,000 sq mi), and former state, central Vietnam. The region extended nearly 1290 km (800 mi) along the South China Sea between Tonkin (N) and Cochin China (S). The capital was HUE. After more than 2000 years of contact with the Chinese the peoples of the Red R. valley came under Chinese rule in 111 BC. The Annamese drove out the Chinese in AD 939 and maintained their independence until the French conquest in the 19th cent. Conflict between ruling dynasties dominated this long period, ending with the establishment (1802) of the empire of VIETNAM by Nguyen-Anh, who had procured French military aid by ceding the port of DA NANG and the Con Son islands. His authority as emperor was recognized by the Chinese in 1803. Mistreatment of French nationals and Vietnamese Christians by his

successor provided an excuse for French military operations, which began in 1858 and resulted in the establishment of the French colony of COCHIN CHINA and the protectorates of TONKIN and Annam. The three territories were occupied by the Japanese during WORLD WAR II. After an independence struggle against the French, most of Annam became part of South Vietnam in 1954; the rest went to North Vietnam. Annam was incorporated into united Vietnam after the VIETNAM WAR.

**Annapolis,** US city (1980 pop. 31,740), state capital of Maryland, on the Severn R. It is a port of entry and a farm-produce shipping centre with seafood and boat-building industries. Settled in 1649, it has a rich history, including a period (1783–84) as the capital of the US; it has been Maryland's capital since 1694. The city has many 18th-cent. buildings, and is the site of the US Naval Academy and St John's College.

**Annapolis Convention,** 1786, interstate convention to discuss US commerce, held at Annapolis, Maryland. Its call for a meeting to discuss changes in the Articles of CONFEDERATION brought about the FEDERAL CONSTITUTIONAL CONVENTION.

**Annapolis Royal,** town (1980 est. pop. 738), W Nova Scotia, E Canada, on the Annapolis R. One of the oldest settlements in Canada, it was founded as Port Royal by the French in 1605, destroyed (1613) by the British, and rebuilt to become the chief town of French ACADIA. Often fought over in the 1600s by the English and the French, it was finally taken (1710) by colonists from New England and renamed in honour of Queen Anne. The ruins of its fort are in Fort Anne Historic National Park.

**Ann Arbor,** US city (1984 est. pop. 104,000), S Michigan, on the Huron R.; settled 1824, inc. 1851. It is a research and educational centre, with government and industrial research firms and the huge Univ. of Michigan. Products include lasers, computers, and precision machinery. The city is also a medical centre with several hospitals.

**Anne,** 1665–1714, queen of England, Scotland, and Ireland (r.1702–07), later queen of Great Britain and Ireland (r.1707–14); daughter of JAMES II; successor to WILLIAM III. The last STUART ruler and a devout Protestant, in 1683 she married Prince George of Denmark. Her reign was one of transition to parliamentary government, but intrigue and the queen's favour could still make and unmake cabinets. The dominant event was the War of the SPANISH SUCCESSION (1701–13). Despite victories won by the duke of MARLBOROUGH (whose wife was long a favourite of the queen), the war's high cost caused political friction. None of Anne's children survived her, and by the Act of SETTLEMENT (1701) GEORGE I succeeded her. Anne's reign was marked by intellectual awakening, the popularization of Palladian architecture, and the growth of parliamentary government, and she herself displayed considerable political talents in the furtherance of her objectives.

**Anne,** 1950–, British princess; daughter of ELIZABETH II. In 1973 she married a British army officer, Mark Phillips. They have two children. In 1988 she was given the title Princess Royal.

**annealing,** process in which materials, principally glass and metals, are treated to render them less brittle and subject to cracking. The material is heated to just below melting point and held there for a period of time dependent on the mass, size, and type of material. The heating is then reduced so that the material cools very slowly. Annealing removes the internal strains that might lead to brittle fracture. In metals the process also increases ductility which allows easier working.

**Anne Boleyn,** queen of England: see BOLEYN, ANNE.

**Annecy,** city (1982 pop. of agglomeration 112,632), capital of Haute-Savoie dept., SE France. Situated at the northern end of Lake Annecy, it commands a routeway through the Pre-Alps and serves as market and service centre of a prosperous farming district, the plain of Rumilly. The lake and the old town with its medieval castle, gardens, and canals have made it a tourist centre.

**annelid worm,** member of the phylum Annelida, which includes the EARTHWORMS, LEECHES, and marine worms. Also called segmented worms; they are soft-bodied, bilaterally symmetrical, and segmented. Distributed worldwide, they live in protected habitats, often in tubes manufactured by their own secretions. Reproduction is sexual or asexual; some species are HERMAPHRODITES. They range from 0.5 mm (¹/₃₂ in) to 3 m (10 ft) in length.

**Anne of Austria,** 1601–66, queen of France. The daughter of PHILIP III of Spain, she married (1615) the French king LOUIS XIII and gained the enmity of Cardinal RICHELIEU, Louis's chief minister. As regent (r.1643–51) for her son LOUIS XIV, she entrusted the government to Cardinal MAZARIN.

**Anne of Brittany,** 1477–1514, queen of France, consort of CHARLES VIII (1491–98) and LOUIS XII (1499–1514). As duchess of Brittany from 1488, she tried to preserve independence from France by marrying by proxy (1490) Maximilian of Austria (later Holy Roman Emperor MAXIMILIAN I). Besieged (1491) by the French, she was forced to annul her marriage and to marry Charles VIII. Widowed in 1498, she then married Louis XII, and Brittany was eventually incorporated (1532) by France.

**Anne of Cleves,** 1515–57, fourth queen of HENRY VIII of England. She was the daughter of a powerful German Protestant prince, and Henry married her in 1540 for political reasons. Finding her dull and unattractive, he divorced her that same year.

**Anne of Denmark,** 1574–1619, queen of JAMES I of England.

**annexation,** in INTERNATIONAL LAW, formal act by which a state asserts its sovereignty over a territory previously outside its jurisdiction. Under the UN charter, self-determination by inhabitants of a territory is the only basis for transfer of sovereignty. In the UK, it also describes the process whereby church lands are appropriated by the CROWN.

**annual,** plant that propagates itself by seed and undergoes its entire life cycle within one growing season, as distinguished from a BIENNIAL or PERENNIAL. Some cultivated annuals will blossom during a season only if started under glass and set out as young plants; others bloom where sown.

**annual rings,** growth layers of WOOD produced yearly in the stems and roots of trees and shrubs. When well-marked alternation of seasons occurs (e.g., either cold and warm or wet and dry), a sharp contrast exists between the early- and late-season growth, the wood cells are larger earlier when growing conditions are better. In uniform climates, there is little visible difference between annual rings. The number of annual rings reflects the age of a tree; the thickness of each ring reflects environmental and climatic conditions.

**Annunzio, Gabriele D':** see D'ANNUNZIO, GABRIELE.

**anode:** see ELECTRODE.

**anointing of the sick,** SACRAMENT of the Orthodox Eastern Church and the ROMAN CATHOLIC CHURCH; formerly known as **extreme unction.** In it a person who is in danger of death is anointed on the eyes, ears, nostrils, lips, hands, and feet by a priest while he recites absolutions for sins. In the Eastern churches it is normally given by three priests and may be administered to the healthy to prevent sickness.

**anomie,** a term drawn from the writings of the French sociologist Emile DURKHEIM. Anomie is a pathological state of existence, characterized by feelings of aimlessness or lack of belonging, generated in the individual when the moral regulation of society is either excessively weak, or when two or more moral precepts conflict. See also ALIENATION.

**anorexia nervosa,** eating disorder, occurring more commonly among adolescent women. Patients become overconcerned with weight and diet, fears fatness, and has a distorted body image. With continuous dieting, strenuous exercise, and abuse of laxatives or forced vomiting, they become emaciated and cease to menstruate. Some die of self-starvation, but many recover completely, often after undergoing PSYCHOTHERAPY, or, more typically, have repeated relapses and recoveries sometimes combined with periods of excess eating (BULIMIA). Anorexia is a result of the interaction between an emotional disorder and nutritional deterioration.

**Anouilh, Jean** (an‚wee), 1910–87, French dramatist. His many popular works contrast the worlds of romantic dreams and harsh reality. Among his best-known dramas are *Antigone* (1944) and *La valse des torédors* (1952; tr. The waltz of the Toreadors).

**Anschluss** [Ger., = annexation], German incorporation of Austria into HITLER's Reich on 12 Mar. 1938. Although most of the Austrian people welcomed it, it was carried out under the threat of military force.

**Anselm, Saint,** 1033?–1109, Italian prelate, archbishop of Canterbury, Doctor of the Church. He succeeded (1093) his friend LANFRANC as archbishop of Canterbury. In England, he quarrelled with WILLIAM II and HENRY I over lay INVESTITURE and was exiled twice. An influential theologian, he was a founder of SCHOLASTICISM. His famous ontological proof deduces God's existence from man's notion of a perfect being in whom nothing is lacking. Feast: 21 Apr.

**Anshan** or **An-shan,** city (1985 est. pop. 2,583,000), central LIAONING prov., NE China. Its huge integrated iron and steel complex is the largest in China and in 1984 produced 16% of China's output of crude steel. Other manufacturing industries produce machinery, chemicals, construction materials, and textiles. There is a developing electronics industry. The Anshan area was taken by Japan following the Russo-Japanese war of 1905. Japanese industrialists built the Anshan Steel Works in 1917 and later enlarged it.

**Ansky, Shloime,** pseud. of **Solomon Seinwil Rapoport,** 1863–1920, Russian Yiddish writer. He incorporated folk elements into his stories of peasants and HASIDIM, e.g., *The Dybbuk* (1916), a tale of demonic possession.

**ant,** insect (family Formicidae) belonging to the same order as the BEE and WASP, but ground-living and distinguished by a stalk (petiole), joining the abdomen and thorax. All 15,000 known species are social and their semipermanent colonies consist of one or more queens (reproductive females) and, seasonally, males. Only the short-lived males and the reproductive females are winged, but the latter break theirs off soon after the mating flight. All ants have biting mouthparts and some are ferocious carnivores, e.g., the Australian bull-dog ants (*Myrmecia*). Most species are omnivorous but harvester ants (e.g., *Messor*) of Mediterranean countries live on seeds which they gather and store, while the leaf-cutters (tribe Attini) of South America feed on fungi, cultivated on composted plant material. Ants like sweet things and drink not just nectar but also the 'honey dew' produced by APHIDS and SCALE INSECTS, whose colonies they guard and manage. Tropical driver and army ants (Dorylinae) are nomadic and utilize any shelter available, but most species have nests in galleries underground, in tree stumps, or in mounds of vegetable matter. Galls (hollow inflated bases of thorns), on the whistling thorn (*Acacia*), provide homes for some African ants (*Crematogaster*), while the Indian tree ant (*Oecophylla*) forms nests by sewing leaves together with silk produced by its larvae, handled like shuttles by workers. Many ants have stings they can use for defending the nest, others simply spray poisons, such as formic acid, from the end of their abdomens, and until recently they were the only source of that chemical. The 'ants eggs' used as aquarium fish food are not their eggs but pupae in cocoons. Because of the protection they provide for aphid and scale-insect colonies, many ants are serious agricultural pests while some, like the pharaoh's ant (*Monomorium pharaonis*) from Africa and the Argentine ant (*Iridomyrmex humilis*) from South America, are now widespread pests in buildings, not only in Europe, including Britain, but also in Australia and New Zealand.

Australian bull-dog worker **ants** (*Myrmecia gulosa*) tending larvae

**antacid,** substance which relieves excessive gastric acidity. Antacids, often compounds of calcium, aluminium, or magnesium, act by neutralizing the hydrochloric acid in digestive juices. They are used to relieve pain and promote healing in cases of peptic ULCER.

**Antakya:** see ANTIOCH.

**Antalya,** city (1980 pop. 173,501), capital of Antalya prov., SW Turkey, on the Mediterranean coast. It is the market for an irrigated plain, handles chrome and other ores, and has related textile and metallurgical industries. Founded in the 2nd cent. BC, it was capital of the ancient Pamphilia prov.

**Antananarivo** or **Tananarive,** city (1985 pop. 662,585), capital of Madagascar. The country's largest city and economic and communications centre, it serves a productive agricultural region whose main crop is rice. A railway connects the city with Tamatave, the chief port. Manufactures include clothing, soap, and footwear. Founded c.1625, Antananarivo became (1797) the residence of the Merina rulers. It was taken by the French in 1895. Today it is a modern city, built on a ridge; at its top stands the old royal residence.

**Antarctica,** fifth largest continent, 14,245,000 km² (c.5,500,000 sq mi), asymmetrically centred on the SOUTH POLE and located almost entirely S of the ANTARCTIC CIRCLE (66° 30'S). It consists of two major regions: Lesser (or West) Antarctica, including the mountainous Antarctic Peninsula, which is structurally related to the ANDES of South America and connected to them by way of the Scotia Arc (South Georgia, South Sandwich islands, and South Orkney); and Greater (or East) Antarctica, a continental shield area (see PLATE TECTONICS) with a rock surface near sea level. These two regions are joined into a single continental mass by an ice cap up to 4000 m (13,000 ft) thick that covers 98% of Antarctica. Vinson Massif (4897 m/16,066 ft) is the continent's highest peak. Great ice shelves up to 1220-m (4000-ft) thick block the southern limits of the ROSS and WEDDELL seas, and a belt of nearly continuous pack-ice surrounds most of the rest of the continent. Average summer temperatures (Jan.) are unlikely to be warmer than − 18°C (0°F); winter mean temperatures are − 57°C (− 70°F). Roald AMUNDSEN (Norwegian) was the first explorer to reach the South Pole, on 14 Dec. 1911, followed by R.F. SCOTT (British) on 17 Jan. 1912. The first to fly over the pole was Richard E. BYRD (US), on 29 Nov. 1929. The success of international scientific cooperation in Antarctica during the International Geophysical Year (IGY) of 1957–58 led to the ANTARCTIC TREATY, which prohibits military operations, nuclear explosions, and the disposal of radioactive wastes south of latitude 60°S, exclusive of the high seas. See map in separate section.

**Antarctic Circle,** imaginary circle on the earth's surface at 66° 30'S lat., marking the southernmost point at which the sun can be seen at the summer SOLSTICE (about 22 June) and the northernmost point of the southern polar regions at which the midnight sun is visible.

**Antarctic Peninsula,** glaciated mountain region of Lesser ANTARCTICA, extending 1930 km (c.1200 mi) north towards South America. It is composed of Palmer Land in the southern and Graham Land in the northern part. The first landing was probably made by a US sealer, John Davis, Feb. 1821 (the first landing on the Antarctic Continent). John Biscoe claimed it for Britain in 1832 and it was later claimed by Argentina (1943) and by Chile (1940). As it is the warmest and most accessible part of Antarctica it has the highest concentration of research stations.

**Antarctic Treaty,** international treaty covering all land and floating ice S of lat. 60°S. It was developed as a result of scientific cooperation after the International Geophysical Year (1957–58); the 12 nations then working in Antarctica initialled it in 1959 and it came into force in 1961. By 1987, there were 25 member countries. The treaty is to last indefinitely, but may be reviewed in 1991. The principal provisions include demilitarization of Antarctica, free exchange of information, placing sovereignty claims in abeyance, prohibiting thermonuclear bombs or disposal of radioactive waste in the treaty limits, and freedom of inspection by designated observers. Agreements on the conservation of seals, other marine species, and specially conserved areas have been made under the treaty, and a regime for mineral exploitation is being negotiated.

**anteater,** toothless MAMMAL of three genera of the order Edentata found in tropical Central and South America. It feeds on ants, termites, and other insects. The great anteater, or ant bear (*Myrmecophaga*), has an elongated snout, a coarse-haired body about 1.2 m (4 ft) long, and a long, broad tail; the arboreal collared, or lesser, anteater (*Tamandua*) is less

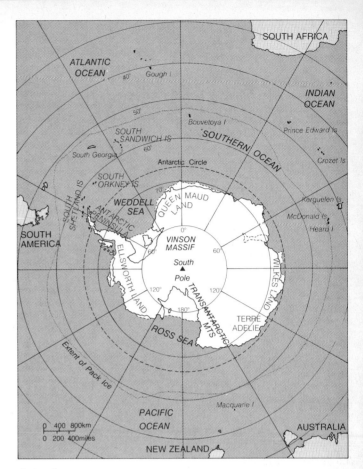

Antarctica

than half the size of the great anteater; and the arboreal two-toed anteater (*Cyclopes*) is about the size of a squirrel.

**antelope,** any of various hoofed ruminant MAMMALS of the CATTLE family. True antelopes are found only in Africa and Asia. Antelopes usually stand 90–120 cm (3–4 ft) at the shoulder, but range from the 30-cm (12-in) pygmy antelope to the 180-cm (6-ft) giant eland. Antelope horns, unlike DEER horns, are unbranched and are not shed. Species of antelope include the bushbuck, with its spiral horns and oxlike body; the addax, a large desert antelope of N Africa; the horselike oryx, found in Africa and Arabia; the GNU and its close relative the hartebeest, a swift, horselike animal with U-shaped horns; and the GAZELLE.

**antenna:** see AERIAL.

**Antheil, George** (ˌantiel), 1900–59, American composer. He moved to Europe, and his early work was influenced by Stravinsky. In 1927 a performance of his *Ballet mécanique,* scored for eight pianos, player piano, car horns, aeroplane propellers, etc., caused a furore in New York City. His later orchestral and dramatic works, film and ballet scores, were more conservative.

**anthem,** short nonliturgical choral composition used in Protestant services, usually accompanied and with an English text. Early anthems, which arose in the Anglican Church, included those by Thomas TALLIS and William BYRD. In the 17th cent. Henry PURCELL and John Blow wrote anthems including solo parts (*verse anthems*); G.F. HANDEL composed *full anthems,* for voice only. The term *anthem* also means 'national anthem', e.g., 'God Save The Queen'.

**Anthony, Mark:** see ANTONY.

**Anthony, Michael,** 1932–, Trinidadian novelist. He celebrates the everyday existence of ordinary people, especially in rural and semi-urban societies, in *The Year in San Fernando* (1965) and *Green Days by the River* (1967), as well as the impact of socioeconomic change in *Streets of Conflict* (1976).

**Anthony, Saint**, 251?–c.350, Egyptian hermit. Living in seclusion, he resisted the many temptations of the devil. A colony of hermits grew up about him, and he ruled them as a community before going away to the desert. He was the father of Christian MONASTICISM. Feast: 17 Jan.

**Anthony, Susan B(rownell)**, 1820–1906, American leader of the WOMEN'S SUFFRAGE movement. She organized the first women's temperance association, the Daughters of Temperance, and with Elizabeth Cady STANTON secured the first laws in New York guaranteeing women rights over their children and control of property and wages. In 1863 she was co-organizer of the Women's Loyal League to support Lincoln's government, but after the Civil War she opposed granting suffrage to freedmen without also giving it to women. She was president of the National American Woman Suffrage Association from 1892 to 1900 and helped compile vols. 1–3 of *The History of Woman Suffrage* (1881–86).

**anthrax**, infectious bacterial disease of animals that can be transmitted to humans through contact or the inhalation of spores. Primarily affecting sheep, horses, pigs, cattle, and goats, anthrax in humans is usually restricted to people who handle hides of animals (e.g., farmers, butchers, and veterinarians) or who sort wool. The disease, usually fatal to animals but not humans, is notifiable. Bacterial spores are formed in air if the carcass of an infected animal is cut or damaged, and carcasses are always buried intact. Louis PASTEUR developed a method of vaccinating cattle against anthrax, but the main official method of control is the slaughter of infected animals.

**anthropology**, study of the origin, development, and varieties of human beings and their societies. Emerging as an independent science in the late 18th cent., it developed two main divisions: physical anthropology, which focuses on human EVOLUTION and variation, using methods of PHYSIOLOGY, anthropometry, GENETICS, and ECOLOGY; and social anthropology (see CULTURE), which draws upon the neighbouring disciplines of ARCHAEOLOGY, PSYCHOLOGY, and LINGUISTICS Among the important schools in anthropology are FUNCTIONALISM, STRUCTURALISM, and STRUCTURAL FUNCTIONALISM.

**antibiotic**, any of a variety of substances, usually obtained from microorganisms, that inhibit the growth of or destroy certain other microorganisms. The foundation for the development and understanding of antibiotics was laid during the 19th cent. when Louis PASTEUR proved that one species of microorganism can kill another, and Paul EHRLICH developed the idea of selective toxicity: that a specific substance can be toxic to some organisms, e.g., infectious bacteria, but harmless to others, e.g., human hosts. Further pioneering work in the 20th cent. by Alexander FLEMING, René DUBOS, and Selman WAKSMAN led to the discovery of PENICILLIN (1939) and streptomycin (1944). Mass production of antibiotic drugs began during World War II with streptomycin and penicillin. Today antibiotics are produced by various methods, including staged fermentation in huge tanks of nutrient media, synthesis in the laboratory, and chemical modification of natural substances. Antibiotics can be classified according to chemical structure, microbial origin, mode of action, or effective range. The tetracyclines are broad-spectrum drugs, effective against a wide range of bacteria (both gram-positive and gram-negative; see GRAM'S STAIN), rickettsias, and the psittacosis virus. The antibiotics bacitracin, penicillin, and the erythromycins are usually used against gram-positive organisms. Newer cephalosporins are used against gram-negative organisms. Polymyxins and other narrow-range antibiotics are effective against only a few species. Antibiotic drugs may be injected, given orally, or applied to the skin. Some, like penicillin, are allergenic and can cause rashes or SHOCK. Others, like the tetracylines, can alter the intestinal environment, encouraging superinfection (reinfection or secondary infection with the same type of organism) by fungi or other microorganisms. Many antibiotics are less effective than formerly because resistant strains of microorganisms have evolved. Antibiotics have been used to enhance the growth of animals reared for food, but some authorities question the practice because it encourages the development of resistant strains of bacteria infecting animals, and because continuous low exposure to antibiotics can sensitize human beings, making them unable to take such drugs later to treat infection.

**antibody:** see IMMUNITY.

**Antichrist**, in Christian belief, a person who will lead the forces of evil on earth against the forces of Christ. He will be destroyed by Christ at the Second Coming (1 John 2.18–22; 4.3; 2 John 7; and Rev. 13).

**anticline:** see FOLD.

**anticoagulant**, agent that inhibits blood clotting. Anticoagulants are used to treat blood clots in leg and pelvic veins, in order to reduce the risk of the clots travelling and obstructing blood flow to vital organs (e.g., the heart and lungs) and causing THROMBOSIS or STROKE. Heparin is an anticoagulant that occurs in the body naturally. Warfarin is a commonly used anticoagulant drug that has also been used as rat poison.

**Anti-Corn Law League**, British popular agitation with middle-class leadership. It was founded in Manchester in 1839 and dedicated to the repeal of the corn laws on imported grain: these were claimed to raise the price of food and add to unemployment. When the duties were repealed by PEEL in 1846 he paid a tribute to Richard COBDEN, the main leader of the agitation.

**antidepressant**, drug used to alleviate depression. There are two main groups of drugs: the tricyclics and related antidepressants, and the monoamine-oxidase inhibitors (MAOI). The former (e.g., imipramine), are more effective and the latter have dangerous interactions with some foods. The drugs elevate mood, counter suicidal thoughts, and increase the effectiveness of psychotherapy, although the exact mechanisms of their action are unknown. Side effects include dry mouth, dizziness, and fatigue. See also LITHIUM.

**antifreeze**, substance added to a solvent to lower its freezing point. Antifreeze is typically added to water in the cooling system of an internal combustion engine so that it may be cooled below the freezing point of pure water (0°C or 32°F) without freezing. Antifreezes for use in car engines include ethylene glycol (the most widely used), methanol, ethanol, isopropyl alcohol, and propylene glycol.

**antigen:** see IMMUNITY.

**Antigone** (an‚tigɔnee), in Greek legend, daughter of OEDIPUS. She looked after her blind father in exile, as told in SOPHOCLES' *Oedipus at Colonus*. When her brothers Eteocles and Polynices killed each other, Creon, king of THEBES, forbade the rebel Polynices' burial. Antigone disobeyed him, performed the rites, and was condemned to death (but committed suicide). The story of her conflict of duties has been dramatized by, among others, Sophocles (*Antigone*) and ANOUILH (*Antigone*, 1944).

**Antigua** or **Antigua Guatemala**, town (1973 est. pop. 17,692), S central Guatemala. Now a trading centre in a coffee-growing area, it was once the capital of Spanish Guatemala and, in the 16th cent., one of the richest cities in the New World. Antigua was founded in 1542, after a flood and earthquake destroyed the earlier capital, Ciudad Vieja, but was itself levelled by earthquakes in 1773. The capital was then moved to GUATEMALA City. Today Antigua is a major tourist centre with fine Spanish buildings.

**Antigua and Barbuda**, island nation (1986 est. pop. 80,000), 442 km² (171 sq mi), West Indies, in the Leeward Islands. It consists of Antigua (280 km²/108 sq mi) and two smaller islands, sparsely populated Barbuda and uninhabited Redonda. The capital is St John's. Antigua is a hilly island with estates that grow some sugarcane and cotton. The GDP is US$161 million and the GDP per capita is US$2037. The population is predominantly black and of African origin. The island was discovered by Christopher COLUMBUS in 1493. Following brief periods under the Spanish and French, it was first successfully settled in 1632 by the British, who introduced sugar planting; the industry went into decline with the abolition of slavery in 1834 and it has been almost moribund for the last decade. Tourism is the economic mainstay. Antigua, with Barbuda and Redonda as dependencies, became an associated state of the COMMONWEALTH in 1967 and, despite Barbuda's wish to secede achieved full independence on 1 Nov. 1981. The islands' post-war political life has been dominated by the Antigua Labour Party, led by Vere C. Bird Sr (prime minister) and his family. The US maintains two military bases in Antigua and Barbuda, which in 1983 participated in the US-led invasion of Grenada.

**antihistamine:** see ALLERGY; HISTAMINE.

**Antilles:** see WEST INDIES.

**Anti-Masonic Party**, American political party founded to counter the supposed political influence of FREEMASONRY. It arose in W New York state after the disappearance (1826) of William Morgan, a former Mason who had written a book purporting to reveal Masonic secrets. Freemasons were said, without proof, to have murdered him. At Baltimore, in 1831,

Anti-Masons held the first national nominating convention of any party, and issued the first written party platform. In 1834 they helped form the WHIG PARTY.

**antimatter,** material composed of antiparticles, which correspond to ordinary protons, electrons, and neutrons but have the opposite electrical charge and magnetic moment (see MAGNETISM). When matter and antimatter collide, both may be annihilated, and other ELEMENTARY PARTICLES, such as photons and pions, are produced. In 1932 Carl D. Anderson, while studying cosmic rays, discovered the positron, or antielectron, the first known antiparticle which had been predicted by DIRAC in 1928. Any antimatter in our part of the universe is necessarily very short-lived because of the overwhelming preponderance of ordinary matter, by which the antimatter is quickly annihilated.

**antimony** (Sb), semimetallic element, first described by Nicolas Lemery in 1707. It is silvery blue-white, brittle and easily powdered, and conducts heat and electricity poorly. Chief uses are as a constituent of alloys and compounds in storage batteries, cable sheathing, and paint pigments. See ELEMENT (table); PERIODIC TABLE.

**Antioch** or **Antakya,** city (1975 pop. 77,518), S Turkey, on the Orontes R., near the Mediterranean Sea. It is a trade centre for a farm area where grains, cotton, and vegetables are grown. Founded (c.300 BC) by Seleucus I, king of ancient Syria, it was an important military, commercial, and cultural centre under Rome and was an early centre of Christianity. It fell (AD 637) to the Arabs but was retaken (1098) by the Crusaders and became a powerful principality under BOHEMOND I. It later became (1516) part of the OTTOMAN EMPIRE, was incorporated into the French mandate of Syria after World War I, and was restored to Turkey in 1939. Many important archaeological finds have been made in or near the city.

**antiparticle:** see ANTIMATTER.

**Antipas,** in the Bible: see HEROD.

**Antipater** (an‚tipətə), d. 319 BC, Macedonian general under ALEXANDER THE GREAT; regent of MACEDON (334–323 BC). After Alexander's death he defeated Perdiccas in a struggle for the regency (321). He held the kingdom together; his death was followed by the wars of the DIADOCHI.

**Antipater,** in the Bible: see HEROD.

**antipope,** person elected pope whose election was later declared uncanonical and in opposition to a canonically chosen legitimate pontiff (see PAPACY).

**anti-psychiatry,** a general term for a group of radical critiques of psychiatric practices and institutions, largely developed in the 1960s and after by R.D. LAING and others in Great Britain, Thomas Szasz in the US and R. Castel in France. Anti-psychiatry criticizes the 'pseudo-scientific' nature of conventional psychiatric practices, the dehumanizing and oppressive nature of psychiatric institutions, and the function of psychiatry as social control.

**antique,** term formerly applied only to objects of preclassical and classical cultures of the ancient world, but now applied in common usage to artifacts of historic, aesthetic, and monetary value that are more than 100 years old. Antique collecting began with the preservation of religious objects in antiquity, but today includes a vast range of decorative objects and memorabilia.

**anti-Semitism,** prejudice against JEWS. Before the 19th cent. anti-semitism was largely religious, based on the belief that Jews were responsible for the crucifixion of Jesus Christ. It was expressed at various times by sporadic persecutions and expulsions (such as those from England in 1290 and from Spain in 1492). In 1753 an Act of Parliament in England to naturalize Jews led to anti-Semite demonstrations on the streets of London. The association—in the popular mind—of Jews with money-lending activities began at an early time and may have come about due to Christian strictures aginst usury. Certainly, Jews have long been forced into certain economic activities and locations (see GHETTO). With the decline of feudalism and the attendant process of secularization, religious and economic anti-Semitism were gradually replaced by racial prejudice. This acted to further justify the exclusion of Jewish people from certain occupations and the holding of public office. Within the Jewish community itself, the richest groups attempted to gain acceptance into gentile society (e.g., Gerson Bleichroder became a Prussian baron in 1872 and Lionel Rothschild an English baronet in 1847 and a baron in 1885). The cultural isolation of Orthodox Jews, the collapse of world markets in the late 1890s, a rising European tide of nationalism, pseudoscientific theories of Aryan racial superiority, and spurious charges of Jewish domination, all encouraged anti-Semitism. Its first institutional manifestation in England was probably the British Brothers' League established in 1900 in London. In the 1930s Sir Oswald Mosley and his British Union of Fascists exploited the tide of feeling against Jews that culminated in the 'battle' of Cable St on the 5 Oct. 1936. At the same time in Germany, Adolf Hitler created the National Socialist Party (see NATIONAL SOCIALISM) and laid the seeds for the extermination of 6 million Jews in the holocaust of WORLD WAR II. Even after this, anti-Semitism is still a powerful force in many nations of the world.

**antiseptic,** agent which destroys or inhibits the growth of microorganisms on living material, used to clean the skin before procedures such as injections or surgery. Many antiseptics are specific in their action—affecting only one or a small number of microorganisms. Agents which destroy microorganisms on nonliving matter (e.g., walls and surgical instruments) are usually referred to as disinfectants.

**antislavery movement:** see ABOLITIONISTS; SLAVERY.

**antitoxin:** see TOXIN.

**antitrust laws,** legislation under which the US government has acted to break up any large business combination alleged to be acting monpolistically to suppress competition (see TRUST, CORPORATE MONOPOLY). The first of these laws was passed in 1890, and further enactments followed in 1914 and 1936. They have operated by declaring illegal contracts, conspiracies, and price-fixing agreements that freeze out competition. During the period 1880–1905, corporate trusts grew rapidly, in response to which Pres. Theodore ROOSEVELT launched his famous 'trust-busting' campaigns. Antitrust action then declined, until it was vigorously renewed by Pres. F.D.ROOSEVELT in the 1930s. In recent years enforcement of antitrust legislation has been complicated by the growth of huge conglomerates that control many companies in various, sometimes interrelated industries. For UK equivalent see MONOPOLIES AND MERGERS COMMISSION.

**Antoine, André,** 1858–1943, French theatre director, manager, and critic. In 1887 he founded the Théâtre Libre (see THEATRE, table) to present works of NATURALISM. His work became a model for experimental theatres.

**Antonello da Messina,** c.1430–1479, Italian painter. His handling of oils shows strong Flemish influence. Messina's works include the *Virgin Annunciate* (c.1476; Galleria Nazionale della Sicilia, Palermo). He was also an excellent portraitist: his *Portrait of a Man* (1476; Museo Cirico, Turin) combines an Italian sense of structure with northern realism of surface and texture.

**Antonescu, Ion,** 1882–1946, Romanian marshal and leader. Against the background of the loss of N Transylvania to Hungary and Bessarabia to the Soviet Union, he was called upon by King CAROL II to form a government in Sept. 1940 and invested with supreme power. The king abdicated in favour of his son MICHAEL and Antonescu formally allied Romania to the AXIS. He commanded the Romanian armies in the attack on the USSR to regain Bessarabia in June 1941. The Russian advance into Romania prompted King Michael to arrest Antonescu on 23 Aug. 1944. He was tried as a war criminal and executed on 1 June 1946.

**Antonine Wall,** a defensive wall of turf and stone built by men of the Roman Legions across the 60-km (38-mi) gap between the Firth of Forth and the Firth of Clyde in Scotland. With 19 forts along its line, the wall was intended to secure the northern frontier of the Roman Empire in Britain during the 2nd cent. AD. It was abandoned by the end of that century. See also HADRIAN'S WALL.

**Antonioni, Michelangelo,** 1912–, Italian film director. In such films as *L'Avventura* (1959), *Red Desert* (1964), *Blow-Up* (1966), and *The Passenger* (1975) he depicted modern alienation, subordinating dialogue to visual images.

**Antony** or **Mark Antony,** Lat. *Marcus Antonius,* c.83–30 BC, Roman politician and soldier. He was of a distinguished family related to Julius CAESAR, who made him a protégé. In 49 BC Antony became tribune. He and Quintus Cassius Longinus (see CASSIUS, family), another tribune, vetoed the bill to deprive Caesar of his army. Caesar then crossed the Rubicon, and the civil war began. After Caesar's assassination (44 BC), Antony, then consul, aroused the mob against the conspirators. Octavian (later AUGUSTUS) joined forces with him, but they soon fell out. However, Octavian arranged the Second TRIUMVIRATE with Antony and Marcus Aemilius Lepidus (see LEPIDUS, family). At Philippi, in 42 BC, Antony and Octavian crushed the republicans, and the triumvirate ruled the empire for five years. Antony met CLEOPATRA in 42 BC, and their love affair began. When Antony's wife, Fulvia, died (40 BC), he married Octavian's sister, OCTAVIA. In 37 BC, Antony settled in Alexandria as the acknowledged lover of Cleopatra. In 32 BC the senate deprived Antony of his powers, thus making civil war inevitable. In the following year Octavian's forces defeated Antony and Cleopatra in the naval battle at Actium, and Antony returned to Egypt. When Octavian came there (30 BC), Antony committed suicide, and Cleopatra killed herself soon afterward. Of the many dramas on the tragedy, the best known by far is SHAKESPEARE's *Antony and Cleopatra*.

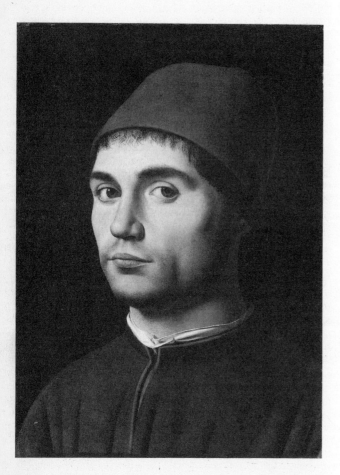

Antonello da Messina, *Portrait of a Man*, 1476. National Gallery, London.

**Antrim,** former county in the N of Northern Ireland, 2815 km² (1098 sq mi), bordering on the North Sea in the N and Lough Neagh in the S. The R. BANN forms much of the E boundary of the county, and the R. Lagan forms much of the boundary in the SE. The county town is BELFAST. The W of the county is mainly low-lying. In the W are the mountains of Antrim which reach 554 m (1817 ft) in Mt Trostan. Most of the county is underlain by basalt which is exposed on the N coast in the spectacular GIANT'S CAUSEWAY. Mixed agriculture is practised in rural areas and Belfast, Lisburn, Ballymena, and Larne are manufacturing towns. Metal and linen manufacturing are important, and Belfast is a seaport.

**Antwerp,** city (1985 pop. 486,576), Flemish N Belgium, on the Scheldt R. It is one of the busiest European ports and a major centre of finance, industry, and the diamond trade. Europe's chief commercial city by the mid-16th cent., it declined after its sacking (1576) by the Spanish and the closing (1648) of the Scheldt to navigation. Its modern expansion dates from 1863. In the 20th cent. it was twice occupied and heavily damaged by the Germans. Antwerp has many notable buildings, e.g., its Gothic

cathedral (14th–16th cent.), and houses many important paintings, e.g., by RUBENS, MASSYS, VAN DYKE.

**anxiety,** an unpleasant but unfocused emotional state, characterized by apprehension, uneasiness, distress and dread. Anxiety differs from fear in that it is objectless, but may manifest itself in similar physiological symptoms (increased pulse rate, blood pressure, and respiration; sweating and dryness of the mouth). Pathological anxiety states are instances of neuroses (see NEUROSIS).

**ANZAC,** originally the Australian–New Zealand Army Corps which fought in WORLD WAR I, notably in the GALLIPOLI CAMPAIGN. ANZAC Day commemorates the first landing at Gallipoli on 25 Apr. 1915. The abbreviation ANZAC is also used for other joint ventures between the two countries, including the **ANZAC Agreement,** signed in 1944 and providing for defence and security cooperation in the South Pacific, and the **ANZAC Free Trade Area** (est. 1966).

**Anzac Day,** 25 Apr., celebrated each year in Australia and New Zealand to commemorate the dead of World War I and II from those countries. It was the date of the landing at Gallipoli (1915) of the Australian and New Zealand Army Corps.

**ANZUS Pact,** security treaty between Australia, New Zealand, and the US. It was signed in San Francisco in 1951 and has been in force since 1952. Each signatory is committed to resisting an armed attack in the Pacific area on either of the others. New Zealand's participation in the alliance was suspended in 1985 because of the new Labour government's refusal to allow US nuclear-armed warships into its ports.

**Apache Indians,** NORTH AMERICAN INDIANS of the Southwest, six culturally related groups; most spoke dialects of Athabascan (see AMERICAN INDIAN LANGUAGES). Their ancestors entered the area c.1100. The NAVAHO INDIANS were once joined to the Apaches. Historically the Apaches subsisted on wild game, seed and fruit gathering, livestock, and some horticulture. Men lived with and worked for their wives' families. The Apaches, known as fierce fighters, resisted the Spanish advance but increasingly fought the COMANCHE INDIANS and other tribes with captured Spanish horses and arms. After the mid-19th cent. COCHISE, GERONIMO, MANGAS COLORADAS, and others led them in strong but futile efforts to stop white expansion westward. Today they live on reservations totalling over 3 million acres in Arizona and New Mexico and retain many tribal customs. Cattle, timber, tourism, and the development of mineral resources provide income. In 1982 the Apaches won a major Supreme Court test of their right to tax resources extracted from their lands.

**apartheid** [Afrik., = apartness], system of racial segregation and white supremacy peculiar to the Republic of SOUTH AFRICA. First formalized in the 1948 Afrikaner Nationalist Party platform, apartheid separates whites from nonwhites, nonwhites—Coloureds (mixed white and black descent), Asiatics (mainly of Indian ancestry), and Africans (called Bantu) —from each other, and one group of Bantu from another. Under Prime Min. Hendrik VERWOERD a policy of 'separate development' established nine BANTUSTANS (later 10), or homelands, totalling about 14% of the country's land, most of it too poor in quality to support the designated population (roughly 70% of all South Africans). On the reservations Bantu can exercise certain rights; elsewhere their activities are strictly curtailed. They cannot vote, own land, travel or work without permits, and spouses are often forbidden to accompany workers to urban areas. The economy of the affluent white community is entirely dependent on nonwhite labour. The policy of apartheid has generated international and domestic protest. In 1961 South Africa withdrew from the COMMONWEALTH in dispute over apartheid. Economic and political pressure has since led to some improvements for Africans, including limited representation for Coloureds and Asiatics (but not blacks); but many feel that apartheid will end only by force from within or without. See AFRICAN NATIONAL CONGRESS; MANDELA, NELSON.

**apatite,** phosphate mineral [$(Ca,Pb)_5(PO_4)_3(F,Cl,OH)$], transparent to opaque in shades of green, brown, yellow, white, red, and purple. Apatite, a minor constituent of many types of rock, is mined in Florida, Tennessee, Montana, N Africa, Europe, and the USSR. Large deposits are mined for use in making phosphatic fertilizers, and two varieties are used to a limited extent in jewellery. Apatite is the chief constituent of animal bones and teeth.

**ape,** PRIMATE of the family Pongidae. There are five living ape groups, including the family Hominidae, or human beings. The small apes, the GIBBON and siamang, and the smallest of the great apes, the ORANG UTAN, are found in SE Asia; the other great apes, the GORILLA and the CHIMPANZEE, are found in Africa. They vary in size from the 1-m (3-ft), 6.8-kg (15-lb) gibbon to the 1.8-m (6-ft), 227-kg (500-lb) gorilla. All the non-human apes are forest dwellers and spend at least some time in trees; unlike MONKEYS, they can swing hand-over-hand. Their brains, similar in structure to the human brain, are capable of fairly advanced reasoning.

**Apeldoorn**, city (1985 pop. 144,807), Gelderland prov., central Netherlands. It is a tourist centre on the edge of the Veluwe (badlands) region, with a famous zoo. Pure water flowing from the Veluwe sands encouraged the growth of a paper-making industry. Nearby is the royal summer palace of Het Loo.

**Apelles**, fl. 330 BC, Greek painter, the most famous in antiquity, now known only through descriptions. Perhaps his most famous work was a painting of Aphrodite rising from the sea. BOTTICELLI painted *Calumny of Apelles* (Uffizi) from ALBERTI's description.

**Apennines**, mountain system c.1350 km (840 mi) long and up to c.130 km (80 mi) wide, extending the entire length of the Italian Peninsula and continuing into Sicily. The earthquake-prone mountains, long since denuded of their original forest cover, reach a high point of 2914 m (9560 ft) in Mt Corno.

**aphasia**, language disturbance caused by BRAIN damage (usually to the left cerebral hemisphere) causing partial or total impairment in the individual's ability to speak, write, or comprehend the meaning of spoken or written words. Treatment consists of reeducation; the methods used include those employed in the education of the deaf.

**aphelion:** see APSIS.

**aphid**, **greenfly** or **plant louse** (‚ayfid), tiny (1–4mm/$\frac{1}{25}$–$\frac{1}{6}$ in), sometimes winged but often wingless, pear-shaped BUG (suborder Homoptera). They are recognized by a pair of horns (cornicles) near the end of the abdomen through which a waxy substance is secreted, as a defence against predators. A great many species occur in northern temperate areas but very few in the tropics. Aphids, like all other Homoptera, are sap-suckers and the excess water and sugars in their diet is excreted as 'honey dew'. This attracts many insects, including ANTS, with which some species live symbiotically. Most aphids overwinter as eggs, but during the spring and summer numerous young are produced alive by PARTHENOGENESIS. Serious infestations of crop plants can therefore build up very quickly. Some aphids (e.g., peach-potato aphid) are also economically important as vectors of VIRUS diseases of cultivated plants. Among the aphids which live in swellings of plant tissue (galls), during at least part of their life cycle, is the vine phylloxera, *Viteus vitifolii*, a serious pest of vines.

**Aphrodite**, in Greek mythology, goddess of love, beauty, and fertility. She was either the daughter of ZEUS and Dione (as Homer suggests), or she emerged from the sea foam. Married to HEPHAESTUS, she loved and had children by other gods and mortals, e.g., Harmonia was fathered by ARES, and AENEAS was the son of Anchises. Aphrodite was awarded the apple of discord by PARIS, leading to the TROJAN WAR. Probably of Eastern origin, she was similar in attributes to the goddesses ASTARTE and ISHTAR. A statue of her by PRAXITELES was his most celebrated work; although it does not survive there are dozens of copies from classical times. The Romans identified her with VENUS.

**Apia**, city (1979 est. pop. 35,000), capital and chief port of WESTERN SAMOA.

**APL:** see PROGRAMMING LANGUAGE.

**Apocrypha**, appendix to the Authorized (King James) Version of the Old Testament, containing the following books or parts of books: First and Second ESDRAS; TOBIT; JUDITH; ESTHER 10.4–16.24; WISDOM; ECCLESIASTICUS; BARUCH; DANIEL 3.24–90, 13, 14; Prayer of Manasses (see under MANASSEH); and First and Second MACCABEES. All except the Prayer of Manasses and First and Second Esdras are included in the Western canon. While Anglicans read them for edification, Protestants follow the Jewish tradition in treating these books as uncanonical. Jewish and Christian works resembling biblical books but not in the Western or Hebrew canon are called pseudepigrapha.

**apogee:** see APSIS.

**Apollinaire, Guillaume**, 1880–1918, French poet and critic; b. Wilhelm Apollinaris de Kostrowitzky. He was an influential innovator, whose lyric poems, e.g., those collected in *Alcools* (1913) and *Calligrammes* (1918), blend modern and traditional verse techniques. He is credited with introducing CUBISM to literature. *Les mamelles de Tirésias* (1918; tr. The Breasts of Tiresias), a play, is an early example of SURREALISM.

**Apollo**, in Greek mythology, one of the most important OLYMPIAN gods; son of ZEUS and Leto, twin brother of ARTEMIS. He was concerned especially with prophecy, medicine (he was the father of ASCLEPIUS), music and poetry (he was also the father of ORPHEUS and the patron of the MUSES), and the pastoral arts. A moral god of high civilization, he was associated with law, philosophy, and the arts. He was most widely known as a god of light, Phoebus Apollo; after the 5th cent. BC he was often identified with the sun god HELIOS. Apollo's oracles had great authority; his chief shrine was at DELPHI, where he was primarily a god of purification. The island of DELOS, his birthplace, is sacred to him. In art he was portrayed as the perfection of youth and beauty. The most celebrated statue of him is the **Apollo Belvedere**, a marble copy of the original Greek bronze, now in the Vatican in Rome.

**Apollo asteroid:** see ASTEROID.

**Apollonius Rhodius**, fl. 3rd cent. BC, EPIC poet of ALEXANDRIA and RHODES; librarian at Alexandria. His *Argonautica* is a four-book Homeric imitation on the Argonaut theme (see GOLDEN FLEECE; JASON).

**apoplexy:** see STROKE.

**apostle** [Gr., = envoy], one of the original missionaries of Christianity. The disciples of JESUS who were chosen to be his Twelve Apostles were PETER, ANDREW, JAMES (the Great), JOHN, THOMAS, JAMES (the Less), JUDE (or Thaddaeus), PHILIP, BARTHOLOMEW, MATTHEW, SIMON, and JUDAS ISCARIOT, who was later replaced by MATTHIAS. St PAUL and sometimes a few others, e.g., St BARNABAS, are also classed as apostles.

**apostrophe:** see PUNCTUATION.

**apothecaries' weights:** see ENGLISH UNITS OF MEASUREMENT; WEIGHTS AND MEASURES (table).

**apothecary**, formerly, someone who prepared drugs and other substances for medical treatment. In the 18th cent. apothecaries were also general medical practitioners. The Apothecaries Act 1815, which imposed the requirement of a licence awarded by the Society of Apothecaries after a period of training, was an attempt to eliminate charlatanism. The society still awards medical qualifications although the preparation of medicines is now carried out by pharmacists.

**Appalachian Mountains**, major North American mountain system extending c.2570 km (1600 mi) SW from Canada's Quebec prov. to Alabama, US, with Mt Mitchell (2037 m/6684 ft), in North Carolina, the highest point. Their rugged hills and valleys, the much-eroded remnants of a very old mountain mass, posed a major barrier to westward expansion in the early years of the US. Industries include coal mining (in the west) and tourism (see BLUE RIDGE).

**appeal**, legal procedure by which a superior court reviews and, if it thinks fit, alters, a lower court decision. It is often necessary to get the leave (permission) of the lower court, before an appeal can be made. The party appealing is called the appellant, the other party the respondent. Ordinarily, only errors in applying legal rules, not factual findings, may be reviewed. The reviewing court may affirm, modify, or reverse the lower court's decision, or may dismiss the case. If an error is found, a retrial may ensue. See COURT SYSTEM IN ENGLAND AND WALES.

**Appel, Karel**, 1921–, Dutch painter. A member of the Cobra group (i.e., Copenhagen, Brussels, and Amsterdam) from 1949, he painted in the 1940s and 50s in an abstract-expressionist style, using a thick impastoed paint layer in violent colours. His images are of masks and animal and fantasy figures which suggest terror and fear.

**appendix** or **vermiform appendix**, small, narrow tube, closed at one end, projecting from the large intestine into the lower right abdominal cavity. It has no apparent function and may be a remnant of a previous digestive organ. Appendicitis can occur if accumulated and hardened waste matter becomes infected; rupture of such an appendix can spread infection to the peritoneum (abdominal membrane), causing peritonitis. Inflammation of the appendix is a frequently diagnosed cause of acute abdominal illness.

**Appia, Adolphe,** 1862–1928, Swiss theorist of stage lighting and decor. His employment of light and shade when staging WAGNER's operas revolutionized modern scene design and stage lighting.

**Appian Way,** Lat. *Via Appia,* most famous of the ROMAN ROADS, built (312 BC) under Appius Claudius Caecus (see CLAUDIUS, Roman gens). It connected Rome with Capua and was later extended to Brundisium (Brindisi), being the chief highway to Greece and the East. Alongside it are many Roman monuments and some of the CATACOMBS.

**Appius Claudius:** see CLAUDIUS, Roman gens.

**apple,** any tree (and its fruit) of the genus *Malus* of the ROSE family. The common apple (*M. sylvestris*) is the best-known and commercially most important temperate fruit. It is native to W Asia, but has been widely cultivated from prehistoric times. Thousands of varieties exist, e.g., Golden Delicious, Cox's Orange Pippin, Granny Smith, and Bramley. The fruit is consumed fresh or cooked, or is used for juice. Partial fermentation of apple juice (sweet cider) produces hard cider (from which calvados is made); fully fermented juice yields vinegar. The hardwood is used in cabinetmaking and as fuel. The fruit of crab apple trees (which are cultivated as ornamentals) is used for preserves and jellies.

**Appomattox,** US town (1980 pop. 1345), central Virginia; inc. 1925. Confederate Gen. Robert E. LEE surrendered to Union Gen. U.S. GRANT at nearby Appomattox Courthouse on 9 April 1865, virtually ending the CIVIL WAR. The site of the surrender has been made a national historical park.

**apricot,** tree (*Prunus armeniaca*) of the ROSE family and its fruit, native to Asia. In the US, it is cultivated chiefly in California. The fruit is used raw, canned, preserved, and dried, and in making a cordial and a brandy.

**April:** see MONTH.

**apse,** projecting recess at the end of a building, particularly the sanctuary end of a church; generally vaulted and semicircular, sometimes square or polygonal. In Roman temples and basilicas (see TEMPLE; BASILICA), was a recess holding the statue of the deity. Early Christian churches placed the altar in the apse, at the eastern end. Because of its function, the apse became the architectural climax of the interior, and was often highly decorated. Chapels sometimes radiated from it.

**apsis,** point in the ORBIT of a smaller body where it is at its greatest or least distance from a larger body to which it is attracted. In an elliptical orbit these points are called the apocentre and pericentre; corresponding terms for elliptical orbits around the Sun, the Earth, and a star are, respectively, aphelion and perihelion, apogee and perigee, and apastron and periastron. The line of apsides, a straight line connecting the two apsides of an elliptical orbit, may shift because of gravitational influences of other bodies or through relativistic effects (see RELATIVITY).

**apteryx:** see KIWI.

**Apuleius, Lucius,** fl. 2nd cent. AD, Latin writer. His romance *The Golden Ass* or *Metamorphoses* is the only entire Latin novel surviving. The story of a man transformed into an ass, it influenced the development of the NOVEL.

**Aqaba, Gulf of,** northern arm of the RED SEA, 190 km (118 mi) long and c.16 km (10 mi) wide, between ARABIA and Egypt's SINAI peninsula. The gulf, which gives Israel direct access to the INDIAN OCEAN, is entered through the Straits of Tiran. At its head are the ports of ELAT (Israel) and AQABA (Jordan). It was declared an international waterway by the UN in 1958 after Arab states opposed to Israel blockaded it (1949–56). It was blockaded again by Egypt in 1967, which resulted in the Six Day War.

**aquamarine,** transparent blue to bluish-green variety of the mineral BERYL, used as a GEM. Sources include Brazil, the USSR, Madagascar, and parts of the US. Oriental aquamarine is a transparent bluish variety of CORUNDUM.

**aqua regia** [Lat., = royal water], corrosive, fuming, yellow liquid prepared by mixing one volume of concentrated NITRIC ACID with three to four volumes of concentrated HYDROCHLORIC ACID. It was so named by the alchemists because it dissolves gold and platinum, the 'royal' metals, which do not dissolve in nitric and hydrochloric acid alone.

**aquarium,** name for any supervised exhibit of living aquatic animals and plants. Aquariums are known to have been built in ancient Rome, Egypt, and the Orient. Large, modern public aquariums were made possible by the development of glass exhibit tanks capable of holding over 375,000 litres (100,000 gal) of water. Aquarium maintenance requires careful regulation of temperature, light, food, oxygen, and water flow; removal of injurious waste and debris; and attention to the special requirements of the individual species. Freshwater and saltwater aquariums are often maintained for research and breeding purposes by universities, marine stations, and wildlife commissions.

**aquatint,** etching technique. A metal plate is coated with resin through which acid bites to create an evenly pocked surface. When printed, it produces tonal effects that resemble wash drawings. Aquatint is often combined with other types of etchings, as in GOYA's series of mixed aquatint etchings.

**aqueduct,** any artificial work to enable water from a source to be distributed to places where it is required for domestic purposes, agricultural irrigation, or for power. It can be partly open to the air, tunnelled through rocks, or piped in soft soils and can, in places, be pumped using water towers to produce pressure. In original form an aqueduct consisted of high-level arched masonry where the flow was dependent on gravity. The Greeks first built these in the 7th cent. BC but the Romans became expert and introduced them all over the Roman Empire. Five surviving examples can be seen at Nîmes in France, Segovia and Tarragona in Spain, and Istanbul. By AD 100 Rome itself was served with drinking water by 11 aqueducts from different sources, the longest being 100 km (62 mi).

Aqueduct near Caesarea, Israel

**aquifer:** see ARTESIAN WELL.

**Aquitaine,** former duchy and kingdom in SW France. Conquered (56 BC) by the Romans, it fell to the VISIGOTHS in the 5th cent. AD. In 507 Aquitaine was added to the Frankish kingdom by CLOVIS I, but later regained some independence. CHARLEMAGNE made (781) Aquitaine into a kingdom that was ruled by his son Louis (later Emperor LOUIS I). Late in the 9th cent. it became a duchy enfeoffed to the French crown. ELEANOR OF AQUITAINE's marriage (1152) to the future HENRY II of England gave Henry and his heirs control of the duchy as vassals of the French crown. France completed the recapture of Aquitaine from the English during the HUNDRED YEARS WAR.

**Ar,** chemical symbol of the element ARGON.

**Arabi** or **Urabi, Ahmed Pasha,** 1841–1911, Egyptian nationalist. Born of *fellah* [indigenous peasant] stock, he rose through the ranks of the army to become the Egyptian minister of defence during the early 1880s. He tried to oppose increasing European intervention in his country's affairs. In 1882 pro-Arabi forces were defeated by the British at Tel el Kebir and de facto British rule introduced. After a period of exile Arabi returned to Egypt in 1901. By the time of his death he was already being proclaimed as the father of modern Egyptian nationalism.

**Arabia,** peninsula, c.3,237,000 km² (1,250,000 sq mi), SW Asia, containing the world's largest known reserves of oil and natural gas. It is politically divided between SAUDI ARABIA (the largest state), YEMEN, Southern Yemen (see YEMEN, SOUTHERN), OMAN, the UNITED ARAB EMIRATES,

QATAR, BAHRAIN, KUWAIT, and several neutral zones. JORDAN and IRAQ are to the north, the RED SEA to the west, and the PERSIAN GULF to the east. The highest areas are the west and southwest, where mountains rise to c.3700 m (12,000 ft), and in Oman in the southeast where the JEBEL AKHDAR Mts reach c.3000 m (9800 ft). From the higher areas the land slopes gradually to lowlands along the Persian Gulf and to a sandy depression (the RUB AL KHALI) in the southeast. Only in the mountains is there significant rainfall, and much of the interior and the east coast is desert with less than 10 cm (4 in). of annual precipitation.

**Arabian art and architecture:** see ISLAMIC ART AND ARCHITECTURE.

**Arabian music,** the urban musical tradition of the Arabic-speaking regions of the Middle East and North Africa. The tradition is founded on an amalgamation of musical systems practised in the Middle East prior to the Islamic conquests of the 7th and 8th cent., to which Byzantine, Persian, and Syrian sources contributed heavily. The chief characteristics are the use of diverse intervals with which a wealth of modes (*maqāms*) are constructed, florid ornamentation, and modal rhythms. Today's Arabian music is usually performed in the form of a *nauba*, a 'suite' of vocal and instrumental pieces, composed or improvised, in a given *maqām*. The principle instruments of Arabian music are the *ud* [lute], *qānun* [psaltery], and *rebāb* [viol].

**Arabian Nights:** see THOUSAND AND ONE NIGHTS.

**Arabian Sea,** ancient *Mare Erythraeum,* northwestern marginal sea of the INDIAN OCEAN, between Arabia and India. Its principal arms include the Gulf of ADEN, extended by the RED SEA, and the Gulf of Oman, extended by the PERSIAN GULF. ADEN, KARACHI, and BOMBAY are the chief ports.

**Arabic languages,** members of the Semitic subdivision of the Hamito-Semitic family of languages. See AFRICAN LANGUAGES (table); ALPHABET (illustration).

**Arabic literature,** literature written in Arabic by Turks, Persians, Africans, and Jews, as well as Arabs. The first significant Arabic literature was the lyric poetry of the 4th to 7th cent., strongly personal *qasidas* (odes) that treat tribal life and the themes of love, combat, and the chase. The Prophet MUHAMMAD was not interested in poetry, so with the rise of ISLAM, Arabic poetry declined, replaced by the study of the KORAN. Literature again flourished in the Arabic–Persian culture of BAGHDAD in the 8th and 9th cent. A group of young poets, including ABU NUWAS, established a new, sophisticated court poetry; typical is the precise, formal, yet exaggerated work of MUTANABBI (d. 965). In the work of later writers, such as HARIRI (11th cent.), the style approached preciosity, and eventually the prose romance became the principal literary form. The THOUSAND AND ONE NIGHTS is the greatest example of this genre. During the Middle Ages MASUDI and IBN KHALDUN produced great works on history and geography, al GHAZALI on theology and philosophy, and AVICENNA on medicine. The Arabic culture of Spain also produced fine poets and scholars, but they were dwarfed by the great philosophers AVERROES and Ibn Tufayl. After 1300, however, Arabic literature again declined. In the late 1800s growing Western influences stimulated a nationalistic vernacular literature in Syria and Egypt. Since then, the novel, the short story, and drama have been adopted and developed, in spite of a reaction against Western models in modern Arabic literature. Notable 20th-cent. writers include the novelist Nagib MAHFUZ, the playwright Tawfiq al-HAKIM, and the poets Ahmad SHAWQI, Hafiz IBRAHIM, and Badr Shakir al-SAYYAB.

**Arabic numeral:** see NUMERAL.

**Arab–Israeli Wars,** conflicts in 1948–49, 1956, 1967, 1973–74, and 1982 between ISRAEL and the Arabs. **1** The 1948–49 war reflected the opposition of the Arab states to the formation of a Jewish state in what they considered Arab territories. Newly created Israel was invaded by forces from Egypt, Syria, Transjordan (later Jordan), Lebanon, and Iraq. A UN-sponsored truce was arranged, but fighting has broken out periodically since then over the basic issue of the existence of Israel. **2** In 1956 Israel, joined by France and Great Britain, attacked Egypt after that country had nationalized the Suez Canal. Intervention by the UN, supported by the US and the USSR forced a cease-fire. **3** In 1967, in the Six-Day War, Israel responded to Egyptian provocation with air attacks and victories on the ground. The result was a humiliating defeat for Egypt, Jordan, and Syria. **4** In the Yom Kippur War of 1973–74, Egypt, Syria, and Iraq attacked Israel on the Jewish holy Day of Atonement, catching the Israelis off guard. Israel recouped quickly, however, and forced the

Arab troops back from their initial gains, but at great cost to both sides. Again, a cease-fire stopped the fighting. **5** In 1978 Palestinian guerrillas, from their base in LEBANON, launched an air raid on Israel; in retaliation, Israel sent troops into S Lebanon to occupy a 10-km (16-mi) strip and thus protect Israel's border. Eventually a UN peace-keeping force was set up there, but occasional fighting continued. In 1982 Israel launched a massive attack to destroy all military bases of the PALESTINE LIBERATION ORGANIZATION in S Lebanon; after a 10-week siege of the Muslim sector of West BEIRUT, a PLO stronghold, Israel forced the Palestinians to accept a US-sponsored plan whereby the PLO guerrillas would evacuate Beirut and go to several Arab countries that had agreed to accept them. Israeli forces withdrew from Lebanon in 1985, leaving pro-Israeli Lebanese Christian militia in control of the sensitive border area.

**Arab League,** association of states formed (1945) to give common expression to the political interests of Arab nations. Its members are Algeria, Bahrain, Djibouti, Iraq, Jordan, Kuwait, Lebanon, Libya, Mauritania, Morocco, Oman, Qatar, Saudi Arabia, Somalia, Sudan, Syria, Tunisia, the United Arab Emirates, North Yemen, South Yemen and the PALESTINE LIBERATION ORGANIZATION. Opposed to the formation of a Jewish state in Palestine, league members jointly attacked Israel in 1948 (see ARAB–ISRAELI WARS). In 1979 Egypt was suspended after its peace agreement with Israel and the headquarters of the league was transferred from Cairo to Tunis; however, in 1987–88 moves were initiated to readmit Egypt. Attempts to coordinate Arab economic life are among the league's chief activities; the **Arab Common Market** was set up in 1965 and the **Arab Monetary Fund** in 1977.

**Arabs,** name originally applied to the Semitic peoples of the Arabian peninsula (see SEMITE); now used also for populations of countries whose primary language is Arabic, e.g., Algeria, Egypt, Iraq, Jordan, Lebanon, Libya, Morocco, Syria, and Yemen. Socially, Arabs are divided into the settled *fellahin* (villagers) and the nomadic BEDOUIN. The invasions of Muslims from Arabia in the 6th and 7th cent. diffused the Arabic language and ISLAM, the Arabic religion. At its peak the Arab empire extended from the Atlantic Ocean across North Africa and the Middle East to central Asia. A great Arab civilization emerged in which education, literature, philosophy, medicine, mathematics, and science were highly developed. In Europe the Arab conquests were particularly important in Sicily, from the 9th to late 11th cent., and in Spain, in the civilization of the MOORS. In the 20th cent., Arab leaders have attempted to unite the Arab-speaking world into an Arab nation. Since 1945 most Arab countries have joined the ARAB LEAGUE. In 1982 member nations had a total population estimated at 43 million. Several of these countries control two thirds of the world's oil reserves and are members of OPEC (see ORGANIZATION OF THE PETROLEUM EXPORTING COUNTRIES). Since 1948 disputes with the state of ISRAEL have resulted in ARAB–ISRAELI WARS.

**Aracajú** (ara͵kahooh), city and port (1980 pop. 287,934), NE Brazil, capital of Sergipe state. Situated 10 km (6 mi) upstream from the mouth of the Sergipe R., on the Atlantic coast, it is the third largest port of the NE coast of Brazil and a major administrative and commercial centre for its sugar-producing hinterland. It was founded in 1855.

**arachnid** (ə͵raknid), mainly terrestrial ARTHROPOD of the class Arachnida, including the SPIDER, SCORPION, MITE, TICK, and HARVESTMAN. The arachnid's body is divided into a cephalothorax with four pairs of walking legs and two pairs of feeding appendages, and an abdomen. Most are carnivorous, and some use the appendages to crush and kill prey feeding. Arachnids have simple eyes and sensory bristles; they have no antennae. Respiration is through air tubes or primitive structures called lungbooks.

**Arad,** city (1983 pop. 171,198), near the Hungarian border of W Romania. It occupies a defensive site on the Mureş R. and has textile, railway engineering, and food industries.

**Arafat, Yasir,** 1929–, Palestine commando leader; b. Jerusalem. Head of the guerrilla group Al Fatah, he became (1969) leader of the PALESTINE LIBERATION ORGANIZATION (PLO). In 1974 Arab leaders recognized the PLO as the 'sole legitimate' spokesman for the Palestinian people. The PLO was considerably weakened when Arafat and his guerrillas were forced to leave their stronghold in West BEIRUT, Lebanon, after the 1982 Israeli siege of the city (see ARAB–ISRAELI WARS). In the mid-1980s his leadership of the PLO was strongly contested by extremist Palestinian factions, but by early 1987 he had reestablished his authority. In 1988 he declared the PLO's willingness to recognize Israel in return for a just settlement of the Palestinian question.

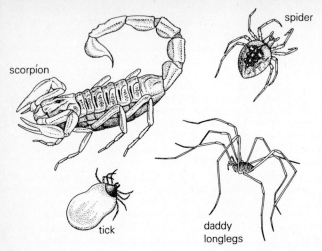

scorpion

spider

tick

daddy
longlegs

Arachnid

**Aragón**, region, 47,609 km² (18,382 sq mi), and former kingdom, NE Spain, bordered in the north by France. Much of Aragón is sparsely populated and desertlike. Grains, sugar beets, and other crops are grown in oases and irrigated areas. Food-processing is the most important industry. The kingdom was founded (1035) on land won from the MOORS, and in the 12th cent. ZARAGOZA became its capital. Aragón annexed NAVARRE in 1076 and was united with CATALONIA in 1137. Its rulers (see ARAGÓN, HOUSE OF) pursued (13th–15th cent.) an expansionist policy in the Mediterranean. The marriage (1479) of Ferdinand of Aragón (later Spanish King FERDINAND V) to ISABELLA I of Castile led to the union of Aragón and Castile.

**Aragón, house of,** ruling family of ARAGÓN and other territories in the Middle Ages. Founded (1035) by Ramiro I, the house during the 12th cent. conquered much territory from the MOORS in Spain and also in S France. In the 14th and 15th cent. it acquired SICILY, SARDINIA, and the kingdom of NAPLES. These possessions were usually held by various branches of the house and were seldom united under one ruler as they were under ALFONSO V in 1442–58. The union of the crowns of Aragón and Castile took place in 1479, after the Spanish king FERDINAND V married ISABELLA I of Castile.

**Aragon, Louis,** 1897–1982, French writer. A founder of SURREALISM, he later turned to realistic social and political fiction after becoming a communist. His works include the surrealist novel *Le paysan de Paris* (1926; tr. Nightwalker), the war poems in *Le crève-coeur* (1941; tr. Heartbreak), and the series of love poems (1953, 1959, 1963) to his wife, the novelist Elsa Triolet.

**Aral Sea,** inland sea, the world's 4th largest lake, c.67,300 km² (26,000 sq mi), in Soviet Central Asia. The sea, which is fed by the AMU DARYA and SYR DARYA rivers, is generally less than 70 m (220 ft) deep and is only slightly saline. It was known to medieval Arab geographers as the Khorezm or Khwarazm Sea and to early Russian explorers, who reached it in the 17th cent., as the Sine [Blue] Sea.

**Aramaic** ('arə,mayik), Hamito-Semitic language that flourished in SYRIA and the FERTILE CRESCENT around the time of Christ. See LANGUAGE (table).

**Aramburu, Pedro Eugenio** (ahrahm,boohrooh), 1903–70, president of Argentina (1955–58). An army general, he participated in the overthrow of Juan PERÓN. As president, he ruled by decree, removed Peronists from important posts, and returned the country to constitutional monarchy. He was kidnapped and murdered by Peronist guerrillas in 1970.

**Arany, János** (ə,ronyə), 1817–82, Hungarian poet. His greatest works are his ballads and the epic trilogy *Toldi* (1847), *Toldi's Eve* (1854), and *Toldi's Love* (1879). His powerful, simple style is often reminiscent of folk song.

**Arapaho Indians:** see NORTH AMERICAN INDIANS.

**Ararat,** mountain, E Turkey, with two peaks, Little Ararat 3925 m (12,877 ft.) and Great Ararat 5165 m/16,945 ft. According to tradition, it was the landing place of Noah's ark. The **kingdom of Ararat** (fl.

c.9th–7th cent. BC), called the Assyrian Urartu, was located near Lake Van in present-day E Turkey.

**Araucanian Indians,** many tribes of South American agricultural people (see SOUTH AMERICAN INDIANS) occupying most of S central Chile before the Spanish conquest (1540) and speaking languages of the Araucanian group (see AMERICAN INDIAN LANGUAGES). The INCA invaded them (c.1448–82) but were never a strong influence. The Araucanians stoutly resisted the Spanish, rebelling periodically until 1881. Some Araucanians, especially in the 18th cent., had fled to Argentina, where with captured wild horses they became plains wanderers. The Araucanians in Chile today number over 200,000; they are divided between assimilated urban dwellers and those who retain many of their traditional ways.

**arbitration, industrial:** see under COLLECTIVE BARGAINING.

**Arblay, Madame d':** see BURNEY, FANNY.

**arboretum:** see BOTANICAL GARDEN.

**arborvitae:** see WESTERN RED CEDAR.

**Arbuthnot, John,** 1667–1735, Scottish writer, scientist, and physician. He is best remembered for his five 'John Bull' pamphlets (1712), allegorical satires on Whig policy that introduced the character John Bull, the typical Englishman. A member of the SCRIBLERUS CLUB, he also wrote medical works.

**arbutus,** common and generic name for group of shrubs and trees, e.g., the strawberry tree, with profuse white flowers and globular, red fruits.

**arc,** in mathematics, any part of a CURVE that does not intersect itself; in particular, a portion of the circumference of a CIRCLE.

**Arcadia,** region of ancient GREECE, in the central PELOPONNESUS. Its inhabitants, the Arcadians, lived a pastoral life. The largest city was Megalopolis.

**Arcadius,** c.377–408, Roman emperor of the East (395–408); son of THEODOSIUS I. His brother HONORIUS inherited the West, which began the division of the empire. During Arcadius's weak reign ALARIC I invaded Greece (395–97).

**Arcagnolo:** see ORCAGNA.

**Arc de Triomphe de l'Étoile** (ahk də treeawnhf də laytwahl), triumphal arch in Paris, in the centre of the Place de l'Étoile [the star],

Arc de Triomphe de l'Etoile

which is formed by the intersection of 12 avenues, one of them the Champs Élysées. It was built (1806–36) to commemorate NAPOLEON I's victories, from the designs of J.F. Chalgrin. In 1920 the body of an unknown French soldier was buried there.

**arch,** structure spanning a wall opening, consisting of separate units (e.g., bricks or blocks) assembled into an upward curve that maintains stability through the mutual pressure of a load and the separate pieces. The weight of the load is converted into downward pressures (thrusts) received by the piers (abutments) flanking the opening. The blocks forming the arch are usually wedge-shaped. The arch was used by the Egyptians, Babylonians, and Greeks, chiefly for drains, and by the Assyrians in vaulted and domed chambers. The oldest known arch in Europe is a Roman drain, the Cloaca Maxima (c.578 BC). The Roman semicircular arch, drawn from Etruscan structures, was continued in early Christian, Byzantine, and Romanesque architecture. The pointed arch (used by the Assyrians) came into general use in the 13th cent. Possibly rediscovered independently in Europe, it became essential to the Gothic system of design. The round arch regained dominance in the RENAISSANCE. The 19th-cent. invention of steel beams for wide spans relegated the arch to a supplementary or decorative function.

**archaeoastronomy,** the study of prehistoric astronomy, especially as applied to astronomical alignments in MEGALITHIC MONUMENTS. Research at STONEHENGE, NEW GRANGE, CARNAC, and other sites suggests that prehistoric peoples oriented structures to specific positions of the Sun, Moon, or stars. The potent linkage of famous ancient monuments with controversial research has created world-wide interest—and many extravagant claims of the discovery of sophisticated ancient observatories.

**archaeology,** systematic study of material remains of human cultures to derive knowledge about prehistoric times and social processes. Research into the life and culture of the past began in 15th-cent. Italy with the excavation of ancient Greek sculpture. Knowledge of the Classical world was advanced in the 18th cent. by excavations at HERCULANEUM and POMPEII while antiquarians continued to ponder the mysteries of the MEGALITHIC MONUMENTS of Northern and Western Europe. The growing awareness that there were aboriginal peoples living outside the world described by the Bible stimulated interest in a remote European past that was slowly emerging in stone tools, sometimes found with the bones of extinct animals, and the pottery and metal objects of BARROWS and middens. In the 19th cent. archaeology caught the public imagination as the ELGIN MARBLES were brought from Greece and legendary cities were unearthed by Heinrich SCHLIEMANN at Troy and Arthur EVANS in Crete; and Egyptology was born with the discovery of the ROSETTA STONE. Without the inscriptional and documentary evidence that guided Classical and BIBLICAL ARCHAEOLOGY, prehistoric research was little more than the collecting of curios until the Danish archaeologist Christian Thomsen developed a classification system that ordered artifacts by their material substance into the Stone, Bronze, and Iron Ages (see THREE-AGE SYSTEM). The late 19th and early 20th cent. saw advances in recording and excavation as exemplified by the work of Gen. PITT-RIVERS, and as the century progressed, concern with the prehistoric landscape and the way that people adapted to it began to emerge in studies of settlement pattern, ECOLOGY, and food production, enhanced by improved field techniques and new DATING methods. The recent interest in the study of existing aboriginal groups—and the contemporary world as a whole—have provided new ways of understanding the complex role of material culture as a social tool in the activities of daily life. In order to see how the past has been shaped, archaeologists have now become students of the present. See also RESCUE ARCHAEOLOGY; UNDERWATER ARCHAEOLOGY.

**Archangel:** see ARKHANGELSK.

**archdeacon,** originally the principal deacon on a bishop's staff. The title has become largely honarary in the Roman Catholic and Orthodox Churches, but in the Anglican Church it denotes a senior cleric to whom the bishop delegates certain administrative functions.

**archery,** sport of shooting with bow and arrow. The four main types are target, field, flight, and crossbow shooting. In target shooting, the object is to score the most points with arrows aimed at the 'bull's-eye', the innermost of five to ten concentric circles. Once an important military and hunting skill, archery was revived as a sport in Europe in the 17th cent.

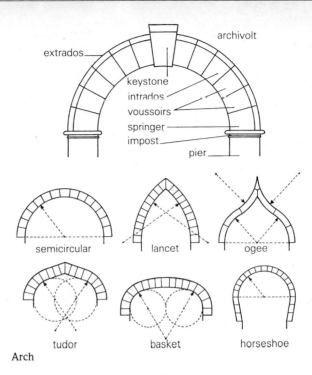

Arch

**Archilochus** (ahki,lokus), fl. c.650 BC, Greek poet; b. Paros. He wrote short poems in a variety of metres, and is most famous for the violent personal invective of some of them.

**Archimedes,** c.287–212 BC, Greek mathematician, physicist, and inventor. His reputation in antiquity was based on several mechanical contrivances, which he is alleged to have invented, e.g., ARCHIMEDES' SCREW. One legend states that during the Second PUNIC WAR he protected his native Syracuse from the besieging armies of Marcus Claudius MARCELLUS for three years by inventing machines of war, e.g., various ballistic instruments and mirrors that set Roman ships on fire by focusing the sun's rays on them. In modern times, however, he is best known for his work in mathematics, mechanics, and hydrostatics. In mathematics, he calculated that the value of $\pi$ (see PI) is between $3\frac{10}{71}$ and $3\frac{1}{7}$; devised a mathematical exponential system to express extremely large numbers; proved that the volume of a sphere is two-thirds the volume of a circumscribed cylinder; and, in calculating the areas and volumes of various geometrical figures, carried the method of exhaustion (invented by EUDOXUS OF CNIDUS) far enough in some cases to anticipate the invention (17th cent.) of the CALCULUS. One of the first to apply geometry to mechanics and hydrostatics, he proved the law of the lever entirely by geometry and established ARCHIMEDES' PRINCIPLE. In another legendary story, the ruler Hiero II requested him to find a method for determining whether a crown was pure gold or alloyed with silver. Archimedes realized, as he stepped into a bath, that a given weight of gold would displace less water than an equal weight of silver (which is less dense than gold); and he is said, in his excitement at his discovery, to have run home naked, shouting *'Eureka! Eureka!'* ['I have found it! I have found it!']. He was killed by a Roman soldier, supposedly while absorbed in mathematics.

**Archimedes' principle,** principle that states that a body immersed in a fluid is buoyed up by a force equal to the weight of the displaced fluid. The principle applies to both floating and submerged bodies, and to all fluids. It explains not only the buoyancy of ships but also the rise of a helium-filled balloon and the apparent loss of weight of objects under water.

**Archimedes' screw,** simple mechanical device used to lift liquids and powders composed of small particles from one level to another; used for water, sludge and slurries, grain, and sand. From his own drawings (3rd cent. BC) it is evident that Archimedes designed such devices and he is given the credit for the original idea. The device consists of a large continuous screw inside a cylinder. When the screw is turned the material is lifted inside the cylinder by the spiral threads.

**Archipenko, Alexander,** 1887–1964, Ukrainian–American sculptor. He recognized the aesthetic value of negative form (the void), as in the bronze figure *Dance* (1912). Although influenced by cubist ideas and similar work by LAURENS, LIPCHITZ, and DUCHAMP-VILLON, Archipenko claimed that the geometric nature of his work derived from simplification of form rather than cubist dogma (see CUBISM). He exhibited at the 1912 Section d'Or, and went to America to teach in 1923.

**Arctic, the,** northernmost area of the Earth, centred on the NORTH POLE. It may be defined as embracing all lands located N of the ARCTIC CIRCLE (lat. 66°30′N) or all lands located N of the 10°C (50°F) July isotherm, which is roughly equivalent to the tree line. It therefore generally includes the ARCTIC OCEAN; the northern reaches of Canada, Alaska, the USSR, and Norway; and most of Greenland, Iceland, and Svalbard. Ice sheets and permanent snow cover regions where average monthly temperatures remain below 0°C (32°F) all year; TUNDRA, which flourishes during the short summer season, covers areas where temperatures are between 0° and 10°C (32°F and 50°F) for at least one month. Day length ranges from a maximum of 24 hours of constant light at the summer solstice on the Arctic Circle to six months at the North Pole throughout summer; conversely, in winter, nights last from a maximum of 24 hours of darkness at the winter solstice on the Arctic Circle to six months at the North Pole. The Arctic is of great strategic value as the shortest route between North America and USSR. Its rich oil and natural-gas deposits have been discovered since the International Geophysical Year (1957–58) on Alaska's North Slope (see PRUDHOE BAY), Canada's northern archipelago (1972), and the northern areas of Siberia, in the USSR. F.A. Cook in 1908 and R.F. Peary in 1909, both from the US, claimed to have been the first to reach the North Pole; there are serious doubts about these claims. The first expedition definitely to have stood at the North Pole was led by P.A. Gordiyenko (USSR) in 1948, and the first surface journey there was made by R. Plaisted (US) with snow-scooters in 1968.

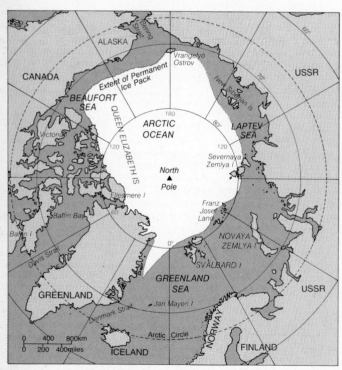

Arctic

**Arctic Circle,** imaginary circle on the earth's surface at 66°30′N lat., marking the northernmost point at which the sun can be seen at the winter SOLSTICE (about 22 Dec.) and the southernmost point of the northern polar regions at which the midnight sun is visible.

**Arctic Ocean,** the world's smallest ocean, 13,986,000 km² (c.5,400,00 sq mi), centring on the NORTH POLE and connecting with the Pacific through the Bering Strait and with the Atlantic through the Greenland Sea and Baffin Bay. It is covered with ice up to 4 m (14 ft) thick all year, except in fringe areas.

**Ardashir I,** d. 240, king of PERSIA (226?–240), founder of the Sassanid dynasty. He reunited Persia and established ZOROASTRIANISM as the state religion. His costly victory (232) over Roman Emperor Alexander Severus consolidated Persian power.

**Ardennes,** wooded plateau, from 488 to 701 m (1600 to 2300 ft) high, in SE Belgium, N Luxembourg, and N France. A traditional battleground, the Ardennes saw heavy fighting in both world wars, notably in the Battle of the Bulge (1944–45).

**Arendt, Hannah,** 1906–75, American political theorist; b. Germany. Fleeing the Nazis in 1941, she came to the US and taught at leading universities. In *The Origins of Totalitarianism* (1951), which established her as a major political thinker, Arendt traced Nazism and Communism to 19th cent. IMPERIALISM and ANTI-SEMITISM. Other works include *The Human Condition* (1958), *Eichmann in Jerusalem* (1963), and *The Life of the Mind* (1977).

**Arequipa,** city (1981 pop. 447,431), capital of Arequipa dept., S Peru. The commercial centre of S Peru and N Bolivia, it produces leather goods, alpaca wool, textiles, and foodstuffs. Founded in 1540 on an INCA site, it was largely destroyed by an earthquake in 1868 but has been restored. It is called 'the white city' because of the light-coloured stone, sillar, used as a building material.

**Ares** (ˌɛəreez), in Greek mythology, OLYMPIAN god of war; son of ZEUS and HERA. The Romans identified him with MARS.

**Argentina,** officially Argentine Republic, republic (1986 est. pop. 31,000,000), 2,776,889 km² (1,072,157 sq mi), S South America, bordered by Chile (W); Bolivia (N); Paraguay, Brazil, and Uruguay (NE); and the Atlantic Ocean (SE). The second largest nation of South America, it stretches c.3700 km (2300 mi) from the subtropics south to TIERRA DEL FUEGO. Major cities include BUENOS AIRES (the capital), CÓRDOBA, and ROSARIO. Argentina consists of six geographical regions: (1) the Paraná Plateau in the NE, a wet, forested area; (2) the GRAN CHACO, a flat alluvial plain; (3) the Pampa (see under PAMPAS), a vast grassland between the Atlantic and the Andean foothills; (4) the Monte, an arid region dotted with oases; (5) PATAGONIA, in the S, a bleak plateau that is the chief oil-producing region; and (6) the ANDES Mts, extending the length of the western border and including ACONCAGUA (6960 m/22,835 ft), the highest point of South America. Most important of these is the Pampa, the chief agricultural and industrial area and site of most of the principal cities. Argentina's economy is a diversified mix of agriculture and industry. Grains and livestock are the basis of the nation's wealth; wheat, maize, flax, oats, beef, mutton, hides, and wool are the major exports. Domestic oil and gas production makes the nation virtually self-sufficient in energy. The industrial base is highly developed, providing nearly all of its consumer goods requirements. Food processing (meat packing, flour milling, canning) is the principal industry; leather goods and textiles are also important. In 1984 GDP was US$66.9 thousand million or US$2188 per capita. The population is overwhelmingly of European descent (especially Spanish and Italian), and about 90% are Roman Catholic. Spanish is the official language.

*History.* The first European explorers, notably Juan Díaz de Solís, Ferdinand MAGELLAN, and Sebastian Cabot (see under CABOT, JOHN), arrived in the early 16th cent. Buenos Aires was founded in 1536, abandoned after Indian attacks, and refounded in 1580. The city was made the capital of a Spanish viceroyalty in 1776. The successful struggle for independence (1810–16) was led by generals Manuel BELGRANO, J.M. de Pueyrredón, and José de SAN MARTÍN. A protracted period of civil war ensued, lasting until the dictatorship of J.M. de ROSAS (1829–52). A new constitution was adopted in 1853 and, with major amendments, remained in effect until 1949, but Argentina continued to suffer political instability and military coups. It belatedly entered (1945) WORLD WAR II on the Allied side after four years of pro-Axis 'neutrality'. Juan PERÓN, an army colonel who, with a group of colonels, seized power in 1944, won the elections of 1946 and established a popular dictatorship with the support of the army, nationalists, and the Roman Catholic Church. His second wife, the popular Eva Duarte de Perón (see under PERÓN, JUAN) won the backing of trade unions; her enormous popularity among the industrial working class was the major pillar of support for the Perón regime. Her death in 1952, followed by an economic downturn, led to Perón's removal (1955) by the military. Government during the next 18 years had to contend with the continuing popularity of the Peronist movement. In 1973, Perón returned from exile and won election as president. His third wife, Isabel Martínez de Perón, was elected vice president; she succeeded him upon his death in 1974. During her presidency terrorism by the left and right grew, and inflation worsened; in 1976 she was overthrown in a military coup that established a repressive military junta. In 1982, with Gen. Leopoldo GALTIERI as president, Argentina occupied the FALKLAND ISLANDS, which it had long disputed with Britain. The Argentine defeat in the ensuing war with Britain led to Galtieri's resignation and to strong public criticism of the military government. Civilian rule was restored after elections in 1983 which resulted in victory for the Radical Civic Union (UCR). In 1989 Carlos Menem (Peronista Party) won the presidential elections.

**Post-war Argentine presidents**
Juan Domingo Perón (Peronist), 1946–55
Eduardo Lonardi (military), 1955
Pedro Eugenio Aramburu (military), 1955–58
Arturo Frondizi (Radical), 1958–62
José María Guido (non-party), 1962–63
Arturo Illía (Radical), 1963–66
Juan Carlos Ongañía (military), 1966–70
Roberto Marcelo Levingston (military), 1970–71
Alejandro Agustín Lanusse (military), 1971–73
Héctor Cámpora (Peronist), 1973
Juan Domingo Perón (Peronist), 1973–74
Isabel Martínez de Perón (Peronist), 1974–76
Jorge Rafael Videla (military), 1976–81
Roberto Eduardo Viola (military), 1981
Leopoldo Galtieri (military), 1981–82
Reynaldo Bignone (military), 1982–83
Raúl Alfonsín (Radical), 1983–89
Carlos Menem (Peronist), 1989–

Argentina

**argon** (Ar), gaseous element, discovered in 1894 by Sir William RAMSAY and Lord RAYLEIGH. An odourless, tasteless, and colourless INERT GAS, it makes up 0.93% of the atmosphere by volume. Argon is used to provide a nonreactive atmosphere in light bulbs and neon signs, in refining reactive elements, and in arc welding. See ELEMENT (table); PERIODIC TABLE.

**Argonauts:** see GOLDEN FLEECE; JASON.

**Argus** or **Argos**, in Greek mythology. 1 Many-eyed monster who guarded IO after she was changed into a heifer. 2 Builder of the ship on which JASON and the Argonauts sailed in quest of the GOLDEN FLEECE.

**Århus**, city (1985 pop. 252,071), central Denmark, on Århus Bay. Founded by the 10th cent., it is a prosperous cultural centre and a commercial and shipping centre, manufacturing beer, textiles, and machinery. Among its landmarks are its theatre and the 12th-cent. Cathedral of St Clemens.

**aria**, elaborate and often lengthy solo SONG with instrumental accompaniment, especially in an OPERA, ORATORIO, or CANTATA. The three-part *aria da capo* was developed in the 17th and 18th cent. by A. SCARLATTI, J.S. BACH, HANDEL, and others. More than 15 types of aria were distinguished. The arias of W.A. MOZART often combined dramatic and lyrical elements. Later composers fused aria and RECITATIVE and tended to abandon the *aria da capo* because it halted the flow of the drama.

**Ariadne**, in Greek mythology, Cretan princess; daughter of MINOS and Pasiphaë. With her help THESEUS killed the MINOTAUR and escaped from the Labyrinth. He left with her but deserted her at Naxos. There she married DIONYSUS, who is said to have set her bridal crown among the stars; this scene has often been painted, e.g., by TITIAN (*Bacchus and Ariadne*; 1517–23, Nat. Gall., London).

**Arianism**, Christian heresy arising from the teaching of the Alexandrian priest Arius, c.256–336. To Arius, Jesus was a supernatural being, not quite human, not quite divine, who was created by God. Arianism spread and was condemned by the First Council of NICAEA (325). The conflict went on, however, and several bishops and emperors sided with Arius. The Catholic tenets of Rome and ATHANASIUS finally triumphed, and the First Council of CONSTANTINOPLE (381) upheld the decrees of Nicaea.

**Arias de Ávila, Pedro,** known as **Pedrarias,** c.1440–1531, Spanish colonial administrator. He succeeded (1514) BALBOA as governor of Darien (now in PANAMA), quarrelled with him, and ordered (1517) his execution. He founded (1519) Panama City and extended Spanish dominions.

**Ariel,** in astronomy, satellite of URANUS.

**Arion,** Greek poet, fl. late 7th cent. BC, inventor of the literary DITHYRAMB. His rescue from drowning by a dolphin charmed by his music is told by HERODOTUS.

**Ariosto, Ludovico,** 1474–1533, Italian poet and playwright. His *Orlando Furioso* (1532), the greatest of the Italian romantic epics, features the enamoured ROLAND's temporary insanity and exalts the ESTE family, in whose service the author spent most of his life. His four classical comedies (1508–28) are an early milestone in modern European drama.

**Aristarchus of Samos,** fl.c.310–c.230 BC, Greek astronomer. He is said to have been the first to propose a heliocentric theory of the universe, anticipating Copernicus by 18 centuries (see COPERNICAN SYSTEM). His only surviving work, *On the Sizes and Distances of the Sun and Moon,* is celebrated for its geometric argument, even though crude observation data led to faulty estimates.

**Aristogiton:** see HARMODIUS AND ARISTOGITON.

**Aristophanes** ('aris,tofəneez), b. c.445 BC, d. after 388 BC, Athenian comic poet, the greatest ancient writer of COMEDY. His plays mix political, social, and literary SATIRE. Invective, burlesque, and direct attack on persons made them suitable for the festival of DIONYSUS. Typically, his characters act naturally in preposterous circumstances; his language is economical, inventive, and beautiful. Eleven surviving plays include *The Clouds, The Wasps, Lysistrata,* and *The Frogs.*

**Aristotle,** 384–322 BC, Greek philosopher. He studied (367–347 BC) under PLATO and later (342–339 BC) tutored ALEXANDER THE GREAT at the Macedonian court. In 335 BC he opened a school in the Athenian Lyceum. During the anti-Macedonian agitation after Alexander's death Aristotle fled (323 BC) to Chalcis, where he died. His extant writings, largely in the form of lecture notes made for his students, include the *Organum* (treatises on logic); *Physics; Metaphysics; De anima* [on the soul]; *Nicomachean Ethics* and *Eudemian Ethics; Politics; De poetica; Rhetoric;* and works on biology and physics. Aristotle held philosophy to be the discerning, through the use of systematic LOGIC as expressed in

SYLLOGISMS, of the self-evident, changeless first principles that form the basis of all knowledge. He taught that knowledge of a thing requires an inquiry into causality and that the 'final cause' the purpose or function of the thing is primary. The highest good for the individual is the complete exercise of the specifically human function of rationality. In contrast to the Platonic belief that a concrete reality partakes of a form but does not embody it, the Aristotelian system holds that, with the exception of the Prime Mover (God), form has no separate existence but is immanent in matter. Aristotle's work was lost following the decline of Rome but was reintroduced to the West through the work of Arab and Jewish scholars, becoming the basis of medieval SCHOLASTICISM.

**arithmetic,** branch of mathematics (and the part of ALGEBRA) concerned with the fundamental operations of addition, subtraction, multiplication, and division of numbers. Conventionally, the term *arithmetic* covers simple numerical skills used for practical purposes, e.g., computation of areas or costs. The study of arithmetic also deals abstractly with the laws and properties (e.g., the ASSOCIATIVE LAW, the COMMUTATIVE LAW, and the DISTRIBUTIVE LAW) governing various mathematical operations.

**arithmetic mean,** the commonest sort of AVERAGE used in STATISTICS to indicate a value which is representative of a collection of individuals, and usually derived from a SAMPLE of the total POPULATION. It is calculated by dividing the sum of all the known values by the number of individuals. While the arithmetic mean is easy to calculate, it tends to be distorted by extreme values.

**arithmetic progression:** see PROGRESSION.

**Arizona,** state of the US (1984 est. pop. 3,053,000), area 295,024 km² (113,909 sq mi), situated in the SW and bordered by Utah (N), New Mexico (E), Mexico (S) and Nevada and California (W). The capital is PHOENIX, around which half the population live; other large cities are Tucson and Flagstaff. The northern and eastern parts of the state are within the arid COLORADO PLATEAU, through which the Colorado R. flows in the GRAND CANYON. The south and west lie in flat desert basins and parts of the Basin and Range region. Manufacturing is the main economic activity, especially machinery, electronic products, and electrical and transport equipment. Arizona is the leading US producer of copper; large irrigated areas in the south produce cotton, vegetables, and fruit, while livestock and dairying are also important. Tourism centres on the spectacular scenery. In 1980 66% of the population was non-Hispanic white, 16% was of Spanish origin, and 6% was native American. The region was first controlled by Spanish missions in the late 17th cent. and came under Mexican control after 1821. The northern part passed to the US territory of New Mexico at the end of the Mexican War in 1848, and the southern strip with the Gadsden Purchase in 1853. Arizona became a separate territory in 1863 and the Apache Indian wars ended in 1866. In 1911 the Roosevelt Dam encouraged industrial development, but expansion has been limited by the scarcity of water. In 1968 Congress authorized a scheme to bring water from the Colorado to Phoenix and Tucson. Combined with the spread of air conditioning, this has allowed the population to increase rapidly.

Coon Butte crater, **Arizona**

**ark,** in the BIBLE. **1** Boat built by NOAH at God's command to save his family and certain animals from the Flood. Gen. 6–9. **2** Ark of the Covenant, the sacred, gold-covered, wooden chest, believed by the Hebrews to represent the presence of God. Touching it meant death. It was carried into battle, as its presence implied victory, and was once captured by the Philistines. Restored many years later, it was placed in SOLOMON's temple. Ex. 25.10–21; 1 Sam. 4–7; 1 Chron. 13; 15; 16; 2 Chron. 5.

**Arkansas,** state of the US (1984 est. pop. 2,349,000), area 137,539 km² (53,104 sq mi), situated in the SE and bordered by Tennessee and Mississippi (E), Louisiana (S), Texas and Oklahoma (W), and Missouri (N). The capital is LITTLE ROCK; other important cities are Fort Smith and Pine Bluff. The northern and western parts of the state are formed by the OZARKS and Ouachita Mts, and the eastern and southern parts are lowlands with many lakes and hot springs. Manufacturing is the main source of state income, led by processed foods, electronic equipment, and paper and wood products. Oil, bauxite, bromine, and natural gas are also found in Arkansas. The leading agricultural commodities are soybeans, rice, cotton, poultry, and cattle. The lakes and hot springs attract tourism. In 1980 82% of the population was non-Hispanic white and 16% black. The original inhabitants were Quapaw, Osage, and Caddo Indians, and in 1803 the area was sold by the French to the US in the LOUISIANA PURCHASE. Arkansas became a state in 1836 and joined the Confederacy in 1861. Oil brought prosperity in the 1920s but farming was severely affected during the GREAT DEPRESSION. In 1957 Gov. Orval Faubus gained worldwide attention for blocking the desegregation of public schools, while in 1981 the federal courts overturned a state law providing for equal teaching of creationism and evolution in public schools. Arkansas has an uncertain economic future, and despite having some features of the SUN BELT it was hit hard by recession in the 1980s.

**Arkhangelsk** or **Archangel,** city (1985 pop. 408,000), NW European USSR, on the Northern Dvina near its mouth on the White Sea. It is a leading port; though icebound much of the year, it can generally be made usable by icebreakers. Major exports are timber and wood products; other industries are fishing and shipbuilding. Founded as Novo-Kholmogory (1584), it was renamed (1613) after the monastery of the Archangel Michael. An Allied supply port in World Wars I and II, it was occupied (1918–20) by Allied and anti-Bolshevik forces.

**Arkwright, Sir Richard,** 1732–92, English inventor and pioneer of the INDUSTRIAL REVOLUTION in England. His industrial work was contemporary with that of James HARGREAVES but neither seemed to be aware of the other's work. His spinning machine for cotton replaced handspinning and brought about the introduction of factories and the abolition of the 'home' industry. He also developed a machine for the manufacture of cotton ribbed hosiery. In 1786 he was knighted by King George II and made a High Sheriff of Derbyshire. He died famous and wealthy.

**Arles, kingdom of,** was formed in 933, when Rudolf II united his kingdom of Transjurane BURGUNDY with Provence or Cisjurane Burgundy. The German Emperor CONRAD II annexed the kingdom to the empire in 1034, but its component parts gradually broke away. In 1378 the Emperor CHARLES IV ceded the realm to the French dauphin (later CHARLES VI), and the kingdom for all practical purposes ceased to exist.

**Arlington,** US city (1984 est. pop. 214,000), N Texas, midway between DALLAS and FORT WORTH; inc. 1884. Located in a rapidly growing industrial area, it produces motor vehicle parts, containers, rubber products, and other manufactures. Arlington is noted for Six Flags over Texas, a huge historical amusement park, and is the home of the Texas Rangers baseball team.

**Arliss, George,** 1868–1946, English actor. He often played suave villains, as in *The Green Goddess* (1921), and was acclaimed in *Disraeli* (stage, 1911; film, 1930).

**Arlt, Roberto,** 1900–42, Argentine novelist, short-story writer, and dramatist. His powerful novels include *Los siete locos* (1929; tr. The Seven Madmen) and *El amor bruja* (1932; tr. Love the Magician).

**Armada, Spanish,** 1588, fleet launched by PHILIP II of Spain for the invasion of England. Commanded by the duque de Medina Sidonia and consisting of 130 ships and about 30,000 men, the Armada was delayed by storms and finally set sail from Lisbon in May. The English fleet, under Charles Howard, sailed from Plymouth and inflicted long-range damage on the Armada but did not break its formation. Anchoring off Calais, Medina Sidonia intended to pick up Alessandro FARNESE's army in Flanders and convey it to England. But on 7 Aug. the English sent fire ships into the anchorage to scatter the Armada and then attacked the fleeing ships at close range off Gravelines. The battered Armada escaped northward, sailed around Scotland and Ireland while buffeted by storms, and returned to Spain after losing about half its ships.

**armadillo,** armoured MAMMAL (order Edentata) found in the S US and Latin America. The head and body are almost entirely covered by an armour of bony, horny plates. Armadillos are usually nocturnal and, although omnivorous, eat mostly insects. The largest species, the giant armadillo (*Priodontes giganteus*), is about 120 cm (4 ft) long; the smallest, the fairy armadillo (*Chlamyphorus truncatus*), about 15 cm (6 in) long.

**Armagh,** former county in N Ireland, 1254 km² (489 sq mi), bordering on Lough Neagh in the N and the Republic of Ireland in the S. The county town is ARMAGH. Other main towns are Lurgan and Portadown. It is low-lying in the N and mountainous in the S, rising to 575 m (1886 ft) in Slieve Gullion. It is drained by the R. Blackwater, the R. BANN, and their tributaries. Potatoes, flax, and other crops are grown. Metal and linen manufacture are important industries.

**Armagh,** town (1981 pop. 12,700), in district of Armagh, N Ireland. Formerly the county town of Co. Armagh, it is an industrial town whose most famous industry is the manufacture of linen. There is a Protestant and a 19th-cent. Roman Catholic cathedral within the town, which is the seat of both Roman Catholic and Protestant bishops. It was the ecclesiastical metropolis of Ireland from the 5th to the 9th cent.

**Armah, Ayi Kwei,** 1939–, Ghanaian novelist, university teacher, journalist and television script writer. His initial explorations of disillusion with post-independence Ghana produced *The Beautiful Ones are Not Yet Born* (1969) and *Fragments* (1970). *Why Are We So Blest?* (1972) has led to an attempt to remythologize the African past in *Two Thousand Seasons* (1973) and *The Healers* (1979).

**armature:** see GENERATOR; MOTOR, ELECTRIC.

**Armenia,** region and former kingdom of Asia Minor. It includes NE TURKEY, the ARMENIAN SOVIET SOCIALIST REPUBLIC, and parts of Iranian Azerbaijan. Under Persian rule from the 6th to the 4th cent. BC, it was conquered in 330 by ALEXANDER THE GREAT but after his death fell to Syria. Armenia was independent from 189 BC to 67 BC, when it became tributary to Rome. Christianity was adopted in the 3rd cent. AD; under Persian rule later in that century many Christians were martyred. Persia and Rome partitioned the kingdom in 387; it achieved autonomy in 886 but was invaded in the mid-11th cent. by the Byzantines, Seljuk Turks, and Mongols. Pushed westward, one group founded Little Armenia, in CILICIA. In 1386–94 the Mongols, under TAMERLANE, seized Greater Armenia and massacred much of the population. The Ottoman Turks invaded in 1405 and by the 16th cent. held all of Armenia. Though most Armenians experienced religious persecution, Armenian merchants played an important role in the economy of the OTTOMAN EMPIRE. Eastern Armenia was long disputed by Turkey and Persia; in 1828 Persia ceded to Russia the present Armenian SSR. From 1894 on, a plan for Armenian extermination was pursued under Sultan ABD AL-HAMID II, culminating in the massacre of 1915. In 1918 Russian Armenia became independent under German auspices (see BREST-LITOVSK, TREATY OF), but in 1920 an autonomous Greater Armenia was created from the Turkish and Soviet Russian areas. In that year, however, Russian Armenia fell to the Communists and was made a Soviet republic; the 1921 Russo-Turkish Treaty established the present boundaries, ending Armenian independence. In 1988 it suffered a severe earthquake.

**Armenian language,** member of the Thraco-Phrygian subfamily of the Indo-European family of languages. See LANGUAGE (table).

**Armenian Soviet Socialist Republic,** constituent republic (1985 pop. 3,320,000), 29,785 km² (11,500 sq mi), SE European USSR, in the S Caucasus. The smallest Soviet republic, it is a mountainous region bounded by Turkey (W); the Azerbaijan SSR (E); Iran (S); and Georgia (N). YEREVAN is the capital. Major bodies of water are Lake SEVAN and the Araks and Razdan rivers. Industries include fishing, mining, and wine-making. Grapes, cotton, and tobacco are important agricultural products. In addition to the Armenian majority there are Azerbaijani, Russian, and Kurdish minorities. For history, see ARMENIA.

**Armidale,** city (1986 pop. 19,525), New South Wales, E Australia. The centre for the NEW ENGLAND farming region, Armidale was named (1839) by early Scottish settlers after the home of the MacDonalds on the Isle of Skye. It is the site of the Univ. of New England.

**Arminianism:** see ARMINIUS, JACOBUS.

**Arminius,** d. AD 21, German chief. When the Romans pushed E toward the Elbe, he surprised Publius Quintilius Varus with a great force and destroyed his army (AD 9). Rome never again tried to absorb land E of the Rhine.

**Arminius, Jacobus,** 1560–1609, Dutch Reformed theologian. Born Jakob Hermansen, he became a professor at the Univ. of Leiden after 1603; there, he developed his teaching, called **Arminianism.** As fully formulated after his death by Simon Episcopus, it opposed the Calvinist doctrine of predestination by asserting the compatibility of divine sovereignty and human freedom and by denying the irresistibility of God's grace. The teaching was later adopted by John WESLEY.

**Armistice Day,** the official commemoration of the ending of WORLD WAR I, 11 Nov. 1918. Parades and prayers are made throughout Europe on the nearest Sunday to that date, often in memory of the dead of World War II as well.

**Armory Show,** art exhibition held in 1913 at the 69th-regiment armoury in New York City. Including works of the European avant-garde, e.g., DUCHAMP's *Nude Descending a Staircase,* it was a sensational introduction of modern art into the US. One of the most important art shows ever held in the country, it helped to change the direction of American painting.

**armour,** protective covering for persons, steeds, or vehicles. Early body armour of leather, shells, wood, or basketwork was replaced by metal in the ancient Middle East; by the Middle Ages the metal helmet, cuirass, and greaves of the Greeks and Romans had evolved into full body armour of chain mail or plate. Heavy and cumbersome, it disappeared after warfare became more mobile and firearms more effective. Steel helmets and protective clothing (e.g., bullet-proof vests) were reintroduced in the 20th cent., and armour is still used extensively on ships, TANKS, and aircraft.

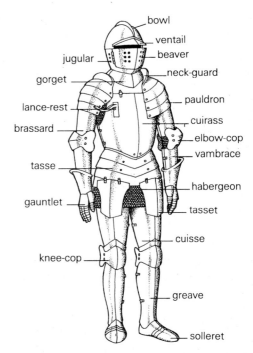

Armour

**arms, coats of :** see BLAZONRY; HERALDRY.

**Armstrong, (Daniel) Louis 'Satchmo,'** 1900–71, black American jazz trumpeter, singer, and bandleader. In New Orleans and, after 1922, in Chicago and New York City, he became known for improvisational genius and strongly influenced the melodic development of JAZZ. Armstrong was in large part responsible for the rise of the soloist in jazz.

**Armstrong, Neil Alden,** 1930–, American astronaut. During the *Apollo 11* lunar-landing mission (16–24 July 1969), which he commanded, he and Buzz ALDRIN (the lunar-module pilot) became the first and second persons, respectively, to walk on the Moon (see SPACE EXPLORATION, table). He later served as deputy associate administrator for aeronautics (1970–71) at NASA and professor of aeronautical engineering (1971–79) at the Univ. of Cincinnati.

**army,** armed land force under regular military organization, as distinguished from the horde, or armed mass of all able-bodied men in a tribe. The earliest known professional army was that of Egypt, followed by those of Assyria and Persia. Military service became obligatory for citizens of Greece. The Roman army evolved from a citizen soldiery into a professional standing army increasingly composed of barbarian mercenaries. In the Middle Ages, the armed KNIGHT and YEOMAN owed a set number of days of military service each year to a great lord; but with the decline of FEUDALISM and the advent of firearms, this system also gave way to the service of mercenaries. In the 17th cent. Louis XIV of France organized a national standing army that set the pattern for all of Europe: a highly disciplined, professional body set apart from civilian life. The concept reached a harsh perfection under Frederick II of Prussia. It was the introduction of CONSCRIPTION during the French Revolutionary Wars that set in motion the development of modern mass armies built around a professional nucleus and organized into specialized units for combat and support. The term *army* generally applies to all armed land forces of a nation (e.g., the French army); it can also designate a self-contained fighting force in a given area (e.g., the Army of the Potomac in the American Civil War) or a unit of c.100,000 men composed of two or more corps. A corps in turn is composed of two or more divisions (usually about 15,000 men). Traditionally, an army was made up of major INFANTRY, CAVALRY, and ARTILLERY commands, but these gave way to more complex forms of organization. Today, each division typically includes infantry, airborne, mechanized, and other specialized battalions or brigades. See also MILITARY SCIENCE.

**Arnauld, Antoine** (ah,noh), 1612–94, French logician and theologian. The author of the fourth set of *Objections* (1641) to DESCARTES' *Meditations*, he criticized the circularity of Descartes' validation of clear and distinct ideas, and challenged his account of the mind–body relation. He wrote the PORT ROYAL LOGIC with Pierre Nicole, and attacked MALEBRANCHE's doctrine of vision in God.

**Arne, Thomas Augustine,** 1710–78, English composer who wrote music chiefly for the theatre. He is best known for his song 'Rule Britannia' which was written for the masque *Alfred* (1740).

**Arnhem,** city (1985 pop. 128,145, agglomeration 292,802), Gelderland prov., central Netherlands. As a Hanse town, it was a flourishing centre of medieval trade. Modern industries include the manufacture of artificial silk, steel-making, and tin-smelting. It was the scene of a British troop landing in Sept. 1944 which resulted in great loss of life.

**Arnhem Land,** region of Northern Territory, Northern Australia. A plateau extending over 130,000 km² (50,000 sq mi) from E of DARWIN to the Gulf of Carpentaria. Named after a Dutch ship which explored the area in 1623, it includes the bauxite deposits on Gove Peninsula, manganese deposits on Groote Eylandt, the Katherine Gorge, KAKADU national park, with large, rich deposits of uranium being mined at Jabiru by Ranger. In 1976 the Aboriginal Land Rights (Northern Territory) Act gave title to the Aboriginal people to the whole of Arnhem Land. Many Aborigines now live in community settlements or on outstations following a traditionally oriented lifestyle.

**Arnim, Achim** or **Joachim von,** 1781–1831, German writer of the romantic school. He is best remembered for his work with his brother-in-law, Clemens BRENTANO, on the folk-song collection *Des Knaben Wunderhorn* (1806–08; tr. The Boy's Magic Horn) and for his historical novels, notably *Isabella of Egypt* (1812). His wife was Bettina BRENTANO.

**Arno,** river, 240 km (150 mi) long, which unites the interior basins of TUSCANY, N central Italy. It rises in the APENNINES and follows a complicated course before entering its lowland section at the city of FLORENCE. Its once-extensive marshes have been drained to create alluvial flats which support a rich agriculture. The old port of PISA is now several km from the sea due to the silting of the river mouth.

**Arnold, Benedict,** 1741–1801, American general and traitor in the AMERICAN REVOLUTION. After excellent service in the colonial assault on Quebec (1775–76) and the SARATOGA CAMPAIGN, he felt slighted regarding promotion. His plot with John ANDRÉ to betray (1780) the American post

at WEST POINT was discovered, but Arnold escaped and later fought for the British.

**Arnold, Malcolm,** 1921–, British composer. Until 1948 he played the trumpet in London orchestras. He has written music for films, ten concertos and seven symphonies, and several chamber works, all in a tuneful and often boisterous diatonic idiom.

**Arnold, Matthew,** 1822–88, English poet and critic; son of Thomas ARNOLD. He was an inspector of schools (1851–86) and professor of poetry at Oxford (1857–67). Arnold wrote superb poetry, usually dealing with the themes of loneliness and pessimism. Among his best-known verses are 'Isolation: To Marguerite' (1852), 'The Scholar Gypsy' (1853), and 'Dover Beach' (1867). His books of literary criticism include *On Translating Homer* (1861) and *Essays in Criticism* (1865; Ser. 2, 1888). *Culture and Anarchy* (1869) and *Literature and Dogma* (1873) are volumes of social criticism and religion, respectively. Arnold stressed the necessity for objectivity and advocated a culture based on the best that has been thought and said in the world.

**Arnold, Thomas,** 1795–1842, English educator. As head of Rugby school (1827–42) he added mathematics, modern languages, and modern history to the classical curriculum, and strengthened the role of the older boys in student self-government. His reforms were adopted by many English secondary schools. A classical scholar, he wrote *History of Rome* (3 vol., 1838–43), among other works. Matthew ARNOLD was his son.

**aromatic compound,** any of a large class of organic compounds including BENZENE and compounds that resemble benzene in chemical properties. Aromatic compounds contain unusually stable ring structures, often made up of six carbon atoms arranged hexagonally. Some of the compounds, however, have rings with more or fewer atoms, not necessarily all carbon. Furan, for example, has a ring with four atoms of carbon and one of oxygen. Also, two or more rings can be fused, as in naphthalene. The characteristic properties of the class, notably the stability of the compounds, derive from the fact that aromatic rings permit the sharing of some electrons by all the atoms of the ring, which increases the strength of the bonds.

Aromatic compound

**Aron Kodesh,** the Holy Ark. This is the focal point of the Synagogue, housed against, or inset into, the eastern wall, called *mizrah*. It is the repository for the Scrolls of the Law. Suspended in front of the Aron Kodesh is the Ark Curtain or *paroket*. This is drawn aside to reveal the inside of the Ark at certain key parts of the service, either to take out the scrolls or to invest the compositions recited while the Ark is open with greater importance and respect. Members of the congregation are given the honour of opening (*petihah*) or closing the Ark.

**Arp, Jean** or **Hans,** 1887–1966, French sculptor and painter. He exhibited in the 2nd BLAUE REITER exhibition and was involved in the founding of the Zurich DADA group is 1916. His abstract compositions with curvilinear shapes were derived from experiments with AUTOMATISM and random factors.

**Arran, Isle of,** island in Strathclyde region, Scotland, on W side of Firth of Clyde, separated from the mainland by the Kilbrannan Sound. It is a mountainous island, whose area is c.430 km² (166 sq mi). The highest point is Goat Fell at 874 m (2866 ft). The main town is Brodick on the E coast, and the chief economic activities are tourism and the grazing of sheep and cattle.

**arrest,** seizure and detention of a person suspected of committing a CRIME, in order to bring that person before a court, or to otherwise administer the law. Except where a law officer witnesses or suspects an arrestable offence, a warrant is usually required. In addition, any citizen can, without a warrant, arrest anyone he or she reasonably suspects of having committed an offence. Reasonable force may be used in making most arrests. Anyone who has been wrongfully arrested can usually sue in the TORT of false imprisonment. Release may be obtained through HABEAS CORPUS, REMAND on BAIL, or through dismissal of the charge or acquittal.

**Arrhenius, Svante August** (ah,rayneeəs), 1859–1927, Swedish chemist. For his theory of electrolytic dissociation, or ionization, he won the 1903 Nobel Prize for chemistry. He also investigated osmosis and toxins and antitoxins. He became (1905) director of the Nobel Institute for Physical Chemistry, Stockholm. In later life, Arrhenius devoted much time applying physicochemical principles as a means of understanding geological, astronomical, meteorological, and immunological phenomena.

**arrowroot,** plant (genus *Maranta*) of the family Marantaceae, found mainly in warm, swampy forests of the Americas. The term *arrowroot* also applies to the easily digested starch obtained from the true, or West Indian, arrowroot (*M. arundinacea*). Plants from other families produce similar starches, e.g., East Indian arrowroot (GINGER family); Queensland arrowroot (Canna family); Brazilian arrowroot, or tapioca (SPURGE family); and Florida arrowroot, or sago. In cookery, arrowroot is used to thicken sauces.

**arrowworm,** common name for Chaetognatha, a phylum of slender-bodied, transparent PELAGIC marine invertebrate animals widely distributed, but preferring warm, shallow seas. Most are less than 2.5 cm (1 in) long. They are PREDATORS. The head is well-developed, with eyes and other sensory organs, grasping spines, teeth, and a protective hood. Arrowworms reproduce sexually.

**Arsaces** (,ahsəseez), fl. 250 BC, founder of the Parthian dynasty of the **Arsacids,** which ruled Persia from c.250 BC to AD 226.

**arsenic** (As), semimetallic element, first described by ALBERTUS MAGNUS in the 13th cent. Arsenic has several allotropic forms (see ALLOTROPY); the most stable is a silver-grey, brittle, crystalline solid that tarnishes in air. Arsenic ores include realgar (used by the ancients in their decorative arts) and arsenopyrite. Combined with other elements, arsenic forms strong poisons; organic compounds of arsenic are used medically to treat syphilis and yaws. The metal is used in the manufacture of lead shot and transistorized circuits. See ELEMENT (table); PERIODIC TABLE.

**arson,** in law; the reckless or intentional destruction of PROPERTY by fire. Because of the unique dangers of fire, and its ability to cause widespread destruction or loss of life, arson has always been punished severely. In the UK, in the 18th cent., arson carried the death penalty. It remains a separate offence under the Criminal Damage Act 1971, punishable by life imprisonment.

**Artaxerxes** ('ahtə,zuhkseez), name of several ancient Persian kings. **Artaxerxes I,** d. 425 BC (r.464–425 BC), was a member of the ACHAEMENID dynasty. Artaxerxes is the Greek form of the name Ardashir the Persian. He succeeded his father, XERXES I, in whose assassination he had no part. The later weakness of the Persian empire is commonly traced to his reign. **Artaxerxes II,** d. 358 BC (r.404–358 BC), was the son and successor of DARIUS II. CYRUS THE YOUNGER attempted to overthrow him but was crushed (401 BC). During his reign the provinces of the empire became restless. His son, **Artaxerxes III,** d. 338 BC (r.358–338 BC), gained the throne by a general massacre of his brother's family. Throughout his reign he continued a policy of terror, and he was finally poisoned by one of his ministers.

**art deco,** name taken from the 1925 Paris Exposition Internationale des Arts Decoratifs et Industriels Modernes, which was used to describe the consciously modern and streamlined style of the decorative arts of the 1920s and 30s. Individuality, fine craftsmanship, and expensive materials, especially in lacquered furniture, were its main characteristics.

**Artemis,** in Greek mythology, goddess of the hunt. She was the daughter of ZEUS and Leto and the twin sister of APOLLO. Artemis is associated with chastity, marriage, children, wildlife, and, as a complement to the sun god Apollo, with the moon. Her temple at EPHESUS, the Artemision, was one of the SEVEN WONDERS OF THE WORLD; it contained a statue of her covered with breasts. The Romans identified her with DIANA.

**arteriosclerosis** (ah'tiəriohskli,rohsis), general term for a condition characterized by thickening, hardening, and loss of elasticity of the walls of the arteries. In its most common form, atherosclerosis, fatty deposits,

e.g., CHOLESTEROL, build up on the inner artery walls; in some cases calcium deposits also form. The blood vessels narrow, blood flow decreases, and blood pressure is raised; THROMBOSIS, CORONARY HEART DISEASE, HEART FAILURE, and STROKE may result. Control of predisposing factors, such as HYPERTENSION, SMOKING, DIABETES, and OBESITY, and improvement in the diet are usually recommended.

**artery:** see CIRCULATORY SYSTEM.

**artesian well,** deep well drilled into an inclined aquifer (layer of water-bearing porous rock or sediment), where water is trapped under pressure between impervious rock layers. When a well is drilled into the aquifer through the overlying impervious rock, pressure forces water to rise in the well. Artesian water is usually desirable for drinking. The largest artesian system is in Australia.

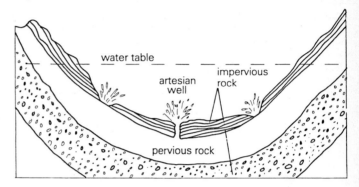

water table

artesian well

impervious rock

pervious rock

Artesian well

**Artevelde, Jacob van,** c.1290–1345, Flemish statesman. A conflict between the count of Flanders and EDWARD III of England cut off English wool imports, ruining the Flemish weavers and merchants. Ghent rebelled, and Artevelde, as head of its government, signed a commercial treaty with England (1338). In 1340 he had the Flemish towns recognize Edward as king of France and thus suzerain of Flanders. He was killed in a riot. His son, **Philip van Artevelde,** 1340–82, led a weavers' revolt against the count of Flanders (1379), taking Bruges and most of Flanders before being killed by the French.

**art history,** the study of works of art and architecture. It was raised to an academic discipline in the mid 19th cent. by Jacob BURCKHARDT, who related art to its cultural environment, and by idealists such as Heinrich WÖLFFLIN, who explored art in terms of formal analysis. Both approaches remain important in contemporary art history. Major 20th-cent. art historians include Bernard BERENSON, Kenneth Clark, Henri Focillon, Ernst Gombrich, Émile Mâle, and Erwin Panofsky.

**arthritis,** inflammation of one or more joints of the body, usually producing pain, swelling, redness, and restriction of movement. It disables more people than any other chronic disorder. A common form is osteoarthritis, a degenerative disease of the joints that commonly occurs with aging. Rheumatoid arthritis, an AUTOIMMUNE DISEASE of unknown cause, is a progressive, crippling joint disorder most common in women between 25 and 50. Initial treatment for arthritis includes use of heat, physiotherapy, and mild analgesics, such as ASPIRIN; in more severe cases, gold salts and CORTISONE are given, but they often have undesirable side effects. See also GOUT.

**arthropod,** invertebrate animal, having a segmented body covered by a jointed EXOSKELETON with paired jointed appendages; member of the phylum Arthropoda, the largest and most diverse invertebrate phylum. The exoskeleton is periodically shed (moulted) to permit growth and METAMORPHOSIS. Arthropods make up more than 80% (800,000) of all known animal species; they include TRILOBITES, HORSESHOE CRABS, ARACHNIDS, SEA SPIDERS, CRUSTACEANS, INSECTS, CENTIPEDES, and MILLIPEDES.

**Arthur,** king of Britain: see ARTHURIAN LEGEND.

**Arthur,** dukes of Brittany. **Arthur I,** 1187–1203?, duke 1196–1203?, was the son of Geoffrey, fourth son of HENRY II of England. After the death of RICHARD I of England, Arthur's claim to the English crown was passed over in favour of his uncle JOHN. Arthur allied himself with PHILIP II of France, who invested Arthur with Richard's fiefs in France. Fighting ensued, and Arthur was captured (1202) by John, who is suspected of murdering him. Arthur's story is told in Shakespeare's *King John*. **Arthur III**, 1393–1458, duke 1457–58, was known as comte de Richemont before his accession. As constable of France in the HUNDRED YEARS WAR, he captured (1436) Paris from the English and helped to regain Normandy for France.

**Arthur, Chester Alan**, 1830?–86, 21st president of the US (1881–85). A lawyer, he was appointed (1871) collector of the port of New York. His removal (1878) by Pres. HAYES angered Sen. Roscoe Conkling and other 'Old Guard' Republicans, but they were placated in 1880 by Arthur's nomination as vice president on the Republican ticket with James A. GARFIELD. Succeeding to the presidency after Garfield's assassination, Arthur had an honest, efficient, and dignified administration. By supporting the civil service reform act of 1883, he belied his reputation as a mere machine politician.

**Arthurian legend**, mass of stories, popular in medieval lore, concerning King Arthur of Britain and his knights. The earliest reference to Arthur is in the Welsh poem *Gododdin* (c.600), although later sources place him at the Battle of Mt Badon, mentioned by Gildas c.540. In Nennius (c.800) he appears as a Celtic victor over Saxon invaders. The legend was greatly elaborated by GEOFFREY OF MONMOUTH in his *Historia* (c.1135), which represents Arthur as the conqueror of Western Europe. Wace's *Roman de Brut* (c.1155) infuses the story with the spirit of chivalric romance, and the *Brut* of LAYAMON (c.1200) pictures Arthur as national hero. The 12th-cent. French poet CHRÉTIEN DE TROYES introduced in *Perceval* the theme of the quest for the Holy Grail. GOTTFRIED VON STRASSBURG, a medieval German poet, wrote the first great treatment of the TRISTRAM AND ISOLDE story. The Middle English *Sir Gawain and the Green Knight* (c.1370) embodied the ideal of chivalric knighthood. Sir Thomas MALORY's *Morte d'Arthur* (1485) was the last important medieval treatment. Since Malory, the legend has appeared in the work of TENNYSON, SWINBURNE, William MORRIS, T.H. WHITE, and others, and was set to music by WAGNER in *Tristan and Isolde* (1865) and *Parsifal* (1882). It is generally accepted that the Arthurian legend developed out of Celtic mythology, as collected in the Welsh MABINOGION. The stories may have coalesced around Irish hero tales and were probably carried to the Continent by Breton minstrels before 1000. Despite innumerable variations, the basic story has remained the same. Arthur, the illegitimate son of Uther Pendragon, king of Britain, wins recognition after his father's death by removing a sword from a stone. Merlin, the court magician, then reveals his parentage. Reigning at CAMELOT, Arthur proves a mighty and noble king. He possesses the great sword Excalibur, given him by the mysterious Lady of the Lake. His enemies include his sorceress sister, Morgan le Fay, and Sir Mordred, usually his nephew, who fatally wounds him. The dying king is borne away to Avalon, whence he will someday return. Among the knights in Arthur's court are Sir Lancelot and Sir Tristram, both involved in illicit and tragic unions, Lancelot with Arthur's wife, Guinevere, and Tristram with Isolde, the wife of his uncle, King Mark. Other figures include Sir Pelleas and Sir Gawain; Sir Galahad, Lancelot's son; Sir Percivale (or Parsifal); and other knights of the Round Table.

**artichoke**, name for two plants of the COMPOSITE family, both having edible parts. The French, or globe, artichoke (*Cynara scolymus*), of S Europe, is a thistlelike plant whose immature, globular flower heads are used as vegetables; only the lower parts of the fleshy bracts ('leaves') and the centre ('heart') are eaten. The other artichoke plant is the JERUSALEM ARTICHOKE.

**artificial insemination** (AI), technique of artificially injecting sperm-containing semen from a male into a female to cause pregnancy. The technique is widely used in the propagation of cattle, especially to produce many offspring from one prize bull. Artificial insemination is also used in humans when normal fertilization cannot be achieved, as with INFERTILITY or IMPOTENCE in the male or anatomical disorders in the female. The semen, which is either obtained from the patient's husband (AIH) or from a frozen bank of semen received from unknown donors (AID), is introduced high up into the vagina at the time of ovulation in order to establish conception. See also IN VITRO FERTILIZATION.

**artificial intelligence** (AI), the use of COMPUTERS to model the behavioural aspects of human reasoning, learning, and perception. Research in AI is concentrated in some half-dozen areas. In *problem solving,* one must proceed from a beginning (the initial state) to the end (the goal state) via a limited number of steps; AI here involves an attempt to model the reasoning process in solving a problem, such as the proof

of a theorem in EUCLIDEAN GEOMETRY. In *game theory* (see GAMES, THEORY OF), the computer must choose among a number of possible 'next' moves to select the one that optimizes its probability of winning; this type of choice is analogous to that of a chess player selecting the next move in response to an opponent's move. In *pattern recognition,* shapes, forms, or configurations of data must be identified and isolated from a larger group; the process here is similar to that used by a doctor in classifying medical problems on the basis of symptoms. Similar problems are involved in speech recognition. *Natural language processing* is an analysis of current or colloquial language usage without the sometimes misleading effect of formal grammars; it is an attempt to model the learning process of a translator faced with the phrase 'throw mama from the train a kiss', or needing to parse the two phrases ' time flies like an arrow' and 'fruit flies like an orange'. CYBERNETICS is the analysis of the communication and control processes of biological organisms and their relationship to mechanical and electrical systems; this study could ultimately lead to the development of 'thinking' robots (see ROBOTICS). *Machine learning* occurs when a computer improves its performance of a task on the basis of its programmed application of AI principles to its past performance of that task. An *expert system* is a computer program that emulates the performance of an expert on a well-defined task which, if performed by a person, would require expert skill and knowledge. AI programs have been found to require a very large amount of processing power and memory. *Fifth-generation machines* and declarative PROGRAMMING LANGUAGES, such as PROLOG and LISP are associated with AI.

**artificial kidney:** see DIALYSIS.

**artificial respiration**, any measure that causes air to flow in and out of a person's lungs when natural breathing is inadequate or ceases. Respiration can be taken over by mechanical devices such as the artificial lung. In emergency situations, mouth-to-mouth (or, in the case of a small child, mouth-to-nose) procedures, known as the 'kiss of life', are often used. The patient's mouth is cleared of any obstruction and the head is tilted back. Holding the nostrils tightly shut, the person administering artificial respiration places his or her mouth over that of the patient and blows air into the lungs, allowing for exhalation after each breath. Twelve vigorous breaths are administered per minute for an adult, 20 shallow breaths per minute for a child. See also CARDIOPULMONARY RESUSCITATION.

**Artigas, José Gervasio** (ah,teegahs), 1764–1850, Uruguayan independence leader. He joined (1811) the revolution against Spanish rule and became leader in the Banda Oriental (now URUGUAY). Artigas agitated against the territory's annexation (1820) by Brazil and went into exile.

**artillery**, a term now applied to heavy firearms, as distinguished from SMALL ARMS. It came into use in the mid-14th cent. with the introduction in Europe of GUNPOWDER, which had been discovered many centuries earlier in China. First employed mainly against fortifications, artillery was increasingly used in the field from the early 17th cent. It was characteristically smooth-bore and muzzle-loaded, firing solid, round shot, until the late 19th cent., when breech-loaded, rifled, and shell-firing artillery became standard. Modern artillery includes a variety of long-range guns that fire their shells with rapid muzzle-velocity in a low arc; *howitzers*, which fire on a high trajectory at relatively nearby targets; *antiaircraft guns*, which fire rapidly and at high angles; armour-piercing *antitank guns*; and many field-artillery pieces used in support of infantry and other ground operations. Mobility has become a key factor in the usefulness of heavy firearms, most of which now either are self-propelled or can be towed.

**Art Institute of Chicago**, museum and art school; inc. 1879. Its famous collections include early Italian, Dutch, Spanish, and Flemish paintings, among them works by El GRECO, REMBRANDT, and HALS. The Institute is also rich in 19th-cent. American and French paintings, as well as modern American and European paintings.

**art nouveau**, decorative art movement begun in Western Europe that lasted from the 1880s to World War I. It was characterized by a richly ornamental, asymmetrical style of sinuous lines, reminiscent of twining plant tendrils, and was most successfully expressed in furniture, jewellery, and book design and illustration. Its themes were symbolic and often erotic. Chief exponents included the illustrators Aubrey BEARDSLEY and Walter Crane in England; the architect and artist Charles Rennie MACKINTOSH in Scotland; the architects Henry van de Velde and Victor HORTA in Belgium; the architect Hector Guimard and the jewellery

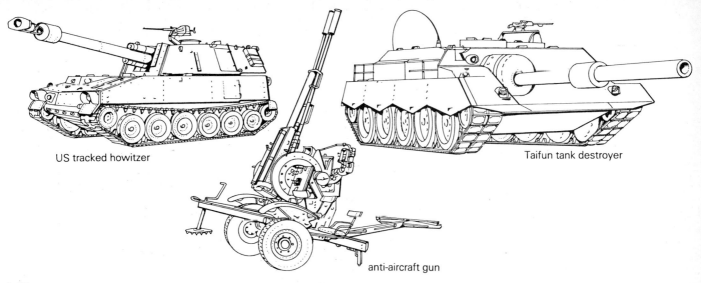

US tracked howitzer

anti-aircraft gun

Taifun tank destroyer

Artillery

designer René LALIQUE in France; the painter Gustav KLIMT in Austria; the architect Antonio GAUDÍ in Spain; the illustrator Otto Eckmann and the architect Peter BEHRENS in Germany; and the glassware designer Louis C. TIFFANY and the architect Louis SULLIVAN in the US.

**arts and crafts,** term for the field of the designing and hand fabrication of functional and decorative objects. The term was invented in late-19th-cent. England to refer to a movement, begun by William MORRIS and others, to revive the handcrafting techniques almost obliterated by industrialization.

**Aruba,** island (1984 est. pop. 67,000), 179 km² (69 sq mi) in the Leeward group off Venezuela. Formerly part of the Netherlands Antilles, Aruba achieved separate status on 1 Jan. 1984, as an autonomous component of the Kingdom of the Netherlands, with full independence being scheduled for 1996. Tourism, now that oil is no longer refined, is the major source of of revenue. Oranjestad is the capital.

**arum,** common name for the Araceae, a family of chiefly tropical and subtropical herbaceous herbs. The characteristic inflorescence consists of a single fleshy spike (spadix), which bears small flowers, and a typically showy flowerlike bract or modified leaf (spathe) surrounding the spadix. *A. maculatum,* known as cuckoo-pint or lords-and-ladies, is the common wild arum in Britain and much of Europe. Its rootstock is edible and its extracted starch used for stiffening cloth. The largest plant inflorescence known belongs to the Sumatran krubi (*Amorphophallus titanum*) of this family; its spadix reaches a height of 4.6 m (15 ft). Among other members of the family are the decorative arum lily, or calla (genus *Zantedeschia*); the smaller, showy water or bog arum (*Calla palustris*); the climbing shrub philodendron (genus *Philodendron*), a popular houseplant; and the decorative *Anthurium* and *Caladium.* Many species in this family have large, starchy edible rootstocks (corms). A major food source in the Pacific and Far East, the corms of elephant's ear (*Colocasia esculenta*), or taro, are the main ingredient of poi. Corms of the arum Indian bread were eaten by natives of E North America.

**Aryans,** speakers of Indo-European or Indo-Iranian languages. In the 2nd millennium BC, waves of warlike nomadic Aryan tribes spread from S Russia and Turkistan to Mesopotamia and Asia Minor. They invaded India c.1500 BC, colonizing the PUNJAB. The subsequent Indo-European period was characterized by a pastoral–agricultural economy and the use of bronze objects and horse-drawn chariots. In the 20th cent., NAZI racist propaganda idealized the Aryan conquest and claimed German descent from the Aryans.

**Asante** (a̱santee): see ASHANTI.

**asbestos,** common name for any of a group of fibrous silicate minerals resistant to acid and fire. Asbestos usually occurs as veins in rocks and seems to be a product of METAMORPHISM. Chrysotile asbestos ($H_4Mg_3Si_2O_9$), a form of SERPENTINE, is the main commercial asbestos. Asbestos is produced chiefly in Canada; asbestos products include yarn

and rope, pipe covering, brake linings, fire-fighting equipment, and insulating materials. Studies have shown that asbestos particles in the air can cause lung cancer and the lung disease asbestosis.

Hardy **arum** (*genus Zantedeschia*)

**Asbury, Francis,** 1745–1816, American Methodist bishop; b. England. Arriving as a missionary in 1771, he promoted the circuit rider system as being particularly well suited to American frontier conditions. He became a bishop in 1784 and did much to establish Methodism throughout the United States.

**Ascension,** volcanic, largely barren island (1980 est. pop. 1,013), 88 km² (34 sq mi), in the S Atlantic, part of the British colony of SAINT HELENA.

It is the site of a US air base, a BBC transmitter, and a missile- and satellite-tracking station.

**Ascension,** name given to the ascent of JESUS to heaven, as described in Luke 24.51, etc. **Ascension Day,** a major feast for most Christians, commemorates the event and occurs on the 40th day after Easter.

**Ascham, Roger** (ˌaskəm), 1515–68, English humanist. A leading intellectual figure of the Tudor period, he became Latin secretary to MARY I and continued in this office under ELIZABETH I, to whom he had been tutor some years earlier. He had a famous encounter with the 13-year-old Lady Jane GREY in 1550. His *Toxophilus* (1545) was a highly successful treatise on archery: *The Scholemaster* (1570) is a treatise on education remarkable for Ascham's theory of 'double translation'—Latin into English, then back into Latin—and for his humane approach to the subject, in particular his rejection of corporal punishment.

**Asclepius** (askˌleepeeɔs), legendary Greek physician and god of medicine; son of APOLLO and Coronis. The sick were treated in his temples; the serpent and cock were sacred to him.

**ascorbic acid:** see VITAMINS AND MINERALS.

**Ascot,** town (1981 pop. 17,930 Sunningdale and Ascot), Berkshire, S England, 10 km (6 mi) SW of WINDSOR across Windsor Great Park. The famous Ascot racecourse was laid out in 1711 by order of Queen Anne. The Royal Ascot race meeting is held annually in June.

**ASEAN:** see ASSOCIATION OF SOUTHEAST ASIAN NATIONS.

**Asgard,** in Norse mythology, home of the gods. Also called Aesir, it consisted of luxurious palaces and halls. One of the most beautiful was Valhalla, the hall of dead heroes.

**ash,** tree or shrub (genus *Fraxinus*) of the OLIVE family, mainly of north temperate regions. The ashes have small clusters of greenish flowers and winged, wind-dispersed fruits. The common ash (*F. excelsior*) occurs throughout Europe and Asia minor. It is a valuable timber tree with a very resilient hardwood timber used for sporting goods, tool handles, and furniture. The mountain ash and prickly ash are not true ashes.

**Ashanti,** or **Asante,** historic and present-day region in central GHANA, inhabited by the Ashanti, one of Ghana's major ethnic groups. In the 17th cent. the Ashanti confederation was forged, with its capital at KUMASI and with the chieftain of the Oyoko clan as king. Ashanti came into conflict with the British colonies along the coast, and the Anglo-Ashanti wars (19th cent.) culminated in the dissolution of the confederation in 1896. In 1901 Ashanti became part of the British colony of the Gold Coast. The Ashanti people are noted for their goldwork and their colourful Kente cloth. (See also GHANA, ancient empire.)

Gold jewellery (18–19th cent.), cast by lost wax method, worn as insignia by senior servants of the **Ashanti** kings.

**Ashbery, John,** 1927–, American poet and art critic. His poems are often experimental, narrative, and strongly visual. His collections include *Some Trees* (1956), *The Double Dream of Spring* (1970), *Self-Portrait in a Convex Mirror* (1975), *As We Know* (1979), and *Shadow Train* (1981).

**Ash Can school,** a group of American realist painters centred around Robert HENRI and the group of The EIGHT. They shared an interest in subjects taken from everyday life of the city, and were part of the general interest in social realism in New York in the first decade of the 20th cent.

**Ashdod,** city and port (1986 est. pop. 71,100), S Israel, on the Mediterranean coast, between GAZA and TEL AVIV. An artificial harbour constructed between 1956 and 1965 has made it the second port of the country. Ashod exports minerals from the NEGEV.

**Ashdown, Paddy (John Jeremy Durham),** 1941–, British politician, leader of the SOCIAL AND LIBERAL DEMOCRATS (1988–). Having entered parliament in 1983 as a LIBERAL PARTY member, Ashdown supported full merger with the SOCIAL DEMOCRATIC PARTY, as proposed by Liberal leader David STEEL immediately after the 1987 elections. Following the completion of the merger (1988), he was elected leader of the new party.

**Asher:** see ISRAEL, TRIBES OF.

**Ashes, the,** cricketing term for a series of Test matches played between England and Australia. It originated in 1882, when England were beaten by Australia for the first time on English soil, and a mock obituary written by Shirley Brooks appeared in the *Sporting Times* as follows: 'In affectionate remembrance of English cricket which died at the Oval August 29, 1882. Deeply lamented by a large circle of sorrowing friends and acquaintances. R.I.P. N.B. The body will be cremated and taken to Australia.' The following year, some Melbourne women burned a bail and presented it in an urn to Lord Darnley, whose English team had beaten the Australians. The urn is now kept permanently at LORD'S.

**Ashkenazim** (ˈashkəˌnahzim), Jews whose ancestors hailed from central and eastern Europe. They developed their own distinctive language, Yiddish (Jewish-German), containing a large admixture of Hebrew vocabulary. Ashkenazi Jewry developed its own Hebrew culture and religious traditions which differed significantly in many areas from their Sephardi (see SEPHARDIM) counterparts. Ashkenazi traditions developed particularly through the influence of the great rabbinic centres in Franco-Germany, Poland, and Russia from the 11th–19th cent.

**Ashley, Laura,** 1926–85, Welsh designer. She designed textiles, wall-coverings, and clothes in a Victorian, floral, romantic idiom, which had enormous impact on British popular taste, dominated up till then by functionalism especially in interior design. The chain of shops under her own name spread throughout Britain in the late 1960s and early 70s, and from the mid 70s onwards to Europe, America, and Australia.

**Ashton, Sir Frederick,** 1904–88, English dancer. After studying with Léonide MASSINE and Dame Marie RAMBERT, he joined (1935) Sadlers Wells (now Royal) Ballet as choreographer, then director (1963–70). His style is lyrical, musical, and classical.

**ashura** [Arab., = the tenth], the tenth day of the Muslim month of Muharram. In SHI'ISM an annual commemoration of the death of HUSAYN is held. HUSAYN, the grandson of MUHAMMAD and son of 'ALI, was killed when his companions were routed at Karbala in Iraq in 680. The annual commemoration entails the performance of a passion play called the *ta'ziya*, and a procession which involves forms of ecstatic self-mortification, such as flagellation.

**Ash Wednesday:** see LENT.

**Asia,** the world's largest continent, c.44,390,000 km² (17,139,000 sq mi), joined in the west with Europe (which may be considered a peninsula of Asia) to form the great Eurasian land mass. It ranges in elevation from 8848 m (29,028 ft) at Mt EVEREST, the world's highest mountain, to 394 m (1292 ft) below sea level at the DEAD SEA, the world's lowest point. It is traversed from east to west by a massive central highland region containing the Tibetan Plateau, the HIMALAYAS, the HINDU KUSH, and other great mountain systems. The continent has every type of climate, from tropical to polar and from desert to rainy. The countries of Asia are Afghanistan, Bahrain, Bangladesh, Bhutan, Burma, China, Cyprus, India, Indonesia, Iran, Iraq, Israel, Japan, Jordan, Kampuchea, North Korea, South Korea, Kuwait, Laos, Lebanon, Malaysia, the Maldives, the Mongolian People's Republic, Nepal, Oman, Pakistan, the Republic of the Philippines, Qatar, Saudi Arabia, Singapore, Sri Lanka, Syria, Taiwan (the Republic of China), Thailand, Asian Turkey, the Asian USSR, the United Arab Emirates, Vietnam, Yemen, and Southern Yemen; other political units are Brunei, Hong Kong, and Macao (see separate articles). Asia was the site of some of the world's earliest civilizations and today contains nearly 60% of the world's population. Some of the world's greatest population densities are found in S and E Asia, particularly in the great alluvial river valleys of the GANGES, in India, and the YANGTZE and HUANG HE, in China. See map of Asia in separate section.

**Asia Minor,** peninsula, W Asia, forming the Asian part of Turkey. Most of the peninsula is occupied by the Anatolian plateau, which is crossed by numerous mountains interspersed with lakes. The first civilization established there (c.1800 BC) was that of the HITTITES. The site of TROY and other ancient cities, Asia Minor was subjugated by·many invaders, including the Persians, Macedonians, Romans, and Crusaders. Conquered by the Turks between the 13th and 15th cent. AD, it was part of the OTTOMAN EMPIRE until the establishment of modern Turkey after WORLD WAR I.

**Asimov, Isaac,** 1920–, American biochemist and author; b. USSR. He taught biochemistry at Boston Univ., but he is most widely known for his science fiction (e.g., *I, Robot,* 1950, a short-story collection; and *The Foundation Trilogy,* 1951–53; sequel, 1982) and for popular introductions to science and other topics.

**Asmara,** city (1984 est. pop. 275,385), capital of Eritrea prov., N Ethiopia. A commercial and industrial centre, it is connected by rail with the Red Sea port of Massawa. Manufactures include textiles, pharmaceuticals, and food canning. The city was occupied (1889) by the Italians, became (1900) the capital of their colony of Eritrea, and was a base for the Italian invasion of Ethiopia (1935–36). It was taken by the British in 1941. In the late 1970s Asmara was briefly besieged by Eritrean guerrillas fighting to secede from Ethiopia.

**Asoka,** d. c.232 BC, Indian emperor (c.273–c.232 BC) of the MAURYA dynasty. One of the greatest of the ancient rulers, he brought nearly all of INDIA together. However, he sickened of war, turned (c.257 BC) to BUDDHISM, and thereafter professed nonviolence. He sent Buddhist missionaries as far afield as Greece and Egypt, thus initiating the transformation of Buddhism into a world religion.

**asp,** popular name for several species of VIPER, one of which, the European asp (*Vipera aspis*), is native to S Europe. It is also a name for the Egyptian COBRA (*Naja haje*); this was probably Cleopatra's asp.

**asparagus,** perennial garden vegetable (*Asparagus officinalis*) of the LILY family, native to the E Mediterranean area, cultivated from antiquity and now grown in much of the world. Its green stems function as leaves, and the true leaves are reduced to scales. Its edible shoots are cut in the spring. Related species, the asparagus fern (*A. plumosus*) and smilax (*A. asparagoides*), are used for decoration.

**aspen:** see POPLAR.

**asphalt,** brownish black substance used in road making, roofing, and waterproofing. A naturally occurring mixture of HYDROCARBONS, it is commercially obtained as a residue in the DISTILLATION or refining of PETROLEUM. Asphalt varies in consistency from a solid to a semisolid, melts when heated, and has great tenacity. Used in paints and varnishes, it imparts an intense black colour. Crushed asphalt rock, a natural mixture of asphalt, sand, and limestone, is used as road-building material. Large natural lakes of asphalt are found in Trinidad.

**asphodel,** hardy, stemless herbs (genera *Asphodelus* and *Asphodeline*) of the LILY family, native to India and the Mediterranean. Both have showy flower spikes. Other asphodels include the false asphodel (genus *Tofieldia*).

**aspirin,** acetylsalicylic acid (discovered in Germany in 1899), commonly used to lower fever; relieve headache, muscle, and joint pain; and reduce inflammation, particularly that caused by rheumatic fever and arthritis. A small daily dose of aspirin reduces the risk of heart attack through its effect on blood clotting. Known side effects are nausea, vomiting, and gastrointestinal bleeding, but aspirin remains one of the most effective and safe medicinal drugs. See also ANALGESIC; PARACETAMOL.

**Asquith, Herbert Henry:** see OXFORD AND ASQUITH, HERBERT HENRY ASQUITH, 1st EARL OF.

**ass,** hoofed, herbivorous MAMMAL (genus *Equus*), related to, but smaller than, the HORSE. Unlike the horse, the ass has a large head, long ears, and small hooves. The two living species are the sandy-coloured wild Asian ass (*E. hemonius*), now endangered, and the larger, grey African ass (*E. asinus*), from which domestic donkeys are descended.

**Assad,** lake, 80 km (50 mi) long, N Syria on the EUPHRATES R., formed by water retained behind the Tabqa Dam. Completed in 1975, it was named after Pres. Hafez al Assad of Syria, under whose government the dam was built with Soviet financial and technical assistance.

**Assad, Hafez al-,** 1928–, president of SYRIA. He was defence minister before leading the 1965 military coup that made him president. A strong anti-Zionist, he is a major supporter of the PALESTINE LIBERATION ORGANIZATION. In 1976 he committed Syrian troops as part· of an Arab peace-keeping force in LEBANON.

**Assamese** ('asə,meez), language belonging to the Indic group of the Indo-Iranian subfamily of the Indo-European family of languages. See LANGUAGE (table).

**assassination,** the killing of a prominent person. The term derives from the 'Assassins', a fanatical Shi'ite muslim sect who murdered Christian princes in the 11th- 13th cent. Assassinations are usually carried out to advance political ends, though personal hatred may also be the motive. One of the most infamous assassinations of the 20th cent. was that of Austrian Archduke Ferdinand in Sarajevo, 1914, which started the chain of events that lead to World War I. In the US, lax gun laws make assassination a more common phenomenon. Pres. J.F. KENNEDY was assassinated in 1963, whilst Presidents FORD and REAGAN have both been the target of attempted assassinations. In the UK, the most notorious recent assassination attempt was by the Irish Republican Army, when they tried to blow up the entire cabinet in Brighton, in 1984.

**Assassins,** militant branch of the medieval ISMA'ILIS, established at Alamut in Northern Iran by Hasan-i Sabbah (d. 1124). The word 'Assassin' derives from the epithet *hashishiyyin* (hashish-users), perhaps given to them by their opponents.

**assault,** in law, intentional attempt to use violence to do bodily harm to another. The victim must reasonably believe the perpetrator capable of such violence. See BATTERY.

**assemblage:** see COLLAGE.

**Assemblies of God:** see PENTECOSTALISM.

**Assis, Joaquim Maria Machado de:** see MACHADO DE ASSIS, JOAQUIM MARIA.

**Assisi,** town (1984 est. pop. 24,000), Umbria, central Italy. A walled, hilltop town, it was the home of St Francis. He founded (1209) the Franciscan Order and Assisi is full of monuments to him: the convent of San Francesco with its two churches, one built above the other, contains frescoes by Giotto depicting 'The Life of St Francis'.

**Assiut:** see ASYÛT.

**association,** a term in philosophy and psychology, denoting a learned connection between two or more elements. Empiricist philosophers claim that knowledge is derived from the association of similar ideas, in which complex ideas arise from the association of simpler ideas and sensations; hence 'associationism'. See also BEHAVIOURISM.

**association football:** see SOCCER.

**Association of South-East Asian Nations** (ASEAN), organization established by the Bangkok Declaration (1967), initially linking Indonesia, Malaysia, the Philippines, Singapore, and Thailand; Brunei became a member in 1984. It seeks to promote social and economic progress and regional stability through cooperation in the economic and political spheres. ASEAN has a permanent secretariat located in Djakarta (Indonesia).

**associative law,** in mathematics, law holding that for a given operation combining three quantities, two at a time, the initial pairing is arbitrary. Addition and, in most cases, multiplication are associative; thus $(a + b) + c = a + (b + c)$ and $(a \times b) \times c = a \times (b \times c)$ for any three numbers $a$, $b$, and $c$. An exception is the multiplication of VECTORS, for which the associative law does not generally hold. Subtraction and division are not associative.

**assonance:** see RHYME.

**Assurbanipal,** or **Ashurbanipal** d. 626? BC, king of ancient ASSYRIA (r.669–626 BC), son and successor of Esar-Haddon. He was the last of the great kings of Assyria. Under him Assyria reached the height of sumptuous living, and art and learning flourished. A few years after his reign ended, Assyria succumbed to the Medes and the Persians. His great expenditures in wars to preserve the state contributed somewhat to its collapse.

**Assurnasirpal II,** d. 860? BC, king of ancient ASSYRIA (884–860? BC). He conquered considerable territory and helped to create a centralized state.

**Assyria,** ancient empire of W Asia, originating around the city of Ashur, on the upper Tigris R., S of its later capital, NINEVEH. At first a small Semitic city-state, Assyria flourished briefly under Tiglathpileser I (d. c.1074 BC). Its real importance, however, began in the 9th cent. with the conquests of ASSURNASIRPAL II, who set up an imperial administration. Later kings such as Shalmaneser III, Tiglathpileser III, and Sargon gained hegemony in the Middle East. SENNACHERIB consolidated their holdings, and Esar-Haddon (r.681–668 BC) defeated the Chaldaeans and conquered Egypt. Under his successor, ASSURBANIPAL (r.669–626 BC), Assyria reached its height of learning, art, and splendour. But Egypt broke away, and Assyria's decline was rapid. Soon after Assurbanipal's death Nineveh was sacked (612 BC) and Assyria was absorbed, first by Babylonia and then by the Persian empire.

**Assyrian art.** An Assyrian artistic style, as distinct from that of BABYLONIA, began to emerge c.1500 BC and lasted until the fall of Nineveh in 612 BC. Assyrian artistic tradition, whilst originally depending on Babylonian models, incorporated a number of elements of the art and techniques of its western neighbours, Aramaens, Hittites, etc. The Assyrian palaces of the 9th–7th cent. (Nimrud, Khorsabad, and Nineveh) were decorated with polychrome carved gypsum reliefs. The scenes depicted the achievements of the king, chiefly in hunting, war and the reception of tribute, but also in his cultic role, as the gods' representative on earth; the latter scenes included representations of magical and protective genies. Guarding the doorways were colossal figures carved partly in the round, of protective composite monsters. Human figures were comparatively rigid, though minutely detailed. Animal forms, particularly horses and lions, were represented in great detail and amongst the finest examples of Assyrian art are the hunting scenes of Assurbanipal (7th cent.), from Nineveh which are in the British Museum. Carvings from the palace of Sargon at Khorsabad may be seen in the Louvre.

Assyrian art: Hunting scenes of Assurbanipal

**Assyrian language,** Hamito-Semitic language of ancient times, in the Akkadian group. See LANGUAGE (table).

**Astaire, Fred,** 1899–1987, American actor, dancer, and choreographer; b. Frederick Austerlitz. After dancing in VAUDEVILLE with his sister, Adele, he made many films, often with Ginger Rogers, in which he displayed an elegant style of tap dance. His films include *Flying Down to Rio* (1933), *Top Hat* (1935), and *Silk Stocking* (1957).

**Astarte,** Semitic goddess of fertility and love. Dominant in ancient Eastern religions, she was the most important goddess of the Phoenicians,

corresponding to the Babylonian ISHTAR and the Greek Aphrodite. See also GREAT MOTHER OF THE GODS.

**astatine** (At), semimetallic radioactive element, discovered in 1931 by Fred Allison and E.J. Murphy. The heaviest known HALOGEN, it is believed to be similar to iodine in its chemical properties. Astatine-211 (half-life 7.21 hr) is used as a radioactive tracer because it collects in the thyroid gland. See ELEMENT (table); PERIODIC TABLE.

**Astell, Mary,** 1666–1731, English writer. She is best known for her writings on the education and difficult position of women in her *Reflections Upon Marriage* (1706) and her *Serious Proposal to the Ladies* (Pt I 1696, Pt II 1697), in which she suggested that women should set up separate households.

**aster,** widely distributed, wild and cultivated perennial flowering plants (genus *Aster*) of the COMPOSITE family. Most species have white, pink, blue, or purple flowers that bloom in autumn. The China aster (*Callistephus chinensis*), the common aster of florists and flower gardens, and the chamomile or golden aster (genus *Anthemis*) are in the same family.

**asteroid,** or **minor planet,** small, usually irregularly shaped body orbiting the Sun, most often found part of the time between the orbits of Mars and Jupiter. Ceres is the largest asteroid (diameter: 750 km/470 mi) and was the first discovered (1801). Of the more than 2000 asteroids known, most have been discovered photographically; their paths appear as short lines in a time exposure. Asteroids may be fragments of a planet shattered in the remote past; material that failed to condense into a single planet; or material from the nuclei of old comets. The Trojan asteroids revolve in the same orbit as Jupiter, kept by perturbation effects in two groups 60° ahead of and 60° behind Jupiter. The Apollo asteroids cross the Earth's orbit.

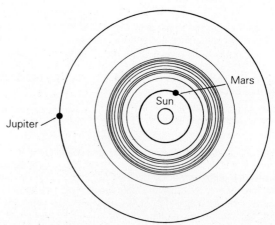

The **asteroid** belt lies between the orbits of Mars and Jupiter

**asthma,** chronic respiratory disorder characterized by paroxysmal attacks of breathlessness and wheezing resulting from obstructed and constricted air passages. Although asthma usually results from an allergic reaction (see ALLERGY), specific allergy-producing substances are not always identifiable. Illness and emotional or physical stress may precipitate an attack. For acute attacks ADRENALINE injections and oxygen therapy bring immediate relief. Long-term control includes use of bronchodilators, STEROIDS, breathing exercises, and, if possible, the identification and avoidance of allergens.

**astigmatism,** common visual defect resulting from irregular curvature of the cornea or lens of the eye, preventing light rays from converging on the retina (see EYE). With astigmatism, some light rays focus on the retina, while others focus in front of or behind it. Congenital or caused by disease or injury, astigmatism can occur in addition to LONGSIGHTEDNESS and SHORTSIGHTEDNESS. It may be alleviated with corrective lenses.

**Astor, John Jacob,** 1763–1848, American merchant; b. Germany. At 21 he arrived in Baltimore, penniless; later he opened a small fur shop in New York City. Shrewd and ambitious, he became a leader of the China trade. His American Fur Company (1808) exercised a virtual monopoly on the fur trade in US territories, and at his death Astor was the wealthiest man in the country. His great-grandson **William Waldorf Astor,** 1st

Viscount Astor, 1848–1919, was an American-British financier. In 1890 he moved to England, where he contributed huge sums to public causes. He was made baron in 1916 and viscount in 1917. His elder son, **Waldorf Astor**, married **Nancy Witcher (Langhorne) Astor, Viscountess Astor**, (see separate article).

**Astor, Nancy Witcher (Langhorne), Viscountess**, 1879–1964, British political leader who became the first woman to sit in PARLIAMENT. As a conservative member (1919–45) she espoused temperance and reforms in women's and children's welfare. In the 1930s she and her husband Waldorf Astor (see under ASTOR, JOHN JACOB) were prominent members of the Cliveden set, which supported Prime Min. Neville CHAMBERLAIN's appeasement policy.

**astrobleme**, [Gk., = star wound], the scar of a pre-Pliocene meteorite impact on the earth's surface. Wolf Creek Crater in NW Australia is a classic impact crater.

**astrolabe**, instrument of ancient origin that measured altitudes of celestial bodies and determined their positions and motions. It typically consisted of a wooden or metal disc with the circumference marked off in degrees, suspended from an attached ring. Angular distances were determined by sighting with the alidade a movable pointer pivoted at the disc's centre and taking readings of its position on the graduated circle. Skilled mariners used astrolabes up to the 18th cent. to determine latitude, longitude, and time of day.

Astrolabe (AD 1054) from the Jagellonian Museum

**astrology**, form of DIVINATION based on the theory that movements of the celestial bodies (stars, planets, Sun, and Moon) influence human affairs and determine events. The Chaldaeans and Assyrians, believing all events to be predetermined, developed a nondeistic system of divination. The spread of astrological practice was arrested by the rise of CHRISTIANITY, with its emphasis on divine intervention and free will; but in the RENAISSANCE astrology regained popularity, in part due to rekindled interest in science and ASTRONOMY. Christian theologians warred against astrology, and in 1585 SIXTUS V condemned it. At the same time the work of KEPLER and others undermined astrology's tenets, although the practice has continued. One's horoscope is a map of the heavens at the time of one's birth, showing the positions of the heavenly bodies in the ZODIAC.

**astronaut** or **cosmonaut**, crew member on a US or Soviet manned spaceflight mission. The early astronauts and cosmonauts were generally trained aircraft test pilots; later astronauts and cosmonauts, however, have included scientists and physicians. As far as is possible, all conditions to be encountered in space, e.g., the physiological disorientation arising from weightlessness (see SPACE MEDICINE), are simulated in ground training. Using trainers and mock-ups of actual spacecraft, astronauts and cosmonauts rehearse every manoeuvre from lift-off to recovery; every conceivable malfunction and difficulty is anticipated and prepared for. Prominent Soviet cosmonauts include Yuri GAGARIN, Valentina TERESHKOVA, and Aleksei LEONOV. Prominent US astronauts include Neil ARMSTRONG and Buzz ALDRIN. The USSR and the US have flown a number of foreign nationals on their spacecraft, including astronauts or cosmonauts from Bulgaria, Canada, Cuba, Czechoslovakia, France, East Germany, West Germany, Hungary, India, Mexico, Mongolia, the Netherlands, Poland, Romania, Saudi Arabia, Syria, and Vietnam.

**Astronomer Royal**, position created by King Charles II of England to determine the positions of the stars in order to improve navigation. John FLAMSTEED became the first Astronomer Royal in 1675 and established the Greenwich Observatory near London to fulfil his task. His successors have included Edmund HALLEY, James BRADLEY, and many other great British astronomers. Until Martin RYLE became Astronomer Royal in 1972, the post was invariably combined with that of Director of the Royal Greenwich Observatory.

**astronomical coordinate systems**, four basic systems used to indicate the positions of celestial bodies on the celestial sphere. The latter is an imaginary sphere that has the observer at its centre and all other celestial bodies imagined as located on its inside surface.

*Equatorial.* The celestial equator is the projection of the Earth's EQUATOR onto the celestial sphere, and the celestial poles are the points where the Earth's axis, if extended, intersects the celestial sphere. *Right ascension* (R.A.) is the angle (in hours, minutes, and seconds, with 1 h = 15°) measured eastward from the vernal EQUINOX to the point where the hour circle (the great circle passing through the celestial poles and the body) intersects the celestial equator. *Declination* is the angle (in degrees, minutes, and seconds, as are all other angles defined hereafter) measured north (+) or south (−) along the body's hour circle between the celestial equator and the body.

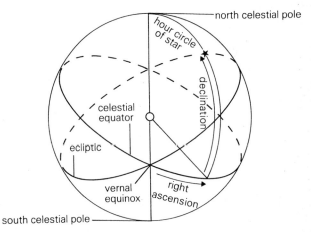

Equatorial **astronomical coordinate system**

*Horizon or Altazimuth.* Altitude is the angle measured above (+) or below (−) the observer's celestial horizon (the great circle on the celestial sphere midway between the points zenith and nadir directly above and below the observer) to the body along the vertical circle passing through the body and the zenith. *Azimuth* is the angle measured along the celestial horizon from the observer's celestial meridian (the vertical circle passing through the nearest celestial pole and the zenith) to the point where the body's vertical circle intersects the horizon. The earth's rotation constantly changes a body's altitude and azimuth.

*Ecliptic or Celestial.* The ecliptic poles are the two points at which a line perpendicular to the plane of the ECLIPTIC and passing through the Earth's centre intersects the celestial sphere. *Celestial latitude* is the angle measured north (+) or south (−) from the ecliptic to the body along the latitude circle through the body and the ecliptic poles. *Celestial longitude* is the angle measured along the ecliptic from the vernal equinox to the latitude circle, in the same sense as R.A.

*Galactic.* The galactic equator is the intersection of the mean plane of our galaxy with the celestial sphere, and the galactic poles are the two points at which a line perpendicular to the mean galactic plane and passing through the Earth's centre intersects the celestial sphere. *Galactic latitude* is the angle measured north (+) or south (−) from the galactic equator to the body along the great circle passing through the body and the galactic poles. *Galactic longitude* is the angle measured eastward along the galactic equator from the galactic centre.

**astronomical unit** (AU), mean distance between the Earth and the Sun. One AU is c. 149,604,970 km (92,960,000 mi).

**astronomy,** branch of science that studies the motions and natures of celestial bodies, such as PLANETS, STARS, and GALAXIES; more generally, the study of matter and energy in the universe at large. Astronomy is perhaps the oldest of the pure sciences. In many primitive civilizations the regularity of celestial motions was recognized, and attempts were made to keep records and predict events. Astronomical observations provided a basis for the CALENDAR by determining the units of MONTH and YEAR. Later, astronomy served in navigation and timekeeping. The earliest astronomers were priests, and no attempt was made to separate astronomy from the pseudoscience of ASTROLOGY. Astronomy reached its highest development in the ancient world with the Greeks of the Alexandrian school in the Hellenistic period. ARISTARCHUS OF SAMOS determined the sizes and distances of the MOON and SUN and advocated a heliocentric (sun-centred) cosmology. ERATOSTHENES made the first accurate measurement of the actual size of the Earth. The greatest astronomer of antiquity, HIPPARCHUS, devised a geocentric system of cycles and epicycles (a compounding of circular motions) to account for the movements of the Sun and Moon. Using such a system, PTOLEMY predicted the motions of the planets with considerable accuracy (see PTOLEMAIC SYSTEM). One of the landmarks of the scientific revolution of the 16th and 17th cent. was Nicholas COPERNICUS's revival (1543) of the heliocentric theory (see COPERNICAN SYSTEM). The next great astronomer, Tycho BRAHE, compiled (1576–97) the most accurate and complete astronomical observations yet produced. Johannes KEPLER's study of Brahe's observations led him to the three laws of planetary motion that bear his name (see KEPLER'S LAWS). GALILEO Galilei, the first to make astronomical use of the TELESCOPE, provided persuasive evidence (e.g., his discovery of the four largest moons of JUPITER and the phases of VENUS) for the Copernican cosmology. Isaac NEWTON, possibly the greatest scientific genius of all time, succeeded in uniting the sciences of astronomy and PHYSICS. His laws of motion and theory of universal GRAVITATION, published in 1687, provided a physical, dynamic basis for the merely descriptive laws of Kepler. The discovery of the ABERRATION OF STARLIGHT (1729) by James BRADLEY was the first unambignous test showing the Earth to be in orbital motion. By the early 19th cent. the science of CELESTIAL MECHANICS had reached a highly developed state through the work of Alexis Clairaut, Jean d'ALEMBERT, Leonhard EULER, Joseph LAGRANGE, Pierre LAPLACE, and others. In 1838, Friedrich BESSEL made the first measurement of the distance to a star (see PARALLAX). Astronomy was revolutionized in the second half of the 19th cent. by techniques based on photography and the SPECTROSCOPE. Interest shifted from determining the positions and distances of stars to studying their physical composition (see STELLAR EVOLUTION). With the construction of ever more powerful telescopes (see OBSERVATORY), the boundaries of the known universe constantly increased. Harlow SHAPLEY determined the size and shape of our galaxy, the MILKY WAY. Edwin HUBBLE's study of the distant galaxies led him to conclude that the universe is expanding (see HUBBLE'S LAW). Various rival theories of the origin and overall structure of the universe, e.g., the big bang and steady state theories, were formulated (see COSMOLOGY). Most recently, the frontiers of astronomy have been expanded by SPACE EXPLORATION (see SPACE ASTRONOMY) and observations in new parts of the spectrum, e.g., gamma-ray astronomy, RADIO ASTRONOMY, ultraviolet astronomy, and X-ray astronomy. The new observational techniques have led to the discovery of strange new astronomical objects, e.g., PULSARS, QUASARS, and black holes (see GRAVITATIONAL COLLAPSE).

**astrophysics,** application of the theories and methods of physics to the study of stellar structure, STELLAR EVOLUTION, the origin of the SOLAR SYSTEM, and related problems of COSMOLOGY.

**Asturias,** region and former kingdom, NW Spain, S of the Bay of Biscay. The major occupations are the mining of coal, iron, and other resources; steel-making; cattle-raising; fishing; and the growing of apples for cider. When the MOORS conquered 8th-cent. Spain, Christian nobles fled to the Asturian mountains, formed a kingdom, and began the long reconquest of Spain. In the 10th cent. León became the capital of the kingdom, then known as Asturias and León. The kingdom was united (1230) with CASTILE.

**Asturias, Miguel Ángel,** 1899–1974, Guatemalan writer. His major works are his novels, including *El señor Presidente* (1946; tr. The President), a study of a dictatorship, *Papa verde* (1954; tr. Green Pope), and *Los ojos de los enterrados* (1960; tr. The Eyes of the Interred), about banana exploitation in the Caribbean. He also wrote stories and poetry. He received the 1967 Nobel Prize for literature.

**Asunción,** city (1982 pop. 455,517), S Paraguay, capital of Paraguay, on the Paraguay R. It is the nation's principal port and chief industrial and cultural centre. Meat-packing is the largest industry. One of the oldest cities in South America, founded in 1537, it retains a colonial aspect. It became a centre of early Jesuit missionary activity and was the most important town in the Río de la PLATA region until it was partially eclipsed by BUENOS AIRES during the 18th cent.

**Aswan High Dam,** one of the world's largest dams, on the Nile R., in Egypt, built (1960–70) c.6.4 km (4 mi) S of the smaller Aswan Dam (completed, 1902; enlarged, 1934). It is 114 m (375 ft) high and 3600 m (11,811 ft) long. The dam has a hydroelectricity capacity of 10,000 million kilowatt-hours and stores sufficient water in impounded Lake Nasser to irrigate more than 2,809,400 hectares (7 million acres) of farmland. The USSR provided funding and engineers for the project.

Aswan High Dam

**asylum,** refuge, most often granted by a nation to a fugitive from another nation. Asylum is usually reserved for victims of political, religious, or other discrimination. See also EXTRADITION.

**Asyût** or **Assiut,** city (1987 pop. 213,752), N Egypt, situated on the Nile R. c.350 km (217 mi) upstream of Cairo. It is noted for pottery, ornamental wood, and ivory work. Asyût Univ. was founded in 1949 and opened in 1957.

**At,** chemical symbol of the element ASTATINE.

**Atacama,** the largest desert of South America. It extends over the provinces of Atacama and Antofagasta in N Chile, the territory of Los Andes in NW Argentina, and SW Bolivia. It is a mountainous region with volcanic peaks ranging from 2100 to 4200 m (7000 to 14,000 ft). It is also highly mineralized and has attracted considerable mining activity, particularly of copper and nitrates.

**Atacama, Desert of,** extremely arid plateau, c.600 (2000 ft) high, in N Chile. It is c.970 km (600 mi) long and has great nitrate and copper wealth. Chile gained sole control of the area from Peru and Bolivia in the 1880s (see PACIFIC, WAR OF THE).

**Atalanta,** in Greek mythology, fleet huntress who joined the Calydonian boar hunt (see MELEAGER). She demanded that each of her suitors race her, the winner to be rewarded with marriage, the losers to die. Hippomenes finally won her by dropping three golden apples that she stopped to retrieve. The story is told in OVID's *Metamorphoses.*

**Atangana, Charles,** 1885–1943, ruler of the Ewondo of Yaoundé, S central CAMEROON. He collaborated with both German and, after World War I, French colonial masters to become the most powerful chief in French Africa. He supplied conscripted labour for imperial projects such as the Doula–Yaoundé railway and made use of the labour himself to start extensive plantations of food crops, cocoa and palm trees. A modernizer, he encouraged the cultivation of cocoa as a cash crop and helped in the fight against sleeping sickness in Cameroon.

**Atatürk, Kemal,** 1881–1938, founder and first president of modern TURKEY (1923–38). Originally known as Mustafa Kemal, he was an army officer who took part (1908) in the Young Turk movement, distinguished himself in WORLD WAR I, and, after the collapse of Ottoman power, founded the Turkish Nationalist Party. With the Allies controlling the government at Constantinople (Istanbul), he set up a rival government at Ankara. He expelled the Greeks who were occupying Anatolia (1921–22), abolished the sultanate (1922), and forced the European powers to recognize the Turkish republic. He ruled the new republic for 15 years as a virtual dictator, changing Turkey profoundly. He instituted widespread internal reforms in his efforts to Westernize his nation; those changes included abolishing the CALIPHATE (1924), which in effect disestablished Islam; women were emancipated, enjoying equal legal rights and being no longer obliged to be veiled in public; universal education was introduced. In foreign affairs he pursued a moderate policy, maintaining friendly relations with Turkey's neighbours, especially the USSR, with whom he established the Balkan Entente; he took Turkey into the LEAGUE OF NATIONS.

**Atget, Eugène** (atzhay), 1857–1927, French photographer. At 47 he began to produce his evocative record of Paris and its environs. He sold his work to printers and to the Paris historical monuments society. His images of the parks, vendors, bridges, and prostitutes of Paris go beyond documentation.

**Athanasius, Saint,** c.297–373, patriarch of ALEXANDRIA (328–73), Doctor of the Church. At the first Council of NICAEA (325) he took part in the debate against the heresy of ARIANISM. He continued to defend the Nicene orthodoxy, especially in *Discourses Against the Arians,* and was exiled from his see five times between 335 and 365. The Athanasian CREED is no longer ascribed to him but to a 4th-cent. Western writer. Feast: 2 May.

**atheism,** denial of the existence of God or gods and of any supernatural existence, to be distinguished from AGNOSTICISM, which holds that the existence cannot be proved. Since the 19th cent. atheism has been advanced by such movements as Marxism and Logical Positivism.

**Athelstan** or **Æthelstan,** d. 939, king of the southern English (r.924–39). He welded together the West Saxon and Mercian people and extended his supremacy over the western and northern kings of Britain. He was also intimately associated with the leading western European rulers of his time. He issued a notable series of royal charters and law codes.

**Athena** or **Pallas Athena,** in Greek mythology, one of the most important OLYMPIAN deities, sprung from the forehead of ZEUS. She was the goddess of war and peace, a patron of arts and crafts, a guardian of cities (notably Athens), and the goddess of wisdom. Her most important temple was the PARTHENON and her primary festival the Panathenaea. A virgin goddess, Athena is represented in art as a stately figure, armoured, and wielding her breastplate, the aegis. In later art she is associated with the owl, which appeared on Athenian coins. The Romans identified her with MINERVA.

**Athenaeus,** fl. early 3rd cent. AD, Greek writer. His work *Deipnosophists* [professors at the dinner table] is a valuable source of information about the cultural life of his time, and of earlier literature, especially COMEDY.

**Athens,** city (1981 pop. 3,027,331 in Greater Athens), capital of Greece, E central Greece. Greater Athens, a transportation hub including the Aegean port of PIRAIÉVS, accounts for most of the country's industry, including textiles, machine tools, and ships. Tourism is also important. Early Athens, the centre of ancient Greek civilization, was rigidly governed by aristocratic archons until the reforms of SOLON (594 BC) and CLEISTHENES (506 BC) established a democracy of its freemen. It emerged from the PERSIAN WARS (500–449 BC) as the strongest Greek city-state, and reached its cultural and imperial zenith in the time of PERICLES (443–429 BC). Its citizens included SOCRATES, AESCHYLUS, SOPHOCLES, and EURIPIDES. After defeat by its arch-rival Sparta in the PELOPONNESIAN WAR (431–404 BC) it began a long decline that continued under the Macedonians and Romans; yet it could still boast such citizens as ARISTOTLE, ARISTOPHANES, and PLATO. Captured (395 AD) by Visigoths, it became the capital of the BYZANTINE EMPIRE, then came in turn under French, Spanish, and Ottoman Turkish rule before becoming (1834) the capital of newly independent Greece. The city escaped damage in World War II. The first modern OLYMPIC GAMES were held there in 1896. Overlooking the city is its foremost landmark, the ACROPOLIS, where the ruins of the PARTHENON, the Propylaea, and the ERECHTHEUM are located.

Maison Close by Eugène **Atget**

**athlete's foot:** see RINGWORM.

**athletics,** sports or exercises engaged in by athletes. TRACK EVENTS consist of running races over set distances (e.g., 100 m, 200 m, 800 m, 1500 m), or running and jumping races (hurdling). See also DECATHLON; FIELD EVENT; MARATHON RACE; and PENTATHLON.

**Athos** or **Akte,** peninsula, NE Greece, in the Aegean Sea. At its southern tip is **Mount Athos,** also called Hagion Oros, a religious community (c.80 km²/30 sq km) of about 20 Eastern Orthodox monasteries of the Order of St. Basil. Founded c.963, it enjoyed administrative independence under the Byzantine and Ottoman empires and was made (1927) a theocratic republic under Greek suzerainty. Women and female animals are barred.

**Atkin, James Richard, Lord,** 1867–1944, British barrister and judge. He became HIGH COURT judge (1913), and later sat in the Court of Appeal (1919), and House of Lords (1928–44). His judgments are learned and respected, and include the classic definition of NEGLIGENCE in DONOGHUE v.

STEVENSON (1932). He was concerned about the rights of ordinary people, and did much to bridge the gap between practising and academic lawyers.

**Atlanta,** capital and largest city, (1984 est. pop. 426,000) of Georgia, US; settled 1837, inc. as a city 1847. Located in one of America's fastest-growing urban areas, it is the largest commercial, industrial, and financial centre in the SE US and the largest city in Georgia, as well as a transport hub and a convention centre. Many facilities of the federal government are located in the area, which also produces textiles, chemicals, automobiles, aircraft, clothing, and a wide variety of other goods. The city is also a centre of international trade and commerce. Atlanta was captured and burned (1864) by Gen. William T. SHERMAN; rebuilt, it prospered and became the state capital in 1868.

**Atlantic Charter,** programme of peace aims enunciated on 14 Aug. 1941, by US Pres. F. D. ROOSEVELT and British Prime Min. Winston CHURCHILL. Included among the aims was the list of human rights known as the FOUR FREEDOMS.

**Atlantic City,** US city (1980 pop. 40,199), SE New Jersey, an Atlantic resort and convention centre; inc. 1854. On Absecon Island, a sandbar 16 km (10 mi) long, it was a fishing village until 1854, when the railway began to transform it into a fashionable resort. It is known for its 9.7-km (6-mi) boardwalk, its convention hall, and its Steel Pier (built 1898; burned 1982). After the state legalized casino gambling there (1976), the city entered a new era of prosperity.

**Atlantic Ocean,** world's second largest ocean, c.82,362,000 km² (31,800,000 sq mi), separating North and South America from Europe and Africa. It is narrowest c.2575 km (1600 mi) off NE Brazil and deepest (c.8530 m/28,000 ft) in the Milwaukee Deep, N of Puerto Rico. The generally narrow continental shelf reaches its greatest widths off NE North America, SE South America, and NW Europe. The ocean is divided lengthwise by the Mid-Atlantic Ridge, a submarine mountain range c.480–970 km (300–600 mi) wide that extends c.16,100 km (10,000 mi) from Iceland to near the Antarctic Circle. This ridge, which has a few peaks that emerge as islands, is constantly widening, filling with molten rock, and pushing the bordering continents farther apart (see PLATE TECTONICS).

**Atlantis,** in Greek mythology, large island in the western sea. PLATO describes it as a UTOPIA destroyed by an earthquake. Questions as to its existence have provoked speculation over the centuries. One theory holds that it was a part of the Aègean island of THERA that sank c.1500 BC.

**Atlas,** in Greek mythology, a TITAN. After the defeat of the Titans by the OLYMPIANS, he was condemned to hold the sky upon his shoulders for all eternity.

**Atlas Mountains,** mountain system, NW Africa, c.2410 km (1500 mi) long. It is widest and most rugged in Morocco, where Jebel Toubkal reaches a high point of 4167 m (13,671 ft). The mountains are rich in phosphates, coal, iron, and oil.

**atmosphere,** the mixture of gases and other substances surrounding a celestial body with sufficient gravity to maintain it. Although some details about the atmospheres of the other planets and some satellites are known (see articles on individual planets), a complete description is available only for the earth's atmosphere, the study of which is called METEOROLOGY. The gaseous constituents of the earth's atmosphere are not chemically combined, and thus each retains its own physical and chemical properties. Within the first c.65 to 80 km (40 to 50 mi) above the earth, the mixture is of uniform composition (except for a high concentration of OZONE at 50 km/30 mi). This whole region contains more than 99% of the total mass of the earth's atmosphere. Based on their relative volumes, the gaseous constituents are nitrogen (78.09%), oxygen (20.95%), argon (0.93%), carbon dioxide (0.03%), and minute traces of neon, helium, methane, krypton, hydrogen, xenon, and ozone. Additional atmospheric constituents include water vapour and particulate matter, such as various forms of dust and industrial pollutants. The earth's atmosphere is separated into certain distinct regions, each having a different temperature range. The troposphere, where air is in constant motion (see WIND), extends from the earth's surface to an altitude of 8 km (5 mi) at the poles and 16 km (10 mi) at the equator. Clouds and other WEATHER phenomena occur here (see also CLIMATE). All forms of the earth's animal and plant life exist in the troposphere or in the waters beneath it. Above the troposphere, the stratosphere extends to about 50 km (30 mi),

followed by the mesosphere, up to about 80 km (50 mi), the thermosphere, up to about 640 km (400 mi), and finally the exosphere. The ionosphere is in the range (80 to 640 km/50 to 400 mi) that contains a high concentration of electrically charged particles (ions), which are responsible for reflecting radio signals. Above it, out to about 64–65,000 km (40,000 mi) in a region called the magnetosphere, electrically charged particles are trapped by the earth's magnetic field (see AURORA; VAN ALLEN RADIATION BELTS). The atmosphere protects the earth by absorbing and scattering harmful radiation and causing extraterrestrial solid matter (see METEOR) to burn from the heat generated by air friction.

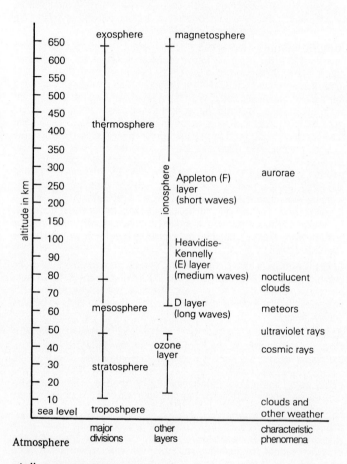

Atmosphere

**atoll:** see CORAL REEF; ISLAND.

**atom,** the smallest unit of a chemical ELEMENT having the properties of that element. An atom contains several kinds of particles. Its central core, the nucleus, consists of positively charged particles, called PROTONS, and uncharged particles, called NEUTRONS. Surrounding the nucleus and orbiting it are negatively charged particles, called ELECTRONS. Each atom has an equal number of protons and electrons. The nucleus occupies only a tiny fraction of an atom's volume but contains almost all of its mass. Electrons in the outermost orbits determine the atom's chemical and electrical properties. The number of protons in an atom's nucleus is called the ATOMIC NUMBER. All atoms of an element have the same atomic number and differ in atomic number from atoms of other elements. The total number of protons and neutrons combined is the atom's MASS NUMBER. Atoms containing the same number of protons but different numbers of neutrons are different forms, or ISOTOPES, of the same element. See also ATOMIC WEIGHT.

*History.* In the 5th cent. BC the Greek philosophers DEMOCRITUS and Leucippus proposed that matter was made up of tiny, indivisible particles in constant motion. Aristotle, however, did not accept the theory, and it was ignored for centuries. Modern atomic theory began with John DALTON, who proposed (1808) that all atoms of an element have exactly the same size and weight, and that atoms of elements unite chemically in simple numerical ratios to form compounds. In 1911 Ernest RUTHERFORD explained an atom's structure in terms of a positively charged nucleus surrounded by negatively charged electrons orbiting around it. In 1913

Niels BOHR used QUANTUM THEORY to explain why electrons could remain in certain allowed orbits without radiating energy. The development of quantum mechanics during the 1920s resulted in a satisfactory explanation of all phenomena related to the role of electrons in atoms and of all aspects of their associated spectra (see SPECTRUM). The quantum theory has shown that all particles have certain wave properties. As a result, electrons in an atom cannot be pictured as localized in space but rather should be viewed as a cloud of charge spread out over the entire orbit. The electron clouds around the nucleus represent regions in which the electrons are most likely to be found. Physicists are currently studying the behaviour of large groups of atoms (see SOLID-STATE PHYSICS), and the nature of and relations among the hundreds of ELEMENTARY PARTICLES that have been discovered in addition to the proton, neutron, and electron.

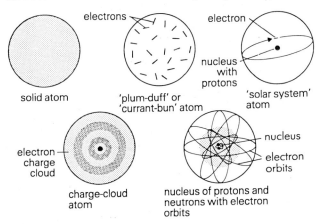

Development of the **atom** model since 1808, when the idea of a solid atom as a fundamental building block of all matter was first proposed

**atomic bomb,** weapon deriving its great explosive force from the sudden release of NUCLEAR ENERGY through the fission, or splitting, of heavy atomic nuclei. The first atomic bomb was successfully tested by the US near Alamogordo, New Mexico, on 16 July 1945 (see MANHATTAN PROJECT). In the final stages of WORLD WAR II the US dropped atomic bombs on Hiroshima on 6 Aug. 1945, and on Nagasaki. Atomic bombs were subsequently developed by the USSR (1949), Great Britain (1952), France (1960), China (1964), and India (1974). An atomic bomb is detonated by assembling rapidly by means of chemical explosives, a sufficiently large and dense mass of fissionable material. The ensuing explosion produces great amounts of heat, a shock wave, and intense neutron and gamma radiation. The region of the explosion becomes radioactively contaminated, and wind-borne radioactive products may be deposited elsewhere as fallout. See also CARCINOGENS; DISARMAMENT, NUCLEAR; HYDROGEN BOMB; MUTAGENS.

**atomic clock:** see CLOCK.

**atomic energy:** see NUCLEAR ENERGY.

**atomic mass:** see ATOMIC WEIGHT.

**atomic mass unit:** see ATOMIC WEIGHT.

**atomic number,** often represented by the symbol $Z$, the number of PROTONS in the nucleus of an ATOM. Atoms with the same atomic number make up a chemical ELEMENT. The elements are arranged in the PERIODIC TABLE in the order of their atomic numbers.

**atomic weight,** mean (weighted average) of the masses of all the naturally occuring ISOTOPES of a chemical ELEMENT; the atomic mass is the mass of any individual isotope. Atomic weight is usually expressed in atomic mass units (amu); the atomic mass unit is defined as exactly one-twelfth the mass of a carbon-12 atom. Each proton or neutron weighs about 1 amu, and thus the atomic mass is always very close to the MASS NUMBER (total number of protons and neutrons in the nucleus). Because most naturally occurring elements have one principal isotope and only insignificant amounts of other isotopes, most atomic weights are also very nearly whole numbers. For the atomic weight of individual elements, see PERIODIC TABLE.

**atonality,** systemic avoidance of harmonies and melodies that imply a keynote (see KEY). The term designates a method of composition in which the composer deliberately rejects the principle of TONALITY in favour of another principle of order, such as the 12-tone system (see SERIAL MUSIC). The move toward atonality has been apparent since the 19th cent., when WAGNER, Richard STRAUSS, and DEBUSSY obscured basic tonalities in their music. Atonal composers of the 20th cent. include SCHOENBERG, BERG, WEBERN and IVES.

**Atonement, Day of:** see under JEWISH HOLIDAYS.

**ATP:** see ADENOSINE TRIPHOSPHATE.

**Atreus,** in Greek mythology, king of Mycenae; son of PELOPS, father of AGAMEMNON and MENELAUS. In retaliation for his brother Thyestes' seduction of his wife, Atreus murdered three of Thyestes' sons and served them to him at a feast. Thyestes then laid a curse on the house of Atreus. Thyestes' son AEGISTHUS killed Atreus, and Thyestes became king.

**atrium,** in architecture, an interior court in Roman houses; also a type of entrance court in early Christian churches, and a major feature in modern commerical and hotel buildings. The Roman atrium was an unroofed or partially roofed area with rooms opening from it. In early times it held a hearth in its centre; later a tank collected rainwater. In more luxurious Roman dwellings, individual chambers had courts of their own, called peristyles. The ruins of POMPEII display atria in various forms.

**Attar** (aht̩tah): see FARID AD-DIN ATTAR.

**Attenborough, Sir David,** 1926–, English naturalist, broadcaster, and traveller who has brought natural history into the homes of the general public through films and television, receiving numerous awards for his work. Joining the BBC in 1952 as a trainee producer, he participated in many zoological and ethnographic filming expeditions all over the world between then and 1975. In 1969 he became Director of Programmes (Television) and a member of the Board of Management of the BBC, and a member of the Nature Conservancy Council in 1973. The television series *Life on Earth* was written and presented by David Attenborough, an excellent example of how the theories of palaeontologists, botanists, ecologists, and zoologists can be presented so that the lay public can understand them.

**attendance centre,** in the UK, place where young, usually first-time, offenders may be ordered to attend, on conviction by a Magistrates' Court. They are divided between junior centres, for offenders under 17, and senior centres for those between 17 and 21. Offenders are required to attend on a part-time basis, e.g., every Saturday afternoon, for a prescribed period. They are run by PRISON officers, with the help of POLICE officers in their free time. The regime at the centres focuses on physical training and constructive work, allowing the offender to develop his or her talents. During the 1970s, they became popular with the courts, and were frequently used for convicted football 'hooligans' in order to prevent them going to football matches on a Saturday.

**Attica,** region of ancient Greece around ATHENS. It has a varied landscape of mountain, plain and coast. According to legend the 12 states of Attica were united by Theseus.

**Attila,** d. 453, king of the HUNS (r.434–53). From 434 he extorted tribute from the Eastern and Western Roman emperors. In 450 MARCIAN of the East and VALENTINIAN III of the West refused to pay. Valentinian's sister Honoria proposed an alliance with Attila, who took this as a marriage offer and demanded half the Western empire as dowry. Refused, he attacked Gaul but was defeated (451) by the Romans. He invaded (452) Italy but spared Rome, apparently because of a shortage of supplies and an outbreak of pestilence in his army. Although feared for his savagery, he was a just ruler.

**Attlee, Clement Richard,** 1ST EARL, 1883–1967, British statesman. A lawyer and social worker, he became the leader of the Labour Party in 1935. During World War II he served in Winston CHURCHILL's coalition cabinet (1940–45), and in 1945 he became prime minister. His government nationalized the Bank of England and parts of British industry; enacted many social reforms, including the National Health Service; and granted independence to Burma, India, Pakistan, Ceylon, and Palestine. Attlee left office in 1951. He led the opposition until 1955, when he received the title Earl Attlee.

**Attorney-General,** in England and Wales, one of the two law officers of the CROWN (see DIRECTOR OF PUBLIC PROSECUTIONS). He or she is head of the bar, and the government's chief legal adviser. The Attorney-General is usually a member of PARLIAMENT, and of the PRIVY COUNCIL, and is occasionally a member of the CABINET. As the government's legal adviser, he or she will advise on important matters, especially INTERNATIONAL LAW and consitutional law, as well as undertaking important prosecutions for the crown. The appointment is a party political one and the holder will change upon a change of government. Most COMMONWEALTH countries employ a legal officer performing similar functions, though they are occasionally carried out by a Minister of Justice. In Scotland, the equivalent tasks are assigned to the Lord Advocate (see SCOTLAND, LEGAL SYSTEM IN).

**Atwood, Margaret,** 1939– , Canadian poet and novelist. Her powerful symbolic novels often treat the alienation and destructiveness of human relations. They include *The Edible Woman* (1969), *Surfacing* (1972), and *Bodily Harm* (1981). Among her volumes of poetry is *Selected Poems* (1978).

**Au,** chemical symbol of the element GOLD.

**Auber, Daniel François Esprit** (oh,beə), 1782–1871, French operatic composer. In collaboration with librettist Augustin SCRIBE he wrote many witty, popular works, including *Fra Diavolo* (1830) and *The Mute Girl of Portici* (1828; also known as *Masaniello*).

**aubergine** or **eggplant**, garden vegetable (*Solanum melongena*) of the NIGHTSHADE family. Native to Southeast Asia, it is a perennial shrub, although it is often grown in warm climates as an annual herb. It is cultivated for its ovoid fruit, which varies in size and may be purple, white, or striped. Aubergines are an essential ingredient in French ratatouille, Greek moussaka and Turkish Imam Bayeldi.

**Aubrey, John,** 1626–97, English antiquarian and biographer. He published studies of antiquities, folklore, and natural history, including his *Miscellanies* (1696) in his lifetime, but his most celebrated work, *Lives of Eminent Men* (better known as *Brief Lives*)—gossipy, sharply-observed and amusing anecdotes—were not published till the 19th cent.

**Auckland,** city (1981 pop. 825,703), NW North Island, New Zealand, on an isthmus between the Pacific Ocean and the Tasman Sea. It is the country's largest city and its chief port, industrial centre, and naval base. Frozen meats and dairy products are important exports. Industries include shipbuilding, food processing, oil refining, car assembly, and the manufacture of chemicals. Auckland was founded in 1840 and was the capital of New Zealand until replaced (1865) by WELLINGTON. The Univ. of Auckland is among the city's educational institutions.

**Auden, W(ystan) H(ugh),** 1907–73, Anglo-American poet, a major 20th-cent. literary figure. His poetry of the 1930s, collected in *The English Auden*, ed. Edward Mendelson (1977), brilliantly combines political foreboding with psychological unease. At this time he was associated with SPENDER, MACNEICE, and ISHERWOOD; with the last he wrote the verse plays *The Dog Beneath the Skin* (1935), *The Ascent of F6* (1936), and *On the Frontier* (1938). His move to the US in 1939 was followed by conversion to Christianity. His wide-ranging later volumes include *New Year Letter* (1941), *The Age of Anxiety* (1948), *Nones* (1951), and *About the House* (1965). He also wrote critical essays and opera librettos. A US citizen from 1946, Auden divided his last years among England, Italy, Austria, and New York.

**audiovisual aids,** nonverbal as well as verbal materials, particularly pictures and sounds, used to promote learning. Audiovisual devices, formerly limited to static materials such as maps, graphs, and textbook illustrations, were used successfully as instructional tools by the US armed forces during World War II. As technology developed, audiovisual instruction began to include films, photographs, sound and video recordings, and television, as well as PROGRAMMED LEARNING provided through computers and other types of teaching machines. Instructional television is widely used in all learning situations with the use of cable television and electronic audio and video equipment, it is available in the home as well. Interactive video links video and the computer for learning purposes.

**auditing:** see under ACCOUNTING.

**Audubon, John James,** 1785–1851, American ornithologist, b. Haiti. After arriving in the US in 1803, he began the extensive ornithological observations that would lead to the publication of his bird drawings and paintings as *The Birds of America* (1827–38). The accompanying text, called the *Ornithological Biography* (5 vol., 1831–39), was written in collaboration with the Scottish naturalist William MacGillivray.

Audubon's drawings and paintings remain one of the great achievements of American intellectual history.

**Aue, Hartmann von:** see HARTMANN VON AUE.

**Augsburg,** city (1984 pop. 246,000), capital of Swabia, West Germany, on the Lech R. It is an important centre of textile manufacture and machine-making. The first diesel engine was made here. Founded by the Emperor AUGUSTUS in 15 BC as Augusta Vindelicorum, it became a free Imperial city in 1276 and was noted for its fairs. It was the home of wealthy merchants and bankers in the 15th and 16th cent., including the Fugger family, who built beautiful houses in a Renaissance style. It is the birthplace of Holbein.

**August:** see MONTH.

**Augusta,** US city (1980 pop. 21,819), state capital of Maine on the Kennebec R.; inc. as a city 1849. Shoes, fabrics, and paper products are among its manufactures. The Plymouth Company established a trading post on the site in 1628; Fort Western was built in 1754. In 1837 manufacturing began with the building of a dam. The Capitol building (1829) was designed by Charles Bulfinch and later enlarged.

**Augustine, Saint,** 354–430, Doctor of the Church, bishop of Hippo (near present-day Annaba, Algeria); b. Tagaste, N Africa. Brought up as a Christian by his mother, St Monica, Augustine gave up his religion while at school in Carthage, then converted to MANICHAEISM. He taught rhetoric in Rome (after 376) and Milan (after 384). In Milan he was drawn to the teachings of St AMBROSE and to NEOPLATONISM, and finally embraced Western Christianity, returning (387) to a monastic life in Tagaste. In 391 he was ordained a priest in Hippo, where he remained for the rest of his life, serving as bishop from 396. St Augustine's influence on Western Christianity was immense, and theologians, both Roman Catholic and Protestant, look upon him as the founder of theology. His polemics against Manichaeism, Donatism, and Pelagianism are well known, and his autobiographical *Confessions* is a classic of Christian mysticism. *On the Trinity* systematized Christian doctrine, and *The City of God,* his monumental defence of Christianity against paganism, is famous for its Christian view of history. Feast: 28 Aug.

**Augustine of Canterbury, Saint,** d. c.605, Italian missionary, called the Apostle of the English, first archbishop of Canterbury (from 601). A BENEDICTINE, he was sent by Pope GREGORY I to England, where he converted King ÆTHELBERT and introduced Roman monastic practices. Feast: 27 May (26 May in England and Wales).

**Augustus,** 63 BC–AD 14, first Roman emperor; a greatnephew of Julius CAESAR. Born Caius Octavius, he became on adoption by the Julian gens (44 BC) Caius Julius Caesar Octavianus (Octavian); Augustus was a title of honour granted (27 BC) by the senate. Caesar made the boy his heir without his knowledge, and after Caesar was killed (44 BC), Octavian became dominant at Rome. He made an alliance with ANTONY and Lepidus (d. 13 BC; see LEPIDUS, family) known as the Second TRIUMVIRATE and with Antony defeated the army of Marcus Junius Brutus (see BRUTUS, family) and Caius Cassius Longinus (see CASSIUS, family) at Philippi (42 BC). Octavian's forces next defeated Sextus Pompeius (son of POMPEY) at Mylae (36 BC). After the naval victory at Actium (31 BC) over Antony and CLEOPATRA, Octavian controlled all of the Roman territories. The senate in 29 BC made him *imperator* [Lat., = commander; from it is derived emperor] and in 27 BC *augustus* [august, reverend]. The month Sextilis was renamed Augustus (August) in his honour. Augustus enacted many reforms in Rome and in the provinces and tried to hold the Roman borders set by Caesar. His attempt to make a buffer state in German territory led to the revolt of ARMINIUS, in which a Roman army was destroyed. Augustus lavished expenditures on ROMAN ROADS, beautified Rome, and was generous to arts and letters. He was a patron of VERGIL, OVID, LIVY, and HORACE. He also established the concept of the Pax Romana [Roman peace]. He was succeeded by his stepson TIBERIUS.

**Augustus,** Polish kings. **Augustus II,** 1670–1733, was king of POLAND (r.1697–1733) and, as Frederick Augustus I, elector of Saxony (r.1694–1733). He was elected with Russian support, which continued throughout the disastrous NORTHERN WAR, turning Poland into a virtual Russian Protectorate. His death led to the War of the POLISH SUCCESSION. The victor was his son, **Augustus III,** 1696–1763, who succeeded him as king of Poland (r.1735–63). He was also, as Frederick Augustus II, elector of Saxony (r.1733–63). One of the unsuccessful claimants of the Habsburg lands, he opposed Maria Theresa for part of the War of the AUSTRIAN SUCCESSION.

**auk,** swimming and diving BIRD of the family Alcidae, which includes the PUFFIN and guillemot. Clumsy on land, auks seldom leave the water except to nest; they return to the same nesting site every year. The largest species, the flightless great auk (*Pinguinus impennis*), was hunted for its flesh, feathers, and oil; it became extinct c.1844.

**Aurangabad,** town (1981 pop. 298,937), Maharashtra state, C India, near the source of the Dudna R. It is a district and divisional, administrative and commercial centre. Set in the poor region known as Marathwada, it has a university and attracts tourists because of its historic fort (founded in the 17th cent.) and even more because of its nearness to the famous caves of Ellora (8th cent.).

**Aurangzeb** or **Aurangzib** (ˌawrəngˈzeb, -ˈzib), 1618–1707, Mogul emperor of INDIA (1658–1707), son and successor of SHAH JAHAN. He ascended the throne after defeating his three brothers and imprisoning his father. The MUGHAL Empire reached its greatest extent under him, but excessive expansion created administrative problems. These, along with agrarian disturbances and long wars with the Mahrattas, weakened the empire. He also abandoned the policy of religious toleration in the latter half of his reign.

**Aurelian** (Lucius Domitius Aurelianus), c.212–275, Roman emperor (r.270–75). He succeeded Claudius II and defended the empire vigorously against the barbarians and ambitious rulers (e.g., Zenobia of Palmyra). One of Rome's greatest emperors, Aurelian regained Britain, Gaul, Spain, Egypt, Syria, and Mesopotamia and revived the glory of Rome. He was murdered, and Marcus Claudius Tacitus succeeded him.

**Auriol, Vincent** (awˌryol), 1884–1966, French statesman, first president (1947–54) of the Fourth Republic. A Socialist until 1959, he was finance minister (1936–37) under Léon BLUM and a member of the provisional government (1945).

**Aurobindo, Sri,** 1872–1950, a mystic philosopher of modern India, a Vedantin and propounder of 'integral yoga'.

**aurochs:** see CATTLE.

**aurora,** luminous display of various forms and colours in the night sky. The aurora borealis (northern lights) and aurora australis (southern lights) are usually visible at latitudes within, respectively, the Arctic Circle and Antarctic Circle, but they are sometimes seen in middle latitudes. Both are seen most frequently at the time of the equinoxes and at times of great sunspot activity. Auroras occur at altitudes of c.55 to 950 km (35 to 600 mi) and are thought to be caused by high-speed particles from the sun excited to luminosity after colliding with air molecules.

**Auschwitz,** now **Oświęcim,** Poland: see CONCENTRATION CAMP.

**Ausonius** (Decimus Magnus Ausonius), AD 310–c.395, Latin poet; b. Bordeaux. His travel verses (*Mosella*), family sketches (*Parentalia*), and *Ordo nobilium urbium* (Order of Noble Cities), on 20 Roman cities, give portraits of people and places.

**Austen, Jane,** 1775–1817, English novelist. She spent her first 25 years at her father's Hampshire vicarage, writing novels published much later. *Northanger Abbey,* written early, appeared posthumously (with *Persuasion*) in 1818. Published in her lifetime were *Sense and Sensibility* (1811), *Pride and Prejudice* (1813), *Mansfield Park* (1814), and *Emma* (1816), comedies of manners, depicting the self-contained world of the English counties. Jane Austen's work is noted for polished irony, moral firmness, impeccable construction and vivid characterization. Her novels enjoyed only a modest popularity during her life, but today she is regarded as one of the masters of the English novel.

**Austerlitz,** Czech *Slavkov u Brna,* town, S Czechoslovakia, in Moravia. An agricultural centre with sugar refineries and cotton mills, it was a seat of the ANABAPTISTS from 1528. At Austerlitz, NAPOLEON I won (2 Dec. 1805) his greatest victory by defeating the Russian and Austrian armies. The town has an 18th-cent. castle and a 13th-cent. church.

**Austin,** US city (1984 est. pop. 397,000), state capital of Texas, on the Colorado R.; inc. 1839. It is the commercial heart of a ranching, poultry, dairy, cotton, and grain area. Hydroelectric development (beginning in the 1930s) has spurred enormous industrial growth; the city now manufactures a wide variety of products, and is a centre for electronic and scientific research. The main campus of the Univ. of Texas is in Austin. State capital since 1870, it was capital (1839–42) of the Texas Republic.

**Austin, John,** 1790–1859, British jurist. He was appointed professor of Jurisprudence at the newly formed Univ. of London (1826), only to resign (1835) in a dispute as to whether JURISPRUDENCE was an integral part of legal education. He is considered the founding father of modern jurisprudence and legal POSITIVISM.

**Austin, J(ohn) L(angshaw),** 1911–60, English philosopher. He held with WITTGENSTEIN, that everyday language was misunderstood and misused in philosophical debate on common beliefs. His distinction between 'performative' and 'constative' utterances developed into *How to Do Things with Words* (1962), in which he exemplified and defined performative as those utterances which do something by their statement, like promising or baptizing, and constative as those which convey information about something. 'A Plea for Excuses' (1956), reprinted in *Philosophical Papers* (1961) is representative of his work, which though enormously influential at the time has since passed into disrepute.

**Austin, Stephen Fuller,** 1793–1836, American colonizer, known as the Father of Texas. He took up the colonizing plans of his father, **Moses Austin,** 1761–1828, and began (1822) planting settlements in Texas between the Brazos and Colorado rivers. He later supported the Texas Revolution (1836) and was briefly secretary of state of the Republic of Texas.

**Australasia,** islands of the South Pacific, including AUSTRALIA, NEW ZEALAND, NEW GUINEA, and adjacent islands. The term sometimes includes all of OCEANIA.

**Australia,** smallest continent, 3860 km (c. 2400 mi) E to W and 3220 km (c. 2000 mi) N to S, only continent occupied by a single nation, the Commonwealth of Australia (1986 pop. 16,018,400), 7,686,810 km² (2,967,877 sq mi). Subdivisions of the nation incl the offshore island state of TASMANIA; the five mainland states of QUEENSLAND, NEW SOUTH WALES, VICTORIA, SOUTH AUSTRALIA, and WESTERN AUSTRALIA; the NORTHERN TERRITORY; and the AUSTRALIAN CAPITAL TERRITORY, containing CANBERRA, the federal capital. External territories include CHRISTMAS ISLAND, the COCOS (KEELING) ISLANDS, the CORAL SEA ISLANDS, NORFOLK ISLAND, the HEARD AND MCDONALD ISLANDS, Ashmore and Cartier Islands and the Australian Antarctic Territory. See map in separate section.

*Geography.* Australia is the flattest of the continents, as well as the oldest and most isolated. Elevations range from 12 m (39 ft) below sea level at Lake EYRE, the lowest point, to a high point of 2230 m (7316 ft) at Mt KOSCIUSKO, in the AUSTRALIAN ALPS near the New South Wales–Victoria border; much of the ancient western plateau is under 610 m (2000 ft). Two-thirds of the continent is either desert or semiarid. Humid climates are restricted to eastern coastal areas and to Tasmania. Alternating wet winters (June–Aug.) and dry summers (Nov.–Mar.) occur in small areas of South Australia and Western Australia, and dry winters and wet summers alternate along the tropical northeastern coast. The MURRAY R. and its major tributaries, the DARLING and MURRUMBIDGEE, form the principal river system. Plant and animal life is distinctive, including many species, such as the EUCALYPTUS, KOALA, KANGAROO and DUCK-BILLED PLATYPUS, found only in Australia.

*Economy and People.* Australia is the world's leading producer of wool and bauxite, and a significant supplier of iron ore, uranium, wheat, meat, dairy products, sugar, and fruit. In the late 1970s important deposits of diamonds were discovered. Manufacturing is highly developed and concentrated mainly in the coastal regions of Victoria and New South Wales. Iron, steel, motor vehicles, aircraft, electrical equipment and appliances, chemicals, and textiles are leading manufactures. The GDP for 1985–86 was $A231,977 million (US$364,429) and GDP per capita $A14,498.6 (US$22,777). SYDNEY, MELBOURNE, BRISBANE, ADELAIDE, and NEWCASTLE, all located along the SE coast, are the largest commercial and industrial centres. New South Wales and Victoria are the most populous states. Most Australians are of British or European ancestry. The indigenous population, the Australian ABORIGINES and Torres Strait Islanders, totalled 227,641 in 1986. Immigration contributes significantly to population growth; more than 3.5 million 'New Australians' entered the country between 1945 and 1980. Racially discriminatory immigration policies were officially ended in 1973.

*History and Government.* The Aborigines are thought to have come to Australia from Southeast Asia at least 40,000 years ago. The area was first visited by Europeans in the 17th cent. but attracted little interest until

Captain James COOK sailed (1770) into BOTANY BAY and claimed the entire eastern coast for Great Britain. The first settlement, a penal colony for 'transported' British convicts, was established in 1788 where Sydney now stands. By the middle of the 19th cent. free colonization had replaced the old penal settlements, and the colonies of Tasmania (1825), Western Australia (1829), South Australia (1834), Victoria (1851), and Queensland (1859) had been formally established although numerous small settlements pre-dated the formal declaration, or separation, of the colonies which provided for responsible government. Wool and wheat were early exports, and gold rushes in the 1850s in New South Wales and 1890s in Victoria and Western Australia attracted new settlers. In 1901 the colonies were federated as states of the Commonwealth of Australia, and in 1927 the seat of government was transferred from Melbourne to Canberra. As prominent member of the COMMONWEALTH, Australia fought on the side of Britain in both world wars. In WORLD WAR II the Japanese bombed or shelled DARWIN, Port Jackson, and Newcastle, and the Allied victory in the battle of the CORAL SEA (1942) probably averted an invasion of Australia. Australia joined regional defence alliances after the war, notably the ANZUS PACT, and sent troops to aid the US in the Korean and VIETNAM WARS. The nation has a popularly elected bicameral parliament. Executive power rests with the governor-general (representing the crown) and a cabinet and prime minister. In 1975 the Labour government of Prime Min. Gough WHITLAM was dismissed by the governor-general in a controversial move. A Liberal–National coalition, led by John Malcolm FRASER, won the subsequent elections. In 1983, however, a Labour government came to power under Robert (Bob) HAWKE and retained a majority in further elections in 1984 and 1987. In 1986 legislation was enacted giving Australia full legal independence from the UK, although Queen ELIZABETH II remained sovereign.

## Post-war Australian Prime ministers

Benedict Chifley (Labour), 1945–49
Robert Menzies (Liberal), 1949–66
Harold Holt (Liberal), 1966–67
John McEwen (Liberal), 1967–68
John Gorton (Liberal), 1968–71
William McMahon (Liberal), 1971–72
Gough Whitlam (Labour), 1972–75
Malcolm Fraser (Liberal), 1975–83
Robert (Bob) Hawke (Labour), 1983–

Australia

**Australian Alps,** mountain chain, SE Australia, forming the southern part of the EASTERN HIGHLANDS, high plains rather than individual mountain peaks. It reaches a high point of 2230 m (7316 ft.) at Mt KOSCIUSKO, the highest peak in Australia. The Alps provide winter ski-fields and summer hiking at several major alpine resorts.

**Australian Ballet:** see DANCE (table).

**Australian ballot,** system of voting by secret ballot. It was first advocated in Britain but introduced for the first time in 1856 in the Australian colonies. The description 'Australian ballot' became common in the US which subsequently adopted the practice.

**Australian Capital Territory,** (1986 pop. 258,900), 2432 km² (939 sq mi), SE Australia, an enclave within NEW SOUTH WALES containing CANBERRA, the capital of Australia. Most of it was ceded to the federal government by New South Wales in 1911 for use as the future capital; a small section on the E coast, at Jervis Bay, was ceded for use as a port in 1915. The territory is administered by the federal government and has an 18-member elected House of Assembly with advisory responsibilities.

**Australian languages,** aboriginal languages spoken by perhaps 130,000 persons on the continent of Australia. These languages, estimated at 100 to 600 in number, do not seem to be related to any other linguistic family and have no writing of their own. Many are already or nearly extinct.

**Australopithecus,** genus of early African hominids. It is characterized by erect trunk and bipedal locomotion, brain of 400–500 cm³ (24½–30½ cu in, chimpanzee/gorilla size), large jaws, and teeth which although large are human rather than ape-like in proportions and pattern of wear. First discoveries were from South Africa (e.g., at STERKFONTEIN), hence the name [Gr., = southern ape] and represent two species: the earlier, lighter ('gracile') *Australopithecus africanus* (around 2.5 to 3.0 million years ago) and the later, heavier *A. robustus* (around 1.5 to 2.0 million years) with enlarged cheek teeth and powerful chewing muscles. Louis LEAKEY and others later recovered East African evidence of a hyper-robust form *A. boisei* ('Zinjanthropus') with even larger cheek teeth, from OLDUVAI GORGE, TURKANA, and other sites well dated between 1.5 and 2.0 million years; a recent discovery at TURKANA suggests early *A. boisei* at 2.6 million years. Specimens from LAETOLI, Tanzania (3.6 million years) and HADAR, Ethiopia (2.8 to 3.3 million years) with larger front and smaller cheek teeth then *A. africanus* have been assigned to *A. afarensis*; the best-known specimen is the partial skeleton 'Lucy', some detailed features of which suggest arboreal climbing. The overall pattern, however, is of a ground-dwelling creature that walked upright, which is confirmed by the 3.6 million years old hominid footprints preserved at Laetoli. The South African fossils, from caves once thought to be living sites, are now regarded as due to leopard predation whereas East African finds are generally from open sites, stream beds, or lake margins. Gracile specimens are from savannah with some bush/tree cover; the robust specimens' environments were drier with fewer trees, suggesting long-term adaptation to arid seasonal conditions by exploiting terrestrial vegetation, whereas, HOMO HABILIS and HOMO ERECTUS, which coexist at some sites, occupied different niches. There are no definite tools associated with *A. africanus/afarensis*, although it is likely that they used or made tools, given modern ape behaviour. Tools are known from *A. robustus/boisei* sites, but are generally assumed to have been made by *H. habilis/erectus*, although there is no compelling evidence that this was so. See also HUMAN EVOLUTION.

**Austria,** Ger. *Österreich,* officially Republic of Austria, federal republic (1985 est. pop. 7,487,000), 83,849 km² (32,374 sq mi), central Europe; bordered by Yugoslavia and Italy (S), Switzerland and Liechtenstein (W), West Germany and Czechoslovakia (N), and Hungary (E). VIENNA is the capital; principal cities include SALZBURG, INNSBRUCK, GRAZ, and LINZ. The ALPS traverse Austria from W to E and occupy three-quarters of the country; the highest peak is the Grossglockner 3798 m (12,460 ft). Austria is drained by the DANUBE R. and its tributaries. Forestry, cattle-raising, and dairying are the main sources of livelihood in the alpine provinces. In the rest of the country tillage agriculture predominates; the chief crops are potatoes, sugar beets, barley, wheat, rye, and oats. Manufacturing (steel, chemicals, foodstuffs, textiles, and machinery) and mining (graphite, iron, magnesium, and lignite) employ nearly half of the labour force. Tourism is very important. The GNP is $69,830 million and the GNP per capita is $9210 (1983). Divided into nine provinces, Austria has a mixed presidential-parliamentary form of government. The population is predominantly German-speaking and Roman Catholic.

*History.* Located at the crossroads of Europe, Austria has been from earliest times a thoroughfare and a battleground. Settled by Celts, the area was conquered (15 BC–AD 10) by Rome; overrun (from the 5th cent.) by Huns, Goths, Lombards, and Bavarians; conquered (788) by CHARLEMAGNE; taken (after 884) by the Moravians (see MORAVIA)and then the MAGYARS; and reconquered (955) by Holy Roman Emperor OTTO I, who bestowed it (976) on the house of Babenberg. Acquired in 1251 by Ottocar II of BOHEMIA, it was claimed (1282) by RUDOLF I of Habsburg, King of the Germans, and from that time until its fall in 1918, Austrian history is that of the house of HABSBURG. (See AUSTRIAN SUCCESSION, WAR OF THE; AUSTRO-HUNGARIAN MONARCHY; AUSTRO-PRUSSIAN WAR; VIENNA, CONGRESS OF; FRENCH REVOLUTIONARY WARS; GERMAN CONFEDERATION; HOLY ALLIANCE; HOLY ROMAN EMPIRE; METTERNICH; SEVEN YEARS' WAR; THIRTY YEARS' WAR.) Following the collapse of the Austro-Hungarian monarchy at the end of WORLD WAR I, German Austria was proclaimed (1918) a republic. The Treaty of Saint-Germain (1919), which fixed its boundaries, reduced it to a small country of 7 million inhabitants, and deprived it of its raw materials, food, and markets. Chronic unemployment, bankruptcy, and political unrest followed, and in 1934 a corporative totalitarian regime was established under Engelbert DOLLFUSS (who was later assassinated) and his successor, Kurt von SCHUSCHNIGG. The nation became part of the German Third Reich in 1938, when it was occupied by German troops. After its capture (1945) by US and Soviet troops, Austria was restored as a republic. Divided into zones, it was occupied by the Allied powers until 1955, when a peace treaty declared it a sovereign and neutral power. By the 1960s the country was enjoying unprecedented prosperity. Politically, a nearly equal balance of power between conservatives and socialists resulted in a succession of coalition governments until 1966, when the conservative People's Party won a clear majority. The party was ousted in the 1970 elections by the Socialists, who, under Chancellor Bruno KREISKY, held power into the 1980s in coalition with the small Freedom Party in 1983–86. In 1983 Kreisky was succeeded by Fred Sinowatz, who himself resigned in 1986 following the presidential election victory of Kurt WALDHEIM amid controversy over his wartime record. The 1986 elections resulted in the formation of a grand coalition of the Socialist and People's parties under Chancellor Franz Vranitzky.

## Post-war Austrian presidents
Karl Renner (Socialist), 1945–50
Theodor Körner (Socialist), 1951–57
Adolf Schärf (Socialist), 1957–65
Franz Jonas (Socialist), 1965–74
Rudolf Kirchschläger (independent), 1974–86
Kurt Waldheim (independent), 1986–

## Post-war Austrian chancellors
Karl Renner (Socialist), 1945
Leopold Figl (People's Party), 1945–53
Julius Raab (People's Party), 1953–61
Alfons Gorbach (People's Party), 1961–64
Josef Klaus (People's Party), 1964–70
Bruno Kreisky (Socialist), 1970–83
Fred Sinowatz (Socialist), 1983–86
Franz Vranitzky (Socialist), 1986–

Austria

**Austrian Succession, War of the,** 1740–48, European war precipitated by the succession of MARIA THERESA to the Habsburg lands by virtue of the PRAGMATIC SANCTION. She was challenged by the elector of

Bavaria (who became Emperor CHARLES VII in 1742), PHILIP V of Spain, and AUGUSTUS III of Poland. FREDERICK II of Prussia, claiming part of Silesia, opened hostilities by invading that region. Prussia was joined by France, Spain, Bavaria, and Saxony. After being promised its Silesian claim, Prussia made a separate peace in 1742. Saxony went over to Austria in 1743, and England (at war with Spain), the United Provinces, and Sardinia became Austrian allies. Fearing Maria Theresa's growing power, Prussia reentered the war in 1744. Maria Theresa's husband was elected emperor, as FRANCIS I, in 1745, on the death of Charles VII. France defeated the English at Fontenoy, but GEORGE II defeated the French-supported Jacobites. The war dragged on in other areas, including North America (see FRENCH AND INDIAN WARS). In 1748 the Treaty of Aix-la-Chapelle ended the war. Maria Theresa's throne was safe, but Prussia had emerged as a major European power, gaining Silesia.

**Austro-Hungarian Monarchy** or **Dual Monarchy,** the HABSBURG empire from the constitutional compromise (*Ausgleich*) of 1867 until its fall in 1918. The empire was divided into two states. Cisleithania (lands W of the Leitha River) comprised Austria proper, Bohemia, Moravia, Austrian Silesia, Slovenia, and Austrian Poland. Transleithania included Hungary, Transylvania, Croatia, and part of Dalmatia. The Habsburg monarch ruled Cisleithania as emperor of Austria and ruled Transleithania as king of Hungary. Both states elected separate parliaments for internal affairs and had independent ministries, but a common cabinet dealt with foreign affairs, defence, and finances. Despite this constitutional division, the monarchy remained weakened by ethnic diversity in an age of increasing nationalism. Czech, Italian, Slavic, and Romanian minorities desired autonomy and later sought to break free of the empire. Archduke FRANCIS FERDINAND apparently had a plan for a South Slavic partner in the monarchy, but his assassination (1914) cut short this hope and precipitated WORLD WAR I. In foreign affairs Austria–Hungary allied (1879) with Germany (see TRIPLE ALLIANCE AND TRIPLE ENTENTE) and in 1908 angered SERBIA by annexing BOSNIA-HERCEGOVINA over which it had secured occupation rights (1878) at the Congress of Berlin (see BERLIN, CONGRESS OF). The empire was dissolved at the end of World War I, and Emperor CHARLES I abdicated (1918). The Treaty of Trianon and other treaties established the boundaries of the successor states.

**Austronesian,** name sometimes used for the Malayo-Polynesian languages. See LANGUAGE (table).

**Austro-Prussian War** or **Seven Weeks' War,** 15 June–23 Aug. 1866, between Austria (seconded by the various German states) and Prussia (allied with Italy). It was provoked by BISMARCK as a way of expelling Austria from the GERMAN CONFEDERATION, thereby assuring Prussian hegemony there. The pretext was a dispute between Prussia and Austria over the administration of SCHLESWIG–HOLSTEIN. Prussia quickly overran Holstein and the German states allied with Austria, and was victorious in Bohemia and Italy. The Treaty of Prague ended the war. Austria was excluded from German affairs and forced to cede Venetia to Italy. Prussia demanded no territory from Austria but annexed Hanover, Hesse, Nassau, and Frankfort, laying the groundwork for the establishment (1871) of the German empire.

**authoritarian personality,** a term denoting a character trait in which subservience to authority is associated with the belief in social conformism and with racial prejudice. The concept was developed by members of the Frankfurt School, especially Adorno, in their analysis of the rise of Fascism.

**Authorized Version,** the English translation of the BIBLE, including the APOCRYPHA, made on the orders of King James I (hence often called the 'King James' Version') and published in 1611. It was never formally authorized, but the title page bears the words 'appointed to be read in Churches'.

**autism** (ˌawtizəm), a PSYCHOPATHOLOGY in which the subject fails to relate normally and realistically to the outside world. More specifically, infantile autism is a rare but seriously psychologically impairing childhood condition associated with communicative delay, obsessional behaviour, and resistance to environmental change. The view that infantile autism is a primarily emotional disturbance has given way to the belief that it is a specific innate cognitive disability (see COGNITION).

**autograft:** see under TRANSPLANTATION, MEDICAL.

**autoimmune disease,** general term for any of a growing number of diseases in which the body produces antibodies (see IMMUNITY) against one or more of its own substances, resulting in tissue injury. For example, in systemic lupus erythematosus, individuals develop antibodies to their own nucleic acids and cell structures, causing dysfunction of many organs, including the heart, kidneys, and joints. Autoimmune diseases are treated by a variety of nonspecific IMMUNOSUPPRESSIVE DRUGS and STEROIDS.

**automatic control,** branch of knowledge dealing with self-regulating and self-correcting systems. It originated with the World War II developments in the automatic aiming and firing of very large guns at targets detected and pinpointed by radar. Britain was protected from the worst assault of missiles by 90% destruction over the English Channel using automated gunnery, where human skill and operation would have been ineffective. At sea the Italian fleet was attacked and destroyed at night at about 27.5-km (17-mi) range (Cape Matapass, Mar. 1941), a feat totally impossible before automatic control. It became apparent that all regulation and control in whatever sphere depended on common fundamental principles, some of deep mathematical sophistication, and some, like FEEDBACK, of amazing simplicity. Research in the understanding of control took place in physiology, psychology, sociology, and economics as well as in science and engineering. In the engineering field the application of automatic control enabled the AUTOMATION of many manufacturing and production processes, using devices to make and execute decisions without employing human operators. It has had a major impact in all industries from paper manufacture to newspaper printing. Robots, very flexible, computer-controlled machine tools, provide automatic skill in mass production, especially in the car industry (see ROBOTICS). Automatic control is also invaluable in hazardous environments, such as the inside of nuclear reactors, or in probes in space taking measurements of climate and features of the planets. The wider branch of knowledge covering all fields has been called cybernetics; the physiological, medical, and biological branches are classed as biocybernetics.

**automation,** the application of automatic control theory to enable systems and processes, mainly industrial, to operate without the use of human skills and operators. The system must be self-correcting and regulatory, with multiple sensing and with computers using the signals fed back from the sensing devices to make decisions and adjustments. Computers controlling large numbers of robotic arms capable of assembling components are now in standard use in the car industry. See also AUTOMATIC CONTROL, ROBOTICS.

**automatism,** term used in SURREALISM for the strategy of suppressing conscious control over composition in order to give free rein to the subconscious in the creation of a work. Often induced, either by alcohol, drugs, starvation, or hyperventilation, it is a flawed technique in that some conscious decisions as regards the work have to be made. The term is also applied to methods which exploit the element of chance, e.g., ARP's compositional method of dropping scraps of paper onto the floor.

**automobile:** see MOTOR CAR.

**autonomic nervous system:** see NERVOUS SYSTEM.

**autumnal equinox:** see EQUINOX.

**avalanche,** rapidly descending mass of snow and ice loosened from a mountain slope. Sudden and often destructive, avalanches result from the addition of a heavy snowfall to an insecure mass of ice and snow, from the melting or erosion of part of the base of the mass, or from sudden shocks such as those caused by explosions or earth tremors.

**Avebury,** a massive ceremonial site constructed in Wiltshire, S England, during the 3rd millennium BC. The HENGE consists of an outer bank and ditch, lined with a circle of 98 stones, and two smaller circles set in the central area. Two additional rows of standing stones lead from one of the four entrances to another structure about 2.5 km (1½ mi) away. Current interest in Avebury and the other great late NEOLITHIC monuments, STONEHENGE and SILBURY HILL, concerns the question of how these massive projects were integrated into a social strategy and what kind of social organization was able to marshall together and control the labour necessary to create them.

**average,** used in STATISTICS to indicate some representative value, and often derived from a SAMPLE of the total POPULATION. The ARITHMETIC MEAN is the most usual average calculated, but the MODE or the MEDIAN may be

more appropriate under certain conditions. While most attention is often given to average values in presenting statistics, the variability of the values may be more important for their interpretation. Thus, the average time that a patient has to wait for treatment in hospital may be only a few weeks, but the fact that this waiting time may range from one day to three years is probably more significant.

The stone circle at **Avebury**

**Averroës** (aˌveroheez), 1126–98, Arabic *Ibn Rushd,* Spanish–Arabian philosopher. His greatest work, his commentaries on ARISTOTLE, remained influential in the West well into the Renaissance. Averroës held that the domains of faith and reason did not conflict, and that philosophic truth derives from reason rather than faith (see SCHOLASTICISM). In this he was opposed by St THOMAS AQUINAS.

**Avesta,** sacred scripture of ZOROASTRIANISM comparable with the Vedas of early Hinduism.

**Avestan** (əˌvestən), language belonging to the Iranian group of the Indo-Iranian subfamily of the Indo-European family of languages. See LANGUAGE (table).

**aviation:** see AEROPLANE; AIR FORCES; AIR TRANSPORT; FLIGHT, POWERED.

**Avicenna** (ˈaviˌsenə), Arabic *Ibn Sina,* 980–1037, Persian philosopher and physician, the most renowned philosopher of medieval Islam. His interpretation of ARISTOTLE followed that of the Neoplatonists (see NEOPLATONISM). Avicenna's *Canon of Medicine,* a classic text, was particularly influential from 1100 to 1500.

**Avignon,** city (1982 pop. 91,474), capital of Vaucluse dept., SE France, on the Rhône R. It has a wine trade and many manufactures. The papal see during the Babylonian Captivity (1309–78), it was later (1378–1408) the residence of several antipopes (see PAPACY and SCHISM, GREAT). Avignon was joined to France after a plebiscite (1791). Medieval ramparts and the papal palace are highlights of the city.

**Ávila,** town (1981 pop. 86,584), capital of Ávila prov., central Spain. A market and administrative centre, it is principally known for its remarkable encircling walls, constructed of granite between the years 1097 and 1101. It is the birthplace of St TERESA.

**Ávila Camacho, Manuel** (ˌahveelah kahˌmahchoh), 1897–1955, president of MEXICO (1940–46). A general and a political moderate, he consolidated the reforms begun by Pres. CÁRDENAS.

**avocado,** tropical American broad-leaved evergreen tree (genus *Persea*) of the LAUREL family, and its pear-shaped fruit. The fruit has a tough, inedible, usually dark green skin and an oily flesh surrounding a large, hard seed. The flesh is eaten fresh, chiefly in salads.

**Avogadro, Amadeo, conte di Quaregna,** 1776–1856, Italian physicist. In 1811 he advanced the hypothesis (since known as Avogadro's law) that equal volumes of gases under identical conditions of pressure and temperature contain the same number of molecules. This hypothesis led to the determination by other physicists of the value of Avogadro's number, i.e., the number of molecules in one MOLE of any gas, and by extension, the number of particles in one mole of any substance. Its value is $6.022\,52 \times 10^{23}$.

**Avogadro's number:** see MOLE, in chemistry.

**avoidance relationship,** in anthropology, a relationship (e.g., mother-in-law/son-in-law, brother/sister) defined by strict decorum governing the interaction of the people concerned or even complete avoidance. Such ritualized distancing has been analysed in a variety of ways: in STRUCTURAL FUNCTIONALISM it is seen as expressing the tension and conflict implicit in such relationships in a specific society; in STRUCTURALISM, as the structural opposition between two relationships. It has also been understood, within the context of the analysis of symbolic systems, as a response to relationships or phenomena that are anomalous in the indigenous CLASSIFICATORY SYSTEM. See JOKING RELATIONSHIP.

**avoirdupois weights:** see ENGLISH UNITS OF MEASUREMENT; WEIGHTS AND MEASURES, table.

**Avon,** county, SW England (1984 est. pop. 939,800), 1345 km² (525 sq mi), bordering on the Bristol Channel. It was formed in 1974 from SW Gloucestershire and NE Somerset, and includes the towns of BRISTOL and BATH. It contains the southern part of the COTSWOLD HILLS in the east and is crossed by the R. AVON. Agriculture is an important economic activity within the county, but there is also a concentration of industry around the port at Avonmouth. Avon is connected with S Wales by the Severn road bridge (opened 1966).

**Avon, Lower,** or **Bristol Avon,** river in SW England, approximately 120 km (75 mi) long. It rises on the E slopes of the COTSWOLD HILLS, near Tetbury, Gloucestershire, and flows along a curved course past Chippenham, Melksham, Bradford-on-Avon, BATH, and BRISTOL, finally entering the Bristol Channel at Avonmouth. It is navigable by large vessels up to Bristol, and tidal to Swineford, which is E of Keynsham.

**Avon, Upper,** or **Warwickshire Avon,** river in W central England, approximately 154 km (96 mi) long. It rises near Swinford, Leicestershire, and flows generally SW past RUGBY, WARWICK, STRATFORD-UPON-AVON, and Evesham, joining the R. SEVERN at Tewkesbury.

**Awami League,** political party in PAKISTAN and BANGLADESH. Founded in 1949, it became the vehicle for the political interests of East Pakistan. When East Pakistan won independence (1971) as Bangladesh, the league became the new nation's dominant political party. However, in 1981 the National party defeated the league in national elections.

**axiom,** in MATHEMATICS and LOGIC, general statement accepted without proof as the basis for logically deducing another statement (THEOREM). Examples of axioms used widely in mathematics are those related to equality (e.g., 'If equals are added to equals, the sums are equal') and those related to operations (e.g., the ASSOCIATIVE LAW). A postulate, like an axiom, is a statement that is accepted without proof; it deals, however, with specific subject matter (e.g., properties of geometrical figures), not general statements.

**Axis,** 1936–45, coalition of countries in WORLD WAR II headed by Germany, Italy, and Japan. The coalition was sealed by the Tripartite Pact of 1940 but in fact there was minimal cooperation between the European Axis powers and Japan. They were opposed and defeated by the Allies, headed by Great Britain, the US, the Soviet Union, and China.

**Axminster,** type of patterned carpet with a thick soft tufted pile in a mixture of colours. Axminster carpets were first made by Thomas Whitty in the late 1700s at Axminster, in Devon, England. One of the first large-scale machine-weaving carpet factories, it supplied the carpets for Carlton House, London in 1790 and for the Brighton Pavilion in 1810. In modern Axminsters the pile is machine-threaded to a backing in a continuous fibre according to a predetermined pattern and then cut. A variation known as Chenille Axminster uses a woven wool strip for the weft. After weaving with this already woven material the weft is teased into fur. It is virtually double woven and of fine quality.

**Ayacucho,** city (1972 pop. 34,593), capital of Ayacucho dept., S central Peru. It is a commercial and tourist centre in a region of rich gold, silver, and nickel mines. On the nearby plains of Ayacucho, Antonio José de SUCRE won (1824) a military victory that secured Peru's independence from Spain and assured the liberation of South America.

**Ayala, Ramón Pérez de:** see PÉREZ DE AYALA, RAMÓN.

**Ayatollah Ruhollah Khomeini:** see KHOMEINI, AYATOLLAH RUHOLLAH.

**Ayckbourn, Alan,** 1939–, English playwright. He is known for such ingenious antibourgeois FARCES as *How the Other Half Loves* (1970); *Absurd Person Singular* (1973); *The Norman Conquests* (1974), a trilogy; and *Bedroom Farce* (1975). Later plays include *Season's Greetings* (1980), *Way Upstream* (1982), *A Chorus of Disapproval* (1984), and *Henceforward* (1987). He is artistic director of the Stephen JOSEPH theatre and has been an associate director of the NATIONAL THEATRE.

**Ayer, Sir Alfred Jules,** 1910–, English philosopher. His *Language, Truth and Logic* (1936), until recently the best-selling philosophy book of all time, introduced LOGICAL POSITIVISM to British philosophy. Although a lifelong adherent of the VERIFICATION PRINCIPLE, he tried to lessen its impact in his later works *The Foundations of Empirical Knowledge* (1940) and *The Problem of Knowledge* (1956).

**Ayers Rock,** sandstone monolith in Northern Territory, central Australia. Standing 960 m (2870 ft.) above sea level and 380 m (1143 ft.) above the surrounding land, this feature has served as a landmark for both European and Aboriginal travellers. The Aboriginal name 'Uluru' achieved general acceptance with the declaration of the Uluru National Park and granting of a freehold title to the Park in 1986 to the Pitjantjatjara people, traditional custodians of the sacred site. The base of the Rock measures 9 km (6 mi) with numerous caves containing Aboriginal paintings on the walls. Unusual rock features have been sculptured by water and wind erosion. A new tourist resort, Yulara, has been built outside the Park to accommodate visitors.

Ayers Rock

**Ayler, Albert,** 1936–70, black American jazz saxophonist and composer. Using excessive vibrato, the emotional intensity of his tenor saxophone playing was startlingly direct, ranging from tenderness to ferocity. A central figure in 1960s musical avant-garde, he was found dead in mysterious circumstances in New York's East R.

**Aylesbury,** county town (1981 pop. 51,999) of Buckinghamshire, S England, on plain below N escarpment of the Chiltern Hills. There are various light industries in the town, including food processing and printing. It was formerly famous for ducks and lace. There are many historic buildings and streets, including the church of St Mary (mainly 13th cent.).

**Aymara,** SOUTH AMERICAN INDIANS of the Lake TITICACA basin in Peru and Bolivia. Their language is classified as a separate unit (see AMERICAN INDIAN LANGUAGES). Believed to be the originators of the great culture seen in the ruins of TIAHUANACO, they were subjugated by the INCA (15th cent.) and by the Spanish (16th cent.) but retained their pastoral civilization and patrilineal society. Still dominant in the region today, the Aymara have adopted some aspects of Spanish culture and Christian belief.

**Ayr,** town (1981 pop. 48,493), Strathclyde region, SW Scotland, on Firth of Clyde at mouth of R. Ayr. A small resort town, its industries include engineering and the manufacture of agricultural implements and electrical equipment. The nearby village of Alloway is the birthplace of Robert BURNS. Prestwick Airport is just to the N of the town.

**Ayub Khan, Muhammad,** 1907–74, president (1958–69) of PAKISTAN. After 1951 he was commander of the Pakistani armed forces, and in 1958 he led a military coup and became president. Despite his reelection in 1965, he bowed to pressure and resigned in 1969.

**azalea,** shrubs (genus *Rhododendron*) of the HEATH family, distinguished by typically deciduous leaves and large clusters of pink, red, orange, yellow, purple, or white flowers. Most grow in damp acid soils of hills and mountains, and are native to North America and Asia. Many of the garden varieties now grown are hybrids. Most of the brilliantly flowered garden varieties are from China and Japan.

**Azaña, Manuel** (ah,thahnyah), 1880–1940, president of Spain (1936–39). A leader of the republican revolution of 1930, he served as premier (1931–33) in the first republic. He headed the Loyalist government in the SPANISH CIVIL WAR but did not play a major role in it.

**Azerbaijan Soviet Socialist Republic** or **Azerbaidzhan** ('azəbie,jahnee), constituent republic (1985 pop. 6,614,000), 86,579 km² (33,428 sq mi), SE European USSR, in Transcaucasia. It is bounded by the Dagestan Republic (N); Iran (S), where the Araks R. divides it from Iranian Azerbaijan; the Caspian Sea (E); and the Armenian SSR (W). The capital is BAKU. The area is sheltered from moist west winds from the Black Sea by parts of the Caucasus Mts, and thus has a continental climate prone to drought. Three-quarters of cultivated land is irrigated, and cotton is the major crop. The area is rich in oil, iron ore, and other minerals. Oil is the most important industry, centred around Baku on the western shore of the Caspian Sea. In addition to the Turkic-speaking Shiite Muslim Azerbaijani majority, there are Russian, Armenian, and other minorities. Under Persian and Mongol rule from ancient times, the region was acquired by Russia from Persia between 1813 and 1828. It became a Soviet republic in 1920, and a constituent republic in 1936.

**Azhar,** an important mosque. Founded in Cairo by the FATIMIDS as a centre for propaganda and devotion for the ISMA'ILIS in the 10th cent., it became a major centre of SUNNISM after SALADIN reestablished it as the official creed. Since then, it has been one of the major international centres of Muslim learning, and its educational functions have now been organized as a modern university.

**azimuth:** see ASTRONOMICAL COORDINATE SYSTEMS.

**Azoic time:** see GEOLOGICAL ERAS (table).

**Azores,** island group belonging to Portugal (1984 est. pop. 250,699), 2344 km² (905 sq mi), located in the Atlantic Ocean, 1,448 km (900 mi) west of mainland Portugal. The nine main islands are São Miguel (the largest) and Santa Maria in the SE; Terceira, Pico, Fayal, São Jorge, and Graciosa in the centre; and Flores and Corvo in the NW. Ponta Delgado, on São Miguel, is the largest city. The islands are divided into three districts named after their capitals: Ponta Delgado, Angra do Heroísmo (on Terceira), and Horta (on Fayal).

**Azorín:** see MARTÍNEZ RUIZ, JOSÉ.

**Aztec,** MIDDLE AMERICAN INDIANS dominating central Mexico at the time of the Spanish conquest (16th cent.), with a Nahuatlan language of the Uto-Aztecan stock (see AMERICAN INDIAN LANGUAGES). Until the founding of their capital, Tenochtitlán (c.1325), the Aztec were a poor nomadic tribe in the valley of Mexico. In the 15th cent. they became powerful, subjugating the Huastec to the north and the MIXTEC and Zapotec to the south, and achieving a composite civilization based on a TOLTEC and Mixteca–Puebla heritage. Engineering, architecture, art, mathematics, astronomy, sculpture, weaving, metalwork, music, and picture writing were highly developed; agriculture and trade flourished. The nobility, priesthood, military, and merchant castes predominated. War captives were sacrificed to the many Aztec gods, including the god of war, Huitzilopochti. In 1519, when CORTÉS arrived, many subject peoples willingly joined the Spanish against the Aztecs. Cortés captured MONTEZUMA, who was subsequently murdered, and razed Tenochtitlán. Many Mexicans and Mexican-Americans today retain an awareness of their Aztec heritage.

**Azuela, Mariano,** 1873–1952, Mexican novelist. *Los de abajo* (1916; tr. The Underdogs), tracing the career of an Indian, grew out of his service as a surgeon with VILLA's revolutionary forces. Other novels of Mexico's 20th-cent. social conflicts include *Las mascas* (1918; tr. The Flies) and *San Gabriel de Valdivias* (1938).

**B,** chemical symbol of the element BORON.

**Ba,** chemical symbol of the element BARIUM.

**Ba, Ma,** c.1820–67, Muslim religious leader and ruler of the kingdom of Baddibu in the Senegambia region of W Africa. He conquered the kingdoms of Saloum and Niumi but died attempting to take the kingdom of Sine.

**Bā, Mariama,** 1929–81, Senegalese feminist and educationist. Her epistolary novel *Une si longue lettre* (1979; tr. *So Long a Letter*, 1981) won international acclaim for superb insights into African male exploitation of women.

**Baade, Walter** (ˌbɑhdə), 1893–1960, German-American astronomer. He presented evidence for the existence of two different stellar populations of older and newer stars. Baade knew that, at the then-accepted distance of the Andromeda galaxy, cluster-type variable stars should have appeared on photographs that he took with the 5.08-m (200-in) telescope at Palomar Observatory. From this and other evidence he established that the previous estimate of the distance to all galaxies should be at least doubled.

**Baader–Meinhof gang,** popular name for the Red Army Faction, a West German left-wing urban terrorist group responsible for many violent actions in the 1970s. Its two original leaders, Andreas Baader and Ulrike Meinhof, both died in prison (suicide verdicts were returned), and many other activists were brought to justice. In the 1980s the movement, although still operational, has been less prominent.

**Baal,** plural **Baalim** (bahl), [Semitic, = possessor], the OLD TESTAMENT term for the deity or deities of CANAAN. First applied to local gods, it was later the name of the chief deity. His cult practised holy PROSTITUTION and child sacrifice. In Israel it was denounced by Hebrew Prophets. The name is synonomous with evil, hence Beelzebub (see SATAN).

**Baal-Shem-Tov** [Heb., = master of the good name, i.e., the name of God], c.1698–1760, Jewish founder of modern HASIDISM; b. Poland as Israel ben Eliezer. He was called Baal-Shem-Tov because of his reputation as a miracle healer. Central to his teachings is the notion that spirituality is not necessarily dependent upon rabbinic distinction, but can infuse the soul of simple, uneducated, but righteous-living, folk. Also, that one must worship God in all activities and with joy. He had a large circle of followers from which developed communities of modern Hasidism.

**Baath Arab Socialist Party:** see IRAQ; SYRIA.

**Babbage, Charles,** 1792–1871, English mathematician, given the credit for the invention of computing machines. He worked on the theory of logarithms and developed plans for an 'analytical engine', a mechanical computer which could be 'programmed' from punched cards to store digits and perform addition and subtraction; although it was decimal rather than binary in conception, it clearly anticipated the modern digital COMPUTER. He was helped in his work by Ada, countess Lovelace, daughter of Byron, herself a keen mathematician and writer of papers on the novelty of using machines to aid computation, who supported Babbage both intellectually and financially in building his mechanical computing engine now in the Science Museum, Kensington, London. Babbage also wrote on mass production and on what is now called OPERATIONAL RESEARCH; he became professor of mathematics at Cambridge Univ.

**Babbitt, Milton,** 1916–, American composer; b. Philadelphia. His 'total serialization' attempts to apply serialism to all the elements of composition: dynamics, timbre, and rhythm, as well as melody and harmony (see SERIAL MUSIC; TWELVE-TONE MUSIC).

**Babel** (ˌbaybəl), in the BIBLE, Babylonian city where NOAH's descendants (who spoke one language) tried to build a tower reaching to heaven. For this presumption they lost the ability to speak intelligibly to each other. Gen. 11.1–9.

**Babel, Isaac Emmanuelovich** (ˌbabil), 1894–1941, Soviet writer. A brilliant stylist, he won fame with *Odessa Tales* (1923–24), depicting Jewish ghetto life, and *Red Cavalry* (1926), which drew on his Civil War experiences. His works also include the novel *Benia Krik* (1927), about a Jewish bandit, and the plays *Sunset* (1928) and *Maria* (1935). He was arrested in 1939 and died in a Soviet labour camp.

**Bab el Mandeb,** strategic strait between Arabia and NE Africa, 27 km (17 mi) wide, connecting the RED SEA with the Gulf of ADEN. It is a vital link in the MEDITERRANEAN SEA–SUEZ CANAL–INDIAN OCEAN sea lane. The eastern shore is occupied by Southern Yemen (S) and Yemen (N) and the western shore by Djibouti (S) and Ethiopia (N). PERIM Island is situated in the middle of the strait.

**Babenberg** (ˌbahbənbeək), ruling house of AUSTRIA (976–1246). As margraves and later dukes of Austria, the family extended its rule eastwards by colonization and kept peace by intermarriage with the ruling families of Bohemia and Poland.

**Babeuf, François Noël** (baˌbuhf), 1760–97, French revolutionary activist. In 1794 he founded a political journal that argued for economic as well as political equality. Imprisoned in 1795, he emerged even more convinced of his communist views. He formed a secret society called the Conspiracy of Equals and plotted to overthrow the government of the DIRECTORY. The plot was discovered, and Babeuf was executed.

**Babington, Anthony,** 1561–86, English conspirator. He was executed for plotting the murder of ELIZABETH I and the freeing of MARY QUEEN OF SCOTS. The evidence against him convinced Elizabeth that it was necessary to behead Mary.

**Babism,** a 19th-cent. Persian sect, an outgrowth of Shi'ite Islam that was founded by Mirza Ali Muhammad of Shiraz, who proclaimed himself the Bab [gate] in 1844. Babism, incorporating elements of SUFISM, GNOSTICISM, and SHI'ISM, centred on a belief in the coming of the Promised One. Oppressed from 1845, the movement declared its complete secession from ISLAM in 1848, and in 1863 the Babists were expelled from Persia. After 1868 a division had its centre in Acre, under the leadership of BAHA ULLAH, the founder of BAHA'ISM.

**Babits, Mihály,** 1883–1941, Hungarian poet, novelist, and essayist. His studied verse used the classical and West European traditions. The novel *The Calif Stork* (1916), while derivative, introduced psychoanalytical thought into Hungarian literature. His *History of European Literature* (1935) remains a work of exquisite literary-critical synthesis.

**baboon,** large, powerful, ground-living MONKEY (genus *Papio*), also called dog-faced monkey, related to the MANDRILL. Found in the open country of Africa and Asia, baboons have close-set eyes under heavy brow ridges, long, heavy muzzles, powerful jaws, cheek pouches for storing food, and sharp, tusklike upper canine teeth. Baboons have a highly developed social structure.

**Babur,** 1483–1530, founder of the MOGUL empire in INDIA. A descendant of TAMERLANE, he invaded India from Afghanistan. He defeated (1526) the sultan of Delhi, captured Agra and Delhi, and later conquered most of N India. Babur was a poet; his autobiography is his major work.

**Babylon,** ancient city of Mesopotamia, on the Euphrates R. It became one of the most important cities of the ancient Near East when HAMMURABI made it the capital of his kingdom of BABYLONIA. The city was destroyed (c.689 BC) by the Assyrians under SENNACHERIB, but it was rebuilt. The brilliant colour and luxury of Babylon became legendary from the days of NEBUCHADNEZZAR (d. 562 BC). The Hanging Gardens were one of the SEVEN WONDERS OF THE WORLD. The Persians captured the city in 538 BC.

**Babylonia,** ancient empire of Mesopotamia. Historically the name refers to the first dynasty of Babylon established by HAMMURABI (c.1750 BC) and to the Neo-Babylonian period after the fall of the Assyrian empire. Hammurabi, who had his capital at BABYLON, issued a famous code of laws for the management of his large empire. Babylonian religion and cuneiform writing were derived from the older culture of SUMER and the quasi-feudal society was divided into classes. These Babylonian institutions influenced ASSYRIA and so contributed to the later history of the Middle East and of Western Europe. Babylonia degenerated into anarchy (c.1180 BC), but flourished once again as a subsidiary state of the Assyrian empire after the 9th cent. BC. Later, Nabopolassar established (625 BC) what is generally known as the Chaldean or New Babylonian empire, which reached its height under his son NEBUCHADNEZZAR. In 538 BC the last of the Babylonian rulers surrendered to CYRUS THE GREAT of Persia.

**Babylonian art:** see SUMERIAN AND BABYLONIAN ART.

**Babylonian captivity,** in the history of Israel, the period from the fall of Jerusalem (586 BC) to the reconstruction in Palestine of a new Jewish state (after 538 BC). Following the capture of the city by the Babylonians, thousands of Jews were deported to Mesopotamia. In 538 BC the Persian King CYRUS THE GREAT decreed the restoration of worship at Jerusalem. The century following this decree was the time of Jewish reintegration into a national and religious unit (see also EZRA).

**baby's breath,** name for plants of the genus *Gypsophila* of the PINK family, with profuse small, usually white flowers.

**Bacău** (ˌbacow), city (1983 pop. 156,891), MOLDAVIA, E Romania, on the Bistriţa R. The city has utilized resources of water and water-power and of local timber to develop woodworking, paper and cellulose industries.

**Bacchanalia,** in Roman religion, festival honouring BACCHUS, god of wine. Originally a religious ceremony, it led to drunken, licentious excesses and was outlawed (186 BC).

**Bacchus** (ˌbakəs), in Greek and Roman mythology, god of wine, vegetation, and fertility. His name is the Lydian version of DIONYSUS. His worship was celebrated in orgiastic rites such as the Bacchanalia; these were especially popular with women, and were dramatized by EURIPIDES in the *Bacchae.*

**Bacchylides** (baˌkilideez), fl. c.470 BC, Greek LYRIC poet. He was a competent writer of DITHYRAMBS, but he lacked the inspiration of his contemporary PINDAR.

**Bach,** family of distinguished musicians who lived in central Germany from the 16th through to the 18th cent., its most renowned member being **Johann Sebastian Bach** (see separate article). **Johannes, or Hans, Bach,** 1580–1626, was a carpetweaver and musical performer at festivals. His sons and descendants were noted organists and composers. One grandson, **Johann Ambrosius Bach,** 1645–95, a musician, was the father of Johann Sebastian Bach. **Johann Christoph Bach,** 1671–1721, Johann Sebastian's eldest brother, was an organist; he took his younger brother in and taught him after their parents' death. Of the 20 children of Johann Sebastian, several were noted as musicians. The eldest son, **Wilhelm Friedemann Bach,** 1710–84, was a brilliant organist and well-known composer, but his life ended in poverty. A younger son was **Carl Philipp Emanuel Bach,** 1714–88, also a composer and for 28 years (1740–68) the harpsichordist of Frederick the Great. He wrote an important treatise, *Essay on the True Art of Playing Keyboard Instruments* (1753). The youngest son, **Johann Christian Bach,** 1735–82, known as

the 'English Bach', became (1762) music master to King GEORGE III. A popular composer in the rococo style, he influenced the young MOZART.

**Bach, Alexander,** 1813–93, Austrian politician. As minister of the interior (1849–59) he centralized and Germanized Habsburg lands and ended internal tariffs. His system met with opposition, especially in Hungary, and was replaced after 1859.

**Bach, Johann Sebastian,** 1685–1750, German composer and organist. Born into a gifted family, Bach was trained in music from childhood by his father, Johann Ambrosius, and later by his brother Johann Christoph. He held a variety of posts from 1703, serving as organist in Arnstadt (1703–7), Mühlhausen (1707–8), and Weimar (1708–17) before becoming (1717) musical director for Prince Leopold at Cöthen. After the death (1720) of his first wife, Maria Barbara Bach, he married (1721) Anna Magdalena Wilcken. Of his 20 children, 12 died in infancy and several became noted musicians (see separate article). In 1723, Bach became cantor and music director of St Thomas Church, Leipzig, a post that he held until his death in 1750. In his instrumental and choral works, Bach perfected the art of POLYPHONY and brought the era of BAROQUE music to its culmination. During his lifetime he was better known as a virtuoso organist than as a composer, but since the 19th cent. his genius has been recognized, and his reputation has grown steadily. In his early years as organist, he composed a series of works for organ that culminated in the great preludes and FUGUES written at Weimar. At Cöthen he focused on instrumental compositions, such as the Brandenburg Concertos, and keyboard works, such as Book I of the celebrated *Well-Tempered Clavier* (1722). His superb religious compositions from the period in Leipzig include the *St John Passion* (1724), the *St Matthew Passion* (1727), the *Mass in B Minor* (1747), and some 300 sacred CANTATAS, of which nearly 200 are extant. His last notable pieces are the *Musical Offering,* composed (1747) for Frederick the Great, and the *Art of the Fugue* (1749).

**bachelor's buttons,** popular name for several plants usually characterized by small, rounded flowers, especially *Ranunculus acris.*

**Bachmann, Ingeborg,** 1926–73, Austrian poet and novelist. Her two early, highly-praised volumes of poetry, *Die gestundete Zeit* (1953; tr. Time Hour by Hour) and *Anrufung des grossen Bären* (1956; tr. Appeal of the Great Bear) are rich elaborations on the themes of hurt love, and personal and national silence and guilt. With *The Thirtieth Year* (1961) she moved into prose fiction and autobiography. A long creative crisis, registered in the poem *Keine Delikatessen* (1964, pub. 1968; tr. No Delicacies) culminated in prose fictions portraying women harmed by men, collected as *Kinds of Death* (1978). These, as much as her poetry, are the basis of her posthumous reputation.

**Back, Sir George,** 1796–1878, British sailor and explorer. A naval officer, he accompanied and led a number of important expeditions to the N American Arctic in the early 19th cent., including exploration of the Coppermine, Mackenzie, and Great Fish rivers. He received the medal of the Royal Geographical Society in 1835 and was made a baronet in 1838, the year after his retirement.

**backbencher,** ordinary elected member of British parliament, or other representative assembly; as opposed to government ministers or opposition party leaders who customarily sit on the front benches.

**backbone:** see SPINAL COLUMN.

**backgammon,** game of chance and skill played by two persons on a specially marked board divided by a space (bar) into two 'tables', each of which has 12 alternately coloured points (elongated triangular spaces) on which each player places 15 counters in a prescribed formation. Two dice are thrown to determine moves. The object is to be the first to move one's pieces around and off the board. The game has very ancient roots in the Middle East.

**Bacon, Francis,** 1561–1626, English philosopher, essayist, and statesman. After his opposition (1584) to Queen Elizabeth I's tax programme retarded his political advancement, he was favoured by the earl of Essex, whom Bacon later helped to prosecute (1601). Under James I he advanced from knight (1603) to attorney general (1613) to lord chancellor (1618). In 1621 he pleaded guilty to charges of accepting bribes and was fined and banished from office; he spent the rest of his life writing in retirement. Bacon's best-known writings are his aphoristic *Essays* (1597–1625). He projected a major philosophical work, the *Instauratio magna,* but completed only two parts: the *Advancement of*

Learning (1605), later expanded in Latin as *De augmentis scientarum* (1623); and the *Novum organum* (1620). His major contribution to philosophy was his application of INDUCTION, the approach used by modern science, rather than the a priori method of medieval SCHOLASTICISM.

**Bacon, Francis,** 1910–, British painter; b. Ireland. Self-taught, with his first large work, *Three Studies* for the base of a *Crucifixion* (1944; Tate Gall., London), he became one of the most controversial of postwar British painters. His figures, distorted and blurred, 'like a snail leaving a trail', and located in ambiguous space frames explore the ugly, horrific, and disgusting side of humanity.

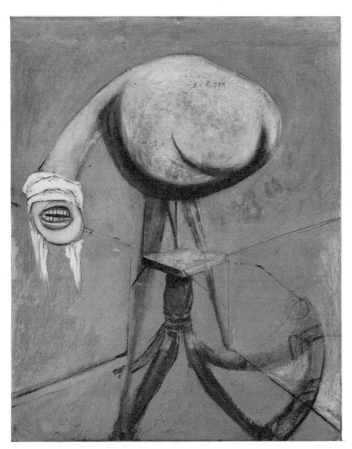

Francis **Bacon**, centre panel from the *Three Studies for the Base of a Crucifixion*, 1944. Oil and pastel on hardboard, 98 × 73.5 cm. Tate Gallery, London.

**Bacon, Nathaniel,** 1647–76, American leader of Bacon's Rebellion in colonial Virginia. Dissatisfied with the regime of the governor, Sir William BERKELEY, and its neglect of frontier defence, Bacon led (1676) a popular uprising. He drove Berkeley from JAMESTOWN, but his sudden death from malaria ended the revolt.

**Bacon, Roger,** c.1214–94?, English scholastic philosopher and scientist, a FRANCISCAN. A celebrated teacher at Oxford, Bacon had an interest far in advance of his times in natural science and accurate observation of phenomena, without, however, abandoning his faith. Three of his most important works, summarizing his studies, were written for Pope CLEMENT I in one year (1267–68): the *Opus majus, Opus minor,* and the *Opus tertium.* Deeply interested in alchemy, Bacon was credited by contemporaries with great learning in magic. Many discoveries have been attributed to him, including the invention of gunpowder and the first examination of cells through a microscope, but much doubt has been cast on the authenticity of such claims.

**bacteria,** microscopic, unicellular organisms having typical forms: rod-shaped (bacillus), round (coccus), spiral (spirillum), comma-shaped (vibrio), or corkscrew-shaped (spirochaete). The cytoplasm of most bacteria is surrounded by a cell wall; the nucleus contains DNA but lacks the nuclear membrane found in higher plants and animals (see CELL). Many forms are motile, propelled by filamentlike appendages (flagella).

Reproduction is chiefly by simple division of cells (MITOSIS), but conjugation (transfer of genetic material between two cells) and other forms of genetic recombination also occur. Some bacteria (aerobes) can grow only in the presence of free or atmospheric oxygen; others (anaerobes) cannot grow in its presence; and a third group (facultative anaerobes) can grow with or without it. In unfavourable conditions, many species form resistant spores. Different types of bacteria are capable of innumerable chemical metabolic transformations, e.g., PHOTOSYNTHESIS and the conversion of free nitrogen and sulphur into AMINO ACIDS. Bacteria are both useful and harmful to humans. Some are used for soil enrichment with leguminous plants (See NITROGEN CYCLE), in pickling, in alcohol and cheese fermentation, to decompose organic wastes (in septic tanks and the soil), and in GENETIC ENGINEERING. Others, called pathogens, cause a number of plant and animal diseases, including CHOLERA, SYPHILIS, TYPHOID FEVER, and TETANUS.

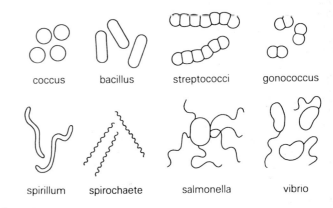

coccus    bacillus    streptococci    gonococcus

spirillum    spirochaete    salmonella    vibrio

Bacteria

**bacteriological warfare:** see BIOLOGICAL WARFARE.

**bacteriophage** or **phage** (bak͵tiəriə'fayj), VIRUS that attacks BACTERIA, sometimes destroying them. A phage has a head composed of PROTEIN and an inner core of NUCLEIC ACID. It invades by attaching itself by its tail to the bacterial cell wall and injecting nucleic acid (DNA) into its host, in which it then grows and replicates. Eventually the bacterial cell is destroyed by lysis, or dissolution, releasing the phage particles to infect other cells. Phages are highly specific, with a particular phage infecting only certain species of bacteria; they are important tools in studies of bacterial genetics and cellular mechanisms.

**Bactria** (͵baktreeə), ancient Greek kingdom in central Asia. Its capital was Bactra (now Balkh, in N Afghanistan). A satrapy of the Persian Empire, it fell to ALEXANDER THE GREAT in 328 BC. It declared its independence in 256 BC and became a powerful state, carrying its conquests deep into N India. Later Bactria fell (c.130 BC) to the nomadic Sakas and did not rise again as a state.

**Badajoz** ('bada͵hoths), city (1981 pop. 114,361), capital of Badajoz Prov., W Spain. The old capital of Estremadura, it is close to the Portuguese frontier in the valley of the Guadiana. It has suffered many sieges because of its border position, notably in the PENINSULAR WAR when it fell to the French and was liberated with great loss of life by Wellington in 1812. Its 13th-cent. cathedral is large and defensive.

**Baden-Baden,** city (1984 pop. 52,600), in BLACK FOREST region of Baden-Württemberg, West Germany. Its mineral springs have been known since Roman times and it is one of the best-known health resorts in Europe.

**Baden-Powell of Gilwell, Robert Stephenson Smyth Baden-Powell,** 1st **baron,** 1857–1941, British soldier, founder of the BOY SCOUTS. For his work in organizing (1908) the Boy Scout and GIRL GUIDE movements, he received a peerage in 1929.

**badger,** any of several related members of the WEASEL family. Most are large, nocturnal burrowers with broad, heavy bodies, long snouts, sharp claws, and long, grizzled fur. The Old World badger (*Meles meles*), found in Europe and N Asia, weighs about 13 kg (30 lb) and feeds on earthworms, rodents, insects, and plants. The smaller American badger (*Taxidea taxus*) has short legs and a white stripe over the forehead and around each eye. Badgers' extensive underground homes, called setts, are large, well organized, and kept very clean. A sett may be as deep as 9 m (30 ft) below ground level.

**badlands,** a term used to describe an area deeply dissected by ravines and gullies where the rate of erosion is relatively high and vegetation sparse or absent. Originally badlands were attributed to intense fluvial erosion though other nonfluvial processes such as mass-wasting are now regarded as influential. Badlands are characteristically formed on unconsolidated sediments that have little resistance to erosion and in semiarid climates. Removal of vegetation cover can initiate their development.

**badminton,** game played by two or four persons in which a shuttlecock (small, cork hemisphere with feathers) is volleyed over a net with light, gut-strung rackets. For singles play the court measures 13.40 by 5.18 m (44 by 17 ft); the doubles court is .91 m (3 ft) wider. The game, which is generally similar to tennis, probably originated in India.

**Badoglio, Pietro** (ba,dolyoh), 1871–1956, Italian soldier and premier (1943–44). In 1936 he brought the conquest of Ethiopia to a victorious end. After the fall of MUSSOLINI he became premier and negotiated an armistice (1943) with the Allies.

**Baeda** : see BEDE, SAINT.

**Baedeker, Karl,** 1801–59, German publisher of travel guides. Translated into many languages, the 'Baedekers' provided historical data. Auto touring guides were issued after 1950.

**Baer, Karl Ernst von,** 1792–1876, Estonian biologist. Considered a founder of modern embryology, he discovered the notochord as well as the mammalian egg in the ovary. In his *History of the Development of Animals* (2 vol., 1828–37), Baer presented the theory of embryonic germ layers (consisting of cells from which body tissues and organs develop) and showed that early embryonic development is similar in all animals.

**Baffin, William,** c.1584–1622, English Arctic explorer. Although he failed to find the NORTHWEST PASSAGE on two expeditions (1615–16), he discovered BAFFIN BAY. His belief that the Northwest Passage did not exist delayed Arctic exploration for a time.

**Baffin Bay,** ice-clogged body of water with hazardous icebergs, 1130 km (c.700 mi) long, between Greenland and Baffin Island (NE Canada), linked with the N Atlantic Ocean by the Davis Strait. Visited (1585) by John Davis and explored (1616) by William BAFFIN, it was an important whaling ground in the 19th cent.

**Baffin Island,** 476,068 km² (183,810 sq mi), NE Canada, largest island in the Arctic Archipelago and fifth largest in the world. Largely tundra in the W and mountains in the E, it is inhabited mainly by ESKIMO. Frobisher Bay (Iqaluit), in the SE, is the largest settlement. Early explorers were Sir Martin FROBISHER (1576–78) and William BAFFIN (1616).

**Bagehot, Walter** (,bajət), 1826–77, English social scientist. Editor (1860–77) of the highly regarded *Economist,* he studied the English banking system (*Lombard Street,* 1873) and economy (*Economic Studies,* 1880). His classic *English Constitution* (1867) distinguished effective government institutions from those which were merely ceremonial, while *Physics and Politics* (1872) was an early application of DARWINISM to the social sciences. Bagehot was also a noted literary critic (*Literary Studies,* 1879).

**Baghdad** or **Bagdad,** city (1981 est. pop. 3,500,000), capital and largest city of Iraq, central Iraq, on both banks of the Tigris R. Most of Iraq's industries are in Baghdad; they include the making of carpets, leather, textiles, and cement. The present city was founded (AD 762) by the ABBASIDS and became their capital. Under the caliph HARUN AR-RASHID it developed into one of the great cities of Islam. The Mongols sacked Baghdad in 1258; it became (1638) part of the Ottoman Empire, and during World War I it was captured (1917) by the British. In 1921 the city was made the capital of newly created Iraq. Baghdad is rich in archaeological remains and has several museums. It has suffered some damage from air and rocket attacks during the recent Iran-Iraq War.

**bagpipe,** an ancient musical instrument, most widely used in Ireland and Scotland, but many different types are indigenous from the Atlantic coast of Europe to the Caucasus, and outside Europe to Tunisia and India. It consists of an inflated bag, usually leather; one or two chanters (or chaunters), melody pipes with finger holes; and one or more drones, which produce one tone each.

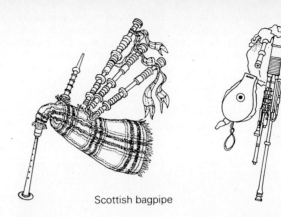

Scottish bagpipe          Irish bagpipe

Bagpipe

**Baha'ism,** religion founded by BAHA ULLAH, a doctrinal outgrowth of BABISM, with Baha Ullah as the Promised One of the earlier religion. Emphasizing simplicity and charity, Baha'ists believe in the unity of all religions, in universal education, in world peace, and in the equality of men and women, and also advocate an international language and government. In the 20th cent. Baha'i teachings have spread across the world, particularly to Africa. The administrative centre of the world faith is in Haifa, Israel.

**Bahamas,** officially Commonwealth of the Bahamas, independent nation (1984 est. pop. 228,000), 13,900 km² (5400 sq mi), in the Atlantic Ocean, consisting of some 700 islands and islets and about 2400 cays, beginning c.80 km (50 mi) off SE Florida and extending c.970 km (600 mi) SE, nearly to Haiti. Most of the islands are low, flat, and riverless, and many are uninhabited. The capital is NASSAU, on New Providence island, which, although smaller than many of the other islands, is the major population centre. Other islands, called 'out islands', include Grand Bahama, Great and Little Abaco, the Biminis, and Great and Little Inagua. The Bahamas' fine beaches, lush vegetation, and colourful coral reefs have made it one of the hemisphere's most popular winter resort areas. Tourism is the major industry, although sugar and oil refining industries have been added to diversify the economy. The GDP is US$1609 million and the GDP per capita is US$7061. The population is about 85% black and mulatto, and the language is English.

*History.* Christopher COLUMBUS first set foot in the New World in the Bahamas (1492), presumably on the island of San Salvador. The British settled the Bahamas in the 1600s and imported blacks to work cotton plantations, which disappeared in the mid 19th cent., after the slaves were freed. Black Bahamians won control of the government from the white minority in the 1960s, and independence was granted in 1973, with the Bahamas becoming a member of the COMMONWEALTH. The Progressive Liberal Party, led by Lynden Oscar PINDLING, has been in power since 1967. In the early 1980s the government sought to preserve the character of the islands by restricting the sale of property to foreigners and stemming immigration from HAITI.

**Bahasa Indonesia,** another name for Indonesian, one of the Malayo-Polynesian languages. See LANGUAGE (table).

**Baha Ullah** or **Baha Allah,** 1817–92, Persian religious leader, originally named Mirza Husayn Ali Nuri. One of the first disciples of BABISM, in 1863 (shortly before being exiled to Constantinople) he declared himself to be the Promised One expected by Babists. He then founded BAHA'ISM and wrote its fundamental book, *Kitabi Ikan* (tr. *The Book of Certitude,* 1943).

**Bahrain** or **Bahrein** (bah,rayn), officially the State of Bahrain, independent sheikhdom (1983 est. pop. 384,221), 598 km² (231 sq mi), an archipelago in the PERSIAN GULF between the Qatar Peninsula and Saudi Arabia. The two main islands are Bahrain and Al Muharraq. The capital and chief port is AL MANAMAH. Flat and sandy, with a few low hills, Bahrain has a hot, humid climate. The economy is based on oil, and oil revenues have financed extensive modernization projects, particularly in health and education. However, oil reserves are expected to be depleted before the end of the 20th cent., and steps are being taken to diversify the nonagricultural sector of the economy. The GNP is US$4612 million and the GNP per capita is US$11,530 (1983). The majority of the population are Muslim Arabs. Ruled successively by Portugal (16th cent.) and Persia (intermittently from 1602), Bahrain became a sheikhdom in 1783 and a British protected state in 1861. Independence was declared in 1971. A constitution, adopted in 1973, limited the powers of the sheikh and granted women the right to vote, but in 1975 the sheikh dissolved the National Assembly. In the early 1980s the generally pro-Western government of Sheikh Isa bin Sulman al-Khalifa established closer ties with neighbouring states within the framework of the GULF COOPERATION COUNCIL, although relations with Qatar have been aggravated by a longrunning territorial dispute.

**Bai Juyi,** 772–846, Chinese poet. A prolific author, he wrote in simple, clear language. *Everlasting Wrong* (806), his most noted poem, recounts the sufferings of Emperor Ming Huang (685–762) and Yang Guifei, his ill-fated concubine.

**Baikal, Lake:** see BAYKAL.

**bail,** in law, the release of an accused person awaiting trial. The granting of bail dates back to Anglo-Saxon times, though the first English act was not until 1876. In the UK, it is now governed by the Bail Act 1976. When released on bail, the accused is placed in the hands of sureties, who deposit money with the court as a guarantee for bringing the defendant to court on a specified day. The granting of bail is usually subject to conditions imposed on the accused, e.g., that they surrender their passport or report regularly to the police. Bail may be granted by the police or a court, though it can be refused and the accused remanded in custody. Failure to surrender to the court at the end of the period of bail is a criminal offence. See REMAND.

**Bailey, David,** 1938–, British photographer. Born in the East End of London, he first worked as assistant to the fashion photographer John French. Bailey's fresh and irreverent approach to fashion photographs launched his career as a fashion photographer and made him a leader of style in the emergent pop culture of the 1960s.

**bailiff,** in UK law, a person appointed by a court with responsibility to carry out the business of the court. Historically in the UK and currently in the Channel Islands, a bailiff is a legal officer entrusted with the administration of justice in a local area, known as a bailiwick. The modern functions of the bailiff include the serving of documents, summoning juries, and enforcing court judgments. A bailiff is entitled both to take away goods and evict people under a court order.

**bailiwick:** see BAILIFF.

**Bairiki,** town (1979 est. pop. 1,800) on TARAWA atoll, capital of KIRIBATI.

**Baja California** or **Lower California** (ˌbaha), peninsula, NW Mexico, separating the Gulf of California from the Pacific Ocean. It is c.1220 km (760 mi) long and 48 to 241 km (30 to 150 mi) wide, and is divided between the states of Baja California (N) and Baja California Sur (S). The peninsula is generally mountainous and arid, with some irrigated agriculture in the N, around Mexicali. Resort ranches, new roads, and deep-sea fishing facilities along the scenic coasts support a growing tourist industry. US forces occupied (1847–48) the peninsula during the MEXICAN WAR.

**Ba Jin,** pseud. of **Li Feigan,** 1904–, Chinese writer. Born in Sichuan to a wealthy gentry family, Ba Jin identified early with the anarchist movement. He studied for two years in Paris (1927–29). His most famous novel is *Jia* [family] (1931), the first volume of a semiautobiographical trilogy *Ji Liu*. He has continued to write essays and short stories and has sat on various cultural committees since 1949.

**Bakelite** [after its inventor, Leo Baekeland], a synthetic thermosetting phenol-formaldehyde RESIN with an unusually wide variety of industrial applications ranging from billiard balls to electrical insulation.

**Baker, Dame Janet,** 1933–, English mezzo-soprano. Acclaimed as an ORATORIO and LIEDER singer, she has also appeared in such operas as Berlioz's *The Trojans,* and Mozart's *Così fan tutte* and Handel's *Julius Caesar.*

**Baker, Sir Samuel White,** 1821–93, English explorer. After founding an agricultural colony in Ceylon (now Sri Lanka), he set out in 1861 to discover the source of the Nile. He was the first European to sight the Albert Nyanza and to find that the Nile flowed through it. His wife, Florence von Sass, accompanied him on his explorations.

**baking soda:** see SODIUM BICARBONATE.

**Bakke Case:** see UNIVERSITY OF CALIFORNIA REGENTS V. BAKKE.

**Bakst, Leon,** 1866–1924, Russian painter and stage designer. He went to Paris in 1893, returning to St Petersburg in 1900 to establish himself as society portraitist and stage designer. He ran his own school which CHAGALL and NIJINSKY attended. In 1908 he designed a number of ballet sets for FOKINE and then went on to Paris to work with DIAGHILEV. He combined the influences of Oriental art and Russian peasant art to produce spectacular sets that revolutionized European stage design.

**Baku,** city (1985 pop. 1,693,000), capital of the AZERBAIJAN SOVIET SOCIALIST REPUBLIC, SE European USSR, on the Caspian Sea. Baku is the fifth-largest city in the USSR and a major port. It is a centre for oil drilling and refining, and shipbuilding. Until World War II it was the leading source of Soviet oil. Under independent Shirvan shahs the city was a medieval centre of trade and crafts. It was under Persian rule from 1509 to 1806 when it was annexed by Russia. In 1920 it became part of the USSR.

**Bakunin, Mikhail** (bəˌkoohnin), 1814–76, Russian revolutionary and leading exponent of ANARCHISM. After taking part (1848–49) in revolutions in France and Saxony, he was sent back to Russia and exiled to Siberia. He escaped (1861) to London, where he worked with Aleksandr HERZEN. In the first International Workingmen's Association he clashed with Karl MARX and was expelled (1872); their philosophical split led to the dissolution (1876) of the organization. Bakunin held that human beings are inherently good and deserve absolute freedom; he advocated the violent overthrow of existing governments. His works include *God and the State* (1882).

**Balaguer, Joaquin** (bahlahˌgayə), 1907–, president of the DOMINICAN REPUBLIC (1960–62, 1966–78, 1986–). He served in dictator TRUJILLO MOLINA's government as vice president (1957–60) and president until ousted (1962) by the military. During his second tenure, he restored financial stability, but political chaos led him to resort to repression. He ran unsuccessfully for president in 1982 but gained victory in the 1986 elections as candidate of the Social Christian Reform Party.

**Balakirev, Mili Alekseyevich** (baˌlakeerif), 1837–1910, Russian composer and conductor, leader of the group called the FIVE. His music, combining ROMANTICISM with Russian folk songs, includes the symphonic poem *Tamara* (1867–82) and the piano fantasy *Islamey* (1869).

**balalaika,** a Russian folk instrument belonging to the GUITAR family, with three strings and a triangular body. Balalaikas are made in different sizes, and are played with a plectrum.

**Bala Lake** or **Llyn Tegid,** largest natural lake in Wales. It is situated in Gwynedd, with the town of Bala at the NE end. It is c.6 km (4 mi) long and 1 km wide.

**balance of payments,** relation between all payments in and out of a country over a given period, the balance on the current and capital accounts. It is an outgrowth of the concept of BALANCE OF TRADE, which it includes; it also includes the movement of government and private capital between countries (e.g., investments and debt payments). The International Monetary Fund (see UNITED NATIONS) was created (1945) to deal with problems relating to the balance of payments. The overall balance of payments in the UK has been healthy since 1982. Traditionally the UK has a deficit on visible trade which is offset by a surplus on invisible trade. In 1986, however, there was a small deficit on the current account which persisted in 1987.

**balance of power,** system of international relations in which nations shift alliances to maintain an equilibrium of power and prevent dominance by any single state. Its modern development began in the 17th cent. with efforts of European countries to contain the France of LOUIS XIV. The balance of power was of primary concern to European nations from 1815 to 1914, particularly to contain the rising power of GERMANY, and was attacked as a cause of WORLD WAR I. It declined with the rise of the US and the USSR as superpowers after 1945, but after the 1960s, with the emergence of China, the THIRD WORLD, and a revived Europe, it seemed to be reemerging as a component of international relations.

**balance of trade,** relation between the value of a nation's exports and imports. The concept first became important in the 16th and 17th cent. with the growth of MERCANTILISM, whose theorists held that a nation should have an excess of exports over imports (i.e., a favourable balance);

although challenged by Adam SMITH and other economists, the idea is still widely believed. The balance of trade is a major element in the current account of a nation's BALANCE OF PAYMENTS.

**Balanchine, George,** 1904–83, American choreographer and ballet dancer; b. Russia. A member of DIAGHILEV's Ballets Russes (1924–28), he moved (1933) to the US and helped to found the School of American Ballet. From 1948 he was artistic director and principal choreographer of the New York City Ballet. His many works have emphasized form and are often abstract; he is considered one of the greatest choreographers in the history of ballet. See also BALLET; DANCE.

**Balassi, Bálint,** 1554–94, Hungarian poet and playwright. A Renaissance nobleman whose life was spent chasing women, his fortune, and the Turks, Balassi fathered Hungarian lyric poetry, both in terms of form (the Balassi stanza, rhyming AABCCBDDDB) and content (personal address both to lovers and to God, and poems praising nature and frontier life). His complete works were published in 1961.

**Balaton, Lake,** largest lake in central Europe, 591 km² (231 sq mi), W Hungary. Owing its origin to faulting, it is a relatively shallow feature, rarely exceeding 4 m in depth; it freezes in winter. The sunny south-facing slopes are given over to vineyards and residences. The southern shore has popular beaches.

**Balboa, Vasco Núñez de,** c.1475–1519, Spanish CONQUISTADOR, discoverer of the PACIFIC OCEAN. Fleeing HISPANIOLA in 1510, he hid in a vessel that took the explorer Enciso to Panama. After reaching Darien, he seized command from Enciso and, with the aid of friendly Indians, marched across the isthmus. He reached the Pacific in Sept. 1513, claiming it and its shores for Spain. He was later accused of treason and beheaded.

**bald cypress:** see SWAMP CYPRESS.

**Balder,** beautiful and gracious Norse god of light; son of Odin (see WODEN) and FRIGG. Invulnerable to everything but mistletoe, he was killed by a mistletoe dart made by LOKI. He is the subject of Matthew ARNOLD's poem 'Balder Dead' (1855).

**Baldung** or **Baldung-Grien, Hans** (bəldoong-green), c.1484/5–1545, German religious and mythological painter. His style reveals his interest in brilliant colour, light, and twisted forms. He is best known as a painter of disturbing subjects, e.g., *Death and the Maiden* (1517; Offentlich Kunstsammlung, Basel).

**Baldwin,** Latin emperors of CONSTANTINOPLE. **Baldwin I,** 1171–1205 (r.1204–05), was a leader in the Fourth CRUSADE as count of Flanders. Elected emperor of Constantinople, he was taken in battle by the Bulgarians (1205) and died in captivity. His brother, HENRY OF FLANDERS, succeeded him. **Baldwin II,** 1217–73 (r.1240–61), was the last Latin emperor of Constantinople. To obtain funds, he sold part of the True Cross to LOUIS IX of France and pawned his own son to the Venetians. When MICHAEL VIII of Nicaea stormed Constantinople, Baldwin fled to Italy.

**Baldwin,** Latin kings of Jerusalem. **Baldwin I,** 1058?–1118 (r.1100–18), was a brother of GODFREY OF BOUILLON, whom he accompanied in the First CRUSADE. He gained the chief ports of Palestine and aided other Latin rulers against the Muslims. His cousin and successor, **Baldwin II,** d. 1131 (r.1118–31), was also in the First Crusade. As king he warred with the Turks in N Syria. During his reign TYRE and Antioch became Jerusalem's dependents. **Baldwin III,** 1130–62 (r. 1143–62), the son of Fulk of Anjou, ruled as Latin power in the East began to decay. Edessa fell (1144) to the Muslims, the Second Crusade failed, and the Turkish sultan Nur ad-Din took (1154) N Syria. His nephew **Baldwin IV** (the Leper), c.1161–85 (r.1174–85) defended his kingdom constantly against SALADIN. When his leprosy became worse, he had his child-nephew crowned (1183) **Baldwin V** (d. 1186).

**Baldwin, James,** 1924–87, black American author. His works, dealing largely with American blacks and relations between the races, include novels, e.g., *Go Tell It on the Mountain* (1953), *Another Country* (1962), and *Just Above My Head* (1979); essay collections, e.g., *Notes of a Native Son* (1955), *The Fire Next Time* (1963); plays; and short stories.

**Baldwin, Robert,** 1804–58, Canadian statesman. He proposed (1836) representative government for the entire country and after the reunion (1841) of Upper and Lower Canada, Baldwin and Sir Louis LaFontaine

formed a coalition government (1842), which won an overwhelming victory in the 1847 election, established responsible Canadian government and reformed local government in ONTARIO.

**Baldwin, Stanley,** 1867–1947, British statesman. A Conservative, he was three times prime minister (1923–24; 1924–29; 1935–37). He broke the 1926 GENERAL STRIKE and secured the ABDICATION of EDWARD VIII. An able politician, Baldwin has been criticized for his apparent blindness to the threat to peace indicated by the rise of fascism in Europe.

**Balearic Islands,** archipelago (1981 pop. 685,088) in the W Mediterranean Sea, forming Baleares prov. of Spain. The three principal islands are Majorca, Minorca, and Ibiza. All have a mild climate and are popular tourist centres. The Balearics were occupied by Moors in the 8th cent. and captured (1229–35) by James I of Aragón. They were included (1276–1343) in the independent kingdom of Majorca and reverted to the Aragonese crown under Peter IV.

**Balenciaga, Cristóbal,** 1895–1972, spanish FASHION designer. Based first at Eisa (Spain) and then in Paris, he designed clothes for the royalty and aristocracy of Europe. His hallmarks were fine tailoring and, for evening wear, dramatic colours, especially black and dark pink. His sack dress of the late 1950s was influential.

**Balfe, Michael William,** 1808–70, Irish composer and singer. He made his debut in Paris as a baritone in 1827. He sang at La Scala, Milan, during the 1830s and took the part of Papageno in the first London performance of Mozart's *The Magic Flute* in 1838. The best known of his many operas is *The Bohemian Girl* (1843). His setting of Tennyson's ballad 'Come into the garden, Maud' was a great favourite in Victorian drawing-rooms.

**Balfour, Arthur James Balfour,** 1st **earl of,** 1848–1930, British statesman. A Conservative, he held many cabinet positions and was prime minister from 1902 to 1905. As foreign secretary under LLOYD GEORGE (1916–19), he issued the Balfour Declaration (1917), pledging British support for a Jewish national home in Palestine.

**Bali,** island and (with two offshore islets) province (1971 pop. 2,120,338), S Indonesia, c.5700 km² (2200 sq mi), separated from JAVA (W) by the narrow Bali Strait. The lushly fertile, scenic, and densely populated island is largely mountainous and volcanic, reaching a high point of 3142 m (10,308 ft) at Mt Agung. Rice, vegetables, fruits, and coffee are grown, and livestock is important. Industries include food processing, tourism, and handicrafts. The Balinese people retain their Hindu religion in a predominantly Muslim nation and are known for their physical beauty and their uniquely ritualistic forms of music, folk drama, dancing, and architecture.

**Balikesir,** city (1980 pop. 124,051), capital of Balikesir prov., NW Turkey. It is a communications centre and acts as market to a region of farming and metalliferous-ore mining.

**Balinese music,** includes vocal and instrumental genres, called *tembang* and *gamelan* respectively. *Gamelan* is a general word used in Indonesia and Malaysia for an orchestra of tuned percussion, and in Bali typically includes suspended gongs; rows, or single items, of mounted gongs, keyed metallophones and/or xylophones; cymbals, drums, and a bamboo flute. *Gamelans* range in size from the *gender wayang* quartet to the *gong gede* ensemble with up to 40 instruments. Most *gamelans* are tuned to the five-tone *pelog* scale whose pitches approximate (not precisely) to E, F, G, B, C, though a few ensembles use the *slendro* system of tuning, whose five pitches are spaced more or less equidistantly. Musical compositions are cyclical, with a nuclear melody (*pokok*) whose most important notes are stressed at regular intervals by the gongs and largest metallophones. This nuclear melody forms the basis for elaborate interlocking figurations on the smaller metallophones and gong chimes. Vocal music, of which there are numerous genres, is generally less rigidly structured. Music is closely linked with dance and drama, and an integral part of ritual and social life, although commercial performances for tourists are increasingly a regular feature of everyday life. The size and repertoire of Balinese orchestras have changed considerably since the turn of the 20th cent., and much music that is loosely described as 'traditional' has in fact been composed and developed in performance by master-musicians whose individual contributions are known and recognized in Bali. There are two major music academies where pupils and teachers are trained.

**Balkan Peninsula,** generally mountainous land area, SE Europe, projecting S from the line of the Sava and Danube rivers between the Black, Aegean, Mediterranean, Ionian, and Adriatic seas. It comprises all or part of six countries—Albania, Greece, Bulgaria, Turkey, Yugoslavia, and Romania—collectively referred to as the **Balkan states**. The peninsula, which had once been ruled by Rome and Byzantium as well as by a number of local and central European empires, fell largely under Ottoman rule from the late 15th cent. The Serbian and Greek revolutions of the early 19th cent. marked the beginning of the Turks' gradual retreat, a process completed by the BALKAN WARS in 1912–13.

**Balkan Wars,** two short wars (1912, 1913) fought for possession of the European territories of the declining OTTOMAN EMPIRE. In the first war, Serbia, Bulgaria, Greece, and Montenegro expelled the Turks from all but Istanbul. The second war ensued when Bulgaria, unable to enforce its pre-war agreement with Serbia over the division of Macedonia, attacked the Serbs, who were then joined by the Greeks, Romanians, and Turks. Bulgaria lost and was forced to cede territories to all four victors. The Balkan Wars heightened nationalism in the area and provoked a diplomatic crisis among the great powers, so contributing to the making of WORLD WAR I.

**Balla, Giacomo,** 1871–1958, Italian artist. In 1910 Balla signed the manifesto of futurist painters and became associated with FUTURISM and its ideas, especially that of depicting movement. Influenced by the philosophy of BERGSON concerning time and memory, and by the photography of Anton Bragaglia, Balla attempted to convey the impression of movement by blurred outlines and multiple images, e.g., *Dynamism of a Dog on a Leash* (1912) and *The Flight of Swifts* (1912).

**ballad,** in literature, short narrative poem usually relating a dramatic event. Folk ballads date from about the 12th cent., literary ballads from the 18th. The anonymous folk ballad was originally sung, passed along orally and changed greatly in transmission. It was short, simple, and formulaic, often with a stock refrain. From the late 18th cent. hundreds were collected; historical, romantic, supernatural, nautical, or heroic. American ballads deal with cowboys, outlaws, folk heroes, and blacks. Mid-20th cent. folk music has drawn on the tradition. The literary ballad is a more elaborate imitation of the type, a prime example being S.T. COLERIDGE's *Rime of the Ancient Mariner.*

**ballade,** in literature, French 14th–15th cent. verse form, usually consisting of three eight-line stanzas and a concluding four-line envoy (a summary or address). Ballades by François VILLON and, in English, by Geoffrey CHAUCER are famous.

**Ballarat,** city (1986 pop. 63,802), Victoria, SE Australia. Today a major provincial centre, the city was established during the gold rush of the 1850s. In 1854 the 'Eureka Stockade' led to bloodshed when miners rioted against police trying to enforce compulsory licences. Industry which developed from the needs of the mines gave the city economic stability later and now supports a large urban population and rural community. Sovereign Hill, S of the city, is the re-creation of a town of the goldrush era, opened to tourists in 1971.

**Ballek, Ladislav,** 1941–, Slovak writer. In 1983 he became secretary of the Slovak Writers' Association. A fine stylist with an accomplished sense of the bizarre, he has written wittily and sensitively about cosmopolitan Southern Slovakia, notably in his sensualist novels, *The Butcher's Assistant* (1977) and *Acacias* (1981).

**ballet,** [It., *ballare*, = to dance], classic, formalized solo or ensemble dancing of a disciplined, dramatic, or abstract nature, performed to music. Foreshadowed in mummeries and masquerades, it emerged as a distinct form before the 16th cent. The first ballets combining poetry, music, dance, decor, and special effects were presented in Italy, and then at the French court of Catherine de' MEDICI. The 17th-cent. court ballet (featuring only males) included poetry, singing, drama, and dance, but by the beginning of the 18th cent. a gradual separation took place to establish the two distinct art forms OPERA and DANCE, which manifested itself in the form of *Ballet d'action* which sought to tell story through dance and mime action, thus breaking with vocalic content of *Ballet de cour*. Through international influence the ballet began to evolve as we know it today. Italy contributed the mimetic tradition of *Commedia Dell' Arte*, with a more virtuoso, elevated dance technique, and France grace and charm as well as some codification of steps, such as the five basic positions of the feet. Early in the 18th cent. Marie Camargo and Marie Salle established

the two dance styles that have provided choreographic resources ever since. Camargo was brilliant in virtuosity, shortening her skirt to show technique; Salle was lyrical and expressive, with a strong dramatic sensitivity (she was also the first female choreographer). Modern ballet technique stressing the turned-out leg and resulting movements was established by the end of the 18th cent., and set down by Carlo Blasis in 1820. With *La Sylphide* (1832) the romantic period (see ROMANTICISM) began, and with it ballet enjoyed an international boom in popularity, and a rivalry between countries for the perfection of ballet took place, leading to advancement in all areas of the art. Under the pressure of NATURALISM in the theatre, ballet declined in mid-cent., but after 1875 a renaissance in romantic ballet began in Russia, where PETIPA and others created many of the standards of the romantic repertoire, e.g., *Sleeping Beauty* (1890). In 1909 the Russian impresario DIAGHILEV brought his Ballets Russes to Paris and revolutionized the ballet world, fusing the modern trends of dance, music, and art. Male dancing, which had fallen into a decline in the second half of the 19th cent., except in Denmark and Russia, has enjoyed a resurgence in the 20th cent. principally through dancers such as NIJINSKY, NUREYEV, and BARYSHNIKOV. Today, the classical training is regarded even by practitioners of MODERN DANCE as an essential training of the body for all kinds of dance.

first             second             third

fourth           fourth             fifth
arms *en avant*  arms *en haut*     arms *en haut*
feet *ouverte*   feet *croisee*

The five classical positions of **ballet**

**Ballet Folklórico de México:** see DANCE (table).

**Ballets Russes:** see DANCE (table).

**Balliol, John de,** d. 1269, English nobleman; founder of Balliol College, Oxford. A regent for ALEXANDER III of Scotland, he was removed from office and later fought for HENRY III of England in the BARONS' WAR. His third son, **John de Balliol,** 1249–1315, king of Scotland (1292–96), claimed the throne at the death of MARGARET MAID OF NORWAY. EDWARD I of England supported him over ROBERT I in return for feudal overlordship, and he was crowned. In 1296 he renounced his oath of fealty, was defeated, and surrendered to Edward. He was imprisoned until 1299, when he retired to France. His son, **Edward de Balliol,** d. 1363, king of Scotland, invaded Scotland (1332) with the aid of EDWARD III and defeated supporters of DAVID II. After David's return from France (1341), he never held power.

**ballistics,** science of projectiles, such as bullets, bombs, rockets, and missiles. Interior ballistics deals with the propulsion and motion of a projectile within a gun or firing device. Exterior ballistics is concerned with the motion of the projectile while in flight, and includes the study of the trajectory, or curved flight path, of the projectile. Terminal ballistics is concerned with the phenomena occurring at the termination of the projectile's flight; such termination may result from impact on a solid target or explosion of the projectile. In criminology, the term *ballistics* is applied to the identification of the weapon from which a bullet was fired. Microscopic imperfections in a gun barrel make characteristic scratches and grooves on bullets fired through it.

**balloon,** usually spherical, lighter-than-air AIRCRAFT inflated with hot air or gas and not equipped with power for horizontal flight. The first practical balloon, made by the brothers MONTGOLFIER, rose near Lyons, France, to a height of about 1800 m (5900 ft) on 4 June 1783. A larger Montgolfier hot-air balloon achieved the first manned ascent on 21 Nov. 1783, and the first man-carrying hydrogen balloon flew on 1 Dec. 1783, both in Paris. Thereafter, ballooning became a popular sport. The English Channel was first crossed by balloon on 7 Jan. 1785. Balloons were crucial during the seige of Paris in the FRANCO-PRUSSIAN WAR (1870–71), carrying 155 passengers and 9 tons of mail (see AIR MAIL) out of the city. Tethered balloons were used extensively for artillery observation during World War I and as a barrage against low-lying aircraft over major cities in World War II. A revival of hot-air ballooning came about in the 1950s through the use of gas-fired controllable hot-air burners. The height record of almost 35,000 m (114,000 ft, or over 21 mi) was made in the US in 1961.

**Balmaceda, José Manuel** ('balma,saydhə), 1840–91, president of CHILE (1886–91). He became chief of state when Chile was profiting from the enormous nitrate wealth it gained from the War of the Pacific (see PACIFIC, WAR OF THE). His presidency saw a massive increase in public works such as railways but he quarrelled both with Congress and the foreign nitrate capitalists. A constitutional crisis in 1890 led to civil war in 1891 when the congressional majority took up arms against him and he was defeated. He committed suicide but left behind a reputation as a nationalist and visionary.

**Balmoral Castle,** royal castle, Grampian region, Scotland. It is situated on the S bank of the R. DEE, 11 km (7 mi) E of BRAEMAR. Built by Prince Albert in the 19th cent. on the site of an earlier castle, it is a private home of British monarchs. It is built in white granite in 'Scottish baronial' style. Balmoral Forest, a deer forest, is situated to the S of the castle.

**balsa:** see BOMBAX.

**Balthasar:** see WISE MEN OF THE EAST.

**Balthus, Balthasar Klossowski de Rola,** 1908–, French painter. Encouraged by BONNARD and DERAIN, he painted street scenes and interiors in a style of poetic naturalism. After World War II his later works were of adolescent girls which explored the interests and stresses of adolescent sexuality.

**Baltic languages,** a subfamily of the Indo-European family of languages. See LANGUAGE (table).

**Baltic Sea,** N Europe, arm of the Atlantic Ocean, c.422,170 km² (163.000 sq mi), bordered by Denmark, Finland, Germany, Poland, Sweden, and the USSR. Shallow and partly frozen in winter, it is connected to the Atlantic by several straits, including the KATTEGAT and SKAGGERAK, and by the Kiel Canal. Principal arms of the Baltic are the gulfs of Bothnia, Finland, and Riga.

**Baltimore,** US city (1984 est. pop. 764,000), N Maryland on the Patapsco R. estuary, a branch of CHESAPEAKE BAY; settled early 17th cent., inc. 1745. One of the ten largest US cities, Baltimore is a major seaport, industrial centre, and railhead. Shipbuilding, food processing, metal and oil refining, and the production of aircraft, missiles, and chemicals are among the leading industries. The city grew phenomenally with the opening (1818) of the National Road and the founding (1827) of the Baltimore & Ohio Railroad. Largely rebuilt after a fire in 1904, it became famous for its red-brick terraced houses. Johns Hopkins Univ., Baltimore Museum of Art, and the Peabody Conservatory of Music are among the city's many educational institutions. H.L. MENCKEN, Babe RUTH, and Billie HOLIDAY were among Baltimore's best-known natives.

**Baltimore, George Calvert,** 1st **baron:** see CALVERT, GEORGE.

**Balts,** peoples of the E coast of the Baltic Sea, namely the Latvians, Lithuanians, and now-extinct Old Prussians. The Estonians are related to the Finns rather than to the Balts. In the 13th cent. the TEUTONIC KNIGHTS and Livonian Brothers of the Sword conquered and Christianized Estonia and Latvia, which remained under German economic dominance until the 20th cent. The Lithuanians, who resisted annexation and adopted

Christianity in 1387, formed a powerful state that united (1569) with Poland. Estonia passed in 1561 to Sweden and in 1721 to Russia, which by 1795 controlled all the Baltic lands. Independent after World War I, LATVIA, LITHUANIA, and ESTONIA were forcibly incorporated into the USSR 1940.

**Baluchi** (bə,loohchee), language belonging to the Iranian group of the Indo-Iranian subfamily of the Indo-European family of languages. See LANGUAGE (table).

**Balzac, Honoré de,** 1799–1850, French writer, among the great masters of the NOVEL. Half starving in a Paris garret, he began his literary career by writing sensational novels to order under a pseudonym. His great work, called 'La comedie humaine', written over a 20-year period, is a vast collection of interrelated novels and short stories recreating French society of the time, picturing in precise detail individuals of every class and profession. Chief among them are *Eugénie Grandet* (1833), *Le père Goriot* (1835), and *La Cousine Bette* (1847).

**Bamako,** city (1976 pop. 404,000), capital of Mali, a port on the Niger R. It is a major regional trade centre connected by rail to DAKAR, on the Atlantic Ocean. Manufactures include processed meat, textiles, and metal goods. Bamako was a centre of Muslim learning under the MALI empire (c.11th–15th cent.). It became (1908) the capital of the French Sudan. A picturesque city, it has a botanical and zoological park, gardens, and several educational institutions.

**Bamba, Ahmadou,** c.1850–1927, Senegalese Muslim religious leader. He was exiled (1895–1907) to Gabon and Mauritania by the French who were fearful of his large religious following. When he was allowed to return to Senegal he founded the Muridiyya Islamic sect and cooperated with the French in developing the interior of Senegal. He encouraged his followers (100,000 in 1927) to grow groundnuts and helped recruit soldiers for World War I.

**Bambata,** ZULU chief and guerila leader. In 1906 he led a rebellion against the government of Natal, in South Africa, after the imposition of a new poll tax on the Zulu in 1905. Lacking the approval of the Zulu king, Dinizulu, the rebellion did not become general. Bambata was killed at the battle of Mome valley in June 1906.

**bamboo,** plants of several genera, e.g., *Arundinaria, Bambusa, Phyllostachis,* etc., of the GRASS family, chiefly of warm or tropical regions. The group contains the largest grasses, sometimes reaching 30 m (100 ft). Bamboo stalks are hollow, usually round, and jointed, with deciduous leaves. Bamboo is used as wood, and for construction work, furniture, utensils, fibre, paper, fuel, and innumerable other articles. Bamboo sprouts and the grains of some species are eaten.

**bamboo curtain,** boundary between communist and noncommunist countries in E Asia, especially between the People's Republic of China and its noncommunist neighbours, and the perceived closed nature of societies on the communist side of the boundary. Once used in the same sense as IRON CURTAIN in the European context, the term has become less applicable in recent years as China has become more open to the Western world.

**banana,** name for a family of tropical herbs (the Musacae), for a genus (*Musa*) of herbaceous plants, and for the fruits they produce. Bananas are probably native to tropical Asia, but are widely cultivated. They are related to the economically valuable MANILA HEMP and to the BIRD-OF-PARADISE FLOWER. Banana plants have a palmlike aspect and large leaves, the overlapping bases of which form the so-called false trunk. Only female flowers develop into the banana fruit (botanically, a berry), each plant bearing fruit only once. The seeds are sterile; propagation is through shoots from the rhizomes. Bananas are an important food staple in the tropics.

**Bancroft, George,** 1800–1891, American historian and public official. Secretary of the navy (1845–46) founder of the US Naval Academy, he served as minister to Britain (1846–49) and Prussia (1867–74). An antislavery Democrat he supported Pres. LINCOLN in the AMERICAN CIVIL WAR. Bancroft's patriotic *History of the United States* (10 vol., 1834–74) remains valuable because of its extensive use of source materials.

**Bancroft, Hubert Howe,** 1832–1918, American historian. A wealthy publisher, he produced, with a staff of researchers and writers, a prodigious history of the US West, Central America, and Mexico (39 vol.,

1874–90). In 1905 he presented his collection of 60,000 books, manuscripts, maps, and personal narratives, known as the Bancroft Library, to the Univ. of California.

**Bancroft, Marie Effie Wilton, Lady,** 1839–1921, English actress and manager, together with her husband, **Sir Squire Bancroft,** 1841–1926. By producing the realistic dramas of Thomas Robertson and following the stage reforms of Mme VESTRIS, they introduced REALISM to the English stage.

**band,** in music, a group of musicians playing mainly on WOODWIND, BRASS and PERCUSSION INSTRUMENTS, often outdoors. Early such groupings in medieval and Renaissance Europe were the town bands and military bands, integral to the civic and social life of the community. In the mid 19th cent. the concert band developed, with a repertory including marches, flourishes, and music transcribed from other mediums. Leading bandmasters include J.P. SOUSA and E.F. GOLDMAN. The BRASS BAND is a British phenomenon. Modern bands include marching bands, dance bands, JAZZ bands, and rock bands (see ROCK MUSIC).

**band,** in social anthropology, a form of social organization characteristic of hunter–gatherer societies. Bands are extremely flexible, egalitarian groups occupying a particular territory, usually composed of from between 50 and 300 persons. They have no formalized kinship or leadership rules and little property. Such leaders as do exist—headmen —are chosen by consensus, and what power they exercise is usually based on personal characteristics and consensual support. Conflicts within bands tend to be resolved by the band splitting, or individuals leaving and joining other bands. In the evolutionary scheme that has been most widely developed in the US the band is the first major stage in sociocultural EVOLUTION.

**Banda, Hastings Kamuzu,** 1902?–, president of MALAWI (1966–). A physician, he was a leading nationalist in Nyasaland and was imprisoned by the British during the country's struggle for independence. He became president for life when it became independent as Malawi.

**Bandaranaike, Sirimavo** (bahndrah‚niekee), 1916–, prime minister (1960–65, 1970–77) of SRI LANKA (formerly Ceylon). She was largely responsible for the constitution of 1972 that transformed Ceylon into the republic of Sri Lanka. In 1980 she was expelled from Parliament and stripped of her civil rights because of alleged abuses as prime minister; however, in 1986 she was pardoned and her civil rights were restored. She unsuccessfully contested the 1988 presidential elections.

**bandicoot,** MARSUPIAL of Australia, Tasmania, and New Guinea, member of the family Paramelidae. There are several genera of bandicoots, ranging from 22 to 40 cm (9 to 16 in) long, some herbivorous, feeding on bulbs, roots, and seeds, and others carnivorous, feeding on insects, molluscs, and worms. They are nocturnal animals, some, like the bilby (*Thylacomys*), digging burrows in which they spend their days, others, like the pig-footed bandicoot (*Chaeropus*), making nests of grass and sticks in forest undergrowth. Bandicoots are rapidly disappearing as their habitats are reduced, they are exterminated accidentally along with RABBITS, and they have to compete with the mammals introduced by humans.

**Bandung** or **Bandoeng,** city (1980 pop. 1,461,000), capital of West Java prov., Indonesia, 120 km (75 mi) SE of Djakarta. Founded by the Dutch in 1810, it became the administrative and military headquarters of the Netherlands East Indies. Third largest city in Indonesia, Bandung is an industrial hub, a famous educational and cultural centre, and a tourist resort. It is a textile centre and site of the country's quinine industry.

**Bandung Conference:** see NON-ALIGNED MOVEMENT.

**Bangalore,** city (1981 pop. 2,628,593), capital of Karnataka state, S central India. It is an industrial centre producing electronic equipment, aircraft, engineering products, textiles, and other manufactures. Founded in 1537, it became the administrative seat of the princely state of Mysore in 1831. The city has many parks and several institutes of learning.

**Banghazi:** see BENGHAZI.

**Bangkok,** city (1984 pop. 5,174,682), capital of Thailand, S central Thailand, on the east bank of the Chao Phraya R., near the Gulf of Siam. Thailand's largest city, its financial and industrial hub, and a leading city of Southeast Asia, Bangkok lies in the heart of the country's rice-growing region. Rice, tin, teak, and rubber are shipped from the city's port. Industrial plants include rice mills, textile mills, sawmills, oil refineries,

and shipyards. The city is also a famous jewellery-trading centre. Ethnic Chinese dominate commerce and industry. A city that contrasts ancient and modern structures, Bangkok contains the vast, walled Grand Palace and over 400 Buddhist temples. It is the site of five universities, as well as the National Museum. It became the nation's capital in 1782. **Thon Buri,** part of metropolitan Bangkok, is an industrial city on the river's west bank. It was the capital of Siam (1769–82).

**Bangladesh,** officially the People's Republic of Bangladesh, republic within the Commonwealth, formerly East Pakistan (1981 pop. 89,912,000), 143,988 km² (55,598 sq mi), S Asia, bordered by India (W, N, and E), Burma (SE), and the Bay of Bengal (S). Principal cities are DHAKA (the capital), formerly Dacca, and CHITTAGONG. A low-lying alluvial region, Bangladesh is composed mainly of the combined delta of the GANGES, BRAHMAPUTRA, and Meghna rivers. The climate is tropical monsoonal, and there are frequent, devastating floods. The economy is predominantly agricultural; jute (of which Bangladesh produces more than half the world supply), rice, and tea are the principal crops. Natural gas is tapped, and there are jute, cotton, and fertilizer factories. The GNP is $12,753 million and the GNP per capita is $130 (1984). Bangladesh has the highest rural population density in the world. The majority of the people are Bengalis, and about 80% are Sunni Muslims.

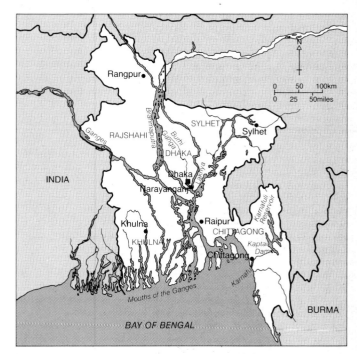

Bangladesh

*History.* Governed for centuries by Afghan and Mogul rulers, the area that is now Bangladesh became part of British India in 1857. When Pakistan achieved independence in 1947, Bangladesh, then called East Bengal and, after 1955, East Pakistan, became an eastern province of Pakistan, from which it is separated by more than 1600 km (1000 mi). A movement for greater autonomy was spearheaded by Sheikh Mujibur Rahman, whose AWAMI LEAGUE won a majority in the federal Pakistani assembly in 1970. The government postponed assembly sessions, and on 26 Mar. 1971, following an army crackdown, the Awami League declared the province independent as Bangladesh (which became a separate member of the COMMONWEALTH). Civil war ensued, and an estimated one million Bengalis were killed before India intervened on Bangladesh's behalf and Pakistan was defeated in December 1971. Widespread famine and political unrest plagued the new nation, led by Sheikh Mujibar Rahman until his assassination in a military coup in 1975. Two countercoups quickly followed, ultimately bringing to power Gen. Ziaur Rahman, who was elected president in 1978. He brought some stability to the country and reintroduced civilian rule, but was killed in an abortive coup in 1981. Another coup, and the introduction of martial law, followed in 1982, bringing to power Gen. Hossain Mohammad ERSHAD. Moves to reestablish civilian rule culminated in 1986 in the election of Ershad to the presidency as leader of the ruling National Party. Parliamentary elections in 1988 were boycotted by the opposition parties.

**Bangor,** cathedral town (1981 pop. 12,244), Gwynedd, NW Wales, at N end of Menai Strait. It is popular as a holiday resort. It is the seat of the Univ. College of North Wales, a constituent college of the Univ. of Wales, which was founded in 1884. The cathedral was built in the 15th and 16th cent., and restored in the late 19th cent.

**Bangui** (ban,gee), city (1981 pop. 387,100), capital of the Central African Republic. A port and light industrial centre on the Ubangi R., it handled most of the country's international trade until 1978, when an overland route was opened through Cameroon. The city is being developed as a tourist centre for the country's large wildlife reserves and national parks. Bangui was founded in 1890 on the trade route between Chad and the Congo–Ubangi river network. It has a university (est. 1970).

**Banja Luka,** city (1981 pop. 183,618), Bosnia, N central Yugoslavia, on the Vrbas R. It is a regional centre with varied industries. Banja Luka means 'Baths of St Luke', and there are remains of Roman baths. The finest monument to Turkish rule is the 16th-cent. mosque. The bazaar dates from the period of the pashas (1580–1640).

**banjo,** a plucked STRINGED INSTRUMENT, played either with a plectrum or with the fingers. The body is circular, with the upper side covered with parchment, and the neck is fretted. The banjo has five or six strings and is used in JAZZ and folk music.

**Banjul,** formerly Bathurst, port city (1978 est. pop. 45,600), capital of Gambia, on St Mary's Island where the Gambia R. enters the Atlantic Ocean. It is Gambia's only large city and its administrative and economic centre. Peanut processing, the chief industry, provides the leading export. The city was founded (1816) by the British as a trading post and a base for suppressing the slave trade.

**Bank for International Settlements (BIS),** financial institution established (1930) in Basel, Switzerland, by bankers and diplomats of Europe and the US. As a meeting place for the governors of West European céntral banks, the BIS serves to promote international financial cooperation. It is the representative of several important West European financial enterprises and holds the accounts of the European Coal and Steel Community (see EUROPEAN COMMUNITY). The BIS is run by a board composed of eight West European central bank governors and five other financiers.

**banking,** in the simplest terms, the business of accepting money (deposits), transferring such money to other accounts for withdrawal in notes or coin, and lending money to other bank customers. Banking, in the form of making loans at interest, dates back to antiquity. Modern banking developed rapidly in the 18th and 19th cent. to support the expansion of industry and trade. In the UK and most other developed countries, many other financial intermediaries transact basic functions including building societies, discount houses, insurance companies, investment and unit trusts, and finance houses, but these are not normally known as bankers in the traditional sense. All banks in the UK are supervised and report regularly to the BANK OF ENGLAND which is the country's central bank. The banking system includes the clearing banks, sometimes known as commercial banks. Their main service to business and individuals is traditionally the provision of current accounts and loans, either on an overdraft basis or fixed-term loan (which is less flexible). But the clearing banks in recent years have become increasingly involved in all financial services such as trade finance, syndicated loans, stockbroking, insurance, and foreign-exchange dealings. The expansion of their activities has eroded some of the merchant banks' competitiveness. These banks were traditionally concerned with trade finance: in return for bills of exchange merchant banks provided finance to companies. The bill once accepted could be discounted; this practice led to some merchant banks becoming known as accepting houses. Merchant banks have also increased the scope of their operations to offer many of the services provided by the clearing banks; they do not, however, have the same large networks of branches. The UK has a worldwide reputation for its expertise in banking and has attracted many overseas banks, which have branches or representative offices there. Many of them do not offer the services of the clearing banks, particularly

the current account facilities, but concentrate on foreign exchange activities and trade finance provision. Savings and investment banks are not normally included in the banking system, although of course their activities are concerned with banking.

**Bank of England,** central bank of the UK. Created in 1694 to enable the government to finance war against France, by 1766 it was banker to the government and most departments of state. The first branch of the bank was opened in Gloucester in 1826 since when a further six have been opened in major English cities, and a small representative office in Glasgow. Since the Bank Charter Act 1844 the Bank of England has been the only note-issuing bank in England and Wales and although Scottish and Northern Irish banks issue their own notes, these are largely backed by Bank of England notes. In 1946 the bank was nationalized under the Bank of England Act. It is responsible for the execution of monetary policy and takes appropriate action in the money, capital, and foreign-exchange markets to preserve a stable banking and financial climate. Although the Exchange Control Regulations were abolished in 1979, the bank continues to operate the Exchange Equalization Account by which it can intervene in foreign-exchange markets to influence the value of sterling against other currencies.

**bankruptcy,** legal proceeding to deal with the liabilities of an insolvent debtor (individual or business). Its purpose is to distribute the bankrupt's assets equitably among the creditors and, in most cases, to free the bankrupt from further liability. Bankruptcy may be instituted by the debtor (voluntary) or by the creditors (involuntary).

**Banks, Sir Joseph,** 1743–1820, English naturalist and patron of the sciences. He accompanied Capt. James COOK on his voyage (1768–71) around the world, collecting biological specimens, most previously unclassified. He was chiefly responsible for making KEW GARDENS an important botanical centre and was president (1778–1820) of the Royal Society.

**banksia,** shrub or small tree (genus *Banksia*) of the Protea family. Of about 50 species, the genus is native to Australia, and grown elsewhere for its spectacular flowers in a range of colours from white to scarlet.

**Bann,** river in Northern Ireland, c.128 km (80 mi) long. It rises in the Mourne Mts as the Upper Bann, in the SE of the country, and flows N past Portadown into Lough Neagh. The Lower Bann flows from the N end of the Lough, through Lough Beg and past Coleraine, entering the Atlantic Ocean at the N end of Lough Foyle. It is well known for salmon fishing.

**Banna, Hassan al-,** 1906–49, Egyptian Islamic reformer. His foundation of the MUSLIM BRETHREN (1925) was an important step in the development of modern Islamist politics.

**Bannister, Sir Roger (Gilbert),** 1929–, English athlete and doctor. He was the first man to run the mile in under 4 min, clocking 3 min 59.4 sec at Oxford in 1954. He was knighted in 1975.

**Banting, Sir Frederick Grant,** 1891–1941, Canadian orthopaedic surgeon and physiologist. He and John MACLEOD won the 1923 Nobel Prize for physiology or medicine for isolating (1921), together with Charles BEST and James COLLIP, the pancreatic hormone later called INSULIN. He made valuable studies of the cortex of the adrenal glands, of cancer, and of silicosis. He was knighted in 1934.

**Bantu,** ethnic and linguistic group of Africa, numbering about 70 millión. They inhabit most of Africa S of the Congo R., except the extreme southwest. The classification is primarily linguistic, and there are almost 100 Bantu languages, including Luganda, Zulu, and Swahili. Few cultural generalizations concerning the Bantu can be made. There were some highly developed Bantu states, and several Bantu confederations were formed in the 19th cent., e.g., the Zulu and the Basuto. Other Bantu tribes include the Matabele and the Mashona. In South Africa the term *Bantu* is commonly used to refer to the native African population, which is subject to the policies of APARTHEID.

**Bantu languages,** group of African languages forming a subdivision of the Benue-Niger division of the Niger-Congo branch of the Niger-Kordofanian language family. See AFRICAN LANGUAGES (table).

**bantustan,** territory set aside by the Republic of SOUTH AFRICA for blacks and given nominal independence in stages. The 10 bantustans, covering 14% of the country's land, were created from the former 'native reserves'. Four of them have been proclaimed independent: TRANSKEI (1976), BOPHUTHATSWANA (1977), VENDA (1979), and CISKEI (1981). No foreign government has recognized the new 'states', and the policy has been condemned as an extension of APARTHEID because blacks in the independent bantustans (8 million thus far) lose their limited rights as South African citizens.

**baobab,** huge tree (*Adansonia digitata*) of the BOMBAX family, native to Africa but occurring widely in India and Australia. The trunk diameter of this relatively short tree is exceeded only by that of the SEQUOIA, and the trunks of living trees are hollowed out for dwellings. The bark is used for rope and cloth, the leaves yield condiments and medicines, and the gourdlike fruit (monkeybread) is eaten.

**Bao Dai** (bow die), 1913–, emperor (1926–45) of ANNAM. He was emperor under French colonial rule and cooperated with the Japanese in World War II. He abdicated (1945) but returned (1949) as chief of state of VIETNAM. Bao Dai was ousted (1955) by Ngo Dinh Diem, who became president of South Vietnam.

**baptism** [Gr., = dipping], in most Christian churches a SACRAMENT. Usually required for membership in a church, it is a rite of purification by water, invoking the grace of God to regenerate a person and cleanse him or her of sin. Formal baptism is performed by immersion (as among the BAPTISTS) or by pouring or sprinkling water on the person to be baptized. Most churches baptize infants; some withhold baptism until a relatively mature age.

**baptistery,** part of a church, or a separate connected building, used for administering BAPTISM. At first it was simply a pool or basin set in the floor. Later a separate structure was set aside for the ceremony; the earliest example still in existence is in the Lateran basilica (4th cent.) at Rome. Most early baptisteries, found in Italy and in Asia Minor, were circular or octagonal. When immersion was no longer practised, standing fonts took their place. In Italy separate baptisteries continued to be built, e.g., at Florence, in the 12th–15th cent.

**Baptists,** denomination of Protestant Christians holding that baptism is only for believers and solely by immersion. Begun (c.1608) by English SEPARATISTS in Amsterdam, it now has a membership of some 35 million worldwide. There are some 250,000 Baptist members in Britain. They are much the largest Protestant denomination in the US, and also in the USSR. A Baptist World Alliance was formed in 1905.

**bar:** see LEGAL PROFESSION.

**Barabbas,** bandit whom the mob demanded be released from punishment by PONTIUS PILATE instead of JESUS. Mat. 27.15–18; Mark 15.6–15; Luke 23.13–25; John 18.39, 40.

**Bárány, Robert,** 1876–1936, Austrian otologist. His work on the mechanism of the inner ear (see EAR) was rewarded by the 1914 Nobel Prize for physiology or medicine.

**Barbados,** island state (1984 pop. 252,600), 430 km² (166 sq mi), WEST INDIES, E of St Vincent in the Windward Islands. The capital is Bridgetown. Lying to the east of the major islands in the Windward chain, Barbados is generally low-lying, rising to no more than 336 m (1104 ft), with no rivers, but ample rainfall from June to December. The porous soil and moderate warmth are ideal for the growing of sugarcane, traditionally the island's major crop. Rum and molasses are exported, there is commercial fishing, and some light industry was introduced in the 1970s and early 1980s. However, the largest source of foreign exchange is tourism, the island having long been a favourite resort area. The GDP is US$1154 million and the GDP per capita is US$4570. The population is mostly rural and about 95% of African origin. The Portuguese probably discovered and named Barbados, but it was settled in the early 1600s by the British. The sugar economy that they introduced survived the abolition of slavery in 1834, and for a time Barbados served as the administrative capital of the Windward Islands. It became a separate colony of Britain in 1885 and an independent state and member within the COMMONWEALTH in 1966; since then political power has alternated between the Democratic Labour and Barbados Labour parties, the former winning the 1986 elections. In 1983 Barbados participated in the US-led invasion of Grenada.

**Barbarians,** a RUGBY UNION touring club formed in 1890 at Bradford, Yorkshire, N England. Membership by invitation only is extended to outstanding players from all countries. There are six principal annual fixtures, v. Penarth, Cardiff, Swansea, Newport, Leicester, and East Midlands. Since 1948 it has been the custom of major touring sides to conclude their tour with a match against the Barbarians. The match against the New Zealanders in 1973, which the Barbarians won 23–11, is remembered as one of the greatest games in rugby history. Their motto is: 'Rugby Football is a game for gentlemen in all classes, but never for a bad sportsman in any class.'

**Barbarossa,** c.1466–1546, Turkish corsair. He and his brother Aruj seized Algiers from Spain in 1518, and placed it and the other BARBARY STATES under Turkish suzerainty. As admiral of the Turkish fleet under SULAYMAN I, he twice defeated (1533, 1538) the Italian admiral DORIA and ravaged the coasts of Greece, Italy, and Spain.

**Barbarossa, Frederick:** see FREDERICK I under FREDERICK, rulers of the Empire.

**Barbary,** European name sometimes still applied to the coastal region of Africa, W of Egypt. It is equivalent to the Arabic term MAGHREB which is now preferred. The name is rooted in the indigenous Berber population of the region.

**barbary ape,** Old World monkey of the macaque family Cercopithecidae, the last wild primate to live in Europe. Barbary apes are found in Gibraltar and along the coast of NE Africa. In their natural habitat, they are mountain forest dwellers. The Gibraltar apes are fed with fruit, leaves and roots, and they catch small invertebrates. Despite their name, they are monkeys, not apes, but their tails are very small and not apparent until they are handled.

**Barbary States,** term historically applied to the North African states of Tripolitania, TUNISIA, ALGERIA and MOROCCO. In the 16th cent., led by the corsair BARBAROSSA, they came under Turkish suzerainty despite efforts by Holy Roman Emperor Charles V to defeat the Turks. As Turkish hold on them weakened, they became the home base for pirates who demanded booty, ransom, and slaves from raids on Mediterranean (and occasionally Atlantic) shipping and ports. The major European naval powers in general found it more convenient to pay tribute to the Barbary States than to try to destroy them. By the 19th cent., however, opposition to them was strong, and the TRIPOLITAN WAR reflected US opposition. In 1830 France captured Algiers, and c.1835 Morocco was forced to abandon plans to rebuild its fleet in effect ending Barbary Coast piracy.

**Barber, Samuel,** 1910–81, American composer. His music is lyrical and generally tonal. Among his major compositions are *Adagio for Strings* (1936); *Knoxville: Summer of 1915* (1948), for soprano and orchestra; and the operas *Vanessa* (1958) and *Antony and Cleopatra* (1966), commissioned to open the new METROPOLITAN OPERA House, at LINCOLN CENTER, in New York City.

**Barbican Centre,** cultural complex, E central London. Opened in 1982, it is a large complex of theatres, concert halls, cinemas, and art galleries, as well as bars and restaurants. The facilities include the Barbican Theatre, which is now the London home of the Royal Shakespeare Company, and the Barbican Hall, which is the home of the London Symphony Orchestra. The centre is near the financial and business district of the City of London.

**bar billiards:** see BILLIARDS.

**Barbirolli, Sir John,** 1899–1970, English conductor and cellist. He succeeded TOSCANINI as conductor of the New York Philharmonic (1937–42), and conducted the Hallé Orchestra (1943–70). He transcribed early music for the modern orchestra.

**barbiturate,** any depressant drug derived from barbituric acid. In low doses, barbiturates have a tranquillizing effect; their medical use is now replaced by the safer BENZODIAZEPINE tranquillizers. Increased doses are hypnotic or sleep-inducing, and still larger doses act as anticonvulsants and anaesthetics. Barbiturates were commonly taken as sleeping pills (e.g., phenobarbitone) but because of their dangers (addiction, overdose, and interaction with alcohol) they are now used only in epilepsy and anaesthesia. Barbiturates do not relieve pain.

**Barbizon school,** an informal association of French landscape painters that flourished c.1830–c.1870. Its name derives from the village of Barbizon, a favourite residence of members of the group. Théodore ROUSSEAU led the group, which also included Jules Dupré, Narciso Diaz de la Peña, Constant Troyon, and Charles DAUBIGNY. They rendered landscape from direct observation of nature, in a straightforward, anticlassical manner much influenced by 17th-cent. Dutch masters, including RUISDAEL and HOBBEMA. COROT and MILLET, although often linked with the group, stand outside its main line of development. The Barbizon school influenced late-19th- and early-20th-cent. American LANDSCAPE PAINTING.

**Barbour, John**, c.1316?–95, Scottish poet. His romance, *The Bruce* (1375), is a celebration of Scotland's gaining of its independence from England under Robert the Bruce.

**Barbuda:** see ANTIGUA AND BARBUDA.

**Barca**, surname of members of a powerful Carthaginian family: see HAMILCAR BARCA; HANNIBAL; HASDRUBAL.

**Barcelona**, city (1981 pop. 1,754,900), capital of Barcelona prov. and the chief city of CATALONIA, NE Spain, on the Mediterranean Sea. It is Spain's second largest city and largest port. Among its manufactures are textiles and machinery. Founded by settlers from CARTHAGE, it was held by the Romans and Visigoths; fell to the MOORS (8th cent.) and to CHARLEMAGNE (801); and was ruled from the 9th cent. by the counts of Barcelona, a title later borne by the kings of Spain. Around 1400 it reached its peak as a centre of trade, banking, and cloth-making. The centre of the Catalan revolt against Spain (1640–52), it was the capital of the Catalan autonomous government (1932–39) and the seat of the Spanish Loyalist government (1938–39) (see SPANISH CIVIL WAR). Barcelona is a handsome, modern city with striking new buildings. Notable older structures include the Cathedral of Santa Eulalia (14th–15th cent.) and the Church of the Holy Family (Sp. *Sagrada Familia*) (begun 1882), designed by Antonio GAUDÍ.

**Barcelona/Puerto La Cruz**, city (1980 est. pop. 275,000), E Venezuela, capital of Anzoátegui state on the Neveri R. 5 km (3 mi) from the Atlantic. The city's recent rapid growth has been closely associated with its proximity to Caracas by paved highway and the recent shift in oil production to E Venezuela.

**Barclay, Arthur**, 1856–1938, president of LIBERIA; b. Barbados. He migrated with his family to Africa as a boy and settled in Liberia. After training as a lawyer he was appointed a judge in 1883 and became Secretary of State in 1892. In 1904 he was elected president, and was re-elected in 1906, 1908, and 1912. He is best remembered for his efforts to bring about unity between the Americo-Liberians and the indigenous people of Liberia.

**Barclay, Edwin J.**, 1882–1955, president of LIBERIA (1930–43). During his 13 years as president he fought off US-inspired efforts to make Liberia a League of Nations mandate, and largely resolved Liberia's economic problems engendered by her indebtedness to the US multinational, Firestone.

**Bardeen, John**, 1908–, American physicist. He is known for his studies of semiconductivity (see SEMICONDUCTOR) and other aspects of SOLID-STATE PHYSICS. The first person to win a Nobel Prize twice in the same field, Bardeen shared the 1956 physics prize with Walter Brattain and William Shockley, for work in developing the TRANSISTOR, and the 1972 physics prize with Leon Cooper and John Schreiffer, for their theory of SUPERCONDUCTIVITY.

**Bareilly**, town (1981 pop. 394,938), Uttar Pradesh state, N India. It is a district administrative, communications, and trading centre, with cotton mills, rice mills, engineering, and agricultural implement works, and other industries. It fell to the British, who made it a district headquarters, in 1801.

**Barenboim, Daniel**, 1942–, Israeli pianist and conductor; b. Argentina. He made his debut in Buenos Aires at seven. In 1967 he married the English cellist Jacqueline DU PRÉ. Barenboim has made many recordings and concert appearances as a soloist and has played CHAMBER MUSIC. Since 1975 he has been music director of the Orchestre de Paris.

**Barents Sea**, an arm of the Arctic Ocean, off N Norway and E USSR, partially enclosed by Frantsa-Iosife Zemlya (N), Novaya Zemlya (E), and SVALBARD (W). Remnants of the North Atlantic Drift, a continuation of the GULF STREAM, keep its ports, including MURMANSK and Vardö, ice-free throughout the year.

**Barentz** or **Barents, Willem**, d. 1597, Dutch navigator. He made three expeditions to the Arctic (1594, 1595, 1596–97) in search of the NORTHWEST PASSAGE. His importance lies in the extent of his explorations and the accuracy of his charts.

**Bari**, city (1984 pop. 368,216), Apulia, S Italy, on the Adriatic coast. It is an important commercial centre and seaport with engineering and oil-related industries. Established by the Romans, it was the place of departure of the First Crusade. The old town has the 11th-cent. Romanesque basilica of St Nicholas and a 13th-cent. castle.

**barite:** see BARYTES.

**baritone:** see VOICE.

**barium** (Ba), metallic element, isolated by electrolysis in 1808 by Sir Humphry DAVY. One of the ALKALINE-EARTH METALS, it is soft and silver-white. Its principal ore is BARYTES. Various barium compounds are used as paint pigments, rat poison, a drying agent, and a water softener, and in pyrotechnics. See ELEMENT (table); PERIODIC TABLE.

**bark**, outer covering of the STEM of woody plants, composed of waterproof CORK cells (the outer bark) protecting a layer of food-conducting tissue (the inner bark or phloem). As the stem grows in size (see CAMBIUM), the outer bark gives way by splitting, shredding, or peeling in patterns typical of the species. Various barks are sources of textile fibres (e.g., HEMP, FLAX, and JUTE), tannin, cork, dyes, flavourings (e.g., CINNAMON), and drugs (e.g., QUININE).

**Barker, George (Granville)**, 1913–, English poet. His highly dramatic poems often treat themes of remorse and pain. Published works include *30 Preliminary Poems* (1933), *The True Confession of George Barker* (1950) and *Villa Stellar* (1978).

**Barker, Harley Granville-:** see GRANVILLE-BARKER.

**Barking and Dagenham**, London borough (1981 pop. 148,979), on N side of R. Thames downstream from the centre of London. There are various industries here, including vehicle manufacture, rubber, chemical, and paint production.

**Bar Kokba, Simon** (ˌkohkhbə), d. AD 135, Hebrew hero and leader of a major but unsuccessful revolt against Rome (AD 132–135). In recent excavations at MASADA, Israeli archaeologists have found letters in his handwriting.

**Barlach, Ernst** (ˌbahlakh), 1870–1938, German sculptor. His visit to Russia in 1906 stimulated his interest in peasant art; from this and from German medieval wood carving he took both aesthetic and spiritual ideas. His figures, solid and block-like, with the appearance of coarsely carved wood (even when cast in bronze) expressed man's aberration and spiritual emptiness, typical of German EXPRESSIONISM. His works were denounced as DEGENERATE ART, and many were destroyed.

**barley**, cereal plant (*Hordeum vulgare*) of the GRASS family. It is a cool climate cereal with the USSR being the main producer. Winter barley is sown in autumn to become established before the worst of the winter weather, whereas spring barley consists of those varieties unable to survive very harsh conditions and is sown in spring. Varieties are classed according to the number of rows of GRAINS in the seed head, e.g., 6-, 4-, and 2-row barleys, the last group appearing to have a flattened seed head. Most varieties are 'bearded', having long, stiff bristles called awns on the grains. In addition to being crushed for stock feed, barley is important as the basis of the brewing industry, where the grain is partly germinated to break down the starches to sugars before fermentation to produce beer and spirits. Pearl barley has the dry floral parts removed and the resulting grain polished as with white RICE, and is used for human consumption. In some countries, barley may be milled to produce a flour for cooking, e.g., for chapatis in India.

**bar mitzvah**, Jewish ceremony in which a young male (traditionally at age 13) is initiated into the religious community and performs his first act as an adult, reading in the synagogue from the weekly portion of the Torah (see under SEFER TORAH). The **bat mitzvah**, or *bat hayyil*, is a comparable 20th-cent. ceremony for girls of 12 or 13.

**Barnabas, Saint**, Cypriot Christian apostle, relative of St. MARK; companion of St. PAUL on his first missionary journey. An epistle attributed to him is in the pseudepigrapha.

**barnacle**, sedentary marine animal (subclass Cirripedia), a CRUSTACEAN. The larval stages are PELAGIC. Adult barnacles are attached permanently to a substrate by means of an adhesive cement. They secrete a calcareous shell around themselves and form conspicuous encrusting colonies on rocks, pilings, boats, and some marine animals (e.g., whales, turtles). The attached end of the animal is the head; jointed legs (cirri) sweep food particles through the shell opening to the mouth. Some barnacles lack shells and are PARASITES of other invertebrates.

legs (cirri)

Barnacle

**Barnard, Christiaan Neething,** 1923–, South African surgeon. In 1958 he was appointed director of surgical research at Groote Schuur Hospital, Cape Town, where on 3 Dec. 1967, he completed the first human heart transplant. Barnard has designed artificial heart valves and developed surgical procedures for organ transplants.

**Barnard, Edward Emerson,** 1857–1923, American astronomer. An astronomer at Lick and Yerkes observatories, he discovered 16 comets, Jupiter's satellite Amalthea (1892), and Barnard's star (1916), a star having the largest observed proper motion.

**Barnard, Henry,** 1811–1900, American educator. He and Horace MANN became leaders in the reform of the country's common schools, and Barnard did pioneer work in school inspection, recommendation of textbooks, and organization of teachers' institutes and parent–teacher associations. The first US commissioner of education (1867–70), he edited and published the *American Journal of Education* (31 vol., 1855–81), a leading compilation of educational scholarship.

**Barnardo, Thomas John,** 1845–1905, British physician and philanthropist, b. Ireland. He was founder of the first Boys' Home (1870) in E London for homeless and destitute children, which was followed by the Girls' Village Home (1876) in Essex. Many Barnardo homes were subsequently established and are still responsible for caring for orphaned and forsaken children.

**Barnaul,** city (1985 pop. 578,000), W Siberian USSR, on the Ob R. It is a major regional industrial centre and rail junction within the rich agricultural lands of the Kulunda Steppe. Industries produce cotton, rayon, and other synthetic fibres, clothing, agricultural machinery, motor-vehicle tyres, and milled grain. Founded in 1738, Barnaul became a town in 1771.

**Barnburners,** radical element in the New York state Democratic Party (1842–48), opposed to the conservative HUNKERS. The name derives from a fabled Dutchman who burned his barn to kill the rats; by implication, Barnburners favoured destroying corporations and public works to rid them of abuses. They opposed the extension of slavery. Among their number were Martin VAN BUREN and S.J. TILDEN. In 1848 some Barnburners joined the FREE-SOIL PARTY though most returned to the Democratic fold after the COMPROMISE OF 1850.

**Barnes, Djuna,** 1892–1982, American author. She is best known for *Nightwood* (1936), a novel marked by a sense of horror and decay. Other works include the novel *Ryder* (1928), poetry, short stories, and a verse tragedy, *Antiphon* (1958).

**Barnet,** London borough (1981 pop. 290,197), outer N London. It contains the districts of Chipping Barnet, East Barnet, Friern Barnet, High Barnet, and New Barnet.

**Barneveldt, Johan van Olden:** see OLDENBARNEVELDT, JOHAN VAN.

**Barnsley,** town (1981 pop. 76,783), S Yorkshire, N Midlands of England, on R. Dearne 19 km (12 mi) N of SHEFFIELD. It is an industrial town, known especially for coal-mining and engineering as well as a range of manufacturing industries.

**Barnum, P(hineas) T(aylor),** 1810–91, American showman. In 1842 he opened his American Museum in New York City and immediately became famous for his extravagant advertising and his exhibits of freaks, including 'Gen. Tom Thumb' and the original SIAMESE TWINS. Barnum managed the hugely successful US tour of the Swedish singer Jenny LIND in 1850. In 1871 (after a brief political career) he opened his famous circus, 'The Greatest Show on Earth'. Merged with its chief competitor in 1881, it continued as Barnum & Bailey.

**Barocchio, Giacomo:** see VIGNOLA, GIACOMO DA.

**Baroja y Nessi, Pío** (bah,rohah ee haysee), 1872–1956, Spanish novelist from the BASQUE PROVINCES. His popular cyclical works include *La lucha por la vida* (3 vol., 1904; tr. The Struggle for Existence), about the Madrid underworld, and *Memorias de un hombre de acción* (22 vol., 1913–34; tr. Memoirs of a Man of Action), about 19th-cent. Spain.

**barometer,** instrument for measuring atmospheric pressure. Originally of the mercurial type, modern barometers are almost invariably of the aneroid type. The mercurial barometer consists of a mercury-filled glass tube that is sealed at one end and inverted in a cup of mercury. Pressure on the surface of the mercury in the cup supports the mercury in the tube, which varies in height depending on variations in atmospheric pressure. At 0° C (32° F), standard sea-level pressure (1 standard atmosphere) is 101,325 newtons/m² (14.7 lb/sq in), which is equivalent to a column of mercury 760 mm in height. In meteorology the usual unit of pressure is the millibar (mb). 1000 mb is a pressure of exactly 100,000 newtons/m. The aneroid barometer contains a sealed, partially evacuated metallic box. As the air pressure on it varies, one of its surfaces expands or contracts; this motion is transmitted by a train of levers to a pointer, which shows the pressure on a graduated scale. In WEATHER forecasting, a rising barometer usually indicates fair weather; a rapidly falling barometer, stormy weather.

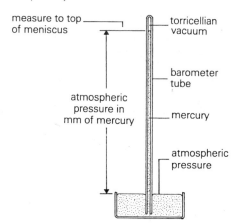

measure to top of meniscus

torricellian vacuum

barometer tube

mercury

atmospheric pressure in mm of mercury

atmospheric pressure

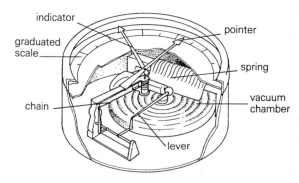

indicator

graduated scale

chain

pointer

spring

vacuum chamber

lever

Barometer

**Barons' War,** in English history, war of 1263–67 between HENRY III and his barons. In 1261 Henry reasserted his power and renounced the PROVISIONS OF OXFORD. Led by Simon de MONTFORT, the barons resorted to arms and won the Battle of Lewes (1264). They failed to establish control over the crown but helped to prepare for the constitutional developments in the reign of EDWARD I.

**baroque,** in art and architecture, style developed in Europe, England, and Latin America during the 17th and 18th cent. Its essential characteristic is an emphasis on a dynamic unity created by a balance among diverse parts. Architecture took on the plastic aspects of sculpture and, along with sculpture, was enhanced by the chiaroscuro (high-contrast) effects of painting. Works in all media were produced on a grand scale. Illusionism increased an unequalled sense of drama, energy, and mobility of form. Baroque buildings, e.g., VERSAILLES and Christopher WREN's churches, compelled order upon overwhelming multiple forms. Throughout Europe undulating facades and complex ground plans abounded. Fountains burst forth as joyous geysers and cascades. Deep PERSPECTIVE was developed in painting, e.g., by RUISDAEL and de HOOCH. Chiaroscuro intensified the works of CARAVAGGIO, ZURBARÁN, Georges de LA TOUR, and REMBRANDT. Colour was superbly exploited to diverse effect by VERMEER, RUBENS, CLAUDE LORRAIN, and Pietro da CORTONA. Sculptors used multiple materials for a single work, e.g., BERNINI's *Ecstasy of St Theresa,* which also exemplifies the baroque fascination with intense emotional states. Landscape subjects were ennobled by the CARRACCI, Ruisdael, HOBBEMA, Rembrandt, Salvator ROSA and Claude Lorrain, and GENRE and STILL LIFE by Vermeer, STEEN, de Hooch, and the LE NAINS. In the *Early Baroque* (c.1590–c.1625), the Roman artists Caravaggio, the Carracci, DOMENICHINO, and Guido RENI were preeminent; their influence spread widely to RIBERA, TERBRUGGHEN, and Rubens. The *High Baroque* (c.1625–c.1660) was dominated by Bernini, BORROMINI, Pietro da Cortona, and Claude Lorrain, and outside Italy by Rembrandt, Rubens, VELÁZQUEZ, Vermeer, HALS, VAN DYCK, Ruisdael, and Zurbarán. In the *Late Baroque* (c.1660–c.1725) Italy lost her dominant position to France. Painters such as MURILLO used lighter colours and softer forms, and the baroque style gradually gave way to the ROCOCO.

**baroque,** in music, the period and style of composition and performance prevailing from c.1600–c.1750. The 16th-cent. revolt against the POLYPHONY of the Renaissance gave rise to an emphasis on the character of individual voices and instruments and also on the use of HARMONY in composition. Use of the older church modes was replaced by major and minor TONALITY as the basis of composition. Principal forms of vocal writing of the period included the OPERA, ORATORIO, and CANTATA; instrumental writing included the SONATA, CONCERTO GROSSO, CONCERTO, and OVERTURE. Later baroque forms were the FUGUE, choral prelude, and the toccata, a free form for keyboard instruments. Famous composers of the period include MONTEVERDI, SCHÜTZ, A. SCARLATTI, VIVALDI, A. CORELLI, J.S. BACH, PURCELL, HANDEL, and LULLY.

**Barossa Valley,** region of South Australia. A major wine-producing area 64 km (40 mi) N of ADELAIDE, with main towns of Tanunda, Angaston, and Nuriootpa, it was originally settled by German migrants in 1838. Many traditional customs, festivals, and foods have been retained. The district was named after the Andalusian battlefield, Barossa.

**Barozzi, Giacomo:** see VIGNOLA, GIACOMO DA.

**Barquisimeto** (ˌbahkisee'metoh), city (1980 est. pop. 489,000), highlands of W Venezuela, capital of Lara state. It was founded in 1552 and was almost totally destroyed by earthquake in 1812. Its traditional role as the centre of an important agricultural region has now been supplemented by increasing industrialization.

**barracuda,** slender, elongated, ferocious FISH (family Sphyraenidae) with a long snout and projecting lower jaw edged with large, sharp teeth. Found in tropical seas, barracudas will strike at anything that gleams and are excellent game fish. The great barracuda (*Sphyraena barracuda*), up to 3 m (10 ft) in length, is reported to be dangerous to swimmers.

**Barranquilla,** city (1979 est. pop. 855,195), N Colombia, on the Magdalena R., 13 km (8 mi) from the Caribbean Sea. Founded in 1629, it developed as a port in the mid 19th cent., with the advent of steam navigation, and is now Colombia's principal port. Manufactures include aluminium sheets, chemicals, processed foods, ships, and automobiles. The city's carnivals are renowned.

**Barrault, Jean-Louis** (bah‚roh), 1910–, French actor and director. He led an outstanding avant-garde theatre company and is known for his role as the mime in the 1944 film *Les Enfants du paradis.*

**Barrie, Sir J(ames) M(atthew),** 1860–1937, Scottish playwright and novelist. Best remembered for his play *Peter Pan* (1904), a fantasy about a boy who refused to grow up, Barrie was a journalist and published Scottish sketches before the success of his novel *The Little Minister*

(1891). Its dramatization (1897) established him as a playwright. Other notable plays include *The Admirable Crichton* (1902), *What Every Woman Knows* (1908), and *Dear Brutus* (1917).

**Barrington, Jonah,** 1940–, English squash-rackets player. He won the Open Championship in 1966, 1967, and 1969–72, and the amateur title in 1966–69. He has also won the amateur championships of Australia, South Africa, and the United Arab Republic. He first played for Ireland in 1966 and turned professional in 1969. He was the first professional to play exhibition squash matches worldwide.

**barrister:** see LEGAL PROFESSION.

**Barron, James,** 1769–1851, US naval officer; b. Hampton, Va. He was court-martialed for failing to clear his ship, the *Chesapeake,* for action during an 1807 incident with the British ship *Leopard.* In 1820 he mortally wounded Stephen DECATUR in a duel.

**Barrow,** river in SE Republic of Ireland, c.192 km (120 mi) long. It rises in the Slieve Bloom Mts in Co. Laois and flows E then S past CARLOW to Waterford Harbour. It is navigable up to Athy, 104 km (65 mi) upriver, and is connected to DUBLIN by canal.

**barrow,** in archaeology, burial mound, built usually of earth and stone or timber. In W Europe long barrows date from the NEOLITHIC and round barrows from the early BRONZE AGE, although barrow burials persisted in some areas into later periods—most notably, the Saxon barrow cemetery at SUTTON HOO in Suffolk, England.

**Barrow, Sir John,** 1764–1848, British geographer. As second secretary of the admiralty, he promoted scientific voyages and instigated Arctic expeditions by John ROSS and William Parry. He helped found (1830) the Royal Geographical Society. Point Barrow, Cape Barrow, and Barrow Strait bear his name.

**Barrymore,** Anglo-American family of actors. The first of the name, **Maurice Barrymore,** 1847–1905, was an Englishman; b. India as Herbert Blythe. A handsome leading man, he went to the US in 1875 to appear with Augustin Daly's company. His American wife, **Georgiana Drew Barrymore,** 1856–93, was a great comedienne. She began her career with the company of her parents, Louisa and John Drew, and acted with her husband in Mme Modjeska's troupe. Their elder son, **Lionel Barrymore,** 1878–1954, was a much admired character actor remembered for his film roles in *A Free Soul* (1931; Academy Award), *Dinner at Eight* (1933), and *You Can't Take It with You* (1938), and for his annual radio portrayal of Scrooge in *A Christmas Carol.* His sister, **Ethel Barrymore,** 1879–1959, an actress of dignity and warmth, achieved success in *Captain Jinks of the Horse Marines* (1901) and is remembered for *The Corn Is Green* (1940) and the film *None but the Lonely Heart* (1944; Academy Award). Their brother, **John Barrymore,** 1882–1942, a handsome, tempestuous matinee idol, was also a distinguished actor, famous for his electrifying *Hamlet* (1922). His films include *Grand Hotel* (1932) and *Twentieth Century* (1934).

**Barth, Heinrich,** 1821–65, German explorer. After attending Berlin University, Barth started travelling in 1845. His first trip of two years is described in *Wanderung durch die Küstenländer des Mittelmeeres* (1849). His second expedition was made for the British government to open up commercial relations with the states of the Sudan and lasted from 1850 to 1855. It was described as 'one of the most fruitful expeditions ever undertaken in inner Africa' and the resulting book, *Travels and Discoveries in North and Central Africa* (1857–58), is still considered one of the best of its kind. He continued to travel until made professor of geography at Berlin University in 1863.

**Barth, John,** 1930–, American novelist. His experimental novels combine satire and parody with serious philosophical concerns. They include *The Sot-Weed Factor* (1960), *Giles Goat-Boy* (1966), *Letters: A Novel* (1979), and *Sabbatical: A Romance* (1982).

**Barth, Karl,** 1886–1968, Swiss Protestant theologian, one of the leading thinkers of 20th-cent. Protestantism. A Swiss minister, he became a professor (1921–35) in Germany, and opposed the Nazi regime. Deported to Switzerland, he later taught at Basel, where he continued to expound his views, known as dialectical theology or theology of the word. Barth sought to reassert the principles of the Reformation. He saw the central concern of theology as the word of God and His revelation in Jesus Christ, which he thought was the only means for God to reveal

Himself to humans, who must listen in awe, trust, and obedience. His (incomplete) *Church Dogmatics* (vol. I–IV, 1932–62) has been hailed by theologians of all creeds as a 20th-cent. classic.

**Barthelme, Donald,** 1931–, American writer. He uses idiosyncratic language and symbol to fit his vision of an absurd reality. His work includes the novels *Snow White* (1967) and *The Dead Father* (1975) and the short-story collections *City Life* (1971), *Sadness* (1972), *Great Days* (1979), and *Sixty Stories* (1981).

**Barthes, Roland** (baht), 1915–80, French literary critic, the major theorist of semiology (see SEMIOTICS; STRUCTURALISM). In *Le degré zéro de l'écriture* (1953; tr. Writing Degree Zero) he attempted to distinguish the act of writing, from conventional categories of language and style. He followed that work in *Mythologies* (1957) with controversial studies of aspects of French culture. In *Eléments de sémiologie* (1964), Barthes systematized the study of signs proposed earlier by Ferdinand de SAUSSURE. In his other works he applied his theories in stylish essays on clichés of national culture, the work of individual writers, photography, autobiography, and other topics.

**Bartholomew, Saint,** one of the Twelve Disciples; identified with NATHANAEL. By tradition he was a missionary in India.

**Bartlett, Sir Frederick:** see SCHEMA.

**Bartók, Béla,** 1881–1945, Hungarian composer and ethnomusicologist. Utilizing the essence of folk melodies and rhythms without quoting them, as well as ATONALITY and traditional techniques, he achieved an original modern style that has had great influence on 20th-cent. music. Bartók became known for his compositions for piano, *Mikrokosmos* (1926–27) and the *Sonata* (1926); for his *Music for Strings, Percussion, and Celesta* (1936), *Concerto for Orchestra* (1943) six string quartets, three piano concertos and two violin concertos. His first popular success was the orchestral *Dance Suite* of 1923. In 1940 he emigrated to the US.

**Barton, Clara,** 1821–1912, American humanitarian; b. Oxford, Mass. Called the Angel of the Battlefield, she set up a supply service during the CIVIL WAR, was nurse in army camps and on battlefields, and led searches for the missing. After working behind German lines for the International Red Cross in the FRANCO-PRUSSIAN WAR, she organized (1881) the American RED CROSS, which she headed until 1904.

**Barton, Sir Derek Harold Richard,** 1918–, English organic chemist. He shared the 1969 Nobel Prize for chemistry with Odd Hassel for work centred on conformational analysis, a technique that illuminates the three-dimensional structure and reactivity of molecules, including steroids, terpenes, and carbohydrates.

**Baruch,** book included in the OLD TESTAMENT of the Western canon and the Septuagint but not in the Hebrew Bible, and placed in the APOCRYPHA in the Authorized Version. Named after a Jewish prince, Baruch (fl. 600 BC), a friend of the prophet JEREMIAH and the editor of his book, it includes a message from exiled Jews to those still at home, a famous messianic allusion, a consolation, and a letter of Jeremiah.

**Baruch, Bernard Mannes,** 1870–1965, US financier and government adviser. An industrial and economic adviser to the government during both world wars, Baruch was US representative (1946) to the UN Atomic Energy Commission.

**baryon:** see ELEMENTARY PARTICLES.

**Baryshnikov, Mikhail,** 1948–, Russian ballet dancer. After being soloist at the Kirov Ballet (1969–74), he went to the US in 1974. After dancing with the American Ballet Theatre (1974–78) and Ballet (1978–79) he became director of the former (1980). He has made many guest appearances, and has done film work; he is considered the leading male dancer of the early 1980s.

**barytes, barite** or **heavy spar,** white, yellow, blue, red, or colourless barium sulphate mineral ($BaSO_4$). Abundant worldwide in tabular crystals or in granular or massive form, barytes is used as a commercial source of the element BARIUM, as a filler in the manufacture of linoleum, oilcloth, rubber, and plastics, and as a mud for sealing oil wells during drilling.

**basal metabolic rate** (BMR), minimum amount of energy expended by the body to maintain all vital processes while at rest (see METABOLISM). It is expressed in joules per square metre of body surface per hour and measured by taking total body consumption of oxygen and calculating energy expenditure relative to body surface area.

**basalt,** fine-grained igneous ROCK of volcanic origin, with a high percentage of iron and magnesium, in a range of dark colours. Its texture varies depending on conditions of cooling. Most of the world's great LAVA flows (e.g., the COLUMBIA PLATEAU in the NW US and the Deccan Plateau in India) are basalt. It underlies the sediment cover in the world's oceans and is believed to underlie the CONTINENTS as well. Many of the lunar rocks obtained by the Apollo astronauts are basalt.

**base,** in chemistry: see ACIDS AND BASES.

**baseball,** the 'national game' of the US popular also in Japan and in Cuba, Puerto Rico, Mexico, and other Latin American countries. It derives its name from the four bases, spaced 27.43 m (90 ft) apart on the inner playing field (the diamond). Cowhide-covered hard balls, wooden bats, and padded gloves constitute the basic equipment. A game is played by two opposing teams of nine players each: a pitcher, a catcher, four infielders, and three outfielders. To win, a team must score more runs in nine innings than its opponent, a run being a complete circuit of the bases. Extra innings are played to resolve ties. A form of baseball derived from the English games of CRICKET and rounders, was played in the US in the early 19th cent. Two main professional associations form the major US leagues. The National League (organized in 1876) and the American League (1900) comprise a total of 26 teams representing US and two Canadian cities. Champions of each league meet annually in the World Series.

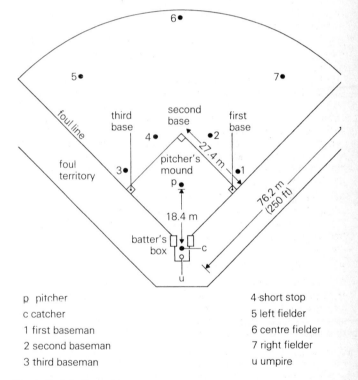

| | |
|---|---|
| p  pitcher | 4 short stop |
| c  catcher | 5 left fielder |
| 1 first baseman | 6 centre fielder |
| 2 second baseman | 7 right fielder |
| 3 third baseman | u umpire |

**Baseball** pitch dimensions

**Basel** or **Basle** (ˌbahzəl, bahl), city (1984 pop. 176,200), N Switzerland, divided by the Rhine R. A river port and financial centre, it is the seat of the Swiss chemical and pharmaceutical industries. Founded by the Romans, it became (7th cent.) an episcopal see and (11th cent.) a free imperial city. It was the residence of prince–bishops, expelled after Basel accepted (1523) the Reformation. Its university attracted ERASMUS (who is buried in the 11th-cent. cathedral), HOLBEIN the Younger, John CALVIN, and NIETZSCHE. The city houses a valuable collection of Holbein's work. It is the birthplace of the mathematician Loonhard Euler (1707–83).

**Basel, Council of,** 1431–49, council of the Roman Catholic Church. Called primarily to discuss the HUSSITE heresy it accepted the conciliar theory that ultimate authority in the church rests in the council and not with the pope. After being denounced (1437) by Pope EUGENIUS IV those who remained in Basel, deposed him and elected (1439) AMADEUS VIII (Antipope Felix V). Lacking support, Felix resigned (1449); the council then recognized Eugenius's successor Nicholas V and dissolved.

**base lending rate,** published rate of interest to which most bank lending is linked. The rate actually charged to the borrower will depend on his status—a large reputable company might secure a loan only 1 percentage point above base rate while a less prestigious company or private individual may be charged several percentage points above. The margins applied by the banks reflect their own cost of funds, provision for debt, administrative and other costs and profit.

**Bashō,** (Matsuo Bashō), 1644–94, usually considered the foremost Japanese HAIKU poet. He did not in fact write haiku but composed stanzas of *haikai no renga* (a sequence of linked verses, usually by a group of poets). The 17-syllable opening, and most important, stanza (*hokku*) was later separated as the verse form haiku. A master of both *hokku* and the integration of verses in a sequence, Bashō imbued what was formerly a social pastime with the spirit of ZEN BUDDHISM, attending to the often lowly details of everyday life in the context of the eternal, e.g., in *Narrow Road to the Deep North* (1694; tr. 1966).

**BASIC:** see PROGRAMMING LANGUAGE.

**basidiomycete** (bə'sidioh͵mieseet), class of advanced FUNGI in which sexual reproduction results in the formation of spores from special cells (basidia) formed in the familiar fruiting bodies of MUSHROOMS or toadstools, puff balls, and bracket fungi.

**Basie, Count** (William Basie), 1904–84, black American JAZZ pianist and bandleader. He worked in New York City and in Kansas City, where he formed (1935) a highly influential band that presented a powerful yet relaxed style of music featuring his own laconic piano.

**Basil,** Byzantine emperors. **Basil I** (the Macedonian), c.813–86 (r.867–86), was the favourite of and co-ruler (866) with MICHAEL III, whose murder (867) he ordered. Basil reformed finance and law, protected the poor, and restored the empire's military prestige. Art and architecture flourished during his rule. He tried to prevent an open break between the Eastern and Western churches. **Basil II,** c.958–1025 (r.976–1025), followed the usurpers NICEPHORUS II and JOHN I as co-ruler with his debauched brother, Constantine VIII. Basil suppressed rebellious landowners and strengthened the laws against them. He annexed (1018) Bulgaria and extended the empire east to the Caucasus. The schism between the Eastern and Western churches increased during his reign.

**basil,** tender herb or small shrub (genus *Ocimum*) of the MINT family, cultivated for the aromatic leaves. Common, or sweet, basil (*O. basilicum*) is used for seasoning. Holy basil and bush basil are related plants.

**Basildon,** town (1981 pop. 94,800), Essex, SE England, 42 km (26 mi) E of London. It is a New Town, designated in 1949 and formed in 1955 from the townships of Billericay, Laindon, Pitsea and Wickford. A range of light industries are carried out here.

**basilica,** large Roman building used to transact business and legal matters. Often rectangular, with a roofed hall, it usually had an interior colonnade, with an APSE at one or both ends. The wide central aisle was usually higher than the flanking aisles, so that light could penetrate through the clerestory windows. Early examples are in Rome and

Pompeii. In the 4th cent. Christians began to build places of worship related in form in Europe and the Middle East, e.g., the Church of the Nativity at Bethlehem (6th cent.). The massive Romanesque churches still retained the fundamental plan of the basilica.

**Baskerville, John,** 1706–75, English printer and, with CASLON, one of two great 18th-cent. English TYPE designers. His typefaces introduced the modern pseudoclassical style, emphasizing the contrast of light and heavy lines. Books made by Baskerville are typically large, with wide margins, and made with excellent paper and INK. Printer for Cambridge Univ. after 1758, he produced a famous folio Bible (1763) and fine editions of Milton, Congreve, Addison, Virgil, Juvenal, Horace, Catullus, and the Greek New Testament.

# ABCDEFGHIJKLMNOPQRSTUV
# abcdefghijklmnopqrstuvwxyz

The **Baskerville** typeface

**basketball,** game played generally indoors by two opposing teams of five players each. At each end of the court, usually about 26 by 14 m (84 by 46 ft) is a bottomless basket made of cord net and suspended from a metal ring attached 3.05 m (10 ft) above the floor to a backboard. The ball may be passed, batted, or dribbled (bounced), but the players may not run holding it. players of one team attempt to shoot the ball through one basket while seeking to keep the opposition from scoring through the other basket. Each field goal, or basket, scores two points (sometimes three points in professional basketball); foul shots, awarded mostly for illegal body contact, count for one point. Overtime periods are played to break ties. Basketball was originated (1891) in Springfield, Mass. by Dr. James Naismith of the YMCA. It quickly grew into a leading US school and college sport and spread throughout the world, becoming (1936) a part of the OLYMPIC GAMES.

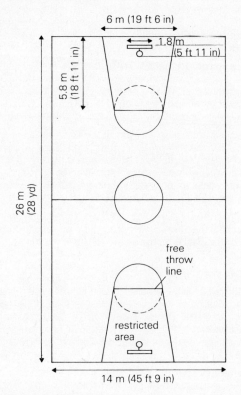

Basketball court dimensions

**basketry,** art of weaving or coiling flexible materials to form utensils for the preparation, storage, or serving of food; boats; huts; traps; apparel; and other objects. Twigs, roots, hide, bamboo, cane, raffia, grass, or straw are used. In antiquity, Egyptians (4000–5000 BC) used baskets for

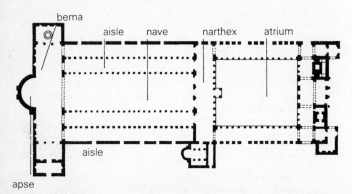

Floor plan of a **basilica**

storing grain, and North American Indians of the Southwest (c.1500 BC) covered baskets with clay and baked them to create fireproof cooking vessels, anticipating pottery. In some parts of the world pottery preceded basketry.

**Basque Provinces,** comprising the provinces of Álava, Guipúzcoa, and Vizcaya, N Spain, on the Bay of Biscay, bordering France in the northeast. In Álava and Guipúzcoa the major occupations are the mining of iron, lead, copper, and zinc; shipbuilding; metalworking; and fishing. Álava is largely agricultural. Nationalism is strong among the BASQUES, and in 1980 the provinces were granted regional autonomy. Basque terrorists, however, continue to press for total independence.

**Basques,** people of N Spain and SW France, numbering 2 million. Probably the oldest ethnic group in Europe, they preserve their ancient, unique language, and their customs and traditions. Since Palaeolithic times the Basques have been genetically and culturally distinct. Mostly peasants, shepherds, fishermen, navigators, miners, and metalworkers, they have produced such famous figures as St IGNATIUS OF LOYOLA and St FRANCIS XAVIER. The Basques accepted Christianity late (3rd–5th cent.). In the 6th cent. they expanded northward into Gascony, to which they gave their name. The kingdom of NAVARRE, founded in 824, united almost all Basques, but after its conquest (1512) by CASTILE Basque prosperity declined. Of the Basque provinces, only Navarre supported the Franco forces in the SPANISH CIVIL WAR (1936–39). Basque nationalism in Spain, often involving violent incidents, continued into the 1980s.

**Basra,** city (1977 est. pop. 1,000,000), SE Iraq, on the SHATT AL ARAB. Iraq's only port, it has a commercially advantageous location near oil fields and 121 km (75 mi) from the PERSIAN GULF. Since 1948 many oil refineries have been built in the city. Basra was founded (AD 636) by the caliph Umar I and was a cultural centre under HARUN AR-RASHID. Since 1982 the area around Basra has been the scene of heavy fighting in the Iran-Iraq War.

**bass,** any of various FISH of the families Serranidae (sea basses) and Centrarchidae (black basses and sunfishes). Sea basses, a large, diverse family of fishes with oblong, rather compressed bodies, inhabit warm and temperate seas worldwide and are highly valued as food and sport fish. The largest sea basses are GROUPERS. The common bass or sea perch (*Morone labrax*) is found from British waters to the Mediterranean. Like most bass, it feeds on CRUSTACEANS and small fishes. Wreckfish or stone bass (*Polyprion americanum*) are found associated with wrecks on the sea bed, and with floating logs.

**bass:** see VOICE.

**Bassano, Jacopo,** c.1517–1592, Venetian mannerist painter (see MANNERISM); b. Jacopo da Ponte. Primarily a painter of biblical themes, he introduced vignettes of country life into his works, e.g., *Annunciation to the Shepherds* (National Gall., Washington, DC). His sons **Francesco Bassano,** 1549–92, and **Leandro Bassano,** 1558–1623, were also painters.

**bassoon,** a WOODWIND instrument with a double reed and a conical bore. It is the bass instrument of the OBOE family, with a range of over three octaves upwards from the B♭ below the bass stave. The bassoon has been a member of the orchestra since the 18th cent.; it is not much used as a solo instrument. The double bassoon (or contrabassoon) is pitched an octave lower than the ordinary bassoon.

**Bass Strait,** strait separating the mainland of Australia from the island state of Tasmania. Two larger islands, King and Flinders, and smaller islands are occupied by small farming communities, remnants of early whaling and sealing bases. Regular ferries travel between Melbourne and Devonport, transporting passengers, vehicles and cargo. On the mainland side Australia's major oil and gas fields operate offshore.

**Bastille,** fortress and prison in Paris, begun c.1369, now demolished. The Bastille became a hated symbol of absolutism because it was used for arbitrary and secret imprisonment by the crown. On 14 July 1789, a Parisian mob stormed the prison, hoping to seize its store of ammunition, but found only seven prisoners. This marked the start of popular participation in the FRENCH REVOLUTION. July 14, Bastille Day, became a national holiday in France.

**bat** or **flitter mouse,** the only MAMMAL (order Chiroptera) capable of true flight. Numbering between 1000 and 2000 species, bats range in size from less than 2.5 cm (1 in) to 45 cm (15 in), with a wingspan of from less than 5 cm (2 in) to 150 cm (5 ft). The body is furry and mouselike, with the forelimbs and extensions of the skin of the back and belly modified to form wings. Bats are most abundant in the tropics, and temperate species often hibernate or migrate to warmer areas in the winter. The 5-cm (2-in) common pipistrelle (*Pipistrellus pipistrellus*) ranges from Britain and Europe across Asia to Japan, with other species in Australasia. Most species frequent crevices, caves, or buildings, and are active at night or twilight; they roost during the day, often in large numbers and usually hanging by their feet. Most bats see well but depend on echo location to navigate in the dark. Bats are fructivores like the flying foxes of Indonesia and Australia which can grow to 30 cm (1 ft) long, or insectivores; one species, the South American vampire bat, feeds exclusively on the blood of living animals, chiefly mammals.

Long-eared **bat** (*Plecotos auritus*)

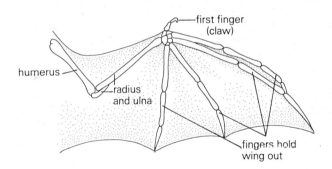

Bat wing

**Bataan,** peninsula and province (1981 pop. 321,860), W Luzon, the Philippines, between Manila Bay and the South China Sea. The capital is Batanga. A mountainous jungle region with bamboo forests, Bataan has a pulp and paper mill, fertilizer plant, and oil refinery. Subsistence farming is also carried on. US and Filipino troops captured on Bataan (Apr. 1942) by the Japanese in WORLD WAR II underwent a brutal 'death march' to a prison camp; thousands died.

**Batavian Republic,** name for the United Provinces of the Netherlands (1795–1806) after their conquest by the French in the FRENCH REVOLUTIONARY WARS. In 1806 NAPOLEON I made Batavia into the kingdom of Holland under his brother Louis Bonaparte (see BONAPARTE, family).

**Bates, Daisy May,** 1863–1951, Australian philanthropist. She worked among the ABORIGINES in the early 20th cent. and aroused the white conscience.

**Bates, Henry Walter,** 1825–92, English naturalist and explorer. His pioneering theory of mimicry, explaining similarity among species, was used by Charles DARWIN as a proof of his theory of natural selection. During travels (1848–59) along the upper Amazon R., he collected specimens of nearly 15,000 animal species (mostly insects), more than 8000 previously unclassified.

**Bates, H(erbert) E(rnest)**, 1905–74, English author. A talented storyteller and describer of the English countryside, he wrote *Fair Stood the Wind for France* (1944), *The Jacaranda Tree* (1949), and *The Triple Echo* (1970).

**Bateson, Gregory**, 1904–80, American biologist, anthropologist, and psychologist; b. England. Bateson's research encompassed subjects as diverse as animal behaviour and psychiatry, in which he developed the 'double bind' theory of schizophrenia which influenced the work of R.D. LAING, and the development of family therapy. In his writings on anthropology, he drew on psychoanalysis and cybernetics to explore the unconscious codings of culture. His lasting preoccupation, reflected in his books *Steps to an Ecology of Mind* (1972) and *Mind and Nature* (1979), was the development of an evolutionary theory capable of bridging the biological and social sciences. He was married to Margaret MEAD.

**Bath**, city (1981 pop. 84,283), Avon, SW England. In the 1st cent. AD the Romans built elaborate baths at the natural hot springs. Bath became England's most fashionable spa in the 18th cent., and the Georgian architecture and Roman baths remain tourist attractions. The University (founded in 1966) is situated to the E of the City.

The Royal Crescent, Bath

**Bath, Order of the:** see DECORATIONS, CIVIL AND MILITARY.

**bat hayyil:** see under BAR MITZVAH.

**Bathoeng I**, c.1850–1910, king of the Bangwaketse (r.1889–1910), one of the eight principal ethnic groups of BOTSWANA. Together with KHAMA III and SEBELE I, he visited England in 1895 to protest against the annexation of their territories, nominally under British protection since 1885, by Cecil RHODES's British South Africa Company.

**batholith**, enormous mass of igneous ROCK, granitic in composition, with steep walls and without visible floors. Batholiths commonly extend over thousands of square kilometres. Their method of formation is a controversial subject; most appear to have moved up through the earth's crust in a molten state, shattering and incorporating the overlying country rock.

**Báthory** (ˌbahtawree), Hungarian noble family. **Stephen Báthory**, 1477–1534, a supporter of JOHN I of Hungary, was made (1529) *voivode* [governor] of Transylvania. His younger son, **Stephen Báthory**, became (1576) king of Poland and was succeeded as prince of Transylvania by his brother, **Christopher Báthory**, 1530–81. Christopher's son and successor, **Sigismund Báthory**, 1573–1613, was mentally unbalanced. He abdicated (1597, 1599) for brief periods, and finally in 1602. **Gabriel Báthory**, 1589–1613, became (1608) prince of Transylvania and was killed in a revolt by nobles against his rule.

**Bath-sheba,** in the BIBLE, wife of Uriah the Hittite. DAVID seduced her, effected the death of her husband, and married her. She was the mother of SOLOMON. 2 Sam. 11; 12; I Kings 1–2.

**Bathurst,** city (1986 pop. 22,237), New South Wales, SE Australia. The oldest inland city in Australia, founded in 1815, it has an important rural service centre for the agricultural hinterland. In 1974 it was established as a growth centre with adjacent Orange (1986 pop. 28,935), New South Wales. Gold was discovered near the town in 1851.

**batik,** method of decorating fabric used for centuries in Indonesia. With melted wax, a design is applied to the cloth (cotton or, sometimes, silk), which is then dipped in cool vegetable dye. Areas covered by wax do not receive the dye and display a light pattern on the coloured ground. The process may be repeated several times. When the design is complete, the wax is removed in hot water. A crackling effect occurs if dye has seeped into cracks of hardened wax. The same or similar patterns have been used for c.1000 years. Batik was brought to Europe by Dutch traders, was adopted in the 19th cent. by Western craftsmen, and is still widely used.

**Batista y Zaldívar, Fulgencio,** 1901–73, Cuban dictator (1933–44, 1952–59). An army sergeant, he took part in the 1933 military coup and, as army chief of staff, became de facto ruler of CUBA and its elected president (1940–44). He accepted his candidate's defeat in 1944, but in 1952 he seized power and had himself elected president (1954, 1958). His corrupt rule caused popular discontent, and he fled (1959) the country during the CASTRO revolution.

**Batlle y Ordóñez, José** (ˌbahtyay ee awˌdohnyays), 1856–1929, president of URUGUAY (1903–7, 1911–15). He initiated laws to increase public welfare and to replace anarchy with orderly government. He influenced the constitution of 1917, which curbed executive power and introduced a welfare state.

**bat mitzvah:** see under BAR MITZVAH.

**Baton Rouge,** [Fr., = red stick], US city (1980 pop. 219,486), state capital of Louisiana, on the Mississippi R.; inc. 1817. A deepwater port and trade centre, it is a major site of petrochemical production with large refineries and machine shops. The city was founded in 1719 and was in turn French, English, and Spanish. Acquired by the US in 1815, it became state capital in 1849. The old (1882) and new (1932) capitols, many antebellum homes, and Louisiana State Univ. are among the points of interest.

**Batory:** see BÁTHORY.

**Batten, Jean,** 1909–82, New Zealand aviator. Trained as a pianist, she moved to England in 1929. In 1934, on her third attempt, she flew solo from England to Australia in record time: 14 days 22 hrs. Her return flight (1935) was the first solo by a woman from Australia to England. She made the first direct flight from England to New Zealand, in 1936, in which year she was awarded the CBE.

**Battenberg,** German princely family, issued from the morganatic union of Alexander, a younger son of Louis II, grand duke of Hesse-Darmstadt, and countess Julia von Hauke, who was created princess of Battenberg in 1858. Their oldest son, Louis (1854–1921), an admiral in the British navy, was created marquess of Milford Haven and married a granddaughter of Queen VICTORIA. During World War I, he anglicized his name to Mountbatten. He was the father of Louis MOUNTBATTEN and the grandfather of Philip, duke of EDINBURGH. Alexander's second son was Prince Alexander of Bulgaria. A third son, Henry, married Beatrice, daughter of Queen Victoria; their daughter, Victoria, married ALFONSO XIII of Spain.

**battered baby syndrome,** nonaccidental injury of childhood. The state of an infant showing bruises, wounds, or fracture as a result of violence inflicted by a parent or step-parent. It is not always obvious that the injuries are nonaccidental.

**Battersea,** former metropolitan borough of SW London, now in Borough of WANDSWORTH, on S side of R. Thames. Battersea Park is situated between the Albert (1873) and Chelsea (1937) bridges. The Thames is also crossed here by the Battersea Bridge (1890). Battersea power station at Nine Elms was one of the largest in Europe, but is now closed. The Battersea Dogs' Home is a famous sanctuary for abandoned dogs.

**battery,** unlawful touching by an aggressor of another person. Like ASSAULT, battery is a TORT. 'Assault and battery' is a CRIMINAL LAW charge combining the two elements.

**battery, electric:** see CELL, in electricity.

**Battle of Britain,** air battle over S England, July–Oct. 1940, now seen as one of the decisive battles not only of World War II but also of world history. After 16 weeks of intensive air fighting the German Luftwaffe, under Hermann GOERING was defeated by the Royal Air Force under Sir Hugh DOWDING, and in consequence Hitler abandoned plans to invade. The main assault took place between 8 Aug. and 30 Sept., involving 1030 German fighters and 1330 German bombers, which were met by an initial strength of 630 British fighters. By the end of the battle, German losses were about 4000 aircrew killed or missing, and 1733 aircraft destroyed; Britain had lost 50 pilots killed or missing and 1139 aircraft destroyed (during the four months July–Oct. 1940 these aircraft losses had been replenished by the production of 1836 Hurricanes, Spitfires, and Defiants).

**baud** (bawd), [after Emil Baudot, Fr. inventor, d.1903], a measure of the speed with which a signal travels over a telecommunications link. It is expressed in terms of the number of events that take place in one second, e.g., in COMPUTER input/output, one baud is equal to one bit per second.

**Baudelaire, Charles** (bohd,leə), 1821–67, French poet whose work has been a major influence on Western poetry. His poems, classical in form, introduced symbolism (see SYMBOLISTS). Baudelaire was moody and rebellious, imbued with an intense religious mysticism, and his work reflects an unremitting inner despair. His main theme is the inseparable nature of beauty and corruption, especially in modern life. His major work, *Les fleurs du mal* (1857; tr. The Flowers of Evil), originally condemned as obscene, is recognized as a masterpiece, especially remarkable for the brilliant phrasing, rhythm, and expressiveness of its lyrics. He also was a perceptive art critic.

**Baudouin,** 1930–, king of the Belgians (1951–). He joined his father, LEOPOLD III, in exile (1945–50) in Switzerland and became king when Leopold abdicated. He married Fabiola Mora y Aragon in 1960; the couple have no children.

**Bauhaus,** German school of art, architecture, and design. Founded in 1919 at Weimar by the architect W. GROPIUS, the school moved to Dessau in 1925 to a new building designed by Gropius, and then to Berlin in 1932, only to be closed by the Nazis in 1933. It was the main centre for modern design in the 1920s, and explored new teaching techniques. The emphasis was largely expressionist in its early years under the influence of ITTEN, but when in 1923 MOHOLY-NAGY replaced him, a redirection towards constructionist ideas took place. Among the artists who taught at the Bauhaus were Itten, Lyonel FEININGER, Oskar SCHLEMMER, Paul KLEE, Wassily KANDINSKY, and Josef ALBERS.

**bauxite,** mixture of hydrated aluminium oxides usually containing oxides of iron and silicon. A noncrystalline substance formerly thought to be a mineral, bauxite is claylike, ranging from white to brown or red in colour, and is the chief source of ALUMINIUM and its compounds. It is widely distributed, with important deposits in Africa, South America, France, the USSR, the West Indies, and the US.

**Bavaria,** Ger. *Bayern,* state (1984 est. pop. 10,951,544), 70,549 km² (27,239 sq mi), S West Germany. It is the largest state of West Germany. Forestry and agriculture are important occupations, and much of its industry is centred in MUNICH, the capital. The region, whose boundaries have varied, was conquered (15 BC) by the Romans and invaded (6th cent. AD) by the Baiuoarii, who set up a duchy. In 788 CHARLEMAGNE added Bavaria to his empire. It was ruled (788–911) by the CAROLINGIANS and in 1070 passed to the GUELPH family. In 1180 the Holy Roman Emperor bestowed the duchy on the WITTELSBACH family, who ruled it until 1918. In 1806 it became a kingdom. Bavaria joined the German Empire in 1871 and became the chief German state after Prussia. The monarchy was overthrown in 1918, and Bavaria later joined the Weimar Republic. Following World War II, Bavaria became (1949) part of West Germany.

**Bavarian Succession, War of the,** between Austria and PRUSSIA, 1778–79. In 1777 Charles Theodore, the duke of Bavaria, in a secret treaty with JOSEPH II, the Holy Roman emperor, ceded Lower BAVARIA to Austria. The Bavarian heir apparent, advised by FREDERICK II of Prussia,

protested the transfer. The resulting war, with no significant engagements, ended with Austria's renunciation of all but a small portion of Lower Bavaria.

**Bax, Sir Arnold,** 1883–1953, English composer. Among his early tone poems, inspired by the spirit of Celtic legend, were *The Garden of Fand* (1913-16) and *Tintagel* (1917–19). Thereafter he wrote seven symphonies (1923–39), three string quartets, and four piano sonatas, as well as concertos and choral works. His gentle, lyrical compositions, with their moments of high tragedy, deserve more frequent performances. But Bax's style was too esoteric and unfashionable to appeal to a wide audience. He was appointed Master of the King's Musick in 1942.

**Baxter, Richard,** 1615–91, English nonconformist clergyman. After serving as a chaplain in Cromwell's army, he sought under Charles II to keep moderate dissenters within the Church of England. After the Act of Uniformity (1662), Baxter left the Church of England, but continued to preach despite persecution.

**Bayamón,** city (1980 pop. 185,087), NE Puerto Rico, a residential and industrial suburb of San Juan. Bayamón was established in 1772. Fruit is a major product; manufactures include clothing, furniture, and metal products.

**bayberry,** common name for the Myricaceae, a family of chiefly temperate and subtropical aromatic trees and shrubs. The waxy grey berries of some species (mainly *Myrica cerifera*) are used to make candles, scented soap, and sealing wax. Sweet gale (*M. gale*) yields tannic acid from the bank, a condiment from the fruit, and insect repellent from the leaves.

**Bayeux tapestry** (bay,uh), an embroidery chronicling the Norman conquest of England (see under WILLIAM, kings of England). It is a strip of linen, 70 m by 51 cm (230 ft by 20 in) in the Bayeux Museum, France. Generally thought to be an almost contemporary product made in England, it is a valuable document on the history and costumes of the time.

**Bayezid,** sultans of the OTTOMAN EMPIRE (Turkey), also spelt Beyazid, Bajazet, and Bayazit. **Bayezid I,** 1354–1403 (r.1389–1402), triumphed over Byzantine Emperor Manuel II, the Turkish rulers of E Anatolia, and Sigismund of Hungary, who was on a crusade, but he was defeated (1402) by TAMERLANE, who routed his armies and took him prisoner. **Bayezid II,** 1447–1512 (r.1481–1512), was a peace-loving monarch who did little to advance Ottoman power but much to further Ottoman culture. With the aid of the JANISSARIES he put down a revolt of his brother Jem, but he failed to gain Cilicia from the Mamelukes of Egypt.

**Baykal** or **Baikal** (bie,kahl), lake, SE Siberian USSR. Nearly 650 km (400 mi) long, it is the largest (31,494 km²/12,160 sq mi) freshwater lake in Eurasia. It is also believed to be the deepest lake in the world, its maximum known depth being 1742 m (5714 ft). The lake is in danger of pollution because of recent industrial development near its shores.

**Bay of Pigs Invasion,** 1961, unsuccessful invasion of Cuba by US-backed Cuban exiles. On 17 Apr. 1961, about 1500 Cuban exiles landed in Cuba in the Bahía de Cochinos (Bay of Pigs) with the aim of ousting the Communist regime of Fidel CASTRO. They had been trained in Guatemala by the CIA, supplied with US arms. Most were soon captured or killed by the Cuban army. The US government was severely criticized for the attack at home and abroad. In Dec. 1962, Cuba traded 1113 captured rebels for $53 million in food and medicine raised by private donations in the US.

**Bayonne,** city (1982 pop. of agglomeration 127,477), SW France, on the Adour R. The chief port of the Basque country, it handles timber from the Landes and sulphur from the natural gas field of Lacq. The agglomeration includes the fashionable resort of Biarritz and the industrial centre of Le Boucau at the river mouth. There is a Gothic cathedral of the 13th–14th cent. Bayonne's company of armourers invented the bayonet in the 17th cent.

**Bayreuth** (,bieroyt), city (1984 pop. 70,000), SE West Germany, in a mountainous region of BAVARIA. Founded in 1194, it was controlled by the Hohenzollern family (1248-1807). The residence of Richard Wagner from 1872 to 1883, it is celebrated for its international Wagner music festivals. The magnificent opera house was built (1744–48) on the instructions of Wilhelmine, sister of FREDERICK THE GREAT of Prussia.

The opera house at **Bayreuth**

**bazooka,** military weapon consisting of a portable, lightweight tube that serves as a rocket launcher, usually operated by two men. Developed by the US as an INFANTRY weapon for use against TANKS, pillboxes, and bunkers, it was widely employed during World War II and the Korean War but was later superseded by more powerful, accurate weapons, notably recoilless weapons and antitank missiles.

**BCG** [Fr., *bacille Calmette–Guérin*], vaccine for immunization against tuberculosis. The French bacteriologists L.C.A. Calmette and C. Guérin grew a strain of tubercle bacillus which has reduced power to cause the disease at the Pasteur Inst., Paris, and the living vaccine prepared from it was introduced into medicine in 1921. Its effectiveness lasts for 7 to 10 years. It has had a dramatic effect in reducing the incidence of tuberculosis in the West.

**Be,** chemical symbol of the element BERYLLIUM.

**Beachy Head,** headland in E Sussex, S England, on English Channel coast. The chalk headland ends in cliffs c.174 m (570 ft) high, and forms the easternmost extremity of the S Downs. It was the scene of a naval battle in 1690 in which the English and Dutch were defeated by the French. There is a lighthouse at the foot of the cliffs.

**Beaconsfield, Benjamin Disraeli,** 1st **earl of:** see DISRAELI, BENJAMIN.

**Beadle, George Wells,** 1903–, American geneticist. For their work on the bread mould *Neurospora crassa,* which showed that genes control cellular production of enzymes and thus the basic chemistry of cells, Beadle and Edward TATUM shared the 1958 Nobel Prize for physiology or medicine with Joshua LEDERBERG.

**Beale, Dorothea,** 1831–1906, pioneer of women's education. She was a tutor at Queen's College, London (1849–56), and principal of The Ladies' College, a proprietary school in Cheltenham, from 1858 until her death. She taught and wrote about the teaching of mathematics, science, English language and literature, and other subjects. She gave evidence on girls' education to the Schools' Inquiry Commission (which reported in 1868), including on the teaching of geometry without rote learning. She resisted excessive commitment to examinations, and opposed the competitive spirit. She was one of those who, like Frances Mary BUSS, built a system of secondary education for middle-class girls in the second half of the 19th cent.

**bean,** name for kidney-shaped, laterally flattened seeds of plants of the PULSE family, especially the genus *Phaseolus.* Cultivated worldwide, beans are an important food staple. They are high in protein and often used as a meat substitute, especially the soybean (*Glycine max*).

**bear,** large MAMMAL of the family Ursidae, found almost exclusively in the Northern Hemisphere. Bears have large heads, bulky bodies, short, powerful, clawed limbs, and coarse, thick fur; almost all are omnivorous. In cold climates, bears do not hibernate (see HIBERNATION) but sleep most of the winter; their metabolism remains normal, and they may wake and emerge during warm spells. Brown bears occur from Europe, across Asia to NW North America, and include the Kodiak bear the grizzly, and the black bear. The American black bear, (*Euarctos americanus*) is the original teddy bear hunted by and kept as a pet by Theodore (Teddy) Roosevelt. The largest bear is the polar bear (*Thalarctos maritimus*) which averages 225 kg (500 lb) and is about 2.25 m (7½ ft) long. This powerful bear has been found swimming over 70 km (45 mi) from land in the Arctic seas. The smallest bear is the 120-cm (4-ft) sun bear which lives in the forests of southern Asia and some Indonesian islands. Sun bears (*Helarctos malayanus*) spend most of their lives in the tree tops.

**Beard, Charles A(ustin),** 1874–1948, American historian. As a professor at Columbia Univ. he taught that history encompasses all aspects of civilization. He was particularly interested in the relationship of economics and politics and in 1913 published *An Economic Interpretation of the Constitution,* an iconoclastic study of the economic interests of the makers of the FEDERAL CONSTITUTION. Beard helped to found the New School for Social Research. With his wife, Mary Ritter Beard (1876–1958), he wrote *The Rise of American Civilization* (2 vol., 1927) and its sequels (Vol. 3 and Vol. 4) *America in Midpassage* (1939) and *The American Spirit* (1943).

**Bearden, Romare,** 1914–, American painter raised in Harlem. Rendered in vibrant, flat planes, often with collage, his works deal with the black experience in America. Bearden is represented in many museum collections.

**Beardsley, Aubrey Vincent,** 1872–98, English illustrator and writer. His highly sophisticated ART NOUVEAU style was influenced by Greek vase painting, Japanese woodcuts, and the French ROCOCO. He developed a superbly artificial, flat, linear, black-and-white style, illustrating macabre, often erotic themes for books, e.g., Oscar WILDE's *Salome* (1894), and periodicals, e.g., *The Yellow Book* (1894–96), for which he was art editor. He died at 26 of tuberculosis.

*The Climax* (1894) from Oscar Wilde's *Salome* by Aubrey **Beardsley**

**bearing,** machine part used to reduce FRICTION between moving surfaces and to support moving loads. There are two principal types. A *plain,* or *journal, bearing* is a cylinder that supports a rotating shaft such as a motor shaft; its inner lining, the bush, or bushing, is usually made of a metal softer than that of the shaft, so that any slight misalignment of the shaft can be adjusted by an equivalent wearing of the bush. Babbit metal, alloys of tin, antimony, and copper with low frictional properties, may also be used. An *antifriction bearing* is a cylinder containing a movable inner ring of small steel balls (the ball bearings used primarily in light machinery) or larger cylindrical rollers. The rotating machine part fits into a centre of the ring, which takes up the motion of the rotating part, distributing and reducing friction through the movement of its bearings.

**beat generation,** certain American artists and writers popular in the 1950s. Influenced by Eastern religions, e.g., ZEN BUDDHISM, and the rhythms of 'progressive' JAZZ, they rejected traditional forms and sought expression in intense experiences and beatific illumination. Novelists in the movement included William Burroughs and Jack KEROUAC. Among the 'beat' poets were Kenneth Rexroth, Allen GINSBERG, and Lawrence Ferlinghetti.

**Beatitudes,** eight blessings spoken by Jesus at the beginning of the Sermon on the Mount (Mat. 5.3–12). Luke 6.20–26, a parallel passage, names four blessings and four woes.

**Beatles, The,** English rock music group (1950s–70). The members were John Lennon (1940–80), Paul McCartney (1942–), George Harrison (1943–), and Ringo Starr (Richard Starkey) (1940–), all from Liverpool. Influenced by Americans like Chuck BERRY, the Beatles dominated ROCK MUSIC in the 1960s with their wit, stage presence, and music that evolved from tight rhythm and blues to allusive lyricism. The lyrics and music for their songs were written mostly by Lennon and McCartney. The group recorded numerous albums, made films, and toured widely.

**Beaton, Sir Cecil,** 1904–80, English stage and costume designer, photographer, writer, and painter. His credits include the designs for the Broadway shows *My Fair Lady* (1956) and *Coco* (1969), and photographic portraits of many famous people.

Charles James's evening dresses photographed by Sir Cecil **Beaton**

**Beatrice,** the lady of DANTE's *Vita Nuova* and *Divine Comedy,* generally assumed to have been a Florentine woman, Bice Portinari (1266–90).

**Beatrix,** 1938–, queen of the NETHERLANDS (1980–). She ascended the throne when her mother, JULIANA, abdicated. She is married to a German, Claus von Amsberg, and has three sons.

**Beatty, Warren,** 1938–, American film actor, director, writer, and producer. He has starred in such films as *Bonnie and Clyde* (1967), *Shampoo* (1975), and *Heaven Can Wait* (1978). In *Reds* (1981), for which he won an Academy Award as director, he portrayed the American journalist John REED.

**Beaufort scale,** a system for estimating WIND speeds without the use of instruments. The behaviour of smoke, waves, trees, etc., is rated on a scale from 1 ( = calm) to 12 ( = hurricane). It was devised in 1806 by the British Adm. Sir Francis Beaufort (1774–1857); further numbers 13–17 were added in 1955.

| **BEAUFORT SCALE** | | | |
|---|---|---|---|
| NUMBER | WIND | SPEED | |
| | | miles per hour | metres per sec. |
| 0 | calm | < 1 | < 0.3 |
| 1 | light air | 1–3 | 0.3–1.5 |
| 2 | light breeze | 4–7 | 1.6–3.3 |
| 3 | gentle breeze | 8–12 | 3.4–5.4 |
| 4 | moderate breeze | 13–18 | 5.5–7.9 |
| 5 | fresh breeze | 19–24 | 8.0–10.7 |
| 6 | strong breeze | 25–31 | 10.8–13.8 |
| 7 | moderate gale | 32–38 | 13.9–17.1 |
| 8 | fresh gale | 39–46 | 17.2–20.7 |
| 9 | strong gale | 47–54 | 20.8–24.4 |
| 10 | whole gale | 55–63 | 14.5–28.4 |
| 11 | storm | 64–75 | 28.5–32.6 |
| 12 | hurricane | ≥75 | ≥32.7 |

**Beaufort Sea,** an arm of the Arctic Ocean between Point Barrow, Alaska, and the Canadian Arctic archipelago. The MACKENZIE R. flows into the sea, which is covered with pack-ice during the winter.

**Beauharnais, Alexandre, vicomte de** (bohah,nay), 1760–94, French general. He fought in the AMERICAN REVOLUTION and in the FRENCH REVOLUTIONARY WARS. After he was guillotined in the REIGN OF TERROR, his widow married NAPOLEON I and became the Empress JOSEPHINE. His son, **Eugène de Beauharnais,** 1781–1824, was also a French general who served with distinction under his stepfather, Napoleon. Made viceroy of Italy in 1805, he retired to Munich after Napoleon's fall. Eugène's sister, **Hortense de Beauharnais,** 1783–1837, married Louis BONAPARTE and was queen of Holland (1806–10).

**Beaumarchais, Pierre Augustin Caron de,** 1732–99, French dramatist. His brilliant comedies, *Le barbier de Séville* (1775; tr. The Barber of Seville) and *Le marriage de Figaro* (1784), are the bases for celebrated operas by ROSSINI and MOZART, respectively. Distinguished by their clever dialogue and intricate plots, they satirize the privileges and foibles of the upper class. Beaumarchais was frequently in litigation, and the pamphlets he wrote about his cases were witty and effective.

**Beaumont, Francis,** 1584?–1616, English dramatist, best known for collaborations with John FLETCHER. They have become known as the major exponents of the romantic tragicomedy. Sole authorship of *The Woman Hater* (1607) and the burlesque *Knight of the Burning Pestle* (c.1607) is usually ascribed to Beaumont.

**Beauvoir, Simone de** (boh,vwah), 1908–86, French author. A leading exponent of EXISTENTIALISM, she was a close associate of SARTRE. Chief among her novels interpreting the existential dilemma is *The Mandarins* (1955). Her most celebrated works include *The Second Sex* (1949), a profound analysis of the status of women and an important influence on the ideas of the WOMEN'S MOVEMENT in Europe; *Old Age* (1970), on society's treatment of the aged; and a lively series of memoirs. Until her death she remained an exemplary figure of women's independence.

**beaver,** large, aquatic RODENT (*Castor fiber*). Once widespread in the Northern Hemisphere, beavers are from 90 to 120 cm (3 to 4 ft) long, including the distinctive broad, flattened tail; they usually weigh about 25 kg (60 lb). Known for their engineering feats, beavers create ponds by building dams of sticks, logs, and mud; they build habitations, or lodges, in the same way.

**Beaverbrook, William Maxwell Aitken**, 1st **Baron** 1879–1964, British statesman and newspaper owner; b. Canada. He amassed a fortune in business before going to England in 1910. There he gained control of the *Daily Express* (1916) and the *Evening Standard* (1923), and began the *Sunday Express* (1918); these newspapers trumpeted his imperialist, isolationist views. A Conservative, he held several posts in Winston CHURCHILL's wartime cabinet (1940–45).

**Beccaria, Cesare Bonesana, marchese di**, 1738–94, Italian criminologist, economist, and jurist. His famous *Essay on Crimes and Punishments* (1764), arguing against CAPITAL PUNISHMENT and cruel treatment of criminals, influenced Jeremy BENTHAM and the utilitarians and stimulated penal reform throughout Europe. As an economist, Beccaria anticipated the wage and labour theories of Adam SMITH.

**Becker, Carl Lotus**, 1873–1945, American historian. He taught at Cornell Univ. for many years (1917–41). Becker's forte was the analysis of philosophy in action. His works include *The Declaration of Independence* (1922) and *The Heavenly City of the Eighteenth-Century Philosophers* (1932).

**Becket, Thomas:** see THOMAS BECKET, SAINT.

**Beckett, Samuel**, 1906–, French novelist and playwright; b. Ireland. He won the 1969 Nobel Prize in literature. His novels, e.g., *Murphy* (1938) and *Molloy* (1951), portray an individual's entrapment by grotesque situations in an apparently normal world. In his theatre of the absurd, typified by the popular but controversial *En attendant Godot* (1952; tr. Waiting for Godot) and *Fin de partie* (1957; tr. Endgame), Beckett combines poignant humour with an overwhelming sense of anguish and loss.

**Beckford, William**, 1760–1844, English writer. He is most famous for his novel *Vathek* (1786) which he first wrote in French and then translated into English; it amalgamates orientalist voluptuousness and Arabist scholarship, and is believed to have influenced novelists including MEREDITH and HAWTHORNE. He built an immense Gothic place (Fonthill Abbey, Wiltshire, S England) designed by James WYATT; the most extraordinary house in England at the time, it is now in ruins.

**Beckmann, Max**, 1884–1950, German painter. He was influenced by German primitives, especially BOSCH, and by contemporary Neue Sachlichkeit artists, with whom he exhibited in 1925. However, unlike those of GROSZ and DIX, his paintings were not so straightforwardly satirical, but attempted to treat more philosophical themes, such as lust and cruelty, in a symbolic way.

**Bécquer, Gustavo Adolfo** (bayˌkeə), 1836–70, Spanish romantic poet and prose writer. His *Rimas* (1871; tr. Rhymes), published after his death, are among the finest 19th-cent. LYRIC poetry. His prose includes the atmospheric *Legendas* (1860–64; tr. Legends).

**Becquerel, Antoine Henri** (bekəˌrel), 1852–1908, French physicist. Professor at the École Polytechnique, Paris, from 1895, he discovered RADIOACTIVITY in URANIUM in 1896. Further investigations of the phenomenon were made by Pierre and Marie CURIE, and the three shared the 1903 Nobel Prize for physics.

**bedbug**, small, flatbodied, blood-sucking BUG (*Cimex lectularius*) of the family Cimicidae. Distributed worldwide, bedbugs are parasites of warm-blooded animals. They are reddish-brown and about 6 mm (¼ in) long.

**Beddoes, Thomas Lovell**, 1803–49, English poet and dramatist. His writings, inclined towards the macabre and grotesque, include the verse work *The Improvisatore* (1821) and two plays, *The Bride's Tragedy* (1822) and *Death's Jest-Book* (1850).

**Bede, Saint** or **Baeda**, 673?–735, English historian, a Benedictine monk, also called the Venerable Bede. His *Ecclesiastical History of the English Nation*, in Latin, is an invaluable primary source for English history from 597 to 731.

**Bedford**, county town (1981 pop. 75,632) of Bedfordshire, E England, on R. Ouse, 74 km (46 mi) N of London. Industries in the town include engineering and brick-making. John BUNYAN wrote parts of *The Pilgrim's Progress* while in Bedford jail.

**Bedford, John of Lancaster, duke of**, 1389–1435, English nobleman, son of HENRY IV of England and brother of HENRY V. Made protector of HENRY VI in 1422, he devoted himself to English affairs in France.

**Bedfordshire**, inland county, S Midlands (1984 est. pop. 515,700), 1235 km² (487 sq mi). The county town is BEDFORD. It is mainly low-lying and drained by the Great Ouse R. Hilly areas are found in the S in the Chiltern Hills. Wheat cultivation and market gardening are common forms of agriculture in the county and industry is developed around LUTON.

**Bednár, Alfonz**, 1914–, Slovak prose writer whose first novel *The Glass Mountain* (1954) began 'the Thaw' in Czechoslovakia. His short stories *The Hours and the Minutes* (1956) concern the similarity between Nazi and Stalinist oppression. He conceives of violence as abhorrently natural in humanity; his trilogy *A Handful of Change* (1970–81) studies the undercurrent of violence in the affluent society.

**Bedouin** [Arab., = desert dwellers], primarily nomad Arab peoples of the Middle East. Of Semitic stock, they are devout believers in ISLAM. Camel- and sheep-breeding provide their main livelihood. Roving tribal groups, headed by a sheikh, traditionally travelled a defined area of land. However, the settlement policies of various governments in the 20th cent. have forced many Bedouins into a sedentary life.

**bee**, flying INSECT of the order Hymenoptera (superfamily Apoidea), all of which are nectar- and pollen-feeders: nectar is converted into HONEY in part of the digestive tract. All female bees have a sting but this is vestigial in the tropical stingless bees. These, like the bumble bees (*Bombus*) and honey bees (*Apis*), are social but the majority of species are solitary; a few (*Psithyrus*) are parasites in the nests of other bees. A typical colony of social bees has an egg-laying queen, sexually undeveloped females (workers), and, seasonally, fertile males (drones). Workers, whose numbers range from a dozen to more than 50,000 depending on species, gather pollen and nectar and, in the honey bee, communicate the location where these were obtained by performing precise dances. Their duties include making honey, fabricating wax cells both for food storage and for larvae, looking after these and the queen, and guarding the nest. Honey-bee colonies are perennial and from time to time new queens are reared; the old queen then leaves the hive with a swarm of workers to set up a home elsewhere. A new queen, after a marriage flight, on which she mates with several drones, returns to the hive and spends the rest of her life (usually several years) laying eggs. Honey bees were originally Old World insects and have been semidomesticated for several thousand years because of the honey and wax they produce. Recently they have also been kept as pollinators, since the natural populations of many other crop-pollinating insects have declined through habitat change and misuse of pesticides.

**beech**, common name for the Fagaceae, a family of trees and shrubs mainly of temperate and subtropical regions in the Northern Hemisphere, also including OAK and CHESTNUT. Many species are important hardwood timber trees, and some are also grown for their fruits and as ornamentals. The beeches have smooth, silvery grey bark and pale green leaves and the fruits are three-sided. The timber is highly suitable for funiture-making, especially for turned items, such as chair legs.

**Beecham, Sir Thomas**, 1879–1961, English conductor. He organized (1932) the London Philharmonic Orchestra and (1946) the Royal Philharmonic Orchestra of London. He was the champion and friend of the composer Frederick DELIUS.

**Beecher, Lyman**, 1775–1863, American Presbyterian minister. A preacher on temperance and a leading revivalist, he was a founder of the American Bible Society (1816) and later president (1832–52) of Lane Theological Seminary, Cincinnati. Among his 13 children were Harriet Beecher STOWE and **Henry Ward Beecher**, 1813–87, American Congregational preacher, orator, and lecturer. After serving congregations in Indiana, he became pastor of the Congregational Plymouth Church in Brooklyn, New York, in 1847. He championed reforms, especially the abolition of slavery and woman suffrage, and advocated the theory of evolution. Accusations of adultery by one of his parishioners led to a civil suit for damages and a long and sensational trial (1875) which ended in jury disagreement. Beecher's popularity suffered but he continued in his influential position for the rest of his life.

**Beeching, Richard, Baron,** 1913–85, Chairman, British Railways Board from 1963–65. His report marked the transition of British Railways from a common carrier to a more specialized mode of transport in which the railway concentrates on those aspects in which it is competitive with other modes of transport. The report led to many closures of rural lines and local stations and its more positive findings concerning the future role of the railway are often forgotten.

**bee-eater,** colourful insect-eating BIRD of the family Meropidae. These spectacular, attractive Old World birds live mainly in tropical Africa, Asia, and Australia. There is one European species, the 28-cm (11-in) *Merops apiaster* which, very rarely, nests in southern Britain. They do eat bees, the technique of the Australian bee-eater (*M. ornatus*) having been studied. The bird catches a bee in its bill, shifts its grip to just behind the sting, and rubs the sting against its perch, which must get rid of either the sting or the venom. The bird only treats stinging insects in this way.

**Beelzebub,** in the Bible: see SATAN.

**beer,** one of the oldest known alcoholic beverages. At first brewed chiefly in the household and monastery, it has been a commercial product since late medieval times and is made today in most industrialized countries. Colour, flavour, and alcoholic content (usually 3%–6%) may vary, but the process in brewing is similar: a mash of malt (usually barley), cereal adjunct (e.g., rice and maize), and water is heated and agitated. The liquid is boiled with hops and cooled. YEAST is then added, and fermentation occurs. Lager, brewed by slow fermentation, is light in colour; bitter, heavily flavoured with HOPS, is darker. Porter is a strong, dark ale brewed with roasted malt; stout (e.g., Guinness) is darker, stronger, and maltier than porter. From the 1970s in the UK the Campaign for Real Ale (CAMRA) has struggled to preserve traditional beer in the face of market domination by the breweries' mass-produced national brands. Brewing beer at home became legal in the UK in 1963, and immediately became widely popular not only as a cheap way to provide drinks but also as an intriguing hobby.

**Beerbohm, Sir Max,** 1872–1956, English essayist, caricaturist, and parodist. Best known today for his witty caricatures of late Victorian writers, e.g., D.G. ROSSETTI and WILDE, he also wrote brilliant parodies, e.g., *A Christmas Garland* (1912), and a popular satire on Oxford, *Zuleika Dobson* (1911).

**Beersheba** or **Be'er Sheva,** city (1983 est. pop. 110,800), S Israel, principal city of the NEGEV Desert. Beersheba is a trading centre, and its manufactures include chemicals and textiles. Once one of the southernmost towns of biblical PALESTINE, Beersheba contains a well believed to have been dug by ABRAHAM. It is the seat of Israel's Arid Zone Research Institute.

**beeswax:** see WAX.

**beet,** biennial or annual root vegetable (*Beta vulgaris*) of the goosefoot family, cultivated since pre-Christian times. Numerous varieties exist, e.g., red, or garden, beetroot; sugar beet; and Swiss chard. Both the roots and foliage of the red beet are edible, as is the foliage of the Swiss chard. The widely cultivated sugar beet, containing up to 20% sucrose, provides about one third of the world's sugar supply.

**Beethoven, Ludwig van,** 1770–1827, German composer. Young Beethoven's musical gifts were acknowledged by MOZART and HAYDN, and his piano virtuosity and extraordinary compositions won him the generous support of the Viennese aristocracy despite his notoriously boorish manners. Despite the onset (1801) of deafness, which became progressively worse and was total by 1817, his creative work was never restricted. Beethoven's work may be divided into three distinct periods. The early works, influenced by the tradition of Mozart and Haydn, include the First and Second Symphonies (1801 and 1804), the first three piano concertos (1795–1803), and a number of piano sonatas, including the Pathétique (1798). From 1802, his work broke the formal conventions of classical music. This most productive middle period included the Third Symphony (Eroica) (1805); the Fourth (1807) to Eighth (1814) Symphonies; his one Violin Concerto (1806); and his sole opera, *Fidelio* (1805–14). Beethoven's final period, dating from about 1816, is characterized by works of great depth, including the Piano Sonatas Op.106–11 (1817–22); the *Missa Solemnis* (1823); the monumental Ninth Symphony, with its choral finale based on SCHILLER's *Ode to Joy* (1824); and the last five string quartets (1823–26). A prolific composer, Beethoven produced numerous smaller works besides his major symphonies, concertos, sonatas, and quartets. His work crowned the classical period and initiated the romantic era in European music.

**beetle,** mainly terrestrial INSECT (order Coleoptera) with leathery or hard, opaque fore wings (elytra), which meet along the mid-line, covering hind (flight) wings and abdomen (except in rove beetles, family Staphylinidae). Adults and larvae both having biting mouthparts and generally feed on plant material, but there are many predatory species and a few are parasites of other insects (e.g., *Stylops*). Some beetles have bright, often metallic colours, e.g., leaf beetles (Chrysomelidae), but most are rather sombre. They range in size from 0.27 to 150 mm (1/100 in to nearly 6 in) and are the largest group of insects, with well over 300,000 known species (4000 in Britain). Many are of great economic importance as crop pests, e.g., wireworms, the larvae of click beetles (Elateridae); both larvae and adults of the Colorado beetle (*Leptinotarsa decemlineata*); CHAFERS; and many WEEVILS. Serious pests of both growing and sawn timer include the larvae of longhorn beetles (Cerambycidae), but ground beetles (Carabidae) and LADYBIRDS are highly beneficial as predators on a wide range of insect pests, and SCARABS and dung beetles (Geotrupidae) usefully recycle animal waste products. After the introduction of cattle into Australia serious difficulties were experienced because the indigenous dung beetles, all of which were adapted to feeding on marsupial pellets, were unable to utilize cow pats, which were therefore not being recycled. This problem was overcome by the successful introduction of several species of African dung beetle. See CHAFER; LADYBIRD; SCARAB; WEEVIL.

**beet sugar:** see BEET; SUCROSE.

**Begin, Menachem,** 1913–, prime minister of ISRAEL (1977–83); b. Poland. In the years before Israeli independence, he commanded the Irgun, an anti-British terrorist group. He sat in the Knesset after 1949. In 1977 he formed a right-wing coalition government. Begin signed a peace treaty with Egypt in 1979 (see CAMP DAVID ACCORDS), and he and Egyptian President Anwar al-SADAT shared the 1978 Nobel Peace Prize. In 1982 he authorized a massive Israeli invasion of LEBANON in order to destroy military bases of the PALESTINE LIBERATION ORGANIZATION located there (see ARAB–ISRAELI WARS). Israeli soldiers then occupied West BEIRUT, and Begin's government (particularly Defence Minister Ariel SHARON) was criticized for allowing the massacre of hundreds of Palestinian civilians by Israel's Lebanese Christian allies.

**begonia,** common name for the Begoniaceae, a family of succulent, perennial herbs of the American tropics, and for members of the genus *Begonia.* Begonia species are common houseplants and summer bedding plants, some grown for their showy, variously coloured leaves (e.g., *B. rex*) and others for their white, pink, red, or yellow flowers (e.g., *B. semperflorens*).

**Behan, Brendan,** 1923–64, Irish dramatist. An outspoken man jailed for Irish Republican Army activities, he is noted for his prison drama *The Quare Fellow* (1956); *The Hostage* (1958), a farce; and his autobiography, *Borstal Boy* (1958).

**behaviourism,** an approach within psychology which regards its only legitimate subject matter to be the observable and measurable behaviour of organisms. Behaviourism as a programme for psychology was proposed in 1913 by J.B. WATSON, who denounced both the method of INTROSPECTION, and any attempt to talk about mental states, as unscientific. Behaviourism is also an extreme environmentalist theory in which animal and human behaviour is controlled by LEARNING through ASSOCIATION. Behaviourism thus incorporates the main tenets of positivism and empiricism. Although it dominated North American psychology for most of the 20th cent., since the rise of COGNITIVE SCIENCE behaviourism has been in decline.

**behaviour modification** or **behaviour therapy,** a method of treating behavioural and other psychiatric and developmental disorders, based upon operant conditioning (see LEARNING). Because of the emphasis upon the control of overt behaviour, and upon reward and punishment, behaviour modification has been criticized as both undesirable and superficial. There is however evidence that behaviour modification can be an effective therapy in a variety of psychiatric and educational circumstances.

**Behmen, Jakob:** see BOEHME, JAKOB.

**Behn, Aphra,** 1640–89, first professional English female writer. She wrote verse under the pseudonym Astraea, adopted during a career as a spy. *The Rover* (1677), a bawdy political comedy, brought her fame as a playwright which was consolidated by later comedies such as *The Lucky Chance* (1686). *Oroonoko* (1688) was the first English philosophical novel.

**Behrens, Peter** (‚bayrəns), 1868–1940, German architect. His utilitarian style was both clear and impressive. He is known for his factory buildings, which based a simple, effective design on the frank terms of modern construction. LE CORBUSIER, GROPIUS, and MIES VAN DER ROHE were his students.

Peter **Behrens'** AEG Turbine Factory

**Behring, Emil Adolph von,** 1854–1917, German microbiologist and serologist. A pioneer in serum therapy (treatment of disease using blood serum containing antitoxins), he received the first Nobel Prize for physiology or medicine in 1901 for his work on immunization against diphtheria (1890) and tetanus (1892) by injections of antitoxins (a word he introduced).

**Beihai,** city, (1984 pop. 172,000), S GUANGXI ZHUANG, S China, on the Beibu Gulf (Gulf of Tonkin). Beihai is to develop as a port and industrial centre based on oil exploration and development in the Beibu Gulf. In 1984 it was designated as one of the 14 coastal cities given special privileges to encourage foreign investment.

**Beijing** or **Peking** [Chin., = northern capital], city (1984 pop. 9,450,000), capital of the People's Republic of China. It is located in central HEBEI prov., N China, but administered directly by the central government. The second-largest city in China (after Shanghai), Beijing is the political, financial, educational, and transport centre of the country. It has become a major industrial area, with factories producing an array of heavy and light industrial goods, such as iron and steel, textiles, machinery, chemicals, and electronic equipment. The historic centre was laid out along the north–south axis. Inside the main avenues were narrow lanes and intricate residential courtyards. Much of the traditional building is now being replaced by modern Western style construction. Major landmarks include the Forbidden City, Tien An Men Square, the Imperial Palace, and the Gate of Heavenly Peace. Beijing has a famous opera, a ballet, the national library, many educational institutions, outstanding museums, a renowned zoo, and a modern international airport. Serving (13th cent.) as Kublai Khan's capital, the city was China's capital from 1421 to 1911. It was the site of important events such as the BOXER UPRISING (1900), the MAY FOURTH MOVEMENT (1919), the founding of the People's Republic of China and its reestablishment as capital (1949), and the deaths (1976) of Zhou Enlai and Mao Zedong and the political turmoil that followed.

**Beirut,** city (1980 est. pop. 702,000), W Lebanon, capital of Lebanon, on the Mediterranean Sea. An important port, Beirut became a major financial centre with food-processing industries. It was a Phoenician city and was called Berytus in ancient times. A prominent city under both the Seleucids and Rome, Beirut was captured by the Arabs in AD 635. It was part of the Latin Kingdom of Jerusalem from 1110 to 1291. After 1517 the DRUZES controlled the city under the OTTOMAN EMPIRE. It fell (1918) to France in World War I and became the capital of Lebanon in 1920 under the French mandate. After the establishment of Israel in 1948 Beirut became the major financial and commercial centre of the Arab Middle East, but this ended with the Lebanese civil war between the Muslims and Christians in 1975–76. Since then conditions have worsened as sporadic fighting between Palestinian refugees, Christians, Muslims, and Druze has continued. Despite two invasions of Lebanon by Israeli forces, an occupation of parts of Beirut by Syrian forces, and an ill-fated intervention by an international peace keeping force (composed of American, French, Italian, and British troops) conditions in Beirut remain anarchic. There is a *de facto* division of the city into a Muslim western sector and a Christian eastern sector. Many of the PLO guerillas were expelled from the city in 1982 and shortly afterwards some 1000 Palestinian refugees were massacred by Lebanese Christian forces.

The Gate of Heavenly Purity, **Beijing** Imperial Palace

**Béjart** or **Béjard** (bay‚zhah), French family of actors in a company associated (after 1643) with MOLIÈRE. The eldest was **Joseph Béjart,** c.1616–1659. His sister **Madeleine Béjart,** 1618–72, a fine actress, was Molière's mistress. Their sister, **Geneviève Béjart,** 1624–75, and brother, **Louis Béjart,** 1630–78, also acted in the company. **Armande Grésinde Béjart,** c.1640–1700, Madeleine's sister or daughter, married Molière in 1662 and played most of his heroines. After merging with two other companies, the troupe became the Comédie Française (see THEATRE, table).

**Béjart, Maurice,** 1928–, French BALLET and opera director; b. Maurice Berger. His eclectic style incorporates JAZZ and avant-garde music, nontraditional dance forms (e.g., acrobatics), and unusual settings. He founded (1959) the highly influential Ballet of the XXth Century (see DANCE, table).

**Bekaa,** valley: see BIQA, AL.

**Bektashis,** a Sufi order of DERVISHES. Of obscure and probably legendary origins, this order found favour among the JANISSARIES of the Ottoman Empire, and grew in influence in proportion to the influence that its members enjoyed at Istanbul. Its doctrines derive mainly from esoteric SUFISM but contain strong elements of SHI'ISM.

**Béla Kun:** see KUN, BÉLA.

**Belau,** formerly Palau, self-governing Micronesian island group (1980 pop. 12,177), c.497 km² (192 sq mi), in the W Pacific Ocean at the extreme western end of the Caroline Islands, administratively part of the

US Trust Territory of the PACIFIC ISLANDS. It consists of c.200 small islands (8 are inhabited), of which Babelthaup (the largest) and Koror (the capital) are the most important. Most of the population is Micronesian. The economy is based on subsistence farming, with some commercial production of tuna fish and copra. Spain held the islands for about 300 years and sold them to Germany in 1899. Japan seized them in WORLD WAR I, administered them as a mandate for the League of Nations, and in WORLD WAR II used them as a major naval base. US forces captured the islands in 1944, and in 1947 they became part of the trust territory placed under US administration by the UNITED NATIONS. Voters approved (1979) a local constitution, notable for its provision that Belau should be a nuclear-free zone. The islands became (1981) self-governing as the Republic of Belau and in 1982 a 'compact of free association' with the US was signed, giving the government full control over internal and external affairs, while the US retained responsibility for defence and security and also obtained 50-year rights to military facilities on the islands. However, ratification of the compact has been delayed because its military provisions in favour of the US are regarded by many opponents as being inconsistent with Belau's non-nuclear constitution. Belau's president, Haruo Remeliik, was assassinated in June 1985 and succeeded by Lazarus Salii.

**Belaúnde Terry, Fernando** (bay͵lahoohday ͵tayree), 1912–, president of PERU (1963–68, 1980–85). An architect, he effected social, educational, and land reforms in his first term as president. In 1968 he was deposed by an army coup and went into exile. Restored to the presidency in 1980, he attempted to combat inflation by denationalizing industries and encouraging foreign investment in the petroleum industry.

**bel canto** [It., = beautiful singing], style of singing featured particularly in late 18th and early 19th-cent. Italian OPERA. It emphasizes vocal technique and beauty of tone, shown in arias with attractive rather than dramatic melodies, lavishly decorated with trills, scales, etc. After being neglected during the first half of the 20th cent., the style has been revived lately, a leading exponent being Dame Joan SUTHERLAND.

**Belém** or **Pará**, city (1980 pop. 755,984), N Brazil, capital of Pará state, on the Pará R. It is the chief commercial centre and port of the AMAZON R. basin. Founded by the Portuguese in 1616, it prospered during the rubber boom of the late 19th cent. and again after World War II with the development of rail and highway links. The Goeldi museum holds ethnological and zoological collections of the region.

**Belfast**, capital city (1981 pop. 302,988) of Northern Ireland, on an inlet of the Irish Sea, at the mouth of the R. Lagan. A port and industrial centre, Belfast is known for its shipyards and linen industry. Agricultural and livestock products are the chief exports. The city was founded in 1177. French HUGUENOT settlers, who arrived in the late 17th cent., stimulated the growth of the linen industry. Since the 19th cent. the city has been scarred by violent strife between the majority Protestants and the minority Catholics. In recent years there has been frequent guerrilla fighting between the IRISH REPUBLICAN ARMY and British troops. It is the birthplace of the scientist Lord KELVIN and the site of Queen's Univ.

**Belgaum**, town (1981 pop. 274,430), Karnataka state, S India. It is a district administrative and communications centre where Maratha and Kannada cultures meet. It has a cotton industry. It was a strong fortress in the 15th cent. and became a British district capital.

**Belgium**, Flemish *België*, Fr. *La Belgique*, officially the Kingdom of Belgium, constitutional kingdom (1985 est. pop. 9,880,000), 30,513 km² (11,781 sq mi), NW Europe; bordered by the Netherlands and the North Sea (N), West Germany and Luxembourg (E), and France (W and SW). BRUSSELS is the capital and ANTWERP the chief commercial centre and port. Low-lying, except for the forested Ardennes Mts in the south, Belgium is crossed by the MEUSE and SCHELDT rivers and a network of canals. It is one of the most densely populated and heavily industrialized nations in Europe, but while the emphasis is on heavy industry, such as production of steel, chemicals, and petrochemicals, the traditional industries of lace-making and diamond-cutting continue to flourish. Coal, zinc, copper, and lead are important minerals. Belgium is a leader in shipping, and its economy depends on its exports. Agricultural activities include cattle-raising and dairying; cereals are the chief crops, and food processing is a major source of income. Tourism is important. The economy entered a recession in 1974 that continued into the 1980s. The GNP is $90,540 million and the GNP per capita is $9160 (1983). Belgium is divided culturally and ethnically into Flemish-speaking

Flanders in the N and French-speaking Wallonia, or Wallony, in the S. Virtually the entire population is Roman Catholic.

*History.* The Franks first appeared in the Roman province of Belgica in the 3rd cent. AD, and the area became the cradle of the CAROLINGIAN dynasty. After the death (814) of CHARLEMAGNE, most of the region was made part of LOTHARINGIA and, later, of Lower Lorraine. By the 12th cent. this had broken up into the duchies of Brabant and LUXEMBOURG, and the histories of these feudal states and of FLANDERS and Hainaut constitute the medieval history of Belgium. In the 15th cent. the area of present-day Belgium passed to the dukes of Burgundy and then to the HABSBURGS (see NETHERLANDS, AUSTRIAN AND SPANISH). Annexed by France in 1797, the region was given to the Netherlands by the Treaty of Paris (1815). Resentment of Dutch rule led (1830) to rebellion, and an independent (1831), 'perpetually neutral' (1838) state was established. Under LEOPOLD I and LEOPOLD II there was rapid industrialization and also colonization, notably in the Congo (see ZAÏRE). Belgian neutrality was violated by the Germans, who occupied the country in WORLD WAR I and WORLD WAR II. Following World War II the unpopular LEOPOLD III, who had surrendered the country unconditionally to the Germans in 1940, abdicated (1951) in favour of his son BAUDOUIN. Postwar recovery was rapid, but crises arising from longstanding tensions between the Flemish- and French-speaking elements toppled several governments in the 1960s. A constitutional reform (1971) in effect federalized the country by creating three partially autonomous regions (Flanders, Wallonia, and Brussels), but ethnic discord between Flemish and French speakers has continued, causing frequent governmental crises. In 1981 a centre-right coalition of the Flemish and French-speaking Christian Social parties and the two wings of the Liberal Party came to power, but was replaced in 1988 by a centre-left coalition of the Christian Socials, the two Socialist parties and the Flemish nationalist People's Union. Belgium is a member of the BENELUX ECONOMIC UNION, and Brussels is the headquarters of the EUROPEAN COMMUNITY and of the NORTH ATLANTIC TREATY ORGANIZATION.

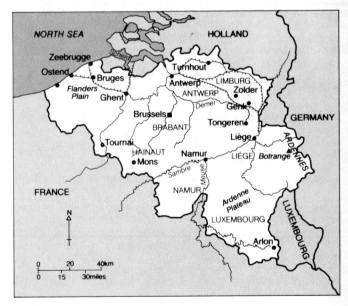

Belgium

**Post-war Belgian prime ministers**
Hubert Pierlot (Christian Social), 1944–45
Achille van Acker (Socialist), 1945–46
Paul-Henri Spaak (Socialist), 1946
Achille van Acker (Socialist), 1946
Camille Huysmans (Socialist), 1946–47
Paul-Henri Spaak (Socialist), 1947–49
Gaston Eyskens (Christian Social), 1949–50
Jean Duvieusart (Christian Social), 1950
Joseph Pholien (Christian Social), 1950–52
Jean van Houte (Christian Social), 1952–54
Achille van Acker (Socialist), 1954–58
Gaston Eyskens (Christian Social), 1958–61
Théo Lefèvre (Christian Social), 1961–65

Pierre Harmel (Christian Social), 1963–66
Paul Vanden Boeynants (Christian Social), 1966–68
Gaston Eyskens (Christian Social), 1968–72
Edmond Leburton (Socialist), 1973–74
Léo Tindemans (Christian Social), 1974–78
Paul Vanden Boeynants (Christian Social), 1978–79
Wilfried Martens (Christian Social), 1979–81
Marc Eyskens (Christian Social), 1981
Wilfried Martens (Christian Social), 1981–

**Belgrade**, Serbo-Croat *Beograd,* city (1981 pop. 1,470,073), capital and largest city of Yugoslavia and of its constituent republic SERBIA, at the confluence of the Danube and Sava rivers. It is the political and communications hub of the federation and an industrial, financial and cultural centre as well. Manufactures include metals, chemicals and textiles. A harbour for Rome's Danubian fleet, it was later held by the Byzantines, Bulgars, Serbs, and Hungarians. After 1521 it was a major Ottoman fortress and administrative centre. Belgrade became capital of the Serbian principality in 1841 and of Yugoslavia in 1918. Severely damaged by German and Allied air raids in World War II, Belgrade is noted for its parks, museums, theatres, and restaurants. The Kalemegdan citadel is now a military museum.

**Belgrano, Manuel**, 1770–1820, Argentine revolutionist. A political figure and journalist, he was a leader of the May 1810 revolution and a member of the first patriot governing junta. Later he commanded the Army of the North (1812–14, 1816–19). A battleship named after him was sunk by the British navy in the Falklands War (1982).

**belief system**, the ways in which any given social group conceptualizes its universe. Belief systems not only provide answers to some of the most fundamental existential questions: how the world came to be, why humans die, why they succeed and fail, they also explain the way in which human beings can relate to and communicate with the unseen powers and forces that are believed to control the operations of the universe. Social relations and religious beliefs validate and regulate human behaviour, and offer a model for and of the world. A close relationship exists between any society's belief system and its forms of social organization: religious ideologies tend to reflect, reinforce, and perpetuate dominant forms of political power, and the exercise of that power is revealed in the way that belief systems operate, e.g., ancestor worship is characteristic of societies with segmentary power systems, whereas centralized political systems tend to have a high god, or a centralized pantheon of gods. See MYTH.

**Belinsky, Vissarion Grigoryevich** (bi‚linskee), 1811–48, Russian literary critic. Although he championed the works of GOGOL, LERMONTOV, and DOSTOYEVSKY, his repudiation of art for art's sake and his emphasis on the social and political uses of literature laid the foundation for later Soviet critical theory and SOCIALIST REALISM.

**Belisarius**, c.505–565, Byzantine general under JUSTINIAN I. He suppressed (532) the Nika riot caused by internal political strife, and defeated (533–34) the Vandals, a Germanic tribe in North Africa. In command (535) of the war against the OSTROGOTHS in Italy, he took NAPLES and ROME (536), as well as MILAN and RAVENNA (540). Justinian replaced him (548) with NARSES, but Belisarius returned (559) to drive the Bulgarians out of Constantinople. After a brief political imprisonment (562) he returned to favour.

**Belize** (bə‚leez), formerly British Honduras, independent nation within the Commonwealth (1983 est. pop. 157,700, increasing at 1.8% per year) 22,965 km² (8867 sq mi), Central America; bordered by Mexico (N), Guatemala (S and W), and the Caribbean Sea (E). The land is generally low-lying, forested, and undercultivated, with a swampy coastline and some low mountains in the S. The capital is BELMOPAN, and the chief port is Belize City. The major products are sugarcane, citrus fruits, bananas and timber. The traditional exports, mahogany and other woods, are declining due to overharvesting. In 1983 GDP was US$1759 million or US$1099 per capita. The population is mostly of black African descent, with sizable Spanish-American and Mayan Indian minorities. Once a part of the MAYA civilization, the region was probably traversed by CORTÉS on his way to HONDURAS, but the Spanish made no attempt at colonization. Buccaneers founded Belize City in the early 1600s and were followed by British Jamaicans who moved into the area to exploit its timber. Spain long contested British possession. British Honduras was granted internal self-government in 1964, but full independence was delayed by GUATEMALA's claim that it had inherited the territory from

Spain. The dispute remains to be settled by negotiation. On 21 Sept. 1981, British Honduras, as Belize, became the last British crown colony on the American mainland to achieve full independence within the COMMONWEALTH. The centre-left People's United Party was politically dominant until 1984, when it was defeated in elections by the centre-right United Democratic Party led by Manuel Esquivel.

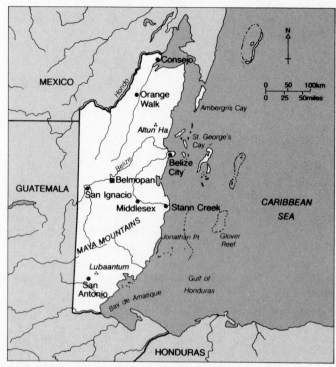

Belize

**bell**, in music, a PERCUSSION INSTRUMENT consisting of a hollow metal vessel set into vibration by a blow from a clapper within or a hammer without. Apparently originating in Asia, bells have been used in connection with all major religions except Islam. A portable set of bells tuned to the intervals of the major scale is called a chime. A carillon is a larger stationary set of up to 70 bells with chromatic intervals played from a keyboard. It developed in the Low Countries and reached a peak there in the 17th cent., while in England the art of CHANGE RINGING evolved. Carillon playing declined at the end of the 18th cent., but was revived in the 20th cent. following the rediscovery of older tuning secrets and the development of improvements in construction.

**Bell, Alexander Graham**, 1847–1922, American scientist, b. Scotland, inventor of the TELEPHONE. For many years he worked on the problems involved in teaching the deaf to speak, conducting his own school of vocal physiology in Boston. In 1865 he conceived the idea of transmitting speech by electric waves, and in 1876 he perfected and demonstrated the first telephone apparatus. Under Bell's influence the magazine *Science* was founded (1880); his patronage of scientists interested in aviation resulted in the development of the HYDROFOIL.

**Bell, Andrew**, 1753–1832, Scottish educator. He developed the MONITORIAL SYSTEM after superintending an orphan asylum in Madras, India. His *Experiment in Education* (1797) described this system, and Joseph LANCASTER, a Quaker, established a school based on similar principles and copied by many nonconformists. Bell's monitorial schools taught the principles of the Established Church.

**Bell, Clive**, 1881–1964, British critic and writer associated with the BLOOMSBURY GROUP. With Roger FRY he was responsible for introducing POST-IMPRESSIONISM to Britain. His art theory relied upon the notion of 'significant form', which stated that it was the purely formal aspects, rather than the subject matter, of a painting that could produce a unique aesthetic emotion in the viewer. This elitist aesthetic theory which sees art as an autonomous and universal formal activity was very influential, but is now discredited.

**Bell, Gertrude Margaret Lowthian,** 1868–1926, English traveller and writer, one of the builders of modern IRAQ. As liaison officer of the Arab Bureau in Iraq she was largely responsible for the selection of FAISAL I as king. She translated many works from Arabic and Persian and her *Letters* (2 vol., 1927) are interesting even though severely edited for publication.

**belladonna,** in botany, the specific name of *Atropa belladonna*, of the NIGHTSHADE family. It is also the common name for the prepared herb and drug extracted from the plant. Growing in woods and shady places throughout Britain and Europe, it bears lurid violet and greenish flowers and black berries. The whole plant is highly poisonous due to its ALKALOID content, but is used medically as an antispasmodic in bronchitis, for heart arrhythmia and nervous complaints, as an anti-emetic in motion sickness, and for the dilation of the pupil of the eye. Its name refers to its former use for removing freckles and blemishes from the skin ('fair lady'). It is not related to the so-called belladonna lily (see AMARYLLIS).

**Bellary,** town (1981 pop. 201,579), Karnataka state, S India, E of the Hagari R. It is a district administrative and railway centre with engineering works and mills processing agricultural produce. It was a fortress in the 17th cent. and later a British district headquarters.

**Bellay, Du:** see DU BELLAY.

**Bell Beaker,** a type of pottery vessel widely distributed in Europe c.2500–2200 BC. The speed and extent of the adoption of Beakers has suggested to many that a 'Beaker folk' spread across Europe. As these vessels are usually found in graves, often under a BARROW, along with bronze weapons or other status objects, their appearance may indicate the movement of a prestige item for social elites rather than the migration of a people.

Bell Beaker pottery of early Bronze Age

**Bellerophon** (bə‚leərəfon), hero in Greek mythology. Given a number of seemingly impossible tasks by King Iobates, he performed them all. Most notable was the killing of the monster Chimera, accomplished with the aid of the winged horse PEGASUS. Grown proud, Bellerophon attempted to ride Pegasus to Mt OLYMPUS, but was thrown, crippled, and blinded.

**Belli, Giuseppe Gioacchino,** 1791–1863, Italian poet. His c.2400 *Roman Sonnets,* the most impressive body of verse ever produced in the Roman dialect, portray the life of the people in the decadent, priest-ridden city of the 1830s and 40s.

**Bellini,** illustrious family of Venetian painters of the RENAISSANCE. **Jacopo Bellini,** c.1400–70, was the father and teacher of Giovanni and Gentile. Few of his works survive, but two of his notebooks dealing with problems of perspective, landscapes, and antiquity are his most important legacy. **Gentile Bellini,** 1429–1507, painted contemporary Venetian life. After his visit to Constantinople in 1479, a distinct Oriental flavour appeared in his paintings, including the portrait of Muhammad II (National Gall., London). **Giovanni Bellini,** c.1430–1516, was the outstanding artist of the family, who became the teacher of TITIAN and GIORGIONE. His works are characterized by serenity, majesty, and luminous colour. They include the altarpieces of the Frari (1488) and San Zaccaria (c.1505) in Venice; and various mythological scenes. He painted many tender pictures of the Madonna and Child, e.g., *The Madonna of the Meadow* (c.1505; National Gall., London).

Giovanni **Bellini,** altarpiece of the Frari 'Madona and Child', 1488. Venice.

**Bellini, Vincenzo,** 1801–35, Italian opera composer. His most celebrated works, *La Sonnambula* and *Norma* (both: 1831), exemplify the virtuosic BEL CANTO tradition of 18th-century vocal composition (see VOICE). His last OPERA, *I Puritani* (1835), was influenced by the dramatic style of French grand opera. He was much admired for his melodies, and had a great impact outside Italy, especially on Chopin. He directed the *bel canto* tradition towards greater naturalism of expression.

**Bellman, Carl Michael,** 1740–95, Swedish poet and writer of popular songs, a protégé of King Gustav III who gave him a sinecure post as director of the national lottery. His most important collections of songs are *The Epistles of Fredman* (1790), with its overtones of Biblical parody and burlesque, and *Songs of Fredman* (1791). The songs are still immensely popular throughout Scandinavia, and there is a long-standing Bellman Society in Sweden devoted to his memory.

**Belloc, Hilaire,** 1870–1953, English author; b. France. A Catholic apologist, he wrote poetry, satire, and essays, including *Bad Child's Book of Beasts* (1896) and *The Path to Rome* (1902). With G.K. CHESTERTON he propounded distributism, a political doctrine opposed to the socialism of SHAW and WELLS.

**Bello Muhammadu,** 1781–1837, sultan of the Sokoto caliphate, N Nigeria. He was the son of Usman DAN FODIO who designated Bello as the supreme leader of the Sokoto caliphate. Although better known for his military conquests during the Sokoto jihad [holy war], he was also a great Muslim scholar, writer, and teacher.

**Bellow, Saul,** 1915–, American novelist; b. Canada. Moral in tone, his novels reflect a concern for the individual in an indifferent society. They include *The Adventures of Augie March* (1953), *Herzog* (1964), *Mr. Sammler's Planet* (1970), *Humboldt's Gift* (1975), and *The Dean's December* (1982). Bellow was awarded the 1976 Nobel Prize in literature.

**Bellows, George Wesley,** 1882–1925, American painter. A student of Robert HENRI, Bellows is known for his direct, unselfconscious realism. *Forty-two Kids* (Corcoran Gall., Washington, DC) and *Stag at Sharkey's* (Mus. Art, Cleveland) are characteristic paintings. Bellows was also noted for his lithographs (see LITHOGRAPHY), e.g., *Dempsey and Firpo.*

**Bell's palsy,** sudden paralysis of the muscles on one side of the face. The cause of the condition is unknown but recovery is usually spontaneous. The condition is named after the Scottish anatomist and surgeon, Sir Charles Bell (1774–1842) who described the condition in 1830.

**Belmondo, Jean-Paul,** 1933–, French actor. He is a heavyweight leading man, whose battered good looks have kept him a French box-office favourite since the early 1960s. His films, many for director

Jean-Luc GODARD, include *Breathless* (1960), *Is Paris Burning* (1966), and *Borsalino* (1970).

**Belmonte, Juan** (bel,montay), 1892–1962, Spanish matador. Often called the greatest matador of all time, he is said to have 'invented' modern BULLFIGHTING with his daring style. He retired in 1936 after a 24-year career.

**Belmopan,** city (1980 pop. 2932), E Belize, capital of Belize (formerly British Honduras) since 1970. A new city, it was constructed on the Belize R., 80 km (50 mi) inland from the former capital, the port city of Belize, after that city's near destruction by a hurricane in 1961. Of note is the National Assembly Building, whose design is based on an ancient Mayan motif.

**Belo Horizonte,** city (1980 pop. 1,442,483), E Brazil, capital of Minas Gerais state. It is a distribution and processing centre for agricultural goods and the gold, manganese, and precious stones mined in the state; a banking centre; and the hub of a burgeoning industrial complex, with steel, motor vehicle, and textile manufacturing. Brazil's first planned metropolis (built 1895–97), laid out with spacious avenues and plazas, it is a cultural centre and a popular resort.

**Belorussia, Byelorussia** or **Belorussian Soviet Socialist Republic** (byelə,rooh'seeə), constituent republic (1985 pop. 9,941,000), c.207,600 km² (80,150 sq mi), W central European USSR. It borders Poland (W); the Russian Soviet Federated Socialist Republic (E); the Ukraine (S); and Lithuania and Latvia (N). MINSK is the capital. It is flat and marshy in the south, with hilly terrain N of Minsk. Since the RUSSIAN REVOLUTION, agriculture has been developed as swamps have been drained. Major crops include flax, sugar beet, and potatoes. Industry, almost completely destroyed during World War II, is based on producing machinery for manufacturing and agriculture. The majority of the people are Belorussians; Russians and Ukrainians are among the minorities. Settled by East Slavic tribes (5th–8th cent.), the region became part of KIEVAN RUSSIA (12th cent.), of the grand duchy of Lithuania (14th cent.), and of the Russian Empire (18th cent.). Belorussia was devastated by the Russian-Polish wars (16th–18th cent.), the Napoleonic invasion (1812), World War I (1914–18), and the Soviet-Polish war (1919–20), which ended with W Belorussia ceded to Poland and the eastern part becoming the Belorussian SSR. In 1939, W Belorussia was occupied by Soviet troops. During the German occupation (1941–44), Belorussia's large Jewish population (dating from the 14th cent.) was decimated. After 1945 most of W Belorussia remained part of the Belorussian SSR. The republic has its own UN seat. It is sometimes called White Russia.

**Belshazzar,** in the BIBLE, the son of NEBUCHADNEZZAR and the last king of Babylon. At his feast, handwriting appeared on the wall that was interpreted by DANIEL as a sign of doom. That night Babylon fell to Cyrus. Dan. 5.

**Belvedere,** court of the VATICAN connecting it to a villa built (1485–87) for INNOCENT VIII. It was designed (1503–04) by BRAMANTE for JULIUS II, and was to include a number of buildings. It was only partially completed. Now a museum, the Belvedere contains the *Laocoön* and the *Apollo Belvedere* as well as other rare works of classical antiquity.

**Bely, Andrei** (,byelee), pseud. of **Boris Nikolayevich Bugayev,** 1880–1934, Russian writer of the SYMBOLIST school. He attempted to fuse all the arts in the poetic *Symphonies* (4 vol., 1901–08). His best prose is contained in the novels *The Silver Dove* (1910), *Petersburg* (1912), and the experimental, Joycean *Kotik Letayev* (1917).

**Bemis Heights, battle of:** see SARATOGA CAMPAIGN.

**Benares:** see VARANASI.

**Benavente y Martínez, Jacinto,** 1866–1954, Spanish dramatist, author of 172 plays. Of his sparkling social SATIRES, the best known are *Los intereses creados* (1907; tr. Vested Interests) and *La malquerida* (1913; tr. The Passion Flower). His plays introduced a more natural diction. He received the 1922 Nobel Prize for literature.

**Ben Bella, Ahmed,** 1919–, Algerian prime minister (1962–65). A leader of the Algerian nationalist movement, he headed Algeria's first government after independence. In 1965 his government was toppled in a coup led by BOUMÉDIENNE. He was imprisoned from 1965 until 1980, and subsequently formed an opposition movement.

**Bendigo,** city (1986 pop. 53,944), Victoria, SE Australia. Important as a goldfield in 1890, the city is now a service centre for the farming district.

An old pottery still in operation, and a eucalyptus-oil distillery, attract tourists.

**bends:** see DECOMPRESSION SICKNESS.

**Benedict, Saint,** c.480–c.547, Italian monk, originator of Western MONASTICISM and founder of the BENEDICTINES; b. Nursia, in Umbria. He became a hermit and later founded the first Benedictine monastery, at Monte Cassino. He devised the Rule of St Benedict, the chief rule of Western MONASTICISM. Feast: 11 July.

**Benedictines,** monks of the Roman Catholic Church following the rule of St BENEDICT [Lat. abbr., = OSB]. Unlike earlier groups, they stress moderation rather than austerity. Their waking hours are spent in worship and work, educational as well as manual. The first Benedictine abbey was at Monte Cassino (founded c.529), Italy. Benedictines such as St GREGORY I, St AUGUSTINE OF CANTERBURY, and St BONIFACE spread the order's influence across Europe. The Cluniac and the Cistercian orders resulted from 10th- and 11-cent. reforms among the Benedictines.

**Benedict XIII,** antipope: see LUNA, PEDRO DE.

**Benedict XIV,** 1675–1758, pope (1740–58), an Italian named Prospero Lambertini. Renowned for his learning, he suppressed pagan practices accepted by missionaries in the East, and called for more humane treatment of the Indians in Paraguay. An admirable administrator and realistic politician, he won the respect of Protestants as well as Catholics.

**Benedict XV,** 1854–1922, pope (1914–22), an Italian named Giacomo della Chiesa. In World War I he kept the Vatican neutral and worked strenuously to restore peace. He founded the Vatican service for prisoners of war.

**Benediktsson, Bjarni,** 1908–70, Icelandic statesman. A leading advocate of independence from Denmark, he was elected mayor of REYKJAVIK in 1940. Later he held various cabinet posts, including that of prime minister (1963–70).

**benefit of clergy,** in English law, the privilege granted to clerics allowing them to avoid trial in the criminal courts. The accused was handed to the ecclesiastical courts for trial, but usually acquitted. In the 18th cent. certain offences, e.g., high TREASON, were excluded, and the privilege was fully abolished in 1827.

**Benelux Economic Union,** economic treaty (signed 1958, in force since 1960) linking Belgium, the Netherlands and Luxembourg, on the basis of close cooperation dating from 1944. The treaty promotes economic integration between the members through free movement of workers, capital, goods, and services. The Benelux countries also pursue these aims within the broader EUROPEAN COMMUNITY. Belgium and Luxembourg have a bilateral economic and monetary union dating from 1922.

**Beneš, Edward** (,benesh), 1884–1948, Czechoslovakian president (1935–38, 1946–48). He was a follower of T.G. MASARYK and succeeded him as president in 1935. A liberal and a nationalist, he resigned after the MUNICH PACT. He returned from exile after World War II, but the Communist coup of 1948 brought his presidency to an end.

**Benet, Juan,** 1927–, Spanish novelist and short-story writer. His best-known novel is *Volverás a Región* (1967; tr. You Will Return to Región). The stories in *Sub rosa* (1973) are highly experimental.

**Ben Ezra:** see IBN EZRA, ABRAHAM BEN MEIR.

**Bengal,** region, 200,000 km² (77,000 sq mi), E India and Bangladesh, on the Bay of Bengal. Its inland mountains fall to the fertile GANGES–BRAHMAPUTRA alluvial plains and delta. The heavy monsoon rains and warm climate make possible more than one harvest a year. From the empire of ASOKA (3rd cent. BC) Bengal passed to the Buddhist Pala kings, the Hindu Sena dynasty, and Muslims of Turki descent. It was in MOGUL hands when Portuguese and British traders arrived (16th–17th cent.). The latter, under Robert CLIVE, defeated the Muslims in 1757 and formed the Bengal presidency. When India became independent in 1947, **West Bengal** (1981 pop. 54,580,647), 87,752 km² (33,880 sq mi), mainly Hindu, was created as a state in India, with CALCUTTA as its capital. It has jute and cotton mills, steel plants, chemical and engineering industries, and mineral reserves. **East Bengal,** overwhelmingly Muslim, became East Pakistan in 1947 and gained independence as BANGLADESH in 1971.

**Bengal, Bay of,** arm of the INDIAN OCEAN, off E India and W Burma, separated from the Andaman Sea by the Andaman and Nicobar islands. It is some 2090 km (1300 mi) long and 1600 km (1000 mi) wide, and is generally shallow. Coastal areas are subject to heavy monsoon rains and destructive cyclones. MADRAS, CALCUTTA, CHITTAGONG and RANGOON are the chief ports.

**Bengali,** language belonging to the Indic group of the Indo Iranian subfamily of the Indo-European family of languages. See LANGUAGE (table).

**Benghazi** or **Banghazi,** city (1985 est. pop. 650,000), NE Libya, a Mediterranean seaport on the Gulf of Sirte. It is an administrative and commercial centre. Manufactures include processed food, textiles, and cement. Benghazi was cocapital of Libya (with TRIPOLI) from 1951 to 1972. The site of Hesperides, a Greek colony (7th cent. BC), the city was conquered by the Romans (1st cent. BC), Vandals (5th cent. AD), Arabs (7th cent.), and Ottoman Turks (mid-16th cent.). Italy held Benghazi from 1911 until it fell (1942) to the British during WORLD WAR II.

**Ben-Gurion, David,** 1886–1973, statesman and first prime minister of ISRAEL. (1949–53, 1955–63); b. Poland as David Grün. He settled in Palestine in 1906, devoted his life to ZIONISM, and was a founder of the Mapai (later Labour) Party. During the struggle (1947–48) for independence he headed Israel's defence efforts, and once independence was achieved he became prime minister.

**Benin,** officially People's Republic of Benin, formerly Dahomey, republic (1984 est. pop. 3,825,000), 112,622 km² (43,483 sq mi), W Africa, bordered by Togo (W), Burkina Faso and Niger (N), Nigeria (E), and the Bight of Benin, an arm of the Gulf of Guinea (S). PORTO NOVO is the capital; COTONOU is the largest city and chief port. There are four major geographical zones: a narrow, lagoon-fringed coastal area in the south; a flat, fertile area crossed by the wide Lama marsh further north; forested mountains in the northwest; and savanna-covered highlands in the northeast. Benin's economy is largely agricultural, with most workers engaged in subsistence farming. The chief crops are palm oil, cotton, maize, cassava, and sorghum. Although there are rich mineral deposits, notably of offshore petroleum, chromite, and iron ore, only limestone is extracted on a large scale. Manufacturing accounts for less than 10% of total output. The GNP is US$994 million, and the GNP per capita is US$260 (1985). The population is made up of black Africans of four main linguistic groups: the Ewe, the Yoruba, the Voltaic, and the Fulani. French is the official language. Most of the people follow traditional religions, but there are large Roman Catholic and Muslim minorities.

*History.* According to oral tradition S Dahomey (now Benin) was settled (12th or 13th cent.) by a group of Ewe-speaking people called the Aja. The kingdom they founded, Great Ardra, reached its height in the 16th and early 17th cent. The Aja gradually mixed with the local people to form the Fon, or Dahomey, ethnic group. By the late 17th cent. the Dahomey were raiding their neighbours for slaves to be sold to European traders, a practice that continued until the late 19th cent. Dahomey came under French influence in 1851 and was made part of FRENCH WEST AFRICA in 1899. Under the French, a port was constructed at Cotonou, railways were built, and the output of palm products increased. In 1958 Dahomey became an autonomous state within the FRENCH COMMUNITY; it gained full independence in 1960. Independent Dahomey was plagued by government instability caused by economic insufficiency, ethnic rivalries, and social unrest. Beginning in 1963 a series of military coups produced several short-lived regimes. A three-man presidential council was established in 1970 but overthrown by the army, led by Major Mathieu Kérékou, in 1972. The country was renamed the People's Republic of Benin in 1975. A new constitution was promulgated, providing for a national revolutionary assembly, but Benin remained essentially a one-party military dictatorship under the leadership of Kérékou, who was elected president in 1980 as the candidate of the Benin People's Revolutionary Party, the only legal political formation.

**Benin** (be͵neen), former kingdom, situated in present-day SW Nigeria. Ruled by the *oba* (to whose family human sacrifices were made) and by a sophisticated bureaucracy, the black African state flourished from the 14th to the 17th cent. Benin traded in slaves as well as ivory, pepper, and cloth with Europeans. After a period of decline, it revived in the 19th cent. with a trade in palm products. The modern Nigerian city of Benin served as the capital and was conquered and burned by the British in 1898. Iron work, carved ivory, and bronze busts made in Benin rank with the finest art of Africa.

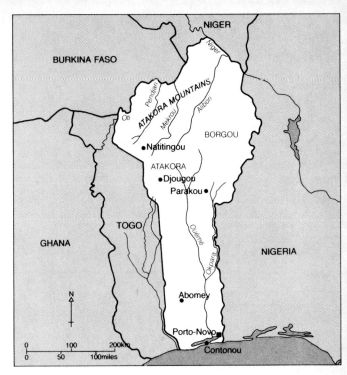

Benin

**Benjamin,** in the BIBLE, youngest son of JACOB and RACHEL, ancestor of one of the 12 tribes of Israel (See ISRAEL, TRIBES OF). He was the favourite of his family. The name survived in the High Gate of Benjamin of the Temple at Jerusalem. SAUL was the most noted son of the House of Benjamin. Gen. 35.18; 42–46.

**Benjamin, Walter,** 1892–1940, German essayist and critic. Now regarded as one of the most perceptive cultural critics of the century, Benjamin has been described as having a 'two-track mind', metaphysical and materialist. Though adopting Marxism in 1925, he did not lose touch with Jewish mysticism. At once nostalgic historian and contemporary social critic, he went in search of the submerged history of the losers. He published only two works in his lifetime, *One-way Street*, i.e., from metaphysics to Marxism (1928; tr. 1979), a montage of essays and aphorisms, and his dissertation *The Origins of German Tragic Drama* (1928; tr. 1977); but his prolific scattered essays, e.g. on Kafka, on allegory, on Paris as the capital of the 19th cent., on translation, are contributions to an unachieved magnum opus on modernity. Many have been collected and translated in ad-hoc volumes: *Illuminations* (1968; including the much-revised *The Work of Art in the Age of its Mechanical Reproduction*, 1936), *Charles Baudelaire* (1973), and *Reflections* (1978). Benjamin died by his own hand in France, en route for American exile.

**Ben Macdui,** second highest mountain in Britain after Ben Nevis, in Grampian region, Scotland. It is situated in the Cairngorms, 15 km (9 mi) SE of Aviemore, and reaches a height of 1309 m (4296 ft).

**Benn, Gottfried,** 1886–1956, German poet. Benn is the ultimate Nietzschean aesthete. His early Expressionist collections of poems, *Morgue* (1912) and *Gehirne* (1916; tr. Brains), present gross medical images drawn from his profession as army doctor in forms of scrupulous exactness. A fanatic for form and energy, Benn at first welcomed National Socialism, but during World War II retreated into the army; 'the aristocratic form of emigration' was how he put it. He had the distinction of being banned by both the Nazis and the Allies. His later collections of poems, *Statische Gedichte* (1949) and *Destillationen* (1953), posit an absolute lyrical self in an empty universe. He published an autobiography, *Doppelleben* (tr. Double Life), in 1950.

**Benn, Tony,** (Anthony Wedgwood (Tony) Benn), 1925–, British politician. He instigated the Peerage Act (1963) which enabled him to renounce his title, Viscount Stansgate, and regain his Labour seat in the House of Commons. He held several cabinet posts under Harold WILSON, including those of minister of technology (1966–70) and secretary for energy (1975–79), a post he also held under James CALLAGHAN. He is leader of the Labour party's radical left wing.

**Bennett, Arnold,** 1867–1931, English novelist, noted for his realistic novels set in the industrial midlands. Influenced by ZOLA'S NATURALISM, Bennett depicted regional life in depth in *Anna of the Five Towns* (1902), *The Old Wives' Tale* (1908), and *Clayhanger* (1910). Later novels include *The Card* (1911) and *Riceyman Steps* (1923). He was an influential critic and reviewer, and wrote a number of plays. His *Journals* (4 vol., 1930–33) reflect his avid, gregarious and businesslike approach to authorship.

**Bennett, James Gordon,** 1795–1872, American newspaper proprietor; b. Scotland. His New York *Herald,* started in 1835 as a penny paper of four four-column pages, made many innovations in American journalism—editorials critical of all political parties; new fields of news, notably Wall Street finance; use of European correspondents (1838); extensive use of the TELEGRAPH; and illustrations for news articles. It gained an excellent reputation for accurate reporting, especially in the CIVIL WAR. His son, **James Gordon Bennett,** 1841–1918, took over management of the *Herald* in 1867 and maintained its reputation. He financed (1869–71) Henry M. STANLEY's expedition to find David LIVINGSTON in Africa and also supported (1879–81) the ill-fated expedition of the explorer George Washington De Long to the Arctic.

**Bennett, Louise,** 1929–, Jamaican poet and actress. She combines her professional training as an actress with oral tradition and folk idiom to create a popular critique of her society. Best known for *Laugh with Louise* (1960) and *Jamaica Labrish* (1966), her other works include *Jamaica Dialect Verses* (1942, expanded 1951) and *Miss Lu Sez* (1948). She has also made several records of her own and traditional songs.

**Bennett, Richard Bedford,** 1870–1947, Canadian prime minister (1930–35). As Conservative leader during the GREAT DEPRESSION, he signed (1932) preferential trade agreements with Britain and the dominions, and proposed (1934) reform social legislation at home. In 1941 he was created a viscount.

**Bennett, Richard Rodney,** 1936–, English composer. He has produced several fine film scores, such as that for *Far from the Madding Crowd,* as well as chamber works, symphonies, concertos and operas. Several of his works have been specially commissioned, such as the operas *The Mines of Sulphur* (1965) and *A Penny for a Song* (1969) by Sadlers Wells.

**Ben Nevis,** highest mountain in Britain, in Highland region of Scotland. It is situated in Lochaber district, 7 km (4 mi) E of Fort William, and reaches a height of 1344 m (4408 ft). It overlooks the picturesque Glen Nevis.

**Benny, Jack,** 1894–1974, American comedian; b. Benjamin Kubelsky. His shows on radio (1932–55) and television (1950–65) made famous his miserliness, reproachful silences, and violin. His films include *To Be or Not to Be* (1942).

**Benozzo Gozzoli:** see GOZZOLI, BENOZZO.

**Bentham, Jeremy,** 1748–1832, English philosopher, jurist, political theorist; founder of UTILITARIANISM. Educated as a lawyer, Bentham devoted himself to the scientific analysis of morals and government. His *Introduction to the Principles of Morals and Legislation* (1789) held that the greatest happiness of the greatest number does and should govern our judgment of every institution and action. The 19th-cent. reforms of English criminal law, of judicial organization, and of the parliamentary electorate owe much to Bentham's active work in English legislative reform, and his thought strongly influenced that of John Stuart MILL.

**benthos,** aquatic plants and animals that live on the sea bed, from the shallow waters of the continental shelf to the extreme depths of the abyssal plains, as opposed to those that are PELAGIC. They may be fixed, like seaweeds and CORALS, or mobile like the crustaceans, and fishes such as skates and RAYS. Some fishes, such as SALMON and HERRING, lay heavy eggs that sink to the bottom; these are described as demersal eggs.

**Ben Yehudah, Eliezer,** 1858–1922, Jewish scholar; b. Lithuania. He settled in Palestine in 1881. A leader in the revival of Hebrew as the national language, he compiled the *Dictionary of Ancient and Modern Hebrew* (16 vol.).

**Benz, Karl,** 1844–1929, German engineer, credited with building (1885) the first MOTOR CAR powered by an INTERNAL-COMBUSTION ENGINE. His car had three wheels, an electric ignition, and differential gears. In 1926, Benz's company merged with that of Gustave DAIMLER and became the manufacturer of the Mercedes-Benz motor car.

**benzene** ($C_6H_6$), colourless, flammable toxic liquid with a pleasant aromatic odour, discovered by Michael FARADAY. A HYDROCARBON, benzene is the parent substance of the aromatic class of organic compounds (see AROMATIC COMPOUND). It consists of an unusually stable hexagonal ring of six carbon atoms, each of which is attached to a hydrogen atom. Derivative compounds include toluene, phenol, and aniline. Obtained from coal tar and petroleum, benzene and its derivatives are used in making dyes, drugs, and plastics.

**benzodiazepine** ('benzohdie,azipin), any of a group of drugs, including diazepam (trademark Valium) and chlordiazepoxide (trademark Librium), with anticonvulsant, muscle relaxant, and sedative properties. They are used as minor tranquillizers (see TRANQUILLIZER), as sedative and HYPNOTIC drugs, and in the treatment of alcohol withdrawal symptoms. Overprescription and consequent addiction is a major (if undramatic) drug-abuse problem in the West.

**Ben-Zvi, Yitzhak** (ben,zvee), 1884–1963, president of ISRAEL (1952–63); b. Russia as Issac Shimshelevitz. He settled in Palestine in 1907 and was one of the creators of the Jewish state. In 1952 he succeeded Chaim WEIZMANN as president. He was a historian and a scholar in the field of Jewish ethnology.

**Beowulf** (,baywoolf), oldest English epic, probably composed in the early 8th cent. by a Northumbrian bard, and drawn from Scandinavian history and folk sources. It recounts Beowulf's struggle with the water monster Grendel and Grendel's mother; the hero's victory in old age over a dragon; and his death and funeral. The poem, in alliterative verse, fuses Christian elements with a picture of old Germanic life.

**Berbers,** aboriginal Caucasoid peoples of N Africa who today form a large part of the populations of Libya, Algeria, and Morocco. Except for the nomadic Tuareg, they are small farmers living in loosely joined tribal villages. Local industries are mining, pottery, weaving, and embroidery. They are SUNNI Muslims, speaking languages of the Hamitic group. Despite a history of conquests, they maintain a culture dating from before 2400 BC In classical times they formed such states as MAURETANIA and NUMIDIA. Most were Christians until the 7th-cent. Arab conquest. In the 9th cent. they supported the FATIMID dynasty; when the Fatimids left N Africa, fighting among the Berbers reduced the region to anarchy until the ALMORAVIDS and ALMOHADS imposed order. The plains Berbers were eventually absorbed by the Arabs; the mountain Berbers, however, retained their warlike traditions, fiercely resisting French and Spanish occupation of N Africa and in the 1960s helping to drive the French from ALGERIA.

**Berenson, Bernard,** 1865–1959, American art critic and connoisseur; b. Lithuania. A conversationalist, wit, and arbiter of taste, Berenson selected work for many art collectors, much of it now in museums, e.g., the Isabella Stewart GARDNER Mus. Many of his judgments in art history, made in his early books, have been criticized by later scholars. His works include *Venetian Painters of the Renaissance* (1894), *Drawings of the Florentine Painters* (1903), and *Rumor and Reflection* (1952).

**Berg, Alban,** 1885–1935, Austrian composer. A pupil and close friend of Arnold SCHOENBERG, he adopted ATONALITY and later combined the 12-tone system (see TWELVE-TONE MUSIC) with the lyric and dramatic qualities of the Viennese romantic tradition. His opera *Wozzeck* (based on dramatic fragments by BÜCHNER) was completed in 1921 and first staged in 1925. It immediately established Berg's reputation and gave him financial security. Other major works are the Chamber Concert (1923–5), the Lyric Suite (1925–26), *Der Wein* (1929), the haunting Violin Concerto (1935), and the opera *Lulu* (completed posthumously by Cerha and performed in 1979).

**Bergamo,** city (1984 pop. 119,991), Lombardy, N Italy. A foothill settlement, its traditional industry is textiles. The old town (*città alta*) has fortifications and Renaissance buildings. It has been the seat of a bishop since the 4th cent. It is the birthplace of the opera composer DONIZETTI (1797–1848).

**Bergen,** city (1985 pop. 207,416), SW Norway. On North Sea inlets, it is a major shipping and shipbuilding centre. Founded c.1070 by OLAF III, it was medieval Norway's largest city and a royal residence. From c.1350 to 1560 the HANSEATIC LEAGUE imposed unpopular rule on the city. Bergen was Norway's foremost city until the rise of OSLO in the 19th cent. Impressive monuments of its medieval past include Haakon's Hall (1261; largely rebuilt after World War II) and several churches.

**Berger, Victor Louis,** 1860–1929, US Socialist leader; b. Austria–Hungary. A Milwaukee journalist, Berger was (1911–13) the first Socialist member of Congress. He was reelected (1918, 1919), but Congress excluded him for sedition, for which he was sentenced to a 20-year prison term. The US Supreme Court reversed (1921) that decision, and he returned (1923–29) to Congress.

**Bergman, Hjalmar,** 1883–1931, Swedish writer. His many popular works, characterized by insight into the ambivalence of human emotions, include the novel *God's Orchid* (1919) and the play *The Swedenhielm Family* (1926).

**Bergman, Ingmar,** 1918–, Swedish film director. His films, often treating man's search for God, are usually studies of human loneliness. They include *The Seventh Seal* (1956), *Wild Strawberries* (1957), *The Silence* (1963), *Cries and Whispers* (1972), *Autumn Sonata* (1978), and *Fanny and Alexander* (1982).

**Bergman, Ingrid,** 1915–82, Swedish film actress. A radiant, gifted actress, she made such films as *Casablanca* (1942), *For Whom the Bell Tolls* (1943), *Notorious* (1946), *Anastasia* (1956; Academy Award), and *Autumn Sonata* (1978).

**Bergson, Henri,** 1859–1941, French philosopher. He became a professor at the Collège de France in 1900. Bergson's dualistic philosophy holds that the world contains two opposing tendencies, the life force and the resistance of matter against that force. The individual knows matter through intellect but through intuition perceives the life force and the reality of time, which is not a unit of measurement but duration in terms of life experience. Bergson was awarded the 1927 Nobel Prize for literature. Among his works are *Time and Free Will* (1889) and *The Creative Mind* (1934).

**Beria, Lavrenti Pavlovich,** 1899–1953, Soviet leader. He became Communist Party secretary in Georgia and the Transcaucasus in 1931, head of the Soviet secret police (NKVD) in 1938, and a member of the politburo in 1946. In the power struggle following the death of Joseph STALIN he was executed.

**beriberi,** disease caused by a deficiency of thiamine (vitamin $B_1$), resulting in inflamation and degeneration of the nerves, numbness, muscular weakness, and heart failure. It occurs in rice-eating communities in which polished rice is the staple diet and in chronic alcoholics who eat little food. See table under VITAMINS AND MINERALS.

**Bering, Vitus Jonassen,** 1681–1741, Danish explorer in Russian employ. He explored the far northeast of SIBERIA for PETER I. In 1728 he sailed through the BERING STRAIT. In 1741 Bering landed a party on the Alaskan coast. The expedition was later wrecked on Bering Island, where he died.

**Bering Sea,** c.2,274,000 km² (878,000 sq mi), northern arm of the Pacific Ocean, screened from the Pacific proper by the ALEUTIAN ISLANDS. It is usually frozen from October to June. Its migratory seal herd, threatened with extinction at the time of the **Bering Sea Fur-Seal Controversy** (1886), has gradually been rebuilt following an international agreement (1911) regulating open-ocean sealing.

**Bering Strait,** 90 km (c.55 mi) wide, connecting the Arctic Ocean and the Bering Sea and separating Siberia and Alaska. The Diomede Islands are in the strait, which is usually frozen from October to June.

**Berio, Luciano,** 1925–, Italian composer. He was introduced to SERIAL MUSIC by Luigi DALLAPICCOLA in 1952 and composed ELECTRONIC MUSIC from 1954. His works include a series of *Sequences* (1957–1975), each for a different instrument; *Sinfonia* (1968) and *Coro* (1976), for orchestra and voices.

**Berkeley, Busby,** 1895–1976, American film director; b. William Berkeley Enos. In such musicals as *42nd Street* (1933), *Footlight Parade* (1933), and *The Gang's All Here* (1942), directing either the dance sequences or the entire production, he created a striking, often surreal visual style.

**Berkeley, George** (ˌbahklee, ˌbuh-), 1685–1753, English philosopher and clergyman; b. Ireland. Reacting against the views of John LOCKE, he argued that we cannot make sense of mind-independent material substance, being unable to abstract away the mind's contribution to what it perceives. His IDEALISM therefore holds that material objects are collections of mental states; the observing mind of God who shares his ideas with us makes possible the apparent continued existence of material objects. Among his more important works are his *Essay towards a New Theory of Vision* (1709), *A Treatise Concerning the Principles of Human Knowledge* (1710), and *Three Dialogues between Hylas and Philonous* (1713).

**Berkeley, Sir Lennox,** 1903–, British composer and teacher. He studied with Nadia BOULANGER, and his early work has a distinctly Gallic poise and elegance, clear texture, and rhythmic neoclassical style, e.g., the *Serenade for Strings* (1939), *Sonatina* for recorder and piano (1940), and *Six Preludes* for piano (1945). His later compositions added a greater intensity to these qualities: the opera *Nelson* (1954), the *Missa Brevis* (1959), and the *Third Symphony* (1969).

**Berkeley, Sir William,** 1606–77, British colonial governor of Virginia (1642–52, 1660–77). Poor frontier defence and favouritism to his friends in his second term led to the rebellion (1676) of Nathaniel BACON, which he so ruthlessly suppressed that he was recalled.

**berkelium** (Bk), synthetic radioactive element, discovered in 1949 by Glenn Seaborg, S.G. Thompson, and Albert Ghiorso by alpha-particle bombardment of americium-241. It is in the ACTINIDE series; nine isotopes exist. See ELEMENT (table); PERIODIC TABLE.

**Berkman, Alexander,** 1870?–1936, US anarchist; b. Russia. He emigrated to the US c.1887 and attempted (1892) to kill industrialist H. C. FRICK. He was imprisoned for 14 years. Deported (1919) to Russia with Emma GOLDMAN and other alien radicals, he became disillusioned with the Bolsheviks, left Russia, and later committed suicide in France.

**Berkshire,** inland county, S England (1984 est. pop. 715,300), 1259 km² (491 sq mi), bounded in the N by the R. Thames. The county town is READING. The Berkshire Downs cross the county from E to W. Mixed agriculture is prevalent. New light industries have developed around Reading and SLOUGH. The historic towns of ETON and WINDSOR are situated in the E of the county.

**Berlin,** city, former capital of Germany and Prussia, is now divided into East Berlin (German Democratic Republic) and West Berlin, on the Spree and Havel rivers. In 1945 it was divided into British, American, and French occupation zones (now West Berlin) and a Soviet sector (now East Berlin). Formed from two villages chartered in the 13th cent., Berlin was a leading member of the HANSEATIC LEAGUE and became prominent as a commercial, cultural, and communications centre of Central Europe. It was the capital of the German Empire after 1871 and of the Weimar Republic (see GERMANY) after WORLD WAR I. During WORLD WAR II it was badly damaged by Allied bombing and a Soviet artillery attack. The status of divided Berlin became a major COLD WAR issue, and in 1948–49 the Western powers carried out a large-scale airlift to supply West Berlin during a Soviet land and water blockade. In 1949 East Berlin was made the capital of East Germany; in 1950 West Berlin was established as a state within, and the de jure capital of, the Federal Republic of Germany (West Germany), with BONN as the de facto capital. In Aug. 1961 East German authorities erected a 47-km (29-mi) wall along the line of partition to halt the exodus of refugees to the West. Accords between the two Germanies were finally reached in 1972. **West Berlin** (1984 est. pop. 1,851,800), over 161 km (100 mi) inside East Germany, has such industries as electrical equipment, clothing, and tourism. Its cultural institutions include the Berlin Philharmonic and the gallery of the Charlottenberg Palace, with its many Rembrandts. **East Berlin** (1984 pop. 1,196,871), slower to recover from the war, has electrical, chemical, and other industries. Among its museums is the Pergamum, known for classical art.

**Berlin, Conference of,** 1884–85, international meeting aimed at settling colonial problems in Africa. Attending were all European nations, with the US and Turkey. In effect, the conference legitimized the sovereignty these nations were already exercising over their African colonies.

**Berlin, Congress of,** 1878, a conference convened to deal with the EASTERN QUESTION at the end of a war between Russian and Turkey (1877–78). It was presided over by BISMARCK in the purported role of an 'honest broker'. Britain was represented by DISRAELI. The congress recognized the independence of Romania and Serbia, created a new 'small Bulgaria' instead of an independent 'large Bulgaria', which victorious Russia had earlier compelled Turkey to concede by the Treaty of San Stefano, and arranged for Austro–Hungarian occupation and administration of Bosnia–Hercegovina and Montenegro. It did not settle the Eastern Question.

**Berlin, Irving,** 1888–, American songwriter; b. Russia as Irving Baline. Composer of nearly 1000 songs, 'Alexander's Ragtime Band' (1911) was his first big hit. He wrote for Broadway reviews and wrote musical and film scores. 'God Bless America' is perhaps his best-known song.

**Berlin, Sir Isaiah,** 1909–, English political philosopher and historian of ideas; b. Latvia. He was a professor of social and political theory at Oxford Univ. (1957–67). He rejects deterministic views of history, especially Marxist ones, and emphasizes the pluralistic nature of moral and political values. His major works are *Karl Marx* (1939), *Historical Inevitability* (1954), and *Two Concepts of Liberty* (1959).

**Berlinguer, Enrico,** 1922–84, Italian politician. A member of the Italian Communist Party from 1944, he entered the Italian chamber of deputies in 1958, and became secretary general of the party in 1972. He was noted for his willingness to cooperate with other political parties and for his espousal of 'Eurocommunism', which rejected the leading role of the Soviet party in the international Communist movement.

**Berlioz, Louis-Hector,** 1803–69, French romantic composer. He abandoned medical study to enter the Paris Conservatory. His *Symphonie fantastique* (1830) marked a new development in programme music, and that year Berlioz won the Prix de Rome. In the next decade he wrote the symphonies *Harold in Italy* (1834) and *Romeo and Juliet* (1839). Other works included the operas *The Damnation of Faust* (1846) and *The Trojans* (1856–59) and the successful ORATORIO *The Childhood of Christ* (1854). Berlioz's ideas of orchestration influenced many later composers.

**Bermuda,** British dependency (1980 pop. 54,670), 52 km² (20 sq mi), comprising 300 coral rocks, islets and islands, in the Atlantic Ocean, c.1050 km (650 mi) SE of Cape Hatteras, North Carolina. The capital is Hamilton. Tourism is the mainstay of Bermuda's economy. Probably discovered by the Spanish in the early 16th cent., the islands remained uninhabited until colonists bound for Virginia were shipwrecked there in 1609. Bermuda's government became the responsibility of the British crown in 1684; internal self-government was granted in 1968. The US operates a naval and air force base there. Elections in 1985 returned to power the United Bermuda Party led by John Swan.

**Bermuda Triangle,** area in the Atlantic Ocean off Florida where a number of ships and aircraft have vanished. Also known as the Devil's Triangle, it is bounded at its points by Melbourne, Florida; Bermuda; and Puerto Rico. Storms are common in the region, and investigations to date have not produced scientific evidence of any unusual phenomena involved in the disappearances.

**Bern** or **Berne,** city (1984 pop. 140,600), capital of Switzerland and of Bern canton, W central Switzerland, within a loop of the Aare R. A university, administrative, and industrial centre, it manufactures such products as precision instruments, textiles, and machinery. It is the seat of the Universal Postal Union, the International Copyright Union, and other world agencies. Said to have been founded in 1191, it joined the Swiss Confederation in 1353 and became its leading member. Bern accepted the REFORMATION in 1528 and adopted a liberal constitution in 1831. It became the Swiss capital in 1848. Its historic buildings include a medieval clock tower and a 15th-cent. town hall.

**Bernadette of Lourdes,** 1844–79, French saint who had visions of the Virgin Mary. LOURDES is a place of pilgrimage by the sick, many of whom claim cure as a result of visiting the shrine of Our Lady of Lourdes.

**Bernadotte, Count Folke,** 1895–1948, Swedish internationalist. Active in the Swedish RED CROSS, which he headed after 1946, he arranged (1945) the evacuation of Danish and Norwegian prisoners from Germany. He was assassinated by Jewish extremists while serving as UN mediator in Palestine.

**Bernadotte, Jean Baptiste Jules** (Charles XIV): see under CHARLES, kings of Sweden.

**Bernanos, Georges,** 1888–1948, French author. His novels *The Star of Satan* (1926) and *Journal d'un curé de campagne* (1936; tr. The Diary of a Country Priest) reflect his mystical, Catholic bent. A Royalist until the Spanish civil war, Bernanos condemned FRANCO's policies in *Les grands cimetières sous la lune* (1938; tr. A Diary of My Times).

**Bernard, Claude** (beə‚nah), 1813–78, French physiologist. One of the great scientific investigators, he is known as the founder of experimental medicine through his work on the digestive process, especially the discovery of the glycogenic function of the liver and of the action of pancreatic juice, and his work on the vasomotor mechanism (control of blood vessel diameter by nerves).

**Bernard, Emile,** 1868–1941, French painter. He met GAUGUIN at Pont-Aven in 1886, and evolved a style known as 'cloisonnisme,' so called due to its resemblance to cloisonné enamels, which used heavy black/blue outlines enclosing flat areas of strong colour. These ideas were influential for Gauguin in the development of his synthetist ideas. In 1889, with Gauguin and other Pont-Aven painters he exhibited at the synthetist group show at the Café Volpini.

**Bernard, Saint:** see BERNARD OF CLAIRVAUX, SAINT.

**Bernard of Clairvaux, Saint,** 1090?–1153, French churchman. He founded (1115) a Cistercian monastery at Clairvaux, where he remained as abbot for the rest of his life, despite efforts to move him higher. His holiness, and eloquence made him one of the most powerful figures of his day; he brought about the condemnation of Peter ABELARD and preached the Second CRUSADE. His writings exerted a profound influence on Roman Catholic spirituality, especially that known as *devotio moderna*. He was canonized in 1174 and declared Doctor of the Church in 1830. Feast: 20 Aug.

**Bernhard, Thomas,** 1931–89, Austrian dramatist and novelist. Obsessed with sickness and death, Bernhard represents the Austrian family and the Austrian province as the worst of all possible worlds, but in a fine, musically organized prose and with a grim relish which belie his themes. His dramas include *The Hunting Party* (1974), *Force of Habit* (1974), *The President* (1975), and *Eve of Retirement* (1979); his novels *The Lime Works* (1970), *Correction* (1975), and *Concrete* (1982). Between 1975 and 1982 he wrote five dark autobiographical works about his childhood, collected and translated as *Gathering Evidence* (tr. 1985). His *roman à clef, Felling Timber, a Scandal* (1984), has caused just that in Viennese cultural circles.

**Bernhardt, Sarah,** 1844–1923, French actress; b. Rosine Bernard. Called 'the divine Sarah' by Oscar WILDE, she was considered the queen of French romantic and classical tragedy. She became famous for her superb portrayals in *Phèdre* (1874), in Victor HUGO's *Ruy Blas* (1872) and *Hernani* (1877), and in *Adrienne Lecouvreur* (1880). She also starred in works by SARDOU and ROSTAND, and wrote some of her own vehicles. She made tours of Europe and the US, including many 'farewell tours' after her leg was amputated in 1915. She played Hamlet at her own Théâtre Sarah Bernhardt in 1899.

**Bernini, Giovanni Lorenzo** or **Gianlorenzo,** 1598–1680, Italian sculptor and architect, the dominant figure of the Italian BAROQUE. Working for the major patrons of his day, he produced brilliantly vital, dynamic sculpture in reaction against mannerist traditions (see MANNERISM) and dramatic, impressive works of architecture enriched with sculpture. For Cardinal Borghese he produced *David* (1623–24), *Rape of Proserpine* (1622), and *Apollo and Daphne* (1625; all: Borghese Gall., Rome). He designed churches, chapels, fountains, monuments, tombs, and statues for the popes. In 1629 he became architect of ST PETER'S CHURCH, lavishly decorating the interior and creating the great, embracing, elliptical piazza in front of the church. His other Roman works include the Cornaro Chapel, with the *Ecstasy of St Theresa* (1645–52; Santa Maria della Vittoria), Sant'Andrea al Quirinale, and the *Fountain of the Four Rivers* in the Piazza Navona.

**Bernoulli,** Swiss family distinguished in scientific and mathematical history. **Jakob, Jacques,** or **James Bernoulli,** 1654–1705, was one of the chief developers of both the ordinary calculus and the calculus of variations. His *Ars conjectandi* (1713) was an important treatise on the theory of probability. His brother, **Johann, Jean,** or **John Bernoulli,** 1667–1748, was famous for his work on integral and exponential calculus; he was also a founder of the calculus of variations and contributed to the study of geodesics, complex numbers, and trigonometry. His son, **Daniel Bernoulli,** 1700–82, has often been called the first mathematical physicist. His greatest work was his *Hydrodynamica* (1738), which included the principle now known as

Giovanni **Bernini**, *The Ecstasy of St Theresa*, 1645–52. Santa Maria della Vittoria, Rome.

Bernoulli's principle (see AERODYNAMICS) and anticipated the law of conservation of energy and the kinetic–molecular theory of gases developed a century later. He also made important contributions to probability theory, astronomy, and the theory of differential equations. Other members of the family were noted in the fields of mathematics, physics, astronomy, and geography.

**Bernstein, Basil Bernard,** 1924–, British sociologist of education. From the late 1950s he developed theories of the social determinants of language usage, and his analysis of the 'language codes' of children from different social backgrounds was influential particularly in Britain and the United States, and made a major contribution to the development of the sociology of education. His main writings are collected in *Class, Codes and Control* (3 vol., 1971–77).

**Bernstein, Leonard,** 1918–, American composer and conductor. He has composed symphonic works (*Kaddish Symphony*, 1963); CHAMBER MUSIC; ballets (*Fancy Free*, 1944); MUSICALS (*On the Town*, 1944; *Candide*, 1956; *West Side Story*, 1957); and choral music (*Chichester Psalms*, 1965). From 1958 to 1970 he was musical director of the New York Philharmonic.

**Berrettini, Pietro:** see CORTONA, PIETRO DA.

**Berry, Chuck,** (Charles Edward Berry), 1931–, black American rock/blues singer, guitarist and composer. Between 1955 and 1964 he wrote and recorded a number of records which were enormous hits and became rock standards, e.g., 'Roll Over Beethoven' (1956), 'Rock 'n Roll Music' (1957), 'Sweet Little Sixteen' and 'Johnny B. Goode' (1958), and 'No Particular Place to Go' (1964). In 1972 he had his first British no. 1 with the risqué novelty number 'My Ding-a-Ling'. Countless groups including the BEATLES and the ROLLING STONES were inspired by his romantically rebellious repertoire.

**Berryman, John,** 1914–72, American poet. His verse is complex, dramatic, and personal, often mirroring the anguish of a trivial age. Among his works are *Homage to Mistress Bradstreet* (1956), *77 Dream*

*Songs* (1964), *His Toy, His Dream, His Rest* (1968), and *Delusions, etc.* (1972).

**Berthelot, Pierre Eugène Marcelin** (beətə‚loh), 1827–1907, French chemist. Professor at the École Supérieure de Pharmacie and later at the Collège de France, he became a member of the French Academy in 1900. A founder of modern organic chemistry, he was the first to synthesize organic compounds (e.g., methanol, ethanol, benzene, and acetylene), thereby dispelling the old theory of a vital force inherent in organic compounds. He also worked in thermochemistry and in explosives.

**Berthollet, Claude Louis, Comte** (beətoh‚lay), 1748–1822, French chemist. Noted for his ideas on chemical affinity and his discovery of the reversibility of reactions, he supported Antoine LAVOISIER's theory of combustion and collaborated with him in reforming chemical nomenclature. He analysed ammonia and prussic acid and discovered the bleaching properties of chlorine.

**Bertolucci, Bernardo** ('beərto‚loohchee), 1940–, Italian film director. He is noted for his visually rich, poetic visions of public and private trauma. His films include *The Conformist* (1970), *Last Tango In Paris* (1972), and *La Luna* (1979).

**beryl,** extremely hard beryllium and aluminium silicate mineral ($Be_3Al_2Si_6O_{18}$), occurring in crystals that may be of enormous size and are usually white, yellow, blue, green, or colourless. It is commonly used as a GEM, the most valued variety being the greenish EMERALD; the blue to bluish-green variety is AQUAMARINE. Beryl is the principal raw material for the element BERYLLIUM and its compounds.

**beryllium** (Be), metallic element, first isolated in 1828 independently by Friedrich WÖHLER and Antoine Bussy. One of the ALKALINE EARTH METALS, it is silver-grey, light, strong, high-melting, and resistant to corrosion. It is used as a window material for X-ray tubes and as a shield and a moderator in nuclear reactors. See ELEMENT (table); PERIODIC TABLE.

**Berzelius, Jöns Jakob, Baron,** 1779–1848, Swedish chemist. He developed the modern system of symbols and formulas in chemistry, made a remarkably accurate table of atomic weights, analysed many chemical compounds, and discovered the elements SELENIUM, THORIUM, and CERIUM. He coined the words *catalyst, isomerism, allotropy,* and *protein.*

**Besançon,** city (1982 pop. 119,687), capital of Doubs dept., E France on the Doubs R. It lies on a major valley routeway which links the basins of the RHÔNE and the RHINE, and at the junction of mountains (JURA) and plain. A regional service centre, it has varied industries. Artificial silk (rayon) was first produced here on a commercial scale (1891). It was a free imperial city until incorporated into Franche-Comté (1648) of which it became capital following French annexation from the Spaniards. It has houses of the 16th and 17th cent. (one where Victor HUGO was born) and a citadel erected by Vauban.

**Besant, Annie (Wood),** 1847–1933, English socialist, theosophist, and women's rights advocate. With her friend Charles Bradlaugh she was tried for immorality after publishing a pamphlet on birth control, *The Fruits of Philosophy* (1875); in 1879 her children were taken away from her by court order. In 1885 she joined the FABIAN SOCIETY and Social Democratic Federation and was the leading organizer of the Bryant and May matchgirls' strike in 1888. She later (1899) converted to theosophy and went to India, where she was active in demands for home rule.

**Bessarabia,** historical province, E Romania. The eastern half of the historical province of MOLDAVIA annexed by Czar Alexander I of Russia in 1812. In 1918 a national council representing the majority Romanian population voted for its union with ROMANIA. In 1940 the USSR seized the province after delivering an ultimatum to the Romanian government but a year later it was reconquered by Romanian and German armies. Recovered by the Red Army in 1944, the greater part of it was added to the MOLDAVIAN SSR.

**Bessel, Friedrich Wilhelm,** 1784–1846, German astronomer and mathematician. His discovery of the parallax of the fixed star 61 Cygni, announced in 1838, was the first fully authenticated measurement of a star's distance from the earth. By 1833 Bessel had increased to 50,000 the number of stars whose positions and proper motions were accurately determined. He established a class of mathematical functions, named after him, as a result of his work on planetary perturbation. These functions give the solution of Bessel's equation which is used in the description of such phenomena as vibrations, waves, buckling of columns, scattering of sound, etc.

**Bessemer process,** industrial process for the manufacture of STEEL from wrought iron, invented by Henry Bessemer, 1813–98, a French Huguenot who fled from the French Revolution and settled in England. PIG IRON and WROUGHT IRON are heated until molten in a large vessel, called a Bessemer converter, and air is then pumped through perforations in the bottom. The resulting oxidation of the impurities generates sufficient heat to keep the material molten without further external heat. The impurities float on the surface and more wrought iron is added through a narrow opening at the top. When the correct carbon content has been achieved the whole vessel is tipped and the steel poured into moulds. Bessemer steel, which is used to make machinery, tools, wire, and nails, and is the modern structural steel used in steel-framework buildings, has transformed manufacturing industry.

**Best, Charles Herbert,** 1899–1978, Canadian physiologist. He, with Sir Frederick BANTING, James COLLIP, and John MACLEOD were the first to isolate (1921) the hormone INSULIN from the pancreas and demonstrate its use in the treatment of DIABETES. Best discovered the antiallergic enzyme histaminase, the blood-clotting substance heparin, and the vitamin choline.

**beta blocker,** drug that reduces the symptoms connected with HYPERTENSION, abnormal heart rythyms (arrhythmias), MIGRAINE headaches, and other disorders related to the central NERVOUS SYSTEM. Within the sympathetic nervous system, beta receptors are located mainly in the heart, lungs, kidneys, and blood vessels. Beta blockers compete with ADRENALINE for these receptor sites and interfere with the action of adrenaline, lowering blood pressure and heart rate, stopping arrhythmias, and preventing migraine headaches. Propranolol is a commonly used beta blocker. These drugs may cause constriction of air passages in the lungs.

**beta decay,** one of the three forms of natural RADIOACTIVITY in which an ELECTRON (or a POSITRON) and an antineutrino (or a NEUTRINO) are emitted. It is a manifestation of the weak interaction of ELEMENTARY PARTICLE physics. The charged particles emitted are referred to as beta particles or beta rays. See also ALPHA DECAY; GAMMA DECAY.

**Betancourt, Rómulo** (betahn‚kaw), 1908–81, president of VENEZUELA (1945–48, 1959–64). He founded (1935) the left-wing party that became Acción Democrática. When he came to power (1945) by a military coup, he instituted universal suffrage, social reforms, and oil royalties for the government. After his exile (1948–58) by a junta, he was elected president (1959) and continued to promote his reform programme.

**bet din,** ecclesiastical court, comprising three *dayyanim* [judges]. Such courts are established in cities of significant Jewish population. Its judges act as consultants to congregational rabbis, arbitrators in small disputes, and overseers of ritual slaughtering and dietary law adminstration. They also act as ultimate authorities in all matters of Jewish law and tradition, with special responsibilities for applying the latter to modern problems, issues and situations.

**betel,** masticatory made from seeds of the betel palm (*Areca catechu*). Slices of the seeds (also called betel nuts), together with other aromatic flavourings and lime paste, are smeared onto a betel pepper (*Piper betle*) leaf, which is then rolled up and chewed. Betel contains a narcotic stimulant and has been chewed in S Asia since ancient times.

**Bet Ha-Mikdash,** Heb. term to denote the ancient Temple at Jerusalem. Traditionally the site where the Patriarch Jacob had his dream of angels ascending and descending the ladder between heaven and earth (Gen. 28:12). The first Temple was built by King Solomon (965–28 BC), and destroyed by the Babylonians in 586 BC. A benign Persian rule enabled the Temple to be rebuilt by the governor of Judah, Zerubbabel (c.515 BC). It was destroyed by the Romans in the year AD 70, after which date animal sacrifices were phased out of the religious ritual. Orthodox Jews pray daily for the restoration of the Temple, though there is no agreement as to how this is to be effected: whether by ordinary political endeavour or by miraculous, divine intervention. There is also doubt as to whether or not it will presage the resumption of the sacrificial system.

**Bethany,** village at the SE foot of the Mount of Olives, modern Ali-'Ayzariyah (Israeli-administered West Bank) 3.2 km (2 mi) E of Jerusalem. Home of LAZARUS, Martha, and MARY, it was frequently visited by JESUS and is closely associated with the final scenes of his life. John 11.

**Bethlehem,** town (1971 est. pop. 25,000), Jordan, on the WEST BANK; the birthplace of JESUS. It is a place of pilgrimage and the trade centre of a farming area. The biblical book of RUTH is set in Bethlehem, and it was DAVID's home. CONSTANTINE I built the Church of the Nativity (completed 333) on the traditional site of Jesus' birth. There St JEROME produced the Vulgate text of the BIBLE. Crusaders held the town from 1099 to 1187. Annexed to the Ottoman Empire in 1571, it was part of Britain's Palestine mandate (1922–48) and then of Jordan. Israel occupied it in 1967.

**Bethlen, Stephen, Count,** 1874–1947?, Hungarian premier (1921–31). He prevented (1921) the return of Austrian Emperor CHARLES I to avoid military intervention by the LITTLE ENTENTE. His foreign policy focused on revising the post–World War I Treaty of Trianon. In 1945 he was taken to the USSR, where he reportedly died in prison.

**Beti, Mongo,** pseud. of **Alexandre Biyidi,** 1932–, Kamerun novelist. His work satirizes French colonialism: *Le pauvre Christ de Bomba* (1956; tr. *The Poor Christ of Bomba,* 1971), *Mission terminée* (1957; tr. *Mission to Kala,* 1964), and *Le roi miraculé: chronique des Essazam* (1958; tr. *King Lazarus,* 1960), as well as post-independence corruption, leading to civil war and resistance, including *Perpetué ou l'habitude du malheur* (1974; tr. *Perpetua and the Habit of Unhappiness,* 1978); and *Remember Reuben* (1974; tr., 1980). Some of his texts have been banned in both France and the Kamerun.

**Betjeman, Sir John,** 1906–84, English poet. He combines a witty appraisal of the present with nostalgia, and was noted for his lifelong enthusiasm for Victorian architecture. His verse includes *Mount Zion* (1931) and *Collected Poems* (1958, subsequently expanded). *Ghastly Good Taste* (1933) was the first of his architectural works. He was POET LAUREATE (1972–84).

**Betterton, Thomas,** 1635?–1710, English actor and manager of the RESTORATION stage. He was a great Hamlet and Macbeth with the producer William D'Avenant's company. As a manager he presented and played in adaptations of SHAKESPEARE, notably by DRYDEN and himself. His company opened the Haymarket Theatre in 1705. His wife, **Mary Saunderson Betterton,** d. 1712, was the first woman to play Shakespeare's great female roles.

**Betti, Ugo** (‚bettee), 1892–1953, Italian dramatist and poet. A judge who gained literary recognition late in life, he is ranked second only to PIRANDELLO among 20th-cent. Italian dramatists. His plays, often pessimistic and moralizing, include *La padrona* (1927; tr. The Mistress), *Frano allo scalo nord* (1936; tr. Landslide at the North Station), *Il diluvio* (1943; tr. The Flood), and *Delitto all'i-sola della capre* (1950; tr. Crime on Goat Island).

**Betto, Bernardino di:** see PINTURICCHIO.

**Beuys, Joseph,** 1921–87, German sculptor. He used a wide variety of waste material, bricks, scrap metal, etc., in his sculpture. He used the strategy of the HAPPENING to break up and then recreate his assemblages, as well as various other approaches that constantly challenged and questioned the public's and the galleries' conception and definition of sculpture.

Joseph **Beuys,** *Bed.* Bronze sculpture, 24.8 × 20 × 52.4 cm. Tate Gallery, London.

**Bevan, Aneurin,** 1897–1960, British politician responsible for introducing the NATIONAL HEALTH SERVICE. The son of a Welsh miner, he became a member of Parliament in 1929 and was made Minister of

Health and Housing under the Labour Government of 1945. Under his supervision, the National Health Service Act, based largely on the 1942 BEVERIDGE report, was passed in 1946 and the National Health Service came into being two years later.

**Beveridge, Sir William Henry,** 1879–1963, British economist; b. India; knighted in 1919. An authority on social problems and unemployment, Beveridge was the director of the London School of Economics (1919–37). In *Social Insurance and Allied Services* (1942), also known as the Beveridge report, he proposed a social security system 'from the cradle to the grave' for all British citizens, and many of his ideas were put into practice by the postwar Labour government as the basis of the NATIONAL HEALTH SERVICE. He was made 1st Baron Beveridge of Tugwell in 1946.

**Beverley,** town (1981 pop. 19,368), Humberside, E England, 12 km (8 mi) N of Hull. It is a market town with brewing, tanning, and other industries. There is a 13th-cent. minster, built in Early English to Perpendicular styles, a 14th-cent. parish church, and a 15th-cent. gateway.

**Bevin, Ernest,** 1881–1951, British trade unionist and statesman. He was an orphan who had earned his living from childhood. In 1921 he merged his dock workers' union with others to form the powerful Transport and General Workers' Union. A member of the Labour Party, he was minister of labour in Winston CHURCHILL's wartime cabinet (1940–45). As foreign minister in the Labour government (1945–51), he worked to build up Western Europe and to establish NATO.

**Bewick, Thomas** (ˌbyoohik), 1753–1828, English wood engraver. He revived the art of original wood engraving. His chief works include illustrations for John GAY's *Fables* (1779) and for Ralph Beilby's *General History of Quadrupeds* (1790) and *Chillingham Bull* (1789).

**Bexley,** London borough (1981 pop. 214,355) on S side of R. Thames. It was the home of William MORRIS for several years.

**Beyle, Marie Henri:** see STENDHAL.

**Bhagalpur,** town (1981 pop. 225,062), Bihar state, NE India. It is a divisional and district administrative centre on the south bank of the GANGES (Ganga) R. with important trading functions and handicrafts. It is the site of the ancient city of Champa.

**Bhagavad-Gītā** [Skt., = song of the Lord], most well-known book of HINDUISM, part of the epic, the Mahābhārata. It consists of a dialogue between KRSNA and Prince Arjuna on the eve of the battle of Kuruksetra. Arjuna is overcome with anguish when he sees his kinsmen and friends in the opposing army, but Krsna persuades him to fight by instructing him in spiritual wisdom and the means of attaining union with God (see YOGA) through selfless action, knowledge, and devotion. The *Gītā* is essentially related to the UPANISADS in content and has influenced many modern thinkers, eastern and western, such as GANDHI, AUROBINDO, SCHOPENHAUER, EMERSON, and THOREAU.

**Bhatpara,** town (1981 pop. 265,419), West Bengal state, E India, on the Hugli (Hooghly) R. It is essentially a northern industrial suburb of CALCUTTA, with a large number of jute mills and a few other industries.

**Bhattacharya, Bhabhani,** 1906–, Indian novelist, journalist, and translator. His novels, written in English, deal with India's social problems. They include *So Many Hungers!* (1948), *A Goddess Named Gold* (1960), and *Shadow from Ladakh* (1966).

**Bhave, Vinoba,** 1895–1982, Indian religious figure. He was a disciple of Mohandas GANDHI and after Gandhi's death (1948) was widely accepted as his successor. In 1951 he founded the Bhoodan, or land-gift, movement, seeking donations of land for redistribution to the landless.

**Bhavnagar** (bˈə,havnəgahr), town (1981 pop. 308,642), Gujarat state, W India, on the E coast of the Kathiawad peninsula. It is a district administrative centre and minor port, subject to siltation, shipping cotton and oilseeds, which it also mills. It makes ceramics. It was formerly the capital of a small princely state.

**Bhilainagar,** town (1981 pop. 369,450), Madhya Pradesh state, E India, on the Seonath R. Situated in Durg dist., this new town was created to house workers and services associated with one of independent India's new integrated steel works.

**Bhopal,** city (1981 pop. 671,018), Madhya Pradesh state, central India. It became the capital of Madhya Pradesh in 1956, since when it has grown rapidly and has become the site of a number of modern industries, notably heavy electrical engineering, cotton, and chemicals. It was a disaster at a chemical works that caused many fatalities and injuries in 1984. Bhopal lies on the main railway line from Bombay to Delhi. At nearby Sanchi is the famous sacred place of ancient Buddhism where there still stands a pillar erected by the emperor ASOKA (3rd century BC). In British times Bhopal was the capital of a princely state of the same name in which Muslim Nawabs (or Begums) ruled over a population that was mainly Hindu or 'tribal'.

**Bhubaneswar,** town (1981 pop. 219,211), Orissa state, E India. It is the capital of Orissa, and has grown rapidly as a planned new town since Indian independence. Its functions are almost entirely administrative, though it also attracts pilgrims because of the famous ancient Hindu temples within its boundaries and in neighbouring places such as Puri and Kanarak.

**Bhutan** (boohˌtahn), officially the Kingdom of Bhutan, kingdom (1985 est. pop. 1,286,000), 47,000 km² (18,147 sq mi), E Asia, in the Himalayas, bordered by India (S and E), the Tibet region of China (N), and Sikkim (W). The capital is Thimbu. Bhutan is a land of great mountain ranges, rising in the north to Kula Kangri, 7554 m (24,784 ft), and intensively cultivated valleys. The climate ranges from humid subtropical at the lower altitudes to temperate in the high mountains. Small-scale subsistence farming, with rice the main crop, and the raising of livestock dominate the economy. Metal, wood, and leather working; papermaking; and weaving are also important. The GNP is US$190 million (1985), and GNP per capita US$160 (1985). Bhutan's people are mostly Bhotias, ethnically related to Tibetans. Their religion is closely related to TIBETAN BUDDHISM; many Bhutanese live in monasteries.

*History.* In the 16th cent. the Tibetans conquered Bhutan's native tribes, and in 1720 China established suzerainty over the area. British interests in Bhutan dated from the arrival of a trade mission in 1774. Britain annexed part of Bhutan in 1865, and in 1910 Bhutan's first hereditary king agreed to let Britain direct the country's foreign affairs; this role was assumed by India in 1949. After Chinese Communist forces occupied (1950) Tibet, Bhutan became a point of contest between China and India, and the China–Bhutan border was closed. Jigme Singhe Wangchuk became king in 1972 (crowned 1974), and has since asserted full control over Bhutan's external policies.

**Bhutto, Zulfikar Ali** (ˌboohtoh), 1928–79, president (1971–73) and prime minister (1973–77) of PAKISTAN. He came to power after Pakistan's defeat in the war over BANGLADESH's independence. He was overthrown (1977), tried for state crimes, and executed (1979). His daughter, **Benazir Bhutto,** maintained his populist political ideals through a decade of military rule, until in 1988 she became prime minister after democratic elections.

**Bi,** chemical symbol of the element BISMUTH.

**Biafra, Republic of,** former African secessionist state, formed in SW Nigeria. Biafra was established in 1967 by Ibos, an ethnic group who feared they could not survive within Nigeria. The new state was led by Lt Col. C.O. Ojukwu. Soon after secession, fighting erupted between Nigerian and Biafran forces. More than one million Biafran civilians are believed to have died of starvation during the war, which ended with Biafra's defeat in 1970.

**Bialik, Hayyim Nahman,** 1873–1934, Ukrainian poet and novelist who wrote mainly in Hebrew. His style sometimes majestic, sometimes simple had a great effect on modern Hebrew literature. His poems include 'In the City of Slaughter' (1903). As an editor and publisher in Odessa, Berlin, and Tel Aviv, Bialik spread the ideas of the *Haskalah,* the renaissance of Jewish culture.

**Bialowieza** (beeˌyowoh veeˈyezhə), national park (1921) on the Soviet border of E Poland. Formerly a royal hunting forest, it preserves the European bison as well as bear and deer.

**biathlon,** athletic event in which cross-country skiers race across a hilly, 20-km (c.12½-mi) course, stopping periodically to fire rifles at fixed targets. Penalty minutes for missed targets are added to the competitor's time for the distance. Biathlon has been a Winter Olympics event since 1960.

**Bialystok,** city (1984 pop. 240,000), NE Poland. Administrative and commercial centre of Bialystok voivodship, it is a centre of textile (especially cotton) production and also has engineering industries. The city has been largely rebuilt after destruction in World War II.

**Bible,** book of sacred writings in Christianity and Judaism. (For the composition and canon of the Bible, see OLD TESTAMENT, NEW TESTAMENT, APOCRYPHA, and articles on individual books.)

*Christian Bible.* The traditional Christian view is that the Bible was written under the guidance of God and is, therefore, entirely true, literally or couched in allegory. Interpretation of the Bible is a main point of difference between Protestantism, which holds that individuals have the right to interpret the Bible for themselves, and Roman Catholicism, which teaches that individuals may read the Bible only as interpreted by the church. In recent times, many Protestants have been influenced by biblical criticism that has applied scientific and historical methods to Bible study ('higher criticism'); in reaction, FUNDAMENTALISM has emphasized the absolute inerrancy of the Bible. Noted extant manuscripts of the Bible include Codex Vaticanus (Greek, 4th cent.), at the Vatican; Codex Alexandrinus (Greek, 5th cent.), in the British Museum; and Codex Bezae (Greek and Latin, 6th cent.), at Cambridge, England. Among the DEAD SEA SCROLLS are the oldest fragments of the Hebrew text known; the New Testament has come down to us in Greek. The first great translation of the whole Bible was the Latin Vulgate of St JEROME. The Greek text generally accepted in the East is, for the Old Testament, the Septuagint. Great names in the history of the English Bible are John WYCLIF (d. 1384), whose influence inspired early translations of it; William TYNDALE, whose New Testament (1525–26) was the first English translation to be printed; and Miles Coverdale, who published (1535) a translation of the entire Bible. The greatest English translation was the Authorized Version (AV), or King James Version (KJV), of 1611, made by a group of churchmen and scholars led by Lancelot Andrewes. The Rheims–Douay Version was produced by Roman Catholic scholars at Rheims (New Testament, 1582) and Douai (Old Testament, 1610), France. In the 19th cent., the Authorized Version was revised as the English Revised Version and the American Revised Version (pub. 1880–90). American scholars published (1952) the influential Revised Standard Version (RSV). New translations are the New English Bible (1970) and such Roman Catholic translations as the Westminster Version and the New American Bible (1970); an English translation of the French Catholic Bible de Jerusalem appeared as the Jerusalem Bible (1966).

*Jewish Bible.* The Hebrew Bible is divided into three major sections: *Torah*, comprising the Pentateuch or Five Books of Moses (see TORAH); *Neviim* [prophetic writings], embodying the historical books (Joshua, Judges, Samuel, and Kings), the major prophets (Isaiah, Jeremiah, and Ezekiel) and the 12 minor Prophets; and *Ketuvim* [sacred writings], containing Psalms, Proverbs, and Job, the five Scrolls (Song of Songs, Ruth, Lamentations, Ecclesiastes, and Esther), the books of Daniel, Ezra, and Nehemiah (set in the Persian period 5th–4th cent. BC), and Chronicles. The order of books in the Hebrew Bible differs in a number of respects from that adopted by the Church. The popular Jewish name for the Bible is *Tanak*, an acronym from the initial letters of its three major divisions.

**biblical archaeology,** ARCHAEOLOGY of the ancient Middle East, intended to verify Biblical accounts or augment the cultural setting outlined in the BIBLE. This task was a prime motivation for the archaeological exploration of the Middle East in the 19th cent., especially in Palestine (see MEGIDDO and SAMARIA). More recent discoveries have revealed the historical accuracy of some Old Testament accounts and pushed back the date of Gospels (see DEAD SEA SCROLLS).

**bibliography,** listing of writings based on some organizational principle, such as a subject, an author, a library or collection. The earliest examples, lists of the contents of early libraries, have been found at NINEVEH, ALEXANDRIA, and PERGAMON. Modern bibliography began with the invention of the PRINTING press and the trade lists issued by publishing houses, comparable to today's *Trade List Annual* and the various 'books in print' volumes. By the 19th cent. there had developed an interest in descriptive bibliography, i.e., the description of a book as a physical object, which in turn led to textual bibliography, the critical examination of the book and its production history to determine the authority of the text. Mechanization has introduced machines to aid the bibliographer, e.g., the COMPUTER and the Hinman collator. Bibliographies of holdings are now published by national libraries, e.g., the British Library and the Library of Congress. Bibliographies of bibliographies include Theodore Besterman's *World Bibliography of Bibliography* and the *Bibliographic Index,* issued semiannually.

**bicameral system:** see LEGISLATURE.

**bicarbonate of soda:** see SODIUM BICARBONATE.

**bicycle,** light, two-wheeled vehicle driven by pedals. A model using pedals, cranks, drive rods, and handlebars was introduced c.1839 in Scotland; it was followed by the development of the hollow steel frame, ball bearings, metal wheel spokes, and rubber-rimmed wheels. The front wheel, directly powered by the pedals, was at one time much larger than the rear wheel. The first bicycle with a sprocket-chain drive powering an equal-size rear wheel was made in England in 1885; the pneumatic tyre was invented in Scotland in 1888. Later improvements included handlebar-mounted brake cables and gear change systems to facilitate changes in speed. The bicycle's popularity brought about major improvements in roads in 19th-cent. Europe and America, and the vehicle continues to be far more widely used than the motor car in many parts of the world today. In advanced countries, the bicycle used to be (pre-World War II) the means of transport of the poorer classes who could not afford a car; it is now enjoying a great revival as an optional means of transport for well-off well-educated urban people concerned both for environmental pollution and their own physical fitness.

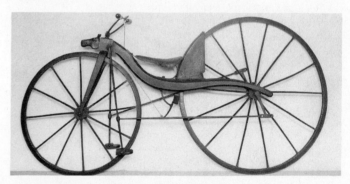

Drive rod **bicycle** introduced in Scotland c.1839

**Bidault, Georges** (bee,doh), 1899–, French political leader. A leader of the French underground in WORLD WAR II, Bidault was a postwar premier (1949–50) and was several times foreign minister. He joined the terrorist opponents of Algerian independence and fled (1962) into exile. He returned to France in 1968.

**Biddle, John,** 1516–62, founder of English UNITARIANISM. After losing his belief in the TRINITY, he stated his conclusions in *Twelve Arguments Drawn Out of Scripture,* for which he was imprisoned (1647). He was banished for publishing his *Two-fold Catechism* (1654). Returning in 1658, he taught and preached until again imprisoned (1662).

**Biedermeier,** style of German furniture, 1816–48. The name derives from a humorous pseudonym used by several German poets. Comfortable and inexpensive, it featured simplified forms of the EMPIRE STYLE and the DIRECTOIRE STYLE and of some 18th-cent. English styles. Black lacquer substituted for costly ebony, and peasant-style painted decoration was applied.

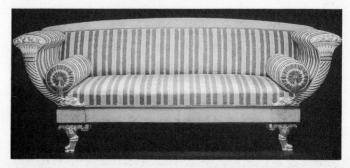

An example of **Biedermeier** furniture showing English influence

**Bielefeld**, city (1984 pop. 303,900), North Rhine–Westphalia, N West Germany. It has a long-established industrial tradition based on textiles and the making of sewing machines. Other industries include the manufacture of electrical and printing equipment.

**biennial**, plant requiring two growing seasons to complete its life cycle, as distinguished from an ANNUAL or PERENNIAL. In the first year the plant produces leaves and a fleshy root; in the second year it produces flowers and seeds, and then dies. Some biennials will bloom in the same growing season if sown early.

**Bierce, Ambrose Gwinett**, 1842–1914?, American writer. After Civil War service he turned to journalism, eventually becoming the literary arbiter of the West Coast. Bierce achieved real distinction in his short stories, collected in such volumes as *In the Midst of Life* (1891) and *Can Such Things Be?* (1893). He is equally famous for a collection of sardonic definitions, *The Devil's Dictionary* (1906). His work is marked by distilled satire, crisply precise language, and a realistically developed sense of horror. He disappeared in Mexico in 1913.

**bigamy**, the offence of marrying another person whilst already married. The offence is mainly prevalent in Western society where the dominant value is monogamous marriage. As extramarital relationships in general are not criminal, bigamy can be said to be more an offence against the institution of marriage rather than against the injured person, although sometimes bigamy is committed with intent to defraud.

**'big bang'**, name commonly given to the deregulation of the STOCK EXCHANGE in the UK in Oct. 1986. The deregulation was prompted by the threat of increasing foreign competition and the greater use of high technology. The changes involved the abolition of minimum scales of commission on transactions of securities; and dual capacity was introduced which meant that the roles of jobbers and brokers need no longer be separate functions. Requirements for membership of the Stock Exchange were relaxed so that companies could take over existing members and become members themselves, without having to conform to the previously rigorous membership requirements. After the 'big bang' membership of the Stock Exchange moved from the relatively small partnerships to large financial institutions, many of them banks and non-British anxious to fully exploit London's time advantage in dealing in New York, Tokyo and other stock exchanges around the world. During 1986 and 1987 the rush to get into the market caused many pressures to build up both in terms of finance and skills, and in some cases professional standards of competence and probity were not adhered to.

**big bang theory:** see COSMOLOGY.

**Big Ben**, the bell in Parliament tower (Westminster Palace), London; also the tower clock. Installed in 1856, it was named after the commissioner of works, Sir Benjamin Hall.

**Bigfoot:** see YETI.

**bighorn** or **Rocky Mountain sheep**, wild SHEEP (*Ovis canadensis*) of W North America. It is a heavy, greyish brown animal with a white patch on the hindquarters; the male has curling horns. Once plentiful, it is diminishing in number as a result of indiscriminate hunting. It is related to the MOUFLON, argali and urial in Eurasia.

**big man**, used to refer to a kind of political leader (and political system) in Melanesia. A big man accedes to no formal, inherited position of authority, but constructs his own following, his own reputation as a potential leader in a factional political system. This he does through acquiring personal prestige by manipulating wealth and political advantage in open status competition with other potential and existing big men. Such leaders act as focal points for exchanges between local communities and in this way the system of conspicuous display and exchange acts as a stimulus to production.

**bignonia**, common name for the Bignoniaceae, a family of woody vines, shrubs, and trees of the tropics. Members of the family include the tropical calabash tree, which bears large fruits used as carrying gourds (called calabashes) and whose wood is used to make pipes; and the ornamental shade trees of the genus *Catalpa*, also used for timber.

**Bigordi, Domenico:** see GHIRLANDAIO, DOMENICO.

**Bikaner**, town (1981 pop. 256,057), Rajasthan state, NW India. It is a district administrative and commercial centre set in desert or semidesert which nevertheless has attracted factories making woollen goods,

Big Ben and Westminster Bridge

carpets, steel pipes, and other products. In British days it was the capital of a princely state of the same name.

**Bikini**, atoll, c.5 km² (2 sq mi), W central Pacific Ocean, in the MARSHALL ISLANDS, US Trust Territory of the PACIFIC ISLANDS. Comprising 36 islets on a reef 40 km (25 mi) long, it was used (1946–58) for US nuclear-bomb tests. Bikinians, evacuated in 1946, were allowed to return in 1969, but they were reevacuated in 1978 when new data showed high levels of residual radioactivity.

**Bilbao**, city (1981 pop. 433,030), capital of Vizcaya prov., N Spain. The largest city of the Basque Provinces, it was founded as a port on the estuary of the Nervión R. in 1300, but remained small until the late 19th cent. Utilizing local iron ores, Bilbao has become a major centre of iron and steel and engineering industries, including shipbuilding.

**bilberry**, common name for *Vaccinium myrtilis* of the HEATH family, also called whortleberry or blaeberry. Native to Britain and N Europe.

**Bilderdijk, Willem** (ˌbildədiek), 1756–1831, Dutch poet. Ranked among the great Dutch poets, he is best known for an unfinished epic, *The Destruction of the First Creation* (1820), and other religious verse. His translations catalysed the romantic movement in Dutch literature.

**bile**, bitter, alkaline fluid of a yellow, brown, or green colour that aids in the digestion of fats (see DIGESTIVE SYSTEM). Composed of water, bile salts, bilirubin (a pigment), cholesterol, and lecithin, bile is secreted by the LIVER and stored in the GALL BLADDER. It is emptied into the upper intestine to break down fats and enable them (and fat-soluble vitamins) to be absorbed through the intestinal wall. Bile is also a route of excretion for cholesterol, haem, and many drugs. JAUNDICE may result if the flow of bile is impeded.

**bilharziasis, bilharzia** or **schistosomiasis**, infestation with parasitic worms (genus *Schistosoma*) which inhabit the veins draining the bladder and lower bowel causing chronic ill-health. The disease is common in poor parts of the world with inadequate sanitation. Eggs are excreted into water by an infected person and larvae develop within water snails to emerge and penetrate the skin of anyone bathing in the infected water.

**billiards,** any one of several games played with a leather-tipped stick (cue) and various numbers of balls on an oblong, cloth-covered table with raised, cushioned edges. The version known simply as *billiards* is played with three balls on a table having six pockets let into the corners and the two longer sides. *Pool* is played with a cue ball and 15 object balls on a table with six pockets. SNOOKER is similar to pool but with 21 object balls. In *bar billiards*, balls are struck into holes on the table. Variants of billiards were popular in England and France in the 16th cent.

**Billings, John Shaw,** 1838–1913, American surgeon and librarian. Under his direction (1864–95) the National Library of Medicine became one of the great medical library systems in the world. He initiated the *Index Catalogue* and *Index Medicus* and compiled (1889) the *National Medical Dictionary*. He also directed development of the New York Public Library, suggested what became punched-card technology, and supervised the 1880 and 1890 US censuses.

**bill of exchange,** an order in writing from one person (the drawer) to another person (the drawee) ordering him or her to pay the holder (payee), a fixed sum on a specified date. A bill of exchange is a special type of NEGOTIABLE INSTRUMENT. A bill is negotiated, by the payee endorsing it to another person, at any time before payment is due. Bills of exchange are the most common form of payment for goods in international trade. A cheque is a type of bill of exchange drawn on a banker, to which special rules apply.

**Bill of Rights,** 1689, in British history, one of the fundamental instruments of constitutional law. It incorporated by statute the Declaration of Rights accepted by WILLIAM III and MARY II, and registered the results of the struggle between the STUART kings and PARLIAMENT. The Bill of Rights stated that no Roman Catholic would rule England; it gave inviolable civil and political rights to the people and political supremacy to Parliament. It was supplemented (1701) by the Act of SETTLEMENT.

**Bill of Rights,** in US history: see under CONSTITUTION OF THE UNITED STATES.

**Billy the Kid,** 1859–81, American outlaw. A large-scale cattle rustler in New Mexico from 1878, he was hunted and fatally shot. Billy's real name was William H. Bonney.

**bimah,** central synagogue platform, from which the Cantor intones the services and the sacred scrolls are read.

**bimetallism,** in economic history, a monetary system in which two commodities, usually gold and silver, were used as a standard and coined at a fixed ratio. The system was designed to create a monetary unit with more stability than one based on a single metal. In a bimetallic system, the ratio, which is determined by law, is expressed in terms of weight, e.g., 16 oz of silver equal 1 oz of gold, or a ratio of 16 to 1. The legal ratio has no relationship to the commercial value of the metals, which fluctuates constantly. This discrepancy between the commercial and face values of the two metals made bimetallism too unstable for most modern nations. The system was practised in the US and other countries (except England, where gold was used) in the 18th and 19th cent.

**binary number,** a number that makes use of only two numerals, 0 and 1. Because these numerals can be represented by the 'on' or 'off' state of an electrical system (see BIT), this is the numbering system normally used in computers. As examples $1 = 1, 2 = 10, 3 = 11, 4 = 100, 5 = 101$. An example of addition, $7 = (4 + 3), = (100 + 11), = 111$. See NUMERATION, DIGITAL SYSTEM.

**binary star,** pair of stars that are held together by their mutual gravitational attraction and revolve about their common centre of mass. True binary stars are distinct from optical doubles — pairs of stars that lie along nearly the same line of sight from the Earth but are not physically associated. A visual binary is a pair of stars that can be seen be direct telescopic observation to be a distinct pair in orbital motion. A spectroscopic binary cannot normally be distinguished telescopically as two separate stars, but spectral lines from the pair show a periodic DOPPLER EFFECT that indicates mutual revolution. An eclipsing binary has the plane of its orbit lying in the line of sight and shows a periodic fluctuation in brightness (see VARIABLE STAR) as one star passes in front of the other.

**binary system:** see NUMERATION.

**binding energy,** energy needed to dissociate (or partially dissociate) an ATOM, MOLECULE, or NUCLEUS into its component parts. The binding energy of the hydrogen atom is the energy needed (13.6 eV) to remove the orbiting ELECTRON. Nuclear binding energies are much larger and, except

for very heavy or very light nuclei, energies of around 8 MeV are needed to remove a NEUTRON or PROTON from a nucleus.

**bindweed:** see MORNING-GLORY.

**Binet, Alfred** (bee nay), 1857–1911, French psychologist. He is best known for devising (with T. Simon) the first INTELLIGENCE test. PIAGET also worked in Binet's laboratory at the beginning of his career, his dissatisfaction with the test method leading him to develop his clinical method.

**Bingham, George Caleb,** 1811–79, American painter and politician. His vigorous GENRE scenes accurately picture their time and locale. They include *Fur Traders Descending the Missouri* (Metropolitan Mus., New York) and *Raftsmen Playing Cards* (City Art Mus., St Louis). Bingham was active in Missouri politics, holding several state offices, and many of his pictures are on political subjects.

**bingo,** lottery game developed in the 1890s from LOTTO. Known as housey-housey in the British Army and tombola in the Royal Navy, it is played principally for cash prizes. Numbers ranging from 1 to 90 or 1 to 99 are drawn at random from a bag by the person running the game. Each participant has a card printed with a selection of different numbers. The first person to cross out all the numbers on their card in accordance with the numbers called is the winner.

**binoculars,** small optical instrument, consisting of a pair of telescopes mounted on a single, usually adjustable frame, that is used for magnifying distant objects. Light entering each TELESCOPE through its objective LENS is bent by a pair of prisms before passing through one or more additional lenses in the eyepiece. The prisms turn the image inverted by the objective lens right side up again and allow the distance between the objective lenses to be twice as far apart as that between the eyepieces, thus enhancing the viewer's perception of depth. The usually less powerful opera and field glasses are also classed as binoculars, although both use Galilean telescopes, which do not employ prisms.

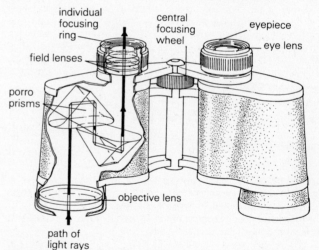

Binoculars

**binomial distribution,** is used in statistics to calculate the probabilities of the various numbers of successes in a series of $n$ independent trials in each of which the chance of a particular outcome is equal to $p$. The name of the DISTRIBUTION is derived from the fact that the relative frequencies are derived from the expansion of the binomial expression $(p + q)^n$ where $q = (1 - p)$. The arithmetic mean of the binomial distribution is $np$ and the variance is $npq$. Most data which are presented as proportions or percentages can be represented by the binomial distribution, e.g., birth and death rates. The percentages of customers buying a given product may also be represented by the binomial distribution in studies of market research.

**binomial nomenclature,** the use of two names to identify a species, after the system devised by LINNAEUS. The generic name is followed by the specific name, and indicates that the animal is related to those with the same generic name (see CLASSIFICATION). The two names may be followed by a third, indicating a particular race of that species.

**Bintley, David**, 1957–, English dancer and choreographer. After training at the Royal Ballet School, he danced with Sadlers Wells Royal Ballet (1976) where he is now resident choreographer.

**biochemistry**, science concerned chiefly with the chemistry of biological processes, e.g., METABOLISM. From its roots in chemistry, chiefly organic and physical chemistry, biochemistry has broadened to encompass any biological problem amenable to the investigative techniques of both chemistry and physics. A milestone in biochemical research was the elucidation of the structure of DNA (1953).

**biocybernetics:** see AUTOMATIC CONTROL; CYBERNETICS.

**bioengineering**, use of engineering and biological principles for the identification of the functions of living systems and for the development of (1) therapeutic devices, especially artificial body parts and systems, e.g., artificial blood vessels, PACEMAKERS, DIALYSIS equipment, and artificial limbs that function like their prototypes; and (2) equipment for monitoring the performance of healthy and diseased organisms.

**biofeedback**, method for learning to increase one's ability to control biological responses, such as blood pressure, muscle tension, and heart rate. Sophisticated instruments are often used to measure physiological responses and make them apparent to the patient, who then tries to alter and ultimately control them without the aid of monitoring devices. Biofeedback programmes have been used to teach patients to relax muscles or adjust blood flow in the case of headache, to help partially paralysed stroke victims activate muscles, and to alleviate anxiety in dental patients.

**biography**, reconstruction in print of the lives of real people. With the autobiography, an individual's interpretation of his or her own life, it shares a venerable tradition. Ancient Egyptian and Assyrian inscriptions proclaimed the deeds of kings. Among the first biographies of ordinary men, the Dialogues of PLATO (4th cent. BC) reveal its subject, SOCRATES, by letting him speak for himself. A balanced assessment of character is achieved in PLUTARCH's *Parallel Lives* (2nd cent. AD), where subjects are paired, e.g., DEMOSTHENES with CICERO. In the medieval lives of saints, human flaws were bypassed for saintly traits, but the few secular biographies of the period, e.g., Einhard's *Life of Charlemagne* (9th cent.), contain lively portraits of real people. The RENAISSANCE interest in worldly power and self-assertion is reflected in CELLINI's *Autobiography* (16th cent.). By the 17th cent. informality and intimacy had been introduced, e.g., John AUBREY's *Brief Lives*. In the 18th cent. Dr. JOHNSON's *Lives of the Poets* (1780–81) set the example for literary biographies, notably James BOSWELL's *Life of Samuel Johnson* (1791). The first definitive biography, it was drawn from personal recollection, letters, memoirs, and interviews. Later developments include the psychoanalytic biography, e.g., Sigmund FREUD's *Leonardo Da Vinci* (1910); the debunking biography, e.g., Lytton STRACHEY's *Eminent Victorians* (1918); and the thematic biography, e.g., Thomas MERTON's *Seven Storey Mountain* (1948), which follows the analogue of DANTE's *Inferno*.

**biological clock**, name given to the internal mechanism that originates the changes which result in BIORHYTHM in plants and animals. The mechanism is not yet understood precisely and is influenced by external changes such as changing daylight hours, light intensity, or tides. The biological clock governs the opening of flower petals in plants, the time of urine production, the rise of plankton through the water, and migratory journeys in birds, among other observable responses.

**biological warfare, bacteriological warfare**, or **germ warfare**, employment in war of microorganisms to injure or destroy human beings, animals, or crops. Although 'first use' of both biological and chemical weapons (see CHEMICAL WARFARE) was prohibited by the 1925 Geneva Convention, several nations (including the UK) subsequently conducted research into detection and defence systems, and developed microorganisms (including strains of smallpox and the plague) suitable for military retaliation. Such organisms can be delivered by animals, especially rodents or insects, or by AEROSOL packages built into artillery shells or the warheads of ground-to-ground or air-to-ground missiles and released into the atmosphere to infect by inhalation. Research in this area did not end after 1972, despite an agreement that year by more than 100 nations to prohibit the development, testing, and stockpiling of biological weapons.

**biology**, science dealing with living things, broadly divided into ZOOLOGY, the study of animal life, and BOTANY, the study of plant life. Subdivisions include ANATOMY and PHYSIOLOGY; GENETICS; molecular biology, the study of cells (cytology), tissues (histology), embryonic development (see EMBRYO), and microscopic forms of life; as well as CLASSIFICATION, EVOLUTION, ECOLOGY (the study of interaction between living things and their environments), and palaeontology (the study of FOSSIL forms of life).

**bioluminescence**, production of light by living organisms resulting from the conversion of chemical energy to light energy. Bioluminescent plants include certain MUSHROOMS that emit light continuously. The dinoflagellates, a group of marine algae, produce light when disturbed giving a phosphorescent wake to boats at night. Some BACTERIA are bioluminescent when decomposing organic remains, such as wood. Bioluminescent animals include the COMB JELLY, ANNELID WORMS, MOLLUSCS, insects such as the FIREFLY, and FISHES. Some animals use luminescence in courtship and mating, to divert predators, or to attract prey.

**biomass energy:** see ENERGY, SOURCES OF.

**biome:** see ECOLOGY.

**Bion**, fl. 2nd cent.? BC, Greek bucolic poet, an imitator of THEOCRITUS. The *Lament for Adonis* (attributed to him) was the model for SHELLEY's *Adonais.*

**bionics**, study of living systems with the intention of applying their principles to the design of engineering systems. Drawing on interdisciplinary research in the mechanical and life sciences, bionics has been used to develop audiovisual equipment based on human eye and ear function, to design air and naval craft patterned after the biological structure of birds and fish, and to incorporate principles of the human neurological system in data-processing systems.

**biophysics**, application of various tools, methods, and principles of physical science to the study of biological problems. In biophysics, physical mechanisms and mathematical and physical models have been used to explain life processes such as the transmission of nerve impulses, the muscle contraction mechanism, and the visual mechanism.

**biopsy**, examination of cells or tissues removed from a living organism to aid medical diagnosis. Samples may be removed surgically, as in excision of breast tissue, or by withdrawal of cells through a special needle, from the liver, kidney, or bone marrow, for instance.

**biorhythm** or **biological rhythm**, cyclic pattern of changes in physiology or in activity of living organisms, often synchronized with daily, monthly, or yearly environmental changes. Rhythms that vary according to the time of day (circadian rhythms), in part a response to daylight or dark, include the opening and closing of flowers and the night-time increase in activity of nocturnal animals. Circadian rhythms also include activities that occur often during a 24-hour period, such as blood pressure changes and urine production. Annual cycles, called cirannual rhythms, respond to changes in the relative length of periods of daylight and include such activities as migration and animal mating. Marine organisms are affected by tide cycles. Although the exact nature of the internal mechanism is not known, various external stimuli including light, temperature, and gravity influence the organism's internal biological clock; in the absence of external cues, the internal rhythms gradually drift out of phase with the environment. In humans, long, quick journeys to the east or west upset the internal rhythm, producing 'jet lag'.

**biosphere**, irregularly shaped envelope of the earth's air, water, and land, encompassing the heights and depths at which living things exist. The biosphere is a closed and self-regulating system (see ECOLOGY) sustained by grand-scale cycles of energy and materials.

**Biqa, Al**, upland valley of Lebanon and Syria, 160 km (100 mi) long and 8–14.5 km (5–9 mi) wide, between the Lebanon and Anti-Lebanon ranges. It is also spelt El Bika, El Bekaa, or El Baqa. It is a continuation in Asia of Africa's GREAT RIFT VALLEY. The southern part of Al Biqa, drained and irrigated by the Litani R., is one of the most productive farming areas in the Lebanon. It has always been an important north–south routeway. Wars have been fought for its control since the dawn of history.

**birch**, common name for some members of the Betulaceae, a family of about 40 deciduous trees or shrubs widely distributed in the Northern Hemisphere, growing as far North as the Arctic zone. Some birches are valued for their fine hardwoods, e.g., the yellow birch (*Betula lutea*). The birches are often used as ornamentals, for their graceful form and silvery-white bark. The bark of the paper birch (*B. papyrifera*) of the N US and Canada was used by Indians for canoes and baskets. Various birches produce edible fruits, sugar, vinegar, tea from leaves, and birch beer from sap.

**bird,** warm-blooded, egg-laying VERTEBRATE of the class Aves, having its body covered with FEATHERS and its forelimbs modified into wings. Like MAMMALS, birds have a four-chambered heart; they have a relatively large brain and acute hearing but little sense of smell. Believed to have evolved from REPTILES (or perhaps DINOSAURS), birds are highly adapted for flight. Their feathers, though light, protect against cold and wet and have great strength. Intricate courtship displays are performed by many species during breeding season, when birdsong is most pronounced; singing ability is usually restricted to, or superior in, the male. Most birds build some kind of nest for their eggs, which vary in size, shape, colour, and number according to species. The chief domestic birds are the CHICKEN, DUCK, GOOSE, TURKEY, and guinea fowl. Among the game birds hunted for food and sport are GROUSE, PHEASANT, QUAIL, and duck.

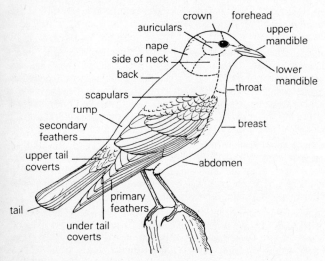

General anatomy of a **bird**

**bird-eating spider** or **tarantula,** name for several species of large, hairy SPIDERS of the family Aviculariidae, found in the Americas. The spider's body may measure 7.5 cm (3 in) long and, with legs extended, up to 25 cm (10 in) across. The largest may kill small vertebrates, but most feed on ARTHROPODS. Its bites, although painful, are not usually dangerous to humans. Although called TARANTULAS in America, they are not truly tarantulas, which are European.

**bird of paradise,** member of the BIRD family Paradisaeidae, all famous for the beauty of their plumage. Birds of paradise live in the forests of New Guinea and mountainous NE Australia. The males use their gorgeous feathers in courtship dances to impress the drabber females. They are fruit-eating birds, but will also take small tree animals. These birds have always been hunted for their feathers, and many species are now rare because of this. We do not know how many went into extinction. All the birds of paradise are protected today. The legend of the phoenix is believed to have arisen from the practice of exporting bird-of-paradise skins, wrapped in scorched banana leaves to keep away moths, to Phoenicia, over 2000 years ago.

**bird-of-paradise flower,** large tropical herb (*Strelitzia reginae*) of the BANANA family, native to S Africa. Its blue and orange blossom resembles an exotic bird of that name.

**Birdseye, Clarence,** 1886–1956, American inventor and founder of the frozen-food industry. His successful experiments with food-freezing processes led to the founding (1924) of the General Foods Co. By 1949, Birdseye had perfected the anhydrous process, which reduces the time needed for food freezing from 18 to 1½ hr. See FOOD PRESERVATION.

**Bird Woman:** see SACAJAWEA.

**birefringence:** see POLARIZED LIGHT.

**Birkenhead,** town (1981 pop. 99,075), Merseyside, NW England, on Wirral peninsula near mouth of R. Mersey. It is an industrial town and port, whose industries include ship-building and ship-repairing, both now

Examples of **birds** from different ecological groups

Bird of paradise

Bird of paradise flower (*Strelitzia reginae*)

in decline. It is connected to LIVERPOOL by a rail tunnel and two road tunnels across the R. MERSEY. The docks were opened in 1847 and led to great expansion of the town.

**Birkhoff, George David**, 1884–1944, American mathematician. He is known for his work on linear DIFFERENTIAL EQUATIONS and difference equations. His introduction of the concepts of minimal or recurrent sets of motion and establishment of their existence under general conditions began a new era in the study of dynamic systems. He also wrote on the foundations of relativity and quantum mechanics.

**Birmingham,** second largest British city (1981 pop. 1,013,995), W Midlands, England. It is a major industrial, service, and transport centre with many growing high-tech and light industries. A market town by the 15th cent., Birmingham developed rapidly in the 17th and 18th cent. because of nearby iron and coal deposits. In the 1870s the city underwent extensive municipal improvement, and much of the centre was rebuilt after being bombed in WORLD WAR II. There are two universities, and a notable symphony orchestra. The National Exhibition Centre is located near Birmingham Airport.

**Birmingham,** US city (1984 est. pop. 280,000), north-central Alabama, in the Jones Valley, near the southern end of the Appalachians; inc. 1871. The largest city in Alabama, it is the leading iron and steel centre in the South. The area's coal, iron, and other resources supply its plants and factories. Its industry has diversified, and it manufactures a wide range of products, including transport equipment, chemicals, and processed food. Birmingham is also a governmental, research, and trade centre, connected by canal with the Gulf of Mexico. It is the site of several colleges and cultural institutions.

**Birney, James Gillespie**, 1792–1857, American abolitionist. After freeing (1834) his inherited slaves, he helped organize (1835) the Kentucky Anti-Slavery Society and was active in the American Anti-Slavery Society. The acknowledged leader of ABOLITIONISTS favouring political action, he ran for president as a Liberty Party candidate in 1840 and 1844.

**Biró, Laszlo**, 1900–85, Hungarian sculptor, painter, journalist, and inventor of the ballpoint pen. Wanting a pen that did not dry up for his art work, Biro, together with his brother Georg, an industrial chemist, developed and patented their revolutionary ballpoint pen in 1938. On the approach of war they both escaped to the Argentine and from there licensed their patent in many countries. One of the advantages of the pen was that, unlike fountain pens, it did not leak at high altitudes and low atmospheric pressure. In 1942 the US Army Quartermaster General ordered the 'biro' as a standard issue. Since the war the ballpoint pen has become the universal writing implement, though its supremacy was challenged by the arrival in the 1960s of the fibre-tipped pen.

**birth control,** practice of preventing conception for the purpose of limiting the number of births; also called contraception and family planning. The modern movement for birth control began in Britain, where the writings of MALTHUS stirred interest in the problems of overpopulation. The first birth-control clinic in Britain was opened in 1921 by birth-control leader Marie STOPES. On an international level, birth control is led by the International Planned Parenthood Federation (founded 1952), and in some countries (e.g., Sweden, Japan, and many Communist nations) the government provides birth-control assistance to its people in order to limit population growth. The Roman Catholic Church has provided the main opposition to the birth control movement, approving only the so-called rhythm method, or abstinence from intercourse around the time of ovulation. Other contraceptive methods include, for males, withdrawal before ejaculation; use of a condom, or rubber sheath over the penis; and sterilization by VASECTOMY. Contraception for women includes precoital use of spermicidal vaginal suppositories, foams, and jellies; use of a diaphragm, a cup-shaped rubber device inserted into the vagina before intercourse to prevent sperm from travelling to the egg; use of an INTRAUTERINE DEVICE; and 'the pill' (see ORAL CONTRACEPTIVE). Surgical sterilization for women includes tubal ligation (severing or sealing of the Fallopian tubes). See also ABORTION; POPULATION.

**birth defects:** see CONGENITAL ABNORMALITIES.

**Birtwistle, Harrison**, 1934–, British composer. His uncompromising use of serial techniques and harsh sonorities is combined with an expressive power that has helped his work appeal to a variety of audiences. After the opera *Punch and Judy* (1968), Birtwistle formed with Maxwell DAVIES the Pierrot Players (renamed The Fires of London in 1970), for whom he wrote several works. In later compositions he has developed more expansive forms, as in the opera *The Masque of Orpheus*

(1973–82), *Earth Dances* (1987), and *Endless Parade* (1988) for trumpet and orchestra.

**bisexuality:** see SEXUAL ORIENTATION.

**Bishop, Elizabeth,** 1911–79, American poet. Her penetrating and detached poetic vision is evident in such volumes as *Poems: North and South—A Cold Spring* (1955), *Complete Poems* (1969), and *Geography III* (1976).

**Bishop, Isabel,** 1902–, American painter. Noted for their delicate treatment of light and shade, her works often have working women as subject matter.

**Bishops' Wars,** two brief campaigns (1639, 1640) of the Scots against CHARLES I of England. Opposing his attempt to impose episcopacy, the COVENANTERS pledged a return to Presbyterianism. They invaded England and forced Charles to sign the Treaty of Ripon (Oct. 1640). See also ENGLISH CIVIL WAR.

**Bismarck,** US city (1980 pop. 44,485), state capital of North Dakota, on hills over the Missouri R.; inc. 1873, territorial capital from 1883. Bismarck developed in the 1870s when the Northern Pacific Railroad reached a steamboat port there. The trade centre for the region, it is a major wheat, grain, and livestock producer.

**Bismarck, Otto von,** 1815–98, German statesman, known as the Iron Chancellor; premier of Prussia (1862–90) and chancellor of Germany (1871–90). He established his political reputation as a hard-line anti-liberal, and upon becoming premier he unconstitutionally dissolved parliament and illegally levied taxes for the army. In order to expel Austria from the GERMAN CONFEDERATION (as a first step toward unification of the German states), he provoked war with Denmark (1864) and Austria itself (1866) over the SCHLESWIG–HOLSTEIN question. The AUSTRO–PRUSSIAN WAR resulted in a quick defeat of Austria, and Bismarck then formed the North German Confederation, from which Austria was excluded. The FRANCO–PRUSSIAN WAR (1870–71), which ended in France's humiliating defeat, facilitated the bringing together of the German states under the crown of Prussia, and William was proclaimed emperor with Bismarck as his first chancellor. His intricate system of alliances and alignments made him the acknowledged leader of Europe (see THREE EMPERORS' LEAGUE; BERLIN, CONGRESS OF; TRIPLE ALLIANCE AND TRIPLE ENTENTE). All his interest lay in Europe, but in 1884 he made a successful bid for overseas colonies. Meanwhile, the increasingly industrialized German economy flourished. Bismarck's struggle with the Church, the '*Kulturkampf*', won him liberal support (1871–76), when he gained a parliamentary majority, and after 1878 when the liberals broke with him he followed a protectionist policy. Later, partly to weaken the appeal of the socialists, he initiated (1883–87) far-reaching social reforms, including child labour laws, maximum hours legislation, and extensive old age, illness, and unemployment insurance. The accession (1888) of WILLIAM II, a longtime critic, brought Bismarck's career to a close; the new emperor dismissed him in 1890.

**bismuth** (Bi), metallic element, established as a separate element by Claud J. Geoffroy in 1753. The silver-white element is the poorest heat conductor of all the metals except mercury. Its soluble compounds are poisonous; its insoluble compounds are used to treat certain gastric disorders and skin injuries. See ELEMENT (table); PERIODIC TABLE.

**bison,** hoofed MAMMAL (genus *Bison*) of the CATTLE family, with short horns and heavy, humped shoulders. The European wisent (*B. bonasus*) is larger than the North American bison (*B. bison*), commonly called BUFFALO, which may reach a shoulder height of 1.5 m (5 ft) and a weight of 1100 kg (2500 lb). Bison roamed America in vast herds until slaughter by settlers for sport and meat reduced them to near extinction; they are now protected and thriving.

**Bissau,** city (1979 pop. 109,214), capital of Guinea-Bissau, on the Geba estuary, off the Atlantic Ocean. It is the country's largest city, major port, and administrative centre. Exports include peanuts, hardwood, palm oil, coconuts, and shellfish, and there is some transit trade. Food and beverage processing is the main industry. Founded (1687) by the Portuguese as a fortified port and trading centre, the city was the capital (1942–74) of Portuguese Guinea.

**bit:** see COMPUTER.

**Bithynia,** ancient country of NW Asia Minor, in present-day Turkey. At first an independent Thracian state, it became part of the Persian empire,

and after the death of ALEXANDER THE GREAT, it was an independent kingdom (3rd–1st cent. BC). King Nicomedes IV willed it to Rome (74 BC). Joined with Pontus as a single province soon afterwards, Bithynia declined in the 2nd cent. AD.

**bittern,** migratory BIRD of the HERON family. Bitterns have a worldwide distribution. The common bittern (*Botaurus stellaris*) is found in Europe, Asia, and parts of Africa, sharing the range with other bitterns. They are secretive birds, nesting in reeds and sedges, feeding on amphibians, fishes, and insects. The male's mating call is a distinctive booming sound.

**bittersweet,** plant (*Solanum dulcamara*) of the NIGHTSHADE family; also called the woody nightshade. Its shoots yield a medicinal narcotic poison similar to belladonna and have been used for skin dieases, asthma, and jaundice. The berries are poisonous.

**bivalve,** MOLLUSC (class Bivalvia or Pelecypoda) with a laterally compressed body and an external shell consisting of two dorsally hinged valves. Bivalves lack eyes and tentacles; in most, a muscular foot, used for burrowing, protrudes from the valves in front of the body. Shells range in size from 2 mm (1/16 in) to over 120 cm (4 ft). Bivalves are an important food source. See CLAM; COCKLE; SHIPWORM; SCALLOP; MUSSEL; OYSTER.

**Bizet, Georges** (ˌbeezay), 1838–75, French composer. He is celebrated for his immensely popular opera *Carmen* (1875), based on a story by MÉRIMÉE. His other works include the opera *The Pearlfishers* (1863), the Symphony in C Major (1868), and incidental music to DAUDET's *L'Arlesienne* (1872).

**Bjerknes, Vilhelm Frimann Koren** (ˌbyeəknes), 1862–1951, Norwegian physicist and pioneer in modern meteorology. He applied hydrodynamic and thermodynamic theories to atmospheric and hydrospheric conditions in order to predict future weather conditions. His work in meteorology and on electric waves was important in the early development of wireless telegraphy. He and his son **Jakob Bjerknes,** 1897–1975, evolved the polar-front theory of cyclones, i.e., that cyclones originate as waves in polar fronts separating warm and cool air masses.

**Bjoørnson, Bjoørnstjerne** (ˌbyuhnsohn), 1832–1910, Norwegian writer and statesman. He was a seminal figure in 19th-cent. Norwegian literature and a lifelong champion of liberal causes. He sought to free the Norwegian theatre from Danish influence and to revive Norwegian as a literary language. As director of Bergen's Ole Bull Theatre (1857–59) and of the Oslo Theatre (1863–67), he recreated Norway's epic past in sagalike dramas, e.g., the trilogy *Sigurd Slembe* (1862). He was named national poet of Norway, and his poem 'Yes, We Love this Land of Ours' became the national anthem. Other major works include the novel *The Fisher Girl* (1868), the epic poem *Arnljot Gelline* (1870), and the play *Pastor Sang* (1893). He received the 1903 Nobel Prize for literature.

**Björnsson, Sveinn** (ˌbjuhnsawn), 1881–1952, Icelandic diplomat and political leader. He served as minister to Denmark (1920–41), regent of Iceland (1941–44), and, after independence from Denmark, Iceland's first president (1944–52).

**Bk,** chemical symbol of the element BERKELIUM.

**Blache, Vidal de la P.** (blahsh), 1845–1918, French geographer, concerned with the relationship between geographical causes and historical effects. He became professor of geography at Nancy and then at Paris after working in the French School in Athens. He lectured widely and founded and edited the periodical *Annales de Géographie*. His main works were: *Tableau général de la géographie de France* (1903) and *Atlas général: histoire et géographie* (1894).

**Black, Hugo Lafayette,** 1886–1971, American politician and associate justice of the US SUPREME COURT (1937–71). As a US senator (1927–37), he was an ardent supporter of the NEW DEAL. Although his appointment to the Supreme Court was strongly opposed because he had been a member of the KU KLUX KLAN, Black led the Court in the battle for civil liberties.

**Black, Joseph,** 1728–99, Scottish chemist and physician; b. France. Professor of chemistry at Glasgow and then at Edinburgh, he is best known for his theories of LATENT HEAT and SPECIFIC HEAT. He discovered carbon dioxide ('fixed air') and helped establish chemistry as an exact science.

**black Americans** or **Afro-Americans,** people of the US whose ancestors came from sub-Saharan Africa; referred to historically as Negroes or coloured people. In 1980 there were c.26.5 million blacks in the US, forming 11.7% of the population. Black people have been in the Americas since the early 16th cent., when Spanish planters began to transport them from Africa to the West Indies as slaves. The first blacks on the North American mainland were brought to Virginia (1619) as indentured servants. With the success of tobacco planting, Negro SLAVERY was legalized in Virginia and Maryland, becoming the foundation of the Southern agrarian economy. After 1700 slave importations rose rapidly and by 1776 blacks accounted for more than 40% of the population of the Southern plantation colonies. Although there were also slaves in the Northern colonies, the institution there did not become especially profitable. During the AMERICAN REVOLUTION slavery was gradually abolished in the North, but the US Constitution (ratified 1788) implicitly recognized slavery and protected the importation of slaves, while the invention of the COTTON GIN (1793) greatly increased the demand for them in the South. By 1830 there were more than 2 million black slaves in the US. Slave revolts were rare and were quickly suppressed, the most serious being that led by Nat TURNER and other ABOLITIONISTS. Although some slaves escaped north via the UNDERGROUND RAILROAD and a few purchased their freedom or received testamentary manumission (freedom granted under the terms of a master's will), the total slave population continued to grow. During the AMERICAN CIVIL WAR nearly 200,000 blacks fought in the Union Army in segregated units led by white officers and some 38,000 lost their lives. Pres. Abraham LINCOLN's EMANCIPATION PROCLAMATION (1863) and Union victory (1865) freed almost 4 million slaves. During RECONSTRUCTION (1865–77) the former slaves rceived the vote and 16 blacks served in Congress, but both then and later extreme poverty became the lot of most black Americans under the SHARECROPPING system in the South. Resented by poor whites as economic competitors, they were often harassed and sometimes killed (see LYNCHING) by mobs. Following Reconstruction Tennessee became (1875) the first of many states to enact segregationist laws, and blacks were also disenfranchised by such devices as the POLL TAX, the GRANDFATHER CLAUSE, and arbitrary literacy tests. Segregation received federal sanction when the Supreme Court ruled (1896) that it was legal if equal accommodations were provided for blacks and whites. By the early 1900s many blacks were seeking better conditions by migrating to northern cities, where they found work chiefly as domestics and unskilled labourers and lived in crowded, segregated GHETTOS. After World War I black Americans began to make some progress in business, the professions, and the arts, aided by the NATIONAL ASSOCIATION FOR THE ADVANCEMENT OF COLORED PEOPLE (founded 1910) and the National Urban League (1911). Some northern ghettos, notably HARLEM, in New York City, became centres of a growing black middle class (see HARLEM RENAISSANCE). World War II stimulated a new wave of black migration to metropolitan areas, where many worked in defence plants. The postwar era brought the end of segregation in the armed services (1953), but economic progress remained slow. The CIVIL RIGHTS movement gained impetus when the Supreme Court ordered (1954) the elimination of segregation in schools, overturning the separate-but-equal rule (see BROWN V. BOARD OF EDUCATION). In 1955 the Montgomery (Alabama) bus boycott brought Dr Martin Luther KING, Jr, to the forefront of the fight for equal rights, and growing white support led to congressional passage (1964, 1965) of sweeping civil rights and voting rights bills. Nonetheless, many young blacks were drawn in the 1960s to the black separatist ideal espoused by MALCOLM X, the BLACK MUSLIMS, and others. Tension and frustration produced riots in Rochester, New York State (1964), the Watts district of Los Angeles (1965), Detroit (1967), and, after Dr King's assassination (1968), in more than 100 US cities. The civil rights movement of the 1970s increasingly became a struggle for economic advancement, and, early in the 1980s, such measures as AFFIRMATIVE ACTION and school busing to achieve racial balance were being tested in the courts. Blacks in public office in 1980 included 182 mayors, 323 state legislators, 17 members of Congress, and 1 Supreme Court justice, but with the median income of blacks far below that of whites and unemployment much higher (especially among youth), full equality of opportunity remained a distant goal. See also biographies of individual black Americans.

**Black and Tans,** semi-regular British military force. They were recruited by the British government to combat the Irish nationalist force SINN FEIN between 1918 and 1920. The name came from their uniforms, a combination of dark police jackets and khaki trousers. See also IRELAND.

**Blackbeard,** d. 1718, English pirate. His name was probably Edward Teach or Thatch. Originally a privateer in the War of the SPANISH SUCCESSION, he preyed on the West Indies and along the Atlantic coast. He was killed by the British.

**blackberry:** see BRAMBLE.

**blackbird,** perching BIRD (*Turdus merula*) belonging to the family Turdidae, related to THRUSHES and ROBINS. The glossy, black male is 25 cm (10 in) long with a bright golden bill but the female is brown with a brownish bill. Blackbirds are insect- and worm-eaters; they have adapted to town life and are common in parks and gardens, nesting in bushes and shrubs.

**black body,** in physics, an ideal substance that absorbs all and reflects none of the radiant energy falling on it. An approximate black body is lampblack (a finely powdered almost pure form of carbon), which reflects less than 2% of incoming radiation. A study of black body radiation led Max PLANCK to develop QUANTUM THEORY in 1900.

**black body radiation,** electromagnetic radiation emitted by a black body. A black body is one which absorbs all radiation falling onto it, for example a small hole in a cavity. The FREQUENCY distribution of black body radiation depends only on the TEMPERATURE of the black body and the value of PLANCK's and BOLTZMANN's constants. Black body radiation with a characteristic temperature of about 3°K pervades the universe and is believed to be a remnant of the BIG BANG which initiated the universe some $10^{10}$ years ago.

**Blackburn,** town (1981 pop. 109,564) in Lancashire, NW England, on R. Darwen and Leeds and Liverpool canal, 34 km (21 mi) NW of Manchester. An industrial town, it is famous for textiles, the manufacture of textile equipment, and general engineering. The church of St Mary's was rebuilt in the 19th cent. and became the cathedral in 1926.

**Black Death:** see PLAGUE.

**black English,** the development of a specific DIALECT among black immigrants, most notably in the US and UK, developing from a PIDGIN in the US and various CREOLES in the UK. African slaves in the US speaking many different languages developed a pidgin, mixing mainly English vocabulary and African syntax. The predominantly West Indian migrants to the UK in the 1950s and 1960s spoke one of the developed Caribbean creoles. In the US, a social, rather than regional dialect exists and in the UK, the second and later generations have adopted a variety mainly based on Jamaican creole. In both countries black English tends to carry prestige as a youth language giving its role in education an element of controversy.

**Blackett, Patrick Maynard Stuart Blackett, Baron** 1897–1974, English physicist. He worked in London and Manchester and was president of the ROYAL SOCIETY. He was awarded the 1948 Nobel Prize for physics for his development of the Wilson cloud chamber (see PARTICLE DETECTOR) and his discoveries in the fields of nuclear physics and cosmic radiation, which included the observation of the positron.

**black-eyed pea, cowpea,** or **black-eyed bean,** annual leguminous plant (*Vigna sinensis*) of the PULSE family, native to the Old World but now cultivated in the S US, where it is used in cooking and, especially, as a catch crop and major forage plant. It is also grown commercially in India and China.

**black-eyed Susan,** weedy biennial North American daisylike wildflower (*Rudbeckia hirta*) of the COMPOSITE family, with yellow rays and a dark brown centre. This and other species in the genus are also called yellow coneflowers. Hybridization and selection have given the modern garden 'Gloriosa' daisies, with large yellow and bronze flowers.

**Blackfoot Indians,** NORTH AMERICAN INDIANS of the Plains, who spoke an Algonquian language (see AMERICAN INDIAN LANGUAGES). The Blackfoot, so called because they wore black-dyed moccasins, were unremittingly hostile to most other tribes and usually to white men, efficiently repelling intrusion. In the early 19th cent. they lived in a large territory around the upper Missouri and N Saskatchewan rivers, but the killing off of the buffalo by the white man brought the Blackfoot almost to starvation. Today they are mostly farmers and ranchers, living in Montana and Canada.

**Black Forest,** block mountain range, SW West Germany, extending c.145 km (90 mi) along the Rhine rift valley. It is named for its cover of dark pine forests. A popular resort area, it is known for its cuckoo clock and toy industries. Baden-Baden and Freiburg are the chief cities.

**Black Friday,** 24 Sept. 1869, in US history, day of financial panic. In a drive to corner the gold market, speculators, including Jay GOULD and

James FISK, sought the support of federal officials of the GRANT administration. The attempt failed when government gold was released for sale. The drive ended on a Friday, when thousands were ruined. Other days of financial panic have also been called Black Friday.

**Black Hills,** forested mountains rising above the GREAT PLAINS in SW South Dakota and NE Wyoming, US. Harney Peak (2207 m/7242 ft) is the highest point. Gold mining (begun in 1874) and tourism are chief industries.

**black hole:** see GRAVITATIONAL COLLAPSE.

**black lead:** see GRAPHITE.

**blackleg** or **black quarter,** acute infectious bacterial disease of cattle and sheep, characterized by muscle inflammation and pain in the affected areas. TOXINS formed by the BACTERIA (genus *Clostridium*) produce severe muscle damage without external symptoms, and mortality is high.

**black-letter,** medieval type which reproduces the *Textura* book-script used for formal writing and liturgical purposes, in use 12th–15th cent. — 'Gothic' typeface. Black-letter was essentially an attempt to reproduce handwriting in print form. Replaced by Latin type in the Renaissance, it remained in use in Germany for books and newspapers until well into the 20th cent.

𝔄𝔅ℭ𝔇𝔈𝔉𝔊ℌℑ𝔍𝔎𝔏𝔐𝔑𝔒𝔓𝔔ℜ𝔖
abcdefghijklmnopqrstuvwxyz

The **Black Letter** typeface

**black lung disease:** see PNEUMOCONIOSIS.

**Black Madonna:** see CZĘSTOCHOWA.

**blackmail,** in law, the offence of obtaining from a person, money or property not legally owed, by the use of threats. The threat can be to inflict physical injury, reveal damaging or false information, or accuse of committing a criminal offence. The offence originated in the 19th cent. and derived from the paying of 'black money', e.g., rent under fear of physical injury. In the UK, a similar offence of extortion was abolished in 1968.

**black market,** trading in currencies or goods, which may be prohibited, above legal price or quantity ceilings. To circumvent rationing and price controls, World War II black marketeers traded in clothing, food, and alcohol in Britain and meat, sugar, and petrol in the US; during PROHIBITION, BOOTLEGGING was also a black-market operation. Fears of inflation, unrealistic official exchange rates or prices, or shortages of convertible currency have led to the development of black markets in foreign exchange in many countries. Centrally planned economies and developing countries, which are particularly prone to shortages of essential goods and foreign exchange, are frequently afflicted by black or 'unofficial' markets.

**Blackmore, Richard Doddridge,** 1825–1900, English novelist. Though he published 14 novels, some poetry, and translations of Latin classics, his fame rests on a single book, *Lorna Doone* (1869), a striking historical novel about the gigantic farmer John Ridd and his long struggle with a colony of outlaws on Exmoor.

**Black Muslims,** popular name for members of a black nationalist movement in the US. Founded (1930) in Detroit, the sect, then called the Nation of Islam, was led (1934–75) by Elijah MUHAMMAD, under whom the sect greatly expanded. In the 1960s tension between Muhammad and MALCOLM X, a Black Muslim minister, developed. Malcolm X's assassination (1965) may have been instigated by Muhammad's followers. The Black Muslims live austerely and advocate a separate autonomous nation within the US for their adherents. Wallace D. Muhammad succeeded his father as leader in 1975 and steered the sect (renamed the World Community of Islam in the West and later the American Muslim Mission) away from these beliefs and toward orthodox Islam. A splinter group, known by the original name, the Nation of Islam, has continued to follow the teachings of Elijah Muhammad.

**Black Panther party,** US black militant political organization (founded 1966) advocating violent revolution to achieve black liberation. Its members became involved (late 1960s) in clashes with the police, and, after close FBI scrutiny, Huey Newton and Bobby Seale, the party's founders, were tried in a number of court cases, but were acquitted.

Another leader, Eldridge Cleaver, left (1975) the party, which was torn by rival factions. By the 1980s the Black Panther party had ceased to play an important part in the black movement.

**Blackpool,** town (1981 pop. 146,297), Lancashire, NW England, on Irish Sea, 24 km (15 mi) W of Preston. A famous coastal resort town, it has recently become established as an important conference centre. Confectionery is made here, and there is also some engineering. The Blackpool Tower, which is a famous landmark, is modelled on the Eiffel Tower in Paris.

**Black Prince:** see EDWARD THE BLACK PRINCE.

**black quarter:** see BLACKLEG.

**Black Sea,** c.413,360 km² (159,600 sq mi), SE Europe, connected with the MEDITERRANEAN SEA via the DARDANELLES and BOSPORUS. Bordered by the USSR (N,E), Turkey (S), and Bulgaria and Romania (W), it is c.1200 km (750 mi) wide at its greatest extent and has a maximum depth of 2245 m (7364 ft). Almost tideless, it is ice-free in winter. The CRIMEA, a peninsula on its northern shore, is a major Soviet resort area. ODESSA and Constanţa are the chief ports.

**Blackstone, Sir William,** 1723–80, British jurist. At Oxford, after 1758, he was the first at a British university to teach English, as opposed to Roman, law. In his great work *Commentaries on the Laws of England* (1765–69) Blackstone ordered and elucidated the bulk of English law, showing it to be comparable to Roman law and to the civil law of the Continent. Although criticized, by BENTHAM among others, for a failure to analyse social and historical factors, Blackstone's work had tremendous effect on the profession and study of law, both in Britain and in the US.

**black studies:** see ETHNIC STUDIES.

**black swan,** only SWAN endemic to Australia; *Cygnus atrata* has also been introduced into New Zealand and Europe as an ornamental bird. Like the rest of the family Anatidae, it is primarily a freshwater bird, building untidy platform nests in shallow water and eating water plants and small animals. It is a very popular bird, chosen as the symbol for Western Australia.

**Black Watch** or **Royal Highland Regiment,** Scottish infantry regiment. It was formed (1739–40) to watch Scottish rebels and keep the peace. It became known as the Black Watch because of the dark colours of the regimental tartan.

**Blackwell, Alice Stone,** see under STONE, LUCY.

**Blackwell, Elizabeth,** 1821–1910, American physician; b. England. An 1849 graduate of the Geneva (New York) Medical College, she was the first woman in the US to receive a medical degree and the first woman to be placed on the British Medical Register. She helped to found the New York Infirmary for Women and Children (1857) and its Women's Medical College (1868), and she was appointed professor of gynaecology and obstetrics at the London School of Medicine for Women (1875). She was a pioneer in the cause of women's education.

**Blackwell, Henry Brown:** see under STONE, LUCY.

**black widow,** poisonous SPIDER (genus *Latrodectus*) found in the Americas. Adults are black with a red to orange hourglass-shaped abdominal marking. The female is about 1.25 cm (½ in) long; she may eat the smaller male after mating. The bite venom, a neurotoxin, is sometimes fatal to children.

**bladder:** see URINARY SYSTEM.

**Blaine, James Gillespie,** 1830–93, American politician. He was a US representative from Maine (1863–76), Speaker of the House (1869–75), US senator (1876–81), and US secretary of state (1881, 1889–92). Blaine failed to capture the 1876 Republican presidential nomination after it was alleged that he had improperly secured a land grant for an Arkansas railroad. The leader of the 'Half-Breed' Republicans who opposed the regular or 'Stalwart' faction, he was the party's nominee in 1884. He was defeated by Grover CLEVELAND, in part because he failed to disavow a supporter's remark that characterized the New York Democrats as the party of 'rum, Romanism, and rebellion'. As secretary of state, he fostered close US–Latin American relations and brought about the first Pan-American Congress.

**Blair, Eric Arthur:** see ORWELL, GEORGE.

**Blake, Nicholas:** see DAY LEWIS, CECIL.

**Blake, Peter,** 1932–, English painter. He studied European folk art, and in the 1950s painted images of children and circus people in a naive style. In the 1960s he included elements of POP ART, consumer goods, pin-up girls, magazine images, etc., into his work.

**Blake, William,** 1757–1827, English poet and artist who exerted a great influence on English ROMANTICISM. His first book, *Poetical Sketches* (1783), was the only one printed conventionally during his life. With the help of his wife, Catherine Boucher, he illustrated and published all his other major poetry himself. *Songs of Innocence* (1789) and *Songs of Experience* (1794), containing 'The Lamb', 'The Tyger', and 'London', are written from a child's point of view, directly, simply, and unsentimentally. Blake was a visionary and a mystic, and in his 'Prophetic Books', including *The Book of Thel* (1789), *The Marriage of Heaven and Hell* (1790-93), *Milton* (1804–08), and *Jerusalem* (1804–08), he created his own mythology in which love, energy, and imagination vie with the forces of reductive rationalism and repression. Blake's paintings and engravings, notably his illustrations of his own works, works by Milton, and the Book of Job, are realistic in their representation of human anatomy and other natural forms, but also radiantly imaginative, often depicting fanciful creatures in exact detail. As in the case of Christopher SMART and John DONNE, Blake's work has been valued highly by the 20th cent.

**Blakey, Art,** (Muslim name Abdullah ibn Buhaina), 1919–, black American jazz drummer and bandleader. His dynamic playing powered a number of swing bands in the 1940s before he formed the first of his Jazz Messengers in 1955, which has nurtured many famous players. He is one of the most explosive accompanists and soloists in the history of jazz.

**Blanc, Louis** (blahnh), 1811–82, French socialist and journalist; b. Spain. In his *Organization of Work* (1840) he outlined an ideal social order based on the principle 'From each according to his abilities, to each according to his needs.' As a first stage he advocated a system of 'social workshops' controlled by workers. A member of the 1848 provisional government, he was implicated in a workers' revolt and fled to England, where he wrote his *History of the French Revolution* (12 vol., 1847–64). On his return to France (1871) he became a member of the national assembly.

**Blanco, Antonio Guzmán:** see GUZMÁN BLANCO.

**blank verse:** see PENTAMETER.

**Blantyre,** city (1985 pop. 355,200), S Malawi, in the Shire Highlands. It is Malawi's main commercial and industrial centre and is connected by rail to the Indian Ocean port of Beira, Mozambique. Manufactures include cement and textiles. Founded in 1876 by Scottish missionaries, it was named after the birthplace of the explorer David LIVINGSTONE.

**Blasco Ibáñez, Vicente** (,blaskoh ee,banyeth), 1867–1928, Spanish novelist and politician. For his anti-monarchist activities he was imprisoned 30 times. His World War I novel *Los cuatro jinetes del Apocalipsis* (1916; tr. The Four Horsemen of the Apocalypse), the best known of his many in the naturalistic vein, made him world famous, but his Valencian regional novels are his best work.

**blast furnace,** structure used chiefly in SMELTING, i.e., extracting METAL, mainly IRON and COPPER, from its ORE. The principle involved is that of the reduction of the ores by the action of CARBON MONOXIDE, i.e., the removal of oxygen from the metal oxide in order to obtain the metal. PIG IRON prepared in the blast furnace is converted to STEEL by the BESSEMER PROCESS. Copper ore treated in a blast furnace yields a copper sulphide mixture, which is usually further refined by electrolytic methods (see ELECTROLYSIS).

**Blaue Reiter, Der** (dea ,blowə ,rietə) [Ger., = the blue rider], German expressionist art movement lasting from 1911 to 1914. The movement was led by KANDINSKY, KLEE, MARC, and MACKE, in Munich. Their works ranged from pure abstraction to romantic imagery, attempting to express spiritual truths. A number of their illustrations and articles were published as the '*Blaue Reiter*' Almanac (1911).

**Blavatsky, Helena Petrovna,** 1831–91, Russian philosopher of religion. After extensive travels she was converted to Buddhism and allegedly acquired supernatural powers. In New York she founded (1875) the Theosophical Society (see THEOSOPHY). Her books, e.g., *Isis Unveiled* (1877), set out her views on theology, science, and universal brotherhood.

**blazonry,** science of describing or depicting armorial bearings. Since the Middle Ages the science has grown very complicated. Its chief part is the description of the shield of a coat of arms, including the color of the field on which devices are displayed. Arms are identified by their charges; the most common of these, the ordinaries, have lines of division, heraldic animals, and flowers. Blazonry also involves descriptions of the crest above the shield and of the motto. In England blazonry is regulated by the HERALDS' COLLEGE. See also HERALDRY.

**Bleriot, Louis** (blea,ryoh), 1872–1936, French aviator and inventor. Trained as an engineer, he began his career inventing and manufacturing motor-car headlights. He began to experiment with aircraft in 1901, and by 1908 had developed a successful powered monoplane (see FLIGHT, POWERED). On 25 July 1909 he became the first person to fly the English Channel in a heavier-than-air machine. He went on to become a leading manufacturer of aircraft over the next three decades, and Bleriot aircraft held records in the 1930s for both duration and distance.

**Bleuler, Eugen:** see SCHIZOPHRENIA.

**Bligh, William,** 1754–1817, British admiral. He is chiefly remembered for the mutiny on his ship, the BOUNTY, in 1789. He was later governor of NEW SOUTH WALES (1805–08).

**blight,** any sudden, severe plant disease characterized by the withering and death of the plant; also, the causative agent of such a disease. Most blights are caused by BACTERIA (e.g., bean blights), VIRUSES (e.g., soybean bud blight), or FUNGI (e.g., potato blight).

**blimp:** see AIRSHIP.

**blindness,** partial or complete loss of sight. Blindness may be congenital or caused by injury or disease. Lesions of the brain, CATARACT, GLAUCOMA, or retinal detachment can result in loss of vision, as can changes in the EYE associated with disorders such as DIABETES and HYPERTENSION. Most of the world's 42 million sightless people live in the Third World where blindness is caused by two parasitic infections, trachoma (bacterial infection of the conjunctiva) and anchocerciasis; vitamin A deficiency; and leprosy. The BRAILLE system enables the blind to read and write. See GUIDE DOG; see also COLOUR BLINDNESS.

**Bliss, Sir Arthur,** 1891–1975, British composer. His military experiences in World War I and the death of his brother in action inspired the symphony *Morning Heroes* (1930). Although an early flirtation with the style of the European avant-garde was short-lived, Bliss's music retained piquant harmonies and dynamic rhythms characteristic of Stravinsky, as in his Piano Concerto and his Second String Quartet. Particularly successful was his music for the film *Things to Come* (1934–35), and for the ballets *Checkmate* (1937) and *Miracle in the Gorbals* (1944). His single opera, *The Olympians* (1949), with a libretto by J.B. PRIESTLEY, was less successful and has not been revived. Bliss was appointed Master of the King's Musick in 1953.

**Blitz, the:** see WORLD WAR II.

**blitzkrieg:** see MECHANIZED WARFARE.

**Blixen, Karen:** see DINESEN, ISAK.

**Bloch, Ernest** (blok), 1880–1959, American composer; b. Switzerland. His music is classical, but personal and Hebraic in tone, e.g., the Hebrew rhapsody *Schelomo,* the symphonic poem *Israel* (both: 1916), and the Sacred Service, *Avodath Hakodesh* (1930–33). He also wrote concertos, string quartets, and pieces for chorus and orchestra.

**Bloch, Konrad Emil,** 1912–, American biochemist; b. Germany. For his discoveries concerning the mechanism and regulation of cholesterol and fatty-acid metabolism, he shared with Feodor Lynen the 1964 Nobel Prize for physiology or medicine.

**Bloch, Marc,** 1886–1944, French historian of French–Alsatian Jewish descent. An authority on medieval feudalism, he wrote *Feudal Society* (1939, 1940), a brilliant synthesis of the subject, and in 1929 was a founder of the ANNALES group. His other works include *French Rural History* (1931) and *The Historian's Craft* (1949), a stimulating introduction to the subject. A courageous soldier in World War I and an active member of the French Resistance during World War II, he was tortured and executed by the Germans.

**block book,** book printed from engraved wooden blocks, one for each page. Although produced in Europe before and after the invention of PRINTING, block books have a richer history in China and Japan, where the large number of written characters made printing from movable type impractical.

**Bloemfontein** (‚bloohmfon'tayn), city (1980 pop. 230,688), capital of the Orange Free State and judicial capital of South Africa. It is a transportation and industrial centre. The city was founded in 1846 and was captured (1900) by the British during the SOUTH AFRICAN WAR (Boer War). It was the site of negotiations that led to the founding (1910) of the Union of South Africa.

**Blois** (blwah), town (1982 pop. 49,422), capital of Loir-et-Cher dept., central France, known for its trade in wine and brandies. From the 10th cent. the counts of Blois were France's most powerful lords. With the accession (1498) of Louis XII (who was born in its Renaissance chateau), Blois passed to the French crown. The town was a favourite royal residence.

**Blok, Aleksandr Aleksandrovich,** 1880–1921, Russian poet, considered the leading Russian SYMBOLIST. Influenced by SOLOVIEV, he voiced mysticism and idealistic passion in *Verses about the Beautiful Lady* (1904). *The Unknown Woman* (1906) expresses his later despair. He celebrated the RUSSIAN REVOLUTION in *The Twelve* (1918) and *The Scythians* (1920).

**blood,** fluid that is pumped by the HEART and circulates through the body via arteries, veins, and capillaries, carrying oxygen and nutrients to the body tissues, and carbon dioxide and wastes away from them (see CIRCULATORY SYSTEM). It is also involved in tissue repair, cell METABOLISM, resistance to infection, and other life-sustaining activities. Blood is made up of plasma, a pale amber, sticky fluid containing red blood cells (erythrocytes), which carry on oxygen–carbon dioxide exchange; white blood cells (leucocytes), which defend the body against infectious and harmful agents; platelets that function in blood clotting; HORMONES; and essential salts and PROTEINS. There are about 5 litres (9 pt) of blood in an average-sized adult male. Blood is classified into BLOOD GROUPS. A deficiency of red blood cells is ANAEMIA; abnormal proliferation of leucocytes is known as LEUKAEMIA. See also BLOOD BANK; BLOOD TRANSFUSION; HAEMOPHILIA.

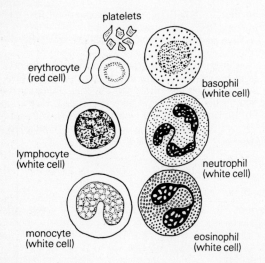

The three types of **blood** cell (erythrocyte shows side and surface view)

**blood bank,** site for collecting, processing, typing, and storing whole BLOOD and blood products. Donors (unpaid volunteers in the UK) are screened for various diseases, including AIDS and HEPATITIS. Whole blood may be preserved at low temperature for up to 21 days without losing its usefulness in BLOOD TRANSFUSIONS; an anticoagulant is added to it to prevent clotting. Blood plasma, the fluid portion of the blood, may be frozen and stored indefinitely.

**blood groups,** classifications of human BLOOD based on individual immunological properties. The most widely used blood classification system is the ABO system, described by LANDSTEINER. It divides blood into A, B, AB, and O groups, depending on the presence of specific chemical substances on the surface of the red blood cells (A, B, or AB), or their absence (O). These substances act antigenically, i.e., cause the formation

of specific antibodies when injected into a recipient (see IMMUNITY). Because the formation of antibodies can create a potentially dangerous condition in an individual receiving a BLOOD TRANSFUSION, the blood of a donor must be compatible with that of the recipient. Another blood-group system important in blood transfusion compatibility is the RHESUS FACTOR.

**blood poisoning:** see SEPTICAEMIA.

**blood pressure,** force exerted by blood upon the walls of the arteries. It is initiated by the pumping action of the heart, and pressure waves can be felt at the wrist and other PULSE points. Blood pressure is strongest in the aorta, where the blood leaves the HEART, and diminishes progressively in the smaller vessels. Contraction of the heart (systole) produces the highest pressure, while heart relaxation (diastole) reduces the pressure to its lowest point. Pressure is measured at the brachial artery in the forearm (for consistency) in millimetres of mercury; pressures of about 120/80 (systolic/diastolic) are considered normal in young people. See HYPERTENSION; STROKE.

**bloodstone** or **heliotrope,** green CHALCEDONY spotted with red, used as a GEM. It is found in India, the US, Brazil, and Australia.

**blood transfusion,** transfer of blood from the venous system of one person to that of another, or from one animal to another of the same species. Transfusions are performed to replace a large loss of blood (as in haemorrhage, SHOCK, and severe BURNS) and as supportive treatment in certain disorders (e.g., HAEMOPHILIA). In whole blood transfusions, the BLOOD GROUPS (including the RHESUS FACTOR) must be compatible with that of the recipient; if not, red blood cells will rupture and clump, a condition that can result in JAUNDICE, kidney damage, and death. People with blood group O are universal donors, having blood that is compatible with all other groups; those with blood group AB are universal recipients, able to accept blood from all other groups. When whole blood is not needed or is unavailable, various components of the blood may be given.

**Bloody Assizes:** see JEFFREYS OF WEM, GEORGE JEFFREYS, 1st BARON.

**Bloody Sunday,** epithet given to several incidents over the past 100 years in which demonstrators have been killed on the Christian sabbath in clashes with government forces. First applied to a clash between left-wing demonstrators and police in London in Nov. 1887, the term was also used to describe an incident in St Petersburg (Czarist Russia) in Jan. 1905 when over 100 demonstrators were killed. More recently, Irish nationalists used the term to describe a clash in Londonderry (Northern Ireland) in Jan. 1972 in which British troops shot dead 13 civilians during a demonstration in favour of Irish unification.

**Bloomer, Amelia Jenks,** 1818–94, American reformer. She edited (1848–54) the *Lily,* dedicated to women's rights and temperance. In 1851 she adopted the full trousers that became known as the Bloomer costume, or bloomers.

**Bloomfield, Leonard,** 1887–1949, American linguist. His major work, *Language* (1933), is a clear statement of principles that were axiomatic for the American Structuralists: that language study must always be centred on the spoken language; that the definitions used in grammar should be based on the forms of the language; and that a given language at a given time is a complete system of sounds and forms existing independently of the past, so that the history of a form does not explain its meaning. See LINGUISTICS.

**Bloomsbury Group,** a group of writers, critics, and artists centred around Virginia WOOLF and Vanessa Bell in their house at 46 Gordon Square, Bloomsbury, London. Its members included Lytton STRACHEY, Leonard Woolf, E.M. FORSTER, V. Sackville-West, Roger FRY, Clive BELL, and John Maynard KEYNES.

**Blücher, Gebhard Leberecht von** (bly:khǝ), 1742–1819, Prussian field marshal. He helped to defeat NAPOLEON I at Leipzig (1813) and at Laon (1814). Napoleon defeated him at Ligny (15 June 1815), but Blücher's timely arrival at WATERLOO three days later helped the duke of WELLINGTON to turn that battle into a great victory.

**blue baby:** see CONGENITAL ABNORMALITIES.

**blueberry,** widely distributed shrubs or small trees (genus *Vaccinium*) of the HEATH family, usually found in acid soils. They are related to CRANBERRY. Blueberries are a popular food and are commercially important. The most cultivated are the high-bush blueberry (*V. corymbosum*) and the low-bush blueberry (*V. angustifolium*).

**blue-green algae,** single-celled or filamentous, primitive, and mainly freshwater ALGAE, in which the blue pigment phycocyanin masks the green plant colour. The cells are enclosed in a gelatinous sheath. Many are able to fix atmospheric nitrogen and so increase soil fertility. RICE paddy fields rely to a large extent on nitrogen fertilizer fixed by the blue-green algae.

**Blue Riband (of the Atlantic),** distinction awarded to the vessel making the fastest crossing of the Atlantic. Holders have included Brunel's *Great Western* (1838), and the ocean liners *Mauretania* (1907–27), *Queen Mary* (1938–52), and *United States* (from 1952). In 1986 *Virgin Atlantic Challenger*, a British power boat, broke the record that had stood since 1952 but was not awarded the trophy as it was held to be ineligible, not being a passenger ship.

Blue Riband: Richard Branson's *Virgin Atlantic Challenger*

**Blue Rider:** see BLAUE REITER, DER.

**Blue Ridge,** eastern range of the APPALACHIAN MOUNTAINS, extending S from S Pennsylvania to N Georgia, US. Heavily forested and long a barrier to early colonial expansion, the area is noted for its resorts and its scenery.

**blues:** see JAZZ.

**blue whale:** see WHALE.

**Blum, Léon** (bloohm), 1872–1950, French Socialist statesman. He was premier (1936–37) in the first Popular Front government (a coalition of Radical Socialists, Socialists, and Communists) and passed important labour reforms. Arrested (1940) by the VICHY government, he was imprisoned by the Germans until 1945. Blum grew more moderate in his later years and was again premier (1946–47) in a Socialist government.

**Blumlein, Alan Dower,** 1903–42, British engineer. After graduating in 1930 he worked with the Gramophone Co. and with EMI where he was responsible for many of the Marconi–EMI TELEVISION system patents. By 1936 he was chief engineer of the company's research laboratories. He was renowned for his inventiveness which is demonstrated by the 128 patents that carry his name, one for every six weeks of his working life. Many of them were highly significant, such as the 405-line television waveform and the stereo system for sound broadcasting that is now in use. During World War II he worked on defence projects and was sadly killed in an air crash, while testing a wartime development.

**Blunt, Anthony Frederick,** 1907–83, English art historian. He was director of the Courtauld Institute, professor of art at the Univ. of London, and Surveyor of the Queen's Pictures. His major writings include *Artistic Theory in Italy, 1450–1600* (1940), *Art and Architecture in France, 1500–1700* (1953), and, with others, *Baroque and Rococo* (1978). Knighted in 1956, Blunt was divested of the title in 1979, when it became known that he had been a Soviet agent.

**Blunt, Wilfrid Scawen,** 1840–1922, English writer. An advocate of Indian and Irish independence, he was a poet of emotional force, as in *The Love Sonnets of Proteus* (1880).

**Blyden, Edward Wilmot,** 1832–1912, Liberian educationalist, journalist, and politician; b. Virgin Islands. He migrated to Liberia in 1851 and taught at Liberia College as well as editing *The Negro* of Freetown.

He believed strongly that Christianity had retarded development in Africa. He served as ambassador to Britain in 1877–78, 1892, and 1905; but his views often conflicted with government policy, and he was finally recalled and retired to Sierra Leone.

**boa,** OVOVIVIPAROUS constrictor SNAKE of the family Boidae, which also includes the PYTHONS, found mostly in the Americas. Boas feed on large lizards, birds, and small mammals. They suffocate their prey by squeezing it. Best known are the boa constrictor, which lives in terrestrial habitats from S Mexico to central Argentina and averages 1.8–2.7 m (6–9 ft) and the South American anaconda, the longest (up to 8 m/25 ft).

**Boadicea:** see BOUDICCA.

**boar:** see PIG.

**Boas, Franz,** 1858–1942, American anthropologist; b. Germany. No one has more greatly influenced American anthropology. Boas reexamined the premises of physical anthropology and pioneered the use of statistical methods. He stressed the importance of the collection of detailed ethnographic data, covering all aspects of social life and drawing on neighbouring disciplines such as linguistics and archaeology. His field work began with observations of the Central Eskimos (1883) and of British Columbian Indians (1886). He became (1899) the first professor of anthropology at Columbia Univ., a position he held for 37 years. In his studies of AMERICAN INDIAN LANGUAGES Boas stressed the importance of internal linguistic structure, and the strict methodology of his contributions gave them scientific value. Among his works are *The Mind of Primitive Man* (1911, rev. ed. 1938), *Primitive Art* (1927), *Race, Language and Culture* (1940), and *Race and Democratic Society* (1945).

**Boat Race,** annual rowing race on the R. Thames between eights from Oxford and Cambridge Univs. It was first raced at Henley-on-Thames in 1829; Oxford won. The next race, in 1836, was rowed between Westminster and Putney, but in 1845 the course became fixed between Putney and Mortlake, a distance of 6.8 km (4¼ mi). In 1839, the race became an annual event. The record time of 16 min 58 sec was set by Oxford in 1976. The only dead heat was in 1877.

**Boaz:** see RUTH.

**bobcat:** see LYNX.

**Bobrowski, Johannes,** 1917–65, East German poet and novelist. His poems invoke the landscapes and mythology of 'Sarmatia', the old Baltic–Slav areas of Lithuania and East Prussia where he was born, and their long history of invasions and suppressions. This interconnectedness of mankind, landscape, and history is also to be found in his novels *Levins Mill. Thirty-four Statements about my Grandfather* (1964) and *Lithuanian Pianos* (1966). His fundamental values are markedly Christian. Bobrowski's formal range is wide, from short symbolic poems to extended Alcaic and Sapphic odes connecting him with KLOPSTOCK and HÖLDERLIN. His collections of poems include *Pruzzian Elegy* (1955), *Sarmatian Tide* (1961), *Shadowland Streams* (1962), and *Signs of the Weather* (1967).

**bobsleighing,** sport in which a bobsleigh (an open, steel-bodied vehicle with runners) hurtles down an icy, steeply banked, twisting course. Sleighs accommodate either two or four persons, including a driver and brakeman in each type, and can attain speeds of 145 km (90 mi) per hr. Bobsleighing has been an Olympic event since the first Winter Games (1924).

**Boccaccio, Giovanni** (bok,kahchoh), 1313–75, Italian poet, storyteller, and humanist. His early works include *Filocolo* (c.1336), a vernacular prose romance; *Filostrato,* a poem infusing the Troilus and Cressida legend with a Neapolitan court atmosphere; the allegorical *Amorosa visione,* imitative of DANTE; and a psychological romance, *Fiammetta.* From 1349 to 1351 he completed his great secular classic, the *Decameron,* a collection of 100 witty and often licentious tales set against the sombre backdrop of the Black Death. In the *Decameron,* medieval courtly themes began to give way to the voice and mores of modern society; the masterly style of the work became a model for later Italian prose. In 1350 Boccaccio met PETRARCA, who inspired him to devote his later life to the study of Greek and other humanistic concerns, producing influential Latin compilations in biography and mythology.

**Boccherini, Luigi,** 1743–1805, Italian composer and cellist. His masterful classical style is often compared to that of HAYDN. Boccherini wrote more than 400 works, including 4 cello concertos, some 90 string quartets, and about 125 string quintets.

**Boccioni, Umberto** (bot͵chohnee), 1882–1916, Italian futurist painter, and sculptor. He was the major figure of FUTURISM (1910–14). His meeting with MARINETTI led to the 'Manifesto of Futurist Painters' (1910) and the formation of a group of Futurist painters. They believed in the positive nature of rapid industrial growth in Italy and saw collective action of the masses as overthrowing the old order and artistic traditions. Boccioni used the word 'unanimism' to express this collective sentiment and illustrated this in his *Riot in the Gallery* (1910), and the *City Rises* (1910). Boccioni also experimented with sculpture, attempting to illustrate the philosopher BERGSON's ideas on movement, as in *Unique Forms of Continuity in Space* (1913; Tate Gall, London).

Umberto **Boccioni**, *Unique Forms of Continuity in Space*, 1913. Bronze. Tate Gallery, London.

**Bochum** (͵bohkhum), city (1984 pop. 387,100), North Rhine–Westphalia, West Germany. An industrial centre of the RUHR coal-mining district, its manufacturing includes car assembly, steel, engineering, and chemicals. Ruhr Univ. was founded here in 1961.

**Bocskay, Stephen**, 1557–1606, Hungarian noble, *voivode* [governor] (1604–06) and prince (1605–06) of Transylvania. In 1604, with Turkish support, he led a revolt against Holy Roman Emperor RUDOLF II's attempt to impose Roman Catholicism on Hungary. In 1606 he negotiated a treaty at Vienna legalizing the partition of Hungary among the HABSBURGS, the Turkish sultan, and the prince of Transylvania. It guaranteed constitutional and religious freedom to Hungary.

**Bode's law:** see TITIUS–BODE LAW.

**Bodin, Jean** (baw͵danh), 1530?–1596, French social and political philosopher. A lawyer, he was dismayed by the chaos resulting from conflict between Roman Catholics and Huguenots (see RELIGION, WARS OF) and argued in his most important work, *Six Books of the Republic* (1576), that the well-ordered state required religious toleration and a fully sovereign monarch. His writings made a major theoretical contribution to the rise of the modern nation-state.

**Bodley, Sir Thomas,** 1545–1613, English scholar and diplomat, organizer of the Bodleian Library at Oxford Univ. He offered (1598) to restore Duke Humphrey's library and spent most of his life and fortune on it.

**Bodoni, Giambattista,** 1740–1813, Italian printer. His stately quartos and folios, in pseudo-classical typefaces, with impressive title pages and luxurious margins, were coldly elegant and frankly made to be admired rather than read. He was relatively indifferent to the accuracy of the text.

# ABCDEFGHIJKLMNOPQRSTUVWX
## abcdefghijklmnopqrstuvwxyz

The **Bodoni** typeface

**Boehme, Böhme** or **Behmen, Jakob** (bo:mə), 1575–1624, German religious mystic. In *De signatura rerum* and *Mysterium magnum* (1623), he describes God as the abyss, the nothing and the all, from which the creative will struggles to find manifestation and self-consciousness. Evil results when single elements of the Deity strive to become the whole. Boehme had many followers in Germany, Holland, and England.

**Boeing,** aircraft manufacturing company founded (1917) by William Edward Boeing (1881–1956) at Seattle, Washington, US. The first commercial Boeing aircraft was a three-seat biplane flying boat which in 1919 carried the first sack of AIR MAIL to be flown from Canada to the US. Boeing built up its successes with many contracts for the US government, notably for its B-17 Flying Fortress, which was the chief US bomber in World War II. Major commercial development came with the Boeing 707 of 1954, the leading aircraft of its time in AIR TRANSPORT. It was followed by the B-727, B-737, and the B-747 or 'jumbo jet', the first of a new category of wide-bodied transport aircraft. By the end of 1986, more than 5000 Boeing jet transport aircraft had been delivered to commercial airlines throughout the world.

The **Boeing** Flying Fortress of the US Air Forces

**Boeotia,** region of ancient GREECE, N of the Gulf of Corinth. The Boeotian League, formed (c.7th cent. BC) by the cities of the region, was dominated by THEBES, which fought many battles to prevent encroachment by the other great CITY-STATES. The league was disbanded when the Greeks besieged Thebes for supporting the Persian enemy (479 BC) and after a brief revival was defeated by ATHENS (457 BC), which annexed the Boeotian cities. Thebes resumed leadership of the league in 446; after Thebes defeated Sparta (371) the history of Boeotia became for a time that of Thebes. Boeotia was the home of the poets HESIOD and PINDAR.

**Boer,** inhabitant of SOUTH AFRICA of Dutch or French Huguenot descent. Boers are also known as Afrikaners.

**Boerhaave, Hermann** (͵booəhahvə), 1668–1738, Dutch physician and humanist. An influential clinician and professor of medicine at Leiden, he established the method of learning from the patient. The modern medical curriculum of natural science, anatomy, physiology, and pathology is derived from his teaching. His works include *Institutiones Medicinae* (1708) and *Elementa Chemiae* (1732), long used as standard texts.

**Boer War:** see SOUTH AFRICAN WAR.

**Boethius, Anicius Manlius Severinus** (boh͵eetheeəs), c.480–524, Roman philosopher and statesman. Consul in 510, he became minister under Emperor Theodoric but was falsely accused of treason and sentenced to death. As a philosopher, he has been described as 'the last of the Romans; the first of the Scholastics'; he straddles the ancient and medieval worlds. His translations of ARISTOTLE and Porphyry began the medieval controversy over universals; his insistence on the importance of logic and method fuelled the whole tradition of SCHOLASTICISM; and his *Consolation of Philosophy*, written in prison, was the most discussed work of the next 800 years. In it he tackles the problem of evil and argues that divine foreknowledge is compatible with free will. His treatise on music was for many centuries the unquestioned authority on Western music.

**Bogarde, Dirk,** 1921–, English film actor; b. Derek van den Bogaerde. He first made his name in British comedy films, e.g., *Doctor in the House* (1953), but in the 1960s he formed a strong and highly productive working relationship with Joseph LOSEY, for whom he acted in *The Servant* (1963), *Modesty Blaise* (1966), and *Accident* (1967), among other films. He was later taken up by directors in the more active continental film industry and worked with Alain Resnais (*Providence*, 1977), R.W. FASSBINDER (*Despair*, 1978), and L. VISCONTI (*The Damned*, 1970; *Death in Venice*, 1971).

**Bogardus, James,** 1800–74, American architect. He was among the first to use cast iron in constructing facades. The Iron Building, New York City, is the best known of his commercial building designs.

**Bogart, Humphrey (DeForest),** 1899–1957, American film actor. He played tough, cynical heroes in such films as *The Maltese Falcon* (1941), *Casablanca* (1942), and *The African Queen* (1954; Academy Award).

**Boğazköy** (baw͵azkuhee), site in Central Turkey of a large citadel that became the vast walled city of the HITTITE empire c.1400–1200 BC. More than 10,000 inscribed clay tablets were discovered in the excavation of the citadel, providing important insights into Hittite life.

**bogie,** device to enable long railway vehicles to traverse curved track. Invented by William Chapman in 1813, the railway bogie has the wheels mounted in sub-frames which can swivel with respect to the body thus following the track. The practical development of the bogie, or truck, was largely carried out in the US but its use is extremely wide throughout the world on all forms of RAILWAY vehicle.

Bogie

**Bogotá,** city (1981 est. pop. 4,300,000), central Colombia, capital of Colombia. Built on a high plateau (c.2610 m/8560 ft), it is the financial, political, and cultural centre of the republic. Manufactures include beverages, foodstuffs, and metal goods. Founded in 1538, it was long the capital of the Spanish colonial viceroyalty of New Granada and a leading Latin American religious and intellectual centre. It became the capital of the independent confederation called Greater Colombia in 1819 and of what was later called Colombia in 1830. A picturesque, spacious city, it is known for its colonial architecture, its collection of pre-Colombian gold art, and its bookshops.

**Bohemia,** historic region, 52,753 km² (20,368 sq mi), and former kingdom, W Czechoslovakia, bordered by Austria (SE), West and East Germany (W, NW), Poland (N, NE), and Moravia (E). The traditional capital is PRAGUE. Bohemia is Czechoslovakia's most urbanized and industrialized area, with such manufactures as machinery, munitions,

and textiles. Grains, sugar beets, hops, and other crops are grown, and coal, silver, and other resources are mined. Bohemia emerged (9th cent.) under the Premysl dynasty and became part (950) of the HOLY ROMAN EMPIRE. It became a kingdom within the empire in 1198 and under Emperor CHARLES IV (r.1355–78) was the empire's seat. In the 15th cent. Bohemia was the scene of the HUSSITE religious movement. The HABSBURG dynasty of Austria dominated the kingdom after 1526; a revolt (1618) against Habsburg rule began the THIRTY YEARS WAR . In 1627 the kingdom was demoted to an imperial crown land. After WORLD WAR I it became the core of the new nation of Czechoslovakia. The MUNICH PACT (1938) transferred the SUDETEN area to Germany, which occupied all of Bohemia in Mar. 1939. Bohemia was abolished as a province of Czechoslovakia in 1948; in 1960 it was divided into five regions and the city of Prague.

**Bohemond I,** c.1056–1111, prince of Antioch, Turkey (r.1099–1111), the son of ROBERT GUISCARD and a leader in the First CRUSADE. Breaking his oath of fealty to Byzantine Emperor ALEXIUS I, he made himself prince of Antioch. Defeated (1108) in a crusade against Alexius, he acknowledged the emperor's suzerainty. He retired and TANCRED became regent.

**Bohr, Niels Henrik David,** 1885–1962, Danish physicist and one of the foremost scientists in modern physics. He was professor of theoretical physics at the Univ. of Copenhagen and was later director of its Institute for Theoretical Physics, which he helped to found. Bohr was awarded the 1922 Nobel Prize for physics for his work on atomic structure. Classical theory had been unable to explain the stability of the nuclear model of the ATOM, but Bohr solved the problem by postulating that electrons move in restricted orbits around the atom's nucleus and explaining how the atom emits and absorbs energy. He thus combined the QUANTUM THEORY with this concept of atomic structure. He also gave a theory of nuclear fission, and during World War II escaped from occupied Denmark to advise on the development of the nuclear bomb.

**boiler,** device for generating steam. Two types are common: fire-tube boilers, containing long steel tubes through which the hot gases from a furnace pass and around which the water to be changed to steam circulates, and water-tube boilers, in which the conditions are reversed. A boiler must be equipped with a safety valve for venting steam if pressure becomes too great.

**boiling point,** the temperature at which a substance boils, or changes from a liquid to a vapour or gas (see STATES OF MATTER), through the formation and rise to the surface of bubbles of vapour within the liquid. In a stricter sense, the boiling point of a liquid is the temperature at which its vapour pressure is equal to the local atmospheric pressure. Decreasing (or increasing) the pressure of the surrounding gases thus lowers (or raises) the boiling point of a liquid. The quantity of heat necessary to change 1 g of any substance from liquid to gas at its boiling point is known as its latent heat of vaporization.

**Boise** (͵boysee, -zee), US city (1984 est. pop. 107,000), state capital of Idaho, on the Boise R.; inc. 1864. It is the largest city in Idaho, and a trade and transport centre. Food processing, steel, timber, light manufacturing, and government offices provide employment. In its early years a gold-mining trade centre, it later became oriented towards the agriculture of the region.

**Boito, Arrigo** (͵boheetoh), 1842–1918, Italian composer and librettist. His opera *Mefistofele* (1868, rev. 1875), influenced by Richard WAGNER's music-drama, became very popular. Boito wrote several LIBRETTOS, including those for VERDI's *Otello* and *Falstaff*.

**Bokaro Steel City,** town (1981 pop. 224,099), Bihar state, NE India, in the valley of the Damodar R. Situated in Hazaribagh district, this town was created, as its name implies, entirely to house workers and services associated with one of independent India's steel-works.

**Bokassa, Jean Bedel,** 1921–, president of the CENTRAL AFRICAN REPUBLIC (1966–79). An army officer, he overthrew David DACKO in 1966 and assumed the presidency. In 1976 he declared the country the Central African Empire, calling himself Emperor Bokassa I. He was thrown out of office in 1979, and the country became a republic again. In 1986 he was put on trial for having indulged in cannibalism and other excesses while in power; in 1987 his death sentence was commuted to forced labour for life.

**Boldrewood, Rolf,** pseud. of **Thomas Alexander Browne,** 1826–1915, London-born Australian novelist. The most famous of his novels of bush-ranging adventures based on real-life outlaws was *Robbery Under Arms* (1882–23).

**Boleslaus,** Polish rulers. **Boleslaus I,** c.966–1025, king of POLAND (r.992–1025), was the first Polish ruler to style himself king. He succeeded his father, Mieszko I, duke of Poland. As king, he greatly expanded Polish territories. **Boleslaus II,** c.1039–1081, duke (r.1058–76) and king (r.1076–79) of Poland, sided with the pope against the Holy Roman emperor but was deposed after killing the bishop of Kraków. **Boleslaus III,** 1085–1138, duke of Poland (r.1102–38), reunited Poland by defeating (1109) his brother Zbigniew, who had the support of Holy Roman Emperor HENRY V. He added (1135) Pomerania and Rügen to his domains.

**Boleyn, Anne,** 1505–36, second queen of HENRY VIII of England; mother of ELIZABETH I. Henry divorced KATHARINE OF ARAGÓN to marry her. The marriage was unpopular, and when she did not produce a male heir, his ardour cooled. She was executed for alleged adultery and incest.

**Bolingbroke, Henry of:** see HENRY IV under HENRY, kings of England.

**Bolívar, Simón,** 1783–1830, revolutionary leader who liberated much of South America from Spanish rule; b. Caracas, Venezuela. He joined (1810) the Venezuelan revolution against Spain and won notable victories in COLOMBIA before a royalist army crushed (1815) his forces. After fleeing to Jamaica and Haiti, he invaded (1816) VENEZUELA and met disaster, forcing his return to Haiti. Recalled (1817) to command the rebel forces, he and his guerrillas occupied the lower Orinoco basin. In 1819 he boldly surprised and defeated the Spanish at Boyacá, and he became president of Greater Colombia. Cooperating with such other rebel leaders as SUCRE and SAN MARTÍN, he won further victories, culminating (1824) in PERU at Junín and AYACUCHO, which sealed the triumph of the revolution. Now the most powerful man of the continent, Bolívar organized (1824) the government of Peru and created (1825) BOLIVIA. His vision of a united South America was not to be, however, for his dictatorial methods were widely resented and separatist movements shook the union. Venezuela and ECUADOR seceded from Greater Colombia, and he resigned (1830) as president. Although bitterly hated at the time of his death, today Bolívar is revered as Spanish America's greatest hero and as its liberator.

**Bolivia,** officially Republic of Bolivia, republic (1985 est. pop. 6,400,000), 1,098,581 km² (424,162 sq mi ), W South America. One of the two inland countries of the continent, it is bordered by Chile and Peru (W), Brazil (E, N), Paraguay (SE), and Argentina (S). SUCRE is the legal capital, but LA PAZ is the administrative capital and seat of government. Bolivia's topography is one of sharp contrasts. In the W are the ANDES, whose snow-capped peak of Ilampú reaches 6485 m (21,276 ft), and a high plateau (ALTIPLANO), 3660 m (12,000 ft) above sea level, which is the population centre of the country. The E is dominated by tropical rain forests, which, in the SE, merge into the plains of the GRAN CHACO. In the N, on the border with Peru, is Lake TITICACA, the largest freshwater lake in South America; this region, with its ruins of TIAHUANACO, was the home of one of the great pre-Columbian civilizations. Bolivia has some of the richest mineral resources in the world; it is one of the leading producers of tin; and silver, copper, tungsten, bismuth, antimony, and zinc are also produced. Production from recent discoveries of oil and natural gas provide three-quarters of the nation's energy requirements. Despite these mineral riches, most Bolivians live by subsistence farming, growing sugarcane, potatoes, maize, wheat, and rice. In 1983 GDP was US$5371 million or US$895 capita. More than half the population is pure Indian, although the whites and those of mixed blood dominate political power. Most of the people are Roman Catholic.

*History.* The Aymara Indians of Bolivia had been absorbed into the INCA empire long before the Spanish conquest of Bolivia (1538) by Gonzalo and Hernando PIZARRO. Attracted by Bolivia's mineral wealth, Spanish exploiters poured into the area, developing mines, textile mills, and great estates all with forced Indian labour. Bolivia was attached to the viceroyalty of Peru until 1776 and later to that of La Plata. Revolt against Spanish rule first erupted in 1809, but Bolivia remained Spanish until the campaigns of José de SAN MARTÍN and Simón BOLÍVAR and the victory by Antonio José de SUCRE at AYACUCHO in 1824. Independence was formally proclaimed in 1825. A series of disastrous border wars, including the War of the Pacific (1879–84) against Chile and the Chaco War (1932–35) against Paraguay, cost Bolivia valuable territory, including its outlet to the sea. In 1952 the nationalistic, pro-miner National Revolutionary

Movement (MNR) won control of the government, nationalizing the tin mines and launching a programme of agrarian reform. They were overthrown by the military in 1964, and Bolivia resumed its history of political strife and instability, marked by recurring military coups that continued into the early 1980s. In 1982, however, a civilian government headed by Pres. Hernán Siles Zuazo assumed leadership of the country. Elections in 1985 resulted in Gen. Hugo Bánzer of the Democratic Nationalist Alliance winning the most votes, but not an absolute majority; the Bolivian congress then proceeded to elect Víctor Paz Estenssoro (of the Historic MNR faction) to his third term as president.

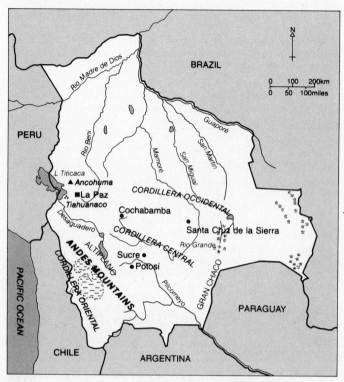

Bolivia

**Böll, Heinrich** (buhl), 1917–85, German novelist. From his first novel, *The Train was on Time* (1949), to his last, *Women in River Landscape* (1985), Böll has been the critical chronicler of the Federal Republic, from the Economic Miracle to the New Conservatism. He has given his generous sympathy to private people under threat from public powers: the war machine in *Wo warst du, Adam?* (1951; tr. Adam, Where Art Thou?), the Catholic Church in *And Never Said a Word* (1953) and *The Clown* (1963), the press and the police in *The Lost Honour of Katharina Blum* (1974), and the interacting 'Them' in authority in *End of a Mission* (1966). Böll is a natural short-story writer and satirist, and favours the short novel with single narrative focus. His major novels, *Billard um halb zehn* (1959; tr. Billiards at Half Past Nine) and *Gruppenbild mit Dame* (1971; tr. Group Portrait with Lady), more ambitious and complex in form and scope, explore the effects of the guilty past on the present moment. Böll was awarded the Nobel Prize for literature in 1972.

**Bologna,** city (1984 pop. 442,307), capital of Emilia-Romagna, N central Italy, at the foot of the Apennines. It is a commercial and industrial centre, with such manufactures as steel and food products. An Etruscan town, it came under Roman (189 BC), Byzantine (6th cent.), and papal rule. Its famous university (founded c.1088) made it an intellectual centre. Political control turned on rivalries among great families (13th–15th cent.) until papal rule was restored, lasting, nearly unbroken, from 1506 until Italian unification (1860). The city has many notable medieval and Renaissance buildings. It is the birthplace of Marconi.

**Bologna, Giovanni** or **Giambologna,** 1529–1608, Flemish sculptor who worked mainly in Florence as chief sculptor to the MEDICI family. His virtuoso *The Rape of the Sabine* (1579–83; Loggia dei Lanzi, Florence) with its spiralling forms and multiple viewpoints, is a seminal work of

Giovanni **Bologna**, *Mercury*, c.1564. Bronze statue. Bargello, Florence.

mannerist sculpture (see MANNERISM). He made many elegant, highly finished bronzes, e.g., *Mercury* (c.1564; Bargello, Florence).

**Bolshevism and Menshevism**, the two main branches of Russian socialism from 1903 to 1918. In 1903 the Russian Social-Democratic Workers' party split into two factions. One, led by LENIN, had a temporary majority and was thereafter known as the *Bolsheviki* [majority members]; their opponents, led by PLEKHANOV, were dubbed *Mensheviki* [minority members]. The Bolsheviks favoured a small party of professional revolutionaries and the establishment of a dictatorship of the proletariat and peasantry. The Mensheviks wanted a loosely organized mass party and held that before reaching socialism Russia must progress through a bourgeois-democratic stage. In the 1917 RUSSIAN REVOLUTION the Mensheviks took part in the KERENSKY provisional government, which was overthrown by the Bolsheviks in the October Revolution. The Bolsheviks became the Russian Communist Party in 1918 and had suppressed all rival political groups by 1921. In 1952 the party adopted its present name, the Communist Party of the Soviet Union.

**Bolshoi Ballet:** see DANCE (table).

**Bolton**, town (1981 pop. 143,960), Greater Manchester, NW England, on R. Croal, 17 km (10 mi) NW of Manchester. The major industries within the town are textiles, aero-engineering, and tanning. The town was known for its woollen manufactures from the 14th cent. and became a major cotton-manufacturing town in the late 18th cent. It is the birthplace of Samuel CROMPTON, inventor of spinning machinery, and of the first Lord Leverhulme.

**Boltzmann, Ludwig**, 1844–1906, Austrian physicist, known for his important contributions to the KINETIC THEORY OF GASES. By investigating the relationship between the temperature and the energy distribution of molecules in a gas, he laid the foundations of statistical mechanics. In 1883 he demonstrated theoretically a law (sometimes called the Stefan–Boltzmann law) describing the radiation from a BLACK BODY that had earlier been found experimentally by the Austrian physicist Josef Stefan. Boltzmann's constant is named after him.

**Bolyai, János** or **Johann** (ˌbohlyoy), 1802–60, Hungarian mathematician. In 1823 he independently developed hyperbolic geometry, a form of NON-EUCLIDEAN GEOMETRY. His father, **Farkas**, or **Wolfgang, Bolyai**, 1775–1856, was also a Hungarian mathematician. Farkas's *Tentamen* (1823–33), a systematic treatment of geometry, arithmetic, algebra, and analysis, contains as an appendix his son's theory of absolute space.

**Bolzano**, city (1984 pop. 102,643) N Italy, in the upper Adige valley. Abundant hydroelectric power supports electrochemical, aluminium, and engineering industries. It is situated in the South Tyrol which belonged to Austria until 1919 and still has a sizable German-speaking population.

**bombax**, common name for the Bombacaceae, a family of tall, thick-trunked deciduous trees, found chiefly in the American tropics. Many members of the family are commercially important, yielding, e.g., balsa wood and KAPOK.

**Bombay**, former state, W central India, on the Arabian Sea. Much of Bombay was part of the Buddhist Maurya empire (320–184 BC). Its Hindu rulers (5th–13th cent.) gave way to the MUGHALS (13th–18th cent.). Bombay passed (1661) from Portugal to Britain, becoming the headquarters (1668–1858) of the EAST INDIA COMPANY. Britain supplanted Portugal as the leading foreign power and formed (19th cent.) the Bombay presidency. Bombay became a state when India gained independence in 1947; it was split into the states of Gujarat and Maharashtra in 1960. The city of **(Greater) Bombay** (1981 pop. 8,243,405), India's largest city and the capital of Maharashtra state, occupies two islands off the coast. It has the only natural deepwater harbour in W India. Manufactures include textiles, chemicals, and petroleum products, and the city is the centre of the Indian film industry. It has the largest community of PARSIS in India. Many people in Bombay live in extreme poverty.

**Bonaparte**, Ital. *Buonaparte*, family name of NAPOLEON I of France. Besides Napoleon, this Corsican family produced many other notable figures. Napoleon's older brother, **Joseph Bonaparte**, 1768–1844, was king of Naples (r.1806–08), but he proved to be an inefficient administrator. As king of Spain (r.1808–13), he failed to cope with the PENINSULAR WAR and was forced to abdicate. He lived from 1815 to 1841 in the US, but died in Italy. Napoleon's brother **Lucien Bonaparte**, 1775–1840, helped Napoleon to overthrow the DIRECTORY in the coup of 18 Brumaire (1799), but later criticized him. They were reconciled while Napoleon was on Elba, and Lucien supported his brother during the Hundred Days. Another brother, **Louis Bonaparte**, 1778–1846, reluctantly married (1802) Hortense de BEAUHARNAIS; their son became NAPOLEON III. Louis was king of Holland (r.1806–10), but Napoleon forced him to abdicate for ignoring France's Continental System in favour of Dutch interests. Napoleon's youngest brother, **Jérôme Bonaparte**, 1784–1860, king of Westphalia (r.1807–13), was extravagant and irresponsible. On a visit to the US he married (1803) Elizabeth Patterson, but Napoleon had the marriage annulled and married him to a German princess. Jérôme commanded a division at Waterloo and later received honours at the court of his nephew, Napoleon III.

**Bonaventure** or **Bonaventura, Saint,** c.1217–74, Italian scholastic theologian, cardinal, Doctor of the Church, called the Seraphic Doctor. He became a Franciscan in 1243. After teaching at the Univ. of Paris, he was made (1257) minister-general of the FRANCISCANS. His writings reconcile ARISTOTLE's learning with Augustinian Christianity. His later mystical works bring the teachings of BERNARD OF CLAIRVAUX to full flower. Feast: 15 July. See also AUGUSTINE, SAINT; SCHOLASTICISM.

**bond,** in finance, a formal certificate of indebtedness issued by local or national governments and business corporations in return for loans. It bears a fixed rate of interest and promises to repay the funds borrowed after a certain period, usually between 10 and 30 years. A bond is generally protected by security; debentures are bonds unsecured by a pledge against specific assets. Bond also describes goods in a warehouse on which customs duties have not yet been paid.

**Bond, Edward,** 1934–, English dramatist. His plays include *The Pope's Wedding* (1962), *Saved* (1965), *Early Morning* (1968), *Human Cannon* (1984), and *The War Plays* (1985). Through the complexities of his plays and the clarity of his prefaces, Bond makes clear his concern for humanity and his outrage at its leaders.

**bone,** hard substance that forms the SKELETON in vertebrate animals. Bone consists of a gelatinous organic material called collagen, together with minerals (mainly calcium and phosphorus). In the very young, the mineral content is low and the bones are mostly cartilage, which is pliable. With age, as their mineral content increases, bones become more brittle. Bone tissue has a three-layered structure: the spongy inner layer; the compact layer surrounding the inner layer, providing support for the body; and the tough outer membrane. The inner spaces of long bones, as those in the arms and legs, are filled with marrow, important in the formation of BLOOD cells. In birds, some of the larger bones contain air-chambers which are connected to the lungs.

**bone-black,** form of charcoal used in industry for its highly absorbent properties. It is manufactured by heating animal bones to a high temperature and then grinding them into fine powder. Chemically it contains only approximately 10% carbon, the rest being phosphates, particularly calcium phosphate. It readily absorbs poisonous gases and was used in gas masks for the first time in World War I. More sophisticated industrially it is used for the recovery or extraction of various substances from liquids and gases.

**Bonheur, Rosa** (bɔˌnuh), 1822–98, French painter of animals. Her pictures are realistic and detailed. Her best-known work is *The Horse Fair* (Metropolitan Mus., New York).

**Bonhoeffer, Dietrich** (ˌbonhuhfə), 1906–45, German Protestant theologian. Influenced very early by Karl BARTH, he urged a conformation to the form of Christ as the suffering servant in a total commitment of self to others. He was imprisoned for two years and hanged for his role in a plot to overthrow HITLER. His writings, published posthumously, called for a Christianity stripped of much of its traditional apparatus.

**Bon Homme Richard:** see JONES, JOHN PAUL.

**Boniface,** d. 432, Roman general. In AFRICA as a semi-independent governor, he was named count of Africa by VALENTINIAN III. Recalled to Rome in 427, he rebelled, causing a civil war between Africa and Rome. The struggle prepared the way for the invasion of Africa by the Vandals under GAISERIC. After a truce was arranged, Boniface attacked the Vandals and was defeated and besieged (430) at Hippo. He died of wounds received in a battle with a rival Roman general, Aetius.

**Boniface, Saint,** c.675–754, English missionary monk and martyr, called the Apostle of Germany. From 718 he devoted himself to the conversion of pagan Germany, where he founded many bishoprics and abbeys. He was named metropolitan of Germany (732) and archbishop of Mainz (c.745). He was martyred by pagans in Friesland. Feast: 5 June.

**Boniface VIII,** c.1235?–1303, pope (1294–1303), an Italian named Benedetto Caetani. Boniface became pope after the abdication of CELESTINE

V, and, to avoid schism, he imprisoned Celestine for life. Trying to assert papal authority, Boniface interfered unsuccessfully in Sicily and further aggravated the quarrel of the GUELPHS AND GHIBELLINES. He was involved in a bitter struggle with PHILIP IV of France. The pope tried to prevent Philip from his illegal levies on the clergy with the bull *Clericis laicos* (1296), but was forced to back down. The struggle was renewed after new troubles, and Boniface issued *Ausculta fili* (1301) and *Unam sanctam* (1302), the latter being an extreme statement regarding the duty of princes to be subject to the pope. As a result, Philip sent an agent to depose Boniface at Anagni, but after the agent's companion struck the pope, the outraged townspeople drove the emissaries out. Boniface died soon afterwards and was succeeded by Benedict XI. Philip later forced Pope CLEMENT V to repudiate many acts of Boniface. An able administrator and canon lawyer, Boniface issued (1298) a fresh volume of authoritative legal texts called the *Sext.*

**Bonifácio, José** (bonee,fahseeoh), 1763–1838, Brazilian scientist and architect of Brazilian independence. An eminent geologist, he influenced the Portuguese prince regent, Dom Pedro, to declare (1822) Brazil an independent monarchy with himself as Emperor PEDRO I. Bonifácio served as first minister (1822–23) of the new empire, and many of his ideas were included in the 1824 constitution.

**Bonington, Richard Parkes,** 1802–28, English landscape painter who worked mainly in France. Bonington travelled widely and painted many landscapes in oil and watercolour which are distinguished by their brilliant colour and fluent technique. He was a friend of DELACROIX, and also painted small historical pictures of medieval and oriental themes. Fine examples are in the Wallace Coll., London.

**Bonin Islands,** volcanic island group, c.100 km² (40 sq mi), in the W Pacific Ocean, c.800 km (500 mi) S of Tokyo. Principal products of the sparsely populated archipelago are sugarcane, cocoa, bananas, and pineapples. The islands were claimed by Britain (1827) and Japan (1875). A Japanese stronghold in WORLD WAR II, the Bonins were captured (1945) by the US. They were returned to Japan in 1968.

**Bonn,** city (1984 pop. 291,700), capital of the Federal Republic of Germany, North Rhine–Westphalia, W West Germany, on the Rhine R. It is the administrative centre of West Germany. Manufactures include chemicals and pharmaceuticals. Founded (1st cent. AD) by the Romans, it was later (1238–1794) the residence of the electors of Cologne. In 1949 it became the capital of West Germany (see under GERMANY). BEETHOVEN was born in Bonn.

**Bonnard, Pierre** (bo,nahd), 1867–1947, French painter, lithographer, and illustrator. He excelled at domestic interiors that emphasized light effects similar in exuberance to those of IMPRESSIONISM, e.g., *Bowl of Fruit* (1933; Philadelphia Mus. Art). His late works are intensely colourful.

**Bonneville Salt Flats,** desert area in Tooele co., NW Utah, US, c.22.5 km (14 mi) long and 11 km (7 mi) wide. It is part of Great Salt Lake Desert, the former bed of Lake Bonneville, whose area, once c.50,500 km² (19,500 sq mi), shrank at the end of the Pleistocene epoch. The smooth salt surface of the Flats is ideal for motor racing, and several world speed records have been set there.

**Bonnie Prince Charlie:** see under STUART, JAMES FRANCIS EDWARD.

**bonsai,** the art of cultivating artificially dwarfed trees, and the plants developed by this method. Bonsai, developed over 1000 years ago in Japan, derives from the Chinese practice of growing miniature plants. In bonsai cultivation, the plants are kept small and in true proportion to their natural models by growing them in small containers, pruning, and forming branches to the desired shape by applying wire coils. The selection of containers, the plant's position in a container, and the choice of single plants or a group are important aesthetic considerations.

**booby,** dagger beaked, streamlined BIRD of the family Sulidae. Boobies live in the southern hemisphere, their northern relatives being called gannets. The family are all fish-eaters, hunting over the open sea for part of the year. They dive into the sea with partly-closed wings after their prey. They are colonial nesters, gannets (*Sula bassana*) choosing rocks, the red-footed booby (*S. sula*) trees and bushes. The Peruvian booby (*S. variegata*) is an important GUANO producer.

**bookbinding.** The practice of bookbinding began with the protection of parchment manuscripts with boards. Parchment sheets had been folded and sewn together from the 2nd cent. AD. In the Middle Ages, the art of fine binding rose to great heights. Books were rare and precious and many were covered exquisitely. Techniques of folding and sewing sheets together in small lots, taping the lots together, and adding outside protection changed little from the medieval monastery to the modern bindery. The invention of PRINTING greatly increased the demand for binding, however. In machine binding, called casing, the cover, or case, is made separately from the book and then glued to it. With the development of mass-production processes and new materials, new methods of binding have become popular; 'perfect' binding uses glue without sewing. The finest binding is still done by hand, often to restore damaged books.

Example of a **bonsai** (genus *Acer*)

**Book of Changes (Yi jing),** classic ancient Chinese book of prophecy and wisdom. Its earliest parts are thought to date from the century before CONFUCIUS. It consists of variants on eight trigrams, corresponding to the powers of nature. They are used to interpret the future with the textual help of supplementary definitions, intuitions, and Confucian commentary.

**Book of Common Prayer,** title given to the service book used in the Church of ENGLAND and in other churches of the ANGLICAN COMMUNION. The first Prayer Book (1549), mainly the work of Thomas CRANMER, was essentially derived from the breviary and the missal. This was revised (1552), but was suppressed under MARY I. Revised under ELIZABETH I, it was again suppressed (1645–60) by the Commonwealth and the Protectorate. A new revision was made compulsory by the Act of Uniformity (1662). Revisions of the book have been carried out at various times in all the branches of the Anglican Communion. The one in use in the Church of England since 1980 is *The Alternative Service Book*; it uses present-day English, addresses God as 'you', and recasts the communion service on primitive lines.

**book of hours,** form of devotional book developed in the 14th cent. containing prayers and meditations appropriate to seasons, months, days, and hours. Many are masterpieces of ILLUMINATION; among the greatest is *Très Riches Heures* (c.1415; Musée Condé, Chantilly), made by the LIMBOURG BROTHERS and other artists for the renowned collector Jean, duc de Berry.

**Book of the Dead,** Egyptian funerary literature. The texts consist of charms, spells, and formulas for use by the deceased in the afterworld. At first inscriptions, the texts were later papyrus rolls placed inside the mummy case. Essential ideas of Egyptian religion are known through them. The earliest collection dates from the XVIII dynasty (1580–1350 BC).

**book publishing.** The term *publishing* usually means the issuing of printed materials, such as books, magazines, and PERIODICALS, and is therefore closely related both to PRINTING and to the retailing of printed materials. Although the practice of making extra copies of manuscripts goes back to ancient times, it was the introduction of printing into Europe in the 15th cent. that caused publishing to spring into lively existence (see TYPE). The differentiation of printer, publisher, and bookseller began astonishingly early. In 1583 the first important publishing house, that of the Elzevir family in Holland (see ELZEVIR, LOUIS), published its first book. With a steadily broadening mass of readers, great publishing houses slowly appeared in cities such as Leipzig, Vienna, Florence, Zürich, Paris, London, and Edinburgh. In the US, Boston, Philadelphia, and especially New York City took the lead in publishing. During the 19th cent. specialization became increasingly evident. Music publishing became almost a separate business, as did map publishing. Specialization also grew within the houses themselves in the 20th cent. Editorial departments became distinct from production departments, and both were quite separate from the sales, promotion, and distribution departments. Publishers also specialized according to the subject matter of their books and the means by which they were distributed. Thus, trade books are fiction and nonfiction books sold to readers primarily through bookshops (or the trade), whereas textbooks are directed toward university, college, and school teachers for use by students in the classroom. Moreover, with the proliferation of book clubs (supported by individuals who order through the post), many books are issued with this market in mind. During the 1930s and 1940s the paperbound, pocket-sized book rose meteorically in popularity in English-speaking countries; by the 1980s one third of all books sold were paperbacks. Publishing has traditionally been an industry of small, family-owned firms. After the 1960s, however, firms were continually being bought by and consolidated with other companies; often they were taken over by conglomerate companies in quite different lines of business; US publishing firms bought up smaller companies in other countries. In the late 1980s this trend was reversed in the UK, with a revival of small firms, sometimes in the form of management buy-outs. The advent of new technologies for the transmission, storage, and distribution of data, once the prerogative of book publishing, had become a problem for the industry; television screens and data bases became symbols of the challenges to editors and publishers alike (see COMPUTER; INFORMATION STORAGE AND RETRIEVAL). The increasing use of sophisticated copying machines posed new problems to the need of publishers and authors to protect their property by COPYRIGHT. The impact of computing on publishing has been—and will continue to be—considerable. Word processing and computing have revolutionized compilation, collating, and indexing, and render the editing of texts a much smoother operation than hitherto. Desk-top publishing, in which a microcomputer can cheaply produce laser-printed material comparable in quality to conventionally printed books, with copies run out virtually on demand, opens up a whole new area of academic and semi-professional publishing, where print-runs are often so short as to make the normal publishing procedure uneconomic.

**Boole, George,** 1815–64, English mathematician and logician. BOOLEAN ALGEBRA, his form of symbolic LOGIC, is central to the study of the foundations of pure mathematics and is the basis of computer technology. Boole wrote *An Investigation of the Laws of Thought* (1854), as well as works on calculus and differential equations.

**Boolean algebra,** an abstract mathematical system primarily used in COMPUTER science and in expressing the relationships between mathematical sets (groups of objects or concepts; see SET). The notational system was developed by the English mathematician George BOOLE about 1850 to permit an algebraic manipulation of logical statements. Such manipulation can demonstrate whether or not a statement is true and show how a complicated statement can be rephrased in a simpler, more convenient form without changing its meaning. When used in set theory, Boolean algebra can demonstrate the relationship between groups, indicating what is in each set alone, what is jointly contained in both, and what is contained in neither. The expression of electrical networks in Boolean notation has aided the development of switching theory and the design of computers.

**Boone, Daniel,** 1734–1820, American frontiersman. In March 1775, as advance agent for the Transylvania Company (an association formed to colonize Kentucky and Tennessee), he blazed the WILDERNESS ROAD and founded Boonesboro, Kentucky. His legendary adventures, many disproved by historical scholarship, were popularized in a so-called autobiographical account (1784) by John Filson.

**Boorman, John,** 1933–, British film director. His most successful films have been tight, suspenseful action pictures, strong on a sense of place and with mythical elements in the drama. His films include *Point Blank* (US; 1967), *Deliverance* (US; 1972), and *Zardoz* (1974).

**Booth,** family prominent in the SALVATION ARMY. **William Booth,** 1829–1912, was an evangelist in London, where he and his wife, **Catherine Mumford Booth,** 1829–90, established (1865) a movement that became (1878) the Salvation Army. Their eldest son, **William Bramwell Booth,** 1856–1929, succeeded his father in 1912 as general of this organization. Another son, **Ballington Booth,** 1859–1940, was commander of the Salvation Army in Australia (1885–87) and in the US (1887–96), withdrawing (1896) to found the Volunteers of America. A daughter, **Evangeline Cory Booth,** 1865–1950, commander of the Salvation Army in Canada (1895–1904) and the US (1904–34), was general (1934–39) of the international Salvation Army.

**Booth, Herbert Cecil,** 1871–1955, English mechanical engineer best known for his invention of the vacuum cleaner. He studied engineering at the City and Guilds College in London, and started his own engineering firm in 1901. At that time industrial cleaning was achieved by compressed air blowers: dust was dislodged from difficult corners, but then had to be swept up by brush. His first suction cleaning machines were very large, on four wheels, and powered by a petrol engine. The machine was left in the road and the flexible tubes passed into the rooms to be cleaned via the windows. His name became famous when he was hired to clean the carpets in Westminster Abbey in preparation for the Coronation of Edward VII in 1902. Booth made a study of dust-related diseases and felt that his machines were combatting these ailments. His other interest was in big structures; he built the big wheels at London, Blackpool, and Vienna, and the Great Wheel of Paris, 61 m (200 ft) in diameter.

**Booth, Junius Brutus,** 1796–1852, American actor; b. England. After making a name for himself in London, especially with Edmund Kean in *Othello* and *King Lear* in the 1820 season at Drury Lane, he went to the US in 1821 and became the foremost tragic actor of his day. His son **Edwin Booth,** 1833–93, toured with his father and scored great successes in Shakespearean tragedies. His 100-night run of *Hamlet* in New York City in 1864 was famous. The next year he retired briefly from the stage because of the scandal involving his brother (see below). He built Booth's Theatre in New York City (1869) and was the founder (1888) and first president of the Players' Club. Another son, **John Wilkes Booth,** 1838–65, won acclaim in Shakespearean roles but is best known as the assassin of Abraham LINCOLN. A Southern sympathizer (unlike the rest of his family) during the CIVIL WAR, he plotted with six fellow conspirators to assassinate Union leaders. On 14 Apr. 1865, he shot Pres. Lincoln during a performance of *Our American Cousin* at Ford's Theater in Washington, DC, vaulted onto the stage (breaking a leg), and escaped. A search party cornered him in a burning barn near Bowling Green, Virginia, on 26 Apr. and Booth was fatally shot, either by himself or by one of his pursuers.

**bootlegging,** the illegal production or distribution of proscribed or highly taxed goods. Historically, the term is most often applied to illegal dealing in alcohol during PROHIBITION in the US. By 1930, alcohol bootlegging had become a large industry dominated by gangsters such as Al CAPONE. Its association with graft and violence was a major factor in prohibition's repeal.

**Bophuthatswana** ('bohpoonhaht‚swahnə), black African homeland or BANTUSTAN (1980 est. pop. 1,300,000), 40,330 km² (15,571 sq mi), declared independent by the Republic of South Africa in 1977, but not recognized internationally. Mmabatho is the capital. The 'state', which consists of seven separate areas (six along the Botswana border), is the designated homeland for the Tswana people.

**Bopp, Franz,** 1791–1867, German philologist. He demonstrated the relationships among the Indo-European languages in his *Comparative Grammar* (1833–52).

**borage,** common name for *Borago officinalis,* of the family Boraginaceae, widely distributed as herbs and tropical shrubs and trees.

Borage is used as a potherb, and a flavouring for drinks. The family also includes forget-me-not (*Myosotis*).

**Borah, William Edgar,** 1865–1940, US senator from Idaho (1907–40). He was a Republican noted for his independent stands and his interest in foreign policy. A fervent nationalist, he opposed the LEAGUE OF NATIONS, but advocated disarmament. Borah also opposed economic monopolies and the growth of big government.

**borax** or **sodium tetraborate decahydrate,** chemical compound ($Na_2B_4O_7 \cdot 10H_2O$) occurring as a colourless, crystalline salt or a white powder. Borax is used as an antiseptic, cleansing agent, water softener, corrosion inhibitor in antifreeze, and flux for silver soldering, and in the manufacture of fertilizers, heat-resistant glass, and pharmaceuticals.

**Bordeaux,** city (1982 pop. 211,197, agglomeration 640,012), capital of Gironde dept., SW France, on the Garonne R. It is a busy port, accessible to the Atlantic, with motor vehicle and other industries. Wine is its major product, with Bordeaux the generic name of the region's wine. A prosperous Roman city, it flourished (11th cent.) as the seat of the dukes of AQUITAINE. ELEANOR OF AQUITAINE precipitated war between France and the English, who ruled the city (1154–1453). The city reached its height of prosperity in the 18th cent. It was the temporary seat of French government in 1914 and 1940.

**Borden, Gail,** 1801–74, American inventor. His process (patented 1856) of evaporating MILK was found to be of great value for the army during the Civil War, and its use spread rapidly afterwards. Borden subsequently also patented processes for concentrating fruit juices and other beverages. See FOOD PRESERVATION.

**Borden, Sir Robert Laird,** 1854–1937, Canadian prime minister (1911–20). He headed the Conservative government (1911–17) and a Union coalition (1917–20) during World War I. It was largely through his efforts that CANADA and other British dominions attained new self-governing status.

**Borders,** region in S Scotland (1985 est. pop. 101,256), 4672 km² (1857 sq mi), bordering on England in the S and the North Sea in the NE. It was formed in 1975 from the counties of Berwickshire, Roxburghshire, Selkirkshire, Peebleshire, and SW Midlothian. The administrative headquarters are in Newtown St Boswells which is in the centre of the region. Most of the region is hilly, including the Lammermuir Hills in the N. It is drained by the R. Tweed and its tributaries. Sheep-rearing and the manufacture of woollen goods are important economic activities.

**Bordet, Jules** (baw‚dəy), 1870–1961, Belgian microbiologist. He received the 1919 Nobel Prize for physiology or medicine for his work in immunity. With Octave Gengou he proved (1900) the diagnostic value of complement-fixation tests (tests to detect specific antibodies; applied by August WASSERMANN to the diagnosis of syphilis) and isolated (1906) the bacterium that causes whooping cough.

**Borg, Björn,** 1956–, Swedish tennis player. As a teenage star he led (1975) Sweden to its first Davis Cup victory. Before losing to John MCENROE in 1981, he captured five successive WIMBLEDON titles, a tournament record.

**Borges, Jorge Luis** (‚bawhays), 1899–1986, Argentine poet, critic, and short-story writer. Perhaps the foremost contemporary Spanish American author, he wrote his early poetry, beginning with *Fervor de Buenos Aires* (1923), under the influence of *ultraísmo,* a movement for pure poetry that followed MODERNISMO. Borges's highly imaginative poetry is collected in *Selected Poems: 1923–1967* (1968). His philosophical and literary essays appear in such collections as *Otras inquisiciones* (1952; tr. Other Inquisitions). He is probably best known for his strikingly original short fiction, ranging from physical allegories through fantasies to sophisticated detective yarns, e.g., *Historia universal de la infamia* (1935), *Ficciones* (1944; tr. Fictions), *El libro de los seres imaginarios* (1957; tr. The Book Of Imaginary Beings), and *The Book of Sand* (1975).

**Borghese** (baw‚gayzay), noble Roman family. It produced one pope, Paul V; several cardinals; and many prominent citizens.

**Borgia,** (‚bawjah), a Spanish–Italian noble family originating from Valencia. Its members included the popes CALIXTUS III and ALEXANDER VI and the Jesuit St Francis Borgia. **Cesare Borgia,** c.1475–1507, a son of Alexander VI, was an able and ruthless political and military leader. He was made a cardinal in 1493. Between 1499 and 1501 he captured a number of cities in the Romagna. Appointed duke of the Romagna by his father, he ruled his territory with cruel efficiency until the death of his father and the election of a hostile successor, JULIUS II. Cesare was forced to flee the Papal States and he ended his short life as a soldier in the service of the King of Navarre. His posthumous reputation owes much to the discussion of his career in MACHIAVELLI's *Prince*. His sister was **Lucrezia Borgia**, 1480–1519, daughter of Alexander VI, was married in turn to Giovanni Sforza, ruler of Pesaro; to Alfonso of Aragon (murdered in 1500, probably by the orders of her brother Cesare); and to Alfonso d'Este, who became Duke of Ferrara (1505). Her beauty and liberality attracted to her court many distinguished artists and writers, notably the humanist Pietro Bembo. The stories about her loose morals are as unfounded as most of the Borgia family legend.

**Borgia, Rodrigo:** see ALEXANDER VI.

**Boris**, rulers of Bulgaria. **Boris I**, d. 907, khan [ruler] of Bulgaria (r.852–89), was a Christian convert and introduced Byzantine Christianity into Bulgaria. In 889 he abdicated, entering a monastery. **Boris III**, 1894–1943, czar (r.1918–43), ruled constitutionally until 1935 and thereafter as a dictator. He joined the Axis in 1940 and died mysteriously soon after visiting HITLER in Berlin.

**Borlaug, Norman Ernest**, 1914–, American agronomist. Associated with the Rockefeller Foundation in Mexico from 1944, he headed a team of scientists experimenting with improvement of grains. He won the 1970 Nobel Peace Prize for his efforts to eradicate hunger and build international prosperity. His 'green revolution', using improved wheat seed, new types of higher-yield rice, and more efficient use of fertilizers and water, improved food production throughout the world.

**Bormann, Martin**, 1900–45, German NAZI leader. In 1942 he became HITLER's private secretary. Although he was rumoured to have escaped to Argentina in 1945, his skeleton was unearthed and identified in West Berlin in 1973.

**Born, Max**, 1882–1970, German physicist. For his statistical interpretation of quantum mechanics (see QUANTUM THEORY), he shared the 1954 Nobel Prize for physics. Born was head (1921–33) of the physics department at the Univ. of Göttingen. After Nazi policies forced him to leave Germany, he taught at Cambridge Univ. and the Univ. of Edinburgh before returning to Germany in 1954.

**Borneo**, island (1983 pop. 10,398,000), SE Asia, world's third largest island, c.743,330 km² (287,000 sq mi), in the Malay Archipelago. It is divided among Indonesia, which holds about 70% of the island (called Kalimantan), Brunei, and the Malaysian states of Sabah and Sarawak. Dense jungles and rain forests cover much of the mountainous island, which reaches a high point of 4101 m (13,455 ft) at Mt Kinabalu. The hot, humid climate is marked by a prolonged monsoon season lasting generally from November to May. Primitive DYAKS occupy the sparsely populated interior; Malays predominate in coastal regions. Oil, discovered in 1888, is the chief resource.

**Bornholm**, island (1984 est. pop. 47,000), 400 km² (227 sq mi), Denmark, in the Baltic Sea. Most of the island consists of old, hard, granitic rocks which yield a useful building stone. Some coal was once worked but the main activities now are agriculture, fishing, and tourism. The principal town and port is Ronne.

**Bornu**, emirate and province (1983 est. pop. 4,901,000), NE Nigeria. It lies in the zone of savanna vegetation. Maiduguri is the provincial capital. The emirate forms the central part of the former Bornu empire of the Kanuri people. In the 18th cent. Bornu was attacked by FULANI tribesmen and by the Sudanese. It was partitioned among the British, French, and Germans in the late 19th cent. The area which now falls within Nigeria was given the status of emirate by the British.

**Borodin, Aleksandr Porfirevich**, 1833–87, Russian composer. He was one of the group known as The FIVE. His principal works include two completed symphonies, three string quartets, the SYMPHONIC POEM *In the Steppes of Central Asia* (1880) and the unfinished opera *Prince Igor*.

**Boroimhe, Brian:** see BRIAN BORU.

**boron** (B), nonmetallic element, isolated by Sir Humphry DAVY in 1807. As a dark-brown to black amorphous powder, boron is more reactive than its jet-black to silver-grey crystalline metallike form. BORAX and boric acid are common compounds. Boron is used in the shielding material and in some control rods of nuclear reactors. See ELEMENT (table); PERIODIC TABLE.

**Borowczyk, Walerian**, 1923–, Polish animator and film director. A leading animation film-maker, who went to France in the late 1950s. From 1968 onwards he has concentrated on live action features, usually about sexual desire and obsession. His animation films include *Le Theatre de Monsieur et Madame Kabal* (1967). His live action films include *Goto, Isle of Love* (1969), *Blanche* (1971), and *The Beast* (1976).

**Borromini, Francesco**, 1599–1677, major Italian BAROQUE architect. His innovations in palace and church architecture were influential in Italy and N Europe. Among his buildings is San Carlo alle Quattro Fontane, Rome, noted for its undulating rhythm of architectural elements within a geometric plan.

*San Carlo alle Quattro Fontane* by Francesco **Borromini**

**Borrow, George Henry**, 1803–81, English writer. He travelled widely in Europe and the East as an agent for the British and Foreign Bible Society, becoming an expert linguist and a friend of the gypsies. His books, all of which are based on his travels, include *The Bible in Spain* (1843), *Lavengro* (1851), and *The Romany Rye* (1857).

**Boru, Brian:** see BRIAN BORU.

**Bosch, Carl**, 1874–1940, German technologist and developer of chemical fertilizer. The use of agricultural land was revolutionized by the availability of fertilizers derived from AMMONIA, formed from atmospheric nitrogen by the HABER process. Bosch developed this process commercially, and for devising chemical high-pressure methods he was awarded the 1931 Nobel Prize for chemistry.

**Bosch, Hieronymus**, c.1450–1516, Flemish painter; real name probably Jerom van Aeken. Bosch is celebrated for the grotesque and fantastic imagery—hideous plants bearing strange fruits, monsters, instruments of torture set in fiery landscapes—that fill his pictures; he perhaps drew his themes from contemporary proverbs and folklore, or from moralizing religious literature or visionary poetry. His pictures satirize human folly and suggest the snares laid by the devil for unwary man. The temptations of hermits and holy men were a favourite theme, as in *The Temptation of St Anthony* (c.1500; Museu Nacional de Arte Antigua, Lisbon). His most celebrated work is the *Garden of Earthly Delights* (c.1505–10), which was one of several pictures collected by Philip II; this collection is now in the Prado, Madrid.

Bosch, *Garden of Earthly Delights* – Right panel: Hell, c.1505–10. Panel, 220 × 97 cm. Museo del Prado, Madrid.

**Bose, Sir Jagadis Chunder,** 1858–1937, Indian physicist and plant physiologist. Professor of physical science (1885–1915) at Presidency College, Calcutta, he is noted for his researches in plant life, especially his comparison of the responses of plant and animal tissue to various stimuli. One of his inventions is the crescograph, a device for measuring plant growth.

**Bose, Subhashchandra,** 1897–1945, militant Indian nationalist. He led the youthful and radical elements in the Indian National Congress in the late 1920s and 30s, jointly with Jawaharlal NEHRU. Repeatedly imprisoned by the British, he escaped from India during the War and, with Japanese help, built up the Indian National Army mainly with Indian prisoners of war. His army's invasion of NE India was easily defeated. Bose died in an air crash.

**Bosnia-Hercegovina** (ˌbozneeə heətsəgoˌveenə), constituent republic of Yugoslavia (1981 pop. 4,124,256), 51,129 km² (19,741 sq mi), W central Yugoslavia. Bosnia is to the north of Hercegovina. The capital is SARAJEVO. Despite rich mineral deposits, this multinational republic remains one of the poorer areas of Yugoslavia. About half of its largely mountainous terrain is forested; one quarter is cultivated, with grains, tobacco, and vines among the major crops. The region was settled (7th cent.) by Slav tribes and was a state of some power from the late 12th cent. to its conquest by the Ottomans in 1463. Large numbers of Slavs converted to Islam. Occupied (1878) and annexed (1908) by Austria–Hungary, the province became a principal bone of contention between Vienna and Serbia and the focus of nationalist rivalries among its Serb, Croat, and Muslim populations. The assassination (1914) of Austrian Archduke FRANCIS FERDINAND and his wife by a Serb student in Sarajevo precipitated the outbreak of WORLD WAR I. Bosnia–Hercegovina entered the Yugoslav state in 1918. During WORLD WAR II it was joined to the Axis puppet state of CROATIA (1941–45) and was the scene of extensive fighting. Afterwards it became one of Yugoslavia's six republics, in which the Serb, Croat, and South Slav Muslim peoples were each recognized as having a stake.

**Bosporus,** strait, c.30 km (20 mi) long and c.640 m (2100 ft) wide at its narrowest, separating European and Asian Turkey. The fortified strait connects the Black Sea with the Sea of Marmara. As a part (with the DARDANELLES) of a passage linking the BLACK and MEDITERRANEAN seas, it is a critically important shipping lane for the USSR. A bridge (1074 m/3524 ft) long spans the Bosporus at Istanbul, near the southern end of the strait.

**Boston,** US city (1984 est. pop. 571,000), state capital of Massachusetts, on Boston Bay; inc. 1822. The largest city of New England, it is a major financial, government, and educational centre, and a leading port. Industries include publishing, food processing, and the manufacture of shoes, textiles, machinery, and electronic equipment. Established by John WINTHROP as the main colony of the MASSACHUSETTS BAY COMPANY in 1630, Boston was an early centre of American PURITANISM, with a vigorous intellectual life. A focus of opposition to the British, it was the scene of several actions in the AMERICAN REVOLUTION. The city prospered in the 19th cent., and shipbuilding, commercial, and industrial magnates such as the Cabots, Lowells, and Lodges patronized the arts, making Boston the 'Athens of America'. The arrival of many immigrants (at first mainly Irish) helped transform Boston into an industrial metropolis with expanded city limits. Boston's great cultural institutions include its Museum of Fine Arts, Symphony Orchestra, Public Library, and Athenaeum. Boston Univ., Northeastern Univ., New England Medical Center, and Harvard Medical School are among the institutions that make Boston world famous as an educational, medical, and research centre.

**Boston Massacre,** 1770, incident prior to the AMERICAN REVOLUTION in which five members of a rioting crowd were killed by British soldiers sent to Boston to maintain order and enforce the TOWNSHEND ACT.

**Boston Tea Party,** Boston, Massachusetts, US, 16 Dec. 1773, a protest against the British Tea Act (1773). Angry colonists disguised as Indians boarded three tea ships and threw the tea into Boston harbour.

**Boswell, James,** 1740–95, Scottish writer. The son of a judge, he reluctantly studied law and practised throughout his life. His true interest was in a literary career and in associating with the great men of the time. He met Samuel JOHNSON in 1763 and, having himself achieved fame with his *Account of Corsica* (1768), produced *Journal of a Tour of the Hebrides with Samuel Johnson, LLD* (1785). His great work, *The Life of Samuel Johnson, LLD* appeared in 1791. Boswell recorded Johnson's conversation so minutely that Johnson is better remembered today for his sayings than for his own literary works. The curious combination of Boswell's own character and his genius at biography has led later critics to call him the greatest of all biographers. Masses of Boswell manuscript, discovered in the 20th cent. in Dublin, have enhanced his reputation.

**botanical garden,** public place where plants are grown both for display and for scientific study. They are often arranged in cultural or habitat groups such as rock gardens, desert gardens, and tropical gardens. An *arboretum* is a botanical garden devoted chiefly to woody plants. Botanical gardens collect and cultivate plants from all over the world, conduct experiments in plant breeding and hybridization (see HYBRID), and maintain libraries and HERBARIUMS (see KEW GARDENS).

**botany,** science devoted to the study of plants, a major branch of BIOLOGY. In the 17th cent. the work of LINNAEUS on the CLASSIFICATION of organisms contributed greatly to the growth of the science, and the introduction of the MICROSCOPE marked the beginning of the study of plant anatomy and cells. Modern botany has expanded into all areas of biology, e.g., plant breeding and GENETICS. Practical areas of botanical study include AGRICULTURE, AGRONOMY, FORESTRY, and HORTICULTURE.

**Botany Bay,** inlet, New South Wales, SE Australia, just S of Sydney. It was visited in 1770 by Capt. James COOK and named after the interesting flora on its shores. Australia's first penal colony, often called Botany Bay, was at Sydney.

**Botev, Khristo,** 1848–76, Bulgarian poet. As a student in Russia he absorbed socialist ideas. In 1875 a volume of his patriotic lyrics and ballads appeared. He was killed leading a band of rebels against Turkish rule.

**Botha, Louis** (ˌbohtə), 1862–1919, South African soldier and statesman. He commanded the Boer troops in the SOUTH AFRICAN WAR (1899–1902). He was prime minister (1907–10) of the Transvaal and, as leader of the Unionist party, prime minister (1910–19) of the Union of SOUTH AFRICA.

**Botha, Pieter Willem,** 1916–, South African politician, prime minister (1978–84) and state president since 1984. A member of the National Party, he has worked for limited reforms in his nation's policy of APARTHEID and has continued the creation of BANTUSTANS as homelands for the black population. Botha also served (1965–80) as defence minister.

**Botham, Ian,** 1955–, English cricketer. One of the outstanding all-rounders in the history of the game, and the most controversial player of his generation. He captained Somerset and England, and between 1977 and 1984 made 65 consecutive Test appearances. In 1985, for Somerset against Warwickshire, he made 100 off 50 balls in 49 minutes and from 26 scoring strokes—94 in boundaries. During that season, he hit 80 sixes. For England against Pakistan in 1978 he took 8 wickets for 34 runs, and against the West Indies in 1984 (both matches were at LORD'S) 8–103.

**Bothnia, Gulf of,** part of the Baltic Sea, extending for some 550 km (350 mi) between the shores of Sweden and Finland. Its coastline, indented and island-strewn, shows evidence of having emerged from the sea since the Ice Age. Rivers draining to the Gulf provide floatways for timber and there are numerous pulp factories and saw mills along the coast. Ports include Vassa and Oulu in Finland and Luleå in Sweden, all of which are closed by ice in winter.

**Bothwell, James Hepburn,** 4th **earl of,** 1536?–78, Scottish nobleman, third husband of MARY QUEEN OF SCOTS. After the murder of her secretary RIZZIO by conspirators, among them her husband, Lord DARNLEY, Mary trusted only Bothwell. Accused of murdering Darnley, Bothwell was acquitted in a rigged trial and married Mary (1567). The Scottish aristocracy attacked him and forced Mary to give him up. He fled to Denmark, where he was imprisoned and died insane.

**Botswana,** officially Republic of Botswana, formerly Bechuanaland, republic (1981 pop. 941,027), 600,372 km² (231,804 sq mi), S central Africa, bordered by Namibia (South West Africa; W and N), Zambia (N), Zimbabwe (E), and South Africa (S and E). GABORONE is the capital. The terrain is mostly a semi-arid plateau (c.910 m/3000 ft high) of rolling land, with hills in the east, the KALAHARI Desert in the south and west, and the Okavango Swamp in the northwest. Cattle-raising and the export of beef are the chief economic activities. Farm production is severely hampered by lack of water. Botswana has vast mineral resources,

discovered in the 1960s, and mining is being rapidly developed. Diamonds have become the principal export, and copper, nickel, and coal are also being extracted. Because of its landlocked location, however, the country remains economically dependent on its neighbours, SOUTH AFRICA and ZIMBABWE (which controls the railway through Botswana). The GNP is US$790 million, and the GNP per capita is US$840 (1985). The population is mainly Tswana, who are divided into eight principal Bantu-speaking groups. English and Tswana are the official languages. There is no official religion; both traditional and Christian religions are followed.

*History.* The region was originally inhabited by the San (Bushmen), who were supplanted by the Tswana in the 18th cent. In the early 1800s Khama, chief of the largest Tswana tribe, curbed expansion by Zulu and Ndebele tribesmen into the territory and established a fairly unified state. A new threat arose in the late 19th cent. when, after gold was discovered in the region (1867), neighbouring Transvaal sought to annex parts of Botswana. This move was opposed by the British, who took the area under supervision (1885) as a protectorate called Bechuanaland. A British plan to incorporate Bechuanaland into the Union of South Africa was eventually abandoned because of South Africa's APARTHEID policy, and in 1966, as Botswana, it gained full independence within the COMMONWEALTH. Led by its first president, Sir Seretse KHAMA (grandson of Khama) until his death (1980), Botswana has established itself as a stable, democratic, nonracist nation committed to a moderate foreign policy. Under the presidency of Quett Masire (of the dominant Botswana Democratic Party), Botswana has in the 1980s come into increasing confrontation with the white regime in neighbouring South Africa.

Botswana

**Böttger, Johann Friedrich** (ˌbuhtgə), 1682–1719, German alchemist and originator of MEISSEN porcelain. In 1709 he produced a glazed hard-paste PORCELAIN, the first in Europe. Later he improved the paste and glaze, and introduced decoration in enamel-colours.

**Botticelli, Sandro,** c.1444–1510, Florentine RENAISSANCE painter; b. Alessandro di Mariano Filipepi. He was a student of Fra Filippo LIPPI, whose influence can be seen in the delicate colours of his early work. He became a favourite of the MEDICI family and was influenced by their Neoplatonic circle. Botticelli was a master of rhythmic line. His mythological scenes, *Primavera* (1477–78), *Birth of Venus* (1485–90; both: Uffizi, Florence), and *Mars and Venus* (1483–85; National Gall., London) perhaps allude to the triumph of love and reason over brutal instinct. In his last years, his popularity probably declined, and he turned to religious scenes. His late works, e.g., *Mystic Nativity* (1490–97;

National Gall., London) and *Pieta* (1490; Alte Pinakothek, Munich) are dramatic and highly expressive. In the 19th cent. he was rediscovered by RUSKIN and Walter Pater.

Sandro **Botticelli**, *Primavera*, 1477–78. Galleria Uffizi, Florence.

**botulism**, acute, often fatal food poisoning from ingestion of food containing botulin, a TOXIN produced by *Clostridium botulinum* bacteria. Most cases are caused by tinned meat and fish that has been improperly processed; the toxin is easily destroyed by heat but bacterial spores are more heat-resistant. The disease causes disturbances in vision, speech, and swallowing and, ultimately, paralysis of respiratory muscles, leading to suffocation. Treatment involves the administration of antitoxin as soon as possible after exposure to contaminated food.

**Bouaké** or **Bwake**, city (1983 est. pop. 230,000), central Côte d'Ivoire. It is a commercial and transport centre linked by rail to ABIDJAN. Tobacco is processed in the town, and gold and manganese are found nearby.

**Boucher, François** (booh,shay), 1703–70, French painter. Boucher's art reflected the spirit of his day: elegant, frivolous, and artificial. A prodigy, he was influenced by WATTEAU and became the most fashionable and prolific artist of his day, producing a vast number of pictures, decorations, tapestry designs, stage settings for ballet and opera, and fine etchings. His best-known works are brilliant, voluptuous decorations, e.g., those in the Frick Collection (New York City). FRAGONARD was his pupil.

**Boucher de Crèvecœur de Perthes, Jacques**, 1788–1868, French archaeologist, the first to show that man had existed in the Pleistocene epoch (see GEOLOGIC ERAS, table).

**Boucicault, Dion** (,boohsikoh), 1822–90, Anglo-Irish dramatist and actor. In the US after 1853, he wrote or adapted over 300 comedies and MELODRAMAS (often acting in them), notably *The Octoroon* (1859), *The Colleen Bawn* (1860), and *The Shaughraun* (1874).

**Boudicca**, d. AD 61, British queen of the Iceni (of Norfolk). She led the Iceni in revolt against the Romans and was at first successful, taking Colchester, London, and Verulamium (St Albans). Finally, her army was crushed, and she took poison.

**Boudin, Eugène Louis** (booh,danh), 1824–98, French painter. His small paintings of Normandy beach scenes are noted for their fresh response to light and weather. He painted from nature and greatly influenced MONET. Examples of his work are in the Musée Boudin, Honfleur.

**Bougainville, Louis Antoine de** (boohganh,veel), 1729–1811, French navigator. He was an aide-de-camp to Gen. MONTCALM in Canada. From 1767 to 1769 he made a voyage around the world, rediscovering the SOLOMON ISLANDS, the largest of which is named after him. In the AMERICAN REVOLUTION he fought Adm. Hood at Martinique. His *Description of a Voyage around the World* (2 vol., 1771–72) popularized the theories of ROUSSEAU.

**bougainvillea** or **bougainvillaea**, chiefly tropical plant (genus *Bougainvillaea*) of the family Nyctaginaceae. Bougainvilleas are woody

*Madame de Pompadour* by François **Boucher**

vines with brilliantly-coloured, massed bracts. A very wide range of colours exists as named varieties.

**Boulanger, Georges Ernest** (booh,lahnhzhay), 1837–91, French general and reactionary politician. He served in the FRANCO-PRUSSIAN WAR and was minister of war (1886–87). Envisioning himself as a dictator, he attracted opponents of the Third Republic and was elected (1889) as a parliamentary deputy. A military coup seemed probable, but Boulanger failed to act. Accused of treason, he fled into exile and killed himself.

**Boulanger, Nadia**, 1887–1979, French conductor and musician. She was noted for her teaching of composition, through which she influenced a whole generation of musicians, notably the American Aaron COPLAND. She was also known for her conducting of choral works.

**Boulez, Pierre** (booh,lez), 1925–, French composer and conductor. His works apply the techniques of SERIAL MUSIC not only to melody and COUNTERPOINT but also to RHYTHM and dynamics. They include *Le marteau sans maître* (1953–55), *Pli selon pli* (1962) and *Mémoriales* (1975). From 1969 to 1977 he was music director of the New York Philharmonic. Since the mid 1970s, Boulez has devoted much time to directing his Institut de Recherche et Coordination Acoustique/Musique in Paris. Its aim is to bring musicians and scientists together in developing new musical material.

**Boulle, André-Charles**, 1642–1732, French cabinetmaker. He collaborated with Jean Bérain, the designer, to produce furniture for Louis XIV, as well as for private clients. He specialized in decoration with MARQUETRY of brass, pewter, and tortoiseshell.

**Boulogne**, city (1982 pop. of agglomeration 98,566), a port in Pas-de-Calais dept. on NE coast of France. It is the country's leading fishing port and has cross-Channel ferry links with England. The Romans sailed across the Channel from here in AD 43 to conquer Britain.

Cupboard by André-Charles **Boulle**

**Boult, Sir Adrian,** 1889–1983, English conductor. He conducted the BBC Symphony Orchestra (1930–50) and the London Philharmonic (1950–57). His handbook on the technique of conducting appeared in 1968.

**Boumédienne, Houari** (boohmedee·,en), 1932?–78, president and prime minister of ALGERIA (1965–78). He came to power in a coup that toppled Ahmed BEN BELLA. His government assumed a rigorous anti-Israeli stance.

**Bounty,** British naval ship, scene of a noted mutiny (1789) while on a trading voyage in the Pacific. Capt. BLIGH and 18 crew members were set adrift in a small boat; they sailed 5822 km (3618 mi) to TIMOR. Some of the mutineers were captured; others settled on PITCAIRN ISLAND.

**bouquet garni,** a small bunch of dried HERBS, i.e., parsley, thyme, and a bay leaf, tied up in a piece of muslin. It is used in soups and stews to give flavour, and is removed before serving.

**Bourbaki, Nicolas,** collective pseudonym of a group of French mathematicians who in 1939 began publishing a general survey of mathematics. The writers, whose identities remain secret, have attempted to develop mathematics from a few broad axioms and have divided it into general structural categories, rather than adhering to traditional mathematical classifications. Their work has been highly influential.

**Bourbon,** royal family that ruled in France, Spain, the TWO SICILIES, and Parma; a cadet branch of the CAPETIANS. It takes its name from the now ruined castle of Bourbon in France. In 1272 Robert of Clermont, sixth son of LOUIS IX of France, married the heiress of Bourbon. His son Louis was created (1327) 1st duc de Bourbon. A younger son of the first duke founded the line of Bourbon-Vendôme. His descendant Antoine de Bourbon, 1518–62, duke of Vendôme, became king of Navarre by marrying (1548) Jeanne d'Albret, later queen of NAVARRE. From his brother Louis descend the houses of CONDÉ and Conti. Antoine's son became (1589) the first Bourbon king of France as HENRY IV. His direct descendants ruled France (except from 1792 to 1814) until 1830, when CHARLES X was deposed, and died out in 1883 with Henri, comte de

Chambord. The younger branch of Bourbon-Orléans gave France King LOUIS PHILIPPE. The house of **Bourbon-Spain** began in 1700 when LOUIS XIV's grandson PHILIP V ascended the Spanish throne. The succession in Spain was contested (19th cent.) by the CARLISTS against ISABELLA II. ALFONSO XIII was deposed in 1931, but the monarchy was restored in 1975 with his grandson JUAN CARLOS I. The house of **Bourbon-Sicily,** sprung from the Spanish line, was founded (1759) by Ferdinand I of the Two Sicilies and ceased to rule when Francis II was deposed (1860). The house of **Bourbon-Parma** was founded (1748) in the duchy of Parma by a younger son of Philip V of Spain. Robert, the fifth duke in the line, was deposed in 1859.

**Bourdelle, Émile Antoine,** 1861–1929, French sculptor. He began his career as Rodin's assistant (1893–1908) and Rodin's influence is clear in his bronze studies of *Beethoven*. Later he was more influenced by ancient Greek art. The Musée Bourdelle in Paris has versions of almost all his works.

**bourgeoisie,** name given in Europe to the middle class. Emerging among the merchants and craftsmen of medieval cities, it played a major role in the 16th cent. in hastening the collapse of FEUDALISM, in the 17th cent. in challenging the traditional power of the landed aristocracy, and from the late 18th cent. in spearheading democratic reform. Following the INDUSTRIAL REVOLUTION, the high bourgeoisie (industrialists and bankers) came to be distinguished from the petty bourgeoisie (tradespeople and white-collar workers). In the works of MARX and ENGELS the term is applied to one of the two great classes of CAPITALISM.

**Bourguiba, Habib,** 1903–, president of TUNISIA (1957–87). As leader of Tunisia's nationalist movement after 1934, he was several times imprisoned and forced to leave the country. He became premier when Tunisia achieved independence in 1956. A year later he deposed the bey and assumed the presidency. He himself was deposed on the grounds of his senility.

**Bournemouth,** town (1981 pop. 142,829), Dorset, on S Coast, of England, 39 km (24 mi) SW of Southampton. It is a major holiday resort which benefits from a mild climate; it developed in the 19th cent. from a village as seaside holidays became fashionable. The town has also become an important conference centre and there are many retirement and nursing homes. A range of light industries are carried out.

**Bournonville, Auguste,** 1805–79, Danish dancer and choreographer. After studying with Auguste VESTRIS in Paris, he joined (1828) the Royal Danish Ballet. As a soloist and choreographer of over 50 works, he developed a distinctive romantic style noted for precise technique especially in male dancing.

**bourse:** see STOCK EXCHANGE.

**Bouts, Dierick, Dirk,** or **Thierry,** c.1420–1475, early Flemish painter. He was influenced by the van EYCK brothers. His luminous *Last Supper* altarpiece (1464–68; St Peter's, Louvain, Belgium) shows his sensitive treatment of changing colour and light and reveals a loving care for detail.

**Bouvetøya,** small volcanic island in the Southern Ocean, S of Africa, Norwegian dependency discovered in 1739. Uninhabited and mostly covered with glaciers, it is the remotest island in the world.

**Bovet, Daniel,** 1907–, Italian pharmacologist; b. Switzerland. He was awarded the 1957 Nobel Prize for physiology or medicine for work in developing antihistamines, and CURARE derivatives and other muscle relaxants. He also studied the effects of mental illness on the brain's chemistry.

**Bow Bells,** in the church of St Mary-le-Bow, London, England. Tradition says that only one who is born within their sound is a true Londoner, or Cockney.

**Bowdler, Thomas,** 1754–1825, English editor. His prudish textual expurgations, especially of Shakespeare and the Bible, gave rise to the term *bowdlerize.*

**Bowen, Edward George,** 1911–, British astronomer. After outstanding contributions to the British development of radar during World War II, he became Chief of the Radiophysics division of Australia's Commonwealth Scientific and Industrial Organization and, with Joseph L. PAWSEY, established and fostered Australian radio astronomy to its outstanding position.

**Bowen, Elizabeth,** 1899–1973, Anglo-Irish author; b. Dublin. Her complex psychological novels include *The Hotel* (1927), *The House in Paris* (1935), *The Death of the Heart* (1938), and *The Heat of the Day* (1949). She also wrote short stories and reminiscences.

**Bowie, David,** (David Jones), 1946–, English rock singer, composer and instrumentalist. Since the mid 1960s he has written and performed a body of work rarely if ever surpassed in the rock world for its inventiveness in style (adopting a number of theatrical guises) from 'Space Oddity' (1969) his first big hit, through to 'Ziggy Stardust' and 'Diamond Dogs' in the 1970s and 'Let's Dance' in the 1980s.

**Bowie, James,** c.1796–1836, American adventurer and Texas hero. He was a leader of the Americans in TEXAS who opposed Mexican rule. A colonel in the Texas Revolution (1835–36), he died at the ALAMO. Legend credits him with inventing the bowie knife.

**Bowles, Paul,** 1910–, American author. Originally a composer, he is best known for his fiction. A longtime resident of Morocco, Bowles often records the collision between the civilized and the primitive. Among his many works are the novel *The Sheltering Sky* (1949) and the short-story collection *The Delicate Prey* (1950). His wife, **Jane Auer Bowles,** 1917–73, was also a writer. Her original, idiosyncratic works include *Two Serious Ladies* (1943), a novel, and *In the Summer House* (1954), a play.

**bowling,** indoor sport, also called **tenpins,** in which a ball is rolled at 10 maple pins down an alley of polished wood. A regulation alley is 104.1 to 106.7 cm (41–42 in) wide and 18.3 m (60 ft) from the foul line to the head pin. A ball, usually weighing 7.26 kg (16 lb) and having three finger-holes, is rolled at the pins, set up in a triangular array. Scoring is based on the number of pins knocked down; a perfect game is 300 points. Duck pins, candle pins, and barrel pins are similar games played with much smaller balls and pins. SKITTLES is played with nine pins.

**bowls,** game played on a long flat lawn with spheres of hard wood made so as to run with a bias. The object of the game is to place the bowl as close as possible to a target ball (jack). Bowls may be knocked on or away by other bowls. Points are scored for each bowl placed nearer to the jack than the opponent's nearest bowl. In singles, each player rolls four bowls; in foursomes, the players roll two bowls each. It is said that Sir Francis Drake was playing bowls on Plymouth Hoe when the Spanish Armada was sighted in 1588.

**Bowman, Isaiah,** 1878–1950, American geographer; b. Canada. He taught at Yale (1905–15), was director of the American Geographical Society (1915–35), and was president of Johns Hopkins Univ. (1935–48). He was an adviser to Pres. Wilson at Versailles and an adviser to the Dept of State in World War II. One of the great modern authorities on political geography, he wrote on many subjects, including the Andes, the Atacama desert, and forest physiography.

**box,** common name for the Buxaceae, a family of trees and shrubs with leathery green leaves, native to tropical and subtropical regions. Boxes (genus *Buxus*) are widely cultivated as hedge plants and for their close-grained, strong hardwood. Boxwood takes a high polish and is used for wood engraving, carving, and turning, and for making musical instruments.

**Boxer Uprising,** 1898–1900, antiforeign movement in China. By the late 19th cent. the West and Japan had wide interests in China. The dowager empress TZ'U HSI favoured expelling the foreigners and encouraged an antiforeign society called Yi he quan [Chinese, = righteous, harmonious fists] or, in English, the Boxers. The movement grew menacing in 1899, and in June 1900 some 140,000 Boxers occupied Beijing and besieged Westerners and Chinese Christians there. The siege was lifted in August by an international force of British, French, Russian, US, German, and Japanese troops. In 1901 China was compelled to pay an indemnity of $333 million, to amend commercial treaties in favour of foreign nations, and to allow foreign troops to be posted in Beijing.

**boxing,** sport of fighting with fists, also called pugilism and prizefighting. Boxers compete in a roped-off area, or ring, 6.1 m (20 ft) square, and fight for a prescribed number of 3-min rounds, separated by 1-min rest periods. Bouts may be decided by a knockout, when a floored contestant is unable to rise within 10 sec, or by the decision of the officials. Professional boxers are divided into eight weight classes, ranging from flyweight (under 50.81 kg/112 lb) to heavyweight (over 79.38 kg/175 lb). Modern boxing began with the code of rules introduced (1865) by the marquess of QUEENSBERRY, which called for the use of gloves. Boxing has been an Olympic sport since 1904.

**boyars,** upper nobility in Russia from the 10th to the 17th cent. They occupied the highest state offices, advising the princes of Kiev through a council. Although they retained their influence after power shifted (14th–15th cent.) to Moscow, it was gradually eroded; PETER I abolished the rank.

**Boyce, William,** c.1710–1779, English composer. The major English-born composer of his day, he wrote symphonies, stage works, and much vocal music. His *Cathedral Music* (3 vol., 1760, 1768, 1773) is a compilation of English church music.

**boycott,** usually, concerted economic ostracism exercised by one group against another. The term was coined in 1880 when Captain Charles Boycott, a ruthless English land agent in Ireland, was ostracized by his victims. The most common form of boycott is for individuals or groups to refuse to purchase, handle, or consume the products of a company or nation which is offensive to them on political or moral grounds. After World War II it was common for citizens of European nations which had been occupied by the Germans to refuse to purchase German cars and other goods. More recently, there have been repeated calls from those opposed to APARTHEID to boycott South African exports.

**Boyd, Arthur Merric Bloomfield,** 1920–, Australian artist. He received little formal training, but learnt much from other members of his family (including William Merric Boyd and Theodore Penleigh Boyd). In the 1940s he was a member of the Angry Penguins artists' group which also included Sidney NOLAN, Albert Tucker, and John Perceval. His painting was figurative, recasting biblical themes in order to constitute an aggressive social realism. Like Nolan, Boyd settled in Britain during the 1960s. His recent work is more introspective, combining mythological imagery and views of the Australian landscape.

**Boyd, Louise Arner,** 1887–1972, American Arctic explorer. She led a series of scientific explorations on the east coast of GREENLAND (1933–41). In 1955 she became the first woman to fly over the NORTH POLE.

**Boyd Orr, Sir John,** 1880–1971, Scottish nutritionist and agronomist. He made notable contributions to the science of nutrition and to the solution of world food problems, winning the 1949 Nobel Peace Prize for advocating a world food policy based on need rather than trade interests. He was director-general (1946–47) of the UN Food and Agriculture Organization.

**Boyle, Robert,** 1627–91, Anglo-Irish physicist and chemist. Often referred to as the father of modern chemistry, he separated chemistry from alchemy and gave the first precise definitions of a chemical element, a chemical reaction, and chemical analysis. He invented a vacuum pump and used it in the discovery (1662) of what is known as Boyle's law (see GAS LAWS). His diverse experimental and theoretical work supplemented Sir Isaac NEWTON's achievements in establishing the dominance of mechanistic theory.

**Boyle's law:** see GAS LAWS.

**Boyne, Battle of the,** Irish battle (1690) in which WILLIAM III defeated JAMES II. William's victory resulted in his conquest of Ireland.

**Boys' Brigade,** a voluntary organization for boys, founded in Glasgow in 1883, which, using military-style uniform and drill, seeks to inculcate Christian principles and moral discipline. It has branches in the Commonwealth and US as well as Britain. The companies are usually attached to local churches.

**Boy Scouts,** organization of boys from 7 to 18–20 years of age, founded (1908) in Great Britain by Sir Robert BADEN-POWELL. The founding document of the movement was Baden-Powell's *Scouting for Boys* (1908). He became World Chief Scout in 1920. Activities of the Boy Scouts aim at mental, moral, and physical development, stressing outdoor skills and training in citizenship and life-saving. The basic Scout unit is a troop of about 15 boys, under the leadership of a volunteer adult scoutmaster; the unit for work is a 'patrol' of 6–8 boys. A junior section of 'Cubs' is for boys of about 8–10 years, and 'Venture Scouts' are for 16–20-year-olds. There are now more than 16 million Scouts and leaders in 119 national Scout organizations in more than 150 countries and territories. See also GIRL GUIDES.

**Bozeman Trail**, a shortcut through Indian lands from the East to the goldfields of Colorado and Montana, made by John M. Bozeman in 1862–63. The trail was used by a few parties, but after the Fetterman Massacre (1866) it was abandoned.

**BP**, (Before the Present), term used in archaeology, palaeontology, etc, to express dates. It replaces BC for dates before about 10,000 years ago. See also DATING.

**Br**, chemical symbol of the element BROMINE.

**Brabazon, John Theodore Cuthbert Moore-Brabazon** (1st Baron Brabazon of Tara), 1884–1964, British aviator and politician. Through his friendship with Charles ROLLS he became interested in flying, and became the first Englishman to make a sustained and controlled powered flight (2 May 1909). Moore-Brabazon gave up flying on the death of his friend Rolls, but continued to be associated with aviation; in World War I he developed (1915) the first air cameras. After the war he became an MP and was Minister of Transport (1940–41) and of Aircraft Production (1941–42). He was made baron in 1942. He chaired the two Brabazon Committees (1943, 1943–45) which drew up the guidelines for the postwar development of British civil transport aircraft. He was president of the ROYAL AERONAUTICAL SOCIETY (1935) and of the ROYAL INSTITUTION (1948–63).

**Bracciolini, Poggio**, 1380–1459, Italian humanist. Chancellor and historiographer of the republic of Florence, he rediscovered many classical works, e.g., LUCRETIUS' *On the Nature of Things*. His *Facetiae* (1438–52) is a collection of earthy fables and anticlerical satires.

**Brachychiton**, genus of colourful Australian flowering trees with clusters of bell-shaped flowers produced in late spring. The flowers are from white to flame-red and deep rose-colour.

**brackets:** see PUNCTUATION.

**Bracton, Henry de**, d. 1268, English writer on law. Originally an ecclesiastic, he probably learnt his law as a royal clerk, and later became a judge (1248–1257). His *On the Laws and Customs of England* is often considered the most important English legal treatise before that of BLACKSTONE, and shows the influence of ROMAN LAW. A previously unknown manuscript of his notes on English cases was found in the British Museum and published in 1877 as *Bracton's Notebooks*. Though unfinished, it is probably the first systematic statement of English law.

**Braddock, Edward**, 1695–1755, British general in the FRENCH AND INDIAN WARS. While on an expedition (1755) to take Fort Duquesne from the French, he was set upon by a force of some 900 French and Indians at the Monongahela R. Many of his men bolted; more than half were killed, and he was mortally wounded.

**Bradford**, city (1981 pop. 293,336), West Yorkshire, N central England. A centre of the worsted industry since the Middle Ages, Bradford now also produces synthetic fabrics, machinery, motor vehicles, and other manufactures. It is the birthplace of Frederick DELIUS.

**Bradford, William**, 1590–1657, governor of PLYMOUTH COLONY; b. England. He succeeded John CARVER as governor in 1621 and remained governor for most of his life, being reelected 30 times. He was largely responsible for the success of the colony. His famous *History of Plymouth Plantation* was not published until nearly 200 years after his death.

**Bradley, Francis Herbert**, 1846–1924, English philosopher. His metaphysics was influenced by HEGEL. In *Appearance and Reality* (1893) he held that IDEALISM, in which the world of appearance is characterized by apparent contradictions, is opposed to the absolute, in which all contradictions are transcended.

**Bradley, James**, 1693–1762, English astronomer. He discovered the ABERRATION OF STARLIGHT (announced in 1729) and the NUTATION, or 'nodding', of the Earth's axis (announced in 1748). Bradley became Astronomer Royal and director of the Royal Greenwich Observatory in 1742.

**Bradley, Omar Nelson**, 1893–1981, US general. During WORLD WAR II, he led the US 1st Army in the invasion of Normandy (1944). He was chairman (1949–53) of the Joint Chiefs of Staff and became general of the army in 1950.

**Bradman, Sir Donald George**, 1908–, Australian cricketer. He was cricket's most successful batsman and, with Dr W.G. GRACE, the most influential figure the modern game has known. He played for New South Wales 1927–34, for South Australia 1935–49, and for Australia 1928–48 (capt. 1936–48). His batting average for all first-class games was 95.14, and his Test match average 99.64. He made 117 first-class centuries, including one innings of 452 not out. After he was knighted in 1949 he served as chairman of the Australian Cricket Board for three years. In 1981 he was made a Companion of the Order of Australia.

**Bradstreet, Anne (Dudley)**, c.1612–72, American poet; b. Northampton, England; went to Massachusetts with her father and husband, both later governors of the colony. The first important woman author in America, she is known for poems that, while derivative and formal, are often realistic and genuine. Her volumes of verse include *The Tenth Muse Lately Sprung Up in America* (1650) and *Several Poems* (1678).

**Braemar**, village in Grampian region, Scotland, on Clunie Water, near its confluence with R. DEE. It is an important tourist centre, most famous for the Highland Games which are held in September. Braemar Castle dates from the 17th cent.

**Braga, Teófilo**, 1843–1924, Portuguese intellectual and political leader. His teachings and writings, e.g., his general history of Portuguese literature (10 vol., 1870–71), exerted a great influence on Portuguese intellectual life. A republican and anticlericalist, he was the first president of the new republic of Portugal (1910–11; 1915).

**Braganza**, royal house that ruled PORTUGAL (1640–1910) and BRAZIL (1822–89). The line was descended from Alfonso, the natural son of JOHN I, and its first king was JOHN IV. The family's Brazilian rulers were PEDRO I and his son, PEDRO II.

**Bragg, Sir William Henry**, 1862–1942, English physicist. He was on the faculties of the Univ. of Adelaide, Australia, the Univ. of Leeds and the Univ. of London, and director from 1923 of the ROYAL INSTITUTION's research laboratory. With his son, **Sir William Lawrence Bragg**, 1890–1971, he shared the 1915 Nobel Prize for physics for studies, with the X-ray spectrometer, of X-ray spectra and of crystal structure. The younger Bragg was professor of physics at Victoria Univ. (Manchester) and Cambridge, and was director (1938–53) of the Cavendish Laboratory, Cambridge.

**Brahe, Tycho** (brah), 1546–1601, Danish astronomer. His exact observations (before the invention of the telescope) of the planets were the basis for KEPLER'S LAWS of planetary motion. Studies of the Moon's motion and of a supernova (1572) and improvements of instruments were among his contributions. Brahe never fully accepted the COPERNICAN SYSTEM, compromising between that and the PTOLEMAIC SYSTEM. In his system, the Earth was the immobile body around which the Sun revolved, and the five planets then known revolved around the Sun.

**Brahmā**, one of the supreme gods of HINDUISM; in the Hindu trinity he is the creator (see also ŚIVA; VIṢṆU).

**Brahman** or **Brahma**, in the UPANIṢADS, the ultimate reality or the universal Soul. In VEDĀNTA, it is the Self from which the world has come into being. It is also said to be identical with the individual soul or *ātman*. See HINDUISM.

**Brāhmaṇa** or **Brahmin**. 1 Member of the highest, or priestly, caste of the Hindus; see HINDUISM. 2 The prose section of the Vedic scriptures. See also MANTRA.

**Brahmaputra**, major river of S Asia, flowing c.2900 km (1800 mi) from the Kailas range of the Himalayas to join the GANGES (Ganga) R. at a vast delta on the Bay of Bengal. It is called Yarlung Zangbo in Tibet (where it is the principal river valley), the Brahmaputra in Assam (NE India), and the Jamuna (Jumna) in Bangladesh. The river's lower course is sacred to Hindus. Large craft navigate the river nearly 1300 km (800 mi) upstream.

**Brahms, Johannes** 1833–97, German composer. He earned a living in Vienna as a moderately successful composer, incorporating the romantic impulse with classical spirit. His conservative style sparked controversy between his supporters (among them his close friends Robert and Clara SCHUMANN) and those of the dramatic romantic style of LISZT and Richard WAGNER. His four SYMPHONIES are considered among the greatest in symphonic music. Other well-known works are the *German Requiem* (1866), the Violin Concerto in D (1878), The Double Concerto for Violin and Cello (1887), and the Piano Concertos in D minor (1854–58) and in B Flat (1878–81). He composed in almost every genre except opera, devoting special attention to chamber music and song. His LIEDER are worldwide favourites.

**Brahui,** Dravidian language of Baluchistan. See LANGUAGE (table).

**Brăila** (ˌbrielə), city (1983 pop. 214,561), Walachia, SE Romania, on the lower Danube R. It handles grain, builds river vessels, and utilizes reeds from the delta to manufacture cellulose. The city was laid out to a formal plan in the 19th cent.

**Braille, Louis,** 1809?–1852, French inventor of the Braille system of printing and writing for the blind. Blind from an accident at age 3, he attended and later taught at the Institution des Jeunes Aveugles, Paris. He evolved a system of writing with points based on Charles Barbier's method, though much simpler. The **Braille system** consists of six raised points used in 63 possible combinations; it is in use, in modified form, for printing, writing, and musical notation.

**brain,** supervisory centre of the NERVOUS SYSTEM in all vertebrates. The brain controls both conscious behaviour (e.g., walking and thinking) and most involuntary behaviour (e.g., heartbeat and breathing). In higher animals, it is also the site of emotions, memory, self-awareness, and thought. It functions by receiving information via nerve cells (neurones) from every part of the body, evaluating the data, and then sending directives to muscles and glands or simply storing the information. Information, in the form of electrical and chemical signals, moves through complex brain circuits, which are networks of the billions of nerve cells in the nervous system. A single neuron may receive information from as many as 1000 other neurons. Anatomically, the brain occupies the skull cavity (cranium), floating in cerebrospinal fluid, and is enveloped by three protective membranes (meninges). The adult brain weighs about 1400 g (50 oz) and constitutes approximately 2% of total body weight. It has several parts, each with a loosely associated function. The brainstem (hindbrain), monitoring involuntary activity (e.g., breathing), and the cerebellum, coordinating muscular movements and posture, are together the basic machinery for survival and reproduction. The forebrain, composed of the limbic system and cerebral cortex, regulates higher functions. The limbic system (including the thalamus, hypothalamus, pituitary, amygdala and hippocampus, and olfactory lobe) is associated with vivid emotions, memory, sexuality, and smell. The forebrain's cerebral cortex, in the uppermost portion of the skull, has some areas concerned with muscle control and the senses and others concerned with language and anticipation of action. The cerebral cortex is split into two hemispheres, each controlling the side of the body opposite to it. In addition, the right hemisphere is associated with perception of melody, nonverbal visual patterns, and emotion, while the left hemisphere is associated with verbal skills. Brain function is monitored by ELECTROENCEPHALOGRAPHY.

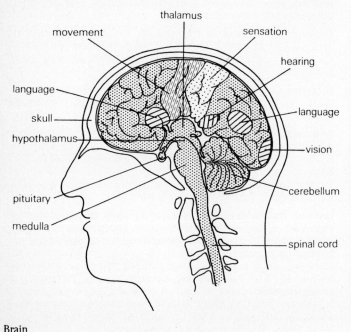

Brain

**Brain Trust,** an academic group of close advisers to Franklin Delano ROOSEVELT as N.Y. governor and as U.S. president. His advisers on the NEW DEAL included Columbia professors Raymond Moley, Adolf A. Berle, Jr., and Rexford G. Tugwell.

**Braithwaite, (Lawson) Edward Kamau,** 1930–, Barbadian poet–historian and cultural critic of the 'Black Diaspora'. His sophisticated imagination is especially evident in *Rites of Passage* (1967) and *The Arrivants* (1973). His critical writings include *The Folk Culture of the Slaves of Jamaica* (1970) and *Contrary Omens: Cultural Diversity and Integration in the Caribbean* (1974).

**brake,** device used to slow or stop the motion of a mechanism or vehicle. Friction brakes, the most common kind, operate on the principle that friction can be used to convert the mechanical energy of a moving object into heat energy, which is absorbed by the brake. Friction brakes consist of a rotating part such as a wheel, axle, disc, or brake drum and a stationary part that is pressed against the rotating part to slow it or stop it. The stationary part usually has a lining, called a brake lining, that can generate a great amount of friction yet give long wear. The simplest brake form is the single-block brake, a wooden block shaped to fit against the rim of a wheel or drum. In disc brakes, two blocks press against either side of a disc that rotates with the wheel. Drum brakes have two semicircular brake shoes inside a rotating brake drum; when actuated, they press against the inner wall of the drum. Motor vehicles use hydraulic pressure to power disc and drum brakes. Additional braking pressure may be supplied by a 'power' brake, which utilizes the vacuum created within the running engine to hold a brake shoe away from a drum. The air brake, invented (1868) by George WESTINGHOUSE, uses compressed air to power block brakes on trains.

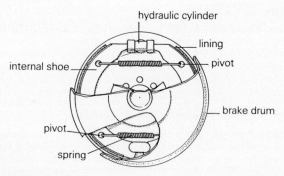

Drum **brake**

**Bramante, Donato,** 1444–1514, Italian architect and painter. His buildings in Rome are considered the most characteristic examples of High Renaissance style. He favoured plans based round a central space and a sense of noble severity. He designed much of Santa Maria presso San Satiro, Milan, painting its choir in perspective to give the illusion of depth. From 1499 he was in Rome, where his works include the Tempietto in the courtyard of San Pietro in Montorio; the BELVEDERE courtyard at the Vatican; and the original central plan for St Peter's.

**bramble,** plants (genus *Rubus*) of the ROSE family, with representatives worldwide. Members include the blackberries, raspberries, loganberries, boysenberries, and dewberries. The plants are typically shrubs with prickly stems (canes) and edible fruits that botanically are not berries but aggregates of drupelets (see FRUIT). The underground parts of brambles are perennial and the canes biennial; only second-year canes bear flowers and fruits. Berries are grown commercially for sale as fresh, frozen, and canned fruit, and for use in preserves, beverages, and liqueurs. Other thorny shrubs are also called brambles.

**bran,** outer coat of cereal GRAINS such as wheat, rye, and maize. Various brans are used as food and livestock feed, and are important in dyeing and calico printing. Nutritionally, bran is an important source of DIETARY FIBRE.

**Brancusi, Constantin,** 1876–1957, Romanian sculptor. He went to Paris in 1904 and after an initial influence of RODIN turned to more simple abstract and organic forms, e.g., *Maiastra* (1910–12). He was also interested in direct carving, i.e., not using studio craftsmen to carry out his designs, as well as primitive sculpture, which influenced works like *Caryatid* (1915).

*The Tempietto*, San Pietro in Montorio, by Donato **Bramante**

**Brandeis, Louis Dembitz** (bran͵dies), 1856–1941, associate justice of the US Supreme Court (1916–39). As a US attorney, he revolutionized legal practice by introducing sociological and economic facts, (the 'Brandeis Brief'), into his arguments before the Supreme Court, in *Muller v. Oregon* (1908). Later as a Supreme Court Justice he gained a reputation for liberalism and after 1933 he was one of the few justices to uphold the NEW DEAL legislation. The UK courts have never accepted the 'Brandeis Brief', and will only hear legal argument.

**Brandenburg**, province of central East Germany. POTSDAM was the capital. A Slavic principality, it was acquired (12th cent.) by the German margrave Albert the Bear and was later ruled by electors of the HOLY ROMAN EMPIRE. In 1417 it passed to the HOHENZOLLERN family, who added (1618) the duchy of Prussia (later EAST PRUSSIA) to their holdings. The later history of Brandenburg is that of PRUSSIA.

**Brandes, Georg Morris Cohen**, 1842–1927, Danish literary critic. He exposed Scandinavia to contemporary European thought. A disciple of TAINE and an opponent of ROMANTICISM, he helped direct Scandinavian literature toward REALISM and social consciousness. A major work is *Main Currents in Nineteenth-Century Literature* (6 vol., 1872–90).

**Brando, Marlon**, 1924–, American film actor. He is noted for the method-inspired naturalism of his acting. His films include *A Streetcar Named Desire* (1952), *On the Waterfront* (1954; Academy Award), *The Godfather* (1972; Academy Award), and *Apocalypse Now* (1979).

**Brandt, Bill (William)**, 1904–83, British photographer. After spending his youth in Europe, including a period of study under Man RAY, he settled in England. He made his name during the 1930s and in World War II (as an official photographer) for his documentary studies of contrasts between rich and poor and of the Blitz. After the war he concentrated on portraits and landscapes in black-and-white, with strongly contrasting tones to create a monumental style.

**Brandt, Willy**, 1913–, German political leader; b. Herbert Ernst Karl Frahm. A Social Democrat, he opposed HITLER and fled (1933) to Norway. Returning after World War II, he was elected mayor of West Berlin (1957). He became chancellor of WEST GERMANY in 1969 and instituted peace talks with E European countries, including East Germany. He was awarded the 1971 Nobel Peace Prize. Brandt resigned as chancellor in 1974 after an East German spy was discovered within his administration, but remained chairman of his party until 1987. In 1976 he was elected president of the Socialist International (see SECOND INTERNATIONAL) and subsequently chaired the 'North–South Commission' on international development issues (1977–83).

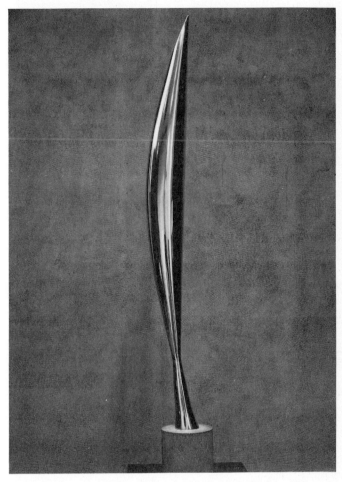

Constantin **Brancusi**, *Bird in Space*, c.1928. Bronze, 137.2 cm high. Museum of Modern Art, New York.

**brandy**, strong alcoholic spirit distilled from wine. Manufactured in many countries, brandy is most notable in the form of cognac, made from white grapes in the Charente district of France. Most fine brandies are distilled in pot stills, blended and flavoured, and stored in casks (preferably oak) to mellow. Brandies are also made from fruits other than the grape, such as plum (slivovitz) or peach.

**Brant, Joseph (Thayendanegea)**, 1742–1807, influential Mohawk (see IROQUOIS CONFEDERACY) chief who bound Indians to the British side in the AMERICAN REVOLUTION. He fought at Oriskany (1777) in the Saratoga campaign and joined Walter Butler in the Cherry Valley Massacre (1778). An educated man and a Christian, Brant translated the BOOK OF COMMON PRAYER and the Gospel of MARK into Mohawk.

**Braque, Georges**, 1882–1963, French painter. A member of the Fauve group (see FAUVISM), he later met PICASSO (1907), and the two explored form and structure, primarily in landscape and still-life compositions. These were derived from an analysis of the work of CÉZANNE. Braque and Picasso worked in near isolation between 1909–14, developing CUBISM. Braque introduced the use of a stencil type of lettering into analytical Cubist works in 1911 and the use of glued-on paper, *papier collé*, in 1912. Braque's interest, like Picasso's, was to use radical techniques in his work, but also always to maintain links with reality by the use of *signifiers* [clues], often items taken from mass culture. After World War I Braque continued to work in a synthetic Cubist idiom which he loosened and developed in his later works from the 1920s onwards.

Georges **Braque**, *The Round Table*, 1929. Oil on canvas. Phillips Collection, Washington.

West End Shelter by Bill **Brandt**

**Brasília,** city and federal district (1980 pop. 1,176,908), E central Brazil, capital of Brazil. One of the world's newest cities, it was laid out (1957) in the shape of an aeroplane by the Brazilian architect Lúcio Costa and replaced RIO DE JANEIRO as capital in 1960. The sparsely settled region is dominated by ultramodern public buildings designed by Oscar NIEMEYER. Extensive residential developments were built in the 1960s, and highways linking Brasília with the major cities of southern and central Brazil were completed in 1982.

**Braşov** (brah‚shov), city (1985 est. pop. 346,640), central Romania, in Transylvania, at the foot of Transylvanian Alps (Carpathian chain). It is an industrial centre known for tractors and textiles, and a winter-sports centre. Founded in the 13th cent. by Saxon settlers, it was an important commercial and cultural centre of Transylvania. Its 'Black Church' dates from the 14th cent.

**brass,** ALLOY having copper (55% to 90%) and zinc (10% to 45%) as its essential components. Its properties vary with the proportion of copper and zinc and with the addition of small amounts of other elements. Cartridge brass is used for cartridge cases, plumbing and lighting fixtures, rivets, screws, and springs. Aluminium brass has greater resistance to corrosion than ordinary brass. Brass containing tin (naval brass) resists seawater corrosion. Brass can be forged or hammered into various shapes, rolled into thin sheets, drawn into wires, and machined and cast. See also SOLDER.

**brass band,** musical groups formed, in contrast to MILITARY BANDS (which contained almost as many woodwind) with the development of valved brass instruments. The *Posaunenchor* had been, and still is, used in Germany for the performance of religious music and especially chorales, and bands have also been popular in Switzerland and France (where they are called *fanfare*), and during the latter half of the 19th cent. in the US. Brass bands became a national institution in the UK, especially as a focus of activity in the factories that sponsored them or in working men's clubs, quite soon after the founding of the Stalybridge Old Band in Lancashire in

1814. Bands usually used the CORNET, saxhorn, TROMBONE, TUBA and various PERCUSSION INSTRUMENTS. National contests were established in 1853, and by 1900 there were over 20,000 bands in the country. Brass bands have also been part of the life of the Salvation Army since 1878. Elgar wrote a suite for brass band, the *Severn Suite* (1930), but later composers have neglected this medium.

**brasses, monumental** or **sepulchral,** memorials to the dead, in use in European churches in the 13th cent. and for several centuries thereafter. Engraved with a figure of the deceased, they are usually set in the pavement. Those that still exist are of native design and show costumes and genealogy of the time.

**brass instruments,** a group of musical instruments made of metal whose sound is produced by a vibrating column of air activated by the player's lips. The mouthpiece may be either funnel-shaped (e.g., FRENCH HORN) or cup-shaped (most other brass) and the bore is either cylindrical (TROMBONE, TRUMPET) or conical (CORNET). Used in the ORCHESTRA to give a brilliant and not always aggressive sound, brass is the mainstay of the MILITARY BAND and BRASS BAND, and is also widely used in JAZZ.

**Brătianu, Ion** (‚bratsee'ahnooh), 1864–1927, a member of the founding family of the Romanian National Liberal Party of which he was president (1909–27). Prime minister on several occasions (1914–18, 1918–19, 1922–26, 1927), Brătianu identified Romania's interests with those of France and Britain. He took his country into World War I on the Entente side in 1916 and led the Romanian delegation to the Paris Peace Conference (1919–20) from which Romania emerged with TRANSYLVANIA, BESSARABIA, BUKOVINA, and Dobrogea.

**Bratislava,** Ger. *Pressburg,* Hung. *Pozsony,* city (1984 pop. 401,000), S Czechoslovakia, on the Danube R. near the Austrian and Hungarian borders. The second largest Czechoslovak city and the traditional capital of SLOVAKIA, it is a major Danubian port, with industries such as mechanical engineering and oil refining. A Roman outpost by the 1st cent. AD, it was later ruled (9th cent.) by MORAVIA. From 1541 to 1784 it

The Black Church, **Braşov**

was the capital of Hungary. It became part of Czechoslovakia in 1918. Landmarks include several 13th-cent. buildings, e.g., St Martin's Cathedral.

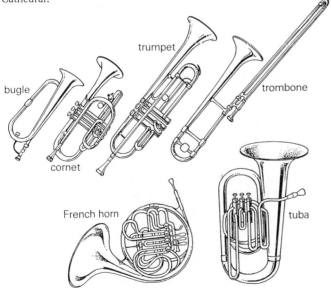

Brass instruments

**Braudel, Fernand Paul,** 1902–, French historian. He taught history in Algiers and Brazil as well as in France before establishing his reputation as

a 'total historian' in the ANNALES tradition with his *The Mediterranean and the Mediterranean World in the Age of Philip II* (1949; tr. 1972–73). He was a professor at the Collège de France (1949–72), and was greatly admired abroad for his studies of the origins and early history of 'material civilization' and capitalism.

**Braun, Eva,** 1912–45, mistress and later wife of German dictator Adolf HITLER. She entered Hitler's household in 1936, but they were married just a few days before their double suicide. She had no influence on the Nazi government.

**Brauwer, Adriaen:** see BROUWER, ADRIAEN.

**Brazil,** Port. *Brasil,* officially Federative Republic of Brazil, republic (1983 est. pop. 129,662,000), 8,511,965 km² (3,286,470 sq mi), E South America, bordered by Venezuela, Guyana, Suriname, and French Guiana (N); Colombia, Peru, and Bolivia (W); Paraguay, Argentina, and Uruguay (SW); and the Atlantic Ocean (E). It is a federation of 24 states, two territories, and the federal district of Brasília. The capital is BRASÍLIA, and principal cities include SÃO PAULO, RIO DE JANEIRO, RECIFE, BELO HORIZONTE, and SALVADOR. The largest South American country, Brazil occupies nearly half the continent and has a greatly varied topography and climate, ranging from tropical in the rainforests of the great AMAZON basin in the north to temperate in the highlands of the heavily populated E and S, which make up two-thirds of the country's land and contain its chief economic centres. Despite rapid industrialization beginning in the 1960s, Brazil still depends heavily on agriculture, which accounts for nearly 50% of its exports. It is an important cattle producer; major commercial crops are coffee (of which it is the world's leading producer), cocoa, cotton, sugarcane, citrus fruit, maize, tobacco, bananas, and soya beans. Expanding industrial production is led by motor vehicles (Brazil ranks fifth in world production), steel, cotton textiles, paper, fertilizer, cement, and machinery. The country's vast mineral wealth includes some of the iron resources in the world, as well as coal, manganese, chromium, industrial diamonds, uranium, and platinum. Only 15% of its petroleum needs are produced domestically, but hydroelectric and nuclear power are being developed. In 1985 GDP was US$234,300 million or US$1748 per capita. The population is diverse in origin, and Brazil boasts that the new 'race' of Brazilians is a successful amalgam of Indian, black, and European strains. About 200,000 Indians of several tribes live in the Amazon basin. Portuguese is the official language and Roman Catholicism the predominant religion.

*History.* Although the Spaniard Vicente Yáñez Pinzón (see under PINZÓN, M.A.) and possibly others visited the coast earlier, the Portuguese, under Pedro Alvares CABRAL, claimed the land in 1500. The first permanent settlement, at São Vicente in present-day São Paulo, was not made until 1532; development of the region now known as the Northeast began at the same time. Portuguese claims did not go unchallenged: French HUGUENOTS had to be expelled from a base in Rio de Janeiro harbour in 1567, and the Dutch held the Northeast for almost 20 years before they were driven out in 1654. When NAPOLEON invaded Portugal, Portugal's king, JOHN VI, fled (1807) to Brazil, and on his arrival (1808) in Rio de Janeiro that city became the capital of the Portuguese empire. In 1821 John returned to Portugal, leaving behind as regent his son, who in 1822 declared Brazil independent and himself Emperor PEDRO I. Forced by his restrictive policies to abdicate, he was succeeded by his son, the popular PEDRO II, whose long reign (1831–89) saw the development of Brazil as a modern nation. Wars with Argentina (1851–52) and Paraguay (1865–70) brought little benefit to Brazil, however. The abolition of slavery (1888) helped bring on a bloodless revolution that established Brazil as a republic in 1889. Large-scale European immigration, an expanding coffee market, and a wild-rubber boom brought wealth to Brazil in the late 19th and early 20th cent. Later, under the presidency of Getúlio VARGAS (1930–45, 1950–54), who came to power in a revolution (1930), stress was laid on industrial expansion and diversification of agriculture. Brazil joined the Allies in World War II (as it had in World War I), enjoying a new boom (chiefly in rubber and minerals). To spur development of the interior, Juscelino KUBITSCHEK, elected president in 1955, undertook the building of the planned city of Brasília, which replaced Rio de Janeiro as the national capital in 1960; he also inaugurated an ambitious programme of highway and dam construction. Political strife and economic chaos led to a coup in 1964 and the installation of a rightist military regime, which, headed by a succession of generals who served as presidents, ruled into the 1980s. A move toward democratization began in the late 1970s, and free nationwide elections, the first in 17 years, were held in 1982. Indirect elections in 1985 resulted in the return of the opposition candidate, Tancredo de Almeida Neves, as the first civilian president since 1964; however, he fell terminally ill on his inauguration day, so that José Sarney (elected as vice president) became president. Congressional gubernatorial elections in 1986 were won overwhelmingly by the Party of the Brazilian Democratic Movement.

## Post-war Brazilian presidents
Eurico Gaspar Dutra (Social Democrat), 1946–50
Getulio Vargas (Labour), 1950–54
Joâo Café Filho (Social Progressive), 1954–55
Juscelino Kubitschek (Social Democrat), 1956–61
Janio Quadros (centre-left), 1961
João Goulart (Labour), 1961–64
Humberto Castelo Branco (military), 1964–67
Artur da Costa e Silva (military), 1967–69
Emilio Garrastazú Médici (military), 1969–74
Ernesto Geisel (military), 1974–79
João Baptista Oliveira Figueiredo (military), 1979–85
José Sarney (Liberal), 1985–

Brazil

**Brazil nut,** common name for the Lecythidaceae, a family of tropical trees. Members include the West Indian anchovy pear (*Grias cauliflora*); several lumber trees of South America, e.g., the cannonball; and the Brazil nut trees (genus *Bertholletia*). Brazil nut trees are found chiefly along the Amazon and Orinoco rivers. The edible nuts are oil-rich seeds that grow clumped together in hard, grapefruit-sized, woody seed pods.

**Brazzaville,** city (1983 pop. 456,383), capital of the People's Republic of the Congo. The country's largest city, and an important port on the Zaïre R., it receives wood, rubber, and agricultural products from the region and ships them by rail to POINTE-NOIRE on the Atlantic Ocean. Motorboats connect Brazzaville with KINSHASA, Zaïre, across Pool Malebo (Stanley Pool). The city was founded (1880) by Savorgnan de Brazza as a base for French territorial claims in the area. It was the capital of FRENCH EQUATORIAL AFRICA from 1910 to 1958. A meeting there in 1944 began the process of independence for France's African colonies.

**bread,** an ancient and universal staple food made from WHEAT or RYE flour. Bread was first made from flour ground by hand in a quern, then between stones turned by a wind or watermill (hence the term 'stoneground'). Nowadays nearly all flour is produced by commercial roller milling and

the extraction rate of the flour from the grain determines the type of loaf; wholemeal 95–100%, wheatmeal or brown 85%, white bread with all the bran and wheatgerm removed. In 1962 the Chorleywood bread process was introduced and replaced the slow method of FERMENTATION and kneading with a method involving fast, hard mixing, an oxidizing agent, and increased YEAST content. This quick method uses a cheaper, weaker flour and a softer loaf is produced which stales more slowly. 11 million large loaves are sold in the UK each day, 80% of which are made by this process. The use of different flours such as rye and maize and various different added ingredients, methods of making, and baking mean that there are a very large number of different sorts of bread such as: bagel, croissant, brioche, pitta, chapati, sour dough, and soda bread. Bread contributes PROTEIN, CARBOHYDRATE, DIETARY FIBRE, and VITAMIN B to the DIET.

**breadfruit,** East Indian tree (*Artocarpus altilis*) of the MULBERRY family, producing a large fruit of high nutritional value.

**Breakspear, Nicholas:** SEE ADRIAN IV.

**Bream, Julian,** 1933–, British guitarist and lutenist. He made his London debut in 1950 and played a major role in editing and reviving works for lute and in promoting contemporary English compositions for guitar. He has made numerous recordings and performed at concerts and festivals in many parts of the world.

**breast:** SEE MAMMARY GLAND.

**breast feeding,** nourishing a baby from its mother's (or another woman's) breast. It has several advantages over feeding a baby on a formula milk. In the first few days after birth the breasts produce colostrum which gives the baby important antibodies as well as nourishment; breast-fed babies are unlikely to grow fat or to get gastroenteritis. It appears to be a feature of advanced societies that mothers find prestige in not breastfeeding their own infants. Where once a wet-nurse would have been found, the modern practice is to use a specially-prepared formula milk. This has had disastrous effects when promoted by unscrupulous food manufacturers in the Third World, where mothers do not have adequate facilities for preparing the milk hygienically. The World Health Organization has attempted to control this process by restrictions on advertising, but in a notable case the manufacturer Nestlé was subject to strenuous campaigning by religious, union, and consumer organizations for five years (1977–82) before they would abandon their promotions of formula milk in the Third World. In 1988 manufacturers decided to desist from including formula milk in the pack of free products given to new mothers in hospital.

**breathalyser,** a device used by POLICE to test the amount of alcohol in the blood of vehicle drivers. It works on the principle that a certain amount of air (breath) passing through a chemical solution will change colour in proportion to the amount of alcohol in the breath. In Britain, a breathalyser test can only be given to a driver either suspected of having a high blood-alcohol level, or after having committed a traffic offence. Other countries have introduced random breath testing, which has a greater effect in reducing the number of accidents.

**Brébeuf, Jean de, Saint** (bray,buhf), 1593–1649, French Roman Catholic missionary, one of the JESUIT Martyrs of North America. A missionary to the HURON INDIANS, Brébeuf with his colleague Gabriel Lalemant was killed by the Iroquois. Feast: 19 Oct. (worldwide since 1969).

**Brecht, Bertolt,** 1898–1956, German dramatist and poet. After Expressionist beginnings with *Baal* (1918), Brecht early developed a cooler demonstrative style, as in his adaptation from MARLOWE, *Edward II* (1924) and *Mann ist Mann* (1926; tr. Man Equals Man), which he developed into his distinctive 'epic', or 'non-Aristotelian', theatre, working out experimental didactic techniques aimed at relativizing the events represented and inducing in actors and audience an attitude of critical freedom. 'Change the world, it needs it', is his sole aesthetic and political dogma. In this respect, he has been the most transforming single influence in the modern theatre, though by now what was innovation has turned into orthodoxy. His highly successful operatic collaborations with Kurt WEILL include *Die Dreigroschenoper* (1928; tr. The Threepenny Opera), a modern version of John GAY's *The Beggar's Opera*, and *The Rise and Fall of the City of Mahagonny* (1930), both of which represent the morality of capitalism in terms of highway robbery. His adoption of Marxism (1928–29) produced a number of didactic pieces too stylized in form and ambivalent in their ideological position to win the approval of the Communist Party (*The Measures Taken*, 1930; *The Exception and the Rule*, 1930). During the NAZI period he went into exile first in Denmark and later in the US, where he wrote many of his finest pieces: *Mutter Courage und ihre Kinder* (1941; tr. Mother Courage and her Children), *Der gute Mensch von Sezuan* (1943; tr. The Good Woman of Sezuan), *Galilei* (1943), and *Der Kaukasische Kreidekreis* (1948; tr. The Caucasian Chalk Circle), as well as his most important theoretical work, *Little Organon for the Theatre* (1948). In 1949 he returned to settle in East Germany, where most of his energies went into setting up the Berliner Ensemble, production, adaptation, and more of the poetry which he had been writing all his life.

**Breda** (ˌbraydə), city (1985 pop. 118,974), Noord Brabant prov., S Netherlands. An old castle and market town, it is now one of the principal centres of the industrialized North Brabant region. Industries include textiles, brewing, and the processing of local market-garden produce.

**Bredero, Gerbrand Adriaenszoon,** 1585–1618, Dutch dramatist and poet, the first Dutch master of COMEDY. *The Spaniard from Brabant* (1617), a realistic comedy of Amsterdam life, is his masterpiece.

**breech presentation,** position of the infant in the uterus such that it has to be delivered buttocks first, instead of the normal head-first position. This can cause a difficult delivery, sometimes requiring a CAESAREAN SECTION, but it is sometimes possible to turn the infant around during labour.

**breeder reactor:** see NUCLEAR REACTOR.

**breeding,** the deliberate selection of certain parent plants and animals for propagation in order to adapt them to human needs. Plants and animals have been bred selectively since their domestication in the Neolithic period. Among plants, pure lines are established by self-pollination, planting the resultant seed, and repeating the process through several generations. Crosses of pure lines produce hybrids of great vigour and uniformity. Pure-bred animals show a breeding uniformity approaching that of pure-line plants. New varieties are developed by hybridization and by breeding individuals that have developed MUTATIONS. See GENETICS; HYBRID.

**Breed's Hill:** see BUNKER HILL, BATTLE OF.

**Bremen,** city (1984 pop. 535,800), N West Germany, on the Weser R. It is the oldest German port city and West Germany's second largest port. Shipbuilding and steel-making are among its industries. Made an archbishopric in 845, it became a leading member (1358) of the HANSEATIC LEAGUE and a free imperial city (1646). It prospered as an overseas trading centre during the 18th and 19th cent. During WORLD WAR II it was badly damaged, but such structures as the Gothic city hall (1405–9) and the Romanesque–Gothic cathedral (begun 1043) remain.

**Bremerhaven,** city (1984 pop. 135,800), BREMEN, N West Germany, on the WESER estuary. Many emigrants to the US passed through the port which still handles cruise liners. It has been modernized to accommodate bulk carriers of iron ore. Shipbuilding and fish-processing are the main industries.

**Brenner Pass,** Alpine Pass, 1370 m (4495 ft) high, connecting Innsbruck, Austria, with Bolzano, Italy. The lowest of the principal passes in the ALPS, it was an important Roman route through which many invasions of Italy were made.

**Brent,** London borough (1981 pop. 251,238), to the N of central London. It contains the districts of Wembley and Willesden. It is largely residential, but there are several industries including electrical engineering and food-processing. Wembley Stadium is the venue of the English FA cup final (see FOOTBALL) and other sporting events. It was the site of the Olympic Games in 1948.

**Brentano, Bettina,** 1785–1859, German writer, sister of Clemens BRENTANO, married (1811) to Achim von ARNIM. One of the most vital of the German Romantics, Bettina enjoyed three careers: as brilliant *enfant terrible*, as chatelaine and mother of seven, and as novelist and publicist. The result of her enthusiastic pursuit of GOETHE and Goethe's mother is her lively mixture of fact and fiction *Goethe's Correspondence with a Child* (1835). Her memoir of her friendship with the poet Karoline von Günderode (d. 1806), *Die Günderode* (1840) is similarly made up of authentic correspondence restructured into fiction. Towards the end of her life she took an active interest in liberal politics, and as an independently-minded aristocrat was well placed to protest on behalf of the exploited poor and the politically victimized in *This Book Belongs to the King* (1843) and *Conversations with Demons* (1852).

**Brentano, Clemens,** 1778–1842, German poet of the romantic school; brother of Bettina von Arnim (see BRENTANO, Bettina). With Achim von ARNIM he collaborated on *Des Knaben Wunderhorn* (1806–08; tr. The Boy's Magic Horn), a folk-song collection that influenced EICHENDORFF, HEINE, and the brothers GRIMM. Brentano wrote plays, lyric poems, fairy tales, and novellas.

**Brentano, Franz,** 1838–1917, German philosopher and psychologist. He is looked upon as the founder of 'Act Psychology'. In opposition to WUNDT's 'content' focus, Brentano argued that the fundamental data of psychology are mental processes, conceived as acts. His students included HUSSERL and Sigmund FREUD.

**Brescia** (ˌbresheeə), city (1984 pop. 202,095), Lombardy, N Italy. Its economic importance rested formerly on the making of weaponry and armour. This metal-working tradition continues and now includes the manufacture of commercial vehicles and motor cycles. There is much evidence of the city's Roman past.

**Bresson, Robert** (breˌsonh), 1907–, French film director. His austere films on spiritual themes include *Diary of a Country Priest* (1950), *Pickpocket* (1959), *The Trial of Joan of Arc* (1961), *Mouchette* (1966), and *Lancelot of the Lake* (1976).

**Brest,** city (1982 pop. 160,355), Finistère dept., NW France, on an inlet of the Atlantic Ocean. It is a commercial port and naval station. Clothing and electronics equipment are the chief manufactures, and there is a national engineering school. The spacious, landlocked harbour was created in 1631. During WORLD WAR II Brest was a major German submarine base and was almost completely destroyed by Allied bombing.

**Brest-Litovsk, Treaty of,** separate peace treaty of WORLD WAR I, signed by SOVIET RUSSIA and the Central Powers on 3 Mar. 1918, at present-day Brest, USSR. It required Russia to cede large areas of the former Czarist empire, and to pay a huge indemnity. It caused a major crisis between LENIN and TROTSKY, who, nonetheless, took part in the negotiations. It was renounced by the general ARMISTICE of Nov. 1918.

**Breton, André** (brəˌtawnh), 1896–1966, French poet and writer. He was the founder and main theorist of SURREALISM, writing the surrealist manifestos of 1924, 1930, and 1942. Trained as a doctor, he read FREUD's theories of the unconscious while treating soldiers with psychiatric conditions during World War I. These theories of psychoanalysis he combined with his Marxist politics to develop a theory of radical art and literature.

**Breuer, Josef** (ˌbroyə), 1842–1925, Austrian physiologist. Breuer first devised the 'method of catharsis' (the orignal 'talking cure', which Sigmund FREUD used as the basis for PSYCHOANALYSIS) in the treatment of HYSTERIA. Breuer and Freud jointly published *Studies on Hysteria* (1895), but thereafter their collaboration ceased, Breuer being unable to accept Freud's hypothesis that every hysteria has a sexual basis.

**Breuer, Marcel Lajos,** 1902–81, American architect and furniture designer; b. Hungary. In the 1920s he was associated with the BAUHAUS and won fame for his tubular chair. In the US he was associated (1937–41) with Walter GROPIUS in building houses. Among his well-known buildings is the Whitney Museum, New York (1966).

**Breughel,** family of painters: see BRUEGEL.

**Breuil, Henri,** known as **Abbé Breuil** (ˌbruhyə), 1877–1961, French priest, archaeologist, and palaeontologist, one of the first to record and interpret PALAEOLITHIC ART and European and African ROCK CARVINGS AND PAINTINGS.

**breviary,** the liturgical book containing the daily offices prescribed to be read by clergy and members of religious orders in the Roman Catholic Church. The breviary in current use is a thorough revision carried out in 1971 as a result of the Second VATICAN COUNCIL.

**Brewster, Sir David,** 1781–1868, Scottish physicist and natural philosopher. His invention of the kaleidoscope was one result of his notable light-polarization studies. He improved the spectroscope and was responsible for the introduction of the lightweight Fresnel lens in British lighthouses. Among his prolific writings was a major biography (1855) of Sir Isaac NEWTON.

Armchair designed by Marcel Lajos **Breuer** (1933)

**Breytenbach, Breyten,** 1939–, white South African painter, poet and translator. He scandalized white society by marrying a Vietnamese woman. Imprisoned for seven years for treason, he wrote *Mouroir: Mirrornotes of a Novel* (1983; tr. 1984). Other works include *A Season in Paradise* and *The True Confessions of an Albino Terrorist*.

**Brezhnev, Leonid Ilyich,** 1906–82. Soviet leader. Rising through the Communist Party, he became chairman of the presidium of the Supreme Soviet (i.e. president) in 1960 and, when Nikita KRUSHCHEV fell in 1964, first secretary (later general secretary) of the party. He shared power with Alexei KOSYGIN (prime minister) initially, but emerged as the chief Soviet leader. In 1977, retaining his party post, he again became president of the USSR. Brezhnev's hard line toward democratic or independent trends in neighbouring countries, evidenced by the Soviet invasions of Czechoslovakia (1968) and Afghanistan (1979), often conflicted with his attempts at DÉTENTE with the West. After Mikhail GORBACHEV became Soviet leader (1985), the Brezhnev era was condemned as a time of stagnation and corruption.

**Brian Boru** or **Brian Boroimhe** (bə‚rooh, bəroh), 940?–1014, king of Ireland. A clan prince, he became high king by subjugating all Ireland. He annihilated the coalition of the Norse and his Irish enemies at Clontarf in 1014, but he was murdered soon after. His victory ended Norse power in Ireland, but the country fell into anarchy.

**Briand, Aristide** (bree‚ahnh), 1862–1932, French statesman. He was premier 10 times between 1909 and 1921. After WORLD WAR I; he emerged as a leading proponent of international peace and cooperation. As foreign minister (1925–32) Briand was the chief architect of the LOCARNO PACT (1925) and the KELLOGG–BRIAND PACT (1928). He shared the 1926 Nobel Peace Prize with Gustav STRESEMANN and advocated a plan for a United States of Europe.

**bribery,** in law, the offence of accepting bribes (usually money) in return for certain favours or acts; bribery is usually committed by people in authority, e.g., police officers, judges, or other public officials. The favours requested include the rigging of elections, the granting of honours, or the acquittal of certain offenders. Bribery rarely comes to light because, if successful, both parties are likely to keep it secret.

**brick,** building material made by shaping clay into blocks and then hardening them in a KILN. Sun-dried bricks are among the most ancient building materials. Examples from c.5000 years ago have been discovered in the Tigris–Euphrates basin. The Romans faced brick buildings with stone or marble, but Byzantine and later European builders used the brick itself to provide a decorative surface. The many varieties of modern brick include firebrick, made of special clays that can withstand very high temperatures, high-strength engineering bricks, and commons used for general building work.

**bridewealth,** payments made on marriage by a husband (and sometimes the husband's kin) to his wife's father or kin. These payments are seen as establishing rights over a women's reproductive, sexual, and physical services. It is usually found associated with unilineal systems of inheritance. See DOWRY; LINEAGE.

**bridge,** engineering structure for the purpose of carrying a path, road, railway, or canal across a river or valley, or across other highways and railways at different levels. Early bridges ranged from suspended rope walkways to wood, stone, and brick structures. The first long bridges were timber superstructures on stone piers. The Roman emperor Trajan, in AD 104, completed such a bridge 1220 m (4000 ft) long across the R. Danube. In the early railway pioneering days, deep ravines were crossed using brick or stone foundations and timber trestle erections. Masonry enabled the arch principle to be used where every stone is in compression, mortar joints having no tensile strength. This principle gave rise to the beautiful medieval bridges, many still in use today. The development of cast and wrought iron in the 18th cent. enabled solid iron bridges to be built. The first in Britain was made on site at Ironbridge in Shropshire. Completed in 1779, and still in use, it is a semicircular arch 305-m (1000-ft) span across the R. Severn. The mass production of steel simplified smaller bridge construction. Simple girders up to about 15 m (50 ft), and in truss form up to about 90 m (300 ft), could be used. Special steel arches supporting a roadway suspended by rods or cables were designed, early examples being Bayonne, New York, and Sydney Harbour Bridge, Australia. Cantilever bridges are an alternative steel structure design giving spans up to 610 m (2000 feet) and high clearance for shipping. Tubular railway bridges in which the train and single track lay inside a tube was a novel development of Robert STEPHENSON. He constructed (1854–59) the Victoria Bridge over the St Lawrence R. at Montreal, in which the tracks were completely enclosed in parallel iron tubes. For many years it was the longest bridge in the world. The design of a suspension bridge requires two tall towers, one at each side of the span, with a continuous chain or steel rope starting at an anchor some distance from the tower, rising to the top of the tower, hanging as a catenary between the two towers, rising to the opposite tower, and then down, finishing at a second anchor. From two such parallel cables is hung the deck or roadway. The earliest short-span suspension bridges using steel chains were designed by Thomas TELFORD, e.g., the Menai Strait Bridge, completed in 1826. Once steel rope could be manufactured in any length and diameter, very long suspension bridges were able to be constructed, the most famous being the GOLDEN GATE BRIDGE at San Francisco, which was completed in 1937, and is 1280 m (4200 ft) long with 244-m (800-ft) towers. The use of computer-aided design has enabled the old heavy solid I-shaped steel girders to be replaced by hollow box-section girders. These are of much lighter construction but equivalent in strength and can be used for spans greater than the old steel-girder bridges. The construction of box-girder bridges is more difficult, however, because there is little strength in the structure until the last section has been fitted. Several serious accidents have occurred during their construction which initially made this type of bridge less favoured by commissioning authorities. See also AQUEDUCT; BROOKLYN BRIDGE; VERRAZANO-NARROWS BRIDGE.

**bridge,** card game derived from whist, played with 52 cards by four players in two partnerships. It probably originated in the Middle East. In contract bridge, a now popular form, the cards rank from ace down to two; in bidding, suits rank spades, hearts, diamonds, and clubs. After all the cards are dealt, the auction begins. Players bid to win a stated number of tricks over six (a trick being the three cards played in rotation after the lead) with a named suit as trump or with no-trump. The highest bid becomes the contract after three consecutive passes end the bidding. The player who first named the suit (or no-trump) is the declarer; the partner's hand is dummy and is played face-up by the declarer who attempts to win enough tricks to fulfil the contract and as many additional tricks as possible. Duplicate bridge, in which prearranged hands are played, is the main form of competitive bridge. The governing principles of bidding were delineated by Ely CULBERTSON, and the currently popular point-counting system in bidding was introduced by Charles H. GOREN.

**Bridge, Frank,** 1879–1941, British composer, conductor, and chamber-music player. Although many of his compositions written before

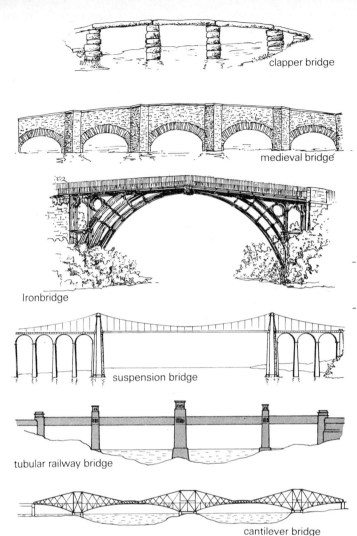

clapper bridge

medieval bridge

Ironbridge

suspension bridge

tubular railway bridge

cantilever bridge

Types of bridges

World War I, especially for the piano, were often played, his later works came to be appreciated only in the 1960s. He taught and influenced Benjamin BRITTEN. Important compositions are two string quartets Nos. 3 and 4 (1926, 1937), the tone-poem *Enter Spring* (1927), and the cello concerto *Oration* (1930).

**Bridge of Sighs,** enclosed bridge built c.1593, connecting the Doge's Palace in Venice to the prison (hence its name), crossing a typical Venetian canal between the buildings. It is supported on an elliptical arch and is decorated with rusticated pilasters and a number of heraldic devices in stone frames. The idea of a Bridge of Sighs seems to have attracted scholars during the Romantic movement; there is one at Oxford (crossing a street), and a more elegant one at Cambridge that crosses the Cam.

**Bridges, Harry,** 1901– , American labour leader; b. Australia, as Alfred Renton Bridges. Arriving in San Francisco in 1920, he became a longshoreman and militant labour organizer. In 1937 he set up the International Longshoremen's and Warehousemen's Union (ILWU), serving as its president for the next 40 years. Efforts by the US government to deport him as a Communist alien failed, and he became a citizen in 1945. Bridges was convicted and sentenced (1950) to prison for perjury in denying Communist party membership, but the US Supreme Court overturned the conviction in 1953. Bridges led his last major strike in 1971–72.

**Bridges, Robert Seymour,** 1844–1930, English lyric poet. The philosophical poem *The Testament of Beauty* (1929) is considered his greatest work. Bridges also wrote two major works on prosody and published the poems of his friend G.M. HOPKINS.

**Bridgetown,** city (1980 pop. est. 100,000), capital of BARBADOS.

**Bridgman, Percy Williams,** 1882–1961, American physicist. A professor at Harvard, he won the 1946 Nobel Prize for physics for his work on high pressures. He also studied electrical conduction in metals and the properties of crystals, and wrote on the philosophy of modern science.

**Bright, John,** 1811–89, English statesman and orator. A quaker, noted for his LAISSEZ-FAIRE views, he was, with COBDEN, the greatest 19th-cent. champion of the middle classes. In 1839 he helped found the ANTI-CORN-LAW LEAGUE and used his formidable oratory to urge repeal of the CORN LAWS. A member of Parliament for many years (1847–57, 1858–89), he strongly opposed the CRIMEAN WAR. He served in GLADSTONE's governments (1868–70, 1873–74, 1880–82).

**Bright, Richard,** 1789–1858, English physician. He worked at Guy's Hospital, London and was appointed physician-extraordinary to Queen Victoria in 1837. He made a special study of dropsy (oedema) and showed it to be a symptom of injury or disease rather than a disease itself. In 1827 he described Bright's disease, a disease of the kidney now known as acute glomerulonephritis, whose symptoms include oedema and the presence of protein in the urine.

**Brighton,** town (1981 pop. 134,581), E Sussex, S England, on English Channel. A famous seaside resort, it is also an important commercial centre and has recently developed as a conference centre. It became popular as a seaside resort in the 18th and early 19th cent. and there are still many Regency buildings. The famous Royal Pavilion was built in 1817 in oriental style for the Prince Regent. The Univ. of Sussex (1959) is situated nearby.

**Brillat-Savarin, Anthelme,** 1755–1826, French lawyer and gastronomist. He is famous for writing *Physiologie du goût* (1825), a compendium of the art of dining.

**brimstone:** see SULPHUR.

**Brindisi,** city (1984 est. pop. 83,000), Apulia, S Italy. It has close links with Greece as a car-ferry port. Nearby are large oil-refinery and petrochemical installations. At the end of the APPIAN WAY, it was a naval

Bridge of Sighs, Venice

The Royal Pavilion, **Brighton**

port in Roman times and later a place of embarkation for the Crusades. After a long period of eclipse it revived with the opening of the Suez Canal in 1869.

**Brindley, James,** 1716–72, English engineer, famous as a canal builder. Born of working-class parents, he received no education whatsoever and never learned to read or write throughout the whole of his life. He had an inventive turn of mind however and made a simple water engine for draining a coal mine in 1752 which attracted the attention of the duke of Bridgewater who became his patron. In 1759 the duke employed Brindley to design and supervise the building of canals, the first being the Manchester to Worsley canal, a very difficult exercise which Brindley successfully completed. All his calculations were done mentally at night as he lay in bed. Other canals he successfully completed were the Grand Trunk Canal and the Brimingham to Chesterfield. He died at the age of 56 having completed 587 km (365 mi) of canals.

**Brisbane,** city (1986 pop. 1,037,815), urban agglomeration, capital and chief port of Queensland, E Australia, on the Brisbane R., above Moreton Bay. Founded in 1824, it was named after Governor Brisbane who succeeded Macquarie in 1821. The third largest city in Australia, it has shipyards; oil refineries; and food-processing, textile, and motor vehicle industries. Sugar, bananas, and bauxite are exported. Brisbane was first settled (1824) as a penal colony. The Univ. of Queensland and Griffith Univ. are in the city.

**Bristol,** city (1981 pop. 413,861), Avon, SW England. A leading international port, Bristol has been a trading centre since the 12th cent. It now manufactures a wide range of machinery, aircraft, and tobacco and food products. Although the city was heavily bombed during WORLD WAR II, many historic buildings remain.

**Britain:** see UNITED KINGDOM.

**britannia metal,** ALLOY of tin with antimony, copper, and, sometimes, bismuth and zinc. Similar in appearance to PEWTER but harder, it is used in manufacturing tableware.

**British Aerospace** (B.Ae), Europe's largest aerospace company, founded 1977. B.Ae's pedigree goes back to the original 12 pioneering British aircraft firms from the time of World War I (see Geoffrey DE HAVILLAND and A.V. ROE), plus the dozen or so famous names (e.g., Gloster, Hawker, SOPWITH) of the inter-war years. Among its immediate forerunners was the British Aircraft Corporation, which developed CONCORDE. B.Ae was privatized in May 1985 and by the late 1980s had a turnover of about £3.5 billion (70% in military contracts) and a workforce of some 75,000 people. Its products are military and civil aircraft, guided weapons, and satellites.

**British Airways,** principal British AIRLINE, founded in its present form in 1972. The original British Airways Ltd was formed in 1933 as an amalgam of four earlier small AIR TRANSPORT companies, and for six years operated on a relatively small scale alongside the state-owned Imperial Airways. It

ceased to exist in Apr. 1940 when, with Imperial Airways, it was absorbed into BOAC (The British Overseas Airways Corporation), joined later by British European Airways (founded 1946). BOAC flew the world's first scheduled jet service (2 May 1952); BEA was the most successful airline in Europe. BOAC and BEA were merged (against the recommendations of the Edwards Committee) in 1972, and commenced operation as British Airways in 1974; the company was privatized in 1987. It ranks fifth in world airlines in terms of passenger/kilometres flown (40 billion) and sixth in passenger numbers (17 million).

**British Association for the Advancement of Science,** founded in 1831 at York, England, as a forum for scientists to discuss their work with their colleagues, and a means of explaining to the public the importance of science. With the increasing specialization of professional work, the second of these roles has become of increasing importance, especially at the large annual meeting held in a city in the UK or the British Commonwealth.

**British Columbia,** province of Canada (1984 est. pop. 2,865,100) area 948,596 km² (366,252 sq mi), situated in the W, bordered by Yukon Territory (N), Alberta (E), Montana, Idaho, and Washington, US (S), and the Pacific Ocean and Alaska, US (W). VICTORIA is the capital and VANCOUVER is the dominant city. British Columbia is almost totally mountainous, with the Rocky Mts in the E and the Coast Mts along the Pacific, separated by the uplands of the Interior Plateau. The coast is deeply indented with many offshore islands, including Vancouver Island. The Fraser and Upper Columbia Rivers drain most of the state southwards, providing water and hydroelectricity. Nearly 75% of the land is covered with forests, and timber and related enterprises are major industries. The province is also rich in minerals, including copper, coal, precious metals, iron ore, zinc, and lead. It has the largest fishing industry of any province. Most of British Columbia is sparsely populated, and 75% of the population lives along the coastal strip; 80% lives in urban areas. There is a small native American population and a growing Asian community. When the British and Spanish competed for control of the area in the late 18th cent. the inhabitants were Indians of the Pacific Northwest. Fur traders of the North West Company and Hudson's Bay Company arrived shortly after. In 1846 the US–Canadian border was set and in 1866 the two separate colonies of Vancouver Island and the mainland merged, joining the confederation in 1871. In the late 19th cent. the Canadian Pacific Railroad arrived and Vancouver became a major port, and later a financial and commercial centre of the Pacific Rim. The interior was opened up first by the search for gold, then salmon fisheries and timber, and more recently by the use of hydroelectric power for aluminium smelting and other industries.

**British Council,** an independent body to promote Britain abroad. It was founded (1934) as the British Committee for Relations with Other Countries, and gained its Royal Charter in 1940. The Council is financed mainly by government grants and has offices in more than 80 countries, to promote English teaching and cultural relations. It assists overseas tours by British drama, ballet, and opera companies, promotes exhibitions, runs libraries and helps to market books and software. It sponsors overseas students, and supports visits by scholars to and from Britain. More than half of its annual budget of over £200 million is devoted to bringing visitors to Britain, and 7% of its resources is spent on the arts. The largest fraction of its expenditure is for work carried out on British government programmes overseas, mainly for the Overseas Development Administration.

**British East India Company:** see EAST INDIA COMPANY, BRITISH.

**British Empire,** overseas territories linked to Great Britain in a variety of constitutional relationships. Established over three centuries, the empire resulted primarily from commercial and political motives, and from emigration. At its height in the late 19th and early 20th cent. it included 25% of the world's population and area.

*The First British Empire.* The foundations of the empire were laid in the late 16th cent. by the chartered companies, commercial ventures encouraged by the crown. In the 17th cent. sugar and tobacco plantations were founded in the Caribbean and in SE North America, and religious dissenters emigrated to NE North America. An integrated imperial trade arose, involving the exchange of African slaves for West Indian molasses and sugar, English cloth and manufactures, and American fish and timber. The theories of MERCANTILISM were implanted by the NAVIGATION ACTS. The British EAST INDIA COMPANY furthered expansion into India, and during the SEVEN YEARS WAR (1756–63) Britain ousted France from Canada and India. The financial burdens of the war, however, caused difficulties in the American colonies, and the success of the AMERICAN REVOLUTION marked the end of the first British Empire.

*The Second British Empire.* The voyages of James COOK and further conquests in India began a new phase of British expansion. The FRENCH REVOLUTIONARY WARS and Napoleonic Wars (see NAPOLEON I) added further possessions, e.g., the Cape Colony, Ceylon, British Guiana, and Malta, and Britain's INDUSTRIAL REVOLUTION lent greater force to the ideas of free TRADE. Humanitarian concerns led to the abolition of the slave trade (1807) and of slavery (1833). The BRITISH NORTH AMERICA ACT of 1867, which granted CANADA internal self-rule as a dominion, inaugurated a pattern by which Britain surrendered its direct governing powers in European-settled colonies, e.g., AUSTRALIA and NEW ZEALAND. Concurrently, Britain assumed greater responsibility in Africa and India.

*From Empire to Commonwealth.* WORLD WAR I brought the British Empire to the peak of its expansion. Imperial contributions had considerably strengthened the British war effort, and victory brought Britain mandates over new territories, e.g., Palestine, Iraq, and German territories in Africa. In 1931 the statute of Westminster officially recognized the independent and equal status under the crown of the former dominions within a British COMMONWEALTH OF NATIONS. After WORLD WAR II, self-government advanced rapidly in all parts of the empire. In 1947 India was partitioned and independence was granted to the new states of INDIA and PAKISTAN. Other parts of the empire, notably in AFRICA, gained independence and subsequently joined the British Commonwealth. Britain still administers many dependencies throughout the world, e.g., BERMUDA, GIBRALTAR, and HONG KONG.

PEACE

The "Boar" comes under the folds of the old Flag at last.

British Empire: 'The "Boar" comes under the folds of the old flag at last' (*Punch* 1902)

**British Expeditionary Force,** name given to the army units sent to the continent to oppose Germany in WORLD WAR I and WORLD WAR II.

**British Honduras:** see BELIZE.

**British Imperial System of weights and measures** see ENGLISH UNITS OF MEASUREMENT; WEIGHTS AND MEASURES, table.

**British Indian Ocean Territory,** archipelago (1981 est. pop. 2,500), c.1900 km (1180 mi), NE of Mauritius, in the central Indian Ocean. The islands, which form the Chagos Archipelago, were administered by MAURITIUS before they became a British dependency in 1965. Their importance is strategic; the US maintains a major naval facility on the main island, DIEGO GARCIA.

**British Medical Association** (BMA), professional organization established in 1832 to protect the interests of physicians. It has nearly 70,000 members in the UK, or nearly three-quarters of practising British doctors. It seeks better pay and conditions of service and it campaigns for improved public health.

**British Museum,** London, the first public museum of secular art in the world, founded 1753. It was based on Sir Hans Sloane's collection of 'plants, fossils, minerals, zoological, anatomical and pathological specimens, antiquities and artificial curiosities, prints, drawings and coins, books and manuscripts', purchased for the nation with funds raised by public lottery. Medieval illustrated manuscripts, including the *Lindisfarne Gospels,* BEOWULF, and MAGNA CARTA, were acquired from the Cotton and Harley collections. In 1756 the first Egyptian exhibits were donated and in 1816 the ELGIN MARBLES were purchased. King GEORGE III's books were donated in 1822, and a new building was designed to house the library. Over the next 30 years the present building was erected, designed by Robert Smirke, completed in 1848 with the neo-classical facade designed by Sydney Smirke, who also designed the circular Reading Room in 1854, where Karl MARX wrote *Das Kapital.* Today the Museum's departments include: Coins and Medals; Prehistoric, Egyptian, Greek, Roman, Roman–British, Medieval, Oriental, and Western Asiatic Antiquities; Prints, Drawings, and Manuscripts.

**British North America Act,** 1867, law providing for the unification of CANADA that functioned as the dominion's constitution until 1982. It spelt out provisional powers and granted residual authority to the dominion government. Under it, the power of amendment was nominally vested in the British Parliament, which in practice acted only at the request of Canada's Parliament.

**British Standards Institution,** (BSI), British body, independent of government, that sets standards for safety, health, and compatibility with other manufacturers. Set up in 1901 by the British Institution of Civil Engineers to set standards in steel girders and bridge building, it expanded with the help of the other engineering institutions to cover all branches of engineering and manufacturing. The 'kite mark' is displayed on goods that conform to the Institution's standards. It received its present name under a Royal Charter in 1929 and now has over 2600 standing committees on different topics. The Institution library contains the publications from other countries who have similar organizations. In the US the equivalent organization is the American Standards Association Inc.

**British thermal unit** (Btu), unit of energy equal to 1055.06 J or 251.997 cal; the energy required to raise the temperature of 1 lb of water by 1°F.

**brit milah,** circumcision. This is performed, according to biblical law, on all Jewish males when they are eight days old. The ritual operation for the removal of the foreskin is performed by a professional *mohel* (circumciser), and the ceremony is accompanied by special blessings recited by the father of the child to signify the entry of his son into 'the covenant of Abraham'. The child is given his Hebrew name at this ceremony.

**Brittany,** region and former province, NW France, a peninsula between the English Channel and the Bay of Biscay. Its economy is based on farming, fishing, and tourism. Breton, a Celtic language, is spoken in some rural traditionalist areas. Brittany got its modern name when it was settled (c.500) by Britons whom the ANGLO-SAXONS had driven from Britain. It struggled for independence from the FRANKS (5th–9th cent.), from the dukes of Normandy and the counts of Anjou (10th–12th cent.), and finally from England and France. Brittany was absorbed by France after the accession (1488) of ANNE OF BRITTANY and was formally incorporated into France in 1532.

**Britten, Benjamin, Baron Britten of Aldeburgh,** 1913–76, British composer, pianist, and conductor, and the leading British musician of his generation. His most popular works include *A Ceremony of Carols* (1942), *Hymn to St Cecilia* (1942), and *Serenade* for tenor, horn, and strings (1943). *A Young Person's Guide to the Orchestra* (1945), and the great *War Requiem* (1962). He composed many fine instrumental works, but after the huge success of *Peter Grimes* (1945) he turned increasingly to opera. His other operas include *Billy Budd* (1951), *The Turn of the Screw* (1954), and *Death in Venice* (1973). With Sir Peter PEARS he established the Aldeburgh Festival (1948).

**brittle star,** marine invertebrate animal (class Ophiuroidea). An ECHINODERM with planktonic larvae, it has five long, slender arms that radiate from a central disc, and the water-vascular system and tube feet common to echinoderms. Their arms break off readily, but new arms are easily regenerated. Most brittle stars are less than 2.5 cm (1 in) across the central disc. They live on the sea bed, both scavenging and filter-feeding. They are able to live at great depths, brittle stars being found at the bottom of the MARIANAS TRENCH.

**Brno** (ˌbuhnoh), Ger. *Brünn,* city (1984 pop. 381,000), central Czechoslovakia, at the confluence of the Svratka and Svitava rivers. The third largest Czechoslovak city and MORAVIA's chief city, it produces textiles, tractors, and other manufactures. Brno flourished (13th–14th cent.) as a free city within the kingdom of BOHEMIA. The Spielberg castle in Brno was a notorious HABSBURG prison (1740–1855).

**Broads, The,** a series of shallow lakes in E England. Most of the area is in the county of Norfolk, the rest in Suffolk. The lakes are mostly connected by channels with the rivers Bure, Waveney, and Yare, and originated mainly from medieval peat digging. The whole area is very popular for boating holidays, and the large wetland area attracts many types of waterfowl.

**Broadway,** street in New York City. The world's longest street, it extends c.241 km (150 mi) from lower Manhattan N to Albany. Its theatre district is known as the 'Great White Way' for its dazzling electric lights and signs. The world-famous intersection of Times Square is formed by Broadway, Seventh Ave., and 42nd St.

**broccoli,** variety of CABBAGE grown for the edible immature flower panicles. It is the same variety as cauliflower (*Brassica oleracea botrytis*) and similarly cultivated.

**Broch, Hermann** (brohkh), 1886–1951, Austrian novelist and cultural critic. His trilogy *Die Schlafwandler* (1932; tr. The Sleepwalkers) deals with loss of values in the modern world. His masterpiece, the extended inner monologue *The Death of Virgil* (1945), deals with the relationship between art and society; *The Spell* (1953, tr. 1987) is an elaborate allegorical treatment of the interaction between evil charismatic leader and mass following. His major essays include *James Joyce and the Present* (1936) and *Hofmannsthal and his Time* (1936).

**Brodsky, Joseph,** 1940–, Russian émigré poet. He has lived in the US since 1972. Brodsky is highly regarded for the formal technique, depth, irony, and wit displayed in his poetry, which often treats the themes of loss and exile. Among his volumes of poetry in English translation are *Joseph Brodsky: Selected Poems* (tr. 1973) and *A Part of Speech* (tr. 1980).

**Broederbond** (ˌbroohdeərˈbond), semi-secret and influential society of the Afrikaner elite in SOUTH AFRICA. Its members are active in the government and in industrial and commercial concerns, promoting the ideals and politics of APARTHEID.

**Broglie, Louis Victor, prince de,** 1892–1987, French physicist. From his hypothesis that particles should exhibit certain wavelike properties, wave mechanics, a form of quantum mechanics, was developed (see QUANTUM THEORY). Experiments proved (1927) the existence of these waves and he won the 1929 Nobel Prize for physics for his theory.

**Broken Hill,** city (1986 pop. 24,460), New South Wales, near the South Australia border. It is the site of one of the world's richest silver-lead and zinc deposits (first developed in 1884). Water is provided from the Menindee Lakes on the Darling R.

**broker,** term in anthropology for the type of middle man, found above all in peasant communities, who as a result of his strategic position in relation to the two worlds, mediates between national and local social, political, and economic levels, a relationship that is frequently found in conjunction with PATRON–CLIENT ties.

**bromeliad,** common name for some members of the pineapple family Bromeliaceae, chiefly epiphytic herbs and small shrubs native to the American tropics and subtropics. A typical bromeliad has strap-shaped leaves clustered in a rosette around a central cup; the flowers are found in the central cup or above it on a spike. The central cup retains water, enabling tropical bromeliads to survive dry spells. Bromeliad species such as those of the genus *Aechmea* and *Billbergia* are often grown as house and conservatory plants for their colourful flowers and foliage.

**bromine** (Br), volatile liquid element, discovered in 1826 by Antoine J. Balard. A HALOGEN, it is a reddish-brown fuming liquid with an offensive odour. Bromine is very corrosive, and its vapour irritates the eyes and the membranes of the nose and throat. The only nonmetallic element that is liquid under ordinary conditions, bromine occurs in compounds in seawater, mineral springs, and salt deposits. Its compounds are used in photographic film, in flame retardants, and in conjunction with an antiknock compound in petrol. See ELEMENT (table); PERIODIC TABLE.

**Bromley,** London borough (1981 pop. 294,526). A large borough in SE London which is mainly residential. H.G. WELLS was born here.

**bronchitis,** inflammation of the bronchial tubes (the larger air passages of the lung) caused by viral or bacterial infection or by the inhalation of irritating fumes (e.g., tobacco smoke and air pollutants). Symptoms include the coughing up of excessive mucus, fever, and chest pains. Acute bronchitis may subside, or, particularly with continued exposure to irritants, may persist and progress to chronic bronchitis or PNEUMONIA. Acute bronchitis can be treated with antihistamines, cough suppressants, bronchodilators, or ANTIBIOTIC drugs. Chronic bronchitis causes disability and premature death.

**Brontë, Charlotte,** 1816–55, **Emily Jane Brontë,** 1818–48, **Anne Brontë,** 1820–49, English novelists and poets. As children in a Yorkshire parsonage, the sisters wrote about the imaginary kingdoms of Angria and Goudal. In 1846 they published the pseudonymous collection, *Poems by Currer, Ellis and Acton Bell.* Charlotte's novel *Jane Eyre,* portraying a friendless and independent-minded governess loved by her rugged employer Mr Rochester, was published in 1847 and was an immediate success and a lasting influence on the plots of innumerable English novels, and on English women's idea of themselves. *Shirley* (1849) and *Villette* (1853), based on her experiences as a teacher in Brussels from 1842–44, followed. She married her father's curate, Arthur Bell Nichols, in 1854 but died a year later. *The Professor,* written first but not published in her lifetime, appeared in 1857. Emily's only novel, *Wuthering Heights* (1847) portrays with passionate intensity and great narrative skill the almost demonic love between Heathcliff and Catherine Earnshaw, in an isolated moorland setting. Her stoic and visionary poems, of which 'The Prisoner' and 'No Coward Soul Is Mine' are the best known, are now rated far above the poetry of her sisters. Anne's *Agnes Grey* (1847) is a realistic account, based on her own experience, of the unhappy situation of Victorian governesses, and *The Tenant of Wildfell Hall* (1848) describes the attempts of a wife to escape from her alcoholic husband. She was the gentlest and most religious of the three Brontë sisters.

**bronze,** ALLOY of copper and tin, often with small amounts of other elements such as zinc and lead. It is harder than BRASS, and its properties depend on the proportions of its components. Leaded bronze is cast into heavy-duty bushes and bearings, silicon bronze is used for telegraph wires and chemical containers, and bronze with 20% to 24% tin is also used for casting bells. Bronze is also used for coins, medals, and GUNMETAL, and in artistic castings, engravings, and forgings. The term may also be used of copper-rich alloys which contain no tin. ALUMINIUM bronze, with its high strength and corrosion resistance, is used for bearings, valve seats, and machine parts.

**Bronze Age,** technological period when metals were first used to make tools and weapons (see THREE-AGE SYSTEM). The earliest phase, when pure copper was predominant, has been called the Copper Age. Copper was used from the 5th millennium BC in the Balkans and the Near East and the 4th millennium BC in Iberia, with the metallurgical process developing

Bromeliad (*Aechmea weiusachii*)

from cold hammering of native copper to the smelting and then CASTING of copper ores. Bronze casting was established in the Middle East by 3500 BC and in Europe it was highly specialized by 2000 BC; in the New World bronze was used in northern Argentina before 1000 BC, and then it developed in Peru with the rise of the INCA empire. The use of copper and bronze occurred during a period of increasing social differentiation and metal became primarily a social tool, as suggested by the high degree of craftsmanship in weaponry and the extent of its deposition in burials and hoards. By the end of the Bronze Age, metal was being used increasingly for practical tools, laying the foundation for the IRON AGE.

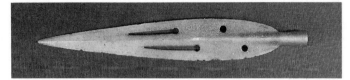

Late **Bronze Age** spearhead

**bronze sculpture.** Bronze is an ideal alloy for casting, engraving, and repoussé work. When melted, it flows into the crevices of a mould, reproducing every detail; once hardened, it is easily worked with a tool. The ancient Egyptians used bronze for utensils, armour, and statuary, and outstanding Oriental bronzes have been made since ancient times. Unexcelled in bronze sculpture, the Greeks created such masterpieces as *The Zeus of Artemesium* (National Mus., Athens) and *The Delphic Charioteer* (Delphi Mus.). Copying Greek models, the Romans made thousands of bronze sculptures, as well as utilitarian objects. Most medieval bronzes were utensils and ornaments. During the RENAISSANCE, Italian sculptors wrought magnificent bronzes, such as the GHIBERTI doors to the baptistery of Florence and sculpture by DONATELLO, VERROCCHIO, and CELLINI. In the 18th cent. France was well known for gilded bronze furniture mounts. Major modern sculptors who have worked in bronze include RODIN, EPSTEIN, BRANCUSI, Henry MOORE, and Jacques Lipchitz.

**Bronzino, Il,** 1503–72, Florentine mannerist painter (see MANNERISM); b. Agnolo di Cosimo di Mariano. He is known for *Venus, Cupid, Folly, and Time* (1545; National Gall., London) and his cold, sophisticated portraits, e.g., *Lucrezia Panciatichi* (c.1540; Uffizi, Florence).

**Brook, Peter,** 1925–, English theatrical director. Since 1962 he has been codirector of the Royal Shakespeare Company. His innovative, controversial productions include Peter WEISS's *Marat/Sade* (1965) and *A Midsummer Night's Dream* (1970). He has also directed films, e.g., *Lord of the Flies* (1963) and *King Lear* (1971). In 1970 he founded the International Centre of Theatre Research in Paris.

**Brooke, Sir James,** 1803–68, rajah of Sarawak. He was made (1841) rajah for helping the sultan of Brunei to suppress rebel tribes. He was succeeded by his nephew, **Sir Charles Anthony Johnson Brooke,** 1829–1917, who made the country prosperous. His son and successor, **Sir Charles Vyner Brooke,** 1874–1963, was forced out of Sarawak by the Japanese in WORLD WAR II. He ceded (1946) the country to Britain.

**Brooke, Rupert,** 1887–1915, English poet. His social charm, wit, and tragic death during World War I made him a legend. He wrote *Poems* (1911) and *1914 and Other Poems* (1915). The romantic patriotism of his war poems contrasts sharply with the bitterness of OWEN, ROSENBERG and SASSOON.

**Brook Farm,** 1841–47, Utopian community at West Roxbury, Massachussets, founded by the Unitarian minister George Ripley. It was based on cooperative living and the principles of TRANSCENDENTALISM and fostered shared manual labour and a stimulating intellectual life. Nathaniel HAWTHORNE was a member, and visitors included R.W. EMERSON, Margaret FULLER, and Horace GREELEY. Brook Farm adopted the ideas of Charles FOURIER in 1844. It was disbanded shortly after its central building burned in 1846.

**Brooklyn,** borough of NEW YORK CITY, US, (1984 est. pop. 2,254,000), 184 km² (71 sq mi), at the SW extremity of LONG ISLAND; settled 1636, chartered as part of New York City 1898. The largest of New York's five boroughs, it has diverse industries and a waterfront handling foreign and domestic commerce. From Dutch and Walloon settlements it became the village of Brooklyn Ferry (1816) and the city of Brooklyn (1834), absorbing as it grew settlements like Flatbush and Gravesend; it became

Bronzino, *Lucrezia Panciatichi*, c.1540. Galleria Uffizi, Florence.

(1855) the third largest US city. Points of interest include Prospect Park, the Brooklyn Botanic Garden, Coney Island, Brooklyn Heights, and the New York Naval Shipyard.

**Brooklyn Bridge,** the first steel-wire suspension bridge in the world, built 1869–83, over the East R., linking the boroughs of Manhattan and Brooklyn in New York City. Designed by J.A. and W.A. ROEBLING, it was the world's longest suspension bridge at the time of its completion.

Brooklyn Bridge

**Brooks, Louise,** 1906–85, American film actress. A silent star of extraordinary beauty, and magnetic naturalism, she appeared in such films as *A Girl in Every Port* (1928), *Pandora's Box* (1929), and *Diary of a Lost Girl* (1929).

**Brooks, Phillips,** 1835–93, American Episcopalian bishop. He began (1869) his ministry at Trinity Church, Boston, and became one of the most influential clergy of his time. In 1891 he was consecrated bishop of Massachusetts. Brooks wrote the hymn 'O little town of Bethlehem.'

**Brooks, Van Wyck,** 1886–1963, American critic. An extremely prolific writer, he concentrated in his early work on the influence of Puritanism on American culture, e.g., *The Wine of the Puritans* (1909), and on critical biography, e.g., *The Ordeal of Mark Twain* (1920). His masterpiece, the series *Makers and Finders: A History of the Writer in America, 1800–1915,* which began with the Pulitzer Prize-winning *The Flowering of New England* (1936), is a humanistic interpretation of American literary history.

**Broome,** town (1986 pop. 5778), Western Australia. Located on the coast 2500 km (1560 mi) N of Perth in the Kimberley region on the Indian Ocean, the area was first sighted by William Dampier in 1699. Before World War II pearl diving was the main activity, with a large Japanese population, but in the post-war period Malay divers replaced the Japanese. The largest pearl found in these waters was the 'Star of the West' which sold in London for £14,000 in 1917. Today the collection of pearl shell is more important but oysters are gathered for a Japanese-based cultured-pearl farm. Tropical cyclones regularly threaten the coast and, in 1935, 142 lives were lost when the lugger fleet was caught at sea.

**Brouwer, Adriaen** (ˌbrowə), 1606–38, Flemish painter. Brouwer introduced a new kind of realistic, low-life GENRE; his pictures show coarse peasants drinking, smoking and brawling in rough taverns. *The Smokers* (c.1637; Metropolitan Mus., New York) includes a self-portrait amongst the merrymakers.

**Brown, Charles Brockden,** 1771–1810, considered America's first professional novelist. His most popular work, *Wieland* (1799), foreshadowed the psychological novel. His other works include *Edgar Huntley* and *Ormond* (both: 1799).

**Brown, Ford Madox,** 1821–93, English historical painter; b. France. Closely affiliated with the PRE-RAPHAELITES, he painted *Work* (1852–63; Manchester Art Gall.) and 12 FRESCOES (in the town hall of Manchester) showing the city's history.

**Brown, George,** 1818–80, Canadian journalist and statesman. After emigrating from Scotland at the age of 24 he founded (1844) the Toronto *Globe* and made it a powerful political journal. A member of the Canadian assembly (1851–67), he worked for political representation by population and for the confederation of CANADA.

**Brown, John,** 1800–1859, American ABOLITIONIST. In 1856, in retaliation for the sack of LAWRENCE, he led the slaughter of five pro-slavery men on the banks of the Pottawatamie R., asserting that he was an instrument in the hand of God. On 16 Oct. 1859, having initiated a plan to liberate Southern slaves through armed intervention, Brown and 21 followers captured the US arsenal at HARPER'S FERRY. It was taken the next morning by Robert E. LEE, and Brown was hanged on 2 Dec. The dignity and sincerity that he displayed during his widely reported trial led many to regard him as a martyr.

**Brown, Robert,** 1773–1858, Scottish botanist and botanical explorer. He went as a naturalist and collector to Australia (1801) and described its flora in his *Prodromus florae Novae Hollandiae* (1810). Librarian to the Linnaean Society and British Museum curator, he observed BROWNIAN MOVEMENT in 1827 and discovered the cell nucleus in 1831.

**Browne, Sir Thomas,** 1605–82, English physician and master of ornate prose. Greatly respected for his holiness and his learning, he practised in Oxford and Norwich, was knighted by Charles II in 1671, and wrote, among other books, the great philosophical and medical classic, *Religio medici,* published without his knowledge in 1642 and officially published in 1643.

**brown haematite:** see LIMONITE.

**Brownian movement** or **motion,** irregular, zigzag motion of minute particles of matter suspended in a fluid. First studied by the botanist Robert Brown after observing (1827) with a microscope the movement of pollen grains suspended in water, the effect is a result of collisions between the particles and the fluid molecules, which are in constant thermal motion.

**Browning, Elizabeth Barrett,** 1806–61, English poet. She first became well known with the publication of *The Seraphim, and Other Poems* (1838). *Poems* (1844) raised her reputation to the point where she was recommended to succeed WORDSWORTH as poet laureate in 1850, and

also put her in touch with Robert BROWNING whom, defying ill health and a tyrannical father, she married in 1846. Her *Sonnets from the Portuguese* (1850) celebrated their courtship. Her most considerable work, *Aurora Leigh* (1857), a novel in verse, explored the position of women and of artists in society. She shocked some of her contemporaries by her radical opinions and her daring prosodic experiments.

**Browning, Robert,** 1812–89, English poet. His *Paracelsus* (1835) was well received but *Sordello* (1840), criticized for obscurity, depressed his reputation till the publication of *Men and Women* (1855) and *Dramatis Personae* (1864). He was master of the dramatic monologue, e.g. 'My Last Duchess', 'Fra Lippo Lippi', 'The Bishop Orders His Tomb'. His masterpiece is *The Ring and the Book* (4 vol., 1868–69). His psychological portraits in verse and his experiments in diction and rhythm have made him an important influence on 20th-cent. poetry. In 1846, after a secret courtship, he married the poet Elizabeth Barrett BROWNING and took her to Italy. After her death in 1861, Browning returned to England. He died in his son's house in Venice in 1889.

**Brownshirts,** name given to the NAZI Party's *Sturmabteilung* [storm troopers], SA for short, or private army. HITLER relied heavily on this force in the years of conflict before he took power in 1933, but its influence greatly declined after he had its leader, Ernst Röhm, murdered in Aug. 1934.

**Brown v. Board of Education of Topeka, Kansas,** case decided in 1954 by the US SUPREME COURT, holding that de jure segregation in public schools was a violation of the equal protection clause of the 14th amendment to the US CONSTITUTION. A unanimous Court stated that racial separation, no matter how equal the facilities, branded minority children as inferior, thus hindering their development. The 'separate but equal' doctrine of Plessy v. Ferguson was reversed. In 1955 the Court added that schools must desegregate 'with all deliberate speed'. The *Brown* decision gave impetus to the civil-rights movement of the 1950s and 60s, and hastened the end of segregation in all public facilities.

**Bruce,** Scottish royal family, descended from an 11th-cent. Norman noble, Robert de Brus, who aided WILLIAM I in his conquest of England. In the struggle following the death of MARGARET MAID OF NORWAY, the Bruces claimed succession to the Scottish throne. Robert the Bruce was a claimant in 1290, rivalled by John de Baliol. His grandson was the famous Robert the Bruce, ROBERT I of Scotland. Edward Bruce, brother of Robert I, was crowned king of Ireland in 1316. The youngest son of Robert I succeeded him as DAVID II. He was succeeded by his nephew, ROBERT II, the first STUART king.

**Bruce, Christopher,** 1945–, English dancer and choreographer. Trained at the Ballet Rambert school, he joined the company in 1963, becoming associate director (1975–79), then associated choreographer. From 1987 he has been resident choreographer of the London Festival Ballet.

**Bruce, earls of Elgin:** see ELGIN, THOMAS BRUCE, 7th EARL OF.

**Bruce of Melbourne, Stanley Melbourne, Viscount,** 1883–1967, Australian prime minister (1923–29). He advocated close relations between Australia and the empire and was later Australian delegate to the LEAGUE OF NATIONS. He was Australian high commissioner in London (1933–45) and served during World War II in the British War cabinet.

**Bruch, Max** (brookh), 1838–1920, German composer. His Violin Concerto in G Minor (1868) and his variations on the *Kol Nidrei* (1881) for cello and orchestra are well known, as well as his *Scottish Fantasy* (1880) for violin and orchestra, which was first performed when he was conductor of the Liverpool orchestra (1880–83).

**Brücke, Die** (dee ˌbrykə), [Ger., = the bridge], German Expressionist art movement lasting from 1905 to 1913 (see EXPRESSIONISM). Founded in Dresden by KIRCHNER, SCHMIDT-ROTTLUFF, PECHSTEIN, and HECKEL. The group at first lived and worked communally, developing an intense, violent style with primitive qualities. Their exhibits, influenced by *Jugendstil* (the German equivalent of ART NOUVEAU) and VAN GOGH, displayed brutally deformed, boldly coloured subjects, a reaction against IMPRESSIONISM and REALISM. The group disbanded in 1913 because of disagreements over a statement of its aims.

**Bruckner, Anton,** 1824–96, Austrian composer and organist. Influenced by Richard WAGNER's orchestral grandeur and use of the chromatic SCALE, he employed complex, extended melody in such works as the MASSES in D Minor (1864), E Minor (1866), and F Minor (1867–71); a *Te Deum* (1881–84); and nine monumental symphonies.

**Bruegel, Brueghel** or **Breughel**, (ˌbruhgəl), family of Flemish painters. The foremost, **Pieter Bruegel, the Elder**, c.1525–1569, painted landscapes and GENRE with a new grandeur and seriousness. His early works are paintings and drawings of moralizing subjects which draw on proverb and parable and look back to BOSCH, e.g., *Netherlandish Proverbs* (1559; Staatliche Mus., Berlin). His most celebrated pictures are a series of majestic, panoramic landscapes that represent the months, e.g., *Hunters in the Snow* (1565; Kunsthistorisches Mus., Vienna) and a group of pictures of peasant life, e.g., the *Peasant Wedding Feast* (1566; Kunsthistorisches Mus.). His son **Pieter Bruegel, the Younger**, 1564–1638, often copied his father's works and was called 'Hell Bruegel' after his pictures of the infernal regions. His brother, **Jan Bruegel**, 1568–1625, called 'Velvet Bruegel', was a more original artist; he painted small-scale cabinet pictures, exquisitely finished and minutely detailed, of flowers and idyllic landscapes, e.g., *Paradise* (Mauritshuis, the Hague).

Pieter **Bruegel**, *Peasant Wedding Feast*, 1566. Panel, 114 × 63 cm. Kunsthistorisches Museum, Vienna.

**Bruges**, city (1985 pop. 117,747), NW Flemish Belgium, connected by canal to the North Sea. Founded in the 9th cent., it was (13th cent.) a major port of the HANSEATIC LEAGUE. At its zenith (14th cent.) it was a great commercial centre, particularly for the wool industry. It has revived as a commercial and tourist centre in this century. Once (14th–15th cent.) the cradle of Flemish art, its churches and museums house many works by such masters as Jan van EYCK and Gerard DAVID.

**Bruhn, Erik**, 1928–86, Danish ballet dancer. He joined the Royal Danish Ballet in 1947. Known for his dramatic, precise style in, e.g., *Giselle* and *Swan Lake*, he was considered throughout his career to have been among the best of the world's male dancers.

**Brumaire:** see FRENCH REVOLUTIONARY CALENDAR.

**Brummell, Beau** (George Bryan Brummell), 1778–1840, English dandy and wit. A friend of the prince regent (later George IV), he popularized dark, simply cut clothes, elaborate neckwear, and trousers rather than breeches.

**Brunehaut**, Frankish queen: see BRUNHILDA.

**Brunei**, independent sultanate (1985 est. pop. 220,000), 5765 km² (2226 sq mi) NW Borneo, surrounded by SARAWAK, Malaysia. The capital and major port is Bandar Seri Begawan. A British protectorate from 1888, it was granted self-government in 1971 and became an independent member of the COMMONWEALTH on 1 Jan. 1984. Oil is the chief export. Although a majority of the population are Malays, the small Chinese community dominates the economy. The government is headed by the Sultan, Sir Hassanal Bolkiah.

**Brunel, Isambard Kingdom**, 1806–59, English engineer. A gifted engineer (like his father Marc Isambard Brunel, 1769–1849), Brunel was the engineer to the Great Western Railway (1838), the advocate of Broad Gauge (2.13 m/7 ft) track. He also designed the *Great Western* (1838) which was the first steamship to cross the Atlantic in regular passenger service and the *Great Britain* (1845) which was the first large iron ship with screw propellers. His *Great Eastern* (1858) was the largest ship in the world for 40 years.

**Brunel, Sir Marc Isambard**, 1769–1849, English engineer and inventor; b. France. His most important work was the construction of the Thames Tunnel (begun 1825), in which a shield was used for the first time (see TUNNEL). His son, **Isambard Kingdom Brunel**, 1806–59, an English civil engineer, worked (1825–28) as resident engineer on the Thames Tunnel project before being appointed as engineer at the Bristol Docks. He designed docks at Monkwearmuth, Brentford, Milford Haven, and Plymouth, and in 1833 was appointed chief engineer to the Great Western Railway. He is best known for his design and construction of suspension bridges at Clifton (1834), Hungerford (1845), and Saltash (1859), and of three oceangoing STEAMSHIPS: the *Great Western* (1838), the first transatlantic steam vessel; the *Great Britain* (1845), the first ocean-going steamship driven by screw propeller; and the *Great Eastern* (1858), the largest steam vessel of its time.

**Brunelleschi, Filippo** (broohnelˌleskee), 1377–1446, first great Italian Renaissance architect, a Florentine. After his trial panel (1401) for the bronze doors of the Florence baptistery was not accepted (he was defeated by GHIBERTI), he concentrated on architectural planning. His Church of San Lorenzo, Florence, with its systematic use of perspective, and his Foundling Hospital, with its series of arches supported on columns, were tremendously influential. In 1420 he began a great octagonal ribbed DOME for the cathedral in Florence, one of the great domical constructions in architectural history.

Florence cathedral dome by Filippo **Brunelleschi**

**Bruner, Jerome Seymour**, 1915–, American psychologist. With George MILLER he was one of the first proponents of the cognitive approach to psychology (see COGNITIVE SCIENCE). He is best known for his work in developmental psychology, particularly the development of language and communication, in which he has done much to popularize the ideas of VYGOTSKY outside the USSR.

**Brunhes, Jean,** 1869–1930, French geographer. A founder of human geography, he wrote *La Géographie humaine* (1910), which was translated into English and had a major influence on the development of the subject in Britain and the US.

**Brunhild, Brünnehilde** or **Brynhild** (bruhnə͵hildə, ͵brinhild), in Germanic mythology and literature, mighty female warrior. In the medieval NIBELUNGEN epic she is the queen of Iceland, defeated by SIEGFRIED, whose death she contrives. In the Icelandic Volsungasaga she is Brynhild, chief of the VALKYRIES. Loved and later deserted by Sigurd, she brings about his death, and destroys herself on his funeral pyre. As Brünnehilde, a Valkyrie, she figures in Richard WAGNER's operatic cycle *Ring of the Nibelungs.*

**Brunhilda** or **Brunehaut,** d. 613, Frankish queen, wife of Sigebert I of Austrasia. She was the real ruler, through her son and grandsons, of Austrasia and BURGUNDY. She played a leading part in the bloody war (567–613) against Neustria. Clotaire I of Neustria, her nephew, put her to death.

**Bruno, Giordano,** 1548–1600, Italian philosopher. A DOMINICAN, Bruno was accused of heresy, left the order (c.1576), and became a wandering scholar. His works continued to be regarded as heretical, and he was arrested (1591), tried before the INQUISITION, and burned at the stake. His major metaphysical works, *On the Infinite Universe and Worlds* and *The Infinite* (both 1584), drew heavily from Hermetic gnosticism and other works on magic and the occult. His defence of Copernicus was based not on mathematics but on animist and religious grounds. Bruno held that there are many possible modes of viewing the world and that therefore we cannot postulate absolute truth. He was the first to state what is now called the cosmic theory: that the physical world is composed of irreducible elements (monads) in constant motion, and that the universe is infinite in scope. This view, reflected in the works of LEIBNIZ and SPINOZA, accounts for Bruno's position as a forerunner of modern science.

**Brunswick,** Ger. *Braunschweig,* city (1984 pop. 255,400), LOWER SAXONY, eastern West Germany, on the Oker R. The rich agricultural surroundings yield wheat, sugar beet, and other crops which are the basis of canning and processing industries. It is also a centre for engineering, publishing, and the manufacture of optical goods. Its town charter dates from the 12th cent. and it succeeded WOLFENBÜTTEL as capital of the Duchy of Brunswick in 1753. Medieval buildings, many restored following damage in World War II, include the 12th-cent. cathedral and 15th-cent. fountain.

**Brussels,** Fr. *Bruxelles,* city (1985 pop. 980,196), capital of Belgium. An important manufacturing centre, it is also the seat of the EUROPEAN COMMUNITY and of the NORTH ATLANTIC TREATY ORGANIZATION. Brussels was inhabited by the Romans and later (7th cent.) by the Franks. It developed into a centre of the wool trade in the 13th cent. and became (1430) the seat of the dukes of Burgundy and later (1477) of the governors of the Spanish (after 1714, Austrian) Netherlands. In 1830 it became the capital of an independent Belgium. Its historic buildings include the Maison du Roi (13th cent.), Gothic city hall (15th cent.), and parliament building (18th cent.).

**Brussels sprouts,** variety (*gemmifera*) of CABBAGE, producing small edible heads (sprouts) along the stem. Cultivated like cabbage, it was first developed in Belgium and France in the 18th cent.

**Brut, Brute** or **Brutus,** a Trojan, the legendary first king of England, a descendant of AENEAS. His name titles long poems by Wace and LAYAMON.

**Brutus,** in ancient Rome, a surname of the Junian gens. **Lucius Junius Brutus,** fl. 510 BC, was the founder of the Roman Republic. Roman historians tell how he led the Romans in expelling the TARQUINS after the rape of Lucrece and how he executed his sons for plotting a Tarquinian restoration. **Marcus Junius Brutus,** 85?–42 BC, was the principal assassin of Julius CAESAR. He had sided with POMPEY, but after the battle of Pharsalia (48 BC), Caesar pardoned him. Nevertheless, he joined Caius Cassius Longinus (see CASSIUS, family) in the plot against Caesar. After Caesar's murder (44 BC), Brutus went E and was defeated at Philippi in 42 BC by Octavian (later AUGUSTUS) and Antony. Brutus then committed suicide. His character has long been disputed. A lesser member of the conspiracy was **Decimus Junius Brutus,** d. 43 BC, a partisan of Caesar against Pompey and a favourite of the dictator. After Caesar's death, Brutus was killed by ANTONY.

The European Parliament, **Brussels**

**Brutus, Dennis** 1924–, South African poet; b. Zimbabwe. He writes about the impact of APARTHEID and is one of the key figures in the boycott in sport against his native country, for which he was imprisoned, and later, exiled, and which marks his works, e.g., *Letters to Martha, and Other Poems from a South African Prison* (1969) and *Stubborn Hope* (1978).

**Bryan, William Jennings,** 1860–1925, American political leader. He was a member (1891–95) of the US House of Representatives. At the 1896 Democratic national convention he made his famous 'Cross of Gold' speech in defence of free silver. He was nominated for president but lost to MCKINLEY that year and in 1900; in 1908 he lost to W.H. TAFT. In 1912 he helped to elect Woodrow WILSON, who named him secretary of state (1913–15). Bryan resigned in 1915, believing that Wilson's insistence on traditional neutral rights after the sinking of the *Lusitania* might lead to war. An advocate of religious FUNDAMENTALISM and an opponent of the teaching of evolution, he appeared for the prosecution in the 1925 Scopes Trial. Although he won the case his beliefs were ridiculed in court and he died five days later.

**Bryce, James, Viscount,** 1838–1922, British historian and statesman; b. Northern Ireland. A professor of law at Oxford, he wrote monumental works in several fields; the first was his *History of the Holy Roman Empire* (1864). He became a leader of the Liberal party, held several government posts, and was a popular ambassador to the US (1907–13). His treatise *The American Commonwealth* (1888) is admired.

**Bryophyta** (brie͵ofitə), division of the plant kingdom consisting of the MOSSES and LIVERWORTS.

**Brythonic** (bri͵thonik), group of languages belonging to the Celtic subfamily of the Indo-European family of languages. See LANGUAGE (table).

**Brzezinski, Zbigniew** (brə͵zhinskee), 1928–, American political scientist and public official. While teaching (1960–77) at Columbia Univ., he became an acknowledged expert on political affairs in the Communist world. As Pres. CARTER's national security adviser (1977–81), he advocated a harder line toward the USSR. He returned to Columbia in 1981.

**Btu:** see BRITISH THERMAL UNIT.

**bubble chamber:** see PARTICLE DETECTOR.

**Buber, Martin,** 1878–1965, Jewish philosopher; b. Austria. He taught Jewish philosophy and religion in Germany until he was forced (1938) to leave the country; he settled in Jerusalem. The mysticism of the HASIDIM and the Christian existentialism of KIERKEGAARD influenced him. His major work, *I and Thou* (1923), which posited a personal and direct dialogue between God and the individual, has had a great impact on contemporary Christian and Jewish theology.

**bubonic plague:** see PLAGUE.

**Bucaramanga,** city (1979 est. pop. 402,379), N Colombia, capital of Santander dept. Its growth since the 19th cent. from a former Indian settlement has been associated with its role as commercial centre for one of Colombia's principal coffee-growing districts.

**Bucer** or **Butzer, Martin** (ˌbyoohsə, ˌboohtsə), 1491–1551, German Protestant reformer. Influenced by LUTHER's preaching, he joined (1523) the REFORMATION movement in Strasbourg. He promoted Protestant education and brought about (1536) the Wittenberg Concord on the doctrine of the Eucharist. At the invitation of Thomas CRANMER, he spent his last years in England, teaching at Cambridge.

**Buchan, John,** 1st **Baron Tweedsmuir,** 1875–1940, Scottish author and statesman. He wrote history, biography, and popular adventure novels, including *The Thirty-nine Steps* (1915). In 1935 he was appointed governor general of Canada.

**Buchanan, James,** 1791–1868, 15th president of the US (1857–61). At first a Federalist, he became a conservative Democrat and was Pres. POLK's secretary of state (1845–49) during the MEXICAN WAR. Under Pres. PIERCE, he was (1853–56) minister to Great Britain and helped draft the OSTEND MANIFESTO. In 1856 he was elected president. Believing slavery was morally wrong but not unconstitutional, he hoped to end the slavery agitation by implementing the policy of SQUATTER SOVEREIGNTY in the territories. Under Southern influence, however, he favoured the pro-slavery settlers in Kansas, thereby infuriating Northern opponents of slavery and splitting his own Democratic party. After the 1860 election was won by Abraham LINCOLN, Buchanan was faced with the crisis of secession. Believing that states did not have the right to secede nor the federal government the right to coerce them if they did, he remained inactive when seven Southern states seceded and formed the CONFEDERACY. He retired from the presidency in March 1861, leaving the crisis for Lincoln to deal with.

**Bucharest,** Romanian *Bucureşti,* city (1985 est. pop. 1,975,808) capital and largest city of Romania, on the Dîmboviţa R., a tributary of the Danube. It is Romania's chief industrial centre and produces machinery, petroleum products, and textiles. It became the capital of WALACHIA in 1654 and of Romania after the Union of WALACHIA and MOLDAVIA in 1859. During World War II it was bombed by both the Allies and the Germans. Bucharest contains over 300 churches. Extensive demolition and rebuilding characterizes its centre.

**Buchman, Frank Nathan Daniel,** 1878–1961, American evangelist. After preaching 'world-changing through life-changing' at Oxford in 1921, he became the head of a movement called the Oxford Group or Buchmanism. In 1938 he founded the controversial Moral Re-Armament Movement (MRA).

**Büchner, Georg** (ˌbyːkhnə), 1813–37, German dramatist. Student of medicine and political activist, materialist and sceptic, Büchner was a writer before his time. His small dramatic output has been one of the most innovative forces on the modern stage: Naturalism, Expressionism, documentary and absurdist drama have all drawn on him. He died of typhus at 23, leaving a powerful historical drama *Danton's Death* (1835, first perf. 1902), the only work to be published in his lifetime; an intense fragment of low-life *Woyzeck* (pub. 1850 as *Wozzeck*; first perf. 1913; adapted by Alban BERG for his opera in 1925) and a romantic comedy *Leonce and Lena* (pub. 1842, first perf. 1895). Caught in a tension between revolution and despair, Büchner presents a world in which man is the puppet of forces—social, historical, biological, metaphysical—beyond his control.

**Buck, Pearl S(ydenstricker),** 1892–1973, American author. Until 1924 she lived in China, where she, her parents, and her first husband were missionaries. She is famous for her vivid, compassionate novels about life in China, the finest of which is thought to be *The Good Earth* (1931). Buck published over 85 books, including novels, children's books, plays, biographies, and non-fiction. She was awarded the Nobel Prize in literature in 1938.

**Buckingham, George Villiers,** 1st **duke of,** 1592–1628, English nobleman, a royal favourite. He arrived (1614) at the English court as JAMES I was tiring of Robert Carr and rose rapidly, becoming lord high admiral in 1619. By 1620 he was dispensing the king's patronage. He gained popularity with Parliament by urging war with Spain, then lost it by negotiating CHARLES I's marriage to HENRIETTA MARIA, a Catholic princess of France. He remained powerful after Charles came to the throne. After the failure of several expeditions, notably one against Cádiz (1625), he was impeached by Parliament, but the king dissolved Parliament to prevent his trial. Villiers was at Portsmouth preparing an expedition to relieve the HUGUENOTS at La Rochelle when he was killed by a discontented naval officer. His son, **George Villiers,** 2nd **duke of Buckingham,** 1628–87, was a royalist in the ENGLISH CIVIL WAR. He served CHARLES II in exile, but intrigues and his marriage to the daughter of a Puritan lord caused estrangement. He regained favour after the RESTORATION and became an extremely powerful courtier. Vain and ambitious, he was noted for his temper, recklessness, and dissoluteness. He was a member of the CABAL but was dismissed for misconduct in 1674. Despite earlier opposition to JAMES II, he regained favour in 1684. A scholar with exquisite tastes, he wrote poetry and plays, including *The Rehearsal* (1671).

**Buckingham Palace,** residence of British sovereigns since 1837, Westminster, London. Built (1703) by the Duke of Buckingham, it was purchased (1761) by GEORGE III and remodelled (1825) by John NASH. The palace has nearly 600 rooms.

Buckingham Palace

**Buckinghamshire,** inland county, in S Midlands of England (1984 est. pop. 594,600), 1883 km² (734 sq mi), bordering on Greater London in the SE. The county town is AYLESBURY. The Chiltern Hills are found towards the S of the county and the land descends sharply on their N slopes into the Vale of Aylesbury. Mixed agriculture is found in the N of the county. HIGH WYCOMBE has manufacturing industry (especially furniture) and much of the S of the county is part of the LONDON commuter belt.

**Buckle, Henry Thomas,** 1821–62, English historian. Using a so-called scientific method, he undertook the ambitious plan of writing a history of civilization rather than of battles and wars. At the time of his death, he had completed the first two volumes of his *History of Civilization in England* (1857–61).

**buckthorn,** common name for some members of the Rhamnaceae, a family of widely distributed woody shrubs, small trees, and climbing vines. The buckthorns (some species of the genus *Rhamnus*) and the jujube (*Zizyphus jujuba*) are cultivated as ornamentals. Jujube is also used as a flavouring and in confectionery. Some members of the family yield dyes; others are used for timber. *R. purshiana* yields the purgative cascara sagrada.

**buckwheat,** common name for some members of the Polygonaceae, a family of herbs and shrubs found chiefly in north temperate areas and having a characteristic pungent juice containing oxalic acid. Members of the family include the knotweeds and smartweeds (genus *Polygonum* or *Persicaria*), some sorrels (the common name used also for the unrelated OXALIS), and the economically important rhubarb (genus *Rheum*) and buckwheat (genus *Fagopyrum*).

**bucolics:** see PASTORAL.

**Budapest,** city (1985 est. pop. 2,072,000), capital and largest city of Hungary, N central Hungary, on both banks of the Danube R. About half of Hungary's industrial output comes from Budapest and its suburbs;

major products include machinery, chemicals, and iron and steel. One of the capitals of the AUSTRO-HUNGARIAN MONARCHY, the city was formed in 1873 by the union of Buda and Óbuda, on the right bank of the Danube, with Pest, on the left bank. The area may have been settled in the Neolithic era. Under Roman rule from the 1st cent. AD, the cities were destroyed by the Mongols in 1241. Buda became the capital of Hungary in 1361 and fell to the Turks in 1541. After 1686 the cities were under HABSBURG rule. During World War II Budapest was occupied (1944–45) by the Germans and was largely destroyed during a 14-week siege by Soviet troops. It became the capital of the Hungarian People's Republic in 1949. In 1956 it was the centre of an unsuccessful uprising against the Communist regime.

**Buddha,** [Skt., = the enlightened one], title given to the founder of BUDDHISM, Siddhārtha Gautama, c.563–c.483 BC; b. S Nepal. A soothsayer is said to have predicted at Siddhārtha's birth that he would become a world ruler or a world teacher. His father, King Śuddhodana, of the warrior caste, raised him in great luxury, but at the age of 29 Siddhārtha renounced the world to become a wandering ascetic and search for a solution to the problems of death and human suffering, i.e., old age, disease, and decay. After six years of spiritual discipline, he achieved supreme enlightenment at the age of 35 while meditating under a pipal tree at Bodh Gayā. He spent the rest of his life teaching his doctrines and establishing a community of monks, the *sangha,* to continue his work.

**Buddhism,** religion and philosophy founded in India in the 6th and 5th cent. BC by Siddhārtha Gautama, called the BUDDHA. One of the great Asian religions, it teaches the practice of MEDITATION and the observance of moral precepts. The basic doctrines include the 'four noble truths' taught by the Buddha: existence is suffering; the cause of suffering is desire; there is a cessation of suffering, called NIRVĀNA, or total extinction; and there is a path leading to this extinction of suffering, the 'eightfold path' of right views, right resolve, right speech, right action, right livelihood, right effort, right mindfulness, and right concentration. Buddhism defines reality in terms of arising and disappearing of momentary events, where the preceding one conditions the succeeding one. It accepts the doctrine common to Indian religions of *samsāra,* or bondage to the repeating cycle of births, deaths and rebirths according to one's physical and mental actions (see KARMA). The ideal of early Buddhism was the perfected saint, *arhant* or *arhat,* purified of all desires. Of the various Buddhist schools and sects that arose, the *Theravāda* [doctrine of the elders] school of Sri Lanka is generally accepted as representative of early Buddhist teaching. *Mahāyāna* [great vehicle] Buddhism has as a central concept the potential Buddhahood innate in all beings. Its ideal for both layman and monk is the *bodhisattva,* the perfected one who postpones entry into *nirvāna* (although meriting it) until all others may be similarly enlightened. Buddhism was greatly strengthened in the 3rd cent. BC by the support of the Indian emperor AŚOKA, but it declined in India in succeeding centuries and was virtually extinct there by the 13th cent., while it spread and flourished in Sri Lanka (3rd cent. BC) and Tibet (7th cent. AD) (see TIBETAN BUDDHISM). In the 1st cent. AD, Buddhism entered China, where it encountered resistance from CONFUCIANISM and TAOISM, and from there spread to Korea (4th cent. AD) and to Japan (6th cent. AD). Two important sects that became established in the 5th cent. AD and have greatly increased in popularity are ZEN BUDDHISM, featuring the practice of meditation to achieve 'sudden enlightenment', and Pure Land Buddhism, or Amidism, a devotional Mahāyāna sect centred on the worship of the Buddha Amitābha, who vowed to save all sentient beings by bringing them to rebirth in his realm, the 'Western Paradise'. Buddhism still flourishes in Asia and has an influence in the modern Western world.

**budgerigar** or **budgerygah,** (*Melopsittacus undulatus*) commonest member of the Australian PARAKEETS, and a popular cage-bird in Europe. It is a nomadic, gregarious BIRD which is a pest to agriculture in the wild. It is about 17 cm (7 in) long. Budgerigars nest in mallee scrub, digging a hole and using rotten wood and wood dust as nesting material. Females cannot lay eggs unless they have a totally dark nest to hide in.

**budget,** a list of proposed expenditures and expected receipts for a definite period, usually one year. The governmental budget originated in England during the late 18th cent. Budgets are essential for the planning and controlling of government or business finances. National budgets estimate income and expenditure for the forthcoming financial year and

in the UK are presented to the British parliament by the chancellor of the exchequer, usually in late March/early April. At this time, any changes in taxation are usually made. Interim budgets are sometimes drawn up to cope with radical changes in economic conditions. Budget deficits are usually met by increased levels of borrowing. In the UK there is normally a deficit—in 1986/87 this was £9.7 billion which necessitated public borrowing of £3.3 billion.

**Buenos Aires,** city and federal district (1980 pop. 2,908,001; metropolitan area pop. 9,927,404), E Argentina, capital of Argentina, on the Río de la Plata. It is one of the largest cities of Latin America, a major world port, and Argentina's commercial and social centre. Heavily industrialized, the city is one of the world's leading exporters of processed foods. It was founded in 1536, abandoned, then resettled in 1580, and was the first Latin American city to revolt (1810) against Spanish rule. Officially independent in 1816, it became the capital of a united Argentina in 1862. It grew into an urban colossus in the late 19th cent., when railways into the agriculturally abundant PAMPA to the west began to supplement the great inland river transport system that linked the city with Uruguay, Paraguay, and Brazil, and immigrants from Europe swelled its population. Famous landmarks include the 19th-cent. cathedral, the opera house, and the many beautiful municipal parks.

**Buero Vallejo, Antonio** (ˌbweəroh'valyekhoh), 1916–, Spanish dramatist. He came to prominence with *Historia de una escalera* (1949; tr. Story of a Staircase), a polemical social drama. His numerous historical dramas include *Las meninas* (1960; tr. The Ladies-in-Waiting). *El concierto de San ovidio* (1962), and *La llegada de los dioses* (1971; tr. Arrival of the Gods). His most recent works are *Caimán* (1981; Alligator) and *Diálogo secreto* (1985; tr. Secret Dialogue).

**Buffalo,** US city (1984 est. pop. 339,000), W New York, on Lake Erie and the Niagara and Buffalo rivers; inc. 1832. One of the major grain-distributing ports in the US and centre of a rail-network, it has automobile, electrochemical, electrometallurgical, and steel industries. Laid out in 1803, it was almost entirely destroyed by fire in the WAR OF 1812. Transport, particularly after the opening (1825) of the ERIE CANAL, was a key factor in the city's development. Its central commercial area underwent major renewal in the 1970s and early 80s. Buffalo is the site of a branch of the State Univ. of New York, the Albright-Knox Art Gallery, and other noted institutions. The Peace Bridge (1927) connects it with Fort Erie, Canada.

**buffalo,** name commonly applied to the North American BISON but correctly restricted to related African and Asian hoofed MAMMALS of the CATTLE family. The water, or Indian, buffalo (*Bubalus bubalis*) is a large, strong, dark grey animal with widespread curved horns, domesticated for draft. Wild forms live near rivers, where they wallow; they feed on grass and have fierce tempers.

**Buffalo Bill** (William Frederick Cody), 1846–1917, American scout and showman; b. near Davenport, Iowa. He worked as an army scout and hunted buffalo for railroad camps. He organized (1883) and then toured with Buffalo Bill's Wild West Show.

**buffer,** solution that can keep its *p*H, i.e., its relative acidity or alkalinity, constant, despite the addition of strong acids or bases (see ACIDS AND BASES). Buffer solutions contain either a weak acid or weak base and one of their salts. See article on *p*H.

**Buffon, George Louis Leclerc, comte de** (byfawnh), 1707–88, French naturalist and author. From 1739 he was keeper of the Jardin du Roi (later Jardin des Plantes) in Paris, making it a centre of research during the Enlightenment. His works include his monumental compendium on natural history, *Histoire naturelle* (44 vol., 1749–1804). On his reception into the French Academy in 1753, he delivered his famous *Discours sur le style.*

**bug,** name correctly applied to any INSECT of the order Hemiptera, although other insects are colloquially referred to as bugs. True bugs all have piercing-sucking mouthparts in the form of a rostrum (proboscis). Most feed on plant juices, e.g., froghoppers (Cercopidae), but some, e.g., assassin bugs (Reduviidae) suck the blood of other insects and a few that of birds and mammals, including man, e.g., bedbug. A number of species are aquatic (see WATER BUG), but the vast majority are terrestrial. Many bugs are important crop pests because of the direct damage they cause or the diseases they transmit, e.g., capsids (Miridae) and APHIDS, while triatomid bugs are, in South America, the vectors of Chaga's disease (a form of TRYPANOSOMIASIS) in humans.

**Buganda:** see UGANDA.

**bugle,** a BRASS INSTRUMENT resembling the cornet but without valves. It is used in brass and military bands, and for signalling.

**building society,** an institution which accepts savings from the public and makes loans for house purchase in the form of mortgages. In the UK, they grew out of FRIENDLY SOCIETIES in the late 17th cent. and were regulated by the Building Societies Act 1874 which was superseded by several acts which increased regulatory controls. Building societies are important generators of housing funds and recipients of domestic savings; shares and deposits in them (including 'save-as-you-earn') attract interest rates according to the type of account, which may permit withdrawals on demand or at the end of a period lasting as much as several years. In 1950 UK building societies accounted for only 10% of retail savings but by 1980 the share had reached 50% and they had secured 75% of the market for mortgages. Their development was helped by the fact that they were not subjected to the same controls as other financial institutions. In 1980 controls on banks were lifted which enabled them to compete on equal terms in the mortgage market with building societies, and as a result the latter's share of the market grew only slowly between 1980 and 1986. The Building Societies Act 1986 marked the end of their traditional role and gave societies increased powers and scope to carry out business previously closed to them. From 1987 the services they were able to offer included unsecured credit, foreign exchange, insurances, PERSONAL EQUITY PLANS, personal pension schemes management, estate agency, and conveyancing services. At the end of 1986 there was a total of 53.6 million accounts held with building societies in the UK, an average of very nearly one per head of population.

**Buisson, Ferdinand Édouard** (bwee,sawnh), 1841–1932, French educator and 1927 Nobel Peace Prize winner. A professor of pedagogy at the Sorbonne, he produced the *Dictionnaire de pédagogie* (1882–93) and was an ardent pacifist and civil-liberties worker.

**Bujumbura,** city (1979 pop. 172,201), capital of Burundi, W Burundi. A port on Lake TANGANYIKA, it is the country's largest city and economic centre, and has a growing tourist industry. Coffee, cotton, hides, and skins are shipped via the lake to Tanzania and Zaïre. The city became (1899) a military post in German East Africa. After World War I it was the administrative centre of Ruanda-Urundi, a Belgian MANDATE. It was called Usumbura until 1962.

**Bukhari, Muhammad Ibn Ismail,** 810–70, Muslim traditionist. Author of the most authoritative of the six authoritative works of HADITH, Bukhari culled out from the 600,000 hadith narratives at his disposal 2762 for which he found the authority to be unquestionable and arranged them under various thematic headings.

**Bukharin, Nikolai Ivanovich** (booh,kahrin), 1888–1938, leading Russian Bolshevik and Marxist theoretician whose work was much admired by LENIN. He was the co-author of the *ABC of Communism* (1920), and editor of the newspaper *Pravda*. After the failures of 'war communism' (of which he had been an enthusiastic proponent) he at first deplored the New Economic Policy (NEP), which introduced or legalized some private production and trade in 1921; he later spoke more favourably of market arrangements and the economic incentives they provided, suggesting that socialism might develop at a 'snail's pace'. He was a full member of the Politburo after 1924, but lost his major party positions in 1929, when he opposed the rapid collectivization of agriculture proposed by Stalin. Along with other leading Bolsheviks he was accused of anti-Soviet activities, and was executed in 1938. In 1987, as part of the liberalization of the Soviet Union under GORBACHEV, Bukharin's name was rehabilitated as a patriot and hero of the revolution.

**Bukovina** ('boohko,veena), historical region, NW ROMANIA. Annexed by Austria in 1775, this region of NW MOLDAVIA was renamed Bukovina and in 1790 united with GALICIA. Later separated, it was in 1849 declared a duchy and crown land of the Habsburg Empire. In 1920 the declaration by its Romanian population of union with Romania was recognized by the Allied powers. In 1940 the northern part of the region was seized by the USSR and incorporated into the UKRAINIAN SSR. Reconquered by the Romanian army in 1941, Northern Bukovina was recovered in 1944 by the Red Army and restored to the Ukrainian SSR.

**Bulawayo,** city (1982 pop. 413,800), Matabeleland North Prov., SW Zimbabwe, on the Matsheumlope R. The country's second largest city, it is an important commercial, railway, and industrial centre that produces textiles, asphalt, agricultural equipment, and electrical goods. The city was founded by the British in 1893. Nearby are the 18th-cent. African ruins of Khami.

**bulb,** thickened, fleshy plant bud, usually formed below the soil surface, which stores food from one blooming season to the next. Bulbs have either layers of leaf bases (e.g., onion and hyacinth) or fleshy scales (e.g., some lilies). Structures that serve similar functions include the TUBER of the potato and the RHIZOMES of some irises.

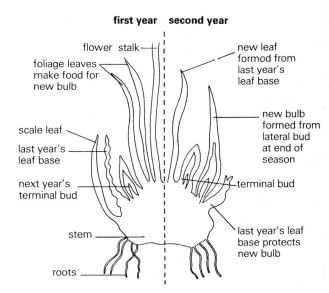

Section through a **bulb** showing growth cycle

**Bulgakov, Mikhail Afanasyevich,** 1891–1940, Russian writer. *The White Guard* (1925), a novel, and *The Days of the Turbines* (1926), a play, are about the RUSSIAN REVOLUTION (1917). His masterpiece is *The Master and Margarita* (published in a censored edition in 1967–68; tr. 1967), a satiric, philosophical fantasy about Satan's visit to Moscow.

**Bulganin, Nikolai Aleksandrovich,** 1895–1975, Soviet leader. He was mayor of Moscow (1931–37), chairman of the state bank (1937–41), and defence minister under STALIN and MALENKOV, whom he succeeded as premier (1955). In 1958, forced from office by KHRUSHCHEV, he was expelled from the Communist Party central committee.

**Bulgaria,** officially the People's Republic of Bulgaria, republic (1985 est. pop. 9,220,000, increasing at 0.47% per year) 110,912 km² (42,823 sq mi), SE Europe, on the E BALKAN PENINSULA. It is bordered by the Black Sea (E), Romania (N), Yugoslavia (W), Greece (S), and European Turkey (SE). SOFIA is the capital. Central Bulgaria is traversed from E to W by the Balkan Mts; the Rhodope range, with the country's highest peak, Musala Mt (2923 m/9592 ft), is in the SW. The principal river is the DANUBE. Bulgaria has been considerably industrialized since World War II, but agriculture (chiefly wheat, maize, barley, sugar beets, grapes, and livestock) remains the principal occupation. Most of the land was collectivized in 1958. The leading industries are food-processing, engineering, metallurgy, and the production of machinery, chemicals, and fertilizers. GNP per capita (1980) is US$4150. The population consists chiefly of Bulgars (86%) and Turks (9%); the EASTERN ORTHODOX CHURCH is the predominant religion.

*History.* In AD 679–80 ancient THRACE and Moesia, site of modern Bulgaria, were conquered by the predominantly Turkic Proto-Bulgars, who gradually merged with earlier Slavic settlers and adopted their language. The first Bulgarian empire was established in 681, introduced to Christianity by BORIS I (r.852–89) in 865, at the height of its power under SIMEON I (r.893–927), and subjugated by the Byzantines in 1018. The second Bulgarian empire rose in 1186 and reached its apogee under Ivan II (r.1218–41). In 1396 it was absorbed by the OTTOMAN EMPIRE, which ruled it for almost five centuries as a core province of the empire. By the 19th cent., however, economic change and Ottoman decay had stimulated the growth of Bulgarian nationalism. The Ottomans' suppression of a Bulgarian revolt (1876) was one of the causes of the RUSSO-TURKISH WAR of 1877–78. The Treaty of San Stefano, imposed by Russia on Turkey, created a large autonomous Bulgarian state, but was revised by the Congress of BERLIN. MACEDONIA was returned to the Ottomans, and Bulgaria was reduced to an autonomous principality north of the Balkan Mts and the Ottoman-administered province of Eastern Rumelia to the south. Alexander BATTENBERG was named prince under a liberal constitution, but lost Russian support and was forced to abdicate when he sanctioned Bulgaria's unification with Eastern Rumelia and defeated Serbia in war (1885). FERDINAND of Saxe-Coburg-Gotha was elected prince in 1887 and proclaimed Bulgaria's full independence in 1908 with himself as czar. The country was enlarged significantly by the BALKAN WARS (1912–13), but the failure to acquire Macedonia led Ferdinand to side with the Central Powers in WORLD WAR I. Defeat caused Ferdinand to abdicate in favour of his son, BORIS III (r.1918–43), but the country was often in political turmoil during and after the peasant regime of Alexander STAMBOLIISKI (1918–23). Boris established a personal dictatorship in 1935 and allied Bulgaria once more with Germany in WORLD WAR II. The Soviet Union occupied the country in 1944, and permitted the Communist-dominated Fatherland Front to seize power, but Bulgaria was forced again to yield up the bulk of Macedonia to Yugoslavia and Greece. The monarchy was abolished, and a republic proclaimed in 1946. Bulgaria became a member of COMECON and the WARSAW TREATY ORGANIZATION, and in 1968 participated in the Soviet-led invasion of Czechoslovakia. It is governed by a 1971 constitution that provides for a unicameral national assembly, council of state, and cabinet of ministers, but actual power resides in the Communist Party (led since 1954 by Todor ZHIVKOV) which has proved a faithful ally of the USSR.

Bulgaria

**Bulgarian language,** member of the South Slavic group of the Slavic subfamily of the Indo-European family of languages. See LANGUAGE (table).

**Bulgars, Eastern,** Turkic-speaking people who appeared on the middle Volga R., E European Russia, by the 8th cent.; also called Volga or Kama Bulgars. One branch moved west into the Balkans, and, merging there with the Slavs, gave rise to the modern Bulgarians. The Eastern Bulgars accepted ISLAM in the 10th cent. and founded a powerful state; it survived the Mongol conquests of 1237 and 1361 but disappeared after its capture by the grand duke of Moscow in 1431.

**bulimia,** eating disorder found almost exclusively among young women, in which the person consumes enormous amounts of food (sometimes several thousand calories within an hour) and then attempts to rid the body of the food by inducing vomiting or taking laxatives. Bulimia often accompanies ANOREXIA NERVOSA, another eating disorder. The recommended treatment is PSYCHOTHERAPY.

**bull,** letter containing an important pronouncement of the pope. In modern times encyclicals (letters to all bishops) are usually used for doctrinal statements, whereas bulls are employed for solemn or grave pronouncements.

**bullfighting,** national sport of Spain, also popular in Mexico and other Latin American countries. The object is for one of the bullfighters, the matador, to kill an untamed bull with a sword in a manner largely prescribed by tradition. The matador is assisted by two mounted picadors and three capemen on foot (*banderilleros*), who sting the bull with lances and barbed sticks to spur his charge. In the final act, the matador makes passes at the bull with his cape, or *muleta,* before thrusting his sword between the animal's shoulderblades into the heart. Although a matador's performance is often one of grace and beauty, critics have denounced bullfighting as an inhumane spectacle. The Portuguese practise a style of bullfighting from horseback in which the bull is not killed.

**Bull Moose party:** see PROGRESSIVE PARTY.

**Bull Run,** small stream, NE Virginia, US; the site of two Union defeats in the AMERICAN CIVIL WAR. The **first battle of Bull Run** (or Manassas) was the first major clash of the war, on 21 July 1861. On 16 July the Union general Irvin McDowell advanced on Manassas Junction but the Confederate general Stonewall JACKSON checked the Union advance and, reinforced, routed the raw Union troops. In the **second battle of Bull Run,** 29–30 Aug. 1862, Jackson was attacked by the Union general John Pope just as Gen. James LONGSTREET arrived with reinforcements; together they twice repulsed Pope, who withdrew to Washington.

**Bülow, Hans Guido, Freiherr von** (by:lov), 1830–94, German pianist and conductor. He studied with LISZT, married his daughter Cosima (who left him to marry Richard WAGNER), and became a champion of BRAHMS. He was the first modern virtuoso conductor (see CONDUCTING).

**Bultmann, Rudolf Karl,** 1884–1976, German existentialist theologian. Influenced by Martin HEIDEGGER, he is best known for his work on the New Testament, which he reduced with the exception of the Passion to basic elements of myth. His approach is termed 'demythologization'. His classic work is *Theology of the New Testament* (tr. 1952–55).

**Bulwer-Lytton, Edward George Earle Lytton,** 1st **baron Lytton,** 1803–73, English novelist. His prolific output included novels of fashionable society such as *Pelham* (1828), studies of criminal psychology such as *Eugene Aram* (1832), tales of the occult and science fiction, plays including the very successful *Lady of Lyons,* and historical novels of which *The Last Days of Pompeii* (1834) was the most celebrated. He was a Member of Parliament, and Colonial Secretary (1858–9).

**Bunau-Varilla, Philippe Jean** (buhno-vahree͵yah), 1859–1940, French engineer. He organized the company that built the PANAMA CANAL. He was a leader in the conspiracy that successfully wrested PANAMA from Colombia. As minister of the new Panamanian republic, he negotiated the treaty (1903) that gave the US control of the waterway. See also GOETHALS; George WASHINGTON.

**Bunbury,** city (1986 pop. 23,031), Western Australia. Located 180 km (110 mi) S of Perth on the Indian Ocean, it is the third largest urban centre in Western Australia. It is a port for coal, timber, meat, fruit, and the mineral ilmenite, which is extracted from local mineral beach sands.

**Bunche, Ralph Johnson,** 1904–71, US diplomat. He was (1945) the first black person to be a division head in the US Department of State. For his work (1947) as principal secretary of the UN Palestine Commission he was awarded (1950) the Nobel Peace Prize. He later served as undersecretary general for special political affairs (1958–71).

**Bundaberg,** city (1986 pop. 33,368), Queensland, NE Australia. Situated on the Burnett R., the city is surrounded by sugar canefields, is the centre for the manufacture of mechanical cane-harvesting machinery, and has a rum distillery.

**Bundestag,** lower house of the parliament of the Federal Republic of Germany (West Germany). It is a popularly elected body that elects the chancellor, passes all legislation, and ratifies the most important treaties. It can remove the chancellor by a vote of no confidence, but only if it simultaneously elects a new chancellor. The Bundesrat (federal council), the upper house, represents the states.

**Bunin, Ivan Alekseyevich** (͵boohnin), 1870–1953, Russian émigré writer. He came to world attention with *The Village* (1910), a pessimistic novel of peasant life. Best known are his short stories, e.g., the title story in the collection *The Gentleman from San Francisco* (1916), an ironic study of vanity and death; and his autobiographical novel *The Well of Days* (1930). An aristocrat, he lived in exile after 1919. He received the 1933 Nobel Prize for literature.

**Bunker Hill, battle of,** battle in the AMERICAN REVOLUTION, 17 June 1775; actually fought on nearby Breed's Hill, Charlestown, Massachusetts. Colonial militia defended the height against Gen. William Howe (see under HOWE, RICHARD HOWE, EARL) until their powder gave out. The British victory failed to break the Patriots' siege of Boston, and the gallant American defence heightened colonial morale and resistance.

**Bunsen, Robert Wilhelm,** 1811–99, German scientist. A professor (1852–89) at Heidelberg, he studied organic compounds of arsenic and developed a method of gas analysis from studies on blast furnaces. With Gustav KIRCHHOFF he discovered by spectroscopy the elements CAESIUM and RUBIDIUM. He invented and improved various kinds of laboratory equipment. The Bunsen burner was developed by him, based on earlier variants by Michael FARADAY.

**Bunshaft, Gordon,** 1909–, American architect. He was responsible for Lever House, New York City's first glass-wall SKYSCRAPER (1952), which was widely imitated. Among his other works is the Albright-Knox Art Gallery, Buffalo, New York State, and the Hirshhorn Museum, Washington, District of Columbia.

Gordon **Bunshaft**: Lever House, New York

**Buñuel, Luis,** 1900–83, Spanish film director. His critical, often witty, studies of social hypocrisy include *Un Chien andalou* (1928), *L'Age d'or* (1930), *Los Olvidados* (1949), *The Exterminating Angel* (1962), and *That Obscure Object of Desire* (1977).

**Bunyan, John,** 1628–88, English writer. A tinker by trade and a Parliamentary soldier, he became a Baptist lay preacher and wrote to defend his beliefs. Arrested in 1660 for unlicensed preaching, he spent 12 years in prison. There he wrote his spiritual autobiography, *Grace Abounding to the Chief of Sinners* (1666), and other books. Imprisoned a second time, he wrote his masterpiece, *The Pilgrim's Progress* (1678, second part 1684), an allegory of the soul of man on its life journey to the Celestial City, written in everyday but heart-searching language. For two centuries it was, next to the Bible, the most universally-read and owned book in English. Bunyan was a prolific writer, his other chief works being *The Life and Death of Mr Badman* (1680) and *The Holy War* (1682).

**bunyip aristocracy,** derisive term coined in Australia during the constitutional debates of the 1850s over the form of future self-government. It was applied to those who proposed the creation of an order of hereditary colonial baronets, from which a second chamber would be drawn. The proposal was defeated.

**Buonaparte:** see BONAPARTE; NAPOLEON I.

**Buonarroti, Michelangelo:** see MICHELANGELO.

**Buoninsegna, Duccio di:** see DUCCIO DI BUONINSEGNA.

**buoyancy:** see ARCHIMEDES' PRINCIPLE.

**Burbage, Richard,** 1567?–1619, first great English actor. He originated the title roles in SHAKESPEARE's *Hamlet, King Lear, Othello,* and *Richard III.* He also acted in the premieres of many plays by Thomas KYD, BEAUMONT and FLETCHER, Ben JONSON, and John WEBSTER. His father, **James Burbage,** built England's first public playhouse in 1576.

**Burbidge, (Eleanor) Margaret,** 1925–, Anglo-American astronomer. She was (1972–73) the first woman appointed director of the Royal Greenwich Observatory and was named (1982) president of the American Association for the Advancement of Science. Burbidge, her husband Geoffrey Burbidge, William Fowler, and Sir Fred Hoyle showed (1956) that all the elements heavier than helium are synthesized from hydrogen and helium in stars (see NUCLEOGENESIS).

**Burckhardt, Jacob Christoph,** 1818–97, Swiss historian, one of the founders of the cultural interpretation of history. A thoughtful and stimulating writer, his *Civilization of the Renaissance in Italy* (1860) remains the great classic on the Renaissance.

**bureaucracy,** term normally used to define a form of governmental institution, but also covering the forms of administration and management associated with large organizations (including government itself). The sociologist Max WEBER produced an 'ideal type' of bureaucratic organization characterized by the following traits: the existence of a formal, written body of rules that govern the way the institution functions; the principle that the individual and the post they occupy are separate; the existence of a formally recognized chain of command, in which each individual is aware of their area of responsibility and competence; the establishment of recognized standards for entrance and promotion within the institution; the keeping of written records of the activity and decisions of the institution; the establishment of impersonal relationships between the institution and its clients; the paying of a fixed salary for duties done. For Weber the spread of such forms of organization was intimately linked with the process of rationalization of human activity with the spread of CAPITALISM.

**Bureh Bai,** c.1840–1908, resistance leader in colonial SIERRA LEONE; also known as Kebalai. He was a chief of the Kesse people and between 1890 and 1898 led the Temne against the establishment of British control over the interior of Sierra Leone. He was captured during the Hut Tax War of 1898 and deported to Ghana. He returned to Sierra Leone in 1905.

**Burgas,** city (1983 pop. 183,477), Bulgaria, on the BLACK SEA. It is a busy port with oil-refining, chemical, and railway engineering industries. It is the point of arrival for visitors to nearby Black Sea resorts.

**Burgess, Anthony,** 1917–, English novelist and critic. Of his surreal, darkly comic novels, the best known is the futuristic thriller *A Clockwork Orange* (1962). Others include *Inside Mr Enderby* (1963), *MF* (1971), and *Earthly Powers* (1980).

**Burghley** or **Burleigh, William Cecil, 1st baron,** 1520–98, English statesman. He was chief adviser to ELIZABETH I, whom he served faithfully for 40 years as her chief spokesman in Parliament (1558–98) and as secretary (1558–72) and lord treasurer (1572–98). A supporter of the Anglican church and able administrator, he suppressed Catholic revolts and persuaded Elizabeth to execute MARY QUEEN OF SCOTS.

**burglary,** in England and Wales, the offence of entering a building as a trespasser with intent to commit a CRIME, e.g., THEFT, RAPE, or grievous bodily harm. If the offender possesses a weapon the offence is aggravated burglary. In Scotland, the equivalent offence is called housebreaking.

**Burgos,** city (1981 pop. 156,449), capital of Burgos prov., N central Spain. It commands important routeways, especially that of the Arlanzon valley between VALLADOLID and the French frontier. It has paper and chemical industries and serves as a military base. Established in the 9th cent., it was an early capital of CASTILE during the reconquest from the Moors, being succeeded by TOLEDO in 1087. The early 13th-cent. cathedral is a fine example of Gothic architecture.

**Burgoyne, John,** 1722–92, British general. A hero of the SEVEN YEARS WAR, he was elected to Parliament in 1761. In the AMERICAN REVOLUTION he led a poorly equipped army in the SARATOGA CAMPAIGN and surrendered in Oct. 1777.

**Burgundy,** historic region, E France. DIJON is the historic capital. Burgundy, centred in the fertile Saône and upper Rhone river valleys, is famous for its fine wines. The Burgundii, a tribe from Savoy, conquered (c.480) the area from Rome and established the First Kingdom of Burgundy, comprising SE France and W Switzerland. Burgundy was partitioned after it fell (534) to the Franks, but it was later united to form (933) the kingdom of ARLES. The duchy of Burgundy, roughly the area of the present region, was created in 877. In 1364 JOHN II of France bestowed it upon his son, PHILIP THE BOLD. Under Philip and his successors, JOHN THE FEARLESS, PHILIP THE GOOD, and CHARLES THE BOLD, Burgundy became a great power and acquired vast territory, including much of the Low Countries. After the accession (1477) of MARY OF BURGUNDY, most of Burgundy's possessions came under HABSBURG rule; the duchy itself was incorporated into France.

**Burke, Edmund,** 1729–97, British political writer and statesman; b. Ireland. He was a member of Samuel JOHNSON's literary circle. His early writings concerned aesthetics and philosophy. In 1765 he became private secretary to the marquess of Rockingham (then prime minister) and entered Parliament. In *Thoughts on the Cause of the Present Discontents* (1770) he was the first to argue the value of political parties. As a member of Parliament he called for conciliation with the American colonists and warned against taxing them excessively. Attempting to reform the English EAST INDIA COMPANY in the 1780s, he instigated the impeachment of Warren HASTINGS, governor general of India, on corruption charges. His most famous work, *Reflections on the Revolution in France* (1790), attacked the abstract theorizing of the revolutionaries and predicted the collapse into dictatorship which was to occur under NAPOLEON Bonaparte. Burke is most famous for the elaboration in his political writings of an eloquent philosophy of CONSERVATISM, defending tradition and evolutionary progress, which greatly influenced 19th-cent. conservatism and all subsequent writers on the subject. What is distinctly modern about Burke's conservatism is his attempt to combine an organic and hierarchical view of society with a commitment to liberal economics, which involves the somewhat contradictory values of freedom and individualism.

**Burke, Robert O'Hara,** 1820–61, Australian explorer; b. Ireland. In 1860, with W.J. Wills (1834–61) he set out from Cooper Creek to cross Australia from south to north. They reached the Gulf of Carpentaria, but died of hunger on the return journey; they are remembered as tragic heroes.

**Burkina,** formerly Upper Volta, officially Burkina Faso, republic (1985 est. pop. 7,919,895), 274,200 km² (105,869 sq mi), W Africa, bordered by Mali (W and N), Niger (NE), Benin (SE), and Togo, Ghana, and Côte d'Ivoire (S). The capital is OUAGADOUGOU. The country is made up of vast, semidesert plains except in the southwest, where the low hills are covered by savanna. Rainfall is sparse, and the soil is of poor quality. Burkina is an impoverished agricultural nation, with the great majority of its workforce engaged in subsistence farming or stock-raising. Cotton, oil seeds, karité nuts, live animals, meat, and hides are exported. Large reserves of manganese, limestone, phosphates, and bauxite have not been fully exploited. The country is economically dependent on foreign aid and on remittances from some 500,000 Burkina nationals who work in Côte d'Ivoire and Ghana. The GNP is US$1188 million, and the GNP per capita is US$150 (1985). The population consists of black Africans, of whom the Mossi is the largest ethnic group. French is the official language. Most people adhere to traditional religious beliefs, but there are about a million Muslims and 220,000 Roman Catholics.

*History.* Mossi invaders from present-day Ghana conquered the region around AD 1100 and, although far outnumbered by their subjects, created powerful states that endured for more than 500 years. France gained control of Upper Volta in the 1890s, administering it as part of Soudan until 1919, when it became a separate protectorate. The country gained full independence in 1960 and was dominated for two decades by Pres. Sangoule Lamizana. He was overthrown by a military coup in 1980 and further coups followed in 1982 and 1983, the second bringing to power Capt. Thomas Sankara, who in 1984 changed the country's name. In late 1985 Burkina fought a brief war with Mali over a disputed border area. In late 1987 Sankara was overthrown and killed in a military coup led by Capt. Blaise Compaoré.

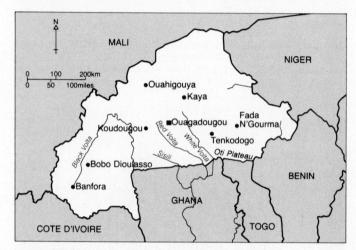

Burkina Faso

**Burleigh, William Cecil, 1st baron:** see BURGHLEY.

**burlesque** [Ital., = mockery; from the *burleschi* of Francesco Berni, a 16th-cent. Italian poet], an entertainment that, unlike COMEDY or FARCE, works by caricature, ridicule, and distortion, but, unlike SATIRE, has no ethical element. Early English burlesque often ridiculed celebrated literary works or sentimental drama, e.g., GAY's *Beggar's Opera* (1728). Extravaganza and burletta were similar to burlesque; the latter was a musical production. American burlesque (from 1865) began as a variety show characterized by vulgar dialogue and broad humour; Al Jolson, Fanny Brice, and W.C. FIELDS were famous stars. By 1920 the term had come to mean a 'strip-tease' show. Burlesque fell victim to the popularity of nightclubs, films, and television.

**Burlington,** town (1980 est. pop. 112,722), SE Ontario, Canada, part of the regional municipality of Halton (1979 est. pop. 234,892). Located on Lake ONTARIO, it is part of the rapidly growing lakefront industrial area between TORONTO and HAMILTON.

**Burma,** officially the Socialist Republic of the Union of Burma, republic (1986 est. pop. 37,000,000), 678,033 km² (261,789 sq mi), SE Asia, bordered by India, Bangladesh, and the Bay of Bengal (W), China (N and NE), Laos and Thailand (E), and the Andaman Sea (S). Principal cities include RANGOON, the capital, and MANDALAY. Except for the centrally located IRRAWADDY valley and delta, where most of the people live, the terrain is mountainous. The climate is mostly tropical monsoonal. About 65% of the labour force is employed in agriculture (mostly rice cultivation) and forestry (especially teak and rubber production). Rich mineral resources, not fully exploited, include petroleum, tin, copper, zinc, and coal. The nationalized industrial sector is small but expanding. Burma's developing economy, depressed by past political turmoil, began to make a recovery in the 1980s. The GNP is US$6460 million (1983), GNP per capita is US$180 (1983). Burmans, a Mongoloid people, constitute about 70% of the predominantly rural population; important minorities are the Karens, Shans, Kachins, Chins, Indians, Chinese, and Bangladeshi. The majority is Buddhist. The official language is Burmese, but more than 100 distinct languages are spoken.

*History.* The Burmans moved into the area from Tibet before the 9th cent.

AD, when they established a kingdom in Upper Burma. Under King Anawratha, who introduced Hinayana Buddhism, they gained (11th cent.) supremacy over the rival Mon kingdom and the Irrawaddy delta. The Burmese capital, Pagan, fell (1287) to the Mongols, and the area was then divided among local rulers. The Burmese Toungoo dynasty united the area in the 16th cent. A resurgence (18th cent.) of Mon rule was checked (1758) by Alaungapaya, who extended Burmese influence to India. During three Anglo-Burmese Wars (1824–26, 1852, 1885) Burma was annexed piecemeal to British India and did not receive limited self-government until 1937. Occupied by Japan in World War II, Burma achieved complete independence in 1948, with U NU as prime minister. Economic chaos and opposition by insurgent minorities plagued the new government, and in 1958 leadership passed to Gen. NE WIN, who restored order. U Nu was returned to power in 1960, but conditions continued to deteriorate, and in 1962 Ne Win staged a successful military coup. A new constitution, making Burma a one-party socialist republic under the Burma Socialist Programme Party (BSPP), was adopted in 1974. In 1981 Ne Win resigned the presidency but retained party leadership. He was succeeded as president by retired army chief San Yu, who in 1985 also became deputy leader of the BSPP. In 1988 Ne Win also stood down as party leader, but amid serious political unrest he retained considerable influence over government.

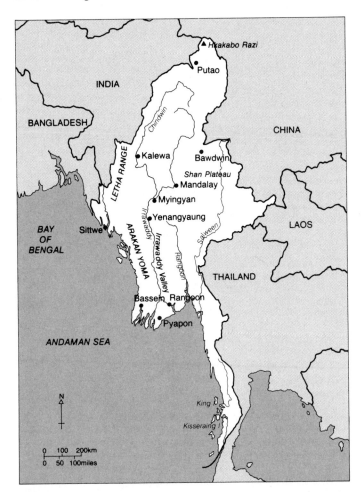

Burma

**Burma Road,** road extending c.1150 km (700 mi) from Kunming, Yunnan prov., S China, to Lashio, a railhead in Burma. A major feat of engineering, it was built (1937–38) over mountainous terrain by the Chinese. It achieved its greatest importance during WORLD WAR II, when Japan controlled the E Asian coast and it served as a vital artery for the transport of Allied military supplies to China.

**Burmese,** language belonging to the Tibeto-Burman subfamily of the Sino-Tibetan family of languages. See LANGUAGE (table).

**burn,** tissue injury resulting from exposure to heat, electricity, radiation, or caustic chemicals. First-degree burns, characterized by simple reddening of the skin, can be treated locally with ice baths and ointments. Second-degree burns, characterized by formation of blisters, may require the care of a doctor to prevent infection. Third-degree burns, with destruction of upper and lower SKIN layers, are serious and often fatal; they require prompt medical attention to reduce pain and prevent SHOCK and infection. BLOOD TRANSFUSION may be necessary to replace body fluids; long-term treatment may include skin grafting (see TRANSPLANTATION, MEDICAL).

**Burne-Jones, Sir Edward,** 1833–98, English painter and decorator. A second-generation PRE-RAPHAELITE and lifelong friend of William MORRIS, he described a dreamlike, medieval world in such popular paintings as *King Cophetua and the Beggar Maid* (1884; Tate Gall., London).

**Burnet, Sir (Frank) Macfarlane,** 1899–, Australian physician. An expert on viruses, he made notable contributions to the understanding of influenza and the development of immunity against it. For work in immunological tolerances, specifically the reactions of the body to the transplantation of foreign living tissues, he shared with Peter MEDAWAR the 1960 Nobel Prize for physiology or medicine.

**Burnet, Gilbert,** 1643–1715, English bishop and writer. The bishop of Salisbury under WILLIAM III and MARY II, he wrote *History of My Own Times* (1723–24), an informative account of the reign of JAMES II.

**Burnett, Frances Eliza Hodgson,** 1849–1924, American author; b. England. She is known for her children's books, particularly *Little Lord Fauntleroy* (1886) and *The Secret Garden* (1911).

**Burney, Fanny,** later **Madame D'Arblay,** 1752–1840, English novelist. *Evelina* (1778) made her famous, and she became part of Samuel JOHNSON's circle. She later wrote *Cecilia* (1782), *Camilla* (1796), and *The Wanderer* (1814). Her novels, in epistolary form, introduced a more realistically awkward and impulsive, though always virtuous, type of heroine, and showed much witty observation of grotesque characters. Her diaries and letters give a revealing picture of the Royal Household, where she was employed by Queen Charlotte, and of French émigré society after her marriage in 1793 to General D'Arblay.

**Burnham, Daniel Hudson,** 1846–1912, American architect and city planner. With John W. Root, he built many major buildings in Chicago. The 20-storey Masonic Temple Building (1892) was the first important skeleton SKYSCRAPER. Other projects included the 'Rookery', the first suitably planned modern office building.

**Burnham Committee,** a national joint committee first established in 1919 to negotiate teachers' salary scales in maintained schools and in further education. The machinery laid down in the Remuneration of Teachers Act 1965 comprised representatives of the LOCAL EDUCATION AUTHORITIES and the Secretary of State on one side, and teachers on the other side. There was provision for arbitration. After a breakdown of negotiations over salaries and conditions the Secretary of State discontinued the Burnham committees in 1987.

**Burnie,** city (1986 pop. 20,665), Tasmania, S Australia. A port on the N coast of the island state, it is important for paper-pulp and timber industries, also being the main rural service centre for local beef, dairy, and vegetable production.

**Burnley,** town (1981 pop. 76,365), Lancashire, NW England, 36 km (22 mi) N of Manchester. An important although declining industrial town, its industries include coal-mining, engineering, and textiles. It became an important cotton-manufacturing town in the late 18th cent.

**Burns, Robert,** 1759–96, Scottish poet. Raised on a farm, as a boy he read Scottish poetry, including Robert FERGUSSON, as well as POPE, LOCKE, and SHAKESPEARE. He wrote early but did not publish until, in 1786, hoping to emigrate to Jamaica, he sold *Poems, Chiefly in the Scottish Dialect,* which became an immediate success. Burns did not emigrate and spent the rest of his life in Scotland, failing as a farmer but producing hundreds of songs, among them 'Flow Gently, Sweet Afton', 'My Heart's in the Highlands', 'Auld Lang Syne', and 'Comin' thro' the Rye'. Burns is noted for his humour and understanding of class conflict and for the descriptive power he brings to bear on Scottish rural life. Burns wrote in Scots and in English mixed with Scots. 'Burns Night' is celebrated all over the world by patriotic Scots on his birthday, 25 Jan.

**Burr, Aaron,** 1756–1836, American political leader. After service in the AMERICAN REVOLUTION, he was (1791–97) US senator from New York. He tied with Thomas JEFFERSON in the presidential election of 1800. Through the efforts of Alexander HAMILTON, the House of Representatives named Jefferson president and Burr vice president. Hamilton's hostility also figured in Burr's defeat (1804) for governor of New York. His political career ended when he mortally wounded Hamilton in a duel. Burr plotted with Gen. James Wilkinson to colonize the Southwest, and was tried (1807) for treason; he was found not guilty, and retired from public life.

**Burra, Edward John,** 1905–76, British painter. Burra painted scenes of social realism (usually in watercolour or gouache) in sharp clear colours with precise angular outlines. These were influenced by GROSZ whom he admired. In the mid 1930s his imagery became more bizarre with surrealist overtones.

**Burroughs, William,** 1914–, American author. His most famous work is *The Naked Lunch* (1959), a nightmare vision of the modern world based on the author's experience of drug addiction. His experiments with improvising writing techniques have influenced many modern American writers. Later works include *The Soft Machine* (1961), *Nova Express* (1964), and *The Wild Boys: A Book of the Dead* (1971).

**Bursa,** city (1980 pop. 445,113), capital of Bursa prov., NW Turkey. It has a long history of silk and textile manufacture. Founded about the 3rd cent. BC, it became the capital of the OTTOMAN EMPIRE during the 14th cent. It has fine mosques and monuments to the early Ottoman period.

**bursitis,** acute or chronic inflammation of a bursa, a fluid-filled sac located close to a joint. Caused by infection, injury, repeated pressure, or diseases such as ARTHRITIS and GOUT, the inflammation produces pain, tenderness, and restricted motion. Treatment includes rest, application of heat, use of ANALGESIC and CORTICOSTEROID drugs and occasionally surgery.

**Burton, Richard,** 1925–84, Welsh actor; b. Richard Jenkins. He starred in many Shakespearean plays in Britain and the US; in the musical *Camelot* (1960, 1980); and in numerous films, e.g., *The Robe* (1953) and *Becket* (1964).

**Burton, Sir Richard Francis,** 1821–90, English explorer, linguist, and writer. Fluent in Arabic, he journeyed (1853) in disguise to the forbidden cities of MECCA and MEDINA. In 1858 he and J.H. SPEKE tried unsuccessfully to find the source of the NILE R. In 1865 he explored Santos, in Brazil. His works include a translation of the *Arabian Nights* (1885–88).

**Burton, Robert,** 1577–1640, English clergyman and scholar. His *Anatomy of Melancholy* (1621), on the causes and effects of melancholy, written in an idiosyncratic and labyrinthine style, was rich in recondite historical anecdotes and allusions which have been a gold mine to many later English writers.

**Burundi,** officially Republic of Burundi, republic, (1984 est. pop. 4,537,000), 27,834 km² (10,747 sq mi), E central Africa, formerly part of Ruanda-Urundi, bordered by Rwanda (N), Tanzania (E), Lake Tanganyika (SW), and Zaïre (W). BUJUMBURA is the capital. The three main geographic zones are a narrow area, part of the GREAT RIFT VALLEY, in the west; a central region of mountains reaching a height of c.2680 m (8800 ft); and, in the east, an area of broken plateaus and somewhat lower elevations (c.1370–1830 m/4500–6000 ft), where most of the people live. Burundi is one of the smallest, most densely populated, and poorest countries in Africa. It relies almost exclusively on coffee for its income. Deposits of nickel, cobalt, and copper could be important in the future. The GNP is US$1043 million, and the GNP per capita is US$230 (1985). The two main ethnic groups are the Hutu (about 85% of the population) and the Tutsi (about 14%), who, despite their relatively small numbers, dominate the government and maintain a virtual lord-serf relationship with the Hutu. The remaining 1% are the Twa, who are PYGMIES. French and Kurundi are the official languages. About half the people are Christian (mostly Roman Catholic); the rest follow traditional religions.

*History.* The original inhabitants, the Twa (Pygmies), were followed (c.1200) and then outnumbered by the Hutu, who in turn gave way to the migrating Tutsi in the 15th cent. By the 19th cent. the Tutsi had established dominance, and a Tutsi king (*mwami*) ruled the country. In 1890 Burundi was incorporated into German East Africa. During WORLD WAR I it was occupied by Belgian forces, and in 1919 it became part of the Belgian League of Nations mandate of RUANDA-URUNDI (made a UN trust territory in 1946). Burundi became an independent kingdom in 1962,

but the monarchy was overthrown in 1966 and a military republic established. The years following independence have been marked by bitter fighting between the Tutsi and Hutu, resulting in thousands of Hutu deaths in the 1970s. The early 1980s saw a trend toward reduced military influence and efforts at Tutsi–Hutu reconciliation. Pres. Jean-Baptiste Bagaza, who seized power in 1976, was reelected unopposed in 1984 as candidate of the Union for National Progress, the country's sole legal party under the 1981 constitution. In late 1987 Bagaza was deposed by Maj. Pierre Buyoya.

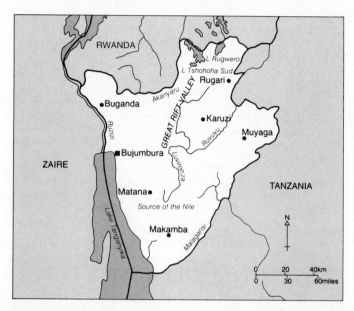

Burundi

**Bush, Alan,** 1900–, British composer, teacher, pianist, and writer. His commitment to Communism has influenced the character and topics of his compositions, such as the operas *Wat Tyler* (1948–51) and *The Sugar Reapers* (1966).

**Bush, George Herbert Walker,** 1924–, 41st president of the US (1989–). A graduate of Yale Univ., he was a Navy fighter pilot in World War II and after 1953 headed an oil drilling firm in Texas. In 1966 he was elected to the first of two terms in the US House of Representatives. He later served as ambassador to the UN (1971–73), chairman of the Republican National Committee (1973–74), chief of the US liaison office in China (1974–75), and director of the CIA (1976–77). After losing the 1980 Republican presidential nomination to Ronald REAGAN, Bush became his running mate and served two terms as vice president. In 1988 he secured the Republican nomination and easily defeated the Democratic nominee, Michael DUKAKIS, in the presidential election. He was sworn in early in 1989.

**bushbuck:** see ANTELOPE.

**Bushell's Case,** English case decided in 1670, where the court granted a writ of HABEAS CORPUS, freeing the chairman of a JURY, who had been imprisoned for non-payment of a fine, imposed after he had delivered a verdict contrary to the judge's direction. The case is important in that it laid down for the first time, the right of jurors to reach verdicts independently of the judge.

**Bushnell, Horace,** 1802–76, American Congregational minister. As pastor of the North Church, Hartford, Connecticut (1833–59), he repudiated the austerity of Calvinism and stressed the divine in humanity and nature. He had profound influence on liberal Protestant thought.

**bushranger,** initially applied to those who achieved mastery of the Australian countryside, the term came to mean rural criminals. The first bushrangers were mainly escaped convicts; a second wave, after 1850, preyed on gold convoys. Ned KELLY (1855–80) was one of the last bushrangers and achieved legendary status.

**Busoni, Ferruccio Benvenuto** (booh͵zohnee), 1866–1924, Italian pianist and composer. Influenced by LISZT, he taught widely, transcribed

J.S. BACH's organ works for piano, edited Bach's *Well-tempered Clavier,* composed piano music, and wrote four remarkable operas which have rarely been performed.

**Buss, Frances Mary,** 1827–94, pioneer of women's education. She founded the North London Collegiate School for Ladies (from 1871 Girls) in 1850, of which she was headmistress. Like Dorothea BEALE she gave evidence to the Schools' Inquiry Commission. She was actively engaged in promoting the education of girls, and teacher education and other opportunities for women to be self-supporting. She was strongly in favour of girls' competing in examinations on the same footing as boys.

**Bustamante, Sir Alexander,** 1884–1977, Jamaican politician, prime minister (1962–67). Of Irish and black descent, he founded the country's largest trade union and (1943) the Jamaica Labour Party. He served as chief minister (1953–55) and became prime minister in 1962, the year Jamaica gained independence within the British Commonwealth. He launched an ambitious programme of public works and land reform.

**Bustamante, Antonio Sánchez de,** 1865–1951, Cuban jurist. He was a member of the HAGUE TRIBUNAL (from 1908) and a judge of the WORLD COURT (1921–39). Bustamante also served as president of the Pan American Congress (1928), which ratified his monumental code of private international law pertaining to the security of person and property.

**butcher bird:** see SHRIKE.

**Butenandt, Adolf Frederick Johann,** 1903–, German chemist. He studied under WINDAUS in Göttingen, and was director (1936–60) of the Max Planck Institute for Biochemistry, Berlin. Butenandt is largely responsible for our knowledge of the structure and synthesis of sex HORMONES. He isolated oestrone in 1929, progesterone in 1934, and testosterone in 1939, the year he received the Nobel Prize for chemistry. His contributions subsequently formed the basis for the large-scale production of the drug CORTISONE.

**Butler, Benjamin Franklin,** 1818–93, American politician and Union general in the AMERICAN CIVIL WAR. He was made military governor of NEW ORLEANS (1862), but his harsh rule caused his removal. He commanded (1864) the Union expedition to seize Fort Fisher, North Carolina, but it failed, and he was removed from command. As a US representative from Massachusetts he favoured the radical Republican policy of RECONSTRUCTION and led the impeachment proceedings against Pres. Andrew JOHNSON.

**Butler, (Fredrick) Guy,** 1918–, white South African playwright, poet and critic. His chief aim in the poems such as *Stranger to Europe* (1952; augmented, 1960) is to contrast his feelings of 'European clarity' with 'African instinct'. His plays include *The Dam* (1953), *The Dove Returns* (1956), and *Take Root or Die* (1970), all on race issues.

**Butler, Josephine Elizabeth (Grey),** 1828–1906, English social reformer and moral campaigner who led the crusade for the repeal (1886) of the Contagious Diseases Acts. These penalized women with imprisonment if they refused compulsory medical examinations intended to regulate prostitution.

**Butler, Reg(inald),** 1913–81, British sculptor. Trained as an architect, he began sculpture in 1944. He won first prize in an International competition (1953) for a monument to 'The Unknown Political Prisoner'; a project that was never realized. He worked in metal, sculpting female nudes and constructivist forms and was one of the leading sculptors of the generation following Henry MOORE.

**Butler, Richard Austen (later baron),** 1902-82, British politician; b. Attock Serai, India. He was a Conservative Member of Parliament from 1929 and held a variety of important Cabinet posts, including Home Secretary (1957–62) and Foreign Secretary (1963–64). From 1965 to 1978 he was Master of Trinity College, Cambridge, and he was Chancellor of Sheffield and Essex Universities. As President of The Board of Education 1941–44 he was responsible for planning the Education Act 1944 and became the first Minister of Education (1944). The 'Butler Act' established for the first time a nation-wide structure of primary, secondary, and further education, putting an end to all-age 'elementary'' schools, and bringing voluntary 'aided' and 'controlled' schools (religious foundations) firmly into a national system of education. Butler is given the credit for negotiating the settlement of religious interests involved in this legislation.

**Butler, Samuel,** 1612–80, English poet and satirist. His best-known work is *Hudibras* (in three parts 1663, 1664, 1678), a venomous satire against the Puritans given as the mock-heroic story of the 'Presbyterian knight', Sir Hudibras.

**Butler, Samuel,** 1835–1902, English author, painter, and composer. After amassing a fortune in New Zealand as a sheep rancher, he returned to England, where he did work in the arts and in biology. He is best known as a writer. *Erewhon,* a satirical utopian novel, appeared in 1872 and *Erewhon Revisited* in 1901. His autobiographical novel *The Way of All Flesh* (1903) is a powerful and at times savage indictment of Victorian life and values.

**Butor, Michel** (by: ‚taw), 1926–, French novelist. His experimental novels often make use of shifting time sequences and the interior monologue. They include *Passage de Milan* (1954) and *Degrés* (1960).

**Butskellism** (‚butskelism), term used to characterize the post-war consensus in Britain over the main elements of government policy, arrived at between the Tory and Labour parties (the word is a compound of the names of the Conservative politician R.A. BUTLER and the Labour leader Hugh GAITSKELL). Broadly speaking, this consensus included acceptance of the WELFARE STATE; a 'mixed economy' of both private and nationalized industries; the belief in the application of Keynesian economic policies by the government (see KEYNES, J.M.); the commitment to full employment (see UNEMPLOYMENT). This consensus has been seriously challenged since the election in 1979 of the Conservative government of Mrs THATCHER, which argued for a rolling-back of the state in order to stimulate free enterprise.

**butte,** an isolated hill with steep sides and a flat top, resulting from the more rapid erosion of the surrounding areas. Many occur in the plains of the W US. See MESA.

**butter,** dairy product obtained by churning milk or cream until its fat solidifies. Cow's milk is generally the basis for butter, but milk from goats, sheep, and mares has also been used. Butter was known by 2000 BC, and as it became a staple food various kinds of hand churns were developed. Traditional butter-making involves cooling milk in pans, allowing the cream to rise and skimming it off, letting the cream ripen by natural fermentation, then churning it. Farm-made until 1850, butter has since then increasingly become a factory product. Commercially-made butter usually contains 80% to 85% milk fat, 12% to 16% water, and 2% salt, or it can be unsalted. The world's leading butter producers are the USSR, France, West Germany, the US, and India. Clarified butter (butterfat with milk solids removed) is widely used in Egypt and in India, where it is known as ghee. Butter, especially that from Normandy, is highly regarded in cookery for its delicate taste and smooth texture. It is an important ingredient in many sauces, cakes, and biscuits. Butter can be an important source of vitamin A and vitamin D in the diet, but it also contains a high percentage of saturated animal fat. See FATS AND OILS.

**buttercup** or **crowfoot,** common name for some members of the Ranunculaceae, a family of chiefly annual or perennial herbs of cool regions of the Northern Hemisphere. Primitive plants, they typically have a simple flower structure. The buttercups and crowfoots comprise the largest genus (*Ranunculus*). Found mainly in the arctic, north temperate, and alpine regions, most have glossy yellow flowers and deeply cut leaves. The family also includes many other wildflowers and cultivated ornamentals. Some of these are the ANEMONE, CLEMATIS, COLUMBINE, LARKSPUR, and PEONY.

**butterfly,** day-flying INSECT with two pairs of membranous wings. The wings are large in relation to the size of its body, wingspan 14–218 mm (½–8½ in), and covered with coloured overlapping scales (modified hairs) that also clothe the body and appendages. The antennae are long and slender with a distinct club or knob at the end. All adults feed on nectar and other liquids through a long suctorial proboscis, that is coiled when not in use. The caterpillar (larva) is a leaf-eater and, in addition to three pairs of true legs has five pairs of abdominal prolegs. When fully grown it changes into a chrysalis (pupa) having a hard integument on which the outline of the wings, eyes, legs, and antennae are visible (see METAMORPHOSIS). Butterflies (Papilionoidea) are one of the 21 superfamilies that make up the order Lepidoptera. The skippers (Hesperoidea) are often grouped with butterflies but the other 19 superfamilies are all MOTHS. Butterflies can be distinguished from moths because a butterfly's wings are linked together by having a basal extension of the leading edge of the hind wing projecting under the fore wing (amplexiform coupling), whereas most moths have a 'clip' system (frenlar coupling). The larvae of both the large and small white butterflies, *Pieris brassicae* and *P. rapae*, cause considerable damage to cabbages and other crucifers, not only in Western Europe but, in the case of the small white, also in Australia, New Zealand, and North America, following accidental introduction.

**butternut:** see WALNUT.

**buttonwood:** see PLANE TREE.

**buttress,** mass of masonry built against a wall to strengthen it, particularly when a vault or arch places a heavy load or thrust on one section. The decorative possibilities were known in Mesopotamia (3500–3000 BC). In larger Roman buildings, internal buttresses served as partitions; the basilica of Constantine in Rome is typical. Buttresses evolved from simple piers in the 11th cent. to bold and complex Gothic structures. The flying buttress, a masonry arch, starts from a detached pier and joins the wall to resist the thrust of the vaulting. Buttresses were often enriched with gables and sculpture; pinnacles were added to increase their weight.

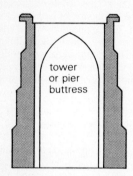 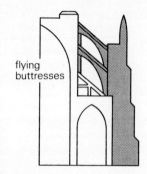

tower or pier buttress

flying buttresses

Types of **buttress**

**Buvelot, Abram Louis** (boohv̩loh), 1814–88, Swiss and Australian artist. He studied at the Lausanne Academy, Switzerland, and in Paris (1834), before travelling to Brazil where he worked as court painter for Dom Pedro II. After a brief return to Switzerland, in 1859, and visits to India and the East Indies, he migrated to Melbourne, Victoria, in 1865. He is best known for his landscapes, which betray the influence of the BARBIZON SCHOOL. Towards the end of his life, he became a source of inspiration to many younger Australian painters—in particular, Julian Ashton, Tom ROBERTS, and other members of the HEIDELBERG SCHOOL.

**Buxtehude, Dietrich** ('booksta̩hoohda), 1637–1707, Danish composer and organist. From 1668 he was organist at Lübeck, where his concerts attracted musicians from all over Germany, including J.S. BACH, whom he greatly influenced.

**Buzău** (booh:zow), city (1983 pop. 120,419), SE Romania, where the Carpathians Mts meet the Danubian Plain. It has oil-related industries, including the manufacture of plastics.

**buzzard,** HAWK of the genera *Buteo* and *Pernis*. Honey buzzards (*Pernis*) feed on insects, wasp and bumblebee larvae, and small reptiles. The term *buzzard* is often incorrectly applied to various hawks and New World VULTURES.

**Bwake** (̩bwahkay): see BOUAKÉ.

**Bydgószcz** (bid̩gosh), city (1984 pop. 358,000) capital of the provincial voivodship of Bydgószcz, N Poland, on the Brda R. There are canal links with the VISTULA and the ODER Rs. It is an important centre of timber-working but also has chemical, electrical, and other industries. Prussian from 1772 to 1919, it was known as Bromberg.

**Byelorussia:** see BELORUSSIA.

**Byng, Julian Hedworth George,** 1st **viscount Byng of Vimy,** 1862–1935, British general. In WORLD WAR I Canadian troops under his command stormed (1917) Vimy Ridge, in N France. He was later governor general of Canada (1921–26).

**Bynkershoek, Cornelius van** (bing̩keashook), 1673–1743, Dutch writer on INTERNATIONAL LAW. He is best known for his classic *De dominio maris* (1702), on MARITIME LAW.

**Byrd, Richard Evelyn,** 1888–1957, American explorer. He was a naval flier. In 1926 he and Floyd Bennett became the first men to fly over the NORTH POLE. Byrd is remembered mainly for his five expeditions to ANTARCTICA: 1930, 1933, 1939–40, 1946–47, 1955–56. He was promoted to rear admiral in 1930 and set up a base, Little America, in Antarctica; from there he conducted major explorations. In 1933 he spent several months close to the South Pole alone; *Discovery* (1935) and *Alone* (1938) are records of this trip. He was made commander of all US Antarctic activities in 1955. His explorations form the basis of US claims in Antarctica.

**Byrd, William,** 1543–1623, English composer and organist. He was favoured by ELIZABETH I, and, although Catholic, wrote MASSES, ANTHEMS, and other music for both English and Roman services. He performed and published music with TALLIS. He was the leading English composer of his time, and he had a profound influence on his contemporaries and successors.

**Byrnes, James Francis,** 1879–1972, American public official; b. Charleston, S.C. A Democrat, he served in the House of Representatives (1911–25); in the Senate (1931-41), where he advised on the NEW DEAL budget; and on the Supreme Court (1941–42). He headed several wartime agencies. As secretary of state (1945–47), Byrnes tried to mend postwar differences with the USSR, but later became extremely anti-Soviet. As governor (1951–55) of South Carolina, he opposed racial integration.

**Byron, George Gordon Noel Byron, 6th baron,** 1788–1824, one of the great English romantic poets. In his life and in his poetry, Lord Byron epitomizes ROMANTICISM. Born with a clubfoot, he grew to be a dark, handsome man, whose many love affairs before and after his ill-fated marriage (1815–16) to Anne Isabella Milbanke (notably with Lady Caroline Lamb, wife of Viscount MELBOURNE, with Claire Clairmont, SHELLEY's sister-in-law, and with his own half-sister Augusta Leigh) made him notorious. When an early work, *Hours of Idleness* (1807), was ridiculed by the *Edinburgh Review,* he replied with *English Bards and Scotch Reviewers* (1809), a satire that made him famous. His renown was

Byzantine art and architecture: 10th- or 11th-cent. silver pectoral cross

confirmed by *Childe Harold's Pilgrimage* (1812-18) and the verse romances *The Bride of Abydos* (1813), *The Giaour* (1813), *The Corsair* (1814) and *Lara* (1814). In 1816 he and his wife separated, and he left England, to which he was never to return. He lived mainly in Italy, often in company with SHELLEY and his family and acquired his last mistress, Countess Teresa Guiccioli. *Manfred* (1817), *Beppo* (1818), and *Mazeppa* (1819) followed, and his masterpiece, the satirical epic *Don Juan*, was published in 1819–20. In 1823 he became deeply committed to the cause of the independence of Greece (where he had travelled 12 years earlier) from Turkish rule, and in 1824 he landed at Missolonghi to aid the Greek insurgents by his prestige and financial support. He died there three months later of fever. His reputation, both as poet and as romantic hero, was of immense, almost archetypal importance all over Europe.

**byte:** see COMPUTER.

**Bytom** (ˌbitom), Ger. *Beuthen*, city (1984 pop. 230,000), Upper Silesia, S Poland. A mining and manufacturing city based on a medieval core, it was transferred from Germany to Poland in 1945.

**Byzantine art and architecture,** include not only works done in the city of Byzantium (Istanbul) after it became the capital of the Roman Empire (AD 330), but also work done under Byzantine influence, as in Italy, Syria, Greece, Russia, and other Eastern countries. A blend of Hellenistic and Oriental traditions, Byzantine art emphasized decorativeness and flat line harmony. Except for the interruption of ICONOCLASM (726–843), when content was restricted to ornamental forms and symbols such as the cross, the style persisted until the fall of CONSTANTINOPLE in 1453. The pillaging of Istanbul (Constantinople) in 1204 was followed by a late flowering of Byzantine art that brought impressive achievements in MOSAIC decoration. Mosaics depicting sacred personages placed in descending order of importance were applied to all available surfaces in Byzantine churches. The stylized gestures of the figures and luminous shimmer of the gold backgrounds made the entire church a tangible evocation of celestial order. The cult of icons (see

ICONOGRAPHY) also played a leading role in Byzantine art. The icons were made using the encaustic technique. Little scope was given to individuality since the effectiveness of the image was held to depend on its fidelity to prototype. A large group of icons has been preserved in the monastery of St Catherine on Mt Sinai. The development of Byzantine painting can also be seen in manuscript ILLUMINATION, e.g., the 9th cent. Homilies of Gregory Nazianzus and the 10th-cent. Paris Psalter. Byzantine enamel, ivory, and metalwork objects such as reliquaries, devotional panels, and ivory caskets were highly prized throughout the Middle Ages. Byzantine architecture was based on the great legacy of Roman formal and technical achievements. The 5th cent. BASILICA of St John of the Studion is the oldest extant church in Istanbul and an early example of Byzantine reliance on traditional Roman models. The most imposing example of Byzantine architecture is the Church of Holy Wisdom (HAGIA SOPHIA), Istanbul which is the culmination of several centuries of experimentation with a unified space of monumental dimensions. These centrally planned religious structures were greatly favoured and had in common a central domed space flanked by smaller domes and half-domes spanning the peripheral spaces. Two of the many great achievements of Byzantine architecture are the Italian octagonal church of San Vitale in Ravenna (547) and ST MARK'S CHURCH in Venice. In its later phases, the Byzantine prototype became more ornate, e.g., the Moscow Cathedral. Byzantine secular architecture has left few traces. Best known are the ruins of the 5th-cent. walls of Istanbul, consisting of an outer and an inner wall, each of which was originally studded with 96 towers, of which some can still be seen.

**Byzantine Empire,** successor state to the Roman Empire (see ROME), also called the Eastern or East Roman Empire. It was named after ancient Byzantium, which CONSTANTINE I rebuilt in AD 330 as his capital, Constantinople. The Roman Empire split permanently (395) into East and West, but after the Western Empire fell (476) the Eastern Empire claimed the entire Roman world. Boundaries shifted, but the core of the Byzantine Empire was ASIA MINOR and the S BALKAN PENINSULA. Throughout its 1000

---

**RULERS OF THE BYZANTINE EMPIRE** (*including dates of reign*)

| | | |
|---|---|---|
| Constantine I (the Great), 330–37 | Constantine V Copronymus, 741–75 | Isaac I Comnenus, 1057–59 |
| Constantius, 337–61 | Leo IV (the Khazar), 775–80 | Constantine X Ducas, 1059–67 |
| Julian (the Apostate), 361–63 | Constantine VI, 780–97 | Michael VII Ducas (Parapinaces), |
| Jovian, 363–64 | Irene, 797–802 |   1067–68 |
| Valens, 364–78 | Nicephorus I, 802–11 | Romanus IV Diogenes, 1068–71 |
| Theodosius I (the Great), 379–95 | Stauracius, 811 | Michael VII Ducas (restored), 1071–78 |
| Arcadius, 395–408 | Michael I, 811–13 | Nicephorus III Botaniates, 1078–81 |
| Theodosius II, 408–50 | Leo V (the Armenian), 813–20 | Alexius I Comnenus, 1081–1118 |
| Marcian, 450–57 | Michael II (the Stammerer), 820–29 | John II Comnenus, 1118–43 |
| Leo I (the Great or the Thracian), 457–74 | Theophilus, 829–42 | Manuel I Comnenus, 1143–80 |
| Leo II, 474 | Michael III (the Drunkard), 842–67 | Alexius II Comnenus, 1180–83 |
| Zeno, 474–75 | Basil I (the Macedonian), 867–86 | Andronicus I Comnenus, 1183–85 |
| Basiliscus, 475–76 | Leo VI (the Wise or the Philosopher), | Isaac II Angelus, 1185–95 |
| Zeno (restored), 476–91 |   886–912 | Alexius III Angelus, 1195–1203 |
| Anastasius I, 491–518 | Alexander, 912–13 | Isaac II (restored) and Alexius IV Angelus, |
| Justin I, 518–27 | Constantine VII Porphyrogenitus, 913–19 |   1203–04 |
| Justinian I (the Great), 527–65 | Romanus I Lecapenus, 919–44 | Alexius V Ducas, 1204 |
| Justin II, 565–78 | Constantine VII (restored), 944–59 | Theodore I Lascaris, 1204–22 |
| Tiberius II Constantinus, 578–82 | Romanus II, 959–63 | John III Vatatzes or Ducas, 1222–54 |
| Maurice, 582–602 | Basil II Bulgaroktonos, 963 | Theodore II Lascaris, 1254–58 |
| Phocas, 602–10 | Nicephorus II Phocas, 963–69 | John IV Lascaris, 1258–61 |
| Heraclius, 610–41 | John I Tzimisces, 969–76 | Michael VIII Palaeologus, 1259–82 |
| Constantine III and Heracleonas, 641 | Basil II (restored), 976–1025 | Andronicus II Palaeologus, 1282–1328 |
| Heracleonas, 641 | Constantine VIII, 1025–28 | Andronicus III Palaeologus, 1328–41 |
| Constans II Pogonatus, 641–68 | Zoë and Romanus III Argyrus, 1028–34 | John V Palaeologus, 1341–76 |
| Constantine IV, 668–85 | Zoë and Michael IV (the Paphlagonian), | John VI Cantacuzenus (usurper), 1347–55 |
| Justinian II Rhinotmetus, 685–95 |   1034–41 | Andronicus IV Palaeologus, 1376–79 |
| Leontius, 695–98 | Zoë and Michael V Calaphates, 1041–42 | John V Palaeologus (restored), 1379–91 |
| Tiberius III, 698–705 | Zoë and Theodora, 1042 | John VII Palaeologus (usurper), 1390 |
| Justinian II (restored), 705–11 | Zoë, Theodora, and Constantine IX | Manuel II Palaeologus, 1391–1425 |
| Philippicus Bardanes, 711–13 |   Monomachus, 1042–50 | John VII Palaeologus (restored as |
| Anastasius II, 713–15 | Theodora and Constantine IX, 1050–55 |   coemperor), 1399–1412 |
| Theodosius III, 716–17 | Theodora, 1055–56 | John VIII Palaeologus, 1425–48 |
| Leo III (the Isaurian or the Syrian), 717–41 | Michael VI Stratioticus, 1056–57 | Constantine XI Palaeologus, 1449–53 |

years of existence the empire was continually beset by invaders. Also, there was constant religious controversy (see EASTERN ORTHODOX CHURCH; ICONOCLASM; MONOPHYSITISM; MONOTHELETISM) and internal political strife. Nevertheless, despite a complex administration, gross violence, and moral decay, the empire carried on the Graeco-Roman civilization blended with Oriental influences while the West was in chaos. It regained vigour in the 6th-cent. reign of JUSTINIAN I, under whom Byzantine art and architecture reached their peak. But his successors lost vast lands to the LOMBARDS and ARABS. The schism between the Eastern and Western churches arose soon after CHARLEMAGNE became emperor of the West (800). The reigns of BASIL I (9th cent.) and his successors brought renewed imperial splendour and vigour, until the defeat by the Seljuk TURKS (1071) and the loss of Asia Minor. The empire was further weakened by the attacks of the Norman leaders ROBERT GUISCARD and Bohemond. After a brief resurgence under ALEXIUS I, a century of decay ended with the Fourth CRUSADE, the fall of Constantinople (1204), and the breakup of the empire into NICAEA, TREBIZOND, and EPIRUS. The weak Latin empire in Constantinople was conquered by the Nicaean emperor MICHAEL VIII, who restored the Byzantine Empire. Gradually, however, the OTTOMAN Turks encircled the empire, and despite a desperate defence under CONSTANTINE XI Constantinople fell (1453) to MEHMED II. The modern era is traditionally reckoned from that date.

**Byzantine music,** music of the BYZANTINE EMPIRE (4th to 15th cent.), composed to Greek texts as ceremonial festival or church music. Elements were derived from Syrian, Hebrew, and Greek sources. Although Greek instruments were used, the ORGAN was the main one. Almost all surviving Byzantine music is sacred; its major form was the HYMN. Byzantine chant was monodic, in free RHYTHM. Notation was first a series of symbols to remind the singer of a melody he already knew; later a staffless notation indicating starting note and subsequent intervals of a melody was used (see MUSICAL NOTATION).

**Byzantium,** ancient city of Thrace, on the site of present-day Istanbul, Turkey. Founded by Greeks in 667 BC, it was chosen (AD 330) by CONSTANTINE I as the site for Constantinople, later the capital of the BYZANTINE EMPIRE.

**C**, chemical symbol of the element CARBON.

**Ca**, chemical symbol of the element CALCIUM.

**Cabal,** inner circle of advisers to CHARLES II of England. Their initials form the word: Clifford of Chudleigh, Ashley (Lord Shaftesbury), BUCKINGHAM (George Villiers), Arlington (Henry Bennet), and Lauderdale (John Maitland). One or more of this group dominated court policy from 1667 to 1673.

**cabala:** see KABBALAH.

**cabbage,** leafy garden vegetable of many widely dissimilar varieties, all probably descended from the wild, or sea, cabbage (*Brassica oleracea*) of the MUSTARD family, found on European coasts. Cabbage is used as food for humans and animals. Varieties include BROCCOLI, BRUSSELS SPROUTS, CAULIFLOWER, KALE, and kohlrabi. All grow best in cool moist climates. Chinese cabbage is a separate species.

**Cabeza de Vaca, Álvar Núñez** (kǝh‚baythah day ‚vahkah), c.1490–c.1557, Spanish explorer. During an expedition to FLORIDA in 1528 he was shipwrecked on a TEXAS island and enslaved by Indians. He escaped and wandered over the Southwest, reaching Mexico in 1536. His reports of the PUEBLO INDIANS gave rise to the myth of the Seven Cities of Cibola. He was later governor of a region of PARAGUAY but was deposed in 1544.

**cabildo,** Spanish autonomous municipal council, important in governing Spanish America from the 16th cent. Presided over by an ALCALDE, it exercised considerable legislative, executive powers. In the 19th cent. it was an important forum for voicing nationalist ideas.

**Cabinda,** province (1970 pop. 81,265), SW Africa exclave of Angola, from which it is separated by Zaïrian territory. Situated on the Atlantic Ocean, Cabinda has produced oil from large offshore reserves since 1968, accounting for 85% of Angola's output. It was the scene of heavy fighting during the war for independence from Portugal (1961–75) and became part of Angola after independence was won in 1975.

**cabinet,** group of advisers to the head of government, who are usually also the heads of major government ministries and departments. In Great Britain, where cabinet ministers are drawn from the majority party in the House of Commons and the Lords, except on rare occasions, such as a national (all-party) government in time of war. Before the emergence of the office of PRIME MINISTER, monarchs used to call meetings of their senior ministers; Queen Anne was the last monarch to attend cabinet meetings and play a decisive part. In Britain, the prime minister appoints and dismisses cabinet ministers, chairs cabinet meetings, and controls the agenda. Discussion is secret and the accepted principle of collective responsibility is that ministers must defend cabinet decisions in public, whatever their personal views, or resign. A modern British cabinet has about 20 members. The conventional wisdom is that with the increase in disciplined party working, effective political power in the British system has passed from the Commons to the cabinet; and from the cabinet, some would add, to the prime minister and a small 'inner cabinet' of trusted ministers. In multi-party systems, such as those of Italy, France, and Germany, coalition governments, and hence coalition cabinets, are the norm; the power of the prime minister is much reduced because coalition partners are in a position to demand cabinet posts and a say in policy-making.

**cable,** usually, high-strength wire cord or heavy metal chain used for hauling, towing, supporting the roadway of a suspension bridge, or securing a large ship to its anchor or mooring. Electric cables are conductors used for the transmission of electrical signals. A coaxial cable, virtually immune to external electromagnetic interference, consists of a tube of copper or other conducting material, the centre of which contains another conductor. The two conductors are separated by an insulator. By means of coaxial cables a large number of telegraph and telephone messages, as well as television images (see CABLE TELEVISION), can be simultaneously transmitted. An intertwined and insulated group of wires that conducts electricity from generator to consumer is called a cable.

**cable railway,** or cable-way, aerial ropeways in which loads were suspended from a moving rope or cable were used from the Middle Ages for the transport of goods and, occasionally, passengers. The first cable railway to be operated up a mountain was at the Wetterhorn, Switzerland and was opened in 1908. The difference in level was 420 m (1375 ft). Modern cable railways have as much as 1000 m (3250 ft) difference in level and single spans of 3600 m (12,000 ft). In a funicular railway the vehicle runs on a track and is hauled by a cable attached to winding gear at one of the stations.

**cable television,** in general, term covering several ways in which television pictures can be transmitted by means of signals through a cable instead of broadcast and picked up by aerial. In the US coaxial cable can transmit up to 50 television channels. Transmitting data or information needs a narrower band width than television pictures so more signals of this kind can be delivered on one channel. Underground cable systems were laid in Britain before World War II in order to transmit TV to areas which had weak off-air reception and this was continued in the 1950s. The commercial potential of cable TV was not really exploited until the late 1970s. In 1982 the British government appointed the Information Technology Advisory Panel which recommended that the cable TV networks should be developed commercially and the Hunt Report, released in September the same year, recommended the wiring up of the nation. Such a development would involve very serious qualifications of the concept of 'public service' broadcasting, and the duopoly of the BBC and IBA would be in jeopardy, should broadcasting be deregulated as a result of cable. Britain has pioneered the use of fibre-optic cable network television, but it is likely that the cable television in this country will combine coaxial and fibre-optic systems; the older system will be used for the trunk routes, and fibre-optic cable to connect to individual homes. See SATELLITE TELEVISION.

**Cabora Bassa Dam,** dam on the Zambezi R. near Songo, W Mozambique. The associated hydroelectric project began full commercial operations in 1979. The station can generate c.2075 megawatts. Total output is purchased by South Africa.

**Cabot, John,** fl. 1461–98, English explorer; probably b. Genoa, Italy. Under a patent granted by HENRY VII, he sailed W from Bristol in 1497, probably seeking access to the riches of the Far East, and touched the North American coast. His second expedition (1498) disappeared. English claims in NORTH AMERICA were based on his discovery. His son, **Sebastian Cabot,** b. 1483–86?, d. 1557, was an explorer in both English and Spanish service. In 1509 he was part of an expedition in search of the NORTHWEST PASSAGE and may have reached HUDSON BAY. Later he explored (1526–30) the Río de la Plata region of BRAZIL for the Spanish. In 1548 he became governor of a joint-stock company in England (later the MUSCOVY COMPANY), which negotiated a commercial treaty with Russia.

**cabotage,** the exclusive reservation by a state of all air traffic rights between any two points in its own territories, even when those territories are separated by the territories of other states. Hence, the traffic between the UK and Gibraltar and between the UK and Hong Kong are exclusively reserved to aircraft registered in the UK or in those two colonies. All domestic air traffic in the UK comes under the cover of cabotage. See AIR, FREEDOMS OF THE.

**Cabral, Pedro Alvares** (kə‚bral), c.1467–c.1520, Portuguese navigator. On an expedition to INDIA in 1500, he went far west of his course and reached the coast of BRAZIL, which he claimed for Portugal. He finally reached India, but his high-handed practices in trade and religion angered the Indians, and he returned to Portugal. His landing in Brazil, accidental or prearranged, was not the first European visit there, though the question of who actually discovered Brazil is still debated.

**Cabrera Infante, Guillermo,** 1929–, Cuban novelist and short-story writer. His novel *Tres tristes tigres* (1967; tr. Three Sad Tigers) chronicles the last months of BATISTA's decadent regime in Havana.

**cacao,** tropical tree (*Theobroma cacao*) of the sterculia family, native to South America and now widely cultivated in the Old World. The fruit is a pod that contains a sweet pulp with rows of embedded seeds (the cocoa 'beans' of commerce). Cocoa is obtained by fermenting the pods and then curing and roasting the extracted seeds. The resulting clean kernels, or cocoa nibs, are then processed. CHOCOLATE is one product. Cocoa products have high food value due to their fat, carbohydrate, and protein content. Other uses are in cosmetics and medicines.

**cactus,** common name for the Cactaceae, a family of succulent plants found almost entirely in the New World. Cactus plants have fleshy green stems that function as leaves (the leaves are typically insignificant or absent), and, usually, spines of various colours, shapes, and arrangements. The large, showy, delicate flowers are commonly yellow, white, red, or purple. Cactus fruits are berries, some of which are edible. The reduced surface area and fleshy stem make cacti well fitted for water storage and retention. An extensive, ramified root system makes the plants adaptable to hot, dry regions, although cacti are not restricted to the desert. Most cacti blossom briefly in the spring, sometimes for only a few hours. Blossoms are especially sensitive to light, and different species bloom at different times of the day, e.g., the night-blooming cereus, whose fragrant blossoms unfold after sunset and last one night. Many species are cultivated for food or as ornamentals; the hallucinatory drug peyote comes from a cactus of the genus *Lophophora*.

The cactus *Pseudolobivia kermesina*

**Cadbury Castle,** a large HILLFORT in Somerset, England, dating from the IRON AGE. For centuries it has been popularly identified as the Camelot of the tales of King ARTHUR. Excavations in the 1960s could not be expected

to enhance the legend, but they did reveal a fortification from the Arthurian times of the 6th cent. AD.

**Cader Idris,** mountain ridge in Gwynedd, W Wales, 5 km (3 mi) SW of Dolgellau. It forms a sharp ridge, which rises to 893 m (2927 ft) in its summit, Pen y Gadair. There is a beautifully formed cwm (or cirque, a glacially-formed, armchair-shaped hollow) in the steep slope down to Llyn y Cau. The area is frequently described in Welsh tales and legends.

**Cadillac, Antoine de la Mothe** (kah‚deeahk), c.1658–1730, French colonial governor in North America; founder (1701) of Detroit. In 1711 he became governor of Louisiana, but after quarrels in his administration he was recalled (1716).

**Cádiz** (‚kahdeeth), city (1981 pop. 157,766), capital of Cádiz prov., SW Spain, in Andalusia, on the Bay of Cádiz. It is a port with such industries as shipbuilding and fishing. Founded c.1100 BC by the Phoenicians, it passed to Carthage (c.500 BC), Rome (3rd cent. BC), the Moors (AD 711), and ALFONSO X of Castile (1262). It became a centre for New World trade but declined when Spain lost its American colonies. The clean, white city has palm-lined promenades and parks and a 13th-cent. cathedral.

**cadmium** (Cd), metallic element, discovered in 1817 by Friedrich Stromeyer. Cadmium is a silver-white, lustrous, malleable, ductile metal. Its major use is as an electroplated coating on iron and steel to prevent corrosion. Some of its compounds are used as pigments to give bright colours (red and yellow) to pottery, ceramics, and tableware. See ELEMENT (table); PERIODIC TABLE.

**Cadmus,** in Greek mythology, son of Agenor; founder of THEBES. He killed the sacred dragon that guarded the spring of ARES. As instructed by ATHENA, he sowed the dragon's teeth; from them sprang the Sparti, ancestors of the Theban nobility. Cadmus was married to Harmonia, daughter of Ares and APHRODITE.

**caduceus,** wing-topped staff, wound about by two snakes, carried by HERMES. In earlier cultures, notably the Babylonian, the intertwined snakes symbolized fertility, wisdom, and healing. The staff was carried by Greek officials and became a Roman symbol for truce and neutrality. Since the 16th cent. it has served as a symbol of medicine.

**caecilian,** legless, burrowing tropical AMPHIBIAN (family Caecilidae). Most are about 30 cm (1 ft) long. Resembling earthworms superficially, but having vertebrate characteristics such as jaws and teeth, caecilians eat animals like termites and earthworms and are found in swampy places. Their eyes are nearly functionless; a groove on either side of the head contains a retractable sensory tentacle. They may lay eggs, or produce live young, which escape into water where they spend their larval stage.

**Caedmon,** fl. 670, English poet, said by BEDE to have written early English versions of OLD TESTAMENT stories. A herdsman reputed to have received poetic powers through a vision, he later became a lay brother at the abbey of Whitby.

**Caen** (kon), city (1982 pop. 117,119, agglomeration 183,526), capital of Calvados dept., lower Normandy, N France, on the Orne R. Favoured by the Dukes of Normandy, it has always had close links across the Channel with England. It serves as market centre of a varied agricultural hinterland. Building stone and iron ore for steel-making are worked in the vicinity. It also has light industries related to the growth of its university and scientific research laboratories. Notable 11th-cent. abbey and church buildings survived the destruction of World War II.

**Caernarvon** or **Caernarfon,** town (1981 pop. 9271) in Gwynedd, NW Wales, near SW end of Menai Strait at mouth of R. Seiont, 13 km (8 mi) SW of Bangor. A small port and resort town, it is built near the site of the Roman fort of Segontium. There is a medieval castle built by Edward I, where Prince Charles was invested as the 21st Prince of Wales in 1969.

**Caesar,** name used by a patrician family of Rome. The careers of Julius CAESAR and the adopted AUGUSTUS led to giving the name an imperial character. In the later Roman Empire it was the title given to the subemperor, who would presumably later become the emperor. The title reappeared later as the German *kaiser* and the Russian *czar* or *tsar*.

**Caesar, (Caius) Julius,** 102?–44 BC, Roman statesman and general. Although he was born into the Julian gens, one of the oldest patrician families in Rome, Caesar was always a member of the democratic or popular party. In 82 BC, SULLA proscribed Caesar, who fled from Rome (81 BC). On Sulla's death, Caesar returned (78 BC) to Rome and began his political career as a member of the popular party. In 69 BC he helped

POMPEY to obtain the supreme command for the war in the East. He himself returned to Rome from Spain in 68 BC and continued to support the enactment of popular measures and to prosecute senatorial extortionists. In 63 BC, as *pontifex maximus*, he undertook the reform of the calendar with the help of Sosigenes; the result was one of his greatest contributions to history, the Julian CALENDAR. In 60 BC he organized a coalition, known as the First TRIUMVIRATE, made up of Pompey, commander in chief of the army; Marcus Licinius Crassus (see CRASSUS, family), the wealthiest man in Rome; and Caesar himself. In the years 58 to 49 BC he firmly established his reputation in the GALLIC WARS. Caesar made explorations into Britain in 55 and 54 BC and defeated the Britons. By the end of the wars Caesar had reduced all Gaul to Roman control. These campaigns proved him one of the greatest military commanders of all time and also developed the personal devotion of the Roman legions to Caesar. Crassus's death (53 BC) ended the First Triumvirate and set Pompey and Caesar face to face. In 50 BC the senate ordered Caesar to disband his army, but two tribunes faithful to Caesar, Mark ANTONY and Quintus Cassius Longinus, vetoed the bill. They fled to Caesar, who assembled his army and got the support of the soldiers against the senate. On 19 Jan. 49 BC, Caesar crossed the Rubicon, the stream bounding his province, to enter Italy, and civil war began. His march to Rome was a triumphal progress. At Pharsalia in 48 BC, Caesar defeated Pompey, who fled to Egypt, where he was killed. Caesar, having pursued Pompey to Egypt, remained there for some time, living with CLEOPATRA and establishing her firmly on the Egyptian throne. On his return to Rome, he set about reforming the living conditions of the people by passing AGRARIAN LAWS and by improving housing accommodations. In 44 BC he became dictator for life. His dictatorial powers had aroused great resentment in his enemies, but when a conspiracy was formed against him, it was made up of his friends and protégés, among them Cimber, Casca, Cassius, and Marcus Junius Brutus (see BRUTUS, family). On 15 Mar. (the Ides of March) 44 BC, he was stabbed to death in the senate house. His will left everything to his 18-year-old grandnephew Octavian (later AUGUSTUS). Caesar made the Roman Empire possible by uniting the state after a century of disorder, by establishing an autocracy in place of the oligarchy, and by pacifying Italy and the provinces. He has always been one of the most controversial characters of history, either considered the defender of the rights of the people against an oligarchy or regarded as an ambitious demagogue who forced his way to power and destroyed the republic. That he was gifted and versatile there can be little doubt. His commentaries on the Gallic Wars (seven books) and on the civil war (three books) are literary masterpieces as well as classic military documents. He was married three times: to Cornelia, to Pompeia, and to CALPURNIA. His life and character have often been portrayed, most notably by SHAKESPEARE (following PLUTARCH), HANDEL, and MANTEGNA.

**Caesarean section,** delivery of an infant by surgical removal from the uterus through an abdominal incision. It is usually performed when childbirth is considered hazardous to mother and/or infant; for example, if the mother's pelvis is too narrow, if the fetus is in a breech position (see BREECH PRESENTATION), or if the placenta obstructs the cervix. It is also performed in cases of prolonged, ineffectual labour. Legend has it that Julius Caesar was born in this way but the operation may be named after a Roman law enforcing the procedure in the event of a woman dying in labour.

**caesium** (Cs), metallic element, discovered by spectroscopy in 1860 by Robert BUNSEN and Gustav KIRCHHOFF. Ductile, soft as wax, and silver-white, it is the most alkaline element (see ALKALI METALS) and the most reactive metal. Caesium metal is used in photoelectric cells and various optical instruments; caesium compounds, in glass and ceramic production. Along with barium, strontium, and ruthenium, it is one of the major products of the fission of URANIUM. The caesium-137 radioactive isotope is used to treat cancer. See ELEMENT (table); PERIODIC TABLE.

**Caetano, Marcello** (kie‚tahnoh), 1906–80, Portuguese statesman. A law professor and close associate of António SALAZAR, he helped to plan Portugal's corporate state and served as prime minister (1968–74). His government was overthrown by a military coup, and he was exiled.

**caffeine,** odourless, slightly bitter ALKALOID found in COFFEE, TEA, COLA nuts, MATÉ, and cocoa (see CACAO). In moderation, caffeine is a mild stimulant that increases urination and the heart rate and rhythm. Excessive intake can cause restlessness, insomnia, heart irregularities, and delirium.

**Cage, John,** 1912–, American composer. He is famous for his controversial theories, experimental compositions, and performances, featuring percussion instruments that include a piano 'prepared' with objects attached to the strings. Cage has also experimented with aleatory or 'chance' music, e.g., *Music of Changes* (1951), in which certain elements were derived by use of charts from the *I Ching*. His famous *Imaginary Landscape No. 4* (1951) is scored for 12 radios tuned at random. Other orchestral works include *Child of Tree* (1975) and *Telephones and Birds* (1977).

**Cagliari,** city (1984 pop. 224,007), capital of the island of SARDINIA, Italy. It is a trading, commercial and administrative centre. There are extensive salt pans in the vicinity. Founded by Phoenicians, it has Roman remains and fortifications from the time it was ruled from Pisa. Its university dates from 1606.

**Cagney, James,** 1904–86, American film actor. A sadistic tough guy in such films as *Public Enemy* (1930) and *White Heat* (1949), he also made musicals, e.g., *Yankee Doodle Dandy* (1942; Academy Award).

**Caillaux, Joseph** (kie‚oh), 1863–1944, French statesman. He was finance minister (1899–1902, 1906–9, 1913–14) and won great unpopularity for his income-tax legislation. As premier (1911–12), Caillaux concluded a peaceful settlement of the MOROCCO crisis with Germany. He resigned (1914) as finance minister after his wife shot and killed a journalist who had attacked Caillaux's private life. Caillaux's pacifist views during WORLD WAR I led to his imprisonment for involvement with the enemy. He later served again as finance minister (1925, 1926) and was a senator.

**Cain,** in the BIBLE, eldest son of ADAM and EVE, a tiller of the soil. In jealousy he killed his brother ABEL and became a fugitive. Gen. 4.

**Caine, Michael,** 1933–, British film actor; b. Maurice Micklewhite. A versatile and popular international star, his films include *Zulu* (1964), *The Ipcress File* (1965), *The Man Who Would be King* (1975), and *Hannah and Her Sisters* (1986).

**Cairngorms, The,** mountain range in Scotland, situated between Aviemore in Highland region and BRAEMAR in Grampian region. It is part of the Grampian Mts. A popular area for climbing, walking, and skiing, it contains the second highest mountain in Britain (BEN MACDUI, 1309 m/4296 ft). It also includes the peaks of Cairn Toul at 1293 m (4241 ft) and Cairn Gorm at 1245 m (4084 ft).

**Cairns,** city (1986 pop. 54,862), Queensland, NE Australia. The centre of tourism for the local Far North and the northern base for visitors to the GREAT BARRIER REEF, the city is backed by the Atherton Tableland, part of the Great Dividing Range. Day trips to Green Island enable visitors to view the underwater coral gardens. At the mouth of the Barron R. are extensive areas of mangroves. Much of the city's economy is centred on the sugar-cane industry (first established by the Chinese in 1882), and the port has a major bulk-handling terminal taking sugar from local mills.

**Cairo,** Arab., *El Qâhira* city (1984 est. pop. [metropolitan area] 9,500,000), capital of Egypt, N Egypt, a port on the Nile R., near the head of its delta. Cairo is Egypt's administrative centre and, along with ALEXANDRIA, the heart of its economy. Manufactures include textiles, food products, and chemicals. It was founded in AD 642 by the Arabs of El Fustat, and a new capital was established in AD 969 by the FATIMID dynasty as capital of Egypt. In 1517 it became part of the OTTOMAN EMPIRE. Cairo fell to NAPOLEON I in 1798 and to the British in 1801. During WORLD WAR II it was the Allied headquarters in the Middle East. In the late 1970s Cairo became important as a Middle Eastern financial and commercial centre. Egyptian–Israeli talks took place (1977) in Cairo, and the headquarters of the ARAB LEAGUE was moved (1979) from Cairo to TUNIS. Cairo has many mosques, palaces, museums (e.g., the Egyptian National Museum), and universities.

**caisson,** boxlike chamber of wood, steel, or concrete used in constructing underwater foundations or piers. It can be floated and positioned before being flooded so that it sinks to the sea bed. Once on the bottom, it can be filled with concrete. Alternatively, it can be anchored and the water removed by compressed air allowing operators to work under an airtight bulkhead.

**Calabar,** formerly Old Calabar, city and port (1981 est. pop. 256,000), SE Nigeria, on the Calabar R. The capital of Cross River state, it is one of

Nigeria's main export ports trading in palm products. The city was founded in the 18th cent. as a market centre and a major slave-trading depot.

**Calais,** city (1982 pop. 76,935), N France, on the Strait of Dover. An industrial centre, it has been a major seaport and communications link with England since the Middle Ages. England held it from 1347 to 1558, when the Duke of GUISE recovered it. Calais was almost razed in World War II.

**Calamy, Edmund,** 1600–1666, English Presbyterian preacher. He became a chaplain to King Charles II but was ejected from the ministry by the Act of Uniformity (1662). His grandson **Edmund Calamy,** 1671–1732, a nonconformist minister in London, is chiefly remembered for his *Account of the Ministers . . . Ejected by the Act for Uniformity* (1702).

**calcite,** widely distributed calcium carbonate mineral ($CaCO_3$) that ranges from white or colourless to a great variety of colours, owing to impurities. Its crystals are noted for their perfect cleavage. Calcite also occurs in a number of massive forms, including MARBLE, LIMESTONE, and CHALK. Other forms include ICELAND SPAR, STALACTITE AND STALAGMITE formations, Oriental ALABASTER, and marl. It is used as a building stone and is the raw material for quicklime (CALCIUM OXIDE) and CEMENT.

**calcium** (Ca), metallic element, first isolated in 1808 by Sir Humphry DAVY. One of the ALKALINE-EARTH METALS, it is silver-white, soft, and malleable. The fifth most abundant element (about 3.6%) of the earth's crust, it is not found uncombined but occurs in numerous compounds, e.g., CALCITE, DOLOMITE, ICELAND SPAR, LIMESTONE, and MARBLE. Calcium acts as a reducing agent (see OXIDATION AND REDUCTION) in the preparation of other metals. It occurs in most plant and animal matter, and is essential for the formation and maintenance of strong bones and teeth (see APATITE). Calcium helps to regulate the heartbeat and is necessary for blood clotting. See ELEMENT (table); PERIODIC TABLE.

**calcium carbonate:** see CALCITE; CHALK; LIMESTONE.

**calcium oxide** or **calcia,** chemical compound (CaO), also called lime, quicklime, or caustic lime. A colourless crystalline or white amorphous substance, it has wide industrial uses, e.g., in making porcelain and glass; in purifying sugar; in preparing bleaching powder, calcium carbide, and calcium cyanamide; in water softeners; in mortars and cements; and in treating acidic soil (liming).

**calculator, electronic,** electronic device for performing numerical computations. Electronic calculators became available in the early 1960s, and in the early 1970s miniature types, some of them pocket-size, were marketed as consumer items. Electronic calculators have ten keys (0–9) that can be used to enter numbers into the machine; additional keys are provided to enable the user to perform a range of operations, from basic arithmetic in simple devices to the generation of complex mathematical functions in more advanced types. The results of an operation are either shown on an electronic display or printed. Some of these machines are actually small COMPUTERS with limited memory and programming capabilities.

**calculus,** branch of MATHEMATICS that studies continuously changing quantities. It was developed in the 17th cent. independently by Sir Isaac NEWTON and G.W. LEIBNIZ. The calculus is characterized by the use of infinitesimal processes, involving passage to a LIMIT. The *differential calculus* arises from the study of the rate at which a FUNCTION, usually symbolized by *y* or *f*(*x*), changes relative to a change in the independent variable, usually *x*. This relative rate can be computed from a new function, the derivative of *y* with respect to *x*, denoted by *dy/dx*, $y_,$ or $_,(x)$, which is arrived at by a process called *differentiation*. Formulas have been developed for the derivatives of all commonly encountered functions. For example, if $y = x^n$ for any real number *n*, then $y_, = nx^{n-1}$, and if $y = \sin x$, then $y_, = \cos x$ (see TRIGONOMETRY). In physical applications, the independent variable is frequently time, e.g., if $s = f(t)$ expresses the relation between the distance, *s*, travelled and the time, *t*, elapsed, then $s_, = f_,(t)$ represents the rate of change of distance with time, i.e., the speed at time *t*. Geometrically, the derivative is interpreted as the slope of the line tangent to a curve at a point. This view of the derivative yields applications, e.g., in the design of optical mirrors and lenses and the determination of projectile paths. The *integral calculus* arises from the study of the limit of a sum of elements when the number of such elements increases without bound while the size of the elements

diminishes. Conventionally, the area *A* under the curve $y = f(x)$ between the two values $x = a$ and $x = b$ is symbolized by $A = \int_a^b f(x)dx$, called the definite integral of $f(x)$ from *a* to *b*. The area is approximated by summing the products of $f(x)$ and *dx* for each of the infinitely small distances (*dx*) that comprise the measurable distance between *a* and *b*. This method can be used to determine the lengths of curves, the areas bounded by curves, and the volumes of solids bounded by curved surfaces. The connection between the integral and the derivative is known as the Fundamental Theorem of the Calculus, which, in symbols, is $\int_a^b f(x)dx = F(b) - F(a)$, where $F(x)$ is a function whose derivative is $f(x)$. Calculus has been developed to treat functions not only of a single variable but also of several variables and is the foundation for the larger branch of mathematics known as ANALYSIS.

**calculus of finite differences.** This deals with the properties of $f(x+w) \cdot f(x)/w$ not with the limit of this expression as $w \to 0$, as does the infinitesimal calculus. Only a series of functional values is given and from these the subject seeks to determine the value of the function at intermediate points, the values of the derivative of the function at a point and of the integral of the function between specified limits.

**Calcutta,** city (1981 pop. 3,305,006), capital of West Bengal state, E India, on the Hooghly R. It is India's second largest city, and the chief port and industrial centre of E India. Jute is milled, and textiles, chemicals, and metal and engineering products are manufactured. Nearly 60 languages are spoken in the city, which suffers from poverty, overcrowding, and high unemployment. It was founded c.1690 by the British EAST INDIA COMPANY. In 1756 the nawab of Bengal captured the garrison, many of whom died when imprisoned in a small, stifling room known as the 'black hole'. Robert Clive retook the city in 1757. It was the capital of India from 1833 to 1912. Its museum houses one of the world's best natural history collections.

**Caldecott, Randolph,** 1846–86, English artist. His charming coloured illustrations for 16 picture books, e.g., *The House That Jack Built* and *The Grand Panjandrum Himself,* inspired the Caldecott Medal for children's-book illustration.

**Calder, Alexander,** 1898–1976, one of the most innovative modern American sculptors. Famous for his MOBILES, brightly coloured constellations of moving shapes, he is also known for his witty wire portraits, imaginative jewellery, colourful and complex miniature zoo (1925; Whitney Mus., New York City), and abstract immobile sculptures called stabiles.

Alexander **Calder,** *Antennae with Red and Blue Dots,* 1960. Kinetic sculpture, 111 × 128.3 × 128.3 cm. Tate Gallery, London.

**caldera,** a large, circular volcanic depression perhaps 1, 2 or more km (½–1 mi) in diameter which may contain a number of smaller volcanic vents and a crater lake. It represents the main vent and surrounding area of a dormant or inactive volcano and is usually explained by collapse or subsidence, possibly following an explosive eruption.

**Calderón de la Barca, Pedro,** 1600–81, Spanish dramatist, last major figure of the GOLDEN AGE. He wrote more than 100 plays, including 70 *autos sacramentales* (one-act religious plays) for the Corpus Christi festival; cloak-and-dagger thrillers, mainly on the theme of honour; and comedies of manners like *El alcalde de Zalamea* (c.1640; tr. The Mayor of Zalamea). His philosophical drama *La vida es sueño* (1635; tr. Life Is a Dream) is considered a masterpiece.

**Caldwell, Erskine,** 1903–87, American author. His realistic, earthy novels of the rural South include *Tobacco Road* (1932) and *God's Little Acre* (1933). His short stories appear in many collections, e.g., *Jackpot* (1940).

**calendar,** system of reckoning time usually based on a recurrent natural cycle, such as the cycle of the Sun through the seasons (see YEAR) or the moon through its phases (see MONTH). Because the solar year is 365 days 5 hr 48 min 46 sec and the lunar year (12 synodic months of 29.53 days) is 354 days 8 hr 48 min, people have been confronted since ancient times with the problem of the discrepancy. The year not being exactly divisible by months and days, the practice arose of making arbitrary divisions and inserting extra (intercalary) days or months. The ancient Chinese lunar calendar (in use by the 2nd millennium BC) was based on a period of 60 days; 60 such periods made up a complete cycle, i.e., 3600 days or just under 10 years. There was also a solar year, divided into 24 periods of 15 days, corrected by intercalation. The Maya calendar, and those of various other civilizations of Central America, had a 260-day cycle for ritual purposes, plus a solar year of 18 months each of 20 days with 5 extra days, considered unlucky, at the end of the year. The system of naming the days and months on a cycle of 20 names and numbering them on a cycle of 13 meant that each of the 18,980 days in 52 years had a unique combination of name and number. The Gregorian calendar, in general use today, evolved from the Roman calendar reformed (46 BC) by Julius CAESAR. In the Julian calendar April, June, September, and November had 30 days, February 28 (29 days every fourth, or leap, year), and all other months 31 days. The date was computed by counting backwards from the Kalends (the 1st day), the Nones (the 7th day in March, May, July, and October, otherwise the 5th), the Ides (the 15th day in March, May, July, and October, otherwise the 13th); thus 10 Jan. was the 4th day of the Ides of January. Because the Julian year was too long, by the 16th cent. the vernal equinox had become displaced from 21 Mar. to 11 Mar. Pope GREGORY XIII ordained that 10 days be dropped in 1582 and that years ending in hundreds be leap years only if divisible by 400. The non-Roman Catholic countries were slow to adopt the Gregorian calendar; it was adopted in England in 1752 and by the Eastern churches in the 20th cent. The Muslim calendar is lunar, and has a year of 354 days consisting of 12 months of 30 and 29 days alternately. There is no intercalation, so the months alter in relation to the seasons. The Jewish calendar has a solar year but lunar months; a 13th month of 30 days is intercalated in the 3rd, 6th, 8th, 11th, 14th, 17th, and 19th years of the 19-year cycle. See also FRENCH REVOLUTIONARY CALENDAR.

**Calgary,** city (1984 est. pop. 619,814), S Alberta, Canada, at the confluence of the Bow and Elbow rivers. It is a major centre for the region's rapidly expanding oil and natural gas industry, and also an agricultural processing and wholesaling centre. The Calgary Stampede, inaugurated in 1912, is a popular annual rodeo usually held in July. Built at the site of a fort established (1875) by the Northwest Mounted Police, Calgary is now one of Canada's fastest-growing cities.

**Calhoun, John Caldwell,** 1782–1850, American statesman. He was the great defender of the agrarian South against the industrial North, and of the doctrine of STATES' RIGHTS. After serving in the House of Representatives (1811–17) and as secretary of war (1817–25), he was vice president (1825–32) under J.Q. ADAMS and Andrew JACKSON. He and Jackson disagreed, however, over the nature of the Union, and Calhoun openly aided South Carolina's opposition to and ultimate NULLIFICATION (1832) of an increased tariff inimical to its interests. As a US senator (1832–43, 1845–50), he eloquently defended slavery and SECESSION. As secretary of state (1844–45) under Pres. TYLER, he secured the admission of Texas to the Union as a slave state.

**Cali,** city (1981 est. pop. 1,400,000), W Colombia, capital of Valle del Cauca dept., on the Cali R. It is an industrial centre, exporting minerals, timber, and food products and manufacturing tyres, textiles, and building materials. Founded in 1536, it has doubled its population since 1950, largely because of a regional hydroelectric power project.

**Caliari, Paolo:** see VERONESE, PAOLO.

**California,** state of the US, most populous (1984 est. pop. 25,622,000), area 411,015 km² (158,693 sq mi), situated in the SW and bordered by the Pacific Ocean (W), Oregon (N), Mexico (S), and Nevada and Arizona (E). The capital is SACRAMENTO; other major cities are LOS ANGELES, (the second largest in the nation), SAN DIEGO, SAN FRANCISCO, SAN JOSE, Long Beach, and Oakland. The mountainous coastal regions are separated from the SIERRA NEVADA mountains in the west by the fertile Central Valley, in which flow the Sacramento and San Joaquin Rs. The eastern part is largely hot desert and includes DEATH VALLEY, while the SAN ANDREAS FAULT runs along the coast causing occasional earthquakes and tremors. The state has a wide range of climatic and environmental conditions. Its economy is the most productive in the US, leading in both manufacturing and agriculture. California is a major producer of aerospace products; electronic and electrical equipment; machinery; and processed foods. The farms, two-thirds of which are irrigated, grow a wide variety of fruits and vegetables, while cotton and cattle are also important. There is oil and natural gas, and the state leads the nation in the production of asbestos, boron, gypsum, tungsten, and other minerals. Tourism is a major industry, centred on natural features, such as Yosemite Valley and the giant sequoia trees, and on Disneyland. The population is ethnically diverse: in 1980 67% of the population was non-Hispanic white, 19% of Spanish origin, 5% black, 5% of Asian ancestry, and 1% native American (representing the largest community in absolute numbers of any state). The Spanish explored the coast in the mid-16th cent. and established missions in the late 18th cent. In 1848 California was ceded by Mexico to the US and the discovery of gold attracted American settlers. Railway construction and agriculture attracted migrants from Asia and Mexico. During World War II industry expanded rapidly, especially in defence, motion pictures, and later, television. Santa Clara Co., known as Silicon Valley, and Orange Co. are major world centres of high-technology industry. California is the most popular destination for immigrants to the US, and in recent years some ethnic tensions have developed. Future expansion depends partly upon the provision of water, and California faces many environmental problems.

**California, Gulf of,** arm of the Pacific Ocean, NW Mexico. It is c.1130 km (700 mi) long and 80–209 km (50–130 mi) wide, and it separates the states of BAJA CALIFORNIA and Baja California Sur from the Mexican mainland. The gulf, which is part of a structural depression that extends north to the Coachella Valley of S California, reaches a maximum depth of c.2590 m (8500 ft) in the south.

**californium** (Cf), synthetic, radioactive, metallic element, produced in 1950 by Glenn Seaborg and colleagues by alpha-particle bombardment of curium-242. It is in the ACTINIDE SERIES. Californium-252, produced in nuclear reactors, is a neutron source. See ELEMENT (table); PERIODIC TABLE.

**Caligula,** AD 12–41, Roman emperor (r.AD 37–41), son of Germanicus Caesar and Agrippina I. His real name was Caius Caesar Germanicus; as a small child he wore military boot, whence his nickname [*caligula* = little boots]. On the death of TIBERIUS the army helped make Caligula emperor. Shortly afterward he became severely ill; it is widely believed that he was thereafter insane. He earned a reputation for ruthless and cruel autocracy. The often-repeated story that he made his horse consul is not true. He was assassinated, and CLAUDIUS I succeeded to the throne.

**caliphate,** [Arab., = office of deputy], a historical and legal institution within SUNNISM. Historically, the caliphal title was assumed by the sovereigns of Muslim dynasties claiming authority over the whole of ISLAM; very rarely was it assumed by provincial potentates, and even then as with the Hafsids it was premissed on ambitions to universal authority. Four caliphs were elected to the caliphal title at Medina after the death of MUHAMMAD. The Umayyad caliphate was then established in Damascus (661–750), after which the ABBASID dynasty established itself, first briefly in Kufa in Iraq and later in Baghdad (749–1258). A branch of the Abbasids was then established under the tutelage of the MAMELUKES in Cairo until the eradication of the Mamluk state by the OTTOMANS in 1517. A branch of the Umayyads fled from the Abbasids and established a caliphate at Cordoba, which lasted until 1031. The states of the ALMORAVIDS and ALMOHADS were also caliphates, as was the dynasty of the FATIMIDS, and Ottoman sultans also assumed the caliphal title until its abolition by Kemal ATATURK in 1924. Some Islamist political groups have since called for the re-establishment of the institution. Legally, a caliph has to fulfill a number of conditions pertaining to majority, learning, and, according to the classical theory, descent from the tribe of Quraish, to which Muhammad belonged. According to classical theory, a caliph is the ultimate political, legal, religious, and economic authority of Islam. But classical theory also caters for a functional division of labour between a caliph and a stronger political and military authority under whose tutelage the office sometimes fell. This provided for the ratification of a military *status quo* by the Caliph provided authority over legal and religious matters was vested in the Caliph and enforced by the stronger partner.

**Calixtus I, Callixtus I,** or **Callistus I, Saint,** c.160–222, pope (217–222), a Roman. As archdeacon to Pope Zephyrinus, he established the famous Calixtus Cemetery in Rome. As pope, Calixtus was opposed by the antipope Hippolytus and extended absolution to many classes of sinners previously thought to be beyond forgiveness. Feast: 14 Oct.

**Calixtus II, Callixtus II** or **Callistus II,** d. 1124, pope (1119–24), named Guy, son of the count of Burgundy and related to the royal houses of Germany, France, and England. Succeeding Gelasius II, Calixtus triumphed over the antipope Gregory VIII and secured an end to the INVESTITURE controversy when the Emperor HENRY V signed (1122) the Concordat of Worms. Calixtus then called (1123) the First Lateran Council which ratified the Concordat.

**Calixtus III, Callixtus III** or **Callistus III,** 1378–1458, pope (1455–58), a Spaniard named Alfonso de Borja (Ital., Borgia). He supplied aid to John HUNYADI and SCANDERBEG to fight the Turks and quarrelled with ALFONSO V of Aragon. Calixtus's nepotism firmly established the BORGIA family in Italy.

**Callaghan, Sir (Leonard) James,** 1912–, British statesman. He was elected a Labour member of Parliament in 1945. Later he served as chancellor of the exchequer (1964–67), resigning when forced to accept devaluation of the pound; home secretary (1967–70); and foreign secretary (1974–76). Upon the resignation of Harold WILSON in 1976 he became prime minister. His government was plagued by inflation, unemployment, and its inability to restrain unions' wage demands. He lost the 1979 election to Margaret THATCHER and resigned the Labour Party leadership in 1980; he was knighted in 1987.

**Callaghan, Morley,** 1903–, Canadian novelist. Callaghan writes from a Christian point of view. His best-known works include the novels *Such Is My Beloved* (1934) and *The Many Colored Coat* (1960), and *That Summer in Paris* (1963), a reminiscence about his friendship with HEMINGWAY, FITZGERALD, and others.

**Callao** (kah‚yoh), city (1981 pop. 441,374), capital of Lima dept., W Peru, on Callao Bay of the Pacific Ocean. It is 13 km (8 mi) W of the Peruvian capital, LIMA, and, as Peru's chief seaport, handles well over half of the nation's foreign trade. Callao has survived foreign attack, tidal waves, and at least two major earthquakes, in 1746 and 1940.

**Callas, Maria,** 1923–77, American operatic soprano; b. New York City to Greek parents. She made her debut at Verona, Italy, in 1947 and at the METROPOLITAN OPERA in 1956. Noted for her dramatic intensity, she excelled in CHERUBINI's *Medea,* BELLINI's *Norma,* and PUCCINI's *Tosca.*

**Calles, Plutarco Elias** (‚kahyes), 1877–1945, president of MEXICO (1924–28). His revolutionary administration initiated economic reforms, enforced anticlerical laws, and unified the government under the National Institutional Revolutionary Party (PRI). After leaving office he remained political chieftain of the nation until he opposed CÁRDENAS and was exiled (1936–41).

**Callicrates,** 5th cent. BC, Greek architect. With ICTINUS he built (447–432 BC) the PARTHENON at Athens. At Athens he also designed (c.427) the Temple of Nike.

**calligraphy** [Gr., = beautiful writing], skilled penmanship practiced as a fine art. Papyrus fragments from the 4th cent. BC show two early European types of handwriting: a cursive script, used for letters and records, and a more polished style, called uncials, used for literary works. This style was developed after the 1st cent. AD, giving rise to many splendid scripts throughout the RENAISSANCE. With the establishment of the printing press, the use of calligraphy declined until the 20th cent., when

interest in the art was revived by the work of Owen Jones and William MORRIS. Calligraphy has always been valued by Far Eastern peoples as a major aesthetic expression, greater perhaps than painting, and in early Japanese imperial society a man was not taken seriously unless he had a good hand. Islamic calligraphy has become very highly developed, partly because painting and decorative arts are restricted by the ban on representing creatures.

**Callimachus,** fl. c.265 BC, Greek poet and critic. At ALEXANDRIA he drew up a catalogue constituting a full literary history. Among his over 800 hymns, epigrams, and poems is *Aetia* [causes], a collection of legends connected with the origins of certain beliefs, practices, and events.

**Calliope:** see MUSES.

**Callisto,** in astronomy, satellite of JUPITER.

**Callistus:** see CALIXTUS.

**Callixtus:** see CALIXTUS.

**Callot, Jacques** (ka‚loh), 1592/3–1635, French etcher and engraver. In Florence, for Duke Cosimo II, he did many etchings, both of elegant courtiers and festivals, and of hunchbacks and beggars; in Nancy, in 1633, he produced his celebrated *The Great Miseries of War,* a response to the horrors of the Thirty Years' War.

**Calonne, Charles Alexandre de,** 1734–1802, French statesman and controller general of finances (1783–87). His spending policy, designed to restore public credit, ended in disaster and hastened the FRENCH REVOLUTION.

**calorie,** (cal), unit of energy equal to 4.1840 J; the energy required to raise the temperature of 1g of water by 1°C (from 14.5° to 15.5°C). Nutritionists use the kilocalorie (1000 cal) to state the energy content of food, and thus to describe its potential for providing the body with energy to be used or stored as body fat.

**Calpurnia,** d. after 44 BC, Roman matron. The daughter of Lucius Calpurnicus Piso Caesoninus, she was married to Julius CAESAR in 59 BC. She was loyal to him despite his many infidelities and his neglect.

**Calvary,** or **Golgotha,** [Lat., = a skull] place where JESUS was crucified, outside the wall of JERUSALEM. Its location is not certainly known. The traditional site was AD c.1130 included in the newly-built Church of the Holy Sepulchre.

**Calvert, George,** 1st **baron Baltimore,** c.1580–1632, English colonizer in America. After holding high offices in England, he was granted (1623) Avalon peninsula in Newfoundland, but the colony he founded there did not prosper. In 1632 James I granted him territory that eventually became Maryland, but Calvert died before the colony's charter was accepted.

**Calvin, John,** 1509–64, French Protestant theologian of the Reformation; b. Noyon, Picardy. Having studied theology and law, he experienced (1533) a 'sudden conversion' and turned his attention to the cause of the REFORMATION, for which he was persecuted and hunted. His work in Geneva began in 1536, but the system he tried to impose was rejected, and he was banished (1538). After a stay at Basel and Strasbourg, he was welcomed back to Geneva in 1541. Calvin had begun the work of systematizing Protestant thought in his *Institutes of the Christian Religion* (1536). His theology diverged from Catholic doctrine in such fundamental ways as rejection of papal authority and acceptance of justification by faith alone, and the doctrine of PREDESTINATION. He also maintained that the Bible was the sole source of God's law, and that it was man's duty to interpret it and to preserve the orderly world that God had ordained. It was such a system that he sought to realize at Geneva by founding a government based solely on religious law. From his teachings grew one of the principal Christian religious systems, CALVINISM. His impact on PROTESTANTISM, not least through his lucid and exhaustive commentaries on Scripture, has been incalculable.

**Calvin, Melvin,** 1911–, American chemist. He was awarded the 1961 Nobel Prize for chemistry for his elucidation of the chemical pathways of PHOTOSYNTHESIS. He fed radioactively labelled carbon dioxide to plants, and, by elegant analytical techniques, including CHROMATOGRAPHY, identified the compounds in which it was first incorporated. Calvin has also contributed to debates on the origin of life.

**Calvinism,** term used in several different senses. It can mean the teachings of John CALVIN himself; all that developed from his doctrine and practice in Protestant countries in social, political, ethical, and theological aspects of life and thought; or the system of doctrine, distinctive in its rejection of consubstantiation in the Eucharist and in its doctrine of PREDESTINATION, that was accepted by the Reformed churches (see PRESBYTERIANISM). Calvinism aimed at a church-dominated society which monitored the behaviour of citizens. It stressed that only those whom God elects are saved, and that man does nothing to effect his salvation. The doctrine challenged LUTHERANISM in Europe, spread to Scotland, and influenced the Puritans of England and New England. It receded under rationalism in the 18th and 19th cent., but has found new expression in the Reformed theology of Karl BARTH.

**Calvino, Italo**, 1923–85, Italian novelist; b. Cuba. He cultivated a variety of genres and styles, showing a preference for allegorical fantasy. Among his works are *The Path to the Nest of Spiders* (1947), a realistic novel about the anti-Fascist resistance; *Our Forefathers* (1960), a trilogy of ironic fables of chivalry; *Cosmicomics* (1965), 12 'science fiction' tales; and *If on a Winter's Night a Traveller* (1979), a novel composed of fragments of 10 stylistically different novels.

**Calvo, Carlo**, 1824–1906, Argentine diplomat and historian, writer on INTERNATIONAL LAW. His principle known as the **Calvo Doctrine** would prohibit diplomatic intervention to enforce private claims before local remedies had been exhausted. The **Calvo Clause** found in statutes, treaties, and contracts is the concrete application of his doctrine.

**Calvo Sotelo, Leopoldo**, 1926–, Spanish engineer and political leader. After leading the Union of the Democratic Centre to victory in the 1981 elections, he was confirmed as prime minister despite an abortive military coup in which the parliament was seized. He resigned before the 1982 elections in which the Socialist Party, led by Felipe GONZÁLEZ, was victorious.

**Calydonian hunt:** see MELEAGER.

**Calypso**, in greek mythology, nymph, daughter of ATLAS, in HOMER's *Odyssey*. She entertained ODYSSEUS on the island of Ogygia for seven years before he rejected her offer of immortality and continued home.

**Camacho, Manuel Ávila:** see ÁVILA CAMACHO, MANUEL.

**Camagüey**, city (1981 pop. 245,235), E Cuba, capital of Camagüey prov. The island's third-largest city, it is a commercial centre with meat-packing and other food-processing industries. Founded in the early 16th cent., it produced salted beef for Spanish fleets and was often sacked by pirates. It has retained a Spanish colonial atmosphere.

**Camargue**, delta of the RHONE R., S France. This wetland of lakes, marshes, and salt-steppe has a rich wildlife and was made a regional park in 1970. Many migrating birds visit the area and the flamingo is a common sight. Commercial activities include salt pans, eel-catching, and the raising of black bulls which are herded by 'cowboys' on white horses. Rice is grown in the north near the city of Arles.

**cambium**, thin layer of regenerative tissue lying between the BARK and the wood of a STEM, most active in woody plants. In herbaceous plants the cambium is usually inactive; in monocotyledons (see ANGIOSPERM) it is absent. Producing thin layers of phloem on the outside and xylem on the inside (see WOOD), cambium growth increases the diameter of the stem. Its seasonal growth is responsible for ANNUAL RINGS.

**Cambodia:** see KAMPUCHEA.

**Cambrai, Treaty of:** see ITALIAN WARS.

**Cambrian period:** see GEOLOGICAL ERA (table).

**Cambridge**, city (1981 pop. 87,111), Cambridgeshire, E central England, on the Cam R. An ancient market town that now has some light and high-tech industry on its outskirts, it is famous as the site of Cambridge Univ. (est. 12th cent.). In addition to the magnificent college buildings, the city abounds in medieval churches (but has no cathedral), old inns, and narrow, winding streets.

**Cambridge**, US city (1980 pop. 95,322), E Massachusetts, across the Charles R. from BOSTON; settled 1630 as New Towne, inc. as a city 1846. A famous educational and research centre, it is the seat of Harvard Univ. (est. 1636). Its industries include electrical and scientific manufactures, and rubber and glass goods. Printing has been important since c.1639. The city, which was the home of such notable people as H.W. LONGFELLOW and J.R. LOWELL, has numerous historic sites.

Cambridge

**Cambridgeshire**, inland county in E England, (1984 est. pop. 609,200), 3409 km² (1329 sq mi), bordering on Lincolnshire in the N. The county town is CAMBRIDGE. Since the 1974 local government reorganization it has included the Isle of Ely, Huntingdonshire, and the Soke of Peterborough. It is mainly flat and low-lying, apart from low hills in the S. Much of the county lies within the FENS. There is much fertile agricultural land and some light industry developed around Cambridge and PETERBOROUGH.

**Cambridge University**, at Cambridge, England. It originated in the early 12th cent., possibly earlier than OXFORD UNIV., and was organized into residential colleges by the end of the 13th cent. There are 31 colleges, 27 of which admit undergraduates. Almost all of the traditionally male colleges and some of the women's colleges now admit both men and women. Cambridge was a centre of the new learning in the Renaissance and of Reformation theology. In modern times it offers a wide range of subjects, excelling in science. Many of the world's outstanding physicists have worked at the university's famous Cavendish Laboratory of experimental physics (opened 1873). The Cambridge University Press dates from the 16th cent.

**Camden**, London borough (1981 pop. 161,098), N of R. Thames. It includes the districts of Holborn, Hampstead, and St Pancras. In the S of the borough are the railway termini of Euston, St Pancras, and King's Cross; the British Museum; and many office blocks. There are several open spaces here, including Hampstead Heath and part of Regent's Park.

**Camden Town group**, a small group of artists formed by SICKERT in 1911. The members had in common a dislike of academic art and an interest in ordinary everyday subject matter. GILMAN and GORE were the principal figures in it. The group merged with other smaller groups to form the LONDON GROUP in 1913. They are sometimes referred to as the 'English post-impressionists'.

**camel**, hoofed ruminant (family Camelidae). The family consists of the true camels of Asia, the wild guanaco and domesticated ALPACA and LLAMA of South America, and the vicuña of South America. The two species of true camel are the single-humped Arabian camel (*Camelus dromedarius*), a domesticated animal of Arabia and N Africa, which includes a special breed, the dromedary; and the two-humped Bactrian camel (*C. bactrianus*) of central Asia. Their humps are storage places for fat. Ranging in colour from white to dark brown, camels are well adapted for desert life and can go without water for several days. There are wild Bactrian camels living in the Gobi desert.

**camel**, in marine engineering, large device used for raising sunken vessels. In construction it is similar to a CAISSON, consisting of a watertight box made of steel and concrete that is slowly filled with water until it can be lowered to the site of the sunken vessel. Divers secure the camels to the vessel and then have the water pumped out by compressed air. The total buoyancy must be sufficient to lift camels and vessel.

**camellia**, evergreen shrub or small tree (genus *Camellia*) of the TEA family, native to Asia, now widely cultivated for the white, red, or variegated showy blossoms and glossy, dark-green foliage. Tea-seed oil, from the seeds of *C. sasanqua,* is used in cooking, and in soap and textile manufacturing.

**Camelot,** in ARTHURIAN LEGEND, the seat of King Arthur's court, frequently located in Somerset or Monmouthshire.

**cameo,** small relief carving, usually on striated precious or semiprecious stones or on shell. The design, often a portrait head, is cut in the light-coloured vein; the dark vein becomes the background. Glass of two colours in layers may also be cameo-cut. The art originated in Asia and spread to ancient Greece and Rome; it was revived during the Renaissance and in the Victorian era.

**camera,** in PHOTOGRAPHY, device for recording an image on film or some other light-sensitive material. It consists of a lightproof box; a LENS through which light enters and is focused; a shutter that controls the size of the lens opening and the length of time it is open; a mechanism for moving the film between exposures; and a viewfinder, or eyepiece, that shows the user the image the lens sees. The camera developed from the Greek **camera obscura** [Lat., = dark chamber], an artist's tool dating from the Middle Ages. It was a light-tight box with a convex lens at one end and a screen that reflected the image at the other; the artist traced the image. Joseph Nicéphore NIÉPCE produced the first negative image in 1816. See also PHOTOGRAPHY, STILL; POLAROID CAMERA.

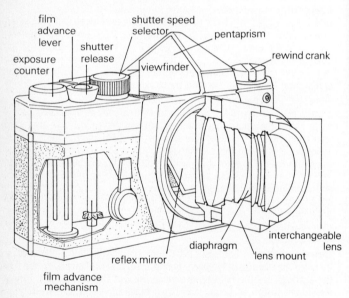

Cross section through a single-lens reflex **camera**

Camera obscura

**Cameron, Julia Margaret,** 1815–79, English pioneer photographer; b. India. In 1864 she began to photograph her many illustrious friends, e.g., Alfred, Lord TENNYSON and Ellen TERRY. Her superb portraits appeared as *Victorian Photographs of Famous Men and Fair Women* (rev. ed., 1973).

*The Passing of King Arthur* (c.1874) by Julia Margaret **Cameron**

**Cameroon,** officially, United Republic of Cameroon, republic (1987 est. pop. 10,106,000), 475,442 km² (183,568 sq mi), W central Africa, bordered by the Gulf of Guinea (W, SW), Nigeria (NW), Chad (NE), the Central African Republic (E), and the Congo, Gabon, and Equatorial Guinea (S). Major cities include YAOUNDÉ (the capital) and DOUALA. Cameroon consists of a coastal region of swamps and dense rain forests, an interior plateau covered with forests and savanna, and an arid northern region. Volcanic peaks near the coast rise to 4070 m (13,354 ft). The economy is based on a varied agriculture that makes the country self-sufficient in food. Cameroon is a leading producer of cocoa which, along with coffee, bananas, palm products, cotton, rubber, timber, and aluminium, constitute the chief exports. Aluminium-smelting, using hydroelectric power, is the principal industry. Petroleum is being produced in increasing quantities. The GNP is US$7424 million, and the GNP per capita is US$810 (1985). Cameroon's diverse population includes more than 150 ethnic groups. French and English are the official languages. Traditional religious beliefs are dominant, but there are large minorities of Christians and Muslims, the latter in the north.

*History.* The first Europeans to arrive in the region were the Portuguese (1472), who developed a large-scale slave trade in which the Spanish, Dutch, French, and English also took part. By the 19th cent. palm oil and ivory had become the main items of commerce. The British established commercial hegemony over the coast in the early 1800s, but were supplanted by the Germans, who made the area a protectorate in 1884. The area was occupied by French and British troops in WORLD WAR I, after which it was divided into French and British mandates under the League of Nations. These became UN trust territories in 1946. In the 1950s guerrilla warfare, sparked by demands for independence, raged in the French Cameroons; the French granted self-government in 1957 and independence in 1960. Following a UN plebiscite in 1961, the southern zone of British Cameroons was incorporated into the new country (the northern zone joined NIGERIA), which became a federal republic with two prime ministers and two legislatures but a single president. A new constitution adopted in 1972 created a unitary one-party state to replace the federation, although the oil boom in English-speaking W Cameroon in the early 1980s brought calls for a return to the federal system. (See also CAMEROONS.) After succeeding Ahmadou Ahidjo as president in 1982, new leader Paul Biya relaunched the ruling party as the Cameroon People's Democratic Movement in 1985.

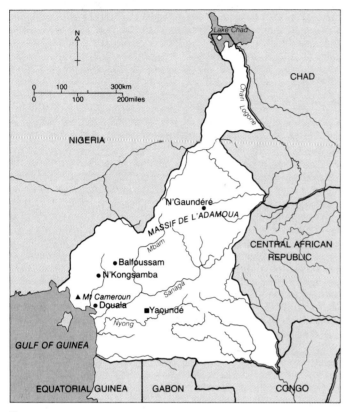

Cameroon

**Cameroons,** former German colony, W Africa, in the region that is now Cameroon and Nigeria. After World War I the colony was divided into British Cameroons and French Cameroons, both League of Nations mandates. Both colonies became UN trust territories and then achieved independence after World War II. French Cameroons and the southern part of British Cameroons became the United Republic of CAMEROON, and the northern section of British Cameroons joined NIGERIA.

**Camm, Sir Sydney,** 1893–1966, British aircraft designer. After building wooden aeroplanes for the Martinsyde Co. in World War I, he joined the Hawker Engineering Co. in 1923 and designed their most successful military aircraft—the Hart bomber, the Fury fighter biplane, and the Hurricane fighter (see BATTLE OF BRITAIN). With the arrival of the jet engine, Camm produced the Sea Hawk and the Hunter; and his final work (1960) was the world's first VERTICAL TAKEOFF AND LANDING AIRCRAFT, later developed as the Harrier. Camm was knighted in 1953, and was president of the ROYAL AERONAUTICAL SOCIETY in 1954–55.

**Camões** or **Camoens, Luís Vaz de** (ˌkamohˈens), 1524?–80, Portugal's national poet and greatest literary figure. Among the events of his turbulent life were study at the Univ. of Coimbra; banishment from court (1546); loss of an eye in the Moroccan campaign; imprisonment for street-fighting; military service in India; dismissal from an official post in Macao; and shipwreck on his return (1570) to Portugal. *The Lusiads* [Port. *Os Lusíadas* = sons of Lusus, i.e., the Portuguese] (1572), a Vergilian epic encompassing the voyage of Vasco da GAMA and much of Portuguese history, is one of the masterpieces of the Renaissance. Camões received a meagre royal pension but died in poverty. His highly regarded plays, sonnets, and lyrics appeared posthumously.

**Campaign for Nuclear Disarmament** (CND), organization founded in the late 1950s to oppose the development of the British hydrogen bomb. Its activities range from mass demonstrations and direct action to lobbying MPs, journalists, and members of the public at local and national levels. The 'first wave' of CND, from its foundation on 16 Jan. 1958 until the mid-1960s, is now remembered chiefly for CND's first president, Bertrand RUSSELL, and for the annual Easter marches between London and the nuclear warhead factory at Aldermaston, Berkshire. Nonviolent direct action or civil disobedience was an important part of the first wave of anti-nuclear-weapons campaigning; it was organized by a separate Direct Action Committee (and, after 1960, by the Committee of 100). Eclipsed by the Vietnam war in the years 1964–76, CND returned to prominence in 1979 with the NATO decision to deploy Pershing 2 and Cruise missiles in Europe. A CND-sponsored demonstration in London in October 1980 drew 100,000 people opposed to the siting of a new generation of nuclear missiles in the UK. Large demonstrations of 250,000 people in the following two years were accompanied by the establishment (1982) of the women's peace camp at GREENHAM COMMON and peace camps at several other nuclear bases and installations. Unsuccessful at preventing the installation of Cruise, the Campaign remains the focus for anti-nuclear campaigning in the UK, concerning itself with nuclear energy as well as nuclear weapons. CND is the largest of many Western European peace movement organizations.

**Campana, Dino,** 1885–1932, Italian poet. From 1918 he was confined to a mental hospital. His intensely subjective *Orphic Songs* (1914), indebted to the ideas of NIETZSCHE and dedicated to the KAISER, are now seen as the work of a major innovator. Lyrics such as 'The Chimaera' and 'Autumn Garden' are unsurpassed in the Italian poetry of the period.

**campanile,** Italian form of bell tower, chiefly medieval. Built in connection with a church or town hall, it served as belfry, watch tower, and often civil monument. The campanile generally stands as a detached unit. In the 8th cent., square campaniles succeeded the earlier round towers. GIOTTO's campanile in Florence (1334) is entirely faced in marble and ornamented with sculptures.

**Campbell, Alexander,** 1788–1866, American clergyman, cofounder of the Disciples of Christ; b. Ireland. His father, **Thomas Campbell,** 1763–1854, emigrated to the US in 1807 and settled in Pennsylvania, where he withdrew his congregation from the Presbyterian Church. Alexander went to the US in 1809 and joined his father's followers, known as Campbellites. Nominally Baptists (c.1812–c.1827), they advocated a return to scriptural simplicity and later became the Disciples of Christ.

**Campbell, Mrs Patrick,** 1865–1940, English actress; b. Beatrice Stella Tanner. She won fame in PINERO's *Second Mrs Tanqueray* (1893). A friend of G.B. SHAW, she created the part of Eliza Doolittle in his *Pygmalion* (1913).

**Campbell, Robert:** see ROB ROY.

**Campbell, Robert,** 1808–94, Canadian explorer; b. Scotland. As a fur trader for the HUDSON'S BAY COMPANY he explored (1834–52) the Mackenzie R. region and discovered the Pelly R. At its junction with the Lewes R. to form the YUKON R. he established (1848) Fort Selkirk. Later (1850–51) he followed the Yukon as far as Fort Yukon.

**Campbell, Roy,** 1901–57, white South African poet and translator. He became a Fascist, fought for Franco in the Spanish Civil War, but also served in the British Army in North Africa in World War II. He is best known for his long, symbolic poem *The Flaming Terrapin* (1924) and the self-regarding lyric *Adamastor* (1930), but he has still not been forgiven by white South Africans for his attack on some leading figures in *The Wayzgoose* (1928). His translations include works of Lorca and St John of the Cross.

**Campbell-Bannerman, Sir Henry,** 1836–1908, British statesman. A Scottish Liberal, he served as secretary to the admiralty (1882–84), secretary of state for Ireland (1884), and secretary of state for war (1886, 1892–95). He was prime minister from 1905 to 1908, backed by a huge majority and furthered many liberal measures, including self-government for the Transvaal and the Orange Free State. He also favoured domestic reforms.

**Camp David accords,** popular name for the agreement leading to the 1979 peace treaty between Israel and Egypt, named after the US presidential retreat (Camp David) in Maryland where the accords were agreed in September 1978. The treaty was signed 26 Mar. 1979, in Washington, DC, by Menachem BEGIN of Israel and Anwar al-SADAT of Egypt, with US Pres. Jimmy CARTER signing as a witness. Under the pact, which was denounced by other Arab states, Israel agreed to return the SINAI to Egypt, a transfer that was completed in 1982. In a joint letter the two sides also agreed to negotiate Palestinian autonomy measures in the occupied WEST BANK and GAZA STRIP, but virtually no progress was made on this issue before Sadat's assassination in 1981. After Israel's siege of BEIRUT in 1982 to force the PALESTINE LIBERATION ORGANIZATION out of Lebanon, US Pres. Ronald REAGAN put forth a proposal for Palestinian autonomy, but this secured little Arab support. See also ARAB–ISRAELI WARS.

**camphor** ($C_{10}H_{16}O$), white, crystalline solid with a pungent odour and taste. It can be obtained from the camphor tree or synthesized from oil of TURPENTINE. Camphor is used to make CELLULOID and lacquers. In medicine it is used as a stimulant, a diaphoretic, and an inhalant; camphor ice, a mixture chiefly of camphor and WAX, is applied externally. The alcoholic solution is known as spirits of camphor.

**Campi, Giulio,** c.1500–72, Italian painter and architect, founder of a school of painters at Cremona. Influenced by CORREGGIO and RAPHAEL, he did many altarpieces in Milan and Cremona. His pupils included his brothers Cavaliere **Antonio Campi,** c.1536–91; **Vincenzo Campi,** 1532–91, a painter of portraits and still lifes; and **Bernardino Campi,** 1522–c.1590, known for frescoes in San Sigismondo, Cremona.

**Campin, Robert,** c.1378–1444, Flemish painter who, with the van EYCK brothers, was a founder of the Flemish school. His dramatic power, robust realism, and concern for details of daily life broke with the aristocratic elegance of international Gothic.

Robert **Campin,** *Merode Altarpiece.* Cloisters, New York.

**Campinas,** city (1980 pop. 566,627), SE Brazil, in the state of São Paulo, 90 km (55 mi) from the city of São Paulo. It is the most important collection centre for the state's coffee estates and has experienced rapid recent industrial growth. It has Brazil's leading agricultural research institute, a noted symphony orchestra and a modern university.

**Campion, Saint Edmund,** 1540–1581, English JESUIT martyr. He early found favour with ELIZABETH I, but had open Roman Catholic leanings and fled to the Continent, where he joined (1573) the Society of Jesus. He returned (1580) to England as a Jesuit missionary and converted many, but was arrested, tortured, and executed. He was canonized in 1970. Feast: 1 Dec.

**Campion, Thomas,** 1567–1620, English poet and composer. He studied law and practised as a physician. He wrote court masques, Latin poems, and lute music, e.g., five *Books of Airs* (1601–17); a treatise on COUNTERPOINT (1614); and a treatise on poetry, *Observations on the Art of English Poesie* (1602), in which he defended the use of classical measures in English.

**camp meeting,** outdoor religious gathering, held usually in the summer over several days. A prominent institution of the American frontier, it originated (c.1800) under the preaching of James McGready in Kentucky and spread rapidly with the revival movement. Camp meetings were held by evangelical sects, e.g., Methodists and Baptists, and were characterized by emotional fervour that followed upon 'conversion'.

**Campo Grande** (ˌkompoh ˌgrandee), city (1980 pop. 282,857), central W Brazil, capital of Mato Grosso do Sul state. Its position on the rail link from São Paulo to Bolivia has caused the city to be an important centre for the forest clearance and agricultural colonization schemes in W Brazil.

**Campos,** city (1980 pop. 268,034), SE Brazil, on the Paraíba R. This modern industrial city previously was an important centre of the coffee-farming frontier which spread from the Paraíba R. though São Paulo state during the 19th cent. It is now a manufacturing town and the centre of Brazil's most important sugar-producing zone. Significant oil discoveries have recently been made.

**Camus, Albert** (kaˌmy), 1913–60, French writer and thinker; b. Algeria. His belief in the absurdity of the human condition identified him with EXISTENTIALISM, but his courageous humanism distinguished him from that group. The characters in his novels and plays, although keenly aware of the meaninglessness of the human condition, assert their humanity by rebelling against their circumstances. His best-known works are the novels *L'étranger* (1942; tr. The Stranger), *La peste* (1947; tr. The Plague), and *La chute* (1956; tr. The Fall) and the essays *Le mythe de Sisyphe* (1942; tr. The Myth of Sisyphus) and *L'homme révolté* (1951; tr. The Rebel). Camus was awarded the 1957 Nobel Prize in literature.

**Cana,** ancient town of Galilee. Here JESUS performed his first miracle by turning water into wine at a wedding. John 2.

**Canaan,** name for ancient PALESTINE. It was the Promised Land of the Israelites, which they conquered after their delivery from Egypt. Its inhabitants, who were probably related to the Amorites, were called Canaanites.

**Canada,** officially Dominion of Canada, independent nation (1985 est. pop. 25,360,000), second largest country in the world (9,922,330 km²/3,831,012 sq mi), occupying all of North America east of Alaska and north of a 8892–km-long (5335-mi) border with the US, and including adjacent islands of the Arctic Archipelago. It comprises 10 provinces and two federal territories. The provinces are ALBERTA, MANITOBA, and SASKATCHEWAN, collectively known as the Prairie Provinces; NEW BRUNSWICK, NOVA SCOTIA, PRINCE EDWARD ISLAND, and NEWFOUNDLAND, known as the Atlantic Provinces (the first three also being called the Maritime Provinces); and BRITISH COLUMBIA; ONTARIO; and QUEBEC. The territories are the YUKON and the NORTHWEST TERRITORIES. Canada is a member of the COMMONWEALTH. Its capital is OTTAWA.

*Land and People.* Occupying more than half of the nation's land area in the east and north is the vast CANADIAN SHIELD, a sparsely populated expanse of ancient, metamorphic rocks locally rich in iron, nickel, gold, and other minerals. Its rim extends from Labrador in the east, along the northern edge of Canada's urban–industrial heartland (the SAINT LAWRENCE R. valley and the peninsula of S Ontario), through WINNIPEG, the GREAT SLAVE LAKE, and the GREAT BEAR LAKE to the ice-clogged ARCTIC OCEAN in the north. Southeast of the Shield, occupying the Maritime Provinces and the island of Newfoundland, are the worn-down northern ranges of the APPALACHIAN MOUNTAINS system. To the west, in SW Manitoba and most of Alberta and Saskatchewan, are the great wheat-growing, oil-rich plains, or prairies, underlain by sedimentary rock in the Interior Lowlands region. The plains continue north through the PEACE R. and Athabasca districts to the area at the mouth of the MACKENZIE R., in the far north. West of the plains, along the western boundary of Alberta and in British Columbia and the Yukon, is the c.800-km-wide (500-mi) complex of high mountains and plateaus known as the Western Cordillera. It includes the ROCKY MOUNTAINS (E) and COAST MOUNTAINS (W), and reaches an elevation of 6050 m (19,850 ft) at Mt LOGAN, Canada's highest point, in the Yukon. Canada's climate ranges from temperate, with short, mild winters, in the southwest, to bitter, Arctic cold. It is temperate, with long, cold, and usually snowy winters in E Canada and the Prairie Provinces. Climatic conditions become progressively harsher to the north, where permafrost severely limits development. The population is predominantly of British or French origin, with smaller minorities of other Europeans, some Asians, and an indigenous population of c.300,000 Indians on reservations and c.23,000 Inuit (ESKIMO). Most Canadians live along the southern edge of the nation, within 160 km (100 mi) of the US border. More than half are concentrated in S Ontario and S Quebec. French (spoken by a majority in Quebec) and English are both official languages. MONTREAL, TORONTO, VANCOUVER, and EDMONTON are the largest urban areas.

*Economy.* Manufacturing, heavily concentrated in S Quebec and Ontario, is the chief economic activity, with major manufactures including motor vehicles, processed food, petrochemicals, aluminium, and iron and steel. Canada, which ranks first among world mineral exporters, produces zinc, asbestos, silver, and nickel for export, and also mines potash, sulphur, uranium, copper, and iron. Coal, oil, and natural gas are abundant in Alberta and to a lesser extent in Saskatchewan. Huge hydroelectric installations on the St Lawrence, Churchill, COLUMBIA, Peace, and other rivers supply additional energy in fuel-deficient regions.

The extensive forest cover just north of the settled fringe supports large exports of newsprint, pulp and paper, and other forest products; and there are major exports of wheat and other grains from the Prairies, as well as fruit and meat. The US is the leading trading partner and principal foreign investor. The GREAT LAKES–SAINT LAWRENCE SEAWAY is the chief trading artery.

*Government.* Canada's constitution was patriated (i.e., returned to full Canadian control by the British Parliament in London) in 1982. It is derived from the British North America Act of 1867. Under the constitution the head of state is the British monarch, acting in Canada through an appointed governor general. Legislative power is vested in a bicameral Canadian Parliament, consisting of a House of Commons (282 elected members) and a Senate (104 appointed members). The head of government is the prime minister, a member of the House. Each province has its own parliament.

*History.* Newfoundland and the eastern seaboard were discovered for England in 1497 by John CABOT and the mouth of the St Lawrence R. and the GASPÉ PENINSULA for France in 1524 by Jacques CARTIER. Port Royal (now ANNAPOLIS ROYAL), Canada's first known permanent mainland settlement, was founded by the French in 1605, and, travelling out from the colony of New France (made a royal colony in 1663), French fur traders, explorers, and missionaries rapidly extended French influence deep into the North American interior. British interest was sparked by the commercial efforts of the HUDSON'S BAY COMPANY after 1670. Through the 18th cent. Anglo-French hostility in Europe kept spilling over into the New World (see FRENCH AND INDIAN WARS). In 1713 Britain gained control of Nova Scotia (the heart of the French colony called ACADIA), Newfoundland, and the Hudson Bay region. The rest of French Canada fell to the British in 1763, following the defeat (1759) of Gen. MONTCALM by James WOLFE on the Plains of Abraham, near the city of Quebec. French residents, then in the majority, were granted rights to their own language

and religion and given other concessions under the Quebec Act of 1774. Tensions mounted, however, as British settlement accelerated, especially after the American Revolution, with an influx of loyalists from the former American colonies (see UNITED EMPIRE LOYALISTS). In an effort to deal with the growing Anglo-French antagonism, Quebec was divided (1791) into English-speaking Upper Canada (now Ontario) and French-speaking Lower Canada (present-day Quebec). Following revolts in both colonies and the report by the earl of DURHAM in 1839, Upper and Lower Canada were again merged (1841) to form a single colony called Canada Province. The union lasted until confederation: the creation (1867), under the British North America Act, of a self-governing Dominion of Canada. Ontario and Quebec (as separate provinces), New Brunswick, and Nova Scotia were the four founding members at confederation. They were later joined by Manitoba (1870), British Columbia (1871), Prince Edward Island (1873), Alberta and Saskatchewan (1905), and Newfoundland (1949). The Northwest Territories were purchased from the Hudson's Bay Company to become (1869) a federal territory, from which the Yukon was created as a separate territory in 1898. After WORLD WAR II Canada became a founder member of the NORTH ATLANTIC TREATY ORGANIZATION and has regional defence arrangements with the US. A strong, sometimes violent French Canadian separatist movement in Quebec, seeking independence or sovereignty for the province, gathered momentum in the late 1960s. In the 1970s new regional strains arose as residents of the rapidly developing western provinces (especially oil-rich Alberta) chafed under a federal system that, in their view, deprived them of the full benefits of their resources. The Quebec separatist challenge faded after a 1980 referendum decision against giving the provincial Parti Québécois government a mandate to negotiate 'sovereignty-association' with the rest of Canada. Nevertheless, such controversies pointed to the need for reform of the traditional federal–provincial power arrangement and led to agitation for the patriation of the constitution. In 1982 Canada's constitution was returned to the Canadians, together with an

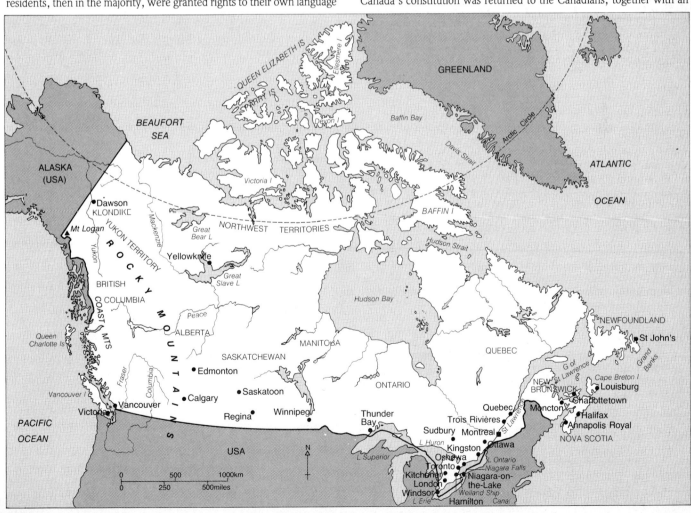

amending formula and a nationally applicable 'charter of rights'. In the same year, despite challenges by eight of the provinces, first steps toward the redistribution of federal and provincial powers were taken by Prime Min. Pierre TRUDEAU's Liberal Party government. Trudeau retired in mid-1984, soon after which 21 years of almost uninterrupted Liberal rule ended with the Progressive Conservatives under Brian MULRONEY winning a landslide election victory. In 1987 the 'Meech Lake Agreement' established a basis for solving longstanding provincial-federal tensions, in particular by recognizing Quebec as a 'distinct society' within the confederation.

**Post-war Canadian prime ministers**
William Mackenzie King (Liberal), 1935–48
Louis St Laurent (Liberal), 1948–57
John Diefenbaker (Prog. Conservative), 1957–63
Lester Pearson (Liberal), 1963–68
Pierre Trudeau (Liberal), 1968–79
Joseph Clark (Prog. Conservative), 1979–80
Pierre Trudeau (Liberal), 1980–84
John Turner (Liberal), 1984
Brian Mulroney (Prog. Conservative), 1984–

**Canada Company,** land settlement company chartered in 1826 that acquired government land along the Lake Huron side of the ONTARIO peninsula. Its first secretary in Canada was the Scottish novelist John GALT. It remained in existence until the 1950s.

**Canada First movement,** short-lived political party founded after Canada's confederation (1867) to promote Canadian nationalism, and to encourage immigration and native industry. Its ideals were absorbed by older political parties.

**Canadian football:** see under FOOTBALL.

**Canadian Shield** or **Laurentian Plateau,** a region of ancient, mostly metamorphic rock forming the geological nucleus of North America. Rich in minerals and water-power potential, it occupies E Canada, from the Great Lakes and the St Lawrence N to the Arctic Ocean. It also covers much of Greenland and extends S into the US as the ADIRONDACK MOUNTAINS and the Superior Highlands.

**canal,** an artificially constructed waterway. Since earliest times irrigation canals fed from rivers or reservoirs have maintained life and allowed agricultural development in unfavourable climates. The Murray Basin in Victoria and the Great Valley of California are examples of modern irrigation canal systems. The oldest canal dug for navigation and still in use today is the Grand Canal in China. Begun in 485 BC and built in stages till AD 1283, it was rebuilt 1958–72, and is the third largest in the world. The system extends for 1780 km (1105 mi), from Tianjin to Hangzhou, and connects with Huang He (Yellow River). The world's largest waterway system is the St Lawrence in Canada, which covers some 3770 km (2340 mi). Many large canals, such as the St Lawrence and the Panama Canal take advantage of and link lakes and rivers. In Britain canal-building was spurred by the early Industrial Revolution. The Manchester–Bridgewater canal (1761–76), built by the engineer James BRINDLEY to carry coal to Manchester, was the first in an inland waterway network covering 4000 km (2500 mi) and linking industrial centres. By the mid 19th cent. canals had been largely overtaken by the railways as a faster means of moving freight. Only a tiny fraction of freight in Britain is now carried by waterways. In Northern Europe and the USSR, however, waterways have been extended to carry an increasing volume of freight. Canal links and better waterway connections between the ports of Rotterdam and Marseilles, and Rotterdam and Constanza, on the Black Sea, are currently under construction, while in the USSR the 2300-km (1500-mi) Baltic–Volga waterway, begun in 1964, will link the Baltic with the Black Sea.

**Canal, Antonio:** see CANALETTO.

**Canaletto,** 1697–1768, Venetian painter; b. Antonio Canal. Unsurpassed as an architectural painter, he executed such finely detailed works as *View on the Grand Canal* (National Gall., London), *View of Venice* (Uffizi, Florence), and *The Piazzetta, Venice* (Metropolitan Mus., New York.). He also produced superb etchings and drawings that were not preparatory but complete in themselves. His nephew and pupil, Bernardo Bellotto, was also called Canaletto.

**canary,** small BIRD of the FINCH family, descended from either the wild serin finch or the wild canary (*Serinus canarius*) of the CANARY ISLANDS,

Canaletto, *Grand Canal: Looking South-West from the Scalzi, with San Simeone Piccolo.* Oil on canvas, 124 × 204 cm.

MADEIRA ISLANDS, and AZORES. The wild birds are usually grey or green; breeding has yielded plain and variegated birds, mostly yellow and buff. Captive canaries are trained to sing and can live for 15 years or more.

**Canary Islands,** group of seven volcanic islands, c.7500 km² (2894 sq mi), some 112 km (70 mi) off the coast of NW Africa. Spanish since the 15th cent., they comprise two provs. of Spain: Las Palmas of which the largest island is Gran Canaria, and Santa Cruz de Tenerife of which the largest island is Tenerife. A wide range of tropical and temperate crops are grown and there is an export trade in bananas and tomatoes. The largest cities are Las Palmas (1981 pop. 366,454) and Santa Cruz de Tenerife (1981 pop. 190,784) which have a thriving tourist industry.

**canasta:** see RUMMY.

**Canberra,** city (1986 pop. 249,044), capital of Australia, in the AUSTRALIAN CAPITAL TERRITORY, SE Australia. The site chosen (1908) for the capital was developed by the American architect Walter Burley Griffin, whose plans won an international competition held in 1911. Parliament first met in Canberra in 1927. The federal government is the city's largest employer, and there are many embassies and consulates. The Australian National Univ., the National War Memorial, Library, Art Gallery, High Court of Australia, and the Defence Forces Academy are located in the capital, as well as the official residences of the Prime Minister and the Governor.

**cancer,** common term for malignant tumours (see TUMOUR) characterized by uncontrolled and invasive growth. Unlike normal cells, cancer cells are atypical in structure and do not have specialized functions. They compete with normal cells for nutrients, eventually killing normal tissue by depriving it of nutrition. Cancerous tissue can remain localized, invading only neighbouring tissue, or can spread via the LYMPHATIC SYSTEM or blood to form secondary growths in other tissues or remote organs, a process known as metastasis. Virtually all tissues and organs are susceptible, including the blood system (see LEUKAEMIA). Cancer symptoms, which are often nonspecific, include weakness and loss of appetite and weight. There are many causative factors of cancer, some of which are known. They include cigarette smoke (lung cancer), ASBESTOS (mesothelioma), ionizing radiation (thyroid cancer and LEUKAEMIA), and sunlight (skin cancer). Viruses are implicated in the development of some cancers (e.g., cervical cancer), as is hormonal imbalance, sometimes caused by drugs. Diet is thought to be important; hereditary factors and sexual activity can also be involved; and many chemicals and compounds are carcinogenic (cancer-inducing). Methods of detection include visual observation, palpation, X-ray study, COMPUTERIZED AXIAL TOMOGRAPHY, ULTRASOUND, and BIOPSY. Tumours caught early, before metastasis, have the best cure rates. Cancer is treated by surgery, CHEMOTHERAPY, and RADIOTHERAPY. The branch of medicine concerned with diagnosis, treatment, and research into the causes of cancer is known as oncology.

**candle,** cylinder of wax or tallow containing a wick, used for illumination, for ceremonies (primarily religious), or as ornamentation. Used in ancient times, candles became common in Europe by the Middle Ages. Tallow, beeswax, and vegetable wax were supplemented by spermaceti in the late 18th cent., stearine c.1825, and paraffin c.1850.

Originally handmade by dipping, moulding, or pouring, candles are now generally machine-made. They are often scented.

**candytuft,** low-growing annuals or sub-shrubs (genus *Iberis*) of the MUSTARD family, often cultivated as a rock garden and border ornamental. Candytufts have flat-topped or elongated clusters of small, white or variously coloured flowers.

**cane,** in botany, name for a hollow or woody, usually slender, jointed plant stem (e.g., RATTAN and some bamboos) and for some tall GRASSES (e.g., SUGARCANE and SORGHUM).

**cane sugar:** see SUCROSE; SUGAR.

**Canetti, Elias,** 1905–, German writer; b. Bulgaria. He has lived in England since 1938. Canetti is principally known for two works: *Auto da fé* (1935), a grotesque novel representing the destructive division of intellect and vitality, and *Crowds and Power* (1960), a study of mass psychology. His other works include plays and essays; a study of KAFKA, *The Other Trial: Kafka's Letters to Felice* (1969); and the autobiographical works, *The Tongue Set Free* (1977) and *The Torch in My Ear* (1980). He was awarded the 1981 Nobel Prize for literature.

**cannabis:** see MARIJUANA.

**Cannes,** city (1982 pop. of agglomeration 295,525), SE France, on the Côte d'Azur. A fashionable resort, there are numerous hotels, marinas, and casinos and an international film festival. Flowers and herbs are grown in the vicinity, supporting the perfume industry of the nearby town of Grasse.

**cannibalism,** practice of eating human flesh, found in Africa, South America, the South Pacific islands, and the West Indies. In *endocannibalism* part of a kinsman's corpse is eaten as a gesture of respect for the deceased. Members of enemy groups may be ritually eaten as a rite of power-transfer. Eating dead humans to survive (e.g., after an air crash) is shocking to the Western mind, so that accurate estimates of its occurrence are hard to come by.

**canning,** process of hermetically sealing cooked food for future use, including meat and poultry, fish, fruits and vegetables, milk, preserves, pickles, and jams. Developed early in 19th-cent. France by Nicolas Appert, a chef, the method spread to other European countries and to the US, where it was patented around 1815. The process was widely used to provide foodstuffs to soldiers during the American Civil War. The early glass and tin containers were ultimately supplanted by tin-plated steel cans. In home as in factory canning, the process involves cleaning and preparing the raw product (with rapid handling necessary to prevent vitamin loss, bacterial spoilage, or enzyme-induced changes). Once filled, the containers are passed through a hot water or steam bath to release gases, then sealed and subjected to heat to destroy any microorganisms. Canned food requires no addition of preservatives but the process destroys the original texture of the food.

**Canning, George,** 1770–1827, British statesman. A TORY supporter of William PITT and anti-Jacobin writer, he went on to serve (1807–09) as foreign minister during the wars against NAPOLEON . After the suicide of CASTLEREAGH, he was again foreign minister (1822–27). He refused to cooperate in the suppression of European revolutions, recognized the independence of Spanish colonies in America, and arranged the Anglo-French-Russian agreement that resulted in Greek independence. He was a strong supporter of CATHOLIC EMANCIPATION and was for a brief period prime minister in 1827.

**Cannizzaro, Stanislao,** 1826–1910, Italian chemist. Professor at Palermo and then at Rome, he is known for his discovery of cyanamide and for his method of synthesizing alcohols (Cannizzaro's reaction). He also explained how atomic weights could be determined on the basis of Avogadro's law and distinguished from molecular weights.

**cannon,** in warfare: see ARTILLERY.

**canoe,** long, narrow watercraft with sharp ends, propelled by paddle, sail, or, recently, outboard motor. Used by most primitive peoples, canoes vary in materials and construction. North American Indians used birchbark, stretched hides, or hollowed logs; the Oldtown, or Penobscot, Indians in Maine developed canvas-covered wooden craft. In the South Pacific, large sailing canoes with outriggers were made for ocean journeys. The Eskimo kayak features a sealskin covering that fits snugly around the paddler. Modern canoes, generally used for recreational journeys or fixed-distance racing, are made of aluminum alloy, wood, or glass fibre. Sport canoeing is generally credited to John MacGregor, an English barrister who founded (1865) the Royal Canoe Club. There are now Olympic events for kayaks and Canadian (North American) canoes.

**canon,** in music, a type of COUNTERPOINT in which all the instruments or voices have the same melody, beginning at different times, with successive entrances at the same or different pitches. A well-known vocal form is the round, of which the earliest known example is the medieval song *Sumer is Icumen in*. The canon is an essential device for SERIAL MUSIC.

**canonization:** see SAINT.

**canon law,** in the ROMAN CATHOLIC CHURCH, law of the church courts, based on legislation of councils, popes, and bishops. It deals primarily with the governance of the clergy and the church, including administration of the sacraments. The present code was promulgated in 1917, and again in a revised form in 1983. The EASTERN ORTHODOX CHURCH and the churches of the ANGLICAN COMMUNION also have their codes of canon law. In the CHURCH OF ENGLAND a revised code of canons was published in 1964–69.

**Canova, Antonio,** 1757–1822, Italian sculptor. Leading examples of neo-classicism, his statues and bas-reliefs, e.g., *Paolina Borghese as Venus* (1805–07; Borghese Gall., Rome) and *Clement XIII* (1792; St Peter's, Rome), are executed with grace, polish, and purity of contour. His portraits include a bust and two nudes of Napoleon I as a Roman emperor.

Antonio **Canova**, *Paolina Borghese as Venus*, 1805–07. Borghese Gallery, Rome.

**Cantabrian Mountains,** range of mountains, extending for over 240 km (150 mi) behind the N coast of Spain. The highest peak (Peña de Cerredo) reaches 2678 m (8786 ft) in the Picos de Europa of the Asturias. They contain valuable deposits of coal and iron ore.

**cantaloupe:** see GOURD; MELON.

**cantata,** composite musical form similar to a short unacted opera or brief ORATORIO, developed in Italy in the BAROQUE period. In France and Italy the secular cantatas included arias and recitatives; the sacred cantatas of Germany had choral and instrumental sections. J.S. BACH utilized hymn verses in his chorale cantatas.

**Canterbury,** city (1978 est. pop. 34,546), Kent, SE England, on the Stour R. The seat of the primate of the Church of England and long the spiritual centre of the country, it is a major tourist attraction. Following his arrival (597) in England, St AUGUSTINE founded an abbey there and became the first archbishop of Canterbury. After the murder (1170) of THOMAS BECKET, the city became the object of pilgrimage, as described in CHAUCER's *Canterbury Tales*. The magnificent cathedral (1070–1180; 1379–1503) embodies the styles of several periods. Although the city was bombed during WORLD WAR II, the cathedral and many other historic buildings survive.

**Canterbury Tales:** see CHAUCER, GEOFFREY.

**Canth, Minna,** 1844–97, Finnish playwright. The most powerful and typical writer of the Finnish REALISM school, her best-known plays are *A*

*Working-Class Wife* (1885) and *Children of Misfortune* (1888). Later she turned to Tolstoyan psychological dramas about women, of which the outstanding example is *Anna Liisa* (1895).

**Canticles:** another name for the SONG OF SOLOMON.

**Canton:** see GUANGZHOU.

**Cantor, Georg,** 1845–1918, German mathematician; b. Russia. His work on transfinite numbers (see INFINITY) and SET theory revolutionized mathematics and led to a critical investigation of its foundations.

**Canute,** (kə͵njooht), 995?–1035, king of England, Norway, and Denmark. The younger son of Sweyn of Denmark, he invaded England with his father in 1013 and forced Æthelred to flee to Normandy. On Sweyn's death (1014) he withdrew to Denmark. He reinvaded England in 1015 and, after the Danish victory at the battle of Assendun, divided the country with EDMUND IRONSIDE. On Edmund's death (1016), Canute was accepted as sole king, and subsequently married Emma, widow of Æthelred. Canute gave England peace, supported the arts, and restored the authority of the church and the power of law. In 1018 he succeeded to the throne of Denmark. After several expeditions to Norway, he deposed OLAF II in 1028, thus becoming ruler of three kingdoms. He made his son Harthacanute king of Denmark and his son Sweyn king of Norway. He played an important diplomatic role in Europe and established close relations with the HOLY ROMAN EMPIRE.

**Cao (Xueqin),** 1715–63, Chinese writer. He was born into a family of high officials in Nanjing which later suffered a loss of fortune and prestige. He wrote most of the highly important novel *Hong lou meng* (tr. as The Dream of the Red Chamber *or* The Story of the Stone); it was first published in 1791 in 120 chapters, though earlier manuscripts had only 80 and the authorship of the last 40 chapters is still a subject for debate. Cao's family home and past riches form the setting of a story of decline (both in wealth and morals). The 'hero' is a strange child born with a magic jade in his mouth and his fortune and fate well established in heaven; part of a constant shift between the world of men and immortals in the novel. Though metaphysical themes are prominent, there is also a wealth of social detail in the novel which illustrates the complex life within a great mansion full of servants, gardens, dramas, and intrigues.

**Cao Yu,** pseud. of **Wan Jiabao** (ca͵ohyooh), 1910–, Chinese Playwright. He studied western literature at Qinghua Univ. and translated Galsworthy and Shakespeare's *Romeo and Juliet*, amongst other plays. Between 1935 and 1941, he had six great stage successes, including *Lei yu* [thunderstorm], *Ri chu* [sunrise], and a stage adaptation of BA JIN's novel *Jia* [family].

**capacitance,** the ability of an electric system to store electric CHARGE when a voltage is applied. It is determined by the disposition of the conducting elements and the insulating material supporting them mechanically. There is a linear relationship between voltage and charge, such that doubling the voltage doubles the stored charge. Capacitance, in units of farads, is expressed as the ratio of charge (in coulombs) to applied potential difference (in volts) and is a constant for a given configuration. In many cases, such as telephone lines and power transmission lines, the capacitance is inevitable but undesirable. In circuitry there is often a need to store charge at a prescribed position; a circuit device designed to store charge is called a CAPACITOR. If an alternating voltage is applied to a circuit then the capacitance is charged one way and then another in phase with the voltage. The pumping of charge in this way forms an alternating current offering reactance or IMPEDANCE to flow.

**capacitor** or **condenser,** device for storing electric CHARGE. Simple capacitors usually consist of two plates of metal separated by insulating material such as glass, paraffin wax, mica, mineral oils, or even air. In radio use capacitors are often constructed from two long strips of metal foil separated by wax-impregnated paper and then rolled up to form a small cylinder. The charge-storing ability, or CAPACITANCE, of the device depends on the geometrical configuration, principally the area of the plates and the distance of separation. It is also dependent on a property of the insulating material known as the dielectric constant. The larger the constant the greater the capacitance. Air has the lowest constant, wax has a constant twice that of air, glass some eight times greater, and solids made from compressed barium titanate, a thousand times greater. When a capacitor is charged by the application of an electric voltage, current flows initially until the charge is established. Energy is consumed and this is recoverable at a later time by connecting the capacitor to a circuit. The energy involved is stored in the insulating material. This can be demonstrated in a simple construction by sliding the charged insulating material from between the plates and inserting it into a set of uncharged plates. These become charged and can be discharged by connecting to a circuit.

**Cape Breton Island,** (1981 pop. 170,088), 10,282 km², (3970 sq mi), in NE Nova Scotia, separated from the Canadian mainland by the Gut (or Strait) of Canso. It was discovered by the English navigator John CABOT in 1497. Under French control (1623–1763), it was renamed Île Royale and fortified (at LOUISBURG) by French loyalists (the Acadians) after the rest of NOVA SCOTIA passed to the English in 1713. It was a separate colony from 1784 to 1820, with its capital at Sydney.

**Cape Canaveral,** low promontory, E Florida, US (called Cape Kennedy, 1963–73). Since 1947 it has been the chief US launching site for long-range test missiles and manned space flights.

**Cape Cod,** hook-shaped, sandy peninsula, SE Massachusetts, US, extending 105 km (65 mi) E and N into the Atlantic Ocean. It is a popular resort area. Parts of it constitute the **Cape Cod National Seashore** (18,050 hectares/44,600 acres; est. 1961). **Cape Cod Canal,** built 1910–14, cut the New York–Boston shipping distance by 121 km (75 mi).

**Čapek, Karel** (͵chapek), 1890–1938, Czech writer. He is best known for two satirical plays attacking technological and materialist excess: *R.U.R.* (*Rossum's Universal Robots,* 1921), which introduced the word *robot;* and *The Insect Play* (1921), written with his brother Josef. His other works include *The Makropoulos Affair* (1922), a play on which JANÁČEK based an opera; *The War with the Newts* (1936), a satirical science-fiction attack on totalitarianism; and a book of conversations with Thomas MASARYK (1928–35). **Josef Čapek,** 1887–1945, was a writer and painter.

**Cape Kennedy:** see CAPE CANAVERAL.

**caper,** common name for members of the family Capparidaceae, chiefly Old World tropical plants closely related to the MUSTARD family. The pickled caper, used as a condiment, is the flower bud of *Capparis spinosa,* cultivated in the Mediterranean area. The family also includes the spiderflower (*Cleome spinosa*), a common garden annual.

**Capetians** (kə͵peeshənz), royal house of France, named after HUGH CAPET, who became king in 987. His direct descendants ruled France until the death of CHARLES IV in 1328. The throne then passed to the collateral branch of VALOIS.

**Cape Town** or **Kaapstad,** city (1985 pop. 776,617; metropolitan area 1,911,521), legislative capital of South Africa and capital of Cape prov. It is an important port on the Atlantic Ocean and a commercial and industrial centre, linked by road, rail, and airlines to other South African cities. Situated at the foot of Table Mt. (c.1090 m/3570 ft), Cape Town is a tourist resort with fine beaches and a pleasant climate. The city, was founded in 1652 by Jan van Riebeck as a victualling station for The Dutch East India Co. It was occupied by The British in 1795. Notable buildings are a fortress, church, and museum, dating to the early Dutch settlement.

**Cape Verde,** Port. *Ilhas do Cabo Verde,* officially Republic of Cape Verde, republic (1985 est. pop. 350,000), c.4040 km² (1560 sq mi), W Africa, in the Atlantic Ocean, about 480 km (300 mi) W of Senegal. Cape Verde is an archipelago made up of 10 islands and 5 islets divided into two main groups, the Barlavento, or Windward, in the north, which include Santo Antão, São Vicente, Santa Luzia, São Nicolau, Boa Vista, and Sal; and the Sotavento, or Leeward, which include São Tiago, Fogo, Maio, and Brava. Praia, the capital, is located on São Tiago, the largest island. The islands are mountainous and of volcanic origin; the only active volcano, and the archipelago's highest point, is Cano (c.2830 m/9300 ft), on Fogo. Farming, the main economic activity, is limited by the small annual rainfall. Occasionally, severe drought, such as that experienced in the 1970s and 80s, further reduces production of the main crops (maize, bananas, sweet potatoes, beans, sugarcane, and coffee). Tuna and lobster are the major fishing catches. The mineral resources are puzzolana (used in mortar) and salt. Many of the islanders work in Portugal and the US, and their remittances, along with foreign assistance, help to support the weak economy. The GNP is US$150 million, and the GNP per capita is US$430 (1985). About 60% of the population is of mixed black African and European descent; most of the rest are black Africans.

*History.* Cape Verde was discovered in 1456 by Luigi da Cadamosto, a navigator in the service of Portugal. Portuguese colonists began to settle in the islands, which were probably uninhabited, in 1462, and soon began importing blacks from W Africa as slaves. Slavery was abolished in the islands in 1876. Cape Verde became an overseas province in 1951 and gained its independence in 1975. A movement for union with Guinea-Bissau (formerly Portuguese Guinea, administered as part of the Cape Verde islands until 1879) was blocked by a 1980 coup in Guinea-Bissau, which brought to power leaders opposed to such close ties with Cape Verde. Under the 1980 constitution the sole legal party is the African Party for the Independence of Cape Verde, headed by Pres. Arístides Maria Pereira. Of overriding concern to the new nation has been a prolonged drought, causing staggering economic problems resulting in large-scale emigration, an unemployment rate of 80%, and the need to import nearly all of the country's food supply.

**Cape York Peninsula,** peninsula in Queensland, NE Australia. This most northerly tip of Australia is separated from Papua by the Torres Strait. Rivers drain W from the GREAT DIVIDING RANGE into the Gulf of Carpentaria. From the small offshore Possession Island, Captain Cook claimed (1770) the E coast of Australia for Britain. Early discoveries of gold and tin attracted settlers but the main land use today is beef cattle raising based on the drought- and tick-resistant Brahman breed. The population of Thursday Island collects pearl-shell, and more recently have developed the culture of pearls. Weipa, a former Aboriginal mission station, now has one of the world's largest bauxite mines, producing aluminium ore.

**capillarity** or **capillary action,** phenomenon in which the surface of a liquid is elevated or depressed when it comes in contact with a solid. The result depends on the outcome of two opposing forces, ADHESION AND COHESION. Adhesion between glass and water causes the water to rise along a glass wall until this force is balanced by the cohesive force acting to minimize the liquid's surface area (see SURFACE TENSION). When adhesion is less than cohesion, as with glass and mercury, the surface is lowered. The upward flow of water in soil and in plants is partially caused by capillarity.

**capital gains tax,** levy on profits earned by the sale of capital assets, such as stocks, bonds, and real estate. In the UK, the tax is not applied to personal belongings, including cars and principal residence, and there is a substantial annual exemption (£6300 in 1986/87). There is a single-rate tax (30%), against which capital losses may be set.

**capitalism,** technically, an economic system in which the greater part of the means of production and distribution are owned by private individuals or institutions and run for profit; in which there is competition and a relatively free market; and in which prices and consumer decisions determine the allocation of resources. More generally, capitalism is used to refer to the combination of political arrangements (liberal democracy) and social life (consumer society) associated with this economic pattern in modern industrialized countries in the West. The emergence of capitalism as an economic world system (see WORLD-SYSTEM THEORY) dates from the 16th cent.; some historians trace its development through phases of agrarian capitalism and commercial capitalism to industrial capitalism and then finance capitalism. Industrial capitalism is associated particularly with the era of the INDUSTRIAL REVOLUTION in the 18th and 19th cent., and with the rise of the BOURGEOISIE, the class of merchants, bankers, and manufacturers, who rivalled and then replaced the traditional landed aristocracy in power. In the 20th cent., capitalism has created a vast credit, manufacturing, and distribution system around the world, whose social and economic effects are transforming world culture. Capitalism and SOCIALISM are the two major economic systems in the world; both systems are subject to attack and defence as part of the ideological propaganda of the COLD WAR. Thus the defenders of capitalism point to its historical association with freedom, to its capacity to reward individual initiative, to the efficiency of the market as an automatic mechanism for adjusting supply and demand, and to the incentive to innovation provided by the profit motive. More generally, it is held to harness the pursuit of individual interest to the public interest, in a way which is of benefit to all. Critics of capitalism follow MARX in pointing to its exploitation of those without personal capital, who are forced to sell their labour simply as another commodity in the market; to the economic inequalities, both within nations and between nations, that are produced and exacerbated by world capitalism; to the relentless pursuit of industrial growth, which

threatens the environment; and to the international competition for markets and resources, which has led to IMPERIALISM and COLONIALISM, and to war. In practice, there are no examples of completely free markets, every 'capitalist' economy exhibits a public sector of industries which are state-owned or controlled, substantial state intervention in the economy, and some attempt at national planning. Similarly, socialist economies experiment continually with the reintroduction of individual incentives and market forces in different forms, and all have a distinct official or unofficial private sector. See also CORPORATISM; LAISSEZ-FAIRE; MARXISM; MONOPOLY.

**capital punishment,** imposition of the death penalty by the state. Applied from ancient times in most societies, it has been used as punishment for crimes ranging in gravity from petty THEFT to murder. In the UK, early capital punishment took place by strangulation, later replaced by public hanging, until this was ended in 1868. During the 18th cent. over 200 capital offences existed, mainly involving crimes against PROPERTY. At this time opposition to capital punishment arose in France, and by the 20th cent. most countries had abolished it. In the UK, the last executions took place in 1964, and capital punishment was abolished in 1965 except for TREASON. Since then pressure for its reintroduction has been maintained, especially for terrorists and child murderers. It is still widely used in Islamic countries, e.g., Iran, and in recent years it has been increasingly used in some states in the US.

**capital transfer tax,** in the UK, a tax on gifts, or other transfers of value made during the lifetime or on the death of the owner. The tax is payable either by the person making the gift, or the deceased's estate. It was introduced in 1974, replacing estate duty. Gifts between spouses and gifts to charity are exempted from the tax.

**capitance,** measure of the ability of a system (a capacitor) to store electric CHARGE. The unit of capitance is the farad (see ELECTRIC AND MAGNETIC UNITS).

**Capitol,** seat of the US government, at Washington, DC, built on an elevated site chosen by George WASHINGTON and Major Pierre L'Enfant. The building is the work of several architects. William Thornton's 1792 plan was initiated with the setting of the cornerstone in 1793. E.S. Hallet, George Hadfield, and James Hoban succeeded Thornton. In 1814 the British burned the uncompleted building, and B.H. Latrobe and Charles Bulfinch restored and completed it (1818–30). The House and Senate wings and the dome were added (1851–65) by T.U. Walter. The dome is 90 m (288 ft) high.

**Capitoline Hill** or **Capitol,** highest of the seven hills of ancient Rome, historic and religious centre of the city in ancient times. In the Middle Ages the Capitol remained the political centre of Rome, and it is the centre of municipal government in modern Rome. In the 16th cent. MICHELANGELO designed the Capitol's present plan.

**Capone, Al(phonse),** 1899–1947, American gangster. His crime syndicate terrorized Chicago in the 1920s, controlling gambling and prostitution there. In 1931 he was sentenced to prison for federal income-tax evasion.

**Capote, Truman,** 1924–84, American author. His fiction often reflects a world of grotesque and strangely innocent people. He has written novels, e.g., *The Grass Harp* (1951); short stories, e.g., *Breakfast at Tiffany's* (1958); nonfiction; the 'nonfiction novel' *In Cold Blood* (1966); and the miscellaneous collection *Music for Chameleons* (1980).

**Cappadocia** (kapə,dohshə), ancient region of Asia Minor, in present E central Turkey. The name was applied at different times to territories of varying size. Before 1800 BC, Cappadocia was the heart of an old HITTITE state; later, it was controlled by the Persians. During the 3rd cent. BC it gradually developed as an independent kingdom. In AD 17 Rome annexed the region as a province. Cappadocia is remarkable for the formations into which its soft rocks have been eroded. Whole villages, including churches, have also been carved into the rocks. The churches of Göreme are famous for their frescoes.

**Capra, Frank,** 1897–, American film director; b. Sicily. *It Happened One Night* (1934), *Mr Deeds Goes to Town* (1936), and *You Can't Take It with You* (1938), mixing 'screwball' comedy and populism, won Academy Awards. Among his other films is *It's a Wonderful Life* (1946).

The churches of Göreme, **Cappadocia**

**Capri,** small, rocky island, 14 km² (5½ sq mi), off the Bay of Naples, S Italy. The views from the island, its sunshine and clear air, have made it a popular tourist resort. It was associated with the emperors Augustus and Tiberius. The Blue Grotto is a cave partially occupied by the sea with curious light effects.

**Caprivi Strip,** area of NE Namibia, 480 km (300 mi) long and 80 km (50 mi) wide, between Botswana (S) and Angola and Zambia (N). It was obtained from Great Britain by Germany in 1890 to give German South West Africa (now NAMIBIA) access to the ZAMBEZI R.

**capybara,** largest living RODENT, reaching a length of 120 cm (4 ft) and a weight of 35–45 kg (75–100 lb). Found in Central and much of South America, it has coarse, scant, brownish hair flecked with yellow. An expert swimmer, the capybara is also called water hog.

**Caracalla,** 188–217, Roman emperor (r.211–17); son of Septimius SEVERUS. His real name was Marcus Aurelius Antoninus; he received his nickname from the *caracalla,* a hooded Gallic tunic he regularly wore. His reign was infamous for its cruelty and bloodshed. Caracalla did pacify the German frontier and extended Roman citizenship to all free inhabitants of the empire. The impressive ruins of the Baths of Caracalla can still be seen in the forum at Rome. In 217 he was murdered by his successor, Macrinus.

**Caracas,** city (1980 est. pop. 2,900,000) N Venezuela, capital and largest city of Venezuela. An extremely cosmopolitan city, it is a major industrial centre, shipping through the nearby Caribbean port of La Guaira. Caracas was founded in 1567 and was the base for Spanish colonization of Venezuela. It was the birthplace of the liberators Francisco de MIRANDA and Simón BOLÍVAR. Caracas retains an old section, with many examples of colonial architecture. The oil boom of the 1950s made possible massive public building projects, transforming much of Caracas into an ultramodern metropolis famed for such futuristic complexes as University City and the Centro Bolívar government centre. The city is the site of a large performing arts centre (1981), three orchestras, an opera, a ballet, and three major art museums.

**Caramanlis, Constantine:** see KARAMANLIS, CONSTANTINE.

**carat** [Arab. *qirat* = bean pod]. **1** Unit of purity of gold equal to ¹/₂₄ part of gold in an alloy. **2** Unit of weight of a gemstone equal to 200 mg.

**Caratacus,** fl. AD 40–50, British chieftain, a son of CUNOBELINUS. He escaped to S Wales after the first stage of the Roman conquest of Britain, and from there led a brave resistance until defeated by the Romans (AD 51). He was handed over to Rome by another tribal ruler, Queen Cartimandua of the Brigantes, and ended his days in honourable captivity.

**Caravaggio, Michelangelo Merisi da** (kara͵vajoh), 1571–1610, Italian painter. His stormy and rebellious character introduced a new kind of artistic persona. He came from Lombardy but settled in Rome in the early 1590s. His early works are GENRE pictures, with erotic undertones, of elegant youths with fruit and flowers or making music e.g., *Concert of*

*Youths* (Metropolitan Mus., New York). Later he turned to religious works; major Roman commissions, as the *Life of St Matthew* (1599–1602; S. Luigi dei Francesi, Rome) and the *Death of the Virgin* (Louvre, Paris) introduced a new and bold NATURALISM to Roman painting. His models, drawn from lower walks of life, are unidealized, and his settings contemporary; dramatic contrasts of light and dark emphasize the physical presence of his figures. In 1606 he fled from Rome having killed a man, and later worked in Naples, Sicily, and Malta.

**caraway,** biennial plant (*Carum carvi*) of the CARROT family, cultivated in Europe and North America for its aromatic, spicy seeds. The seeds are used to flavour bread, cabbage, sausage, cheese, and liqueurs.

**Carazo Odio, Rodrigo** ('karə͵thohdeeoh), 1926–, president of COSTA RICA (1978–82). An economist, he founded (1976) the coalition party Unidad and was elected president two years later. His administration was plagued with economic problems.

**carbohydrate,** any member of a large class of chemical compounds that includes sugars, starches, cellulose, and related compounds. Carbohydrates are produced naturally by green plants from carbon dioxide and water (see PHOTOSYNTHESIS). Important as foods, they supply energy and are used to make fats. The three main classes of carbohydrates are monosaccharides, which are the simple SUGARS, e.g., FRUCTOSE and GLUCOSE; disaccharides, which are made up of two monosaccharide units and include LACTOSE, MALTOSE, and SUCROSE; and polysaccharides, which are polymers with many monosaccharide units and include CELLULOSE, GLYCOGEN, and STARCH.

**carbon** (C), nonmetallic element, known since ancient times. Pure carbon forms are amorphous carbon (found in such sources as CHARCOAL, COAL, COKE, LIGNITE, and PEAT) and the crystals GRAPHITE, a very soft, dark-grey or black, lustrous material, and DIAMOND, the hardest substance known. ORGANIC CHEMISTRY is the study of carbon compounds. All living organisms contain carbon. Carbon has seven isotopes; carbon-12 is the basis for determining ATOMIC WEIGHT; carbon-14, with a half-life of 5730 years, is used to trace chemical reactions and to date geological and archaeological specimens (see DATING). See CARBON CYCLE; CARBON DIOXIDE; CARBON MONOXIDE; ELEMENT (table); PERIODIC TABLE.

**carbon-14 dating,** in ARCHAEOLOGY, the most common method of direct dating. All living things absorb the radioactive form of carbon, carbon-14, through the food chain. While the organism lives, the proportion of carbon to carbon-14 remains constant; at death, however, this process ceases and the carbon-14 begins to decay, reducing in proportion to carbon. As the rate of decay of carbon-14 (half-life) is known, the proportion at the time of measurement can be used to calculate how long the carbon-14 has been decaying and, hence, the age of the specimen. Since the amount of carbon-14 available for organisms has varied over time, the accuracy of radiocarbon dates must be qualified. Tree-ring dating (see DENDROCHRONOLOGY) has provided an index of absolute dates against which to improve the accuracy of radiocarbon sequences. A new method of measuring carbon-14 was developed in the early 1980s. In place of the traditional measurement of radioactivity, which requires a relatively large sample of carbon often resulting in the destruction of the object, accelerator mass spectrometry requires as little as 1 mg of carbon.

**carbon cycle,** in biology, the exchange of carbon between living organisms and the nonliving environment. Carbon, the central element in the compounds of which organisms are composed, is derived from free carbon dioxide which is about 0.03% of the atmosphere. It is also dissolved in water. Plants incorporate carbon into carbohydrates and other complex organic molecules by means of PHOTOSYNTHESIS; during RESPIRATION, or OXIDATION, they combine oxygen with portions of the carbohydrate molecule, releasing carbon in the form of carbon dioxide and water. Carbon is also returned to the environment when plants die and their organic material is broken down by bacteria and other microorganisms. Animals obtain carbon by feeding on plants and other animals; they release carbon dioxide into the air through respiration and, after death, indirectly through the respiration of microorganisms that consume them.

**carbon dioxide** ($CO_2$), chemical compound, occurring as a colourless, odourless, tasteless gas that is about 1½ times as dense as air under ordinary conditions. It does not burn and will not support combustion of ordinary materials. Its weakly acidic aqueous solution is called CARBONIC ACID. The gas, easily liquefied by compression and cooling, provides the

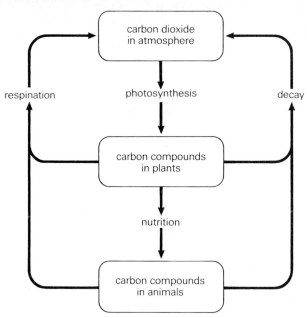

Carbon cycle

sparkle in carbonated drinks. Solid carbon dioxide, or dry ice, is a refrigerant. Dough rises because of carbon dioxide formed by the action of yeast and baking powder. Carbon dioxide is the raw material for PHOTOSYNTHESIS in green plants, and is a product of animal RESPIRATION and of the decay of organic matter. It occurs both free and combined in nature, and makes up about 1% of the volume of dry air. It can cause death by suffocation if inhaled in large amounts.

**carbonic acid,** a weak acid ($H_2CO_3$), formed when CARBON DIOXIDE dissolves in water; it exists only in solution. With bases it forms the carbonate and bicarbonate salts.

**Carboniferous period:** see GEOLOGICAL ERA (table).

**carbon monoxide,** chemical compound (CO), a colourless, odourless, tasteless, extremely poisonous gas that is less dense than air under ordinary conditions. It burns in air with a characteristic blue flame, producing carbon dioxide. It is a component of the artificial fuel producer gas (carbon monoxide, nitrogen, and hydrogen), WATER GAS, and synthesis gas or syngas (carbon monoxide and hydrogen). As a reducing agent, it removes oxygen from many compounds and is used in the reduction of metals from ores (see OXIDATION AND REDUCTION). When air containing as little as 0.1% carbon monoxide by volume is inhaled, the oxygen of haemoglobin is replaced by the carbon monoxide, resulting in fatal oxygen starvation throughout the body.

**carburettor,** device in a petrol engine that vaporizes the petrol and mixes it with a regulated amount of air for efficient combustion in the engine cylinders. Land vehicles, boats, and light aircraft have a float carburettor, in which a float regulates the fuel level in a reservoir from which the fuel is continuously sucked into the intake manifold at a restriction called a venturi. When there is an individual spray for each cylinder and the injection is an intermittent, timed, metered spurt, the device is called a fuel injector. See also INTERNAL-COMBUSTION ENGINE; RICARDO, Harry Ralph.

**Carcassonne** (‚kahrka'sohnay), city (1982 pop. 42,450), capital of Aude dept., SW France. It is the centre of an important wine-producing district. The strategic location of Carcassonne, on the land route from the Mediterranean to Aquitaine, has been recognized from Roman times. There are two parts separated by the Aude R.: the medieval part has double fortifications, mainly 11th–13th cent. in date, which were restored (19th cent.) by the architect Eugène VIOLLET-LE-DUC and are now a tourist attraction.

**carcinogens,** chemical or physical agencies causing the conversion of normal body cells to a state of uncontrolled division and growth in a cancerous manner. Carcinogenic substances include mineral oils and tars involved in skin cancer, cigarette smoke in lung cancer, dyestuffs in

bladder cancer, hydrocarbon derivatives from overheated fats and grilled meat, some constituents of smoked meat and fish, and nitrosamines derived from nitrates used in FOOD PRESERVATION. Cancer may also be induced by physical means such as ULTRAVIOLET RADIATION and Ionizing Radiation. UV light affects mainly the exposed parts of the body, causing cancer of the skin, especially on the face, neck, and hands, and also the legs in Western women. Outdoor workers are most susceptible, and especially whites living in areas of high-intensity sunlight. X-RAYS and GAMMA RADIATION affect also the deep-seated tissues of the body, and information on radiation-induced cancers has been derived from the use of radiation in medical treatments. Most tumours are probably caused by known external agencies, and many of those thought to be spontaneous may in fact be due to the general background radiation which occurs naturally. Because of the range of materials suspected of inducing cancer, the mode of action of carcinogenic substances is not known. Testing is expensive and long-term and the results are often open to question and accused of causing unnecessary public concern; e.g., although it can be shown that there is a link between cancer and certain food additives such as the artificial sweeteners saccharin and cyclamates (now banned in some countries), the effect is only found after prolonged and heavy doses, very unlikely to be ingested in any diet. Also, different animals vary widely in response to treatment with suspected carcinogens, some of which become ineffective because of detoxification in the body. There is also public concern that an unacceptable risk to public health comes with the use of NUCLEAR ENERGY; although the evidence of raised incidence of leukaemia near nuclear power stations is highly controversial, there can be no doubt that the result of an accident such as the one at CHERNOBYL is to cause substantial numbers of cases of cancer.

**cardamom:** see GINGER.

**Cárdenas, Lázaro,** 1895–1970, president of MEXICO (1934–40). He fought (1913–17) as a general in the Mexican revolution and held political posts before being elected president. He expropriated foreign-held properties, distributed land to peasants, and instituted social reforms to benefit Indians and Mexican workers. His political influence in advancing orderly constitutional processes was great.

**Cardiff,** city (1981 pop. 262,313), S Glamorgan, S Wales, on the Bristol Channel. The capital, largest city, and chief port of Wales, it produces iron and steel, machinery, ships, road vehicles, paper, and other manufactures. Cardiff was one of the world's greatest coal-shipping ports in the 19th and early 20th cent. The ruins of Cardiff Castle, built (1090) on the site of a Roman fort, are of special interest.

**Cardigan,** town (1981 pop. 3815), in Dyfed, S Wales, on R. Teifi estuary, Cardigan Bay. Formerly a port, it suffered a decline owing to the silting of the river mouth and the advent of large steamships. It is now a market town. There are the remains of a 12th cent. castle.

**Cardin, Pierre,** 1922–, French FASHION designer. He has been influential since the 1960s, more for his ready-to-wear clothes than for his haute couture. His fashions for men have been particularly important.

**cardinal,** a member of the highest body within the Roman Catholic Church below the pope—the college of cardinals, having the duty of electing the pope (since 1059) and all the duties of a privy council to him. Its members are appointed by the pope and are of three classes: cardinal bishops, bishops of the seven sees around Rome and the Eastern rite patriarchs; cardinal priests, mostly archbishops outside the Roman province; and cardinal deacons, priests with functions within papal government. A cardinal's insignia resemble those of a bishop except for the red, broad-brimmed, tasselled hat, which is conferred by the pope but not subsequently worn. Pope SIXTUS V set the number of cardinals at 70, but since the pontificate of JOHN XXIII, the number has steadily increased to over 150.

**cardiopulmonary resuscitation** (CPR), emergency procedure used to treat victims of cardiac and respiratory arrest. Special training is recommended for CPR, which combines external heart massage (to keep the blood flowing through the body) with ARTIFICIAL RESPIRATION (to keep air flowing in and out of the lungs). When CPR is to be performed, the victim is placed face up and prepared for artificial respiration. The person administering CPR places his or her hands (one on top of the other, with fingers interlocked) heel down on the patient's breastbone, leans forward, and presses down rhythmically about 60 times a minute. This procedure is alternated with mouth-to-mouth artificial respiration.

**Cardozo, Benjamin Nathan,** 1870–1938, associate justice of the US SUPREME COURT (1932–38). A New York attorney and judge of considerable stature, in the Court he was an eloquent and influential supporter of liberal social and economic views. His published lectures are considered classics of JURISPRUDENCE.

**Carducci, Giosuè,** 1835–1907, Italian poet, scholar, and critic. Professor of literature at the Univ. of Bologna from 1860 to 1904, he became poet laureate of the new kingdom of Italy, and was awarded the 1906 Nobel Prize for literature. His verse, classic in spirit and design, but with great emotional range, ranks him among leading Italian poets. His works include *Inno a Satana* (1865; tr. Hymn to Satan), *Rime nuove* (1887; tr. New Rhymes), *Odi barbari* (1877–89; tr. Barbarian Odes), and *Rime e ritme* (1899).

**Caréme, Marie-Antoine,** 1784–1833, French chef and patissier. From an impoverished background he rose to work for Talleyrand, the Czar Alexander, the Prince Regent, Louis XVIII, and the Rothschild family. He is known as the inventor of many of the classic dishes of French cuisine.

**Carew, Jan Rynveld,** 1925–, Guyanese novelist and poet. His novels, e.g., *Black Midas* (1956) and *The Third Gift* (1974), are concerned with the history (of slavery and colonialism) as well as myth (El Dorado) that make up the complex past of the Caribbean. The same themes recur in his poetry, *Streets of Eternity* (1952) and *Sea Drums in my Blood* (1980).

**Carew, Thomas,** 1595?–1639?, English poet. He was briefly a diplomat and then a courtier of CHARLES I. One of the Cavalier poets, he is best known for courtly, amorous lyrics like 'Ask me no more where Jove bestows', as well as for 'An Elegy on the Death of Dr Donne' and the highly erotic 'Rapture'.

**Carey, Peter,** 1943–, Australian novelist and short-story writer. His surreal, often macabre stories and novels give a new and distinctive shape to the traditional Australian theme of the 'battler' or underdog in a hostile society. His novels include *Bliss* (1981), the huge picaresque *Illywhacker* (1985), which won five major literary awards, and *Oscar and Lucinda* (1988), which won the Booker Prize.

**cargo cults,** millenarian movements characteristic of early 20th-cent. Melanesia. It was believed that, through the use of the right ritual and supernatural means, Western consumer goods would be obtained directly by the indigenous population, and confer on their possessors the same power as they evidently conferred on white colonialists. See MILLENARIANISM.

**cargo system,** a hierarchy of religious and political offices through which individuals pass as temporary office-holders. Holders of cargo positions must spend considerable sums to enable the performance of essential cultural and religious duties and rituals. The system is derived from Spanish imposed systems of political control and authority, which were in turn based on Aztec and Mayan forms of social organization.

**Caribbean Community** (CARICOM), intergovernmental organization (est. 1973) seeking economic integration of English-speaking Caribbean countries. Members are (1986) Antigua and Barbuda, the Bahamas, Barbados, Belize, Dominica, Grenada, Guyana, Jamaica, Montserrat, St Christopher and Nevis, St Lucia, St Vincent and the Grenadines, and Trinidad and Tobago. Based in Georgetown (Guyana), CARICOM operates a Caribbean Common Market (successor to the Caribbean Free Trade Association).

**Caribbean Sea,** tropical sea, c.1,942,500 km² (750,000 sq mi), an arm of the Atlantic Ocean bordered by the West Indies (N, E), South America (S), and Central America (W). Its waters are clear and warm (averaging 24°C/75°F), with almost no tidal range. Bartlett Trench (6946 m/22,788 ft below sea level), between Cuba and Jamaica, is the deepest point. After its discovery (1492) by Christopher COLUMBUS the sea was controlled by Spain, but other European nations later established colonies in the Greater Antilles—Jamaica and St Domingue (Haiti)—and on its western fringe in the Lesser Antilles. Since the MONROE DOCTRINE of 1823, and especially after the opening (1914) of the PANAMA CANAL, the US has tried to exclude foreign powers from this strategic area (see CUBAN MISSILE CRISIS) and has often intervened in the region's domestic affairs, e.g., in the DOMINICAN REPUBLIC in 1965. See also WEST INDIES.

**caribou,** name in North America for the DEER (genus *Rangifer*) from which the REINDEER was domesticated. Found in arctic and subarctic regions, caribou are the only deer of which both sexes have antlers. They feed on grasses, sedges, and shrubs and can digest the lichen called reindeer moss.

**caricature,** a satirical portrait in art or literature that, through exaggeration and distortion of features, makes its subject appear ridiculous. The comic tradition in art was established in 17th-cent. Italy by the CARRACCI. Caricature flourished in 18th-cent. England in the works of HOGARTH, ROWLANDSON, and James Gillray. Expanding to include political and social satire, the genre developed into the CARTOON. Caricature was extremely popular in European and American periodicals of the 19th cent., many of which included work by such artists as DAUMIER, CRUIKSHANK, TENNIEL, and Art Young. Notable modern caricaturists include BEERBOHM, Ronald Searle, Al Hirschfeld, and David Levine. In literature, caricature has been a popular form since the ancient Greeks. Perhaps the most striking and pervasive use of literary caricature in English is in the work of Charles DICKENS.

**caries,** common form of tooth decay generally believed to be caused by acids formed by the action of bacteria on CARBOHYDRATE in the mouth. Frequent consumption of sugars is the most important dietary factor contributing to the condition, which can be prevented by FLUORIDATION of the water supply.

**carillon,** in music: see BELL.

**Carinthia** or **Karinthia,** region, S Austria. The basin of the Drave (Drau) R., it is flanked by mountains which rise to 3798 m (12,457 ft) in the Gross Glockner on the border of the East Tyrol. The glaciated mountain scenery attracts many visitors and there is some ore mining.

**Carlisle,** city (1981 pop. 72,206), Cumbria, NW England, at confluence of R. Eden and R. Caldew. It is a major commercial and industrial centre for the area, whose industries include the manufacture of metal goods, biscuits, and textiles. The service sector is now the major employer within the town. The cathedral was originally an Augustinian priory built in the 12th cent., and was enlarged in the 13th and 14th cents. The remains of HADRIAN'S WALL runs through the N suburbs.

**Carlists,** partisans of Don Carlos (1788–1855) and his successors in their claims to the Spanish throne. After FERDINAND VII changed the law to enable his daughter, ISABELLA II, to succeed him (1833), his brother, Don Carlos, claimed the throne and initiated an unsuccessful civil war (1833–40). The conservative, clericalist Carlists revived the claim (1860) for Don Carlos's son, Don Carlos, conde de Montemolin (1818–61), and again (1869, 1872) on behalf of the latter's nephew, Don Carlos, duque de Madrid (1848–1909). They seized most of the Basque provinces and other territory and fought another civil war (1873–76), which failed. The Carlists supported the Nationalists in the SPANISH CIVIL WAR (1936–39), but FRANCO ended the Carlists' dynastic claim in 1969 by naming the Bourbon prince, JUAN CARLOS, as his successor.

**Carlos.** For Spanish rulers thus named, see CHARLES.

**Carlos, Don:** see CARLISTS.

**Carlow,** county in SE of Republic of Ireland (1986 pop. 40,958), 887 km² (346 sq mi), in the province of Leinster. The county town is CARLOW. Much of the county is gently undulating, rising to 795 m (2,608 ft) in the Blackstairs Mts in the extreme SE. The R. Barrow crosses the county from N to S in the W, and the R. Slaney crosses in the E. Agriculture is the main economic activity, including dairy farming and the cultivation of oats and potatoes.

**Carlow,** county town (1986 pop. 11,502) of Co. Carlow, Republic of Ireland. It is situated at the confluence of the R. Burren and the R. BARROW. It is a small market town, whose industries include food-processing and brewing. It contains the ruins of an ancient castle, and a 19th-cent. Roman Catholic cathedral.

**Carlson, Chester Floyd,** 1906–68, American inventor. A patent lawyer, he invented (1938) xerography (see PHOTOCOPYING), a method of electrostatic printing, and made a fortune from royalties and stockholdings in the Haloid Co. (later the Xerox Corp.). The first Xerox copier was marketed in 1959.

**Carlsson, Ingvar,** 1934–, prime minister of SWEDEN (1986–). After serving as a minister under Olof PALME, he became chairman of the Social Democratic Party and prime minister following Palme's assassination early in 1986.

**Carlstadt, Karlstadt,** or **Karolstadt,** c.1480–1541, German Protestant reformer, originally named Andreas Rudolph Bodenstein. During LUTHER's stay at the Wartberg (1521–22), Carlstadt became the leader at Wittenberg and implemented his radical beliefs. Luther later accused him of betrayal. Accused of revolutionary political activity, Carlstadt fled to Switzerland, where he taught theology at Basel.

**Carlyle, Thomas,** 1795–1881, Scottish writer. He first gained attention as an interpreter of German ROMANTICISM with his *Life of Schiller* (1825) and a translation of Goethe's *Wilhelm Meister* (1824). In 1826 he married Jane Baillie Welsh, an ambitious woman and notable letter-writer who did much to aid his career. A trenchant critic of the materialism of the age, with the voice of a prophet he expressed his views in an autobiographical work, *Sartor Resartus* (1833–34), in essays, tracts for the times, and in his *French Revolution* (1837). He attacked laissez-faire theory, questioned parliamentary democracy and stressed his belief in strong government and great men in *On Heroes, Hero-Worship, and The Heroic In History* (1841), *Past and Present* (1843), in an edition of the writings of Oliver CROMWELL (1845), and in a biography of Frederick the Great (1858–65). Carlyle had great influence on the literary world of his day; his distinctive style, complex yet powerful, is unique.

**Carman, Bliss,** 1861–1929, Canadian poet. His emotional, impressionistic poetry appears in *Behind the Arras* (1895), *Pipes of Pan* (1902–05), and *Echoes from Vagabondia* (1912). He also published (1926) lectures on Canadian literature.

**Carmarthen,** town (1981 pop. 13,860), in Dyfed, SW Wales, on R. Towy. Built on the site of the Roman fort of Moridunum, it is now a market and industrial town. Industries found here include milk processing and the manufacture of agricultural implements. There are the remains of a Norman castle within the town, and a church which dates back to the 14th cent.

**Carmelites,** Roman Catholic order of mendicant friars. Originating apparently as hermits on Mt Carmel in Palestine, they were made into a Western order by St Simon Stock (d. 1265) and became prominent in university life. An enclosed order of Carmelite nuns was established. After a decline, the Carmelites were revived by the reforms of St TERESA of Ávila and St JOHN OF THE CROSS in 16th-cent. Spain. The now larger reformed order is known as the Discalced Carmelites.

**Carmichael, Hoagy** (Hoagland Howard Carmichael), 1899–1981, American songwriter. His melodies reflect early JAZZ influence. 'Stardust' (1929) is his best-known song; others include 'Georgia on My Mind' and 'Skylark.' He also appeared in films, e.g., *To Have and Have Not* (1944).

**Carnac,** the site in Brittany of a vast complex of stone alignments and MEGALITHIC MONUMENTS and tombs of NEOLITHIC age. Almost 3000 standing stones are set in three groups of 10 to 13 parallel rows several kilometres long, some ending in semicircular structures. It has been contended that Carnac was a lunar observatory (see ARCHAEOASTRONOMY).

The prehistoric aligned stones at **Carnac**

**Carnap, Rudolf,** 1891–1970, American philosopher; b. Germany. The most influential exponent of LOGICAL POSITIVISM, he made major contributions to logic, semantics and the philosophy of science. He taught at Vienna Univ. (1926–31) and was a member of the Vienna Circle before emigrating to the US in 1935. In *The Logical Construction of the World* (1928) he offered a logical reduction of all knowledge to experiences of similarity. Influenced by the early writings of WITTGENSTEIN, he aimed to eliminate metaphysics by showing that all philosophical problems are pseudo-problems. Regarding the logical analysis of language as the only legitimate role of philosophy, he attempted in *The Logical Syntax of Language* (1934) to construct an entirely general formal language. *Meaning and Necessity* (1947) is an important contribution to modal logic, and *Logical Foundations of Probability* (1950) is a systematic treatment of the concept of confirmation, which he used to replace the VERIFICATION PRINCIPLE.

**Carnarvon,** town (1986 pop. 6847), Western Australia. Located 980 km (610 mi) N of Perth, on the Indian Ocean, at the mouth of the Gascoyne R., the town was a whaling base until 1963, and today has an important prawn-fishing industry. Irrigated plantations produce tropical fruits with bananas the main crop. The US has a space-vehicle tracking station near the town.

**Carnarvon, George Edward Stanhope Molyneux Herbert,** 5th **earl of,** 1866–1923, British Egyptologist who, with Howard CARTER, excavated (1906–22) in the Valley of the Kings, Luxor, Egypt. The tomb of TUTANKHAMEN was their final discovery (1922).

**Carnarvon Gorge,** valley in the Carnarvon Range in central Queensland, NE Australia. This deep and narrow gorge, running 32 km (20 mi) into the mountains, forms part of the Carnavon National Park. Outstanding examples of Aboriginal stencil art are preserved on the sandstone walls. The nearest settlement is Roma, 100 km (65 mi) to the S, site of Australia's first viable oilflow (1964).

Aboriginal stencil art on rock walls at **Carnarvon Gorge**

**carnation:** see PINK.

**Carné, Marcel,** 1909–, French film director. A poetic, romantic film maker, his greatest films were made in collaboration with writer Jacques Prévert and include *Drôle de drame* (1937), *Quai des brumes* (1938), and *Les enfants du paradis* (1945).

**Carnegie, Andrew,** 1835–1919, American industrialist and philanthropist; b. Scotland, emigrated to the US 1848. As a superintendent (1859–65) for the Pennsylvania railway he invested heavily in iron manufactures. In 1873 he began to acquire firms that were later consolidated into the Carnegie Steel Co., which by 1900 was producing one quarter of the steel in the US and controlled iron mines, ore ships, and railways. His partnership with Henry C. FRICK aided his success. In 1901 he sold all his interests to the US Steel Corp. and retired. Believing that wealth should be used for the public good, he made donations of c.$350 million, establishing such philanthropic organizations as the Carnegie Corp. of New York, the Carnegie Endowment for International Peace, and over 2800 libraries.

**carnivore,** term applied to any animal whose diet consists primarily of animal matter. In animal systematics, it refers to members of the mammalian order Carnivora, which contains aquatic and terrestrial species, including the dog, cat, seal, and other families. Carnivorous mammals' teeth are designed to hold and to kill prey and to tear and shear flesh. Those carnivores with specialized diets may be referred to as piscivores (fish-eaters) or insectivores (insect-eaters). Non-carnivorous animals may be HERBIVORES, OMNIVORES, or DETRIVORES.

**carnivorous plants:** see PITCHER PLANT; VENUS'-FLYTRAP.

**Carnot, Lazare Nicolas Marguerite** (kah‚noh), 1753–1823, French revolutionary. He organized the republican armies and masterminded a successful strategy in the FRENCH REVOLUTIONARY WARS. A member of the DIRECTORY, he later held high posts under NAPOLEON I and wrote a classic work on fortification (1810).

**Carnot, (Nicholas Léonard) Sadi,** 1796–1832, French physicist, son of Lazare CARNOT. He studied the relation between heat and mechanical energy and devised an ideal engine whose series of operations showed that even under ideal conditions a heat engine must reject some heat energy instead of converting it all into mechanical energy. This illustrates the second law of THERMODYNAMICS, formulated later.

**Caro, Anthony,** 1924–, British sculptor. He was an assistant to Henry MOORE (1951–53), and in 1959 visited Mexico and the US and was impressed by the work of M. LOUIS, K. NOLAND, and D. SMITH. He subsequently began to work with prefabricated metal elements welded together and sprayed with bright enamel paint. The combination of shapes and colour in these large works were used to help convey a mood as suggested by the title, e.g., *Early One Morning* (1962; Tate Gall., London).

**Caro, Joseph ben Ephraim,** 1488–1575, Jewish codifier of law; b. Spain, d. Palestine. His most well-known work is *Shulhan Arukh* [the set table] (see SHULHAN ARUKH), still regarded as authoritative for Orthodox religious and legal decisions, though his magnum opus remains the *Bet Yoseph*, a commentary to Jacob B. Asher's Code of Law, the *Tur*. Caro was also a kabbalist (see KABBALAH).

**carob,** evergreen tree (*Ceratonia siliqua*) of the PULSE family, native to the Mediterranean but cultivated in other warm areas. Its large, red pods have been a food source since prehistoric times, and the pods and their extracts have many common names, e.g., St John's bread and locust bean gum. Carob is used as a food stabilizer and a caffeine-free chocolate substitute; carob pods are used as livestock feed.

**Carol,** kings of Romania. **Carol I** or **Charles I,** 1839–1914, prince (1866–1881) and first king (r.1881–1914), was a Hohenzollern born at Sigmaringen. He was in many respects the maker of his adopted country for he won independence for his realm as the commander of the victorious joint Russo-Romanian forces in the Russo-Turkish war of 1877–78, established national finance, built up a considerable export trade, and fostered industrial development. **Carol II,** 1893–1953, was a nephew of Carol I. His first marriage in 1918 to Ioana Lambrino at Odessa was annulled by the Romanian Supreme Court on his father, King Ferdinand's, instructions. In 1921 he married Princess Helen of Greece with whom he had a son, MICHAEL. Carol's infatuation with Helen Tìmpeanu (Madame Lupescu) led him to renounce his right to the throne in 1925. When Ferdinand died in 1927, Michael succeeded, but in 1930 Carol returned to Romania, was proclaimed king and largely took the affairs of the country into his own hands. In 1938 he instituted a personal dictatorship but the loss of N Transylvania and Bessarabia forced him to abdicate in 1940 in favour of Michael.

**carol,** popular, joyful HYMN, celebrating an occasion such as EASTER or CHRISTMAS. English carols date from the 15th cent. Like the FOLK SONG, the carol is characterized by directness of thought and expression.

**Caroline of Brunswick,** 1768–1821, consort of GEORGE IV of England. She married George in 1795, separated from him in 1796, and lived abroad after 1814. When George became king in 1820, she returned to claim her rights as queen. The king instituted divorce proceedings on the grounds of adultery, but after Caroline's apparent persecution by a profligate husband aroused popular sympathy, particularly among radicals, they were dropped.

**Carolingian architecture and art.** In the 8th cent. under CHARLEMAGNE changes in Western culture and art reached their apex. In architecture, the small, boxlike structures of the Merovingian period gave way to the spacious BASILICAS built round a central space. Of incalculable importance to the later Middle Ages was the new emphasis given to the western facade of the church, called the westwork. Its function is still debated, but it was flanked by symmetrical towers and was several storeys high. A vaulted vestibule was below, and the room above may have been a chapel for dignitaries. The outstanding Carolingian structure still in existence is the palatine chapel at Aachen (805), in W Germany, which may have been based partly on the 5th-cent. church of San Vitale in Ravenna, Italy (see BYZANTINE ART AND ARCHITECTURE). The best-preserved artistic works of the period are illumina manuscripts, ivory carving, and metalwork. They show a fusion of Anglo-Saxon and Irish ornamental motifs with figures derived from antiquity, e.g., the Gospel book by Godescalc (783). The illustrations of the Utrecht Psalter, full of flickering movement, are unparalleled in early Western art. Carved ivory book covers are rare, and metalwork is rarer, but the gold altar of Sant' Ambrogio (835, Milan), the portable altar of Arnulf (Munich), several splendid book covers, and other sumptuously decorated objects provide insights into the artistic accomplishments of the period, which ended in the late 9th cent.

Carolingian architecture and art: The Gospel book by Godescalc, 783

**Carolingians,** Frankish dynasty founded (7th cent.) by PEPIN of Landen. They ruled as mayors of the palace under the MEROVINGIANS until 751, when Pepin the Short made himself king. His son, CHARLEMAGNE, who was crowned emperor in 800, brought the dynasty to its zenith. On the death of LOUIS I in 840, the Treaty of Verdun (843) split the empire among his three sons: Lotharingia went to Lothair I; Germany went to Louis the

German; and France went to Charles II. In 870 Lotharingia was divided between Louis and Charles. The dynasty died out in Germany in 911 and in France in 987.

**carp,** freshwater, bottom-feeding member of the carp family Cyprinidae. *Cyprinus carpio* was native to Asia but is now found throughout Europe and America. Carp may be up to 90 cm (3 ft) long and 11 kg (25 lb) in weight. They have four 'whiskers' (barbels) around the mouth, and are usually dark greenish or brown with red on the fins. Carp have been farmed since Roman times in Europe and were part of the stock in the fish ponds of religious houses.

**Carpaccio, Vittore,** c.1460–c.1525, Venetian painter. He is most famous for his cycles of colourful narrative paintings, which are crowded with picturesque details of Venice and of the pageantry of contemporary Venetian life. Among them are scenes from the *Legend of St Ursula* (1490; Academy, Venice) and the *Lives of Sts George, Jerome, and Tryphonius* (1502–08), painted for the Scuola di San Giorgio degli Schiavoni, Venice.

**Carpathian Mountains,** or **Carpathians,** major mountain system of central and E Europe, c.1500 km (930 mi) long. A continuation of the Alps, they curve in a great arc through Czechoslovakia, Poland, and the USSR, and extend into Romania as the Transylvanian Alps, or Southern Carpathians. Gerlachovka 2663 m (8737 ft) is the highest point.

**Carpeaux, Jean-Baptiste,** 1827–75, French sculptor and painter. Freedom and force distinguish his sculptures, e.g., *Ugolino* (1860–62; Louvre, Paris), *The Dance* for the façade of the Opéra: the original (1866–69) is in the Louvre.

**Carpentier, Alejo,** 1904–80, Cuban novelist. His politically-conscious novels include *El reino de este mundo* (1949; tr. The Kingdom of this World), *Los pasos perdidos* (1953; tr. The Lost Steps), and *Concierto barroco* (1974; tr. Baroque Concert).

**carpet** or **rug,** stiff, stable, strong, hardwearing fabric, most commonly used for floor coverings. Originally warps were made of jute, hemp, flax, or cotton with lustrous good quality wool for weft pile, but often now man-made yarns are used or a mixture of natural with man-made and synthetic yarns. Rugs and carpets have been woven in Middle Eastern countries since early Christian times, both flat woven rugs known as Kilims and hand-knotted pile rugs. Two principle methods of carpet knotting are used: (1) Ghiordes knot used in Turkish, Caucasian, Western Persian, and English carpets; (2) Sehna knot used in Persian, Turkestan, and Chinese carpets. All types of hand-woven rugs and carpets are still imported into Europe from Middle Eastern countries. With the introduction of Brussel looms in the 18th cent., pile carpets could be woven mechanically. The pile consisted of rows of loops formed over bladed wires inserted weft-wise during weaving; subsequently the bladed wires were withdrawn, thus cutting the loops to produce pile carpets known as Wilton. With the invention of the Axminster loom (1876) carpets were produced with unlimited number of colours. Endless chains of spools carry lengths of coloured yarns wound in a predetermined order from which short pieces are cut and inserted during weaving to form pile tufts known as spool Axminster. European carpets, with many outstanding examples from France in the 17th cent. and England in the 18th cent., were handmade until the introduction of the power loom by Erasmus Bigelow in 1841. Although handmade rugs are still produced in the Near and Far East and are highly prized, contemporary Western carpet manufacturing is a highly mechanized industry that employs a wide variety of methods to produce floor coverings.

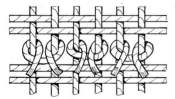

Turkish/Ghiordes knot          Senneh/ Persian knot

Two examples of **carpet** knotting

**carpetbaggers,** Southern term for Northerners who went to the South during RECONSTRUCTION following the Civil War. Named after the carpetbags in which they carried their belongings, they were regarded as transients although most intended to settle in the South and make money there. The black vote won them important posts in Republican state governments. Those who were corrupt made the term synonymous with outsiders who profit from an area's political troubles.

**Carrà, Carlo,** 1881–1966, Italian painter. A member of the futurist group of artists and co-signatory of the 1910 manifesto of FUTURISM. He painted unanimist works of which his large *Funeral of the Anarchist Gali* (1911) is the most important. It also shows the influence CUBISM had on Carrà after his visit with other futurists to Paris in 1911, in areas that he repainted with fragmented interlocking planes. After World War I he moved away from futurism, looking first (1915) at Giotto and then at CHIRICO's *Scuola Metafisica* ideas when they met in 1917.

**Carracci** (ka͵rachee), family of Italian painters, founders of an important school of painting. **Lodovico Carracci** (1555–1619) established with his cousins a school of painting in Bologna that sought to unite in one system the best characteristics of the great masters; the school laid fresh emphasis on the practice of drawing from life. The academy was one of the outstanding schools in Italy, and its noted pupils include DOMENICHINO. Lodovico's paintings are distinguished by their tender feeling; e.g., *The Baragellini Madonna* (1588; Pinacoteca Nazionale, Bologna). His cousin, **Agostino Carracci,** 1557–1602, was more important as a teacher and engraver. Agostino's brother, **Annibale Carracci,** 1560–1609, was the outstanding artist of the three. His art broke with the artificiality of late MANNERISM and restored glowing colour to Italian painting. His decoration of the ceiling of a gallery in the Farnese palace, Rome (1597–1600), with its feigned architecture, rich colour, and exuberant pagan subject matter, was immensely influential and became the cornerstone of BAROQUE painting.

**Carranza, Venustiano,** 1859–1920, Mexican political leader. He fought in the Mexican revolution and helped to overthrow (1914) Gen. HUERTA. He became president (1914) and, aided by Gen. OBREGÓN, survived a civil war (1915). When he did not enforce the reform constitution of 1917 and tried to prevent Obregón from becoming president, the latter revolted (1920). Carranza fled the capital and was murdered.

**Carrara,** marble quarries in the Apuanian Alps of Tuscany, N central Italy. The marble was worked as early as Roman times and has become famous for its use in sculpture. It is also now used for tombstones.

**Carrel, Alexis,** 1873–1955, French surgeon and physiologist. For his work at the Rockefeller Inst., New York, on the development of methods of suturing blood vessels, he received the 1912 Nobel Prize for physiology or medicine. With Charles LINDBERGH he invented an artificial heart, to culture and preserve living tissue outside the body.

**Carrera, Rafael,** 1814–65, dictator of GUATEMALA (1840–65). He overthrew (1840) the liberal government and restored the power of the Roman Catholic Church. Becoming president for life in 1854, he interfered in other Central American states to install or restore conservative regimes.

**Carrick-on-Shannon,** county town (1986 pop. 2037) of Co. Leitrim, Republic of Ireland, on R. SHANNON. It is a small market town and fishing centre.

**Carroll, John,** 1735–1815, American Roman Catholic churchman, the first Roman Catholic bishop in the US. A JESUIT, he supported the AMERICAN REVOLUTION and was a friend of Benjamin FRANKLIN. In 1784 he became superior of the missions in the US. In 1790 he was made bishop of Baltimore and in 1808 archbishop. Carroll fought anti-Catholic feeling in the US and founded various educational institutions, including Georgetown Univ.

**Carroll, Lewis,** pseud. of **Charles Lutwidge Dodgson,** 1832–98, English writer and mathematician. He lectured on mathematics at Oxford for many years, but his fame rests on the children's tales *Alice's Adventures in Wonderland* (1865) and *Through the Looking Glass* (1872). These books grew out of the stories he told to children, among them Alice Liddell, the daughter of H.G. Liddell, dean of Christ Church, Oxford. *The Hunting of the Snark* (1876) and the verses in *Sylvie and Bruno* (1889–93) showed his poetic dexterity and surrealist fantasy. An amateur photographer, Carroll took many fine photographs of children.

**carrot**, common name for some members of Umbelliferae (also called parsley family), a family of mainly perennial or biennial herbs of north temperate areas. Most are typified by aromatic foliage, a dry fruit that splits when mature, and an umbellate inflorescence (in which the floret stems of the flattened flower cluster arise from the same point, like an umbrella). The seeds and leaves of many of these herbs are used for seasoning or as greens, e.g., ANISE, CARAWAY, CORIANDER, CUMIN, DILL, FENNEL, and PARSLEY. The carrot, CELERY, and PARSNIP are commercially important vegetables. The common carrot (*Daucus carota sativa*) is a root crop, probably derived from the wild carrot (or QUEEN ANNE'S LACE). Carrots are rich in carotene (vitamin A), especially when cooked; in antiquity they were used medicinally. A few members of the family, e.g., POISON HEMLOCK, produce lethal poisons.

**Carrucci, Jacopo:** see PONTORMO, JACOPO DA.

**carrying capacity,** the maximum number of users that can be sustained by a given set of land resources. The users may be plants, animals, or humans. The carrying capacity of an area will vary according to the management of the land and its inherent quality, and if exceeded environmental degradation will result.

**Carson, Edward Henry,** Baron, 1854–1935, Irish politician and lawyer. As a trial lawyer he cross-examined Oscar WILDE (1895). Before World War I he led the movement in Ulster to oppose HOME RULE for Ireland. During the war he served as attorney general (1915) in Herbert ASQUITH's coalition government, and as first lord of the admiralty (1916–17) and member of the war cabinet (1917–18) under David LLOYD GEORGE.

**Carson, Kit** (Christopher Carson), 1809–68, American frontiersman. In 1825 he went to New Mexico and served as cook, guide, and hunter for exploring parties, including those of FRÉMONT. In 1853 he became an Indian agent. Carson was a Union general in the CIVIL WAR.

**Carson, Rachel Louise,** 1907–64, American writer and marine biologist. Her book *Silent Spring* (1962) was an influential study on the dangers of insecticides. Some of her other popular works include *The Sea Around Us* (1951) and *The Edge of the Sea* (1954).

**Cartagena,** city (1981 est. pop. 450,000), NW Colombia capital of Bolívar dept., a port on the Bay of Cartagena, in the Caribbean Sea. Oil-refining and the manufacture of sugar and tobacco are major industries, and there is an expanding petrochemical complex. Founded in 1533, Cartagena became the treasure city of the SPANISH MAIN, where precious New World minerals awaited transshipment to Spain. It was often sacked despite its massive fortifications, some of which still stand. It declared its independence from Spain in 1811 and was incorporated into Colombia in 1821. Its rapid development in the 20th cent. was due largely to the discovery of oil in the Magdalena basin. One of the most picturesque of Latin American cities, with shady plazas and cobblestone streets, Cartagena attracts many tourists.

**Cartagena,** city (1981 pop. 172,751), Murcia prov., SE Spain. At the head of a sheltered inlet, it is Spain's leading naval base and arsenal. The commercial port handles the iron, lead, silver, and other minerals obtained from nearby hills. Industries include mineral smelting and oil refining. Founded c.243 BC by HASDRUBAL, as Carthago Nova, it was the principal seat of Carthaginian power in Spain until taken by Romans in 209 BC. It was largely rebuilt in the 16th cent.

**cartel,** national or international organization of producers who act in concert to fix prices, limit supply, divide markets, or set quotas. Basically, the cartel seeks to achieve maximum profits by driving out competition and by limiting production in times of oversupply. Like the TRUST and the MONOPOLY, it is most often criticized for eliminating the price benefits of competition. Defenders argue that it distributes risks, stabilizes markets, and protects weak members. The system sometimes fails because member firms or nations deviate from the rules of the cartel to serve their own interests. In Germany before World War II nearly all industry was controlled by cartels. In the US cartels are illegal, except for export associations. The most successful cartel of recent times is the ORGANIZATION OF THE PETROLEUM EXPORTING COUNTRIES (OPEC).

**Carter, Elliott,** 1908–, American composer. His mature music is organized into highly intellectualized contrapuntal patterns. He characteristically uses TEMPO as an element of form. His works include the ballet *Pocahontas* (1936–39), three string quartets (1951, 1959, 1971),

a brass quintet (1974) and a *Piano Concerto* (1964–65), a *Concerto for Orchestra* (1969), and a *Symphony of Three Orchestras* (1976–77).

**Carter, Howard,** 1873–1939, British Egyptologist who excavated for many years in the Valley of the Kings at THEBES. In 1922 he found the tomb of TUTANKHAMEN, hidden from ancient looters under the rubble of a later tomb.

**Carter, Jimmy** (James Earl Carter, Jr), 1924–, 39th president of the US (1977–81). A graduate of the US Naval Academy (1946), he served in the US navy and in 1953 returned to his family's peanut farm, which he built into a prosperous business. As governor of Georgia (1970–75), he reorganized the state executive branch and sponsored consumer and land-use legislation. After a spectacularly successful campaign for the 1976 Democratic presidential nomination, Carter, although a Southerner and political outsider, narrowly defeated the Republican candidate, Pres. Gerald FORD; his running mate was Walter MONDALE. Carter's presidency was plagued by difficult relations with Congress, which ratified his two Panama Canal treaties (1977) giving eventual control of the canal to Panama, but would not ratify his arms-limitation treaty with the Soviet Union (1979). He was successful, however, in effecting (1979) a peace treaty between Egypt and Israel (see CAMP DAVID ACCORDS). During Carter's term of office the US suffered high interest rates, inflation, and then recession, all of which he had little success in controlling. In Nov. 1979 a group of Muslim militants in Teheran, Iran, took some 50 US citizens hostage and held them until Jan. 1981. Carter's failure to attain their release contributed to his defeat in the 1980 presidential election by the Republican candidate, Ronald REAGAN.

**Carteret, Sir George,** c.1610–80, British proprietor of East Jersey, part of New Jersey, US. He commissioned his fourth cousin, **Philip Carteret,** 1639–82, as the first governor (1665–76) of New Jersey.

**Cartesian coordinates,** system for representing the relative positions of points in a plane or in space. In a plane, the point *P* is specified by the pair of numbers (*x, y*) representing the distances of the point from two intersecting straight lines, referred to as the *y*-axis and the *x*-axis, respectively. The point of intersection of these axes, which are called the coordinate axes, is known as the origin. If the axes are perpendicular, as is commonly the case, the coordinate system is called rectangular; otherwise it is oblique. In either type the *x*-coordinate, or abscissa, of *P* is measured along a line parallel to the *x*-axis, and the *y*-coordinate, or ordinate, along a line parallel to the *y*-axis. A point in space may be similarly specified by the three numbers (*x, y, z*) representing the distances from three planes determined by three intersecting straight lines not all in the same plane. Named after the French philosopher and scientist René DESCARTES, Cartesian coordinates allow certain questions in geometry to be transformed into questions about numbers and resolved by means of ANALYTICAL GEOMETRY.

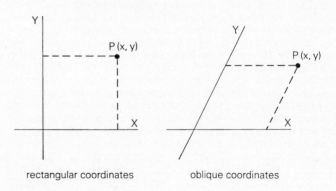

rectangular coordinates          oblique coordinates

**Cartesian coordinates**

**Carthage,** ancient city of N Africa, on the Bay of Tunis and near modern Tunis. Founded (traditionally by DIDO) by Phoenicians from Tyre in the 9th cent. BC, it eventually grew to be a mercantile CITY-STATE under an oligarchy, with explorers (e.g., Hanno) going far and wide to gather trade. Carthage's greatest weakness lay in the rivalry of two blocs of leading families who contended for control. By the 6th cent. BC the Carthaginians had established themselves on Sardinia, Malta, and the Balearic Islands, and later in Spain. Their attempt to conquer Sicily in the

5th cent. BC was set back by the victory of Gelon of Syracuse at Himera (480 BC). Later Carthaginian excursions into Sicily led to the PUNIC WARS. The contest between Rome and Carthage was hotly pursued, and the greatest general involved was a Carthaginian, HANNIBAL. Nevertheless, Carthage was finally defeated at the battle of ZAMA (202 BC), and the Carthaginian empire fell. The city itself was destroyed by Scipio Africanus Minor at the end of the Third Punic War (146 BC). A new city was founded in 44 BC and under AUGUSTUS became an important centre of Roman administration. Carthage was later (AD 439–533) the capital of the Vandals, a Germanic tribe, and was briefly recovered (533) for the Byzantine Empire by Belisarius. Although practically destroyed by the Arabs in 698, the site was populated for many centuries afterward. LOUIS IX of France died there (1270) while on crusade.

**Cartier, Sir Georges Étienne,** 1814–73, Canadian statesman. A leader of the French Canadians, he was chiefly responsible for persuading them to accept the proposals for CANADA's confederation (1867).

**Cartier, Jacques** (ˌkɑhtiay), 1491–1557, French explorer in CANADA, discoverer of the SAINT LAWRENCE R. In three voyages between 1534 and 1542 he discovered the Magdalene Islands and PRINCE EDWARD ISLAND, and ascended the St Lawrence to the modern sites of Quebec and Montreal. French claims to the St Lawrence valley were based on his explorations.

**Cartier-Bresson, Henri** (kɑhtiˌay breˌsonh), 1908–, French photojournalist. His superbly composed images of individuals and events convey a strong sense of the rush of time arrested. Among his many books are *The Decisive Moment* (1952) and *Henri Cartier-Bresson: Photographer* (1979).

**cartoon,** in the fine arts, a full-sized preliminary drawing, whose outlines are copied or can be transferred, for a work in fresco, oil, mosaic, stained glass, or tapestry. Some Italian Renaissance painters, e.g., RAPHAEL, made complete cartoons for their frescoes, and many are considered masterpieces in themselves. The use of the term *cartoon* to mean a humorous or satirical drawing began in the mid 19th cent. The first political cartoons preceded the terminology by some three centuries, appearing in 16th-cent. Germany during the Reformation. In 18th-cent. England the cartoon was an integral part of journalism. By the mid 19th cent. editorial cartoons had become regular features of American newspapers, with the work of Thomas NAST particularly influential. With the development of the colour press in the late 19th cent., humorous nonpolitical cartoons became popular, soon evolving into narrative comic strips. Some noted 20th-cent. cartoonists are Bill MAULDIN, Herblock, Charles ADDAMS, Saul Steinberg, and James THURBER.

**Cartwright, Edmund,** 1743–1823, English inventor of a power loom (patented 1785) that made possible the weaving of wide cotton cloth and led to the development of the modern loom. Cartwright also invented a wool-combing machine (1789), a ropemaking machine (1792), and an alcohol-fuelled engine (1797) and, with Robert FULTON, experimented with steam navigation.

**Caruso, Enrico,** 1873–1921, Italian operatic tenor. The beauty, range, and power of his voice made him one of the greatest of all singers. He sang more than 50 roles in Europe, the US, and Latin America, excelling in works by VERDI and PUCCINI. After his death his recordings perpetuated his fame.

**Cary, (Arthur) Joyce (Lunel),** 1888–1957, English author. He is best known for two trilogies exploring English social change. The first consists of *Herself Surprised* (1941), *To Be a Pilgrim* (1942), and *The Horse's Mouth* (1944). The second includes *Prisoner of Grace* (1952), *Except the Lord* (1953), and *Not Honour More* (1955).

**caryatid,** sculptured female figure serving as an ornamental support, in place of a column or pilaster. It was a frequent motif in architecture, furniture, and garden sculpture during the Renaissance, the 18th cent., and, notably, the CLASSIC REVIVAL of the 19th cent., when caryatids were popular as mantelpiece supports. Caryatids appeared in Egyptian and Greek architecture, the most celebrated example being the Porch of the Caryatids at the ERECHTHEUM.

**Casablanca,** city (1982 pop. 2,158,349), W Morocco, on the Atlantic coast. It is the country's largest city and major commercial centre, handling over two-thirds of its commerce and trade, particularly exports of phosphates and imports of petroleum products. Almost destroyed by an earthquake in 1755 and rebuilt in 1757, Casablanca was occupied by the French in 1907. In WORLD WAR II it was a site for the Allied invasion (1942)

Caryatid

of N Africa and for a conference (Nov. 1943) between F.D. Roosevelt and Winston Churchill.

**Casablanca Conference,** 12–14 Jan. 1943, WORLD WAR II meeting of US Pres. F.D. ROOSEVELT and British Prime Min. Winston CHURCHILL at Casablanca, French Morocco. The policy of unconditional AXIS surrender was enunciated there.

**Casals, Pablo (Pau),** 1876–1973, Spanish cellist and conductor. He began his concert career in 1891 and conducted his own orchestra in 1919. He was especially noted for his performance of J.S. BACH's unaccompanied suites and for the music festivals he directed at Prades, France, and after 1956 in Puerto Rico.

**Casanova, Giacomo,** 1725–98, Venetian adventurer and writer. He travelled widely and supported himself by such means as gambling and spying. In 1756 he escaped from Venice's state prison; in Paris, he became director of the lottery and amassed a fortune. In 1785 he retired to the castle of Dux, Bohemia, where he worked as a librarian. A man of wide interests, learning, and taste, his reputation rests on his memoirs (*History of my Life*, in French and not published in full until 1960), which are primarily his account of a remarkable series of sexual exploits.

**Casas, Bartolomé de las:** see LAS CASAS.

**Cascade Range,** forested mountain chain in the western part of the North American Cordillera, extending c.1130 km (700 mi) from British Columbia to N California. Prominent peaks include Mts Rainier (the highest, 4392 m/14,410 ft), Shasta, and Hood, and volcanically active Lassen Peak and Mt SAINT HELENS.

**case,** in language, one of the several possible forms of a given noun, pronoun, or adjective that indicates its grammatical function (see INFLECTION), usually by a series of suffixes attached to a stem, as in Latin *amicus*, 'friend' (nominative), *amicum* (accusative), *amici* (genitive), and *amico* (ablative and dative). The hypothetical ancestor of the Indo-European languages had eight cases: nominative, referring to a person performing an action; possessive or genitive, indicating a possessor; dative, indicating the secondary recipient of an action; accusative, referring to the entity directly affected by an action; ablative, indicating separation or locating place and time; vocative, referring to a person addressed; instrumental, indicating means or instrument; and locative, referring to location. Old English used the nominative, accusative, dative, genitive, and instrumental cases, but modern English only uses two cases, e.g., *person* (common or nominative) and *person's* (possessive or genitive). Some pronouns have three, e.g., *she* (nominative), *her* (objective), and *hers* (possessive). The Altaic and Finno-Ugric language families also use case systems. German has four cases, Russian six, and Finnish sixteen.

**casehardening,** in metallurgy, a process to harden steel by increasing the percentage of carbon at its surface. This is done by packing the STEEL in charcoal and then heating it; by heating it in a furnace with a hydrocarbon gas atmosphere; or by heating it in a molten-salt bath containing potassium and sodium cyanides.

**casein,** a type of protein found in milk, providing many essential nutrients. When milk is treated with acid, casein separates as an insoluble white curd; it is used in adhesives and water paints. Casein produced when milk is curdled with rennet is used to make cheese and also a plastic from which imitation gemstones and other objects are made.

**Casey, Richard Gardiner, Baron,** 1890–1976, Australian politician. He was a member of the governments of J.A. LYONS and R.G. MENZIES, and served the British war cabinet as minister of state in the Middle East during World War II. From 1965 to 1969 he was governor-general of Australia.

**cashew,** tropical American tree (*Anacardium occidentale*) of the SUMAC family, valued chiefly for its kidney-shaped nut, whose sweet, oily kernel is used for food and yields an oil used in cooking. The nut grows at the end of a red, white, or yellow pear-shaped fleshy stalk, or cashew apple, which is also eaten or pressed to extract the juice, which may be fermented to make wine. The acrid sap of the cashew tree is used to make a varnish that protects woodwork from insects.

**Casimir,** Polish rulers. **Casimir I,** c.1015–58, duke of POLAND (r.c.1040–58), reunited the Polish lands under the hegemony of the Holy Roman Empire. **Casimir II,** 1138–94, duke of Poland (r.1177–94), deposed his brother and secured for his descendants the hereditary right to the crown. **Casimir III,** 1310–70, king of Poland (r.1333–70), known as **Casimir the Great,** extended Polish territories, codified the law, improved the lot of peasants and Jews, founded (1364) Kraków Univ., and in general greatly increased royal power. **Casimir IV,** 1424–92, king of Poland and Lithuania (r.1447–92), successfully ended (1466) the war with the Teutonic Knights.

**casino** or **cassino,** card game played with a full 52-card deck by two to four players. Four cards are dealt to each player, four open cards to the table. Each player 'takes in' cards, principally by matching their cards with cards of corresponding indices on the table. The game ends after all the cards are dealt. The object is to take the greatest total number of cards; the greatest number of spades; and the point-scoring cards, namely, the aces, the 10 of diamonds (big casino), and the 2 of spades (little casino).

**Caslon, William,** 1692–1766, English TYPE designer. His individual letters were less impressive than those of BASKERVILLE or BODONI, but were regular, legible, and of sensitive proportion. His typefaces were used for most important printed works c.1740 to c.1800; some are still in use.

**Caspar:** see WISE MEN OF THE EAST.

**Caspian Sea,** world's largest lake, c.373,000 km² (144,000 sq mi) in the USSR and Iran, on the traditional border between Europe and Asia. The salty lake is 28 m (92 ft) below sea level and reaches a maximum depth of 980 m (3200 ft) in the south. More than 75% of its waters are derived from the VOLGA R., whose flow is now diminished by dams and lakes. Beluga caviar is a major product of the shallow waters in the north. BAKU and Astrakhan are the chief ports.

**Cassander,** 358–297 BC, king of MACEDON (r.316–297 BC); one of the DIADOCHI. The son of ANTIPATER, he deposed the regent, Polyperchon. To consolidate his power, he procured the murder (316) of OLYMPIAS, mother of ALEXANDER THE GREAT, and (311) of Alexander's widow, Roxana, and their son; he married Alexander's half-sister, Thessalonica (316). One of a coalition that defeated Antigonus and DEMETRIUS I at Ipsus (301), he ruled Macedonia and Greece.

**Cassandra,** in Greek mythology, Trojan princess; daughter of Priam and HECUBA. She was given the power of prophecy by APOLLO, but when she spurned him he decreed that she should never be believed. A slave of AGAMEMNON after the TROJAN WAR, she was killed with him by CLYTEMNESTRA.

**Cassatt, Mary,** 1845–1926, American painter. Most of her life was spent in France, where she became a member of the Impressionist group (see IMPRESSIONISM). Her paintings are simple, vigorous, and pleasing in colour. Cassatt's favourite subject was motherhood, e.g., versions of *Mother and Child* (Metropolitan Mus., New York; Mus. Fine Arts, Boston). She also excelled in etching and PASTELS.

**cassava** or **manioc,** plant (genus *Manihot*) of the SPURGE family, native to Brazil. The roots are the source of cassava starch, cassava flour, and tapioca; they are also fermented to make an alcoholic beverage and have other uses. The raw roots of bitter cassava (*M. esculenta*), chief source of cassava flour, contain potentially lethal amounts of prussic acid, which must be dispelled in preparation. Sweet cassava roots contain less acid and can be eaten raw. Cassava is the dominant staple food in Africa.

**Cassini, Gian Domenico,** 1625–1712, Italian–French astronomer. He determined rotational periods for the planets Jupiter, Mars, and Venus, discovered four of Saturn's satellites, and studied the division in Saturn's ring system that is named after him. He and three generations of descendants directed the Royal Observatory in Paris from its founding (1669) to the time (1793) of the French Revolution.

**Cassiopeia,** in Greek mythology: see ANDROMEDA.

**Cassirer, Ernst,** 1874–1945, German philosopher. A neo-Kantian, he devoted himself, in *Substance and Function* (1910), to a critical–historical study of the problem of knowledge. In *Philosophy of Symbolic Forms* (3 vol., 1923–29) he characterized the human being as a 'symbolic animal', holding that all cultural achievements (including language, art, myth, and science) are the result of the human ability to conceptualize experience in artificial signs, or symbols.

**Cassius,** ancient Roman family. **Quintus Cassius Longinus,** d. 45 BC, served with ANTONY as a tribune, and in 49 BC they vetoed the attempts of the senate to deprive Julius CAESAR of his army. Cassius died in a shipwreck. The best-known family member was **Caius Cassius Longinus,** d. 42 BC, leader in the successful conspiracy to assassinate Julius Caesar on the Ides of March in 44 BC. When the people were aroused by Antony against the conspirators, Cassius went to Syria and joined Marcus Junius Brutus (see BRUTUS, family); Antony and Octavian (later AUGUSTUS) met them in battle at Philippi in 42 BC. In the first engagement, Cassius, thinking the battle lost, committed suicide.

**Cassius Dio** or **Dio Cassius** (Claudius Cassius Dio Cocceianus), fl. late 2nd–early 3rd cents. AD, Greek historian of Rome. A native of Bithynia (on the S shore of the Black Sea), he became a Roman senator, and wrote a history of Rome from the beginning to AD 229, much of which survives. Uneven in quality, it still preserves valuable information.

**Casson, Sir Hugh,** 1910–, English architect. He came into prominence as director of architecture for the Festival of Britain in 1951, coordinating the work of young architects designing pavilions for the exhibition on the South Bank in London. Informal and cheerful, rich with colour and plants, and unusual in shape, these buildings popularized the modern movement in architecture in Great Britain and introduced a new liveliness into the drab environment that survived World War II. He has designed many civic and academic buildings, e.g., in Cambridge Univ. He was the professor of environmental design (1953–75) and provost (1980–86) at the Royal College of Art, London and President of the Royal Academy of Art (1971–84).

**cassowary,** flightless forest BIRD of Australia and the Malay Archipelago, standing 175 cm (about 6 ft) tall. The plumage is dark and glossy, with a brilliantly-coloured head and neck. Nocturnal and mostly herbivorous, they are fast runners. Cassowaries are wary birds, rarely seen. The male, which incubates the eggs, has a long claw on the inner toe of each foot. One recorded story of a youth being killed by a threatened cassowary has led to tales of the birds being vicious killers.

**Castagno, Andrea del,** c.1423–57, Florentine painter. One of the leading artists to follow Masaccio, his art is distinguished by its energy and passion. In c.1445 he began the Passion of Christ cycle for the church of Sant' Apollonia in Florence. Best known of these scenes is *The Last Supper* with its harsh perspective and metallic light.

**castanets:** see PERCUSSION INSTRUMENT.

**Castel Branco, Camilo,** 1825–90, Portuguese writer. Many of his novels, e.g., *Where is happiness?* (1856), are based on incidents in his colourful and scandalous life. He also wrote historical and satirical novels. Always popular for his narrative accomplishment, he was made a viscount in 1885. He committed suicide when his sight failed him.

**Castellón de la Plana,** city (1981 pop. 126,464), capital of the province of the same name, Valencia, E Spain. The population of Castellón moved from a hill-top site to the plain in the 13th cent., giving the city its modern name. Oranges are extensively grown.

Andrea del **Castagno**, *The Last Supper*. Sant'Appolonia, Florence.

**Castelo Branco, Humberto** (kəsh‚teeloo‚brangkoo), 1900–67, president of BRAZIL (1964–67). An army officer, he helped to oust (1964) Pres. Goulart in a coup and became provisional president. He curtailed political freedoms but imposed economic reforms that spurred the country's growth.

**caste system,** type of social organization found particularly in the Indian subcontinent. A caste system is characterized by the existence of corporate, ranked, closed social groups, members of which share common descent, are restricted to certain specified occupations, and practise endogamous marriage (see ENDOGAMY). Hindu ideology states that each caste (*jati*) shares certain physical substances which can be polluting to members of other castes. Caste boundaries have therefore to be controlled, ordered, and maintained by correct conduct. Caste conduct is most strictly enforced in connection with appropriate in-marriage, the consumption of food, and the organization of service relationships between castes. The term caste is also used loosely to refer to any very rigidly demarcated social group.

**Castiglione, Baldassare, Count** (kastil‚yohnay), 1478–1529, Italian writer and diplomat. His dialogues *Libro del cortegiano* (1528; tr. The Courtier) discuss the qualifications for the perfect courtier and contributed to a Renaissance ideal of aristocracy embodied in the life of Sir Philip SIDNEY.

**Castile,** region and former kingdom, central and N Spain, traditionally divided into Old Castile (N) and New Castile (S). It is a vast, generally underdeveloped area surrounding the highly industrialized city of MADRID. In Old Castile grains are grown and sheep raised. The fertile areas, especially in New Castile, produce olive oil and grapes. Castile became a kingdom in 1035 and was united with LEÓN in 1230. Castilian kings were prominent in the fight against the MOORS, from whom they wrested New Castile. The privileges of the nobles were limited by PETER THE CRUEL (r.1350–69). In 1479 a personal union of Castile and ARAGÓN was established by ISABELLA I of Castile and her husband, Spanish King FERDINAND V. Castile was the core of the Spanish monarchy, centralized in Madrid (the capital after 1561).

**casting** or **founding,** the shaping of METAL by melting and pouring into a mould. Most castings are made in sand moulds. Sand, mixed with a binder to hold it together, is pressed around a wooden pattern that leaves a cavity in the sand. Molten metal is poured into the cavity and allowed to solidify. *Investment casting* is used for small, complex shapes. Wax or plastic replicas of the parts are covered with sand in a box. When the whole mould is heated, the replica melts, leaving behind a cavity into which the metal is poured. *Die casting,* in which molten metal is forced under pressure into metal moulds, is used to make large numbers of small, precise parts with metals of low melting points.

**cast iron,** form of IRON made from pig iron remelted in a small cupola furnace and poured into moulds to make castings. It usually contains from 2% to 6% carbon, and scrap iron or steel is often added to vary the composition. Cast iron is used extensively to make machine parts, engine cylinder blocks, stoves, pipes, radiators, and many other products.

**castle,** fortified dwelling characteristic of the Middle Ages. In the 9th cent. feudal lords began to develop private fortress-residences suitable to conditions of endemic warfare and housing both the lords and their retainers and families. The castle of W Europe was a Norman creation, an outgrowth of the 10th- and 11th-cent. mound or motte castle, which was essentially an artificial mound of earth (a motte), surrounded by a ditch, and surmounted by a blockhouse and palisade. Until the 12th cent., the only English development was the addition of a masonry keep inside the

palisade, e.g., the TOWER OF LONDON. As sieges became more successful provisions for effective defence were needed. Outer masonry walls came into use, with gates, flanking towers, and earthworks. Subterranean passages and curving walls were developed. Castles were, in general, designed for security rather than comfort. Defenders operated from galleries on top of the walls during a siege; with successive series of defences, the loss of one did not mean complete defeat, as those inside could retreat until they were within the keep. Gunpowder and the development of artillery rendered the castle obsolete. It was replaced by the manor house, but its effect on architecture continues to the present day.

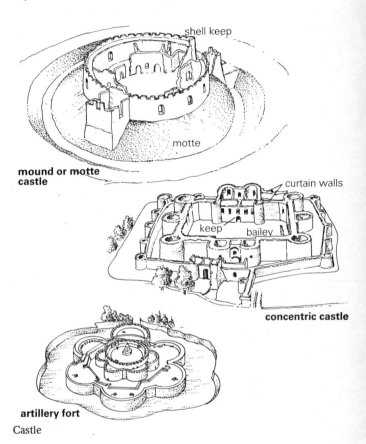

Castle

**Castlebar,** county town (1986 pop. 6349) of Co. Mayo, Republic of Ireland, at E end of Castlebar Lough. It is a small market town.

**Castle Hill uprising,** a rebellion of Irish convicts at Castle Hill, near Sydney, Australia, in 1804. The rebels were defeated and eight of them executed. This was the first battle between Europeans in Australia and left a lasting fear of a convict uprising.

**Castlereagh, Robert Stewart, 2nd Viscount** (‚kahsəlray), 1769–1822, British statesman; b. Ireland. As acting chief secretary for Ireland, he was responsible for suppressing the French-aided rebellion of 1798 and for the Act of Union of 1800. He was secretary of war (1805–06, 1807–09) during the wars with NAPOLEON I, coordinating British land and sea power and, after early disasters in the PENINSULAR WAR, putting the duke of WELLINGTON in command. He resigned (1809) after what he considered to be a political betrayal by George CANNING (with whom he fought a duel). As foreign secretary (1812–22), he helped form the 'concert of Europe' against Napoleon, later confirmed by the QUADRUPLE ALLIANCE. He advocated a moderate peace settlement for France, and was a dominant figure at the Congress of VIENNA. A great statesman abroad, Castlereagh was never popular at home. He committed suicide in 1822.

**Castor and Pollux,** in classical mythology, twin heroes called the Dioscuri; Castor was the son of LEDA and Tyndareus, Pollux the son of Leda and ZEUS; they hatched from a single egg. Castor was a skilled horseman, Pollux a boxer. They were famous warriors, noted for their devotion to each other. In one legend, Zeus created the constellation

Gemini in their honour. Patrons of mariners, the Dioscuri were especially honoured by the Romans.

**castrato:** see VOICE.

**Castries,** city (1981 pop. 50,000), capital of SAINT LUCIA.

**Castriota, George:** see SCANDERBEG.

**Castro, Fidel,** 1926–, Cuban revolutionary and premier of CUBA (1959-). He opposed the BATISTA dictatorship and unsuccessfully attacked an army post on 26 July 1953. After being imprisoned and released (1955), he went to Mexico, where he organized the 26th of July revolutionary movement. He invaded (1956) SE Cuba and, with his brother Raúl, 'Che' GUEVARA, and nine other rebels, hid out in the Sierra Maestra Mountains, from where they attracted supporters and fought a guerrilla campaign that toppled (1959) Batista. A brilliant propagandist and charismatic orator, Castro declared himself a Marxist–Leninist, nationalized industry, confiscated foreign-owned property, collectivized agriculture, and increasingly depended on the economic assistance of the Soviet Union. He weathered the severance of economic and political ties by the US and Latin American nations, the BAY OF PIGS INVASION (1961), a US economic blockade, and the CUBAN MISSILE CRISIS (1962). He has supported revolutionary movements in other Latin American countries and in Africa, and he has remained the symbol of revolution and social change in Latin America, despite the economic failures of his regime.

**Castro, Inés de,** or **Inez de Castro,** d. 1355, Spanish noblewoman at the Portuguese court. Her love affair with the crown prince, Dom Pedro (later PETER I), ended in tragedy; she bore him four children but was murdered with the connivance of his father ALFONSO IV to preserve the legitimate succession to the throne. Her life has been a favourite theme of Portuguese and Spanish writers.

**cat,** carnivorous MAMMAL of the family Felidae, including the domestic cat (*Felis catus*), the great cats, e.g., LION, TIGER, LEOPARD, and CHEETAH, and the smaller wild cats, e.g., the LYNX and the European wild cat (*F. sylvestris*). Highly adapted for hunting by sight and sound, cats have flexible, well-coordinated, muscular bodies, short muzzles, and rounded faces with large eyes and highly sensitive whiskers. Their retractile claws are used in holding prey and in climbing. Cats have very acute hearing in the high-frequency range, and their eyes are specially adapted to low light intensities. Lions and cheetahs live in groups called prides, but most other species are solitary. Domestic cats are about 70 cm (27 in) long, including a 24 cm (10 in) tail, and weigh up to about 7 kg (15 lb). They are thought to have been domesticated in ancient Egypt, and are derived from the African bushcat (*F. libica*), with some European wild cat admixture. The domestic cat is more similar to its wild ancestors in both form and behaviour than is the case with the DOG, and often retains complete independence from humans, e.g., on farms. Breeds have been selected, mostly short-haired, with a range of coat colours. Siamese cats have pure white kittens turning to pale fawn when adult, with dark brown ears, nose, mouth, feet, and tail, and with intensely blue eyes. Abyssinian cats have reddish-brown coats with dark banding on each hair, and large yellow eyes. The Russian blue has a soft, seal-like coat of bright blue-grey, and green eyes. The Persian is a very popular breed, of a range of coat colours with long, silky hair, prominent neck ruffs, and a bushy tail. Other breeds include the Burmese, which is related to the Persian, the Cyprus, and the Rex. The Manx cat, not native to the Isle of Man but originating in the Far East, is tailless, and its hind legs are longer than the forelegs, giving it a typical stance. Most breeds are sexually mature at about 10 months. The breeding season is mainly December to March, but may extend through to summer. The gestation period is about 65 days, and commonly up to 8 kittens are born, blind and deaf, and with little hair. The eyes open at between 4 and 10 days. The cat was sacred in ancient Egypt, and has been associated with witchcraft and magic in many cultures.

**catacombs,** large underground vaults and galleries serving as cemeteries for early Christians, who did not follow the Greek and Roman practice of cremation. They were built in Italy, N Africa, Asia Minor, and other Christian areas from the 1st to the 5th cent. AD. The main ones, outside the city gates of Rome, lie from 7 to 20 m (22 to 65 ft) below ground and occupy 240 hectares (600 acres) of space in multilevel passages lined with tiers of niches for bodies. Plaster walls and ceilings were frescoed. Goths and later invaders plundered the catacombs; by the 8th cent. most bodies had been transferred to churches and the labyrinths

forgotten. Rediscovery began in 1578, and preservation is now controlled by the papacy.

**Catalan language,** member of the Romance group of the Italic subfamily of the Indo-European family of languages. See LANGUAGE (table).

**Çatal Hüyük,** a town on the Konya plain in Anatolia, Turkey, dating from the 7th millennium BC. It was a thriving agricultural and trade centre with specialized production in prestige crafts such as obsidian flaking and polishing. Its secular and sacred architecture were remarkable. Houses were packed together like cells, requiring access through the roof. The many shrines had walls with elaborate paintings and relief carvings and contained displays of bull horns and skulls.

Çatal Hüyük

**catalogue,** descriptive list of the contents of a library, displayed on cards, in a book, on microfilm, or on-line (see COMPUTER). ASSURBANIPAL'S library at Nineveh was catalogued on shelves of slate. The first known subject catalogue was compiled by CALLIMACHUS at the library in ALEXANDRIA (3rd cent. BC). An early union catalogue of British monastic libraries was compiled in 1472. In the 19th cent. Sir Anthony PANIZZI began the printing of the British Museum Catalogue; Charles Cutter devised the modern dictionary catalogue (with author, title, and subject entries arranged in one alphabet); and Melvil DEWEY devised his decimal classification system. In 1901 the US Library of Congress began to print its catalogue entries on small cards, distributing them to other libraries inexpensively and thus providing libraries with a standardized format, call numbers, and subject headings. Libraries are now cooperating in networks to develop computerized cataloguing systems that will offer a more extensive and efficient catalogue with a greater variety of formats and access points.

**Catalonia,** region, NE Spain, stretching from the Pyrenees at the French border southward along the Mediterranean Sea. BARCELONA is the historic capital. Catalonia produces one third of Spanish wines; grows olives and grains; and manufactures textiles, cars, aeroplanes, and other products. The counts of Barcelona emerged (9th cent.) as the most powerful lords of the region, and in 1137 Catalonia was united with ARAGÓN. In the 13th and 14th cent. Catalan traders rivalled those of GENOA and VENICE. Catalonia briefly won autonomy in the 1930s; in 1980 regional autonomy was restored.

**catalpa:** see BIGNONIA.

**catalyst,** term first used by BERZELIUS to describe a substance that causes a change in the rate of a chemical reaction without itself being consumed by the reaction. Catalysts, which work by changing a reaction's activation energy, or minimum energy needed for the reaction to occur, are used in numerous industrial processes. Substances that increase the reaction rate are called positive catalysts, or simply catalysts, whereas substances that decrease the reaction rate are called negative catalysts, or inhibitors. The presence of a small amount of an acid or base may catalyse some reactions. Finely divided metals (e.g., platinum, copper, iron, palladium, rhodium) or metal oxides (e.g., silicon dioxide, vanadium oxide) may also serve as catalysts. Certain ZEOLITES catalyse the decomposition (cracking) of PETROLEUM; others the synthesis of petrol from methanol. Biological catalysts are called ENZYMES.

'**Cat and Mouse Act**', name by which the Prisoners, Temporary Discharge for Health, Act (1913) was known. It was introduced by the Liberal government of Herbert ASQUITH in response to the hunger strikes of suffragettes in prison. It freed them while making them liable for re-arrest once they had recovered their health. See WOMEN'S SOCIAL AND POLITICAL UNION.

**Catánia**, city (1984 pop. 377,707), Italy, on E coast of SICILY. It is principally a market and commercial centre, with an old-established university (1445), and cultural and administrative activities. Founded as a Greek colony (Katane) in the 8th cent. BC, it was captured by the Romans in 263 BC. Lying on the southern slopes of ETNA, it has suffered damage from earthquakes and lava flows, and it was largely rebuilt to a formal plan in the early 18th cent. Historic buildings include the Greek theatre and a 13th-cent. Germanic castle.

**cataract**, opacity of the lens of the EYE, causing gradual, painless loss of sight. It is the greatest single cause of BLINDNESS worldwide. Most commonly caused by aging, cataracts may also be congenital or result from eye inflammations, injury, or certain diseases, such as DIABETES. Cataracts are treated by surgical removal of the lens, implantation of an artificial lens, and the use of corrective lenses.

**catastrophism**, originally, the outdated geological doctrine that the physical features of the earth's surface, e.g., mountains and valleys, were formed during violent worldwide cataclysms, e.g., earthquakes and floods. This theory, easily correlated with religious beliefs, was systematized by Georges CUVIER, who argued that all living things were destroyed and replaced with wholly different forms during these cataclysmic events. In the 18th cent. the doctrine was attacked by James HUTTON, who advanced the doctrine of UNIFORMITARIANISM. Geologists now use the term *catastrophe* to refer to a more localized, relatively milder event in earth history.

**catchment area** or **drainage basin**, area drained by a stream or other water body. The amount of water reaching a RIVER, reservoir, or LAKE from its catchment area depends on the size of the area, amount of precipitation, and loss through evaporation and absorption.

**Cateau-Cambrésis, Treaty of:** see ITALIAN WARS.

**catechism**, originally oral instruction in religion, later written instruction. Catechisms, usually in the form of questions and answers, were used for the instruction of converts and children. Famous catechisms include the Lutheran Small Catechism (1529), the Anglican catechism contained in the BOOK OF COMMON PRAYER, the Presbyterian Westminster Catechism (1647), and for Roman Catholics the recent Dutch Catechism.

**catecholamine**, any of several structurally related compounds occurring naturally in the body that help regulate the sympathetic NERVOUS SYSTEM. They include ADRENALINE, NORADRENALINE, and dopamine substances that prepare the body to meet emergencies such as cold, fatigue, and shock. Synthetic catecholamines are used as drugs to treat diseases such as EMPHYSEMA, BRONCHITIS, and ASTHMA.

**categorical imperative:** see KANT, IMMANUEL.

**caterpillar:** see BUTTERFLY.

**catfish**, freshwater fishes of the family Siluridae with barbels, or whiskers, around a broad mouth, fleshy, rayless posterior fins, scaleless skin, and sharp defensive spines on the pectoral and dorsal fins. The wels or European catfish (*Silurus glanis*) lives in the rivers of E Europe and W Asia. Catfish range in size from about 5 cm (2 in) to 4 m (13 ft) or more. Omnivorous feeders and scavengers, they are important food fish and are raised on fish farms. The related marine catfish of the family Ariidae are mouth breeders. Other marine catfish have poisonous spines.

**cathedral**, church in which a bishop presides, regardless of size or magnificence. Romanesque cathedrals (see ROMANESQUE ARCHITECTURE AND ART) were massive, domed, heavily vaulted structures based on the BASILICA form, reflecting the style dominant in Europe from c.1050 to c.1200. The tall, wide nave was flanked by narrow side aisles, crossed by transepts, and illuminated by a clerestory pierced with small windows. The great cathedrals of the 13th and 14th cent. are the crowning achievement of GOTHIC ARCHITECTURE AND ART. These buildings were elaborated to house the liturgical life of the Church and are distinctive in their use of the ribbed VAULT, pointed ARCH, ROSE WINDOW, BUTTRESS, geometric tracery, and STAINED GLASS, combined in a rich and complex design. In the intricacy of the glass, exterior facade, and buttresses, the building's structure is expressed through elaborate detail. Among the most important cathedrals are: *France* Amiens, Beauvais, Chartres, Notre-Dame de Paris, Rheims, Rouen; *England* Canterbury, Durham, Ely, Winchester, York; *Germany* Cologne, Ulm; *Belgium* Louvain; *Italy* Florence, Milan; *Spain* Ávila, Toledo; *Sweden* Lund, Uppsala. A noted modern adaptation of the form is at Coventry, England (1962) by Sir Basil SPENCE. Later cathedrals are more revolutionary in plan and designed for community worship, e.g., the cathedral in Brasília (1970) designed by Oscar NIEMEYER.

**Cather, Willa Sibert**, 1876–1947, American author. She was reared in Nebraska, the setting of her first major novel, *O Pioneers!* (1913). She also celebrated frontier settlers in such novels as *My Ántonia* (1918) and *A Lost Lady* (1923). Another Cather theme, the artist's need for freedom from inhibiting influences, is important in *The Song of the Lark* (1915) and *Lucy Gayheart* (1935). Cather later turned to the North American past for *Death Comes for the Archbishop* (1927), considered her masterpiece, and *Shadows on the Rock* (1931). In both novels she blended history and religion with loving characterizations. She also wrote short stories, collected in *Youth and the Bright Medusa* (1920) and others, and several essays on fiction. Her own fiction—clear, charming, and stately in style—is considered among the finest in 20th-cent. American literature.

**Catherine**, czarinas of Russia. **Catherine I**, 1683?–1727 (r.1725–27), was born Martha Skavronskaya, a Livonian peasant. She became the mistress of MENSHIKOV, an advisor to PETER I, and then of Peter, who married her in 1712 and had her crowned czarina in 1724. When he died without naming a successor she was raised to the throne by Menshikov, who dominated her rule. PETER II succeeded her; her daughter ELIZABETH became czarina in 1741. **Catherine II** or **Catherine the Great**, 1729–96 (r.1762–96), b. Princess Sophie of Anhalt-Zerbst, married the future PETER III in 1744. She became thoroughly Russian and was popular with powerful groups opposed to her eccentric husband. In June 1762, conspirators headed by Grigori Orlov, her lover, deposed Peter and proclaimed her ruler; shortly afterwards Peter was murdered. Catherine's rule began with projects of reform, but after the peasant uprising led by PUGACHEV (1773–74) and the FRENCH REVOLUTION she strengthened serfdom and increased the privileges of the nobility within a system of provinces that survived until 1917. Her foreign policy was imperialistic: she increased Russian control of the Baltic provinces and Ukraine; began colonization of Alaska; annexed the Crimea and in two wars with Turkey made Russia dominant in the Near East; and secured for Russia the major share in the partitions of Poland (1772, 1793, 1795). A patron of art and literature, she corresponded with VOLTAIRE and other French thinkers, and wrote memoirs, comedies, and stories. Of her many lovers, only Orlov and POTEMKIN influenced her policies. Her son, PAUL I, succeeded her.

**Catherine de' Medici**, 1519–89, queen consort of HENRY II of France, daughter of Lorenzo de' MEDICI, duke of Urbino. Married in 1533, she was neglected in the reigns of Henry and her eldest son, FRANCIS II, but was regent (1560–63) and adviser (1563–74) for her son CHARLES IX. At first conciliatory toward the French Protestants, she later viewed their political demands as dangerous. HENRY III was her son.

**Catherine of Braganza**, 1638–1705, queen of CHARLES II of England; daughter of JOHN I of Portugal. Her dowry included Bombay and Tangier. A Roman Catholic, she was never popular. Titus OATES accused her unfairly of plotting to poison the king, but Charles protected her. After his death, she returned home and acted as regent for her brother, PETER II.

**Catherine of Siena, Saint**, 1347–80, Italian DOMINICAN, mystic and diplomat, Doctor of the Church. In response to a vision she entered public life and in 1376 influenced Pope GREGORY XI to end the 'Babylonian captivity' of the PAPACY and return to Rome. She was later papal ambassador to Florence. Catherine caused a spiritual revival almost everywhere she went, and her mysticism contains an overwhelming love of God and humanity. She dictated *The Dialogue,* a notable mystical work. Feast: 29 Apr.

**Catherine of Valois**, 1401–37, queen consort of HENRY V of England; mother of HENRY VI; daughter of CHARLES VI of France. Some time after Henry V's death (1422), she married Owen TUDOR. The Tudor kings descended from them.

**Catherine the Great** (Catherine II): see CATHERINE, czarinas of Russia.

**cathode:** see ELECTRODE.

**cathode-ray tube,** ELECTRON TUBE in which electrons are accelerated by high-voltage anodes, formed into a beam by focusing ELECTRODES, and projected toward a phosphorescent screen that forms the face of the tube. The electron beam leaves a bright spot wherever it strikes the screen. To form the screen display, or image, the electron beam is deflected in the vertical and horizontal directions either by the electrostatic effect of electrodes within the tube or by magnetic fields produced by coils located around the neck of the tube. Some cathode-ray tubes, as those for a COMPUTER TERMINAL, OSCILLOSCOPE, or TELEVISION receiver, can produce multiple beam of electrons and have phosphor screens that are capable of displaying more than one colour. See also RADAR.

**Catholic Emancipation,** term applied to the process by which Roman Catholics in the British Isles were relieved of civil disabilities, dating back to HENRY VIII. In 1791 most of the disabilities in Great Britain were repealed. Agitation in Ireland, led by Daniel O'CONNELL, resulted in the Catholic Emancipation Act (1829), which lifted most other restrictions.

**Catiline** (Lucius Sergius Catilina), c.108–62 BC, Roman politician and conspirator. In 66 BC he was barred from candidacy for the consulship by accusations of misconduct in office, charges that later proved false. Feeling with some justification that he had been cheated, he concocted a wild plot to murder the consuls. He and the other conspirators were acquitted (65 BC). When in 63 BC he ran again for consul, he found CICERO, the incumbent, and the conservative party anxious to stop his election at any cost. Catiline was defeated, prompting him to try for the consulship by force. Learning of the plot, Cicero arrested the conspirators still in Rome, but Catiline had fled. On 5 Dec. they were condemned to death and executed, in spite of an appeal from Julius CAESAR to use moderation. Catiline did not surrender; he fell in battle at Pistoia a month later.

**cation:** see under ION.

**catnip** or **catmint,** strong-scented perennial herb (*Nepeta cataria*) of the MINT family, native to Europe and Asia. Catnip, best known for its stimulating effect on cats, is also used to make a home-remedy tea for use in gastrointestinal complaints. The garden form is a hybrid (*N. x Faassenii*).

**Cato the Elder** or **Cato the Censor** (Marcus Porcius Cato), 234–149 BC, Roman statesman and moralist. He fought in the Second PUNIC WAR and later served as consul (195) and censor (184). Cato the Elder was renowned for his devotion to the old Roman ideals simplicity of life, honesty, and courage. He told the senate to destroy Carthage and thus helped to bring on the Third Punic War, in which Carthage was destroyed. He also wrote many works, most of which are now lost. **Cato the Younger** or **Cato of Utica** (Marcus Porcius Cato), 95–46 BC, Roman statesman, was the great-grandson of Cato the Elder. He showed an intense devotion to the principles of the early republic. He had one of the greatest reputations for honesty and incorruptibility of any man in ancient times, and his Stoicism put him above the graft and bribery of his day. His politics were extremely conservative. Thus he opposed Julius CAESAR and supported POMPEY. After Pompey's defeat at Pharsalia in 48 BC, Cato went to Africa to continue the struggle and took command at Utica. When Caesar clearly had gained power, Cato committed suicide, bidding his people make their peace with Caesar.

**CAT scan:** see COMPUTERIZED AXIAL TOMOGRAPHY.

**Catt, Carrie Chapman,** 1859–1947, American suffragist. As an organizer and president (from 1900) of the National American Woman Suffrage Association, she campaigned for a constitutional amendment on WOMEN'S SUFFRAGE. When the 19th amendment to the US CONSTITUTION passed (1920), she organized the League of Women Voters and later worked for the peace movement.

**cattail** or **reed mace,** perennial herb (genus *Typha*), found in open marshes. Cattails have long, narrow leaves and one tall stem with tiny male flowers above the female flowers. Pollinated female flowers form the familiar cylindrical spike of fuzzy brown fruits; the male flowers drop off. The starchy rootstocks are edible.

**cattle** ruminant MAMMALS, genus *Bos*, especially the domesticated species *B. taurus*. Western domestic cattle are descended from the wild auroch, *B. primigenius*, which was hunted to extinction by the mid 17th cent. In India fossil remains suggest that a form of the wild auroch *B. primigenius namadicus* gave rise to the humped ZEBU cattle, *B. indicus*,

widespread in India and Africa, and kept in small numbers elsewhere. European breeds of cattle are in general unsuccessful in most parts of Africa as they are subject to diseases such as sleeping sickness. Several species of cattle are of great economic importance in E Asia, such as the YAK and the water buffalo. With European cattle the grown male is called a bull; the grown female, a cow; an infant, a calf; a female which has not given birth, a heifer; and a young castrated male is called a steer. A grown castrated male, used for draught purposes, is called an ox, although this term is sometimes loosely used. Cattle are often selectively bred for meat (beef), for dairying, and in many societies, for use as a draught animal. Beef breeds include the hornless Aberdeen Angus, an ancient Scottish breed; the Hereford, originally developed for ploughing; the Charolais, from central and SE France; and the picturesque horned West Highland cattle of Scotland. Dairy breeds include the Ayrshire; the Jersey and Guernsey both from the Channel Islands; the Holstein–Friesian from Holland; and the Brown Swiss. The Brahman (Brahma) cattle of India are ZEBU, and are sacred to the Hindu, who is not allowed to harm or to sell them. Many cattle of continental Europe are general-purpose, e.g., the Simmental, of Austria, the Switz, and the Charolais are used for beef, milk, and also as draught animals. Large areas of central and E Africa, and W and E Asia do not produce milk and the adult humans living there are in general unable to digest LACTOSE, which ferments in the digestive tract, causing pain.

**Cattleya,** brilliant-flowered genus of ORCHIDS of Brazilian origin. They are much used for hybridization by orchid breeders.

**Catullus** (Caius Valerius Catullus), 84?–54? BC, Roman poet, one of the greatest LYRIC poets. His poems, addressed to the faithless Lesbia, his friend Juventius, and others, include elegies (see ELEGY), EPIGRAMS, an epyllion (minor epic), and other pieces and range from gay and tender to obscenely derisive. 'On the Death of Lesbia's Sparrow' is well known.

**Caucasian** and **Caucasoid:** see RACE.

**Caucasian languages,** family of languages spoken by about five million people in the CAUCASUS region of the USSR. See LANGUAGE (table).

**Caucasus,** great mountain system, SW USSR, extending c.1210 km (750 mi) between the Black and Caspian seas, forming part of the traditional border between Europe and Asia. Mt ELBRUS (5633 m/18,481 ft) is the highest peak. The mountains are usually divided into N Caucasia, a region of semiarid northern slopes, and the southern slopes of Transcaucasia. The Caucasus are inhabited by a great variety of ethnic and linguistic groups, including Armenians, Georgians, and Azerbaijani in the S and Ossetians, Circassians, and Dagestani in the N. Russia gained control in the 19th cent. after a series of wars with Persia (now Iran) and Turkey. Oil is a major resource.

**Cauchy, Augustin Louis, Baron,** 1789–1857, prolific French mathematician who did influential work in every branch of MATHEMATICS. In CALCULUS, he propounded the notion of continuity, gave the first adequate definition of the definite integral as a limit of sums, and defined improper integrals. Cauchy provided the first comprehensive theory of complex numbers (see NUMBER), established fundamental theorems on complex functions, published the first comprehensive treatise on determinants (see MATRIX) and founded the mathematical theory of elasticity.

**Caulfield, Patrick,** 1936–, British painter. He was influenced by POP ART and artists like Roy LICHTENSTEIN. As well as popular illustrations, he developed a style in which interiors, still lifes, etc. were drawn in regular black outlines on flat coloured grounds and coloured in with bright unmodulated colour.

**cauliflower,** variety of CABBAGE (var. *botrytis*), with an edible head of condensed flowers and stems. Another cultivation of the same variety is broccoli. Both have been grown since Roman times.

**Cavafy, Constantine,** 1863–1933, Greek poet; b. Egypt. He lived most of his life in Alexandria. The background of his poetry is a mythic, Hellenistic world peopled with historical and imaginary figures. Many of his poems treat homosexual love. Although his output was small (about 150 poems), Cavafy is ranked among the great modern Greek poets.

**cavalry,** mounted troops trained to fight from horseback. In use since the time of the ancient Hittites, horsemen remained at a disadvantage against well-disciplined INFANTRY until the introduction (4th cent. AD) of the saddle. In medieval Europe the mounted KNIGHT became the typical warrior. Despite the invention of SMALL ARMS, cavalry remained important in warfare until the end of the 19th cent. The elite of the fighting forces in Europe, it was often recruited from the nobility and landed gentry. On the African, US, and British Indian frontiers the cavalry's mobility was essential against the lightly armed natives (the French used some camel cavalry in N Africa), but its value was drastically diminished by the development of rapid-fire rifles and machine guns. It was ultimately superseded by mobile TANK units in World War II.

**Cavan,** county (1986 pop. 53,881), 1872 km² (730 sq mi), N of Republic of Ireland, bordering on Northern Ireland in the N. It is in the province of Ulster. The county town is CAVAN. Most of the land in the NE and SW is hilly, rising to 667 m (2188 ft) in Mt Cuilcagh in the NW. The main rivers are the Erne and the Annalee. There are several loughs, and much of the low-lying areas are boggy and infertile. Potato-farming and the rearing of cattle and pigs are the most important economic activities.

**Cavan,** county town (1986 pop. 3341) of Co. Cavan, in N of Republic of Ireland, located near Lough Oughter. It is a small market town with a modern Roman Catholic cathedral. There is a ruined Dominican abbey.

**cave,** a hollow in earth or ROCK. Caves are formed by the chemical and mechanical action of water on soluble rock, by volcanic activity (the formation of large gas pockets in lava or the melting of ice under lava), and by earthquakes. LIMESTONE formations, because of their solubility, almost invariably have caves, some notable for their STALACTITES AND STALAGMITES. See also SPELEOLOGY.

**cave art:** see PALAEOLITHIC ART; ROCK CARVINGS AND PAINTINGS.

**Cavell, Edith** (ˌkavəl), 1865–1915, English nurse. The matron of a hospital in Brussels in WORLD WAR I, she was shot by the Germans for aiding Allied prisoners.

**Cavendish, Henry,** 1731–1810, English physicist and chemist; b. France. He determined the specific heats for numerous substances (although these heat constants were not recognized until later), did research on the composition of water and air, and studied the properties of a gas that he isolated and described as 'inflammable air' (later named HYDROGEN). In a now-famous experiment (1798), he determined the value of the proportionality constant in Newton's law of GRAVITATION.

**Cavendish, Margaret, duchess of Newcastle,** 1623–1773, English writer of plays, philosophical and scientific prose, tales, and verse. Writing and publishing during the CIVIL WAR, Cavendish was regarded by contemporaries as an eccentric. Nevertheless, she was invited to attend the ROYAL SOCIETY after her reputation became established. Until recently she was best known for her biography of her husband, the duke of Newcastle, but she published extensively: *Poems and Fancies* (1653), *Playes* (1662), and her writings on science in both *Philosophical Fancies* (1653) and *Philosophical and Physical Opinions* (1655).

**Cavour, Camillo Benso, conte di,** 1810–61, Italian statesman, premier of Sardinia (1852–59, 1860–61). Cavour introduced liberal internal reforms and for domestic reasons involved Sardinia in the CRIMEAN WAR. He was a skilful politician and became the chief architect of Italian unification under VICTOR EMMANUEL II (see RISORGIMENTO).

**Caxton, William,** c.1421–91, English printer, the first to print books in English. Apprenticed as a mercer, he was later a diplomat, and learned printing in Cologne, Germany, in 1471–72. At Bruges, Belgium (1475), he printed with Colard Mansion *The Recuyell of the Historyes of Troye,* the first book printed in English. At Westminster (1477) he printed *Dictes or Sayengis of the Philosophres,* the first dated book printed in England. He is known to have printed about 100 books, having translated about one-third of them himself.

**Cayenne,** city (1982 pop. 38,135), capital of FRENCH GUIANA, on Cayenne Island. It exports timber and rum, and gives its name to cayenne pepper, found on the island. Founded (1643) by France, it was held (1808–16) by Britain and Portugal. Many residents are descended from inmates of French prison colonies (1851–1946).

**Cayley, Arthur,** 1821–95, English mathematician and lawyer. His researches included the theory of matrices (see MATRIX) and the theory of invariants (quantities, relationships, etc., unaltered by a particular mathematical operation).

**Cayley, Sir George,** 1773–1857, British inventor, called 'the father of British aeronautics'. He built, in 1849, a triplane glider which flew well enough to carry a 10-year-old boy, and in 1852 his monoplane glider carried his coachman a distance of about 500 m (550 yd). In his studies on the principles of flight, he experimented with wing design; distinguished between lift and drag; and formulated the concepts of vertical tail surfaces, steering rudders, rear elevators, and air screws. Cayley wrote in 1809 that 'aerial navigation would form the most prominent feature in the progress of civilization'.

**Cayman Islands,** British dependency (1984 est. pop. 19,000), c.259 km² (100 sq mi) sq km), West Indies, consisting of three main islands, of which Grand Cayman is the largest. The capital is George Town. Discovered (1503) by Christopher COLUMBUS, the islands are now tourist attractions.

**CB radio:** see RADIO.

**Cd,** chemical symbol of the element CADMIUM.

**CD ROM** or **compact disc read-only memory,** an optical, digital, data storage device. CD ROMs developed from the COMPACT DISC developed for audio reproduction. In a compact disc dimples in a reflective track embedded in protective transparent plastic are used to encode sounds digitally (see DIGITAL SYSTEM). It was soon realized that a similar system could be used to record any type of data digitally, provided that the disc was read by a device that would interpret the pattern of dimples on it as the strings of 0s and 1s that a computer is accustomed to handle. The technology of optical disc manufacture does not allow the dimple pattern on the tracks of a disc to be changed, so CD ROMs are only suitable for storing data that will not be modified. One of the most promising applications for these devices is for holding database-like information. Records with an associated index structure can be encoded on a CD ROM and accessed by a personal computer-cum-disc player with database manipulation software. This method of accessing information can be much cheaper than using an on-line database when the information held does not need to be changed.

**Ce,** chemical symbol of the element CERIUM.

**Ceauşescu, Nicolae** (chowˌcheskooh), 1918–, Romanian Communist leader and president of ROMANIA (1974–). A protégé of GHEORGHIU-DEJ, he rose steadily in the party ranks after the Communist takeover in 1948 and succeeded to the party leadership upon the former's death in 1965. He expanded his predecessor's policy of semi-autonomy from the USSR and developed economic ties with the West whilst maintaining an authoritarian regime internally. A debt crisis in the early 1980s led him into increased reliance upon the USSR.

**Čech, Svatopluk** (chekh), 1846–1908, Czech patriot, poet, and novelist. Among his works are the two novels satirizing the Czech petty bourgeois character, *Mr Brouček's True Excursion to the Moon* (1888) and *Mr Brouček's New Epoch-Making Excursion, This Time into the Fifteenth Century* (1888), on which JANÁČEK based his opera.

**Cecil, Robert:** see SALISBURY, ROBERT CECIL, 1st EARL OF.

**Cecil, Robert Arthur Talbot Gascoyne:** see SALISBURY, ROBERT ARTHUR TALBOT GASCOYNE-CECIL, 3rd MARQUESS OF.

**Cecil, William:** see BURGHLEY, WILLIAM CECIL, 1st BARON.

**cedar,** common name for a number of mostly coniferous evergreen trees. The true cedars (genus *Cedrus*), of the PINE family, are all native to Asia and N Africa, but the cedar of Lebanon (*C. libani*) and the fragrant deodar cedar (*C. deodara*), are widely cultivated. True cedar timber, which is fragrant and durable, is rare, the term 'cedar' being applied commercially to a range of timber types which are not true cedars. See WESTERN RED CEDAR.

**ceilidh** (ˌkayli), a word common to Scottish and Irish languages widely used to refer to an informal gathering for music, dancing, songs, and stories. The houses of musical families, where such events are common, are often described as 'ceilidh houses'.

**Cela, Camilo José** (ˌthaylah), 1916–, Spanish novelist. His brutally realistic works include *La familia de Pascual Duarte* (1942), *La colmena* (1951; tr. The Hive), *San Camilo, 1936* (1969), and *Mazurka para dos muertos* (1983; tr. Mazurka for Two Dead Men).

**Celan, Paul,** pseud. of **Paul Ancel,** 1920–70, German poet and translator. Celan is arguably the most important postwar poet writing in German, the language from which he was cast out. His poetry draws on Jewish mysticism and French symbolism and connects with the German tradition by way of HÖLDERLIN and RILKE. The metaphor in the title of one of his collections, *Sprachgitter* (1959; tr. Language Grille), indicates how he sees his medium: as a grid, a framework which provides a scheme for utterance and a filter and net to salvage meaning, but which also obscures and imprisons. His early verse is richly metaphorical and rhythmical, as in his famous 'Death-fugue' from the collection *Poppy and Memory* (1952), but his later works tend towards minimalist intensity and silence. Other collections are *The Sand from the Urns* (1948), *From Threshold to Threshold* (1955), *Nomansrose* (1963), and several posthumous volumes. He died in Paris by his own hand.

**Celebes** or Sulawesi, island (1980 pop. 10,410,000), largest island in E Indonesia, c.189,070 km² (73,000 sq mi), separated from BORNEO by the Makasar Strait. Irregular in shape, it comprises four large peninsulas. The terrain is almost wholly mountainous, with many active volcanoes. Valuable stands of timber cover much of the island; mineral resources include nickel, gold, diamonds, and sulphur. The inhabitants are Malayan, with some primitive tribes in the interior. The Dutch took control of Celebes from the Portuguese in the 1600s. In 1950 it became a province of the newly created Indonesia. Makasar is the chief city and port.

**celery**, biennial plant (*Apium graveolens*) of the CARROT family, widely distributed and cultivated in north temperate areas. Once used as a medicine and flavouring, it is now used chiefly as a food, especially in soups and salads; the seeds are still used for seasoning.

**celesta:** see PERCUSSION INSTRUMENT.

**celestial equator** and **celestial horizon:** see ASTRONOMICAL COORDINATE SYSTEMS.

**celestial mechanics,** the study of the motions of astronomical bodies as they move under the influence of their mutual GRAVITATION. The solution is readily arrived at for two isolated bodies (Sun and one planet as described by KEPLER'S LAWS, Earth and Moon, a pair of binary stars), but if more gravitating bodies must be taken into account, analytical solutions cannot be found. The problem of three bodies was a prime object of study for generations, as was the detailed analysis of motions in the solar system when mutual perturbations between the planets (and between planets and satellites) were allowed for. With modern computing power coming to aid the analytical efforts, a much better understanding has been gained. This is essential for predicting with precision the complex orbits of spacecraft, especially for close encounters with the Moon, planets, or a comet. In addition to being now able to work out accurately the perturbations, due to bodies other than the Sun, of planetary orbits, it has become possible to show that certain trajectories, while unstable in the long run, have long dwell times in some regions, mimicking thereby proper stability.

**celestial meridian, celestial pole,** and **celestial sphere:** see ASTRONOMICAL COORDINATE SYSTEMS.

**Celestine I, Saint,** d. 432, pope (422–432), an Italian. He advanced orthodoxy by sending a delegation to the Council of Ephesus to oppose NESTORIANISM. Feast: 27 July.

**Celestine V, Saint,** c.1209–96, pope (5 July–13 Dec. 1294), an Italian named Pietro del Morrone. Elected to end the two-year deadlock in finding a successor to Nicholas IV, Celestine was a hermit who had attracted a following of extremists (called Celestines). His papacy was chaotic and was dominated by Charles II of Naples; it lasted but five months before he resigned. His successor, BONIFACE VIII, confined Celestine for life to avert schism. Feast: 19 May.

**Céline, Louis Ferdinand** (say,leen), 1894–1961, French author; b. Louis Ferdinand Destouches. He wrote sensationally misanthropic but influential novels, e.g., *Voyage au bout de la nuit* (1932; tr. Journey to the End of Night) and *Mort à crédit* (1936; tr. Death on the Instalment Plan). Based on his experiences during World War I and as a suburban doctor, they portray the vileness of humanity through frank, often obscene, language which imitates popular speech, and has been a major influence over contemporary French style. Céline later wrote a chaotic trilogy (1957–61) recounting the last days of the Third Reich in Germany where he fled as a collaborationist.

**cell,** in biology, the unit of structure and function of which all plants and animals are composed. The cell is the smallest unit in the living organism that is capable of carrying on the essential life processes of sustaining METABOLISM for producing energy and reproducing. Many single-celled organisms (e.g., PROTOZOA) perform all life functions. The cell is

differentiated into the cytoplasm; the cell membrane, which surrounds it; and the nucleus, which is contained within it. Plant cells also have a thickened cell wall, composed chiefly of CELLULOSE. Included in the cytoplasm are mitochondria, which produce energy; lysozymes, which digest; Golgi apparatuses, which synthesize, store, and secrete substances; ribosomes, the sites of protein synthesis; and CHLOROPLASTS (in green plants only), in which PHOTOSYNTHESIS occurs. The nucleus contains chromosomes, which store the information for the metabolic functions of the whole cell and pass on their information to daughter cells by replicating themselves exactly. In higher organisms groups of cells are differentiated into specialized tissues.

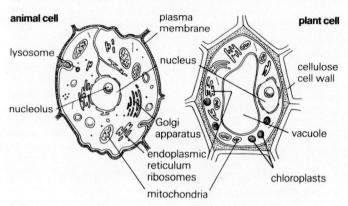

Cell

**cell,** in electricity, device that operates by converting chemical energy into electrical energy. A cell consists of two dissimilar substances, a positive ELECTRODE and a negative electrode, and a third substance, the ELECTROLYTE, that acts chemically on the electrodes. A group of cells connected together is called a battery. The ELECTROMOTIVE FORCE, or voltage produced between the positive and negative electrodes, depends on the chemical properties of the substances used but not on the size of the electrodes or the amount of electrolyte. When the electrodes are connected externally by a piece of wire, electrons flow out of the negative electrode, though the wire, and into the positive electrode. There are several kinds of cells, differing in electrode material and electrolyte. The Leclanché cell has a zinc negative electrode, a carbon positive electrode, and an electrolyte consisting of ammonium chloride solution. It is the basis of the common dry cell, so called because the electrolyte is in the form of a paste instead of a liquid. An alkaline dry cell, which can operate up to ten times longer than common dry cells, has a zinc negative electrode, a manganese dioxide positive electrode, and an electrolyte of potassium hydroxide. A mercury dry cell, with a zinc negative electrode, a mercuric oxide positive electrode, and a potassium hydroxide electrolyte, has a constant output voltage and may be stored for many years.

**Cellini, Benvenuto** (che,leenee), 1500–71, Florentine sculptor and goldsmith. His career in the service of Renaissance popes and the king of France (1523–45) is vividly recorded in his *Autobiography* which, first published in 1728, in the following century came to be seen as epitomizing the brilliance of the Italian RENAISSANCE. BERLIOZ's opera *Benvenuto Cellini* (1838) was inspired by it. Though most of his works have perished, the famous gold and enamel saltcellar of FRANCIS I of France and the gold medallion of *Leda and the Swan* (both: Vienna Mus.) still remain. His late Florentine sculptors include the bust of Cosimo I (Bargello, Florence) and *Perseus with the Head of Medusa* (Loggia dei Lanzi, Florence).

**cello:** see VIOLONCELLO.

**cellophane,** thin, transparent sheet or tube of regenerated CELLULOSE. Used in packaging and for DIALYSIS, cellophane is made by mixing alkali-treated cellulose with carbon disulphide to form viscose. After aging, the viscose is forced through a slit into dilute acid. The regenerated cellulose that results has a lower molecular weight and a less orderly structure than cellulose.

**cellular radio,** mobile telephone communications by means of short-wave radio. The service introduced in Britain in 1985 consists of a

Gold saltcellar by Benvenuto **Cellini**, Kunsthistorisches Museum, Vienna.

network of short-range radio transmitters and receivers dividing the country into 'cells'. These are relatively unobtrusive: one is sited in the tower of Ely Cathedral. When a call is made to a cell phone a computer first locates the apparatus by 'paging' it over all transmitters. Having located it, a frequency is selected for the call which is routed through the nearest transmitter/receiving station. Stations and frequencies can be changed automatically in the course of a call as the cell phone moves from one cell to another, e.g., when the call is being made from a car travelling along a motorway. The service has rapidly grown into something more than an up-market executive toy: it has been estimated that up to 50% of telephone traffic in the UK could be handled by means of radio frequencies by the end of the century.

**celluloid,** transparent, colourless synthetic PLASTIC made by treating CELLULOSE nitrate with CAMPHOR and alcohol. The first important synthetic plastic, celluloid was widely used as a substitute for more expensive substances, such as ivory, amber, and tortoiseshell. It is highly flammable and has been largely superseded by newer plastics.

**cellulose,** a carbohydrate of high molecular weight that is the chief constituent of the CELL walls of plants. Raw cotton is 91% cellulose. Other important natural sources are FLAX, HEMP, JUTE, straw, and WOOD. Cellulose has been used to make PAPER since the 2nd cent. AD. Cellulose derivatives include guncotton (fully nitrated cellulose), used for EXPLOSIVES; CELLULOID (the first PLASTIC); and cellulose acetate, used for plastics, lacquers, and fibres such as RAYON.

**Celsius temperature scale:** see TEMPERATURE.

**Celtic Church,** name given to the Christian church founded 2nd or 3rd cent. in the British Isles before the mission (597) of St AUGUSTINE OF CANTERBURY from Rome. It spread in the 5th cent. through the work of St Ninian in Scotland, St Dyfrig in Wales, and St PATRICK in Ireland, but was all but extinguished in England by the Saxon invasions, beginning c.450. At the Synod of Whitby (664) differences in Celtic and Roman church practices were largely resolved.

**Celtic languages,** subfamily of the Indo-European family of languages. See LANGUAGE (table).

**Celts,** Indo-European-speaking tribal groups who dominated central Europe during the IRON AGE, developing the LA TÈNE culture. Mounted raiders with iron weapons, they spread rapidly over Europe in the 6th and 5th cent. BC from their home in SW Germany, reaching the British Isles, France, Spain, Italy, Macedonia, and Asia Minor. Their social hierarchy included kinglike chiefs and priests known as DRUIDS. A richly ornamental art and colourful folklore were their important cultural legacies. The term *Celts* also refers to natives of areas where a Celtic language is (or was until recently) spoken, i.e., Ireland, the Scottish Hebrides and Highlands, the Isle of Man, Wales, Cornwall, and Brittany.

**cement, hydraulic,** building material typically made by heating a mixture of limestone and clay until it almost fuses and then grinding it to a fine powder. Once it is mixed with water, cement will harden. The

most common cement, Portland cement, is made by mixing and then heating substances containing lime, silica, alumina, and iron oxide, with gypsum added during the grinding process. Quick-setting aluminous cement is made from limestone and bauxite. See also CONCRETE.

**cenotaph** [Gk., = empty tomb], tomb or monument honouring a person or group of people whose remains are elsewhere. Cenotaphs originated during the first two dynasties of ancient Egypt. The pharoah having two tombs, one in Lower Egypt and the other in Upper Egypt, only one could be occupied by his body; thus the other became a cenotaph. Some pyramids were in effect cenotaphs, such as that at Der-el-Bahari in Thebes (2065 BC). Cenotaphs were also popular in ancient Rome. The most celebrated example is the **Cenotaph** in Whitehall, London, designed (1920) by Sir Edwin LUTYENS, who also named it. It commemorates the dead from World War I; on the Sunday nearest to Armistice Day (11 Nov.) a ceremony is held there, attended by members of the royal family, politicians, and survivors of the war.

**Cenotes** (the nohtez), underground caverns and sinks formed by subsurface erosion in the limestone rock of the Yucatán peninsula in SE Mexico. Many have become famous archaeological sites becuase of the relics they contain from the city-states of the late Mayan Empire.

**Cenozoic era:** see GEOLOGICAL ERA (table).

**censorship,** the official restriction of any expression believed to threaten the social, moral, or political order. Censorship takes many forms. Centres of power face a complex and baffling paradox. They need publicity in order to exist, their continuing as political beings depends upon the public's awareness of their existence as political realities; but the powerful feel their security threatened by public questioning and debate, which they often perceive as subversion. Direct censorship, such as that exercised by the Star Chamber until the English Revolution in the 17th cent., involved the submission before publication of all material for public consumption. Items deemed offensive to the powers that be were cut out. This was replaced during the Commonwealth by the Licensing Act, under which only those likely to publish material favourable to the status quo were allowed to continue in business. After 1695 this was superseded by a brief period of complete freedom. The Stamp Act 1712 placed a government duty on publications, based on the assumption that the well-to-do (who would be the only readers able to afford a costly press) would not be likely to conspire the overthrow of a system in which they themselves were the elite. In addition to this the reporting of parliamentary proceedings was actually physically forbidden: would-be reporters were firmly shown the door. Politicians such as John WILKES and William COBBETT fought against such restrictions. It was not until 1855 that all duties and restrictions were removed and Britain had a 'free' press. Even so there are still legal restrictions on the press, such as legislation covering official secrets (see D NOTICE; PRESS, FREEDOM OF THE) and the reporting of cases *sub judice*). In totalitarian states censorship is overt. Moral censorship of creative works is practised in most countries, whether on a religious or secular basis. In the UK plays for public performance used to be subject to censorship by the Lord Chamberlain, with particular attention being paid to sexual activities; since 1968 plays no longer needed to be licensed in this way. Films in the UK are censored by the British Broad of Film Censors; this was established (1912) by the film industry itself, and has no statutory authority or responsibilities towards films; it does, however, issue certificates to videos under the terms of the Video Recording Act 1984. Printed publications are covered by the Obscene Publications Act 1964; publications being imported into the UK may also be controlled under customs regulations.

**census,** a periodic SURVEY of population or of certain aspects of the activities of any one or more nation-states. Censuses have been taken in some countries since biblical times, when their main function was to provide a register for taxation, and other forms of assessment. In Britain a census has been held every 10 years since 1801 (except 1941), conducted by the Office of Population and Censuses. Governments make use of the demographic information created to plan future state activities (e.g., provision of school places). The enumerator's returns (only available 100 years after the date of the census) are an invaluable source of information for economic and social historians, as well as those wishing to trace their genealogy. Some social theorists have argued that the wide practice of census-taking, coming as it did at the same time as the emergence of industrial capitalism, can be seen as an attempt by one class to gain knowledge of—and thereby control over—another (see SOCIAL CONTROL). See also DEMOGRAPHY, GENERAL HOUSEHOLD SURVEY.

**centaur,** in Greek mythology, a creature half man, half horse, descended from Ixion. Most were savage followers of DIONYSUS, but some, like CHIRON, were teachers of men.

**centigrade temperature scale:** see TEMPERATURE.

**centimetre:** see METRIC SYSTEM; WEIGHTS AND MEASURES (table).

**centipede,** invertebrate animal of the class Chilopoda, an ARTHROPOD. The flattened body is divided into a head and trunk comprised of segments (somites). The average number of legs is 35 pairs, one pair per segment except for the first one and last two. The appendages of the first segment are modified into claws equipped with poison glands, used to capture prey. The largest tropical species may reach 30 cm (12 in) in length; temperate species are usually about 2.5 cm (1 in) long.

**Central,** region in central Scotland (1985 est. pop. 273,515), 2631 km² (1,026 sq mi), bordering on Strathclyde in the W. The administrative centre is STIRLING. It was formed in 1975 from Clackmannanshire, most of Stirlingshire, the S of Perthshire, and a small part of W Lothian. Much of the region is mountainous. Loch Lomond is on the W border. It is drained by the R. FORTH. Coalmining, agriculture, and whisky distilling are important economic activities. Falkirk is an iron-working town and there are oil refineries at Grangemouth.

**Central African Republic,** republic (1982 est. pop. 2,442,000), 622,983 km² (240,534 sq mi), central Africa, bordered by Chad (N), Sudan (E), Zaïre and the Congo Republic (S), and Cameroon (W). BANGUI is the capital. Situated on a savanna-covered plateau 610–910 m (2000–3000 ft) above sea level, the country has tropical forests in the south and a semidesert area in the east. Of the numerous rivers, only the Ubangi is commercially navigable. Agriculture is the chief economic activity, engaging about 90% of the people, mostly in subsistence farming. The principal cash crops and exports are cotton and coffee; other exports include diamonds and timber. The GNP is US$635 million, and the GNP per capita is US$260 (1985). There are no railways and few adequate paved roads; rivers are the chief means of transportation. The chief ethnic groups are the Mandjia-Baya, the Banda, the Mbaka, and the Zandé. French is the official language, but Sangho is the lingua franca. More than half the population practises traditional animist religions; most of the rest are Christian.

*History.* In the 19th cent. various tribes fleeing the slave trade arrived in the region. The French occupied the area in 1887 and organized it (1894) as the colony of Ubangi-Shari; it was united administratively with CHAD in 1906 and incorporated into FRENCH EQUATORIAL AFRICA in 1910. Despite periodic rebellions sparked by French concessionaires' use of forced labour, the population supported the Free French forces in WORLD WAR II. The colony was given its own territorial assembly in 1946, received autonomy and took its present name in 1958, and gained full independence in 1960 under Pres. David DACKO. In 1965 the parliamentary government was overthrown in a military coup led by Col. Jean-Bédel BOKASSA, who in 1976 changed the country's name to Central African Empire and had himself crowned Emperor Bokassa I. During his brutal regime it was alleged that he personally took part in a 1979 massacre of children who were protesting against human-rights violations. Shortly thereafter, control was regained by Dacko, who restored republican government but was ousted again (1981) in a military coup led by Gen. André Kolingba. In 1985 Kolingba dissolved the ruling Military Committee for National Recovery and formed a new government with greater civilian representation. A death sentence passed on Bokassa in 1987 was, the following year, commuted to forced labour for life.

**Central America,** collective term applied to the six nations of North America lying SE of Mexico: BELIZE, COSTA RICA, EL SALVADOR, GUATEMALA, HONDURAS, and NICARAGUA and usually also including PANAMA, on the Isthmus of Panama. The region is predominantly mountainous in the interior, with an active zone of volcanoes and earthquakes marking the junction of North America's mountain systems and outliers of South America's ANDES chain. Tajumulco (4210 m/13,846 ft), a volcano in Guatemala, is the highest point. The climate varies with altitude from tropical to cool, with heavy rainfall occurring in the east. Bananas, coffee, sugar, and cotton are the chief commercial crops. The population is mainly Spanish-speaking, Roman Catholic, and mestizo (of mixed Spanish and native Indian extraction). Though rich culturally, the area

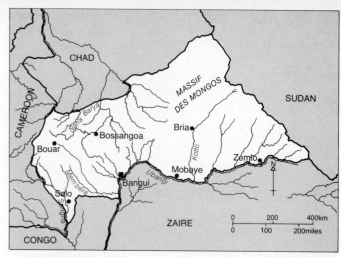

Central African Republic

has suffered chronic political and economic problems, due largely to the persistence of a landholding system that leaves a vast gap between rich and poor.

**Central American Federation,** political confederation (1825–28) of the republics of Central America—Costa Rica, El Salvador, Guatemala, Honduras, and Nicaragua. Enmity between the states frustrated later attempts to revive it as such. The **Organization of Central American States** and the **Central American Common Market,** established by the same countries in 1951 and 1961 respectively, have implemented some cooperative measures and greatly increased regional trade, but have failed to develop into a close political or economic union.

**central bank,** financial institution designed to regulate and control a nation's fiscal and monetary activities. Usually state-owned, central banks issue notes to be used as legal tender, maintain adequate reserve backing for the nation's banks, and control the flow of money and precious metals. By regulating the supply of MONEY and CREDIT they influence INTEREST rates and, to some extent, the whole national economy. Most central banks are modelled on the BANK OF ENGLAND (1694), the first to fill a central banking role.

**Central Intelligence Agency** (CIA), US agency established (1947) by the National Security Act. It conducts intelligence and counterintelligence activities outside the US (see INTELLIGENCE GATHERING). It also engages in domestic counterintelligence operations, but only in coordination with the FEDERAL BUREAU OF INVESTIGATION and subject to the attorney general's approval. These limitations were mandated by a 1978 executive order, issued in the wake of abuses related to the WATERGATE AFFAIR and of a presidential commission's charge (1975) that the CIA had engaged in 'unlawful' domestic spying. The CIA has also been criticized for taking an active role in the internal affairs of foreign governments.

**Centre National d'Etudes Spaciales** (ˌsontrə ˌnatseeonal ˌdaytyoohd), the French space agency, established in 1962 to develop launch vehicles, satellites, and support facilities. In 1966, it established a launch site at Kourou, in French Guiana, which, being just 5° N of the equator, is ideally placed to take maximum advantage of the Earth's rotational speed to assist launch vehicles on their way to orbit. This launch site is currently used by the European Ariane launch vehicle (see ROCKET).

**centre of gravity:** see CENTRE OF MASS.

**centre of mass,** the point at which the mass of a body (or group of objects) may be considered to be concentrated from the point of view of its behaviour under the influence of an external FORCE (or forces). If the external force is GRAVITATION this point is also called the centre of gravity and is the point at which all the WEIGHT of the body may be considered to be concentrated. The motions of several colliding elementary particles, or of the Earth and Moon around the Sun, are sometimes analysed from the point of view of the centre of mass of the entire system of objects.

**centrifuge,** device using centrifugal force to separate substances of different density, e.g., cream from milk. Substances are placed in containers that are spun at speeds high enough to cause the heavier elements to move to the periphery of the containers. The first successful centrifuge was built in 1883 by the Swedish engineer Carl G.P. de Laval.

**centripetal force and centrifugal force,** action–reaction force pair associated with circular motion. Centripetal ('centre-seeking') force is the constant inward force necessary to maintain circular motion. The centripetal force $F$ acting on a body of mass $m$ is given by the equation $F = mv^2/r$, where $v$ is its velocity and $r$ is the radius of its path. The centripetal force, the action, is balanced by a reaction force, the centrifugal ('centre-fleeing') force, which acts not on the circling object but on the source of centripetal force, usually located at the circle's centre. The two forces are equal in magnitude and opposite in direction.

**cephalopod,** free-swimming MOLLUSC (class Cephalopoda) with a long body with a ring of sucker-bearing arms (tentacles) encircling the mouth. The head is large, with prominent eyes. Only the NAUTILUS has an external shell; in the SQUID and CUTTLEFISH the shell is internal and reduced, and in the OCTOPUS it is completely absent. Most cephalopods are aggressive carnivores that move by means of a kind of jet propulsion.

**Cepheid variables,** small class of VARIABLE STARS that brighten and dim in regular periods ranging from 1 to 50 days. The periods of Cepheids, which are yellow supergiant stars, are found to be linked to their intrinsic brightness, or absolute MAGNITUDE: the brighter the star, the greater its period. By comparing the Cepheid's absolute magnitude to its apparent magnitude, one can determine its distance. The period-luminosity relation of Cepheids make them invaluable in estimating interstellar and intergalactic distances.

**Cerberus** (ˌsuhbərəs), in Greek mythology, many-headed dog with a mane and a tail of snakes; guardian of HADES. One of the 12 labours of HERCULES was to capture him.

**cerebral dominance:** see LATERALITY.

**cerebral palsy,** disorder in which muscular control and coordination are impaired, and speech and hearing problems and mental retardation may occur. It is most commonly caused by brain damage occurring before or during birth, and varies greatly in severity. Treatment involves physical, occupational, and speech therapy; braces; orthopaedic surgery; and drugs to reduce muscle stiffness and spasticity.

**cerebrovascular accident:** see STROKE.

**Ceres** (ˌseereez), in Roman mythology, goddess of grain; daughter of SATURN and Ops. Her worship involved fertility rites and rites for the dead, and her chief festival was the Cerealia. She was identified with the Greek DEMETER.

**Ceres,** in astronomy: see ASTEROID.

**cerium** (Ce), metallic element, purified in 1875 by W.F. Hillebrand and T.H. Norton. Iron-grey, soft, and malleable, it is the most abundant of the RARE-EARTH METALS. It is used as a core for the carbon electrode of arc lamps. Cigarette-lighter flints are cerium alloys. Cerium dioxide is a vital component of certain catalysts used in converting car exhausts into harmless products such as water vapour, carbon dioxide, and nitrogen. See ELEMENT (table); PERIODIC TABLE.

**CERN:** see EUROPEAN ORGANIZATION FOR NUCLEAR RESEARCH.

**certificate of deposit** (CD), in banking, a receipt acknowledging the deposit of funds. Demand CDs do not attract interest and are payable on demand. Time CDs are interest-bearing and are payable after a fixed date. Cheques may not be drawn against them. Introduced in 1961, CDs are a major source of investment capital in the UK. CDs became especially attractive during the high-interest economy of the late 1970s and early 1980s, after they were brought (1978) within the means of smaller investors and made competitive with MONEY-MARKET FUNDS. In the UK, sterling CDs were introduced in 1968; they are controlled by the Bank of England. CD futures are actively traded on the COMMODITY MARKET.

**Cervantes Saavedra, Miguel de** (sə‚vanteez sahvedrah), 1547–1616, Spanish novelist, dramatist, and poet, author of *Don Quixote.* Little is known of Cervantes's youth. In 1569, in the service of a cardinal, he went to Italy, where he studied literature and philosophy. At the naval battle of Lepanto (1571) his left arm was permanently crippled. Returning to Spain (1575), he was captured by Barbary pirates and sold as a slave. After many escape attempts he was ransomed at ruinous cost from the viceroy of Algiers in 1580. As a government purchasing agent (1588–97) he was jailed twice for financial irregularities. His first published work was *La Galatea* (1585), a PASTORAL romance in prose and verse. Part I of his masterpiece, *Don Quixote de la Mancha* (1605), was an immediate success. The addled idealism of Don Quixote, a country gentleman who has read too many chivalric romances, and the earthy acquisitiveness of his squire, Sancho Panza, propel them into a series of adventures involving characters from every level of society. The appearance of a spurious sequel prompted Cervantes to publish Part II in 1615. The work had an indelible effect on the development of the European NOVEL. Among his other works are poems; many plays; the *Novelas ejemplares* (1613; tr. Exemplary Novels), a collection of 12 tales; and *Los trabajos de Persiles y Sigismunda* (1617; tr. The Travails of Persiles and Sigismunda), a prose epic.

**cervical smear,** specimen of cells obtained from the cervix (neck of the uterus) and examined microscopically to detect the presence of cancer. The test is used as a screening procedure to detect early cell changes in healthy women so that the disease may be caught at a curable stage.

**Cetswayo** ((t)ets‚wieyoh), c.1825–84, king of the ZULU (1872–84). He was recognized as heir to the throne only after defeating his brother, Mbuyazi, in battle in 1856. His reign was marked by constant clashes with the British, culminating in the Anglo-Zulu war of 1879 and the British forces' capture of the Zulu capital, Ulundi. Cetswayo was exiled to Cape Town and his kingdom dismembered. Though he was reinstalled as king in 1883 he ruled over only a small fraction of his former lands and people.

**Ceuta** (thay‚oohtah), city (1985 est. pop. 70,172), c.18 km² (7 sq mi), NW Africa, a Spanish possession, on the Strait of Gibraltar. An enclave in Morocco administered as part of Cádiz prov., Spain, Ceuta is a free port with such industries as fishing and food processing. An ancient city, it was seized (1415) by Portugal and in 1580 passed to Spain.

**Cézanne, Paul,** 1839–1906, French painter. Strongly influenced by PISSARRO, he became a leading figure in the revolution toward abstraction. His early work is marked by heavy use of the palette knife; these fantastic, dreamlike scenes anticipate the expressionist idiom of the 20th cent. (see EXPRESSIONISM). After meeting MANET and the impressionist painters Cézanne became interested in using colour to create perspective (see IMPRESSIONISM), but he was utterly unconcerned with transitory light effects. *La Maison du pendu* [the suicides's house] (1873; Musée d'Orsay, Paris) is characteristic of his impressionist period. He sought to 'recreate nature' by simplifying forms and utilizing colour and distortion, as in *Mont Sainte-Victoire* (1885–87; Phillips Coll., Washington, DC), *The Kitchen Table* (1888–90; Musée d'Orsay, Paris), *The Card Players* (c.1892; Courtauld Coll., London), and vital portraits. He also developed a new type of spatial pattern, portraying objects from shifting viewpoints. His simple forms are always represented with almost classical structural stability, as in *The Bathers* (versions 1906; National Gall., London, and Philadelphia Mus. Art), a monumental embodiment of several of his visual systems. Cézanne's influence on the course of modern art, particularly CUBISM, was enormous and profound, and his theories spawned a whole new school of aesthetic criticism.

Paul **Cezanne,** *Lac d'Annecy* 1896. Oil on canvas, 64.8 × 81.3 cm. Musee d'Orsay, Paris.

**Cf,** chemical symbol of the element CALIFORNIUM.

**cgs system:** see METRIC SYSTEM.

**Chabrier, Alexis Emmanuel** (chabree͵ay), 1841–94, French composer, best known for the orchestral rhapsody *España* (1883); an opera, *The King Despite Himself* (1887); and piano pieces. He influenced RAVEL and SATIE.

**Chabrol, Claude,** 1930–, French film director. A leading member of the French 'New Wave' of the 1960s, his films, which usually expose the sins of the petty bourgoisie, include *Les biches* (1968), *Le Boucher* (1970), and *Violette Nozière* (1978).

**Chad,** Fr. *Tchad,* officially Republic of Chad, republic (1985 est. pop. 5,000,000), 1,284,000 km² (495,752 sq mi), N central Africa, bordered by the Central African Republic (S), Sudan (E), Libya (N), and Cameroon, Niger, and Nigeria (W). N'DJAMENA is the capital. The terrain in the south is wooded savanna, becoming brush country near Lake Chad, on the western border. Northern Chad is a desert that merges with the S SAHARA and includes the mountainous Tibesti region. Chad's backward economy is based largely on subsistence farming, livestock-raising, and fishing. The single important cash crop is cotton, which also supports a textile industry. Deposits of petroleum, tungsten, and uranium have not been exploited. The population is made up of two distinct, often hostile, groups: agricultural black Africans, mostly animists, with some Christians, in the politically dominant south; and seminomadic or nomadic Muslim tribesmen, who engage in herding, in the north. French is the official language.

*History.* Long a focal point for trans-Saharan trade routes, the region was penetrated in the 7th cent. by Arab traders. Shortly thereafter nomads from N Africa established the state of Kanem, which reached its peak in the 13th cent. The successor state of Bornu was joined by the rival Wadai and Bagirmi empires, all of which fell to the Sudanese conqueror Rabih by the early 1890s. French expeditions moved into the region in 1890 and by 1913 had defeated the Sudanese and conquered Chad, which became a colony in FRENCH EQUATORIAL AFRICA. It gained autonomy in 1958 and full independence in 1960. Internal strife between the Muslim north and the black south has dominated the new country's affairs, flaring into guerrilla warfare (with the main Muslim group receiving active support from LIBYA, which occupied part of N Chad in 1973) and precipitating numerous changes of government. The country's first president, Ngarta Tombalbaye, was ousted in a coup and assassinated in 1975. In 1979 a coalition government, headed by Goukouni Oueddei, a former rebel from the north, assumed power, but fighting broke out again in 1980. Libyan troops were withdrawn in late 1981 and replaced by a peace-keeping force dispatched by the ORGANIZATION OF AFRICAN UNITY. The political situation remained unsettled, and in 1982 Oueddei's government was overthrown by the forces of former prime minister Hissène Habré. Despite having French military support, the new government lost control of large areas of N Chad to pro-Oueddei rebels backed by Libya. In 1984 the Chad government created a new political organization called the National Union for Indpendence and Revolution. By early 1988 the central government had reestablished its authority in the northern area, leading Libya to declare its recognition of Hissène Habré and an end to the war.

**Chadli, Bendjedid** (kal͵dee), 1929–, army officer and president of ALGERIA (1979–). Col. Bendjedid played a part in the coup which brought Houari BOUMEDIENNE to power in 1965 and became president following the latter's death, as well as secretary general of the ruling National Liberation Front.

**Chadwick, Sir James,** 1891–1974, English physicist. He worked on radioactivity under Ernest RUTHERFORD and was assistant director (1923–35) of radioactive research at Cavendish Laboratory, Cambridge. For his discovery of the NEUTRON he received the 1935 Nobel Prize for physics. He moved to Liverpool where he developed a school of nuclear physics. During World World II he was responsible for Anglo-American cooperation in the development of the atomic bomb.

**chafer** or **cockchafer,** a fairly large to large (15–45 mm/½–1½ in) plant-eating BEETLE (Scarabaeidae). In addition to the dung-feeding SCARABS belonging to this family there are many more (about 9000) plant-eating chafers (subfamily Melolonthinae). One of the best known is the large and very substantial brown-and-black cockchafer (*Melolontha*) of Western Europe. Its larvae, during the 3–4 years needed to complete their

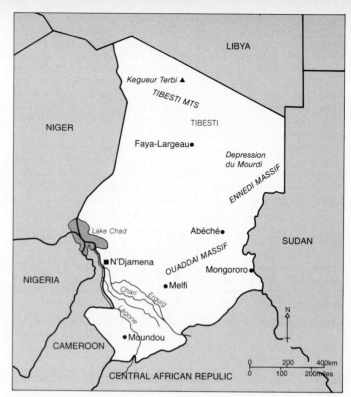

Chad

development, live underground and feed on the roots both of trees and herbaceous plants, including grasses and cereals. The adults are leaf-, flower-, and fruit-eaters and they too can damage crops, a habit shared with many species worldwide, some of which are serious agricultural pests, e.g., the grey-back *Dermolepida albohirtum* which attacks sugar-cane in Queensland. A few European and many tropical species have a brilliant brassy green or blue coloration which is due not to pigments but to the absorption by the cuticle of light of all wavelengths other than those reflected. Even more spectacular, but being nocturnal more rarely seen, are the essentially tropical Dynastinae, which includes the world's largest insects, e.g., the goliath (*Goliathus*) of Africa and the hercules (*Dynastes*) beetles of South America, which may be up to 180 mm (7 in) long. A somewhat smaller species is the rhinoceros beetle (*Oryctes*), a major pest of coconuts.

**chaffinch,** one of the commonest of all BIRDS, a member of the FINCH family. It lives as far north as the Scandinavian tree line, east to Tomsk and south to the level of North Africa. Chaffinch song is unusual in that it varies from district to distict, the young birds learning the version of their district from older songsters. The bird is 15 cm (6 in) long, and the male, with brown back and pinkish breast, is more brightly coloured than the female. The chaffinch is one of the birds that has learned to live with humans, both around farms and in town parks and gardens.

**Chagall, Marc,** 1889–1985, Russian painter. He lived in France for most of his life. He repeatedly drew subject matter from Jewish life and folklore and rendered it with deceptive fairy-tale naiveté, as in *I and the Village* (1911; Mus. Mod. Art, New York City). He was in Paris from 1910 to 1914 and was influenced by CUBISM. He returned to Russia (1914–1923) and after the Revolution became Commissar of Fine Arts in Vitebsk for a short while before disagreeing with Malevich and resigning. He designed sets and costumes for STRAVINSKY's ballet *The Firebird* (1945); 12 stained-glass windows (1962) for Hadassah-Hebrew Univ. Medical Center synagogue, Jerusalem; and two vast murals for New York City's Metropolitan Opera House (1966). A museum of his work opened in Nice in 1973.

**Chain, Sir Ernst Boris,** 1906–79, English biochemist; b. Germany. For their work in isolating and purifying penicillin, he and Sir Howard FLOREY shared with Sir Alexander FLEMING the 1945 Nobel Prize for physiology or medicine. Chain held various professorial and research positions in Berlin, Rome, and London and at Oxford and Cambridge.

Cockchafer (*Melolontha melolontha*)

Marc **Chagall**, *I and the Village*, 1911. Oil on canvas, 192.1 × 151.4 cm. Museum of Modern Art, New York.

**chain reaction:** see NUCLEAR ENERGY.

**Chalcedon, Council of,** AD 451, 4th ecumenical council. It stated that Christ's divine nature and human nature are distinct, but inseparably united; Christ is both true God and true man. This definition refuted EUTYCHES, and since the 7th cent. has been accepted as orthodox by most Christians.

**chalcedony,** form of QUARTZ with microscopic crystals. Some varieties of chalcedony are AGATE, BLOODSTONE, JASPER, and ONYX.

**chalcopyrite** or **copper pyrites,** copper and iron sulphide mineral ($CuFeS_2$), brass yellow and sometimes with an iridescent tarnish. It is found in crystal form but is most often massive. Occuring worldwide in igneous and metamorphic rocks, it is an important ore of COPPER.

**Chaliapin, Feodor Ivanovich** (sha,lyahpin), 1873–1938, Russian operatic bass. He lived outside the USSR after 1921. His powerful voice, tremendous physique, and acting ability made him one of the great performers in operatic history. He was particularly effective in MOUSSORGSKY's *Boris Godunov*.

**chalk,** a calcium carbonate mineral, similar in composition to limestone but softer. Chalk has been deposited throughout geological time. The chief constituents are the shells of minute animals called foraminifera; however, the dominant component of the best-known formations, the Cretaceous chalks (e.g., the White Cliffs of Dover, England), are coccolith algae. Chalk is used to make putty, plaster, cement, quicklime, and blackboard chalk. Harder forms are used as building stones, and poor soils with high clay content are sweetened with chalk.

**Challoner, Richard,** 1691–1781, English Roman Catholic bishop. A convert, he worked hard to win toleration for Catholics in England. His revision of the Douai version of the BIBLE became the standard one chiefly used by English-speaking Catholics. He also wrote devotional works.

**Chamberlain, (Arthur) Neville,** 1869–1940, British statesman. A former Conservative chancellor of the exchequer (1923–24, 1931–37), he succeeded Stanley BALDWIN as prime minister in 1937. His belief that HITLER was a rational statesman resulted in the policy of 'appeasement' of the AXIS powers that culminated in the MUNICH PACT (1938). He remained in office following the outbreak of WORLD WAR II, but he resigned (1940) after the British debacle in Norway.

**Chamberlain, Joseph,** 1836–1914, British politican. He served his political apprenticeship as reforming mayor of Birmingham (1873–76) before entering Parliament as a radical. He served with great ability under GLADSTONE (1880–86), but broke with him on home rule, and became leader of the Liberal Unionists, joining a SALISBURY Cabinet as colonial secretary (1895–1903). In that post he pursued as active a set of policies as he had previously advocated in home affairs. Having split the Liberal Party, he went on to split the Conservative Party in 1903 when he advocated protection. He suffered a stroke in 1906, from which he never recovered.

**Chamberlin, Thomas Chrowder,** 1843–1928, American geologist. With the American astronomer F.R. Moulton he formulated the planetesimal hypothesis of the origin of the SOLAR SYSTEM. His works include *The Origin of the Earth* (1916) and *Two Solar Families* (1928).

**chamber music,** ensemble music for small groups of instruments, with only one player to each part. Originally played by amateurs in courts, it began to be performed by professionals in the 19th cent. with the rise of the concert hall. The main BAROQUE type was the trio SONATA. The STRING QUARTET (two violins, viola, and cello) arose c.1750 and, as developed by HAYDN and MOZART, became the principal form of chamber music, used by classicists (BEETHOVEN, SCHUBERT), romantics (MENDELSSOHN, SCHUMANN, DVOŘÁK), and early 20th-cent. composers (DEBUSSY, RAVEL). Modern composers, such as SCHOENBERG, BARTOK, WEBERN, and STRAVINSKY, have also composed chamber music.

**chamber of commerce,** business association promoting commercial and community interests. It works to attract new business and tourism to its area. The first organization to use the name was established (1599) in

Marseilles, France; the first in the UK was in Jersey (1768) followed by Glasgow and Belfast (1783); Edinburgh and Leeds (1785); Manchester (1794); Birmingham (1813). In the UK the Association of British Chambers of Commerce is the central lobbying and coordinating body —its membership of 90 includes most of the major chambers in the UK, of which there are several hundred. The International Chamber of Commerce was founded in 1920; it is a world federation of business organizations and companies.

**Chambers, Sir William,** 1723–96, English architect. He designed decorative architecture for KEW GARDENS. The foremost official architect of his day, he continued the neo-Palladian tradition, notably at Somerset House, London (begun 1776).

**chameleon,** small- to medium-sized LIZARD of the family Chamaeleonidae, found in sub-Saharan Africa, with a few species in S Asia. Chameleons have laterally flattened bodies ornamented with crests, horns, or spines and bulging, independently rotating eyes. Their skin changes colour in response to stimuli such as light, temperature, and emotion, not simply in response to background colour. The so-called common chameleon (*Chamaeleo chamaeleon*) is found around the Mediterranean. Chameleon range from the 5-cm (2-in) dwarf chameleon to the largest 60-cm (2-ft) specimens. They all move very slowly in trees and shrubs, capturing insects, lizards, mammals, and even birds by shooting out their extending, sticky tongues to stick to the prey and pull it back into their jaws. The American chameleon, not a true chameleon, belongs to the IGUANA family.

**Chamisso, Adelbert von,** 1781–1838, German poet and naturalist; b. France as Louis Charles Adelaïde de Chamisso. His poetic cycle *Frauenliebe und Leben* (1830) was set to music by SCHUMANN. His tale of Peter Schlemihl, the man who sold his shadow to the devil (1814), has become legend.

**chamois,** hollow-horned, hoofed MAMMAL (*Rupicapra rupicapra*) found in the mountains of Europe and the E Mediterranean. About the size of a large GOAT, it is brown with a black tail and back stripes; its horns are erect with terminal hooks. The skin was the original chamois leather, a name now also given to the skins of other animals.

**chamomile** or **camomile,** name for some herbs of the COMPOSITE family, especially the perennial English, or Roman, chamomile (*Anthemis nobilis*) and the annual German, or wild, chamomile (*Matricaria chamomilla*). The former is the chamomile most used for ornament and for a tea, made from the dried flower heads containing a volatile oil. The oil from wild chamomile flowers is chiefly used as a hair rinse.

**Champa,** kingdom of the Chams in Vietnam, fl. 2nd cent. AD–17th cent. The Chams warred successively with China, the KHMER EMPIRE, and ANNAM. The Cham kingdom finally fell to the Annamese, and its people were scattered.

**Champagne,** region, NE France. Champagne is a generally arid, chalky plateau cut by the Aisne, Marne, Seine, Aube, and Yonne rivers. Agriculture and sheep-grazing are the traditional activities. A small fertile area around Rheims and Epernay produces virtually all of France's celebrated champagne wine. Champagne enjoyed an early commercial prosperity, and in the Middle Ages its great fairs, particularly those at Troyes and Provins, attracted merchants from all over W Europe. Cultural life also flourished, culminating in the work of CHRÉTIEN DE TROYES and in the Gothic cathedral at RHEIMS. The county of Champagne passed to the counts of Blois in the 11th cent., and was incorporated into the French royal domain in 1314. WORLD WAR I devastated much of the region, but recently efforts have been made to reforest the area.

**champagne,** sparkling white wine, traditionally made from a mixture of grapes grown in the old French province of Champagne; the best is from the Marne valley. It was reputedly developed in the 17th cent. by a monk, Dom Perignon. The fermented and blended wine is bottled, then sweetened and allowed to ferment further. The carbonic acid left in the bottle after the final fermentation gives champagne its sparkle.

**Champagne, Philippe de,** 1602–74, French painter; b. Belgium. His early work was influenced by the Flemish BAROQUE; in his later works, which include solemn religious scenes and sober portraits, he developed a restrained and classical style. Outstanding works are his portraits of Richelieu and his austere *Ex Voto* (1662; Louvre, Paris) painted for the cure of his daughter, a nun at Port Royal.

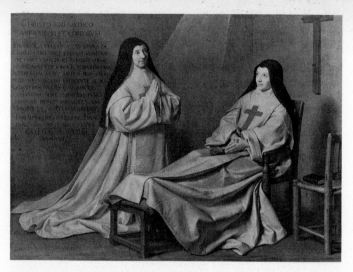

Philippe de **Champagne,** *Ex Voto,* 1662. Louvre, Paris.

**Champlain, Lake,** mainly in NE US, fourth largest freshwater lake in the country (1269 km²/490 sq mi), extending S 201 km (125 mi) from S Quebec to form part of the New York–Vermont border. Its maximum width is 23 km (14 mi). Discovered (1609) by Samuel de CHAMPLAIN, it was the scene of battles in the FRENCH AND INDIAN WAR, the AMERICAN REVOLUTION (Crown Point and Ticonderoga), and the WAR OF 1812.

**Champlain, Samuel de,** 1567–1635, French explorer. In 1605 he founded Port Royal, in NOVA SCOTIA, and in 1608 brought his colonists to QUEBEC. He explored as far W as Lakes Huron and Ontario, and S to Lake CHAMPLAIN, in New York, which bears his name. He extended French claims as far W as WISCONSIN.

**Champollion, Jean François,** 1790–1832, French Egyptologist. The founder of Egyptology, he discovered the key to Egyptian HIEROGLYPHICS while deciphering (1821) the ROSETTA stone. Sometimes called Champollion le jeune, he was trained in archaeology by his elder brother, **Jean Jacques Champollion-Figeac,** 1778–1867.

**Chandigarh,** city (1981 pop. 379,600), Union territory, N India. It was built as a new town, spaciously and with distinguished architecture by LE CORBUSIER, to be the capital of India's Punjab state after the separation of Pakistan. With the partition of this state into Punjab and Haryana it became the capital of both states. Its future status is uncertain. Its functions are almost entirely administrative, though it has a university and some industry.

**Chandler, Raymond T(hornton),** 1888–1959, American writer. His well-plotted, wittily written, brutally realistic detective novels, all featuring the tough yet honourable Philip Marlowe, include *The Big Sleep* (1939) and *The Long Goodbye* (1953).

**Chandragupta** (Chandragupta Maurya), fl. c.321–c.298 BC, Indian emperor, founder of the MAURYA dynasty and grandfather of ASOKA. He conquered the Magadha kingdom in N India, defeated (305 BC) the invading army of Seleucus I, and may have expelled the last of ALEXANDER THE GREAT's army from India.

**Chanel, Gabrielle (Coco),** 1883–1970, French FASHION designer. She was of great influence between the two World Wars. Her box-jacket suits with contrasting binding, known as 'Chanel suits', are still imitated, as is the junk jewellery that she designed to be worn with them. The 'little black dress', at one time almost obligatory party-wear, was created by her. Chanel No. 5, one of many designed by her, is the most famous perfume ever.

**Changamire,** title taken by the kings of the most powerful state (the Changamire, or Rozvi, empire) in what is now S Zimbabwe, during the 16th to the 19th cent. The kingdom was founded by Changa in the late 15th cent. when he revolted from the MWENE MUTAPA empire. His son became known as Changamire after the Arab traders of the east coast gave him the title of 'emir'. The Changamire rulers gradually gained control over the gold and ivory trade with the east coast which had been the source of the power and wealth of the Mwene Mutapa empire.

Coco **Chanel** modelling one of her suits (1929)

Changamire power itself disappeared in the wake of the Nguni invasions of the early 19th cent.

**Changchun** (chahngchoohn), city (1984 pop. 5,842,300), capital of JILIN prov., NE China. The former capital of the Japanese puppet state of Manchukuo (1932–45), Changchun is a major industrial city and the centre of China's motor vehicle industry. It also produces machinery, motors, and textiles. The city is a major educational and cultural centre; the Changchun Film Studio is one of China's leading film centres.

**change ringing**, a form of BELL-ringing that developed during the 17th cent. in England simultaneously with the development of carillon playing in the Low Countries. A group of ringers, each ringer controlling the rope pull of one bell, uses a peal (set) of 5 to 12 bells tuned to the diatonic scale; the bells are rung full circle in various predetermined orders, but without repeating any order. The result is a sound that is not melodious, but complex and compelling.

**Changjiang:** see YANGTZE.

**Changkiakow:** see ZHANGJIAKOU.

**Changsha**, city (1984 pop. 4,969,500), capital of HUNAN prov., S China, on the Xiang R. Changsha is an agricultural distribution and market centre. Founded in the 3rd cent. BC, the city was known as an important literary and educational centre as early as the Song dynasty. In 1904 an Open Door Treaty between Japan and China opened up Changsha to foreign trade. Mao Zedong spent much of his early life here, particularly as a student and teacher at Hunan teacher-training school.

**Channel Islands**, archipelago (1981 est. pop. 134,000), 194 km² (75 sq mi), 16 km (10 mi) off the coast of France in the English Channel. The principal islands are Jersey, Guernsey, Alderney, and Sark. Agriculture and tourism are the mainstays of the economy. The islands became possessions of the duke of Normandy in the 10th cent. and were joined to the English crown at the NORMAN CONQUEST. They were occupied by the Germans during WORLD WAR II.

**Channel Tunnel**, rail/road route under the English Channel. The possibility of such a tunnel was first put forward by Napoleon I in 1802, and several abortive starts have been made on its construction. A treaty between the Governments of Britain and France was signed on 12 Feb. 1986 and following this a concession was signed with one English and one French company to finance, construct, and operate the Channel Tunnel.

Two main rail tunnels (diameter 7.3 m/24 ft) and a service tunnel (diameter 4.5 m/15 ft) will be constructed and the total length will be nearly 50 km (30 mi). As a feat of engineering, the tunnel requires 8 million cubic metres of waste to be removed and 1.8 million tonnes of concrete and steel installed in its place. Construction started in 1987 and the Tunnel is due to open to traffic in 1993. It will convey road vehicles across the Channel in specially built ferry trains, carrying 4000 vehicles per hour and also trains between Paris, Brussels, and London and between other centres, including HIGH SPEED TRAINS. The journey time across the Channel from terminal to terminal will be 35 min, while the journey time between London and Paris will be about 3¼ hr. In early 1989 the total cost of the project was expected to be £4.7 billion.

**Channing, William Ellery**, 1780–1842, American minister and author. A great preacher, called 'the apostle of Unitarianism', he advocated humanitarianism and tolerance in religion. His lucid writings on slavery, war, labour problems, and education were in advance of his time and influenced many American authors, including EMERSON and other exponents of TRANSCENDENTALISM, HOLMES, and BRYANT.

**chansons de geste** [Fr., = songs of deeds], a group of epic poems of medieval France written from the 11th to the 13th cent. The oldest extant chanson, and also the best and most famous, is the *Chanson de Roland* [song of Roland], composed c.1098–1100.

**chant**, general name for one-voiced, unaccompanied liturgical music, usually referring to melodies of the Orthodox, Roman Catholic, and Anglican branches of Christianity. The texts of Anglican chant are from the BOOK OF COMMON PRAYER, and its melodies, unlike the Roman Catholic PLAINSONG, are harmonized. The term is also applied to the recitation of the Koran, and the singing of sacred Buddhist texts.

**chanty** or **shanty**, work song with marked rhythm, particularly one sung by sailors at work, but also by shore gangs or lumberjacks. It often has solo stanzas sung by a leader, alternating with a chorus by the entire group.

**Chanukah:** see Hanukkah under JEWISH HOLIDAYS.

**Chao Phraya, Mae Nam Chao Phraya,** or **Menam Chao Phraya,** chief river of Thailand, formed by the confluence of the Nan and Ping rivers at Nakhon Sawan. It flows generally S c.230 km (140 mi) past the capital city of Bangkok to a large delta on the Gulf of Thailand. Its valley is the country's main rice-producing region.

**Chaos,** in Greek mythology, the vacant, unfathomable space from which everything arose. In the OLYMPIAN myth GAEA sprang from Chaos and became the mother of all things.

**chaos** or **chaology**, an increasingly active branch of science and mathematics which concerns itself with systems whose development over time, although governed by deterministic equations such as NEWTON's laws of motion, is very sensitively dependent on the initial conditions. Starting from a particular state, the behaviour of such a system rapidly becomes unpredictable (i.e., chaotic) although it may be possible to specify certain general statistical features of this chaotic behaviour. Many systems are of this kind—physical, biological, meteorological, epedemiological, ecological, economic—and it is impossible to make long-term predictions about their behaviour.

**chaparral,** type of plant community in which shrubs are dominant, occurring usually in areas drier than forests and wetter than deserts. The species of shrub vary in different areas. The chaparral in Colorado, E Utah, and N New Mexico is mostly deciduous, while that of S California, Nevada, and Arizona is primarily evergreen. Chaparral is well exemplified in the W and SW US, but similar growth is found in many other parts of the world, e.g., the garrigue and maquis of the Mediterranean lands.

**chapbook,** early form of popular printed literature. Chapbooks were publications circulated for ordinary people—popular stories, farces, travels, religious tracts, biographies, folk and nursery tales. The industry was established in the BLACK-LETTER tracts of Wynken de Worde and was flourishing by the end of the 15th cent. Much material was translated from French originals. These publications were circulated by dealers or 'chapmen' all over England, Scotland, and the American colonies, and the survival of much traditional vernacular literature is the direct legacy of the chapbook industry. Samuel PEPYS had a collection of chapbooks.

**chapel,** subsidiary place of worship, either an alcove or chamber within a church, or a room set apart in a secular building (e.g., a school, college, or hospital); or a small separate building for worship away from the parish church (e.g., a chapel-of-ease or a chapel at a cemetery). Chapels in churches became necessary after the early Middle Ages with the increase of relics and devotions at altars sacred to various saints. At first they appeared as minor apses flanking the main APSE. After the 10th cent. a complex series of radiating chapels developed behind the high altar. In the 13th cent. chapels were added to side aisle bays. Peculiar to English cathedrals are small chantry chapels, built either by individuals for private masses or to enclose the tombs of bishops and other churchmen. A **Lady Chapel** is dedicated to the Blessed Virgin Mary and was from the 14th cent. frequently the most sumptuous part of English cathedrals; there are fine examples at Ely and Gloucester. Medieval lords established private chapels, over which episcopal jurisdiction was enforced as completely as possible. Chapel is also used to denote the places of worship of various non-conforming churches in England and Wales; they were often built to severe classical design. The two main chapels at the VATICAN are the Pauline Chapel (1540) and the Sistine Chapel (1473). Notable modern chapels are at Vence, decorated by Henri MATISSE, and at Ronchamp (by LE CORBUSIER).

**Chaplin, Charlie,** 1899–1977, British actor, director, producer, screen writer, and composer. Possibly the most famous film actor in the world, he was renowned for his creation of the 'little tramp' in such films as *The Kid* (1921), *City Lights* (1931), and *Modern Times* (1936).

**Chapman, George,** 1559?–1634, English poet, playwright, and translator. His earliest published poems are *The Shadow of Night* (1594), and in 1598 his six-book continuation of MARLOWE's *Hero and Leander* was published. His plays include *Eastward Ho* (1605), in collaboration with Ben JONSON and John MARSTON, which led to a short spell of imprisonment for all three dramatists because of some anti-Scottish jokes. From 1598 onwards Chapman was engaged in translating the works of HOMER, a project which was completed in 1616 as *The Whole Works of Homer, Prince of Poets*. Chapman is one of several candidates for the role of 'Rival Poet' alluded to in the *Sonnets* of SHAKESPEARE.

**Chapultepec** (chah,poohltaypek), fortified hill, S of Mexico City. A traditional home of Spanish viceroys and Mexican rulers, it was the site of a brave defence to the death by Mexican cadets (the 'boy heroes') when it was stormed and taken (1847) by US forces during the MEXICAN WAR. The castle is maintained as a historical museum.

**char:** see SALMON.

**Charcas,** Spanish colonial territory, also known as Upper Peru, roughly corresponding to present-day BOLIVIA but including parts of Argentina, Chile, Peru, and Paraguay. Established in 1559, the territory was often disputed and fought over by neighbouring colonies or states.

**charcoal,** nonvolatile residue obtained when organic matter, usually wood, is heated in the absence of air. Largely pure CARBON, charcoal yields more heat per volume than wood. Charcoal obtained from bones is called bone black or animal charcoal. Finely divided charcoal, with its porous structure, efficiently filters solids from solution, and gases by ADSORPTION. Charcoal is used in sugar refining and in water and air purification.

**Charcot, Jean Martin** (shah,koh), 1825–93, French neurologist. He developed at the Salpêtrière, Paris, the greatest clinic of his time for diseases of the nervous system. His insight into the nature of hysteria was credited by Sigmund FREUD, his pupil, as having contributed to early psychoanalytic formulations on the subject.

**Chardin, Jean-Baptiste-Siméon** (shah,danh), 1699–1779, French painter. He favoured simple still lifes and unsentimental domestic interiors. His muted tones and ability to evoke textures are seen in *Benediction* and *Return from Market* (both: Louvre, Paris) and *Blowing Bubbles* and *Mme Chardin* (both: Metropolitan Mus., New York.). His unusual geometric compositions had great influence.

**charge,** in ELECTRICITY, property of matter that gives rise to all electrical phenomena. The basic unit of charge is usually denoted by $e$ and has the value $e = 1.6 \times 10^{-19}$ COULOMB. It is the magnitude of the charge of the ELECTRON and the PROTON; that on the proton is designated as positive $(+e)$ and that on the electron is designated as negative $(-e)$. All other charged ELEMENTARY PARTICLES have charges equal to $+e$, $-e$, or some whole number times one of these, with the exception of QUARKS whose charges have magnitudes $\frac{1}{3}e$ and $\frac{2}{3}e$. Every charged particle is surrounded by an

Jean-Baptiste-Simeon **Chardin,** *The Laundress*. Hermitage Museum, Leningrad.

electric FIELD of force such that it attracts any charge of opposite sign brought near it and repels any charge of like sign. The magnitude of this force is described by COULOMB'S LAW. This force is much stronger than the gravitational force between two particles and is responsible for holding protons and electrons together in ATOMS and in chemical bonding. Any physical system containing equal numbers of positive and negative charges is neutral. Charge is a conserved quantity; the net electric charge in a closed physical system is constant. Although charge is conserved, it can be transferred from one body to another. Electric current is the flow of charge through a conductor (see CONDUCTION).

**Charlemagne (Charles the Great)** or **Charles I** (shahlə,mayn), 742?–814, emperor of the West (r.800–814), Carolingian king of the Franks (r.768–814). The son of PEPIN THE SHORT, he consolidated his rule in his own kingdom, invaded Italy in support of the pope, and in 774 was crowned king of the Lombards. He took NE Spain from the MOORS (778), annexed Bavaria (788), and in a series of wars in the 790s destroyed the Avar kingdom. After a long struggle (772–804) he subjugated and Christianized the Saxons. In 800 he restored LEO III to the papacy and was crowned emperor by him on Christmas Day, thus laying the basis for the HOLY ROMAN EMPIRE and finalizing the split between the Byzantine and Roman empires. Charlemagne ruled through a highly efficient administrative system. He codified the law in his various dominions, and his court at AACHEN was the centre for an intellectual and artistic renaissance. The end of his reign was troubled by raids by the NORSEMEN. His son, LOUIS I, was named co-emperor in 813 and succeeded on his father's death. Charlemagne's legend soon enhanced and distorted his actual achievements, and he became the central figure of a medieval romance cycle.

**Charleroi,** city (1985 pop. 211,943), Hainaut prov., S Belgium, in the valley of the Sambre R. It is a leading centre of iron, steel and glass manufacture in the coalfield industrial region. Growth of employment in engineering industries has helped to compensate for the decline in coal-mining. It was an important fortress in the 17th and 18th cent.

**Charles,** emperors (see HOLY ROMAN EMPIRE). **Charles II** or **Charles the Bald,** 823–77, emperor of the West (875–77) and king of the West Franks (840–77), was the son of Emperor LOUIS I by a second marriage. Louis's attempts to create a kingdom for Charles were responsible for the almost constant warfare with Charles's elder brothers, LOTHAIR I and LOUIS THE GERMAN. In 843 Charles received what is roughly modern France, and in 870 he divided LOTHARINGIA with Louis. Charles became emperor upon the death of his nephew LOUIS II. His brief reign saw the rise of the power of the nobles and serious threats by the NORSEMEN. **Charles III** or **Charles the Fat,** 839–88, emperor of the West (881–87), king of the East Franks, or Germany (882–87), and king of the West Franks, or France (884–87), was the son of Louis the German. He inherited Swabia (876) and was crowned king of Italy (881). When he became king of France, he briefly reunited the empire of Charlemagne. A weak ruler, he was deposed in 887 after he failed to stop the inroads of the Norsemen. **Charles IV**, 1316–78, Holy Roman emperor (1355–78). In 1347 he succeeded his father, John of Luxembourg, as king of BOHEMIA and was elected anti-king to Emperor Louis IV, after whose death he made his claim. As emperor he promulgated the Golden Bull (1356), which strengthened the German ELECTORS at the expense of the emperor. He founded Charles Univ. at PRAGUE. **Charles V**, 1500–1558, Holy Roman emperor (1519–58) and, as Charles I, king of Spain (1516–56), was the son of PHILIP I and JOANNA of Castile, and grandson of Emperor MAXIMILIAN I and MARY OF BURGUNDY. Charles was the greatest of all HABSBURG emperors. He inherited a vast empire: the Spanish kingdoms, Spanish America, Naples, Sicily, the Low Countries, and the hereditary Austrian lands. The chief problems he faced were the Protestant REFORMATION in Germany; the dynastic conflict with FRANCIS I of France, particularly for supremacy in Italy; and the Ottoman Turks, then at the height of their power. He also had difficulties with his Spanish subjects, who at first regarded him as a foreigner. Initially successful against the Protestant princes in Germany, he eventually was forced to compromise with them and to accept (1555) the Peace of Augsburg. He was more successful in promoting the Catholic REFORMATION. Charles's bitter struggle with the French kept them out of Italy. His efforts to halt the advance of the Ottomans under SULAYMANI were not completely successful, but Vienna survived a siege in 1529 and Austria did not collapse as Hungary had done. As king of Spain, he was triumphant. The conquest of Mexico and Peru represented the high point of the Spanish empire. In 1556 Charles abdicated all his titles and retired to a monastery. His son PHILIP II received Spain, America, Naples, and the Netherlands; and his brother became emperor as FERDINAND I. **Charles VI**, 1685–1740, Holy Roman emperor (1711–40) and, as Charles III, king of Hungary (1712–40), son of Leopold I, was, before his accession, involved in the War of the SPANISH SUCCESSION. The PRAGMATIC SANCTION, whereby he settled his Habsburg lands on his daughter MARIA THERESA, was challenged after his death. **Charles VII**, 1699–1745, Holy Roman emperor (1742–45) and, as Charles Albert, elector of BAVARIA (1726–45), refused to recognize the Pragmatic Sanction, and joined the coalition against Maria Theresa in the War of the AUSTRIAN SUCCESSION. He was elected emperor, but lost his own Bavaria to Austrian occupation.

**Charles**, kings of England, Scotland, and Ireland, of the STUART house. **Charles I**, 1600–49 (r.1625–49), was the son and successor of JAMES I. Upon his accession, he offended his Protestant subjects by marrying HENRIETTA MARIA, a Catholic French princess. Also, the foreign ventures of his favourite, the duke of BUCKINGHAM, were unsuccessful and expensive. His reign soon became the bitter struggle between king and Parliament for supremacy that resulted in the ENGLISH CIVIL WAR. Charles supported the Anglican bishops under LAUD. Parliament, largely Puritan, controlled money grants and developed the tactic of withholding money until its grievances were redressed. Charles dismissed Parliament in 1625 and 1626, but called it again in 1628 and signed the PETITION OF RIGHT in return for a subsidy. After 1629 he ruled without Parliament. The period of the Personal Rule was one of stability, but Charles's religious policies were unpopular with some. A crisis was reached when Charles's attempt to force episcopacy upon Scotland resulted in the BISHOPS' WARS. Eventually the Long Parliament (1640) was called. Led by John Hampton, PYM, and VANE, it secured itself against dissolution and caused the death of the earl of STRAFFORD, the abolition of STAR CHAMBER courts, and the end of arbitrary taxation. Fear of the king and of Catholics mounted, and civil war broke out. Defeated at Marston Moor (1644) and Naseby (1645), Charles surrendered to the Scottish army (1646) and finally fell into the hands of the English. He was tried by a high court controlled by his enemies, convicted of treason, and beheaded. Often obstinate, Charles brought about his own downfall as much by his weakness of character as by his religious and political beliefs. His son, **Charles II**, 1630–85 (r.1660–85), fled to France in 1646. On his father's death, he was proclaimed king of Scotland and, after accepting the terms of the COVENANTERS, was crowned there in 1651. He then marched into England but was defeated by Oliver CROMWELL at Worcester and escaped to France. In 1660 he issued the conciliatory Declaration of Breda. Later that year, Gen. MONCK engineered Charles's RESTORATION to the throne. He made the earl of CLARENDON his chief minister. Episcopacy was restored and nonconformity weakened by the CLARENDON CODE, although the king favoured toleration. The great London plague (1665) and fire (1666) took place during the second DUTCH

WAR (1664–67). In 1667 the CABAL ministry replaced Clarendon. As a result of a secret treaty with LOUIS XIV of France, Charles entered the third Dutch War in 1672. It was unpopular, and he was forced to approve the TEST ACT (1673) and make peace (1674). His French alliance was broken by the marriage of his niece Mary to William of Orange. He intervened in the Titus OATES affair to protect the queen, CATHERINE OF BRAGANZA. In 1681 he dissolved Parliament to block passage of the Exclusion act that prevented his brother, the duke of York (later JAMES II), from succeeding him, and ruled absolutely thereafter. Although he fathered illegitimate children by several mistresses (e.g., Nell GWYN), he had no legitimate children and was succeeded by James II. His reign, the brilliant Restoration period, was marked by the rise of political parties, and advances in colonization and trade.

**Charles**, kings of France. **Charles I**: see CHARLEMAGNE. **Charles II** (the Bold) and **Charles III** (the Fat): see CHARLES II and CHARLES III, emperors of the West. **Charles III** (the Simple), 879–929 (r.893–923), was the son of LOUIS II and joint king with Eudes, count of Paris, until 898. He ceded (911) part of Normandy to the Norse leader Rollo and was defeated and imprisoned (923) by nobles who made Raoul of Burgundy king. **Charles IV** (the Fair), 1294–1328 (r.1322–28), succeeded his brother PHILIP V and was the last king of the CAPETIAN dynasty. **Charles V** (the Wise), 1338–80 (r.1364–80), was the son of JOHN II and was regent during John's captivity (1356–60, 1364) in England. As regent Charles dealt with the JACQUERIE and the reformist movement of Étienne Marcel. During his reign his general Bertrand DU GUESCLIN nearly drove the English out of France. With his ministers, Charles strengthened royal power, founded a standing army, reformed taxation, and patronized the arts. His son **Charles VI** (the Mad or the Well Beloved), 1368–1422 (r. 1380–1422), was intermittently insane after 1392. France was ruled and plundered by his uncle PHILIP THE BOLD and by his brother Louis d'ORLÉANS. Their rivalry led to a civil war that laid France open to an invasion (1415) by HENRY V of England. By the Treaty of Troyes (1420) Charles named Henry his successor. His disinherited son **Charles VII** (the Victorious or the Well Served), 1403–61 (r. 1422–61), repudiated the treaty. Still called the DAUPHIN, he ruled indolently over what parts of France remained to him S of the Loire, but in 1429 JOAN OF ARC spurred him to action and had him crowned king at Rheims. In 1435 he won the alliance of Burgundy against England, and in 1453 he ended the HUNDRED YEARS WAR by expelling the English from most of France. He reorganized the army and, with the help of Jacques CŒUR, restored the finances. The PRAGMATIC SANCTION of Bourges (1438) and the suppression of the Pragurie (1440), a revolt of the nobility, strengthened royal authority. Charles's last years were troubled by the intrigues of his son, the future LOUIS XI. **Charles VIII**, 1470–98 (r.1483–98), was the son of Louis XI. His sister Anne de Beaujeu was regent during his minority and arranged his marriage (1491) to ANNE OF BRITTANY. In 1495 Charles began the ITALIAN WARS with the short-lived conquest of Naples. **Charles IX**, 1550–74 (r.1560–74), was at first under the regency of his mother CATHERINE DE' MEDICI. Later he chose Gaspard de COLIGNY as chief adviser, but was persuaded to take part in the massacre of SAINT BARTHOLOMEW'S DAY (1572). **Charles X**, 1757–1836 (r.1824–30), was known as the comte d'Artois before he succeeded his brother, LOUIS XVIII, in 1824. He led the powerful ultraroyalist group before his accession and as sovereign had reactionaries as premiers. Liberal and capitalist forces joined to bring about the JULY REVOLUTION of 1830. Charles abdicated and died in exile.

**Charles**, kings of Hungary. **Charles I**, 1288–1342 (r.1308–42), was the grandson of CHARLES II of Naples and son-in-law of Stephen V of Hungary. In 1308 he was elected king by the Hungarian diet and thus founded the Angevin dynasty in Hungary. He reorganized the army on a feudal basis and increased the privileges of the cities. His eldest son became King Louis I of Poland. **Charles II**: see CHARLES III, king of Naples. **Charles III**: see CHARLES VI, Holy Roman emperor. **Charles IV**: see CHARLES I, emperor of Austria.

**Charles**, rulers of Naples. **Charles I** (Charles of Anjou), 1227–85, king of Naples and Sicily (r.1266–85), was a brother of LOUIS IX of France. Charles championed the papal cause against MANFRED in Naples and Sicily, and as a reward the pope crowned him (1266) king. He founded the Angevin dynasty in Naples. Heavy taxes to support his wars against the Byzantine Empire led to a rebellion (1282) in Sicily (see SICILIAN VESPERS). The ensuing war with PETER III of Aragón, who was chosen king by the rebels, continued into the reign of his son, **Charles II** (the Lame), 1248–1309, king of Naples (r.1285–1309). Charles II's great-grandson,

**Charles III** (Charles of Durazzo), 1345–86, king of Naples (r.1381–86), was adopted by Joanna I of Naples, who later repudiated him in favour of Louis of Anjou (later Louis I of Naples). Charles deposed Joanna, was crowned king (1381), and repulsed Louis's attacks. In 1385 Charles was elected king of Hungary over Holy Roman Emperor SIGISMUND, but he was assassinated soon afterwards.

**Charles,** kings of Spain. **Charles I:** see CHARLES V, Holy Roman emperor. **Charles II,** 1661–1700, king of Spain, Naples, and Sicily (r.1665–1700), was both mentally and physically handicapped; his mother, Mariana of Austria, ruled as regent for him. During his reign Spain continued to lose influence abroad and to suffer a decline in its economy and intellectual life. His choice of an heir provoked the War of the SPANISH SUCCESSION. **Charles III,** 1716–88, king of Spain (r.1759–88) and of Naples and Sicily (r.1735–59), was Spain's greatest BOURBON king. He conquered and ruled NAPLES and SICILY before becoming king of Spain. By involving Spain in the SEVEN YEARS' WAR on the side of the defeated French, he lost Florida to England. But he fought on the colonists' side in the AMERICAN REVOLUTION and thereby regained (1783) Florida. His reign was noteworthy for Spain's prosperity and for his expulsion of the JESUITS. **Charles IV,** 1748–1819 (r.1788–1808), was an ineffective ruler who allowed his chief minister, GODOY, to pursue disastrous policies. Spain suffered major naval defeats by England at Cape Saint Vincent (1797) and TRAFALGAR (1805), and it suffered reverses (1808) in the PENINSULAR WAR, as the result of which he was forced to abdicate.

**Charles,** kings of Sweden. **Charles IX,** 1550–1611 (r.1604–11), was the youngest son of GUSTAVUS I. As regent after the death of his brother, John III, he made Lutheranism the state religion. By his efforts the Catholic heir, SIGISMUND III of Poland, was deposed (1599). Charles became king after Sigismund's brother, John, renounced the Swedish crown. In 1600 he began the Polish–Swedish wars that ended only in 1660. His son, GUSTAVUS II, succeeded him. **Charles X,** 1622–60 (r.1654–60), was the nephew of Gustavus II. He succeeded on the abdication of his cousin, CHRISTINA. He invaded Poland (1655) but soon suffered reverses. After Denmark and Russia entered the war, Charles forced the Danes (1658) to cede territory that extended Sweden's southern boundaries to the sea. His son **Charles XI,** 1655–97 (r.1660–97), succeeded him. A council of regency ruled until he was 17. In the third of the DUTCH WARS he was defeated by FREDERICK WILLIAM of Brandenburg (1675). Under Charles, royal power was increased at the nobles' expense. **Charles XII,** 1682–1718 (r.1687–1718), was the son of Charles XI. Facing (1699) a coalition of Russia, Poland, and Denmark in the NORTHERN WAR, he forced Denmark to make peace (1700); invaded Poland and had STANISLAUS I enthroned (1704); and, with MAZEPA, invaded Russia, where his army was crushingly defeated (1708). He fled to Turkey and persuaded AHMED III to declare war on Russia (1710). After Turkey and Russia made peace (1711), Charles refused to leave Turkey and was imprisoned. At Swedish-occupied Stralsund (1714–15) he fought the Prussians and Danes. When Stralsund fell, he fled to Sweden and invaded (1716) Norway, where he was killed in battle. His sister, Ulrica Leonora, succeeded him under a new constitution that strengthened the nobles and clergy. **Charles XIII,** 1748–1818, was king of Sweden (1809–18) and Norway (1814–18). He was regent for his nephew, GUSTAVUS IV, after the assassination (1792) of his brother GUSTAVUS III. Called to the throne at the forced abdication of his nephew, Charles accepted a new constitution limiting royal power, signed treaties with Denmark and France, and ceded Finland to Russia. **Charles XIV** (Charles John; Jean Baptiste Jules Bernadotte), 1763–1844, king of Sweden and Norway (r.1818–44), was a French Revolutionary general. He served under Napoleon in Italy (1796–97), was French ambassador at Vienna (1798), and was minister of war (1799). In 1810 the aging and childless Charles XIII of Sweden adopted him, and he was elected crown prince by the Riksdag. He allied Sweden with England and Russia against NAPOLEON I and took part in his defeat at Leipzig (1813). In 1814 he forced Denmark to cede Norway, which was united with Sweden under a single king. He succeeded to the throne in 1818, having held the reins of government since 1810. His son, Oscar I, succeeded him. **Charles XV,** 1826–72 (r.1859–72), was the son of Oscar I. A liberal ruler, he agreed to such reforms as a bicameral parliament. He was succeeded by his brother, Oscar II. **Charles XVI Gustavus** (Carl Gustaf), 1946– (r.1973–), is the grandson and successor of GUSTAVUS VI and the son of Prince Gustaf Adolf of Sweden. A new Swedish constitution, passed shortly before his grandfather's death and effective in 1975, made the king a ceremonial figurehead.

**Charles,** 1948–, prince of Wales, eldest son of ELIZABETH II of Great Britain and heir apparent to the British throne. He was created prince of Wales in 1958. In 1981 he married Lady Diana Spencer (see DIANA, princess of Wales). They have two sons, Prince William (b. 1982) and Prince Henry ('Harry', b. 1984).

**Charles,** 1771–1847, archduke of Austria, brother of Holy Roman Emperor FRANCIS II. Despite his epilepsy, he was an able Austrian commander. In 1809 he defeated NAPOLEON I at Aspern (May) but was beaten at Wagram (July).

**Charles I,** 1887–1922, last emperor of Austria and, as Charles IV, king of Hungary (1916–18). After his accession during WORLD WAR I, he put out peace feelers, causing friction between Germany and Austria. After Austria's defeat he was unable to save the AUSTRO-HUNGARIAN MONARCHY, and abdicated (Nov. 1918). In 1921 he tried twice to regain the Hungarian throne, without success.

**Charles I,** king of Spain: see CHARLES V under CHARLES, emperors.

**Charles II** (the Bad), 1332–87, king of Navarre (r.1349–87). He carried on a long feud with his father-in-law, JOHN II of France, and allied himself with EDWARD III of England. Charles helped to suppress the JACQUERIE (1358) and was chosen by Étienne Marcel to defend Paris against the DAUPHIN (later King CHARLES V), but he betrayed this trust.

**Charles, Jacques Alexandre César** (shahl), 1746–1823, French physicist. He discovered (1787) Charles's law (see GAS LAWS); invented a thermometric hydrometer; and was the first to use hydrogen gas in balloons.

**Charles, Ray** (Ray Charles Robinson), 1930–, black American musician and composer. Blinded at the age of seven, he rose to fame in the 1950s singing rhythm-and-blues songs to the accompaniment of his piano and orchestra. His work, rooted in GOSPEL MUSIC, influences, and is influenced by, JAZZ.

**Charles Edward Stuart:** see under STUART, JAMES FRANCIS EDWARD.

**Charles Martel,** 688?–741, Frankish ruler, illegitimate son of PEPIN of Heristal and grandfather of CHARLEMAGNE. Although never king, he ruled as mayor of the palace (714–41). He united all MEROVINGIAN kingdoms under his rule and halted the European invasion of the MOORS. His sons, PEPIN the Short and Carloman, divided the Frankish lands at his death.

**Charles's law:** see GAS LAWS.

**Charles the Bold,** 1433–77, duke of BURGUNDY (1467–77), son of PHILIP THE GOOD. He opposed the growing power of LOUIS XI of France and allied himself with England. Master of the Low Countries, Charles dreamed of reestablishing the kingdom of LOTHARINGIA, to which end he tried to acquire Alsace and Lorraine. The Swiss, roused by his actions, routed him at Grandson and Morat (1476) and in 1477 defeated and killed Charles at Nancy. Burgundy then disintegrated.

**Charles the Great,** Frankish king, emperor of the West: see CHARLEMAGNE.

**Charleston.** 1 city (1980 pop. 69,510), SE South Carolina, US; founded 1680, inc. 1783. On a peninsula between the Ashley and Cooper rivers, it is a major southeastern port. US naval operations provide much employment; chemicals, steel, and other products are manufactured. The oldest city in the state, it was the scene of the first incident of the CIVIL WAR, the firing on Fort Sumter (12 Apr. 1861); it fell to Gen. SHERMAN's army in 1865. A major tourist centre, Charleston is famous for its picturesque streets, houses, and other 18th-cent. monuments, reminders of its early importance as a prosperous, cosmopolitan port. 2 US city (1980 pop. 63,968), state capital of West Virginia, on the Kanawha R. where it meets the Elk R.; inc. 1794. The largest city in the state, it is a major chemical, glass, and metal producer. The region provides salt, coal, natural gas, clay, sand, timber, and oil for the city's manufactures. The city, which grew around Fort Lee (1788), was the home (1788–95) of Daniel BOONE. It was state capital 1870–75 and after 1885.

**Charlotte,** US city (1984 est. pop. 331,000), S North Carolina; inc. 1768. It is the largest city in North Carolina, the commercial and industrial centre of the Piedmont region, and a distribution hub for the Carolina textile manufacturing belt, which utilizes Catawba R. hydroelectric power. An early centre of rebellion against British rule, it was the site of the signing of the Mecklenburg Declaration of Independence (May 1775).

**Charlotte Amalie,** city (1980 pop. 11,585), on St Thomas, capital of the US VIRGIN ISLANDS.

**Charlottetown,** city (1984 est. pop. 15,282), capital, chief port, and only city of Prince Edward Island, E Canada. Food processing is a major industry. Charlottetown was laid out by the British in 1768 and named after George III's queen. It was noted in the mid-1800s for the sailing ships built there. The Charlottetown Conference (1864) was the first step toward Canadian confederation. The Charlottetown Festival, held every summer in the Confederation of the Arts Centre (built 1960s), is a major cultural event.

**Charon,** in astronomy, natural satellite of PLUTO.

**Chartism,** British working class movement. The first organization of its kind, it was born in economic depression and named after the People's Charter, drafted by the London Working Men's Association in 1838. It had six demands: universal manhood suffrage; equal electoral districts; voting by ballot; annually elected parliaments; payment of members of parliament; and abolition of property qualifications for members of parliament. Its chief leader Feargus O'CONNOR, despite having many critics, had large mass support, but neither petitions to parliament, drawn up in 1839, 1842, and 1848, nor strong local organization met with any immediate success. Chartism collapsed after 1848, but left strong and lasting memories. Most of the Chartist demands were subsequently granted.

**Chartres,** city (1982 pop. 39,243), capital of Eure-et-Loir dept., NW France. The probable site of DRUIDS' assemblies, it became a royal possession (1286) and a duchy (1528). Its magnificent Gothic cathedral (12th–13th cent.) is renowned for its spires and stained-glass windows; there the Second Crusade was preached (1146) and Henry IV crowned (1594).

Chartres cathedral

**Charybdis:** see SCYLLA AND CHARYBDIS.

**Chase, Salmon Portland,** 1808–73, 6th chief justice of the US SUPREME COURT (1864–73). A zealous abolitionist, he served as US senator (1849–55; 1861) and as governor of Ohio (1855–59). As chief justice he presided over the impeachment trial of Pres. Andrew JOHNSON with scrupulous fairness. His greatest achievement, however, was as secretary of the treasury (1861–64), when he created a national bank system.

**Chase, William Merritt,** 1849–1916, American painter. He is best known for his spirited portraits and still lifes in oil, e.g., *Carmencita* and *Lady in Black* (Metropolitan Mus., New York). Chase was also an important art teacher.

**château,** royal or seignorial residence and stronghold of medieval France, counterpart of the English CASTLE. The fortified château culminated in the late 15th cent., e.g., Pierrefonds, near Compiègne. 16th-cent. châteaux, with gardens and outbuildings, usually had a moat, but were little fortified. Notable châteaus are those of the Loire, Indre, and Cher valleys, e.g., Chambord, Amboise, Chenonceaux.

**Chateaubriand, François René, vicomte de** (shatohbree͵anh), 1768–1848, French writer. A founder of ROMANTICISM in French literature, he visited the US in 1791 and until 1800 was an émigré in England. A Royalist, despite his liberal sympathies, he was minister of foreign affairs (1823–24). He made his mark with *La génie du Christianisme* (1802) and two tragic love stories set in a novel about American Indians, *Atala* (1801) and *René* (1805), exemplifying the melancholy, poetic style that became typical of romantic fiction. He spent his final years with the celebrated beauty and social figure Mme Récamier, composing his *Mémoires d'outre-tombe* (1849–50; tr. Memoirs from beyond the Tomb).

**Chattanooga,** US city (1984 est. pop. 164,000), E Tennessee, on both sides of the Tennessee R. near the Georgia border; inc. 1839. From a trading post (est. 1810) the port city grew into a major shipping point for salt and cotton. It was of great strategic importance in the CIVIL WAR. Textile and metal industries are important. The city is surrounded by mountains, and is a tourist centre.

**Chatterjee, Bankim Chandra,** 1838–94, Indian nationalist writer. His historical novels, written in Bengali, include *Anandamath* (1882), from which India's national anthem was derived, and *Krishna Kanta's Will* (tr. 1895).

**Chatterton, Thomas,** 1752–70, English poet. At age 12 he was composing the 'Rowley poems' and claiming they were copies of 15th-cent. manuscripts. He came to London, failed to get his work published, and killed himself at 17. After his death dispute began about the composer of the Rowley poems, leading to their publication. An original genius as well as an adept imitator, he used 15th-cent. language but a modern approach. He was a hero to the Romantics.

**Chaucer, Geoffrey,** c.1343–1400, English poet. Chaucer's biography is fragmentary. A London vintner's son, he served as a court page, in the army, and on frequent diplomatic missions, then held various official positions in London. His earlier work is derived largely from French models, including the *Roman de la rose,* which he partially translated. His first poem of importance is the allegorical dream poem *The Book of the Duchess* (1368). Later he used Italian models, primarily DANTE and BOCCACCIO. Dante's influence is first seen in the *House of Fame,* an unfinished vision of love and the grounds of reputation. *The Parliament of Fowls,* on the mating of birds on St Valentine's Day, may possibly celebrate the betrothal of RICHARD II to Anne of Bohemia. His philosophical seriousness is indicated by his prose translation of BOETHIUS. *Troilus and Criseyde* (c.1385), based on Boccaccio, is one of the great love poems in English; in it he perfected the seven-line stanza later called rhyme royal. The unfinished *Legend of Good Women* treats classical heroines as Cupid's saints, and introduced the rhymed heroic couplet. Chaucer's final work is his masterpiece, *The Canterbury Tales.* This unfinished work, about 17,000 lines, is one of the major poems of world literature. In it a group of pilgrims travelling to the shrine of St Thomas à Becket decide to pass the time by telling stories. The tales include a variety of medieval genres, from the humorous FABLIAU to the serious homily, and vividly depict medieval attitudes toward love, marriage, and religion. From his lifetime onwards, with scarcely a break, Chaucer was regarded as one of the greatest English poets.

**Chausson, Amédée-Ernest,** 1855–99, French composer. His compositions were at first influenced by MASSENET and WAGNER, and later by FRANCK and DEBUSSY. Several of his works are gaining wider recognition, such as the heroic opera *Le Roi Arthur* (1886–95), *Poème* for violin and orchestra, the Symphony in B♭ (1889–90) and the Piano Quartet (1897). His premature death in a cycling accident struck him down at the height of his powers.

**Chavannes, Puvis de:** see PUVIS DE CHAVANNES.

**Chávez, Carlos**, 1899–1978, Mexican composer and conductor. He established (1928) the Symphony Orchestra of Mexico, which he conducted until 1948. Chávez used Mexican Indian elements in his *Xochipilli Macuilxochitl* (1940). Other works include the ballet-symphony *H.P.* [horsepower] (1926–27); *Sinfonía Antigona* (1933); and *Invention,* for string trio (1965).

**Cheddar Gorge**, a deep limestone gorge in the southern part of the Mendip Hills, Somerset, SW England. The largest and most spectacular gorge in England, it is a popular tourist spot, with steep limestone cliffs and nearby caves.

Cheddar Gorge

**cheese**, food known from ancient times, consisting of the curd of MILK separated from the whey. Although milk from various animals has been used for making cheese, today milk from cows, sheep, and goats is most common. In making cheese, casein, the chief milk protein, is coagulated by enzyme action, by lactic acid, or by both. The many kinds of cheeses depend for their distinctive qualities on the kind and condition of the milk, the processes used in their making, and the method and extent of curing. There are two main kinds of cheeses: hard cheeses, which improve with age, and soft cheeses, made for immediate consumption. Hard cheeses include Cheddar (originally from England), Emmental (Switzerland), and Parmesan (Italy). Among the semisoft cheeses are Gruyère (Switzerland), Edam (Holland), and Münster (Germany). Soft cheeses may be fresh (unripened), e.g., cream and cottage cheeses, or may be softened by microorganisms in a ripening process that develops flavour, e.g., Camembert, Brie, and Limburger. Blue cheeses, e.g., Stilton (England), Gorgonzola, (Italy), develop extra flavour from moulds growing inside the maturing cheeses. Cheese is a valuable source of protein, insoluble minerals, and, when made from whole milk, vitamin A, but it can also have a high fat content.

**cheetah**, CAT (*Acinonyx jubatus*) found in Africa, SW Asia, and India although it may be extinct there in the wild. The swiftest four-footed animal, it runs down its prey at speeds of over 95 kph (60 mph), the only cat to hunt this way. Cheetahs have tawny coats with many round, black spots; the average adult weighs 45 kg (100 lb). Cheetahs are unique among cats in having nonretractile claws. Hunting has greatly reduced their numbers.

**Cheever, John,** 1912–82, American author. A moralist whose works are often comic or surreal, he wrote of life in America's affluent suburbs. His novels include *The Wapshot Chronicle* (1957), *Falconer* (1977), and *Oh What A Paradise It Seems* (1982). Many of his stories are in *The Stories of John Cheever* (1978).

**Chefoo:** see YANTAI.

**Chekhov, Anton Pavlovich,** 1860–1904, Russian writer and physician. The son of a grocer and grandson of a serf, he helped support his family, while he studied medicine, by writing humorous sketches. His reputation as a master of the short story was assured when in 1888 'The Steppe', a story in his third collection, won the Pushkin Prize. *The Island of Sakhalin* (1893–94) was a report on his visit to a penal colony in 1890. Thereafter he lived in Melikhovo, near Moscow, where he ran a free clinic for peasants, took part in famine and epidemic relief, and was a volunteer census-taker. His first play, *Ivanov* (1887), had little success, but *The Seagull* (1898), *Uncle Vanya* (1899), *The Three Sisters* (1901), and *The Cherry Orchard* (1904) were acclaimed when produced by the Moscow Art Theatre. In 1901 Chekov married the actress Olga Knipper, the interpreter of many of his characters. Three years later he died of tuberculosis. The style of his stories, novels, and plays, emphasizing internal drama, characterization, and mood rather than plot and focusing on the tragicomic aspects of banal events, had great influence.

**Chekiang:** see ZHEJIANG.

**Chelčický, Petr** (ˌhelsikee), c.1390–c.1455, Czech philosopher. His writings expressed a philosophy of total nonviolence and of anarchist communism. He is traditionally considered the founder of the Bohemian Brethren and, hence, the Moravian Church, which now survives mainly in the US and South America.

**Chelmsford,** county town (1981 pop. 91,109) of Essex, SE England, on R. Chelmer, 48 km (30 mi) NE of London. The main industries of the town are the manufacture of radio and electrical equipment. St Mary's parish church (completed 1424) was rebuilt after partially collapsing in 1800, and became a cathedral in 1914.

**Cheltenham,** town (1981 pop. 87,188), Gloucestershire, SW England, on R. Chelt (tributary of R. Severn). It is mainly a residential town whose industries include the manufacture of aircraft components. It became famous as a spa after the discovery of mineral springs in 1716. There are three public schools within the town, Cheltenham College (1841), and Cheltenham Ladies' College (1853), and Dean Close (1886). There are many Regency and Victorian buildings. It is the birthplace of Gustav HOLST.

**Chelyabinsk,** city (1985 pop. 1,096,000), W Siberian USSR, in the southern foothills of the Urals and on the Mias R. A major industrial centre, it processes ore and produces steel and farm machinery. Founded in 1736 as a Russian frontier outpost, it lies on the TRANS-SIBERIAN RAILWAY.

**chemical pollutants:** see POLLUTION; WASTE DISPOSAL.

**chemical warfare,** employment in warfare of toxic substances to damage or kill plants, animals, or human beings. POISON GAS was effectively used during WORLD WAR I, when chlorine gas and later mustard gas inflicted heavy casualties on both sides. After the war the major powers continued to develop and stockpile chemical agents for possible future use, but lethal types were not employed during World War II. Thousands of synthetic toxins and naturally occurring poisons have since been tested. Besides potentially lethal chemicals that attack the skin, the blood, the nervous system, or the respiratory system, there are also nonlethal incapacitating agents that cause temporary physical disability or mental effects such as confusion, fright, or stupor. Such agents, e.g., tear gas, are used in civil disturbances as well as warfare. Various forms of HERBICIDES and defoliants were used during the VIETNAM WAR to destroy crops and clear away vegetation. In the early 1980s there were persistent reports that a lethal agent, popularly called 'yellow rain', was being used in SE Asia. Modern delivery systems artillery shells, grenades, missiles, and aircraft and submarine spray systems have increased the potential effectiveness of chemical warfare, as they have that of BIOLOGICAL WARFARE, in which micro-organisms are the toxic agents.

**chemistry,** branch of science concerned with the properties, composition, and structure of substances and the changes they undergo when they combine or react under specified conditions. Inorganic chemistry deals mainly with components of mineral origin. ORGANIC CHEMISTRY was first defined as the study of substances produced by living organisms; it is now defined as the study of the compounds of CARBON. PHYSICAL CHEMISTRY is concerned with the physical properties of materials; its subcategories are ELECTROCHEMISTRY; thermochemistry, the investigation of the changes in ENERGY and ENTROPY that occur during chemical reactions and phase transformations (see STATES OF MATTER); and chemical kinetics, which is concerned with the details of chemical reactions and of how equilibrium is reached between the products and reactants. Analytical chemistry is a collection of techniques that allows exact laboratory determination of the chemical composition of a given sample of material.

**Chemnitz:** see KARL-MARX-STADT.

**chemotherapy,** treatment of disease with chemicals or drugs; the term is now most often used to refer to the pharmacological treatment of CANCER using cytotoxic (poisonous to living cells) drugs in contrast to radiotherapy. In current approaches, drugs are used in combination to create a synergistic effect more powerful than that produced by the individual drugs used separately, and doses are scheduled to attack rapidly proliferating cells, such as cancer cells, during their vulnerable phase.

**Chengchow:** see ZHENGZHOU.

**Chengdu** or **Chengtu** (chungdooh), city (1984 pop. 8,539,000), capital of SICHUAN prov., SW China, at the confluence of the Nan and Fu rivers. It is an important regional centre for machinery production, metallurgy, and electronics. Once an ancient walled city, it was the capital of the Shu kingdom (3rd cent. AD). The cultural hub of SW China, it is the site of Sichuan Univ., and home of the Sichuan opera.

**Chengtu:** see CHENGDU.

**Chénier, André** (shay,nyay), 1762–94, French poet; b. Constantinople. His pamphlets denouncing the excesses of the REIGN OF TERROR led to his execution. His poems, perhaps the greatest in 18th-cent. France, range from the lyrical, e.g., *La Jeune Captive* (1795) and *Élégies* (1819), to the satirical.

**Cheops:** see KHUFU.

**Chepstow,** town (1981 pop. 9039), Gwent, SW Wales, on R. Wye, 24 km (15 mi) E of Newport. A market town and river port, it contains several historic buildings. The ruined castle dates mainly from the 14th cent. The ruins of Tintern Abbey are nearby.

**Chernenko, Konstantin,** 1911–85, Soviet political leader, general secretary of the ruling Communist Party (CPSU) and president of the Soviet Union (1984–85). Born the son of a Siberian peasant, he rose to prominence as a party administrator in the 1940s, becoming a close associate of Leonid BREZHNEV. Following the latter's elevation to the party leadership in 1964, Chernenko became a central committee member (1971), a central committee secretary (1976), a candidate member of the politburo (1977) and a full member (1978). Although believed to be Brezhnev's favoured successor as party leader, this post went to Yuri ANDROPOV when Brezhnev died in 1982; but following Andropov's death in 1984 Chernenko became CPSU general secretary, apparently as a transitional phase to a new leadership generation. As party leader he continued, albeit more cautiously, the campaign against corruption and inefficiency begun by Andropov.

**Chernobyl,** site of a nuclear power complex in the Ukraine, USSR, 24 km (15 mi) NW of the town of Chernobyl and 110 km (70 mi) N of Kiev. On 26 Apr. 1986 during the conduct of an unauthorized experiment reactor no.4 suffered a runaway chain reaction causing the reactor power to rise to between 100 and 500 times its design power. The resultant rise in the steam pressure lifted a 1000-ton cover plate and blew apart the reactor core starting fires and releasing a large quantity of radioactive material into the environment. The Soviet Union estimates that 3% of the heavy elements, 13% of the caesium and 20% of the iodine in the core was released resulting in a worldwide radiation dose estimated at between 8 and 210 million-person rems (see RADIOLOGY). The number of extra cancer deaths that will have been caused by the release has been variously estimated at between 8000 and 80,000. The net irradiation was approximately equivalent to the fallout from the explosion of a very large atmospheric atomic bomb. Soviet authorities evacuated 135,000 people from a zone 35 km (22 mi) surrounding Chernobyl. The radioactive cloud emanating from the disaster affected many parts of eastern and northern Europe and led to the need to destroy considerable amounts of agricultural produce that had become unfit for human consumption. In a number of areas, such as parts of N England and Wales, where heavy rain at the worst moment contaminated hill sides, the grazing of sheep continues to be affected. In western countries it is argued that through more safety-conscious design and tighter control of operations, no such accident could occur there.

Vehicles at the **Chernobyl** nuclear power station were given frequent decontamination sessions. More than 200 vehicles were treated in eight hours.

**Cherokee Indians,** once the outstanding NORTH AMERICAN INDIAN group in the SE US. They spoke an Iroquoian language (see AMERICAN INDIAN LANGUAGES). By the 16th cent. they had an advanced agricultural culture, but soon after 1750 half the tribe died in a smallpox epidemic. In 1827 they established themselves as the Cherokee Nation, with a constitution providing for an elected, republican government. The syllabary devised by SEQUOYAH contributed to their progress. When gold was discovered on their lands, a fraudulent treaty obtained by whites bound the tribe to move West, and they were forcibly removed in 1838 to land in what is now Oklahoma, and thousands of Cherokees died on the way. In Oklahoma they became the most important of the FIVE CIVILIZED TRIBES. Today, nearly 45,000 Cherokees live in Oklahoma, while some 5000 remain on a reservation in North Carolina.

**cherry,** name for various trees and shrubs (genus *Prunus*) of the ROSE family, and for their fruits. Botanically, the small red-to-black fruits are drupes, or stone fruits, closely related to the PEACH, APRICOT, and PLUM. Hundreds of varieties of sweet (*P. avium*) and sour (*P. cerasus*) cherries, believed to be native to Asia Minor, are widely cultivated. Sour cherries are mostly self-fertile, and are hardier and more easily grown than sweet cherries, which must be cross-pollinated. The fruit is popular eaten raw, and in preserves, pies, ciders, and liqueurs. Species of *flowering cherry* are cultivated for their beautiful, usually double flowers; *cherry laurel* species are also cultivated as ornamentals, e.g., American cherry laurel, or mock orange (*P. caroliniana*). The wood of the wild black cherry (*P. serotina*), fine-grained and usually reddish in colour, is prized for cabinetwork.

**chert,** cryptocrystalline variety of QUARTZ, commonly occurring in nodules. Flint—the dark variety of chert—was used by primitive peoples to make knives and spearheads, because, although it is very hard, it is easily shaped by flaking off the edges. It was long used with steel for lighting fires and later for setting off the powder in flintlock firearms.

**Cherubini, Luigi,** 1760–1842, Italian composer. He lived in Paris after 1788 and wrote operas of broad dramatic scope in the French tradition, e.g., *Médée* (1797) and *Les Deux Journées* (1800), and sacred music. In 1805, Beethoven described him as Europe's foremost dramatic composer.

**Chesapeake Bay,** major inlet on the Atlantic shoreline of the US. About 320 km (200 mi) long and up to 48 km (30 mi) wide, it is the drowned lower course of the Susquehannah R. and separates the Delmarva Peninsula from mainland sections of E Maryland and E Virginia. The bay is crossed by the Chesapeake Bay Bridge-Tunnel. BALTIMORE, Maryland, is the chief port. Rivers feeding into the bay include the POTOMAC and the James, on which JAMESTOWN, the first permanent English settlement in the Americas, was founded in 1607. The bay was explored and charted (1608) by Capt. John SMITH.

**Cheshire,** county in NW England, (1984 est. pop. 937,400), 2328 km² (908 sq mi), bordering on the Mersey estuary and WALES in the W. The county town is CHESTER. Most of the county is low-lying with many small meres or lakes. It is drained by the DEE and Weaver rivers, as well as several canals. Dairy farming is an important activity, and the county has long been famous for its cheese. Around Northwich, Middlewich, and other towns, salt is extracted to be used in the chemical industry.

**chess,** game for two players played on a square board composed of 64 small squares, alternately dark and light in colour. Each player is provided with 16 pieces, or chessmen, either white or black. Various pieces are set down in a designated order in the two ranks closest to the player. Each piece is moved according to specific rules and is removed from the board when it is displaced by the move of one of the opposing pieces into its square. The objective in chess is to checkmate, or trap, the opponent's king, a piece whose mobility is limited. Chess probably originated in India. By the 13th cent. it was played throughout Europe. The first modern international chess tournament was held in London in 1851. There have been recognized world chess champions since, and recent championship matches, such as those in which Bobby FISCHER took the title from Boris Spassky (1972), Anatoly KARPOV defeated Viktor KORCHNOI (1978, 1981), and Garik KASPAROV defeated Karpov (1985) have received worldwide media coverage. Soviet players have dominated world chess since the late 1940s.

**Chester,** county town and cathedral city (1981 pop. 80,154), in Cheshire, NW England, on R. Dee 54 km (34 mi) SW of Manchester. It is an important railway centre which contains various industries, including light engineering and the manufacture of electrical components. Built on the site of the Roman town of Deva, it contains many ancient buildings, including the cathedral, which dates from Norman times, and several 16th- and 17th-cent. timbered houses. The medieval town walls are very well preserved. It was the last English city to fall to WILLIAM THE CONQUEROR (1066). In the English Civil Wars the city was conquered by the Parliamentarians after a long siege (1643-46).

**Chesterfield, Philip Dormer Stanhope,** 4th **earl of,** 1694–1773, English statesman and writer. He was a noted wit and orator whose literary fame rests on letters to his illegitimate son Philip Stanhope (pub. 1774), aimed at educating a young man, and on letters to his godson (pub. 1890).

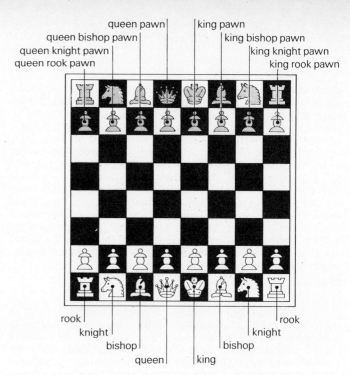

Chess piece positions

Bishop Lloyd's House, **Chester**

**Chesterton, G(ilbert) K(eith),** 1874–1936, English author, conservative, and Catholic apologist. A prolific writer, he produced studies of Browning (1903) and Dickens (1906); novels, including *The Napoleon of Notting Hill* (1904); detective fiction featuring the intuitive

Father Brown; poems; and essays, collected in *Heretics* (1905) and elsewhere. With BELLOC he propounded the economic theory of Distributism.

**chestnut,** deciduous tree (genus *Castanea*) of the BEECH family, with thin-shelled, sweet, edible nuts borne in bristly burrs. It is widely distributed in the Northern Hemisphere, having been introduced into many countries by the Romans. Edible chestnuts are now mostly imported from Italy. It forms a magnificent specimen tree but does not produce good timber outside the Mediterranean area. See also HORSE CHESTNUT.

**Chevalier, Maurice** (shə͵valyay), 1888–1972, French singer, dancer, and actor. He had tremendous success as a MUSIC-HALL entertainer and also appeared in such American films as *Gigi* (1958) and *Fanny* (1961).

**Cheyenne,** US city (1980 pop. 47,283), alt. 1848 m (6062 ft), state capital of Wyoming; inc. 1868. A market and transport centre for a ranching area, it grew with the arrival (1867) of the Union Pacific railway and was made territorial capital in 1869. Its annual Frontier Days celebration (in July; first held 1897) is a famous tourist attraction.

**Cheyenne Indians,** NORTH AMERICAN INDIANS of the Plains, speaking an Algonquian language (see AMERICAN INDIAN LANGUAGES). After acquiring horses (c.1760) they became nomadic buffalo hunters. The tribe was friendly to whites until prospectors swarmed into their lands when gold was found in Colorado. Aroused by an unprovoked massacre at Sand Creek (1864), the Cheyenne waged bitter war that culminated in the Battle of the Little Bighorn (1876), where Cheyenne massacred the cavalry of Gen. George CUSTER. In 1877, however, the sick and starving Cheyenne surrendered and were moved first to Oklahoma, then to Montana. About 3000 live on reservations.

**Chiang Ch'ing:** see JIANG QING.

**Chiang Ching-kuo** (jang jing gwaw), see under CHIANG KAI-SHEK.

**Chiang Kai-shek** (jang kieshek), 1887–1975, Chinese Nationalist leader and president of TAIWAN (1950–75). He became prominent in the KUOMINTANG after the death (1925) of SUN YAT-SEN and in 1926 launched the Northern Expedition, in which the Nationalists captured Hankou, Shanghai, and Nanjing. Chiang cooperated at first with Chinese Communists, but in 1927 reversed himself and began a long civil war with the Communists. He headed the National Government from 1928 and in 1937 formed a united front with the Communists against the Japanese in the Second SINO-JAPANESE WAR (1937–45). In 1949, however, the Communists drove Chiang and the Nationalists from the mainland to Taiwan. There he reorganized his military forces with US aid, became (1950) president of Nationalist China (Taiwan), and instituted limited democratic political reforms. He continued to promise reconquest of the mainland, but his position was hurt when Taiwan was expelled (1972) from the UN in favour of Communist China. His son, **Chiang Ching-kuo,** 1910–88, was Nationalist China's defence minister (1965–72), premier (1972–78), and president (1978–88). He was succeeded by Vice Pres. Lee Teng-Hui.

**Chiba,** city (1986 est. pop. 784,811), capital of Chiba prefecture, Honshu, Japan, on Tokyo Bay, E of Tokyo. It is the seventh largest international trade port in Japan and the centre of an industrial complex built round the site of a large steel-works. In the surrounding area there are two international facilities, New Tokyo International port and Makahari Messe.

**Chicago,** US city (1984 est. pop. 2,992,000), NE Illinois, third largest US city, centre of a vast metropolitan area, (1984 est. pop. 8,035,000), on Lake Michigan; inc. 1837. A major GREAT LAKES port and the leading commercial, financial, industrial, and cultural centre of the nation's interior, Chicago is a leader in steel production, printing, radio and television, and the manufacture of plastics, confectionery, industrial and electrical machinery, and musical instruments. It is also a major financial centre with stock, mercantile, and commodity exchanges. Downtown Chicago ('The Loop') has a dramatic skyline with some of the world's tallest skyscrapers, e.g., the SEARS TOWER and the John Hancock Tower. The North Side, mainly residential, stretches more than 30 km (c.20 mi) along the lake. The West Side is a mix of European ethnic neighbourhoods that developed in the 19th and early 20th cents. The heavily industrialized South Side is the home of most of the city's 1,197,000 blacks. Leading cultural institutions include the ART INSTITUTE OF CHICAGO, Natural History Museum, Chicago Symphony Orchestra, and

Univ. of Chicago. The city's modern development dates from the opening (1825) of the ERIE CANAL and the arrival (1852) of the railways. A fire destroyed much of Chicago in 1871. Labour troubles, e.g., the 1886 HAYMARKET SQUARE RIOT and the 1894 Pullman strike (see DEBS, EUGENE V.; ALTGELD, JOHN P.), followed rapid industrialization. In the 1920s PROHIBITION brought a reputation for gang warfare. The SAINT LAWRENCE SEAWAY opened Chicago to ocean shipping after 1959. The 1980s have seen a period of intense political conflict within the Democratic Party, surrounding the election of the city's first black mayor (1983).

**Chicano,** term used to describe Mexican-Americans. Originally pejorative, it was adopted with a sense of pride by militant Mexican-American youths in the 1960s and has since been generally accepted by members of the ethnic group. Chicanos first migrated to the US, either legally or illegally, as seasonal farm labourers, but after World War II large numbers settled in cities, especially in Los Angeles and in S Texas; 8.7 million Chicanos now live in the US, many in Mexican neighbourhoods called *barrios.* In the 1960s and 70s Chicanos grew politically active, demanding equal employment opportunities and pressing for voter registration. Cesar Chavez organized (1962) the United Farm Workers, scoring victories against large California growers. La Raza Unida, a party formed in 1970, has won local elections.

**Chichén Itzá,** archaeological site in central YUCATÁN, Mexico. Probably founded c.514 by precursors of the Itzá, it was alternately abandoned and reoccupied until it was deserted for the last time in 1194. Spanning two great periods of MAYA civilization, it displays Classic and Post-Classic architectural styles and shows a strong TOLTEC influence.

Chichén Itzá

**Chichester,** county town (1981 pop. 26,050) of W Sussex, near head of Chichester harbour, to E of Hayling Island. It is a market town with little industry. The town is built on the site of the Roman town Noviomagus. There is a cathedral, which was begun in the late 11th cent., and a 16th-cent. market cross. The Festival Theatre was opened in 1962. The famous Goodwood racecourse is nearby.

**chickadee:** see TIT.

**Chickasaw Indians:** see FIVE CIVILIZED TRIBES.

**chicken,** chief POULTRY bird, probably derived from a SW Asian jungle fowl. They are bred and selected for meat or egg production, and their physiology has been the subject of intensive scientific investigation. Chickens are raised commercially in highly-mechanized systems with closely-controlled environments of daylength, light intensity, humidity, and temperature, which maximize and regulate egg and meat production to a fine degree. Daylength (period of illumination) controls rate of growth, size of egg, and rate of laying through its effect on the production of gonadotrophic HORMONES. Low light intensities regulate physical activity, and are important to prevent self-mutilation by pecking. The cage or floor area allowed for each bird has been reduced over the years for economic reasons and is a major source of contention between farmers and animal-rights movements. However, the methods have been responsible for the relative cheapness of poultry meat and the consequent rise in consumption. During the 1980s over 600 million chickens have been produced each year for meat in the UK alone, and changes in methods would lead to large price increases. Over the same period the number of laying birds has steadily decreased partly owing to falling demand for eggs, but also due to increases in egg production per bird.

**chicken pox** or **varicella**, mild, highly infectious disease caused by the herpes zoster virus that also causes SHINGLES. Usually a disease of childhood, chicken pox is characterized by an itchy rash of blisterlike lesions that appear two to three weeks after infection, accompanied by fever and malaise. When the lesions have crusted over, the disease is no longer communicable. Topical medication is often given to relieve the itching. Since an attack in childhood confers lifelong immunity, chicken pox is rare among adults.

**chick-pea,** annual plant (*Cicer arietinum*) of the PULSE family, cultivated since antiquity for the edible, pealike seed. Chick-peas are used as food for humans and animals. They are boiled or roasted, and have been used as a coffee substitute.

**Chiclayo,** city (1981 pop. 280,244), N Peru, capital of Lambayeque dept. It is the centre of the country's most important rice- and sugar-producing regions.

**chicory** or **succory,** herb (*Cichorium intybus*) of the COMPOSITE family, native to the Mediterranean and widely grown in North America and Europe. The roasted and powdered root is used as a coffee substitute and adulterant. Chicory is also used as a seasoning and in salads. French endive is the type that is blanched for salad. True endive, or escarole (*C. endivia*), a salad vegetable since antiquity, is cultivated in broad- and curly-leaved varieties.

**chiefdom,** in schema of sociocultural EVOLUTION the stage which follows the tribal stage (see TRIBE; BAND), and is characterized by an increasingly specialized division of labour, the beginning of formalized social divisions, and redistribution as the major form of exchange. The term is more widely and unspecifically used to refer to a political system characterized by formal centralized authority which has no military or repressive apparatus and in which power is exercised by an individual chief uniting different kin groups.

**chigger:** see MITE.

**Chihuahua** (chi̱wahwah), city (1979 est. pop. 385,953), NW Mexico, capital of Chihuahua state. It was founded in 1703 as a mining town and retains its importance as the focus for an important region of mining and cattle ranching. During the Mexican Revolution 'Pancho' VILLA operated in the surrounding countryside and captured and lived in the city.

**Chikamatsu Monzaemon** (cheekaẖmatsooh), 1653–1725, Japanese dramatist. He wrote primarily for the puppet theatre, sometimes on events of the immediate past, e.g., *The Battles of Coxinga* (Kokusenya Kassen, 1715; tr. 1951) and *The Love Suicides at Amijima* (Shinjū Ten no Amijima, 1721; tr. 1961); or on love affairs with courtesans of the pleasure quarters. He wrote more than 100 puppet plays and over 30 *kabuki*, including *The Love Suicides at Sonezaki* (Sonezaki Shinjū, 1703; tr. 1961).

**Child, Lydia Maria,** 1802–80, American author and abolitionist. In 1826 she established the *Juvenile Miscellany*, the first American monthly periodical for children. She later identified herself with the antislavery cause; she wrote widely-read pamplets on the subject and edited (1841–49) the influential *National Anti-Slavery Standard*.

**childbirth:** see PREGNANCY AND BIRTH.

**Childe, Vere Gordon**, 1892–1957, British archaeologist; b. Australia. In his seminal work, *The Dawn of European Civilization* (1925), and in such popular works as *What Happened in History* (1942), he brought the study of prehistory from its traditional focus on local developments to a view that took in the whole of Europe. His idea that the prehistoric world consisted of distinct and dynamic cultures, defined by patterns of artifacts and transformed by migration, dominated archaeology until well into the 1970s.

**children's literature.** Much early literature for adults, chiefly oral ballads, sagas, and epics recounting myths and legends, came to be read as children's literature. The first writing expressly for children, however, Latin texts by BEDE and others, was instructional. More enjoyable material

appeared when William CAXTON printed (1484–85) AESOP's *Fables* and Sir Thomas MALORY's *Morte d'Arthur*. The hornbook and chapbook, from the same period, taught the alphabet, numbers, and prayers. The first distinctly juvenile literature in English, for Puritan boys and girls, consisted of gloomy, pious tales. Later, Daniel DEFOE's *Robinson Crusoe* and Jonathan SWIFT's *Gulliver's Travels* were adapted for children. In 1729 Charles PERRAULT's *Mother Goose* became popular in England. The bookseller John NEWBERY was the first to publish exclusively for children. By the end of the 18th cent. didactic works, intellectual and moralistic, predominated. In contrast, ROMANTICISM produced a body of fantasy and adventure genuinely appealing to children. GRIMM's folk tales appeared in English in 1823, and Hans Christian ANDERSEN's fairy tales in 1846. During the 19th cent. the poetry of Edward LEAR and Robert Louis STEVENSON, the inspired lunacy of Lewis CARROLL, and the fully developed characters and interesting plots of novels by Louisa May ALCOTT, Mark TWAIN, and Stevenson set high standards for juvenile literature as did translations of such foreign works as J.D. WYSS's *Swiss Family Robinson* (tr. from the German, 1814) and Carlo COLLODI's *Pinocchio* (tr. from the Italian, 1892). Fantasy continued to be well-represented in 20th-cent. children's literature, e.g., L. Frank Baum's *Wonderful Wizard of Oz* (1900), A.A. MILNE's *Winnie-the-Pooh* (1927), P.L. Travers's *Mary Poppins* (1934), J.R.R. TOLKIEN's *The Hobbit* (1937), E.B. WHITE's *Charlotte's Web* (1952) and *The Trumpet of the Swan* (1970), and Madeleine L'Engle's work of science fiction *A Wrinkle in Time* (1962). The novel for children became increasingly sophisticated, incorporating many of the elements of adult literature, a trend accelerated in the 1960s and 1970s by the appearance of more books dealing with 'mature' social and psychological themes. The novels of Judy Blume, for example, treat the emotional, sexual, and spiritual problems of adolescence; they include *Are You There God? It's Me, Margaret* (1970) and *Starring Sally J. Freedman As Herself* (1977). The Newbery Medal (1922) is one of many awards fostering the growth of children's literature.

**Chile,** officially Republic of Chile, republic (1986 est. pop. 12,300,000), 756,945 km² (292,256 sq mi), S South America, bordered by Peru (N), Bolivia (NE), Argentina (E), and the Pacific Ocean (W). Long and narrow, Chile stretches 4630 km (2880 mi) from N to S, but is only 430 km (265 mi) at its widest point. Major cities include SANTIAGO (the capital), VALPARAISO, and CONCEPCIÓN. The ANDES Mts extend the entire length of eastern Chile; Ojos del Salado (6870 m/22,539 ft), the second highest point in South America, is found here. Chile has three main natural regions: the arid north, which includes the Atacama Desert (see ATACAMA, DESERT OF); the cold and humid south, with dense forests, snow-covered peaks, glaciers, and islands; and the fertile central area, Mediterranean in climate, which is the most populous, economically advanced, and cultural heart of the nation. Located along an active zone in the earth's crust, Chile is subject to devastating earthquakes. With an economy based on its mineral wealth, Chile is one of the world's leading exporters of copper; other minerals include nitrates, iron ore, manganese, lead, and zinc. Manufactures include processed foods, fish meal, textiles, and iron and steel. Chief crops are wheat, potatoes, maize, grapes, and sugar beet, but Chile is not self-sufficient in food. Sheep raising, fishing, and timber production are also important. In 1984 GDP was US$19,500 million or US$1615 per capita. The majority of Chile's population is mestizo, but a sizable number are of European origin. Spanish is the official language. More than 85% of the people are Roman Catholic.

*History.* Upon arrival in the area that is now Chile, the Spaniards met stout resistance from the ARAUCANIAN INDIANS who lived there, but in 1541 Pedro de VALDIVIA succeeded in establishing the first Spanish settlement at Santiago. Despite continued Indian hostility, not fully subdued until the late 19th cent., the colonists established a pastoral society. In 1810 a struggle for independence from Spanish rule was initiated and finally, in 1818, following a decisive victory at Maipú by José de SAN MARTÍN, independence was proclaimed, and Bernardo O'HIGGINS, a revolutionary leader, was established as ruler. In 1879 long-standing border disputes with Bolivia and Peru led to the War of the Pacific; Chile, victorious, gained valuable mineral-rich territory. Exploitation of mineral resources, accompanied by industrialization, brought prosperity. Politically, Chile was one of the most stable and democratic nations in South America. In 1970 Salvador ALLENDE GOSSENS, of the (Marxist) Socialist Party, was elected president. His attempt to transform Chile into a socialist state ended in 1973 with a bloody military coup, in which Allende lost his life.

A repressive military junta, headed by Gen. Augusto PINOCHET, was in control into the 1980s. In 1984 the regime announced that political parties would be allowed to operate under certain conditions. The following year, amid growing internal violence and demonstrations, it rejected demands for a speedy transition to full democracy. However, in 1988 a national plebiscite showed a majority against continued rule by Gen. Pinochet beyond early 1990. Chile's longstanding territorial dispute with Argentina over three islands in the Beagle Channel was resolved (1984) on the basis of mediation by the Vatican.

**Post-war Chilean presidents**
Juan António Ríos (Radical), 1942–46
Gabriel González (Radical), 1946–52
Carlos Ibañez (centre-left), 1952–58
Jorge Alessandri (independent right), 1958–64
Eduardo Frei (Christian Democrat), 1964–70
Salvador Allende (Socialist), 1970–73
Augusto Pinochet (military), 1973–

Chile

**chilli:** see PEPPER.

**chime,** in music: see BELL.

**chimpanzee,** black-haired APE (genus *Pan*) of the equatorial forests of central and W Africa, including the common chimpanzee (*P. troglodytes*) and pygmy chimpanzee (*P. paniscus*); considered the most intelligent of apes. The common chimpanzee is covered with long, black hair and may reach 1.5 m (5 ft) in height and 70 kg (150 lb) in weight. Captive chimpanzees have been taught to communicate by using SIGN LANGUAGE or a computer console.

**China,** officially People's Republic of China, Chinese *Zhongguo Renmin Gongheguo,* people's republic (1987 pop. 1,060,000,000) 9,561,000 km² (3,691,502 sq mi), E Asia; the most populous country in the world. It is bounded by the USSR and North Korea (E), the USSR and the Mongolian People's Republic (N), the USSR and Afghanistan (W), and Pakistan, India, Nepal, Bhutan, Burma, Laos, and Vietnam (S). A coastline c.6440 km (4000 mi) long borders the Yellow and East China seas (E) and the South China Sea (S). The capital is BEIJING (Peking); other important cities include SHANGHAI, TIANJIN, and GUANGZHOU (Canton). China is the world's third-largest country (after the USSR and Canada). The terrain is generally rugged, with broad plains along the rivers and the southern coast. The Tibetan plateau occupies SW China and is separated from the Tarim basin of XINJIANG to the north by the massive Kunlun Mts. N China contains the vast tableland of INNER MONGOLIA, as well as the eastern highlands and central plain of Manchuria. The two main rivers are the YELLOW RIVER in the north, and the Changjiang (YANGTZE) R. in central China. The climate, harsh in the north and subtropical in the south, is mainly temperate.

*Economy.* China has a centrally planned economy and economic development is coordinated in five-year plans. Since the late 1970s market forces have played an increased role, particularly in agriculture. Despite rapid industrialization in recent years, China remains a predominantly agricultural country, with about 75% of the work force engaged in agricultural activities. However, cultivation is limited by natural conditions to about 15% of the land surface. Principal crops are food grains, including rice, wheat, corn, millet, barley, and kaoliang (a form of sorghum); peanuts, sweet potatoes, soya beans, cotton, tobacco, and tea are also important. Pigs and poultry are widely raised, and both inland and marine fishing are important. China is one of the world's major mineral-producing countries. Reserves of coal, its most abundant mineral and principal energy source, rank among the world's largest. Once an importer of petroleum, China is now the world's 10th-ranked oil producer, and oil exports are an increasingly important source of foreign exchange, used to finance industrial modernization. China also has extensive deposits of iron, tungsten, tin, mercury, magnesite, salt, uranium, gold, and zinc. The country's enormous hydroelectric potential is being rapidly developed; the largest project, Gezhouba Dam, on the Yangtze R., opened in 1981. China's manufactures include agriculture-related products, such as farm machinery, as well as machine tools, iron and steel, and construction materials. In recent years light industrial and consumer items have increased greatly in importance. Rivers and canals are important arteries of transport.

*People.* The population is relatively homogeneous, with the Han ethnic Chinese constituting 94% of the total. Putonghua [common language] is uniformly spoken in the north, but in the south, many dialects, mainly Cantonese, but also Wu and Hakka, are spoken; the written language is universal. Non-Chinese minorities include the Zhuang, Huis, Uighurs, and Mongols. Traditionally, most Chinese followed a mixture of Confucianism, Buddhism, and Taoism, but religious practice is not encouraged.

*History.* A protohuman toolmaker known as Pekin man (*Homo erectus;* see HUMAN EVOLUTION) lived in N China about 500,000 years ago. Modern man first appeared in the region around 20,000 years ago, establishing primitive agricultural villages by 5000 BC. The first documented Chinese civilization was the **Shang** (or Yin) dynasty (c.1480–c.1050 BC), which had cities, bronze metallurgy, and a system of writing. It was succeeded by the often turbulent **Zhou** dynasty (c.1122 BC–221 BC), which nevertheless gave rise to China's golden age of philosophy, highlighted by the works of CONFUCIUS, LAO-ZI, and Mencius. The **Qin** dynasty (221–206 BC) united China under a centralized imperial system; construction of the GREAT WALL was begun during this period. The **Han** dynasty (202 BC–AD 220), considered China's imperial age, was notable for its long, peaceable rule, territorial expansion, and technological and artistic achievement. There followed four centuries of warfare among petty states and invasions by the Huns; however, despite the chaos, the arts and sciences flourished, and BUDDHISM and TAOISM developed as important Chinese religions. Political reunification, begun under the **Sui** (581–618), paved the way for the glorious age of the **Tang** dynasty (618–907), which at its height controlled an empire stretching from Korea to Turkistan. Prosperity continued under the **Song** dynasty (960–1279), a time of scholarly studies and artistic progress, marked by the invention of movable type. In the 13th cent. N China fell to the MONGOLS led by JENGHIZ KHAN. His grandson KUBLAI KHAN founded the **Yuan** dynasty (1276–1368) and subdued (1279) the Song. Kublai's vast realm was visited and described by Marco POLO. After a massive peasant rebellion (14th cent.) ethnic Chinese rule was restored with the establishment of the **Ming** dynasty (1368–1644). However, in 1644 foreigners from the north, the Manchus, once again conquered China, establishing the **Qing** (MANCHU) dynasty (1644-1912), the last in China's history.

*Foreign Intervention.* In a relaxation of China's traditional isolationist policy, Guangzhou was opened to limited overseas trade in 1834. Dissatisfied with this restricted arrangement, Great Britain provoked the OPIUM WAR (1839–42) and easily defeated China. The Treaty of Nanking ceded HONG KONG to Britain, forced China to open several ports to unrestricted trade, and established the principle of EXTRATERRITORIALITY, by which Britons in China were granted immunity from local law enforcement. France, Germany, and Russia soon won similar concessions. The Qing regime was further weakened by a series of internal rebellions, particularly the TAIPING REBELLION (1850–64), a radical military–religious movement; by defeat in the First Sino-Japanese War (1894–95); and by the subsequent further partitioning of China into foreign spheres of influence. The BOXER UPRISING (1898–1900), a final desperate effort to resist foreign influence, was crushed by an international force and China became, in effect, a subject nation.

*Internal Struggles.* These events added impetus to growing anti-Manchu sentiment, and despite belated domestic reforms, a revolution (1911) overthrew the Qing, and a republic, led by SUN YAT-SEN, was established in 1912. With the death (1916) of Sun's successor, YUAN SHIKAI, Chinese warlords gained control of the government; they were finally ousted in 1926, after years of civil war, by the nationalist KUOMINTANG, led by CHIANG KAI-SHEK and aided by the Communists. In 1927 Chiang inaugurated the long Chinese civil war when he purged his Communist allies, eventually forcing them on the LONG MARCH (1934–35) to Shaanxi, where they established their base. In 1931 Japan had occupied Manchuria, and in 1937 it mounted a full-scale attack against China (see SINO-JAPANESE WAR, SECOND). An uneasy coalition of Nationalists and Communists fought the Japanese, but following victory in 1945, civil war once again erupted, with the US supporting the Nationalists. Beijing, followed by the other major cities, fell to the Communists in 1949, and on 1 Oct. the People's Republic of China was proclaimed with MAO ZEDONG as chairman and ZHOU ENLAI as premier. Chiang Kai-shek fled to TAIWAN, where he established a Nationalist, Republic of China.

*The People's Republic.* Under the Communists, high inflation was brought under control, a land-reform programme introduced, industry nationalized and expanded with Soviet aid, and agriculture gradually collectivized. The Chinese entered the KOREAN WAR against UN forces in 1950, participating on a large scale until the armistice of 1953. A liberal 'hundred flowers' period (1957) was followed by a crackdown on intellectuals and the Great Leap Forward (1958–60), a massive industrial development programme that was intended to transform China's economy overnight but that ended in failure. At about the same time a growing ideological rift between China and the USSR led to withdrawal

## CHINESE DYNASTIES

| Dynasty | Characteristics and History | Dynasty | Characteristics and History |
|---|---|---|---|
| Hsia c.1994– c.1523 BC | Semilegendary Emperor Yu built irrigation channels, reclaimed land. Bronze weapons, chariots, domestic animals used. Wheat, millet cultivated. First use of written symbols. | Sui 581–618 | Reunification; centralized government re-established. Buddhism, Taoism favoured. Great Wall refortified; canal system established. |
| Shang or Yin c.1480 c.1050 BC | First historic dynasty. Complex agricultural society with a bureaucracy and defined social classes. Well-developed writing, first Chinese calendar. Great age of bronze casting. | Tang 618–907 | Territorial expansion. Buddhism temporarily suppressed. CIVIL SERVICE examinations based on Confucianism. Age of great achievements in poetry (LI BAI, BAI JUYI, DU FU), sculpture, painting. |
| Zhou c.1122– 221 BC | Classical age (CONFUCIUS, LAO-ZI, Mencius) despite political disorder. Written laws, money economy. Iron implements and ox-drawn plough in use. Followed by Warring States period, 403–221 BC. | Five Dynasties and Ten Kingdoms 907–960 | Period of warfare, official corruption, general hardship. Widespread development of printing (see TYPE); paper money first printed. |
| Qin 221–206 BC | Unification of China under harsh rule of Shih Huang-ti. FEUDALISM replaced by pyramidal bureaucratic government. Written language standardized. Roads, canals, much of GREAT WALL built. | Song 960–1279 | Period of great social and intellectual change. Neo-Confucianism attains supremacy over Taoism and Buddhism; central bureaucracy reestablished. Widespread cultivation of tea and cotton; gunpowder first used militarily. |
| Han 202 BC– AD 220 | Unification furthered, but harshness lessened and CONFUCIANISM made basis for bureaucratic state. BUDDHISM introduced. Encyclopedic history, dictionary compiled; porcelain produced. | Yuan 1276–1368 | MONGOL dynasty founded by KUBLAI KHAN. Growing contact with West. Confucian ideals discouraged. Great age of Chinese playwriting. Revolts in Mongolia, S China end dynasty. |
| Three Kingdoms AD 220–265 | Division into three states: Wei, Shu, Wu. Wei gradually dominant. Confucianism eclipsed; increased importance of TAOISM and Buddhism. Many Indian scientific advances adopted. | Ming 1368–1644 | Mongols expelled. Confucianism, civil service examinations reinstated. Contact with European traders, missionaries. Porcelain, architecture (see CHINESE ARCHITECTURE), the novel and drama flourish. |
| Tsin or Chin 265–420 | Founded by a Wei general; gradual expansion to the southeast. Series of barbarian dynasties ruled N China. Continued growth of Buddhism. | Qing or Manchu 1644–1912 | Established by the MANCHUS. Territorial expansion but gradual weakening of Chinese power; decline of central authority. Increasing European trade; foreign powers divide China into spheres of influence. OPIUM WAR; HONG KONG ceded; BOXER UPRISING. Last Chinese monarchy. |

of Soviet aid and technical assistance. Evidence of internal tension began to surface in the 1960s, culminating in the CULTURAL REVOLUTION of 1966–69, a massive upheaval launched by Mao to purge the Communist Party. Tension increased again in the early 1970s with the revelation that Lin Biao, China's defence minister and Mao's designated heir, had died (1971) in a plane crash after an attempt to assassinate Mao. In international affairs, China's progress towards recognition as a world power was aided by its explosion of an atomic bomb (1964) and the launching of its first satellite (1970). An easing of relations with the West led to the admission of China to the UN in 1971 and to a visit to China by Pres. Richard Nixon in 1972. Zhou Enlai and Mao Zedong died in 1976. Following the assumption of power by HUA GUOFENG, the country was shaken by the arrest of Mao's widow, JIANG QING, and three colleagues (the GANG OF FOUR); Jiang was sentenced to death in 1981 but granted a renewable two-year reprieve. The Third Plenum of the Communist Party's Eleventh Central Committee in 1978 marked the consolidation of power by DENG XIAOPING and his associates and adopted a programme of rapid economic modernization. Liberal economic and trade policies were instituted, and the US and China normalized diplomatic relations on 1 Jan. 1979. ZHAO ZIYANG replaced Hua Guofeng as premier in 1980 and HU YAOBANG was appointed general secretary of the Communist Party. In 1981 the Communist Party severely criticized Mao Zedong's policies in the last years of his life in a public document, and in 1982 Maoist ideology and political structure were curbed through the adoption of new party and national constitutions. The restructuring of the commune system in the countryside followed in 1983 and LI XIANNIAN was appointed president of the People's Republic of China. Britain and China signed an agreement in

1984 for the return of Hong Kong to China in 1997. Queen Elizabeth II in 1986 became the first British monarch to visit China. Discussions on democratic reforms and student demonstrations in 1986 led to a political backlash and the fall of Hu Yaobang in 1987. Deng's modernization policies continue, however, but in 1989 student protest on an unprecedented scale, backed by other groups in Beijing, was followed by severe repression. The hardline government, led by LI PENG, stripped Zhao Ziyang (general secretary of the Communist Party since 1987) of his power, and Qiao Shi, previously in charge of security, emerged as a key figure.

### Post-war Chinese Communist Party leaders*
Mao Zedong (1935–76)
Hua Guofeng (1976–81)
Hu Yaobang (1982–87)
Zhao Ziyang (1987–)
*Chairman until 1982, general secretary since then

### Post 1949 Chinese premiers
Zhou Enlai (1949–76)
Hua Guofeng (1976–80)
Zhao Ziyang (1980–)

### Post-1949 Chinese heads of state*
Mao Zedong (1949–59)
Liu Shaoqi (1959–68)
Li Xiannian (1983–88)
Yang Shangkun (1988–)
*Position did not exist between 1968 and 1983

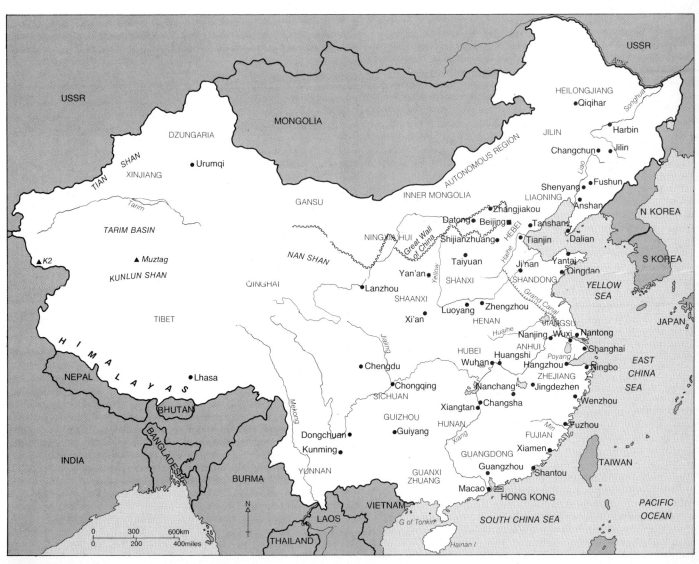

China

**China, Great Wall of:** see GREAT WALL OF CHINA.

**China, Republic of:** see TAIWAN.

**chinchilla,** small, burrowing RODENT that lives in colonies up to 4250 m (15,000 ft) high in the Andes of Bolivia, Chile, and Peru. Its soft grey pelt is one of the costliest of all furs, and the wild chinchilla was nearly exterminated before protective laws were passed.

**chinchona:** see CINCHONA.

**Chinese,** subfamily of the Sino-Tibetan family of languages. See LANGUAGE (table).

**Chinese architecture.** Few buildings exist in China predating the Ming dynasty (1368–1644). Wars, invasions, and insubstantial construction (wood and rice-paper) account for most of the loss. An exception is the Great Wall of China. Mid-20th-cent. architectural finds have clarified some of the history of Chinese architecture. As early as the Neolithic period, the basic principle of supporting a roof with spaced columns rather than walls was established. Walls served merely as enclosing screens. The typical Chinese roof probably dates from c.1500 BC, but it is known only from the Han dynasty (202 BC–AD 220), when it appeared in the familiar form—graceful, overhanging, sometimes in tiers, and with upturned eaves. It rested on brackets which rested in turn on columns. Roof tiles were colourfully glazed and brackets elaborately carved and painted. A characteristic ground plan has remained constant in Chinese and Japanese palaces and temples. Inside an external wall, the building complex is arranged along a central axis and is approached through a series of gates. Next comes a public hall and finally the private quarters. Each residential unit was built around a central court with a garden, which became an art form in itself. The coming of BUDDHISM did not affect the style. The only distinctly Buddhist building was the PAGODA, simple and square at first, later more elaborate. A distinctive pagoda style emerged in the 11th cent. Built in three stages, it had a base, shaft, and crown, surmounted by a spire, and was often octagonal. In the Ming period the complex of courtyards, parks, and palaces became labyrinthian. BEIJING's Forbidden City remains a spectacular achievement of intricacy and decoration. Since the late 19th cent. the Chinese have adopted European styles, particularly Soviet, with a trend towards the massive and clearly functional in public buildings.

**Chinese art,** the oldest in the world, has its origins in remote antiquity (see CHINA). Excavations in Gansu and Henan have revealed a Neolithic culture with pottery painted in dynamic swirling or lozenge-shaped patterns. Bronze vessels from the Shang dynasty (2nd millennium) indicate an advanced culture as well as a long period of prior experimentation. Bronzes were mainly made using piece-moulds rather than the CIRE PERDUE method and were decorated with severe abstract as well as naturalistic representations. The advent of BUDDHISM (1st cent. AD) brought works of sculpture, painting, and architecture of a distinctly religious nature. Representations of the BUDDHA and the bodhisattvas became great themes in sculpture. The forms of these figures came from India, but by the 6th cent. AD Chinese artists had developed their own sculpture style, which reached its greatest distinction in the Tang dynasty (618–907). Buddhist sculpture continued to flourish until the Ming dynasty (1368–1644). The origins of Chinese painting are largely lost until the 5th cent. AD. The Caves of a Thousand Buddhas, near Dunhuang, contain frescoes and scrolls dating from the 5th to 8th cent. Chinese painting achieves its effects through mastery of the line and silhouette rather than through PERSPECTIVE or the rendering of light and shadow. The art of figure painting reached its peak in the Tang dynasty, which also saw the rise of Chinese LANDSCAPE PAINTING. In the Song dynasty (960–1276) landscape painting reached its peak, reflecting contemporary Taoist and Confucian views. The human figure was diminished so as not to intrude on the orderly magnitude of nature. The monumental detail also began to emerge—a single bamboo, flower or bird became the subject for a painting. The Ch'an (Zen) sect of Buddhism used rapid brush strokes and ink splashes to create intuitive works of great vigour. With the Yuan dynasty (1276–1368) and Mongol rule, a flourishing of landscape and bamboo painting, as well as underglaze painted procelain, was led by native Chinese who retired from office. In the Ming dynasty the Wu school of amateur scholar painters reacted against the professionals of the Che school (1368–1644). During the Qing (1644–1912) dynasty a level of technical competence was developed that lasted until the 19th cent., but there was little innovation in painting apart from the Individualist painters of the late 17th cent. By the 19th cent. reliance on calligraphic techniques had produced sterile formulas in painting. The development of Chinese POTTERY-making followed that of painting, reaching perfection in the Song dynasty and extreme technical elaboration in the Ming. In the minor arts, e.g., ENAMEL ware, lacquer ware, jade, ivory, and textiles, the world owes an incalculable debt to the influence of Chinese art.

Chinese art: early 15th-cent. blue and white Ming flask, 30.8 cm high.

**Chinese exclusion,** policy initiated in 1882 banning US entry to Chinese labourers. After the US acquisition (1848) of California, there arose a need for cheap labour, and Chinese flocked there to work on the railroads. By 1867 they numbered 50,000; their number increased after the Burlingame Treaty of 1868, which permitted Chinese immigration but not naturalization. Anti-Oriental prejudice and the competition with American workers led to anti-Chinese riots (1877) in San Francisco, then to the Chinese Exclusion Act of 1882, which banned Chinese immigration for 10 years. In a new treaty of 1894, China accepted another 10-year exclusion, which Congress unilaterally continued until the 1924 immigration law that excluded all Asians. In 1943 a new law extended citizenship rights, and permitted an annual immigration of 105 Chinese. The quota was abolished in 1965.

**Chinese literature,** Most of the earliest surviving written works from China are administrative records of the Shang (c.16th cent. BC to c.1066 BC) inscribed on bone and historical works including the *Chun qiu* [spring and autumn annals], a chronological record of the State of Lu, 722–481 BC. An early folk tradition has, however, survived in the *Shi jing* [book of poetry], a verse anthology covering c.11th to 6th cent. BC, including love songs, folk songs, ritual hymns, and political poems. These two formed part of the 'Five Classics' traditionally associated with *Confucius* and a later body of Confucian commentary and interpretation grew up on the basis of the Classics. More literary writings, associated with the early Taoist philosophers LAO ZI and ZHUANG ZI, contrast with the concrete, historical nature of many of the texts associated with Confucius, in a dichotomy that was to persist in the later scholarly tradition. The short, lyrical poems of the *Shi jing* gave way to longer, more personal verse in the *Chu ci* anthology associated with QU YUAN (c.340–278 BC) and to the five-syllable regulated verse style of the Han period (221 BC–AD 220), although the golden age of Chinese poetry is considered to be the Tang dynasty (AD 618–907), its greatest exponents LI BAI, WANG WEI, and DU FU.

During the Tang, poetic composition formed part of the civil-service examinations; poetic skill was an essential requirement for the scholar, and the absorption of the poetic legacy created an allusive style firmly based in tradition. In the period before the Tang, fiction began to develop beyond the simple folk story into the more complex *chuanqi* stories of the Tang and Song, often love stories involving penniless young scholars trying to pass the civil-service examination or tales of the supernatural. The *hua ben* [storyteller's script] of the Song (960–1279) and Yuan (1276–1368) with natural breaks in the narrative flow developed into the full-scale novel of the Ming (1368–1644) and Qing (1644–1912) periods with chapter divisions and narrative devices that recall the storyteller's art. Major themes continue those of the *chuanqi* but also include historical novels, satires like *Ru lin wai shi* [the scholars] by Wu Jingzi (1701–54), novels of the heroic (*Shui hu zhuan* [the water margin], ?15th cent.), novels of the supernatural including *Xi yu ji* [journey to the west] (an imaginative and allegorical version of a famous pilgrimage where the real-life monk is accompanied by a monkey and a pig), detective stories and the famous *Hong lou meng* [tr. as The Dream of the Red Chamber *or* The Story of the Stone] by CAO XUEQIN (1715–63) which combines romance with manners, morals and the supernatural against the background of an aristocratic family in decline. Prose writing flourished at the same time as the novel in the *suibi* (informal essays of scholars and connoisseurs). The stylization of later Chinese poetry and the distance of the written language from the spoken vernacular, combined with radical ideas of political change in the period after the Republican Revolution in 1911, led intellectuals like Hu Shi and the satirical essayist and short-story writer LU XUN to reject the classical style and write in *bai hua* [everyday speech]. Novels by BA JIN, LAO SHE, MAO DUN, and (the more complex) Qian Zhongshu, as well as the short stories of SHEN CONGWEN and Lu Xun reflect the best of the pre-1949 literature. In 1944, Mao Zedong's 'Talk at the Yan'an Forum for Art and Literature' laid down new rules for literature which should guide and uplift and serve the Communist Party and the masses. Despite restrictions, DING LING, Wang Meng, and others, as well as some of the pre-1949 writers generally managed to maintain the *bai hua* realist tradition until the CULTURAL REVOLUTION (1966–76). Since 1976, younger writers and poets, to some extent influenced by western models, have been trying to experiment with free verse, stream of consciousness and surrealism, etc.

**Chinese music** can be traced to the third millennium BC. Most of its early history is lost. In China music and philosophy were always inseparably bound. Musical theory was symbolic and was stable through the ages. The single tone was more significant than melody and was an attribute of the substance producing it. Music had cosmological and ethical connotations comparable to GREEK MUSIC. The Chinese SCALE is pentatonic. Vocal melody is limited by the fact that, in Chinese, inflection affects a word's meaning, and also because quantitative RHYTHMS are not easily adaptable to the language. The ancient hymns were slow and solemn, accompanied by large orchestras. Opera originated in the 14th cent. In the 20th cent. Western harmony has been influential. Since 1949 the Peking Opera has produced numerous new works in traditional performance style.

**chinoiserie**, decoration influenced by Chinese art. Medieval travellers brought Eastern art back to Europe, and by the 17th cent. Dutch ceramics showed the influence of Chinese blue-and-white porcelains. In the mid-18th cent., interiors, furniture, and textiles were decorated with Chinese-inspired motifs of human figures, scenery, pagodas, and exotic birds and flowers. In France, chinoiserie blended with the ROCOCO Louis XV style. In England, the style influenced furniture made by CHIPPENDALE. Chinoiserie was also popular in the American colonies, especially in wallpaper designs.

**Chios:** see KHIOS.

**chip:** see INTEGRATED CIRCUIT.

**chipmunk:** see GROUND SQUIRREL.

**Chippendale, Thomas**, 1718–79, English cabinetmaker. His designs, popularized through his book *The Gentleman and Cabinet-Maker's Director* (1754), were so widely followed that much 18th-cent. English furniture is grouped under his name, but only those pieces for which the original bills survive (e.g., for Harewood House) can be assigned unquestionably to his workshop. To the sober design and fine construction of the Queen Anne and Georgian styles he added Chinese (see CHINOISERIE), Gothic, and ROCOCO motifs. He made chairs of many types, from geometrical to sumptuously carved; desks; mirror frames; china cabinets and bookcases; and tables with fretted galleries and cluster-column Gothic legs.

Design for a bookcase from Thomas **Chippendale's** *The Gentleman and Cabinet-Maker's Director*

**Chirac, Jacques** (ˌshirak), 1932–, French conservative political leader, prime minister of FRANCE (1974–76, 1986–88). After a rapid rise in the political establishment, he was appointed prime minister by Pres. Valéry GISCARD D'ESTAING in 1974 at the age of 41, but resigned two years later amid policy differences. He then reorganized the Gaullist party under his own leadership and was elected mayor of Paris in 1977. After unsuccessfully contesting the 1981 presidential elections, he became the dominant opposition figure during the subsequent period of left-wing government (1981–86). In the 1986 parliamentary elections he led the centre-right parties to a narrow overall majority, thus becoming prime minister again under the continued presidency of François MITTERRAND of the Socialist Party. He unsuccessfully opposed Mitterrand in the 1988 presidential elections and was obliged to surrender the premiership.

**Chirico, Giorgio de** (ˌkeereekoh), 1888–1978, Italian painter; b. Greece. In hospital after World War I he met CARRÀ and they formed the *Scuola Metafisica* (1917). His powerful, disturbing paintings employ steep PERSPECTIVE, mannequin figures, empty space with long cast shadows, and forms out of context to create an atmosphere of mystery and loneliness. Train stations and time are recurrent themes in these works and were an influence on early SURREALISM. By 1930 however he had abandoned his earlier ideas and he attempted a reworking of the technical and thematic interests of the old masters.

**Chiron** (ˌkieron /-ən), in Greek mythology, a centaur; son of CRONUS. He was a wise physician and prophet whose pupils included HERCULES, ACHILLES, JASON, and ASCLEPIUS. After receiving an incurable wound, he gave his immortality to PROMETHEUS and died. ZEUS turned him into the constellation Sagittarius.

**chiropody**, profession concerned with the care of the feet. Of particular benefit to elderly and disabled people, chiropody deals with such common conditions as corns, bunions, and ingrowing toenails as well as minor surgery and prescription of medication.

**chiropractic**, system of treatment of disease by manipulation, based on the theory that disease results from a disruption of nerve function. This interference is thought to stem from the incorrect alignment of bones, primarily displaced vertebrae, which chiropractors massage and manipulate manually in order to relieve pressure on nerves. X-rays are used to aid diagnosis.

**Chisholm Trail**, route over which herds of cattle were driven to railheads in Kansas after the Civil War. In 1866, Jesse Chisholm, an Indian trader, cut the trail by carting a heavy load of buffalo hides from Oklahoma to Kansas. Drovers followed the trail for 20 years with hundreds of thousands of Texas longhorn cattle; it became celebrated in frontier stories and ballads. The trail fell into disuse as railways and wire fencing developed, but traces of it survive.

**chitin,** main constituent of the shells of ARTHROPODS. Analogous in structure to CELLULOSE, chitin contributes strength and protection to the organism. The cell walls of some fungi also contain chitin.

**chiton,** marine MOLLUSC (class Amphineura). The chiton has a low oval body covered dorsally by a slightly convex shell of eight overlapping plates. It clings tightly to hard surfaces with its broad flat ventral foot; it crawls by means of muscular undulations of the foot. The mouth, located in front of the foot, contains a toothed scraping organ, the radula. Chitons range from 1.2 to 30 cm (½ to 12 in). They graze on the algae growing on rocks.

**chiton,** the gown worn by men and women in classical Greece. The two main types have been distinguished as the *Doric*, a single length of fabric, turned down at the top, wrapped around the body, and secured at the shoulders with pins or brooches, and the *Ionic*, a two-piece gown, stitched together at the shoulders.

**Chittagong,** city (1981 pop. 1,391,877), capital of Chittagong division, SE Bangladesh, on the Karnafuli R. near the Bay of Bengal. An important rail terminus and administrative centre, it is the chief port of Bangladesh, with modern facilities for oceangoing vessels. Oil (offshore installations and refineries) and cotton- and jute-processing are among its important industries. A port known since the early centuries AD, it was controlled successively by the Hindus, Arakans, Moguls, and British.

**Chitungwiza** (chitung,weeza), city (1983 est. pop. 202,000), on the southern outskirts of HARARE, Zimbabwe. A dormitory suburb for the capital, it has grown rapidly since political independence in 1980.

**chivalry,** system of ethical ideals that grew out of FEUDALISM and had its zenith in the 12th and 13th cent. Chivalric ethics originated chiefly in France and Spain and spread rapidly. They represented a fusion of Christian and military concepts of morality, and they still form the basis of gentlemanly conduct. The chief chivalric virtues were piety, honour, valour, courtesy, chastity, and loyalty. The knight's loyalty was due to God, to his suzerain, and to his sworn love. Love in the chivalrous sense was largely platonic. The ideal of militant knighthood was greatly enhanced by the CRUSADES, and the monastic orders of knights, the KNIGHTS TEMPLARS and KNIGHTS HOSPITALLERS, produced soldiers sworn to uphold the Christian ideal. Besides the battlefield, the tournament became an arena in which the virtues of chivalry could be proved. The code of COURTLY LOVE was developed in France and Flanders. In practice, chivalric conduct was never free from corruption, and the outward trappings of chivalry declined in the 15th cent. Medieval secular literature, such as the ARTHURIAN LEGEND and the CHANSONS DE GESTE, was concerned primarily with knighthood and chivalry. In the 19th cent. ROMANTICISM brought about a revival of chivalrous ideals.

**chive:** see ONION.

**Chivor Dam,** dam on the Bata R. in Colombia, completed in 1975. It is the highest dam in Latin America at 237 m (778 ft).

**chlorine** (Cl), gaseous element, discovered in 1774 by Karl SCHEELE, who thought it was an oxygen compound, and identified as an element by Sir Humphry DAVY in 1810. Chlorine is a greenish-yellow, poisonous gas with a disagreeable, suffocating odour. A HALOGEN, it occurs in nature in numerous and abundant compounds, e.g., sodium chloride (common salt). Chlorine is soluble in water; chlorine water has strong oxidizing properties (see OXIDATION AND REDUCTION). Chlorine is used in water purification, as a disinfectant and antiseptic, and as a bleaching agent in the textile industry. Chlorinated hydrocarbons (e.g., DDT) are long-lasting pesticides. Many poison gases contain chlorine. Chlorine compounds used medically include chloroform, formerly used as a general anaesthetic, and chloral hydrate, a sedative drug. See ELEMENT (table); PERIODIC TABLE.

**chlorophyll,** green pigment in plants that gives most their colour and enables them to carry on the process of PHOTOSYNTHESIS. Chlorophyll, found in the CHLOROPLASTS of the plant cell, is able to trap and store the energy of sunlight. The light absorbed by chlorophyll molecules is mainly in the red and blue-violet parts of the visible spectrum; the green portion is not absorbed but reflected and transmitted, and thus chlorophyll appears green.

**Chlorophyta,** division of the plant kingdom consisting of green ALGAE.

**chloroplast,** complex, discrete, lens-shaped structure, or organelle, contained in the cytoplasm of plant cells. Chloroplasts have submicroscopic, disclike bodies, called grana, composed of layered membranes that house CHLOROPHYLL and are the central site of the process of PHOTOSYNTHESIS.

**Chocano, José Santos,** 1875–1934, Peruvian poet and revolutionary. An exponent of MODERNISMO, he emphasized Indian and native themes, e.g., in *Alma América* (1906). He was murdered in Chile.

**chocolate,** term for products of the seeds of the CACAO tree, used for making beverages or sweets. Chocolate is prepared by a complex process of cleaning, blending, and roasting the beans, which are then ground and mixed with sugar, cocoa butter, and milk solids. A chocolate drink known to the Aztecs came to Europe through Spanish explorers c.1500, and was a fashionable beverage in 17th- and 18th-cent. England. The process for making milk chocolate was perfected in Switzerland c.1876.

**Choctaw Indians:** see FIVE CIVILIZED TRIBES.

**choir 1** A group of singers, most commonly singing religious music as part of a church service (see CHORUS). Choirs have participated in church services for many centuries; at first they sang only PLAINSONG in unison, but with the advent of POLYPHONY choir music began to be written for parts. **2** The division of an organ used to accompany singers. **3** A section of a chorus or orchestra, as brass choir.

**cholera,** acute epidemic disease caused by the bacterium *Vibrio cholerae* and characterized by devastating intestinal loss of fluid and electrolytes. The disease is contracted from faecally contaminated food and water and causes severe vomiting and diarrhoea (known as ricewater stools), and, if untreated, death. Treatment consists of replacement of fluid and electrolytes. The disease, which occurs only in humans, remains prevalent in regions of Asia where public sanitation is poor. See SNOW, JOHN.

**cholesterol,** fatty substance found in vertebrates and in foods from animal sources. A STEROID, cholesterol is found in large concentrations in the brain and spinal cord, as well as in the liver, the major site of cholesterol biosynthesis. Cholesterol is the major precursor in the synthesis of vitamin D and the various steroid HORMONES. It sometimes crystallizes in the GALL BLADDER to form gallstones. A high level of cholesterol in blood serum is associated with atherosclerosis (see ARTERIOSCLEROSIS) and cardiovascular disease.

**Chomsky, Avram Noam,** 1928–, American linguist, philosopher, and political thinker. He was profoundly influenced by Zellig Harris and is mainly assoicated with the theory of TRANSFORMATIONAL–GENERATIVE GRAMMAR, which reacted against the linguistic theories of American Structuralism (see LINGUISTICS), and sought to prove linguistics an integral part of modern psychology and philosophy. His most important works are *Syntactic Structures* (1957), *Cartesian Linguistics* (1966), and *Reflections on Language* (1975). His works on current politics include *The Washington Connection and Third World Fascism* (1979), with Edward S. Herman.

**Chongqing** or **Chungking** (choohng ching), city (1984 pop. 13,944,800), SICHUAN prov., SW China, at the junction of the Yangtze and Jialing rivers. A major inland port, rail, and air centre, with important metallurgical, engineering, chemical, and textile industries, it is now also developing as a telecommunications centre. Chongqing became a treaty port in 1891. In 1938 it became the war-time capital of Chiang Kai-shek's Kuomintang government. After 1949 it became central to the industrialization of SW China and in 1983 was singled out as a centre for encouraging economic reforms and modernization.

**Chonju,** city (1984 pop. 421,751), capital of Cholla Pukto prov., SW South Korea. It was originally the principal market and service centre of a major rice-growing province. The traditional industries of bamboo fan-making, paper, boots, textiles, and food-processing have been augmented by plastics, tyres, and agricultural implements.

**Chopin, Fryderyk Franciszek** (shoh,panh), 1810–49, Polish composer. He brought romantic piano music to unprecedented heights of expressiveness. In the 1830s he settled in Paris; although he remained a Polish nationalist, he never returned home. He associated with literary and artistic figures, notably George SAND, with whom he had a liaison from 1837 to 1847, when a long illness developed into tuberculosis. Chopin established the PIANO as a solo instrument free from choral or orchestral influence. In his piano CONCERTOS in E Minor (1833) and F Minor (1836), the piano dominates the orchestra. Other major works are 24 studies (1832 and 1834); 24 preludes (1838–39); SONATAS in B Flat Minor (1840) and B Minor (1845); many nocturnes and four scherzos; and, expressing Polish nationalism, many polonaises and mazurkas.

**Chopin, Kate O'Flaherty**, 1851–1904, American author. Her novel *The Awakening* (1899) caused great controversy because of her treatment of female sexuality but is now highly regarded. She also wrote sketches of Creole life collected in *Bayou Folk* (1894) and *A Night in Acadie* (1897).

**chorale**, any of the traditional, strophic congregational hymns of the German Protestant Church. The form was developed after the Reformation to replace the earlier PLAINSONG. J.S. BACH harmonized nearly 400 chorales and composed 30 new ones.

**chordate**, common name for an animal having three unique features at some stage of its development: a notochord (dorsal stiffening rod) as the chief internal support, a tubular nerve cord (spinal cord) above the notochord, and GILL slits leading into the pharynx (anterior part of the digestive tract). Grouped in the phylum Chordata, chordates are mainly vertebrates, animals of the subphylum Vertebrata (the FISHES, AMPHIBIANS, REPTILES, BIRDS, and MAMMALS), in which a backbone of bone or cartilage forms around the notochord; the rest are small aquatic invertebrates of the subphyla Urochordata (TUNICATES) and Cephalochordata (LANCELETS), in which there are no backbones.

**chorea**, involuntary jerky, arrhythmic movement of the face, limbs, or entire body. The childhood disease **Sydenham's chorea**, or **St Vitus's dance**, which causes chorea, is usually a complication of RHEUMATIC FEVER. The condition develops slowly, sometimes up to six months after the acute infection has occurred, but it resolves completely. In **Huntington's chorea**, a hereditary disease of adulthood, the jerky movements characteristic of the disorder result from progressive degeneration of the central NERVOUS SYSTEM. The disease is invariably fatal.

**choreography**, the art of inventing or composing dances. Used originally to describe the notation of the movements of the feet in the early 18th cent. Anthropologists have shown, however, that choreography in its creative sense existed in primitive societies; it is thus much older than Western dance historians have maintained. The art remained male-dominated until the 20th cent., when dancers such as Ninette de VALOIS, Doris HUMPHREY, and Martha GRAHAM established women as important choreographic artists. Regarded until recently as a very rare talent, it is acknowledged now to be rare only if referring to work of the highest theatrical quality. There are many other kinds and levels of choreographic activity, in musical theatre, opera, television, films, festivals, education and community productions, all of which can claim to be creative. Choreography is now taught in schools, higher education institutions, and in community situations. See also BALLET; DANCE; MODERN DANCE.

**chorus**, in ancient Greek drama, the group that sang and danced to accent the action and to represent a more public dimension of it. The tragic chorus seems to have arisen from the singing of the DITHYRAMB and to have become a true dramatic chorus when THESPIS introduced the actor in the 6th cent. BC. As TRAGEDY developed, the size and role of the chorus diminished while that of the actor increased. By the 2nd cent. BC it had ceased to have anything to do with the action, and it eventually disappeared.

**chorus**, in music, large group of singers performing in concert; a group singing religious music is a CHOIR. Much choral music stems from religious and folk music. As a musical form, the chorus is integral to OPERA. Since the 19th cent., it has been written into symphonies and other compositions.

**Chorzów** (ˌhawjoohf), city (1984 pop. 145,000) in Upper Silesia, S Poland. It is a mining and manufacturing centre, especially for fertilizers in the KATOWICE industrial region. Iron production utilizing coke dates from 1802.

**Chou En-Lai**: see ZHOU ENLAI.

**Chrétien de Troyes** or **Chrestien de Troyes** (kray,tyanh də ,trwah), fl. 1170, French poet, author of the first great literary treatments of the ARTHURIAN LEGEND. His narrative romances, imbued with the ideals of chivalry, include *Érec et Énide*, *Cligès*, and *Perceval*.

**Christchurch**, city (1981 pop. 321,373), E South Island, New Zealand. It is the commercial centre of the productive Canterbury Plains and the third largest city in New Zealand. Lyttleton is its port. Perhaps the most English of New Zealand's cities, it has such landmarks as Hagley Park and Christchurch Cathedral. It was settled in 1850 and is the site of the Univ. of Canterbury (est. 1873).

**Christian**, Danish kings. **Christian I**, 1426–81, king of Denmark (1448–81), Norway (1450–81), and Sweden (1457–64), was the founder of the Oldenburg dynasty of Danish kings. In 1460 he also succeeded to Schleswig and Holstein. A weak monarch, he made concessions to the Danish nobles and lost his authority over Sweden. He was succeeded by his son John, whose son was **Christian II**, 1481–1559, king of Denmark and Norway (1513–23) and Sweden (1520–23). His massacre of Swedish nobles led to the accession of GUSTAVUS I of Sweden and the end of the KALMAR UNION. Christian was deposed (1523) by the Danish nobles in favour of his uncle, Frederick I, and imprisoned (1532) until his death. **Christian III**, 1503–59, king of Denmark and Norway (1534–59), was the son of Frederick I. With Gustavus I of Sweden he defeated the German city of LÜBECK (1536), breaking the power of the HANSEATIC LEAGUE. He established (1536) Lutheranism in Denmark. Never elected king of Norway, he declared it a Danish dependency. He was succeeded by his son Frederick II. **Christian IV**, 1577–1648, king of Denmark and Norway (1588–1648), was the son of Frederick II. He made war (1611–13, 1643–45) on CHARLES IX of Sweden and had a major part in the THIRTY YEARS WAR. His son FREDERICK III succeeded him. Frederick's son was **Christian V**, 1646–99, king of Denmark and Norway (1670–99). His minister, GRIFFENFELD, dominated his reign. His son FREDERICK IV succeeded him. **Christian VI**, 1699–1746, king of Denmark and Norway (1730–46), was the son of Frederick IV. A Pietist, he carried out a peaceful foreign policy. In 1733 he established a form of serfdom. His son FREDERICK V succeeded him. **Christian VII**, 1749–1808, king of Denmark and Norway (1766–1808), was Frederick V's son. Because he was mentally ill, power was held first by his ministers and then by his son and successor, FREDERICK VI, as regent. Their reforms included the end of serfdom. **Christian VIII**, 1786–1848, king of Denmark (1839–48) and Norway (1814), was the cousin and successor of Frederick VI. He accepted a liberal Norwegian constitution. In 1836 Danish rule of SCHLESWIG-HOLSTEIN became an issue. His son FREDERICK VII succeeded him. **Christian IX**, 1818–1906, king of Denmark (1863–1906), succeeded Frederick VII, last of the Oldenburg line. In war (1864) with Prussia and Austria he lost Schleswig and Holstein. During his rule there was pressure for a more democratic constitution. His son FREDERICK VIII succeeded him. A younger son became GEORGE I of Greece. **Christian X**, 1870–1947, king of Denmark (1912–47) and Iceland (1912–44), was the son of Frederick VIII and the brother of HAAKON VII of Norway. He granted (1915) a new constitution enfranchising women. During the German occupation (1940–45) he was placed under house arrest (1943). His son FREDERICK IX succeeded him.

**Christian Aid**, a charitable agency, established in 1950 under the auspices of the British Council of Churches and operating mainly in Third World countries, which enables the denominations belonging to the council to cooperate effectively in relief work. The projects it supports include refugee resettlement, disaster relief, and economic development through agricultural, health, education, and community schemes. While working closely with equivalent organizations in the US and many other countries, it also carries out in Britain, through churches, schools, and universities, an educational programme concerned with poverty and development.

**Christian Democrat International** (CDI), world coordinating body of about 50 Christian democratic parties. It was formed in 1982 as successor to the Christian Democratic World Union (est. 1961). The CDI has two regional organizations: the Christian Democratic Organization of the Americas (est. 1949) and the European Christian Democratic Union (est. 1965). The Christian democratic parties of the EUROPEAN COMMUNITY are federated in the European People's Party.

**Christianity**, all doctrines and religious groups based on the teachings of JESUS Christ. Jesus is held by Christians to be the Son of God, the second person of the TRINITY, and the Saviour of mankind. This teaching is embodied in the Bible, particularly in the New Testament. Rooted in JUDAISM, Christianity was founded in the 1st cent. in Palestine by disciples of Jesus. It was spread, despite sporadic persecution, through the Roman

Empire by missionaries, notably St PAUL, and was recognized (313) by CONSTANTINE I. The early church was plagued by heresies concerning the nature of Christ (e.g., ARIANISM, NESTORIANISM, MONOPHYSITISM), which were condemned at councils such as the First Council of NICAEA (325). MONASTICISM arose in Egypt in the 3rd and 4th cent. and was organized in the East by St Basil the Great and in the West by St BENEDICT. Christian writers, notably ORIGEN, St ATHANASIUS, St JEROME, and St AUGUSTINE helped to determine and preserve the text of the Bible. In the East the church became centred in Constantinople and was largely subordinate to the emperor; in the West the PAPACY at Rome remained an independent force. From both centres Christianity grew to embrace all Europe, but in the 7th and 8th cent. lost Asia Minor and N Africa to ISLAM. Gradually, a break developed between East and West (see ROMAN CATHOLIC CHURCH; EASTERN ORTHODOX CHURCH), and became more or less permanent after 1054. In the West the growing power and corruption of the church contributed to the Protestant REFORMATION, which splintered Christianity into numerous sects (see PROTESTANTISM). In the 20th cent. the ECUMENICAL MOVEMENT was begun to promote Christian unity.

**Christian Science,** religion founded upon principles of divine healing and laws expressed in the acts and sayings of JESUS Christ, as discovered and formulated by Mary Baker EDDY and practiced by the Church of Christ, Scientist. The sect denies the reality of the material world, arguing that sin and illness are illusions to be overcome by the mind; thus, its members refuse medical help in fighting sickness. Mrs Eddy's *Science and Health with Key to the Scriptures* is the textbook of the doctrine. The church was founded in 1879 and is centred in Boston, Massachusetts.

**Christian socialism,** term used in Great Britain and the US for a kind of socialism growing out of the clash between Christian ideals and the effects of competitive business. In Europe it usually refers to a party or trade union directed by religious leaders in contrast to socialist unions and parties. Begun (1848) in England and led by Frederick Denison MAURICE and Charles KINGSLEY, it sought to encourage the labouring masses and the church to cooperate against capitalism. It was influenced by the Fourierists (see FOURIER, CHARLES), rather than by MARX.

**Christie, Dame Agatha,** 1890–1976, English detective-story writer. Most of her over 80 books feature one of two detectives, Hercule Poirot or Jane Marple. Her novels include *The Murder of Roger Ackroyd* (1926) and *Murder on the Orient Express* (1934). Among her plays is the long-running *Mousetrap* (1952).

**Christina,** 1626–89, queen of Sweden (r.1632–54), daughter of GUSTAVUS II. Until 1644 she was under a regency headed by OXENSTIERNA. Her interest in state affairs gave way to her zeal for learning, and she attracted to her court musicians, poets, and such scholars as DESCARTES. She refused to marry, naming her cousin, later CHARLES X, as her successor. In 1654 she abdicated, becoming a Catholic and settling in Rome. On the death (1660) of Charles X she returned to Sweden but failed to regain the throne. She is buried at St Peter's in Rome.

**Christmas** [Christ's Mass], in the Christian calendar, the feast of the nativity of JESUS Christ (25 Dec.). It ranks after EASTER, PENTECOST, and EPIPHANY in liturgical importance and did not become widespread until the 4th cent. The customs of the yule log, carolling, mistletoe, and gifts at Christmas are English. Elsewhere, gifts are given at other times, as at Epiphany in Spain. Christmas cards appeared c.1846. The concept of Santa Claus (see NICHOLAS, SAINT) as the kindly patron of children was first made popular in 19th-cent. New York. The Christmas tree was a medieval German tradition. Midnight Mass is a familiar religious observance among Roman Catholics and some Protestants.

**Christmas Island,** tropical island (1986 pop. 178), 155 km² (60 sq mi), external territory of Australia, in the Indian Ocean, 2620 km (c.1630 mi) NE of PERTH. Most of the inhabitants are Chinese and Malays who work the island's extensive phosphate deposits; there is no indigenous population. Christmas Island was annexed by Great Britain in 1888 and transferred to Australian rule in 1958.

**Christo,** 1935–, Bulgarian artist; b. Christo Javacheff. His art involves the wrapping of objects, thus transforming the everyday into the ambiguous. In his large environmental projects Christo alters urban structures or landscapes, giving them a temporary, artificial skin that both conceals and reveals. His work includes *Running Fence* (1976), a fabric curtain that ran 39 km (24 mi) through the California countryside.

**Christ of the Andes,** statue of Christ in Uspallata Pass, the ANDES. Dedicated on 13 Mar. 1904, it commemorates a series of peace and boundary treaties between Argentina and Chile.

Christ of the Andes

**Christophe, Henri** (krees͵tof), 1767–1820, Haitian revolutionary leader. A freed black slave, he helped TOUSSAINT L'OUVERTURE to liberate HAITI and plotted the assassination of DESSALINES. A tyrant, he ruled (1806–20) N Haiti as King Henri I. He committed suicide.

**Christopher, Saint,** supposedly a martyr c.250 in Asia Minor. In legend he carried a child across a river and felt the child's weight almost too heavy to bear; the child was JESUS, who was holding the world in his hands. Christopher is the patron of travellers. His feast, 25 July, was dropped from the Roman Catholic liturgical calendar in 1969; but may be observed locally.

**Christus,** or **Cristus, Petrus** d. c.1473, Flemish painter. A follower and probable pupil of the van EYCK brothers, he was noted for his introspective treatment of figures and rendering of geometric perspective. Many of his compositions are simplifications of Jan van Eyck's. They include *Lamentation* (c.1448; Museé Royal, Brussels) and *St Eligius and Two Lovers* (1449; Metropolitan Mus., New York).

**chromatography,** resolution of a chemical mixture into its component compounds by passing it through a system, called a chromatograph, that retards each compound to a varying degree. The retarding substance is usually a surface adsorbent, such as ALUMINA, CELLULOSE, or SILICA. In column chromatography the adsorbent is packed into a column, and a solution of the mixture is added at the top and washed, or eluted, down with an appropriate solvent; each component of the mixture passes through the column at a different speed. In paper chromatography the mixture to be separated is allowed to soak along the paper by capillary action, the cellulose in the paper acting as the adsorbent. The gas chromatograph is a system in which a liquid with a high boiling point is impregnated on an inert solid support packed into a thin metal column, and helium gas is allowed to flow through it. The solution to be analysed is injected into the column, immediately volatilized, and swept by the helium gas through the column, where the mixture is resolved into its

Christus, *Portrait of a Young Man*

components. Other variants, including affinity-chromatography, and gel-permeation chromatography have recently been developed. These play a vital role in the separation, identification, and characterization of macromolecules, especially those of biological origin.

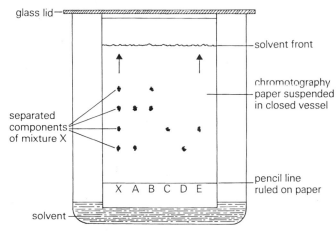

Chromatography

**chromium** (Cr), metallic element, discovered in 1797 by L.N. Vauquelin. A lustrous, silver-grey metal, it is comparatively rare and occurs only in compounds; the chief source is the mineral chromite. Hard and nontarnishing, chromium is used to plate other metals. In alloys (e.g., STEEL) with other metals it contributes hardness, strength, and heat resistance. Chromium compounds are used as paint pigments, in tanning, and in dyeing. See ELEMENT (table); PERIODIC TABLE.

**chromosome**, structural carrier of hereditary characteristics, found in the cell nucleus. The number of chromosomes is characteristic of each species; in sexually reproducing species, chromosomes generally occur in pairs. In MITOSIS, or ordinary cell division, each individual chromosome is duplicated and each daughter cell receives all chromosomes, a set exactly like its parent's. In MEIOSIS, the process by which sex cells (OVUM and SPERM) are formed, each daughter cell receives half the number of chromosomes, one of each pair. A fertilized egg contains two sets of chromosomes, one set from each parent. Chromosomes are made of PROTEIN and NUCLEIC ACID. They represent the linear arrangement of GENES, the units of inheritance.

**chromosphere:** see SUN.

**Chronicles** or **Paralipomenon**, [Gr., = things left out], two books of the OLD TESTAMENT, originally a single work in the Hebrew canon. The books contain a history of the Jewish kingdom under DAVID (1 Chron. 10–29) and SOLOMON (2 Chron. 1–9), and, after the division of the kingdom, a history of the southern kingdom of JUDAH, including the BABYLONIAN CAPTIVITY (2 Chron. 10–36).

**chronometer,** mechanical instrument for keeping highly accurate time. The perfection of the chronometer in 1759 by the English clockmaker John Harrison allowed navigators at sea to determine longitude accurately for the first time. A marine chronometer is a spring-driven escapement timekeeper, like a watch, but its parts are more massively built and it has devices to compensate for changes in the tension of the spring caused by changes in temperature. See CLOCK.

**chrysanthemum,** annual or perennial herb (genus *Chrysanthemum*) of the COMPOSITE family, long grown in the Orient. The chrysanthemum is a national flower of Japan and the floral emblem of the Japanese imperial family. The red, white, yellow, or bronze flowers range from single daisylike heads to large rounded or shaggy heads. They are commercially important. Innumerable horticultural types exist, most varieties of *C. morifolium.* The pyrethrum, which produces a commercially-important insecticide; feverfew, used medicinally for migraine; and the marguerite belong in the same genus.

**Chrysler, Walter Percy,** 1875–1940, American industrialist, founder of the Chrysler Corp. Initially a machinist's apprentice, he became (1916) a vice president of the General Motors Corp. and in 1924 brought out the first Chrysler car. The Chrysler Corp., founded the next year, quickly became one of the major US car manufacturers.

**Chrysophyta,** division of the plant kingdom consisting of the golden ALGAE, the best known of which are the DIATOMS.

**Chrysostom:** see JOHN CHRYSOSTOM, SAINT.

**chrysotile:** see ASBESTOS; SERPENTINE.

**Chun Doo Hwan,** 1931–, Korean military leader, president of South KOREA (1980–88). An army officer, Chun rose to power after the murder (1979) of South Korean Pres. PARK CHUNG HEE. As president, Chun banned many of his opponents from politics and passed (1980) a new authoritarian constitution. In 1981 he lifted martial law, in effect since 1979. After he vacated the presidency (1988), the alleged repression and corruption of his administration came under strong public criticism.

**Chungking:** see CHONGQING.

**Chuquicamata** ('choohkee̩kahmatə), the world's largest open-cast mine. Situated in the deserts of N Chile copper has been mined here since the beginning of the 20th cent.

**Church, Frederick Edwin,** 1826–1900, American painter. A member of the HUDSON RIVER SCHOOL, he preferred exotic foreign landscapes to native views. His large canvases are noted for their crystalline portrayal of light.

**Church Army,** an organization of lay evangelists, male and female, founded for the Church of England in 1882 on the model of the nondenominational SALVATION ARMY. Its officers help local clergy, run missions to seaside resorts and prisons, and engage in a wide range of social and rehabilitation work among the underprivileged. It has daughter societies in many other countries (e.g., the US and many Commonwealth countries) where the ANGLICAN COMMUNION operates.

**Church Commissioners,** a statutory body set up in 1948 to administer the estates and revenues of the CHURCH OF ENGLAND. Comprising eminent lay persons as well as the archbishops, bishops, and certain other clergy, with day-to-day business transacted by a small Estates and Finance Committee, the Commissioners are responsible for the payment of clergy stipends and pensions, for help in providing clergy houses and churches in new housing areas, and for pastoral organization. Their income from all sources for the year 1984 amounted to almost £127 million.

**Churchill, John:** see MARLBOROUGH, JOHN CHURCHILL, 1st DUKE OF.

**Churchill, Sarah:** see under MARLBOROUGH, JOHN CHURCHILL, 1st DUKE OF.

**Churchill, Sir Winston Leonard Spencer,** 1874–1965, British statesman, soldier, and writer. Son of a politician and a graduate of Sandhurst, he fought in India, the Sudan, and South Africa, where he made his reputation. In 1900 he was elected to Parliament, changing sides and serving alongside LLOYD GEORGE in the Liberal ministries (1906–1914). He was the first lord of the admiralty (1911–15) in WORLD WAR I until discredited by the failure of the GALLIPOLI CAMPAIGN which he had championed. He later served in several cabinet positions in the Coalition government of Lloyd George. A Conservative after 1924, he was chancellor of the exchequer from 1924 to 1929; his revaluation of the pound was as controversial in retrospect as his handling of the general strike of 1926. Out of office from 1929 to 1939, Churchill issued repeated but unheeded warnings of the threat of Nazi Germany. In 1940, seven months after the outbreak of WORLD WAR II, he replaced Neville CHAMBERLAIN as prime minister. His stirring leadership, powerful oratory, inspiring energy, and unequivocal refusal to make peace with HITLER were crucial to maintaining British resistance from 1940 to 1945. He believed

" CHEER UP! THEY WILL FORGET YOU BUT THEY WILL REMEMBER ME ALWAYS "

THE LEADER OF HUMANITY

'Two **Churchill's**', a cartoon by Low which appeared in the *Evening Standard* after Winston Churchill's election defeat in 1945.

passionately in an Anglo–American alliance, but gave full, if not always fully appreciated, help to the Soviet Union after Hitler attacked it. He twice addressed the US Congress, twice went to Moscow, and attended a series of international conferences (e.g., YALTA CONFERENCE). After the postwar Labour victory in 1945, he became leader of the opposition. In 1951 the conservatives returned to power and he was again appointed prime minister; he was knighted in 1953 and retired in 1955. Churchill was the author of many histories, biographies, and memoirs, and in 1953 he was awarded the Nobel Prize for literature for his writing and his oratory.

**Church of Christ, Scientist:** see CHRISTIAN SCIENCE.

**Church of England:** see ENGLAND, CHURCH OF.

**Church of Scotland:** see SCOTLAND, CHURCH OF.

**Church Slavonic,** language belonging to the South Slavic group of the Slavic subfamily of the Indo-European family of languages. It is the first Slavic tongue known to be recorded in writing. From the 9th to 11th cent. AD the language is termed Old Church Slavonic, Old Church Slavic, or Old Bulgarian. The later Church Slavonic flourished as a literary language before the 18th cent. It is still the liturgical language of most branches of the EASTERN ORTHODOX CHURCH, but is extinct as a spoken tongue. See LANGUAGE (table).

**churchwardens,** elected lay representatives, male or female, of the parishioners of an English parish church. Normally two in number, they

are responsible for the moveable property of the church, and also for maintaining order in it and in the churchyard.

**Churriguera, José Benito** (choohree‚geərə), 1665–1725, Spanish architect and sculptor. He won fame for his design (1689) for the great catafalque for Queen Maria Luisa and for his ornate retables. Associated with his brothers, he served as architect for the cathedral of Salamanca and built a private palace and the urban complex Nuevo Baztán in Madrid. The term **Churrigueresque** describes late-17th- and early-18th-cent. Spanish architecture, marked by extravagance of design and capricious use of Renaissance motives. Its influence was important in the missions of Spanish colonial North America.

Jose Benito **Churriguera:** Cartuja chapel, Granada

**Chu Teh** (jooh day): see ZHU DE.

**CIA:** see CENTRAL INTELLIGENCE AGENCY.

**Cibber, Colley,** 1671–1757, English dramatist and actor-manager. After successes playing RESTORATION comedy, he wrote *Love's Last Shift* (1696), the first sentimental COMEDY. He wrote 30 more plays and was made poet laureate in 1730. An unpopular man, he was attacked by Alexander POPE in *The Dunciad*.

**cicada** (si‚kahdə, -‚kaydə), medium to very large (18–110 mm/³⁄₄–4¹⁄₄ in long), noisy, usually tree-living, and often gregarious BUGS (suborder Homoptera). The males have a pair of tambourine-like organs (tymbals) at the base of the abdomen which, when caused to vibrate, produce loud, shrill, species-specific songs to attract females. Both adult and nymphs (larvae) are sap-suckers; the latter, whose fore legs are modified for digging, live underground, usually feeding on tree roots, and can take several years to complete their development. Some North American periodical cicadas (genus *Magicicada*) take as long as 17 years. The adults are generally short-lived. Females have long, substantial ovipositors and can cause appreciable damage to young trees through cutting slits in the bark for egg-laying.

**Cicero** (Marcus Tullius Cicero) or **Tully,** 106 BC–43 BC, greatest Roman orator, also a philosopher. As senatorial party leader he prosecuted CATILINE, but was later exiled himself by CLODIUS; recalled by POMPEY, he

Cicada emerging from shell

opposed Julius CAESAR. He answered Mark ANTONY in the senate with his first and second PHILIPPICS, defending the Republic. After Octavian (AUGUSTUS) took Rome, Cicero was executed. To the modern reader, his letters, to his brother and friends, are perhaps most interesting. His philosophical works are influenced by Stoic ethics (see STOICISM). He is best known for his *Orations against Catiline, Against Verres, On the Manilian Law,* and others. His mastery of Latin prose is unsurpassed.

**Cid** or **Cid Campeador** (sid), 1043–99, Spanish soldier whose exploits were romanticized in many literary works. He fought against the MOORS but ALFONSO VI distrusted and banished (1081) him. The Cid then served the Muslim ruler of Saragossa, fighting against Moors and Christians alike. In 1094 he conquered VALENCIA and ruled there until his death.

**CID:** see CRIMINAL INVESTIGATION DEPARTMENT.

**cilia,** minute, hairlike filaments, found on the surface of cells and tissues, which give their name to a class of PROTOZOANS, the ciliates. The unicellular ciliates are covered by cilia which beat in regular waves and propel them through the water. Cilia are also found in multicellular animals, beating to set up a feeding current or to transport strings of mucus, with food entangled in them, into the digestive tract.

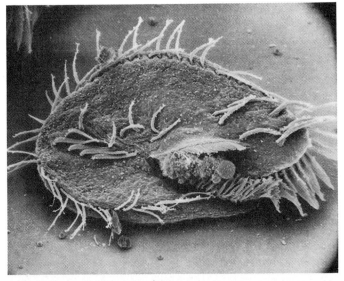

Scanning electron micrograph of *Oxytricha sp.*, a ciliate protozoa. The body is decorated with individual or groups of **cilia** which help in locomotion and feeding.

**Cilicia,** ancient region of SE Asia Minor, between the Mediterranean and the Taurus range. Part of the Assyrian empire and then of the Persian empire, it was later hellenized. Roman and Byzantine rule followed. Cilicia was invaded (8th cent. AD) by the Arabs, and in 1080 an Armenian state (later called Little Armenia) was set up. This lasted until the area was conquered by the Turks in 1375.

**Cimabue, Giovanni** (cheemah,boohay), d. c.1302, Florentine painter; b. Cenni di Pepo or Peppi. His works constitute the transition from formal Byzantine painting to the greater naturalism of the 14th cent. His only documented work is a mosaic in Pisa Cathedral (1301–02). His attributed works include the *Madonna Enthroned* (c.1280; Uffizi, Florence) a *Crucifixion* (c.1285; Santa Croce, Florence), and some frescoes at Assisi.

Giovanni **Cimabue,** *Madonna Enthroned,* c.1280. Galleria Uffizi, Florence.

**Cimarosa, Domenico** cheemah,rohzah), 1749–1801, Italian opera composer. He worked in Venice, St Petersburg, and Vienna, before returning to Naples (scene of his first successes) in 1793. He was one of the leading composers of *opera buffa* in his time and was considered a serious rival to Mozart. His greatest work is *Il matrimonia segreto* (1792).

**Cimmerians,** ancient and little-known people who were driven (8th cent. BC) from the CRIMEA to the Lake Van region in present E Turkey.

They swept across Asia Minor (late 7th cent.), plundering Lydia and weakening Phrygia.

**cinchona** or **chinchona**, evergreen tree (genus *Cinchona*) of the MADDER family, native to mountainous areas of South and Central America and widely cultivated elsewhere for its bark, the source of QUININE and other antimalarial alkaloids. The tree was named for the Countess of Chinchón, said to have been cured of a fever in 1638 by a preparation of the bark.

**Cincinnati**, US city (1984 est. pop. 370,000), SW Ohio, on the Ohio R.; founded 1788, inc. as a city 1819. It is the industrial, commercial, and cultural centre of a large area of Ohio and neighbouring Kentucky, and a major river port and transport centre. Machine tools, transport equipment (automobile and aircraft engines and parts), chemicals, and cosmetics are among its manufactures. The city was the first seat (1799) of the legislature of the NORTHWEST TERRITORY. The city is noted for its cultural institutions, e.g., its conservatory, opera, museums, and symphony orchestra. William Howard TAFT and Robert A. TAFT were born there, and it is the site of the Taft Museum.

**Cincinnatus** (Lucius or Titus Quinctius Cincinnatus), fl. 5th cent. BC, Roman patriot. He was consul (460 BC) and dictator twice (458 and 439). According to tradition, he was called from his farm to defend Rome twice, first against foreign invaders, then against the plebeians.

**Cinderella**, heroine of a famous folktale in which she is ill-used by her stepmother and sisters, helped by a fairy godmother, and marries a prince. Dating from 9th-cent. China, the story exists in many versions and is included in the tales of Charles PERRAULT and the GRIMM brothers. ROSSINI's opera (1817) also tells the story.

**cinema**, film-making as an art and an industry, including its production techniques, its creative artists, and the distribution and displaying of its products (see CINEMATOGRAPHY and CAMERA). Experiments in photographing movement were made in the US and Europe well before 1900. The first motion pictures made with a single camera were by E.J. Marey, a French physician, in the 1880s. In 1889 Thomas EDISON developed the kinetograph, using rolls of coated celluloid film, and the kinetoscope, for peep-show viewing. The LUMIÈRE brothers, in France, created the Cinématographe (1895). Projection machines were developed in the US and first used in New York City in 1896. The first film theatre, a 'nickelodeon', was built in Pittsburgh in 1905. Films developed simultaneously as an art form and an industry. They had enormous immediate appeal, and were established as a medium for chronicling contemporary attitudes, fashions, and events. The camera was first used in a stationary position, then panned from side to side and moved close to or away from the subject. With the evolution of sound films in the late 1920s, language barriers forced national film industries to develop independently. In the US a separation of cinema crafts had developed by 1908, and actors, producers, cinematographers, writers, editors, designers, and technicians worked interdependently, overseen and coordinated by a director. Hollywood, California, became the American film capital after 1913. Films were at first sold outright to exhibitors and later distributed on a rental basis. By 1910 the 'star system' had come into being. Directors became known for the individual character of their films and were as famous as their stars. During World War I the US became dominant in the industry. In 1927 dialogue was successfully introduced in *The Jazz Singer.* Early colour experiments were achieved by hand-tinting each frame. In 1932 Technicolor, a three-colour process, was developed. The film industry in its heyday (1930–49) was managed by a number of omnipotent studios producing endless cycles of films in imitation of a few successful original types. In those great years Hollywood gave employment to a host of talented actors, e.g., Ingrid BERGMAN, Humphrey BOGART, Joan CRAWFORD, Bette DAVIS, Cary GRANT, Katharine HEPBURN, Spencer TRACY, and John WAYNE. In the 1950s the overwhelming popularity of TELEVISION began to erode studio profits, necessitating technological innovations such as wide-screen processes, stereophonic sound systems, and three-dimensional cinematography (3-D). By 1956 studios were compelled to produce films made expressly for television reruns. In the 1960s many filmmakers began to work independently of the studio system, producing low-budget films departing from the glamorous, celebrity-packed works of earlier years. Costly and elaborate science fiction productions and horror films attained unprecedented popularity in the late 1970s and early 1980s. Among the great directors of the cinema are D.W. GRIFFITH, Mack SENNETT, John FORD,

Howard HAWKS, and Alfred HITCHCOCK in the US, Jean RENOIR and Jean-Luc GODARD in France; Ingmar BERGMAN in Sweden; F.W. MURNAU and Rainer Werner FASSBINDER in Germany; Lucino VISCONTI, Michelangelo ANTONIONI, and Federico FELLINI in Italy; Sergei EISENSTEIN and Aleksandr DOVZHENKO in the USSR; Satyajit RAY in India; and KUROSAWA AKIRA in Japan.

**cinematography**, photographic arts and techniques involved in making films. The motion-picture CAMERA evolved from multi-image stop-action devices that recorded the parts of a continuous movement. D.W. GRIFFITH gave the medium its first cohesive language of camera techniques; his innovations included the close-up, a device by which he heightened the emotional impact of his film. Silent pictures brought cinematographic art to its greatest heights: expressive devices were developed for silent films, such as cutting (the reorganization of film footage by means of the removal of unwanted frames) and MONTAGE (the creative cutting of images that, when juxtaposed, create a meaning absent from the single images, devised by the Russian director Sergei EISENSTEIN). The German directors Fritz LANG and F.W. MURNAU evolved a highly subjective film style, expressive of psychic and emotional states, using distorted images presented by the camera as if seen from the principal character's vantage point. VON STERNBERG combined spectacular sets with soft focus to create a sense of fantasy and mystery. Smooth sound synchronization was achieved in the 1930s. Orson WELLES's *Citizen Kane* (1941) was a milestone among sound films, a showcase for numerous technical innovations copied and adapted throughout film's subsequent history. Colour processes, in existence since the 1920s, were perfected in the 1930s and 40s. In the 1950s and 60s various cinematographic gimmicks were developed, e.g., three-dimensional photography, split-screen processes, Aromarama (in which audiences were bombarded with scents deemed appropriate to what they were watching), and several wide-screen processes, of which only CinemaScope was extensively used. Film techniques have been greatly refined in the past 50 years, largely through experimentation by gifted cameramen and their assistants. The foremost American cinematographers include Karl Freund, Gregg Toland, Charles Rosher, James Wong Howe, Lee Garmes, Vilmos Zsigmond, Caleb Deshanel, and Gordon Willis. The French directors of the 'new wave' of the 1960s (e.g., François TRUFFAUT and Jean-Luc GODARD) evolved an influential intimate camera style. A choppy style termed *cinéma vérité,* characterized by frequent jump cutting, enjoyed a brief vogue in the 1960s in low-budget films such as John Cassavetes's *Shadows* (1960). Intensely personal, highly expressive cinematographic styles are the hallmark of the works of Alfred HITCHCOCK, Ingmar BERGMAN (working with the cameramen Gunnar Fischer and Sven Nykvist), Luis BUÑUEL, Michelangelo ANTONIONI, Rainer Werner FASSBINDER, and Werner HERZOG.

**Cinna** (Lucius Cornelius Cinna), d. 84 BC, Roman politician. When SULLA left Italy, Cinna as consul (87–84 BC) opposed him, and slaughtered many of Sulla's followers. After Sulla set out for Rome, and before the civil war began, Cinna was murdered in a mutiny at Brundisium. His daughter Cornelia was the first wife of Julius CAESAR.

**cinnabar,** deep-red mercury sulphide mineral (HgS). Used as a pigment, it is principally a source of the metal MERCURY. Cinnabar is mined in Spain, Italy, and California.

**cinnamon,** tree or shrub (genus *Cinnamomum*) of the LAUREL family. Cinnamon spice, obtained by drying the bark of the tropical Ceylon cinnamon (*C. zeylanicum*), has been used since biblical times. *C. camphora* is the source of CAMPHOR.

**Cinque Ports,** a group of towns on the south coast of England which in former times combined for defence. In the 11th cent. the towns were given privileges in return for furnishing the English crown with ships in times of war. Originally there were five towns within the group, i.e., HASTINGS, Romney, Hythe, DOVER, and Sandwich, although further towns were added later. Their importance declined in the 17th and 18th cent. The Cinque Ports are under the jurisdiction of a Lord Warden, who is admiral of the ports and governor of Dover Castle.

**Cintra,** town (1984 pop. 15,994) west of Lisbon, Portugal, on wooded slopes. It is famed for the beauty of its situation which has inspired writers. It was a favourite residence of Portuguese kings and preserves a royal palace of the 15th–16th cent.

**Cione, Andrea di:** see ORCAGNA.

**Circe** (,suhsee), in Greek mythology, enchantress; daughter of HELIOS. In HOMER's *Odyssey* she turned ODYSSEUS' men into swine, but was forced to break the spell.

**circle,** closed plane CURVE consisting of all points at a given distance from a fixed point, called the centre. A radius of a circle is any line segment connecting the centre and the curve; the word *radius* is also used for the length *r* of that line segment. Both the circle itself and its length *C* are referred to by the term *circumference*. A line segment whose two ends lie on the circumference is a *chord;* a chord through the centre is a *diameter.* The circumference of a circle is given by $C = 2\pi r$. The area $A$ bounded by a circle is given by $A = \pi r^2$. In the religion and art of many cultures the circle frequently symbolizes heaven, eternity, or the universe. See also CONIC SECTION.

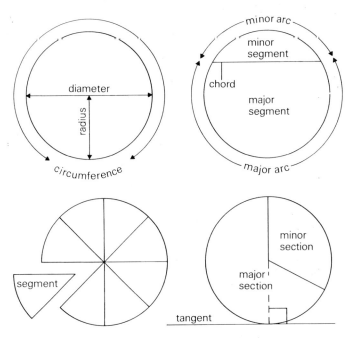

Parts of a **circle**

**circuit breaker,** electric device for interrupting the current in an ELECTRIC CIRCUIT when there is a fault. Used in power transmission lines, the detection of a fault, its location, and its isolation are all achieved at high speed by instruments and computers. In the high voltage transmission of power, the grid system allows for alternative routing and the isolation of the fault to await repair. In some circuit breakers compressed gas is used pneumatically to operate the arms of the breaker. When a fault occurs excessive currents flow and the breakers operate, those on either side of the fault remaining open until the fault is located; the remainder can be closed and supply resumed. Under computer operation the whole process can take less than three cycles of the 50 to 60 cycles per second alternating current. Domestically one sees this as a flicker in the lighting. Some circuit breakers also have their own detecting mechanisms. These usually depend on balanced bridge circuits which trip when unbalanced, or on heat generated in a special detector or on the change of strength of the magnetic field produced by the current.

**circulatory system,** group of organs that transport blood and the substances it carries to and from all parts of the body. In humans the circulatory system consists of vessels (arteries and veins) that carry the blood, and a muscular pump, the HEART, that drives the blood. Arteries carry the blood away from the heart; the main arterial vessel, the aorta, branches into smaller arteries, which in turn branch into still smaller vessels that reach all parts of the body. In the smallest blood vessels, the capillaries, which are located in body tissue, gas and nutrient exchange occurs: the blood gives up nutrients and oxygen to the cells and accepts carbon dioxide, water, and wastes (see RESPIRATION). Blood leaving the tissue capillaries enters converging large vessels, the veins, to return to the heart. The human heart has four chambers and a dividing wall, or septum, that separates the heart into right and left sides. Oxygen-poor, carbon dioxide-rich blood from the veins returns to the right side of the

heart. The heart contracts to pump the blood through pulmonary arteries to the LUNGS, where the blood receives oxygen and eliminates carbon dioxide. Pulmonary veins return the oxygen-rich blood to the left side of the heart. The left side then pumps the oxygenated blood through the branching aorta and arteries to all parts of the body. An auxiliary system, the LYMPHATIC SYSTEM, collects lymph, or tissue fluid, from body tissues and returns it to the blood. See also ARTERIOSCLEROSIS; BLOOD PRESSURE; CORONARY HEART DISEASE; HEART FAILURE; SHOCK; STROKE.

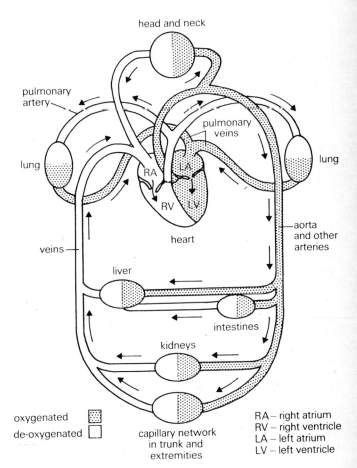

Diagram of circulatory system

**circumcision,** operation to remove the foreskin covering the glans of the penis. Dating from prehistoric times, it is performed by Jews as a sacramental operation on the eighth day after the birth of a male child. It is also practised among Muslims and other peoples and is now widely performed as a sanitary measure. Female circumcision—excision of all or part of the external genitals—is a mutilating procedure, often involving removal of the clitoris. Found in Islam and in certain communities in Africa, South America, and elsewhere (it is far more widespread than male circumcision), it causes severe physical and emotional distress and difficulty in childbirth. Both male and female circumcision usually form part of the INITIATION of children into social adulthood.

**circumpolar star,** a star whose apparent daily path on the celestial sphere lies completely above or below an observer's horizon. A star whose declination (see ASTRONOMICAL COORDINATE SYSTEMS) is greater than 90° minus an observer's latitude will always remain above the horizon for that observer.

**circus** [Lat., = circle], associated historically with the horse and chariot races, gladiatorial combats, and brutal athletic contests known in ancient Rome as the Circensian games. The Roman circus was a round or oval structure, with tiers of spectators' seats enclosing the area where the action took place. The modern circus, which originated in performances of equestrian feats in a horse ring, dates from the late 18th cent. It is a tent show featuring wild and trained animals, acrobats, and clowns. The three-ring circus was originated by James A. Bailey. With the growing movement of protest against the use of animals in circus, a New Circus has developed which relies solely on human skills such as juggling, unicycling, tumbling, fire-eating, stilt-walking, and acrobatics.

**cire perdue** [Fr., = lost wax], process of hollow metal casting. A plaster or clay model is coated with wax and covered with a mould of perforated plaster or clay. Heat is applied, the wax melts and runs out of the holes, and molten metal (usually bronze) is poured into the space formerly occupied by the wax. When the metal is cool, the mould is broken and the core removed. Probably of Egyptian origin, the method was introduced into Greece in the 6th cent. BC and was used extensively from the 5th cent. The process, employed worldwide, was brought to China c.200 BC and was later used in casting the Benin bronzes of Africa. The great bronze masterpieces of the RENAISSANCE were produced by the cire perdue method.

**cirrhosis,** degeneration of LIVER tissue, resulting in the formation of fibrous tissue and nodules. There are a variety of causes and types, one of which is correlated with prolonged, excessive consumption of alcohol; other causes include infections, such as HEPATITIS, obstruction of BILE flow, and chronic HEART FAILURE. Cirrhosis can result in gastrointestinal disturbances, emaciation, JAUNDICE, and oedema. It is irreversible, but its progress may be halted if the cause can be removed.

**Cisalpine Republic,** 1797–1802, Italian state created by Napoleon Bonaparte, who united the two republics he had established (1796) N and S of the Po R. A French protectorate, it became the Italian Republic (1802) and, with the addition of Venetia, the Napoleonic kingdom of Italy (1805), which was broken up by the Congress of VIENNA (1815).

**Ciskei,** black African homeland or BANTUSTAN (1981 est. pop. 660,000), 8500 km² (3280 sq mi), declared independent (1981) by the Republic of South Africa, but not recognized internationally. Bisho is the capital; the largest city is Mdantsane. Half of the Xhosa-speaking black inhabitants were moved to Ciskei from white areas in Cape Province in the 1970s. The population density is extremely high, and economic conditions are among the worst in South Africa.

**Cisleithania:** see AUSTRO-HUNGARIAN MONARCHY.

**Citizens' Advice Bureaux (CABx),** in the UK, local, publicly-funded advice agencies offering free legal and general advice to the public. Established during World War II to impart government information to the public, they have since developed both in role and number, and there are now over 840 bureaux. CABx generally handle the problems of the poorer sections of society, such as social security or consumer disputes. They are staffed both by trained advice workers and volunteers, and many employ solicitors (see LEGAL PROFESSION) on a rota basis. CABx workers can also represent clients at a TRIBUNAL. See LAW CENTRE.

**citizens band radio:** see RADIO.

**citric acid cycle:** see KREBS CYCLE.

**citron,** small evergreen tree (*Citrus medica*) of the ORANGE family, and its fruit, the first of the CITRUS FRUITS introduced to Europe from the Orient. Citrons are grown in the Mediterranean, West Indies, Florida, and California. The large yellow-green, thin-rinded, and furrowed fruit contains a thick, white, and tender inner rind and a small acid pulp. The juice is used as a beverage and syrup, and the candied, preserved rind is used in confectionery and cookery.

**citrus fruits,** edible fruits of trees of the orange, or RUE, family; almost all native to Southeast Asia and the East Indies. The fruits are rich in vitamin C, citric acid, and sugars; the rind and blossoms yield ESSENTIAL OILS. Citrus fruits include the ORANGE, GRAPEFRUIT, LEMON, LIME, and KUMQUAT.

**city-state,** in ancient GREECE, autonomous political unit consisting of a city and the surrounding countryside. The Greek world included several hundred city-states, with a variety of governments ranging from absolute monarchy to pure democracy. Only citizens participated in the government of the city-state, and citizenship was limited to adult males born of citizen parents. A large proportion of the population consisted of slaves. The organization of Greece into separate city-states left it open to foreign attack by large centralized states, to which it eventually became subject.

**Ciudad Guayana,** city (1980 est. pop. 206,000), central Venezuela, on the Orinoco R. This planned modern metropolis is designed as the industrial centre for the processing of major local resources such as the iron ore of the Cerro Bolívar open-cast mines and the 600-megawatt capacity of the Guri hydroelectric plant, completed in 1986.

**Civic Trust,** trust founded (1957) with the object of improving the quality of the environment in Britain and promoting high standards in architecture and planning. It is supported by voluntary contributions from individuals and industry and has associated trusts in Scotland, Wales, and the north of England. It played a major part in the drafting of the Civic Amenities Act 1967, which resulted in the setting up of 'conservation areas', i.e., areas of buildings and landscape which it is desirable to both preserve and enhance. The Trust also makes annual awards for good development work.

**civil defence,** nonmilitary measures designed to protect civilians in wartime. In response to the use and destructiveness of military aircraft, civil defence greatly expanded in World War II. Measures to meet the threat of nuclear weapons have been controversial and include a warning system, survival planning, shelter construction, and stockpiling of necessities. Such measures have been criticized as being ineffectual in principle and as serving to encourage unilaterism in foreign relations.

**Civilian Conservation Corps** (CCC), founded in 1933 by the US Congress to provide work and job training for unemployed young men in conserving and developing the nation's natural resources. It was abolished by Congress in 1942.

**civil law,** legal system based on ROMAN LAW; also the body of law dealing with relationships between individuals, as opposed to CRIMINAL LAW, which deals with offences against the state. After the collapse of the Roman Empire, the legal ideas and concepts of Rome were kept alive in the CANON LAW of the medieval church and the *Corpus juris civilis* (6th cent.) of JUSTINIAN I. There are many later codifications of civil law principles. The most famous is the *Code Napoléon* (1804), the codification of the civil law of France, which has strongly influenced the law of continental Europe and Latin America, where civil law is prevalent. In contrast to COMMON LAW, prevalent in English-speaking countries (including England and Wales, most Commonwealth countries, and the US) civil law judgments are based on codified principles rather than on PRECEDENTS, and civil law courts do not generally employ trial by jury or the law of EVIDENCE.

**civil liberties,** rights protecting a person against arbitrary or discriminatory treatment. In the UK most civil rights (e.g., freedom of speech) are not protected by statute, but are COMMON LAW rights, whose existence depends on the political will of the government not to restrict them. However, in recent years, a number of statutes have been passed protecting the rights of minorities, e.g., Race Relations Act 1968, prohibiting discrimination in the provision of goods and services on the grounds of race. The National Council for Civil Liberties was established in 1934, and has since operated as a non-party political pressure group, campaigning for the protection and extension of civil liberties. Unlike the US and many other countries, the UK does not have a BILL OF RIGHTS protecting basic liberties from government infringement. However, in 1950, the British government signed the European Convention on Human Rights, and since then a UK citizen has been able to go the European Court of Human Rights in Strasbourg if he or she thinks a British law is infringing the Convention. The courts decisions have resulted in changes in British law on CONTEMPT OF COURT, corporal punishment and telephone tapping. In many countries, citizens do not enjoy basic civil liberties, e.g., in South Africa, where they are denied to the majority black population. In Communist countries such as the USSR social rights, e.g., the right to work, are considered more important.

**civil rights,** rights claimed by groups and individuals as citizens, including legal and political equality, free access to all public facilities, and the right to be protected against arbitrary or discriminatory treatment on the grounds of race, religion or sex. In the US there has been a historic campaign to achieve (or extend) full civil rights for blacks, led by the NATIONAL ASSOCIATION FOR THE ADVANCEMENT OF COLOURED PEOPLE, Martin Luther KING, and others. It has been instrumental in achieving civil rights acts (1964 and 1968) and a voting rights act (1965) expressly prohibiting discrimination in public housing, schools, employment, and voting, for reasons of colour, race, religion, or national origin. Although it has not eliminated the racial prejudice in the US which gave rise to the discrimination, this movement has also had a profound educative effect on public opinion. In Europe, the most prominent contemporary struggle for civil rights has been in Northern Ireland, where the Protestant majority community undoubtedly abused their control of regional government by discriminating against Roman Catholics in areas such as employment and public housing. In the 1970s the Catholic-supported Civil Rights Association won reforms from the British government, which at one point reintroduced direct rule over the province from London, but the injustices complained of were only part of a wider religious and political confrontation between the communities, which remains not only unsolved, but violent.

**civil service,** entire body of those employed in civil administration, as distinct from the armed forces, but excluding elected officials. Historically, civil service appointments were an enormous source of patronage and there were many sinecures. The rise of the modern NATION-STATE produced a great increase in the size of central governments, in their tax 'take', and in the popular conception of what they could and should undertake. This made necessary an enlarged professional civil service selected on merit. In Europe it was Prussia, under FREDERICK THE GREAT, and France, under NAPOLEON, who led the way in the development of efficient civil administrations. Recruitment by competitive examination, first seen in ancient China, was not introduced in Britain until 1854. In some nations, including Britain, there is a strong tradition of political neutrality in the civil service, but in others, e.g., the US and France, political appointments are made, especially to the higher ranks of the service. In W Germany, members of political groups held to be hostile to the constitution, such as Communists, have been refused civil-service appointments, or fired from them. This practice, known as *berufsversbot*, was a government response to the activities of the terrorist Red Army faction. Senior civil servants in most countries work in areas related to their specialist qualifications and also receive a professional training in administration, but in Britain there is a belief that highly intelligent 'generalists', usually educated in the humanities, are best able to judge the public interest, taking specialist advice where necessary. It has been argued that this 'cult of the amateur' has contributed to Britain's relatively poor postwar performance as an advanced industrial and trading nation in an era of high technology.

**civil time:** see SOLAR TIME.

**Civil War, American:** see AMERICAN CIVIL WAR.

**Civil War, English:** see ENGLISH CIVIL WAR.

**Civil War, Russian,** 1918–22, struggle between the Bolshevik 'Reds' and an assortment of anti-Bolshevik 'Whites' following the second RUSSIAN REVOLUTION of Oct. 1917. The Bolsheviks held the advantage of dictatorial power in central Russia, whilst their adversaries were hampered both by geographical dispersal and by deep political divisions amongst the competing factions. The conflict was complicated by the activities of local non-Russian nationalist movements in each of the main regions, and by the presence of foreign forces of intervention—the Germans in Ukraine, the British at Murmansk in N Russia, the French on the Black Sea coast, the Americans and Japanese in the Far East. As a result, multisided contests proliferated on the periphery, while the hard-pressed Bolsheviks could nonetheless pick off their main opponents in turn. In these circumstances, the organization and expansion of the Red Army under TROTSKY represented a major achievement. The Bolshevik war effort was also bolstered by the militarization of the economy under so-called 'War Communism', and by the application of unrestricted terror. In 1918, the Don Cossacks, the Ukrainian Directorate, Gen. Denikin's 'Volunteer Army' in the south, and Admiral Kolchak in Siberia all took to the field without lasting success. In 1919, Gen. Yudenich was held on the approaches to Petrograd from Estonia; the Poles were engaged in Lithuania and Byelorussia; Kolchak was routed in Siberia; and Denikin came within a hundred miles of Moscow before being repulsed. In 1920, the Red Army turned to the general offensive, building up a massive strike-force in the West (see POLISH-SOVIET WAR) and destroying Denikin's successor, Wrangel, in Crimea. In 1921–22, the conquest of the Caucasus was completed, in 1923–24 the domination of Central Asia.

**Ci Xi,** 1834–1908, dowager empress of China (1861–1908) and regent (1861–73, 1874–89, 1898–1908). Consort of Emperor Xian Feng (d. 1861), she bore his successor, Tong Zhi, and after his death (1875) named her nephew, Guang Xu, to the throne. In 1898 she resumed the regency after he had tried to enact political reforms. She encouraged the BOXER UPRISING against foreigners.

**Cl,** chemical symbol of the element CHLORINE.

**Clair, René** (kelə), 1898–1981, French film director. His films, noted for wit and fantastic satire, include *Sous le toits de Paris* (1929), *Le million* (1931), *À nous la liberté* (1932), *The Ghost Goes West* (1936), and *Les belles de nuit* (1952).

**clam,** name for some BIVALVE molluscs, especially marine species that live buried in mud or sand and have shells (valves) of equal size. Clams burrow by means of a muscular foot, which can be extruded through the valves. The giant clam is found in shallow tropical waters where it can grow to 120 cm (4 ft) across. Clams are highly valued as food. Some freshwater bivalves are also called clams. See also MOLLUSC.

**clan,** a unilineal DESCENT group which recognizes shared descent either through a shared male (patriclan) or female (matriclan) ANCESTOR, but in which actual kinship links are not known.

**Clare,** county in SW of Republic of Ireland (1986 pop. 91,343), 3156 km² (1231 sq mi), bordering on the Atlantic. It is located between Galway Bay in the N and the Shannon estuary in the S, within the province of Munster. The county town is ENNIS. It is hilly in the N (including the Slieve Aughty Mts) and the E where the land rises to 533 m (1748 ft) in Slieve Bernagh. The S and central parts of the county are low-lying and fertile. Lough Derg forms part of the eastern boundary. Agriculture is an important economic activity here, with dairy-farming and the cultivation of oats and potatoes common. There is some manufacturing industry in Ennis. SHANNON AIRPORT is situated on the Shannon estuary in the S of the county.

**Clare, John,** 1793–1864, English poet. His poor, rural childhood is reflected in *Poems Descriptive of Rural Life and Scenery* (1820) and succeeding volumes. After 1837, except for one brief escape, he was confined to mental institutions, in which, however, he wrote some of his best poetry.

**Clarendon, Constitutions of,** 16 articles issued in 1164 by HENRY II of England at the Council of Clarendon. Important in the development of English law, the Constitutions extended the jurisdiction of civil over church courts. After the pope condemned them, THOMAS BECKET, the archbishop of Canterbury, repudiated them, but for the most part they remained the law.

**Clarendon, Edward Hyde,** 1st **earl of,** 1607–74, English statesman and historian. A monarchist, he aided CHARLES I and went into exile with CHARLES II. After the RESTORATION, he was lord chancellor. Although he favoured religious toleration, he was forced by Parliament to enforce the CLARENDON CODE limiting the expression of religious nonconformity. In 1667 Charles made him the scapegoat for various failures in the second DUTCH WAR and he was removed him from office and died in exile. He wrote an impressive *History of the Rebellion.* His daughter Anne married JAMES II.

**Clarendon Code,** 1661–65, group of English laws passed after the RESTORATION of CHARLES II to strengthen the position of the Church of ENGLAND. Four in number, the laws decreased the followers of dissenting sects, especially Presbyterians. They were named after the earl of CLARENDON, who opposed but enforced them. Charles tried to court popularity with dissenters by his unsuccessful declarations of indulgence (1662, 1672). The Code was largely superseded by the TEST ACT (1673).

**Clarín:** see ALAS, LEOPOLDO.

**clarinet,** a WOODWIND instrument with a single reed and a conical bore, usually in B♭ or A. It has a range of over three and a half octaves upwards from the D or C♯ below middle C. The clarinet became a member of the orchestra in the late 18th cent., and also has considerable solo and chamber repertoire. The bass clarinet is pitched an octave lower than the B♭ clarinet, and the basset horn (now obsolete) was a tenor clarinet, pitched in F.

**Clark, Joe** (Charles Joseph Clark), 1939–, prime minister of CANADA (1979–80). He entered the Canadian House of Commons from Alberta in 1972 and became leader of the Progressive Conservative Party (PCP) in 1976. In the 1979 elections he led his party to victory and briefly replaced Pierre TRUDEAU as prime minister. His election represented the new political importance of W Canada, especially oil-rich Alberta. He was replaced as PCP leader (1983) by Brian MULRONEY, but became minister of external affairs following the PCP election victory the following year.

**Clarke, Arthur C(harles)**, 1917–, British scientist. His perceptive paper in the *Wireless World* in 1945 first described how world-wide communications could be ahieved with three geostationary SATELLITES, 37,000 km (23,000 mi) above, and equally spaced round, the Earth, each carrying relay transmitters powered by light cells. He showed how, through these satellites, communications would be possible between any two locations on the Earth's surface and calculated that reception would be achieved with parabolic dishes just 30 cm (1 ft) in diameter. Apart from writing many technical papers on the subject of rocket propulsion and books on underwater exploration, Arthur Clarke is a noted writer of SCIENCE FICTION. His *2001:A Space Odyssey* was filmed in 1984 by Stanley KUBRICK.

**Clarke, David**, 1938–76, British archaeologist. Clarke heralded the turn away from the idea that archaeology was the description of the history of cultures. In his seminal work, *Analytical Archaeology* (1968), he stressed the need to develop explicit theories and a more scientific approach to the collection of prehistoric information.

**Clarke, Marcus**, 1846–81, Australian novelist. His major work was the massive convict novel *His Natural Life* (1870–72), powerful, sometimes melodramatic; following the terrible sufferings of the wrongly convicted hero, Rufus Dawes, the novel is a scarifying indictment of the convict era in Australia.

**Clarke, Michael**, 1962–, English dancer and choreographer. After training at the Royal Ballet school, he joined Ballet Rambert at 17, leaving (1981) to pursue an independent career. He formed Michael Clarke and Co. in 1984.

**class**, group or division of society in which individuals enjoy a similar degree of wealth, status, or influence. The concept of class is one which has continued to develop as different writers applied it to changing historical circumstances. Perhaps the most influential account of class was given by Karl MARX for whom class meant essentially economic class: the relation of a group to the means of production, distribution, and exchange. He believed that the owners of capital necessarily exploited those who had only their labour-power to sell, that as a result of this inequality class conflict between the capitalist and working classes was inevitable, and that such conflict was the chief 'motor' of historical progress (see CAPITALISM). Max WEBER accepted the importance of economic class, which he defined in terms of sets of individuals having similar 'life-chances', or opportunities to achieve wealth and position, but he stressed that individuals also belonged to status groups (such as the castes in India) and political parties, and that these were equally important in the analysis of power in society. Some societies, including both the US and the USSR, have claimed to be classless. The USSR has indeed largely abolished private ownership of the means of production, but there are nevertheless obvious distinctions of wealth and opportunity between the ordinary worker or peasant and the higher bureaucrats and members of the Communist Party. Milovan DJILAS has argued that the latter constitute 'a new class', based on status and political position. Seen from the point of view of PLURALISM, a class analysis of the US is not really appropriate, because competition between rival elites and pressure-groups ensures that power is exercised by a constantly changing set of interests. However, this has been disputed by C. Wright Mills and others who have sought to show the existence of an interlocking power elite of political, business, and military leaders whose influence is decisive in national affairs. In Britain, despite the introduction of progressive taxation and a WELFARE STATE, class distinctions are perpetuated by large inequalities of wealth and income, a divided educational system, and the survival of a traditional aristocracy. Some writers have argued that this damages industrial relations, others that it disfigures social life with a subtle and pervasive snobbery. Academic research has shown that the extent to which individuals are conscious of themselves as members of a class is less than might be expected; also, that knowledge of an individual's class position is of limited value in predicting political behaviour; and that class privileges tend to persist across generations. Further analyses of class in terms of differences in lifestyle and values indicate that, whatever the disagreements over its definition and use, the concept is likely to remain central to social and political discussion.

**class action**, in the US, lawsuit in which one or more persons represent a group (class) too large for individual suits to be practical. The decision binds all members of the group. Class action suits often involve major social issues, e.g., women seeking equal pay for equal work. They are not recognized in UK courts, where each person would have to sue individually.

**classicism**, term meaning clearness, elegance, symmetry, and repose produced by attention to traditional forms; absence of emotionalism, subjectivity, and excess enthusiasm; and, more precisely, admiration of Greek and Roman models. Renaissance writers, for example, looked to CICERO. In England, Francis BACON in prose and Ben JONSON in poetry strove for classical style. The movement reached its apex with Alexander POPE and the Augustans. In France neoclassicism found its highest expression in the dramas of Pierre CORNEILLE and Jean RACINE. The works of RENAISSANCE painters and of the composers F.J. HAYDN and W.A. MOZART particularly reveal the classical impulse. Classicism and ROMANTICISM are generally contrary tendencies.

**classic revival**, widely diffused phase of taste ('neoclassic') influencing architecture and the arts in Europe and the US in the last years of the 18th and first half of the 19th cent. Enthusiasm for antiquity and for archaeological knowledge was stimulated by the excavation of POMPEII and by investigations in Greece. James Stuart and Nicholas Revett's *Antiquities of Athens* (1st vol., 1762) was extremely influential. In general, Roman influence predominated at first. In France, the Empire style sponsored by NAPOLEON I brought imitation of ancient Rome to a peak. In the US the same spirit was seen in public buildings, e.g., Thomas JEFFERSON's Virginia capitol design (1785). Eventually a Graeco-Roman form emerged. It dominated in no country more than in the US, where classic colonnades were seen even on country farmhouses.

**classification**, in biology, the systematic categorization of organisms. One aim of modern classification, or systematics, is to show the evolutionary relationships among organisms. The broadest division of organisms is into kingdoms, traditionally two—Animalia (animals) and Plantae (plants). Fairly widely accepted today are three additional kingdoms: the Protista, comprising protozoans and some unicellular algae; the Monera, bacteria and blue-green algae; and the Fungi. From most to least inclusive, kingdoms are divided into the following categories: phylum (usually called *division* in botany), class, order, family, genus, and species. The relationship of species to those closely related to them is made clear by BINOMIAL NOMENCLATURE. The species, the fundamental unit of classification, consists of populations of genetically similar, interbreeding or potentially interbreeding individuals that share the same gene pool (collection of inherited characteristics whose combination is unique to the species).

**classificatory system**, in anthropology, the ordering of the social and physical world into distinct categories, which are frequently elaborated in terms of oppositions. The understanding and interpretation of the principles which underlie classificatory systems are crucial to much of social and cultural anthropology. E. DURKHEIM and M. MAUSS argued that all logical classificatory schema were extensions of the fundamental classification, that of persons and social groups. Structural functionalist anthropologists built on this, arguing that such systems were extensions of features of the social order. Structuralist anthropolgists on the other hand focus on the binary logic and opposition underlying such systems, while others (e.g., Mary DOUGLAS) are concerned with the significance of those categories that are marginal in such schema. See STRUCTURAL FUNCTIONALISM; STRUCTURALISM.

**Claudel, Paul** (kloh͵del), 1868–1955, French dramatist, poet, and diplomat. He was ambassador to the Far East (1921–27), the US (1927–33), Belgium (1933–35), etc. His writings reflect his profound and mystical Catholicism. His finest works include the play *L'annonce faite à Marie* (1912; tr. Tidings Brought to Mary) and the rich lyric verse of *Cinq grandes odes* (1910; tr. Five Great Odes).

**Claude Lorrain** (klohd lo͵ranh), whose original name was **Claude Gelée** or **Gellée**, 1600–82, French painter. He worked in Rome and became the foremost ideal landscape painter of his time and amongst the greatest 17th-cent. draughtsmen. His early works include harbour and coast scenes and wooded pastoral landscapes which perfectly convey the mood of VIRGIL's bucolic poetry; his later works, often inspired by the Bible, e.g., *The Expulsion of Hagar* (1668; Munich) or by the *Aeneid*, became increasingly monumental and heroic. Claude's outstanding originality lay in his treatment of light; he opened up unlimited vistas, introducing lyrical variations of light to dissolve forms and lead the eye into vast panoramas.

Chemically, clay minerals are hydrous aluminium silicates with various impurities. Clays are most commonly formed by surface weathering. In the form of BRICKS, clay has been indispensable to architecture since prehistoric times. Clays are of great industrial importance, e.g., in the manufacture of tile and pipe. Clay is one of the three principal types of soil; the others are SAND and loam.

**Clay, Cassius Marcellus, Jr:** see ALI, MUHAMMAD.

**Clay, Henry,** 1777–1852, American statesman. He served Kentucky as US senator (1806–7, 1810–11, 1831–42, 1849–52) and member of the House of Representatives (1811–14, 1815–21, 1823–25). A leader of the 'war hawks', Clay helped to bring on the WAR OF 1812. His 'American system' was a national programme of federal aid for internal improvements, a protective tariff, and a rechartering of the Bank of the United States. Secretary of state (1825–29) under Pres. John Quincy ADAMS, he opposed the succeeding Jackson administration, especially on the bank issue. He was the presidential candidate of the National Republican party in 1832 and of the WHIG PARTY in 1844. Clay pushed the MISSOURI COMPROMISE (1820–21) through the House, and, denouncing extremists in both North and South, he was the chief shaper of the COMPROMISE OF 1850. He was called the Great Pacificator and the Great Compromiser.

**clay-pigeon shooting,** also known as trap-shooting. Spinning clay saucers are spring-catapulted into the air and shot at with a 12-gauge open bore shotgun. There are two distinct types: 'down-the-line'—or 'trench', or 'Olympic trench'—and the more recent 'skeet', designed to simulate more realistically the shooting of game birds.

**Clayton–Bulwer Treaty,** concluded at Washington, DC, on 19 Apr. 1850, between the US, represented by Secretary of State John M. Clayton, and Great Britain, represented by Sir Henry Bulwer. US–British rivalries in CENTRAL AMERICA, particularly over a proposed isthmian canal, led to the treaty which checked British expansion in Central America but prevented the US from building and politically controlling a canal. The treaty remained effective until it was superseded by the Hay–Pauncefote Treaty of 1901.

**cleft palate:** see CONGENITAL ABNORMALITIES.

**Cleisthenes,** fl. 510 BC, Athenian statesman; head of the family Alcmaeonidae. The undisputed ruler of ATHENS after 506 BC, he instituted democratic reforms that ended civil strife there.

**clematis,** herb or vine (genus *Clematis*) of the BUTTERCUP family. The vines are usually profuse and varied bloomers. The Jackman clematis (*C. jackmanii*) is a large purple hybrid; the Japanese clematis (*C. paniculata*) has small white flowers. Other names for clematis are virgin's bower, traveller's joy, and old-man's-beard.

**Clemenceau, Georges** (klaymahnh,soh), 1841–1929, French premier (1906–9, 1917–20), called 'the Tiger'. As a journalist, he passionately defended Dreyfus in the DREYFUS AFFAIR. His coalition cabinet in World War I, by reinvigorating French morale, facilitated the Allied victory. At the Paris Peace Conference, he forcefully opposed Woodrow WILSON, believing that the Treaty of VERSAILLES would not adequately protect France. Ironically, he lost the 1920 presidential election because of his perceived leniency towards Germany.

**Clemens, Samuel Langhorne:** see TWAIN, MARK.

**Clementi, Muzio,** 1752–1832, English composer, pianist, and conductor; b. Italy. His more than 100 piano SONATAS set the definitive form, and he had a great influence on all aspects of piano music. He is remembered for his series of études, *Gradus ad Parnassum* (1817).

**Clement I, Saint,** or **Clement of Rome,** d. AD c.101, pope (AD c.91–c.101), said to have been a martyr. Highly esteemed in his day, he may have known Sts PETER and PAUL. His letter to the Corinthians was considered canonical by some until the 4th cent. and is notable for the authority Clement assumes. He was the first Christian writer to use the phoenix as an allegory of the Resurrection. Feast: 23 Nov.

**Clement V,** c.1260–1314, pope (1305–14), a Frenchman named Bertrand de Got. As archbishop of Bordeaux, he gained the favour of the French king PHILIP IV, who engineered his election as pope. He settled (1309) in Avignon, thus beginning the long 'captivity' of the PAPACY. Dominated by Philip, he strove to resist attempts to condemn Pope BONIFACE VIII posthumously, but was forced to agree to the suppression of the KNIGHTS TEMPLARS. He issued an important collection of canon law.

Claude Lorrain, *Landscape with Aeneas at Delos*. National Gallery, London.

**Claudian** (Claudius Claudianus), b. c.AD 370 in Alexandria, d. c. AD 404 in Rome, a Greek who wrote poetry in (very good) Latin. He produced, under imperial patronage, panegyrics and other occasional poems for his patrons, EPIC poems on historical and mythological subjects (e.g., *On the Rape of Proserpina*), and a variety of short poems. His work has both historical and literary value.

**Claudius,** ancient Roman gens. **Appius Claudius Sabinus Inregillensis** or **Regillensis** was a Sabine; he came (c.504 BC) with his tribe to Rome. As consul (495 BC) he was known for his severity. **Appius Claudius Crassus** was *decemvir* (451–449 BC). Legend says that his attempt to rape VIRGINIA caused a revolt in which he was killed and which led to the fall of the *decemvirs*. **Appius Claudius Caecus,** censor (312–308 BC), constructed the first Roman aqueduct and began construction of the APPIAN WAY. **Publius Claudius Pulcher,** consul (249 BC), attacked the Carthaginian fleet at Drepanum and was defeated. **Appius Claudius Pulcher,** d. c.48 BC, consul (54 BC), joined POMPEY in the civil war and died before the battle at Pharsalia (48 BC).

**Claudius I** (Tiberius Claudius Drusus Nero Germanicus), 10 BC–AD 54, Roman emperor (r.AD 41–54), son of Nero Claudius Drusus Germanicus (see DRUSUS, family) and thus nephew of TIBERIUS. When CALIGULA was murdered (AD 41), Claudius was proclaimed emperor by the PRAETORIANS. Despite suffering from a type of paralysis, he consolidated and renewed the empire. Claudius caused MESSALINA, his third wife, to be executed. He was in turn supposedly poisoned by her successor, Agrippina II, after she had persuaded him to pass over his son Britannicus as heir in favour of NERO, her son by a former husband. Claudius was much reviled by his enemies; however, he seems to have had considerable administrative ability. His life is described in two novels by Robert GRAVES.

**Clausewitz, Karl von** (,klowzəvits), 1780–1831, Prussian general and writer on military strategy. After serving in the wars against NAPOLEON I, he was appointed (1818) director of the Prussian war college. His masterpiece, *On War,* expounded the doctrines of 'total war' and war as a political act (a continuation of diplomacy by other means). Published after his death, it not only had a major impact on military strategy and tactics but also greatly influenced political thinking.

**Clausius, Rudolf Julius Emanuel** (,klowzeeoos), 1822–88, German mathematical physicist. He introduced the concept of entropy and restated the second law of THERMODYNAMICS to assert that heat cannot of itself pass from a colder to a hotter body. Through investigations of heat, electricity, and molecular physics, he developed the KINETIC THEORY OF GASES and formulated a theory of ELECTROLYSIS.

**claustrophobia:** see PHOBIA.

**clavichord:** see PIANO.

**clay,** common name for a number of fine-grained, earthy materials that are plastic when wet. They are easily moulded into a form they retain when dry, and become hard and hold their shape when subjected to heat.

**Clement VI**, 1291–1352, pope (1342–52), a Frenchman named Pierre Roger. Completely pro-French, he kept an elegant court at Avignon. When the PLAGUE known as the Black Death struck (1348–50) Europe, he did much to help the sufferers and tried to stem the subsequent wave of anti-Semitism. In Roman affairs he at first favoured but then opposed Cola di RIENZI.

**Clement VII**, 1478–1534, pope (1523–34), a Florentine named Giulio de' Medici, a member of the MEDICI family. Weak and timorous, he seemed unaware of the threat that the REFORMATION posed to the church. Allied with FRANCIS I of France, Clement quarrelled with Holy Roman Emperor CHARLES V and was captured (1527) when imperial troops sacked Rome. Peace was restored in 1529, and Clement crowned Charles emperor. Clement vacillated in the matter of granting an annulment for HENRY VIII of England and was unable to prevent Henry's break with Rome.

**Clement VIII**, 1536–1605, pope (1592–1605), a Florentine named Ippolito Aldobrandini. Reversing papal policy, he allied the Holy See with France instead of Spain and was friendly with the French king HENRY IV. He was also known for piety.

**Clement XI**, 1649–1721, pope (1700–21), an Italian named Giovanni Francesco Albani. He became involved in the War of the SPANISH SUCCESSION, supporting first the claims of PHILIP V and then those of Charles of Hapsburg. Clement was known for his great learning and issued (1713) the bull *Unigenitus* condemning Jansenism (see under JANSEN, CORNELIS).

**Clement XIV**, 1705–74, pope (1769–74), an Italian named Lorenzo Ganganelli, a Conventual Franciscan. Bowing to the wishes of the Bourbon monarchs of France and Spain, Clement issued (1773) a brief suppressing the JESUITS.

**Clement of Alexandria** (Titus Flavius Clemens), d. c.215, Greek theologian. A convert to Christianity, he was one of the first to attempt a synthesis of Platonic and Christian thought. He attacked GNOSTICISM, but he has himself been called a Christian gnostic for his efforts to state the faith in terms of contemporary thought. ORIGEN was his pupil.

**Clement of Rome:** see CLEMENT I, SAINT.

**Cleon**, d. 422 BC, Athenian statesman. An antagonist of SPARTA, he won a great victory at Sphacteria (425 BC) but was killed in the defeat at Amphipolis. His reputation as a vulgar demagogue is due to accounts by his enemies THUCYDIDES and ARISTOPHANES.

**Cleopatra**, 69–30 BC, queen of EGYPT. The daughter of PTOLEMY XI, she was married (as was the custom) to her younger brother, PTOLEMY XII. By revolting against him, with the aid of Julius CAESAR, she won the kingdom, although it remained a vassal of Rome. After her husband died, she married another brother, Ptolemy XIII; but she was the mistress of Caesar, and in Rome she bore a son, Caesarion (later Ptolemy XIV), said to be his. Returning to Egypt after the murder of Caesar, she was visited by Mark ANTONY, who fell in love with her. She seems to have hoped to use him to reestablish her throne's power; they were married in 36 BC. But the Romans were hostile, and Octavian (later AUGUSTUS) defeated Antony and Cleopatra off Actium in 31 BC. Failing to defend themselves in Egypt, Antony and Cleopatra killed themselves. PLUTARCH, SHAKESPEARE, and G.B. SHAW are among the writers who have described Cleopatra's remarkable life.

**Cleopatra's needles,** popular name for two red granite OBELISKS from Egypt. Originally erected at Heliopolis (c.1475 BC) by THUTMOSE III, they were sent separately as gifts of ISMAIL PASHA to England (1878) and the US (1880).

**Clerk-Maxwell, James:** see MAXWELL, JAMES CLERK.

**Clermont-Ferrand,** city (1982 pop. 151,092, agglomeration 256,189), capital of Puy-de-Dôme dept., central France. Ancient capital of Auvergne, it lies on the edge of the fertile plain of the Limagne. The town's early prosperity was based on leather-working and food industries. Tyre manufacture is now its principal industry, employing many thousands. It has a fine Romanesque church and Gothic cathedral. Dominating the city to the west is the ancient volcanic core of Puy de Dôme.

**Cleveland,** US city (1984 est. pop. 547,000), NE Ohio, on Lake Erie, at the mouth of the Cuyahoga R.; laid out 1796, chartered 1836. Ohio's largest city, it is a major ore port and GREAT LAKES shipping point, one of the nation's leading iron and steel centres, and a major producer of metal products. It has diverse light and heavy manufacturing, including the production of machine tools, chemicals, oil refining, and electrical goods, and houses government and corporate research facilities. The arrival of the canal (1827) and railway (1851) spurred the city's growth; its location between the Pennsylvania coal and oil fields and the Minnesota iron mines led to industrialization. John D. ROCKEFELLER began his oil dynasty there.

**Cleveland,** county in NE England (1984 est. pop. 562,700), 583 km² (227 sq mi), around the Tees estuary on the North Sea coast. It was formed in 1974 and includes the urban areas of MIDDLESBROUGH, HARTLEPOOL, Guisborough, and Stockton-on-Tees. Most of the county is urbanized and industrial, the iron and steel and chemical industries being especially important.

**Cleveland, (Stephen) Grover,** 1837–1908, 22nd (1885–89) and 24th (1893–97) president of the US. He was mayor of Buffalo, New York State (1882–83) and governor of New York State (1883–85). An enemy of machine politics, he was named the Democratic candidate to oppose James G. BLAINE in 1884, and was elected after a bitter campaign. As president he pursued his conscientious, independent course, offending the zealots of his party by his moderate use of the spoils system. In the 1888 election, Cleveland campaigned for a lower tariff, but in spite of a popular majority he lost the election to Benjamin HARRISON. The panic of 1893 struck a hard blow at his second administration, and he angered radical Democrats by securing repeal of the SHERMAN SILVER PURCHASE ACT. The party rift widened when he refused to sign his tariff measure as altered by the protectionist Sen. A.P. Gorman. In the Pullman strike (1894), he sent in troops and broke the strike on grounds that the movement of the US mail was being halted. In foreign affairs he took a strong stand on the VENEZUELA BOUNDARY DISPUTE, and refused recognition to a Hawaiian government set up by Americans.

**client-centred therapy:** see ROGERS.

**climate,** average weather conditions in an area over a long period of time, taking into account temperature, precipitation, humidity, wind, atmospheric pressure, and other phenomena. The major factor governing climate is latitude; this is modified by one or more secondary factors including position relative to land and water masses, altitude, ocean currents, topography, prevailing winds, and prevalence of cyclonic storms. The earth is divided into climatic zones based on average yearly temperature and average yearly precipitation. The study of climate is called climatology.

**Clinton, Sir Henry,** 1738?–1795, British general in the AMERICAN REVOLUTION; b. Newfoundland, Canada. Knighted in 1777, he was (1778–81) supreme commander in America. He took Charleston (1780) but failed to aid in the YORKTOWN CAMPAIGN.

**Clio:** see MUSES.

**Clisthenes:** see CLEISTHENES.

**Clive, Kitty,** 1711–85, English singer and actress; b. Catherine Raftor. GARRICK's leading lady, she was notable in comedies by GAY, FIELDING, and CIBBER and, as a singer, in HANDEL's *Samson*. She was a friend of Samuel JOHNSON.

**Clive, Robert, Baron Clive of Plassey,** 1725–74, British soldier and statesman. In the military service of the English EAST INDIA COMPANY, he won a series of brilliant victories against the French that broke French power in INDIA. He brought BENGAL under British control after his victory over the last nawab, Sirajuddaulah, at Plassey, 1757 and was its first governor. In his second term as governor (1765–67), he reduced corruption and inefficiency and formally assumed responsibility for the civil government of Bengal, nominally under the Mughal emperor. On his return to England in 1767, he was accused by Parliament of having unlawfully enriched himself while in India. He was acquitted in 1773, but, broken in health, committed suicide.

**clock,** mechanical, electrical, or atomic instrument for measuring and indicating time. Predecessors of the clock were the sundial, the hourglass, and the clepsydra. The operation of a mechanical clock depends on a stable oscillator, such as a swinging PENDULUM or a mass connected to a spring, by means of which the energy stored in a raised weight or coiled spring advances a pointer or other indicator at a controlled rate. The heavy and bulky weight-driven clock may first have been built in the 9th cent. The introduction (c.1500) of the coiled spring made possible the construction of smaller, lighter-weight clocks. The Dutch scientist Christiaan HUYGENS invented (1656 or 1657) a pendulum clock, probably the first. Electric clocks, first made in the late 19th cent., are powered by an electric motor synchronized with the frequency of alternating current. The quartz clock, invented c.1929, uses the vibrations of a quartz crystal to drive a synchronous motor at a very precise rate. An atomic clock (invented 1948), even more precise, is indirectly controlled by atomic or molecular oscillations. Digital clocks and watches dispense with the hour-marked dial and display time as a numerical figure.

**Clodius** (Publius Clodius Pulcher), d. 52 BC, Roman politician. In 62 BC, disguised as a woman, he took part in the women's mysteries of Bona Dea in the house of Julius CAESAR, thus leading Caesar to divorce his wife Pompeia. In 58 BC he became tribune of the people and proved to be a demagogue, seeking popularity in every way. His gang of hired ruffians changed the complexion of Roman politics. He was killed by a rival gang hired by the tribune Milo.

**cloisonné,** method of decorating metal surfaces with enamel. Filaments of metal are attached to the surface of the object, outlining the design and forming compartments that are filled with coloured paste enamels. When the piece is heated the enamels fuse onto the metal, forming a glossy, coloured surface. Probably invented in the Middle East, cloisonné was perfected by the Chinese, Japanese, and French.

**cloister,** part of a religious establishment, a vaulted passageway of continuous colonnades or arcades opening onto a court. It is characteristic of monastic institutions, serving both as sheltered access to rooms and for recreation. Cloisters were built in some English examples and in some churches. Superb Romanesque examples remain in S France, Italy, and Spain; of the Gothic period, the English examples are particularly fine, e.g., Gloucester cathedral and WESTMINSTER ABBEY. Renaissance cloisters are chiefly Italian and Spanish, while 16th-cent. cloisters exist in California, Cuba, and Mexico.

**Cloncurry,** town (1986 pop. 2297), Queensland, NE Australia. Linked by rail with TOWNSVILLE, the town was part of the 1918 copper boom but has declined in importance as nearby Mt Isa (1986 pop. 23,348) has grown. It now services the beef-cattle industry of the Channel Country. In 1927 the inaugural flight of the Royal Flying Doctor Service (SEE FLYING DOCTOR) was made from Cloncurry. Radio networks and the 'School of the Air' are still based at Cloncurry, providing a 'mantle of safety' for isolated communities and pastoral properties.

**clone,** group of organisms descended from a single individual through asexual REPRODUCTION. Except for changes in hereditary material due to MUTATION, all members of a clone are genetically identical. Experiments resulting in the development of a frog from a somatic cell of an adult animal and the laboratory fertilization of human eggs have raised questions about the eventual possibility of cloning identical humans from cells of a preexisting individual.

**Clonmel,** county town (1986 pop. 11,737) of Co. Tipperary, Republic of Ireland, on R. SUIR. It is a market town, whose industries include various forms of food-processing. It is also famous as a centre for horseracing, hunting, and fishing. It is the birthplace of Lawrence STERNE.

**closed shop,** popular name for a 'Union Membership Agreement'. It is an agreement between an employer and a TRADE UNION stipulating that only trade-union members may be employed at that place of work. The closed shop has benefitted both employer and union, in that the employer can enter into COLLECTIVE BARGAINING with just the one union, and the union has a better chance of achieving its objectives through solidarity. In the UK the closed shop was given statutory protection in 1975; however, legislation passed by the Conservative government in 1980 has made closed shops more difficult to establish and maintain. Even where there is a closed shop, a worker may still avoid joining a trade union on the grounds of conscience, or other deeply held personal conviction.

**Clotho:** see FATES.

**cloud,** aggregation of minute particles of water or ice suspended in the air. Clouds are formed when air containing water vapour is cooled below a critical temperature called the DEW point and the resulting moisture condenses into droplets on microscopic dust particles (condensation nuclei) in the atmosphere. The air is normally cooled by expansion during its upward movement. Clouds may be classified according to appearance, altitude, or composition. Each cloud type is formed by specific atmospheric conditions and is, therefore, indicative of forthcoming weather. *Cirrus* clouds, generally white, and delicate and fibrous in appearance, are the highest clouds and are made of ice crystals. *Stratus* clouds, layered in appearance, are the lowest clouds and are associated with stormy weather. *Cumulus* clouds, which are vertically developed, usually with a horizontal base and a dome-shaped upper surface, are intermediate in height and are associated with fair weather. Combinations of these cloud names are common. *Cirrostratus* clouds, for example, are high-altitude layered clouds that often indicate rain or snow. Prefixes and suffixes are also used. For example, *nimbus* means rain, and *cumulonimbus* clouds, commonly called thunderheads, indicate rain showers.

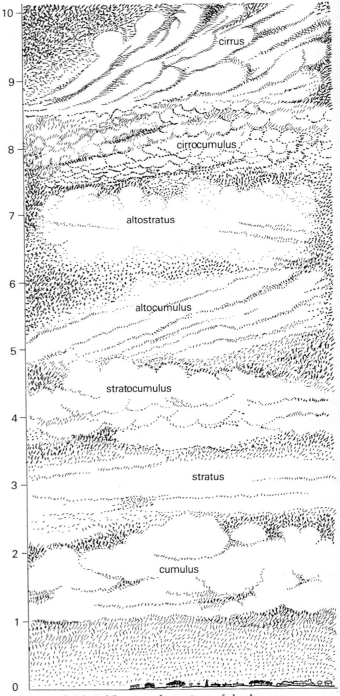

Approximate height in kilometers of some types of **clouds**

**cloud chamber:** see PARTICLE DETECTOR.

**Cloud of Unknowing,** anonymous English prose text of the late 14th cent., sometimes attributed to Walter HILTON. It is a spiritual work of great intellectual intensity and demanding difficulty.

**Clouet, Jean** (klooh͵ay), c.1485–c.1540, court painter to FRANCIS I of France. He is thought to have been Flemish. A group of softly modelled portrait drawings (Musée Condé, Chantilly) are usually attributed to him; a few pictures have been associated with these. His son, **François Clouet,** c.1510–72, inherited his father's position as court painter. His clear, precise draughtmanship can be seen in his portraits of Francis I and Elizabeth of Austria (both: Louvre, Paris).

**Clough, Arthur Hugh** (kluf), 1819–61, English poet. His main works were two long poems *The Bothie of Tober-na-Vuolich* (1848) and *Amours de Voyage* (1858) but he is best remembered for his lyric 'Say not the struggle naught availeth'. Clough is the subject of 'Thyrsis', an elegy written by his close friend Matthew ARNOLD.

**clove,** small tropical evergreen tree (*Syzygium aromaticum* or *Eugenia caryophyllata*) of the MYRTLE family and its unopened flower bud, an important spice. The buds, whose folded petals are enclosed in four toothlike lobes of the calyx, are dried and used whole or ground for cooking. Clove oil is used in flavourings, perfumes, and medicines.

**clover,** plant (genus *Trifolium*) of the PULSE family, mainly native to north temperate and subtropical areas. Clovers are cultivated for hay and are excellent honey plants. They enrich the soil by fixing atmospheric nitrogen as fertilizer. The dried flowers and seed heads of the common white clover (*T. repens*) were used to make bread during famines in Ireland, and the leaves are used for salads in some parts of the US. Sweet clover is a related plant.

**Clovis I,** c.466–511, Frankish king (r.481–511), founder of the MEROVINGIAN monarchy. He rose from tribal chief to sole leader of the Salian FRANKS by dint of patience and murder. He won Gaul and SW Germany by fighting the Romans, Alemanni, Burgundians, and Visigoths. His wife, St Clotilda, encouraged his conversion (496) to Christianity.

**club foot:** see CONGENITAL ABNORMALITIES.

**club moss,** living member of LYCOPSIDA, a class of primitive vascular plants that reached their zenith in the Carboniferous period and are now almost extinct. They resemble the more primitive, nonvascular true mosses. Club mosses are usually creeping or epiphytic; many of them inhabit moist tropical or subtropical regions. Reproduction is by spores, which are clustered in small cones or borne in the axils of the scalelike leaves. Some species of *Lycopodium,* called ground pine, resemble miniature hemlocks with flattened fan-shaped branches. Spores of *L. clavatum* are sold as lycopodium powder, or vegetable sulphur, a flammable yellow powder used in pharmaceuticals and fireworks. Species of *Selaginella* are grown as ornamentals.

**Cluj-Napoca,** Hung. *Kolozsvár,* Ger. *Klausenburg,* city. Cluj was founded (12th cent.) and settled by Saxon colonists and Hungarians. From the 16th cent. it became a major cultural, religious, and administrative centre. Incorporated with Transylvania into România in 1920, it was awarded as part of N Transylvania to Hungary in 1940 and restored to Romania in 1944 following its recapture by Soviet and Romanian forces. The city was officially rechristened Cluj-Napoca in 1975.

**Cluny Museum,** Paris, 14th- and 15th-cent. Gothic and Renaissance structure built on the site of the Roman baths of Emperor Julian. Acquired and converted by the antiquarian Du Sommerard, it was left to the state at his death (1842). Its 24 galleries display medieval works of carved wood, metalwork, textiles, and stained glass, as well as superb 15th- and 16th-cent. tapestries.

**cluster, star,** group of neighbouring stars that resemble each other in certain characteristics that suggest a common origin. Galactic, or open, clusters typically contain from a few dozen to about a thousand loosely scattered stars and exist in regions rich in gas and dust, such as the spiral arms of the galaxy. More than 1000 galactic clusters, including the Hyades and Pleiades in the constellation Taurus, have been catalogued in the Milky Way. Globular clusters are spherical aggregates of thousands or millions of densely concentrated stars and exist in the outer halo of the galaxy. The brightest of the more than 100 globular clusters so far detected in the galaxy are Omega Centauri and 47 Tucanae, both seen with the unaided eye in the southern skies.

Stag's Horn **club moss** (*Lycopodium clavatum*)

**Clwyd,** county in NE Wales (1984 est. pop. 396,300), 2477 km² (966 sq mi), borders on the Irish Sea in the N and the Dee estuary in the NW. It was formed in the local government reorganization of 1974 from Flintshire, most of Denbighshire, and NE Merionethshire. It is mainly mountainous or hilly, with several fertile and beautiful valleys, e.g., that of the R. Clwyd. The Clwydian Hills lie towards the E of the county. Agriculture is important, and there is a declining industrial area towards the E. The main towns are Wrexham (associated with coal production), Colwyn Bay, Rhyll, and Langollen (tourist centres).

**Clyde,** one of the major rivers of Scotland, c.170 km (106 mi) long. It rises S of Abington in the Strathclyde region and flows generally N past Lanark, Hamilton, GLASGOW, Clydebank, and Dumbarton. At Dumbarton it widens into the Firth of Clyde. Near Lanark there is a series of waterfalls known as the Falls of Clyde, whose former impressiveness has been reduced by the construction of a hydroelectricity scheme. Oceangoing ships can reach as far as Glasgow, and the river is lined with shipyards around here.

**Clytemnestra,** in Greek mythology, daughter of LEDA and Tyndareus. The wife of AGAMEMNON, she was the mother of ORESTES, ELECTRA, and IPHIGENIA. She and her lover, AEGISTHUS, murdered Agamemnon and, in revenge, were slain by Orestes. HOMER portrayed Clytemnestra as a noble woman, misled by her lover, but the Greek tragedians, particularly AESCHYLUS, depicted her as remorseless and vengeful.

**Cm,** chemical symbol of the element CURIUM.

**CND:** see CAMPAIGN FOR NUCLEAR DISARMAMENT.

**Co,** chemical symbol of the element COBALT.

**coal,** fuel substance of plant origin, composed largely of CARBON with varying amounts of mineral matter. Coal belongs to a series of carbonaceous fuels that differ in the relative amounts of moisture, volatile matter, and fixed carbon they contain; the most useful are those containing the largest amounts of carbon and the smallest amounts of moisture and volatile matter. The highest grade of coal is anthracite, or hard coal, which is nearly pure carbon and is used as a domestic fuel. Bituminous coal, or soft coal, with a lower carbon content, is used as an industrial fuel and in making COKE. LIGNITE is the second lowest and PEAT the lowest in carbon content. Large amounts of coal were formed in the Carboniferous period of geological time (345 to 280 million years ago). It is thought that great quantities of vegetable matter collected and underwent slow decomposition in SWAMPS similar to present-day peat bogs and in lagoons. The peat that formed was converted to lignite and coal by METAMORPHISM. The pressure of accumulated layers of overlying sediment and rock forced out much of the volatile matter, leaving beds or seams of compact coal interstratified with shales, clays, or sandstones. Higher grades of coal were produced where the stress was greatest. Major US coal fields are found in Appalachia, the Midwest, the Rocky Mts region, and along the Gulf Coast. The chief coal-producing countries of Europe are Germany, Britain, the USSR, Poland, France, and Belgium. Valuable coal deposits also exist in China, India, South Africa, and Australia. See also COAL MINING.

**coal mining,** physical extraction of COAL resources to yield coal; also, the business of exploring for, developing, mining, and transporting coal in any form. OPEN-CAST MINING is the process in which the earth and rock material overlying the coal is removed to expose a coal seam or bed; the coal is then removed in a separate operation. Underground coal mining is the extraction of coal from below the surface of the earth. The coal is worked through tunnels, passages, and openings connected to the surface for the purpose of removing the coal. Mechanical equipment breaks up the coal to a size suitable for transporting. Alternatively, the coal is drilled, and the resultant holes are loaded with explosives and blasted to break up the coal. To protect miners and equipment, much attention is paid to the buildup of poisonous and explosive gases and to maintaining and supporting a safe roof system in underground mines. The latest coal-cutting equipment is remote-controlled by computer and can be used for seams too thin to be tackled by traditional methods. See also MINING.

**Coalport,** English porcelain factory in Shropshire. Founded c.1797, it initially produced hard-paste porcelain, much of it decorated with Oriental blue-and-white patterns. During the 1820s and 30s the factory became known for bone china with painted and encrusted floral decoration in rococo revival style. In the 1840s it introduced table and ornamental ware in imitation of SÈVRES. High standards were maintained during the late 19th cent., but financial losses in the early 20th cent. led to the sale of the business and closure of the original factory. Coalport is now part of the Wedgwood Group and the old factory has been restored as a museum.

**coal tar:** see TAR AND PITCH.

**coastguard,** body responsible for monitoring coastal shipping, watching for vessels in distress, oil slicks, smuggling, etc. The British Coastguard (now under the Board of Trade) was founded after the Napoleonic Wars (1805–15) originally to combat smuggling. The US Coast Guard, set up in 1915, has wide-ranging duties including law-enforcement on the high seas, maintenance of lighthouses, patrolling the seas for ice, and operating a LIFEBOAT service.

**Coast Mountains,** western range of the North American Cordillera, extending c.1610 km (1000 mi) N from W British Columbia into SE Alaska. Geologically distinct from the COAST RANGES, the range reaches a high point at Mt Waddington (4042 m/13,260 ft).

**Coast Ranges,** series of geologically related ranges forming the western edge of the North American Cordillera. The highest peaks are in the St Elias Mts (Alaska). Other ranges are the Olympic Mts and the Coast Ranges (Oregon), the Klamath Mts and Coast and Los Angeles Ranges (California), and the mountains of BAJA CALIFORNIA.

**coat of arms:** see BLAZONRY; HERALDRY.

**Coatzacoalcos** (koh,ahthakoh,alkos), city (1985 est. pop. 350,000), SE Mexico, on the mouth of the Coatzacoalcos R. The recent explosive growth of this city is closely associated with the offshore discoveries and mining of oil and natural gas in the Gulf of Mexico. Its petrochemical industries and the oil refineries of Minatitlán (1985 est. pop. 200,000) are the basis of rapid local industrial growth and the influx of population from the surrounding areas.

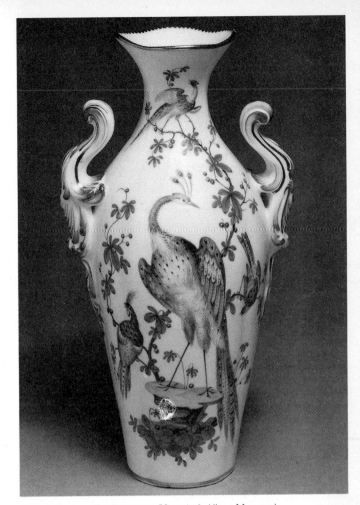

Early 19th-cent. **Coalport** vase (Victoria & Albert Museum)

**coaxial cable:** see CABLE.

**cobalt** (Co), metallic element, discovered in 1735 by Georg Brandt. It is silver-white, lustrous, and hard, and can be magnetized. It is combined with other metals in the ores cobaltite and smaltite. Cobalt alloys are used in very hard cutting tools, high-strength permanent magnets, and jet engines. Radioactive cobalt-60 is used in cancer therapy and to detect flaws in metal parts. See ELEMENT (table); PERIODIC TABLE.

**Cobb, Ty(rus Raymond),** 1886–1961, American baseball player. Cobb was the first player elected (1936) to the National Baseball Hall of Fame. An outfielder, the 'Georgia Peach' is considered by many to be the greatest player in the history of the game. In a 24-year career (Detroit Tigers, 1905–26; Philadelphia Athletics, 1927–28) he set numerous major-league records, such as his lifetime batting average of .367, and 12 batting championships. His career aggregate of 4191 hits was, however, exceeded in 1985 by Pete Rose of the Cincinnati Reds. A daring base runner, he stole 892 bases. He was manager of the Tigers from 1921 to 1926.

**Cobbett, William,** 1763–1835, British journalist and reformer. After seven years in the Army, and a period in America, he returned to England (1799) and became a radical working-class leader and champion of agrarianism, founder of the influential journal *Cobbett's Political Register*, advocate of Parliamentary reform and, from 1832, Member of Parliament for Oldham. His *Rural Rides* (1830) documented his horseback travels to investigate the spoliation of the countryside.

**Cobden, Richard,** 1804–65, British politician, a leading spokesman for the MANCHESTER SCHOOL. After making a fortune as a calico printer, he became a major influence in the repeal of the CORN LAWS. With John BRIGHT and Robert PEEL, he managed the ANTI-CORN-LAW LEAGUE. As a member of Parliament, Cobden negotiated the 'Cobden Treaty' for reciprocal tariffs with France (1859–60), and favoured the Union in the US Civil War.

**COBOL:** see PROGRAMMING LANGUAGE.

**cobra,** venomous SNAKE of the family Elapidae equipped with an inflatable neck hood, found in Africa and Asia. The king cobra (*Ophiophagus hannah*), or hamadryad, the largest poisonous snake, is found in S Asia; it may reach a length of 5.5 m (18 ft). Other species include the Indian cobra (*Naja naja*) and the Egyptian cobra (*Naja haje*), also called the ASP. The family also includes CORAL SNAKES.

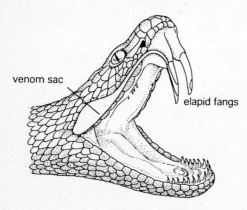

venom sac

elapid fangs

Cobra – showing how elapid fangs are connected to venom sac

**coca,** plant (genus *Erythroxylon,* particularly *E. coca*) found mainly in upland regions and on mountain slopes of South America and in Australia, India, and Africa. Certain South American Indians chew the leaves mixed with lime, which acts with saliva to release COCAINE from the leaves. In this form and concentration, the DRUG acts as a stimulant. A cocaine-free extract of the leaves is used in some soft drinks. Coca is grown commercially in Sri Lanka, Java, and Taiwan.

**cocaine,** ALKALOID drug derived from COCA leaves, producing euphoria and temporary increases in physical energy. It acts as a local anaesthetic and is a strongly addictive central NERVOUS SYSTEM stimulant (see DRUG ADDICTION AND DRUG ABUSE). Withdrawal from the drug can produce severe depression. Its medical use is confined to pain relief in terminal illness.

**Cochabamba,** city (1982 est. pop. 281,962), W central Bolivia, c.2560 m (8400 ft) high in the Andes. Centre of a productive agricultural region, it was founded as Villa de Oropeza in 1574 and renamed in 1786.

**Cochin,** city (1981 pop. 551,567), Kerala state, S India, where a great backwater enters the Arabian Sea. It is in fact a grouping of several distinct settlements: Cochin proper, a port developed by the Portuguese and Dutch; Mattancheri, an ancient Indian port; Alwaye; and Ernakulam. Cochin has grown as a modern port (the sixth most important in India) thanks to engineering operations, and is now able to accommodate any ships that can traverse the Suez Canal. It exports local agricultural produce and imports petroleum, machinery, and other goods. It has developed industries from the base provided by traditional boat-building: these include modern ship-construction, oil-refining, aluminium, and electrical engineering. Cochin proper was the first European settlement in India (1500). In British times Cochin was the capital of a princely state of the same name.

**Cochin China,** historic region, c.68,600 km² (26,500 sq mi), S Vietnam, bounded by Cambodia (NW, N), Annam (NE), the South China Sea (E, S), and the Gulf of Siam (W). The capital and chief city was Saigon (now HO CHI MINH CITY). Cochin China included the MEKONG delta, one of the world's great rice-growing areas, and, in the northeast, plantations where rubber, coffee, tea, oil palms, and sugarcane were grown. Originally part of the KHMER EMPIRE, Cochin China fell to ANNAM in the 18th cent. and became (1862–67) a French colony. The Japanese occupied it during WORLD WAR II. In 1954, after an independence struggle against the French, Cochin China became part of South Vietnam. At the end of the VIETNAM WAR it was incorporated into united Vietnam.

**Cochise,** c.1815–74, chief of the Chiricahua APACHE INDIANS in Arizona, US, noted for his courage, integrity, and military skill. From 1861, when soldiers unjustly hanged some of his relatives, he warred relentlessly against the US army. Peace talks in 1872 promised him a reservation on his native territory, but after he died his people were removed.

**Cockaigne** or **Cockayne, Land of,** country in medieval tales where delicacies were to be had for the taking. *The Land of Cockaigne* is a 13th-cent. satire on monastic life.

**cockatoo,** colourful member of the PARROT family found in Australasia. Cockatoos are recognized by the crest of feathers on their heads, which they can raise at will. They are gregarious birds in the wild, living in large flocks, feeding on seeds and fruits. This makes them pests in some areas. Their bright plumage and clever mimicry makes them popular cage-birds, condemning very social birds to a solitary life. Cage-birds that escape often join flocks of local birds, with a recorded case of a sulphur-crested cockatoo (*Kakatoe galerita*) living with rooks on Wimbledon Common, in London.

**cockchafer:** see CHAFER.

**Cockcroft, Sir John Douglas,** 1897–1967, English physicist. After serving as professor of natural philosophy at Cambridge, he directed (1946–59) the British Atomic Energy Research Establishment at Harwell. He shared with Ernest Walton the 1951 Nobel Prize for physics for their pioneer work in transmuting atomic nuclei by bombarding elements with artificially accelerated atomic particles. He was the first Master of Churchill College, Cambridge, named in honour of Sir Winston.

**Cockerell, Sir Christopher Sydney,** 1910–, English radio engineer and inventor and developer of the hovercraft. The first person to invent a means of producing and containing a cushion of air, he filed his first patent in 1953 and proved his invention and obtained the fundamental principles using small power models. He has wide-ranging engineering interests and has done much research on airborne navigational electronic equipment. He was awarded the International James Watt gold medal in 1983.

**cock-fighting,** match or fight between cocks, once considered a sport but banned in 1835 and now considered barbaric. It was possibly introduced to Britain by Roman soldiers. By the 17th cent. the natural weapons of a cock (beak and spur) had been augmented by a metal spur. Among those who campaigned for the abolition of cock-fighting in the early 19th cent. were the playwright Richard Brinsley SHERIDAN and the reformer William WILBERFORCE.

**cockle,** heart-shaped marine BIVALVE mollusc (superfamily Cardiacea), having ribbed, brittle shells. The spiny cockle moves with a jumping motion produced by means of a large, muscular foot. Most species do not exceed 7.5 cm (3 in) in length. Cockles burrow in sand or mud in shallow water. Several species, particularly the European cockle (*Cerastoderma edule*), are edible.

**cockney,** a native of London, especially the East End; strictly, a person born within the sound of Bow Bells, the bells of St Mary-le-Bow in the City of London. The word also means the dialect associated with that area, noted for its RHYMING SLANG.

**cockroach,** largely nocturnal, ground-living flat-bodied, oval INSECT of the order Dictyoptera (suborder Blattaria). Cockroaches range in size from 3 to 75 mm (¹⁄₁₀ to 3 in), have long thin antennae, long spiky legs adapted for running, and the dorsal surface of the first thoracic segment (pronotum) expanded to cover both thorax and head. Most species can fly. They have biting mouthparts and the majority feed on decaying vegetable matter. Several species, mostly of African origin despite their misleading names (e.g., American, German, and oriental cockroaches), have become serious cosmopolitan pests in food storage and handling facilities. Cockroaches also infest household drains, toilet facilities, and sewers. There they feed on faecal material and are often implicated in outbreaks of food-poisoning and gastroenteritis caused by *Salmonella* bacteria. Cockroaches are an ancient and successful group and were already abundant in the tropical forests which grew during the upper Carboniferous period, 335 to 270 million years ago.

**cocoa:** see CACAO.

**coconut,** edible fruit of the coco palm tree (*Cocos nucifera*) of the PALM family, widely distributed throughout the tropics. The coco palm, which grows to a height of 18 to 30 m (60 to 100 ft) and has a crown of frondlike leaves, is one of the most useful trees in existence. It is a source of timber, and its leaves are used in baskets and for thatch. The coconut itself is a single-seeded nut with a hard, woody shell encased in a thick, fibrous husk. The hollow nut contains coconut milk, a nutritious drink, and its white kernel, a staple food in the tropics, is eaten raw and cooked.

Common **cockroach** (*Blatta orientalis*)

Commercially valuable coconut oil is extracted from the dried kernels, called copra, and the residue is used for fodder. Husk fibres are used in cordage and mats, and nutshells are made into containers.

**Cocos (Keeling) Islands,** external territory of Australia (1986 pop. 676), 14.2 km² (5.5 sq mi), consisting of two separate atolls, West Island (administrative centre and airport) and Home Island (Cocos–Malay community), with 27 coral islets in the Indian Ocean. The islands were settled (1827) and developed by the Clunies-Ross family for copra. They were a dependency of Britain's Singapore colony from 1946 to 1955, when they were transferred to Australia. Australia purchased the Clunies-Ross interests in 1978 and leased the copra plantation to a cooperative run by Cocos–Malay which chose to integrate with Australia in 1984 in an Act of Self-Determination.

**Cocteau, Jean** (kok‚toh), 1889–1963, French author and filmmaker. Unrivalled in the 20th cent. for versatility in the arts, he experimented in almost every artistic medium, producing poetry, fiction, drama, films, ballets, drawings, and operatic librettos. Surrealistic fantasy suffuses his work. He is best known for the novel *Les enfants terribles* (1929; film 1950); the plays *Orphée* (1926; film 1949) and *La machine infernale* (1934); and the films *Le sang d'un poète* (1932; tr. The Blood of a Poet) and *La belle et la bête* (1945; tr. Beauty and the Beast).

**cod,** marine, bottom-feeding FISH (family Gadidae), among the most important and abundant food fishes. The Atlantic cod (*Gadus morhua*) averages 5–10 kg (11–24 lb), but specimens up to 90 kg (200 lb) have been reported. The haddock (*Melanogrammus aeglefinus*), one of the most important food fish in the Atlantic, is smaller, reaching a weight of 15 kg (33 lb). The cod and the haddock populations are both suffering from overfishing.

**code,** in communications, set of symbols and rules for their manipulation by which the symbols can be made to carry information. For telegraphic work, codes such as the MORSE CODE are used. All written and spoken languages are codes of some degree of efficiency. Certain arbitrary codes are used to ensure diplomatic and military secrecy of communication. The science of translating messages into cipher or code is termed *cryptography* [Gr., = hidden writing].

**codeine,** ALKALOID drug derived from OPIUM. A NARCOTIC with effects like those of MORPHINE, codeine is prescribed as an ANALGESIC and cough suppressant. It is less addictive than morphine (see DRUG ADDICTION AND DRUG ABUSE).

**Code Napoléon:** see CIVIL LAW.

**Cody, William Frederick:** see BUFFALO BILL.

**Coe, Sebastian,** 1956–, English middle-distance runner. At the Moscow Olympic Games in 1980 he won a silver medal in the 800 m and a gold medal in the 1500 m. In 1981 he broke three world records: the 800 m (1 min 41.73 sec); the 1000 m (2 min 12.18 sec); and the mile (3 min 47.33 sec). At the Los Angeles Olympics in 1984 he again won a silver medal in the 800 m and a gold medal in the 1500 m He was made an MBE in 1982.

**coeducation,** the education of both sexes in the same institution. Historically this has been common at nursery and primary levels, less so at higher levels until the late 19th and 20th cent. The first coeducational public school in Britain was Bedales, founded in 1893. Universities and colleges did not begin to admit women to lectures until the second half of the 19th cent. (see WOMEN'S EDUCATION). Only since World War II has

there been a growth of mixed teacher education colleges. Since the 1960s there has been research and debate about the advantages of mixed and single-sex schools, with some evidence to suggest that girls do better academically in single-sex schools in some subjects.

**coelacanth** or **lobefin,** name for several lunged, fleshy-finned, bony FISHes, predecessors of the AMPHIBIANS. Coelacanths were considered extinct until 1938, when a live one (*Latimeria chalumnae*), was caught in the sea off S Africa. Coelacanths are brown to blue and 150 cm (5 ft) long, with circular, overlapping scales, a laterally flattened three-lobed tail, a spiny dorsal fin, and a vestigial lung.

**coelenterate,** radially symmetrical, predominantly marine invertebrate animal of the phylum Cnidaria (also called Coelenterata), having a three-layered body wall, tentacles, and specialized stinging cells (nematocysts). Members of the phylum have a primitive nervous system and no specialized organs for excretion or respiration. The phylum includes the SEA ANEMONES, CORALS, JELLYFISH, and hydroids (see HYDRA). See also POLYP and MEDUSA.

**coenzyme,** a relatively small, nonprotein, organic molecule that constitutes the active part of some ENZYME complexes. Coenzymes participate in chemical reactions catalyzed by enzymes; although often structurally altered in the course of the reaction, the coenzymes are always restored to their original form after it. Many coenzymes are chemically related to vitamins (especially those of the B group) and are vital to the biochemical reactions in the body.

**Coeur, Jacques** (kuh), c.1395–1456, French merchant and chief adviser to CHARLES VII of France. He amassed a fabulous fortune with which he financed the last campaigns of the HUNDRED YEARS WAR. Arrested (1451) on the concocted charge of having poisoned Agnès SOREL, the king's mistress, he escaped (1454–55) to Rome and died fighting the Turks.

**coffee,** name for an evergreen shrub or tree (genus *Coffea*) of the MADDER family, its seeds, and the beverage made from them. The mature, red fruit (a drupe) typically contains two seeds, or coffee beans. Varieties of Arabian coffee (*C. arabica*) supply the bulk of the world's crop; Liberian coffee (*C. liberica*) and Congo coffee (*C. robusta*) are of some commercial importance. Coffee plants require a hot, moist climate and rich soil. The harvested seeds are cleaned and roasted; heat acts on the essential oils to produce the aroma and flavour. Roasts range from light brown to the very dark Italian roast. Coffee contains CAFFEINE, a stimulant that can cause irritability, depression, and indigestion if taken in excess. The coffee plant was known before AD 1000 in Ethiopia, where its fruit was used for food and wine. A beverage made from ground, roasted coffee beans was used in Arabia by the 15th cent., and by the mid 17th cent. it had reached most of Europe and had been introduced into North America.

**Coffs Harbour,** city (1986 pop. 18,074), New South Wales, E Australia. A subtropical tourist resort, the area is important for its banana production and vegetable growing. It is also one of Australia's major timber-shipping ports.

**cognac:** see BRANDY.

**cognate,** a bilateral kinsman or woman; cognatic DESCENT is reckoned through both male and female ancestors.

**cognition,** the set of activities or functions of mind which involve reasoning, judgment, MEMORY, problem-solving, language, symbolic and conceptual thought; in general, the 'higher mental functions' which go beyond PERCEPTION.

**cognitive science,** the interdisciplinary study of the human mind and mental processes (see COGNITION). Cognitive science has its roots in developments after World War II in psychology, linguistics, and computer science, in all of which the inadequacy of BEHAVIOURISM to explain complex behaviour became increasingly evident, together with the need for an explicit theory of mind. Cognitive science now also draws upon contributions from philosophy of mind, neurosciences, and ARTIFICIAL INTELLIGENCE. Cognitive science as a broad interdiscipline can be distinguished from cognitive psychology, a subfield of psychology whose major research topic is MEMORY, usually studied with an INFORMATION PROCESSING framework. The development of cognitive science has been deeply influenced by the notion that the mind can be viewed in terms of computational processes, but this emphasis is not exclusive.

**cohesion:** see ADHESION AND COHESION.

**Cohn, Ferdinand,** 1828–98, German botanist. Considered a founder of bacteriology, he developed theories of the bacterial causes of infectious disease and recognized bacteria as plants. His writings cover such subjects as fungi, algae, insect epidemics, and plant diseases.

**Coimbatore** ('kwəmbaˌtawr), city (1981 pop. 704,514), Tamil Nadu state, S India. It is a district administrative, communications, and commercial centre and has a justly famous Agricultural Univ. Its cotton mills date from the 1880s, and saw rapid growth in numbers and production after 1920. More recently the town has acquired other industries, including oil mills and engineering works. Coimbatore was the site of a fort of some antiquity, and was annexed by the EAST INDIA COMPANY in 1799. It became a district headquarters in British days.

**Coimbra** (koyˌimbrə), city (1984 pop. 74,616) and former capital of Portugal. Of Roman origin, it was occupied by the Moors from the 8th cent. to 1064 and subsequently became capital of Portugal from 1139 to 1385. The university, founded in Lisbon in 1290, was transferred to Coimbra in 1307 and makes the city an important centre of cultural activities. The former cathedral of Sé Velha is a fine example of 12th-cent. Romanesque architecture.

**coin,** piece of metal, usually a disc of gold, silver, nickel, bronze, copper, or a combination of such metals, issued by a government for use as MONEY. State coinage, said to have originated in Lydia in the 7th cent. BC, enabled governments to make coins whose nominal value exceeded their value as metals. See also NUMISMATICS.

**coke,** hard, grey, porous fuel with a high CARBON content. It is the residue left when bituminous COAL is heated in the absence of air. Coke is used in extracting metals from ores in the BLAST FURNACE; it is also capable of being converted, by high temperature treatment, to GRAPHITE.

**Coke, Sir Edward** (kook) or (kohk), 1552–1634, English jurist and political leader. After a rapid rise in Parliament he became (1593) attorney general, gained a reputation as a severe prosecutor, and was favoured at the court of JAMES I. As chief justice of common pleas (from 1606) and of the king's bench (from 1613) he championed the common law against the royal prerogative. Collisions with the king and political enmities led to his dismissal in 1616. By 1620 he had returned to Parliament, where he led popular opposition to the Crown. He was prominent in drafting the PETITION OF RIGHT (1628). Coke's writings include his *Reports* (on common law) and the *Institutes*.

**cola** or **kola,** tropical tree (genus *Cola*) of the sterculia family, native to Africa but grown in other tropical areas. The fruit is a pod containing CAFFEINE-yielding seeds. Cola nuts are chewed for this stimulant. They are also exported for use in soft drinks and medicine.

**Colbert, Jean Baptiste** (kolˌbeə), 1619–83, French statesman. Appointed (1665) controller general of finances by LOUIS XIV, he aimed to make France economically self-sufficient through the practice of MERCANTILISM. He encouraged industry by subsidies and tariffs, regulated prices, built roads, canals, and harbours, and expanded the navy and France's commercial potential. His power declined with the opening of Louis XIV's wars.

**Colchester,** town (1981 pop. 87,476) in Essex, SE England, on R. Colne, 82 km (51 mi) NE of London. Industries within the town include engineering and the manufacture of agricultural equipment. The town dates from the Iron Age. It was the first Roman capital of Britain (Camulodunum), and there are many Roman remains. There is a Norman castle, which is now a museum. The oyster fisheries nearby at the mouth of the R. Colne have been famous for several centuries. The Univ. of Essex (founded 1961) is located 4 km (2 mi) SE of the town.

**cold** or **common cold,** viral inflammation of the mucous membranes of the upper respiratory tract, especially the nose and throat. There are numerous viruses that cause the common cold. Transmission occurs by coughing and sneezing. No specific remedy yet exists for this common and annoying affliction, which can prove serious in patients with preexisting heart and lung disabilities. Treatment of symptoms includes fluids to prevent dehydration, analgesics (e.g., ASPIRIN) to lessen fever, and decongestants to shrink swollen mucous membranes. Some believe that large doses of vitamin C may be helpful in prevention.

**cold sore:** see HERPES.

**cold war,** term used to describe the political and economic struggle between the capitalist, democratic Western powers and the SOVIET BLOC after WORLD WAR II. The cold war period was marked by massive military buildups (including nuclear weaponry) by both sides and by intensive economic competition and strained, hostile diplomatic relations. The origins of the Cold War lay in the forcible Soviet takeover of Eastern Europe, particularly POLAND and CZECHOSLOVAKIA. Further disagreement between East and West occurred over the intended reunification of Germany, which proved to be impossible. The one major 'hot war' of the period was the KOREAN WAR. Communications between the two sides virtually ceased, and an IRON CURTAIN descended between them. The US rallied the other Western powers by sponsoring a series of strategic actions, including the MARSHALL PLAN, the NORTH ATLANTIC TREATY ORGANIZATION (NATO), and other regional pacts. Within the Communist bloc the USSR maintained tight political, economic, and military control over its satellites, for example, by suppressing the Hungarian Revolution of 1956; by instituting (1955) the WARSAW TREATY ORGANIZATION; and by supporting Communist takeovers of CHINA, parts of SE Asia, and CUBA. By the early 1960s tensions had relaxed somewhat, and a measure of DÉTENTE was apparent. Most observers felt that East and West were entering into more complex relations to which the term cold war could no longer apply.

WHAT A HEADACHE SOMETIMES TO BE WITH AMERICA

BUT TO BE WITHOUT IT— O LOR!

Cold War

**Cole, Thomas,** 1801–48, American painter; b. England. He specialized in painting the spectacular scenery of New York State, becoming a leader of the HUDSON RIVER SCHOOL. A characteristic painting is *Catskill Mountains* (Mus. Art, Cleveland). Other famous but less successful works are neo-classical in style.

**Coleman, Ornette,** 1930–, black American musician and composer. After playing saxophone in rhythm-and-blues bands, he emerged at the end of the 1950s as the most controversial figure in the JAZZ avant-garde. His impassioned, atonal music continued to exert great influence in the 1980s.

**Coleridge, Samuel Taylor,** 1772–1834, English poet and man of letters. After an erratic university career, he planned with Robert SOUTHEY to found a utopian 'Pantisocratic' community in the US, but the project did not materialize. In 1797 he met William WORDSWORTH, and they were neighbours in Somerset where they published *Lyrical Ballads* (1798), a volume whose experiments in language and subject matter (and the prefaces to later editions) make it a seminal work of English ROMANTICISM. Coleridge contributed 'The Rime of the Ancient Mariner', his best-known work. In 1800 he followed the Wordsworths to the Lake District, where he shared a house with Southey (the two men had married sisters), wrote the ode *Dejection* (1802) and became increasingly addicted to opium. A brilliant conversationalist, Coleridge lectured (notably on SHAKESPEARE), wrote plays, edited and contributed to newspapers and journals on religion, philosophy, and politics. His *Biographia Literaria*, which includes accounts of his literary life and also critical essays, appeared in 1817, and his poems *Christabel* and *Kubla Khan* were published in 1816, though written much earlier. His *Notebooks*, meditative diaries never published in his lifetime, are now among his most admired work. From 1816 he lived in London at the home of

Dr James Gilman, who helped to control his opium addiction. Though many of his literary projects were uncompleted, and he has been accused of some plagiarism from German philosophers, Coleridge was a major influence on 19th cent. religion and philosophy, and on literary criticism, and, at his best, a great poet.

**Coleridge-Taylor, Samuel,** 1875–1912, British composer, teacher, and conductor, the son of a doctor from Sierra Leone and an English mother. The most popular and successful of his many compositions were his settings of poems by Longfellow, *Hiawatha's Wedding Feast* (1898), *The Death of Minnehaha* (1899), and *Hiawatha's Departure* (1900).

**Colette,** 1873–1954, French novelist; b. Sidonie Gabrielle Colette. Her numerous novels, e.g., *Chéri* (1920), *La chatte* (1933; The Cat), and *Gigi* (1945), are famed for their sensitive observations of women, nature, and eroticism. Colette's early *Claudine* books were published under the name of her first husband, Willy (pseud. of Henry Gauthier-Villars).

**colcus,** tropical plant (genus *Coleus*) of the MINT family, native to Asia and Africa. Some, with large, colourful leaves, are cultivated as houseplants and for summer bedding.

**Coligny, Gaspard de Châtillon, comte de** (kohleen,yee), 1519–72, French Protestant leader, admiral of France. With Louis I de CONDÉ, he commanded the HUGUENOTS in the Wars of Religion (see RELIGION, WARS OF) and negotiated a peace in 1570. He became a favourite adviser of CHARLES IX, thus arousing the enmity of CATHERINE DE' MEDICI. Coligny was the first victim in the massacre of SAINT BARTHOLOMEW'S DAY.

**Coliseum:** see COLOSSEUM.

**collage,** [Fr., = pasting], technique in art consisting of cutting natural or manufactured materials and pasting them to a painted or unpainted surface; also, a work of art in this medium. PICASSO and BRAQUE were the first to use real objects, such as newspaper, in their works. Collage often involves playing and punning on levels of reality within the finished painting, where illusion and reality compete with each other. DADA artists used collage for social and ideological purposes in their works, and surrealists (see SURREALISM) exploited collage to juxtapose disparate images, e.g., ERNST's collage *La Femme 100 Têtes* (1929).

**collective bargaining,** in labour relations, procedure whereby an employer agrees to discuss working conditions by bargaining with employee representatives, usually a trade union. First developed in the UK in the 19th cent., it became a widely adopted practice as trade unionism played an increasing and growing role. The process is now accepted in most Western industrialized countries as the basic method of settling disputes about wages, hours, job security, health and safety issues, and other matters. Industrial **arbitration** is a last resort, implying the need for a third party to resolve the dispute and impose a decision on both sides (see ACAS).

**collective farm,** an agricultural producers' cooperative. In the USSR, collectivization of agriculture was initiated by STALIN in 1929. A collective farm's land and equipment is owned by the state, which decides what will be produced. Farm workers share in state-guaranteed profits and have small private plots where they can grow goods for free-market sale. In China, the commune (first established 1958) is similar to the Soviet collective farm. Land and equipment are owned by the commune, which oversees fulfillment of government quotas by production teams (small groups of workers). There are private plots, and profits are shared. Both China and the USSR also have state farms, whose workers are paid wages. The best-known type of Israeli collective farm is the KIBBUTZ.

**college of arms:** see HERALDS'S COLLEGE.

**colleges,** various kinds of institution in higher, and in some cases, secondary education. The term has four main educational connections. **1** Associated historically with some PUBLIC SCHOOLS (e.g., Dulwich College, Eton College), it is now a synonym for school. **2** In FURTHER EDUCATION it means colleges which provide post-secondary, non-higher education (colleges of further education, technical colleges). **3** It is used for the component institutions of some UNIVERSITIES. This derives historically from the associations of colleges which in the medieval period became CAMBRIDGE UNIVERSITY and OXFORD UNIVERSITY, and in those two instances the colleges remain the unit for students to enter the university, for residence, meals, and tutorial relationships. Other universities such as LONDON UNIVERSITY and the Univ. of Wales, also became federations of colleges. Some of the new universities created in the 1950s (such as the Univ. of

York) also divided themselves for residential, social, and some academic purposes into 'colleges'. **4** The 19th-cent. teacher-training colleges became 'colleges of education' after the Robbins report on *Higher Education* (1963) recommended that all teacher education should be at least three years and result in a Bachelor of Education. These, together with some other further education colleges which had not become POLYTECHNICS, became 'Colleges (or in some cases Institutes) of Higher Education' in the mid-1970s. Colleges of Higher Education, like polytechnics and universities, are mainly degree-level institutions.

**colligative properties,** properties of a SOLUTION that depend on the number of solute particles present, but not on the chemical properties of the solute. Colligative properties of a solution include its freezing and boiling points (see STATES OF MATTER) and osmotic pressure (see OSMOSIS).

**Collingwood, Robin George,** 1889–1945, English historian and philosopher. Collingwood taught philosophy at Oxford and was Waynflete professor of metaphysics (1935–41). He became an authority on the history and archaeology of Roman Britain with his *Roman Britain* (1921); later with J.N.L. Myers he wrote the first volume of the *Oxford History of England—Roman Britain* (1936). His autobiography appeared in 1939 and among his distinctive philosophical works were *Speculum mentis* (1924) and *The Idea of History* (1946).

**Collins, Michael,** 1890–1922, Irish revolutionary leader. A member of the SINN FEIN, he organized the guerrilla warfare that forced the British to sue for peace. With Arthur GRIFFITH he set up the Irish Free State. He was assassinated.

**Collins, (William) Wilkie,** 1824–89, English novelist. The author of some 30 novels, he is best known for *The Woman in White* (1860) and *The Moonstone* (1868), considered the first full-length detective novel in English.

**Collip, James Bertram,** 1892–1965, Canadian biochemist who together with BANTING, BEST, and MACLEOD discovered INSULIN. When the 1923 Nobel Prize for physiology or medicine went to Banting and Macleod, the latter shared the prize money with Collip, and Banting shared his with Best.

**Collodi, Carlo,** pseud. of **Carlo Lorenzini,** 1826–90, Italian writer. A journalist, he also wrote didactic tales for children, the most famous of which is *The Adventures of Pinocchio* (1883).

**colloid,** a mixture in which one substance is divided into minute particles (called colloidal particles) and dispersed throughout a second substance. Colloidal particles are larger than molecules but too small to be observed with a microscope; however, their shape and size (usually between $10^{-7}$ and $10^{-5}$ cm) can be determined by electron microscopy. In a true SOLUTION the particles of dissolved substance are of molecular size and thus smaller than colloidal particles. In a coarse mixture (e.g., a SUSPENSION) the particles are much larger than colloidal particles. Colloids can be classified according to the phase (solid, liquid, or gas) of the dispersed substance and of the medium of dispersion. A gas may be dispersed in a liquid to form a *foam* (e.g., shaving lather) or in a solid to form a solid foam. A liquid may be dispersed in a gas to form an AEROSOL (e.g., FOG), in another liquid to form an *emulsion* (e.g., homogenized milk, mayonnaise, ice-cream, luncheon meat, and low-fat spreads), or in a solid to form a *gel* (e.g., jellies). A solid may be dispersed in a gas to form a solid aerosol (e.g., dust or smoke in air), in a liquid to form a *sol* (e.g., INK), or in a solid to form a solid sol (e.g., certain ALLOYS). Colloids are distinguished from true solutions by their inability to diffuse through a semipermeable membrane (e.g., cellophane) and by their ability to scatter light (the TYNDALL effect). In the Middle Ages colloidal GOLD was used in the treatment of certain ailments, a practice which is still continued in many parts of the world.

**Cologne,** Ger. *Köln,* city (1984 pop. 932,400), North Rhine–Westphalia, W West Germany, on the Rhine R. It is a river port and an industrial centre producing iron, steel, and other manufactures. Founded (1st cent. BC) by the Romans, it flourished (4th–13th cent.) under powerful archbishops. It became a free imperial city (1475) and a member (15th cent.) of the HANSEATIC LEAGUE. The city was badly damaged in WORLD WAR II. However, such buildings as its Gothic cathedral (begun 1248) and Romanesque Church of St Andreas still stand.

**Colombia,** offically Republic of Colombia, republic (1985 est. pop. 29,190,000), 1,138,914 km² (439,735 sq mi) NW South America. The only South American country with both Pacific and Caribbean coastlines,

Colombia is bordered by Panama (NW), Venezuela (NE), Ecuador and Peru (S), and Brazil (SE). Major cities include BOGOTÁ (the capital), MEDELLÍN, and CALI. By far the most prominent physical features are the three great Andean (see ANDES) mountain chains (CORDILLERAS) that fan N from Ecuador, reaching their highest point in Pico Cristóbal (5775 m/ 18,947 ft). The Andean interior is the heart of the country, containing the largest concentration of population as well as the major coffee-growing areas. In pre-Columbian days this was the site of the advanced civilization of the Chibcha Indians. To the east of the Andes lies more than half of Colombia's territory, a vast undeveloped lowland, including the tropical rainforests of the AMAZON basin and the grasslands (LLANOS) of the ORINOCO basin. Agriculture is the chief source of income: Besides coffee, Colombia's leading export crops are bananas, cotton, sugarcane, and tobacco. Rich in minerals, Colombia produces petroleum and natural gas, iron, coal, gold, nickel, and emeralds. The growing manufacturing sector is led by processed foods, textiles, metal products, and chemicals. In 1985 GDP was US$36,600 million or US$1262 per capita. About two thirds of the population are mestizos. Spanish is the official language, and most of the people are Roman Catholic.

*History.* Conquered by the Spanish in 1530s, the region that is now Colombia became the core of the Spanish colony of NEW GRANADA, which included Panama and most of Venezuela. The struggle for independence from Spain began in 1810, lasting nine years, and ending with the victory of Simón BOLÍVAR at Boyacá in 1819. Bolívar set up the new state of Greater Colombia, which included all of New Granada and (after 1822) Ecuador. Political differences soon emerged, however, and the union fell apart. Venezuela and Ecuador became separate nations; the remaining territory eventually became the Republic of Colombia (1886), from which Panama seceded in 1903. During the 19th and into the 20th cent., political unrest and civil strife racked Colombia. Strong parties developed along conservative (centrist) and liberal (federalist) lines, and civil war frequently erupted between the factions. As many as 100,000 people were killed before the conservatives emerged victorious in a civil war of unprecedented violence that raged from 1899 to 1902. And, again, after a four-decade hiatus of political peace, in 1948 bloody strife rent the nation, costing hundreds of thousands of lives. Orderly government was finally restored as the result of a compromise between liberals and conservatives in 1958 under which the two sides agreed to share power. The situation began to deteriorate in the 1970s, and unrest and guerrilla activity continued into the 1980s, some of the violence being associated with drug industry death squads. In 1984 Pres. Belisario Betancur concluded a cease-fire with the main guerrilla groups; however, amid continuing official and unofficial violence the truce with the significant April 19 Movement (M-19) broke down in 1985. Virgilio Barco Vargas (Liberal Party) was elected president in 1986.

**Post-war Colombian presidents**
Alberto Lleras Camargo (liberal), 1945–46
Mariano Ospina Pérez (conservative), 1946–50
Laureano Gómez (conservative), 1950–51
Roberto Urdaneta Arbelaez (conservative), 1951–53
Laureano Gómez (conservative), 1953
Gustavo Rojas Pinilla (military), 1953–57
Alberto Lleras Camargo (liberal), 1958–62
Guillermo León Valencia (conservative), 1962–66
Carlos Lleras Restrepo (liberal), 1966–70
Misael Pastrana Borrero (conservative), 1970–74
Alfonso López Michelsen (liberal), 1974–78
Julio César Turbay Ayala (liberal), 1978–82
Belisario Betancur (conservative), 1982–86
Virgilio Barco Vargas (liberal), 1986–

**Colombo,** largest city (1981 pop. 585,771) and capital of Sri Lanka, on the Indian Ocean near the mouth of the Kelani R. It has one of the world's largest man-made harbours, with facilities for containerized cargo. Noted for its gem-cutting and ivory-carving, Colombo also has oil-refining and other industries. A port since Greco-Roman times, it was settled by Muslims in the 8th cent. The Portuguese built (16th cent.) a fort to protect their spice trade. The city passed (17th cent.) to the Dutch and then to the British, who made it (1802) the capital of their colony of Ceylon. The city has several colleges and universities and many churches, mosques, and temples.

**Colombo Plan,** officially Colombo Plan for Cooperative, Economic and Social Development in Asia and the Pacific, intergovernmental

Colombia

organization founded in 1951, initially as a regional grouping of the COMMONWEALTH and later expanded to include non-Commonwealth countries. Area members (1988) are Afghanistan, Bangladesh, Bhutan, Burma, Fiji, India, Indonesia, Iran, Kampuchea, South Korea, Laos, Malaysia, Maldives, Nepal, Pakistan, Papua New Guinea, Philippines, Singapore, Sri Lanka and Thailand. Developed countries in membership are Australia, Canada, Japan, New Zealand, the UK and the US.

**colon,** in writing: see PUNCTUATION.

**Colonial Conference, British:** see IMPERIAL CONFERENCE.

**colonialism:** see COLONIZATION; IMPERIALISM.

**colonization,** extension of political and economic control over an area by an occupying state that usually has organizational or technological superiority. The colonizer's nationals may migrate to the colony because of overpopulation or economic or social distress at home, but IMPERIALISM has been a major colonizing force. The colony's population must be subdued or assimilated to the colonizer's way of life, or a modus vivendi otherwise imposed. Colonization dates back at least to the Phoenicians, but it is most important historically as the vehicle of European expansion from the 15th cent. into Africa, the Americas, and Asia. The Spanish, Portuguese, English, French, and Dutch established colonies worldwide that have, for the most part, obtained independence from imperial systems only in the 20th cent. Today classic colonialism is widely considered immoral. See also MANDATES; TRUSTEESHIP, TERRITORIAL.

**Colonna,** a leading noble Roman family from the 12th to the 16th cent. **Sciarra Colonna,** d. 1329, was a bitter enemy of Pope BONIFACE VIII and led, with Chancellor Nogaret, the French expedition that captured (1303) Boniface. The family also produced Pope MARTIN V. **Fabrizio Colonna,** d. 1520, was a general of the HOLY LEAGUE against LOUIS XII of France in the ITALIAN WARS. His cousin **Prospero Colonna,** 1452–1523, defeated the French at La Biocca (1522). **Marcantonio Colonna,** 1535–84, duke of Paliano, led the papal forces at LEPANTO.

**colony:** see COLONIZATION.

**Colorado,** state of the US (1984 est. pop. 3,178,000), area 270,000 km² (104,247 sq mi), situated in the W and bordered by Wyoming (N),

Nebraska (NE), Kansas (E), Oklahoma and New Mexico (S), and Utah (W). The capital is DENVER; other major cities are Colorado Springs and Pueblo. The high parts of the GREAT PLAINS in the east area are separated by the Front Range from the ROCKY MTS in the west; Colorado has the highest mean elevation of any state (c.2100 m/6800 ft). In the westernmost part of the state the COLORADO PLATEAU is drained by the deep canyons of the COLORADO R. The economy is led by manufacturing, including food processing, nonelectrical machinery and instruments, metal refining, and printing. Agriculture is dominated by raising cattle and sheep, but irrigated crops such as corn, wheat, hay, and sugar beets are also important. Colorado has the world's largest deposits of molybdenum and extensive deposits of petroleum, coal, and uranium. In 1980 77% of the population was non-Hispanic white and 12% was of Spanish origin. Most of the population live within 30 miles of the Front Range. Spain claimed the area in 1706 from the cliff-dwelling tribes, and in 1803 it passed to the US, first in the LOUISIANA PURCHASE and then after the Mexican–American War in 1848. The discovery of precious meals in the late 19th cent. became the basis for development, once water was transferred from the west to the east.

**Colorado,** chief river of the arid SW US. It flows 2335 km (1450 mi) from the Rocky Mts of N Colorado to the Gulf of Mexico, c.1610 km (1000 mi) of its course cutting through deep canyons, including the spectacular GRAND CANYON. Use of the river, whose flow is controlled by HOOVER, Davis, Imperial, Parker, Glen Canyon, and other dams, is allocated by treaties with Mexico and by compacts between states.

**Colorado Plateau,** physiographic region of the SW US, covering c.385,000 km² (150,000 sq mi) in Arizona, Utah, Colorado, and New Mexico. The broad, sparsely vegetated, and semiarid plateau surfaces one-third located within Indian reservations are cut by great canyons, including the GRAND CANYON and Canyon de Chelly.

**Colorado Springs,** US city (1984 est. pop. 248,000), central Colorado, on Monument and Fountain creeks, at the foot of Pikes Peak; founded 1859, inc. 1886. It is a year-round vacation and health resort, with industries producing electronic, mining, and aerospace equipment. The US Air Force Academy is nearby.

**Colosseum** or **Coliseum,** common name for the Flavian AMPHITHEATRE in Rome, built AD c.75–80 under VESPASIAN and TITUS. Much of the four-storeyed oval, 188 m (617 ft) by 156 m (512 ft), still stands. Tiers of marble seats accommodated about 45,000 people. In the arena gladiatorial combats were held until AD 404, and according to tradition, Christians were thrown to beasts.

The **Colosseum** interior

**Colossians,** EPISTLE of the NEW TESTAMENT. It was written to Christians of Colossae and Laodicea (Asia Minor) by St PAUL (AD c.60), apparently to warn his readers against gnostic tendencies current in the churches addressed. Like EPHESIANS, it emphasizes the doctrine of the mystical body of Christ.

**colossus,** name given in antiquity to a statue of very great size. Examples include the Athena Parthenos on the ACROPOLIS at Athens and the **Colossus of Rhodes,** one of the SEVEN WONDERS OF THE WORLD. Among colossi of later times, the Great Buddha at Kamakura, Japan, and the Statue of LIBERTY in New York harbour are notable. Two colossal figures of Christ are in South America, one at Rio de Janeiro and the other, CHRIST OF THE ANDES, on the boundary of Argentina and Chile.

**colour,** visual effect resulting from the eye's ability to distinguish the different wavelengths or frequencies of light. The apparent colour of an object depends on the wavelength of the light that it reflects. In white light, an opaque object that reflects all wavelengths appears white and one that absorbs all wavelengths appears black. Any three primary, or spectral, colours can be combined in various proportions to produce any other colour sensation. Beams of light are combined 'additively', and red, blue, and green are typically chosen as primaries. Pigments, however, combine by a 'subtractive' process, i.e., by absorbing wavelengths, and artists generally choose red, blue, and yellow as their primaries. Two colours are called complementary if their light together produces white.

**colour blindness,** inability to distinguish certain colours, an inherited trait occurring almost exclusively in males. The most common form is red–green colour blindness. Those who are completely red–green colour-blind see both colours as shades of yellow, yellowish-brown, or grey. Totally colour-blind people see only black, white, and shades of grey.

**colour field painting,** abstract art movement begun by painters of the 1960s. Working toward a more intellectual aesthetic than that of ABSTRACT EXPRESSIONISM, colour field painters dealt with their conception of the fundamental formal elements of abstract painting: pure areas of untempered colour; flat, two-dimensional space; monumental scale; and the varying shape of the canvas. Painters associated with the movement include Ellsworth KELLY, Morris LOUIS, Kenneth NOLAND, and Frank STELLA.

**Colt, Samuel,** 1814–62, American inventor. His revolving breech pistol (patented 1835–36) was one of the standard SMALL ARMS of the world in the last half of the 19th cent. Colt also invented a submarine battery used in harbour defence and a submarine telegraph cable.

**Coltrane, John,** 1926–67, black American musician. Rising to prominence with the Miles DAVIS quintet in the mid-1950s, he was until his death the dominant tenor and soprano saxophonist of the JAZZ avant-garde.

**Columba, Saint,** or **Saint Columcille,** 521–97, Irish missionary to Scotland, called the Apostle of Caledonia. He established a monastic centre at IONA in 564 and eventually Christianized all of N Scotland. Feast: 9 June.

**Columbia,** US city (1980 pop. 99,296), state capital of South Carolina, on the Congaree R.; inc. 1805. The largest city in the state, it is the trade centre for a farming region, and manufactures such products as textiles, plastics, and electronic equipment. Most of the city was burned by Gen. SHERMAN's troops in 1865. The Univ. of South Carolina and several other colleges are located there.

**Columbia,** chief river of the NW US, c.1950 km (1210 mi) long, including 748 km (465 mi) in SW Canada. It flows generally south in British Columbia and Washington and then west, forming the Washington–Oregon boundary and entering the Pacific Ocean W of Portland, Ore. Numerous dams, including the GRAND COULEE DAM, provide hydroelectricity and irrigation. The Columbia, whose volume is greatly increased by the SNAKE and other major tributaries, was the early focus of American settlement in the Oregon country.

**Columbia Plateau,** physiographic region of the NW US, covering c.260,000 km² (more than 100,000 sq mi) in Washington, Oregon, and Idaho. Most of it is underlain by thick, nearly horizontal beds of lava (mainly basalt) and partly covered with fertile loess. Arid areas south of the GRAND COULEE DAM are irrigated as part of the Columbia Basin project.

**columbine,** perennial plant (genus *Aquilegia*) of the BUTTERCUP family. Columbines have delicate foliage and red, white, yellow, blue, or purple flowers with long, nectar-secreting spurs on the petals. *A. vulgaris* is poisonous and the ingested seeds can be fatal.

**columbium:** see NIOBIUM.

**Columbus,** US city (1984 est. pop. 566,000), state capital of Ohio, on the Scioto R.; founded 1797, inc. as a city 1834. A major industrial and trade centre in a rich farm region, it took over state government from Chillicothe in 1816. Transport has been key to its development: canals, the national road (reaching Columbus in 1833), and the railway (1850) all brought growth. The city manufactures appliances, machinery, vehicle parts, and other products. Ohio State Univ. is located there, as is the Columbus Gallery of Fine Arts.

**Columbus, Christopher,** 1451–1506, discoverer of America; b. Genoa, Italy. In Portugal, he became a master mariner and was determined to reach India by sailing west. After eight years of supplication, he received the backing of the Spanish monarchs FERDINAND V and ISABELLA I. On Oct. 12, 1492, his ships, the *Niña, Pinta,* and *Santa María,* reached Watling Island, in the Bahama group; later they touched CUBA and HISPANIOLA. He was made an admiral and governor general of all new lands. In 1493 he set sail with 17 ships, discovering PUERTO RICO and the Leeward Islands, and founding a colony in Hispaniola. In 1498 he explored VENEZUELA, realizing that he had found a continent. Because of disreputable conditions in Hispaniola, he was replaced as governor in 1500 and returned to Spain in chains. On his last voyage (1502) he reached Central America. Although he is considered a master navigator today, he died in neglect, almost forgotten.

**Columcille, Saint:** see COLUMBA, SAINT.

**column,** vertical architectural support, circular or polygonal in plan. It is generally at least four times as high as its diameter or width; stubbier masses are usually called piers or pillars. Shape, proportions, and materials of columns vary widely. Columns arranged in a row form a colonnade. The Egyptians used massive columns, closely spaced, for inner courtyards and halls. Early Greek columns had a cushionlike cap and tapering shaft. By the 7th cent. BC, the Greek Doric had been established. In Greek, Roman, and Renaissance architecture, the various column types, with their entablatures, form the classical ORDERS OF ARCHITECTURE. The classical column has three fundamental elements: base, shaft, and capital. The capital provides a structural and decorative transition between the circular column and the rectangular ENTABLATURE. In Greek buildings columns were usually indispensable, but Roman and Renaissance architects used them also as a decorative feature, mostly following fixed rules of proportions. Romanesque, Gothic, and Byzantine columns were usually structural elements, and were without canons of proportioning. Chinese and Japanese columns had, instead of capitals, ornamented brackets.

**coma,** state of complete unconsciousness from which a person cannot be aroused even by the most painful stimuli. Its severity is sometimes graded according to pupillary and corneal responses. It may be caused by severe brain injury, DIABETES, MORPHINE or BARBITURATE poisoning, SHOCK, or haemorrhage. Treatment is directed at the cause of the condition.

**Comanche Indians,** NORTH AMERICAN INDIANS of a nomadic Plains culture, who ranged the Southwest US from the 18th cent. They spoke a Shoshonean language (see AMERICAN INDIAN LANGUAGES). Excellent horsemen and warriors, they killed more whites in proportion to their numbers than any other tribe and kept their territory unsafe for whites for more than a century. Today some 3500 live in Oklahoma.

**combinations,** in mathematics: see PERMUTATIONS AND COMBINATIONS.

**comb jelly** or **sea gooseberry,** solitary marine invertebrate (phylum Ctenophora) having eight radially arranged rows (combs) of ciliated plates (ctenes) on the spherical body surface and specialized adhesive cells (colloblasts) used for capturing PLANKTON. Comb jellies are carnivorous, bioluminescent (see BIOLUMINESCENCE), and HERMAPHRODITE. They are weak swimmers but possess a unique sense organ controlling equilibrium (statocyst). Usually transparent, comb jellies vary from 0.5 cm (¼ in) to more than 30 cm (1 ft) in length and look very much like JELLYFISH.

**COMECON:** see COUNCIL FOR MUTUAL ECONOMIC ASSISTANCE.

**Comédie Française** or **Théâtre Française,** state theatre of France, Paris, est. 1680 by LOUIS XIV, merging troupes of Hôtel Guénégaud and Hôtel de Bourgogne. It was reorganized (1803) under NAPOLEON I. The company performs finest French drama in generally traditional repertory, and has no star system; all permanent associates enjoy equal status.

**comedy,** literary work, usually dramatic, aiming chiefly to amuse. Whereas TRAGEDY seeks to engage the emotions, comedy strives to entertain through ridicule of characters, customs, and institutions or through a resolution of contretemps thrown up by the plot. Dramatic comedy had its origins in Greek fertility rites. Old Comedy, culminating in ARISTOPHANES, was a series of scenes using FARCE, fantasy, parody, and SATIRE, with a final lyric celebration of unity. New Comedy (from c.4th cent. BC) was more realistic and romantic, less satirical and critical. MENANDER in Athens, PLAUTUS and TERENCE in Rome were its leading

Comb jellies (*Pleurobrachia pileus*); one on its side and one end-on showing eight rows of comb plates.

practitioners. In the Middle Ages comedy survived in folk plays and in the Italian COMMEDIA DELL'ARTE. In the RENAISSANCE, Elizabethan comedy drew in part on Latin comedy to produce the caustic satires of Ben JONSON and the romantic comedy of SHAKESPEARE. Classical and commedia dell'arte elements blended in France in MOLIÈRE's brilliant work. After the Puritan suppression of the theatre, witty, artificial comedy reappeared during the English RESTORATION in the work of William CONGREVE and William WYCHERLEY. It descended into sentiment by the end of the 17th cent. but revived late in the 18th cent. with Oliver GOLDSMITH and R.B. SHERIDAN. Oscar WILDE typified the late-19th-cent. comedy of manners, G.B. SHAW the comedy of ideas. Twentieth-century trends include the romantic comic fantasies of J.M. BARRIE and Jean GIRAUDOUX; the native Irish comedy of J.M. SYNGE and others; the absurdist works of Samuel BECKETT and Eugène IONESCO; and the so-called black comedy (the darkly humorous treatment of serious themes) of Joe ORTON and others. Masters of nondramatic comedy include, among many, BOCCACCIO, RABELAIS, CERVANTES, VOLTAIRE, Henry FIELDING and Charles DICKENS.

**Comenius, John Amos,** Czech *Jan Amos Komenský,* 1592–1670, Czechoslovakian churchman and educator. Relating education to everyday life, he advocated systematizing all knowledge, teaching in the vernacular rather than Latin, and establishing a universal system of education with opportunities for women. One of his major works, *Didactica magna* (1628–32; tr. M.W. Keatinge, 1896), expounds these principles.

**comet,** mostly gaseous body of small mass and enormous volume that can be seen from Earth for periods ranging from a few days to several months. A comet head, on the average about 31,000 km (80,000 mi) in diameter, contains a small, bright nucleus (theorized to be ice and frozen gases interspersed throughout with particles of heavier substances) surrounded by a coma, or nebulous envelope of luminous gases. As the comet approaches the Sun, the particles and gases are driven off, forming a tail as long as 160 million km (100 million mi). Pushed by the SOLAR WIND, the tail always streams out away from the Sun. J.H. OORT hypothesized (1950) a shell of more than 100,000 million comets surrounding the solar system and moving very slowly at a distance of as much as 150,000 times the Sun–Earth distance; a passing star, however, may gravitationally perturb a few into orbits that approach the Sun closely. Some, such as HALLEY'S COMET, return periodically.

**Cominform:** see under COMINTERN.

**Comintern,** acronym for Communist International. This organization was also known as the 'Third International' because it followed the First (1864–76) and the Second (founded in 1889, effectively destroyed in 1914); it brought together the Communist parties of the world under the leadership of the Communist Party of the Soviet Union. Founded in 1921 by LENIN, it followed various changes in the foreign policy of the Soviet Union (see POPULAR FRONT), before being dissolved by STALIN in 1943 as a gesture of conciliation towards his western allies in WORLD WAR II.

**comma:** see PUNCTUATION.

**Commagene** (komə‚jeenee), ancient district of N Syria, on the Euphrates R. and S of the Taurus range, now in SE Asiatic Turkey. Once

Comet Bennett, clearly showing the tail of the comet as two distinct streamers trailing out thousands of miles.

part of the Assyrian empire and later of the Persian Empire, it became independent in 162 BC. The Roman emperor Vespasian permanently annexed Commagene in AD 72.

**Commager, Henry Steele,** 1902–, American historian. He taught at Columbia Univ. (1938–56) and at Amherst College (1956–). His many works include *The Growth of the American Republic,* with S.E. MORISON (1930); *Majority Rule and Minority Rights* (1943); and *Jefferson, Nationalism, and the Enlightenment* (1975). He has been a strong advocate of Anglo-American friendship.

**Commandos,** originally the units raised by the Boers in the SOUTH AFRICAN WAR. The Term is now used for a highly mobile amphibious force, especially that attached to the Royal Marines.

**commedia dell'arte,** (koh͵maydeeah del͵ahtay), popular form of comedy in Italy from the 16th to 18th cent. Using improvised dialogue and masked actors in satiric song, dance, and farce, it gave rise to such traditional PANTOMIME characters as Harlequin and Columbine. Its influence on European theatre, particularly French pantomine and English harlequinade, was great.

**commensalism,** relationship between members of two different species of organisms in which one individual is usually only slightly benefited while the other is not affected at all. In many cases, commensalism cannot be distinguished from parasitism (see PARASITE). See also SYMBIOSIS.

**commercial paper,** type of short-term NEGOTIABLE INSTRUMENT, usually an unsecured promissory note, that calls for the payment of money at a specified date. Because it is not backed by collateral, commercial paper is usually issued by major firms with strong credit ratings and sold to other business firms. An important source of cash for the issuing firm, it is usually payable at a lower rate of interest than the prime discount rate. In the UK a new sterling commercial paper market started in May 1986 with any company having assets (net) of more than £50 million which is listed on the STOCK EXCHANGE able to issue paper. The minimum issue was set as £500,000 with a maturity of between 7 days and one year. The Bank of England has to be advised of all issues. By the end of 1986 £527 million of commercial paper was outstanding.

**Committee on Safety of Medicines,** body established in 1972 to advise the British government on the safety, quality, and usefulness of therapeutic items or drugs. It collects information on adverse reactions to drugs and may ask that a drug already on the market be withdrawn. It also advises on the issue of product licences without which a drug may not be marketed in the UK. Health ministers have the final responsibility for decisions.

**commodity market,** organized traders' exchange market in which contracts for delivery of certain products are bought and sold. Most trading is done in futures contracts—agreements to deliver goods at a

future date for a specified price. Such trading allows both hedging against serious losses in a declining market and speculation for gain in a rising market. Spot contracts, a less widely used form of trading, call for immediate delivery. In the UK, commodity markets deal in a wide range of products, such as tea, coffee, cotton, rubber, sugar, and gold. Trading in financial futures, such as Treasury bills and CERTIFICATES OF DEPOSIT, increased greatly in the 1980s.

**Common Agricultural Policy (CAP),** system of agricultural support adopted by the COMMON MARKET. The main aims of the CAP as identified by Article 39 of the Treaty of Rome are to increase productivity; to ensure a fair standard of living, particularly for the agricultural community; to stabilize markets; and to ensure that supplies are available to consumers at reasonable prices. The policy is implemented by means of support prices, import levies, and the subsidized export of surpluses. The CAP covers over 75% of farm output including most cereals, sugar, dairy products, beef, veal, pigmeat, fish, wine, and some fruit and vegetables. Common prices are set each year by the Council of Ministers on the recommendation of the Commission, which give producers an indication of what to expect under normal market conditions. Support prices are fixed at about 7% below the basic prices and are the point at which the EEC authorities intervene through their agencies and buy produce offered to them. These surpluses are stored for possible use in the event of an EEC shortage, or exported with an export refund to compensate the exporter for the difference between EEC and world market prices. EEC farmers are protected against cheaper imports by the imposition of levies which raise the import prices to those in the EEC. The existence of the CAP is a continuing cause of controversy for a number of reasons. The objective of self-sufficiency in many agricultural products was achieved quickly as farms increased their production. The cost of supporting uneconomic farmers and financing unwanted surpluses proved prohibitive and in the 1980s the CAP accounted for 70% of the entire EEC budget. In early 1986 EEC intervention stocks were valued at £5.7 billion. Although subsidized food surpluses may have benefitted poor consumers in the Third World, at the same time they have eroded the markets of developing countries which depend for their livelihood on food exports.

**common cold:** see COLD.

**common law,** system of law based on custom and PRECEDENT established by court decisions. Developed in medieval England and so called because it represented common, rather than local, custom, the common law prevails in most English-speaking nations, including England and Wales, most Commonwealth countries, and the US. The formality and inflexibility of early common law often led to injustice, and in 15th-cent. England the chancellor issued the first of many decrees to restore 'equity' (fairness); this was the beginning of the modern body of EQUITY law, later merged with the common law in many jurisdictions. The slowness of common-law procedure has led to adoption of numerous statutes that supersede the common law, notably in the fields of commercial, administrative, and CRIMINAL LAW.

**Common Market,** officially the European Economic Community (EEC), established (1958) to promote the social and economic integration of Western Europe through gradual elimination of internal tariff and customs barriers and development of common price levels and a monetary union. An outgrowth of the European Coal and Steel Community, the Common Market was an important step toward the creation (1967) of the EUROPEAN COMMUNITY. The original members Belgium, France, Italy, Luxembourg, the Netherlands, and West Germany were joined by Great Britain, the Republic of Ireland, and Denmark in 1973, and by Greece in 1981. In January 1986 Spain and Portugal became members.

**Commons, House of:** see PARLIAMENT.

**Commonwealth,** or **Commonwealth of Nations,** voluntary association of the UK, its dependencies and associated states, and 48 (1988) sovereign states that were once under British rule. The purpose of the Commonwealth (founded in 1931 as successor to the BRITISH EMPIRE) is consultation and cooperation in the political, economic, and cultural spheres. The British monarch is the symbolic head of the Commonwealth and head of state of about half the member countries (most of the others being republics). Collective decisions of the Commonwealth are not binding and member countries may withdraw at any time (as South Africa did in 1961 and Pakistan in 1972). Members are linked economically, but the system of preferential tariffs was phased out after the UK joined the EUROPEAN COMMUNITY in 1973. The Commonwealth has a permanent secretariat in London; its many subsidiary bodies include the Commonwealth Parliamentary Association (dating from 1911) and the Commonwealth Fund for Technical Cooperation (est. 1971). Commonwealth heads of government meet in conference every two years.

**Commonwealth, legal systems in the,** law and legal systems relating to and applicable in COMMONWEALTH countries. Historically, the British PARLIAMENT had jurisdiction over the British colonies, and the sovereign appointed a governor-general to exercise the powers of Royal Prerogative. English COMMON LAW was applied in the colonies, but statutes only applied if expressly provided for. However, in some countries colonized by Britain, the existing legal system continued to be applied (e.g., Spanish Law in Trinidad). By the begining of the 20th cent. many colonies had gained self-governing status (e.g., NEW ZEALAND) as the 'Dominions'. The Statute of Westminster 1931 provided that no British act of Parliament would be applicable in the Dominions. Most Commonwealth countries have a written CONSTITUTION, though many have modelled their parliamentary systems on the Westminster parliament. New Zealand adopted a written constitution in 1852, INDIA in 1950, and CANADA in 1982. India, and to a lesser extent AUSTRALIA have adopted rigid constitutions and established a supreme court (High Court in Australia) along the lines of the US SUPREME COURT. The New Zealand constitution provides for a unicameral parliamentary system. Canada, Australia and India have adopted FEDERAL constitutions on US lines. Most Commonwealth countries operate under a COMMON LAW system, with the courts following decisions of their own courts, and often the English Court of Appeal and House of Lords (see COURT SYSTEM IN ENGLAND AND WALES). The New Zealand courts can follow the decisions of the courts in any foreign common law jurisdiction. Initially, many Commonwealth countries adopted the Judicial Committee of the PRIVY COUNCIL as their final appeal court; however, most have since abolished this practice (e.g., Canada in 1949). However, much of the substantive English law has been incorporated into Commonwealth legal systems and much legal education relies on English law textbooks. The vast majority of Commonwealth countries have a unified LEGAL PROFESSION.

**commune** or **communal group,** community or household of individuals, often unrelated by blood or marriage, who are brought together by shared values in an attempt to implement an alternative lifestyle outside conventional society. Historically, communes have taken the form of religious communities, such as those set up by the SHAKERS, MORMONS, and ANABAPTISTS, and secular utopian communities, such as those set up in the 19th cent. by the followers of Robert OWEN, e.g., New Lanark in Scotland, or Charles FOURIER, e.g., BROOK FARM in the US. Contemporary forms include the successful COLLECTIVE FARMS or kibbutzim of Israel, and the generally less stable rural or urban communes set up in Europe and the US as a 'counter-culture' in the radical ferment of the 1960s. The latter represented different ways out of the established order and were often deemed threatening, or were persecuted because they challenged such institutions as capitalism, the nuclear family, Christiantity, and sexual monogamy. Most failed to survive over a generation.

**Commune of Paris,** an insurrection against the French government at the end (1871) of the FRANCO-PRUSSIAN WAR. Having suffered from a four month siege by the Germans, the leaders and rank and file of the Paris commune opposed the national government led by Adolphe THIERS at VERSAILLES as too conservative and too ready to accept humiliating peace terms. Versailles troops laid siege to Paris, against which the *communards* (whose aims included economic reforms and whose members comprised radical republicans, socialists, anarchists, and Marxists) put up a desperate defence. Before their defeat (28 May) they shot hostages and burned the TUILERIES and the palace of justice. Severe reprisals followed, with more than 17,000 people executed, a repression that lastingly embittered French political life. The memory of the Commune was an inspiration to Marxists during and after the RUSSIAN REVOLUTION.

**communicable disease,** disease that can be transmitted from one infected person to another. Many diseases are spread by airborne microorganisms through contact or proximity (e.g., INFLUENZA, MEASLES, and WHOOPING COUGH). Some are spread through contaminated food or water (e.g., CHOLERA, TYPHOID), while others are transmitted by an animal or insect carrier (e.g., MALARIA, RABIES). Still others are transmitted under special circumstances, such as sexual contact (e.g., SYPHILIS, AIDS) or infected instruments or blood transfusion (e.g., HEPATITIS). Control of communicable disease includes isolation of infected people, immunization, personal hygiene, and stringent public health and sanitation measures.

**communications protocol,** the set of rules needed to allow communication between computers across communications links. Protocols must handle corrupted data, the opening and closing of connections and the flow of the data (see DATA TRANSMISSION). Agreement must be established on the format of information to be communicated and the relative timing of the control and data messages to be exchanged. Although any interworking between computers requires a protocol, those of particular interest are associated with general applications in solving a large class of problems. Examples are file transfer protocols, document transfer protocols, electronic mail transfer protocols and MAP (Manufacturing Applications Protocol). These application protocols are supported by lower level protocols for data transmission across a COMPUTER NETWORK.

**communications satellite,** artificial SATELLITE that provides a worldwide linkup of RADIO and TELEVISION transmissions and TELEPHONE service; three such satellites above the equator in a geostationary orbit equally spaced round the earth can provide worldwide communications. The first communications satellite was NASA's *Echo 1*, an uninstrumented inflatable sphere that passively reflected radio signals back to earth. Later satellites, starting with NASA's Relay satellites and the American Telephone and Telegraph Co.'s Telstar satellites, carried with them electronic devices for receiving, amplifying, and rebroadcasting signals to earth. The US launching (1963) of the first synchronous-orbit satellite (*Syncom 1*) paved the way for the formation of the International Telecommunications Satellite Organization, whose successive series of Intelsat geostationary satellites have steadily lowered the cost of transoceanic communications. Domestic communications

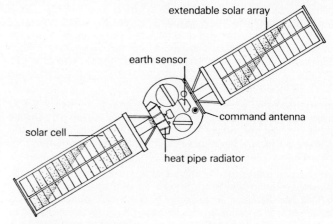

Communications satellite

satellite systems, also geostationary, have been developed by Canada, the USSR, Indonesia, and several US firms. Communications satellites are also used for military purposes.

**communion,** a SACRAMENT for most Christians, a partaking of bread and wine that repeats the actions of JESUS at the LAST SUPPER. Some of them, especially Roman Catholics, believe that the substances actually and miraculously become the body and blood of Christ (transubstantiation). Others believe that the sacrament is symbolic; but all believe that the recipient is united mystically with Christ. Most Christians call the sacrament the Eucharist, but many Protestants prefer the name the Lord's Supper.

**communism,** system of social organization based on the communal ownership of property. Some undeveloped human societies provide examples of 'primitive communism', and historically the principle has been exemplified in religious communities and in radical societies such as the 16th-cent. Münster ANABAPTISTS. The concept also recurs in fictional accounts of an ideal society, from PLATO's *Republic* to St Thomas MORE's UTOPIA. But by far the most significant influence on the theory of contemporary communism was provided by Karl MARX, who, with Fredrich ENGELS, published the *Communist Manifesto* in 1848. He set out a theory of history based upon the inevitability of CLASS struggle, and of a process leading, via the overthrow of CAPITALISM, and an interim stage of SOCIALISM, to a classless communist society. In this highest stage of human development, according to Marx, the state with its apparatus of coercion would ultimately 'wither away', and with it the restrictions on individual, social, and material development necessarily associated with the exploitative structure of capitalism. The ethos of such a society was characterized by the phrase 'From each, according to his ability, to each, according to his needs.' Until World War I, the terms communist, socialist, and social democratic were all in use, more or less interchangeably, to describe movements and parties committed to the overthrowing of capitalism on the basis of egalitarian ideas heavily indebted to Marx. Not until after their triumph in the 1917 RUSSIAN REVOLUTION, did the Bolsheviks, led by LENIN and TROTSKY, form the Communist Party (1918) and the COMINTERN (1919) which claimed leadership of the world socialist movement. In applying the term Communist to themselves and the other parties who joined the Comintern, Lenin sought to distinguish revolutionary Communism, from the increasingly reformist socialist and social democratic (see SOCIAL DEMOCRACY) parties of Western Europe, who were pursuing similar ideals by means of electoral politics within parliamentary democracies. Since that time the term Communist is usually taken to refer to those parties and states which accept Lenin's account of MARXISM and the leadership of the Soviet Union, although it is important to note that ruling Communist parties for the most part describe the systems over which they preside as being in the socialist stage of development, albeit in transit to the higher stage of communism under the direction of the party (see COMMUNIST PARTY). Since 1917, Communist parties have taken power all over the world, notably in China, since 1949 under MAO ZEDONG, and in Eastern Europe after World War II, in Poland, Hungary, Czechoslovakia, Romania, Yugoslavia, Albania, Bulgaria, and East Germany. Although paying homage to Marxism–Leninism, and in most cases owing their existence to Soviet help or Soviet military pressure, none of these states have exhibited in their development the scheme outlined by Marx, and the many variations in their ideology and political practice are rather to be explained by the reaction of a radical NATIONALISM with a particular set of historical circumstances. However, they do have important common features, notably the absence of such liberal institutions as competing parties, a free press, and a free market. Typically a powerful state directs a centralized Command Economy and a highly regimented social life by means of a vast administrative bureaucracy. Clearly this approach to TOTALITARIANISM represents an utterly different state of affairs from that envisaged as communism by Marx. So far from withering away, the state has become omnipresent. Whether this is an inevitable feature of attempts to achieve communism in the modern world, or represents a transitory phase, and how far the ideals of Marx have been realized in other respects, remain matters of debate.

**Communist Party**, a particular form of party, devoted to MARXISM–LENINISM, also characterized by its military-style discipline where every member is sworn to obey the orders of the higher organs. When a communist party takes power, it automatically assumes the role of the executive branch of government, with the party's general secretary acting as chief executive. According to the principles of *democratic centralism*, the organs of the ruling party duplicate and control the main institutions of the state. The POLITBURO is thereby enabled to exercise dictatorial power over all branches of government, and via the NOMENKLATURA over all appointments. The party's central committee and secretariat control the council of ministers and the state legislature. The party's local and regional committees control all local and regional state councils. See also COMMUNISM.

**community care**, the care of ill or handicapped people other than in institutions. The term is used particularly with reference to policies within the National Health Service in Britain. Enlightened attitudes in PSYCHIATRY from the 1960s onwards led to the idea that many mental patients would do better by being de-institutionalized. This well-meant and fairly successful initiative has been turned into the pretext under Thatcher's Conservative governments for the wholesale running down of provision

for in-patient treatment for the mentally ill and handicapped: between 1971 and 1984 the number of beds for such people fell by 33% while their attendance as outpatients increased by some 20%. Well over 40 million patients with mental illness or handicap were being treated in the community by the mid 1980s.

**Community Health Council** (CHC), body set up in each health district in 1973 to represent the view of patients under the NATIONAL HEALTH SERVICE. District Health Authorities must consult CHCs on all matters affecting the provision of local health services. The councils consist of 18–24 members who also act in an advisory capacity when patients wish to submit a complaint.

**community service**, unpaid part-time work in the community, carried out by a convicted offender as an alternative to imprisonment. Used in various countries, it was introduced in the UK in 1972 following the proposals of the Wootton Report (1970) on non-custodial sentences. A community service order is issued by a Magistrates' Court, against any offender over 16, who has been convicted of an imprisonable offence; the offender must, however, be willing to do the work. Community service involves some work in the community that allows the offender to be engaged in constructive tasks, while repaying his or her debt to society. In recent years, especially in the US, it has involved the offender doing work for the victim of the CRIME, thus also involving an element of compensation.

**commutation of sentence:** see SENTENCE.

**commutative law,** in mathematics, law holding that for a given operation combining two quantities, the order of the quantities is arbitrary. Addition and, in most cases, multiplication are commutative; thus, $a + b = b + a$ and $a \times b = b \times a$ for any two numbers $a$ and $b$. An exception is the multipliction of matrices (see MATRIX), for which the commutative law does not generally hold. Subtraction and division are not commutative.

**commutator:** see GENERATOR; MOTOR, ELECTRIC.

**Comnenus** (kom͵naynəs), dynasty of Byzantine emperors: ISAAC I, ALEXIUS I, JOHN II, MANUEL I, ALEXIUS II, and Andronicus I.

**Comoros, The,** officially Federal Islamic Republic of the Comoros, independent nation (1985 est. pop. 469,000), 1862 km² (718 sq mi), occupying most of the Comoro Islands, an archipelago in the Indian Ocean, between the E African coast and Madagascar. The capital is Moroni. It consists of three main islands Njazidja, Nzwani, and Mwali (formerly Grand Comore, Anjouan, and Mohéli, respectively), as well as numerous coral reefs and islets. A fourth island, MAYOTTE, is administered by France. Because of poor soil, lack of natural resources, and overpopulation, the islands have severe economic problems. Most of the population is engaged in subsistence agriculture and the production of vanilla, copra, and essential oils for export. The GNP is US$112 million, and the GNP per capita is US$240 (1985). African peoples dominate the population, but there are large Arab and Indian minorities. French and Arabic are the official languages, but most people speak a blend of Swahili and Arabic. The state religion is Islam.

*History.* Originally populated by immigrants from Africa, Indonesia, and Arabia, the islands were ceded to the French between 1841 and 1909. After occupation by the British in WORLD WAR II, they were granted administrative autonomy within the French Union (1946) and internal self-government (1968). In 1975 the Comoros unilaterally declared their independence; the island of Mayotte, however, voted to remain under French control, and its ultimate status is in dispute. In 1978 The Comoros was proclaimed a federal Islamic republic; shortly thereafter, a one-party state was proclaimed and the Comorian Union for Progress (UPC) formed. In 1984 Pres. Ahmed Abdallah Abderrahman, the sole candidate, was reelected for a further six-year term; the following year an unsuccessful coup attempt was staged by local leftists.

**compact disc**, thin plastic disc 12 cm (4¾ in) in diameter carrying audio recordings in a digital form. The digital audio information is encoded in 'dimples' in the record tracks which are read by a laser beam. Since the dimples lie at the bottom of tracks and are overlaid with plastic, there is no wear on the disc, and the recorded sound thus cannot deteriorate. In technical performance compact discs are much superior to records. Because the digital system depends upon either the presence or absence of digital pulses there is no non-linear distortion and with no mechanical connection to the disc surface there is a complete absence of noise during periods of silence. Similarly there is no background noise to interfere with quiet passages and very high dynamic ranges can therefore be achieved. The data from the disc is fed into a memory store from which it is clocked out by a crystal oscillator. The audio output is therefore not changed by any variations in the speed of rotation of the disc which only affects the writing speed into memory. See also CD ROM.

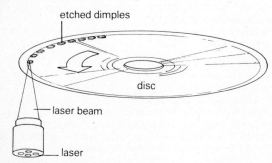

Compact disc

**compadrazgo**, ritual co-parenthood. Found in Latin American societies, it is a form of fictive kinship in which godparents, often those in a more powerful social position than the parents, establish bonds of co-parenthood with the parents of the godchild. The relationship has strong associations of sacredness and entails ritual respect and formalized reciprocity. Incest taboos are extended to the *compadrazgo*.

**comparative linguistics:** see LINGUISTICS.

**compass**, in navigation, an instrument for determining direction. The mariner's compass, probably first used by European seamen in the 12th cent., consists of a magnetic needle freely suspended so that it turns to align itself with the magnetic north and south poles. The **gyrocompass** is a more accurate form of navigational compass, unaffected by magnetic influences, that came into wide use on ships and aircraft during World War II. It consists essentially of a rapidly spinning, electrically driven rotor suspended in such a way that its axis automatically points along the geographical meridian.

**complementary medicine:** see HOLISTIC MEDICINE.

**complex**, a term used in PSYCHOANALYSIS to refer to a cluster of unconscious memories, ideas or feelings, with a strong emotional charge, resulting from repressed infantile experiences and psychic conflicts. The Oedipus complex, in Sigmund FREUD's theory, resolves the conflict engendered by the child's sexual desire for the parent of the opposite sex, and hostility towards the parent of the same sex, through identification with the same-sex parent and repression of the desire for the other-sex parent. This partial resolution of the Oedipal conflict through the establishment of the Oedipus complex is said to occur at the age of about 3–4 years. Many neurotic symptoms, according to Freud, could be traced to incomplete resolution of Oedipal conflicts and to biographical vicissitudes in the development of Oedipus complex. In a quite unrelated usage in VYGOTSKY's developmental psychology, a complex is a mental class or category which is less systematic than a concept.

**composite**, common name for the Compositae, the daisy family, which is one of the largest families of plants, mostly herbs and a few shrubs, trees, and climbing plants. The family includes many edible salad plants (e.g., LETTUCE, endive, CHICORY, salsify, and ARTICHOKE), many cultivated species (e.g., ASTER, DAISY, CHRYSANTHEMUM, MARIGOLD, and ZINNIA), and many common weeds and wildflowers. The typical composite flower, e.g., a sunflower, is composed of a multiflowered head. The outer ring consists of the conspicuous, but sterile, often petallike ray florets which serve to attract insects for pollination. The central part of the head is composed of minute tubular disc florets, usually with both stamens and pistils. A series of modified leaves (bracts) arising from the base of the flower stalk supports the head. Many composite FRUITS are highly adapted to dispersal by animals (e.g., the burr plants such as burdock and cocklebur) or by wind (e.g., the DANDELION).

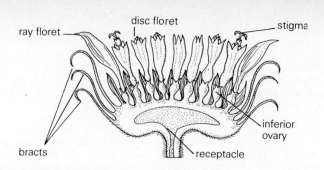

Vertical section of a sunflower, a member of the **composite** family

**compost**, substance composed mainly of partly decayed organic material, used to fertilize the SOIL and increase its HUMUS content. Usually made from plant materials (e.g., grass clippings, leaves, and PEAT), manure, and soil, compost can include chemical FERTILIZERS and lime.

**compound**, in chemistry, a substance composed of ATOMS of two or more ELEMENTS in chemical combination, occurring in fixed, definite proportion and arranged in fixed, definite structures. A compound has unique properties that are distinct from the properties of its elemental constituents and of all other compounds. A compound differs from a mixture in that the components of a mixture retain their own properties and may be present in many different proportions. The components of a mixture are not chemically combined; they can be separated by physical means. A molecular compound, e.g., WATER, is made up of electrically neutral MOLECULES, each containing a fixed number of atoms. An ionic compound, e.g., SODIUM CHLORIDE, is made up of electrically charged IONS that are present in fixed proportions and are arranged in a regular, geometric pattern or crystalline structure (see CRYSTAL), but are not grouped into molecules.

**compressor**, machine that decreases the volume of air or gas by the application of pressure. Compressor types range from the simple hand PUMP and the piston-equipped compressor used in petrol stations to inflate tyres, to machines that use a rotating, bladed element to achieve compression. Compressed air exerts an expansive force that can be used as a source of power to operate pneumatic tools or to control such devices as air brakes (see BRAKE). Air under compression can be stored in closed cylinders.

**Compromise of 1850**, an attempt at solving North–South tensions in the US over the extension of slavery, specifically into territory gained by the US in the MEXICAN WAR. The WILMOT PROVISO of 1846, prohibiting slavery in land acquired from Mexico, caused contention. Compromise measures, largely originating with Henry CLAY, were guided through the Senate by Stephen A. DOUGLAS. The compromise proposed was to admit California as a free state, use popular sovereignty to decide free or slave status for New Mexico and Utah, prohibit the slave trade in the District of Columbia, pass a more stringent fugitive slave law, and settle Texas boundary claims. Chances for acceptance of these proposals were enhanced by a famous speech by Daniel WEBSTER (7 Mar. 1850), and even more by the succession of Millard FILLMORE, a supporter of the compromise, after the death of Pres. Zachary TAYLOR. The proposals were passed as separate bills in Sept. 1850. The Compromise of 1850 was not, as had been hoped, a final solution to the question of slavery in new territories; that issue arose again in 1854 (see KANSAS–NEBRASKA ACT).

**Compton-Burnett, Dame Ivy**, 1884–1969, English novelist. Relying almost completely on highly stylized conversation, her witty novels, including *Brothers and Sisters* (1929) and *Mother and Son* (1955), with undercurrents of Greek tragedy, picture a hypocritical Edwardian world.

**computer**, device that can be programmed to perform desired computations on a set of data, giving results that can be predetermined to be of any level of accuracy. There are theoretical limits to the calculations that can be performed, which were first stated by Alan TURING in the 1930s. The term is now almost exclusively used for electronic digital computers. Historically, the first all thermionic-valve computer, ASCC (Automatic Sequence Controlled Calculator), was begun in 1930 but was never fully operational. ENIAC (Electronic Numerical Integrator And Calculator), which used 20,000 valves and could handle 10,000 digits, was completed at the Univ. of Pennysylvania in 1946. It was a special-purpose machine designed to solve the trajectory problems of high altitude, where variations of atmospheric pressure and gravity made hand calculations impossible. It was not completed in time to be of use during World War II. After the war attention was focused on making general-purpose digital electronic computers that could be programmed to solve any type of problem. The Manchester Mark 1, under the guidance of F.C. Williams, used his invention of cathode-ray-tube storage. The EDSAC at Cambridge (UK), under the guidance of M.V. Wilkes, used mercury delay line storage. Both became operational in 1949. Shortly afterwards, Turing's ACE at the National Physical Laboratory which also used mercury delay lines was operational as were A.D. Booth's LEO machines at Lyons. The UNIVAC (Universal Automatic Computer) in 1951 was the first complete machine in the US. All of these were enormous machines which took up large volumes for their accommodation and consumed upwards of 50 kW power for the thermionic valves. However their computing power and memory capability were limited. Today a small microprocessor less than a postage stamp in size and requiring only microwatts of power would be faster and have greater capacity (see COMPUTER GENERATIONS). The size and cost of these pioneering machines led to the thought that the future lay in the development of a few very large machines in computing centres, which one would be able to use by direct private contact by phone. In practice, the reverse has happened: miniaturization and the fall in cost has made possible the possession of considerable computing power in a small free-standing PERSONAL COMPUTER of modest cost. The four major physical subdivisions, or hardware, of a computer are the central processing unit (CPU), the high-speed internal memory, auxiliary storage, and the input/output devices which constitute the interface between the machine and people. A modem ('*modulator–demodulator*') enables the direct linking of a telephone line to the computer. The development of memory devices is almost the history of the computer, from using vacuum tubes, cathode-ray-tube storage, mercury-acoustic delay lines, and magnetic drums to the capability of the silicon chip to hold 100,000 digits. Research continues for greater storage in smaller volume with rapid access. The latest rival fields are magnetic bubbles, optical fibres, laser holography and, at the molecular level, polarized polymers. In all machines (since ENIAC which was decimal) data are expressed in binary digital form (see NUMERATION) using 0 or 1 (known as a 'bit'). A standard word is made up of eight such numbers, such as 11001001, and since the 1 or 0 can appear in any one of the eight places there are $2^8$ or 256 different patterns. This eight-block unit is known as a 'byte'. The COMPUTER PROGRAM, or software, which can be typed in manually or, more generally, fed in from a magnetic disc, controls the functioning of the computer and directs its operation. See also ANALOGUE-TO-DIGITAL CONVERSION; ARTIFICIAL INTELLIGENCE; BAUD; BOOLEAN ALGEBRA; DIGITAL-TO-ANALOGUE CONVERSION; PROGRAMMING LANGUAGE; VIDEOTEX.

**computer-aided design**, (CAD), interactive computer assistance for the design of a wide range of artifacts such as cars, aeroplanes, buildings, and electronic components, in particular integrated circuit layout. A CAD system allows experts to input design criteria such as component sizes and tolerances and allows standard components to be inserted into a design from a software library. A design may be modified interactively and tested by simulation software which shows the behaviour of a device over time for a given set of inputs. Output takes the form of printed charts and artwork (hard-copy) but also computer readable files which are used in computer-aided manufacture, for example, chip fabrication (see INTEGRATED CIRCUIT).

**computer-assisted instruction:** see PROGRAMMED LEARNING.

**computer generations**, term used to describe, somewhat loosely, the major technological advances in the development of computers. *First-generation* programmable electronic computers dating from the early 1940s into the 1950s were general-purpose machines using vacuum tubes for the central processor unit. Very large in size, often filling large laboratories, they could only handle up to 20,000 bits of information with the speed of 100,000 additions per second. In the *second-generation computers* of the mid-1950s to mid-1960s vacuum tubes were replaced by individual transistors which enabled greater capacity and faster speeds up to one million operations per sec. These machines were supplanted by the *third-generation computers* of the mid-1960s and 1970s, in which the use of the silicon microchip to house thousands of effective transistors

miniaturized the electronics by a factor of a thousand. The computer philosophy was basically the same as the first generation. In the 1980s the introduction of VERY LARGE-SCALE INTEGRATION (VLSI), whereby many thousands of transistors and their circuitry of microscopic size can be manufactured on a small single silicon chip, has revolutionized both the size and design of *fourth-generation computers*. The desk top computer of enormous power and capacity is now an accepted piece of equipment in the modern office. They operate free-standing, or can be interconnected throughout a firm or connected to a large mainframe computer for access to a wide range of data. The concept of *fifth-generation computers* utilizes the full potential of VLSI in enabling ARTIFICIAL INTELLIGENCE to be incorporated. Such computers, whose development began in the 1980s, will be able to interrogate, learn by experience, and make decisions. They will be useful, for example, in tactics in the armed services, in diagnostic medicine, and in literate translations from one language to another; they will also be the kernel of the electronic office. Most large computer firms predict that these machines will be available before the end of the century. Futuristic *sixth-generation computers* for the next century may incorporate biological components which mimic the brain and will certainly use new mechanisms of rapid-access storage of large quantities of data together with developments in artificial intelligence. Their conceptual ability will enable them to tackle deep problems beyond man's capability. They will also read and understand handwriting and listen and understand the human voice, thus transforming the interface between machine and person beyond present recognition.

**computer graphics**, the transfer of pictorial data into and out of a COMPUTER. Using ANALOGUE-TO-DIGITAL CONVERSION techniques, a variety of devices such as curve tracers, digitizers, and light pens connected to graphic COMPUTER TERMINALS can be used to store pictorial data in a digital computer. By reversing the process through DIGITAL-TO-ANALOGUE CONVERSION techniques, the stored data can be output on a mechanical plotting board, or plotter, or on a television-like graphic display terminal. Sophisticated COMPUTER PROGRAMS allow the computer to manipulate the stored graphic image either automatically or under the control of a designer, engineer, or architect. This last feature, called COMPUTER-AIDED DESIGN (CAD), has enhanced the productivity of those involved in professions that call for drafting. More recently, as colour display terminals and plotters have become readily available, computer graphics have become a popular contemporary art form. See also ELECTRONIC GAME. Two-dimensional graphics may take the form of histograms, graphs, or diagrams. Three-dimensional graphics requires a large amount of processing power and memory and may take the form of contour lines or fully shaded solids. Movement and animation is obtained by operations such as rotation and displacement. Perspectives from different angles and hidden lines may be shown. Zooming in on a selected area and displaying it in a window in an enlarged form is possible. Software may carry out smoothing during the enlargement.

**computerized axial tomography** (CAT), technique for producing an image of a cross-section of any part of the head or body. X-ray beams scan the specific area of the head or body at a series of angles. The images produced are coordinated by a computer and a composite readable image constructed. A CAT scan (or CT scan) permits safe and rapid diagnosis of disease in previously inaccessible areas.

**computer network**, a set of autonomous computer systems, interconnected to allow interaction between any pair of systems. Interconnection may be for data sharing or transfer, DATABASE access, resource sharing (e.g., US east-coast computers may be used by west-coast workers during east-coast night time), remote program execution (a powerful supercomputer may be used remotely), human communication by computer mail, document transfer and connection of parts of companies which are dispersed across countries or continents. Computer networks are broadly classified as LOCAL AREA NETWORKS (LAN) and Wide Area Networks (WAN). The connected computers may be homogeneous (all the same types), or heterogeneous (a mixture of types). An initiative of ISO, the International Standards Organization, has been to develop standards for COMMUNICATIONS PROTOCOLS to allow 'open systems interconnection' so that dissimilar computers may interwork. In connecting computer systems, use is frequently made of public facilities, e.g., operated by British Telecom in the UK, ranging from simple connections to complex message handling circuits. These services are usually contained within an Integrated Services Digital Network (ISDN), which has the ability to accommodate voice, data, and facsimile. Circuits may be leased for private use, usually by large companies, e.g., banking networks. In the US there are some 2000 private communications companies, controlled by a federal government agency, which offer these services.

**computer program,** a series of instructions that a COMPUTER can execute or obey in order to carry out some task. Programs are loaded into the memory of digital electronic computers (also called stored program computers) and from there, instructions are fetched into the processing hardware and executed. Programs are called software to distinguish them from hardware, the physical electronic devices that comprise the computer system. Programs are written in a PROGRAMMING LANGUAGE which may be a low level language, closely associated with a specific computer, or a high level language which is application orientated and machine independent. Programs are classified as *systems* or *applications* software. Systems programs are those that control the operation of the computer hardware and create a system suitable for the end user. Chief among these is the operating system (also called executive, supervisor, or monitor) which schedules the execution of other programs, allocates system resources to programs and controls input and output operations. Language translators decode source programs, written in a programming language, and produce object programs in machine language which directly control the computer hardware. Translators include *assemblers*, which translate programs in symbolic languages that in general have a one-to-one relation with machine language; *compilers*, which translate programs in a high level language into object programs which may be stored for later execution; and *interpreters*, which translate single source language statements within programs into object language for immediate execution. An *Integrated Program Support Environment* (IPSE) is system software comprising a number of programs which assist the user in creating, editing, debugging (correcting), and testing programs. Assistance is also provided in managing and maintaining large software systems which evolve over time and which may be developed and maintained by a team of programmers. Applications programs typically perform commercial, industrial, government, or scientific functions.

**computer terminal,** a device that enables a COMPUTER to receive or deliver data. Computer terminals vary greatly depending on the format of the data they handle. For example, a simple terminal comprises a typewriter keyboard for input and a typewriter printing element for ALPHANUMERIC output. A similar device includes the keyboard for input and a televisionlike screen to display the output. The screen can be a CATHODE-RAY TUBE or a gas plasma panel, the latter involving an ionized gas (sandwiched between glass layers) that glows to form dots which, in turn, connect to form lines. Such displays can present a variety of output, ranging from simple alphanumerics to complex graphic images used as design tools by architects and engineers. Under program control, these graphic terminals can rotate the images to show 'hidden' parts and even compile parts lists from the design. Other familiar terminals include supermarket checkout systems that deliver detailed printed receipts and use laser scanners to read the bar codes printed on food packages, automatic money-dispensing terminals in banks, and sorters that read the magnetic-ink numbers printed on bank cheques. Modern *intelligent* terminals exploit inexpensive processing power and memory to provide sophisticated *user interfaces* with multiple *windows* representing the range of activities of interest to the user. For example, windows may be used to display sections of programs, to give commands and to observe the results of the program when it is run. A 'mouse' pointing device supplements the keyboard and is used to move between windows. *Icons* may also be used to stand in place of documents, files, mailboxes, printers, etc. In such a system a file is deleted by moving its icon to a wastebasket icon, a file is printed by moving its icon to the printer icon, etc.

**Comstock, Anthony,** 1844–1915, American morals crusader. He secured strict New York and federal legislation against obscene matter. As organizer and then secretary (1873–1915) of the New York Society for the Suppression of Vice, he was responsible for the destruction of 160 tons of literature and pictures.

**Comte, Auguste,** 1798–1857, French philosopher and sociologist, founder of the school of philosophy known as POSITIVISM. Comte was primarily a social reformer; his goal, as set forth in *The Course of Positive Philosophy* (1830–42), was a society in which both individuals and nations could live in harmony and comfort. He regarded sociology (a term he originated) as the method by which this harmony and well-being could be achieved. Comte formulated a theory of three stages of social development: theological (belief in the supernatural), metaphysical (belief in ideas as reality), and positive (phenomena are explained by observation, hypothesis, and experimentation).

**Conakry,** city and port (1980 pop. 763,000), capital of Guinea, on the Atlantic Ocean. It is Guinea's largest city and its administrative, economic, and communications centre. Situated on Tombo island, it is connected with the mainland by a causeway. Conakry's economy is based on its modern port, which ships iron ore, bauxite, fruit, and agricultural produce. The city was occupied by the French in 1887. Since World War II it has grown into a modern city with wide boulevards.

**Conant, James Bryant,** 1893–1978, American chemist and educationalist. His early work concerned the uptake of oxygen by haemoglobin. At an early age (in 1933) he became the president of Harvard Univ., from which position he profoundly influenced American scientific policy. To a wider audience he advocated that schooling should be used as an instrument of national purpose. He was US ambassador to West Germany (1955–57).

**concentration,** in chemistry, measure of the relative proportions of two or more quantities in a mixture (see COMPOUND). Concentrations may be expressed in a number of ways. The simplest is in terms of a component's percentage by weight or volume. Mixtures of solids or liquids are frequently specified by weight-percentage concentrations, whereas mixtures of gases are usually specified by volume percentages. Very low concentrations, such as those of various substances in the atmosphere, are expressed in parts per million (ppm). The *molarity* of a SOLUTION is the number of MOLES of solute per litre of solution. The *molality* of a solution is the number of moles of solute per 1000 grams of solvent. The *mole fraction* of a solution is the ratio of moles of solute to the total number of moles in the solution.

**concentration camp,** prison camp outside the regular criminal system, first introduced by the British during the BOER WAR for the internment of civilians. Under the Nazis (see NATIONAL SOCIALISM) camps for political prisoners were set up after 1933 in Germany: Dachau, Buchenwald, Ravensbrück (for women), etc., and after 1939 in Nazi-occupied Poland: Auschwitz I, Majdanek, etc., where several million prisoners, mainly Poles, Soviets, and Jews, died from gross maltreatment, malnutrition, and disease. In addition, the Nazis organized several death-camps, notably Treblinka, Auschwitz II (Birkenau), Sobibor, and Belsen, whose sole function was to kill the inmates, overwhelmingly Jews. In the Soviet Union, the system of slave-labour camps, which proliferated under STALIN, was organized on an even vaster scale (see GULAG).

**Concepción,** city (1984 pop 213,818) S Central Chile, capital of Concepción prov., near the mouth of the Bío-Bío R. It is a major industrial centre. Founded in 1550, it was levelled or severely damaged by at least six major earthquakes in the period from 1570 to 1960. The frequent rebuilding of the city has given it a modern aspect.

**conceptual art,** a term used to describe works of the 1960s that emphasized the point that a work of art is primarily an 'idea' or a 'concept', rather than merely a physical object produced by the artist. The work of Sol Le Witt and Victor Burgin have been thus categorized.

**concerto,** musical composition usually for orchestra and soloist (most often piano or violin) or a group of soloists. The *concerto grosso,* for a small group of soloists with full orchestra, was developed by Giuseppe Torelli, VIVALDI, and CORELLI. The BAROQUE concerto was most fully developed by J.S. BACH and G.F. HANDEL. Toward the end of the 18th cent. the solo concerto displaced the *concerto grosso,* and was fixed by W.A. MOZART in its classical form of three movements. In the 19th cent. BEETHOVEN gave greater importance to the orchestra, and LISZT unified the concerto form through the use of repeated themes.

**conch,** name for some tropical, marine GASTROPODS having beautiful, heavy, spiral shells, the whorls of which overlap each other. The typical gastropod foot is reduced in size and the horny plate (operculum) located at the end of the foot has the appearance and function of a claw. They feed on seaweed. Their shells range in colour from white to red. Conchs are a valuable food source and their shells are used to make trumpets. The Greek god Triton carried a conch trumpet.

**Concord, 1** US town (1980 pop. 16,293), E Massachusetts, on the Concord R.; inc. 1635. Electronic and wood products are made. The site of the 1775 battle (see LEXINGTON AND CONCORD, BATTLES OF) is marked by Daniel Chester FRENCH's bronze *Minuteman*. Concord's fine old houses were the homes of EMERSON, the ALCOTTS, HAWTHORNE, and THOREAU, among others. **2** US city (1980 pop. 30,400), state capital of New Hampshire on the Merrimack R.; settled 1725–27, inc. 1733 as Rumford, Massachusetts, inc. 1765 as Concord, New Hampshire; became state capital in 1808. Its granite quarries are famous. The city also produces electrical and leather goods and foods.

**concordat,** formal agreement, specifically between the pope in his spiritual capacity and the temporal authority of a state. The earliest so-called concordat was the Concordat of Worms (1122) which ended the INVESTITURE controversy. The most famous was the **Concordat of 1801,** reached between Napoleon and Pope PIUS VII. It reestablished the Roman Catholic Church in France and provided for the nomination of bishops by the state and the conferral of office by the pope.

**Concorde,** world's first successful supersonic commercial transport aeroplane. Designed and built jointly by the British Aircraft Corporation (see BRITISH AEROSPACE) and Aerospatiale of France. The concept of a supersonic airliner was first considered in 1956, and by 1961 designs had been drawn up. The name 'Concorde' was announced by Pres. de Gaulle in 1963. The French prototype flew on 2 Mar. 1969 and the British on 9 Apr. 1969. The first services were flown on 21 Jan. 1976, British Airways flying London to Bahrain and Air France, Paris to Rio; flights to the US began the same year. BA and Air France each have seven planes in service, which can cruise at speeds of up to Mach 2.25. After the writing off of development costs Concorde became profitable in British Airways from 1985.

Concorde

**concrete,** structural masonry material made by mixing broken stone or gravel with sand, CEMENT, and water, and allowing the mixture to harden into a solid mass. Concrete has great strength under compression, but its tensile strength must be increased by embedding steel rods (reinforced concrete) or CABLES under tension (prestressed concrete) within the concrete structural member.

**concrete music:** see ELECTRONIC MUSIC.

**Condé** (kawnh day), French princely family, cadet branch of the house of BOURBON. It originated with **Louis I de Bourbon, prince de Condé,** 1530–69, Protestant leader and general. He tried to topple the GUISE family from power in the conspiracy of Amboise (1560) and commanded the HUGUENOTS in the Wars of Religion (see RELIGION, WARS OF). He was slain at the battle of Jarnac. His great-grandson **Louis II de Bourbon, prince de Condé,** 1621–86, called the Great Condé, won major victories in the THIRTY YEARS WAR at Rocroi (1643), Freiburg (1644), Nördlingen (1645), and Lens (1648). In the FRONDE he turned against the government by taking command of the rebellious army of the princes in 1651 and of the Spanish army in 1653. Defeated in the battle of the Dunes (1658), he was pardoned (1659) by LOUIS XIV, for whom he fought successfully (1672–78) in the DUTCH WARS. His great-grandson **Louis Joseph de Bourbon, prince de Condé,** 1736–1818, formed the emigré 'army of Condé' (dissolved

1801), which fought in alliance with France's enemies against French Revolutionary forces.

**condensation:** see STATES OF MATTER.

**condenser:** see CAPACITOR.

**conditioning:** see LEARNING.

**condor,** VULTURE found in the high peaks of the Coast Range of S California and the ANDES. Condors are the largest flying birds alive today, nearly 125 cm (50 in) long with wingspans of 275–300 cm (9–10 ft). Voracious eaters, they prefer carrion but will attack living animals as large as deer. Condors are extremely rare and near extinction.

**Condorcet, Marie Jean Antoine Nicolas Caritat, marquis de** (kawnhdaw say), 1743–94, French mathematician, philosopher, and political leader. He did notable work (1785) on the theory of PROBABILITY. His best-known work is *Sketch for a Historical Picture of the Progress of the Human Mind* (1795), in which he traced human development through nine epochs to the French Revolution and predicted in the tenth epoch the ultimate perfection of the human race.

**conducting,** in music, the art of unifying the efforts of a number of musicians simultaneously engaged in musical performance. In the Middle Ages and Renaissance the conductor was primarily a time beater. During the BAROQUE era the harpsichordist and then the first violinist became the leader. The principles of modern conducting were laid down by Richard WAGNER; Hans von BÜLOW was the first of the virtuoso conductors. Modern conducting requires mastery of baton and hand gestures, thorough knowledge of the instruments and repertory, and sensitivity to the needs of the performers. Outstanding conductors of the 20th cent. include Arturo TOSCANINI, Sir Thomas BEECHAM, Bruno WALTER, Herbert von KARAJAN, and Bernard Haitink. Many soloists (esp. pianists or violinists) now conduct as they play, e.g., Daniel BARENBOIM, though this practice is not universally approved by orchestras.

**conduction,** transfer of HEAT or ELECTRICITY through a substance, resulting, in the case of heat, from a difference in TEMPERATURE between different parts of the substance or, in the case of electricity, from a difference in electric POTENTIAL. Heat may be conducted when the motions of energetic (hotter) molecules are passed on to nearby, less energetic (cooler) molecules, but a more effective method is the migration of energetic free electrons. Conduction of electricity consists of the flow of CHARGE. Metals are thus good conductors of both heat and electricity because they have a high free-electron density.

**Confederacy,** name commonly given to the Confederate States of America (1861–65), the government established by the southern states of the US after their secession from the Union. When Pres. LINCOLN was elected (Nov. 1860), seven states—South Carolina, Georgia, Louisiana, Mississippi, Florida, Alabama, and Texas—seceded. A provisional government was set up at Montgomery, Alabama, and a constitution was drafted; it resembled the US CONSTITUTION but had provisions for STATES' RIGHTS and SLAVERY. After the firing on Fort Sumter and Lincoln's call for troops, four more states—Arkansas, North Carolina, Virginia, and Tennessee—joined. Richmond, Virginia, became the capital, and Jefferson DAVIS and A.H. STEPHENS were elected president and vice president. The story of the Confederacy is the story of the loss of the AMERICAN CIVIL WAR. It was refused recognition by England and France. Volunteers for its army were insufficient; conscription was used but opposed. Financial troubles were heavy, and its paper money became worthless. Mounting Union victories made defeat inevitable. The Confederacy fell after R.E. LEE's surrender in Apr. 1865.

**Confederate States of America:** see CONFEDERACY.

**Confessing Church,** German Protestant movement. Founded (1933) by Martin NIEMOELLER in opposition to the Nazi-sponsored German Christian Church, it was later driven underground. It continues as a separate group within the German Evangelicals.

**confirmation,** Christian rite confirming an individual's prior initiation into the church by BAPTISM. In the Roman Catholic and Orthodox Eastern Churches, it is a SACRAMENT. In the West it is ordinarily conferred by a bishop and consists of the laying on of hands and anointing with chrism, a mixture of oil and balm. Priests confer it in the East. Lutherans and Anglicans also use confirmation.

**Confucianism,** moral and religious system of China. Its origins lie in the collection of sayings known as the *Analects* (see CHINESE LITERATURE), attributed to CONFUCIUS, and in ancient commentaries such as that of Mencius. Before the 3rd cent. BC, Confucianism was a system of ethical precepts for the management of society, based on the practice of *ren*— sympathy or 'human-heartedness'—as shown in one's relations with others and demonstrated through adherence to *li*, a combination of etiquette and ritual. A person who wishes to be properly treated when in a subordinate role must, according to the Confucian belief, treat his own inferiors with propriety. Confucianism, with its practical social precepts, was often challenged by the supernatural religious systems of TAOISM and BUDDHISM and was to some extent eclipsed by them from the 3rd to the 7th cent. AD. The Song dynasty (960–1279) saw the development of neo-Confucianism, a metaphysical system that drew on the beliefs of Taoism and especially of ZEN BUDDHISM; during the Ming period (1368–1644) it stressed meditation and intuitive knowledge. Thereafter the system gradually weakened, and with the overthrow of the monarchy (1911–12) Confucianism declined, a process accelerated by the Communist revolution (1949). Much of traditional Chinese culture derives from Confucianism and still persists.

**Confucius,** Chinese *Kong fu zi*, c.551–479? BC, Chinese sage. Legend surrounds his life, but modern scholars base their accounts mainly on the *Analects,* a collection of sayings and dialogues apparently recorded by Confucius's disciples. He was born in the feudal state of Lu, in modern Shandong province. He held only minor governmental posts throughout his life, but in the midst of the warfare and tyranny that were rife at the time, he urged a system of morality and statecraft to bring about peace, stability, and just government. His supposed doctrines are embodied in CONFUCIANISM.

**congenital abnormalities,** physical or mental abnormalities present at or soon after birth. The commonest major abnormalities which occur in about 1.5% of all births (rising to 5% when infants are observed for one year) are talipes (club foot), congenital heart disease (blue babies), spina bifida (see NEURAL TUBE DEFECT), anencephaly (absence of part or most of the brain), cleft lip and palate, DOWN'S SYNDROME (mongolism), hydrocephalus (water on the brain), and congenital hip dislocation. Most congenital abnormalities seem to be caused by both genetic and environmental factors, although Down's syndrome, HAEMOPHILIA, and some other rare syndromes are completely genetically determined. The list of environmental factors includes hormones, drugs (e.g., THALIDOMIDE), infectious diseases (e.g., RUBELLA), and radiation. The mother's nutritional status and alcohol and smoking habits can also affect the developing fetus. AMNIOCENTESIS can detect the presence of certain abnormalities.

**conglomerate,** a large corporation whose growth comes mainly through acquisition of, or merger with, firms in unrelated fields. Although corporate mergers and acquisitions were common earlier, the modern conglomerate did not emerge until the 1960s, when it quickly became popular among investors. By diversifying its interests, the conglomerate seeks to protect itself against changing markets and economic conditions.

**Congo** or **Zaïre,** great river of Africa, flowing c.4380 km (2720 mi) generally north and west through Zaïre to the Atlantic Ocean in NW Angola. It drains much of central equatorial Africa. Its upper course, above Boyoma (Stanley) Falls, is known as the Lualaba R. Its lower course widens near Kinshasa to form lakelike Pool Malebo (Stanley Pool), from which the river descends 267 m (876 ft) through a series of rapids (Livingstone Falls) to the port of Matadi. Called the Congo after the historic KONGO kingdom near its mouth, the river was explored in the 19th cent. by David LIVINGSTONE and Henry STANLEY.

**Congo,** officially People's Republic of the Congo, republic (1985 pop. 1,912,429), 342,000 km² (132,046 sq mi), W central Africa, bordered by Gabon (W), Cameroon and the Central African Republic (N), Zaïre (E and SE), and Cabinda (an exclave of Angola) and the Atlantic Ocean (SW). Major cities include BRAZZAVILLE (the capital) and POINTE-NOIRE. The country is largely covered by tropical rain forests and stretches of wooded savanna, and is drained by tributaries of the CONGO and Ubangi rivers. The Congo serves as the commercial and transport hub of central Africa, with important road, river, and rail systems connecting inland areas with the Atlantic. Forestry and agriculture are the chief economic activities, providing sugarcane, palm oil, coffee, cocoa, and timber for export, and

serving as the basis of most of the country's industry. Mining is increasingly important, with petroleum and potash the principal exports. The GNP is US$2122 million, and the GNP per capita is US$1110 (1985). The Bakongo, the major ethnic group, are Bantu-speaking, as are the other principal tribes, the Bateke, Mbochi, and Sanga. French is the official language. Most of the people practice animist religions, but about 30% are Roman Catholic.

*History.* The region probably was first inhabited by PYGMIES, followed (15th cent.) by the Bakongo, Bateke, and Sanga. After the Portuguese navigator Diego Cão explored the coast in 1482, a slave trade developed between Europeans and the coastal African states. Portuguese traders predominated throughout the 17th cent., although French, English, and Dutch merchants competed for commercial opportunities. From 1889 the area (called French Congo and later Middle Congo) was administered by French concessionaires, who exploited the rubber and ivory resources, until it became a colony in FRENCH EQUATORIAL AFRICA in 1910. In 1946, after serving as a bastion for Free French forces in WORLD WAR II, the Congo was granted a territorial assembly. It gained autonomy within the FRENCH COMMUNITY in 1958 and full independence in 1960. Its first president, Fulbert Youlou, was ousted in 1963, and a government with a Marxist-Leninist ideology was established. This was, in turn, overthrown in 1968, but the new military regime continued the previous government's socialist policies. Following a presidential assassination in 1977, a military council governed until elections in 1979 installed another military government, with Col. Denis SASSOU-NGUESSO as president and leader of the Congolese Party of Labour, the country's only legal party.

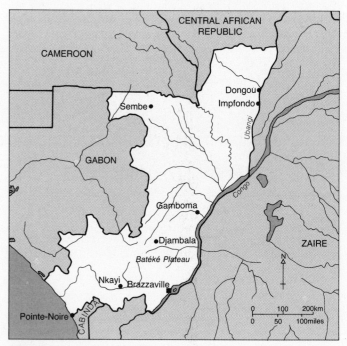

Congo

**Congregationalism,** a type of Protestant church organization in which each congregation, or local church, has free control of its own affairs, with Jesus Christ alone as its head. The movement arose (16th–17th cent.) in England in a SEPARATIST revolt against formalized worship. Pilgrims brought Congregationalism to America in 1620, and it later spread to most English-speaking countries. Since the 1950s it has engaged in several mergers, e.g., in England in 1972 to form the United Reform Church.

**Congress of Racial Equality** (CORE), civil rights organization founded (1942) in Chicago by James FARMER. It seeks, through nonviolent direct action, to end discrimination in public accommodation, housing, and other areas. CORE first gained national recognition with the 1961 Freedom Rides, in which interracial groups travelled south by bus. It later moved toward a more separatist policy, calling for black economic independence within the US.

**Congress of the United States,** legislative branch of the federal government, instituted (1789) by Article 1 of the CONSTITUTION OF THE UNITED STATES. It comprises two houses, the Senate and the House of Representatives. The Senate consists of two senators from each state, who serve six-year terms. Senators were elected by state legislatures until 1913, when the 17th amendment to the Constitution required that they be chosen by popular election. Every two years one third of the Senate is elected. The House of Representatives consists of 435 members apportioned among the states according to their population in the federal CENSUS. Representatives are elected from congressional districts drawn up by the state legislatures and serve two-year terms. The House traditionally elects its presiding officer, the Speaker, by consensus of the majority party. The vice president of the US is the presiding officer of the Senate, but the agenda is set by the majority leader. Most of the work in both houses is transacted by standing committees in which both majority and minority members are represented. Each chamber has an equal voice in legislation, although revenue bills must originate in the House. The Senate must ratify all treaties by a two-thirds vote; it also confirms important presidential appointees. A presidential VETO of congressional legislation can be overridden by a two-thirds vote in each house. Whenever an item of legislation is approved in varying forms by the two houses, the differences are reconciled by a joint (or conference) committee that includes members of both chambers. See also EXECUTIVE; CABINET; COURT SYSTEM IN THE UNITED STATES; SUPREME COURT, UNITED STATES.

**Congreve, William,** 1670–1729, English dramatist. After publishing a novel, *Incognita* (1692), and translations, he turned to the stage. His first comedy, *The Old Bachelor* (1693), was a great success and was followed by *The Double Dealer* (1693), *Love for Love* (1695), and a tragedy, *The Mourning Bride* (1697). His masterpiece, *The Way of the World*, appeared in 1700. Congreve's plays are considered the apex of RESTORATION comedy. With brilliant language and complex plots they present amused, cynical portraits of people more concerned with manners than morals.

**conic section** or **conic,** curve formed by the intersection of a plane and a right circular cone, or conical surface. The ordinary conic sections are the CIRCLE, the ellipse, the parabola, and the hyperbola. When the plane passes through the vertex of the cone, the result is a point, a straight line, or a pair of intersecting straight lines; these are called degenerate conic sections. In ANALYTICAL GEOMETRY every conic section is the graph of an equation of the form $ax^2 + bxy + cy^2 + dx + ey + f = 0$, where $a, b, c, d, e,$ and $f$ are constants and $a, b,$ and $c$ are not all zero.

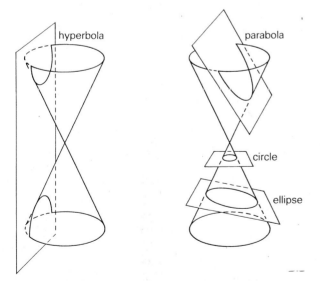

Conic sections

**conifer,** cone-bearing tree or shrub of the GYMNOSPERMS. The group contains many softwood timber trees of great economic importance, including the PINE and CYPRESS.

**Coniston Water,** lake in the Lake District, Cumbria, NW England, to the W of Lake WINDERMERE. It is situated at the foot of the mountain called the Old Man of Coniston, which is 802 m (2631 ft) high. The lake is 9 km (5 mi) long, and less than 1 km wide. In 1939 Sir Malcolm Campbell set a world water speed record on the lake. His son, Donald Campbell, set a new record here in 1959.

**conjugation:** see INFLECTION.

**conjunction:** see PART OF SPEECH.

**conjunction,** in astronomy: see SYZYGY.

**conjunctivitis,** infection of the conjunctiva, the membrane that covers the eyeball and lines the eyelid; also called 'pink eye'. Producing redness, discharge, and itching of the eyes, conjunctivitis can be treated with ANTIBIOTIC drugs. Before the use of silver nitrate drops in the eyes of newborn babies, conjunctivitis due to infection (e.g., gonorrhoea in the mother) was a major cause of blindness in infants.

**Connacht,** province in W of Irish Republic (1986 pop. 430,726), 17,122 km² (6678 sq mi). It is situated between the Atlantic Ocean in the W and the R SHANNON in the E. It contains the counties of Galway, Leitrim, Mayo, Roscommon, and Sligo.

**Connecticut,** state of the US (1984 est. pop. 3,154,000), area 12,793 km² (5009 sq mi), situated in the NE and bordered by Massachusetts (N), Rhode Island (E), Long Island Sound (S), and New York (W). The capital is HARTFORD, a major insurance centre; the other major cities are Bridgeport and NEW HAVEN. The state consists of rolling hills except for the coastal strip and the central valley of the Connecticut R. The major industries are fabricated metals, machinery, munitions, and transport equipment. The small agricultural sector is dominated by dairying and shade-grown tobacco. The population was 90% metropolitan in 1980. Although discovered by the Dutch in 1614, Connecticut was first settled by English Puritans in the 1630s. It joined the American Revolution and the economy suffered from British protectionism in the early 19th cent. Slavery was abolished in 1848 and the state supported the Union in the Civil War. The economy has flourished in the 20th cent., and Connecticut is the largest defence contractor per capita in the US.

**connective tissue,** supportive tissue binding or separating specialized tissues. Consisting mainly of substances secreted by certain cells, it contains relatively few cells. The connective tissue that forms TENDONS and LIGAMENTS consists mainly of white inelastic fibres of collagen (a protein). Cartilage, vital to the skeletal system of vertebrates, is fibrous collagen in a gel, firm but flexible. Connective tissue found under the skin and supporting most organs contains collagen in addition to fibres of the yellow elastic protein elastin. BONE connective tissue is made up largely of collagen fibres and calcium salt crystals; its structure is strong and rigid.

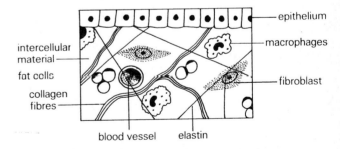

Connective tissue

**Connery, Sean,** 1930–, British film actor. Famed worldwide as the first James Bond, he has also pursued a versatile career in other roles. His films include *Dr No* (1962), *The Wind and the Lion* (1975), and *The Name of the Rose* (1987).

**conquistador,** military leader of the Spanish conquest of the New World in the 16th cent. Francisco PIZARRO and Hernán CORTÉS were the greatest conquistadors. The word can mean any daring, ruthless adventurer.

**Conrad,** rulers of the Holy Roman German Empire and its predecessor state. **Conrad I,** d. 918, German king (r.911–18), succeeded Louis the Child, but was plagued by feuds and rebellions in Lorraine, Swabia, and Bavaria. His failure to halt the continuing Hungarian invasions and the alienation of his nobles almost dissolved the kingdom. **Conrad II,** c.990–1039, emperor and German king (r.1024–39), was the first of the Frankish Salian dynasty. His election as German king was contested by

Swabia, Lotharingia, and Italy; but he was crowned after three years of conflict. His reign was marked by constant revolts, but he added Burgundy to his dominions and greatly increased commerce. **Conrad III,** c.1093–1152, emperor and German king (r.1138–52), founder of the HOHENSTAUFEN dynasty, was set up as anti-king to Emperor LOTHAR II in 1127 but submitted to Lothar in 1135. He was elected king at Lothar's death by those opposing Henry the Proud of Bavaria and his brother Guelph, thereby setting in force the struggle between the GUELPHS AND GHIBELLINES. Conrad was never crowned. **Conrad IV,** 1228–54, emperor and German king (r.1237–54), king of Sicily and of Jerusalem (r.1250–54), was made king by his father Emperor FREDERICK II, but the struggle between Frederick and Pope INNOCENT IV kept him from being crowned. He was excommunicated in 1254 and died shortly thereafter of fever.

**Conrad,** d. 1192, Latin king of JERUSALEM (1192), marquis of Montferrat, a leader in the Third CRUSADE. He saved TYRE from the Saracens and became (1187) its lord. To gain the throne of Jerusalem he married the daughter of AMALRIC I, but he was immediately murdered, probably by Muslim assassins. The title passed eventually to AMALRIC II.

**Conrad, Joseph,** 1857–1924, English novelist; b. Poland, as Jósef Teodor Konrad Walecz Korzeniowski. After a period at sea (during which he became a British subject), he began (1894) writing novels in English, an acquired language, and eventually became one of the greatest prose stylists in English literature. Notable early works include *The Nigger of the Narcissus* (1897), *Lord Jim* (1900), and the novellas *Youth* (1902), *Heart of Darkness* (1902), and *Typhoon* (1903). A master at creating character and atmosphere, Conrad acutely portrayed individuals suffering from isolation and moral disintegration, and the clash between primitive cultures and modern civilization. His best works include *Nostromo* (1904), *The Secret Agent* (1907), *Under Western Eyes* (1911), *Chance* (1913), and *Victory* (1915).

**consanguinity:** see KINSHIP.

**Conscience, Hendrik** (kawnhsee ahnhs), 1812–83, Flemish novelist, a founder of modern Flemish literature. His many historical novels are romantic but powerful in the tradition of Sir Walter SCOTT. *The Lion of Flanders* (1831) is famous.

**conscientious objector,** person who, on grounds of conscience, refuses military service. Resistance based on religious or humanitarian convictions, as among Quakers (see FRIENDS), is usually distinguished from political opposition to particular wars. In World Wars I and II, the US and Britain allowed objectors who were members of recognized pacifist religious denominations to substitute nonmilitary service, but imprisoned other pacifists. In the 1970s the US Supreme Court allowed conscientious objection based on deeply held ethical as well as religious beliefs, but refused to accept opposition to the VIETNAM WAR as a basis for exemption.

**conscription,** compulsory enrolment, in war or peace, in the armed forces. The idea of compulsory military service by all of a nation's able-bodied men was introduced in the late 18th cent. during the French Revolution and enabled Napoleon, several years later, to raise huge armies. Other European countries adopted such a system during the 19th cent; the UK ended its conscription ('National Service') in 1960, but many European countries retain it. In the US wartime conscription was used in the Civil War and both world wars, and a peacetime draft was maintained from 1945 to 1973. Israel is unusual in having conscription into active-serving units for women as well as men.

**Conseil de l'Entente** (kon sayl del en tentay), intergovernmental organization formed in 1959. It comprises five French-speaking West African states (Benin, Burkina Faso, Côte d'Ivoire, Niger, and Togo) and promotes economic cooperation and integration.

**conservation,** a term in PIAGET's development psychology denoting the understanding that certain quantitative attributes of a STIMULUS array (such as length, volume, weight) are unaffected by changes in the location and disposition of the stimuli. Piaget devised conservation experiments, such as the 'test of conservation of liquid volume', on the basis of which he concluded that conservation, a mark of 'operational thinking', does not appear until the age of 7–8 years. The conservation tests have been both widely replicated and widely criticized for underestimating the child's cognitive competence.

**conservation laws,** in physics, basic laws that maintain that the total value of certain quantities remains unchanged during a physical process.

Conserved quantities include MASS (or matter), ENERGY, linear MOMENTUM, angular momentum, and electric CHARGE; the theory of RELATIVITY, however, combines the laws of conservation of mass and of energy into a single law. Additional conservation laws have meaning only on the subatomic level.

**conservation of natural resources,** informed restraint in the human use of the earth's resources. The term *conservation*, which came into use in the late 19th cent., referred to the management, mainly for economic reasons, of such valuable natural resources as timber, fish, game, topsoil, pastureland, and minerals. It referred also to the preservation of forests, wildlife (see NATURE RESERVE), parkland, WILDERNESS, WATERSHED areas, and ENDANGERED SPECIES. Conservationism, a movement based on aesthetics, a sense of awe, and a pragmatic, non-aggressive approach to the use of natural resources, came into being around the turn of the century. In the UK one of the earliest conservation bodies was the Royal Society for the Protection of Birds, which started life with a campaign to stop the destruction of egrets and other birds whose feathers were used to decorate hats. In the US the first president with a true awareness of and concern for conservation was Theodore ROOSEVELT, who was responsible for the 1902 Newlands Reclamation Act, the first major stimulus to the movement in America. Britain's first statutory body in conservation was the Nature Conservancy (now Nature Conservancy Council), set up shortly after World War II. The International Union for the Conservation of Nature and Natural Resources (IUCN), based in Gland, Switzerland, was founded in 1948 and represents more than 100 countries. A union of governments, government agencies, and conservation groups, it seeks to determine the scientific priorities for conservation action. The World Wide Fund for Nature (WWFN) was established in 1961, largely to provide the IUCN with adequate money. Conservation has several strands, including the management, rational use, and safeguarding of water, wildlife, and raw materials, ENERGY conservation, the development of environmentally benign technologies, and the prevention of POLLUTION. Crucial to all these aspects is population control. In the 1960s and 70s a related movement—ENVIRONMENTALISM—arose and measures were taken in many countries to protect the environment and its resources. The UNITED NATIONS Environmental Programme (UNEP) was established in 1972 with the aim of preventing deforestation, erosion, and desertification worldwide. In 1980, the IUCN and the WWF, together with UNEP, produced a World Conservation Strategy, based on the conviction that conservation principles must play a part in all successful development programmes.

**conservatism,** the disposition to maintain or conserve the existing order; the principles and practice of conservative political parties. Modern political conservatism emerged in the 19th cent. as a reaction against the political and social changes associated with the FRENCH REVOLUTION and the INDUSTRIAL REVOLUTION. Writers such as Edmund BURKE and Joseph de Maistre expressed scepticism about the idea of progress and the perfectibility of human nature. They stressed the significance of tradition, the importance of law and order, the necessity of an established church, the inevitability of social inequality, and the social responsibilities of an enlightened aristocracy, and in the rightful political ascendancy of men of property. Strictly speaking, the conservative does not oppose change which is cautious, limited, and traditional in form, only that which is rapid, far-reaching, and undertaken according to abstract principles. Clearly this is a stance which is congenial to those who benefit most from existing arrangements. Conservative instincts are not, however, confined to the rich: since being enfranchised by DISRAELI at the end of the 19th cent., a consistent one-third of the British manual working class has voted for the Conservative Party. As society itself changes, so do the composition of its ruling class, and the ideas with which they defend their interests. As the 19th cent. progressed, and the new captains of industry joined the landed interest in power, so a new emphasis on individualism and economic LAISSEZ-FAIRE grew up alongside the Christian paternalism of an earlier generation of conservatives. The tension between these two sets of ideas, and a willingness to bend in order not to break, explains the history of modern conservatism. In Britain, as in other European nations, parties of the Right have in fact accommodated themselves to reforms they once opposed, such as universal suffrage, an extended WELFARE STATE, and the increased taxation necessary to pay for it. This was consistent with the traditional notion that the leaders of society had a moral responsibility to the masses, and in any case the older conservatism had no hesitation over the use of state power. But the emphasis of recent (1980s) conservative governments in Europe and the US has swung back to a neo-liberal attack on the welfare state in the name of freedom and individualism. It is important to notice that this emphasis on freedom does not extend to the social sphere. On the contrary, the peculiar character of modern conservatism lies in combining economic liberalism with very traditional attitudes towards work, the family, and religion.

**Conservative Judaism:** see JUDAISM.

**Conservative Party,** officially Conservative and Unionist Party, major British political party, the other being the LABOUR PARTY. The successor of the TORY Party, it came into being after the REFORM BILL of 1832 and advocated the Tory policies of defence of the Church of England and protection of agricultural interests. Later, it strongly supported imperialism. The repeal of the protectionist CORN LAWS (1846) by the Conservative leader Sir Robert PEEL caused a split in the party and its exclusion from power for most of the period 1846–73. Under Benjamin DISRAELI's 'Tory democracy' (1874–80), the party wooed the broadening electorate with social legislation. The dominant party under Stanley BALDWIN, during the 1920s and 30s, it lost prestige with the failure of Neville CHAMBERLAIN's appeasement of Nazi Germany (1937–40), but the country rallied to his successor, Sir Winston CHURCHILL who headed an all-party coalition government, during WORLD WAR II. Heavily defeated by Labour in 1945, the Conservative Party returned to power in 1951, being led by Churchill until 1955 and then by Sir Anthony EDEN (1955–57), Harold MACMILLAN (1957–63), and Sir Alec DOUGLAS-HOME (1963–64); during those 13 years the free-market economy was given its head, although Labour's welfare state structure was maintained. In opposition from 1964, the party unexpectedly won the 1970 elections under Edward HEATH, who successfully negotiated Britain's entry into the EUROPEAN COMMUNITY (1973). Amid major industrial unrest, the Conservatives went into opposition in 1974 but returned to power in 1979 under Margaret THATCHER, who became Britain's first woman prime minister. Distinctly right-wing in policy orientation, Thatcher led the party to a further election victories in 1983 and 1987. The Conservative Party has organizational links with the Official Unionist Party of Northern Ireland.

**Considérant, Victor Prosper** (kawnhseeday,rahnh), 1808–93, French socialist. Leader of Fourierism after the death (1837) of Charles FOURIER, he took part in the JUNE DAYS uprising (1848), was forced to flee to Belgium, and later tried unsuccessfully to establish (1855–57) a Fourierist colony in Texas. His books include *Principles of Socialism* (1847).

**consideration:** see CONTRACT.

**Constable, John,** 1776–1837, leading English landscape painter. The originality of Constable's landscapes lay in their naturalism, in his close observation of a particular scene (often in the Suffolk countryside around his boyhood home or, later, in Salisbury or on Hampstead Heath) and of particular effects of light and weather. His use of broken colour and his

John **Constable,** *The Hay Wain*, 1821. Oil on canvas, 130.5 × 185.5 cm. National Gallery, London.

free sketchy brushwork were new; his preparatory sketches, e.g., *Weymouth Bay* (National Gall., London), are spontaneous and vigorous. His most famous work, *The Haywain* (1821; National Gall., London) was admired in France, especially by DELACROIX, and his work later influenced painters of the BARBIZON SCHOOL.

**Constance,** Ger. *Konstanz,* city (1984 pop. 68,300), Baden-Württemberg, West Germany, on Lake Constance. Its industries include the manufacture of textiles and clothing. Originating as a Roman fort in the 4th cent., it was an episcopal see by the late 6th cent., and was made a free imperial city in 1192. The Council of Constance held its meetings here (1414–18) and John HUSS was burned to death in 1415 in the city. Awarded to Austria in 1548, it passed to Baden in 1815. Historic buildings include an 11th-cent. minster, the Dominican monastery where the Council met, and the House of Huss.

**Constance, Council of:** see SCHISM, GREAT.

**Constance, Lake,** Ger, *Bodensee,* lake, 530 km² (208 sq mi), bordered by Switzerland, West Germany and Austria, on the Rhine R. The shores are popular with tourists. CONSTANCE (Germany) is the largest town on its shores and is a popular tourist centre.

**Constant, Benjamin,** 1767–1830, French political writer and novelist; b. Switzerland. Through Germaine de STAËL he became interested in politics, and his affair with her took him to Paris (1795). He served (1799–1801) as a tribune under NAPOLEON I but lived in exile (1802–14) with de Staël after she was expelled from France. During the Bourbon restoration he served (1819–22, 1824–30) in the chamber of deputies, earning a reputation as a liberal. His most important work is the semiautobiographical novel *Adolphe* (1816).

**Constanţa** (kon,stantsah), city (1985 est. pop. 323,236), SE Romania, on the Black Sea. It is Romania's principal port, shipbuilding centre and naval base. In the 1960s it was developed as a major industrial centre and in 1984 linked to the DANUBE R by canal. Founded (7th cent. BC) by the Greeks, it came under Roman, Byzantine, and Turkish authority before passing to Romania in 1878 following the Russo-Turkish War.

**Constantine,** Roman emperors. **Constantine I** or **Constantine the Great,** 288?–337 (r.310–337), was born at Naissus (now Nis, Yugoslavia), the son of Constantius I and St HELENA. When Constantius died at York in 306, his soldiers proclaimed Constantine emperor, but much rivalry for the vacated office ensued. Before the battle at the Milvian or Mulvian Bridge near Rome in 312, Constantine, who was already sympathetic toward Christianity, is said to have seen in the sky a flaming cross as the sign by which he would conquer. He adopted the cross and was victorious. The battle is regarded as a turning point for Christianity. Constantine ruled in the West and LICINIUS in the East as co-emperors until they fell out in 324. Licinius lost his life in the struggle, leaving Constantine sole emperor. In a reign of peace, Constantine rebuilt the empire on a basis of absolutism. In 325 he convened the epoch-making Council of NICAEA. In 330 he moved the capital to Constantinople, a city dedicated to the Virgin. As the founder of the Christian empire, Constantine began a new era. He was baptized on his deathbed. **Constantine II,** 316–40 (r.337–40), was the son of Constantine. When the empire was divided at his father's death (337), he received Britain, Gaul, and Spain. Feeling cheated, he warred with his brother Constans I, but he was killed while invading Italy.

**Constantine,** Byzantine emperors. **Constantine I** Constantine, Roman emperors. **Constantine IV** (Pogonatus), c.652–685 (r.668–85), repelled the Muslims but had to cede land to the Bulgars. He called the Third Council of Constantinople (680-81), which condemned MONOTHELETISM. **Constantine V** (Copronymus), 718–75 (r.741–75), was a capable general and administrator. His support of ICONOCLASM and opposition to MONASTICISM lost him Rome. **Constantine VI,** b. c.770 (r.780–97), reigned first with his mother, IRENE, as regent and then as co-ruler (792). In 797 she had her cruel and unpopular son deposed and blinded. **Constantine VII** (Porphyrogenitus), 905–59 (r.913–59), had his reign interrupted by the usurpation of ROMANUS I (919–44). He fostered learning, law reform, and the fair distribution of land. **Constantine XI** (Palaeologus), 1405–53, was the last Byzantine emperor (r.1449–53). He proclaimed the union of the Eastern and Western churches. After a long siege Constantinople fell (1453) to Ottoman sultan MEHMED II. Constantine died in the battle.

**Constantine,** kings of the Hellenes (Greece). **Constantine I,** 1868–1923 (r.1913–17, 1920–22), opposed the Allies in World War I and was forced to abdicate in favour of his second son, ALEXANDER. He was restored after Alexander's death, but in 1922 a military rebellion forced him to abdicate again, this time in favour of his eldest son, GEORGE II. **Constantine II,** 1940– (r.1964–73), succeeded his father, PAUL, but in 1967 was forced into exile by a military junta. He was formally deposed in 1973.

**Constantine,** formerly Quacentina, city (1987 pop. 408,578), chief town of Constantine prov., N Algeria. An administrative and commercial centre, it trades in textiles, leather, and grain. Its industries include flour milling. It was captured by the French in 1837.

**Constantinople,** former capital of the BYZANTINE EMPIRE and of the OTTOMAN EMPIRE, called ISTANBUL since 1930. It was founded (AD 330) at BYZANTIUM as the new capital of the Roman Empire by CONSTANTINE I and became the largest, most splendid medieval European city. Built on seven hills above the BOSPORUS, it had such magnificent buildings as the church of HAGIA SOPHIA and the emperors' palace (a city in itself), and many artistic and literary treasures. It was conquered in 1204 by Crusaders (see CRUSADES), in 1261 by MICHAEL VIII, and in 1453 by MEHMED II. Almost depopulated when it fell to the Turks, the city recovered quickly, and was embellished by the Ottoman sultans with palaces and mosques. After WORLD WAR I Constantinople was occupied (1918–23) by the Allies. In 1923 Kemal ATATÜRK made ANKARA Turkey's capital.

**Constantinople, Councils of,** four church councils, all recognized as ecumenical by the Roman Catholic Church. The First Council of Constantinople (381) was called to confirm the victory over ARIANISM and established the orthodox teaching of the Trinity. It also condemned the heresy of Apollinarianism. The second council (553) was called by Byzantine Emperor JUSTINIAN I and was dominated by him; it condemned Nestorian writings (see NESTORIANISM) and encouraged MONOPHYSITISM. The third (680) condemned MONOTHELETISM and a former pope, HONORIUS I. The fourth council (869–70) confirmed the condemnation of PHOTIUS. The fourth council is not accepted as ecumenical by the Orthodox Church.

**Constantinople, Latin Empire of,** 1204–61, feudal empire in the S Balkans and Greek archipelago, founded by the leaders of the Fourth CRUSADE. Its government was divided between the Crusaders and their Venetian creditors. The rulers were BALDWIN I, HENRY OF FLANDERS, ROBERT OF COURTENAY, and BALDWIN II. The empire at once began to decline from internal strife and attacks by the Bulgars, Turks, and Greek states of NICAEA and EPIRUS. It was taken (1261) by MICHAEL VIII of Nicaea, who restored the Byzantine Empire. However, Venice retained most of the Greek Isles, the Villehardouin family of France kept Achaia, and Athens came under Catalan rule.

**constellation,** in common usage, group of stars (e.g., URSA MAJOR) that are imagined to form a configuration in the sky; in astronomy, the term is used to denote a definite region of the sky in which the configuration of stars is contained. The entire celestial sphere is divided into 88 such regions, with boundaries fixed by international agreement along lines of right ascension and declination. The 12 constellations located along or near the ecliptic, or apparent path of the Sun through the heavens, are known as the constellations of the ZODIAC.

**constitution,** fundamental principles of government of a nation, either implied in its laws, institutions, and customs, or embodied in one or more documents. The British constitution, an unwritten, flexible code, comprises the whole body of common and statutory law, conventions and customs that have evolved there; it can be modified simply by an ACT OF PARLIAMENT, although major decisions, such as whether Britain should join the EUROPEAN COMMUNITY, have been decided by referendum. The US CONSTITUTION, which is written, has superior sanction to ordinary laws and can be changed only through an elaborate process of amendment. It remains abreast of the times, however, through statutes passed by CONGRESS and interpretations and rulings of the SUPREME COURT. Many nations have constitutions which are not realized in their political practice. In the USSR, for example, post war dissidents have been persecuted for exercising or claiming their constitutional rights.

**Constitution Act 1982,** Canadian law that superseded the BRITISH NORTH AMERICA ACT of 1867 as the basic constitution of Canada. Also known as the patriation bill, it gives Canadians the power to make their own constitutional changes, whereas the previous act had required the formal approval of the British Parliament. Despite protests from Canadian Indians and from Quebec Prov., the act was signed into law by Queen ELIZABETH II in Ottawa on 17 Apr. 1982.

**Constitutional Convention:** see FEDERAL CONSTITUTIONAL CONVENTION.

**Constitutional Union party,** in US history, formed when the conflict between North and South broke down older parties. Organized just before the election of 1860, it recognized 'no political principle but the Constitution of the country, the union of the states, and the enforcement of laws.' Party candidates John Bell and Edward EVERETT carried Kentucky, Tennessee, and Virginia in the presidential election won by Lincoln.

**constitution of the United Kingdom,** rules and practices developed over the centuries governing how Britain is run. Unlike most modern constitutions, the UK constitution is not embodied in a single document, but is to be found in various sources such as statutes, cases, conventions, and books by writers of authority (see A.V. DICEY). The constitution is therefore flexible and can be amended merely by passing an Act of Parliament. Some of the more important statutes are the BILL OF RIGHTS 1689, limiting the power of the sovereign, and the Act of Union 1707, establishing a PARLIAMENT for the UK. An important constitutional case is ENTICK V. CARRINGTON (1765), limiting the arbitrary power of government. The constitution also recognizes some important principles. The most fundamental of these is the sovereignty of PARLIAMENT, stating that parliament has the power to pass any law. Unlike in the US, UK courts cannot strike down a statute as unconstitutional. Other important constitutional principles are the RULE OF LAW and the Separation of Powers. In recent years discussion has been increasing over whether the UK should adopt a written Bill of Rights and a written constitution.

**Constitution of the United States,** document embodying the principles on which the American nation is governed. It establishes a federal REPUBLIC with sovereignty balanced between the national government and the states. Within the national government, power is separated among three branches, the EXECUTIVE, legislative (see CONGRESS), and judicial (see SUPREME COURT, UNITED STATES). The US Constitution is the supreme law of the land; no other law, state constitution or statute, federal legislation, or executive order can operate in conflict with it. Drawn up at the FEDERAL CONSTITUTIONAL CONVENTION of 1787 in Philadelphia and ratified by the required nine states by 21 June 1788, the Constitution began to function in 1789, superseding the Articles of Confederation (1781). It is relatively brief and concise, consisting of a preamble, seven articles, and (to 1982) 26 amendments. The BILL OF RIGHTS, comprising the first nine amendments to the constitution, was added in 1791 to provide adequate guarantees of individual liberties. The US Constitution is an example of a written constitution, embodied in a single document.

**constructivism,** a term used to cover a broad spectrum of artistic and ideological issues. In the context of post-Revolutionary Russia it generally refers to an aesthetic that denied simulation, investigated the properties, aesthetic and practical, of modern materials, and emphasized the social usefulness of art. TATLIN, RODCHENKO, LISSITZKY and MALEVICH were participants in this fusion of the roles of artist and industrial designer. GABO and PEVSNER in their *Realistic Manifesto* (1920), however, believed that creative art must be non-social and non-utilitarian. The exhibition of Russian art in 1922 in Berlin, organized by Lissitzky, introduced Soviet constructivism into Europe, as well as Pevsner and Gabo who left Russia in 1921. Constructivist ideas were introduced into the teaching of the BAUHAUS in 1923 by the arrival of MOHOLY-NAGY. International constructivism, which could be seen to encompass Elementarism and Purism, had a far less specific artistic and ideological direction.

**Consumer Price Index:** see INDEX NUMBER.

**consumer protection,** actions by government, business and private groups to safeguard the interests of the buying public. In recent times consumers' rights have been extended to such broad areas as product information and safety, satisfaction of grievances, advertising claims, and a voice in governmental decisions affecting the consumer. In the UK the consumer is well protected by numerous official regulations and qualitative standards, and inspection systems which are imposed on many products. A government body, The Consumer Protection Advisory Committee, is appointed to look at consumer trade practices which may adversely affect the economic interests of UK consumers (established under the Fair Trading Act 1973). Within the Common Market there has been increasing interest in consumer protection; in 1986 the EEC adopted the Commission's 'New Impetus for Consumer Policy' which sets policy guidelines for the future.

**consumption:** see TUBERCULOSIS.

**contact lenses,** thin lenses of hard or soft plastic (originally glass), worn on the eyeball and used instead of spectacles to improve vision or, in certain cases, to treat disorders. The widely used corneal lenses cover just the cornea of the eye and can correct LONGSIGHTEDNESS, SHORTSIGHTEDNESS, and ASTIGMATISM. Those made of soft and gas-permeable plastic can be worn for considerably longer periods of time than the hard lenses, which are removed at night. Lenses, sometimes covering the entire eye, are occasionally used to treat eye injuries or infections.

**Contadora Group,** informal group formed by the governments of Colombia, Mexico, Panama, and Venezuela in 1983 to find a political solution to the Central American conflict, particularly with regard to the situations in Nicaragua and El Salvador. The group drew up (1984) a draft peace treaty, but acceptance by all the parties concerned was not forthcoming.

**contagious disease:** see COMMUNICABLE DISEASE.

**contempt of court,** in law, interference with the functioning of a court, either direct (occurring before a judge) or constructive (actions obstructing justice, e.g., disobeying an INJUNCTION, or publishing information about a case against a judge's instructions). Contempt is punished to enforce a party's rights (civil contempt) or to vindicate authority (criminal contempt). The court may impose a fine or imprisonment; in the case of direct contempt, no hearing is required.

**continent,** largest unit of land on the earth. The continents are Eurasia (EUROPE and ASIA), AFRICA, NORTH AMERICA, SOUTH AMERICA, AUSTRALIA, and ANTARCTICA. More than two-thirds of the continental regions are in the Northern Hemisphere. Continental areas bounded by the sea-level contour comprise about 29% of the earth's surface. All continents contain interior plains, or PLATEAUS, underlain by the oldest rocks; where exposed to the surface, these rocks are called continental shields, or cratons. The oldest of these rocks dated by radioactivity are 3800 million years old, indicating that the cratons formed with the solidification of the earth's crust. The continents have grown by accretion on their edges, where huge plates of crust converge, creating MOUNTAIN belts (see CONTINENTAL DRIFT; PLATE TECTONICS).

**Continental Congress,** 1774–89, federal legislature of the THIRTEEN COLONIES and later of the United States under the Articles of CONFEDERATION. After England passed the INTOLERABLE ACTS, the First Continental Congress met (5 Sept.–26 Oct. 1774) in Philadelphia and petitioned the king. When the Second Continental Congress met there on 10 May 1775, armed conflict had begun (see LEXINGTON AND CONCORD, BATTLES OF), but the Congress still moved only gradually toward independence. It finally created the Continental Army, named George WASHINGTON commander in chief, and adopted (4 July 1776) the DECLARATION OF INDEPENDENCE.

**Continental Divide,** the drainage divide separating rivers flowing to different sides of a continent. In the US, where it is also called the Great Divide, it follows the crest of the Rocky Mts and separates rivers draining to the Arctic, Atlantic, and Pacific oceans.

**continental drift,** the theory that the positions of the earth's continents have changed considerably through geological time. The first comprehensive theory of continental drift was proposed by the German meteorologist Alfred WEGENER in 1912. On the basis of the jigsaw fit of the opposing Atlantic coasts and geological and paleontological correlations on both sides of the Atlantic, he advanced the theory that c.200 million years ago there was one supercontinent, Pangaea, which split into two vast land masses, Laurasia and Gondwanaland. The present continents separated in the next geological era (the Mesozoic). A plastic layer in the interior of the earth accommodated this process, in which the earth's rotation caused horizontal alterations in the granitic continents floating on the 'sea' of the basaltic ocean floors. The frictional drag along the leading edges of the drifting continents created MOUNTAINS. Wegener's theory met controversy until 1954, when it was revived by British geophysicists

seeking to explain the phenomenon of polar wandering (see MAGNETIC POLE). Since then, the modern theory of PLATE TECTONICS has evolved from and replaced Wegener's original thesis.

180 million years

65 million years

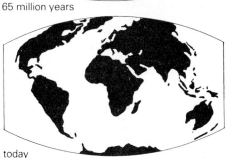

today

Continental drift

**continuing education:** see ADULT EDUCATION.

**contrabassoon:** see BASSOON.

**contraception:** see BIRTH CONTROL.

**contract,** in law, enforceable agreement between two or more persons to perform, or refrain from performing, a specified act. A contract is made when one party submits an offer that is accepted by the other. Generally, the parties must be mentally sound, of legal age, and acting with free will. A contract must not have an immoral or criminal purpose, or be against public policy. Certain types of contracts must be in writing. A contract must involve consideration—something of value (e.g., money or a promise) given by each party to the other. A contract is terminated when its terms have been fulfilled or when special circumstances, e.g., the death of one party, make fulfillment impossible or unlawful. The law provides several remedies for breach (failure to carry out the terms) of a contract, most often the award of monetary damages for losses incurred.

**contraction,** in writing: see ABBREVIATION.

**contralto:** see VOICE.

**convection,** transfer of heat by the flow of a liquid or gas. A fluid expands when heated and thus undergoes a decrease in density. The warmer, less dense regions of a fluid tend to rise, in accordance with ARCHIMEDES' PRINCIPLE, through the surrounding cooler fluid. If the heat continues to be supplied, the cooler fluid that flows in to replace the rising fluid will also become heated and will rise, setting up a convection current.

**Conwy,** town (1981 pop. 3649), Gwynedd, N Wales, on W bank of R. Conwy estuary. A resort town, small port, and market town, it has many historic remains. There is a 13th-cent. castle and remains of the town walls. The river is crossed here by a road suspension bridge designed by Thomas TELFORD (1826), and a tubular railway bridge designed by Robert STEPHENSON (1848).

**Coober Pedy,** town (1986 pop. 2103), South Australia. Located 950 km (600 mi) N of Adelaide, in the Stuart Range, the town has been a major opal mining district since 1915. Many people live in underground homes, known locally as 'dug outs'. One of the country's first solar desalination plants was installed here to process saline artesian water to supply residents with potable water.

**Cook, James,** 1728–79, British explorer. As a Royal Navy officer he commanded the astronomical expedition which observed the transit of Venus from Tahiti. He then explored the coasts of AUSTRALIA and NEW ZEALAND. In 1776 he rediscovered the Sandwich Islands and searched the west coast of NORTH AMERICA for a passage to the Atlantic. He is credited with preventing scurvy among his crew through proper diet. Cook was killed by the islanders of Hawaii.

**Cook, Thomas,** 1808–92, English travel agent who originated the guided tour. He founded his travel agency in 1841. In 1884 he transported an 18,000-man expeditionary force up the Nile to try to relieve Gen. Charles George GORDON.

**Cooke, Alistair,** 1908–, American broadcaster; b. England. Educated Cambridge, Yale and Harvard, he became film critic for the BBC (1934–37); he then wrote for *The Times* (1937–41). During World War II Cooke was correspondent for the *Daily Herald* and the *Manchester Guardian* (now *The Guardian*). Since 1942 he has broadcast regularly from the US, and his 'Letter from America' over these years has achieved wide recognition as outstanding radio journalism. His numerous publications include *A Generation on Trial* (1950) (about the Hiss case), *Around the World in 50 Years* (1966), and several collections of the 'Letters from America'. His television series *America—A Personal History of the United States* (1972–73) was widely acclaimed. Polished and urbane, Cooke's journalism is not remarkable for its controversy.

**Cooke, Jay,** 1821–1905, American financier. His Philadelphia banking house, Jay Cooke and Company, successfully marketed huge government loans to the public to finance the AMERICAN CIVIL WAR. His subsequent failure to raise $100 million to finance construction of the Northern Pacific Railroad led to the collapse of his firm (1873) and precipitated the Panic of 1873.

**Cook Islands,** self-governing dependency of New Zealand (1979 est. pop. 18,200), 234 sq km (90 sq mi), consisting of two groups of coral islands in the South Pacific Ocean. They were proclaimed a British protectorate in 1888, passed to New Zealand in 1901, and achieved self-government in 1965. The Cook Islands Party was in power until 1978, when it was replaced by the Democratic Party. Cook Islanders are MAORIS and hold New Zealand citizenship. Major products include citrus fruits, copra, and handicrafts.

**Coolidge, Calvin,** 1872–1933, 30th president of the US (1923–29). As governor of Massachusetts (1919–20) he became nationally known for using the militia to end a Boston police strike. He was US vice president (1921–23) before becoming president upon the death of Warren G. HARDING. Coolidge's New England simplicity and personal honesty were appealing. His faith in laissez-faire business, economy in government, and tax cuts, and his opposition to agricultural price fixing all reflected the national mood. Through his public statements he encouraged the stock market speculation of the late 1920s and left the nation unprepared for the economic collapse that followed.

**Cooper, Gary,** 1901–61, American film actor. b. Frank James Cooper. His films include *Mr Deeds Goes to Town* (1936), *For Whom the Bell Tolls* (1943), and *High Noon* (1952; Academy Award).

**Cooper, James Fenimore,** 1789–1851, first major American novelist. His literary career began in 1820 and covered a period of 30 years, during which he published more than 50 works. He first achieved success with the American Revolutionary novel *The Spy* (1821). Cooper's most important novels comprise *The Leatherstocking Tales,* named for their chief character, the frontiersman Natty Bumppo, nicknamed Leatherstocking. Notable for their descriptive power, mastery of native background, and idealization of the American Indian, they are (in narrative order): *The Deerslayer* (1841), *The Last of the Mohicans* (1826), *The Pathfinder* (1840), *The Pioneers* (1823), and *The Prairie* (1827). Cooper is also known for his romances of American life on land

and sea, e.g., *The Pilot* (1823), *The Red Rover* (1827), and *The Water-Witch* (1830). An apologist for the US during his years abroad (1826–33) in works such as *Notions of the Americans* (1828), he was repelled by the abuses of democracy on his return and wrote several critical novels, e.g., *Homeward Bound, Home as Found* (both: 1838), which earned him violent criticism and many enemies. Cooper's late novels include the Littlepage trilogy (1845–46), a study of conflict between the landed and landless in New York state.

**cooperative,** nonprofit economic enterprise for the benefit of those using its services. Cooperatives are common today in such areas as insurance, food, banking and credit (see CREDIT UNION), and housing. The cooperative movement grew out of the philosophy of Robert OWEN, Charles FOURIER, and others. The first permanent consumer cooperative was founded (1844) in Britain, and workers and farmers in the US formed producer cooperatives soon after (see GRANGER MOVEMENT). Cooperatives of various kinds are important in Scandinavia, Israel, China, the USSR, and France. See also COLLECTIVE FARM; COMMUNE.

**Coornhert, Dirck Volckerszoon** (ˌkawnheət), 1522–90, Dutch humanist. His translation of the first 12 books of HOMER's *Odyssey* (1561) is the first major poetic work of the Dutch RENAISSANCE. A supporter of religious tolerance, he also wrote comedies, morality plays, and a philosophical treatise (1586).

**Coorong,** inlet in S Australia. A tidal lagoon 140 km (90 mi) long, formed at the mouth of the MURRAY R. The wetlands provide an important nesting and breeding ground for local and migratory birds. Large shell middens are evidence of extensive past Aboriginal occupation. A system of barrages, completed in 1940, prevents salt water from entering Lakes Albert and Alexandrina at the mouth of the MURRAY R. and has enabled extensive areas of the lower floodplains to be developed under irrigation for dairy pastures.

**coot,** water fowl of the RAIL family living in both the Old World and the New World. They have unusual lobed toes which act as paddles in water, making them excellent swimmers. The European coot (*Fulica atra*) is black, 38 cm (15 in) long, and easily recognized by its white bill and frontal shield. It is the most widespread coot, breeding across Europe, southern Africa, and Asia to Australia. The moorhen (*Gallinula gallinula*) is a coot. The group includes the flightless New Zealand takahe (*Notornis mantelli*) which was believed to be extinct until rediscovered on South Island in 1948.

**Cope, Edward Drinker,** 1840–97, American palaeontologist. He was the first to provide comprehensive descriptions of Eocene vertebrates. He and the palaeontologist Othniel Marsh, with whom he disputed on priority and other matters for 20 years, discovered the first complete dinosaur remains. Cope believed that evolution was caused by an organism's inner urge to attain a higher state of being.

**Copeau, Jacques** (ko,poh), 1879–1949, French theatrical producer and critic. A founder (1909) and editor (1912–14) of the PERIODICAL *Nouvelle Revue française,* he also founded the experimental Théâtre du Vieux Colombier in Paris (1913–24) in order to produce poetic drama of artistic worth.

**Copenhagen,** city (1985 pop. of Greater Copenhagen 1,358,540), capital of Denmark. It is a major commercial, fishing, and naval port, and Denmark's chief commercial and cultural centre, with such industries as brewing, furniture, and the pottery known as Copenhagen Ware. Founded by the 11th cent., it survived attacks by the HANSEATIC LEAGUE and Sweden, became Denmark's capital in 1443, and expanded as a prosperous trade hub in the 16th and 17th cent. During WORLD WAR II the city was occupied (1940–45) by the Germans. Its landmarks include the 17th-cent. Charlottenborg Palace, the 19th-cent. palaces on Amalienborg Square, the round tower used by Tycho BRAHE as an observatory, and the statue of Hans Christian ANDERSEN's Little Mermaid.

**Copernican system,** the first modern European heliocentric theory of planetary motion; it placed the sun motionless at the centre of the solar system with all the planets, including the Earth, revolving around it. COPERNICUS developed his theory (which replaced the PTOLEMAIC SYSTEM) in the early 16th cent. from a study of ancient astronomical records. His system explained RETROGRADE MOTION in a natural way.

**Copernicus, Nicholas,** 1473–1543, Polish astronomer. After studying law and medicine at the Univ. of Cracow and at Bologna, Padua, and plumbing, and refrigerator and air-conditioner coils. Copper alloys include BRASS and BRONZE. Copper compounds are used as insecticides, fungicides, and paint pigments, and in electroplating. Many of them, especially the oxides of yttrium–barium–copper, are superconducting at high temperatures (c.95 K). CHALCOPYRITE is the principal ore. Copper is essential for normal metabolism and haemoglobin synthesis in humans. See ELEMENT (table); PERIODIC TABLE.

**Copper Age:** see BRONZE AGE.

**copperhead:** see PIT VIPER; TIGER SNAKE.

**Copperheads,** in the US CIVIL WAR, reproachful term for Southern sympathizers in the North. Led by Clement Laird Vallandigham, they were especially strong in Illinois, Indiana, and Ohio. The term was often used by Republicans to label all Democratic opponents of the Lincoln administration.

**copper pyrites:** see CHALCOPYRITE.

**Coppola, Francis Ford,** 1939–, American film director, writer, and producer. Among his films are *The Godfather,* in two parts (1972, 1974; Academy Awards), a study of an Italian–American crime family; *The Conversation* (1974), and *Apocalypse Now* (1979).

**copra:** see COCONUT.

**Copt,** member of the native Christian minority (5%–10%) of Egypt that has resisted conversion to ISLAM. Most Copts belong to the Coptic Church, an autonomous sect that adheres to MONOPHYSITISM. The Coptic language, now extinct, was the Egyptian language spoken in early Christian times.

**Coptic art,** Christian art in the upper Nile Valley of EGYPT. Reaching its mature phase in the late 5th and 6th cent., Coptic art was influenced by Islamic art after the Arab conquest of Egypt between 640 and 642. It shows a high degree of stylization verging on abstraction. The themes represent both Roman and Christian sources with flattened-out forms and decorative motifs. Remains of wall paintings reveal Old and New Testament scenes and images of the Madonna and Child. Representative examples of Coptic art are found in sculpture, ivory, textiles, and ILLUMINATION.

The Little Mermaid statue, **Copenhagen**

Ferrara, he took up (1512) his duties as canon of a cathedral in Frauenberg, East Prussia. Copernicus laid the foundation for modern astronomy with his heliocentric theory of planetary motion (see COPERNICAN SYSTEM). This theory, first presented (1512 or earlier) in a short form in his unpublished manuscript 'Commentariolus', was probably completed by 1530 and was published in his immortal work *De revolutionibus orbium coelestium* (1543).

**Copland, Aaron,** 1900–, American composer. The American character of his music is apparent in his use of JAZZ and folk elements, as in the ballets, *Billy the Kid* (1938), *Rodeo* (1942), and *Appalachian Spring* (1944), and in some music for films, e.g., *Of Mice and Men* (1939). His major orchestral works are *El Salón México* (1936) and the Third Symphony (1946). Other works include *12 Poems of Emily Dickinson* (1950) and a tone poem (see SYMPHONIC POEM), *Inscape* (1967). Copland has lectured and written widely on music.

**Copley, John Singleton,** 1738–1815, American painter. Considered the greatest early American portraitist, he painted in Boston, New York City, and Philadelphia, producing many brilliant portraits. In 1774 he settled in London, where he spent the rest of his life, enjoying many honours. In England his style gained in subtlety and polish but lost most of the vigour and individuality of his early work. His modern reputation rests on his early American portraits, which are treasured for their pictorial qualities and as powerful records of their time and place. Among his outstanding portraits are those of Paul Revere, Samuel Adams (both: Mus. Fine Arts, Boston), and Daniel Hubbard (Art Institute, Chicago).

**copper** (Cu), metallic element, known to humans since the BRONZE AGE. The reddish, malleable, ductile metal is a good conductor of heat and electricity. It has low chemical reactivity. In moist air it forms a patina, a protective, greenish surface film. The chief commercial uses are in electrical apparatus and wire, roofing, utensils, coins, metalwork,

Coptic art: Fresco from Gondar, Ethiopia (Abyssinia)

**copyright,** statutory right of the creator to exclusive control of an original literary or artistic production. Copyright laws first appeared in the 15th cent., when PRINTING began in Europe. The earliest British statute was passed in 1709. The copyright holder may reproduce the work or may license others to do so and receives payments for each performance or copy. Copyright is indicated in books by the symbol © followed by the name of the copyright holder and the date of publication. In the UK copyright protection is for the author's lifetime plus 50 years. Unlike a PATENT, copyright arises automatically and does not need to be applied for. Titles cannot be copyright but where a title can be identified with a particular writer/work then the original author may obtain an injunction and/or damages. Ideas or plot lines cannot be copyright. Although it is usually asserted that no part of a publication may be reproduced in any form without permission from the copyright-holder, it is legitimate to quote from copyright work for the purposes of 'criticism or review' provided 'sufficient acknowledgment' is given. The first international agreement on copyright was the Berne Convention (1886), with mainly European signatories. In 1952 the Universal Copyright Convention stated that each country would give authors of other member countries the same rights as its own; most countries are now signatories. In spite of these international agreements 'piracy' (as infringement of copyright is known) is carried out on an ever-increasing scale, both in the way of business and by individuals making illegal use of such devices as photocopiers, cassette-recorders, and video recorders.

**copyright library,** a library in the UK designated to receive copies of British published works. The system of copyright libraries dates from an informal arrangement in 1610 between the diplomat and scholar Sir Thomas BODLEY, founder of the Bodleian Library in Oxford, and the Stationers Company. An Act of 1662 stipulated that three libraries (the Royal Library and those at the universities in Oxford and Cambridge) should receive copies of all new works. In 1710 the number was increased to 9 as a result of the Act of Union with Scotland; the Act of Union with Ireland brought the number to 11; and the Imperial Copyright Act 1911 included the National Library of Wales. The law now requires that one copy of every new book published in the UK must be deposited at the British Museum within 12 months of publication, and if written request is made to the publisher then four copies must be sent to the agency named on behalf of the Bodleian Library, Oxford; the University Library, Cambridge; the National Library of Scotland; and Trinity College, Dublin. A further copy may be demanded for the National Library of Wales.

**Coquelin, Benoît Constant** (kok‚lanh), 1841–1909, French actor. A member of the COMÉDIE FRANÇAISE, he achieved his greatest success in the title role of ROSTAND's *Cyrano de Bergerac*.

**coral,** small, sedentary marine animal of the class Anthozoa, having a horny or calcareous skeleton, also called coral. Most corals form colonies by budding, but solitary corals also exist. In both, the individual animal (polyp) secretes a cup-shaped skeleton around itself; in colonial corals, the skeleton and a thin sheet of living tissue are attached to other individuals. They feed like the related SEA ANEMONE. As a colonial coral produces more polyps, the lower members die, and new layers are built up on the old skeletons, forming CORAL REEFS. The greatest structure made by living things is made by corals, not humans. It is the 2000-km (1250-mi) long Great Barrier Reef in Australia. A precious red Mediterranean coral is used for jewellery.

**coral reef,** limestone formation produced by living animals, found in shallow, tropical marine waters. In most, the predominant animals are stony CORALS, which secrete skeletons of calcium carbonate (limestone) that build up into a massive formation. Coral reefs are formed only in the tropics where the water is warmer than 22°C (72°F). Coral reefs are classified as fringing reefs (platforms continuous with the shore), barrier reefs (separated from the shore by a wide, deep lagoon), or atolls (surrounding a lagoon). Reefs formed by other organisms are also called coral reefs.

**Coral Sea,** southwest arm of the Pacific Ocean, between NE Australia, New Guinea and Vanuatu (formerly the New Hebrides). It was the scene of a US victory (1942) that checked the southward expansion of Japanese forces in WORLD WAR II.

**Coral Sea Islands,** external territory of Australia, comprising scattered small islands and reefs spread over 780,000 km² (c. 300,000 sq mi) of the South Pacific Ocean, E of the GREAT BARRIER REEF, off NE Australia. The islands, uninhabited except for a three-man meteorological station on Willis Island, became a territory in 1969 and were declared a nature reserve in 1982.

**coral snake,** New World poisonous SNAKE of the same family as the COBRAS. The venom of coral snakes, like that of cobras, is especially potent, and the mortality rate among bitten humans is high. The Australian coral snake (*Rhychoelaps australis*) is not a true coral snake and is harmless to humans. Coral snakes are marked by alternating bands of black edged with yellow, and red; the harmless milk snake copies the coral snake's colouring, but the pattern is alternating bands of yellow edged with black, and red.

**Corday, Charlotte,** 1768–93, French assassin of Jean Paul MARAT. A sympathizer of the GIRONDISTS, she gained access to Marat, a critic of the Girondists, under false pretences and stabbed him (1793) in his bath. She was arrested and guillotined.

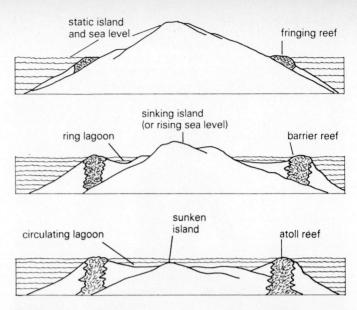

Coral reef

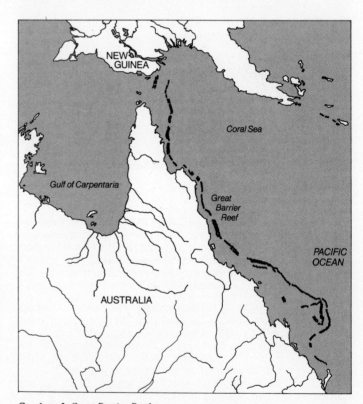

Coral reef: Great Barrier Reef

**Cordeliers,** French revolutionary club. Instrumental in the fall (1793) of the GIRONDISTS, it originally included men like Georges DANTON. Later it drifted to the extreme left under J.R. HÉBERT. It dissolved (1794) after the extremists were executed in the REIGN OF TERROR.

**cordial:** see LIQUEUR.

**Cordilleras** (Span., originally = little string), general name for the chain of mountains in W North America, from N Alaska to Nicaragua, including the ROCKY MTS, the COAST RANGES, and the SIERRA MADRE. Some geographers use the term for any extensive group of mountain systems.

**Córdoba,** city (1980 pop. 990,007), central Argentina, on the Río Primero. It is a commercial metropolis near a major dam that has transformed the surrounding area from a ranching centre to a land of grain fields, orchards, and vineyards. Settled in 1573, Córdoba was an early Argentine cultural centre with a university (est. 1613). Many colonial buildings, e.g., the former city hall, remain.

**Córdoba** or **Cordova**, city (1981 pop. 284,737), capital of Córdoba prov., S Spain, in Andalusia, on the Guadalquivir R. Its industries include brewing and metallurgy. Of Iberian origin, it flourished under Rome. As the seat (756–1031) of an emirate comprising most of Moorish Spain, it was a centre of Muslim and Jewish culture and was renowned for its wealth, crafts, and architecture, e.g., the great mosque (begun 8th cent. and now a cathedral). Córdoba passed to Seville in 1078 and to Castile in 1236.

**Corelli, Arcangelo,** 1653–1713, Italian composer and violinist. He was a noted virtuoso whose technique was perpetuated by his students and in his SONATAS. He also helped to establish the typical form of the CONCERTO grosso.

**Corfu.** see KÉRKIRA.

**Cori, Carl Ferdinand,** 1896–1984, and **Gerta Theresa,** 1896–1957, American medical biochemists. They married after graduation in Prague and then emigrated to the US, where they worked together on the metabolism of carbohydrate. They were awarded the 1947 Nobel Prize for physiology or medicine with Bernardo HOUSSAY.

**coriander,** annual herb (*Coriandrum sativum*) of the CARROT family, cultivated for its fruits. The dried seed is used as a spice, and contains an aromatic oil used as a flavouring, as a medicine, and in liqueurs.

**Corinna,** fl. c.500? BC, Greek poet. Her verse, fragments of which remain, deals with mythological themes and is written in the dialect of BOEOTIA.

**Corinth** or **Kórinthos,** city (1981 pop. 22,658), S Greece, in the NE Peloponnesus, on the Gulf of Corinth. Founded after the destruction of Old Corinth by an earthquake (1858) and rebuilt after another earthquake in 1928, the modern city is a port and trading centre for olives, raisins, and wine. Ancient Corinth was one of the oldest and most powerful of the Greek CITY-STATES, dating from Homeric times. Athenian assistance to its rebellious colonies was a direct cause of the PELOPONNESIAN WAR (431–404 BC). Destroyed by the Romans in 146 BC, it was restored by Julius CAESAR in 46 BC. Later it passed to the Byzantine Crusaders, the Venetians, and the Ottoman Turks before being captured (1822) by Greek insurgents. Ruins at Old Corinth include the Temple of Apollo.

**Corinthian order:** see ORDERS OF ARCHITECTURE.

**Corinthians,** two EPISTLES of the NEW TESTAMENT. They were written to the church at CORINTH by St PAUL. First Corinthians (AD 55?) is one of the longest, most important epistles. It begins with an attack on factionalism and condemns various practices, e.g., litigation among Christians. The epistle closes with five famous passages: the institution of the Eucharist (11); the doctrine of the mystical body of Christ (12); a panegyric on Christian love (13); the functions of prophecy among Christians (14); and a chapter on Christ's resurrection (15). The shorter Second Corinthians focuses on Paul's apostleship, authority, and motives, closing with a defence of his mission. See also SACRAMENT.

**Coriolanus** (Gnaeus Marcius Coriolanus), Roman patrician, fl. 5th cent. BC. According to legend he was expelled from Rome because he demanded the abolition of the people's tribunate in return for distributing state grain to the starving plebeians. He led (491? BC) the Volscians against Rome. Only the tears of his wife and his mother caused him to spare the city. The angry Volscians killed him. His tragedy is told by SHAKESPEARE, and inspired an overture by BEETHOVEN.

**Coriolis effect** (after Gaspard Coriolis), tendency for any moving body on or above the earth's surface to drift sideways from its course because of the earth's rotational direction (west to east) and speed, which is greater for a surface point near the equator than toward the poles. In the Northern Hemisphere the drift is to the right of the motion; in the Southern Hemisphere, to the left. In most human-operated vehicles, continuous course adjustments mask the Coriolis effect. The Coriolis effect must be considered, however, when plotting ocean currents and wind patterns (see CYCLONE) as well as trajectories of free-moving projectiles through air or water.

**Cork,** county in SW of Republic of Ireland (1986 pop. 412,623), 7385 km² (2880 sq mi), bordering on the Atlantic Ocean in the S. It is the largest county in Ireland, and is situated in the province of Munster. The

The Temple of Apollo at Old **Corinth**

county town is CORK. Much of it is hilly or mountainous, including the Derrynasaggart Mts, the Boggeragh Mts, and the Nagles Mts which are all in the N. The coastline is deeply indented with bays and estuaries. The county is crossed from W to E by the rivers Blackwater, Lee, and Bandon, in whose fertile valleys agriculture is concentrated. Potatoes are cultivated and dairy farming is common. There used to be an important port and oil terminal at Bantry Bay, but this was closed in the early 1980s.

**Cork,** city (1986 pop. 133,196), county town of Co. Cork, S Republic of Ireland, on the Lee R. at Cork Harbour. The second largest city in the nation, it has such industries as vehicle manufacturing and whisky distilling. Its exports are largely agricultural. Probably founded in the 7th cent., Cork was occupied by the Danes (9th cent.) and passed to English control in 1172. It was prominent in the nationalist disturbances of 1920. University College is located there.

**cork,** protective, waterproof outer covering of the stems and roots of all woody plants, produced by the cork CAMBIUM. Cork cells have regularly arranged walls impregnated with a waxy material, called suberin, that is resistant to water and gas. Cork is buoyant, resilient, light, and chemically inert; it is used for bottle stoppers and insulating materials, and in many household and industrial items. The cork OAK (*Quercus suber*), which has a thick cork layer, is the source of commercial cork.

**Corman, Roger,** 1926–, American film producer and director. Famous for producing fast, cheap genre pictures since the late 1950s, his films are all distinctive. As a producer, he has nurtured many young directors who have later become famous. His films include *The Mask of the Red Death* (as director) (1964), *Targets* (as producer) (1968), and *Piranha* (as producer) (1978).

**cormorant** or **shag,** mainly sea BIRDS of the family Phalacrocoridae. The two names are used indiscriminately except in the British Isles, where *Phalacrocorax carbo* is the cormorant and *P. aristotelis* the shag. *P. carbo* ranges from Greenland, across Europe, Asia, and Africa to Australia. Fish-eaters, they dive for food from the surface. The Galapagos cormorant (*Nannopteris harrisi*) cannot fly. Cormorants are important guano producers, and have been trained to catch fish for humans in China and Japan.

**corn,** in botany, name given to the leading cereal crop of any major region. In England, corn means WHEAT; in Scotland and Ireland, oats. In America, corn is the grain called maize, or Indian corn (*Zea mays*).

**Cornaro, Caterina,** 1454–1510, queen of Cyprus. A noted Venetian beauty, she married James II of Cyprus and ruled (1474–89) after his death. Venice recalled her and took Cyprus. Her portrait by TITIAN is in the Uffizi, Florence.

**Corneille, Pierre** (kaw͵nay), 1606–84, French dramatist, a master of classical TRAGEDY. His masterpiece, *Le Cid* (1637), based on a Spanish play (see CID), took Paris by storm. Among the finest of his other tragedies are *Horace* (1640), *Cinna* (1640), and *Polyeucte* (1643). The comedy *Le*

Cork trees and bark, Portugal

*menteur* (1643; tr. The Liar) also had great success. A master of the grand style, Corneille exalted the will, celebrating the subordination of passion to duty. His old age was embittered by the rise of RACINE, who replaced him in popular favour.

**cornel:** see DOGWOOD.

**cornet,** a BRASS INSTRUMENT similar to the trumpet but with a conical bore. It has a range of about two and a half octaves upwards from the E below middle C. It is an important solo instrument in BRASS BANDS.

**cornflower,** common herb (*Centaurea cyanus*) of the COMPOSITE family. The long-stemmed, blue flower heads have radiating vase-shaped florets that yield a juice used as a dye when mixed with alum.

**Cornish,** dead language belonging to the Brythonic group of the Celtic subfamily of the Indo-European family of languages. See LANGUAGE (table).

**corn laws,** regulations imposed in the UK from the 12th cent. to regulate exports and imports of grain, finally repealed in 1846 by the government of Sir Robert PEEL. The main struggle before 1846 was that of the ANTI-CORN-LAW LEAGUE against the corn law of 1815, introduced by a parliament consisting of landowners who wanted to keep up home corn prices. Shortly afterwards, Robert PEEL was influential in the 1846 repeal of all Corn Laws.

**Cornwall and Isles of Scilly,** county in SW England (1984 est. pop. 439,000), 3564 km² (1390 sq mi), bordering on the English Channel in the S and the Atlantic in the N and W. The county town is Bodmin. Much of the county is hilly, with Bodmin Moor rising to 419 m (1375 ft). The coastline is mainly rugged and picturesque, with high cliffs interspersed with sheltered bays. Dairy farming is important as well as the production

of early vegetables and flowers. The county was famous for tin and copper mining which have now declined, but there is still some china-clay mining. LAND'S END is the most westerly point in England. Tourism is now one of the greatest sources of revenue.

**Cornwallis, Charles Cornwallis,** 1st **Marquess,** 1735–1805, British general. He led British forces in the AMERICAN REVOLUTION, and his defeat in the disastrous YORKTOWN CAMPAIGN ended the fighting. Later he was governor general of India (1786–94, 1805) and viceroy of Ireland (1798–1801).

**corollary:** see THEOREM.

**Coronado, Francisco Vásquez de** (koro,nahdhoh), c.1510–1554, Spanish explorer. In search of the Seven Cities of Cibola, he was the first to explore ARIZONA and NEW MEXICO. Though he found no gold, he acquainted the Spanish with the PUEBLO INDIANS and opened the Southwest to colonization.

**coronary heart disease,** or **ischaemic heart disease,** heart disease resulting from narrowing of the coronary arteries due to fibrous and fatty tissue deposits (atherosclerosis). This condition is the most common underlying cause of heart disease which is a major cause of death in the West. Factors contributing to coronary heart disease include HYPERTENSION, high CHOLESTEROL levels, and cigarette smoking. See ARTERIOSCLEROSIS.

**coroner,** in the UK, an officer of the CROWN, who inquires into deaths whose causes are sudden, violent, unnatural, or unknown. The coroner is a solicitor or barrister of at least five years' standing, who exercises his or her powers in a coroner's court, sometimes with the assistance of a JURY. Previously, coroners had the power to find a person guilty of MURDER or MANSLAUGHTER, but this was abolished in 1977. They also have minor powers relating to TREASURE TROVE. In the US and COMMONWEALTH countries, corroners exercise similar functions though in the US they are frequently elected.

**coronet,** circular head ornament of a noble of high rank, worn on state occasions. It is inferior to the CROWN. Dukes wore coronets by the 14th cent., and in the reign of Elizabeth I patterns were adopted for other peers.

**Corot, Jean-Baptiste Camille,** 1796–1875, French landscape painter. One of the most influential 19th-cent. painters, he celebrated the countryside without romanticizing farm labour or peasants. His Roman works have simplicity of form and clarity of lighting, as in the *Coliseum* and *Forum* (both: 1826, Louvre, Paris). Using sketches made directly from nature, he painted his later landscapes in shades of grey and green. His delicate lighting is seen in *La Femme à la perle* (c. 1869; Louvre, Paris) and *Interrupted Reading* (1865–70; Art Inst., Chicago).

**corporation tax,** a tax on company profits. In the UK the tax is applied to limited companies and, in some cases, to unlimited companies and certain associations. The assessment is for an accounting period which cannot exceed 12 months and usually corrresponds to the company's financial year. The rate of corporation tax declined from 52% in 1982 to 35% in 1986; it is calculated net of interest, Inland Revenue allowances, and before distribution of *dividends*.

**corporatism,** system of economic representation in which governments recognize representatives of the main occupational groups in society rather than members of a legislature elected for a given geographical area. Originally conceived in the late 19th cent. as an alternative to the extension of the franchise, corporatism was put into effect by Fascist governments (see FASCISM) in Italy (1933), Portugal (1933), Austria (1934), Spain (1939), Brazil (1937), and Argentina, under PERÓN (1943–55). The corporations set up under these governments were nominally vocational associations representing the professions, the workers, or both workers and employers, in each branch of industry. They were conceived as the most efficient possible instruments of economic control, replacing both capitalist and socialist forms, and rendering representative political institutions superfluous. These corporations had, on the whole, a short life, failing to survive the regimes which created them. They were not, in reality, historical groups advancing the interests of sections of society or the workforce, as in classical corporatist theory, but in effect administrative agencies of the state designed to keep a tight centralized grip on the workers. However, corporatist arrangements have by no means been confined to Fascist states. In the first quarter of the 20th cent. many European nations, including Germany and Britain, also set up institutions in which organized labour, big business, and the government could discuss and coordinate industrial policy, with the twin aims of improving national economic performance and avoiding industrial conflict. These institutions, existing alongside parliamentary democracy, have, to a greater or lesser extent, remained part of public life in virtually every liberal democracy; occasionally, as in Britain during the 1960s, appearing to take a leading role in policy-making in respect of the economy. This phenomenon of major interest groups in society not only bargaining directly with government but appearing to be incorporated into an extended state, is considered by some to represent a new state form, entailing a tilting of power and influence away from the political parties and parliamentary institutions. The belief that with these developments the management of capitalism was entering a new phase appears to be undermined, in Britain at least, by the fact that conservative governments in the 1980s have reverted to a neo-liberal stance on the economy, involving minimal government intervention in the market, and an abrupt end to corporatist consultation.

**Corpus Christi,** US city (1984 est. pop. 258,000), S Texas; inc. 1852. It is a petroleum and natural-gas centre, with such heavy industries as refineries, smelting plants, and chemical works. Shrimp and fish processing is important, as is tourism. The first settlers arrived in the 1760s; a trading post (est. 1839) boomed in the MEXICAN WAR. The fast-growing area has a busy port and military facilities.

**Corpus juris civilis:** see ROMAN LAW.

**Correggio** (kə‚rejoh), c.1494–1534, Italian High RENAISSANCE painter; b. Antonio Allegri, called Correggio after his birthplace. His early works, e.g., the *Marriage of St Catherine* (National Gall., Washington), were greatly influenced by the styles of MANTEGNA and LEONARDO DA VINCI. Among his many mythological scenes are the sensual *Io* (1530s; Vienna) and *Antiope* (1530s; Louvre, Paris). His most famous project, *Assumption of the Virgin* (1524–30; Parma cathedral), used daring foreshortening. His illusionistic ceiling decorations, with their sense of grace and tenderness and soft play of light and colour, were widely imitated in the 17th cent.

**Corregidor,** historic fortified island (c.5 km²/2 sq mi) at the entrance to Manila Bay, just off BATAAN, the Philippines. It was a fortress from Spanish times; its defences were greatly elaborated by the US after the SPANISH-AMERICAN WAR (1898). During WORLD WAR II the Japanese bombarded Corregidor for five months, finally forcing the surrender (May 1942) of 10,000 US and Filipino troops. The island was retaken by US forces in 1945.

**correlation,** used in STATISTICS to indicate the degree of association between two or more variables. Several coefficients have been developed for measuring the degree of correlation between variables, and the simplest of these coefficients assumes that the relationship between the variables is linear. It is important to stress that a correlation between two or more variables does not necessarily indicate causation, i.e., that one of the variables causes the others to vary in some way. Thus, although there is a strong correlation between the smoking of cigarettes and the incidence of lung cancer, that correlation does not prove that smoking actually causes lung cancer. The cause may be some factor which is associated with both cigarette smoking and the incidence of lung cancer.

**correspondence principle,** in QUANTUM THEORY, the statement that the predictions of quantum mechanics agree with those of classical mechanics in the limiting case of large (as compared with atomic) masses and dimensions.

**corset,** an undergarment worn to support or mould the figure, sometimes worn by men but mainly by women. In use by the 16th cent., they were then known as stays. Stiffened with cane, cord, or whalebone, and adjusted and fastened with lacing, they covered the body from breast to hips. Since the late 19th cent., rubberized fabrics have been used to give corsets extra strength and flexibility. In the past, their ability to constrict the figure with tight lacing has often been abused, and they have been alleged to be the cause of female ill-health. There was a brief return to tight-waisted corsetry at the introduction of the 'New Look' by the couturier Christian DIOR in 1947, but current attitudes make the general adoption of any style involving extreme body distortion unlikely. See also FASHION; UNDERWEAR.

Correggio, *Antiope*, 1530s. Louvre, Paris.

A CORRECT VIEW OF THE NEW MACHINE FOR WINDING UP THE LADIES

Corset

**Corsica,** island (1984 est. pop. 244,600), 8721 km², (3367 sq mi) a territorial collectivity of metropolitan France, in the Mediterranean Sea SE of France. The capital is Ajaccio. Much of the island is wild, mountainous, and covered with *maquis,* the flowers which have earned it the name 'the scented isle'. The island was granted by the Franks to the papacy in the late 8th cent., and Pope GREGORY VII ceded (1077) it to Pisa; it was taken over by Genoa in the 15th cent. Genoese rule was harsh and unpopular, and following a rebellion led (1755) by Pasquale PAOLI the island was ceded (1768) to France. With British support Paoli expelled the French and from 1794 to its recapture in 1796 it was controlled by the British. French possession was confirmed by the Congress of VIENNA in 1815. Blood feuds between clans and banditry have persisted into modern times. Most Corsicans speak a dialect of Italian. In recent years a serious security threat has been posed by the violent actions of pro-independence extremist groups, notably The Corsican National Liberation Front (which was banned in 1983). Electoral politics have nevertheless been dominated by parties favouring Corsica's French status and the substantial autonomy granted in 1982.

**Cort, Henry,** 1740–1800, English inventor. He revolutionized the British IRON industry with his use of grooved rollers to finish iron, replacing the process of hammering, and through his invention of the puddling process, which involved stirring the molten PIG IRON in a reverberatory furnace until the decarbonizing action of the air produced a loop of pure metal.

**Cortázar, Julio** (kaw,tahzah), 1914–84, Argentine writer; b. Belgium. An exponent of SURREALISM who often depicts life as a maze, he is known for the novels *The Winners* (1960), *Hopscotch* (1963), and *62: Modelo para armar* (1968; tr. *62: A Model Kit*), and such short-story collections as *Final del juego* (1956; tr. *End of the Game*) and *A Change of Light and Other Stories* (tr. 1980).

**Cortes,** representative assembly of SPAIN. From the 12th to the 19th cent. each region, e.g., LEÓN and CASTILE, had its own cortes. The first national Cortes met (1810) during the PENINSULAR WAR against Napoleonic rule and voted (1812) a liberal constitution revoked (1814) by the king. The Cortes was Spain's parliament (1931–39) after the fall of the monarchy but was stripped of power under Francisco FRANCO. After his death (1975) it emerged as an important element in Spanish democracy.

**Cortés, Hernán,** or **Hernando Cortez,** 1485–1547, Spanish CONQUISTADOR, conquerer of MEXICO. Under a commission of the Cuban governor, Diego de VELÁZQUEZ, Cortés sailed from Cuba in 1519 to conquer the AZTEC empire of MONTEZUMA. He founded the city of Vera Cruz, burned his ships to prevent his men from turning back, and enlisted the help of the Tlaxcalans after defeating them. Believing the Spanish to be descendants of the god QUETZALCOATL, Montezuma received them. Cortés took him hostage and ruled through him. Velázquez tried to recall Cortés, who returned to the coast and defeated a force sent to retrieve him. When he returned to the capital, Tenochtitlán, he found the Aztecs in rebellion. In a famous battle known as *noche triste* [sad night], he retreated from the city with heavy losses. He returned the next year; after a three-month siege, the city fell, and with it the empire. As Captain-General, Cortés extended his conquest to most of Mexico and N Central America. Though CHARLES V of Spain made Cortés a marqués, he refused to make him governor of Mexico. Cortés returned to Spain in 1540, where, neglected by the court, he died.

**corticosteroid,** any of a group of STEROID hormones produced by the cortex of the ADRENAL GLANDS, or a synthetic analogue. Corticosteroids occur in two groups, gluco corticoids (e.g., CORTISONE, hydrocortisone, prednisolone) and mineralocorticoids (e.g., aldosterone). The first group are widely used in hormone replacement therapy and to treat ARTHRITIS and other rheumatoid diseases, ASTHMA, allergic and inflammatory eye disorders, systemic lupus erythematosus (see AUTOIMMUNE DISEASE), and HODGKIN'S DISEASE and some other forms of cancer. Both groups are used in the treatment of ADDISON'S DISEASE. Their anti-inflammatory, anti-allergic, itch-suppressing, and vasoconstrictive properties make corticosteroids useful in relieving eczema, psoriasis, and insect bites.

**cortisone,** steroid HORMONE whose main physiological effect is on carbohydrate metabolism. It is synthesized from cholesterol in the outer layer, or cortex, of the ADRENAL GLANDS and is necessary for life. Failure of the adrenal gland to synthesize cortisone (ADDISON'S DISEASE) is fatal unless cortisone is administered. The anti-inflammatory effect of the hormone makes it useful in treating asthma and other allergic reactions, arthritis, and various skin diseases.

**Cortona, Pietro Berrettini da,** 1596–1669, Italian BAROQUE painter and architect. His most celebrated work, *Allegory of Divine Providence and Barberini Power* (1633–39), a vast ceiling fresco in the Barberini Palace, Rome, is an example of the overwhelming illusionism of the Roman High BAROQUE.

**Coruña, La** or **Corunna,** city (1981 pop. 232,356), capital of Coruña prov., Galicia, NW Spain on the Mero R. The port has passenger ferry as well as freight services, some fishing, and various light industries. A port in Roman times, it was attacked by Drake in 1598, and in 1809 was the scene of the PENINSULAR WAR battle in which Sir John Moore was fatally injured.

**corundum,** aluminium oxide mineral ($Al_2O_3$) occurring in both GEM and common varieties. The transparent gems, chief of which are RUBY and SAPPHIRE, are colourless, pink, red, blue (Oriental AQUAMARINE), green (Oriental EMERALD), yellow, and violet. Common varieties, used as ABRASIVES (e.g., emery), are blue-grey to brown. Corundum is found in North Carolina, Georgia, Montana, Burma, Sri Lanka, India, Thailand, South Africa, and Tanzania.

**corvee,** labour demanded as a form of tribute or taxation from the subjects of a political authority. Such labour is often employed in the creation or maintenance of public works, roads, buildings, etc. Most frequently found in feudal type societies (e.g., the Inca empire) and in some colonial systems.

**Corvinus, Matthias:** see MATTHIAS CORVINUS.

**Cosenza,** city (1984 pop. 106,333), Calabria, S Italy. In the Crati valley, it was the capital of the ancient Brutii. It is an administrative and market centre of interior Calabria, handling the fruit grown in the area, especially figs. A new university has re-established its historic role as a place of learning. It has a Norman castle and a 13th-cent. Gothic cathedral.

**Cosimo de' Medici:** see under MEDICI, family.

**cosmetics,** preparations applied to enhance the beauty of skin, lips, eyes, hair, and nails. Body paint has been used for ornamental and religious purposes since prehistoric times. Ancient Egyptian tombs have yielded cosmetic jars (kohl pots) and applicators. Thought to have originated in the Orient, cosmetics were used in ancient Greece; in imperial Rome, ladies required the services of slaves adept in applying them. Medieval Europe also used oils and PERFUMES brought from the East by returning Crusaders. In the Renaissance white-lead powder and vermilion were used extravagantly. From the 17th cent. cosmetic recipes abounded, often using dangerous compounds, and professional cosmetologists began to appear, a significant part of whose work was to conceal the effects of disfiguring diseases. After the French Revolution cosmetics virtually disappeared. Since 1900, however, particularly with the growth of the advertising industry, their manufacture and use have grown to huge proportions. Cosmetics are inextricably linked with sexuality, so that their use by different sexes is not the same (e.g., either sex may, in the West, dye its hair, but only women may use lipstick). This consideration has not prevented the promotion of provocative cosmetics to girls in the primary school age-group.

**cosmic rays,** high-energy particles bombarding the earth from outer space. The extraterrestrial origin of cosmic rays was determined (c.1911) by Victor Hess; they were so named by Robert MILLIKAN in 1925. Primary cosmic rays consist mainly of PROTONS; alpha particles (see ALPHA DECAY); and lesser amounts of nuclei of carbon, nitrogen, oxygen, and heavier atoms. These nuclei cause showers of secondary cosmic rays by colliding with other nuclei in the Earth's atmosphere. Some cosmic rays have energies one thousand million times greater than those that can be achieved in particle accelerators; cosmic rays of lower energy, however, predominate. The processes by which cosmic rays attain high energy are still a matter of debate.

**cosmology,** the subject dealing with the structure, the evolution, and the origin of the entire universe (cosmogony is a term occasionally used for the latter aspects). The universe used to mean the solar system (which was accounted for by first the PTOLEMAIC and then the COPERNICAN SYSTEMS) but as the range of astronomy increased the term came to refer to the totality of fixed stars which were shown by William HERSCHEL to make up our GALAXY, the Milky Way. The fixed stars occur in huge numbers, separated by enormous distances. Still later it became clear that our galaxy was only one amongst many millions of galaxies and nowadays the term universe generally means the universe of galaxies. Each of these is 10,000–100,000 light-years across and separated from is neighbours by distances of the order of a million light-years. Following pioneering findings by SLIPHER, Edwin HUBBLE and Milton HUMASON established in the

1920s that, correlated with the distance of a galaxy (as inferred by its apparent faintness), there is a RED SHIFT of the lines of its SPECTRUM, the only plausible interpretation of which is a velocity of recession, so that its velocity is proportional to its distance (HUBBLE'S LAW). This fitted in with theoretical work (started by de Sitter) that showed that such motion was not only uniquely compatible with the idea of the homogeneity of the universe (i.e., it looks the same on average from each galaxy) but is demanded by our theoretical understanding. All major theories agree both on this uniformity in space and on the universal motion of recession. The most widely studied model of the universe is the *big bang*, according to which this motion of recession began in a tremendous explosion when all the content of the universe was densely packed. The discovery in the 1960s of a universal weak background radiation, interpreted as the highly red-shifted flash of the big bang, greatly strengthened support for it and counted against its rival, the *steady-state* theory, which added unchanging character in time to the homogeneity in space. This assumption implies a process of continual creation of matter, so that in spite of the universal motion of recession the mean density of matter is constant. Though no longer favoured, in the 1950s the steady-state theory stimulated the work that accounts satisfactorily for the origin of all the elements heavier than helium (see NUCLEOGENESIS).

**Cosmos,** blanket name for a wide range of USSR scientific and military SATELLITES. By 1986 over 1700 Cosmos satellites had been launched.

**Cossa, Baldassare,** c.1370–1419, Neapolitan churchman, antipope (1410–15) as John XXIII. A cardinal, he deserted Pope GREGORY XII and supported the Council of Pisa, which was intended to end the schism (see SCHISM, GREAT) between Rome and Avignon. When the antipope Alexander V died, Cossa was elected (1410). He sought the aid of SIGISMUND and helped to elect him Holy Roman emperor, then allied himself with Louis II of Anjou against Ladislas of Naples. Pressured by Sigismund, he convened the council of Constance (1414–18) and promised to abdicate if the rival popes would do so. Then, secretly, he fled, hoping to keep his position; but he was forced to return and was deposed (1415).

**Cossacks,** peasant-soldiers in the Russian empire who held certain privileges in return for military service. They were descended from Russians and Poles, including many runaway serfs, who settled along the Dnepr and Don rivers in the 15th and 16th cent. For taking part in 17th- and 18th-cent. peasant revolts they lost much of their early autonomy and were integrated into the Russian military. Most Cossacks fought against the Red Army in the 1918–20 civil war. Their communities were collectivized (1928–33), but many of their traditions survive.

**Costa Rica,** officially Republic of Costa Rica, republic (1986 est. pop. 2,660,000), 50,700 km² (19,575 sq mi), Central America; bordered by Nicaragua (N), the Caribbean Sea (E), Panama (S), and the Pacific Ocean (W). The capital is SAN JOSÉ. The coastal areas are hot, humid, heavily forested, and sparsely populated. A massive chain of volcanic mountains, rising to over 3600 m (12,000 ft), traverses the country from NW to SE; nestled within it lies the *meseta central,* a broad plateau with a springlike climate, where most Costa Ricans live. Costa Rica is an agricultural nation, exporting coffee, sugar, meat, and bananas. In 1982 GDP was US$2593 million or US$1054 per capita. It is also one of the most politically stable of Latin American countries, with a long democratic tradition, a literacy rate of over 90%, and no army as such. The people are mainly of Spanish descent, and the language is Spanish.

*History.* Conquest of the area by Spain began in 1563, with the founding of Cartago. The early colonists were mainly small landowners. Gaining independence in 1821, Costa Rica was successively part of the Mexican Empire and of the CENTRAL AMERICAN FEDERATION (which also included GUATEMALA, HONDURAS, NICARAGUA, and EL SALVADOR), before becoming a sovereign republic in 1838. Coffee growing was initiated on the plateau in the early 1800s, and banana cultivation was introduced on the coast (by US interests) in 1874. Costa Rica's history of orderly, democratic government began in 1889, and has been interrupted only by brief periods of junta rule, in 1917–19 and in 1948–49, after a disputed election sparked a six-week civil war. Less fortunate economically, the nation has been subject to balance-of-payments squeezes, as in the early 1980s, when the cost of importing manufactured goods and oil far exceeded the income received for agricultural exports. In recent decades political power has alternated between the (social democratic) National Liberation Party (PLN) and conservative alliances. PLN candidates were

successful in both the 1982 and the 1986 presidential elections, the victor on the latter occasion being Oscar Arias Sánchez. The latter won the Nobel Peace Prize in 1987 for his efforts to resolve the Central American conflict.

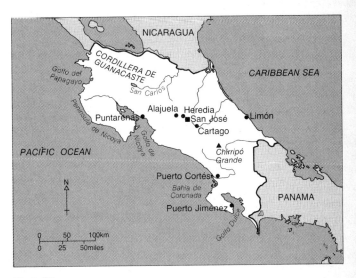

Costa Rica

**cost of living,** amount of money needed to buy the goods and services necessary to maintain a specified STANDARD OF LIVING. The figure is based on the cost of such items as food, clothing, housing, fuel, recreation, transport, and medical services. Since World War II many employers and unions have agreed to use the cost-of-living index (see INDEX NUMBER) as a basis for wage rates and subsequent adjustments. SOCIAL SECURITY payments and some PENSION plans are also pegged to the cost-of-living index. A closely watched cost-of-living measurement is the retail price index.

**costume,** the term for all dress at its most basic, or that which does not conform to FASHION in its conventional Western form. There have been many theories to explain why human beings took to wearing costume, and most are based on an alleged desire for sexual display or status, modesty (the traditional Judaeo-Christian view), or the need for protection against extremes of weather. No society has been found that does not have some form of costume: body decoration or distortion and hairstyles are involved as well as clothes and JEWELLERY, and the results are extraordinarily diverse. The earliest forms of dress were made from animal skins, but textiles had come into use by the Bronze Age. Unstructured (draped) clothes were worn by the ancient Egyptians, Greeks, and Romans (see CHITON; TOGA); structured (cut-and-sewn) clothes are thought to have originated in central Asia, as did also the separate leg covering or trouser. Clothes differ according to climate, area, religion, etc; all cultures have changes of style with time, though often the rate of change is so slow as to be invisible to the outside observer. Clothes usually convey and often emphasize status and sexual attributes (see UNIFORM; VESTMENTS). In ancient Rome and medieval Europe sumptuary laws regulated what garments, colours, or materials might be worn by persons of different rank. The slowly evolving and extremely differentiated clothes worn in some countries and communities are sometimes referred to as peasant dress; as it is not necessarily worn by agricultural workers, a more apt term is regional dress. Such clothing can usually be traced back to fashionable forms which have developed along different lines through being in comparative cultural isolation. Since it is often uncomfortable and expensive, regional dress tends to be replaced by more modern styles as opportunity offers, a process somewhat restrained by nationalist feelings; revivals are often displayed as part of the tourism industry. Specially elaborate and expensive clothes, often in a bygone style, are worn in most cultures for weddings, as is sober clothing for funerals. Colours have significance, e.g., white for mourning in many eastern cultures, purple for royalty in Europe.

**cot death:** see SUDDEN INFANT DEATH SYNDROME.

**Côte d'Ivoire,** Eng. Ivory Coast, republic (1986 est. pop. 10,000,000), 322,463 km² (124,503 sq mi), W Africa, bordered by the Gulf of Guinea

(S), Liberia and Guinea (W), Mali and Burkina Faso (N), and Ghana (E). The capital and chief port is ABIDJAN. The country consists of a coastal lowland in the south, a densely forested plateau in the interior, and high savannas in the north. Rainfall is heavy, especially along the coast. One of the most prosperous W African countries, Côte d'Ivoire has enjoyed a high economic growth rate since independence. Predominantly agricultural, the country is one of the world's largest coffee and cocoa producers. Timber from mahogany and other forests is a valuable export. Industrialization has been steady since the 1960s; flour, palm oil, petroleum, textiles, and cigarettes are produced. Oil was discovered offshore, and, although it is being developed slowly as a resource, the country was practically self-sufficient in petroleum by the mid 1980s and expects to become a major oil exporter. The GNP is US$6430 million, and the GNP per capita is US$660 (1985).

*History.* Precolonial Côte d'Ivoire was dominated by native kingdoms. Beginning in the 16th cent., the Portuguese and other Europeans engaged in a flourishing trade in slaves and ivory along the coast. The French began systematic conquest in 1870, proclaiming a protectorate in 1893. However, strong tribal resistance delayed occupation of the interior, and although Côte d'Ivoire was nominally incorporated into FRENCH WEST AFRICA in 1904, effective French control was not established until after World War I. In 1946 a mounting desire for independence led Félix HOUPHOUËT-BOIGNY to form an all-African political party. Côte d'Ivoire voted for autonomy within the FRENCH COMMUNITY in 1958 but in 1960 withdrew and declared itself independent. A one-party state, Côte d'Ivoire was headed after independence by Houphouët-Boigny, who was reelected to a fifth term as president in 1980. Côte d'Ivoire was one of the few African states to recognize Biafra during the Nigerian Civil War (1967–70); this action, as well as Houphouët-Boigny's advocacy of dialogue with white-ruled South Africa, estranged the country somewhat from other black African states. In 1985 Houphouët-Boigny was elected to a sixth five-year presidential term as sole candidate of the Democratic Party, which later that year adopted the country's French name as the only officially-recognized version.

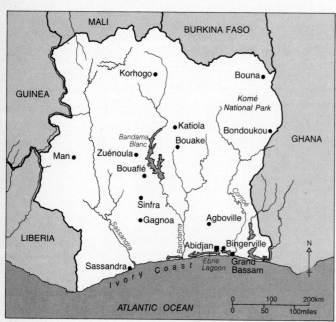

Cote d'Ivoire

**Cotman, John Sell,** 1782–1842, English watercolour artist who, after training in London, became a leading member of the Norwich School. His most famous watercolours, amongst them *The Drop Gate, Duncombe Park* and *Greta Bridge* (both: British Mus., London) were painted in Yorkshire c.1803–5 and are distinguished by their sense of abstract design. His later works include watercolours of picturesque architecture in French towns.

**Cotonou,** city (1982 est. pop. 487,020), S Benin, a seaport on the Gulf of Guinea. Although PORTONOVO is the capital, Cotonou, Benin's largest

city, is the unofficial seat of government and commercial centre. Its air, road, and rail connections also make it the country's communications hub. The seaport has been expanded to handle increased transit trade for Niger and Nigeria. Its economic activities include sawmilling, trade in agricultural produce and the manufacture of soap and vegetable oils. Offshore oil-drilling is carried on nearby. Cotonou was a small state controlled by Dahomey (later Benin) before coming under French rule (1883–1960).

**Cotswold Hills,** range of hills in SW England, extending from Edge Hill, NW of Banbury, Oxfordshire to the R. Avon valley, at Bath, Avon, and occupying much of the eastern part of Gloucestershire. The limestone hills rise to a height of 330 m (1083 ft) in Cleeve Hill. There are many picturesque villages and small towns here, built mainly of the local limestone, e.g., Bourton-on-the-Water, Stow-on-the-Wold, and Burford.

**Cottbus,** city (1984 pop. 122,886), Lower Lusatian region of Brandenburg, southern East Germany on the Spree R. As an important railway junction it is a centre of brown-coal working, electricity generation, and textile manufacture.

**cotton,** name for a shrubby plant (genus *Gossypium*) of the MALLOW family, for the fibres surrounding the seeds, and for the cloth woven from the spun fibres. Each of the seeds, which are contained in capsules, or bolls, is surrounded by white or cream-coloured downy fibres that flatten and twist naturally as they dry. Cotton is tropical in origin but is now cultivated worldwide. It has been spun, woven, and dyed since prehistoric times. Most commercial cotton in the US is from *G. hirsutum*, and the chief cultivated species in Asia are *G. arboreum* and *G. herbaceum*. Cotton is planted annually by seed. Diseases and insect pests are numerous, e.g., the boll weevil, responsible for enormous losses, particularly of the highly susceptible, silky-fibred sea-island cotton, which was the leading type of cotton before the advent of this pest. Cotton is separated from its seeds by a COTTON GIN. Manufacture of cotton into cloth, TEXTILES, and yard goods involves carding, combing, and SPINNING. Cotton is a source of CELLULOSE products, fertilizer, fuel, plastic reinforcing, pressed paper, cardboard, and cottonseed oil (used, e.g., in cooking, cosmetics, soaps, candles, detergents, oilcloth, paints, and artificial leather), which is pressed from the seeds. Used in Egypt, China, and India before the Christian era, cotton has long played a significant role in world industry. Britain's need for imported cotton dictated much of its sea-domination policy as an imperial nation, and in the US, cotton was a principal economic cause of the CIVIL WAR.

**Cotton, John,** 1584–1652, Puritan clergyman in England and Massachusetts; b. England. When vicar of St Botolph's Church, Boston, Lincolnshire, he was summoned (1632) to court for his Puritanism. Fleeing (1633) to Massachusetts Bay, he became a leading figure of the colony. Cotton was the author of some 50 works, including the historically important *The Way of Congregational Churches Cleared* (1648).

**Cotton, Sir Robert Bruce,** 1571–1631, English antiquary. His collection of books, manuscripts, coins, and antiquities became part of the BRITISH MUSEUM in 1753.

**cotton gin,** machine for separating COTTON fibres from the seeds. American inventor Eli WHITNEY invented (1793) the saw gin, which was especially suited to short- and medium-staple cotton. In a modern gin, which still uses Whitney's basic design, seeds are removed as the fibres are pulled through a grid by a series of circular saws; an air blast or suction carries the clean fibres off the saws to a condenser and, finally, to the baling apparatus.

**Coughlin, Charles Edward,** 1891–1979, Roman Catholic priest in the United States; b. Canada. While pastor of the Shrine of the Little Flower near Detroit, Michigan in the 1930s, he won a huge radio following with addresses attacking bankers for causing the GREAT DEPRESSION. In 1934 he organized the national Union for Social Justice which denounced the New Deal and advocated silver inflation and the nationalization of banks and utilities. His magazine *Social Justice* become increasingly pro-Fascist and anti-Semitic and was barred from the mails (1942) for violation of the Espionage Act.

**coulomb** (C), unit of electric CHARGE. The amount of charge transferred in 1 sec by a current of 1 AMPERE, i.e., 1 ampere-second.

**Coulomb, Charles Augustin de,** 1736–1806, French physicist. He is known for his work on electricity, magnetism, and friction, and he invented a magnetometer (instrument for measuring magnetic intensity) and a torsion balance that he employed in determining torsional elasticity (see STRENGTH OF MATERIALS) and in establishing COULOMB'S LAW. The unit of electric charge, the coulomb, is named after him.

**Coulomb's law,** physical law stating that the electrostatic force between two point charges in free space is proportional to the product of the amount of CHARGE on each body divided by the square of the distance between them. If the bodies are oppositely charged, one positive and one negative, they are attracted towards each other; if the bodies are similarly charged, both positive or both negative, they repel one another.

**council, ecumenical,** council of church authorities accepted by the church as official. Roman Catholics recognize the following ecumenical councils (listed with their starting dates): (1) 1 Nicaea, 325; (2) 1 Constantinople, 381; (3) Ephesus, 431; (4) Chalcedon, 451; (5) 2 Constantinople, 553; (6) 3 Constantinople, 680; (7) 2 Nicaea, 787; (8) 4 Constantinople, 869; (9) 1 Lateran, 1123; (10) 2 Lateran, 1139; (11) 3 Lateran, 1179; (12) 4 Lateran, 1215; (13) 1 Lyons, 1245; (14) 2 Lyons, 1274; (15) Vienne, 1311; (16) Constance, 1414; (17) Basel and Ferrara–Florence, 1431, 1438; (18) 5 Lateran, 1512; (19) Trent, 1545; (20) 1 Vatican, 1869; (21) 2 Vatican, 1962. The Orthodox Church recognizes only the first seven councils and the continuation of 3 Constantinople (the Trullan Synod), while Anglicans and most Protestants accept the first four. The purpose of the first eight councils was to determine whether specific theological concepts were orthodox or heretical. The remaining councils, all held in Western Europe, have dealt chiefly with church discipline. Two of them, 2 Lyons and Ferrara–Florence, attempted to reconcile the Eastern and Western churches. In the Great SCHISM the conciliar theory developed, which held that an ecumenical council was superior to the pope; this theory was in its heyday at the Council of Constance. The 21st ecumenical council, called by Pope JOHN XXIII, held out the reunion of all Christians as the ultimate goal (see VATICAN COUNCILS).

**Council for Mutual Economic Assistance,** (COMECON), international governmental organization for the coordination of economic policy within the Communist bloc. Founded in 1949, it adopted a formal charter in 1959 and became active in the 1960s. Its first members were Albania (which left in 1961), Bulgaria, Czechoslovakia, Hungary, Poland, Romania, and the USSR. Later adherents were East Germany (1950), Mongolia (1962), Cuba (1972), and Vietnam (1978). Yugoslavia is an associate member, and observer status is held by Afghanistan, Angola, Ethiopia, North Korea, Laos, Mozambique, Nicaragua, and South Yemen.

**Council for National Academic Awards,** British educational body (est. 1964) for granting awards to students following courses of study at institutions other than universities. It therefore 'validates' courses in COLLEGES and POLYTECHNICS, and from 1987 has 'accredited' those of its associated institutions which have developed sufficiently to validate their own courses. CNAA-related institutions have a total enrolment of over 200,000 students, and include more than half of the undergraduates in British higher education.

**Council of Europe,** international organization (est. 1949) promoting political, social, legal, and cultural cooperation between democratic European states. Members (1988) are Austria, Belgium, Cyprus, Denmark, France, West Germany, Greece, Iceland, Ireland, Italy, Liechtenstein, Luxembourg, Malta, the Netherlands, Norway, Portugal, Spain, Sweden, Switzerland, Turkey, and the UK. Located in Strasbourg, the council has a ministerial committee and a parliamentary assembly; it also encompasses the European Court of Human Rights, which rules on alleged violations of the European Convention for the Protection of Human Rights and Fundamental Freedoms, in force since 1953.

**counterfeiting:** see FORGERY.

**counterintelligence:** see INTELLIGENCE GATHERING.

**counterpoint,** in music, the art of combining melodies each of which is independent though forming part of a homogeneous texture. The academic study of counterpoint established in the 18th cent. examined five 'species' of counterpoint, or ways in which two lines of music could be interwoven: note against note; two notes against one; four notes against one; syncopation (a shifting of metrical accent in one of the lines); and florid counterpoint, which combined the other species. Early masters of contrapuntal music include PALESTRINA, LASSO, and William BYRD.

**Counter-Reformation,** 16th-cent. reform of the Roman Catholic Church, largely in response to the Protestant Reformation; sometimes called the Catholic Reformation. Since the time of St CATHERINE OF SIENA (14th cent.) there had been a growing demand in the church for reform, but it was hampered by church quarrels, notably the Great SCHISM. Consequently the church became home to many ills such as SIMONY, worldliness, and corruption among the higher clergy, ignorance in the priesthood, and general spiritual apathy. It was not until 1534, when PAUL III became pope and St IGNATIUS OF LOYOLA founded the Jesuits (see JESUS, SOCIETY OF) that major reform began. Paul summoned the Council of TRENT, which was the central feature of the Counter-Reformation; the Jesuits became the reform's crusaders. The council uprooted simony, standardized worship, reorganized church administration, set educational requirements for priests, and scrutinized the morals of the clergy. A new spirit entered the church, as seen in the work of Saints Charles Borromeo, TERESA of Ávila, and VINCENT DE PAUL, and Catholicism reclaimed its initiative in Europe.

**countertenor:** see VOICE.

**country and western music,** American popular form originating in the SE (country) and in the W and SW (western), coalescing in the 1920s when recorded material became widely available. It is directly descended from the folk music of the English, Scottish, and Irish settlers of the SE US. Country music tends toward simpler forms, western toward a band style verging on swing. The music, depicting the life experience of poor rural (and recently urban) whites, has gained a national audience, largely through the 'Grand Old Opry' radio broadcasts from Nashville. Although black GOSPEL MUSIC and blues have been influential, performers and audiences are almost all white. Noted performers include Hank Williams, Merle Haggard, Johnny Cash, and Loretta Lynn.

**country house,** the most distinctive type of English dwelling in the 'age of elegance'. The country house, which came after the CASTLE as a place of residence, developed from the later castles and especially the fortified manor houses which followed them and which were partly defensive. Other influences were the uniquely English 'prodigy houses' of Elizabethan times and the French châteaus of the 16th century. The mature country house was the product of the 18th and 19th cent. It included courts of service buildings, lodges, and other facilities in a surrounding park. The first complete country houses were the BAROQUE buildings of VANBRUGH and HAWKSMOOR, e.g., Castle Howard (1701). The most typical houses however were in Palladian style, e.g. Holkham (Kent 1734) (see PALLADIO) and the original neoclassic style of the ADAM brothers, e.g., Kedleston (1765–70). The romantic movement heralded the revival of the Gothic style (see GOTHIC ARCHITECTURE AND ART). Country houses became even bigger and grander in the Victorian and Edwardian periods, e.g., Bear Wood (1874), their golden age ending only with World War I.

**county court:** see COURT SYSTEM IN ENGLAND AND WALES.

**Couperin, François** (koohpə,ranh), 1668–1733, French harpsichordist and composer and the most famous of a family of musicians. His graceful, delicate music represents the apex of French rococo, the reaction against BAROQUE style. He published four books of harpsichord SUITES (1713–30) and also composed much ORGAN music.

**Courbet, Gustave** (kooə,bay), 1819–77, French painter. Courbet was the foremost Realist painter (see REALISM) who, always at odds with aesthetic and political authority, audaciously chose politically disturbing subjects from everyday life which he presented with all the grandeur of history painting; the most famous are the *Stonebreakers* (1849; destroyed) and *Funeral at Ornans* (1850; Musée d'Orsay, Paris). Later he painted the self-congratulatory allegory, the *Painter's Studio* (1855; Musée d'Orsay, Paris). He also painted seascapes, landscapes, hunting scenes, nudes, and still-lifes; his work is vigorous and solidly constructed.

**coureurs de bois,** unlicensed traders during the French regime in Canada who stimulated the fur trade and exploration of the country.

**Courrèges, André,** 1923–, French FASHION designer. Two of his designs made enormous impacts in the 1960s: in 1964 he was the first to show a miniskirt (it was in a formal geometric design, and worn with peep-toe white calf-length boots), and later the same year he showed a trouser-suit for women.

**courtly love,** aristocratic philosophy of love that flourished in France and England during the Middle Ages, probably derived from OVID's works, various Oriental ideas, and TROUBADOR songs. The code required a man to fall in love with a married woman of equal or higher rank, and, before consummating this love, to commit daring exploits proving his devotion; the lovers then pledged themselves to secrecy and fidelity. In reality, the code was little more than rules governing adultery. More important as a literary convention, it appears in the works of CHRÉTIEN DE TROYES and CHAUCER. See also CHIVALRY.

**court-martial,** a court established for the purpose of trying members of the armed forces accused of offences under either the CRIMINAL LAW, or the force's disciplinary code. In the UK, the accused can be assisted by a civilian lawyer or an officer. A judge will advise the court on procedure and law. Trial by court-martial constitutes an exception to the DOUBLE JEOPARDY rule, as the accused can later be tried for the same offence in the ordinary courts.

**courts of love:** see CHIVALRY; COURTLY LOVE.

**court system in England and Wales,** the judicial branch of government, which applies and interprets the law. The court system is divided between civil and criminal cases, though many courts hear both types of cases (see Table). The system is hierarchical, and decisions are made on the basis of PRECEDENT. In civil cases, the lowest court is the County Court, though Magistrates' Courts (see MAGISTRATE) will deal with some civil disputes. County Courts, consisting of circuit judges and part-time judges known as recorders, have jurisdiction to hear a wide range of civil disputes, including CONTRACT, TORT, ADOPTION, and LANDLORD AND TENANT cases. An APPEAL from the County Court will go to the High Court, which was established in 1873 incorporating the former courts of COMMON LAW and EQUITY. The High Court comprises 80 judges and consists of three divisions: the Chancery Division, dealing with PROPERTY and TRUST disputes; the Family Division, dealing with DIVORCE and WARD proceedings; and the Queen's (or King's) Bench Division, presided over by the LORD CHIEF JUSTICE, dealing largely with JUDICIAL REVIEW. Any of the three divisions may, in certain cases, sit with two or three judges as the Divisional Court. An appeal from the High Court will go to the civil division of the Court of Appeal (est. 1873) and from there to the House of Lords (see LAW LORDS). Appeal to the House of Lords usually requires the leave (permission) of the Court of Appeal. A number of specialist civil courts also exist, including the Small Claims Court (a branch of the County Court dealing informally with low-value DEBT enforcement), the BANKRUPTCY Court (dealing with bankruptcy only in London), and the Restrictive Practices Court. TRIBUNALS also deal mostly with civil disputes. The lowest court for criminal cases is the Magistrates' court, which hears committal proceedings for indictable offences, and hears summary offences in full (see CRIMINAL LAW). A branch of this court is the JUVENILE COURT (est. 1908), which hears both criminal and civil cases involving persons under 17 and has to take account of both the protection of the community and the welfare of the child. Appeal from the Magistrates' Court, for either sentence or conviction, will go to the Crown Court,

established in 1971 replacing the Court of Quarter Sessions. The Crown Courts sit in six circuits and consist of High Court judges, circuit judges, and recorders. Sitting with a judge and JURY they have conclusive jurisdiction to hear criminal cases on INDICTMENT. The Crown Court for Greater London is popularly known as the 'Old Bailey'. If convicted, the defendant may appeal to the criminal division of the court of Appeal (est. 1966, replacing the Court of Criminal Appeal) on a matter of law, and then to the House of Lords. If an issue of law of the EUROPEAN COMMUNITY arises in any court, the court may refer the matter to the Court of Justice of the European Community for a ruling, which will then be applied by the English or Welsh court. See also SCOTLAND, LEGAL SYSTEM IN.

**court system in the United States,** the judicial branch of government, which applies and interprets the law. It is divided into separate federal and state systems. The federal court system consists of three levels. At the lowest level there are district courts, which have original jurisdiction in most cases involving federal law. There are 91 districts, with at least one in each state. The court of appeals system (est. 1891), on the second level, consists of 11 judicial circuits, which hear appeals from district courts and also deal with cases involving federal regulatory agencies. The US SUPREME COURT is the ultimate arbiter of the law of the land. While individual state court systems vary, they are also built on a hierarchical principle. At the lowest level are the inferior courts, which may include magistrate, municipal, traffic, and other courts that deal with petty civil and criminal cases. Superior courts, in which JURY trials are common, handle more serious cases. The highest state court, variously called the appellate court, court of appeals, or supreme court, hears appeals from the lower courts. There are also special state courts, such as juvenile, divorce, probate, and small claims courts.

**cousin,** a person descended from the same grandparent as oneself, an important relationship in anthropological study. A *cross cousin* is the child of the individual's mother's brother, or father's sister (a relationship that is frequently the prescribed marriage pattern in elementary systems); a *parallel cousin* is linked to the individual's parents by same-sex ties, i.e., he is the father's brother's or mother's sister's child. See KINSHIP TERMINOLOGY.

**Cousin, Victor** (kooh‚zanh), 1792–1867, French educational leader and philosopher, founder of eclecticism. Becoming (1840) minister of public instruction, he reorganized and centralized the French primary system and established philosophical freedom in the universities. As an eclectic he combined the psychological insights of the French philosopher Maine de Biran, the common sense philosophy of the Scottish school, and the idealism of HEGEL and SCHELLING. His works include a history of philosophy (8 vol., 1815–29) and a translation of Plato.

**Cousteau, Jacques-Yves,** 1910–, French oceanographer and inventor. In 1943, with Emil Gagnan, he invented the self-contained underwater breathing apparatus (scuba). He founded (1945) the French navy's undersea research group, and since 1951 he has gone on annual oceanographic expeditions and produced many books and documentary films.

**couvade,** custom observed in some societies in which a father acts out the labour and childbirth that are actually being experienced by his wife. This may include retiring to bed, observing TABOOS, and/or appearing to feel pain. Couvade has been known since antiquity and practised, in such places as Europe and South America, into the 20th cent. It may have begun as a way of asserting paternity or as an attempt, through MAGIC, to draw the attention of evil spirits away from the mother and child.

**covenant,** in the Bible and theology, a voluntary agreement of God with mankind; in law, a contract under seal or an agreement by deed; in Scottish history, a pact by opponents of episcopacy (see COVENANTERS). The Old Testament tells of several covenants between God and Israel, e.g., that culminating in the delivery of the Law of Moses. In English common law, covenants follow the same rules as other contracts; variously classified, all contain an explicit promise by the covenanter to the covenantee.

**Covenanters,** in Scottish history, groups of Presbyterians bound by oath to sustain one another in the defence of their religion. The first formal Covenant was signed in 1557, by Protestants trying to seize control of Scotland, and was later renewed at times of crisis, especially in the 17th cent. The Covenanters particularly opposed the imposition of the

| COURT SYSTEM IN ENGLAND AND WALES | |
|---|---|
| CIVIL | CRIMINAL |
| House of Lords | House of Lords |
| Court of Appeal (Civil Division) | Court of Appeal (Criminal Division) |
| High Court (Divisional Court) *Chancery Family Queen's Bench* | |
| County Court | Crown Court |
| | Magistrates' Court (Juvenile Court) |

episcopate in Scotland and the use of the English Book of Common Prayer. After the GLORIOUS REVOLUTION (1688), the Presbyterian Church became the official church in Scotland.

**Covent Garden,** area in London known as the former site of the city's principal produce market and home of the Royal Opera. The market was established (1671) on the site of a convent garden. In 1974 it was removed to Nine Elms, on the River Thames. The Royal Opera was erected on the site of the Theatre Royal built (1732) by John Rich; it was rebuilt after fires in 1808 and 1856. The Royal Ballet began performances there in 1946. The area has recently become a fashionable shopping area, with the redevelopment of the former market site.

Covent Garden

**Coventry,** city (1981 pop. 318,718), West Midlands, central England. It is an industrial centre noted for the production of motor vehicles and aeroplanes. The city grew around a Benedictine abbey founded by Lady GODIVA and her husband in 1043. During WORLD WAR II a massive air raid (1940) destroyed the city's centre and its 14th-cent. cathedral. A new cathedral (by Sir Basil SPENCE) was built alongside the ruins in 1962.

**cover crop,** green temporary crop grown to prevent or reduce EROSION and to build up the soil's nitrogen and general organic content. GRAINS, LEGUMES (e.g., CLOVER), and some vegetables are used. Cover crops often are the first means used to rehabilitate neglected or misused land.

**cow:** see CATTLE; DAIRYING.

**Coward, Sir Noel,** 1899–1973, English playwright, actor, composer, director, and producer, known for his wit and sophistication. His works include comedies, e.g., *Hay Fever* (1925), *Private Lives* (1930), and *Blithe Spirit* (1941); musicals, e.g., *Bitter Sweet* (1929); films, e.g., *In Which We Serve* (1942) and *Brief Encounter* (1946); and many popular songs.

**Cowley, Abraham,** 1618–67, English METAPHYSICAL POET. In the scriptural epic *Davideis* (1656) he developed the use of the couplet as a vehicle for narrative verse. Among his principal works are the love cycle *The Mistress* (1647), influenced by DONNE; *Poems* (1656), including Pindaric odes and elegies; and *Verses on Several Occasions* (1663).

**Cowper, William** (ˌkoohpə ˌkowpə), 1731–1800, English poet. Always melancholic and convinced that he was a lost soul, and at times insane, he led a quiet life in Bedfordshire with a parson's family who adopted him. His poems included lyrics and hymns, the ballad 'John Gilpin', a translation of Homer, and a long poem, *The Task*, which foreshadowed 19th-cent. ROMANTICISM in its descriptions of country life. He was a playful and moving letter-writer.

**Cowper, William Cowper,** 1st **Earl** (ˌkoohpə), 1664–1723, British barrister and jurist. Called to the bar in 1688, he practised successfully as a barrister. He was a leading negotiator in the union of England and Scotland in 1707, and then became first LORD CHANCELLOR of Great Britain (1707–10, 1714–18). As a judge his decisions tended to be conservative, though he was thought of as fair and honourable. He was a major contributor to the modern system of EQUITY.

**Cox, David,** 1783–1859, English landscape watercolourist. He painted in Europe, but is most closely associated with North Wales; his broadly painted views evoke the bleak grandeur of a rainswept Welsh landscape. After 1840 Cox painted in oils, e.g., *Rhyl Sands* (1854–55; Birmingham City Art Gall.).

**Coxey, Jacob Sechler,** 1854–1951, American social reformer. After the panic of 1893 he gained fame by leading **Coxey's Army,** a band of jobless men who marched across the country from Ohio to Washington, DC, to demonstrate for measures to relieve unemployment. On its arrival (May 1894), the 'army' numbered only 500 instead of the threatened 100,000, and it disbanded anticlimactically when its leaders were arrested for walking on the Capitol lawn.

**coyote** or **prairie wolf,** small, swift WOLF (*Canis latrans*) found in deserts, prairies, open woodlands, and brush country. Resembling a medium-sized dog with a pointed face, thick fur, and a black-tipped, bushy tail, the coyote is common in the central and W US and ranges from Alaska to Central America and the Great Lakes; it is occasionally seen in New England. Considered dangerous to livestock, coyotes are killed each year by the thousands.

**Cozens, Alexander,** c.1717–86, English draftsman; b. Russia. A landscape painter and drawing master, Cozens explained his system of making accidental 'blot' drawings to suggest subjects in *A New Method of Assisting the Invention in Drawing Original Compositions of Landscape* (c.1785). His son, **John Robert Cozens,** 1752–97, is known for poetic watercolour landscapes.

**CPU:** see COMPUTER.

**Cr,** chemical symbol of the element CHROMIUM.

**crab,** chiefly marine animal (a CRUSTACEAN) of the order Decapoda, with an enlarged cephalothorax covered by a broad, flat shell (carapace). Extending from the cephalothorax are five pairs of legs, the first pair bearing claws (pincers). Crabs have a pair of eyes on short, movable stalks and many mouthparts. They tend to move sideways, but can move in all directions. The edible crab or chancre (*Cancer pagurus*) and the spider crab (*Maia squirado*) are eaten in Europe. The giant Japanese spider crab, with a 30-cm-wide (1-ft) carapace and legs about 120 cm (4 ft) long, is the largest arthropod.

**Crab Nebula,** diffuse gaseous NEBULA surrounding an optical PULSAR in the constellation Taurus. It is the remnant of a SUPERNOVA explosion observed in 1054 and is a strong emitter of radio waves and X-rays.

Crab Nebula in Taurus photographed in red light

**crafts :** see ARTS AND CRAFTS.

**Craig, Edward Gordon,** 1872–1966, English stage designer and producer; son of Ellen TERRY. His innovative theories and designs (e.g., *Hamlet,* 1912, for the Moscow Art Theatre), which strove for the poetic and the suggestive, were an important influence on modern theatre.

**Craigie, Sir William A.,** 1867–1957, Scottish lexicographer. Generally considered the foremost lexicographer of his time, Craigie worked on the *New English Dictionary* (commonly called the *Oxford Dictionary*) from 1897 and was joint editor from 1901 to 1933. In the US he was chief editor of *A Dictionary of American English on Historical Principles* (4 vol., 1938–43).

**Craiova** (kray͵ovə), city (1983 pop. 243,117), capital of Oltenia, S Romania. Situated on the northern edge of the Walachian plain and of Roman origin, it commands routeways from the Transylvanian Alps. Brown coal is worked nearby and it has important chemical industries and manufactures tramway equipment.

**Cranach,** or **Kranach, Lucas** the Elder, 1472–1553, German painter and engraver. From 1505 Cranach was court painter to three electors of Saxony; for them he painted richly patterned portraits and mythological scenes in which the erotic effect of slender nudes is heightened by jewellery and dashing hats. He painted several fine portraits of LUTHER and executed propaganda woodcuts for him. His son and pupil **Lucas Cranach,** the Younger, 1515–86, inherited his style.

**cranberry,** low, creeping, evergreen bog plant (genus *Oxycoccus*) of the HEATH family. The tart red berries are used for sauces, jellies, pies, and beverages. The native American, or large, cranberry (*O.* or *V. macrocarpus*) is commercially cultivated. The unrelated high-bush cranberry, or cranberry tree, is in the HONEYSUCKLE family. Cranberries are often classified in the blueberry genus *Vaccinium*.

**crane,** large, wading marsh BIRD of the Northern Hemisphere and Africa, related to the RAIL family. Cranes are known for their loud, trumpeting call and graceful, high-spirited dancing. The common crane *Grus grus* is the most widespread, ranging from Scandinavia to North Africa. It is 115 cm (45 in) high. The Manchurian crane, *G. japonicus*, was almost extinct in 1924 but has been saved by rigorous protection. It is a symbol of longevity in China and Japan.

**Crane, (Harold) Hart,** 1899–1932, American poet. Although he published only two volumes, he is considered one of the most original poets of his time. His first collection, *White Buildings* (1926), was inspired by New York City. His most ambitious work, *The Bridge* (1930), is a series of long poems on the US, in which the Brooklyn Bridge serves as a mystical unifying symbol. An alcoholic and a homosexual, plagued by personal problems, Crane jumped overboard while returning from Mexico to the US and was drowned.

**Crane, Stephen,** 1871–1900, often considered the first modern American writer. He introduced REALISM into American fiction with his grim and unpopular first novel, *Maggie: A Girl of the Streets* (1893). Crane achieved fame with his next novel, *The Red Badge of Courage* (1895), a remarkable account of a young CIVIL WAR soldier. Later a war correspondent in Cuba and Greece, he also wrote superb short stories, e.g., 'The Open Boat' (1898) and 'The Monster' (1899), and poetry. Vilified because of his domestic life, Crane spent his last years in Europe.

**Cranmer, Thomas,** 1489–1556, English churchman. He came to the attention of HENRY VIII in 1529 by suggesting that the king might further his efforts to divorce KATHARINE OF ARAGÓN by collecting favourable opinions from the universities. He was made archbishop of Canterbury in 1533 and was completely subservient to Henry's will. While serving EDWARD VI, he shaped the doctrinal and liturgical transformation of the Church of England. He placed the English Bible in churches, and in 1552 he revised the BOOK OF COMMON PRAYER. Under the Roman Catholic MARY I, he was tried for treason, convicted of heresy, and burned at the stake.

**Crashaw, Richard,** 1612?–49, English METAPHYSICAL POET. The son of an ardent Puritan minister, he converted to Catholicism and lived on the Continent. His fame rests on his intense religious verse, which combines sensuality with mysticism in a manner suggestive of baroque art. *Steps to the Temple* (1646), his major volume of poems, was enlarged to include *Delights of the Muses* (1648).

**Crassus,** ancient Roman family, of the plebeian Licinian gens. **Lucius Licinius Crassus,** d. 91 BC, a noted orator and lawyer (much admired by Cicero), was consul in 95 BC. He proposed the Licinian law to banish from Rome all who had gained Roman citizenship by illegal means. This helped bring on the Social War (90–88 BC). **Marcus Licinius Crassus,** d. 53 BC, was the best-known member of the family. Charming, avaricious, and ambitious, he became the principal landowner in Rome by organizing his private fire brigade, buying burning houses cheaply, and then putting out the fire. He gained immense prestige along with POMPEY for suppressing the uprising of SPARTACUS. He and Julius CAESAR drew closer together and, with Pompey, formed the First TRIUMVIRATE (60 BC), but Crassus and Pompey did not get along. Avid for military glory, Crassus undertook a campaign against the Parthians. His army was routed at Carrhae (modern Haran) in 53 BC, and he was treacherously murdered.

**crater:** see METEORITE.

**Crawford, Joan,** 1908–77, American film actress; b. Lucille Le Sueur. For many years a major Hollywood star, she made such films as *Grand Hotel* (1932), *Mildred Pierce* (1945; Academy Award), and *Humoresque* (1946).

**Crawley,** town (1981 pop. 80,113) in W Sussex, England, 43 km (27 mi) S of London. It was designated a New Town in 1947. There is a variety of light industry within the town. GATWICK AIRPORT is located 4 km (2½ mi) to the N.

**crayfish** or **crawfish,** edible freshwater CRUSTACEAN smaller than, but structurally similar to, the LOBSTER. Crayfish are found in ponds and streams in most parts of the world except Africa. They are scavengers and grow to 7 to 10 cm (3 to 4 in) in length. Crayfish are usually brownish green; some cave-dwelling forms are colourless. In British coastal waters, the spiny lobster (*Palinurus vulgaris*) is often called a crayfish.

**Crazy Horse,** d. 1877, revered chief of the Oglala SIOUX INDIANS. Resisting encroachment of whites in the mineral-rich Black Hills of South Dakota, he repeatedly defeated US troops. He joined SITTING BULL and Gall to defeat CUSTER at Little Bighorn (1876), but finally he and 1000 starving followers had to surrender. He was stabbed to death trying to escape from prison.

**creationism,** 1 Belief in the view, set out in the BIBLE, that the origin of matter and of biological species is to be attributed to the creative act of God. 2 The doctrine that God creates a fresh soul for each human individual at his conception or birth. The latter is opposed both to Traducianism, which teaches that the soul is generated with the body, and to any doctrine of the soul's pre-existence.

**credit,** granting of goods, services, or money in return for a promise of future payment, usually accompanied by an INTEREST charge. The two basic forms of credit are business and consumer. The chief function of business credit is the transfer of capital from those who own it to those who can use it, in the expectation that the profit from its use will exceed the interest payable on the loan. Consumer credit permits the purchase of retail goods and services with little or no down payment in cash. In installment buying and selling, the consumer agrees to make payments at specific intervals in set amounts. *Credit cards* are issued by local and national retailers and by banks. Cardholders usually pay an annual fee and a monthly interest charge on the unpaid balance. The major bank cards also provide short-term personal loans. See CREDIT CARDS; DEBT.

**credit cards,** form of credit account whereby the holder of a plastic card issued by a bank or other business enterprise obtains goods or services on credit. They originated in the USA during the 1920s when they were introduced by major companies, such as hotel chains, to facilitate more convenient payment by their customers. In 1950 Diners Club Inc. initiated the first card which could be used at a number of outlets. The UK experienced a rapid expansion in credit-card turnover, which tripled between 1980 and 1985 to £17.5 billion. Bank credit cards are widely accepted throughout the world and competition in plastic cards on the domestic market increased as more major retail stores issued their own. Card operators benefit both from the extra business generated and from the high interest rates which they charge on unpaid balances of the monthly accounts they issue. Disadvantages of the widespread use of credit cards include their effect in increasing the MONEY SUPPLY, the ease with which they can be fraudulently used, and their tendency to increase indebtedness especially among the poor.

**Crédit Mobilier of America,** ephemeral construction company, involved in a major 19th-cent. US financial scandal. Stockholders of the Union Pacific Railroad set up (1867) the Crédit Mobilier and awarded themselves contracts for construction on the Union Pacific that netted profits estimated at from $7 million to $23 million. To forestall investigations or interference by Congress, they sold or assigned shares of stock to members of Congress at par, though the shares were worth twice as much. The scandal broke during the 1872 presidential campaign and resulted in a Congressional investigation that issued censures, but there were no prosecutions.

**credit union,** cooperative financial institution that makes low-interest personal loans to its members. It is usually composed of persons from the same occupational group or the same local community, such as company employees or members of labour unions and churches. Funds for lending come from members' savings deposits. The Credit Union National Association (CUNA) is an international federation of credit union leagues formed in 1934 to promote credit unions.

**creed,** summary of basic doctrines of faith. The following are some of the historically important Christian creeds. **1** The **Nicene Creed,** usually said to be a revision by the First Council of CONSTANTINOPLE (381) of a creed adopted by the First Council of NICAEA (325). **2** The **Athanasian Creed,** a 5th-cent. statement, no longer ascribed to St ATHANASIUS, on the Trinity and the Incarnation. **3** The **Apostles' Creed,** the creed used in the West at baptism, dating in its present form to c.650.

**Cree Indians:** see NORTH AMERICAN INDIANS.

**Creek Indians,** confederacy of 50 NORTH AMERICAN INDIAN towns or tribes of the Eastern Woodlands, who spoke a Muskogean language (see AMERICAN INDIAN LANGUAGES). So named for their villages on creeks or rivers, they lived a settled agricultural life, mainly in Georgia and Alabama. Certain villages were reserved for war ceremonies, others for peace celebrations. They governed themselves democratically, holding land in common and setting aside portions of individual crops for public use. They were friendly to the British in colonial times, but later white encroachment aroused their hostility. They rebelled in the Creek War of 1813–14, but were subdued by Andrew JACKSON and lost two thirds of their territory. They were eventually moved to INDIAN TERRITORY, where they became one of the FIVE CIVILIZED TRIBES. Today they live largely in Oklahoma.

**Creeley, Robert,** 1926–, American poet. His spare, elegant, lyrical poems are included in such collections as *Pieces* (1969) and *Hello* (1978), a 'journal' in verse. He has also written a novel, *The Island* (1963), and short stories.

**cremation,** disposal of a corpse by fire, widely practised in some societies, notably India and ancient Greece and Rome. The rise of Christianity ended the custom in Europe, but it revived as cities grew and cemeteries became crowded. Belief in the purifying properties of fire, a desire to light the way of the dead, and fear of the return of the dead may have been among early motivations for cremation. The practice is not sanctioned by the Roman Catholic Church or traditional Judaism.

**Crémazie, (Joseph) Octave** (krayma,zee), 1822–79, French Canadian poet, 'the father of French Canadian poetry.' His poem 'Le Vieux Soldat canadien' (1855) made him famous. His poetry is patriotic and was influenced by French ROMANTICISM.

**Cremona,** city (1984 pop. 82,169), Lombardy, N Italy, close to the Po R. It acts as market for a rich agricultural region, handling rice and cheeses. STRADIVARIUS helped to establish the city's reputation for stringed musical instruments. Modern industry is based on nearby deposits of natural gas. The 12th-cent. cathedral is Gothic in style, as is the Torrazzo campanile (111 m/364 ft) which dates from the mid 13th cent.

**creole,** a language developing from a PIDGIN which becomes the mother-tongue of a community. It expands its vocabulary and develops a more elaborate syntactic system as the needs of that community evolve.

**Crerar, Henry Duncan Graham,** 1888–1965, Canadian general. During WORLD WAR II he commanded (1941–44) with distinction a Canadian army division and then (1944–46) the 1st Canadian Corps in the Allied invasion of Europe.

**Cresta Run,** winding, steeply banked channel of ice built each year at St Moritz, Switzerland, for toboggans. The rider lies face down on the toboggan and holds on to the upper bow of the metal runners.

**Cretaceous period:** see GEOLOGICAL ERA (table).

**Crete,** island (1981 pop. 502,165), 8380 km² (3235 sq mi), SE Greece, in the E Mediterranean Sea and marking the southern limit of the Aegean Sea. It is now a popular tourist region composed mainly of small farms growing grains, olives, and oranges, and raising livestock. Crete was the site of the MINOAN CIVILIZATION, which reached its peak c.1600 BC. Invaluable archaeological finds have been made at the ruins of the palace at the ancient city of KNOSSOS. Although the island later flourished as a trading centre, it played no important political role in ancient Greece. It was conquered by the Romans (68–67 BC) and by the Ottoman Turks (1669), but a series of revolts finally forced (1898) the Turks to evacuate. The island officially joined modern Greece in 1913, as a result of the BALKAN WARS. A British military base in WORLD WAR II, it was attacked by Germany in the first and only successful all-air invasion of the war.

**cretinism:** see DWARFISM.

**Crèvecoeur, J. Hector St John,** 1735–1813, American author and agriculturist; b. France. After settling in Orange co., New York, he wrote *Letters from an American Farmer* (1782) and other agricultural articles that described US rural life of the time. He introduced the culture of the American potato into Normandy and of European crops, notably alfalfa, into the US. He returned to France in 1790.

**Crick, Francis Harry Compton,** 1916–, English scientist. He shared with Maurice WILKINS and James WATSON the 1962 Nobel Prize for physiology or medicine for their work in establishing the function and double-helix structure of DNA, the key substance in the transmission of hereditary characteristics.

**cricket,** very small to large (6–80 mm/¼–3 in), essentially nocturnal, omnivorous INSECT (order Orthoptera). They usually have long and powerful hind legs for jumping, biting mouthparts, thin body-length antennae, and hearing organs (tympana) in the front legs. Most females have a conspicuous ovipositor for egg-laying. Males produce mating 'songs' (stridulate) by rasping one of their specially modified fore wings (tegmina) across the other while closed. Best known, often by its chirping, is the house cricket (*Acheta domestica*) of N African origin that, by infesting heated buildings (e.g., bakeries), advanced across Europe during the Middle Ages or possibly earlier. From there it later spread to North and South America, South Africa, Australia and New Zealand. Today it is uncommon in buildings in Britain, but occurs on many municipal rubbish dumps. Each kind of cricket has its own distinctive songs and in many parts of southern Europe species such as the Italian cricket (*Oecanthus pellucens*), which is noted for its pleasant singing, have been kept in little cages, as pets; this practice was even more widespread in Japan. Bush crickets (Tettigonidae), or long-horned grasshoppers, are agricultural pests; the few British species are harmless but in France the large brown *Ephippiger provincialis* often does considerable damage to vines. By far the smallest crickets are the myrmecophelines which inhabit ants' nests (see INQUILINE), absent from Britain but widespread in Europe and elsewhere. An interesting form of sexual dimorphism exists in those robust and heavily armoured New Zealand crickets called wetas (*Deinacrida*) and in Australia's king crickets (*Australostoma*), the males having disproportionately large heads and formidable mandibles. The name katydid, sometimes used instead of bush cricket, is derived from the song 'Katy did Katy didn't' of the seldom-seen but often heard New England species *Pterophylla camellifolia*. See GRASSHOPPER.

**cricket,** bat-and-ball game played by two sides each of 11 players. The playing area may be of any size, but must have at or near its centre a pitch of 20.12 m (22 yd) with three wooden stumps topped by two wooden bails at either end (wickets). Each side bats and fields in turn, with the object of scoring more runs than the other side. Batsmen score runs when, defending one wicket, they strike the ball, delivered by a bowler from the other wicket, and run the length of the pitch one or more times; or when they hit the ball across the boundary of the playing area. A batsman may be dismissed in 10 different ways, of which the most common are bowled, caught, and leg before wicket. Test matches (international matches) customarily last five days. The origins of cricket are obscure; the first definite reference dates from the 16th cent. The first code of laws was drawn up in 1744. The game is played chiefly in Britain and Commonwealth or former Commonwealth countries. The countries participating in Test matches are Australia, England, India, New Zealand, Pakistan, Sri Lanka, and West Indies. The British counties having 'first-class' teams are Derbyshire, Essex, Glamorgan, Gloucestershire, Hampshire, Kent, Lancashire, Leicestershire, Middlesex, Northamptonshire, Nottinghamshire, Somerset, Surrey, Sussex, Warwickshire, Worcestershire, and Yorkshire.

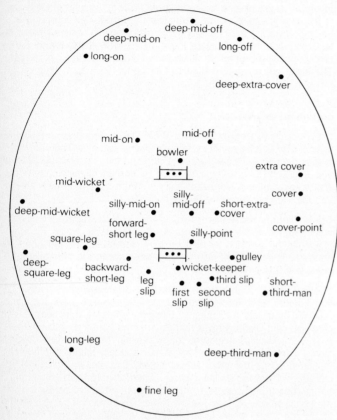

Fielding positions for **cricket**

**crime,** the recorded violation of major rules of social behaviour codified in CRIMINAL LAW. Such law varies from one culture to the next, reflecting differences in social norms. Crime, its causes, and its prevention are the subject of criminology, a subdivision of sociology that also draws on psychology, economics, and other disciplines. One of its branches is penology, which deals with PRISON management and the rehabilitation of convicted offenders. The causes of crime may include psychological predisposition, emotional disorders, environment, or other factors. Crime tends to rise during periods of economic DEPRESSION and social upheaval and is most common in poverty areas, often as juvenile delinquency; so-called white-collar crime is committed by those of higher economic status. Crimes of violence traditionally draw the heaviest penalties, whereas 'victimless crimes' (such as PROSTITUTION) are often virtually decriminalized through the failure of the authorities to prosecute. See ORGANIZED CRIME.

**Crimea,** peninsula and oblast of the Ukraine, c.25,900 km² (10,000 sq mi), SW European USSR linked with the mainland by the Perekop Isthmus and bounded by the Black Sea (S, W) and the Sea of Azov (NE). Major cities include Simferopol (capital of the oblast), SEVASTOPOL, Kerch, and Yalta. The north is a semiarid steppe that supports wheat, corn, and cotton crops; in the south rises the Crimean or Yaila range. The subtropical shore along the Black Sea, the 'Soviet Riviera', is famed for its resorts. Heavy industry in the Crimea includes ironworks and plants producing machinery and chemicals. In ancient times the peninsula was inhabited by a CIMMERIAN people called Tauri, who were expelled (8th cent. BC) by the Scythians. In the 5th cent. BC the kingdom of the Cimmerian Bosporus emerged, later coming under Greek, then Roman, influence. The area, overrun between the 3rd and 13th cent. by the Goths, Huns, Khazars, Cumans, and Mongols, became an independent TATAR khanate in the 15th cent. It was annexed by Russia in 1783. The peninsula was a battleground in the CRIMEAN WAR (1853–56), the RUSSIAN REVOLUTION, and both world wars.

**Crimean War,** 1853–56, between Russia and the allied powers of Turkey, Britain, France, and Sardinia. It arose out of what contemporaries called the EASTERN QUESTION; its pretext was a quarrel between Russia and France over guardianship of holy places in Palestine. Turkey declared war on Russia after the latter occupied Moldavia and Walachia; Britain, France, and Sardinia joined later. The fighting centred on SEVASTOPOL, the heavily fortified base of the Russian fleet. After a long, bloody siege, the city fell in 1855 and the war ended. The war, popular in Britain while it lasted, is particularly remembered for the futile Charge of the Light Brigade, and for the heroic nursing reforms of Florence NIGHTINGALE. It stimulated radical criticism of the whole machinery of government.

**Criminal Injuries Compensation Board,** a scheme established in the UK in 1964 to compensate victims of CRIME. Any person who has suffered personal injury as a direct result of a criminal offence or trying to prevent a criminal offence or trying to arrest an offender can apply to the board for compensation. The money is paid from public funds, not by the offender, and can be paid even if the crime remains undetected. If the injury is fatal, the person's dependents can apply for compensation. The board consists of qualified lawyers and holds its hearings in private; there is no APPEAL against its decisions.

**Criminal Investigation Department (CID),** originally the detective section of the London Metropolitan Police, established in 1878 and based at SCOTLAND YARD. Since its inception it has grown rapidly, now containing over 4000 staff working in various departments. Each UK police force now has its own CID. Its tasks include investigating serious CRIME, keeping criminal records and fingerprints of convicted offenders, and studying criminal methods. The Special Branch, a section of the CID, deals with offences against the state and has developed sophisticated techniques for surveilling subversive individuals or groups (see SECRET POLICE).

**criminal law,** body of law that defines offences against the state and regulates their prosecution and punishment. It is distinguished from CIVIL LAW, which is concerned with relations between private parties. In the UK, power to define CRIME rests with PARLIAMENT, though some common-law crimes still exist. Since World War II there has been an increasing trend toward codification. In England and Wales, criminal procedure differs between more serious, indictable offences, and less serious, summary offences. Indictable offences begin with committal proceedings before a MAGISTRATE who will decide whether sufficient EVIDENCE exists to send the accused for trial before judge and JURY in the Crown Court (see COURT SYSTEM IN ENGLAND AND WALES). A barrister from the Crown Prosecution Service presents the case, and a barrister represents the accused. The prosecution must prove their case beyond all reasonable doubt. Summary offences are tried before a Magistrates' Court. The same burden of proof exists, but legal representation is not guaranteed and the vast majority of defendants plead guilty. Over 90% of criminal cases are tried before a magistrate. In both situations, if the accused is found innocent, he or she is discharged; if found guilty, the judge or magistrate pronounces SENTENCE (though if the magistrate's powers are insufficient he or she may send the defendant to the Crown Court to be sentenced). If convicted, the defendant may appeal; the prosecution, however, under the prohibition against DOUBLE JEOPARDY, cannot appeal against an acquittal.

**criminology:** see CRIME.

**crinoid,** member of the class (Crinoidea) of marine invertebrate animals (ECHINODERMS) that includes the sea lilies and feather stars. Most sea lilies remain stalked and sessile for their entire lives, while feather stars break off the stalk and become mobile as adults. All crinoids live with their oral side upward with a ring of arms encircling the mouth. Most have 10 arms, but some sea lilies have up to 40 and some feather stars up to 200. Their larvae live in the PLANKTON.

**crinoline,** a fabric made from horsehair alone or in combination with other fibres, and used for stiffening. The term is derived from the Fr. *crin* [horsehair] and *lin* [thread]. In the mid 19th cent., the term was applied to the stiff petticoat which distended the large fashionable skirt. The most popular type was made from graduated hoops of spring steel, suspended from tapes attached to a belt at the waist. See UNDERWEAR.

**Cripps, Sir Stafford,** 1889–1952, British statesman. A successful lawyer, he was knighted in 1930 on becoming solicitor general in the

Labour government (1930–31). In 1939 he was expelled from the Labour Party for urging a POPULAR FRONT with the Communists. Under Winston CHURCHILL he served as ambassador to the USSR (1940–42) and lord privy seal and leader of the House of Commons (1942). In 1945 he was readmitted into the Labour Party and appointed president of the board of trade in the new Labour government. He initiated Britain's postwar austerity programme. As minister of economic affairs and chancellor of the exchequer (1947–50), he virtually controlled Britain's economy until ill health forced his resignation.

**Cristus, Petrus:** see CHRISTUS, PETRUS.

**critical mass:** see NUCLEAR ENERGY.

**critical point**, point, specified by volume, TEMPERATURE, and PRESSURE, at which it is impossible to distinguish between the gaseous and liquid phases of a substance. Above the critical temperature it is impossible to liquify a gas however high the pressure.

**Crittenden Compromise**, unsuccessful last-minute effort to avert the AMERICAN CIVIL WAR. It was proposed in Dec. 1860 by Sen. John J. Crittenden of Kentucky as a series of constitutional amendments guaranteeing federal noninterference with slavery in the states where it already existed and extending the MISSOURI COMPROMISE line to California to divide free and slave territories. It was defeated (Jan. and Mar. 1861) in Congress.

**Croatia** (kroh,aysha), Croatian *Hrvatska*, constituent republic of Yugoslavia (1981 pop. 4,601,469), 56,524 km² (21,824 sq mi), NW Yugoslavia. ZAGREB is the capital. The second largest and second most developed Yugoslav republic, Croatia supplies most of the country's petroleum, natural gas, ships and synthetics, as well as large portions of its chemicals, textiles and electronics. Banking and foreign trade are important, as is tourism, especially on the ADRIATIC coast. The population is 75% Croat, 12% Serb and 8% declared 'Yugoslav'. Formerly part of the Roman province of Pannonia, Croatia was a kingdom from the 10th cent., but entered a dynastic union with Hungary in 1102. It passed in 1572 into Habsburg hands, while remaining constitutionally subordinate to Hungary. The Turks held much of Croatia from the 16th to the 18th cent. Magyarization policies in the 19th cent. produced the Illyrian and Yugoslav movements, which looked forward to South Slav unification either inside or outside the Habsburg empire (see YUGOSLAVISM). Other Croats aspired to independence; but at the end of World War I Croatia's leaders opted to join the Kingdom of Serbs, Croats, and Slovenes, although the form of union was later rejected by many. In World War II the Axis powers set up an enlarged 'Independent State of Croatia' under the fascist USTAŠE movement. This state collapsed in 1945 when Croatia was reunited with Yugoslavia under communist auspices.

**Croce, Benedetto**, 1866–1952, Italian philosopher, historian, and literary critic. His *Aesthetic as Science of Expression and General Linguistic* (1902), the first part of his major work *Philosophy of the Spirit* (1902–17), was a landmark of modern IDEALISM. Croce was renowned for his works of literary criticism and AESTHETICS, cultural history, and historical methodology. A staunch anti-Fascist, he became a Liberal party leader in 1943.

**crochet**, construction of fabric by interlocking loops of thread or yarn using a hook. The chain stitch is used to cast on a foundation chain of the desired length, into which successive rows of stitches are worked. All stitches and patterns derive from single and double crochet. Like KNITTING, crochet produces a fabric that stretches. When a fine hook and thread are used, crochet can be used to produce a form of LACE.

**Crockett, Davy** (David Crockett), 1786–1836, American frontiersman. He was elected to the US Congress as a representative from Tennessee (1827–31, 1833–35) and died defending the ALAMO. Known for his backwoods humour, he is the supposed author of several autobiographical works, although their idiom does not match that of his own letters.

**Crockford**, abbreviated name for *Crockford's Clerical Directory*, a reference book listing the names, careers, and benefices of the clergy of the Church of England and certain other Anglican churches (now only those of Scotland and Wales). First issued in 1858 by John Crockford (d. 1865), it was originally published annually, but in recent years has appeared only at irregular intervals.

**crocodile**, carnivorous REPTILE (order Crocodilia) found in tropical and subtropical regions, distinguished from the ALLIGATOR by greater aggressiveness, a narrower snout, and a long, lower fourth tooth, which protrudes when the mouth is closed. Crocodiles have flattened bodies, short legs, and powerful jaws. The saltwater crocodile is often 4 m (14 ft) long, while the Nile, American, and Orinoco crocodiles are commonly 3.5 m (12 ft) long. They lay eggs in nests, either digging pits for them or building a mound of leaves. The female guards the nest and uncovers the hatching eggs. The young feed on insects, the older crocodiles feeding on birds and mammals.

**crocus**, perennial herb (genus *Crocus*) of the IRIS family, native to the Mediterranean and SW Asia. Crocuses usually bear a single yellow, purple, or white flower and have small, grasslike leaves. One species, (*C. sativus*) is cultivated commercially as a yellow dye (see SAFFRON). The unrelated meadow saffron, or autumn crocus, is in the LILY family.

**Croesus** (,kreesas), d. c.547 BC, last king of Lydia (560–c.547 BC), noted for his great wealth. He allied himself with Egypt and Babylonia against CYRUS THE GREAT of Persia, but he was defeated and captured.

**Crommelynck, Fernand** (krohma,lanhk), 1886–1970, Belgian dramatist who wrote in French. His tragic farce *The Magnificent Cuckold* (1921) and other plays reveal expert craftsmanship and strong lyric power.

**Crompton, Samuel**, 1753–1827, English inventor (1779) of a SPINNING machine that for the first time allowed the production of fine strong cotton yarns. Crompton's mule spinner, or muslin wheel, combined the best features of Richard ARKWRIGHT's spinning frame and James HARGREAVES's spinning jenny.

**Cromwell, Oliver**, 1599–1658, lord protector of England. A Puritan, he entered Parliament in 1628, standing firmly with the opposition to CHARLES I. During the first civil war (see ENGLISH CIVIL WAR), he rose rapidly to leadership because of his military ability and genius for organization. His own regiment, the Ironsides, distinguished itself at Marston Moor (1644). In 1645 he became second in command to Sir Thomas Fairfax in the New Model Army, which defeated the king at Naseby (1645). After Charles's flight to Carisbrooke (1647), Cromwell lost hope of dealing moderately with him. In the second civil war, he repelled the Scottish royalist invasion at Preston (1648). His was the leading voice demanding execution at the king's trial in 1649. After the republican Commonwealth was proclaimed, Cromwell led a cruelly punitive expedition into Ireland, where he initiated a policy of dispossessing the Irish. He defeated the Scottish royalists at Dunbar (1650) and CHARLES II at Worcester (1651). In 1653 Cromwell dissolved the Rump Parliament and replaced it with the Nominated (Barebones) Parliament, which he himself appointed. That same year the Protectorate was established and Cromwell was named lord protector. In 1657 he declined the crown. Cromwell's foreign policy was governed by the need to expand English trade and prevent the restoration of the Stuarts. He approved the Navigation Act of 1651, which led to the first (1652–54) of the DUTCH WARS; his war with Spain (1655–59) was over trade rights. Opinions of Cromwell have always varied. Although he favoured religious toleration, he tolerated only Jews and non-Anglican Protestants. His military genius and force of character are recognized, but the necessities of government forced him into cruelty and intolerance. His son **Richard Cromwell**, 1626–1712, succeeded him. The army and Parliament struggled for power until the Protectorate collapsed and the Commonwealth was reestablished in 1659. He lived abroad (1660–80) and later in England under an assumed name. A man of virtue and dignity, he was forced into a situation beyond his talents.

**Cronaca, Il:** see POLLAIUOLO, family.

**Cronkite, Walter**, 1916–, American journalist. From 1962 to 1981 he served as anchorman of the Columbia Broadcasting System's evening television news programme and was regarded as the most trusted newsman in the US.

**Cronus**, in Greek mythology, the youngest TITAN; son of URANUS and GAEA. He led the Titans in a revolt against Uranus and ruled the world. By his sister RHEA, he fathered the great gods ZEUS, POSEIDON, DEMETER, HERA, HADES, and HESTIA. Fated to be overthrown by one of his children, he tried unsuccessfully to destroy them. Zeus later led the OLYMPIAN gods in defeating him in a battle, described by HESIOD, called the Titanomachy. Cronus is equated with the Roman god SATURN.

**Crookes, Sir William**, 1832–1919, English chemist and physicist. Noted for his work on radioactivity, he invented the spinthariscope (used to make visible the flashes produced by bombarding a screen, coated with certain sensitive minerals, with the alpha rays of a particle of radium), the radiometer (used to measure the intensity of radiant energy), and the Crookes tube (a highly evacuated tube through which is passed an electrical discharge). He founded (1859) *Chemical News* and discovered the element THALLIUM.

**croquet**, lawn game in which players hit wooden balls with wooden mallets through a series of 6 wire arches (hoops). Developed in France in the 17th cent., the game is popular, with varying rules, in Britain and the US.

**Crosby, Bing**, 1904–77, American singer and film actor; b. Harry Lillis Crosby. His crooning voice was heard on radio and records. His many films include *Going My Way* (1944; Academy Award).

**cross**, widely used symbol found in such diverse cultures as those of ancient India, Egypt, and the American Indians. Its most important use is among Christians, to whom it recalls the crucifixion of JESUS and humanity's redemption thereby. The oldest Christian remains contain drawings of crosses. Their use was attacked by Byzantine ICONOCLASM, but was vindicated at the Second Council of NICAEA (787). There are many types of crosses. The Latin cross, the commonest, has its upright longer than its transom. With two transoms it is called a patriarchal or archiepiscopal cross; with three, it is a papal cross. The Greek cross has equal arms. A crucifix is a cross with the figure of Christ upon it.

**croup**, acute obstructive inflammation of the larynx in young children. Symptoms include difficulty in breathing and a high-pitched, barking cough due to swelling or spasm. The cause may be an infection (in the past DIPHTHERIA was a common cause), ALLERGY, or obstruction by a swallowed object. Treatment is directed at the cause.

**crow**, black BIRD (family Corvidae) related to the RAVEN, MAGPIE, JACKDAW, and JAY and among the most intelligent of birds. Known for its throaty 'caw,' the carrion crow *Corvus corone* is about 48 cm (19 in) long. As its name suggests, it is a scavenger, but is an adaptable feeder, taking plant as well as animal food. It is found in Europe and Asia.

**Crow Indians**, NORTH AMERICAN INDIANS of the Plains, who ranged the Yellowstone R. region and spoke a Siouan language (see AMERICAN INDIAN LANGUAGES). A hunting tribe, they cultivated only tobacco. Their highly complex social system stressed care of children. They helped the white men in the SIOUX wars. Today most Crows live in Montana, near the LITTLE BIGHORN, where tourism, ranching, and mineral leases provide tribal income.

**crown**, circular head ornament worn by sovereigns. (The CORONET is worn by nobles.) In ancient Greece and Rome crowns were merely wreaths, sometimes made of leaves, awarded in athletic or poetic contests, or in recognition of public service. The use of the crown as a symbol of royal rank is of ancient tradition in Egypt and the Orient. The medieval and modern crown, an elaboration of the DIADEM, is usually made of metal, often gold, inlaid with gems. Famous historic crowns include the Lombard iron crown (Monza, Italy), the crown of Charlemagne (Vienna, Austria), and the crown of St Stephen of Hungary. The triple crown of the pope, known as a tiara, dates from the 14th cent.

**Crown, the,** in the UK, term used to describe the queen (or king) as head of state; more generally used to refer to government in its widest sense. The queen as head of state has potentially wide powers under the Royal Prerogative (e.g., to dissolve PARLIAMENT). However, they are limited by convention and in practice are carried out on the advice of government ministers. In its widest sense the Crown includes the government, parliament, the head of the judiciary and the head of the armed forces. All government action in the UK is carried out in the name of the Crown. All criminal prosecutions are brought by the Crown, through the Crown Prosecution Service in England and Wales and the Lord Advocate in Scotland.

**crown court:** see COURT SYSTEM IN ENGLAND AND WALES.

**Crown–Derby** collectors' term for Derby porcelain. It derives from the crowned D mark adopted by the factory in the mid 1770s, and which after c.1782 incorporated crossed batons and six dots between the crown and D. It should only be applied to pieces produced between 1786 and 1811, but is often used to describe porcelain in the style of that period, made in Derby from the closure of the original firm in 1848 to the present.

**Crown land,** land belonging to the CROWN. In Anglo-Saxon times this included the king's private estates, crown demesne (e.g., palaces), and rights in the ordinary land of the country. Following the Norman Conquest, these three were merged as the crown's estate. In the reign of George III revenue from crown lands was surrendered to Parliament in return for a sum of money, the Civil List, and this practice has continued ever since. Crown lands are vested in the sovereign but managed by the Commissioners of Crown Lands.

**Croydon**, London borough (1981 pop. 316,306), S of R. Thames. It is a large residential and commercial centre, with various light industries. The first London airport was here, until it was replaced by Northolt.

**crucifix:** see CROSS.

**crucifixion**, hanging on a cross, an ancient method of execution. It was used in the Middle East, but not by the Greeks. The Romans may have borrowed it from Carthage and reserved it for slaves and despised criminals. A prisoner was either nailed or tied to the cross, and, to induce more rapid death, his legs were often broken.

**crude oil:** see PETROLEUM.

**Cruft, Charles**, 1852–1939, British originator of the internationally-famous annual Cruft's Dog Show. He joined the dog-food manufacturing firm of Spratts in 1876, and became a salesman, organizing various dog shows from 1886. The first Cruft's Dog Show was held in 1891, and became an annual event. After his death in 1939, the shows were continued by his widow, and their management was taken over by the Kennel Club of Great Britain from 1948. The award 'Best in Show' at Cruft's is regarded as the world's highest accolade in dog breeding. Even to be entered for the show, a dog must have 'qualified' by winning specified awards at other shows.

**Cruikshank, George**, 1792–1878, English caricaturist, illustrator, and etcher. The most popular caricaturist of his day, he illustrated more than 850 books and contributed to the *Meteor,* the *Scourge,* and the *Satirist.* Among his best works are illustrations for *Oliver Twist* and his woodcuts *The Drunkard's Children.*

**cruise liner,** luxurious ocean-going passenger vessel. The heyday of transatlantic ocean liners lasted from about the beginning of the 20th cent. till the 1930s. From the 1940s they were increasingly superseded by commercial airliners, which cut travel costs by half and could traverse the Atlantic in 15 hours, compared with the fastest liner, which took just over three days. In 1969 *United States*, launched in 1952 and holder of the BLUE RIBAND for the fastest crossing, with a speed of 30 knots, stopped operating. Other great ocean-going liners such as Britain's *Queen Mary* (launched 1936) and *Queen Elizabeth* (launched 1940 and later, in 1972, destroyed by fire) were decommissioned and sold off as pleasure ships or tourist attractions. Between the 1950s and mid 1980s the number of transatlantic liner passengers fell by 90%. At the same time the passenger liner has experienced a revival, through a new class of luxury vessels, such as the *Achille Lauro*, which cruise the Mediterranean and deliver tourists to winter vacation resorts. Britain's last great ocean liner, *QEII*, launched 1968, now divides its time between crossing the Atlantic and serving as a pleasure-cruise ship.

**Crusades,** wars undertaken by European Christians between the 11th and 13th cent. to recover the Holy Land from the Muslims. At the Council of Clermont (1095) Pope URBAN II exhorted Christendom to war, and the Crusaders took their name from the crosses distributed there. Religious motives dominated the Crusades at first, but worldly aims were never absent. The nobles hoped to capture land and loot; the Italian cities looked to expand trade with the Near East. The **First Crusade**, 1096–99, was led by Raymond IV, count of Toulouse, GODFREY OF BOUILLON, BOHEMOND I, and his nephew TANCRED. Their victorious campaign was crowned by the conquest of Jerusalem (1099). The establishment of the Latin Kingdom of JERUSALEM and the orders of the KNIGHTS HOSPITALLERS and the KNIGHTS TEMPLARS followed. The **Second Crusade**, 1147–49, preached by St BERNARD OF CLAIRVAUX after the Christians lost EDESSA (1144) to the TURKS, ended in dismal failure. After SALADIN captured (1187) Jerusalem for Islam, the **Third Crusade**, 1188–92, led by Emperor FREDERICK I, PHILIP II of France, and RICHARD I of England, failed to recapture the city. A three-year truce, however, gave Christians access to Jerusalem. The

**Fourth Crusade,** 1202–04, was diverted for the benefit of Venice, and the Crusaders seized Constantinople (see CONSTANTINOPLE, LATIN EMPIRE OF). In the pathetic **Children's Crusade** (1212), thousands of children set out for the Holy Land, only to be sold as slaves or to die of hunger or disease. The **Fifth Crusade,** 1217–21, was aimed at Egypt, but failed. The truce arranged with the Muslims by Emperor FREDERICK II in the **Sixth Crusade,** 1228–29, was short-lived. Three later crusades in the 13th cent. failed to reverse the Muslim gains. In 1291 the last Christian stronghold of Akko (Acre) fell.

**crustacean,** invertebrate animal (class Crustacea), an ARTHROPOD. Primarily aquatic, they have bilaterally symmetrical segmented bodies covered by a chitinous exoskeleton that is periodically shed. In most, the head and thorax are fused as a cephalothorax and protected by a shield-like carapace. The head typically has two pairs of antennae, three pairs of biting mouthparts, and usually one medial and two lateral eyes. Thoracic appendages are often modified into claws and pincers with gills at their bases. They lay eggs which hatch into larvae, passing through several stages before becoming adults. Crustaceans include SHRIMP, CRAYFISH, LOBSTERS, CRABS, and BARNACLES.

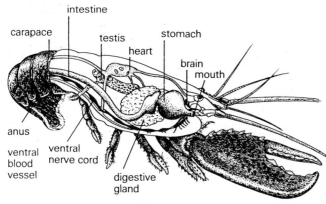

Internal anatomy of a **crustacean**

**Cruz, Juana Inés de la** (kroohth), see JUANA INÉS DE LA CRUZ.

**cryogenics:** see LOW-TEMPERATURE PHYSICS.

**cryolite,** sodium and aluminium fluoride mineral ($Na_3AlF_6$), usually pure white or colourless but sometimes tinted pink, brown, or even black and having a waxy lustre. Cryolite is used principally as a flux in the smelting of aluminium, but it is also a source of soda, aluminium salts, fluorides, and hydrofluoric acid. Discovered (1794) in Greenland, it occurs almost nowhere else.

**cryptography,** science of translating messages into ciphers or codes. The science of breaking codes and ciphers without the key is called cryptanalysis. Cryptology is the science embracing both cryptography and cryptanalysis. The beginnings of cryptography can be traced to the HIEROGLYPHICS of early Egyptian civilization (c.1900 BC). Ciphering has always been considered vital for diplomatic and military secrecy. The widespread use of computers and data transmission in commerce and finance is making cryptography very important in these fields as well. Recent successes in applying certain aspects of computer science to cryptography have stimulated progress in this area, and seem to be leading to more versatile and more secure systems in which the ciphering or coding is implemented with sophisticated digital electronics.

**crystal,** solid body often bounded by natural plane faces that are the external expression of a regular internal arrangement of constituent atoms, molecules, or ions. The particles in a crystal occupy positions with definite geometrical relationships to each other, forming a kind of scaffolding called a crystalline lattice. On the basis of its chemistry and the arrangement of its atoms, a crystal falls into one of 32 classes; these in turn are grouped into seven systems according to the relationships of their axes.

**Crystal Palace,** building designed by Sir Joseph Paxton, erected at Hyde Park, London, for the Great Exhibition in 1851. It was removed to

Sydenham and used as a museum until destroyed by fire in 1936. The iron, glass, and wood structure greatly influenced late 19th-cent. architecture.

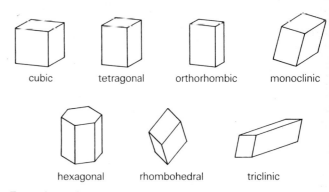

Types of **crystal**

Crystal Palace: Interior view by R. Cuff, 1851

**Cs,** chemical symbol of the element CAESIUM.

**CT Scan:** see COMPUTERIZED AXIAL TOMOGRAPHY.

**Cu,** chemical symbol of the element COPPER.

**Cuba,** officially Republic of Cuba, republic (1986 est. pop. 10,400,000), 114,524 km² (44,218 sq mi), in the Caribbean Sea, 145 km (90 mi) S of Florida. It consists of Cuba, the largest island in the WEST INDIES, and many small adjacent islands. Principal cities are HAVANA (the capital), CAMAGÜEY, SANTIAGO DE CUBA, and GUANTÁNAMO. The main island has three mountain regions, including the rugged Sierra Maestra in the east, but is predominantly level or gently rolling. The climate is subtropical. Coffee, rice, corn, citrus fruits, and an excellent tobacco are grown; nickel is mined; and there is a fishing industry. However, despite all efforts to diversify the base, Cuba's economy remains overwhelmingly dependent on the planting and processing of sugar. The people are of Spanish, African, and mixed Spanish-African descent, but mostly white or pass-as-white, and their language is Spanish. Roman Catholicism, the major religion, is tolerated by the regime, a one-party Marxist government dominated by its founder, Fidel CASTRO.

*History.* Christopher COLUMBUS discovered the island of Cuba in 1492, and Spain colonized it from 1511, using it as a base for New World exploration and as an assembly-point for its treasure fleets. Called the 'Pearl of the Antilles', Cuba prospered in the 1600s and 1700s, its population swelled by immigrants from Spain and African slave labourers. When most of Spain's American possessions became independent republics in the early 1800s, Cuba remained a colony. Slavery, a major prop of the sugar-based economy, was not abolished until 1886. A TEN YEARS WAR for independence (1868–78) was inconclusive. In 1895 a new struggle led by José MARTÍ, culminated in the SPANISH-AMERICAN WAR and separation from Spain (1898) followed by full independence (from the US) in 1903. The new nation suffered recurrent periods of dictatorship during which reformist zeal gave way to corruption and repression, notably under Gerardo MACHADO (1925–33) and his successor, Fulgencio BATISTA Y ZALDÍVAR. After a guerrilla campaign, Batista was supplanted by Fidel Castro on 1 Jan. 1959. Castro introduced agrarian reform and a highly successful literacy programme. An unsuccessful US-supported attempt by anti-Castro exiles to invade Cuba at the BAY OF PIGS in 1961 was followed by Castro's declaration of his government as Marxist-Leninist; in 1962 a US-Soviet confrontation was sparked by Soviet introdution of offensive weapons onto the island (see CUBAN MISSILE CRISIS). The US has maintained a trade embargo against Cuba provoked by Cuban alliance with the USSR and its support of revolutionary movements in Latin America and, later, in Africa. Domestically, Castro has built up the educational and health systems but has failed to develop the economy, which continues to require massive Soviet aid (Cuba being a member of the COUNCIL FOR MUTUAL ECONOMIC ASSISTANCE). A new constitution adopted in 1976 described Cuba as 'a socialist state of working people and other manual and intellectual workers', and recognized the leading role of the Communist Party. Opposition to the Castro government comes mainly from right-wing Cuban émigrés living in the US.

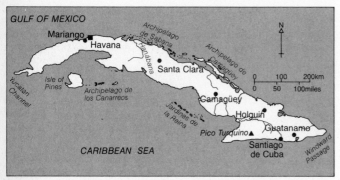

Cuba

**Cuban Missile Crisis,** 1962, major COLD WAR confrontation between the US and the Soviet Union. Following the US-sponsored BAY OF PIGS INVASION, the USSR, at the request of the Cuban government, began building launching sites in Cuba for missiles carrying nuclear warheads. After the construction was detected by US reconnaissance flights, US Pres. KENNEDY demanded (22 Oct.) the withdrawal of the missiles, and imposed a naval blockade on Cuba. The Soviets agreed (28 Oct.) to dismantle the missile sites, and the crisis ended as suddenly as it had begun.

**cubism,** art movement, primarily in painting, that originated in Paris c.1907. In intellectual revolt against the sensual, emotional art of previous eras, the cubists used an analytical system in which three-dimensional subjects were fragmented and redefined from several different points of view simultaneously. Work from this analytic phase (1907–12), as by Pablo PICASSO and Georges BRAQUE, appealed to the intellect and has been termed 'analytical cubism' because it shows objects as the mind, not the eye, perceives them. During the synthetic phase (1913 through the 1920s) works were composed of fewer and simpler forms, in brighter colours, and many artists introduced the *trompe l'oeil* effect of COLLAGE, as in the works of Juan GRIS. Other major exponents of cubism included Jean METZINGER, Marcel DUCHAMP, and Fernand LÉGER.

**cuckoo,** BIRD of the family Cuculidae. The name comes from the call of the common cuckoo (*Cuculus canorus*), living in Europe and Asia. This bird is 33 cm (13 in) long, and like the rest of the Old World subfamily is parasitic, laying its eggs in other birds' nests. The second subfamily, which extends to the New World, is not parasitic; it includes the road runner (*Geococcyx californianus*).

**cuckoo-pint:** see ARUM.

**cucumber,** herbaceous vine (*Cucumis sativus*) of the GOURD family. Its greenish, generally cylindrical fruit is eaten fresh as a salad and pickled.

**Cuenca,** city (1982 pop. 272,397), capital of Azuay prov. in the ALTIPLANO of S Ecuador. Founded in 1557 the city centre retains a strongly

Young **cuckoo** (*Cuculus canorus*) ejecting egg from nest of Tree Pipit

colonial atmosphere though a fine modern cathedral has been constructed in the main square.

**Cueva, Juan de la** (‚kwayvan), 1550?–1610?, Spanish dramatist. Of his 14 plays, the most famous is the comedy *El infamador* (1581; tr. The Scoundrel). By introducing national themes he laid the foundation for the drama of Spain's GOLDEN AGE.

**Cui, César Antonovich** (ky‚ee), 1835–1918, Russian composer and critic. He was the nationalistic champion of The FIVE. Cui's best-known works were SONGS and short salon pieces. His operas are rarely performed.

**Culbertson, Ely,** 1893–1955, American authority on contract BRIDGE; b. Romania. A champion bridge player himself, he introduced the first successful system of bidding, wrote many books and a syndicated newspaper column on the game, and edited *Bridge World* magazine. After World War II, he wrote and lectured widely on world peace.

**Culloden,** battle (1746) in Scotland in which the Jacobite army under Charles Edward STUART was defeated by the Duke of Cumberland, second son of George II.

**cult,** ritual worship of the supernatural or its symbolic representations. It is often associated with a particular deity; for example, a cult of the ancient Middle East was that of the GREAT MOTHER OF THE GODS. The term is now often used to refer to contemporary religious groups whose beliefs and practices depart from the conventional norms of society. These groups vary widely in doctrine, leadership, and ritual, but most stress direct experience of the divine and duties to the cult community. Cults tend to proliferate during periods of social unrest; most are transient and peripheral. Many of those emerging in the US since the late 1960s have been marked by renewed interest in MYSTICISM and Oriental religions. Such major US cults as the Rev. Sun Myung MOON's Unification Church and HARE KRISHNA, a movement derived from Hinduism, have stirred wide controversy. Popular hostility toward religious cults was aroused by the mass suicide in 1978 of more than 900 cultists in Jonestown, Guyana.

**Cultural Revolution,** (1966–69), mass campaign in CHINA begun by MAO ZEDONG to revitalize the nation's revolutionary fervour and renew its basic institutions. Allied with the army, revolutionary RED GUARDS recruited from the youth attacked so-called bourgeois elements in cultural circles and in the bureaucracy. Lin Biao and JIANG QING were other leaders of the movement, which resulted in widespread disorder and violence. The revolution led to the fall of LIU SHAOQI and many other Communist Party officials.

**culture,** 1. In sociology, the collection of meanings, values, morals, modes of thinking, patterns of behaviour, idioms of thought or speech, ways of life, etc., that identify a particular nation–state, group, or social category. Thus, one may speak of 'working-class' or 'middle-class culture', meaning the core set of values and norms to which the majority of the group concerned subscribes and that make them distinctive from other groups. Distinctive patterns of values, meanings or styles, within larger cultural groupings, are sometimes called 'subcultures' (e.g., deviant, criminal, or professional subcultures; postwar youth groupings, such as mods, skinheads, hippies, or punks). 2. In anthropology, the forms of speech or language, the categories and classifications, symbols, concepts, and meanings which are used in society to make sense of their world or to organize and represent experience. Forms of discourse (art, media, literature, etc.) which embody those interpretive frameworks would be included in this definition, as would economic organization and material culture (e.g., tools, musical instruments, clothing). 3. A particular level of intellectual or artistic cultivation, as in 'high culture'. Often this usage assumes that the level of culture can only be experienced by a small minority. The emergence of popular or 'mass culture', is then viewed as a fundamental threat to the values of high culture, and therefore to the values of society as a whole. Contemporary debate often divides between the three principal uses outlined above; also, as to the degree to which culture is autonomous and universal, or historically-specific and determined by other factors (class, education, ethnicity, etc.).

**Cumans** or **Kumans,** nomadic East Turkic people. Coming from NW Russia, they conquered the Black Sea steppes and Walachia in the 11th cent. From their state along the Black Sea they traded with the Orient and Venice. After their defeat by the MONGOLS (13th cent.) many Cumans fled to Bulgaria and Hungary, and others joined the Empire of the GOLDEN HORDE.

**Cumberland Gap,** mountain pass through the Cumberland Mts of the Appalachians, near Middlesboro, Kentucky, US, discovered in 1750 by Dr Thomas Walker. Daniel BOONE's WILDERNESS ROAD to the 'Old West' ran through the gap, and it was an important military objective of both sides in the CIVIL WAR. The pass was designated a national historical park in 1940.

**Cumbre** or **Transandine Summit,** tunnel in the Andes on the border between Chile and Argentina. Constructed in 1910 it carries the principal rail connection between the two countries and at 3.17 km (1.97 mi) it is the longest tunnel in South America.

**Cumbria,** county, NW England (1984 est. pop. 483,600), 6810 km² (2656 sq mi), bordering on Scotland in N, and Irish Sea and Solway Firth in W. It was formed in 1974 from Cumberland, Westmorland, and Furness. The chief town is CARLISLE. In the NW of the county is the broad plain of Carlisle. The land rises in the E to the PENNINES and in the NE to the Cheviot Hills. The S of the county is occupied by much of the picturesque and mountainous LAKE DISTRICT. Dairy farming and mixed arable farming are undertaken in the lowlands, with sheep farming important in the uplands. Granite and limestone are quarried within the county. Britain's first atomic power station was opened at Calder Hall in 1956.

**cumin** or **cummin,** low annual herb (*Cuminum cyminum*) of the CARROT family, long cultivated in the Old World for the aromatic, seedlike fruits. Cumin is an ingredient of curry powder. It yields an oil used in liqueurs and veterinary medicines. Related to the CARAWAY, cumin has similar uses in cooking.

**cummings, e e** (Edward Estlin Cummings), 1894–1962, American author. His lyrical verse, eccentric in typography and language, is included in such volumes as *Tulips and Chimneys* (1923), *Is 5* (1926), and *95 Poems* (1958). *The Enormous Room* (1922) is an exceptional prose account of his World War I internment in France.

**cuneiform** [Lat., = wedge-shaped], system of WRITING developed before the last centuries of the 4th millennium BC in the lower Tigris and Euphrates valley, probably by the Sumerians. The characters consist of arrangements of wedge-like strokes, generally on clay tablets. The history of the script is strikingly like that of the Egyptian HIEROGLYPHIC (see also ALPHABET). Normal Babylonian and Assyrian writing used from 300 to 600 arbitrary cuneiform symbols for words and syllables, some originally pictographic. There was also an alphabetic system that made it possible to spell out a word, but because of the adaptation from Sumerian, a different language, there were many ambiguities. Cuneiform writing was used outside Mesopotamia, notably in ELAM and by the HITTITES, but was not common after the Persian conquest of Babylonia (539 BC). A late use was that of the ACHAEMENIDS of Persia (mid-6th–4th cent. BC). H.C. Rawlinson and G.F. Grotefend were noted cuneiform scholars.

**Cunningham, Merce,** 1919–, American dancer, choreographer, and teacher. He danced with the Graham Co. (1939–45), and had a close collaboration with composer John CAGE from 1944 onwards. He performed solo programmes until the formation (1952) of his own company. He considers music, design, and dance as being independent of one another, thus breaking with the traditional concepts of choreography. He is the most influential figure in modern dance in the later 20th cent., and his dance technique has become recognized as an important tool in the training of today's dance artists.

**Cunobelinus** or **Cymbeline,** d. AD c.40, British king. His conquest of the Trinovantes (of Essex) made him the wealthiest and most powerful ruler in SE England. His son CARATACUS led resistance against the Romans. Cymbeline gives his name, and little else, to SHAKESPEARE's play.

**Cupid:** see EROS.

**Curaçao** ('kyooərə,soh), island (1981 est. pop. 147,388), 461 km² (178 sq mi), in the NETHERLANDS ANTILLES. Willemstad is the capital of the island group. Its refineries, among the world's largest, process oil from nearby Venezuela. Discovered in 1499, it was settled (1527) by the Spanish and captured (1634) by the Dutch. Many African slaves were imported.

**curare,** extract of any of several ALKALOID plants originally used by South American Indians as a poison on the ends of arrows . Curare produces paralysis by interfering with the transmission of nerve impulses in skeletal muscle. In recent years curare has been used medically as an adjunct to general anaesthesia and in diagnosing MYASTHENIA GRAVIS.

**Curia Regis:** see PARLIAMENT.

**Curie,** family of French scientists. **Pierre Curie,** 1859–1906, scientist, and his wife, **Marie Sklodowska Curie,** 1867–1934, chemist and physicist, b. Poland, married 1895, are known for their work on radioactivity and on radium. Pierre discovered (1883) and, with his brother Jacques, investigated piezoelectricity (a form of electric polarity) in crystals. Following Antoine BECQUEREL's discovery of RADIOACTIVITY, Marie began to study URANIUM, a radioactive element found in pitchblende. Together, the Curies discovered POLONIUM and RADIUM and determined their atomic weights and properties. For their work on radioactivity, they shared with Becquerel the 1903 Nobel Prize for physics. Marie Curie became the first person to be awarded a second Nobel Prize when she received the 1911 chemistry prize for the discovery of polonium and radium. The French scientists **Frédéric Joliot-Curie,** 1900–1958, formerly Frédéric Joliot, and **Irène Joliot-Curie,** 1897–1956, daughter of Pierre and Marie Curie, were married in 1926. They received the 1935 Nobel Prize for chemistry for artificially producing radioactive substances by bombarding elements with alpha particles. The Joliot-Curies investigated (1940) the chain reaction in nuclear fission and filed three patents for nuclear explosives. In 1946 they helped to organize the French atomic energy commission, of which Frédéric was the first chairman (1946–50).

**Curitiba,** city (1980 pop. 843,733) SE Brazil, capital of Paraná state. It handles the products of an expanding agricultural and ranching area through the Atlantic port of Paranaguá, c.110 km (70 mi) away. Founded in 1654, the city became important when immigrants developed the Paraná hinterland from the late 19th cent. The city has grown rapidly since 1950.

**curium** (Cm), synthetic element, first produced by alpha-particle bombardment of plutonium-239 by Glenn Seaborg and colleagues in 1944. It is a silvery metal and a very radioactive element in the ACTINIDE series. Curium accumulates in bones and disrupts red blood cells. See ELEMENT (table); PERIODIC TABLE.

**curlew,** migratory BIRDS of the family Scolopacidae, usually living in open country near water. The whimbrel (*Numenius phaeopus*) breeds across Europe, Asia, and North America and migrates as far as South America and Australia. Curlews have long, probing beaks to search for worms and shellfishes. They also take fishes, frogs, berries, and seeds.

**currant,** northern shrub (genus *Ribes*) of the SAXIFRAGE family. The gooseberry bush belongs to the same genus. The tart black, white, or red currant berries and the green and purple gooseberries are both eaten fresh or used in preserves, sauces, and pies. Dried currants were used by native Americans in making pemmican, a travel food. Today's commercial 'dried currant' is a raisin (see GRAPE).

**currency:** see MONEY.

**currency lads and lasses,** the name given to native-born Australians in the early colonial period to distinguish them from convicts. Contemporaries discerned in them qualities that promised well for a future nation.

**current,** in ELECTRICITY, the flow of electric CHARGE through a conductor (see CONDUCTION). The SI (see METRIC SYSTEM) unit of current is the AMPERE.

**Currier & Ives,** American lithographers and publishers who produced highly popular hand-coloured prints of 19th-cent. scenes and events in American life. **Nathaniel Currier,** 1813–88, founded the business (1835) in New York City and formed (1857) a partnership with the artist and businessman **James Merritt Ives,** 1824–95. The business closed in 1907.

**Curtin, John Joseph,** 1885–1945, Australian prime minister. As a socialist he opposed conscription for overseas military service during World War I. As prime minister (1941–45) during World War II he persuaded his Labor Party to allow conscription, and provided national leadership against the threat of Japanese invasion.

**Curtiss, Glenn Hammond,** 1878–1930, American inventor and aviation pioneer. He made (1908) the first public flights in the US, established (1909) the first US flying school, and made (1910) a spectacular flight from Albany to New York City. He invented (1911) ailerons (see AEROPLANE) and after World War I made other radical improvements in the design of both planes and aero-motors.

**curve,** in mathematics, the path of a point moving in space. In ANALYTICAL GEOMETRY, a plane curve, i.e., a curve that lies in one plane, is usually considered as the graph of an equation or function (for some examples, see CONIC SECTION). A skew, twisted, or space curve is one that does not lie all in one plane, e.g., the helix, a curve having the shape of a wire spring.

**Curzon Line,** cease-fire line proposed by the British in July 1920 during the Polish–Soviet war, named after the British Foreign Secretary of the day (Lord Curzon). At that time it was rejected by both sides, and Poland was subsequently able to extend its borders in the east as a result of its military successes. During World War II these territories once again became the object of disagreement between Poland and the USSR, being initially (in Sept. 1939) occupied by the Red Army, and reoccupied by Soviet troops in 1944. At the Teheran conference of the 'Big Three' (Dec. 1943) it was agreed that the Curzon Line would form the basis of Poland's postwar eastern frontier.

**Cush,** ancient kingdom of NUBIA, in what is now SUDAN. It flourished from the 11th cent. BC to the 4th cent. AD and in the 8th cent. BC included Egypt in its domain. Meroe, its capital, was overrun by the Ethiopians in the 4th cent., and the kingdom came to an end. The ruins of many pyramids —royal tombs—remain.

**Cushing, Harvey Williams,** 1869–1939, American neurosurgeon. A noted brain surgeon, he wrote a classic biography of Sir William OSLER. **Cushing's syndrome** first described by him, is caused by hyperactivity of the cortex of the ADRENAL GLANDS and affects more women than men. Symptoms include weakness, obesity, hypertension, hirsutism, and diabetes. Treatment is by removal of one or both adrenal glands, or, if the pituitary body is involved, by X-ray therapy or surgery.

**Cushitic** (kə,shitik), group of languages belonging to the Hamitic subfamily of the HAMITO-SEMITIC family of languages. See LANGUAGE (table).

**Custer, George Armstrong,** 1839–76, US Army officer. During the AMERICAN CIVIL WAR he became (1863) the youngest general in the Union army. Later he commanded the 7th Cavalry. During a campaign against the SIOUX INDIANS in 1876, Custer and an entire detachment of over 200 men were killed by Indians on the Little Bighorn R. His spectacular death made him a popular but controversial hero.

**customary law,** term used to describe the practices and procedures of a particular area or country, that became so firmly established as to amount to law. In medieval Europe, the Germanic tribes were mostly regulated by customary law (see GERMANIC LAW), more coercive law playing only a small part in the tribes' life. In England, prior to the development of the COMMON LAW in the 13th cent., most of the country was run according to local customary law, which differed from area to area. The king's justices, who developed the common law, applied the best of these customs nationally, and customary law thus served as an important source of the original common law. Customary law persists in some countries, e.g., in southern Africa where it is important in the laws of marriage and inheritance; however, efforts are being made to phase it out because of its discrimination against women.

**customs and excise,** part of the indirect taxation system. In the UK customs duties are charged under the Common Customs Tariff of the EEC. Some goods may be imported free or at reduced rates from certain countries under TARIFF quotas. Excise duty is a tax on goods or services consumed within a country. In the UK it is applied to most alcoholic drinks, tobacco products and matches, and most types of hydrocarbon oil; various forms of betting and gaming are also subjected to excise duties. With VALUE-ADDED TAX (not really an excise tax although it is an internal tax), these are administered by the Board of Customs and Excise, whereas direct taxation (see INCOME TAX) is administered by the INLAND REVENUE.

**Cuttack,** town (1981 pop. 295,268), Orissa state, E India. It is a district administrative, communications, and commercial centre in a strategic position at the head of the MAHANADI delta, a densely populated rice-growing region. There is an important rice-breeding station at Cuttack. The town was taken from the *bhonsla* of NAGPUR by the (British) East India Company in 1803 and became the capital of the province of Orissa when this was created in 1935.

**cuttlefish,** mollusc (order Sepioidea) that has ten tentacles, eight bearing muscular suction cups on their inner surface and two longer ones for grasping prey. A CEPHALOPOD, the cuttlefish has a reduced internal shell embedded in the mantle; in some there is a degenerate internal shell of lime called cuttlebone. The body is short, broad, and flattened with lateral fins, similar to the SQUID. When disturbed, cuttlefish eject a dark ink, which hides them from predators.

**Cutty Sark,** 19th-cent. sailing ship, now preserved at Greenwich dock, London. Built in 1869, the *Cutty Sark* was among the most famous of the fast tea clippers that raced to China to collect its cargo and then back to Europe to sweep the market in advance of competitors. The name, which is Scottish for 'short shirt', is taken from the witch in Robert Burns's poem 'Tam O'Shanter'.

**Cuvier, Georges Léopold Chrétien Frédéric Dagobert,** (kyv,yay), 1769–1832, French naturalist. A pioneer in comparative anatomy, he originated a system of zoological classification based on structural differences of the skeleton and organs. His reconstruction of the soft parts of fossils deduced from their skeletal remains greatly advanced palaeontology, and he identified and named the flying reptile pterodactyl. He rejected evolutionary theory in favour of CATASTROPHISM.

**Cuvilliès, François de** (kyvee,yees), 1695–1768, French architect, decorater, and engraver. He introduced French ROCOCO decoration into Germany. His Residenz-Theater (1751–53) and Amalienburg pavilion, in the park of Nymphenburg, both at Munich, represent the apex of German rococo decoration.

**Cuyp** or **Kuyp, Aelbert** (koyp), 1620–91, the most distinguished of a family of Dutch painters, and one of the foremost Dutch landscapists. He is famous for his simple but richly coloured pastoral scenes; among the best are *Piper with Cows* and *Promenade* (both: Louvre, Paris), and *Horseman and Cows in a Meadow* (1650s?; National Gall., London).

**Cuza, Alexander Ioan,** 1820–73, first prince of the United Principalities of Walachia and Moldavia (1859–62) and of ROMANIA (1862–66) which emerged from this union. The emancipation of the serfs (1864) was the most notable of a number of reforms instituted by Cuza. Abandoned by his boyars he was forced to abdicate in 1866.

**Cuzco** or **Cusco,** city (1981 pop. 181,604), S Peru, capital of Cuzco dept. It is an agricultural trading centre and has woollen mills. Said to have been founded by MANCO CAPAC, it was the capital of the INCA empire, with massive, gold-decorated palaces and temples. After it was plundered by Francisco PIZARRO in 1533, the Spaniards raised a colonial city within the old walls, many of which remain visible. The city was devastated by

The **Cutty Sark** at Greenwich

an earthquake in 1950, but most of the historic buildings have been restored. The ruins of an Inca fortress are nearby.

**cyanide,** salt or ester of hydrogen cyanide (HCN) formed by replacing the hydrogen with a metal or a radical. The most common and widely used (those of sodium and potassium) are employed as insecticides, in making pigments, in metallurgy, and in gold and silver refining. Most cyanides are deadly poisons that cause respiratory failure. Symptoms include a breath odour of bitter almonds, dizziness, convulsions, collapse, and, often, froth on the mouth.

**Cyaxares** (sie͵aksəreez), d. 585 BC, king of MEDIA (r.c.625–585 BC). He made the kingdom of the Medes a major power in the Middle East. In 612 BC Cyaxares took NINEVEH and completely defeated the Assyrians by 605 BC.

**Cybele,** in ancient Asiatic religion, GREAT MOTHER OF THE GODS. The chief centers of her early worship were Phrygia and Lydia. In the 5th cent. BC her cult spread to Greece and later to Rome. She was primarily a nature goddess, responsible for maintaining and reproducing the wild things of the earth. Her annual spring festival celebrated the death and resurrection of her beloved Attis, a vegetation god.

**cybernetics,** term used by Norbert Wiener in 1948 to refer to the general analysis of control systems and communication systems in living organisms and machines. Analogies are drawn between the functioning of the brain and nervous system and that of the COMPUTER and other electronic systems. Cybernetics overlaps the fields of AUTOMATIC CONTROL and AUTOMATION, computing machinery, INFORMATION THEORY, and neurophysiology.

**Cybulski, Zbigniew** (si͵boohlskee), 1927–67, Polish film actor; b. Ukraine. Famous in the West for his angry-young-man roles in the mid 1950s, his films include *A Generation* (1954), *Ashes and Diamonds* (1958), and *The Saragossa Manuscript* (1965).

**cycad,** palmlike plant of the Cycadales, an order of mostly tropical and subtropical cone-bearing evergreens. Cycads, known from the Permian period, are the most primitive of the living SEED-bearing plants. Some have tuberous, underground stems and crowns of leathery, glossy, fernlike leaves arising from ground level; others have high, columnar stems. Some cycads, e.g., the fern palm of the Old World tropics and the Australian nut palm, bear edible, nutlike fruits. Sago is a starch from the pith of the sago

palm (*C. revoluta*). The order comprises nine genera with fewer than a hundred species.

**Cyclades,** island group (1981 pop. 88,458), c.2590 km², (1000 sq mi), SE Greece, in the Aegean Sea. It includes about 220 islands, the most important of which are Tínos, Ándros, Mílos, Náxos, Kéa, and Páros. Largely mountainous, the islands are agricultural areas and tourist centres. In 1829 they passed from the OTTOMAN EMPIRE to Greece.

**Cycladic art,** BRONZE AGE art of the central Aegean Cycladic islands. Early tomb remains include jugs, pots, and bowls decorated in geometric designs, as well as marble female fertility figures. These are frontal and geometric in style. Figures of musicians have also been found. Considerable Minoan (see MINOAN CIVILIZATION) influence is seen in the pottery of the 17th cent. BC found at Phylakopi in Melos.

**Cycladic art:** Calyx-shaped marble kylix with trumpet-shaped foot, 2800–2000 BC

**cyclamate,** either of two compounds, sodium or calcium cyclamate, used as artificial sweeteners, being 30 times as sweet as sugar and stable when heated. The use of cyclamates in foods was banned in 1969 when it was reported that massive doses caused cancer in rats.

**cyclamen,** Mediterranean herbs (genus *Cyclamen*) with tuberous roots. Cyclamens are widely cultivated as greenhouse plants for their colourful flowers and decoratively-marked leaves (forms of *C. persicum*) and as naturalized garden plants (e.g. *C. neapolitanum*).

**cycles,** the constant re-use of the elements that make up living things. Cycles play a vital role in the living processes as elements pass out of the soil and the atmosphere, through the biosphere and back to the inanimate world. The OXYGEN CYCLE, CARBON CYCLE, and NITROGEN CYCLE describe the stages through which those elements pass as they are extracted from the air, taken into living material, and released again. Minerals also circulate from the soil, and calcium, iron, and potassium cycles can be drawn up. The physical processes which move water about the planet are also described in the water cycle. Life histories of plants and animals can be described as life cycles. Those organisms with complex patterns of development, which involve intermediate stages between the egg and the adult, have life cycles: ferns, insects, crustaceans and amphibians are some examples.

**cyclone,** region, often called a 'low', of low central atmospheric pressure relative to the surrounding pressure. The resulting pressure gradient, combined with the CORIOLIS EFFECT, causes air to circulate about the centre, or core, in a counterclockwise direction north of the equator and a clockwise direction south of it. The frictional drag on near-surface air moving over land or water causes it to spiral inward toward lower pressures; this movement is compensated for near the centre by rising currents, which are cooled by expansion when they reach the lower pressures of higher altitudes. The cooling, in turn, characteristically increases the relative HUMIDITY greatly and produces cloudiness. An **anticyclone** has the opposite characteristics: a 'high', or region of high central pressure relative to the surrounding pressure; clockwise circulation north of the equator and counterclockwise circulation south of it; descending and diverging air that is warmed by compression as it encounters higher pressure at lower altitudes; and characteristic low humidity and little cloudiness. Both cyclones and anticyclones move across the land at speeds of 800 to 1600 km/day (500 to 1000 mi/day).

**Cyclops,** plural **Cyclopes,** in Greek mythology, immense one-eyed beings. According to HESIOD, they were skilled smiths, sons of URANUS and GAIA, who gave ZEUS the lightning bolts that helped him defeat CRONUS. In HOMER, they were a barbarous people, one of whom (POLYPHEMUS) was encountered by ODYSSEUS in his wanderings.

**cyclotron:** see PARTICLE ACCELERATOR.

**cymbals:** see PERCUSSION INSTRUMENT.

**Cymbeline:** see CUNOBELINUS.

**Cynewulf** (kumiwoolf), fl. early 9th cent. Anglo-Saxon religious poet to whom are ascribed four didactic poems: *Juliana, The Ascension, Elene,* and *The Fates of the Apostles.*

**cypress,** common name for the genus *Cupressus,* a widely distributed member of the PINE family of coniferous shrubs and trees, some yielding valuable timber. The true cypresses found in S Europe, the Far East, and W North America, are resinous evergreens with a fragrant, durable wood and scalelike leaves and include the widely grown Monterey cypress (*Cupressus macrocarpa*). Trees of the genus *Chamaecyparis,* also commonly called cypresses, comprise some important timber trees, e.g., the Lawson cypress, (*Chamaecyparis lawsoniana*).

**Cyprian, Saint,** 200?–258, Father of the Church, bishop of CARTHAGE (c.248). While agreeing with Pope Cornelius that Christians who had apostatized under persecution could be readmitted to the church, he rejected the view of Pope Stephen I that baptism administered by heretics and schismatics was valid. He was martyred in the persecution of the Roman emperor Valerian. Feast: 16 Sept.

**Cyprus,** Gr. *Kypros,* officially the Republic of Cyprus, republic (1985 est. pop. 667,000), 9267 km² (3578 sq mi), an island in the E Mediterranean Sea, c.60 km (40 mi) S of Turkey. The capital is NICOSIA. Two mountain ranges traverse the island from E to W; the highest peak is Mt Olympus 1953 m (6406 ft), in the SW. Between the ranges lies a wide plain, where grapes (used for wine), cereals, olives, tobacco, and cotton are grown. Fishing, tourism, and the raising of livestock are also important. Copper is the chief mineral resource. The GNP is $2691 million and the GNP per capita is $4035 (1984). Nearly 80% of the population is Greek, and about 18% is Turkish.

*History.* Excavations have revealed the existence of a Neolithic culture on Cyprus from 4000 to 3000 BC. Influenced by the Middle East and, after 1500 BC, by Greece, Cyprus fell to a succession of rulers, including Assyria, Egypt, Persia, and Rome. After eight centuries (from AD 395) of Byzantine control, it was conquered (1191) by RICHARD I of England, who bestowed it on the French Lusignan dynasty. Annexed (1489) by VENICE and conquered (1571) by the Turks (see OTTOMAN EMPIRE), it came under British administration in 1878 and was annexed outright by the UK in 1914. The movements among Greek Cypriots for self-rule and union *(enosis)* with GREECE were a source of constant tension, erupting in 1955 into violence that was tantamount to civil war. The conflict was aggravated by Turkish support of Turkish Cypriot demands for partition of the island. In 1959, a settlement, precluding both *enosis* and partition, provided for independence in 1960 as a member of the COMMONWEALTH; MAKARIOS III, leader of the Greek Cypriot nationalists, was elected president. The British retained two sovereign military enclaves, Akrotiri and Dhekelia. Large-scale fighting continued, however, and a UN peacekeeping force was sent to Cyprus in 1965. In 1974 the national guard, dominated by Greek army officers, overthrew the Makarios regime. Citing its responsibility to protect the Turkish Cypriot community, Turkey invaded Cyprus and established a 'Turkish Federated State of Cyprus' in the northern third of the island, which, in 1983, was declared the independent TURKISH REPUBLIC OF NORTHERN CYPRUS. Since 1975 Cyprus has been a divided state, with a self-governing Turkish community in the north and a Greek community in the south; mediation efforts by the UNITED NATIONS have made little progress. In 1983 Pres. Spyros Kyprianou was reelected for a further five-year term as candidate of a centre-left alliance. He was succeeded in 1988 by Georgios Vassiliou, who was elected president with the backing of the island's Communist Party.

**Cyrene,** ancient city near the northern coast of Africa, in Cyrenaica (now E Libya). A Greek colony (7th cent. BC), it was a city-state with much

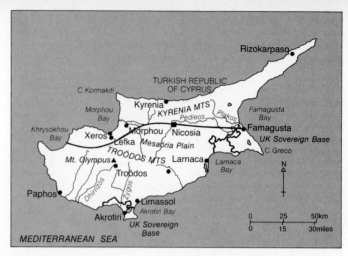

Cyprus

commerce with Greece and some development of art. Cyrene became powerful over other cities and held nominal independence until the marriage of Berenice (d. 221? BC) to PTOLEMY III of Egypt. It was later the centre of a Roman province. The Roman emperor TRAJAN's punishment of Cyrene because of Jewish uprisings led to its decline.

**Cyril and Methodius, Saints,** d. 869 and 885 respectively, Greek missionaries, brothers, called Apostles to the Slavs and fathers of Slavonic literature. Sent (c.863) to MORAVIA, they won papal approval for the use of Slavonic in church liturgy. The **Cyrillic alphabet,** used in Russia and elsewhere, is named after St Cyril but was probably the work of his followers. Feast: 14 Feb. (11 May in the East).

**Cyrillic script:** see ALPHABET.

**Cyrus the Great,** d. 529 BC, king of Persia, founder of ACHAEMENID power and the Persian empire. He conquered MEDIA between 559 and 549 BC, Lydia (see CROESUS) in 547, and BABYLONIA in 538. In EGYPT he laid the basis for future Persian victories. Because he placed Jews in power in PALESTINE, creating a buffer state between Persia and Egypt, he is spoken of approvingly in the Old Testament, e.g., Dan. 6.28. He respected the religion and customs of each part of his empire.

**Cyrus the Younger,** d. 401 BC, Persian prince, younger son of DARIUS II and Parysatis. His mother obtained several satrapies for him in Asia Minor when he was very young. In the PELOPONNESIAN WAR he helped LYSANDER to build a victorious fleet. When Darius died (404 BC) Cyrus was accused of a plot to kill his elder brother, the heir, ARTAXERXES II. Saved by his mother, he raised an army to overthrow Artaxerxes but died in battle. XENOPHON's *Anabasis* describes the revolt.

**cystic fibrosis,** inherited disorder of the exocrine glands (see GLAND), affecting infants and children. It is characterized by secretion of a thick, sticky mucus from glands throughout the body, especially affecting the pancreas, lungs, and liver. Respiratory infections are common and severe. The sweat contains excessive sodium and chloride, which aids diagnosis. Treatment consists of a low-fat, high-protein diet, vitamins, pancreatin, and ANTIBIOTIC drugs to ward off infection.

**cytochrome,** any of a class of iron-containing proteins, discovered in 1886. Cytochromes play a vital role in the energy-producing reactions of cell RESPIRATION, transporting electrons generated by oxidative biochemical reactions (particularly those of the KREBS CYCLE), by undergoing successive oxidation and reduction (loss and gain of electrons). An oxygen molecule is the ultimate electron acceptor.

**Czartoryski, Prince Adam Jerzy** ('chahrtaw‚riskee), 1770–1861, Polish statesman and politician. He was adviser to Czar Alexander I and Russian minister for foreign affairs (1804–08). Czartoryski was a Polish patriot and favoured a Russian solution to the Polish problem rather than the Napoleonic. As a Russian representative at the Congress of Vienna (1815) he was able to defend Polish interests. He became head of the National Government at the Polish Uprising of 1830–31, but following its suppression by Russian troops sought exile abroad. He went to Paris where he became the leading figure of the conservative wing of Polish exile politics, and also used his considerable personal fortune to sponsor artistic and literary endeavours.

**Czech language,** in the past sometimes also called Bohemian, member of the West Slavic group of the Slavic subfamily of the Indo-European family of languages. See LANGUAGE (table).

**Czech Legion,** 1918 20, a military force of some 40,000–50,000 men formed in Russia largely from Czech and Slovak prisoners-of-war of the Austro-Hungarian Army. In the course of an epic withdrawal across Siberia to the Far East, they fought against the Bolsheviks in the Russian CIVIL WAR.

**Czechoslovakia,** Czech *Československo,* officially the Czechoslovak Socialist Republic, federal republic (1985 est. pop. 15,648,000) 127,869 km² (49,370 sq mi), central Europe; bordered by East Germany and Poland (N), West Germany (W), Austria and Hungary (S), and the USSR (E). Major cities include PRAGUE (the capital), BRNO, and BRATISLAVA. The three main geographic regions are the Bohemian plateau, the Moravian lowland, and mountainous Slovakia. The country is landlocked, and the chief rivers the DANUBE, ELBE, Vltava (Moldau), and Oder are economically important. The GNP per capita (1980) is US$5820. The republic comprises Slovakia and the traditional Czech lands of Bohemia, Moravia, and Czech SILESIA. The population is largely Slavic, consisting chiefly of Czechs (64%) and Slovaks (30%). Czech and Slovak are the official languages. Roman Catholicism is the majority religion, but there are sizable Protestant (notably HUSSITE), Eastern Orthodox, and Uniate groups. Czechoslovakia is highly industrialized; major manufactures include machinery and machine tools, metal-working and transport equipment, iron and steel, chemicals, food products, textiles, and footwear. The country has large reserves of bituminous coal and lignite and some iron ore. Agriculture is collectivized; major crops include sugar beets, potatoes, wheat, and barley.

*History.* Czechoslovakia emerged in 1918 from the ruins of the AUSTRO-HUNGARIAN MONARCHY as an independent republic. It was largely the creation of its first and second presidents, Thomas Garrigue MASARYK and Eduard BENEŠ. Economically the most favoured of the Habsburg successor states, it also benefited from a liberal, democratic constitution (1920) and able leadership. Its weakness lay in the disaffection of the German and Magyar minorities and agitation for autonomy in Slovakia. Vehemently backed by HITLER, the German nationalist minority demanded union with Germany. Faced with the threat of war, the West pursued a policy of appeasement and signed (1938) the MUNICH PACT, by which Germany obtained the Bohemian borderlands (Sudetenland). The truncated state was dissolved in 1939, when Germany made Bohemia and Moravia a 'protectorate', Slovakia gained nominal independence, and Ruthenia was awarded to HUNGARY. After liberation by US and Soviet forces at the end of WORLD WAR II, Czechoslovakia was restored to its pre-Munich status

(except for Ruthenia, which was ceded to the USSR) and the German population was expelled. A communist-dominated coalition government ruled until 1948, when the communists gained control and established a Soviet-style state. Czechoslovakia was a founder member of both COMECON and the WARSAW TREATY ORGANIZATION. A trend toward liberalization, begun in 1963, reached its climax in 1968 with the installation of reformers Alexander DUBČEK as party leader and Ludvik Svoboda as president. In August the USSR with four Warsaw Pact allies invaded Czechoslovakia, forcing the repeal of most of the reforms and replacing Dubček with the staunchly pro-Soviet Gustav HUSÁK, who became Communist Party leader in 1969 and president of the republic in 1976. The Husák regime maintained a firm grip on power, although internal dissident movements continued to be active. Increasing pressure for liberalization from 1985 led to the replacement of Husák as party leader by Milos JAKES in 1987. (For history prior to 1918, as well as more detailed geographic and economic information, see BOHEMIA; MORAVIA; SLOVAKIA.)

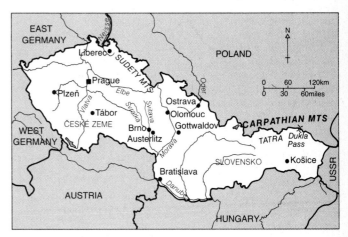

Czechoslovakia

**Czerny, Karl** (ˌcheənee), 1791–1857, Austrian pianist, teacher and prolific composer. He taught LISZT and is best known for his technical studies for the piano.

**Częstochowa** ('chenstokˌhohva), city (1984 pop. 244,000), S Poland, on the Warta R. Since World War II it has become a centre of iron and steel production based on local ores. The monastery of Jasna Góra [shining mountain] is a place of pilgrimage because it withstood the besieging Swedes in 1655. There, a painting of the Black Madonna (Our Lady of Częstochowa) is venerated as a symbol of national survival.

# D

**Dacca:** see DHAKA.

**Dachau,** West Germany: see CONCENTRATION CAMP.

**Dacia,** ancient region roughly corresponding to Rumania, whose people were called Getae by the Greeks, Daci by the Romans. They had an advanced material culture. DOMITIAN tried to subdue them but ended by paying them tribute (AD 90). Under TRAJAN, Dacia became (AD 105) a Roman province, but AURELIAN lost it to the invading Goths (250–70). The main Roman legacy to Dacia was the Romance tongue Romanian.

**Dacko, David,** 1930–, president of the CENTRAL AFRICAN REPUBLIC (1960–66, 1979–81). He was a leader in the independence movement in French Equatorial Africa and became the first president of the newly independent Central African Republic. He was toppled from power in 1966 by J.B. BOKASSA but was reinstated in a 1979 coup. Reelected president, he was overthrown by a military junta in 1981.

**Dada,** an artistic movement that had various simultaneous manifestations in Europe and America (Zurich, Berlin, Cologne, Hanover, Paris, and New York), during and shortly after World War I. Dada's ideology was a reaction against the senseless barbarities of the war and was generally more subversive and negative than positively revolutionary. By developing a strategy of anti-art, as exemplified by DUCHAMP's ready-made urinal (1917), and his *Mona Lisa* decorated with a moustache and the obscene caption *LHOOQ* (which when read out sounds like 'She has hot pants'), Dada artists sought to undermine traditional artistic and social values. By 1922 Dada, as a state of mind rather than as a style, was no longer valid and so the movement came to an end. Many of the artists then aligned themselves with SURREALISM. Artists associated with Dada are ARP, ERNST, GROSZ, HEARTFIELD, and SCHWITTERS.

**Daddi, Bernardo,** fl. 1312–48, Italian painter of the Florentine school. First influenced by GIOTTO, he later adopted the delicate line of the Sienese painters. His only documented work is the *Virgin and Child enthroned* (1346–47; Or San Michele, Florence).

**daddy long legs, crane fly** or **leatherjacket,** name given to long legged flies (family Tipulidae) in Britain, where they invade houses in the summer months. Some species' LARVAE, which are laid in the soil, develop into the destructive leatherjackets which feed on the roots and lower stems of crops and garden plants. The American daddy long legs is a HARVESTMAN.

**Daedalus,** in Greek mythology, craftsman and inventor. He built the MINOTAUR's labyrinth in Crete. When King MINOS refused to let him leave, Daedalus built wax and feather wings for himself and his son Icarus. They flew away, but when Icarus came too close to the sun his wings melted and he fell to his death. Daedalus escaped to Sicily. Daedalus has given his name to the hero of James JOYCE's *A Portrait of the Artist as a Young Man* (1916).

**Daejeon:** see TAEJON.

**daffodil:** see NARCISSUS.

**Daguerre, Louis Jacques Mandé** (daˌgeə), 1789–1851, French scene painter and physicist, inventor of the daguerreotype. Known first for his illusionistic stage sets, he was also the inventor, with C.M. Bouton, of the diorama (pictorial views seen with changing lighting). The daguerreotype, a photograph produced on a silver-coated copper plate treated with iodine vapour, was developed with J. Nicéphore NIÉPCE and ceded to the Academy of Sciences in 1839.

*The artist's studio* by **Daguerre,** 1837

**Dahl, Robert,** 1915–, American political scientist. He has undertaken a detailed analysis of the operation of Western liberal democracies. His classic accounts of PLURALISM in *A Preface to Democractic Theory* (1956), *Who Governs: Democracy and Power in an American City* (1961), and *Polyarchy, Participation and Opposition* (1971), led him to conclude that power in US society was not concentrated in a ruling CLASS, but distributed among competing elites, interests, and pressure-groups. In *A Preface to Economic Theory* (1985), however, Dahl expresses worries about the inequalities produced by the power of corporate capitalism which, he now believes, distort the democratic process (see CORPORATISM).

**dahlia,** tuberous-rooted, half-hardy perennial plant (genus *Dahlia*) of the COMPOSITE family, native to Mexico and widely cultivated. Most of the thousands of horticultural varieties are thought to be developed from one species (*D. pinnata*), the garden dahlia. Dahlias are stout, woody plants with colourful, late-blooming flowers.

**Dahomey:** see BENIN.

**Daimler, Gottlieb,** 1834–1900, German engineer, inventor, and designer of an advanced INTERNAL-COMBUSTION ENGINE. He learned his engineering part-time at the polytechnic in Stuttgart whilst working in an engineering factory at Strasbourg. In 1881, in the summerhouse of his home, he produced his first 900 rpm, high-speed, single-cylinder engine. In 1889 he built two cars, well in advance of his contemporaries. The Paris to Rouen car race in 1894, the first international, was won by a Daimler engine in a racing-car body.

**daimyo** [Jap., = great name], barons or territorial rulers of the SAMURAI class. Under the TOKUGAWA shogunate they enjoyed considerable autonomy and independence within their domains.

**Dairen:** see DALIAN.

**dairying,** industry concerned with producing, processing, and distributing MILK and milk products. About 90% of the world's milk comes from CATTLE; the rest comes from GOATS, BUFFALO, SHEEP, REINDEER, YAKS, and other ruminants. In the UK domestic use of liquid milk has fallen from about 60% to less than 45% of total milk production over the last 12 years, and the number of producers has declined. The remainder of the milk is used for BUTTER and CHEESE-making, dried and condensed milk, cream and ice-cream, and for the production of substances such as LACTOSE and CASEIN for the chemicals industry. The rise of modern, large-scale dairying paralleled the growth of urban populations and was stimulated by the discovery of PASTEURIZATION.

**daisy,** name for several common wild flowers of the COMPOSITE family. The common daisy (*Bellis perennis*) is a lawn weed, but has given rise to several cultivated forms. Other species include the common, white, or oxeye, daisy (*Chrysanthemum leucanthemum*). Other plants called daisy include the Gloriosa daisy (see BLACK-EYED SUSAN), and the Michaelmas daisy, an ASTER.

**Dakar,** largest city and port (1979 pop. 978,553), capital of Senegal, on Cape Verde Peninsula, on the Atlantic Ocean. It is an economic centre for a market-gardening region, and its expanding industries produce pharmaceuticals, textiles, cement, ground nut oil, plastics, and soap. The city is the busiest port in W Africa, also serving Mali and Mauritania, and is linked by rail and air with other Senegalese cities. Dakar became the capital of FRENCH WEST AFRICA in 1902 and was occupied by US forces in World War II. It has been the capital of Senegal since 1958. The modern city is an educational and cultural centre.

**Daladier, Édouard** (dalad,yay), 1884–1970, French premier (1934, 1938–40). A leading Radical Socialist throughout the 1930s, Daladier signed the MUNICH PACT with HITLER in 1938 and presided over France's fortunes in the early months of WORLD WAR II, until overthrown by his failure to aid Finland. After France's fall (1940) he was arrested by the VICHY government and was tried (1942) in the war-crimes trials at Riom. In the Fourth Republic he served (1946–58) in the national assembly.

**Dalcroze, Jaques,** 1865–1950, Swiss music teacher and theoretician. He developed a system of musical perception through the translation of rhythm into bodily movements, called *gymnastique rhythmique*. He trained many of the members of the German MODERN DANCE movement at his 'Institute for Applied Rhythm' (Dresden, later Geneva). His teaching was a source of inspiration to many of the 20th-cent. dance pedagogues.

**Dale, Sir Henry Hallett,** 1875–1968, English physiologist and pharmacologist. For his study of ACETYLCHOLINE as an agent in the chemical transmission of nerve impulses, he shared with Otto LOEWI the 1936 Nobel Prize for physiology or medicine. Dale also investigated the pharmacology of ergot (a potent fungus) and histamine shock. He was knighted in 1932.

**d'Alembert, Jean le Rond** (dalanh,beə): see ALEMBERT, JEAN LE ROND D'.

**Dali, Salvador,** 1904–89, Spanish painter. He became a member of the Surrealist group (see SURREALISM) in 1929 but did not take on their implicit Marxist political interests and was expelled in 1938. He developed his 'paranoic critical' method, where he attempted to make 'real', by the use of a highly finished technique influenced by VERMEER, dream sequences and Freudian imagery (see FREUD). Often objects in these works can take on several meanings and identities, as in *The Metamorphosis of Narcissus* (1936; Tate Gall.), where Narcissus can simultaneously be read as either a figure or a rock formation.

**Dalian** or **Talien,** city (1984 pop. 4,807,600), NE China, on the southern tip of the Liaodong Peninsula, LIAONING prov. A major industrial and transport centre, Dalian has a deep, natural harbour which is silt- and ice-free, and by tonnage is China's largest foreign trade port. It is a major rail centre and is developing as an important air link. The city has been known by a variety of names: Dalian, Dairen, Lushun, and Luda. Lushun originally was a separate settlement comprising the old Port Arthur. Dalian has a diverse industrial base and has been designated a centre of high technology development and foreign investment. It is a very recently created city. During the last phase of the Qing dynasty it was the base of the northern navy (at Port Arthur). In 1894 Japan seized the Liaodong Peninsula which became a centre for rivalry with Czarist Russia. In 1930 Japan completed construction of the port. By the Yalta Agreement of 1945, control of Dalian passed to the USSR who did not leave the city

Salvador **Dali**, *Metamorphosis of Narcissus*, 1936. Oil on canvas, 50.8 × 78.2 cm. Tate Gallery, London.

until 1954, five years after the establishment of the Peoples Republic, an indication of the city's strategic and industrial importance.

**Dalin, Olof von** (da,leen), 1708–63, Swedish historian, poet, and journalist, the foremost figure of the Swedish ENLIGHTENMENT. His prose masterpiece, the allegorical *Tale of the Horse* (1740), uses folk material to satirize the relations between the Swedish people and the monarchy.

**Dallapiccola, Luigi,** 1904–75, Italian composer. The first Italian to use ATONALITY and TWELVE-TONE serialism, he is noted for his operas *The Prisoner* (1944–48) and *Odysseus* (1968); the ORATORIO *Job* (1950); and the Christmas CONCERTO (1956) for soprano and orchestra.

**Dallas,** US city (1984 est. pop. 974,000), N Texas, on the Trinity R.; inc. 1871. A French settlement c.1841 and a cotton market in the 1870s, it later developed into the principal financial and commercial city of the southwest. Oil refineries; diverse manufactures, particularly aircraft and electronics; meat-packing plants; corporate headquarters for oil, gas, insurance, and banking companies; and governmental offices are of major importance in its economy. The city attracts tourists and hosts numerous conventions. Dallas is noted as a centre of fashion and of cultural and educational institutions such as the Dallas Theatre Center and Baylor Univ. The rapidly expanding Dallas–Fort Worth area had a 1980 metropolitan population of over 2.9 million.

**Dalmatia,** (dal,mayshə), historic province of CROATIA and region of YUGOSLAVIA extending along the ADRIATIC SEA from Zadar to the Gulf of Kotor. Split is the major city and DUBROVNIK the most popular tourist centre. Consisting of a coastal strip and offshore islands backed by the Dinaric Alps, Dalmatia is an area of great scenic beauty. Besides tourism, other economic activities include viniculture, fishing, and ship-building. A Roman province, Dalmatia was divided by the 10th cent. between the kingdom of Croatia and Byzantium. By 1420 Venice held most of the region. Various parts of Dalmatia passed (16th–20th cent.) to Hungary, the Ottomans, France, and finally, Austria. A centre of pro-Yugoslav feeling in the late 19th cent., Dalmatia joined the Kingdom of Serbs, Croats, and Slovenes in 1918. Most of the region was occupied by Italy in World War II.

**Dalton, John,** 1766–1844, English scientist. He taught mathematics and physical sciences at New College, Manchester. Dalton revived the atomic theory of matter (see ATOM), which he applied to a table of atomic weights and used in developing his law of partial pressures (Dalton's law). He was colour-blind and studied that affliction, also known as Daltonism.

**dam,** barrier, commonly across a watercourse, to hold back water, often forming a reservoir or lake. Modern dams may be built for multiple purposes: to provide water for irrigation, aid flood control, furnish hydroelectric power, and improve the navigability of waterways. Rock-fill and earth dams are built with a central core, usually clay or cement respectively, that is impervious to water. Gravity dams, usually made of concrete, use their own weight to provide resistance to the pressure of water. Single-arch concrete dams are curved upstream and are usually constructed in narrow canyons where the rocky side walls are strong enough to withstand the tremendous thrust of the dam, caused by the pressure of the water. Multiple-arch dams consist of a number of single arches supported by buttresses. See also ASWAN HIGH DAM; GRAND COULEE DAM; HOOVER DAM.

**Damanhūr,** city (1987 pop. 170,633), N Egypt, in the Nile delta. Situated on the railway E of ALEXANDRIA, it is associated with the cotton industry.

**Damascene, John:** see JOHN OF DAMASCUS, SAINT.

**Damascus,** city (1981 est. pop. 1,112,000), capital of Syria, SW Syria. The largest city in Syria, it stands in an oasis between mountains and desert and is bisected by the Barada R. As a terminus of caravan routes across the Syrian desert its importance was increased in the late 19th and early 20th cent. by the construction of railways to ALEPPO, BEIRUT, HAIFA, and MEDINA. Manufactures include textiles, sugar, and glass. Inhabited before 2000 BC, it may be the oldest continuously occupied city in the world. From the 2nd millennium BC to AD 395 it was ruled by the Egyptians, the Israelites, the Assyrians, the Persians, Alexander the Great, the Seleucids, and the Romans. A thriving commercial city, it early adopted Christianity. St PAUL was converted on the road to Damascus. A provincial Byzantine capital, it fell to the Arabs in 635 and became Islamic. Under the Ummayed dynasty (660–750) it was the capital of the Arab Empire, then at its greatest extent. It was subsequently attacked and occupied by the Abbasids, Seljuk Turks, Egyptians and Mongols and sacked once more by Tamerlane in 1401. In 1516, together with most of Syria, it was occupied by the Ottoman Turks and it remained part of the Ottoman Empire until 1918. T.E. LAWRENCE and his Arab irregular forces under Emir Faisal helped the British take it in 1918. The French then ruled it as part of a League of Nations mandate until Syria became independent (1941). Landmarks include the Great Mosque, one of the world's largest.

**Damien, Father,** 1840–89, Belgian missionary priest; b. Joseph de Veuster. After working as a missionary (1863–73) among the natives of Hawaii, he was transferred to the leper colony on Molokai, where he laboured until he himself died from leprosy.

**Damocles** (ˌdaməkleez), in classical mythology, courtier of DIONYSIUS THE ELDER at SYRACUSE. In order to show the precariousness of power and rank, Dionysius gave a banquet at which a sword was suspended over Damocles' head by a hair.

**Damon and Phintias,** two youths whose loyalty to each other symbolizes true friendship. When Phintias, condemned to death by the Syracusan tyrant DIONYSIUS THE ELDER, was released to arrange his affairs, Damon stayed on as pledge. On Phintias's return, Dionysius freed them both.

**Dampier, William,** 1651?–1715, English explorer. After a buccaneering expedition against the Spanish (1679–81), he sailed around the world and was marooned on the Nicobar Islands. He wrote of his experiences in *Voyages and Discoveries* (1699), which includes a masterly treatise on hydrography. He later commanded an expedition to the Pacific (1703–7), and discovered Dampier Island and Dampier Strait.

**damselfly,** very slender, long-bodied, day-flying, predatory INSECT of the order Odonata (suborder Zygoptera). Damselflies have a somewhat fluttering flight and usually occur along the banks of ponds and slow-moving streams. Both pairs of wings are identical and, when at rest, are often closed vertically above the body. The widely separated eyes and biting mouthparts are adaptions to a predatory way of life, but unlike the DRAGONFLY which feeds on flying insects, damselflies often pick resting insects off leaves. The juvenile stage is an aquatic carnivore.

**Dan:** see ISRAEL, TRIBES OF.

**Dana, Richard Henry,** 1787–1879, American author. A lawyer, poet, critic, and essayist, he was a founder of the *North American Review* and is best known for his poem *The Buccaneer* (1827). His son, **Richard Henry Dana,** 1815–82, was a writer and lawyer who wrote a classic of the days of sailing ships in *Two Years before the Mast* (1840), based on his experiences as a common sailor. *The Seaman's Friend* (1841), a manual of maritime law, grew out of his legal practice.

**Da Nang,** formerly Tourane, city (1971 est. pop. 437,700), E Vietnam, a port on the SOUTH CHINA SEA. It has an excellent deep-water harbour. Copper, coal, and gold are mined nearby. The scene (1535) of the first European landing in Vietnam, it was ceded to France by ANNAM in 1787. During the VIETNAM WAR it was the site of a huge US military base.

**dance,** art of precise, expressive, and graceful human movement, usually performed in accord with musical accompaniment. It developed as a natural expression of united feeling and action. Many primitive dances have survived in the FOLK DANCE of modern times. American Indian dances, usually of a ritualistic and ceremonial nature, illustrate many of the purposes of primitive dancing. The dance of religious ecstasy, in which hypnotic and trancelike states are induced (characteristic of Africa and the Orient), was represented in America by the remarkable Indian GHOST DANCE. American Indian dancing is always performed on the feet, but in islands of the Pacific and the Orient, dances are performed in a sitting posture, with only the hands, arms, and upper parts of the body being used. In Japan, the early dances became institutionalized with a national school of dancing in the 14th cent. Soon dance became associated with the famous No drama (see ORIENTAL DRAMA). In medieval Europe, the repeated outbreaks of dance mania, associated with epidemics of bubonic plague, are reflected in the ALLEGORY of the Dance of Death. Dancing as a social activity and a form of community expression is shown by anthropologists to be very recent in origin. In the Middle Ages, social dancing was a feature of the more enlightened courts. The BALLET first appeared at the Italian and French courts in the 16th cent. Among formal social dances of the 17th cent. were the MINUET and the GAVOTTE. Popular national dances include the mazurka and polonaise, from Poland; the fandango and bolero, from Spain; and the WALTZ, from Germany. The US initiated such dances as the cake walk, the Virginia reel, the fox trot, and the Charleston often arising from Negro culture. Since the 1920s the US has seen a number of dance crazes, e.g., the Lindy Hop of the 1930s, the jitterbug of the 1940s, the rock "n' roll of the 1950s, the go-go dances of the 1960s, and the disco dances of the 1970s usually spreading to Europe and other parts of the world, with some exception, notably the dances of the Punk movement in the UK, the Slam and the Pogo. More recent developments in 'street dance' crazes include Body-breaking, Popping, and Robotics, largely practised by younger members of society both on the streets and off. See tables of major dance companies accompanying this article; see also CHOREOGRAPHY; MODERN DANCE.

**dance notation,** written systems through which the recording of dance and movements is made possible. The roots of dance notation are traceable to the mid 15th cent. Today there are two main systems of notation in use; **Labanotation** developed by Rudolf von LABAN, Kurt JOOSS,

---

## DANCE COMPANIES

| | |
|---|---|
| **American Ballet Theatre**<br>Formerly (1937–40) Mordkin Ballet and (1940–56) Ballet Theatre. Presents newly staged classics and dances with American themes both in US and internationally. BALANCHINE, DE MILLE, ROBBINS, TUDOR among choreographers. BARYSHNIKOV artistic director since 1980. | **Bat-Dor Dance Company, Israel**<br>Founded 1963 and now backed by state of Israel. Martha GRAHAM was the original artistic advisor; Bat-Dor performed some of her works including *Dream* (1974) which she created especially for them. Tours extensively. |
| | **Ballet Folklorico de Mexico**<br>Founded 1952 by Amalia Hernandez at the National Inst. of Fine Arts, Mexico City, to produce for television dances based on Mexican, e.g., Aztec, folklore. Artistic excellence led to recognition as Mexico's national company. One of the greatest of the "ethnic" companies. Tours world. |
| **Australian Ballet**<br>Drew on the tradition est. 1940 by Edouard Borovansky of Ballet Russes. Began 1962 with Peggy Van Praagh as director. Based in Melbourne, linked to Royal Ballet in style. | |

## DANCE COMPANIES *(continued)*

### Ballet di Teatro alla Scala, Milan
In the 19th cent. La Scala was the centre of European ballet under the great classical teacher and choreographer Carlo Blasis. During this cent. the Italian school of ballet has declined steadily, but La Scala remains Italy's most important company.

### Ballet Nacional de Cuba
Founded (1948) in Havana by Alicia Alonso. After the Cuban revolution, the company received support from Castro's government, becoming an international standard-bearer for the regime. Technically brilliant, its repertoire includes the standard classics as well as folklore and modern works.

### Ballet of the XXth Century
Founded (1960) in Brussels by Maurice BÉJART. Popular choreography; favouring the male dancer, although some criticism of substance and misuse of music. Company moved to Switzerland (1987). Works include *Bolero* (1960), *Mass for the Present Time* (1967), and *Les Illuminations* (1979).

### Ballet Rambert
See RAMBERT, DAME MARIE.

### Ballets Russes
See DIAGHILEV, SERGEI PAVLOVICH.

### Bolshoi Ballet
Dancing school (1773), Moscow. Bolshoi theatre, opened 1856; competed with Maryinsky, St Petersburg. Alexander Gorsky revitalized (early 20th cent.) with dramatic realism, today its dramatic and ensemble skills are famous.

### Central Ballet of China
Founded (1959) in Beijing. Originally based on Soviet methods and teaching, the company suffered greatly during the cultural revolution. It has now been revived and enjoys official support. As well as Chinese choreography, performs classical and western Romantic repertoire.

### Dance Theater of Harlem
First black classical company est. 1968 by Arthur Mitchell of New York City Ballet. First full-length New York season 1974. Repertoire mainly classics; choreography by Mitchell, ROBBINS, TUDOR and others. Company tours extensively, offers community dance courses at home.

### Dutch National Ballet
Formed in 1961, based Amsterdam, under direction of Rudi Van Dantzig and choreographers Van Manen and Van Schayk. Succeeds in balancing classical and modern idioms in its repertoire.

### Extemporary Dance Co.
British modern dance group est. 1976. The membership of the company varies according to the demands or subject of the choreography. From 1981 directed by Emlyn Claid.

### Kirov Ballet
Originally Imperial Russian Ballet, St Petersburg (now Leningrad); dating from ballet school founded in 1738; based Maryinsky Theatre from 1889. Under PETIPA premiered *Sleeping Beauty* (1890) and *Swan Lake* (1895). The teaching of Agrippina Vaganova (from 1935) helped to reestablish its school as supreme exponents of classical elegance and beauty.

### Les Grandes Ballets Canadiens
Founded (1956–57) in Montreal and until recently under the direction of Ludmilla Chiriaeff. Large classical and contemporary repertoire, inc. its founder's rock ballet *Tommy*.

### London Contemporary Dance Theatre
Founded 1967 by Robin Howard and Robert Cohan of the Graham Co. with Martha GRAHAM's approval, as an attempt to develop a British school of modern dance. Has been largely successful, and the associated school has produced such choreographers as Richard ALSTON, Siobhan DAVIES, and Robert NORTH.

### London Festival Ballet
Founded (1950) by Dame Alicia Markova, Anton Dolin, and Julian Braunsweg, originally as a commercial company, with artistic policy aimed at popular appeal based on popular classical repertoire. Under Peter Schaufuss company has broadened its horizons, with the inclusion of more contemporary works.

### National Ballet of Canada
Founded (1951) by Celia Franca, based Toronto. Modelled on SADLERS WELLS ROYAL BALLET. Repertoire grounded on classics; tours extensively.

### Netherlands Dance Theatre
Founded (1959) by American Benjamin Harkarvy, with choreographer Hans Van Manen. Experimental and iconoclastic in character. Directed by Jiri KYRIAN (from 1975), the company has enjoyed international success.

### New York City Ballet
Founded (1946) by BALACHINE and Lincoln Kirstein as Ballet Society; based at Lincoln Center, New York. Balanchine developed American style, combining European tradition, austere emotion, and musicality. Later directors include Jerome ROBBINS and Peter Martins.

### Paris Opera Ballet
Oldest classical ballet company in the world, founded 1669 by Louis XIV; first to incorporate female dancers (1681). Produced one of the greatest teachers, Auguste Vestris (1760–1842), due to whose work Paris was pre-eminent in ballet until arrival of DIAGHILEV's Ballets Russes. Directed (1930–39) by Serge Lifar the company regained some of its lustre. Present director Rudolf NUREYEV.

### Royal Ballet
Founded (1931) by Ninette de VALOIS as Vic–Wells Ballet, at Sadlers Wells Theatre. Moved to Royal Opera House (1946). De Valois director until 1963; later directors include Sir Frederick ASHTON and Kenneth MACMILLAN. Balances 3-act classical dramas with shorter often controversial works. Its school considered one of the world's leading classical schools.

### Royal Danish Ballet
Est. Copenhagen (1748). Vincenzo Galeotti director 1775–1816, Auguste Bournonville 1828–79. Bournonville's works and teaching established tradition of excellence in Danish male dancing. Style noted for light precise footwork.

### Royal Winnipeg Ballet
Oldest of Canada's three companies, founded 1938. Since 1953 director has been Arnold Spohr, responsible for its rise in standard and eclectic repertory. Tours widely.

### Sadlers Wells Royal Ballet
Although part of the Royal Ballet's organization in London, the company, based at Sadlers Wells Theatre, has acquired a distinct repertory of its own under the direction of Peter Wright since 1970. Launched (1964) first ballet education group "Ballet for All".

### Scottish Ballet
Originally Western Theatre Ballet. Moved to Glasgow (1969) to become Scottish Theatre Ballet, then Scottish Ballet (1974). Now the national company of Scotland.

### Stuttgart Ballet
First major German company; became prominent in the 1960s under John Cranko. On his death (1973) Glen Tetley succeeded, followed by Haydee as artistic director. Focuses on full-length story productions, e.g., *Romeo and Juliet*, *Eugene Onegin*. Tours extensively.

### Tokyo Ballet
Founded (1964) by Tagatsugu Sasaki, largely influenced by Soviet style and classics. Has toured widely in Europe and America, and has recently augmented its classical repertory with more modern works by Maurice BÉJART and Jiri KYLIAN.

and Albrecht Knust and **Benesh dance notation** developed by Rudolf and Joan Benesh. See also CHOREOGRAPHY.

**Dance Theater of Harlem:** see DANCE (table).

**dandelion,** perennial herb (genus *Taraxacum*) of the COMPOSITE family, widely distributed in temperate regions. It has a rosette of deep-toothed leaves and a bright yellow head followed in fruit by a round head of white down for wind distribution. The common dandelion (*T. officinale*) is often considered a lawn pest but is cultivated for food and medicine in some places. The leaves are used in salads and as a seasoning; the roots are used as a coffee substitute, as a bitter tonic, and as a laxative; the flower heads are used for making dandelion wine and as forage for bees. The dandelion plant contains a white latex, a hydrocarbon that can be converted into a combustible fuel. One species (*T. bicorne*) is grown commercially for latex in the USSR and Argentina.

**Danegeld** (‚dayn'geld), medieval land tax originally raised to buy off raiding Danes and later used for military expenditures. In England the tribute was first levied in 868 and then in 871 by ALFRED. Under ÆTHELRED (978–1016) it became a regular tax, and was collected by later rulers until the 12th cent.

**Danelaw** (‚dayn'law), originally the body of law that prevailed in the part of England occupied by the Danes after the treaty of King ALFRED with Guthrum in 886. It soon came to mean also the area in which Danish law obtained. The Danelaw had four main regions: NORTHUMBRIA; the areas around and including Lincoln, Nottingham, Derby, Leicester, and Stamford; EAST ANGLIA; and the SE Midlands.

**dan Fodio, Usman,** 1754–1817, Nigerian Muslim scholar and founder of the Sokoto caliphate. He launched the first of the 19th-cent. Fulani *jihads* [holy wars] in 1804 against the King of Gobir. The Sokoto *jihad*, as it is popularly known, turned into a people's war against Hausa aristocratic oppression and ended with the formation of a far-flung political empire, the Sokoto caliphate, in N Nigeria. In his latter years, dan Fodio devoted his energies to writing and meditation and left the governance of the caliphate to his brother Abdullahi and his son BELLO.

**Daniel,** book of the OLD TESTAMENT. It relates events and visions from the life of Daniel, a Jew of the 6th cent. BC. Daniel and his friends, taken to BABYLON, remain faithful to the TORAH (1); Daniel interprets a dream of NEBUCHADNEZZAR (2); Nebuchadnezzar tries to punish three recalcitrant Jews (the Three Holy Children) in the fiery furnace (3); Daniel interprets a second dream of Nebuchadnezzar to foretell the latter's madness (4); Daniel interprets the handwriting on the wall at BELSHAZZAR's feast (5); he escapes from the lions' den (6); he has four apocalyptic visions (7–12). The story of Susanna and the elders, and also the stories of Daniel's revelation of the fraud connected with the Babylonian idol Bel and of his killing a dragon and subsequent miraculous escape after being thrown to lions, are in the version of Daniel in the APOCRYPHA. Most modern scholars think that the book was written between 168 and 165 BC.

**Daniel, Samuel,** 1563–1619, English poet and dramatist. His earliest work was *Delia* (1592), a sonnet sequence. His verse epic on the Wars of the Roses, *Civil Wars*, was completed in 1609. Plays include the classically-based *Cleopatra* (1594) and *Philotas* (1604), and many court masques and pastorals. He contributed to the Elizabethan debate about poetry with his verse dialogue *Musophilus* (1599) and his prose treatise *A Defence of Ryme* (1603). Though successful in his own time, and admired by many later poets, including WORDSWORTH and COLERIDGE, Daniel has not enjoyed a revival of interest in the 20th cent.

**Danish language,** member of the North Germanic, or Scandinavian, group of the Germanic subfamily of the Indo-European family of languages. See LANGUAGE (table).

**D'Annunzio, Gabriele,** 1863–1938, Italian poet, novelist, dramatist, and military hero. The sensuous imagery of his early poetry, from *Canto nuovo* (1882) to *Alcione* (1904), displayed unrivalled craftsmanship. His novels, e.g., *Il piacere* (1889; tr. The Child of Pleasure) and *Il trionfo della morte* (1894), show the same control of language but are shallow and theatrical. Two of his plays, *La Gioconda* (1899) and *Francesca da Rimini* (1902), were written for Eleonora DUSE; their affair he described in the novel *Il fuoco* (1900; tr. The Flame of Life). In World War I, D'Annunzio's oratory had much to do with Italy's entry on the Allied side. In Sept. 1919, with a band of volunteers, he seized Fiume (Rijeka), and established an illegal government. He contributed, by his extreme nationalism, to the rise of Fascism but did not participate in the Fascist revolution or regime. See also IRREDENTISM.

**Dante Alighieri** (‚dantee alee‚gyeəree), 1265–1321, Italian poet, author of the *Divine Comedy*. A Florentine patrician, he fought on the side of the GUELPHS but later supported the imperial party. In 1290, after the death of his exalted BEATRICE, he sought consolation in the study of philosophy. Politically active in Florence from 1295, he was banished in 1302 and thereafter led a wandering existence, dying at his last refuge, Ravenna. The *Divine Comedy*, a vernacular poem in 100 cantos (more than 14,000 lines), was composed in exile. It is the tale of the poet's symbolic journey to God through a tour of Hell and Purgatory (guided by VIRGIL) and through his vision of Paradise in the company of Beatrice, the agent of his salvation. Written in *terza rima* (eleven-syllable lines arranged in triplets), it is a magnificent synthesis of poetry and philosophy uniquely encapsulating the religious world-view of the middle ages. Through it Dante established Tuscan as the literary language of Italy and gave rise to a vast literature. His works also include the *Vita nuova* (c.1292), a collection of lyrics, with a linking prose narrative, celebrating his ideal love for Beatrice; treatises on language, philosophy, and politics; eclogues; and epistles.

**Danton, Georges Jacques** (‚dantən), 1759–94, French Revolutionary leader. A lawyer who won immense popularity through his powerful oratory, he exercised power as a member of the Legislative Assembly (1791–92), the COMMUNE OF PARIS, and the CORDELIERS, and through his participation in the overthrow (1792) of the monarchy. In the new republic he was virtual head of the Provisional Executive Council and came to dominate the first Committee of Public Safety (1793) created by the Convention. Although initially Danton had sought foreign wars in order to spread French institutions, with France's military reverses he advocated a conciliatory foreign policy and the relaxation of the REIGN OF TERROR at home. Eclipsed by ROBESPIERRE and the extremists, he was arrested on a charge of conspiracy in 1794, subjected to a mock trial, and guillotined.

**Danube,** chief river of central and SE Europe, c.2850 km (1770 mi) long, second-longest European river after the Volga. It rises in the Brege and Brigach rivers in the BLACK FOREST of SW West Germany and crosses or forms part of the borders of Austria, Czechoslovakia, Hungary, Yugoslavia, Romania, Bulgaria, and the USSR before entering the BLACK SEA through a large (c.2590 km²/1000 sq mi), swampy delta. The river is navigable by barges to Ulm (West Germany) and is connected to N Europe by the Rhine–Main–Danube Canal. The Sip Canal bypasses the rapids at Iron Gate gorge in the Romanian–Yugoslavian section.

**Danzig:** see GDAŃSK.

**Daphne,** in Greek mythology, a nymph loved by APOLLO. When she was pursued by him, she prayed for rescue and was transformed by GAIA into a laurel tree. She is often represented in art, e.g., in a sculpture by BERNINI (*Apollo and Daphne*; 1622-24, Borghese Gall., Rome).

**Daphnis and Chloë:** see LONGUS.

**Da Ponte, Lorenzo,** 1749–1838, Italian librettist, teacher and memorialist. He wrote the librettos to MOZART's *Marriage of Figaro* (1786), *Don Giovanni* (1787), and *Così fan tutte* (1790). He lived in England (1792–1805) before moving to America, where he became a teacher of Italian language and culture, and was involved in attempts to establish opera in New York. In old age (1823–27) he published four volumes of memoirs.

**DAR:** see DAUGHTERS OF THE AMERICAN REVOLUTION.

**D'Arblay, Madame:** see BURNEY, FANNY.

**Dardanelles,** narrow strait, known as the Hellespont in ancient times, c.60 km (40 mi) long and 1.6–6.4 km (1–4 mi) wide, linking the Sea of Marmara and the Mediterranean Sea, and separating European and Asian Turkey. It forms, with the Sea of Marmara and the BOSPORUS, the only outlet of the BLACK SEA, controlling access of Soviet ships to the great MEDITERRANEAN SEA–SUEZ CANAL–INDIAN OCEAN sea lane. International access by all merchant ships and by warships in peacetime was guaranteed by the Montreux Convention (1936), which also recognized Turkey's right to fortify the strait.

**Dardic languages,** group of languages belonging to the Indo-Iranian subfamily of the Indo-European family of languages. See LANGUAGE (table).

**Dare, Virginia,** b. 1587, first child born of English parents in America. She was a member of the 'lost colony' of ROANOKE ISLAND that disappeared c.1591.

**Dar-es-Salaam,** largest city (1985 est. pop. 880,000) and former capital of Tanzania, on the Indian Ocean. It is the country's chief port and economic centre, connected by rail to Kigoma, in the west, and (since 1975) to LUSAKA, Zambia. The city has a variety of industries including oil refining, food processing, textiles, and pharmaceuticals. Founded in 1866 by the sultan of ZANZIBAR, it became the capital of German East Africa in 1891 and grew rapidly after World War II. Today it is a modern city with a university and several colleges. DODOMA is the new Tanzanian capital.

**Darién,** coastal region on the N side of the Isthmus of Panama which was the site of one of the earliest Spanish settlements on the mainland of America. The settlement of Sta María La Antigua Darién was founded close to the present boundary between Panama and Colombia in 1510 and from here Balboa crossed the isthmus to discover the Pacific in 1513.

**Darío, Rubén,** 1867–1916, Nicaraguan poet and diplomat; b. Félix Rubén García Sarmiento. His first book, *Azul* (1888; tr. Blue), heralded the founding of MODERNISMO. Other works include *Prosas profanas* (1896), *El canto errante* (1907; tr. The Wandering Song), and *Poema del otoño* (1910; tr. Autumn Poem), perhaps his masterpiece. His influence on all Spanish-language writers was enormous. He served as a diplomat in many European and Latin American countries.

**Darius,** several kings of ancient PERSIA. **Darius I** (the Great), d. 486 BC (r.521–486 BC), proved to be one of the most able of the ACHAEMENIDS by perfecting a highly efficient system of administration. Around 500 BC, when the Ionian cities rebelled against Persian rule, Darius put down the rebels and set out to punish the Greek city-states that had aided the insurrection. The expedition met defeat in the memorable battle of MARATHON (490 BC); however, he consolidated Persian power in the East. He also continued Cyrus the Great's policy of restoring the Jewish state. **Darius II,** d. 404 BC (r.423?–404 BC), was not popular or successful, and he spent much time in quelling revolts. He lost Egypt (410) but secured influence in Greece. **Darius III,** d. 330 BC (r.336–330 BC), seriously underestimated the strength of ALEXANDER THE GREAT when the Macedonians invaded Persia. Darius was defeated by Alexander in several major battles and was forced to flee to Bactria, where the satrap had him murdered. These events brought the Persian empire to an end and marked the beginning of the Hellenistic period in the E Mediterranean.

**Dark, Eleanor,** 1901–, Australian novelist. She is best known for her historical trilogy *The Timeless Land* (1941), *Storm of Time* (1948), and *No Barrier* (1953), which traces the development of European settlement in Australia 1780–1814 and the conflict between the timeless continent of Australia and the time-governed civilization of Europe.

**Dark Ages:** see MIDDLE AGES.

**Darlan, Jean François,** 1881–1942, French admiral and politician. The leading member of Marshal PÉTAIN's Vichy government in WORLD WAR II, he strengthened France's collaborationist ties with Germany. Later, as commander of all French forces, he was in N Africa during the Nov. 1942 Allied landings and brought French N and W Africa over to the Allied side. He was assassinated on 28 Dec.

**Darling,** longest river in Australia, flowing 2,739 km (1702 mi) generally SW across the semiarid plains of NEW SOUTH WALES to join the MURRAY R. at Wentworth. An important source of irrigation water, it rises in the rainy EASTERN HIGHLANDS and receives many tributaries; occasionally it runs dry.

**Darmstadt,** city (1984 pop. 135,600), and former seat of the ruling family of HESSE, West Germany. It is situated above the RHINE between FRANKFURT and MANNHEIM where routes converge. Chemical industries predominate and there is a technological university founded in 1863.

**Darnley, Henry Stuart** or **Stewart, Lord,** 1545–67, second husband of MARY QUEEN OF SCOTS and father of JAMES I. Son of the powerful earl of Lennox, he claimed succession to the English throne through his grandmother Margaret TUDOR. His Catholic sympathies, his claim to the throne, and perhaps his handsome appearance induced Mary to marry him in 1565. He proved to be a disappointment, and she did not make him royal consort. Jealous of David RIZZIO, Darnley and others killed him. A plot was formed to murder Darnley, probably under the earl of BOTHWELL. On 9 Feb. 1567, the house near Edinburgh where he was staying was blown up; he was found strangled in an adjoining garden the next day.

**Dart, Thurston,** 1921–71, British musicologist and harpsichordist. He was a leading figure in the revival of early music and in research into performance practice. He wrote numerous articles, made many recordings, and edited much 17th-cent. music. He was appointed professor of music at Cambridge in 1962, but took up the new chair at King's College, London in 1964.

**Dartmoor,** upland region in Devon, SW England. It is a large area, (over 770 km²/300 sq mi in extent), of wild moorland scenery. There are many isolated masses of granite on the moors, known as 'tors'. The highest point is at High Willhays, where the land rises to 621 m (2039 ft). Most of the Devonshire rivers rise here, and there are several boggy areas. Cattle, sheep, and half-wild ponies graze the moor. Dartmoor prison, founded in 1805, is on the moor, near Princetown. Much of the area is now a national park.

**darts,** indoor game in which players throw small arrows at a board having a diameter of 0.34 m (13½ in). The board is divided into 20 numbered wedge-shaped sectors with an inner central ring or 'bull's-eye' worth 50 pts and an outer central ring worth 25 pts. A ring round the circumference of the board and another half way between the circumference and the centre respectively double or treble the score. The game is played widely in Britain, especially in public houses, and has become even more popular through being televised. The most common form of competition is to reduce the score from 501 or 301 to 0, beginning and ending on a double. The board is mounted with its centre 1.72 m (5 ft 8 in) above the floor, and players throw from a line 2.43 m (8 ft) away.

**Darwin,** city (1986 pop. 72,937), capital of the Northern Territory, N Australia, on an inlet of the Timor Sea. It is the chief port and administrative centre for the sparsely settled tropical north coast. Called Palmerston until 1911, it was renamed for Charles DARWIN, who discovered its site in 1839 on a voyage of the *Beagle*. It has been largely rebuilt since a devastating tropical cyclone *Tracey* in 1974. It is the tourist centre for the 'Top End', servicing Kakadu National Park, Katherine Gorge and the Ord R. In 1872, with the completion of the submarine cable and the Overland Telegraph Line, the northern port linked Australia with the world through the electric telegraph.

**Darwin, Charles Robert,** 1809–82, English naturalist, grandson of Erasmus DARWIN. He firmly established the theory of organic EVOLUTION. His position as official naturalist aboard the H.M.S. *Beagle* during its world voyage (1831–36) started Darwin on a career of accumulating and assimilating data that resulted in the formulation of his concept of evolution; he was also stimulated by the writings of MALTHUS. In 1858 he and Alfred Russel WALLACE simultaneously published summaries of their independently conceived notions of evolution by NATURAL SELECTION; a year later Darwin set forth the structure of his theory and massive support for it in his *Origin of Species*. This was supplemented by later works, notably *The Descent of Man* (1871) and *The Expression of the Emotions in Man and Animals* (1872). Darwin also formulated a theory of the origin of coral reefs, wrote a standard text on the barnacles, and wrote about mechanisms of fertilization in plants.

**Darwin, Erasmus,** 1731–1802, English physician and poet; grandfather of Charles DARWIN. His long poem *Botanic Garden* (1789–91) expounded the Linnaean system. *Zoonomia* (1794–96) explained organic life in evolutionary terms, anticipating later theories.

**Darwinism:** see NATURAL SELECTION.

**dash:** see PUNCTUATION.

**database,** An INFORMATION STORAGE AND RETRIEVAL SYSTEM recording data relating to some common enterprise. Examples include medical, police, and social services records, vehicle registration records, medical and legal information, stock market and banking systems, cataloguing systems, booking systems for airlines, etc. A *database management system* (DBMS) is a software system which supports the storage and retrieval of data in a database. The data is defined by means of a *schema* and the detailed structure of its components is described in a *data dictionary*. A *database administrator* is a person responsible for all aspects of the design, implementation, and operation of the database. *Database* languages are provided for defining and accessing the database. A query language, for example, might be used to retrieve a simple fact 'list the owner of car ABC

123', or data items satisfying complex relationships 'list the owners of all red Ford cars manufactured between 1975 and 1980' (which have an entry in this (police) database). A given database may be used over a wide geographic area, even worldwide, and may be stored on many separate computers connected by a COMPUTER NETWORK forming a distributed database.

**data processing (DP),** the operation of handling, merging, sorting, and computing performed upon data in accordance with strictly defined procedures. The term is usually associated with commercial, industrial, or government organizations and is typically carried out within a DP department under the control of a DP manager. DP software is applications software relating to employees (payroll and personnel records), customers and suppliers (order processing, stock control), and general business support (accounting, forecasting, investment, planning, and control). A central DP department may increasingly be replaced, at least partially, with a distributed *office system*, in which employees use workstations to support their activities. A company may also be dispersed geographically in which case a COMPUTER NETWORK is used to allow interworking of the various DP activities.

**Data Protection Act,** in the UK, act of Parliament designed to protect a person (data-subject) who has information held on him or her on a computer, by another person (data-user). The Act allows the data-subject access to the data (e.g., to check its accuracy), and prevents the data-user passing it to others without the data-subject's permission. The Act was passed in order to stem the threat to privacy caused by the growth of computers. All data-users must by law register with the Data Protection Register, whose job it is to enforce the Act. If an unauthorized disclosure is made by the data-user, the data-subject can claim compensation for any loss caused. The Act does not cover information held manually, e.g., on file.

**data transmission,** the exchange of information between computers, or between a computer terminal and a computer according to some COMMUNICATIONS PROTOCOL. Speeds vary widely: 150 characters per sec. is common, and distances might be local (within a room or building: see LOCAL AREA NETWORK) or over a wide geographic area which normally require public transmission facilities. World-wide connections are now common (see COMPUTER NETWORK). The elements of data transmission are a transmitter, a channel, and a receiver, and, for two-way operation (full-duplex, both ways simultaneously; half-duplex, both ways but not simultaneously), these elements must be duplicated. A feature of all data transmission is the effect of and the control of errors (data corruptions). As a general rule modern communication systems are reliable and virtually error-free and consequently only simple protocols are required. Conventional data transmission between computer systems uses error detection together with some form of a repeat transmission request, in other cases, for example deep space probes, the repeat request is not practical and more complex error correction techniques are used.

**date,** name for a PALM (*Phoenix dactylifera*) and for its edible fruit, probably native to Arabia and North Africa and long a major food source in desert and tropical regions. The sweet, nutritious fruits grow in heavy clusters; a tree may produce up to 90 kg (200 lb) annually. Sugar and a fermented drink are made from the sap of the tree, and the seeds are sometimes used as a coffee substitute. The wood of the trunk is used in construction, and mats and baskets are woven from the leaves.

**dating,** in ARCHAEOLOGY, the primary means by which the past is organized. A guiding principle is that as cultural material is deposited over time, older material is covered by more recent material, thereby providing a way to sort buried artifacts into a relative chronology. The principle holds generally, but studies of site deformation after deposit (taphonomy) show that many natural and cultural factors can alter the stratification of a deposit. More precise dating is obtained by analysing cultural materials directly. Tree-ring dating (DENDROCHRONOLOGY) may be used to obtain an absolute date on wooden objects; relatively precise dates may be obtained through processes involving measurement of the decay of radioactive impurities in organic and inorganic substances (see CARBON-14). Dating remains essential to archaeology as a technique, but the goal of establishing cultural chronologies is now being replaced by a concern with how and why cultures change.

**dative:** see CASE.

**Daubigny, Charles-François** (dohbeen,yee), 1817–78, French landscape painter. A member of the BARBIZON SCHOOL, he was best known for his paintings of the banks of the Seine and the Oise. Daubigny was particularly successful in his atmospheric depiction of dawn, twilight, and moonlight.

**Daudet, Alphonse** (doh,day), 1840–97, French author. He is noted for his gently naturalistic portrayals of French life, as in the Provence-inspired collection of short stories, *Lettres de mon moulin* (1869; Letters from my Mill). His semiautobiographical novel, *Le Petit Chose* (1868), touchingly describes his life at boarding school. His son, **Léon Daudet,** 1867–1942, editor of the right-wing Catholic paper *Action française,* was the author of an extensive and valuable series of memoirs.

**Daughters of the American Revolution** (DAR), patriotic society founded 1890 in Washington, DC, and open to women with one or more ancestors who aided the cause of the AMERICAN REVOLUTION. It has over 209,000 members and has done much to preserve and mark historic places. The DAR has been criticized for its conservative political stance.

**Daumier, Honoré** (doh,myay), 1808–79, French caricaturist, painter, and sculptor. Daumier was the greatest social satirist of his day. His bitterly ironic approach mercilessly ridiculed bourgeois society in realistic graphic style. He produced almost 4000 lithographs. His oil paintings, e.g., *Third-Class Carriage* (Metropolitan Mus., New York), have the same dramatic intensity. His sculpture includes caricature heads.

**dauphin** (,dawfin), [Fr., = dolphin], French title. It was borne first by the counts of Vienne and after 1350 by the eldest son of the king of France. If the dauphin died before the king, the title went to the dauphin's eldest son.

**Davenport, John,** 1597–1670, Puritan clergyman; b. England. For theological reasons he fled to New England in 1637. The following year he helped to found New Haven in Connecticut. Davenport became minister at the First Church, Boston, in 1668.

**David,** d. c.972 BC, king of the ancient Hebrews (r. c.1012–c.972 BC), successor of SAUL and one of the greatest of Hebrew national heroes. To him were ascribed many of the PSALMS. There are many narratives in the BIBLE dealing with the story of David, e.g., the fight between David and GOLIATH; the friendship of David and Saul's son, Jonathan; David's love for BATH-SHEBA; and the revolt of ABSALOM.

**David,** kings of Scotland. **David I,** c.1085–1153 (r.1124–53), fought without success for MATILDA, his niece, in the struggle for the English crown between STEPHEN and Matilda. He did realize his main aim, securing Northumberland. His rule of Scotland was felicitous. **David II** (David Bruce), 1324–71 (r.1329–71), went to France after EDWARD III and Edward de BALLIOL invaded Scotland in 1332. He invaded England in 1346, was captured, and held until ransomed in 1357.

**David** or **Davit, Gerard,** c.1460–1523, Flemish painter, who developed the tradition of MEMLING and van der WEYDEN. The *Baptism of Christ* (c.1500–08; Musée Comunale des Beaux Arts, Bruges) shows his union of Italian grandeur with northern detail.

**David, Jacques-Louis** (dha,veed), 1748–1825, French painter. David was the leading artist of the neo-classical movement (see CLASSICISM). His severe *Oath of the Horatii* (1785; Louvre, Paris), an exemplar of Republican virtue, broke with his early ROCOCO style and established his dominance. There followed other major works, as the *Death of Socrates* (1787; Metropolitain Mus., New York) and *The Lictors bringing Brutus the body of his sons* (1789; Louvre, Paris), which celebrate the stern heroes of antiquity. During the Revolution he became the virtual art dictator of France; his *Marat assassinated* (1793; Brussels) is his most moving memorial to a martyr of the Revolution. Later he became first painter to Napoleon.

**David, Saint,** d. c.600, patron saint of WALES, first abbot of Menevia (now St David's) in Wales. His shrine was an important place of pilgrimage in the Middle Ages, and the national Welsh festival is still celebrated on his feast, 1 Mar.

**Davidson, Donald,** 1930–, American philosopher. His work links the philosophy of language, action, and mind. He argues that the way to understand meaning is to study the process of 'radical translation' in which speakers' utterances are interpreted within the framework of a TARSKI truth-theory so as to show how the meanings of sentences depend systematically on the meanings of their parts. Actions, he thinks, are

Jacques-Louis **David**, *Oath of the Horatii*, 1785. Louvre, Paris.

events caused by reasons, so that our everyday psychological explanations are irreducible to scientific explanation, although he also holds that mental events are physical events. His papers are collected in *Essays on Actions and Events* (1980) and *Inquiries into Truth and Interpretation* (1984).

**Davies, Sir John,** 1569–1626, English poet. His major works are the long poem *Nosce Teipsum* (1599), on the immortality of the soul; *Orchestra; or, A Poem of Dancing* (1596), on the order of the universe; and *Hymns of Astraea* (1599).

**Davies, Sir Peter Maxwell,** 1934–, British composer. He has been influenced by serial techniques and medieval music. The music of John Taverner inspired two orchestral fantasias (1962 and 1964) and the opera *Taverner* (1962–70, performed 1972). Maxwell Davies has been Director of the Summer School of Music at Dartington, Devon, and has written much music for schools. He composed many works for the Fires of London (originally founded with BIRTWISTLE as the Pierrot Players), most notably *Eight Songs for a Mad King* (1969). Since 1971 he has lived in Orkney, which has influenced the music of his three symphonies and other works. He also founded in 1977, and has since directed, the St Magnus Festival in Orkney.

**Davies, Robertson,** 1913–, Canadian novelist. He came to international attention with the Deptford trilogy of novels *Fifth Business* (1970), *The Manticore* (1972), and *World of Wonders* (1975) a richly plotted study of three people's journey to self-discovery, replete with humor, mystery, magic, Jungian ideas, and grotesque characters. His other novels include *Tempest-Tost* (1951), *Leaven of Malice* (1954), *A Mixture of Frailties* (1958), and *The Rebel Angels* (1982).

**Da Vinci, Leonardo:** see LEONARDO DA VINCI.

**Davis, Angela Yvonne,** 1944–, American black activist. She taught (1969–70) philosophy at UCLA despite state efforts to oust her for being a Communist. In 1970 she went into hiding after being accused of aiding a group that killed four persons in an attempted courtroom escape. She was apprehended and tried (1972), but was acquitted of all charges. A member of the Communist Party since 1968, she was its vice-presidential candidate in the 1980 US election.

**Davis, Bette,** 1908–, American film actress; b. Ruth Elizabeth Davis. An enduring Hollywood star, she has made such films as *Jezebel* (1938; Academy Award), *Dark Victory* (1939), and *All About Eve* (1950). Later she played grotesque older women, e.g., in *Whatever Happened to Baby Jane* (1963).

**Davis, Sir Colin,** 1927–, English conductor. He conducted the BBC Symphony Orchestra (1967–71) and the Royal Opera, Covent Garden Orchestra (1971–86).

**Davis, Jack,** 1918–, Australian Aboriginal poet and dramatist. His writings concentrate on the injustices endured by his people, their melancholy sense of loss and cultural alienation in white society. His plays, which constitute a history of race-relations from an Aboriginal point of view, are *The Dreamers* (1982), *No Sugar* (1985), *Barungin* (1988), constituting a trilogy called *The First Born*.

**Davis, Jefferson,** 1808–89, American statesman, president of the CONFEDERACY (1861–65). A US senator from Mississippi (1847–51, 1857–61) and US secretary of war (1853–57), Davis left Washington after the secession (Jan. 1861) of Mississippi. As president of the Confederacy, he assumed strong centralized power, weakening the STATES' RIGHTS policy for which the South had seceded. During the AMERICAN CIVIL WAR, he was involved in many disputes with Confederate generals. Captured (1865) by Union forces, he was imprisoned for two years but was released (1867) without prosecution.

**Davis, Miles,** 1926–, black American musician. He worked with Charlie PARKER in the 1940s, was a catalyst of 'cool' JAZZ around 1950, led influential small bands through the 1960s, and produced a jazz–rock blend in the 1970s and 80s. His warm, often muted trumpet style is famous.

**Davis, Stuart,** 1894–1964, American painter. A jazz enthusiast, he often incorporated jazz tempos into the vibrant patterns of his paintings. In the 1920s Davis came under the influence of CUBISM and created, in such works as *Colonial Cubism* (Walker Art Center, Minneapolis), a brightly coloured, distinctly American interpretation of the movement.

**Davis, William Morris,** 1850–1934, American geographer and geologist. He systematized the study of geography (particularly of geomorphology) and enlarged its scope; his methods of description and analysis and use of maps and block diagrams revolutionized its teaching.

**Davit, Gerard:** see DAVID, GERARD.

**Davy, Sir Humphry,** 1778–1829, English chemist and physicist. He was professor (1802–13) at the ROYAL INSTITUTION, London, where his electrochemical researches led to his isolation of the chemical elements sodium and potassium (1807) and barium, boron, calcium, and magnesium (1808). He showed chlorine to be an element, theorized that acids characteristically contain hydrogen, and classed chemical affinity as an electrical phenomenon. He was the inventor of the renowned Davy lamp which has saved the lives of countless miners who work in atmospheres rich in firedamp (METHANE). For this service to humanity, Czar Alexander II of Russia sent him a special gilded ornament, still in use at the Royal institution.

**Dawes Plan,** presented (1924) by the committee headed by US vice president C.G. Dawes to the Allied Reparations Commission and accepted that year. It provided for the reduction of Germany's REPARATIONS after WORLD WAR I and the stabilization of German finances. See also YOUNG PLAN.

**Dawson** or **Dawson City,** city (1979 est. pop. 838), W Yukon, N Canada, at the confluence of the Yukon and Klondike rivers. A famous gold rush town whose population reached c.20,000 in 1898, it was the territorial capital until replaced by WHITEHORSE in 1952.

**day:** see SIDEREAL TIME; SOLAR TIME.

**Day, John,** 1522–84, English printer. His types included musical notes and the first Anglo-Saxon type. He printed the first English book of church music (1560) and the first English edition of FOXE's *Book of Martyrs* (1563).

**Dayan, Moshe** (die͵ahn), 1915–81, Israeli military leader; b. Palestine. He directed the 1956 Sinai campaign as chief of staff and the 1967 Six-Day War as defence minister. Blamed for Israeli unpreparedness in the 1973 October War, he resigned (1974) with Golda MEIR. Later (1977–79) he was Israeli foreign minister. See also ARAB–ISRAELI WARS.

**Day Lewis, C(ecil),** 1904–72, English author. His verse was at first didactic and social, reflecting his leftist leanings, later more personal and metaphysical. His works include *Collected Poems* (1954); a translation of Virgil's *Aeneid* (1952); and detective stories written under the pseudonym Nicholas Blake. He was POET LAUREATE (1968–72).

**daylight saving time** (DST), time observed when clocks and other timepieces are set ahead, usually by 1 hr, so that the sun will rise and set later in the day as measured by civil time (see SOLAR TIME). DST conserves lighting power and provides more usable daylight hours for afternoon and evening activities.

**Dayton,** US city (1984 est. pop. 181,000), SW Ohio, on the Great Miami R.; inc. 1805. It is a port and trading hub for a fertile farm area, and an aviation centre. Chief manufactures are cash registers, appliances, and automobile parts. The city grew with the extension of canals (1830s–40s) and railways, and with the industrial demands of the CIVIL WAR. The WRIGHT brothers, Dayton natives, returned there after their historic first flight and established a research aircraft plant.

**Dazai Osamu,** (‚dahzie ‚shoohjee), 1909–48, Japanese novelist. He was noted for his obsession with suicide, his ironic and gloomy wit, and his brilliant fantasy. His masterpiece, *Setting Sun* (1947), depicts the decline of Japan's nobility after World War II.

**DBS** or **direct broadcasting by satellite,** SATELLITE transmission aimed at direct home reception. The satellite power necessary to achieve this is 100 W, some five times greater than the power used in communication satellites relying upon very large dishes at ground reception stations, which allows receiving dishes no more than 90 cm (3 ft) in diameter to be used. In most areas of Britain dishes of only 45 cm (18 in) will suffice, allowing them, since the broadcasting satellites are in orbit above the equator, to be mounted on the south-facing walls of houses. DBS transmissions use a special method of encoding TV signals, known as MAC, and so need a decoder to provide signals to feed existing TV receivers.

**DC:** see ELECTRICITY; GENERATOR; MOTOR, ELECTRIC.

**D Day:** see WORLD WAR II.

**DDT:** see INSECTICIDE.

**deacon, 1** In the Roman Catholic, Eastern Orthodox, and Anglican churches the lowest rank of the threefold ministry of bishops, priests, and deacons. **2** In certain Protestant bodies a lay official, often with financial responsibilities, who assists the minister of a congregation.

**deadly nightshade:** see BELLADONNA; NIGHTSHADE.

**Dead Sea,** salt lake, c.1010 km² (390 sq mi) in the arid Jordan trough of the GREAT RIFT VALLEY, on the Israel-Jordan border. At 396 m (1300 ft) below sea level, it is the lowest point on earth. The lake, which has no life and owes its high salinity to rapid evaporation, derives most of its inflow (now diminished because of irrigation) from the JORDAN R. It is rich in mineral salts. Potash and bromine are commercially extracted.

**Dead Sea Scrolls,** documents of great historical and scholarly value, found in 1947 and later in caves above the NW Dead Sea. Archaeologists have shown that the scrolls stored in jars in the first cave at QUMRAN were written or copied between the 1st cent. BC and the first half of the 1st cent. AD. Chief among the scrolls are two copies of the Book of Isaiah, almost 1000 years older than any Hebrew biblical manuscript previously known. Another important scroll was a *Manual of Discipline* for the ascetic community of Qumran, which has been closely identified with the Essenes, a Jewish religious sect living an ascetic communal agricultural life in that region between the 2nd cent. BC and 2nd cent. AD. Startling parallels between the Qumran scrolls and the New Testament suggest a tie between the Essenes and the early Christians, and have led to the much-disputed suggestion that Jesus and John the Baptist may have been Essenes. More biblical and other manuscripts have been found elsewhere in the Dead Sea area, some even more ancient than those at Qumran.

**deafness,** partial or total loss of hearing. It may be present at birth (congenital) or acquired any time thereafter. Conductive deafness, one of the two major types of deafness, involves a disturbance in the transmission of sound to the nerve receptors of the inner ear. This type of deafness may be caused by infection (otitis media), impacted wax, perforation of the eardrum, or otosclerosis, a hereditary disorder in adults, that restricts the vibration of the bone leading to the inner ear. These conditions can usually be treated with ANTIBIOTIC drugs, surgery, hearing aids, and other techniques. The other major type of deafness, perceptive deafness, involves damage to neural receptors in the inner ear, to nerve pathways to the brain, or to the area of the brain concerned with hearing. Usually permanent, it can be caused by injury, infection, old age, tumours, or excessive noise, or it may be present at birth, for example if the mother was affected with German measles during pregnancy. Those who cannot be helped to hear may communicate through lip reading and SIGN LANGUAGE. See EAR.

Fragment of the **Dead Sea Scrolls**, photographed by ordinary light (left) and by infrared (right)

**Deak, Francis** (‚deahk), Hung. *Deák, Ferenc* (dĕ‚äk), 1803–76, Hungarian politician. He advocated the continued union of Austria and Hungary, but sought recognition of Hungary as a separate kingdom. In 1867 he negotiated the *Ausgleich* [compromise], which established the AUSTRO-HUNGARIAN MONARCHY.

**Deakin, Alfred,** 1856–1919, Australian statesman. A liberal and visionary nationalist, he aided the fight for Australian federation and was prime minister (1903–04, 1905–08) of liberal governments. His last period as prime minister (1909-10) saw a fusion of the non-Labor parties.

**Dean, James,** 1931–55, American film actor; b. James Byron. After only three leading roles, he became the embodiment of the rebelliousness of young Americans in the 1950s. His death in a car crash served to heighten the mythology surrounding him. His main films are *East of Eden* (1955), *Rebel Without a Cause* (1955), and *Giant* (1956).

**death,** cessation of all life processes. Traditionally, death was defined as the cessation of the heart beat and RESPIRATION. However, with advances in organ transplantation techniques (see TRANSPLANTATION, MEDICAL), the need has arisen for a more precise definition of death, since the death of a donor must be established before transfer of an organ can be undertaken. Artificial ventilation and fluid intake can maintain heart beat and some organ and tissue viability. Brain death is therefore used to define death, with a group of signs indicating irreversible brain damage. Death is followed by a number of irreversible changes which are of legal importance in estimating time of death (e.g., rigor mortis, rigidity of the body caused by changes in muscle tissue, occurring 10 min to several hours after death).

**Death Valley,** protected desert region, US, 836,757 hectares (2,067,628 acres), S California and S Nevada, location of the lowest point (86 m/282 ft below sea level) in the Americas. It receives less than 5 cm (2 in) of rain a year and has recorded some of the world's highest air temperatures (57°C/134°F) and ground temperatures (74°C/165°F). The unusual plants and animals found there are of considerable scientific interest. Death Valley was a major source of borax in the late 19th cent.

**debenture:** see BOND.

**Debrecen** (‚debretsən), city (1986 est. pop. 186,000), E Hungary. Activities are mainly agricultural, and there is a university. The centre of the Hungarian Calvinist Church since the 16th cent., Debrecen has been identified with movements for national independence in modern times. The Habsburg dynasty was declared dethroned in the town church in Apr. 1849.

**de Broglie, Louis Victor, prince:** see BROGLIE.

**Debs, Eugene Victor,** 1855–1926, American Socialist leader. An advocate of industrial unions and a pacifist, Debs was imprisoned in 1895 for breaking an injunction during the Pullman railway strike. Later, he was jailed (1918–21) for violating the Espionage Act. He helped to form the Socialist Party and was its presidential candidate five times after 1900. Debs was widely revered as a martyr to his principles.

**debt,** obligation in services, money, or goods owed by one party (the debtor) to another (the creditor). A debt usually involves the payment of INTEREST. If a debtor fails to pay, a court may assign payment out of the debtor's property. In ancient times debt was associated with slavery, because the insolvent debtor and his household were often turned over to the creditor to perform compulsory services. Imprisonment for debt, which once filled prisons, was ended as such in Europe and the US by laws enacted in the 19th cent., although imprisonment on related charges, such as concealment of assets, may still occur. The laws of BANKRUPTCY are designed to distribute a debtor's assets to the creditors.

**debt, public,** indebtedness of a government expressed in money terms. It is also known as the national debt. The public debt increases whenever public spending exceeds public revenues, producing budget deficits. To finance such deficits, the government must borrow from private or institutional investors or from other governments. Public loans may be in the form of short-term instruments, such as treasury certificates, long-term government bonds, or various other notes. Governments may incur debts for several reasons, two major ones being the financing of wars and the combating of the effects of recessions. Heavy government borrowings exert upward pressures on INTEREST rates and may be harmful to the general economy. Public debt in the UK fell steadily as a percentage of GROSS NATIONAL PRODUCT from 70% in 1974 to an estimated 53% in 1987. This was in contrast to most other industrialized countries where the share grew—from 40% to 51% in the US, from 18% to 69% in Japan and from 58% to an estimated 107% in Italy—over the same comparative period.

**Debussy, Claude Achille** (dǝ‚byoohsee/daybyoohsee), 1862–1918, French composer, exponent of musical IMPRESSIONISM. He employed the whole-tone SCALE and other original devices to create nuances of mood and expression, exploring unusual harmonies and dissonances. He is best known for the tone poem (see SYMPHONIC POEM) *Prelude to the Afternoon of a Faun* (1894), inspired by a poem of MALLARMÉ. Other orchestral works include *Nocturnes* (1899) and *La Mer* (1905). His piano works include *Suite Bergamasque* (1905), including *Clair de lune; Estampes* (1903); two books of *Préludes* (1910 and 1913), 12 *Études* (1915) and the two-piano suite *En blanc et noir* (1915).

**Debye, Peter Joseph Wilhelm,** 1884–1966, Dutch physical chemist. Early in his career he taught physics at universities in Zurich, Göttingen, and Leipzig before becoming director of the Kaiser Wilhelm Institute in Berlin. In 1940 he moved to the Baker Chemical Laboratories of Cornell University, US. His work was wide-ranging and emphasized the essential unity of the physical sciences. He studied quantization of electron energies, X-ray scattering, electrolyte solutions, dipole moments, shape of polymer molecules, and vibrations in crystals. In 1936 he was awarded the Nobel prize for chemistry.

**Decadence,** term widely used to signify a period of moral and artistic decline, and specifically to describe a movement among late 19th-cent. artists and writers. This movement originated in France where artists and writers, reacting against bourgeois materialism, cultivated a taste for the sensuous and artifical and explored an often morbid eroticism. It developed from BAUDELAIRE's *Les Fleurs du Mal* (1857), and the hero of Huysmans' novel, *À Rebours* (1884), became the archetypal Decadent. The movement spread to England in the 1890s, where its main exponents were SWINBURNE, Oscar WILDE, and BEARDSLEY.

**Decameron:** see BOCCACCIO, GIOVANNI.

**decathlon,** a contest comprising 10 track-and-field events: long jump; high jump; discus; shot put; javelin; 100-m, 400-m and 1500-m races; 110-m hurdles; and pole vault. An Olympic event since 1912, it has been dominated by Americans. The winner gains the traditional title 'world's greatest athlete'. See PENTATHLON.

**Decatur, Stephen,** 1779–1820, American naval officer. During the TRIPOLITAN WAR, he led (1804) a daring raid into Tripoli harbour to burn the captured US frigate *Philadelphia*. In the WAR OF 1812, Decatur commanded the *United States* and captured (1812) the British frigate *Macedonian*. Known for his reckless bravery and stubborn patriotism, he was mortally wounded in a duel with James BARRON.

**Deccan,** region of India. It is sometimes used in a wide sense for all of India S of the Narmada R. and sometimes, more specifically, for the area of rich black soils and basalt-covered plateaus in the northern part of the peninsula between the Narmada and Krishna rivers.

**December:** see MONTH.

**Decembrists,** Russian officers who rose against Czar NICHOLAS I in Dec. 1825. Influenced by liberal ideals while serving in W Europe during the Napoleonic Wars (see NAPOLEON I), they advocated representative democracy but disagreed on its form. Their poorly organized rebellion was crushed, but it led to increased revolutionary activity among the educated classes and an accompanying rise in police terrorism.

**De Chirico:** see CHIRICO, GIORGIO DE.

**decibel** (dB), unit of sound intensity. The faintest audible sound is arbitrarily assigned a value of 0 dB, and the loudest sounds that the human ear can tolerate are about 120 dB. The difference in decibels between any two sounds is equal to $10 \log_{10} (P_1/P_2)$, where $P_1$ and $P_2$ are the two power levels.

**decimal system** [Lat., = of tenths], NUMERATION system based on powers of 10 and using the digits 0, 1, 2, 3, 4, 5, 6, 7, 8, and 9. A NUMERAL in the decimal system is written as a row of digits, with each position in the row corresponding to a specific power of 10 (see EXPONENT). A decimal point in the row divides it into increasing positive powers of 10 for positions to the left, and increasing negative powers of 10 for positions to the right. For example, 103 represents $(1 \times 10^2) + (0 \times 10^1) + (3 \times 10^0)$, or $100 + 0 + 3$; and 1.03 corresponds to $(1 \times 10^0) + (0 \times 10^{-1}) + (3 \times 10^{-2})$, or $1 + 0 + \frac{3}{100}$. The decimal system was introduced into Europe c.1300. Its positional system made it an improvement over Roman numerals and simplified arithmetic computation. The METRIC SYSTEM of weights and measures is based on the decimal system, as are most systems of national currency.

**Declaration of Independence,** adopted July 4, 1776, by delegates of the THIRTEEN COLONIES, announcing their separation from Great Britain and creation of the United States. It was written almost totally by Thomas JEFFERSON. The opening paragraphs state the American ideal of government, based on the theory of natural rights. The Declaration of Independence is the most important of all American historical documents; its combination of general principles and an abstract theory of government with a detailed enumeration of specific grievances and injustices makes it one of the great political documents of the West.

**Declaration of London:** see LONDON, DECLARATION OF.

**Declaration of Rights:** see BILL OF RIGHTS.

**Declaration of the Rights of Man and Citizen,** historic French document. It was drafted (1789) by Emmanuel SIEYÈS and embodied as the preamble in the French constitution of 1791. Influenced by the US DECLARATION OF INDEPENDENCE and the ideas of the ENLIGHTENMENT, it asserted the equality of all men, the sovereignty of the people, and the inalienable rights of the individual to liberty, property, and security.

**declension:** see INFLECTION.

**declination:** see ASTRONOMICAL COORDINATE SYSTEMS.

**decompression sickness,** physiological disorder caused by rapid decrease in atmospheric pressure that results in the release of nitrogen bubbles from the blood into body tissues. This causes nausea, pain in the joints and chest, and, in severe cases, shock, paralysis, and death, unless the bubbles are forced back into solution by recompression. Also known as the bends, or altitude sickness, it affects deep-sea divers, aeroplane pilots, and others working in compressed air. Use of a decompression chamber allows for a gradual reduction of pressure, according to a strict time schedule, permitting the elimination of nitrogen through the lungs.

**Decorated:** see GOTHIC ARCHITECTURE AND ART.

**Deconstruction:** see DERRIDA, Jacques.

**Dedekind, Julius Wilhelm Richard,** 1831–1916, German mathematician, perhaps best known for the 'Dedekind cut', whereby real numbers can be defined in terms of rational numbers (see NUMBER). A student of Carl GAUSS, he led the effort to formulate rigorous definitions of basic mathematical concepts.

**deduction, 1** In traditional LOGIC the process of drawing, by reasoning, particular conclusions from more general principles assumed to be true. The Aristotelian SYLLOGISM is the classic example of deductive logic in the tradition. 2 In contemporary logic, any statement derived by a transformed rule upon an axiom; more generally, the term now refers to a process of deriving theorems from axioms, or conclusions from premises, by formal rules (transformation rules). See also INDUCTION.

**Dee,** Welsh *Dyfrdwy*, river in Wales and W England, approximately 112 km (70 mi) long. It rises at the NE end of Bala Lake, Gwynedd, and flows circuitously past Corwen, Llangollen, and CHESTER, entering the Irish Sea between the Point of Air and Hoylake. It has a long and wide estuary, which forms a huge expanse of sand at low tide.

**Dee,** river in E Scotland, approximately 145 km (90 mi) long. It rises at Pools of Dee in the Cairngorms, in SW of Grampian region and flows E past BRAEMAR, BALMORAL CASTLE, Ballater, and Aboyne to the North Sea at ABERDEEN. It is connected to the North Sea at Aberdeen by an artificial channel. Well-known for salmon fishing, it has also supplied Aberdeen with water since the late 19th cent.

**Dee, John,** 1527–1608, English mathematician, astrologer, and occultist. Acquitted of a charge of sorcery against Queen Mary I, he became a favourite of Queen Elizabeth I, for whom he drew up valuable scientific studies about newly discovered lands. His occult studies led to his claim of having discovered the secret of ALCHEMY, which he practised abroad.

**Deep Sea Drilling Project,** US programme, begun in 1964, to investigate the evolution of ocean basins by drilling and studying cores of ocean sediments and underlying oceanic crust. It uses the *Glomar Challenger,* an elaborately equipped ship capable of drilling through great water depths.

**deer,** ruminant MAMMAL of the family Cervidae, found worldwide except for Australia. Deer range in size from the ELK or MOOSE, which may be about 2 m (7 ft) high at the shoulder, to the pudu of South America, which is 30 cm (12 in) high. Antlers, bony outgrowths of the skull used as weapons during the breeding season, develop in males of most species and are shed and renewed annually. In deer lacking antlers, such as the Chinese water deer and the muntjac, long, upper canine teeth are used for fighting. The red deer (*Cervus elephas*) and its close relatives are found right across Europe and Asia. The fallow deer (*Dama dama*), wild in Mediterranean Europe, are often kept in British parks or on country estates, and escapees flourish in Europe and North America.

**defence mechanism,** a term in PSYCHOANALYSIS referring to the UNCONSCIOUS processes underlying reactive behaviours whose object is to reduce or eliminate ANXIETY. Some commonly cited defence mechanisms are: repression, the 'censoring' of memories, associations or wishes from consciousness; displacement, the redirection or substitution of activity; projection, the attribution of one's own unconscious wishes or anxieties to another; and sublimation, the investment of sexual or destructive energies in creative or socially valued activities.

**deferent:** see PTOLEMAIC SYSTEM.

**deficiency disease,** disorder caused by lack of a particular vitamin, mineral, or other essential micronutrient, such as an essential AMINO ACID or fatty acid (component of fats and oils). The classic deficiency diseases include SCURVY, PELLAGRA, BERIBERI, and RICKETS. Strict vegetarianism and ANOREXIA NERVOSA can also create deficiencies. Recommended Dietary Allowances (RDAs) of most micronutrients essential for health have been drawn up, but there is controversy as to optimum intakes, with RDAs in the US being set at a higher level than those in the UK. A diet selected from a wide variety of foodstuffs including sufficient protein and plenty of fruit and vegetables should also provide adequate amounts of vitamins and minerals for health and growth. See also VITAMINS AND MINERALS (table).

**De Filippo, Eduardo,** 1900–, Neapolitan actor and dramatist. Born into an acting family, he directed a series of successful companies to become Italy's best-known dialect playwright of this century, with such works as *Napoli milionaria* (1945; tr. Naples' Millionaires), *The Voices from Within* (1948), *Saturday, Sunday, Monday* (1959), which project a tragi-comic world-view centred on the family in a typically Neapolitan setting.

**deflation:** see under INFLATION.

**Defoe** or **De Foe, Daniel,** 1660?–1731, English prose writer. His poem *The True-born Englishman* (1701), a defence of William III, brought fame, but an ironic satire, *The Shortest Way with Dissenters* (1702), brought a prison term. Called the father of modern journalism, he was associated with 26 periodicals, and he wrote and published

(1704–13) *The Review,* a journal, singlehandedly. His three great novels *The Life and Strange Surprising Adventures of Robinson Crusoe* (1719), based in part on the experience of Alexander SELKIRK; the picaresque *Moll Flanders* (1722); and *A Journal of the Plague Year* (1722) all appeared as memoirs, intended to be taken as true. Defoe's narrative tension, straight-forward prose, and sharp-eyed observation of detail have made *Robinson Crusoe* one of the most widely read and loved English books, endlessly imitated and often considered the first true NOVEL in English.

**defoliant:** see HERBICIDE.

**De Forest, Lee,** 1873–1961, American inventor. A pioneer in the development of wireless telegraphy, sound pictures, and television, he invented the triode (1906), which made the amplification of signal necessary for transcontinental telephony practicable, and led to the foundation of the radio industry.

**Degas, Edgar (Hilaire Germain Edgar Degas)** (ˌdəgah), 1834–1917, French painter and sculptor. Degas strove to unite the discipline of classical art with the immediacy of IMPRESSIONISM. His favourite subjects were ballet dancers, women at their toilette, café life, and race-course scenes. He combined his portrayal of contemporary life with such daring compositional innovations as accidental cutoff views, off-centre subjects, and unusual angles. His innovative achievement of balance is seen in *Woman with Chrysanthemums* (1865; Metropolitan Mus.) and *Foyer of the Dance* (1872; Louvre). Degas gradually turned from oils to pastels and charcoal, perhaps because of failing eyesight. His works in sculpture include dancers and horses. He profoundly influenced such later artists as TOULOUSE-LAUTREC and PICASSO. Many of his most

Edgar **Degas,** *The Little Dancer of Fourteen,* 1880–81. Bronze statue, 98 cm high. Musee d'Orsay, Paris.

celebrated works, e.g., *The Bellelli Family* (1859), *The Rehearsal* (1882), and *Two Laundresses* (1882), are in the Louvre.

**De Gasperi, Alcide** (day ‚gahspayree), 1881–1954, prime minister of ITALY, founder of the Christian Democratic Party. From 1945 to 1953 he was premier of eight successive coalition cabinets dominated by the Christian Democrats. De Gasperi championed close cooperation with the US and led Italy into the NORTH ATLANTIC TREATY ORGANIZATION.

**De Gaulle, Charles,** 1890–1970, French general and statesman, first president (1959–69) of the Fifth Republic. Opposing the Franco-German armistice in WORLD WAR II, he fled (1940) to London and there organized the Free French forces and rallied several French colonies to his movement. In 1943 he became co-president (with Henri Honoré Giraud) of the French Committee of National Liberation at Algiers, and in 1945 he was elected provisional president of France. He resigned (1946) when it became apparent that the Fourth Republic's constitution would not provide for a strong executive. He became (1947) head of a new party, Rally for the French People (RFP), but dissolved it in 1953 and retired. In 1958, during the political crisis created by the civil war in ALGERIA, De Gaulle became premier with the power to rule by decree for six months. A new constitution that strengthened the presidency was drawn up, and in 1959 De Gaulle became president of the new Fifth Republic. As president, he reached (1962) a settlement for Algerian independence, developed France's nuclear potential, and withdrew (1966) from the military structure of the NORTH ATLANTIC TREATY ORGANIZATION. He supported French participation in the EUROPEAN COMMUNITY but opposed British membership as a potential threat to French interests. Nearly overthrown (1968) by worker–student demonstrations, he resigned in 1969 after defeat on constitutional reform.

**Degenerate Art,** term coined by the leaders of the NATIONAL SOCIALIST Party who from 1933 onwards carried out their ideological battles in the domain of art, proposing a politically indoctrinated academic art as the true artistic expression of German life and culture. All modern art was suppressed, many modern artists being forbidden to paint at all. In 1936 an exhibition of *Entartete Kunst* [degenerate art] was mounted in Munich, which sought to ridicule all modern, especially expressionist, tendencies in art. More than 16,500 works were expropriated from German galleries, many of them being burnt in Berlin in 1939.

**De Grasse, François Joseph Paul, comte:** see GRASSE, FRANÇOIS JOSEPH PAUL, COMTE DE.

**de Havilland, Sir Geoffrey,** 1882–1965, British aircraft designer. Having taught himself to fly in an aeroplane he built, he was already an established aircraft designer at the outbreak of World War I, in which nearly 9000 of his aeroplanes were used. The world's first regular scheduled international air service (see AIR TRANSPORT) used de Havilland's aircraft. His aeroplanes, including the wooden Mosquito and the Vampire jet fighter, were important in World War II. After the war he was responsible for the first jet airliner, the Comet (1949) as well as jet and piston aero engines. De Havilland was knighted in 1944.

**Dehra Dun,** town (1981 pop. 220,530), Uttar Pradesh state, N India. It is set in a *dun*, or valley, leading to the gorge of the GANGES (Ganga) where it bursts forth from the foothills of the HIMALAYAS at Hardwar. It is a district administrative and trading centre which has grown rapidly. It has textile, saw-milling, and other industries. Dehra Dun is mainly remarkable as the site of a number of defence, research, and other government establishments, including the Survey of India and the Indian Military Academy. Dehra was founded by a Sikh dissident in 1676, in the reign of Aurangzeb.

**dehydrated food:** see FOOD PRESERVATION.

**Deimos,** in astronomy, natural satellite of MARS.

**Deirdre,** heroine of Irish legend. Intended as the wife of Conchobar, king of Ulster, she fell in love with Naoise and fled to Scotland with him and his brothers. On their return home Conchobar killed Naoise, and Deirdre died on his grave. The story was popular with writers of the Irish literary renaissance, e.g., W.B. YEATS and J.M. SYNGE.

**deists,** rationalist thinkers of the 17th and 18th cent., who held that the course of nature demonstrates the existence of God, while they rejected formal religion and claims of supernatural revelation. VOLTAIRE, J.J. ROUSSEAU, Benjamin FRANKLIN, and Thomas JEFFERSON were deists. See also ENLIGHTENMENT.

**Deken, Agatha:** see WOLFF, ELISABETH.

**Dekker, Thomas,** 1572?–1632?, English dramatist and pamphleteer. His most famous play, *The Shoemaker's Holiday* (1599), about a shoemaker who becomes lord mayor of London, is notable for its realistic depiction of London life. He collaborated with John WEBSTER, Thomas MIDDLETON (*Honest Whore,* Pt I, 1604), Philip MASSINGER, and others. Most of his works have been lost. His pamphlets include *The Seven Deadly Sins of London* (1606) and *The Gull's Handbook* (1609).

**de Kooning, Willem,** 1904–, American painter and leader of ABSTRACT EXPRESSIONISM; b. Netherlands. De Kooning painted huge canvases slashed with colour and charged with great energy. He is particularly known for his monumental 1950s series entitled *Woman,* e.g., the ferocious *Woman I* (Mus. Mod. Art, New York City).

**Delacroix, Eugène (Ferdinand-Victor-Eugène Delacroix)** (dəlah‚kwah), 1798–1863, French painter. He was the foremost painter of the romantic movement in France (see ROMANTICISM) and was particularly influential as a colourist. His first major work, *The Bark of Dante* (Louvre), brought him recognition as the leader of the opposition to the neoclassical school of DAVID. His dramatic interpretation of scenes from mythology, literature, political, religious, and literary history was lavish and exuberant. He was influenced by English painting and a trip to Morocco that provided him with much exotic material, e.g., *Women of Algiers* (1834; Louvre). He did many portraits of notable contemporaries, e.g., George SAND (Copenhagen), and his animals in motion, e.g., *Tiger Attacking a Horse* (Louvre), are compelling.

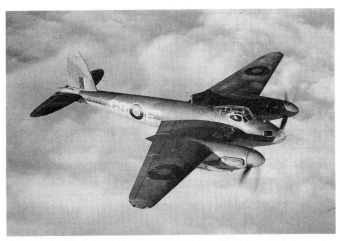

The **de Havilland** DH98 Mosquito MkVII Fighter Bomber (1944).

**De Hooch** or **De Hoogh, Pieter:** see HOOCH, PIETER DE.

Eugene **Delacroix,** *Tiger Attacking a Horse.* Louvre, Paris.

**de la Madrid Hurtado, Miguel** ('delama,drid), 1934–, Mexican public official, president of MEXICO (1982–88). As minister of planning and budget in the cabinet of José LÓPEZ PORTILLO, he was influential in planning the utilization of Mexico's oil wealth to promote economic growth. Known as a conservative technocrat, he was chosen (1981) as the candidate of the ruling Institutional Revolutionary Party and was elected in 1982 for a six-year term.

**de la Mare, Walter,** 1873–1956, English poet and novelist. His writing often delights in the shadowy world between the real and unreal. His poetry includes *The Listeners* (1912), his fiction *Henry Brocken* (1904) and *The Return* (1910). *Peacock Pie* (1913) is among his many books for children.

**Delaunay, Robert** (dəloh,nay), 1885–1941, French painter. He was a major figure in the movement that APOLLINAIRE termed ORPHISM. His amalgam of fauve colour (see FAUVISM), futurist dynamism (see FUTURISM), and analytical CUBISM is best seen in his series of paintings of the EIFFEL TOWER.

**Delaware,** state of the US (1984 est. pop. 613,000), second smallest in area 5328 km² (2057 sq mi), situated on the mid-Atlantic coast and bordered by Maryland (W,S), the Delaware Bay and New Jersey (E), and Pennsylvania (N). The state occupies the eastern half of a low-lying peninsula. The capital is DOVER and the only large city is Wilmington in the northern tip of the state. The heavily industrialized economy is dominated by the Du Pont chemical industry, but food processing, petroleum refining, and metals and plastics manufacture are also important. Half of Delaware's agricultural income is from broiler chickens, and other products include corn, soybeans, and dairy products. The local inshore fishing industry is declining. In the 17th cent. the Dutch, Swedes, and finally the British contested the area, which was inhabited by the Delaware Indians. Delaware was one of the thirteen colonies to sign the Declaration of Independence and the first to ratify the new Constitution. It remained loyal to the Union in the Civil War, although it was split between an urban north and a rural south. Industry has expanded in the 20th cent. as Du Pont has branched out and many corporations have established headquarters there.

**Delaware,** a major river of the E US, flowing c.450 km (280 mi) from sources in the Catskill Mts, SE New York, past Trenton, New Jersey (the head of navigation), Philadelphia, Pennsylvania, and Wilmington, Delaware, into Delaware Bay and the Atlantic Ocean. The Delaware River Basin Compact (1961) regulates water use by the heavily industrialized states through which the river flows.

**Delaware Indians,** the English name for a group of NORTH AMERICAN INDIAN tribes of the Eastern Woodlands, with an Algonquian language (see AMERICAN INDIAN LANGUAGES). Calling themselves the Lenni-Lenape, they claimed ancient occupation of the Delaware R. region, where most Algonquian tribes had originated, and by those tribes were respectfully addressed as *Grandfather*. In 1682 they made a treaty of friendship with William PENN, but in 1720 the Iroquois forced them to move into Ohio. The Delaware sided with the British in the AMERICAN REVOLUTION; afterwards they moved successively to Kansas, Texas, and INDIAN TERRITORY. A few still live on reservations, mainly in Oklahoma.

**Deledda, Grazia,** 1871–1936, Italian novelist; b. Sardinia. Her works, e.g., *Elias Portolu* (1903), *Cenere* (1904; tr. Ashes), and *La madre* (1920; tr. The Mother), show some affinity to VERGA's naturalism, combining sympathy and humour with occasional violence. She was awarded the 1926 Nobel Prize for literature.

**delegated legislation,** in government, secondary legislation made under the authority of an initial statute. In the UK, the majority of delegated legislation is made by government minsters in the form of statutory instruments, in order to implement in detail the provisions of an Act of Parliament. Statutory instruments are laid before PARLIAMENT and pass into law automatically if no Member of Parliament objects within 40 days. Orders in Council are a form of delegated legislation issued by the PRIVY COUNCIL. They are generally issued without the prior consent of parliament to deal with emergencies, and are ratified later. Local government bye-laws are also a form of delegated legislation passed under powers granted by central government. Since World War II, the development of the WELFARE STATE has resulted in a massive growth in the number of statutory instruments used to implement law in complex areas (e.g., social security).

**Delhi,** union territory and city, N central India. It is located on a hot, arid plain, but irrigation supports agriculture. From ancient times the region, a crossroads, was the key to empire, and the remains of many dynasties survive. The chief cities are NEW DELHI, the capital of India, and Delhi, or Old Delhi (1981 metropolitan area pop. 5,157,870), on the Jamuna (Jumna) R. SHAH JAHAN made Old Delhi the MOGUL capital in 1638. The MAHRATTAS held the city from 1771 to 1803, when the British took it. Points of interest include Shah Jahan's Red Fort.

The Diwan-i-khas in Shah Jahan's Red Fort, Old **Delhi**

**Delhi Sultanate,** the rule of the five Turko-Afghan dynasties who established a pan-Indian empire (1192–1526), which at its height (c.1315) encompassed almost the entire subcontinent. It was founded by Qutb ud-Din, a general in the service of Muhammad of Ghur, ruler of Afghanistan, who proclaimed himself sultan in 1192. Under constant challenge, particularly by Rajput forces, it was finally destroyed in 1526 by Babur.

**Delian League,** confederation of Greek states under the leadership of ATHENS. The first Delian League (478–404 BC) was formed by Athens and a number of Ionian states to oppose Persia, an object accomplished in the PERSIAN WARS. Dissent arose within the league, but by a mixture of force and persuasion Athens established supremacy, and the league in effect became an Athenian empire. The alliance was unstable, however, and with Athens' defeat (404 BC) in the PELOPONNESIAN WAR it came to an end. After Conon reestablished Athenian mastery of the sea, the second Delian League was formed (378 BC). It lasted, despite Athenian–Theban quarrels, until utterly destroyed by the victory of PHILIP II of Macedon at Chaeronea (338 BC).

**Delibes, Léo** (də,leeb), 1836–91, French composer. He wrote melodic, vividly orchestrated works, e.g., the ballets *Coppélia* (1870) and *Sylvia* (1876) and the opera *Lakmé* (1883).

**Delibes, Miguel** (day,leebays), 1920–, Spanish novelist, short-story writer, and journalist. He depicts rural life and demonstrates a mastery of psychological analysis in such novels as *El camino* (1950; tr. The Path), *Las ratas* (1962; tr. Smoke on the Ground), *Cinco horas con Mario* (1966; tr. Five Hours with Mario), *Parábola del náufrage* (1969; tr. Parable of the Drowning Man), and *Los santos inocentes* (1981; tr. The Innocent Saints).

**Delilah:** see SAMSON.

**delirium tremens:** see ALCOHOLISM.

**De Lisser, Herbert George,** 1877–1944, Jamaican novelist. An underrated but influential popular novelist and newspaper editor (*The Gleaner*), he adopted a policy of publishing his books first in Jamaica, then in England. He is best remembered for his delineation of working-class life, e.g., *Jane's Career* (1914) and *Susan Proudleigh* (1915), and historical romances.

**Delius, Frederick,** 1862–1934, English composer, of German parentage. Influenced by GRIEG, he combined ROMANTICISM and

IMPRESSIONISM in music characterized by free structure and rich chromatic HARMONY. His best-known works include *Brigg Fair* (1907), *On Hearing the First Cuckoo in Spring* (1912), and *North Country Sketches* (1914). He wrote five operas, including *Koanga* (1904) and *A Village Romeo and Juliet* (1907), four concertos, and five choral works such as *A Mass of Life* (1905) and *Song of the High Hills* (1911).

**Della Robbia** (delah ˌrobeeə), Florentine family of sculptors and ceramicists famous for their enamelled terra-cotta or faience. **Luca della Robbia,** 1400?–82, founder of the workshop, was the outstanding artist of the family. He is best known for the marble *Singing Gallery* (1431; Cathedral Mus., Florence), decorated with charming child musicians. He later perfected a method of creating polychrome-glazed terra-cottas, which became the major output of his workshop. The family tradition was continued by his nephew **Andrea della Robbia,** 1435–1525, and by Andrea's sons. Andrea did the famous medallions on the Foundling Hospital, Florence, showing babies against a blue background.

Luca **Della Robbia,** *Singing Gallery,* 1431. Cathedral Museum, Florence.

**Deller, Alfred,** 1912–79, English countertenor. His unusual voice was suited especially to Renaissance music, HANDEL, and PURCELL (see VOICE). He founded (1948) the Deller Consort, specializing in medieval and Renaissance recitals.

**Delon, Alain,** 1935–, French film actor and director. He is a handsome, cool leading man who has remained very popular with French audiences for over two decades. His films include *The Leopard* (1963), *The Samourai* (1967), and *Mr Klein* (1976).

**Deloney, Thomas,** 1560?–1600, one of the earliest English writers of popular fiction. His four novellas, of which the best known are *Jacke of Newberie* and *Thomas of Reading,* depict the worldly and romantic success of hard-working craftsmen and apprentices. He also wrote ballads on contemporary events, such as the defeat of the Spanish Armada (1588).

**Delorme** or **de l'Orme, Philibert** (dəˌlawm), c.1510–70, French architect, one of the greatest Renaissance architects. Most of his work has been destroyed. After Italian travels he introduced into France a classical style that endured to the mid-18th cent. Among his works were the tomb of FRANCIS I at Saint-Denis, the TUILERIES, and the gallery at the chateau of Chenonceaux.

**Delos,** island, of c.3.5 km² (1.4 sq mi), in the CYCLADES Islands, Greece. In Greek legend the birthplace of Apollo, it achieved great religious and commercial importance from the 7th cent. BC. Temples, villas and meeting places continued to be built until the island's population was finally defeated and massacred by MITHRIDATES of Pontus in 88 BC. The ruins of six countries of Greek culture, including the famous Terrace of the Lions, attract many visitors.

**Delphi,** town in Phocis, GREECE, near the foot of Mt Parnassus. It was the seat of the Delphic ORACLE, the most famous and powerful oracle of ancient Greece. The oracle, which originated in the worship of an earth-goddess, possibly GAIA, was the principal shrine of APOLLO. It was housed in a temple built in the 6th cent. BC. The oracular messages were spoken by a priestess in a frenzied trance and interpreted by a priest, who usually spoke in verse. The oracle's influence prevailed throughout Greece until

Hellenistic times. Delphi was the meeting place of the Amphictyonic League and the site of the PYTHIAN GAMES. It was later pillaged by the Romans, and the sanctuary fell into decay.

**delphinium:** see LARKSPUR.

**delta,** the alluvial plain formed at the mouth of a river where the stream loses velocity and drops part of its sediment load. No delta is formed if the coast is sinking or if ocean or tidal currents prevent sediment deposition. A deltaic plain is usually very fertile but subject to floods. The three main varieties of delta are the arcuate (e.g., that of the Nile), the bird's-foot (e.g., that of the Mississippi), and the cuspate (e.g., that of the Tiber).

**Delta Plan,** flood control and reclamation project, S Netherlands, in the Rhine R. delta. Built in 1957–81, it involved construction of four major dikes (up to 40 m/131 ft high) across the Rhine's four estuaries on the North Sea, three auxiliary dams, and a storm-tide barrage 11.5 m (38 ft) high and 80 m (262 ft) wide across the IJssel R. The project shortened the Dutch coastline by c.700 km (440 mi), reclaimed 15,000 hectares (6,100 acres), and created a freshwater lake (85 km²/33 sq mi). Two navigable waterways to Antwerp and to Rotterdam and Europoort were left open.

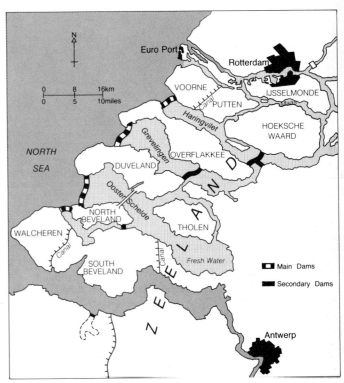

Delta Plan

**Deluge:** see NOAH.

**Delvaux, Paul,** 1897–, Belgian painter. He was influenced by the metaphysical painting of CHIRICO and by MAGRITTE. By the mid 1930s he had developed his mature style of surrealist images of women in a meticulously painted dreamlike world with a mood of menace and unease. He was not a member of the surrealist movement (see SURREALISM), disagreeing with its political function.

**De Mabuse, Jan:** see MABUSE, JAN DE.

**demersal:** see BENTHOS.

**Demeter** (diˌmeetə), in Greek mythology, goddess of harvest and fertility; daughter of CRONUS and RHEA; mother of PERSEPHONE by ZEUS. She and her daughter were the chief figures in the ELEUSINIAN MYSTERIES, and her primary festival was the Athenian Thesmophoria. The Romans identified her with CERES.

**Demetrius,** in Russian history: see DMITRI.

**Demetrius I,** (Demetrius Poliorcetes), c.337–283 BC, king of MACEDON. He aided his father, Antigonus I, in the wars of the DIADOCHI until their defeat (and Antigonus's death) at Ipsus (301 BC). He recovered ATHENS (295) and, after murdering his competitors, seized the throne of Macedon

(294). Driven out by PYRRHUS, he took refuge (285) with King Seleucus I of Syria. His son, Antigonus II, made good his claim to the throne of Macedon.

**De Mille, Agnes,** 1909?–, American dancer and choreographer; niece of Cecil B. DE MILLE. She created (1942) the first major American ballet, *Rodeo* (to music by Aaron COPLAND), and brought ballet techniques to musicals such as *Oklahoma!* (1943; see Richard RODGERS and Oscar HAMMERSTEIN). She created *Fall River Legend* (1948) for the American Ballet Theatre. She wrote books on dance and autobiographical works but her significance is that she broke the hegemony of Russian classical ballet in the US.

**De Mille, Cecil B.,** 1881–1959, American film director. His many 'spectacle' films include *The Ten Commandments* (1923; 1956), *King of Kings* (1927), *The Crusades* (1935), *Union Pacific* (1939), and *The Greatest Show on Earth* (1952).

**De Mita, Ciriaco,** 1927–, Italian Christian Democratic (DC) politician, prime minister (1988–). A minister in the 1970s, he became DC secretary-general (1982) and succeeded to the premiership (1988) at the head of a centre-left coalition, Italy's 48th postwar government.

**democracy,** rule by the people rather than by a minority or a single person. Both the definition of democracy and the best means of giving it political effect have been disputed throughout history. Everything depends on what is meant by 'rule', and who are to count as 'the people'. The celebrated democracy of classical Athens (5th cent. BC) did not extend to the slaves by whom the economy of the city-state was supported. Among the first to argue for a modern conception of democracy was J. J. ROUSSEAU, who held that all individuals should be regarded as equal in rights and should be entitled to participate in discussions and decisions which affected their lives. However, he felt that only *direct democracy*—the settling of public affairs at public meetings of the whole citizenry—was worthy of the name, and concluded that true democracy was impossible in any community larger than Corsica. The size of modern nations has meant that only indirect or *representative democracy* is practicable, and many variations exist on the basic principle that individuals vote for representatives to act on their behalf in national legislative assemblies. Until the 19th cent. most European nations which had such assemblies restricted the vote to substantial landowners. The rise in economic power of the BOURGEOISIE (17th–18th cent.) and later pressure from the new working class created by the INDUSTRIAL REVOLUTION (19th cent.) led to a cautious extension of the vote, first to the middle class, then to all adult males, and finally to women. Female suffrage was not achieved in Britain until 1928; in some cantons of Switzerland they still await it. The *liberal democracy* of Western nations is based on a number of presuppositions: that there exists an educated citizenry with freedom of speech and association, that there is FREEDOM OF THE PRESS, that elections are regular and free (with no intimidation of voters), that there is a genuine choice between rival candidates and parties, that opposition parties may campaign against the government and, if successful, replace it by a nonviolent constitutional process. Although one-party Communist states lack most of these features, and hence are not considered democratic by the West, they nevertheless claim to be democratic in the sense that they represent the popular will. In fact almost all modern political systems claim that in some sense the will of the people is sovereign, calling themselves democracies, people's republics, and so on. Socialist critics of Western liberal democracy argue that formal political and legal equality for citizens is meaningless in the face of the inequalities of wealth and opportunity associated with a CLASS system under CAPITALISM. They recommend the extension of democracy from the political sphere to the economic, involving either public ownership, or at least a minimum standard of living for all, and popular participation in the control of the workplace (*industrial democracy*) and other areas of social life.

**Democratic Party,** American political party. The party traces its origins to the group of anti-Federalists who gathered around Thomas JEFFERSON in the 1790s in opposition to Alexander HAMILTON's financial programme and who came to call themselves Republicans. Standing for personal liberty, STATES' RIGHTS and the limitation of the powers of the federal government, the Republican party, consisted, as have its successors, of a loose coalition of Southern agrarians and Northern city-dwellers. After Jefferson was elected president in 1800, the Republican party retained the presidency until 1824, though as Federalism waned the Republicans abandoned their traditional hostility to centralized power and loose construction. The split which developed in the Republican ranks in 1824 resulted in the supporters of John Quincy ADAMS and Henry CLAY becoming known as National Republicans, while Andrew JACKSON's followers emerged as Democratic Republicans. From the time of their overwhelming triumph in the 1828 presidential election, however, the Jacksonians were known simply as Democrats. More avowedly egalitarian than the Republican party from which it had sprung, Jackson's Democratic party nonetheless continued to champion the old Jeffersonian virtues of frugality, fiscal solvency, and limited government. Between 1828 and 1860 it won every presidential election except those of 1840 and 1848. But in the 1850s disputes over the status of slavery in the territories created sharp divisions within the party, and the AMERICAN CIVIL WAR deepened the split. The party had revived by the time of the disputed election of 1876, when it won a plurality of popular votes, and although it won the presidency only twice between 1860 and 1912, it often controlled one or both houses of Congress and had wide success in the states. In this period the Democratic party had become basically an alliance of the 'solid South' and the immigrant population of the big Northern cities. In the late 19th cent. the Democrats could be characterized as the party of agrarianism and cheap money and of hostility to protective tariffs. Yet many Democrats found radical economic and agrarian schemes no less distasteful than did the Republicans. Hence the nomination (1896) of William Jennings BRYAN on a FREE SILVER platform again split the party and illustrated the difficulty of reconciling its diverse elements. The years between 1896 and 1932 were lean ones for the Democrats at the national level. They regained the presidency in 1912 only because the Republican vote was split and were again in eclipse in the 1920s. However the Great Depression swept the Democrats under Franklin D. ROOSEVELT into office in 1932 and the NEW DEAL he initiated kept the presidency in Democratic hands for the next 20 years. The Democrats kept control of Congress throughout EISENHOWER's presidency and continued to do so during the Democratic administrations of John F. KENNEDY and Lyndon B. JOHNSON. American involvement in the VIETNAM WAR produced growing criticism of Pres. Johnson from members of his own party, while his civil rights legislation alienated many Southern Democrats. These divisions contributed to Democratic defeats in the presidential elections of 1968 and 1972 and although the WATERGATE AFFAIR enabled the Democrats to elect Jimmy CARTER in 1976, they remained an uneasy coalition of trade unionists, minorities, middle class reformers and Southern Democrats, whose disunity led to Carter's defeat by Ronald REAGAN in 1980.

**Democritus,** c.460–c.370 BC, pre-Socratic Greek philosopher. His atomic theory of the nature of the physical world, developed from the earlier work of LEUCIPPUS, and known to us through ARISTOTLE's writings, was the most scientific theory proposed up to his time. He held that all things are composed of tiny indivisible particles, called atoms, and that their constant motion explains the creation of the universe: the heavier atoms clustered together to form the Earth, while the lighter ones formed the heavenly bodies.

**demography,** the study of human populations and their change over time. By studying birth and death rates, population distribution, and marital and migration patterns, demography ascertains trends and predicts possible changes.

**Demosthenes,** 384–322 BC, Greek orator. His reputation as the greatest of the Greek orators rests mainly on his orations arousing ATHENS against PHILIP II of Macedon—three PHILIPPICS (351–341 BC) and three *Olynthiacs* (349). Philip triumphed (338), and Demosthenes' cause was lost. His other orations include *On the Peace* (346), *On the False Legation* (343), and *On the Crown* (330). In 324 BC Demosthenes was exiled for his involvement in an obscure affair involving money taken by a lieutenant of ALEXANDER THE GREAT. Recalled after Alexander's death (323), he failed in his attempt to free Greece from Macedon, fled, and took poison to avoid capture by ANTIPATER.

**demotic:** see HIEROGLYPHIC.

**Dempsey, Jack** (William Harrison Dempsey), 1895–1983, American boxer. The 'Manassa Mauler' won the heavyweight title by knocking out Jess Willard in 1919 and lost it to Gene TUNNEY in 1926. In a controversial rematch (1927) Dempsey knocked Tunney down in the seventh round, but the count (now known as the 'long count') was delayed by Dempsey's failure to go to his corner and Tunney won a 10-round decision.

**Demuth, Charles,** 1883–1935, American painter. Known for his translucent WATERCOLOURS of fruits and flowers, Demuth was also one of the first painters to draw inspiration from the geometric shapes of modern technology.

**dendrochronology** or **tree-ring dating,** in ARCHAEOLOGY, the dating of wood according to the pattern of growth rings. Environmental conditions govern the size of the annual growth rings of trees. Sequences of growth ring patterns may be built up in a region, using living trees, timbers, and other preserved wood, and if part of the sequence can be matched to a calendrical date, then the entire sequence becomes a means of absolute dating. The most ancient of living things, the bristlecone pine, has provided a sequence of almost 10,000 years in California, and oaks have been charted in long sequences in Europe. Dendrochronology has an important use in verifying carbon-14 dates (see CARBON-14 DATING).

**Deneuve, Catherine,** 1943–, French film actress. Her exquisite beauty, combined with an extreme detachment, has ensured her status as a top star of French and international films, which include *Repulsion* (1965), *Belle du jour* (1967), and *Hustle* (1975).

**dengue fever,** acute infectious disease caused by a virus and transmitted by the *Aëdes* mosquito. It occurs in tropical and subtropical climates. Symptoms include headache, fever, and intense joint pain, followed by a generalized irritating rash. Complete recovery is usual, although debilitation can be marked. Aspirin relieves the pain and calamine lotion soothes the rash.

**Deng Xiaoping** (dung sheeowping), 1904–, Chinese Communist leader and 'elder statesman'. Twice purged from power (1967, 1976) and twice rehabilitated (1973, 1977), Deng was deputy premier under HUA GUOFENG. He soon became (1977) powerful as Communist Party deputy chairman, and in 1979 visited the US to seek closer US–Chinese ties. In 1981 Deng strengthened his position in China by replacing Hua as party chairman (later general secretary) with his own protégé, HU YAOBANG. At the 1982 Communist Party congress he was named to lead the newly created Central Advisory Commission. In 1986–87, however, Deng's liberalization policies and 'opening to the West' came under challenge from conservative elements alarmed by student demonstrations in favour of greater democracy and Hu was replaced as party general secretary by ZHAO ZIYANG. Nevertheless, Deng's influence remained preeminent, as demonstrated at the 13th party congress (1987), when he was reelected chairman of the powerful military commission despite giving up his other leadership posts because of his advancing years.

**De Niro, Robert,** 1943–, American film actor. One of the finest American film actors to emerge in the 1970s, he specializes in violent, often psychotic types in such films as *Mean Streets* (1973), *Taxi Driver* (1976), and *The Deer Hunter* (1978).

**Denis, Maurice** (ˌdenis/dəˌnee), 1870–1943, French painter and writer who was a founding member of the Nabis group. His paintings, often on religious themes, were not as influential as his art theories. His writings include *Theories* (2 vol., 1920, 1922) and *History of Religious Art* (1939).

**Denmark,** Dan. *Danmark,* officially the Kingdom of Denmark, country (1985 est. pop. 5,144,000), 43,069 km² (16,629 sq mi), N Europe; bordered by West Germany (S), the North Sea (W), the Skagerrak (N), and the Kattegat and the Øresund (E). The southernmost of the Scandinavian countries, Denmark includes most of the JUTLAND peninsula as well as more than 450 islands. The FAEROE ISLANDS and GREENLAND, which are semiautonomous, lie to the NW. COPENHAGEN is the capital and chief industrial centre; other important cities are ÅRHUS, ODENSE, and ÅLBORG. Denmark, which is almost entirely low-lying, has traditionally been an agricultural country; after 1945, however, it greatly expanded its industrial base. The main commodities raised are livestock and poultry, root crops, and cereals. The leading manufactures include meat and dairy products, chemicals, and ships. Fishing and shipping are also important. The GNP is $58,850 million and the GNP per capita is $11,490 (1983). Nearly all the inhabitants speak Danish, and most belong to the established Lutheran Church. Denmark is a constitutional monarchy, governed under the 1953 constitution. Legislative power is vested in a unicameral, 179-member *Folketing* [parliament]; executive authority rests with the monarch and the appointed prime minister and cabinet. The reigning monarch is Queen MARGARET II, who succeeded her father, Frederick IX, upon his death in 1972.

*History.* The Danes probably settled Jutland by c.10,000 BC, but little is known of Danish history before the 9th to 11th cent. AD, when the Danes had an important role in the VIKING raids on W Europe. Harold Bluetooth (d. c.985) was the first Christian king of Denmark, and his son, Sweyn, conquered England. Danish hegemony over N Europe was first established (12th–13th cent.) by WALDEMAR I and WALDEMAR II. Queen MARGARET I achieved (1397) the KALMAR UNION of Denmark, Sweden, and Norway; the union with Sweden was largely ineffective and ended in 1523, but that with Norway lasted until 1814. The house of Oldenburg, from which the present dynasty is descended, acceded in 1448 with CHRISTIAN I, who also united Schleswig and Holstein with the British crown. Participation in the THIRTY YEARS WAR (1618–48) and the wars (1657–1660) of FREDERICK III with Sweden caused Denmark to lose prestige. Under the Treaty of Kiel (1814) Denmark lost Norway to Sweden, and following its defeat (1864) by Prussia and Austria it was deprived of SCHLESWIG-HOLSTEIN. Of more lasting importance was the internal reform of the 19th cent. that transformed Denmark's poor peasantry into the most prosperous small farmers in Europe. Denmark was occupied (1940–45) by German forces in WORLD WAR II. In 1949 it broke a long tradition of neutrality and joined the NORTH ATLANTIC TREATY ORGANIZATION, and in 1973 it joined the EUROPEAN COMMUNITY. The Social Democratic Party has been dominant in the postwar era, although at times ruling in a coalition or as a minority government. However, a centre-right coalition government of the Conservatives, Venstre Liberals, Centre Democrats, and Christian People's Party was formed in 1982 under Poul Schlüter, and continued in office after the 1984, 1987, and 1988 general elections.

**Post-war Danish prime ministers**
Vilholm Buhl (Social Democrat), 1945
Knud Kristensen (Liberal), 1945–47
Hans Hedtoft (Social Democrat), 1947–50
Erik Eriksen (Liberal), 1950–53
Hans Hedtoft (Social Democrat), 1953–55
H.C. Hansen (Social Democrat), 1955–60
Viggo Kampmann (Social Democrat), 1960–62
Jens Otto Krag (Social Democrat), 1962–68
Hilmar Baunsgaard (Radical), 1968–71
Jens Otto Krag (Social Democrat), 1971–72
Anker Jørgensen (Social Democrat), 1972–73
Poul Hartling (Liberal), 1973–75
Anker Jørgensen (Social Democrat), 1975–82
Poul Schlüter (Conservative), 1982–

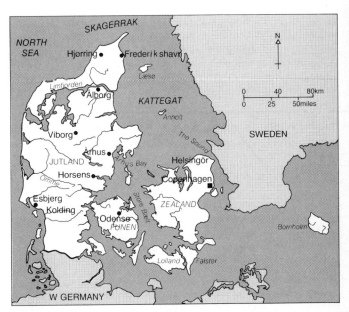

Denmark

**Denning, Alfred Thompson, Lord,** 1899–, British barrister and judge. He became a HIGH COURT judge (1944), before joining the Court of Appeal (1948) and later becoming MASTER OF THE ROLLS (1962–82). A controversial judge, he was often more interested in achieving what he saw as a just result to the case, rather than adhering to the rigid rules of PRECEDENT. His many books include *Discipline of Law* (1979).

**Dennis, C.J.**, pseud. of **Clarence Michael James**, 1876–1936, Australian writer of a series of verse narratives. The most famous is the *Songs of a Sentimental Bloke* (1915). These extremely popular expressions of Australian nationalism employed many colloquialisms in an exaggerated idiom, expressing both humour and pathos, earning an affectionate place in Australia's folk literature.

**density**, ratio of the MASS of a substance to its volume. Because all substances, especially gases, can be compressed into a smaller volume by increasing the pressure acting on them, the temperature and pressure at which the density is measured are usually specified. See RELATIVE DENSITY.

**dentistry**, treatment and care of the TEETH and associated oral structures. Dentists are concerned with tooth decay (CARIES), diseases of the supporting structures (the jaws and the gums), faulty growth of the teeth, and tooth replacements, as well as prevention of these problems. Specialized fields of dentistry include orthodontics (corrective dentistry) and periodontics (treatment of gum diseases; see GINGIVITIS; PERIODONTITIS). In the UK a dentist must be registered with the General Dental Council unless he or she holds a medical qualification.

**Denver**, US city (1984 est. pop. 505,000), state capital of Colorado, on the South Platte R.; inc. 1861. Colorado's largest city, Denver is a processing, shipping, and distributing point for a large agricultural area. It is the chief financial and administrative city of the ROCKY MOUNTAIN region, and a centre for the development of the West's energy resources. Numerous federal agencies have offices there. Denver has stockyards, canneries, mills, and many diversified industries, including electronics. Tourism is also important. In the 1870s and 1880s it was the metropolis of a gold and silver boom. Its development into a major modern city began in the 1890s. In the post-war period Denver became a major centre of oil exploration and production activities.

**Depardieu, Gerard**, 1948–, French film actor. He is a strong, husky actor who has inherited the mantle of Jean Gabin, while remaining offbeat in his choice of roles. His films include *Les Valseuses* (1974), *Préparez vos mouchoirs* (1978), and *The Return of Martin Guerre* (1983)

**Department of Education and Science** (DES), department of central government responsible for educational policy and planning in England. Responsibility for other parts of the UK is devolved to the appropriate Secretary of State. The DES, acting under the Secretary of State for Education and Science, itself spends only some 3% of national expenditure on education, financial support for the LOCAL EDUCATION AUTHORITIES (LEAs) coming from the Exchequer (nearly half of the LEAs' budgets). The DES establishes priorities and advises on the distribution of resources; the detailed operation of the system is in the hands of the LEAs.

**Department of Health and Social Security**, (DHSS), British government department under several ministers headed by the Secretary of State for Social Services, responsible for policy-making and financial control of the NATIONAL HEALTH SERVICE. Equivalent departments support ministers of health in Scotland, Wales, and Northern Ireland. The DHSS is staffed by civil servants and is directly accountable to Parliament.

**De Patinir, De Patenier**, or **De Patiner, Joachim:** see PATINIR, JOACHIM DE.

**dependency**, term used to describe the relationship between Third and First World societies. Dependency theorists argue that the processes of imperialism and colonialism that allowed the West to develop created underdevelopment in the colonized world and that, because of the unequal relationship between the two worlds, the same processes are still in operation. Thus it is not internal factors that prevent the development of the Third World but the dependent relationship itself. Such nations need to break economic relations with the West in order to achieve any degree of autonomy and independence.

**depreciation**, in ACCOUNTING, reduction in the value of fixed assets as a result of use, damage, or obsolescence. It can be estimated in several ways. In the straight-line method, annual depreciation is simply the cost of the asset (minus its value, if any, as scrap) divided equally over its estimated lifetime. Decreasing-charge methods assign higher depreciation costs to the early years. In recent years other methods have been introduced which take into account the fact that the replacement cost may be very much higher than the original because of inflation. Depreciation allows companies to cut costs of capital investment through tax savings.

**depression**, in economics, a period of economic crisis in commerce, finance, and industry, characterized by falling prices, restriction of credit, reduced production, numerous bankruptcies, and high unemployment. A less severe crisis is usually known as a downturn, or **recession**. Depressions tend to become worldwide in scope because of the international nature of trade and credit. Such was the case in the most severe economic reversal of the 20th cent., the GREAT DEPRESSION of the 1930s, which began in the US and quickly spread to Europe as US loans were withdrawn. The industrial slump which ensued caused a fall in demand for raw materials and food and the depression quickly became worldwide. Since that time, governments have acted to stabilize economic conditions in an effort to prevent depressions, using tax and fiscal measures as well as tighter controls over BANKING and the STOCK EXCHANGES. Job-training programmes, youth employment schemes, and increased public welfare are other steps taken to alleviate economic slumps.

**depression**, in PSYCHIATRY, a disproportionately intense reaction to difficult life situations, characterized by strong feelings of loss, sadness, worthlessness, or rejection. It may be accompanied by such physiological symptoms as tense posture, persistent frowning, slowing of activity, fatigue, lack of appetite, and insomnia. The depressed individual's tendency toward self-recrimination, self-punishment, and guilt may ultimately lead to SUICIDE. See also PSYCHOSIS.

**depth charge**, explosive device used against submarines and other underwater targets. Delivered from surface ships, it is either rolled into the water or propelled by special throwers. The charge is detonated by water pressure at a predetermined depth and, if it explodes near enough, can destroy the target by concussion.

**De Quincey, Thomas**, 1785–1859, English essayist. The autobiographical *Confessions of an English Opium-Eater* (1822) brought him literary eminence. His prolific contributions to various journals included *Recollections of the Lake Poets* (1834–39), *Autobiographic Sketches* (1834–41) and *Suspiria de Profundis* (1845). He was a pioneer in exploring the subconscious mind through dreams, and a powerful influence on later opium addicts.

**Derain, André** (də,ranh), 1880–1954, French painter. In 1904, he and his friend MATISSE encountered divisionist colour theories, and both Derain and Matisse lightened and brightened their palette and used a broad divisionist brushstroke. Derain was one of the group of artists exhibiting at the 1905 autumn salon that gave rise to the name FAUVISM. After World War I Derain started to paint in a classical style, following other artists in a general 'return to order' after the expressionist excesses of the pre-war years.

**Derby**, county town and industrial city (1981 pop. 218,026) in Derbyshire, Midlands of England, on R. Derwent, 56 km (35 mi) NE of Birmingham. Industries found in the town include engineering and the manufacture of aero-engines and electrical equipment. It is also well known for the manufacture of porcelain. All Saints' church, which has a 16th-cent. tower, but mainly dates from the 18th cent., became a cathedral in 1927.

**Derby, Edward Stanley**, 14th **Earl of**, 1799–1869, British statesman. He led the Conservative Party from 1846 to 1868, three times serving as prime minister (1852, 1858–59, 1866–68). He had served in Earl GREY's predominantly Whig cabinet (1831–32), but while supporting parliamentary reform, joined DISRAELI in 1846 opposing repeal of the CORN LAWS. He disliked the drudgery of office and relied on Disraeli's political skills just as Disraeli relied on his social power.

**Derby, the**, known as the Blue Riband of the turf, the Derby is a flat race for three-year-old colts and fillies run annually over 2.413 km (1½ mi) on Epsom Downs, usually on the last Wednesday in May or the first in June. It was first run on 4 May 1780 and is named after the 12th earl of Derby (1752–1834). There have been two dead heats: in 1828 between Cadland and The Colonel; and in 1884 between Harvester and St Goatien. Lester PIGGOTT has won it a record nine times. In the 1913 Derby Miss Emily Davison threw herself in front of King George V's Anmer in the cause of women's suffrage and died of her injuries.

**Derbyshire,** county in N Midlands of England (1984 est. pop. 911,700), 2630 km² (1026 sq mi), bordering on S Yorkshire in the N. The county town is DERBY. It is mountainous in the N and NW at the S end of the Pennines, and flatter in the S and E. It is drained by the Derwent, Dove, Wye, and TRENT rivers, and Buxton and Bakewell are towns noted for their mineral springs. Sheep are farmed in the upland areas and dairy farming is important in the lowlands. Coalmining is important in the E and S, where there are several industrial towns specializing in iron manufacture, engineering, and textiles.

**derivation,** in grammar: see INFLECTION.

**derivative:** see CALCULUS.

**Derrida, Jacques,** 1930–, French philosopher. He is concerned with the 'deconstruction' of Western rationalist thought. In *Writing and Difference* (1967) and *On Grammatology* (1967) he set forth his theories, based on a broad reading of the Western tradition. In opposition to the theory of SAUSSURE (see SEMIOTICS), Derrida challenges the primacy of spoken language, emphasizing the written language's ability to alter speech and thought, creating rather than merely transmitting meaning. His writings have analysed the work of HUSSERL, HEGEL, and other major philosophers, and have themselves influenced writers and philosophers.

**dervish,** [Pers., = beggar], term preferentially used by Europeans with reference to SUFIS and mendicant mystics.

**Derwent Water,** lake in LAKE DISTRICT, Cumbria, NW England, just S of Keswick. It is formed by the R. Derwent, which enters at the S end of the lake and leaves at the N end, to connect it with Bassenthwaite lake. The lake is about 5 km (3 mi) long, and up to 2 km wide. It is surrounded by beautiful mountain scenery, has several small islands in the centre, and the Falls of Lodore at the S end.

**Derzhavin, Gavril Romanovich** (dyiəz̧hahvin), 1743–1816, Russian poet. An innovator in the age of classicism, he dedicated *Felitsa* (1783) to CATHERINE II, leading to his appointments as poet laureate and then minister of justice. His most famous lyric is the *Ode to God* (1784).

**Desai, Morarji Ranchhodji** (de̦sie), 1896–, prime minister (1977–79) of INDIA. As leader of the Janata [people's] Party, he became prime minister after Indira GANDHI's fall from power. He was unable to maintain a working majority, however, and resigned in 1979, thereby clearing the way for Mrs Gandhi's return to power.

**desalination,** process of removing soluble salts from water to render it suitable for drinking, irrigation, or industrial uses. In *distillation,* salt water is heated in one container to make the water evaporate, leaving the salt behind. The desalinated vapour is then condensed to form water in a separate container. Although known about for many years, distillation has found limited application in water supply because of the fuel costs involved in vaporizing salt water. Other desalination techniques include *electrodialysis,* the use of porous membranes to filter out negatively and positively charged salt ions; *freezing,* based on the principle that water excludes salt when it crystallizes to ice; *ion-exchange,* in which water passes through a bed of specially treated synthetic resins that are capable of extracting ions of the salt from the solution and replacing them with ions that form water; and *reverse osmosis,* in which pressure, generated by the presence of salt in the water, forces water through a membrane which allows only pure water to pass through it.

**De Sanctis, Francesco,** 1817–83, essayist, educator, and politician, the father of modern Italian criticism. His brilliant synthesis, *Storia della letteratura italiana* (1870–71), has been dubbed 'the finest history of any literature ever written' (R. Wellek).

**Descartes, René,** 1596–1650, French philosopher, mathematician, and scientist. His philosophy is called Cartesianism (from *Cartesius,* the Latin form of his name). He is often called the father of modern philosophy, and his work is generally regarded as the bridge between SCHOLASTICISM and all philosophy that followed him. Primarily interested in mathematics, he was the founder of ANALYTICAL GEOMETRY and originated the CARTESIAN COORDINATES and Cartesian curves. To algebra he contributed the treatment of negative roots and the convention of exponent notation. Descartes also made important contributions to science, including works on optics, physiology, and psychology. His *Discourse on Method* (1637), *Meditations* (1641), and *Principles* (1644) contain his important philosophical theories. Reacting against the scepticism of MONTAIGNE, he hoped to show that knowledge by the highest standards is possible.

Beginning with the certainty of *cogito* [I think] and *sum* [I exist], he extended knowledge step by step to admit the reliability of clear and distinct ideas, the existence of God, the immortality of the soul, and the reality of the physical world, which he held to be purely mechanistic. His mind–body dualism holds that selves are non-material non-spatial substances which nonetheless can causally interact with human brains.

**descent,** a principle through which membership of groups is established through common descent from a shared ancestor/ancestress. Groups established through descent traced through one sex only are *unilineal* descent groups; where the socially recognized line of descent is from father to son these groups are *patrilineal*, while mother-to-daughter ties are *matrilineal*; in double descent systems both kinds coexist. Non-unilineal descent systems (bilateral or cognatic groups) trace descent through both sexes. See also LINEAGE; COGNATE.

**desegregation:** see INTEGRATION.

**desert,** arid region, usually partly covered by sand, supporting a limited and specially adapted plant and animal population. So-called cold deserts, caused by extreme cold and often covered perpetually by snow or ice, form about one-sixth of the earth's surface. Warm deserts form about one-fifth of it. The world's largest desert areas lie between 20° and 30° north and south of the equator in regions where mountains intercept the paths of the trade winds or where atmospheric conditions limit precipitation. An area with an annual rainfall of 25 cm (10 in) or less is considered a desert, although some deserts and semideserts exist in areas of higher precipitation where moisture is lost by runoff or evaporation. The two largest deserts in the world are the SAHARA in Africa and the great desert of central and W Australia.

**desertification,** the spread of desert-like conditions in arid or semiarid areas owing either to man's influence or to climatic change. This has been one of the most contentious environmental issues of recent years. Clearing vegetation for cultivation or cutting trees for firewood, together with overgrazing and burning, set in train such phenomena as soil erosion, deflation, increased water runoff from the ground surface, and dune reactivation.

**De Sica, Vittorio,** 1901–74, Italian film director and actor. His *Shoeshine* (1946), *Bicycle Thieves* (1948), and *Umberto D.* (1952) are classics of postwar Italian neorealism. Among his later works is *The Garden of the Finzi-Continis* (1971). He starred in ROSSELLINI's *General Della Rovere* (1959) and many other films.

**design of experiments,** one of the most important branches of STATISTICS, dealing with the efficient design of investigations and trials of all kinds, essential in all branches of science. Much of the theory underlying the design of experiments was originally developed for agricultural experiments, but has since been greatly extended to include industrial and commercial applications, in addition to those in the physical and biological sciences. Good experimental design requires REPLICATION and RANDOMIZATION of the experimental treatments, and enables the experimenter to investigate the INTERACTION between treatment factors. While many experiments can be performed under closely controlled situations in laboratories or factories, others have to be performed in less ideal conditions in order to determine, for example, the effects of acid rain on forests or on fish in lakes and rivers, or the long-term effects on human health of radioactivity from nuclear power stations.

**Des Moines,** US city (1980 pop. 191,003), state capital of Iowa, on the Des Moines and Raccoon rivers; chartered 1857. Iowa's largest city, it is a major Corn Belt industrial and transport centre. Publishing and printing, food processing, insurance, and diverse manufactures are important.

**De Soto, Hernando,** c.1500–1542, Spanish explorer. After serving with Francisco PIZARRO in PERU, he was named governor of CUBA. In 1539 he set out to conquer Florida. In search of treasure, his group explored much of GEORGIA, the Carolinas, TENNESSEE, ALABAMA, and OKLAHOMA. They were probably the first white men to see (1541) the MISSISSIPPI R. De Soto died on the journey and was buried in the Mississippi.

**Despard, Charlotte (French),** 1844–1939, Scottish suffragette, socialist, and Irish Republican. In the 1890s she worked in London's East End as a social reformer and activist in the Independent Labour Party. After joining the WOMEN'S SOCIAL AND POLITICAL UNION, she left, alienated by its undemocratic leadership, to found (1907) the Women's Freedom League. She worked for equal suffrage until 1928 and after World War I was involved in the struggle for Irish independence.

**Des Prés, Josquin:** see JOSQUIN DESPREZ.

**Dessalines, Jean Jacques** (desah,leen), c.1758–1806, emperor of HAITI (1804–6). Born a black slave, he became a shrewd general who defeated (1803) French forces and, upon Haiti's independence (1804), ruled as a despot until he was assassinated.

**destructive distillation:** see DISTILLATION.

**detective story,** type of popular fiction in which a crime, usually a murder, is solved by a detective professional or amateur who logically interprets the evidence. The modern detective story, complete with its conventions, is considered to have emerged in E.A. POE's 'Murders in the Rue Morgue' (1841). Wilkie COLLINS's *The Moonstone* (1868) is probably the first full-length detective novel. In 1887 Arthur Conan DOYLE, in 'A Study in Scarlet,' introduced Sherlock Holmes, the most famous of all sleuths. Subsequent writers, too, have often used one detective in a series of works. Especially famous are G.K. CHESTERTON's Father Brown, Earl Derr Biggers's Charlie Chan, Rex Stout's Nero Wolfe, Dorothy SAYERS's Lord Peter Wimsey, and Agatha CHRISTIE's Hercule Poirot. Many writers incorporate the conventions of the detective story into the NOVEL, producing works that are witty, erudite, and filled with interesting characters. Such writers include Margery Allingham, Ngaio MARSH, C. DAY LEWIS, Josephine Tey, P.D. James, Peter Dickinson, and Ruth Rendell. More specialized types of detective fiction include the 'police procedural', by such writers as Freeman Wills Crofts, Ed McBain, and Maj Sjöwall and Per Wahlöö, which focus on the technical aspects of crime-solving; the 'hard-boiled' story, such as those of Dashiell HAMMETT, Raymond CHANDLER, and Ross MACDONALD, featuring tough but honorable 'private eyes'; and the psychological, like the novels of Georges Simenon, in which motivation and ambience are more important than the solution to the crime. Espionage novels involving international intrigue share many conventions of detective fiction. Masters of this genre include Eric AMBLER, Graham GREENE, Ian Fleming, and John LE CARRÉ.

**detector:** see PARTICLE DETECTOR.

**détente,** relaxation of tensions between nations, applied particularly to a phase of improved relations between the US and USSR that began in the 1960s. Following the period of hostility known as the COLD WAR, détente flourished in such agreements as the Nuclear Nonproliferation Treaty (1968), Strategic Arms Limitation Treaty (SALT I; 1972), and the Helsinki accords (1975). After the Soviet invasion of Afghanistan (1979), relations between the two superpowers worsened. The crisis in Poland, an escalation of the arms race, and Pres. REAGAN's anti-Soviet stance left détente in abeyance during the early 1980s. It was revived in 1985 with a series of summit conferences between Reagan and the new Soviet leader, Mikhail GORBACHEV, leading to the signature (1987) of a treaty for the reduction of intermediate-range nuclear forces (INF).

**detention centre,** a place of confinement for young offenders, who have been convicted of a CRIME for which an adult could have been sent to PRISON. Introduced in the UK in 1948, following a debate going back to the 1920s, they are designed to give inmates a 'short, sharp, shock'. Offenders spend between three weeks and four months in the centres, during which time they are subject to a regime of strict discipline and vigorous training. In the 1980s, detention centres have been at the forefront of the UK government's penal policy. However, there is little evidence they they reduce the reconviction rate and it has been argued they merely produce a fitter, more determined criminal.

**determinant:** see MATRIX.

**detrivore,** animal that feeds on detritus, which is the name given to the remains of plants and animals normally found on the soil surface or at the bottom of bodies of water. Many of the deep-sea animals are detrivores, feeding on the remains drifting down from the PLANKTON and NEKTON of the surface waters. Detrivores play an important role in the decomposition processes.

**Detroit,** US city (1984 est. pop. 1,089,000), SE Michigan, on the Detroit R., between Lakes St Clair and Erie; inc. as a city 1815. It is Michigan's largest city, the nation's sixth largest, and a major GREAT LAKES shipping and rail centre. Its early carriage industry helped Henry FORD and others to make it the 'automobile capital of the world'. It continues to be the headquarters of major vehicle manufacturers, but declines in the field have caused severe unemployment in the city and its environs. Other industries include steel, pharmaceuticals, and food processing. A producer of foundry products and machine tools, tyres, paint, and chemicals, it also has extensive salt mines. Detroit is the oldest city in the Midwest. After a devastating 1805 fire, the city was rebuilt to a plan by L'Enfant and grew to great commercial importance in the mid-1800s. In July 1967 race riots caused several deaths and many injuries, as well as some $150 million in property damages. The present-day city is the site of many ambitious modern building projects, e.g., the Renaissance Center. The city's educational and cultural institutions include Wayne State Univ., the Univ. of Detroit, the Detroit Inst. of the Arts, and the Detroit Symphony Orchestra. An international bridge and a vehicular tunnel link Detroit with WINDSOR, Ontario.

**Deucalion** (dyooh,kayleeən), in Greek mythology, son of PROMETHEUS; father of HELLEN. Only he and his wife Pyrrha survived the flood that ZEUS caused in anger at mankind's irreverence. Later an oracle told them to cast behind them the stones of the earth. These stones became human and repopulated the world.

**deuterium:** see HYDROGEN.

**Deuteronomy** (dyoohtə,ronəmee), book of the OLD TESTAMENT ascribed by tradition to MOSES. According to the text it gives the final words of Moses to his people, and includes a review of the history of Israel since the exodus from Egypt and a number of general and particular moral principles. The book concludes with a blessing by, and the death of, Moses. Its main themes are monotheism and God's love to his people.

**Deutsch, Helene,** 1884–1982, pioneering female disciple of FREUD, she produced (1944) a two-volume work, *The Psychology of women*, which is to this day the only systematic study of feminine psychology.

**De Valera, Eamon** (devə,leərə), 1882–1975, Irish statesman; b. US. He took part in the Easter Rebellion of 1916; sentenced to life imprisonment, he was released under an amnesty in 1917 and elected president of SINN FÉIN. Again imprisoned in 1918, he escaped to the US, where he raised funds for Irish independence. While away, he was elected president of the revolutionary assembly, Dáil Eireann; he returned in 1920. In 1922, De Valera repudiated the treaty between Britain and Ireland that established the Irish Free State because it did not give Ireland absolute freedom or unity, and left the Dáil. In 1927 he reentered the Dáil with his party, FIANNA FÁIL. As prime minister (1932–48, 1951–54, 1957–58), he made Ireland a sovereign state and maintained neutrality in WORLD WAR II. He was also president of Ireland (1959–73).

**devaluation,** decreasing the official value of one country's currency relative to gold or the currencies of other nations. It is usually undertaken to correct a trade deficit on the BALANCE OF PAYMENTS. The object is to make exports cheaper, and imports more expensive on the home market. Decisions to devalue are not taken lightly, however, since they do not always achieve their objectives. A decision to devalue the £ sterling, for example, would achieve its objective only if the export price could be maintained. This would be difficult if the product contained an imported element which the devaluation had made more expensive. For the same reason, devaluations may have inflationary effects.

**development,** the sequence of changes over the lifespan of an individual organism, also known as ontogenesis (to distinguish it from the sequence of changes undergone by a species in evolution, or phylogenesis). Development is generally understood as the sequence of changes which is common to members of the same species, but the study of development also includes individual differences in development. Development is a complex process of interaction between heredity and environment. Developmental disorders of psychological and neurological functions are distinguished from acquired disorders by not being occasioned by some specific accident, but by being the result of factors affecting the course of development.

**developmental cycle,** a concept developed by M. FORTES to describe the variation in the composition of different domestic groups, through linking the notion of the individual life-cycle to the creation of groups. The developmental cycle is thus the process through which domestic groups form, dissolve, and re-form. A domestic group originates at the marriage of the couple, increases with the birth of children, disperses as the children leave, and breaks up at the death of the parents. Domestic groups vary therefore in size and social and economic significance at different stages in the developmental cycle.

**Devereux, Robert:** see ESSEX, ROBERT DEVEREUX, 2nd EARL OF.

**deviance,** in sociology, the infringement of any socially-defined norm or convention, whether embodied in law (e.g., drug use) or in custom and morality (e.g., bad language). Some explanations of deviance tend to focus on the physical, mental, or genetic constitution of the individual, others look to environmental causes (e.g. bad housing, poverty, etc.). More recent explanations stress the social construction of the category of deviant: it is society which labels certain behaviours 'deviant'. The labelling of deviance is a process undertaken from the perspective of the dominant moral and social order, often by powerful institutions (the law, government, police, courts, the church), directed towards socially marginalized groups. Once identified, deviants may be (or will feel themselves to be) excluded from normal social activities and acceptability and will start to conform to the modes of behaviour supposed to characterize the deviant group or subculture (see CULTURE) thus completing a self-fulfilling circle.

**devil fish,** fish of the RAY family. The largest is the manta ray or greater devil fish which is 6.7 m (22 ft) across, weighing 2270 kg (5000 lb). The Australian pigmy devil fish is only 60 m (2 ft) across and is the smallest. They live in the surface waters, 'flying' through the water by flapping the enormous pectoral fins. They can also fly through the air for short distances, even the giant manta ray. Devil fish are mostly harmless planktonic feeders, although some have poisonous spines on their tails with which to defend themselves.

Manta ray; the **devil fish** of the Red Sea

**Devils Island,** most southerly of the Îles du Salut, in the Caribbean Sea, off FRENCH GUIANA. It was the site of a penal colony (1852–1951) used mostly for political prisoners, such as Capt. Alfred Dreyfus (see DREYFUS AFFAIR). Its name was synonymous with the system's horrors.

**Devlin, Patrick Arthur, Lord,** 1905–, British barrister and judge. He became a HIGH COURT judge (1948), and was later a member of the Court of Appeal (1960) and the House of Lords (1961–64). A conservative judge, he believed that society was held together by a common bond of morality, which the law had the right to protect. His many books include *The Judge* (1979).

**Devolution, War of,** 1667–68, between France and Spain over the Spanish Netherlands. On the basis of a complicated legal claim, LOUIS XIV of France overran the Spanish Netherlands and Franche-Comté. The United Provinces, in alarm, formed the Triple Alliance with England and Sweden, and France was forced to make peace.

**Devon,** county in SW England (1984 est. pop. 978,300), 6711 km² (2617 sq mi), bordering on the English Channel in the S and the Bristol Channel in the N. The county town is EXETER. Much of the county is upland moorland, including EXMOOR in the NE, DARTMOOR in the S, and the Blackdown Hills in the E. The chief rivers are the Tamar, EXE, Dart, and Teign. The attractive scenery (both inland and along the coast) coupled with a mild climate has led to tourism becoming the main industry. Beef and dairy cattle are farmed and Devon is famous for its clotted cream and cider. PLYMOUTH is a port and naval town.

**Devonian period:** see GEOLOGICAL ERA (table).

**Devonport,** city (1986 pop. 22,645), Tasmania, S Australia. Located on the N coast of the island state, it is the terminal port for the BASS STRAIT ferries between MELBOURNE, on the mainland, and Tasmania. Situated at the mouth of the Mersey R. it has an important textile and carpet industry.

**de Vries, Hugo,** 1848–1935, Dutch botanist. He rediscovered (1900) Gregor MENDEL's laws of heredity and developed the theory of MUTATION, expounded in *The Mutation Theory* (1901–03) and in *Plant-Breeding* (1907). De Vries introduced the experimental method to the study of evolution, and maintained that new species develop via mutations and that each quality subject to change is represented by a single physical unit (which he called a pangen). His work on osmosis is also important; he coined the term *isotonic.*

**dew,** thin film of water that has condensed on the surface of objects near the ground. Dew forms when objects cool during the night, causing the layer of air in contact with them to cool, and then causing the condensation of the water vapour in that layer of air. Condensation occurs because the capacity of air to hold water vapour decreases as the air is cooled. FROST forms if the dew point, or temperature at which condensation begins, is below 0°C (32°F).

**Dewar, Sir James,** 1842–1923, Scottish chemist and physicist. Professor at the ROYAL INSTITUTION, London, and later director of the Davy–Faraday Research Laboratory there, he was knighted in 1904. Best known for his work on the properties of matter at very low temperatures and the liquefaction of gases, he liquefied and solidified hydrogen, and invented the DEWAR FLASK, and the explosive cordite.

**Dewar flask** [after Sir James Dewar], container for storing hot or cold substances, e.g., liquid air. It consists of two flasks, one inside the other, separated by a vacuum. The vacuum greatly reduces the transfer of heat. The common household vacuum flask is an adaptation of the Dewar flask.

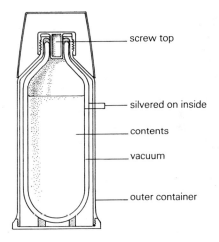

screw top

silvered on inside

contents

vacuum

outer container

Dewar flask

**Dewey, John,** 1859–1952, American philosopher and educator. He rejected authoritarian teaching methods, regarding education in a democracy as a tool to enable the citizen to integrate his or her culture and vocation usefully. To accomplish those aims, both pedagogical methods and curricula needed radical reform. Dewey's philosophy, called instrumentalism and related to PRAGMATISM, holds that truth is an instrument used by human beings to solve their problems, and that it must change as their problems change. Thus it partakes of no transcendental or eternal reality. Dewey's view of democracy as a primary ethical value permeated his educational theories. He had a profound impact on PROGRESSIVE EDUCATION and was regarded as the foremost educator of his day. He lectured all over the world and prepared educational surveys for Turkey, Mexico, and the Soviet Union. Among his works are *Democracy and Education* (1916) and *Logic* (1938).

**Dewey, Melvil,** 1851–1931, American library pioneer, originator of the Dewey decimal system. As acting librarian of Amherst College (1874) he evolved his system of book classification, using the numbers 000 to 999 to cover the general fields of knowledge and narrowing the system to fit special subjects by the use of decimals. While at Columbia Univ. he established the first library school. Dewey was also librarian of the New

York State Library at Albany, where he founded another important library school. He was a founder of the American Library Association.

**De Witt, Jan:** see WITT, JAN DE.

**dextrose:** see GLUCOSE.

**Dhahran,** city (1980 est. pop. 15,000), NE Saudi Arabia, near the Persian Gulf. Since the discovery (1938) of oil nearby, it has grown rapidly into a modern city. In Dhahran are the headquarters of the Arabian American Oil Co. (ARAMCO), the office of the Saudi petroleum ministry, and the Univ. of Petroleum and Minerals (1964). It has an international airport and an oil pipeline to Bahrain.

**Dhaka** (formerly **Dacca**), city (1981 pop. 3,430,312), capital of Bangladesh, on the Burhi Ganga R. It is the nation's industrial, commercial, and administrative centre, with an active trade in jute, rice, and tea. Among its manufactures are textiles, jute products, and paper, and, in cottage industries, confectioneries, jewellery, and other handicrafts. The city achieved glory as the 17th-cent. MOGUL capital of BENGAL, passed under British rule in 1765, and became capital of the newly formed Bangladesh in 1971. Historic buildings include the Bara Katra palace (1644) and Lal Bagh fort (1678).

**dharma.** 1 In Hinduism, the religious and ethical duties of the individual; virtue, right conduct. 2 In Buddhism, religious truth, namely, Buddhist teaching. The plural, *dharmas,* refers to the constituent qualities and phenomena of the empirical world. In fact, a number of fundamental *dharmas* [ultimate phenomena] are said to constitute our world of experience.

**dhimmi,** member of a non-Muslim religious community. FIQH works have elaborate provisions for dhimmis, entailing protection of life, property, and liberty of worship in return for loyalty, submission, and a poll tax. Deriving from early Islamic practice, ordinances concerning dhimmis were rarely applied with any rigour in the history of Islam.

**dhoti,** a term used in India for a man's garment which consists of a cloth wrapped around, then drawn up between the legs, and tucked in at the waist, and sometimes having the loose end draped over the shoulders. The garment was given prestige by Mahatma GANDHI, for nationalist reasons and to promote the Indian cotton trade.

**DHSS:** see DEPARTMENT OF HEALTH AND SOCIAL SECURITY.

**Dhulia,** town (1981 pop. 210,759), Maharashtra state, central India, on the Panjhra R. It is a district administrative and commercial centre set in the region known as Khandesh, and has some cotton textile mills. As a market town it is of long standing.

**diabetes** or **diabetes mellitus,** common chronic disorder in which a deficiency of INSULIN secretion leads to high blood sugar (hyperglycaemia) and altered fat and protein metabolism. Long-term complications of diabetes include thickening of the arteries, which can affect the eyes (diabetic retinopathy) and cause blindness. A milder form of the disease can develop later in life, over the age of 40. This type of diabetes, which has a tendency to be inherited and is associated with obesity, can often be managed by weight loss and diet regulation, although sometimes insulin or oral drugs which lower blood sugar may be needed. Diabetics unable to produce their own insulin are known as insulin-dependent and must receive injections of the hormone daily. The term diabetes is sometimes used to refer to the condition *diabetes insipidus*, a disorder of the PITUITARY GLAND; symptoms include intense thirst and excretion of large amounts of urine.

**diadem,** in ancient times, the fillet of silk, wool, or linen tied around the head of a king, queen, or priest; later, a band of gold, which gave rise to the CROWN. In heraldry, the diadem is one of the arched bars supporting the crown.

**Diadochi** (die‚adəkee) [Gr., = successors], subordinates of ALEXANDER THE GREAT who, after his death (323 BC), struggled for control of his empire. Chief among them were Antipater, Perdiccas, Eumenes, Craterus, Antigonus, Ptolemy, Seleucus, and Lysimachus. The major events of the wars of the Diadochi were the victory of Antipater over Perdiccas for the regency (321 BC), the defeat of Antigonus by Lysimachus, Ptolemy, and Seleucus at Ipsus (301), and the victory of Seleucus over Lysimachus at Corupedion (281). At the end of the period Alexander's empire was irrevocably split, with power divided among the descendants of Ptolemy, Seleucus, and Antigonus.

**Diaghilev, Sergei Pavlovich,** 1872–1929, Russian impresario and art critic. With Michel FOKINE and others, he founded (1909) the Ballets Russes in Paris. His lavish productions, incorporating asymmetry and perpetual motion, revolutionized BALLET. Artists of the first rank worked with him: among dancers, PAVLOVA, KARSAVINA, and NIJINSKY; choreographers, Fokine, Nijinsky, MASSINE, and BALANCHINE; designers, Benois, BAKST, PICASSO, and MATISSE; composers, STRAVINSKY, RAVEL, and DEBUSSY. After his death the dispersal of his company established and nourished ballet throughout the world.

**Diagne, Blaise,** 1872–1934, Senegalese politician and French civil servant; b. Senegal. He won election to the French Assembly in 1914 as its first African deputy. As a junior minister in Prime Min. Clemenceau's war government he helped recruit over 60,000 men in French West Africa; in return he obtained from France the exemption of ex-servicemen from taxes, promises to build agricultural and medical training schools in Senegal, and confirmation of French citizen rights to all residents of Senegal's four communes. After the war he was elected president of the Pan-African Congress in 1919 and founded the Republican-Socialist Party which won control of all municipal councils in Senegal. Shortly before his death he was made Undersecretary of State for the Colonies.

**dialect,** variety of a LANGUAGE used by a group of speakers within a particular speech community. Every individual speaks a variety of his language called an idiolect. Dialects are groups of idiolects with a common core of similarities in pronunciation, grammar, and vocabulary. Adjacent dialects are mutually intelligible, yet with increasing distance differences may accumulate to the point of mutual unintelligibility. For example, in the Dutch–German speech community, there is a continuum of intelligibility from Flanders to Schleswig and from there to Styria, but Flemish and Styrian dialects are mutually unintelligible. The methods of comparative linguistics, using written texts, and of modern linguistic geography, using informants, have been used to study dialects. In recent years linguists have focused increasingly on social dialects that reflect occupations or life-styles.

**dialectical materialism,** the belief that all social, natural, and intellectual development takes place through the reconciliation of contradictions. The dialectical process involves thesis (the thing), antithesis (its opposite), and synthesis (the combination of the two). ENGELS took the concept from the work of HEGEL, who had used it in an idealist sense, and applied it to explaining change in the material world. The concept had been used by MARX but only to explain social and historical events; this application is called historical materialism.

**dialysis,** in chemistry, transfer of dissolved solids (solute) across a semipermeable membrane, which permits or hinders diffusion of molecules according to their size. Dialysis is frequently used to separate different components of a solution. For example, in artificial kidney machines dialysis is used to purify the blood of people whose KIDNEYS have ceased to function. In the machine, blood is circulated on one side of a semipermeable membrane, while dialysis fluid containing substances necessary to the body and closely matching the chemical composition of the blood is circulated on the other side. Metabolic waste products, such as urea, diffuse through the membrane into the dialysis fluid and are discarded, while the diffusion of substances necessary to the body is prevented. See also OSMOSIS.

**diamagnetism:** see MAGNETISM.

**diamond,** mineral, one of two crystalline forms of the element CARBON. It is the hardest substance known, and inferior stones are used as ABRASIVES, in certain types of cutting tools, and as gramophone needles. GEM diamonds were first found in streambeds in India and Borneo; most now come from volcanic pipes in South Africa. Famous diamonds include the Koh-i-noor, now among the English crown jewels; the Cullinan, from which 105 stones were cut; and the blue Hope diamond. Synthetic diamonds, produced since 1955, are now widely used in industry. Diamond knives are used in cutting thin sections for examination by electron microscopy, and are increasingly used in surgery.

**Diana,** in Roman mythology, goddess of the moon, forests, animals, and women in childbirth. Both a virgin goddess and an earth goddess, she was identified with the Greek ARTEMIS.

**Diana,** 1961–, princess of Wales, wife of CHARLES, prince of Wales, and heir to the British throne. Daughter of the 8th Earl Spencer, she was known as Lady Diana Frances Spencer and worked as a kindergarten teacher in London before her marriage in 1981.

**Diane de Poitiers** (pwah,tyay), 1499–1566, mistress of HENRY II of France. She maintained friendly relations with the queen, CATHERINE DE' MEDICI, while completely eclipsing her. She supported the king's anti-Protestant policy.

**diaphragm:** see RESPIRATION.

**diary** [Lat., = day], a daily record of events and observations. It derives its impact from its immediacy, unlike the retrospective memoir. Diaries interest historians because they depict everyday lives in a given time and place. Three of the most famous are those by Samuel PEPYS, who bore witness to the plague (1665) and great fire (1666) then sweeping London; Mary Chesnut, who chronicled in personal terms the fate of the CONFEDERACY in the American CIVIL WAR; and Anne Frank, a young German-Jewish girl who, before she died in a World War II CONCENTRATION CAMP, recorded her experiences while hiding in Holland. Important literary diaries include those of John EVELYN, André GIDE, Franz KAFKA, and Virginia WOOLF.

**diatom,** single-celled, microscopic plant that secretes and is enclosed by an often intricate, round-to-elongated silica shell. Golden ALGAE, diatoms are found in fresh and salt water, in moist soil, and on the moist surfaces of other plants; they are the principal constitutent of PLANKTON, an important food source for aquatic animals. Most exist singly, but some form colonies. When the aquatic forms die, their shells collect in the ooze on the bottom, eventually forming the material called diatomaceous earth (kieselguhr) or the more compact, chalky, light-weight rock called diatomite, used in sound and heat insulation, in making explosives, and for filters and abrasives. Much PETROLEUM is of diatom origin.

**Díaz, Porfirio,** 1830–1915, Mexican dictator. In 1876 he lost the presidential election, revolted, and seized power. He ruled MEXICO ruthlessly for 35 years in the interest of the few and at the expense of the peons. He promoted prosperity by encouraging foreign investments. Growing popular discontent culminated in the 1910 revolution led by MADERO. Díaz fled and died in exile.

**dice** [plural of *die*], small cubes used in games, usually made of ivory, plastic, or similar materials. The six sides are numbered by dots from 1 to 6, placed in such a way that the sum of the dots on opposite sides equals 7. Dice games have been popular since ancient times. In the simplest form of play, each player throws, or shoots, for the highest sum. In craps, a popular gambling game in the US, the 'shooter' rolls two dice, winning on the first roll if 7 or 11 is thrown and losing if the sum is 2, 3, or 12. If any other number is thrown, the player continues to shoot until that number is duplicated, for a win, or a 7 is rolled, for a loss.

**Dicey, Albert Venn,** 1835–1922, British jurist. He practised as a barrister for many years before being appointed professor of English law at Oxford Univ. (1882–1909). His classic *Introduction to the Study of the Law of the Constitution* (1885), considered important enough to be part of the CONSTITUTION OF THE UNITED KINGDOM, outlined the principle of the RULE OF LAW, and established Dicey as a firm believer in LAISSEZ-FAIRE and the limited role of government.

**Dickens, Charles,** 1812–70, English novelist, one of the great fiction writers in English. After a childhood of poverty, during which he had to work for a time in a blacking warehouse (a humiliation he never forgot), Dickens became a court stenographer and parliamentary reporter. His early sketches of London life were collected in *Sketches by Boz* (1836). *The Posthumous Papers of the Pickwick Club* (1836–37), a series of connected humorous sketches, promptly made Dickens famous, and the major novels that followed established him as the most popular writer of his time. They include *Oliver Twist* (1838), *Nicholas Nickleby* (1839), *The Old Curiosity Shop* (1841), *Barnaby Rudge* (1841), *Dombey and Son* (1848), *David Copperfield* (1850), *Bleak House* (1853), *Hard Times* (1854), *Little Dorrit* (1857), *A Tale of Two Cities* (1859), *Great Expectations* (1861), *Our Mutual Friend* (1865), and *The Mystery of Edwin Drood* (1870; unfinished). After an American tour in 1842, he wrote sharply about the US in *American Notes* (1842) and in the novel *Martin Chuzzlewit* (1843). Working ceaselessly, Dickens gave highly successful readings from his works, edited two magazines, wrote Christmas stories, e.g., *A Christmas Carol* (1843), and managed amateur theatricals. He married Catherine Hogarth in 1836, but despite their 10 children, it was not a happy union, and they separated in 1858. Although

sometimes marred by sentimentality, Dickens's novels are remarkable for their rich portraits of all aspects of society, their crusades against abuses (imprisonment for debt, legal delays, bad education), and their sharply drawn, eccentric characters, whose names Mr Micawber, Uriah Heep, Ebenezer Scrooge have become household words for generations of readers.

**Dickinson, Emily,** 1830–86, one of the greatest poets in American literature. The daughter of a prominent lawyer, she spent almost all of her life in her birthplace, gradually withdrawing from local activities, and spending her later years as a virtual recluse in her father's house. She composed over 1000 unique lyrics dealing with religion, love, nature, death, and immortality, only seven of which were published during her lifetime. Her verse, noted for its aphoristic style, its wit, its delicate metrical variation, and its bold and startling imagery, has had great influence on 20th-cent. poetry. Her posthumous fame began with the first editions of her poems (1890, 1891) and her correspondence (2 vol., 1894). While her work has gone through many editions, a definitive edition of Dickinson did not appear until the 1950s, when T.H. Johnson published her poems (3 vol., 1955) and her letters (3 vol., 1958).

**Dickinson, John,** 1732–1808, American Revolutionary statesman. He wrote *Letters from a Farmer in Pennsylvania* (1767–68) to protest against the TOWNSHEND ACTS. A conservative member of the CONTINENTAL CONGRESS, he championed the rights of the small states at the FEDERAL CONSTITUTIONAL CONVENTION.

**Dicksonia,** a tree-fern, up to 10m high (35 ft), native to Tasmania and spread throughout Australasia. Unlike most tree-ferns, which are tropical or sub-tropical, some members of this genus grow well in temperate regions, even withstanding frost.

*Dicksonia fibrosa*, tree ferns in New Zealand

**dicotyledon:** see ANGIOSPERM.

**dictionary,** published list, in alphabetical order, of the words of a language, explaining or defining them, or, in the case of a bilingual dictionary, translating them into another language. Modern dictionaries usually also provide hyphenation, synonyms, derived forms, and etymology. Dictionaries were produced in China, Greece, Islam, and other earlier cultures. English dictionaries began in Anglo-Saxon times developing as glosses for Latin texts. By 1450 recognizable English–Latin dictionaries were being made. It was not until the early 17th cent. that dictionaries giving English definitions for English words appeared. The first attempt at a comprehensive English dictionary along etymological lines was published in 1721 by Nathan Bailey, the *Universal Etymological English Dictionary*, on whose revised form (1730) Samuel JOHNSON based his *Dictionary of the English Language* (1755) which remained the authoritative dictionary for English well into the 19th cent. In 1828 Noah WEBSTER, published an *American Dictionary of the English Language* which has been skilfully and successfully revised over the years, thus retaining its popularity in the US. Discussions in the (English) Philological

Society in 1857 prompted the development of the *New English Dictionary* (later known as the *Oxford English Dictionary*) which aimed to give more information than any previous work. It was eventually published in 1928 and remains an outstanding achievement in lexicography. Two major shorter editions exist: *The Concise Oxford Dictionary of Current English* and the *Shorter Oxford English Dictionary*. In the 20th cent. many smaller general dictionaries have been published and found popular acclaim as have dictionaries explaining terms in specialized subject areas.

**Diderot, Denis** (,deedəroh), 1713–84, French encyclopedist and materialist philosopher. He was enormously influential in shaping the rationalist thought of the 18th cent. His life work, the ENCYCLOPÉDIE, for which he enlisted the leading French talents of the time, epitomized the spirit of the ENLIGHTENMENT. Also a novelist, satirist, and playwright, he produced *The Father of the Family* (1758), the first 'bourgeois drama'. He wrote many philosophical works and in his *Salons* pioneered in modern art criticism. In his later years, he enjoyed the patronage of CATHERINE II of Russia.

**Dido** (,diedoh), in Roman mythology, founder and queen of CARTHAGE. Of the several versions of her story the most famous is in VERGIL's *Aeneid*, in which she loves AENEAS. When he leaves her to continue his journey to Italy, she destroys herself on a burning pyre. The story is told in the operas *Dido and Aeneas* (PURCELL, 1689) and *The Trojans* (BERLIOZ, 1856–59).

**Didot, François**, 1689–1757, French printer, the first of his family to win fame in his craft. His son **François Ambroise Didot**, 1730–1804, influenced by BASKERVILLE, designed pseudoclassical type and in turn influenced BODONI. He improved and established the point system of measuring and naming type sizes. His sons, **Pierre Didot**, 1761–1853, and **Firmin Didot**, 1764–1836, continued the family tradition, producing conscientiously edited texts that met the general reader's requirement for good but inexpensive books. Firmin Didot was the first in France to print from stereotype plates, reducing costs. He improved and named the process.

**Didymus:** see THOMAS, SAINT.

**Diefenbaker, John George**, 1895–1979, prime minister of CANADA (1957–63). He was leader of the Progressive Conservatives and led them to a major election victory in 1958. He instituted agricultural reforms, but a recession contributed to his party's defeat by the Liberals in 1962; his government fell the following year.

**Diego Garcia**, coral island, Indian Ocean, largest island of the Chagos Archipelago, SW of Sri Lanka. Part of the British Indian Ocean Territory, it is also claimed by Mauritius. The 28-km² (11-sq-mi) island, leased (1970) to the US, was later developed as a major US naval base to guard the PERSIAN GULF oil routes and to counter increased Soviet military activities in S Asia and Africa.

**dielectric**, material that does not readily conduct electricity, i.e., an insulator (see INSULATION). A good dielectric resists breakdown under high voltages, does not draw appreciable power from the circuit, and has reasonable physical stability. Dielectrics are used to separate the plates of a CAPACITOR. The dielectric strength is a measure of the maximum voltage (see POTENTIAL, ELECTRIC) that a dielectric can sustain without significant CONDUCTION.

**dielectric constant:** see CAPACITOR.

**Dienbienphu** (,dyen,byen,fooh), former French military base, NW Vietnam, near the Laos border. It was the scene (May 1954) of the last great battle between the French and the VIET MINH, whose victory after a 56-day siege marked the end of French power in INDOCHINA.

**Dieppe**, city (1982 pop. of agglomeration 35,360), Seine-Maritime dept., N France. A fishing port and resort on the English Channel, it has passenger links with Newhaven, in the UK, and imports fruit and vegetables. It was the scene (August 1942) of the Canadian Commando Raid in World War II.

**diesel engine**, type of INTERNAL-COMBUSTION ENGINE patented (1892) by the German engineer Rudolph Diesel. The diesel is heavier and more powerful than the petrol engine and uses heavier oils instead of petrol. It differs from the petrol engine in that the ignition of fuel is caused by such high compression that the temperature of the gas in the cylinders at the high compression point is sufficient to cause ignition. The heavy oil burns and produces a pressure stroke, unlike petrol which when ignited by a spark explodes, thus producing pressure on the piston. The speed and power of the diesel are controlled by varying the amount of fuel injected into the cylinder not the amount of air admitted, as in the petrol engine. Diesels are widely utilized to power industrial and municipal electric generators, continuously-operating pumps such as those used in oil pipelines, and ships, locomotives, and some motor vehicles (especially buses and heavy goods vehicles).

**diet**, an individual's total intake of food and drink. There is no single optimal diet for everybody and recommendations as to the daily amounts of individual nutrients needed have varied dramatically (see NUTRITIONAL SCIENCE). It is probable that over a very wide range of variation there are no effects of diet upon health. However, in certain diseases the diet directly causes the symptons (e.g., coeliac disease) and in others it may have an indirect effect (e.g., surplus calories lead to obesity which is associated with coronary heart disease); dietary deficiencies, especially of VITAMINS, may also lead to disease. There are many factors which will influence an individual's diet. Amongst these are income, religious beliefs, cultural patterns, seasonal changes, advertising and marketing influences, knowledge about nutrition, cookery skills, and the amount of choice and control the individual is able to exercise.

**dietary fibre**, the structural component of all the plants (fruit, vegetables, nuts, and cereals) included in the human diet. The fibre, mostly composed of CELLULOSE, lignin, and pectin, is largely indigestible to humans, but is useful because it speeds the passage of food along the gastrointestinal tract and makes the faeces more bulky. It is believed that a DIET high in dietary fibre (30 g per day) helps to prevent various diseases, including diverticulitis, cancer of the colon, and obesity-related conditions. See DIGESTIVE SYSTEM; NUTRITION.

**diethylstilboestrol** (DES) or **stilboestrol**, synthetic female sex hormone having the same physiological effects as OESTROGEN. Effective even when taken orally, DES was formerly used in pregnant women to prevent miscarriage. During the 1970s the drug was linked to vaginal cancer in some women whose mothers had taken DES during pregnancy. The use of DES as a growth accelerator in beef cattle is controversial because small amounts of DES may persist in the carcass and thus be eaten.

**Dietrich, Marlene** (,deetrikh), 1901–, American film actress; b. Germany. She played the sultry, ageless femme fatale. Her films include *The Blue Angel* (1930), *Shanghai Express* (1932), *The Scarlet Empress* (1934), *A Foreign Affair* (1948), and *Witness for the Prosecution* (1957).

**difference equation:** see DIFFERENTIAL EQUATION.

**differential calculus:** see CALCULUS.

**differential equation**, equation containing derivatives (see CALCULUS) that expresses a relation between a dependent variable $x$, and an independent variable, e.g., time, $t$, both of which are continuous. In many problems the rates of change of a quantity are linked with the quantity itself. Thus in the oscillation of a pendulum the force on, and thus the acceleration of, the bob of the pendulum are dependent on its position and, if air resistance is to be taken into account, also on its velocity. Thus the acceleration $d^2x/dt^2$ is a function of $x$ (position) and $dx/dt$ (velocity). Such a relation is expressed by a differential equation. The solution is not a unique function $x(t)$, but involves arbitrary constants usually derived from initial conditions (e.g., the starting position and starting velocity of the bob of the pendulum). In other problems the value of a function may depend upon specific previous values. Thus, for example, $y(t)$ may be a function of $y(t-1)$ and $y(t-2)$. In a case such as this, the relation between these quantities is called a *difference equation*.

**diffraction**, bending of radiation (such as light) around the edge of an obstacle or by a narrow aperture. Diffraction results from the INTERFERENCE of light waves that pass an opaque body, producing a fuzzy region between the shadow area and the lighted area that, upon close examination, is actually a series of light and dark lines. A **diffraction grating** contains many fine, parallel slits or scratches (about 12,000 per cm or 30,000 per in.) and disperses light into its colours. Such a grating is used in a diffracting SPECTROSCOPE. The atomic and molecular structure of crystals is examined by X-ray diffraction.

**diffusion**, the spread of elements of one culture to another. Early 20th-cent. anthropological research was particularly interested in tracing the supposed routes of such cultural spread, and at that time archaeologists also related different cultures according to how particular developments (e.g., in metal technology) might have diffused. More recently there has been more emphasis on parallel but separate evolution as a general process.

**diffusion,** in physics and chemistry, the spreading of different liquids or gases into each other due to the thermal motion of the molecules.

**digestive system,** in animals, a group of organs that digest food and eliminate waste. Digestion converts the major components of food (PROTEINS, FATS AND OILS, and CARBOHYDRATE) into a form that can be absorbed into the CIRCULATORY SYSTEM and distributed to tissues throughout the body. Digestion begins in the mouth, where chewing reduces the food to a fine texture, saliva moistens it, and an enzyme (amylase) in saliva begins the conversion of starch into simple sugars. The swallowed food passes through the PHARYNX and through a long tube, the oesophagus, into the STOMACH, where digestive enzymes and acid gastric juice are secreted, and sugars and alcohol are absorbed directly through the stomach wall into the bloodstream. The remainder, in the form of a thick liquid (chyme), is pushed onwards by peristalsis (contractions of the muscles forming the outer walls of the digestive tract) and passes into the first section of the small INTESTINE (the duodenum). There digestive enzymes from the PANCREAS break down fats into glycerol and fatty acids, starch into sugars, and proteins into amino acids. The LIVER supplies BILE, which makes fat globules smaller and more easily digested. Small glands in the intestinal wall also secrete enzymes that continue digestion. Digested food is absorbed through villi (small projections of the intestinal wall) into the blood and lymph (see LYMPHATIC SYSTEM). Undigested material passes into the large intestine and is excreted through the anus (see EXCRETION).

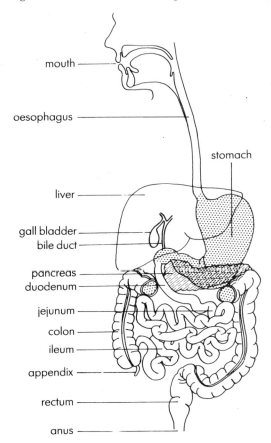

Digestive system

**Di Giacomo, Salvatore** ('deejeeya,kohmoh), 1860–1934, Italian poet, playwright, and short-story writer, b. Naples. His plays and stories portray a world of poverty, the Camorra, and typically Neapolitan characters and customs, but his naturalism (rooted in *verismo* and the example of VERGA) is mitigated by a vein of fantasy and a marked lyrical tendency. *The Vow* (1910) and *Assunta Spina* (1910) are generally considered to be his best plays. His poetry (definitive edition 1926), often set to music, has enriched the repertoire of Neapolitan song.

**digital circuit,** ELECTRIC CIRCUIT in which the output currents or voltages are interpreted as having one of several (often two) values, depending on which of a corresponding number of ranges they fall into. Such circuits are used to implement logical operations or operations on representations of discrete numbers, often in binary form. See also ANALOGUE CIRCUIT.

**digital computer:** see COMPUTER.

**Digitalis,** generic name for several herbs commonly called foxglove, especially *Digitalis purpurea*, which is cultivated commercially and horticulturally. It is poisonous due to glycosides, which stimulate heart muscle. Digitalis also refers to any of several chemically similar drugs, including digitoxin, digoxin, and ouabain, used to treat heart failure and abnormalities of heart rhythm.

**digital system,** one depending solely on the binary representation of information expressed by means of the presence or absence of discrete signals. Thus a continuous waveform, such as human speech, or music, can be converted to a digital form by sampling its amplitude at regular intervals of time and expressing the amplitude at each interval point as a BINARY NUMBER. The accuracy of the digital reresentation depends upon the sampling interval, i.e., the sampling frequency, and the number of bits used to determine the amplitude. An amplitude accuracy of 0.4% is obtained with 8-bit samples and 14-bit samples will give an accuracy of 0.006%. The significant advantage of a digital system is that signals can be handled by computer techniques, stored in computer memory, and reconstituted without loss of signal quality. Digital processing is used in control systems whether they are for major industrial plants or for domestic appliances.

**digital-to-analogue conversion,** the process of changing discrete data into a continuously varying signal. The most common use is to present the output of a digital COMPUTER as a graphic display (see COMPUTER GRAPHICS) or as audio output, as in computer-generated music. See also ANALOGUE-TO-DIGITAL CONVERSION.

**dihedral,** angle between the horizontal, span-wise, axes of the mainplanes (wings) of an AEROPLANE, designed to provide a measure of inherent lateral aerodynamic stability. Positive dihedral, on modern aeroplanes is usually 1°–5° upwards, so that the wingtips are higher than the wing roots in relation to the fuselage. Tailplanes are sometimes set at a negative dihedral angle to keep them out of the slipstream (or the jet efflux) from the engines.

**Dijon,** city (1982 pop. 145,569, agglomeration 215,865), capital of Côte-d'Or dept., E central France. A Roman town and capital of the former Duchy of BURGUNDY, it emerged in the 19th cent. as an important railway centre. It is involved in the wine trade of the Côte d'Or and has long-established food and drink industries; it is famous for its mustard. Notable buildings include the 12th-cent. ducal palace, 13th-cent. cathedral and other churches, the 16th-cent. palace of justice, and many Renaissance houses.

**dill,** annual or biennial plant (*Anethum graveolens*) of the CARROT family, native to Europe. Its pungent, aromatic leaves and seeds are used for pickling and for flavouring sauces, salads, and soups.

**Dillinger, John** (1902?–34), American bank robber and murderer. After his second jailbreak, he and his gang terrorized the Midwest with hit-and-run bank robberies in 1933. He was held responsible for 16 killings and was declared 'public enemy number one' by the FBI, whose agents gunned him down on a Chicago street (July 1934).

**Dilthey, Wilhelm,** 1833–1911, German philosopher. A strict proponent of EMPIRICISM, Dilthey based what he called his 'philosophy of life' on a foundation of descriptive and analytical psychology. He rejected transcendental considerations in his study of all aspects of human activity. His influence on early sociological theory is especially evident in the works of Max WEBER. Dilthey's major work is *Einleitung in die Geisteswissenschaften* [introduction to the human sciences] (1883).

**dime novels,** swift-moving thrillers, mainly about the AMERICAN REVOLUTION, the frontier period, and the CIVIL WAR. First sold in 1860 for 10 cents, the books featured such real life adventurers as BUFFALO BILL, Ned Buntline, and Deadwood Dick and such fictional characters as Nick Carter. The quality of the novels dropped in the 1880s, and they were eclipsed by other series, pulp magazines, and comic strips in the 1890s.

The image labels (from top to bottom): mouth, oesophagus, stomach, liver, gall bladder, bile duct, pancreas, duodenum, jejunum, colon, ileum, appendix, rectum, anus.

**dimension**, in mathematics, number of parameters or coordinates required to describe points in a mathematical (usually geometric) object. The space we inhabit, having height, width, and depth, is three-dimensional; a plane or surface is two-dimensional; a line or curve is one-dimensional; and a point is zero-dimensional. By means of a coordinate system, e.g., CARTESIAN COORDINATES, one can specify any point with respect to a chosen origin (and coordinate axes through the origin, in the case of two or three dimensions). By analogy, an ordered set of four, five, or more numbers is defined as representing a point in a space of four, five, or more dimensions.

**Dimitrov, Georgio** (di,meetrof), 1882–1949, Bulgarian and international Communist leader, premier of Bulgaria (1946–49). A founder of the Bulgarian Communist Party, he took part in the abortive 1923 rising, after which he fled abroad to work as a professional revolutionary for the COMINTERN. In 1933 the NAZIS charged him with setting the REICHSTAG on fire, and his trial made him an anti-fascist hero. Released on account of his Soviet citizenship, he became Comintern general secretary (1935–43) and presided over the adoption of the united front strategy. He returned to Bulgaria in 1945 to become head of the Communist-dominated Fatherland Front government.

**D'Indy, Vincent** (danh,dee), 1851–1931, French composer, pupil of FRANCK. In 1894, he helped to found the Schola Cantorum, Paris, and directed it (1911–31). His compositions include *Symphony on a French Mountain Air* for piano and orchestra (1886), several musical dramas, and the symphonic variations *Istar* (1896).

**Dine, Jim**, 1935–, American painter. A prominent figure in American POP ART, he is best known for his combination of real objects, household appliances, etc., set against backgrounds of abstract painting textures. He pioneered the HAPPENING and performance art of the 1960s and 70s.

**Dinesen, Isak**, pseud. of **Baroness Karen Blixen** (,dinisən), 1885–1962, Danish author who wrote primarily in English. She is best known for her imaginative tales, which contain romantic and supernatural elements. Collections include *Seven Gothic Tales* (1934), *Winter's Tales* (1942), and *Last Tales* (1957). *Out of Africa* (1937) is an autobiographical account of her years on a coffee plantation in Kenya.

**Dingaan**, c.1795–1840, ruler of the ZULU kingdom (r.1828–40). He assassinated his brother SHAKA, the founder of the Zulu kingdom, in order to succeed to the throne. His reign was marked by unsuccessful wars against the Boers, the Ndebele, and the Swazi. He was killed by the Swazi having been defeated in battle by an alliance of the Boers and his brother Mpande who then succeeded him.

**Ding Ling**, 1902–86, Chinese writer; one of several pen-names of a writer of short stories and novels. Born into a remarkable family in Changsha where her widowed mother defied convention and became a teacher, Ding Ling's own life was one of uncoventionality and passion. Her lover, Hu Yebin, a Communist poet, was executed and she was imprisoned in 1933. She went to the Communist base in Yan'an in 1936 but in 1942 wrote a critical essay on the sexist attitude of Mao Zedong and others. Her second short story, *Shafei nushi de riji* [Miss Sophie's diary], depicts a passionate and sensitive girl dying of tuberculosis; a great success, it was followed by many others about young intellectuals and intellectual struggles until *Shui* [flood] (1931), a story of peasant heroism particularly praised as 'proletarian literature' by Communist critics. She won the Stalin Prize for *Taiyang zhao zai Sanggan he shang* [the sun shines over the Sunggari River] (1951) but was attacked as an anti-rightist in 1957 and not rehabilitated until after 1976, probably because of her outspoken manner and essays, rather than her fiction.

**dingo**, wild DOG of Australia; shoulder height about 60 cm (2 ft). Probably introduced by aboriginal settlers thousands of years ago, it was the only large carnivorous mammal found in Australia by the first European colonists. It has large, erect ears, a wolflike head, and long legs, and is usually yellowish red, with white markings. A nocturnal hunter, it preys on small animals and often kills livestock.

**Diniz** (dee,neesh), Port. *Dinis* 1261–1325, king of Portugal (1279–1325). He stimulated farming and commerce and restricted the Roman Catholic Church's acquisition of land. A poet and patron of literature, he founded (1290) a university at Lisbon during his relatively peaceful reign.

**dinoflagellates:** see PYRROPHYTA.

**dinosaur**, any of a large group of extinct REPTILES (subclass Archosauria) that dominated the earth for nearly 150 million years in the Mesozoic era. Dinosaurs ranged in length from the 60-cm (2-ft) *Compsognathus* to the 27-m (90-ft) *Diplodocus*, and in weight up to the 75-ton *Brachiosaurus*. They are traditionally classified as cold-blooded reptiles, but recent evidence on posture, skeleton, and eating habits suggests some may have been warm-blooded. They are all thought to have been egg-layers. Saurischian (order Saurischia), or lizard-hipped, dinosaurs included meat-eating bipeds, e.g., *Allosaurus* and *Tyrannosaurus*, and plant-eating quadrupeds, e.g., *Brontosaurus* and *Diplodocus*. Ornithischian (order Ornithischia), or bird-hipped, dinosaurs included plant-eating bipeds, e.g., *Iguanodon* and the duckbills, and armoured dinosaurs, e.g., the plated *Stegosaurus* and horned *Triceratops*. It is not known why dinosaurs died out. Most theories postulate that changes in geography, climate, and sea level were responsible, and one recent theory suggests that an asteroid impact caused the changes that led to their extinction.

Triceratops
Stegosaurus
Apatosaurus (Brontosaurus)
Tyrannosaurus

Dinosaur

**Diocletian** (Caius Aurelius Valerius Diocletianus), 245–313, Roman emperor (r.284–305); b. Salona (now Split, Yugoslavia). An army commander of humble birth, he was chosen to succeed Numerian as emperor and became sole ruler after his co-emperor, Carinus, was killed (285). Diocletian appointed Maximian as his co-emperor and Constantius I and Galerius as caesars (subemperors). Each of the four men was given a district of the empire to rule. Under this reorganization the empire throve; Britain was restored (296), and the Persians were subjugated (298). Diocletian's unsuccessful economic policies and his persecution of Christians marred his splendid reign. In 305 he retired to his castle at Salona, whose impressive ruins later influenced Robert ADAM.

**diode**, device with two electrodes that has a very high resistance to current flow in one direction and a very low resistance in the reverse direction. When an alternating voltage is applied to a circuit containing a diode, current flows when the voltage is of one polarity but is blocked when the voltage reverses. Thus in the circuit itself, current, albeit pulsed, is unidirectional. This is called rectification (see RECTIFIER) and converts alternating current (AC) into direct current (DC). A combination of diodes with switching mechanisms can be used to convert DC into AC. Some diodes are also sensitive to light, in the visible, ultraviolet, and infrared ranges, and this phenomenon can be usefully applied (see

PHOTOELECTRIC CELL; PHOTOVOLTAIC CELL). A light-emitting diode (LED) produces light as current passes through it; some LEDs can act as lasers. A thermistor is a special SEMICONDUCTOR diode whose conductivity increases with temperature.

**Diogenes,** c.412–323 BC, pre-Socratic Greek philosopher. He taught that the virtuous life is the simple life, a maxim he dramatized by living in a barrel. Condemning the corruption of his contemporaries, he went about the streets looking for 'an honest man'. None of his writings survives.

**Dione,** in astronomy, natural satellite of SATURN.

**Dion of Syracuse** 409?–354? BC, Greek political leader in Syracuse, brother-in-law of DIONYSIUS THE ELDER. A friend of PLATO, he opposed tyranny. Leading a force from Athens, he overthrew (357 BC) DIONYSIUS THE YOUNGER and ruled Syracuse until he was assassinated.

**Dionysius of Halicarnassus,** fl. late 1st cent. BC, b. Halicarnassus (Bodrum), Greek rhetorician and historian. He came to Rome in 30 BC, and there wrote *Roman Antiquities*, a history of Rome down to the First PUNIC WAR, and some works of literary criticism, including studies of THUCYDIDES and DEMOSTHENES. His criticism is often shrewd and sensitive, and his history is well researched.

**Dionysius the Elder,** c.430–367 BC, tyrant of SYRACUSE. Gaining influence by supporting the poorer classes, he became (405 BC) TYRANT. He maintained power by exploiting Syracusan fear of the Carthaginians, leading expeditions against them in Sicily, and against Italian cities. He was succeeded by his son, **Dionysius the Younger,** fl. 368–344 BC. Unsuited for the position by both training and temperament, he was overthrown by DION OF SYRACUSE (357). The murder of Dion permitted his return, but he was finally expelled in 344.

**Dionysus** (dieə,niesəs) in Greek mythology, god of fertility and wine, later considered a patron of the arts. Probably of Thracian origin, Dionysus was one of the most important Greek gods and the subject of profuse and contradictory legends. He was thought to be the son of either ZEUS and PERSEPHONE or of Zeus and Semele. Dionysus was attended by a carousing band of SATYRS, MAENADS, and NYMPHS. He taught mankind to grow vines but was capable of dreadful revenge upon those (e.g., ORPHEUS and Pentheus) who denied his divinity. His worship was characteristically drunken and orgiastic. The chief figure in the ORPHIC MYSTERIES and other cults, Dionysus had many festivals in his honour. From the music, singing, and dancing of the Greater Dionysia in Athens developed the dithyramb and, ultimately, Greek drama. The Romans identified him with Liber and BACCHUS, who was more properly the wine god.

**Diop, Birago Ishmael,** 1906–, Senegalese writer, veterinary scientist, and diplomat. He is best known for his collections of aphoristic stories based on African folk tales, *Contes d'Amadou Koumba* (1947; tr. *Tales of Amadou Koumba*, 1966), and *Leurres et lueurs* (1960; tr. *Lures and Glimmers*, 1960). His play *L'Os de Mor Lam* was performed in Senegal in 1967–68, and was later included in the repertory of Peter BROOK's troupe of the Bouffes du Nord Théâtre in Paris.

**Dior, Christian,** 1905–57, French FASHION designer. His was the first house to achieve international market and celebrity after World War II. He designed the wasp-waisted 'New Look' with full skirt, narrow shoulders, which was welcomed after the austerity of the war years. His other innovation was the triangular unwaisted A-line, 1956. He made finely-finished opulent clothes for a wealthy, traditional clientele, and his clothes were not available ready-to-wear. On Dior's death, Yves SAINT-LAURENT became designer of the house.

**Dioscuri:** see CASTOR AND POLLUX.

**diphtheria,** acute, dangerous, contagious disease caused by the bacterium *Corynebacterium diphtheriae*. It is spread through respiratory droplets of infected individuals. The bacteria, lodging in the mucous membranes of the throat, secrete a potent toxin, which causes tissue destruction and the formation of a grey membrane in the upper respiratory tract that can loosen and cause asphyxiation. The toxin may also spread via the blood and affect the heart and peripheral nervous system. Treatment of the disease, which can cause death within four days, involves antitoxin and PENICILLIN. An effective immunization programme has now made diphtheria rare in the West.

**Dirac, Paul Adrien Maurice,** 1902–76, English physicist. He formulated (1928) a version of quantum mechanics (see QUANTUM THEORY) that took into account the theory of RELATIVITY. This theory showed that the electron must have a fourth degree of freedom (fourth characteristic way in which it could have or take up energy)—the property of spin—and implied the existence of an antiparticle (see ANTIMATTER) to the electron; the antiparticle was discovered later and named the positron. His equation of a particle's motion is a relativistic modification of Erwin SCHRÖDINGER's basic equation of quantum mechanics. Dirac and Schrödinger shared the 1933 Nobel Prize for physics. Dirac also helped to formulate the Fermi–Dirac statistics which state the relations and properties obeyed by one group of ELEMENTARY PARTICLES, and contributed to the quantum theory of electromagnetic radiation.

Christian **Dior** took his collection, insured for £60,000, to Scotland in 1955

**direct broadcasting by satellite:** see DBS.

**direct current:** see ELECTRICITY; GENERATOR; MOTOR, ELECTRIC.

**Directoire style,** in French interior decoration and costume, the manner prevailing at the time of the DIRECTORY (1795–99). Influenced by Greco-Roman design, it departed from the sumptuous LOUIS PERIOD STYLES and forecast the EMPIRE STYLE. Furniture became more angular and severe; painted and waxed wood replaced marquetry. Women adopted a slim-fitting gown, with low neckline and high waistline, and men wore tight breeches and coats with long tails and wide lapels.

**Director of Public Prosecutions (DPP),** in the UK, one of the government's chief legal officers, and head of their department of lawyers. His or her job is to institute important criminal proceedings and to give advice as to whether certain prosecutions should be undertaken. Advice is sought by government departments, the POLICE, and magistrates. In certain cases, usually involving serious crimes, the police must refer the case to the DPP, who will inquire as to whether sufficient EVIDENCE exists to bring a prosecution. At all times he or she works under the supervision of the ATTORNEY-GENERAL.

**Directory,** five men who held (1795–99) executive power in France during the FRENCH REVOLUTION. They were chosen by the legislature and each year one director was replaced. The Directory was riddled by corruption and torn by internal squabbles. After the military reverses of 1799, the Abbé SIEYÈS, who became a director that year, helped NAPOLEON I stage the coup of 18 Brumaire (9 Nov. 1799), which replaced the Directory with the Consulate.

**disarmament, nuclear.** The first ATOMIC BOMB dropped (1945) on Japan by the US in WORLD WAR II demonstrated the terrible threat to humanity posed by the possibility of nuclear war. Therefore the first resolution (1946) of the General Assembly of the UNITED NATIONS set up the UN Atomic Energy Commission to make proposals for control of atomic energy. The US-sponsored Baruch Plan proposed an international agency to control all destructive uses of atomic power. Intensification of the COLD

WAR made agreement impossible, and the Soviet Union became the second nuclear power (1949). After both the US (1952) and the USSR (1953) exploded the HYDROGEN BOMB, UN disarmament talks were revived, and a subcommittee of the commission was established. Its Western members—the US, Canada, Great Britain, and France—advocated an international control system with on-site inspection. The USSR called for an immediate ban on nuclear weapons with possible later controls. The US, Great Britain, and the USSR began discussions on the formulation of a nuclear test-ban treaty in 1958 and agreed to suspend nuclear testing for one year. These talks, continued under the US Pres. John F. KENNEDY and Soviet premier Nikita KHRUSHCHEV, led to the first test-ban treaty (1963), the Moscow Agreement, which banned testing in the atmosphere, in outer space, and under water. This treaty rapidly reversed the growth in the radioactivity of the atmosphere due to atmospheric nuclear tests, although these were continued by France and China for some years. Underground testing by the nuclear weapon states is continuing, though there are agreements to limit the size of underground nuclear explosions. A comprehensive test ban treaty would end all testing. The Non Proliferation Treaty (which originated with the UK, US, and USSR) attempted to limit the spread of nuclear weapons by distinguishing between nuclear weapon states, who agreed not to export nuclear weapons or materials or knowledge relevant to them, and to negotiate to reduce their own nuclear arsenals, and nonnuclear weapon states who agreed not to acquire nuclear weapons and to accept international inspection ('safeguards'') of all their nuclear facilities by the International Atomic Energy Agency, and in return were offered assistance with the development of peaceful nuclear power. Though the large majority of all countries have acceded to this treaty, some of the most important nuclear-capable states have not (India, Pakistan, Israel, South Africa, Brazil, Argentina). The US and USSR began holding Strategic Arms Limitation Talks (SALT), which resulted in the signing (1972) of the SALT I treaty: the two powers agreed to limit antiballistic missiles and reached an interim accord on limiting offensive nuclear weapons. The SALT II talks led to an agreement tentatively approved by the US Pres. Jimmy CARTER and Soviet premier Leonid BREZHNEV. Ratification of the plan by the US Senate, however, was shelved (1980) after the Soviet invasion of Afghanistan. In 1982 the US and USSR began a new set of talks, called START (STrategic Arms Reduction Talks). In Dec. 1987 US Pres. Ronald Reagan and Soviet leader Mikhail Gorbachev signed a treaty to destroy all intermediate-range nuclear warheads (i.e., those in Europe controlled by the NATO powers and by the Warsaw Pact forces); although a historic step in that it represented the first reduction of nuclear weaponry, the treaty achieved a reduction of only 3% of the world's stock of nuclear warheads. Many people in both East and West oppose the total abolition of nuclear weapons by the nuclear powers since this would be an invitation to use conventional military power wherever a nation thought it had superiority, and would give immense power to even a minor country that chose to evade the ban. Yet there is a very widespread feeling that the number of nuclear weapons can be reduced in a balanced manner without causing dangerous feelings of international insecurity to arise. See also CAMPAIGN FOR NUCLEAR DISARMAMENT.

**Disarmament Conference,** 1923–37, series of international meetings for the discussion of general disarmament. Participants were the members of the LEAGUE OF NATIONS, the US, and the USSR. The first meeting (Feb. 1932–June 1933), in Geneva, was marked by disagreement over definitions of the categories of war materials, the reluctance of France to agree to any arms limitations, and Germany's insistence on a military parity with the other powers. The session ended in deadlock. The second session (Oct. 1933) met in Germany, but when Adolf HITLER withdrew Germany from the League of Nations, the Conference again adjourned. Thereafter, it met only sporadically until it went out of existence in 1937. By then a general military buildup preparatory to WORLD WAR II was already under way, and all hopes of disarmament had vanished.

**discourse,** in sociology, term referring to both sets of ideas and to material practices through which it is possible to achieve knowledge of and power over certain areas of human activity. For example, the French philosopher M. FOUCAULT writes of the discourses of sexuality: ways of talking (or not talking) about organizing and constructing modalities of human sexuality which have changed over time and represent different strategies of power over the human body.

**discourse analysis,** the attempt to discover regularities within a stretch of language longer than a sentence using grammatical, phonological,

syntactic, and semantic criteria. The classification of discourse criteria and context is often carried out by sociolinguists when looking at different types of language use, e.g., jokes, narratives, ritual, monologues versus dialogues, teacher–pupil or doctor–patient interaction. It is also called conversational analysis when only working within phonology and the spoken word.

**discus throwing,** athletics FIELD EVENT in which the competitor throws a discus (weighing 2 kg (4 lb 6⅔ oz) for men and 1 kg (2 lb 3¼ oz) for women) as far as possible by revolving within a circle, gaining momentum before release.

**Disney, Walt(er Elias),** 1901–66, American film producer, a pioneer in animated cartoons. He began his career as a cartoonist in 1920. In 1928 he created the character of Mickey Mouse in the cartoon short *Steamboat Willie.* His *Snow White and the Seven Dwarfs* (1938) was the first full-length animated cartoon. Others include *Fantasia* (1940) and *Alice in Wonderland* (1951). After 1950 he also produced adventure stories and semidocumentary nature films. Disneyland, a gargantuan amusement park in Anaheim, California, opened in 1955; Walt Disney World opened near Orlando, Florida, in 1971 and Epcot Center, on adjoining grounds, opened in 1982.

**displaced person:** see REFUGEE.

**Disraeli, Benjamin, 1st earl of Beaconsfield,** 1804–81, British statesman and author. Of Jewish descent, he was baptized a Christian in 1817. His political essays and novels, e.g., *Coningsby* (1844) and *Sybil* (1845), earned him a permanent place in English literature. Elected to Parliament in 1837, he developed into an outstanding politician. In 1846 he opposed the free trade policy of his leader PEEL, attacking him personally with caustic wit. He quietly abandoned protectionism, however, after 1852 when he became chancellor of the exchequer in the tory government of DERBY, under whom he also served in minority governments (1858–59, 1866–68). Always imaginatively daring, he 'educated his party' (now the Conservative Party) to pass the REFORM BILL of 1867, which enfranchised some 2 million men, largely of the urban working class. He became prime minister in 1868, but lost the office to GLADSTONE that same year after the extended electorate returned a Liberal majority. His second ministry (1874–80) produced many domestic reforms but is noted for its aggressive foreign policy. The annexation of the Fiji islands (1874) and the Transvaal (1877), and the wars against the Afghans (1878–79) and the ZULUS (1879), proclaimed England an imperial world power. Disraeli's purchase of controlling shares of the Suez Canal strengthened British interests in the Mediterranean. After the Russo-Turkish War, he induced Turkey to cede Cyprus to Great Britain, and through the Congress of Berlin he reduced Russian power in the Balkans. A favourite of Queen VICTORIA, he had her crowned empress of India in 1876. His policy of democracy and imperialism revitalized his party. His father, **Isaac D'Israeli,** 1766–1848, was a writer, best known for *Curiosities of Literature* (6 vol., 1791–1834).

**dissenters:** see NONCONFORMISTS.

**distaff:** see SPINNING.

**distance learning,** a form of education not requiring residence or attendance, and using various forms of communication between the student and the centre concerned. The oldest form of such learning is by correspondence course—in Britain for qualifications from GCE to university level, including preparation for the LONDON UNIVERSITY external degree. Modern technologies enabled the OPEN UNIVERSITY to structure courses round multiple forms of communication. An Open College, at further education level, has developed an adapted, nationally diffused version of the OU model. Other countries have experimented with 'open' or distance learning: the Télé-université du Québec began courses in 1974, Deakin Univ. in Australia started an ambitious off-campus programme in 1978, and a Dutch Open University began operation in 1982. International consortia for distance learning have been established, and developments in adult education particularly are taking place by distance learning in Africa, Europe, the Middle East, Australasia, North, Central and Latin America.

**distillation,** process used to separate the substances composing a mixture; it involves a change of state, as of liquid to gas, and subsequent condensation (see STATES OF MATTER). A simple distillation apparatus consists of three parts: a flask in which the mixture is heated, a condenser in which the vapour is cooled, and a vessel in which the condensed vapour, called the distillate, is collected. Upon heating, the substances with a higher boiling point remain in the flask and constitute the residue. When the substance with the lowest boiling point has been removed, the temperature can be raised and the process repeated with the substance having the next lowest boiling point. The process of obtaining portions (or fractions) in this way is called *fractional distillation*. In *destructive distillation* various solid substances, such as wood, coal, and oil shale, are heated out of free contact with air, and the portions driven off are collected separately. Distillation is used in refining PETROLEUM and in preparing alcoholic drinks.

**distribution,** used in STATISTICS to indicate the frequencies with which observed values occur in designated class intervals. The distributions derived from samples of large populations are often compared with theoretical distributions, including the NORMAL DISTRIBUTION, the BINOMIAL DISTRIBUTION, and the POISSON DISTRIBUTION. The identification of distributions often requires the use of large samples, such as those derived from national censuses of populations.

**distributive law,** in mathematics, a law governing the interaction of certain pairs of operations. The distributive law of multiplication over addition states that the equation $a \times (b + c) = (a \times b) + (a \times c)$ holds for all numbers a, b, and c.

**District of Columbia,** federal district of the US and coextensive with the nation's capital, WASHINGTON, DC, established in 1790–91 on the east bank of the Potamac R., bordered by Maryland (E) and Virginia (W), area 170 km² (69 sq mi). The District is governed by a mayor and city council, but all legislation is reviewed by Congress. Since 1960 residents have been able to vote in presidential elections and since 1970 they have had a nonvoting delegate to Congress.

**dithyramb,** in ancient Greece, hymn to the god DIONYSUS, an antiphonal choral LYRIC out of which TRAGEDY probably grew. It developed into the form used by poets such as BACCHYLIDES. Later it became freer in metre and more musical.

**Dittersdorf, Karl Ditters von,** 1739–99, Austrian composer and violinist. A prolific composer and an important precursor of MOZART in operatic and symphonic forms, his best-remembered and most successful work was the comic opera *Doktor und Apotheker* (1786).

**diuretic,** any agent that increases the volume of urine formed by the kidney, thus eliminating excess sodium and water from the body. Diuretics are given to treat high blood pressure, glaucoma, and heart insufficiencies. Some diuretics (thiazides) cause potassium deficiency, which is corrected by administration of potassium salts.

**diurnal circle,** apparent path followed by a star due to the Earth's rotation on its axis. The stars appear to move from east to west on the celestial sphere in concentric circular paths centred at the celestial poles (see ASTRONOMICAL COORDINATE SYSTEMS).

**diverticulitis,** inflammation and irritation of the colon. A common and distressing condition in the developed world, which may be relieved by improving the diet to include a higher proportion of fibre (see FIBRE, DIETARY).

**dividend,** the part of the net earnings, or profits, of a company that is distributed to its shareholders after deduction of income tax at standard rate. Dividends are declared by the board of directors, usually at regular intervals. Holders of preference shares and debentures must be paid their dividends before anything is paid on common stock. Dividends are normally declared as a percentage of the nominal value of the share capital, or as an absolute amount per share.

**divination,** a means of acquiring knowledge, e.g., of the future or of the perpetrator of an act, through divine sources, omens, or oracles. It is based on the belief that revelations are offered to humans in extrarational forms of knowledge: ancient Chaldeans studied birds' flight and patterns in water or entrails; the Greeks put their trust in the ORACLE. Present-day forms of divination include crystal-gazing, palmistry, and astrology.

**Divine Comedy:** see DANTE ALIGHIERI.

**divine right:** see under MONARCHY.

**diving, deep-sea,** descent into deep water for extended periods, used in a variety of commercial, scientific, and military activities. Helmeted diving suits were first devised in England in the 17th cent., and improved versions are still in use today. The scuba (acronym for self-contained underwater breathing apparatus), invented by J.-Y. COUSTEAU, which enables divers to carry their own air supply, allows much greater mobility. The bathyscaphe, developed by Auguste PICCARD, was the first self-contained diving craft. Skin diving, a popular sport, is done with a face mask and snorkel (plastic tube) just below the surface, or with a scuba at greater depths.

**diving, springboard and platform,** sport of entering the water from a raised position, often while executing tumbles and other acrobatic manoeuvres. Springboard diving is done from a flexible plank either 1 or 3 m (about 3 ft 3 in or 9 ft 10 in) above the water. Platform diving (or high diving) is usually done from a rigid platform projecting from a tower 10 m (32 ft 10 in) high. Both types are marked on the basis of form, execution, and difficulty of the dive. Competitive diving, a part of most aquatic sports meets, is an Olympic event for men (since 1904) and women (since 1912).

**divisional court:** see HIGH COURT.

**divisionism:** see POSTIMPRESSIONISM.

**division of labour,** the allocation of different kinds or categories of work to different classes or kinds of people, most fundamentally classified on the basis of generation or gender. The division of labour tends to become increasingly specialized with increasing economic and political complexity (see EVOLUTION, SOCIOCULTURAL). The breaking down of productive activity into discrete tasks, which are then combined under supervision, is generally characteristic of labour under CAPITALISM; see TAYLORISM and Fordism.

**divorce,** in law, the dissolution of marriage by court judgment, nowadays on application by either party. Partial dissolution leaving the parties married but allowing non-cohabitation, is judicial separation. In the UK, prior to 1857 divorce could only be granted by an Act of Parliament and was therefore restricted to the most privileged class. Since then judges have been able to grant divorces, e.g., because of adultery, which were easier for men to obtain than women. Since 1969, the sole ground for divorce is that the marriage has irretrievably broken down; this can be shown on a number of grounds, e.g., cruelty, desertion or adultery. The court will determine the issues of custody of the children, PROPERTY distribution, and the award of maintenance to one party (usually the wife). After the divorce decree is final, both parties are free to re-marry. In countries where the legal code is strongly influenced by religious beliefs (especially Islam or Roman Catholicism) divorce is either forbidden or restricted, e.g. in the Republic of Ireland where it is prohibited in the constitution.

**Dix, Dorothea Lynde,** 1802–87, American social reformer. A pioneer in the movement for specialized treatment of the insane, she influenced the founding of state hospitals for the insane in the US, Canada, and Europe. Dix also did notable work in penology.

**Dix, Otto,** 1891–1969, German painter and draftsman. Associated with the NEUE SACHLICHKEIT group, his interests were to depict the social horrors of post-World War I German society, where beggars, disfigured soldiers, and prostitutes were seen as exemplar figures of a corrupt and decadent society.

**Diyarbakir,** city (1980 pop. 235,617), capital of Diyarbakir prov., SE Turkey, on the upper Tigris R. It is a commercial and administrative centre with carpet weaving and other industries. Successor to the Roman town of Amida, it preserves its encircling medieval walls.

**Djakarta** or **Jakarta,** city (1980 pop. 6,480,000), capital and largest city of Indonesia, NW JAVA. It is the administrative, commercial, industrial, and transportation center of the country; industries include food-processing, ironworks, automobile assembly, textiles, and chemicals. Resembling a Dutch town, with its many canals and drawbridges, Djakarta has an old quarter and a new suburb. Its port, largest in Indonesia, handles most of the country's export-import trade. Founded (c.1619) as the Dutch EAST INDIA COMPANY fort of Batavia, it became capital of the newly established nation in 1949 and was renamed Djakarta. It is the seat of the Univ. of Indonesia. Notable museums include the National Museum with its superb collection of Asian porcelain and the Djakarta Museum (the former Batavia City Hall).

**Djibouti** (ji,boohtee), officially Republic of Djibouti, republic (1986 est. pop. 360,000), c.22,020 km² (8500 sq mi), E Africa, formerly the French Territory of the Afars and Issas (1967–77), and French Somaliland

(1896–1946), bordered by Ethiopia (N and W), the Somali Republic (S), and the Gulf of Aden (E). DJIBOUTI is the capital. Largely a stony desert, the country is economically underdeveloped. Nomadic animal-herding is the chief occupation, but the government is attempting to develop agriculture and fisheries. Exports include hides, cattle, and coffee (transshipped from Ethiopia), and some revenue is derived from the port of Djibouti. The small-scale industry includes the building and repairing of ships, production of compressed or liquid gas, and food processing. The population is almost equally divided between Somali (including Issas) and Afars (of Ethiopian origin), the former being slightly preponderant. Both groups are Muslim and speak Cushitic languages.

*History.* Djibouti is important for its strategic situation on the strait between the Gulf of ADEN and the RED SEA. France obtained a foothold in the area in 1862 and organized it as a colony, French Somaliland, in 1896. The colony gained territorial status in 1946. In a 1967 referendum the Afars voted to continue ties with France, while the Somali voted for independence and eventual reunion with SOMALIA. Djibouti became independent in 1977 under Pres. Hassan Gouled Aptidon, who heads the ruling Popular Rally for Progress. Friction between the two ethnic groups created immediate problems, and cabinet shuffles to give the Afars greater voice in the government failed to end their claims of discrimination.

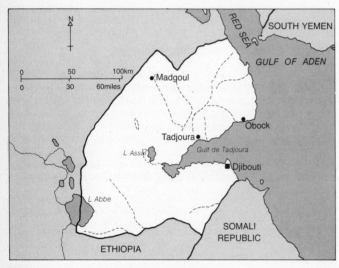

Djibouti

**Djibouti,** town, (1985 est. pop. 200,000), capital of the Republic of Djibouti. A strategically located port on the Gulf of ADEN, it is the country's only large town and the mainstay of its economy. The port, linked by railway to ADDIS ABABA, derives most of its revenue from the Ethiopian transit trade. Founded (c.1888) by the French, the city was the capital of French Somaliland (1892–1945) and of the French territory of the Afars and Issas (1945–77) until the nation became independent.

**Djilas, Milovan,** (ˌjeelahs), 1911–, Montenegrin-born Yugoslav politician, writer, and dissident. A member of the Communist Party's inner leadership from the mid-1930s, he fell foul of TITO in 1953 for advocating an end to the Party's monopoly of power in a series of newspaper articles. He was jailed in 1956 for supporting the Hungarian uprising, and his term was extended when *The New Class*, his critique of the Communist oligarchy, was published in the West in 1957. Released in 1961, he was again imprisoned between 1962 and 1966. His other works include *Conversations with Stalin* (1962), *Wartime* (1977), *Tito* (1980), *Rise and Fall* (1985), and *Of Prisons and Ideas* (1986).

**Dmitri** or **Demetrius,** 1582–91, czarevich, son of IVAN IV of Russia (Ivan the Terrible). Dmitri's brother, Feodor I, succeeded Ivan, but Boris GODUNOV ruled in actuality. Dmitri was killed in 1591, possibly by Boris's order. Boris became czar when Feodor died in 1598. Four pretenders later assumed Dmitri's name. The first invaded Russia with Polish help in 1604, was crowned when Boris died suddenly, but was killed in 1606. The second invaded in 1607 and was killed in 1610. Two men claiming to be Dmitri's son were executed, in 1612 and 1613. The coronation of

Michael ROMANOV in 1613 ended the chaotic period, known as the Time of Troubles.

**Dmowski, Roman** (ˌd(ə)movˈskee), 1864–1939, right-wing Polish politician and political theorist. Dmowski was instrumental in turning the Liga Polska (Polish League) into a weapon of nationalist struggle. He was opposed to the workers' movement and socialist ideals. His 'exclusive' vision of a state dominated by ethnic Polish culture and values contrasted with PILSUDSKI's hopes for a wider, federalist structure which would have had a place for the non-Polish minorities. Leader of the Polish National Committee in Paris (1914–18) and of the Polish delegation at the Paris Peace Conference, he never held office in Poland. The right-wing National Democratic movement which he inspired grew in strength during the interwar period and took on fascist overtones, exerting strong pressure on minorities such as the Jews and Ukrainians.

**DNA** or **deoxyribonucleic acid,** NUCLEIC ACID found in the nuclei of CELLS. It is the principal constituent of CHROMOSOMES, the structures that transmit hereditary characteristics. The amount of DNA is constant for all typical cells of any given species of plant or animal, regardless of the size or function of that cell. Each DNA molecule is a long, two-stranded chain made up of subunits, called nucleotides, containing a sugar (deoxyribose), a phosphate group, and one of four nitrogenous bases: adenine (A), guanine (G), thymine (T), and cytosine (C). In 1953 J.D. WATSON and F.H. CRICK proposed that the strands, connected by hydrogen bonds between the bases, were coiled in a double helix. Adenine bonds only with thymine (A—T or T—A) and guanine only with cytosine (G—C or C—G). The complementarity of this bonding ensures that DNA can be replicated, i.e., that identical copies can be made in order to transmit genetic information to the next generation.

**Dnepr** or **Dnieper,** major river of the W USSR, flowing generally S c.2300 km (1430 mi) into the Black Sea. The river, which rises W of Moscow and is the chief river of the UKRAINE, was made navigable for virtually its entire length by construction (1932) of the Dneproges Dam at Zaporozhye. Known to the ancients as Borysthenes, the river was (9th–11th cent.) an important commercial link between the Slavs and Byzantines.

**Dnepropetrovsk** (dəˈnyeeprəpiˌtrofsk), city (1985 pop. 1,153,000), S European USSR, in the UKRAINE, on the Dnepr R. A hub of rail and water transport, it is a leading producer of iron, steel, heavy machinery, chemicals, and rolling stock. Nearby is the Dneproges hydroelectric station. Founded (1787) as Ekaterinoslav, the city was occupied (1941–43) by German forces.

**Dnestr,** river, c.1370 km (850 mi) long, SW USSR. It rises in the CARPATHIAN MOUNTAINS and flows generally SE through the Ukraine and the Moldavian Republic to an estuary on the BLACK SEA SW of Odessa. The Dnestr formed the Romanian–Soviet border from 1918 to 1940, when the USSR recovered Bessarabia.

**D-notice,** a system of voluntary CENSORSHIP of the media on the grounds of national security, established in the UK in 1912. A D-(for defence) notice is a formal letter sent to publishers, televison, radio and press editors, asking them not to publish anything on a specified matter. The notice is issued at the request of a government department by the Services, Press and Broadcasting Committee, consisting of both politicians and media representatives. Because of their secrecy it is difficult to establish either the number of D-notices issued, or their contents; however, they are usually accompanied by a warning about prosecution under the Official Secrets Act 1911 if they are ignored. One of the most famous breaches of a D-notice was the publication by the *Sunday Times* in 1967 of a story about the spy Kim Philby.

**Dobell, Sir William,** 1899–1970, Australian artist. He studied as an architect before attending the Julian Ashton School of Art, Sydney (1924–29). He then travelled to Europe where he worked for 10 years, exhibiting at the Royal Academy. He returned to Sydney where he established a reputation as Australia's leading portrait and genre painter. His portrait of fellow artist, Joshua Smith, with which he won the Archibald Portrait Prize (Sydney) in 1943, outraged the local art establishment and resulted in a notorious court case. In later years his artistic achievements were acknowledged with a major retrospective exhibition (Sydney, 1964) and a knighthood (1966).

**Döblin, Alfred** (döˈblin), 1878–1957, German novelist. By profession a psychiatrist in a poor quarter of Berlin, Döblin introduced modernist techniques to the German novel. He is often compared with DOS PASSOS and James JOYCE, especially for his best-known novel *Berlin Alexanderplatz* (1929), a portrait of a city by means of shifts of perspective, stream of consciousness, reportage, montage, simultaneity. His range includes the *Bildungsroman* with *Die drei Sprünge des Wang-lun* (1915; tr. The Three Leaps of Wang-Lun); the sceptical historical novel with *Wallenstein* (1920) and the trilogy *November 1918* (1948–50; partly tr. as *Karl and Rosa*, 1983); and science fiction with *Mountains, Oceans and Giants* (1924). His last work, a novel of return, was *Hamlet, or, The Long Night has an End* (1956).

**Dobrogea** (dobro͵gayə), region of SE Romania and NE Bulgaria. A low plateau between the Danube R. and the Black Sea, it is largely in agricultural use, producing wine, flax for oil, and sheep. CONSTANŢA is the largest city in Romanian Dobrogea. Southern Dobrogea (largest city TOLBUKHIN) was ceded to Romania in 1913 but recovered by Bulgaria in 1940 under the Treaty of Craiova.

**Dobzhansky, Theodosius** (dob͵zhanskee), 1900–75, American geneticist; b. Russia. After his emigration to the US in 1927, he taught at Columbia (1940–62) and at Rockefeller Univ. (1962–71). He was known for his research in genetics and for his work with the fruit fly *Drosophila*. His most important writings were *Genetics and the Origin of Species* (1937) and *Mankind Evolving: The Evolution of the Human Species* (1962).

**Dodecanese**, island group (1981 pop. 145,071), SE Greece, in the Aegean Sea between Asia Minor and Crete, c. 2580 km², (1035 sq mi). Despite its name ('twelve islands'), the Dodecanese group consists of some 20 islands, notably RHODES (site of the administrative centre), Kós, Kárpathos, Kálimnos, and Pátmos. Part of ancient Greece, the islands were occupied by the Ottoman Turks (1522–1912) and by Italy before being captured by the Allies in WORLD WAR II. In 1947 they were ceded to Greece.

**Doderer, Heimito von,** 1896–1966, Austrian novelist. Doderer is a critical but affectionate chronicler of Viennese society at all levels between the two World Wars. His novels are large-scale, with several interlocking strands. *The Strudelhof Steps* (1951) uses a single place in the Viennese suburb of the Alsergrund as its focus; *The Demons* (1956) the crucial day in July 1927 when the Viennese Palace of Justice was burnt down. His last major novel was *The Merowings, or, the Total Family* (1962).

**Dodgson, Charles Lutwidge:** see CARROLL, LEWIS.

**dodo,** flightless BIRD of the PIGEON family which lived on islands in the Indian Ocean. The dodo (*Raphus cucullatus*) was about 120 cm (4 ft) long with blue-grey feathers. It finally became extinct between 1790 and 1800 on Rodriguez, having gone from Mauritius by 1680, a victim of the introduction of pigs, dogs, and rats by Europeans as much as of over-hunting by hungry sailors.

**Dodoma,** city (1978 pop. 45,703) and capital of Tanzania. A centrally situated transport hub, it was designated (1975) the administrative capital to replace DAR-ES-SALAAM, on the coast. Administrative functions are in the process of being transferred. Dodoma is linked by road and rail to other cities.

**Doenitz, Karl** (͵dö:nits), b. 1881–1980, German admiral. He was chief naval commander during WORLD WAR II. After HITLER's death (1945) he headed the German government that negotiated the unconditional surrender to the Allies. He was imprisoned (1946–56) as a war criminal.

**Doesburg, Theo van,** 1883–1931, Dutch painter and architect. He met MONDRIAN in 1915 and rapidly developed his style from post-impressionist through to abstraction. In 1917 he started the de STIJL journal, and wrote and lectured on the ideas of neo-plasticism. In 1924 he started using diagonal elements in his works, called 'counter-compositions', thus departing from the ideas of Mondrian. He was also interested in the application of his artistic idea to the total environment and collaborated on architectural projects with Oud, Van Esteren, and Richveld. He lectured at the BAUHAUS (1922–24).

**dog,** carnivorous, domesticated MAMMAL (*Canis familiaris*) of the family Canidae, containing also the WOLF, COYOTE, FOX, DINGO etc. The species is distributed throughout the world in close association with man. The dog was domesticated some 14 or 15 thousand years ago, and is probably descended from the wolf and the JACKAL, with which the domestic dog is still able to interbreed. The species shows enormous variability of form and behaviour, having been selected for many specialist purposes such as hunting, guarding, fighting, as draught animals (illegal in the UK), and as companions. There are many systems in use for the classification of dogs, based on convenience for breeding and show purposes and not on scientific fact. Breeds are usually divided into *sporting* and *nonsporting* dogs, and the Kennel Club of Great Britain further divides these into six classes: the sporting dogs consisting of HOUNDS, GUN DOGS, and TERRIERS, and the nonsporting group containing the WORKING DOGS, the TOY DOGS, and the so-called UTILITY DOGS, this last group containing those breeds not readily accommodated in the five definitive classes. A purebred dog is one conforming to the standards of a recognized breed, and whose pedigree is acceptable, whereas a dog of mixed origin is called a mongrel. The female is able to mate at about 6-month intervals; the gestation period is approximately 9 weeks, and a litter commonly contains up to about 12 puppies.

**dogtooth violet,** common name for *Erythronium dens canis* and extended to other members of the same genus. They are often delicately ornamental and are used in rock gardens and for naturalizing.

**dogwood** or **cornel,** common name for some members of the family Cornaceae, mostly trees or shrubs (genus *Cornus*) chiefly of north temperate and tropical mountain regions. Dogwoods have inconspicuous flowers surrounded by large, showy bracts, often mistaken for petals. The flowering dogwood (*C. florida*) and the red-bark dogwood (*C. sanguinea*) are cultivated as ornamentals. Their bark, rich in tannin, is used as a QUININE substitute. The dwarf cornel (*C. canadensis*), is a low, herbaceous flower with bunches of bright red fruits. The cornelian cherry (*C. mas*) with yellow flowers and bright red edible fruits, is of special merit as an ornamental.

**Doha,** city (1982 est. pop. 190,000), capital and main port of Qatar, SE Arabia, on the Persian Gulf. A fishing village before oil production began (1949) in Qatar, it has become a modern city containing almost three quarters of Qatar's population.

**Dohnányi, Ernst von** 1877–1960, Hungarian composer, pianist, and conductor. He directed the Budapest Conservatory from 1919. In 1948 he left Hungary and settled in the US. His compositions, influenced by BRAHMS, include the suite *Ruralia Hungarica* (1924), operas, piano music, and the popular *Variations on a Nursery Song* for piano and orchestra (1913).

**doldrums** or **equatorial belt of calms,** area around the earth, centred slightly north of the equator between the two belts of trade winds. The large amount of solar radiation at these latitudes results in various forms of severe weather, e.g., HURRICANES, as well as calms (periods of no wind) that can strand sailing vessels for weeks.

**Dolin, Sir Anton,** 1904–83, English ballet dancer. He joined DIAGHILEV's company in 1921, and formed his own company in 1927. He had a long partnership with MARKOVA, and was artistic director of the London Festival Ballet until 1961.

**doll,** small figure of a human being, usually a child's toy. In ancient Egypt, Greece, and Rome, dolls were used symbolically and probably also as children's playthings. In Europe, from the 15th cent., fashion dolls given as gifts by monarchs and courtiers helped spread costume styles. By the 17th cent. both boys and girls played with dolls. Sonneberg, Germany, was noted for the manufacture of wooden dolls (17th cent.) and of dolls' china heads (19th cent.). In Paris, dolls were made that could speak and close their eyes. In the 19th cent. dolls were made of papier-mâché, china, wax, hard rubber, or bisque; by the 20th cent. doll manufacturing was an important industry in developed countries, including crude attempts to represent black or Asian babies as well as white.

**Dollfuss, Engelbert** (͵dolfoohs), 1892–1934, Austrian chancellor (1932–34). He opposed the National Socialists and the Social Democrats, and sought support from Austrian Fascists and from Italy. In Apr. 1934 Austria became a corporative state with a one-party, authoritarian system. He was assassinated (25 July) by Austrian Nazis.

**Döllinger, Johann Joseph Ignaz von** (͵dölingə), 1799–1890, German theologian, historian, leader of the OLD CATHOLICS. Ordained (1822) a Roman Catholic priest, he was long associated with the Univ. of Munich and was a leading member of the Catholic party in the Frankfurt Parliament (1848–49). He spurned the dogma of papal infallibility promulgated by the First VATICAN COUNCIL (1870) and was

**gun dogs**

cocker spaniel

pointer

**hounds**

dachshund

bloodhound

**terriers**

smooth-haired
fox terrier

Airedale

**working dogs**

German shepherd

corgi

**toy dogs**

toy poodle

Pekingese

**utility dogs**

bulldog

chow chow

The six classes of **dogs**

excommunicated (1871). While closely identified with the Old Catholics, he never intended a separate sect to grow from the movement and saw its role as the reuniting of divided Christendom.

**Dolmetsch, Arnold,** 1858–1940, Swiss musician and maker of early instruments, who emigrated to England in 1883. He came from a family of instrument makers, but it was not until 1889 that he began the research into English VIOL music which led to his giving concerts of music on 'authentic' instruments and to making LUTES, CLAVICHORDS, and HARPSICHORDS, as well as RECORDERS and viols. Through his recordings, publications, and the manufacture of instruments, he was a pioneer in the revival of interest in early music and its performance on original instruments.

**dolomite.** 1 White, grey, brown, or reddish calcium magnesium carbonate mineral [CaMg(CO$_3$)$_2$], commonly crystalline. 2 Carbonate rock composed chiefly of the mineral dolomite, similar to LIMESTONE but harder and heavier. Dolomite formations are widespread and are notable in the region of the Alps called the Dolomites, where the rock was first studied. Dolomite is used chiefly as a building stone, for the manufacture of refractory furnace linings, and as basic magnesium carbonate for pipe coverings.

**Dolomites,** Alpine mountain region of N Italy, close to the border with Austria. Its name is derived from the mineral dolomite, principal constituent of Magnesian Limestone. The rock has been weathered into sharp-edged pinnacles and ridges and the dramatic scenery, which includes forests and lakes, attracts many tourists, rock climbers, and winter skiers. Resorts include Cortina d'Ampezzo.

The Staunies Pass, near Cortina, in the **Dolomites**

**dolphin,** aquatic MAMMAL, any of the small, toothed, gregarious WHALES of the family Delphinidae. They include the beaked dolphin, the killer whale, the PILOT WHALE, and 12 freshwater species in South America and S Asia. Fishlike in form, dolphins breathe air through a dorsal blowhole. They propel themselves by means of powerful flukes, steering with a dorsal fin and navigating with the aid of echolocation. Dolphins are exceptionally friendly toward humans, and their high order of intelligence and their complex language have long been the subject of study. There are also two species of fish called dolphins, *Coryphaena hippurus* and *C. equiselus*, predatory fish living in tropical seas, which leap out of the sea after FLYING FISH.

bottlenose
dolphin

common
dolphin

Dolphin

**Domagk, Gerhard** (ˌdohmahk), 1895–1964, German chemist and pathologist. Because of a Nazi decree, he had to decline the 1939 Nobel Prize for physiology or medicine, awarded for his discovery of the efficacy of prontosil, the forerunner of the SULPHONAMIDE drugs, in treating infections with streptococcal bacteria. He received the Nobel Prize medal (but not the prize money) in 1947.

**dome,** a roof, circular or (rarely) elliptical in plan and usually hemispherical in form, placed over a square, circular, or other space. Ancient examples are found at Mycenae and in Sicily, but the Romans apparently were the first developers of the form. Their constructions culminated in the PANTHEON (2nd cent. AD). The use of the pendentive, essential to placing a dome over a square, was discovered by the Byzantine builders of HAGIA SOPHIA at Istanbul (AD 532–37). Islamic architects, under Byzantine influence, built many domes, e.g., the Dome of the Rock, Jerusalem. The Persian or onion dome is best seen at the TAJ MAHAL. Roman and Byzantine influences converged in the designers of the Italian RENAISSANCE. A circular drum was usually interposed between pendentive and dome, to give greater elevation; the dome was then topped with a lantern. Noted domes include the one in HAGIA SOPHIA (6th cent.), BRUNELLESCHI's for the cathedral at Florence (1420–36), and MICHELANGELO's for St Peter's, Rome (completed 1590). Modern domes employ a wide variety of materials and designs.

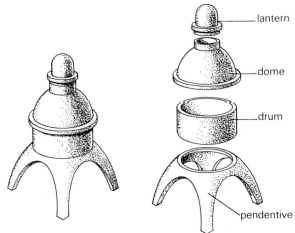

lantern

dome

drum

pendentive

Parts of a **dome**

**Domenichino** or **Domenico Zampieri** (dohmaynee ̩keenoh), 1581–1641, Italian painter. His severely classical FRESCO cycles, as his scenes from the **Life of St Cecilia** (1615–17; S. Luigi dei Francesi, Rome), dominated Roman painting in the early years of the century. He painted some portraits, and his heroic, rocky landscapes introduced ideal landscape painting.

**Domenico Veneziano** (venetsy ̩ahnoh), c.1400–1461, Italian painter. His work, with its light, atmospheric colour, and his name suggest that he came from Venice. His masterpiece, the *St Lucy Altarpiece* (c.1445; central panel, Uffizi, Florence), reveals an innovative use of space; in it, he disposed of the Gothic hierarchical order and introduced figures (deity and saints) in a harmonious group.

Domenico Veneziano, *St Lucy Altarpiece*, c.1445. Galleria Uffizi, Florence.

**Dome of the Rock,** earliest important Islamic monument, erected in Jerusalem by the Umayyad Caliph 'Abd al-Malik in 691/2. It is a shrine, not a mosque, and should not therefore be referred to by its common name of Mosque of 'Umar. Muslim tradition has come to associate the Dome of the Rock with Muhammad's famous ascension to Paradise, but modern scholarship has queried whether this was the intention when it was first built.

**Domesday Book,** the surviving record of a census of England made (1085–86) by order of WILLIAM I. It contains extensive information on English land division and its use, on inhabitants, and also on economic resources in the country. It is a major historical source.

**domestic group,** a group of people, usually kin (see KINSHIP), or those seen as kin, who share the same cooking pot, the procreation and rearing of children, and who are frequently although not inevitably co-resident. The term is most often used as synonymous with a household. In certain agricultural communities the domestic group is the main unit of production, with control over the means of production and the labour process. It has been argued by M SAHLINS that these economies constitute a domestic mode of production which is characterized by the fact that the domestic group acts as an autonomous economic unit and tends to produce only to the limits of its own immediate requirements; any surplus production has then to be forced from such groups by external political pressure which the domestic group will tend to resist. This argument has been criticized for its tendency to overemphasize the degree to which such production units can ever be independent of the wider community.

**Domingo, Placido,** 1941–, Spanish operatic tenor, who moved to Mexico in 1950. His first major tenor role was as Alfredo in *La Traviata* (1962). He sang with the Israeli National Opera (1962–65), and made his New York debut at the City Opera in 1966 in the first North American performance of Ginastera's *Don Rodrigo*. Since then he has sung leading roles in many countries and earned a reputation of being one of the finest operatic tenors of his time.

**Dominic, Saint,** 1170?–1221, Castilian churchman, founder of the DOMINICANS. Dominic successfully preached to the ALBIGENSES in S France. In 1216 he was given a house at Toulouse for his growing band of preachers and won the consent of Pope Honorius III to form a new order. Tradition says that the rosary was given to him by the Virgin Mary in a vision. Feast: 8 Aug.

**Dominica,** officially Commonwealth of Dominica, island nation (1986 est. pop. 83,300), c.750 km² (290 sq mi), West Indies, between Guadeloupe and Martinique, largest of the Windward Islands. Dominica is mountainous and forested; of volcanic origin, it has fertile soil, a mild climate, and plentiful rainfall. The capital and chief port is Roseau. The nation exports bananas, coconuts, and citrus fruits and is a tourist resort. The GDP is US$85 million and the GDP per capita is US$1105. English is the official language, but a French patois is widely spoken. Most of the people are descendants of black slaves brought in to work plantations in the 18th cent. There are also a few Carib Indians, whose ancestors delayed European settlement of the island. It became a British colony in the late 1700s, after a long struggle for control between Britain and France. It has been a fully independent member of the COMMONWEALTH since 1978. Dominica is subject to frequent hurricanes, one of the worst of which, in 1979, left some 60,000 people homeless. In 1980 the Dominica Freedom Party led by Mary Eugenia Charles came to power, and in 1983 Dominica participated in the US-led invasion of Grenada.

**Dominican Republic,** Span. *Republica Dominicana,* republic (1986 est. pop. 6,700,000), 48,734 km² (18,816 sq mi), West Indies, on the eastern two thirds of the island of HISPANIOLA, which it shares with HAITI. The land ranges from mountainous to gently rolling, with fertile river valleys; the climate is subtropical. The capital and chief port is Santo Domingo. The economy has long been dominated by sugar, which still produces up to 50% of the country's foreign exchange, despite recent establishment of varied light industries and vigorous promotion of nickel mining and tourism. Cocoa, coffee, bananas, and tobacco are also exported. The GDP is US$8235 million and the GDP per capita is US$1350. About two thirds of the population is mulatto, and one quarter is black. Spanish is spoken, and Roman Catholicism is the state religion.

*History.* Part of the Spanish colony of SANTO DOMINGO during the 16th and 17th cent., and then under Haitian rule after 1821, the Dominican Republic was proclaimed in 1844 but sustained continuously in independence only after 1865. Its history has been unusually turbulent, with recurrent dictatorships and rebellions. Bankrupted by civil strife after the murder of the dictator Ulises Heureaux in 1899, the republic came under US domination; US marines occupied the country in 1916–24 and the US exerted fiscal control until 1941. In 1930 Rafael TRUJILLO MOLINA began 30 years of corrupt dictatorship, which ended with his assassination in 1961. Democratic elections in 1962 brought to power a reform president, Juan Bosch, but right-wing opposition led to his removal a year later. In 1965 civil war between pro- and anti-Bosch forces broke out, and US troops intervened again. In 1966, elections supervised by the Organization of American States restored a degree of normality; Joaquín BALAGUER defeated Bosch, and under his regime (1966–78) considerable progress was made towards stabilizing the economy. Economic stability was also pursued by his successors, Antonio Guzmán Fernández and Jorge Blanco. In the 1986 presidential election Balaguer returned to power as candidate of the Social Christian Reform Party.

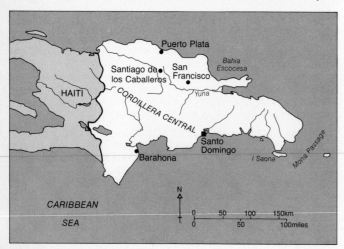

Dominican Republic

**Dominicans,** Roman Catholic religious order, officially named the Order of Preachers (O.P.). Founded (1216) by St DOMINIC, the order preached against the heresy of the ALBIGENSES and produced many eminent theologians, notably St THOMAS AQUINAS. Members are accepted not into a specific house, but into the whole order, and wear a white habit with a black mantle (worn when preaching). There is a contemplative order of nuns and a widespread third order, including many teachers.

**Dominion Day** (July 1), Canadian national holiday. It commemorates the creation (1867) of the Dominion of Canada.

**Domino, Fats,** (Antoine Domino), 1928–, black American singer, composer and pianist. With his bluesy voice and thumping piano style over instrumental riffs, he was one of the founding fathers of rock and roll. His first hit was 'The Fat Man' (1949) and was followed by a string of others in the 1950s, including 'Blueberry Hill', 'Blue Monday', 'My Blue Heaven', 'I'm Ready', through to 'Walkin' to New Orleans' in the 1960s.

**Dominoes,** game played with small rectangular pieces of wood. The face of each of these is divided into two sections that bear from one to six dots arranged as on dice faces, except that some faces are blank. Players put the dominoes down in turn, usually by matching dots. In China dominoes date back to around the 12th cent.

**domino theory,** notion that if one country becomes communist, other states in the region will probably follow, like falling dominoes in a line. The analogy, first applied (1954) to SE Asia by Pres. EISENHOWER, was adopted in the 1960s by supporters of the US role in the VIETNAM WAR. The theory was revived in the 1980s to characterize the threat perceived by the US from left-wing movements and governments in Central and South America.

**Domitian** (Titus Flavius Domitianus), AD 51–96, Roman emperor (r. AD 81–96). On the death of his brother TITUS, he succeeded to the throne. His rule became increasingly despotic and plots were formed against him. Finally his wife Domitia had him murdered.

**Don,** river, c. 1930 km (1200 mi) long, SW USSR. It rises near Tula and flows SE to within 105 km (65 mi) of the VOLGA R., to which it is connected by canal, then southwest into the Sea of Azov. It is an important artery for grain, timber, and coal shipments and is the outlet for the industrial Donets Basin. The Don is navigable for c. 1370 km (850 mi) to ROSTOV-NA-DONU, its chief city and port.

**Donatello,** c. 1386–1466, Florentine sculptor, a major innovator in Renaissance art; b. Donato di Niccolo di Betto Bardi. He worked as assistant to GHIBERTI; a series of sculptures for the Or San Michele and Florence cathedral, amongst them *St Mark* (1411–12; Cathedral Mus., Florence) and *St George* (1415–20; Bargello, Florence), show his break with Gothic forms and his development of a new, vital realism influenced by classical art. The relief beneath the St George, of *St George and the Princess* (c. 1420), is one of the earliest uses of linear perspective; he developed a shallow relief technique (schiacciato) with which he achieved effects of spatial depth. His *David* (Bargello, Florence) is the first free-standing, life-size bronze of the Renaissance. He was in Padua from 1443 to 1453, where his two outstanding works were the equestrian statue of *Gattemalata* (1443–47) and the high altar for the church of St Anthony. His later Florentine works, including the polychrome wood *Magdalene* (1453–55; Cathedral Mus., Florence) and the reliefs for the pulpits in San Lorenzo, are dramatic and highly expressive.

**Doncaster,** town (1981 pop. 74,727), in S Yorkshire, E Midlands, on R. Don, 27 km (17 mi) NE of Sheffield, on eastern edge of the S Yorkshire coalfield. Industries found within the town include railway engineering and the manufacture of confectionery. The town is built on the site of the Roman fort of Danum. Nearby is the Town Moor racecourse where the St Leger is run.

**Donegal,** county in extreme NW of Republic of Ireland, (1986 pop. 129,428), 4782 km² (1865 sq mi), bordering on the Atlantic ocean in the N and W, and Northern Ireland in the E. It is in the province of Ulster. The county town is LIFFORD. The coast is rocky and indented, including the large inlets of Donegal Bay and Lough Swilly. There are many offshore islands, including Aran and Tory Islands. The county also includes Malin Head which is the northernmost point in Ireland. Much of the inland part of the county is mountainous and picturesque, including the Derryveagh Mts in the NW. The major rivers are the Finn, Foyle, and Erne. The land is generally not very fertile, but there is some mixed agriculture. Near Ballyshannon in the S there are hydroelectric power stations on the R. Erne.

**Donetsk** (də̩nyetsk), city (1985 pop. 1,073,000), S European USSR, in the UKRAINE, on the Kalmius R. The hub of the Donets Basin industrial region, it has coal mines, iron and steel mills, machinery works, and chemical plants. It was founded (1870) as Yuzovka and renamed in 1961.

David **Donatello**. Life-size bronze. Bargello, Florence.

**Don Giovanni:** see DON JUAN.

**Donizetti, Gaetano,** 1797–1848, Italian composer. Influenced early by ROSSINI, he later developed his own melodic, often sentimental style. His best-known operas include *Lucrezia Borgia* (1833), *Lucia di Lammermoor* (1835), and *Don Pasquale* (1843), all with fine BEL CANTO parts. *The Daughter of the Regiment* (1840) is a comic opera.

**Don Juan,** legendary profligate. There are many versions of his story, but the Spanish is the most widespread. In it, Don Juan seduces the daughter of the commander of Seville and kills her father in a duel. When he jeeringly invites a statue of his victim to a feast, it comes to life and drags Don Juan to hell. The earliest-known dramatization of the story is by TIRSO DE MOLINA. Other famous treatments are by MOLIÈRE, MOZART, BYRON, and G.B. SHAW.

**donkey:** see ASS.

**Donne, John,** 1572–1631, English divine and greatest of the METAPHYSICAL POETS. Born a Roman Catholic, he later renounced his faith, took part in naval expeditions and became a Member of Parliament. His early writing was mainly cynical, realistic and sensuous lyrics, essays and satires. His secret marriage in 1601 ended his prospects of a political career, and in 1615 he took holy orders in the Anglican Church. His later poetry, including his *Holy Sonnets* and *Devotions*, sounded a deepening religious note. He became one of the great preachers of his day, and from 1621 to his death he was Dean of St Paul's, London. All of his poetry —his love sonnets, and religious and philosophical verse—is marked by a striking blend of passion and reason. His love poetry treats metaphorically the breadth, physical and spiritual, of the experience. The devotional poems are deeply concerned with death and the possibility of

the soul's union with God. Original, witty, and erudite, his style is characterized by a brilliant use of paradox, hyperbole, and image. Neglected for 200 years, Donne was rediscovered in the 20th cent. and greatly influenced such poets as W.B. YEATS, T.S. ELIOT, and W.H. AUDEN.

**Donner Party,** group of emigrants to California who met with tragedy in 1846–47. The party, named for its two Donner families, was trapped by snow in Oct. 1846 in the Sierra Nevada near what is today called the Donner Pass. The survivors resorted to cannibalism before their rescue, and only about half of the original party of 87 reached California.

**Donoghue v. Stevenson,** English case decided in 1932, where the House of Lords granted damages to a woman who contracted illness after drinking a bottle of ginger beer containing a decomposing snail. The English court, for the first time, held that a manufacturer owed a duty of care to ensure the ultimate consumer was not injured by his or her products, even in the absence of a CONTRACT. It was the foundation case for the development of NEGLIGENCE in the UK.

**Donoso, José,** 1925–, Chilean novelist and short-story writer. His work ranges from ironically realistic studies of decadent Chilean life, e.g., *Coronación* (1957; tr. Coronation), to surrealistic portrayals of bizarre subjects, written in a dense and powerful style, e.g., *El obsceno pájaro de la noche* (1970; tr. The Obscene Bird of Night) and *Casa de campo* (1978; tr. Country House).

**Don Quixote de la Mancha:** see CERVANTES SAAVEDRA, MIGUEL DE.

**Doolittle, Hilda,** pseud. **H.D.,** 1886–1961, American poet. She lived abroad after 1911 and was married to Richard ALDINGTON. One of the most original of the IMAGISTS, she wrote such volumes of verse as *Sea Garden* (1916), *The Walls Do Not Fall* (1944), and *Bid Me to Live* (1960).

**Doomsday Book:** see DOMESDAY BOOK.

**Doppler effect,** change in the wavelength (and frequency) of a wave as a result of the motion of either the source or receiver of the wave. If the source and the receiver are approaching each other, the frequency of the wave as measured by the receiver will increase and the wavelength will be shortened, sounds will be higher in pitch, and light will be bluer. If the source and receiver are moving apart, sounds will become lower-pitched, and light will appear redder (see RED SHIFT). Astronomers analyse Doppler shifts of light and radio waves to measure the velocities and (indirectly) distances of remote objects.

**Dorchester,** county town (1981 pop. 13,734) of Dorset, SW England on R. Frome, 12 km (7 mi) N of Weymouth. It is a market town, built on the site of the ancient town of Durnovaria. The town is famous mainly for its associations with Thomas HARDY. His birthplace is nearby, and the town is immortalized as 'Casterbridge' in his Wessex novels. There are many prehistoric and Roman remains nearby, including the earthworks of Maiden Castle.

**Dordogne** (daw,doyn), region and former province of SW France. It is noted for its cuisine based on paté de foie gras and preserves, and its wines, especially Monbazillac. There is now much tourism. The principal town and administrative centre is Périgueux. Cave paintings at Lascaux and Les Eyzies, which date from the Palaeolithic period, bear witness to the antiquity of human settlement. Fortified towns (*bastides*) and a large number of castles date from the time when this region was disputed between the French and English crowns.

**Dordrecht,** city (1985 pop. 107,274) Zuid Holland prov., W Netherlands. Once the leading port of Holland, it was an important centre of sea and river navigation, with fishing and shipbuilding industries. Having lost this role, it is now an outlier of the ROTTERDAM industrial region, manufacturing cranes and port equipment. It has a Gothic church of the 14th cent.

**Doré, Gustave,** 1832–83, French illustrator, engraver, painter, and sculptor. He is best known for his fantastic, imaginative, wood-engraved illustrations for some 120 books, including *Don Quixote* (1862); his most famous work is his set of realistic engravings of London slums (1872).

**Doria, Andrea,** b. 1466 or 1468, d. 1560, Italian admiral and statesman. He fought for France in the ITALIAN WARS until 1528, when he went over to Holy Roman Emperor CHARLES V. Doria became (1528) virtual dictator of Genoa but did not destroy the republican constitution. He aided Charles in taking Tunis (1535), and, with French aid, he recovered Corsica for Genoa (1559).

**Dorians,** people of ancient GREECE. They arrived in the PELOPONNESUS between 1100 and 950 BC, drove out the Achaeans (see ACHAEA), and rapidly extended their influence. SPARTA and CRETE were Dorian centers. The Dorians' arrival inaugurated a period of Greek decline, but they did contribute to Greek culture, particularly in the Doric style of architecture.

**Doric order:** see ORDERS OF ARCHITECTURE.

**dormancy,** seasonal inactivity in growth which can only be relieved by specific environmental conditions recognized by the plant, e.g., chilling (just above freezing point), daylength, or drying. Usually connected with the formation of special organs, e.g., SEEDS, winter buds, BULBS, and corms.

**dormouse,** Old World nocturnal RODENT of the family Gliridae. European species hibernate for nearly six months. The hazel dormouse (*Muscardinus avellanarius*) of Europe and W Asia is up to 10 cm (4 in) long with rounded ears, large eyes, and thick, reddish brown fur; it eats insects, nuts, and berries. The edible dormouse (*Glis glis*) was fattened in small earthenware pots by the Romans and eaten at feasts. It is illegal now in Britain to eat dormice.

**Dorset,** county, SW England (1984 est. pop. 617,800), 2654 km² (1035 sq mi), bordering on the English Channel. The county town is DORCHESTER. Much of the county is low-lying, crossed by the chalk uplands of the N and S Dorset Downs. Agriculture is the predominant economic activity, but there is some light industry in POOLE. There are several tourist resorts along the picturesque coast including BOURNEMOUTH. Portland stone is quarried within the county. Thomas HARDY portrayed many parts of Dorset in his Wessex novels.

**Dortmund,** city (1984 pop. 584,800), North Rhine–Westphalia, W West Germany, a port on the Dortmund–Ems Canal. An industrial centre with such manufactures as iron and steel, it is located in the RUHR industrial district. It flourished (13th–17th cent.) as a member of the HANSEATIC LEAGUE. The city was badly damaged during WORLD WAR II, but such buildings as the Reinold church (begun in the 13th cent.) remain.

**Dos Passos, John Roderigo,** 1896–1970, American novelist. In works such as *Manhattan Transfer* (1925) and his major opus, the trilogy *U.S.A.* (1937) *The 42nd Parallel* (1930), *1919* (1932), and *The Big Money* (1936) he developed a kaleidoscopic technique to portray American life, combining narration, STREAM OF CONSCIOUSNESS, biographies, and quotations from newspapers and magazines. The left-wing views that coloured his early works gave way to a conservatism that is evident in his less powerful later novels, e.g., his second trilogy, *District of Columbia* (1952).

**Dostoyevsky,** or **Dostoevsky, Feodor Mikhailovich** ('dostoyˌefskee), 1821–81, Russian writer, one of the great figures of world literature. Shortly after completing an engineering education, he published his first novel, *Poor Folk* (1846), to wide acclaim. Though less successful, his next novels, *The Double* (1846) and *White Nights* (1848), nevertheless showed the profound insight into character that marks his greatest works. Arrested in 1849 for membership in a secret political group, he was exiled to Siberia, and there served four years at hard labour and five as a soldier. His harsh experiences (recorded in *The House of the Dead,* 1862) transformed his youthful liberalism into a fervent religious orthodoxy. The existentialist *Notes from the Underground* (1864), the first major work following his return to St Petersburg in 1859, inaugurated his most fruitful literary period. It coincided with the death of his first wife and increasing financial burdens. *Crime and Punishment* (1866), a brilliant portrait of sin, remorse, and redemption through sacrifice, was followed by *The Idiot* (1868), the story of a failed Christ-figure. It was written in Germany, where Dostoyevsky had gone with his new wife, Anna Grigoryevna Snitkina, whose love and practicality enriched his later years. In *The Possessed* (1871–72) he denounced the alienated radicalism that characterized contemporary Russia. *A Raw Youth* (1875) described decay within family relationships and the inability of science to answer man's deepest needs. These themes were central to his masterpiece, *The Brothers Karamazov* (1880), in which with rare psychological and philosophical insight Dostoyevsky plumbed the depths and complexities of the human soul.

**Dou, Dow,** or **Douw, Gerard** or **Gerrit,** 1613–75, Dutch GENRE and portrait painter. An apprentice of REMBRANDT, he executed detailed scenes of domestic life that were very popular, e.g., *The Mother* (1658; Mauritshuis, The Hague).

**Douai,** city (1982 pop. of agglomeration 202,613) NE France, on the Scarpe R. Originating as a small Flemish market settlement, it became a centre of coal-mining and related industries in the 19th cent. There is now a motor-car assembly works. Douai College was founded in 1568 by exiled English Roman Catholic priests; the Douai Bible was prepared there. Despite wartime damage the city's character owes much to its 18th-cent. rebuilding.

**Douala,** formerly Kamerunstadt, city (1984 est. pop. 784,000), chief town of Littoral prov., United Republic of Cameroon, on the Wouri R. estuary. The economic capital and major port of Cameroon, it is a commercial and transport centre handling most of the country's exports (chiefly cocoa, coffee, and tobacco) as well as transit trade from Chad. Its industries include oil exploration, food processing, brewing, and the manufacture of cement and chemicals. Douala developed as a centre of the slave trade after the Portuguese arrived in 1472. It later became capital of the German CAMEROONS (1885–1901) and then of the French Cameroons (1904–46).

**double bass,** a STRINGED INSTRUMENT descended from the VIOL family, and like them tuned in fourths. The lowest of its four strings is the third E below middle C; some basses have one more string, normally tuned to the C below the E. Although the double bass has very little solo music and is not much used in chamber music (not being a member of the string quartet), it is an indispensable member of the ORCHESTRA, providing a foundation under all the other sounds. It is also used in JAZZ.

**double-bind situation:** see Gregory BATESON; SCHIZOPHRENIA.

**double jeopardy,** in law, prosecution twice for the same criminal offence. The general principle exists that a person cannot be tried twice for the same offence. In the US, it is prohibited by the US CONSTITUTION. A second trial is not precluded, however, if at the first trial there were procedural errors, or the JURY failed to reach a verdict. In the UK, a member of a profession (e.g., a doctor) or member of the armed forces, can be tried for the same offence both under a professional code of discipline and the CRIMINAL LAW.

**double refraction:** see POLARIZED LIGHT.

**double star:** see BINARY STAR.

**Doughty, Charles,** 1843–1926, English author and traveller. He is best known for *Travels in Arabia Deserta* (1888), about his life with the Bedouins.

**Douglas, Gavin,** c.1475–1522, Scottish poet and bishop. His greatest work is the first complete translation into English of Virgil's *Aeneid*.

**Douglas, Sir James de, lord of Douglas,** 1286?–1330, Scottish nobleman, called the Black Douglas and Douglas the Good. In the war of independence against England, he joined ROBERT I and made himself the terror of the border. He led a force at Bannockburn (1314) and in 1327 succeeded in ending the English campaign. After Robert died, Douglas started for Palestine to bury the king's heart but was killed fighting Moors in Spain.

**Douglas, Mary,** 1921–, British anthropologist. Trained at Oxford Univ., she has worked in the US since 1981. Using the framework of STRUCTURAL FUNCTIONALISM she writes of the cultural symbols present in RITUAL, POLLUTION beliefs, sexual prohibitions, etc. Her best-known book is *Purity and Danger* (1966), exploring the ritual symbolism of the body.

**Douglas, Stephen Arnold,** 1813–61, American statesman. A Democratic congressman (1843–47) and senator (1847–61) from Illinois, he thought sectional disputes between North and South could be solved peacefully by SQUATTER SOVEREIGNTY and incorporated that concept into the COMPROMISE OF 1850 and the KANSAS–NEBRASKA ACT. Seeking Senate reelection in 1858, he engaged his opponent, Abraham LINCOLN, in the famous Lincoln–Douglas debates. At the Freeport (Illinois) debate, Douglas asserted that territories could exclude slavery, a doctrine that made him anathema to the South. The Democrats nominated him for president in 1860, but he ran second to Lincoln in the popular vote. A great orator, Douglas was long in the shadow of the Lincoln legend but is now held to have had a truly national vision.

**Douglas, William Sholto, Lord Douglas of Kirtleside,** 1893–1969, Marshal of the Royal Air Force. After distinguished service in the Royal Flying Corps in World War I, he became a commercial pilot. He rejoined the Royal Air Force in 1920, and was already an Air Vice Marshal before the outbreak of World War II. In the war he held some of the highest commands: Commander-in-Chief Fighter Command (1941; in succession to Sir Hugh DOWDING), Commander-in-Chief Middle East Command (1942), and Commander-in-Chief Coastal Command (1944). After the war he served (with distaste) as Commander-in-Chief British Air Forces in Germany. Raised to the peerage in 1948, he become chairman of British European Airways (1940) which he ran successfully for 15 years (see BRITISH AIRWAYS).

**Douglas fir,** tree (*Pseudotsuga menziesii,* formerly *P. taxifolia*) of the PINE family, native to British Columbia. One of the tallest trees known (up to 117 m/385 ft), it is the leading timber-producing tree of the N American continent and is exported as British Columbian or Oregon pine. Its usually hard, strong wood is of great commercial importance in construction. Because of its rapid growth and high productivity, it is grown throughout Europe and also in New Zealand.

**Douglas-Home, Sir Alec** (Alexander Frederick) (Baron Home of the Hirsel), 1903–, British politician. A Conservative, he entered Parliament in 1931 and later served in various government and cabinet posts, including that of foreign secretary (1960–63, 1970–74). An hereditary peer of the realm, he renounced his title on becoming prime minister in Oct. 1963. Defeated in the 1964 general elections, he relinquished the Conservative Party leadership in 1965. After again serving as foreign secretary (1970–74), in 1974 he was made a life peer.

**Douglass, Frederick,** c.1817–1895, American ABOLITIONIST. Escaping from slavery in 1838, he took the name Douglass from Sir Walter Scott's *Lady of the Lake.* In 1845 he published his *Narrative of the Life of Frederick Douglass,* and in 1847, after English friends had purchased his freedom, he established the *North Star* (Rochester, New York State), which he edited for 17 years, advocating abolition through political activism. During the CIVIL WAR he urged blacks to join the Union ranks, and during and after RECONSTRUCTION he held several government posts.

**Douro,** river, c.760 km (475 mi) long, rising near Soria in N central Spain and flowing W across Old Castile and Portugal to the Atlantic Ocean at OPORTO.

**dove:** see PIGEON.

**Dove, Arthur Garfield,** 1880–1946, American painter. His abstract style flowered in the 1930s in fluid, poetic canvases based on natural forms. Dove is recognized as a precursor of ABSTRACT EXPRESSIONISM.

**Dover,** town (1981 pop. 33,461), Kent, S England, on English Channel. It is an important port, with a ferry service to Calais, France. In 1984 the port handled 9.0 million tonnes of goods. Industries found within the town include furniture and paper manufacture. The town is built on the site of the ancient Dubris. There is a Roman lighthouse and a Norman castle. Dover is one of the CINQUE PORTS.

**Dovzhenko, Aleksandr** (dov,zhenkoh), 1894–1956, Ukrainian film director and writer. He was the main pioneer of Ukrainian national cinematography and together with Sergei EISENSTEIN and Vsevolod Pudovkin one of the fathers of Soviet cinema. His films include *Earth* (1930), ranked by an international jury in 1958 among 12 best films in world cinematography, *Ivan* (1932), and *A Poem about the Sea* (1956). Dovzhenko showed great skill and imagination in exploiting the film's and cinema's artistic possibilities which earned him the title of 'the first poet of the cinema'. In the 1930s he was severely criticized for his alleged nationalist deviations and experienced some persecution.

**Dowding, Hugh Caswall Tremenheere, Dowding,** 1st **Baron,** 1882–1970, British air chief marshall. He was commander-in-chief of RAF Fighter Command (1936–40) during the Battle of Britain, in which his tactical and strategic expertise was instrumental in the defeat of the Luftwaffe. He retired in 1942 and the following year was created baron.

**Dow Jones Index,** the most widely-quoted indicator of general trends and prices of stocks and bonds on the US stockmarket (WALL STREET). It is based on 30 selected industrial stocks. The financial news publisher Dow Jones & Co. began computing 'averages' of stock prices on Wall Street in 1897.

**Dowland, John,** 1562–1626, English composer and lutenist. His books of *Songs or Ayres* (1597–1603) made him the foremost SONG composer of his time.

**Down,** former county in the SE of N Ireland, 2441 km² (952 sq mi), bordering on the Irish Sea in the E. The R. Lagan forms much of the N border and the Newry canal forms much of the W border. The county

town is DOWNPATRICK. Strangford Lough is a large inlet on the E coast. The Mourne Mts are in the S and reach a height of 850 m (2788 ft) in Slieve Donard. It is drained by the R. BANN and the R. Quoile. Mixed agriculture is important in the fertile lowlands and valleys. Banbridge, Newry, DOWNPATRICK, and Bangor are manufacturing towns. Linen and metals are produced.

**Downpatrick,** town (1981 pop. 8245), in district of Down, N Ireland. Formerly the county town of Co. Down, it is a small market town. Industries found here include the manufacture of linen, and brewing. St Patrick and St Columba are said to be buried here. Nearby are the remains of the 12th-cent. Inch Abbey.

**Down's syndrome** or **trisomy 21,** congenital disorder characterized by moderate to severe MENTAL HANDICAP, slow physical development, and flattish skull and facial features, giving an 'Oriental' appearance (hence the former name for the condition, mongolism). The syndrome is usually caused by genetic transmittance of an extra chromosome. The risk of transmission increases significantly with maternal age, particularly if the mother is over 40. AMNIOCENTESIS can be used to detect the disorder in the fetus. Few people with Down's syndrome survive beyond the age of 35.

**dowry,** property given by a bride's kin to her, or her children, her husband or his kin group, at marriage. It has been seen as a kind of anticipated inheritance, and it has been argued (e.g., by J. Goody) that dowry is characteristic of hierarchical, monogamous social systems (e.g., in Europe and India). See BRIDEWEALTH.

**Doyle, Sir Arthur Conan,** 1859–1930, English author and creator of Sherlock Holmes, best known of all fictional detectives. The brilliantly deductive Holmes and his stolid companion, Dr Watson, appear in *A Study in Scarlet* (1887), *The Memoirs of Sherlock Holmes* (1894), *The Hound of the Baskervilles* (1902), and others. Doyle also wrote historical and other romances, e.g., *The White Company* (1891) *The Lost World* (1912), and a *History of Spiritualism* (1926).

**D'Oyly Carte, Richard,** 1844–1901, British impressario and theatre manager. His long and successful collaboration with GILBERT and SULLIVAN (he presented nearly all their comic operas) enabled him to build the Savoy Theatre, the first theatre in London to be lit by electricity. He later founded the D'Oyly Carte Company for the sole purpose of producing the works of Gilbert and Sullivan.

**Drabble, Margaret,** 1939–, English novelist. She is best known for her realistic portrayal of the dilemmas of modern women in, e.g., *The Millstone* (1966), and *The Needle's Eye* (1972). Her critical works include a biography of BENNETT (1974).

**Draco** or **Dracon,** fl. 621 BC, Athenian politician and law codifier. Draco's code appears to have prescribed the death penalty for even trivial offences, and Draconian has become a synonym for harshness in legislation.

**Dracula:** see STOKER, BRAM.

**Drago, Luis María** (,drahgoh), 1859–1921, Argentine statesman and jurist. His protest against coercion of Venezuela by Great Britain, Italy, and Germany (1902) became known as the **Drago Doctrine;** it stated that no public debt could be collected from a sovereign American state by armed force or through occupation of American territory by a foreign power. It was adopted in modified form at the HAGUE CONFERENCE (1907).

**dragon,** mythical beast, usually represented as a huge, winged, fire-breathing reptile; prominent in the folklore of many peoples. The highest achievement of a hero in medieval legend, e.g., St GEORGE, was slaying a dragon. The beast is usually associated with evil; the dragon of the Book of REVELATIONS gave rise to its use as a symbol of SATAN. However, it can also be benevolent, as in Chinese culture.

**dragonfly,** large predatory, day-flying INSECT of the order Odonata (suborder Anisoptera). They have very big eyes covering most of the head, biting mouthparts, two pairs of similar net-veined wings which cannot be closed, and elongate abdomens. Their nymphs live in still or slow-moving water and are also predators. The adults, which are strong fliers and can be found well away from water, catch and eat on the wing the many small insects on which they feed. The Odonata are widely distributed but most numerous in South America and the Far East. In contrast to the largest of the present-day dragonflies (*Megaloprepus coerulatus*), whose females have a wingspan of 190 mm (7½ in), one ancestral species (*Meganeura monyi*), alive during the upper

Carboniferous period (approximately 280 million years ago), had a wingspan of 60 cm (2 ft). See DAMSELFLY.

**drainage basin:** see CATCHMENT AREA.

**Drake, Sir Francis,** 1540–96, English navigator, the first Englishman to circumnavigate the globe (1577–80). He was a leader of the marauding campaign against Spanish vessels and settlements. On one such voyage in 1577, he navigated the Strait of MAGELLAN in his ship the *Golden Hind,* and pillaged the coasts of South and North America. He sailed across the Pacific and reached England in 1580, bearing treasure of great value. He was knighted by ELIZABETH I. Drake was an admiral in the fleet that defeated the Spanish ARMADA. He was defeated by the Spanish in the WEST INDIES (1595) and died off Portobello.

**draughts,** game for two players. It is played on a square board composed of 64 small squares, alternately dark and light in colour, with all play conducted on the dark squares. On each turn, players on opposite sides of the board may move one of their 12 pieces diagonally in a forward direction. Kings (pieces 'crowned' by reaching the last rank of the board) may move either backwards or forwards diagonally. The object is to eliminate an opponent's pieces by 'jumping' them (jumping over the squares that they occupy). The game has been played in Europe since the 16th cent., and a similar game is known to have been played in ancient times. Its US name is checkers.

**Dravidian languages,** family of about 20 languages that appears to be unrelated to any other known language family. They are spoken by people living in S India and N Sri Lanka. See LANGUAGE (table).

**drawing,** art of the draughtsman, commonly used to denote works in pen, pencil, crayon, charcoal, PASTEL, or similar media in which line and form, rather than colour, are emphasized. Often vigorous and spontaneous, drawings are made as preparatory studies (see CARTOON) or as finished works. Among the many artists known for their drawings are LEONARDO DA VINCI, MICHELANGELO, RAPHAEL, DÜRER, REMBRANDT, RUBENS, WATTEAU, INGRES, DEGAS, PICASSO, and MATISSE. (See also ILLUSTRATION.)

**Drayton, Michael,** 1563–1631, English poet. A prolific writer, though otherwise of obscure life, he produced pastorals, e.g., *The Shepherd's Garland* (1593); a sonnet sequence, *Idea's Mirror* (1954); poems in the form of love-letters (1597); and the topographical *Poly-Olbion* (1612–13, 1622), his longest work. His best-known poems are the *Ballad of Agincourt* and the sonnet 'Since there's no help, come let us kiss and part'.

**dream,** mental activity associated with the rapid-eye-movement (REM) period of sleep. It generally consists of visual images and may reflect bodily disturbances (e.g., indigestion) or external stimuli (e.g., the ringing of an alarm clock). REM sleep accounts for about half of the newborn's total sleeping time, but the proportion decreases with age to about two hours for every eight-hour period of the adult's sleep. In primitive and ancient cultures, dreams played an extensive role in myth and religion. Sigmund FREUD emphasized dreams as interpretative keys to the makeup of the individual. He distinguished between the experienced content of a dream and the actual meaning of the dream, which is largely concealed from the dreamer in the subconscious. JUNG held that dreams are not limited to the personal UNCONSCIOUS but may also be shaped by universal symbols called archetypes, that originate in the collective unconscious of the human species.

**dreaming,** name given to the beliefs and mythology of the Australian ABORIGINES. It tells of the creation of the land and its creatures, and fixes principles that guide Aborigines in their religious and social practices.

**Drebbel, Cornelis Jacobszoon,** 1572–1634, Dutch inventor, physicist, and mechanician. Among his many inventions were the first navigable SUBMARINE, a scarlet dye, and a thermostat for a self-regulating oven.

**Dred Scott Case,** case argued before the US SUPREME COURT in 1856–57 involving the status of SLAVERY in the federal territories. Scott, a slave, had been taken to Illinois and Wisconsin territory, where slavery was prohibited by the MISSOURI COMPROMISE. Later, in Missouri, he sued for his freedom on the basis of his residence in a free state and territory. The Supreme Court's mainly Southern majority declared that the Compromise was unconstitutional and that Congress had no power to limit slavery in the territories. Three justices also held that a Negro descended from slaves had no rights as an American citizen and thus no

standing in court. The decision further inflamed the sectional controversy leading to the CIVIL WAR.

**Dreiser, Theodore** (,driesə), 1871–1945, American novelist. A pioneer of NATURALISM in American literature, Dreiser wrote novels reflecting his mechanistic view of life, which held man as the victim of such ungovernable forces as economics, biology, society, and even chance. Among his novels are *Sister Carrie* (1900) and *Jennie Gerhardt* (1911), both about 'fallen women'; *The Financier* (1912), *The Titan* (1914), and *The Stoic* (1947), a trilogy concerning a ruthless industrialist; and *The Genius* (1915) and *The Bulwark* (1946), both about an American artist. *An American Tragedy* (1946), considered his greatest work, tells of a poor young man's futile attempts to achieve social and financial success. Dreiser also wrote short stories, autobiographical works, and nonfiction commentaries on the USSR and the US.

**Dresden,** city (1984 pop. 520,061), capital of Dresden district, SE East Germany, on the Elbe R. It is an industrial and cultural centre and an inland port. Originally a Slavic settlement, it was settled (13th cent.) by Germans and later occupied by Prussia. From the 17th cent. until it was heavily bombed by the Allies in WORLD WAR II, Dresden was a showplace of art and of BAROQUE and ROCOCO architecture. It has been extensively rebuilt since 1945.

**dressage,** [Fr., = training], equestrian event that tests the training and physique of a horse through a series of specified manoeuvres to be carried out in an arena. Scoring is by penalty points given for inaccuracy or incorrectness of style, or for exceeding the specified time. The Olympic Grand Prix de Dressage was first competed for in 1912. See EVENTING.

**Dreyer, Carl Theodor,** 1889–1968, Danish film director. *The Passion of Joan of Arc* (1928) typifies his austere style. Among his other films are *Vampyr* (1932), *Day of Wrath* (1943), *Ordet* (1955), and *Gertrud* (1964).

**Dreyfus Affair.** In 1894 Capt. Alfred Dreyfus (1859–1935), a French officer, was convicted of treason by a court-martial, sentenced to life imprisonment, and sent to Devil's Island. The case had arisen with the discovery in the German embassy of a handwritten *bordereau* (schedule) that listed secret French documents and was addressed to Maj. Max von Schwartzkoppen, German military attaché in Paris. The French army was at the time permeated by anti-Semitism, and suspicion fell on Dreyfus, an Alsatian Jew. Although Dreyfus protested his innocence, interest in the case lapsed until 1896, when evidence was discovered pointing to Maj. Ferdinand Walsin Esterhazy as the real author of the *bordereau*. After the army's attempt to suppress this information failed, Esterhazy was tried (Jan. 1898) by court-martial, but there was a sense of scandal when he was acquitted within minutes. Émile ZOLA, a leading supporter of Dreyfus, published an open letter accusing the judges of following orders from the military. Zola was sentenced to jail for libel, but fled to England. Meanwhile, the case had become a major political issue. Royalist, militarist, nationalist, anti-Semitic and Roman Catholic elements joined the anti-Dreyfus group, while republican, socialist, and anticlerical forces allied to defend Dreyfus and to discredit the rightist government. In 1898 it was learned that much of the evidence against Dreyfus had been forged by Col. Henry of army intelligence. After Henry's suicide (Aug. 1898) and Esterhazy's flight to England, a revision of Dreyfus's last sentence became imperative. A new court-martial was ordered, but the military court, unwilling to admit error, once more found Dreyfus guilty and sentenced him to 10 years in prison. He was pardoned by Pres. Émile Loubet, and in 1906 the supreme court of appeals exonerated Dreyfus. A year earlier widespread antimilitarism and rabid anticlericalism generated by the case led the separation of church and state in France.

**drift,** deposit of clay, gravel, sand, and boulders, transported and laid down by glaciers. Some drift is stratified, or sorted by size, with coarser particles nearer the point of origin. Till, the greater part of drift, consists of unstratified heaps of rocks. Drifts can take many forms (e.g., DRUMLINS, ESKERS, MORAINES). Large sections of North America and continental Europe are covered by drift.

**drive,** a term in psychology referring to a motivational state of an organism oriented to the satisfaction of a need or wish. 'Primary' drives, such as those for food, water, sex, warmth, avoidance of pain, arising directly from the physiological character of the organism, are frequently associated with instinct; while other 'secondary' drives are acquired rather than innate.

**dromedary:** see CAMEL.

**Droste-Hülshoff, Annette Elisabeth, Freiin von** (drostǝ,hylshof), 1797–1848, German poet. She wrote a fine short novel, *Die Judenbuche* (1842; tr. The Jew's Beech Tree); masterful religious verse, *Das geistliche Jahr* (1850; tr. The Spiritual Year); and nature poetry.

**drought,** a period of dry conditions resulting from a lack of rainfall. Often this shortage results in the depletion of water reserves stored on the surface or within the ground; prolonged periods of drought may have serious repercussions such as famine. In the UK an official drought is defined as a period of at least 15 days on none of which more than 0.25 mm of rain has fallen.

**drug addiction and drug abuse,** chronic or habitual use of any chemical substance to alter states of body or mind for other than medical purposes. Among the drugs with potential for abuse are NARCOTICS, including MORPHINE, OPIUM, HEROIN, and METHADONE; depressants, such as ALCOHOL, BARBITURATES, and sedatives; stimulants, such as COCAINE and AMPHETAMINES; hallucinogenic drugs; and MARIJUANA. Nicotine and CAFFEINE can also be abused. An individual is said to be addicted if a physical dependence on a given drug develops and if withdrawal symptoms are experienced when the drug is discontinued or its dose decreased. True physical addiction is known to occur with the narcotics, depressants, and stimulants; psychological dependence, with or without physical symptoms, can develop with many other drugs, such as TRANQUILLIZERS. The hallucinogens can cause traumatic experiences and trigger psychotic reactions, including paranoia. Treatment for drug addiction includes methadone programmes and participation in therapeutic communities with other addicts who are giving up drugs (see also ALCOHOLISM). The question of what constitutes drug abuse depends on the cultural and social context. In some countries, narcotic use in the form of opium smoking is common and not considered a serious drug problem; in others, hashish (marijuana) or related compounds are widely used. In most industrialized nations, however, the use of most of these drugs is illegal.

**drugs,** substances used for medicinal purposes. Before 1900, only a few drugs were used scientifically, among them alcohol, ether, MORPHINE, DIGITALIS, QUININE, IRON, IODINE, MERCURY, diphtheria antitoxin, and smallpox vaccine. Since then, and particularly since World War II, many new drugs and classes of drugs have been developed. Such drugs include ANTIBIOTICS; SULPHONAMIDES; cardiovascular drugs, including BETA BLOCKERS; DIURETICS; ANTICOAGULANTS; whole blood, plasma, and blood derivatives; various smooth-muscle relaxants and smooth-muscle stimulants; IMMUNOSUPPRESSIVE DRUGS; HORMONES, such as thyroxine, INSULIN, and OESTROGEN; CORTISONE and other CORTICOSTEROIDS; ORAL CONTRACEPTIVES; vitamins; ANALGESICS; poison antidotes; and various stimulants and depressants, among them NARCOTICS, AMPHETAMINES, and BARBITURATES (see also ANAESTHESIA). Drugs are derived from many sources, organic and inorganic. ALKALOIDS, hormones, vaccines, and antibiotics come from plants and animals; other drugs are synthesized in the laboratory. There are two marketing classes of drugs; those for which prescriptions are needed, and those which are sold over the counter without prescription (see PATENT MEDICINE). Most drugs have more than one name: in addition to their chemical description they are given an approved or generic name by the British Pharmacopoeia Commission (see PHARMACOPOEIA) as well as any proprietary names given by manufacturers. New drugs are licensed for sale in the UK by the COMMITTEE ON SAFETY OF MEDICINES. The scientific study of drugs, their actions, and effects is PHARMACOLOGY.

**Druids,** an IRON AGE Celtic priesthood or learned class, known primarily from classical sources. The sources tended to paint a lively, but harsh, picture of a tribal society that indulged in barbarous rites, including human sacrifice. The connection of STONEHENGE and other NEOLITHIC monuments with Druidic rites was first voiced in the 17th cent., but as artifacts associated with the Druids are almost nonexistent, Druid rites and the Druids themselves remain chiefly in legend.

**drum,** in music, PERCUSSION INSTRUMENT consisting of a frame over which one or more membranes or skins are stretched, and which acts as a resonator when the membrane is struck. The kettledrum, a metal bowl with a membrane stretched over the open side, can be tuned to a definite pitch by adjusting the tension of the head. In the snare drum, wire-covered gut strings are stretched across the head; these rattle when the drum is struck. The tom-tom is a high-pitched, tunable hand drum. The tambourine is a single-headed, small drum, usually with jingles attached to the frame, which is shaken or struck by hand. In addition to these standard orchestral instruments, there are many African and Asian drum types and ensembles. Sets of tuned drums inspire virtuoso performances in Nigeria and Uganda.

**drumlin,** smooth, oval hill of glacial DRIFT, elongated in the direction of the movement of the ice that deposited it.

**Drummond, William Henry,** 1854–1907, Canadian poet; b. Ireland. His verse, collected in such volumes as *Poetical Works* (1912), portrays French Canadians in their own English dialect.

**Drusus,** Roman family of the gens Livius. An early distinguished member was **Marcus Livius Drusus,** d. 109? BC, tribune of the people (122) with Caius Sempronius Gracchus (see GRACCHI). He successfully attacked Gracchus in the senate and became consul in 112. His son, **Marcus Livius Drusus,** d. 91 BC, was also a leader of the senatorial party. By a general increase in the franchise he won the support of the Romans and of the Italians, but the senate annulled Drusus's laws and brought on the Social War (90–88 BC) between Rome and the Italians. Drusus was assassinated. **Nero Claudius Drusus Germanicus,** 38 BC–9 BC, was the stepson of AUGUSTUS and father of CLAUDIUS I. He ravaged Germany E and N of the Rhine, but failed to subdue the Germans permanently. He died in Germany. His brother was the emperor TIBERIUS. Tiberius's son, **Drusus Caesar,** d. AD 23, earned the jealousy of Sejanus, Tiberius's minister, who tried to turn Tiberius against his son. Drusus died, perhaps of poisoning by Sejanus or by his wife under Sejanus's influence.

**Druze,** Muslim sect derived from SHI'ISM. It grew out of the entourage of Caliph al-Hakim bi-Amr Allah, of the FATIMIDS, whom the Druze considered to be God incarnate. When al-Hakim disappeared outside Cairo in 1021 and was presumed dead, the Druze disputed this and claimed he had gone to India. Among the beliefs of the Druze are an elaborate cosmology involving a correlation between spiritual and earthly hierarchies with the notion of souls successively occupying different (not necessarily human) bodies and a strict distinction between lay and initiated members of the community. The Druze today live in mountainous regions of Lebanon and Syria and are strictly forbidden to intermarry with other groups.

**dryads:** see NYMPH.

**dry cell:** see CELL, in electricity.

**Dryden, John,** 1631–1700, English poet, dramatist, and critic. He first came to notice with *Heroic Stanzas* (1659), commemorating the death of Oliver CROMWELL, but in 1660 he celebrated the restoration of Charles II with *Astraea Redux. Annus Mirabilis,* a long poem on the Dutch war, appeared in 1667, and in 1668 he became poet laureate. His plays include the heroic *Conquest of Granada* (1670–71); the comedy *Marriage à la Mode* (1672); and his blank-verse masterpiece, *All for Love* (1677). His great political SATIRE, *Absalom and Achitophel,* appeared in two parts (1681, 1682), and his attack on Thomas Shadwell, *MacFlecknoe,* in 1682. Five years after publishing *Religio Laici* (1682), a poetical exposition of the Protestant layman's creed, he announced his conversion to Roman Catholicism in *The Hind and the Panther.* Dryden lost his laureateship with the accession of William III. Throughout his life, he wrote brilliant critical prefaces and discourses, notably the *Essay of Dramatic Poesy* (1668). His last years were occupied chiefly with translating Juvenal, Virgil, and others.

**dry ice:** see CARBON DIOXIDE.

**drypoint,** INTAGLIO printing process in which lines are scratched directly into a metal plate with a needle; also, the print made from such a plate. The method is often used in combination with etching. In drypoint, the burr raised by the needle produces a rich, velvety effect and allows relatively few good prints to be made. Among the greatest masters of the technique are REMBRANDT, WHISTLER, and PICASSO.

**dry rot,** fungus disease of timber, typified by the destruction of CELLULOSE, with discoloration and eventual crumbling of the wood. Dry rot requires moisture for growth and occurs in improperly seasoned wood or where ventilation is poor or humidity high. See also FUNGI.

**Drysdale, Sir George Russell,** 1912–81, Australian artist; b. England. He emigrated to Australia as a child. He studied art at the George Bell School in Melbourne (1931, 1935–38) before travelling to Paris and London, where he became acquainted with the work of Henry MOORE, Graham SUTHERLAND, and John PIPER. After his return to Australia in 1940, he produced pictures of the drought-stricken outback of New South

Wales. These landscapes, inhabited by Aborigines, stockmen, and their families, profoundly influenced the work of later Australian artists.

**Dual Alliance:** see TRIPLE ALLIANCE AND TRIPLE ENTENTE.

**dualism,** in philosophy and theology, system that explains all phenomena in terms of two distinct and irreducible principles, e.g., ideas and matter (as in PLATO, ARISTOTLE, and modern METAPHYSICS) or mind and matter (as in psychology). In theology the term refers to a concept of opposing principles, e.g., good and evil. See also MONISM.

**Dual Monarchy:** see AUSTRO-HUNGARIAN MONARCHY.

**Duarte, José Napoleón** (dooh,wahtay), 1925–, president of EL SALVADOR (1980–82, 1984–). A Christian Democrat, he was mayor of San Salvador (1964–70). In 1972 Duarte was elected president, but was exiled by the army. He was allowed to return (1979) and in 1980 was named to the ruling military junta, which later named him president. Duarte ruled, jointly with the junta, during a period of civil war when the government was seriously opposed by leftist rebels. After the 1982 elections, he was forced from office by a coalition of right-wing parties. However, he returned to power as a result of the 1984 presidential elections and sought to hold negotiations with left-wing guerrilla forces. In mid-1988 Pres. Duarte was diagnosed as having terminal cancer.

**Dubai,** small state on the Arabian shore of the PERSIAN GULF. See UNITED ARAB EMIRATES.

**Du Barry, Jeanne Bécu, comtesse,** 1743–93, mistress of LOUIS XV of France. A courtesan of illegitimate birth, she was installed (1769) at court and retained her influence until the king's death (1774). During the FRENCH REVOLUTION she was arrested for treason and guillotined.

**Dubbo,** city (1986 pop. 25,796), New South Wales, SE Australia. This rural service centre for the northwest wheatlands has developed as a regional centre and transport node for road and rail networks, with a rate of population growth at 3.8% (1981).

**Dubček, Alexander** (,doobchek), 1921–, Czechoslovak Communist leader. In 1968 he replaced NOVOTNÝ as party first secretary, and in his brief term of office he instituted reform policies that promised a gradual democratization. In Aug. 1968 Soviet-led forces invaded and a hardline government was reinstated. Dubček was removed from office in 1969.

**Dube, John Langalibalele** (doohɔbe), 1871–1946, South African politician and journalist. A Methodist minister, he founded the first Zulu newspaper in Natal (1904) and in 1912 was elected the first president of the South African Native National Congress (renamed the AFRICAN NATIONAL CONGRESS in 1923). His influence waned in the 1930s as more radical opinions prevailed.

**Du Bellay, Joachim,** 1522?–1560, French poet of the Pléiade (see under PLEIAD), author of their manifesto. Some of his finest poems, in *Les regrets* (1558) and *Les antiquités de Rome* (1558), written while he was in Rome, convey his impressions of that city and his nostalgia for France.

**Dubinsky, David,** 1892–1982, American labour leader; b. Russian Poland. Sent to a Siberian prison (1908) for union activity, he escaped and reached the US in 1911. He worked as a cloak cutter and rose rapidly in the International Ladies' Garment Workers Union, becoming its president (1932–66). In 1936 he took the union out of the American Federation of Labour (AFL), of which he was a vice president, and into the Congress of Industrial Organizations (CIO), but he broke with the CIO in 1938 and rejoined the AFL in 1940. Dubinsky was prominent in the 1950s in AFL-CIO efforts to stamp out union corruption and racketeering.

**Dublin,** city (1986 pop. 502,337), capital of the Republic of Ireland and county town of Co. Dublin, on Dublin Bay at the mouth of the LIFFEY R. It is Ireland's chief commercial, cultural, and administrative centre. Its major industries include brewing, textile manufacturing, distilling, and shipbuilding. Dublin's turbulent early history was marked by the rule of the Danes, Irish, and English, who held the city from 1170 until 1800. It prospered in the late 18th cent., but declined after the Act of Union of 1800. In the 19th and early 20th cent. the city saw great bloodshed in connection with nationalist efforts to free Ireland from British control. It also became the centre of a Gaelic renaissance; the Gaelic League was founded (1893) there and the Abbey Theatre (see THEATRE, table) began producing Irish plays. Dublin is the seat of the Irish legislature, the Dáil Éireann. Its notable institutions include the Univ. of Dublin (Trinity College), University College, and a national museum. It is the birthplace of many famous people, including the writers James JOYCE, George Bernard SHAW, Jonathan SWIFT, J.M. SYNGE, Oscar WILDE and W.B. YEATS, and the Duke of WELLINGTON.

**Dublin,** county in E of Republic of Ireland (1986 pop. 1,020,796), 913 km² (356 sq mi), bordering on the Irish Sea in the E. It is situated in the province of Leinster. The county town is DUBLIN. Most of the county is low-lying, but the land rises in the S within the Wicklow Mts. The main river is the LIFFEY and there are two nearby canals, the Grand Canal and the Royal Canal. Oats and potatoes are cultivated and dairy farming is common. DUN LAOGHAIRE is an important seaport.

**Du Bois, W(illiam) E(dward) B(urghardt),** 1868–1963, black American civil rights leader and author. Earning a Ph.D. from Harvard (1895), he taught economics and history at Atlanta Univ. (1897–1910; 1932–44) and was one of the first exponents of full and immediate racial equality. He cofounded (1909) the National Negro Committee, which became (1910) the NATIONAL ASSOCIATION FOR THE ADVANCEMENT OF COLORED PEOPLE, and edited the NAACP magazine, *The Crisis,* until 1932. Late in life he promoted worldwide black liberation and pan-Africanism and, in 1961, joined the Communist Party and moved to Ghana. His many writings include an autobiography (1968).

**Dubos, René Jules** (dy,boh), 1901–81, American microbiologist; b. France. Associated with Rockefeller Univ. from 1927, he isolated, in crystalline form, the ANTIBIOTIC gramicidin, which destroys gram-positive bacteria (see GRAM'S STAIN). This discovery laid the basis for later developments in antibiotics. His works include *So Human an Animal* (1969).

**Dubrovnik,** It. *Ragusa,* city (1981 pop. 43,990), on the S Dalmatian coast of Yugoslavia. Today a major tourist resort, the walled city and its adjacent island and coastal territories comprised an effectively independent republic and an important trading, manufacturing, and cultural centre for much of its history. Founded by Roman colonists as Ragusium in the 7th cent., by the 12th cent. it had become a maritime and overland trading power. Under Venetian rule between 1205 and 1358, the city–state both adopted its form of patrician oligarchy and was gradually Slavicized. Thereafter a republic of nobles, Dubrovnik established a unique and mutually advantageous relationship with the Ottoman Empire from 1397 which allowed it to flourish as a commercial and cultural bridge between east and west: the city was as famed for its Renaissance arts, science, and diplomacy as it was for its enterprise. Devastated by an earthquake in 1667, the city declined thereafter along with the Ottoman empire until its independence was extinguished by Napoleon in 1806. Acquired by Austria at the Congress of Vienna (1814–15), Dubrovnik was ruled from Vienna with the rest of Dalmatia until it became part of the Yugoslav state in 1918.

**Dubuffet, Jean** (dyby,fay), 1901–85, French painter and sculptor. His primitive, childlike, humorous paintings are often done in thick impastoes of asphalt, pebbles, and glass to enrich the surface texture. He was inspired by graffiti on walls as well as by the work of the mentally ill, and thus attacked traditional values of art by replacing them with forms, materials, and subjects taken from sources not associated with High Culture.

**Ducas,** dynasty of Byzantine emperors: Constantine X, Michael VII, ALEXIUS V, and JOHN III.

Duccio di Buoninsegna, *The Madonna and Child from the Maesta,* 1308–11. Cathedral Museum, Siena.

**Duccio di Buoninsegna** (ˌdoohchoh dee bwohneenˌsaynyah), fl. 1278–1319, Italian painter; the first great Sienese painter. His art is distinguished by its jewel-like colour and graceful line; the vitality and tenderness of his narrative scenes enriched the Byzantine style. *The Rucellai Madonna* (1285; Uffizi, Florence) is attributed to him; his only documented work is the *Maestá* (1308–11; Cathedral Museum, Siena) painted for Siena cathedral, and one of the most celebrated panel paintings of the era. On the front, in a blaze of gold, is the Madonna and Child with angels and saints; on the back, small, lively scenes of the Passion of Christ. Duccio's influence on later painting was profound.

**Duchamp, Marcel** (dyˌshahnh), 1887–1968, French painter; brother of Raymond DUCHAMP-VILLON, half-brother of Jacques VILLON. He is particularly noted for his cubist–futurist work *Nude Descending a Staircase* (1912), depicting continuous action with a series of overlapping figures (see CUBISM; FUTURISM). A cofounder of the DADA group, he invented ready-mades (commonplace objects), e.g., the urinal entitled *Fountain*, and signed R. Mutt, 1917, which he exhibited as works of art. His major work, the *Large Glass: The Bride Stripped Bare by her Bachelors Even* (1915–23) [broken in 1926—a copy is now in the Tate Gall.], fuses machine elements to human functions in a complex imaginary system of reproduction and is extensively documented by Duchamp.

Marcel **Duchamp**, *The Bride Stripped Bare by her Bachelors Even*, 1915–23. Oil and lead wire on glass, 277.5 × 175.6 cm. Philadelphia Museum of Art.

**Duchamp-Villon, Pierre-Maurice-Raymond** (ˌdoohshom'veeyon), 1876-1918, French sculptor, brother of Jacques VILLON and Marcel DUCHAMP. After 1910 he abandoned his naturalistic style and started to sculpt in a cubist style (see CUBISM). His best-known work was *The Horse* (1912–14), a semi-abstract, machine-like representation of the movements and rhythms of a horse in motion. He was a member of the SECTION D'OR group.

**duck,** wild and domestic waterfowl of the family Anatidae, which also includes the GOOSE and SWAN. It is hunted and bred for its meat, eggs, and feathers. Strictly speaking, *duck* refers to the female; the male is a *drake*. Ducks range from 36 to 56 cm (16 to 22 in) in length and have waterproof feathers, with a thick layer of down underneath, and webbed feet. They are usually divided into three groups: surface-feeding such as the mallard, wigeon, and teal, which frequent ponds and quiet waters; diving such as the tufted duck and eider, found on bays, rivers, and lakes; and fish-eating, or mergansers, which also prefer open water.

**duck-billed platypus,** semiaquatic egg-laying MONOTREME (*Ornithorhynchus anatinus*), of TASMANIA and E Australia. It has a rubbery, duckbill-shaped muzzle, no teeth, and no external ears. Its head, body, and tail are broad, flat, and covered with dark-brown fur; its feet are webbed. The adult male is about 60 cm (2 ft) long with a poisonous spur on his hind leg for defence. The platypus eats small freshwater animals and lives in burrows along stream banks.

**Dudley, Robert:** see LEICESTER, ROBERT DUDLEY, EARL OF.

**Dufay, Guillaume** (geeˌyohm dyˌfay), c.1400–1474, founder and leading composer of the Burgundian school of music and the most acclaimed musician of the 15th cent. A singer in the papal chapel in Rome and elsewhere, he wrote chansons, MASSES, and MOTETS in the northern French tradition, with English and Italian elements.

**Du Fu,** 712–70, Chinese poet. One of the greatest of all China's poets, Du Fu was an official in the government, failing to gain high office because of his outspokenness. Living in turbulent times, he wrote poetry reflecting social conditions and the suffering of victims of poverty, war, and disgrace; there are also many poems on the theme of friendship.

**Dufy, Raoul** (dyˌfee), 1877–1953, French painter, illustrator, and decorator. Turning to FAUVISM c.1905, he executed glittering landscapes, seascapes, and witty views of society, painted with swift, stenographic brush strokes.

**dugong:** see SIRENIAN.

**Du Guesclin, Bertrand** (dy gekˌlanh), c.1320–80, French soldier, constable of France (1370–80). In the service of CHARLES V of France, he defeated CHARLES II of Navarre, and in the HUNDRED YEARS WAR reconquered much of France from the English. He was the greatest French soldier of his time.

**Duhem, Pierre Maurice Marie,** 1861–1916, French physicist and philosopher. He developed a formalist account of scientific theories, on which they are merely devices for predicting. His views on holism (the doctrine that evidence bears on the whole of a theory, not just isolated parts) and underdetermination (the idea that any body of evidence can be accounted for equally well by conflicting theories) were a major influence on QUINE.

**Duisburg** (doohisboook), city (1984 pop. 528,000), North Rhine–Westphalia, W West Germany, at the confluence of the Rhine and Ruhr rivers. It is Europe's largest inland port and a steel-making centre. Founded in Roman times, it passed to the duchy of Cleves (1290) and to Brandenburg (1614). During WORLD WAR II it was an armaments centre and was heavily bombed.

**Dukakis, Michael S(tanley),** 1933–, US Democratic politician. Educated at Harvard Law School, he practised as an attorney before entering the Massachusetts house of representatives (1962–70). After serving as governor of the state in 1975–79, he was elected for further successive terms beginning in 1983 and 1987, gaining a reputation for sound financial management and economic expansion. After securing the Democratic presidential nomination by a comfortable margin, he was defeated by the incumbent Republican vice-president, George BUSH, in the 1988 election.

**Dukas, Paul** (dyˌkah), 1865–1935, French composer and critic. Influenced by Richard WAGNER and DEBUSSY, he is best known for his SYMPHONIC POEM *The Sorcerer's Apprentice* (1897).

Duck-billed platypus diving to river bed

**Dukhobors** or **Doukhobors**, [Russ., = spirit wrestlers], religious sect, prominent in Russia from the 18th to the 19th cent., originally called Christians of the Universal Brotherhood. Doctrinally somewhat like the Quakers, they rejected outward symbols of Christianity, promoted a communal, absolutely democratic attitude, and preached equality. Persecuted in Russia, many eventually moved (1898–99) to W Canada. There they prospered, but had difficulties with the Canadian government on several occasions. In 1945 they formed two groups, the Union of the Dukhobors of Canada and the Sons of Freedom.

**dulcimer:** see STRINGED INSTRUMENT.

**du Lhut, Daniel Greysolon, sieur:** see DULUTH.

**Dulles, John Foster,** 1888–1959, US secretary of state (1953–59). After serving (1945–49) as US delegate to the UN, he negotiated (1951) the Japanese peace treaty formally ending World War II. As secretary of state under Pres. EISENHOWER, Dulles emphasized the collective security of

the US and its allies through foreign economic and military aid. He encouraged the development of nuclear weapons capable of 'massive retaliation'. His brother, **Allen Welsh Dulles,** 1893–1969, was director (1953–61) of the CIA.

**Duluth** or **du Lhut, Daniel Greysolon, sieur** (də‚loohth), 1636–1710, French explorer. His explorations won the Lake SUPERIOR and upper MISSISSIPPI R. regions for France. He is remembered for his just treatment of the Indians.

**duma,** Russian representative body established after the 1905 RUSSIAN REVOLUTION. The first (1906) and second (1907) dumas were dissolved by NICHOLAS II after a few months, because of their political hostility. The third (1907–12) and fourth (1912–17) were the last before the 1917 Revolution.

**Dumas, Alexandre,** known as **Dumas père** (dy‚mah), 1802–70, French author. After several successful historical dramas, he produced his great triumphs, *Les trois mousquetaires* (1844; tr. The Three Musketeers) and its sequels and *Le comte de Monte Cristo* (1845). Although these highly romantic novels, written with the aid of collaborators, are sometimes scorned by critics, they have delighted generations of readers and have been translated into nearly every language. His illegitimate son, **Alexandre Dumas,** known as **Dumas fils** (fēs), 1824–95, is famed for his play *La Dame aux camélias* (1852), known in English as *Camille.* Portraying the tragic love affair of a courtesan, the play became the vehicle for many famous actresses and was the basis of VERDI's opera *La Traviata.* Dumas fils was the chief creator of the 19th-cent. comedy of manners.

**Du Maurier, George Louis Palmella Busson,** 1834–96, English artist and novelist. A noted *Punch* illustrator, he also wrote the novels *Peter Ibbetson* (1891) and *Trilby* (1894). His granddaughter **Daphne Du Maurier,** 1907–89, is the author of *Rebecca* (1938).

**Dumfries and Galloway,** region in SW Scotland (1985 est. pop. 145,502), 6370 km² (2484 sq mi), bordering on the Solway Firth and England in the SE and the Irish Sea in the SW. The administrative centre is Dumfries. It was formed in 1975 from the counties of Wigtownshire, Kirkcudbrightshire, and Dumfriesshire. Much of the N of the region is upland, descending toward the coastal plain. The main rivers are the Nith, Annan, Dee, and Esk. Agriculture is the main economic activity, with sheep farming in the hills and mixed agriculture in the more fertile lowlands.

**Dumouriez, Charles François** (dymoohree‚ay), 1739–1823, French general in the FRENCH REVOLUTIONARY WARS. He won victories at Valmy and Jemappes in 1792. Defeated at Neerwinden (1793), he opened negotiations with the Austrians. After turning over to them the commissioners sent from Paris to investigate his defeat, he deserted to the Austrian lines.

**Dunant, Jean Henri** (dj‚nahnh), 1828–1910, Swiss philanthropist. His published description (1862) of the suffering of wartime wounded and his plea for organizations to care for them led to the establishment (1864) of the International RED CROSS. Dunant shared the first Nobel Peace Prize (1901) with Frédérick PASSY.

**Dunbar, William,** c.1460–c.1520, Scottish poet. He wrote at the court of King James IV; his skilful and vigorous work covers an extraordinary range of forms and themes, ranging from courtly allegory (*The Thrissill and the Rois*) to scurrilous satire (*The Tua Mariit Wemen and the Wedo*).

**Duncan, Isadora,** 1878–1927, American dancer. Her dances based on Greek classical art had great success in Europe which she toured extensively and with greater acclaim than in America. Duncan danced barefoot in a revealing modified Greek tunic with flowing scarves, to complex music. Her concerts, schools, and dynamic personality greatly influenced MODERN DANCE.

**Dundalk,** county town (1986 pop. 26,581) of Co. Louth, Republic of Ireland, on Irish Sea coast, near the mouth of R. Castletown. Industries found here include the manufacture of linen, engineering, and brewing. In 1315 Edward Bruce declared himself to be king of Ireland here.

**Dundee,** city (1981 pop. 172,294), Tayside region, E Scotland, on N side of Firth of Tay. It is a seaport, and used to be the centre of the British jute industry. Recently, industrial diversification has taken place. The city is linked to the S across the Firth of Tay via a railway bridge (1888) and a road bridge (1966). There is a university, and an episcopal cathedral on the site of the old castle.

**dune,** a deposit of sand particles which may greatly vary in size and shape, characteristically found in deserts and on sea coasts. The grains are deposited and shaped by the wind (aeolian processes) and the subsequent landforms are often mobile.

**Dunkirk,** town (1982 pop. 73,618, agglomeration 195,705), N France, on the North Sea. It is a major port and an important centre for iron, steel, and other industry. Fought over for centuries, ruled by many, it was bought (1662) from England by Louis XIV and restored to France. In 1940, during WORLD WAR II, more than 300,000 Allied troops, cut off from land retreat by the Germans, were rescued from there by British ships and boats.

**Dun Laoghaire** (dun,liaree), town (1986 pop. 54,495), in Co. Dublin, Republic of Ireland, on Irish Sea coast. Previously it has been called Dunleary or Kingstown. It is the passenger seaport for Dublin, with ferry services to the British mainland. It is also a popular resort and yachting centre.

**dunnock:** see HEDGE SPARROW.

**Duns Scotus, John,** c.1266–1308, Scottish scholastic philosopher, known as the Subtle Doctor. A FRANCISCAN, he adapted Aristotelian thought to Christian theology and founded the school of SCHOLASTICISM known as Scotism, which opposed the Thomism of the followers of THOMAS AQUINAS. Duns Scotus denied that individuality comes from matter. Modifying St ANSELM's ontological proof of the existence of God, he argued that God's possible existence must be demonstrable from sense experience. His best-known works are *On the First Principle* and two commentaries on the *Sentences* of the Italian theologian Peter Lombard.

**Dunstable, John,** 1390–1453, English composer, the most outstanding of the 15th cent. His music is known chiefly from collections in Italy and Germany, and there survive polyphonic masses, motets (mostly for three or four voices), and a few secular songs. His special ability was to use the prevailing techniques of the time in a more flexible way, and also to create a richer texture of voices by introducing intervals of thirds and sixths as well as fourths, fifths, and octaves.

**Duoala Manga, Prince Rudolph,** 1873–1914, king of the Duoala of CAMEROON (1897–1913). Educated in Germany, he led his people in their resistance against forced removal by the Germans from Duoala. The colonialists wanted to create a European settlement on the left bank of the R. Wouri on the Jos plateau. He was removed from the throne by the Germans in 1913 and hanged the following year.

**Du Pré, Jacqueline** (,dyooh'pray), 1945–87, British cellist. After winning several prizes, she made her debut at the Wigmore Hall in 1961. Her feeling for style and her fine technique, and her recordings, especially of the Elgar and Schumann concertos, soon earned her an international reputation. She married Daniel BARENBOIM in 1967. In 1973 she had to abandon her concert career because of multiple sclerosis, though she continued to teach.

**Duque de Caxias** (,doohkay day ,kayseeas), city (1980 pop. 306,243), S Brazil, in Rio Grande do Sul state. It was established in the late 19th cent. by Italian immigrants and despite its recent growth as a modern city its inhabitants remain primarily of Italian descent. It is the centre of the Brazilian wine industry.

**duralumin,** ALLOY of aluminium with copper, magnesium, and manganese. Heat treatment causes a reaction between the ALUMINIUM and MAGNESIUM, increasing hardness and tensile strength. Because of its lightness and other properties, duralumin is widely used in the aircraft industry.

**Duras, Marguerite** (dy,rah), 1914–, French novelist; b. Indochina (now Vietnam). Her novels became increasingly experimental and include *Un barrage contre le Pacifique* (1950; tr. The Sea Wall), *Détruire dit-elle* (1969; Destroy, She Said), and *L'amant* (1984; The Lover). She has also written plays and screenplays, e.g., *Hiroshima mon amour* (1959), and has directed films.

**Durban,** city (1985 pop. 634,301; metropolitan area 982,075), Natal prov., E South Africa, on Durban Bay, an arm of the Indian Ocean. It is an industrial centre, a major seaport, and a year-round resort. Industries include shipbuilding, petroleum refining, distilling, and the manufacture

of chemicals, fertilizers, and textiles. About 40% of the population is of Indian and Pakistani descent. The city was settled as Port Natal by the British in 1824 and was renamed after Sir Benjamin D'Urban in 1835. It is the site of several educational and cultural institutions.

**Dürer, Albrecht** (,dyrə), 1471–1528, German painter, engraver, and theoretician, the most influential artist of the German school. The son of a goldsmith, he was apprenticed to his father and the painter Michael Wolgemut. After travel in Switzerland and Italy he settled in Nuremburg. On further trips to Italy and the Netherlands he became the first German artist to achieve renown outside Germany. Dürer's foremost achievement was to adapt the principles of the Italian RENAISSANCE to the Northern taste. A gifted draughtsman, he produced a vast number of woodcuts (see WOODCUT AND WOOD ENGRAVING) and engravings, achieving an unsurpassed technical mastery and expressive power in graphic media. His highly rational system of perspective and proportion served equally well his penchant for both realistic detail and visionary fantasy. His series of woodcuts of the *Apocalypse* was issued in 1498, followed by two cycles of the *Passion of Christ* and *Life of the Virgin*. After 1500 he developed as an art theoretician and produced greatly detailed engravings. From 1510 onwards he concentrated on the translation of lighting and tonal effects into graphic works. His humanistic inclinations were revealed in such works as *Knight, Death and the Devil, St Jerome in his Cell,* and *Melencolia I* (all: 1514). Dürer usually signed his works, and his many self-portraits reveal a self-awareness rare for his time. He produced some important altarpieces, many sensitive watercolours of wildlife and landscapes, several decorative projects, and treatises on human proportions, applied geometry, and fortifications.

*Knight, Death and the Devil,* an engraving by Albrecht **Dürer,** 1514

**Durgapur,** town (1981 pop. 311,798), West Bengal state, E India, on the Damodar R. It is a new town developed to service a post-independence integrated steel-works, and forms the lower end of an industrial belt stretching up the Damodar valley to Asansol.

**Durham,** county in NE England (1984 est. pop. 603,700), 2436 km² (950 sq mi), bordering on the North Sea in the E. The county town is DURHAM. The county is hilly in the W where it rises to the Pennines. In the

E there is a coastal plain and an important coalfield. Sheep farming is practised in the upland areas and mixed arable farming is important in the fertile valleys. Boundary changes in 1974 meant that the county lost many of the industrial towns formerly in the E of the county, whose heavy industries were based on the coalfield.

**Durham,** cathedral city and county town (1981 pop. 38,103) in county of Durham, NE England, on R. Wear. The Durham coalfield is nearby, but there is little industry within the town. The cathedral is mainly Norman and is the burial place of St Cuthbert and the Venerable BEDE. There is also a medieval castle, which is now used by the Univ. of Durham. The university (founded 1832) is collegiate.

**Durham, John George Lambton, 1st earl of,** 1792–1840, British statesman. A Whig member of Parliament (1813–32), he was one of the leading promoters of the REFORM BILL of 1832. As governor general of Canada, he prepared the masterly *Report on the Affairs of British North America* (1839), supporting Canadian self-government and reforms but opposing French Canadian nationalism.

**duricrust,** a hard deposit formed at or near the ground surface by the zonal concentration of minerals in solution and their subsequent deposition as solids. It is most commonly found in tropical or arid regions.

**Durkheim, Émile,** 1858–1917, French sociologist, considered one of the founders of modern SOCIOLOGY. Durkheim attempted (carrying on the work of SAINT-SIMON and COMTE) to establish the distinctive basis of sociology by applying the methods of natural science, particularly empirical evidence and statistics. Durkheim's method of correlating different social characteristics with different roles provided the model for one of the principal methods of explanation in social science. He debated the consequences of the DIVISION OF LABOUR and individualism for modern society in *The Division of Labour in Society* (1893). In *The Rules of Sociological Method* (1895) Durkheim argued that the legal system of any society constitutes a social fact because it embodies formal rules that are not dependent on any one incidence of law enforcement for their exisitence. His study *Suicide* (1897) proposed that suicide was not an individual act, but could be explained in terms of the degree and forms of social solidarity obtaining in the particular society.

**Durrell, Lawrence,** 1912–, English novelist and poet; b. India. His *Alexandria Quartet* (1957–60), a novel-sequence, is celebrated for its rich, ornamental language and romantic evocation of the variety of cultures encountered by English expatriates in Egypt. Many of Durrell's other books have Mediterranean settings. They include poetry, travel books, and a subsequent novel-sequence, the *Avignon Quintet* (1974–85).

**Dürrenmatt, Friedrich,** 1921–, Swiss dramatist. Much-acclaimed writer of highly theatrical black comedies such as *The Marriage of Mr Mississippi* (1952), *Der Besuch der alten Dame* (1956; tr. The Visit), a grotesque parable of the power of money, and *The Physicists* (1962), Dürrenmatt has declared tragedy no longer appropriate to the modern world (see *Theatre Problems*, 1955). His stories are similarly informed by ironical chance, not by meaningful destiny: *The Pledge* (1958), *The Quarry* (1951). Later dramas include the apocalyptic *Portrait of a Planet* (1971), described as an 'endgame for actors', and *Achterloo* (1983), which presents world history as a madhouse.

**Durrës** (ˌdawrez), city (1984 pop. c.60,000), port on the Adriatic coast of Albania. It is the hub of the Albanian rail network and has varied industries. Founded as a Greek colony (Epidamnus) in the 7th cent. BC, it became important in Roman times (now Dyrrachium) as the start of the Via Egnatia to the east. Its 5th-cent. walls were rebuilt under the Venetians in the 14th cent. There are remains of a Roman amphitheatre and baths.

**Dušan, Stephen:** see STEPHEN DUŠAN.

**Duse, Eleonora** (ˌdoohzə), 1859–1924, Italian actress. From her Juliet at age 14 to her farewell appearance (1923) in IBSEN's *Lady from the Sea,* she projected tremendous emotional power; she was BERNHARDT's only rival. For years a romantic attachment existed between her and D'ANNUNZIO.

**Dušek, Dušan** (ˌdoohshek), 1946–, Slovak prose writer. He is concerned with the multiplicity of perception and looks for fairy-tale behaviour in his fellow human beings whom he treats with kind irony.

The short stories in *A Place on His Heart* (1982) and *Thimble* (1985) are representative.

**Dushanbe,** formerly Stalinabad, city (1985 pop. 552,000), capital of the TADZHIK SOVIET SOCIALIST REPUBLIC, Soviet Central Asia, in the Gissar Valley of the Tien Shan Mts. Dushanbe is the processing centre for the agricultural products of the irrigated valley surrounds. There is a large cotton mill, as well as silk-winding and meat-packing industries, and plants producing superphosphate fertilizers and machinery. The modern city is built on the site of an old Tadzhik village.

**Düsseldorf,** city (1984 pop. 570,700), capital of North Rhine–Westphalia, W West Germany, at the confluence of the Rhine and Düssel rivers. It is an inland port and an industrial centre producing iron and steel, machinery, and other manufactures. Chartered in 1288, it was (14th–16th cent.) a ducal residence. HEINE was born in Düsseldorf.

**Dust Bowl,** collectively, those areas of the US prairie states subject to dust storms or the removal of unprotected topsoil by strong winds. It covered c.65,000 km² (25,000 sq mi) at its greatest extent in the 1930s, when grasslands that had been ploughed for wheat in the 1920s were abandoned or returned to grazing. Irrigation, regrassing, contour farming, and other conservation measures are now widely used.

**dust storm,** climatic event in which dust particles are picked up by the wind and suspended in the atmosphere. A dust storm is said to exist if visibility is reduced to 1000 m (c.3300 ft) or less as a result of the density of dust particles. During windy conditions particles may be carried up to great heights—up to 3000 m (10,000 ft)—and over long distances. Although dust storms usually originate in arid or semiarid regions, the load carried in the atmosphere may reach other areas: Saharan dust has been recorded as falling in the UK and the US. Dust storms are associated with conditions of high temperature, low humidity, and high electrical tension and can constitute a serious long- and short-term hazard.

**Dutch East India Company:** see EAST INDIA COMPANY, DUTCH.

**Dutch elm disease,** disease caused by a fungus (*Ceratocystis ulmi*) which has devastated the ELM tree population in Holland and parts of N America. An epidemic in the 1970s changed the landscape of the English western counties by killing the field elms (*Ulmus procera*). The fungal spores are carried from tree to tree by the elm-bark beetle (*Scolytus*). Research into the subject has become mainly centred on the selection and breeding of resistant species and varieties.

**Dutch language,** member of the West Germanic group of the Germanic subfamily of the Indo-European family of languages. See LANGUAGE (table).

**Dutch Reformed Church,** the Afrikaans-speaking church of the Reformed tradition in South Africa which traces its origins to the white settlers who came from the Netherlands in the early 17th cent.

**Dutch Wars. 1** 1652–54, war between the English and the Dutch. The long-standing rivalry between the two nations as competitors in world trade erupted into war after the British closed their possessions to Dutch traders. After a sea fight (Nov. 1652) the Dutch gained control of the English Channel, but in 1653 the English broke the control and blockaded the Dutch coast. The Dutch were defeated (31 July 1653) and were forced to accept a humbling peace treaty. **2** 1665–67, another war between the English and the Dutch. The fortunes of battle were mixed. The English took various Dutch colonies, including New Netherlands (later New York and New Jersey). Despite some English advances, domestic problems, the plague, and the great fire made them eager for peace. The resulting Treaty of Breda was a blow to English prestige. **3** 1672–78, the first of the great wars of LOUIS XIV of France. Louis was determined to crush Holland and end Dutch commercial rivalry; with secret support from CHARLES II of England, he invaded the Netherlands but was unable to take Amsterdam. CHARLES abandoned the struggle in 1674. After five years of fighting with Spain, the Holy Roman emperor, and various other powers coming to Holland's aid, Louis was unable to crush Holland. France did gain some territory, including Franche-Comté, but ended up with a severely depleted treasury.

**Dutch West India Company,** 1621–1791, trading and colonizing company chartered by the States-General of the Dutch republic in 1621 and organized in 1623. Given jurisdiction over a wide range of coast in Africa and the Western Hemisphere, it fought (1624–54) Portugal unsuccessfully for control of NE Brazil. The company founded (1626)

Fort Amsterdam, which grew to be called New Amsterdam (now New York City).

**Du Toit, Stephanus Jacobus,** 1850?–1911, Afrikaner nationalist, theologian, and journalist. He was ordained a minister in the Dutch Reformed Church (1875) and in the following year founded the first Afrikaans-language newspaper, *Die Afrikaanse Patriot.* In 1877 he published an Afrikaans history of South Africa and during the British occupation of the Transvaal (1877–81) was a fierce advocate of resistance, for which he is remembered as a founding father of Afrikaner nationalism.

**Duun, Olav,** 1876–1939, Norwegian novelist. He was the most important representative of new Norwegian writing in Landsmaal between the wars. His major achievement was the great series of saga-like novels about the district of Namdalen, *The People of Juvik* (6 vol., 1918–23).

**Duvalier, François** (dyval͵yay), 1907–71, dictator of HAITI (1957–71). A physician, he served in the government and was elected president (1957) with army backing. After his reelection (1961), 'Papa Doc', declared himself (1964) president for life. His long regime was a brutal reign of terror. Upon his death his son, **Jean-Claude Duvalier,** 1951–, became 'president-for-life' (1971). Known as 'Baby Doc', he pursued somewhat more enlightened policies (without slackening dictatorial controls) but was overthrown in 1986 and forced into exile in France.

**Dvořák, Antonín** (͵dvawzhahk), 1841–1904, Czech composer. Rising from humble origins, Dvořák became one of the most successful and internationally known composers of his day. Influenced by the music of WAGNER and BRAHMS, he developed an original style whose melody and rhythm were profoundly influenced by the music of his own country. During his stay in America as director of the National Conservatory of Music in New York, he became interested in Negro SPIRITUALS and plantation songs. These influenced the composition of his Ninth Symphony in E minor, *From the New World* (1893) and his F major String Quartet (1893). He also wrote eight other symphonies, chamber works, a violin concerto, a cello concerto, OVERTURES and seven operas.

**dwarfism,** condition in which an animal or plant is smaller than normal size; in humans, it usually results from a combination of genetic factors and endocrine malfunction (see ENDOCRINE SYSTEM). Pituitary dwarfism is caused by a deficiency of pituitary growth hormone. Typically, a person with this condition has normal body proportions, mental capacity, and sexual development. Cretinism is a type of dwarfism accompanied by mental retardation and body distortion, resulting from an insufficiency of thyroid hormone.

**Dwight, John,** 1633/36–1703, English potter. Dwight settled at Fulham in 1671, and in 1672 was granted a patent for the manufacture of stoneware, then known as 'Cologne ware'; he was the first English potter to make STONEWARE successfully for a prolonged period. Dwight made mainly bottles, mugs and jars of brown, marbled or white salt-glazed stoneware, and teapots of dry-bodied (unglazed) red stoneware. A few highly accomplished busts and figures were fired at the factory. These are among the earliest English ceramic figures.

**Dy,** chemical symbol of the element DYSPROSIUM.

**Dyak** or **Dayak,** indigenous people of BORNEO, numbering over 1 million. Modern civilization has made little change in their customs and mode of life, including intertribal warfare and head-hunting. A whole village lives in a few enormous longhouses, and crops of rice, yams, and sugarcane are grown communally. The Dyak also fish and hunt, using blowguns and poison darts. Their religious cults are animistic and shamanistic.

**Dyck, Sir Anthony van:** see VAN DYCK, SIR ANTHONY.

**dye,** natural or synthetic substance used to colour various materials, especially textiles, leather, and food. Natural dyes are obtained from plants (e.g., indigo), from animals (e.g., cochineal), and from minerals (e.g., ochre). They are known to have been used in pre-dynastic Egypt, and cochineal was used to produce the expensive royal scarlet of Roman times. The Picts used woad for body decoration. Natural dyes have been largely replaced by synthetic dyes, first made in the 19th cent. Most of these are made from coal tar (see TAR AND PITCH). Although some materials, e.g., silk and wool, can be coloured simply by being dipped in the dye, others, including cotton, require a mordant. The process by which dyes

Marbled stoneware bottle by John **Dwight** (c.1690; Fitzwilliam Museum)

become 'attached' to the material they colour is not fully understood. It is thought either that a chemical reaction takes place between the dye and the fibre or that the dye is absorbed.

**Dyfed,** county in SW Wales (1984 est. pop. 335,000), 5768 km² (2249 sq mi), bordering on the North Sea (in the N and W) and the Bristol Channel (in the S). It was formed in the local government reorganization of 1974 from Pembrokeshire, Cardiganshire, and Carmarthenshire. It is mountainous in the E, rising to 753 m (2470 ft) in Plynlimon. The main rivers are the TEIFI and Towy. Agriculture and stock rearing are important economic activities. In the extreme SE coalmining and metal industries are found centred on Llanelli, although these have declined in recent years. MILFORD HAVEN in the SW is an important oil port. The coastline is attractive, particularly in the W, and Tenby and ABERYSTWYTH are popular holiday resorts.

**Dylan, Bob,** 1941–, American singer and composer; b. Robert Zimmerman. In the 1960s he gained recognition through his lyrics, capturing the alienation of American youth, and his harsh, insistent delivery. Influenced by Woody GUTHRIE, among others, Dylan himself exercised a profound influence on folk and ROCK MUSIC, his style evolving from folk to folk-rock to country. Enigmatic and reclusive, he became something of a cult figure.

**dynamics,** branch of mechanics that deals with the MOTION of objects; it may be further divided into *kinematics*, the study of motion (see FORCE) without regard to the forces producing it, and *kinetics*, the study of the relation between the motion of objects and the forces acting on them (see FORCE). The principles of dynamics are used to solve problems involving work and energy, the motion of bodies in space (planets, satellites, space vehicles), and to explain the pressure and expansion of gases. Special branches of dynamics treat the particular effects of forces and motions in fluids (see FLUID MECHANICS); these include AERODYNAMICS—the study of gases in motion, and hydrodynamics—the study of liquids in motion.

Land **Dyak** children on the bamboo platform of a longhouse at Benuk Segu, near Kuching, Sarawak

**dynamite,** explosive made from NITROGLYCERINE and various amounts of an inert, absorbent filler, e.g., sawdust. Often ammonium nitrate or sodium nitrate is added. Invented in 1866 by Alfred B. NOBEL, dynamite is usually pressed into cylindrical forms and wrapped in an appropriate material, e.g., paper or plastic. The charge is set off either by a long fuse which can be lit by a match at a safe distance, or by a detonator which, by the action of a manually operated plunger, produces a pulse of high voltage which is carried by electric cable to the charge forming a spark and igniting the dynamite.

**dyne:** see FORCE.

**dysentery,** inflammation of the large intestine (colon), causing severe diarrhoea, usually with blood and mucus. Amoebic dysentery is caused by the AMOEBA *Entamoeba histolytica* and is mainly confined to tropical and subtropical countries. Bacillary dysentery is most often caused by the *Shigella* bacillus and can give rise to epidemics. Spread by faecal contamination of food and water, both forms are common where sanitation is poor. Treatment of bacillary dysentery is with a broad-spectrum ANTIBIOTIC; a combination of an antibiotic and an amoebicide is necessary for successful treatment of amoebic dysentery.

**dysgraphia,** a specific developmental disability of writing, frequently associated with DYSLEXIA. *Acquired dysgraphia* is frequently referred to as agraphia.

**dyslexia,** a specific developmental disability of reading, not the consequence of a more general intellectual or sensory disability. Dyslexia is sometimes used inclusively to refer to a disability of both reading and writing (see DYSGRAPHIA). *Acquired dyslexia* is frequently referred to as alexia.

**dysprosium** (Dy), metallic element, discovered (but not isolated) in 1886 by P.E. Lecoq de Boisbaudran. One of the RARE-EARTH METALS and a member of the LANTHANIDE SERIES, dysprosium is lustrous, silvery, and soft. It is used in magnetic alloys and in nuclear-reactor control rods. See ELEMENT (table); PERIODIC TABLE.

**Dzungaria,** steppe and desert region of NW China, in XINJIANG Uygur Autonomous Region; also known as Jungaria, Sungaria, or Zungaria. Since 1953 large numbers of Chinese have moved there to work the deposits of coal, iron ore, and oil. The Dzungarian Gate, used for centuries by central Asian conquerors as an invasion route to China, is a pass at the eastern end of the Ala-Tau, a mountain chain that marks part of the USSR–China border.

# E

**e,** irrational NUMBER occurring widely in mathematics and science, approximately equal to the value 2.71828; it is the base of the natural, or Napierian, LOGARITHM system. Like π (see PI), e is transcendental, i.e., not a ROOT of any algebraic equation. It is defined as the LIMIT of the expression $(1 + \frac{1}{n})^n$ as $n$ becomes infinitely large. Expressions of the form $e^x$, known as the *exponential function*, occur in applications ranging from statistics to nuclear physics. Certain combinations of exponential functions give the *hyperbolic functions*—a set of six functions analagous to the trigonometric functions (see TRIGONOMETRY) but defined in terms of the hyperbola. The hyperbolic sin of $x$, denoted by sinh $x$, is given by $(e^x - e^{-x})/2$, and cosh $x$ by $(e^x + e^{-x})/2$.

**Ead-.** For some Anglo-Saxon names beginning thus, see ED-; e.g., for Eadgar, see EDGAR.

**eagle,** name given to a number of large BIRDS of prey. True eagles are recognized by their feathered legs. The commonest eagle is the tawny eagle (*Aquila rapax*). It is over 66 cm (26 in) in length and is found in Africa and Asia. The golden eagle (*A. chrysaetos*) is larger, 76 cm (30 in) or more in length and with a wingspan of 2 m (6 ft), and lives in mountainous parts of the northern hemisphere. Sea eagles, fishing eagles, and harpy eagles look like true eagles, with hooked beaks and curved talons, but they have scaly legs.

**Eakins, Thomas** (,aykinz), 1844–1916, American painter, photographer, and sculptor. Eakins is considered the foremost American portraitist and one of the greatest 19th-cent. artists. He sought to describe reality with absolute honesty, his study of anatomy and perspective providing a means of painting exterior reality. Eakins revived US portraiture with his extraordinarily penetrating paintings and, as a teacher of artists such as HENRI, SLOAN, and GLACKENS, founded a school of native American art. Also a photographer, he used the medium as an art form, as an aid in painting, and to study motion. His paintings include *The Gross Clinic* (1875; Jefferson Medical College, Philadelphia), *The Clinic of Professor Agnew* (1889; Univ. of Pennsylvania), and portraits of Mrs Frishmuth (1900; Philadelphia Mus.) and Miss Van Buren (1891; Phillips Coll., Washington, DC).

**Ealing,** London borough (1981 pop. 278,677), in W London. It is made up of the former London boroughs of Acton, Ealing, and Southall. It is mainly residential, although there is some engineering and other industry. It is the birthplace of Thomas HUXLEY.

**Eanes, António dos Santos Ramalho** (ay,anesh), 1935–, Portuguese army officer and president of PORTUGAL (1976–86). In 1975 Eanes, then a colonel, headed the army group that crushed an attempted left-wing coup. A centrist, he was elected (1976) president with the support of all the major parties except the Communists. He carried out democratic and economic reforms and was reelected in 1980.

**ear,** organ of hearing and equilibrium. The human ear consists of outer, middle, and inner parts. The outer ear, the visible portion, includes the skin-covered flap of cartilage (pinna) and the auditory canal, which leads to the eardrum. The middle ear contains three small bones, or ossicles, known because of their shapes as the hammer (or malleus), anvil (incus), and stirrup (stapes). The eustachian tube connects the middle ear to the throat. The inner ear contains the cochlea, which houses the sound-analysing cells, and the vestibule, with the organs of balance. In the course of hearing, sound waves enter the auditory canal and strike the

eardrum, causing it to vibrate. The waves are concentrated as they pass through the ossicles to a small opening leading to the inner ear. The vibration sets in motion fluid within the cochlea. This agitates a delicate membrane, stimulating thousands of sensory hair cells, which in turn stimulate the auditory nerve to send impulses to the brain. Three fluid-filled semicircular canals and two sac-like organs, the utriculus and the sacculus, are the chief organs of balance and orientation; as with hearing, stimulation of sensory hair cells in these organs stimulates nerve impulses.

Thomas Eakins, *The Gross Clinic*. Jefferson Medical College, Thomas Jefferson University.

**Earhart, Amelia,** (,eəhaht), 1897–1937, American aviator. She was the first woman to fly across the Atlantic (1928), to fly the Atlantic alone (1932), and to fly nonstop across the American continent (1932). She was the first person to achieve the crossing from Hawaii to California (1935). In 1937 she and Frederick J. Noonan attempted to fly round the world, but having completed 22,000 miles with 7000 miles left to go, they disappeared mysteriously after leaving New Guinea.

**Early Christian art and architecture.** Among the earliest manifestations of Christian art still in existence are the early 3rd-cent. paintings of biblical figures on CATACOMB walls in Rome. Among the main themes portrayed are the hope of resurrection and immortality

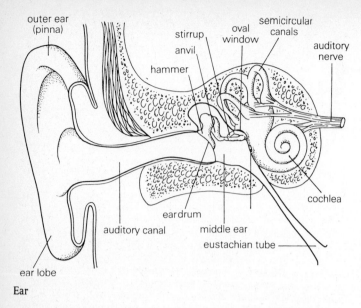

outer ear (pinna)

semicircular canals

oval window

stirrup
anvil
hammer

auditory nerve

cochlea

eardrum

auditory canal

middle ear

eustachian tube

ear lobe

**Ear**

symbolized by fish and peacock motifs. After the Edict of Toleration (313) the scope of Christian art was radically enlarged. BASILICAS were covered with elaborate MOSAIC narrative cycles, e.g., Santa Maria Maggiore and Santa Pudenziana in Rome and Sant'Appollinare Nuovo in Ravenna. In Christian art the ILLUMINATION of sacred texts assumed great importance. Fragments of silver and gold biblical text on purple vellum with sumptuous illuminations are still preserved, e.g., the Vienna Genesis from the first half of the 6th cent. The elaborate sculpture of the stone sarcophagus was extensively practised, often depicting the life of Christ. Ivory carvers decorated book covers and reliquaries and such large objects as the throne of Maximianus in Ravenna (6th cent.). After legal recognition of the faith, imposing cult edifices were erected throughout the Roman Empire. As with other art forms, Christian architecture adapted and modified existing structures from the pagan world. Church structure became centralized, emphasizing round, polygonal, or cruciform shapes. The BAPTISTERY and memorial shrine (martyry) followed the Roman style. A distinct type of Christian art and architecture was evolved in Egypt (see COPTIC ART). In the East the Byzantine emperors supported the developments of the Early Christian artistic tradition (see BYZANTINE ART AND ARCHITECTURE).

**Early Christian art and architecture:** Sant'Appollinaire Nuovo in Ravenna, mosaic narrative cycle.

**Early English:** see GOTHIC ARCHITECTURE AND ART.

**Earp, Wyatt Berry Stapp,** 1848–1929, lawman and gunfighter of the American West. After serving as a policeman in Kansas, Earp was involved (1881) in the controversial gunfight at the O.K. Corral in Tombstone, Arizona.

**ear shell, sea-ear, ormer, abalone, paua,** or **'oreille de mer',** GASTROPOD in the abalone family, spread through temperate and warm seas round the world, easily recognized by the single shell with its line of respiratory holes along one side. It lives on rocks, moving slowly over them, scraping algae from the surface with its rasping tongue (radula). The fleshy foot is a great delicacy in many parts of the world and the pearly shell lining is used to make mother-of-pearl decorations.

**Earth,** fifth largest PLANET of the SOLAR SYSTEM and the only one known to support life. Its mean distance from the SUN is c.150 million km (93 million mi). The change of seasons is caused by the tilt (23.5°) of the Earth's EQUATOR to the plane of the orbit. The Earth is surrounded by an envelope of gases, mostly oxygen and nitrogen, called the ATMOSPHERE. Gravitational forces have moulded the Earth into a spherical shape that bulges slightly at the equator (equatorial diameter: c.12,756 km/7926 mi; polar diameter: 12,714 km/7900 mi). Studies indicate that the Earth consists of concentric layers that differ in size, chemistry, and density. The outer shell, or crust, consists of the CONTINENTS and the OCEAN basins. The crust is broken into vast plates that slide around on a plastic zone, or asthenosphere, within the middle shell, or mantle (see CONTINENTAL DRIFT; PLATE TECTONICS). At the centre of the Earth is an outer core, believed to be liquid, and an inner, solid core. The Earth is estimated to be 4550 million years old, and its origin continues to be a controversial subject. The Earth has one natural satellite, the MOON.

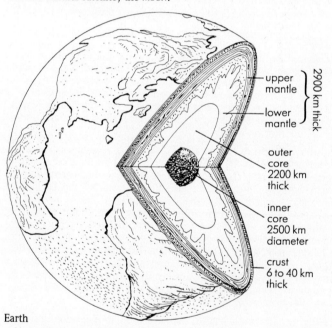

upper mantle

lower mantle

2900 km thick

outer core 2200 km thick

inner core 2500 km diameter

crust 6 to 40 km thick

**Earth**

**earthquake,** trembling or shaking movement of the earth's surface. Great earthquakes usually begin with slight tremors, rapidly increase to one or more violent shocks, and diminish gradually. The immediate cause of most shallow earthquakes is the sudden release of stress along a FAULT, or fracture, in the earth's crust, resulting in the movement of opposing blocks of rock past one another. This causes vibrations to pass through and around the earth in wave form (see TSUNAMI). The subterranean origin of an earthquake is its focus; the point on the surface directly above the focus is the epicentre. Waves generated by earthquakes are of three types. Both P, or primary, waves, which are compressional and are the fastest, and S, or secondary, waves, which cause vibrations perpendicular to their motion, are body waves that pass through the earth. L, or long, waves travel along the surface and cause damage near the epicentre. Seismologists (see SEISMOLOGY) have deduced the internal structure of the earth by analysing changes in P and S waves. The magnitude and intensity of earthquakes are determined by the use of scales, e.g., the Richter scale, which describes the amount of energy released at the focus of an earthquake.

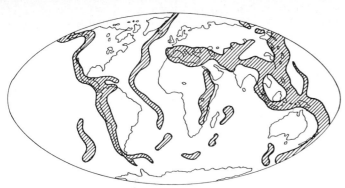

Worldwide pattern of **earthquake** activity

**earthworks,** art form of the late 1960s and early 1970s using elements of nature in situ. Often vast in scale, the works are subject to changes in temperature and light. Robert Smithson's *Spiral Jetty* (1970), a huge spiral of rock and salt crystal in the middle of the Great Salt Lake, Utah, is a characteristic example of the earthwork form.

**earthworm,** cylindrical, segmented worm (see ANNELID WORM) of the class Oligochaeta. Ranging from 2.5 cm (1 in) to a 330-cm (11-ft) long Australian species, earthworms burrow in the ground and swallow soil from which organic matter is extracted in the gizzard. They are important to agriculture in aerating and mixing the soil. Earthworms deposit fine earth on the surface. They are burying to a depth of 17 cm (7 in) per century.

**easement,** in law, a right enjoyed by the owner of land, over the land of his or her neighbour, e.g., a right of access, or right of light. An easement can be positive, giving the owner the right to do something, or negative, preventing the neighbour from doing something. Easements can be created by statute, express grant, or prescription (long use). Interference with an easement is actionable in TORT, as a private NUISANCE.

**East Anglia,** kingdom of Anglo-Saxon England, comprising the modern counties of Norfolk and Suffolk. Settled in the late 5th cent. by Angles, it was one of the most powerful English kingdoms of the late 6th cent. It became an underkingdom of MERCIA, against which it later rebelled (825), only to become a dependency of WESSEX. The Danish invading army, quartered in East Anglia (865–66), later (869) conquered the state entirely. The treaty of 886 confirmed the region as part of the DANELAW. After 917 East Anglia was an earldom of England.

**East China Sea,** arm of the Pacific Ocean, c.1,243,200 km² (480,00 sq mi), bounded by China (W), Japan and the Senkaku and Ryukyu Islands (E), and Taiwan (S). Vast oil deposits, first indicated in 1980, are believed to underlie much of the shallow sea floor.

**Easter** [from Old Eng. *Eastre,* name of a spring goddess], chief Christian feast, commemorating the resurrection of JESUS Christ after his crucifixion. In the West it falls on a Sunday between 22 Mar. and 25 Apr. inclusive (see CALENDAR). Preceded by the penitential season of LENT, Easter is a day of rejoicing. The date of Easter is calculated differently in the Orthodox Eastern Church and usually falls several weeks after the Western date.

**Easter Island,** 119 km² (46 sq mi), in the South Pacific Ocean, W of Chile, which annexed it in 1888. The origin of the island's unusual hieroglyphs and gigantic carved heads, some weighing more than 50 tons, has been the subject of much speculation by the American psychologist Werner Wolff, the French ethnologist Alfred Métraux, and others. Thor HEYERDAHL theorized that the heads were carved by fair-skinned invaders from the East prior to the arrival (c.1680) of the island's present Polynesians.

**Eastern Highlands,** mountains and plateaus in E Australia that extend roughly parallel to the E and SE coasts and into TASMANIA for 3860 km (c. 2400 mi). They form the continental divide and are sometimes referred to as the Great Dividing Range. Mt KOSCIUSKO in the SE is Australia's highest peak. Sections of the highlands are widely known by local names, including the SNOWY MOUNTAINS, AUSTRALIAN ALPS, Blue Mountains, Grampians, Atherton Tableland, and New England Range. Generally rugged, with few gaps and many gorges, the Eastern Highlands long hindered westward expansion across the continent.

Stone statues at Ranc Raraku quarry, **Easter Island**

**Eastern Orthodox Church,** community of Christian churches, independent but mutually recognized, originating in E Europe and SW Asia through a split with the Western church. They agree in accepting the decrees of the first seven ecumenical councils and in rejecting the jurisdiction of the pope. Orthodox and Roman Catholics view each other as schismatic, but consider the Nestorian, Coptic, Jacobite, and Armenian churches heretical. The split between East and West began in the 5th cent. and became definite only with the condemnation of the patriarch of Constantinople by Pope LEO IX (1054). The CRUSADES embittered feelings, and many attempts at reunion since have failed. Eastern church liturgy is always sung and is not usually celebrated daily as in the West, and communion is given in a spoon. Parish priests may marry; bishops and monks may not. The term *Greek Church* may be used very loosely and is best confined to the patriarchate of Constantinople, the Church of Greece, and churches using the Byzantine rite (liturgy in Greek). Among the national churches, the most ancient is the Church of Cyprus, and the most important is the Russian Orthodox Church. The latter was first under Constantinople, but a patriarchate was set up in Moscow in 1589. The rite is in Old Church Slavonic. After the Russian Revolution the church suffered greatly and went into an eclipse, but a new patriarch was elected in 1943; the succession has been maintained since then with Pimen being elected patriarch in 1971. After World War II, Communist influence greatly weakened the Orthodox churches in Bulgaria, Yugoslavia, Romania, and Poland. There are approx. 300,000 Orthodox in Britain, and over 3.5 million in the US. Several observers from Orthodox churches attended the Second VATICAN COUNCIL in 1962, and since then there has been steadily increasing rapport between Orthodoxy and the Holy See.

**Eastern Question,** problem of the fate of the European territory, especially the Balkans, controlled by the decaying OTTOMAN EMPIRE (Turkey) in the 18th, 19th, and early 20th cent. For much of that time the Great Powers (Austria, Britain, Prussia, Russia, and France) were involved in either diplomatic intrigue or actual armed warfare to protect their national interests there. RUSSIA, in particular, was eager to expand into the area, looking for warm-water ports accessible to the Mediterranean. The other powers, especially Great Britain, were chiefly involved in thwarting Russia's ambitions. However, there were considerable shifts in alliances. The RUSSO-TURKISH WARS, in particular, resulted from the Eastern Question. In the 19th cent. the problem was exacerbated by the national aspirations of the individual Balkan peoples, who were aided or discouraged by the Great Powers, depending on what their own national interests were deemed to be. In the CRIMEAN WAR, Britain and France successfully aided Turkey in warding off Russian advances. Turkey's position, however, continued to decline. The BALKAN WARS (1912–13) set the stage for the final dissolution of the Ottoman Empire in WORLD WAR I. See also ATATÜRK, KEMAL.

**East India Company, British,** 1600–1858, company chartered by the Crown for trade with Asia. It acquired unequalled trade privileges from the Mughal emperors in India, and began to reap large profits by exporting Indian textiles and Chinese tea. As Mughal power declined, the company intervened in Indian political affairs. Its agent, Robert CLIVE, defeated (1751–60) the rival French East India Company, and in the days of Warren HASTINGS, the first governor-general of British India, it came under the control of King-in-Parliament. Britain took over directly India's administration after the INDIAN MUTINY of 1857, and the company was dissolved.

**East India Company, Dutch,** 1602–1798, chartered by the States-General of the Netherlands. Granted a monopoly on Dutch trade E of the Cape of Good Hope and W of the Strait of Magellan, the company subdued local rulers; drove the British and Portuguese from Indonesia, Malaya, and Ceylon; and dominated trade with the Spice Islands. When it was dissolved its possessions became part of the Dutch empire in the Far East.

**East India Company, French,** 1664–1769, commercial enterprise chartered by LOUIS XIV to trade in the Eastern Hemisphere. It was merged (1719–23) into the Compagnie des Indes as part of John LAW's Mississippi Scheme. From 1741 the company pursued an active course in India, but was dissolved after the French defeat by the British under Robert CLIVE.

**East Indies,** name, now seldom used, first applied to India, then to SE Asia, and finally to the islands of Indonesia.

**Eastman, George,** 1854–1932, American inventor and industrialist. He invented a dry-plate photographic process, roll film, and the Kodak camera (1888), as well as a process for colour photography (1928). The Eastman Kodak Co. (founded 1892) was one of the first US firms to mass-produce a standardized product, greatly stimulating the development of photography as a popular hobby. Eastman's philanthropies exceeded $100 million.

**East Prussia,** former province of NE Germany. Königsberg (now KALININGRAD) was the capital. The area was conquered (13th cent.) by the TEUTONIC KNIGHTS from the Borussi, or Prussians. From 1525 to 1657, a fief of Poland, and linked from 1618 with BRANDENBURG, it was held by the Hohenzollerns who in 1701 founded the kingdom of Prussia. From 1701 to 1945 East Prussia shared the history of Prussia. In 1945 East Prussia was divided between the USSR and Poland.

**East Sussex,** county in S England (1984 est. pop. 678,400), 1795 km² (700 sq mi), bordering on the English Channel in the S. It is the eastern portion of the former county of Sussex. The South Downs run E to W in the S of the county, ending in the cliffs at BEACHY HEAD. To the N of the county is the Weald, including Ashdown Forest. The Weald was famous for iron manufacture from the Roman times until the early 19th cent. Much of the county is farmed, with fruit and hops especially famous. BRIGHTON, Hove, HASTINGS, and Eastbourne are important resort towns and NEWHAVEN is a port with a cross-Channel ferry service.

**Eastwood, Clint,** 1930–, American film actor and director. After making his name as a laconic gunslinger in Italian 'spaghetti' westerns, he built an even greater success in Hollywood and is now one of the very few leading men in cinema history who have directed themselves in their own films. His films include *A Fistful of Dollars* (1964), *Dirty Harry* (1971), and *The Outlaw Josey Wales* (1976).

**Ebbinghaus, Hermann von,** 1850–1909, German psychologist. He was an early exponent of experimental psychology and of the associationist theory of MEMORY.

**Ebert, Friedrich,** 1871–1925, president of Germany (1920–25). A saddler by trade, and later elected to the Reichstag, Ebert became chairman of the German Social Democratic Party in 1914. He supported the German government in WORLD WAR I, and was head of the provisional government in 1918–19 and then the first president of the WEIMAR REPUBLIC.

**Ebla,** ancient city near Aleppo, Syria. The palace archive contained more than 15,000 clay tablets, which revealed that Ebla had been a major commercial centre trading with much of the Middle East. The texts, written in a Semitic language (Eblaite), date from c.2500 BC.

**ebony,** common name for the Ebenaceae, a family of trees and shrubs widely distributed in warm climates. The genus *Diospyros* includes the ebony and persimmon trees. Ebony wood, from the tree *D. ebenum*, valued since ancient times, is dark, hard, and very heavy, and is used extensively in cabinetmaking and for piano keys and woodwind instruments. Some species (e.g., *D. hirsuta*) have wood striped with black or shades of brown (called variegated ebony). The persimmon (*D. virginiana*) bears edible fruit that when unripe is astringent and when ripe is soft and pulpy. Persimmon wood has a limited use in the manufacture of objects (e.g., golf club heads) requiring very hard wood.

**Eboué, Félix Adolphe** (e‚bway), 1884–1944, French colonial governor of CHAD (1938–40) and of FRENCH EQUATORIAL AFRICA (1940–44). As France's first black colonial governor, he attempted to develop the region's economy while retaining the society and customs of the Africans.

**Ebro,** river, c.745 km (465 mi) long, which gathers the drainage of one-sixth of the Spanish peninsula. Rising in the CANTABRIAN MOUNTAINS it flows south of the PYRENEES to a delta in the MEDITERRANEAN SEA. There are extensive irrigation systems, some of great antiquity. ZARAGOZA is the largest city of the Ebro basin.

**eccentricity,** in astronomy: see ORBIT.

**Ecclesiastes,** book of the OLD TESTAMENT. It is traditionally ascribed to SOLOMON but clearly written much later (3rd cent. BC or as late as 160 BC). A philosophical essay, it opens with the theme that since 'all is vanity', life should be enjoyed. This is followed by praise of wisdom and mercy, an emphasis on the universality of death, and a brief epilogue on the fear of God's judgment.

**Ecclesiasticus,** book included in the OLD TESTAMENT of the Western canon and the Septuagint but not in the Hebrew Bible, and placed in the APOCRYPHA in the Authorized Version. It is also called the Wisdom of Jesus the Son of Sirach. The original Hebrew text dates from 200–180 BC and was translated perhaps in 132–131 BC. Its theme is the excellence of wisdom, and it consists largely of moral and practical maxims.

**ECG:** see ELECTROCARDIOGRAPHY.

**Echegaray, José** (aychaygah‚rie), 1832–1916, Spanish dramatist, mathematician, economist, and cabinet minister. His 68 plays range from romances to melodramatic problem plays like *El gran galeote* (1881; tr. The Great Galeoto). He shared the 1904 Nobel Prize for literature with Frédéric MISTRAL.

Echidna

**Echeverría, Esteban** ('ahchayvay‚reeah), 1805–51, Argentine poet, novelist, and revolutionary. He introduced ROMANTICISM into Argentina with his poem *Elvira* (1832). *La cautiva* (1837; tr. The Captive), extolling the PAMPAS, was his most successful poem. An opponent of Juan Manuel de ROSAS, he spent his late years in Uruguay, where he attacked the dictator in his short novel *El matadero* (1871; tr. The Abattoir).

**Echeverría Álvarez, Luis** (‚aylvahrəys), 1922–, president of MEXICO (1970–76). A member of the Institutional Revolutionary Party, he held numerous government posts, including secretary of the interior (1964–69). As president he attempted reforms but was faced with inflation, unemployment, and political violence.

**echidna** or **spiny anteater**, primitive, egg-laying MONOTREME, of NEW GUINEA, E Australia, and TASMANIA. Covered with sharp quills, the greyish-brown echidna protects itself by rolling into a ball. It may reach 45 cm (18 in) in length. The New Guinea echidna (*Zaglossus*) is larger, growing to 97 cm (39 in). A rapid burrower, the echidna probes for ants and termites with its sensitive muzzle and long, sticky tongue.

**echinoderm,** marine invertebrate animal of the phylum Echinodermata, having external skeletons of calcareous plates just under the skin, no head, and a unique water-vascular (ambulacral) system with tube-feet. Echinoderms are radially symmetrical, lack specialized excretory organs, and reproduce sexually. They have extensive powers of regeneration of lost or injured parts. All members of the phylum live on the sea floor. The phylum includes the STARFISH, BRITTLE STARS, SEA URCHINS, SEA CUCUMBERS, and CRINOIDS.

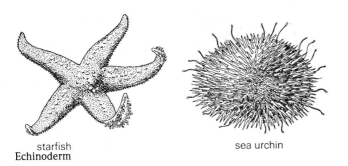

starfish                  sea urchin
**Echinoderm**

**Echo,** in Greek mythology, mountain NYMPH. She incurred HERA's wrath with her chatter and, as punishment, could only repeat the last words said by others. In unrequited love for NARCISSUS, she pined away until her voice alone remained. The story is told in OVID's *Metamorphoses*.

**echo,** reflection of a sound wave back to its source in sufficient strength and with a sufficient time lag (at least 0.1 sec) to be separately distinguished by the human ear. The term is also used in connection with electromagnetic waves (e.g., in radar).

**echo sounder,** also known as sonar, a device for the location of submerged objects and for submarine detection and communication at sea. Capable of rotation, it can scan a surrounding area. The device projects subsurface sound waves and, as a HYDROPHONE, listens for returning echoes, determining the range and bearing of submerged targets. Returning signals may be audibly sounded through a loudspeaker and/or visually displayed by a CATHODE-RAY TUBE. Simpler echo sounding devices are used as depth finders and to locate schools of fish.

**Eck, Johann Maier von,** 1486–1543, German Roman Catholic theologian. Although he held humanistic ideas, he is known as the theologian who forced LUTHER, with whom he disputed publicly at Leipzig (1519), into a position of open opposition to the Roman Catholic Church and thus obtained his excommunication.

**Eckhart, Meister,** c.1260–1327, German mystical theologian. A DOMINICAN, he communicated in various ways his burning sense of God's nearness to men and began a popular mystical movement in 14th-cent. Germany. Formally charged with heresy in 1326, he appealed to the papal court at Avignon, and 28 of his propositions were condemned (1329) as heretical by Pope John XXII. He was perhaps the first writer of speculative prose in German, which became thereafter the language of popular tracts.

**eclampsia:** see TOXAEMIA.

**eclipse,** phenomenon in which a celestial body becomes invisible because another body intervenes between it and the observer or between it and the source of light illuminating it. Thus Jupiter from time to time eclipses one of its satellites passing behind it, or one companion of a binary star eclipses the other by passing across the line of sight from it to the Earth. A **solar eclipse** occurs when the Moon happens to pass directly between the Sun and the Earth (at the time of the new moon). In some parts of the Earth's surface the Sun then wholly disappears for some minutes (total solar eclipse) or, more rarely, only its very rim is visible (annular eclipse), if the Moon is particularly far from the Earth. Over larger regions one observes a partial solar eclipse with the Moon obscuring only part of the Sun's disc. Total solar eclipses afford the astronomer the possibility of viewing the atmosphere of the Sun, or looking past it, without the tremendous glare, permitting a test of GENERAL RELATIVITY and other observations. A **lunar eclipse** occurs when the Moon passes through the Earth's shadow, thus cutting out its illumination wholly (total lunar eclipse) or in part.

**lunar eclipse**

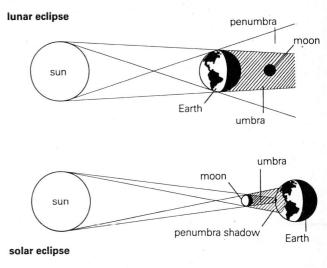

penumbra

moon

sun

Earth

umbra

umbra

moon

sun

penumbra shadow       Earth

**solar eclipse**

Eclipse

**ecliptic,** the great circle on the celestial sphere (see ASTRONOMICAL COORDINATE SYSTEMS) that lies in the plane of the Earth's ORBIT. Because of the Earth's yearly revolution around the Sun, the Sun appears to move in an annual journey along the ecliptic. The obliquity of the ecliptic is the inclination (about 23½°) of the plane of the ecliptic to the plane of the celestial equator. The constellations of the ZODIAC are those through which the ecliptic passes.

**Eco, Umberto,** 1932–, Italian critic, semiotician, and novelist. Currently professor of semiotics at Bologna and in N America, he extended an original interest in aesthetics (*The Aesthetic Problem in Thomas Aquinas,* 1956) to contemporary art-forms and popular culture (*The Open Work,* 1962), before achieving international celebrity as a semiotician (*The Absent Structure,* 1968; *A Theory of Semiotics,* 1976; *Lector in fabula,* 1979, etc.) and latterly as author of the best-selling novel *The Name of the Rose* (1980).

**ecology,** study of the interrelationships of organisms and the physical environment. Within the BIOSPHERE, the basic unit of study is the ecosystem —a community of plants and animals in an environment supplying the raw materials for life, i.e., chemical elements (or food) and water. An ecosystem is delimited by climate, altitude, latitude, water, and soil characteristics, and other physical conditions. The energy for fuelling life activities reaches the earth in the form of sunlight. By PHOTOSYNTHESIS green plants capture that light energy and store it in the chemical bonds of carbohydrates, fats, and proteins. Some of the energy is acquired by plant-eating animals, and a fraction of it is passed on to predatory animals. Such sequences, called food chains, overlap at many points. Once spent, the energy for life cannot be replenished except by further exposure of green plants to sunlight. Recently discovered exceptions are the communities of organisms found near the mid-ocean ridges (see PLATE TECTONICS), where heat and chemicals from the depths of the earth provide the energy for BACTERIA to grow, providing the basis for the

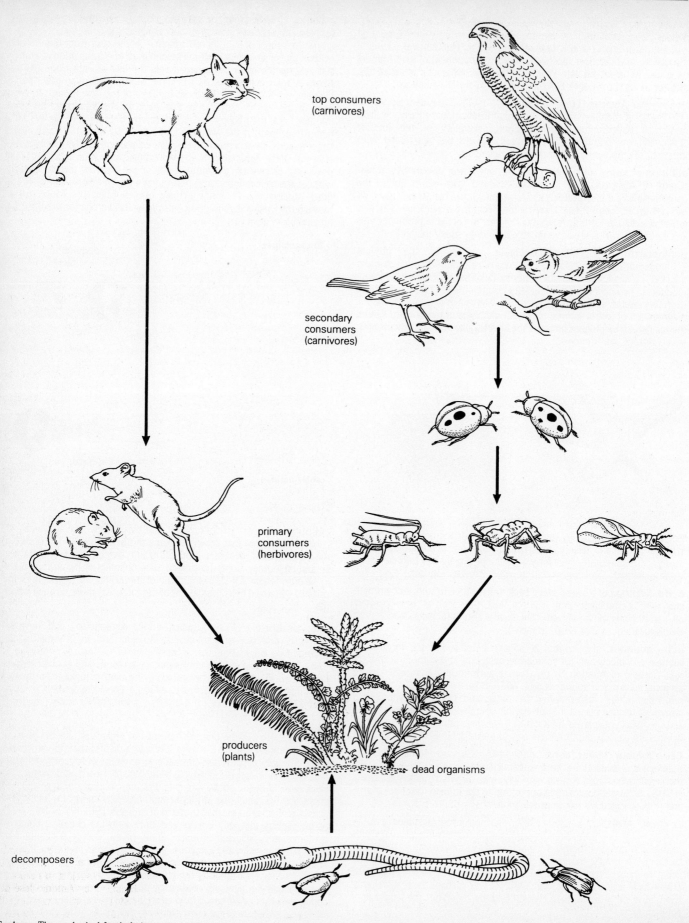

top consumers
(carnivores)

secondary
consumers
(carnivores)

primary
consumers
(herbivores)

producers
(plants)

dead organisms

decomposers

**Ecology:** The ecological food chain

only ecosystem yet known which is not dependent on sunlight. The chemicals of life are continually recycled by such processes as photosynthesis, RESPIRATION, and nitrogen fixation (see NITROGEN CYCLE). Disruption of these cycles by natural causes such as drought or by POLLUTION can disturb the balance of an entire ecosystem. An ecosystem that has reached a stable and self-perpetuating stage is known as a *climax community*. When extensive and well-defined, the climax community is called a *biome*. Examples are TUNDRA, SAVANNA (grassland), DESERT, and forests. Stability is attained through a process known as succession, whereby a relatively simple community, such as lichen- and algae-covered rocks, gives way over time to one more complex, such as a forest or tundra (see SUCCESSION THEORY).

**econometrics,** a technique of economic analysis that combines economic theory with statistical and mathematical methods of analysis. It is an attempt to improve economic forecasting and to make possible successful policy planning. In econometrics, economic theories are expressed as mathematical relations and then tested empirically by statistical techniques. The system is used to create models of the national economy that endeavor to predict such basic factors as GROSS NATIONAL PRODUCT, levels of unemployment, inflation rate, and budget deficits. The use of econometrics is growing, even though its forecasts have not always attained a high degree of accuracy.

**economic botany,** the study of economically important plants from a botanical, rather than an agricultural or horticultural point of view.

**Economic Community of Central African States,** intergovernmental organization. It was created in 1983 by Burundi, Cameroon, Central African Republic, Chad, Congo, Equatorial Guinea, Gabon, Rwanda, São Tomé and Príncipe, and Zaïre to facilitate economic cooperation.

**Economic Community of West African States** (ECOWAS), intergovernmental organization (est. 1976) linking Benin, Burkina Faso, Cape Verde, Côte d'Ivoire, The Gambia, Ghana, Guinea, Guinea–Bissau, Liberia, Mali, Mauritania, Niger, Nigeria, Senegal, Sierra Leone, and Togo.

**economics,** the study of how human beings allocate scarce resources to produce various commodities and how those goods are distributed for consumption among the people in society. The essence of economics lies in the fact that resources are scarce, or at least limited, and that not all human needs and desires can be met. How to distribute these resources in the most efficient and equitable way is a principal concern of economists. The field of economics has undergone a remarkable expansion in the 20th cent. as the world economy has grown increasingly large and complex. Today, economists are employed in large numbers in private industry, government, and higher education. The development of computer sciences has further enhanced the importance of economics in modern society. Economics is usually divided into two broad categories and a number of lesser ones. **Macroeconomics** involves the study of the whole economic picture, as opposed to the parts. It analyses aggregate data in such areas as GROSS NATIONAL PRODUCT (GNP) and national income, general price levels, and total employment. It also examines the interplay of these forces with each other and the results of any imbalances among them. **Microeconomics,** on the other hand, looks at economic activity in the individual case, whether it be a single corporation, commodity, or consuming unit, and attempts, for example, to determine how productive resources are allocated among competing producers and how incomes are distributed among the various sectors of an economy. It is especially concerned with the price levels of particular goods and services. Some economists list a third major category, that of economic growth and development. All of these fields today make use of ECONOMETRICS, a branch dealing with statistical analysis and forecasting. The history of economics has roots in the writings of the ancient Greeks. Economics was developed from the 17th cent. onwards, and was established as a major field of study after Adam SMITH in the 19th cent. by the so-called classical school. David RICARDO was the first great theorist. Not all classical economists accepted the concept of LAISSEZ-FAIRE (allowing business to follow freely the 'natural laws' of economics), but J.M. KEYNES in the 20th cent. developed theories that have led to governmental attempts to control business cycles and the level of economic activity. Opposing the Keynesian school are the monetarists, such as Nobel Prize winner Milton FRIEDMAN, who believe that the money supply exerts a

dominant influence on the economy. See also BANKING; CREDIT; DEPRESSION; INFLATION; INTEREST; MONEY; SUPPLY AND DEMAND; TAXATION.

**ecosystem:** see ECOLOGY.

**ECT:** see ELECTROCONVULSIVE THERAPY.

**ectopic pregnancy,** development of a foetus outside the uterus, usually in the fallopian tube. The pregnancy is usually curtailed but it may cause an acute emergency by rupturing the tube. Occasionally a live infant can be delivered by CAESAREAN SECTION.

**Ecuador,** officially Republic of Ecuador, republic (1986 est. pop 10,500,000), 270,670 km² (104,505 sq mi), W South America, bordered by Colombia (N), Peru (S and E), and the Pacific Ocean (W). QUITO is the capital, and GUAYAQUIL is the largest city and chief port. The ANDES Mts dominate the landscape, extending from N to S in two parallel ranges and reaching their highest point in the peak of Chimborazo (6272 m/20,577 ft). There are numerous active volcanoes, and earthquakes are frequent, and often disastrous, in this area. Within the mountains are high, often fertile, valleys, which support the main bulk of the population and house the major urban centres. E of the Andes is a region of almost uninhabited tropical jungle, through which run the tributaries of the Amazon R., while to the W are the hot, humid lowlands of the Pacific coast. Since completion of a trans-Andean pipeline in 1972, Ecuador has become one of the largest oil producers and exporters in Latin America. Other exports include bananas, coffee, seafood, and cocoa. Industry expanded rapidly in the 1970s in such areas as food products, textiles, pharmaceuticals, and cement. Forestry and fishing are also important. Many foodstuffs and other needs must be imported, however. In 1984 GDP was US$12,600 million or US$1400 per capita. The majority of the population is Indian or part Indian, but there are many blacks and mulattoes in the coastal region. Spanish is the official language, although many Indians speak Quechua or Jarvo. Roman Catholicism is the predominant religion.

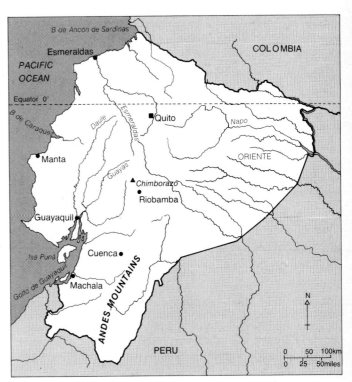

Ecuador

*History.* Entering the region that is now Ecuador in 1533, the Spanish CONQUISTADORS did not find the wealth they sought and moved on. The area became a colonial backwater, at various times subject to Peru and NEW GRANADA. It was liberated from Spanish control by Antonio José de SUCRE in the battle of Pichincha in 1822, made part of the newly formed state of Greater Colombia by Simón BOLÍVAR, and became a separate state (four times its present size) in 1830. Boundary disputes led to frequent invasions by Peru in the 19th and 20th cent., and some of them have still not been settled. Politically, Ecuador became divided between conservatives, who supported entrenched privileges and a dominant Church, and liberals, who sought social reforms; and its history in the 19th cent. was marked by bitter internecine struggles between the two factions. Political instability continued in the 20th cent., bringing a bewildering number of changes in government. Military coups in support of various rival factions have been common. The most recent junta, installed after a coup in 1976, promised true democracy for Ecuador. In 1979 a new constitution was promulgated, and popular presidential and legislative elections were held. The new president, the progressive Jaime Roldós Aguilera, died in a plane crash in 1981 and was succeeded by the more conservative Vice Pres. Oswaldo Hurtado Larreo. The 1984 elections installed a conservative government under Pres. Léon Febres Cordero of the Social Christian Party. He was succeeded in 1988 by Rodrigo Borja Cevallos of the moderate Democratic Left.

**ecumenical council:** see COUNCIL, ECUMENICAL.

**ecumenical movement,** the movement, initially among Protestants but later including Eastern Orthodox and Roman Catholics, which aims at the unification of all Christians. The Edinburgh Missionary Conference of 1910 was its modern starting-point, and this led to the formation first of the World Conference on Faith and Order at Lausanne (1927), and then of the World Council of Churches (1948). The Eastern Orthodox Church has participated fully in the latter since 1961, and since the Second VATICAN COUNCIL (1962–65) the Roman Catholic Church has shown an increasing concern for ecumenism. On the practical plane the movement has resulted in numerous mergers of churches, the most noteworthy being the creation (1947) of the Church of South India (see SOUTH INDIA, CHURCH OF), the first example of the reunion of episcopal and non-episcopal bodies.

**Edda** (ˌedə), title of two works in Old Icelandic. The *Poetic* (or *Elder*) *Edda* (AD c.800–c.1200) is a collection of 37 mythological and heroic poems and lays reaching back to the roots of Germanic mythology and legend. The *Prose* (or *Younger*) *Edda* (c.1220), written by Snorri STURLUSON, is a compendium of Norse mythology using older poetic sources, and a treatise on the art of Icelandic poetics.

**Eddington, Sir Arthur Stanley,** 1882–1944, English astronomer. He made major contributions to Einstein's general theory of relativity, including its first major observational test at the solar eclipse of 29 May 1919. He made the first modern analysis of the structure of the stars, and discovered the connection between mass and luminosity. In addition to many contributions to astronomy and cosmology he wrote popular as well as academic books on these subjects.

**Eddy, Mary Baker,** 1821–1910, founder of the CHRISTIAN SCIENCE movement. In frail health from childhood, she became interested in healing and faith, especially after meeting P.P. Quimby, a mental healer, in 1862. She later discarded his methods and began (1866) the Christian Science movement. *Science and Health,* the movement's textbook, appeared in 1875, and she planned the *Church Manual* and the upbuilding of the sect. As pastor emeritus of the Mother Church, Boston, and head of the whole church, she exercised great influence, even in retirement. In 1908 she founded the *Christian Science Monitor,* a daily newspaper.

**eddy currents,** electric currents induced in a metal by a varying magnetic field. In a transformer core they are a cause of energy loss, and are greatly inhibited by using laminated cores consisting of alternate sheets of metal and insulator. See MAGNETISM.

**edelweiss,** perennial plant (*Leontopodium alpinum*) of the COMPOSITE family, found at high altitudes in the mountains of Europe, Asia, and South America. It has woolly, white floral leaves and small yellow disc flowers surrounded by silvery bracts. It is esteemed as a symbol of purity, and in Switzerland is protected by law.

**Eden, Sir Anthony,** 1895–1977, British statesman. A Conservative, he was foreign secretary from 1935 to 1938 but resigned in opposition to Neville CHAMBERLAIN's 'appeasement' of the AXIS powers. Again foreign secretary in Winston CHURCHILL's war cabinet (1940–45), he was instrumental in establishing the UN. After Labour's defeat in 1951, he once again became foreign secretary. He succeeded Churchill as prime minister in 1955. His decision to use armed intervention in the SUEZ CANAL crisis in 1956 provoked much controversy. In poor health, he resigned in 1957. He was made an earl in 1961.

**Eden, Garden of,** in the BIBLE, the first home of human beings. God established the garden, with its trees of knowledge and of life, as a dwelling place for ADAM and EVE, until, having eaten of the forbidden fruit, they were banished. Gen. 2; 3. It has been located variously, especially in Mesopotamia.

**Edessa,** ancient city of Mesopotamia (modern Urfa, Turkey). Around 137 BC it became the capital of the kingdom of Osroene and later came under Roman and Byzantine rule. In AD 639 it fell to the Arabs. Edessa was captured by the Crusaders in 1097 (see CRUSADES) but passed into Muslim hands again in 1144.

**Edgar** or **Eadgar,** 943–75, king of the English (r.957–75). His reign was peaceful and prosperous. He encouraged substantial monastic reforms, and his coronation fixed the order for all subsequent English monarchs. He was acknowledged as supreme ruler by all the kings in Britain, but he granted legal autonomy to his Scandinavian subjects. His son was ÆTHELRED the Unready.

**Edgar, David,** 1948–, English dramatist. After working as a journalist, he wrote for political fringe companies, but is better known for works produced by the Royal Shakespeare Company, e.g., *Destiny* (1976), the collaborative adaptation *Nicholas Nickleby* (1981), and *Maydays* (1983).

**Edgeworth, Maria,** 1767–1849, Irish novelist. She is best known for her realistic novels of Irish life *Castle Rackrent* (1800) and *The Absentee* (1812) and for books for and about children, including *The Parent's Assistant* (1796–1800).

**Edinburgh,** capital city (1985 est. pop. 446,165) of Scotland and royal burgh. The city is divided into two sections: the Old Town, on the slope of Castle Rock, dates from the 11th cent.; the New Town spread to the north in the late 18th cent. Most industry, which includes brewing, publishing, paper-producing, and engineering, is situated near the city's port, Leith. Edinburgh grew up around its 11th-cent. castle and became Scotland's capital in 1437. It blossomed as a cultural centre in the 18th and 19th cent., with such figures as David HUME, Robert BURNS, and Sir Walter SCOTT. It remains a cultural and educational centre, and is the site of the annual Edinburgh International Festival of Music and Drama.

**Edinburgh, Duke of:** see PHILIP, PRINCE.

**Edison, Thomas Alva,** 1847–1931, American inventor. Edison was a genius in the practical application of scientific principles and one of the most productive inventors of his time, despite only three months of formal schooling and an increasing deafness throughout most of his life. Among his most important inventions were the carbon MICROPHONE (1877), the RECORD PLAYER (patented 1878), and the Kinetoscope (see CINEMA). His most significant contributions, however, were his development of the first commercially practical incandescent lamp (1879) and his design for a complete electrical distribution system for lighting and power, culminating in the installation (1881–82) of the world's first central electric-light power plant in New York City. His New Jersey workshops were forerunners of the modern industrial research laboratory, in which teams of workers, rather than a lone inventor, systematically investigate a problem.

**Edmonton,** city (1984 est. pop. 560,085), capital of Alberta, W Canada, on the North Saskatchewan R. It is one of Canada's largest and fastest-growing cities, and the chief centre for Alberta's expanding oil and petrochemical industries. Edmonton is also an important agricultural processing and wholesaling centre, and serves as the gateway to the developing Peace R. and Athabasca frontier country. Founded (1795) as Fort Edmonton, it was a major western fur trading post in the 19th cent.

**Edmund, Saint,** 1170?–1240, English churchman, archbishop of Canterbury. His zeal for reform antagonized HENRY III, who secured from Rome a papal legate sympathetic to himself, with jurisdiction over Edmund. Feast: 16 Nov.

**Edmund Crouchback:** see under LANCASTER, HOUSE OF.

**Edmund Ironside,** d. 1016, king of the English (r.1016), son of ÆTHELRED the Unready. He was prominent in the fighting against CANUTE. On Æthelred's death, Edmund was proclaimed king although Canute received the support of over half of England. After the battle of Assandun (18 Oct. 1016), he and Canute came to terms and partitioned England, but Edmund died the next month. His courage earned him the name Ironside.

**Edom:** see ESAU.

**education:** a process involving the acquisition of experience and knowledge, formally in schools or informally in other social contexts. The earliest forms of education consisted of learning in religious and community settings, in the court or manor, in the family and in apprenticeship, and increasingly in schools of various kinds and with varied purposes. The education of free men—as opposed to slaves—in Plato's Greece pointed to a conception of citizenship and moral quality; in early Christian Europe it pointed towards forms of service to church or state. Private endowment, church or other patronage, gave place in Europe and elsewhere to coordinated educational systems, and from the early 19th cent. in particular, with models developed by Prussia and Napoleonic France, to state provision. Education was a prime commitment of Confucian China or early Islam. Basic controversies have surrounded the nature and purposes of education, and what it is designed to achieve governs the content of the curriculum—whether it be designed to produce an elite or 'lady' or 'gentleman', a skilled workforce, or a flexible citizenry adaptable to changing social and economic conditions. Controversy has also surrounded VOCATIONAL EDUCATION as against 'liberal' or 'general' education, the extent to which education should be available to girls (see WOMEN'S EDUCATION), who should have access to secondary and higher education, and structures and curricula. In some countries higher education is still scarcely available to girls, and in others it is biased towards certain kinds of provision. In some advanced countries, including Britain, only a small proportion of children from lower income groups reach higher education. In advanced countries education is one of the main items in national budgets, and in less developed countries educational campaigns—e.g., for universal primary education—have been frequent but often difficult in recent decades. Although education is now thought of mainly in terms of formal provision in schools, it remains a process which takes place throughout life in many ways—hence the term 'continuing education'. See also ADULT EDUCATION; COLLEGES; DISTANCE LEARNING; EDUCATION ACTS; EXAMINATIONS; FURTHER EDUCATION; POLYTECHNICS; PROGRESSIVE EDUCATION; SPECIAL EDUCATION; UNIVERSITIES.

**Education Acts,** British laws which, in the 19th and 20th cent. have brought central government into the planning, financing, and oversight of an increasingly complex educational system. The first Act affecting education throughout England and Wales was the Elementary Education Act 1870 (FORSTER's Act), which required directly elected School Boards to provide elementary schooling where voluntary provision was insufficient; attendance was made compulsory in 1880 and elementary schooling was made free in 1891. The Education Act 1902 (Balfour Act) transferred control of elementary education from the School Boards to comprehensive local authorities, which were also empowered to provide secondary education. The Education Act 1918 established a minimum school leaving age of 14. The Education Act 1944 (BUTLER's Act) created a unified system of primary and secondary education for all, compulsory and free to age 15 (implemented in 1947) and 16 (implemented in 1972). The 1988 Baker National Education Act covers all levels of education.

**Edward,** kings of England. **Edward I,** 1239–1307 (r.1272–1307), was the son and successor of HENRY III. He gained new claims to France through his marriage (1254) to Eleanor of Castile and was responsible for his father's victory in the BARONS' WAR. As king, his conquest of Wales (1277–82) was followed by a long and futile campaign against Scotland (1290–1307). Edward's legal reforms, notably the statutes of WESTMINSTER, earned him the title 'English Justinian'. He restricted private and church courts and controlled land grants to the church. His Model Parliament (1295) marked greater participation by the barons, merchants, and clergy whose resistance to war taxation had forced him to confirm previous charters (e.g., MAGNA CARTA). His son, **Edward II,** 1284–1327 (r.1307–27), was a weak king, dissipated and self-indulgent. His reign was characterized by internal dissension and the loss of Scotland. His insistence on having his favourite, Piers Gaveston, at court caused rebellion among the barons, who eventually had Gaveston killed. Edward's later favourites, Hugh le Despenser and his son, virtually ruled England (1322–26). They made a truce with ROBERT I and recognized him as king of Scotland. Edward's wife, Queen ISABELLA, refused to return from France while the Despensers ruled. She entered into an adulterous

alliance with Roger de MORTIMER and invaded England. The Despensers were executed and Edward forced to abdicate. He was imprisoned and almost certainly murdered by henchmen of Isabella and Mortimer. His son, **Edward III,** 1312–77 (r.1327–77), was dominated by Isabella and Mortimer until Edward seized power in a coup in 1330, putting Mortimer to death and forcing his mother into retirement. He supported Edward de BALLIOL against the young Scottish king DAVID II, but despite his victory at Halidon Hill in 1333, the Scottish question remained unsettled. In 1337 the HUNDRED YEARS WAR began; it would dominate Edward's reign. He and his son EDWARD THE BLACK PRINCE took an active part in the war, the first phase of which ended with the treaty of London in 1359. The war was renewed after various treaties and truces, but, like the Scottish wars, was inconclusive in Edward's reign. There were many constitutional developments in Edward's long reign. The most important of these was the emergence of the Commons as a distinct and powerful group in PARLIAMENT. The king's constant need for money for his wars enabled the Commons to assert its power to consent to all lay taxation. The Black Death (see PLAGUE) decimated the population, producing a labour shortage that enabled the lower classes to demand higher wages and social advancement. Edward quarrelled with the church, and the resulting religious unrest found a spokesman in John WYCLIF. There was rivalry between a court party headed by Edward's son JOHN OF GAUNT and the parliamentary party, headed by the Black Prince. Edward was succeeded by RICHARD II. **Edward IV,** 1442–83, son of Richard, duke of York, became king (r.1461–70, 1471–83) as leader of the York party (see ROSES, WARS OF THE) after his defeat of the Lancastrians and capture of HENRY VI. Edward's marriage to Elizabeth WOODVILLE (1464) and his favouritism to her family angered his cousin Richard Neville, earl of Warwick, who rebelled and fled to France, where he formed an alliance with MARGARET OF ANJOU, wife of the deposed Henry VI. They returned to England with troops and placed Henry on the throne. Their defeat by Edward (1471) led to Henry's death in the Tower (1471) and a peaceful end to Edward's region. His son, **Edward V,** 1470–83?, was king in 1483. He was a pawn in the conflicting ambitions of his uncles, earl Rivers and the duke of Gloucester. Gloucester had Rivers arrested, confined the king and his young brother in the Tower, had them declared illegitimate, and took the throne as RICHARD III. The boys disappeared and were presumed to have been murdered. One of the oldest and most prevalent theories that they were smothered in their sleep by order of Richard III is now considered anti-York propaganda of the TUDORS. **Edward VI,** 1537–53 (r.1547–53), succeeded his father HENRY VIII as king at the age of nine. He ruled under a council of regency controlled by his uncle and protector, Edward Seymour, duke of SOMERSET. During his reign Tudor absolutions was relaxed by a liberalization of the treason and heresy laws, and the government moved slowly toward Protestantism. Somerset's sympathy to the peasants led to his overthrow as regent by John Dudley, duke of Northumberland. Dudley gained ascendancy over the young king, now dying of tuberculosis, and persuaded him to settle the crown on Dudley's own daughter-in-law, Lady Jane GREY. The ensuing struggle ended with the victory of MARY I. **Edward VII,** 1841–1910, king of Great Britain and Ireland (r.1901 10), was the eldest son of Queen VICTORIA. Prince of Wales for 60 years, he was a leader of fashionable society. As king, he cooperated reluctantly in Herbert Asquith's attempt to limit the veto power of the House of Lords. He improved international understanding by travelling on the continent and by promoting an alliance with France. He and his wife, ALEXANDRA, were the parents of GEORGE V, whose eldest son, **Edward VIII** (1894–1972) was king in 1936. He was extremely popular until his announced intention of marrying Wallis Warfield Simpson (see WINDSOR WALLIS, WARFIELD, DUCHESS OF), an American suing her second husband for divorce, precipitated a crisis with the cabinet, then headed by Stanley BALDWIN. Edward insisted that he had the right to marry the woman of his choice, though her marital background made her unacceptable. The government saw in his challenge a threat to constitutional procedure and forced his abdication in 1936. As duke of Windsor, he married Wallis Warfield in 1937. He was governor of the Bahamas (1940–45), then lived in France for the rest of his life.

**Edwards, Jonathan,** 1703–58, American theologian and metaphysician. In 1729 he took sole charge of a congregation in Northampton, Massachusetts, where he soon gained a wide following by his forceful preaching and powerful logic in support of Calvinist doctrine. A revival that he held (1734–35) effectively brought the GREAT AWAKENING to New England. His stern demands for strict orthodoxy and his unbendingness in a membership controversy resulted in his dismissal (1750) from Northampton. At Stockbridge, Massachusetts, he completed his masterpiece, *The Freedom of the Will* (1754), which set forth metaphysical and ethical arguments for determinism. He is often regarded as the last great New England Calvinist.

**Edward the Black Prince,** 1330–76, eldest son of EDWARD III of England. He was created duke of Cornwall in 1337, the first duke ever to be created in England, and prince of Wales in 1343. Joining his father in the battles of the HUNDRED YEARS WAR, he fought at Crécy and Calais and in 1356 won the battle of Poitiers and captured JOHN II of France. It was apparently the French who first called him the Black Prince, perhaps because he wore black armour. Edward III made his French holdings a principality, and the Black Prince maintained a brilliant court at Bordeaux after 1363. He aided Peter I of Castile and León, but the taxes he was forced to levy in Aquitaine resulted in war with CHARLES V of France. Bad health forced him to resign his principalities in 1372. He opposed his brother JOHN OF GAUNT, who had become the virtual ruler of England with the ageing of Edward III. The Black Prince died before his father, but his son succeeded to the throne as RICHARD II.

**Edward the Confessor,** d. 1066, king of the English (1042–66), son of ÆTHELRED the Unready. He grew up in Normandy and returned to succeed Harthacnut. He was an able but not very energetic ruler, and his strife with the powerful noble Earl Godwin was heightened by his support of the Normans in England. Godwin and his family were exiled (1051) but soon returned. During their absence, Edward apparently made William, duke of Normandy (later WILLIAM I), his heir. Since both William and Harold III of Norway had claims to the English throne, Edward eventually recognized Godwin's warlike son HAROLD as his heir to avoid bloodshed. Edward's piety was responsible for his name the Confessor. He was canonized in 1161. Feast: 13 Oct.

**Edward the Elder,** d. 924, king of WESSEX (r.899–924). The son and successor of ALFRED, he fought with his father against the Danes and was apparently joint king with him. He gradually became ruler of all England S of the Humber.

**EEC:** see COMMON MARKET.

**EEG:** see ELECTROENCEPHALOGRAPHY.

**eel,** any of a large order (Anguilliformes) of FISH with a long, snakelike body, elongate dorsal and anal fins, no pelvic fins, and scales either lacking or embedded in the skin. The European eel (*Anguilla anguilla*) shows its sex difference in size. The male grows to about 50 cm (20 in), the female to 150 cm (5ft). Most, including the morays and conger eels, are marine; one family, Anguillidae, is partially freshwater. All eels spawn in the sea, the eggs hatching into transparent, ribbonlike larvae that drift about feeding until they metamorphose into small eels, or elvers; freshwater species typically undertake long migrations to spawn in the sea. The European eel migrates to the Sargasso sea, the elvers returning to Europe. Freshwater eels are an important food item in some parts of the world.

**eel, electric:** see ELECTRIC FISH.

**Égalité, Philippe:** see under ORLÉANS, family.

**Egbert,** d. 839, king of WESSEX (r.802–39). He secured the submission at various times of KENT, EAST ANGLIA, MERCIA, and NORTHUMBRIA, but he was only effectively in control of Wessex and Mercia. His reign marked an important stage in the process of unifying the English.

**egg:** see OVUM.

**Egil's Saga,** one of the Old Icelandic SAGAS (c.1220–30). It describes the colourful life of Egil Skallagrímsson, Icelandic chieftain and the greatest poet of the Viking Age, telling of his adventures at home and abroad in the 10th cent., and his clashes with King Eirik Blood-Axe in Norway and in the Viking city of York, in England. It contains all of Egil's surviving poetry, especially the deeply moving *Sonatorrek* [on the loss of sons], a powerful expression of grief and religious turmoil. *Egil's Saga* was in all probability written by Snorri STURLUSON.

**Egmont, Lamoral, count of,** 1522–68, Flemish general and statesman. Although a Catholic, he opposed the persecution of Protestants in the Low Countries. His beheading by order of the duke of ALBA helped to embitter relations between Spain and the local aristocracy. He is the hero of GOETHE's tragedy *Egmont*, with music by BEETHOVEN.

**ego,** the 'Self' or 'I' at the core of conscious psychic life. In PSYCHOANALYSIS, one of the components of Sigmund FREUD's model of the psychic aparatus, together with the ID and the SUPEREGO. The ego forms that part of the psyche responsible for consciousness and which represents reality. It is also the seat of the DEFENCE MECHANISMS, and in the adult mediates between the demands of the Id and the prohibitions of the superego, in the light of the 'reality principle'.

**egocentrism,** in common usage, a tendency to self-preoccupation and insensitivity to the needs of others. In the developmental psychology of PIAGET, the limited cognitive competence displayed by the young child in freeing him- or herself from his or her own perceptual viewpoint. See also PERCEPTION.

**egret,** name for several HERON species. Egrets were nearly exterminated by hunters seeking their white, silky plumage (which develops during the mating season) for millinery. The cattle egret *Ardeola ibis* is interesting both for its association with CATTLE and other grazing animals, following them and feeding on insects disturbed by their feet, and for the rapid spread of the species across the world. Most egrets feed on small water animals.

**Egypt,** Arab. *Misr,* biblical *Mizraim,* officially Arab Republic of Egypt, republic (1987 est. pop. 48,500,000), 1,001,449 km² (386,659 sq mi), NE Africa, bordered by the Mediterranean Sea (N), Israel and the Red Sea (E), Sudan (S), and Libya (W); the Sinai peninsula, the only part of Egypt located in Asia, is separated from the rest of the country by the Suez Canal. Major cities include CAIRO (the capital) and ALEXANDRIA. The principal physiographic feature is the NILE R., which flows the length of the country from south to north and separates the Libyan (Western) and Arabian (Eastern) deserts that comprise 90% of the land area. Bordering the Nile between Aswan and Cairo are narrow strips of cultivated land, home of the vast majority of Egypt's inhabitants. Although the country's industrial base has been increased considerably in the 20th cent., the economy has been severely strained by the Arab-Israeli Wars, and Egypt in the early 1980s remained predominantly agricultural. The country depends on the Nile for its fertility; completion of the ASWAN HIGH DAM in 1970 greatly increased the arable land. Cotton is the leading cash crop. Major manufactures include refined petroleum, chemicals, textiles, and processed foods. The Suez Canal and, to a lesser extent, tourism are major sources of foreign exchange. Most of the population is of a complex racial mixture, being descended from the ancient Egyptians, Berbers, black Africans, Arabs, Greeks, and Turks. The majority are SUNNI Muslims, but there is a large minority of Coptic Christians (see COPT). Arabic is the official language.

*Ancient Egypt.* Egyptian civilization, one of the world's oldest, developed in the valley of the Nile over 5000 years ago. The rival kingdoms of Upper and Lower Egypt were united as a centralized state c.3200 BC by a king named Menes, who established his capital at MEMPHIS. A high culture developed early, and the use of writing was introduced. During the Old Kingdom (3110–2258 BC) Egyptian culture and commerce flourished, and the great pyramids were built. Its fall introduced a period of anarchy, which ended c.2000 BC with the establishment of the Middle Kingdom, with its capital at THEBES. Civilization again flourished until in 1786 BC weak rulers allowed the country to pass under the rule of foreign nomads, known as the HYKSOS. The Hyksos were expelled c.1570 BC, and the New Kingdom was established. During the XVIII dynasty (1570–c.1342 BC) ancient Egyptian civilization reached its zenith; a vast empire was established and THEBES and MEMPHIS became the political, commercial, and cultural centres of the world. After the XX dynasty (1200–1085 BC) Egypt came increasingly under foreign domination, with periods of rule by Libya, Sudan, Assyria, Nubia, and Persia. Following a brief reestablishment of native power in 405 BC, Egypt fell without a struggle to ALEXANDER THE GREAT in 332 BC. After Alexander's death (323 BC) Egypt was inherited by his general, PTOLEMY, who founded the dynasty of Ptolemies and under whom the new city of ALEXANDRIA became the intellectual and religious centre of the Hellenistic world. The Ptolemies maintained a formidable empire for more than two centuries until, weakened by internal dynastic disputes, Egypt fell to Rome in 30 BC. Christianity was readily accepted in Egypt, which became part of the Byzantine Empire about AD 395. However, with the Arab conquest (639–42) Egypt became an integral part of the Muslim world.

*Modern Egypt.* After 500 years as part of the CALIPHATE, Egypt was seized by the MAMELUKES in 1250 and the Ottoman Turks in 1517. The first close

## DYNASTIES OF ANCIENT EGYPT

### Old Kingdom (*or Old Empire*)

| DYNASTY | YEARS | FAMOUS RULERS |
|---|---|---|
| I | 3110–2884 BC | Menes |
| II | 2884–2780 BC | |
| III | 2780–2680 BC | Snefru |
| IV | 2680–2565 BC | KHUFU (Cheops), Khafre, Menkaure. Age of the great pyramids. |
| V | 2565–2420 BC | |
| VI | 2420–2258 BC | Pepi I, Pepi II |

### First Intermediate Period

| | | |
|---|---|---|
| VII, VIII | 2258–2225 BC | An obscure period. |
| IX, X | 2225–2134 BC | Capital at Heracleopolis. |
| XI | 2134–c.2000 BC | Capital at THEBES. |

### Middle Kingdom (*or Middle Empire*)

| | | |
|---|---|---|
| XII | 2000–1786 BC | AMENEMHET I, Sesostris I, Amenemhet II, Sesostris II, Sesostris III, Amenemhet III, Amenemhet IV |

### Second Intermediate Period

| | | |
|---|---|---|
| XIII–XVII | 1786–1570 BC | The HYKSOS. An obscure period. |

### New Kingdom (*or New Empire*)

| | | |
|---|---|---|
| XVIII | 1570–c.1342 BC | AMENHOTEP I, THUTMOSE I, THUTMOSE II with Hatshepshut, THUTMOSE III, Amenhotep II, THUTMOSE IV, Amenhotep III, Amenhotep IV (IKHNATON), TUTANKHAMEN |
| XIX | c.1342–1200 BC | Horemheb, RAMSES I, Seti I, RAMSES II, Merneptah, Seti II |
| XX | 1200–1085 BC | RAMSES III with TIY. New Kingdom declines. |
| XXI | 1085–945 BC | Tanite dynasty (capital at Tanis). |
| XXII | 945–745 BC | Sheshonk I. Libyan dynasty (capital at Bubastis). |
| XXIII | 745–718 BC | Nubian dynasty with invasion of Piankhi (capital at Bubastis). |
| XXIV | 718–712 BC | Saïte dynasty (capital at Saïs). |
| XXV | 712–663 BC | Taharka. Assyrian invasions begin foreign domination. |
| XXVI | 663–525 BC | Psamtik, NECHO, Apries, Amasis II (capital at Saïs). |
| XXVII | 525–405 BC | The ACHAEMENIDS of Persia in control. Cambyses II to DARIUS II. Egypt revolts. |
| XXVIII, XXIX, XXX | 405–332 BC | NEKHTNEBF I, Nekhtnebf II. Last native dynasties, ending with conquest of ALEXANDER THE GREAT. Capital at Saïs, then at Mendes, then at Sebennytos. |

French–British commission to manage its financial affairs. The British consolidated their control between 1883 and 1907, and during WORLD WAR I, when Turkey joined the Central Powers, Great Britain declared Egypt a British protectorate, which lasted until 1937.

*Independent Egypt.* After World War II Egypt bitterly opposed the UN partition of Palestine in 1948 and played an important role in the ARAB-ISRAELI WARS that followed. In 1952 the Egyptian army deposed King FAROUK in a coup d'état; a republic was established in 1953, and Col. Gamal Abdel NASSER became president. For a brief period Egypt and Syria merged (1958) in the UNITED ARAB REPUBLIC, then were joined by Yemen in the United Arab States; the union was dissolved in 1961. Inaugurating a programme of economic and social reform, modernization of the army, and construction of the Aswan High Dam, Nasser, with the aid of the USSR, strove to make Egypt the undisputed leader of the Arab world. His rallying-cry was denunciation of Israel; in 1967 Egypt lost much territory in the Six-Day War, which also shattered its economy and armed forces. Nasser died in 1970 and was succeeded by Anwar al-SADAT, who regained much of Egypt's lost territory in the Yom Kippur War (1973) and reversed a 20-year trend by ending Soviet influence and seeking closer ties with the West. In 1977 Sadat angered his Arab allies by travelling to Jerusalem as a conciliatory gesture to Israel; the two nations signed a peace treaty in 1979 (see CAMP DAVID ACCORDS). In 1981 Sadat was assassinated by Muslim fundamentalists, and Hosni MUBARAK, who pledged to continue Sadat's policies, became president. The Israeli withdrawal from the Sinai and its return to Egypt, which began in 1979, was completed in 1982, but many other crucial problems remained unsolved. President Mubarak has maintained Sadat's democratization process, with his own National Democratic Party dominating political life, although opposed by a resurgent Wafd Party and the fundamentalist Moslem Brotherhood.

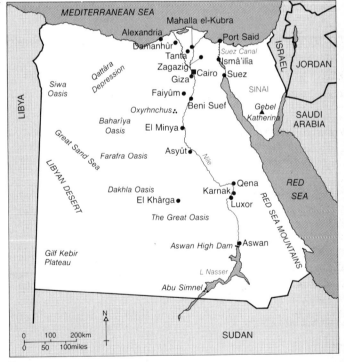

Egypt

contact with the West occurred in 1798, when French forces under NAPOLEON occupied the country; they were expelled in 1801 by combined Ottoman and British troops. In 1805 MUHAMMAD ALI, a common soldier, was appointed pasha of Egypt; under his rule the foundations of the modern state of Egypt were established. The construction of the SUEZ CANAL (1859–69) put Egypt deeply into debt, and, although nominally still part of the OTTOMAN EMPIRE, the country was forced to appoint a

**Egyptian architecture**, was formulated prior to 3000 BC. Abundant clay and scarce wood led to the early development of ceramic arts and brickwork. A massive, static, serene architecture emerged. Walls were immensely thick; columns were confined to halls and inner courts. Exterior walls had few openings and were covered with HIEROGLYPHICS and pictorial carvings in brilliant colours, with symbolic motifs such as the scarab beetle. The capacity of sculptors to integrate decoration into structure was highly developed. Flat stone block roofs were supported by walls or by closely spaced internal columns. No dwellings, only tombs and temples, survive. Belief in the afterlife led to massive, impressive sepulchral architecture. Of the Old Kingdom (2680–2258 BC) remains, the MASTABA is the oldest remaining form of sepulchre. The PYRAMID of a ruler was begun as soon as he ascended the throne. Middle Kingdom (2134–1786 BC) tombs were tunnelled out of Nile cliffs. In temples of the New Kingdom (1570–1085 BC), the doorway was flanked by great pylons or towers, often with statues or obelisks in front. The temple was screened from the common people by a high wall. The hall had immense columns arranged in a nave and side aisles; behind were small, restricted sanctuaries. New Kingdom temples were also carved from rock, e.g., ABU SIMBEL. Egyptian architecture consistently resisted foreign influences.

**Egyptian art.** The art of predynastic EGYPT (c.4000–3200 BC), known from funerary offerings, was largely painted pottery and figurines, ivory carvings, slate cosmetic palettes, and flint weapons. Towards the end of the predynastic period, sculptors carved monolithic figures of the gods from limestone, e.g., the Min at Coptos. In the protodynastic and early dynastic periods (3200–2780 BC), Mesopotamian motifs appeared. The stone bowls and vases of these periods are remarkable for fine craftsmanship. During the Old Kingdom, centred at Memphis (2680–2258 BC), the stylistic conventions that characterize Egyptian art were developed, notably the law of frontality, in which the human figure is represented with head in profile, the eye and shoulders in front view, and the pelvis, legs, and feet in profile. There was little attempt at linear perspective or spatial illusionism. Relief was shallow, e.g., the palette of Namer (Cairo), a masterpiece of the I dynasty showing battle scenes. In sculpture as well as in painting, the law of frontality was strictly followed. Working with the most durable materials they had, artists decorated tombs with domestic, military, hunting, and ceremonial scenes to enable the dead to attain a happy continuation of their previous lives. Chief examples of Old Kingdom sculpture are the *Great Chephren,* in diorite; the *Prince Ra-hetep and Princess Neferet,* in painted limestone; and the *Sheik-el-Beled,* in painted wood (all: Cairo). Painting was generally employed as an accessory to sculpture. In the Middle Kingdom, based at Thebes (2000–1786 BC), the forms of the Old Kingdom were retained, but the unity of style was broken to admit a new formalism and delicacy. The tomb paintings at Bani Hasan are remarkable for freedom of draughtsmanship. The sculptured portraits of Sesostris III and Amenemhet III (both: Cairo) are exceptional in their revelation of inner feelings. New Kingdom art (1570–1342 BC) was the final development of classic Egyptian style, with monumental forms, bold design, and a controlled vitality. During the Amarna period (1372–1350 BC) a naturalistic style developed in sculpture, e.g., the colossal statue of IKHNATON (Cairo) and the magnificent painted limestone bust of Queen NEFERTITI (Berlin Mus.). The rich sophistication of the period is exemplified by the furnishings from the tomb of TUTANKHAMEN. The Ramesside period (1314–1085 BC) saw an unsuccessful attempt to return to New Kingdom styles, but the vitality of that period was lost. The following period of decline (1085–730 BC) is characterized by mechanical repetition of earlier forms and by satirical drawings in the papyri. In the Saite period (730–663 BC) a coarse, brutal style predominated. After the Assyrian conquest of Egypt (663 BC), all the arts but metalworking declined. Egypt proved resistant to foreign influence in art through the Ptolemaic dynasty (332–30 BC). Architecture remained vital, e.g., at Idfu and Philac, and the minor arts continued to flourish.

**Egyptian language,** extinct language of ancient Egypt that is generally classified as a member of the Hamitic subfamily of the Hamito-Semitic family of languages. See AFRICAN LANGUAGES (table).

**Egyptian religion.** Ancient Egyptian worship is remarkable for its reconciliation and union of conflicting beliefs. The earliest predynastic tribes venerated many deities who were at first embodied in animals (such as the sacred cat of Bubastis), but who were later gradually humanized. The most widely accepted creation myth was that of the great sun god RA (Re), who appeared out of Chaos to create a race including OSIRIS and ISIS, and their son HORUS. When a national religion arose at the end of the predynastic period (c.3200 BC), various priesthoods attempted to systematize the gods and myths. The reign of IKHNATON established a monotheistic cult, but POLYTHEISM was restored after his death. The most important of the many forms of Egyptian worship were the cults of Osiris, king and judge of the dead, protector of all; the sun god Ra (symbolized by the PYRAMID), said to be the direct ancestor of the kings of Egypt; and AMON, Egypt's greatest god by the XIX dynasty. With no established book of teachings such as the Bible or Koran, Egyptian conduct was guided by human wisdom and the belief in *maat,* the principle of divine justice and order, held to be reflected in civil order as administered by the state under

Egyptian art: Painted limestone bust of Queen Nefertiti. Berlin Museum

the pharaoh. While the priesthoods and state cult grew, the populace found its expression of religious feeling in the strict rites prescribed by funerary cults (see BOOK OF THE DEAD).

**Ehrenburg, Ilya Grigoryevich** (ˌeərənbooək), 1891–1967, Soviet writer. From 1909 to 1917 and 1921 to 1941 he lived in W Europe, where he wrote such novels as *The Extraordinary Adventures of Julio Jurenito* (1922), *The Love of Jeanne Ney* (1924), and *Out of Chaos* (1933). Returning to the Soviet Union in 1941, he became a war correspondent. His best-known novel, *The Fall of Paris* (1941–42), deals with the decay of French society, while *The Thaw* (1954) was the first work to discuss Stalinist repression.

**Ehrlich, Paul,** 1854–1915, German immunologist, haematologist, and pharmacologist. For his work in immunology he shared with Élie METCHNIKOFF the 1908 Nobel Prize for physiology or medicine. He introduced the arsenic-containing drug Salvarsan for the treatment of syphilis and made valuable contributions in haematology, cellular pathology, cancer study, and the use of dyes in microscopy.

**Eichendorff, Joseph, Freiherr von** (ˌiekhəndooəf), 1788–1857, German poet, a leader of the late romantics. His lyric verse was set to music by SCHUMANN, MENDELSSOHN, and others. His poetic dreams are expressed in the delightful short novel *Aus dem Leben eines Taugenichts* (1826; tr. Memoirs of a Good-for-Nothing).

**Eichmann, Adolf** (ˌiekhman), 1906–62, German NAZI official. As head of the Gestapo's Jewish section, he oversaw the maltreatment, deportation to concentration camps, and murder (especially by the use of gas chambers) of millions of JEWS. After World War II, he escaped to Argentina, but he was located and abducted by Israeli agents in 1960. He was tried and hanged in Israel for crimes against the Jews.

**Eiffel Tower,** structure designed by the French engineer Alexandre Gustave Eiffel (1832–1923) for the Paris Exposition of 1889. The tower is 300 m (984 ft) high and consists of an open iron framework on four

Eiffel Tower

masonry piers; these piers support four columns that unite to form the shaft.

**Eigen, Manfred,** 1927–, German biophysical chemist. He shared, with Ronald Norrish and George PORTER, the 1967 Nobel Prize for chemistry, for developing techniques for following the course of rapid reactions. He has contributed to the debate on self-replicative entities and the origin of life.

**Eight, the,** group of American artists in New York City, formed in 1908 to exhibit paintings. Men of widely different tendencies, they were bound by common opposition to academism and, because of their portrayal of everyday American life, were stigmatized as the ASH CAN SCHOOL. They organized the ARMORY SHOW of 1913, which introduced modern European art to a reluctant but curious America.

**eight-hour day,** a working day of eight hours, won by the stonemasons of Melbourne, Australia, in 1856. Thereafter, the labour movement celebrated the achievement with an annual parade held in all principal centres. The eight-hour day became a rallying-point for Australian trade unions during the later 19th cent., and is still marked by a public holiday.

**Eijkman, Christiaan** (ˌaykman), 1858–1930, Dutch physician. For his work on the cause of BERIBERI, which led to the isolation of thiamine (vitamin B₁) he shared with Sir Frederick HOPKINS the 1929 Nobel Prize for physiology or medicine.

**Eilat:** see ELAT.

**Eilshemius, Louis Michel** (ielˌsheemeeəs), 1864–1941, American painter. He is known for his imaginative, atmospheric American landscapes. *New York at Night* (1917; Metropolitan Mus., New York) is an excellent example.

**Eindhoven,** city (1985 pop. 191,675, agglomeration 374,974), Noord Brabant prov., S Netherlands. A leading centre of manufacturing industry, its early importance was based on cotton textiles and tobacco. To these was added the manufacture of light bulbs in the 1890s. Today the Philips company employs many thousands and has diversified its activities to include radio and television components, and electronic equipment. The company operates large research establishments and plays a major part in the social life of the city, providing housing and other services.

**Einstein, Albert,** 1879–1955, American theoretical physicist; b. Germany; recognized as one of the greatest physicists of all time. He became (1914) titular professor of physics and director of theoretical physics at the Kaiser Wilhelm Institute in Berlin. The Nazi government confiscated (1934) his property and revoked his German citizenship because he was Jewish, and in 1940 Einstein became an American citizen; in 1933 he was appointed a life member of the Institute for Advanced Study in Princeton. Although an ardent pacifist, he urged Pres. Franklin Roosevelt to investigate the possible use of atomic energy in bombs. In one of three important papers (1905), he explained BROWNIAN MOVEMENT on the basis of his study of the motion of atoms. His special theory of RELATIVITY (1905) dealt with systems or observers in uniform (unaccelerated) motion with respect to one another. He asserted (1911) the equality of GRAVITATION and INERTIA and formulated (c.1916) a general theory of relativity that included gravitation as a determiner of the curvature of a SPACE–TIME continuum. Einstein contributed to the development of QUANTUM THEORY, postulating (1905) light quanta (see PHOTON), on which he based his explanation of the PHOTOELECTRIC EFFECT, and developing the quantum theory of specific heat. Working on a unified field theory which would account for all (four) interactions or forces between particles, he attempted to explain gravitation and electromagnetism with one set of laws. For his work in theoretical physics, notably on the photoelectric effect, he received the 1921 Nobel Prize for physics.

**einsteinium** (Es), radioactive element, discovered in 1952 by A. Ghiorso and colleagues in residue from a thermonuclear explosion. A member of the ACTINIDE SERIES, weighable amounts have since been prepared by neutron bombardment of plutonium. See ELEMENT (table); PERIODIC TABLE.

**Einthoven, Willem,** 1860–1927, Dutch physiologist; b. Java. He received the 1924 Nobel Prize for physiology or medicine for his invention of a sensitive string galvanometer to produce the electrocardiogram (ECG), a graphic record of the action of the heart (see ELECTROCARDIOGRAPHY).

**Eisenhower, Dwight David,** 1890–1969, American general and 34th president of the US (1953–61); his nickname was 'Ike'. A West Point graduate, he had a meteoric rise as a military commander during WORLD WAR II. In 1942 he became chief of army operations in Washington, DC. Later that year he was named US commander of the European theatre of operations, and in 1943 he became supreme commander of the Allied Expeditionary Force. Eisenhower was responsible for coordinating and directing the Allied invasion of Europe in June 1944. In Dec. 1944 he was made general of the army (five-star general) and upon his return to the US became army chief of staff (1945–48). He was president of Columbia Univ. from 1948 to 1950 and in 1950 was named supreme commander of the Allied forces in Europe. After organizing the defence forces of the North Atlantic Treaty Organization (NATO), Eisenhower resigned (1952) from the army to campaign for the Republican presidential nomination. Popularity as a World War II hero brought him an easy victory over his Democratic opponent, Adlai E. STEVENSON. One of Eisenhower's first moves as president (July 1953) was to fulfil a campaign promise to end the KOREAN WAR. He and his secretary of state, John Foster DULLES, continued the TRUMAN administration's policy of containing Communism. In domestic affairs, Eisenhower remained aloof from the legislative process and took few initiatives. Despite a heart attack (1955) he easily won reelection in 1956. His administration then took a more active role in the growing CIVIL RIGHTS movement. In 1957 federal troops were sent to Little Rock, Arkansas, to enforce a court-ordered school desegregation decision, and later Congress enacted federal civil-rights legislation. Also in 1957, the president promulgated the so-called Eisenhower doctrine, which committed the US to an active role in the Middle East to protect the region from Communist aggression. Tensions with the Soviet Union increased, however, and a summit meeting with Nikita KHRUSHCHEV ended abruptly because of conflict over US espionage flights over the USSR. In 1959 the coming to power of the Communist Fidel CASTRO in Cuba posed further problems, and Eisenhower broke diplomatic relations with Cuba just before leaving office in Jan. 1961.

**Eisenstein, Sergei Mikhailovich,** 1898–1948, Russian film director. Ranked with D.W. GRIFFITH as a cinematic genius, he pioneered the use of MONTAGE in such works as *Potemkin* (1925), *October* (1928), and *Alexander Nevsky* (1938).

**eisteddfod** (ie͵stedfəd), (literally 'session') Welsh festival involving contests in ARTS AND CRAFTS with special emphasis on music and poetry. The National Eisteddfod is held for a week in August; local festivals are held throughout the year. It dates from the 12th cent., but declined with the decline of the bards. It was revived in 1880.

**Ekelöf, Gunnar** (͵aykəlö:f), 1907–68, Swedish poet, considered the most important Swedish poet of the 20th cent. His verse, philosophic and mystical, reflects his interest in the French SYMBOLISTS and Oriental literature. Volumes in English translation include *Selected Poems* (tr. 1971) and *A Mölna Elegy* (tr. 1979).

**Ekelund, Vilhelm** (͵aykə'lund), 1880–1949, Swedish writer. He wrote poems, e.g., *Stella Maris* (1906), and a long series of essays, e.g., *Classical Ideal* (1909). Although not widely read, his work influenced Scandinavian MODERNISM.

**Ekwensi, Cyprian,** 1921–, Nigerian novelist. A prolific writer, who aims at a mass market, he is fascinated by, yet warns about, the dangers of urban society in *People of the City* (1954), *Jagua Nana* (1961), and *Beautiful Feathers* (1965). He has also written two novels about the Nigerian civil war and its aftermath: *Survive the Peace* (1976) and *Divided We Stand* (1980).

**Elam,** ancient Asiatic country, N of the Persian Gulf, now in W Iran. A civilization began there in the late 4th millennium BC, and in the early 2nd millennium BC Elam overthrew Babylonia. Its golden age came after 1300 BC. Around 645 BC Elam fell to the Assyrian king ASSURBANIPAL. Its capital was Susa.

**eland:** see ANTELOPE.

**elasticity:** see STRENGTH OF MATERIALS.

**elastic limit:** see STRENGTH OF MATERIALS.

**Elat** or **Eilat,** city (1986 est. pop. 22,700), S Israel, a port at the head of the Gulf of AQABA. It is strategically located near Egypt, Jordan, and Saudi Arabia and is Israel's gateway to Africa and the Far East. The city is a centre for tourism and small industry. An ancient port (perhaps identical with the 10th-cent. Ezion-geber), Elat was resettled in 1949, and its deepwater harbour was opened in 1965.

**Elba,** island, 223 km² (86 sq mi), in the Tyrrhenian Sea, 9.7 km (6 mi) W of the Italian peninsula. Controlled at times by Pisa, Spain, and Naples, it was an independent principality (1814–15) under the exiled NAPOLEON I prior to his escape and return to France. Following his final defeat, Elba passed to TUSCANY.

**Elbe,** river, central Europe, flowing c.1170 km (725 mi) from NW Czechoslovakia and through East Germany before entering the North Sea through a 97-km (60-mi), two-armed estuary at Cuxhaven, West Germany. Navigable for c.845 km (525 mi), the river was internationalized in 1919. Traffic declined after Germany repudiated (1938) internationalization, and the division of Germany (1945) made the river part of the boundary between East and West Germany.

**Elbrus, Mount,** highest mountain of the CAUCASUS, SW USSR, considered the highest point in Europe by those who regard the area as part of that continent. Its twin peaks are extinct volcanic cones 5633 m (18,481 ft) and 5595 m (18,356 ft) high.

**Elburz Mountains,** mountain range of N Iran, extending 800 km (500 mi) from Ardabil to Gorgan, between the CASPIAN SEA and the central Iranian plateau. It has an average width of 100 km (60 mi), and its highest peak is Mt Demavend (5601 m/18,370 ft). The northern slopes are rainy and forested; the southern slopes are steppe and desert.

**El Cordobés** (el kawdoh͵vays), 1936?–, Spanish bullfighter; b. Manuel Benítez Pérez. The highest paid matador in history, he rose to national fame in the early 1960s because of his courage and personal magnetism. He retired in 1971.

**elder,** in botany, common name for shrub or small tree (*Sambucus nigra*) of the HONEYSUCKLE family. Flowers and FRUITS are widely used for wine-making. All parts of the plant have a purgative action.

**elder,** in anthropology, person in whom authority and power is vested in a LINEAGE group. The eldest men in the lineage have control over the allocation of labour, over goods produced, distributed, and exchanged, and over certain forms of knowledge. They are in charge of marriage exchanges and of ritual and/or worship. In the Presbyterian Church the elder is a key lay officer.

**El Dorado,** legendary land of the Golden Man, a place of gold and plenty sought by Spanish CONQUISTADORS in the New World from the early 16th cent. Its location shifted as new regions were explored. Similar legends appeared in the W US.

**Eleanor of Aquitaine,** 1122–1204, queen consort first of LOUIS VII of France and then of HENRY II of England; daughter of William X, duke of Aquitaine. Her marriage to Louis was annulled in 1152 and shortly thereafter she married Henry, then duke of Normandy, uniting her vast possessions with his. Two of her sons RICHARD I and JOHN became kings of England. Henry's many infidelities caused her to establish her own court (1170) at Poitiers, which became the scene of much artistic activity. She supported her sons in their unsuccessful revolt (1173) against Henry and was confined by Henry until his death. In 1189 she helped Richard secure the throne.

**electors,** the German princes who had the right to elect the German king, who was generally crowned emperor (see HOLY ROMAN EMPIRE). The number of electors varied, but in 1356 Emperor CHARLES IV issued the Golden Bull, an edict that regularized election procedures and named the electors as the archbishops of Cologne, Mainz, and Trier, the king of Bohemia, the count palatine of the Rhine, the duke of Saxony, and the margrave of Brandenburg. Later, the duke of Bavaria and the ruler of Hanover were added. After 1438 only members of the house of HABSBURG were elected. The electoral function disappeared with the end of the Holy Roman Empire in 1806.

**Electra,** in Greek mythology, daughter of AGAMEMNON and CLYTEMNESTRA. She aided her brother ORESTES in avenging the murder of their father by their mother and AEGISTHUS. The tale was dramatized by AESCHYLUS, SOPHOCLES, and EURIPIDES. It is also the subject of Eugene O'NEILL's play *Mourning Becomes Electra* (1931) and the opera *Elektra* (1909) by Hugo von HOFMANNSTHAL and Richard STRAUSS.

**electric and magnetic units,** units used to express the magnitudes of various quantities in electricity and magnetism. The SI system of units (based on mks units; see METRIC SYSTEM) is commonly used for all scientific and technical work. The basic electrical unit is the AMPERE (for electric current); others are the VOLT (for POTENTIAL), OHM (for RESISTANCE), WATT (for POWER), farad (for CAPACITANCE), and HENRY (for INDUCTANCE). Two other systems, now nearly abandoned but used on occasions, are both based on the cgs system. Electrostatic units (cgs-esu) are defined in a way that simplifies the description of interactions between static electric charges; there are no corresponding magnetic units in this system. Electromagnetic units (cgs-emu), on the other hand, are defined especially for the description of phenomena associated with moving electric charges, i.e., electric currents and magnetic poles.

**electric circuit,** path along which an electric current may flow. The simplest example is in domestic wiring where the supply through the meter switch and fuses is wired to lights and power sockets made active by individual switches. More complex circuitry involves the three passive elements, resistors, conductors, and capacitors, together with switch diodes and transistors. They may all be fabricated on a small silicon chip. LOGIC CIRCUITS comprise an arrangement of gates and FLIP-FLOPS which perform the logical functions required in computing.

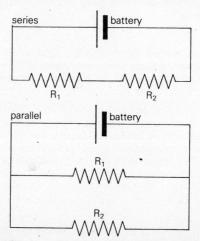

Electric circuit

**electric fish,** any of many unrelated species of FISH that have electric organs, usually made of modified muscle tissue, that are capable of producing from 450 to 600 volts of electricity. This electricity is used to detect and paralyse prey, repel enemies, navigate, and possibly communicate. Important electric fish include the electric EEL, the electric CATFISH, and the electric RAY, or torpedo.

**electricity,** class of phenomena arising from the existence of CHARGE. According to modern theory, most ELEMENTARY PARTICLES of matter possess charge, either positive or negative. Two particles of like charge, both positive or both negative, repel each other; two particles of unlike charge are attracted (see COULOMB'S LAW). The electric FORCE between two charged particles is much greater than the gravitational force between the particles. Many of the bulk properties of matter are ultimately due to the electric forces among the particles of which the substance is composed. Materials differ in their ability to allow charge to flow through them. Those that allow charge to pass easily are conductors (see CONDUCTION), whereas those that allow extremely little charge to pass through are called insulators (see INSULATION), or DIELECTRICS. A third class of materials, called SEMICONDUCTORS, is intermediate. Electrostatics is the study of charges, or charged bodies, at rest. When positive or negative charge builds up in fixed positions on objects, certain phenomena can be observed that are collectively referred to as static electricity. The charge can be built up by rubbing certain objects together, such as silk and glass or rubber and fur; the friction between these objects causes electrons to transfer from one to another with the result that the object losing electrons acquires a positive charge and the object gaining electrons acquires a negative charge (see ELECTRON). Electrodynamics is the study of charges in motion. A flow of electric charge constitutes an electric current. In order for a current to exist in a conductor, there must be an ELECTROMOTIVE FORCE (emf), or difference in POTENTIAL, between the conductor's ends. An electric CELL, a PHOTOVOLTAIC CELL, and a GENERATOR are all sources of emf. An emf source with an external conductor connected from one of the source's two terminals to the other constitutes an ELECTRIC CIRCUIT. Direct current (DC) is a flow of current in one direction at a constant rate. Alternating current (AC) is a current flow that increases in magnitude from zero to a maximum, decreases back to zero, increases to a maximum in the opposite direction, decreases to zero, and then repeats this process periodically. The number of repetitions of the cycle occurring each second is defined as the FREQUENCY, which is expressed in hertz (Hz). The frequency of ordinary household current in the UK is 50 cycles per sec (50 Hz), and electrical devices must be designed to operate at this frequency. In a solid, the current consists not of a few electrons moving rapidly but of many electrons moving slowly; although this drift of electrons is slow, the impulse that causes it moves through the circuit, when the circuit is completed, at nearly the speed of light. The movement of electrons in a current is not steady; each electron moves in a series of stops and starts. In a direct current, the electrons are spread evenly through the conductor; in an alternating current, the electrons tend to congregate along the conductor surface. In liquids, gases, and semiconductors, current carriers may be positively or negatively charged.

**electrocardiography,** science of recording and interpreting the electrical activity of the HEART by means of a device called an electrocardiograph. Electrodes (leads) attached to the extremities and the left side of the chest pick up electrical currents from heart muscle contractions. The currents are registered in wave patterns on an electrocardiogram (ECG) which may be analysed automatically by computer. Deviations in the normal height, form, or duration of the wave patterns indicate specific disorders, so the ECG is an important aid in diagnosing many heart diseases. The first practical device for recording the activity of the heart was developed by W. EINTHOVEN in 1903, for which he won (1924) the Nobel Prize for physiology or medicine.

**electrochemistry,** science dealing with the relationship between electricity and chemical changes; it was founded by the pioneering work of VOLTA, GALVANI, DAVY, and especially FARADAY. Of principal interest are the reactions that take place between ELECTRODE and the ELECTROLYTE in electric and electrolytic cells (see ELECTROLYSIS), and that take place in an electrolyte as electricity passes through it.

**electroconvulsive therapy** (ECT), treatment of severe mental disorders with electricity to produce convulsions. Although there is no general agreement as to the overall value of ECT, and there are many who strongly oppose its use, it has been used successfully in certain types of DEPRESSION. ECT has now largely been replaced by tranquillizing drugs (see TRANQUILLIZER).

**electrode,** terminal, usually in the form of a wire, rod, or plate, through which electric current passes between metallic and nonmetallic parts of an ELECTRIC CIRCUIT. The electrode through which current passes from the metallic to the nonmetallic conductor is called the anode; that through which current passes from the nonmetallic to the metallic conductor is called the cathode. An electrode may be made of a metal, e.g., copper, lead, platinum, silver, or zinc, or of a nonmetal, commonly carbon.

**electroencephalography,** science of recording and analysing the electrical activity of the BRAIN. The recording, known as an electroencephalogram, or EEG, is made through electrodes by an electroencephalograph and appears as characteristic wave patterns. An important aid in diagnosing brain disorders and malfunctions, it has contributed to understanding normal brain function, SLEEP, the effects of drugs, and such activities as BIOFEEDBACK. The electrical activity of the brain was first demonstrated by the German psychiatrist Hans Berger in 1929.

**electrolysis,** passage of an electric current through a conducting solution or molten salt (either is a type of ELECTROLYTE) that is decomposed in the process. When a cathode, or negative electrode, and an anode, or positive electrode, are dipped into a solution, and a direct-current source is connected to the electrodes, the positive ions migrate to the negative electrode and the negative ions migrate to the positive electrode. At the negative electrode each positive ion gains an electron and becomes neutral; at the positive electrode each negative ion gives up an electron and becomes neutral. The migration of ions through the electrolyte constitutes the electric current flowing from one electrode to the other. Electrolysis is used in the commercial preparation of various substances, e.g., chlorine by the electrolysis of a solution of common salt, and hydrogen by the electrolysis of water. The electrolysis of metal salts is used for plating. In the early 1830s Michael FARADAY reported his discovery by experiment of the fundamental laws of electrolysis, which state: (1) the mass of a substance produced by a cathode or anode reaction in electrolysis is directly proportional to the quantity of electricity passed through the cell; and (2) the masses of different substances produced by the same quantity of electricity are proportional to the equivalent masses of the substances. See also ELECTROCHEMISTRY.

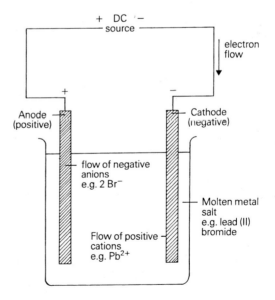

Electrolysis

**electrolyte,** electrical conductor in which current is carried by IONS rather than free electrons (as in a metal). Electrolytes include water solutions of acids, bases (see ACIDS AND BASES), or SALTS; certain pure liquids; and molten salts. See also ELECTROLYSIS.

**electromagnet,** device in which an electric current, passing through a wire coil wrapped around a soft iron core, produces a magnetic field. The magnetic-field strength produced depends on the number of turns of the coil of wire, the size of the current, and the magnetic permeability of the core. Electromagnets lose their magnetism when the current is discontinued. See also SUPERCONDUCTIVITY.

**electromagnetic radiation,** energy radiated in the form of a WAVE comprising an electric field combined with a magnetic field. Electromagnetic radiation is the result of the acceleration of a charged particle. It does not require a material medium, and can travel through a vacuum. The theory of electromagnetic radiation was developed by James Clerk MAXWELL and published in 1865, although his ideas were not accepted until Heinrich HERTZ proved the existence of radio waves in 1887. In order of decreasing wavelength and increasing frequency, the various types of electromagnetic radiation are RADIO waves, MICROWAVES, INFRARED RADIATION, visible LIGHT, ULTRAVIOLET RADIATION, X-RAYS, and GAMMA DECAY. The possible sources of electromagnetic radiation are directly related to wavelength; long radio waves are produced by large antennas such as those used by broadcasting stations; much shorter, visible light waves are produced by the motion of charges within atoms; the shortest waves, those of gamma radiation, result from changes within the nucleus of the atom. The individual quantum of electromagnetic radiation is known as the PHOTON.

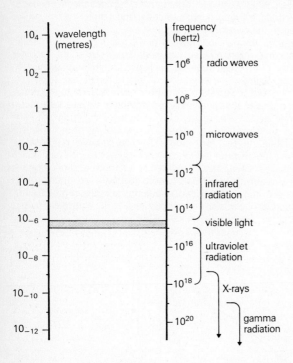

Electromagnetic radiation

**electromotive force** (emf), difference in electric POTENTIAL, or voltage, between the terminals of a source of electricity. The unit of measurement is usually the VOLT.

**electron,** ELEMENTARY PARTICLE carrying a negative electric CHARGE of magnitude *e* and an intrinsic SPIN of magnitude ½ (in unit of $h/2\Pi$). An ATOM consists of a small, dense, positively charged nucleus surrounded by moving electrons that form a cloud of CHARGE. Ordinarily there are just enough negative electrons to balance the positive charge of the nucleus, and the atom is neutral. If electrons are added or removed, a net charge results, and the atom is said to be ionized (see ION). Atomic electrons are responsible for the chemical properties of matter (see VALENCY). The electron was discovered in 1897 by Joseph John THOMSON, who showed that cathode rays are composed of the particles now called electrons. The electron is the lightest known particle having a non-zero rest mass. The positron, the electron's antiparticle (see ANTIMATTER), was discovered in 1932.

**electronegativity,** in chemistry, tendency for an atom to attract a pair of electrons that it shares with another atom. If the pair of electrons is not shared equally, i.e., if they spend more time with one atom than with the other atom, the favoured atom is said to be more electronegative. Nonmetals have much higher electronegativities than metals; of the nonmetals, fluorine is the most electronegative, followed by oxygen, nitrogen, and chlorine.

**electronic game,** device that challenges eye–hand coordination in a setting designed to provide entertainment and, sometimes, education. Made possible by the development of the MICROPROCESSOR, electronic games are marketed in various sizes, such as hand-held, one-player models, home-video types consisting of cartridges that are inserted in modules attached to television sets, and freestanding arcade versions. Most of their appeal comes from the COMPUTER PROGRAM that synchronizes flashing lights and a variety of rhythmic auditory stimuli with the action portrayed on a graphic display (see COMPUTER GRAPHICS). The games may be contested among several players, or an individual may engage in a test of skill against the COMPUTER. Game subjects include sports (e.g., baseball and football); action warfare, often space-oriented; and such classics as contract bridge, chess, and poker.

**electronic music,** term applied to compositions whose sounds are either produced or modified electronically. The early examples of electronic compositions, called concrete music, were taped montages of electronically altered sound obtained by microphone from nonelectronic sources, such as voices and street noise. After the perfection of the tape recorder in the 1940s, music was composed with tones that were electronically produced as well as electronically manipulated. In 1955 the synthesizer was developed, a single unit with numerous generating and modifying capacities that enable composers to generate new sounds and to combine these sounds with great precision. Contemporary composers of electronic music include Karlheinz STOCKHAUSEN, Luciano BERIO, and Pierre BOULEZ. Since the 1950s, composers such as John CAGE, Milton BABBITT, and others have also experimented with COMPUTER-generated music. Many rock musicians play electronic instruments, i.e., the instrument is connected to an amplifier and its sound is fed through speakers (see ROCK MUSIC).

**electronics,** a branch of electrical engineering; the science and technology based on and concerned with the controlled flow of electrons or other carriers of electric charge, especially in the ELECTRON TUBE and SEMICONDUCTOR devices. The miniaturization (see MICROELECTRONICS) and savings in power brought about by the invention (1948) of the TRANSISTOR and the subsequent development of the INTEGRATED CIRCUIT have allowed ELECTRIC CIRCUITS to be packaged more densely, making possible compact computers, advanced RADAR and navigation systems, more reliable RADIO and TELEVISION receivers, advanced sound-reproducing systems, and electronic automotive accessories.

**electron microscope,** instrument that produces a highly magnified image of a small object, using an accelerated electron beam held within a vacuum to illuminate the object, and electromagnetic fields to magnify and focus the image. (By contrast, the optical MICROSCOPE uses visual light for illumination, and glass lenses for magnifying and focusing.) First developed in Germany c.1932, the transmission electron microscope exploits the very short (de BROGLIE) wavelengths of accelerated electrons, which are thousands of times shorter than those of light, to magnify an object up to one million times without losing definition. Images produced by the microscope are thrown onto a fluorescent screen or are photographed. The more recently developed scanning electron microscope constructs an image on a CATHODE-RAY TUBE as the surface of a specimen is gradually scanned by the electron beam, as in a television system.

**electron tube** or **thermionic valve,** device consisting of a sealed enclosure in which electrons flow between ELECTRODES separated either by vacuum (in a vacuum tube) or by an ionized gas at low pressure (in a gas tube). The two principal electrodes of an electron tube are called the anode and cathode. The simplest vacuum tube, the DIODE, contains only these two electrodes. When the cathode is heated, it emits a cloud of electrons, which are attracted to the positive polarity of the anode and constitute the current through the tube. Because the anode is not capable of emitting electrons, no current can flow in the reverse direction, and the diode acts as a RECTIFIER. In the vacuum triode, small signals applied to a third electrode, called a grid, placed between the cathode and anode cause large fluctuations in the current between the cathode and anode. A triode can thus act as a signal AMPLIFIER. Although formerly the key elements of ELECTRIC CIRCUITS, electron tubes have been almost entirely displaced by SEMICONDUCTOR devices. See also CATHODE-RAY TUBE.

**electron-volt** (eV), unit of ENERGY used in atomic, nuclear and elementary particle physics; 1 eV is the energy transferred in moving an electric charge, positive or negative and equal in magnitude to the charge of the electron, through a potential difference of 1 V. 1 eV = $1.60 \times 10^{-19}$ J. In nuclear physics energies are measured in MeV (= $10^6$ eV), and in elementary particle physics in GeV (= $10^9$ eV).

**electroweak interaction:** see UNIFIED THEORIES.

**electrum,** an ALLOY or solid SOLUTION of silver in gold. It occurs naturally and can be readily made by mixing aliquots of the two metals in the melt. The ancient Egyptians varied the hue of gold by converting it to electrum.

**elegy,** in Greek and Roman poetry, type of verse (in hexameter and pentameter couplets), written by THEOCRITUS, OVID, CATULLUS, and others; in English, a reflective poem of lamentation or regret, of no set metrical form, mourning one person, e.g., P.B. SHELLEY's 'Adonais', or all mankind, e.g., Thomas GRAY's 'Elegy in a Country Churchyard'. The pastoral elegy, of which John MILTON's 'Lycidas' is the best known, has a classical pastoral setting.

**element,** in chemistry, substance composed of ATOMS all having the same number of PROTONS in their nuclei. This number, called the ATOMIC NUMBER, defines the element and establishes its place in the PERIODIC TABLE. Each element is assigned a symbol of one or two letters (see table). The total number of protons and NEUTRONS in the nucleus of an atom is called the MASS NUMBER. Although all atoms of an element have the same number of protons in their nuclei, they may not all have the same number of neutrons. Atoms of an element with the same mass number make up an ISOTOPE of the element. All elements have isotopes; over 1000 isotopes of the elements are known. As of 1982, 108 elements were known. Only 92 elements occur naturally on earth; the others are produced artificially (see SYNTHETIC ELEMENTS; TRANSURANIC ELEMENTS). The chemical properties of an element are due to the distribution of electrons around the nucleus, particularly the outer, or VALENCY, electrons (the ones involved in chemical reactions). Chemical reaction does not affect the nucleus and thus does not change the atomic number. For this reason an element is often defined as a substance that cannot be decomposed into simpler substances by chemical means. See also ATOMIC WEIGHT; COMPOUND; MOLECULE.

**elementary particles,** very small bits of matter assumed to be the most basic constituents of the universe. Certain elementary particles combine to form an ATOM, which is the basic unit of any chemical ELEMENT and from which all forms of naturally occurring matter are built. The first elementary particle to be discovered was the ELECTRON, identified in 1897 by Joseph John THOMSON. The nucleus of ordinary hydrogen was subsequently recognized as a single particle and was named the PROTON. The third basic particle in an atom, the NEUTRON, was discovered in 1932. Neutrons and protons are the basic constituents of the atomic NUCLEUS. Although models of the atom consisting of just these three particles are sufficient to account for all forms of chemical behaviour of matter, QUANTUM THEORY predicted the existence of additional elementary particles. A search for the positron, or antiparticle (see ANTIMATTER) of the electron, led to its detection in 1932, but a search for a particle predicted by YUKAWA in 1935 led to the unexpected discovery of the mu meson, or muon, the following year. Yukawa's particle was finally discovered in 1947 and named the pi meson, or pion. Both the muon and the pion were first observed in COSMIC RAYS. As the list of particles and antiparticles grew, through further study of cosmic rays and the study of the results of particle collisions produced by the PARTICLE ACCELERATOR, four basic categories of particles were distinguished, according to their SPIN and their behaviour with regard to the four fundamental forces or interactions of nature: gravitational, electromagnetic, strong, and weak. The electromagnetic interaction is experienced only by particles having an electric CHARGE or a magnetic moment (see MAGNETISM). It is transmitted by the PHOTON. The strong interaction, which is transmitted by gluons, and the weak interaction are very short ranged and are only experienced over nuclear distances. Of the four classes of particles, the smallest is that of the massless bosons, which include the photon, eight types of gluons, and the hypothetical graviton (hypothesized to transmit the gravitational interaction). The lepton class includes 12 particles: the electron, the positron, the positive and negative muons, the tauon and its antiparticle, and the neutrino or antineutrino associated with each of these particles.

The leptons all have spin ½ and are not strongly interacting. Members of the meson class are more massive than the leptons and have integer spins; the lightest member of this class is the pion. The largest class comprises the baryons which have half-integer spins and include as the lightest members the PROTON and the NEUTRON; the heavier members are known as hyperons. Baryons and mesons experience both the strong and the weak interactions and are referred to collectively as hadrons. A theory independently proposed in 1964 by Murray Gell-Mann and George Zweig explains the properties of all known hadrons according to the assumption that hadrons are built up of other, still more fundamental particles called QUARKS.

**elephant,** largest living land MAMMAL, of Africa and Asia. It has a massive head, thick legs, and tough, grey skin. The upper lip extends into a long, flexible trunk used for drinking, spraying, conveying food to the mouth, and touching; the large ears provide an extensive cooling surface. African bull elephants may measure 4 m (13 ft) high at the shoulder and weigh 5500–7000 kg (6–8 tons). Hunted for their great, curved ivory tusks, they have become endangered. Highly intelligent, Indian elephants are used in foresting and trained as circus and zoo performers. See also MAMMOTH, MASTODON.

Indian elephant

African elephant

Elephant

**elephantiasis,** gross enlargement of any part of the body due to obstruction of the lymph vessels (see LYMPHATIC SYSTEM). Characteristically, the legs or scrotum are affected. In tropical countries, the most common cause is filariasis, obstruction of the lymph vessels by small parasitic roundworms.

**Eleusinian Mysteries,** principal religious MYSTERIES of ancient Greece, held at ELEUSIS. The secret rites, which celebrated the abduction of PERSEPHONE and her return to her mother DEMETER, symbolized the annual cycle of death and rebirth in nature, as well as the immortality of the soul. DIONYSUS was also much honoured at the festival.

**Eleusis** (i,loohsis), ancient city of Attica, GREECE, NW of ATHENS. It was the seat of the ELEUSINIAN MYSTERIES, dedicated to DEMETER. The Eleusinian games were also held there.

**El Faiyûm:** see FAIYÛM.

**Elgar, Sir Edward William,** 1857–1934, English composer. Among his outstanding compositions are *Variations on an Original Theme* (or *Enigma Variations,* 1899), *The Dream of Gerontius* (1900), two symphonies (1908 and 1911), the *Pomp and Circumstance* marches, the Violin and Cello Concertos (1910 and 1919), and a String Quartet and Piano Quintet (1919).

**Elgin, Thomas Bruce,** 7th **earl of,** 1766–1841, British diplomat. While on a diplomatic mission in Constantinople (1799–1803), he arranged for the so-called ELGIN MARBLES to be brought to England. His son **James Bruce,** 8th earl of Elgin, 1811–63, was governor-general of Canada (1847–54). He implemented the plan for responsible government outlined by his father-in-law, the earl of DURHAM, and personally negotiated the reciprocity treaty of 1854 with the US. His son, **Victor Alexander Bruce,** 9th earl of Elgin, 1849–1917, was viceroy of India (1894–99) and colonial secretary (1905–08).

**Elgin Marbles,** ancient sculpture taken from the Acropolis of Athens to England in 1806 by Thomas Bruce, 7th earl of Elgin. The PARTHENON frieze and sculpture from the pediments by PHIDIAS are on view at the British

## ELEMENTS

| Element | Symbol | Atomic Number | Atomic Weight[1] | Melting Point (Degrees Centigrade) | Boiling Point (Degrees Centigrade) |
|---|---|---|---|---|---|
| actinium | Ac | 89 | 227.0278 | 1050. | 3200. $\pm$ 300 |
| aluminium | Al | 13 | 26.98154 | 660.37 | 2467. |
| americium | Am | 95 | (243) | 994. $\pm$ 4 | 2607. |
| antimony | Sb | 51 | 121.75 | 630.74 | 1950. |
| argon | Ar | 18 | 39.948 | $-189.2$ | $-185.7$ |
| arsenic | As | 33 | 74.9216 | 817. (28 atmospheres) | 613. (sublimates) |
| astatine | At | 85 | (210) | 302. (est.) | 337. (est.) |
| barium | Ba | 56 | 137.33 | 725. | 1640. |
| berkelium | Bk | 97 | (247) | – | – |
| beryllium | Be | 4 | 9.01218 | 1278. $\pm$ 5 | 2970. |
| bismuth | Bi | 83 | 208.9804 | 271.3 | 1560. $\pm$ 5 |
| boron | B | 5 | 10.81 | 2079. | 2550. (sublimates) |
| bromine | Br | 35 | 79.904 | $-7.2$ | 58.78 |
| cadmium | Cd | 48 | 112.41 | 320.9 | 765. |
| calcium | Ca | 20 | 40.08 | 839. $\pm$ 2 | 1484. |
| californium | Cf | 98 | (251) | – | – |
| carbon | C | 6 | 12.011 | $\sim$3550. | 4827. |
| cerium | Ce | 58 | 140.12 | 799. | 3426. |
| caesium | Cs | 55 | 132.9054 | 28.40 | 669.3 |
| chlorine | Cl | 17 | 35.453 | $-100.98$ | $-34.6$ |
| chromium | Cr | 24 | 51.996 | 1857. $\pm$ 20 | 2672. |
| cobalt | Co | 27 | 58.9332 | 1495. | 2870. |
| copper | Cu | 29 | 63.546 | 1083.4 $\pm$ 0.2 | 2567. |
| curium | Cm | 96 | (247) | 1340. $\pm$ 40 | – |
| dysprosium | Dy | 66 | 162.50 | 1412. | 2562. |
| einsteinium | Es | 99 | (252) | – | – |
| erbium | Er | 68 | 167.26 | 1522. | 2863. |
| europium | Eu | 63 | 151.96 | 822. | 1597. |
| fermium | Fm | 100 | (257) | – | – |
| fluorine | F | 9 | 18.998403 | $-219.62$ | $-188.14$ |
| francium | Fr | 87 | (223) | (27) (est.) | (677) (est.) |
| gadolinium | Gd | 64 | 157.25 | 1313. $\pm$ 1 | 3266. |
| gallium | Ga | 31 | 69.72 | 29.78 | 2403. |
| germanium | Ge | 32 | 72.59 | 937.4 | 2830. |
| gold | Au | 79 | 196.9665 | 1064.43 | 3080. |
| hafnium | Hf | 72 | 178.49 | 2227. $\pm$ 20 | 4602. |
| helium | He | 2 | 4.00260 | $< -272.2$ | $-268.934$ |
| holmium | Ho | 67 | 164.9304 | 1474. | 2695. |
| hydrogen | H | 1 | 1.00794 | $-259.14$ | $-252.87$ |
| indium | In | 49 | 114.82 | 156.61 | 2080. |
| iodine | I | 53 | 126.9045 | 113.5 | 184.35 |
| iridium | Ir | 77 | 192.22 | 2410. | 4130. |
| iron | Fe | 26 | 55.847 | 1535. | 2750. |
| krypton | Kr | 36 | 83.80 | $-156.6$ | $-152.30 \pm 0.10$ |
| lanthanum | La | 57 | 138.9055 | 921. | 3457. |
| lawrencium | Lw | 103 | (260) | – | – |
| lead | Pb | 82 | 207.2 | 327.502 | 1740. |
| lithium | Li | 3 | 6.941 | 180.54 | 1342. |
| lutetium | Lu | 71 | 174.967 | 1663. | 3395. |
| magnesium | Mg | 12 | 24.305 | 648.8 $\pm$ 0.5 | 1090. |
| manganese | Mn | 25 | 54.9380 | 1244. $\pm$ 3 | 1962. |
| mendelevium | Md | 101 | (258) | – | – |
| mercury | Hg | 80 | 200.59 | $-38.842$ | 356.58 |
| molybdenum | Mo | 42 | 95.94 | 2617. | 4612. |

[1] Parentheses indicate most stable isotope.

Museum; there is pressure from the Greek government for them to be returned.

**El Giza:** see GIZA.

**El Greco:** see GRECO, EL.

**Elijah** or **Elias,** fl. c.875 BC, Hebrew PROPHET in the reign of King AHAB and an outstanding figure in the OLD TESTAMENT. Elijah's mission was to

## ELEMENTS *(Continued)*

| Element | Symbol | Atomic Number | Atomic Weight[1] | Melting Point (Degrees Centigrade) | Boiling Point (Degrees Centigrade) |
|---|---|---|---|---|---|
| neodymium | Nd | 60 | 144.24 | 1021. | 3068. |
| neon | Ne | 10 | 20.179 | −248.67 | −246.048 |
| neptunium | Np | 93 | 237.0482 | 640. ± 1 | 3902. (est.) |
| nickel | Ni | 28 | 58.69 | 1453. | 2732. |
| niobium | Nb | 41 | 92.9064 | 2468. ± 10 | 4742. |
| nitrogen | N | 7 | 14.0067 | −209.86 | −195.8 |
| nobelium | No | 102 | (259) | − | − |
| osmium | Os | 76 | 190.2 | 3045. ± 30 | 5027. ± 100 |
| oxygen | O | 8 | 15.9994 | −218.4 | −182.962 |
| palladium | Pd | 46 | 106.42 | 1554. | 2970. |
| phosphorus | P | 15 | 30.97376 | 44.1 (white) | 280. (white) |
| platinum | Pt | 78 | 195.08 | 1772. | 3827. ± 100 |
| plutonium | Pu | 94 | (244) | 641. | 3232. |
| polonium | Po | 84 | (209) | 254. | 962. |
| potassium | K | 19 | 39.0983 | 63.25 | 760. |
| praseodymium | Pr | 59 | 140.9077 | 931. | 3512. |
| promethium | Pm | 61 | (145) | ∼1168. ± 6 | 2460. |
| protactinium | Pa | 91 | 231.0359 | < 1600. | − |
| radium | Ra | 88 | 226.0254 | 700. | 1140. |
| radon | Rn | 86 | (222) | −71. | −61.8 |
| rhenium | Re | 75 | 186.207 | 3180. | 5627. (est.) |
| rhodium | Rh | 45 | 102.9055 | 1966. ± 3 | 3727. ± 100 |
| rubidium | Rb | 37 | 85.4678 | 38.89 | 686. |
| ruthenium | Ru | 44 | 101.07 | 2310. | 3900. |
| samarium | Sm | 62 | 150.36 | 1072. ± 5 | 1791. |
| scandium | Sc | 21 | 44.9559 | 1541. | 2831. |
| selenium | Se | 34 | 78.96 | 217. | 684.9 ± 1.0 |
| silicon | Si | 14 | 28.0855 | 1410. | 2355. |
| silver | Ag | 47 | 107.8682 | 961.93 | 2212. |
| sodium | Na | 11 | 22.98977 | 97.81 ± 0.03 | 882.9 |
| strontium | Sr | 38 | 87.62 | 769. | 1384. |
| sulphur | S | 16 | 32.06 | 112.8 | 444.674 |
| tantalum | Ta | 73 | 180.9479 | 2996. | 5425. ± 100 |
| technetium | Tc | 43 | (98) | 2172. | 4877. |
| tellurium | Te | 52 | 127.60 | 449.5 ± 0.3 | 989.8 ± 3.8 |
| terbium | Tb | 65 | 158.9254 | 1356. | 3123. |
| thallium | Tl | 81 | 204.383 | 303.5 | 1457. ± 10 |
| thorium | Th | 90 | 232.0381 | 1750. | ∼4790. |
| thulium | Tm | 69 | 168.9342 | 1545. ± 15 | 1947. |
| tin | Sn | 50 | 118.69 | 231.9681 | 2270. |
| titanium | Ti | 22 | 47.88 | 1660. ± 10 | 3287. |
| tungsten | W | 74 | 183.85 | 3410. ± 20 | 5660. |
| unnilennium | Une | 109 | (266) | − | − |
| unnilhexium | Unh | 106 | (263) | − | − |
| unnilpentium[2] | Unp | 105 | (262) | − | − |
| unnilquadium[3] | Unq | 104 | (261) | − | − |
| unnilseptium | Uns | 107 | (262) | − | − |
| uranium | U | 92 | 238.0289 | 1132.3 ± 0.8 | 3818. |
| vanadium | V | 23 | 50.9415 | 1890. ± 10 | 3380. |
| xenon | Xe | 54 | 131.29 | −111.9 | −107.1 ± 3 |
| ytterbium | Yb | 70 | 173.04 | 819. | 1194. |
| yttrium | Y | 39 | 88.9059 | 1522. ± 8 | 3338. |
| zinc | Zn | 30 | 65.38 | 419.58 | 907. |
| zirconium | Zr | 40 | 91.22 | 1852. ± 2 | 4377. |

[1] *Parentheses indicate most stable isotope.*
[2] *Other proposed names are nielsbohrium (USSR) and hahnium (US).*
[3] *Other proposed names are kurchatovium (USSR) and rutherfordium (US).*

destroy the worship of foreign gods and to restore justice, and his zeal brought about a temporary banishment of idolatry. His story in the Bible has many incidents, such as his raising the widow's son from the dead, his being fed by ravens, his experience of the still, small voice on Mt Horeb, and his departure from earth in a chariot of fire enveloped in a whirlwind. 1 Kings 17–19; 21; 2 Kings 1–2. His disciple was ELISHA. In

Elgin Marbles: Horsemen in panathenaic procession, North frieze of Parthenon XXXIX, c.440 BC.

Jewish tradition, Elijah is the herald of the MESSIAH. He is also prominent in the KORAN.

**Elijah ben Solomon,** 1720–97, Jewish scholar, called the Gaon [Eminence] of Vilna; b. Lithuania. Although a student of the KABBALAH, he fought the spread of HASIDISM among the Jews of Lithuania and Poland, fearing that it would weaken the Jewish community. His major writings were on the HALAKAH.

**Elin Pelin,** pseud. of **Dimitr Ivanov,** 1878–1949, Bulgarian prose writer. He was a patriotic satirist, but also a master of characterization, e.g. in his *Tales* (1904–11). He also wrote compelling studies of peasant life, e.g., *Soil* (1922).

**Eliot, George,** pseud. of **Mary Ann** or **Marian Evans,** 1819–80, English novelist. She defied convention to live with G.H. LEWES till his death in 1878. Two years later she married Walter Cross, 20 years her junior; she died seven months later. Starting as a translator from the German to the *Westminster Review,* she first made a name (the pseudonym George Eliot) with *Scenes of Clerical Life* (1857). *Adam Bede* (1859) established her as a major novelist of powerful intellect, and was followed by *The Mill on the Floss* (1860), *Silas Marner* (1861), *Romola* (1862–63), *Felix Holt* (1866), her masterpiece *Middlemarch* (1871–72) and *Daniel Deronda* (1874–76). English rural communities were the scene of most of her novels, and the individual's moral responsibility and integrity were her main themes. Her reputation waned after her death, but she is now rated among the greatest English novelists. She edited and contributed to the *Westminster Review.*

**Eliot, T(homas) S(tearns),** 1888–1965, English poet, one of the most influential literary figures of the 20th cent.; b. St Louis, US. Living in London from 1914, he became a British subject in 1927, the same year he espoused Anglo-Catholicism. He was associated with the periodicals *The Egoist* (1917–19) and his own *Criterion* (1922–39), and he had an active career in publishing. Eliot's early poems *Prufrock and Other Observations* (1917), *Poems* (1920), and *The Waste Land* (1922) express the anguish and barrenness of modern life. Breaking completely with the Victorian and Edwardian poetic tradition, they drew on the 17th-cent. METAPHYSICAL POETS, along with DANTE, Jacobean drama, and the French SYMBOLISTS. The complex, meditative later verse of *Ash Wednesday* (1930) and *Four Quartets* (1935–42) reflects his religious conversion. He explored the relationship of poetry and society in critical books such as *The Sacred Wood* (1920), *Selected Essays* (1932), and *Notes Towards the Definition of Culture* (1948). His plays, attempts to revitalize the verse drama, include *Murder in the Cathedral* (1935), *The Family Reunion* (1939), and *The Cocktail Party* (1950). He was awarded the 1948 Nobel Prize in literature.

**Elisabeth:** see ELIZABETH.

**Elisha** or **Eliseus** (ee‚lieshə, eli‚seeəs), Hebrew prophet. He continued the work of ELIJAH, but was more diplomatic and of a milder nature. Unlike Elijah, he headed a band of prophets. 2 Kings 1–13.

**elite,** a minority group who occupy a privileged position in the institutional orders of society and who are socially recognized as superior in some way (the managerial or military elites, the government, industrial or union leaderships). The essential issue is whether democracies are open political and economic structures or whether they are governed by one or more self-perpetuating elite groups (though the notion of an elite group need not indicate complete social isolation from the rest of society). Some elite-group theorists have seen the ease of entry into elite groups as an indicator of their compatibility with democracy. Although the terms elite and CLASS are often used interchangeably, they should not be confused: elites need not be united by a common economic interest and are normally identified more by their ability to exercise power. Traditionally America has been seen as a society that is ruled by various competing elite groups (pluralism). The resulting balance of forces between these groups is said to ensure that no single group emerges in a socially dominant position.

**Elizabeth,** 1837–98, empress of Austria and queen of Hungary, consort of FRANCIS JOSEPH. Her life was marred by tragedy, notably the death of her only son, Archduke RUDOLF. She was assassinated in Geneva by an Italian anarchist.

**Elizabeth,** 1709–62, czarina of Russia (1741–62); daughter of PETER I and CATHERINE I. She gained the throne by overthrowing the young IVAN VI. Violently anti-German, she sided against FREDERICK II of Prussia in the SEVEN YEARS WAR. She gave the nobles greater power over their serfs and in local government, while decreasing the service they owed the state.

**Elizabeth,** queens of England. **Elizabeth I,** 1533–1603, queen of England (1558–1603), the daughter of HENRY VIII and Anne BOLEYN, was declared illegitimate after her mother's execution; in 1544 Parliament reestablished her in the succession. Imprisoned as a rallying point for discontented Protestants, she regained some freedom by outward conformity to Catholicism. On her succession in 1558 England's low fortunes included religious strife, a huge government debt, and failure in wars with France. Her reign took England through one of its greatest eras: a period that produced such men as William SHAKESPEARE, Edmund SPENSER, Francis BACON, and Walter RALEIGH; a period that saw the country united to become a first-rate European power with a great navy; a period in which commerce and industry prospered and colonization began. Elizabeth's Tudor concept of strong rule and the need for popular support helped her select excellent counsellors, such as Sir William Cecil (Lord BURGHLEY) and Sir Francis Walsingham. She reestablished Anglicanism, and measures against Catholics grew harsher. Important legislation enacted in her reign included stabilization of labour conditions, currency reforms, poor laws, and acts to encourage agriculture, commerce, and manufacturing. Elizabeth began a policy of peace, and her diplomatic manoeuvers eventually defeated Spain and stalemated France. The Treaty of Edinburgh (1560) started a policy of supporting Protestant lords against Catholics. After the abdication of MARY QUEEN OF SCOTS from the Scottish throne, Elizabeth gave her refuge, kept her prisoner, and executed her only after numerous plots to seat Mary on the English throne. Although she had many favourites, notably the earl of LEICESTER, Elizabeth never married, but she used the possibility of marriage as a diplomatic tool. By marriage negotiations with FRANCIS, duke of Alençon and Anjou, she secured (1572) a defence alliance against Spain and, later, French aid for the Dutch against Spain, who now emerged as England's main enemy. PHILIP II of Spain, whose marriage offer Elizabeth had refused in 1559, planned the Spanish ARMADA as a reprisal for English raids against Spanish shipping. The defeat of the Armada (1588) broke the power of Spain and strengthened England's national pride. Elizabeth's last years were darkened by the rash uprising of her favourite, Robert Devereux, 2nd earl of ESSEX. She was succeeded by James VI of Scotland, son of Mary Queen of Scots, who became JAMES I of England. Vain, fickle in bestowing favours, prejudiced, vacillating, and parsimonious, she was nonetheless a great monarch, highly aware of the responsibility of rule and immensely courageous. **Elizabeth II,** 1926–, queen of Great Britain and Northern Ireland, succeeded her father, GEORGE VI, in 1952. In 1947 she married Philip Mountbatten, duke of EDINBURGH. They have four children: Prince CHARLES, Princess ANNE, Prince Andrew (b. 1960), and Prince Edward

(b. 1964). In 1977 she celebrated her Silver Jubilee, the 25th anniversary of her accession to the throne. Her mother, **Elizabeth**, 1900–, queen consort to George VI, was the daughter of the 14th earl of Strathmore.

**Elizabeth**, 1843–1916, queen of ROMANIA, consort of CAROL I, also known as Elizabeth of Wied. Under the pseudonym of Carmen Sylva she wrote extensively in several languages.

**Elizabethan style**, in architecture and decorative arts, transitional style of the English RENAISSANCE. During the period large manor houses were built. Plans tended towards symmetry, although many characteristics of TUDOR STYLE remained. The great hall was retained, and many features were added, notably broad staircases and long galleries. A famous example is Longleat, Wiltshire. Owners often designed houses themselves, and carpenters and masons amplified the plans. Renaissance, mannerist, and Flemish motifs were haphazardly adapted with no attempt at a unified classical style.

**Elizabeth Woodville:** see WOODVILLE, ELIZABETH.

**elk**, any of several members of the DEER family. It most properly designates the largest member of the family, *Alces alces*, found across Northern Europe and Asia to China. Elk are nearly 3 m (9 ½ ft) long with antlers up to 200 cm (6 ½ ft) across. In N North America, it is called MOOSE. The name *elk* is used in North America to designate a different animal, the WAPITI.

**Ellice Islands:** see TUVALU.

**Ellington, Duke** (Edward Kennedy Ellington), 1899–1974, black American jazz pianist and composer. He formed a band in 1918 and became nationally famous while appearing in Harlem nightclubs. His orchestra, playing his own often complex compositions, made many innovations in the JAZZ idiom. Ellington's compositions include 'Solitude', 'Mood Indigo', and hundreds more, as well as long concert works like *Black, Brown, and Beige* (1943).

**ellipse:** see CONIC SECTION.

**elliptic geometry:** see NON-EUCLIDEAN GEOMETRY.

**Ellis, Alexander John**, 1814–90, English philologist and mathematician, who has been called 'the father of ethnomusicology' because of his scientific measurements of the scales of several Asian musical systems (1885) and the revolutionary conclusions that he drew from this. He abandoned an earlier theory that music was governed by the natural laws of the constitution of musical sound worked out by von Helmholtz (whose book *Die Lehre von den Tonempfindungen* he had translated in 1875), and he claimed that SCALES were diverse and artificial. Musical systems are symbol systems that have been developed as a result of individual choice and social conventions: there are therefore no natural laws which determine what people shall regard as consonant or dissonant.

**Ellis, (Henry) Havelock**, 1859–1939, English physician, psychologist, and pioneering sexologist. His major work was *Studies in the Psychology of Sex* (7 vol., 1897–1928).

**Ellis Island**, c.10.9 hectares (27 acres), in Upper New York Bay, US. Government property since 1808, it served (1892–1943) as the chief entry station for immigrants to the US. It is now part of the Statue of Liberty National Monument.

**Ellison, Ralph**, 1914–, black American writer. His classic novel, *Invisible Man* (1952), details the struggles of a nameless young black man in a hostile society. Ellison has also written short stories and essays.

**elm**, tree of the family Ulmaceae, found chiefly in the Northern Hemisphere. Elm trees (genus *Ulmus*) are tall and graceful, with fan-shaped crowns of finely subdividing branches and twigs. The American, or white, elm (*U. americana*, difficult to grow outside N America) and the English, or common, elm (*U. procera*) of Eurasia are widely planted as ornamental and shade trees. Both species are highly susceptible to the fungus causing the fatal DUTCH ELM DISEASE.

**El Mahalla el-Kubra:** see MAHALLA EL-KUBRA.

**El Mansûra:** see MANSÛRA.

**Elohim:** see GOD.

**elongation**, the angular distance between two points in the sky as measured from a third point. As viewed from a third body, the elongation of two celestial bodies will be 0° when they are in conjunction and 180°

when in opposition (see SYZYGY); quadrature occurs when the two bodies have an elongation of 90°. As viewed from the Earth, the greatest elongations with respect to the Sun of the inferior planets Mercury and Venus are 28° and 47°; the Moon and the superior planets can range from 0° to 180°.

**El Paso**, US city (1984 est. pop. 464,000), extreme W Texas, on the RIO GRANDE, opposite JUÁREZ, Mexico, and near the N Mexico border; inc. 1873. Located in a region of cattle ranches and farms, the city is a port, and a commercial, industrial, and mining centre. Manufactures include refined petroleum, copper, clothing, and machinery. The dry climate attracts tourists. The largest of the border cities, El Paso has a history bound up with that of MEXICO; the arrival of railway service in 1881 initiated the border town's growth into a modern city.

**El Salvador**, officially Republic of El Salvador, republic (1986 est. pop. 4,860,000), 21,393 km² (8260 sq mi), Central America; bordered by the Pacific Ocean (S), Guatemala (W), and Honduras (N and E). The capital is SAN SALVADOR. Two volcanic ranges traverse the country from W to E. In between are the broad, fertile valleys that are the nation's heartland. The densely populated country is the smallest of the Latin American republics, with a weak economy overly dependent on fluctuation in the world market price for coffee, the principal export. Cotton and sugar are also exported while oil and manufactured goods are imported. Maize is the main subsistence crop. Light industry includes textile manufacture and food processing. In 1982 GDP was US$5606 million or US$1177 per capita. The Spanish-speaking, Roman Catholic population is predominantly mestizo.

*History.* Spaniards conquered the area in 1524. El Salvador declared independence in 1821 followed by a brief period as part of the Mexican Empire (1821–23) and then of the CENTRAL AMERICAN FEDERATION (1825–38). After becoming a separate republic in 1839 it was plagued by frequent interference from nearby states, notably GUATEMALA and NICARAGUA. The establishment of coffee cultivation in the late 19th cent. created an inequitable distribution of wealth that became the basis for future unrest and, consequently, of several repressive dictatorships. Overpopulation is a major 20th-cent. problem. Failure of land reform in the 1970s brought increasing left–right polarization and guerrilla warfare, with some US and Cuban involvement. In 1982 the left boycotted but failed to prevent voting in a widely publicized election, which brought to power a right-wing coalition. Presidential elections in 1984 were won by José Napoléon DUARTE (Christian Democrat). Alfredo Christiani, the right-wing candidate (Nationalist Republican Alliance), was elected president in 1989.

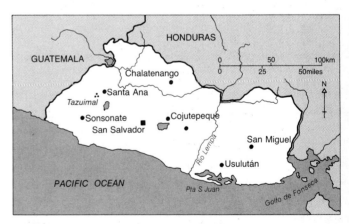

El Salvador

**Elsheimer, Adam** (ˌelshiemə), 1578–1610, German painter. Best known for his small paintings on copper of biblical subjects, he excelled at landscape and light effects and influenced Dutch painters. His *Rest on the Flight to Egypt* (1609) is in the Alte Pinakothek, Munich.

**Elsinore:** see HELSINGØR.

**Elssler, Fanny**, 1810–84, Austrian ballet dancer. One of the most famous dancers of the romantic ballet, personifying its earthy, sensual, and dramatic side. She made her debut in Naples (1825), and subsequently danced in all the leading capitals of Europe and the US.

**Ely,** cathedral city (1981 pop. 9006) in Cambridgeshire, E England, on R. Ouse, 23 km (14 mi) NE of Cambridge. It is a market town with some industry, including the manufacture of agricultural equipment. The cathedral dates from the 11th cent. Ely is the centre of a large agricultural area within the FENS.

**Elysian fields** or **Elysium,** in Greek mythology, happy otherworld in the west for heroes favoured by the gods. The Champs Elysées in Paris are called after them.

**Elytis, Odysseus,** pseud. of **Odysseus Alepoudelis,** 1911–, Greek poet; b. Crete. His poetry, joyful and sensuous, is replete with imagery of the sunny Aegean Islands. *The Sovereign Sun* (1974) is a selection of his poems in English translation. He was awarded the 1979 Nobel Prize in literature.

**Elzevir, Louis,** 1540–1617, Dutch publisher, whose name also appeared as Elsevier or Elzevier. His family concern, from his first published book in Leiden (1583) to the death of the second Abraham Elzevir in 1712, was, in its best years, the greatest publishing business in the world. Businessmen rather than printers or scholars, the Elzevirs owned presses and employed good editors and printers in Leiden, Amsterdam, Utrecht, and The Hague. Elzevir agencies functioned in cities from Denmark to Italy. Their books were typically legible, sturdy, and inexpensive, rather than elegant.

**Emancipation, Edict of,** 1861, edict by which Czar ALEXANDER II freed all Russian SERFS (one third of the population). Serfdom was abolished, and peasants were to receive land from landlords and pay them for it. The system of payment and of land distribution, cumbersome and unjust, was reformed by STOLYPIN in 1906 in an effort to stem discontent.

**Emancipation Proclamation,** in US history, the presidential proclamation purportedly abolishing SLAVERY in territory controlled by the CONFEDERACY. Pres. LINCOLN refrained at the start of the AMERICAN CIVIL WAR from issuing any edict freeing slaves lest it alienate the loyal border slave states. But after the successful Antietam Campaign, Lincoln issued a preliminary edict and, on 1 Jan. 1863, the formal Emancipation Proclamation. It did not free all slaves in the US, but only those residing in territory in rebellion 'as a fit and necessary war measure for suppressing said rebellion'. It was designed to deplete the Southern manpower reserve in slaves and to enhance the Union cause abroad, especially in Britain.

**embalming,** preservation of the body after death by means of chemical compounds that delay putrefaction. It was highly developed in ancient EGYPT, where immersion in a soda solution and filling of body cavities with resins and spices were common. Modern embalming (routinely used in the US) developed from 17th-cent. attempts to preserve anatomical specimens. Formaldehyde, infused to replace the blood, is the most common embalming agent.

**embargo,** prohibition by a country of the departure of ships or certain types of goods from its ports. Instances of confining all domestic ships to port are rare, and the EMBARGO ACT OF 1807 passed because of the molestation of US ships by France and the UK is a rare example. The detention of foreign vessels, however, has often occurred as an act of reprisal or in anticipation of war. Embargoes on goods for economic and strategic purposes are also common. Both the LEAGUE OF NATIONS and the UNITED NATIONS have recognized the use of embargoes, e.g., the League's sanctions (1935) against Italy for its aggression in Ethiopia and the UN call for an oil and arms embargo against Rhodesia (now Zimbabwe). In the 1980s many countries have imposed partial trade embargoes in South Africa reflecting their opposition to South Africa's apartheid policy.

**Embargo Act of 1807,** passed 22 Dec. 1807, by the US Congress in answer to British and French restrictions on neutral shipping during the Napoleonic Wars (see NAPOLEON I). It virtually forbade all international trade to and from American ports in an attempt to persuade Britain and France of the value and rights of neutral commerce. Britain and France stood firm, however, and enforcement was difficult, especially in New England. The Nonintercourse Act (1 Mar. 1809) and Macon's Bill No. 2 (1810) which substituted nonintercourse for the embargo, proved equally ineffectual.

**Embden–Meyerhof pathway:** see GLYCOLYSIS.

**embezzlement:** see FRAUD.

**embolism:** see STROKE.

**embroidery,** decorative needlework applied to all types of fabrics and worked with linen, cotton, wool, silk, or metallic thread. Beads, shells, feathers, leather, or gems may be added. The art is mentioned in the Hindu Vedas and in the Old Testament; it probably antedates WEAVING. Through the spread of religion the tradition of embroidery was adopted into Europe. Opus Anglicanum is the generic name for ecclesiastical embroidery in England from the 12th–14th cent. which probably was the finest period of English embroidery; both men and women participated in its production. It was the technical excellence of underside couching and the expressive use of split stitch that created the demand for large quantities of embroidery in Europe. With the reorganization of the guild system women were excluded from workshop practice, and after the Renaissance, women became largely responsible for secular embroidery for domestic consumption. During the 19th cent. embroidery became a lady's accomplishment using commercially produced embroidery patterns. With the invention of the sewing machine, machine embroidery was initially used to imitate hand embroidery; since the mass production of the sewing machine (c. 1950) machine embroidery has offered a range of textures and stitches used by the embroiderer in conjunction with hand embroidery. Peasant embroidery which has long flourished in Eastern Europe, Asia, and South America, is to be found in the major collections of Britain.

**embryo,** name for the developing young of an animal or plant. Embryology, the scientific study of embryonic development, deals with the period from fertilization until hatching or birth of an animal or, in plants, germination. In animals, early divisions produce a hollow ball one cell thick (a blastula), which later becomes a two-layered cuplike gastrula. In higher animals, a third (middle) layer of cells develops from one or both of the first two layers. The outer layer (ectoderm) gives rise to skin, scales, feathers, hair, nails, and the nervous system; the innermost layer (endoderm) forms the digestive glands and lining of the alimentary tract and lungs; the middle layer (mesoderm) develops the skeletal, muscular, and connective tissue and circulatory, excretory, and reproductive systems.

**Emecheta, Buchi** (emay̩che̩tə), 1944–, Nigerian novelist. Since moving to London she has depicted the real lives of black people in Britain, e.g., *Second Class Citizen* (1976) and *The Joys of Motherhood* (1979). Her other works rebut the idealized portrayal of women by male novelists, e.g., *The Bride Price* (1976) and *The Slave Girl* (1977).

**Emei Shan,** mountain, SICHUAN prov., China, 3000 m (8197 ft) high, 168 km (105 mi) E of the city of Chengdu. It is one of China's sacred mountains, the others being Putuo, Wutai, and Jiuhua. Taoist and later Buddhist temples have been built here since the 2nd cent. AD. It became a sacred place for Buddhist pilgrims from all over China. When not clouded in mist and cloud the view from the top is outstanding. It is now a favoured tourist site.

**emerald,** highly valued GEM, green variety of the mineral BERYL. The finest emeralds are found in Colombia; other sources are the USSR, Zimbabwe, and Australia. The Oriental emerald is the transparent green variety of CORUNDUM.

**Emerson, Ralph Waldo,** 1803–82, one of America's most influential authors and thinkers. A Unitarian minister, he left his only pastorate, Boston's Old North Church (1829–32), because of doctrinal disputes. On a trip to Europe Emerson met Thomas CARLYLE, S.T. COLERIDGE, and WORDSWORTH, whose ideas, along with those of PLATO, the Neoplatonists, Oriental mystics, and SWEDENBORG, strongly influenced his philosophy. Returning home (1835), he settled in Concord, Mass., which he, Margaret FULLER, THOREAU, and others made a center of TRANSCENDENTALISM. He stated the movement's main principles in *Nature* (1836), stressing the mystical unity of nature. A noted lecturer, Emerson called for American intellectual independence from Europe in his Phi Beta Kappa address at Harvard ('The American Scholar', 1837). In an address at the Harvard divinity school (1838), he asserted that redemption could be found only in one's own soul and intuition. Emerson developed transcendentalist themes in his famous *Journal* (kept since his student days at Harvard), in the magazine *The Dial*, and in his series of *Essays* (1841, 1844). Among the best known of his essays are 'The Over-Soul', 'Compensation', and 'Self-Reliance'. He is also noted for his poems, e.g., 'Threnody', 'Brahma', and 'The Problem'. His later works include *Representative Men* (1850), *English Traits* (1856), and *The Conduct of Life* (1870).

**emery:** see CORUNDUM.

**Emigrant Aid Company,** formed (1854) to promote organized antislavery immigration to KANSAS from the US Northeast. It hoped to use the concept of SQUATTER SOVEREIGNTY in the KANSAS–NEBRASKA ACT to ensure that Kansas became a free state. Conceived by Eli Thayer, the company sent out 1240 settlers. The movement did little towards making Kansas a free state, but it captured public attention and engendered much of the bitterness that contributed to theAMERICAN CIVIL WAR.

**emigration:** see IMMIGRATION.

**Eminescu, Mihail** (yemee‚neskooh), 1850–89, Romanian poet. The lyrical, passionate, and revolutionary work of Eminescu, considered the leading Romanian poet of his century, is typified by 'Calin', extolling nature and simple peasant life.

**Emmanuel Philibert,** 1528–80, duke of Savoy-Piedmont (1553–80), called Ironhead. He succeeded his father, who had been dispossessed of Savoy by the French and the Swiss. Serving Spain, he defeated the French at Saint-Quentin (1557), and by the Treaty of Cateau-Cambrésis (1559) most of Savoy was restored to him. He increased ducal authority in his territories and moved his capital to Turin, thus stressing the Italian character of his state.

**Empedocles,** c.495–c.435 BC, pre-Socratic Greek philosopher. He held that everything in existence is composed of four underived and indestructible substances — fire, water, earth, and air — and that atmosphere is a corporeal substance, not a mere void. He believed that motion is the only sort of change possible and that apparent changes in quantity and quality are in fact changes of position of the basic particles underlying the observable object.

**emphysema,** abnormal enlargement and distension of the air sacs of the lungs, causing breathlessness. Usually chronic and progressive, pulmonary emphysema is associated with heredity, smoking, and long-standing respiratory ailments such as chronic bronchitis. There is no specific treatment and management is aimed at increasing lung capacity and preventing and treating infection, a common complication. Surgical emphysema is the presence of air in the tissues after surgery.

**Empire State Building,** in New York City, US, on Fifth Avenue, between 33rd St and 34th St. It was designed by Shreve, Lamb, and Harmon, and built in 1930–31. With 102 storeys, it was for years the tallest building in the world.

Empire State Building

**Empire style,** in French interior decoration and costume, the manner prevailing in the reign of Napoleon I (1804–14), largely created for him by the architects FONTAINE and PERCIER and the artist J.-L. DAVID. Furniture was chiefly of mahogany. Walls were decorated with stucco, or with classical motifs and such imperial symbols as the emperor's monogram and representations of military trophies. There was greater formality in etiquette and dress. Women's gowns were high-waisted with trimming at the hem and shoulders. Men wore tail coats and high cravats, and the top hat was introduced.

**empiricism,** philosophical doctrine holding that all knowledge is derived from experience, whether of the mind or of the senses. Thus it opposes the rationalist belief in the existence of innate ideas. A doctrine basic to the scientific method, empiricism is associated with the rise of experimental science after the 17th cent. It has been a dominant tradition in British philosophy, as in the works of LOCKE, HUME, and George BERKELEY. Most empiricists acknowledge certain a priori truths (e.g., principles of mathematics and logic), but John Stuart MILL and others have treated even these as generalizations deduced from experience.

**Empson, Sir William,** 1906–86, English poet and literary scholar. His *Seven Types of Ambiguity* (1930) and *Some Versions of Pastoral* (1935) are classics of literary criticism. His poetry is witty, learned, and tautly-expressed.

**Ems,** river, 330 km (206 mi) long, rising in the Teutoburger Hills and flowing NW across the West German Plain to the North Sea. Its broad estuary is known as the Dollart. The Dortmund–Ems Canal follows it for much of its length below MÜNSTER. Natural-gas reserves are found between its lower course and the Dutch border (the Emsland).

**Ems dispatch,** 1870 communication between King William of Prussia (later German Emperor WILLIAM I) and his premier, Otto von BISMARCK. In June 1870 the Spanish throne had been offered to Prince Hohenzollern–Sigmaringen. France having protested, the prince refused this offer, but the French ambassador, Comte Benedetti, meeting William at Ems, demanded further assurance. William rejected the request, and Bismarck made public an edited version of the king's report of the conversation. France declared war on 19 July, and the FRANCO-PRUSSIAN WAR began.

**emu,** large, flightless Australian BIRD (*Dromiceius novaehollandiae*) related to the CASSOWARY and OSTRICH. A swift runner, it is 150–180 cm (5–6 ft) tall. Its brownish plumage is coarse and hairlike. Emus live in deserts, plains, and open forest. They are very inquisitive birds. They normally feed on fruits, insects, and larvae, but have been seen to take coins, keys, and nails.

**emulsion:** see COLLOID.

**enamel,** a siliceous substance that fuses onto metal. Transparent or opaque, clear or coloured, it is usually employed to add a decorative surface. Enamel was used in making jewellery in ancient Greece, and Rome, and was perfected in the Byzantine world, often in the CLOISONNÉ technique. Fine enamel-work was created in 12th-cent. France and Spain. The most famous enamellist was the 16th-cent. French artist Léonard LIMOUSIN. In England from the 17th cent. on, enamel was used for miniature portraits. Enamel-work declined in the 19th cent. but was revived in the 1960s.

**Enceladus,** in astronomy, natural satellite of SATURN.

**encephalitis,** general term used to describe an inflammation of the brain and spinal cord, characterized by headache, drowsiness (hence its popular name sleepy, or sometimes sleeping, sickness), and convulsions. Mumps, rabies, and HERPES viruses, among others, are common causes. For many forms of encephalitis there is no treatment, although herpes encephalitis responds to the antiviral drug adenine arabinoside.

**Encina** or **Enzina, Juan del** (ayn‚theenah), 1469?–c.1530, Spanish poet and court musician. His *Églogas* [pastoral plays], which together with musical compositions and a treatise on poetry appear in *Cancionero* (1496), made him the father of Spanish RENAISSANCE drama.

**enclosure of land:** see INCLOSURE.

**encomienda,** system of tributary labour in Spanish America to supply adequate and cheap labour. Indians were required to pay tribute from their lands in return for Spanish protection. The hardships of the system soon decimated the Indian population, however, and it was abandoned gradually after 1542.

**encyclical:** see BULL.

**encyclopedia,** a compendium of knowledge, either general or specialized, i.e., within one field. A dictionary is basically devoted to words, an encyclopedia to data on and discussion of each subject covered. An almanac is a periodical publication containing much ephemeral data. Although attempts at comprehensive knowledge began with ARISTOTLE, the *Natural History* of PLINY the Elder is considered the first true encyclopedia. There were various compendia during the Middle Ages, including Vincent of Beauvais's *Mirror of the World,* printed in English translation in 1481. The modern encyclopedia—alphabetically arranged, and often with bibliographies—is usually said to have begun with John Harris's *Lexicon technicum* (1704) and Ephraim Chambers's *Cyclopaedia* (1728). The most renowned and influential of all encyclopedias, the French ENCYCLOPÉDIE, was completed in 1772 by Denis DIDEROT and other philosophes. The *Encyclopaedia Britannica,* first published (1771) in three volumes, grew in size and reputation and is now published in the US. The famous French Larousse encyclopedias date from 1865, and the first noteworthy American encyclopedia, the *Encyclopedia Americana,* from 1829–33. Encyclopedias increased in usefulness in the 19th and 20th cent. as knowledge in various fields grew more complex and specialized. Notable national encyclopedias today include the *Encyclopedia Italiana* (1929–39), the *Great Soviet Encyclopedia* (1926–47, 3rd ed. 1980), and the French *Universal Encyclopedia* (1968–74). Some specialized encyclopedias are in many volumes. They include *Encyclopedia of the Social Sciences, Encyclopedia of Islam, Encyclopedia of Science and Technology,* and *Encyclopedia of World Art.* The first one-volume general encyclopedia in English was the *Columbia Encyclopedia* (1935).

**Encyclopédie,** influential 28-volume French encyclopedia, edited by Denis DIDEROT and Jean d'ALEMBERT, with the aid of QUESNAY, MONTESQUIEU, VOLTAIRE, J.J. ROUSSEAU, TURGOT, and others. It was published between 1751 and 1775. Its famous 'preliminary discourse', signed by Alembert, indicated its aims and then presented definitions and histories of science and the arts. Despite attacks by the JESUITS and unofficial censorship by the printer, the *Encyclopédie* was an immediate success. There were 4000 subscribers to the first edition. It championed the scepticism and rationalism of the ENLIGHTENMENT and played a major role in the intellectual preparation for the FRENCH REVOLUTION. In 1780 a five-volume supplement and two-volume index were added. Most cultural historians would agree that it was an effect of the scientific enlightenment rather than one of its causes.

**endangered species,** any species of animal or plant whose ability to survive is seriously in question. Human activities can contribute to such decline: for example, by deliberate extermination to protect livestock; unrestricted hunting to obtain hides, feathers, or food; or the use of PESTICIDES to protect crops. Humans have contributed to the destruction of entire habitats through, e.g., STRIP-MINING, oil spills, water POLLUTION, and the draining of swamps and levelling of forests for industrial and residential development. In this way the usual prey of an animal may also be removed. Any or all of these disturbances to patterns of existence can endanger the lives and breeding grounds of a large number of species simultaneously. Though action to protect endangered species dates back at least to the early years of the century (e.g., the international agreement in 1911 between Canada, the US, the USSR, and Japan to protect the remaining stocks of sea otters), more concerted efforts have been made in recent years in response to an increasingly critical situation: currently animal and bird species are disappearing at the rate of one per year and many more are threatened. The International Union for the Conservation of Nature and Natural Resources (IUCN) publishes Red Data books on endangered species of plant and animal, and was largely responsible for CITES, the Convention on International Trade in Endangered Species of Wild Fauna and Flora (1975), which seeks to control or halt altogether international trading in plants and animals and in the products derived from them. Together with the World Wild Fund for Nature, the IUCN has fostered the development of national parks and reserves (e.g., Africa, the Americas) and launched international appeals to save particular species or habitats (e.g., tropical rainforests 1975, Operation Tiger 1972, Rhino Project 1979). The USSR, the US, Canada, Denmark, and Norway have signed an Agreement for the Conservation of Polar Bears (1976), which guarantees a high degree of protection to the species and its ecosystems. The International Whaling Commission declared a worldwide moratorium on commercial whaling, beginning in 1986, though it met with objections from Japan and the USSR. The killing of whales continues under the guise of 'scientific whaling', over which there is no control. Thanks to the efforts of Sri Lanka, the Indian Ocean has been established as a sanctuary for marine mammals. The problem of endangered species remains acute: despite careful management, breeding programmes, and the reintroduction of animals into the wild, there are, for example, fewer than 70 Javan rhino in existence, the number of right whales has dwindled from about 100,000 to only 3000 in 60 years, and about 250,000 dolphins die each year by accident when they are caught in tuna-fishing nets. Of equal concern is the destruction of flora, especially of rainforests, the home to a variety of people and animal species, an environment of enormous genetic richness, and source of many vital drugs and medicines. The world's rainforests are being cleared or seriously degraded at the rate of 40 ha (100 acres) per minute. See also CONSERVATION: NATURE RESERVE.

**endive:** see CHICORY.

**endocrine system,** body control system composed of a group of glands that keep the internal environment stable by producing hormones, chemical regulatory substances that exert a specific effect on the activity of cells in other parts of the body (see HORMONE). In humans the major endocrine organs are the PITUITARY GLAND, THYROID GLAND, PARATHYROID GLANDS, ADRENAL GLANDS, THYMUS GLAND, PINEAL BODY, PANCREAS, ovaries, and testes (see REPRODUCTIVE SYSTEM); the KIDNEYS are also sometimes included. The endocrine, or ductless, glands secrete the hormones they produce directly into the internal environment from where they are transmitted via the bloodstream or by diffusion to distant points in the body. Some hormones, such as thyroxine from the thyroid gland, affect nearly all body cells; others, such as PROGESTERONE from the female ovary, which regulates the uterine lining and ovulation, affect only a single organ. The pituitary, sometimes called the master gland, secretes hormones that regulate many of the other endocrine glands. The regulation of body function depends on the existence of specific receptor cells in target organs, cells that respond in specialized ways to minute hormonal stimuli. The hormones act by regulating cell metabolism: by accelerating, slowing, or maintaining enzyme activity in receptor cells, they control growth and development, metabolic rate, sexual rhythms, and reproduction. The quantities of hormones are maintained by feedback mechanisms that depend on interactions between the endocrine glands, blood levels of hormones, and activities of the target organs. See HYPOTHALAMUS.

**endogamy,** in anthropology, the practice of MARRIAGE between partners of the same LINEAGE. It is not so widespread as its opposite, *exogamy,* the practice of finding a marriage partner in another lineage.

**endometriosis,** condition in which fragments of tissue resembling that lining the uterus are found in other organs (e.g., the ovaries) and tissues. These fragments go through the same cyclical changes as the uterus lining, giving rise to extreme pain before and during menstruation.

**endorphin,** any of a group of proteins produced by the pituitary gland, affecting mood, perception of pain, memory retention, and learning. Often referred to as natural opiates, endorphins were searched for and found in the 1970s after the discovery that MORPHINE works by attaching itself to specific receptor sites in the brain. Endorphins also attach to these receptors and appear to be the brain's own natural 'painkillers'. It is thought that ACUPUNCTURE reduces pain, at least in part, by stimulating the body to produce endorphins.

**Endō Shūsaku,** 1923–, Japanese writer. He discusses Catholic themes in 16th cent. Japan in his novels *Chinmoku* [Silence] (1966; tr. 1969), the story of a Portuguese priest who is imprisoned by the shogunate and apostasizes, and *Shi* [The Samurai] (1980; tr. 1982). He also writes comic short stories.

**endoskeleton:** see SKELETON.

**energy,** in physics, the ability or capacity to do WORK. Forms of energy include HEAT, chemical energy, and, according to the theory of RELATIVITY, MASS (see NUCLEAR ENERGY); other forms of energy are associated with the transmission of LIGHT, SOUND, and ELECTRICITY. Energy and work are measured in the same units: joules, ergs, electron-volts, calories, foot-pounds, or some other, depending on the system of measurement being used. When a force acts on a body, the work performed (and the energy expended) is the product of the force and the distance over which the body is moved by the force. Potential energy is the capacity for doing work that a body possesses because of its position or condition. For example, a weight lifted to a certain height has potential energy because of its position in the Earth's gravitational field. Kinetic energy, the energy a body possesses because it is in motion, is equal to $\frac{1}{2}mv^2$, for linear motion with velocity $v$ and $\frac{1}{2}Iw^2$ for rotational motion with angular velocity $w$ where $m$ is the MASS and $I$ the MOMENT OF INERTIA of the body (see MOTION). The average kinetic energy of the atoms or molecules of a body is related to the TEMPERATURE of the body. Energy (or its equivalent in mass) can be neither created nor destroyed (see CONSERVATION LAWS), but it can be changed from one form into another.

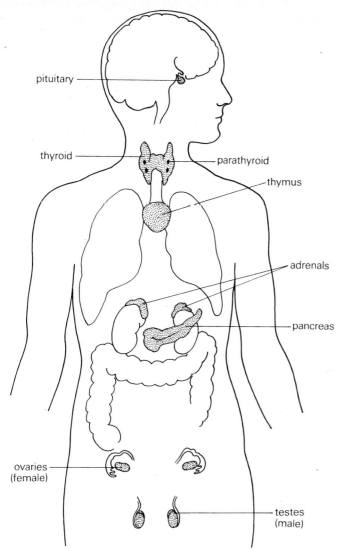

pituitary

thyroid — parathyroid

thymus

adrenals

pancreas

ovaries (female)

testes (male)

Endocrine system

**energy, sources of.** In the physical world energy is that fundamental entity that provides the power for doing work; in dimensional terms work and energy are synonymous, the former being one emanation of the latter. William Thomson (Lord Kelvin) introduced (1848) the concept of 'conservation of energy', i.e., that if all the energy in different forms, such as heat, light, sound, kinetic energy, etc., are taken into account when work is achieved by use of energy, then the total is the same after the event as before. Nowadays this is understood to be applicable only when there are no changes in the masses of the objects involved. In atomic and nuclear energy phenomena where some mass is destroyed, energy is created from the mass lost by an amount predicted by EINSTEIN's formula $E = mc^2$, where $E$ is energy, $m$ is mass, and $c$ is a constant equal to the velocity of light. Energy sources are of two basic types, renewable and nonrenewable. Most of the industrial world is presently powered by the nonrenewable fossil fuels COAL, PETROLEUM, and NATURAL GAS that, once used, cannot be replaced. Fission NUCLEAR REACTORS are fuelled by uranium or plutonium, themselves finite energy sources. Spent uranium can be converted to fissile plutonium in a breeder reactor, however, a process that makes nuclear energy almost infinitely renewable. Nuclear technology, however, has not yet developed either failproof reactors or a safe method for disposing of nuclear wastes (see WASTE DISPOSAL). The development of nuclear fusion (whose end products are harmless) has so far been hindered by the difficulties of containing the fuels (the abundant heavy form of hydrogen) at the extremely high temperatures necessary to initiate and sustain fusion. Renewable energy sources include the energy from water and wind (see TURBINE; WATER WHEEL; WINDMILL); geothermal energy, the earth's internal heat that is released naturally in

GEYSERS and VOLCANOES; tidal energy, the power released by the ebb and flow of the ocean's tides; biomass, the use of certain crops (including wood) or crop wastes either directly as fuel or as a fermentable source of fuels such as alcohol or methane; and SOLAR ENERGY, which can be stored and used directly as heat, or transformed into electricity through the use of a PHOTOVOLTAIC CELL. All these renewable energy sources are presently being tapped in some form, but none can replace fossil fuels without huge advances in the technologies needed to exploit them.

**Enewetak, Enewetok** or **Eniwetok,** circular atoll, central Pacific, in the MARSHALL ISLANDS, part of the US Trust Territory of the PACIFIC ISLANDS. Consisting of c.40 islets surrounding a large lagoon c.80 km (50 mi) in circumference, it was used (1948–54) by the US for nuclear-bomb tests. Former residents, evacuated before the tests started, began returning in the early 1970s, and the island was declared free of residual radioactivity in 1980. Because of damage inflicted by the tests and continuing need for US aid, residents requested (1981) that the UN trusteeship relationship with the US be continued after the rest of the trust territory becomes independent in the 1980s.

**Enfield,** London borough (1981 pop. 257, 154), in outer N London. Industries found here include the manufacture of metal goods and electrical equipment. It was once a market town, which has now become a largely residential suburb of London. Enfield Chase, a large rural area, is just to the NW.

**Engel, Marian,** 1933–, Canadian novelist. A major contemporary Canadian writer, Engel introduced elements of feminism into such works as *No Clouds of Glory* (1968), *The Honeyman Festival* (1970), *Bear* (1976), *The Glassy Sea* (1979) and *Lunatic Villas* (1981).

**Engels, Friedrich,** 1820–95, German social philosopher and revolutionary; with Karl MARX a founder of modern COMMUNISM and SOCIALISM. He was the son of a textile manufacturer, and after managing a factory in Manchester, England, he wrote his first major work, *The Condition of the Working Class in England in 1844* (1845). In 1844 he met Marx in Paris, beginning a lifelong collaboration. He and Marx wrote the *Communist Manifesto*, (1848) and other works that predicted the inevitable triumph of the working class. When the REVOLUTIONS OF 1848 failed, Engels settled in England. With Marx he helped found (1864) the International Workingmen's Association. Engel's financial aid enabled Marx to devote himself to writing *Das Kapital* (3 vol., 1867–94); after his death Engels edited vol. 2 and 3 from Marx's drafts and notes. Engels had enormous influence on the theories of MARXISM and DIALECTICAL MATERIALISM. His major works include *Anti-Dühring* (1878) and *The Origin of the Family, Private Propety, and the State* (1884).

**engine:** see DIESEL ENGINE; INTERNAL-COMBUSTION ENGINE; MOTOR CAR; STEAM ENGINE; TURBINE.

**engineering,** profession devoted to designing, constructing, and operating the structures, machines, and other devices of industry and everyday life. Before the INDUSTRIAL REVOLUTION, the field was confined to the military engineer, who built fortifications and weapons, and the civil engineer, who built bridges, harbours, aqueducts, buildings, and other structures. During the early 19th cent., mechanical engineering developed to design and build manufacturing machines and the engines to power them. Major modern engineering fields include the allied pursuits of mining, metallurgical, and petroleum engineering; electrical engineering, encompassing the generation and transmission of electric power and the design of all the devices that use it; electronics engineering, dealing mainly with computers and communications equipment; chemical engineering, dealing with the design, construction, and operation of plants and machinery for making such products as acids, dyes, drugs, plastics, and synthetic rubber; and aerospace engineering, comprising the design and production of aircraft, spacecraft, and missiles. Industrial, or management, engineering is concerned with efficient production and the design of methods and processes to achieve it. The chartered engineer is concerned with the development and use of new technologies, the promotion of advanced design and design methods, the introduction of new and more efficient production methods, and the generation and pioneering of new engineering services. Before being eligible for chartered status (C.Eng.) the engineer must have obtained a good honours degree on an accredited course, have a minimum of two years' experience attached to a chartered engineer, and then have some years of responsible practice.

**England,** largest (130,357 km²/50,334 sq mi) and most populous (1984 est. pop. 46,956,000) political division of the United Kingdom of Great Britain and Northern Ireland. Separated from the continent of Europe by the ENGLISH CHANNEL, the Strait of Dover, and the NORTH SEA, it is bounded by Wales and the Irish Sea (W) and Scotland (N). The Isle of WIGHT and the SCILLY ISLES are part of England. Inland from the white chalk cliffs of the southern coast lie gently rolling downs and wide plains. The lowlands of the east coast extend north to the reclaimed marsh of the FENS. Northern England, above the Humber R., is generally mountainous; the chief highlands are the Cumbrian Mts and the PENNINES, and the famous LAKE DISTRICT, in the Cumbrians, is the site of England's highest points. In Central England the Midlands is a large plain, interrupted and bordered by hills. In the west and southwest the terrain is high and hilly. The THAMES and the SEVERN are the longest rivers. Among the principal cities are LONDON, the capital of the United Kingdom; BIRMINGHAM and MANCHESTER, both industrial centres; and LIVERPOOL and BRISTOL, important ports. Despite its northerly latitude, England has a mild climate. Most of the region is subject to wet weather and some of it to severe cold, but in general life in England is conducive to a wide variety of agricultural and industrial pursuits. (For government, economy, and history of England, see UNITED KINGDOM.)

**England, Church of,** the established church in England and the mother church of the ANGLICAN COMMUNION. Christianity, brought by the Romans, was established in Britain by the 4th cent., but it was nearly destroyed by invasions of pagan Anglo-Saxons beginning in the 5th cent. The mission of St AUGUSTINE OF CANTERBURY began (597) the reconversion of England and the reestablishment of its ties to the papacy. Conflicts between church and state during the Middle Ages culminated with HENRY VIII's break with Rome. The pope's refusal to annul Henry's marriage to KATHARINE OF ARAGÓN led Henry to issue the Act of Supremacy (1534), which declared the king to be the head of the Church of England. Henry suppressed the monasteries and authorized the Great Bible (1539). Under Archbishop CRANMER the First BOOK OF COMMON PRAYER was produced and adopted (1549). MARY I returned the English church to communion with Rome, but with the accession of ELIZABETH I, an independent church was restored and steered along a middle ground between Roman Catholicism and Calvinism. During the ENGLISH CIVIL WAR the Long Parliament established (1646) PRESBYTERIANISM, but with the RESTORATION (1660), the episcopacy was restored and the Prayer Book was made the only legal service book by the Act of Uniformity (1662). Since that time, despite internal controversies, e.g., the OXFORD MOVEMENT, the church has held firm. The Archbishop of Canterbury is the chief leader (primate) of the church. In polity, the High Church party lays stress on sacramental worship and apostolic succession, the Low Church party on the Bible, preaching, and salvation by faith in Christ's death. In the 1980s there has been much debate about the admission of women to the ministry.

**English Channel,** arm of the Atlantic Ocean between France and Great Britain. Up to c.240 km (150 mi) wide in the west, it narrows to 34 km (21 mi) in the east, where it is connected to the North Sea by the Strait of Dover. Train and motor transport ferries, along with hovercraft, provide regular Channel crossings. Construction of a long-discussed tunnel crossing was begun in 1974, but was postponed shortly thereafter for lack of funds. In 1986 the French and British governments reached agreement that the project should go ahead as soon as privately-raised funds were made available.

**English civil war,** 1642–48, the conflict between CHARLES I of England and a large body of his subjects, generally called the 'parliamentarians', that culminated in the defeat and execution of the king and the establishment of a republican Commonwealth. The struggle has been called the Puritan Revolution because many of the king's opponents were Puritans, and the king's defeat was accompanied by the abolition of episcopacy. The more important constitutional issue in the war was between a king who claimed to rule by divine right and a Parliament that claimed the right to govern the nation independent of the crown. Charles's father, JAMES I, temporized with Parliament because of his need for money. Sir Edward COKE upheld Parliament's rights and was dismissed by the king; Sir Francis BACON upheld the royal prerogative and was impeached by Parliament. James's last Parliament granted money with specific directions for its use. Charles I proved more intractable. Parliament tried hard to limit his power; it refused his subsidy until he signed the PETITION OF RIGHT. Charles still levied forced taxes, dissolved Parliament, and governed alone for 11 years, but his financial needs in the

BISHOPS' WARS forced him to recall Parliament in 1640. This was the **Long Parliament,** the remnant of which was dissolved by Cromwell in 1653. Parliament recited the evils of Charles's reign in the Grand Remonstrance and tried to gather an army with a militia bill. The king organized an army himself and refused Parliament's final 19 demands. War became inevitable, and both sides bid for popular support. Charles was aided by the nobles, Anglicans, and Catholics, Parliament by the trading and artisan classes and the Scottish COVENANTERS. After initial indecisive campaigns, the victories of Oliver CROMWELL at Marston Moor and Naseby led to the king's surrender in 1645 and the end of the first civil war. His escape caused the second civil war (1647); it failed quickly. Pride's purge (see under PRIDE, THOMAS) expelled from Parliament all those opposed to the army. The remainder, known as the Rump Parliament, sentenced and beheaded Charles for treason (1649). A quasi-democratic commonwealth was followed by Cromwell's domination in the Protectorate. The English civil war led to the temporary defeat of the Stuarts, but the weakness of Parliament's position in 1681-88 (see under JAMES, kings of England) indicates the extent to which the civil war's consequences were temporary.

**English horn:** see OBOE.

**English language,** member of the West Germanic group of the Germanic subfamily of the Indo-European family of languages. See LANGUAGE (table).

**English-Speaking Union,** organization founded in 1918 by Sir Evelyn Wrench, to promote the advancement of education of English-speaking peoples around the world. It organizes educational exchanges, courses and conferences, and promotes English-language study to facilitate international communication and understanding.

**English units of measurement,** principal system of a few nations, the only major industrial one being the US. The English system actually consists of two related systems the US Customary System, used in the US and dependencies, and the British Imperial System (see WEIGHTS AND MEASURES, table). Great Britain, the originator of the latter system, is now gradually converting to the METRIC SYSTEM. The names of the units and the relationships between them are generally the same in both systems, but the sizes of the units differ, sometimes considerably. The basic unit of length is the yard (yd); the basic unit of mass (weight) is the pound (lb). Within the English units of measurement there are three different systems of weights (avoirdupois, troy, and apothecaries'), of which the most widely used is the avoirdupois. The troy system (named after Troyes, France, where it is said to have originated) is used only for precious metals. Apothecaries' weights are based on troy weights; in addition to the pound, ounce, and grain which are equal to the troy units of the same name other units are the dram and the scruple. For liquid measure, or liquid capacity, the basic unit is the gallon. The British imperial gallon is the volume of 10 lb of pure water at 62°F and is equal to 277.42 cubic inches (cu in). The US gallon, or wine gallon, is 231 cu in. The British units of liquid capacity are thus about 20% larger than the corresponding American units. The British imperial bushel of 2219.36 cu in is about 3% larger than the US bushel, or Winchester bushel of 2150.42 cu in. A similar difference exists between British and US subdivisions. The barrel is a unit for measuring the capacity of larger quantities and has various legal definitions depending on the substance being measured. Since 1965 in Britain, the yard and pound and all units derived from them have begun to be superseded by the introduction of the metric units of length and mass, the metre (m) and the kilogram (kg); the equivalent values are 1 yd = 0.9144 m and 1 lb = 0.45359237 kg. The English units of measurement have many drawbacks: the complexity of converting from one unit to another, the differences between British and American units, the use of the same name for different units (e.g., *ounce* for both weight and liquid capacity, *quart* and *pint* for both liquid and dry capacity), and the existence of the three different systems of weights.

**Eniwetok:** see ENEWETAK.

**enkephalin,** substance with opiate and ANALGESIC properties that occurs naturally in the nervous system and other tissues. Enkephalins, which belong to the ENDORPHIN group of substances, are thought to act as neurotransmitters in the processing of pain.

**Enlightenment,** term for the rationalist, liberal, humanitarian, and scientific trend of 18th-cent. Western thought; the period is also sometimes known as the Age of Reason. The enormous scientific and intellectual advancements made in the 17th cent. by the EMPIRICISM of Francis BACON and LOCKE, as well as by DESCARTES, SPINOZA, and others, fostered the belief in NATURAL LAW and universal order, promoted a scientific approach to political and social issues, and gave rise to a sense of human progress and belief in the state as its rational instrument. Representative of the Enlightenment are such thinkers as VOLTAIRE, J.J. ROUSSEAU, MONTESQUIEU, Adam SMITH, SWIFT, HUME, KANT, G.E. LESSING, BECCARIA, and, in America, Thomas PAINE, Thomas JEFFERSON, and Benjamin FRANKLIN. The social and political ideals they presented were enforced by 'enlightened despots' such as Holy Roman Emperor JOSEPH II, CATHERINE II of Russia, and FREDERICK II of Prussia. DIDEROT's *Encyclopédie* and the US CONSTITUTION are representative documents of the Age of Reason.

**Ennis,** county town (1986 pop. 6106), of Co. Clare, Republic of Ireland, situated on R. Fergus, 30 km (19 mi) NW of Limerick. It is a small town, with brewing and distilling industries. There is a 13th-cent. Franciscan abbey.

**Enniskillen,** town (1981 pop. 10,429), district of Fermanagh, N Ireland. It was formerly the county town of Co. Fermanagh, and is a market town. It is situated on an island in R. Erne, between Upper and Lower Lough ERNE. Historically, it is well known as a Protestant stronghold.

**Ennius, Quintus,** 239–169 BC, Calabrian poet, regarded by the Romans as the father of Latin poetry. He introduced quantitative hexameter and the elegiac couplet. Though he wrote in many forms, his masterpiece is the EPIC *Annales,* a poetic history of Rome.

**Enoch,** in the BIBLE, father of METHUSELAH. It was said of him that he walked with God, a phrase also used of NOAH, and that like ELIJAH he was translated to heaven.

**Enquist, Per Olov,** 1934–, Swedish playwright and novelist. His best-known work for the theatre is a collection of three plays published in 1981 under the title *Triptych,* comprising *Lesbian Night* (about Strindberg and his wife), *To Phaedra,* and *The Life of the Slow-Worms* (about Hans Christian Andersen). His major novel to date is *The Legionaries* (1968), a controversial documentary about the expulsion of Baltic refugees to Russia after the war.

**Enschede,** city (1985 pop. 144,566, Enschede-Hengelo agglomeration 247,939), Overijssel prov., E Netherlands. Centre of the Twente region, it has a long history of textile manufacture, especially of cotton cloth which was exported to the colonies of the Dutch East Indies. The need to adapt to changing circumstances has brought new industries, including tyres and chemicals.

**Ensor, James Ensor, Baron,** 1860–1949, Belgian painter and etcher. Containing bizarre and powerful imagery, his early work, such as the nightmarish *Entry of Christ into Brussels* (1888), was rejected as scandalous. He produced his most inventive and original works, with weird, often gruesome compositions, until about 1900. Among his masterpieces is *The Temptation of St Anthony* (1887; Mus. Mod. Art, New York City). His sources included the grotesque fantasies of BOSCH and BRUEGEL; he often used masks and skeletons. Ensor was one of the great innovators of the 19th cent.; his art opened the way for SURREALISM and EXPRESSIONISM.

**entablature,** the entire unit of horizontal members above columns or pilasters in classical architecture. Its height in relation to that of the column varies with the three Greek ORDERS OF ARCHITECTURE: Doric, Ionic, and Corinthian. In Roman and Renaissance architecture it is about one quarter of the column height. Components are the architrave, which rests directly on the column cap, the frieze, and the cornice, or topmost member.

**Entebbe,** town (1969 pop. 21,096), S Uganda, on VICTORIA NYANZA (Lake Victoria), near KAMPALA. Founded in 1893, it was the administrative capital (1894–1962) of the British Uganda protectorate. It is the site of a major international airport, where in 1976 Israeli airborne commandos staged a daring rescue of 91 passengers aboard a hijacked plane.

**Entente:** see TRIPLE ALLIANCE AND TRIPLE ENTENTE.

James **Ensor,** *The Temptation of St Antony,* 1887. Oil on canvas, 117.8 × 167.6 cm. Museum of Modern Art, New York.

**Entente Cordiale,** agreements, falling short of an alliance. The term was first used to describe the agreement between Britain and France on matters of foreign, including colonial, policy, taking shape in and after 1904.

**enterprise zones,** areas designated by government for the encouragement of industrial and commercial activity. They are usually located in economically depressed areas. Private investment is attracted by means of tax and other financial incentives. In the UK, the first eleven zones were designated in 1981–82, a second batch of 14 in 1983–84, and extensions to three of the first round zones, during 1983–85. At the beginning of 1986 businesses in the 25 UK zones employed 53,500, with 6600 of the jobs in Welsh zones and 7000 in Scotland, and some 2330 enterprises had been established. An important objective of the UK government was to revitalize urban areas following the rundown of traditional industries. Particularly noteworthy was the Isle of Dogs development (in London's docklands) which by 1988 had been transformed into one of the country's 'boom' areas.

**Entick v. Carrington,** English case decided in 1765, where the court held that King's messengers, who had entered Entick's house and siezed his papers without a valid warrant, had committed a trespass. An important constitutional case deciding that private PROPERTY could not be seized without legal authority, thereby curbing the arbitrary power of government.

**entomology,** the study of INSECTS for aesthetic, practical, or professional reasons which must have begun with that of potentially useful species. The earliest known entomological illustration is a cave painting of around 7000 BC, in Valencia (N Spain), showing someone raiding a honey bee's nest in a tree. Using SILK, from MOTH cocoons, for making thread began well before 4700 BC, as by then SILKWORMS were being reared in China. Evidence of the early Egyptian interest in insects was the allocation of the hornet (see WASP) as the symbol for Lower Egypt by Narmer who founded the I dynasty in about 3100 BC, and the personification of the god Kheper in the SCARAB. The first European literary reference to insects is in Homer, at about 850 BC. A considerable understanding had however been achieved by about 340 BC, when ARISTOTLE introduced the term 'entoma' and produced a classification based on wings and mouthparts. Further advances had been made by AD 77, when PLINY wrote *Historia naturalis,* but it was not until the publication in Bologna in 1602 of *De animalibus insectis* by Aldrovandi that entomology was established as a science in its own right. 1658 saw the publication of *The Theatre of Insects,* Topsell's English version of an earlier work in Latin, which marked the beginning of an ever-increasing flood of books on every aspect of entomology. In 1833 the (now Royal) Entomological Society was instituted, and the study of insects in British universities was placed on a firm footing by the foundation in 1849 of the Hope Department of Entomology at Oxford. Because of the rapid expansion of human populations and the demand for a higher standard of living, ever-increasing efforts are being made to find more economically viable and environmentally acceptable means of combatting the insect pests which damage crops, destroy stored products, and transmit human and livestock diseases. Considerable use is also made of some insects, because of their rapid rate of reproduction, for genetical and physiological research into human problems.

**entropy,** quantity specifying the amount of disorder or randomness in a system bearing energy or information. In THERMODYNAMICS, entropy indicates the degree to which a given quantity of thermal energy is available for doing useful work; the greater the entropy, the less available the energy. According to the second law of thermodynamics, during any process the change in entropy of a system and its surroundings is either zero or positive; thus the entropy of the universe as a whole tends towards a maximum. In INFORMATION THEORY entropy represents the 'noise', or random errors, occurring in the transmission of signals or messages.

**Enugu,** city (1981 est. pop. 256,000), S Nigeria. Chief town of Anambra state, it is a coal mining centre and its industries include the manufacture of glass and bricks, sawmilling, and railway engineering. Enugu developed after the discovery of coal in 1909.

**environmentalism,** movement to preserve the quality and continuity of life on earth. Conservationists began working early in the 1900s towards the CONSERVATION OF NATURAL RESOURCES and the establishment of NATIONAL PARKS, NATURE RESERVES, and forests. In the decades following World War II, growing concern about POLLUTION, dwindling energy resources, and the dangers of pesticides and radiation, and, later, about the values and ideology underlying the industrial culture, gave rise to environmentalism. This holistic approach embraces the concept of conserving the earth itself by protecting its capacity for self-renewal (see BIOSPHERE; ECOLOGY). Environmentalism is informed by the realization that environmental issues must be interlinked with economics and that many also have political implications which call for political solutions. Radicals in the movement assert the need for a post-industrial society; the more conservative element, the need for increased resources to be devoted to environmental planning and pollution control. The movement has generated extensive legislation, notably laws regulating air quality, water quality, noise, pesticides, toxic substances, and ocean dumping; laws to protect ENDANGERED SPECIES and wilderness areas; and agencies and coordinating bodies in key regions of the world. In some countries, e.g., the US, private citizens may sue government and industry for failure to comply with statutory standards. Numerous voluntary organizations, such as the World Wild Fund for Nature (1961), Friends of the Earth (1971), Greenpeace (begun in Canada 1971, UK 1976), the National Trust (UK, 1895), the Royal Society for the Protection of Birds (1904, Europe's largest conservation pressure group), and the Sierra Club and National Audubon Society (US), continue to lobby and litigate to preserve and extend environmental safeguards. Environmentalism is, equally importantly, a grassroots movement, as exemplified by the Australian Aborigines defending their land against uranium-mining companies, Lapps their reindeer grazing land in Norway, and Japanese mounting a sometimes violent struggle (1966–78) to prevent the building of Narita airport. Concern for the environment often conflicts with the vested interests of farmers and landowners, developers and industrialists, and the defence interests of the major, especially nuclear, powers.

**Enzensberger, Hans Magnus,** 1929–, German poet, essayist, and journalist. One of the most intelligent writers of the postwar generation. Enzensberger's three careers are all marked by acute social and historical awareness: as a lyric poet of great wit and virtuosity (see his collections: *Defence of the Wolves*, 1957; *Local Language*, 1960; and *Blind Writing*, 1964); as an acute critic of the media and the German political scene (his essays on newspaper-language in *Details*, 1962, 1964 were epoch-making; tr. as *The Consciousness Industry*, 1974); and as editor: in 1965 he founded the influential left-wing journal *Kursbuch*, declaring at the height of the student revolution in 1968 that literature had lost any social function and that henceforth he would devote himself to Germany's political education—as he did, for example, in his documentary drama *The Havana Inquiry* (1970). He has subsequently returned to lucid, critical poetry. His long narrative poem, *The Sinking of the Titanic* (1978), he translated into English himself.

**Enzina, Juan del:** see ENCINA, JUAN DEL.

**enzyme,** protein functioning as a biological CATALYST. Enzymes accelerate (often by several orders of magnitude) chemical reactions in the cell without being used up in the process. Most enzymes demonstrate great specificity, reacting with only one or a small group of closely related chemical compounds (substrates); thus, sometimes several enzymes are required for efficient catalytic function. Some enzymes depend on the presence of a COENZYME for their function. Over 1000 different enzymes have been identified. Enzymes are involved in all metabolic processes and play an important role in heredity. They function by attaching the substrate molecule to a specific molecular site, so that the electrostatic forces of nearby atoms sharply reduce the energy needed to cleave and reform the appropriate chemical bonds. Enzymes are typically named by adding *-ase* to their substrate (e.g., amylase) or type of action (e.g., dehydrogenase) except where older names (e.g., pepsin) have been retained.

**Eocene epoch:** see GEOLOGICAL ERA (table).

**Eos,** in Greek mythology, goddess of dawn. Daughter of Hyperion and Theia, she was the sister of the sun god HELIOS, and the mother of the winds. The Romans called her Aurora.

**Epaminondas** (epami,nondas), d. 362 BC, Theban statesman and general. He became prominent after his city expelled the Spartans (379/8 BC), and won unrivalled fame by defeating the full Spartan army, hitherto reckoned invincible, at Leuktra in 371. Thereafter he led four invasions of the Peloponnese, reaching the gates of Sparta itself, liberating MESSENIA after three centuries of subjection and founding a new city at Messene, and founding also a new capital for the Arcadian confederacy at Megalopolis. He was killed in the act of winning another victory over the Spartans at Mantinea (362).

**ephedrine,** mild, slow-acting ALKALOID drug used to treat moderate atacks of bronchial asthma and to relieve nasal congestion from hay fever or infection of the upper respiratory tract. Nonaddictive, ephedrine may cause insomnia and restlessness.

**ephemeris,** table listing the positions of one or more celestial bodies for each day of the year. Early national ephemerides include the French *Connaissance des temps* (begun 1679) and the British *Nautical Almanac and Astronomical Ephemeris* (begun 1767). Since 1958 the US and Great Britain have jointly published solar, lunar, planetary, and satellite ephemerides in identical publications (the US *American Ephemeris* and the British *Astronomical Ephemeris*).

**Ephesians,** EPISTLE of the NEW TESTAMENT. Tradition ascribes it to St PAUL (AD c.60), but some hold it to be a circular letter written by a disciple AD c.90. The most profound of the Pauline epistles, it is pervaded with the doctrine of the mystical body of Christ, Paul's analogy of the perfect union of Christians. It contains a famous metaphor of the Christian as soldier (6:10–17).

**Ephesus** (,efəsəs), ancient Ionian Greek city of ASIA MINOR, in modern TURKEY. A wealthy seaport, it was captured in turn by Lydia, Persia, and Macedonia. It passed to Rome in 133 BC and was the leading city of the province of Asia. Its temple of Artemis (Diana) was one of the SEVEN WONDERS OF THE WORLD. Ephesus later became a centre of Christianity and was visited by St PAUL.

**Ephraim:** see ISRAEL, TRIBES OF.

**epic,** long, narrative poem, usually on a serious, or exalted theme, centred on a heroic figure. Early epics, e.g., the Babylonian *Gilgamesh,* HOMER's *Iliad* and *Odyssey,* and the Anglo-Saxon BEOWULF, were shaped from the legends of expanding nations. Literary epics, e.g., VIRGIL's *Aeneid* and John MILTON's *Paradise Lost,* consciously imitate the earlier form. Epic conventions include a hero embodying national ideals, the performance of great deeds, the depiction of an era, divine intervention, and concern with eternal human problems. A mock epic is a satire based on an incongruous treatment of the trivial in epic terms, e.g., Alexander POPE's *Rape of the Lock.*

**Epictetus,** AD c.50–c.138, Stoic philosopher of Phrygia (part of Asia Minor), once a slave. His STOICISM taught that the true good is within oneself and is not dependent on external things, and he emphasized the doctrine of brotherhood. His teachings, set down by his disciple Arrian in the *Encheiridion* [handbook] and *Discourses,* influenced MARCUS AURELIUS.

**epic theatre:** see BRECHT, BERTOLT; PISCATOR, ERWIN.

**Epicurus,** 341–270 BC, Greek philosopher, founder of Epicureanism. He defined philosophy as the art of making life happy and subordinated METAPHYSICS to ETHICS, naming pleasure the highest and only good. For Epicurus, however, pleasure was not the heedless indulgence advocated by the followers of HEDONISM, but rather the serenity (*ataraxia*) resulting from the absence of pain. He also prescribed a code of social conduct that advocated honesty, prudence, and justice in dealing with others (because such conduct would save the individual from society's retribution, or pain). Only fragments of his writings are extant; the finest exposition of his ideas is contained in *On the Nature of Things* by the Roman poet LUCRETIUS.

**epicycle:** see PTOLEMAIC SYSTEM.

**Epidaurus,** Gr. *Epídavros,* ruins of an ancient city in the Argolis peninsula of Peloponnesus, Greece. Associated with the god of healing, ASCLEPIUS, it was a place of pilgrimage for those seeking cures The magnificent theatre of the 3rd cent. BC has excellent acoustics and is still used for plays during the summer season.

**epidemic:** see EPIDEMIOLOGY.

**epidemic parotitis:** see MUMPS.

**epidemiology,** field of medicine concerned with the study of epidemics, outbreaks of disease that affect large numbers of people. Epidemiologists, using sophisticated statistical analyses, field investigations, and complex laboratory techniques, investigate the cause of a disease, its distribution (geographic, social, and ethnic), method of spread, and measures for control and prevention. Epidemiological investigations once concentrated on such communicable diseases as TUBERCULOSIS, INFLUENZA, and CHOLERA, but now encompass CANCER, CORONARY HEART DISEASE, and other diseases affecting large numbers of people.

**Epigoni:** see SEVEN AGAINST THEBES.

**epigram,** short, polished saying, usually in verse, often with a satirical or paradoxical twist. Established by MARTIAL, the form of English is particularly associated with John DONNE, Alexander POPE, Lord BYRON, and S.T. COLERIDGE. Among the most brilliant epigrammatists was Oscar WILDE, whose works are studded with epigrams, e.g., 'A cynic is a man who knows the price of everything, and the value of nothing'.

**epilepsy,** disorder of the brain characterized by sudden, brief, partial seizures or muscle spasms (petit mal) or by widespread convulsive seizures involving loss of motor control and consciousness (grand mal). The development of epilepsy may be idiopathic (of unknown cause) or symptomatic (with the cause identified). Infantile epilepsy may result from developmental abnormalities, metabolic disease, or birth injury. In adults, causes of epilepsy include trauma, tumours, and organic brain disorders. Drug therapy includes the use of anticonvulsants such as phenytoin and phenobarbitone.

**Epiphany** [Gr., = showing], a leading Christian feast, celebrated 6 Jan. It commemorates the baptism of Jesus, the visit of the Wise Men to Bethlehem, and the miracle of Cana. Its eve is Twelfth Night.

**epiphyte** or **air plant,** plant that grows not in the soil but on another plant, depending on it only for physical support; an epiphyte makes its own food, thus differing from a PARASITE. Epiphytes obtain moisture from the air or moisture-laden pockets on the host plant. Well-known examples are many ORCHIDS and BROMELIADS.

**Epirus,** ancient country of W GREECE, on the Ionian Sea. It reached its height in the 3rd cent. BC, under PYRRHUS. It sided with MACEDON against Rome, was sacked (167 BC), and passed under Roman rule. In AD 1204 the independent despotate of Epirus emerged, but the Turks took it over in the 15th cent. In the late 18th cent. ALI PASHA established an independent state in Epirus and Albania.

**Episcopal Church, Protestant,** in the United States of America, a part of the ANGLICAN COMMUNION. Anglican (Church of England) services were first held in America at Jamestown, Virginia, in 1607, but after the American Revolution, it was necessary for American Anglicans to organize a national church. Samuel SEABURY was consecrated (1784) as the first bishop, and the first General Convention (1789) approved the name and constitution of the church and revised the BOOK OF COMMON PRAYER for use in America. The church follows the doctrinal lines of the Anglican Communion, although the Thirty-nine Articles have been modified to fit American conditions. Since 1976 its priesthood has been open to both men and women. In 1980 church membership was reported to be 2,786,004.

**episiotomy,** surgical incision of the vagina and perineum (area between vagina and anus) in order to enlarge the outlet at the time of giving birth.

The procedure was believed by surgeons to be preferable to spontaneous tearing of this area.

**epistemology,** branch of philosophy dealing with the origin and nature of knowledge, a fundamental theme since the 17th cent. The rationalist view, led by DESCARTES, SPINOZA, LEIBNIZ, and others, sought to integrate a belief in the existence of certain innate ideas with an acceptance of the value of data received by experience. EMPIRICISM, expounded by HUME, LOCKE, and John Stuart MILL, denied the existence of innate ideas altogether, maintaining that all knowledge comes from human experience. KANT attempted to combine the two views. In later theories the split was reflected in IDEALISM and MATERIALISM. The empirical view has been central to PRAGMATISM, as taught by C.S. PEIRCE, William JAMES, and John DEWEY, and to the development of the modern scientific approach.

**epistle,** in the BIBLE, a letter of the NEW TESTAMENT. The Pauline Epistles (ascribed to St PAUL) are ROMANS, First and Second CORINTHIANS, GALATIANS, EPHESIANS, PHILIPPIANS, COLOSSIANS, First and Second THESSALONIANS, First and Second TIMOTHY, TITUS, PHILEMON, and HEBREWS. JAMES, First and Second PETER, First, Second, and Third JOHN, and JUDE are traditionally called Catholic, or General, Epistles.

**Epsom salts,** a water-soluble, bitter-tasting compound ($MgSO_4 \cdot 7H_2O$) that occurs as white or colourless needle-shaped crystals. It is used as a medicinal purgative, in leather tanning, in mordant dyeing, and as a filler in cotton goods and paper. It is found in waters of mineral springs and as the mineral epsomite.

**Epstein, Sir Jacob,** 1880–1959, English sculptor; b. New York City. After studying with RODIN in Paris, he revolted against the ornate and pretty in art, producing bold, often harsh and massive forms in stone and bronze. His best-known pieces include the Oscar Wilde Memorial (1911; Père-Lachaise, Paris), and a *Madonna and Child* (Convent of the Holy Child Jesus, London).

**Equal Opportunities Commission,** set up by the British government (1975) to monitor the workings of the SEX DISCRIMINATION ACT and the EQUAL PAY ACT, to fight discrimination and promote equal opportunities. Feminists have often criticized the limited extent of its powers and resources to carry out this brief.

**Equal Pay Act 1970,** in the UK, law providing for equal pay and other conditions of employment between men and women. It was passed in 1970 and came into force in 1975 along with the SEX DISCRIMINATION ACT. The original Act applied to men and women in the same employment, doing 'like work' or 'work rated as equivalent'. In 1983, under pressure from the EUROPEAN COMMUNITY it was extended to cover 'work of equal value'. These categories have been hard for claimants to prove. A claimant takes his or her case to an industrial TRIBUNAL and if successful will get an equality clause inserted into their contract of employment, remedying the past discrimination. Despite the Act, women's pay remains on average about 66% of men's.

**Equal Rights Amendment:** see CIVIL RIGHTS.

**equation,** a statement, usually in symbols, that two quantities or mathematical expressions are equal, e.g., $x + 3 = 6 - y$ or $sin^2\theta = 1 - cos^2\theta$. A numerical equation contains only numbers, e.g., $2 + 3 = 6 - 1$; a literal equation contains some letters, representing unknowns or variables. An *identity* is an equation that is true no matter what value is substituted for the variables, such as $x^2 - 1 = (x - 1)(x + 1)$; a *conditional equation* is true for only certain substitutions, e.g., only the values $+1$ and $-1$ make true the equation $x^2 - 1 = 0$. See also ALGEBRA; ROOT.

**equation of state:** see GAS LAWS.

**equation of time:** see SOLAR TIME.

**equator,** imaginary great circle around the earth, equidistant from the two geographical poles and forming the base line from which LATITUDE is reckoned. Measuring c.38,600 km (24,000 mi), the equator intersects N South America, central Africa, and Indonesia. See also ASTRONOMICAL COORDINATE SYSTEMS.

**Equatorial Guinea,** officially Republic of Equatorial Guinea, republic (1986 est. pop. 390,000), 28,051 km² (10,830 sq mi), W central Africa, formerly Spanish Guinea, consisting of a mainland section, Río Muni, bordered by Cameroon (N), Gabon (E and S), and the Gulf of Guinea (W); and several islands, the most important of which is Bioko (formerly Fernando Po), in the Gulf of Guinea. MALABO, on Bioko, is the capital.

Río Muni, with 93% of the nation's land and 75% of the population, comprises a low-lying coastal area that rises in the interior to c.1100 m (3600 ft); forests of okoume, mahogany, and walnut grow along the coast. Bioko is made up of three extinct volcanoes, the highest of which rises to c.3010 m (9870 ft); the island has abundant fertile volcanic soil. The economy of Equatorial Guinea is almost exclusively agricultural, with cocoa beans (from Bioko), coffee, palm oil, and timber the principal cash crops. The population is black African, notably the Fang in Río Muni and the Bubi on Bioko. Spanish is the official language, but most people speak a Bantu language. Traditional tribal religions and Roman Catholicism are both practised.

*History.* The island now called Bioko was discovered by Fernão do Po, a Portuguese navigator, in 1472, but Portugal ceded it to Spain in 1778. Spain formally acquired Río Muni in 1885. The boundaries of the possession were defined in a 1900 treaty, and Bioko and Río Muni, as well as several other islands, were grouped together as Spanish Guinea. In 1968 nationalist demands resulted in the granting of limited autonomy and then full independence. The first president, Francisco Macías Nguema, imposed a brutal and despotic rule over the new nation; by the late 1970s thousands of refugees had fled to neighbouring countries, and the economy was virtually ruined. In 1979 a military coup overthrew Macias, who was tried for treason and other crimes, and was executed. Under a new constitution promulgated in 1982, coup leader Teodoro Obiang Nguema Mbasogo was to remain head of state for a further seven years.

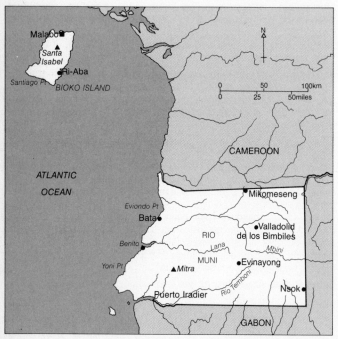

Equatorial Guinea

**equestrian events:** see DRESSAGE; EVENTING; SHOWJUMPING.

**equilibrium:** see STATICS.

**equinox,** either of two points on the celestial sphere where the ECLIPTIC and the celestial equator intersect (see ASTRONOMICAL COORDINATE SYSTEMS). The vernal equinox is the point at which the sun appears to cross the celestial equator from south to north; the autumnal equinox, the point where it appears to cross from north to south. These crossings occur about 21 Mar. and 23 Sept. and mark the beginnings of northern hemisphere spring and autumn. On either date night and day are of equal length (12 hr each) in all parts of the world. The equinoxes are not fixed points, but move westward along the ecliptic (see PRECESSION OF THE EQUINOXES).

**equity,** body of legal principles, developed by the English Court of Chancery to correct the injustices of the COMMON LAW. 'Equity' implies the application of justice and what seems right, rather than strict rules of law. It developed in the 15th cent. as a result of the formality and rigidity of the common law, which was felt to be out of touch with the needs of

society. Equity is responsible for many features of law which the common law did not recognize (e.g., TRUST, INJUNCTION). During the 16th cent. equity and common law came into conflict; this was settled by James I (1603–25) in equity's favour. In England in 1873, the court of common law and equity were joined, and today the courts administer both common law and equity. In a dispute between the principles of common law and equity, those of equity always prevail.

**Er,** chemical symbol of the element ERBIUM.

**era of good feelings,** period (1817–23) in US history after the decline of the FEDERALIST PARTY when there was little open party feeling, at least at the national level. Under the surface, however, vast sectional issues and personal rivalries were developing, to break loose in the campaign of 1824.

**Erasistratus,** fl. 3rd cent. BC, Greek physician. He was born on the island of Keos and became leader of a school of medicine in Alexandria. Erasistratus suggested that air carried from the lungs to the heart is converted into a vital spirit distributed by the arteries, and he also developed a reverse theory of circulation (veins to arteries). He studied brain convolutions, named the trachea, distinguished between motor and sensory nerves, and considered plethora (hyperaemia, excess blood in particular vessels) to be the primary cause of disease.

**Erasmus** or **Desiderius Erasmus,** 1466?–1536, Dutch humanist. One of the great figures of the RENAISSANCE, he taught throughout Europe, influencing European letters profoundly from 1500. An ordained priest of the Roman Catholic Church, he edited the Latin and Greek classics and the writings of the Fathers of the Church, and made a Latin translation of the New Testament based on the original Greek. Among his original, satirical works, written in Latin, are *In Praise of Folly* (1509) and *The Education of a Christian Prince* (1515). He was intimate with most of the scholars of Europe; his English friends included Henry VIII and Thomas MORE. Erasmus combined vast learning with a fine style, keen humour, moderation, and tolerance. He championed church reform but opposed the Protestant Reformation and remained a loyal Catholic. As a result, he and Martin LUTHER became bitter opponents, and in *On the Freedom of the Will* he denounced Luther's position on predestination.

**Erastus, Thomas,** 1524–83, Swiss Protestant theologian, originally named Lüber, Lieber, or Liebler. He opposed Calvinist doctrine and the power of the church to impose punishments, even ecclesiastical ones. The term **Erastianism** has come to represent approval of the dominance of civil authority in punitive matters and, by extension, complete dominance of state over church.

**Erato:** see MUSES.

**Eratosthenes,** c.275–c.195 BC, Greek scholar. The author of works on literature, mathematics, astronomy, geography, and philosophy, he devised a world map and a system of chronology and measured the Earth's circumference and tilt and the size and distance from Earth of the Sun and Moon.

**erbium** (Er), metallic element, discovered by Carl G. Mosander in 1843 in the mineral gadolinite. Silvery and malleable, erbium is one of the RARE-EARTH METALS and a member of the LANTHANIDE SERIES. The rose-coloured oxide erbia is used as a colouring agent in glazes and glass. See ELEMENT (table); PERIODIC TABLE.

**Ercilla y Zúñiga, Alonso de** (eətheelyah ee thoohnyeegah), 1533–94, Spanish poet. His *La Araucana* (1569–89), about the conquest of the Araucanian Indians of Chile (in which he took part), is the finest EPIC of the Spanish GOLDEN AGE.

**Erechtheum,** temple on the Acropolis, Athens, a masterpiece of Greek architecture. Built between c.421 BC and 405 BC, it is sometimes ascribed to the architect MNESICLES. It contained sanctuaries to Athena, Poseidon, and the Athenian king Erechtheus. Of the Ionic order (see ORDERS OF ARCHITECTURE), the temple has three porticos; the southern one is the famous Porch of the CARYATIDS.

**Erenburg, Ilya Grigoryevich:** see EHRENBURG.

**Erfurt,** THURINGIA, southern East Germany. The centre of a horticultural district, its industries include footwear, clothing and the manufacture of office machinery. Erfurt is one of Germany's oldest cities, its bishopric having been founded by St Boniface in AD 741. A university was established in 1392 and was later attended by Luther. Amongst notable buildings are the 13th-cent. cathedral and Church of St Severus.

Erechtheum

**erg:** see WORK.

**ergot**, disease of rye and other cereals caused by a fungus (*Claviceps purpurea*), which appears on heads of rye as dark purple structures called ergots. The ergots, which resemble rye seeds, contain certain active substances (ALKALOIDS) that are poisonous. Ergot poisoning was epidemic in the Middle Ages, for example, because bread was often made from ergot-contaminated rye. The ergots also contain alkaloids used as drugs: e.g., ergotamine to treat migraine headaches and ergonovine to stop postpartum uterine bleeding.

**Erhard, Ludwig**, 1897–1977, West German political leader and economist, chancellor (1963–66). As economics minister (1949–57) he oversaw the resurgence of the West German economy. A Christian Democrat, he succeeded Konrad ADENAUER as chancellor.

**Ericsson, Leif:** see LEIF ERICSSON.

**Eric the Red**, fl. 10th cent., Norse chieftain; discoverer and colonizer of Greenland. He discovered Greenland c.982 and led (c.986) a group of 500 colonists there, founding Brattahlid. The colony may have lasted four or five centuries.

**Erie, Lake**, fourth largest (25,745 km²/9940 sq mi) of the GREAT LAKES, separating Canada (at Ontario) and the US (at New York). It is 388 km (241 mi) long, 48–92 km (30–57 mi) wide, 174 m (572 ft) above sea level, and up to 64 m (210 ft) deep. Discharge of municipal and industrial wastes from lakeshore cities, although banned since 1972, has left much of the lake polluted. Lake Erie was discovered by JOLLIET in 1669. British and French and, later, British and Americans fought for its control in the 18th and 19th cents.

**Erie Canal**, historic artificial waterway (opened 1825) between Lake ERIE and the HUDSON R., US, providing a link between the Atlantic Ocean and the Great Lakes. Its use declined after 1850, as traffic was diverted to the railways. It was replaced (1918) by the larger New York State Barge Canal.

**Erikson, Erik**, 1902–, Danish-American psychoanalyst; b. Germany. He became a MONTESSORI teacher in Vienna after 1927 and trained under Sigmund and Anna FREUD, specializing in child analysis. After emigrating to the US (1933) he became engaged in varied clinical work, widening the scope of psychoanalytic theory to take greater account of social, cultural, and other environmental factors. In his most influential book, *Childhood and Society* (1950), he divided the human life cycle into eight psychosexual stages of development. His famous psychohistorical studies, *Young Man Luther* (1958) and *Gandhi's Truth* (1969), explore the convergence of personal and social history.

**Erinyes:** see FURIES.

**Eritrea** (eriˌtrayə), province (1980 est. pop. 2,426,200), c.124,320 km² (48,000 sq mi), N Ethiopia, on the Red Sea. ASMARA is the capital. Most of Eritrea is sparsely populated by pastoral nomads, but there is settled agriculture in valleys of the central plateau. Products include citrus fruits, cereal grains, and cotton. Part of an ancient Ethiopian kingdom until the 7th cent., Eritrea remained under Ethiopian influence until it fell to the Ottoman Turks in the mid-16th cent. It became an Italian colony in 1890 and was the main base for the Italian invasion of Ethiopia (1935–36); it was captured by the British in 1941. Since 1962, when it was annexed by Ethiopia, secessionist movements have sought to end the union. In the late 1970s Eritrean guerrillas held most of the province before Ethiopian forces, aided by the USSR and Cuba, regained control.

**Erlander, Tage Fritiof**, 1901–85, prime minister of SWEDEN (1946–69). Leader of the Social Democratic Party, he helped further the development of the Swedish welfare state. His foreign policy emphasized Sweden's neutrality in the COLD WAR and subsequently.

**Erlanger, Joseph**, 1874–1965, American physiologist. He collaborated with Herbert S. GASSER to work on studies of single nerve fibres, for which they received jointly the 1944 Nobel Prize for physiology or medicine.

**ermine:** see STOAT.

**Erne, Lough,** lake in SW of Northern Ireland, consisting of Upper Lough Erne in the S and Lower Lough Erne (also known as Lough Erne) in the N. The two lakes are connected by the R. Erne. Both of them have many islands within them.

**Ernst, Max**, 1891–1976, German painter. A member of the DADA group in Cologne in 1919, he moved to Paris in 1922 and became involved with the Surrealist group (see SURREALISM). He developed technical strategies of collage and FROTTAGE, which enabled him to include unlikely juxtapositions, chance, and automatism into his works.

**Eros**, in Greek mythology, god of love in all its manifestations. According to some legends, he was one of the oldest of the gods, born from CHAOS but personifying harmony. In most stories he was the son of APHRODITE and ARES and was represented as a winged youth armed with bow and arrows. He was the lover of PSYCHE. In Roman myth, under the name Cupid or Amor, he was the naked infant son and companion of VENUS. The statue of him in Piccadilly Circus, London, is a memorial to Lord SHAFTESBURY.

**erosion**, general term for the processes by which the surface of the earth is constantly worn away, principally by the abrasive action of running water, waves, GLACIERS, and wind. Streams and ocean waves, for example, erode bedrock by their own impact or by the abrasive action of the debris they carry. Rock surfaces are eroded by glaciers moving over them or by wind driving sand and other particles against them. Erosion is also caused by strip mining and the removal of vast areas of plant cover, e.g., by careless land developers. Some methods of preventing soil erosion are reforestation, terracing, and special ploughing techniques.

**Erskine, Thomas**, 1st **Baron Erskine**, 1750–1823, British jurist. Earlier a noted commercial lawyer, Erskine is best known as a defender of radicals at the time of the French Revolution. He defended Thomas PAINE's publication of *The Rights of Man* against a charge of SEDITION.

**Erskine May, Sir Thomas**, 1815–86, British barrister. He devoted his life to work at PARLIAMENT, being assistant clerk (1856–71) and clerk (1872–86) to the House of Commons. His *A Practical Treatise, on the Law, Privileges, Proceedings and Usage of Parliament* (1844), also known as May's *Parliamentary Practice*, runs to many editions, and is considered the authoritative work on PARLIAMENTARY LAW. It is used as a guide for many COMMONWEALTH legislatures.

**Erzberger, Matthias**, 1875–1921, German political leader. He headed the German delegation that signed the armistice at the end of World War I. He was vice chancellor and finance minister of the republican government formed in 1919, but he resigned after ruthless attacks by conservatives and reactionaries.

**Erzurum**, city (1980 pop. 190,241), capital of Erzurum prov., E Anatolia, Turkey. Situated at an altitude of 1900 m (5900 ft), it commands an ancient W–E routeway and historically has played an important strategic role. It serves as market to a predominantly livestock-producing region. In addition to its castle, it has imposing mosques and minarets.

**Es**, chemical symbol of the element EINSTEINIUM.

**Esau** (ˌeesaw), in the BIBLE, son of ISAAC. He sold his birthright for pottage to his younger twin, JACOB, who also tricked him out of their father's blessing. Gen. 25–28. Also known as Edom, Esau was the ancestor of the Edomites, a tribe consistently hostile to the Jews.

**Esbjerg,** city (1985 pop. 80,514) and largest settlement along the W coast of Danish JUTLAND. The new town and port of Esbjerg was planned in the 1860s to take advantage of growing trade links with England. Exports include bacon and dairy products. It is home port for an extensive fishing fleet and has fish processing industries.

**escape velocity,** the velocity that a body must be given in order to escape the gravitational hold of some other larger body, e.g., the earth, moon, or sun. Escape velocity depends on the mass of the larger body and the distance of the smaller body from its centre. The escape velocity from the earth's surface is about 11.3 km/sec (7 mi/sec).

**escarole:** see CHICORY.

**Eschenbach, Wolfram von:** see WOLFRAM VON ESCHENBACH.

**Escher, Maurits Cornelis,** 1898–1970, Dutch artist. Primarily a graphic artist, he composed ironic works, often visual riddles that play with the pictorially logical and the visually impossible.

**Escoffier, Georges Auguste,** 1846–1935, French chef. After being chef to Napoleon III he worked mainly in England, at the Savoy and Carlton hotels. He invented many dishes, e.g., the Pêche Melba, created for Dame Nellie when she stayed at the Savoy in 1893. Among his many books is *Guide to Modern Cookery* (1903).

**Escorial** or **Escurial,** monastery and palace, in central Spain, near Madrid. It was built (1563–84) by PHILIP II to commemorate a victory over the French. A sombre, massive granite pile, it includes a monastery, church, palace, mausoleum, college, and library. Designed by Juan Bautista de Toledo and Juan de Herrera, it has a famous art collection.

**Esdraelon** ('esdray,eelon), plain, N Israel, c.520 km² (200 sq mi), extending SE c.40 km (25 mi) between the coastal plain, near Mt Carmel, and the Jordan R. valley. Once a swampy, malarial lowland, it has been drained, irrigated, and turned into one of Israel's most fertile agricultural regions. Esdraelon is also called the plain of Jezreel or of Megiddo.

**Esdras,** two pseudepigraphic texts included in the Western canon and the Septuagint but placed in the APOCRYPHA in the Authorized Version, where they are called First and Second Esdras. The Western canon calls EZRA and Nehemiah First and Second Esdras respectively, and the terms Third and Fourth Esdras are then used for the pseudepigraphic books. These are a series of apocalyptic visions and revelations to Ezra. Third Esdras dates from before 100 BC; most critics date Fourth Esdras as a whole after AD 100.

**Esenin, Sergei Aleksandrovich:** see YESENIN.

**Esfahan** or **Isfahan,** city (1982 est. pop. 926,600), central Iran, on the Zayandeh R. The third city of Iran and an important centre of modern industry, Esfahan has long been known for its fine carpets, hand-printed textiles, and metalwork. A noteworthy city from SASSANID times, Esfahan reached the height of its glory under Persian Shah ABBAS I, who made it his capital in 1598 and embellished it with many fine buildings, e.g., the beautiful imperial mosque, the Lutfullah mosque, and the great royal palace. The city declined after its capture (1723) by the Afghans.

**Eshkol, Levi,** 1895–1969, Israeli statesman; b. Ukraine as Levi Shkolnik. Prominent in the Mapai (later Labour) Party, he served in David BEN-GURION's cabinet as minister of finance from 1952 to 1963, when he became prime minister. He led Israel in the Six-Day War (1967) and died in office. See also ARAB–ISRAELI WARS.

**esker,** long (up to many kilometres), narrow, winding ridge of stratified sand-and-gravel DRIFT, deposited in the beds of streams flowing through or beneath GLACIERS. Eskers occur in Scandinavia, Ireland, Scotland, and New England.

**Eskimo,** Algonquian and European name for the **Inuit,** native inhabitants of the coast from the Bering Sea to Greenland and of the Chukchi Peninsula, in NE Siberia. They have remained largely of pure stock and, despite their wide dispersal, are extremely uniform in language (dialects of Eskimo-Aleut), physical type (Mongoloid), and culture. Probably of Asian origin, the Eskimo first appeared in Greenland in the 13th cent. Adapting to a severe environment, they get their food, clothing, oil, tools, and weapons from sea mammals. Fish and CARIBOU are also important. Summer shelters are tents of caribou or seal skins, while cold-weather shelters are built of sod, wood, or stone; the igloo, or snow

Lutfullah mosque, **Esfahan**

hut, is seldom used. Travel is by dog sled or kayak. The Eskimo live in small bands, and almost all property is communal. Their religion has a rich mythology, and their art, which includes soapstone, ivory, and bone carvings, is skilfully rendered and well developed (see ESKIMO ART).

**Eskimo art.** The art of the Eskimo, or Inuit, peoples arose some 2000 years ago in the Bering Sea area and in Canada. Traditional art consisted of small utilitarian objects, such as weapons and tools, as well as diminutive animals, carved and incised in walrus ivory, bone, and stone. The subjects of Eskimo art reflected their lives as hunters and fishermen as well as their extensive mythology. Carved and painted wooden masks of the 19th cent. were used in various rituals. Modern Eskimo art dates from the late 1940s, when Canadians encouraged the development of art by native craftsmen working in traditional modes. Contemporary Eskimo art consists mainly of carved figures in smooth soapstone, ivory, and rough-surfaced whalebone, and lithographs printed with local stone that represent the Eskimo hunters and their quarry by simplified abstract forms.

**Eskişehir,** city (1980 pop. 309,431), capital of Eskişehir prov., NW Anatolia, Turkey. An important centre of communications, it serves as market for a grain-growing district. Metallic ores are mined in the area. Its varied industries include food-processing, textiles and engineering.

**ESP:** see PARAPSYCHOLOGY.

**Esperanto:** see INTERNATIONAL LANGUAGE.

**Espinel, Vicente Martínez** (ayspee,nel), 1550–1624, Spanish novelist, poet, and musician, who helped to popularize the guitar. His major work is the picaresque, semiautobiographical novel *Relaciones de la vida del escudero Marcos de Obregón* (1618; tr. History of the Life of the Squire Marcos of Obregón), the source of much of LE SAGE's *Gil Blas.*

**espionage:** see under INTELLIGENCE GATHERING.

**Espronceda, José de** ('espron,thayda), 1808–42, Spain's major romantic poet. His best poems, such as 'El verdugo', 'Canción del pirata', and 'El canto del cosaco', vigorously extol individual liberty. He was much influenced by BYRON.

**essay,** relatively short literary composition in prose in which the writer discusses a topic or tries to persuade the reader to accept a point of view. PLUTARCH and CICERO, among classical authors, wrote essays, but the term was first used by MONTAIGNE (1580) and Francis BACON (1597), two of the greatest essayists. The informal essay is personal, conversational, relaxed, and, frequently, humorous. Charles LAMB, William HAZLITT, and Mark TWAIN are among its masters. The formal essay, as written by Joseph ADDISON, Matthew ARNOLD, John Stuart MILL, Walter PATER, and others, is dogmatic, systematic, and expository.

**Essen,** city (1984 pop. 628,800), North Rhine–Westphalia, W West Germany, on the Ruhr R. An industrial centre of the RUHR district, it is the site of the KRUPP steelworks and West Germany's chief producer of electricity. The city grew up around a 9th-cent. Benedictine convent and

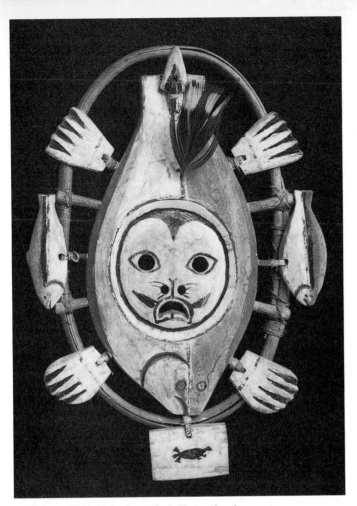

Eskimo art: Mask in the form of a halibut and seal

was a small imperial state until it passed (1802) to Prussia. Badly damaged during WORLD WAR II, it was rebuilt after 1945. Landmarks include the cathedral (9th–14th cent.).

**essential oils,** volatile oils that occur in plants and in general give the plants their characteristic odours, flavours, or other such properties. Generally complex mixtures of organic compounds, they are used in perfumes, flavourings, and medicines. Among the plants notable for their essential oils are members of the following plant families: CARROT (e.g., ANISE, DILL, angelica), GINGER (cardamom), LAUREL (CINNAMON, CAMPHOR), MINT (peppermint, THYME), MYRTLE (CLOVE), and ORCHID (VANILLA). See also FATS AND OILS.

**Essex,** one of the kingdoms of Anglo-Saxon England. Probably settled by Saxons in the early 6th cent., Essex eventually approximated in size the modern counties of Essex, London, and Hertfordshire. King Sæbert of Essex accepted Christianity c.604, but the kingdom lapsed for a time into heathenism. Long dominated by MERCIA, Essex submitted (825) to WESSEX and became an earldom. It became part of the DANELAW in 886 but was retaken (917) by Edward the Elder of Wessex.

**Essex,** county, in SE England (1984 est. pop. 1,496,700), 3672 km² (1432 sq mi), bordering on the R. Thames in the S and the North Sea in the E. The county town is CHELMSFORD. It is mainly low-lying and flat, with a marshy coastline indented with estuaries. There are undulating, low hills in the NW. The N of the county is mainly agricultural, whereas much of the S and SW is urbanized and forms part of the LONDON commuter belt. SOUTHEND-ON-SEA and Clacton are popular seaside towns and HARWICH and Tilbury are ports.

**Essex, Robert Devereux, 2nd earl of,** 1567–1601, English courtier. After distinguishing himself as a cavalry officer in the Netherlands (1585–86), serving under his stepfather, the earl of LEICESTER, he became a favourite of ELIZABETH I and a rival of Sir Walter RALEIGH. In 1590 he angered the queen by his secret marriage to the young widow of Sir Philip

SIDNEY. Advised by Francis BACON, he entered politics, hoping to seize power from the ageing Lord BURGHLEY, but Elizabeth conferred power on Burghley's son, Robert Cecil, instead. On his own demand, Essex was made lord lieutenant of Ireland and was sent there to quell the rebellion of the earl of Tyrone. He failed utterly and on his return was confined and later banned from court. He attempted a coup to establish his own party around the queen, but it failed and he was arrested. Elizabeth signed the warrant for his execution.

**Esson, Louis,** 1878–1943, Australian playwright. Influenced by the Abbey Theatre, Dublin, he was a founder of the Pioneer Players, Melbourne, the first attempt to create a national theatre in Australia. His *The Time Is Not Yet Ripe* (1912) is occasionally revived.

**estate,** in law, term applied to the rights and interests that may be held in PROPERTY; also applied to the property itself. Interests in property may range from absolute ownership, to mere possession. Examples of estate include a freehold, a LEASEHOLD, and a tenancy. A LICENCE is not an interest in land; it merely gives the licensee the right of occupation, with the licensor's permission. In England and Wales since 1926 only two legal interests in land are capable of existing: absolute ownership in possession, and a fixed term of years in possession. All other estates are recognized in EQUITY only.

**Estates-General:** see STATES-GENERAL.

**estate tax:** see INHERITANCE TAX.

**Este** (ˌestay), Italian noble family, rulers of Ferrara (1240–1597) and of Modena (1288–1796), celebrated patrons of the arts. **Azzo d'Este II,** 896–1097, founded the family's greatness, and acquired Milan. His son, **Guelph d'Este IV,** d. 1101, founded the German line of GUELPHS. Among the Italian branch, **Azzo d'Este VII,** 1205–64, became (1240) chief magistrate of Ferrara. **Obizzo d'Este II,** d. 1293, was made perpetual lord of Ferrara (1264) and lord of Modena (1288). **Beatrice d'Este,** 1475–97, married Ludovico SFORZA; her sister **Isabella d'Este,** 1474–1539, was an important patron of Renaissance art. **Alfonso d'Este I,** 1476–1534, second husband of Lucrezia BORGIA (see BORGIA, family), fought for France in the ITALIAN WARS (1494–1559). Pope JULIUS II declared (1510) his fiefs forfeited, but Alfonso aided Holy Roman Emperor CHARLES V against Pope CLEMENT VII, who was forced to recognize (1530) Alfonso's claims. His brother, **Ippolito I, Cardinal d'Este,** 1479–1520, was a patron of ARIOSTO. Alfonso's son, **Ippolito II, Cardinal d'Este,** 1509–72, built the Villa d'Este at Tivoli. In 1597 the direct male line died out, and Pope CLEMENT VIII annexed (1598) Ferrara to the papal states. Another branch ruled Modena until deposed (1796) by the French.

**Esterházy** (ˌesteəhahzee), princely Hungarian family. **Paul, Fürst Esterházy von Galantha,** 1635–1713, took part in the defence of Vienna (1683) and the reconquest of Hungary from the Turks. His grandson, **Nikolaus Joseph, Fürst Esterházy von Galantha,** 1714–90, made (1766) F.J. HAYDN chief musical director at Eisenstadt and built the celebrated Esterházy palace there. His nephew, **Nickolaus, Fürst Esterházy von Galantha,** 1765–1833, was offered (1809) the crown of Hungary by NAPOLEON I, but refused it.

**Esther,** book of the OLD TESTAMENT. It is the story of the beautiful Jewish woman Esther (Hadassah), chosen as queen by the Persian king Ahasuerus (see XERXES) after he has repudiated his previous wife, Vashti. Esther and her cousin Mordecai thwart the courtier Haman, who plots to massacre the Jews; Haman is hanged, and Mordecai becomes the king's chief minister. The feast of Purim (see JEWISH HOLIDAYS) celebrates this event. The historicity of the book is in question.

**Estienne, Étienne** (ay,tyen), or, Latinized, **Stephanus,** family of Parisian and Genevan printers and scholars of the 16th and 17th cent. **Henri Estienne,** d. 1520, was established in Paris by 1502, and issued more than 100 books, some of great beauty. His son **Robert Estienne,** b. 1498 or 1503, d. 1559, devoted himself to printing scholarly works, classics, and critical editions of the Bible, many of which he edited. He was the French king FRANCIS I's printer for Latin, Hebrew, and Greek. Claude GARAMOND and probably Geofroy TORY worked for him. A humanist, he was driven by attacks on him to Geneva, Switzerland, in 1550 and established a press there. His Latin dictionary (1531) and his grammatical treatises in French are major works. A brother, **Charles Estienne,** c.1504–64, succeeded Robert at Paris (1551). Educated in medicine and the classics, he produced an early ENCYCLOPEDIA, and many other works. One of Robert's sons, the second **Henri Estienne, 1531?–98,** the greatest scholar in the family, discovered, edited, and printed at Geneva numerous Greek and Latin works, including his *Thesaurus graecae linguae* (1572). He championed the use of French, notably in *La Précellence du langage françois* (1579). The Estienne family remained prominent as printers until late in the 17th cent.

**Estonia** or **Estonian Soviet Socialist Republic,** constituent republic (1985 pop. 1,529,000), 45,100 km² (17,413 sq mi), W European USSR. It borders on the Baltic Sea (W); the gulfs of Riga and Finland (SW and N); Latvia (S); and the Russian Soviet Federated Socialist Republic (E). The capital is TALLINN. Estonia is situated on a low-lying plain, about one-fifth of which is forest. Agriculture and dairy farming are the most important economic activities. Meat, milk, eggs, potatoes, and vegetables are the main products. Sawmills, and furniture, match, and pulp industries utilize the forest resource, while other important manufacturing industries include engineering and shipbuilding. Rich shale deposits are located in the NE, and gas produced from shale is supplied by pipeline to Tallinn and Leningrad. In addition to the Estonian majority, there are Russian and other minorities. The Estonians, ethnically and linguistically close to the Finns, settled the region before the 1st cent. AD. Between the 13th and 18th cent. it was ruled by Denmark, the Livonian Knights, Sweden, and Russia. Independent after 1920, it was annexed by the USSR in 1940 and was under German occupation from 1941 to 1944. Incorporation into the USSR has been recognized *de facto* by the British Government, but not by the US Government which still recognizes an Estonian consul-general in New York.

**estuary,** partly enclosed coastal body of water, open to the ocean so that fresh and salt water are mixed. Estuaries are extremely sensitive and ecologically important habitats, providing waterfowl sanctuaries and breeding and feeding grounds for many desirable life forms. They are often excellent harbours, and many large international ports are located in them. The human impact on estuaries (e.g., landfill, sewage pollution, industrial effluents) can destroy the very properties of the estuary that facilitated development of the region.

**Eteocles:** see SEVEN AGAINST THEBES.

**ethanol** or **ethyl alcohol** (CH₃CH₂OH), a colourless liquid with characteristic odour and taste, commonly called grain alcohol or, simply, ALCOHOL. Ordinary ethanol is about 95% pure, the remaining 5% being water, which can only be removed with difficulty to give pure or absolute ethanol. Ethanol is the alcohol in beer, wine, and spirits, and can be made by the FERMENTATION of sugar or starch. Denatured alcohol, for industrial use, is ethanol with toxic additives. Ethanol is used as a solvent in the manufacture of varnishes and perfumes; as a preservative; in medicines; as a disinfectant; and as a fuel. Ethanol is sleep-inducing; if its presence in the blood exceeds about 5%, death usually occurs. Behavioural changes, impairment of vision, or unconsciousness occur at lower concentrations. See ALCOHOLISM.

**Ethelfleda:** see ÆTHELFLED.

**ether** or **aether,** in physics, a hypothetical medium for transmitting ELECTROMAGNETIC RADIATION, filling all unoccupied space. The theory of RELATIVITY eliminated the need for such a medium, and the term is used only in a historical context.

**Etherege, Sir George,** 1634?–91, English dramatist. His witty *Comical Revenge; or, Love in a Tub* (1664), *She Wou'd If She Cou'd* (1668), and *The Man of Mode; or, Sir Fopling Flutter* (1676) set the tone for the RESTORATION comedy of manners.

**ethics,** in philosophy, the study of ways of life in the light of rules of conduct. The discipline divides roughly into two parts. *Meta-ethics* is a branch of METAPHYSICS which studies the form, nature, and status of moral judgments, e.g., the problem of the objectivity of morals, the distinction between moral and factual beliefs, the connection between moral beliefs and action. KANT's account of the categorical imperative and G.E. MOORE's account of the good are examples of meta-ethical doctrines. *Normative ethics* studies the content of moral judgments and attempts to articulate a framework within which ethical thinking can take place. Philosophers differ widely on what this should be. For PLATO, ethics is a matter of acquaintance with timeless Platonic ideals; for ARISTOTLE it is the exercise of natural faculties in the pursuit of excellence; for HOBBES, the pursuit of self-interest; for KANT, obedience to the categorical imperative—a rule independent of any desire, including happiness; for HEGEL and MARX,

subordination to the state; for BENTHAM and J.S. MILL it is the maximization of human happiness; in EXISTENTIALISM, the attempt to create ourselves and our values.

**Ethiopia,** formerly Abyssinia, independent state (1986 est. pop. 43,350,000), 1,221,900 km² (471,776 sq mi), NE Africa, bordered by the Red Sea (N), Djibouti (NE), Somalia (E and SE), Kenya (S), and Sudan (W). ADDIS ABABA (the capital) and ASMARA are the principal cities. Ethiopia may be divided into four geographic zones: from west to east they are the Ethiopian Plateau, a highland region including more than half the country and reaching a height of 4620 m (15,158 ft) at Ras Dashan; the GREAT RIFT VALLEY, containing the Danakil Desert and several large lakes; the Somali Plateau, with heights of more than 4267 m (14,000 ft) in the Urgoma Mts; and the Ogaden Plateau, which is mostly desert. The Blue NILE (called the Abbai in Ethiopia) flows through the centre of the Ethiopian Plateau from its source, Lake Tana, Ethiopia's largest lake. The economy is almost entirely agricultural, with most of the labour force engaged in subsistence farming. Coffee accounts for 70% of export earnings; other leading exports are oilseeds, hides and skins, and grain. Industry is limited to production of basic consumer needs. Some minerals are extracted on a small scale. The GNP is US$4638 million and the GNP per capita is US$110 (1985). The Muslim Galla, who constitute about 40% of the population, are the largest ethnic group, and there are significant numbers of Somali, but the Amhara and Tigrinya (33% combined), who are Coptic Christians, are politically dominant. Amharic is the official language, but English is widely spoken.

*History.* According to tradition, the kingdom of Ethiopia was founded (10th cent. BC) by Menelik I, Solomon's first son, supposedly by the Queen of Sheba. The first recorded kingdom, however, is that of Aksum (Axum), probably founded (1st cent. AD) by traders from S Arabia and converted to Coptic Christianity in the 4th cent. With the rise of Islam in the 7th cent., Aksum lost control of the Red Sea routes, and a period of chaos followed. Order was restored in the 13th cent., with the founding of a new Solomonian dynasty. However, a war to expel the encroaching Somali, while successful (1543), exhausted the nation, which for the next two centuries was beset by ruinous civil wars. Finally, in 1889, MENELIK II, supported by Italy, instituted a strong rule. Claiming that Menelik had agreed to the establishment of a protectorate, Italy invaded Ethiopia in 1895 but was decisively defeated at Adowa (1896). HAILE SELASSIE, who ascended the throne in 1930, faced a renewed Italian threat, which culminated in a full-scale invasion in 1935. Ethiopia was incorporated into ITALIAN EAST AFRICA until 1941, when it was liberated by the British. In 1974 Haile Selassie was overthrown by military officers who proclaimed a socialist state and nationalized the economy. The military regime has been plagued by serious political and economic problems, particularly a secessionist movement in ERITREA, a territorial dispute with Somalia in OGADEN, and a famine-threatening drought, and has been dependent on outside support from the Soviet Union and its allies. In 1984 the Workers' Party of Ethiopia was established as the sole legal party, with head of state Lt.-Col. MENGISTU Haile Mariam as its leader.

**Ethiopic,** extinct language of Ethiopia belonging to the Semitic subfamily of the Hamito-Semitic family of languages. See AFRICAN LANGUAGES (table).

**ethnic group,** a group of people defining themselves in terms of shared history, language, and culture (sometimes also geographical location). Ethnic identity acts as a powerful political and cutural focus for minority groups who perceive themselves as socially, politically, or economically disadvantaged (e.g., in Britain, Sikhs, Bangladeshis or Afro-Caribbeans; Basques in Spain; Tamils in Sri Lanka; Kurds in Afghanistan). Ethnicity should not be confused (though it often is) with RACE as a defining characteristic.

**ethnic studies,** in American education, courses of instruction in the history and culture of US minority groups. As a result of the BLACK AMERICAN protest movement of the 1960s, courses in areas such as black history and literature were added to the curricula of educational institutions. Other ethnic minorities, especially CHICANOS and other HISPANIC AMERICANS, have obtained similar course offerings, but to a lesser extent. See also MULTICULTURAL EDUCATION.

**ethnocentrism,** the belief that a group's mode of living, values, and patterns of adaptation are superior to those of other groups. It may manifest itself in attitudes of superiority or hostility toward members of other groups and is sometimes expressed in discrimination, proselytizing, or violence.

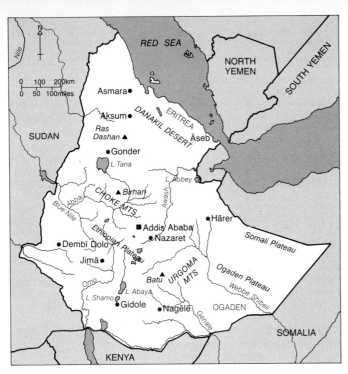

Ethiopia

Etruscan art: Bride and Groom, 6th cent BC life-size terracotta sculpture sarcophagus

**ethnology,** scientific study of the origin and functioning of humans and their cultures, usually considered a branch of cultural ANTHROPOLOGY. In the 19th cent. historical ethnology attempted to explain extant cultures by examining their early development. In the 20th cent. the comparative study of cultures has predominated. See EVOLUTION, SOCIOCULTURAL.

**ethology,** study of animal behaviour, especially its physiological, ecological, and evolutionary aspects. Originally, an organism's actions were classified as either instinctive behaviour (actions not influenced by the animal's previous experiences, e.g., common reflexes) or learned behaviour (actions dependent on earlier experiences, e.g., problem-solving). Current emphasis is on the interaction between environmental and genetically determined responses, particularly during early development.

**ethyl alcohol:** see ETHANOL.

**ethyne:** see ACETYLENE.

**Etna** or **Aetna,** frequently active volcano, 3340 m, (10,958 ft), the highest in Europe, on the E coast of Sicily, S Italy. Snowcapped for much of the year, the volcano towers over and constantly threatens a densely populated agricultural area at its base. It last erupted in 1986.

**Étoile, Place de l':** see ARC DE TRIOMPHE DE L'ÉTOILE.

**Eton,** town, Berkshire, central England, on the Thames R. It is known chiefly for **Eton College** (est. 1440), the largest and most famous of the English public schools.

**Etruria** (i,trooəreeə), ancient country, W Italy, now Tuscany and W Umbria. It was the centre of ETRUSCAN CIVILIZATION.

**Etruscan art,** the art of Etruria, a mysterious nation whose civilization prospered in central Italy from the 8th to the 2nd cent BC. The bronze and clay sculptures and carvings of the Etruscans owe much to Greek sources but have an idiosyncratic, naturalistic character of their own. The Etruscans excelled in portraiture and metalwork. Their sepulchral art was highly developed in centres such as Caere (Cerveteri), Veii (Veio), and Tavxuna (Tarquinia); several sarcophagi show reclining couples on their tombs feasting in the after life, and painted frescoes, especially at Tarquinia, show hunting, dancing, and banqueting scenes. There is an important collection of Etruscan art at the Villa Giulia, Rome, which includes the *Apollo of Veii* (c.500 BC).

**Etruscan civilization,** highest civilization in Italy before the rise of Rome. Modern research tends to uphold the tradition of HERODOTUS that the Etruscans migrated to Italy from Lydia in Asia Minor in the 12th cent.

BC. A distinctive Etruscan culture evolved about the 8th cent. BC, developed rapidly during the 7th cent., achieved its peak of power and wealth during the 6th cent., and declined during the 5th and 4th cent. Etruria comprised a loose confederation of city-states, including Clusium (now Chiusi), Tarquinii (Tarquinia), Veii (Veio), Volterra, and Perusia (Perugia). The Estruscans' wealth and power were in part based upon their knowledge of metalworking. They also made fine pottery. The Etruscan language cannot be classified into any known group of languages.

**etymology** (eti,moləjee), branch of linguistics that investigates the origin and development of words. This study revealed the regular relations of sound in the Indo-European languages (as described in GRIMM'S LAW), and led to the historical study of language in the 19th cent. Modern linguists are particularly interested in investigating the meaning of a form within the specific context of a given time and place. The term *etymology* has been replaced by *derivation* for the creation of combinations used in a language, such as new nouns formed with the ending *-ness*.

**Eu,** chemical symbol of the element EUROPIUM.

**Euboea:** see ÉVVOIA.

**eucalyptus,** tree or shrub (genus *Eucalyptus*) of the myrtle family, a prominent feature of the Australian vegetation and widely planted elsewhere. *E. globulus,* the blue gum, is a 22-m (75-ft) tree, one of the most valuable timber trees of the Southern Hemisphere. The strongly antiseptic oil of eucalypt is obtained from members of this genus. Eucalypts are grown in gardens in Britain and elsewhere for their delicately blue-tinted foliage.

**Eucharist:** see COMMUNION.

**Euclid,** fl. 300 BC, Greek mathematician whose treatment of elementary plane GEOMETRY serves as the basis for most first courses on the subject. His great contribution was the use of a deductive system of proof in his *Elements,* a presentation of the mathematics of his day in 13 books. Studies of his work in the 19th cent. gave rise to several types of NON-EUCLIDEAN GEOMETRY.

**Euclidean geometry,** set of propositions in geometry that can be derived by rigorous logical steps from the five postulates stated by EUCLID at the beginning of his *Elements.* The first three postulates state that it is possible (1) to draw a straight line from any point to any point, (2) to produce a finite straight line continuously in a straight line, and (3) to describe a circle with any centre and radius. The fourth postulate states that 'All right angles are equal to one another', and the fifth posits that 'If a straight line falling on two straight lines makes the interior angles on the same side less than two right angles, the two straight lines, if produced indefinitely, will meet on that side on which are the angles less than two right angles.' A NON-EUCLIDEAN GEOMETRY replaces the fifth postulate with either of two alternative postulates.

**Eudoxus of Cnidus** (yoo͵doksəs), 408?–355? BC, Greek astronomer, mathematician, and physician. He was the first Greek astronomer to explain the movements of the planets scientifically, holding that a number of concentric spheres supported the planets in their paths. It is claimed that he calculated the length of the solar year, indicating a calendar reform like that made later by Julius CAESAR, and that he was the discoverer of some parts of geometry included in EUCLID's work.

**Eugene III, Blessed,** d. 1153, pope (1145–53), a Pisan named Bernard. He was driven (1146) from Rome by the agitation of Arnold of Brescia and the republicans. Eugene was a friend of BERNARD OF CLAIRVAUX and promoted the disastrous Second CRUSADE.

**Eugene IV,** 1383–1447, pope (1431–47), a Venetian named Gabriele Condulmaro. Eugene at first opposed the Council of BASEL, but after being driven by rebellion from Rome to Florence (1434), he became conciliatory. He removed (1437) the council to Ferrara, where it proclaimed (1439) the reunion of the Eastern and Western churches (see COUNCIL, ECUMENICAL).

**Eugene of Savoy,** 1663–1736, prince of the house of Savoy and general in the service of the Holy Roman Empire. He is regarded as one of the great military commanders of the modern age. He was a leading participant in the War of the SPANISH SUCCESSION, and he and the duke of MARLBOROUGH won the great battle of Blenheim (1704). He also fought the French for Austria in the War of the POLISH SUCCESSION, and defeated the Turks on a number of occasions.

**eugenics,** the attempt to 'improve' the racial stock through the selective encouragement (*positive eugenics*) or suppression (*negative eugenics*) of certain human traits. At the height of its popularity (in the 1880s and 1890s), eugenics was associated with the emerging discipline of social statistics and with broader humanitarian concerns about the physical and moral health of the population. Because of its implicit assumption of racial superiority, eugenics has often been associated with the political right (e.g., fascist ANTI-SEMITISM), though it has also been espoused by radical groups (e.g., the SUFFRAGETTE and FABIAN movements). Like other 'sciences of human engineering', eugenics poses serious ethical questions. Eugenic issues are very pertinent in contemporary debates around such questions as the abortion of 'defective' foetuses, sterilization of the mentally handicapped, discouraging the under-class from having too large families, etc.

**Eugénie** (yoo͵jeenee), 1826–1920, empress of the French (1853–70), consort of NAPOLEON III. A Spanish noblewoman of great beauty and a leader of fashion, she married the emperor in 1853 and took an active part in government. After Napoleon III's deposition (1870) during the FRANCO-PRUSSIAN WAR, she fled to England.

**Euglenophyta,** small division of the plant kingdom consisting of photosynthetic, aquatic organisms. Most are unicellular; many have flagella and are motile. They resemble plants in that they have CHLOROPLASTS, but they also have gullets and lack cell walls, like animals. The most characteristic genus is *Euglena,* common in ponds and pools.

**Eulenspiegel, Till** (͵oylən'shpeegəl), a north German peasant clown of the 14th cent., immortalized in CHAPBOOKS describing his practical jokes. He is celebrated in Richard STRAUSS's tone poem and in stories and verse throughout Europe.

**Euler, Leonhard** (͵oylə), 1707–83, Swiss mathematician. A highly prolific mathematician, he worked at the St Petersburg Academy of Sciences, Russia (1727–41, 1766–83), and at the Berlin Academy (1741–66). Euler contributed to numerous areas of both pure and applied mathematics, including calculus, analysis, number theory, topology, algebra, geometry, trigonometry, analytical mechanics, hydrodynamics, and the theory of the moon's motion.

**euphorbia:** see SPURGE.

**Euphrates,** major river of arid SW Asia, formed by the confluence of the Kara and Murad rivers in E Turkey. It flows generally south, then southeast for c.2740 km (1700 mi) through deep canyons and narrow gorges in its upper course to a wide flood plain in Syria and Iraq. Upstream of BASRA the river joins with the TIGRIS R. to form the SHATT AL ARAB, which enters the PERSIAN GULF. The Euphrates drains a large highland area of E Turkey where rainfall is heavy and the winter severe. Spring snow melt causes a large annual flood from April to May. Dams on the river in Turkey, Syria and Iraq now provide some control over the flow and generate hydroelectric power. An important source of irrigation for modern Syria and Iraq, the Euphrates contributed significantly to the development of many great civilizations in ancient MESOPOTAMIA.

**euphuism,** an elaborate, artificial English prose style, derived from John LYLY's *Euphues,* that flourished in the 1580s. The term now means preciosity.

**Eurasia,** name of the great land mass that comprises the continents of EUROPE and ASIA.

**Eureka,** a protest movement on the Eureka goldfield, Ballarat, Australia, in 1854 against the colonial administration. The aggrieved miners swore allegiance to a Southern Cross flag and barricaded themselves in a stockade, which was captured by troops, with the death of 30 'diggers' and five soldiers. Eureka became a symbol of democracy in Australia and the Southern Cross is now part of the Australian flag.

**Euric,** d. c.484, king of the VISIGOTHS (r.466–c.484). He conquered the Iberian peninsula and S Gaul, made Toulouse his capital, and codified (475) Visigothic law.

**Euripides,** b. 480 or 485 BC, d. 406 BC, major Greek tragic poet. He wrote perhaps 92 plays, of which 18 are extant, including *Alcestis, Medea, Hippolytus, Andromache,* the *Trojan Women, Iphigenia in Tauris,* the *Phoenician Women, Orestes, Iphigenia in Aulis,* and the *Bacchae.* More realistic than AESCHYLUS or SOPHOCLES and rationalistic and iconoclastic toward the gods, he was interested in less-than-heroic characters. He often used the *deus ex machina* [god from a machine] to end his plots, and may have invented the device, which in his hands is not mechanical nor undramatic. See also TRAGEDY.

**Europa,** in astronomy, natural satellite of JUPITER.

**Europe,** 6th largest continent, c.10,360,000 km² (4,000,000 sq mi), including adjacent islands (1980 est. pop. 686,000,000). Actually a vast peninsula of the Eurasian landmass, it is conventionally separated from Asia by the URALS and Ural R. (E); the CASPIAN SEA and CAUCASUS (SE); and the BLACK SEA, BOSPORUS and DARDANELLES straits, and the Sea of Marmara (S). The MEDITERRANEAN SEA and Strait of GIBRALTAR separate it from Africa. The huge, young Alpine mountain chain, which includes the PYRENEES, ALPS, APENNINES, CARPATHIANS, and Caucasus, traverses the continent from W to E. MONT BLANC 4807 m (15.771 ft) in the Alps and Mt ELBRUS 5633 m (18,481 ft) in the Caucasus are the highest points. The fertile European plain stretches from the Atlantic coast of France to the Urals. The climate is mild and generally humid in the W and NW, dry in summer (Mediterranean type) in the S, and humid with cool summers in the E. Except for the N, Europe is densely populated. The countries of Europe are Albania, Andorra, Austria, Belgium, Bulgaria, Czechoslovakia, Denmark, Finland, France, East Germany, West Germany, Greece, Hungary, Iceland, the Republic of Ireland, Italy, Liechtenstein, Luxembourg, Malta, Monaco, the Netherlands, Norway, Poland, Portugal, Romania, San Marino, Spain, Sweden, Switzerland, European Turkey, the United Kingdom (Great Britain and Northern Ireland), the European USSR, Vatican City, and Yugoslavia (see separate articles). LONDON, MOSCOW, and PARIS are the largest cities. See map of Europe in separate section.

**European Atomic Energy Community,** (EURATOM), economic organization established in 1958 as the 3rd member of the EUROPEAN COMMUNITY. Its members are pledged to the common development of Europe's nuclear energy resources through coordination of their nuclear research and development programmes. EURATOM is vested with wide powers, e.g., to obtain raw materials and set safety standards. It operates nuclear reactors and research centres at Culham (England), Ispra (Italy), Geel (Belgium), Petten (the Netherlands), and Karlsruhe (West Germany).

**European Coal and Steel Community:** see EUROPEAN COMMUNITY.

**European Community,** officially the European Communities, the collective name given to the consolidation (1967) of three supranational groups: the European Coal and Steel Community established (1952) when six nations pooled their coal and steel resources to create unified products and labour markets; the European Economic Community (or Common Market, est. 1958), the principal aspects of which are a common external tariff, a common agricultural policy, the EUROPEAN MONETARY SYSTEM and the LOMÉ CONVENTIONS with developing African, Caribbean and Pacific states; and the European Atomic Energy

Community, or Euratom (est. 1958), pledged to the common development of member states' nuclear resources. The European Community grew out the efforts of such statesmen as Jean MONNET and Robert SCHUMAN of France and Paul Henri SPAAK of Belgium, who envisaged a unified Europe. It consists of a Council of Ministers of its member nations, an executive Commission, a European Parliament (whose members were directly elected by voters in the member states for the first time in 1979), and a Court of Justice. The six original members (Belgium, France, West Germany, Italy, Luxembourg, and the Netherlands) were joined by Denmark, Ireland, and the UK in 1973, by Greece in 1981 and by Portugal and Spain in 1986. Under the 1986 Single European Act, all internal barriers to economic activity within the Community are supposed to be dismantled from 1992.

Edward Heath led the UK into the **European Community** in 1973 (E.M.M. Wood *Daily Mail*)

**European Currency Unit (ECU)**, official monetary unit of the EEC. It is based on a basket of the EUROPEAN MONETARY SYSTEM's ten members' currencies (Deutschemark, French franc, pound sterling, Italian lira, Dutch guilder, Belgian franc, Danish krone, Greek drachma, Irish punt, and Luxembourg franc), which are weighted according to their national GDP and amount of intra-EEC trade. The ECU is the standard against which EMS exchange-rate fluctuations are measured, as well as being a unit of account and reserve instrument. Members deposit 20% of their gold and dollar reserves to the credit of the European Monetary Cooperation Fund (FECOM). The composition of the ECU is examined every five years, or more often if requested, but only one change was made up to 1986; the next examination is due in 1989 when the Spanish and Portuguese currencies are expected to be included. The use of ECUs grew rapidly in the 1980s. In the public sector they are used for settlements between central banks and in the private financial markets for loans, trade, and investment. The ECU bond market also developed strongly after the first issues were made in 1981. Since October 1985 non-EEC central banks have been allowed to hold ECUs.

**European Free Trade Association (EFTA),** a customs union and trading bloc formed (1960) by Austria, Denmark, Norway, Portugal, Sweden, Switzerland, and the UK to promote free trade among members and to seek the broader economic integration of Europe. Iceland joined EFTA in 1971; Denmark and the UK left in 1973 to join the EUROPEAN COMMUNITY, as did Portugal in 1986. Finland, hitherto associated with EFTA, became a full member in 1986. EFTA has strong trade links with the EEC and final agreement was reached in 1984 on free trade in industrial goods, thereby creating the world's largest free trade area, and a simplified customs system took effect from Jan. 1988. Other areas identified for joint cooperation included the setting of common standards and elimination of unfair trade practices. Non-trade cooperation is growing and apart from research and development covers environmental and industrial issues. EFTA has no supranational powers and member countries make their own decisions. The EFTA secretariat is located in Geneva.

**European Monetary System (EMS)**, set of provisions to bring about financial cooperation and monetary stability in Europe. The EMS was formed in 1979 in the wake of the 1974 oil crisis which brought disruption to the European economies not least because of the floating exchange rates. The key provision of the EMS is the Exchange Rate Mechanism (ERM) in which all EEC members participate except for the UK, Greece, Spain, and Portugal, and whose purpose is to eliminate exchange-rate fluctuations between participating countries. To achieve this a central rate in the EUROPEAN CURRENCY UNIT (ECU) is agreed for each participant and that currency is allowed to fluctuate within a specified band. If it moves outside this the government concerned must intervene and change its policies to avert the trend, or realign the central rate. The UK is a member of the EMS only in so far as sterling is one of the 'basket' of currencies upon which the ECU's value is based.

**European Organization for Nuclear Research** (CERN), principal European centre (est. 1954) for research in the physics of elementary particles. Twelve European countries sponsor the activities of the centre, which straddles the Franco-Swiss border W of Geneva.

**European People's Party:** see CHRISTIAN DEMOCRAT INTERNATIONAL.

**European Recovery Programme:** see MARSHALL PLAN.

**European Security Conference**, officially the Conference on Security and Cooperation in Europe (CSCE), also known as the Helsinki Conference, held in 1975 between 33 E and W European states plus the US and Canada. The Helsinki 'final act', adopted unanimously, incorporated measures to prevent accidental conflict between the Soviet and Western blocs; proposals for greater East–West cooperation; and a blueprint for closer contact between the peoples of the participating states. Specific provisions included acceptance that existing frontiers were inviolable and that basic human rights should be observed by signatory states. Formal CSCE follow-up meetings have been held in Belgrade (1977–78), Madrid (1980–83) and Vienna (from late 1986), interspersed with numerous lower-level sessions on specific questions. Among the latter, the Stockholm conference (1985–86) produced agreement on a set of confidence and security building measures in the military field.

**European Space Agency** (ESA), European agency concerned with developing, launching and operating satellites, space probes, manned orbiting laboratories and space platforms (see SATELLITE, ARTIFICIAL; SPACE PROBE; SPACE PLATFORM), and with the development of launch vehicles such as Ariane (see ROCKET). Succeeding the earlier European Space Research Organization (beginning in 1962) which built many successful satellites, and other joint European efforts, the 11-nation consortium was formed in 1975 to promote the peaceful exploration of space. Member nations are: Belgium, Denmark, France, Germany, Ireland, Italy, the Netherlands, Spain, Sweden, Switzerland, and the UK. The Agency's headquarters are in Paris, its technical centre in the Netherlands, and its operations centre is in Darmstadt, West Germany.

**europium** (Eu), metallic element, purified by Eugène Demarcay in 1901. Silvery-white and one of the RARE-EARTH METALS, it has physical properties like those of other LANTHANIDE SERIES members, but its chemical properties resemble those of calcium. Europium is used in nuclear-reactor control rods. See ELEMENT (table); PERIODIC TABLE.

**Eurydice:** see ORPHEUS.

**eustasy,** the phenomenon of absolute changes in sea level on a global scale. The most important type of sea-level change is glacio-eustasy where the proportion of water in the global water budget stored as ice varies between glacials (periods of extensive freezing in an ice age) and interglacials (warmer periods between glacials). It is thought that sea levels have been lowered by as much as 175 m (575 ft) below present levels during glacials of the Pleistocene ice ages, and the melting of the Greenland and Antarctic ice caps could raise present sea levels by 66 m (216 ft).

**Euterpe:** see MUSES.

**euthanasia,** either painlessly putting to DEATH (positive euthanasia) or failing to postpone death from natural causes (passive or negative euthanasia) in cases of terminal illness. The term *passive euthanasia* has come to mean withdrawal of extraordinary means (e.g., intravenous feeding, respirators, and artificial kidney machines) used to preserve life. Positive euthanasia is illegal in most countries, but in some doctors may lawfully refuse to prolong life when there is extreme suffering or where brain death has occurred. In Holland doctors involved in *voluntary euthanasia* at the request of the patients are not charged with murder, and have received negligible sentences. Debate centres around whether measures used to keep the terminally ill alive are routine, and justifiable, or extraordinary. Those seeking to legalize positive euthanasia assert that a patient has a right to decide to refuse treatment even though that may result in death. The problem of incapacitation can be solved, it is held, by a living will, in which a person expresses, in writing, preferences concerning medical treatment and death.

**eutrophication,** ageing of a lake or slow-moving stream by biological enrichment of its water. In a young lake, the water is cold and clear, supporting little life. With time, plant and animal life burgeon, and organic remains begin to be deposited. As the lake grows shallower and warmer, marsh plants take root and begin to fill in the basin. Eventually the lake gives way to bog, finally becoming dry land. The natural ageing of a lake may span thousands of years. However, wastes from human activities can accelerate the ageing process, as with water POLLUTION. The prime pollutants are nitrates and phosphates, which greatly stimulate the growth of algae, producing a pungent surface scum. The decomposition of dead algae reduces the water's dissolved oxygen content, adversely affecting fish and other aquatic life forms typical of a mature lake.

**Eutyches** (,yoohtikees), c.378–c.452, archimandrite in CONSTANTINOPLE, sponsor of Eutychianism (the first phase of MONOPHYSITISM) and leader of the opponents of NESTORIANISM. He taught that Christ's humanity was absorbed in his one divine nature. Eutyches was deposed (448), but was reinstated (449) by the Robber Synod at Ephesus. The Council of CHALCEDON (1451) ended Eutychianism.

**Evald, Johannes:** see EWALD, JOHANNES.

**Evangelical Alliance,** an association of individual Evangelical Christians of many denominations and countries, founded (1846) in London. Since 1951 its branches in different countries have been linked by the World Evangelical Fellowship.

**evangelist** [from Gr., = Gospel], title given to saints MATTHEW, MARK, LUKE, and JOHN. The title is now applied to Protestant preachers who preach personal conversion. Notable examples are John WESLEY, George WHITEFIELD, George FOX, Dwight Moody, and Billy GRAHAM.

**Evans, Sir Arthur John,** 1851–1941, British archaeologist. Keeper (1884–1908) of the Ashmolean Museum, Oxford, he excavated at KNOSSOS on Crete for over 30 years. He gave the world a vivid picture of this ancient Cretan culture, which he called MINOAN CIVILIZATION, in *The Palace of Minos* (4 vol., 1921–35).

**Evans, Dame Edith,** 1888–1976, English actress. Her distinguished career included stage and film work ranging from Elizabethan to modern drama. She was particularly memorable as Lady Bracknell in *The Importance of Being Earnest.*

**Evans, Gil,** (Ian Ernest Gilmore Green), 1912–88, Canadian jazz arranger, composer, pianist and bandleader. Best known for his enriching arrangements of others' compositions, he has provided the bedrock for a number of seminal recordings, including fruitful collaborations with Miles DAVIS on 'Birth of the Cool' and 'Porgy and Bess'. He has embraced rock compositions and rhythms in recent years with his own bands, without compromising the sophisticated orchestral texturing which is his trademark.

**Evans, Mary Ann** or **Marian:** see ELIOT, GEORGE.

**Evans, Oliver,** 1775–1819, American inventor. Evans developed and patented a number of grain-handling machines, including an elevator and a conveyor system, that later became standard equipment in US mills. He was a pioneer in the design of high-pressure steam engines, and in 1804 he built the first land vehicle in the US that moved under its own power, an engine-equipped dredge.

**Evans-Pritchard, Sir Edward Evan,** 1902–73, English social anthropologist. An early student of B. MALINOWSKI, he left FUNCTIONALISM to concentrate on demonstrating the rationality of subjective culture, shown most clearly in his treatment of WITCHCRAFT in *The Azande* (1971). A specialist on Africa, he wrote *The Nuer* (1940), a classic of ethnography, and *Theories of Primitive Religion* (1965). He became professor of anthropology at Oxford Univ. in 1946, succeeding RADCLIFFE-BROWN.

**evaporation:** see STATES OF MATTER.

**Evatt, Herbert Vere,** 1894–1965, Australian politician. After serving (1930–40) as justice of the high court of Australia, Evatt, a Labor Party member, was (1941–49) attorney general and foreign minister. He was president (1948–49) of the UN General Assembly, and subsequently (1951–60) leader of the Labor Party.

**Eve,** in the BIBLE, the first woman, wife of ADAM, mother of CAIN, ABEL, and Seth. Led by the serpent to eat of the forbidden tree of knowledge, Eve tempted Adam to eat of the tree also. As punishment, they were banished from the Garden of EDEN. Gen. 2–4.

**Evelyn, John,** 1620–1706, English diarist and writer. A founder of the ROYAL SOCIETY (1660), he wrote on reforestation, natural science, art history, and numismatics. He is best known for his lifelong DIARY (pub. 1818), full of historical information on 17th-cent. England.

**evening primrose,** common name for a plant of the family Onagraceae, distributed worldwide. More specifically, it refers to a yellow, evening-flowering annual or biennial of the genus *Oenothera*. The family also includes the FUCHSIA.

**eventing,** equestrian sport that tests the all-round ability of horse and rider. An event is a competition in three parts. The first, DRESSAGE, tests the horse's obedience and suppleness. Second comes the tough cross-country jumping; the course typically includes one or more water jumps and 'drop' fences where the landing side is much lower than the take-off. Penalties are exacted for falls or refusals to jump, and for exceeding the specified time. In the SHOWJUMPING phase there are penalties for knocking fences down and refusals, and for exceeding the time limit. At championship and international level the event takes place over three days (**three day event**), and the cross-country phase includes a steeplechase course and a slow trek along roads and tracks as well as a jumping course of up to 32 km (about 20 mi). The best-known three-day event is the one at Badminton House, Gloucestershire, S England, held annually since 1949. In team competitions each nation is allowed to enter four riders but only the top three scores count. Eventing is an Olympic sport, and men and women riders compete on equal terms.

**Everest, Mount,** 8848 m (29,028 ft) high, highest mountain in the world, located in the central HIMALAYAS, on the Tibet–Nepal border. Named after Sir George Everest, the surveyor of the Himalayas, it was first climbed in 1953 by Sir Edmund HILLARY and TENZING NORGAY, after at least eight earlier attempts to scale it had failed.

Mount Everest

**Everett, Edward,** 1794–1865, American orator and statesman. His long public career included service as congressman from Massachusetts (1825–35), governor of the state (1836–39), minister to England (1841–45), and US senator (1853–54). During the CIVIL WAR he travelled throughout the North, speaking for the Union cause. He gave the principal speech at Gettysburg on the same occasion that produced Lincoln's famous GETTYSBURG ADDRESS.

**Everglades,** marshy, low-lying tropical area (maximum elevation 2.1 m/7 ft), S Florida, covering c.13,000 km² (5000 sq mi). It is an area of solidly packed mud and sedges, interspersed with small areas of slightly higher ground with fertile soil, and is rich in wildlife. The local Seminole Indians were driven out in the 1830s. From the late 19th cent., large tracts of land were drained with a view to cultivation, but most such plans were abandoned after great fires occurred in 1939.

**Everyman,** late-15th-cent. English morality play. Summoned by Death, Everyman can persuade none of his friends—Beauty, Kindred, Worldly Goods—to go with him, except Good Deeds.

**evidence,** in law, material submitted to a court or other inquiring body to prove the facts in a legal dispute. The admissibility of evidence is governed by various rules. Particular evidence may be excluded on the grounds that it is irrelevant (having no bearing on the dispute), immaterial (having no impact on the substance of the dispute), or incompetent (outside the knowledge of the witness, e.g., hearsay). Rules of personal privilege excuse a witness from giving evidence relating to certain communications, e.g., between husband and wife; witnesses may also withhold self-incriminating evidence, and criminal defendants may refuse to testify. Evidence may be direct, such as that arising from personal observation, or it may be circumstantial, arising from facts that tend to prove other facts by inference. The kinds of evidence usually produced are physical objects (real evidence); written statements and documents (documentary evidence); oral testimony of the parties to the dispute or of other persons directly involved (personal evidence); and technical or other specialized testimony (expert evidence). The burden of proof, i.e., the responsibility to establish a disputed fact, shifts according to the nature of the controversy: in a civil suit, each party must prove its case on the balance of probabilities; in a criminal suit, the burden of proof rests on the prosecution, which must prove each element of its case beyond all reasonable doubt.

**evolution,** concept embodying the belief that existing organisms descended from a common ancestor. This theory, also known as descent with modification, constitutes organic evolution. Inorganic evolution deals with the development of the physical universe from unorganized matter (see COSMOLOGY). Organic evolution conceives of life as having begun as a simple, primordial protoplasmic mass from which arose, through time, all subsequent living forms. The first clearly stated theory of evolution, that proposed by Jean LAMARCK in 1801, included the inheritance of ACQUIRED CHARACTERISTICS as the operative force in evolution. Subsequently (1858), Alfred Russel WALLACE and Charles DARWIN independently set forth a scientifically credible theory of evolution based on NATURAL SELECTION, focusing on the survival and reproduction of those species best adapted to the environment. This theory had a profound effect on scientific thought and experimentation. Although it has undergone modification in light of later scientific developments, the theory of evolution still rests on essentially the grounds emphasized by Darwin, supported by research in GENETICS as well as by comparative anatomy, embryology, geography, palaeontology, and, recently, biochemistry. It has been challenged by those believing in the creation theory of the universe (see CREATIONISM). See also MUTATION.

**evolution, sociocultural,** ways of accounting for the historical progression from simple to increasingly complex forms of social organization. Evolutionary theories dominated late 19th-cent. anthropology, and proposed unilineal progression: a single series of developmental stages; contemporary hunter–gatherers were therefore seen as survivals of past stages. The new anthropology introduced in the US by F. BOAS and in the UK by B. MALINOWSKI rejected such 'speculative histories' and defined the task of anthropology as being to provide a detailed understanding of particular societies which were to be seen as functioning totalities. Theories of social evolution are still however an aspect of anthropology, the most important work in this sphere being done in the US, which stresses multilinear evolution within an overall scheme, which is subject to considerable ecological modifications, of progression from BAND to TRIBE to CHIEFDOM to STATE; the same idea is found within some schools of MARXIST anthropology.

**Evtushenko, Evgeny:** see YEVTUSHENKO.

**Évvoia** or **Euboea,** island (1981 pop. 188,410), c. 3800 km², (1467 sq mi), SE Greece, separated from the mainland by the Evripos strait. Its main industries are agriculture, magnesite and lignite mining, and marble quarrying. Settled by the ancient Greeks, it was divided among seven CITY-STATES, including Eretria, and later passed to Rome, Venice, and the Ottoman Turks before its incorporation (1830) into Greece.

**Ewald** or **Evald, Johannes** (ˌayvahlt), 1743–81, Danish poet and dramatist, the leading poet of his time. His works include the tragedy *Balder's Death* (1774) and the operetta *The Fishermen* (1779), containing the Danish national anthem.

**Ewing, (William) Maurice,** 1906–74, American geophysicist. Ewing's oceanographic work was critical to the acceptance of the theory of PLATE TECTONICS. In the late 1930s he conducted the first seismic studies (1935) and the first photographing (1939) of the ocean floor.

**examinations,** a means by which students' knowledge and understanding are assessed, and a basis for the award of qualifications. Written examinations became a prominent feature of British education during the 19th cent, starting with Oxford and Cambridge 'locals' in the 1850s. This system of 'school leaving' examinations led to the School Certificate and Higher School Certificate (1917), which were replaced (1951) by the General Certificate of Education (GCE) at Ordinary (O) and Advanced (A) levels. A Certificate of Secondary Education (CSE) was introduced in 1965, which was combined with O-level to form (1988) the General Certificate of Secondary Education (GCSE). In the late 19th cent. the Royal Society of Arts and the City and Guilds of London Institute developed systems of examinations, which have continued to the present, in areas of technical, scientific, commercial, and arts training. In higher education, the most common examinations at undergraduate level are for Bachelor of Arts (BA) and Bachelor of Science (BSc) awards, normally at the end of three years' full-time study, and a Bachelor of Education (BEd) which normally takes four years. The most common post-graduate degrees by examination are the MA and MSc, following one or two year's full-time or two or three years part-time study. The 'examination' for the doctorate (PhD) is by thesis and is only rarely accompanied by written examinations. A variety of professional bodies conduct examinations through which students qualify to practise. Competitive examinations for entry to the civil service, a notable feature of Chinese civilization, were introduced in Britain in the 1850s.

**excess profits tax,** levy on any profit above a standard level, usually imposed during wartime to prevent businesses from making unreasonable profits. Both the UK and the US levied such taxes during the world wars. A 'windfall profits' tax on banking profits was imposed in the UK by the Thatcher government in 1981.

**exchange,** in anthropology, the giving and receiving in return of goods, rights, and valuables (see GIFT). Such exchanges occur between individuals and groups. All relationships involve some kind of exchange, and their form and patterns are thus central to the creation and maintenance of social relationships, as they are to the whole subject of anthropology. In structural anthropology the exchange of words, goods, and women tend to be seen as expressing the same underlying models of social relationships (see STRUCTURALISM).

**exchange rate:** see FOREIGN EXCHANGE.

**excise:** see CUSTOMS AND EXCISE.

**exclamation mark:** see PUNCTUATION.

**exclusion principle:** see PAULI.

**excommunication,** formal expulsion of a person from a religious community, especially from the Roman Catholic Church. It involves a formal decree (or anathema) and public exclusion from the church, sacraments, and society. An excommunicate may return to the church on repentance.

**excretion,** process of eliminating from an organism the waste products of metabolism and other materials of no use. In one-celled organisms wastes are discharged through the cell's surface. Higher plants eliminate gases through the stomata, or pores, on the leaf surface, and multicellular animals have special excretory organs. In vertebrates, including humans, the main excretory organs are the KIDNEYS and other organs of the URINARY SYSTEM, through which URINE is eliminated, and the large intestine, from which solid wastes are expelled (see DIGESTIVE SYSTEM). Excretion also takes place in the SKIN, which eliminates water and salt in the form of sweat, and the LUNGS, which expel water vapour and carbon dioxide.

**Exe,** river in SW England, approximately 96 km (60 mi) long. It rises on EXMOOR in Somerset, flows E to Exton, and then S past Tiverton to EXETER.

It widens out into an estuary at Topsham, and enters the English Channel at Exmouth.

**executive,** the branch of government charged with enacting laws, as distinguished from the legislative (see PARLIAMENT) and judicial (see COURT SYSTEM IN ENGLAND AND WALES) branches. A further distinction is sometimes made between executives who decide policy and the body of civil servants who implement it. Executive areas include directing foreign policy, commanding the armed forces and generally directing the policy of government. In the UK the executive includes the sovereign (a nominal head of state), the PRIME MINISTER, CABINET, and other government ministers. According to the doctrine of separation of powers, members of the executive are supposed to be independent of members of the legislature and judiciary. However, in the UK, executive ministers also sit in the LEGISLATURE (Parliament).

**Exeter,** city (1981 pop. 88,235), capital of Devon, SW England, on the Exe R. It is the market and distribution centre for SW England. Strategically located, it was besieged by the Danes (9th, 11th cent.), by William the Conqueror (1068), and by Yorkists (15th cent.). Its many historic sites include Roman ruins and the massive Norman cathedral, whose library contains the famous Old English Exeter Book. The city's centre was rebuilt after heavy bombings in WORLD WAR II.

**existentialism,** any of several philosophical systems of the 20th cent., all centred on the individual and the individual's relationship to the universe or to God. Søøren KIERKEGAARD developed a Christian existentialism that recognized the concrete ethical and religious demands confronting the individual, who is forced each time to make a subjective commitment. The necessity and seriousness of these decisions cause him dread and despair. Following Kierkegaard, HEIDEGGER and SARTRE, both students of HUSSERL, were the major thinkers of the movement. Heidegger rejected the label of existentialism, describing his philosophy as an investigation of the nature of being in which the analysis of human existence is only a first step. For Sartre, the only self-declared existentialist among the major thinkers, existence precedes essence: there is no God and no fixed human nature; thus man is totally free and entirely responsible for what he makes of himself. It is this responsibility that accounts for his dread and anguish. Sartre's thought influenced the writings of CAMUS and de BEAUVOIR. A Christian existentialism was developed in France by Gabriel Marcel, a Roman Catholic. The religious thinkers Karl BARTH, Paul TILLICH, Reinhold NIEBUHR, and Martin BUBER, and the philosopher Karl JASPERS are often included within the orbit of existentialism.

**Exmoor,** high moorland region, in Somerset and Devon, SW England. It was largely covered in forest until the 19th cent., but is now covered with heather, bracken, and grass. It is bounded in the N by the Bristol Channel. The highest point is Dunkery Beacon which rises to 520 m (1706 ft). The area was immortalized in the book *Lorna Doone,* by R.D. Blackmore. It is now a national park, with the Brendon Hills.

**exobiology,** the study of the possibility of and the search for extraterrestrial life within the solar system and throughout the universe. Philosophical speculation that there might be other worlds similar to ours dates back to the ancient Chinese and Greeks. Six basic parameters determine whether an environment is suitable for life as we know it: temperature, pressure, salinity, acidity, water availability, and oxygen content. Advanced life is restricted to a narrow range of these parameters, but primitive micro-organisms can exist over a much wider range. Data already collected by SPACE PROBES essentially rule out advanced life on other planets of our solar system. Some scientists, however, have estimated that as many as 50,000 planets in our galaxy have Earth-like conditions and that a substantial fraction of these are likely to have cultures as technologically advanced as our own; efforts to detect radio emissions from these civilizations have so far been unsuccessful. A continuing effort is being made to detect primitive life within our solar system, e.g., the surface landings (1976) on Mars of the Viking space probes.

**Exodus,** second book of the OLD TESTAMENT and of the PENTATEUCH, ascribed by tradition to MOSES. It is a religious history of the JEWS during their flight from Egypt, when they began to receive the Law. The events include the bondage in Egypt and God's preparations for liberation through the agency of Moses (1–11); the exodus proper, with the institution of the Passover (see JEWISH HOLIDAYS) and the crossing of the Red Sea (12–18); and the divine legislation at Mt Sinai (19–40), including the giving of the TEN COMMANDMENTS.

**exogamy:** see ENDOGAMY.

**exorcism,** ritual driving out of evil spirits, as distinguished from rites of propitiation or evocation. It may be applied to a person, place, or thing by use of holy water, incense, incantation, or various rites. The New Testament records Christ's ability to drive out devils. The Roman Catholic Church carefully regulates exorcism of demons from persons.

**exoskeleton:** see SKELETON.

**expansion,** in physics, the increase in size of a substance when its temperature is raised. The increase is generally proportional to the change in temperature and the constant of proportionality is known as the *expansion coefficient.*

**explosive,** a substance that undergoes rapid decomposition or combustion, evolving much heat and producing a large volume of gas. The heat evolved causes the gas to expand greatly, exerting the enormous pressure of explosions. Important explosives include TNT (trinitrotoluene), DYNAMITE, and NITROGLYCERINE. Chemical explosives are of two general kinds. Some, e.g., GUNPOWDER, are mixtures of readily combustible but not necessarily explosive substances, which, when set off (by ignition), undergo very rapid combustion. Others, called high explosives (e.g., TNT), are compounds whose molecules are unstable and can undergo explosive decomposition (detonation) without burning. The latter kind is used in warfare (e.g., in bombs, explosive shells, torpedoes, and missile warheads) and for blasting rock in mining and construction work. Nondetonating explosives, e.g., gunpowder and modern smokeless powders, are used as propellants for bullets and in fireworks. Nuclear explosives release energy by transformation of the atomic nucleus (see ATOMIC BOMB; HYDROGEN BOMB; NUCLEAR ENERGY).

**exponent,** in mathematics, a number or algebraic expression written above and to the right of another number or algebraic expression called the base. In the expressions $x^2$ and $x^n$, the number 2 and the algebraic letter $n$ are the exponents, respectively, of the base $x$. A positive whole number as exponent indicates the power, or how many times the base is to be taken as a factor (e.g., $2^3 = 2 \times 2 \times 2 = 8$). Fractional and negative exponents indicate, respectively, the ROOT and reciprocal (e.g., $8^{\frac{1}{3}} = \sqrt[3]{8}$ and $x^{-2} = \frac{1}{x^2}$). A zero exponent makes any quantity equal to 1.

**exponential function:** see article on e.

**expressionism,** term used to describe works of art and literature in which the representation of reality is distorted to communicate an inner vision, transforming nature rather than imitating it. 1 In painting and the graphic arts, certain movements such as the BRÜCKE (1905) and BLAUE REITER (1911) are described as expressionist. In addition, certain independent artists e.g., ROUAULT, SOUTINE, VLAMINCK, KOKOSCHKA, and SCHIELE, did personal visionary paintings. GAUGUIN, ENSOR, VAN GOGH, and MUNCH were the spiritual fathers of expressionism, as were such earlier artists as El GRECO, GRÜNEWALD, and GOYA, whose works show striking parallels to modern expressionist sensibility. See also NEOEXPRESSIONISM. 2 In literature, expressionism is often considered a revolt against realism and naturalism, seeking to achieve a psychological or spiritual reality rather than to record external events. In the novel, the term applies to KAFKA and JOYCE (see STREAM OF CONSCIOUSNESS). In drama, STRINDBERG is the forerunner of the group of early 20th-century dramatists to which the term is applied, e.g., KAISER, Toller, and WEDEKIND. Their work was often characterized by a bizarre distortion of reality. The movement, though short-lived, gave impetus to a free form of writing and of theatrical production.

**extortion:** see BLACKMAIL.

**extradition,** delivery of a person, suspected or convicted of a crime, by the country of refuge to the country asserting jurisdiction. Its purpose is to prevent criminals from escaping punishment by fleeing to another jurisdiction. Extradition became common policy in the 19th cent., but since under INTERNATIONAL LAW it is not obligatory without a treaty, virtually all extradition occurs under the authority of specific bilateral treaties between nations; these may vary widely. Most European countries will surrender a criminal fugitive upon simple demand. The UK will only extradite a suspect if it has a reciprocal treaty with the demanding country. Like many nations, the UK will not surrender a fugitive wanted for a political crime (see ASYLUM).

**extrasensory perception:** see PARAPSYCHOLOGY.

**extraterritoriality,** privilege of immunity from local law enforcement enjoyed by certain aliens while present in the territory of a foreign nation. It is extended to most diplomats and their families, who are considered by customary INTERNATIONAL LAW to be under the legal jurisdiction of their home countries and thus exempt from civil and criminal action, ARREST, lawsuits, and, often, the payment of personal and property taxes. Certain transgressions, however, can result in an alien being declared *persona non grata* and expelled from the host country. Extraterritoriality also extends to public (i.e., state-owned) vessels in foreign territorial waterways and ports, and to air space over national territory, although air space remains regulated by bilateral agreements because uniform standards of jurisdiction have not been established (see AIR, LAW OF THE).

**extraversion–introversion,** a pair of terms in psychology, originally introduced by C.G. JUNG, denoting a dimension of personality. The pole of extraversion is characterized by the tendency to direct oneself outwards and by sociability, while the pole of introversion is characterized by the tendency to contemplation, solitude, and withdrawal.

**extreme unction:** see ANOINTING OF THE SICK.

**Eyck, Hubert van,** (iek), c.1370–1426, and **Jan van Eyck** c.1390–1441, Flemish painters, brothers. Little is known of Hubert, who may have worked (1414–17) for Duke William of Bavaria and did settle in Ghent, Belgium. He is tentatively credited with an *Annunciation* and a stunningly detailed miniature diptych of the *Crucifixion and Last Judgment* (both: Metropolitan Mus., New York). Jan worked in the courts of Count John of Holland (1422–25) and Philip of Burgundy. His paintings are minutely descriptive, realistic depictions of portrait subjects and religious scenes replete with contemporary GENRE details. His oil technique reveals an unprecedented richness and intensity of colour for

Jan Van **Eyck**, *Giovanni Arnolfini and his Bride*, 1434. National Gallery, London.

the medium. The two brothers probably collaborated on their masterwork, the altarpiece of the Church of Saint Bavon in Ghent (completed by Jan in 1432). One or both brothers illuminated (see ILLUMINATION) parts of the *Heures de Turin* manuscript. Jan's portrait oils include *Portrait of an Unknown Man* (1432) and *Man with the Red Turban,* perhaps a self-portrait (both: London), and the wedding picture *Giovanni Arnolfini and his Bride* (1434; National Gall., London). His splendid *Annunciation* is in Washington, (National Gall.). Jan van Eyck's influence on the development of European painting is enormous.

**eye,** organ of sight. Like a camera, it has a diaphragm and variable focusing. The eyeball has three covering layers: the sclera, choroid, and retina. The sclera, the outermost layer, is partially visible as the 'white' of the eye. In the centre of the sclera and projecting slightly is the cornea, a transparent membrane that acts as the window of the eye. The choroid, the layer lying beneath the sclera, is composed of dense pigment and blood vessels. Near the centre of the visible part of the eye the choroid forms the ciliary body, the muscles of which change the shape of the lens. The ciliary body merges with the iris, a muscular diaphragm that regulates the size of the pupil, the round opening through which light enters the eye. The iris, where it is not covered by the sclera, reveals the choroid's pigmentation, usually brown or blue (giving the eye its colour). Behind the iris is the lens, a transparent, elastic, but solid ellipsoid body that bends light rays, focusing them on the retina, the third tissue layer. The retina is a network of nerve cells, notably the rods and cones, which send impulses along the optic nerve to the brain. The rods provide vision in dim light, while the cones respond best in bright light and provide colour vision. See also ASTIGMATISM; BLINDNESS; COLOUR BLINDNESS; LONGSIGHTEDNESS; GLAUCOMA; SHORTSIGHTEDNESS.

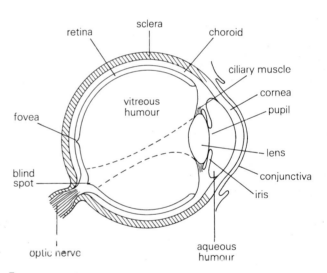

Eye

**Eyre, Lake,** largest lake in Australia, located in the continent's arid interior. It forms the continent's lowest point, 12 m (39 ft) below sea level, and it completely fills only about twice a century. Its waters are salty. Nearby Cooper Basin is an important oil and natural-gas exploration area.

**Ezekiel** or **Ezechiel** (ee‚zeekeeəl), book of the OLD TESTAMENT. It recounts the prophecies of Ezekiel, who preached (592–570 BC) to the Jews of the BABYLONIAN CAPTIVITY. It centres on the fall of JERUSALEM (586 BC): chapters 1–32 prophesy doom; 33–48, looking to restoration, end with a vision of the ideal Temple. Ezekiel stresses individual responsibility, and is noted for its symbolic passages.

**Ezra** or **Esdras** and **Nehemiah** (‚ezrə, ‚ezdrəs, neeə‚miəə), two books of the OLD TESTAMENT. They tell the history of the JEWS from 538 to 432 BC, from the decree of CYRUS THE GREAT permitting the return from the BABYLONIAN CAPTIVITY to the dedication of JERUSALEM's new walls. The book of Ezra concerns the return of one group, the rebuilding of the Temple, and the return of Ezra 'the priest, the scribe' with orders to restore Jewish Law. Nehemiah tells of the return of Nehemiah, who was a cupbearer to ARTAXERXES I, the rebuilding of the walls, and the reading of the Law and signing of a covenant.

**Ezra,** charismatic religious reformer and leader of the Palestinian Jewish community in the period following the return from the BABYLONIAN CAPTIVITY. Ezra restored the walls of Jerusalem, intensified religious life, rooted out the widespread practice of intermarriage, and initiated a renaissance of scribal activity and Jewish learning. His name forms the title of the biblical book covering this period.

**Ezzelino da Romano** ('etsay,leenoh dah roh,mahnoh), 1194–1259, Italian Ghibelline leader (see GUELPHS AND GHIBELLINES). He held Verona and other cities, and after 1237 he was the greatest power in N Italy. He was defeated (1258) at Milan. Placed by DANTE in the *Inferno,* he is remembered as a cruel tyrant.

**F,** chemical symbol of the element FLUORINE.

**Fabergé, Peter Carl,** 1846–1920, Russian goldsmith. As head of the studio established by his father, he was responsible for the design of elegant jewellery and objets d'art. Fabergé was particularly well known for the richly imaginative jewelled and enamelled Easter eggs he created for the Russian royal family. He died in exile in Switzerland.

**Fabian Society,** British organization founded (1884) to promote evolutionary socialism. Its members included George Bernard SHAW, Sidney and Beatrice WEBB, and H.G. WELLS. The Fabians rejected Marxism and denied the need for violent class struggle. Instead they recommended practical reforms which the State should undertake to relieve poverty. After publication of the *Fabian Essays* (1889) they gained widespread recognition. The Fabian Society played a leading role in the creation of the LABOUR PARTY, of which it remains an affiliated agency for research and the discussion and publication of ideas.

**Fabius,** ancient Roman gens. **Quintus Fabius Maximus Rullianus** or **Rullus,** d. c.291 BC, was renowned as a general, especially for his victory over the Etruscans, the Samnites, and their allies at Sentinum (295). His descendant, **Quintus Fabius Maximus Verrucosus,** d. 203 BC, the opponent of HANNIBAL, was called Cunctator [Lat., = delayer] because of his delaying tactics, from which the term 'Fabian', referring to a waiting policy, is derived (e.g., the FABIAN SOCIETY). Tired of his masterly inaction, the Romans replaced him (216 BC) and were defeated at Cannae.

**fable,** brief, allegorical narrative, in verse or prose, illustrating a moral thesis or satirizing human behavior. The characters are usually animals who talk and act like people while retaining animal·traits. The oldest known fables are in the Sanskrit *Panchatantra* and by AESOP. LA FONTAINE, G.E. LESSING, John DRYDEN, and John GAY continued the tradition, as did James THURBER and George ORWELL in the 20th cent.

**fabliau,** plural **fabliaux,** short comic, often bawdy verse tale realistically satirizing middle- or lower-class life, marriage, or the clergy. It flourished in France in the Middle Ages, and appears in the work of CHAUCER and BOCCACCIO.

**Fabriano, Gentile da:** see GENTILE DA FABRIANO.

**fabric:** see TEXTILES.

**Faeroe Islands** or **Faröe Islands** (ˌfeəroh), group of volcanic islands (1984 pop. 45,464), 1400 km² (540 sq mi), Denmark, located in the N Atlantic Ocean c.1370 km (850 mi) from mainland Denmark. There are 17 inhabited and 5 uninhabited islands; Steymoy, with Tórshavn as the capital, and Oøsteroø are the largest islands. Fishing is the chief economic activity. Settled by Norsemen in the 8th cent., the islands became part of Norway in the 11th cent. and passed to the Danish crown in 1380. They became a British protectorate (1940–45) in World War II and gained self-government (1948) after an aborted independence movement.

**Faes, Pieter van der:** see LELY, SIR PETER.

**Fahd ibn Abdul Aziz,** 1922–, king of SAUDI ARABIA (1982–). A son of IBN SAUD, the founder of Saudi Arabia, Fahd served (1962–75) as interior minister and was named (1975) crown prince by his half-brother King KHALID. He was a powerful shaper of Saudi foreign and domestic policy under Khalid, on whose death (1982) he succeeded to the throne.

**Fahrenheit temperature scale:** see TEMPERATURE.

**Fairbanks, Douglas,** 1883–1939, American film actor; b. Julius Ullman. He starred in such swashbucklers as *The Mark of Zorro* (1920), *The Thief of Baghdad* (1924), and *The Black Pirate* (1926). His son, **Douglas Fairbanks, Jr.,** 1909–, is an actor whose films include *The Prisoner of Zenda* (1937), *Gunga Din* (1939), and *The Fighting O'Flynn* (1949).

**Fair Isle:** see KNITTING.

**fairy,** in folklore, one of a variety of supernatural beings having magical powers. Belief in fairies has existed from earliest times, but the concept and description of the creatures varies widely, from the tiny old men, or leprechauns, of Irish legend, to beautiful enchantresses like the Germanic Lorelei, to man-eating giants, or ogres. Particular kinds of fairies include the Arabic JINNI, the Scandinavian troll, the Germanic elf, and the English pixie. Although usually represented as mischievous and capricious, they could also be loving and bountiful. Among the great adapters of popular fairy tales were Charles PERRAULT, the brothers GRIMM, and Hans Christian ANDERSEN.

**Faisal** or **Feisal,** kings of Iraq. **Faisal I,** 1885–1933 (r.1921–33), joined (1916) with T.E. LAWRENCE in the Arab revolt against the Turks. The British, largely through the efforts of Gertrude BELL, named him king. He was generally pro-British and was succeeded by his son, Ghazi. Ghazi's son, **Faisal II,** 1935–58 (r.1939–58), was generally pro-Western in his short majority reign. He was killed in a revolution that overthrew the Iraqi monarchy.

**Faisalabad,** (formerly **Lyallpur**), city (1981 est. pop. 1,092,000), NE Pakistan. The commercial centre of a region which grows cotton and wheat, it produces textiles, pharmaceuticals, and other manufactures. The city was founded c.1895 by Sir James Lyall, a British civil servant and Orientalist.

**Faisal ibn al Saud,** 1905–75, king of SAUDI ARABIA (r.1964–75). A son of IBN SAUD, he forced the abdication of his brother, King Saud, in 1964 and assumed the throne. He used his country's vast oil revenues to finance far-reaching economic and social development plans. He was assassinated by a deranged nephew.

**faith healing:** see HEALING.

**Faiyûm,** city (1987 pop. 166,910), N Egypt, c.112 km (70 mi) SW of Cairo. It lies in an area rich in archaeological objects. Modern industries include cotton ginning and tanning.

**Falange** [Span., = phalanx], Spanish political party, founded 1933. Adhering to FASCISM, the Falange, through its militia, joined the Nationalist forces of Francisco FRANCO in the SPANISH CIVIL WAR (1936–39). The party's founder, José António Primo de Rivera, son of the dictator Miguel PRIMO DE RIVERA, was executed by the Loyalists in the civil war. In 1937 Franco took control of the Falange, making it the official party of his regime. By the 1970s its power had waned.

**Falashas** [Ethiopic, = emigrant], group of approximately 30,000 Ethiopians who practise a form of JUDAISM. They believe in the Old Testament, certain apocryphal books, and some traditions that correspond to those found in the MIDRASH and the TALMUD. In modern times there have been POGROMS against the Falashas.

**falcon,** long-winged BIRD of prey of the family Falconidae, which includes the KESTREL, merlin, and hobby. Widely distributed, falcons are typified by notched beaks. They range in size from the 16-cm (6½-in) falconet to the 60-cm (24-in) gyrfalcon. Falcons are one of the fastest flying birds in the world. They feed on birds, bats, and insects, which they take on the wing. Falcons lay their eggs on the ground, on cliff ledges, or in deserted HAWK or CROW nests. The PEREGRINE FALCON and gyrfalcon are used in falconry.

**falconry,** sport of hunting with a falcon or a hawk, especially the peregrine, or occasionally an eagle. Attacking its quarry is natural to the falcon, so the skill of the falconer lies in training the bird to respond to commands. The bird may be flown direct from the fist or allowed to soar freely in alliance with a dog that flushes out the prey.

**Faliscan** (fə‚liskən), extinct language belonging to the Italic subfamily of the Indo-European family of languages. See LANGUAGE (table).

**Falkland Islands,** Span. *Islas Malvinas,* British crown colony (1984 est. pop. 1900 and a garrison of 4000 British troops), 11,961 km² (4618 sq mi), S Atlantic. Consisting of two large islands and some 200 small ones, they are economically dependent on sheep-raising. The capital is Stanley. Under British rule since the 1830s, the islands are also claimed by Argentina. On 3 April 1982 they were seized by Argentina and retaken on 14 June by British troops. Dependencies of the colony include SOUTH GEORGIA and the South Sandwich islands.

**Falla, Manuel de** (‚fahlyah), 1876–1946, Spanish composer. He was influenced by the IMPRESSIONISM of DEBUSSY and RAVEL, but in his early works he used Spanish characteristics derived from his study of *cante jondo,* a type of popular Spanish song, characterized by much repetition of notes, melodic ornamentation, and 'non-European' intervals. His works include *Nights in the Gardens of Spain* (1916; for piano and orchestra) and the ballets *El Amor Brujo* (1915) and *The Three-Cornered Hat* (1917).

**Fälldin, Thorbjörn** (‚feldin), 1926–, prime minister of SWEDEN (1976–78, 1979–82). With the support of a three-party coalition, including his own Centre Party, he became the first non-socialist prime minister in 44 years. The coalition dissolved (1978), but in 1979 it was returned to power with Fälldin as prime minister. In 1981, after another coalition rift, Fälldin formed a two-party minority government, which lasted until 1982, when parliamentary elections enabled the Social Democrats, led by Olof PALME, to form a government. Fälldin resigned as Centre Party leader in 1986.

**fall line,** line where waterfalls occur in rivers passing from areas of relatively hard rocks (as in the Piedmont of the E US) to areas of softer rock (as in the Atlantic Coastal Plain). It is usually the head of navigation.

**fallout:** see ATOMIC BOMB; HYDROGEN BOMB.

**falsetto:** see VOICE.

**family,** universally assumed to be one of the fundamental units of society. An exact definition has proved elusive, but it is recognized that while the unit is created through KINSHIP it is not necessarily the same as the DOMESTIC GROUP or household. One common definition distinguishes between pre-industrial and industrial forms of the family unit. Here, 'pre-industrial' means that a number of generations of the family live either in the same house or in close proximity to each other (*extended family*). In contrast, in the *nuclear family* unit (a product of the INDUSTRIAL REVOLUTION), the family unit is small—typically, mother, father and two children—and highly mobile. However, some recent research suggests that in village life under FEUDALISM, the family unit was closer to the nuclear type than the extended, and studies of working class life carried out in the 1950s and 60s showed that the extended family was the norm. The 'Western' family performs many social functions: it provides mutual services between its members; it acts as a unit of consumption; it enables the care and socialization of the young to take place; and it regulates sexuality within monogamous marriage. Its forms vary in different periods and amongst different social classes. Nuclear families are popularly regarded as the lynch-pin of a stable social order; however, they have also been criticized for the relative social isolation associated with domesticity, their rigid separation of gender roles (patriarchal/matriarchal functions), and their effect in isolating women from the wider world. In the 20th cent., the state has taken over many of the functions once performed by families, at least in advanced industrial societies. Nevertheless, the family continues to change (e.g., the growth of 'one-parent families'), and recent surveys suggest that only 20% of the UK population now are in a family of mother, a few children, and father as the single breadwinner.

**Family Compact,** popular name for a small clique of wealthy, powerful men who dominated Upper Canada (see ONTARIO) from the late 18th to the mid-19th cent. New settlers who were thus denied political opportunity formed an opposition which became the Reform Party.

**Family Expenditure Survey,** the longest running multipurpose SURVEY in Britain (founded 1957). Organized jointly by the Department of Employment and the Office of Population Censuses and Surveys, the FES samples 11,000 households annually. With a response rate of 68–70%, roughly 7000 households are actually surveyed. The sampling is continuous over the course of the calandar year with any one household being studied for two weeks. Individual members of the household over the age of 16 are interviewed on expenditure and asked to keep a diary of how much they spend and on what. All major items of individual and household expenditure are covered by the survey including the cost of housing, telephone bills, insurance premiums, travel, food and drink, clothes, entertainment, books and newspapers, children's pocket money, and any large items of expenditure on household goods that occur during the two-week period (e.g., furniture, televisions, etc.).

**family planning:** see BIRTH CONTROL.

**family therapy:** see PSYCHOTHERAPY.

**famine,** extreme shortage of food over a protracted period, usually due to crop failure or overpopulation. Drought is a common cause of famine and it frequently occurs in arid and semiarid areas; flooding in low-lying areas is also a cause. In India and China famine has been associated with overpopulation although this problem has diminished in recent years with the rise in agricultural production. Human causes of famine include the political control of the means of production and distribution of basic foodstuffs, and the failure of politicians to allow the transport of food, when it is made available in areas in need. In the late 20th cent. famine has ceased to be a problem in the European countries, the US, and other developed countries. In the developing world the problems of famine persist but have been alleviated by increased world food trade in food and international activity, particularly on the part of relief organizations, when famine is reported. Severe drought at the end of the 1970s badly affected the Sahel and eastern and southern Africa and caused much loss of life in the early 1980s. Latin America, central Africa and Asia remain vulnerable to problems of famine.

**Fanfani, Amintore,** 1908–, Italian political leader. A Christian Democrat, he served as foreign minister (1965, 1966–68), president of the Senate (1968–73, 1976–82), and as premier (1954, 1958–59, 1960–63, 1982–83, 1987).

**Fantin-Latour, Henri** (fan‚tanla'taw), 1836–1904, French painter, who is best known for his flower pictures, e.g., *Roses* (1890; Nat. Gall., London). He was associated with the most progressive artists of his era, whom he commemorated in group portraits, amongst them *Homage to Delacroix* (1864) and *A Studio at Batignolles* (1870; both Musée d'Orsay, Paris).

**Farabi, al-,** c.870–950, Islamic philosopher, full name Abu-Nasr Muhammed al-Farabi. Known as 'the second master', ARISTOTLE being the first, he wrote commentaries on PLATO and Aristotle, and his major work, *The Virtuous City,* a study of justice and the good life, was inspired by Plato's *Republic.*

**Faraday, Michael,** 1791–1867, English scientist. Despite little formal education he laid the foundations of classical FIELD theory, later fully developed by James Clerk MAXWELL. Faraday worked (1813–62) at the laboratory of the ROYAL INSTITUTION in London, becoming its director in 1825. He developed the first dynamo (in the form of a copper disk rotated between the poles of a permanent magnet), the precursor of the modern dynamo and GENERATOR. From Faraday's and Joseph HENRY's independent discoveries (1831) of electromagnetic INDUCTION stemmed a vast development of electrical machinery for industry. In 1825 Faraday discovered the compound BENZENE. He formulated (1834) Faraday's law, which states that the number of moles of substance produced at an electrode during ELECTROLYSIS is directly proportional to the number of moles of electrons transferred at that electrode. The unit of CAPACITANCE in the SI system (see METRIC SYSTEM) is called the *farad* in his honour.

**Faraday constant,** the amount of electricity corresponding to one MOLE of electrons. It is the product of Avogadro's number and the electronic charge: 96,487 coulombs per mole. See ELECTROLYSIS.

**Farah, Nuruddin,** 1945– , Somali writer. He is acclaimed for writing some of the most sensitive texts about the status of women in Africa, e.g., *From a Crooked Rib* (1970) and *Maps* (1986). Having lived mostly abroad (India, West Germany, England, Nigeria), Farah chooses to write in English as a statement of opposition to the post-independence Somali regime.

**farce,** light theatre piece with characters and events exaggerated to produce broad, simple humour. An element in the plays of ARISTOPHANES, PLAUTUS, and TERENCE, it appeared as a distinct genre in 15th-cent. France. Nicholas UDALL's *Ralph Roister Doister* (1566) is an early English example. Broad, ribald humour, absurdity, and buffoonery are also found in works not considered farces, e.g., the plays of MOLIÈRE.

**Far East,** term commonly used today in a restricted sense for the region comprising E Asia (i.e., CHINA, JAPAN, KOREA, MONGOLIA) and the SOVIET FAR EAST (E SIBERIA). It is also sometimes extended to include SOUTHEAST ASIA. As used in the 19th cent., the term denoted those portions of the Asian continent farthest removed by sea from the W European maritime powers trading there.

**Farel, Guillaume** (fah͵rel), 1489–1565, French religious reformer, associate of John CALVIN. He was a fearless and eloquent evangelist; in 1535, he won over Geneva to the REFORMATION. With Calvin, he instituted reforms there that proved too sudden and strict, and in 1538 they were forced to leave. Calvin returned to Geneva in 1541, but Farel went to live in Basel and then Neuchâtel.

**Faridabad,** town (1981 pop. 330,864), Haryana state, N India, near the Jamuna (Jumna) R. Situated just S of the boundary of the Union territory of Delhi, Faridabad is a 'new town' developed as an industrial centre for a wide range of industries, from engineering and chemicals to refrigerators and glassware. Its growth has been remarkable, and accomplished in a short period of time.

**Farid ad-Din Attar** (aht͵tah), d. c.1229, Persian poet, one of the greatest Muslim mystic poets. Of his many and varied works his masterpiece is *Conference of the Birds,* an allegory surveying the philosophy and practices of SUFISM.

**Farley, James Aloysius,** 1888–1976, American political leader. As Democratic National Committee chairman, he managed (1932, 1936) F.D. ROOSEVELT's presidential campaigns. He served (1933–40) as US postmaster general.

**Farmer–Labor Party,** US political organization founded (1919) to unite agrarian and organized labour interests. It promoted nationalization of various industries and resources but garnered little support and dissolved after 1924. The Minnesota Farmer–Labor Party, unaffiliated with the national party, elected a governor and several US senators and congressmen in the 1920s and 30s. It merged (1944) with the Minnesota Democratic Party.

**Farnese** (fah͵nayzay), Italian noble family that ruled Parma and Piacenza from 1545 to 1731. In 1534 Alessandro Farnese became pope as PAUL III. He created (1545) the duchy of Parma and Piacenza for his illegitimate son, **Pier Luigi Farnese,** 1503–47, who was assassinated by nobles. His son and successor, **Ottavio Farnese,** 1520–86, married MARGARET OF PARMA. Their son, **Alessandro Farnese,** 1545–92, duke 1586–92, was a general in the service of PHILIP II of Spain. Appointed (1578) governor in the rebellious Netherlands, he took Tournai, Maastricht, Breda, Bruges, Ghent, and Antwerp from the rebels. In 1590 he entered France to aid the Catholic League against HENRY IV of France and relieved Paris (1590) and Rouen (1592). He is considered one of the age's greatest generals. The last duke of the line, Antonio, died in 1731. His niece, **Elizabeth Farnese,** 1692–1766, married (1714) PHILIP V of Spain and for a time virtually ruled Spain. She secured (1748) Parma and Piacenza for her son Philip, who founded the line of BOURBON-Parma.

**Faröe Islands:** see FAEROE ISLANDS.

**Farouk,** 1920–65, king of EGYPT (r.1936–52), son and successor of Fuad I. He was regarded as a corrupt playboy and was deposed by the 1952 military coup led by Gamal Abdal NASSER. His infant son, Fuad II, succeeded him briefly.

**Farquhar, George,** 1678–1707, English dramatist; b. Ireland. The geniality of such plays as *The Constant Couple* (1699), *The Recruiting Officer* (1706), and his masterpiece, *The Beaux' Stratagem* (1707), mark Farquhar as a transitional figure between RESTORATION and 18th-cent. drama.

**Farragut, David Glasgow,** 1801–70, American admiral. In the AMERICAN CIVIL WAR he sailed (1862) up the Mississippi R. past Confederate forts and defeated an enemy flotilla, enabling Union forces to take New Orleans. In 1864, uttering the famous cry 'Damn the torpedoes [mines]', he forced the defences of Mobile, Alabama, and defeated a Confederate fleet. The outstanding naval commander of the war, Farragut was the first officer in the US navy to receive the ranks of vice admiral (1864) and admiral (1866).

**Farrell, James T(homas),** 1904–79, American novelist. In the tradition of NATURALISM, his fiction deals mainly with life in Chicago's Irish Catholic slums. His work includes the novels of the Studs Lonigan trilogy (1932–35) and Danny O'Neill pentalogy (1936–53), many short stories, and essays.

**farrier,** craftsman, also called blacksmith, who fits iron shoes to horses and other hoofed animals, and who makes other articles from iron by forging. Farrier is derived from the Latin *ferrum* [iron]. The horny part of the hoof is cleaned, shaped and trimmed, and the iron shoe is shaped at high temperature and fastened to the hoof with nails. Some defects in a horse's movement can be corrected by the farrier, by means of trimming the foot or fitting specially shaped or weighted shoes.

**farthing,** a bronze ('copper') coin in the UK which ceased to be legal tender in 1961. It was worth one-quarter of an old penny, or 1/480th of a pound.

**farthingale,** a skirt support used all over the fashionable Western world from the mid 16th to the early 17th cent. It took its name from the Fr. version of the Span. word for one of the types of stiffening used, *verdugo* [rod or stick]. In the mid 16th cent., they were cone-shaped, and in the later period, bolster-like, giving a cylindrical outline to the skirt. See UNDERWEAR.

**fascism,** political movement or system of government characterized by: a para-military character; extreme NATIONALISM; opposition to parliamentary democracy; violent anti-Communism; a cult of action, in particular the use of violence to achieve political aims; belief in a one-party authoritarian state directed by a charismatic leader with dictatorial powers; and an aggressive foreign policy. Anti-Semitism and theories of racial supremacy were notable features of German Nazism, but not of all fascist movements. The term was first used by the party started by MUSSOLINI which ruled Italy from 1922 until the Italian defeat in 1943, and is usually applied also to NATIONAL SOCIALISM under HITLER in Germany, and the FALANGE under FRANCO in Spain. In the social upheaval and economic depression following World War I in Europe, fascism appealed to ex-soldiers of the defeated nations unable to adjust to civilian life; to the unemployed, by promising work; to members of the middle classes whose security was threatened by inflation; and to major financial and commercial interests hostile to the organized working class, whether trade unionist or communist. While retaining class divisions and usually protecting the capitalist and landowning interests, fascist states attempted to exert totalitarian control over social life (see TOTALITARIANISM), by means of mass PROPAGANDA and terroristic special police forces. In the economy, trade unions were usually destroyed and in some cases economic CORPORATISM was set up. Since the defeat of the fascist states in World War II, fascism has existed only in the form of negligible minority parties in Europe, though features of fascism may be discerned in several South American states.

**fashion,** the prevailing mode affecting modifications in COSTUME, most noticeable in the prosperous and swiftly changing societies of modern Europe and the US. European fashions used to be set by the aristocracy and prominent persons, and were copied more or less slowly by the rest of the community according to their social standing and income. This process was much accelerated in the 19th cent. with the introduction of the sewing machine and cheap textiles, which made factory-based mass production of clothing feasible. Since the later 18th cent., news of changing styles had been professionally gathered and disseminated, mainly by fashion-plate illustrations. Fashion magazines became increasingly important when cheaper printing techniques and wider literacy enlarged their potential market in the later 19th cent. Paris was the leading arbiter of fashion from the mid 17th cent., a role strengthened by the development of the high-class designer dress trade (*haute couture*) in the mid 19th cent. Fashion clothes were still always made to order for clients by artisan tailors and dressmakers, and continued to be so until well into the 20th cent. Since World War II a large international clothing industry has grown up, which continually stimulates comsumer demand with sophisticated marketing via not only magazines but also films, television, and video. The target market since the 1960s has increasingly been the young with their growing spending power, and in the 1980s the older career-woman, for the same reason. Sometimes distinctive styles developed by the young as 'street fashion' and spread by pop groups or film stars are picked up by the fashion industry and produced for the mass market. The modern tendency is to display wealth and status by wearing clothes that can be recognized as the work of a particular designer, to facilitate which many garments are now made with the designer's name prominently but discreetly shown on the outside.

**Fassbinder, Rainer Werner,** 1946–82, German film director. His over 40 films, many of which portray post-World War II German life, include *Why Does Herr R. Run Amok?* (1969), *Effi Briest* (1974), *Despair* (1978), *The Marriage of Maria Braun* (1979), *Lola* (1982), and *Veronika Voss* (1982).

**fast food,** food brought to be eaten straight away. Known all over the world for centuries (pie-men in England, herring-stalls in Holland, grilled corn-cobs in S Africa), this way of eating has become increasingly popular in the West. Over 1000 hamburger establishments, 1350 pizza parlours, and over 650 chicken outlets have opened in the UK in the past 10 years. These are mainly run on a concessionary basis from the parent company. These companies have achieved international success with a clean, dynamic image (regularly updated to remain fashionable) and by producing a uniform, reliable product quickly and repetitively. Three-quarters of their labour force is under 21 and they have a staff turnover of 70% per year due to the extremely routine nature of the work. Fast food appeals particularly to the young to middle-age group and to families with young children, all of whom appear to have a less rigid attitude to mealtimes than is traditional.

**Fatehpur Sikri** or **Fathpur Sikri** (fətə‚pooə ‚sikree), historic abandoned city, Uttar Pradesh state, N India. It was founded (1569) by AKBAR as his capital and is unique in India as a largely intact masterpiece of Mogul architecture.

**Fates,** in Greek mythology, three goddesses who controlled human life; also called the Moerae or Moirai. They were: Clotho, who spun the web of life; Lachesis, who measured its length; and Atropos, who cut it. The Roman Fates were the Parcae; the Germanic Fates were the NORNS.

**Fathers of the Church,** Christian writers of antiquity whose work is generally considered orthodox. A convenient definition includes all such writers up to and including St GREGORY I in the West and St JOHN OF DAMASCUS in the East. The Christian church also recognized **Doctors of the Church** who exhibited great holiness and learning. The eight ancient doctors are Sts Basil the Great, GREGORY NAZIANZEN, JOHN CHRYSOSTOM, and ATHANASIUS in the East; and Sts AMBROSE, JEROME, AUGUSTINE, and GREGORY I in the West.

**Fátima,** hamlet near the episcopal town of Leiria in W Portugal. Here, in May 1917, shepherd children claimed that the Virgin Mary appeared to them. The nearby shrine of Our Lady of the Rosary has become a major centre of pilgrimage.

**Fatimids,** a Muslim dynasty, founded in Tunisia in 909 with Mahdiyya as capital. After the conquest of Egypt they founded Cairo in 969, which remained their capital until the dynasty was dealt a *coup de grace* by SALADIN in 1171 with his procalamation of allegiance to the ABBASIDS. Claiming descent from Fatima, a daughter of MUHAMMAD, the Fatimids originally grew out of the sect of the ISMA'ILIS and their caliphs assumed a semi-divine character. The Fatimids were a major maritime power in the Mediterranean, the Red Sea, and the Indian Ocean, and such prosperity produced a court of almost legendary opulence. The Fatimids also became a major power in Syria and were a serious threat to the Abbasids in the 11th cent.

**fats and oils,** group of organic substances that form an important part of the diet and are used in industry. Generally, fats are solid and oils liquid at ordinary room temperatures. Vegetable oils, e.g., those from CORN, PEANUTS, and linseed (see LINSEED OIL), are made by pressing crushed fruits or seeds. The highest grade oils, used in food, are cold

pressed. Subsequent warm pressing or extraction with solvents yields industrial-grade oil, used, for example, in making SOAP. Most animal fats, e.g., BUTTER and lard, are saturated fats, i.e., compared with unsaturated fats or oils, they contain more hydrogen relative to carbon and do not become as easily rancid. Hardening, the conversion of unsaturated liquid oils into more saturated solid fats by hydrogenation, is an important chemical industry. Although fats and oils are nutritionally important as energy sources, forming part of the structure of all cell membranes, medical research indicates that saturated fats may contribute to the incidence of ARTERIOSCLEROSIS by increasing the blood's level of CHOLESTEROL, a substance deposited in the arteries. Fats and oils are often in emulsified form (see COLLOID) and have a significant effect on the texture and palatability of food. They are responsible for providing the fat-soluble vitamins A and D. Some fat is essential in the DIET to provide the essential fatty acids, linoleic and linolenic. See also ESSENTIAL OILS; PETROLEUM.

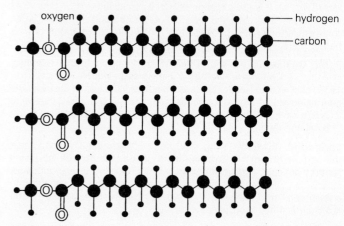

Fats and oils: Composition of a typical fat

**fatwa:** see MUFTI.

**Faulkner, William,** 1897–1962, American novelist. One of the great American writers of the 20th cent., he explored primarily the loss of traditional values and the decay and anguish of the post-Civil War South, using the imaginary Yoknapatawpha county as a microcosm of Southern life. A brilliant literary technician, Faulkner was master of a rhetorical, highly symbolic style. He was awarded the 1949 Nobel Prize in literature. His best-known novels include *The Sound and the Fury* (1929), *Light in August* (1932), *The Hamlet* (1940), *A Fable* (1954), and *The Reivers* (1962). He also published short stories, essays, and poems.

**fault,** in geology, a fracture in the earth's crust in which the rocks on each side move in relation to each other. This movement can be vertical, horizontal, or oblique. Horizontal faults showing lateral displacement of points originally directly opposite each other, such as the SAN ANDREAS FAULT in California, are called strike-slip. Another type of horizontal fault, the transform fault, occurs on the ocean floor between offset portions of the

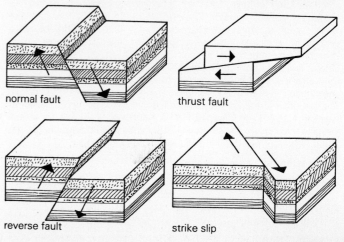

normal fault        thrust fault

reverse fault        strike slip

Types of **faults**

mid-ocean ridge (see PLATE TECTONICS). Altered positions of rocks due to faulting can mislead the geologist, because one rock layer can appear twice in the same cross-section or disappear entirely. See also EARTHQUAKE.

**Faunus,** in Roman mythology, woodland deity, protector of herds and crops; identified with the Greek PAN. He was attended by fauns—mischievous creatures, half man, half goat.

**Fauré, Gabriel Urbain** (foh‚ray), 1845–1924, French composer and teacher of RAVEL. His works include refined, intimate piano and CHAMBER MUSIC, a *Requiem* (1888), an orchestral suite *Pelléas et Mélisande* (1898), an opera *Pénélope* (1907–12) and SONGS, e.g., 'Clair de Lune'.

**Faust,** or **Faustus, Johann,** fl. 16th cent., learned German doctor who performed magic and who died under mysterious circumstances. According to legend he sold his soul to the devil (Mephistopheles) in exchange for youth, knowledge, and magical power. Literary treatments of the story include the *Volksbuch* of Johannes Spies (1587), Christopher MARLOWE's *Dr. Faustus* (1593), GOETHE's masterpiece *Faust* (1808, 1833), and Thomas MANN's *Doctor Faustus* (1947). The legend inspired many composers of musical works, including BERLIOZ, GOUNOD, LISZT, SCHUMANN, and BOITO.

**Faustus:** see FAUST.

**fauvism** (‚fohvizəm), [Fr., *fauve* = wild beast], name given by the critic Vauxcelles to the group of artists, led by MATISSE, exhibiting in the central gallery of the 1905 autumn salon in Paris. It jokingly referred to a painting of a lion by ROUSSEAU in the same gallery (hence 'wild beast') and was used to highlight the group's use of exaggerated colour. They developed the ideas of the post-impressionists, esp. VAN GOGH and GAUGUIN, extending the subjective element in painting. The group, which included Matisse, ROUAULT, DERAIN, VLAMINCK, BRAQUE and DUFY, never developed a joint programme and by 1908 the artists had divergent interests.

**Fawcett, Millicent (Garrett),** 1847–1929, English woman suffragist, sister of Elizabeth Garrett ANDERSON. She was president of the NATIONAL UNION OF WOMEN'S SUFFRAGE SOCIETIES after its grouping in 1897 of suffrage societies all over Britain.

**Fawkes, Guy:** see GUNPOWDER PLOT.

**fax** [from *facsimile*], system of transmission of documents, consisting of text, diagrams, or monochrome pictures, over the telephone network. The document to be transmitted is placed in a fax machine where it is mechanically scanned so that a point-by-point digital signal is generated to correspond to the presence of print and its degree of darkness. After transmission over the telephone line similar equipment at the receiving end will scan a sheet of thermal sensitive paper with a thermal writing head in sympathy with the originating scan and will provide a photocopy of the document. The time it takes to transmit and print a document will depend upon the degree of complexity of the material and whether it is handling various grades of shade in a picture: an A4 sheet of text would take about 20 seconds and a picture with different tones may take some two minutes. The early lack of universal standards for equipment made by different manufacturers delayed its introduction on a widespread scale. However the newest generation of fax machines are compatible with one another and are posing a serious threat to TELEX as the main form of non-voice business communication, particularly as they operate over the existing telephone network, both nationally and internationally, and do not need dedicated communications links or special lines. The sales of fax machines overtook the sales of telexes for the first time in the UK in 1988.

**FBI:** see FEDERAL BUREAU OF INVESTIGATION.

**Fe,** chemical symbol of the element IRON.

**feathers,** outgrowths of the skin that constitute the protective and decorative plumage of birds and are thought to have evolved from reptilian scales in Mesozoic times. Feathers grow only along defined tracts; full grown, they lack a blood supply and have hollow shafts. Typically, barbs radiate from the distal part of the shaft (the rachis) and interlock via smaller cross-linking barbules to form a web, which gives the feather flexibility and durability. Down feathers of young birds and the protective undercoats of aquatic birds lack webs. Specializations (e.g., crests, ruffs, and topknots) and modifications (e.g., bristles) exist. Most feather colours (e.g., red, yellow, brown) are due to pigment in the

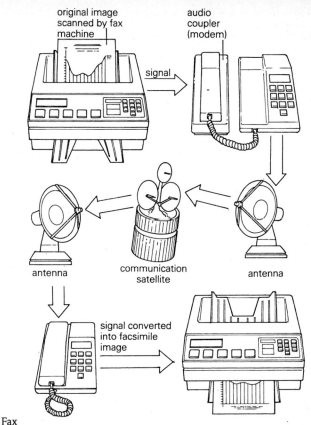

Fax

feather; some (e.g., green and violet), as well as iridescent effects, are due to reflection and diffraction of light. The most important roles of feathers are in flight, heat retention, and sexual display.

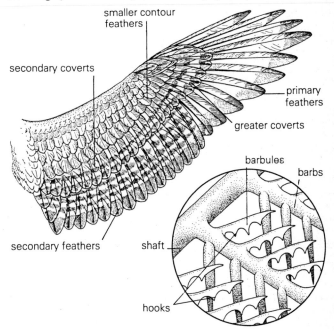

Wing **feathers** and structure of a feather

**feather star:** see CRINOID.

**February:** see MONTH.

**February Revolution,** 1848, French revolution that followed an economic crisis (1846–47), and led to the overthrow of the monarchy of LOUIS PHILIPPE and the Second Republic. There was general dissatisfaction with the policies of the king and his minister François GUIZOT, and after the government forbade a banquet to promote political opposition, street fighting began and government troops fired (23 Feb. 1848) on the demonstrators, setting off the revolution. Louis Philippe abdicated on 24 Feb. A provisional government was formed and a republic was proclaimed, with LAMARTINE as one of its leaders, but the differing aims of the bourgeois revolutionaries and the radicals and socialists contributed to the revolution's eventual failure. To meet workers' demands, the right to work was guaranteed and national workshops were established by Louis BLANC, but mismanagement and the election of a more moderate government led to the dissolution of the workshops in May. The resulting workers' rebellion, known as the JUNE DAYS, was crushed. After the completion of the republican constitution, Prince Louis Napoleon (later NAPOLEON III) was elected president. The revolution set off similar uprisings in Europe, but they failed virtually everywhere (see REVOLUTIONS OF 1848).

**February Revolution,** 1917, in Russian history: see RUSSIAN REVOLUTION.

**Febvre, Lucien,** 1878–1956, French historian. Educated at the École Normale Supérieure in Paris, Febvre's first field of historical study was the relationship between history and geography. He was a co-founder of ANNALES (1929). During World War II he published three books from his country house, and after the war, when his 'new history' was becoming increasingly popular, he helped to reorganize the *École des hautes études.* The first volume of his collected and wide-ranging essays, *Combats pour l'histoire,* was published when he was 75; in it he emphasized that history was a 'human science' and that 'structures' had to be analysed, not just described.

**Fechner, Gustav** (ˌfekhnə), 1803–87, German physiologist and psychologist. He was one of the founders of experimental PSYCHOPHYSICS.

**Federal Bureau of Investigation** (FBI), division of the US Dept of Justice charged with investigating all violations of federal law except those specifically assigned to other federal agencies. The FBI investigates espionage, sabotage, KIDNAPPING, bank robbery, drug trafficking, terrorism CIVIL RIGHTS violations, and fraud against the government, and conducts security clearances. Created in 1908, the bureau greatly increased its scope under the directorship (1924–72) of J. Edgar HOOVER, gaining wide popularity in the 1930s for its fight against criminal desperadoes such as John DILLINGER and against World War II saboteurs. During Hoover's controversial final years, the FBI came under attack for what many considered political bias and violation of the constitutional rights of citizens. See also INTELLIGENCE GATHERING.

**Federal Constitutional Convention,** in US history, the meeting (May–Sept. 1787) in Philadelphia at which the CONSTITUTION OF THE UNITED STATES was drawn up. The Articles of CONFEDERATION, under which the US had been governed, provided only a weak central government that had trouble conducting foreign policy, quelling internal disorders, and maintaining economic stability. Demand for a more centralized government grew steadily among the wealthy and conservative classes in many states. In 1786 a commercial conference, the ANNAPOLIS CONVENTION, disbanded with a call to convene a meeting in Philadelphia the next year for the purpose of revising the Articles. All states except Rhode Island sent delegates; George WASHINGTON presided. The major dispute at the convention was between large and small states over representation in the new Congress. A compromise proposal (the Connecticut compromise) for a Congress with an upper house in which states were equally represented and a lower house elected by population was proposed by Oliver Ellsworth and Roger Sherman, and finally approved. James MADISON was the chief drafter of the Constitution; Gouverneur MORRIS contributed to its style. Despite opposition, a sufficient number of states ratified the document to make it effective by the end of June 1788.

**federal government** or **federation,** government of a union of states in which sovereignty is divided between a central authority and component state authorities. The central government most often handles the concerns of the people as a whole, including foreign affairs, defence, coinage, and commerce; the local entities retain other jurisdictions. A successful federation usually requires a fairly uniform legal system and broad cultural affinities. The federal system is often accompanied by tensions between the central government (with its need for unity among the states) and state governments (with their desire for autonomy). Modern federations include the US, Switzerland, Australia, and Canada. The USSR is technically a federation, but the component republics have normally been subservient to the central authority.

**Federalist Party,** US political party that supported a strong federal government. During Pres. WASHINGTON's administration (1789–97) political divisions appeared within his cabinet, and the group that gathered around Alexander HAMILTON was called Federalists. They were conservatives who favoured strong centralized government, encouragement of industry, attention to the needs of the great merchants and landowners, and a well-ordered society. They also were pro-British in foreign affairs. The party was strongest in New England, with a sizable element in the Middle Atlantic states. After the Republican party's victory in 1800, the Federalists remained powerful locally, but leadership passed to reactionaries rather than moderates. Federalist opposition to the EMBARGO ACT OF 1807 and to the WAR OF 1812 resulted in the HARTFORD CONVENTION, but the successful issue of the war ruined the party, and by 1824 it was virtually dead.

**Federal Reserve System,** central banking system of the US, established by the Federal Reserve Act (1913). The act created 12 regional Federal Reserve banks, supervised by a Federal Reserve Board. All national banks must belong to the system, and state banks may if they meet certain requirements. Member banks hold the bulk of the deposits of all commercial banks in the country. The most important duties of the Federal Reserve authorities involve the maintenance of national monetary and credit conditions through lending to member banks, open-market operations, fixing reserve requirements, and establishing discount rates. By controlling the credit market, the Federal Reserve System exerts a powerful influence on the nation's economic life. See also CENTRAL BANK.

**federation:** see FEDERAL GOVERNMENT.

**feedback,** term used to describe a situation in which part of an output is sent back to the input to control it and thus modify subsequent output. Feedback forms the basis of AUTOMATIC CONTROL theory and occurs in all self-regulating machines and processes as well as in biological systems, e.g., the production of hormones. In servosystems, which constitute a general class of feedback-controlled mechanisms, the continuous measurement of the actual output quantity and comparison with the desired value forms an error control signal. For example, in the speed control of a motor, without automatic control the speed will vary as the load varies, but if the speed is sensed or measured automatically and fed back to a controller then the actual speed can be compared with the required speed and the difference or error used to actuate the controller of the motor. It this happens rapidly then the speed can be kept virtually constant irrespective of changes of load.

**Fehmgericht:** see VEHMGERICHT.

**Feininger, Lyonel,** 1871–1956, American painter. Living in Europe, he was an illustrator and caricaturist before turning to easel painting in 1907. Feininger exhibited with the BLAUE REITER group and taught at the BAUHAUS in Germany (1919–32). He returned to the US in 1937. Feininger developed a geometric style with interlocking translucent planes, often portraying sailing boats or skyscrapers.

**Feinstein, Moses,** 1895–1986, American rabbi and theologian; b. Belorussia. As President of the Union of Orthodox Rabbis of America, and head of one of the leading American talmudical colleges, Feinstein became one of the most influential authorities on religious matters. His decisions, later collected in his *Iggrot Mosheh* (6 vols.), are accepted as authoritative by Orthodox Jews throughout the world.

**Feisal:** see FAISAL.

**feldspar** or **felspar,** any of a group of minerals that are aluminium silicates of potassium, sodium, or calcium ($KAlSi_3O_8$, $NaAlSi_3O_8$, and $CaAl_2Si_2O_8$) or a mixture of these. The three pure members are called, respectively, orthoclase, albite, and anorthite. As constituents of crystalline rocks, the feldspars form much of the earth's crust. Pure feldspar is colourless and transparent, but impurities commonly make it opaque and colourful. Potassium feldspars are used in making porcelain and as a source of aluminium in making glass. The plagioclase feldspars (those ranging in composition from albite to anorthite) are commonly grey and occasionally red. MOONSTONE is a gem variety.

**Felixstowe,** town (1981 pop. 24,207), in E Suffolk, E England, on North Sea coast, 17 km (11 mi) SE of Ipswich. It is a seaside resort and port. In 1984 the port handled 9.3 million tonnes.

**Felix V,** antipope: see AMADEUS VIII.

**Fellenberg, Philipp Emanuel von,** 1771–1844, Swiss educator and agriculturist. His theory of combining farm training with well-rounded education, encouraging productive labour, and bringing together pupils from different social levels influenced educational theories, especially of manual training and VOCATIONAL EDUCATION.

**Fellini, Federico,** 1920–, Italian film director. His films, noted for their extravagant visual fantasy, include *La Strada* (1954), *La dolce Vita* (1960), *8½* (1963), *Juliet of the Spirits* (1965), *Amarcord* (1974), and *City of Women* (1980). Many feature his wife, the actress Giulietta Massina.

**felspar:** see FELDSPAR.

**Femgericht:** see VEHMGERICHT.

**feminism,** movement and set of ideas committed to the achievement for women of full legal, political, social, economic, and educational equality with men. Early European feminists included Olympe de Gouges, who wrote *The Declaration of the Rights of Women* (1789), and Mary WOLLSTONECRAFT, whose *Vindication of the Rights of Women* (1792) was extraordinarily radical and far-sighted. In the US a women's movement led by Elizabeth Cady STANTON and Susan B. ANTHONY (mid-19th cent.) began the long struggle for women's suffrage, finally achieved in 1920. The first nation to give women the vote was New Zealand (1893) followed by Australia (1903). In England the suffragettes, led by Emily PANKHURST, went to extreme lengths to make their case, but the active role taken by women on the home front during World War I was decisive in making the breakthrough in Britain in 1920 and 1928. In France and Italy the vote was not extended to women until the end of World War II. The publication of Simone de BEAUVOIR's *The Second Sex* (1949) and Betty FRIEDAN's *The Feminine Mystique* (1963) contributed to progressive changes in the climate of public opinion, raising the consciousness of both women and men to feminist issues. Meanwhile the political struggle had shifted to equal pay and equal opportunities, where significant victories were achieved on both sides of the Atlantic, and educational and career prospects for women slowly improved. From the early 1970s books such as Germaine GREER's *The Female Eunuch* (1970) and Kate MILLET's *Sexual Politics* (1970) heralded a more radical women's liberation movement analysing history in terms of the oppression of women by patriarchy, and attacking the pervasive sexism in almost all social institutions and practices. Campaigns to change the laws on marriage, property ownership, child-care, abortion, and birth control, and continued challenges to sexual stereotyping in all forms, have begun to remove the obstacles to a free and equal choice of lifestyle for women in many countries. See WOMEN'S MOVEMENT; WOMEN'S SUFFRAGE; SEXUAL POLITICS.

**fencing,** sport of duelling with foil, épée, and sabre. The weapons and rules of modern fencing evolved from weapons used in warfare. The foil, a light, flexible weapon with a blunted point, was originally used for practice. The épée, or duelling sword, is a straight, narrow, stiff weapon without cutting edges. The sabre, a light version of the old cavalry broadsword, has a flexible, triangular blade with theoretical cutting edges. Fencing matches may be conducted among individuals or between teams, generally of nine players (three for each weapon). Points are made by touching the opponent. Protective clothing includes heavy canvas jackets, wire-mesh masks, and gloves. In women's fencing, only the foil is used. Fencing was first developed as a sport by the Germans in the 14th cent. It was included in the first modern Olympic Games in 1896 and became an Olympic event for women in 1924.

**Fenian movement** (ˌfeeneeən), a secret revolutionary society, organized c.1858 in Ireland and the US to achieve Irish independence from England by force. The famine of the 1840s, which forced vast numbers of Irishmen to emigrate, brought to a crisis Irish discontent with English rule. In Ireland the Fenian movement was led by James Stephens. It appealed to the nonagrarian population and was opposed by the Roman Catholic Church. The various Fenian risings and acts of terrorism led at first to suppression by the British but eventually drew Parliament's attention to Irish problems. The movement in the US was led by the émigré Irish revolutionary John O'Mahony. In 1865 a group of embittered Irish-American Fenians unsuccessfully attempted to invade Canada. The movement continued until 1914 but its influence was largely drawn into new organizations, notably the SINN FEIN.

**Fenians,** a professional military corps that roamed over ancient Ireland (c.3rd cent.) in the service of the high kings. They figure in the legends that developed around FINN MAC CUMHAIL and OSSIAN.

**fennel,** common name for several herbs, particularly those of the genus *Foeniculum* of the CARROT family. Their liquorice-scented foliage and seeds are used for flavouring. Sweet fennel has a thickened leaf base and is eaten like CELERY.

**Fens, the,** also **Fenland,** fertile agricultural district, E England, reclaimed from The Wash, an arm of the North Sea. Romans, then Saxons, attempted to drain the low-lying, original swampland. Effective drainage began in the 17th cent. under Cornelius Vermuyden, a Dutch engineer, and continued into the 19th cent. A drainage-improvement programme was completed in the 1960s to deal with continued land sinkage.

**Fenton, Roger,** 1816–69, English photographer. At first an art student, he turned to photography and became a founder and first secretary in 1852 of what later became the Royal Photographic Society. Official photographer to the BRITISH MUSEUM, he also took portrait photographs of Queen VICTORIA and her family; with the support of Prince ALBERT he was commissioned to photograph scenes from the Crimean War, though not its battles.

Camp of the 4th Dragoon Guards, a scene from the Crimean War in 1855 by Roger **Fenton.**

**feral,** name given to domestic animals that have gone wild. Cats and horses become feral readily. The Australian brumbies are feral horses, being domestic in origin.

**Ferdinand,** rulers of the HOLY ROMAN EMPIRE. **Ferdinand I,** 1503–64, emperor (1558–64), king of BOHEMIA (1526–64) and of HUNGARY (1526–64), was the younger brother of Emperor CHARLES V; he increasingly acted as Charles's agent in the Habsburg lands. In Hungary he fought against rival claimants who had the support of Ottoman Sultan SULAYMAN I, to whom he eventually was forced to pay tribute. In Bohemia, Ferdinand vigorously defended the Catholic church and established HABSBURG absolutism. In Germany he faced princely particularism and the growth of Protestantism and negotiated the Peace of Augsburg (1555). Charles abdicated in his favour in 1558. **Ferdinand II,** 1578–1637, emperor (r.1619–37), king of Bohemia (r.1617–37) and of Hungary (r.1618–37), was the grandson of Ferdinand I. In 1619 the Bohemian nobles rebelled and elected FREDERICK THE WINTER KING, thus beginning the THIRTY YEARS' WAR. Ferdinand defeated Frederick in 1620, but the war spread. Ferdinand was almost certainly responsible for the murder (1634) of his leading general, WALLENSTEIN. **Ferdinand III**, 1608–57, emperor (1637–57), king of Hungary (1626-57) and of Bohemia (1627–57), continued to defend the Imperial position in the Thirty Years' War until the Peace of WESTPHALIA (1648), when the power of the German princes and the Habsburg position in their hereditary lands were both recognized. Ferdinand spent the last years of his reign healing the wounds of war and reforming the imperial bureaucracy.

**Ferdinand**, 1861–1948, prince (1887–1908) and czar (r.1908–18) of Bulgaria. Having outlasted Russian disapproval of his selection as prince and mastered the autonomous principality's politicians, he proclaimed Bulgaria's full independence from the Ottoman Empire and assumed the imperial title in 1908. Failing to win MACEDONIA in both the BALKAN WARS (1912–13) and in WORLD WAR I, he abdicated in favour of his son, BORIS III.

**Ferdinand**, kings of Bohemia and Hungary: see FERDINAND, rulers of the Holy Roman Empire.

**Ferdinand**, kings of Portugal. **Ferdinand I**, 1345–83 (r.1367–83), the son of PETER I, had ambitions for the throne of CASTILE that led to three disastrous wars between 1369 and 1382. In 1372 he allied himself with JOHN OF GAUNT of England, but their two wars against Castile resulted in defeat. The final war ended with the marriage of Ferdinand's daughter, Beatrice, and John I of Castile. The throne of Portugal, after Ferdinand's death and a national revolution, went to his half brother, JOHN I. **Ferdinand II**, 1816–85 (r.1837–53), was the king consort of Maria II of Portugal and was regent for their son, PETER V. He was more interested in his art collection than in governing the country.

**Ferdinand**, 1865–1927, king of ROMANIA (r.1914–27); nephew and successor of CAROL I. He took Romania (1916) into WORLD WAR I on the Allied side. In 1918 he acquired Bessarabia, and in 1919 he successfully intervened in Hungary against the Communist government of Bela KUN. During his reign agrarian reforms and universal male suffrage were instituted.

**Ferdinand**, Spanish kings. **Ferdinand I** (the Great), d. 1065, king of CASTILE (1035–65) and of LEÓN (1037–65), inherited the former kingdom and conquered the latter. He reduced the Moorish kings of Zaragoza, Badajoz, SEVILLE, and TOLEDO to vassalage and introduced church reforms. Prior to his death, he divided his kingdom among three sons. **Ferdinand III**, 1199–1252, king of Castile (1217–52) and León (1230–52), permanently united the two kingdoms in 1230. He crusaded against the MOORS and completed the reconquest of Spain, except for the kingdom of GRANADA, by 1248. **Ferdinand IV**, 1285–1312, king of Castile and León (1295–1312), conquered GIBRALTAR (1310) from the Moors with the help of ARAGÓN, but he failed in his attempt to take Algeciras. **Ferdinand V** (the Catholic), king of Castile and León (1474–1504, jointly with his wife, ISABELLA I), king of Aragón (as Ferdinand II, 1479–1516), king of Sicily (1468–1516), and king of Naples (1504–16), with his wife completed the unification of Spain by conquering Granada in 1492. In that fateful year they also expelled the JEWS and sponsored COLUMBUS's discovery of the New World. Ferdinand fought France in the ITALIAN WARS and captured NAPLES. After Isabella's death (1504), he kept control of Castile by acting as regent for their daughter, JOANNA. He increased the powers of the throne by curbing the nobles and the CORTES. During his reign Spain became an Atlantic power and revolutionized European commerce. He left a vast empire to his grandson, Holy Roman Emperor CHARLES V. **Ferdinand VI**, c.1712–59, king of Spain (1746–59), kept the nation out of the SEVEN YEARS WAR during his lifetime. After the death (1758) of his beloved queen, Maria Barbara de Braganza, Ferdinand did not recover from his grief and died soon afterwards. **Ferdinand VII**, 1784–1833, king of Spain (1808–32), was forced by NAPOLEON I to renounce his throne and was imprisoned in France during the PENINSULAR WAR (1808–14). His name became the rallying cry of Spanish nationalists who resisted the French invaders and proclaimed (1812) a liberal constitution. But when he was restored to the throne (1814), Ferdinand proved to be a thorough reactionary; he abolished the new constitution but was forced to reinstate it by a revolution (1820). Backed by France's military intervention, he revoked the constitution again (1823) and ruthlessly repressed Spanish liberals. Ferdinand's death caused no less trouble than his reign; he had excluded his brother, Don Carlos, from the throne and thus brought on the CARLIST wars.

**Ferdinand**, kings of the TWO SICILIES. **Ferdinand I**, 1751–1825 (r.1816–25), had previously been king of Naples as Ferdinand IV and king of Sicily as Ferdinand III. He had succeeded (1759) to the kingdoms when his father became king of Spain as CHARLES III. He opposed the French, who drove him from Naples to Sicily in 1799 and 1806. Restored (1815) in Naples, he abolished Sicilian autonomy and proclaimed himself king of the Two Sicilies. His rule was despotic. His grandson, **Ferdinand II**, 1810–59 (r.1830–59), initially tried to improve the kingdom's wretched state but soon drifted into absolutism. He bombarded Messina (1848) and Palermo (1849) to quell disorders, thus earning the nickname 'King Bomba'.

**Ferdinand the Catholic** (Ferdinand V): see under FERDINAND, Spanish kings.

**Ferenczi, Sandor**, 1873–1933, Hungarian psychoanalyst and early associate of Sigmund FREUD. Ferenczi was a member of the first 'inner circle' of the psychoanalytic movement (see PSYCHOANALYSIS); his ideas regarding the relationship between evolution and human psychology having a profound influence on Freud's own later 'metapsychology'. Freud was severely critical of Ferenczi's later independent stance on matters of both technique and theory, particularly regarding Ferenczi's collaboration with Otto RANK; and Ferenczi was expelled from the official psychoanalytic movement.

**Fergana** or **Ferghana Valley** (fyeəgə,nah), region, c.22,000 km² (8500 sq mi), in the Uzbek, Tadzhik, and Kirghiz republics of the S USSR. It is one of Soviet Central Asia's most densely populated agricultural and industrial areas, with important oil, coal, natural gas, and iron deposits. The valley belonged to a succession of Central Asian empires until it was acquired by Russia in 1876. It prospered until the 16th cent. from caravan trade along the traditional silk route between China and the Mediterranean.

**Fergusson, Robert**, 1750–74, Scottish poet. The best of his *Poems* (1773) give graphic and amusing pictures of life among the Edinburgh poor. BURNS acknowledged his debt to him.

**Fermanagh**, former county in the SW of N Ireland, 1833 km² (715 sq mi), bordering on the Irish Republic in the S and W. The county town is ENNISKILLEN. It is hilly in the NE and SW. Much of the centre of the county is occupied by Upper and Lower Lough ERNE. It is largely a rural county, with cattle-farming and potato cultivation important activities.

**Fermat, Pierre de** (feə,mah), 1601–65, French mathematician and magistrate. Although his work in mathematics was done for recreation, he was a founder of modern NUMBER THEORY and PROBABILITY theory. Many developments in number theory have resulted from unsuccessful attempts to prove Fermat's Last Theorem, a still unproved conjecture that states that the equation $x^n + y^n = z^n$, where $x$, $y$, and $z$ are nonzero integers, has no solutions when $n$ is an integer greater than 2.

**fermentation**, anaerobic degradation of glucose and other simple sugars in the living cell. Of the many different kinds of glucose fermentation, two kinds predominate: one, in microorganisms and animal cells, produces lactic acid as the sole end product; the other, in brewer's yeast and some bacteria, yields ethyl alcohol and carbon dioxide. Alcoholic fermentation to produce intoxicating beverages was practised in antiquity. By 1500 BC production of beer from germinating cereals (malt) and of wine from crushed grapes was an established technical art in most of the Middle East. The modern science of biochemistry emerged directly from 19th-cent. studies of fermentation.

**Fermi, Enrico**, 1901–54, Italian physicist. He went to the US in 1938 because his wife Laura was Jewish and became a US citizen in 1944. He contributed to the early theory of beta decay and the NEUTRINO and to quantum statistics and discovered the element neptunium. For his experiments with RADIOACTIVITY he was awarded the 1938 Nobel Prize for physics. Fermi and co-workers created (1942) the first self-sustaining chain reaction in uranium and worked on the atomic bomb at Los Alamos (see MANHATTAN PROJECT). He later helped develop the hydrogen bomb and served on the General Advisory Committee of the US Atomic Energy Commission.

**Fermi National Accelerator Laboratory** (Fermilab), physical science research centre (est. 1968) located near Batavia, Ill, US. Universities Research Association operates it under contract to the US Department of Energy. Work at Fermilab is devoted to the study of ELEMENTARY PARTICLES, principally through the use of a synchrotron PARTICLE ACCELERATOR capable of accelerating protons up to energies of 800 GeV.

**fermium** (Fm), radioactive element, discovered in 1952 by Albert Ghiorso and colleagues in residue from a thermonuclear explosion. Its physical properties are largely unknown; its chemical properties are similar to those of other ACTINIDE SERIES members. See ELEMENT (table); PERIODIC TABLE.

**fern**, any plant of the division Pteropsida consisting of several thousand species found worldwide, usually in tropical rain forests. Most common living ferns belong to the polypody family (Polypodiaceae) and are characterized by triangular fronds subdivided into many leaflets (pinnae) and smaller pinnules. Except for ornamentals, the only commercially important ferns are tree ferns (families Dicksoniaceae and Cyatheaceae), which can reach 18m (60ft) in New Zealand, and whose trunks are used in construction; the starchy pith is used as stock food. Ancestors of modern ferns were the dominant vegetation during the Carboniferous era. They, and such relatives as CLUB MOSSES and HORSETAILS, are the most primitive plants to have developed a true vascular system. Ferns reproduce by ALTERNATION OF GENERATIONS, and although no present-day ferns reproduce by seed, there is some fossil evidence that fernlike plants are the ancestors of seed plants (CONIFERS and true flowering plants).

**Ferrara**, city (1984 pop. 146,142), in Emilia-Romagna, N Italy, an industrial and agricultural centre on a marshy plain. It was the site of an ESTE family principality (13th cent.). Its commerce and art flourished during the Renaissance. The 12th-cent. cathedral, 14th-cent. castle, and several palaces are notable.

**Ferrara–Florence, Council of:** see COUNCIL, ECUMENICAL.

**ferret**, domesticated polecat (*Mustela furo*), an albino WEASEL common in the Old World. Used for centuries to hunt rats, mice, and rabbits, the ferret is related to the wild North American black-footed ferret (*M. nigripes*), now nearly extinct.

**Ferrier, Kathleen**, 1912–53, British contralto. She sang the title role in BRITTEN's *Rape of Lucretia* (1946) and was noted for her interpretations of GLUCK, BRAHMS, and MAHLER.

**ferromagnetism:** see MAGNETISM.

**ferry**, short-haul passenger and cargo vessel. Traditionally a small craft used to transport passengers and their belongings across rivers, lakes, and other short stretches of water, the much larger modern ferry can accommodate around 2000 people and 350 motor vehicles, and is designed for longer crossings of, for example, the English Channel, the Baltic, or the Adriatic. Roll-on roll-off ('RO-RO') ferries, built to carry large numbers of motor cars or heavy lorries, as well as passengers, came into service in the late 1940s. These open at the stern or sides to allow motor vehicles to drive on and off, whereas previously they had to be loaded by cranes. Some are also equipped to handle container traffic. A threefold increase in the volume of heavy freight traffic crossing the English Channel since 1975 may be accounted for, in part, by increased use of the RO-RO. These came under a cloud, however, when in 1986, the British vessel *Herald of Free Enterprise* sank off the Belgian coast in calm seas with the loss of 188 lives.

**Ferry, Jules**, 1832–93, French statesman, minister of education (1879–80, 1882), premier (1880–81, 1883–85). He established the modern, secular French educational system. An exponent of imperialism, he directed French colonial expansion into Tunis, Tonkin, Madagascar, and Africa. He was assassinated by a religious fanatic.

**Fertile Crescent**, historic region of the Middle East, flanked by the Nile R. (W) and the Tigris and Euphrates rivers (E). A well-watered area, it includes parts of Israel, Lebanon, Jordan, and Iraq. It was the cradle of many ancient civilizations, e.g., EGYPT and MESOPOTAMIA.

**fertility drug**, any of a variety of substances used to increase the potential for conception and successful pregnancy by correcting various functional disorders. In the male, inadequate sperm production can sometimes be remedied by administering TESTOSTERONE and sometimes pituitary hormones. In the female, failure to ovulate, the most common cause of female sterility, can sometimes be treated with the hormone gonadotrophin and, in some cases, clomiphene citrate. Often inducing more than one ovum in a month, the use of clomiphene may result in multiple births. In cases of repeated miscarriage or bleeding during pregnancy, PROGESTERONE has been found effective.

**fertilization**, in biology, sexual reproductive process involving the union of two unlike sex cells (gametes) the ovum, or egg (female), and sperm (male) followed by fusion of their nuclei. The principle of fertilization is the same in all organisms. The ovum absorbs the first sperm to make successful contact and the two nuclei fuse, combining the hereditary material of both parents; the subsequent EMBRYO develops into a new individual. In lower plants and in all animals, the sperm swims to the egg through an external medium or through fluid in the female reproductive tract. In some higher plants, POLLINATION enables the sperm to contact the egg. In multicellular animals, sperm contact initiates cell division in the fertilized egg (zygote).

**fertilizer**, organic or inorganic material added to the soil to replace or increase plant nutrients. Organic fertilizers including animal manures and COVER CROPS, fish and bone meal, GUANO (seabird excrement), and COMPOST are decomposed by soil micro-organisms, and their elements are freed for plant use (see HUMUS). Most inorganic or chemical fertilizers contain the major nutrients (nitrogen, phosphorus, and potassium) in proportions required by the crops. See also NITROGEN CYCLE.

**Festival of Britain**, a series of national exhibitions of arts and sciences organized in 1951 to coincide with the centenary of Prince Albert's Great Exhibition of 1851 and to celebrate Britain's achievements since the ending of World War II. Some of the buildings on the SOUTH BANK in London were commissioned for the festival, as was the 'Skylon', a temporary steel structure somewhat reminiscent of the Eiffel Tower, which dominated London's skyline that year.

**Festus** (Sextus Pompeius Festus), fl. at some time between AD 100 and 400, Roman lexicographer. His surviving work, *On the Meaning of Words*, an abridgment of the lost glossary of Marcus Verrius Flaccus, is important as a primary source for Roman scholarship and antiquities.

**fetish**, inanimate natural or man-made object believed to have magical power, either from a will of its own or from a god that has transformed the object into an instrument of its desires. A fetish with great power is often declared TABOO. The term is also used in psychology to denote an object, usually inanimate but perhaps a part of the body, that acts as a focus or stimulus for sexual desires.

**Feuchtwanger, Lion** (ˌfoykhtvangə), 1884–1958, German historical novelist. He achieved fame with *The Ugly Duchess* (1923), *Jud Süss* (1925), and the *Josephus* trilogy (1923–42). Feuchtwanger left Germany in 1933 and lived in the US after 1940. His novels are noted for imaginative historical reconstruction and character portrayal.

**feud**, a continuing state of hostility between groups which occasionally erupts into violence or warfare. In blood feuds kin (see KINSHIP) have to avenge the murder of their kin by a retaliatory murder of a member of the group responsible for the murder. This can lead to bouts of revenge killings, which can be carried on through generations.

**feudalism**, a political and social system which can be traced back in Western Europe to the early Middle Ages and the rise of a local agricultural economy with the manor as its unit. In the MANORIAL SYSTEM, the VILLEIN and SERF held land from the lord of the manor, the seigneur or suzerain, in return for services and dues. The king owned all land. Under him came a hierarchy of nobles, the highest holding land from the king and those of lesser rank from the nobles above them. Landholding was by fief and was ceremonially acquired by INVESTITURE. The unsettled conditions of the time necessitated warriors for the lord and protection for the vassal. Gradations of vassalage were based on land-holding and military service, from the single serf to private armies of hundreds. The KNIGHT was the typical warrior, with the squire below him and counts, dukes, and other nobles above him. The system, rooted in the decay of Roman institutions, spread from France to Spain, to Italy, and later to Germany and E Europe. WILLIAM I (the Conqueror) brought (1066) the Norman form of feudalism to England. Feudalism lingered in France until the French Revolution, in Germany and in Russia, although serfdom was abolished officially in 1861, until 1917. The term is often applied to non-European societies, and in Marxist thought represented a distinct phase in social development.

**Feuerbach, Ludwig Andreas**, 1804–72, German philosopher. At first a follower of HEGEL, he abandoned IDEALISM for materialism, a progression that influenced Karl MARX in the development of DIALECTICAL MATERIALISM. Feuerbach rejected the 'illusionistic' nature of religion and established a naturalistic–humanistic ethic that held mankind and nature to be the proper study of philosophy. His best-known work, *The Essence of Christianity* (1841), was translated into English by George ELIOT.

**Feuerbach, Paul Johann Anselm von,** 1775–1833, German jurist. A CRIMINAL LAW theorist, he argued in *Critique of Natural Law* (1796) that law was the positive mandate of the state, and not to be confused with natural morality. Feuerbach saw a dual role for criminal law as protector both of society (through its deterrent function) and of the individual (through its exact definition of crimes). In 1813 he drafted an influential liberal criminal code in Bavaria.

**Feuillade, Louis** (fwee,yahd), 1873–1925, French film director. Director of over 800 silent films, he became famous for his fantasy creations such as *Fantômas* (1914), *Judex* (1916), and *Les Vampires* (1915–16), serials which are the earliest thriller and suspense films.

**Feuillants,** political club of the FRENCH REVOLUTION. Emerging in July 1791, the group advocated a constitutional monarchy. After the fall (Sept. 1792) of the monarchy, it was suppressed by the JACOBINS.

**Fez,** city (1982 pop, 548,206), N central Morocco. It is located in a rich agricultural region. An important religious town, Fez is noted for its Muslim art and handicraft industries. It has given its name to the brimless felt hats worn by Islamic followers. The oldest of Morocco's four imperial cities, it was founded in 808 by Moulay Idris II. New Fez was founded in 1276 by the Merinade dynasty. The city has more than 100 mosques.

**Fianna Fáil,** Irish political party, organized in 1926 by opponents of the Anglo-Irish treaty of 1921 establishing the Irish Free State. Led by Eamon DE VALERA, the party gained control of the government in 1932 and advocated separation from Great Britain. Except for the years 1948–51 and 1954–57, it held power until 1973. It returned to power under John LYNCH (1977–79) and Charles Haughey (1979–81, Mar.–Dec. 1982).

**fiat money:** see MONEY.

**Fibiger, Johannes Andreas Grib,** 1867–1928, Danish pathologist. He discovered that certain species of worm parasites were associated in animals with the development of cancer, and for this discovery he was awarded the 1926 Nobel prize for physiology or medicine.

**Fibonacci, Leonardo** (feeboh,natchee), b. c.1170, d. after 1240; Italian mathematician, known also as Leonardo da Pisa. The Fibonacci SEQUENCE 0, 1, 1, 2, 3, 5, 8, 13, 21 . . ., in which each term is the sum of the two preceding terms, occurs in higher mathematics in various connections.

**fibre,** threadlike strand, usually pliable and capable of being spun into a yarn. Fibres are classified as either natural (including animal, vegetable, and inorganic) or artificial (see SYNTHETIC TEXTILE FIBRES). Animal fibres, e.g., SILK, WOOL, and goat hair (mohair), consist mainly of proteins. Vegetable fibres, e.g., COTTON, consist mainly of cellulose. ASBESTOS is the chief natural inorganic fibre; FIBREGLASS is also of inorganic origin. Artificial fibres are made by either synthesizing a POLYMER, as in nylon, or altering natural fibres, as in RAYON. Fibres are used for textiles, e.g., cotton, silk, wool; cordage, e.g., hemp; brushes, e.g., animal hairs; filling, e.g., horsehair; and plaiting, e.g., sisal. The invention of SPINNING and WEAVING machinery during the INDUSTRIAL REVOLUTION greatly increased the demand for fibres.

**fibreglass,** thread made from glass. Molten glass is forced through a kind of sieve, thus spinning it into threads. Strong, durable, and impervious to many caustics and to extreme temperatures, fibreglass fabrics are widely used in industry. Some, resembling silk and cotton, are used for drapery. Boat hulls and car bodies moulded of fibreglass combined with plastic are rustproof.

**fibre optics,** the study of the behaviour of light in thin strands of glass and its commercial exploitation. If a ray of light is directed down a very thin glass filament it will, since the angle at which it will strike the glass/air interface is very small, be repeatedly reflected along the length of the fibre with very little loss of intensity. This finding was of limited interest and application until the advent of digital communications. However, as soon as it was seen that the digital signal—the binary 0 or 1—could be transmitted as a light pulse, optical fibres came to be seen as offering major advantages over copper cables. These include an optical fibre's ability to carry more digital traffic than a copper wire, the great reduction in the amount of amplification that a light signal requires (electrical signals need to be boosted every 3–4 km, signals in optical fibres, with the very great band width they can handle, have been shown to be still usable 150 km from their starting point), and its freedom from linear distortion and electromagnetic interference. Futhermore silica, the

principal ingredient of glasses, is the most abundant mineral on earth and thus cheap. Optical fibres are now used for all major high-speed communications links, and the trunk network of Mercury Communications, the telecommunications company set up in 1983 to rival British Telecom, is entirely optical fibre laid in gullies alongside railway lines linking major cities. The majority of Britain's trunk network is expected to be optical by 1990, and continental cables are expected to follow suit following the completion of the first such cable between Britain and Belgium in 1987.

**fibrositis:** see RHEUMATISM.

**Fichte, Johann Gottlieb,** 1762–1814, German philosopher. He received early recognition for *A Critique of All Revelation* (1788), erroneously attributed to KANT. His later works, including *The Vocation of Man* (1800), developed a transcendental IDEALISM that considered the individual ego as the source of experience and postulated an absolute ego or moral will of the universe from which everything derives. An important influence on SCHELLING and HEGEL, Fichte is best remembered for his political theories. His *Addresses to the German People* (1808) established him as a leader of liberal nationalism, and he became a hero to the revolutionaries of 1848.

**fiction:** see NOVEL; SHORT STORY.

**Fiedler, Arthur,** 1894–1979, American conductor. He formed (1924) the Boston Sinfonietta, a group dedicated to performing little-heard compositions. Fiedler became director of the Boston Pops Orchestra in 1930; for almost 50 years he led it to enormous international popularity with an astute blend of classical and popular music concerts featuring a wide variety of guest artists.

**fief :** see FEUDALISM.

**field,** in physics, region throughout which a force may be exerted; examples are the gravitational, electric, and magnetic fields that surround, respectively, masses, electric charges, and magnets (see GRAVITATION; ELECTRICITY; MAGNETISM). Fields are used to describe all cases in which two bodies separated in space exert a force on each other.

**Field, Cyrus West,** 1819–92, American promoter of the first Atlantic telegraph CABLE. In 1854 he conceived the idea of the cable and organized English and American companies to lay it. The first message was transmitted on 16 Aug. 1858; the cable failed three weeks later, but he raised new funds and succeeded in laying a new cable in 1866. He later promoted other oceanic cables, notably one via Hawaii to Asia and Australia.

**Field, John,** 1782–1837, Irish composer and pianist. He was a prodigy who became a pupil of CLEMENTI, a friend of Dussek, and one of the finest pianists of his day. He travelled with Clementi to St Petersburg in 1802 and lived happily and fruitfully there and in Moscow until 1831, and then from 1835–37. His piano improvisations inspired him to invent the nocturne, and by 1812 he had published the first three pieces with this title. He wrote some fine piano concertos which presage the style of Chopin, as well as nocturnes, piano sonatas, and chamber music.

**field event,** athletics event other than races: i.e., DISCUS THROWING, HAMMER THROWING, HIGH JUMP, JAVELIN THROWING, LONG JUMP, POLE VAULT, SHOT PUT, TRIPLE JUMP, etc.

**field hockey:** see HOCKEY, FIELD.

**Fielding, Henry,** 1707–54, English novelist and dramatist. *Tom Thumb* (1730) was the most notable of his early comedies, farces, and burlesques. Two satires, *Pasquin* (1736) and *The Historical Register for 1736* (1737), in which he attacked the government of Robert WALPOLE, ended his dramatic career by provoking the Licensing Act of 1737, which introduced stage censorship. In 1748 he became a magistrate, and powerfully influenced standards of judicial probity and the control of criminal activity. His innovative and picaresque novels, which set the course for the English novel and strongly influenced Dickens and Thackeray, included *Joseph Andrews* (1742), *Shamela* (1741) a parody of Samuel RICHARDSON's *Pamela*; *Jonathan Wild* (1743), the ironic history of a highwayman; and his masterpiece, *Tom Jones* (1749), which presents in the foundling Tom and his guardian, Squire Allworthy, Fielding's ideal man, in whom goodness and charity are combined with common sense. Fielding's last works were *Amelia* (1751) and the *Journal of a Voyage to Lisbon* (1755).

**field mouse:** see VOLE.

**Field of the Cloth of Gold,** meeting place of HENRY VIII of England and FRANCIS I of France, near Calais, France (1520). Both kings brought large retinues, and the name given the site indicates the splendour of the pageantry. The political results were negligible, because Henry had decided to ally himself with Holy Roman Emperor CHARLES V rather than with Francis.

**Fields, W.C.,** 1880–1946, American film actor; b. William Claude Dukenfield. Known for his rasping voice and bulbous nose, he played a series of drunken, misanthropic yet wistful rascals in such comedies as *It's a Gift* (1934), *My Little Chickadee* (1940), and *The Bank Dick* (1940).

**fieldwork:** see PARTICIPANT OBSERVATION.

**Fife,** region in E Scotland (1985 est. pop. 341,589), 1307 km² (510 sq mi), bordering on the Firth of Tay in the N, the North Sea in the E and the Firth of Forth in the S. The administrative centre is Glenrothes. It was formed in 1975 from the former county of Fife. Hilly in the W, it is drained by the R. Leven. Agriculture is an important activity on fertile soils within the coastal plain. Coal is mined in the S. Cupar, Kircaldy, and Dunfermline are the main towns, and ST ANDREWS is a seaside resort and university town.

**fifth-generation computers:** see COMPUTER GENERATIONS.

**Fifty-four forty or fight,** in US history, phrase commonly used by American expansionists in the controversy with Great Britain over the OREGON country. They held that US rights extended to lat. 54°40′N, the recognized southern boundary of Russian America. The phrase was used by supporters of Democrat James POLK in the 1844 presidential campaign. In 1846 the boundary was set at 49°N.

**fig,** plant (genus *Ficus*) of the MULBERRY family, comprising over 600 species of vines, shrubs, and trees. Fig plants bear hundreds of tiny female flowers inside a fleshy receptacle, which ripens into a soft, pear-shaped fruit containing masses of tiny seeds. The common fig (*F. carica*), native to the Mediterranean region and cultivated from early times for its commercially valuable fruit, has been naturalized elsewhere in mild, semiarid climates. Some edible varieties can be pollinated only by the fig wasp.

**Figueiredo, João Baptista de Oliveira** (feegay,raydoh), 1918–, Brazilian general and politician, president of BRAZIL (1979–85). He was named (1974) to head the national intelligence service and in 1979 was chosen to succeed Ernesto Geisel as president. Figueiredo liberalized Brazil's military regime and moved the nation cautiously towards the restoration of civilian rule in 1985.

**Figueres Ferrer, José** (fee,gayrays feə,ray), 1906–, president of COSTA RICA (1948–49, 1953–58, 1970–74) and founder of the National Liberation Party. In 1948 he led a revolt to ensure the presidency of newly elected Otilio Ulate and served as provisional president. His administrations enacted social legislation and economic reforms.

**figured bass,** in music, a system of shorthand notation in which figures are written below the notes of the bass part to indicate the chords to be played; also called thorough bass and basso continuo. It arose in the 17th cent. and was widespread until after the time of J.S. BACH as a means of notating an accompaniment on the harpsichord or ORGAN.

**figurehead,** carved decoration, usually a head or figure, placed under the bowsprit of a ship. Ancient ships had beaks on the bow to ram enemy vessels; these were often surmounted by figureheads of national or religious significance. Roman vessels often carried bronze gods' heads, and Viking ships had elaborately carved prows. Dragons, lions, and human forms adorned Renaissance vessels. In the final phase of the art, in the 18th and 19th cent., highly original wood figureheads were carved in the United States.

**Fiji** or **Viti,** independent country (1986 est. pop. 714,000), c.18,130 km² (7000 sq mi), comprising c.320 islands (c.105 inhabited), in the SW Pacific Ocean. The two largest islands are Viti Levu, the site of Suva, the capital; and Vanua Levu. The climate is tropical. Sugarcane, coconuts, pineapples, and bananas are the chief crops, and copra and timber are significant exports. Tourism is important. The original Fijians, of Melanesian origin in the west and Polynesian origin in the east, are now outnumbered by Indians, who first came (1870–1916) to the islands as indentured workers for the British. The islands were discovered (1643) by the Dutch navigator Abel TASMAN and visited (1774) by Capt. James COOK. The first European settlement was established in 1804, and the

islands were annexed by Britain in 1874. Fiji gained independence as a member of the COMMONWEALTH in 1970. After independence successive elections won by the conservative Alliance headed by Ratu Sir Kamisese MARA, until in 1987 a coalition of predominantly Indian parties was elected. A military coup by the Melanesian armed forces quickly followed, led by Brig. Sitiveni Rabuka, and Fiji was declared a republic and ceased to be a member of the Commonwealth.

**filbert:** see HAZEL.

**filibuster,** term used to designate obstructionist tactics, notably speeches of many hours in length, in legislative bodies, especially the US Senate. The term was applied in the 17th cent. to buccaneers who plundered Spanish colonies in the New World, and in the 19th cent. to adventurers who led private forays into friendly countries, e.g., from the US into Cuba and Mexico.

**Filipepi, Alessandro di Mariano:** see BOTTICELLI, SANDRO.

**Fillmore, Millard,** 1800–1874, 13th president of the US (1850–53). A US representative from New York (1833–35, 1837–43), Fillmore was elected (1848) vice president on the WHIG PARTY ticket with Zachary TAYLOR. Succeeding to the presidency on Taylor's death, Fillmore signed the COMPROMISE OF 1850 and tried to enforce the Fugitive Slave Act thereby incurring great unpopularity in the North. In 1852 he was denied renomination by the Whigs, but in 1856 he was the presidential candidate of the KNOW-NOTHING PARTY, running a poor third.

**finch,** BIRD of the family Fringillidae, found worldwide except Australia, considered the most highly developed of birds. Finches are typified by stout, conical bills, used to open the seeds that comprise their main diet; many also eat insects. Highly diversified, finches are classified in three groups: those with triangular bills, e.g., CANARY, SPARROW, and the birds called finch, e.g., CHAFFINCH, bullfinch and goldfinch; those with thick, rounded bills, e.g., cardinal; and those whose mandibles cross at the tips, e.g., crossbill. Because their seed diet does not depend on weather, many finches are year-round residents in colder areas.

**Fingal:** see FINN MAC CUMHAIL.

**fingerprint,** an impression of the underside of the end of a finger or thumb, which has ridges that form a pattern unique to each person. Fingerprinting as an identification device dates from antiquity, but sophisticated modern methods are based on work by the English scientist Sir Francis GALTON and others during the late 19th cent. Fingerprint identification is used extensively in criminal investigation, the armed services, government employment, and banking. The term has also come to mean any process whereby an object can be uniquely identified, e.g., fingerprinting DNA describes the analytical techniques used to determine the sequence bases along a DNA molecule.

**Finiguerra, Maso** or **Tommaso** (feeneegweərah), 1426–64, Florentine goldsmith and engraver during the RENAISSANCE. He collaborated with Antonio Pollaiuolo (see POLLAIUOLO, family) on such works as the baptistery *Crucifixion* in Florence.

**Finland,** Finnish *Suomi*, officially the Republic of Finland, republic (1985 est. pop. 4,875,000), 337,009 km² (130,119 sq mi), N Europe; bordered by the Gulf of Bothnia and Sweden (W), Norway (N), the USSR (E), and the Gulf of Finland and the Baltic Sea (S). HELSINKI is the capital. There are three main geographical zones: a low-lying coastal strip in the S and W that includes most of the major cities; a vast forested interior plateau, dotted with some 60,000 lakes; and a thinly wooded or barren region N of the ARCTIC CIRCLE, part of LAPLAND. Since World War II, manufacturing has replaced agriculture as the principal sector of the economy; the chief manufactures are forest products (about 70% of Finland is forested), processed foods, metal and engineering products, machinery, and chemicals. Finland is also known for its design of glass, ceramics, and stainless-steel cutlery. The GNP is $50,730 million and the GNP per capita is $10,440 (1983). Finnish and Swedish are both official languages, and most of the population belongs to the established Evangelical Lutheran Church. Finland is governed by an elected president and a 200-member unicameral parliament (*Eduskunta*) elected for a four-year term.

*History.* Beginning in the 1st cent AD, Finland was settled by nomadic hunters and fishers, who forced the small number of Lapps living in the central and southern regions to move to the far north, where they live today. Sweden conquered the area in the 13th cent. but allowed the

Finns considerable independence, raising Finland to the rank of grand duchy in 1581. During the Napoleonic Wars, Finland was invaded by Russia, which annexed it in 1809. As a Russian grand duchy, Finland was again allowed wide-ranging autonomy. Finnish nationalism became a strong force early in the 19th cent.; an elected parliament was established in 1906, and Finnish independence was proclaimed in 1917. In the civil war that followed (1918), the nationalist White Guard, led by C.G.E. MANNERHEIM and aided by German troops, defeated the leftist Red Guard, supported by the Soviets. A republic was established in 1919. After the start of WORLD WAR II, Soviet troops invaded Finland (1939), which, despite heroic resistance, was defeated (1940). Hoping to recover territories lost in the conflict, Finland joined the German attack (1941) on the USSR but was forced to capitulate (1944). The armistice required Finland to expel the Germans, and in the ensuing Finnish-German warfare N Finland was devastated. The peace treaty signed in 1947 ceded additional Finnish territory to the USSR. In the postwar era the Social Democrat and Centre (Agrarian until 1965) parties have dominated Finnish politics, although the large Communist Party has also participated in several coalition governments. Mauno KOIVISTO was elected president in 1982 (and reelected in 1988) and pledged to maintain a neutral foreign policy and to pursue good relations with the USSR. Following the 1983 elections a coalition of the Social Democratic, Centre, Swedish People's and Rural parties was formed. After the 1987 elections the Conservatives replaced the Centre Party in the coalition and Harri Holkeri became the first Conservative premier since 1945.

## Post-war Finnish presidents
C.G. Mannerheim (non-party), 1944–46
Juho Paasikivi (non-party), 1946–56
Urho Kekkonen (Agrarian/Central), 1956–82
Mauno Koivisto (Social Democrat), 1982–

## Post-war Finnish prime ministers
Juho Paasikivi (non-party), 1945–46
Mauno Pekkala (Socialist), 1946–48
Karl-August Fagerholm (Social Democrat), 1948–50
Urho Kekkonen (Agrarian), 1950–53
Sakari Tuomioja (non-party), 1953–54
Ralf Törngren (Swedish People's P.), 1954
Urho Kekkonen (Agrarian), 1954–56
Karl-August Fagerholm (Social Democrat), 1956–57
Veino Johannes Sukselainen (Agrarian), 1957
Rainer von Fieandt (non-party), 1957–58
Reino Kuuskoski (non-party), 1958
Karl-August Fagerholm (Social Democrat), 1958–59
Veino Johannes Sukselainen (Agrarian), 1959–61
Martti Miettunen (Agrarian), 1961–62
Ahti Karjalainen (Agrarian), 1962–63
Reino Lehto (non-party), 1963–64
Johannes Virolainen (Agrarian Centre), 1964–66
Rafael Paasio (Social Democrat), 1966–68
Mauno Koivisto (Social Democrat), 1968–70
Teuvo Aura (non-party), 1970
Ahta Karjalainen (Centre), 1970–71
Teuvo Aura (non-party), 1971–72
Rafael Paasio (Social Democrat), 1972
Kalevi Sorsa (Social Democrat), 1972–75
Keijo Liinamaa (Social Democrat), 1975
Martti Miettunen (Centre), 1975–77
Kalevi Sorsa (Social Democrat), 1977–79
Mauno Koivisto (Social Democrat), 1979–82
Kalevi Sorsa (Social Democrat), 1982–87
Harri Holkeri (Conservative), 1987–

**Finnish language,** also called Suomi, member of the Finnic group of the Finno-Ugric languages. These languages form a subdivision of the Uralic subfamily of the URALIC AND ALTAIC family of languages. See LANGUAGE (table).

**Finn mac Cumhail, Fionn mac Cumhail,** or **Finn MacCool** (finmə‚koohl), semimythical Irish hero, celebrated in OSSIAN's narrative poems and in the Fenian ballads, so called after the fighters Finn is said to have led in the 3rd cent.

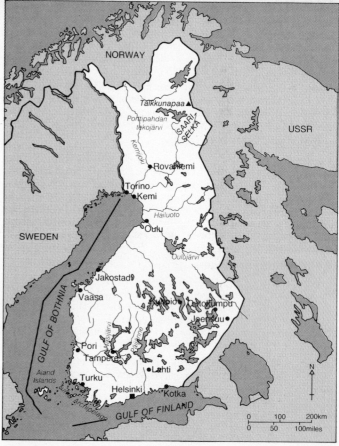

Finland

**Finno-Ugric languages** (‚finoh-‚oohgrik), group of languages forming a subdivision of the Uralic subfamily of the URALIC AND ALTAIC family of languages. See LANGUAGE (table).

**Finsen, Niels Ryberg,** 1860–1904, Danish physician. He proved the healing power of sunlight in tuberculosis of the skin and received the 1903 Nobel prize for physiology or medicine for this work.

**fiord:** see FJORD.

**fiqh,** [Arab., = knowledge, understanding], the system of Islamic law. One of the outstanding intellectual achievements of Islamic culture. Islamic legal theory (*usul al-fiqh*) utilizes the KORAN, HADITH, *ijma'* (consensus), and *qiyas* (analogical and other logical procedures) to derive specific rulings and judgments. Juristic theory also provides for rules concerning the revision of rulings on grounds of considerations of local custom and the public weal. Everything that is not specifically indicated, by permission, interdiction, or otherwise, in the Koran and Hadith is thus open to interpretation, and there are rules governing the particularization and generalizations of statements from these sources. Juristic theory, properly inaugurated by SHAFI'I, reached its systematic consummation in treatises of the 13th cent. SUNNISM produced four durable schools of law which differed in their overall theoretical orientations and in their detailed legislation, although there is a certain basic uniformity between them. These schools were that named after Shafi'i, which is today predominant in Egypt, the school named after MALIK which represented the tradition of Medina and is now predominant in North Africa, the school named after ABU HANIFA which represented the Iraqi tradition and is now predominant throughout Turkey, the Levant, Afghanistan, and the Indian Sub-Continent, and the school that slowly emerged out of the teachings of IBN HANBAL. These four schools are mutually recognized. SHI'ISM has a special body of fiqh whose details are similar to that of the HANAFISM. Theoretically, Shi'ite law differs in its rejection of the notion of consensus, for which is substituted revealed Hadith attributed to the IMAMS; no other hadith is considered by them to have authority. Shi'ite fiqh is sometimes referred to as Ja'farite law, after JA'FAR AL SADIQ. All systems of Islamic law contain provision for private and family law, criminal law, and the commercial law of contract and partnership. Many of these precepts have been absorbed into the body of civil law in the 19th and 20th cent. in Arab and other countries with islamic majorities and traditions. The office entrusted with the dispensation of justice according to Islamic law is that of QADI. See also ULAMA.

**fir,** term generally applied to several CONIFERS but strictly meaning the silver fir, genus *Abies*, of the PINE family, found chiefly in the alpine areas of the Northern Hemisphere. Firs are tall, pyramidal evergreens, with short, flat, stemless needles, and erect, cylindrical cones. The name silver is derived from the white bands of resin on the undersurfaces of the needles. They are highly valued for their fragrance and beauty of form, and are important timber producers on the continent of Europe, where they are the preferred species for use as Christmas trees. Their timber is exported as whitewood.

**Firbank, (Arthur Annesley) Ronald,** 1886–1926, English author. An eccentric aesthete, he wrote unconventional satiric novels, e.g., *Vainglory* (1915), *Valmouth* (1919), *Prancing Nigger* (1924), that influenced WAUGH, COMPTON-BURNETT, and Aldous HUXLEY.

**Firdausi** (fə͵dowsee), c.940–1020, Persian poet, author of the *Book of Kings,* the first great work of Persian literature; b. Abul Kasim Mansur. The *Book of Kings* is an epic poem recounting the history of Persia from the arrival of the Persians to that of the Arabs. It is noted for its even rhyme, stately cadences, and continuous flow.

**firearm:** see ARTILLERY; GUN; MORTAR; SMALL ARMS.

**firefly,** fairly small (5–20 mm, ⅕–¾ in) nocturnal BEETLE (families Lampyridae and Elateridae), with light-producing organs (see BIOLUMINESCENCE). Lampyrid females that retain their larval form are GLOW-WORMS but those insects in which light-producing females are winged or in which males produce light are fireflies. This name is also used for luminescent species of click beetle (Elateridae), a family better known for the damage the larvae (wireworms) cause to the roots and tubers of crop plants. Fireflies and some glow-worms emit light in a series of flashes and both the length of flash and interval between flashes is species-specific. In some, especially SE Asian species, males form mating aggregations on trees and bushes and then synchronize their flashing, with a remarkable degree of accuracy, to reinforce its attractiveness to females.

**Firestone, Harvey Samuel,** 1868–1938, American industrialist. He began to manufacture rubber tyres in 1896. The Firestone Fire & Rubber Co., which he organized in 1900, became a leader of the rubber industry and one of the largest tyre manufacturers in the US.

**Firozabad,** town (1981 pop. 202,338), AGRA district, Uttar Pradesh state, N India, on the Jamuna (Jumna) river. It is chiefly remarkable for its cottage industries, especially the manufacture of glass bangles.

**first aid,** immediate treatment of a victim of sudden illness or injury while awaiting the arrival of medical aid. Essentials of first aid treatment include correct positioning of the patient in the recovery position and ARTIFICIAL RESPIRATION.

**Firth, John Rupert,** 1890–1960, English linguist. The first academic to occupy a chair in general linguistics in Great Britain, he insisted on the development and autonomy of linguistics as an academic subject. He is especially remembered for his contributions to prosodic PHONETICS and his contextual theory of meaning.

**Firth, Sir Raymond William,** 1901–, English social anthropologist; b. New Zealand. A professor at the London School of Economics (1944–68), he conducted research in the Pacific and in West Africa, focusing on social organization and economic systems. His works include *We the Tikopia* (1936, rev. ed. 1957), *Human Types* (1938, rev. ed. 1957), and *Symbols: Public and Private* (1973).

**Fischer, Bobby** (Robert James Fischer), 1943–, American chess player. In 1972 at Reykjavik, Iceland, he won the world chess championship from Boris Spassky of the USSR. Fischer subsequently disputed match rules with the International Federation of Chess, and in 1975 Anatoly KARPOV of the USSR was declared champion by default.

**Fischer, Hermann Emil,** 1852–1919, German chemist. Arguably the greatest organic chemist of all time, he was awarded the Nobel Prize for chemistry in 1902. His early work led to discoveries in carbohydrate chemistry and in synthetic (the triphenylmethane) dyes. He synthesized PURINE in 1898, and many members of the purine family which play a vital

role in NUCLEIC ACIDS. He was the first to synthesize nucleotides, carbohydrates, polypeptides, and proteins, and in so doing he often devised brilliant and elegant methods. More so than any of his contemporaries, Fischer placed the growing field of biochemistry on a sound organic chemical basis.

**Fischer-Dieskau, Dietrich,** 1925–, German baritone. He is one of the foremost singers of German LIEDER, noted for his interpretations of Brahms, Schubert, Schumann, and Wolf.

**Fischer–Tropsch process,** method, discovered (1923) by the German coal researchers Franz Fischer and Hans Tropsch, for the synthesis of HYDROCARBON and other aliphatic compounds. A mixture of hydrogen and carbon monoxide is reacted in the presence of an iron or cobalt catalyst. Much heat is evolved, and such products as methane, synthetic motor fuel and waxes, and alcohols are made, with water or carbon dioxide by-products. In those countries, like South Africa, with no PETROLEUM reserves, petrol and other products, and chemical feedstuffs for the manufacture of textiles and plastics, are synthesized from coal. The latter is gasified with oxygen and steam and thereby converted to the required mixture of CARBON MONOXIDE and hydrogen (termed 'syngas') which, over an appropriate catalyst is converted to petrol and other grades of fuel. It was by this method that Germany produced aviation fuel in World War II.

**fish,** limbless, aquatic, VERTEBRATE animal with fins, internal gills, and skin with a glandular secretion that decreases friction. Most fish have scales and are POIKILOTHERMIC. A typical fish is torpedo-shaped, with a head containing a brain and sensory organs, a muscular-walled trunk with a cavity containing internal organs, and a muscular tail. Most fish propel themselves through the water with weaving movements and control their direction with fins. Although some fish, such as sharks, are OVOVIVIPAROUS, most fish eggs are fertilized and hatch in water. There are over 20,000 species in three classes: Agnatha, the most primitive fishes, jawless and without paired pelvic and pectoral fins (e.g., LAMPREY); Chondrichthyes, cartilaginous fishes, with skeletons of cartilage but no swim bladder or lungs (e.g., SHARK, RAY); and Osteichthyes, bony fishes, the most highly developed. Bony fishes have a bony skeleton and a swim bladder or lungs, and are divided into fleshy-finned (e.g., LOBEFIN, LUNGFISH) and ray-finned fishes (e.g., BASS, TUNA). The largest fish is the whale shark (*Rhincodon typus*), reaching 15 m (50 ft) in length and found worldwide in tropical seas; the smallest is the 1.25-cm (½-in) goby (family Gobiidae) of the Philippines.

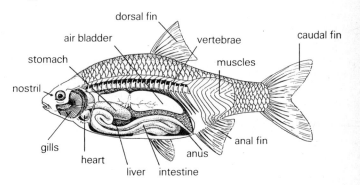

Internal anatomy of a **fish**

**Fish, Hamilton,** 1808–93, American statesman. A Whig congressman (1843–45) and senator (1851–57) from New York, Fish served as Pres. GRANT's secretary of state (1869–77) and was one of the ablest men ever to hold that office. He arranged the Treaty of WASHINGTON (1871), which settled long-standing disputes with Britain, and he kept US-based filibustering expeditions against Cuba from escalating into war with Spain.

**Fishbourne Palace,** site near Chichester in S England of a palatial Roman villa, said to be the residence of the pro-Roman king, Cogidubnus, during the 1st cent. AD. The richly decorated palace, replete with marble, wall paintings, and mosaics, had four wings enclosing an ornamental garden. The political role of the occupant is suggested by the presence of reception and administrative quarters in one of the wings.

**Fisher, Irving,** 1867–1947, American economist. A professor at Yale Univ. (1890–1935), he is known for his pioneering work in monetary economic theory; his theory of the 'compensated dollar' to stabilize purchasing power; and his development of the INDEX NUMBER, a measurement of price levels.

**Fisher, Sir Ronald Aylmer,** 1890–1962, British geneticist and statistician. Appointed as statistician at the Rothamsted Experimental Station in 1919, where he remained until 1933, he developed much of the basis for modern statistical mathematics, especially for the design and analysis of experiments. He was appointed professor of eugenics in London Univ. in 1933, and professor of genetics at Cambridge in 1943, where he established a sound basis for future studies of heritability and schemes of artificial and natural selection. His book *The Genetical Theory of Natural Selection* (1930) was of great importance in first showing how Mendelian genetics underpinned Darwin's theory of evolution. Throughout his life he carried out breeding experiments with the house mouse on polydactyly, recombination, dominance modification, and the extension of Mendel's laws.

**Fisher, Saint John,** c.1469–1535, English prelate, cardinal, bishop of Rochester (1504–34). For opposing the divorce of HENRY VIII and KATHARINE OF ARAGÓN and other acts of the English REFORMATION, Fisher was imprisoned in 1534. To show his support, Pope PAUL III created (1535) Fisher a cardinal, but an enraged Henry quickly had Fisher beheaded. He was canonized in 1935. Feast: June 22.

**Fishguard** or **Abergwaun,** town (1981 pop. 2903), Dyfed, SW Wales at S end of Fishguard Bay. A small town and fishing port, it is also a railway terminus. There are passenger ferries from here to the Republic of Ireland.

**fission:** see ATOMIC BOMB; NUCLEAR ENERGY.

**Fitch, John,** 1743–98, American inventor. An early experimenter with steam engines and steamboats (see STEAMSHIP), he is believed to have designed (1786) the first practical steamboat. Nevertheless, he failed to receive either the opportunity to commercialize his invention or the recognition he justly deserved.

**FitzGerald, Edward,** 1809–83, English author. His masterpiece is his translation of *The Rubaiyat of Omar Khayyam* (1859; rev. 1868, 1872, 1879). He published other translations from Persian and from Spanish, and some essays and anthologies. He was a celebrated letter-writer.

**Fitzgerald, Ella,** 1918–, black American jazz singer. She was a popular big band and solo artist. Principally a JAZZ and blues singer with a sweet and effortless style, she is also a noted interpreter of the songs of George GERSHWIN and Cole PORTER, among others.

**Fitzgerald, F(rancis) Scott (Key),** 1896–1940, American author, one of the great American writers of the 20th cent. Considered the literary spokesman of the 1920s 'jazz age', he wrote about people whose lives resembled his own. He and his wife, Zelda, lived a celebrated life, glittering and dissipated, in New York City and the French Riviera, but his later years were plagued by financial worries and his wife's insanity. Fitzgerald's novels are *This Side of Paradise* (1920); *The Beautiful and Damned* (1922); *The Great Gatsby* (1922), his masterpiece about the corruption of the American dream; *Tender Is the Night* (1934); and *The Last Tycoon* (1941), an unfinished work reflecting his last years in Hollywood. He also published four short-story collections.

**FitzGerald, Garret,** 1926–, prime minister of the Republic of IRELAND (1981–82, 1982–87). Elected leader of the centrist Fine Gael party in 1977, he headed two coalition governments with the Labour Party, during the second of which he signed (1985) the Anglo-Irish Agreement giving the Republic a consultative role in the affairs of Northern Ireland. Defeated in the 1987 elections, he resigned the Fine Gael leadership shortly thereafter.

**Five, The,** a group of 19th-cent. Russian composers. They were BALAKIREV, CUI, MOUSSORGSKY, BORODIN, and RIMSKY-KORSAKOV and drew on Russian history, literature, and folklore to write music of a distinctly national character.

**Five Civilized Tribes,** name used since the mid-19th cent. for the CHEROKEE, Chickasaw, Choctaw, CREEK, and SEMINOLE INDIANS settled in INDIAN TERRITORY under the Removal Act of 1830. Living on communally held land, each tribe had a written constitution, a tripartite government, and a public school system. A later federal policy of detribalization resulted in the loss of their governmental functions, except advisory, and the division of all land into individual holdings.

**Five Nations:** see IROQUOIS CONFEDERACY.

**Five-Power Treaty:** see NAVAL CONFERENCES.

**fives,** hand-and-ball game played as doubles or singles in a court with a front wall and two side walls but no back wall. There are two types of fives, Eton Fives (in which the court has a buttress (or pepper) protruding from the left-hand wall) and Rugby Fives. Players wear gloves and may hit the ball with either hand or both. Round the walls is a ledge, above which the ball must be struck. Only the server can score points. When the server loses a rally, the receiver serves. The first pair or player to reach 12 points wins the game. Matches usually consist of five games.

**Five-Year Plan,** a programme to speed industrialization and the collectivization of agriculture in the USSR, initiated (1928–33) by Joseph STALIN. Now a standard feature of the Soviet bloc, five-year development plans have been adopted widely throughout the world.

**fjords,** long, branching inlets which dissect the west coast of Norway, the result of erosion during the Ice Ages and subsequent flooding by the sea. The largest are the Sognefjord, the Hardangerfjord, and the Trondheimfjord. They are deep and steep-sided, with waterfalls down the sides which are used to generate power for pulp and paper and metallurgical plants.

**flag,** piece of cloth, usually bunting or similar light material, plain, coloured, or bearing a device, varying in size and shape but often oblong or square, used as an ensign, standard, or signal or for display or decorative purposes, and generally attached at one end (the hoist) to a staff or a halyard by which it may be hoisted. The portion from the hoist to the free end is the fly; the top quarter of the flag next to the staff is the canton. Flags have been used since ancient times. Early flags had a religious significance that persisted historically. For example, the ensign of Great Britain, the Union Jack, is formed by the crosses of St GEORGE, St ANDREW, and St PATRICK, the national saints, respectively, of England, Scotland, and Ireland. Armies and navies use flags for signaling: the white flag is used universally for truce; the black in early times was a symbol for piracy; the red symbolizes mutiny or revolution; the yellow is a sign of infectious diseases. Shipping lines have their own flags. Striking a flag signifies surrender, and the flag of the victor is hoisted above that of the vanquished. A flag flown at half-mast is a symbol of mourning. The inverted national ensign is a signal of distress. The first flag of the US was raised at Cambridge, Massachussetts by George WASHINGTON on 2 January 1776. Today, the US flag has 13 stripes, denoting the 13 original colonies, and 50 stars, for the 50 states.

**flagellum,** single, long, hairlike filament which is used to propel single-celled organisms through water. The class of PROTOZOA named Flagellata derive their name from their characteristic flagella, which are found also in unicellular algae and gametes.

**Flagstad, Kirsten,** 1895–1962, Norwegian soprano. In 1935 she appeared at the METROPOLITAN OPERA in Richard WAGNER's *Die Walküre* and thereafter was regarded as the greatest living Wagnerian soprano.

**Flaherty, Robert Joseph,** 1884–1951, American film director. His pioneering documentaries include *Nanook of the North* (1922) and *Man of Aran* (1934).

**flamingo,** large pink or red tropical wading BIRD (order Ciconiiformes), similar to the related HERON and STORK but with webbed feet and a unique, down-bent bill. Ranging in height from 90 to 150 cm (3 to 5 ft), the flamingo has a long neck and legs and a broad wingspan. It has an unusually shaped hair-fringed bill with which it filter-feeds on small aquatic life.

**Flamsteed, John,** 1646–1719, English astronomer who became in 1675 the first ASTRONOMER ROYAL. He developed and used novel methods for establishing the positions of stars and planets with hitherto unavailable accuracy, both for navigational purposes and as data for NEWTON's work.

**Flanders,** former country in the LOW COUNTRIES extending along the North Sea and W of the Scheldt R. It became a French fief in the 9th cent. Virtually independent, it was the hub of medieval Europe's cloth industry but was weakened by civil strife and by rebellion against France. By the

15th cent., although Flemish art and commerce flourished under the Burgundians, it was little more than a French province. It passed in turn to the Spanish Habsburgs and Austria before being partitioned among France (1797), the Netherlands (1815), and Belgium (1830); parts of W Flanders had earlier been annexed (1668–78) to France. Its strategic location has made Flanders a key battleground; occupation by the Germans in WORLD WAR II led to the dramatic British evacuation at DUNKIRK (1940).

**flatfish,** member of the order Pleuronectiformes, bottom-living FISH of the Atlantic and Pacific. Adult flatfish have an unusual, flattened body with both eyes on one side of the head. They lie with the blind, generally whitish, side on the ocean bottom; the eyed, coloured side faces up. Soles are generally small, warm-water flatfishes with small eyes and mouths and few or no teeth. Flounders, generally larger, are known for changing colour to match the background. The European sole (*Solea solea*) and many flounders (*Platichthys* sp.), the plaice (*Pleuronectes platessa*), turbot and brill (*Scophthalmus* sp.), and the large, voracious, cool-water halibuts (genus *Hippoglossus*), are important food fish.

**Flathead Indians** or **Salish Indians:** see NORTH AMERICAN INDIANS.

**flatworm,** soft-bodied, bilaterally symmetrical invertebrate of the phylum Platyhelminthes. Among the most primitive organisms, flatworms are divided into the free-living, primarily aquatic class of turbellarians (including PLANARIANS) and the exclusively parasitic classes of FLUKES and TAPEWORMS.

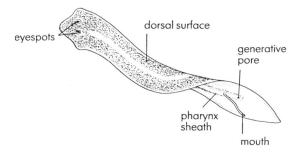

External anatomy of a planarian, a representative **flatworm**

**Flaubert, Gustave** (floh͵beɔ), 1821–80, French novelist, a master of the realistic novel. A scrupulous writer, intent on finding the exact word (*le mot juste*) and achieving complete objectivity, he published his masterpiece, *Madame Bovary,* in 1857, after five years of work. Portraying the frustrations of a romantic young woman married to a dull provincial doctor, it resulted in his prosecution on moral grounds. His other works include the novels *Salammbô* (1862), *L'education sentimentale* (1869), and the satirical *Bouvard et Pécuchet* (1881) and *Trois contes* (1877; tr. Three Tales), one of which is the great novella 'A Simple Heart'.

**flax,** common name for an annual herb of the Linaceae family, especially members of the genus *Linum,* and for the fibre obtained from such plants. Native to Eurasia, flax was the major source of cloth fibre until the growth of the COTTON industry (c.1800). The flax of commerce is obtained from several varieties of *L. usitatissimum.* Exposure to water or dew and sun loosens the fibre from the woody tissue in a process known as retting. After washing, drying, beating, and combing, fibres are obtained for use in making fabric (see LINEN), threads, and cordage. Flax seeds are crushed to make LINSEED OIL, and the remaining linseed cake is used for fodder. Dried seed is also used in medicines, e.g., as a laxative.

**Flaxman, John,** 1755–1826, English sculptor and draftsman. After designing Wedgwood POTTERY, he produced figure drawings influenced by Greek vases to illustrate works by Homer and Dante. He is known for his memorial sculpture, e.g., to Sir Joshua REYNOLDS.

**flea,** small, wingless blood-sucking INSECT of the order Siphonaptera, having a tough laterally-compressed body, piercing and sucking mouthparts, and strong hind legs for jumping. Adult fleas feed only on blood and are external PARASITES of mammals and birds. Their legless, maggot-like larvae feed on organic debris and the droppings of adult fleas in the dens or nests of their hosts, and fleas are therefore rarely found on nomadic mammals. Many fleas infest only one species of host, others

several; e.g., the human flea *Pulex irritans* also occurs on domestic pigs, but its original hosts were apparently fox and badger. At least six diseases are transmitted from other animals to man by fleas, including murine TYPHUS and bubonic PLAGUE, both carried by rat fleas (*Xenopsylla*). Of considerable medical importance, in Africa and tropical America, is the jigger (*Tunga penetrans*), of which the female is a subcutaneous parasite of man and other mammals, especially pigs.

**flèche:** see SPIRE.

**Fleet Street,** thoroughfare between Ludgate Circus and the Strand, London, a collective term for the British Press. Traditionally Fleet Street was the centre of the British press and newspaper industry as so many leading publications had their headquarters there. It was named from the old Fleet River which ran from Hampstead southwards along the line of the Farringdon Road, passing under the Fleet Bridge (now Ludgate Circus) and flowing into the Thames at Blackfriars. Ironic reference is often made to the fact that the River Fleet is now a covered sewer. The street itself was the home of the *Daily Telegraph, Daily Express,* and other papers; many others had their offices close by. Journalists were able to exchange news and gossip in the many pubs in the district. The trend throughout the 1980s has been for newspapers to move out as new technology has been introduced (see MURDOCH, Rupert).

**Fleetwood,** town (1981 pop. 27,899), in Lancashire, NW England, on Irish Sea coast, at mouth of R. Wyre, 13 km (8 mi) N of Blackpool. It is a fishing port, which handled 2.0 million tonnes in 1984. The town contains a range of industries including the manufacture of chemicals and plastics. There are passenger ferries from here to BELFAST, Northern Ireland, and the Isle of MAN

**Fleming, Sir Alexander,** 1881–1955, Scottish bacteriologist. He discovered PENICILLIN (1928) and lysozyme (1922), a natural ANTIBIOTIC found in many body secretions. Professor of bacteriology at the Univ. of London, he shared the 1945 Nobel Prize for physiology or medicine with Ernst CHAIN and Sir Howard FLOREY for work on penicillin. Fleming was knighted in 1944.

**Flemish language,** member of the West Germanic group of the Germanic subfamily of the INDO-EUROPEAN family of languages. It is one of the official languages of Belgium. See LANGUAGE (table).

**Fletcher, John,** 1579–1625, English dramatist, thought to have worked with SHAKESPEARE on *Two Noble Kinsmen* and *Henry VIII.* His most important collaboration was with Francis BEAUMONT. Their chief works *Philaster, The Maid's Tragedy, A King and No King,* and *The Scornful Lady* (1610–13) developed the romantic tragicomedy, to be popular through the 18th cent.

**Fleury, André Hercule de** (flø͵ree), 1653–1743, French Roman Catholic cardinal, chief minister of LOUIS XV. As virtual ruler of France (1726–43), he restored financial order. He strove for peace abroad, but was drawn into the wars of the POLISH SUCCESSION and the AUSTRIAN SUCCESSION.

**flight,** sustained motion through the air, as accomplished by an animal, aircraft, or rocket. Adaption for flight is highly developed in birds and insects. Birds fly by means of semicircular flapping strokes, the wings moving backward on the upstroke and forward on the downstroke. That motion pushes air downward and to the rear, creating a lift and forward thrust. Besides flapping, some birds also use gliding and soaring techniques in flight. In gliding, a bird holds its outstretched wings relatively still and relies on its momentum to keep it aloft for short distances. In soaring, a bird uses rising warm air currents to give it lift. AIRSHIPS and BALLOONS owe their ability to ascend and remain aloft to their inflation with a gas lighter than air. Aircraft, which are heavier than air, are able to remain aloft because of forces developed by the movement of the craft through the air. The development of JET PROPULSION makes high speeds possible, and the ROCKET engine allows flight outside the earth's atmosphere and in interplanetary space. See also AERODYNAMICS; AEROPLANE; FLIGHT, POWERED; GLIDER; HANG-GLIDER; HELICOPTER; SPACE EXPLORATION.

**flight, powered,** propulsion of any AIRCRAFT through the air by mechanical means. The first recorded example of an aero-engine is Leonardo de Vinci's design for a 'bow-string' motor for an ingenious ornithopter; a similar mechanism was used successfully 300 years later, in 1784, to power a model helicopter designed by Launoy and Bienvenu in France. The first aero-engine to power a manned flight was a

3-horse-power steam engine used by Henri Giffard to fly a small AIRSHIP a distance of 27 km (17 mi) near Paris in 1852. Some 30 years later, a Siemens electric motor, fed by 24 batteries and delivering less than 2 horse-power, powered another airship. The petrol INTERNAL-COMBUSTION ENGINE was, however, responsible for the successful development of powered flight. The first such was a single-cylinder 2-horse-power Daimler engine which powered an airship. The first man to leave the ground in a powered heavier-than-air aircraft was the Frenchman Clément Ader (1841–1925) who flew about 50 m (165 ft) in 1890, but the first controlled powered flight was that of the brothers WRIGHT on 17 Dec. 1903. Thereafter for 40 years internal-combustion reciprocating piston engines, both air- and liquid-cooled, were the standard power-plant for every type of aircraft. Piston engines reached their peak of performance with a Pratt and Whitney 28-cylinder engine delivering 3500 brake-horse-power. The jet engine (see JET PROPULSION) was first proposed by A.A. Griffith in 1926 and developed by Frank WHITTLE who ran the prototype in 1937. Hans von Ohain in Germany developed a jet engine independently, and his engine powered the world's first jet flight, at Rostov on 27 Aug. 1939. A ROCKET-powered aeroplane was the first manned aircraft to exceed Mach 1, on 14 Oct. 1941. The fastest aircraft is the North American X-15A2, which achieved Mach 6.72 (8420 kph, 4534 mph) on 30 Oct. 1987; it also achieved the height record of 107,960 m (354,200 ft), on 2 Aug. 1983. The longest distance flown was the 42,960 km (26,678 mi) round the world nonstop achieved by the Voyager, 14–23 Dec. 1986.

**Flinders Petrie, Sir William Matthew:** see PETRIE.

**Flinders Ranges,** mountain chain, South Australia state, Australia. The ranges were discovered by Matthew FLINDERS in 1802 and named by Edward John Eyre in 1839. Aboriginal rangers from a local community are employed in the two national parks, which are renowned for the rugged scenery, Aboriginal art and spring wildflowers. They extend 418 km (260 mi) between Lake Torrens and Lake Frome and reach a high point of 1189 m (3900 ft) at St Mary's Peak. Copper was mined at Oraparinna and processed at Quorn.

**flint:** see CHERT.

**flip-flop,** electronics circuit used for the storage of one binary digit, or bit, i.e., either a 0 or a 1. It can only assume either one of two states to represent the two values of the bit and can easily be triggered to change state.

**Flodden,** battle in Northumberland on 9 Sept. 1513. JAMES IV of Scotland was defeated and killed by the forces of HENRY VIII under Thomas, Earl of Surrey, while invading England in alliance with Louis XII of France.

**Flood,** in the Bible: see NOAH.

**floppy disc,** thin plastic disc coated with a magnetic surface on to which data is recorded or from which data is read off through a read/write magnetic head. Data is held as magnetized or demagnetized areas of circular tracks into which the disc is formatted, each magnetizable section of track being capable of representing one BIT of information. Data read into the disc is permanently retained unless deliberately erased or overwritten. The discs vary in diameter between 7.6 cm (3 in) and 20 cm (8 in) and can hold from 170,000 to 500,000 bits of data. They are the most common form of data storage for a PERSONAL COMPUTER.

**Florence,** Ital. *Firenze,* city (1984 pop. 435,698), capital of TUSCANY, central Italy, on the Arno R. It is a commercial, industrial, and tourist centre known for fine handicrafts. Of Roman origin, it became prominent after gaining autonomy in the 12th cent. It was a centre of GUELPH AND GHIBELLINE strife (13th cent.), but nonetheless grew in size and power through war with other cities. Meanwhile, trade in silks, tapestries, and jewellery brought great wealth. The MEDICI family dominated Florence from the 15th to 18th cent., their rule interrupted by two revolutions (1494–1512, led by SAVONAROLA; and 1527–30). The artistic and intellectual life of the city flowered from the 14th to 16th cent., with DANTE, BOCCACCIO, DONATELLO, LEONARDO DA VINCI, RAPHAEL, and MICHELANGELO among the many born or active there. Florence passed (1737) to the house of Habsburg-Lorraine, was annexed (1860) to Sardinia, and was the capital of Italy (1865–71). Among its many glorious works of architecture are the cathedral of Santa Maria del Fiore; the nearby baptistry; the churches of Santa Croce, Santa Maria Novella, and San Lorenzo; and the Pitti Palace, Palazzo Vecchio, and UFFIZI, all of which house masterpieces of RENAISSANCE art.

The Ponte Vecchio, **Florence**

**Florey, Howard Walter** (Baron Florey of Adelaide and Marston), 1898–1968, British pathologist; b. Australia. For their work in isolating PENICILLIN and demonstrating its effectiveness against harmful bacteria, he and Ernst CHAIN shared with Alexander FLEMING the 1945 Nobel Prize for physiology or medicine. He was professor of pathology at Oxford Univ. from 1935 to 1962 and was made a life peer in 1944.

**Florida,** state of the US (1984 est. pop. 10,976,000), area 151,670 km² (58,560 sq mi), forming a long peninsula between the Atlantic Ocean (E) and the Gulf of Mexico (W), bordered by Georgia and Alabama (N), and closest part of the US to Cuba. The capital is TALLAHASSEE but the dominant city is MIAMI, a leading international trade and financial centre; other large cities are Jacksonville, Tampa, Saint Petersburg, and Fort Lauderdale. Florida is low-lying, the central part contains many lakes, and the EVERGLADES swamp and wilderness area extends over most of the south. The FLORIDA KEYS extend off-shore to the SW. The tropical climate of the southern tip, together with its beaches and islands, and the Walt Disney World and Epcot Centre ensure the profitability of tourism. Florida is a leading agricultural state, producing citrus fruits, winter vegetables, and cattle. Principal industries are agricultural processing and electrical equipment and chemicals manufacturing. In addition, phosphate, petroleum, natural gas, and the shellfish catch provide revenue. In 1980 9% of the population was of Spanish origin, including many Cubans and Central Americans concentrated around Miami, and a further 14% was black. Almost 85% of the population is urban. The Spanish landed in Florida in 1513 and it remained under Spanish control until 1819, when it was ceded to the US. The Seminole Indians were defeated (1835–42) and removed to Oklahoma. The economy grew with real estate speculation in the 19th and 20th cents., and in recent years Florida has had one of the highest rates of population increase (due to retirement migration), and will become the fourth most populous state. Cuban refugees first arrived after the Cuban revolution in 1959 and more recently in 1980, along with many Haitians. In 1947 CAPE CANAVERAL was established as a rocket-launching site. Led by Miami's international financial economy, the state is one of the fastest growing in the SUN BELT.

**Florida Keys,** chain of small islands and reefs extending into Florida Bay c.240 km (150 mi) southwest from the southern shore of Florida, US. A motor causeway traverses the keys, linking the mainland and the city of Key West on the outermost island (Key West), which is c.150 km (90 mi) N of Cuba, separated by the Straits of Florida. The largest of the Florida Keys is Key Largo. Commercial fishing and tourism are the principal industries.

**Florio, John,** 1553?–1625, English writer. He wrote on Italian grammar and compiled an Italian–English dictionary (1598), and is best known for his translation (1603) of MONTAIGNE's *Essays.*

**flotation process,** process for concentrating the metal-bearing mineral in an ORE. Crude ore is ground to a fine powder and mixed with water and reagents. When air is blown through the mixture, mineral particles cling to the bubbles, which rise to form a froth on the surface. The froth is skimmed off and the water and chemicals removed, leaving a clean concentrate. Among the minerals effectively concentrated by this method are sulphide and phosphate ores.

**Flotow, Friedrich von,** 1812–83, German operatic composer. Influenced by French opéra comique, he is best known for *Alessandro Stradella* (1844) and *Martha* (1847).

**flounder:** see FLATFISH.

**flower,** specialized part of seed plants that contains reproductive organs. The basic floral parts (sepal, petal, stamen, and carpel) are modified leaves, typically arranged concentrically and attached at their bases to the tip of the stem. The outermost, green sepals (the calyx) encircle a whorl of usually showy, coloured petals (the corolla), within which POLLEN-bearing stamens surround a central ovary-bearing pistil. After fertilization, each ovule (the part that contains the egg) in the ovary becomes a SEED, and the ovary becomes the FRUIT. The number and arrangement of floral parts (inflorescence) varies greatly among groups of plants and are important bases for classification. In general, the higher a plant is on the evolutionary scale, the greater the flower's complexity and efficiency for reproduction.

**fluid mechanics,** branch of MECHANICS dealing with the properties and behaviour of fluids, or substances that flow, i.e., liquids and gases. The larger part of the field is fluid dynamics (study of fluids in motion), which itself is divided into hydrodynamics (study of liquids in motion) and AERODYNAMICS (study of gases in motion).

**fluke,** FLATWORM of the class Trematoda. Flukes, which are related to the TAPEWORM, are internal and external parasites that cause many diseases. Adults cling to their hosts with sucking discs and bear an external cuticle resistant to digestion by the host. Larval stages pass through intermediate hosts or VECTORS. In Britain the liver fluke (*Fasciola hepatica*) causes liver rot which kills large numbers of sheep. A blood fluke is responsible for the human disease BILHARZIA. Some species of FLATFISH are also called flukes.

**fluorescence,** LUMINESCENCE in which light of a visible colour is emitted from certain substances, called phosphors, when irradiated by electromagnetic radiation, especially ultraviolet light. Unlike PHOSPHORESCENCE, the light is emitted only while the stimulation continues.

**fluoridation,** process of adding a fluoride to a community water supply to preserve the TEETH of the inhabitants. Tooth enamel ordinarily contains small amounts of fluoride, which, when augmented with fluoridated water, can greatly reduce tooth decay (CARIES) in children. While studies have proved fluoridation safe at levels of one part per million, opponents assert that such action constitutes compulsory medication and that those wanting fluoride can take it individually. Fluoridated toothpaste has greatly reduced the incidence of dental caries in Europe and the US.

**fluorine** (F), gaseous element, first prepared in 1886 by Henri Moissan. Fluorine is a yellowish, poisonous, highly corrosive HALOGEN gas. It is the most chemically active nonmetallic element and the most electronegative of all the elements (see ELECTRONEGATIVITY). FLUORITE is its chief commercial source. Soluble fluorides, in a concentration of one part per million are added to public water supplies to reduce tooth decay. Fluorine compounds are used in ceramic and glass manufacturing, in refrigeration and air-conditioning systems, and as AEROSOL propellants. The destructive effect of some fluorine compounds—the chlorofluorocarbons—on the OZONE layer of the upper atmosphere is causing growing concern amongst environmentalists who want to see their manufacture and use curtailed.

TEFLON is an inert, heat-resistant fluorocarbon. See ELEMENT (table); PERIODIC TABLE.

**fluorite** or **fluorspar,** calcium fluoride mineral ($CaF_2$), occurring in various colours in crystal, granular, and massive forms. Its crystals sometimes exhibit fluorescence, and are often intensely coloured, such as the dark violet variety from Bavaria. The colouring agents are finely divided calcium and free fluorine generated within the solid by the radiation from associated uranium-containing minerals. When this fluorite is struck a pungent gas is released. Found mainly in England, Germany, Mexico, Kentucky, and Illinois, fluorite is used as a flux in metallurgy, in preparing hydrofluoric acid, and in making opal glass and enamel. Some colourless crystals are used to make lenses and prisms.

**flute,** a WOODWIND instrument which has existed in various forms since prehistoric times. The modern flute evolved in the 16th cent. It has a cylindrical bore and is played by blowing across an elliptical hole. Today flutes are usually made of metal rather than the traditional wood. The flute has a range of about three octaves upwards from middle C. A member of the orchestra from the 18th cent., the flute is often used as a solo instrument and has a considerable chamber repertoire. The other members of the flute family include the piccolo, pitched 9 notes higher, and the bass flute, an octave lower.

**fly,** name used for a variety of winged INSECTS, but properly restricted to members of the order Diptera. True flies have only one pair of wings, the hind pair being drumstick-like flight stabilizers (halteres). Not all adults feed, but some species are predatory, e.g., robber flies (Asaliae) and some feed on blood, e.g., HORSE FLY. The larvae (maggots) have a very wide range of lifestyles and habitat preferences; some of the plant-eating species are crop pests, e.g., 'leatherjackets' (the larvae of crane flies, Tipulidae), the larvae of gall MIDGES, and those of fungus GNATS. In other species the maggots infest the bodies of domestic animals, e.g., warble fly (*Hypoderma*) larvae under the skin of cattle, nostril fly (*Oestrus*) larvae in the nasal passage of sheep, and bot fly (*Gasterophilus*) larvae in horses' stomachs. Those of the tumbu fly (*Cordylobia*) live under the skin of man, as well as that of most domestic animals.

**flying buttress:** see BUTTRESS.

**flying doctor services,** medical services in remote areas of Australia, Canada, and East Africa provided by means of light aircraft and often piloted by the doctors themselves. The first such service was pioneered in Queensland, Australia in 1928.

**flying fish,** torpedo-shaped FISH (family Exocoetidae) of warm seas with well-developed pectoral fins that can be held rigid and used to glide short distances over the water. Specially adapted tail fins, vibrated in taxiing along the water surface to gain momentum, and (in some species) enlarged pelvic fins also help in 'flight'. The largest species is the 45-cm (18-in) California flying fish. The commonest species, the 25-cm (10-in) *Exocoetus volitans*, is found in all tropical seas.

**flying fox:** see BAT.

**flying lizard:** see AGAMA.

**flying saucer:** see UNIDENTIFIED FLYING OBJECT.

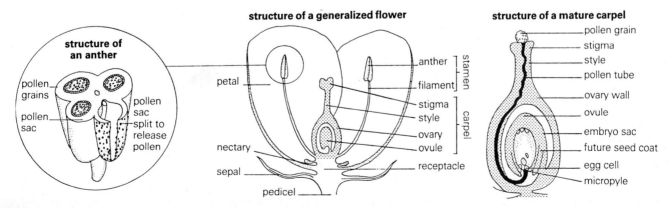

structure of
an anther

pollen grains
pollen sac
pollen sac
split to release pollen

**structure of a generalized flower**

petal
nectary
sepal
pedicel

anther
filament
stigma
style
ovary
ovule
receptacle

stamen
carpel

**structure of a mature carpel**

pollen grain
stigma
style
pollen tube
ovary wall
ovule
embryo sac
future seed coat
egg cell
micropyle

Flower

Flying fish (*Exocetus volitans*)

**flying squirrel**, nocturnal SQUIRREL adapted for gliding; flying squirrels do not actually fly. Most are found in Asia, but there are two North American species (genus *Glaucomys*) and one Eurasian species. The giant flying squirrel of Asia is 120 cm (4 ft) long, but they are usually about 60 cm (2 ft) long. The gliding mechanism is a fold of skin extending along each side of the body. When the animal extends its limbs in leaping, the flaps stretch out taut like a parachute.

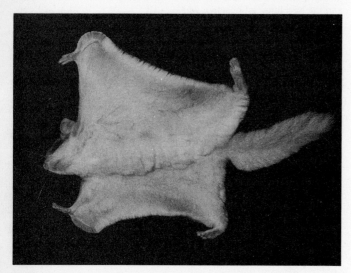

**Flying squirrel**, showing skin extension which enables it to glide

**Fm**, chemical symbol of the element FERMIUM.

**FM:** see MODULATION.

**Fo, Dario**, 1926–, Italian actor, dramist, and theatre activist. Through such pieces as *Comic Mystery* (1969) and *Accidental Death of an Anarchist* (1970) he has become known to a vast public in Italy and abroad for a theatre of social and political satire, rooted in Italian popular comedy and in collectivist ideals, which he has promoted since the 1960s in collaboration with his actress wife Franca Rame.

**foam:** see COLLOID.

**Foch, Ferdinand**, 1851–1929, marshal of France. In WORLD WAR I he halted the German advance at the Marne (1914) and fought at Ypres (1915) and the Somme (1916). In 1917 he became chief of the French general staff, and in Apr. 1918 he assumed the unified command of the British, French, and US armies.

**fog**, aggregation of water droplets just above the earth's surface, i.e., a cloud near the ground. A light or thin fog is usually called a mist. Fog may occur either when the moisture content of the air is increased beyond the saturation point or when the air is cooled below the DEW point. In either case, excess moisture condenses on microscopic dust particles (condensation nuclei) in the atmosphere.

**Foggia**, city (1984 pop. 157,818), Apulia, S Italy. A focus of communications, it serves as the administrative and service centre of a traditionally poor farming region where wheat and pastoralism are the principal concerns. Diesel engines are manufactured. The 12th-cent. Romanesque cathedral has been much restored.

**Fokine, Mikhail**, 1880–1942, American dancer and choreographer; b. Russia. After an early career as a dancer and teacher, he became important as a choreographer. His initial works include *The Dying Swan* (1907) for PAVLOVA. For DIAGHILEV he created *Les Sylphides* (1909), *Firebird* (1910), and *Petrouchka* (1911), among other works. He is considered the founder of modern BALLET; eliminating rigid traditions, he paved the way for expressionism.

**Fokker, Anthony Hermann Gerard** (ˌfokə), 1890–1939, Dutch aircraft manufactuer; b. Java. Not a trained engineer, Fokker experimented with monoplane design, and had achieved enough success by 1914 to gain orders from the German Army and Navy to supply planes (mono-, bi- and triplanes) for World War I. Fokker patented a device for synchronizing the airscrew with a machine gun to enable bullets to be fired through the airscrew disc when neither blade was in the line of fire; this had been devised by engineers on Fokker's staff. Fokker moved to the US in 1925, and made a second fortune with civil aircraft, mostly the work of his best designer Reinhold Platz.

**fold**, in geology, bent or deformed arrangement of stratified rocks. Arches, or upfolds, are known as anticlines; depressions, or downfolds, are called synclines. An imaginary line drawn along the crest of an anticline or the trough of a syncline is its axis; the two sides curving away from the axis are the limbs. The complex causes of folding involve large-scale crustal movements (see PLATE TECTONICS).

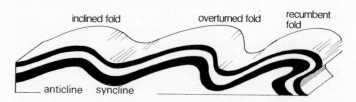

Fold

**folic acid:** see table under VITAMINS AND MINERALS.

**folk art**, art works of a culturally homogeneous people made by artists without formal training. Generally nationalistic in character, folk art often involves craft processes, e.g., in America, QUILTING and sculpture of FIGUREHEADS and cigar-store figures; in Britain, wrought-iron work and the production of horse brasses. Paintings in the tradition of PRIMITIVISM are also in the folk idiom. Much folk art has a rough-hewn, awkward quality often admired and imitated by sophisticated artists.

**folk dance**, primitive, tribal, or ethnic form of the dance, sometimes the survival of an ancient ceremony or festival. The term includes characteristic national dances, country dances, and figure dances in costume. Examples include children's games such as 'The Farmer in the Dell' as well as the Spanish fandango, the Bohemian polka, the Irish jig, and the American Virginia reel. The English musician Cecil James Sharp made a notable collection of English folk songs and dances, and the American Folk Dance Society has preserved American country dances.

**folklore**, body of customs, legends, beliefs, and superstitions passed on by oral tradition, including folk tales, dances, songs, and medicine. The study of folklore became significant in the 19th cent. as a result of the rise of European ROMANTICISM and nationalism. Today most anthropologists see the many manifestations of folklore as imaginative expressions by a people of its desires, attitudes, and cultural values and regard folk heroes (e.g., Paul BUNYAN in the US and ROBIN HOOD in England) as reflections of the civilizations from which they sprang.

**folk song**, music of anonymous composition, transmitted orally. The germ of a folk song is assumed to be produced by an individual, altered in transmission as a group expression but invariably re-composed by individuals. National and ethnic individuality is seen and claimed in folk music, but little is wholly indigenous. That of the US, for example, reveals transplanted European and African sources. Interest in folk music grew in the 19th cent., although earlier scholars had worked in the field. Béla BARTÓK made great contributions in notating the folk music of central Europe and Cecil SHARP collected songs in Britain. The gramophone and tape recorder facilitated transcription and collection of folk song. The music often shows the influence of formal composition, and songs of traceable authorship, e.g., 'Dixie', are often considered folk songs. Since the 1950s folk music has been a significant influence and source for much popular vocal and instrumental music. Types of folk song include the work songs found in all cultures, e.g., sea CHANTYS and SPIRITUALS.

**folk–urban continuum,** a concept designed to account for the difference between urban and rural communities. The ideal-type folk end is characterized by its small scale, the predominance of KINSHIP relations, social homogeneity, heavily ritualized social relations, an oral rather than a literate tradition, and its own cultural forms. Urban society on the other hand is characterized by social heterogeneity, literacy, national culture, etc. Any given society could be located along the two extremes, according to the extent to which it contained characteristics of either end.

**folly,** in architecture, fanciful structure built usually for no purpose other than to satisfy a whim or for theatrical effect. Popular in the 18th and 19th cent., they were a hobby for rich landowners anxious to vary their parks with moments of surprise and wit. Most are eccentric structures, such as imitation grottoes and ruins (real or imitation), gazebos and unexpected seats inscribed with poetry, towers and temples. The most elegant and elaborate are to be found at Stow, Stourhead, and Studley Royal, where the ruins of Fountains Abbey were incorporated in an 18th-cent. pleasure garden.

**Fonda, Henry,** 1905–82, American actor. Among his films are *Young Mr Lincoln* (1939), *The Grapes of Wrath* (1940), *Mr Roberts* (1955), and *On Golden Pond* (1981; Academy Award). His daughter, **Jane Fonda,** 1937–, has starred in such films as *Klute* (1971; Academy Award), *Julia* (1977), *The China Syndrome* (1979), and *On Golden Pond* (1981).

**Fongafale,** town (1973 est. pop. 871), capital of TUVALU.

**Fontaine, Pierre François Léonard** (fawnh,tayn), 1762–1853, French architect. Working from 1794 with Charles PERCIER, he was a developer of the Empire style in France.

**Fontainebleau, school of,** group of 16th-cent. artists who decorated the royal palace at Fontainebleau in France. Chief in importance were Il ROSSO, Francesco PRIMATICCIO, and Niccolo dell' Abate. An Italian development of MANNERISM, the style of the Fountainebleau school was refined to the point of artificiality. Its subjects were allegorical and symbolic in keeping with the tastes of FRANCIS I's court.

**Fontana, Domenico,** 1543–1607, Italian architect. In Rome he designed (1588) the LATERAN palace and the Vatican library. His other work included the fountain Acqua Felice (1587), the erection of an Egyptian obelisk before St Peter's (1586), and the royal palace, Naples (1600).

**Fontane, Theodor** (fon,tahnə), 1819–98, German novelist. The creator of the modern German social novel, Fontane trained as a pharmacist, but turned to literature with historical ballads, and later to journalism. Following a lengthy stay in England, he wrote travel books: *A Summer in London* (1854), *Across the Tweed* (1860, tr. 1965), a loving topography of Prussia, *Travels in the Brandenburg March* (4 vol., 1861–81), which made his reputation. As a war correspondent he was present at each of BISMARCK's wars, and each produced its book. He came to fiction late, with his historical novel *Before the Storm* (1878, tr. 1985), and became the profound, ironical chronicler of the social life of the new capital of Berlin. Discreet and tolerant, he has fine antennae for the connections, often distorting and destructive, between public values and private lives under the Second Empire. His main works are: *Schach von Wuthenow* (1882; tr. *A Man of Honour* 1975); *Irrungen Wirrungen* (1888; tr. *A Suitable Match* 1968); *Beyond Recall* (1891; tr. 1964); *Frau Jenny Treibel* (1892; tr. 1976); his masterpiece *Effi Briest* (1895; tr. 1967); *The Poggenpuhl Family* (1896; tr. 1979); and *Der Stechlin* (1899).

**Fonteyn, Dame Margot** 1919–, English ballet dancer. She was prima ballerina at Sadlers Wells then Royal Ballet (1935–59), after which she became an international guest artist. She had a noted partnership with NUREYEV. In style and musicality she represented the best of the English school of ballet. She has been president of the Royal Academy of Dancing since 1954.

**Foochow:** see FUZHOU.

**food additives,** substances added to food to give desirable properties or to suppress undesirable ones. They fall into several categories: colours; preservatives; anti-oxidants (which prevent fats becoming rancid and cut apples browning), emulsifiers and stabilizers (which prevent mixtures separating), sweeteners, solvents, mineral hydrocarbons (used to make foods shiny and to stop them drying out), modified starches (thickening agents), flavour enhancers (such as monosodium glutamate), propellant gases for food aerosols, bulking agents, anti-foaming substances, and glazing and releasing agents. There are regulations within the European Community governing the use of additives, those considered safe for use in food being given an 'E' number. The two most common additives to food are SALT and SUGAR.

**Food and Agricultural Organization:** see UNITED NATIONS (table 3).

**food chain:** see ECOLOGY.

**food labelling,** a means of identifying the contents of pre-packaged food, a legal requirement in most Western countries. It has become important now that a significant amount of food preparation takes place in factories and not in the home. Under EEC regulations ingredients must be listed in descending order of weight (water need only be listed if the food contains more than 5%), a date mark is usually required, and the average weight must be given. FOOD ADDITIVES must also be listed.

**food poisoning,** acute illness caused by the contamination of food by bacteria, including SALMONELLOSIS, *Staphylococcus aureus, Clostridium perfringens* and *C. botulinum,* and *Bacillus cereus.* Once the food has become infected by unhygienic practises all that is needed is time and a little warmth to allow the bacteria to multiply. In some cases the poisoning is due to infection of the person with the bacteria, in some it is due to a toxin produced by the bacteria; such toxins are heat-tolerant and thus are not destroyed by recooking food that is already infected. Food produced in large kitchens (e.g., in ships or hospitals) is particularly at risk, but the true size of the problem is much greater than the thousands of cases reported each year, as many milder outbreaks go unreported. Botulism is the most severe, but any form of food poisoning may be fatal.

**food preservation.** Because most foods remain edible for only a limited time, food preservation has been practised since the remotest times. Early products of conservation were cheese, butter, wine, bacon, pemmican, raisins, and parched grains. Advances in the methods used came with scientific investigations of the microorganisms that cause food spoilage, especially in the work of Louis PASTEUR. Basic methods of modern food preservation include dehydration, freeze-drying, heating (e.g., CANNING and PASTEURIZATION), refrigeration (both chilled and FROZEN FOODS), hermetic sealing to remove air, and atomic radiation to destroy microorganisms. Such preserving agents as salt, vinegar, SUGAR, smoke, and alcohol are also used, often in combination. Other common preservatives are chemical agents.

**fool's gold:** see PYRITE.

**Foot, Michael,** 1913–, British politician. He entered parliament in 1945 and became a spokesman for the Labour Party's radical left wing. Editor of the leftist organ, the *Tribune,* he served as secretary of state for employment (1974–75) and leader of the House of Commons (1976–79). He succeeded James CALLAGHAN as Labour Party leader in 1980 and attempted to maintain the party's traditional policies in the face of the opposition of right-wing members, who broke away and formed the SOCIAL DEMOCRATIC PARTY. After Labour's defeat in the 1983 general elections, he was succeeded as Labour leader by Neil KINNOCK.

**foot-and-mouth disease,** acute, highly-contagious viral disease of cattle and other cloven-hoofed animals. Symptoms include fever, loss of appetite and weight, and blistering of the mucous membranes of the mouth and digestive tract. The disease is spread by direct contact, and also by contaminated food, water, and soil. The virus is also dispersed in water droplets downwind from farms where infections occur. Humans seldom contract the disease, but may be carriers, as may also rats, dogs, and birds and other wild animals. The disease is notifiable, and although there are vaccines available, epidemics still cause enormous losses. Most countries control the importation of live animals and meat, and operate policies of slaughter on farms where the disease is diagnosed.

**football,** any of several games in which two opposing teams attempt to score points by moving an inflated ball past a goal line or into a goal area. The games, differing greatly in their rules, include SOCCER (association football) and RUGBY, both English games from which **American football** developed. The American game is played by two teams of 11 men each on a field that measures 91.4 by 48.8 m (100 by 53⅓ yd). At each end of the field is an end zone 9.14 m (10 yd) deep, in which stand H-shaped goal posts. Play is directed towards gaining possession of the football and

## E-NUMBERS: STANDARD DESIGNATIONS OF FOOD ADDITIVES AUTHORIZED FOR USE BY THE EUROPEAN COMMISSION

### Colours

| number | name | example of use |
|---|---|---|
| E100 | circumin | confectionery |
| E101 | riboflavin | sauces |
| E102 | tartrazine | soft drinks |
| E104 | quinoline yellow | |
| E110 | sunset yellow FCF | biscuits |
| E120 | cochineal | alcoholic drinks |
| E122 | carmoisine | jams and preserves |
| E123 | amaranth | |
| E124 | ponceau 4R | dessert mixes |
| E127 | erythrosine | glacé cherries |
| E131 | patent blue V | |
| E132 | indigo carmine | |
| E140 | chlorophyll | |
| E141 | copper complexes of chlorophyll and chlorophyllins | |
| E142 | green S | pastilles |
| E150 | caramel | beer, soft drinks, sauces |
| E151 | black PN | |
| E153 | carbon black (vegetable carbon) | liquorice |
| E160(a) | alpha-carotene; beta-carotene; gamma-carotene | margarine; soft drinks |
| E160(b) | annatto; bixin; norbixin | crisps |
| E160(c) | capsanthin; capsorubin | |
| E160(d) | lycopene | |
| E160(e) | beta-apo-8' carotenal | |
| E160(f) | ethyl ester of beta-apo-8'-carotenic acid | |
| E161(a) | flavoxanthin | |
| E161(b) | lutein | |
| E161(c) | cryptoxanthin | |
| E161(d) | rubixanthin | |
| E161(e) | violaxanthin | |
| E161(f) | rhodoxanthin | |
| E161(g) | canthaxanthin | |
| E162 | beetroot red (betanin) | ice-cream |
| E163 | anthocyanins | yoghurt |
| E171 | titanium dioxide | sweets |
| E172 | iron oxides; iron hydroxides | |
| E173 | aluminium | |
| E174 | silver | |
| E175 | gold | cake decorations |
| E180 | pigment rubine (lithol rubine BK) | |

### Preservatives

| number | name | example of use |
|---|---|---|
| E200 | sorbic acid | soft drinks; fruit yoghurt |
| E201 | sodium sorbate | |
| E202 | potassium sorbate | |
| E203 | calcium sorbate | frozen pizza; flour confectionery |
| E210 | benzoic acid | |
| E211 | sodium benzoate | beer, jam, salad cream, |
| E212 | potassium benzoate | soft drinks, fruit pulp, |
| E213 | calcium benzoate | fruit-based pie fillings, |
| E214 | ethyl para-hydroxy benzoate | marinated herring and |
| E215 | sodium ethyl para-hydroxy-benzoate | mackerel |
| E216 | propyl para-hydroxy-benzoate | |
| E217 | sodium propyl para-hydroxy-benzoate | |
| E218 | methyl para-hydroxy-benzoate | |
| E220 | sulphur dioxide | |
| E221 | sodium sulphate | dried fruit, dehydrated |
| E222 | sodium bisulphite | vegetables, fruit juices |
| E223 | sodium metabisulphate | and syrups, sausages, |
| E224 | potassium metabisulphite | fruit-based dairy desserts, |
| E226 | calcium sulphite | cider, beer and wine; also |

| number | name | example of use |
|---|---|---|
| E227 | calcium bisulphite | used to prevent browning of raw peeled potatoes and to condition biscuit doughs |
| E230 | diphenyl | |
| E231 | orthophenylphenol | surface treatment of citrus fruit |
| E232 | sodium orthophenyl-phenate | |
| E233 | thiabendazole | surface treatment of bananas |
| E239 | hexamine | marinated herring and mackerel |
| E249 | potassium nitrite | |
| E250 | sodium nitrite | bacon, ham, cured meats |
| E251 | sodium nitrate | corned beef and some |
| E252 | potassium nitrate | cheeses |
| E280 | propionic acid | |
| E281 | sodium propionate | bread and flour |
| E282 | calcium propionate | confectionery, Christmas |
| E283 | potassium propionate | pudding |

### Antioxidants

| number | name | example of use |
|---|---|---|
| E300 | L-ascorbic acid | fruit drinks |
| E301 | sodium L-ascorbate | |
| E302 | calcium L-ascorbate | |
| E304 | ascorbyl palmitate | scotch eggs |
| E306 | extracts of natural origin rich in tocopherols | vegetable oils |
| E307 | synthetic alphatocopherol | cereal-based baby foods |
| E308 | synthetic gammatocopherol | |
| E309 | synthetic deltatocopherol | |
| E310 | propyl gallate | vegetable oils; chewing gum |
| E311 | octyl gallate | |
| E312 | dodecyl gallate | |
| E320 | butylated hydroxynisole (BHA) | beef stock cubes; cheese spread |
| E321 | butylated hydroxytoluene (BHT) | chewing gum |
| E322 | lecithins | low fat spreads emulsifier in chocolate |

### Emulsifiers and stabilizers

| number | name | example of use |
|---|---|---|
| E400 | alginic acid | ice-cream; soft cheese |
| E401 | sodium alginate | cake mixes |
| E402 | potassium alginate | |
| E403 | ammonium alginate | |
| E404 | calcium alginate | |
| E405 | propane-1,-2-diol alginate (propylene glycol alginate) | salad dressings; cottage cheese |
| E406 | agar | ice-cream |
| E407 | carageenan | jelly mixes; milk shakes |
| E410 | locust bean gum (carob gum) | salad cream |
| E412 | guar gum | packet soups |
| E413 | tragacanth | salad dressings; processed cheese |
| E414 | gum arabic (acacia) | confectionery |
| E415 | xanthan gum | sweet pickle; coleslaw |
| E440(a) | pectin | |
| E440(b) | amidated pectin, pectin extract | jams and preserves |
| E460 | microcrystalline cellulose; alphacellulose | high-fibre bread; grated cheese |
| E461 | methylcellulose | low fat spreads |
| E463 | hydroxypropyl-cellulose | |
| E464 | hydroxypropyl-methylcellulose | edible ices |
| E465 | ethylmethylcellulose | gateaux |

## Emulsifiers and stabilizers *(Continued)*

| *number* | *name* | *example of use* |
|---|---|---|
| E466 | carboxymethylcellulose, sodium salt (CMC) | jelly; gateaux |
| E470 | sodium, potassium and calcium salts of fatty acids | cake mixes |
| E471 | mono- and di-glycerides of fatty acids | frozen desserts |
| E472(a) | acetic acid esters of mono- and di-glycerides of fatty acids | mousse mixes |
| E472(b) | lactic acid esters of mono- and di-glycerides of fatty acids | dessert topping |
| E472(c) | citric acid esters of mono- and di-glycerides of fatty acids | continental sausages |
| E472(e) | mono and diacetyltartaric acid esters of mono- and di-glycerides of fatty acids | bread; frozen pizza |
| E473 | sucrose esters of fatty acids | |
| E474 | sucroglycerides | edible ices |
| E475 | polyglycerol esters of fatty acids | cakes; gateaux |
| E477 | propane-1,2-diol esters of fatty acids | instant desserts |
| E481 | sodium stearoyl-2-lactylate | bread; cakes and biscuits |
| E482 | calcium stearoyl-2-lactylate | gravy granules |
| E483 | stearyl tartrate | |

## Sweeteners

| E421 | mannitol | sugar-free confectionery |
|---|---|---|
| E420 | sorbitol; sorbitol syrup | sugar-free confectionery, jams for diabetics |

## Others

| E170 | calcium carbonate | base, firming agent, release agent, diluent; nutrient in flour |
|---|---|---|
| E260 | acetic acid | acid/acidity regulators (buffers) used pickles, salad cream and bread; they contribute to flavour and provide protection against mould growth |
| E261 | potassium acetate | |
| E262 | sodium hydrogen diacetate | |
| E263 | calcium acetate | firming agent; |
| E270 | lactic acid | acid/flavouring protects against mould growth; salad dressing, soft margarine |
| E290 | carbon dioxide | carbonating agent/packing gas and propellant |
| E325 | sodium lactate | buffer, humectant; used in jams, preserves, sweets, flour confectionery |
| E326 | potassium lactate | buffer; jams, preserves and jellies |
| E327 | calcium lactate | buffer, firming agent; canned fruit pie filling |
| E330 | citric acid | acid/flavourings, sequestrants, emulsifying salts; used in soft drinks, jams, preserves, sweets, UHT cream, processed cheese, canned fruit, dessert mixes, ice-cream |
| E331 | monosodium citrate disodium citrate trisodium citrate | |
| E332 | monopotassium citrate tripotassium citrate | |
| E333 | monocalcium citrate dicalcium citrate tricalcium citrate | |
| E334 | L-(+)-tartaric acid | |

| *number* | *name* | *example of use* |
|---|---|---|
| E335 | monosodium L-(+)-tartrate; disodium L-(+)-tartrate; | acid/flavourings, buffers, emulsifying salts, sequestrants; used in soft drinks; biscuits creams and fillings, sweets, jams, dessert mixes and processed cheese |
| E336 | monopotassium L-(+)-tartrate (cream of tartar); dipotassium L-(+)-tartrate | |
| E337 | potassium sodium L-(+)-tartrate | |
| E338 | phosphoric acid | acid/flavourings; soft drinks, cocoa |
| E339 | sodium dihydrogen orthophosphate; disodium hydrogen orthophosphate; trisodium orthophosphate | buffers, sequestrants, emulsifying salts; used in dessert mixes, non-dairy creamers, processed cheese |
| E340 | potassium dihydrogen orthophosphate; dipotassium hydrogen orthophosphate; tripotassium orthophosphate | |
| E341 | calcium tetrahydrogen diorthophosphate; calcium hydrogen orthophosphate; tricalcium diorthophosphate | firming agent, raising agent; cake mixes, baking powder, dessert mixes |
| E450(a) | disodium dihydrogen diphosphate; trisodium diphosphate; tetrasodium diphosphate; tetrapotassium diphosphate | buffers, sequestrants, emulsifying salts, stabilizers, texturisers, raising agents, used in whipping cream, fish and meat products, bread, processed cheese, canned vegetables |
| E450(b) | pentasodium triphosphate; pentapotassium triphosphate | |
| E450(c) | sodium polyphosphates; potassium polyphosphates | |

moving it (by running or passing) across the opponent's goal line, thereby scoring a touchdown, worth six points. Points are also scored by kicking the ball over the crossbar between the goal posts (a field goal, worth three points); downing a man with the ball behind his own goal line (a safety, worth two points); and a conversion following a touchdown. In professional ball, the conversion is made by kicking the ball over the goal posts (one point); in college and high school ball, the conversion is by a kick (one point) or by a pass or run (two points). The offensive team, led by the quarterback, must gain 9.14 m (10 yd) in four tries (downs) or yield possession of the ball. The defending team tries to stop the ball carrier from advancing by tackling him. Blocking and tackling make American football one of the most rugged of sports, and players must wear heavy protective gear. The annual Super Bowl game for the league championship has been a major sports spectacle since its introduction in January 1967. **Canadian football** is similar to the US game except that the field and the end zone are larger, measuring 100 by 59 m (110 by 65 yd) and 23 m (25 yd) deep, respectively; a team consists of 12 players; and only three downs are allowed. In **Gaelic football,** played primarily in Ireland, the object is to punch, dribble (bounce), or kick the ball into (three points) or directly over (one point) the rectangular goalnet. A team is made up of 15 men. **Australian rules football** is played on a large oval field. Each team of 18 players attempts to kick the egg-shaped ball through a set of goal posts. The ball may be advanced by punches (hand-passes), kicks, or dribbles.

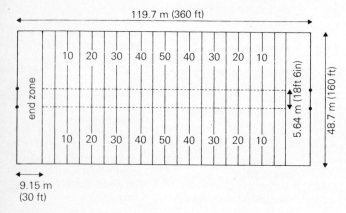

119.7 m (360 ft)

5.64 m (18ft 6in)

48.7 m (160 ft)

9.15 m (30 ft)

American **football** pitch dimensions

**foot-pound:** see TORQUE; WORK.

**footwear,** the most primitive kinds of footwear are the pieces of leather or textile wrapped around the foot, like the brogue of the ancient Celt or the moccasin of the Plains Indian (the modern shoes of the same names bear little resemblance to their early originals). In antiquity and in tropical countries footwear sometimes consists merely of a sole secured to the foot with thongs or straps; such sandals have proved very versatile as Western leisure wear. Whatever the style, most modern Western footwear is made with a vamp to cover the toe and instep and a quarter to cover the heel; they are shaped on a last and stitched together and stitched or glued on to the sole. Handmaking of shoes and boots has largely been taken over by factory methods. The British centres of the trade were Northampton and Norwich, but they are undercut by imported footwear from the Far East and southern Europe, where labour is cheaper. Today, most footwear is made from leather, its plastic imitations, or textiles, and has leather, synthetic or rubber soles. Because of its function, footwear is often highly specialized: dancing and gymnastics shoes are made of particularly flexible leather with nonslip soles, ballet shoes have blocks in the toes, industrial boots have reinforced toe-caps, riding boots are knee-high to protect the legs. In the context of FASHION, the utilitarian function is often compromised, so that high heels of small diameter (the 'stiletto heel' of the 1950s) and pointed toes have been in and out of style since the 17th cent. Nonfunctional design used to be characteristic of both men's and women's shoes, but is now mainly confined to the latter.

**Forain, Jean Louis,** 1852–1931, French painter, etcher, and lithographer. He is best known for his political cartoons and satires of the theatre and courtroom. His work enlivened many publications, including the New York *Herald.*

**Forbidden City:** see CHINESE ARCHITECTURE; BEIJING.

**force,** in physics, a quantity that produces a change in the size or shape (see STRENGTH OF MATERIALS) or the MOTION of a body. Commonly experienced as a 'push' or 'pull', force is a vector quantity, having both magnitude and direction. Four basic types of force are known in nature (see ELEMENTARY PARTICLES). The gravitational force (see GRAVITATION) and the electromagnetic force (see ELECTRICITY; MAGNETISM) both have long range. The strong nuclear force, or strong interaction, is a short-range force holding the atomic nucleus together, and the weak nuclear force, or weak interaction, is a short-range force associated with BETA DECAY and other forms of particle decay. In the METRIC SYSTEM forces are measured in such units as the newton (SI and mks systems) and, formerly, the dyne (cgs system), which cause accelerations of, respectively, $1 \text{ m/sec}^2$ on a 1-kg mass and $1 \text{ cm/sec}^2$ on a 1-gram mass; 1 dyne equals $10^{-5}$ newtons. In nonmetric systems the pound force or the poundal is used. A 1-lb force equals 4.44822 newtons; 1 poundal equals 0.138255 newtons.

**Ford, Ford Madox,** 1873–1939, English author; b. Ford Madox Hueffer. He wrote over 60 works, including novels, poems, criticism, travel essays, and reminiscences, and edited the *English Review* (1908–09) and *transatlantic review* (1924). His novel *The Good Soldier* (1915) is much admired for its irony and mastery of form. His tetralogy *Parade's End* (1924–28) draws on his experiences as an army officer on the French front in World War I.

**Ford, Gerald Rudolph,** 1913–, 38th president of the US (1974–77). A Republican congressman from Michigan (1949–73), he served (1965–73) as Republican minority leader in the House and was (1968, 1972) permanent chairman of the Republican National Convention. In Oct. 1973 Ford was nominated by Pres. NIXON to succeed Spiro T. AGNEW as vice president; on 6 Dec. 1973, he became vice president, the first to be appointed under the procedures of the 25th Amendment to the CONSTITUTION. When Nixon resigned (9 Aug. 1974) amidst the WATERGATE AFFAIR, Ford became president; one month later he issued a pardon to Nixon. As president, Ford continued Nixon's foreign policy and advocated anti-inflationary measures and limited social spending at home. A presidential candidate in 1976, he lost the election to Democrat Jimmy CARTER.

**Ford, Henry,** 1863–1947, American industrialist, pioneer motor vehicle manufacturer. While working as a machinist and engineer with the Edison Co., in his spare time he built (1892) his first motor car. In 1903 he organized the Ford Motor Co. By cutting production costs, controlling raw materials and distribution, adapting the assembly line to motor cars, and featuring an inexpensive, standardized car, Ford became the largest motor car manufacturer in the world. In 1908 he designed the Model T; over 15 million cars were sold before the model was discontinued (1928), and a new design, the Model A, was created to meet growing competition. In 1914 Ford created a sensation by paying his workers five dollars for an 8-hour day, considerably above the average, and by beginning a profit-sharing plan that would distribute up to $30 million annually among his employees. He stubbornly resisted union

Henry **Ford's** early Model T production line

organization until 1941. He retired in 1945. His numerous philanthropies included the FORD FOUNDATION. Henry's grandson, **Henry Ford II,** 1917–, who became president in 1945 and chairman in 1960, modernized the firm, and, for the first time in company history, recruited outsiders for high positions. He retired in 1980.

**Ford, John,** 1586–c.1640, English dramatist. The most important playwright during the reign of Charles I, he wrote many tragedies, of which *'Tis Pity She's a Whore, The Broken Heart,* and *Love's Sacrifice* (all first presented between 1627 and 1633) are generally considered the most important.

**Ford, John,** 1895–1973, American film director. He won Academy Awards for *The Informer* (1935), *The Grapes of Wrath* (1940), *How Green Was My Valley* (1941), and *The Quiet Man* (1952). His many Westerns include *Rio Grande* (1950) and *The Searchers* (1956).

**foreign aid,** economic, military, technical, and financial assistance, usually rendered at the intergovernmental level but also given through international organizations. The US, many nations in Europe, some in the Middle East and Far East have significant aid programmes. In the UK, the Overseas Development Agency deals with aid to overseas countries. This includes both capital aid on concessional terms and technical assistance which is mainly in the form of specialist staff abroad and training facilities in the UK, whether provided directly to developing countries or through the various multilateral aid organizations. International agencies such as the International Bank for Reconstruction and Development (or World Bank) and the International Monetary Fund provide capital, and a number of UN agencies render development assistance (see UNITED NATIONS). Foreign-aid programmes became controversial in the late 1980s when many countries found themselves unable to keep up interest payments on development loans. It was also stated that aid to developing countries was too often merely a device to make those countries buy goods manufactured by Western economies.

**foreign exchange,** methods and instruments used to adjust the payment of debts between two nations that employ different currency systems. A nation's BALANCE OF PAYMENTS has an important effect on the exchange rate of its currency. The rate of exchange is the price in local currency of one unit of foreign currency measured against another and is determined by the relative supply and demand of the currencies in the foreign-exchange market. The chief demand for foreign exchange comes from importers and exporters, purchasers of foreign securities, government agencies, and international corporations. Exchange rates were traditionally fixed under the gold standard and, later, by international agreements, but in 1973 the major industrial nations of the West adopted a system of 'floating' rates that allows for fluctuation within a limited range. See also INTERNATIONAL MONETARY SYSTEM.

**Foreign Legion,** French volunteer armed force composed chiefly, in its enlisted ranks, of foreigners. Its international composition and practice of not inquiring into enlistees' backgrounds surrounded it with an aura of romance. Created by King LOUIS PHILIPPE (1831) to pacify Algeria, it was used throughout the French colonial empire and during both world wars. Today there are c.8000 members stationed in metropolitan France, its overseas departments, and the Republic of Djibouti.

**Foreign Ministers, Council of,** organization of the foreign ministers of the WORLD WAR II Allies the US, the UK, France, and the USSR that in a long series of meetings (1945–72) attempted to reach political settlements after the war. At the third meeting (New York City, 1946) final peace treaties with Italy, Hungary, Romania, Bulgaria, and Finland were drafted, and the TRIESTE problem was advanced. At the next two meetings (Moscow, London, both 1947), unsuccessful attempts were made to reach agreement on Germany and Austria. German unification was again the subject at meetings in Paris (1949) and Berlin (1954). In 1954, in Geneva, the council called for a conference on the KOREAN WAR (see GENEVA CONFERENCE 1). In 1955, in Vienna, an Austrian peace treaty was agreed upon. In 1959 the conference again met in Geneva to consider German unification; but after failing to agree, the conference recessed for an indefinite period. In 1972, however, the foreign ministers regularized BERLIN's status and paved the way for both East and West Germany to enter the UN.

**Forester, C(ecil) S(cott),** 1899–1966, English novelist. He is best known for stories of the Royal Navy in the days of sail, especially for those centring on Capt. Horatio Hornblower. Forester also wrote *The African Queen* (1935).

**forestry,** the management of forests for WOOD, water, wildlife, forage, and recreation. Due to wood's economic importance, forestry has been chiefly concerned with timber management, especially reforestation, maintenance of extant forests, and fire control. Present-day forestry, however, must include the wider aspects of environmental and wild-life conservation. Most countries have an official forestry service, e.g., the FORESTRY COMMISSION in the UK, concerned with the management of state-owned woodlands and forests, their integration with national agricultural policy, and the provision of technical advice for the private sector.

**Forestry Commission,** official body coordinating forestry policy in the UK. It was instituted in 1919 to develop reserves of standing timber for use in time of war or national emergency; to assist with private afforestation; to undertake research and encourage forest-based industries; and to develop a balance between the aesthetic and productive aspects of forestry. More recently it has become concerned with the control of pests and diseases; protection and enhancement of the environment; provision of public recreational facilities, e.g., walking, camping, fishing, boating; and the integration of forestry with agriculture.

**forgery,** in law, fabrication or alteration of a written document with intent to deceive or defraud. Most instances of forgery occur in connection with instruments for payment of money, such as cheques but the CRIME may also involve documents of title (e.g., deeds) or public documents (e.g., birth and marriage certificates). Counterfeiting (the manufacture of false money with intent to deceive) may be regarded as a special variety of forgery.

**forging:** see WELDING.

**Forli,** city (1984 pop. 110,824), Emilia-Romagna, N Italy. It is the centre of a prosperous agricultural district, the Forlivese, and has grain-milling and engineering industries. Nearby Faenza gave its name to faience pottery.

**formaldehyde** or **methanal** (HCHO), a colourless, flammable, poisonous gas with a suffocating odour. Pure gaseous formaldehyde is uncommon, because it readily polymerizes into solid paraformaldehyde. Formalin, a 40% by volume solution of formaldehyde in water, is used as an antiseptic, disinfectant, and preservative for biological specimens. Formaldehyde is also used in DYE, PLASTIC and synthetic RESIN (e.g., Bakelite), manufacture.

**Formosa:** see TAIWAN.

**Forrest, Edwin,** 1806–72, American actor, the nation's first theatrical idol. His New York City debut as Othello (1826) established him as a great tragedian, noted for bold and forceful acting. His rivalry with the English actor W.C. MACREADY resulted in a riot (1849) in New York by Forrest partisans in which many were killed.

**Forrest, John, baron,** 1847–1918, Australian explorer and politician. He was one of the principal explorers of Western Australia and first premier (1890–1901) of the colony when it achieved self-government. He later served as a federal minister.

**Forster, E(dward) M(organ),** 1879–1970, English novelist and essayist. A leading member of the BLOOMSBURY GROUP, his subtle and morally probing novels explore the effect of sexual, cultural and racial barriers on human relationships. *Where Angels Fear to Tread* (1905) was followed by *The Longest Journey* (1907), *A Room with a View* (1908), *Howards End* (1910), and *Maurice* (1913–14, published 1971). His last and best-known novel, *A Passage to India* (1924), consolidated his reputation as a spokesman for liberal humanism. He also published short stories and nonfiction, including *Aspects of the Novel* (1927), and was a noted broadcaster.

**Forster, William Edward,** 1818–86, English politician and educational reformer. He was a Liberal Member of Parliament for Bradford from 1861 until his death. In the Gladstone government of 1868, as Vice-President of the Council, he saw the Endowed Schools Bill of 1869 through the House of Commons, and produced a compromise between the educational views of the two main pressure groups—the church-related National Education League and the radical National Education Union —to produce the Elementary Education Act 1870 (see EDUCATION ACTS).

**forsythia,** shrub (genus *Forsythia*) of the OLIVE family, native to Europe and Asia. Producing abundant bell-shaped yellow flowers, which appear before the leaves, forsythia bushes are often cultivated as ornamentals in hedges and along borders.

**Fortaleza,** city (1980 pop. 648,815), NE Brazil, capital of Ceará state. An Atlantic port at the mouth of the Paejú R., which bisects the city, it ships coffee and other products of Brazil's interior and has processing industries. It is also known for traditional handicrafts, e.g., lace-making. The city first achieved importance in the 17th cent., as a centre of the great colonial sugar plantations.

**Fortes, Meyer,** 1906–83, British anthropologist; b. South Africa. A key figure in the STRUCTURAL FUNCTIONALISM that dominated postwar Africanist anthropology, Fortes developed KINSHIP theory and sought to demonstrate how kinship could structure juridical, moral, and political life in the absence of formal political institutions. He carried out his fieldwork among the Tallensi in Africa. He became professor of anthropolgy at Cambridge Univ. in 1950.

**Forth,** river in Central region, Scotland, c.105 km (66 mi) long. It is formed by the confluence of two headstreams (Avondhu and Duchray water) near Aberfoyle. It then flows E past Stirling and Alloa to Kincardine, where it widens out into the Firth of Forth, which itself is c.82 km (51 mi) long. The Firth of Forth is crossed by a road bridge (built in 1936) at Kincardine, and a rail bridge (completed 1890) and a road bridge (1964), both near Queensferry. Just above the rail bridge is the naval base of Rosyth.

**fortification,** system of defence structures for protection from enemy attacks. The art developed in earliest times with the building of simple earthworks, which soon evolved into walls, palisades, and elaborate stockades. City walls appeared very early in the Middle East, notably in Mesopotamia and Phoenicia. Major advances in permanent fortification were made by the Romans, who built walls along the Danube and Rhine rivers and in Britain, e.g., HADRIAN'S WALL. The GREAT WALL OF CHINA was an even more ambitious undertaking. The advent of siegecraft (see SIEGE), using such devices as battering rams and catapults, reduced the effectiveness of large-scale fortification, but in the Middle Ages CASTLES and citadels remained defensible against all but a lengthy siege. In the 15th cent. the development of ARTILLERY further diminished the value of fixed fortifications, and military engineers had to devise new methods of defence based on detached forts that created an entrenched camp over a wide area. This ring system of fortification failed in Belgium in World War I, however, as did the French MAGINOT LINE in World War II. The development of airpower, heavy artillery, and MECHANIZED WARFARE eventually brought an end to such defence systems. In both the Korean and Vietnam wars the theory of fortification returned to the idea of temporary, even improvised, shelter, intended mainly to delay the enemy's advance.

**Fort Knox,** [after Henry KNOX], US military reservation, 44,515 hectares (110,000 acres), Hardin and Meade cos., N Kentucky, US; est. 1917 as a training camp, became a permanent post 1932. In 1940 it became the site of the US Army Armored Center. The US Depository (built 1936) holds the bulk of the nation's gold bullion in steel and concrete vaults.

The US Government's currency vault at **Fort Knox**

**Fort Lauderdale,** US city (1984 est. pop. 150,000), SE Florida, on the Atlantic coast; settled around a fort built (c.1837) in the Seminole War, inc. 1911. The city has more than 435 km (270 mi) of natural and artificial waterways, and one of the largest marinas in the world. A major beach resort, it also produces electronic devices, boats and yachts, and various light manufactures.

**FORTRAN:** see PROGRAMMING LANGUAGE.

**Fortuny, Mariano Madrazo,** 1871–1949, Italian painter and innovatory textile and dress designer. He was influential in the 1910s and 20s. He introduced the fine, pleated, 'Delphos' dress, popular with an artistic clientele. His dress and textile designs derived from classical, oriental, and mediaeval sources. Some of his textile designs are still used for furnishings.

**Fort Wayne,** US city (1984 est. pop. 165,000), NE Indiana, inc. 1840. It is a railway, wholesale, and distribution centre with electronics and motor vehicle industries. The MIAMI INDIANS had their chief town on the strategic site. A French fort (built before 1680) was replaced by one built (1794) by Anthony WAYNE, who subdued the Indians.

**Fort Worth,** US city (1984 est. pop. 415,000), N Texas, 48 km (30 mi) W of DALLAS; settled 1843, inc. 1873. Established as an army post in 1847, it became a cattle town after the Civil War. Completion (1876) of the railway made it a meat-packing and shipping point. Wheat (late 19th cent.) and oil (discovered 1919 W of the city) furthered its development. Today it is a major N Texas industrial city, with large oil and gas facilities and a huge aircraft industry. The Dallas–Fort Worth airport (opened 1974 between the cities) is one of the world's largest. Texas Christian Univ., the Fort Worth Art Center, and the Amon Carter Museum of Western Art are among the city's well-known institutions.

**Forty-five,** rising: see under JACOBITES.

**Foscolo, Ugo,** 1778–1827, Italian writer. A novel recounting his political disillusionment with Napoleon Bonaparte (see NAPOLEON I), *Last Letters of Jacopo Ortis* (1798–1802), together with his criticism and lyrics (especially *Of Sepulchres,* 1807), strongly influenced Italian letters.

**Fosdick, Harry Emerson,** 1878–1969, American clergyman. He was known as a Modernist leader in the Fundamentalist controversies of the 1920s, and his sermons, books, and radio addresses won wide recognition.

**Fosse Way,** road situated between Lincoln and Exeter, built by the Romans to connect a chain of forts along the original frontier of the British province (see ANTONINE WALL; HADRIAN'S WALL). When the Romans expanded their domain, the road became a major cross-country transport route.

**fossil,** remains or imprint of a plant or animal preserved from prehistoric times by natural methods and found mainly in sedimentary rock, asphalt, and coal. Fossilization of skeletal structures or other hard parts is most common. Conditions for fossilization include quick burial in an originally moist sediment or other material that prevents both weathering and decay. Shells and bones embedded in hardened sediment can be dissolved by water, leaving a natural mould. Sometimes these moulds are filled with mineral deposits, forming natural casts. Fossil footprints and trails, and coprolites, or fossil excrement, can reveal much about the lives and feeding habits of ancient animals. Entire animals of the late Pleistocene have been found, notably in Siberia. In California, the LA BREA tar pits have yielded many skeletons. The study of fossils is palaeontology.

**fossil fuel:** see ENERGY, SOURCES OF.

**Foster, Norman,** 1935–, English architect. An apostle of high-tech building design and an expert in the creation of a controlled internal environment, Foster is best known for the headquarters of Willis Faber & Dumas in Ipswich, with its open-plan interior with linking escalators and its reflective glass envelope; the Sainsbury Centre for Visual Arts at the Univ. of East Anglia, Norwich; and the headquarters of the Hong Kong–Shanghai Bank in Hong Kong, a brilliantly organized building with components from different countries and a structure in which floors are suspended in groups.

**Foster, Stephen Collins,** 1826–64, American songwriter and composer. He had little training. Writing songs for the E.P. Christy minstrel troupe, he acquired a knowledge of Negro life, but sensing prejudice against 'Ethiopian songs' he was reluctant even to put his name to them. Because of their utter simplicity, his Negro dialect songs are often thought of as folk music. His songs include 'Oh! Susannah', 'Camptown Races', 'My Old Kentucky Home', and 'Old Black Joe'.

**foster care,** generally, care of children on a full-time, temporary basis by persons other than their own parents. Also known as boarding-home care, foster care offers a supportive family environment to children whose natural parents cannot raise them because of the parents' physical or

The Hong Kong–Shanghai Bank by Norman **Foster**

mental illness; because of the child's behavioural difficulties; or because of problems within the family environment, e.g., abuse, neglect, alcoholism, or crime. Children may be placed in group homes or with individual foster families, who receive some payment towards care. In some cases, the natural parents retain their parental rights and the child ultimately returns home. Under permanent foster care, the agency has guardianship; the child may then be available for adoption by the foster parents or others.

**Foucault, Jean Bernard Leon** (fooh‚koh), 1819–68, French physicist. Investigating the speed of light, he determined its velocity in air and found that its speed in water and other media decreased in proportion to the index of refraction. He originated the Foucault PENDULUM with which he demonstrated the earth's rotation, invented (1852) the GYROSCOPE, and with the physicist Armand Fizeau took the first clear photograph of the sun.

**Foucault, Michel** (fooh‚koh), 1926–84, French philosopher and historian. A highly original thinker, he attempted to merge history and philosophy by tracing the history of concepts (e.g., madness, health, punishment) to exhibit them as functions of social power structures. Examples of this technique are *Madness and Civilization* (1961), *The Archaeology of Knowledge* (1972), *The Birth of the Clinic* (1973), and *The History of Sexuality* (1976–83).

**Fouché, Joseph** (fooh‚shay), b. 1759 or 1763, d. 1820, French police minister (1799–1802, 1804–10). A lifelong opportunist, he sided with every party in power from the FRENCH REVOLUTION through the BOURBON restoration. He was one of the indispensable men in the empire of NAPOLEON I, who created him duke of Otranto in 1809. Sometimes considered the father of the modern police state, he created a ruthlessly efficient system of criminal and political police. After the second Bourbon restoration, he was exiled and died in obscurity.

**Foucquet:** see FOUQUET.

**founding:** see CASTING.

**Fouquet** or **Foucquet, Jean** or **Jehan** (fooh‚kay), c.1420–c.1481, French painter and illuminator (see ILLUMINATION). Court painter to CHARLES VII and LOUIS XI, he produced religious paintings, court portraits, and an illuminated BOOK OF HOURS for Étienne Chevalier (Chantilly) that is regarded as his masterpiece.

**Four Freedoms.** On 6 Jan 1941, Pres. F.D. ROOSEVELT, in a message to Congress proposing LEND–LEASE legislation, stated that Four Freedoms should prevail throughout the world—freedom of speech and expression, freedom of worship, freedom from want, and freedom from fear. These were substantially incorporated (Aug. 1941) in the ATLANTIC CHARTER.

**Four Horsemen of the Apocalypse,** allegorical figures in the BIBLE. Rev. 6. One interpretation of the rider on the white horse is that he represents Christ. The rider on the red horse may represent war; on the black horse, famine; and on the pale horse, death.

**Fourier, Charles** (fooh‚ryay), 1772–1837, French social philosopher. He held that social harmony could be achieved in a society based on the 'phalanx', an economic unit of 1620 people sharing a communal dwelling and dividing work according to their natural inclinations. The many Fourierist communities included BROOK FARM. After Fourier's death, Fourierism was led by V.P. CONSIDÉRANT.

**Fourier, Jean Baptiste Joseph, Baron,** 1768–1830, French mathematician and physicist, noted for his researches on heat diffusion and numerical equations. He originated the Fourier series, which allowed discontinuous functions to be represented by a trigonometric series.

**Four-Power Treaty:** see NAVAL CONFERENCES.

**Fourteen Points,** formulation of a peace programme, presented (Jan. 1918) by US Pres. WILSON near the end of WORLD WAR I. The programme called for a just, unselfish peace that would offer self-government to the European national groups and pave the way for general disarmament and open agreements between nations. The programme had two purposes: to reach the people and liberal leaders of the Central Powers in the hope that their influence would help shorten the war and also to provide an actual framework for the peace discussions. The first aim was successful; but, despite the enormous moral authority the Fourteen Points conferred on Wilson, the programme's important points were lost in the compromises that came out of the actual peace treaty (see VERSAILLES, TREATY OF).

**fourth-generation computers:** see COMPUTER GENERATIONS.

**Fourth International,** coordinating centre of revolutionary socialist parties founded in the 1930s by TROTSKY as a rival to the SECOND INTERNATIONAL and the COMINTERN (Third International). In the post-war era the Fourth International has experienced serious ideological divisions and its affiliated parties have remained of marginal influence.

**Fourth of July, Independence Day,** or **July Fourth,** US patriotic holiday commemorating the adoption of the DECLARATION OF INDEPENDENCE. Celebration of it began during the AMERICAN REVOLUTION.

**Fowler, Henry Watson,** 1858–1933, English lexicographer. He and his brother, Francis G. Fowler (1870–1918), collaborated on *The King's English* (1906), *The Concise Oxford Dictionary of Current English* (1911), and *The Pocket Oxford Dictionary* (1924). After the death of his brother, H.W. Fowler completed alone the invaluable reference work *A Dictionary of Modern English Usage* (1926).

**Fowles, John,** 1926–, English novelist. A cerebral writer, he is interested in manipulating the novel form. His books include *The Collector* (1963), *The French Lieutenant's Woman* (1969), *Daniel Martin* (1977), and *Mantissa* (1982).

**fox,** carnivorous MAMMAL of the DOG family, found in much of the Northern Hemisphere. It has a pointed face, thick fur, and bushy tail. The arctic fox (*Alopex lagopus*), distributed round the North Pole, has very small ears. The desert fox or fennec (*Fennecus zerda*) has very large ears, to assist in cooling. The European red fox (*Vulpes vulpes*) has adapted to town life, and has been seen in the heart of London.

**Fox, Charles James,** 1749–1806, British statesman and orator, for many years the outstanding parliamentary proponent of liberal reform. A WHIG, he entered Parliament in 1768. He was a close friend of the prince of Wales (later GEORGE IV), a critic of GEORGE III, and a rival of William PITT. Three times foreign secretary (1782, 1783, 1806), Fox opposed British intervention in the FRENCH REVOLUTION and advocated legislative independence for Ireland, enlargement of the franchise, and parliamentary reform. Abolition of the slave trade, which he proposed and urged, was passed in 1807.

**Fox, George,** 1624–91, English religious leader, founder of the Society of FRIENDS. In 1646 he underwent a mystical experience that convinced him that Christianity was an inner light by which Christ directly illumines the believing soul. Beginning to preach in 1647, he was often persecuted and imprisoned, but won many followers and organized his sect in 1668. The first London Yearly Meeting was held in 1671. His journal (1694, with a preface by William Penn), has appeared in various editions.

**Fox, Margaret:** see SPIRITUALISM.

**Foxe, John,** 1516–87, English clergyman, author of the noted *Book of Martyrs.* A Protestant, he fled to the Continent in the reign of MARY I. There, a Latin edition of his history was published in 1559. An expanded English edition (1563) appeared in the reign of ELIZABETH I. The book praised the Protestant martyrs of Mary's reign.

**fox hunting,** field sport in which hunters on horseback follow a pack of hounds in pursuit of a fox. In Britain, the season begins on 1 Nov. and ends in the spring. Leading hunts include the Quorn, the Pytchley, and the Duke of Beaufort's. Traditional clothing for members of a hunt consists of a red ('pink') coat and top hat for men; women riding sidesaddle wear a black habit and top hat, or astride they wear black coat and bowler hat. The principal member of a hunt is called, whether male or female, the Master (MFH: Master of Foxhounds); in the field, the pack is controlled by the huntsman, helped by a whipper-in. When caught, the fox's mask (head), brush (tail), and pads (feet) are taken as trophies, and the remains fed to the hounds. The sport has been practised in England at least since the 13th cent. Stag hunting has similar traditions and practices. Harriers are packs of hounds with mounted followers which hunt hares; beagles and basset hounds also hunt hares but the followers are on foot.

**Foz do Iguaçu** or **Nova Iguaçu,** city (1980 pop. 491,766), situated near to the ITAÍPU on the Paraná R. on the Brazil–Paraguay boundary. Since 1973 it has been the centre for the Brazilian involvement in the construction of the dam and its future is tied closely to the future impact of that project, as is the neighbouring Paraguayan town of Puerto Stroessner and the Argentine town of Puerto Iguazú. Each of these towns now have international airports and each is the centre of a growing tourist industry.

**Fr,** chemical symbol of the element FRANCIUM.

**Fra:** see ANGELICO, FRA; LIPPI, FRA FILIPPO.

**fraction,** in arithmetic, an expression representing a part, or several equal parts, of a unit. In writing a fraction, e.g., ⅖, the number after or below the bar, called the denominator, indicates the total number of equal parts into which the unit has been divided; the number before or above the bar, called the numerator, indicates how many of these parts are being considered. The present notation for fractions is of Hindu origin, but some types of fractions were used by the Egyptians before 1600 BC. The DECIMAL SYSTEM uses another way to represent fractions, e.g., 0.75 for ¾, often simplifying computation.

**fractional distillation:** see DISTILLATION.

**Fragonard, Jean-Honoré** (fragoh͵nah), 1732–1806, French painter. Influenced by BOUCHER, he was admitted to the Académie Royale in 1765 for *Coresus and Callirrhoë* (Louvre, Paris). Thereafter he devoted himself to painting polished, delicately erotic scenes of love for the court of LOUIS XV. Representative works are *The Souvenir* (c. 1775–80) and *The Swing* (1769) (both: Wallace Coll., London), and the *Music Lesson* (c.1769?; Louvre, Paris). He is esteemed for the freedom of his brushstroke, the vitality of his portraiture and landscapes, and his virtuosity in depicting the gaiety and charm of the age of Louis XV.

**Frame, Janet,** 1924–, New Zealand author of such complex, disturbing novels as *Owls Do Cry* (1957), *Faces in the Water* (1961), and *Living in the Maniototo* (1979), and of poems, e.g., *The Pocket Mirror* (1967), and short stories.

**France,** officially the French Republic, republic (1986 est. pop. 55,270,000), 547,026 km² (211,207 sq mi), W Europe; bordered by the English Channel (N), the Atlantic Ocean and Bay of Biscay (W), Spain (SW), the Mediterranean Sea (S), Switzerland and Italy (E, SE), and West Germany, Luxembourg, and Belgium (NE). PARIS is the capital; other major cities include MARSEILLES, LYONS, TOULOUSE and NICE. One of the country's major natural features is the MASSIF CENTRAL, a rugged mountain

Jean-Honore **Fragonard,** *The Swing.* The Wallace Collection, London.

area occupying south-central France. North of this and of the LOIRE R. is the Paris basin, a fertile depression drained by the SEINE and Marne rivers. To the SE is the RHÔNE valley, which widens into a plain near its delta on the MEDITERRANEAN. To the SW is the great Aquitanian plain, drained by the GARONNE and Dordogne rivers. The main mountain ranges are the French ALPS, with France's highest peak, MONT BLANC (4807 m/15,771 ft), the VOSGES and the JURA mountains in the east, and the PYRENEES in the SW.

*Economy.* France is one of the world's major economic powers. Agriculture is important, and about 60% of the land is used for farming. Over half of the value of agricultural output derives from livestock; leading crops are sugar beets, wheat, corn, potatoes, and barley. Only Italy produces more wine. Iron ore and bauxite are the leading minerals. Major industrial products include metals, chemicals, natural gas, foods (particularly cheese), motor vehicles, aircraft, and textiles. Tourism is important, as is the production of luxury goods. The railroads, utilities, many banks, and some key industries are nationally owned. The GNP is $568,690 million and the GNP per capita is $10,390 (1983).

*People.* France has great ethnic diversity. French is the universal language, but Alsatian (a German dialect), Flemish, Breton, Basque, and Catalan are still spoken in various regions. Roman Catholicism is the dominant religion.

*Government.* Metropolitan (European) France is composed of 95 departments (including CORSICA), grouped into 21 regions and subdivided into districts, municipalities, and cantons. Together with the overseas departments and territories, they constitute the French Republic. The Fifth French Republic is governed under a constitution adopted in 1958 and amended in 1962. It provides for a strong president, directly elected to a 7-year term, and a bicameral parliament.

*Early History.* The area known as GAUL was conquered (58–51 BC) by the Romans under Julius CAESAR. Beginning in the 3rd cent. AD, the Gallo-Roman civilization that had developed was overrun by Germanic invaders, including the FRANKS under CLOVIS I, who defeated (486) the last Roman governor. Under the MEROVINGIAN and CAROLINGIAN dynasties the Franks ruled Gaul until 987, when powerful feudal lords established HUGH CAPET as king. Under the Capetian kings, who reigned until 1328, France experienced a rebirth that reached its height in the 13th cent. Its leading role in the CRUSADES established its cultural supremacy in most of Europe, and the HUNDRED YEARS WAR (1337–1453) evicted the English from French soil. The 16th cent. brought religious conflict and civil wars, but in the 17th cent. two great statesmen, Cardinal RICHELIEU and Cardinal MAZARIN, reestablished French power, and under LOUIS XIV (r. 1643–1715) France became the greatest power in Europe.

*The Ancien Régime and the New France.* Burdened by remnants of feudalism and a system of outworn privileges, France under LOUIS XV (r. 1715–74) hovered on the verge of bankruptcy. The SEVEN YEARS WAR (1756–63) drained the treasury and cost France its empire in India and North America. French support of the AMERICAN REVOLUTION proved a financial disaster. The result was the upheaval that shook Europe from 1789 to 1815 (see FRENCH REVOLUTION; FRENCH REVOLUTIONARY WARS; NAPOLEON I). During this time a constitutional monarchy was created (1791); war with much of Europe began, accompanied by the growth of radical factions in France (1792); ROBESPIERRE presided over the REIGN OF TERROR (1793–95); and a reaction ushered in the DIRECTORY (1795–99), which was terminated by Napoleon's coup d'etat. Making himself emperor (1804), Napoleon led his armies as far as Moscow before his final defeat in the WATERLOO CAMPAIGN (1815).

*Modern France.* France emerged as a uniform, bureaucratic state, dominated by the bourgeoisie. The Bourbon Restoration (1814–30) was shortlived. The JULY REVOLUTION of 1830 enthroned LOUIS PHILIPPE, who was overthrown in turn by the FEBRUARY REVOLUTION of 1848. Louis Napoleon headed the Second Republic and later (1852) made himself emperor as NAPOLEON III. Defeat in the FRANCO-PRUSSIAN WAR (1870–71) led to his downfall and the establishment of the Third Republic. In WORLD WAR I, France, led by CLEMENCEAU, bore the brunt of the fighting in the West. In WORLD WAR II, defeat by Germany (1940) was followed by occupation; Marshal PÉTAIN headed the collaborationist VICHY government in unoccupied France, while Gen. Charles DE GAULLE led the 'Free French' resistance. In 1944 the Allies expelled the Germans from France. The Fourth Republic, proclaimed in 1946, was weakened by the defeat (1954) of French troops in INDOCHINA and a war for independence in ALGERIA. De Gaulle was returned to power as first president (1958–69) of the Fifth Republic. Seeking to restore French prestige in world affairs, De Gaulle stressed independence from the US and NATO in military affairs. His conservative policies were continued by his successors, Georges POMPIDOU and Válery GISCARD D'ESTAING. In 1981, after 23 years of Gaullist dominance, François MITTERRAND of the Socialist Party was elected president and embarked on a programme that included administrative decentralization and nationalization of banks and industry. The Socialists lost their parliamentary majority in 1986, and a Gaullist prime minister Jacques CHIRAC, reversed many of their policies, governing in uneasy 'cohabitation' with Pres. Mitterrand. In 1988, however, Mitterrand was reelected president and the left regained a majority, Michel Rocard becoming prime minister of a new government with centrist participation.

**Post-war French prime ministers**
*Provisional*
Charles de Gaulle (Gaullist), 1944–46
Félix Gouin (Socialist), 1946
Georges Bidault (Christian Democrat), 1946
*Fourth Republic*
Léon Blum (Socialist), 1946–47
Paul Ramadier (Socialist), 1947
Robert Schuman (Christian Democrat), 1947–48
André Marie (Radical), 1948
Robert Schuman (Christian Democrat), 1948
Henri Queuille (Radical), 1948–49
Georges Bidault (Christian Democrat), 1949–50
Henri Queuille (Radical), 1950
René Pleven (Left Radical), 1950–51
Henri Queuille (Radical), 1951
René Pleven (Left Radical), 1951–52
Edgar Faure (Radical), 1952
Antoine Pinay (Independent), 1952
René Mayer (Radical), 1953
Joseph Laniel (Republican), 1953–54
Pierre Mendès-France (Radical), 1954–55

Edgar Faure (Radical), 1955–56
Guy Mollet (Socialist), 1956–57
Maurice Bourges-Maunoury (Radical), 1957
Félix Gaillard (Radical), 1957–58
Pierre Pflimlin (Christian Democrat), 1958
Charles de Gaulle (Gaullist), 1958
*Fifth Republic*
Michel Debré (Gaullist), 1959–62
Georges Pompidou (Gaullist), 1962–68
Maurice Couve de Murville (Gaullist), 1968–69
Jacques Chaban-Delmas (Gaullist), 1969–72
Pierre Messmer (Gaullist), 1972–74
Jacques Chirac (Gaullist), 1974–76
Raymond Barre (Centrist), 1976–81
Pierre Mauroy (Socialist), 1981–84
Laurent Fabius (Socialist), 1984–86
Jacques Chirac (Gaullist), 1986–88
Michel Rocard (Socialist), 1988–

France

**France, Anatole,** pseud. of **Jacques Anatole Thibault,** 1844–1924, French author, probably the most prominent French man of letters of his day. His early fiction displayed allusive charm and subtle irony, as in *Le crime de Sylvestre Bonnard* (1881), *Thaïs* (1890), and *La rôtisserie de la Reine Pédauque* (1893; tr. At the Sign of the Reine Pédauque). After the DREYFUS AFFAIR (in which he supported ZOLA), France concentrated more on political satire, notably in the novel *L'Île des pingouins* (1908; tr. Penguin Island), an allegory of French history. He was elected to the French Academy in 1896 and received the Nobel Prize in literature in 1921.

**Franceschi, Piero de':** see PIERO DELLA FRANCESCA.

**Franche-Comté** (ˌfronsh'komtay), region and historic prov., E France. Dole is the historic capital, succeeded by Besançon. It embraces the JURA uplands and the upper basin of the Saône R. Dairy cattle are grazed on the limestone pastures; gruyère cheese is made in cooperative dairies. Other industries were developed by HUGUENOT refugees. Franche-Comté, or the Free County of Burgundy, was created in the 9th cent. Acquired by

Burgundy, and later Spain, it retained a good deal of autonomy until it became absorbed into France in 1678.

**franchise,** type of business in which a group or individual receives a license to conduct a commercial enterprise. Corporate franchises enable a franchisee to market a well-known product or service in return for an initial fee and a percentage of gross receipts. The franchiser usually provides assistance with merchandising and advertising. Major franchise networks, are usually associated with the US. They include fast-food restaurants, petrol stations, motels, car dealerships, and estate agencies, and the system has expanded into many other fields. Government franchises are issued to public utility and transport companies.

**Francia, José Gaspar Rodríguez de,** 1766–1840, Paraguayan dictator (1814–40). Known as *El Supremo,* he successfully achieved PARAGUAY's independence from Spain and ruled the country with an iron hand until his death.

**Francis,** rulers of the HOLY ROMAN EMPIRE. **Francis I,** 1708–65, emperor (1745–65), duke of Lorraine (1729–37), and duke of Tuscany (1737–65), exchanged Lorraine for the reversion to Tuscany in 1735 as part of the settlement of the War of the POLISH SUCCESSION. In 1736 he married MARIA THERESA, heiress to the HABSBURG lands. He became emperor at the end of the War of the AUSTRIAN SUCCESSION, but enjoyed little influence in the Habsburg lands, which were ruled by his wife. **Francis II,** 1768–1835, was the last Holy Roman emperor (r.1792–1806) and, as Francis I, the first emperor of Austria (r.1804–35) and king of Bohemia and Hungary (r.1792–1835). When NAPOLEON I forced the dissolution of the Holy Roman Empire, Francis took the title emperor of Austria. Later he helped defeat Napoleon and, guided by METTERNICH, presided over the Congress of VIENNA. His reign was repressive both of liberalism and nationalism, but encouraged the rise of BIEDERMEIER culture.

**Francis,** kings of France. **Francis I,** 1494–1547 (r.1515–47), was the cousin, son-in-law, and successor of LOUIS XII. He resumed the ITALIAN WARS and recovered Milan by a brilliant victory at Marignano (1515). A candidate for Holy Roman emperor (1519), Francis lost to CHARLES V, who became his lifelong rival. A planned alliance with HENRY VIII of England failed to occur at the FIELD OF THE CLOTH OF GOLD (1520), and Francis was captured in his first war (1521–25) against Charles V. To gain his freedom, Francis renounced many territorial claims. He then created the League of Cognac, consisting of Francis, Henry VIII, Venice, Florence, and the papacy; they were all allied against Charles V, but a second war (1527–29) gained little, and a third war (1536–38) proved inconclusive. In 1542 Francis, allied with the Turkish sultan SULAYMAN I, again attacked Charles, who was supported by Henry VIII. The resulting peace treaties only confirmed earlier French losses. During Francis's reign France was generally peaceful domestically. The king was also known for his support of the arts. He was a patron of François RABELAIS, and LEONARDO DA VINCI worked at his court. Francis was succeeded by his son HENRY II. His grandson, **Francis II,** 1544–60 (r.1559–60), married (1558) MARY QUEEN OF SCOTS, and during his reign the government was run by her relatives the GUISE family. Their persecution of Protestants caused the HUGUENOTS to launch the ill-fated Amboise Conspiracy (1560) in an effort to displace them.

**Francis,** 1554–84, French prince, duke of Alençon and Anjou, youngest son of HENRY II of France. He played a major role in the French Wars of Religion (see RELIGION, WARS OF), and was considered as a husband for ELIZABETH I of England. Offered (1580) the rule of the Low Countries by WILLIAM THE SILENT, leader of the Netherlands' revolt against Spain, he invaded the Netherlands, but withdrew in 1583.

**Francis, Dick,** 1920–, English novelist. Formerly a professional champion steeplechase jockey, he drew on his expert knowledge of the horse-racing world in a series of successful mysteries including *Dead Cert* (1962), *Blood Sport* (1967), and many others.

**Francis, Saint,** or **Saint Francis of Assisi,** 1182?–1226, founder of the FRANCISCANS; b. Assisi, Italy. The son of a wealthy merchant, he underwent a conversion at age 22 and became markedly devout and ascetic. In 1209 he began to preach and was given permission by Pope INNOCENT III to form an order of friars. The friars travelled about Italy and soon began preaching in foreign countries, including (1219–20) the Holy Land. In 1221 Francis gave up command of the order, and in 1224 he became the first known person to receive the stigmata (wounds corresponding to those of the crucified Christ). Francis exemplified

humility, love of poverty, and joyous religious fervour; he is also associated with a simple love of nature and man and is often depicted preaching to birds. Stories about him were collected in *The Little Flowers of St Francis.* Feast: 4 Oct.

**Francis I, emperor of Austria:** see FRANCIS II, Holy Roman emperor.

**Franciscans,** members of several Roman Catholic religious orders following the rule (approved 1223) of St FRANCIS. There are now three orders of Franciscan friars. The Friars Minor (O.F.M.), formerly called Observants, and the Friars Minor Conventual (O.M.C.) split (1517) as a result of a reform. Further reform (1525) created the Capuchins (O.M.Cap.). The Franciscans also include an order of nuns, the Poor Clares, and a third order including both laity and religious members. Franciscans are active in education and as missionaries.

**Francis de Sales, Saint,** 1567–1622, French Roman Catholic preacher, Doctor of the Church, key figure in the COUNTER-REFORMATION in France. He became (1602) bishop of Geneva and is credited with many conversions of Protestants by his eloquent preaching. With St Jane Frances de Chantal he founded the Order of the Visitation for women. His *Introduction to the Devout Life* is a religious classic, and in 1923 he was named saint of journalists and writers. Feast: 24 Jan.

**Francis Ferdinand,** 1863–1914, Austrian archduke, heir apparent to his great-uncle, Emperor FRANCIS JOSEPH. He and his wife, Sophie, were assassinated (1914) in SARAJEVO by Gavrilo Princip, a Serbian nationalist. The consequent Austrian ultimatum to Serbia led directly to WORLD WAR I.

**Francis Joseph** or **Franz Joseph,** 1830–1916, emperor of Austria (1848–1916) and king of Hungary (1867–1916). He subdued Hungary (1849) but lost (1859) Lombardy to Sardinia, and later he lost Venetia to Italy in the AUSTRO-PRUSSIAN WAR of 1866. After reorganization (1867), his empire became the AUSTRO-HUNGARIAN MONARCHY. Francis Joseph joined (1879) in an alliance with Germany (see TRIPLE ALLIANCE AND TRIPLE ENTENTE). Government under him was bureaucratic, but Vienna became increasingly significant as a great cultural capital. His reign was disturbed by the tragic deaths of his son, RUDOLF; his brother, MAXIMILIAN, emperor of Mexico; and his wife, ELIZABETH. He died during World War I and was succeeded by CHARLES I.

**Francistown,** town (1987 pop. 31,065), capital of North-East District, E Botswana. On the Cape Town–Bulawayo railway line, it has a regional airport and is an industrial centre processing livestock products.

**Francis Xavier, Saint,** 1506–52, Basque JESUIT missionary, called the Apostle of the Indies. A friend of St IGNATIUS OF LOYOLA, with whom he and five others formed the Society of Jesus, he spent the last 11 years of his life as a missionary in India, Southeast Asia, and Japan. He is considered one of the greatest Christian missionaries, possessing both profound mysticism and common sense. Feast: 3 Dec.

**francium** (Fr), radioactive element, discovered in 1939 by Marguerite Perey as a disintegration product of actinium. Some of the 21 known isotopes of this rare ALKALI METAL are prepared by bombarding thorium with protons, deuterons, or alpha particles. See ELEMENT (table); PERIODIC TABLE.

**Franck, César Auguste** (franhk), 1822–90, French composer and organist; b. Belgium. As a teacher in Paris he influenced an entire generation of composers. His distinctive music, drawing on the techniques of BACH and LISZT's techniques of thematic transformation includes a String Quartet (1889), a Piano Quintet (1879), a Violin Sonata (1886), and a Symphony in D minor (1886–88).

**Franco Bahamonde, Francisco,** 1892–1975, Spanish general, *caudillo* [leader] of SPAIN (1939–75). An army chief of staff (1934–36) and a political conservative, he joined (1936) the Nationalist rebellion against the republic and invaded Spain from Morocco. He became head of the rebel government (1936) and of the fascist FALANGE party (1937). With German and Italian help, he won the SPANISH CIVIL WAR in 1939, dealt ruthlessly with Loyalist opponents, and established a corporate state. He kept Spain a nonbelligerent in WORLD WAR II, and in 1947 he declared Spain a kingdom with himself regent. He named (1969) JUAN CARLOS as his successor and, despite social unrest, retained power until his death.

**Franconia,** one of the five basic or stem duchies of medieval Germany, S West Germany. It became (9th cent.) a duchy that included the cities of Mainz, Würzburg, Frankfurt, and Worms. Partitioned in 939, it remained politically fragmented. Most of Eastern Franconia passed (1803–15) to Bavaria.

**Francophone Conference,** first held at Versailles (France) in 1986 with the participation of 42 French-speaking countries or regions. Reflecting the desire for a francophone counterpart to the COMMONWEALTH OF NATIONS, the conference adopted measures to protect and promote the French language and culture. Other agencies for francophone cooperation include the High Council of Francophony (est. 1984) and the Agency for Cultural and Technical Cooperation (est. 1970), both based in Paris.

**Franco-Prussian War** or **Franco-German War,** 1870–71, war encouraged by BISMARCK as part of his plan to create a unified German empire. Bismarck correctly surmised that his publication of the EMS DISPATCH would goad the French government into declaring war (on 19 July 1870) on Prussia. As he also expected, the other German states fell into line behind Prussia. A brilliant campaign led by von MOLTKE brought a string of German victories, culminating in the French rout at Sedan, where the emperor, NAPOLEON III, was captured (1 Sept.). In Paris, Napoleon was deposed and a provisional government was formed, but French resistance was made useless after the surrender of the French commander, Marshal Bazaine, at Metz (27 Oct.). Paris, however, held out until Jan. 1871, when the Prussian siege finally succeeded. France was forced to pay a huge indemnity and to give up most of Alsace and Lorraine. Again Paris resisted, until the COMMUNE OF PARIS was crushed militarily by the new French government. The war had far-reaching consequences. The German Empire was proclaimed (at Versailles on 18 Jan 1871), but the so-called Third Republic of France never accepted the loss of Alsace and Lorraine.

**Franc Zone,** currency union between FRANCE (including its overseas departments and territories) and 14 former French dependencies in Africa. The latter form the African Financial Community (CFA), whose CFA franc has a fixed and guaranteed rate against the French franc.

**Frank, Jacob,** c.1726–1791, Polish Jewish sectarian and adventurer; b. Ukraine as Jacob ben Judah Leib. He founded the Frankists, a heretical Jewish sect that was an anti-Talmudic outgrowth of the mysticism of SABBATAI ZEVI.

**Frankenthaler, Helen,** 1928–, American painter. A one-time student of Jackson POLLOCK, she is known for her lyrical and sensuous stained canvases.

**Frankfort,** US city (1980 pop. 25,973), state capital of Kentucky, cut by the Kentucky R.; est. 1786, became capital 1792. In the bluegrass country, it is the trade centre for a tobacco and livestock area, and produces whisky, vehicle parts, and other manufactures.

**Frankfurt** or **Frankfurt am Main,** city (1984 pop. 604,600), Hesse, central W Germany, on the Main R. A port and an industrial centre producing chemicals, pharmaceuticals, and other manufactures, it is the site of major international trade fairs. Founded (1st cent AD) by the Romans, it became a royal residence (8th cent.) under CHARLEMAGNE and the coronation place (1562–1792) of the Holy Roman emperors. In the 19th cent. it was the seat of the diet of the GERMAN CONFEDERATION. The city was the original home of the ROTHSCHILD family and the birthplace of GOETHE.

**Frankfurt an der Oder,** city (1980 pop. 79,679), E East Germany, a port on the Oder R. It is an industrial centre, agricultural market, and railway hub. Manufactures include machinery, wood products, and frankfurter sausages. Chartered in 1253, the city was sacked (1631) by the Swedes in the THIRTY YEARS WAR and was severely damaged in WORLD WAR II.

**Frankfurt Parliament,** 1848–49, national assembly convened as a result of the liberal revolution that swept Germany. Its members were popularly elected, and its aim was the unification of Germany. It offered the imperial crown to FREDERICK WILLIAM IV of Prussia, but he refused the offer because it came from a popularly elected parliament. Thereafter divisions within it multiplied and most members withdrew.

**frankincense:** see INCENSE-TREE.

**Franklin, Benjamin,** 1706–90, American statesman, printer, scientist, and writer. He went (1723) to Philadelphia as a printer and there won attention for his wit and commonsense philosophy, especially as expressed in *Poor Richard's Almanack* (pub. 1732–57). He helped establish (1751) an academy that became the present Univ. of Pennsylvania, and he served as deputy postmaster general of the colonies (1753–74). His famous experiment with a kite in a thunderstorm proved the presence of the electricity in lightning. Franklin proposed a plan of union for the colonies at the ALBANY CONGRESS (1754) and was agent for several colonies in England. Returning (1775) to America during the Revolutionary unrest, he helped draft the DECLARATION OF INDEPENDENCE, which he signed. During the AMERICAN REVOLUTION he was a successful American agent in France and was appointed (1781) a commissioner to negotiate the peace with Britain. Franklin's last great public service was his attendance at the FEDERAL CONSTITUTIONAL CONVENTION (1787). His autobiography is well known.

**Franklin, Sir John,** 1786–1847, British explorer in N Canada. He explored the arctic coast of CANADA on expeditions in 1819–22 and 1825–27, during which he founded Fort Franklin. After serving as governor of Van Diemen's Land (now TASMANIA) (1836–43) he set out to look for the NORTHWEST PASSAGE in 1845. His entire expedition of 129 men was lost, their ships apparently frozen in the ice. The tragedy inspired over 40 searches, from which much geographical information was gained.

**Franklin, Miles ('Brent of Bin Bin'),** 1879–1954, Australian novelist. Her autobiographical novel *My Brilliant Career* (1901) expressed both her feminist ambitions and her intense love–hate relationship with Australian rural life. She also published the pseudonymous 'Brent of Bin Bin' series. She bequeathed her estate to establish what has become one of Australia's most prestigious literary awards, the Miles Franklin Award.

**Franks,** group of Germanic tribes that settled by the 3rd cent. along the Rhine. The Salian Franks, under CLOVIS I, moved into GAUL and overthrew (486) the Romans. Clovis united them with the Ripuarian Franks, and they accepted Christianity and founded the MEROVINGIAN dynasty. Their conquests eventually encompassed most of western and central Europe, including the kingdoms of Neustria, Austrasia, and Burgundy. In the 8th cent. the rule of the CAROLINGIAN dynasty was culminated by the reign of CHARLEMAGNE. In 870 the kingdom of the West Franks became France and that of the East Franks became Germany.

**Franz Joseph:** see FRANCIS JOSEPH.

**Fraser,** major river of British Columbia, Canada, flowing in a zigzag course c.1350 km (850 mi) from a source in the Rocky Mts near Yellowhead Pass, Alberta, to a fertile delta on the Strait of Georgia at Vancouver, British Columbia. The Fraser contains the chief spawning grounds in North America for the Pacific salmon. Early explorers were Sir Alexander MACKENZIE (1793) and the fur trader Simon Fraser (1808).

**Fraser, John Malcolm,** 1930–, prime minister of AUSTRALIA (1975–83). In 1955 he was elected to Parliament. In 1975 he became the leader of the opposition Liberal Party and prime minister after the fall of the Labour government of Gough WHITLAM. In office, Fraser followed a conservative policy, including cuts in government spending.

**Fraser, Peter,** 1884–1950, New Zealand political leader; b. Scotland. Emigrating (1910) to New Zealand, he became Labour Party leader and was prime minister (1940–49).

**fraternity and sorority,** in American colleges, student societies formed for social, literary, or religious purposes, with initiation by invitation and occasionally by a period of trial called hazing. Sororities are for women. Usually named with two or three Greek letters, fraternities and sororities are also known as Greek-letter societies. **Phi Beta Kappa,** the oldest of these societies, was founded (1776) at the College of William and Mary (Williamsburg, Virginia). Because of their entrance policies, which can be discriminatory, fraternities and sororities are forbidden on some campuses.

**fraud,** in law, wilful misrepresentation intended to deprive another of some right. Fraud may be actual (involving actual deceit) or constructive (involving abuse of a relationship of trust). The remedy granted the plaintiff in most cases of fraud is either damages for the loss incurred or cancellation of the fraudulent CONTRACT (or sometimes both).

**Frazer, Sir James George,** 1854–1941, British anthropologist. He is best known for *The Golden Bough* (1890), a comparative study in folklore, magic, and religion that showed parallel beliefs in primitive and Christian cultures. The monumental work had a great impact on early-20th-cent. thought. He also wrote *Totemism and Exogamy* (1910).

**Frederick,** rulers of the HOLY ROMAN EMPIRE. **Frederick I** or **Frederick Barbarossa,** c.1125–90, emperor (r.1155–90) and German king (r.1152–90), was of the HOHENSTAUFEN dynasty, but his mother was a GUELPH and Frederick was chosen emperor in the hope that he could end the discord between the GUELPHS AND GHIBELLINES. His coronation was delayed by unrest in Germany and by the revolutionary commune of Rome (1143–55). He restored peace, placated his Guelph cousin, HENRY THE LION, by restoring Bavaria to him, and was crowned in 1155. He failed in his efforts to restore imperial power in Italy; he was forced to recognize the LOMBARD LEAGUE, and Pope Alexander III, whom he had opposed, excommunicated him. In Germany, however, he succeeded in breaking the power of Henry the Lion in 1180–81. In 1189 he joined the Third CRUSADE and was drowned in Cilicia, in Turkey. His grandson **Frederick II,** 1194–1250, emperor (r.1220–50) and German king (r.1212–20), king of Sicily (r.1197–1250), and king of Jerusalem (r.1229–50), was one of the most arresting figures of the Middle Ages. He was a patron of art and science, and greatly expanded commerce. His intense struggle with the papacy led to the ruin of the house of Hohenstaufen. With his rule the great days of the German empire ended and the rise of states in Italy began. He was the son of Emperor HENRY VI and Constance, heiress of Sicily. Both died while he was an infant and the imperial crown passed him by, but he was made king of Sicily. After OTTO IV became emperor in 1209, he alienated Pope INNOCENT III by asserting imperial authority in Italy, and Innocent retaliated by crowning Frederick as German king (1212). Otto was deposed (1215) and, after long negotiations, Frederick was crowned emperor in 1220. His long-delayed crusade, when it finally took place (1228–29), turned out to be a state visit that culminated in Frederick's being crowned king of Jerusalem. The sporadic fighting between emperor and pope turned into a serious breach in 1239, and INNOCENT IV excommunicated (1245) Frederick and declared him deposed. Just as the war had turned in his favour, Frederick died of dysentery. **Frederick III,** 1415–93, emperor (r.1452–93) and German king (r.1440–93), was generally a weak ruler, but made considerable progress toward reuniting the HABSBURG family lands within his own branch. His greatest success was the acquisition of Burgundy through the marriage of his son, later Emperor MAXIMILIAN I, to MARY OF BURGUNDY, daughter of CHARLES THE BOLD. After 1490 Frederick relinquished most of his duties to Maximilian. He was the last emperor crowned at Rome.

**Frederick,** Danish kings. **Frederick III,** 1609–70, king of Denmark and Norway (1648–70), was the son of CHRISTIAN IV. After disastrous wars (1657–60) with CHARLES X of Sweden, the monarchy was made hereditary and the burghers strengthened at the expense of the nobles. Frederick's son, CHRISTIAN V, succeeded him. **Frederick IV,** 1671–1730, king of Denmark and Norway (1699–1730), was the son of Christian V. In the NORTHERN WAR he failed to recover S Sweden but obtained Schleswig and Lauenburg. His son, CHRISTIAN VI, succeeded him. **Frederick V,** 1723–66, king of Denmark and Norway (1746–66), was Christian VI's son. He encouraged commerce and industry, but the peasants' condition remained poor. His son, CHRISTIAN VII, succeeded him and was the father of **Frederick VI,** 1768–1839, king of Denmark (1808–39) and Norway (1808–14). In the FRENCH REVOLUTIONARY WARS England's attack on Denmark led him to ally himself with NAPOLEON I. At the Congress of Vienna (1814–15) he lost Norway to Sweden. His cousin CHRISTIAN VIII succeeded him. The son of Christian VIII, **Frederick VII,** 1808–63, was king of Denmark and duke of Schleswig, Holstein, and Lauenberg (1848–63). He accepted a constitution ending absolute monarchy. The SCHLESWIG-HOLSTEIN issue continued, leading to war with Prussia under his successor, CHRISTIAN IX. **Frederick VIII,** 1843–1912, king of Denmark (1906–12), was the son of Christian IX. He fought in the 1864 war with Prussia. His son CHRISTIAN X succeeded him. Another son became HAAKON VII of Norway. **Frederick IX,** 1899–1972, king of Denmark (1947–72), was the son of Christian X. Because he had no son, the Danish constitution was amended in 1953 to permit the succession of his daughter, Queen Margaret II.

**Frederick,** German kings: see FREDERICK, rulers of the Holy Roman Empire.

**Frederick II** or **Frederick the Great,** 1712–86, king of Prussia (r.1740–86), son and successor of FREDERICK WILLIAM I. He spent a miserable youth, ill-treated and despised by his father, and at one time was imprisoned for desertion. Once king, however, he displayed unexpected qualities of leadership and decision, becoming one of the great military generals of all time. His exploits in the War of the AUSTRIAN SUCCESSION (1740–48) and the SEVEN YEARS' WAR (1756–63) made Prussia the greatest military power in Europe. He was the prime mover in the first partition of POLAND (1772), which vastly increased his kingdom. He was less successful in the War of the BAVARIAN SUCCESSION (1778–79), in which he was thwarted by Emperor Joseph II. A 'benevolent despot', Frederick promoted important legal and social reforms. He was a great patron of the arts and surrounded himself with intellectuals. He had a marked taste for French culture and a stormy friendship with VOLTAIRE. He was a champion of religious liberty, and his philosophy was materialistic and sceptical. He wrote mediocre poetry and excellent prose (in French); and he composed passable music, especially for the flute, which he played well. He was childless and was succeeded by his nephew, FREDERICK WILLIAM II.

**Frederick Augustus I** and **II,** electors of Saxony: see AUGUSTUS II and AUGUSTUS III under AUGUSTUS, kings of Poland.

**Frederick Barbarossa:** see FREDERICK I under FREDERICK, rulers of the Holy Roman Empire.

**Frederick Henry,** 1584–1647, prince of Orange, son of WILLIAM THE SILENT. He succeeded (1625) his brother MAURICE OF NASSAU as stadtholder of the United Provinces. In 1635 he signed a pact with France and Sweden against the Habsburgs in the THIRTY YEARS' WAR. During his rule commerce, science, and art (see HALS; REMBRANDT) flourished, and his title was made hereditary in his family. His son, WILLIAM II, succeeded him.

**Frederick the Great:** see FREDERICK II, king of Prussia.

**Frederick the Winter King,** 1596–1632, king of Bohemia (r.1619–20, or during one winter; hence his sobriquet) and elector palatine (r.1610–20) as Frederick V. The Protestant diet (parliament) of Bohemia deposed the Catholic King Ferdinand (Holy Roman Emperor FERDINAND II) and named Frederick king, thus precipitating the THIRTY YEARS' WAR. When he did not receive the expected Protestant support, he was defeated (1620) at White Mountain and forced to give up all his lands. He was the father of Prince RUPERT and of the Electress SOPHIA, the forebear of the British ruling family, the Hanoverians.

**Frederick William,** kings of Prussia. **Frederick William I,** 1688–1740 (r.1713–40), created a strong, absolutist state, instituting administrative reforms and rigid economy. He also built up the Prussian army, but except for a brief intervention in the Northern War (1700–21) he observed peace. He was a coarse man who had contempt for his gifted son, who succeeded him as FREDERICK II (Frederick the Great). **Frederick William II,** 1744–97 (r.1786–97), was the nephew and successor of Frederick II (the Great). He was defeated in the FRENCH REVOLUTIONARY WARS and signed a separate peace (1795) with the French. He participated in the second and third partition of POLAND (1793, 1795). He was a patron of MOZART. His son, **Frederick William III,** 1770–1840 (r.1797–1840), suffered crushing defeat by the French, and the Treaty of Tilsit (1807) made Prussia virtually a French vassal. Though he was weak and vacillating, he surrounded himself with able administrators who made valuable reforms. He grew increasingly reactionary in his old age. **Frederick William IV,** 1795–1861 (r.1840–61), was the son and successor of Frederick William III. A romanticist, mystic, and halfhearted liberal, he nonetheless crushed the REVOLUTIONS OF 1848 and refused the imperial crown because it was offered by a popularly elected body, the FRANKFURT PARLIAMENT. In 1857 his mental imbalance necessitated the regency of his brother and successor, William I.

**Frederick William,** known as the **Great Elector,** 1620–88, elector of Brandenburg (r.1640–88). He rebuilt his devastated state after the THIRTY YEARS' WAR and added greatly to his domains. He secured East Pomerania and other territories in 1648, and secured full sovereignty over East Prussia in 1660. He was succeeded by his son Frederick who in 1701 crowned himself 'king in Prussia' and styled himself Frederick I.

**freedom of the press,** liberty to publish information and opinions without official restraint. Freedom of the press is one of the most important CIVIL RIGHTS in a liberal DEMOCRACY and is a precondition for a well-informed and independent electorate. The concept of a free press is usually extended to include editorial independence, and the availability of a variety of publications expressing different viewpoints. Hence a narrowing of the range of newspapers or the concentration of titles in the hands of a few owners is regarded as a cause for concern. Otherwise, press freedom is about CENSORSHIP. John MILTON's *Aeropagitica* (1644) is the most famous statement of the arguments for freedom of publication.

In England the abandonment of official censorship before publication was achieved in 1695 (but see D-NOTICE); in the US it was secured by the 1st Amendment to the Constitution. After publication the publisher, who is legally liable for what is printed, may of course be sued for libel or any other infringement of the laws, such as those involving SEDITION or national security. Restrictions on the freedom of the press occur in wartime to protect military information and national morale. In one-party and totalitarian states (see TOTALITARIANISM), where there is no offical opposition, the press is a vehicle for PROPAGANDA, but there is usually circulation of independent critical views by means of an 'underground' free press.

**free fall,** in physics, the state of a body moving solely under the influence of gravitational forces (see GRAVITATION). A body falling freely toward the surface of the earth undergoes an acceleration (see MOTION) equal to 9.8 m/sec² (32 ft/sec²).

**Freeman, Edward Augustus,** 1823–92, English historian. An authority on medieval history and a staunch liberal, he was regius professor of modern history at Oxford (1884–92). He insisted on the unity of history and the need to base conclusions on a study of sources, but he was capable of error. His major work was a *History of the Norman Conquest* (6 vol., 1867–79).

**Freemasonry,** teachings and practices of the secret fraternal (males only) order known as the Free and Accepted Masons. There are 6 million members worldwide, mostly in the US and other English-speaking countries, and no central authority. Its ideals include fellowship, religious toleration, and political compromise. Drawing on guild practices of medieval stone-masons, the order's first Grand Lodge was organized in London (1717). In America, Masons were active in the Revolution and continued as a force in later politics. In Europe, they included VOLTAIRE, GOETHE, HAYDN, MAZZINI, and GARIBALDI. Freemasonry's identification with 19th-cent. bourgeois liberalism led to a reaction, e.g., in the US, the ANTI-MASONIC PARTY; its anticlericalism brought the hostility of the Roman Catholic Church. Totalitarian states have always suppressed Freemasonry. Masons have a complex systems of rites and degrees, subsidiary organizations for women and children, and lodges noted for their parades and fraternal gatherings.

**freesia:** see IRIS.

**free silver,** in US history, term designating the political movement for the free coinage of silver. Free silver emerged as an issue after the Panic of 1873 and the hard times that followed. Opponents of the deflationary fiscal policy of post-Civil War Republican administrations, having failed to secure currency expansion by means of GREENBACKS, turned instead to the unlimited coinage of silver; silver-mining interests supported the demand. In response to the agitation Congress passed the Bland–Allison Act (1878), which provided for limited quantities of silver bullion to be coined into silver dollars, but this failed either to increase the money supply or to halt the decline in the market price of silver (due to greater production). The return of economic depression in the late 1880s revived the free silver agitation, especially by debt-ridden Southern and Western farmers who saw inflation as the panacea for collapsing farm prices. Congress responded to the political pressure with the SHERMAN SILVER PURCHASE ACT, (1890), which required a doubling of government purchases of silver. But half-measures such as this failed to satisfy silver advocates, many of whom turned to the POPULIST PARTY, whose platform included free silver. The silver forces were enraged when, following the Panic of 1893, the CLEVELAND adminstration forced the repeal of the Sherman Silver Purchase Act, and in 1896 free silver became the chief issue in the presidential campaign when the Democratic candidate William Jennings BRYAN made it the main plank of his platform. McKinley's victories over Bryan in 1896 and 1900, coupled with returning prosperity and an expansion in the money supply consequent upon rising world gold production, thereafter virtually killed free silver as a political issue.

**Free-Soil Party,** US political party born in 1847–48 to oppose the extension of SLAVERY into territories newly gained from Mexico. In 1848 the Free-Soil Party ran Martin VAN BUREN and C.F. Adams (see ADAMS, family) for president and vice president; by polling 300,000 votes it gave New York state to the Whigs and thus made Zachary TAYLOR president. After the COMPROMISE OF 1850 seemed to settle the slavery-extension issue, the group known as the BARNBURNERS left the Free-Soilers to return to the Democratic party, but radicals kept the Free-Soil party alive until 1854, when the new REPUBLICAN PARTY absorbed it.

**Freetown,** city (1985 pop. 469,776), capital of Sierra Leone, W Sierra Leone, on the Atlantic coast. It is the nation's largest city and chief port, exporting such goods as ginger, diamonds, and gold. Industries include ship repair, oil refining, and the manufacture of cement and plastics. A major road link to MONROVIA, in Liberia, was constructed in the early 1980s. Freetown was founded in 1788 as a settlement for freed African slaves. It achieved municipal status in 1893.

**free trade:** see TRADE.

**free verse,** loose term for verse free of conventional limitations and metrical restrictions. Cadence, particularly of common speech, is often substituted. The term comes from the *vers libre* of Jules Laforgue, Arthur RIMBAUD, and others who rejected the classical ALEXANDRINE. The term has been applied to the King James translation of the Bible, and is associated with Walt WHITMAN, Ezra POUND, T.S. ELIOT, and other modern poets.

**free will,** in philosophy, the doctrine that the will of an individual can and does determine some of his acts. PLATO held that actions are determined by the extent of a person's understanding. Christian ethics have long disputed the extent of human dependence on the power of God: St AUGUSTINE, LUTHER, and CALVIN followed the doctrine of predestination or divine grace, while St THOMAS AQUINAS held that God's omnipotence does not include the predetermination of human will. Later advocates of free will have referred to common practice: individuals believe they determine their actions and hold one another accountable for doing so. Modern psychology has introduced the concept of the UNCONSCIOUS as a motivating force.

**freezing:** see STATES OF MATTER.

**Frege, Gottlob,** 1848–1925, German philosopher and mathematician. Frege was one of the founders of modern symbolic logic (see LOGIC) and a major influence on Bertrand RUSSELL and Russell's student WITTGENSTEIN. He aimed to demonstrate that mathematics is derived solely from deductive logic and is not synthetic, as Kant had posited. He also believed that verbal conceptualizations can be translated into logical form. After Russell and others had pointed out some serious contradictions in vol. 2 of his major work, *The Basic Laws of Arithmetic* (1893–1903), Frege virtually ceased to produce original work. Nevertheless, his contributions to the development of modern mathematical theory and the theory of meaning are of prime importance.

**Freiburg im Breisgau** (͵friebawg), city (1984 pop. 179,400), Baden-Württemberg, West Germany, on the edge of the BLACK FOREST. It is a market, university, and ecclesiastical centre. Freiburg, like other towns in the region, was laid out to a plan in the early 12th cent. by the dukes of Zähringen. The university was founded in 1457. Its historic buildings include a magnificent 13th-cent. Gothic cathedral.

**Frei Montalva, Eduardo** ('frayeemon͵talvə), 1911–82, president of CHILE (1964–70). The first Christian Democratic president of Latin America, he pursued a wide-ranging programme of reform, especially on the land, in education, and in housing. But, with a party increasingly divided and without control of the Chilean senate, his government lost popularity and failed to win the presidential election of 1970. He himself, however, stands as an outstanding statesman of modern Latin America.

**Fremantle,** city (1986 pop. 11,798), Western Australia. At the mouth of the Swan R., this is the main port for the city of PERTH, with shipping and heavy industry based here. The 1987 AMERICA'S CUP challenge was held here, hosted by the Royal Perth Yacht Club.

**Frémont, John Charles,** 1813–90, American explorer, soldier, and political leader. His enthusiastic reports of his Western explorations (1841–44) created wide interest in that region. He was a leader (1846) in the revolt of California against Mexico until he quarrelled with S.W. KEARNY in Kearny's contest for command with Robert Stockton. Frémont was US senator from California (1850–51) and Republican candidate for president in 1856. He commanded the Western Department in the AMERICAN CIVIL WAR but was removed because his action in freeing the slaves of rebels conflicted with LINCOLN's policy. The Pathfinder, as he was called, is one of the most controversial figures of Western history.

**French, Daniel Chester,** 1850–1931, American sculptor. After executing his first large work, *The Minute Man* (1875; Concord, Massachusetts), he received many commissions for public statues. His most famous achievement is the heroic figure of Abraham Lincoln (1922) in the LINCOLN MEMORIAL (Washington, DC).

**French and Indian Wars,** 1689–1763, a series of colonial campaigns in North America between England and France, corresponding to wars between European alliances in the worldwide struggle for empire. In America, coastal strongholds and western forts were seized, and the settlers suffered the horrors of Indian border warfare. *King William's War* (1688–97), linked to the War of the GRAND ALLIANCE, consisted chiefly of frontier attacks on the British colonies. *Queen Anne's War* (1702–13) corresponded to the War of the SPANISH SUCCESSION, and *King George's War* (1744–48) to the War of the AUSTRIAN SUCCESSION. The last and most important conflict, called simply the *French and Indian War* (1754–63), was linked to the SEVEN YEARS WAR. Jeffrey Amherst took Louisburg (1758), and Quebec and Montreal also fell (1759–60) to the British. The war ended French control in Canada and the West (see PARIS, TREATY OF). After the wars the American colonies felt less dependent militarily on the British; they began to concentrate on their own problems and institutions, and to think of themselves as American rather than British.

**French Community,** established in 1958 to replace the French Union. Its purpose was to create a political federation into which France and all its overseas departments and territories (colonies) could fit. However, since all of France's African colonies chose total independence, the French Community never achieved its aims. After 1962 it operated primarily as a vehicle for fostering military, economic, technical and cultural cooperation among its members (France and its overseas departments and territories, plus the Central African Republic, Chad, Gabon and Senegal). More recently, French Community countries have participated in broader cooperation between French-speaking countries, notably within the framework of regular Franco-African Conferences and of the FRANCOPHONE CONFERENCE.

**French East India Company:** see EAST INDIA COMPANY, FRENCH.

**French Equatorial Africa,** former French federation of territories in W central Africa (1910–58), comprising what are now GABON, CHAD, the CENTRAL AFRICAN REPUBLIC, and the People's Republic of the CONGO. It was dissolved (1958) when the members became constituent republics within the FRENCH COMMUNITY.

**French Guiana,** Fr. *La Guyane française,* French overseas department (1982 pop. 73,022), 91,000 km² (35,135 sq mi), NE South America, bordered by the Atlantic Ocean (N), Surinam (E), and Brazil (S and E). CAYENNE is the capital. The population, largely Creole, is concentrated along the coast. The economy rests on the export of timber, shrimp, and rum; there are deposits of gold and bauxite. A rocket-launching base for communications satellites is located at Kourou, on the coast. French settlement dates from 1604; following periods of Dutch and British rule, French authority was restored in 1815. Guiana was made an overseas department in 1947. French Guiana was used as a penal colony during the French Revolution, and permanent penal camps were established under Napoleon III; DEVIL'S ISLAND, off the coast, was especially notorious. Agitation in favour of independence developed in the late 1970s, but pro-French parties have dominated in recent elections.

**French horn,** a BRASS INSTRUMENT with a funnel-shaped mouthpiece, a conical bore, and a wide bell. The modern horn has three valves which alter the length of the tubing and allow a full range of notes to be played. Before the valves were invented, horn players used different crooks to enable them to play in different keys. The modern French horn is in F and has a range of over three octaves upwards from the B♭ below the base stave. The horn has been a member of the orchestra since the 18th cent., but its solo and chamber repertoire are limited.

**French language,** member of the Romance group of the Italic subfamily of the Indo-European family of languages. See LANGUAGE (table).

**French Polynesia,** overseas territory of France (1977 pop. 137,382), 105 islands in the South Pacific. The capital is Papeete, on TAHITI. It comprises the Society Islands; Marquesas Islands; Austral Islands; Tuamotu Islands; and Gambier Islands. Tropical fruits are grown, vanilla and copra exported. Under a new 1984 statute the territory has a president and cabinet drawn from an elected assembly, but the French high commissioner retains supreme executive authority. Pro-independence factions are active but pro-French status parties predominate.

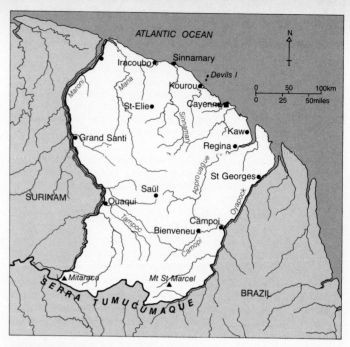

French Guiana

**French Revolution,** political upheaval that began in France in 1789 and eventually affected the whole world. Historians differ widely as to its causes. Some see it as an intellectual movement, born from the liberal ENLIGHTENMENT of the 18th cent.; some, as a rebellion of the underprivileged classes against feudal oppression; others, as the assertion of the new capitalist bourgeoisie against an outdated and restricted social and economic system—in the fixed order of the *ancien régime,* France was still ruled by two privileged classes, the nobility and the clergy, who refused to give up many of their privileges. The immediate cause of the revolution was without doubt the bankrupt state of the public treasury. The wars of the 17th and 18th cent., an iniquitous and inefficient system of taxation, intervention in the AMERICAN REVOLUTION, and waste had resulted in a gigantic public debt, which neither NECKER, nor CALONNE, nor Loménie de Brienne was able to reduce. As a last resort, LOUIS XVI called the STATES-GENERAL, which, it was hoped, would pass the necessary fiscal reforms. It convened at VERSAILLES on 5 May 1789, for the first time since 1614. From the start, the deputies of the third estate—the commons —joined by many members of the lower clergy and by a few nobles, pressed for sweeping political and social reforms that far exceeded the assembly's powers. Defying the king, they proclaimed themselves the National Assembly (17 June ), and, on an indoor tennis court, took an oath not to separate until a constitution had been drawn up. The king yielded and legalized the Assembly, but his dismissal of Necker led to the storming of the BASTILLE by an excited Paris mob (14 July). Louis XVI, ever anxious to avoid bloodshed, gave in once more; Necker was recalled; the commune was established as the city government of Paris; and the National Guard was organized. On 4 Aug. 1789, the Assembly abolished all feudal privileges. Meanwhile, rumours of counterrevolutionary court intrigues were exploited by extremist demagogues, and on 5 Oct. a mob marched to Versailles and forcibly moved the royal family and the Assembly to Paris. There the Assembly drafted a constitution (1791) that created a limited monarchy with a unicameral legislature (the Legislative Assembly) elected by voters who had the requisite property qualifications; the preamble was the famous DECLARATION OF THE RIGHTS OF MAN AND CITIZEN. Earlier, anticlerical legislation had been capped when the clergy was required to take oaths to civil authority (1790), a measure that alienated many pious rural districts from the Revolution. The king decided to join those nobles who had already fled abroad (*émigrés*), but his flight (20–21 June 1791) was arrested at Varennes. Brought back in humiliation to Paris, Louis accepted the new constitution. In the Legislative Assembly, the republican GIRONDISTS and the extreme JACOBINS and CORDELIERS gained the upper hand. 'Liberty, Equality, Fraternity' became a catch phrase. Elsewhere, the *émigrés* were inciting other European courts to intervene. The Declaration of Pillnitz played into the hands of the Girondists, who hoped that a foreign war would rally the nation to the republican cause. With the declaration of war on Austria (20 April 1792), the FRENCH REVOLUTIONARY WARS began. Early reverses and rumours of treason by the king and Queen MARIE ANTOINETTE brought the lower classes, especially those in Paris, into action. In Aug. 1792 a mob stormed the TUILERIES palace and an insurrectionary commune replaced the legally elected one (see COMMUNE OF PARIS); all police power was seized by the Paris commune (dominated by DANTON and MARAT); the Assembly suspended the king and ordered elections for a National Convention to draw up yet another constitution; and hundreds of royal prisoners were killed by 'spontaneous' mobs in the September massacres (2–7 Sept. 1792). On 21 Sept. the Convention abolished the monarchy, set up the First Republic, and proceeded to try the king for treason. Louis's conviction and execution (Jan. 1793) led to royalist uprisings, notably in the Vendée, and was followed by the REIGN OF TERROR, in which ROBESPIERRE and his associates triumphed in turn over the more moderate Girondists and over his rivals DANTON and J.R. HÉBERT. The republican constitution never became active; the Committee of Public Safety and the Revolutionary Tribunal reigned supreme. Robespierre's final excesses frightened the Convention into the *coup d'etat* of 9 Thermidor (27 July 1794), which resulted in his execution and a period of relative reaction. Under the new constitution of 1795, the DIRECTORY came into existence. Its rule was marked by corruption, intrigues, runaway inflation, bankruptcy, and a fatal dependence on the army; it was ended by Napoleon Bonaparte's *coup d'etat* of 18 Brumaire (see NAPOLEON I). With the establishment of the Consulate (followed in 1804 by Napoleon's empire), the victory of the bourgeoisie became final. With the French Revolutionary Wars and the Napoleonic Wars, the French Revolution tore down the medieval structures of Europe, opened the paths of 19th-cent. liberalism, and hastened the advent of nationalism. See also FRENCH REVOLUTIONARY CALENDAR.

**French Revolutionary calendar,** the official CALENDAR of France, 24 Nov. 1793–31 Dec. 1805. Supposedly philosophical in its basis, it was divided into 12 months of 30 days: Vendémiaire (vintage month); Brumaire (fog); Frimaire (sleet); Nivôse (snow); Pluviôse (rain); Ventôse (wind); Germinal (seed); Floréal (blossom); Prairial (pasture); Messidor (harvest); Thermidor or Fervidor (heat); Fructidor (fruit). The remaining five days, called *sans-culottides,* were feast days named for Virtue, Genius, Labour, Reason, and Rewards, respectively. In leap years the extra day, the last of the year, was Revolution Day. There was no week; the months were divided into three decades, with every 10th day *(décadi)* a day of rest.

**French Revolutionary Wars,** 1792–1802, general and prolonged European war precipitated by the FRENCH REVOLUTION, which had aroused in foreign lands the hostility of monarchs, nobles, and clergy, all of whom feared the spread of republican ideas. Some of them looked upon war as the only way to restore LOUIS XVI (still nominally king of France) to his full powers. For their part, some revolutionaries in France looked upon war as a way of making their revolution stronger. In Aug. 1791 Austria and Prussia called for the restoration of Louis, but it was France that declared war on Austria on 20 Apr. 1792. Meeting little resistance at first, Austrian armies invaded France, but the cannonade at Valmy (20 Sept.) marked the limit of their advance and proved a turning point. The French overran the Austrian Netherlands, invaded Germany, and seized Savoy and Nice from Sardinia. Louis XVI was executed (21 Jan. 1793), an act that led to the formation of the First Coalition (Austria, Prussia, Great Britain, Holland, Spain). The French, led by Lazare CARNOT, raised new armies and by the end of 1793 had driven the allies from France. Holland, Prussia, and Spain all made peace in 1795. NAPOLEON Bonaparte contributed stunning French victories in Italy, and by 1797 only Britain remained in the war. Bonaparte's strike against Britain in Egypt was disastrous, however, and the English destroyed (1798) the French fleet at Aboukir. In 1798 a Second Coalition was formed, equally unsuccessful, consisting of Britain, Russia, Austria, Turkey, Portugal, and Naples. The French victory over the Russians at Zürich took Russia out of the war, and after Napoleon Bonaparte, back in France, declared himself First Consul (Nov. 1799), he inflicted a heavy defeat on the Austrians at Marengo (1800), and the Second Coalition collapsed (1801) when Austria consented to the Peace of Lunéville. Once more, only the British persevered, but they too signed the Treaty of AMIENS (1802) which brought the war to an end, if only temporarily, for further coalitions were to be formed against NAPOLEON I. By 1802 the French Revolutionary Wars had transformed the political landscape of Europe. With their victories the French had created a whole series of new political entities: the BATAVIAN Republic (Holland), the Helvetic Republic (Switzerland), the Parthenopian Republic (Naples), the CISALPINE Republic (various Italian states), and the Roman Republic (the Papal States).

**French Southern and Antarctic Lands,** Terres Australes et Antarctiques Françaises, overseas territory of France, including Terre Adélie, which covers 520,000 km² (c.200,000 sq mi) in ANTARCTICA, and a number of islands in the S Indian Ocean. The largest of these is Kerguelen (3414 km²/1318 sq mi). One of 300 islands in the Îles Kerguelen archipelago, it is a base for research, and formerly for sealing and whaling. The Îles Crozet, to the west, and Îles Saint Paul et Amsterdam, to the northeast, are also part of the territory; each group has a research station.

**French West Africa,** former federation of French territories in W Africa (1895–1959) that comprised Dahomey (now Benin), French Guinea (Guinea), French Sudan (Mali), Côte d'Ivoire, Mauritania, Niger, Senegal, and Upper Volta (now Burkina Faso). It was dissolved in 1959 as the territories moved towards independence.

**Freneau, Philip,** 1752–1832, American writer. America's first professional journalist, he was a propagandist for the AMERICAN REVOLUTION and Jeffersonian democracy. His fame rests on such lyrical poems as 'The Wild Honeysuckle', 'The Indian Burial Ground', and 'Eutaw Springs'. His poem *The British Prison Ship* (1781) recorded his captivity on a British brig.

**Freon,** trade name for any of a special class of chemical compounds used as refrigerants, aerosol propellants, and solvents. Freons are HYDROCARBON derivatives that contain FLUORINE and often chlorine and bromine as well. They are generally colourless, odourless, nontoxic, noncorrosive, and nonflammable. Though usually unreactive, freons are now suspected to undergo reactions in the upper atmosphere that may damage the earth's OZONE layer. The most commonly used is Freon-12, or dichlorodifluoromethane ($CCl_2F_2$).

**frequency,** the number of times that a periodic process, such as a vibration, is repeated in unit time. It is usually measured in HERTZ (Hz); 1 Hz is 1 repetition per second. See HARMONIC MOTION; WAVE.

**frequency modulation:** see MODULATION.

**fresco,** painting on plaster. Pure fresco is painted on damp, fresh lime plaster. The binder is in the lime, which, in drying, forms a calcium carbonate that incorporates the pigment with the material of the wall. Fresco is unsuitable for a large range of colours or delicate transitional tones, unlike painting in oil, but its clear, luminous colour and permanence make it ideal for murals. An ancient technique, fresco was probably employed in the Minoan palace at KNOSSOS and used by the Romans for decoration, notably at POMPEII. The great period of fresco began in the 14th cent. with GIOTTO, and in this era the design was drawn in charcoal on the plaster. The technique was brought to perfection by the great masters of the Italian RENAISSANCE, who, by the mid 15th cent. customarily prepared a CARTOON and transferred the design to wet plaster. For large frescoes, the plaster was applied to small sections daily, each painted in a day. Fresco was revived in 20th-cent. Mexico with the work of José Clemente OROZCO, Diego RIVERA, and other artists.

**Frescobaldi, Girolamo,** 1583–1643, Italian composer. He became organist at St Peter's Church, Rome, in 1608, and at the Medici Court, Florence (1628–34). His style travelled to Germany and influenced organists through to J.S. BACH. He wrote many ORGAN works and some instrumental and vocal music.

**Fresnel, Augustin Jean** (fray‚nel), 1788–1827, French physicist and engineer. His investigations of light, especially interference phenomena in POLARIZED LIGHT and double refraction, supported the wave theory of light and the concept of transverse vibrations in light waves. He also devised a way of producing circularly polarized light.

**Fresno,** US city (1984 est. pop. 267,000), south-central California; founded 1872, inc. 1885. It is the financial centre of the San Joaquin Valley. Grapes, figs, cotton, and vegetables are grown in the area, and Fresno co. leads all US counties in the value of agricultural products sold. The city is also a railway, marketing, and processing centre.

**Freud, Sigmund,** 1856–1939, Austrian-Jewish founder of the theory and practice of PSYCHOANALYSIS. Freud trained in Vienna as a physician, his early work in neuroanatomy and physiology being well received. Later he studied in Paris with BRENTANO and Jean-Martin Charcot (1825–1923), returning as a firm supporter of the latter's therapeutic use of HYPNOSIS in the treatment of HYSTERIA. Freud's collaborative investigations of the treatment of hysteria, with BREUER, led to his abandonment of hypnosis and adoption of the therapeutic technique of 'free association', which became the cornerstone of clinical psychoanalytic practice. At the same time, Freud began to elaborate the theory of DEFENCE MECHANISMS, resistance and repression which formed the basis for psychoanalytic theory. During his subsequent association with Wilhelm Fliess (1858–1928), Freud attempted to develop a neurologically-based theory of NEUROSIS; an attempt which he then abandoned, along with his early belief that neuroses were the consequence of early sexual relations between children and adults (the 'seduction theory'). From the publication of *The Interpretation of Dreams* (1900), Freud's work was directed exclusively to the understanding of the psychological (psychoanalytic) processes underlying both normal and PSYCHOPATHOLOGICAL development, and of the role of sexuality in the unconscious. His collected psychoanalytic works were published in English (24 vol.) in 1953-74. Psychoanalysis, despite much criticism, attracted a considerable following. The International Psychoanalytic Association was founded in 1910, but was riven by internal disagreements at an early stage, principally over the issue of the primacy of sexuality in mental life and disorder. In 1938, with the Nazi occupation of Austria, Freud emigrated to England with his daughter **Anna Freud,** 1895–1982, a pioneer in child psychoanalysis, and a major proponent of the variant of psychoanalytic theory known as 'ego psychology'. Her collected works (7 vol.) were published in English (1973).

**Freyja, Freya** (ˌfrayah), Norse goddess of love, marriage and fertility. She was also a deity of the dead and was the sister of the god Frey.

**Freyre, Gilbert** (ˌfrayray), 1900–87, Brazilian historian. Freyre studied in the US, the UK, France, and Germany. His Columbia Univ. dissertation was converted into his great masterpiece *Casa-grande e Senzala* (1934), an exploration of Brazilian identity. This was only one of a large number of impressively imaginative studies of Brazilian social and cultural development, based on every kind of evidence, including buildings and artifacts. He was founding professor of social anthropology at the Univ. of Brazil (1934) and a member of parliament (1946–50). He published one novel, *Mother and Son* (1964).

**Fricker, Peter Racine,** 1920–, British composer, teacher, and director of Morley College (1953–64), until he moved to the Univ. of California, Santa Barbara. Influenced by BARTÓK and HINDEMITH, his music is rigorously polyphonic and often serial in technique. He has written five symphonies and many chamber works.

**friction,** resistance offered to the movement of one body past another body with which it is in contact. The amount of friction depends on the nature of the contact surfaces and on the magnitude of the force pressing the two bodies together, but not on the surface area of the contact surface. The coefficient of friction is the ratio of the force necessary to move one body horizontally over another at a constant speed, to the weight of the body. Fluid friction, observed in the flow of liquids and gases, is minimized in aeroplanes by a modern, streamlined design (see AERODYNAMICS).

**Friday:** see WEEK.

**Friedan, Betty Naomi,** 1921–, American social reformer and feminist. In 1963 she galvanized the contemporary women's movement by publishing *The Feminine Mystique,* an attack on the traditional notion that women find fulfilment only through childbearing and homemaking. Founder of the NATIONAL ORGANIZATION FOR WOMEN (1966), she also helped organize the National Women's Political Caucus (1970) and campaigned vigorously against sexual discrimination. In *The Second Stage* (1981) she revised her earlier critique, arguing for the reform of the family and criticizing the radical demands of the women's movement.

**Friedman, Milton,** 1912–, American economist and a leading spokesman for the monetarist school of economics. A staunch conservative and opponent of the beliefs of J.M. KEYNES, Friedman developed the theory that changes in monetary supply precede, rather than follow, changes in overall economic activity. A professor at the Univ.

of Chicago (1946–77), he received the 1976 Nobel Prize for economics. His writings include *Capitalism and Freedom* (1962) and *Monetary Trends of the United States and the United Kingdom* (1981). See ECONOMICS.

**Friedrich, Caspar David,** 1774–1840, German romantic landscape painter. His mystical, pantheistic attitude toward nature is best seen in *Capuchin Friar by the Sea* and *Man and Woman Gazing at the Moon* (both: Berlin).

**Friel, Brian,** 1929–, Irish playwright. He has gained prominence both at home and abroad for his ability to explore and expound 'the Irish situation' through the medium of theatre. His work includes *Philadelphia Here I Come* (1964), written after observing five months of Tyrone GUTHRIE at work; *Lovers* (1967); *Faith Healer* (1979); *The Communication Cord* (1982); and his most acclaimed piece, *Translations* (1980). Together with the actor Stephen Rea, Friel founded Field Day, a theatre company which premieres its work in Derry, the town in which Friel was born.

**friendly societies,** voluntary mutual-aid organizations to give members financial protection in the event of illness, old age, or death. Established in Britain in the 17th cent., they were the forerunners of other organizations including BUILDING SOCIETIES, life-assurance companies, and TRADE UNIONS. Their activities are free of tax and they offer tax-efficient savings endowment policies which are strictly controlled.

**Friends, Religious Society of,** religious body originating in England in the 17th cent. under George FOX. He believed that a person needed no spiritual intermediary, but could find understanding and guidance through 'inward light'', supplied by the Holy Spirit. Commonly called Quakers, members refused to participate in Church of England services, take oaths, or bear arms, and were often subject to persecution. They spread to Asia and Africa, and to America, where they found refuge in Rhode Island and in a famous colony established (1682) in Pennsylvania by William PENN. Almost alone among Christian denominations the Friends have no ordained ministry or outward observance of sacraments. Their meetings are periods of silent meditation, in which those urged by the spirit can offer prayer or exhortation. Friends are active in education and social welfare and believe in complete equality.

**Friends of the Earth,** worldwide network of independent groups campaigning for environmental protection and conservation, and for greater ecological awareness by people and governments. First established in the US in the 1960s, Friends of the Earth later spread to many other countries, including the UK (1971); such groups are a major component of the anti-nuclear movement.

**Frigg** or **Frigga,** Norse mother goddess and the wife of WODEN. Of great importance in GERMANIC RELIGION, she was queen of the heavens, a deity of love and the household.

**frilled lizard:** see AGAMA.

**Frisch, Karl von,** 1886–1982, Austrian zoologist. For his pioneering work in comparative behaviourial psychology, particularly his studies of the complex communication between insects, he shared the 1973 Nobel Prize in physiology or medicine with Konrad LORENZ and Nikolaas TINBERGEN. An important implication of his work is that behavioural continuity exists between animal communication and human language.

**Frisch, Max,** 1911–, Swiss novelist and dramatist. Originally an architect, Frisch made his early reputation on his political allegories *Biedermann und die Brandstifter (1953; tr. The Firebugs) and Andorra* (1961). His main novels *I'm not Stiller* (1958), *Homo Faber* (1957), *Mein Name sei Gantenbein* (1965; tr. A Wilderness of Mirrors), and *Man in the Holocene* (1980) share the theme of the search for the self in a wilderness of masks, roles and fictions, developed with virtuoso formal inventiveness. A strong tendency to 'compose' his own voice can be seen in his *Sketchbooks 1946–49* and *1966–71* (tr. 1977 and 1974), his drama *Biography* (1968), and the confessional novel *Montauk* (1975).

**Frisch, Otto Robert,** 1904–74, English physicist; b. Austria. He described the fission of uranium under neutron bombardment, in collaboration with his aunt, Lise Meitner. After leaving Germany in 1933, he worked in Cambridge and Copenhagen. With Rudolf PEIERLS, during World War II, he was the first to calculate the critical mass of a uranium bomb, and was thus instrumental in alerting the British

Government of the need to undertake uranium research. From 1947 to 1971 he was Jacksonian professor of natural philosophy, Cambridge Univ.

**Frisch, Ragnar,** 1895–1973, Norwegian economist who, with Jan TINBERGEN, won the first Nobel Prize for economics (1969) for pioneering work in the development of ECONOMETRICS, done while he was a professor at the Univ. of Oslo (1931–65).

**Frisian language,** member of the West Germanic group of the Germanic subfamily of the Indo-European family of languages. See LANGUAGE (table).

**Frobisher, Sir Martin,** 1535?–1594, English mariner. He was licensed by ELIZABETH I for three expeditions to search for the NORTHWEST PASSAGE (1576, 1577, 1578). He reached Frobisher Bay and S BAFFIN ISLAND but erroneously believed that he had found Cathay. He commanded a ship in Sir Francis DRAKE's WEST INDIES expedition (1585) and was knighted for his services in the defeat of the Spanish ARMADA (1588).

**Fröding, Gustaf** (ˌfrøːding), 1860–1911, Swedish lyric poet. His popular volumes of poems, *Guitar and Concertina* (1891), *New Poems* (1894), and *Drops and Fragments* (1896), include songs, meditations, and poems in praise of nature.

**Froebel, Friedrich Wilhelm August** (ˌfrøːbəl, froh-), 1782–1852, German educator and founder of the KINDERGARTEN system. Having little formal schooling himself, he stressed pleasant surroundings, self-activity, and physical training for children. Influenced by SCHELLING, he also insisted upon spiritual training as a fundamental principle. He founded (1816) the Universal German Educational Institute to train teachers, and opened the first kindergarten in 1837. The most important of his several books on education is *The Education of Man* (1826).

**frog,** tailless, freshwater AMPHIBIAN (order Anura) found worldwide. Some frogs are highly aquatic; others, like the related TOADS, are more terrestrial. Frogs have bulging eyes, short, neckless bodies, long, muscular hind legs for jumping, webbed feet for swimming, and smooth skin, usually green or brown. They capture insects and other food with a sticky, extendable tongue. Most frogs lay eggs in early spring which hatch into TADPOLES, and by the end of summer METAMORPHOSIS to a four-legged adult is complete. The so-called true frog belongs to the Ranidae family, which includes the bullfrog (*Rana catesbeiana*), the common frog (*R. temporia*), the edible frog (*R. esculenta*), and the widespread marsh frog (*R. ridibunda*). The group includes the TREE FROGS.

**Froissart, Jean** (frəwahˌsəh), c.1337–1410?, French poet, courtier and chronicler of chivalry. He travelled widely and knew many important people. His famous chronicle covers the history of Western Europe from 1327 to 1400 during the first half of the HUNDRED YEARS WAR. In it he describes events with brilliance and gusto: he also wrote of courtly love.

**Fromm, Erich,** 1900–80, American psychoanalyst and social theorist; b. Germany. He was a major influence on the part of the Frankfurt School's research programme which concerned the synthesis of Marxism and PSYCHOANALYSIS. Fromm's work in what he termed 'analytic social psychology' became increasingly sociological in emphasis, and has sometimes been classed with that of Karen HORNEY as 'neo-Freudian'. Despite later disagreements between Fromm and his former Frankfurt School colleagues, his work drew on the same tradition of 'Left Freudianism' as that of Adorno, MARCUSE, and REICH. His books include *Escape from Freedom* (1941) and *The Crisis of Psychoanalysis* (1970).

**Fronde** (frawnhd), 1648–53, series of outbreaks in France during the minority of LOUIS XIV. They were caused by the efforts of the Parlement of Paris (the chief judicial body) to limit royal authority (as championed by Cardinal MAZARIN), by the ambitions of discontented nobles, and by the excessive fiscal burden on the people. The **Fronde of the Parlement,** 1648–49, began with Parlement's refusal to register a fiscal edict that would have required the magistrates of high courts to give up four years' salary. Parlement then drew up a reform document limiting royal authority. The royal court secretly fled Paris, and government forces under Louis II, prince de CONDÉ, blockaded the city until a compromise peace between Parlement and the monarchy was arranged. The arrest of the overbearing Condé by the order of Mazarin, his former ally, precipitated the much more serious **Fronde of the Princes,** 1650–53. Although Condé was released and Mazarin fled into exile (1651), Condé, with the support of several powerful nobles and the provincial parlements of S France, waged open warfare on the government and even concluded

an alliance with Spain, then at war with France. Defeated at Faubourg Saint-Antoine (1652), Condé was given shelter in Paris. His arrogance soon alienated the Parisians, and the Fronde disintegrated. In 1652 the king returned to Paris, followed by Mazarin in 1653. The last attempt of the nobility to resist the king by arms, the Fronde resulted in the strengthening of the monarchy and the further disruption of the French economy.

**Frondizi, Arturo,** 1908–, president of Argentina (1958–62). A liberal and anti-Peronist, he supported a policy of economic austerity. Because he allowed Peronists to participate in the elections of 1962, outraged anti-Peronist elements in the army arrested him and annulled the elections.

**front,** in meteorology, the boundary between adjacent air masses. If a cold air mass pushes a warm air mass ahead of it, a cold front exists; a warm front is the reverse situation. A stationary front is one in which neither air mass pushes against the other. An occluded front exists when a cold front catches up to a warm front; the warm air mass lying between the two cold air masses is thus forced to rise.

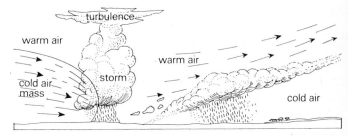

An occluded **front** occurs when a cold front (left) meets a warm front (right)

**Frontenac, Louis de Buade, comte de Palluau et de** (ˌfrontənak), 1620–98, French governor of New France (1672–82, 1696–98). Although his independent policy displeased King LOUIS XIV and his powers as governor were reduced, he advanced French exploration in Canada, established new forts and posts, subdued (1696) the IROQUOIS CONFEDERACY, and held QUEBEC against the British in the first FRENCH AND INDIAN WAR.

**front-line states,** designation applied to Angola, Botswana, Mozambique, Tanzania, Zambia, and Zimbabwe in their joint opposition to the South African government and its APARTHEID policies.

**frost** or **hoarfrost,** ice formed by the condensation of atmospheric water vapour on a surface whose temperature is below 0°C (32°F). In the formation of frost, water vapour is changed directly to a solid (see DEW). Frost appears as a light, feathery deposit of ice, often in a delicate pattern.

**Frost, Robert,** 1874–1963, one of the most popular American poets of the 20th cent. He went to England in 1912 and won his first acclaim there. After publishing *A Boy's Will* (1913) and *North of Boston* (1914), he returned to the US and settled in New Hampshire. While Frost wrote movingly of the people and landscape of New England, his lyrical, dramatic, and often deeply symbolic verse goes far beyond regional poetry. His volumes of poetry include *New Hampshire* (1923), *A Witness Tree* (1942), *Steeple Bush* (1947), and *In the Clearing* (1962). Frost was awarded the Pulitzer Prize for poetry in 1924, 1931, 1937, and 1943. His complete poems were published in 1967.

**frostbite,** tissue injury caused by exposure to cold, usually affecting the hands, feet, ears, or nose. Extreme cold causes the small blood vessels in the extremities to constrict, resulting in slowed circulation and stagnation of the blood, depriving tissues of nutrients. The condition is aggravated by inactivity and dampness. Severe, untreated frostbite may result in GANGRENE.

**frottage** [Fr., = rubbing], a technique in art, especially exploited by the surrealist Max ERNST, to create automatic compositions by rubbing over floorboards or other rough surfaces. The natural abstract patterns so generated can then be used to suggest figurative subject matter in the mind of the artist.

**Froude, James Antony,** 1818–94, English historian. The son of a clergyman, he was educated at Oxford in some of the most exciting years of the OXFORD MOVEMENT. He wrote with enthusiasm, mainly about Tudor

England. His major work was *The History of England from the Fall of Wolsey to the Defeat of the Spanish Armada* (12 vol., 1856–70). Savagely attacked for his errors, of which there were many, he had an enthusiastic readership, and at the very end of his life was briefly regius professor of history in Oxford.

**frozen foods,** foods preserved for human (or sometimes animal) consumption by rapid anhydrous freezing. The technique of freezing foods was discovered by chance by Clarence BIRDSEYE during a hunting expedition in the Arctic at the end of World War I. The first frozen food went on sale in the US in 1933. Fish fingers were introduced into Britain in 1955. Frozen foods have become immensely popular in advanced countries, their convenience being attractive to households where the person who does the cooking also has a job. In Britain in the 1980s over 75% of households with children had a deep-freeze (and 97% a refrigerator), and weekly expenditure on frozen foods averaged 50p per person per week. Frozen food is preserved with no additives and the nutritional value of the fresh food is maintained.

**Fructidor:** see FRENCH REVOLUTIONARY CALENDAR.

**fructose, levulose,** or **fruit sugar,** simple SUGAR found in honey and fruit. Sweeter than SUCROSE, fructose is a carbohydrate with the same formula as GLUCOSE, but with a different structure (see ISOMER). An equimolar mixture of fructose and glucose, called invert sugar, is obtained by the breakdown of sucrose and is the major component of honey.

**fruit,** matured ovary of a FLOWER, containing the seed. After FERTILIZATION takes place and the embryo plantlet has begun to develop, the surrounding ovule becomes a seed, and the ovary wall around the ovule (pericarp) becomes the fruit. Fruits are classified into four types: simple, aggregate, multiple, and accessory. Simple fruits are either fleshy or dry. Fleshy fruits are either berries (the entire pericarp is fleshy, e.g., tomato and banana) or drupes (the inner layer of the pericarp becomes a pit or stone around the seed, e.g., peach and walnut). Dry fruits are divided into those whose hard, papery shells either split to release the mature seeds (dehiscent), e.g., the PEA, or do not split (indehiscent), e.g., the NUT or GRAIN. Aggregate fruits (e.g., raspberry) are masses of small drupes (drupelets), each developed from separate ovaries of a single flower. Multiple fruits (e.g., pineapple) develop from ovaries of many flowers in a cluster. Accessory fruits contain tissue derived from parts other than the ovary, e.g., apple, the edible portion of which is actually a swollen stem.

**fruit strawberry** – is eaten and seeds are distributed in faeces

highly coloured flesh attracts animals

sepal

fleshy receptacle

achenes (the true fruits)

**goosegrass** – attaches itself to animal fur and later falls or is scratched off

hooks

**ash** – relies on the wind to disperse its winged fruit

seed contained in fruit

wing

**peach** – drops when ripe; stone containing seed is released when fruit rots

skin (outer layer)

stone encloses seed and kernal

flesh (middle layer)

**peas** – split and twist when ripe and eject seeds

seed

pod

remains of flower

**poppy** – sways in the wind enabling seeds to be shaken out of capsule

capsule containing seeds

Fruit

**fruit fly,** small (3–5 mm/⅛–⅕ in long) FLY (family Tephritidae), with distinctly patterned wings. In some species the larvae feed inside succulent fruits; the Mediterranean fruit fly (*Ceratitis capitata*), is a serious pest of oranges and other fruit such as apricots, peaches, and plums. Another important horticultural pest is the celery fly (*Philophylla heraclei*), which mines the leaves of celery and parsnips. A second family, sometimes called fruit flies, are the plain-winged, red-eyed Drosophilidae. Some live on and in decaying fruit and many are attracted by the products of fermentation. Among these is the vinegar fly *Drosophila melanogaster*, often used in the laboratory study of GENETICS because it is easy to rear, and has a short life cycle (14 days) and large chromosomes.

**Frunze,** formerly Pishpek, city (1985 pop. 604,000), capital of the KIRGHIZ SOVIET SOCIALIST REPUBLIC, Soviet Central Asia, on the northern slopes of the Tien Shan Mts in the valley of the Chu R. Agricultural machinery, machine tools, and textiles are produced. Wheat, barley, tobacco, and sugar beet from the surrounding agricultural region are also processed here and it has one of the largest meat-packing plants in the USSR. Founded in 1873, it was renamed Frunze (1926) after Mikhail Vasilyovich Frunze, the Bolshevik revolutionary leader who was born there in 1885.

**Fry, Christopher,** 1907–, English dramatist, one of the few 20th-cent. playwrights to employ verse successfully. His plays include *The Lady's Not for Burning* (1949), *Venus Observed* (1950), *A Sleep of Prisoners* (1951), and *Yard of Sun* (1970).

**Fry, Elizabeth (Gurney),** 1780–1845, English prison reformer and philanthropist. A Quaker, she worked from 1813 to improve the conditions of women in Newgate prison. Such innovations as segregation of the sexes and education and employment programmes in British prisons were largely due to her efforts. She also founded soup kitchens in London.

**Fry, Roger Eliot,** 1866–1934, English art critic and painter. A champion of the modern French schools of art (see POSTIMPRESSIONISM), he emphasized analysis of the formal qualities in a work of art. His writings include *Vision and Design* (1920) and *Cézanne* (1927).

**Frye, Northrop,** 1912–, Canadian literary critic. Among his works are *Fearful Symmetry* (1947), a study of William BLAKE, and *Anatomy of Criticism* (1957), a synoptic view of the principles and techniques of literary criticism.

**Fuchs, Klaus Emil,** 1911–88, German physicist; came to England as refugee from the Nazi government. He passed information to the USSR while working on the atomic bomb in the US (1944–45) and in the atomic research centre at Harwell as head of the theoretical physics division. He was arrested in 1950 and imprisoned until 1959, when he was sent to East Germany. He was director of the Institute for Nuclear Physics in Rossendorf from 1959 to 1979.

**fuchsia,** shrub or herb (genus *Fuchsia*) of the EVENING PRIMROSE family, a tropical American plant cultivated for its pendulous, brilliant, red-to-purple and white flowers. Most garden fuchsias are hybrids. Several species are winter-hardy, e.g., varieties of *F. magellanica*.

**fuel cell,** electric CELL in which the chemical energy from the oxidation of a gas fuel is converted directly to electrical energy in a continuous process. In the hydrogen and oxygen fuel cell, hydrogen and oxygen gas are bubbled into separate compartments connected by a porous disc through which an ELECTROLYTE, such as aqueous potassium hydroxide (KOH), can pass. Inert graphite electrodes, mixed with a catalyst such as platinum, are dipped into each compartment. When the two electrodes are electrically connected, an OXIDATION AND REDUCTION reaction takes place in the cell: hydrogen gas is oxidized to form water at the anode; electrons are liberated in this process and flow through the external circuit to the cathode, where the electrons combine with the oxygen gas and reduce it. Fuel cells have been used to generate electricity in spacecraft.

**Fuentes, Carlos** (ˌfwayntays), 1928–, Mexican novelist and short-story writer. He synthesizes reality and fantasy in such experimental novels as *La región más transparente* (1958; tr. Where the Air is Clear), *La muerte de Artemio Cruz* (1962; tr. The Death of Artemio Cruz), *Cambio de piel* (1967; tr. A Change of Skin), *Terra Nostra* (1975), and *Una familia lejana* (1980; tr. Distant Relations).

**Fuessli, Johann Heinrich:** see FUSELI, HENRY.

**Fugard, Athol,** 1932–, South African playwright. An Afrikaner strongly opposed to APARTHEID, Fugard has written of the suffering and common humanity of blacks, Coloureds, and poor whites in his country in such powerful plays as *The Blood Knot* (1961); *People Are Living There* (1968); *Boesman and Lena* (1969), considered his masterpiece; *A Lesson from Aloes* (1981); and *Master Harold . . . and the Boys* (1981); and *The Road to Mecca* (1985). Two of his best-known pieces, *Sizwe Bansi is Dead* (1972) and *The Island* (1973), were devised with the actors John Kani and Winston Ntshona.

**fugue** [from Ital., = flight], in music, a form of composition, originally choral, in which the basic principle is imitative COUNTERPOINT of several voices. Its main elements are: a theme or subject, stated first in one and then in all voices; continuation of a voice after the subject, accompanying the subject statements in other voices; and passages built on a *motif,* a short phrase derived from the subject or countersubject. First established by Flemish composers in the 15th cent., the fugue was highly developed by J.S. BACH. The CANON is a short form of fugue.

**Fujairah,** small state on the Arabian shore of the Gulf of Oman. See UNITED ARAB EMIRATES.

**Fuji, Mount** or **Fujiyama,** volcano 3776 m (12,389 ft) high, highest point on HONSHU, Japan. The mountain, which last erupted in 1707, is considered sacred in Japan and is a traditional place of pilgrimage. A perfectly formed, snow-capped cone, it long has inspired Japanese artists.

Mount **Fuji**

**Fujian** or **Fukien,** province (1985 est. pop. 27,130,000), 121,400 km² (46,872 sq mi), SE China facing Taiwan across the Taiwan (Formosa) Strait. Major cities are FUZHOU, the capital and XIAMEN. Most of the land is mountainous or hilly and there is very limited flat or valley country. The mountain areas support some timber production. The valley areas with their tropical climate have been developed as important rice-producing regions, and in favoured areas rice can be double cropped. Sugarcane, tobacco, and fruits are significant cash crops. The coastal region is important for fishing, and has historically been commercially important because of its links with Japan and the Philippines. Until recently industrialization has been limited; Xiamen is now being developed as a special economic zone to attract foreign investment. Clashes with Western powers have marked Fujian's recent history. In 1842 Fuzhou was one of the treaty ports forced open to Western commerce by the Treaty of Nanjing. In 1958 Chinese troops sought unsuccessfully to regain the offshore islands of MAZU DAO AND JINMEN DAO from the American-backed forces of Chiang Kai-shek.

**Fujiwara,** Japanese family founded in the 7th cent. It exercised power for much of the HEIAN PERIOD through use of the office of regent to control the emperors. The apogee of its successes was the time of Fujiwara no Michizane, whose landholdings and palaces exceeded those of the imperial family. Political decline came partly as a result of neglecting developments in the provinces, particularly the rise of the SAMURAI.

**Fukien:** see FUJIAN.

**Fukuoka** ('foohkooh͵ohkah), city (1986 est. pop. 1,127,253), capital of Fukuoka prefecture, N Kyushu, Japan. A port and major air and rail terminus, it is also the seat of several universities. Hakata dolls and textiles have been made there for centuries. The city has three noted shrines, Dazaiftu, Kushida, and Hakozaki. The ancient port area, Hakata, was in medieval times one of the chief ports of Japan.

**Fukuzawa Yukichi,** 1835–1901, Japanese educator. On the first Japanese mission to the US (1860) and subsequent visits to the West he became convinced of the superiority of Western civilization. He described his experiences abroad in his best-seller *Seiyō Jijō* [Conditions in the West] (1866–70) and devoted the rest of his life to the task of awakening the Japanese people to the importance of Western science and inculcating a spirit of intellectual independence.

**Fulani,** people of W Africa, numbering approximately 7 million. They are of mixed African and Berber origin. First recorded as living in the Senegambia region, they are now scattered throughout the area of the Sudan from Senegal to Cameroon. The Fulani became zealous Muslims (11th cent.) and from 1750 to 1900 engaged in many holy wars in the name of Islam. In the first part of the 19th cent. the Fulani carved out two important empires. One, based on Massina, for a time controlled TIMBUKTU; the other, centred at Sokoto, included the HAUSA States and parts of Bornu and W Cameroon. The Fulani emir of Sokoto continued to rule over part of N Nigeria until the British conquest in 1903.

**Fulbright, J(ames) William,** 1905–, US senator from Arkansas (1945–75). A Democrat, he was elected to the House of Representatives (1942) and then to the Senate (1944). He became known internationally for the Fulbright Act (1946), which provided for the exchange of students and teachers between the US and other countries. As chairman (1959–74) of the Senate Foreign Relations Committee, he opposed the VIETNAM WAR.

**Fuller, Margaret,** 1810–50, American writer and lecturer. One of the most influential literary figures of her day, she was a leading exponent of TRANSCENDENTALISM and edited (1840–42) its journal, *The Dial. Woman in the Nineteenth Century* (1845) expresses her feminist views. Her essays as first literary critic of the New York *Tribune* are collected in *Papers on Literature and Art* (1846). In 1847 she went to Rome, where she married the Marchese Ossoli, a follower of MAZZINI, and with him took part in the REVOLUTIONS OF 1848, writing about it for the *Tribune*. Returning to the US (1850), she, her husband, and their baby were drowned in a shipwreck.

**Fuller, R(ichard) Buckminster,** 1895–1983, American architect and engineer. He is noted for his revolutionary technological designs aimed at deriving maximum output from minimum material and energy—the *Dymaxion* principle. Examples are his self-contained '4-D' house (1928), Dymaxion car (1933), and designs for geodesic domes.

Geodesic dome at Montreal designed by R. Buckminster **Fuller**

**Fuller, Sam,** 1911–, American film director. A former tabloid reporter and infantry soldier in World War II, his films possess a primitive power, whose brutal impact is enhanced by dynamic camerawork. His films include *Park Row* (1952), *Pickup on South Street* (1953), *Forty Guns* (1957), and *The Big Red One* (1979).

**Fuller, Thomas,** 1608–61, English clergyman and writer. He is best known for *Worthies of England* (1662), an invaluable source of antiquarian information on English personalities. His works include *The Church History of Britain* (1655).

**full-stop:** see PUNCTUATION.

**fulmar,** a gull-like BIRD of the PETREL family. Fulmars range the oceans of the world, returning to coastal cliffs to breed. On the nest chicks and adults defend themselves by shooting the evil-smelling contents of their crops over any attacker. The northern fulmar (*Fulmarus glacialis*) feeds on zooplankton, but is also an efficient scavenger, closely associated with whaling and trawling for over 300 years. An increased supply of fish waste from factory ships may explain the increase in the fulmar population in the last 30 years.

Fulmar (*Fulmarus glacialis*) showing tube nose

**Fulton, Robert,** 1765–1815, American inventor, engineer, and painter. A man of many talents and a mechanical genius, he was successively an expert gunsmith, a landscape and portrait painter, and a maker of torpedoes and submarines. In 1807 his *Clermont,* launched on the Hudson, was the first commercially successful steamboat (see STEAMSHIP) in America; although Fulton had predecessors, e.g., John FITCH, he is popularly considered the steamboat's inventor.

**function,** in mathematics, a relation that assigns to each member $x$ of some set $X$ (the domain) a unique member $y$ of another set $Y$ (the range); $y$ is said to be a function of $x,$ usually denoted $f(x)$ (read '$f$ of $x$'). In the equation $y = f(x),$ $x$ is called the independent variable and $y$ the dependent variable. Although a function $f$ assigns a unique $y$ to each $x,$ several $x$'s may yield the same $y;$ e.g., if $y = f(x) = x^2$ (where $x$ is a number), then $f(2) = f(-2) = 4.$ If this condition never occurs, then $f$ is called a one-to-one, or injective, function.

**functional group,** in organic chemistry, group of atoms within a molecule that is responsible for certain properties of the molecule and reactions in which it takes part.

**functionalism,** theory of social organization which explains a social phenomenon or institution in terms of the function it performs in meeting the 'needs' of the organism as a whole, of which it is a part. Writers like Herbert SPENCER viewed societies as analogous, in this way, to biological organisms. Social anthropologists like B. MALINOWSKI and A.R. RADCLIFFE-BROWN viewed tribal societies as sociocultural entities and explained their institutions as functional in meeting the needs (often conceived biologically) of the individuals who made them up. The sociologist DURKHEIM argued that as societies became more complex, they became more heterogeneous and diverse—a drive he explained as functionally necessary to social development. The American sociologist Talcott PARSONS, with his structural functionalist approach, treated society as composed of a set of interdependent systems, each contributing to its cohesion and stability. There are also Marxist versions of functionalism, which explain particular aspects of economic or political life in terms of

their functions relative to the needs of capital. Functionalism explains things in terms of the objective requirements which (it argues) all systems have to reproduce themselves over time, and ignores the meanings which social actors place on their actions. It is frequently criticised because it describes how things function (but not *why* they function in that way) and for its inability to account for change. See also STRUCTURAL FUNCTIONALISM.

**fundamentalism,** term originally applied to conservative Protestantism at the turn of the 19th–20th cent. Its aim is to maintain traditional interpretations of the Bible and what its adherents believe to be the fundamental doctrines of the Christian faith. The emergence of liberal theology attempted to recast Christian teachings in light of new scientific and historical thought. The term is now applied to all religions since a so-called fundamentalist revival from the 1970s onwards.

**Fundy, Bay of,** large inlet of the Atlantic Ocean, c.270 km (170 mi) long and 50–80 km (30–50 mi) wide, NE Canada, between New Brunswick and Nova Scotia. It is famous for its tidal bore and for high tides that reach 12–15 m (40–50 ft), creating the reversing falls of the St John R.

**fungi,** division of simple plants that lack CHLOROPHYLL, true stems, roots, and leaves. Unlike ALGAE, fungi cannot photosynthesize, and live as PARASITES or SAPROPHYTES. The division comprises the SLIME MOULDS and true fungi. True fungi are multicellular (with the exception of YEASTS); the body of most true fungi consists of slender cottony filaments, or hyphae. All fungi are capable of asexual REPRODUCTION by cell division, budding, fragmentation, or SPORES. Those that reproduce sexually alternate a sexual generation (GAMETOPHYTE) with a spore-producing one. The four classes of true fungi are the algaelike fungi (e.g., black bread MOULD and downy MILDEW), sac fungi (e.g., yeasts, powdery mildews, TRUFFLES, and blue and green moulds such as *Penicillium*), basidium fungi (e.g., MUSHROOMS and puffballs) and imperfect fungi (e.g., species that cause athlete's foot and ringworm). Fungi help decompose organic matter (important in soil renewal); are valuable as a source of ANTIBIOTICS, vitamins, and various industrial chemicals; and for their role in FERMENTATION, e.g., in bread and alcoholic beverage production.

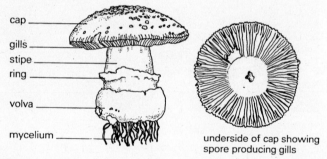

cap
gills
stipe
ring
volva
mycelium

underside of cap showing spore producing gills

Fungus

**fungicide,** substance used to prevent infection by, or to destroy FUNGI. Made from sulphur or copper compounds, organic salts of iron, zinc, and mercury, and other chemicals, fungicides are used on seeds, growing crops, timber, and fabrics, and for human and animal fungal diseases.

**Funk, Casimir** (foongk), 1884–1967, American biochemist; b. Poland; went to US, 1915. Credited with discovering vitamins (see VITAMINS AND MINERALS), he stirred public interest with his 1912 paper on vitamin-deficiency diseases. He coined the term *vitamine* and later posited the existence of four such substances ($B_1,$ $B_2,$ C, and D).

**fur,** hairy covering of an animal, especially that with thick, soft, close-growing underfur next to the skin and a coarse protective layer of guard hair above it. The term includes sheepskins with their hair, and curled pelts, e.g., Persian lamb. Used for clothing since prehistoric times, furs were traditionally luxury goods in the more populous, temperate regions of the world, where wild animals are scarce. The most prized furs include sable, mink, and chinchilla, but many others, e.g., beaver, fox, rabbit, and ocelot, are also valued, and breeding and hunting industries are important in North America and Asia. Following the exploitation (17–19th cent.) of N American and Asian wilderness areas, depleting the sea otter and threatening the fur seal, conservationists and humane groups have protested against trapping for fur, and legislation has followed. The US government was one of the first to ban the import or sale of pelts of such animals as the polar bear, jaguar, and tiger. The Convention on International Trade in Endangered Species of Wild Fauna and Flora (CITES) (1975) prohibits trade not only in plants or animals but also in products derived from them. The UK has in force a ban on wildlife exports. In Britain and the US public pressure and legislation have reduced the demand for spotted cat garments almost to nil; in Japan, West Germany, and other affluent countries, however, trade in furs, even those of the big cats, is flourishing.

**Furies** or **Erinyes** (ee͵rinee -eez), in Greek mythology, goddesses of vengeance. Born from the blood of URANUS, they punished wrongs committed against blood relatives regardless of the motivation, as in the case of ORESTES. Named Megaera, Tisiphone, and Alecto, they were usually represented as hideous old women with bats' wings, dogs' heads, and snakes for hair. They are the heroines of AESCHYLUS's *Eumenides* [the kindly ones].

**furniture,** such movables as chairs, tables, beds, chests, cabinets, and mirrors; the term is also sometimes used to embrace any interior furnishings. Throughout history furniture has most commonly been made of wood but metal and, in recent times, plastics, have also been used. Ornamental techniques include carving, painting, GILDING, LACQUER, INLAY, MARQUETRY, and embellishing with decorative metalwork. Form has been influenced by the customs of the various cultures. In Ancient Egypt furniture was almost non-existent for those other than the rich and powerful and it was customary to sit and sleep on the ground. Consequently chairs and beds were rare and tables were low; more common were stools, some of folding type, while boxes, baskets, and stands also served as furniture. Carved animal hooves or paws often decorated the feet of these. The Greeks used couches and beds for reclining at mealtimes—a custom continued by the Romans. Stools and chairs were more common, the typical Greek chair being the *klismos*, with tapering legs curving to the front and back; small tables and chests were also used. Carved details in the form of animal heads or feet were popular. The Romans based much of their furniture on Greek models but used iron or bronze for some stools, small tables and stands. They introduced the cupboard and marble tables with slab supports carved in the form of fabulous beasts. Outside Europe furniture was in general very sparse, largely as the result of the widespread custom of sitting and sleeping on the floor. Of the various decorative techniques particularly notable was the use in the Far East of colourful LACQUER, which had the added advantage of resistance to attack from insects. In the medieval period in Europe furniture was still sparse, mostly made of oak, sometimes painted or inlaid, and strongly influenced by architectural forms in its ornament; wool, animal hair, feathers, or vegetable matter were used for stuffing chairs and beds. The RENAISSANCE saw the rise of other woods, notably walnut, and greater sophistication in decorative techniques, such as carving and MARQUETRY, alongside an increase in both quantity and type; there was a growing interest in furniture and techniques from the Far East. Fixed upholstery appeared in the Renaissance, using silk, velvet, tapestry, needlework, or leather, attached with nails and sometimes enriched with fringes of silk or gold thread. Greater elegance and refinement were the hallmarks of the 18th cent., with the introduction of concealed mechanisms in the second half. The 19th cent. saw the increased copying of past styles and a tendency to over-elaborate decorative details, which was further stimulated by the introduction of mass-production by machinery. A reaction against this arose in the 1860s, with a return to simpler, traditional designs. Throughout these periods European countries mostly followed similar trends, although each country developed its own special characteristics. The Americans generally produced simplified versions of English models, sometimes with slight influences from other European countries. Peasant furniture, which generally relied on paint for decoration, was only marginally influenced by fashionable styles and traditional forms tended to persist. In the years around 1900 there was a fashion for the sinuous forms of ART NOUVEAU. After World War I the BAUHAUS school of design was an important international influence, notably in the use of steel tubing for supports for chairs and tables, although reproduction styles remained popular too. After World War II elegant, simple, Scandinavian furniture in fine woods achieved wide popularity; sophisticated Italian designs making much use of metal and glass were also influential. Plastics became used, particularly for the moulded shapes of stacking chairs; built-in and unit furniture were also widely developed. Introductions of the 1960s were the throw-away "paper chair' and the inflatable or "blow-up' chair,

made of PVC, but most furniture continues to be made of more traditional materials.

**Furphy, Joseph,** 1843–1912, Australian writer. Using the pseudonym 'Tom Collins', he wrote the unconventional novel *Such is Life* (1903), an idiosyncratic anti-romantic view of bush life which he described as: 'temper, democratic; bias offensively Australian'.

**further education (FE),** post-secondary full- or part-time education below degree level. Such education is most commonly available in further education colleges, of which there are more than 600 in Great Britain. The FE colleges provide mainly 'non-advanced' vocational and prevocational courses, apprenticeship training, and opportunities for GCSE, A-level, Royal Society of Arts, City and Guilds, and other technical and professional EXAMINATIONS, and nonvocational part-time courses. They provide a route back into part-time education for students who dropped out of education and training on leaving school. The FE colleges have developed in parallel with the sixth forms of SECONDARY SCHOOLS, and in some areas these functions have been combined in 'tertiary colleges'.

**Furtwängler, Wilhelm,** 1886–1954, German conductor, in Lübeck, Mannheim, Berlin, and with the New York Philharmonic. He was renowned for his interpretations of such composers as BRAHMS and Richard WAGNER.

**fuse, electric,** safety device used to protect an ELECTRIC CIRCUIT against an excessive current. A fuse consists of a low-melting-point alloy strip enclosed in a suitable housing and connected in series with the circuit that it protects. Because of its electrical RESISTANCE, the alloy strip is heated by electric current; if the current exceeds the safe value for which the fuse was designed, the strip melts, opening the circuit and stopping the current. See also CIRCUIT BREAKER.

**Fuseli, Henry** (͵fyoohzilee), 1741–1825, Anglo-Swiss painter and draftsman, also known as Johann Heinrich Fuessli or Füssli. His paintings were grotesque and visionary, e.g., *Nightmare* (1782). His drawings reveal his romantic fascination with the terrifying and the weird.

**fusel oil,** oily, colourless liquid with a disagreeable odour and taste. A mixture of ALCOHOL and fatty acids formed during the alcoholic FERMENTATION of STARCH, fusel oil may occur as an unwholesome impurity in imperfectly distilled spirits. It is used as a solvent in making lacquers and enamels.

**Fushun** (fooh-shoohn), city (1984 est. pop. 2,088,500), NE LIAONING prov., NE China. The city is sited in a highly industrialized area, 60 km (36 mi) from SHENYANG. It is the coal-mining centre of China and has one of the largest opencast coal mines in the world. Oil production and refining are also major industries. The city was developed by Russia until 1905 and by Japan until 1945.

**fusion,** the release of energy through the fusion of hydrogen nuclei into those of helium (via deuterium and tritium) releases much more energy than fission, and the raw materials (hydrogen or deuterium) are abundant. Though the process occurs naturally at high temperatures in the centres of the stars and is the source of their heat, controlled nuclear fusion has not yet been achieved. Major efforts are continuing in research centres worldwide since, if successful, it would be a source of energy with virtually unlimited fuel producing less radioactive waste than fission. See also HYDROGEN BOMB; NUCLEAR ENERGY.

**Füssli, Johann Heinrich:** see FUSELI, HENRY.

**Fust** or **Faust, Johann,** d. 1466?, printer at Mainz, Germany. He loaned Johann GUTENBERG money, and took over his press and types on his default, carrying on his work. With Peter Schöffer he was the first (1457) to print in colours. They also produced the first dated book, a great psalter, in 1457.

**futurism,** a movement in Italian literature and art, founded by the poet Filippo MARINETTI by his publication of the first futurist manifesto in 1909. The artists (who included BOCCIONI, CARRÀ, RUSSOLO, BALLA, and SEVERINI) aimed to illustrate the excitement and speed of modern urban life that would overthrow the old order of the Italian tradition; in this sense it was nationalistic, as Marinetti and the others wished Italy to compete with Paris and Europe both industrially and artistically. The image of the motor car became a potent symbol for the futurist artists, and the depiction of movement and speed were major themes. The futurist artists travelled to Paris in 1911 and were greatly influenced by CUBISM; a futurist exhibition was held in Paris (1912), which then travelled on to London, Berlin,

Moscow, and other cities in Europe, rapidly spreading the group's ideas. As an artistic movement futurism had lost its momentum by the end of World War I.

**Fuzhou** or **Foochow** (fooh-joh), city (1984 pop. 4,826,500), capital of FUJIAN prov., SE China. A port on the Min R. delta, c.40 km (25 mi) from the coast, it consists of an old walled city, dating from the Tang dynasty, and a modern riverside town. Industries include food-processing (tea, sugar, and fruit), chemicals, and textiles, and a developing electronics industry. The city's lacquerware and handicrafts are famous throughout China. Long a centre for China's foreign commerce, and a treaty port following the Opium Wars (1839–42), in 1979 and in 1984 it was granted special rights to encourage foreign investment.

# G

**G**, force of gravity exercised upon a body. In aircraft this force can be increased, or decreased, substantially upon all the components and occupants as a result of various manoeuvres. In a tight turn, a fast aeroplane can induce a force of up to 9 G, in which all weights, including those of crew and passengers, are increased by nine times and so become virtually immovable. In the opposite direction, such as in a sudden dive, negative gravity can reach zero G or weightlessness; this condition is also maintained during a space flight in orbit. Some military and special aerobatic aircraft are designed to be able to withstand, without damage, gravities from $+9$ to $-6$ G.

**Ga**, chemical symbol of the element GALLIUM.

**Gable, Clark,** 1901–60, American film actor. For years a box-office attraction, he made such films as *It Happened One Night* (1934), *Mutiny on the Bounty* (1935), *Gone with the Wind* (1939), and *The Misfits* (1960).

**Gabo, Naum,** (‚gahboh), 1890–1977, Russian sculptor. The younger brother of Antoine PEVSNER, Gabo abandoned a medical training and studied art, first in Munich under the art historian Wölfflin and then with his brother in Paris in 1913/14. His first construction of 1915 combined features of CUBISM with geometrical abstraction. In 1917 he returned with Pevsner to Russia, publishing the *Realistic Manifesto* in 1920. In this they took to task the 'laboratory art' theoreticians, and argued for an aesthetic that ultimately had no useful purpose. He left Russia for Berlin in 1922; after 1932 he worked in Paris, London, and finally the US. Using transparent perspex, he reworked the basic forms of sphere, column, and spiral in abstract constructions that had apparent weightlessness. He also experimented with kinetic works, e.g., *Kinetic Sculpture* (Standing Wave) (1920; Tate Gall., London).

**Gabon** (ga‚bon), officially Gabonese Republic, republic (1986 est. pop. 1,150,000), 267,667 km² (103,346 sq mi), W central Africa, bordered by the Atlantic Ocean (W), Equatorial Guinea and Cameroon (N), and the Congo Republic (E and S). LIBREVILLE (the capital) and Port-Gentil are the only large cities. Gabon is situated astride the equator. The coastline is a narrow, low-lying strip; the interior is made up of mountain ranges and high plateaus. Much of the country is drained by the Ogooué R., which flows into the Atlantic. The economy is based on oil production, which provides the highest per capita income in sub-Saharan Africa and accounts for two-thirds of export earnings. Output has been declining since the mid-1970s, however, and experts predict that Gabon's oil resources will be exhausted by 1990. Other minerals extracted include manganese, uranium, and gold. Forest products are also important. Agricultural output is low, and much food needs to be imported. The GNP is US$420 million, and the GNP per capita is US$3678 (1985). The inhabitants of Gabon are black Africans, chiefly Fang (the most numerous group), Omiéné, Batoka, and Eshira. French is the official language. Most of the people follow traditional beliefs, but there are many Christians in the cities. Lambaréné, on the Ogooué, is the site of the famous hospital established by Albert SCHWEITZER in 1913.

*History.* The region that is now Gabon was inhabited in Palaeolithic times. The Omiéné were living there by the 16th cent., the Fang by the 18th, and from the 16th to 18th cent. Gabon was part of the Loango empire, which stretched from the Ogooué to the Congo (Zaïre) rivers. Portuguese navigators arrived in the Ogooué estuary in the 1470s, and Gabon soon became an important centre of a slave trade that flourished until the 1880s. By the late 18th cent. the French had gained a dominant position in the area, and, despite resistance from the Fang, Gabon became part of the French Congo in 1889 and of FRENCH EQUATORIAL AFRICA in 1910. Held by the Free French in WORLD WAR II, Gabon became an overseas territory in 1946 and self-governing in 1958. It achieved full independence in 1960, but retained close ties with France. In 1967 the country adopted a one-party political system, and the ruling Gabonese Democratic Party (PDG) led by Pres. Omar Bongo has been unopposed in successive legislative elections. Through the years of PDG rule Gabon has remained one of the most stable black African countries.

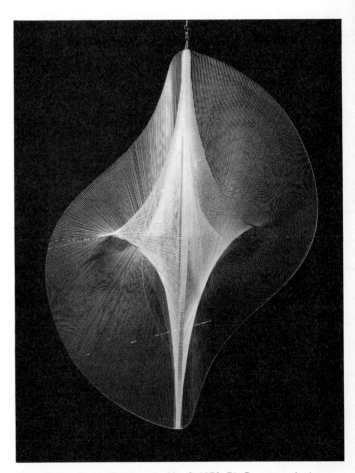

Naum **Gabo**, *Linear Construction No. 2*, 1970–71. Perspex and wire, 83.5 × 114.9 × 83.5 cm. Tate Gallery, London.

**Gaborone,** city (1981 pop. 59,657), capital of Botswana. Primarily an administrative centre, it is located on the country's main rail line and has

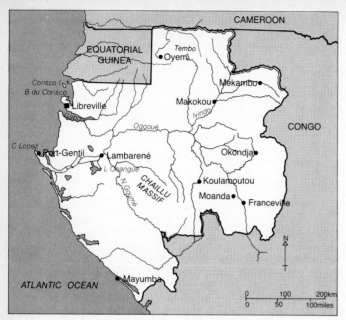

Gabon

a small international airport. The city was founded c.1890 by a black African chief. It became the capital of newly independent BOTSWANA in 1966.

**Gabriel,** archangel, the divine herald. In the BIBLE he appears to DANIEL (Dan. 8–9); to Zacharias, father of JOHN THE BAPTIST; and to the Virgin MARY in the Annunciation (Luke 1). Christian tradition makes him the trumpeter of the Last Judgment. In Islam, Gabriel reveals the KORAN to MUHAMMAD, becoming the angel of truth.

**Gabriel, Jacques Ange** (gabree͵el), 1689–1782, French architect of the ROCOCO. His work is characterized by classical repose, purity of form, and restraint. He worked for 30 years for LOUIS XV at VERSAILLES, Compiègne, and other royal residences. He also designed Place Louis XV (now Place de la Concorde), Paris (1753), and worked on the LOUVRE.

**Gabrieli, Andrea,** c.1510–86, Italian organist and composer. He wrote MADRIGALS, MOTETS, MASSES, *ricercari,* and canzonas for organ and was important in developing multiple-CHOIR technique, which was further refined by his nephew **Giovanni Gabrieli,** c.1555–1612. Giovanni was most important in the development of the CONCERTO style and published (1597) the first printed music with dynamic indications.

**Gadda, Carlo Emilio,** 1893–1973, Italian novelist. His remarkable style combines literary language, slang, dialects, deliberate misspellings, foreign words, and pastiches of various prose styles. *Quer pasticciaccio brutto de via Merulana* (1957; tr. That Awful Mess on Via Merulana) is considered his masterpiece.

**Gaddi,** celebrated family of Florentine artists. **Gaddo Gaddi,** c.1260–c.1333, a painter and mosaicist, is thought to have produced the MOSAIC works in the portico of Santa Maria Maggiore, Rome. His son, **Taddeo Gaddi,** c.1300–c.1366, was a pupil and assistant to GIOTTO and chief Florentine painter after Giotto's death. His works include paintings in Santa Croce and Santa Felicità, Florence. Taddeo's son, **Agnolo Gaddi,** fl. 1369–1396, possessed a somewhat rigid, Giottesque style. His frescoes include *The Story of the Virgin and her Girdle* (1392–95; cathedral, Prato).

**Gaddis, William,** 1922–, American writer. His first and major work is *The Recognitions* (1955), a vast satirical novel which explores every aspect of forgery, fraudulence, and counterfeiting in the modern world. It was a very influential work and is now recognized as one of the greatest modern American novels. Later novels by Gaddis are *JR* (1975) and *Carpenter's Gothic* (1985).

**gadolinium** (Gd), metallic element, extracted in oxide form by J.C.G. de Marignac in 1880. This silver-white, lustrous, malleable, and ductile member of the RARE-EARTH METALS is found in gadolinite, MONAZITE, and

bastnasite. It is paramagnetic at room temperature but becomes strongly ferromagnetic (see MAGNETISM) when cooled. See ELEMENT (table); PERIODIC TABLE.

**Gaelic,** or Goidelic, group of languages belonging to the Celtic subfamily of the Indo-European family of languages. Gaelic is spoken in highland Scotland, in Ireland, and on the Isle of Man. See LANGUAGE (table).

**Gaelic football:** see under FOOTBALL.

**Gagarin, Yuri Alekseyevich,** 1934–68, Soviet cosmonaut. He became the first person to achieve orbital spaceflight when, on 12 Apr. 1961, he circled the Earth once in *Vostok 1.* He died (27 Mar. 1968) in the crash of a jet trainer.

**Gage, Thomas,** 1721–87, British general, commander of the British forces in North America (1763–75). As governor of Massachusetts (1774–75) he tried to enforce the INTOLERABLE ACTS. His coercive measures brought on the battles of LEXINGTON AND CONCORD, which began the AMERICAN REVOLUTION.

**Gaia,** in Greek mythology, the earth; daughter of CHAOS, mother and wife of both URANUS (the sky) and Pontus (the sea). She was mother, by Uranus, of the CYCLOPS, the TITANS, and others, and, by Pontus, of five sea deities. She helped bring about the overthrow of Uranus by the Titans. Gaia was worshipped as the primal goddess, the mother of all things.

**Gaia** or **Gaea,** hypothesis, first formulated by James E. Lovelock, British scientist, that the entire range of living matter on Earth, from whales to viruses, can be regarded as a single entity capable of manipulating its environment to suit its ends. This hypothesis, with its mystical overtones, has guided recent research into the physics and chemistry of planetary atmospheres and the various *elemental cycles* on Earth, and has also appealed to a number of the non-technocratic strands in the environmental movement.

**Gainsborough, Thomas,** 1727–88, English portrait and landscape painter. Greatly influenced by VAN DYCK, he was celebrated for the elegance, vivacity, and refinement of his portraits. His favourite subject, however, was landscape, and he produced some of the first great LANDSCAPE PAINTINGS in England. Gainsborough had few English rivals as a colourist. In his last years he excelled in fancy pictures, a pastoral genre with idealized subjects, e.g., *The Cottage Door* (1780; Huntington Art Gall., San Marino, California). Among his well-known works are *Perdita (Mrs Robinson)* (1781–82; Wallace Coll., London) and *The Blue Boy* (1770?; Huntington Art Gall., San Marino, California).

**Gaiseric** or **Genseric,** c.390–477, king of the Vandals and Alani (r.428–77). He left Spain for Africa (429), subdued a large territory, and took CARTHAGE (439). Recognized as independent of Rome, he persecuted Roman landowners and clergy. In 455 he sacked Rome, and he frustrated Roman expeditions against him. By the time he made peace with ZENO (476), he held N Africa, Sicily, Sardinia, Corsica, and the Balearic Islands.

**Gaitskell, Hugh Todd Naylor,** 1906–63, British politician. During WORLD WAR II he served in the ministry of economic warfare (1940–42) and on the Board of Trade (1942–45). He entered Parliament as a Labour member in 1945 and later was chancellor of the exchequer (1950–51). In 1955 he succeeded ATTLEE as party leader. He favoured moderation of party policies, but opposed Britain's entry into the European community.

**Gaius** (͵giəs) fl. 2nd cent., Roman jurist whose textbook *Institutes* is a major source of our knowledge of early ROMAN LAW.

**galactic cluster:** see CLUSTER, STAR.

**Galápagos Islands,** archipelago of 12 large and several hundred smaller islands on the equator in the Pacific 310 km (500 mi) due W of Ecuador to which they belong. The name of the islands is derived from the Spanish for tortoise and refers to the giant tortoises evolved on the islands. A very large proportion of the fauna are of species unique to the islands and provided Charles DARWIN, during his visit to the islands on the *Beagle* in 1835, with valuable data for the formulation of his theory of evolution.

**Galati,** city (1983 pop. 254,636), Moldavia, SE Romania, on the DANUBE R. A major iron and steel works, completed in the 1960s, supports metallurgical and engineering industries. The Danube Navigation Commission had its headquarters here (1856–1939).

**Galatians,** epistle of the NEW TESTAMENT, possibly the earliest. It was written (AD c.48) by St PAUL to Christians of central Asia Minor. Some scholars date it after AD 52. In answer to the belief that circumcision and

1949–75, except for time spent in government service). An adviser to Pres. J.F. KENNEDY, he served (1961–63) as US ambassador to India. A Keynesian economist (see KEYNES), Galbraith advocated government spending to fight unemployment and using more of the nation's wealth for public services and less for private consumption. His widely read books include *The Affluent Society* (1958; 3rd rev. ed., 1978), *The New Industrial State* (1967; 3rd rev. ed., 1978), and *The Age of Uncertainty* (1977).

**Galdós, Benito Pérez:** see PÉREZ GALDÓS, BENITO.

**Galen,** c.131–c.201, physician and writer; b. Pergamum, Asia Minor, of Greek parents. He resided chiefly in Rome and was personal physician to several emperors. Credited with some 500 treatises (at least 83 extant), Galen correlated earlier medical knowledge with his own discoveries (based on experiments and animal dissections). He showed that arteries carry blood, not air, and added greatly to knowledge of the brain, nerves, spinal cord, and pulse. His virtually undisputed authority discouraged original investigation and hampered medical progress until the 16th cent.

**galena** or **lead glance,** lustrous, blue-grey lead sulphide mineral (PbS). It is the chief ore and principal source of LEAD. Distributed worldwide, it frequently contains silver and other accessory metals.

**Galicia** (gah‚leetheeah), region, NW Spain, on the Atlantic Ocean, S of the Bay of Biscay and N of Portugal. It includes the provinces of La Coruña, Lugo, Orense, and Pontevedra. In this largely mountainous area, fishing and stock-raising are the major occupations. Galicia passed from Rome to the German Suevi (5th–6th cent.), the MOORS, and ASTURIAS (8th–9th cent.).

**Galicia** (gə‚leeʃə), historic region (83,740 km²/32,332 sq mi), now in POLAND and UKRAINE (USSR). Originally one of the principalities of RUTHENIA, it developed within the kingdom of Poland (1340–1775), when it was annexed by Austria at the first Partition of Poland (see POLAND, PARTITIONS OF). The western part (also known as Mapolska) was largely settled by Poles. The eastern part (also known as Red Ruthenia, and latterly as W Ukraine) was largely settled by Ukrainians. There was a very large Jewish community. East Galicia was disputed between Poland and Ukraine (1918–19), but in 1939 was occupied by Soviet forces and incorporated as W Ukraine into the USSR.

**Galilean satellites:** see JUPITER, in astronomy.

**Galilee,** Heb. *Ha Galil,* fertile and hilly region of N Israel, c.2300 km² (900 sq mi), between the Mediterranean and the upper JORDAN valley. Galilee was the chief scene of the ministry of Jesus Christ. After the destruction of Jerusalem (AD 70), it became the main centre of Judaism in PALESTINE. Zionist colonization of the area began at the end of the 19th cent. and accelerated after World War II. The chief city is NAZARETH.

**Galilee, Sea of, Lake Tiberias** or **Lake Kinneret,** lake in NE Israel (168 km²/65 sq mi), on the upper part of the JORDAN R., between the hills of GALILEE (W) and the GOLAN HEIGHTS (E). About 209 m (686 ft) below the level of the Mediterranean, it is a source of freshwater fish. It is fed and drained by the Jordan R. and some of its water is pumped to S Israel for irrigation. Since the outbreak of the Arab-Israeli War (1967) the whole of the lake shore has been under Israeli control.

**Galileo** (Galileo Galilei), 1564–1642, Italian astronomer, mathematician, and physicist. At the age of 19 he discovered the principle of isochronism that each oscillation of a pendulum takes the same time irrespective of amplitude. Soon thereafter he became known for his invention of a hydrostatic balance and his treatise on the centre of gravity of falling bodies. He found experimentally that bodies do not fall with velocities proportional to their weights, a conclusion received with hostility because it contradicted the accepted teaching of ARISTOTLE. Galileo discovered that the path of a projectile is a parabola, and he is credited with anticipating Isaac NEWTON's laws of motion. In 1609 he constructed the first astronomical telescope, which he used to discover the four largest satellites of Jupiter and the stellar composition of the Milky Way, and in 1632 he published his *Dialogue Concerning the Two Chief World Systems,* a work that upheld the COPERNICAN SYSTEM rather than the PTOLEMAIC SYSTEM and marked a turning point in scientific and philosophical thought. Brought (1633) before the INQUISITION in Rome, he was made to

Thomas **Gainsborough**, *Perdita*, 1781–82. The Wallace Collection, London.

the Law of MOSES are essential, Paul argues, in a passage central to Christianity, that salvation can be achieved through faith alone.

**galaxy,** large aggregation of gas, dust, and typically thousands of millions of stars. It is held together by the gravitational attraction between its constituent parts, and its rotational motion prevents it from collapsing on itself. A typical spiral galaxy is shaped like a flat disc, about 100,000 light-years in diameter, with a central bulge, or nucleus, containing old stars; winding through the disc are the characteristic spiral arms of dust, gas, and young stars. Our own Milky Way is such a spiral galaxy, with the Sun and all our astronomical neighbourhood of fixed stars in the plane of its disc (which shows up as the Milky Way) and about 25,000 light-years from its centre. An elliptical galaxy, lacking spiral arms entirely and containing little or no gas and dust, resembles the nucleus of a spiral galaxy. A small minority of galaxies are classified as irregular, i.e., showing no definite symmetry or nucleus. One theory suggests that irregulars evolve into spirals or ellipticals depending on the initial amount of rotational motion. Some galaxies radiate a large fraction of their energy in forms other than visible light, such as radio waves, X-rays, and infrared and ultraviolet radiation; their optical counterparts may be faint or undetectable. Gravitation also holds clusters of galaxies together; the Local Group cluster includes the MILKY WAY (containing the Sun and solar system) and the ANDROMEDA GALAXY, both spirals, and the irregular MAGELLANIC CLOUDS. See also HUBBLE'S LAW.

**Galbraith, John Kenneth,** 1908–, American economist and public official; b. Canada. He taught economics at Harvard (1934–39;

renounce all his beliefs and writings supporting the Copernican theory. His last book, *Dialogues Concerning Two New Sciences* (1638), contains most of his contributions to physics.

**Gall, Franz Joseph,** 1758–1828, Austrian physician. Devoting most of his life to a minute study of the nervous system, he showed that the brain's white matter consists of nerve fibres and he launched the doctrine localizing various mental processes in specific parts of the brain. Gall founded the now discredited science of phrenology, in which traits of character are said to be revealed by protuberances on the skull.

**Galla,** Hamitic pastoral tribes of W and S Ethiopia and Kenya, numbering about 10 million. They are either Muslim, Christian, or pagan. They have inhabited the Ethiopian highlands since the 16th cent., having come there from Somalia. A warlike people, the Galla have historically maintained small-group autonomy from the Ethiopian government.

**Gallatin, Albert,** 1761–1849, US public official and financier; b. Switzerland. A skilful secretary of the treasury (1801–14), whose fiscal accomplishments were wrecked by the EMBARGO and the WAR OF 1812, his financial policy was shaped less by Jeffersonian principles than his earlier criticisms of HAMILTON might have suggested. Thus he defended the Bank of the United States and urged the use of federal money to expand the internal economy. A key figure in negotiating the Treaty of GHENT, he was also minister to France (1816–23) and to Great Britain (1826–27). In 1842 he founded the American Ethnological Society.

**Gallaudet** ('galaw,det), American family of educators of the deaf. **Thomas Hopkins Gallaudet,** 1787–1851, founded (1817) the first free school for the deaf in the US. His oldest son, **Thomas Gallaudet,** 1822–1902, an Episcopal priest, founded St Ann's Church for Deaf-Mutes, New York City and the Gallaudet Home for aged deaf-mutes, Poughkeepsie, New York. The youngest son, **Edward Miner Gallaudet,** 1837–1917, opened a school for deaf-mutes (now Gallaudet College) in Washington, DC.

**gall bladder,** small, pear-shaped sac attached to the LIVER by the hepatic duct. The gall bladder stores and concentrates BILE, which is produced by the liver and functions in fat digestion. Fatty foods stimulate intestinal cells to produce a hormone that causes the gall bladder to contract, forcing the bile into the common bile duct and the intestine, where fats are absorbed. Components of bile sometimes crystallize in the gall bladder, forming gallstones, which may need to be treated by surgery.

**Gallegos, Rómulo** (gah,yaygɔs), 1884–1969, Venezuelan novelist and statesman. In 1948 he was president for 11 months until ousted by a military coup. In *Doña Bárbara* (1929), *Chanticleer* (1934), and other works, he explored Venezuelan life, concentrating on its landscape and customs.

**Galli-Curci, Amelita,** 1889–1963, American coloratura soprano; b. Italy. From her debut in 1909 to her retirement in 1930, she was not excelled by any coloratura of her day.

**Gallic Wars,** campaigns in Gaul led by Julius CAESAR as proconsul of Gaul (58–51 BC). Caesar's first campaign was to prevent the Helvetii from entering SW GAUL. Next, the Aedui asked Caesar's help against the German Ariovistus, whom Caesar routed. In 57 Caesar pacified Belgica (roughly equivalent to modern Belgium). In 56 BC he attacked the Veneti, and in the following year he went to the Low Countries and repelled a German invasion. He invaded (54 BC) Britain and the next winter put down a revolt of Belgian tribes led by Ambiorix. In 53 BC all central Gaul raised a revolt, organized by VERCINGETORIX. With incredible speed and brilliant tactics, Caesar crossed the Alps and suppressed the Gauls. The prime source of the Gallic Wars is Caesar's own commentaries, *De bello Gallico.*

**Gallieni, Joseph Simon** (gahlyay,nee), 1849–1916, French general. As governor general of Madagascar (1896–1905) he solidly established French rule. The military governor of Paris in WORLD WAR I, he contributed greatly to the French victory at the Marne (1914) by urging Gen. JOFFRE to counterattack.

**Gallipoli campaign,** Apr. 1915–Jan. 1916, Allied expedition in Turkey in WORLD WAR I. Planned by Winston CHURCHILL, British first lord of the admiralty, its purpose was to gain the Dardanelles, capture Constantinople, and make contact with Russia. Poor Allied cooperation and strong Turkish resistance forced the Allies into an evacuation that was the only successful operation in a disastrous campaign.

**Gallitzin** (gə,litsin), Russian princely family. **Vasily Vasilyevich Gallitzin,** d. 1619, sent to offer the Russian throne to Prince Ladislaus of Poland, was imprisoned by King SIGISMUND III for refusing to help him gain the throne; he died in prison. **Vasily Vasilyevich Gallitzin,** 1643–1714, was the lover and chief advisor of Sophia Alekseyevna, regent for PETER I. He was exiled to Siberia after her downfall (1689). **Boris Alekseyevich Gallitzin,** 1654–1714, tutor to PETER I, headed the government during Peter's first foreign tour. **Dmitri Mikhailovich Gallitzin,** 1665–1737, helped ANNA, daughter of IVAN IV, gain the throne providing she agreed to limit her power; she began to rule absolutely and sentenced him to death, then exiled him instead. **Dmitri Alekseyevich Gallitzin,** 1735–1803, Russian ambassador at Paris (1765–73), was a friend of DIDEROT and VOLTAIRE. **Aleksandr Nikolayevich Gallitzin,** 1773?–1844, a statesman of liberal tendencies, was a counsellor to ALEXANDER I. **Nikolai Dmitryevich Gallitzin,** 1856–1925, headed the council of ministers of NICHOLAS II from 1916 until the RUSSIAN REVOLUTION of 1917.

**gallium** (Ga), metallic element, discovered spectroscopically by P.E. Lecoq de Boisbaudran in 1875. Solid gallium is blue-grey; the liquid form is silver. It is chemically similar to ALUMINIUM. Gallium compounds, especially gallium arsenide and gallium aluminium arsenide, are used in transistors, lasers, and diodes. See ELEMENT (table); PERIODIC TABLE.

**gallotanic acid:** see TANNIN.

**Gallup, George Horace,** 1901–84, American public-opinion statistician. He founded the American Institute of Public Opinion (1935) at Princeton, New Jersey, and originated the Gallup POLL to measure voter sentiment and to gauge the national mood on various issues.

**Galois, Évariste,** 1811–32, French mathematician. Although killed at the age of 21 in a political duel, he made contributions to NUMBER THEORY and function theory and invented Galois theory, a critical area of modern algebra.

**Galsworthy, John,** 1867–1933, English novelist and dramatist. He is best remembered for his Forsyte novels, grouped in three trilogies, *The Forsyte Saga* (1922), *A Modern Comedy* (1929), and *End of the Chapter* (1934), dealing with three generations of a complacent upper-middle-class family from the 1880s to the 1920s. Galsworthy also wrote highly successful dramas on social problems, including *The Silver Box* (1906), *Strife* (1909), and *Justice* (1910). He was awarded the 1932 Nobel Prize in literature.

**Galsworthy, Olive Edis,** 1876–1955, English photographer. She set up a photographic studio with her sister in Norfolk, eventually moving to London, where she produced portraits of many eminent people, especially notable women such as Elizabeth Garrett ANDERSON and Emmeline PANKHURST. She was commissioned to record the work of women in the World War I battle zones of France and Belgium in 1919. From 1912 she also took beautiful colour portraits using the 'autochrome' process. She became a Fellow of the Royal Photographic Society in 1914.

Tending graves in the cemetery by Olive Edis **Galsworthy,** 1919

**Galt, John,** 1779–1839, Scottish novelist. Known chiefly for his novels of Scottish country life, e.g., *The Ayrshire Legatees* (1821), *Annals of the Parish* (1821), *The Entail* (1823), he also wrote a biography of BYRON (1830).

**Galtieri, Leopoldo Fortunato,** 1927–, Argentine general, president of ARGENTINA (1981–82). Army commander and a member of the ruling military junta, he assumed the presidency in Dec. 1981. He was quickly involved in a conflict with Britain over the British-held FALKLAND ISLANDS, which Argentina occupied in Apr. 1982. After the British recapture (14 June 1982) of the islands, he was forced to resign his posts. In 1986 he was sentenced to 12 years' imprisonment and stripped of his rank for his handling of the Falklands episode.

**Galton, Sir Francis,** 1822–1911, English scientist and cousin of Charles DARWIN. In his *Hereditary Genius* (1869), he presented strong evidence that talent is an inherited characteristic; this finding led him to found the EUGENICS movement. His system of classifying fingerprints is basically that still in use.

**Galvani, Luigi,** 1737–98, Italian physician. A noted surgeon and researcher in comparative anatomy, Galvani concluded, from his observation that a frog's leg contracted when touched by two different metals in a moist environment, that animal tissues generate ELECTRICITY. Although he was eventually proved wrong by Alessandro VOLTA, the controversy stimulated research in electrotherapy and on electric currents. Many electrical terms are derived from Galvani's name.

**galvanizing,** process of coating a metal, usually iron or steel, with a protective coating of ZINC. Galvanized iron is usually prepared by dipping or electroplating. Pure iron, copper iron, and various steels are often galvanized because the zinc coating resists oxidation and moisture.

**galvanometer,** instrument used to determine the presence, direction, and strength of electric current in a conductor. Galvanometers are based on the discovery (1819) by Hans OERSTED that a magnetic needle is deflected by the presence of an electric current in a nearby conductor. When an electric current is passing through the conductor, the magnetic needle tends to turn at right angles to the conductor, so that its direction is parallel to the lines of induction around the conductor and its north pole points in the direction in which these lines of induction flow. In general, the extent to which the needle turns is dependent upon the current strength. In the modern d'Arsonval galvanometer, the magnet is fixed and the coil that carries the current is movable. If a pointer is attached to the moving coil so that it passes over a suitably calibrated scale, the galvanometer can be used to measure quantitatively the current passing through it. A direct current (DC) AMMETER measures direct current by allowing a known percentage of the current to pass through a galvanometer. A DC VOLTMETER measures direct voltage (see POTENTIAL, ELECTRIC) between two points by allowing current to flow through a galvanometer connected in series with a high resistance. The current through the galvanometer is then proportional to the voltage (see OHM'S LAW).

**Galway,** county in W of Republic of Ireland (1986 pop. 178,180), 5879 km² (22293 sq mi), bordering on the Atlantic Ocean in the W. It is situated in the province of Connacht. The county town is GALWAY. Much of the eastern and central area is low-lying. In the S are the Slieve Aughty Mts. The W is mountainous, including the Maumturk Mts and the Twelve Pins, which rise to 730 m (2394 ft). The western area is known as Connemara and contains lakes, bogs, and hills. Lough Mask and Lough Corrib separate this western hilly region from the low-lying easterly part of the county. Agriculture is important and there is some manufacturing industry in Galway town.

**Galway,** county town (1986 pop. 47,008), of Co. Galway, Republic of Ireland, on N shore of Galway Bay. It is situated at the mouth of R. Corrib, which flows from Lough Corrib, just to the N of the town. It is a seaport and centre for the fishing industry. There are several old buildings, including a 14th-cent. church. University College was founded in 1849 and is part of the National Univ. of Ireland.

**Gama, Vasco da,** c.1469–1524, Portuguese navigator, the first European to travel by sea to INDIA (1497–99). At the order of MANUEL I, he commanded four vessels, reached Calicut (1498), and opened up a lucrative spice trade, thus beginning the Portuguese empire. He returned with 20 ships in 1502 and established Portuguese power in India and Africa. His methods were harsh, and he was not a good administrator. He was sent back to India as viceroy in 1524 but soon died.

**Gamaliel of Jabneh,** fl. AD 100, Jewish scholar, head of the SANHEDRIN at Jabneh. He unified the Jewish people after the destruction of Jerusalem, e.g., by regulating the prayer ritual and standardizing the Jewish calendar. The Romans also recognized him as a leader of his people.

**Gambetta, Léon** (gahnhbe͵tah), 1838–82, French republican leader. An opponent of the Second Empire of NAPOLEON III, he was prominent in the provisional government that followed the empire's fall (1870) in the FRANCO-PRUSSIAN WAR. He bitterly fought French capitulation and after 1871 helped to create the Third Republic. He pursued a moderate policy between the radicals and the monarchists and was premier (1881–82).

**Gambia, The,** officially Republic of The Gambia, republic (1983 est. pop. 695,886), 11,295 km² (4361 sq mi), W Africa, the continent's smallest independent state. It is a narrow strip of land on both banks of the Gambia R., bordered by the Atlantic Ocean on the west and surrounded on the remaining three sides by Senegal. The capital is BANJUL, on St Mary's Island, near the mouth of the Gambia R. A low-lying country, it ranges from sandy beaches along the coast to a swampy river valley in the interior. The economy is overwhelmingly dependent on the export of peanuts, which provides 90% of earnings. Tourism is an important source of revenue. The GNP is US$160 million, and the GNP per capita is US$230 (1985). Rice and other grains are produced for local consumption. The population is primarily Muslim black African, of whom the Mandingo are the most numerous; West Indians are an important minority. English is the official language.

*History.* Prior to the arrival of Portuguese explorers in the mid-15th cent., the area that is now Gambia was part of the MALI empire. English merchants won trading rights from the Portuguese in 1588, and in the early 17th cent. British companies founded settlements along the Gambia R. In 1816 the British purchased St Mary's Island, where they established Bathurst (now Banjul), and in 1843 the territory became a crown colony. The French, who controlled the neighbouring interior (now Senegal), failed in negotiations to acquire the Gambia R. settlements, which, in 1894, became a British protectorate. Gambia achieved self-government in 1962 and independence in 1965; it became a republic in the COMMONWEALTH in 1970. Independent Gambia is notable in Africa as a bastion of parliamentary democracy and political stability. The dominant political formation is the People's Progressive Party led by Pres. Sir Dawda K. Jawara. It has close relations with SENEGAL, and in 1981 the two nations joined in a confederation known as Senegambia, which, while maintaining individual sovereignty, aimed at cooperation in foreign policy, security, communications, and monetary and economic affairs.

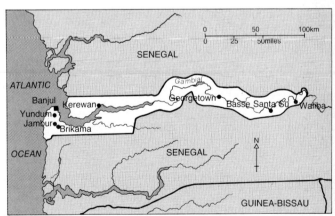

The **Gambia**

**games, theory of,** group of mathematical theories applying statistical logic to the choice of strategies in a game. A game consists of a set of rules governing a competitive situation in which two or more individuals or groups attempt to maximize their own winnings or minimize those of their opponents. Game theory, first developed by John VON NEUMANN, is applied to many fields, e.g., military problems, economics, and the study of evolutionary biology.

**gametophyte,** phase of a plant life cycle in which the egg (see OVUM) and SPERM (gametes) are produced. In many lower plants the gametophyte phase is the dominant life form; for example, the familiar MOSSES are the gametophyte form of the plant. The union of egg and sperm gives rise to the sporophyte phase, in which spores are formed; spores, in turn, give rise to the gametophyte. In mosses the sporophyte is a capsule atop a slender stalk that grows out of the top of the gametophyte. The alternation between the gametophyte and sporophyte phase is known as ALTERNATION OF GENERATIONS.

**gametophyte:** see ALTERNATION OF GENERATIONS.

**gamma decay,** one of the three types of natural RADIOACTIVITY. It involves the emission of the most energetic form of ELECTROMAGNETIC RADIATION, with a very short wavelength of less than $10^{-10}$ m. Gamma rays are essentially very energetic X-RAYS emitted by excited nuclei. They often accompany ALPHA DECAY or BETA DECAY, because following these decays the nucleus may be left in an excited (higher-energy) state. Gamma-ray sources are used in medicine for cancer treatment and for diagnostic purposes, and in industry for the inspection of castings and welds.

**gamma globulin:** see GLOBULIN.

**Gamow, George** (,gamof), 1904–68, American theoretical physicist and author; b. Russia; went to US, 1933. He is best known as an author who popularized abstract physical theories. Gamow devised (1928) a theory of radioactive decay and applied nuclear physics to problems of stellar evolution. He also proposed an important theory on the organization of genetic information in the living cell.

**Gance, Abel,** 1889–1981, French film director. Noted in his time for his silent films of enormous length, he has since been rediscovered with the recent recovery of his full 17-reel *Napoléon*, a film in which can be found, for the first time, virtually every technical accomplishment of the cinema. His other films include *J'accuse* (1919) and *La Roue* (1923).

**Gandhi, Indira,** 1917–84, prime minister of INDIA (1966–77, 1980–84); daughter of Jawaharlal NEHRU. After serving as an aide to her father and rising through the ranks of the INDIAN NATIONAL CONGRESS, she became prime minister on the death of SHASTRI. India's defeat of Pakistan in 1971 assured Indian dominance of the subcontinent. Gandhi's administration, increasingly authoritarian, was marked by stress on social programmes and government planning. Faced with opposition, she declared an 'emergency' in 1975, jailing opponents and suspending civil liberties. Forced from office in 1977, she made a triumphant return in 1980, but was assassinated by a SIKH extremist in 1984. She was succeeded as prime minister by her son **Rajiv Gandhi** (b.1945), a former airline pilot who had become a political adviser to his mother following the death (1980) of his younger brother **Sanjay** (the original heir-apparent of the Gandhi political dynasty).

**Gandhi, Mohandas Karamchand,** 1869–1948, Indian political leader. Born in Gujarat in W India, Gandhi practised as a barrister in London and settled in South Africa where he led the nonviolent struggle for the civil rights of Indians in the 1890s. Later, as the supreme leader of the INDIAN NATIONAL CONGRESS, he applied the technique of *satyagraha* [nonviolent resistance] for the attainment of India's independence, first in the Non-Co-operation-cum Khilafat (1920–22) and later in the Civil Disobedience Movement (1930–34). When negotiations for a political settlement failed, he called upon Indians to launch the Quit India movement (1942) which became a spontaneous rising after the arrest of Gandhi and other leaders. He also worked for programmes of rural reconstruction and abolition of untouchability. He virtually withdrew from politics after independence and was assassinated by a Hindu extremist in the belief that his attitude to Pakistan and the Muslims was a threat to Hindu interest.

**Gandhi, Rajiv,** 1944–, prime minister of India. He was elected with an overwhelming majority following the assassination of his mother, Indira GANDHI. Committed to a free-market ideology and technological revolution, he has lost a substantial part of his initial support especially after allegations of corruption over arms deals.

**Ganges** or **Ganga** (,gangeez), chief river in India, c.2500 km (1560 mi) long, considered sacred by Hindus. It rises in the HIMALAYAS and flows generally E-SE through a wide and densely populated plain to join the BRAHMAPUTRA R. in Bangladesh. The combined river then continues through a vast and fertile delta on the Bay of BENGAL, which it enters as the Padma and other distributaries. Hardwar, ALLAHABAD, and VARANASI (Benares) are especially holy bathing sites along its banks. The Ganges is a major source of water for irrigation in both India and Bangladesh.

**Gang of Four,** JIANG QING and associates, Wang Hongwen, Zhang Chunqiao, and Yao Wenyuan. Also known as the Shanghai Group, they were prominent radicals in the CULTURAL REVOLUTION and leaders of an ultra-left faction in the succession struggle on the death of MAO ZEDONG. Their arrest (1976) and public trial (Dec. 1980–Jan. 1981), was a form of retribution for those persecuted in the Cultural Revolution. Sentences ranged from death (to be commuted upon rehabilitation) to 20 years in prison.

**gangrene,** local death and putrefaction of body tissue associated with a deficiency of blood supply. The causes include injury, atheroma (fatty deposits on artery walls), FROSTBITE, and DIABETES. Dry gangrene results from a simple cessation of local blood circulation. Moist gangrene results from bacterial infection. Treatment includes rest and ANTIBIOTIC drugs; excision of the diseased area or, in advanced cases, amputation of the affected part may be necessary. Gas gangrene, a rapidly spreading gangrene in which gas bubbles form in the dead and dying tissue, is a dangerous complication of extensive wounds, particularly when contaminated with soil, due to infection by bacteria.

**gannet:** see BOOBY.

**Gansu** or **Kansu,** province (1985 est. pop. 20,410,000), 451,000 km² (174,131 sq mi), NW China; bordered by Inner Mongolia (NE) and Qinghai prov. (SW). The upper reaches of the YELLOW RIVER flow through this elongated province. Major cities are LANZHOU, the capital, and Tianshui. SE Gansu is an extension of the eroded SHAANXI plateau. The central Lanzhou basin is important in providing agricultural land, much of the province being unsuitable for agriculture. To the northwest the Gansu corridor runs through mountain ranges, used chiefly for pasture, to XINJIANG prov. In the Gansu corridor only irrigated oasis agriculture is important. In the Lanzhou basin and the eastern loess lands, wheat, kaoliang (a type of sorghum), and millet are grown. The province's historic and contemporary importance is based on its role as a route between China, Mongolia, and Tibet. Part of the historic Silk Road, on which China's trade depended, passed through Gansu, and today Lanzhou is a transport and commercial centre. It is a central site for China's industrialization of its NW provinces and, partly based on a pipeline from Yumen in W Gansu, Lanzhou has developed oil-refining and chemical industries. In the Gobi desert region of the NW is Shuangchengzi, the site of China's missile-testing programme.

**Ganymede,** in astronomy, natural satellite of JUPITER.

**Ganymede,** in Greek mythology, a beautiful youth carried off by ZEUS to be cupbearer to the gods.

**Gaon of Vilna:** see ELIJAH BEN SOLOMON.

**gar, garpike, garfish,** cylindrical, New World freshwater FISH called garpike (family Lepisosteidae) with hard, diamond-shaped scales, a long jaw, and long, sharp teeth. The largest species is the 2.5-m (9-ft) alligator gar (*Lepisosteus spatula*) of the Mississippi valley. This family are living fossils. There are a large group of unrelated Old World fishes called garfishes, mostly marine, living round Britain and Europe, and in the Indian and Malayan waters. The garfish (*Belone belone*) found in British waters is unusual in that it has green bones. The skippers and needlefishes belong to this group.

**Garamond, Claude,** 1480–1561, French designer and maker of printing TYPES. His types were used by the ESTIENNES, Plantin, and BODONI. The ELZEVIR family based their types on his. His roman and italic types were innovative in being designed as metal types, not as imitations of handwriting. He was a chief influence in establishing the roman letter as standard.

**Garbarek, Jan,** 1947–, Norwegian jazz tenor and soprano saxophonist, clarinettist, flautist, bandleader, and composer. Although the Nordic overtones in his playing and composition are frequently cited, his stature as an improviser is firmly rooted in the true jazz tradition, including imaginative handling of blues-based material. A leading international contemporary player who has successfully embraced jazz/rock as well as collaborating with composers outside the jazz field.

**Garbo, Greta,** 1905–, American film actress; b. Sweden as Greta Gustafson. She was noted for her beauty and her dramatic intensity. Her films include *Queen Christina* (1933), *Anna Karenina* (1935), and *Camille* (1936).

**Garborg, Arne**, 1851–1924, Norwegian writer. He championed the use of Landsmaal as a literary language (see NORWEGIAN LANGUAGE). His major works are the naturalistic novels *Peasant Students* (1883), *Tired Men* (1891), and *Peace* (1892), and the verse cycle *The Hill Innocent* (1895).

**García Lorca, Federico** (gah,theeah ,lawkah), 1898–1936, Spanish lyric poet and dramatist. His work reflects the spirit of his native Andalusia and his own passionate response to life. *Romancero gitano* (1928; tr. Gypsy Ballads) made him the most popular Spanish poet of his generation, while *Llanto por la muerte de Ignacio Sánchez Mejías* (1935; tr. Lament for the Death of a Bullfighter) and *Poeta en Nueva York* (1940) showed his growing maturity of thought. His plays, notably the tragedies *Bodas de sangre* (1933; tr. Blood Wedding), *Yerma* (1934), and *La casa de Bernada Alba* (1936; tr. The House of Bernarda Alba), ensure his continuing international reputation. García Lorca was shot by FRANCO's soldiers at the outbreak of the SPANISH CIVIL WAR.

**García Márquez, Gabriel** (gah,seeah məhkays), 1928–, Colombian writer. His works, generally chronicling the physical and moral collapse of Macondo, an imaginary town, include *La hejarasca y otros cuentos* (1955; tr. Leaf Storm and Other Stories) and the novels *Cien años de soledad* (1967; tr. One Hundred Years of Solitude), *El otoño del patriarca* (1975; tr. The Autumn of the Patriarch), and *Crónica de una muerta anunciada* (1981; tr. Chronicle of a Death Foretold). He was awarded the 1982 Nobel Prize for literature.

**García Moreno, Gabriel** (gah,seeah moh,raynoh), 1821–75, president of ECUADOR (1861–65, 1869–75). A fervent Roman Catholic, he guaranteed (1862) the church's independence and granted it control over education. His despotism in crushing liberal opposition led to his assassination.

**García y Iñigues, Calixto** (gah,seeah ee en,yeegays), 1839–98, Cuban revolutionary. He was a leader in the TEN YEARS' WAR (1868–78) and played an important role in the SPANISH-AMERICAN WAR.

**Garcilaso de la Vega** (gahthee,lahsoh day lah ,vaygah), 1501?–36, Spanish lyric poet. He typified the courtly poet–soldier of Spain's GOLDEN AGE. His sonnets, elegies, odes, and eclogues, published after his death in battle, introduced Italian RENAISSANCE poetic forms into Spain.

**Garda, Lake**, 366 km² (143 sq mi), on the edge of the Lombardy Alps in N Italy. It owes its depth (346 m/1135 ft) to glacial erosion in the Ice Ages. The mildness of the lakeshore climate enables olives, almonds, and citrus fruits to be grown. This, and the attractive scenery, draw many visitors. Riva di Trento is a favourite resort.

**garden city**, new town of limited size and moderate density as envisaged by Ebenezer Howard in his *Tomorrow: A Peaceful Path to Real Reform* (1898; reissued 1902 as *Garden Cities of Tomorrow*). A British concept, it was a corrective to the overcrowded and congested industrial cities which had grown at an unprecedented rate during the 19th cent., Howard proposed the building of new towns with populations of between 32,000 and 58,000, surrounded by agricultural land and complete with the facilities to provide a full social and economic life. The system of land ownership had the freehold held in trust for the public. The first garden city was Letchworth, Hertfordshire, founded in 1903, more than 50 km (31 mi) from London. Its population grew to 31,000. The second was Welwyn Garden City, Hertfordshire, founded in 1920. Both were planned to mix elements of both country and town. They were preceded by garden suburbs and garden villages such as New Earswick near York. The logical successor to the garden city was the post-war NEW TOWN.

**gardenia**, evergreen shrub or tree (genus *Gardenia*) of the MADDER family, native to the Old World tropics. Gardenias' heavily fragrant and showy blossoms make them popular corsage and greenhouse plants. Most of the cultivated types are varieties of *G. jasminoides*, also called Cape jasmine but unrelated to true JASMINE.

**Gardiner, Samuel Rawson**, 1829–1902, English historian. His carefully researched history of the ENGLISH CIVIL WAR appeared as several works, later regrouped into three: *The History of England from the Accession of James I to the Outbreak of the Great Civil War* (10 vol., 1863–82), *History of the Great Civil War* (3 vol., 1886–91), and *History of the Commonwealth and Protectorate* (3 vol., 1895–1901).

**Gardner, Percy**, 1846–1937, English classical archaeologist and professor of archaeology (1887–1925) at Oxford, a specialist in Greek art and numismatics. His *Types of Greek Coins* (1883) shows how coinage reflects both the history and art of a period. His brother, **Ernest Arthur Gardner**, 1862–1939, wrote the *Handbook of Greek Sculpture* (1897, rev. ed. 1915).

**Garfield, James Abram**, 1831–81, 20th president of the US (March–Sept. 1881). He served in the Union army until 1863, when he became a Republican member of the US House of Representatives. Elected president in 1880, he declared war on the leading faction of his party by appointing James G. BLAINE secretary of state (passing over the 'Stalwarts' of the influential Roscoe Conkling). But on 2 July 1881, he was shot by a disappointed office seeker, Charles J. Guiteau. Garfield died 19 Sept. and was succeeded by Vice Pres. Chester A. ARTHUR.

**Garibaldi, Giuseppe**, 1807–82, Italian patriot and soldier, a leading figure in the RISORGIMENTO; b. France. He fled to South America (1835) after a republican plot failed and fought (1042–46) in the Uruguayan civil war. Returning to Italy, he fought for Sardinia against Austria (1848) and for MAZZINI's short-lived Roman republic (1849), then found asylum in the US. Returning (1851) to Italy, he renounced his republican views and supported a united Italy under VICTOR EMMANUEL II of Sardinia. In 1860, with Victor Emmanuel's connivance, Garibaldi led 1000 volunteer 'red shirts' in a spectacular conquest of Sicily and Naples. He then relinquished his conquests to Sardinia, and Victor Emmanuel was proclaimed (1861) king of Italy. In 1862 and 1867 he tried unsuccessfully to take Rome, which had remained outside the new kingdom. He was elected (1874) to the Italian parliament.

**Garland, Hamlin**, 1860–1940, American author. Raised in the Midwest, he wrote of the difficulties of prairie life in tales, e.g., *Main-Travelled Roads* (1891); novels, e.g., *A Little Norsk* (1892); and autobiographical works, e.g., *A Daughter of the Middle Border* (1921).

**Garland, Judy**, 1922–69, American singer and film actress; b. Frances Gumm. Her films include *The Wizard of Oz* (1939), *Meet Me in St Louis* (1944), and *A Star Is Born* (1954). Her daughter **Liza Minnelli**, 1946–, is a singer and film actress whose films include *Cabaret* (1972) and *Arthur* (1981).

**garlic:** see ONION.

**Garmisch-Partenkirchen** (,gahmish), town (1984 pop. 27,500), S West Germany, in the Bavarian Alps. It is a fashionable winter resort amongst dramatic mountain scenery, lying at the foot of Zugspitze (2963 m/9720 ft), the highest peak in Germany.

**garnet**, name applied to a group of silicate minerals [(Fe, Mg,Ca,Mn)$_3$(Al,Fe,Cr)$_2$(SiO$_4$)$_3$], used chiefly as GEMS and abrasives. The most common gem varieties are red, but garnets are also yellow, brown, and green. They are found in many types of rock throughout the world.

**Garnett, Richard**, 1835–1906, English author and distinguished librarian at the British Museum (1851–99). He wrote essays, novels, and poems, and biographies of MILTON, CARLYLE, EMERSON, and COLERIDGE, and discovered previously unknown poems by P.B. SHELLEY. His son, **Edward Garnett**, 1868–1937, was a critic who corresponded with and encouraged many writers. Edward's wife, **Constance (Black) Garnett**, 1862–1946, made important translations from Russian of TOLSTOY, DOSTOYEVSKY, and others. Their son, **David Garnett**, 1892–1981, wrote the imaginative *Lady into Fox* (1922) and other novels.

**Garonne**, river of SW France 643 km (402 mi) long, which rises in the high PYRENEES and flows through the basin of AQUITAINE to enter the Bay of Biscay below BORDEAUX. Its fertile river terraces support rich crops of wheat, maize, and orchard fruit. Vines are extensively grown and there are famous vineyards around the Gironde, the common estuary of the Garonne and Dordogne Rs.

**Garrett, João Baptista de Silva Leitão de Almeida**, 1799–1854, Portuguese poet, novelist, and dramatist. Fleeing to England after taking part in the liberal revolt of 1820, he came into contact with ROMANTICISM. When he returned home he once again took an active part in politics, becoming a peer in 1852. His Romantic poetry was influential, and he is particularly remembered for his plays, e.g., *Brother Luis de Sousa* (1844; tr. 1909), which revitalized Portuguese theatre.

**Garrick, David**, 1717–79, English actor, manager, and dramatist, the greatest actor of 18th-cent. England. A pupil of Samuel JOHNSON, he accompanied Johnson to London in 1737. His formal debut (1741) as Richard III made him the idol of London, where his straightforward manner and diction revolutionized acting styles. Noted for his versatility, he played contemporary drama as well as Shakespearean roles; his King Lear was especially praised. As manager (1747–76) of the Drury Lane Theatre, he initiated many reforms in stagecraft.

**Garrison, William Lloyd**, 1805–79, American abolitionist. He founded the *Liberator* in 1831 and for 35 years campaigned for immediate and complete abolition of slavery. Favouring moral persuasion over violence or political involvement, he helped organize (1833) the American Anti-Slavery Society and was its president from 1843 to 1865. He advocated Northern secession from the Union because the Constitution permitted slavery, and he opposed the Civil War until Lincoln issued the EMANCIPATION PROCLAMATION in 1862. Although Garrison was considered the foremost antislavery leader during the 19th cent., historical evidence indicates that less famous ABOLITIONISTS were more effective.

**Garter, Order of the:** see DECORATIONS, CIVIL AND MILITARY.

**Garvey, Marcus,** 1887–1940, American proponent of black nationalism; b. Jamaica. In 1914 he founded the Universal Negro Improvement Association to foster worldwide unity among blacks and establish the greatness of the African heritage. Rejecting any notion of integration in countries where blacks were a minority, he urged a 'back to Africa' movement. Garvey's brilliant oratory and his newspaper, *Negro World*, made him the most influential black leader of the early 1920s, but his influence declined after his misuse of funds intended to establish a Negro steamship company resulted in a mail fraud conviction. He was jailed (1925) and deported to Jamaica (1927), dying in relative obscurity.

**Gary,** US city (1984 est. pop. 143,000), NW Indiana, on Lake Michigan, near Chicago. One of the world's great steel centres, Gary was founded by the US Steel Corp., which bought the land in 1905. Its location midway between western iron ore sources and eastern and southeastern coal areas made it ideal for industry. During the nationwide steel strike of 1919 federal troops occupied the city for several months.

**gas,** in physics: see KINETIC–MOLECULAR THEORY OF GASES; STATES OF MATTER.

**Gasca, Pedro de la** (,gahskah), c.1485–1567, Spanish colonial administrator in PERU (1547–50). Sent by the Emperor CHARLES V to restore order, he repealed the New Laws of LAS CASAS, which were meant to protect Indians, and pardoned their violators. He put down (1548) a revolt by Gonzalo PIZARRO and restored order in Peru.

**Gascoigne, George,** 1534?–77, English soldier–poet. He served with Queen Elizabeth's forces in the Netherlands and wrote in a variety of genres, some traditional, some innovatory. His *Posies* (1575), which had previously been published as *A Hundreth Sundrie Flowres* (1573), included a mixture of lyric and descriptive verse, some heavily influenced by CHAUCER; a prose comedy, *Supposes*, translated from ARIOSTO; a tragedy, *Jocasta*, deriving from Euripides by way of Italian and Latin intermediaries; a short but pioneering account of English versification; and a strange novella about adultery in a country house, *The Adventures of Master F.J.*

**gas constant:** see GAS LAWS.

**Gascony,** region, SW France. The sandy, wooded Landes along the ocean, the Pyrenees, and the hilly Armagnac region are the main geographic areas. Fishing, timber and paper-making, and tourism are the chief industries. Auch is the historic capital. The Vascones, or BASQUES, invaded the area and set up a duchy in 601. In 1154 Gascony, along with AQUITAINE, came under English rule; and France did not recover it completely until the end (1453) of the HUNDRED YEARS WAR. It later passed to Henry of Navarre (later HENRY IV of France) and was united with the royal domain in 1607.

**Gaskell, Elizabeth Cleghorn (Stevenson),** 1810–65, English novelist. *Mary Barton* (1848), *Ruth* (1853), and *North and South* (1855) showed her humanitarian concern for exploited industrial workers and for the outcasts of society. In her most popular work, *Cranford* (1853), and in her unfinished masterpiece, *Wives and Daughters* (1866), she depicted with affectionate insight the idiosyncrasies of country communities. Her *Life of Charlotte Brontë* (1857) was masterly but caused some controversy.

**gas laws,** physical laws describing the behaviour of a gas (see STATES OF MATTER) under various conditions of volume ($V$), pressure ($P$), and absolute, or Kelvin, TEMPERATURE ($T$). Boyle's, (sometimes called Mariotte's) gas law states that under constant temperature $PV = k_1$. Charles's (also called Gay-Lussac's) law states that under constant pressure $V = k_2 T$. A third law states that under constant volume $P = k_3 T$. The constants $k_1$, $k_2$, and $k_3$ are dependent on the amount of gas present and, respectively, on the temperature, pressure, and volume of the gas. These three laws can be combined into a single law, or equation of state: $PV = kT$ or $Pv = RT$, in which $v$ is the specific volume equal to $V/n$, $n$ is the number of moles of the gas, $k$ is a proportionality constant, and $R$ is the universal gas constant, equal to $8.3149 \times 10^3$ joules/kg-mole-degree. These laws are formulated for so-called ideal or perfect gases. Real gases are described more accurately by the VAN DER WAALS equation: $(P + a/v^2)(v - b) = RT$, in which $a$ and $b$ are specific constants for each gas.

**gasoline:** see PETROL.

**Gaspar:** see WISE MEN OF THE EAST.

**Gaspee,** British revenue cutter, burned 10 June 1772, at Gaspee Point, Narragansett Bay, Rhode Island, US. Colonists burned the *Gaspee* in defiance of the enforcement of revenue laws.

**Gaspé Peninsula** or **Gaspésie,** tongue of land, E Quebec, Canada, 97–145 km (60–90 mi) wide, projecting c.240 km (150 mi) E into the Gulf of St Lawrence. The coast is famous for its bold headlands and picturesque settlements. The interior is a mountainous wilderness, completely forested, that reaches a high point of 1268 m (4160 ft) in the Shickshock Mts.

**Gass, William,** 1924–, American writer. He is a philosopher and literary critic as well as a fiction writer and is most interested in problems of style and the workings of language. His works include the novel *Omensetter's Luck* (1966), the collections of essays entitled *Fiction and the Figures of Life* (1970) and *The World Within the Word* (1978), and an extraordinary stylistic meditation on a word, *On Being Blue* (1976).

**Gassendi, Pierre,** 1592–1655, French philosopher. He is best known for his *Objections* (1642) to DESCARTES' *Meditations*, but he also produced a careful study of EPICURUS, which led him to develop an atomistic explanation of the universe in *Syntagma Philosophicum* (1658).

**Gasser, Herbert Spencer,** 1888–1963, American physiologist. Former director of the Rockefeller Inst., he worked with Joseph ERLANGER on nerve impulse conduction, for which they both received the 1944 Nobel Prize for physiology or medicine.

**gastropod,** MOLLUSC of the class Gastropoda. It usually has a coiled or spiralled one-piece shell (univalve), although it may be reduced or absent. The head has sensory tentacles and a mouth with a rasplike tongue (radula). The ventral surface of the animal is modified into a large, flattened foot, which, along with other soft body parts, can be withdrawn into the shell; in most cases, the opening is covered by a plate (operculum). Most gastropods are marine, but there are forms that live in fresh water and on land. The class includes the EAR SHELL, CONCH, SNAIL, SLUG, WHELK, LIMPET, PERIWINKLE, and SEA SLUG.

**Gateshead,** town (1981 pop. 91,429), in Tyne and Wear, NE England, on S bank of R. Tyne, opposite NEWCASTLE UPON TYNE. It is linked to Newcastle by a tunnel and five bridges. The town is an important, although declining, industrial centre, with many heavy industries including engineering and the manufacture of chemicals. In the 1930s an industrial estate was established (the Team Valley Trading Estate) to relieve unemployment.

**Gatling, Richard Jordan,** 1818–1903, American inventor. He invented and manufactured agricultural implements, but is remembered as the creator of a rapid-firing gun, the precursor of the modern machine gun (see SMALL ARMS). He offered it to the Union army, but it was not accepted for use until 1866, after the Civil War had ended.

**Gatti-Casazza, Giulio,** 1869–1940, Italian operatic manager. He was director of La Scala, Milan (1898–1908), and the METROPOLITAN OPERA, New York City (1908–35).

**Gatwick Airport,** international airport, 4 km (2½ mi) N of Crawley and 39 km (24 mi) S of London, in W Sussex, SE England. It is one of two airports serving London, the other being HEATHROW AIRPORT. In 1984 14 million passengers passed through the airport.

**Gaudier-Brzeska, Henri** (goh,dyay bəzhes,kah), 1891–1915, French sculptor. The chief exponent of VORTICISM in sculpture, he is known for his draughtsmanship, animal figures, and abstracts.

**Gaudí y Cornet, Antonio** (,gowdee ee ,kawnet), 1852–1926, Spanish architect, working mainly in Barcelona. He created startling architectural forms paralleling the development of ART NOUVEAU or MODERNISMO. Many of his buildings resemble sculptural configurations, e.g., the undulating facade of Casa Milá (1905–10). His use of colour and mixed materials is seen in his masterpiece, the Expiatory Church of the Holy Family (begun 1882), still unfinished. He also made many technological innovations.

Templo Sagrada Familia, Barcelona by Antonio **Gaudí y Cornet**

**Gauguin, Paul** (goh,ganh), 1848–1903, French painter and woodcut artist; a highly influential founder of modern art. At 35 he left his career as a stockbroker and devoted himself to painting. At first associated with the impressionists (see IMPRESSIONISM), he spent long periods in Brittany, where in 1888 he and Émile Bernard proposed a synthetist theory emphasizing the use of flat planes and bright, non-naturalistic colour with symbolic or primitive subjects. *Vision after the Sermon* (1888; National Gall., Edinburgh) is the key work of this period. In 1891 he went to Tahiti, where he painted some of his finest works and wrote *Noa Noa* (tr. 1947), an autobiographical novel. He returned to France briefly, and died in poverty and despair in the South Seas. Gauguin rejected the tradition of Western NATURALISM, using nature as a starting point from which to abstract figures and symbols. His colour harmonies and profound sense of mystery can be seen in such paintings as *Where Do We Come From? What Are We? Where Are We Going?* (1897; Mus. Fine Arts, Boston), *la Orana Maria* (1891; Metropolitan Mus., New York), and *By the Sea* (1892; Nat. Gall., Washington., DC). He also revived the art of woodcutting, and did some fine ceramics.

Paul **Gauguin**, *The Vision after the Sermon*, 1888. Oil on canvas, 73 × 92 cm. National Gallery of Scotland.

**Gaul**, Lat. *Gallia,* ancient name for the land S and W of the Rhine, W of the Alps, and N of the Pyrenees. The name was extended by the Romans to include N Italy and is derived from its settlers of the 4th and 3rd cent. BC, invading CELTS, called Gauls by the Romans. Julius CAESAR conquered Gaul in the GALLIC WARS (58–51 BC). He is the best ancient source on Gaul, and he has immortalized its three ethnic divisions: Aquitania in the S, Gaul proper (central France), and Belgica in the N. Gaul was rapidly Romanized.

**Gaunt, John of:** see JOHN OF GAUNT.

**Gauss, Carl Friedrich,** 1777–1855, German mathematician, physicist, and astronomer. Considered the greatest mathematician of his time and the equal of ARCHIMEDES and Sir Isaac NEWTON, Gauss made many discoveries before he was twenty. His greatest work was in NUMBER THEORY; his *Disquisitiones arithmeticae* (completed 1798; pub. 1801) is a masterpiece. Extremely careful and rigorous in his work, Gauss refused to publish any result without a complete proof. Consequently, many discoveries were not credited to him and were rediscovered by others later, e.g., the work of János BOLYAI and Nikolai LOBACHEVSKY in NON-EUCLIDEAN GEOMETRY, Augustin CAUCHY in complex variable analysis, Carl JACOBI in elliptic functions, and Sir William Rowan HAMILTON in quaternions. Gauss early discovered, independently of Adrien LEGENDRE, the method of least squares. In 1801, when the asteroid Ceres was discovered by the Italian astronomer Giuseppe Piazzi, Gauss calculated its orbit on the basis of only a few accurate observations, and it was found the next year precisely where he had predicted. His *Theoria motus corporum celestium* (1809) treats the calculation of the orbits of planets and comets from observational data. From 1807 until his death Gauss was director of the astronomical observatory at Göttingen. Geodetic survey work done for the governments of Hanover and Denmark from 1821 led him to an interest in space curves and surfaces, as well as to the invention of the heliotrope, a device to measure distances by means of reflected sunlight. Gauss's collaboration with the German physicist Wilhelm Weber in research on electric and magnetic phenomena led to his invention, in 1833, of the electric telegraph.

**Gautier, Théophile,** 1811–72, French poet, novelist, and critic and exponent of art for art's sake. His finely crafted poems, notably *Emaux et camées* (1852; tr. Enamels and Cameos), foreshadowed the revolt against ROMANTICISM by the PARNASSIANS and SYMBOLISTS. His novel *Mademoiselle de Maupin* (1835) is well known.

**gavotte**, originally a peasant DANCE of the Gavots, in upper Dauphiné, France. A circle dance in 4/4 time with lively, skipping steps, it was used by LULLY in court ballets, and by COUPERIN and J.S. BACH in their keyboard suites.

**Gay, John**, 1685–1732, English playwright and poet, best known for *The Beggar's Opera* (1728), a ballad opera about thieves and prostitutes, and satirizing society and then-fashionable Italian opera. Its sequel, *Polly* (1729), was suppressed by the government. Gay's verse appeared in *Fables* (1727, 1738).

**Gaya,** town (1981 pop. 247,075), Bihar state, NE India. It is a district administrative and trading centre with rice, cotton and oil mills and railway workshops, and a flourishing pilgrim and tourist trade, for nearby is Buddh Gaya, where the Buddha received enlightenment. Gaya itself is an ancient city.

**Gay Liberation:** see HOMOSEXUALITY.

**Gay-Lussac, Joseph Louis,** 1778–1850, French chemist and physicist. He and the French chemist Louis Jacques Thénard were the first to isolate BORON. Gay-Lussac discovered (1802) independently that at constant pressure the volume of an enclosed gas is directly proportional to its temperature, a law known as Charles's law or as Gay-Lussac's law (see GAS LAWS). He was the first to formulate (c.1808) the law of combining volumes, which states that gases combine by volume in simple multiple proportion.

**Gay-Lussac's law:** see GAS LAWS.

**Gaza Strip,** coastal region of the Middle East (1982 est. pop. 500,000), 370 km² (140 sq mi), on the Mediterranean Sea, adjoining Egypt and Israel; largely inhabited by Arab refugees from Israel. It was part of the British mandate for PALESTINE from 1922 to 1948, passed to Egyptian control in 1949, and was occupied by Israel from the time of the 1967 ARAB-ISRAELI WAR. Autonomy for the region was promised by the CAMP DAVID ACCORDS (1978) and the Egyptian-Israeli peace treaty (1979), but was not immediately granted.

**gazelle,** delicate, graceful ANTELOPE (genus *Gazella*) inhabiting arid, open country, usually in Africa. Standing 60–90 cm (2–3 ft) high at the shoulder, the fawn-coloured gazelle often has heavily ringed horns that curve back and inward. Gazelles are powerful jumpers and very swift. Closely related is the reddish-brown **impala** (*Aepyceros melampus*), the most powerful jumper of all antelopes, able to leap 3 m (10 ft) into the air and travel 9 m (30 ft) in a single bound.

**Gaziantep,** city (1980 pop. 374,290), capital of Gaziantep prov., S Turkey. It is the commercial centre of an area famed for its pistachio nuts. Cotton textiles are manufactured. Captured by Saladin in 1183, it is overlooked by the ruins of a medieval fortress.

**Gazira:** see GEZIRA.

**Gd,** chemical symbol of the element GADOLINIUM.

**Gdańsk** or **Danzig,** city (1984 pop. 464,000), N Poland, on a branch of the Vistula R. and on the Gulf of Gdańsk. It is a major port on the BALTIC SEA, with some of the world's largest shipyards. Its other industries include metallurgy and sawmilling. An old Slavic settlement, it was the capital of Pomerelia (see POMERANIA) from the 10th cent. and a member of the HANSEATIC LEAGUE from the 13th cent. Seized by the Teutonic Knights in 1308, it soon became a predominantly German city. From 1466 to 1793, it was the chief port of the kingdom of Poland; and during 1793–1806, 1815–1920, and 1939–45 it was ruled by PRUSSIA. During the Napoleonic era, and again 1920–39, it was a Free City. HITLER's demand for Danzig's return to Germany provoked WORLD WAR II. In 1945–46, the city's German inhabitants were expelled, and it was repopulated with Poles. In 1970 and again in 1980 workers' strikes at Gdansk led to serious political crisis in Poland. In Aug. 1980, the Lenin Shipyard was the site of the birth of SOLIDARITY.

**Gdynia,** city (1984 pop. 240,000), Poland, on the Baltic Sea coast. A new town of the interwar years, it was built at the end of the POLISH CORRIDOR to reduce the country's dependence on GDAŃSK. The port accommodates passenger shipping as well as handling foodstuffs and fishing vessels. Shipbuilding is an important industry.

**Ge,** chemical symbol of the element GERMANIUM.

**gear,** toothed wheel, cylinder, or cone, usually mounted on a shaft, that transmits motion from one part of a machine to another, often with a change of rotational axis. When the teeth of two gears are meshed, the turning of one shaft will cause the other shaft to rotate. By meshing two gears of different diameters, a variation in both speed and torque is obtained dependent on the ratio of diameters. If one of the meshed gears is a flat bar with identical teeth then rotary motion is converted to linear motion or vice versa.

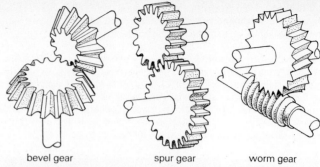

bevel gear                    spur gear                    worm gear

Types of **gear** wheels

**gecko,** any of several LIZARDS, members of the family Geckonidae, recognized by their large eyes and their expanded toes, covered beneath by microscopic hooks which give the group exceptional climbing abilities. There are an enormous number of species of geckos in all the warmer regions of the world, ranging in size from 3.25 cm (1⅓ in) to 35 cm (14 in). They are found in a variety of habitats, in trees, among rocks, and in deserts. All of them are insectivores. The geckos have the ability to break off their tails if threatened, leaving it twitching to distract the predator while the animal makes its escape. A new tail will grow. These engaging lizards have adapted completely to living with humans, amazing watchers by their skill at running up apparently smooth walls and moving upside down across ceilings.

**Geddes, Norman Bel,** 1893–1958, American designer; b. Adrian, Mich. He was known for imaginative designs for the New York City stage, notably *The Miracle* (1924), and for numerous industrial products. His daughter, **Barbara Bel Geddes,** 1922–, is a well-known actress. She has appeared in the television series *Dallas* (1978–).

**Geddes, Patrick,** 1854–1932, Scottish biologist, sociologist, and pioneer of urban studies. He was knighted in 1931.

**Geelong,** city (1986 pop. 125,833), Victoria, SE Australia, on an inlet of Port Phillip Bay, near Melbourne. It is one of Australia's chief ports and industrial centres, with such manufactures as refined oil, motor vehicles, aluminium, glass, and carpets. Deakin Univ. is at Geelong.

**Geertz, Clifford,** 1926–, American anthropologist. He is the main exponent of 'interpretive anthropology', in which society is seen as a text, the different levels of which have to be interpreted by the anthropologist as a critic interprets a novel. His work on symbolic systems in Bali exemplifies this approach. Geertz has been professor of social science at the Inst. of Advanced Studies, Princeton, US, since 1970.

**gegenschein,** brightening of the night sky in the region of the ECLIPTIC directly opposite the Sun's position at the time of observation. It is caused by reflection of sunlight by small particles that lie in the plane of the solar system.

**Geiger counter:** see PARTICLE DETECTOR.

**gelatin** or **animal jelly,** foodstuff obtained from connective tissue (found in hoofs, bones, tendons, ligaments, and cartilage) of vertebrate animals by the action of boiling water or dilute acid. It is largely composed of the protein collagen. Pure gelatin is brittle, transparent, colourless, tasteless, and odourless. It dissolves in hot water and congeals when cooled. Gelatin is widely used to give food a proper consistency as in mousses, jellies, and cold soufflés, in photographic emulsions, and as a coating for pills. Vegetable gelatin, or AGAR, is made from seaweed.

**Gelée, Claude; Gellée, Claude:** see CLAUDE LORRAIN.

**Gellius, Aulus,** b. c.AD 129, Roman writer. His *Noctes Atticae* [Attic nights] is a learned miscellany (see also ATHENAEUS), especially valuable for its quotations from early Latin literature otherwise lost to us, but also for its entertaining stories (e.g., *Androcles and the Lion*), and its reflection of the cultural interests of the author and his time.

**Gell-Mann, Murray,** 1929–, American theoretical physicist. In 1953 he and, independently, the Japanese team of T. Nakano and Kazuhiko Nishijima proposed the concept of 'strangeness' to account for certain particle-decay patterns. In 1961 Gell-Mann and Yuval Ne'eman independently introduced the 'eightfold way', or SU(3) symmetry, a tablelike ordering of all subatomic particles (see ELEMENTARY PARTICLES). The

1964 discovery of the omega-minus particle, which filled a gap in this ordering, brought the theory wide acceptance, and led to Gell-Mann's being awarded the 1969 Nobel Prize for physics. In 1963 Gell-Mann and George Zweig independently postulated the existence of the QUARK, an even more fundamental particle with a fractional electric charge.

**Gelsenkirchen,** city (1984 pop. 290,700), North Rhine–Westphalia, W West Germany. Originating as a centre of RUHR coal-mining in the 19th cent., it benefits from its position as an important rail junction. A coal-based chemical industry was developed which has subsequently been extended into oil-refining and petrochemicals. Clothing is also manufactured.

**gem,** commonly, a mineral or organic substance that is cut and polished and used as an ornament. The qualities sought in gems are beauty, rarity, and durability. The unit of weight used for gems is the metric carat (200 mg). Gems are usually cut to bring out their colour and brilliance and to remove flaws, and gem cutting is a distinct trade. The precious stones are DIAMOND, some forms of CORUNDUM (e.g., RUBY and SAPPHIRE), and EMERALD. The chief semiprecious stones include AMETHYST, AQUAMARINE, GARNET, JADE, MOONSTONE, OPAL, QUARTZ, TOPAZ, TOURMALINE, and TURQUOISE. The organic gems are AMBER, CORAL, PEARL, and jet. Synthetic gems produced using the chemical elements of natural stones include diamonds, emeralds, rubies, and sapphires. See also AGATE; BERYL; BLOODSTONE; JASPER; LAPIS LAZULI; SERPENTINE.

**Gemara:** see TALMUD.

**Gemayel, Amin,** 1942–, president of LEBANON (1982–88). A lawyer and a member of the Christian Phalange Party founded by his father, Pierre (1905–84), he served in the Lebanese parliament from 1970. In 1982, after the assassination of his brother, President-elect Bashir Gemayel, Amin Gemayel was elected president and pledged to work for a united Lebanon.

**gender** [from Lat., *genus* = kind], in grammar, subclassification of nouns or nounlike words, not usually considered to include the classification of number. A two-gender distinction between animate and inanimate is widespread, as in the North American Indian languages. A number of Indo-European languages, such as German, Russian, and Latin, have three genders: masculine, feminine, and neuter. The modern Romance languages such as French, Italian, and Spanish, have only two. In such languages, many nouns referring to males are masculine, e.g., German *der Mann,* the man, and many referring to females are feminine, e.g., German *die Frau,* the woman. This is the classification of natural gender. Other words are assigned grammatical gender, a distinction that does not derive from sex classes, e.g., German *das Mädchen,* the girl (neuter). By the grammatical device of concord or agreement, a word bears a formal signal to show its relationship to the word it accompanies or modifies, as in the agreement of article with noun, e.g., French *la femme,* the woman, or of adjective with noun, e.g., French *la vieille femme,* the old woman. Although gender is present in many languages, it is far from universal.

**gender role,** the pattern of behaviour, expectation, and attitude which is considered appropriate in a given human society for the members of either the male or female sex, and which indicates to others the degree of affiliation to masculinity or femininity. Gender role can also be seen as the social–behavioural manifestation of gender identity, a psychosocial construction which may be experienced independently of biological SEX.

**gene,** ultimate unit by which inheritable characteristics are transmitted to succeeding generations in all living organisms. Genes are contained by, and arranged along the length of, the CHROMOSOME. The gene is composed of deoxyribonucleic acid (see DNA). Each chromosome of each species has a definite number and arrangement of genes, which govern both the structure and metabolic functions of the cells and thus of the entire organism. They provide information for the synthesis of ENZYMES and other PROTEINS and specify when these substances are to be made. Alteration of either gene nature, number, or arrangement can result in MUTATION, a change in the inheritable traits. See GENETICS; GENETIC ENGINEERING.

**General Agreement on Tariffs and Trade:** see UNITED NATIONS (table 3).

**General Assembly :** see UNITED NATIONS (table 2).

**General Household Survey,** British social SURVEY (founded 1971). The General Household Survey provides data on five main areas: family information, housing, education, employment, and health. It is organized by the Social Survey Division of the Office of Population Censuses and is designed to fill the gap in information between the decennial CENSUS. Like its companion survey, the FAMILY EXPENDITURE SURVEY, the GHS is conducted over the course of the calendar year. The GHS samples 15,000 households annually, of which roughly 12,000 are surveyed.

**General Medical Council,** body controlling the registration of doctors in Britain and overseeing medical education. The aim of the Council, which was established in 1858, is to protect the public from unqualified practitioners. It is authorized to remove the names of practitioners found guilty of unprofessional conduct from the Medical Register, the list of all qualified doctors in the UK, which the Council compiles annually.

**general practice,** in Britain, the first line of primary health care, the family practitioner service. The general practitioner (GP) provides continuing medical care under the NATIONAL HEALTH SERVICE to the local population, diagnosing and treating disease, referring patients to specialists where necessary, and promoting the health of patients.

**general relativity:** see RELATIVITY.

**General Strike,** strike action by the entire labour force in a country, or internationally. The idea of a general strike for industrial or political purposes was advocated in the international labour movement from the late 19th cent. onwards. In Britain, the only attempted general strike was on 3–13 May 1926, when all the unions affiliated to the TRADES UNION CONGRESS went on strike in an unsuccessful attempt to support the striking coalminers.

**generator,** device for producing electricity by the conversion of mechanical energy. It operates on the principle of electromagnetic INDUCTION discovered by FARADAY, i.e., if a conductor is moved through a magnetic field a voltage is generated in the conductor. The voltage depends on the speed of movement through the field, the strength of the field, and the length of the conductor in the field. Rotation of a rectangular coil in a magnetic field produces alternating induced voltage because one arm of the rectangle moves through the field first in one direction and then in the opposite direction. The coil thus produces alternating current (AC), moving first in one direction, then in the other, if it is connected to an external circuit via slip ring connections. Large-scale AC generators, or alternators, are designed to rotate synchronously at 50 cycles per sec or 60 cycles per sec depending on the power system. They can be driven by any mechanical means of producing rotation. The largest machines are driven by steam turbines; the combination is called a turbo-alternator and can reach sizes of 500 megawatts. Inefficiency produces heat in the machine; even in a 99.9% efficient machine half a million watts are dissipated per second in the form of heat. Forced cooling, even to the extent of pumping liquid nitrogen round the machine, is essential. To obtain direct current (DC) it is necessary to use a commutator, a device which switches the connection of the rotating coil to the outside circuit automatically with the position of the coil. The commutator, which allows current to flow in one direction only in the external circuit whilst still alternating internally, was perfected by Ernst SIEMENS about the 1870s and is used in small sizes for motor vehicle electricity. The whole assembly carrying the rotating coils is called the armature, or rotor. The stationary parts constitute the stator. Small generators may use permanent magnets, in which case they are referred to as magnetos. Larger generators use electromagnets. The very largest AC generators can produce currents of the order of 100,000 amperes.

**Genesis,** first book of the OLD TESTAMENT and of the PENTATEUCH, ascribed by tradition to MOSES. It tells of the origin of the world and of man (1–11), including the stories of man's disobedience and fall, CAIN and ABEL, and NOAH; the career of God's special servant ABRAHAM (12–24), including the story of Hagar and ISHMAEL, the sacrifice of ISAAC, and Abraham's journey to CANAAN and God's promises to him; the career of Isaac (25–26); and the life of JACOB, called Israel (27–50), with the story of his son JOSEPH and the migration of the family to Egypt. Sources of Genesis include Babylonian and Egyptian folklore. The debate over its interpretation and literary history still continues.

**gene splicing:** see GENETIC ENGINEERING.

**Genet, Jean,** 1910–86, French novelist and dramatist. While in prison, he attracted attention with his narratives about homosexuality and crime, e.g., *Nôtre-Dame des fleurs* (1943; tr. Our Lady of the Flowers). He was pardoned (1948) from a sentence of life imprisonment through the intervention of prominent French literary figures. His plays include *Le balcon* (1956; tr. The Balcony), *Les nègres* (1958; tr. The Blacks), and *Les paravents* (1961; tr. The Screens); they challenge normal values and are among the most technically innovative of the 20th cent.

**genetic engineering,** group of new research techniques that manipulate the DNA (genetic material) of cells. The gene-splicing technique, which produces recombinant DNA, is a method of transporting selected genes from one species to another. In this technique, the genes, which are actually portions of molecules of DNA produced enzymically, are removed from the donor (insect, plant, mammal, or other organism) and spliced into the genetic material of a virus (called a vector); then the vector is allowed to infect a recipient organism, usually a bacterium. In this way the bacteria come to contain both viral and donor genetic material. When the vector replicates within the bacteria, large quantities of the donor as well as viral material are made. The introduction into bacteria of foreign genetic material is an important tool for the study of gene structure and regulation, but it also presents risks that some genetic material would no longer be under natural control. The recipient bacterium in use is a modified form of *E. coli*, a natural inhabitant of human intestines. Recently plants, yeasts, and animals have been shown to act as suitable recipients of donor DNA using appropriate vectors. Other techniques include cell fusion, which has made the mapping of human genes possible, and nuclear transplantation, valuable to the study of factors controlling embryological development. The enzymes used in gene splicing were first studied by microbiologists Werner Arber, of the Univ. of Basel, Switzerland, and Daniel Nathan and Hamilton O. Smith, both of John Hopkins Univ., Baltimore, who shared the 1978 Nobel Prize for physiology or medicine for their work.

**genetic epistemology: see** PIAGET.

**genetics,** scientific study of heredity. The science arose in 1900, with rediscovery of Gregor MENDEL's work on traits that are inherited as if each were a separate, independent unit. Geneticists probing the physical basis of the transmission of inherited characteristics have studied the unit of inheritance, the GENE; the small chemical differences in genes that are expressed as different versions of the same trait (alleles); the array of genes along the CHROMOSOME in the cell nucleus; and the set of genes characteristic of each species (the genome). Since the discovery (1953) of the structure of DNA, work on NUCLEIC ACIDS has explained how genes determine all life processes by directing the synthesis of all cell proteins. It has also explained MUTATION as alterations in gene or chromosome structure. See also GENETIC ENGINEERING.

**Geneva,** city (1984 pop. 159,500), capital of Geneva canton, SW Switzerland, on the Lake of Geneva, divided by the Rhône R. A cultural, financial, and administrative centre, it manufactures watches, jewellery, and precision instruments. The city was settled by the Celts and later held by the Romans. In the 16th cent. it was the focal point of the Reformation under John CALVIN; by the 18th cent. it had become an intellectual centre, the residence of J.J. ROUSSEAU and others. Geneva joined (1815) the Swiss Confederation. The LEAGUE OF NATIONS and the GENEVA CONFERENCES met there. It is the seat of such bodies as the WORLD HEALTH ORGANIZATION and the RED CROSS.

**Geneva, Lake,** Fr. *Léman,* lake on the border between Switzerland and France, on the RHÔNE R. Crescent-shaped, its N shore is 90 km (56 mi) long and its S shore, partly in France, is 70 km (44 mi) long. Its N shore is fringed with vineyards and orchards and there are numerous resorts, including Montreux and Vevey, as well as the larger cities of GENEVA and LAUSANNE. Writers and poets have been attracted by its scenery. Evian and Thonon are spas on the French shore.

**Geneva Conference. 1** International conference held Apr.–July 1954 to bring peace to KOREA and INDOCHINA. The chief participants were the US, the USSR, the UK, France, China, the two Koreas, and various factions from Indochina. No permanent agreement on Korea resulted, but three agreements were reached on Indochina (see VIETNAM; VIETNAM WAR). **2** So-called summit conference, held in July 1955, attended by the leaders of the US, the USSR, the UK, and France. A wide agenda of issues was discussed (e.g., disarmament, unification of Germany, increased cultural and economic ties). Although no substantive agreements resulted, the conference ended on a note of optimism and is regarded as a major step in the ending of the COLD WAR. **3** Conference, beginning Oct. 1958, attended by the US, the USSR and the UK; its purpose was to reach an

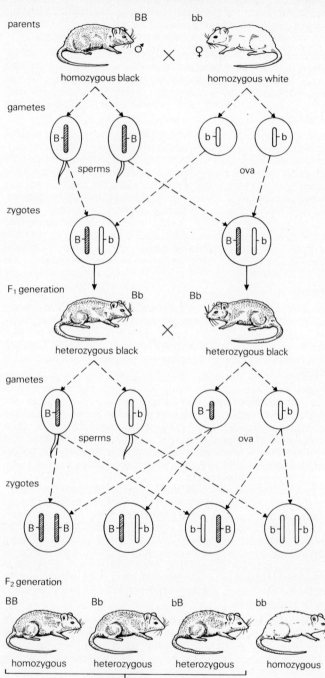

single factor inheritance

parents — BB × bb
homozygous black — homozygous white

gametes — sperms — ova

zygotes

F₁ generation — Bb × Bb
heterozygous black — heterozygous black

gametes — sperms — ova

zygotes

F₂ generation
BB — Bb — bB — bb
homozygous — heterozygous — heterozygous — homozygous
3 black — 1 white

**Genetics:** In single-factor inheritance, when a homozygous black rat mates with a homozygous white one all the F1 generation will be black, since the gene for black is dominant. Mating of this heterozygous F1 generation will produce both black and white F2 generation rats, since each of the parent rats carries a white recessive gene.

accord on the banning of nuclear testing. Since then, most international meetings at Geneva have been concerned with the general problem of nuclear arms. See DISARMAMENT, NUCLEAR.

**Geneva Conventions,** series of treaties signed (1864–1949) in Geneva, Switzerland, providing for humane treatment of combatants and civilians in wartime. The first convention, signed by 16 nations, covered the protection of sick and wounded soldiers and medical personnel and facilities. Later conventions extended (1906) the first to naval warfare and covered (1929) the treatment of prisoners of war. As a result of World War II, particularly of the conduct of Germany and Japan, four conventions were adopted in 1949 to strengthen and codify earlier treaties and safeguard civilians.

**Genghis Khan:** see JENGHIZ KHAN.

**genie:** see JINNI.

**genitive:** see CASE.

**Gennesaret:** see GALILEE, SEA OF.

**Genoa,** city (1984 pop. 738,099), capital of Liguria, NW Italy, on the Italian RIVIERA. Italy's chief port, it handles heavy passenger and freight traffic. Iron and steel, chemicals, oil refineries, and shipyards lead the economy. After it became (10th cent.) a free commune, its maritime power grew; rivalry with Pisa ended (1284) in naval victory. It was the birthplace of Christopher COLUMBUS. In decline, it fell to many hands, including Napoleon's (1805–14). The medieval Cathedral of San Lorenzo and the doges' palace are highlights.

**genocide,** systematic destruction by a government of a racial, religious, or ethnic group. The term was coined in 1944, with particular reference to the attempt of Nazi GERMANY in the 1930s and 40s to destroy European Jewry (see HOLOCAUST; National SOCIALISM). Other instances of genocide exist, however, such as the massacre of Armenians in Ottoman Turkey (1894–96). A 1949 UN convention defines the crime of genocide and provides for prosecution by national or international courts. The US has never ratified the convention, claiming that the provision for international tribunals and the principle of personal liability for national actions violate the concept of SOVEREIGNTY.

## GEOLOGIC ERAS

| Time | Geologic Development | Life Forms |
|---|---|---|
| **Azoic Time.** From the formation of the earth. | | |
| 4550–3800 million years ago | Crust and oceans forming. Lack of ATMOSPHERE allows meteorite bombardment. | No life forms. |
| **Precambrian Time.** Traditionally divided into two eras, Archaeozoic and Proterozoic. | | |
| 3800–700 million years ago | Permanent crust formed, with vast deposits of metallic minerals. Metamorphic rocks in massive formations, e.g., CANADIAN SHIELD. Erosion, sedimentation begin. | Earliest life marine (blue-green ALGAE). PHOTOSYNTHESIS begins to develop oxygen-rich atmosphere. Wormlike forms possible. First recognizable fossils. |
| **Palaeozoic Era.** Age of INVERTEBRATES and marine forms. Six periods. | | |
| Cambrian: 700–500 million years ago | Sedimentary rock (sandstone, shale, limestone, conglomerate) forms in shallow seas over continents. Climate generally mild, but North America tropical. | First FOSSILS of animals with hard parts, e.g., shells, skeletons. All fauna marine; every invertebrate phylum represented. Animal ability to secrete CALCIUM leads to shell, skeleton formation. TRILOBITE dominant. |
| Ordovician: 500–435 million years ago | North America, Europe, Africa moving together (see PLATE TECTONICS; CONTINENTAL DRIFT). Seas at greatest extent over North America. Rocks chiefly sedimentary. | Marine ecosystems develop; fossil evidence of deep-water life forms. MOLLUSCS, some CORALS. Fishlike VERTEBRATES appear. |
| Silurian: 435–395 million years ago | Shallow flooding deposits sediments. Later withdrawal of water leaves oxidized 'red beds', salt deposits. | Earliest land plants. In seas, coral reefs, ARTHROPODS, CRINOIDS. Fish develop first vertebrate jaw. SHARKS appear. |
| Devonian: 395–345 million years ago | Continents drier at beginning. Europe, North America collide, causing mountain building (orogeny). South pole in central Africa. | Fish dominant: armoured fish, lungfish. Towards end of period first land animals, AMPHIBIANS. Plant life, including lowland forests of giant PSILOPHYTA plants, highly developed, uniform over planet. |
| Carboniferous: 345–280 million years ago | Climate warm, moist; COAL-forming sediments laid down in vast swamps. Severe continental collisions cause orogeny, e.g., in URALS. | FERNS, fernlike trees, primitive CONIFERS among flora in swamps. INSECTS, e.g., cockroaches, flourish. First REPTILES appear towards end. |
| Permian: 280–230 million years ago | Land, e.g., E North America, rising. Atmosphere, oceans cooler. Glaciation in southern hemisphere. General aridity. Appalachians thrust up at end. | Insects evolve towards modern types. Reptiles flourish. Ferns, conifers persist in cool air. |
| **Mesozoic Era.** Age of reptiles. Three periods. | | |
| Triassic: 230–195 million years ago | Climate warming; semiarid to arid. Continental plates, joined c.200 million years ago in supercontinent Pangaea, begin to break into continents; FAULTS, tilting widespread. | Fewer species, higher populations. Ammonites, clams, snails present. First DINOSAURS. First MAMMALS may have evolved. |
| Jurassic: 195–140 million years ago | North America, Africa separate; ocean basins open. Erosion reduces Appalachians. Plate subduction (Pacific under North American) causes folding, orogeny in W North America. | Climate warmer than present. CYCADS appear. GINKGOES, HORSETAILS among flora. Reptiles dominant on land, in sea and air. Archaeopteryx, first BIRD, appears. First mammal fossils. |
| Cretaceous: 140–65 million years ago | Extensive submergence of continents leaves overlapping marine rocks. Chalk deposits. South America, Africa separate; North Atlantic widening. Cycles of orogeny. | Dinosaurs, large reptiles climax, then disappear. Snakes, lizards appear. Revolution in plants: flowering plants (ANGIOSPERMS); modern trees. Floral uniformity that lasts into Eocene. |

| GEOLOGIC ERAS *(Continued)* | | |
|---|---|---|
| *Time* | *Geologic Development* | *Life Forms* |
| Cenozoic Era. Age of mammals, modern seed plants. Traditionally divided into two periods, Tertiary (Palaeocene/Eocene, Oligocene, Miocene, and Pliocene epochs) and Quaternary (Pleistocene and Holocene epochs). | | |
| Palaeocene/Eocene: 65–37 million years ago | Seas withdraw; Europe emergent. Volcanism forms Rockies, other ranges. Erosion fills basins, laying BAUXITE deposits in W North America. Greenland, North America split. | Most common modern plants present. Modern birds. Early horses, pigs, rodents, whales. Number of PRIMATE types greatly increases. Hardwoods, redwoods in W North America. Climate warm, humid. |
| Oligocene: 37–23 million years ago | North America largely dry; red bed sedimentation; erosion in Rockies. African, European plates collide, causing Alpine orogeny. Arabia, Africa split at Red Sea rift. California collides with mid-Pacific ridge. | Archaic mammals disappearing. Modern horses, pigs, true CARNIVORES, rhinoceroses, elephants begin to appear. Cats, dogs evolving. Modern grasses. |
| Miocene: 23–5 million years ago | Coastal submergence; volcanism raises CASCADES, western North American plateaus. Himalayas, Alps, Andes built up. South America, Antarctica separate; cold transantarctic current isolates southern continent. | Climate cooler; forests reduced, grassy plains increase. Mammals include hyena, bear, seal, raccoon. Giant ape widespread. Giant hog develops, then disappears. |
| Pliocene: 5–1.8 million years ago | Volcanism creates isthmus between North and South America. Outlines of North America roughly modern. Polar, Alpine ice caps sizable. Uplifting, tilting in W North America continues. | Cooler, drier climate. Life forms begin to take on modern appearance. Climax, maybe initial decline, of mammals. Manlike apes. Earliest human artifacts, OLDUVAI GORGE skeletal finds from this epoch. |
| Pleistocene: 1.8 million–10,000 years ago | Great age of GLACIERS. Polar, Alpine ice advances in many separate glacial periods. Glacial DRIFT widespread. Land forms altered; lakes created by ice retreats. | Extinction of mammals, including mastodon, mammoth, sabretooth carnivores. Rise of man (*Homo sapiens*) c.100,000 years ago; Cromagnon c.35,000 years ago. Horse, camel disappear from Americas. See also STONE AGE. |
| Holocene or Recent: 10,000 years ago to present | Glaciers retreat. Climate warmer; DESERTS form in some areas. Many scientists argue that Holocene is only another interglacial episode of the Pleistocene epoch. | Human civilization; mankind begins to affect climate, geology. Extinction of other species continues. |

**genre,** type of painting dealing with subjects from everyday life. Genre was not seen as worthy independent subject matter until it was popularized by Pieter Bruegel, the Elder (see BRUEGEL, family), in 16th-cent. Flanders. It flourished in 17th-cent. Holland in the work of TER BORCH, de HOOCH, VERMEER, and others, and extended into France and England, where, in the 18th and 19th cent., its practitioners included WATTEAU, CHARDIN, and MORLAND. The French impressionists (see IMPRESSIONISM) often painted genre scenes, as did members of the EIGHT in the US.

**Gentile, Giovanni,** 1875–1944, Italian philosopher. An admirer of MUSSOLINI, and education minister under him, he helped introduce Hegelian idealism to Italy in the early 20th cent. and collaborated with CROCE until they quarrelled over FASCISM. His major work is *The General Theory of the Spirit as Pure Act* (1916).

**Gentile da Fabriano,** c.1370–1427, Italian painter, one of the foremost exponents of the international Gothic style. His elegant, lavishly gilt *Adoration of the Magi* altarpiece (1423; Uffizi, Florence) exhibits his jewel-like colours and courtly style. He worked throughout Italy.

**Gentlemen's Agreement,** an agreement reached between the US and Japan in 1907–08 in response to anti-Japanese agitation in California. Japan was to stop the emigration of labourers to the US and the US was to recognize the rights of Japanese already resident there. This informal agreement came to an end in 1924 when Congress passed an Immigration Act designed to exclude Japanese immigrants, just as had been done already in the case of Chinese immigrants.

**geocentric system:** see PTOLEMAIC SYSTEM.

**geochemistry,** study of the chemistry of the earth, especially the study of the absolute and relative abundances of the elements and their distribution and movement. Such studies have provided insights into the evolution of the oceans and atmosphere, the ages of rocks, the chemical evolution of life, and, more recently, the effects of the massive introduction of pollutants into the environment.

**geodesy** or **geodetic surveying,** subdivision of GEOPHYSICS that determines the earth's size and shape, the position of points on the earth's surface, and the dimensions of areas so large that the curvature of the earth must be taken into account. In a process called triangulation, a base line between two points, many kilometres apart, is measured, and a third point is determined by the angle it makes with each end of the base line. In recent years, triangulation has been done increasingly with geodetic satellites in space.

**Geoffrey IV,** known as **Geoffrey Plantagenet,** 1113–51, count of Anjou (1129–51). He married (1128) MATILDA, daughter of HENRY I of England. On Henry's death (1135), he claimed and conquered (1144) Normandy in his wife's name. After 1139, Matilda tried to conquer England from her cousin King STEPHEN. Her son by Geoffrey became HENRY II of England. In 1147 Geoffrey went on a crusade with LOUIS VII of France.

**Geoffrey of Monmouth,** c.1100–1155, English author. His *Historia Regum Britanniae* (c.1130–38), a supposed chronicle of the kings of Britain, is a major source of ARTHURIAN LEGEND, giving the first coherent account of Arthur.

**Geoffroy Saint-Hilaire, Étienne** (zho͵frwah sanhtee͵leə), 1772–1844, French zoologist. He was professor (1793–1840) at the Museum of Natural History in Paris and a member of Napoleon's scientific staff in Egypt. His theory that all animals conform to a single plan of structure was strongly opposed by the naturalist Georges CUVIER, and they held a widely publicized debate in 1830.

**geological eras,** major units of geological time. For the purpose of dating rock formations and the fossils contained within them, the earth's history has been divided into eras, which are further subdivided into periods and, in some cases, epochs (see table).

**geology,** science of the EARTH's history, composition, and structure. Branches include mineralogy (see MINERAL), PETROLOGY, geomorphology (the origin of landforms and their modification by dynamic processes), GEOCHEMISTRY, GEOPHYSICS, sedimentation, structural geology, economic geology, and engineering geology. Historical geology includes stratigraphy (the interrelationships of layered ROCKS) and palaeontology (the study of FOSSILS). Geological observations have been made since ancient times, but modern geology began in the 18th cent., notably with

James HUTTON's doctrine of UNIFORMITARIANISM, which, in its opposition to CATASTROPHISM, laid the groundwork for much of modern geological science. The systematic survey in the mid-20th cent. of the OCEAN floors brought radical changes in concepts of crustal evolution (see PLATE TECTONICS).

**geometric progression:** see PROGRESSION.

**geometry,** branch of MATHEMATICS concerned with the properties of and relationships between points, lines, planes, figures, solids, and surfaces. Elementary EUCLIDEAN GEOMETRY of two and three dimensions (plane and solid geometry) is based largely on EUCLID's *Elements* (c.300 BC), a systematic presentation of the geometry of its time. Although Euclid's basic assumptions have been judged insufficiently rigorous by David HILBERT and others, his axiomatic method of proof has been adopted throughout mathematics and in other fields as well. In the 17th cent., René DESCARTES invented CARTESIAN COORDINATES to express geometric relations in algebraic form; he thus founded ANALYTICAL GEOMETRY, from which developed algebraic geometry, concerned with geometrical objects defined by algebraic relations between their coordinates. Other branches of geometry include descriptive geometry, which is concerned with the two-dimensional representation of three-dimensional objects; differential geometry, in which the concepts of CALCULUS are applied to curves, surfaces, and other geometrical entities; projective geometry, which is concerned with those properties of geometrical figures that remain unchanged under projection, e.g., from one plane to another; and NON-EUCLIDEAN GEOMETRY. TOPOLOGY, perhaps the most general type of geometry, is often considered a separate branch of mathematics.

**geomorphology:** see GEOLOGY.

**geophysics,** study of the structure, composition, and dynamic changes of the EARTH and its ATMOSPHERE, based on the principles of physics. Applied geophysics uses seismic, electrical, gravimetric, magnetic, and radiometric techniques for geological exploration and prospecting.

**geopolitics,** method of political analysis stressing the importance of geographical factors (e.g., natural boundaries and access to waterways) in determining national interests and international relations. The term received wide attention through the works of the German geographer Karl Haushofer, who popularized H.J. MACKINDER's theory of a Eurasian 'heartland' central to world dominance. The NAZIS used Haushofer's ideas to justify their expansion in central Europe. Geopolitical considerations have been used to justify other expansionist policies, such as MANIFEST DESTINY.

**George,** kings of Great Britain and Ireland. **George I** (George Louis), 1660–1727 (r.1714–27), was the great-grandson of JAMES I. He was the first British sovereign of the house of HANOVER under the ACT OF SETTLEMENT. His dual role as elector of Hanover and king of England, his German manners, and his inability to speak English made him unpopular. His indifference to government led to the first real cabinet and the rise of the WHIGS to power. In 1718 the QUADRUPLE ALLIANCE guaranteed the Hanoverian succession. His son, **George II** (George Augustus), 1683–1760 (r.1727–60), was more active in government than his father. In the War of the AUSTRIAN SUCCESSION, he personally led his troops in battle, the last British monarch to do so. His wife, Caroline of Ansbach, furthered the dominancy of Robert WALPOLE. During his reign, the Whigs united behind the policy of William PITT (the elder) in the SEVEN YEARS WAR. His grandson, **George III,** 1738–1820 (r.1760–1820), ended the long Whig control of government by securing Pitt's resignation in 1761. George wanted to rule personally, and he found an amenable minister (1770–82) in Lord NORTH, whose policy of coercion led to the AMERICAN REVOLUTION. The notable TORY ministry of the younger William PITT (1783–1801) saw the end of royal attempts to control the ministry. George III's reign witnessed a great expansion of empire and trade, the beginning of the INDUSTRIAL REVOLUTION, and a flowering of arts and letters. The king's insanity led to the regency (1811) of his son **George IV,** 1762–1830, prince regent (r.1811–20), then king (r.1820–30). A patron of the arts, who gave his name to a style, Regency, and at first a supporter of the whigs, George IV was a target of radical criticism after 1815, which reached its height in the CAROLINE OF BRUNSWICK case (1820–21). He opposed CATHOLIC EMANCIPATION and parliamentary reform, but had to concede the former in 1827. His death opened the way to the latter when WELLINGTON gave way to GREY in 1830. **George V** (George Frederick Ernest Albert), 1865–1936 (r.1910–36), was the seocond son of EDWARD VII. He was always interested in the affairs of the British empire and in 1911

travelled to India. During WORLD WAR I (1917) he gave up all his German titles and changed the name of the royal house from Saxe-Coburg-Gotha to WINDSOR. His second son, **George VI** (Albert Frederick Arthur George), 1895–1952, king of Great Britain and Northern Ireland (r.1936–52), became king on the abdication of his brother, EDWARD VIII. During WORLD WAR II, he worked to keep up British morale by visiting bombed areas, war plants, and theatres of war. He and his wife, ELIZABETH, had two daughters: ELIZABETH II and Princess MARGARET. Like his father, he was held in deep affection by his people.

**George,** kings of the Hellenes (Greece). **George I,** 1845–1913 (r.1863–1913), was the second son of Christian IX of Denmark and was elected king of Greece after the deposition (1862) of OTTO I. He introduced (1864) a democratic constitution and expanded the Greek domain. He was assassinated. **George II,** 1890–1947 (r.1922–23, 1935–47), did not succeed his father, CONSTANTINE I, but was passed over (1917) because of his pro-German sympathies. The crown fell to his younger brother ALEXANDER. In 1922 he did become king, but hostility towards the dynasty forced him into exile in 1923 and Greece was declared a republic. He was restored in 1935 and instituted a dictatorship under John METAXAS. George was in exile during World War II, and his return to Greece in 1946 failed to halt the civil war then raging. He was succeeded by his brother PAUL.

**George, David Lloyd:** see LLOYD GEORGE, DAVID.

**George, Henry,** 1839–97, American economist, founder of the single-tax movement. His own poverty and his observation of avarice as a newspaperman in San Francisco bolstered his reformist ideas. Believing that the simultaneous growth of poverty and wealth stemmed from the fact that the rental of land and the unearned increase in land values profited only a few individuals, not the community, George proposed a single tax on land to meet all costs of government. His theories, published in *Progress and Poverty* (1879), have influenced tax legislation in many countries.

**George, Saint** (gəy,awgə), 4th cent.?, patron of England. Possibly a soldier in the imperial army who died a martyr in Asia Minor, he was adopted by England in the Middle Ages. In legend he is the slayer of a dragon. Feast: 23 April.

**George, Stefan,** 1868–1933, German poet. He was influenced poetically by Greek classical forms and the French SYMBOLISTS and intellectually by NIETZSCHE. His esoteric, pure verse appeared in such volumes as *Algabal* (1892), *Die Bücher der Hirten* (1895; tr. Book of the Shepherds), *The Soul's Year* (1897), and *Der siebente Ring* (1907; tr. The Seventh Ring). George's aesthetic ideal called for a controlled humanism. He devoted himself to the purifying of German language and culture and had great influence on younger poets through his verse and through *Blätter für die Kunst* (founded 1892), the literary organ of his circle. He died in Switzerland.

**George Town,** city (1976 est. pop. 72,049), N Guyana, capital of Guyana, on the Atlantic Ocean at the mouth of the Demerara R. Guyana's largest city, it exports bauxite and other products of the interior. Settled in the 1600s by the Dutch, who called it Stabroek, it was taken and renamed by the British in 1812. It still has canals and other Dutch features.

**Georgetown,** city (1980 pop. 250,578), capital of Penang State, Federation of Malaysia, NW Malay Peninsula. It is situated on the island of Penang and although George Town is the official name the city is commonly referred to simply as Penang. It is the chief seaport of N Malaysia and has an international airport that serves the thriving tourist industry of Penang. Penang was formerly part of the STRAITS SETTLEMENT; it joined the Federation of Malaysia in 1948.

**Georgia,** state of the US (1984 est. pop. 5,837,000), area 152,489 km² (58,876 sq mi), located in the SE and bordered by Florida (S), Alabama (W), Tennessee and North Carolina (N), and South Carolina and the Atlantic Ocean (E). ATLANTA is the capital, and COLUMBUS, Savannah, and Macon are also major cities. Northern Georgia is part of the APPALACHIAN MTS while the south is a low-lying coastal plain which includes the large OKEFENOKEE SWAMP wilderness area. Industry is the most important economic sector, particularly cotton textiles, clothing, and carpets; other major products are transport equipment, processed foods, and paper. Georgia is heavily forested, and produces timber and related products. Peanuts, tobacco, corn, maize, and cotton are the major agricultural crops. In 1980 72% of the population was white and 27% black. Originally inhabited by Creek and Cherokee Indians, Georgia was settled by the British and partly held during the American Revolution. Following the war, cotton cultivation, based on the plantation system and slavery, dominated the economy. The state joined the Confederacy in the Civil War, and suffered considerable damage as a result of General SHERMAN's destructive march to the sea and the burning of Atlanta. By the 1880s the textile industry had begun to transform the state's economy from agriculture to manufacturing. Atlanta's new affluence has regenerated the state's economy, while the election of a Georgian, Jimmy CARTER, to the presidency (1976–80) signalled a period of political liberalism and racial accommodation.

**Georgia** or **Georgian Soviet Socialist Republic**, constituent republic (1985 pop. 5,203,000), c.69,700 km² (26,900 sq mi), SE European USSR, in W Transcaucasia. It borders the Black Sea (W); the Azerbaijan SSR (E); Turkey and the Armenian SSR (S); and the Russian Soviet Federated Socialist Republic (N). The capital is TBILISI. A largely mountainous region, Georgia has the highest snow-capped peaks of the Caucasus Mts. To the W is a low-lying coastal plain. Western Georgia has a mild, damp climate, which is subtropical on the Black Sea shore. The region is rich in minerals, of which manganese is the most important; others include coal and oil. Georgia grows most of the USSR's tea and citrus fruits, and produces high-quality tobacco and wines. The Black Sea coast has a number of popular holiday resorts. In addition to the Georgian majority, there are Armenian, Russian, and other minorities. The kingdom of Georgia, dating from the 4th cent. BC, reached its height in the 12th and 13th cent. AD. In 1555 W Georgia fell to Turkey and E Georgia to Persia. Under Russian sway after 1783, Georgia was briefly independent (1918–21) before becoming part of the USSR. In 1936 it became one of the constituent republics, and in 1989 was a storm centre of soviet politics.

**Georgian style**, several trends in English architecture during the reigns (1714–1820) of George I, George II, and George III. The first half of the period (c.1710–c.1760) was dominated by Neo-Palladianism (see PALLADIO). Colin Campbell's *Vitruvius Britannicus* (1715) inspired a return to CLASSICISM, based on the works of Inigo JONES and Palladio. His Mereworth Castle, Kent, epitomizes the style. A second generation of architects carried the Palladian tradition through the Georgian period. In the first half of the 18th cent., a BAROQUE countercurrent, stemming from Sir Christopher WREN's designs, was carried on by Sir John VANBRUGH, Nicholas HAWKSMOOR, and James GIBBS. In the second half, the CLASSIC REVIVAL was led by Sir William CHAMBERS, Robert ADAM, and Sir John SOANE. A standard type of town house construction, red brick with white stone courses and cornices and white painted trim, came to be known as Georgian. Notable buildings of the period include Soane's Bank of England and Gibbs's St Martin's-in-the-Fields. American builders of the period followed English models closely, especially those by Gibbs.

**geothermal energy:** see ENERGY, SOURCES OF.

**Gera** (ˌkheərə), city (1984 pop. 131,313), THURINGIA, southern East Germany, on the Elster R. It profited in the 16th cent. from the arrival of Dutch clothiers. Its principal industries are textiles, including carpets, and engineering. Uranium is mined nearby. Before 1918 it was capital of the principality of Reuss.

**Geraldton**, city (1986 pop. 21,726), Western Australia. Located 500 km (310 mi) N of Perth on the Indian Ocean, it is the fourth largest city in the state. Large silos provide bulk handling facilities for wheat from the surrounding farms. A titanium processing plant and crayfish (lobster) fishing are major activities.

**geranium**, herb or shrub of the cranesbill family (Geraniaceae). More commonly the name refers to the popular garden and greenhouse geranium (genus *Pelargonium*), grown for its colourful flowers and ornamental, sometimes scented foliage. The long, beak-shaped fruits give the family the name cranesbill. The family also includes the true geraniums (genus *Geranium*) and the stork's bill (genus *Erodium*). Geraniums are also cultivated for the aromatic oils extracted from their foliage and flowers. In folk medicine they are variously used for diarrhoea, ulcers, and to stop wounds bleeding.

**Gerard, John**, 1512–1612, English surgeon and botanist. He was the author of *Great Herbal* (1597), which was the most popular and influential book on English botany and its connections with medicine. Herbals were the first properly-illustrated books to be produced, and as such are important historically and bibliographically.

**gerbil**, desert RODENT (subfamily Gerbillinae) found in the hot, arid regions of Africa and Asia. Gerbils have large eyes and powerful, elongated limbs upon which they can spring. Sandy, grey, or red-brown, gerbils are 7 to 12 cm (3 to 5 in) long, excluding the long tail, and are popular pets.

**geriatrics**, medical specialty concerned with the medical aspects of old age and the care of old people. For example, aging cells are more susceptible to the accumulation of CALCIUM, CHOLESTEROL, and other substances that may cause tissue deterioration and decreased physiological functioning. Many disabilities of old age are related to CIRCULATORY SYSTEM deterioration. Proper nutrition and exercise can prolong good health and circulation. See also GERONTOLOGY.

**Géricault, Jean Louis André Théodore** (zhayreeˌkoh), 1791–1824, French painter. After studying in Rome he exhibited in Paris his famous *Raft of the Medusa* (1819; Louvre, Paris), a turbulent painting of shipwrecked men at sea that ushered in French ROMANTICISM. He later went to England, where he did such fine horse paintings as *The Lime Kiln* (c.1822; Louvre, Paris). He also modelled small figures and made excellent lithographs.

**German Confederation**, 1815–66, union of 39 German states created by the Congress of VIENNA to replace the old HOLY ROMAN EMPIRE. It comprised 35 monarchies and 4 free cities. It was little more than a loose union for the purpose of mutual defence, with its main organ a central diet under the presidency of Austria. The confederation was dominated by the strong influence of Austria and Prussia. The Austro-Prussian War (1866) destroyed the confederation, and the North German Confederation that replaced it was under the sole leadership of Prussia.

**Germanic languages**, subfamily of the Indo-European family of languages, of which English and German, the standard language of Germany, are members. See LANGUAGE (table).

**Germanic law**, customary laws of the ancient Germans, codified (5th–9th cent.) after the Germanic tribes invaded the Roman Empire. Enacted cooperatively by ruler and people, they deal chiefly with penal law and legal procedure, although there are many laws pertaining to landholding. The Germans regarded law as personal, not territorial, and therefore continued to govern the Romans under their rule by ROMAN LAW.

**Germanic religion**, pre-Christian religious practices among the tribes of W Europe, Germany, and Scandinavia. There was no one religion common to all the Scandinavian and Teutonic peoples, but descriptions from TACITUS and the EDDAS point to certain basic polytheistic features. In early times two groups of gods were worshipped, the Aesir and the Vanir; later they coalesced to form a single pantheon of 12 principal deities, headed by WODEN (Odin) and including Tiw (Tyr), Thor (Donar), Balder, Frey, FREYJA, and FRIGG. Their home was Asgard. There, in the palace Valhalla, Woden and his warrior maidens (the Valkyries) gave banquets to dead heroes. Unlike the gods of most religions, the ancient Nordic deities were subject to Fate (the Norns) and tradition held that they were doomed to eventual destruction by the forces of evil in the form of giants and demons, led by Loki. After a ferocious battle at Ragnarok, the universe would end in a blaze of fire; but a new cosmos was to rise from the ashes of the old, and a new generation of gods and men would dwell in harmony. The Germanic temples were attended by priests, who oversaw magic rites (e.g., divination) and prayer. Conversion of the Germans to Christianity began as early as the 4th cent. AD, but it took many centuries for the new religion to spread throughout N Europe.

**Germanicus Julius Caesar**, 15 BC–AD 19, Roman general. He was adopted by his uncle TIBERIUS, and was the father of CALIGULA. His notable successes in Germany aroused the jealousy of Tiberius, who recalled him and appointed him to command in the East. He died at Antioch in mysterious circumstances, possibly poisoned on Tiberius's orders. He was an able and charismatic figure, compared by contemporaries to Alexander the Great.

**germanium** (Ge), semimetallic element, isolated from argyrodite (a sulphide ore) by Clemens Winkler in 1886. Grey-white, lustrous, and brittle, it is chemically and physically similar to SILICON. It is used as a SEMICONDUCTOR in TRANSISTORS and integrated circuits. The oxide, transparent to infrared radiation, is used in optical instruments, in intruder alarm systems, and in night-vision cameras. See ELEMENT (table); PERIODIC TABLE.

**German language,** member of the West Germanic group of the Germanic subfamily of the Indo-European family of languages. See LANGUAGE (table).

**German measles:** see RUBELLA.

**Germans,** a large ethnic complex of ancient Europe, a basic stock in the composition of the modern peoples of Scandinavia, Germany, Austria, Switzerland, the Low Countries, and England. They lived in N Germany and along the Baltic Sea, expanding south, southeast, and west in the early Christian era. CAESAR and TACITUS wrote of their warlike attributes, culture, and distribution. The Teutons and Cimbri, whom the Roman general Marius defeated (102–101 BC), may have been Germans. German tribes increasingly troubled the Roman Empire, with Vandal attacks in the west and OSTROGOTH attacks in the east. Among the tribes were the Alemanni, the FRANKS, the Angles, the Burgundii, the LOMBARDS, the SAXONS, and the VISIGOTHS. The Scandinavians included the Icelanders, who produced the first Germanic literature.

**Germany,** country of central Europe, divided since 1949 into two independent republics, West and East Germany. In antiquity, Rome conquered (1st cent. BC–1st cent. AD) SW Germany but was stopped from further conquest by Germanic tribes who lived to the northeast. Germanic tribes later (4th–5th cent.) overran most of the Roman Empire, and by the 6th cent. one of these tribes, the FRANKS, had created a vast empire in Germany and Gaul (see MEROVINGIANS; CAROLINGIANS; CHARLEMAGNE). In the 8th cent. Christianity was spread among the Germans by St BONIFACE. A successor state, the HOLY ROMAN EMPIRE, was founded in the 10th cent., but Germany remained a loose federation of small principalities and cities. The Holy Roman Empire, weakened by the Protestant REFORMATION (16th cent.) and the THIRTY YEARS WAR (1618–48), was finally swept aside (1806) by NAPOLEON I. The Congress of VIENNA (1814–15) created the GERMAN CONFEDERATION, another loose federation of German states, in which PRUSSIA and Austria emerged as rivals. Prussia, under Otto von BISMARCK, finally achieved the unification of Germany after victories in the AUSTRO-PRUSSIAN WAR (1866) and the FRANCO-PRUSSIAN WAR (1870–71). In 1871 King WILLIAM I of Prussia was proclaimed emperor of Germany, and the new German empire rapidly became the chief economic and military power on the Continent. Its industrial, colonial, and naval expansion threatened British and French interests and helped bring about WORLD WAR I. Badly defeated, Germany accepted (1919) the harsh Treaty of VERSAILLES and established the Weimar Republic. This was beset from the beginning by extremist agitation, mass unemployment, and severe inflation. In 1933 Adolf HITLER was appointed chancellor, and within a year he had established an absolute dictatorship. WORLD WAR II began with Germany's invasion of Poland (1939) and ended, in Europe, with the German surrender in 1945. The defeated country was divided into four Allied occupation zones, but dissension between the USSR and the West led to the formation (1949) of the Federal Republic of Germany (West Germany) in the US, French, and British zones, and of the German Democratic Republic (East Germany) in the Soviet zone. The precise legal status of West BERLIN has remained in dispute.

**West Germany,** republic (1985 est. pop. 61,106,000) 247,973 km² (95,742 sq mi); bordered by Austria and Switzerland (S), France, Luxembourg, Belgium, and the Netherlands (W), the North Sea and Denmark (N), the Baltic Sea (NE), and East Germany and Czechoslovakia (E). BONN is the seat of government; other important cities include FRANKFURT, HAMBURG, and MUNICH. Geographically, West Germany is made up of parts of the N German plain, the central German uplands, and, in the S, the ranges of the Bavarian ALPS, which rise to the Zugspitze 2963 m (9721 ft). There are many important rivers, including the RHINE, WESER, ELBE, DANUBE, and MAIN. Virtually all the people speak German, and the country is fairly evenly divided between Protestants (in the N) and Roman Catholics (in the W and S). Aided by the MARSHALL PLAN, West Germany recovered quickly from World War II, and by 1970 was one of the world's primary industrial powers. In the late 1970s it maintained the highest growth rate among the major industrial nations, as well as a comparatively low rate of inflation. Leading industrial products include iron and steel, cement, chemicals, motor vehicles, electric and electronic equipment, precision instruments, textiles, refined petroleum, and foodstuffs. Natural resources are limited, with hard coal, potash, and lignite the chief minerals. West Germany carries on a very large foreign trade and usually enjoys a trade surplus. The GNP is $702,440 million and the GNP per capita is $11,420 (1983). The Federal Republic of

Germany was established in 1949, with Konrad ADENAUER as its first chancellor. The country gained most of the attributes of national sovereignty in 1952 and full independence in 1955, when it joined the NORTH ATLANTIC TREATY ORGANIZATION; West Germany was also a founder member of the EUROPEAN COMMUNITY. Politics in the early years were dominated by insistence on reunification, to be achieved through democratic elections, and nonrecognition of East Germany. The government of Willy BRANDT, while upholding the goal of a united Germany, made significant steps toward improving relations with Eastern Europe, including the signing of a nonaggression pact with the USSR (1970) and a treaty with East Germany (1973). Over a decade of political dominance by the Social Democrats ended when the Christian Democrat Helmut KOHL succeeded Helmut SCHMIDT as chancellor in 1982.

West **Germany**

**East Germany,** republic (1985 est. pop. 16,642,000) 107,771 km² (41,610 sq mi) bordered by Czechoslovakia (S), West Germany (S and W), the Baltic Sea (N), and Poland (E). East Berlin is the capital; other major cities include LEIPZIG, DRESDEN, and MAGDEBURG. East Germany is made up largely of a low-lying plain, but there are mountains in the W and S. The chief rivers are the ELBE and the ODER, which, with its tributary, the Neisse, forms most of the eastern boundary. Virtually all the people speak German, and the majority are Protestant. Industrialization has been rapid in the postwar era, and East Germany is now the largest producer of industrial goods, after the USSR, in Eastern Europe. Principal manufactures include steel, chemicals, machinery, and electric and electronic equipment. Lignite and potash are the only important mineral resources. The GNP is $119,489 million and the GNP per capita is $7180 (1983). The German Democratic Republic was established in 1949, with Otto Grotewohl as its first prime minister. Economic hardships led (1953) to a workers' uprising that was suppressed by Soviet forces. Under Walter ULBRICHT, who emerged as leader in the 1950s, the Berlin wall was erected (1961) to halt the flow of millions of East Germans to the West.

East Germany is a member of the COUNCIL FOR MUTUAL ECONOMIC ASSISTANCE and of the WARSAW TREATY ORGANIZATION, and in 1968 participated in the Soviet-led invasion of Czechoslovakia. Beginning in the late 1960s and early 1970s, significant steps were taken toward improving relations with the rest of the world; a treaty with West Germany was signed in 1973, and East Germany was accorded diplomatic recognition by a number of non-Communist countries, including the US (1974). In 1971 Ulbricht was replaced as leader of the ruling Socialist Unity Party by Erich HONECKER, who in 1976 also became head of state.

### Federal German presidents
Theodor Heuss (Free Democrat), 1949–59
Heinrich Lübke (Christian Democrat), 1959–69
Gustav Heinemann (Social Democrat), 1969–74
Walter Scheel (Free Democrat), 1974–79
Karel Carstens (Christian Democrat), 1979–84
Richard von Weizsächer (Christian Democrat), 1984–

### Federal German chancellors
Konrad Adenauer (Christian Democrat), 1949–63
Ludwig Erhard (Christian Democrat), 1963–66
Kurt Georg Kiesinger (Christian Democrat), 1966–69
Willy Brandt (Social Democrat), 1969–74
Helmut Schmidt (Social Democrat), 1974–82
Helmut Kohl (Christian Democrat), 1982–

**germination,** process by which the plant embryo within the SEED resumes growth after a period of dormancy and the seedling emerges. Food stored in the endosperm or in the cotyledons (see ANGIOSPERM) provides energy in the early stages of growth until the seedling can make its own.

**Germiston,** city (1978 pop. 216,123), South Africa, E of Johannesburg. A leading gold-mining and industrial centre founded in 1887, it has the largest railway junction in South Africa. Manufactures include engineering, textiles, furniture, and chemicals. It is named after the Scottish birthplace of John Jack of the Simmer and Jack Mine.

**germ warfare:** see BIOLOGICAL WARFARE.

**Geronimo,** c.1829–1909, leader of the Chiricahua APACHE INDIANS. After the Chiricahua Reservation in Arizona was abolished (1876) he

repeatedly led raids, was captured, and escaped. Finally surrendering in 1886, he was removed to Fort Sill, Oklahoma and became a Christian and a prosperous farmer.

**gerontology,** scientific study of old age and the biological process of aging, concerned with the physical and psychological aspects of aging and the special economic and social problems of the elderly. Gerontology emerged as a major area of study in the 20th cent. as the steady increase in average life expectancy swelled the numbers of older people in the population, first in developed countries and then in developing countries. The medical specialty that focuses on the health and diseases of the elderly is called GERIATRICS.

**gerrymandering,** rearrangement of lines and boundaries of voting districts to favour the party in power. The term, which described this political art as practised by Massachusetts Jeffersonians, originated while Elbridge GERRY was governor.

**Gershwin, George,** 1898–1937, American composer. His scores to MUSICALS, including *Lady, Be Good!* (1924) and *Of Thee I Sing* (1931), made him famous. In his extended compositions, e.g., *Rhapsody in Blue* (1923), Piano Concerto in F (1925), and *An American in Paris* (1928), he blended traditional with folk and JAZZ elements. Gershwin wrote the music for the folk opera *Porgy and Bess* (1935). Among his best-known songs are 'Summertime' and 'I Got Rhythm'. His brother, **Ira Gershwin,** 1896–1983, wrote lyrics to many of his compositions.

**Gesner, Konrad von,** 1516–65, Swiss scientist and bibliographer. He is important as a reviver of the classical school of zoological description that culminated in the work of Carolus LINNAEUS. Gesner's illustrated compendium, *Historia animalium* (5 vol., 1551–58, 1587), influenced both biology and the arts; it is considered the foundation of zoology as a science.

**gesneria,** herb or shrub, chiefly tropical and subtropical, of the family Gesneriaceae, cultivated for its showy, often tubular blossoms. The family includes the AFRICAN VIOLETS; the African Cape primrose (genus *Streptocarpus*); and the florists' gloxinia (*Sinningia speciosa*) of Brazil, not to be confused with the true genus *Gloxinia,* which is seldom cultivated.

**Gestalt psychology,** a school in psychology originating in Germany in the early 20th cent., though its leading theorists fled to the US during the 1930s. Gestalt psychologists argued that the significance of structured phenomena (such as visual figures, or melodies) depend upon the relationships between the parts which make up the whole, or 'Gestalt', and not upon the individual constituent elements. LEARNING was viewed by Gestalt theorists such as Max Wertheimer (1880–1943), Wolfgang Köhler (1887–1967), Kurt Koffka (1886–1941), and Kurt Lewin (1890–1947), not as ASSOCIATION but as restructuring or reorganization, frequently involving insight. Gestalt psychology was hostile to BEHAVIOURISM and advocated instead 'field' theories of behaviour, development, and brain function. Though Gestalt psychology as an organized 'school' no longer exists, many of its ideas are current in contemporary COGNITIVE SCIENCE.

**Gestalt therapy,** a form of PSYCHOTHERAPY, drawing on both psychoanalytic and existential psychiatry, which focuses upon 'restructuring' the experience and perception of interpersonal relationships.

**Gesta Romanorum,** medieval collection of Latin stories, each with a moral, probably older than the extant 14th-cent. manuscript. CHAUCER and others used it as a source.

**gestation,** in MAMMALS, the period between conception and birth in which the developing young animal, or embryo, is carried within the uterus. In humans, gestation is usually called PREGNANCY.

**gestural painting,** a term used generally and not to describe a specific school of painting. It implies both that a work of art records the artist's creative process in the direct action of paint application to the canvas, and that it expresses the artist's emotions in the forms and colours used. It has been used as a synonym for ACTION PAINTING and TACHISM and covers the work of US abstract expressionists like J. POLLOCK and European 'art-informed' artists like Wols, H. Harting, and A. TAPIES.

East **Germany**

**Gethsemane,** olive grove or garden, E of Jerusalem, near the foot of the Mount of OLIVES. It was the scene of the agony and betrayal of JESUS.

**Gettysburg Address,** 19 Nov. 1863, famous speech by Abraham LINCOLN at the dedication of the AMERICAN CIVIL WAR cemetery at Gettysburg, Pennsylvania. Lincoln eloquently stated his grief for the fallen soldiers and the principles for which they had given their lives. The brief address is perhaps the most quoted speech of all time, including among many memorable phrases: 'and that government of the people, by the people, for the people, shall not perish from the earth'.

**Gettysburg campaign,** June–July 1863, a series of battles that marked the turning point of the AMERICAN CIVIL WAR. After his victory at Chancellorsville, the Confederate general Robert E. LEE undertook a second invasion of the North, crossing the Potomac into Pennsylvania. Union forces under George G. MEADE met the Confederates just W of Gettysburg in the greatest battle of the war (1–3 July 1863). Tremendous losses resulted and on 4 July Lee withdrew. Union losses totalled 23,000 killed or wounded; Confederate, 25,000.

**geyser,** HOT SPRING from which water and steam are ejected periodically to heights ranging from a metre or so to a hundred or more. The generally accepted explanation is that rainwater, collected under pressure in hot rocks below ground, turns partly to steam and causes the water above it to overflow, thereby reducing the pressure and forcing an eruption. Notable geysers are found in Iceland; North Island, New Zealand; and Yellowstone National Park, US.

**Gezelle, Guido** (khe‚zelə), 1830–99, Flemish poet; b. Belgium. He was a Roman Catholic priest. A forerunner of the Flemish literary revival, he combined a love of nature, intense religious feeling, and Flemish patriotism in his idiomatic lyrics, e.g., *Necklace of Rhymes* (1897).

**Gezira, Gazira,** or **Al Jazirah,** region in the Sudan, NE Africa, between the White Nile and the Blue Nile, just south of their convergence, at Khartoum. A massive irrigation scheme, begun in 1925, includes two dams and a series of canals that have put nearly 1 million hectares (2.5 million acres) into cultivation. Cotton and wheat are the chief crops.

**Gezo,** 1797–1858, king (r.1818–58) of Dahomey (now BENIN). In 1827 he gained Dahomey's independence from the kingdom of Oyo and spent the rest of his life extending his kingdom, mainly at the expense of Oyo, and reorganizing his country's economy after the abolition of the slave trade. The cash crops cotton and palm oil replaced slaves, though the state-owned plantations still made use of unfree labour. He was succeeded by his son GLELE.

**Ghana,** officially Republic of Ghana, republic (1986 est. pop. 13,500,000), 238,536 km² (92,099 sq mi), W Africa, bordered by the Gulf of Guinea (S), Côte d'Ivoire (W), Burkina Faso (N), and Togo (E). Major cities include ACCRA (the capital) and KUMASI. The coastal region and the far north are savanna areas; in between is a forest zone. Lake Volta, in central Ghana, is one of the world's largest man-made lakes. Cocoa is the principal crop in Ghana's predominantly agricultural economy, accounting for 60% of export earnings; other exports include minerals (gold, diamonds, and bauxite) and timber. Aluminium smelting, food-processing, and timber production are the principal industries, and coffee and peanuts are widely grown. The GNP is US$4826 million, and the GNP per capita is US$380 (1985). The population includes various tribal groups, chiefly the Akan (Ashanti and Fanti), Mole-Dagbani, Ewe, and Ga-Adangme. English is the official language. About 40% of the people are Christians, 10% are Muslims (mainly in the north), and the rest follow traditional religions.

*History.* In precolonial times the region comprised a number of independent kingdoms, including the ASHANTI confederation in the interior and the Fanti states along the coast. The first European fort was established by the Portuguese at Elmina in 1482, and for more than three centuries European nations engaged in a brisk but highly competitive trade in gold and slaves. The expanding Ashanti kingdom forced the withdrawal of the Danes (1850) and the Dutch (1872), but the British allied themselves with the Fanti, defeated the Ashanti in 1874, and organized the coastal region as the Gold Coast colony. After renewed fighting between the British and the Ashanti, Britain made the kingdom a colony in 1901, at the same time declaring a protectorate over the Northern Territories, a region north of Ashanti. After World War I part of the German colony of TOGOLAND, mandated to Britain, was administered with the Gold Coast. In 1951, in the face of rising nationalist activity,

Britain granted a new constitution and held general elections, from which Kwame NKRUMAH, the colony's leading nationalist figure, emerged as premier. The state of Ghana, named after a medieval African empire (see separate article) and including British Togoland, which had voted to join it, became an independent country within the COMMONWEALTH in 1956. In 1960 Nkrumah transformed Ghana into a republic and named himself president for life. Increasingly repressive and beset by a deteriorating economy, Nkrumah was overthrown by a coup in 1966. The ensuing years have seen a succession of coups. By the late 1970s the economy had slid into chaos, and corruption was rife at all levels of society. Elections in 1979 marked a return to civilian government, but conditions failed to improve, and in 1981 the military led by Jerry RAWLINGS again seized power.

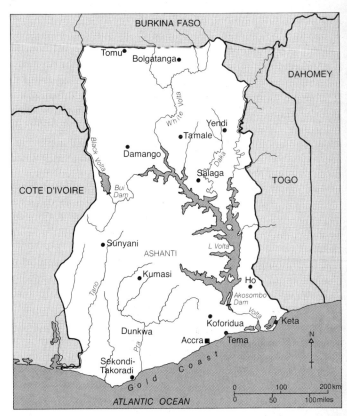

Ghana

**Ghana,** ancient empire of W Africa, in the savanna region now occupied by E Senegal, SW Mali, and S Mauritania. The empire was founded c.6th cent. by Soninke peoples and lay astride the trans-Saharan caravan routes. Its capital was Kumbi Saleh. It prospered from trade, mostly salt and gold, and from tribute. Invaded by the Almoravids in 1076, it disintegrated by the 13th cent. Modern GHANA takes its name from the ancient empire.

**Ghats.** These form the eastern and western edges of the DECCAN plateau, S India. Anai Mudi (2695 m/8841 ft) is the highest point. The **Western Ghats,** c.1600 km (1000 mi) long, extend southeast from near Bombay to the southern tip of India. Their largely forested western slopes receive abundant rainfall from onshore monsoon winds and are the source of many easterly-flowing rivers, including the GODAVARI, KRISHNA, and KAVERI. The **Eastern Ghats,** facing the Bay of Bengal, form a series of discontinuous hills extending c.1450 km (900 mi) SW from the MAHANADI valley.

**Ghazali, Abu Hamid,** 1058–1111, Muslim scholar. Born in eastern Iran, Ghazali studied at the MADRASA in Nishapur, then the major eastern centre of Islamic learning, and taught at the Nizamiyya Madrasa in Baghdad. He represents one of the foremost results of Madrasa consolidation of Sunnite scholarship (see SUNNISM). His works on KALAM, FIQH, SUFISM, heretical beliefs, and his critique of AVICENNA had a momentous impact on subsequent Islamic thought.

**Ghazali, al-,** 1058–1111, Islamic philosopher, considered the greatest theologian in ISLAM, well known in medieval Europe as Algazel. Of Persian origin, he abandoned teaching to wander for 10 years as a Sufi mystic (see SUFISM), attempting to reconcile MYSTICISM with orthodox Islam. His great compendium of Muslim thought, *Restoration of the Sciences of Religion,* outlines an orthodox system for the attainment of unity with God.

**Ghaziabad,** town (1981 pop. 275,815), Uttar Pradesh state, N India, on the Hindan R. It is a railway junction and commercial centre which has grown rapidly, profiting from its proximity to, and good communications with, DELHI. It forms part of an urbanized belt that stretches from Delhi to MEERUT, and has acquired a number of industries.

**ghee:** see BUTTER.

**Ghelderode, Michel de** (geldə͵rohd), 1898–1962, Belgian dramatist. A satirist and exquisite poet, he is considered one the most original French-language playwrights of modern times. A wide variety of influences—MAETERLINCK, medieval morality plays, Flemish painting, puppet theatre, COMMEDIA DELL'ARTE, the Elizabethans, and Edgar Allan POE—reveal themselves in such masterpieces as *Chronicles of Hell* (1929), *Pantagleize* (1929), *Mademoiselle Jaïre* (1934), and *Hop Signore!* (1935).

**Ghent,** city (1985 pop. 234,563), W Belgium, at the confluence of the Scheldt and Leie rivers. It is a major port and a textile- and steel-manufacturing centre. One of Belgium's oldest cities, founded in the 7th cent., it was the capital of FLANDERS. It was a medieval wool-producing city and was virtually independent until 1584. Thereafter it was ruled by the HABSBURGS, until the French Revolution. It is noted for its many medieval and Renaissance buildings.

**Ghent, Treaty of,** 1814, agreement ending the WAR OF 1812 between the US and Great Britain. Stipulating the restoration of territory taken by either party during hostilities, it ignored the maritime and frontier issues which had caused the war.

**Gheorghiu-Dej, Gheorghe** (gay͵awgyoohdayzh), 1901–65, Romanian Communist leader. He became secretary general of the Communist Party (1945–54, 1955–65), premier and president of the State Council (1961–65). He was architect of Romania's semi-autonomous foreign and economic policy within the East European bloc.

**ghetto,** area of European city where the Jews were confined. Within the compulsory ghettos, which originated in 14th-cent. Spain and Portugal, Jews generally had autonomy in all but economic matters: outside it, they were severly restricted. Abolished in Western Europe by the 19th cent., ghettos were reinstituted by the Nazis in World War II (see ANTI-SEMITISM; NATIONAL SOCIALISM). In the social sciences the term is used, more broadly, to designate any densely packed, economically and socially deprived area of a city occupied by an identifiable racial, ethnic, or religious group (e.g., Harlem in New York, Brixton in London).

**Ghibellines:** see GUELPHS AND GHIBELLINES.

**Ghiberti, Lorenzo** (gee͵beətee), 1378–1455, major Florentine sculptor of the early Renaissance. He is famous for two sets of bronze doors for the Baptistery in Florence. In 1401 he won the competition for the first of these, defeating BRUNELLESCHI. These doors, the north portal (1403–24), were designed to match Andrea PISANO's earlier Gothic portal, and show New Testament scenes within quatrefoil frameworks. The second doors (1424–52), dubbed the 'Gates of Paradise', (perhaps by MICHELANGELO) were more modern in form and structure; the ten reliefs of Old Testament scenes are brilliantly decorative, and use complex perspective settings and subtle gradations from high to low relief.

**Ghirlandaio** or **Ghirlandajo, Domenico** (geəlahn͵dahyoh), 1449–94, Florentine painter whose family name was Bigordi. His religious narrative paintings, e.g., *Scenes from the Life of St Francis* (1482–86; Santa Trinità, Florence), reveal a keen eye for contemporary detail. Among his pupils was MICHELANGELO, who probably assisted with Ghirlandaio's FRESCO cycle of the life of Mary and St John the Baptist in Santa Maria Novella, Florence (1485–90). His famous realistic portrait *Grandfather and Grandson* (undated) is in the Louvre, Paris.

**Ghose, Aurobindo** (gohsh), 1872–1950, Indian mystic philosopher, known as Sri Aurobind. He spent his early years as an agitator for Indian independence. He experienced mystic visions, retired from political activism, and formulated what became Purna, or Integral, Yoga. In 1926 he retired into seclusion in his ashram at Pondicherry.

**ghost dance,** ritual central to the messianic religion instituted c.1870 among the PAIUTE INDIANS by their prophet WOVOKA. The religion, which prophesied the end of white expansion westward and the return of land to the Indians, spread to most of the western Indians. The ritual was danced for five successive days and was accompanied by hypnotic trances. The SIOUX performed the ritual prior to their massacre at WOUNDED KNEE in 1890 wearing 'ghost shirts' that they thought would protect them from bullets.

Lorenzo **Ghiberti,** the 'Gates of Paradise' from the Baptistery in Florence, 1424–52.

**Giacometti, Alberto** (jahkoh͵mettee), 1901–66, Swiss sculptor and painter. Associated with SURREALISM in the 1930s, he is known for his bronze sculptures of elongated human figures, e.g., *Standing Woman* figures (1958–59; Tate Gall., London).

**Giambologna:** see BOLOGNA, GIOVANNI.

**giant,** in mythology, manlike being of great size and strength; a brutish power of nature, lacking the stature of gods and the civilization of humanity. In many cultures, e.g., Greek, Scandinavian, and American Indian, giants were believed to be the first race of people that inhabited the earth.

**Giant's Causeway,** promontory on N coast of Northern Ireland, to E of Coleraine. It is made of columnar basalt, which forms spectacular pillars which are mostly hexagonal in shape, and of varying height.

**giant sequoia:** see SEQUOIA.

**Gibanda, Gabanda,** 1865–1932, king of the Bapende of ZAÏRE. Although in the 1920s Gibanda's authority was recognized by King Leopold of Belguim's Congo Free State, forced removals and land confiscation by the colonialists estranged Gibanda and his subjects. In 1931 the Bapende revolted and Gibanda and several other chiefs were

Giant's Causeway

Carving by Grinling **Gibbons**

imprisoned and later executed. The Belgian authorities later admitted that Gibanda had been erroneously condemned for crimes he never committed.

**gibbon,** smallest and most agile of the four APES in the family Pongidae. There are six species of gibbon, all living in SE Asia from Assam to Java. All have long arms and fingers, the ability to swing hand over hand through the trees, known as brachiating, and claw-like nails and long fangs. Four species are in the genus *Hylobates*, all about 90 cm (3 ft) tall, with arms one and a half times the length of their legs. The largest gibbon is the siamang (*Symphalangus syndactylus*), which is about 120 cm (4 ft) tall with an armspan of 150 cm (5 ft). The apes live in family groups in the upper canopy of tropical rain forests. They feed on fruits, eggs, leaves, and insects and have been seen to take birds from the air in mid leap. They keep in touch in the dense leaf cover by calling, which also defines the territory of each family group.

**Gibbon, Edward,** 1734–94, English historian. He is the author of *The History of the Decline and Fall of the Roman Empire* (6 vol., 1776–88), one of the most influential historical works of modern times, as remarkable for its footnotes as for its text. Gibbon was one of the main English figures in the ENLIGHTENMENT. He also wrote a subtle and revealing autobiography. He served in Parliament from 1774 to 1783.

**Gibbons, Grinling,** 1648–1721, woodcarver; b. Holland. After he settled in England c.1667, Gibbons' naturalistic and freely composed limewood carvings of garlands of fruit, flowers, and birds, executed in a virtuoso technique, introduced a new kind of decoration to English country-house interiors. There are documented examples at Sudbury, Badminton, and St Paul's Cathedral, London.

**Gibbons, Orlando,** 1583–1625, English organist and composer. His compositions include English ANTHEMS and services, chamber music, and MADRIGALS.

**Gibbons v. Ogden,** case decided in 1824 by the US SUPREME COURT, which ruled that New York's grant of a steamboat monopoly on the Hudson R. interfered with congressional power over interstate commerce under Article I of the US CONSTITUTION. Chief Justice MARSHALL, rejecting the idea that the states and the federal government are equal sovereignties, held that although federal power is limited, within its sphere Congress is supreme.

**Gibbs, James,** 1682–1754, English architect. An exponent of the GEORGIAN STYLE, he is noted for London churches, e.g., St Mary-le-Strand (1714–17) and St Martin's-in-the-Fields (1721–26). He also designed the circular Radcliffe Camera (1737-49), a library at Oxford.

**Gibbs, Josiah Willard,** 1839–1903, American mathematical physicist. He was professor of mathematical physics at Yale. Gibbs's studies in physical chemistry and thermodynamics have had a profound effect on industry, notably in the production of ammonia. He formulated the concept of chemical potential, was influential in developing vector analysis, and did important work in statistical mechanics.

**Gibraltar,** British dependency (1979 est. pop. 29,760), 5.8 km (2.25 sq mi), on a narrow, rocky peninsula extending into the Mediterranean Sea from SW Spain. The town of Gibraltar lies at the northwest end of the Rock of Gibraltar. Although Gibraltar is a free port with some transit trade, its major importance is strategic, and its status has long been a subject of dispute between Great Britain (which has maintained possession since 1704) and Spain. In 1980 The UK and Spain agreed to open negotiations on Gibraltar, whose land border with Spain (closed since 1969) was reopened in 1985.

**Gibran, Kahlil** (ji,brahn), 1883–1931, Lebanese poet and novelist. He wrote in both English and Arabic. Fusing elements of Eastern and Western mysticism, he achieved lasting fame with such aphoristic, poetic works as *The Prophet* (1923) and *The Garden of the Prophet* (1934).

**Gibson, Charles Dana,** 1867–1944, American illustrator. As an illustrator of various contemporary magazines, he delineated aristocratic social ideals and created an ideal woman, the famous 'Gibson Girl'.

**Gibson, James Jerome,** 1904–80, American psychologist. His theory of 'direct perception' proposes that information processing in PERCEPTION is based upon the INNATE attunement of the organism to the invariant properties and 'affordances' of the environment. Gibson's theory is frequently seen as an alternative to more cognitive and computational theories of perception. His books include *The Ecological Approach to Visual Perception* (1979).

**Gide, André** (zheed), 1869–1951, French author. A leader of French liberal thought, he was one of the founders (1909) of the influential *Nouvelle revue française.* He was controversial for his frank defence of homosexuality and for his espousal (and later disavowal) of communism. In his major novels *L'Immoraliste* (1902), *Les caves du Vatican* (1914; tr. Lafcadio's Adventures), and *Les faux-monnayeurs* (1926; tr. The Counterfeiters) he shows individuals seeking out their own natures, which may be at odds with prevailing ethical concepts. He was also known for his journals (1889–1949). Gide received the Nobel Prize in literature in 1947.

**Gideon, Gedeon** or **Jerubbaal,** in the BIBLE, one of the greater judges of Israel, a strong opponent of the BAAL cult. He refused the kingship because of his belief that God was the king of Israel. He also defeated the Midianite (see MIDIAN) oppressors and appeased the rival Ephraimites (see ISRAEL, TRIBES OF). Judges 6–8.

**Gielgud, Sir John,** 1904–, English actor. He excelled in plays by SHAKESPEARE (notably *Hamlet*), WILDE, and PINTER, and won applause for major film and television roles, e.g., *Arthur* and *Brideshead Revisited* (both: 1981).

**Gierek, Edward,** 1913–, Polish Communist leader. He replaced Wladyslaw GOMULKA as first secretary of the party in 1970, after food riots had broken out. A failing economy, industrial unrest, and the rise of the SOLIDARITY free trade movement caused his resignation in 1980.

**gift,** in anthropology, an essential mode of expression of a relationship. According to M. MAUSS the most basic and fundamental morality is to give, to receive, and to reciprocate, and this is linked to the idea that things remain part of the person offering them as a gift so that therefore a special relationship still exists between them. A gift is a statement about the relationship between the giver and the receiver, and gift giving, receiving, and repaying establishes or maintains a social relationship, which can be one of equivalence (involving reciprocal exchanges) or inequality, the receiver being obliged to reciprocate with tribute or services. Givers and receivers may be either individuals or groups.

**gift tax:** see under INHERITANCE TAX.

**Gijón,** city (1981 pop. 255,969) N Spain, on the Bay of Biscay. One of the country's leading ports, its exports include coal from the Asturian fields. To the older activities of glass-making and ceramics, have been added heavy metallurgical and engineering industries and various food trades. The port dates from pre-Roman times but expanded in the 18th cent. as trade with the Americas grew.

**gila monster,** venomous LIZARD (*Heloderma suspectum*) found in the deserts of the SW US and NW Mexico. It averages 45 cm (18 in) in length, with a large head, stout body, and thick tail that acts as a food reservoir;

The Radcliffe Camera, Oxford (1737–49) designed by James **Gibbs**

its skin is covered with beadlike scales. It and the beaded lizard (*H. horridum*) are the only known venomous lizards.

**Gilbert, Cass,** 1859–1934, American architect. His 60-storey Woolworth Building (1913) in New York City exerted great influence on the growth of the SKYSCRAPER. Among his other conspicuous works are the Federal Courts Building, New York City, and the Supreme Court building, Washington, DC.

**Gilbert, Grove Karl,** 1843–1918, American geologist employed as a surveyor. The formation of the United States Geological Survey in 1876 found Gilbert as one of its top six geologists, but he gave up most of his duties in 1892 to devote more time to geological investigation. His most important work, the *Bonneville Monograph*, was published in 1890; other works such as *Geology of the Henry Mountains* and *History of the Niagara River* were also of great importance in furthering the understanding of geological processes.

**Gilbert, Sir Humphrey,** 1537?–1583, English soldier, navigator, and explorer; half brother of Sir Walter RALEIGH. He was knighted (1570) for services in Ireland. His *Discourse* (1566), arguing the existence of the NORTHWEST PASSAGE, long motivated English exploration. In 1583 he reached NEWFOUNDLAND and claimed it for England. He disappeared at sea near the Azores.

**Gilbert, William,** 1544–1603, English scientist and physician. Noted for his studies of ELECTRICITY and MAGNETISM, he coined the word *electricity* and was the first to distinguish between electric and magnetic phenomena. In his *De magnete* (1600) he described methods for strengthening natural magnets (lodestones) and for using them to magnetize steel rods by stroking, and he concluded that the earth acts like a giant magnet with its poles near the geographic poles. From 1600 he was president of the College of Physicians and court physician to Elizabeth I and James I.

**Gilbert, Sir William Schwenck,** 1836–1911, English playwright and poet. With the composer Sir Arthur SULLIVAN he wrote a series of popular, satirical operettas, including *Trial by Jury* (1875), *H.M.S. Pinafore* (1878), *The Pirates of Penzance* (1879), *Patience* (1881), *Iolanthe* (1882), *Princess Ida* (1884), *The Mikado* (1885), *Ruddigore* (1887), *The Yeomen of the Guard* (1888), and *The Gondoliers* (1889).

**Gilbert Islands,** group of islands in the Pacific Ocean; now part of KIRIBATI.

**gilding,** decoration with gold leaf. With furniture this is generally done on a ground of whitening, size, and linseed oil. The earliest examples were found in the tombs of the pharaohs. In Europe since the Middle Ages two ways of applying the gold leaf have been used; oil-gilding, the simpler process, is more durable but water-gilding can be given a finer lustre by burnishing. See also ORMOLU.

**gilds:** see GUILDS.

**gill,** external respiratory organ of most aquatic animals, the basic function of which is oxygen–carbon-dioxide exchange. Gill structure and location vary among animals of different groups. In fishes, gills are located at the rear of the mouth and contain capillaries; in higher aquatic invertebrates, they protrude from the body surface and contain extensions of the vascular system; in molluscs, they are inside the mantle cavity; in aquatic insects, they occur as projections from the walls of the air tubes. In amphibians, gills are usually present only in the larval stage; in higher vertebrates, they occur merely as rudimentary, nonfunctional gill slits, which disappear during embryonic development.

**Gill, Eric,** 1882–1940, British sculptor, engraver, and writer. A member of the Art Workers' Guild and the Fabian Society, he became converted to Catholicism in 1913 and was commissioned to carve the *Stations of the Cross* for Westminster Cathedral (1914–18). His other best-known work is his *Prospero and Ariel* group for Broadcasting House (1929–31). After World War I he founded the Guild of St Joseph and St Dominic to revive interest in craftsmanship and religious art. In sculpture Gill was one of the leaders in the revival of direct carving and was also responsible for a revival in book design and typography.

**Gillespie, Dizzy** (John Birks Gillespie), 1917–, black American musician. With Charlie PARKER he led the bop movement in JAZZ in the 1940s. His trumpet style blends spectacular facility with taste and intelligence.

**Gilman, Harold,** 1876–1919, British painter. He was a founding member of the CAMDEN TOWN GROUP (1911) and the first president of the LONDON GROUP (1913). He was strongly influenced by Roger FRY's post-impressionist exhibitions (1910 and 1912), and GAUGUIN's work and ideas; he became the main British exponent of synthetism.

**Gilson, Étienne,** 1894–1978, French philosopher and historian. After teaching in Paris, Gilson founded (1929) the Institute of Medieval Studies at the Univ. of Toronto and was long a member of its faculty. He was also one of the leaders of the neo-Thomist movement in Catholic philosophy (see THOMAS AQUINAS, ST). His works include *The Philosophy of St Thomas Aquinas* (1919) and *The Spirit of Medieval Philosophy* (2 vol., 1932).

**gilt-edged securities,** stocks and shares traded on the London stockmarket whose interest and capital are guaranteed by the British government. Depending on the date at which they may be redeemed, they are described as long gilts, without a redemption date for 15 years; medium gilts, for redemption between 5 and 15 years, or short gilts where they may be redeemed within 5 years. Gilt-edged securities are not without risk since their price will fluctuate on the stockmarket. In 1986 they raised £14 billion, or £7.2 billion net of redemptions.

**gin,** strong alcoholic spirit distilled mainly from fermented cereals and flavoured with juniper berries. Of Dutch origin, it is now chiefly made in England and the US. Types of gin include London (highly distilled), and sloe (flavoured with sloes instead of juniper berries).

**Ginastera, Alberto** (heenahs␣tayrah), 1916–, Argentine composer. His early works used Latin American folk material; later compositions utilize serial techniques (see SERIAL MUSIC). Among his best-known works are *Estancia* (1941), a ballet; the *Estudios sinfónicos* (1967), for orchestra; and the operas *Don Rodrigo* (1964) and *Beatrix Cenci* (1971).

**ginger,** common name for perennial herbs of the tropical and subtropical family Zingiberaceae. Many are important for their aromatic oils. Ginger (*Zingiber officinale*) is cultivated for its root, which is an important ingredient in several Eastern cuisines; in the West it is candied or dried for medicines and spice. Turmeric (*Curcuma longa*) and the seeds of cardamom (*Elettaria cardamomum*) are also used as medicines or spices and often combined with ginger to make a curry.

**gingivitis,** inflammation of the gums, characterized by red, swollen, spongy gums that bleed easily. It may be acute, chronic, or recurrent. Chronic gingivitis usually results from bacteria, although other factors, such as poor dentition, prolonged use of the drug phenytoin (used in the treatment of epilepsy), vitamin C deficiency, or DIABETES, may also contribute to it. If left untreated, gingivitis can lead to PERIODONTITIS.

**ginkgo** or **maidenhair tree,** deciduous tree (*Ginkgo biloba*) with fan-shaped leaves. A sacred plant in its native China and Japan, ginkgo is a 'living fossil', the only remaining species of a large order (Ginkgoales) of GYMNOSPERMS that existed in the Triassic period. Today the ginkgo is valued as an avenue tree because of its exceptional tolerance for smoke (although the female plant, with its malodorous fruit, is not as desirable an ornamental as the male). The pollen grains produce swimming sperms. Ginkgo seeds are esteemed as a food in the Orient.

**Ginsberg, Allen,** 1926–, American poet of the BEAT GENERATION. He is best known for *Howl* (1956), a long poem attacking American values. Other volumes include *Kaddish and Other Poems* (1961) and *Mind Breaths* (1978).

**ginseng,** plant (genus *Panax*) of the family Araliaceae. Ginseng (*P. pseudoginseng*) is prized by the Chinese for its curative properties. It is not of interest as an ornamental plant. It and a North American ginseng (*P. quinquefolius*), used as a substitute for true ginseng, have been nearly exterminated by commercial exploitation. It is widely used as a tonic medicine. However, large doses may cause depression, insomnia, and nervous disorders.

**Giono, Jean** (jaw␣noh), 1895–1970, French novelist. His works particularly the pastoral trilogy *Colline* (1920; tr. Hill of Destiny), *Un de Baumugnes* (1929; tr. Lovers Are Never Losers), and *Regain* (1930; tr. Harvest) at first described Provençal life, emphasizing closeness to nature but became increasingly imaginative, and a demonstration of freedom in novelist and character.

**Giordano, Luca** (jaw␣dahnoh), 1634–1705, Italian decorative painter. An immensely prolific and widely travelled artist, he is known for his airy, luminous frescoes in the ESCORIAL (Madrid) and for his many decorations in Neapolitan churches.

**Giordano, Umberto,** 1867–1948, Italian operatic composer. *Andrea Chénier* (1896) and *Fedora* (1898) are among his works.

**Giorgione** (jaw␣johnay), c.1478–1510, Venetian painter. A seminal figure in the development of Italian painting, he greatly influenced the principal painters of his time. Few details remain of his life. He undertook commissions in oil and FRESCO and died of the plague in his 30s. His frescoes are virtually destroyed, and only a few oils are ascribed to him with certainty. His art is dominated by light and colour; he created a new kind of landscape that evokes a dreamy, poetic mood. His work introduced pastoral subjects into Venetian art that were later developed by TITIAN. Among his works are the *Tempest* (c.1504; Accademia, Venice) and *The Three Philosophers* (Kunsthistorisches, Vienna).

Giorgione, *Tempest*, c.1504. Accademia, Venice.

**Giotto** (␣jottoh), (Giotto di Bondone), c.1266 or 1276–c.1337, Florentine painter and architect. More than any other artist he may be said to have determined the course of painting in Europe. Giotto turned from the formulas of Byzantine painting to the study of nature, achieving lifelike, expressive faces and the illusion of volume and space. He designed a great number of works, many of which have disappeared. In Rome in 1300 he executed the MOSAIC of the *Navicella* (now in St Peter's, Rome), and began (c.1305) the 38 FRESCOES in the Scrovegni (Arena) Chapel (Padua). Among the greatest works in Italian art, these scenes from the *Life of the Virgin,* the *Life of Christ,* the *Last Judgment,* and *Virtues and Vices* illustrate Giotto's dramatic sense and power of narration. Returning to Florence, he did the frescoes of *St John the Baptist* and *St John the Evangelist* (1320s?; Peruzzi Chapel, Church of Santa Croce, Florence) and the *Life of St Francis* (Bardi Chapel, Florence). He achieved a remarkable representation of space, allying figures and background harmoniously, without using a system of perspective, e.g., in *Madonna in Glory* (c.1305–10; Uffizi, Florence). Chief architect of the cathedral in Florence, in his last years he designed the CAMPANILE called 'Giotto's Tower'. His reforms in painting were carried throughout Italy by his many pupils and followers, and his popularity is attested in literature by DANTE, PETRARCH, BOCCACCIO, and others.

Giotto, *Descent from the Cross*, one of the frescoes in the Scrovegni Arena, Rome.

**Giovanni Bologna:** see BOLOGNA, GIOVANNI.

**Giovanni di Paolo,** fl. 1420–82, Italian painter of the Sienese school. Like other Sienese painters of his era, he paid scant attention to the artistic innovations made in Florence. He had an inclination toward fantasy and a disregard for perspective. *Paradise* (1445; Metropolitan Mus., New York) and a late series of expressive scenes from the life of St John the Baptist (National Gall., London) are typical of his work.

**Giovanni Gondola:** see GUNDULIĆ, IVAN.

**Gippsland,** region of Victoria, SE Australia. The area extends 130 km (80 mi), between the GREAT DIVIDING RANGE and BASS STRAIT, includes the Latrobe Valley industrial area based on large deposits of brown coal mined by open-cut methods, and was named (1839) after the New South Wales governor Gipps. Wilson's Promontory National Park, the most southerly point on the Australian mainland, has abundant rainforests. The mouth of the Snowy R. is located at Orbost. The main urban centres for the region are Moe-Yallourn (1986 pop. 18,376) and Traralgon (1986 pop. 19,233), birthplace of Sir Macfarlane BURNETT.

**giraffe,** African ruminant MAMMAL (*Giraffa camelopardalis*) living in open SAVANNA S of the SAHARA. The tallest animal (up to 5.5 m/18 ft), the giraffe browses in the tops of ACACIA and MIMOSA trees. The legs and neck are elongated; the skin is patterned in large, sandy-to-chestnut spots on a lighter background. Giraffes travel in small herds.

**Giraudoux, Jean** (zheeroh͵dooh), 1882–1944, French dramatist and novelist. Mostly imaginative interpretations of Greek myths, his plays include *La guerre de Troie n'aura pas lieu* (1935; tr. Tiger at the Gates) and *Electra* (1937). *La folle de Chaillot* (1945; tr. The Madwoman of Chaillot) is a bitter satire on 20th-cent. materialism. In his novels, e.g., *Provinciales* (1909) and *Siegfried et le Limousin* (1922), the provinces are a metaphor for wisdom in a modern age.

**Girl Guides,** community service, recreational, and housecraft movement created in 1910 on the model of the BOY SCOUTS organized by Sir Robert BADEN-POWELL two years earlier. A World Association of Girl Guides and Girl Scouts was established in 1928, and Lady Baden-Powell became World Chief Guide in 1930. In 1914 the Brownie Guides for girls ages 7–11 were created, followed in 1916 by Ranger Guides for 14–20-year-olds. Activities stress good citizenship, service to others, health, kindness to animals, international friendship, and the arts. There are some 7½ million guides in 98 countries, 870,000 of them being in the UK.

**giro,** credit-transfer system whereby a bank or POST OFFICE transfers money from one account to another on receipt of written instructions. In the UK the system was introduced by commercial banks in 1961 and by the Post Office in 1968. Because transactions by giro are simple and not costly to make, the system has become popular and widely used throughout Europe. It is used in the UK for social-security benefits, being a secure way to make payments to people who have no bank account.

**Girondists** or **Girondins** (ji͵rondists), group of moderate republicans in the FRENCH REVOLUTION, so called because their early leaders were mostly from the Gironde dept. Notable members were Jacques Brissot de Warville, Charles DUMOURIEZ, and Jean Marie Roland de la Platière. Representing the educated, provincial middle class, they favoured a constitutional government and a continental war, splitting with the JACOBINS on the second issue. They were unable to prevent the execution of the king, and their position was weakened after the treason of Dumouriez. In June 1793 many Girondists were arrested and executed; the leftist MOUNTAIN was thus assured of complete control.

**Girtin, Thomas,** 1775–1802, English watercolourist, Girtin transformed the art of watercolour landscape, both by the boldness and directness of his colour, applied in superimposed washes, and by the grandeur of his compositions. Among his works are the *White House at Chelsea* (1800; Tate Gall., London) and a group of watercolour studies (British Mus., London) for his *Eidometropolis*, or circular panorama of London, probably in oil (destroyed).

**Giscard d'Estaing, Valéry** (zhees͵kah des͵tanh), 1926–, president of FRANCE (1974–81). A centrist member of the national assembly from 1955, he was finance minister (1962–66, 1969–74) under DE GAULLE and POMPIDOU. His attempts as president to deal with inflation and rising unemployment met with little success. He lost the 1981 election to François MITTERRAND of the Socialist Party.

**Gish, Lillian,** 1896–, American actress. She is best known for her work in such silent films as *The Birth of a Nation* (1915), *Broken Blossoms* (1919), and, with her sister, **Dorothy Gish** (1898–1968), *Orphans of the Storm* (1921). She still acts, notably in *A Wedding* (1978) and *The Whales of August* (1987).

**Gissing, George,** 1857–1903, English novelist. He wrote realistic novels of late Victorian urban life, often with a sardonic twist. His best-known work is *New Grub Street* (1891), depicting the plight of the poor, alienated artist. *The Nether World* (1889) portrays the London working-class, and *The Odd Women* (1893) is a pioneering study of emancipated women. Much of his work, including the autumnal *The Private Papers of Henry Ryecroft* (1903), reflects his own unhappy life.

**Giulini, Carlo Maria,** 1914–, Italian conductor. A disciple of TOSCANINI, he was first known as a conductor of opera, chiefly in Milan and Rome. In 1968 he made his orchestral debut with the New York Philharmonic. After holding posts with the Chicago Symphony and Vienna Symphony he became (1978) musical director of the Los Angeles Philharmonic.

**Giulio Romano,** c.1499–1546, Italian painter, architect, and decorator, a founder of MANNERISM; b. Giulio Pippi. A favourite pupil of RAPHAEL, Giulio painted many frescoes from Raphael's designs. His most famous work, produced whilst in the service of the duke of Mantua, is the Palazzo del Tè, which he decorated with illusionistic and witty frescoes of the story of Psyche and *The Fall of the Giants.*

**Giza** (͵geezə or el ͵jeezah), city (1987 pop. 1,230,446), NE Egypt, on the west bank of the Nile, adjacent to Cairo. There are cotton textiles, footwear, and brewing industries. To the west of the city lie the Sphinx and the great pyramids.

**glacier,** mass of ice formed in high mountains and polar regions by the compacting of snow and kept in constant movement by the pressure of the accumulated mass. The four main types are *valley*, or *mountain, glaciers,* tongues of ice moving from mountain snowfields into stream valleys; *piedmont glaciers,* formed by the spread of one or the convergence of several valley glaciers; *ice caps,* flattened, somewhat dome-shaped glaciers covering mountains and valleys alike; and *continental glaciers,* huge ice sheets that give rise to ICEBERGS. Glaciers alter topography greatly by their erosive action, by their transport of debris, and by the various forms of DRIFT they leave behind.

**Glackens, William James,** 1870–1938, American painter. An illustrator for various periodicals, Glackens first showed his paintings with the EIGHT and is known for his portrayals of the contemporary scene. His dark early style yielded to a brighter palette influenced by French IMPRESSIONISM, e.g., *Chez Mouquin* (1905; Art Inst., Chicago).

**gladiators** [Lat., = swordsmen], in ancient Rome, class of professional fighters, who performed for exhibition. There were various types of gladiators, armed and armoured differently. Gladiators fought each other

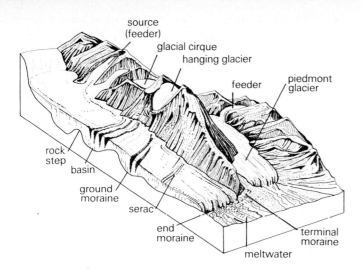

source (feeder)
glacial cirque
hanging glacier
feeder
piedmont glacier
rock step
basin
ground moraine
serac
end moraine
terminal moraine
meltwater

Glacier

and also wild beasts. They were slaves or prisoners, including Christians, or impoverished freedmen. Forbidden by CONSTANTINE I, gladiatorial games continued nonetheless until AD 405.

**gladiolus:** see IRIS.

**Gladstone,** city (1986 pop. 22,033), Queensland, NE Australia. The sheltered deep-water port was first settled in 1847 at Port Curtis, by time-expired convicts from Tasmania. The population increased by 70% between 1961 and 1966 with the establishment of alumina refining of bauxite ores from Weipa on CAPE YORK PENINSULA and processing of local mineral beach sands. The port now ranks fifth in Australia by tonnage of cargo handled. Offshore Heron Island on the GREAT BARRIER REEF is a marine biology research station.

**Gladstone, William Ewart,** 1809–98, British statesman, the dominant personality of the LIBERAL PARTY from 1868 to 1894, although he began his political career as a Tory and served under PEEL. As chancellor of the exchequer (1852–55, 1859–66), he secured measures for economic retrenchment and free trade. He was prime minister four times (1868–74, 1880–85, 1886, 1892–94) and achieved notable reforms: passage of the Irish land act; establishment of competitive examinations for the civil service; vote by secret ballot; abolition of the sale of army commissions; parliamentary reform; and educational expansion. His advocacy of HOME RULE for Ireland (1886) wrecked his third ministry and split the LIBERAL PARTY. A great orator and master of finance, Gladstone was deeply religious and brought a high moral tone to politics, including foreign policy. He disliked government intervention in the economy and an active social policy. He had an enthusiastic following, but never got on well with Queen VICTORIA.

**Glamis Castle,** castle in Tayside, Scotland, 16 km (10 mi) N of Dundee. Just outside the village of Glamis. Mainly of 17th-cent. construction, there are much older parts. It is the birthplace of Queen Elizabeth the Queen Mother, and Princess Margaret. An earlier castle on the site belonged to Macbeth, thane of Glamis, who was the hero of Shakespeare's play.

**gland,** organ that manufactures chemical substances. A gland may vary from a single cell to a complex system. The glands of the ENDOCRINE SYSTEM, e.g., the thyroid, adrenals, and pituitary, secrete hormones directly into the bloodstream. Sweat, salivary, and other exocrine glands secrete substances on to external or internal body surfaces, usually through ducts. Mixed glands such as the LIVER and PANCREAS have both endocrine and exocrine functions.

**glanders,** highly contagious, fatal bacterial disease of horses, mules, and donkeys that can be transmitted to humans. The bacterium, *Actinobacillus mallei,* primarily infects the skin, lungs, and nasal membranes, causing ulcerating nodules to form in the infected area. In countries where the disease occurs infected animals are slaughtered. Glanders does not now occur in the UK, owing to strict control over animal importation.

**glandular fever:** see INFECTIOUS MONONUCLEOSIS.

**Glasgow,** city (1986 est. pop. 774,068), Strathclyde, S central Scotland, on the River Clyde. It is Scotland's leading seaport and largest city, and the centre of the Clydeside industrial belt. Manufactures include ships, metals, machinery, and textiles. Founded in the late 6th cent. by St Mungo (St Kentigern), Glasgow began its modern commercial growth with the tobacco trade in the 18th cent. Nearby coal fields and its location on the Clyde contributed to its industrial growth in the early 19th cent. There is a university and several important museums, including the art collection bequeathed by Sir William Burrell.

**Glasgow, Ellen,** 1873–1945, American novelist. Her realistic fiction presents a history of VIRGINIA since 1850, stressing its changing social order. Her many novels include *The Descendant*(1897), *Virginia*(1913), *Barren Ground* (1925), and *In This Our Life* (1941).

**Glasnost,** (Rus., = openness), term used to encapsulate the policy of greater freedom of expression and debate in the Soviet Union since Mikhail GORBACHEV came to power in 1985. An important component of Gorbachev's reform programme (see PERESTROIKA), glasnost enables the Soviet media to publish criticisms of negative aspects of the Soviet system and has reduced restrictions on the flow of information to and from the outside world.

**glass,** hard substance, usually brittle and transparent, composed chiefly of silicates and an alkali fused at high temperatures. Metallic oxides impart colour. In prehistoric times objects were fashioned from natural glass such as obsidian (a volcanic substance) and rock crystal (a transparent quartz). The oldest extant manufactured glass is from Egypt, c.2000 BC Many types were made in Roman times, but little is known of European glassmaking from the fall of Rome until the 10th cent., when STAINED GLASS appeared. Methods have changed little since ancient times. The materials are fused at high temperatures in seasoned fireclay containers, boiled down, skimmed, and cooled several degrees; then the molten glass is ladled or poured into molds and pressed, or it is blown or drawn. The shaped glass is annealed to relieve stresses caused by manipulation, then slowly cooled. Until the 17th cent. the finest glass was made in Venice; later France and England became centres of glassmaking. In the 20th cent. many new types have been developed, including fibreglass and safety glass, but some uses of glass have been superseded by PLASTIC. Despite mass production, glassmaking by hand remains a valued art.

**Glass, Philip,** 1937–, American composer; b. Baltimore. Influenced by Asian music, his writing blends standard notation and tonality with electronics, is repetitive and of great duration. His best-known works are the operas *Einstein on the Beach* (1976; with Robert Wilson), *Satyagraha* (1980) and *Akhnaten* (1985).

**Glastonbury,** a village of over 60 LAKE DWELLINGS in Somerset, England, dating from the IRON AGE. With unusually good preservation conditions, iron tools retained their wooden hafts and many other wooden objects were found, including baskets, tubs decorated with LA TÈNE-style art, and dugout canoes.

**glaucoma,** disease of the eye characterized by an excess of fluid within the eyeball, causing increased pressure on the retina, pain, and impairment of vision ranging from blurring of the visual image to blindness. It most commonly develops gradually after the age of 40 but can sometimes occur abruptly. It is treated with drugs that decrease pressure in the eyeball.

**Glazunov, Aleksandr Konstantinovich,** 1865–1936, Russian composer. With RIMSKY-KORSAKOV he completed BORODIN's *Prince Igor.* His own early works reflected nationalism, but in his Third (1890) and Fourth (1893) Symphonies, and in later works, he concentrated on a more cosmopolitan, well crafted style.

**Gleizes, Albert Léon** (glez), 1881–1953, French cubist painter, illustrator, and writer. A leading cubist, he used a rich palette and wrote the first tract on the principles of CUBISM, *Du Cubisme* (1912), with Jean METZINGER.

**Glele** (,glelay), c.1830–88, king (r.1858–88) of Dahomey (now BENIN). Like his father, GEZO, he succeeded in expanding the frontiers of his state by military conquest, largely at the expense of the suzerain power of Oyo. In 1886 he conquered the Yoruba kingdom of Ketu.

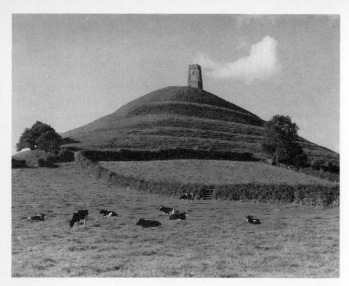

Glastonbury Tor

**Glen Coe,** valley of R. Coe, Highland region of Scotland. It is situated in Lochaber district, running W to Loch Leven, and is about 11 km (7 mi) long. It is flanked by steep mountains including the Three Sisters of Glen Coe (Beinn Fhada, Gearr Aonach, and Aonach Dubh). The glen was the scene of the massacre of the Macdonalds by the Campbells and the English soldiers in 1692.

**Glendower:** see OWEN GLENDOWER.

**Gleneagles,** two popular Scottish hotel golf courses set among the foothills of the Grampians. Here in 1977 heads of Commonwealth governments met to agree the **Gleneagles Principle** which stated that all sporting links with South Africa should be cut off in protest against apartheid: no national teams would visit South Africa nor would South African national teams be received, and any players going independently to South Africa would be barred from representing their country internationally.

**Glen More** or **Great Glen,** valley in Highland region, Scotland. It stretches from Loch Linnie, at Fort William, in the W to the Moray Firth at Inverness in the NE. It is c.97 km (60 mi) long, and contains Lochs Lochy, Oich and Ness. The lochs are linked by canals 35 km (22 mi) long to form the Caledonian Canal. Construction of the canals (designed by Thomas TELFORD) was started in 1803 and completed in 1847. It is now used by small cargo boats and pleasure boats.

**glider,** type of aircraft resembling an aeroplane but without mechanical means of propulsion at all. Modern gliders are mostly made of wood covered with fibreglass, weigh between 180 and 225 kg (400 to 500 lb), and are flown by one person. The most common method of getting them airborne is to tow them behind light aircraft until sufficient height has been gained, though they may also be hauled by a winch; then they use gravity to keep flying and updrafts of air to gain altitude. The first authenticated man-carrying glider was designed by Sir George CAYLEY. Gliding is now an international sport, whose world championships were first held in 1937. See HANG-GLIDER; LILIENTHAL, OTTO.

**Glière, Reinhold Moritzovich** (glee͵eə), 1875–1956, Russian composer and teacher of PROKOFIEV and KHACHATURIAN. His romantic, impressionistic compositions show folk influences. The ballet *The Red Poppy* (1927) is well known and his Harp Concerto (1938) and epic Third Symphony (1909–11) have an assured international reputation.

**Glinka, Mikhail Ivanovich** (͵gleenkah), 1804–57, first of the nationalistic school of Russian composers. His operas *A Life for the Czar* (1836) and *Russlan and Ludmilla* (1842) introduced a characteristically Russian style

**Gliwice** (glee͵veetsə), Ger. *Gleiwitz*, city (1984 pop. 211,000), Upper Silesia, S Poland. It is a mining and industrial centre with important chemical industries; it is linked to the ODER R. by the Gliwice Canal, opened in 1939. The city was founded in 1276 and retains its medieval market core. It was transferred from Germany to Poland in 1945. The first coke-fired blast furnace in Silesia was put into operation here in 1796.

**Globe Theatre,** London playhouse, built 1598, where most of SHAKESPEARE's plays were presented. It burned down in 1613, was rebuilt, and was destroyed by the Puritans in 1644.

**globular cluster:** see CLUSTER, STAR.

**globulin,** any of a very large family of PROTEINS widely distributed in animals and plants. Those in the bloodstream may be divided into immunoglobulins and nonimmune globulins. The gamma globulins belong to the former group and include most of the antibodies of the immune system (see IMMUNITY). Gamma globulin injections are given to people exposed to a disease (e.g., infectious hepatitis) to create a temporary immunity to the disease or reduce its severity.

**glockenspiel:** see PERCUSSION INSTRUMENT.

**Glorious Revolution,** in English history, the events of 1688–89 leading to the deposition of JAMES II and the accession of WILLIAM III and MARY II. James's overt Catholicism and the birth of a Catholic heir led to a conspiracy against him. Seven Whig and Tory leaders sent an invitation to the Dutch prince, William of Orange, and his consort, Mary, the Protestant daughter of James, to come to England. When William and Mary landed, James's army deserted him and he fled to France (Dec. 1688). William and Mary accepted the BILL OF RIGHTS (1689), which assured the ascendancy of Parliamentary power over royal power.

**Gloucester,** county town (1981 pop. 106,526) of Gloucestershire, SW England, on R. Severn, 52 km (32 mi) NE of Bristol. It is a river port, with docks on the Gloucester and Sharpness Canal which connects the town to the Severn estuary at Sharpness. There is some, mainly light, industry in the town, including the manufacture of aircraft components. The town is built on the site of the Roman Glevum. There is a cathedral built in Norman and Perpendicular styles, which hosts the Three Choirs Festival every third year.

**Gloucestershire,** county in SW England (1984 est. pop. 509,200), 2643 km² (1031 sq mi), bordering on the lower Severn R. and its estuary in the W. The county town is GLOUCESTER. The COTSWOLD HILLS form an upland area in the E of the county. The land falls westward into the lower Severn Valley, with the Forest of Dean in the extreme W of the county. Coal was formerly mined in the Forest of Dean, but much of the county is agriculturally based, with dairy and fruit-farming particularly important; Double Gloucester cheese is a famous product. CHELTENHAM is an historic spa town.

**Glover, John,** 1767–1849, British and Australian artist. He was President of the Society of Painters in Watercolour (London 1807) and founding member of the Royal Society of British Artists (1823), before emigrating to Tasmania in 1831, where he lived as a landscape painter and gentleman farmer. His style of painting was transformed by his attempts to render faithfully the unfamiliar landscape and its native inhabitants. He regularly returned to London and exhibited his Australian work at the Royal Academy.

**glow-worm,** fairly small (5–24 mm/⅕–1 in) predatory, nocturnal BEETLE (family Lampyridae) with light-producing organs (see BIOLUMINESCENCE) on the underside of terminal abdominal segments of females, but not all males. Most females are wingless and have retained the grub-like larval form (neoteny) and it is they that emit the much brighter light, hence the name glow-worm. Females emit light to attract the normal, winged males, which fly around in search of them. As well as emitting light to attract a mate, females of the Nova Scotian glow-worm (*Photuris fairchildi*) sometimes mimic the flash frequency of the light produced by other species; any males which are deluded are caught and eaten on arrival. The remarkable insects of the Glow-worm Grotto in Waitomo Cave in New Zealand are not beetles but the larvae of *Botiophila luminosa*, a mycetophilid fly (see GNAT). They produce light not for sexual reasons but to lure small, flying insects which they catch with a fishing line consisting of a silken thread, with sticky, mucoid droplets at intervals along it. A similar species occurs in the Bunadoon Cave, in New South Wales, Australia. See FIREFLY.

**gloxinia:** see GESNERIA.

**glucagon,** polypeptide HORMONE secreted by the islets of Langerhans in the PANCREAS. It tends to counteract the action of INSULIN, i.e., it raises the concentration of glucose in the blood, essentially by promoting GLYCOLYSIS.

**Gluck, Christoph Willibald von** (glook), 1714–87, German-born operatic composer. With *Orfeo ed Euridice* (1762) he revolutionized OPERA, establishing lyrical tragedy as a vital form that unified dramatic, emotional, and musical elements. *Alceste* (1767) followed. In Paris he produced (1774) *Iphigénie en Aulide,* his first serious opera with a French LIBRETTO. His last important work, *Iphigénie en Tauride* (1779), is often considered his masterpiece. Gluck's emphasis on dramatic impact and musical simplicity became incorporated into French operatic tradition.

**glucose** (empirical formula: $C_6H_{12}O_6$), white crystalline SUGAR; somewhat less sweet-tasting than SUCROSE (table sugar), it is found in fruits and honey. Known also as dextrose and grape sugar, glucose is the end product of the metabolic breakdown of carbohydrates, and is the body's major source of energy. It requires no digestion prior to absorption into the bloodstream. A monosaccharide (see CARBOHYDRATE), glucose can be obtained by HYDROLYSIS of a variety of more complex carbohydrates, e.g., MALTOSE, CELLULOSE, or GLYCOGEN. It is commercially made from cornstarch (see STARCH) and is used in sweetening various foods and confectionery. Glucose present in urine may be a symptom of DIABETES.

**glue-sniffing:** see SOLVENT ABUSE.

**gluon:** see ELEMENTARY PARTICLES.

**glutton:** see WOLVERINE.

**glycogen,** highly branched POLYMER of GLUCOSE that is made and stored in the LIVER and MUSCLE cells of humans and the higher animals and in the cells of lower animals. It is the main form in which CARBOHYDRATE is stored in the animal body. During short periods of strenuous activity, energy is released in the muscles by direct conversion of glycogen to lactic acid. See also CARBOHYDRATE.

**glycolysis** or **Embden–Meyerhof pathway,** process in all higher animals and most microorganisms by which glucose is broken down by a series of enzyme-controlled chemical reactions to yield lactic acid (in anaerobic conditions) or pyruvic acid which then enters the KREBS CYCLE (in aerobic conditions). The reactions of glycolysis also generate energy, stored in the form of the high-energy substance ADENOSINE TRIPHOSPHATE (ATP).

**gnat,** term often used to describe any small, delicate, long-legged FLY having many-segmented antennae (suborder Nematocera) but correctly applied only to true gnats (family Dixidae), winter gnats (Trichoceridae), and fungus gnats (Mycetophilidae). All adult gnats are harmless and the males are often seen in swarms, performing aerial dances to attract females. The larvae of several species of fungus gnat (e.g., *Sciara* and *Exechia*) feed on mushrooms and can be serious pests where these are cultivated. The New Zealand and Australian glow-worms are actually the larvae of the two other members of this family (see GLOW-WORM).

**gneiss,** coarse-grained, imperfectly layered metamorphic ROCK, characterized by alternating dark and light bands that differ in mineral content. Gneisses result from the metamorphism of many igneous or sedimentary rocks and are the most common types of rocks found in Precambrian regions.

**Gnetales,** an order of GYMNOSPERM plants of great evolutionary interest. Related to GINKGO and the CONIFERS, they bear structures resembling true flowers. Only three genera exist now, mostly plants of dry places, including *Welwitschia mirabilis,* confined to the Namib desert of SW Africa. The stem of this plant resembles a huge carrot over 1m (3 ft) in diameter. It bears only two strap-shaped leaves which remain on the plant growing throughout its long life, thought to be up to 100 years.

**Gnosticism,** dualistic religious and philosophical movement of the late Hellenistic and early Christian eras. The term designates a wide assortment of sects, all promising salvation through an occult knowledge [Gr. *gnōsis*] that they claimed was revealed to them alone. Christian ideas were quickly incorporated into these syncretistic systems, and by the 2nd cent. AD several posed a serious threat to Christianity; much of early Christian doctrine was formulated in reaction to this danger. Gnosticism taught that the spirit was held captive by evil archons, but that through the use of secret formulas it could be freed at death and restored to the heavenly abode. Gnosticism eventually merged with MANICHAEISM, which adopted many of its ideas. The Mandaeans, in modern Iran and Iraq, are the only Gnostic sect extant.

**GNP:** see GROSS NATIONAL PRODUCT.

**gnu** or **wildebeest,** large ANTELOPE (genus *Connochaetes*) living in herds on African grasslands. A swift runner, it has hindquarters like those of a horse and a head and humped shoulders like those of a buffalo. A beard, mane, long tail, and large curving horns are characteristic of both sexes. The brindled gnu, or blue wildebeest (*C. taurinus*), weighs about 225 kg (500 lb) and stands 135 cm (4½ ft) at the shoulder. They only feed on young grass shoots, and they migrate in the wake of rain to find fresh growth. Gnu is the favourite prey of LIONS.

**goat,** ruminant MAMMAL of the genus *Capra*, family Bovidae. The goat has hollow horns, usually coarse hair with a characteristic 'beard', and is closely related to the SHEEP (skeletally, the two are virtually identical). Goats are extremely hardy, living in mountainous terrain and arid climates throughout the world. They live in herds, and whereas sheep are close-grazing animals, goats browse on tall herbs, bushes, and small trees. They are often included by herders with sheep flocks, as their browsing habit keeps open the grasslands for the sheep, and they are thus often stated to have been the primary cause of the expansion of the desert areas of the Middle East. The domestic goat (*C. hircus*), kept for its milk and its meat, is probably descended from the wild goat (*C. aegagrus*), found throughout the Middle East. The IBEX is a wild goat of high altitudes found in the Alps, the Spanish mountains, and parts of Asia. *C. angorensis* is the Angora goat producing mohair, a long, white, shiny WOOL, used for upholstery fabrics, coats, and knitting yarns.

**goatsucker:** see NIGHTJAR.

**Gobelins, Manufacture nationale des** (gaw blanh), state-controlled TAPESTRY workshop in Paris. Begun as a dye works in the 15th. cent., then merged with a tapestry works, it was bought in 1662 by Louis XIV. The firm is still in operation.

**Gobi,** one of the world's great deserts, c.1,295,000 km² (500,000 sq mi), extending c.1610 km (1000 mi) E to W across Central Asia, in SE Mongolia and N China. It is from 910 to 1520 m (3000 to 5000 ft) high, with cold winters, short hot summers, and fierce sand and wind storms. Grassy fringe areas support a small population of nomadic Mongol herders, and there are important deposits of oil at Yumen (China) and Saynshand (Mongolia) and coal at Tawan-Tolgoi (Mongolia). The Kerulen R. is the largest permanent stream.

**God,** divinity of the three great monotheistic religions, JUDAISM, CHRISTIANITY, and ISLAM. In the Old Testament various names for God are used, *Elohim* most commonly. The four-letter form YHWH is the most celebrated; the Hebrews considered it ineffable and in reading substituted the name *Adonai* [my Lord]. The reconstruction *Jehovah* was based on a mistake, and the form *Yahweh* is not now regarded as reliable. The general conception of God is that of an infinite being (often a personality but not necessarily anthropomorphic) who is supremely good, who created the world, who knows all and can do all, who is transcendent over and immanent in the world, and who loves all human beings. (The Old Testament concept of God is less unified and consistent.) The majority of Christians believe God lived on earth in the flesh as Jesus Christ (see TRINITY). The several famous arguments for the existence of God are based on causality, design and purpose in the universe, and the nature of divine being; many have held, however, that God's existence must be accepted on faith. Some philosophers have extended the name God to such concepts as world soul, cosmic energy, and mind.

**Godard, Jean-Luc** (go dah), 1930–, French film director. Initiator, with others, of the French 'new wave' of the 1960s, his highly personal films are marked by a free-wheeling approach to content and style. *Breathless* (1960), noted for its elliptical editing, was followed by films like *My Life to Live* (1962), *Weekend* (1967), and *Every Man for Himself* (1980).

**Godavari,** river of India flowing c.1400 km (900 mi) SE from the Western GHATS near NASHIK to enter the Bay of Bengal through a large and fertile delta at the head of which stands the town of RAJAHMUNDRY. The Godavari is sacred to Hindus.

**Goddard, Robert Hutchings,** 1882–1945, American physicist and rocket expert. In 1926 he completed and successfully fired the world's first liquid-fuel rocket. Goddard designed and built early high-altitude rockets, the first practical automatic steering device for rockets, and many other rocket devices. He was one of the first persons to develop a general theory of rocket action and to prove experimentally the efficiency of rocket propulsion in a vacuum.

**Gödel, Kurt** (‚gœ:dəl), 1906–78, American mathematician and logician; b. Czechoslovakia. He went to the US in 1940. Gödel is best known for his work in mathematical logic, particularly his proof (1931) of a theorem stating that the various branches of mathematics are based in part on propositions that are not provable within mathematics itself, although they may be proved by means of logical systems external to mathematics.

**Godfrey of Bouillon** (booh‚yonh), c.1058–1100, crusader, duke of Lower Lorraine. He achieved prominence in the First CRUSADE at the siege of Jerusalem (1099) and was elected ruler of the city after its capture. Known for his piety and simplicity, Godfrey was the subject of many legends and CHANSONS DE GESTE. He was succeeded in Jerusalem by his brother BALDWIN I.

**Godfrey of Strasbourg:** see GOTTFRIED VON STRASSBURG.

**Godiva, Lady** (gə‚dievə), fl. c.1040–c.1080, wife of Leofric, earl of Mercia. According to legend, she rode naked through the town of Coventry to persuade her husband to lower the heavy taxes. The only person who looked at her as she rode became known as Peeping Tom.

**Godolphin, Sidney Godolphin,** 1st **earl of,** 1645–1712, English statesman. Possessed of considerable financial knowledge, he early established a friendship with the duke of MARLBOROUGH , and their political fortunes were closely linked. He was first lord of the treasury under CHARLES II, JAMES II, WILLIAM III (1689–96, 1700–01), and Queen ANNE (1702–10).

**Godoy, Manuel de** (goh‚dhoy), 1767–1851, Spanish statesman. As chief minister (1792–97, 1801–08) of CHARLES IV, he made peace with France (1795) and led the Spanish army to victory over Portugal (1801). His alliance with NAPOLEON I against England resulted in the Franco-Spanish naval defeat at TRAFALGAR (1805). An unscrupulous, corrupt politician, he was overthrown (1808) when France invaded Spain in the PENINSULAR WAR and went into exile in France.

**Godunov, Boris** (‚godə'nof), c.1551–1605, czar of Russia (1598–1605). A favourite of IVAN IV, Boris ruled as regent for Feodor I, Ivan's son, and probably had Ivan's younger son, DMITRI, murdered. On Feodor's death Boris was made czar by an assembly of the ruling class. He ruled capably, but popular distrust and famine (1602–4) undermined his reign. In 1604 a pretender claiming to be Dmitri invaded Russia; Boris died, and his son, Feodor II, was unable to defend the throne.

**Godwin, William,** 1756–1836, English writer and political philosopher. Rationalism, materialism, and anarchism mark his *Enquiry Concerning Political Justice* (1793) and his novels, including *The Adventures of Caleb Williams* (1794) and *Fleetwood* (1805). In 1797 he married the feminist Mary WOLLSTONECRAFT. Their daughter, Mary SHELLEY, married the poet P.B. SHELLEY, who was influenced by Godwin's works.

**Godwin Austen, Mount:** see K2.

**Goebbels, Paul Joseph** (‚gœbəls), 1897–1945, German NAZI propagandist. One of HITLER's original followers, he became propaganda minister in 1933, which gave him complete control over the German radio, press, cinema, and theatre; later he also regimented all German culture. A master of the 'big lie', he directed his most virulent propaganda against the JEWS. He killed himself and his family on Germany's defeat in World War II.

**Goehr, Alexander** (guh), 1932–, British composer. Although he was a contemporary of BIRTWISTLE and Maxwell DAVIES at Manchester, Goehr writes music that leans more towards the serialism of SCHOENBERG and to classical structures. He has written chamber and orchestral pieces, an opera *Arden Must Die* (1967), and three theatre pieces (1968–70). Professor of music at Cambridge since 1976, he gave the BBC Reith lectures in 1987.

**Goering** or **Göring, Hermann Wilhelm,** 1893–1946, German NAZI leader. One of HITLER's earliest followers, Goering founded and headed (1933–36) the Gestapo (secret police) after Hitler came to power. He was air minister after 1937, and he directed the German economy as a virtual dictator. Hitler designated him as his successor in 1939. In WORLD WAR II he was responsible for the total air war. He was severely criticized for not being able to counter the Allies' bombing raids, and in 1943 Hitler

relieved him of all duties and offices. He was sentenced to death for his WAR CRIMES at the Nuremberg trials, but he killed himself two hours before he was to be hanged.

**Goes, Hugo van der** (goohs), d.1482, Flemish painter; the outstanding northern artist of his era. His *Monforte Altarpiece* (c.1472; Museum Dahlem, Berlin) reveals a classic sonority in colour and serenity. Later works, e.g., the great *Portinari Altarpiece* (c.1476; Uffizi, Florence), show tension and dissonance in colour and spatial arrangement. His *Death of the Virgin* (c.1480; Musée Comunale des Beaux Arts, Bruges) is remarkable for its staring, melancholy apostles.

Hugo van der **Goes,** *Death of the Virgin,* c.1480. Musée Comunale des Beaux Arts, Bruges.

**Goethals, George Washington** (‚gohthəlz), 1858–1928, American army engineer. After serving on inland water projects, he became (1907) chief engineer of the PANAMA CANAL. After overcoming geological, climatic, and labour problems, he completed (1919) the canal ahead of schedule. For the next two years he was governor of the Canal Zone.

**Goethe, Johann Wolfgang von** (‚gœ:tə), 1749–1832, German poet, dramatist, novelist, and scientist whose genius embraced most fields of human endeavour. His autobiography, *Poetry and Truth* (1811–13), describes his happy childhood. He studied law at Leipzig (1765) and at Strasbourg (1770–71), where he met HERDER, collected folk-songs, and began his lifelong study of plants and animals. Lasting influences from this period were J.J. ROUSSEAU and SPINOZA, who appealed to his feeling for nature. Goethe first won attention with the historical drama *Götz von Berlichingen*, a product of STURM UND DRANG, and *Die Leiden des jungen Werthers* (1774; tr. The Sorrows of Young Werther), the highly influential epistolary novel of sensibility and suicide. In 1775, Goethe was invited to visit Charles Augustus, duke of Saxe–Weimar, at whose court he was to spend the rest of his life. For 10 years Goethe was chief minister of state at Weimar. He escaped to Italy (1786–88), where his encounter with classical art brought creative renewal: he completed the dramas *Iphigenie auf Tauris* (1787), *Egmont* (1788), and *Tasso* (1790), and wrote the love poems *Roman Elegies* (1795). On his return, he joined forces with SCHILLER to establish a German classical literature. *Wilhelm*

*Meisters Lehrjahre* (1796; tr. The Apprenticeship of Wilhelm Meister) became the prototype of the German novel of character development; he wrote the model *Novella* (1827) and established the novel as an art form with the classic psychological novel *Elective Affinities* (1809). The first part of his dramatic poem *Faust*, one of the great works of world literature, was published in 1808; the second, after his death. The collection of love poems *West-Eastern Divan* (1819) also reflects the extension of his range beyond European-centred literature, particularly his reading of the Persian poet HAFIZ. Increasingly aloof in his later years from national or literary partisanship, Goethe more and more was turned into the Olympian divinity to whose shrine at Weimar all Europe flocked. His approach to science combined sensuous empiricism with poetic intuition. He is happiest here in his pursuit of unity and continuity in organic forms, as instanced by his *Metamorphosis of Plants* (1790) and his discernment of the premaxilla in the human species. His *Theory of Colours* (1805–10) stubbornly rejected NEWTON's theory of light. Most of his works have been translated into English, notably by Thomas CARLYLE.

**Gogarty, Oliver St John,** 1878–1957, Irish author. Known as the model for Buck Mulligan in JOYCE's *Ulysses,* he wrote poems and the reminiscences *As I Was Going Down Sackville Street* (1937) and *It Isn't This Time of Year at All!* (1954).

**Gogh, Vincent Van:** see VAN GOGH, VINCENT.

**Gogol, Nikolai Vasilyevich** (͵gohgəl), 1809–52, Russian writer. His first success was *Evenings on a Farm Near Dikanka* (1831–32), a collection of fanciful tales set in his native Ukraine. *Mirgorod* (1835) included 'Taras Bulba', a novella of 17th-cent. COSSACK life. He next wrote several tales of St Petersburg; the most famous is 'The Overcoat'. His fame as a dramatist rests on *The Inspector-General* (1836), a satire on provincial folly. The culmination of his inventive gift was *Dead Souls* (1842), a picaresque novel about a rogue who buys the names of dead serfs in order to mortgage them.

**Goiána** (goy͵ahna), city (1980 pop. 702,858), central W Brazil, capital of Goiás state. Founded in 1933 it is the second (after Belo Horizonte) of Brazil's planned state capitals. It succeeded Goiás Velho as capital of the state of Goiás in 1937 and its rapid growth around its spacious planned centre has been directly associated with the emergence of the surrounding region as Brazil's most important developing area for the production of cattle, coffee, and rice.

**Goidelic:** see GAELIC.

**Golan Heights,** Arab *Jaulan*, strategic upland region, c.1250 km² (500 sq mi), between S Lebanon and S Syria, formally annexed by Israel in 1981. Elevations range from c.2000 m (6500 ft) in the north to below sea level along the Sea of Galilee (Lake Tiberias) and the Yarmuk R. in the south. A fertile, cereal growing region formerly part of Syria, the Golan Heights were fortified and used for artillery attacks on Israeli settlements after the creation of Israel (1948) and were captured and placed under military rule by Israel during the 1967 ARAB-ISRAELI WAR.

**gold** (Au), metallic element, known since prehistoric times. Chemically inactive, this very ductile and malleable METAL can be beaten into thin sheets of gold leaf. Only silver and copper conduct electricity better. Gold is usually hardened by alloying with other metals; it also often occurs in nature as an alloy. The gold content of an alloy is stated in carats; by definition, pure gold is 24 carats, and thus a 75% gold alloy is 18 carats. Gold is found widely distributed, mostly in metallic form as dust, grains, flakes, or nuggets. It occurs in quartz veins or lodes, usually in association with silver or other metals, and in alluvial placer deposits. Possibly the first metal used by humans, gold was valued for ornaments, and magical powers were attributed to it. Alchemists of the Middle Ages tried to transmute baser metals into gold (see ALCHEMY). The search for gold stimulated European exploration of the Western Hemisphere. Colloidal dispersions of gold have been used as medical cures; they continue to be used for colouring and staining glass. For discussion of its monetary function, see BIMETALLISM; COIN; MONEY. See also ELEMENT (table); PERIODIC TABLE.

**Gold, Thomas,** 1920–, American astronomer; b. Austria. Gold worked in both the US and in Britain, where in collaboration with Hermann Bondi and Fred Hoyle he formulated the steady-state theory of the universe (see COSMOLOGY). More recently he has provided the standard theoretical model of a PULSAR.

**Goldberg, Rube** (Reuben Lucius Goldberg), 1883–1970, American cartoonist; b. San Francisco. A humorous and political cartoonist, he is known for drawings of wildly intricate machines that perform simple tasks. He was also a sculptor.

**Gold Coast,** region on the E coast of Australia, extending 32 km (20 mi) from Southport in Queensland to Tweed Heads in New South Wales. Early development of the area was based on the cedar trade but now it has become a winter resort for tourists from the colder southern states. With important resorts such as Surfers Paradise and Coolangatta, the area has a population (1986) of 185,612.

**Golden Age,** first and most perfect of the four Ages of the World, followed by the increasingly harsh Silver, Bronze, and Iron Ages. The Roman poets inherited the concept from the Greeks, Hesiod and Aratus. OVID, in the opening of the *Metamorphoses*, described a Golden Age under Saturn, when Man lived in harmony; Spring was everlasting, and the lovely fertility of the earth, untilled, supplied his simple desires. VIRGIL'S *Fourth Eclogue* set the age in the future; here Virgil celebrated the birth of a boy that shall bring back the race of gold. Renaissance poets and writers, such as Tasso (in the *Aminta* Tasso describes the Golden Age as a paradise of love without shame), Guarini, Montaigne, Ronsard, and Shakespeare, imitated and elaborated these concepts. The term was widely used in courtly eulogy; poets and painters extolled the restored Golden Age of the Medici; and Elizabethan writers and courtiers used the term in praise of the Virgin Queen, who was personified as the Just Virgin, Astraea, whose return heralded the return of the Age of Gold. The term can also be used figuratively, to describe eras distinguished by the brilliance of their cultural achievements, e.g., Elizabethan literature is called the Golden Age of English Poetry and 17th-cent. Dutch painting is known as the Golden Age of Dutch Art. The Siglo de Oro, in Spanish literature, is the period between c.1500 and c.1680. In this period the spirit of the Renaissance invaded its life and letters. Spanish writers assimilated the foreign influences to produce a distinctive literature characterized by patriotism, realism, and occasionally, mysticism. The greatest single work of the period was *Don Quixote de la Mancha* (1605, 1615) by CERVANTES. Other important writers of the Golden Age were ALARCÓN Y MENDOZA, CALDERÓN, ERCILLA, ESPINEL, GARCILASO DE LA VEGA, GONGORA, GRACIÁN, St JOHN OF THE CROSS, LOPE DE VEGA, MORETO, QUEVEDO, ROJAS ZORRILLA, St TERESA of Avila, and TIRSO DE MOLINA.

**Golden Ass, The:** see APULEIUS, LUCIUS.

**golden calf,** in the BIBLE, an idol erected by the Israelites on several occasions. AARON made one while MOSES was on Mt Sinai. (Ex. 32). JEROBOAM I made two, and HOSEA denounced a calf in Samaria (1 Kings 12; Hosea 8). A bull cult was widespread in CANAAN at the time of the Israelite invasion.

**Golden Fleece,** in Greek mythology, magic fleece of the ram that carried Phrixus and Helle from Boeotia. Helle fell into the sea (which became the Hellespont), but Phrixus arrived safely in Colchis. He then sacrificed the ram, which became the constellation Aries. Its fleece, hung in a wood guarded by a dragon, was later sought by JASON and the Argonauts.

**Golden Gate Bridge,** one of the world's longest suspension bridges, built (1933–37) across the entrance (Golden Gate) of San Francisco Bay, California, US. It has a main span of 1280 m (4200 ft) and a total length of 2824 m (9266 ft).

**Golden Horde, Empire of the,** Mongol state comprising most of Russia, founded in the mid-13th cent. by the Mongol leader Batu Khan (see TATARS). The name derives from the magnificence of the Mongol camp on the Volga, where the empire had its capital. The Russian principalities were tributaries of the khan, who confirmed princely succession and exacted taxes. In the early 14th cent. Islam became the official religion of the empire. Warfare among its leaders, and attempts by the Russian princes to end tributary payments, weakened the empire. TAMERLANE conquered it in the late 14th cent.

**goldenrod,** any species of the genus *Solidago* of the COMPOSITE family, chiefly North American weedy herbs with small, mostly yellow flowers growing along a slender stem, which were once incorrectly thought to cause hay fever. Several attractive modern garden forms have been produced. Goldenrod has been used in dyes and teas.

**Golden Rule,** saying of JESUS, 'As ye would that men should do to you, do ye also to them likewise'. Mat. 7.12; Luke 6.31.

**Golden Section:** see SECTION D'OR.

**goldfish,** freshwater FISH (genus *Carassius*) in the CARP family, popular in home aquariums. Native to China, it was domesticated centuries ago from its wild form, an olive-coloured carplike fish up to 40 cm (16 in) long. Marketed goldfish are 2.5 to 10 cm (1 to 4 in) long and most commonly orange in colour; breeders have developed bizarre varieties with unusual tails, double or triple fins, bulging eyes, and a range of colours.

**Golding, Arthur,** 1536?–1605?, English poet. He was a productive English translator from French and Latin, whose version of OVID's *Metamorphoses* was well known to SHAKESPEARE.

**Golding, William,** 1911–, English novelist. A critic of rationalism and ideas of progress, he has portrayed the dark side of human behaviour in novels and romances noted for their poetic language and religious symbolism. The nightmarish *Lord of the Flies* (1954) was followed by *The Inheritors* (1955), *Pincher Martin* (1956), *The Spire* (1964), *Darkness Visible* (1979), a trilogy of sea novels beginning with *Rites of Passage*, and other works. He has also published poetry, plays, essays and travel books. He was awarded the 1983 Nobel Prize for Literature.

**Goldman, Emma,** 1869–1940, American anarchist; b. Russia; emigrated to the US in 1886. With the anarchist Alexander BERKMAN she published the paper *Mother Earth.* Between 1893 and 1917 she was imprisoned several times on such charges as inciting to riot, publicly advocating birth control, and obstructing the draft. She and Berkman were deported (1919) to the USSR; critical of Soviet centralism, she left in 1921.

**Goldoni, Carlo,** 1707–93, Italian dramatist, author of over 250 works, including both comedies and comic opera librettos. He created a new COMEDY of character in place of the outworn COMMEDIA DELL'ARTE, achieving some of his best results in his native Venetian dialect, e.g., *The Boors* (1760), and *The Squabbles at Chioggia* (1762). His best-known work remains *The Mistress of the Inn* (1753).

**gold rush,** influx of prospectors, merchants, and adventurers to newly discovered gold fields. One of the most famous was the California Gold Rush in 1848, when the discovery of gold at Sutter's Mill brought more than 40,000 prospectors to California within two years. Although few of them struck it rich, their presence stimulated economic growth. Other large gold rushes took place in Australia (1851–53); WITWATERSRAND, South Africa (1884); and the KLONDIKE, Canada (1897–98).

**Goldsmith, Oliver,** 1730?–74, Irish writer. One of Samuel JOHNSON's circle, he made his name with *Citizen of the World* (1762), a series of whimsical essays; the philosophical poem *The Traveller* (1764); and the nostalgic pastoral *The Deserted Village* (1770). His best known works are two comedies, *The Good-natur'd Man* (1768) and *She Stoops to Conquer* (1773), and his novel *The Vicar of Wakefield* (1766). The comedies injected realism into the dull, sentimental theatre of the day and, like the novel, are humorous and warm-hearted.

**gold standard,** system whereby a currency is freely convertible into gold. The currency is fixed to the value of gold or the coin is of a certain weight of gold. To operate on the gold standard a country's central bank must be willing to exchange any currency it is offered for gold. In an international gold-standard system, currency exchange rates are fixed to the weight of gold. Gold took over as the standard for the British currency in the 18th cent. largely because the heavy demand for silver in India made the commodity worth more than its mint price. Gold was imported in large quantities and its mint price stood at approximately £3.89 an ounce for some 200 years up to 1914. This was the basis of the international gold standard which was maintained until 1914 and briefly from 1925 until its end in 1931. An international gold standard persisted with the US dollar being fixed to gold at a rate of $37 an ounce until 1973 when it was raised to $42. In 1976, however, the system was abandoned.

**Goldstein, Vida Jane Mary,** 1869–1949, Australian feminist. In 1903 she was the first woman in the British empire to stand for election to a national parliament, though she was unsuccessful on this and subsequent occasions. She formed a Woman's Peace Army that opposed Australian participation in World War I.

**Goldthorpe, John H,** 1935–, British sociologist. Together with David Lockwood he studied the English working and middle class and reported in *The Affluent Worker: Industrial Attitudes and Behaviour* (1968), *The Affluent Worker: Political Attitude and Behaviour* (1968); and *The Affluent Worker in the Class Structure* (1969). The authors claimed to have identified a major cleavage in the working class between an old, traditional proletariat, with its conflictual image of CLASS relationships, living in communities centred on the workplace, and a modern, more privatized, affluent worker, with a more instrumental attitude to consumption and class solidarity. Goldthorpe also did important work on SOCIAL MOBILITY.

**Goldwater, Barry Morris,** 1909–, US senator (1953–65, 1969–87). He was the acknowledged leader of the extreme conservative wing of the Republican party during the 1950s and 1960s. He ran for president in 1964, but was decisively defeated by Lyndon B. JOHNSON.

**golem** [Heb., = something shapeless], in medieval Jewish legend, a robotlike servant made of clay and given life by means of a charm, particularly the name of God.

**golf,** game in which players hit a small, hard ball with specially designed clubs over an outdoor course (links). The object is to deposit the ball in a cup, or hole, using as few strokes as possible. The standard course, usually more than 5500 m (6000 yd) in length, is divided into 18 holes, each consisting of a tee, from which the ball is initially driven; the fairway, bounded by tall grass (the rough) and containing natural or artificial obstacles (hazards) such as water and sand traps (bunkers); and the green, a smooth surface on which the cup (11.43 cm/4.5 in diameter) is located. A set of golf clubs includes 3 or 4 woods, 9 or 10 irons, and a putter for use on the green. Although its origin is unknown, golf is identified with Scotland, where it was played as early as 1457. The four main international competitions, all played over 72 holes, are the British Open (founded in 1860), the US Professional Golfers Association (1916), and the US Masters (1934). Team competitions include the Walker Cup (1922) between British and US male amateurs; the Curtis Cup (1932) between British and US women amateurs; and the Ryder Cup (1927) between US and European professionals.

**Golgi, Camillo** (¸goljee), 1843–1926, Italian pathologist. For his work on the structure of the nervous system he shared with Santiago Ramón y Cajal the 1906 Nobel Prize for physiology or medicine. Golgi stained nerve tissue with silver nitrate to delineate (1883) certain nerve cells (Golgi cells) in the central nervous system; observed (1909) the Golgi apparatus, a part of the cytoplasm distinguishable by staining; and recognized that the three types of malaria are caused by different protozoan organisms.

**Golgotha:** see CALVARY.

**Goliardic songs,** Late Latin poetry (11th–13th cent.) of the 'wandering scholars,' or Goliards, who included university students, poor scholars, unfrocked priests, runaway monks, and clerks who begged and sang their way from place to place. Their existence is seen as a reaction against the medieval ascetic ideal and the strictures of the church. Their songs, in lilting bastard Latin verse with stressed rhymes, mimic the form of medieval hymns and include lusty paeans to love, wine, and the vagabond life as well as skillful attacks on the immorality of church life.

**Goliath,** in the BIBLE, gigantic Philistine who challenged the Israelites. The young DAVID accepted the challenge and killed him with a stone from a sling. 1 Sam. 17.

**Gombrich, Sir Ernst,** 1909–, British art historian; b. Austria. From 1959 to 1976 he was Director of the Warburg Institute and Professor of the History of the Classical Tradition. Three collections of essays on the Italian Renaissance (1966, 1972, 1976) explore questions of style, taste, and patronage; symbolism; and the classical heritage. His works have also interested scientists, and he has written on the psychology of visual perception (*Art and Illusion*, 1960; *The Image and the Eye*, 1982); and in 1984 *Tributes*, a defence of the humanities through a study of celebrated scholars and critics.

**Gombrowicz, Witold** (gom¸brohvich), 1904–69, Polish writer. He lived in Argentina (1939–63) and France (1964–69). His reputation as a satirist and existential innovator with a highly personal vision rests on such novels as *Ferdydurke* (1937), *Trans-Atlantyk* (1953), and *Cosmos* (1965).

**Gómez, Juan Vicente** (ˌgohmes), 1857–1935, dictator of VENEZUELA (1908–35). A guerrilla leader, he seized power (1908) as president and ruled the country as an absolute tyrant until his death. His secret police crushed opponents by means of imprisonment and torture. Gómez brought economic stability to Venezuela and attracted foreign investment in order to build a modern country with railways, highways, and other public works. He enriched himself as well as the nation, which he tried to make a personal fief.

**Gomorrah:** see SODOM AND GOMORRAH.

**Gomullka, Wlladysllaw,** 1905–82, Polish Communist leader. As first secretary of the Communist Party (1943–48, 1956–70) he introduced a measure of liberalization while retaining close ties with the USSR. His return to power in Oct. 1956 marked the start of the 'Polish Road to Socialism'; but enthusiasm for his regime quickly waned.

**Goncharov, Ivan Aleksandrovich** (gənchəˌrof), 1812–91, Russian writer. A government official, he wrote the satirical novel *Oblomov* (1859), a classic study of indolence. Other novels are *A Common Story* (1847) and *The Precipice* (1869).

**Goncourt, Edmond Louis Antoine Huot de,** 1822–96, and **Jules Alfred Huot de Goncourt,** (gawnhkooə), 1830–70, French authors, brothers. Together they wrote social history, art criticism, and influential naturalistic novels, e.g., *Renée Mauperin* (1864) and *Mme Gervaisais* (1869). From 1851 they published the highly successful *Journal des Goncourt,* for 40 years providing an intimate account of Parisian society. Their work paved the way for both NATURALISM and IMPRESSIONISM. In his will, Edmond provided for the founding of the Goncourt Academy and its annual prize for fiction.

**Gondwanaland:** see CONTINENTAL DRIFT.

**gong:** see PERCUSSION INSTRUMENT.

**Góngora y Argote, Luis de** (gohngohrah ee ahgohtay), 1561–1627, Spanish poet. A major figure of Spain's GOLDEN AGE, he wrote sonnets, ballads, and the long pastoral *Soledades* (1613; tr. Solitudes), his masterpiece. His complex, artificial style, characterized by innovative use of metaphor, latinate vocabulary, and classical and mythological allusions, exemplifies the baroque tendencies that came to be known as *Gongorism.*

**gonorrhoea,** infectious disease involving chiefly the mucous membranes of the genitourinary tract, caused by the bacterium *Neisseria gonorrhoeae.* A sexually transmitted disease, gonorrhoea causes inflammation of the genital organs and urethra, and, if untreated, sterility. The disease is treated with PENICILLIN or another ANTIBIOTIC. See VENEREAL DISEASE.

**González, Julio,** 1876–1942, Spanish sculptor. He taught PICASSO iron-welding techniques and was in turn influenced by Picasso's CUBISM. González's ingenious, semiabstract sculptures include *Hombre-Cactus* (1939–40).

**González Márquez, Felipe,** 1942–, prime minister of SPAIN (1982–). A lawyer and first secretary (1974–79, 1979–) of the Spanish Socialist Workers' Party, González led the Socialists to a landslide victory in the 1982 parliamentary elections, becoming head of Spain's first leftist government since the SPANISH CIVIL WAR. He was returned to power in the 1986 elections.

**Good Friday,** anniversary of JESUS's death on the cross, the Friday before Easter. Among Christians it is a day of mourning and penitence. In the Orthodox, Roman Catholic, and Anglican churches, the saying of Mass is suspended.

**Goodman, Benny** (Benjamin David Goodman), 1909–86, American clarinettist and bandleader. He formed a big band in 1934 and went on to fame as the 'King of Swing', performing for radio, motion pictures, and records. He also led famous small ensembles, e.g., with Teddy Wilson (piano), Gene Krupa (drums), and Lionel Hampton (vibraphone). Goodman also achieved success as a classical clarinettist. See also JAZZ.

**Goodyear, Charles,** 1800–60, American inventor and originator of vulcanized RUBBER. He experimented for years to find a way to keep rubber from sticking and melting in hot weather; in 1839 he discovered vulcanization, patenting it in 1844. Goodyear worked and died in poverty.

**goose,** large, wild or domesticated swimming BIRD related to the DUCK and SWAN. Strictly speaking, the term *goose* applies to the female and *gander* to the male. The Canada goose (*Branta canadensis*) is known by its honking call and V-shaped, migrating flocks in spring and autumn. Originally North American, it was brought to Europe in the 17th cent. and has become a familiar sight on ornamental waters. Geese have been domesticated since ancient times; the farmyard goose is descended from the European greylag (*Anser anser*).

**gooseberry:** see CURRANT.

**Goossens, Sir Eugene,** 1893–1962, British composer and conductor, from a musical family which included brother Leon and sisters Sidonie and Marie, who were respectively an oboist and harpists; his father and grandfather were also conductors. After his debut with the Queen's Hall Orchestra, he directed orchestras in Rochester (1923–31) and Cincinnati (1931–46), From 1947–56, he directed both the Sydney Symphony Orchestra and the New South Wales Conservatorium, and he exerted considerable influence on the development of Australian music. His compositions include two operas, orchestral and chamber works, and songs.

**gopher:** see GROUND SQUIRREL.

**Gorakhpur,** town (1981 pop. 307,501), Uttar Pradesh state, N India, on the Rapti R. It is the headquarters of a large, mainly agricultural district in the extreme NE of Uttar Pradesh; also a divisional capital. It is a notable trading and communications centre, owing much to the junction of railways. It has a fertilizer factory and railway workshops, and a number of small industries. It is an ancient town whose nucleus in the 10th cent. lay around the Gorakhnath temple and whose site has moved over the centuries as the Rapti has shifted its course.

**Gorbachev, Mikhail Sergeievich,** 1931–, Soviet political leader, general secretary of the ruling Communist Party, CPSU (1985–). Born the son of a peasant, he studied law at Moscow Univ. before returning to his home region in the N Caucasus and becoming a successful party administrator, specializing in agriculture. Elected a full member of the CPSU central committee (1971), he was called to Moscow in 1978 to take responsibility for agriculture in the party secretariat. He rapidly rose to candidate membership of the CPSU politburo (1979) and to full membership a year later. During the shortlived party leadership terms of Yuri ANDROPOV (1982–84) and Konstantin CHERNENKO (1984–85), Gorbachev achieved greater prominence (being a close supporter of Andropov's drive for greater efficiency and discipline within the party) and was the natural choice to head the party when Chernenko died. As CPSU general secretary (and thus the Soviet political leader), he quickly launched economic reform and political liberalization measures (see PERESTROIKA) and demanded more GLASNOST in the Soviet bureaucracy. He also tabled a series of proposals for East–West nuclear arms control and signed (1987) a treaty limiting intermediate-range nuclear forces (INF) with Pres. REAGAN of the US.

**Gorboduc,** legendary early British king mentioned by GEOFFREY OF MONMOUTH. He divided his kingdom between his sons Ferrex and Porrex, causing great strife. *Gorboduc, or Ferrex and Porrex* (1561), was the first English blank-verse tragedy.

**Gordian,** name of three Roman emperors. Gordian I (Marcus Antonius Gordianus Africanus), d. 238, was made co-emperor (238) with his son. After a reign of only 22 days, he committed suicide after learning that his son and colleague, **Gordian II,** 192–238, had been killed in battle. The latter's son, **Gordian III,** c.223–244, became emperor in 238. Philip the Arabian had him murdered in 244.

**Gordian knot:** see GORDIUS.

**Gordimer, Nadine,** 1923–, white South African writer. She is the pre-eminent portraitist of English-speaking white middle-class life in South Africa, with a particular talent for precise portrayal of psychologically complex moments, especially under the impact of political choices, best displayed in *The Conservationist* (1974), *July's People* (1981), and *A Sport of Nature* (1987), as well as in her collections of short stories, e.g., *The Soft Voice of the Serpent* (1952), *Friday's Footprint* (1960), and *Something Out There* (1984).

**Gordius,** in Greek mythology, king of Phrygia. The pole of his wagon was fastened to the yoke with a knot that defied efforts to untie it. An oracle stated that he who untied this Gordian knot would rule Asia. In time, ALEXANDER THE GREAT simply cut the knot with his sword.

**Gordon, Charles George,** 1833–85, British soldier and administrator. After serving in the CRIMEAN WAR, he went to China in 1860 and commanded the Chinese army that suppressed the TAIPING REBELLION; he had a magnetic personality and afterwards was popularly known as 'Chinese Gordon'. He was governor of the Egyptian Sudan (1877–80), and in 1885, while sent out by GLADSTONE to try to crush the power of the MAHDI, was killed in the siege of KHARTOUM. Parliament had ordered in Aug. 1884 an expedition to rescue the besieged Gen. Gordon; when it arrived on 28 Jan. 1885 it was two days too late. Gladstone's government was severely shaken in consequence.

**Gordon, Judah Leon,** 1830–92, Russian Jewish novelist and poet; b. Lithuania. A leader of the renaissance of progressive culture among the Jews (*Haskalah*), he wrote in classical Hebrew and in Russian historical poems and satirical works attacking traditional Judaism.

**Gore, Spencer Frederick,** 1878–1914, British painter. He studied (1896–99) at the Slade School under TONKS. In 1904 he met SICKERT in France and entered his circle in London. He was the first president of the CAMDEN TOWN GROUP (1911) and a member of the LONDON GROUP (1913). His early landscapes are in the style of SISLEY; Roger FRY's exhibitions (1910 and 1912) introduced the ideas of CÉZANNE and GAUGUIN to his later works.

**Goren, Charles Henry,** 1901–, American expert on contract BRIDGE. He wrote the first of his many books on the game, *Winning Bridge Made Easy,* in 1936, later giving up his law practice to concentrate entirely on bridge. He won two world championships (1950, 1957) and 26 US titles, and his point-count bidding system became standard.

**Gorgon,** in Greek mythology, one of three hideous sisters, Stheno, Euryale, and Medusa (the only mortal one, killed by PERSEUS). Winged and snake-haired, they turned all who looked at them to stone. They were much represented in Greek art.

**gorilla,** largest APE (*Gorilla gorilla*), native to the forests of equatorial W Africa. Males range from 150 to 190 cm (5 to 6 ft) in height and weigh about 200 kg (450 lb) in the wild; they have prominent sagittal crests and brow ridges and enormous canine teeth. Females are about half the size of males and their features are less developed. Their shaggy coats are brown or black. Though extremely muscular and powerful, gorillas are quiet and retiring; they are chiefly vegetarian.

**Göring, Hermann Wilhelm** (ˌgøːring), see GOERING, HERMANN WILHELM.

**Gorky,** formerly Nizhny Novgorod, city (1985 pop. 1,399,000), E European USSR, on the Volga and Oka rivers. A major river port, it has the largest car factory in the USSR, as well as steel-making and other industrial plants. Founded in 1221, it was a centre of trade with the East. In 1932 it was renamed after Maxim GORKY, who was born there.

**Gorky, Arshile,** 1904–48, American painter; b. Armenia. His early work is figurative and refined. Later he was influenced by SURREALISM and began (c.1940) to create abstractions of mysterious organic forms. His work was influential in the development of ABSTRACT EXPRESSIONISM.

**Gorky, Maxim,** or **Maksim,** pseud. of **Aleksey Maximovich Pyeshkov,** (Rus., = bitter), 1868–1936, Soviet writer. Born in poverty, he wandered the Volga region, educating and supporting himself, from the age of eight. *My Childhood* (1913), *In the World* (1916), and *My Universities* (1923) describe his early years. His first story appeared in 1892. In *Sketches and Stories* (1898) he wrote of the vigour and nobility of peasants, workers, and vagabonds. In 1902 *The Lower Depths,* the first and greatest of his 15 plays, was performed by the Moscow Art Theatre. Gorky's friendships with the writers ANDREYEV, CHEKHOV, and TOLSTOY date from this time; he later published memoirs of all three. When the 1905 Revolution failed he was forced into exile. *Mother* (1906), which became the prototype of the revolutionary novel, was written in the US. After living in Capri (1907–13) Gorky returned to Russia in 1914. In the period of turmoil after the RUSSIAN REVOLUTION (1917) he used his friendship with LENIN and his post as head of the state publishing house to aid writers and artists. In 1921 he went abroad again, returning in 1928. *The Life of Klim Samgin* (1927–36), a four-part novel often considered his masterpiece, was unfinished at his death. Gorky's work, vital and optimistic, combines realism with a strong poetic strain. He is considered the father of Soviet literature and the founder of the doctrine of SOCIALIST REALISM.

**Gosnold, Bartholomew,** fl. 1572–1607, English explorer who navigated the northern Atlantic coast of North America and named Cape Cod. In 1606 he commanded the *God Speed,* which carried some of the first settlers to Virginia.

**Gospel,** [Middle English, = good news; cf. *evangel* from Gr., = good news], one of the four narrative accounts of JESUS in the NEW TESTAMENT: MATTHEW, MARK, LUKE, and JOHN. The first three are called Synoptic Gospels because they present a comprehensive view, agreeing in subject matter and order. Many church liturgies include a solemn reading of the Gospel for the day. The honour paid to the Gospels resulted in some of the glories of book ILLUMINATION, e.g., the Book of Kells.

**gospel music,** American musical form that developed in Protestant churches of the South of the US. It is performed today by blacks and whites, but black gospel music is much more important. Rooted in field and work songs, and owing less to the Protestant hymns than do American Negro SPIRITUALS, gospel is an intense, joyful music. Its form derives from the call-and-response singing of preacher and congregation in black churches; the message is conveyed with tight control, at other times with abandon. Gospel and JAZZ were considered antithetical in black society until both forms gained general acceptance by the mid 20th cent.; together they influence 'soul' and ROCK MUSIC. Major gospel performers include Mahalia JACKSON, and Sister Rosetta Tharpe. Gospel-influenced popular artists include Ray CHARLES and Aretha FRANKLIN.

**Gossaert** or **Gossart, Jan:** see MABUSE, JAN DE.

**Göteborg** (yøtə‚bawryə), city (1984 pop. 424,085), capital of Göteborg och Bohus co., SW Sweden, on the KATTEGAT. Sweden's most important seaport, it has shipyards and fisheries as well as such manufactures as iron and steel, and ball bearings. Founded in 1604 by CHARLES IX, it was a major commercial centre from the 17th cent. Early in the 20th cent. it became the terminus of an important transatlantic shipping service.

**Gothic architecture and art.** The character of the Gothic visual aesthetic was one of immense vitality; it was spikily linear and restlessly active. Informed by the scholasticism and mysticism of the Middle Ages, it reflected the religious enthusiasm and the fascination with logical formalism that were the essence of the medieval. The Gothic style was the dominant structural and aesthetic mode in Europe for 400 years. Making its appearance (c.1140) in the Île-de-France, the style owes much to prior experimentation in Normandy (see NORMAN ARCHITECTURE). Ribbed vaulting (see VAULT) and the pointed ARCH had been used in Romanesque construction (see ROMANESQUE ARCHITECTURE AND ART) but without such purposeful and constant application. The important Gothic rib delineated the vaults and clarified the entire structure. Unlike the Romanesque, Gothic construction emphasized light and soaring spaces. The introduction (c.1180) of the flying BUTTRESS reduced wall surfaces by relieving them of part of their structural function, making possible the huge stained glass windows that gave High Gothic church walls the appearance of curtains of light. The High Gothic cathedral was based on the traditional basilican plan (see BASILICA), but single units were integrated into a unified spatial scheme. The exterior view was dominated by twin towers crowning a facade decorated with sculptures. Additional towers, a profusion of flying buttresses, and pinnacles rose around the upper part of the edifice. The first landmark Gothic structure is the ambulatory of the abbey of Saint-Denis, N France (1140–44). The influence of its large areas of glass and use of space was imitated in such cathedrals as those of Sens, Noyon, Laon, and Paris. The High Gothic phase is marked by the Cathedral of Chartres (begun after 1194). In the mid-13th cent., the Rayonnant style (known as the Decorated Gothic style in England) further reduced opaque wall surfaces for windows and stone tracery, e.g., Sainte-Chapelle, Paris. Interesting variations on Gothic style appeared in Western Europe. The Early English style (late 12th–early 13th cent.) retained much of the ponderous mural style of Norman architecture, e.g., Salisbury Cathedral. Romanesque proportions were dominant in Italy, but the French style inspired German churches, e.g., in Cologne, as well as Spanish Gothic architecture. The latter was also influenced by Moorish tradition, e.g., in Toledo. In the 14th and 15th cent. these trends culminated in the flamboyant style, e.g., the Church of Saint-Maclou, Rouen; the Decorated style (c.1250–1370) in England, e.g., Ely Cathedral, in which ornament became more luxuriant; and the even more flamboyant and distinctively English Perpendicular style (c.1300–1540), e.g., the choir of the cathedral at Gloucester, noted for its vertical lines, complex vaults, and panelled windows. After the

14th-cent. economic crises and the Black Death, building slowed, but the Gothic tradition never completely died. It was revived in the 19th cent. (see GOTHIC REVIVAL). The other arts of the Gothic period were basically dominated by architecture and commissioned by the Church. However commissions from private patrons grew in number; portraits of the patrons or donors began to appear in panel paintings and stained glass of the period. Stained glass was integrated into the churches on a grand scale, perhaps the most beautiful and well known example of this being the SAINTE-CHAPELLE in Paris (1243–48). By the 13th cent. sculpture became more important and more humanized. The west front of Wells cathedral (begun 1225) is a stunning example of this. Gradually sculpture became less united with architecture and the tendency toward mannerisms in gesture and greater realism reached monumental form in the *Well of Moses* (1395–1403; Dijon) by Claus SLUTER. Large-scale fresco painting was rare in the Gothic period, though stained glass and tapestry assumed great importance and showed a stylistic development parallel to that of sculpture. The growth of the pilgrimage industry resulted in the wholesale production of smaller artworks such as reliquary caskets and candlesticks. The Mosan and Limoges enamel workshops flourished in the 13th cent. and the style spread fast throughout Europe. Other more elaborate metalwork can be seen to encompass the spirit of Gothic art, linking architecture, sculpture, and metalwork in one piece, such as in the 13th-cent. Crozier belonging to Bishop William of Wykeham, now in New College, Oxford. Illuminated Bibles and psalters appeared in ever-increasing numbers for both the church and private patrons during this period. The Paris school was the centre of Gothic painting and manuscript illumination and its influence was widespread as the manuscripts were easily transported. The *Pietà* of the Avignon School (c. 1460; Louvre, Paris) is noted for its originality of expression. The elegant International Style was developed at this time, and panel painting dominated all other forms of painting. The culmination of Gothic art in the 15th cent. was marked by SCHONGAUER, LOCHNER, FOUQUET, and the van EYCKS.

**Gothic language,** dead language belonging to the Germanic subfamily of the Indo-European family of languages. One of the earliest literary remains in any Germanic tongue is the Gothic Bible of Ulfilas. See LANGUAGE (table).

**Gothic revival,** term designating a return to building styles of the Middle Ages, most important in France, Germany, England, and the US. Early works were in the fanciful late ROCOCO manner of Horace WALPOLE's 'gothick' house, Strawberry Hill (1770). By 1830, architects were copying the originals more literally. A.W.N. PUGIN's *Contrasts* (1836) and *True Principles of Pointed or Christian Architecture* (1841) were two basic texts. In them he advocated adherence to the methods of medieval builders in order to achieve structural clarity. John RUSKIN elaborated on these ideas. The movement came into conflict with the CLASSIC REVIVAL. The Church of England, supporting the Gothic style, provided for the restoration of many medieval religious buildings. In 1840 Sir Charles Barry won a competition with Gothic designs for the Houses of Parliament and recruited Pugin to design the details. VIOLLET-LE-DUC led the exponents of Gothic design in France. In the US the picturesque aspect of the style dominated, Gothic works include James Renwick's St PATRICK's CATHEDRAL, New York City.

**Gothic romance,** type of novel that flourished in late-18th–early-19th-cent. England. Horror-tinged mysteries often involving the supernatural, they were set among ruins and haunted castles. Horace WALPOLE's *Castle of Otranto* (1765) established the type, which included the works of Ann RADCLIFFE, M.L. 'Monk' LEWIS, and Mary SHELLEY. Since the 1960s romantic 'Gothic novels,' seemingly based on Charlotte BRONTË's *Jane Eyre* (1847) and Daphne du Maurier's *Rebecca* (1938), have become popular.

**Goths:** see OSTROGOTHS; VISIGOTHS.

**Gotland,** island, 3000 km² (1158 sq mi), in the Baltic Sea between Sweden and the USSR. It had great importance as a focus of trade routes in late medieval times. Its farms produce dairy and market garden produce for the Stockholm market, and its limestone rocks are quarried for building stone and for making cement. It has been Swedish since 1645.

**Gottfried von Strassburg** (‚gotfreet fən shtrahsbooək), (Godfrey of Strasbourg), fl. 1210, German poet. He was the singer of the chivalric romance *Tristan* (c.1210), the supreme account of the ill-fated lovers Tristan and Isolde at the court of King Mark (see TRISTRAM AND ISOLDE). The

narrative includes moralizing and allegorical passages reflecting on the values of courtly love. Based on earlier *Tristan* texts, it was left incomplete by Gottfried and continued by later courtly poets. It provided the basis for WAGNER's opera *Tristan und Isolde.*

**Gotthelf, Jeremias,** 1797–1854, Swiss writer and clergyman; b. Albert Bitzius. His pen name was that of the hero of his autobiographical novel *Bauernspiegel* (1837). Christian fervour, humour, sincerity, and vigour characterize his many prose works, but his greatest is a chilling tale of evil, *Die schwarze Spinne* (1842; tr. The Black Spider).

**Göttingen,** city (1984 pop. 133,000), LOWER SAXONY, E West Germany. It profited in the Middle Ages from its position in the N–S corridor of the Leine valley. The university, which came to be noted for its science faculty, was founded in 1737 by Elector George Augustus, later GEORGE II of England. The Brothers Grimm were professors of the university in the 1830s. Many of Göttingen's industries have close links with the university and include printing and publishing, and the manufacture of scientific instruments and optical goods.

**Gottlieb, Adolph,** 1903–74, American painter. In 1935 he was one of the founders of the expressionist group 'The Ten', exhibiting with them until 1940. He was influenced by SURREALISM, and used Freudian symbolism in his *Pictographs* (1941–51), where the canvas was divided into compartments each containing symbolic signs. Gottlieb was an important member of the American abstract expressionist movement, his later landscapes becoming increasingly abstract and expressive.

**Gottwald, Klement** (‚gotvalt), 1896–1953, Czechoslovak Communist leader and president (1948–53). He became president after the Communist coup of 1948 and dominated the party and government through a system of brutal purges and trials. He made Czechoslovakia a satellite of the Soviet Union.

**Gottwaldov** formerly Zlin, city (1984 pop. 85,000), Moravia, central Czechoslovakia. Centre of the Czech footwear industry, it grew up around the manufacturing complex established by Tomáš Bat'a between the two world wars.

**gouache:** see WATERCOLOUR PAINTING.

**Gough Island,** isolated small S Atlantic island, dependency of Saint Helena. It was discovered in 1505 and became the site of the southern sealing industry. A South African meteorological station, established in 1955, is the only habitation.

**Goujon, Jean** (gooh‚zhawnh), c.1510–c.1566, French RENAISSANCE sculptor and architect. Reflecting mannerist style, his elegant, elongated forms are seen in the *Fountain of the Innocents* (1547–49; Louvre, Paris), and the *Tribune of Caryatids.* He designed ornaments for the ground floor and attic of the LOUVRE, and columns for the organ loft of the Church of Saint-Maclou, Rouen.

**Goulburn,** city (1986 pop. 21,522), New South Wales, SE Australia. Located 220 km (150 mi) SW of SYDNEY, it is the regional capital of the Southern Tablelands of New South Wales, supporting a major wool market and textile industry.

**Gould, Jay,** 1836–92, American speculator. From country-store clerk he rose to control half the railway mileage in the Southwest, New York City's elevated lines, and the Western Union Telegraph Co. Aided by James Fisk, he defeated Cornelius Vanderbilt for control of the Erie RR, but public protest over Gould's stock manipulations resulted in his expulsion in 1872. He then bought into the Union Pacific and other Western roads, and by sharp practice gained control of four lines that made up the Gould system. His scheming with Fisk to corner the gold market in 1869 caused the BLACK FRIDAY panic, and Gould's name became synonymous with autocratic business practice.

**Gould, Stephen Jay,** 1941–, American palaeontologist and popularizer of science. With Niles Eldredge, Gould proposed (1972) an evolutionary theory of 'punctuated equilibrium' stating that many species may evolve relatively quickly, rather than through a continuous slow accretion of tiny species variations (see EVOLUTION; NATURAL SELECTION), and then persist virtually unchanged for perhaps millions of years. The 'missing links' in evolutionary development sought since the time of Charles DARWIN may thus not exist. Elaboration of these concepts has led to extensive scientific debate. Gould has taught at Harvard Univ. since 1967.

**Gounod, Charles François** (gooh͵noh), 1818–93, French composer of the romantic operas *Faust* (1859) and *Romeo and Juliet* (1867). He also wrote ORATORIOS and CANTATAS.

**gourd,** common name for some members of the Cucurbitaceae family, of tropical, subtropical, and temperate regions. The family is known for its many edible and otherwise useful plants, almost all annual herbs that grow as vines. Among these are *Cucurbita* species, including the PUMPKIN and summer squashes (varieties of *C. pepo*) and the winter squashes (*C. maxima*); and *Cucumis* species, including the CUCUMBERS, gherkins (*C. anguria*), and all MELONS except the WATERMELON (*Citrullus vulgaris*). The edible fruit of the loofah, (*Luffa cylindrica*), is dried for the inner fibrous network, which is used as a scrubbing sponge. The term *gourd* is applied to those members of the family whose fruits have hard, durable shells used for ornament and as utensils, e.g., cups, dippers, and bowls. The genus *Lagenaria* includes the calabash, dipper, and bottle gourds.

**gout,** condition that manifests itself as recurrent attacks of acute ARTHRITIS, distinguished from other forms of arthritis by the presence of increased uric acid in the body. It may become chronic and deforming. Gout, which only occurs in men and post-menopausal women, usually begins with an acute attack of pain, inflammation, extreme tenderness, and redness in the affected joint. Treatment includes high liquid intake and drugs that increase uric acid excretion by the kidneys.

**Gower, John,** 1330?–1408, English poet, a friend of CHAUCER. His three major works are *Speculum meditantis* or *Miroir de l'omme,* an allegorical manual in French; *Vox clamantis,* in Latin; and *Confessio amantis* (begun c.1386), in English, a collection of stories treating love in the context of the Seven Deadly Sins.

**Gowing, Margaret Mary,** 1921–, English historian and writer, and professor of History of Science in the Univ. of Oxford (1973–86). She is the author of books on the history of the British atomic energy project.

**Gowon, Yakubu,** 1934–, Nigerian head of state (1966–75). In 1966 he was appointed commander in chief of the armed forces and head of the military government. He led (1967–70) the fight against secessionist BIAFRA, and after the Nigerian victory he attempted a policy of reconciliation. He was deposed in a bloodless coup in 1975 and went into exile.

**Goya y Lucientes, Francisco José de,** 1746–1828, Spanish painter and graphic artist, the greatest painter of his age. After studying in Saragossa, Madrid, and Rome, Goya designed a series of ROCOCO tapestries full of gaiety and charm, enhanced by earthy realism. The candour of observation revealed in these early works was later to make him the most graphic and savage of satirists. He became court painter to CHARLES III and CHARLES IV, and his royal portraits are painted with extraordinary realism. In 1792 a severe illness left him deaf, and thereafter his works were cheerless. Two of his most celebrated paintings, *Maja Nude* and *Maja Clothed* (both: Prado, Madrid) are from this period, as was his chief religious work, FRESCOES for the Church of San Antonio de la Florida, Madrid. It is in his etchings and AQUATINTS that his disillusionment is clearly seen. His *Caprichos* are a grotesque social satire; his *Disasters of War,* a series of etchings suggested by the Napoleonic invasions of Spain, are an indictment of human evil and corruption. Also inspired by the Napoleonic invasions is his compelling painting, *The Third of May 1808* (1814–15; Prado, Madrid). At 70 Goya retired to his villa, decorating it with 'Black Paintings' of macabre subjects, e.g., *Satan Devouring His Children, Witches' Sabbath,* and *The Three Fates* (all: Prado, Madrid).

**Goyen, Jan Josephszoon van,** 1596–1656, Dutch landscape painter. His greyish-green landscapes of harbours, canals, riverbanks, and winter scenes sacrifice minute detail for atmospheric effects, e.g., *Cottages and Fishermen by a River* (1631; Mus. and Art Gall., Glasgow).

**Goytisolo, Juan** ('goytee͵sohloh'), 1931–, Spanish writer. His novels, often realistic portrayals of post-civil war Spanish society, include *Juegas de manos* (1954; tr. The Young Assassins), *Fin de fiesta* (1962; tr. The Party's Over), *Señas de identidad* (1966; tr. Marks of Identity), *Reividicación del Conde Don Julian* (1970; tr. The Restoration of Count Julian), *Juan sin tierra* (1975; tr. Landless John), *Makbara* (1980), and *Paisajes después de la batalle* (1982; tr. Landscapes after the Battle).

**Gozzano, Guido,** 1883–1916, Italian poet and essayist. Author of the verse collections *Road of the Shelter* (1907) and *Conversations* (1911), and of *Towards the Cradle of the World* (1917), a posthumous account of a voyage to India, his promising career was cut short by tuberculosis.

Goya y Lucientes, *Maja Clothed*, c.1797–98. Oil on canvas, 44 × 31 cm. Museo de Prado, Madrid.

He was a leading exponent of what has been dubbed 'crepuscular poetry', poetry marked by fin de siècle melancholy and influenced by PASCOLI.

**Gozzi, Carlo,** 1720–1806, Venetian playwright and polemicist. An impoverished aristocrat, he waged a life-long crusade against the progressive ideas of the ENLIGHTENMENT, attacking GOLDONI for the subversive realism of his comedies, offering a popular theatre of fantasy in its place, and vindicating his career in the autobiographical *Useless Memoirs* (1797–98), His ten *Fables* (i.e., dramatized fairy-tales, 1761–65), after their initial stage success, won critical acclaim in German translation during the Romantic period, but are now best known through such operatic versions as PROKOFIEV's *The Love of Three Oranges* and PUCCINI's *Turandot*.

**Gozzoli, Benozzo** (͵gottsohlee), c.1421–97, Florentine painter; b. Benozzo di Lese. He was apprenticed to Fra ANGELICO. His famous *Journey of the Magi* (1459–61; Medici Palace, Florence) depicts a magnificent cavalcade crowded with sumptuous detail and with portraits of the Medici family amongst the retinue.

**Gracchi** (͵grakie), two Roman statesmen and social reformers, brothers. **Tiberius Sempronius Gracchus,** d. 133 BC, the elder brother, became alarmed at the growth of wealth of the few. He stood for the tribunate of the people in 133 BC as an avowed reformer and was the author of the Sempronian Law to redistribute the public lands. At the next election Tiberius renominated himself, but the senate had the election postponed. In a great riot on the following day Tiberius was killed. His brother, **Caius Sempronius Gracchus,** d. 121 BC, became the organizer of the reform movement begun by Tiberius. Elected (123 BC) tribune of the people, he initiated a series of remarkable social reforms. Caius was reelected (122 BC) tribune, but the following year was defeated for reelection. Repeal of his measures was proposed, and in the ensuing riots Caius was killed.

**grace,** in Christian theology, the free favour of God toward people, necessary for their salvation. Differing conceptions of grace led to challenges to the church by the 5th-cent. heresy Pelagianism and by 16th-cent. CALVINISM. There is also divergence in Christianity about the role of sacraments. Most traditional Christians hold that sacraments confer grace; strict Protestants, that they are merely signs, not sources, of grace.

**Grace, William Gilbert,** 1848–1915, English cricketer. Generally regarded as the greatest cricketer who ever lived, he raised the game to heights of skill and popularity undreamed of before his day. He played for the All-England eleven aged 15. In 1867, only one professional took more wickets than he did, at the age of 19. In 1895 he made 1000 runs in May and his hundredth 100. He captained England 1888-93, and played his last Test match in 1899 when he was aged 50. During his whole first-class career (1865–1908) he made 54,896 runs and took 2876 wickets. For three decades, with his huge frame and mighty beard, he was the best-known man in England.

**Graces,** in Greek mythology, personifications of beauty and charm; daughters of ZEUS and the oceanid NYMPH Eurynome. Also known as the Charities, they were named Aglaia, Thalia, and Euphrosyne. The Romans called them the Gratiae. They are often represented in art, e.g., the *Primavera* of BOTTICELLI (1478; Uffizi, Florence).

**Gracián, Baltasar** (grahth͵yahn), 1601–58, Spanish JESUIT writer of the GOLDEN AGE. His masterpiece is the allegorical, pessimistic novel *El criticón*

(3 parts, 1651–57), which contrasts an idyllic primitive life with the evils of civilization.

**grackle:** see MYNAH.

**grafting,** horticultural practice of uniting the cambial layers, or CAMBIUM, of two closely related plants so that they grow as one. The scion (the piece grafted onto the stock or rooted part) may be a single bud or a cutting with several buds; the stock may be a whole plant or a decapitated root system. The primary reason for grafting is to propagate HYBRIDS which may be unable to bear seed or do not grow true from seed. It is also used to control fruit-tree size by the grafting of otherwise tall trees onto dwarfing rootstocks, to grow a plant in an unfamiliar environment by using a stock adapted to that environment, and to combat diseases and pests by using resistant stocks.

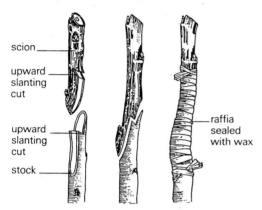

An example method of **grafting**

**Graham, Billy** (William Franklin Graham), 1918–, American evangelist. Ordained (1939) a minister in the Southern Baptist Church, he began his career as an evangelist in 1944. A fiery and persuasive preacher, he has had highly successful evangelistic campaigns that have brought him international attention.

**Graham, Martha** 1894–, American dancer, teacher, and choreographer. She founded her company in 1926, and for them has choreographed over 160 works, many of which are seminal to MODERN DANCE. She became a catalyst of many of the important artistic trends from the 1930s, through her collaboration with leading sculptors, artists, and composers. Her dance school (founded 1927), which teaches the technique that bears her name, nurtured many of the leading talents in modern dance. See also CHOREOGRAPHY.

**Graham, Thomas,** 1805–69, Scottish chemist. His research in diffusion in both gases and liquids led to his formulation of Graham's law. The first to work in colloidal chemistry, he observed that some substances pass through a membrane more slowly than others, thus discovering DIALYSIS. His studies of phosphoric acid led to the present chemical concept of polybasic acids.

**Grahame, Kenneth,** 1859–1932, English author. His charming, humorous works include *The Golden Age* (1895) and, especially, his children's classic, *The Wind in the Willows* (1908).

**grain,** in agriculture, the caryopsis, or dry FRUIT, of a cereal GRASS, the seedlike fruits of BUCKWHEAT and other plants, and the plants bearing such fruits. Grains, whole or ground into meal or flour, are the main food of humans and domestic animals. The food content is mostly carbohydrate, but some protein, oil, and vitamins are present. Low in water content, grains can be stored for long periods. The primary grain crops including WHEAT, RICE, and MAIZE together occupy about half of total world cropland.

**Grainger, Percy,** 1882–1961, Australian composer, pianist, and ethnomusicologist. His compositions are essentially miniatures, often marked by bold harmonies and owing much to his early interest in English folksong. For much of his life he was a US citizen.

**gram:** see METRIC SYSTEM; WEIGHTS AND MEASURES, table.

**grammar,** description of the structure of a language, consisting of the sounds (see PHONETICS); the meaningful combination of these sounds into words or parts of words, called morphemes; and the arrangement of the morphemes into phrases and sentences, called syntax. The list of morphemes and their meanings (see SEMANTICS) in a language is usually not part of a grammar but is isolated in a DICTIONARY. Syntax is also concerned with agreement in a phrase or sentence between concomitant entries, e.g., agreement of subject and verb in number and GENDER. Also studied are sentence transformations such as negativization, interrogation, and passivization. The earliest study of grammar began about the 5th cent. BC in India with PANINI's descriptive grammar of Sanskrit and in Greece with PLATO's dialogue *Cratylus.* Early traditional grammars were devoted primarily to defining the parts of speech semantically. The scientific analysis of language began in the 19th cent. with the genealogical classification of languages by comparative linguists. Grammatical analysis was advanced greatly in the 20th cent. by the theories of structural linguistics and of TRANSFORMATIONAL-GENERATIVE GRAMMAR. School grammar books tend to be prescriptive, that is, they provide rules of what is considered correct and do not take into account common usage and differences, such as those of DIALECT or those in styles and levels of language (such as formal and informal; standard, substandard, and nonstandard).

**Gramme, Zénobe-Théophile,** 1826–1901, Belgian electrical engineer. Model-maker for a Parisian manufacturer of electrical devices, he developed (1869), with little knowledge of electrical theory, an improved, practical direct-current dynamo. By reversing its principle, he invented the electric engine. In 1872, working with others, he transmitted direct-current electricity over a long distance.

**gramophone:** see RECORD PLAYER.

**Grampian,** region in NE Scotland (1985 est. pop. 484,899), 8704 km² (3395 sq mi), bordering on the Moray Firth in the N and the North Sea in the E. The administrative centre is ABERDEEN. It was formed in 1975 from the counties of Aberdeenshire, Kincardineshire, Banffshire, and most of Morayshire. Mountainous in the S and W, it contains part of the Cairngorms, which rise to over 1200 m (4000 ft). The N and E are generally low-lying and fertile. The main rivers are the Don, DEE, and SPEY. Sheep-farming is practised in hilly areas, and cereals and root crops produced in the coastal plain. Much of the upland area is popular with tourists, and there is good salmon fishing in several of the rivers. BRAEMAR is a popular highland resort town, with BALMORAL CASTLE nearby.

**Gramsci, Antonio** (ˌgramshee), 1891–1937, Italian Communist leader and political theorist; probably the outstanding theorist of MARXISM of the 20th cent. Born in Sardinia, Gramsci studied literature and linguistics at Turin Univ. (1911–15), coming under the influence of CROCE. As a political journalist he founded and edited the influential *L'Ordine Nuovo,* as well as becoming practically involved in the workers' movement setting up factory councils in Turin (1919–20). With Amadeo Bordiga he broke away from the Italian Socialist Party in 1921 to found a separate Communist Party, the PCI. In 1923 Mussolini came to power and from 1924 Gramsci, leader of the Communist Party in parliament, attempted to build a popular front of workers and peasants against FASCISM. In 1926 he was arrested for political offences, and in 1928 sent to prison, where he died nine years later. Mussolini's avowed intention to 'prevent this brain from functioning for 20 years' was thwarted by Gramsci's writings, published posthumously as *Letters from Prison* (1947; tr. 1975) and *The Prison Notebooks* (9 vol., 1947–54; extracts tr. 1971). Written in failing health, these established his reputation as one of the most original, learned, and humane Marxist thinkers. He addressed himself particularly to the role of ideas, and of intellectuals, in creating the hegemony, or cultural domination, by means of which the ruling class gained the mass support to achieve its aims. He held that successful political revolution which would preserve, rather than destroy, the best aspects of the existing culture, must be preceded by a passive revolution in the climate of opinion: a process of persuasion in which 'organic intellectuals' of the working class would work to bring about a change of consciousness. Gramsci's ideas, not least his account of the way in which 'historic blocs', or class alliances, could achieve progress by combining to solve particular political problems, have been immensely influential in the postwar Italian Communist Party and Marxist intellectuals in many countries.

**Gram's stain,** laboratory staining technique that distinguishes between two groups of bacteria, gram-negative and gram-positive, by identifying differences in their cell-wall structure. Pinpointing the type of bacterial pathogens involved in disease (see BACTERIA) is valuable in determining ANTIBIOTIC treatment.

**Granada,** city (1981 pop. 262,182), capital of Granada prov., S Spain, in Andalusia, at the confluence of the Darro and Genil rivers and at the foot of the Sierra Nevada. Now the centre of a mineral-rich agricultural region, Granada flourished as the seat (1238–1492) of the kingdom of Granada, the last refuge of the MOORS whom the Christian reconquest of Spain had driven south. The city is dominated by the Alhambra, a Moorish citadel and palace, and also contains a cathedral and the palace of Holy Roman Emperor CHARLES V.

Court of the Lions in the Alhambra, **Granada**

**Granados, Enrique** (grah,nahdhos), 1867–1916, Spanish composer and pianist; b. Cuba. He created the Spanish piano manner later used by FALLA. *Goyescas* (1912–14), a set of piano pieces, is his outstanding work.

**Gran Canaria:** see CANARY ISLANDS.

**Gran Chaco,** extensive lowlands situated between the Andes to the W and the PARANÁ R. to the E. Its E section is covered by grassy savanna and ill-drained swamplands which gives way to thorn scrub and desert in the increasingly arid W. Resources include oil (in the E) and quebracho, a source of tannin. The highest daily temperatures in South America have been registered here.

**Grand Alliance, War of the,** 1688–97, war between France and members of the League of Augsburg (known as the Grand Alliance after 1689). League members included the Holy Roman emperor LEOPOLD I, the German states, Spain, Sweden, the Dutch Netherlands, Savoy, and England (after WILLIAM III ascended the throne). They attempted to thwart the territorial incursions of LOUIS XIV. Despite some English victories, France was generally successful. But as the war dragged on, both sides wearied of it. The Treaty of Ryswick, which ended the war, forced France to give up most of its conquests. See FRENCH AND INDIAN WARS.

**Grand Army of the Republic** (GAR), organization established by Union veterans of the AMERICAN CIVIL WAR in 1866. At its peak in 1890 it had more than 400,000 members. Its principal goals were to aid fellow veterans and their families, obtain pension increases, and preserve the memory of fallen comrades (they secured the adoption of Memorial Day in 1868). They exerted a strong influence on the REPUBLICAN PARTY until 1900.

**Grand Banks,** submarine plateau off SE Newfoundland, Canada. Shallow and frequently fog-bound, the waters in the area are rich in cod, halibut, haddock, and other marine life, making it one of the most important fishing grounds in the world.

**Grand Canal,** world's longest and oldest artificial waterway, extending c.1600 km (1100 mi) from TIANJIN (the port for Beijing) in N China to HANGZHOU and the Yangtze R. in the south. The canal was built to link the productive rice fields of the lower Changjiang (Yangtze) with the poorer (capital) cities of the north. Sections of the system date back to the 6th cent. BC, but the main sections were built in the 6th and 7th cent. AD. Later, in the 13th cent. the northern sections were redredged. Long in decline, it has been dredged, widened, and extended since 1956.

**Grand Canyon,** world-famous gorge cut by the COLORADO R., NW Arizona, US. It is up to 1.6 km (1 mi) deep, 6–29 km (4–18 mi) wide, and more than 320 km (200 mi) long. Multicoloured layers of rock in the canyon wall record more than 2 million years of geological time. Trails wind from the rim of the gorge to its floor. The most spectacular section of the canyon is part of Grand Canyon National Park and is one of the principal tourist attractions in the US, visited each year by more than 2 million people.

Grand Canyon

**Grand Coulee Dam,** concrete dam, 168 m (550 ft) high and 1272 m (4173 ft) long, on the COLUMBIA R., Washington, US. Built 1933–42, it impounds **Franklin D. Roosevelt Lake** (335 km²/130 sq mi), one of the largest reservoirs in the US, and supports a hydroelectric installation that was being expanded during the early 1980s into one of the largest in the world (more than 9.7 MW capacity).

**grandfather clause,** provision in constitutions of seven Southern states (adopted 1895–1910) exempting from rigid economic and literacy requirements those persons eligible to vote on 1 Jan 1867, and their descendants. Since blacks had not yet been enfranchised on that date, the provision effectively barred them from the polls while granting voting rights to poor and illiterate whites. The clause was ruled unconstitutional by the Supreme Court in 1915. The term *grandfather clause* is now applied to any kind of legal exemption based on prior status.

**grand jury:** see under JURY.

**Grand National,** famous steeplechase. It was first contested in 1837, then called the Grand Liverpool Steeplechase, and is now held annually at Aintree, near Liverpool, in the late March or early April. The race is a handicap for geldings and mares six years old and upwards; weights carried range from 76 to 63 kg (12 to 10 stone). It consists of 30 jumps, of which the most famous are Valentine's Brook and Beecher's Brook, over a distance of 7.219 km (4 mi 856 yd), which is twice round the circuit. Seven horses have won the race at least twice: Peter Simple, 1849 and 1853; Abd-el-Kadir, 1850 and 1851; The Lamb, 1868–71; The Colonel, 1869 and 1870; Manifesto, 1897 and 1899; Reynoldstown, 1935 and 1936; and Red Rum, 1973 (in the record time of 9 min 1.9 sec), 1974, and 1977.

**Grand Rapids,** US city (1984 est. pop. 183,000), west-central Michigan, on the Grand R.; inc. 1850. The commercial centre for a farm and orchard area, the city is famous for furniture manufacturing (begun 1859), which is still one of its leading industries. Gravel, gypsum, and appliances are among other products. Grand Rapids is the gateway to a large recreational area of Michigan.

**Grand Union Canal,** artificial waterway in central and S England which connects the R. THAMES at London to the R. Soar S of Leicester, and then the R. Soar to the R. TRENT at Trent Junction, N of Kegworth,

Leicestershire. Another branch of the canal goes from Norton Junction, SE of RUGBY, to BIRMINGHAM, via Leamington Spa, Solihull, and WARWICK.

**Granger movement,** American agrarian movement named after the National Grange of the Patrons of Husbandry, founded in 1867. Originally established for social and educational purposes, the granges became political forums seeking to correct economic abuses through cooperative enterprise. The 'Granger laws', regulating railways and grain storage facilities, established the constitutional principle of public regulation of private utilities. After 1876 other groups adopted the agrarian protest, and the granges reverted to their social role.

**granite,** coarse-grained ROCK composed chiefly of QUARTZ and FELDSPARS, of varying colour. It is commonly believed to be igneous (having solidified from a molten state), but some granites show evidence of being metamorphic in origin (see METAMORPHISM). Formed at depth, granite masses are exposed at the earth's surface by crustal movements or erosion of overlying rocks. Very coarse-grained granite, called pegmatite, may contain minerals and gems of economic value.

**Grant, Cary,** 1904–86, American film actor; b. England as Archibald Leach. Debonair and charming, he appeared in such films as *Bringing Up Baby* (1938), *The Philadelphia Story* (1940), and *North by Northwest* (1959).

**Grant, Ulysses Simpson,** 1822–85, commander in chief of the Union army in the AMERICAN CIVIL WAR, 18th president of the US (1869–77); original name Hiram Ulysses Grant. He graduated from West Point in 1843. Upon the outbreak of the Civil War, he was commissioned colonel, then brigadier general, of a regiment of volunteers. In Feb. 1862 he captured Fort Henry and Fort Donelson in Tennessee, providing the first major Union victory, and he was at once promoted to major general. In Apr. 1862 he barely escaped defeat at the Battle of SHILOH. The VICKSBURG CAMPAIGN (1862–63), which ended Confederate control of the Mississippi, was one of his greatest successes. Called to the supreme command in the West (Oct. 1863), he thoroughly defeated the Confederate forces under Braxton Bragg at Chattanooga. Pres. LINCOLN gave him command of all the Union armies, with the rank of lieutenant general in Mar. 1864. He directed the Union army in the Wilderness Campaign (May–June 1864), wearing out the Confederates by sheer attrition; he received Robert E. LEE's surrender at APPOMATTOX on 9 Apr. 1865. He was made full general in 1866, the first US citizen after Washington to hold that rank. Grant was elected president in 1868, defeating Horatio Seymour, and reelected in 1872, defeating Horace GREELEY. His administration was characterized by corruption, scandal, and special-interest legislation. In foreign affairs, however, much was accomplished by his able secretary of state, Hamilton FISH. Grant's *Personal Memoirs* (2 vol., 1885–86) rank among the great military narratives of history.

**Granville-Barker, Harley,** 1877–1946, English dramatist and critic. A major avant-garde producer of plays in the early 1900s, he also wrote realistic plays, e.g., *Waste* (1907), and *The Madras House* (1910), and the monumental *Prefaces to Shakespeare* (6 vol., 1927–47).

**grape,** common name for plants of the family Vitaceae, about 60 species of mostly climbing shrubs of tropical, subtropical, and temperate zones. The WINE grape, *Vitis vinifera,* is a vigorous, deciduous, woody vine, growing up to 35 m (115 ft) in its natural habitat in the Mediterranean areas. The majority of its 8000 varieties are used for winemaking, with only about 25 being specially bred for table fruit and dried fruit making. It is grown in most temperate areas of the world, and although fruiting may be limited by short summers it is very hardy and will grow in the far north.

**grapefruit,** evergreen tree (*Citrus paradisi*) of the RUE family, and its globular CITRUS FRUIT, which grows in grapelike bunches. It is a hybrid between the pomelo (*C. maxima*) and the sweet orange (*C. sinensis*).

**graph,** figure that shows relationships between quantities. In a bar graph the lengths of bars indicate the quantities to be compared. In a line graph the relationship to be studied is treated as a FUNCTION and is plotted on a coordinate system (for an example, see CARTESIAN COORDINATES). The graph of a function $y = f(x)$, where $x$ and $y$ are numbers, is the set of points in the $xy$-plane with coordinates $[x, f(x)]$. Statistics makes use of both bar graphs and line graphs.

**graphics:** see COMPUTER GRAPHICS; PRINTING; WOODCUT AND WOOD ENGRAVING.

**graphite,** an allotrope (see ALLOTROPY) of CARBON, known since antiquity. Soft, black, and relatively light, it marks papyrus, paper, and stone when pressed against them. It occurs naturally in many parts of the world including Cumbria in England, Sri Lanka, Madagascar, Siberia, and New York State. Synthetic graphite is made by high-temperature treatment of petroleum coke (small graphite crystals in an organic matrix) and coal-tar pitch. Industrially it is used as furnace and crucible linings, electrodes (e.g., for the production of aluminium), as a lubricant, in pencils, and in composites of high strength and low density. Its excellent chemical and mechanical properties, as well as its biocompatibility, has led to its use in artificial heart valves.

**Grappelli, Stephane,** 1908–, French jazz violinist. He developed an individual style which became famous before World War II through the recordings of the Hot Club de France. He has performed on radio and TV and in concerts worldwide, especially with musicians such as Django *Reinhardt* and Johnny Ethridge. In the 1980s he still retained all his personal charm and musical sensitivity in superb performances with players such as Yehudi MENUHIN and Julian BREAM.

**grass,** any plant of the family Gramineae, a widely distributed group of mostly annual and perennial herbs. The grass family is of far greater economic importance than any other. It includes the cereal grasses, e.g., WHEAT, RICE, MAIZE, OATS, BARLEY, and RYE, which provide the GRAIN that is the staple food in most countries and the major type of feed; most hay and pasture plants; SUGARCANE; and species of REED and BAMBOO used for thatching and construction. In addition, plants of the grass family provide raw material for the production of many spirits and PAPER items, form climax vegetation (see ECOLOGY) in areas of low rainfall (see PAMPAS; PRAIRIE; SAVANNA; STEPPE; VELDT), and help to prevent EROSION.

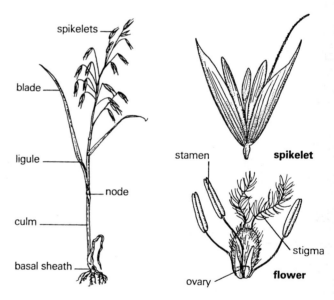

Structure of a typical **grass**

**Grass, Günter** (grahs), 1927–, German writer and artist; b. Danzig. Arguably the most inventive and energetic of the postwar generation of writers, Grass began with poetry and absurdist drama before making his name with the scandal-provoking picaresque novel *Die Blechtrommel* (1959; tr. The Tin Drum), the self-accusatory autobiography of a dwarf with a sceptical view of German history who had survived the Hitler years into the years of the Economic Miracle. It was the first of the so-called Danzig trilogy, which also includes *Cat and Mouse* (1961) and *Hundejahre* (1963; tr. Dog Years). Their location is Grass's lost home town, which he has turned into a literary locale as vivid as JOYCE's Dublin or DÖBLIN's Berlin. A satirical social critic in his fictions, Grass was politically active in the election campaigns of the 1960s on behalf of the SPD and his friend Willi BRANDT. This formed part of the subject-matter of his autobiographical *Aus dem Tagebuch einer Schnecke* (1972; tr. From the Diary of a Snail). His most recent novels *The Flounder* (1977) and *The Rat* (1986) continue the inventive blurring of autobiography and grotesque fiction: the first is a vast history of cooks and an uneasy reckoning with contemporary feminism, the second a vision of the end of the man-polluted world. Trained as a sculptor, Grass has increasingly accompanied his prose texts with his own illustrations and interspersed them with poems. Other works include *Local Anaesthetic* (1969); *The Meeting in Telgte* (1979), an historical–allegorical tribute to his alter ego GRIMMELSHAUSEN and to his patron and friend H.W. RICHTER; the critical travel journal *Headbirths, or The Germans are Dying Out* (1980); and the volume of poems *Flounder, Your Tale Has an Unhappy Ending* (1983). In 1978 he founded a literary prize for the encouragement of new writing.

**Grasse, François Joseph Paul, comte de** (kawnht də grahs), 1722–88, French admiral. His blockade of the York and James rivers during the AMERICAN REVOLUTION effectively contained Gen. CORNWALLIS at Yorktown and led to the great American victory of the YORKTOWN CAMPAIGN.

**grasshopper,** fairly small to large (15–100 mm/½–4 in) diurnal, plant-eating INSECT, order Orthoptera (family Acrididae), with long, powerful hind legs for jumping and initiating flight, a saddle-shaped thorax, chewing mouthparts, and antennae distinctly shorter than body, i.e., 'short-horned'. Female grasshoppers have short, inconspicuous ovipositors. In most species it is only the males which produce mating 'songs' (stridulate), by rubbing their hind legs across the fore wings when closed. Both sexes have a pair of hearing organs (tympana), at the base of the abdomen. Grasshoppers are usually an inconspicuous green or brown, but some southern European and many tropical species have brightly-coloured and often boldly-patterned wings; the sudden flash of colour when a disturbed individual takes flight may serve to distract predators. Being leaf-eaters it is inevitable that some are important agricultural pests, e.g., the small rice grasshoppers (*Oxya*), which attack that crop wherever it is grown in Africa, India, and the Far East. From time to time far greater and more widespread crop damage is caused by those grasshoppers which have, in addition to the normal solitary phase, a gregarious phase (see LOCUST).

**Gratiae:** see GRACES.

**Grattan, Henry,** 1746–1820, Irish statesman. Entering the Irish Parliament in 1775, he became known as a brilliant orator. He helped achieve nominal legislative independence for the Irish Parliament, and he helped gain Catholics the right to vote in Ireland. When hopes that Catholics could sit in Parliament were dashed, he retired (1797). He sat in the British Parliament from 1805, but took little part.

**Graves, Robert,** 1895–1985, English poet and novelist. He is best known for his traditional lyric verse, including many love-poems, and for his war memoir *Goodbye To All That* (1929). He wrote two popular novels on Roman history, *I, Claudius* (1934) and *Claudius the God* (1934), as well as studies of myth, e.g., *The White Goddess* (1948) and *The Greek Myths* (2 vol., 1955). He also produced criticism, and translations of Apuleius and Homer.

**gravitation,** the attractive FORCE existing between any two particles of matter. Because this force acts throughout the universe, it is often called universal gravitation. Isaac NEWTON was the first to recognize that the force holding any object to the earth is the same as the force holding the moon and planets in their orbits. According to Newton's law of universal gravitation, the force between any two bodies is directly proportional to the product of their masses (see MASS) and inversely proportional to the square of the distance between them. The constant of proportionality is known as the gravitational constant (symbol $G$) and equals $6.673 \times 10^{-11}$ newton-m²/kg². The measure of the force of gravitation on a given body on earth is the WEIGHT of that body. In the general theory of RELATIVITY, gravitation is explained geometrically: matter in its immediate neighbourhood causes the curvature of the the four-dimensional SPACE-TIME continuum. See also CELESTIAL MECHANICS.

**gravitational collapse,** in astronomy, theoretically predicted final stage in the life history of a star (see STELLAR EVOLUTION). The ability of a star to resist contraction under its own immense gravitational force depends on the pressures in the interior being sufficiently high. During the middle stages of evolution the pressure is made sufficient by the high temperatures maintained by the heat output of nuclear reactions in the central regions. When the energy-producing nuclear fuels are all used up, further contraction becomes inevitable, though if the star was originally rotating fast it may scatter its material into space. If the mass of the star is not too large (up to 1.4 times the mass of the Sun) it may find a new equilibrium through the resistance to further compression of the electrons

of the material, and then is called a WHITE DWARF. For somewhat larger masses this resistance is insufficient to counter gravitation, but after substantial further contraction and explosive loss of material as a SUPERNOVA all the remaining material assumes the form of neutrons (an energy-absorbing change which turns the contraction into a sudden gravitational collapse), and again, for a range of values of the mass of the body equilibrium may be reached through the resistance of the material (largely neutrons) to further compression becoming strong enough, and thus a NEUTRON STAR may result. However, beyond a certain value of the mass, the neutrons are not strong enough to arrest the collapse which according to our understanding will continue without end. At some stage during this endless collapse the gravitational force on its surface becomes so great that even light does not have a sufficient velocity to escape far from the body, so that all contact with the rest of the universe is lost. The former star is now a **black hole**. Because light and other forms of energy and matter are permanently trapped inside a black hole by the enormous pull of gravitation, a black hole can be observed only indirectly. For example, in some BINARY STAR systems, such as the X-ray source Cygnus X-1, the smaller and invisible companions are strong emitters of X-rays and are suspected of surrounding black holes. Gas flows from the larger component of the binary and forms an accretion disc around the black hole. As the gas from this disc spirals into the black hole, it is accelerated by the collapsed star's enormous gravitational pull; as this happens, the matter becomes compressed and heated to the extreme temperatures at which X-rays are emitted.

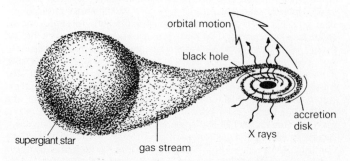

**Gravitational collapse:** The x-ray source Cygnus X-1 is believed to be a black hole orbiting around an optically observed supergiant star (HDE 226868).

**Gray, Asa,** 1810–88, leading American botanist and taxonomist. Professor of natural history at Harvard and a prolific author, he (with the botanist John Torrey) helped to revise LINNAEUS's taxonomy, basing his version mainly on fruit anatomy rather than gross morphology. His writings include the *Manual of Botany*, the standard reference for E US flora; *Structural Botany;* and *The Elements of Botany* .

**Gray, Elisha,** 1835–1901, American inventor. He patented many electrical devices, most having to do with the telegraph. In 1875, experimenting with transmitting musical notes, he hit on the idea of transmitting the human voice. His attempts to patent his work in early 1876 were frustrated by the registration of Alexander Graham BELL's final telephone patent just a few hours earlier.

**Gray, Thomas,** 1716–71, English poet. A scholar of Greek and history, he spent a secluded life at Cambridge. The first important poems of his small output, written in 1742, include 'Ode on a Distant Prospect of Eton College'. The meditative 'Elegy Written in a Country Churchyard' (1751) is his best known work. His friend Horace Walpole published in 1757 his Pindaric odes, which in their strenuous sublimity illustrate the evolution of 18th-cent. English poetry from CLASSICISM to early ROMANTICISM. Gray was a letter-writer of memorable charm and insight.

**Gray's Inn:** see INNS OF COURT.

**Graz,** city (1981 pop. 243,166), capital of Styria prov., SE Austria, on the Mur R. Probably founded in the 12th cent., it was built around the Schlossberg, a mountain peak, on which stand the famous Uhrturm [clock tower] and the ruins of a 15th-cent. fortress. The second largest city in Austria, Graz has iron and steel, paper, and machinery works. Noteworthy are its Gothic structures and the Johanneum museum. The astronomer Johannes KEPLER taught at the university.

**Great Awakening,** series of religious revivals that swept over the American colonies about the middle of the 18th cent. Beginning in the 1720s, Theodorus Frelinghuysen and Gilbert TENNENT made local stirrings in New Jersey. In New England the movement was started (1734) by Jonathan EDWARDS. It was spread by a tour (1739–41) by George WHITEFIELD and reached the South with the preaching (1748–59) of Samuel Davies. The Great Awakening led to bitter doctrinal disputes, but it also resulted in missionary work among the Indians and in the founding of new educational institutions. It encouraged a democratic spirit in religion.

**Great Barrier Reef,** largest coral reef in the world, in the CORAL SEA, off the coast of Queensland, NE Australia. It is 2000 km (c.1250 mi) long and is separated from the mainland by a shallow lagoon up to 161 km (100 mi) wide. The reef is composed of thousands of individual reefs and has many islets, coral gardens, and unusual marine life. In some places it is more than 122 m (400 ft) thick. Marine biological research stations are based on Heron Island and Lizard Island. Illegal poaching is threatening the giant clam and other species of fish.

**Great Basin,** desert region, in Nevada, Utah, US, and parts of adjoining states, forming the northern half of the **Basin and Range** physiographic province. It was explored (1843–45) and named by J.C. FRÉMONT, who recognized it as a basin of interior drainage (i.e., without outlet to the sea). GREAT SALT LAKE, Sevier, and Utah are the chief lakes. The basin is sparsely populated. Industries include mining (copper, silver, gold) and ranching.

**Great Bear Lake,** largest lake of Canada and fourth largest of North America, c.31,800 km² (12,275 sq mi), on the Arctic Circle in the Mackenzie district of the Northwest Territories. The lake, which is ice-bound for eight months of the year, is 310 km (190 mi) long, 40–177 km (25–110 mi) wide, and drains west through the Great Bear R. to the MACKENZIE R. Port Radium, in the east, was a radium-mining boom town in the 1930s.

**Great Britain:** see UNITED KINGDOM.

**Great Britain, Government,** The hereditary monarch plays a largely ceremonial role in the government. The current monarch is Queen ELIZABETH II, who came to the throne in 1952. Supreme legislative power rests in the Parliament, which consists of the House of Commons and the House of Lords. The House of Commons has 650 members, who are elected by universal suffrage for all citizens over the age of 18. Each representative (known as an MP or Member of Parliament) is elected by a 'first past the post' system and represents a constituency. The House of Lords is made up of hereditary and life peers and peeresses (including the LAW LORDS), archbishops, and bishops. Executive authority rests nominally with the Crown, but in practice it is associated with a committee of ministers known as the Cabinet, headed by the prime minister, chosen from the majority party in the House of Commons.

**Great Depression,** the unprecedentedly severe US economic crisis of the 1930s, supposedly precipitated by the 1929 stock market crash. Certain causative factors are generally accepted: overproduction of goods; a tariff and war-debt policy that curtailed foreign markets for American goods; and easy money policies that led to overexpansion of credit and fantastic speculation on the stock market. At the depth (1933) of the Depression, 16 million people, one-third of the labour force were unemployed. The effects were also felt in Europe, and contributed to the rise of Adolf HITLER in Germany. The policies of the NEW DEAL relieved the situation, but complete recovery came only with the heavy defence spending of the 1940s. See also DEPRESSION.

**Great Dividing Range,** crest line of the EASTERN HIGHLANDS of Australia, forming most of that continent's drainage or continental divide. It is also widely used as an alternate name for the Eastern Highlands.

**Great Elector, the:** see FREDERICK WILLIAM.

**Greater Antilles:** see WEST INDIES.

**Greater Manchester,** former metropolitan county of NW England (1984 est. pop. 2,604,763), 129 km² (50 sq mi). Formed in the local government reorganization of 1974, it contained the urban areas of MANCHESTER, BOLTON, Bury, OLDHAM, ROCHDALE, SALFORD, STOCKPORT, and Wigan. The metropolitan county council was abolished in April 1986.

**Great Exhibition,** 1851, a pioneering exhibition held in Hyde Park London in a sequence of 19th- and 20th-cent. international exhibitions.

Its exhibits were arranged and displayed to illustrate the progress of human achievement, particularly in science and technology, and were housed in an innovative building of glass and iron, the CRYSTAL PALACE. A hundred years later the Festival of Britain took up these themes.

**Great Lakes,** group of five connected freshwater lakes, E central North America, together covering c.246,000 km² (95,000 sq mi). The lakes SUPERIOR, MICHIGAN, HURON, ERIE, and ONTARIO and their connecting waterways extend 1876 km (1160 mi) along the US–Canadian border. With the SAINT LAWRENCE SEAWAY they form the **St Lawrence & Great Lakes Waterway,** a major shipping artery that is navigable (except from December to April, when blocked by ice) for 3770 km (2342 mi) by ocean-going vessels of 8.2-m (27-ft) draft. The lakes range in elevation from 183 m (602 ft) in the west to 75 m (246 ft) in the east, the greatest drop (51 m/167 ft) occurring between Lakes Erie and Ontario at NIAGARA FALLS.

**Great Mother of the Gods,** in ancient Middle Eastern religion (and later in Greece, Rome, and W Asia), mother goddess, the great symbol of the earth's fertility. As the creative force in nature she was worshipped under many names, including ASTARTE (Syria), CERES (Rome), CYBELE (Phrygia), DEMETER (Greece), ISHTAR (Babylon), and ISIS (Egypt). The later forms of her cult involved the worship of a male deity (her son or lover, e.g., ADONIS, OSIRIS), whose death and resurrection symbolized the regenerative power of the earth.

**Great Ouse:** see OUSE.

**Great Plains,** semiarid region of level and rolling terrain, located E of the Rocky Mts and extending more than 2415 km (1500 mi) from Texas N into Canada. Elevations range from c.1800 m (6000 ft) in the west to c.450 m (1500 ft) at the eastern boundary, which coincides roughly with the 100th meridian of longitude (running from E Oklahoma through the central Dakotas). Ranching and wheat farming, begun in the late 1800s, ended centuries of habitation by Indians and buffalo. Coal, oil, and natural gas deposits underlie the Plains.

**Great Rift Valley,** huge depression, currently thought to be the product of PLATE TECTONICS, extending c.4830 km (3000 mi) across most of E Africa and into SW Asia. In Africa it consists of an eastern arm, occupied in part by Lakes Rudolf and MALAWI (Nyasa), and a western arm, occupied in part by Lakes TANGANYIKA, Kivu, Edward, and Mobuto Sese Seko (Albert). In SW Asia it forms the RED SEA, the Gulf of AQABA, the DEAD SEA, and the JORDAN and Al BIQA valleys. Flanked in places by high cliffs and volcanoes (Mts KENYA and KILIMANJARO), the floor of the rift ranges in elevation from c.395 m (1300 ft) below sea level, in the Dead Sea, to c.1830 m (6000 ft) above sea level, in S Kenya.

**Great Salt Lake,** largest salt lake in North America, c.2600 km² (1000 sq mi), in NW Utah, US. The shallow lake (c.4 m/13 ft deep) fluctuates in level in response to climatic fluctuations and river diversions. The lake's waters have a salt content of c.276 parts per thousand (greater than sea water) and support no life except brine shrimp and colonial algae.

**Great Slave Lake,** second largest lake of Canada, c.28,400 km² (10,980 sq mi), in the Mackenzie district of the Northwest Territories. The deepest lake (614 m/2015 ft) in North America, it is c.480 km (300 mi) long, 19–109 km (12–68 mi) wide, and drains W through the MACKENZIE R. Gold is mined at YELLOWKNIFE, in the north, and some lead and zinc on the southern shore.

**Great Smoky Mountains,** (or Great Smokies), range of the APPALACHIAN MTS, on the North Carolina–Tennessee border, US, named for a smokelike haze that frequently envelops them. They rise to a high point of 2024 m (6642 ft) at Clingmans Dome.

**Great Wall of China,** fortifications, winding c.2400 km (1500 mi) across N China from Gansu prov. to the Yellow Sea. It is an amalgamation of many walls, first united in the 3rd cent. BC by the Qin dynasty. The present form dates substantially from the Ming dynasty (1368–1644) and averages 7.6 m (25 ft) in height. Successive invasions of China by northern nomads proved the wall to be of little military usefulness.

**Great Yarmouth,** town (1981 pop. 54,777), in Norfolk, E England, on North Sea coast at the mouth of R. Yare. It is a resort town and fishing port. Famous as a herring port it handled 2.8 million tonnes in 1984. Industries carried on in the town include flour milling, engineering and brewing. There are several old buildings in the town, including a 14th-cent. tollhouse, which is now a museum.

Great Wall of China

**grebe,** swimming BIRD found on or near quiet waters in much of the world. Resembling both the related LOON and unrelated DUCK, it has short wings, a vestigial tail, and long, individually webbed toes on feet that are set far back on a short, stubby body. Grebes are poor fliers and clumsy on land. They have complex courtship rituals, including dancing in pairs on the water.

**Greco, El,** c.1541–1614, Greek painter in Spain; b. Candia, Crete, as Domenicos Theotocopoulos. By 1577, he was established in Toledo after having painted in Rome and studied in Venice under TITIAN. He left portraits of Toledo's proud nobility; their ascetic faces are seen in the foreground of the *Burial of the Count Orgaz* (Church of San Tomé, Toledo). El Greco's flamelike lines, accentuated by vivid highlights, elongated and distorted figures, and full, vibrant colour produced dynamic representations of religious ecstasy. Among his great works are *Baptism, Crucifixion,* and *Resurrection* (all: Prado) and a long series of paintings of St. FRANCIS. To his last period belong such works as the *Adoration* and *View of Toledo* (both: Metropolitan Mus.). El Greco undoubtedly influenced VELÁZQUEZ and is ranked among the great inspired, visionary artists.

**Greece,** Gr. *Hellas* or *Ellas,* officially the Hellenic Republic, republic (1985 est. pop. 9,932,000), 131,945 km², (50,944 sq mi) SE Europe. Occupying the S Balkan Peninsula, it is bordered by the Ionian Sea (W), the Mediterranean Sea (S), the Aegean Sea (E), Turkey and Bulgaria (NE), Yugoslavia (N), and Albania (NW). ATHENS is the capital and largest city; other major cities include THESSALONÍKI and PIRAIÉVS. About 75% of the country is mountainous, the major range being the Pindus Mts, in the north. Central Greece includes the low-lying plains of Thessaly, Attica, and Boeotia, as well as Greece's highest point, Mt OLYMPUS 2917 m (9570 ft). The southern portion of the country is the PELOPONNESUS. Of the total land area, almost 20% is in islands, notably CRETE, the DODECANESE (including RHODES), and the CYCLADES. Industry has replaced agriculture as the leading source of income. Principal manufactures include construction materials, textiles, food products, chemicals, and ships. The chief farm products are wheat, fruits, olives and olive oil, grapes, tobacco,

sugar beets, and tomatoes; large numbers of sheep and goats are raised. Tourism is important. The GNP is $39,210 million and the GNP per capita is $3970 (1983). Modern Greek is the official language, and the established religion is Greek Orthodox. Government is by a unicameral parliament of 200 to 300 members, who elect a president for a 5-year term. Greece became a full member of the COMMON MARKET in 1981. The country left the military wing of NATO in 1974, but rejoined it in 1980.

*Ancient Greece.* The region had seen the rise and fall of splendid cultures, e.g., the MINOAN CIVILIZATION and the MYCENAEAN CIVILIZATION, before the arrival of Greek-speaking peoples. By 1000 BC Achaeans, Aeolians, Ionians, and Dorians had settled in the region that is modern Greece, where they developed many independent, often warring, CITY-STATES. Taking to the sea, by the 8th cent. BC they had created a network of colonies from Asia Minor to Spain (see MAGNA GRAECIA). The 5th cent. BC began with attempted invasions of Greece by the Persians. Greek success in the PERSIAN WARS (500–449 BC) ushered in the golden age of Greek history. Prosperous economies were founded on the extensive use of SLAVERY. Athens, in particular, grew dramatically and, in the age of PERICLES (c.495–429 BC), experienced a surge of cultural development rarely equalled in world history. Although Athens succumbed to SPARTA in the PELOPONNESIAN WAR (431–404 BC), Athenian thought prevailed, and the culture that was to be the fountainhead of Western civilization lived on. When PHILIP II of Macedon conquered Greece (338 BC) at Chaeronea, he paved the way for his son, ALEXANDER THE GREAT, who spread Greek civilization across the known world. By 146 BC the remnants of the Greek states had fallen to Rome, but when the Roman Empire was split (AD 395), the BYZANTINE EMPIRE, formed from the eastern portion, was thoroughly Greek in tradition. HELLENISTIC CIVILIZATION, centred at Alexandria and other cities, also preserved the Greek heritage.

*Modern Greece.* Turkish incursions and Norman attacks began in the 11th cent., and Greece was absorbed into the OTTOMAN EMPIRE in 1456. Under Ottoman rule, Greece languished in obscurity and poverty until the successful Greek War of Independence (1821–32) and the establishment of a constitutional monarchy. Greece acquired the Ionian Islands (1864), Thessaly and part of Epirus (1881), and Crete (1913); in the BALKAN WARS (1912–13) it obtained SE MACEDONIA and W THRACE. Pressured by the Allies, Greece entered WORLD WAR I in 1917 and after the war was awarded most of European Turkey and the Bulgarian coast. The period between the world wars was marked by political turmoil: monarchs were enthroned and dethroned; a republic proclaimed in 1924

Greece

collapsed in 1935; and in 1936 a right-wing dictatorship was established under George METAXAS. During WORLD WAR II Greece was occupied (1941–44) by the German army. Civil war erupted in 1946, but massive US and British military and economic assistance ensured the victory of royalist forces over Communist insurgents. Greece joined the NORTH ATLANTIC TREATY ORGANIZATION in 1952, although its participation has frequently been complicated by traditional rivalries with fellow member Turkey. A *coup d'état* by rightist army officers in 1967 resulted in the rise to power of George PAPADOPOULOS at the head of a military junta, which abolished the monarchy in 1973 but which was itself overthrown in 1974 following a disastrous military adventure in Cyprus. Civilian government was restored under Constantine KARAMANLIS and a new constitution adopted in 1975; Greece became a member of the EUROPEAN COMMUNITY in 1981. In the same year the electoral victory of the Pan-Hellenic Socialist Movement (Pasok) led by Andreas PAPANDREOU gave Greece its first socialist government, which was returned to power with a reduced majority in 1985. In 1983 the Papandreou government signed a new five-year defence and economic cooperation agreement with the US.

**Greek Anthology,** collection of epigrammatic poems representing that form of Greek literature from the 7th cent. BC to the 10th cent. AD. It began with Meleager's *Garland* (c.90–80 BC) and was added to by others. A 10th-cent. version, the *Palatine Anthology,* is the chief modern source.

**Greek architecture** arose on the shores of the Aegean Sea. When the Dorians migrated into Greece (c.1000 BC) true Hellenic culture began; by the 6th cent. BC, a definite Dorian system of construction existed. All the great works were produced between 700 BC and the Roman occupation (146 BC). The major masterpieces were erected between 480 BC and 323 BC, including the reign of PERICLES, when CALLICRATES, MNESICLES, and ICTINUS flourished. Of the three great styles or ORDERS OF ARCHITECTURE, the Doric was earliest and the one in which most of the monuments were erected. Early examples (6th cent. BC) are found in Sicily and Paestum in Italy; after 500 BC the Doric was perfected at Athens in the Hephaesteum (465 BC), the PARTHENON (c.447–432 BC), and the Propylaea (437–432 BC). The Greek colonies of Asia Minor evolved the second great order, the Ionic order, stamped with oriental influences. After 500 BC it appeared in Greece proper, challenging with its slender columns and carved enrichments the sturdy, simple Doric. The most important Ionic buildings were at Miletus. In Greece, the ERECHTHEUM was the one major Ionic structure. The third, or Corinthian order, appeared in this period. Even more ornate, it was used more in Hellenistic and Roman periods. Examples are the Choragic monument (c.335 BC) and the Tower of the Winds (100 BC–35 BC), both at Athens. The Greeks used finely cut stone joints rather than mortar. Marble was used after the 5th cent. BC. Earlier, rough stone was covered with a marble dust and lime coating. Although Greek buildings were long thought to have been left white, traces of decorative colouring have been found. Cities often had an acropolis, a citadel and temple site built on a steep hill. The standard Greek temple had a simple rectangular chamber with an entrance porch flanked by columns. The sides and ends would then be surrounded with a colonnade, sometimes doubled. A body of traditional mathematical formulas was developed to ensure harmony of proportions. The Greeks built temples; monumental tombs; agoras, or public meeting places; stoas, or colonnaded shelters; stadiums; palaestrae, or gymnasiums; propylaeas, or city gates; and amphitheatres. After Athens and Sparta declined, the more opulent and florid Hellenistic architecture arose (4th–3rd cent. BC), from which the Romans doubtless acquired their concepts of monumental architecture.

**Greek art.** The Aegean basin was a centre of artistic activity from early times (see AEGEAN CIVILIZATION). Two great cultures the MINOAN CIVILIZATION and the MYCENEAN CIVILIZATION had developed complex and delicate art forms. After the invasion of the Dorians and other barbarians (before 1000 BC), the curvilinear designs and naturalistic representations of the Mycenean age were replaced by geometric schemes with linear patterns. The transformation is seen in late geometric (c.900–700 BC) pottery. Between 700 and 600 BC Oriental influence led to the use of floral and arabesque patterns and monster and animal themes. Then, during the archaic period (c.660–480 BC), sculpture became the principle form of artistic expression. The statues of nude walking youths, *kouroi,* suggesting Egyptian prototypes but distinct in stylization and tension of movement, e.g., *Kouros* (Metropolitan Mus., New York), date from this period. Draped female figures show Near Eastern influence, e.g., *Hera of Samos* (Louvre, Paris). The outstanding Athenian school of black-figure

vase painting led by Éxecias depicted mythological and contemporary scenes. A greater concern with three-dimensional space and naturalistic detail emerged with red-figure vase painting (c.525 BC). Euthymides and Euphronius were early masters. The early classical (or 'Severe') period revealed new insight into the structure of the human form (c.480–450 BC). e.g., the sculptures from the Temple of Zeus at Olympia, the bronze *Charioteer* (museum; Delphi), and the *Zeus* or *Poseidon* (Athens, National Mus.). During the Golden Age, the height of the classical period (450–400 BC), POLYKLEITOS arrived at a rational norm for the ideal figure. The magnificent sculptures from the ACROPOLIS and its PARTHENON, thought to have been designed by PHIDIAS, exemplify this ideal. In the late classical period (400–300 BC) there was more emphasis on emotion in art. The works attributed to PRAXITELES are elegant and graceful; to SCOPAS, strongly emotional; and to LYSIPPOS, individualized, though all are largely adduced through fragments or Roman copies. The works of the painters of the period, e.g., Apollodorus and APELLES, are known only through description. The Hellenistic period began with the conquests of Alexander the Great. Masterpieces of the period include the *Nike* (*Victory*) *of Samothrace* and *Aphrodite of Melos* (both: Louvre, Paris); the *Pergamum Frieze* (Berlin Mus.); the Roman copies of the *Odyssey Landscape* (Vatican), a painting with spatial illusionism; and the *Laocoön* (Vatican). Despite its decline, Greek culture and art inspired Western art throughout history.

Greek art: Kouros, c.570–550 BC. Metropolitan Museum of Art, New York.

**Greek language,** member of the Indo-European family of languages. Modern Greek is derived from the standard Greek or *koinē* of the Hellenistic world, in which the New Testament was written. See ALPHABET (illustration); LANGUAGE (table).

**Greek music.** The music of ancient Greece was inseparable from poetry and dancing. It was monodic (without HARMONY in the modern sense). The musical culture of the Homeric period was looked upon as a golden age. In the 6th cent. BC choral music was used in the drama (see TRAGEDY). The phorminx, a lyre, and later (6th cent. BC) the oboelike *aulos* and the kithara, a large lyre, were the main instruments. Few fragments of ancient Greek music survive. The physical relationships of tones, the basis of harmony, was a Greek discovery, usually attributed to PYTHAGORAS.

**Greek religion.** Although its exact origins are lost in time, Greek religion is thought to date from about the 2nd millennium BC, when the culture of Aryan invaders fused with those of the Aegean and Minoan peoples who had inhabited the region of Greece from Neolithic times. As portrayed in Homer's *Iliad,* the classical Greek pantheon, also called Homeric or Olympian (from Mt Olympus, home of the gods), was a blend of Minoan, Egyptian, Asian, and other elements. The Greek deities had supernatural powers, particularly over human life, but were severely limited by the relentless force of fate (Moira). The gods were most important in their role as guardians of the city-states and as those who could provide information, through divination rites, about one's future on earth. Often the favourable response or reward expected did not materialize, and the civil strife that followed the classical period (from c.500 BC) placed the old gods on trial. The popular religion of the Greek countryside rose, emphasizing the promise of afterlife and elaborate rites offered by such cults as the Eleusinian and ORPHIC MYSTERIES. The Dionysian excesses of these mystery rites were offset by the virtues of moderation ascribed to Apollo. Later Greek philosophical inquiry sought a more logical connection between nature and mankind, leading to the rationalization of the early myths and the final destruction of the Homeric pantheon. The vacuum was eventually filled by Christianity.

**Greeley, Horace,** 1811–72, American newspaper editor. He founded the New York *Tribune* in 1841, and edited the paper for over 30 years, advocating a protective tariff, the organization of labour, temperance, a homestead law, and women's rights, and opposing monopoly, land grants to railways, and SLAVERY. Greeley's editorials were widely quoted and influential; he coined the phrase 'Go West, young man, go West'. He was one of the first members of the new REPUBLICAN PARTY, although he denounced Pres. LINCOLN's delay in issuing an EMANCIPATION PROCLAMATION and embarrassed the administration by his antiwar sentiments. Following the Civil War, he favoured black suffrage but also amnesty for all Southerners. He ran for president in 1872 as the candidate of the LIBERAL REPUBLICAN PARTY, but was soundly defeated by the incumbent, Ulysses S. GRANT.

**Greely, Adolphus Washington,** 1844–1935, American army officer and explorer. Between 1881 and 1884 he commanded the Lady Franklin Bay Expedition to establish one of a chain of Arctic meteorological stations. He and his party mapped a stretch of Greenland's coast, crossed Ellesmere Island, and achieved a northern record of 83°24′N. After two relief efforts failed, a ship found only Greely and six others alive. He directed relief operations after the San Francisco earthquake in 1906.

**Green, Henry,** 1905–73, English novelist; b. Henry Vincent Yorke. His enigmatic, comic novels include *Living* (1929), *Caught* (1943), *Loving* (1945), and *Concluding* (1948). He also published an autobiography, *Pack My Bag* (1940).

**Green, John Richard,** 1837–83, English historian. Educated at Oxford, he became a clergyman, but renounced his orders in 1877. His *Short History of the English People* (1874) made social history lively and popular. He was a friend of E.A. FREEMAN and a serious scholarly researcher.

**Green, Julian,** 1900–, French novelist, of American parentage. His novels, e.g., *The Closed Garden* (1927), *The Dark Journey* (1929), *Moïra* (1950) and *Chaque homme dans sa nuit* (1960; tr. Each in His Darkness) and his autobiography mostly show a struggle between mysticism and sensuality and a strong sense of individual destiny.

**Green, William,** 1872–1952, American labour leader; b. Coshocton, Ohio. He rose through the ranks of the United Mine Workers of America (UMW), serving (1912–24) as secretary-treasurer. In 1924 he was elected president of the AFL (see AMERICAN FEDERATION OF LABOR AND CONGRESS OF INDUSTRIAL ORGANIZATIONS), a post he held until his death. He organized skilled labour into craft unions, and he led the AFL in the struggle with the CIO after the groups split in 1935.

**Greenaway, Kate,** 1846–1901, English illustrator. Her fanciful coloured drawings of child life influenced children's clothing and illustrated books. She provided text and pictures for many books, e.g., *Under the Window* (1879).

**greenback,** popular name for legal tender notes, unsecured by specie, issued (starting in 1861) by the US government during the American CIVIL WAR. The notes were to have been recalled following the war, but following demands, particularly by Western farmers, for an inflated currency through the creation of more greenbacks, a compromise was finally reached in 1869, whereby greenbacks to the amount of $356 million were left in circulation. In 1879 Congress provided that greenbacks then outstanding ($346,681,000) remain a permanent part of the nation's currency.

**Greenback Party,** a US political organization founded (1874–76) to promote currency expansion. Its principal members were Southern and Western farmers stricken by the Panic of 1873. They nominated Peter COOPER for president in 1876, but he received only 81,737 votes. Uniting with labour in the Greenback–Labour party (1878), they polled over 1 million votes and elected 14 representatives to Congress. Thus encouraged, and with a broadened programme that included woman suffrage, federal regulation of interstate commerce, and a graduated income tax, they nominated James B. WEAVER for president (1880). But the return of prosperity had allayed discontent, and their vote declined to a little over 300,000. Following the 1884 election the party dissolved. Many members later joined the Populists.

**green belt,** a British term describing an area of agricultural 'green' land surrounding a town or city, designated by law to prevent the spread of urban development and unplanned growth. The idea of containing towns in this way was known in antiquity, practised in Rome by the device of 'designated fields', and advocated in literature, e.g., Thomas More's *Utopia*. The modern idea stems from the theories of Ebenezer Howard in connection with the concept of the GARDEN CITY, but the practical realization of green belts in Britain was the result of the Town and Country Planning Act 1947, which set up the most complete system of town planning known in history, including provision for the designation of green belts round cities and town. It is often regarded as the single most successful feature of modern British planning. A more selective and less definitive policy is now advocated.

**Greene, Graham,** 1904–, English novelist. A Catholic convert with intense moral concerns, he writes novels that are essentially parables of the damned. Those that are thrillers, e.g., *Stamboul Train* (1932), he calls 'entertainments'. His major works include *Brighton Rock* (1938), *The Power and the Glory* (1940), *The Heart of the Matter* (1948), *The End of the Affair* (1951), and *The Human Factor* (1978). A superb journalist, he has set novels in sites of topical interest, e.g. *The Quiet American* (1955), in Indochina. He is also known for his short stories, plays, film criticism, and film scripts, including *The Third Man* (1950).

**Greene, Robert,** 1558–92, English writer. A prolific author of romances and romantic dramas, he is now best known for his apparent attack on SHAKESPEARE in *Greenes Groats-Worth of Witte* (1592) as 'an upstart Crow, beautified with our feathers'.

**greenfly:** see APHID.

**Greenham Common,** US Air Force base in Berkshire, S England, site of an anti-nuclear-weapons protest. In 1981 a group (mostly women) marched from Cardiff to the base and set up a peace camp in protest against the deployment of Cruise missiles. Although the campers (all women since early 1982) have made many successful demonstrations, including one in which 30,000 people held hands to surround the base, cruise missiles arrived in 1983. The women have continued to infiltrate the base and to stage symbolic protests. See also CAMPAIGN FOR NUCLEAR DISARMAMENT.

**greenhouse effect,** process whereby heat is trapped at the surface of the earth by the atmosphere. Energy from the sun passes through the atmosphere, warming the earth and providing the wavelengths used in PHOTOSYNTHESIS. Much of the incoming energy is reradiated in the form of heat, some directly and some as a result of either the METABOLISM of living things or human industrial activities. This heat (infrared radiation) is prevented from leaving the earth by atmospheric carbon dioxide, water vapour, and ozone (acting like the glass in a greenhouse), and much of it goes back into the ground. An increase in atmospheric carbon dioxide of 10% over the past century has led some authorities to predict a long-term warming of the earth's climate.

**Greenland,** officially Kalâtdlit Nunât (1983 est. pop. 52,000), largest island in the world, c.2,175,600 km² (840,000 sq mi) of which 341,700 km² (131,930 sq mi) are ice-free, semiautonomous overseas state of Denmark, lying largely within the Arctic Circle off NE Canada. The capital is Nuuk (formerly Godthàb). An ice sheet c.4300 m (14,000 ft) deep in places covers more than four fifths of the land area. Most people live along the coast in the SW where the climate is warmed by the North Atlantic Drift. About 10% are Europeans; the others are of mixed Eskimo and Danish ancestry. Fishing, shrimping, and sealing are the principal economic activities. Greenland was named and settled (c.982) as a self-governing colony by ERIC THE RED, a Norseman. The colony was neglected by Norway in the 14th and 15th cent., and the colonists had either died out or had been assimilated with the Eskimos when Greenland was rediscovered, with no trace of the Norsemen, in the 16th cent. by the British explorers Martin FROBISHER and John Davis. It was recolonized, beginning in 1721, by Norway and became a Danish colony in 1815. Greenland became an integral part of Denmark in 1953 with representatives in the *Folketing* (Parliament), and was granted home rule in 1979. Greenlandic names came into common use in 1979, and in 1982 the island independently withdrew from the EUROPEAN COMMUNITY (of which it had become a member in 1973 as a Danish dependency). Elections in 1984 resulted in the formation of a left-wing coalition government of the Forward and Eskimo Community parties, this being continued after the 1987 elections.

**Greenough, Horatio** (͵greenoh), 1805–52, American sculptor and writer. As a writer, he heralded modern concepts of functionalism in architecture. As a sculptor, he is famous for a colossal statue of George Washington (Smithsonian Inst.).

**Green Revolution,** popular term referring mainly to the large increases achieved in GRAIN production in certain underdeveloped areas especially India, Pakistan, and the Philippines in the late 1960s. It was accomplished through the use of high-yielding HYBRIDS, chemical FERTILIZERS, and new crop strategies and harvesting methods.

**Greensboro,** US city (1984 est. pop. 159,000), north-central North Carolina; settled 1749, inc. 1808. The state's second-largest city, it has an important textile industry, produces tobacco and machinery, and is a regional financial, insurance, and distribution centre. The Revolutionary War battle of Guilford Courthouse was fought nearby.

**Greenwich,** borough (1981 pop. 209,873) of Greater London, SE England, on the Thames R. The system of geographical longitude and time-keeping worked out at its old Royal Observatory (1675–1958) have become standard in most of the world; the prime meridian (zero longitude) passes through the observatory. Other points of interest are the Royal Naval College (begun 17th cent.), and the Queen's House (by Inigo JONES), now part of the National Maritime Museum.

**Greenwich Mean Time** (GMT): see SOLAR TIME.

**Greenwich meridian:** see PRIME MERIDIAN.

**Greenwich Village,** district of lower Manhattan, New York City, US. An influx of artists and freethinkers in the early 1900s established the area's reputation for bohemianism.

**Greer, Germaine,** 1939–, Australian writer and critic. Her study of female subordination *The Female Eunuch* (1970) was a lively influence on the emerging WOMEN'S MOVEMENT in Britain. Her other books include *The Obstacle Race: the Fortunes of Women Painters and their Work* (1979) and *Sex and Destiny* (1984).

**Gregorian chant:** see PLAINCHANT.

**Gregory, Lady Isabella Augusta (Perse),** 1859–1932, Irish dramatist, a founder and director of the Abbey Theatre, Dublin. Her plays include *Spreading the News* (1904), *The Gaol Gate* (1906), *The Rising of the Moon* (1907), and *The Workhouse Ward* (1908). Her partnership with W.B. YEATS extended to her assisting him as with *Cathleen Ni Houlihan* (1902) and *King Oedipus* (1928). Her *Our Irish Theatre* (1913) is a key document of the IRISH LITERARY RENAISSANCE.

**Gregory I, Saint** (Saint Gregory the Great), c.540–604, pope (590–604), Doctor of the Church. A Roman prefect, he became a monk and, although he resisted promotion, eventually pope. His rule was notable for the enforcement of papal supremacy and the establishment of the temporal position of the pope. He attacked Donatism in Africa, refused to recognize the title *ecumenical* of the patriarch of

Constantinople (an act that helped split East and West), and treated (592) with the invading LOMBARDS after the Byzantine exarch failed to defend Rome. Gregory encouraged monasticism, made laws for the lives of the clergy, and sent missionaries to England. His writings include letters, commentaries on the Book of Job, saints' lives, and *Pastoral Care*. He also contributed to the development of Gregorian chant or PLAINSONG. Feast: Sept. 3.

**Gregory VII, Saint,** 1020?–1085, pope (1073–85), an Italian named Hildebrand. A Benedictine, he became a notable figure under Pope Gregory VI and under LEO IX launched his reform programme, aimed at correcting the widespread corruption and laxity in the church. As chief figure in the curia under Leo's successors, he transferred the papal election from the Romans to the college of cardinals and formed an alliance with the Normans of S Italy. As pope he pressed his reforms by condemning clerical marriage, simony, and lay INVESTITURE, and he sent papal legates throughout Europe to enforce his actions. Opposition was widespread, and a powerful anti-reform party grew among laymen who feared church domination. In Germany, HENRY IV joined the antireform party and was excommunicated (1076) by Gregory. Losing support, Henry humbled himself before Gregory at Canossa, but in 1080 the two again fell out. Henry, again excommunicated, set up Guibert of Ravenna (Clement III) as antipope, and Gregory's appeal to the Christian world failed. When the German civil war ended, Henry marched into Italy and took Rome (1084). Gregory retired into the Castel Sant' Angelo until the Normans under ROBERT GUISCARD rescued him, then followed the Norman withdrawal and he died in Salerno after a year of exile. His reform was a turning point in church history. It elevated the moral level of the church and began the successful struggle against lay investiture. Feast: 25 May.

**Gregory IX,** 1155?–1241, pope (1227–41), an Italian named Ugolino di Segni and nephew of INNOCENT III. Elected at age 84, he excommunicated (1227) Emperor FREDERICK II for not undertaking a crusade. Imperialists in Rome revolted and forced Gregory into exile until 1230. In a dispute over Italian politics he again excommunicated (1239) Frederick and ordered him dethroned. Frederick blocked Gregory's call for a general council and was preparing to attack Rome when Gregory died at age 86.

**Gregory XI,** 1329–78, pope (1370–78), a Frenchman named Pierre Roger de Beaufort. After receiving prophetic admonitions from St Bridget of Sweden and St CATHERINE OF SIENA, he determined to move the papacy from Avignon back to Rome. But the Avignon court was opposed, and the papal states were in chaos. After sanctioning a foray into Italy by Robert of Geneva, Gregory returned to Rome (Jan. 1377), thus ending the Babylonian Captivity of the popes. The elections after his death began the Great SCHISM.

**Gregory XII,** c.1325–1417, pope (1406–15), a Venetian named Angelo Correr. Gregory negotiated with the Avignon antipope, Benedict XIII (see LUNA, PEDRO DE), to end the Great SCHISM, but failed, whereupon the Council of Pisa elected a second antipope. The Council of Constance accepted Gregory's resignation (1415), deposed the two antipopes, and elected MARTIN V pope (1417).

**Gregory XIII,** 1502–85, pope (1572–85), an Italian named Ugo Buoncompagni, best known for the reformed or Gregorian CALENDAR. He was prominent at the Council of TRENT (1545, 1559–63). As pope he proposed the deposition of Queen Elizabeth I of England and took an interest in the education of the clergy and the conversion of Protestants. He issued a new edition of the canon law and patronized the Jesuits.

**Gregory Nazianzen, Saint** (nayzee͵anzin), c.330–90, Cappadocian theologian, Doctor of the Church, one of the Four Fathers of the Greek Church. Active in the struggle against ARIANISM, he was recognized as bishop of Constantinople by the ecumenical council held there in 381, but retired before it concluded. Feast: 2 Jan. in the West; 25 and 30 Jan. in the East.

**Gregory of Tours, Saint,** 538–94, French historian, bishop of Tours (from 573). His masterpiece, *History of the Franks,* is a universal history with an important account of contemporary events. Feast: 17 Nov.

**Grenada** (gri͵naydə), island nation (1984 est. pop. 92,600), in the West Indies, consisting of the main island of Grenada (311 km²/120 sq mi), the southernmost of the Windward Islands, and the southern group of the sparsely settled archipelago known as the Grenadines. The capital and main port, Saint George's, is on Grenada, which is a volcanic, mountainous island on which bananas, sugar, coconuts, nutmeg and mace, cotton, and limes are grown for export. The GDP is US$87 million and the GDP per capita is US$938. The people, mainly blacks with some mulattos, speak English (the official language) together with a French patois. Settlement of Grenada, delayed by hostile Carib Indians, was begun by the French in 1650, but the island was taken over in 1783 by the British, who established sugar plantations and imported African slaves. Grenada became self-governing in 1967 and an independent state within the COMMONWEALTH in 1974. A coup in 1979 installed a Marxist government, headed by Maurice BISHOP of the New Jewel Movement (NJM), which established close relations with Cuba. In 1983 Bishop was overthrown and murdered by a more extreme NJM faction, whereupon US forces supported by small contingents from neighbouring Caribbean states landed on Grenada and quickly took control. Elections held in 1984 resulted in a victory for the (conservative) New National Party.

**grenade,** small bomb designed to be thrown by hand or shot from a modified rifle or a grenade launcher. It may be filled with gas or chemicals but more often holds an explosive charge that fractures the casing into lethal fragments. First used in the 15th cent. (by 'grenadiers'), the grenade later fell into disuse until the 20th cent., when it became a standard INFANTRY weapon.

**Grenfell, Sir Wilfred Thomason,** 1865–1940, English physician and missionary. After serving as missionary to North Sea fishermen, he spent over 40 years in Labrador and Newfoundland, building hospitals and nursing stations and establishing cooperative stores, agricultural centres, schools, libraries, and orphanages. He also opened (1912) a seamen's institute in Newfoundland.

**Grenoble,** city (1982 pop. 159, 503, agglomeration 392, 021), capital of Isère dept., SE France. A leading resort at the foot of the Alps and site of the 1968 winter Olympics, it is important for its nuclear-research centre, hydroelectric power, and science-based industries and research institutes, linked to the noted University of Grenoble (est. 1339). It passed from the dauphins of Viennois to the crown in 1349.

**Grenville, George,** 1712–70, British statesman. While prime minister (1763–65), he provoked reformers by his persecution of John WILKES and aroused opposition by his attempt to tax the American colonies internally through the STAMP ACT. His son **George Nugent Temple Grenville,** 1st **marquess of Buckingham,** 1753–1813, served as lord lieutenant of Ireland (1782–83, 1787–89). The latter's brother **William Wyndham Grenville, Baron Grenville,** 1759–1834, was foreign secretary to William PITT (1791–1801). In 1806 he formed the 'ministry of all talents', which abolished the slave trade (1807).

**Grenville, Sir Richard,** 1542?–91, English naval hero. In 1585 he commanded the fleet carrying the first colonists to ROANOKE ISLAND. On an expedition to capture Spanish treasure ships off the Azores in 1591, his ship, the *Revenge,* became separated from the rest of the fleet. He tried to break through the Spanish line, but he was mortally wounded and died in Spanish captivity.

**Gresham, Sir Thomas,** 1519?–1579, English merchant and financier. Founder of the Royal Exchange, he accumulated a great private fortune while serving as an adviser to ELIZABETH I. His name was given to **Gresham's law,** the economic principle (actually formulated long before his time) that 'bad money drives out good.' When depreciated, mutilated, or debased coinage (or currency) circulates concurrently with money of high value in terms of precious metals, the good money automatically disappears because of hoarding.

**Gresham's law:** see under GRESHAM, SIR THOMAS.

**Grettir's Saga,** Old Icelandic Saga (early 14th cent.), the last of the 'classical' SAGAS of Icelanders. Its protagonist, Grettir the Strong, is the most renowned outlaw in Icelandic history. He spent 19 years in outlawry, wandering all over Iceland in the desolate mountains and uninhabited valleys, until he was killed on a desert island off the north coast. The saga is rich in folkloristic tales of his superhuman strength and his fights with giants and supernatural beings. Above all, it is a tragic story of a man of outstanding gifts brought low by his failings and ill-fortune.

**Greuze, Jean-Baptiste** (grøz), 1725–1805, French genre and portrait painter. He is best known for his moralizing pictures, e.g., *The Broken Pitcher* (Louvre, Paris). His portraits, e.g., that of his wife (*The Milkmaid*), and J.G. Wille (1763; Musée Jacquemart-André, Paris), are more admired today.

**Greville, Sir Fulke, Lord Brooke,** 1554–1628, English courtier and poet. He was at Shrewsbury School with Sir Philip SIDNEY, to whom he proclaimed a lifelong devotion. His works include a *Life* of Sidney, two tragedies in the manner of Seneca, *Mustapha* and *Alaham,* a verse *Treatise on Monarchy* (1600?), and *Caelica,* a sequence of songs and lyrics initially imitative of his friend's *Astrophel and Stella,* but developing from the amatory to the reflective.

**Grevillea** (grevi,lyay·ə), Australian genus of shrubs and trees of the Protea family. With graceful, silvery foliage and beautiful flower clusters, *G. robusta,* the silky oak, is widely grown as an ornamental.

**Grévy, Jules,** 1807–91, president of France (1879–87). He opposed the Second Empire of NAPOLEON III. A moderate republican, he resigned as president because of a scandal over his son-in-law's traffic in decorations of honour.

**Grey, Charles Grey, 2nd Earl,** 1764–1835, British statesman. In 1806 he became foreign secretary in the 'ministry of all talents' and WHIG leader of the House of Commons, putting through the measure to abolish the slave trade (1807). A lifelong supporter of parliamentary reform, he became prime minister (1830–34), and secured the passage of the REFORM BILL of 1832 by threatening to force WILLIAM IV to create enough Whig peers to carry it in the House of Lords. His grandson, **Albert Henry George Grey, 4th Earl Grey,** 1851–1917, was a Liberal member of the House of Commons (1880–86). Later he was a successful governor general of Canada (1904–11), and was foreign secretary at the beginning of World War I.

**Grey, Sir George,** 1812–98, British colonial administrator. He was governor of South Australia (1841–45), New Zealand (1845–53), and the Cape Colony (1854–60). Recalled to New Zealand as governor (1861–68), he failed to halt warfare between English settlers and MAORI natives. He was later premier (1877–79) of New Zealand.

**Grey, Lady Jane,** 1537–54, queen of England for nine days; grandniece of HENRY VIII. She was married to the son of the duke of Northumberland, who persuaded EDWARD VI to make her his successor. She was proclaimed queen in 1553, but the English people rallied behind MARY I and Jane was imprisoned. Her life might have been spared, but her father, the duke of Suffolk, joined Thomas Wyatt's rebellion, and she was beheaded.

**greyhound racing,** trials of speed in which greyhounds, which possess not only speed and keen sight but the instincts to chase and a poor sense of smell, pursue a mechanically controlled hare round a circular or oval track. Races are usually between five or six animals over distances between 210 m (230 yd) for the sprint and 1097 m (1200 yd) for the marathon, and can be on the flat or over hurdles. An artificial hare was first used in 1876. Betting plays a large part in the sport, which is popular worldwide.

**Griboyedov, Aleksandr Sergeyevich** ('griboy,aydəv), 1795–1829, Russian writer. His best-known work is the verse comedy, *Woe from Wit* (1822–24), in which he gives a satirical picture of Moscow society. Although closely linked with revolutionary circles, he had a brilliant career as a diplomat. After Russia's victory in the war with Persia (1828) he led a mission to Teheran, where he was murdered by a mob storming the Russian Legation.

**Grieg, Edvard Hagerup** (greeg), 1843–1907, Norwegian composer who developed a strongly nationalistic style. He founded (1867) the Norwegian Academy of Music. His best-known works are the Concerto in A Minor for piano and orchestra (1868); the CANTATA *Olav Trygvason* (1873); the SUITE of incidental dramatic music, *Peer Gynt* (1874); and settings of Norwegian FOLK SONGS.

**Grien, Hans Baldung:** see BALDUNG, HANS.

**Griffenfeld, Peder Schumacher, Count,** 1635–99, Danish politician. As secretary to FREDERICK III he drew up (1665) a law making the monarchy absolute. His power under CHRISTIAN V was resented by the army and nobles, who had him sentenced to death for treason, a sentence changed to life imprisonment by the king.

**griffin,** in ancient and medieval legend, creature with an eagle's head and wings and a lion's body. Originating in Middle Eastern legend, it is often found in Persian art. It is thought to have symbolized strength and vigilance.

**Griffith, Arthur,** 1872–1922, Irish statesman, founder of SINN FEIN. Through his newspaper, the *United Irishmen,* he advocated the creation of an Irish assembly. He was the first president (1922) of the Irish Free State.

**Griffith, D(avid) W(ark)**, 1875–1948, American film director. A cinematic genius, he innovated cross-cutting, close-ups, long shots, moving-camera shots, and flashbacks in such films as *The Birth of a Nation* (1915) and *Intolerance* (1916).

**Grillparzer, Franz** (ˌgrilpahtsə), 1791–1872, Austrian dramatist. He wrote a wide range of highly performable dramas on classical and historical themes: *Sappho* (1819); *The Golden Fleece* (1820); *König Ottokars Glück und Ende* (1825; tr. King Ottokar's Rise and Fall); *Des Meeres und der Liebe Wellen* (1831; tr. Hero and Leander); but from 1840, under pressure from censorship and personal inhibition, he wrote nothing for the public stage. After his death, three major plays, unpublished, were found among his papers: *Die Jüdin von Toledo*, *Brothers' Rivalry in Habsburg*, and *Libussa*. A sardonic diarist, Grillparzer was a grim observer of the muted Biedermeier public scene.

**Grimké, Angelina Emily**, 1805–79, and **Grimké, Sarah Moore**, 1792–1873, American abolitionists and feminists. Sisters from an aristocratic slaveholding family, they were converted to the Quaker faith, moved north, and became the first women to speak publicly on the issues of slavery and women's rights. Angelina became a persuasive orator, and Sarah published influential works on abolition (1836) and the equality of the sexes (1838).

**Grimm, Jakob**, 1785–1863, German philologist and folklorist, a founder of comparative philology. Apart from his study of Germanic languages (see GRIMM'S LAW) and his writings on German grammar and mythology, he is best known for the collection of folk tales known as *Grimm's Fairy Tales* (1812–15), compiled with his brother, **Wilhelm Grimm**, 1786–1859.

**Grimmelshausen, Hans Jakob Christoffel von** ('grim.əlsˌhow'sən), 1622–76, German novelist. He served in the THIRTY YEARS' WAR, which provides the setting for much of his picaresque novel *The Adventures of Simplicius Simplicissimus in German* (1669, tr. 1964), the first modern realistic portrayal of an age, and at the same time a Baroque moral and satirical allegory of man in the world. He also wrote a number of related fictions, including *The Full Account of the Marvellous Strange Life of the Sturdy Vagrant and Queen of Cozeners Courasche* (1670, tr. *Mother Courage* 1965). A racy story-teller from dark times, Grimmelshausen has been rediscovered by such modern writers as Bertolt BRECHT and Günter GRASS.

**Grimm's law**, principle of relationships in Indo-European languages, first formulated by Jakob GRIMM in 1822. It demonstrates that the regular shifting of consonants in groups took place once in the development of English and the other Low German languages, and twice in German and the other High German languages. Thus the unaspirated voiceless stops *(k, t, p)* of the ancient, or classical, Indo-European languages (Sanskrit, Greek, Latin) became voiceless aspirates *(h, th, f)* in English and mediae *(h, d, f)* in German; unaspirated voiced stops *(g, d, b)* became voiceless stops *(k, t, p)* in English and voiceless aspirates *(kh, ts, f)* in German; and aspirated voiced stops *(gh, dh, bh)* became unaspirated voiced stops *(g, d, b)* in English and voiceless stops *(k, t, p)* in German.

**Grimsby**, town (1981 pop. 91,532), in Humberside, E England, on the North Sea at the mouth of the R. HUMBER. It is a fishing port and an important centre for the North Sea fishing industry. In 1984 Grimsby and the nearby port of IMMINGHAM handled 26.9 million tonnes of fish. Other industries include flour milling and the importing of timber.

**Gris, Juan** (grees), 1887–1927, Spanish cubist painter; b. José Victoriáno Gonzalez. A developer of synthetic CUBISM, he produced paintings of simple forms that reflect an architectonic design. His later works received a more sumptuous, decorative treatment and included collages or fragments of mirror, etc.

**Grolier de Servières, Jean, vicomte d'Aguisy**, 1479–1565, French bibliophile. Of his collection of some 3000 finely bound books, about 350 are known to be in existence, many in the Bibliothèque nationale.

**Gromyko, Andrei Andreyevich** (grəmeekoh), 1909–, Soviet statesman and head of state (1985–88). After such appointments as ambassador to the US (1943–46), he became foreign minister in 1957, holding the post for an unparalleled 28 years during which he presided over a measure of East-West DÉTENTE. A member of the Soviet Communist

Party's politburo from 1973, he was elected chairman of the Supreme Soviet's Presidium (i.e., head of state) in 1985 on the nomination of the new party leader, Mikhail GORBACHEV, who replaced him in that post three years later.

**Gronchi, Giovanni** (ˌgrohnkee), 1887–1978, Italian politician. He broke (1922) with MUSSOLINI. A founder of the Christian Democratic Party, he was minister for commerce, industry, and labour (1944–46); speaker of the chamber of deputies (1948–55); and president of Italy (1955–62).

**Groningen** (ˌgronigən), city (1985 pop. 168,119), Groningen prov., N Netherlands. A market and service centre, its industries include textiles and clothing. Following the discovery of oil and gas fields, it has become the focus since 1960 of a large natural-gas industry, supplying a number of other European countries. It has been a university town since the early 17th cent

**Gropius, Walter** (ˌgrohpeeoos), 1883–1969, American architect; b. Germany. He was a leader of modern functional architecture. In Germany his glass-wall Fagus factory buildings (1910–11) at Alfeld were among the most advanced works in Europe. In 1918 he became director of the Weimar School of Art and reorganized it as the BAUHAUS. He designed (1926) a complete new set of buildings for it in Dessau, as well as the Staattheater in Jena (1923), residences, and industrial buildings. The village college at Impington, near Cambridge, is his best-known work in England. In the US after 1937, he taught at Harvard until 1952.

**Grosseteste, Robert** (ˌgrohstest), c.1175–1253, English prelate. A founder of the Oxford Franciscan school, he made Oxford a centre of learning. As bishop (1235) of Lincoln, he resisted the efforts of HENRY III to control church appointments and supported the reforms of Simon de MONTFORT. He also censured Pope INNOCENT IV for excessive exactions and for appointing foreigners to English benefices. His writings include treatises on the sciences, pastoral works, and poems; they place him somewhat apart from the SCHOLASTICISM of THOMAS AQUINAS and ALBERTUS MAGNUS.

**gross national product (GNP)**, total market value of a nation's total output of goods and services in a given period, usually one year. The GNP, a closely watched barometer of the national economic performance includes only the final value of a product (e.g., cars, but not the steel that they contain). The four major components of GNP are consumer purchases, private investment, government spending and trade. If income from overseas investments is excluded gross domestic product remains, which measure is commonly used in developing countries.

**Grosz, George** (grohs), 1893–1959, German–American painter; b. Germany. Grosz's early works depict the horrors of life in Berlin in World War I. In 1919 he became a founder member of the German Communist Party. A reading of MARX led him to develop a strategy for a poletarian art form that could participate in the class struggle. This relied upon caricature and satire and resulted in highly critical prints and paintings of the corruption of German bourgeois society. Series of lithographs were also published to help raise class consciousness, e.g., the *Ecce Homo* portfolio of 1923. By the later 1920s and the reestablishment of the German art market Grosz's work became less explicitly Marxist and he increasingly looked towards American culture for escape. He became a US citizen in 1938 and painted traditional landscapes and figures. Deeply affected by the horrors of World War II, he created a symbolic series of ravaged figures, e.g., *Street Scene* (Philadelphia Mus. Art).

**Grotius, Hugo** (ˌgrohshəs), 1583–1645, Dutch jurist and humanist. His *Concerning the Law of War and Peace* (1625) is considered the first definitive text on INTERNATIONAL LAW. Drawing on the Bible and on classical history, Grotius argued that natural law prescribes rules of conduct for nations, as for individuals. While not condemning all war, he maintained that only certain causes justified it, and he devoted much attention to the concept of more humane warfare.

**ground-effect machine:** see HOVERCRAFT.

**ground squirrel**, member of the SQUIRREL family found on or under the ground in Africa, in North America (where they are called prairie dogs, chipmunks, and gophers), and in Eurasia (where they are called susliks and spermophiles). Ground squirrels are between 20 and 80 cm (8 to 31 in) long, coloured greyish, some with lighter coloured spots, others with darker stripes. Their tails may be bushy, but not as bushy as those of tree

George **Grosz**, *The face of the Ruling Class*, Berlin (1921).

squirrels. They are omnivorous, but will also eat carrion. Some burrow, others shelter in hollow logs or trees. The MARMOT is a ground squirrel.

**group,** in mathematics, a collection of elements $x, y, z, \ldots$, which has an operation, o, such that (1) $xoy$ is uniquely defined and belongs to the group; (2) the associative law holds; (3) there is an identity element (element that does not change another element of the set when combined with it by addition, multiplication, etc.); and (4) every element has an inverse. An example of a group is the rational numbers under multiplication. The concept of groups is applicable to many physical phenomena, such as the symmetry of crystals and the relations between subatomic particles.

**grouper,** large, carnivorous FISH of the sea BASS family, abundant in tropical and subtropical seas and highly valued as food. Most have bright markings that change in colour and pattern to match the background. The largest is the Queensland grouper (*Epinephelus lanceolatus*) which grows to 3.5 m (12 ft) in length, and is reported to stalk divers.

**Group of 77,** pressure group set up (1964) to defend the interests of developing countries, particularly within the framework of the UNITED NATIONS. By 1988 the group's original 77 member countries had increased to 120.

**group therapy:** see PSYCHOTHERAPY.

**grouse,** henlike terrestrial BIRD of the family Tetraonidae, found in the colder parts of the Northern Hemisphere. It is protectively plumaged in reds, browns, and greys. The males have elaborate courting dances. They are popular game birds, the red grouse, *Lagopus lagopus scoticus*, being protected during its breeding season on the British grouse moors along with the black grouse, *Lyrurus tetrix*, which lives in the scrub at the edge of moorlands. The ptarmigan (*Lagopus mutus*) is an arctic species that migrates south in winter, when its rusty brown plumage changes to white.

**Grove, Sir George,** 1820–1900, English engineer and writer on music. His *Dictionary of Music and Musicians* (1879–89; 6th ed. 1980) became a standard reference work.

**Grundtvig, Nikolai Frederik Severin** (‚groohntvig), 1783–1872, Danish writer, churchman, and educator. He founded the folk high school, a form of adult education designed to foster patriotism and religious conviction in young adults. His many literary works include the epoch-making *Northern Mythology* (1808), a loose retelling of the Old Norse myths. In his poems, songs, and hymns, he treated historical, mythological, and religious subjects.

**Grünewald, Mathias** (‚grynəvalt), c.1470–1528, German religious painter; b. Mathis Gothart Neithart. Possessed of unique expressive power, he used stylistic components such as silhouette and unusual colour, the striking contrast of light and shadow, and the exaggeration of the human form to convey anguish and terror. His most frequent subject was the crucifixion of Christ, and his masterpiece is the *Isenheim Altarpiece* (1515; Colmar, France).

Mathias **Grünewald**, *The Crucifixion from the Isenheim Altarpiece*, 1515. Colmar, France.

**grunion:** see WHITEBAIT.

**Guadalajara,** city (1980 est. pop. 2,000,000), SW Mexico, capital of Jalisco state. A spacious, beautiful city (called the 'Pearl of the West'), it is Mexico's second-largest city. Although it is a modern metropolis with varied manufactures, it retains many old colonial buildings notably a cathedral and a governor's palace. Its location on a plain more than 1500 m (5000 ft) high and its mild, dry climate have made it a popular health resort. Founded c.1530, Guadalajara was a centre of the movement for independence from Spain. It has suffered several earthquakes.

**Guadalcanal,** island c.6500 km² (2510 sq mi), in the SW Pacific Ocean, largest of the SOLOMON ISLANDS and site of the national capital, Honiara. The largely mountainous and forested island is of volcanic origin. Coconuts are grown, and some gold is mined. In bitter fighting during WORLD WAR II, US forces seized (1942–43) the island and its airstrip, Henderson Field, from Japanese troops.

**Guadalquivir,** river, c.670 km (420 mi) long, in S Spain. Rising in the Sierra de Cazoria, it flows SW across the plain of ANDALUSIA, to enter the Atlantic Ocean below the marshy area of LAS MARISMAS. The principal cities along its length are CORDOBA and SEVILLE, the latter reached by small sea-going vessels. Extensive flood control and irrigation works have been carried out for cotton and other crops.

**Guadalupe Hidalgo, Treaty of,** 1848, peace treaty between the US and Mexico that ended the MEXICAN WAR. It confirmed US claims to TEXAS, and Mexico ceded most of the present SW US for $15 million and the assumption by the US government of claims against Mexico by American citizens.

**Guadalupe Victoria**, 1786?–1843, first president of MEXICO (1824–29); b. Manuel Félix Fernández. A general, he fought against Spanish rule, and after Mexican independence (1821) he and SANTA ANNA overthrew the ITURBIDE regime. His administration was marred by factional strife.

**Guadeloupe**, overseas department of France (1982 pop. 327,000), 1779 km² (687 sq mi), in the Leeward Islands; comprising Basse-Terre, Grande-Terre, and smaller islands. Discovered (1493) by Columbus, it was settled (17th cent.) by the French, who eliminated the native Caribs, imported African slaves, and made it a major sugar producer. Tourism, bananas, and coffee are important. It became a French department in 1946. Agitation for independence, sometimes violent, developed in the 1970s, but pro-independence parties have made little electoral impact.

**Guadiana**, river, 815 km (510 mi) long, flowing across central Spain from its source in the Campos de Montiel. Below BADAJOZ it forms the frontier with Portugal for part of its length to the Gulf of Cadiz.

**Guam**, island (1980 pop. 105,821), 541 km² (209 sq mi), W Pacific, southernmost of the Marianas islands; an unincorporated US territory. Agana is the seat of government. Guam is tropical and partly mountainous. Discovered (1521) by MAGELLAN, it belonged to Spain until it was surrendered to the US in 1898. A major military base, Guam was occupied by the Japanese from 1941 to 1944. Military installations provide much employment, and subsistence agriculture is practised. There is growing tourism and some light industry. Guamanians, who are chiefly of Chamorros (mixed Spanish, Filipino, and Micronesian) stock, are US citizens but cannot vote in US elections. Administered by the US Dept. of the Interior, Guam has an appointed governor and an elected legislature.

**Guanajuato**, city (1979 est. pop. 45,000), central Mexico, capital of Guanajuato state. Until this century it was the second largest city in Mexico. Founded in 1554 its wealth and importance was closely associated with the nearby Valenciana silver mine, for long the world's richest. Its early opulence is reflected in the city's many fine colonial churches and public buildings and one of these, the Alhóndiga, is associated with Spanish resistance to the uprising led by Father Hidalgo in 1810. Today the city is an important centre for tourism and for international cultural festivals.

**Guangdong** or **Kwangtung**, province (1985 est. pop. 62,530,000), 212,000 km² (81,853 sq mi), SE China, having a long coastal section bordering the South China Sea. The capital is GUANGZHOU (Canton); other major cities are Foshan and SHANTOU. Physically, the land is a mixture of mountains, hills, and valleys. The extensive delta and basin of the Pearl R. (see XI JIANG) are agriculturally important; the city of Guangzhou lies on the northern edge of the delta. A long growing season and high moisture makes this area an important subtropical producer of rice (which is double or even triple cropped), wheat, sweet potatoes, and sugarcane. Tea, tobacco, and peanuts are grown on the higher and sandier areas. HAINAN island is developing as a significant producer of tropical crops including bananas, coffee, and natural rubber. The extensive coastline provides a fishing catch of about one-quarter of the national total. Though there are sources of nonferrous minerals, including tungsten and iron shale, industrialization has been hampered by lack of coal and poor communications with the rest of China. As China's links with the outside world increase, so foreign investment is supplementing the traditional light industry in Guangzhou and elsewhere. Shenzhen, China's first 'special economic zone', lies in the province's coastal area and HONG KONG, though still officially a British colony adjacent to Guangdong, is effectively the primary territory of the province. The importance of the province's coastal region may increase if oil exploration in the South China Sea is successful and the disputes over its ownership (with Vietnam and other states) can be resolved.

**Guangxi Zhuang** or **Kwangsi Chuang Autonomous Region** (gwong see jwong), autonomous region (1985 est. pop. 38,730,00), 236,275 km² (91,225 sq mi), China, W of GUANGDONG prov. and bordering Vietnam (SW). Major cities are Nanning, the capital, and Guilin. Much of the land is hilly and mountainous and rivers have cut through the karst topography as they flow southwards to the sea. The climate ranges from tropical in the south to subtropical in the north, and rainfall is generally heavy. The northern hill lands are generally forested,

except for the narrow valleys which are largely given over to rice-growing. In the Southeast of the province two or three crops of rice can be grown and sugarcane is an important crop. The coast has a traditional fishing industry. Despite a wide variety of mineral deposits, including tin and manganese, poor communications have limited industrial development in the region. It is, however, developing as an important tourist area centred around Guilin and the Li R. Guangxi Zhuang was a late southern frontier of Chinese settlement, established as Chinese settlers migrated southwards from their origins around the central YELLOW RIVER. Demographically, these origins are reflected in the large numbers of non-Han Chinese or minority peoples, who total c.15 million, or 40% of the total population. They include the Zhuang people, who are related to the Thai people and live mainly in the west of the province. They are China's largest ethnic minority but through long association with Han Chinese have taken on many Chinese customs.

**Guangzhou** or **Canton**, city (1984 pop. 6,990,000), capital of GUANGDONG prov., SE China, and a major deepwater port on the XI JIANG (Pearl) R. delta. Among the largest cities in the country, Guangzhou is the transport, industrial, and trade centre of S China. It has shipyards, a steel-making complex, and factories producing many heavy and light industrial products. Its principal exports are textiles, paper, cement, and sugar. It has a large international airport and is linked with Hong Kong by the Guangzhou–Kowloon railway and by hovercraft. A modernized electrified railway links Guangzhou with the SHENZHEN special economic zone. Guangzhou became a part of China in the 3rd cent. BC and was later the first Chinese port regularly visited by European traders. The British gunboats attacked the city in the 1840 Opium War; it became one of five Chinese ports opened to foreign trade. The seat (1911) of Sun Yat-Sen's revolutionary movement, Guangzhou was a Nationalist centre in the 1920s and its fall (1949) to Communist armies signalled the Communist victory in all of China. It is a major marketplace for China's foreign trade, and for foreign investment in S China. Its proximity to Hong Kong and the biannual trade fair are central to its success in obtaining foreign contacts.

**guano**, a substance consisting chiefly of the excrement of sea birds. It is rich in nitrogen, phosphates, and potassium, and is used as a fertilizer. There are important deposits on islands off the coasts of Peru and Chile.

**Guantánamo**, city (1981 pop. 167,405), SE Cuba, in Oriente prov. Founded in the 19th cent. by Frenchmen from Haiti, it is now a sugar-processing centre. It is c.32 km (20 mi) inland from its port, Caimanera, on well-protected **Guantánamo Bay**, which is also the site of a large US naval station established in 1903. Since the revolution of 1959, Cuba has refused to accept the token annual US rent for the naval base and has pressed for its surrender.

**Guaraní Indians**, people in N and E South America (see SOUTH AMERICAN INDIANS) of the Tupi–Guaraní linguistic stock (see AMERICAN INDIAN LANGUAGES). Those who live in S Brazil and Paraguay are called Guaraní; those in the Amazon region are called Tupí or Tupinambá. At the time of the Spanish conquest (16th cent.) communities of both groups had a chief and a powerful SHAMAN. The Guaraní grew maize and manioc. In ancient times they practised ritual CANNIBALISM. Although their material culture was not advanced, they had a rich body of folklore. Early Jesuit missionaries founded among them the agricultural settlements called reductions, using Indian labour under the absolute, but usually benevolent, rule of priests. Guaraní is widely spoken in Paraguay; most Tupí have been assimilated into European culture.

**Guardi, Francesco** (,gwahdee), 1712–93, Venetian painter of landscapes and architectural scenes. A follower of CANALETTO, he developed a freer style. His work ranges from architectural scenes to delightful, spontaneous *capricci* (fantastical scenes).

**Guardia, Tomás** (,gwahdeeah), 1832–82, president of COSTA RICA. He led an army revolt and largely ruled the country from 1870 to 1882. Although basically a military strong man, he laid the foundation for the country's stability.

**guardian and ward**, in law, relationship in which one person (the guardian) is entrusted with protecting the rights and interests of another person considered legally incompetent (the ward). The ward is commonly a child, an insane person, or a spendthrift. A guardian may be natural (such as a parent), appointed by will, or chosen by a court. The same person is usually, but not necessarily, guardian of both the person and PROPERTY of the ward.

**Guarnieri, Giuseppe,** 1698–1744, Italian VIOLIN maker, heir to the tradition of his home town of Cremona (see AMATI) where his father and uncle also made violins. His workmanship is not as fine as that of STRADIVARI, but the powerful tone of his violins makes them even more highly prized by many soloists.

**Guatemala,** officially Republic of Guatemala, republic (1987 est. pop. 8,700,000), 108,889 km² (42,042 sq mi), Central America; bordered by Mexico (N and W), Belize and the Caribbean Sea (E), Honduras and El Salvador (SE), and the Pacific Ocean (SW). The capital is GUATEMALA CITY. A highland region occupies the southern half of the country and is the most densely populated area. Much of northern Guatemala is covered by a vast tropical forest, the Petén. Coffee accounts for more than half of the nation's revenue. Cotton (which superseded bananas in the economy in the 1930s), vegetables, fruit, and beef are also exported, and industry is being expanded. In 1983 GDP was US$8720 million or US$1245 per capita. The mainly Roman Catholic population is about evenly divided between Maya Indians and mestizos. The language is Spanish, although many Indians speak only Indian dialects. The literacy rate and per capita income are extremely low.

*History.* After defeat of the Quiché (MAYA) Indians in 1523–24, Spain established a prosperous colony in the area, with its capital (from 1542) at ANTIGUA. After independence (1821), Guatemala became the nucleus of the CENTRAL AMERICAN FEDERATION and, after dissolution of the federation in 1839, a separate republic. Ruled through the 19th cent. by a series of usually repressive dictators, Guatemala alternated in the 20th cent. between economic reform and reaction. A conservative coup in 1954 owed its success to US military intervention. From 1970 the country was dominated by conservative military elements in an atmosphere of terrorism by the right and the left, punctuated by right-wing military coups in 1963, 1982, and 1983, the last of which brought Gen. Oscar Humberto Mejía Victores to power. He called general elections in 1986 which resulted in Vinicio Cerezo (Christian Democrat) being returned as the country's first civilian president since 1970.

Guatemala

**Guatemala City,** city (1981 pop. 754,243), S central Guatemala, capital of Guatemala. The largest city in Central America, it is the nation's commercial and industrial centre, with a cosmopolitan atmosphere and many modern public buildings, as well as Spanish colonial structures and large Indian markets. It was constructed in a highland valley in 1779, after the former capital, ANTIGUA, was destroyed by earthquakes. Guatemala City itself suffered that fate in 1917–18 and has since been completely rebuilt.

**guava,** small evergreen tree or shrub (genus *Psidium*) of the MYRTLE family, native to tropical America and grown for its ornamental flowers and edible fruit. Species include the common tropical guava (*P. guajava*) and the strawberry guava (*P. cattleyanum*). The guava is grown commercially in Florida and California and is made into jellies and beverages.

**Guayaquil,** city (1982 pop. 1,300,868), capital of Guayas prov., W Ecuador, on the Guayas R. near its mouth on the Gulf of Guayaquil, an inlet of the Pacific Ocean. It is the commercial and administrative centre of Ecuador's major region of commercial agriculture. It is Ecuador's largest city and its chief port and manufacturing centre. Founded by Sebastián de Benalcázar in 1535, it was liberated from Spain by Antonio José de SUCRE in 1821, and in 1822 was the site of a meeting between Simón BOLÍVAR and José de SAN MARTÍN that determined the course of South American independence. The climate is hot and humid, and yellow fever was a problem until the early 20th cent.

**Gudrun** or **Kudrun** (ˌgoohdroon, ˌkooh), in Germanic literature. **1** Heroine of the Volsungasaga. **2** Heroine of a Middle High German epic influenced by the Nibelungenlied (see NIBELUNGEN). **3** Principal character of the Icelandic *Laxdaelasaga.*

**Guelphs** (gwelfs), German dynasty of the Middle Ages. It traced its descent from the Swabian count Guelph, or Welf, in the 9th cent. Eventually the Guelphs became the dukes of Bavaria and Saxony, and were the rivals of the house of HOHENSTAUFEN. In Italy, the dynasty was represented by the ESTE family. The Guelphs came to represent the papal faction in the longtime struggle between the GUELPHS AND GHIBELLINES.

**Guelphs and Ghibellines** (ˌgibiˈlienz), opposing political factions in Germany and Italy in the later Middle Ages. The names were used to designate the papal (Guelph) party and the imperial (Ghibelline) party during the long struggle between the papacy and the emperors; they also designated two rival German families, the Welfs or GUELPHS, and the HOHENSTAUFEN. In Germany the rivalry began under Emperor HENRY IV and last flared at the election of Emperor OTTO IV. In Italy the terms were used from the 13th to the 15th cent., and the rival factions plunged the country into internal warfare. Among the Ghibellines were EZZELINO DA ROMANO and the VISCONTI family of Milan. Milan itself was Guelph, as were, generally, Florence and Genoa. Cremona, Pisa, and Arezzo were usually Ghibelline. Venice remained neutral.

**Guercino, Il** or **Giovanni Francesco Barbieri** (gweə,theeno), 1591–1666, Italian painter. He came from Cento, near Bologna. In 1621 Pope Gregory XV summoned him to Rome; over the next two years he produced a series of major works, amongst them the *Burial of St Petronilla* (1622–23; Capitoline Mus., Rome) and the ceiling fresco *Aurora* (1623) in the garden villa of the Cardinal Ludovisi. These works, with their rich, deep colours, surging diagonal movement, and flickering patterns of light and shade, look on to the Roman high BAROQUE. Later Guercino worked at Cento and Bologna, and his style became duller and more classical.

**Guernica** (geər,neeka), town (1981 pop. 17,836), Vizcaya prov., N Spain. A small market centre, it was the place where councils of the Basque peoples were once held. The bombing of Guernica by German planes in 1937 (see SPANISH CIVIL WAR) inspired the famous painting by PICASSO.

**Guernsey:** see CHANNEL ISLANDS.

**Guerrero, Vicente** (gay,rayroh), 1782–1831, Mexican revolutionary leader. He won guerrilla victories over Spanish forces but accepted ITURBIDE's conservative leadership of the Mexican independence movement. He and SANTA ANNA led (1828) a successful revolt against Iturbide, and Guerrero served briefly (1829) as president, but he was forced to retreat and was finally captured and shot.

**guerrilla warfare,** fighting by groups of irregular troops (guerrillas), usually in enemy-held territory. Tactics stress sabotage, unpredictable hit-and-run attacks, and ambush rather than mass confrontation. Guerrilla strategy often relies on a sympathetic population, sometimes won over by propaganda. Such tactics were developed during the American Revolution, but the term *guerrilla* was first applied to Spanish partisans in the PENINSULAR WAR (1808–14). Guerrilla warfare has played an important part in almost every major conflict since that time, e.g., resistance movements in Nazi-occupied Europe in WORLD WAR II, such as the *maquis* in France. It has increasingly been used in peacetime by nationalist groups to challenge governments in power, e.g., Al Fatah, in the Middle East (see PALESTINE LIBERATION ORGANIZATION); the South-West

African People's Organization (SWAPO), in NAMIBIA; and the IRISH REPUBLICAN ARMY provisionals. In many cases such 'nationalists' are manipulated by governments outside a country in order to subvert a legitimate elected regime, e.g., the US support for the Contras in Nicaragua or South Africa's for UNITA in Angola. Notable guerrilla leaders have included Fidel CASTRO; Ernesto ('Che') GUEVARA; Thomas Edward LAWRENCE; and MAO ZEDONG, often called the leading guerrilla theorist in the 20th cent. Such modern 'urban guerrilla' activities as hijacking, KIDNAPPING, and the planting of bombs, are often tinged with elements of TERRORISM.

**Gueux** (gø), [Fr., = beggars], 16th-cent. Dutch revolutionary group. In 1566 over 2000 nobles and burghers vowed to resist Spanish repression in the NETHERLANDS. Called 'these beggars' at the court of the Spanish regent, MARGARET OF PARMA, they adopted the subriquet. The 'Beggars of the Sea', crews of Dutch privateers chartered in 1569 by WILLIAM THE SILENT to harass Spanish shipping, raised the siege of LEIDEN in 1574.

**Guevara, Che (Ernesto)**, 1928–67, Cuban revolutionary leader; b. Argentina. A physician and political activist, he became (1956) Fidel CASTRO's chief lieutenant and a guerrilla leader in the victorious Cuban revolution (1959). He served as minister of industry (1961–65), then left Cuba to foster revolutions in other countries. He was killed in Bolivia.

**Guggenheim**, family of American industrialists and philanthropists. **Meyer Guggenheim**, 1828–1905; b. Switzerland, emigrated (1847) to the US and prospered as a merchant in Philadelphia. Seven sons Isaac, Daniel, Murry, Solomon, Benjamin, Simon, and William contributed to the expansion of the family enterprises. **Simon Guggenheim**, 1867–1941, established (1925), with his wife, the John Simon Guggenheim Memorial Foundation to assist scholars, writers, and artists. **Solomon Robert Guggenheim**, 1861–1949, created a foundation that established (1937) the SOLOMON R. GUGGENHEIM MUSEUM.

**Guggenheim Museum:** see SOLOMON R. GUGGENHEIM MUSEUM.

**Guicciardini, Francesco** (gweetchah,deenee), 1483–1540, Italian historian and statesman. He served in the Florentine government and Pope LEO X before taking up writing. Breaking with medieval tradition, he removed history from the realm of literature and related it to the development of states. His history of Italy (1492–1534) is the masterwork of Italian historical literature of the RENAISSANCE.

**guide dog**, dog trained to lead a blind person. Guide dogs were first trained to lead blinded ex-servicemen in Germany in 1916. The training was further developed in the US, and schools to train such dogs now exist in several countries. In the UK the Guide Dogs for the Blind Association, founded in 1934, is a registered charity. The breeds most commonly used are the Labrador, the German shepherd, and the golden retriever.

**Guidi, Tommaso:** see MASACCIO.

**Guido Reni:** see RENI, GUIDO.

**Guildford**, county town (1981 pop. 61,509), of Surrey, SE England, on R. Wey, 43 km (27 mi) SW of London. It is a market town. There are the remains of a Norman castle keep within the town. A new cathedral was completed in 1936, and the Univ. of Surrey (founded 1966) is situated to the NW of the town centre. It was a royal borough in the Middle Ages.

**guilds or gilds**, economic and social associations of persons engaged in the same business or craft, typical of Western Europe in the Middle Ages. Membership was never by class but by profession or trade. The primary function of guilds was to establish local control over a profession or craft by setting standards of workmanship and price, by protecting the business from competition, and by gaining status in society for guild members. Merchant guilds in some cases developed into intercity leagues for the promotion of trade, such as the medieval HANSEATIC LEAGUE. By the 17th cent. the power of the guilds had withered in England. They were abolished in France in 1791 and elsewhere in Western Europe during the 19th cent.

**guild socialism**, form of socialism in Great Britain, hostile to the state and parliamentary politics, that advocated industrial self-government through national worker-controlled guilds. The theory originated (1906) with Arthur J. Penty, who sought to revive the spirit of medieval craft guilds and argued that workers should strive for control of industry rather than for political reform. Several guilds were started, but the movement ended after an unsuccessful attempt to take over the FABIAN SOCIETY and the

collapse (1922) of the National Building Guild, its most powerful component.

**Guilford, Frederick North, 2nd earl of:** see NORTH, FREDERICK.

**Guillén, Jorge** (geel,yayn), 1893–1984, Spanish poet. He settled in the US in 1939. His difficult, classic verse appears in *Cántico* (1928), *Clamor* (1957), and *Affirmation: A Bilingual Anthology* (1968). He also wrote *Language and Poetry* (1961).

**Guinea**, Fr. *Guinée,* officially People's Revolutionary Republic of Guinea, republic (1986 est. pop. 6,000,000), 245,856 km² (94,925 sq mi), W Africa, bordered by Guinea-Bissau, Senegal, and Mali (N), Côte d'Ivoire (E), Sierra Leone and Liberia (S), and the Atlantic Ocean (W). CONAKRY is the capital. A humid and tropical country, Guinea comprises an alluvial coastal plain; the mountainous Fouta Jallon region; a savanna interior; and the forested Guinea Highlands, which rise to c.1770 m (5800 ft) in the Nimba Mts. Guinea is predominantly agricultural. Coffee, bananas, palm kernels, and pineapples are the leading cash crops; the main subsistence crop is rice. Some of the world's largest bauxite deposits lie in Guinea, the world's third largest producer; iron ore, gold, and diamonds are also mined. Poor transportation has hampered industrialization. Most sectors of the economy are under state control. The GNP is US$1696 million, and the GNP per cpaita is US$320 (1985). The main ethnic groups are the pastoral Fulani and the agrarian Malinké and Susu. Islam is the chief religion, but there are animist and Roman Catholic minorities. French is the principal language.

*History.* Part of present-day Guinea belonged to medieval GHANA and later to the MALI empire. As in other W African states, Portuguese exploration of the Guinea coast in the mid-15th cent. led to the development of a slave trade involving also the French and British. France proclaimed a protectorate over the Boké area of Guinea in 1849 and, after extending its control over much of the rest of Guinea, annexed it under the name Rivières du Sud (rivers of the south). In 1895, as French Guinea, it became part of French West Africa. Exploitation of Guinea's rich bauxite deposits began just before World War II, accompanied by the growth of a radical labour movement led by Sékou TOURÉ. Under his leadership, Guinea was the only French colony to reject (1958) self-government within the FRENCH COMMUNITY and voted instead for full independence. Until his death in 1984, Touré held the presidency and created a one-party socialist state in which he, as head of the government and the ruling Democratic Party of Guinea (PDG), had ultimate authority. A week after his death, the country's armed forces seized power and established a military government headed by Col. Lansana Conté as president.

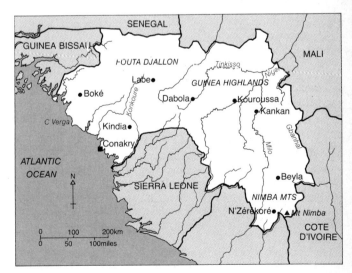

Guinea

**Guinea–Bissau** ('bis,sow), officially Republic of Guinea–Bissau, formerly Portuguese Guinea, republic (1987 est. pop. 890,000), 36,125 km² (13,948 sq mi), W Africa, bordered by the Atlantic Ocean (W), Senegal (N), and Guinea (E and S), and including the Bijagós Archipelago and several islands in the Atlantic. The capital is BISSAU. Guinea-Bissau is largely a low-lying coastal plain, with many rivers and swampy estuaries.

Farming is the leading occupation, producing rice, palm oil, peanuts, and coconuts. Fishing is an increasingly important industry. The GNP is US$144 million, and the GNP per capita is US$180 (1985). Most of the people hold animist beliefs, but about one third are Muslim.

*History.* First visited by the Portuguese in 1446–47, the area that is now Guinea-Bissau developed in the 16th cent. as a slave-trading centre. It was administered as part of the CAPE VERDE islands until 1879, when it became the separate colony of Portuguese Guinea. In 1951 it was constituted an overseas province. A nationalist movement was organized in 1956, and a war for independence began in the early 1960s. After more than 10 years of fighting, independence was proclaimed in 1973 and recognized by Portugal in 1974. The following year, some 100,000 refugees of the war returned. Ties with Cape Verde are very close, and eventual union was contemplated. However, a military coup in 1980, which killed Pres. Luis de Almeida Cabral and brought to power João Bernardo Vieira as head of a revolutionary council, left the future of the unification plan in doubt. Nevertheless, the new regime upheld the pro-unity precepts of the ruling African Party for the Independence of Guinea and Cape Verde (PAIGC).

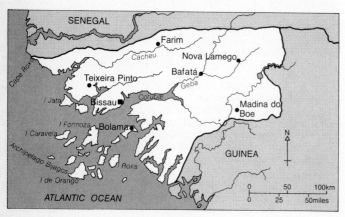

Guinea–Bissau

**guinea pig,** domesticated form of the cavy (*Cavia porcellus*), a South American RODENT unrelated to the pig. Guinea pigs have rounded bodies and large heads, are 15–25 cm (6–10 in) long and weigh 400–900 g (1–2 lb). There are smooth and long-haired varieties and a range of colours in many combinations.

**guinea worm,** parasitic worm *Dracunculus medinensis* which infests various mammals, including humans, and causes chronic ill-health in the developing world. The adult female worm, 60–120 cm (2–4 ft) long, inhabits the connective tissues beneath the skin, causing an ulcer on the skin which discharges larvae into water. The larvae develop in an intermediate host, the water flea, which is then swallowed by humans. The worms frequently have to be extracted manually.

**Guinevere:** see ARTHURIAN LEGEND.

**Guinness, Sir Alec,** 1914–, English actor. Noted for his versatility, he has appeared in such films as *Kind Hearts and Coronets* (1949; he performed eight parts); *The Bridge on the River Kwai* (1957; Academy Award); and, for television, *Tinker, Tailor, Soldier, Spy* (1980) and *Smiley's People* (1982), dramatizations of novels by John LE CARRÉ.

**Güiraldes, Ricardo** (gwee͵rahldays), 1886–1927, Argentine novelist and short-story writer. His major work, the novel *Don Segundo Sombra* (1926), celebrates the life of the gaucho (Argentine cowboy).

**Guise,** French ducal family. The family was founded as a cadet branch of the house of Lorraine by **Claude de Lorraine,** 1st **duc de Guise,** 1496–1550. His daughter, MARY OF GUISE, married JAMES V of Scotland and was the mother of MARY QUEEN OF SCOTS. His sons **François de Lorraine,** 2nd **duc de Guise,** 1519–63, and **Charles de Guise, Cardinal de Lorraine,** c.1525–74, controlled the French government in the reign of FRANCIS II, the first husband of Mary Queen of Scots. They championed the Roman Catholic cause against the Protestant HUGUENOTS and harshly suppressed the Huguenot conspiracy of Amboise (1560). After Francis's death, they opposed the tolerant policies of the regent, CATHERINE DE MEDICI, and helped to provoke the Wars of Religion (see RELIGION, WARS OF).

François's son **Henri de Lorraine,** 3rd **duc de Guise,** 1550–88, helped to plan the massacre of Huguenots on SAINT BARTHOLOMEW'S DAY (1572). He formed the Catholic league to oppose Protestantism and revived the League in 1585 to block the accession of the Protestant Henry of Navarre (later HENRY IV). Because of Guise's designs on the throne, King HENRY III brought about the assassinations of Guise and his brother **Louis de Lorraine, Cardinal de Guise,** 1555–88. Henri was succeeded by his son, **Charles de Lorraine,** 4th **duc de Guise,** 1571–1640. Charles's son **Henri de Lorraine,** 5th **duc de Guise,** 1614–64, was the archbishop of Rheims. He conspired against Cardinal RICHELIEU (1641) and fought in Naples against Spain (1647–48; 1654). He was grand chamberlain at the court of LOUIS XIV.

**guitar,** a plucked STRINGED INSTRUMENT which originated in Spain and spread throughout Europe. The modern guitar usually has six strings, a flat back, a round soundhole, and a fretted neck. It has a range of three octaves upwards from the E below the bass stave. Some guitars have each string doubled, giving a total of 12 strings. The electric guitar is tuned the same as the acoustic guitar but the tone is different as it is electrically amplified. The body of an electric guitar, not providing any resonance, can be of any shape. The bass guitar is an electric guitar tuned in the same way as the DOUBLE BASS. Electric guitars are hardly ever used outside pop music of various types.

**Guitry, Lucien Germain** (͵geetree), 1860–1925, the most versatile French actor of his day. His son, **Sacha Guitry,** 1885–1957, was an actor; popular playwright, e.g., *Nono* (1905); and film director.

**Guiyang** or **Kweiyang** (gway-yahng), city (1984 pop. 1,352,700), capital of GUIZHOU prov., SW central China. A major transport and industrial centre, it produces textiles, fertilizers, machine tools, and petroleum products. The city's population includes minority nationalities.

**Guizhou** or **Kweichow** (gweejoh), province (1985 est. pop. 29,680,000), 174,000 km² (67,181 sq mi), central China, S of SICHUAN prov. The capital is GUIYANG. Much of the land is plateau which has been deeply dissected by rivers, such as the Wu, flowing northwards into the YANGTZE R., and by rivers flowing southwards. This dissected terrain has historically hindered the effective integration of the province into the rest of China. Agriculture is largely restricted to the valley floors where wheat and rice are grown. Much of the land, particularly in the west is given over to forest and pasture. The limited industrialization is mainly centred on Guiyang which has an integrated iron and steel manufacturing plant. The area's demographic history as an area of late Chinese migration is reflected in the Han concentration in the river valleys and the varied minority groups occupying the higher land. The major minority groups are the Buyi (a Thai people), the Dong, and the Miao.

**Guizot, François** (gee͵zoh), 1787–1874, French statesman and historian. A university professor, he served LOUIS PHILIPPE as minister of public instruction (1832–37). Becoming the chief power in the ministry (1840), he was named premier in 1847, but his acceptance of the established order led to his overthrow in the FEBRUARY REVOLUTION of 1848. He devoted the rest of his life to writing. His *History of the Revolution in England* (6 vol., 1826–56) illustrates his critical approach and his admiration for the British experience.

**Gujranwala** (͵goojran'wahlə), city (1981 pop. 654,000), Punjab province, Pakistan. It is in the centre of a fertile and well-irrigated agricultural region for which it performs marketing and other services. It has notable craft industries, especially in textiles and metalwork, and modern textile mills.

**GULAG,** system of forced-labour prison camps in the USSR, from the Russian acronym for Chief Administration of Corrective Labour Camps, a department of the KGB (Soviet SECRET POLICE). Established in 1918, the vast penal network reached its peak under STALIN, when deaths of political prisoners from starvation and other forms of maltreatment were estimated in the tens of millions. The system, which continues on a much-reduced scale today, has been publicized in the writings of SOLZHENITSYN. See also CONCENTRATION CAMP.

**Gulbarga,** town (1981 pop. 221,325), Karnataka state, S India. It is a district administrative centre with some industry. In the 14th cent. it became the first capital of the Bahmani dynasty, which came to rule over a large area in the DECCAN, and whose tombs survive. It later formed part of the dominions of the Nizam of HYDERABAD, and was renamed Ahsanabad.

**Gulf Cooperation Council** (GCC), officially the Cooperation Council of the Arab States of the Gulf, intergovernmental organization. It was founded in 1981 to promote political, economic, and scientific cooperation between Bahrain, Kuwait, Oman, Qatar, Saudi Arabia, and the United Arab Emirates.

**Gulf Stream**, warm ocean current of the N Atlantic Ocean off E North America, originating in the Gulf of Mexico, passing through the Straits of Florida, and moving northeastward until it merges with the NORTH ATLANTIC DRIFT at lat. 40°N and long. 60°W. The Gulf Stream has an average speed of 6.4 km (4 mi) per hour. At its beginning the water temperature is 27°C (80°F), but it decreases as it moves north.

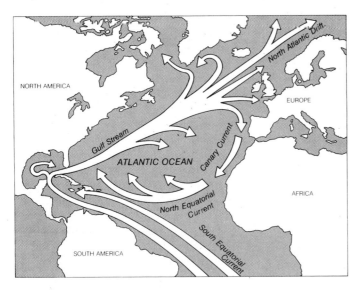

Gulf Stream

**gull**, aquatic BIRD of the family Laridae, which also includes the TERN, found near all oceans and many inland waters. White with grey or black plumage, gulls are larger and bulkier than terns, and their tails are squared rather than forked. They have long, narrow wings adapted for soaring, webbed feet for swimming, and hooked bills. The black-headed gull *Larus ridibundus* has adapted to town life and is found frequenting sewage farms and rubbish dumps.

**Gullstrand, Allvar**, 1862–1930, Swedish ophthalmologist. He was awarded the 1911 Nobel Prize for physiology or medicine for his work on the properties of lenses.

**Gumilyov, Nikolai Stepanovich**, 1886–1921, Russian poet, one of the founders of the ACMEIST school. His early verse contained exotic elements inspired by his travels in Africa; his later poetry is more tragic and prophetic. From 1910–1918 he was married to the poet Anna AKHMATOVA. After 1917 he took an openly anti-Bolshevik stance, and was arrested and shot. His best-known poems include *Agamemnon's Warrior* (1910) and *The Tram that Lost its Way* (1918–21).

**gum tree**, common name for the EUCALYPTUS and other trees forming resins or oils, e.g., sweet gum (WITCH-HAZEL family).

**gun**, a device that discharges shot, shells, or bullets from a straight tube. A gun using the explosion of GUNPOWDER or some other explosive substance to propel the projectile is called a firearm; types include ARTILLERY (large firearms), MORTAR, and SMALL ARMS. Certain other guns use compressed air produced by a spring-operated plunger (e.g., BB gun) or a lever-and-pump system (e.g., air rifle) to propel the projectile.

**gun dog**, class of DOG bred to assist man in hunting by flushing out game, directing the hunter to its position, or retrieving dead and wounded game. The pointer stands rigidly, with nose and body in line with the quarry. Setters were originally bred to hold the quarry at bay, but are now general-purpose shooting dogs. Retrievers recover dead and wounded game. Gun dogs are docile and very trainable, making excellent companion dogs. Breeds include the cocker and springer spaniels, the golden retriever, the weimaraner, and the Irish setter. The Labrador retriever is one of the most popular companion dogs. It is frequently used as a GUIDE DOG, and by the police and customs for the detection of hidden drugs and explosives.

**Gundulić, Ivan**, or **Giovanni Gondola** (goohn‚doohlich or ‚gondəlah), 1588–1638, Croatian poet (from what is now Yugoslavia). His finest work, *Osman* (1626), an epic of the Polish wars against the Turks, shows early Slavic nationalism and the influence of ancient song.

**gunmetal**, a BRONZE, an ALLOY of COPPER, TIN, and a small amount of ZINC. Originally used to make guns, it is now employed in casting machine parts. The percentages of the three elements vary, depending on the intended use.

**Gunnarsson, Gunnar** (‚gynahson), 1889–1975, prolific Icelandic novelist who wrote all his major works in Danish before rewriting them all in Icelandic. His first novel, *The History of the Borg Family* (1912–14, tr. into Eng. as *Guest the One-Eyed* in 1920), became the first Icelandic work to be turned into a film, and helped to interest Europeans in Icelandic culture. His masterpiece, the autobiographical novel *The Church on the Mountain* (1923–28, tr. in 2 vol. as *Ships in the Sky* and *The Night and the Dream*), demonstrates his rich imagination and poetic skill.

**gunpowder**, explosive mixture of saltpetre (75%), sulphur (10%), and charcoal (15%). It is believed to have originated as early as the 9th cent. in China, where it was used for making fireworks, and to have been introduced into Europe in the 14th cent. Its use revolutionized warfare. Gunpowder was the only explosive in wide use until the mid 19th cent., when it was superseded by NITROGLYCERIN-based EXPLOSIVES.

**Gunpowder Plot**, conspiracy to blow up the English Parliament and JAMES I on 5 Nov. 1605, the opening day of Parliament. An uprising of English Catholics was to follow. In preparation, gunpowder was stored in the cellar of the House of Lords. The plot was exposed when a conspirator warned a relative not to attend Parliament that day. One of the plotters, Guy Fawkes, was arrested as he entered the cellar. The others were either seized and killed outright or imprisoned and executed. The plot only worsened the plight of English Catholics. Guy Fawkes Day is celebrated in England on 5 Nov.

**Guntur**, town (1981 pop. 376,699), Andhra Pradesh state, E India, W of delta of the KRISHNA R. It is a district administrative, railway, and trading centre whose population has grown notably in recent years; and has industries dependent on local agriculture. It has been a district headquarters since British times: Guntur district had been a bone of contention between the British and the Nizam of Hyderabad in the 18th cent.

**Gupta** (‚gooptə), Indian dynasty (c.320–c.550) founded by CHANDRAGUPTA (r. c.320–c.330). At its height, the dynasty ruled much of what is modern India.

**Gurkha**, ethnic group of NEPAL. Predominantly Tibeto-Mongolians, they speak Khas, a Rajasthani dialect of Sanskritic origin; practise Hinduism; and claim descent from the RAJPUTS of N India. By the 18th cent. they had expanded E from their small state of Gurkha throughout Nepal. Many Gurkha soldiers have served in Indian and British armies.

**Gustafsson, Lars**, 1936–, Swedish novelist and poet. His doctoral thesis, *Language and Lies* (1978), explored the problem of language as a barrier between experience and understanding, much influenced by Wittgenstein. His outstanding contribution to literature so far has been his series of five novels under the general title *Cracks in the Wall* (1971–78).

**Gustavus**, kings of Sweden. **Gustavus I**, 1496–1560 (r.1523–60), was the founder of the modern Swedish state and the VASA dynasty. After his father, a Swedish senator, was killed (1520) in a massacre ordered by the Danish king, CHRISTIAN II, Gustavus escaped from prison and defeated the Danes. His election as king by the Riksdag (1523) ended the KALMAR UNION of Denmark, Sweden, and Norway. In 1527 he founded a national Protestant Church. With a newly strengthened navy he defeated LÜBECK (1537), freeing Swedish commerce from the power of the HANSEATIC LEAGUE. In 1544 he made the throne hereditary in the Vasa family, ending the election of Swedish kings. His son ERIC XIV succeeded him. **Gustavus II** (Gustavus Adolphus), 1594–1632 (r.1611–32), was the son of CHARLES IX. Aided by his chancellor, OXENSTIERNA, he ended the Kalmar War with Denmark (1613) and forced Russia to cede Ingermanland (1617). In the THIRTY YEARS WAR he obtained much of Polish Livonia and several Baltic ports (1629), then invaded German Pomerania, defeating TILLY near Leipzig (1631). At Lützen (1632) the Swedes defeated WALLENSTEIN, but Gustavus was killed. His daughter, CHRISTINA, succeeded him. **Gustavus III**, 1746–92 (r.1771–92), was the son of Adolphus Frederick. To quell civil strife, he imposed (1772) a new constitution restoring the royal prerogatives lost by his successors. In a war with Russia and Denmark (1788–90) he had limited success. He planned a coalition to aid the French royalists but was assassinated by an agent of the nobles. His son, **Gustavus IV**, 1778–1837 (r.1792–1809), succeeded him under the regency of his uncle, later CHARLES XIII. After he joined (1805) the Third Coalition against NAPOLEON I he lost Swedish Pomerania to France and Finland to Russia (1808). His despotism, mental imbalance, and disastrous policies led to his forced abdication when the Russians threatened Stockholm (1809). Charles XIII became king and made peace with Russia. Gustavus was exiled and his descendants barred from succession. **Gustavus V**, 1858–1950 (r.1907–50), was the son of Oscar II. During his reign Sweden prospered and avoided involvement in two world wars. He was succeeded by his son, **Gustavus VI** (Gustaf Adolf), 1882–1973 (r.1950–73). He participated in archaeological expeditions in Sweden, Greece, and China, and his work as a botanist earned him admission (1958) to the British Royal Academy. His grandson, Carl Gustaf, succeeded him as CHARLES XVI GUSTAVUS.

**Gustavus Adolphus** (Gustavus II): see GUSTAVUS, kings of Sweden.

**Gutenberg, Johann**, c.1397–1468, German printer, believed to have been the first European to print with movable TYPE. Laurens Janszoon Koster of Holland and Pamfilo Castaldi of Italy are thought by some to have preceded him. Gutenberg's name did not appear on any of his work, and details of his life are scant. He is thought to have trained as a goldsmith. He may have invented PRINTING in Strasbourg in 1436 or 1437, but the work attributed to him, including the MAZARIN BIBLE (1455), was done in Mainz. He had to give up his press and types to Johann FUST for debt.

**Guthrie, Sir Tyrone**, 1900–71, English director and producer. Noted for his experimental Shakespearean productions, he headed the Old Vic and Canada's Shakespeare Festival before founding (1963) the Guthrie Theater in Minneapolis. Grandson of Irish actor Tyrone Power and Chancellor of Queen's University, Belfast, Guthrie remembered Ireland in his will, bequeathing the family home, Annaghmakerrig, to the artistes of the nation. Since 1982 it has been a retreat for actors, writers, directors, and artists from all parts of Ireland.

**Guthrie, Woody** (Woodrow Wilson Guthrie), 1912–67, American folk singer, guitarist, and composer. He wrote over 1000 songs, chiefly on social and political themes, and strongly influenced younger performers like Bob DYLAN. His son, **Arlo Guthrie**, 1947–, is also a folk singer and composer.

**Guyana** (gie,ahnə or -,an-), officially Cooperative Republic of Guyana, formerly **British Guiana**, republic within the Commonwealth (1987 est. pop. 900,000 increasing at 2.8% per year), 214,969 km² (83,000 sq mi), NE South America, bordered by the Atlantic Ocean (N), Suriname (E), Brazil (S and W), and Venezuela (W). GEORGETOWN is the capital. The climate is hot and humid, and rainfall is heavy. There is a cultivated coastal plain and a forested, hilly interior. Agriculture and mining are the principal economic activities, with the processing of bauxite (nationalized in the 1970s) and sugarcane the largest industries. In 1983 GDP was US$547 million or US$633 per capita. The population, primarily East Indian and black, with about 4% native Indian, is concentrated along the coast. English is the official language, and Hindi, Urdu and Amerindian languages are also spoken. Christianity, Hinduism, and Islam are the main religions. Originally settled by the Dutch in the 17th cent., the region was awarded to the British in 1815 and united as British Guiana in 1831. Full independence was gained in 1966 within the COMMONWEALTH, and Guyana became a republic in 1970. The People's National Congress, based in the African-descended section of the population, has held power since 1964 under the leadership first of Forbes Burnham and, since his death in 1985, of Pres. Desmond Hoyte.

**Guzmán Blanco, Antonio** (goohs,mahn ,blahnkoh), 1829–99, Venezuelan dictator (1870–88). Instrumental in deposing (1863) PAEZ as dictator, he served (1863–68) as Liberal vice president, and led a counterrevolution (1870) that made him president. A benevolent despot, he reformed government administration and brought about material progress. His regime was overthrown in 1888.

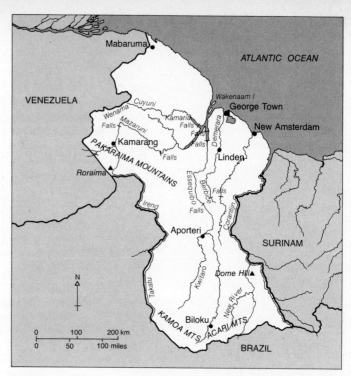

Guyana

**Gwalior**, city (1981 pop. 539,015), Madhya Pradesh state, C India. It is a district administrative and commercial centre and railway junction with a number of industries, notably textiles (traditional and modern), engineering, leather, pottery, and biscuits. Gwalior proper derives its name from a dominating rock fortress founded in the 1st cent. which played a large part in the wars of many of the succeeding centuries until the Scindia Rajputs captured it in the 18th cent. and ruled Gwalior state until India became independent. One of them, Daulat Rao (1794–1827) founded Lashkar as a new capital at the foot of the fort, but still within the (greater) Gwalior described above.

**Gwent**, county in SE Wales (1984 est. pop. 439,700), 1,376 km² (537 sq mi), situated on the English border. It was formed in 1974 in the reorganization of local government from the county of Monmouthshire. It is hilly in the W and drained by the USK and Wye rivers. Orchards and sheep farming are common. In the valleys of the NW coalmining was the dominant industry until recently, when economic stagnation has set in. Light industries have been established to provide employment. NEWPORT is the largest town and a seaport.

**Gwyn** or **Gwynn, Nell** (Eleanor), 1650–87, English actress, notable for her charm in comic roles. From 1669 she was the mistress of CHARLES II, and bore him two sons.

**Gwynedd**, county in NW Wales (1981 pop. 226,212), 3869 km² (1509 sq mi), bordering on the Irish Sea in the N and W. It was formed in the local government reorganization of 1974 from Anglesey, Caernarvonshire, and Merionethshire. The Isle of Anglesey is separated from the rest of the county by the narrow Menai Strait. It is generally mountainous and includes the high peaks of SNOWDON at 3562 ft (1086 m) and Cader Idris at 2929 ft (893 m). The Main rivers are the CONWY and the DEE. Sheep-farming is practised, and formerly there was a slate-quarrying industry, but this has now declined. The beautiful mountain scenery has meant that tourism has become a major industry. The main towns are BANGOR (a university town), CAERNARVON, CONWY and Llandudno (all tourist centres).

**gymnastics**, exercises for the balanced development of the body, usually practised in a gymnasium, named after the training place for the OLYMPIC GAMES of ancient Greece. Modern gymnastics date from the early 19th cent., when several *Turnplätze* were established in Berlin, then spread on the Continent, to England, and to the US. Gymnastics include free calisthenics, the horse, bars, rings, tumbling, and trampoline. Modern rhythmic gymnastics, a recent addition to the female side of the sport, involve exercises with handheld apparatus including ribbons, ropes, hoops, and Indian clubs.

**gymnosperm,** plant in which the SEEDS are exposed during all stages of development, in contrast to ANGIOSPERMS. Gymnosperms, which include the PINES, are woody plants with STEMS, ROOTS and LEAVES, and vascular, or conducting, tissue (xylem and phloem). Gymnosperms are always pollinated by wind, and many have their seed-bearing structures organized into cones. They comprise the CYCADS; the CONIFERS, YEWS, and GINKGOS; and the GNETALES, which contains three families, all of evolutionary interest.

**gynaecology,** branch of medicine specializing in disorders of the female REPRODUCTIVE SYSTEM. Modern gynaecology deals with disorders of MENSTRUATION, menopause, disease and maldevelopment of reproductive organs, hormonal and fertility problems, and BIRTH CONTROL devices. A related branch of medicine is **obstetrics,** which specializes in the treatment of women during PREGNANCY and childbirth.

**Györ,** city (1985 pop. 129,000), NW Hungary, on the Raab R. It is a manufacturing centre with important textile and vehicle manufacturing industries. The cathedral dates from the 12th cent. but was rebuilt in the 17th cent.

**gypsies** or **gipsies,** nomadic people found on every continent, but particularly prominent in Spain and the Balkans. Despite much wandering they have clung to their identity and customs. They travel in small caravans, earning a living as metalworkers, musicians, horse-dealers, mechanics, and fortune-tellers. Most are Roman Catholic or Eastern Orthodox Christian. Their Indo-Iranian language, Romany, and their blood groupings are related to those found in India, where they are thought to have originated. They went to Persia in the 1st millennium AD and divided into the Gitanos, Kalderash, and Manush. They had spread throughout Europe by the 16th cent. and appeared in North America in the late 1800s. Gypsies today are estimated at 5 million; half a million died in Nazi CONCENTRATION CAMPS during World War II.

**gypsum,** the most common sulphate mineral, occurring in many places and forms. It is very soft; the massive variety ALABASTER and the lustrous variety satin spar are easily worked into decorative objects. Plaster of Paris, used to make casts, moulds, and wallboard, is made from gypsum.

**gypsy language:** see ROMANY.

**gyroplane,** powered AIRCRAFT sustained in flight by a freely-rotating, articulated, multiblade rotor mounted on a vertical shaft but not connected to the power plant except for the initial spin-up of the rotor for takeoff. Thrust for forward flight is provided by a tractor or pusher airscrew as in an ordinary aeroplane (see FLIGHT, POWERED). Pioneered by the Spanish engineer Juan de la Cierva y Codorniu, the gyroplane was first demonstrated in 1923; practical gyroplanes built to Cierva's designs were built in Britain, France, Germany, and the US. See also HELICOPTER.

**gyroscope,** symmetrical mass, usually a wheel, mounted so that it can spin about an axis in any direction. A spinning gyroscope will resist changes in the orientation of its spin axis. Gyroscopes are used in ship stabilizers to counteract rolling, and a gyroscope is the nucleus of most automatic steering systems, such as those used in aeroplanes, missiles, and torpedoes. See also COMPASS.

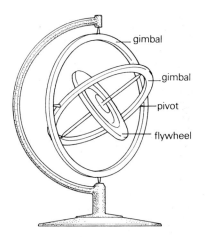

Three-frame **gyroscope**

**H,** chemical symbol of the element HYDROGEN.

**Haacke, Hans,** 1936–, German artist. Trained in Germany and Paris, he worked and taught in the US in the 1960s. His early work, plexiglass containers filled with water that responded to the environment by forming condensation patterns, gave way to interests in spectator participation. His more recent work has focused on the politics of art, and uses photographic reproductions and text to illustrate the political and material values of art production and consumption in the west.

**Haakon** (ˌhahkon), kings of Norway. **Haakon I** (the Good), c.915–61 (r. c.935–61), was the son of HAROLD I. Raised as a Christian in England, he tried unsuccessfully to introduce Christianity into Norway after seizing power from his brother Eric Bloodaxe. Eric's sons succeeded him. **Haakon IV** (Haakon Haakonsson), 1204–63 (r.1217–63), was the illegitimate son of Haakon III. Under him medieval Norway reached its zenith. Iceland and Greenland were acquired, legal reforms were carried out, and Old Norse literature flowered (see STURLUSON). His son, MAGNUS VI, succeeded him. **Haakon VII,** 1872–1957 (r.1905–57), was born Prince Charles, second son of FREDERICK VIII of Denmark. He was chosen king when Norway separated from Sweden. During the German occupation of Norway (1940–45) he headed a government in exile in London. His son, OLAF V, succeeded him.

**Haarlem,** city (1985 pop. 151,025), capital of N Holland prov., W Netherlands. It has heavy industry but is best known as a flower-growing centre and exporter of bulbs, chiefly tulips. Leading masters, e.g., HALS, van OSTADE, and van RUISDAEL, painted there. Among its many historic buildings are the 15th-cent Groote Kerk (church) and the city hall (begun 1250).

**Habakkuk, Habacus** or **Habbacus** (ˌhabəkək), book of the OLD TESTAMENT. It is a set of poems on the punishment of the wicked by God, using the Chaldaeans (Babylonians) as His instrument, and on the triumph of divine justice and mercy.

**habeas corpus,** [Lat., = you should have the body], in law, a writ issued by a court commanding that a person held in custody be brought before a court so that it may determine whether the detention is lawful. Meant to ensure that a prisoner is accorded due process of law, it does not determine guilt or innocence. *Habeas corpus* originated in medieval England and is now protected in the UK by the Habeas Corpus Act 1679. This Act has been temporarily suspended by the government at times of public danger or political necessity, e.g., 1794–1801. In the US, the writ is protected by the US CONSTITUTION.

**Haber, Fritz,** 1868–1934, German chemist. During World War I he directed Germany's chemical warfare activities, which included the introduction of poison gas. In 1920 he became involved in the futile attempt to pay off German war debts by means of gold extracted from sea water. After the Nazi rise to power (1933), he went into exile in England. His last public act was to resign (1933) as director of the Kaiser Wilhelm Institute in Berlin–Dahlem in protest against the dismissal of Jewish scientists. For his discovery of the Haber process for synthesizing ammonia from its elements he won the 1918 Nobel Prize for chemistry. Over 100 million tons of ammonia are produced annually worldwide via the Haber process. Most of it is used for making agricultural fertilizer.

**habitat,** the type of environment within which species live, sufficient to provide all their requirements. Habitats may be on any scale, depending on the scale and requirements of the organism. However, the word is most commonly used to describe a particular, recognizable type of environment, e.g., woodland habitat, grassland habitat. See also ECOLOGY.

**Habsburg** or **Hapsburg,** ruling house of AUSTRIA (1282–1918). The family originally held lands in Alsace and NW Switzerland, and Otto (d. 1111) took the name Habsburg when he was made count. In 1273 Count Rudolf IV became king of the Germans as RUDOLF I; his war with Ottocar II of Bohemia resulted in Ottocar's defeat (1278) and confirmation of Habsburg possession of Austria, Carniola, and Styria. These lands and the Austrian ducal title were declared hereditary in 1282, and in 1335 Carinthia too was claimed. The possessions were divided (1365) between the Albertine and the Leopoldine lines but were reunited under Holy Roman Emperor MAXIMILIAN I in the late 15th cent. Tyrol (1363), NE Istria (1374), and Trieste (1382) were added to the Habsburg domain. From the election (1438) of Albert II as German king, the head of the Habsburgs, with one exception, was chosen German king and Holy Roman emperor. Through marriage the Habsburgs gained most of the Low Countries, and Habsburg power reached its zenith under Emperor CHARLES V, who had inherited (1516) the crown of Spain. Charles was succeeded in Spain by his son, PHILIP II, and in Austria by his brother, Emperor FERDINAND I. The Spanish Habsburgs died out in 1700. In Austria the PRAGMATIC SANCTION (1713) guaranteed the indivisibility of the Habsburg domains and after the death of CHARLES VI's only son (1716) the succession of MARIA THERESA. Her son, Emperor JOSEPH II, began the line of **Habsburg-Lorraine.** In 1806 Holy Roman Emperor FRANCIS II abdicated and assumed the title emperor of Austria. In 1867 the Habsburg empire was reorganized into the AUSTRO-HUNGARIAN MONARCHY, which was dissolved at the end of WORLD WAR I.

**Hackney,** London borough (1981 pop. 179,529), in inner NE London. It includes the districts of Shoreditch and Stoke Newington. Industries found here include furniture-making, clothing, and confectionery. There are many housing estates which were built after World War II. Hackney Marsh is a large open space.

**Hadar,** area in the Afar region, N Ethiopia, with early hominid sites along the Awash R. excavated by D.C. Johanson and associates in the 1970s. Deposits cover the period c.2.8 to 3.3 + million years ago and have yielded numerous fossils of *Australopithecus afarensis* (see AUSTRALOPITHECUS), the best known being the partial skeleton 'Lucy'. See also HUMAN EVOLUTION; LAETOLI.

**haddock:** see COD.

**Hades** (ˌhaydeez), in Greek mythology. **1** The ruler of the underworld, commonly called PLUTO. **2** The world of the dead, ruled by Pluto and PERSEPHONE. Guarded by CERBERUS, it was either underground or in the far west, and was separated from the land of the living by five rivers. One of these was the STYX, across which the dead were ferried. Three judges decided the fate of souls; heroes went to the ELYSIAN FIELDS, evildoers to TARTARUS.

**Hadewijch** (ˌhahdəviekh), fl. early 13th cent., Dutch mystical poet, a nun. Her works are a monument both to early Dutch literature and to Roman Catholic mysticism.

**hadith,** [Arab., = narrative report], pronouncements attributed to the prophet MUHAMMAD. Each hadith consisted of a text and a chain of authorities who transmitted it, and hadith scholars concentrated on the scrutiny of such lines of transmission for judgments upon the veracity of such attributed pronouncements. In the 9th cent., authoritative compilations of authoritative hadith material became established and formed, along with the KORAN, a most important source of precedent and precept for the construction of Islamic law (see FIQH). Hadith material covers a great many spheres of human conduct and Islamic doctrine.

**Hadrian.** For popes of that name, see ADRIAN.

**Hadrian** or **Adrian,** AD 76–138, Roman emperor (r.117–138); b. Spain. His name in full was Publius Aelius Hadrianus. A ward of TRAJAN, Hadrian distinguished himself as a commander and as an administrator. He was chosen as Trajan's successor. Hadrian's reign was vigorous and judicious. Abandoning the aggressive policy of Trajan in Asia, he withdrew to the boundary of the Euphrates in Palestine. In 132 he put down the insurrection of the Hebrew leader BAR KOKBA with great severity. Hadrian travelled extensively in the empire, stabilizing government and adorning the cities. In Germany he built great protective Frontier barriers, and in Britain he had Hadrian's Wall built. He also patronized the arts; his regard for the youth Antinous was recorded by sculptors and architects. As his successor he chose Antoninus Pius.

**Hadrian's Wall,** a stone built by the emperor Hadrian AD c.122–28 to defend the N frontier of Roman Britain. It ran approximately 120 km (75 mi) between the Solway Firth and the Tyne and was protected by a chain of 16 forts and many smaller fortifications. Like other permanent defensive lines (see ANTONINE WALL) it was overrun several times and was finally abandoned about AD 400.

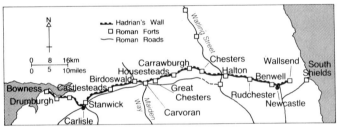

Hadrian's Wall

**Haeckel, Ernst von,** 1834–1919, German biologist and philosopher. He was an early exponent in Germany of Charles DARWIN's theory of EVOLUTION. Based on his interpretations of Darwin's theory, he evolved a mechanical form of MONISM. His theory of recapitulation postulated a hypothetical ancestral form represented by the gastrula stage of individual development. Although many were later proved incorrect, his theories attracted a following and stimulated research.

**haemoglobin,** oxygen-carrying respiratory pigment found in the red blood cells of all vertebrates and some invertebrates (see BLOOD). It is produced in the bone marrow and transports oxygen to the body tissue from the LUNGS. An inadequate amount of circulating haemoglobin results in ANAEMIA.

**haemophilia,** hereditary disorder in which the clotting ability of the BLOOD is impaired and excessive bleeding results. The haemophiliac bleeds uncontrollably externally or internally after a small injury, after rigorous exertion, or even spontaneously, unable to form or maintain a sufficient blood clot and often requiring a BLOOD TRANSFUSION containing the missing clotting factor (factor VIII). The disease is genetically transmitted through females but affects only males.

**haemorrhoids** or **piles,** enlarged veins in or about the anus, often producing itching, bleeding, and pain. A common disorder associated with conditions such as constipation, diarrhoea, and pregnancy, haemorrhoids can be successfully treated, usually by injection or surgery.

**Hafiz,** d. 1389?, Persian poet; b. Shams ad-Din Muhammad. Traditionally interpreted allegorically by Muslims, his poems are passionate lyrics, usually ghazals (groups of rhyming couplets), on such themes as love and drink.

**hafnium** (Hf), metallic element, discovered by X-ray spectroscopy in 1923 by Dirk Coster and Georg von Hevesy. Lustrous, silvery, and ductile, it is chemically similar to ZIRCONIUM; the two elements are among the most difficult to separate. Hafnium is used for nuclear-reactor control rods. See ELEMENT (table); PERIODIC TABLE.

**Hagar,** see ISHMAEL.

**Hagen,** city (1984 pop. 209,500), North Rhine–Westphalia, W West Germany, at the confluence of the Ennepe R. and the Volme R. It has close industrial links with the cities of WUPPERTAL and SOLINGEN, manufacturing special steels and electrical equipment.

**Hagen, Walter,** 1892–1969, American golfer. He won 11 major championships: the US Open twice (1914, 1919) and, during the 1920s, the British Open four times and the Professional Golfers' Association five times. He played in five Ryder Cup teams.

**hagfish,** primitive eel-like descendant of the jawless ostracoderms which gave rise to all modern fishes. Hagfishes are marine parasites found off Europe, South Africa, New Zealand, and the Americas. They grow up to 60 cm (2 ft) long. Their life style and appearance is very like that of the LAMPREY. Hagfishes will eat worms and crustaceans, but they usually attack weakened fishes, boring into their bodies through the skin and rasping away at all the internal organs with their toothed tongues until there is nothing left but a skinful of bones.

Hagfish (*Myxinge Glutinosa*) underwater with slime secretions

**Haggai,** book of the OLD TESTAMENT. Writing in 520–19 BC, the prophet urges the post-exilic community in Judah, and especially their leader Zerubbabel and the high priest Joshua, to press on with the rebuilding of the destroyed Temple of Jerusalem.

**Haggard, Sir Henry Rider,** 1856–1925, English novelist. He is known for his highly popular romantic adventure stories, particularly *King Solomon's Mines* (1885) and *She* (1887).

**Hagia Sophia** [Gr., = Holy Wisdom] or **Santa Sophia,** Turkish *Aya Sofia,* originally a Christian church at Constantinople (now Istanbul), later a MOSQUE, now a museum of Byzantine art. The supreme masterpiece of Byzantine architecture, the present structure was built (AD 532–37) by Anthemius of Tralles and Isidorus of Miletus for the emperor JUSTINIAN I. After the Turkish conquest of Constantinople (1453) it became a mosque. The interior mosaics were obscured under layers of plaster and painted ornament, and Christian symbols were obliterated. Four MINARETS were added at the outer corners. The nave is covered by a lofty DOME carried on pendentives; its weight thus rests on four huge arches and their piers. The E and W arches are extended by half-domes and domed exedrae. A vast oblong interior is thus created. The dome is 31 m (102 ft) in diameter and 56 m (184 ft) high, with a corona of 40 arched windows flooding the interior with light. The original decorations and gold mosaics have been largely restored.

**Hague, The,** city (1985 pop. 443,456, agglomeration 671,830), capital of S Holland; seat of the Dutch government, the Dutch supreme court, and the International Court of Justice (see UNITED NATIONS). It grew around a palace begun c.1250 by William, count of Holland. Seat (from 1586) of the States General of the United Provinces of the Netherlands and residence (17th–18th cent.) of their stadtholders, it became a major

The nave of **Hagia Sophia**

diplomatic and intellectual centre. It was the Dutch royal residence from 1815 to 1948. Site of the HAGUE CONFERENCES, the city is known as a centre for the promotion of peace. Landmarks include the 14th-cent. Gevangenenpoort prison, the 17th-cent. Mauritshuis (containing an excellent collection of paintings), and the Peace Palace (1913).

**Hague Conferences,** two international conferences (1899, 1907), held at The Hague, the Netherlands, on the problems of armaments and the rules of modern warfare. They adopted various conventions that were later ratified by many nations. Although they failed to prevent WORLD WAR I, they furnished an example for both the LEAGUE OF NATIONS and the UN. The first conference created the HAGUE TRIBUNAL.

**Hague Tribunal,** popular name for the Permanent Court of Arbitration, established by the first HAGUE CONFERENCE (1899). Headquartered in The HAGUE, it consists of a permanent group of jurists from which a panel is selected whenever contending nations agree to submit a dispute to arbitration. It has ruled in more than 20 international disputes, including the VENEZUELA CLAIMS (1904). After World War I it was largely eclipsed in importance by the WORLD COURT.

**Hahn, Otto,** 1879–1968, German chemist and physicist. Noted for important work on radioactivity and nuclear fission, he received the 1944 Nobel Prize for chemistry for splitting (1939) the uranium atom and discovering the possibility of nuclear fission chain reactions. The development of the ATOMIC BOMB was based on this work.

**Haidar Ali** or **Hyder Ali,** 1722–82, Indian Muslim ruler. A peasant by birth, he rose through army ranks and by 1761 was the virtual ruler of the state of Mysore. His efforts to expand his domain met with British opposition. He defeated the British in 1769, but in 1781 he was defeated near Madras. His son, Tipu Sultan, continued the war with the British, but was eventually defeated and killed in battle. The bulk of his territory was absorbed into the British Indian empire. The Hindu kingdom of Mysore was established.

**Haifa,** city (1983 est. pop. 225,800), NW Israel, on the Mediterranean Sea sheltered by Mt Carmel. It is a major industrial centre and the main port of Israel. Haifa is known to have existed by the 3rd cent. AD and was destroyed (1191) by SALADIN after which it lost trade to ACCO. The city's revival began in the late 18th cent., development of its port in the 20th cent. led to its main growth. It is the world centre of BAHA,ISM and has two universities.

**Haig, Alexander Meigs, Jr,** 1924–, US general and public official, US secretary of state (1981–82). A career military officer, he served as Pres. NIXON's civilian chief of staff during the WATERGATE AFFAIR. Later he was (1974–79) NATO commander and in 1981 became Pres. REAGAN's secretary of state. His sudden resignation (1982) was attributed to disagreements over foreign policy.

**Haig, Douglas Haig,** 1st **Earl,** 1861–1928, British field marshal. In WORLD WAR I he became (1915) commander in chief of the BRITISH EXPEDITIONARY FORCE in France, but received little support from LLOYD GEORGE. He was much criticized for the staggering losses suffered in the battle of the Somme and the Passchendaele campaign (see YPRES, BATTLES OF).

**haikai no renga:** see BASHO.

**haiku** (,hiekooh), unrhymed Japanese poem recording the essence of a keenly perceived moment linking nature and human nature. Usually consisting of 17 syllables, it was adapted by the IMAGISTS and other Western writers as a three-line poem of five, seven, and five syllables. See BASHO.

**hail,** solid form of precipitation that can occur at any time of year, usually in a cumulonimbus cloud and often during a THUNDERSTORM. Large hailstones are spherical or irregularly spherical in shape and are composed of alternate hard and soft layers of ice. Hail usually forms when raindrops are blown up to high (cold) areas in a cloud and freeze. As they fall, they become coated with more water drops; they are then blown back up and refrozen, adding an additional layer. This process is repeated until the wind currents can no longer support the weight of the hailstone. Hailstones are generally less than 1.25 cm (½ in) in diameter, although larger ones are occasionally observed.

**Hail, Mary,** prayer to the Virgin Mary, universal among Roman Catholics. Its first lines are from Luke 1.28, 42. The prayer is much used in private and public devotions, e.g., in the rosary. Known in Latin as the *Ave Maria,* it has many musical settings.

**Haile Selassie** (,hielee sə,lasee), 1891–1975, emperor of ETHIOPIA (1930–74). The grandnephew of Emperor MENELIK II and a Coptic Christian, he forced (1916) the abdication of Lij Yasu, a Muslim convert, and placed Menelik's daughter, Zauditu, on the throne. In 1928 he was crowned king, and after Zauditu's mysterious death in 1930 he became emperor. During the Italian invasion (1935–36) he personally led the troops against the enemy. He lived in exile in England until 1941, when he returned and claimed the throne. After World War II he instituted social and political reforms, such as establishing a national assembly in 1955. In 1974, however, he was deposed by an army coup, and he died in captivity.

**Hainan,** (,hienan), province and island (1983 pop. 5,710,000) in the South China Sea, 50 km (30 mi) off S China; administratively part of GUANGDONG prov., China. A subtropical zone, it is traditionally one of the poorest parts of the Chinese empire with significant minority groups—the Li and Miao people. Rich in minerals, including iron ore, brown coal, and oil shales, and with a potential for subtropical agricultural produce. In 1988 it was designated a province. (It had previously been administratively part of GUANDONG prov.) It was also designated as China's fifth and largest special economic zone. This granted it greater independent powers to encourage foreign investment, including investment in the area's developing tourist industry. It is an important military base, particularly the west coast, with a key role of defending China's interests in the South China Sea and Beibu Gulf (Gulf of Tonkin). Incorporated into China in the 13th cent. AD, Hainan was occupied by Japan during World War II.

**Haiphong** (hie,fong), city (1979 pop. 1,279,067) NE Vietnam, on a large branch of the Red R. delta c.16 km (10 mi) from the Gulf of Tonkin. One of the largest ports in Southeast Asia, it was developed (1874) by the French and became their chief naval base in INDOCHINA. During the VIETNAM WAR Haiphong was severely bombed (1965–68, 1972) and its harbour mined. Its shipyards, textile mills, cement factories, and other industrial installations have since been rebuilt.

**hair,** slender, threadlike outgrowth from the skin of mammals. Some animals grow a dense profusion of hair known as FUR or WOOL. Insulation from cold, protection against dust and sand, and camouflage are among the functions of hair. Each hair originates in a deep, pouchlike hair follicle, which contains the bulb-shaped root of the hair. The papilla, containing nerves and capillaries that supply the hair, extends into an indentation at the base of the root. Here newly dividing cells force older cells upward, where they die and harden into the hair shaft. The shaft has two layers, the colourless outer cuticle and the cortex, which contains pigment and the protein keratin. Hair is lubricated by sebaceous glands in the follicle. A hair may be raised by a small erector muscle attached to the hair follicle.

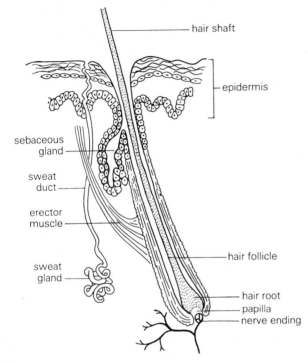

Hair

**hairstyle,** considered an essential of a conventional appearance in most cultures. The cutting off of all or some of the hair to symbolize the breaking-off of relations with the everyday world occurs in many different cultures, e.g., women in Heian Japan cutting their hair to enter a nunnery. Sometimes children have a different hairstyle from adults, and the change from one to the other is an important sign of a person's new status. Long hair has been fashionable for men as well as women, most recently in the 1960s, but it is now usual for Western man to have short hair and for women's to be longer and more variously styled. Most hairdressing is based on curling or straightening the hair with damp and heat, and holding it to shape with pins, or stiffening lotions. Women's hairdressing was especially elaborate between the 1770s and 80s and in the 1830s, when quantities of false hair were used to build up styles. Marcel waving, with curling tongs, which produced a lasting and regular wave, was introduced in the late 19th cent., and permanent waving, for which chemicals and heat were used and which gave a much more durable effect, was introduced in the 1920s. With the application of chemicals and dyes, it is easy to change the colour and texture of the hair, and this has been done from earliest times. To conceal baldness, or as an alternative to styling the natural hair, or for theatrical effect, a WIG can be worn.

**Haiti,** Fr. *Häiti,* officially Republic of Haiti, republic (1987 est. pop. 5,800,000), 27,713 km² (10,700 sq mi), West Indies, on the western third of the island of HISPANIOLA, which it shares with the DOMINICAN REPUBLIC. The capital and main seaport is PORT-AU-PRINCE. The densely populated, mostly mountainous country has the lowest per-capita income in Latin America. It has few manufacturing industries, except those set up by North American companies with tax incentives and cheap labour, and a high rate of emigration. Subsistence farming (cassava, rice, yams) is the

principal occupation; coffee is the main export. About 95% of the population is black, and French and Creole (a French dialect) are spoken. Haiti is a Roman Catholic nation in which *vodun* (voodoo) rites are widely practised.

*History.* Nominally part of the Spanish colony of SANTO DOMINGO from the early 1500s, eastern Hispaniola remained virtually unsettled until the mid-17th cent., when French colonists, importing African slaves, developed sugar plantations in the north. Under French rule from 1697, Haiti (then called Saint-Domingue) became one of the world's richest sugar and coffee producers. However, after the 1780s, rebellion, race war among black, mulatto, and white Haitians, and invasions by French and British forces shredded the nation's social and economic fabric. TOUSSAINT L'OUVERTURE's slave rebellion secured freedom for the blacks and decolonization for the black republic; in 1804 Haiti became the second independent nation in the Americas. Ruled until 1859 by self-styled emperors, it lost control of western Hispaniola in 1845. Haiti's subsequent history is one of economic poverty, dictatorship, and occasional anarchy, with a period of US military occupation (1915–34). In 1957 François 'Papa Doc' DUVALIER was elected president. Supported by a personal police force (*tontons macoutes*), he imposed an especially repressive rule, relaxed to some degree only after his death (1971), when he was succeeded by his son, Jean-Claude Duvalier. 'Baby Doc' married into the mulatto elite which his father had despised, terrorized, and marginalized. Following a popular revolt, however, Duvalier fled the country (to France) in 1986 and a military–civilian government headed by Gen. Henri Namphy took power. After a four-month civilian interlude early in 1988, Gen. Namphy again seized power in June of that year.

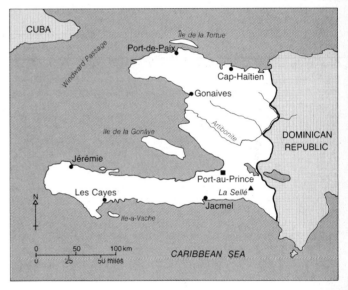

Haiti

**Hajj** [Arab., = pilgrimage], one of the five pillars of ISLAM which every sane, free, financially able Muslim is obliged to undertake at least once in a lifetime. The focal point of the pilgrimage is MECCA and its environs where a number of set rituals, many associated with the prophet Abraham, are performed.

**Hajj, al-, Umar,** 1794–1864, Muslim reformer and founder of an empire in W Sudan. He launched a *jihad* [holy war] in 1851 which resulted in the creation of a caliphate between the rivers Niger and Senegal. He died in battle and his state broke up into three independent states.

**Hakim, Tawfiq al-,** 1898?–87, Egyptian playwright. After studying law and literature in Egypt and France he became famous both for his novels *The Return of the Spirit* (1933) and *Diaries of a Rural Prosecutor* (1937), and as a playwright. He did more than any other writer to establish the drama in modern Arabic literature, and plays such as *People of the Cave* (1933), *Sheherazade* (1934), and *Oh Tree Climber* (1962) have become classics of the Arab theatre.

**Hakluyt, Richard** (͵haklOOt), 1552?–1616, English geographer. He promoted English discovery and colonization, especially in N America, and published many accounts of exploration and travel. His chief work is *The Principal Navigations, Voyages, Traffics, and Discoveries of the English Nation* (3 vol., 1598–1600). The Hakluyt Society (founded 1846) continues to publish narratives of early exploration.

**halakah** or **halachah,** legal portion of the TALMUD and of post-Talmudic literature; Jewish law; rabbinic directives and guidance concerning personal, communal, and international matters.

**halcyon:** see KINGFISHER.

**Hale, George Ellery,** 1868–1938, American astronomer. He was the founder of the Yerkes, Mt Wilson, and PALOMAR OBSERVATORIES (and director of the first two), each in its time housing the largest telescope in the world. His observatories were also laboratories employing the latest in photographic and spectrographic techniques. He invented (1890) the spectroheliograph, which led to the discovery of magnetic fields and vortices in sunspots, and founded (1895) the *Astrophysical Journal,* still the leading publication in its field.

**Halévy, Elie,** 1870–1937, French historian. The son of an opera librettist and producer, Halévy was educated in Paris and studied philosophy before turning to history. His *History of the English People,* the first volume of which appeared in 1912–13, remains the most thorough study of British history from 1815 to 1914, with a gap between the 1850s and 1895. A lecturer at the *École libre des sciences politiques,* he was also an authority on the history of European socialism. He raised as many questions as he answered.

**half-life:** see RADIOACTIVITY.

**Haliburton, Thomas Chandler,** pseud.**Sam Slick,** 1796–1865, Canadian author. A judge and historian, he is best known for his satiric series about the doings of Sam Slick, Yankee peddler, collected in *The Clockmaker* (1836) and later volumes.

**halibut:** see FLATFISH.

**Halicarnassus,** ancient city of Caria, SW Asia Minor (modern Bodrum, Turkey). In the 4th cent. BC the widow of King Mausolus built him a tomb there that was one of the SEVEN WONDERS OF THE WORLD. The historians HERODOTUS and Dionysius of Halicarnassus were born there.

**Halifax,** city (1984 est. pop. 114,594), capital of Nova Scotia, E Canada, overlooking one of the world's great natural harbours. It is the largest city in the Atlantic provinces and Canada's principal ice-free port and naval base on the eastern seaboard. Much of E Canada's trade passes through the port when the Great Lakes–St. Lawrence Seaway is closed by ice in winter. Founded in 1749 by the British as a rival to France's naval stronghold at LOUISBURG, Halifax played a major role in the AMERICAN REVOLUTION and the WAR OF 1812. It continued to be used by the British fleet until 1906 and was a naval base during both world wars. In 1917 a munitions ship was rammed in the harbour and exploded, killing 1800 and destroying the northern part of the city. Major landmarks in Halifax include the Citadel, a massive fortress (built 1794–97), and St Paul's Church (1750), the oldest Anglican church in Canada.

**Halifax,** town (1981 pop. 76,675), W Yorkshire, N Midlands of England, near R. Calder, 11 km (7 mi) SW of Bradford. An industrial town, it is famous for the manufacture of textiles and confectionery, and for its engineering industry. The cloth trade here dates back to the 15th cent.

**Hall, Sir Peter,** 1930–, English theatre director. He founded the Royal Shakespeare Company (1958) and remained its director until 1968. In 1973 he was appointed director of The National Theatre, a position he held until 1987. He has also directed operas, e.g., at Glyndebourne.

**Halle,** city (1984 pop. 236,456), Saxony-Anhalt, southern East Germany, on the Saale R. It is a centre of salt-mining and brown-coal working. Local sugar beet is refined and there are machine-making and extensive chemical industries. The old town developed around a Frankish castle in the early 9th cent. The university was founded in 1693. Halle was the birthplace of Handel and has a music academy and other cultural institutions. Notable buildings include the Gothic Red Tower and Marienkirche.

**Haller, (Victor) Albrecht von,** 1708–77, Swiss anatomist and physiologist. Haller's research in experimental physiology at the new Univ. of Göttingen, on which he based his theory of irritability, or contractility, of muscle tissue, is set forth in *A Dissertation on the Sensible and Irritable Parts of Animals* (1732). Back in his native Bern, he

Halle's market square

continued his research and wrote extensively (including novels and poetry), notably *Elementa physiologiae corporus humani* (8 vol., 1757–66).

**Halley, Edmund,** 1656–1742, English astronomer. He was the first to predict the return of a comet, using Isaac NEWTON's gravitational theory to calculate the orbit of the great comet of 1682 (now known as HALLEY'S COMET). He was also the first to point out the use of a transit of Venus in determining the Sun's parallax. Halley financed the publication (1687) of Newton's *Principia.* In 1720 he became Astronomer Royal.

**Halley's comet,** periodic COMET named for Edmund HALLEY, who observed it in 1682 and identified it with those seen in 1531 and 1607. It returned in 1759, close to the time Halley predicted, as well as in 1835 and 1910. It was sighted again in late 1982 and returned to its closest approach to the Sun in 1986, when the SPACE PROBE *Giotto* encountered it.

**Hallgrímsson, Jónas,** 1807–45, Icelandic poet. The most important creator of modern Icelandic poetry, he brilliantly combined nationalism and intensely lyrical ROMANTICISM. As a student in Denmark he and his friends founded the periodical *Fjölnir* (1835–47), which inspired Iceland's struggle for political freedom from Danish rule. His collected *Poems* were first published in 1847, and his complete *Works* in five volumes in 1929–37.

**Halliday, Michael Alexander Kirkwood,** 1925–, English linguist. He developed a model or GRAMMAR of language, known as Systemic Grammar. In recent years he has concentrated on developing a functional approach to language study. From the early 1970s he has worked in Australia.

**hallmark,** system of marking gold, silver, and more recently, platinum articles, to show that they conform to a legal standard of purity. Precious metals, too soft for domestic wares or jewellery, are alloyed for durability, according to specified standards. In Britain, where hallmarking dates back to the 14th cent., alloy standards are (by weight in parts per thousand): gold 916.6 (22 ct), 750 (18 ct), 585 (14 ct), 375 (9 ct); silver 958.4 (Britannia), 925 (Sterling); and platinum 950. By law, all precious metalwork offered for sale, with few exemptions, must be hallmarked by the Assay Office in London, Birmingham, Sheffield, or Edinburgh. Samples taken from each item submitted by the sponsor/maker, are analysed, and if to standard, the article is stamped with punches denoting the maker, metal, alloy standard, Assay Office, and year (distinguished by different letters in distinctive typographical styles). The International Convention of Assay Offices (Austria; Finland, Ireland, Portugal, Norway, Switzerland, and Sweden) are comparable, their marks being recognized as legal in Britain, excepting lower grades of silver. Other foreign marks lack official scrutiny.

**Halloween:** see ALL SAINTS' DAY.

**hallucinogenic drug,** drug that induces hallucinations; also called psychedelic drug. Hallucinogens include mescaline, or Peyote; psilocin

A typical hallmark showing the sterling mark, the crowned leopard's head (denotes London), the assay mark (in this case 'E' which denotes 1800), the sovereign's head, and the maker's initials (Thom. Wallis).

**Birmingham**
An anchor introduced in 1773.

**Dublin**
The crowned harp with the addition of Hibernia after 1730.

**Edinburgh**
The castle with the thistle which was added in 1759.

     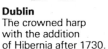

**London**
A leopard's head (crowned between 1478 and 1821)

**Sheffield**
The crown introduced in 1773.

Some other halls with their dates of closure.

**Chester** (1762)     **Exeter** (1883)     **Glasgow** (1965)

**Newcastle-upon-Tyne** (1884)
**Norwich** (1702)
**York** (1858)

**Hallmark**

and psilocybin, from the mushrooms *Psilocybe mexicana* and *Stropharia cubensis;* LSD (lysergic acid diethylamide); BELLADONNA; and MANDRAKE. MARIJUANA has hallucinogenic properties but is pharmacologically distinct. Hallucinogens have been used for centuries by primitive societies in both the Old and New Worlds to facilitate meditation, cure illness, placate evil spirits, and enhance mystical and magical powers. They produce a wide range of effects, from pleasant to extremely disturbing, depending on dosage, potency, and the personality and environment of the drug taker. Effects include altered perception of time and space and of the colour, detail, and size of objects; also the experience of imaginary conversations, music, odours, tastes, and other sensations. Hallucinogens are not physically habit-forming, but tolerance i.e., the need to take increased quantities to induce the original effect may develop.

**halo,** in art: see NIMBUS.

**halo,** in meteorology, circle of light surrounding the moon or sun. A halo occurs when sunlight or moonlight is refracted or reflected by ice crystals in the atmosphere, usually in a thin layer of high cirrostratus clouds. In general, a white halo results when the light is reflected, and coloured rings (showing the colours of the spectrum, with red on the inside) result when the light is refracted.

**halogen,** any of the five chemical elements in group VIIa of the PERIODIC TABLE. FLUORINE, CHLORINE, BROMINE, IODINE, and the radioactive ASTATINE are nonmetallic, monovalent negative ions and exist in pure form as diatomic molecules. The first four elements exhibit an almost perfect gradation of physical properties. Fluorine is the least dense and chemically the most active, displacing other halogens from their compounds and oxygen from water. Iodine is the least active. The halogens form numerous compounds with each other, and with other elements, such as hydrogen halides, metal halides (SALTS), and halocarbons.

**Hals, Frans,** c.1582/3–1666, Dutch painter of portraits and GENRE scenes; b. Belgium. Although his reputation was established early, Hals spent most of his life in poverty. His scenes from everyday life were painted in the first half of his career. In the 1620s and 30s he painted group portraits, e.g., *Banquet of the Officers of the St. George Militia*

(1616; Haarlem) with vivacity and informality, and some important single portraits, e.g., *Lucas de Clercq* (Rijksmuseum, Amsterdam). He worked rapidly, employing brilliantly free brushwork to capture momentary effects. At 84 he painted two masterpieces, *The Governors of the Almshouse* and *Lady Regents of the Almshouse* (both: Haarlem), which have the same brilliant lighting and cool clarity as his gayer canvases. His notable paintings include *The Merry Drinker* (Rijksmuseum, Amsterdam) and *The Laughing Cavalier* (1624; Wallace Coll., London). **Dirk Hals,** c.1591–1656, his brother, specialized in festivals and drinking scenes, e.g., his *A Party at Table* (1626; National Gall., London).

Frans **Hals,** *The Merry Drinker*. 81 × 66.5 cm. Rijksmuseum, Amsterdam.

**Ham:** see NOAH.

**hamadryads:** see NYMPH.

**Hamah** or **Hama,** city (1981 pop. 176,640), W central Syria, on the Orontes R. It is the market centre for an irrigated farm region where cotton, wheat, and barley are grown. Manufactures include textiles, carpets, and dairy products. As Hamath, it is often mentioned in the Bible as the northernmost location of the Israelites. Points of interest include a Roman aqueduct, large water wheels, and the Great Mosque of Djami al-Nuri (until 638 a Christian basilica).

**Hamamatsu,** city (1986 est. pop. 513,904), Shizuoka prefecture, S Honshu, Japan, surrounded by the R. Tenryu (E); Lake Hamana (W); and the Nakatajima Sand Dune (S). Long established as an important cotton mill area, it is now a leading industrial centre producing musical instruments, cars and motorcycles, and optoelectronic devices. Hamamatsu is an old castle town and was a busy trading post on the route between Edo (now Tokyo) and Kyoto. To the north, is the ancient battlefield of Mikatagahara where Tokugawa IEYASU defeated his rival, Takeda Shingen.

**Haman:** see ESTHER.

**Hamasa,** anthology of ARABIC LITERATURE, compiled in the 9th cent. by ABU TAMMAM. Consisting of 10 books of poems grouped by subject, it is one of the treasures of early Arabic poetry. The poems are of exceptional beauty.

**Hamburg,** city (1984 pop. 1,600,300), coextensive with, and capital of, Hamburg state, N West Germany, on the Elbe and Alster rivers. It is

West Germany's largest city and busiest port. Manufactures include ships and machinery. Founded in the 9th cent., it formed (13th cent.) an alliance with LÜBECK that became the basis of the HANSEATIC LEAGUE. The city was largely destroyed by fire in 1842. Severely damaged during WORLD WAR II, it has been rebuilt and is now a modern cultural centre. Felix MENDELSSOHN and Johannes BRAHMS were born in Hamburg.

**Hamhung,** city (1972 pop. 420,000), E central North Korea. An industrial and commercial centre specializing in textiles, it was developed by the Japanese during World War II but severely damaged in the KOREAN WAR. Just SE is the seaport and industrial centre of Hungnam, with important chemical and fertilizer plants.

**Hamilcar Barca,** d. 229 or 228 BC, Carthaginian general, father of HANNIBAL. In the First PUNIC WAR, he gave a good account of himself in Sicily. He ruthlessly put down (238) a revolt of mercenaries and became virtual dictator of CARTHAGE. In 237 he set out to conquer Spain but fell in battle.

**Hamilton,** city (1984 est. pop. 308,102), S Ontario, Canada, on Lake Ontario, part of Hamilton–Wentworth municipality. A major GREAT LAKES shipping port, it is Canada's chief iron and steel centre, and manufactures automobiles and heavy machinery. The city, hemmed into the narrow coastal plain by the Niagara escarpment, was founded in 1778 by UNITED EMPIRE LOYALISTS.

**Hamilton, Alexander,** 1755–1804, US statesman; b. West Indies. In the AMERICAN REVOLUTION he was Gen. WASHINGTON's secretary and aide-de-camp, and served brilliantly in the YORKTOWN CAMPAIGN. As a delegate (1782–83) to the CONTINENTAL CONGRESS, he pressed for a strong national government. After serving as a New York delegate to the FEDERAL CONSTITUTIONAL CONVENTION (1787) he did much to get the Constitution ratified, particularly by his contributions to *The Federalist.* As secretary of the treasury (1789–95) under Pres. Washington, Hamilton sponsored legislation to pay off the debt of the Continental Congress and to charter the Bank of the United States. To raise revenue he advocated a tariff on imported manufactured goods and excise taxes. By these measures he hoped to strengthen the federal government and tie it to men of wealth. In foreign affairs, Hamilton sought close ties with Britain and opposed the FRENCH REVOLUTION. Opposition to Hamilton and his supporters, who were known as Federalists, gathered around Thomas JEFFERSON, and the FEDERALIST PARTY was defeated in the election of 1800. Hamilton was killed in a duel by Aaron BURR, whose bids for the presidency (1800) and for New York governor (1804) Hamilton had thwarted.

**Hamilton, Emma, Lady,** c.1765–1815, English beauty. She was the mistress and, later, wife of Sir William Hamilton, the English ambassador to Naples. After 1798 she was the mistress of Horatio NELSON, whose daughter she bore in 1801. Many portraits of her were painted by George ROMNEY.

**Hamilton, Richard,** 1922–, British painter. He was one of the main artists involved in POP ART in Britain. He took an intellectual and critical approach to popular culture in his paintings, collages, and montages, e.g., *Hommage à Chrysler Corp* (1957), in which the connection between car styling and sex symbolism is used to show up the subtle psychological games and strategies of American advertising. He organized the Tate Gallery's retrospective exhibition (1966) of Marcel DUCHAMP.

**Hamilton, Sir William Rowan,** 1805–65, Irish mathematician. A child prodigy, he had mastered 13 languages by the age of 13. Hamilton was one of the most creative mathematicians of his time. In *Theory of Systems of Rays* (1828) he showed that all systems and problems in the field of optics could be considered and explained in terms of the principle of varying 'action' (a product of time and energy), which he later extended to dynamics and which is of fundamental importance in modern physics, particularly QUANTUM THEORY. His later years were devoted to the development of his theory of quaternions, complex numbers (see NUMBER) with one real and three imaginary components.

**Hamites,** African people of Caucasoid descent, inhabiting the Horn of Africa (chiefly Somalia and Ethiopia), the W Sahara, and parts of Algeria and Tunisia. They are believed to have been the original settlers of N Africa, having come from S Arabia and farther east. Eastern Hamites include the ancient and modern Egyptians, the GALLA, the Somali, and most Ethiopians. Northern Hamites include the BERBERS, the Tuareg of the Sahara, and other groups.

**Hamitic languages,** subfamily of the Hamito-Semitic family of languages. See AFRICAN LANGUAGES (table).

**Hamito-Semitic languages,** family of languages, spoken by people in N Africa, much of the Sahara, parts of E central and W Africa, and W Asia (especially the Arabian peninsula). See AFRICAN LANGUAGES (table); LANGUAGE (table).

**Hamm,** city (1984 pop. 167,600), North Rhine–Westphalia, West Germany. On the NE edge of the RUHR industrial region, it is a major rail junction with the largest marshalling yards in the country. Canals follow the Lippe to the RHINE at Wesel.

**Hammarskjöld, Dag** (ˌhaməˈshoold), 1905–61, Swedish statesman, secretary general (1953–61) of the UNITED NATIONS. He was chairman of the board of the Bank of Sweden (1941–48) and deputy foreign minister (1951) before joining Sweden's UN delegation. As secretary general he greatly extended the influence of the UN with his peacekeeping efforts, particularly in the Middle East and Africa. He was on a mission to the Congo (now ZAÏRE) when his plane crashed in northern Rhodesia (now Zambia) in 1961.

**Hammersmith and Fulham,** London borough (1981 pop. 144,616), on N side of the R. Thames, which is crossed here by Hammersmith, Putney, and Fulham bridges. It is largely residential, with a variety of industries. The BBC television centre and studios are here, as is the Olympia exhibition centre.

**Hammerstein, Oscar, 2nd,** 1895–1960, American lyricist and librettist. He collaborated on many MUSICALS with Vincent Youmans; Rudolf Friml; Sigmund Romberg; Jerome KERN, e.g., *Show Boat* (1927); and, particularly, Richard RODGERS. His grandfather **Oscar Hammerstein,** 1846–1919, was a German-American operatic impresario. He built the Harlem Opera House (1888) and the Manhattan Opera House (1906), in New York City, and introduced many singers to the US.

**hammer throwing,** FIELD EVENT in athletics, in which an iron or brass sphere attached to a steel sprung handle is thrown as far as possible from within a circle (2.13 m/7 ft). The weight of the sphere is 7.26 kg (16 lb) and the overall length of the device 1.21 m (3 ft 11¾ in). Throwers begin at the back of the circle and rotate themselves and the hammer across the circle before release. Sledgehammer throwing became part of local sporting events in the 16th cent. and achieved official recognition at the Oxford Univ. sports of 1860.

**Hammett, Dashiell,** 1894–1961, American writer. He originated the 'hard-boiled' detective novel—realistic, fast-paced, sophisticated. His novels include *The Maltese Falcon* (1930) and *The Thin Man* (1932).

**Hammurabi,** fl. 1792–1750 BC, king of BABYLONIA. He founded an empire that was eventually destroyed by raids from Asia Minor. His code of laws found on a column at Susa is one of the greatest of the ancient codes.

**Hampshire,** county in S England (1984 est. pop. 1,509,500), 3777 km² (1473 sq mi), bordering on the English Channel in the S. The county town is WINCHESTER. In the 1974 boundary changes Hampshire lost BOURNEMOUTH to the neighbouring county of Dorset and the Isle of WIGHT became a separate county. It is crossed by the Hampshire Downs in the N and the South Downs in the SE. The NEW FOREST is situated in the SW. Much of the county is occupied by agricultural land, but industry is important in SOUTHAMPTON and PORTSMOUTH, both also ports.

**Hampton,** part of the Greater London borough of Richmond upon Thames, SE England, on the Thames R. It is the site of **Hampton Court Palace,** begun by Cardinal WOLSEY in 1514. After his fall it was taken by HENRY VIII, and it remained a royal residence until the time of GEORGE II. Much of it is open to the public. The **Hampton Court Conference** was held in 1604, in the reign of JAMES I, to consider reforms of the Established Church for which its Puritan clergy had petitioned. Few concessions were made to the Puritans. The conference authorized the King James version of the BIBLE.

**hamster,** nocturnal RODENT with large cheek pouches for holding food. The common, or European, hamster (*Cricetus cricetus*), about 30 cm (12 in) long, is reddish brown with white patches on the nose, cheeks, throat, and flanks. The Syrian, or golden, hamster (*Mesocricetus auratus*) of E Europe and W Asia is familiar as a laboratory animal and as a pet. Hamsters are serious agricultural pests because their diet consists of fruit, grain, and vegetables.

**Hamsun, Knut** (‚hamsoon), 1859–1952, Norwegian novelist. His youthful wanderings, including two visits to the US, provided the theme for many of his novels, especially *Hunger* (1890), which established him. He is best known for the lyrically beautiful *Pan* (1894), expressing his interest in irrational forces, and for his masterpiece, *The Growth of the Soil* (1917), reflecting his love of nature and concern for the effect of material conditions on the individual spirit. He was awarded the 1920 Nobel Prize for literature, but lost popularity during World War II because of his NAZI sympathies, for which he was fined. His reputation has now been largely rehabilitated.

**Han,** dynasty: see CHINA.

**Hanafism,** Hanafism, school of Sunni Islamic Law. See FIQH.

**Hanbalism,** Hanbalism, school of Sunni Islamic law and theological tendency. See FIQH; KALAM.

**Hancock, John,** 1737–93, political leader of the AMERICAN REVOLUTION. He opposed the STAMP ACT (1765) and advocated resistance to the British. Hancock was a member (1775–80) and president (1775–77) of the CONTINENTAL CONGRESS, and he was the first to sign the DECLARATION OF INDEPENDENCE.

**handball,** hand-and-ball game with 11 players on each side played on a pitch much like a soccer pitch with a goal at either end. A player may catch, throw, or pass the ball in the attempt to score goals, but must not take more than three steps while in possession before either passing or bouncing it. Handball is a no-contact game, so the ball, not its possessor, must be played, and dispossession is achieved largely by interception. Handball was played in antiquity and is now played in more than 50 countries; it has been an Olympic sport since 1932. In the indoor version, the teams have seven players each. Irish handball is played in a four-walled court by two or four people and is closely related to FIVES.

**handedness:** see LATERALITY.

**Handel, George Frederick,** 1685–1759, English composer; b. Germany as Georg Friedrich Handel. By 1705 he had produced two OPERAS in Hamburg; he spent the next four years in Italy, where he absorbed Italian style and became a master of the BAROQUE. Moving to England in 1712, he wrote music, including the celebrated *Water Music* (1717), for GEORGE I. Together with members of the nobility, Handel set up an opera syndicate on strictly commercial lines, called The Royal Academy of Music. When this company went bankrupt in 1728, Handel became an impresario and established his own company. After many successes there came a period of failures. He left England for Dublin in 1741, and a series of successful concerts and the first performance of *Messiah* (1742) ushered in a new period of writing and producing oratorios. Among his 46 operas are *Julius Caesar* (1724), *Atalanta* (1736), and *Xerxes* (1738). The contemplative character of *Messiah* sets it apart from the rest of his 32 oratorios, which include *Acis and Galatea* (1720), *Esther* (1732), *Athalia* (1735), *Saul* (1739), *Belshazzar* (1735), *Judas Maccabeus* (1747), and *Jephtha* (1752). He also composed about 100 Italian solo CANTATAS; numerous orchestral works, among them the Twelve Grand Concertos (1739); harpsichord SUITES; organ CONCERTOS; and the ANTHEM 'Zadok, the Priest' (1727), used at all British coronations since that of George II.

**Handke, Peter,** 1942–, Austrian playwright and novelist. His early avant-garde works represent a deliberately scandalous literary rebellion against the constraints of literary and social convention, and even of words themselves, as in his dramas *Offending the Audience* (1966) and *Kaspar* (1968). He explores the limitations of social role and system in *A Sorrow beyond Dreams* (1972), his work of mourning for the death of his mother; and attempts to escape them in *A Left-Handed Woman* (1976). His most recent works, collected as *Slow Homecoming* (1981), have been subjective and autobiographical.

**Handley Page, Sir Frederick,** 1885–1962, British aeronautical engineer. He was a pioneer of the design of large aircraft in both civil and military fields. His Handley Page 42 civil transport aircraft was one of the leading types of commercial aircraft of inter-war years, flying more than 10 million miles and carrying 644,000 passengers without injury. Between 1916 and 1987 there was never a time when Handley Page aircraft were not in service with the Royal Air Force, the most famous being the Halifax bomber of World War II and the Victor jet bomber.

**Handy, W(illiam) C(hristopher),** 1873–1958, black American songwriter and bandleader. He was among the first to set down the blues (see JAZZ), and became famous with 'Memphis Blues'. Other well-known compositions are 'St Louis Blues' and 'Beale Street Blues'.

**Hangchow:** see HANGZHOU.

**hang-glider,** ultra-light airframe to which is attached a triangular, aerodynamic, fabric lifting-surface under which a pilot is suspended in a harness. A hang-glider is launched into the wind down a steep slope and the flight path is controlled by movements of the pilot's body. Modern hang-gliders were invented and developed from 1972 by Francis Rogallo in the US; a Rogallo wing is 5.5 m (18 ft) in span and weighs 16 kg (35 lb). A much earlier form was invented and flown by Otto LILIENTHAL, starting in 1891. By 1894 Lilienthal had made controlled glides of up to 350 m (1150 ft), but he was killed in 1896 when his hang-glider stalled. His pioneering work was taken over by the Scotsman Percy Pilcher (1867–99) who was killed when his hang-glider suffered structural failure.

**Hangzhou** or **Hangchow** (hahng-joh), city (1984 pop. 5,374,900), capital of ZHEJIANG prov., E China, at one end of the GRAND CANAL. Long a famous silk- and tea-producing centre, Hangzhou has become an important regional industrial complex; producing textiles, iron and steel products, and motor vehicles. The city is also one of China's most popular tourist centres. The scenic West Lake, wooded hills, and shrines and monasteries dating from the 10th cent. are all located in the city. As the capital (1132–1276) of the Southern Song (Sung) dynasty, it was a famous cosmopolitan centre of commerce and culture. Almost destroyed (1861) in the Taiping Rebellion, it was rebuilt as a modern city.

**Hannibal,** b. 247 BC, d. 183 or 182 BC, Carthaginian general. One of the great military geniuses of all time, he was son of HAMILCAR BARCA, of the great Barca family. In 221 BC he succeeded his brother-in-law, HASDRUBAL, as commander in Spain. During the Second PUNIC WAR, he set out to invade Italy with a small force of picked troops, crossed the Alps with a full baggage train and elephants, and with his cavalry overran the Po valley. He wiped out a Roman force and in 217 BC set out toward Rome. After defeating the Romans again at Lake Trasimeno, he went to S Italy and gained many allies. At Cannae (216 BC), he won one of the most brilliant victories in history, but he failed to get proper support from CARTHAGE and could not take Rome. In 207 his brother Hasdrubal was defeated on the Metaurus R., and Hannibal had to draw back. Recalled (203 BC) to defend Carthage against Scipio Africanus Major (see SCIPIO, family), he was decisively beaten at the battle of ZAMA (202 BC). After peace was concluded (201 BC), he was chief ruler in Carthage, governing well, but Rome demanded him as a prisoner, and he went into exile, finally poisoning himself to avoid being given to the Romans.

**Hanoi,** city (1979 pop. 2,145,662), capital of Vietnam, N Vietnam, on the Red R. A major transport and industrial centre, it produces such manufactures as locomotives, machine tools, and chemicals. It became the seat of the Chinese rulers of Vietnam in the 7th cent. and the capital of French INDOCHINA in 1887. When the French withdrew in 1954 Hanoi became the capital of North Vietnam. It was heavily bombed during the VIETNAM WAR, after which it became the capital of united Vietnam. A cultural centre with several universities and institutes, it is noted for its European-style buildings and tree-lined avenues.

**Hanover,** former kingdom and former province of Germany. Its chief cities included Hanover, Osnabrück, and Stade. In 1692 Duke Ernest Augustus of Calenburg became elector of Hanover. His son succeeded (1714) to the English throne as GEORGE I (see also HANOVER, HOUSE OF), thus uniting Britain and Hanover in a personal union. NAPOLEON I broke up the electorate, but in 1813 Britain regained possession. In 1815 it was made a kingdom. On the accession (1837) of Queen VICTORIA, Hanover was separated from Britain because of the SALIC LAW of succession. As a result of the AUSTRO-PRUSSIAN WAR (1866) Hanover was made a Prussian (from 1871 a German) province. After World War II it was incorporated into Lower Saxony.

**Hanover,** city (1984 pop. 517,900), capital of Lower Saxony, N West Germany, on the Leine R. and the Midland Canal. A transshipment and industrial centre with such manufactures as iron and steel, it is noted for its annual industrial fair. It was chartered in 1241 and became a member (1386) of the HANSEATIC LEAGUE and the capital (1692) of the electorate of HANOVER. Badly damaged during WORLD WAR II, the city has been rebuilt since 1945. Historic buildings include the 14th-cent. Marktkirche and the 17th-cent. Leineschloss, which now houses the parliament of LOWER SAXONY.

**Hanover, house of,** ruling dynasty of Hanover (see HANOVER, province), which was descended from the GUELPHS and which in 1714 acceded to the British throne in the person of GEORGE I, elector of Hanover, through a claim based on descent from JAMES I. George I's succession was based on the Act of SETTLEMENT. There were five Hanoverian British kings. With VICTORIA the crowns of Hanover and Britain were separated.

**Hansard,** official record of debates in the British Houses of Parliament since 1774, compiled until 1892 by Messrs. Hansard.

**Hansa towns:** see HANSEATIC LEAGUE.

**Hansberry, Lorraine,** 1930–65, American playwright. Her famous play *A Raisin in the Sun* (1959) deals with the problems of a black family in modern America. Many of her writings were collected in *To Be Young, Gifted, and Black* (1969).

**Hanseatic League,** mercantile league of medieval N German towns. It came into existence gradually as the Hansas, companies of merchants dealing with foreign lands, and the cities from which they operated drew closer together as a way of protecting themselves from foreign competition and piracy. In the 13th cent. more than 70 German cities joined in treaties of mutual protection. The Hanseatic League was formally organized in 1358, and in 1370 it won a trade monopoly in all of Scandinavia. The league prospered in the following centuries but finally went out of existence in the 17th cent. BREMEN, HAMBURG, and LÜBECK are still known as Hanseatic cities.

**Hansen's disease:** see LEPROSY.

**Hanson, Duane,** 1925–, American sculptor. A superrealist (see PHOTOREALISM), he is noted for his life-sized and astonishingly realistic figures, e.g., *Woman with Dog* (1977; Whitney Mus., New York City).

**Hanson-Dyer, Louise,** 1884–1962, Australian music patron. She founded Editions de l'Oiseau-Lyre in Paris in 1932 to publish the works of COUPERIN and other early music. She later issued recordings, among them the first long-playing record made in France.

**Hanukkah:** see under JEWISH HOLIDAYS.

**Haora** (formerly **Howrah**), city (1981 pop. 744,429), West Bengal state, E India, on the Hugli (Hooghly) R. It is essentially a part of the Greater CALCUTTA, or Hugliside, conurbation on the west side of the river. It has a large and important railway station and is a district administrative centre. Its prime function, however, is industrial: it has many textile mills (cotton and jute), chemical works, and metal-working plants (ferrous and otherwise).

**Happening,** a term used in the 1960s to cover a wide variety of art practices in which the traditional values of creativity and craftsmanship were undermined. The production of a work of art was seen as an 'event' in which the spectator was often involved. Yves KLEIN's *Anthropométries* (1960) were created by instructing naked girls to spread paint on their bodies, and then under his direction to press against the canvas, leaving marks. In the US Jim DINE, Claus OLDENBURG, Robert RAUSCHENBERG, and Roy LICHTENSTEIN were involved in its development. In Germany Joseph BEUYS conceived the Happening as a political demonstration, where shock tactics were used to undermine and question establishment values and attitudes.

**Hapsburg,** family: see HABSBURG.

**hara-kiri** [Jap., = belly-cutting], traditional Japanese form of suicide. Performed in circumstances of defeat and dishonour, or as atonement for a transgression, hara-kiri was also used as an honourable form of execution until the 1870s. The most recent occurrences of voluntary hara-kiri were at the end of WORLD WAR II and the spectacular suicide of MISHIMA YUKIO in 1970.

**Harald:** see HAROLD.

**Harare** formerly **Salisbury,** largest city (1982 est. pop. 656,000) and capital of Zimbabwe on the Makabusi R. One of Africa's most modern cities, it is the country's commercial and communications centre and the market for an agricultural region. Industries include the manufacture of polythene products, paint, construction materials, and electrical goods. The city is connected by rail with BULAWAYO and the Mozambique port of SOFALA (formerly Beira). Founded by the British in 1890, it was the capital

of the Federation of Rhodesia and Nyasaland (1953–63). In 1982 it was renamed Harare (after a 19th-cent. leader).

**Harbin,** city (1984 pop. 3,770,900), capital of HEILONGJIANG prov., NE China, on the SONGHUA R. It is the major trade, industrial, and transport centre of NE China and the main port on the Sungari. Harbin is part of the great Manchurian complex of metallurgical, machinery, chemical, oil, and coal industries. It is also an important producer of tractors, paper, and aircraft. Harbin's strong resemblance to Russian cities results from settlers who came to the city after Russia was granted (1896) a concession there, and after the Russian Revolution (1917). Most of its European population, once one of the largest in the Far East, left the city following the rise to power of the Chinese Communists.

**Hardenberg, Friedrich von:** see NOVALIS.

**Hardenberg, Karl August, Fürst von,** 1750–1822, Prussian minister of foreign affairs (1804–06) and chancellor (1810–22). Continuing the reform programmes begun by Karl vom und zum STEIN, he abolished trade monopolies, turned feudal land into freeholds, and emancipated the JEWS. Hardenberg persuaded King William Frederick III to join (1813) the anti-NAPOLEON coalition. He became increasingly reactionary in his later years.

**Harding, Warren Gamaliel,** 1865–1923, 29th president of the US (1921–23). An Ohio Republican, Harding was elected (1914) to the US Senate and was a compromise choice as Republican presidential candidate in 1920. His administration had one achievement: the calling (1921) of the Washington NAVAL CONFERENCE. He had promised to appoint a cabinet of the 'best minds', but in 1923 came rumours of government scandals. Harding died suddenly (Aug. 1923) in San Francisco on his way back from Alaska. He thus was spared the public exposure of the TEAPOT DOME scandal and the humiliation of seeing his cabinet appointees, Albert B. Fall and Harry M. Daugherty, brought to justice. Harding's administration has been called one of the most corrupt in US history.

**Hardouin, Jules:** see under MANSART.

**hardware:** see COMPUTER.

**Hardy, Thomas,** 1840–1928, English novelist and poet, one of the great English writers of the 19th cent. He won success with *Far from the Madding Crowd* (1874). His other major novels are *The Return of the Native* (1878), *The Mayor of Casterbridge* (1886), *The Woodlanders* (1887), *Tess of the d'Urbervilles* (1891), and *Jude the Obscure* (1896). Set in the landscapes of his native Wessex, they are tragic novels in which colourful, romantic heroes and heroines are brought low by their own weaknesses and by a hostile, unforgiving environment. Stung by adverse criticism and accusations of obscenity, after 1896 Hardy abandoned the novel for poetry. His later verse includes *The Dynasts* (written 1903–08), an epic historical drama, and the lyric collections *Wessex Poems* (1898) and *Moments of Vision* (1917), in which his pessimistic outlook and haunting emotional sensitivity are expressed with a plainness of diction which greatly influenced later poets.

**hare,** herbivorous MAMMAL of the family Leporidae, which also includes the RABBIT, native to Eurasia, Africa, and North and Central America. The term *hare* is especially applied to the genus *Lepus,* sometimes called true hares. Hares generally have longer ears and hind legs than rabbits and move by jumping rather than running. They are usually brown or greyish in colour, but northern species acquire a white coat in winter. The brown hare (*Lepus europaeus*) is about 60 cm (24 in) long, and spends the day hiding in a hollow called a form. The young are called leverets, and they each have a form, the doe visiting them. The males, or jacks, indulge in strange pre-mating behaviour, kicking, bucking, and standing on their hind legs to 'box' with one another. This has given rise to the expression 'as mad as a March hare'.

**Hare, Richard Meryyn,** 1919–, English moral philosopher. In *The Language of Morals* (1952) and *Freedom and Reason* (1963) he argues for a sharp distinction between the form and content of moral judgments, holding that moral judgments are disguised imperatives (a doctrine he calls 'prescriptivism') which are universalizable. A staunch defender of UTILITARIANISM, he tries to show in *Moral Thinking* (1981) that it is the only ethic compatible with his logical principles.

**Hare Krishna,** popular name for a modern Hindu sect, the International Society for Krishna Consciousness, that gained prominence in the US and Canada after its founding (1966) by A.C. Bhaktivedanta Swami

Prabhupada (1896–1977). Originally spelt as Hare Kṛṣṇa, it refers to a couplet used for chanting beginning with these two words—*O Hari, O Krishna* (Hare, vocative case of Hari, a name for Krishna). Claiming thousands of followers, the movement teaches devotion to Krishna (see HINDUISM) as a means of attaining spiritual enlightenment, particularly through the practice of chanting the couplet. See also CULT.

**Hargreaves, James,** 1720?–78, English engineer and inventor of the spinning jenny. This machine, invented in 1764, allowed the spinning of many threads simultaneously thereby multiplying production of yarn. Handloom weavers upset by this cheaper competition set fire to his house and machinery at Blackburn, in Lancashire, in 1768. Because of patent litigation which he lost there is some belief that he was not the actual inventor.

**Hari, Mata:** see MATA HARI.

**Haringey,** London borough (1981 pop. 202,650), in N London. It contains the districts of Hornsey, Tottenham, and Wood Green. A mainly residential borough, it has also some varied industry. It contains Alexandra Palace, which was opened in 1873, burned down and reopened in 1878; in use as an exhibition centre, it suffered further fire damage and was again the subject of rebuilding in the 1980s. The first BBC television transmitter was established at Alexandra Palace in 1936.

**Harington, Sir John,** 1561?–1612, English poet and translator. He was a godson to ELIZABETH I, and translated ARIOSTO's *Orlando Furioso* (1591) probably at her request. His *Nugae Antiquae* contain interesting recollections of many individuals at the Elizabethan court.

**Hariri, Abu Muhammad al-Kasim al-** (hah‿reeree), 1054–1122, Arab writer. *Assemblies of al-Hariri,* his principal work and one of the most popular Arabic books, is an episodic tale of an old rogue, Abu Zaid, who earns his living by his wits.

**Harlem,** section of NEW YORK CITY, US. Established (1658) as Nieuw Haarlem by the Dutch, Harlem remained rural until the 19th cent., when it became a fashionable residental district. A rapid influx of blacks beginning c.1910 made it one of the largest black communities in the US, and in the 1920s it became a centre of art and literature (see HARLEM RENAISSANCE). Harlem deteriorated after World War II and the area is now depressed economically, with a high rate of unemployment.

**Harlem Renaissance,** term used to describe a flowering of black American literature that took place in the 1920s. During the great migration of blacks from the rural South to the industrial North (1914–18), some settled in the HARLEM district of New York City, as did the musicians who brought JAZZ from New Orleans, and Harlem became a sophisticated artistic and literary centre. In his magazine *Crisis,* W.E.B. DU BOIS urged racial pride among blacks, and writers, many living in Harlem, began producing fine original works about black life. Their work constituted a fresh, new subject that attracted white readers and publishers. Writers associated with the Harlem Renaissance include Arna Bontemps, Langston HUGHES, Claude McKay, Countee Cullen, James Weldon Johnson, Zora Neale HURSTON, and Jean Toomer. The Renaissance faded with the onset of the Great Depression of the 1930s.

**Harlow, Jean,** 1911–37, American film actress; b. Harlean Carpenter. A wisecracking platinum blonde, she starred in such films as *Red Dust* (1932), *Dinner at Eight* (1933), and *Blonde Bombshell* (1933).

**Harmodius and Aristogiton** (hah‿mohdeeəs, ‿eəristoh‿jietən), d. c.514 BC, Athenian tyrannicides. Their attempt to assassinate the tyrant Hippias and his brother Hipparchus ended with Hipparchus dead but Hippias unhurt. Harmodius was killed instantly; Aristogiton was captured and executed later. Although they had been motivated by a personal quarrel, they became heroes of ATHENS and were given public recognition after the expulsion (510 BC) of Hippias.

**harmonic motion,** regular vibration, or up-and-down motion, in which the acceleration of the vibrating object is directly proportional to the displacement of the object from its equilibrium position, but oppositely directed. A single object vibrating in this manner is said to exhibit simple harmonic motion; examples are a PENDULUM swinging in a small arc, a mass moving backwards and forwards at the end of a spring, and the motion of air molecules when a sound wave passes. Simple harmonic motion is periodic, i.e., it repeats itself at regular intervals. The time required for one complete vibration of the object is the period of the motion. The inverse of the period is the FREQUENCY, which is the number

of vibrations per unit of time. The maximum displacement of the object from its central position of equilibrium is the amplitude of the motion. See WAVE.

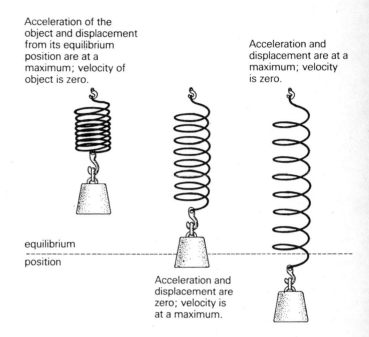

Acceleration of the object and displacement from its equilibrium position are at a maximum; velocity of object is zero.

Acceleration and displacement are at a maximum; velocity is zero.

equilibrium position

Acceleration and displacement are zero; velocity is at a maximum.

Harmonic motion

**harmonic progression:** see PROGRESSION.

**harmony,** in music, simultaneous sounding of two or more tones and, especially, the study of chords and their relations. POLYPHONY, or the interweaving of several independent melodic lines, prevailed in composition until the 16th cent., when interest centred on harmonic chord construction, or the relationship between one tone and the tone or tones being played at the same time. In 1722 Jean Philippe RAMEAU presented the idea that different groupings of the same notes were inversions of the same chord. In the 18th cent. the concept of TONALITY became firmly established. Using the principle of MODULATION, later composers developed freer concepts of tonality, until some in the 20th cent. have discarded traditional tonality altogether. See also ATONALITY; SERIAL MUSIC.

**Harmsworth, Alfred Charles William:** see NORTHCLIFFE, ALFRED CHARLES WILLIAM HARMSWORTH, VISCOUNT.

**Harmsworth, Harold Sidney:** see ROTHERMERE, HAROLD SIDNEY HARMSWORTH, 1ST VISCOUNT.

**harness racing,** also known as trotting, a form of horse race in which standardbreds, not thoroughbreds, pull a jockey and a small lightweight carriage (sulky) round an oval dirt track, usually of 1.609 km (1 mi). There are two types of standard bred horse, the trotter and the pacer. In trotting, the diagonal legs move together; in pacing, the two legs on one side of the horse move together, then the other two. Archeologists have found evidence suggesting that trotting races took place as early as 1350 BC; modern harness racing seems to descend directly from Roman charioteering.

**Harold,** 1020?–66, king of England (r.1066). The son of Godwin, earl of Wessex, he belonged to the most powerful noble family in the reign of EDWARD THE CONFESSOR. After Harold's succession in 1053 to the earldom of Wessex, he aspired to the throne. In c.1064 he was shipwrecked on the French coast and was forced to take an oath (which he later renounced) supporting WILLIAM I's claim to the English throne. In 1065 he sided with the Northumbrians against his brother Tostig. The family was thus divided at the death of the king, who probably named Harold his heir. William at once invaded England from the south and Tostig, with HAROLD III of Norway, invaded from the north. Harold soundly defeated them in a battle in which both Harold III and Tostig were killed. The king then met William in the battle of HASTINGS, fought valiantly, and was killed.

**Harold,** kings of Norway. **Harold I** or **Harold Fairhair,** c.850–c.933 (r.872–c.933), was the son of Halfdan the Black, king of Vestfold (SE Norway). He became Norway's first king by defeating other petty kings. During his reign, raids on Europe and migration to Iceland reached their peak. His son HAAKON I succeeded him by defeating another son. **Harold III** or **Harold Hardrada** [stern council], d. 1066 (r.1046–66), half brother of OLAF II. He joined (1042) the revolt against MAGNUS I and was made joint king (1046), becoming sole king at Magnus's death (1047). After invading N England, he died in battle with HAROLD of England.

**harp,** STRINGED INSTRUMENT of ancient origin, the strings of which are plucked with the fingers. During the 15th cent. the European harp came to be made in three parts, as it is today: sound box, neck, and pillar. The strings are stretched between the sound box and the neck, into which are fastened the tuning pegs. The diatonic harp was perfected c.1810 with the invention of double-action pedals, which can raise pitch by a semitone or a tone. Ethnomusicologists have recorded and described a range of harps and different playing techniques from Asia and Africa, and from Latin America.

**Harpers Ferry,** US town (1980 pop. 361), Jefferson co., easternmost W Virginia, at the confluence of the Shenandoah and Potomac rivers; inc. 1763. The US Arsenal (est. 1796) was seized in the famous raid by John BROWN on 16 Oct. 1859. Because of its strategic SHENANDOAH VALLEY location and its arms production, its industry was repeatedly destroyed by both sides during the CIVIL WAR; the town never recovered. The Harpers Ferry National Historical park preserves Civil War historical sites.

**harpsichord:** see PIANO.

**Harpy,** [Gk., = snatcher], in Greek mythology, a predatory monster with the head of a woman and the body, wings, and claws of a bird.

**harrier,** medium sized migratory BIRD of prey related to EAGLES and HAWKS. Harriers hunt over open ground and swamp land. The marsh harrier (*Circus aeruginosus*) is the largest European example, being 48–55 cm (19–22 in) long. It is found across Europe, Africa, and Asia to Australia. The hen harrier (*C. cyaneus*) was named from the trouble it caused when all hens were free-range. It is called the marsh hawk in North America. The hen harrier population, along with that of the New Zealand swamp harrier, is now increasing. In Britain only careful protection has prevented the disappearance of the marsh harrier, which was reduced to six breeding pairs in 1966. It is now recovering.

**Harriman, W(illiam) Averell,** 1891–1986, American businessman and public official. A Democrat, he was ambassador to the USSR (1943–46), secretary of commerce (1946–48), governor of New York state (1955–59), undersecretary of state (1963–65), and ambassador-at-large (1965–68). He was also (1968) chief US negotiator at the Paris peace talks on Vietnam.

**Harrington, James,** 1611–77, English political philosopher. His *Commonwealth of Oceana* (1656) described a utopian society in which political power rested with the landed gentry. He advocated a written constitution and limitations on the amount of land one individual could hold. His ideas foreshadowed certain doctrines of the American and French revolutions.

**Harris, Sir Arthur Travers,** 1892–1984, Marshal of the Royal Air Force; b. Rhodesia (now Zimbabwe). He served in the Royal Flying Corps in World War I, and continued his career in the Royal Air Force, serving in India, Iraq, and Egypt between the wars. From 1941 he was Commander-in-Chief Bomber Command, directing the night bombing offensive against Germany that was a significant factor in ultimate victory. By 1944 more than half a million tonnes of bombs had been dropped on German cities causing appalling devastation and casualties, at a cost of heavy casualties to Bomber Command (47,000 killed or missing). Harris was created a baronet in 1953.

**Harris, Joel Chandler,** 1848–1908, American regionalist writer. His popular tales, narrated by the former slave Uncle Remus, drew upon black folklore, dialect, and humour to capture the authentic life of Southern blacks. Volumes include *Uncle Remus: His Songs and His Sayings* (1881), *The Tar Baby* (1904), and *Uncle Remus and Br'er Rabbit* (1906).

**Harris, Roy,** 1898–1979, American composer. Vital, melodic, and personal expression is characteristic of his works, including his First Symphony (1934); *When Johnny Comes Marching Home* (1934), a

choral work; Cumberland Concerto (1951); and his Piano Quintet (1936).

**Harris, (Theodore) Wilson,** 1921–, Guyanese writer. He is renowned for his technical experimentation with literary form, and for his attempts to utilize classical myth to elucidate Caribbean experience. His best-known works are *The Guyana Quartet* (1960–64). Resident in England since the early 1970s, he has written about black people in Britain in *Black Marsden* (1972), and *The Angel at the Gate* (1982). His *Carnival* (1985) is a complex work about the tradition of masks in the Caribbean.

**Harris, William Torrey,** 1835–1909, American educator and philosopher. Founder and editor (1867–93) of the *Journal of Speculative Philosophy,* he wrote several books on the psychology of education. He opened (1873) the first permanent public-school KINDERGARTEN in the US and served as US commissioner of education (1889–1906).

**Harrisburg,** US city (1980 pop. 53,264), state capital of Pennsylvania, on the Susquehanna R.; settled c.1710 as a trading post; inc. 1791. A commercial and transport centre, it produces steel and processed foods. Iron and coal mines are nearby. Harrisburg became the state capital in 1812; its capitol building (1906) is noteworthy. A 1979 accident at the nearby Three Mile Island nuclear generating station focused national attention on the area.

**Harrison, Benjamin,** 1833–1901, 23rd president of the US (1889–93). A grandson of William Henry HARRISON, he commanded an Indiana volunteer regiment in the AMERICAN CIVIL WAR, became a corporate lawyer, and served (1881–87) as US senator from Indiana. The Republicans chose him (1888) as presidential candidate against Grover CLEVELAND. After what has been called the most corrupt campaign in US history, he was elected by the electoral college, though Cleveland had won the popular vote. The first Pan-American Conference was held (1889) during his administration. He was defeated (1892) for reelection by Cleveland.

**Harrison, Rex,** 1908–, English actor; b. Reginald Carey. Noted for his insouciant style, he was acclaimed as Professor Henry Higgins in both the stage (1956, 1980) and film (1964) versions of *My Fair Lady* (see G.B. SHAW).

**Harrison, William Henry,** 1773–1841, 9th president of the US (4 Mar.–4 Apr. 1841). Following service against the Indians in the Old Northwest, Harrison was governor (1800–1812) of Indiana Territory and defeated the Indians under TECUMSEH in the battle of Tippecanoe (1811). In the WAR OF 1812 he recaptured Detroit from the British and defeated a combined force of British and Indians in the battle of the Thames (1813). Gaining the WHIG PARTY presidential nomination in 1840, he and his running mate, John TYLER, ran a 'rip-roaring' campaign with the slogan 'Tippecanoe and Tyler too.' After becoming president he selected a brilliant Whig cabinet, but he died after only a month in office. He was the grandfather of Benjamin HARRISON.

**Harrow,** London borough (1981 pop. 196,159), in outer NW London. A largely residential borough, it includes Harrow on the Hill, site of Harrow School (founded 1571), one of England's famous public schools for boys.

**Hart, Basil Henry Liddell:** see LIDDELL HART, BASIL HENRY.

**Hart, Herbert Lionel Adolphus,** 1907–, British barrister and jurist. After practising at the Bar for many years he became professor of Jurisprudence at Oxford Univ. (1952–68). He edited many works of Jeremy BENTHAM, and his *Concept of Law* (1961) is widely considered to be the classic modern statement of legal POSITIVISM (see also JURISPRUDENCE).

**Hart, Lorenz Milton,** 1895–1943, American lyricist. His lyrics were witty, literate, and expressive. He collaborated with Richard RODGERS on such MUSICALS as *Connecticut Yankee* (1927) and *Pal Joey* (1940).

**Harte, (Francis) Bret(t),** 1836–1902, American author. At 19 he went to California, where he helped establish the *Overland Monthly,* in which his short stories and poems first appeared. Harte is best known for his picturesque stories of Western local colour, e.g., 'The Luck of Roaring Camp' and 'The Outcasts of Poker Flat'. He was US consul in Germany and Scotland (1878–85) and spent his last years in England.

**hartebeest:** see ANTELOPE.

**Hartford,** US city (1980 pop. 136,392), state capital of Connecticut, on the Connecticut R.; settled as Newtown 1635–36 on the site of a Dutch trading post (1633), inc. 1784. It is world famous for its insurance companies, and is a commercial, industrial, and cultural centre. Manufactures include aircraft jet engines, firearms, typewriters, and computers. Part of the Connecticut colony (1639), Hartford was an important depot in the AMERICAN REVOLUTION and was the scene of the 1814–15 HARTFORD CONVENTION. The old statehouse (1796), the capitol (1878), and the Wadsworth Atheneum are noteworthy. Harriet Beecher STOWE, Mark TWAIN, and Wallace STEVENS were among its notable residents.

**Hartford Convention,** 15 Dec. 1815–4 Jan. 1815, meeting held in Hartford, Connecticut, US, to consider the problems of New England in the WAR OF 1812. It was an outgrowth of the disaffection of New England Federalists (see FEDERALIST PARTY) with Republican policy and especially the declaration of war. Moderates were in charge and a proposal to secede from the Union was rejected. New England's grievances were aired, but the war's successful conclusion made any recommendation a dead letter. The convention continued the view of STATES' RIGHTS as the refuge of sectional groups and sealed the destruction of the Federalist party, which never regained its lost prestige.

**Hartlepool,** town (1981 pop. 91,749), in Cleveland, NE England, on Hartlepool Bay on the North Sea. It is a port with a range of now declining heavy industries, including engineering. In 1984 the port, combined with other ports at the mouth of the R. TEES, handled 32.6 million tonnes.

**Hartley, Marsden,** 1877–1943, American painter. Reflecting the influence of French and German modernism, his early works are almost entirely abstract. His later paintings, particularly of the people and scenery of Maine, depict the world with forceful simplicity.

**Hartmann von Aue** (ˌhahtman fən ˌowə), c.1170–c.1220, German poet whose name is also spelled von Ouwe. Among his works are the chivalric romances *Erec* and *Iwain,* the religious legend *Gregorius,* and the idyll *Der arme Heinrich* (Poor Henry), used by LONGFELLOW for his *Golden Legend.*

**Harun ar-Rashid,** c.764–809, 5th and most famous ABBASID caliph (786–809). His empire included all of SW Asia and the northern part of Africa. He was a patron of the arts, and during his reign Baghdad was at its apogee. He figures prominently in the *Thousand and One Nights.*

**Harunobu,** (Suzuki Harunobu), 1725–70, Japanese colour-print artist of the *ukiyo-e* school (see JAPANESE ART). He was the first to use a wide range of colours effectively in printing, and in 1765 he developed multicoloured calendar prints from wood blocks. His subjects include actors, courtesans, and domestic life.

**Harvester judgment,** decision by H.B. HIGGINS, president of the Australian Court of Conciliation and Arbitration, in 1907 that determined a 'fair and reasonable' wage and sought to apply it to the employees of the Harvester factory in Melbourne. A notable feature of Higgins's judgment was that it assessed the needs of a family as the determinant of male wages, while it based female wages on the needs of a single woman. By the 1920s these principles were applied to most Australian wage-earners.

**harvest festival,** a service of thanksgiving for the ingathering of the harvest observed by Christian churches of most denominations in the UK, the US, and other countries. In Britain a Sunday in late September or early October is usually chosen, and it is customary to decorate the church with flowers, fruit, and vegetables (tinned or bottled produce often also appears), as well as sheaves of corn, which are later devoted to charitable objectives.

**harvestman,** an ARACHNID with long slender legs, related to the SPIDERS. It has eight legs extending from a rounded or oval body. The harvestman is omnivorous, feeding on plant fluids and animal tissue. In the US the harvestman is called a DADDY LONGLEGS.

**Harvey, Gabriel,** 1550?–1631, English writer. A Cambridge scholar, he is best remembered for his friendship with Edmund SPENSER and literary dispute with Thomas NASHE. His notes reflect early responses to many Eliabethan writers, including SHAKESPEARE.

**Harvey, William,** 1578–1657, English physician, considered by many to have laid the foundation for modern medicine. A physician at St Bartholomew's Hospital in London and to the king, he was the first to demonstrate the function of the heart and the circulation of the blood. His

renowned *On the Movement of the Heart and Blood in Animals* (1628) sets out his theories, which were not fully substantiated until 1827. Harvey also contributed greatly to comparative anatomy and embryology.

**Harwich,** town (1981 pop. 17,245) in Essex, SE England. It is a port for a passenger ferry service to Europe, and for containerized freight. In 1984 the port handled 17.2 million tonnes. It was an important naval base in World War II.

**Harz,** mountain massif, extending some 100 km (62 mi), between the Weser and Elbe Rs., crossing the West and East German border. It is extensively forested and its old rocks are rich in lead, copper, zinc, and silver. The highest point is the Brocken, 1142 m (3747 ft).

**Hasdrubal,** d. 221 BC, Carthaginian general. He succeeded his father-in-law, HAMILCAR BARCA, as commander in Spain, increased the Carthaginian empire, and founded Cartagena. He was succeeded by his brother-in-law HANNIBAL.

**Hašek, Jaroslav,** 1883–1923, Czech prose writer. He was a prolific writer who composed most of his short stories in cafés and pubs—and they often read like that. His chief work was the anti-authoritarian novel, *The Fate of the Good Soldier Švejk in the Great War* (1923), in which a morally repugnant hero creates a funny and disturbing patchwork satire on Austro–Hungarian military life.

**Hasidim,** [Heb., = the pious], term used by the rabbis to describe those Jews who maintained the highest standard of religious observance and moral action. The term has been applied to three distinct movements. **1** The first Hasidim, also called the Assideans or Hasideans, were members of a sect that developed between 300 BC and 175 BC. Rigid adherents of Judaism, they led the resistance to the Hellenizing campaign of Antiochus IV of Syria and were important in the revolt of the MACCABEES. **2** In 12th- and 13th-cent. Germany there arose the *Hasidei Ashkenaz,* a group with messianic and mystical elements, influenced by SAADIA BEN JOSEPH. **3** The third movement of Hasidim was that founded in the 18th cent. by BAAL-SHEM-TOV and known as HASIDISM.

**Hasidism,** Jewish movement founded in Poland in the 18th cent. by BAAL-SHEM-TOV. Its name derives from HASIDIM. The movement arose in reaction to persecutions and to the academic formalism of rabbinical Judaism. It encouraged joyous religious expression through music and dance, and taught that purity of heart was more pleasing to God than learning. Although the Talmudists pronounced Hasidism heretical in 1781, it continues to be a strong force in Jewish life, particularly in New York and Israel. In recent years, adherents of the movement—recognizable by their fur hats, black coats, beards and side-locks—have adopted militant measures against those fellow-Jews whom they regard as violating the basic moral and religious tenets of the faith. The power-base of their movement is located in the Mea Shearim district of Jerusalem.

**Hasmoneans:** see under MACCABEES.

**Hassam, Childe,** 1859–1935, American painter and etcher. Hassam, who studied in Paris, produced sprightly landscapes and interiors that show the strong influence of IMPRESSIONISM, e.g., *Isles of Shoals* (Metropolitan Mus., New York).

**Hassan II,** 1929–, king of MOROCCO (1961–). He succeeded his father, MUHAMMAD V. An abortive coup (1971) led him to yield some of his powers to parliament. After 1976 he sought to establish full Moroccan control over WESTERN SAHARA.

**Hastings,** borough (1981 pop. 74,979), E Sussex, SE England. Today a seaside resort and residential city, it was occupied in Roman times and probably earlier. The battle of Hastings (1066) between the Norman invaders of England and the Anglo-Saxon defenders, the first and most decisive victory of the NORMAN CONQUEST, took place nearby.

**Hastings, Warren,** 1732–1818, first governor-general of British India (1774–1784). His aggressive policy of judicial and economic reform rebuilt British prestige in India but created powerful enemies at home, including Edmund BURKE and Charles James FOX. He was impeached (1787) on charges of extortion and other crimes. After a long and costly trial he was acquitted (1795).

**Hatta, Mohammad,** 1902–80, Indonesian statesman. With SUKARNO, he fought for Indonesian independence from the Netherlands. He served (1945–48, 1950–56) as vice president of Indonesia but broke with Sukarno and resigned in 1956.

**Hatteras, Cape**, promontory on Hatteras Island, North Carolina, US. The site of frequent storms and shipwrecks, it is known as the 'Graveyard of the Atlantic'. The cape is part of **Cape Hatteras National Seashore,** one of the longest stretches of undeveloped shoreline on the US Atlantic coast.

**Hauptmann, Gerhart**, 1862–1946, German dramatist, novelist, and poet. He inaugurated the naturalist movement in German theatre with his plays *Before Dawn* (1889) and *The Weavers* (1892), then turned to the romantic with *Hannele* (1893) and *The Sunken Bell* (1897). His prose works include the novels *The Fool in Christ, Emanuel Quint* (1910) and *The Heretic of Soana* (1918). A leading figure in German literature for three generations, he was awarded the 1912 Nobel Prize for literature.

**Hausa**, black African ethnic group numbering about 9 million, chiefly in N Nigeria and S Niger. The Hausa, who are almost exclusively Muslim, practise agriculture and carry on a widespread trade. Their language is a lingua franca of W Africa. The Hausa are a major force in Nigerian politics.

**Hausa language**, member of the Chad group of languages, frequently assigned to the Hamitic subfamily of the Hamito-Semitic family of languages. See AFRICAN LANGUAGES (table).

**Hausa states**, group of loosely-connected neighbouring states, in what is now N Nigeria. They lay between the SONGHAI empire in the west and BORNU empire in the east. In the 14th cent. Islam was introduced by missionaries from Mali. In the 16th cent. the Hausa states were subsumed by the Songhai empire. Early in the 19th cent. they were conquered by the FULANI and subsequently organized into emirates. At the beginning of the 20th cent. the British took over administration of the region which became part of the northern provinces of the protectorate of Nigeria.

**Hausmann, Raoul**, 1886–1971, Austrian painter. A leading member of the Berlin DADA group, he was an early experimenter with PHOTOMONTAGE, e.g., in his *Tatlin at Home* (1920). He stopped painting in the mid 1920s until 1941 when he settled in France.

**Haussmann, Georges Eugène, Baron**, 1809–91, French civic official and city planner. Noted for his bold plan for PARIS under NAPOLEON III, he is largely responsible for the city's appearance, with its wide streets, broad vistas, parks (including the Bois de Boulogne, laid out by him), and avenues radiating from focal points.

**Havana**, Span. *La Habana,* city (1983 pop. 1,972,000), W Cuba, capital of Cuba and La Habana prov. The largest city and chief port of the WEST INDIES, it is Cuba's political and industrial centre, with oil and sugar refineries, rum distilleries, tobacco factories, and some heavy manufacturing. It is a popular winter resort, although tourism from the US ended after the Cuban revolution of 1959. One of the oldest cities in the Americas, Havana was founded by the Spanish before 1520. It has often been invaded and held by foreign forces. The sinking of the US battleship *Maine* in its harbour sparked (1898) the SPANISH-AMERICAN WAR. The modern part of Havana has wide avenues and impressive public buildings. Much of the old colonial city has been preserved.

**Havel, Václav**, 1936–, Czech dramatist and essayist, leader of the Charter 77 human-rights movement. His first plays, *The Garden Party* (1963) and *The Memorandum* (1965), considered linguistic manipulation in totalitarianism. Since he has been banned by the Czechoslavak authorities (1970) he has become the most mordant Czech analyst of the workings of socialist society. He has spent spells in prison ranging from one day to over three years for antistate activity.

**Havering**, London borough (1981 pop. 239,788), in outer E London. It contains the towns of Rainham, Romford, Upminster, and the village of Havering-atte-Bower. It is mainly residential, with some manufacturing and engineering industry.

**Hawaii**, 50th state of the US, a group of eight major islands and numerous islets in the central Pacific Ocean, c.3380 km (2100 mi) SW of San Francisco.

*Area,* 16,706 km² (6450 sq mi). Pop. (1980), 965,000, a 25.3% increase over 1970 pop. *Capital,* Honolulu. *Statehood,* 21 Aug. 1959 (50th state). *Highest pt.,* Mauna Kea, 4208 m (13,796 ft); *lowest pt.,* sea level. *Nickname,* Aloha State. *Motto, Ua Mau Ke Ea O Ka Aina I Ka Pono* [The Life of the Land Is Perpetuated in Righteousness]. *State bird,* Hawaiian goose. *State flower,* hibiscus. *State tree,* candlenut. *Abbr.,* HI.

*Land and People.* The islands, of volcanic origin, are ringed with coral reefs. Oahu, site of HONOLULU, the capital and only large city, is the most populous and economically important island. On Hawaii Island are located MAUNA KEA, a huge extinct volcano, and MAUNA LOA, a large active volcano in Hawaii Volcanoes National Park. Haleakala, one of the world's largest volcanic craters, on Maui Island, is part of Haleakala National Park. Other principal islands are Kahoolawe, Kauai, Lanai, Molokai, and Nihau. The islands are generally fertile, are largely covered in luxuriant vegetation, and enjoy a mild climate. About 60% of Hawaii's ethnically diverse population is of Asian descent, including people of Japanese, Chinese, and Filipino origin; there is a small minority of indigenous Hawaiians; nearly 33% of the population is white; and 7% is of other races.

*Economy.* Service industries, especially tourism and military installations, dominate the economy of Hawaii. The leading agricultural products are sugarcane and pineapples both cultivated on large corporate plantations and cattle and dairy products. Sugar refining and pineapple canning are the basis of the leading industry, food processing, which is supplemented by petroleum refining and printing and publishing.

*Government.* The constitution (adopted 1950) provides for a governor serving a four-year term. The legislature consists of a senate with 25 members elected to four-year terms and a house with 51 members serving two-year terms. Hawaii sends two representatives and two senators to the US Congress and has four electoral votes.

*History.* It is believed that the Polynesians who first settled the islands had arrived by c.750 AD. The first European to discover (1778) the islands was Capt. James COOK. In 1810 King KAMEHAMEHA I united the islands under his sovereignty, ushering in a prosperous period of agriculture and trade. However, American and European traders introduced devastating infectious diseases that greatly reduced the native population. Missionaries and American planters who arrived in 1820 established sugar plantations and increasingly dominated the islands' economy and government. The monarchy was overthrown in 1893, and Hawaii became a US territory in 1900. On 7 Dec. 1941, Japanese aircraft made a surprise attack on the naval base at PEARL HARBOR, plunging the US into WORLD WAR II. Since the war's end and statehood (1959) Hawaii has enjoyed sustained economic and population growth.

**hawk,** name for smaller members of the Accipitridae family, diurnal BIRDS of prey, distinguished from the related FALCONS by their broader, rounded wings. Hawks have keen sight, sharply hooked bills, and powerful feet with curved talons. The hunting hawks, or accipiters, include the widespread goshawks (*Accipiter*) which feed on small MAMMALS and birds, and the sparrow hawks, and shikras. The European sparrow hawk (*A. nisus*), which ranges across Europe and Asia, is one of the best studied of all birds of prey. Buteos, or BUZZARDS, are a diverse group of larger hawks; they feed on RODENTS and REPTILES. The term *hawk* is also applied to many falcons and a number of unrelated birds.

**Hawke, Robert (Bob) W.,** 1929–, Australian political leader and Labor prime minister (1983–). After serving as president of the Australian Council of Trade Unions (1970–80), he entered parliament (1980) and became leader of the Labor Party (ALP) shortly before the 1983 elections, in which he led the ALP back to power.

**Hawkins** or **Hawkyns, Sir John,** 1532–95, English admiral. As a slave-trader, he sold native Africans at a profit in Spanish ports. As treasurer and comptroller of the navy, he improved ship construction. In the great defeat of the Spanish ARMADA, he commanded the *Victory* and was knighted for his services. His son, **Sir Richard Hawkins,** 1562–1622, served under his father and Sir Francis DRAKE. While on a raiding expedition in South America, he was captured and sent to a Spanish prison (1597–1602). He later served in Parliament.

**Hawkins, Coleman,** 1904–69, black American musician. He established the tenor saxophone as a major JAZZ instrument. His huge tone, vigorous attack, and evolving improvisatory style made his influence pervasive, even among avant-garde musicians, from the 1930s until his death.

**Hawkins, Erick,** 1909–, American dancer, choreographer, and teacher. He joined the American Ballet in 1935, and was the first male member of the Graham Co. (1938–51). He was married to Martha GRAHAM (1948–51). He formed his own company and school developing his own dance technique.

**Hawks, Howard,** 1896–1977, American film director. He stands alongside John Ford as one of the greatest of studio directors during

Hollywood's greatest era. He moved with expert professional ease through all the major genres, displaying a clean, uncluttered style and a penchant for heroes in a dangerous situation and highly capable heroines. His films include *Scarface* (1932), *Bringing Up Baby* (1938), *Only Angels Have Wings* (1939), *His Girl Friday* (1940), *The Big Sleep* (1946), and *Gentlemen Prefer Blondes* (1953).

**Hawksmoor** or **Hawksmore, Nicholas,** 1661–1736, English architect involved in the development of most of the great English BAROQUE buildings. He assisted Sir Christopher WREN at Chelsea Hospital and St Paul's, and Sir John VANBRUGH at Castle Howard and Blenheim Palace. His London churches (1714–30) include St George's, Bloomsbury, and Christ Church, Spitalfields.

**Hawthorne, Nathaniel,** 1804–64, a master of American fiction. Hawthorne created highly symbolic fiction that penetratingly explored complex moral and spiritual conflicts. In early life he wrote the unsuccessful novel *Fanshawe* (1829) and the acclaimed short-story collection *Twice-Told Tales* (1837; 2nd series, 1842). He lived briefly (1841) at BROOK FARM, basing his later novel *The Blithedale Romance* (1852) on the experience. After his marriage (1842) to Sophia Peabody he settled in Concord, where he wrote the tales collected in *Mosses from an Old Manse* (1846). In the novels *The Scarlet Letter* (1850) and *The House of the Seven Gables* (1851) he examined the gloomy, brooding spirit of Puritanism. His last novel, *The Marble Faun* (1860), is set in Italy. His works include two juvenile books, *A Wonder Book* (1852) and *Tanglewood Tales* (1853). He also helped establish the American short story as an art form.

**Haya de la Torre, Víctor Raúl** (ˌahyah day lah ˌtawre), 1895–1979, Peruvian politician. He founded (1924) the reformist American Revolutionary Popular Alliance (APRA) to champion social and economic reforms, especially for Indians, and spent much of his life in exile or in prison. He was elected president of PERU (1962) but was prevented from taking office by a military coup. APRA won the 1978 elections shortly before his death.

**Haydn, Franz Joseph** (ˌhiedən), 1732–1809, Austrian composer. After early struggles, he worked 29 years for the princes Esterházy, received commissions, travelled, and formed a close friendship with MOZART, a bond that influenced the music of both. Haydn wrote over 100 SYMPHONIES, establishing the basic form. Many are called by names, e.g., The Clock Symphony (1794). His string quartets and symphonies expanded C.P.E. BACH's three-part form, affecting the development of classical SONATA form. Two great ORATORIOS, *The Creation* (1798) and *The Seasons* (1801), were written in old age. He wrote over 80 string quartets, over 50 sonatas, and many other pieces. His brother **Michael Haydn,** 1737–1806, was also a composer, known particularly for his church music.

**Hayek, Friedrich August von,** 1899–, Austrian economist and political theorist. During the 1920s and 30s he developed a distinctive explanation of the causes of unemployment which led him to oppose the theories and policy recommendations of J. M. KEYNES, and to warn that Keynesian policies would inevitably result in inflation. In *The Road to Serfdom* (1944) he further argued that the extension of collectivist economic planning would extinguish individual freedom and destory the liberal social order which he saw as the greatest social achievement of Europe, and humanity. His views were at first rejected by most economists, but attracted attention again in the 1970s, a period of high inflation, and in 1974 he was awarded the Nobel Prize in Economics (jointly with Gunnar MYRDAL) for his work in the theory of money and economic fluctuations. Since World War II, Hayek has developed his political philosophy (which refines many of the traditional arguments of LIBERALISM) in the *Constitution of Liberty* (1960) and *Law, Legislation and Liberty* (1973–79). His ideas are central to the neo-Liberalism of the New Right, espoused by the REAGAN and THATCHER gavernments of the US and UK in the 1980s.

**Hayes, Rutherford Birchard,** 1822–93, 19th president of the US (1877–81). A lawyer, he fought in the AMERICAN CIVIL WAR and rose in rank to a major general of volunteers (1865). Hayes served (1865–67) as a Republican in the US Congress and was elected (1867, 1869, 1875) governor of Ohio three times. In 1876, chosen as the Republican candidate for president, he ran against Democrat Samuel J. TILDEN. In the election the returns of South Carolina, Louisiana, Florida, and Oregon were disputed, and Congress created an electoral commission to decide the result. The commission awarded all the disputed returns to Hayes, thus giving him a majority of one in the electoral college. Indignation over this partisan decision weakened Hayes's administration, which was generally conservative and efficient but no more. He withdrew federal troops from Louisiana and South Carolina, ending the RECONSTRUCTION era. An advocate of hard money, he vetoed the Bland-Allison Act allowing the coinage of silver, which was passed nonetheless.

**Haymarket Square riot,** outbreak of violence in Chicago on 4 May 1886. Amid American labour's drive for an eight-hour working day, a demonstration was staged by anarchists in Haymarket Square. A crowd of some 1500 people gathered; when police attempted to disperse them, a bomb exploded and rioting ensued. Eleven people were killed and more than 100 others wounded. Eight anarchists were tried, but no evidence was found to link them to the bomb. They were, however, convicted of inciting violence. Four were hanged, one committed suicide, and three were pardoned in 1893 after having served seven years in prison.

**hazan,** cantor or synagogue prayer leader. In larger congregations he is a ministerial official who, in addition to taking the services on Sabbaths and festivals, also assists the rabbi in discharging pastoral duties. The name is also applied to ordinary laymen who are called upon to lead the weekday (and, in smaller congregations, also the Sabbath) services. Some of the most distinguished cantors, particularly in the US, were also leading tenors of the opera.

**hazel,** shrub or small tree (genus *Corylus*) of the BIRCH family, grown as an ornamental and for its edible nuts. Species include the American hazel (*C. americana*) and European hazels (*C. maxima* and *C. avellana*); hazelnuts, usually known as filberts, are chiefly from the European trees. WITCH HAZEL is not related to hazel.

**Hazlitt, William,** 1778–1830, English essayist and critic. His penetrating literary criticism is collected in *Characters of Shakespeare's Plays* (1817), *Lectures on the English Poets* (1818), *Lectures on the English Comic Writers* (1819), *Table Talk* (1821–22), and *The Spirit of the Age* (1825). His *Dramatic Literature of the Age of Elizabeth* (1820) renewed interest in SHAKESPEARE and Elizabethan drama. His revolutionary sympathies and his tempestuous private life, painfully revealed in his *Liber Amoris* (1823), aroused much hostility, but he is recognised as a pioneering literary critic.

**Hazzard, Shirley,** 1931–, American novelist; b. Australia. Her four novels are *The Evening of the Holiday* (1966), *People in Glass Houses* (1967), *The Bay of Noon* (1970), and *The Transist of Venus* (1980). This last has established her as a major novelist who explores the theme of the quest for love with poise and wit.

**H.D.:** see DOOLITTLE, HILDA.

**He,** chemical symbol of the element HELIUM.

**Head, Bessie,** 1937–86, black South African novelist. In exile in Botswana since the mid-1960s, she charts her experience compellingly in *Maru* (1971), *A Question of Power* (1974), and in her collection of short stories, *The Collector of Treasures* (1977).

**Head, Edith,** 1907–81, American FASHION and costume designer. Working in Hollywood in its most glamorous period, she designed many hundreds of film costumes, and received many Academy Awards. She also influenced American haute couture.

**headman,** the recognized political leader of a small community or BAND. Headmen in hunter–gatherer societies are chosen by consensus, and the obligation on them is to give away, to prove their generosity, their concern for the group. The term is also applied to local leaders in centralized political systems. British colonial rule used or created headmen as a means of establishing local political control.

**Head Start,** US educational programme for disadvantaged preschool children, established under the Economic Opportunity Act of 1964. The programme was essentially aimed at preparing poor children for elementary school, initially (in 1965) by a summer programme, then extended to a full year. Head Start is concerned with both the health and welfare of the child, as well as with preschool education.

**headwear,** an important status symbol, also in some circumstances a functional part of COSTUME. Headwear may be part of UNIFORM or VESTMENTS, e.g., the crown worn by monarchs, the mitre by bishops, or the WIG by judges. In some religions, the wearing of some head-covering is a ritual necessity, e.g., the yarmulke worn at all times by orthodox

Jewish males. The basic types of hat are (1) the cloth draped over or wound round the head, and (2) the shaped hat made of hide in northern regions and woven twigs or leaves in hot regions. In Europe since the 15th cent. most fashionable men's hats have been made of felt. Hats were wide-brimmed in the 17th cent., and in the 18th cent. the brims were turned up ('cocked') either into three points ('tricorne') or two ('bicorne'). In the early 19th cent. men began to wear the cylindrical hat with a high crown known as a top hat, a version of which is still worn for formal occasions. The 19th cent. saw the introduction of a number of different styles for men, including the bowler, the trilby, and the straw boater, all still worn. In the later 20th cent. the convention that men should always wear a hat outdoors has relaxed. Women's head-gear in Europe has been dictated to some extent by the idea that they must keep their hair covered for modesty's sake. By the 15th cent. styles for veils or caps were extreme or elaborate. In the 18th cent. hats or caps became less elaborate as HAIRSTYLES became more so, but in the mid 19th cent. conventions became more rigid and hats became once more an important item of FASHION. Since World War II it has not been essential for a women to wear a hat outdoors.

**healing,** term now used for faith healing or spiritual healing. Healers are believed to possess strong healing powers which they transmit to the sick person by prayer, by laying on hands, by stroking the patient, or by visualizing the patient's aura. See HOLISTIC MEDICINE.

**Health and Safety Commission,** body established in Britain in 1974 to secure the health, safety, and welfare of people at work. It is active in supervising conditions in industry, particularly work with hazardous equipment and dangerous substances, and in regulating the conditions of buildings.

**health insurance,** prepayment plan providing medical services or cash indemnities for medical care; it may be voluntary or compulsory. Compulsory accident and sickness insurance was initiated (1883–84) in Germany by Bismarck and adopted by Britain, France, Chile, the USSR, and other nations after World War I. In 1948 Britain instituted the most comprehensive compulsory health plan to date (see NATIONAL HEALTH SERVICE), including free medical care from any doctor participating in the system; a small charge for some services has been instituted since then for those able to pay. Canada has provided nearly free hospital service since 1958 and more comprehensive coverage since 1967. National health insurance has been widely adopted in Europe and parts of Asia. In the US, where the medical profession opposed government health insurance, voluntary cooperative or commercial programmes developed, offering limited benefits to group or individual subscribers. The US is the only Western industrial nation without some form of comprehensive national health insurance.

**Heaney, Seamus** (ˌheenee), 1939–, Irish poet. Rooted in his own life and in that of Ireland, balanced between the personal and the topical, Heaney's carefully crafted poems are extremely evocative, yet clear and direct. His volumes of verse include *Door into the Dark* (1969), *North* (1975), *Field Work* (1979), and *Station Island* (1984). Many of his critical and autobiographical pieces in prose were collected in *Preoccupations* (1980).

**Heard and McDonald Islands,** two small island groups in the Southern Ocean, S of the Indian Ocean; Australian possessions. Heard Island was possibly sighted in 1833 and 1848, but the first definite report was not until 1853. The islands became a major base for the Antarctic sealing industry for the rest of the century, but are now uninhabited except for occasional visiting scientists.

**hearing:** see EAR.

**Hearn, Lafcadio,** 1850–1904, American author; b. Ionian Islands; went to US, 1869. Partially blind and morbidly discontented, he was skilled at writing about the macabre and exotic, e.g., *Stray Leaves from Strange Literature* (1884). In 1890 he went to Japan, where he became a citizen and wrote 12 books, e.g., *Japan: An Attempt at Interpretation* (1904).

**Hearne, John,** 1926–, Jamaican writer. His main concern is to probe the complexity of social and racial relations in his island and region; he is best known for a series of novels (1956–61) about a mythical island, Cayuna.

**Hearne, Samuel,** 1745–92, British fur trader and explorer of N Canada. Working for the HUDSON'S BAY COMPANY, he explored the Coppermine River area in 1770. He opened up unknown territory and proved that there was no short NORTHWEST PASSAGE.

**Hearst, William Randolph,** 1863–1951, American journalist and publisher. During his lifetime Hearst established a vast publishing empire that included 18 newspapers in 12 cities and 9 successful magazines (including *Good Housekeeping* and *Harper's Bazaar*). His use of flamboyant pictures, shrieking typography, and earthy, mass-appeal news coverage, together with a policy of buying distinctive talent from other papers and selling papers at a penny, made him the leader in 'penny journalism' by 1900. His New York Journal's wild reports of Cuba's struggle for independence from Spain helped bring about the SPANISH–AMERICAN WAR. He served in the House of Representatives (1903–07) but was defected as candidate for mayor of New York city in 1905 and 1909 and for governor of New York in 1906. At first a supporter of public owneship, antitrust laws and trade unions he later in life became stridently conservative. His huge castle at San Simeon, California, is now a state museum. He is said to be the original of Orson WELLES's *Citizen Kane* (1940); he attempted to hinder the film's distribution.

**heart,** muscular organ that pumps blood to all parts of the body. The pear-shaped human heart is about the size of a fist and lies just left of centre within the chest cavity. The contractions of heart muscle, or myocardium, are entirely self-stimulated. The heart is divided into two cavities by a wall of muscle; each cavity is divided in turn into two chambers, the upper ones called atria, the lower ones ventricles. Blood from the veins, high in carbon dioxide but low in oxygen, returns to the right atrium. It enters the right ventricle, which contracts, pumping the blood through the pulmonary artery to the LUNGS. Blood rich in oxygen and poor in carbon dioxide returns from the lungs to the left atrium and enters the left ventricle, which contracts, forcing the blood into the aorta, from where it passes through the smaller arteries and is distributed throughout the body. The blood is prevented from flowing backwards by a series of valves. See CIRCULATORY SYSTEM; see also BLOOD; CORONARY HEART DISEASE; TRANSPLANTATION, MEDICAL.

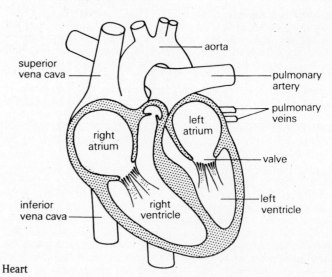

Heart

**heart failure,** condition in which the heart cannot pump sufficient blood to meet the demands of the body. Common causes are coronary THROMBOSIS, HYPERTENSION, chronic disease of the valves, and arrhythmias (disturbances in normal heartbeat). The patient is breathless. Treatment includes rest, DIURETICS, and, where necessary, surgery.

**Heartfield, John,** 1891–1968, German painter; b. Helmut Herzfelde. With his brother Wieland and GROSZ he founded (1917) the Marxist publishing house Malik Verlag. He was a founder member of the Berlin DADA group in 1917 as well as the German Communist Party in 1919. He was a pioneer of the technique of PHOTOMONTAGE, which enabled Heartfield to combine together two different and incompatible images into a new context, thus creating a new 'reality' and a new meaning. He employed this technique to undermine the politic and ideology of NATIONAL SOCIALISM to great effect in the run-up to the elections of 1933, e.g., in *Millions Stand Behind Me*. A militant communist, he moved to E Berlin in 1950.

Photomontage by John **Heartfield**, 1935

**heart-lung machine,** device outside the body that maintains the circulation and oxygen content of the BLOOD. It is used in open-heart surgery to bypass the HEART and LUNGS so that the surgeon can operate on a dry, nonbeating heart. Blood is drawn from the veins, reoxygenated, and pumped into the arterial system. See CIRCULATORY SYSTEM.

**heat,** internal ENERGY of a substance, associated with the positions and motions of its component molecules, atoms, and ions. The average kinetic energy of the molecules or atoms, which is due to their motions, is proportional to the TEMPERATURE of the substance; the potential energy is associated with the state, or phase, of the substance (see STATES OF MATTER). Heat energy is commonly expressed in JOULES, CALORIES, or BRITISH THERMAL UNITS (Btu). Heat may be transferred from one substance to another by three means: CONDUCTION, CONVECTION, and RADIATION. See also HEAT CAPACITY; SPECIFIC HEAT CAPACITY; THERMODYNAMICS.

**heat capacity** or **thermal capacity,** HEAT energy required to raise the TEMPERATURE of a body by one unit; it is usually expressed in joules per kelvin, or sometimes in CALORIES per degree Celsius or BRITISH THERMAL UNITS per degree Fahrenheit. See also SPECIFIC HEAT CAPACITY.

**heath,** common name for some plants of the family Ericaceae, composed chiefly of evergreen shrubs native to the Old World. Heaths form the characteristic vegetation of many regions with acid soils, particularly moors, swamps, and mountain slopes. They are valued for their edible fruit, e.g., CRANBERRY and BILBERRY; as a source of flavouring, e.g., WINTERGREEN; and for their showy blossoms, e.g., RHODODENDRON and AZALEA. The names *heath* and *heather* are often used interchangeably, although true heaths (genus *Erica*) have needlelike foliage and white, rose, or yellow flowers, and heathers, such as the common heather (*Calluna vulgaris*), have scalelike foliage and rose-coloured flowers.

**Heath, Edward Richard George,** 1916–, British statesman. A Conservative, he was prime minister from 1970 to 1974 and led the UK into the EUROPEAN COMMUNITY (1973). His attempts to reduce inflation by enforcing wage controls led to bad relations with the trade unions and a confrontation with the miners' union (Nov. 1973–Feb. 1974) that forced the nation into a three-day working week. Defeated in both the Feb. 1974 and the Oct. 1974 general elections, Heath relinquished the party leadership to Margaret THATCHER in 1975.

**Heath, Roy Aubrey Kelvin,** 1912–, Guyanese writer. His novels, of which the best known is *Orealla* (1984), explore the aspirations of middle-class in Caribbean through several generations. He lives in England.

**heather:** see HEATH.

**Heathrow Airport,** major international airport in London borough of Hillingdon, 23 km (14 mi) W of central London. It is the larger of the two airports serving London, the other being GATWICK AIRPORT. There are four terminal buildings and a London Underground link with central London (Piccadilly Line). In 1984 the airport handled 29.1 million passengers.

**heaven,** in Judaeo-Christian belief, the state of bliss in which the just see God face to face. Many Christians believe that after the RESURRECTION the glorified human body will be reunited forever with the soul in heaven, a realm popularly thought to contain material delights. Islam is often credited with a sensuous doctrine of the life to come, but the passages in the Koran describing it are commonly interpreted symbolically.

**Heaviside, Oliver,** 1850–1925, English physicist. Self-taught in mathematics and science, he solved the general equations of the transmission of electrical signals along long-distance lines, work which made the long-distance telephone and telegraph service practicable. he predicted an ionized layer in the Earth's upper atmosphere and lived long enough for its discovery and confirmation. The layer was named after him.

**heavy spar:** see BARYTES.

**heavy water:** see HYDROGEN.

**Hebbel, Christian Friedrich** (ˌhebəl) 1813–63, German tragic dramatist. Linking romantic and realist drama, his plays often portray the struggle between old and new values. They include *Judith* (1840), *Maria Magdalena* (1844), *Agnes Bernauer* (1852), and the trilogy *The Nibelungs* (1862).

**Hebe** (ˌheebee), in Greek mythology, goddess of youth; daughter of ZEUS and HERA and wife of HERCULES.

**Hebei** or **Hopei** or **Hopeh,** province (1985 est. pop. 55,480,000), 187,693 km² (72,468 sq mi), N China, it encloses the city of BEIJING which is a separate province. Major cities are Shijiazhuang, the capital, and TANGSHAN. Hebei consists mainly of low-lying alluvial land and has a cold, dry winter. Irrigation has enabled dense crop production with winter wheat, maize, and cotton, being important. There are significant mineral deposits, including extensive coal reserves. Iron and steel, and textile manufacture are major industries. In July 1976 the Tangshan area was struck by a massive earthquake (measuring 8.2 on the Richter scale) and over 700,000 people were killed.

**Hébert, Jacques René** (ay ber), 1757–94, French revolutionary. The editor of a virulent paper, *Le Père Duchesne,* he led the CORDELIERS after MARAT's death. He was largely responsible for the price ceilings during the REIGN OF TERROR. His power over the Paris commune threatened ROBESPIERRE, who had him and his followers guillotined on a concocted charge of conspiracy. His fall marked the triumph of the propertied middle class.

**Hébert, Louis,** 1575–1627, French Canadian pioneer. In 1623 he became the first permanent settler and farmer in Canada, settling at the site of Upper Town, QUEBEC.

**Hebrew language,** member of the Canaanite group of the Semitic subdivision of the Hamito-Semitic family of languages. In 1948 it became the official language of Israel. See ALPHABET (illustration); LANGUAGE (table).

**Hebrews.** For history, see JEWS; for religion, see JUDAISM.

**Hebrews,** epistle of the NEW TESTAMENT. It is traditionally ascribed to St PAUL; few modern scholars accept his authorship. It was written before AD 96. Most modern scholars feel it is addressed to Christians lapsing into indifference. The first part (1.1–4.13) argues Christ's superiority to the angels and to MOSES; the second (4.14–10.18) treats Christ's ministry and sacrifice, which supersedes all other sacrifices and serves to expiate sin.

**Hebrides, the,** group of more than 500 islands, W and NW Scotland. Less than a fifth of the islands are inhabited. They form two groups: the Outer Hebrides (known administratively as the WESTERN ISLES) and the Inner Hebrides which are part of Highland region, including SKYE and IONA. The main economic activities are fishing, farming, sheep-grazing, and the manufacture of tweeds and other woollens. The islands were ruled by the Norwegians (8th–13th cent.) and by Scottish chiefs (13th–16th cent.) until they were acquired by the Scottish crown.

**Hebron,** city (1971 est. pop. 43,000), Jordan, on the WEST BANK, near Jerusalem. Grapes, grains, and vegetables are grown in the area, and the main industries include tanning, food processing, and glass blowing. According to the Bible, the cave of Machpelah in Hebron is the burial place of ABRAHAM and his family, and the city was King DAVID's capital for seven years. The Haram al Khalil, the mosque built over the cave, is sacred to Jews and Muslims. Hebron has been occupied by Israel since the 1967 ARAB-ISRAELI WAR.

**Hecate,** in Greek mythology, goddess of ghosts and witchcraft. An attendant of PERSEPHONE, she was a spirit of black magic, able to conjure up dreams and the spirits of the dead. She appears with the three witches in SHAKESPEARE's *Macbeth*. She haunted graveyards and crossroads.

**Heckel, Erich,** 1883–1970, German painter. Heckel was one of the members of the Die BRÜCKE group founded in 1905 in Dresden. In 1911 he settled in Berlin, where he met FEININGER and others. His figures, often depicting sickness and anguish, become more distorted and expressive. During the war he met and was influenced by BECKMANN, but after the war his work became more conventional. He was one of the many artists whose work was considered as DEGENERATE ART by the Nazis in 1937.

**Hector,** in Greek mythology, greatest Trojan hero of the TROJAN WAR, eldest son of Priam and HECUBA, and husband of ANDROMACHE. In HOMER's *Iliad* he was killed by ACHILLES in revenge for the death of Patroclus, and his body was dragged round the walls of Troy.

**Hecuba,** in Greek mythology, queen of TROY; wife of Priam, to whom she bore 19 children including HECTOR, PARIS, Troilus, and CASSANDRA. After the TROJAN WAR she was taken as a slave by ODYSSEUS. She is an important character in EURIPIDES' plays *Hecuba* and *The Trojan Women*.

**hedgehog,** or **hedgepig, urchin,** usually brownish Old World MAMMAL of the family Erinaceidae, related to MOLES and SHREWS. Spiny hedgehogs, of Africa and Eurasia, are covered with stiff spines; they can roll into a ball when attacked, becoming invulnerable to predators. The European hedgehog (*Erinaceus uropaeus*) is nocturnal, living in a burrow (often in hedgerows) and hibernating in winter. It is about 25 cm (9 in) in length. Like a pig, it roots in the ground for food; it eats worms, insects, mice, frogs, and snakes. Hedgehogs have adapted to town life and are often seen in gardens. They will eat tinned petfood and drink milk.

**hedge sparrow,** or **dunnock,** small, insect-eating BIRD of the Accentor (*Prunellidae*) family. The 14.5-cm (5¾-in) hedge sparrow (*Prunella modularis*) is a very common bird, breeding across Europe into Russia. It is often mistaken for a female HOUSE SPARROW, as it has adapted to humans in a similar way. Its slender bill is designed for eating insects and spiders, although the bird will take seeds in winter. It forages beneath hedges and shrubs on the ground.

**Hedin, Sven Anders,** 1865–1952, Swedish explorer. After travelling in Persia, Hedin was attached to the embassy to the shah of Persia which made possible many further expeditions throughout the Asiatic continent. He then directed the Sino-Swedish Expedition to China and spent the remaining years of his life preparing the results for publication as *Scientific Results of the Sino-Swedish Expedition, 1927–1935* (30 vol., 1937–42). He was considered one of the finest Asiatic explorers of his day.

**hedonism,** in philosophy, the doctrine that pleasure is the highest good. Ancient hedonism equated pleasure variously with the gratification of sensual desire (as in the teaching of Aristippus and the Cyreniacs, c.435–360 BC) and with the intellectual serenity brought on by the rational control of desire (as in the teaching of EPICURUS). The psychological hedonism of UTILITARIANISM claims that pleasure is the only thing that humans desire.

**Hegel, Georg Wilhelm Friedrich,** 1770–1831, German philosopher. His all-embracing philosophical system, set forth in such works as *Phenomenology of Mind* (1807), *Science of Logic* (1812–16), *Encyclopedia of the Philosophical Sciences* (1817), and *The Philosophy of Right* (1821), includes theories of ethics, aesthetics, history, politics, and religion. At the centre of the universe Hegel posited an enveloping absolute spirit that guides all reality, including human reason. His absolute IDEALISM envisages a world-soul, evident throughout history, that develops from, and is known through, a process of change and progress now known universally as the Hegelian dialectic. According to its laws, one concept (thesis) inevitably generates its opposite (antithesis); their interaction leads to a new concept (synthesis), which in turn becomes the thesis of a new triad. Thus philosophy enables human beings to comprehend the historical unfolding of the absolute. Hegel's application of the dialectic to the concept of conflict of cultures stimulated historical analysis and, in the political arena, made him a hero to those working for a unified Germany. He was a major influence on subsequent idealist thinkers and on such philosophers as KIERKEGAARD and SARTRE; perhaps his most far-reaching effect was his influence on Karl MARX, who substituted materialism for idealism in his formulation of DIALECTICAL MATERIALISM.

**hegemony,** [GK., = leadership], the means by which a ruling bloc (usually, an alliance of different class factions), manages to maintain its rule by winning the consent of the majority without constantly resorting to force. The Italian Marxist GRAMSCI argued that this was achieved by the ruling bloc presenting its interest and aims as if they were common to all classes in society, thereby creating a collective political will, and maintaining its hegemony over the other dominated classes in that society. Hegemony which depends on securing a position of social authority, moral and intellectual leadership, in many different domains of society, is contrasted with rule by domination and direction.

**Heian period,** 794–1185, period in Japanese history named after the then capital, Heian-kyō (now KYOTO). Chinese influence was on the wane but Japanese literary traditions flourished and many of the classics of court literature were written at this time, including *The Tale of Genji* (c.1010) by MURASAKI SHIKIBU. Political intrigues at court were overshadowed by the rise of the SAMURAI class in the provinces and the court lost political power to MINAMOTO NO YORITOMO.

**Heiberg, Johan Ludvig** (ˌhiebeə), 1791–1860, Danish dramatist, critic, and director of the National Theatre. He composed many musical comedies, of which his masterpiece was *No!* (1836). He was married to the great actress Johanne Luise Heiberg. His romantic play *The Hill of the Elves* (1828) is considered a classic.

**Heidegger, Martin,** 1889–1976, German philosopher. A student of HUSSERL, whom Heidegger succeeded as professor of philosophy at Freiburg, he was also strongly influenced by KIERKEGAARD, DILTHEY, and NIETZSCHE. Heidegger's analysis in his major work, *Being and Time* (1927), of the concepts of 'care', 'mood', and the individual's relationship to death, relates authenticity of being as well as the anguish of modern society to the individual's confrontation with his own temporality. Although he himself rejected the title, Heidegger is regarded as one of the founders of 20th-cent. EXISTENTIALISM, and he influenced the work of SARTRE. His later work included studies of poetry and of dehumanization in modern society.

**Heidelberg,** city (1984 pop. 133,500), Baden-Württemberg, SW West Germany, on the Neckar R. Its manufactures include printing presses and precision instruments. First mentioned in the 12th cent., it was the residence of the electors and capital of the PALATINATE until the 18th cent. Its famous university (est. 1386) is the oldest in Germany. Since 1952 the city has been the headquarters of the US army in Europe.

**Heidelberg School,** group of Australian artists, notably Tom ROBERTS, Arthur STREETON, Federick McCubbin, and Charles Conder, who promoted an impressionist style of painting (see IMPRESSIONISM) during the late 1880s. They first worked in and around the Melbourne suburb of Heidelberg. Their '9 by 5' exhibition (1889), modelled on WHISTLER's 'Notes, Harmonies and Nocturnes' exhibition (London, 1884), brought them public recognition. They sought to express national sentiment by capturing the colour and atmosphere of the Australian landscape. Despite the brevity of its existence, the Heidelberg School had a profound influence on the development of Australian landscape painting in the 20th cent.

**Heidenstam, Verner von** (ˌhaydənstam), 1859–1940, Swedish lyric poet. An opponent of NATURALISM, he was noted for his personal and subjective style, e.g., *Pilgrimage and Wanderyears* (1888) and *Poems* (1895). Other works include historical novels, e.g., *The Tree of the*

*Folkungs* (1905–17), and essays, e.g., 'Renascence' (1889). He received the 1916 Nobel Prize for literature.

**Heifetz, Jascha**, 1901–87, American violinist; b. Lithuania. A child prodigy in Europe, he emigrated to the US in 1917, becoming a greater artist in maturity. He combined reasoned interpretation with virtuoso technique.

**Heijermans, Herman** (ˌhieǝmans), 1864–1924, Dutch dramatist. Much of his work focuses on life among Dutch Jews. His most famous play, *The Good Hope* (1900), celebrates the struggles of Dutch fishermen.

**Heilongjiang** or **Heilungkiang**, province (1985 est. pop. 33,110,000), 469,000 km² (181,081 sq mi), NE China. It borders the USSR (N and E) and the JILIN prov. (S). Major cities are HARBIN the capital, and QIQIHAR. In the north, much of the land is mountainous and forested. To the south, the SONGHUA R. flows through the Manchurian plain. Though the growing season is short, fertile soils have aided crop production, particularly of soya beans, sugar beet, and spring wheat. Animal husbandry is also practised. A wide variety of ferrous and nonferrous metals (including significant gold and graphite deposits) have been discovered, and the discovery of large oil reserves in the south of the province at Daching (Ta'ch'ing) in the 1960s enabled China to develop as a significant oil producer and exporter. Historically and economically the province's development has been linked with the other two NE provinces (see LIAONING).

**Heimlich manoeuvre**, emergency procedure used to treat choking victims whose airway is obstructed by food or another substance. It forces air from the lungs through the windpipe, pushing the obstruction out. With the victim standing, the arms of the rescuer are wrapped around the victim's waist from the back. Then making a fist with one hand and placing the thumb side of the fist against the abdomen just above the navel, the rescuer grasps the fist with the other hand and pulls in with firm, quick, upward thrusts.

**Heine, Heinrich** (ˌhienǝ), 1797–1856, German poet. His early poems, collected as *Buch der Lieder* (1827; tr. Book of Songs), established him as a romantic, and his travel sketches, beginning with *Die Harzreise* (1826; tr. Harz Journey), reveal a mixture of poignant emotion and sceptical wit. A supporter of the social ideals of the FRENCH REVOLUTION, he left Germany for Paris in 1831. From there he continued to disseminate French revolutionary ideas in Germany and his works were banned *in absentia* in 1835. Heine worked in Paris as a journalist, writing *The History of Religion and Philosophy in Germany* (1835) and *The Romantic School in Germany* (1836) for French readers, and *Conditions in France* (1832) and *Lutezia* (1855) for German. His *New Poems* (1844), sharply political, were also written in Paris. He died there after years of agony, having contracted syphilis. His lyrics have been used in some 3000 compositions by SCHUMANN, SCHUBERT, and many others. His later verse satires *Atta Troll: a Summer Night's Dream* (1843) and *Germany: a Winter's Tale* (1844) reflect his response, as a left-wing German of Jewish descent, to German anti-Semitism and reaction. His last collections, *Romanzero* (1851) and *Poems 1853 and 1854*, are among his wittiest and profoundest. Virtually all his work has been translated into English.

**Heinesen, Andreas William**, 1900–, distinguished Faroese poet and novelist from Thórshavn in the Faroe Islands who writes all his works in Danish. His early books of poems all had cosmic associations: *Arctic Elegies* (1921), *Harvest Near the Sea* (1924), *The Stars Awaken* (1930); and his subsequent work is characterized by sharply defined contrasts between intimacy and distance, joy and fear, life and death. His best-known works are *The Errant Musicians* (1950), and his late masterpiece, *The Tower at the Edge of the World* (1976).

**Heisenberg, Werner**, 1901–76, German physicist. A founder of the QUANTUM THEORY, he is famous for his uncertainty principle, which states that it is impossible to determine both the position and momentum of a subatomic particle (such as the electron) with arbitrarily high accuracy. The effect of this principle is to convert the laws of physics into statements about probabilities, instead of absolute certainties. Heisenberg's matrix mechanics, a form of the quantum theory, was shown to be equivalent to Erwin SCHRÖDINGER's wave mechanics. Heisenberg received the 1932 Nobel Prize for physics for his work in the creation of quantum mechanics.

**Hejaz**, district of W. Arabia which includes the cities of Jeddah, MECCA, MEDINA, and Yanbo. In the 19th cent. and early 20th cent. the district was ruled by the Sharif of Mecca, protector of the Holy Places of Islam. It was incorporated into the Kingdom of Saudi Arabia after its capture by Ibn Saud in 1926.

**Hejaz Railway**, railway linking DAMASCUS with AMMAN, Ma'an, and MEDINA. It was constructed by the OTTOMAN EMPIRE (1900–08) to facilitate the travel of Muslim pilgrims to Mecca, and to enable Turkish troops to hold the HEJAZ district. During World War I it became a favourite target of the Arab irregular forces assisted by Lawrence of Arabia; it was damaged in many places. It has not operated south of Ma'an since 1918 in spite of several attempts to rebuild it.

**Hekla** (ˌheklah), active volcano, c.1490 m (4900 ft) high, SW Iceland, on the Mid-Atlantic Ridge. Hekla regularly emits steam and has several craters. The most destructive known eruption occurred in 1766; a recent one happened in 1947.

**Helen**, in Greek mythology, the most beautiful of women; daughter of ZEUS and LEDA, sister of CLYTEMNESTRA and of CASTOR AND POLLUX. Courted by many suitors, she married MENELAUS. When PARIS awarded the apple of discord to APHRODITE, the goddess gave him Helen; he carried her off to Troy, precipitating the TROJAN WAR. After the war she returned to Sparta with Menelaus, by whom she bore Hermione. She also figures in the legend of FAUST.

**Helena**, US city (1980 pop. 23,938), state capital of Montana, on the eastern slope of the CONTINENTAL DIVIDE; inc. 1870. It is a commercial centre in a ranching and mining area, with some manufactures, including machine parts and paints. Helena's main street is the site of Last Chance Gulch, where gold was discovered in 1864.

**Helena, Saint**, c.248–328?, mother of CONSTANTINE I. Converted to Christianity in 313, she is said to have discovered the True Cross while the Church of the Holy Sepulchre was being built in Jerusalem. Feast: 18 Aug.

**helicopter**, powered AIRCRAFT in which the lift and the thrust for forwards, backwards, or sideways movement is derived from mechanically-driven rotating AEROFOILS (rotor blades), mounted on a vertical axis and turning in a horizontal plane which can be inclined in the desired direction of motion. The first person-lifting helicopters were built in France in 1907, but they were not developed. The first practical helicopter was built in Germany in 1936, and it flew for 1 hr 20 mins, attaining a speed of 122 kph (76 mph) and a height of 3400 m (11,243 ft). Helicopters were successfully developed by SIKORSKY from 1939, initially for military use. Helicopters made possible the exploitation of offshore oilfields by floating rigs. Helicopters are now widely used for executive communications, for air-sea rescue operations, for antisubmarine patrols, for police observation work, and as 'gun ships' in land warfare.

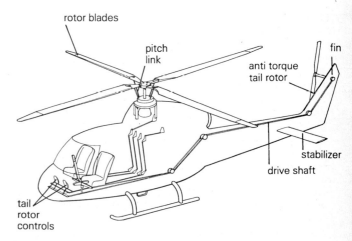

Helicopter

**heliocentric system:** see COPERNICAN SYSTEM.

**Heliopolis,** ancient city, N EGYPT, in the Nile delta, 10 km (6 mi) below Cairo. It was the centre of sun worship, and its god RA or Re was the state deity until THEBES became the capital (c.2100 BC), when the gods AMON and Ra were combined as Amon-Ra. Its famous schools declined after the founding of Alexandria (332 BC)

**Helios** (ˌheeleeos), in Greek mythology, the sun god; son of the TITANS Hyperion and Theia; father of PHAËTHON. Each morning he left a palace in the east and crossed the sky in a golden chariot, then returned along the river Oceanus. He was a national god in Rhodes, where a COLOSSUS represented him; it was one of the SEVEN WONDERS OF THE WORLD. In Rome, where he was known as Sol, he was an important god.

**Helios,** in space exploration: see SPACE PROBE, table.

**heliotrope,** in mineralogy: see BLOODSTONE.

**helium** (He), gaseous element, first observed spectroscopically in the SUN during a solar eclipse in 1868. Its noncombustibility and buoyancy make this extremely unreactive, INERT GAS the most suitable of gases for BALLOONS and AIRSHIPS. Deep-sea divers often breathe a helium-and-oxygen mixture; because helium is less soluble in human blood than nitrogen, its use reduces the risk of the bends (see DECOMPRESSION SICKNESS; DIVING, DEEP-SEA). Liquid helium is essential for low-temperature work (see LOW-TEMPERATURE PHYSICS; SUPERFLUIDITY). Helium is also used in arc welding and gas-discharge lasers. Abundant in outer space, helium is the end product of fusion processes in STARS. See ELEMENT (table); PERIODIC TABLE.

**hell,** in Christian theology, eternal abode of unrepentant sinners. Souls in hell are held by SATAN and deprived forever of the presence of God. In legend it is a place of fire and brimstone, where the damned undergo physical torment. Islam has a similar hell. In the ancient Jewish Sheol or Tophet, souls wander about unhappily, but Sheol later became much like the Christian hell. The ancient Greeks believed souls went to an underworld called Hades.

**Helladic culture:** see MYCENAEAN CIVILIZATION.

**Hellen,** in Greek mythology, ancestor of the Hellenes, or Greeks; son of DEUCALION and Pyrrha. His sons Dorus, Xuthus, and Aeolus were the progenitors of the principal Greek nations the DORIANS, Ionians, Achaeans (see under ACHAEA), and Aeolians.

**Hellenism,** the culture, ideals and pattern of life of classical Greece, especially of Athens during the age of PERICLES; also, later thought and writing drawing on these ideals. It is often contrasted with austere, monotheistic Hebraism.

**Hellenistic civilization,** spread of HELLENISM through the Mediterranean and Near East and into Asia after ALEXANDER THE GREAT's conquests. While the Greek city-states stagnated, their culture flourished elsewhere, notably at ALEXANDRIA. The city's influence on art, letters, and commerce was so great that the era is sometimes called the Alexandrian age. PERGAMON and other cities were also important. Navigators extended the known world and commercial wealth was reflected in ornate, grandiose architecture. Social divisions were extreme, but education was more widespread than ever before, with Greek the language of culture. A division between popular and learned writing appeared. The libraries of Alexandria and Pergamum were great learning centres, and writers like CALLIMACHUS, LUCIAN, and THEOCRITUS flourished. Philosophical disputation abounded, with STOICISM and Epicureanism (see EPICURUS) especially important. The highest achievement of the age may have been the preservation of Greek culture for the Romans. As Rome overshadowed the Mediterranean world, Hellenistic civilization was absorbed rather than extinguished.

**Heller, Joseph,** 1923–, American writer. He is best known for the novel *Catch-22* (1961), a wildly comic tale of military absurdities. He has also written a play and other novels, including *Something Happened* (1974) and *Good as Gold* (1979).

**Hellman, Lillian,** 1905–84, American dramatist. Her finely crafted plays include *The Children's Hour* (1934), *The Little Foxes* (1939), and *Watch on the Rhine* (1941). During her lifetime she was also acclaimed for her autobiographical works, e.g., *An Unfinished Woman* (1969), *Pentimento* (1973), *Scoundrel Time* (1976) but these have now been shown to consist largely of self-glorifying fabrications.

**Helmholtz, Hermann Ludwig Ferdinand von,** 1821–94, German scientist. An investigator of thermodynamics, electrodynamics, and vortex motion in fluids, he extended the application of the law of conservation of energy and in 1847 formulated it mathematically. A pioneer in physiological optics, Helmholtz invented (1851) the ophthalmoscope. He was professor of physics at the Univ. of Berlin.

**Helmont, Jan Baptista van,** 1577–1644, Flemish physician, chemist, and physicist. He attributed physiological changes to chemical causes, but his work was coloured by his belief in mysticism. He introduced the term *gas* in its present scientific sense and discovered carbon dioxide.

**helots:** see SPARTA.

**Helpmann, Sir Robert,** 1909–86, Australian choreographer and dancer. He danced with the Sadlers Wells Ballet from 1933, often as partner to FONTEYN. He was noted for roles in *The Rake's Progress*. He was joint director of the Australian Ballet (1965–76).

**Helsingør** or **Elsinore,** city (1985 pop. 56,388), E Denmark, on the Oresund. It is an industrial centre, fishing port, and summer resort. Known since the 13th cent., it served as a toll port from the 15th to the 18th cent. Kronborg castle (now a maritime museum), the setting of Shakespeare's *Hamlet,* is used to stage performances of the play.

**Helsinki,** city (1984 pop. 484,263, metropolitan area 942,825), capital of Finland, S Finland, on the Gulf of Finland. Though blocked by ice from January to May, it is a natural seaport and the nation's administrative, cultural, and commercial centre, with machine shops, shipyards, and textile mills. Founded in 1550 by GUSTAVUS I of Sweden, it was devastated by fire in 1808 but was rebuilt and became the capital in 1812. Its university became (19th cent.) a centre for Finnish nationalist activity against Russian rule. Landmarks include the railway station (designed by Eliel SAARINEN) and the sports stadium, site of the 1952 OLYMPIC GAMES.

**Hemingway, Ernest,** 1889–1961, one of the great American writers of the 20th cent. With the publication of his novel *The Sun Also Rises* (1926), he was recognized as a leading spokesman of the 'lost generation' of American expatriates in post-World War I Paris. Writing in a direct, terse style, Hemingway focused on courageous people living essential, dangerous lives. His other major novels include *A Farewell to Arms* (1929), a tragic wartime love story, and *For Whom the Bell Tolls* (1940), based on an incident in the SPANISH CIVIL WAR, in which he was a correspondent. He is also famous for his vigorous short stories, e.g., 'The Killers' and 'The Snows of Kilimanjaro'. In 1945 he settled in Cuba, where he wrote the novella *The Old Man and the Sea* (1952). His other writings include the nonfiction works *Death in the Afternoon* (1932) and *Green Hills of Africa* (1935). In 1954 he was awarded the Nobel Prize in literature. He later moved to Idaho where, plagued by illness, he committed suicide.

**hemispheric dominance:** see LATERALITY.

**hemlock,** coniferous evergreen tree (genus *Tsuga*) of the PINE family, native to North America and Asia. The common hemlock of E North America (*T. canadensis*) has small cones and short, dark-green leaves that give the branchlets a flat appearance. The wood of a Western hemlock (*T. heterophylla*), which is of high quality, is used for construction. The name 'hemlock' was given to the trees by early European settlers because the smell of the damaged foliage is similar to that of the POISON HEMLOCK, a herb of the CARROT family. The proper name *Tsuga* is Japanese.

**Hémon, Louis,** 1880–1913, French Canadian novelist; b. France. A journalist, he moved to Quebec after 1911 and wrote four novels, including the classic *Maria Chapdelaine* (1914).

**hemp** or **Indian hemp,** annual herb (*Cannabis sativa*) native to Asia and widely cultivated in Europe. It is often grown for the fibre made from its stems and for the narcotic drugs hashish, cannabis, and MARIJUANA, made primarily from the female flowers. Of major importance in many kinds of cord, hemp fibre, similar to flax, is used in making paper, cloth, and other products.

**Hempel, Carl Custav,** 1905–, American philosopher of science and mathematics, b. Germany. An adherent of CARNAP's LOGICAL POSITIVISM, he developed a more relaxed version of the doctrine. He allowed that observation statements can play an interpretative role, attempted a precise definition of confirmation, and introduced the 'covering law' model of scientific explanation, on which events are explained by being derived from general laws, themselves deduced from higher-order laws. His major works are *Fundamentals of Concept Formation in Empirical Science* (1952) and the collected essays of *Aspects of Scientific Explanation* (1965).

**Henan** or **Honan,** province (1985 est. pop. 77,130,000), 167,000 km² (64,478 sq mi), central China. It borders on six provinces, including SHAANXI to the west. Major cities are ZHENGZHOU, the capital, and LUOYANG. Most of the province lies to the south of the YELLOW RIVER. In the past the river has flooded in these middle reaches but since 1949 the river's course has been strengthened and the threat from flooding has significantly declined. Contrasting physical regions are found in the western mountains and central loess highlands. Agriculture has long been a major industry and Henan is now China's leading producer—by output and sown area—of tobacco, wheat, and sesame. Cotton is also a major cash crop. Since 1949 Henan has become more industrialized; Zhengzhou has developed as a major textile producer, heavy engineering has developed at Luoyang, and steel production at Angyang. The province is rich in mineral resources, particularly coal (including coking coal for the WUHAN steel industry) and bauxite. Historically, Henan has great significance; it was here in c.5000 BC that the Yangshao culture was established. This neolithic culture, based on millet cultivation, developed in villages located on loess terraces of tributaries of the Yellow R. Though recent discoveries have revealed other independent Neolithic cultures, the Yangshao culture is seen as the origins of Chinese culture. The Shang dynasty (c.1480–1050 BC) and the Zhou dynasty (c.1122–221 BC) were both based near Luoyang and Luoyang became the capital of the Zhou in 770 BC. For the next 13 centuries it was periodically to become the capital during both the Han (202 BC–AD 220) and the Tang dynasties (AD 618–907). In the later Han period the city had a population of half a million and was laid out in the Chinese cosmological tradition of a rectangular shape facing the four points of the compass.

**Hench, Phillip Showalter,** 1896–1965, American physician. Working at the MAYO CLINIC, he studied rheumatoid ARTHRITIS, which he treated with cortisone. For this work, he received in 1950, with KENDALL and Reichstein (a Swiss biochemist) the Nobel Prize for physiology or medicine.

**henge,** a form of ceremonial enclosure consisting of an earthen bank and ditch and often with circles of standing stones. They are unique to the NEOLITHIC and early BRONZE AGE of the British Isles; the most outstanding henges are STONEHENGE and AVEBURY.

**Heng Samrin,** 1934–, Kampuchean Communist leader. In 1979, after the Vietnamese invasion of Kampuchea ousted the regime of POL POT and the KHMER ROUGE, Heng became head of the new Vietnamese-backed government in Phnom Penh. His government has faced continued armed resistance from the Khmer Rouge and other forces, and has failed to gain widespread diplomatic recognition.

**Henie, Sonja** (ˌhenee), 1912–69, American figure skater; b. Norway. Ten times the world's figure-skating champion, she won Olympic championships in 1928, 1932, and 1936. She later became a popular professional skater and film actress.

**Henningsen, Agnes,** 1868–1962, Danish author, the Bohemian of turn-of-the-century Danish letters. Her practice of free love and daring erotic novels aroused both outrage and enthusiastic praise. Her *Memoirs,* not published until several decades later (8 vol., 1941–55), are an invaluable document of their times, especially on such subjects as the emancipation of women.

**Henri, Robert,** 1865–1929, American painter. A member of the EIGHT, he rebelled against academic art and excelled in urban GENRE paintings and stylish portraits, e.g., *Spanish Gypsy* (Metropolitan Mus., New York) and *Young Woman in Black* (Art Inst., Chicago). One of the foremost American art teachers, he imbued such students as George BELLOWS, Rockwell KENT, and Edward HOPPER with his dynamic concepts.

**Henrietta Maria,** 1609–69, queen of CHARLES I of England, daughter of HENRY IV of France. Her dealings with the pope, foreign powers, and army officers increased the suspicion of Charles and the fear of a Catholic uprising that helped to precipitate (1642) the ENGLISH CIVIL WAR.

**Henry,** kings of England. **Henry I,** 1068–1135 (r.1100–35), was the youngest son of WILLIAM I. On the death of his brother WILLIAM II, he had himself elected and crowned king while his older brother, ROBERT II, duke of Normandy, was on crusade. In 1101 Robert invaded England, but Henry bought him off. Henry invaded Normandy in 1105, defeated his brother in 1106, and became duke of Normandy. In the meantime, he had been involved in a struggle with ANSELM over lay investiture. His later years were marked by his attempts to obtain the succession for his daughter MATILDA. Under Henry's reign of order and progress, royal justice was strengthened. **Henry II,** 1133–89 (r.1154–89), was the son of Matilda and GEOFFREY IV, count of Anjou. Founder of the Angevin, or Plantagenet, line, he became duke of Normandy in 1150 and in 1152 married ELEANOR OF AQUITAINE, thus gaining vast territories in France. In 1153 he invaded England and forced STEPHEN to acknowledge him as his heir. As king he restored order to war-ravaged England, subdued the barons, centralized the power of government in the crown, and strengthened royal courts. Henry's desire to increase royal authority brought him into conflict with THOMAS BECKET, whom he had made (1162) archbishop of Canterbury. The quarrel, which focused largely on the jurisdiction of the church courts, came to a head when Henry issued (1163) the Constitutions of CLARENDON, defining the relationship between church and state, and ended (1170) with Becket's murder, for which Henry was forced to do penance. During his reign he gained the northern counties from Scotland and increased his French holdings. He was also involved in family struggles. Encouraged by their mother and LOUIS VII of France, his three oldest sons, Henry, RICHARD I, and Geoffrey, rebelled (1173–74) against him. The rebellion collapsed, but at the time of Henry's death, Richard and the youngest son, JOHN, were in the course of another rebellion. **Henry III,** 1207–72 (r.1216–72), was the son of John. He became king under a regency and assumed full powers of kingship in 1227. In 1230, against the advice of the chief justiciar, Hubert de Burgh, he led an unsuccessful expedition to Gascony and Brittany. He dismissed Hubert in 1232 and began a reign of extravagance and general incapacity, spending vast sums on futile wars in France. Henry's absolutism, his reliance on French favourites, and his subservience to the papacy aroused the hostility of the barons. His attempt to put his son, Edmund, earl of Lancaster, on the throne of Sicily (given to Henry by the pope) eventually led to the BARONS' WAR. Simon de MONTFORT, the barons' leader, won at Lewes and summoned (1265) a famous PARLIAMENT, but Henry's son EDWARD I led royal troops to victory at Evesham (1265), where de Montfort was killed. By 1267 the barons had capitulated, Prince Edward, later EDWARD I, ruled the realm, and Henry was king in name only. **Henry IV,** 1366–1413, (r.1399–1413), was the son of JOHN OF GAUNT. In 1387 he joined the opposition to RICHARD II and was one of the five 'lords appellant' who ruled England from 1388 to 1389. In 1398 Richard banished Henry and, after John's death in 1399, seized his vast Lancastrian holdings. Counting on the king's unpopularity and his absence in Ireland, Henry invaded England and successfully claimed the throne, thus establishing the Lancastrian dynasty. His reign was spent suppressing rebellions, notably by Richard's followers; by the Scots; by the Welsh under OWEN GLENDOWER; and by Sir Henry PERCY. He left the kingdom militarily secure but in debt. His son, **Henry V,** 1387–1422 (r.1413–22), presided over the privy council during his father's illness. As prince of Wales (Shakespeare's 'Prince Hal'), he led armies against Owen Glendower and figured largely in the victory over the Percys. The early years of his reign were troubled by difficulties with the Lollards (see LOLLARDY). Determined to regain lands he believed to be his, he invaded France in 1415, thus reopening the HUNDRED YEARS WAR. After announcing his claim to the French throne, he met and defeated a superior French force at the famous battle of AGINCOURT. By 1420 he had conquered Normandy, married CATHERINE OF VALOIS, and persuaded her father, CHARLES VI of France, to name him his successor. He fell ill and died in 1422. As king he ruled with justice and industry, restoring civil order and the national spirit. Though his wars left the crown in debt, his charm, military genius, and care for his less fortunate subjects made him a popular hero. His son, **Henry VI,** 1421–71 (r.1422–61, 1470–71), became king when he was not yet nine months old. During his early years England was under the protectorate of two of his uncles. After their defeat at Orléans by JOAN OF ARC, the English attempted to protect their French interests by crowning Henry king of France at Paris in 1431, but their cause was hopeless. Henry's rule was dominated by factions, and there were many riots and uprisings indicating public dissatisfaction with the government. The struggle between the faction headed by Henry's wife, MARGARET OF ANJOU, and Edmund Beaufort, duke of Somerset, and that headed by Richard, duke of York, developed into the dynastic battle between the LANCASTERS and YORKS known as the Wars of the ROSES. Henry went insane in 1453. In 1455 Somerset was killed in the battle of St Albans, and the Yorkists gained control of the government. Margaret had control from 1456 to 1460, when the Yorkists won a victory at Northampton, and Henry was taken prisoner. York, who had been named Henry's successor, was killed at Wakefield in 1460, but his son EDWARD IV defeated the Lancastrians and was proclaimed king. Later he fled to France, and Henry was briefly (1470–71) restored. In 1471 Edward retook the throne, and Henry was murdered in the Tower. Henry was a mild, honest, pious man, a patron of literature and the arts, and the founder of Eton College (1440) and King's College, Cambridge (1441). He was also unstable, weak-willed, and politically naive. **Henry VII**, 1457–1509 (r.1485–1509), became head of the house of Lancaster at Henry VI's death. In 1485 he invaded England from France and defeated the forces of RICHARD III at the battle of Bosworth Field. The next year he married Edward IV's daughter, Elizabeth, thus uniting the houses of York and Lancaster and founding the TUDOR dynasty. Although his accession marked the end of the Wars of the Roses, the early years of his reign were disturbed by Yorkist attempts to regain the throne, e.g., the impersonations of Lambert SIMNEL and Perkin WARBECK. He consolidated English rule in Ireland (1494) and effected a peace treaty with Scotland (1499), which was followed by the marriage of his daughter Margaret to JAMES IV of Scotland. He established the Tudor tradition of autocratic rule tempered by justice and increased the powers of the STAR CHAMBER court. His son **Henry VIII**, 1491–1547 (r.1509–47), married his brother Arthur's widow, KATHARINE OF ARAGÓN, who bore him a daughter, MARY I. His chief minister (1514–29), Thomas WOLSEY, concluded an alliance with FRANCIS I of France but Henry (despite the FIELD OF THE CLOTH OF GOLD), joined (1522) Emperor CHARLES V in a war against France. England prospered internally under Wolsey, who had almost complete control. The court became a centre of learning and the pope gave Henry the title 'Defender of the Faith' for a treatise he wrote against Martin LUTHER. By 1527 Henry, desiring a male heir, wished to marry Anne BOLEYN, but Pope CLEMENT VII, under the control of Katharine's nephew, Charles V, resisted his demands for a divorce. Wolsey's failure in this affair caused his downfall, and Thomas Cromwell became chief minister. An antipapal policy was adopted, and the subservient Thomas CRANMER became archbishop of Canterbury. He immediately pronounced Henry's marriage to Katharine invalid (1533). Papal powers were transferred to the king (1533–34), who became the supreme head of the English church (1534). The break with Rome was now complete, and an independent Church of ENGLAND was established. Anne, whom Henry immediately married (1533), had one daughter, ELIZABETH I. The marriage ended in 1536 when Anne was convicted of adultery and beheaded. Ten days later Henry married Jane SEYMOUR, who died in 1537 giving birth to EDWARD VI. The king dealt harshly with rebellions against the abolition of papal supremacy and the dissolution of the monasteries. In 1537 he licensed the publication of the Bible in English. His marriage (1540) to ANNE OF CLEVES (whom he disliked and soon divorced) led to the execution of Cromwell. He then married Catherine HOWARD, who suffered (1542) Anne Boleyn's fate. In 1543 Catherine PARR became his sixth queen. In 1542 war with Scotland began again, and Henry made unsuccessful attempts to unite the two kingdoms. Wales was officially incorporated into England (1536), but the conquest of Ireland proved too expensive. The end of Henry's reign saw a gradual move toward Protestantism. Henry's reign witnessed significant political and administrative changes, including a major increase in the importance of Parliament. However, Henry's zeal for conflict led to severe financial problems helping to produce an unsettled end to a generally peaceful, if not placid, reign.

**Henry**, kings of France. **Henry I**, c.1008–60 (r.1031–60), was the son and successor of ROBERT II. He unwisely invested his brother Robert with the duchy of Burgundy, setting up a powerful rival to the French kingdom. Henry also fought with William, duke of Normandy (later WILLIAM I of England). **Henry II**, 1519–59 (r.1547–59), succeeded his father, FRANCIS I. Weak and pliant, he was dominated by Anne de Montmorency, by his mistress DIANE DE POITIERS, and by François and Charles de GUISE. Henry resumed his father's wars against Holy Roman Emperor CHARLES V and continued them against Charles's son PHILIP II of Spain. He was killed accidentally in a tournament and was succeeded by FRANCIS II. **Henry III**, 1551–89 (r.1574–89), was the son of Henry II and CATHERINE DE' MEDICI. He helped his mother plan the SAINT BARTHOLOMEW'S DAY massacre (1572) and was elected (1573) king of Poland. Assuming the French crown on the death of his brother CHARLES IX, Henry was faced with an ongoing civil war between Roman Catholics and Protestants, who were called HUGUENOTS (see RELIGION, WARS OF). In 1576 he made concessions to the Protestants that caused Henri, 3rd duc de GUISE, to form the Catholic League. When the Protestant Henry of Navarre (later HENRY IV of France) became (1584) legal heir to the throne, Guise forced Henry III to suppress Protestantism and to exclude Navarre from the

succession. In the ensuing War of the Three Henrys, Navarre defeated a royal army at Coutras (1587). Guise then revolted against the weakened Henry III, who was expelled (1588) from Paris by the mob. The king arranged the assassination of Guise, joined forces with Navarre, and attempted to retake Paris. During the siege he was assassinated by a fanatical monk, Jacques Clément. Henry was the last male member of the house of VALOIS. **Henry IV**, 1553–1610, king of France (1589–1610) and, as Henry III, king of Navarre (1572–1610), was the first BOURBON monarch of France. Raised as a Protestant, he became (1569) the nominal head of the Huguenots. To save himself from the Saint Bartholomew's Day massacre (1572), Henry renounced his faith. He returned to Protestantism in 1576, however, and led a combined force of Protestants and moderate Catholics against Henry III and the Catholic League (for the resulting conflict see under Henry III, above). Henry became heir to the throne in 1584 and became king after Henry III was assassinated (1589). He defeated the Catholic League at Arques (1589) and Ivry (1590), but was forced to abandon the siege of Paris when the League received aid from Spain. In 1593 Henry again abjured Protestantism, allegedly with the remark 'Paris is well worth a Mass'. He entered the city in 1594 and his conciliatory policy soon won him general support. He waged a successful war (1595–98) against Spain, and by the Edict of NANTES (1598) established political rights and a measure of religious freedom for the Huguenots. The rest of his reign was spent in attempting to restore order, while his minister Sully sought to improve the economy. He was assassinated by a Catholic extremist François Ravaillac on the eve of a potentially dangerous conflict with Spain. In 1600 Henry married MARIE DE' MEDICI, and he was succeeded by their son LOUIS XIII. His reputation for gallantry, wit, and concern for the peasantry has tended to deflect attention from his precarious control of the country and his failure to reform its government appreciably.

**Henry**, German kings: see HENRY, rulers of the Holy Roman Empire.

**Henry**, rulers of the HOLY ROMAN EMPIRE **Henry I** or **Henry the Fowler**, 876?–936, German king (r.919–36), was the first of the Saxon line, precursors to the emperors. After succeeding CONRAD I as German king, he won LOTHARINGIA from its allegiance to France (925), defeated the MAGYARS (933), and fortified his frontiers. St Matilda, his queen, founded many monasteries. **Henry II**, 973–1024, emperor (r.1014–24) and German king (r.1002–24), was the last of the Saxon line. He was duke of Bavaria and succeeded his third cousin, OTTO III. In 1004 he entered Italy and was crowned king of Lombardy. He carried on a long warfare with BOLESLAUS I of Poland. After being crowned (1014) emperor, Henry was forced to assert his control over Italy. Both he and his empress, Kunigonde, are saints of the Roman Catholic Church. **Henry III**, 1017–56, emperor (r.1046–56) and German king (r.1039–56), served jointly as king with his father, CONRAD II, and acceded after his father's death. Under Henry the medieval empire probably attained its greatest power and solidity. He defeated (1041) the Bohemians and maintained control over SAXONY and Lotharingia. The four Germans he named to the papal throne greatly increased the power of the papacy. His son, **Henry IV**, 1050–1106, emperor (r.1084–1106) and German king (r.1056–1106), was the central figure in the long struggle between the empire and the papacy, which had been greatly strengthened by his father. His appointment of bishops in 1075 was condemned by Pope GREGORY VII. Henry declared Gregory deposed, and Gregory in turn excommunicated Henry. Even though Henry recanted, an anti-king, Rudolf of Swabia, was named by a faction of German nobles, and civil war broke out. Henry was against excommunicated, but he invaded Italy, defeated the pope's forces, and was crowned emperor (1084) by the antipope, Guibert of Ravenna. His continuing battles with the pope endangered the monarchy, however, and in 1105 his rebellious son Henry V tried to depose him. **Henry V**, 1081–1125, emperor (r.1111–25) and German king (r.1106–25), tried to force his father to abdicate with the blessing of Pope PASCHAL II, but he soon fell out with the pope and in 1111 took Paschal and his cardinals prisoner. To secure his release, the pope crowned Henry emperor and made other concessions. The conflict continued, but was finally resolved by the Concordat of Worms (1122). **Henry VI**, 1165–97, emperor (r.1191–97) and German king (r.1190–97), was the son and successor of FREDERICK I. As the husband of Constance, heiress of Sicily, he gained control (1194) of that kingdom. He also took RICHARD I of England prisoner and forced him to swear fealty. He died while preparing to lead a Crusade. **Henry VII**, c.1275–1313, emperor (r.1312–13) and German king (r.1308–13), was a count of Luxembourg when he was named king. As emperor he tried vainly to end the strife between the GUELPHS AND GHIBELLINES. He died while on a futile campaign to secure imperial authority in S Italy.

**Henry, Joseph,** 1797–1878, American physicist. A professor of philosophy at Princeton (then the College of New Jersey), he was later (from 1846) the first secretary and director of the Smithsonian Institution. Henry improved the electromagnet, invented and operated the first electromagnetic telegraph, and discovered self-inductance. The unit of electric INDUCTANCE in the SI system (see METRIC SYSTEM, ELECTRIC AND MAGNETIC UNITS) is called the *henry* in his honour. Independently of Michael FARADAY, he discovered the principle of the induced current.

**Henry, Patrick,** 1736–99, political leader in the AMERICAN REVOLUTION. A brilliant orator, he served in the Virginia house of burgesses (1765–74) and the CONTINENTAL CONGRESS (1774–76), and was governor of Virginia (1776–79). The phrases 'If this be treason, make the most of it' and 'Give me liberty or give me death' are attributed to him. He later worked to add the Bill of Rights to the Constitution.

**Henry of Flanders,** c.1174–1216, Latin emperor of CONSTANTINOPLE (r.1206–16) after his brother, BALDWIN I. Ablest of the Latin emperors, he fought off the Bulgarians.

**Henry of Navarre** (Henry IV): see under HENRY, kings of France.

**Henryson, Robert,** c.1425–c.1500, Scottish poet. His works include the *Testament of Cresseid*, a severe and moving alternative conclusion to CHAUCER's *Troilus and Criseyde*, and the learned and humorous *Moral Fables*, based on Aesopian stories.

**Henry the Fowler:** see HENRY I under HENRY, rulers of the Holy Roman Empire.

**Henry the Lion,** 1129–95, Guelph duke of SAXONY (r.1142–80) and of BAVARIA (r.1156–80). Bavaria and Saxony were restored to him by Emperor FREDERICK I in an effort to end the strife between the GUELPHS AND GHIBELLINES. At first he supported Frederick in Italy and Christianized the Wendish lands. By 1180 the growth of his power had alarmed the emperor, who seized his two duchies and subdivided them into small principalities. Henry later regained parts of Saxony (Brunswick and Lüneburg). His son became emperor as OTTO IV.

**Henry the Navigator,** 1394–1460, prince of Portugal, patron of exploration. The son of Portuguese King JOHN I, he established (1416) at Sagres a base for sea exploration, an observatory, and a school for geographers and navigators. Henry's sea captains explored the W African coast, rounding Cape Verde (1444) and reaching as far as present-day Sierra Leone. Their return with gold and slaves made for a lucrative and popular business although he forbade (1455) the kidnapping of Negroes. His promotion of navigation and exploration provided the groundwork for the development of Portugal's sea power and colonial empire.

**Henslowe, Philip,** d. 1616, English theatrical manager. His fame rests on his association with the company the Admiral's Men and its principal actor, Edward ALLEYN, to whom his stepdaughter Joan was married. Pawnbroker, moneylender, and property magnate, Henslowe owned three London playhouses and kept a business diary which has become an important source of information about Elizabethan theatre organization.

**Henze, Hans Werner** (ˌhentsə), 1926–, German composer. He was influenced early by STRAVINSKY, HINDEMITH, and BARTÓK and experimented with TWELVE-TONE MUSIC, but when he settled in Italy in the early 1950s he began to adopt a more melodic and harmonic style which was most developed in *The Bassaride* (1965). His socialist politics are manifested in such works as *Essay on Pigs* (1969). He has written SYMPHONIES and OPERAS, e.g., *The Young Lord* (1964), *La Cubana* (1973), and *We Come to the River* (1976).

**hepatitis,** inflammation of the liver, usually due to a viral infection, that causes nausea, fever, weakness, loss of appetite, and frequently JAUNDICE. Two forms are most common: hepatitis A (infectious), spread through contaminated food or water; and hepatitis B (serum), which can be fatal and is usually transmitted by transfusions of infected blood or use of poorly sterilized medical instruments. Hepatitis can also occur as a complication of other diseases, such as amoebic DYSENTERY, and as a toxic reaction to alcohol, drugs, or other chemicals.

**Hepburn, Katherine,** 1909–, American actress. She has enhanced the screen with her dignified and commanding presence since 1932. Her films include *Little Women* (1933), *The Philadelphia Story* (1940), *The African Queen* (1951), *The Lion in Winter* (1968; Academy Award), and *On Golden Pond* (1981; Academy Award).

**Hephaestus,** in Greek mythology, OLYMPIAN god; son of HERA and ZEUS; husband of APHRODITE. Originally an Oriental fire god, in Greece he was the divine smith and god of craftsmen, worshipped in centres such as Athens. Usually a comic figure, he was represented as bearded, with mighty shoulders, but lame. He made Achilles' armour in the *Iliad* (see TROJAN WAR). He worked at huge furnaces, aided by CYCLOPS. The Romans identified him with VULCAN.

**Hepplewhite, George,** d. 1786, English cabinetmaker. His work is noted for light, curvilinear forms; painted or inlaid decoration with ribbon and rosette motifs; slender, tapering legs; chair backs in shield and oval forms; and the use of satinwood, painted beechwood, and mahogany. His small pieces, e.g., inlaid work tables, are especially prized.

A typical **Hepplewhite** chair

**Hepworth, Dame Barbara,** 1903–75, English sculptor. She was one of the first British abstract sculptors and worked in the circle of B. NICHOLSON and Henry MOORE. Working primarily in stone or bronze, she sought perfection of form and surface technique. In 1939 she settled in St Ives, Cornwall, where her studio is now a museum.

**Hera,** in Greek mythology, queen of OLYMPIAN gods; daughters of CRONUS and RHEA; wife and sister of ZEUS; mother of ARES and HEPHAESTUS. A jealous wife, she plagued Zeus, his mistresses, and his progeny, e.g., HERCULES. Hera was powerful and widely worshipped as the protectress of women, marriage, and childbirth. The Romans identified her with JUNO.

**Heracles, Herakles:** see HERCULES.

**Heraclitus,** c.535–c.475 BC, pre-Socratic Greek philosopher. He taught that there is no permanent reality except the reality of change, a position illustrated by his famous maxim 'You cannot step twice in the same river.'

Thus the only possible real state is the transitional one of becoming. He believed fire to be the underlying substance of the universe and all other elements to be transformations of it.

**Heraclius,** c.575–641, Byzantine emperor (610–41). He recovered provinces from Persia (622–28) but lost them (629–42) to the Arabs. MONOTHELETISM resulted from his efforts to reconcile MONOPHYSITISM with the Orthodox Church. He began the reorganization of the empire into military provinces.

**Herakleion,** Gr. *Iráklio*, city (1981 pop. 101,634), Greece, on N coast of CRETE. It is the principal port and commercial centre of the island. Originating as the outlet for KNOSSOS, it was a Byzantine port and acquired its medieval name of Candia when it was the Venetian capital of Crete. Extensive fortifications were built between the 14th and 17th cent. The museum has an excellent collection of Minoan works of art.

**heraldry,** system in which inherited symbols, or devices, called charges are displayed on a shield, or escutcheon, for the purpose of identifying individuals or families. In the Middle Ages the herald, often a tournament official, had to recognize men by their shields. As earlier functions of the herald grew obsolete, his chief duties became the devising, inscribing, and granting of armorial bearings. Heraldry proper, developed by noblemen using personal insignia on seals and shields, was a feudal institution. It is thought to have originated in Germany in the late 12th cent. and to have been imported into England by the Normans (see NORMAN CONQUEST). The CRUSADES and the tournaments that drew together knights from many countries caused heraldry to flourish in Europe. The embroidering of family emblems on the surcoat worn over chain mail in the 13th cent. accounts for the term 'coat of arms.' The use of armorial bearings spread rapidly thereafter. In England the regulation of heraldry was assigned to the HERALDS' COLLEGE (chartered 1483). Arms were borne by families, corporations, guilds, colleges, cities, and kingdoms, and the tradition still persists. See also BLAZONRY.

**Heralds' College,** body chartered (1483) by RICHARD III of England that assigns new coats of arms and traces lineages to determine heraldic rights and privileges (see HERALDRY). It has collected and combined the rules of BLAZONRY into a system. The college includes the Garter king of arms and the kings of arms of Norroy and of Clarenceux.

**Herat,** city (1979 pop. 140,323), capital of Herat prov., NW Afghanistan, on the Hari Rud. Located in a fertile valley, the city is renowned for its fruits, textiles, and carpets. Its strategic location on ancient trade routes made it an object of conquest. Long part of the Persian empire, Herat fell to Jenghiz Khan (1221), Tamerlane (1383), and the Uzbeks (early 16th cent.). In 1881 it was confirmed as part of a united Afghanistan. During the 1979–89 Soviet occupation of Afghanistan, it was occupied by Soviet troops. Noted for its colourful bazaars, Herat is the site of the 12th-cent. Great Mosque.

**herb,** name for any plant that is used medicinally or as a flavouring, chiefly in savoury dishes. The flavour comes from the aromatic ESSENTIAL OILS in the leaves of plants such as PARSLEY, SAGE, MARJORAM, ROSEMARY, BASIL, THYME, MINT, TARRAGON, and OREGANO. Each herb has a traditional association with certain foods. The leaves are used fresh or dried. See also BOUQUET GARNI. The term is also applied to all herbaceous plants as distinguished from woody plants.

**herbarium,** a systematic collection of dried plant specimens, used as a reference or standard in plant identification, and in studies of botanical classification.

**Herbart, Johann Friedrich,** 1776–1841, German philosopher and educator. He developed the mathematical and empirical, as well as the metaphysical, aspects of psychology. In education he stressed relating new concepts to the experience of the learner. Many of his works have been translated into English, e.g., *Application of Psychology to the Science of Education* (tr. 1892).

**Herbert, George,** 1593–1633, English METAPHYSICAL POET. In youth worldly and ambitious, he became a parish priest of saintly character. His devotional poems, combining spiritual insight with homely but surprisingly and subtle imagery, were published after his death as *The Temple* (1633). Some are now among the best-loved hymns.

**Herbert, Victor,** 1859–1924, cellist, composer, and conductor. Born in Ireland, he went to the US in 1886. He conducted the Pittsburgh Symphony Orchestra from 1898 to 1904. His major successes were melodious OPERETTAS, including *Babes in Toyland* (1903), *The Red Mill* (1906), and *Eileen* (1917). In 1916 he provided the first musical score specifically composed to accompany a film: *The Fall of a Nation*.

**Herbert, Xavier,** 1901–84, Australian novelist. He spent most of his life in northern, tropical Australia which provided the setting and themes for his best-known works, *Capricornia* (1938) and *Poor Fellow My Country* (1975), the longest novel ever published in Australia (some 850,000 words). Herbert's main protagonists are tragically alienated half-castes, victims of the destruction of aboriginal culture and society at the hands of European Australians. His writing is intensely chauvinist, self-righteous and prolix, but also powerful and disturbing to the European conscience.

**herbicide,** substance that kills plants or inhibits their growth. Selective herbicides are designed to affect weeds without permanently harming crops; nonselective ones, generally toxic, are used to clear all plants from areas such as roads, railways, and around buildings. Inorganic compounds such as common salts have long been used as herbicides; certain sulphates, ammonium and potassium salts, and other compounds were first used as selective herbicides. The 1940s saw the development of 2,4-D (2,4-dichlorophenoxyacetic acid), an organic compound that is a highly selective systemic herbicide. Such herbicides are now widely used. One such compound, 2,4,5-T (2,4,5-trichlorophenoxyacetic acid), has been banned in some countries as dangerous. Interest is now expressed in the breeding by GENETIC ENGINEERING of varieties of the major crop plants unaffected by herbicides which therefore kill all other plants in the growing crop.

**herbivore,** name given to plant-eating animals. Herbivores usually have specialized digestive tracts, designed to keep the plant food in contact with digesting bacteria and digestive enzymes for long periods of time. Herbivorous mammals' teeth have flat crowns, designed to grind down tough plant material. Plant material is more difficult to digest than animal material. Herbivores may be further defined as fructivores or fruit-eaters and graminivores or grain-eaters. Herbivorous animals are the secondary producers in ecological energy pyramids, between the primary producers, or plants, and the tertiary producers, the carnivorous animals.

**Herculaneum,** ancient city at the foot of Mt. Vesuvius, S Italy, buried along with POMPEII when Vesuvius erupted in AD 79. Since the first ruins of the popular Roman resort were found in 1709, the most important excavations have been the Villa of the Papyri, a basilica, and a theater.

**Hercules, Heracles,** or **Herakles,** in Greek mythology, most popular hero, famous for strength and courage. The son of Alcmene and ZEUS, he was hated by HERA, who sent serpents to his cradle; he strangled them. Later Hera drove Hercules mad and he slew his wife and children. He sought purification at the court of King Eurystheus, who set him 12 mighty labours: killing the Nemean lion and HYDRA; driving off the Stymphalian birds; cleaning the Augean stables; capturing the Cerynean hind, Cretan bull, mares of Diomed, Erymanthian boar, cattle of Geryon, and CERBERUS; and procuring the girdle of Hippolyte (an AMAZON) and the golden apples of the Hesperides. He was later involved in the Calydonian hunt (see MELEAGER) and the Argonaut expedition (see JASON). At his death he rose to OLYMPUS, where he was reconciled with Hera and married HEBE. Represented as a powerful man with lion's skin and club, he was widely worshipped. He is the hero of plays by SOPHOCLES, EURIPIDES, and SENECA.

**Herder, Johann Gottfried von,** 1744–1803, German philosopher, critic, and clergyman. He was an influential critic and a leader of the STURM UND DRANG movement. While studying at Königsberg, he was influenced by KANT, and later he gained notice with *Fragments Concerning Current German Literature* (1767). He became court preacher at Weimar through the influence of GOETHE, whose work was greatly influenced by Herder's *On the Origin of Language* (1772). At Weimar, Herder became the chief theorist of German ROMANTICISM and produced his anthology of foreign folk songs, *Voices of the People* (1778–79). His vast work *Outlines of the Philosophy of Man* (1784–91) developed a major evolutionary approach to history, propounding the uniqueness of each historical age.

**Heredia, José María** (ayraydheeə), 1803–39, Cuban lyric poet and prose writer. Such poems as 'Niagara' (1825) typify his romantic melancholy and joy in nature. Exiled (1823) as a revolutionary he spent two years in New York before settling in Mexico.

**Heredia, José María de,** 1842–1905, French poet; b. Cuba. His 118 Petrarchan sonnets, *Les Trophées* (1893), almost unparalleled in their reproduction of sensory effects in poetic terms, epitomize the poetic ideals of the PARNASSIANS.

**heredity and environment,** the pair of terms denoting the respective contributions of genetically inherited (INNATE) factors and environmentally experienced factors (including those acquired through LEARNING) in the development and formation of particular characteristics of an organism. There is a long standing opposition, frequently referred to as the 'heredity–environment' or 'nature–nurture' controversy, between 'nativist' and 'environmentalist' conceptions of human psychology; and of 'human nature' in general. The controversy has frequently taken the form of the dispute between EMPIRICISM and Rationalism. In the recent history of psychology, the nativist position is associated with the theories of CHOMSKY who has argued that the 'faculty' of language is innate; and the environmentalist position with BEHAVIOURISM. This debate over universal properties of the human mind should be distinguished from another, more politically and ideologically contentious aspect of the heredity-environment debate. This pertains to the causation of INDIVIDUAL DIFFERENCES and group differences (between ethnic groups, social classes and/or genders), particularly in performance on INTELLIGENCE tests. Although it is clear that many differences between individuals reflect both hereditary and environmental factors, there is no generally accepted evidence that genetic factors are responsible for psychological or behavioural differences between, for example, human males and females, or between different races. The view that behavioural differences are genetically determined is sometimes called 'biological determinism' (see SOCIOBIOLOGY).

**Hereford,** town (1981 pop. 48,277), in Hereford and Worcester, W Midlands of England, on R. Wye. Cider is manufactured here, and it is also an important centre for trade in agricultural products. There is also a cathedral which includes every style from Norman to Perpendicular and is one of the three hosts of the Three Choirs Festival (see also GLOUCESTER and WORCESTER).

**Hereford and Worcester,** county in the W Midlands of England (1984 est. pop. 645,300), 3926 km² (1531 sq mi), bordering on Wales in the W. It was formed in 1974 from the counties of Herefordshire and Worcestershire. Much of the eastern part of the county consists of relatively low-lying valleys. The western part is more hilly with the Malvern Hills in the centre and the Black Mountains in the SW. The county is drained by the rivers WYE, SEVERN, and AVON. Agriculture is important, with dairy and beef cattle farmed and fruit, vegetables, and hops produced. The Vale of Evesham in the E of the county is famous for its plums.

**Her Majesty's Inspectors,** a group of inspectors appointed by Order of the Queen in Council with the main purposes of inspecting schools and advising the Secretary of State for Education and Science. There are over 700 Inspectors in the UK. The first Her Majesty's Inspectors were appointed in 1839 to oversee the effective use of parliamentary grants in support of education. Britain is the only country to have such a system of national inspectors operating independently outside the civil service.

**hermandad** [Span., = brotherhood], federation of Spanish towns in the medieval era that protected the populace against bandits and the lawless nobility by arresting and summarily trying suspects. In the late 15th cent. the crown's Holy Hermandad was effective in ensuring security and order in rural Spain. *Hermandades* survived as modest local constabularies until 1835.

**hermaphrodite,** animal or plant with both female and male reproductive systems, producing both eggs and sperm. Some hermaphrodites undergo self-FERTILIZATION, in which egg and sperm of the same individual fuse, as in self-pollinating plants; others may undergo cross-fertilization, in which egg and sperm of different individuals fuse, as in the EARTHWORM. Protandric hermaphrodites (e.g., OYSTER and sage plant) produce both eggs and sperm but at different times.

**hermeneutics,** branch of philosophy dealing with the theory of understanding and interpretation. 'Understanding' is viewed as a circular process, whereby one can understand the whole only in terms of the parts but the parts only from the whole. First used to interpret biblical texts in the early 19th cent., the theory was extended by SCHLEIERMACHER beyond scriptural interpretation, and by the end of the century DILTHEY construed

it as the general methodology for all the social sciences and humanities. Both held that a universal human capacity for empathy—the personal experience of that which has been expressed by someone else—was the bridge between past and present. In the 20th cent. HEIDEGGER and his student Hans-Georg Gadamer rejected this psychological foundation, instead basing their hermeneutics on the study of linguistic phenomena such as translation and etymology.

**Hermes,** in Greek mythology, son of ZEUS and Maia; messenger of the gods and conductor of souls to HADES. He was also the god of travellers, of luck, music, eloquence, commerce, young men, cheats, and thieves. He was said to have invented the lyre and flute. The riotous Hermaea festival was celebrated in his honour. Hermes was represented (e.g., in a surviving original statue by PRAXITELES) with winged hat and sandals, carrying the CADUCEUS. He is equated with the Roman MERCURY.

**Hermitage Museum,** Leningrad, situated in the former Winter Palace of the Czar, built in 1762 by Francesco Bartolomeo Rastrelli and later extended, one of the most magnificent settings of any museum in the world. Although much damaged in the fire of 1837, parts of the building were restored, including the Alabaster Room. The collection of paintings, arms, coins, and medals was begun by PETER THE GREAT, and a gallery opened in the Winter Palace by the Empress CATHERINE II, who gave it the name of the Hermitage. The Imperial collections were added to by the purchase of other private collections, including the Empress JOSEPHINE's from Malmaison, and include Western European 14th- to 20th-cent. paintings including LEONARDO DA VINCI's *Benois Madonna* and GIORGIONE's *Judith* (bought by Catherine the Great as a RAPHAEL). It was opened to the public in 1852 and taken over by the state in 1917 after the RUSSIAN REVOLUTION, when many more aristocratic collections were acquired for the Museum. It now has exhibits from prehistoric to modern times. Departments opened since the Revolution include the Culture of the East, the History of Primitive Cultures, and the History of Russian Culture.

**hermit crab,** primarily marine animal (a CRUSTACEAN) distinguished from the true CRAB by its long, soft, spirally coiled abdomen terminating in an asymetrically hooked tail. Most occupy the empty shells of GASTROPODS and are marine scavengers. The largest species reaches 30 cm (1 ft) in length.

Hermit crab (*Eupagurus bernhardus*) in common whelk shell

**Hernández, Miguel,** 1910–42, Spanish poet and dramatist. A fervent Loyalist in the SPANISH CIVIL WAR, he died in prison, where *Cancionero y romancero de ausencias* (1938–41; tr. Songbook of Absences) was written. His war poetry includes *El hombre arecha* (1938; tr. Man Lies in Wait).

**Herne,** city (1984 pop. 174,800), North Rhine–Westphalia, W West Germany. A product of 19th-cent. industrialization in the RUHR district, it has a wide range of chemical industries. It is linked by canal to the RHINE.

**hernia,** protrusion of an internal organ or part of an organ through the wall of a body cavity. It may be present at birth or acquired after heavy strain on the musculature in such areas as the lower abdomen (inguinal hernia), diaphragm (hiatus hernia), or region around the navel. Surgery is sometimes recommended to alleviate symptoms and prevent the hernia from becoming caught and strangulated (cut off from the blood supply).

**hero,** in Greek mythology, famous person worshipped after death as quasi-divine. Heroes might be actual great people, real or imaginary ancestors, or 'faded' deities (ancient gods demoted to human status). Most hero worship, performed at night with blood sacrifices, was celebrated at the supposed place of the hero's tomb.

**Hero,** in Greek mythology, a priestess whose lover Leander used to swim across the Hellespont (now the DARDANELLES) to see her. One night the lamp in her temple by which he was guided blew out, and he was drowned. The story has been retold by many poets, e.g., MARLOWE (*Hero and Leander*, 1598)

**Herod,** dynasty reigning in Palestine at the time of Christ. **Antipater,** fl. c.65 BC, was the founder of the family fortune. He was an Idumaean and managed to gain a stronghold in Palestine. His son **Antipater,** d. 43 BC, was favoured by Julius CAESAR, who made him (c.55 BC) virtual ruler of all of Palestine. The son of the second Antipater was **Herod the Great,** d. 4 BC, who gave the family its name. He was friendly with Mark ANTONY, and secured (37 BC–4 BC) the title king of Judaea; after the battle of Actium he made peace with Octavian (later AUGUSTUS), who thereafter showed him great favour. Herod made great efforts to mollify the Jews by publicly observing Hebrew laws and by building a temple, but also promoted hellenization. In his last years Herod became bloodthirsty, and around the time of Jesus's birth, he ordered the massacre of the innocents. His son **Herod Antipas,** d. after AD 39, tetrarch of Galilee and Peraea, was the Herod who executed JOHN THE BAPTIST and who was ruling at Jesus's death. He repudiated his wife to marry his niece Herodias, wife of his half-brother Herod Philip. He was eventually banished by CALIGULA in AD 39. **Herod Agrippa I,** d. AD 44, was the nephew of Herod Antipas and a man of some ability. His son, **Herod Agrippa II,** d. c.AD 100, was a poor ruler who alienated his subjects. The Herods are usually blamed for the state of virtual anarchy in Palestine at the beginning of the Christian era. The prime source is the history by JOSEPHUS.

**Herodotus,** 484?–425? BC, Greek historian, sometimes called the Father of History; b. Halicarnassus, Asia Minor. His history of the PERSIAN WARS, the first comprehensive attempt at sustained narrative history, marks the start of Western historical writing. The work demonstrates his eager curiosity and his wide range of social and cultural interests. It is written in an anecdotal style of great charm and offers a rich diversity of information about the ancient world, its leaders, and its peoples.

**heroic couplet:** see PENTAMETER.

**heroin,** NARCOTIC drug synthesized from MORPHINE. In some parts of the world it is accepted as a powerful ANALGESIC (for relief of pain), particularly for the terminally ill and in other countries its medical use is prohibited because of its extreme addictiveness. In Britain the drug is subject to rigorous controls. Heroin is widely available illicitly and there is a growing problem of misuse and dependence, especially among the young around the world. See DRUG ADDICTION AND DRUG ABUSE.

**heron,** BIRD of the family Ardeidae, large wading birds including the BITTERN and EGRET, found in many temperate regions but most numerous in tropical and subtropical areas. Herons have sharp, serrated bills, broad wings, and long legs. They may have long, showy plumes on their heads, breasts, and backs. The common grey heron *Ardea cinerea* ranges from Western Europe to Indonesia. Like all herons, it has powder down patches. These FEATHERS crumble into powder and help to clean the rest of the plumage of fish slime.

**Heron, Patrick,** 1920–, British painter. His abstract style is close to TACHISM and colourfield painting and emphasizes the purely visual effect of colour.

**Hero of Alexandria** or **Heron** (ˌheeron), fl. AD 62, mathematician and inventor. His origin is uncertain, although he wrote in Greek. He wrote on the measurement of geometric figures and invented many contrivances operated by water, steam, or compressed air, including a fountain and a fire engine.

**herpes,** viral infection of the skin characterized by one or many small blisters. **Herpes simplex** causes a variety of disorders, including the cold sore around the mouth. Genital herpes is caused by herpes simplex type II and is a recurring sexually transmitted disease. **Herpes zoster,** or **shingles,** is an acute infectious disease causing pain along the distribution of a nerve. See also CHICKEN POX.

**Herrera, Francisco de** (eəˌreərah), c.1576–1656, Spanish painter, engraver, and miniaturist. He usually painted religious and GENRE subjects. His broad, dynamic style, expressive distortions, and light-and-dark accents can be seen in the *Triumph of St Hermengild* (Seville). His son, **Francisco de Herrera,** the younger, 1622–85, used a loose technique and bright colours, e.g., *Triumph of St Francis* (Seville Cathedral). He was CHARLES II's court painter.

**Herrera Campíns, Luis,** 1925–, president of VENEZUELA (1979–84). A founder of the moderate Social Christian Party, he was exiled (1952) by dictator M.P. Jiménez, but he returned (1958) after Jiménez's fall and entered the Venezuelan congress. Elected president in 1978, Herrera lost much popularity because of a weak economy.

**Herrick, Robert,** 1591–1674, considered among the greatest of the English Cavalier poets. A country clergyman, he never married, and the many women in his poems are probably fictitious. Most of his work appeared in *Hesperides* (1648), which included the sacred songs called *Noble Numbers*. A disciple of JONSON, Herrick shows classical influence, but his greatness rests on simplicity and sensuousness. Among his best-known lyrics are 'Upon Julia's Clothes' and 'Corinna's Going a-Maying'.

**herring,** important marine food FISH of the family Clupedae, including the SARDINE, pilchard, sprat, menhaden, and shad. Herrings are relatively small but very abundant, although stocks have suffered from overfishing in some areas; they are PELAGIC fish, swimming in large schools. The adult common herring (*Clupea harengus*) of the N Atlantic is about 30 cm (1 ft) long, with silvery sides and blue back. They live in water temperatures of 6–15°C (43–59°F) moving north in the summer, when the water warms up. Smoked herring are kippers.

**Herriot, Édouard** (eryˌoh), 1872–1957, French statesman. As a leader of the Radical Socialist Party, he was three times premier (notably 1924–25 and 1932). In 1932 he sought a conciliatory foreign policy and favoured payment of France's war debt to the US a stand that caused his cabinet's downfall. Imprisoned by the Germans in WORLD WAR II, he later was president of the French National Assembly (1947–54).

**Herschel,** family of distinguished English astronomers. **Sir William Herschel,** 1738–1822, originally Friedrich Wilhelm Herschel, b. Germany, discovered (1781) the planet Uranus, which led (1782) to his position as private astronomer to the king. The large reflecting telescopes that he constructed, including one with a 12.2-m (40-ft) focal length, far surpassed in size those of his contemporaries. He concluded from the motion of double stars that they are held together by gravitation and that they revolve around a common centre, thus confirming the universal nature of Isaac NEWTON's gravitational theory. He discovered the Saturnian satellites Mimas and Enceladus (1789) and the Uranian satellites Titania and Oberon (1787). His research on nebulae suggested a possible origin of new worlds from gaseous matter, and his catalogue of nebulae (including some objects that are now known to be galaxies or star clusters) increased those known from about 100 to 2500. His sister, **Caroline Lucretia Herschel,** 1750–1848, discovered eight comets and three nebulae. For her arrangement of her brother's catalogue of star clusters and nebulae, she received (1828) the Royal Astronomical Society's gold medal. Sir William's son, **Sir John Frederick William Herschel,** 1792–1871, spent four years (1834–38) at the Cape of Good Hope, cataloguing 1707 nebulae and clusters and 2102 pairs of double stars. He published (1864) a consolidated catalogue of 5079 nebulae and clusters; revised by Johann Dreyer as *A New General Catalogue of Nebulae and Star Clusters* (1888; see NEW GENERAL CATALOGUE), it is still a standard reference. In photography, he was the first to use sodium thiosulphate as a fixing agent, and he introduced the terms *positive image* and *negative image*.

**Hertford,** county town (1981 pop. 21,350) of Hertfordshire, in S Midlands of England, on R. Lea 32 km (20 mi) N of London. It is a market town, with some light industry. There are the remains of a 10th-cent. castle.

**Hertfordshire,** inland county in S England (1984 est. pop. 980,300), 1634 km² (637 sq mi), bordering on Greater London in the S. The county town is HERTFORD. Much of the county is low-lying, rising in the N in the

Chiltern Hills. It is drained by the Lea, Stort, and Colne rivers which flow into the R. Thames. Market gardening and mixed agriculture are important in the N, while much of the S is urbanized and industrialized. ST ALBANS and WATFORD are important towns in the S within London's commuter belt.

**Hertz, Heinrich Rudolf,** 1857–94, German physicist. He confirmed James Clerk MAXWELL's electromagnetic theory by producing and studying electromagnetic waves (radio waves), which he showed to be long transverse waves that travel at the speed of light and can be reflected, refracted, and polarized like light. The unit of FREQUENCY, the hertz, is named after him.

**Hertzog, James Barry Munnik,** 1866–1942, South African lawyer, soldier, and statesman. Judge of the Supreme Court of Pretoria (1895) and then a successful general during the SOUTH AFRICAN WAR, he became the unchallenged political leader of the Orange Free State, and served in Louis Botha's cabinet after the formation of the Union in 1910. In 1912 he resigned to form the National Party (with Gen. SMUTS) and served as prime minister from 1924 to 1939. He achieved British recognition of the equality of the Dominions, and won for the Afrikaans language equality with English in South Africa. He resigned from active politics in 1939 after refusing to join the British in the war against Germany.

**Hertzsprung–Russell diagram** [after astronomers Ejnar Hertzsprung and Henry Norris RUSSELL], graph showing the LUMINOSITIES, or absolute MAGNITUDES, of the STARS of a cluster or galaxy plotted against their surface temperatures (or some temperature-dependent characteristic such as SPECTRAL CLASS or colour). It is found that the majority of stars lie on a diagonal band (the main sequence) that extends from hot stars of high luminosity in the upper left-hand corner to cool stars of low luminosity in the lower right-hand corner. The concentration of stars in certain distinct regions of the H–R diagram indicates that definite laws govern stellar structure and STELLAR EVOLUTION.

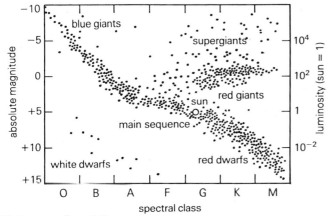

Hertzsprung–Russell diagram

**Herzen, Aleksandr Ivanovich,** 1812–70, Russian revolutionary leader and writer. A major landowner, he was sent to the provinces (1834) for participating in a socialist group. He left Russia permanently in 1847. In England he set up the first free Russian press abroad; his weekly journal *Kolokol* [the bell] (1857–62) was banned in Russia but widely read, even at the czar's court. His books include *My Past and Thoughts* (1855).

**Herzl, Theodor** (ˌheətsəl), 1860–1904, Hungarian Jew, founder of modern ZIONISM. As a newspaper correspondent covering the DREYFUS AFFAIR, he became convinced that the only solution to European ANTI-SEMITISM was the establishment of a Jewish national state. He organized the first Zionist World Congress (1897) and was its president until his death.

**Herzog, Werner,** 1942–, German film director. His visionary, near-hallucinatory films, often treating bizarre historical incidents, include *Aguirre, the Wrath of God* (1972), *Kaspar Hauser* (1974), *Stroszek* (1977), *Heart of Glass* (1977), *Nosferatu* (1979), and *Fitzcarraldo* (1982).

**Hesiod,** fl. late 8th cent. BC, Greek didactic poet, self-described as a Boeotian farmer. His *Works and Days* is filled with maxims for farmers,

to inculcate righteousness and efficiency. Also ascribed to him is the *Theogony,* a genealogy of the gods. Hesiod and HOMER codified much of Greek myth.

**Hess, Moses,** 1812–75, German socialist. He converted ENGELS to SOCIALISM and introduced MARX to the study of social and economic problems. By viewing humanity as initiating history rather than just observing it, he transformed Hegelian theory. In *Rome and Jerusalem* (1862) he urged the founding of a Jewish state in Palestine.

**Hesse** (ˌhesə), state (1984 est. pop. 5,535,185), 24,064 km² (8150 sq mi), central West Germany. Weisbaden is the capital. Hesse is largely agricultural, with heavily forested areas. Fine wines are produced along the Rhine valley. Industries include metallurgy and mining. Hesse emerged (1247) as a landgraviate under the Holy Roman emperor and was divided (1567) among several lines; Hesse–Kassel and Hesse–Darmstadt were the most important. In the 18th cent. the rulers of Hesse raised revenue by letting mercenaries, called Hessians, for hire. Hesse–Kassel was made (1803) an electorate and was annexed (1866) to PRUSSIA. Hesse–Darmstadt joined (1871) the German Empire and was ruled by its own dynasty until 1918.

**Hesse, Hermann,** 1877–1962, German novelist and poet. As a pacifist, he became a Swiss citizen after the outbreak of World War I. The spiritual loneliness of the artist is a major theme in Hesse's symbolic novels, which include *Peter Camenzind* (1904), *Demian* (1919), *Steppenwolf* (1927), and *Narziss and Goldmund* (1930). *Das Glasperlenspiel* (1943; tr. The Glass Bead Game) and *Siddhartha* (1922) reflect his interest in Oriental mysticism. In 1946 he was awarded the Nobel Prize for literature.

**Hesse, Philip of:** see PHILIP OF HESSE.

**Hestia,** in Greek mythology, goddess of the hearth; daughter of CRONUS and RHEA. Widely worshipped, she was a kind deity who represented personal and communal security and happiness. The Romans identified her with VESTA.

**heterosexuality:** see SEXUAL ORIENTATION.

**Hewett, Dorothy,** 1923–, Australian playwright and poet. Her best-known plays are *The Chapel Perilous* (1971) and *The Man From Mukinupin* (1979).

**Hewish, Antony,** 1924–, English radio astronomer. In 1946 he joined a university team headed by Sir Martin RYLE. With Jocelyn Bell he discovered PULSARS in 1947, later identified as small rotating neutron stars (1968). Hewish and Ryle received the 1974 Nobel Prize for Physics for their work.

**Heyerdahl, Thor,** 1914–, Norwegian explorer and anthropologist. Seeking evidence that ancient cultures could have been diffused by transoceanic travellers, he sailed across the Pacific (1947), the Atlantic (1970), and the Persian Gulf (1977) in replicas of primitive craft. He described these voyages in *The Kon-Tiki Expedition* (tr. 1950), *The Ra Expeditions* (tr. 1971), and *The Tigris Expedition* (tr. 1981). His work is controversial.

**Heywood, John,** 1497?–1580?, English actor and dramatist. He wrote didactic interludes and comedies, including *The Four PPs* and *The Play of the Weather,* proverbs, epigrams, and a verse satire *The Spider and the Fly* (1556).

**Heywood, Thomas,** 1574?–1641, English dramatist, best known for *A Woman Killed with Kindness* (1603), one of the finest domestic tragedies. A prolific playwright, he also wrote *Apology for Actors* (1612), a response to Puritan attacks.

**Hezekiah,** d. c.686 BC, king of Judah (r. c.715–c.686 BC). The successor to AHAZ, he resisted two invasions by SENNACHERIB of Assyria. He was one of the best of Judah's kings, abolishing idolatry and listening to ISAIAH and MICAH. 2 Kings 18–20; 2 Chron. 29–32; Isa. 36–39.

**Hf,** chemical symbol of the element HAFNIUM.

**Hg,** chemical symbol of the element MERCURY.

**hiatus hernia:** see HERNIA.

**Hiawatha,** fl. c.1550, legendary chief of the Onandaga Indians, credited with founding the IROQUOIS CONFEDERACY. He is the hero of a well-known poem by Henry Wadsworth LONGFELLOW.

**Hibberd, Jack,** 1941–, Australian playwright. He was originally associated with the PRAM FACTORY in Melbourne. His *Dimboola* (1969), modelled on a country wedding reception, is the most popular Australian play; *A Stretch of the Imagination* (1972), is probably the most influential. His style, influenced by Beckett, has been called 'Ocker baroque'.

**hibernation,** protective practice, among certain animals, of spending part of the cold season (when normal body temperatures cannot be maintained and food is scarce) in a state of relative dormancy. Hibernating animals can store enough food in their bodies to survive this period, during which no growth occurs and body activities are at a minimum. Cold-blooded animals (POIKILOTHERMS) assume the temperature of the environment and must hibernate when temperatures fall below freezing; frogs and fishes, for example, bury themselves in ponds below the frost line. Most warm-blooded animals (HOMOTHERMS) can survive freezing environments by metabolic control of their body temperatures, although many seek insulation in sheltered places, e.g., bears and bats in caves. Some animals undergo a similar device, called AESTIVATION to survive in hot, dry conditions.

**hibiscus:** see MALLOW.

**hiccup,** spasmodic contraction of the diaphragm producing characteristic sound. There is usually no obvious cause although hiccups are occasionally a sign of some pathological irritation of the diaphragm.

**Hickok, Wild Bill** (James Butler Hickok), 1837–76, American frontier marshal. Becoming marshal of Hays (1869) and Abilene (1871), in Kansas, he gained repute as a marksman from his encounters with outlaws. After his murder in Deadwood (now in South Dakota) by Jack McCall, he became a legend.

**hickory,** deciduous, nut-bearing tree (genus Carya) of the WALNUT family, native to E North America and SE Asia. The shagbark hickory (*C. ovata*) is valued for its edible hickory nuts and strong, resilient wood, often used for golf clubs, tool handles, and furniture. The pecan tree (*C. illinoensis*) and the paper-shelled pecans, the cultivated varieties with unusually thin-shelled nuts, yield pecans, among the most popular and commercially important nuts. The trees do not grow well in Europe.

**Hicks, Edward,** 1780–1849, American painter and preacher. Untrained in art, he painted primitive works of great charm and appeal. Hicks's fame rests on the nearly 100 versions of his painting *The Peaceable Kingdom*.

**Hicks, Sir (Richard) John,** 1904–, British economist. He had a distinguished academic career, teaching at the London School of Economics (1926–35) and at Cambridge and Oxford Univs. He made a valuable contribution toward solving the apparent conflict between the equilibrium theory and business-cycle theory in his classic work *Value and Capital* (1939) and, with Kenneth J. Arrow with whom he shared the Nobel Prize for economics (1972), showed that active forces create economic balances when the forces cancel each other out, not passive ones as had been accepted. Hicks's other significant works were *A Revision of Demand Theory* (1956), *Capital and Growth* (1965), *A Theory of Economic History* (1969), and *Causality in Economics* (1979).

**Hidalgo y Costilla, Miguel** (ee,dhalgoh ee kos,teeyah), 1753–1811, Mexican priest and revolutionary hero. In 1810 he rebelled against Spanish rule and with a huge army of Indians won the initial battles. But he was defeated (1811) by a royalist army at Calderón Bridge and was captured, defrocked, and executed.

**Hideyoshi** (heeday,ohshee): see TOYOTOMI HIDEYOSHI.

**hierarchy of needs,** a psychological theory of human motivation developed by Abraham Maslow (1908–70), in which all motives are derived from a hierarchical system of needs, from the 'basic' physiological needs, through 'security and love' needs to aesthetic needs and needs for self-actualization.

**hieratic:** see HIEROGLYPHIC.

**hieroglyphic** [Gr., = priestly carving], type of WRITING used in ancient EGYPT. Similiar pictographic styles of Crete, Asia Minor, and Central America and Mexico are also called hieroglyphics. Interpretation of Egyptian hieroglyphics, begun by J.F. CHAMPOLLION, is virtually complete; the other hieroglyphics are still imperfectly understood. Hieroglyphics are conventionalized pictures used chiefly to represent meanings that seem arbitrary and are seldom obvious. Egyptian hieroglyphics were already

perfected in the first dynasty (3110–2884 BC), but they began to go out of use in the Middle Kingdom and after 500 BC were virtually unused. There were basically 604 symbols that might be put to three uses (although few were used for all three purposes): as an ideogram, as when a sign resembling a man meant 'man'; as a phonogram, as when an owl represented the sign *m,* because the word for owl had *m* as its principal consonant; or as a determinative, an unpronounced symbol placed after an ambiguous sign to indicate its classification (e.g., an eye to indicate that the preceding word has to do with looking or seeing). The phonograms provided a basis for the development of the ALPHABET.

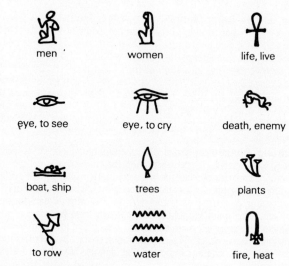

| | | |
|---|---|---|
| men | women | life, live |
| eye, to see | eye, to cry | death, enemy |
| boat, ship | trees | plants |
| to row | water | fire, heat |

Examples of **hieroglyphics**

**Higgins, Henry Bournes,** 1855–1929, Australian politician and judge; b. Ireland. A prominent liberal in the early Commonwealth parliament, he became president of the Court of Conciliation and Arbitration, and delivered the HARVESTER JUDGMENT in 1907.

**High Court:** see COURT SYSTEM IN ENGLAND AND WALES.

**higher education:** see COLLEGES; POLYTECHNICS; UNIVERSITIES.

**high jump,** athletics FIELD EVENT in which the competitor is allowed three attempts to jump over a crossbar. It is an elimination competition. Common techniques are the Western Roll, the Scissors, and the Fosbury Flop (invented by Dick Fosbury who won the Olympic gold medal in 1968).

**Highlands,** region in N Scotland (1985 est. pop. 194,903), 25,391 km² (9902 sq mi) bordering on the Moray Firth in the SE. It is separated from the Western Isles by The Minch, and from Orkney Island Area by the Pentland Firth. The administrative centre is INVERNESS. The region was formed in 1975 from the counties of Caithness, Sutherland, Ross and Cromarty, Nairnshire, Inverness-shire and the N part of Argyllshire. It includes the islands of Skye, Rhum, and Eigg from the Inner HEBRIDES. It is the largest Scottish region, containing not only much of the wildest and most picturesque upland scenery, but also BEN NEVIS which, at 1343 m (4406 ft) is the highest mountain in Britain. Towards the S it is crossed by GLEN MORE (the Great Glen), within which are LOCH NESS, Loch Oioch, and Loch Lochy, which are linked by canals to form the Caledonian Canal. In the extreme N there are more mountainous and moorland areas, but there is some low-lying terrain in the E which is fertile agricultural land. Much of the upland area is used for deer- and sheep-farming. Fishery and distilling are also important.

**Highland Games,** athletics meetings held in the Scottish Highlands since the early 19th cent. The best-known meeting is the Braemar Gathering which features TOSSING THE CABER. The Games include standard track and field events, as well as competitions in Highland dancing and bagpipe playing.

**Highlands, the** historical name for mountainous region of N Scotland, now known as HIGHLAND region. Early history is not well known, but by the 11th cent. the Scottish monarchy was centred in the Lowlands, and the Highland lairds were left to run their own affairs. In the early 18th cent. Highlanders strongly supported the JACOBITE uprisings. During the first half of the 19th cent. many people were removed from their crofts in the Highlands to make way for sheep-farming being developed by absentee landlords (the Highland Clearances). Until the 19th cent. the Scottish Gaelic language was the core of a Highland culture marked by the clan system and distinctive dress (kilt, tartan, etc.).

**high speed train,** fast train used for long-distance passenger services. High speed trains can offer journey times for many intercity distances superior to other modes of transport. Provided there is sufficient traffic (i.e., high population density) to support the expensive infrastructure of the track, signals, and stations, a high speed RAILWAY is economically viable. Whilst growth in speed capability has always been a feature of railway operation, significant growth in railway speeds became apparent in the 1960s when the SHIN KANSEN in Japan was opened, and when incremental speed increases on British Railways suggested that as a rough rule, for a 1% increase in speed there was a 1% increase in traffic. Many railways have increased speeds by making improvements to trains which run on existing tracks. Then minor modifications to track may be carried out, but most investment is in new trains. The fastest diesel-electric trains in service are British Railways' high speed trains operating at 200 kph (125 mph). Existing track can be further exploited by using TILTING TRAINS. Other railways have constructed completely new lines for high speed trains: the SHIN KANSEN in Japan, TGV in France (up to 260 kph/160 mph), and ICE in West Germany. Development of trains for speeds of 300 kph (185 mph) is proceeding in both France and Germany. Further increases in speed are possible using both new tracks and MAGNETIC LEVITATION and LINEAR MOTORS. Experimental installations in Japan and West Germany have demonstrated, respectively, speeds of 501 kph (310 mph) and 400 kph (248 mph). Whilst a new network of high speed trains using this technology is technically feasible, there are severe difficulties in raising finance for the very large investments necessary, and the planning of new routes so as to obtain an acceptable environmental impact is not easy.

**High Wycombe,** town (1981 pop. 69,575), in Buckinghamshire, S England, on R. Wye on S side of Chiltern Hills. There are various industries, including the manufacture of furniture. Just SE of the town centre is the site of a Roman villa.

**Higinbotham, George,** 1826–92, Australian politician and judge; b. Ireland. He achieved legendary status as a fierce upholder of the Australian colonies' powers of self-government while Victorian attorney-general in the 1860s. As chief justice of the Victorian supreme court, he gave public support to the trade unions in a national strike in 1890.

**hijacking,** in law, the illegal seizure and diversion of any vehicle by force or threats; most commonly applied to the seizure of aircraft. Most hijackings are carried out by terrorist groups in order to coerce governments by threatening to kill the passengers. In the past hijackers have demanded ransom money or the release of prisoners, or have merely sought publicity for their cause. The signatories of the Tokyo Convention (1963) have agreed to make every effort to return the aircraft to the pilot. The Hague Convention (1970) provides for the prosecution or EXTRADITION of hijackers by states. The most notorious hijacking campaign was carried out by the PALESTINE LIBERATION ORGANIZATION in the late 1960s and early 70s.

**Hijra** [Arab., = migration], primarily the original flight by MUHAMMAD from MECCA to Medina (622). Later this served as a constant paradigm for any flight from infidelity or pagan territory (*dar al-harb*) to Islam or Islamic lands (*dar al-Islam*). It marks the beginning of the Muslim era, years being numbered with the abbreviation AH (Lat. *anno hogirae*).

**Hilbert, David,** 1862–1943, German mathematician. After work on the theory of invariants, he developed a new approach that foreshadowed 20th-cent. abstract algebra. One aspect of his abstract work is the *Hilbert space,* a VECTOR space whose elements have infinitely many components and which has found applications in quantum theory. Hilbert also made important contributions to algebraic number theory and to functional analysis, particularly in the area of integral equations. His presentation in a 1900 speech of a list of 23 unsolved problems of mathematics stimulated much investigation by 20th-cent. mathematicians. Hilbert taught (1895–1930) at Göttingen Univ., where his breadth of mind and personality attracted to him many students who became important mathematicians.

**Hildebrand:** see GREGORY VII, SAINT.

**Hildesheim,** city (1984 pop. 101,600), Lower Saxony, E West Germany. Important in the Middle Ages, it grew up around its 11th-cent. cathedral, becoming a market, administrative, and ecclesiastical centre. It survived as a prince–bishopric to 1803. Varied industries now include food-processing and mechanical and electrical engineering.

**Hill, David Octavius,** 1802–70, Scottish painter. In 1843 he joined forces in Edinburgh with studio photographer **Robert Adamson** (1821–48), initially to take portrait photographs for Hill's projected painting on the founding of the Free Church of Scotland that same year. The collaboration continued until Adamson's death, producing some 2000 calotypes of Scottish subjects including the fishing village of Newhaven. So excellent was their work that the *Edinburgh Review* in 1843 credited it with 'all the force and beauty of the Sketches of Rembrandt'.

**Hill, Geoffrey,** 1932–, English poet. A professional scholar and teacher, he is noted for his intensely symbolic exploration of themes from English history and legend. His books include *King Log* (1968) and *Mercian Hymns* (1974).

**Hill, Joe,** 1879–1915, Swedish-American union organizer; b. Sweden, as Joseph Hillstrom. He came to the US in 1902 and, as a maritime worker, joined the INDUSTRIAL WORKERS OF THE WORLD in 1910. He wrote many labour songs, including 'Casey Jones' and 'The Union Scab'. Found guilty in 1915 of murdering a prominent Salt Lake City man, Hill was executed. He has since become a legendary hero of radical labour.

**Hillary, Sir Edmund Percival,** 1919–, New Zealand mountain climber and explorer. In 1953 he and TENZING NORGAY of Nepal became the first men to reach the summit of Mt EVEREST. He led (1958) a party in the first successful overland trek to the South Pole since 1912. He was knighted in 1953.

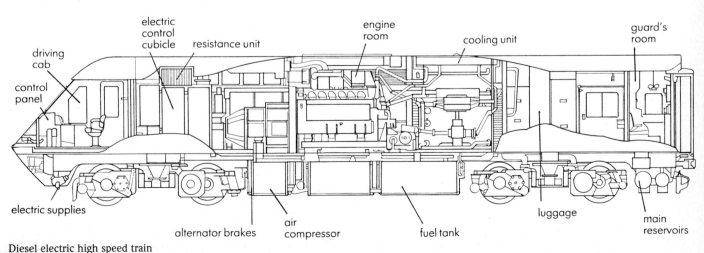

Diesel electric high speed train

A portrait photograph of the Rev. T. Henshaw Jones, one of the many calotypes taken by David Octavius **Hill** and Robert Adamson, c.1845.

**Hillel,** fl. 30 BC–AD 10, Jewish scholar; b. Babylonia. President of the SANHEDRIN, he fostered a systematic and more flexible interpretation of Hebrew Scripture and Jewish law, especially of hermeneutical principles. He was also the spiritual and ethical leader of his generation. SHAMMAI opposed his teachings.

**hillfort,** a fortified hilltop settlement usually protected by earth or stone ramparts and ditches. In Europe, the movement of settlement to defended sites was a feature of the IRON AGE. The periodic unrest of these times is revealed in the complex sequence of defences at MAIDEN CASTLE in SW England.

**Hilli, Jamal al-Din Hasan Ibn Yusuf Ibn al-Mutahhar Al-,** 1250–1325, Shi'ite Muslim theologian and jurist. Born in Hilla in Iraq he later studied under the great philosopher and astrologer Tusi under the aegis of Mongol power. His works on dogmatic theology and on FIQH according to Twelver SHI'ISM are considered authoritative, and still form part of normal formation of Shi'ite ULAMA.

**Hilliard, Nicholas,** 1547–1619, English miniature painter. The first true miniaturist in England, he was court painter to ELIZABETH I and JAMES I. His meticulous portraits on card, vellum, and the backs of playing cards are elegant and subtle, e.g., *Queen Elizabeth* (1572; National Portrait Gall., London).

**Hillingdon,** London borough (1981 pop. 226,263), in outer W London. The borough contains the town of Uxbridge; the districts of Harlington, Harmondsworth, Hayes, Ruislip, W Drayton, and Yiewsley; and HEATHROW AIRPORT. The borough is mainly residential, but there is a variety of industry also.

**Hillman, Sidney,** 1887–1946, American labour leader; b. Lithuania. He emigrated to the US in 1907 and became a garment worker. As president (1914–46) of the Amalgamated Clothing Workers, he introduced such union practices as cooperative housing and banking. One of the founders of the Congress of Industrial Organizations (CIO), he was its vice president (1935–40). Through the CIO Political Action Committee, which he headed (1943–46), he sought support for political programmes favoured by unions. Hillman was a strong backer of Pres. F.D. Roosevelt and a power in the Democratic Party.

**Hilton, Walter,** d.1396, English writer. His finely crafted prose writings, especially the *Scale of Perfection*, had much influence on late-medieval English spirituality.

**Himalayas,** great mountain system of Asia, extending c.2410 km (1500 mi) through Pakistan, India, Tibet, Nepal, Sikkim, and Bhutan. For most of its length it comprises two nearly parallel ranges separated by a wide valley in which the INDUS R. flows W and the BRAHMAPUTRA (Yarlung Zangbo) flows E. The northern range is called the Trans-Himalayas. The southern range has three parallel zones: the perpetually snow-covered Great Himalayas, where Mt EVEREST, the highest mountain in the world, rises to 8848 m (29,028 ft); the Lesser Himalayas, with elevations of 2000 to 4500 m (7000 to 15,000 ft); and the southernmost Outer Himalayas, 600 to 1500 m (2000 to 5000 ft) high. The Himalayas are associated with many legends (e.g., the Abominable Snowman). Simla, Naini Tal, Mussoorie, and Darjeeling are popular summer retreats from the heat of the Indian plains to the south.

**Himeji,** city (1986 est. pop. 449,968), W Honshu, Japan, on the INLAND SEA. An old picturesque castle town, Himeji is now the centre of a designated special industrial area where steel works and chemical factories are located. To the northwest there is a modern technology park where the largest synchrotron in the world is under construction. The shining white five-storeyed castle, popularly known as 'White Heron Castle' because of its beauty, was built in the 16th cent.

**Himeji** castle, built on Himeyama Hill

**Himmler, Heinrich,** 1900–1945, German NAZI leader. He was a Nazi from the founding (1920) of the party, and after HITLER came to power he headed (1936–45) the secret police, or Gestapo. The most ruthless of the Nazi leaders, Himmler was responsible for the death of millions in forced-labour and CONCENTRATION CAMPS. He was also held in fear by members of the Nazi party. In the last years of WORLD WAR II, he was the virtual dictator of German domestic affairs. He was captured by the British in 1945 but committed suicide by taking poison.

**Hims** or **Homs,** city (1981 pop. 354,508), W central Syria on the ORONTES R. Strategically situated at the northern end of the BIQA valley and commanding an important route from interior Syria to the Mediterranean. It is a commercial centre located in a fertile, irrigated plain where cotton, wheat, grapes, and other crops are grown. The city's manufactures include refined petroleum and fertilizer. In ancient times, called Emesa, it was the site of a temple to BAAL and gained prominence when a temple priest, Heliogabalus, became (AD 218) Roman emperor.

The Arabs took the town in 636 and renamed it. From the 16th cent. to 1918 the Ottoman Turks ruled it. The French then held it as part of a League of Nations mandate until Syria gained independence (1941).

**Hindemith, Paul,** 1895–1963, American composer and viola player; b. Germany. He combined traditional and experimental techniques in a distinctive style. The NAZIS banned his compositions (1937) because of their dissonance and modernity, and so he left Germany in 1938 and finally settled in the US in 1940. Hindemith's early compositions are contrapuntal and often atonal (see COUNTERPOINT; ATONALITY). Later he returned to a tonality some have called neoclassical. His best-known work is a symphony (1934) drawn from his opera *Mathis der Maler* (1938). In addition to other operas, sonatas, and chamber works, he wrote *Ludus Tonalis* (1943) for piano, the song-cycle *The Life of Mary* (1923, 1948), *The Four Temperaments* for piano and strings (1940), and the symphony *Die Harmonie der Welt* (1951), which was developed into an opera. He wrote a theoretical work *The Craft of Musical Composition* (1937–38), elaborating a revised system of tonality.

**Hindenburg, Paul von,** 1847–1934, German field marshal and president (1925–34). In WORLD WAR I he won great victories on the eastern front, especially the battle of Tannenberg (1914), making him the greatest German hero of the war. Although a monarchist, he supported the new republican government in 1918 and was elected president in 1925. In the election of 1932 he defeated HITLER and was reelected, but he was persuaded to appoint (1933) Hitler chancellor. He continued as figurehead president until his death.

**Hindi,** language belonging to the Indic group of the Indo-European family of languages. It is one of the official languages of India. See LANGUAGE (table).

**Hinduism,** Western term for the religious beliefs and practices of innumerable sects to which the vast majority of the people of India belong. Arising initially as a synthesis of indigenous religion and the religion brought to India c.1500 BC by the ARYANS, Hinduism developed over a period of 4000 years in syncretism with the religious and cultural movements of the Indian subcontinent. Hindu belief is generally characterized by the CASTE system and the acceptance of the VEDA as the most sacred scripture. The Veda, which comprises the liturgy and interpretation of sacrificial ritual, culminates in the UPANISADS, mystical and speculative works that state the doctrine of BRAHMAN, the absolute reality or Self, and its identity with the individual soul, or *ātman*. The goal of Hinduism, like that of other Eastern religions, is liberation from the cycle of rebirth and the suffering brought about by one's own actions (see KARMA); one of the ways to achieve this is to follow spiritual YOGA, practices leading to knowledge of reality and union with God. Early Brahmanism, dominated by the priests, or Brahmins (who through Vedic ritual sacrifice established a proper credential for achieving heaven—svarga), was challenged in the first millennium BC by non-Vedic systems such as BUDDHISM and JAINISM. To meet the challenge, the Brahmins recognized popular devotional movements and showed greater concern for the people. Writings like the laws of MANU regulated DHARMA (duty) according to one's class (priest, warrior, farmer or merchant, labourer) and stage in life (celibate student, householder, forest recluse, one who completely renounces societal ties). The post-Vedic Purāṇas deal with this structure of individual and social life and also describe the repeating cycle of rebirths and dissolution of the universe, represented by the divine trinity of Brahmā, the creator; Viṣṇu, the preserver; and Śiva, the destroyer. In medieval times, TANTRA and devotional sects flourished, producing poet–saints all over India who wrote religious songs and epics. This literature still plays an essential part in Hinduism, as does the practice of *pūjā*, or ritualistic worship of enshrined deities, such as Viṣṇu and his incarnations Rāma and Kṛṣṇa, Śiva, Gaṇeśa, and Kālī, Sarasvatī, or Lakṣmī. Modern Hindu leaders, e.g., Swami Vivekananda, Mahatma GANDHI, and Aurobindo GHOSE, have stressed the necessity of uniting spiritual life with social concerns.

**Hindu Kush,** one of the highest mountain systems in the world, extending c.800 km (500 mi) west from Pamir Knot, N Pakistan, into NE Afghanistan. Tirich Mir, 7692 m (25,236 ft), is the highest point. Meltwater from the permanently snow-covered peaks feeds the headstreams of the AMU DARYA and INDUS rivers. Several high-altitude passes, followed by trade routes, cross the mountains, once called the Caucasus Indicus.

**Hindu music:** see INDIAN MUSIC.

**Hindustani,** subdivision of the Indic group of the Indo-Iranian subfamily of the Indo-European family of languages. See LANGUAGE (table).

**Hipparchus,** fl. 2nd cent. BC, Greek astronomer; b. Bithynia (present-day Turkey). Ptolemy's geocentric theory of the universe (see PTOLEMAIC SYSTEM) was based largely on the conclusions of Hipparchus. In Ptolemy's *Almagest,* Hipparchus is credited with discovering the PRECESSION OF THE EQUINOXES, the eccentricity of the Sun's apparent orbit, and certain inequalities of the Moon's motions. He also made the first known comprehensive chart of the heavens.

**Hippocrates,** 460–c.370 BC, Greek physician, recognized as the father of medicine. He is believed to have been born on the island of Kós, where he later practised and taught. Hippocrates based medicine on objective observation and deductive reasoning. Although he accepted the belief that disease results from an imbalance of the four bodily humours, he maintained that the humours were glandular secretions and that outside forces influenced the disturbance. He taught that medicine should use diet and hygiene to build the patient's strength, resorting to more drastic treatment only when necessary. The Hippocratic Oath, an ethical code formulated in ancient Greece and still administered to medical graduates in many modern universities, cannot be directly credited to him, but it does represent his ideals and principles.

**Hippolytus:** see PHAEDRA.

**hippopotamus,** river-dwelling MAMMAL (*Hippopotamus amphibius*) of tropical Africa, related to the PIG. The male stands about 160 cm (5 ft) at the shoulder and weighs about 4500 kg (5 tons). The broad, short-legged body has a thick brown or grey hide, and the eyes are near the top of the head so that the animal can see when submerged. Hippopotamuses live in small herds, spending their days in the water. They emerge at night to feed, eating mainly grass. Hunted for meat and hides, they are endangered.

**Hiranuma Kiichirō, Baron** (hee̠rahnoohmooh), 1867–1952, Japanese statesman. Firmly opposed to political parties and Western ideas of democracy and socialism, he founded (1924) a reactionary militaristic society, the Kokuhonsha. He supported Japan's aggressive foreign policy in the 1930s and was prime minister from 1939 to 1940. Arrested (1946) as a war criminal, he was sentenced to life imprisonment and died in prison.

**hire purchase,** a form of credit whereby the purchaser pays a deposit and takes possession of goods under a hire agreement. The balance of the purchase price plus an interest charge is paid by regular instalment over a fixed term. At the end of the term, ownership of the goods passes to the purchaser. This form of credit is extended by finance houses which retain ownership of the goods throughout the hire period. Interest rates in hire-purchase agreements tend to be extremely high since they are calculated on the whole of the sum borrowed for the full term. Being an expensive way of buying goods, it has traditionally only been resorted to by the poor. However, motor cars have been sold this way to most income groups, and still are; offering better terms of hire-purchase is one of the main forms of competition between car makers. Smaller consumer purchases, e.g., electrical goods, tend now to be bought by CREDIT CARD, also expensive but with the advantage that the goods immediately become the property of the purchaser. Businesses often buy equipment such as office machinery by hire purchase.

**Hirohito,** 1901–89, emperor of JAPAN. Made regent in 1921, he succeeded his father, Taisho, as emperor in 1926. Hirohito helped persuade the Japanese government to accept unconditional surrender at the end of WORLD WAR II. In 1946 he renounced the idea of imperial divinity and was stripped of all but ceremonial powers by a new constitution. On his death (1989) he was succeeded by his son, Crown Prince AKIHITO.

**Hiroshige** (Andi-Hiroshige) (hee̠roshee'gəh), 1797–1858, Japanese painter and colour print artist of the *ukiyo-e* school (see JAPANESE ART). Among his many works is a landscape series, *Fifty-three Stages of the Tokaido Highway* (1833), as well as snow, rain, mist, and moonlight scenes that influenced WHISTLER.

**Hiroshima,** city (1986 est. pop. 1,023,022), capital of Hiroshima prefecture, SW Honshu, Japan, on the delta of the R. Ota, which divides the city into six islands. Founded (1589) by powerful local lord Terumoto Mori, Hiroshima manufactures cars, oil-drilling equipment, and ship components, and is the centre of the traditional Japanese needle

Hiroshige, *Ramerzama in Snow* from the Fifty three Stages of the Tokaido Highway, 1833. 22.8 × 35 cm.

manufacturing industry. On 6 Aug. 1945 it became the first city to be the target of an atomic bomb, dropped by the US Air Force. Most of the city was destroyed and over 200,000 people died. Hiroshima is now dedicated to international peace and is the site of a Peace Memorial Museum.

**Hirsch, Samson Raphael,** 1808–88, German rabbi and chief exponent of Neo-Orthodoxy. He sought to combine traditional Jewish studies with secular learning (*Nineteen Letters,* 1836) and condemned the Reform movement (see JUDAISM) for breaking with tradition.

**Hishikawa Moronobu:** see MORONOBU.

**Hispanic Americans,** Spanish-speaking residents of the US. The three largest groups (in order of size) are Mexican-Americans, or CHICANOS, concentrated in Texas and S California; Puerto Ricans, living mainly in the Northeast, especially the New York City area; and Cubans, many of them refugees from the Castro regime who live in Miami, Florida. Dominicans and others from the Caribbean region, as well as Central and South American groups, also have sizable representations. The number of Hispanic Americans, who together constitute the US's fastest-growing ethnic minority, rose sharply during the 1970s, from 9.1 million (4.5% of the total population) to 14.6 million (6.4%) in 1980. Millions of them, however, are believed to lack legal residency status.

**Hispaniola,** subtropical island, 76,483 km² (29,530 sq mi), with abundant rainfall, in the WEST INDIES. It is divided between HAITI (W) and the DOMINICAN REPUBLIC. The island was discovered in 1492 by Columbus and has at times been known as Española and Saint-Domingue. Coffee, cacao, sugarcane, and bauxite are the principal products.

**Hiss, Alger,** 1904–, US public official. He served (1936–47) in the Dept of State, becoming a coordinator of US foreign policy. In 1948, Whittaker Chambers, an editor who confessed to being a Communist courier, accused Hiss of helping to transmit confidential government documents to the Russians. Hiss denied the charges and was indicted for perjury by a grand jury. His first trial ended in a hung jury, but in a second trial (1950) he was found guilty. He was sentenced to five years in prison but was released in 1954.

**histamine,** organic compound derived from the amino acid histidine. Histamine is released from certain cells upon tissue injury or during the activity of certain antibodies (see IMMUNITY). It then causes dilation of blood vessels and contraction of smooth MUSCLE (e.g., in the lungs). It is released in allergic conditions (see ALLERGY), including ASTHMA, and is largely responsible for the allergic reaction of inflammation and irritation to such things as insect venom. Allergic reactions can often be controlled by antihistamine drugs and ointments.

**histology,** study of the groups of specialized cells called tissues, found in most multicellular plants and animals (see TISSUE). Histologists study tissue organization at all levels, from the whole organ to the molecular components of cells. Histological techniques include tissue culture, fixing and staining, light and electron microscopy, and X-ray diffraction.

**historical linguistics:** see LINGUISTICS.

**historiography,** the history of history, covering the work of individual historians, their background, experience, methods, outlook, and relations with other historians and their readers, and the development of the subject, including the increased professionalization of the late 19th cent. and the increased specialization of the 20th cent. Scholarly interest in historiography has given a new dimension to the study of history. Cambridge Univ. has been a centre.

**Hitchcock, Sir Alfred,** 1899–1980, English film director. He worked in Hollywood. A master of suspense, he made such films as *The Lady Vanishes* (1938), *Notorious* (1946), *Strangers on a Train* (1951), *Vertigo* (1958), *Psycho* (1960), and *Frenzy* (1972).

**Hitchens, Ivor,** 1893–1979, British painter. A member of the LONDON GROUP (1931), he exhibited (1934) as an 'objective abstract' artist, which was a form of expressive abstraction which reduced natural appearances into abstract formal components. He remained faithful to this style, developing his use of colour, intensifying it in the 1970s.

**Hitler, Adolf,** 1889–1945, German dictator, founder and leader of NATIONAL SOCIALISM or Nazism; b. Braunau, Upper Austria. In World War I he served in the Bavarian army, was gassed and wounded, and received the Iron Cross (first class) for bravery. The war embittered him, and he blamed Germany's defeat on the Jews and Marxists. Settling in Munich, he joined with other nationalists to found (1920) the Nazi Party. In the famous 'beer-hall putsch' (1923) Hitler attempted to overthrow BAVARIA's republican government, but the army put down the revolt and Hitler was imprisoned. He thus became known throughout Germany and used his nine months in prison to write *Mein Kampf* [my struggle], filled with anti-Semitism, power worship, disdain for morality, and his strategy for world domination. It became the bible of the Nazi Party. The Nazi movement grew slowly until 1929, when the economic depression brought it mass support. Hitler made prime use of his frenzied but magnetic oratory of hate and power, his insight into mass psychology, and his mastery of deceitful strategy, or the 'big lie'. He used his virulent ANTI-SEMITISM and anti-Communism to win the support both of the workers and of the bankers and industrialists. Although he was defeated when he ran for president in 1932, Pres. Paul von HINDENBURG was persuaded to name him chancellor (1933), and the REICHSTAG gave him dictatorial powers. With other Nazi leaders, among them GOERING, HIMMLER, and GOEBBELS, he crushed the opposition and took control of all facets of German life. Anti-semitism was enacted into law, and CONCENTRATION CAMPS were set up to take care of enemies of the state. In 1934, 88% of the voters favoured the union of the presidency and chancellorship in Hitler's person. His aggressive foreign policy, abetted by English and French appeasement, culminated in the triumph of the MUNICH PACT (1938). As he prepared Germany for war, he bullied smaller nations into making territorial concessions. He became allied with MUSSOLINI in Italy, and he helped FRANCO come to power in Spain. Austria was absorbed into the 'Third Reich', and Czechoslovakia was dismembered. In 1939 he signed a nonaggression pact with the Soviet Union, which gave him a free hand to invade Poland. With that act WORLD WAR II began, and Hitler took complete control of Germany's war efforts. At first Germany was triumphant, but the tide turned and by July 1944 the German military situation was desperate. Despite a well-planned assassination attempt against him, in which he was injured, Hitler remained in charge and insisted that Germany fight to the death. As the Third Reich collapsed, Hitler remained in an underground bunker in Berlin as the Russians approached the city. On 29 Apr. 1945, he married his longtime mistress, Eva BRAUN, and on 30 Apr. they committed suicide. He left Germany a devastated nation. Hitler's legacy is the memory of the most dreadful tyranny of modern centuries.

**Hittite,** language belonging to the Anatolian subfamily of the Indo-European family of languages. See LANGUAGE (table).

**Hittites,** ancient people of Asia Minor and Syria, who flourished from 1600 to 1200 BC. The Hittites, a people of Indo-European connection, were supposed to have entered Cappadocia around 1800 BC. The Hittite empire, with its capital at BOĞAZKÖY (then called Hattusas), was the chief power and cultural force in W Asia from 1400 to 1200 BC. It was a loose confederation that broke up under the invasions (c.1200 BC) of the Thracians, Phrygians, and Assyrians. The neo-Hittite kingdom (c.1050–c.700 BC) that followed was conquered by the Assyrians. The Hittites were one of the first peoples to smelt iron successfully.

**Hjartarson, Snorri**, 1906–86, Icelandic poet. He made his debut in Norway with a novel written in Norwegian, *High Soars the Raven* (1934). He returned to Iceland to become one of the most influential poets of post-war Iceland, striking a masterly compromise between traditional and modern poetry distinguished by deeply musical and painterly images. He published only four volumes of poetry, culminating in *Autumn Twilight* (1979), which won the Nordic Council's literary award for 1981.

**Ho**, chemical symbol of the element HOLMIUM.

**Hobart**, city (1986 pop. 127,106), capital and chief port of Tasmania, SE Australia. Founded in 1804 as a penal colony, the city has one of the world's finest harbours. Mt Wellington rises 1270 m (4200 ft) above the city. Manufactures include textiles, chemicals, and glass. It is the site of the Hobart Theatre Royal (1836), Australia's oldest major theatre, and Tasmania's one university is located S of the city near Wrest Point, Australia's first casino. Hobart is the destination of the annual Sydney–Hobart yacht race.

**Hobbema, Meindert** (ˌhobimə), 1638–1709, Dutch painter, considered the last of the great 17th-cent. Dutch landscape painters (see LANDSCAPE PAINTING). His paintings of woodland scenes, country villages, water mills, and other rustic subjects are full of life and luminosity, with bold execution and colour. His best-known work is the *Avenue at Middelharnis* (1689; National Gall., London).

**Hobbes, Thomas**, 1588–1679, English philosopher. Hobbes developed a materialist and highly pessimistic philosophy that was denounced in his own day and later, but has had a continuing influence on Western political thought. His *Leviathan* (1651) presents a bleak picture of human beings in the state of nature, where life is 'nasty, brutish, and short'. Fear of violent death is the principal motive that causes people to create a state by contracting to surrender their natural rights and to submit to the absolute authority of a sovereign. Although the power of the sovereign derived originally from the people, Hobbes said —challenging the doctrine of the divine right of kings—the sovereign's power is absolute and not subject to review by either subjects or ecclesiastical powers. Hobbes's concept of the SOCIAL CONTRACT led to investigations by other political theorists, notably LOCKE, SPINOZA, and J.J. ROUSSEAU, who formulated their own radically different theories. Hobbes also wrote on mathematics.

**Hoby, Sir Thomas**, 1530–66, English translator. He made the first English version of Baldassare CASTIGLIONE's *Il Cortegiano*, published as *The Courtyer* (1561).

**Hoccleve, Thomas**, c.1367–1426, English poet. Chaucer's earliest important disciple, he was a clerk in the Privy Seal office. Several of his works contain interesting autobiographical elements concerning his excessive drinking and a 'nervous breakdown' from which he suffered.

**Ho Chi Minh**, 1890–1969, Vietnamese nationalist leader, president of North VIETNAM (1954–69); b. Nguyen Tat Thank. In 1911 he left Vietnam and lived in London, the US, and France, where he became (1920) a founding member of the French Communist Party. He later lived in Moscow and in 1930 founded the Communist Party of Indochina. He returned to Vietnam in WORLD WAR II and organized a Vietnamese independence movement, the VIET MINH. He raised an army to fight the Japanese, and in the French Indochina war (1946–54) he defeated the French colonial regime. After the Geneva Conference (1954), which divided Vietnam, Ho became the first president of North Vietnam. In his last years he led the North's struggle to defeat the US-supported government of South Vietnam (see VIETNAM WAR).

**Ho Chi Minh City**, formerly Saigon, city (1986 pop. 4,000,000), S Vietnam, on the Saigon R. It is the largest city in Vietnam and a large river port and industrial centre producing textiles, ships, processed foods, and other goods. An ancient settlement in the KHMER EMPIRE, Saigon grew into a city under French rule in the 19th cent. It became the capital of South Vietnam in 1954. Military headquarters for US and South Vietnamese forces during the VIETNAM WAR, it was heavily damaged and faced the overcrowding created by the influx of over 1 million refugees. It was renamed at the end of the war. Built in the European style, it is the seat of several universities.

**hockey, field**, outdoor stick and ball game similar to SOCCER. It is played on a field measuring 46 to 55 m by 82 to 91 m (50–60 yd by 90–100 yd) by two teams of 11 players each. Teams attempt to advance the ball down the field with their wooden sticks. A point is scored by delivering the ball past the goalkeeper through the goal posts, which are joined by a net. Field hockey, of ancient origin, was played in England for centuries before it spread to other countries.

**hockey, ice**, winter skating sport in which players use sticks to propel a rubber disc into a net-enclosed goal. A rough sport, it is played chiefly by men, who wear heavy protective gear. The rink, which is divided into three zones (attacking, neutral, and defending), measures up to 60 m (200 ft) in length and 30 m (98 ft) in width. A team consists of six players, including a goalkeeper, all of whom wear ice skates. Play is directed towards advancing the disc (called a puck) with flat-bladed sticks and striking it into the goals at each end of the rink. A goal counts for one point. A player who violates the rules is removed to the penalty box for two minutes or more while his team plays shorthanded. Ice hockey originated in Canada in the 1870s and later spread to the US and other northern countries. It has been an Olympic event since 1920. The professional National Hockey League (founded 1917) is made up of 21 teams representing US and Canadian cities. The annual Stanley Cup playoffs determine the league championship.

**Hockney, David**, 1937–, English painter. His realistic, witty, clearly illuminated compositions often contain elements of POP ART. Unlike most pop artists, Hockney did not treat mass media and advertising culture as his central theme. The theme of homosexuality became an increasingly important subject. He now lives and paints in California. In the 1980s he has developed the use of polaroid photography, collaged together to create large, almost cubist compositions. A superb draughtsman, he has executed several print series and designed stage sets.

**Hodeida**, city and port (1981 est. pop. 126,386), N Yemen, on the Red Sea coast. It is the second city and the principal port of the country, exporting coffee and cotton. The special variety of Arabian coffee formerly exported through the nearby port of Mocha is now mainly exported from Hodeida.

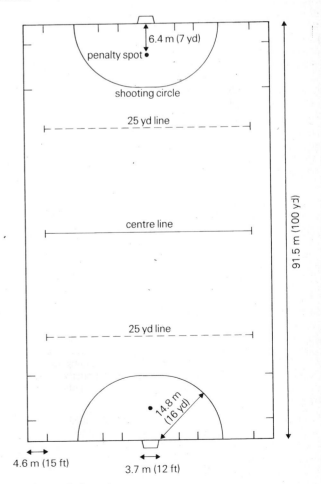

Field **hockey** pitch dimensions

David **Hockney**, *Mr and Mrs Clark and Percy*. Oil on canvas. Tate Gallery, London.

**Hodgkin, Sir Alan Lloyd**, 1914–, English biophysicist. For their work in analysing the electrical and chemical events in nerve-cell discharge, he and Andrew HUXLEY shared with Sir John Eccles the 1963 Nobel Prize for physiology or medicine. He was a research professor of the Royal Society (1952–69) and professor of biophysics at Cambridge Univ. (1970–81).

**Hodgkin, Dorothy Mary Crowfoot**, 1910–, English chemist and X-ray crystallographer; b. Egypt. She received the 1964 Nobel Prize for chemistry for determining the structure of biochemical compounds (particularly of vitamin $B_{12}$) used to control pernicious anemia. In 1933 she and J.D. Bernal made the first X-ray photograph of a protein (pepsin). She was president (1977–78) of the British Association for the Advancement of Science.

**Hodgkin's disease**, chronic malignant disease of the lymph nodes (see LYMPHATIC SYSTEM). Symptoms vary, but often include enlargement of one or more lymph nodes, particularly in the neck region, followed by fatigue, loss of weight, and fever. As the disease progresses, other lymph nodes and organs may become involved. As with some other forms of CANCER, it is often treated effectively with surgery, RADIOTHERAPY, and CHEMOTHERAPY.

**Hoffa, James Riddle**, 1913–75?, American labour leader. In 1957 he became president of the TEAMSTERS UNION, which was expelled from the AFL-CIO that year because of evidence of union corruption. Hoffa's power continued to grow, however, and by 1964 he was able to effect the road haulage industry's first national contract. In the same year he was convicted in two separate trials for jury tampering and fraud. Imprisoned in 1967, he retained the Teamster presidency until 1971, when Pres. Nixon commuted his sentence with the proviso that he not engage in union activity until 1980. Hoffa disappeared in 1975 and is widely assumed to have been murdered.

**Hoffmann, Ernest Theodor Amadeus**, 1776–1822, German romantic novelist and composer. His gothic tales of madness, grotesquerie, and the supernatural include *Die Serapionsbrüder* (1819–21; tr. The Serapion Brethren), *Die Elixiere des Teufels* (1815–16; tr. The Devil's Elixir), and *Lebensansichtendes Katers Murr* (1821–22; tr. Kater Murr, the Educated Cat). OFFENBACH's opera *Tales of Hoffmann* is based on three of his stories.

**Hofmann, Hans**, 1880–1966, American painter; b. Germany. After emigrating to the US in 1930, he opened two art schools (New York City and Provincetown, Massachusetts) that were central to the development of ABSTRACT EXPRESSIONISM. His own exuberant canvases combine violent, clashing colours.

**Hofmannsthal, Hugo von** (‚hohfmanstahl), 1874–1929, Austrian poet and dramatist. He wrote his first 'aesthetic' poems and lyrical dramas (*Death and the Fool*, 1893) while still in his teens. His *Letter from Lord Chandos to Francis, Lord Verulam* (1902) has become the classical document of the modernist crisis of language, which Hofmannsthal resolved by turning to the public genres of drama and opera, with adaptations (of Shakespeare, Calderon, Otway), modern versions of classical themes (*Ödipus and the Sphinx*, 1906), and librettos in collaboration with Richard STRAUSS: *Elektra* (1909); *Der Rosenkavalier* (1911); *Ariadne auf Naxos* (1912); *Die Frau ohne Schatten* (1919); *Arabella* (1933). *The Difficult Man* (1921) is one of the few great German comedies. After World War I, Hofmannsthal was active in founding the Salzburg festival as a reaffirmation of European culture; he revived his adaptation of *Everyman* (1911) and wrote *The Great Salzburg World Stage* (1922) for it. His last major work was the much-revised allegorical tragedy *The Tower* (1927).

**hog:** see PIG.

**Hogan, Ben**, 1912–, American golfer. One of the game's leading money winners, he won nine major championships, beginning with the Professional Golfers' Association title in 1946. His greatest victories, notably a sweep of the US Open, British Open, and Masters crowns in 1953, came after recovery from a near-fatal car accident in 1949. Hogan was the first since Bobby JONES to capture four US Open titles.

**Hogarth, William**, 1697–1764, English painter, satirist, engraver, and art theorist. His first real success came in 1732 with a series of six morality pictures, *The Harlot's Progress*, first painted and then engraved. *The Rake's Progress* (1735) followed. In the series *Marriage à la Mode* (c.1743), he depicts the inane, profligate existence of a fashionable couple with great detail and brilliant characterization. His *Analysis of Beauty* (1753) is a treatise on the ROCOCO aesthetic. In such prints as *Gin Lane* (1751) he satirizes cruelty and stupidity. His portraits *The Shrimp Girl* (National Gall., London) and *Captain Coram* (1740; Foundling Hospital, London) are masterpieces of British painting.

William **Hogarth**, Marriage-à-la-Mode, 1: the Marriage Contract, 1743. Oil on canvas 68.6 × 89 cm. National Gallery, London.

**hog cholera:** see SWINE FEVER.

**Hogg, James**, 1770–1835, Scottish poet, called the Ettrick Shepherd. He is now more celebrated for his *Private Memoirs and Confessions of a Justified Sinner* (1824), than for his rustic poetry. The *Memoirs* is a macabre story of a split personality and a critique of CALVIN's doctrine of PREDESTINATION.

**Hohenstaufen** (ˈhohənˌshtowfən), German princely family of the 11th to 13th cent. They were dukes of Swabia from 1079; German kings and emperors, 1138–1254; and kings of Sicily, 1194–1266. Their chief rivals were the Guelphs (see GUELPHS AND GHIBELLINES), who sided with the papacy in the long struggle between emperor and pope.

**Hohenzollern**, German princely family that ruled from the 11th cent. to 1918. They ruled BRANDENBURG (1415–1918), PRUSSIA (1525–1918), and Germany (1871–1918). They comprised two main branches (the Swabian and the Franconian) and held various titles, including that of burgrave, margrave, duke, and elector. In 1701 Frederick I styled himself 'king in Prussia', and thereafter the members of the Franconian branch held that title. After Germany was unified in 1871, three Hohenzollern emperors (or kaisers), WILLIAM I, FREDERICK III, and WILLIAM II, reigned.

**Hokkaido,** island (1986 est. pop. 5,668,059), Japan, 2nd largest (c.78,040 km²/30,130 sq mi), northernmost, and most sparsely populated of Japan's major islands. It is separated from HONSHU island by the Tsugaru Strait and from SAKHALIN, USSR, by the Soya Strait. SAPPORO is the capital. The rugged, partly volcanic interior reaches a high point of 2290 m (7513 ft) at Asahi-dake. Forests, providing timber, pulp, and paper, cover much of the island, and there were coal, iron ore, and manganese deposits. The AINU, the original inhabitants, became a minority after Japan began a policy of colonizing the island after 1868. Recently, large coastal industrial complexes have been constructed at Tomakomai and Ishikari.

**Hokusai** (Katsushika Hokusai), 1760–1849, Japanese painter, draughtsman, and wood engraver, one of the foremost *ukiyo-e* print designers (see JAPANESE ART). He used over 50 different names. His prodigious output included book illustrations, printed cards, and landscapes in a variety of styles. His technical excellence and observant delineation of contemporary life can be seen in *Mangwa, or Ten Thousand Sketches* (15 vol., 1814–78), and *Views of Mt Fuji*.

**Holbein, Hans** (ˌhohlbien), the Elder, c.1465–1524, German painter and draughtsman. His most important work was the altarpiece of St Sebastian (1516; Munich). He also designed STAINED GLASS windows and silverpoint drawings. His younger son, **Hans Holbein,** the Younger, c.1497–1543, an outstanding portrait and religious painter of the northern RENAISSANCE, started his career early. In Basel, Switzerland, he illustrated ERASMUS's *Praise of Folly* (1515) and in 1519 was admitted to that city's painters' guild. During this period he decorated many buildings and painted the celebrated *Dead Christ* (1521; Offentliche Kunstsammlung, Basel), and his famous *Madonna of the Burgomaster Meyer* (1526; Darmstadt, W Germany). In these works and in the portraits of Erasmus (1523; Louvre, Paris) and Boniface Amerbach (1519; Offentliche Kunstsammlung, Basel), he shows his full genius. The larger conception, monumental composition, and idealization of characters show Italian influence. In England from 1526 to 1528, he painted a fine group of portraits, including one of Sir Thomas More (Frick Coll., New York), all of which reveal his combination of northern detail with Italian grandeur. He returned to England in his last years and did his famous portrait of *The Ambassadors* (1533; National Gall., London). He was also court painter to HENRY VIII and painted numerous portraits of the king and his wives and prospective brides, including Christine of Denmark (1538; National Gall., London). His preliminary drawings and woodcuts are also famous.

**Holberg, Ludvig, Baron** (hohlbeə), 1684–1754, Danish man of letters; b. Norway. An apostle of the ENLIGHTENMENT in Scandinavia, he was professor, consecutively, of Metaphysics, Eloquence, and History at the Univ. of Copenhagen. He wrote many satirical poems, including the mock-heroic epic poem *Pedar Paars* (1719–20). As director of the first Danish theatre which opened in 1721, his comedies earned him the title of the 'Danish Molière', especially *The Political Tinker, The Transformed Peasant*, and *Erasmus Montanus*. Later he turned to history and biography and serious reflective essays.

**Hölderlin, Johann Christian Friedrich** (ˌhøldəleen), 1770–1843, German poet. At the transition between CLASSICISM and ROMANTICISM, Hölderlin's lyrical odes are filled with his sense of mission as the poet of barren times and the celebratory prophet whose vision could reconcile the opposities of Christ and Dionysus, Christianity and paganism. He modelled his modern verse on classical Greek forms: among his elegiac odes are *Bread and Wine*, among his later free Pindaric hymns *The Rhine, Patmos, Celebration of Peace*, all written before he went mad half-way through his life. He also wrote a novel, *Hyperion* (1797–99), and a dramatic fragment *The Death of Empedocles* (1799). Best appreciated in the 20th cent., his *Poems and Fragments* have been translated by Michael Hamburger (1966); some of them, in German, have been set to music by Benjamin BRITTEN.

**holding company:** see TRUST.

**Holiday, Billie,** 1915–59, black American singer; b. Eleanora Fagan. She began singing in 1930 and earned a supreme position among modern JAZZ singers with her emotional impact and highly personal approach to a

Hans **Holbein,** *Benedikt von Hertenstein,* 1495?–1522. Oil on paper, mounted on wood, 52.4 × 38.1 cm. Metropolitan Museum of Art, New York.

song. Her life was complicated by the drug addiction that eventually destroyed her career and hastened her death.

**holidays,** originally feast days of saints or important days in the church calendar, when people would not have to work. Some, e.g., Good Friday, would be kept throughout Christendom but many were particular to a locality or to a trade. Following the injunction in the 4th Commandment, one day of the week is to be a day of rest (see SABBATH). The present 5-day working week is of recent origin, it having been usual for office workers etc. to work for 5½ days including Saturday mornings until at least the 1950s. Two weeks' annual paid holiday was the norm until after World War II, since when the annual allowance has been steadily increasing, especially for white-collar workers and particularly for managerial grades. Greater affluence has meant that more people have been able to take holidays abroad: the number of Britons doing so has risen from 7 million in 1971 to 16 million in 1985.

**Holinshed, Raphael** (ˌholinz-hed), d. c.1580, English chronicler. With the assistance of William Harrison and Richard Stanihurst, he wrote the famous *Chronicles of England, Scotland, and Ireland* (1577), from which SHAKESPEARE and other Elizabethan dramatists drew material for plays.

**holistic medicine,** system of health care based on a concept of the 'whole' person—one whose body, mind, spirit, and emotions are in balance with the environment. Stressing personal responsiblity for health, the holistic approach shuns the notion of the patient with a particular malfunction. Surgery and prescription drugs are generally avoided; instead, patients are encouraged to establish self-regulated regimes to control such risk factors as poor diet, smoking, alcohol intake, and stress. Holistic medicine, often called alternative or complementary medicine, embraces many varied therapies, including CHIROPRACTIC, ACUPUNCTURE, BIOFEEDBACK, faith healing (see HEALING), folk medicine (based on the use of herbal remedies), megavitamin therapy (therapy involving administration of large doses of vitamins), MEDITATION, and YOGA.

**Holland,** former county of the HOLY ROMAN EMPIRE and, from 1579 to 1795, the chief member of the United Provinces of the Netherlands. Its name has been popularly applied to the entire Netherlands. Since 1840 the area has been divided into two provinces, North and South Holland. The original county was created in the 10th cent. and was controlled (14th–15th cent.) in turn by the WITTELSBACH family, BURGUNDY, and the HABSBURGS. Holland led (16th–17th cent.) the struggle for Dutch independence, and its history became virtually identical with that of the Netherlands.

**Hollerith, Herman,** 1860–1929, American mechanical engineer and inventor of the punched-card tabulating machine. After graduating from the Columbia Univ. School of Mines in 1879, he worked as a statistician on the US 1880 census returns. He became interested in the feasibility of automating this work and by the 1890 census had devised a system of cards with punched holes to carry information, and invented the machines to record and count the statistics. In 1896 he founded the Tabulating Machine Company which later became International Business Machines Corporation (IBM).

**holly,** common name for about 300 species of trees and shrubs of the Aquifoliaceae family. Many are cultivated as ornamentals. The English holly (*Ilex aquifolium*) and the American holly (*I. opaca*) are popular for their hard white wood, used, when dyed, as a substitute for EBONY, and for their decorative spiny leaves and red berries. Some hollies are sources of tea, such as MATÉ, and medicinal preparations. Many ornamental forms of the common species are grown.

**Holly, Buddy** (Charles Harden Holley), 1936–59, American singer, songwriter, and guitarist. In the two years before his death in an aeroplane crash at age 22, he, with his group The Crickets, made an indelible mark on the history of melodic rock with a string of hits including 'That'll Be The Day', 'Peggy Sue', 'Maybe Baby', 'Rave On', 'On Boy', etc. He was an outstanding songwriter with a tremulously catchy voice and 'boy-next-door' appeal.

**hollyhock:** see MALLOW.

**Hollywood,** US city on the slopes of the Santa Monica Mts, S California; inc. 1903, consolidated with Los Angeles 1910. Once the centre of the US cinema industry (its first film was made c.1911), it draws many tourists. Television, radio, and recording companies are also located there, and cosmetics are manufactured. Its crowded and lively Hollywood Boulevard and Sunset Strip are famous.

**Holm, Hanya,** 1898–, American choreographer, dancer, and teacher; b. Germany. She studied with Jacques DALCROZE and Mary WIGMAN. After moving to the US (1931), she formed her own school and company (1936–67), one of the foremost MODERN DANCE schools in the US. Her choreographic works are often used as a vehicle for social comment, but she gained popularity as choreographer of Broadway musicals.

**Holmes, Oliver Wendell,** 1809–94, American author and physician; father of Oliver Wendell HOLMES, Jr. A professor at Harvard medical school (1847–82), he wrote a number of important medical papers. His witty series of sketches, originally published in the *Atlantic Monthly,* were collected in *The Autocrat of the Breakfast-Table* (1858) and other volumes. Holmes also wrote poems and pioneering psychological novels, e.g., *Elsie Venner* (1861), and biographies.

**Holmes, Oliver Wendell,** 1841–1935, associate justice of the US SUPREME COURT (1902–32). A profound scholar, Holmes achieved international recognition in 1881 with publication of *The Common Law,* in which he attacked prevailing views of JURISPRUDENCE. In the US Supreme Court, he advocated 'judicial restraint'. From his eloquent and frequent disagreements with his more conservative colleagues over the nullification of social legislation, Holmes came to be known as 'the Great Dissenter'.

**Holmes, Sherlock:** see DOYLE, SIR ARTHUR CONAN.

**Holmes, William Henry,** 1846–1933, American geologist and archaeologist. After creating seminal reports on Yellowstone Park (see NATIONAL PARKS) and the classic illustrations in the GRAND CANYON *Atlas,* Holmes became a pioneer in Southwestern archaeology and the study of Indian art, and was chief (1902–09) of the Bureau of American Ethnology. His later works include *Handbook of Aboriginal American*

*Antiquities* (1919). He was also internationally recognized for his work as curator (1910–20) and director (from 1920) of the National Gallery of Art.

**holmium** (Ho), metallic element, discovered independently by J.L. Soret and M. Delafontaine in 1878 and by Per Teodor Cleve in 1879. The soft, malleable, lustrous, silvery metal is a member of the LANTHANIDE SERIES. Holmium, its oxides, and its salts have no commercial uses. See ELEMENT (table); PERIODIC TABLE.

**Holocaust** [Gk., = burnt whole], name given to the period (1933–1945) of persecution and extermination of European Jews by Nazi GERMANY. After Adolf HITLER's rise to power in 1933, most Jews who did not flee Germany were sent to CONCENTRATION CAMPS. With the outbreak of WORLD WAR II Hitler began to implement his 'final solution of the Jewish question': the extermination of Jews in all countries conquered by his armies. By the end of the war 6 million Jews had been systematically murdered and a creative religious and secular community destroyed. See also ANTI-SEMITISM; NATIONAL SOCIALISM; WAR CRIMES.

**Holocene epoch:** see GEOLOGICAL ERA (table).

**Holofernes:** see JUDITH.

**holography,** method of reproducing a three-dimensional image of an object by means of light-wave patterns recorded on a photographic plate or film. The object is illuminated with a coherent beam of light (light in which the waves are in phase) produced by a LASER. Before reaching the object, the beam is split into two parts: the reference beam is recorded directly on the photographic plate, and the other is reflected from the object and then is recorded. On the photographic plate the two beams create an INTERFERENCE pattern, exposing the plate at points where they arrive in phase. When this photographic recording, called a hologram, is later illuminated with coherent light of the same frequency as that used to form it, a three-dimensional image of the object becomes visible, and the object can be photographed from various angles.

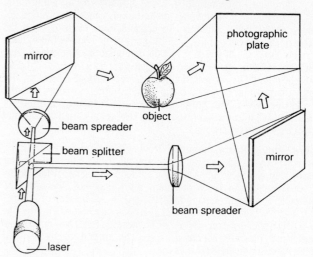

Holography

**Holst, Gustav,** 1874–1934, English composer. GRIEG, Richard STRAUSS, and VAUGHAN WILLIAMS were early influences. His outstanding works are *The Planets* (1914–16), an orchestral SUITE; *The Hymn of Jesus* (1917), for chorus and orchestra; and the orchestral piece *Egdon Heath* (1927). As a teacher, he had a profound influence on many individuals and on the English musical scene of the early 20th cent.

**Holt, Helen Maud:** see under TREE, SIR HERBERT BEERBOHM.

**Holy Alliance,** 1815, agreement between the emperors of Russia and Austria and the king of Prussia, to preserve the social order after the fall of the Napoleonic empire. It was engineered by METTERNICH, and eventually almost all the princes of Europe signed the agreement. Although it accomplished nothing specific, it became a symbol of reaction. It was strongly disliked by liberals, nationalists, and British foreign secretaries.

**Holy Ghost** or **Holy Spirit,** in Christian doctrine, the third person of the TRINITY, sometimes described as the aspect of God immanent in this world, in people, and in the church. Its descent upon the apostles, giving them the gift of tongues (Acts 2), is commemorated on Pentecost (Whit Sunday). The dove is the symbol of the Holy Ghost.

**Holyhead** or **Caergybi,** town (1981 pop. 12,569), Gwynedd, NW Wales, on Holy Island, Anglesey. It is a resort and industrial town, whose industries include engineering and aluminium smelting. There is a passenger ferry service from here to the Republic of Ireland. In 1984 the port handled 1.15 million tonnes.

**Holy Island** or **Lindisfarne,** off the coast of Northumberland, NE England. Tourism, fishing, and farming are important. A church and monastery, built in 635, represented the first establishment of Celtic Christianity in England. The *Lindisfarne Gospels*, an illuminated Latin manuscript now in the British Museum, was written there before 700. A Benedictine priory was set up on the island in 1083.

**Holy League,** alliance formed (1511) by Pope JULIUS II during the ITALIAN WARS to expel LOUIS XII of France from Italy. It included Venice, the Swiss cantons, the Spanish king FERDINAND V, HENRY VIII of England, and Holy Roman emperor MAXIMILIAN I. It fell apart after Julius's death (1513).

**Holyoake, Sir Keith Jacka,** 1904–83, NEW ZEALAND political leader. As National Party leader, he was prime minister (1957, 1960–72). He served (1975–77) as state minister and (1977–80) as governor general of New Zealand.

**holy orders,** in Christianity, the higher grades of the ministry, conferred by the Sacrament of Holy Order. The Roman Catholic Church, like the Church of England, has three orders: bishop, priest, and deacon, and like the Eastern Orthodox churches it has permanent deacons, who serve in local parishes. The bishop heads a diocese consisting of many parishes; a priest may be the head of a parish or a member of a religious order.

**Holy Roman Empire,** somewhat anachronistic designation for the political entity that originated at the coronation as emperor of CHARLEMAGNE in 800, who claimed legitimate succession to the Roman Empire. In theory, just as the pope was the vicar of God on earth in spiritual matters, so the emperor was God's temporal vicar; hence he claimed to be the supreme temporal ruler in Christendom. Various titles were used to describe it, but the title Holy Roman Empire first occurs in 1254 by which time the medieval empire was past its zenith. Actually,

the power of the emperors never equalled their pretensions. Their suzerainty never included the East, and it ceased early over France, Denmark, Poland, and Hungary. Their control over England, Sweden, and Spain was never more than nominal; and their control over Italy was always in contention. The core of the empire was the various German principalities plus Austria, Bohemia, and Moravia. Switzerland, the Netherlands, and parts of northern Italy were at times included. Its rulers were chosen by the princes of Germany until 1356, after which they were elected by a fixed number of ELECTORS. They elected the German king (later known as king of the Romans), who became emperor only when crowned by the pope in Rome. After 1562, however, emperors-elect dispensed with coronation by the pope and were crowned at Frankfurt. Emperors held immediate jurisdiction only over their hereditary family domains (e.g., the Saxon dynasty over Saxony) and over the imperial free cities. The rest of the empire they controlled only to the extent of their influence and power. Important also was the relative power of the papacy at any given period. The conflict between pope and emperor was a never-ending one. A longtime dispute was over the right of INVESTITURE, an issue finally settled in the church's favour by the Concordat of Worms (1122). Political control of Italy was another source of conflict. In addition to being a spiritual leader, the pope was also a great temporal power there; and popes were generally jealous of efforts by the emperors to extend their political control over the various Italian states. The feud between the GUELPHS AND GHIBELLINES dramatized the conflict. Although the emperorship was technically an elective office, after 1438 the HABSBURG dynasty became permanently entrenched. Thereafter, the hereditary domains of the Habsburgs were the primary concerns of the emperors. The domain of CHARLES V, for example, stretched around the globe, far beyond the boundaries of the Holy Roman Empire. The empire was seriously weakened by the REFORMATION, which generally aligned the German Protestant princes often with France against the emperors, who championed Roman Catholicism. The THIRTY YEARS' WAR ended with the significant weakening of the empire in the Peace of WESTPHALIA (1648), which recognized the sovereignty of all the states of the empire. Thereafter, the title was largely honorific; the Habsburg emperors remained powerful monarchs, but because of their hereditary domains and not because of the empire. In the 17th cent. the prestige of the empire was further weakened by the military triumphs of LOUIS XIV of France, whom the emperors opposed. Also, the male Habsburg line died out, creating a crisis that led to the War of the AUSTRIAN SUCCESSION. In the end,

---

### HOLY ROMAN EMPERORS *(including dates of reign)*

**Saxon Dynasty**
Otto I, 936–73
Otto II, 973–83
Otto III, 983–1002
Henry II, 1002–24

**Salian or Franconian Dynasty**
Conrad II, 1024–39
Henry III, 1039–56
Henry IV, 1056–1105
Henry V, 1105–25
Lothair II, duke of Saxony, 1125–37

**Hohenstaufen Dynasty and Rivals**
Conrad III, 1138–52
Frederick I, 1152–90
Henry VI, 1190–97
Philip of Swabia, 1198–1208
*antiking*: Otto IV (Guelph), 1198–1208
Otto IV (king, 1208–12; emperor, 1209–15), 1208–15
Frederick II (king, 1212–20; emperor, 1220–50), 1212–50
Conrad IV, 1237–54
*antiking*: Henry Raspe, 1246–47
*antiking*: William, count of Holland, 1247–56

**Interregnum, 1254–73**
Richard, earl of Cornwall, and Alfonso X of Castile, rivals

**Habsburg, Luxembourg, and Other Dynasties**
Rudolf I (Habsburg), 1273–91
Adolf of Nassau, 1292–98
Albert I (Habsburg), 1298–1308
Henry VII (Luxembourg), 1308–13
Louis IV (Wittelsbach), 1314–46
Charles IV (Luxembourg), 1346–78
Wenceslaus (Luxembourg), 1378–1400
Rupert (Wittelsbach), 1400–10
Sigismund (Luxembourg), 1410–37

**Habsburg Dynasty**

| | |
|---|---|
| Albert II, 1438–39 | Matthias, 1612–19 |
| Frederick III, 1440–93 | Ferdinand II, 1619–37 |
| Maximilian I, 1493–1519 | Ferdinand III, 1637–57 |
| Charles V, 1519–58 | Leopold I, 1658–1705 |
| Ferdinand I, 1558–64 | Joseph I, 1705–11 |
| Maximilian II, 1564–76 | Charles VI, 1711–40 |
| Rudolf II, 1576–1612 | |

**Interregnum, 1740–42**

**Wittelsbach-Habsburg and Lorraine Dynasties**
Charles VII (Wittelsbach-Habsburg), 1742–45
Francis I (Lorraine), 1745–65

**Habsburg–Lorraine Dynasty**

| | |
|---|---|
| Joseph II, 1765–90 | Francis II, 1792–1806 |
| Leopold II, 1790–92 | |

the husband of MARIA THERESA, heiress to the Habsburg lands, became emperor as FRANCIS I. Whatever power remained in the office, however, was exerted by Maria Theresa herself and her advisers. The empire finally came to an end in 1806 as the result of the triumphs of NAPOLEON I in the French Revolutionary Wars. Francis II, grandson of Maria Theresa and Francis I, renounced his title and styled himself Francis I, emperor of Austria. After the fall of Napoleon (1815), no attempt was made to resurrect the Holy Roman Empire.

**Holy Week:** see LENT.

**Home Army** (*Armia Krajowa, AK*), underground resistance force called into existence in Poland during WORLD WAR II by the exiled Polish government. The Home Army was divided into a military and a political wing, both controlled from London. Its tasks were to resist the occupying forces by gathering intelligence, by diversionary and propaganda activities, and later, by armed partisan struggle. Contact with the exiled Polish government in London was maintained both by radio and by courier. Plans for a general insurrection against the Germans were drawn up and set in motion in 1944. However the main efforts of the insurgents became concentrated in the bloody Warsaw Rising launched on 1 Aug. which lasted for 63 days before it was crushed.

**Home Guard,** volunteer force raised to defend Britain against the expected German invasion in WORLD WAR II. Started in 1940, it consisted largely of World War I veterans, and was used for general civil defence duties. It was immortalized in the television serial *Dad's Army*.

**Homer,** principal figure of ancient Greek literature, the first European poet. Two epic poems are ascribed to him, the *Iliad* and the *Odyssey*. Among the greatest works of Western literature, they are the prototype for all later EPIC poetry. Modern scholars generally agree that they were composed for an aristocratic audience, possibly by a single poet in Asia Minor before 700 BC. The *Iliad* tells of an episode in the TROJAN WAR: the wrath of ACHILLES and its tragic consequences, including the deaths of Patroclus and Hector. The *Odyssey,* beginning 10 years after the fall of Troy, tells of ODYSSEUS' wanderings on his way home to Ithaca, of his wife and son's plight, and of their reunion. The atmosphere of adventure and fate contrasts with the heavier tone and tragic grandeur of the *Iliad*. Also attributed to Homer, wrongly, were the HOMERIC HYMNS. According to legend, Homer was blind.

**Homer, Winslow,** 1836–1910, American painter. Homer first won acclaim as a magazine illustrator, especially for his CIVIL WAR reportage. In 1876 he abandoned illustration to devote himself to painting. He found inspiration in the American scene and, above all, in the sea. Homer's paintings are direct and realistic and have a splendid sense of colour. His powerfully dramatic seascapes in watercolour are unsurpassed and hold a unique place in American art, e.g., *Breaking Storm* (Art Institute, Chicago) and *The Hurricane* (Metropolitan Mus., New York).

**Homeric Hymns,** hexameter poems, c.650–400 (or later) BC, addressed to various gods, and wrongly attributed to HOMER by the ancients. They are important sources of knowledge about Greek religion.

**Home Rule,** in Irish and English history, political slogan adopted by Irish nationalists in the 19th cent. to describe their basic objective of self-government for Ireland. The modern movement began in 1870 and was strengthened by the rise of C.S. PARNELL, who unified the Irish Party in Parliament. The First Home Rule Bill, introduced (1886) by GLADSTONE, failed to pass; the Second was passed (1893) by the Commons but defeated by the Lords. In consequence, advocates of constitutional means to Home Rule began to lose ground to republicans and revolutionaries. The Third Home Rule Bill passed (1912) by the Commons led to threats of civil war from Protestant Ulster, and the Lords excluded Ulster from its provisions. The bill never took effect, however, because continuing agitation led to recognition of the Irish Free State with dominion status in 1921, and other ties with Britain were gradually broken (see IRELAND, REPUBLIC OF). The six counties of Northern Ireland remained part of Great Britain, governed under the Fourth Home Rule Bill (1920). See IRELAND, NORTHERN.

**homicide,** killing of one human being by another human being. In law, there are four categories of homicide. Two of them, murder and manslaughter, are criminal; both are homicide committed without justification or excuse, but manslaughter is distinguished from murder by the absence of malice aforethought. Noncriminal homicides are justifiable homicide, which is killing in circumstances authorized by law (e.g., executing a condemned prisoner), and accidental, negligent, or excusable homicide, which is killing unintentionally, by misadventure, or without gross negligence (e.g., in the course of unsuccessful surgery).

**homoeopathy,** alternative therapy based on the principle that like cures like. The system was founded by a German doctor, Samuel Hahnemann (1755–1843). Homoeopaths employ extremely small quantities of those drugs that, in healthy people, produce similar symptoms to the disease being treated. It is questionable whether the patient actually receives a pharmacologically active dose of the drug, but homoeopathy has a substantial following in Europe and in the US. In the UK the therapy is pursued by a small number of doctors under the National Health Service and is popular with many patients.

**Homo erectus,** early human species dating from 0.3 to 1.8 million years ago and known from Africa, Asia, and possibly Europe. Compared with HOMO HABILIS (an earlier human ancestor) the cranium is larger overall and of generally rugged construction, although with lighter jaws and smaller teeth, and with greater brain size (775–1300 cm³/47¼–79¼ cu in; larger specimens are within the lower part of the modern human range); the postcranial skeleton is essentially modern. The earliest specimens are from East Africa, especially around Lake TURKANA, Kenya, and include the virtually complete skeleton of a youth (c.1.6 million years). Other African remains cover the period 0.5 to 1.0 + million years, as do specimens from Java (originally known as Pithecanthropus) and China (originally Sinanthropus). Possible European finds, which some consider archaic HOMO SAPIENS rather than *H. erectus*, are 0.2 to 0.5 million years old. *H. erectus* communities were the first to move beyond the tropics; the African remains are of tall, rugged individuals, whereas those from China are shorter, suggesting polytypic population diversity due to climatic/nutritional differences. Cultural associations include hand-axe (Acheulian) assemblages in Africa, Europe, and parts of Asia, and pebble (chopper) tool industries in the Far East. Fire is known from some sites, e.g., ZHOUKOUDIEN, near Beijing (China), and there is evidence for systematic hunting. See also HUMAN EVOLUTION.

**Homo habilis,** 'Handyman', the earliest and most primitive human species. It is known from finds in East and South Africa dated c.1.5 to 2.0 million years ago. Originally the description of the species was based on fossils discovered by Louis and Mary LEAKEY at Olduvai Gorge, Tanzania, with hand bones indicating an evolved precision grip (as in holding a pen) and associated stone tools; hence the name. Other sites are Koobi Fora (Lake TURKANA/Rudolf) Kenya, and STERKFONTEIN/Swartkrans, South Africa. The brain size was 500–800 cm³ (about 30½–50 cu in, i.e., 33%–50% of the modern human average); face and jaws were of light to moderate construction and cheek teeth smaller than those of the earlier and more primitive AUSTRALOPITHECUS fossil species. Many *H. habilis* sites also yield *Australopithecus robustus/boisei*, and later specimens overlap with HOMO ERECTUS, suggesting a complex pattern of early HUMAN EVOLUTION and adaptive diversity. Because of the faunal remains and artifacts, *H. habilis* has often been reconstructed as a skilful, systematic hunter. This is unlikely; diet was mostly plant items, and any meat was probably scavenged, not hunted.

**Homo sapiens,** human species including modern man (*H. sapiens sapiens*) and immediate precursors from the later Middle and Upper Pleistocene (0.4 million years ago to the present). Early (archaic) *H. sapiens* specimens have a strongly constructed brain case of moderate size (1000–1400 cm³/about 60–85 cu in) and relatively large face. They differ from late HOMO ERECTUS from which they probably evolved, in having a rather higher, more rounded skull vault (especially at the rear), and somewhat thinner cranial bones; the distinction between the two species is largely arbitrary. Important finds are Petralona, Steinheim, Swanscombe and Arago (Europe), Bodo (Africa), Narmada (India), Dali (China), Ngandong (SE Asia), which show differences suggesting polytypic (geographical) diversity. This is more evident in later (30,000–120,000 years ago) specimens such as NEANDERTHAL fossils and the Kabwe and Saldana specimens from southern Africa. Anatomically modern *H. sapiens* fossils with large, globular thin-walled braincase, flat face, small jaws and teeth, and external chin are known from Europe

('Cromagnon Man') 25,000 years ago, and in the Middle East/N Africa at 30,000–40,000 years ago; they are also known from SE Asia and Australia at this time, indicating prior occurrence in more central areas. The earliest anatomically modern *H. sapiens* fossils currently known are from several sub-Saharan sites: Kibish beds, Omo, Ethiopia; Border Cave and Klaasie's River, South Africa. These are probably 50,000–120,000 years old, although technical limitations make precise dating difficult. See also HUMAN EVOLUTION.

**homosexuality:** see SEXUAL ORIENTATION.

**homothermic,** scientific description of warm-blooded animals. Homothermic animals can maintain their bodies at a constant temperature which is independent of their surroundings. Birds and mammals are homothermic, and can live and remain active in much hotter and colder conditions than POIKILOTHERMIC animals.

**Homs:** see HIMS, Syria.

**Honan:** see HENAN.

**Honduras,** officially Republic of Honduras, republic (1986 est. pop. 4,370,000), 112,088 km² (43,277 sq mi), Central America; bordered by the Caribbean Sea (N), Nicaragua (E and S), El Salvador and the Pacific Ocean (SW), and Guatemala (W). The capital is TEGUCIGALPA. Over 80% of the land is mountainous; in the E are the swamps and forests of the Mosquito Coast. Bananas, grown on US-owned plantations established in the 1800s, dominate the economy, accounting for one-third of annual exports. Coffee, timber, meat, cotton, tobacco, and minerals are also exported, and some manufacturing is being attempted, but the general economy remains seriously underdeveloped. In 1983 GDP was US$2450 million or US$612 per capita. The people, of whom about 90% are mestizo, are Spanish-speaking and Roman Catholic.

*History.* At one time an important centre of Mayan Indian culture (see MAYA), the region was colonized after 1524 by the Spanish, who established mines in the highlands. Honduras gained independence in 1821 and, after brief periods as part of the Mexican Empire and the CENTRAL AMERICAN FEDERATION, became a separate republic in 1838. Its history has been turbulent, marked by frequent coups (nearly one a year) and trouble with neighbours: a four-day war with EL SALVADOR (1969) and border clashes with NICARAGUA (1981). Foreign influence and conservative government were the rule from the 1890s to the 1950s, when a labour code and other reforms were adopted. From 1963 to 1981 the country was under almost uninterrupted military rule, usually exercised through the conservative National Party. In 1982 a Liberal government came to power under Roberto Suazo Córdova, albeit under close military supervision in view of the perceived threat posed by the new Sandinista regime in neighbouring Nicaragua and by the activities of left-wing guerrillas in El Salvador. José Simón Azcona (also Liberal) succeeded to the presidency in 1986, this being the first handover between democratically-elected civilian presidents since 1931.

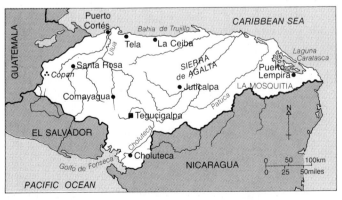

Honduras

**Honecker, Erich,** 1912–, East German Communist leader. The son of a miner, he succeeded Walter Ulbricht as first secretary of the ruling Socialist Unity Party in 1971. The post was renamed general secretary in 1976, in which year Honecker also became chairman of the State Council (i.e., head of state).

**Honegger, Arthur** (ˌhoniɡə), 1892–1955, Swiss composer. One of the Parisian group 'les SIX', he is known for *Pacific 231* (1923), a cycle of five symphonies and the operas *Judith* (1926) and *Antigone* (1927; libretto by COCTEAU). His 'dramatic psalm' *Le Roi David* (1921) and 'dramatic oratorio' *Jeanne d'Arc au bûcher* (1935) are also important.

**honey,** sweet, viscous fluid made by honeybees from the nectar of flowers, containing 70% to 80% sugar. It has been a major sweetening agent since earliest times. The worker bee transforms the sucrose of nectar into the simple sugars fructose and glucose by the enzyme action of its honey sac, and stores the honey to thicken in the wax cells of the hive (called the honeycomb). The excess of the colony's requirement may be extracted by humans for use as food. The flavour and colour of honey depend on the kind of flower that produced the nectar, e.g., clover, orange blossom, heather, or lavender.

**honeydew melon:** see MELON.

**honey locust,** deciduous tree (*Gleditschia triacanthos*) of the PULSE family, native to Asia and N America. Often grown as a shade tree or as an ornamental, the honey locust has fragrant flowers, compound leaves, branching thorns, and brown pods with edible pulp. Its durable wood is used chiefly for fence posts and small construction work.

**honeysuckle,** common name for vines and shrubs of the family Caprifoliaceae. Found in the Northern Hemisphere, the family includes the honeysuckles, ELDERS, viburnums, and weigelas. The true honeysuckles (genus *Lonicera*) include the well-known trumpet honeysuckle (*L. sempervirens*), with fragrant scarlet blossoms, and the Japanese honeysuckle (*L. japonica*), with white to yellow blossoms. Elders and viburnums usually have showy clusters of white flowers, and some produce edible berries.

**Hong Kong,** Chinese *Xiang gang*, British crown colony (1985 pop. 5,588,000), land area 1034 km² (399 sq mi), adjacent to Guangdong prov., SE China; on the estuary of the Pearl R., (see XI JIANG), 64 km (40 mi) E of Macao and 145 km (90 mi) SE of GUANGZHOU (Canton). The colony comprises Hong Kong island, ceded by China in 1842; Kowloon peninsula, ceded in 1860; and the New Territories, a mainland area adjoining Kowloon that was leased in 1898 for 99 years along with Deep Bay, Mirs Bay, and some 235 offshore islands. The capital is Victoria, or Hong Kong, on Hong Kong island. Hong Kong is a free port, a bustling trade centre, a shopping and banking hub, and one of the greatest trading and transshipment centres in the Far East. It has also become a leading light-industrial manufacturing centre, utilizing the abundant cheap labour available. The textile industry is the colony's largest; clothing, plastics, and electronic goods are also produced. Only about one-seventh of the land is arable, and food and water must be imported, much of it from China. Hong Kong was a sparsely populated area when it was occupied by the British during the Opium War (1839–42). As a colony, it prospered as an East–West trading centre and as the commercial gateway to and distribution centre for S China. Conquered (1941) by the Japanese during World War II, it was reoccupied by the British in 1945. Hong Kong is one of the most severely crowded urban areas in the world. Hundreds of thousands of refugees streamed into the urban areas after 1949, and thousands more from Vietnam and S China flooded it in the late 1970s, sparking stringent new controls on the Chinese border (1980). For China, Hong Kong remains a major source of foreign exchange and an important commercial link with the West. However, China has also viewed Hong Kong as a territory seized by a foreign power. Under a declaration signed by the UK and China in 1984 and ratified the following year, Hong Kong will revert to Chinese rule on 1 July 1997, retaining a high degree of local autonomy and its existing legal and economic system remaining unchanged for 50 years after the transfer.

**Honiara,** city (1981 est. pop. 20,000), capital of the SOLOMON ISLANDS, on GUADALCANAL.

**Honolulu,** city (1980 pop. 365,048; Honolulu co. pop. 762,874), capital of HAWAII, on the SE coast of the island of Oahu. The city and county are legally coextensive. Famous for its beauty and ethnic diversity, it is the economic centre of the Hawaiian islands and the crossroads of the Pacific. The first European to see it was an Englishman, Captain William Brown. Honolulu grew into a Hawaiian royal residence and became the capital of the kingdom of Hawaii in 1845. In the 19th cent. it was a busy whaling and trading port occupied successively by Russian, British, and

Hong Kong

French forces. It remained the capital upon US annexation (1898) of the islands and the coming (1959) of statehood. During WORLD WAR II its naval base, PEARL HARBOR, was the staging area for US forces in the Pacific and was the site of the 1941 Japanese bombing. After the war, tourism, industrial diversification, and luxury building accelerated. Defence activities are still important. Sugar processing and pineapple canning are the city's main industries. [Bikiki Beach and nearby Diamond Head crater are famous. Notable institutions include the Univ. of Hawaii, Bishop Museum, Kawaiahao Church (1841), and Iolani Palace (the only royal palace in the US).

**Honorius,** 384–423, Roman emperor of the West (395–423), which he inherited from his father, THEODOSIUS I, as his brother ARCADIUS inherited the East. Honorius had his guardian, STILICHO, murdered (408). After the Visigoths under ALARIC I invaded Italy and sacked Rome (410), Honorius made peace (412) with them. In 421 he was forced to accept as co-ruler his general Constantius, who had married his sister, Galla Placidia. The West declined markedly during his weak reign.

**Honorius I,** pope (625–38), an Italian. He wrote a letter unambiguously supporting the heresy of MONOTHELETISM. The pope and letter were declared heretical at the Third Council of CONSTANTINOPLE. The letter has been explained by supporters of papal infallibility as the result of imprudence rather than heretical intent.

**honour/shame,** an explanatory concept most often used to typify Mediterranean societies. In such societies the FAMILY is the key unit of socio-political identity and the women associated with it become the contested means through which it is defined. Women are confined to particular social contexts such as the domestic sphere and their behaviour within these contexts is closely controlled. The transgression of the appropriate female behaviour patterns constitutes shame. It is the duty of men to defend the boundaries of the family from external threat—a duty enjoined in the concept of honour.

**Honshu,** island (1986 pop. 96,335,179), largest (c.230,510 km²/89,000 sq mi) and most densely populated island in Japan. It is c.1290 km (800 mi) long and from 50 to 240 km (30 to 150 mi) wide, with a climate ranging from subtropical in the south to cold-temperate in the north. Rugged mountains, reaching 3776 m (12,389 ft) at Mt FUJI, cover most of the island. The population is concentrated in a series of small coastal plains along the south, including the Kanto Plain (c.12,950 km²/5000 sq mi), site of the great CHIBA–TOKYO–YOKOHAMA industrial complex, the Kinki district (OSAKA–KOBE), and the Nobi Plain (NAGOYA).

**Honthorst, Gerrit van** (ˌhonthawst), 1590–1656, Dutch portrait, GENRE, and allegorical painter. Influenced by CARAVAGGIO, he was a master of candlelit genre and biblical scenes. He introduced Italianate illusionistic decoration into Dutch interiors. His *Merry Fiddler* (1623) is in the Rijks Mus., Amsterdam.

**Hooch** or **Hoogh, Pieter de** (hohkh), 1629–84, Dutch GENRE painter. His paintings of tranquil interiors, with rooms opening into other rooms

or outdoors, display his ability to handle complicated lighting. One of his finest works is *Courtyard in Delft* (1658; National Gall., London).

**Hood, Thomas,** 1799–1845, English poet, noted for his compassion for the poor and unfortunate in such poems as 'The Song of the Shirt' and 'The Bridge of Sighs'. He also wrote much humorous verse and prose and edited several prominent magazines.

**Hoogh, Pieter de:** see HOOCH, PIETER DE.

**Hooke, Robert,** 1635–1703, English physicist, mathematician, and inventor; considered the greatest mechanic of his age. He improved astronomical instruments, watches, and clocks, and first formulated the theory of planetary movements as a mechanical problem. He devised (1684) a practicable telegraph system; invented the spiral spring in watches and the first screw-divided quadrant; and constructed the first arithmetical machine and Gregorian telescope. He stated Hooke's law on elasticity (see STRENGTH OF MATERIALS) and anticipated the law of universal GRAVITATION.

**Hooker, Sir Joseph Dalton,** 1817–1911, English botanist. He was a Director of KEW GARDENS, as was his father before him. With collaborator George Bentham, he standardized the genera of flowering plants (*Genera Plantarum*) and produced the *Flora of the British Isles* (1870), a standard work until very recent times.

**Hooker, Richard,** 1554?–1600, English theologian and Anglican clergyman. His *Of the Laws of Ecclesiastical Polity* (1593) helped to formulate the intellectual concepts of Anglicanism and influenced civil ecclesiastical government.

**Hooker, Thomas,** 1586–1647, Puritan clergyman in colonial America; b. England. Emigrating (1633) to Massachusetts, Hooker became unhappy with the strict theological rule there. In 1635–36 he and his followers founded HARTFORD, Connecticut.

**Hooke's law:** see STRENGTH OF MATERIALS.

**hookworm,** any of a number of parasitic nematodes, order Strongyloidea, found in tropical and subtropical climates. The hookworm larva usually penetrates exposed skin of humans and other mammals and migrates to the small intestine, where it attaches itself by means of hooks and feeds on the host's blood. Hookworm infestation causes ANAEMIA, diarrhoea, and abdominal pain, and is treated with drugs.

**Hoover, Herbert Clark,** 1874–1964, 31st president of the US (1929–33). Before 1914 he was a mining engineer and consultant. During World War I he headed food and relief bureaus in Europe. As secretary of commerce (1921–29) under HARDING and COOLIDGE, Hoover fostered trade associations and supported such engineering projects as the St Lawrence Waterway and the Hoover Dam. He easily won the 1928 Republican presidential nomination and defeated Democrat Alfred E. SMITH. His administration was dominated by the GREAT DEPRESSION, ushered in by the stock market crash of Oct. 1929. Believing that the economy would regenerate spontaneously, Hoover was reluctant to extend federal activities. But he did begin a large public-works programme, and the RECONSTRUCTION FINANCE CORPORATION was created (1932). Congress, controlled by Democrats after 1930, passed the Emergency Relief Act and created the federal home loan banks. In 1932 some 15,000 ex-servicemen, known as Bonus Marchers, marched on Washington to demand immediate payment of their World War I bonus certificates. Hoover ordered federal troops to oust them from government property. In 1931 Hoover proposed a one-year moratorium on REPARATIONS and war debts to ease the financial situation in Europe. He ran for reelection in 1932 but was overwhelmingly defeated by Franklin D. ROOSEVELT. Later Hoover coordinated (1946) food supplies to war-ravaged countries and headed (1947–49) the Hoover Commission, which recommended administrative reforms of the executive branch of government. He headed a second commission (1953–55), which studied policy and organization.

**Hoover, J(ohn) Edgar,** 1895–1972, US director of the FEDERAL BUREAU OF INVESTIGATION (1924–72). As director, he built an efficient crime-detection system and attacked organized crime. After World War II he targeted Communist activities and became a controversial figure because of his agency's harassment of left-wing dissenters.

**Hoover Dam** known as **Boulder Dam**, (1933–47), one of the world's major dams, c.221 m (726 ft) high and 379 m (1244 ft) long, on the

**Hoover Dam**

COLORADO R. between Nevada and Arizona, US. Built between 1931 and 1936, the multipurpose dam impounds **Lake Mead** and has a hydroelectric capacity of 1.3 MW.

**hop,** herbaceous perennial vine of the MULBERRY family, widely cultivated since early times for brewing purposes. The commercial hop (*Humulus lupulus*), native to Eurasia, is grown for the conelike female flowers, called hops, used to impart a bitter flavour to beer. Oil of hops is used in perfumes, and the stem is used for fibre.

**Hope, A(lec) D(erwent),** 1907–, Australian poet. Professor of English at the Australian National Univ. until his retirement in 1968, he is also a distinguished literary critic, essayist, and reviewer. His many award-winning collections of poems include *The Wandering Islands* (1955), *A Late Picking* (1975), and *The Drifting Continent* (1979). Iconoclastic, frankly sensual, and invariably witty, his poetry is also traditional in its satiric emphasis and employment of myth.

**Hopei** or **Hopeti:** see HEBEI.

**Hopi Indians,** group of PUEBLO INDIANS of the Southwest (see NORTH AMERICAN INDIANS) who occupy several MESA pueblos in NE Arizona. Geographically isolated, they resisted European influence more than other Pueblo tribes and participated in Popé's revolt (1680) against the Spanish. In the 1820s the NAVAHO began to encroach on their lands. Sedentary farmers and sheep herders, they retain clan structure and rituals, including the snake dance; at the same time, the Hopi have a high level of education. In 1975 the federal government began procedures to separate Navaho and Hopi lands, requiring several thousand Navahos to relocate.

**Hopkins, Sir Frederick Gowland,** 1861–1947, English biochemist. Knighted in 1925, he made many wide-ranging researches of great importance. For his work on vitamins he was awarded the 1929 Nobel Prize for physiology or medicine with Christiaan EIJKMAN.

**Hopkins, Gerard Manley,** 1844–89, English poet. His intense poems and experiments in prosody have profoundly influenced 20th-cent. poetry. Hopkins was a convert to Catholicism and a Jesuit priest, and his poems and letters often show his inner conflict and deep dissatisfaction with himself as a poet and a servant of God. His mature work began with 'The Wreck of the *Deutschland*' and includes 'God's Grandeur' and 'The Windhover'. Edited by Robert BRIDGES, his *Poems* was published posthumously in 1918.

**Hopkinson, John,** 1849–98, English electrical engineer and physicist. At 15 he went to Owens College (later Manchester Univ.) to study electrical engineering, then to Cambridge to read mathematics, achieving senior wrangler in 1871. Whilst manager of a glass works he became involved with producing lenses for lighthouses and developed rotating mechanisms for flashing periodically in order to identify the lighthouse. He demonstrated that it was possible to synchronize alternating-current generators so that a number of these could work in parallel, all adding to the total power. Prior to this it was thought that increasing demand for power required the construction of a single machine of larger size. This discovery led eventually to the idea of the power grid system of electrical transmission. In 1890 he was made professor of electrical engineering at Kings College, London. He was a fellow of the Royal Society and was twice elected president of the Institution of Electrical Engineers.

**Hopper, Edward,** 1882–1967, American painter. A student of HENRI, he gained an early reputation with his etchings. His realistic paintings of streets and houses, often without figures, have an atmosphere of loneliness and an almost menacing starkness. A characteristic oil is *Early Sunday Morning* (1930; Whitney Mus., New York City). His works have no overt social propaganda and he disclaimed association with the aims of the ASH CAN SCHOOL and American scene painting school.

**Horace** (*Quintus Horatius Flaccus*), 65 BC–8 BC, Latin poet, one of the greatest LYRIC poets. His benefactor, MAECENAS, gave him the famous Sabine farm where he spent much of his later life, writing poetry reflecting the civilized spirit of the Augustan age and his own genial disposition and love of nature. His poetry consists of two books of *Satires*, four books of *Odes,* the *Epodes,* two books of *Epistles,* the *Carmen Saeculare* (a hymn), and the *Ars Poetica* (on literary matters). Horace's SATIRE was gentler than that of JUVENAL. He was a master of poetic form, and his later verse shows a completely individual adaptation of Greek metres to Latin. Horace has remained a major influence on English poetry.

**Horatius** (Horatius Cocles), legendary Roman hero. With two companions he held Lars Porsena's Etruscan army at bay while the Romans cut the Sublician bridge behind him. He then swam the Tiber to safety. The story is related in MACAULAY's *Lays of Ancient Rome.*

**hormone,** chemical messenger released in minute amounts by the endocrine, or ductless, glands and carried by the bloodstream to target tissues, where it produces either rapid or long-term effects (see ENDOCRINE SYSTEM). Most hormones fall into two major categories: PEPTIDE hormones composed of chains of amino acids, and LIPIDS (including STEROID hormones). Since the lack of any hormone may cause serious disorders, many hormones are now synthesized for use in treating such hormonal deficiencies.

**Hormuz, Strait of,** strategic waterway, 48 to 80 km (30 to 50 mi) wide, between the PERSIAN GULF and the Gulf of Oman, controlling ocean traffic to and from the oil-rich Persian Gulf area. Located in the strait are Qishm Island (Iran) and three other islands Greater Tunb, Lesser Tunb, and Abu Musa seized by Iran (1971) but also claimed by the United Arab Emirates.

**Horn, Cape,** southernmost point of South America, S Chile, known for its strong currents and stormy climate. 'Rounding the Horn' was a great hazard in the era of sailing ships.

**hornbill,** BIRD of the family Bucerotidae, which lives in the tropical rainforests of Africa and Asia. Hornbills are easily recognized by their extraordinarily shaped, enlarged bills. Some of these are combined with apparently heavy casques on the head, but these are actually quite light, being made of spongy bone. Hornbills are fruit-eaters like the similar but unrelated New World birds, the TOUCANS. They nest in hollow trees and in some species the female is walled into the nest with the eggs, to be fed by the male until the eggs hatch.

**Hornbostel, Erich Moritz von,** 1877–1935, Austrian scholar, ethnomusicologist, and teacher. Trained as a chemist, in 1914 he devised (with Curt Sachs) a scheme for the classification of musical instruments. He published many articles and analyses of the world's music, and he trained several scholars in what was then called 'comparative musicology'. Dismissed from his post in 1933 because his mother, the singer Helene Magnus, was Jewish, he went first to New York and then to Cambridge, where he died.

**horned lizard:** see MOLOCH.

**hornet:** see WASP.

**Horney, Karen,** 1885–1952, American psychoanalyst; b. Germany. Though working within the tradition of Freudian PSYCHOANALYSIS, she disagreed with Sigmund FREUD's interpretation of the role of biological factors in the origins of NEUROSIS, emphasizing the importance of society and culture. Horney was one of the earliest feminist critics of Freud's theories of female sexuality. Horney later founded the American Institute

Red-billed **hornbill** (*Tockus erythrorhynchus*)

of Psychoanalysis (1941). Her books include *The Neurotic Personality of Our Time* (1937) and *Neurosis and Human Growth* (1950).

**Horniman, Annie (Elizabeth Fredericka),** 1860–1937, English theatre manager and patron. Her first major success as a patron was to see the Abbey Theatre, Dublin, open in 1904 as a result of her support with its building and equipment. By 1910, disenchanted with the Abbey's nationalistic approach, she had handed it to a board of trustees and turned her attention to the Gaiety Theatre in Manchester, which she had refurbished in 1908. Her name is most commonly linked to the rise of the regional repertory movement in England.

**hornpipe,** an English dance similar to the jig but in 3/2, 2/4, or 4/4 time. Its name may have been derived from an instrument of the same name, a small pipe with up to six holes and two short sections of cow horn serving at either end as mouthpiece and bell. Hornpipes were used in dance suites in the 16th cent., and the dance itself became popular in Wales, Scotland, and Ireland, where a single dancer was accompanied by the fiddle or bagpipes. It is much used in modern Irish traditional music.

**horoscope:** see ASTROLOGY; ZODIAC.

**Horowitz, Vladimir,** 1904–, American virtuoso pianist; b. Russia. He made his Russian debut at 17 and first appeared in the US in 1928. He is noted for his interpretations of CHOPIN, RACHMANINOFF, and LISZT.

**horse,** hoofed, herbivorous MAMMAL, genus *Equus*, of the family Equidae, including the domestic horse, the wild Przewalski's horse, the ASS, and the ZEBRA. They are swift, plains-dwelling herd animals with teeth adapted for grinding coarse grass. The species can interbreed (see MULE), but the offspring are usually sterile. The modern horse evolved in America, where it later became extinct, and spread to other parts of the world. It was domesticated probably by Asian nomads in the 3rd millennium BC. The N American mustangs and the Australian brumbies are domestic escapes which have become established in the wild. In decline for many years because of the replacement of the draught horse by the farm tractor and the driving horse by the motor car, there is now a great increase in interest in the horse for recreational and sporting use. Horses are conveniently grouped according to their uses as heavy draught, light draught, riding horses, and ponies. The heavy draught group includes the Shire horse, which is the largest of all horses (180 cm/ 6 ft at the shoulder), developed in Lincolnshire and adjoining counties, the Clydesdale, the Suffolk Punch, and the French Percheron. Light draught horses, such as the English Hackney, have become more popular with the growth of harness sports; the larger light draught horses include the Cleveland Bay of Yorkshire, originally used for drawing coaches and now once more popular as event horses, and for crossing with Thoroughbreds to produce hunters. The English Thoroughbred is the most famous of all riding horses, used for all sports, but especially for racing. The ponies (see PONY) are generally smaller breeds, but sturdy, very hardy, and typically strong. The smallest living horse is the Shetland pony, about 102 cm (40 in) high.

**horse chestnut,** common name for some trees and shrubs of the family Hippocastanaceae, found in north temperate zones and South America. The horse chestnut tree (*Aesculus hippocastanum*) is usually cultivated as an ornamental tree; its wood is soft and in little demand commercially.

**horse fly,** fairly small to quite large and substantial (7–24 mm/¼–1 in long) FLY (family Tabanidae). Horse flies are usually sombre-coloured but they have beautifully iridescent green, blue, and purple eyes, which are distinctly patterned in the mottled-wing clegs (*Haematopota*). Both males and females feed on nectar but most of the latter are also blood-suckers and can inflict painful bites. In addition to severely harassing humans and domestic animals, horse flies also transmit several human and livestock diseases, e.g., tularaemia to humans in northern temperate areas and loiasis in African rainforests. It is however as vectors of *Trypanosoma*

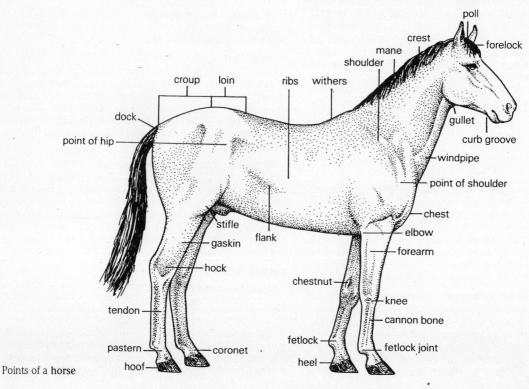

Points of a **horse**

*evansi,* which causes the often-fatal disease surra in camels, horses, cattle, and buffalo, from NW Africa right across to the Philippines, that horse flies are of greatest economic importance.

**horsemanship,** art of riding and handling a horse. Riding as a skilled sport developed in medieval times and now includes diverse styles. Horse shows, which originated (1864) in Ireland, are mainly to display the horses and ponies themselves, but also include competitions to test horsemanship skills in such events as SHOWJUMPING, DRESSAGE, and driving harness horses. Equestrian competition is part of the Olympics.

**horsepower:** see POWER.

**horse racing,** trials of speed between two or more horses. It involves races among harnessed horses with different gaits (pacers and trotters), saddled thoroughbreds along a flat track, and saddled horses over an obstacle course (steeplechase). Horse races are recorded as early as 1500 BC in Egypt. See also POINT-TO-POINT.

**horseradish,** perennial herb (*Armoracia rusticana*) of the MUSTARD family, native to central and S Europe. Once used medicinally against scurvy, today it is grown mainly for its pungent roots, which are used in sauce which is traditionally served with roast beef. It is taken to represent the 'bitter herbs' of Ex. 7:8.

**horsetail,** plant of the genus *Equisetum,* the single surviving genus of a large group of primitive vascular plants that flourished during the Carboniferous period. Found in temperate and tropical regions, horsetails seldom grow to over 91 cm (3 ft), although FOSSIL evidence indicates that many extinct species were treelike in size. Common species, e.g., *E. arvense,* are troublesome weeds which are very difficult to eradicate. They have whorls of small, scalelike leaves around a green, hollow, jointed stem. Some species bear shoots with spore-bearing cones at the top for reproduction. The scouring rushes are common species of horsetails, so called because they have a coarse texture suitable for polishing wood and metal, due to the silica deposited in their tissues.

**Horst, Louis,** 1884–1964, American composer and teacher. He worked as a musical director until 1925, then with Martha GRAHAM (1926–48). He was a leading mentor in the development of the American MODERN DANCE movement, important as a teacher of choreography, and influential as a dance critic.

**Horta, Victor, Baron,** 1861–1947, Belgian architect. His Tassel House, Brussels (1892–93), was the earliest monument of ART NOUVEAU. He also designed the Maison du Peuple (1896–99), a great market and communal complex in Brussels.

**Horthy de Nagybanya, Nicholas** (ˌhawtee də ˌnodyəˈbanyo), 1868–1957, Hungarian admiral and regent. He led (1919) the counterrevolutionary forces in Hungary against Béla KUN and was regent (1920–44). After he tried to make peace with the USSR in WORLD WAR II, the Germans forced him to resign in Oct. 1944 and took him to Germany. He died in Portugal.

**horticulture,** science of cultivating fruits, vegetables, flowers, and ornamental plants; a branch of AGRICULTURE. Although many horticultural practices are ancient, relatively recent knowledge of plant science and its practical application (e.g., in plant breeding) have made horticulture an extremely complex science. It is practised as a commercial enterprise, and also to a large extent for aesthetic purposes in parks, and public and private gardens.

**Horton, Lester,** 1906–53, American dancer, teacher, and choreographer. He formed L.H. Dancers (1934), choreographing many works for the company and his own theatre in Los Angeles (1948). He was important as a teacher, many of his pupils having formed companies of their own.

**Horus,** in ancient EGYPTIAN RELIGION, sky god, god of light and goodness. The son of OSIRIS and ISIS, he avenged his father's murder by defeating Set, the god of evil and darkness.

**Horváth, Ödon von,** 1901–38, Austrian dramatist. Of Austro-German-Magyar background, Horváth was 14 before he wrote his first German sentence. As a dramatist, he revived the popular Viennese 'Volksstück' in a way that was highly critical, focusing on the attenuated and pretentious language of the petty bourgeoisie as a mask for empty brutality, as in *Tales from the Vienna Woods* (1931; tr. 1977), *Casimir and Caroline* (1931), and *Don Juan comes back from the War* (1936; tr. 1978). Losing his audience when the NAZIS came to power, he turned to

Baron Victor **Horta's** Tassel House, Brussels

prose fiction with *A Child of our Time* (1938) and *Youth without God* (1938; tr. *The Age of the Fish* 1978).

**Hosea** or **Osee** (ōsēˌ), book of the OLD TESTAMENT. The writer was a native of the northern kingdom of Israel who prophesied there (c.751–c.721 BC) and interpreted his experience of Gomer, his unfaithful wife, as a parable of God's relationship with ISRAEL. His main theme, God's love for his chosen people, prepared the way for the Christian teaching of God as Father.

**hospice,** place offering humane and supportive care of the terminally ill and their families, a place to house dying patients who can no longer be cared for at home. Staff are committed to meeting the individual needs of the patient and providing physical, emotional, social, and spiritual comfort. Hospice care emphasizes relief from pain, an attractive, noninstitutional environment, and personal and family counselling. The movement was pioneered by Dame Cecily Saunders, founder of St Christopher's Hospice, London, (opened 1967), and furthered by Dr Elisabeth Kübler-Ross's work with the dying. The movement has recently gained importance throughout Europe and in the US as more and more old people live on with incurable disabling diseases.

**hot spring,** natural discharge of groundwater with an elevated temperature. Most hot springs (including GEYSERS) result from water passing through or near recently-formed, hot, igneous rocks. Current energy concerns have spurred an interest in using the geothermal energy of hot springs.

**Hotspur:** see PERCY, SIR HENRY.

**Hottentots:** see KHOIKHOI.

**Houdin, Jean Eugène Robert,** 1805–71, French magician. Famed for his optical illusions, he liked to explain the natural causes of these and other 'magic' tricks.

**Houdini, Harry,** 1874–1926, American magician; b. Hungary as Erich Weiss. He took his stage name from the French magician HOUDIN. He was world-famed for his escapes from every sort of bond and sealed container, and for his exposure of fraudulent spiritualistic mediums.

**Houdon, Jean-Antoine** (ooh͵donh), 1741–1828, French neo-classical sculptor. In creating sculptural documents of his time he also developed a kind of portrait remarkable for elegance, measured realism, and depiction of individuality. He did portrait busts of such statesmen as Thomas Jefferson, Benjamin Franklin, and Prince Henry of Prussia, and the seated figure of Voltaire.

**hound,** class of DOG bred to hunt by scent or sight, mostly of ancient lineage, including the bloodhound, foxhound, bassett hound, beagle, and the dachshund, all of which hunt by scent, and the Afghan hound and greyhound, which hunt by sight. The bloodhound is usually associated with the tracking of humans, and is able to follow a trail more than a week old. The dachshund was bred to track quarry both above and below ground. The Afghan is capable of very high speeds, twisting and turning in a very agile manner, and the modern greyhound is mostly used in the sport of dog-racing.

**Hounslow,** London borough (1981 pop. 198,938), in outer W London. It includes the districts of Heston, Isleworth, Brentford, Chiswick, and Feltham. It was once an important coaching stop on the Great West Road.

**Houphouët-Boigny, Félix** (ooh͵fway ͵bwahnyee), 1905–, president of CÔTE D'IVOIRE, formerly Ivory Coast (1960–). When Côte d'Ivoire became a constituent member of the French Community in 1958, he was its president. Two years later he led the country to full independence and became president of the new republic.

**hour circle:** see ASTRONOMICAL COORDINATE SYSTEMS.

**household:** see DOMESTIC GROUP.

**House of Commons:** see PARLIAMENT.

**House of Lords:** see PARLIAMENT.

**House of Representatives,** United States: see CONGRESS OF THE UNITED STATES.

**Houses of Parliament:** see WESTMINSTER PALACE.

**house sparrow,** small (14 cm/5½ in), seed-eating European BIRD which has become so closely associated with humans that it now lives only in man-made habitats. House sparrows (*Passer domesticus*) followed humans when they colonized other parts of the world and are now established in Africa, Australia, New Zealand, and North and South America. These birds are very adaptable, living and nesting in town centres and feeding on scraps from humans.

**Housman, A(lfred) E(dward),** 1859–1936, English poet and scholar. A failure at Oxford and a recluse, he nevertheless became a leading classicist, editing Manilius, Juvenal, and Lucan. He is best known for the poetry that appeared in two volumes, *A Shropshire Lad* (1896) and *Last Poems* (1922). In such lyrics as 'To an Athlete Dying Young' and 'When I was One-and-twenty', he handled with vivid economy the themes of mortality and the passing of youth. His brother, **Laurence Housman,** 1865–1959, was also a writer, particularly noted for his play *Victoria Regina* (1934).

**Houssay, Bernardo Alberto,** 1887–1971, Argentine physiologist. He received the 1947 Nobel Prize for physiology or medicine with Carl and Gerta CORI for their research in carbohydrate metabolism.

**Houston,** US city (1984 est. pop. 1,706,000), SE Texas, a deepwater port on the Houston Ship Channel; inc. 1837. The fastest-growing urban centre in the US, it is the largest city in the South and Southwest; a focus for commercial, industrial, and financial activity; and one of the world's great oil centres. It has numerous space and science research firms, petrochemical works, shipyards, grain elevators, breweries, mills, and factories. The city is also a major corporate centre. Settled in 1836, it was capital (1837–39) of the Texas Republic. It was a 19th-cent. railhead and grew rapidly after the opening (1914) of the ship channel linking it to the Gulf of MEXICO. Coastal oil fields and other natural resources poured money into Houston. World War II shipbuilding and the opening (1961) nearby of NASA's Manned Spacecraft Center (renamed the Lyndon B. Johnson Space Center, 1973) furthered its growth, although the collapse of oil prices has caused severe problems for government and industry in the 1980s. Houston is noted for its art museums, numerous universities and cultural institutions, and the Astrodome stadium (opened 1965).

**Houston, Samuel,** 1793–1863, Texas statesman. He spent much of his youth with the Cherokee Indians. After serving in Andrew JACKSON's campaign against the Creek Indians (1814), he held several state offices in Tennessee, including the governorship (1827), which he resigned (1829) in order to rejoin the Cherokee, later moving to Texas. After Texas declared its independence from Mexico, Houston commanded the revolutionary troops and defeated the Mexicans at the battle of San Jacinto (21 Apr. 1836). He was the first president of the Republic of TEXAS (1836–38), serving again from 1841 to 1844. After Texas joined the US, he was US senator (1846–59). Elected (1859) governor of Texas, he opposed secession from the Union and was removed from office in 1861.

**hovercraft,** powered transport vehicles, designed to be operated over water, swamps, or unencumbered land surfaces, riding on a low-level cushion of air generated by downwards-vectored fans and enclosed in a flexible 'skirt' or curtain. Hovercraft (as a trade-name) were pioneered by Sir Christopher COCKERELL, who invented the principle in 1953. Hovercraft are now used as vehicle and passenger ferries on short sea crossings, powered by gas turbine or diesel engines, usually driving airscrews mounted on pillars to provide forward thrust.

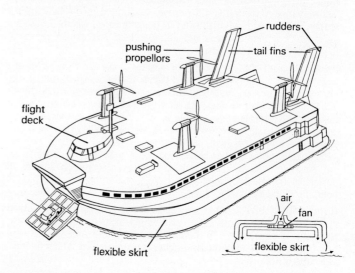

Hovercraft

**Howard, Catherine,** 1521?–42, fifth queen of HENRY VIII of England. Niece of the powerful Thomas Howard, 3rd duke of Norfolk, she married the king in 1540. She was accused of adultery late in 1541 and subsequently beheaded.

**Howard, Henry:** see SURREY, HENRY HOWARD, EARL OF.

**Howe, Elias,** 1819–67, American inventor. He was apprenticed (1838) to a Boston instrument- and watchmaker, at whose suggestion he turned his attention to devising a SEWING MACHINE. He exhibited his first in 1845, patented another in 1846, and sold a third (1846) in England. After several patent infringement suits, he obtained (1854) a judgment for royalty. See also SINGER.

**Howe, Joseph,** 1804–73, Canadian politician. A newspaper publisher, he campaigned for reform and became premier (1860–63) of NOVA SCOTIA. Although he had opposed confederation, he served as president of the council (1869–73) in J.A. MACDONALD's dominion cabinet.

**Howe, Richard Howe, Earl,** 1726–99, British admiral. He defended the English Channel in the SEVEN YEARS' WAR. In the AMERICAN REVOLUTION, he commanded (1776–78) the North American fleet. He is best remembered for his victory over the French fleet in the battle called the First of June in 1794. His brother, **William Howe,** 5th Viscount Howe, 1729–1814, was a British general. In the American Revolution he was commander in chief in the colonies (1775–78). He was successful in the battle of Long Island (1776), defeated WASHINGTON again at the battle of the Brandywine (1777), and captured Philadelphia, but missed several opportunities to crush the Continental army and resigned in 1778.

**Howells, Herbert,** 1892–1983, British composer, organist, and teacher. Much of his earlier music was similar to, and often overshadowed by, that of VAUGHAN WILLIAMS. However, the fine music that he wrote for the liturgy after 1945, such as *Missa sabrinensis* (1953), established him as an independent voice and a leader in that field.

**Howells, William Dean,** 1837–1920, American novelist and critic. A printer, journalist, and biographer of Lincoln, he won recognition with the first of many travel books, *Venetian Life* (1866), written after five years as consul to Venice. On his return to the US, he was associated with such periodicals as the *Atlantic Monthly* and *Harper's Magazine.* In his own novels and in his criticism, Howells was a champion of REALISM in American literature. Among his works, the realistic novels *A Modern Instance* (1882) and *The Rise of Silas Lapham* (1885) are regarded as his major achievements. The friend and editor of Mark TWAIN, Howells sponsored such younger American realists as Stephen CRANE and Frank NORRIS, and his essays on realistic European writers helped to mould American taste. An amazingly prolific writer, he wrote novels, plays, criticism, reminiscences, and short stories.

**howitzer:** see ARTILLERY.

**Hoxha, Enver,** 1908–85, Albanian Communist leader. A founder (1941) of the Albanian Communist Party and political commissar of its National Liberation Army during World War II, Hoxha was premier, foreign minister, and defence minister from 1946 to 1953. Thereafter he chose to rule through the party as first secretary, regularly purging real and imagined rivals and traitors. Although dependent on Yugoslav support before 1948, he took advantage of the split between TITO and STALIN to cast off Belgrade's tutelage in favour of that of Moscow. Devoted to Stalin and Stalinism, he repudiated Soviet patronage for that of China when KHRUSHCHEV pressed for reforms in Albania (1960). The Chinese opening to the US (1972) caused him to consign them, in turn, to the camp of 'revisionists'. Under Hoxha, Albania was an isolated and repressive backwater, despite its claims to be the one truly 'Marxist–Leninist–Stalinist' state in the world.

**Hoyle, Sir Fred,** 1915–, English astronomer. He was one of the originators of the steady state theory of COSMOLOGY and of the theory of NUCLEOGENESIS. He made many contributions to the understanding of stellar evolution and of the interaction between the stars and interstellar matter. He has proposed life as a phenomenon of astronomical origin.

**Hs-.** For some Chinese names beginning thus, see S-; e.g., for Hsi, see SI.

**Hua Guofeng** (hwah gwaw-fung), 1920–, Chinese Communist leader. He succeeded (1976) ZHOU ENLAI as premier and MAO ZEDONG as chairman of the Chinese Communist Party. Hua was ousted as premier (1980) and party chairman (1981) when the followers of DENG XIAOPING consolidated their power. In 1982 Hua was removed from the party's politburo.

**Hua Kuo-feng:** see HUA GUOFENG.

**Huang He** (hwang hə): see YELLOW RIVER.

**Hubble, Edwin Powell,** 1889–1953, American astronomer. As a staff member (from 1919) at Mt Wilson Observatory, Hubble used the 100-in (254-cm) telescope to show conclusively that the spiral nebulae were galaxies far beyond the confines of our own Milky Way and were distributed fairly uniformly over the sky. With Milton HUMASON he also established HUBBLE'S LAW and so laid the observational basis of modern COSMOLOGY.

**Hubble's law,** empirical result that distant GALAXIES invariably show a RED SHIFT of their spectral lines so correlated with their faintness of appearance that if the red shift is interpreted as being due to a velocity of recession (and there is no other acceptable interpretation) and the faintness of a galaxy is used as a measure of its distance, then the velocity is proportional to distance. This is in fact the only type of motion that is compatible with the notion of the uniformity of the universe, as Hubble's law would hold from whichever galaxy the universe was viewed.

**Hubei, Hupei** or **Hupeh,** province (1985 est. pop. 49,310,000), 158,897 km² (61,350 sq mi), central China, E of SICHUAN prov. Major cities are WUHAN, the capital, and Huangshi. Except for a mountainous western section most of the province comprises a low basin occupied by the YANGTZE and Hanshui rivers. In the past flooding has been a problem, though since 1949 this has largely been controlled, with the river water being used for irrigation. Though the waters can be cold for this latitude, the climate is subtropical and the plains have long been a grain surplus region. Winter wheat and rice (often double cropped) are major crops as are soya beans and cotton. It is an important mineral-producing area, particularly of phosphorus, copper, limestone, gypsum, and anthracite coal. However coking coal has to be imported from Henan and Jiangxi provs. Hubei has major hydroelectric power potential, particularly in the Yangtze valley. Industrial production is concentrated in Wuhan, which is a major steel and heavy engineering producer. This section of the Yangtze contains the famous gorge area, including the Three Gorges, namely the Qutang, Wu, and Xiling gorges. They are now one of the sights most prized by foreign tourists.

**Hubli-Dharwad,** town (1981 pop. 527,108), Karnataka state, S India, astride the Gangawali R. It is a twin town; Dharwad (formerly Dharwar) is a district administrative centre and railway junction; and Hubli a commercial centre with growing modern industries, including cotton mills and railway workshops. Dharwar was a district capital under the British.

**Huch, Ricarda** (hookh), 1864–1947, German novelist, historian, and poet. She wrote a number of historical romances on GARIBALDI, *Defeat and Victory* (1906–7), and on the THIRTY YEARS' WAR, *Der grosse Krieg in Deutschland* (1912–14; tr. The Great War in Germany). She is best known now for her pioneering 2 vol. study of ROMANTICISM (1899, 1902), and for her solitary stand against the NAZI takeover of the Writers' Section of the Prussian Academy of Arts in 1933.

**huckleberry,** shrub (genus *Gaylussacia*) of the HEATH family, native to the Americas. Huckleberry, often confused with BLUEBERRY, is grown as an ornamental or for its fruit. The common huckleberry (*G. baccata*) is particularly valued for its blue or black fruit.

**Huddersfield,** town (1981 pop. 147,825), in W Yorkshire, N England, on R. Colne, 17 km (11 mi) S of Bradford. It is an industrial town, whose industries include textile and chemical manufacture and engineering. An important centre of the woollen and worsted industry since the 17th cent., it developed rapidly owing to the presence of coal nearby.

**Hudson,** river in New York State, US, flowing generally south c.510 km (315 mi) from Lake Tear of the Clouds on Mt Marcy in the Adirondack Mts to the Atlantic Ocean at New York City. It is tidal, and navigable by ocean vessels, to Albany, 240 km (150 mi) upstream. First sighted (1524) by VERRAZANO, it was explored (1609) by Henry HUDSON and became part of the first all-water trans-Appalachian route when linked (1825) to the GREAT LAKES by the ERIE CANAL. Many industries are located along its banks, which are also associated with the well-known HUDSON RIVER SCHOOL of painting and Washington IRVING's legend of Rip Van Winkle.

**Hudson, Henry,** fl. 1607–11, English explorer. Sailing for the Dutch EAST INDIA COMPANY in search of the NORTHWEST PASSAGE, he explored (1609) the HUDSON R., giving the Dutch their claims to the area. Sailing for the English, he reached (1610) HUDSON BAY. He was abandoned at sea by a mutinous crew.

**Hudson, William Henry,** 1841–1922, English author and naturalist; b. Argentina of American parents. He described nature with great sensitivity in works such as the romance *Green Mansions* (1904), set in a South American jungle, and the autobiographical *Far Away and Long Ago* (1918).

**Hudson Bay,** shallow sea, N Canada, covered by ice from October to mid-July. Explored and named (1610) by Henry HUDSON, the bay (which extends south as James Bay) is c.1350 km (850 mi) long and c.1050 km (650 mi) wide, and connects with the Atlantic Ocean through Hudson Strait and with the Arctic Ocean through Foxe Channel. The Hudson Bay region has been a rich source of furs since the late 1600s (see HUDSON'S BAY COMPANY).

**Hudson River school,** group of American landscape painters, working from 1825 to 1875. Influenced by European ROMANTICISM's attitude towards nature, they were attracted to the grandeur of the Hudson river valley's scenery and painted its awesome beauty together with other spectacular vistas from the American landscape. Thomas COLE was the leader of the group during its most active years. Other members of the school were Bierstadt, Durand, J.F. Kensett, S.F.B. MORSE, Henry Inman, F.E. CHURCH, and, in his early work, George Innes S.F.B.

**Hudson's Bay Company,** corporation chartered (1670) by the English crown to operate a fur trade monopoly and settlements in the HUDSON BAY region of North America, and to discover a NORTHWEST PASSAGE to the Orient. The company's traders failed to find a passage, but they did establish a monopoly of the Canadian fur trade after the company's amalgamation (1821) with the NORTH WEST COMPANY had ended their violent rivalry (see RED RIVER SETTLEMENT). The united company ruled a vast territory extending from the Atlantic to the Pacific, and its fortunes peaked under Sir George SIMPSON's governorship (1821–56). An internal reorganization (1863) passed its stock from a few to many holders. The company's fur monopoly was curtailed by the transfer (1869) of its territory to the new dominion government in return for £300,000. In the late 19th and early 20th cent. it was transformed from a fur-trading agency to a gigantic corporation with many varied business interests. The company was split up into separate organizations in 1930.

**Hue** (hway), city (1971 est. pop. 199,900), S Vietnam, on the Hue R. near the South China Sea. It is the market centre for a rich farming region and has a cement plant nearby. Hue was probably founded in the 3rd cent. AD. In the 16th cent. it became the seat of the dynasty that ruled ANNAM. The French took Hue in 1883. In 1954 it became part of South Vietnam. During the VIETNAM WAR it was the scene of fighting in which c.4000 civilians were killed and most of the city destroyed. After the war it was incorporated into united Vietnam; it has since been rebuilt.

**Huelva,** city (1981 pop. 127,806), capital of Huelva prov., Andalusia, S Spain, on the Odiel R. It is the principal export route for the copper and pyrites of the Sierra Morena (Rio Tinto mines) to the N. It is a fishing port and has a wide range of chemical industries based on its oil refinery and the use of imported phosphates.

**Huerta, Victoriano** (,weətah), 1854–1916, Mexican president (1913–14). As commander of federal forces he overthrew Pres. MADERO and set up a dictatorship marked by corruption and violence. Numerous revolts forced him to resign (1914) as president and to flee into exile.

**Huggins, Sir William,** 1824–1910, English astronomer. A pioneer in spectroscopic photography, he helped develop the combined use of the telescope, spectroscope, and photographic negative. He adapted the gelatin dry-plate negative for use in astronomical photography, making possible exposures of any length. Huggins proved that while some nebulae are clusters of stars, others are uniformly gaseous. He made (1866) the first spectroscopic observations of a nova.

**Hugh Capet,** c.938–96, king of France (r.987–96), first of the CAPETIANS. He inherited (956) a vast domain in France from his father, Hugh the Great, and in 987 was elected king. He spent much of his reign fighting with Charles I of Lower Lorraine, the ignored Carolingian claimant.

**Hughes, (James) Langston,** 1902–67, black American poet. A major figure in the HARLEM RENAISSANCE, he often depicted urban black life. His collections of verse include *The Weary Blues* (1926) and *One-Way Ticket* (1949). Among his many other works are plays, children's books, and novels.

**Hughes, Richard,** 1900–76, English novelist. He is best known for *A High Wind in Jamaica* (1929), a bizarre novel about a group of children captured by pirates. *The Fox in the Attic* (1961) and *The Wooden Shepherdess* (1972) are part of a projected long novel, *The Human Predicament* (unfinished).

**Hughes, Ted,** 1930–, English poet, appointed POET LAUREATE in 1984. A predominantly rural writer, he evokes the violence and passion of the natural world in tightly controlled verse. His works include *The Hawk in the Rain* (1957), *Wodwo* (1967), *Crow* (1971), and *Moortown* (1980). He was married to Sylvia PLATH.

**Hughes, Thomas,** 1822–96, English author. His novel of school life, *Tom Brown's Schooldays* (1857), is a classic. It idealizes Dr Thomas ARNOLD, the headmaster of Rugby school.

**Hughes, William Morris,** 1864–1952, Australian statesman; b. England. He was minister for external affairs (1904) in the first Labor government and was later attorney general (1908–09, 1910–13, 1914–21). As prime minister (1915–23) of Australia, he gave strong support to Britain in WORLD WAR I, but in 1916 was expelled from the Labor Party for his unsuccessful attempt to introduce military conscription.

**Hugo, Victor Marie, Vicomte** (,hyoohgoh), 1802–85, French poet, dramatist, and novelist and 19th-cent. France's leading literary figure. The preface to his drama *Cromwell* (1827) placed him at the head of the romantic school, and the production of his unconventional poetic drama *Hernani* (1830) produced a riot between champions of ROMANTICISM and CLASSICISM. Other plays are *Le Roi s'amuse* (1832) and *Ruy Blas* (1838). His principal poetic works, e.g., *Les feuilles d'automne* (1831; tr. Autumn Leaves), *Les rayons et les ombres* (1840; tr. Rays and Shadows), and *Les contemplatives* (1856), demonstrate his musical powers and

highly personal voice. His two great epic novels, *Nôtre-Dame de Paris* (1831; tr. The Hunchback of Notre Dame) and *Les Misérables* (1862), for which he is best known in English, portray the sufferings of humanity with great compassion and power. Originally a monarchist, Hugo later became an ardent republican, and his opposition to NAPOLEON III led to his exile in 1851. In 1870 he returned in triumph to Paris, where his final years were marked by public veneration; he is buried in the Panthéon.

**Huguenots** (,hyoohgənohs), French Protestants, followers of John CALVIN. Protestants founded (1559) a Presbyterian church in France and soon became one of the nation's most industrious and economically advanced elements. They engaged with Roman Catholic forces in the Wars of Religion (see RELIGION, WARS OF) (1562–98) and by the Edict of NANTES (1598) received certain religious and political privileges. Cardinal RICHELIEU, however, captured their strongholds and, by the Peace of Alais (1629), stripped them of their political power. In 1685 LOUIS XIV revoked the Edict of Nantes, and countless Huguenots fled to Protestant Europe and to America.

**Huizinga, Johan** (,hoyzingə), 1872–1945, Dutch historian. Noted for his work on the cultural history of the late Middle Ages, he wrote the classic *Waning of the Middle Ages* (1919). He considered the Renaissance the death of the MIDDLE AGES rather than the birth of the modern world.

**Hull, Clark Leonard,** 1884–1952, American psychologist. Hull attempted by means of rigorous mathematical formalisms to overcome the limitations of BEHAVIOURISM, but his approach was superseded by the development of COGNITIVE SCIENCE.

**Hull, Cordell,** 1871–1955, American statesman. A US congressman (1907–21, 1923–31) and senator (1931–33) from Tennessee, he served (1933–44) as secretary of state under Pres. F.D. ROOSEVELT. Hull sought sound international economic relations and in WORLD WAR II backed the creation of a world organization to maintain peace. He was awarded the 1945 Nobel Peace Prize.

**Hull House:** see ADDAMS, JANE.

**Hull (Kingston upon Hull),** city (1981 pop. 322,144), in Humberside, NE England, at confluence of R. Hull and R. Humber, 80 km (50 mi) E of Leeds. It is an important port and centre of the fishing industry. Other industries found within the town include flour and saw mills, and paint and chemical manufacture. In 1984 the port handled 4.0 million tonnes. The Univ. of Hull at Newland started life as University College in 1929 and received its charter in 1954. Much of the city was bombed during World War II and there has been much rebuilding within the city centre. The Humber Bridge, a large single-span suspension bridge, was opened in 1981.

The Humber Bridge, **Hull**

**human evolution,** Modern humans (*Homo sapiens sapiens*) are the only living members of the primate family Hominidae, which also includes precursors and fossil collaterals of humans (genus *Homo*). Molecular and anatomical evidence indicate our closest living relatives to be the African apes—the chimpanzee and gorilla—usually assigned to a separate family, Pongidae. Hominid origins lie within the extensive ape radiation of the middle to late Miocene (8 to 14 million years ago), evidence for which is

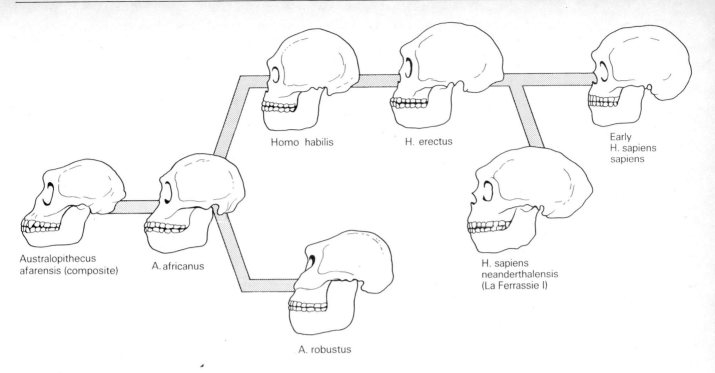

Homo habilis      H. erectus      Early H. sapiens sapiens

Australopithecus afarensis (composite)      A. africanus      H. sapiens neanderthalensis (La Ferrassie I)

A. robustus

**Human evolution:** Australopithecus afarensis was first discovered in 1974. It lived 3–4 million years ago and so is one of the oldest hominids.

drawn from Africa, Europe, the Middle East, India, and China. An initial split at perhaps 10 to 14 million years was between African and Asian lineages: *Ramapithecus*, an Asian fossil, once thought an early hominid, is now considered an ancestor of the orang. Thereafter at about 6 to 10 million years the African lineage split into hominid and pongid lines, perhaps following contrasting adaptations to savannah/grassland and tropical forest environments; the final split in the pongid line between chimpanzee and gorilla was probably less than 3 million years ago, although fossil evidence is lacking. There is fragmentary hominid evidence from the Rift Valley 4 to 6 million years old, but more complete fossils are from South and East Africa 1.5 to 3.5 million years ago. These are of AUSTRALOPITHECUS—erect, bipedal hominids with small brains and large jaws, of which several species are recognized. The later ones overlap with early *Homo* (HOMO HABILIS) at OLDUVAI, Lake TURKANA, and other sites of about 1.5 to 2.0 million years ago. Early HOMO ERECTUS is also present, so that at least three hominid species coexisted—early hominid evolution was evidently complex, with several lineages adapted to contrasting ecological niches. Thereafter diversity is markedly reduced, suggesting only a single lineage; by about 1 million years ago *H. erectus* fossils are known from SE Asia as well as Africa, and by 0.5 million years are present in temperate regions (N China and possibly Europe). Between 0.2 and 0.4 million years ago *H. erectus* populations evolved into HOMO SAPIENS within which geographical diversity (*H.s. neanderthalensis, H.s. rhodesiensis*) is more evident than before. Anatomically modern *H.s. sapiens* had probably evolved by about 100,000 years ago; the oldest specimens currently known are those from sub-Saharan Africa and the Middle East. By 20,000 to 30,000 years ago *H.s. sapiens* groups are known from Europe ('Cromagnon Man') and Australia on the Old World periphery, exploiting marginal environments by means of complex tool kits, and with evidence of accomplished creative and spiritual activities. Human evolution has been claimed as an especially clear example of both the *punctuated equilibria* and *phyletic gradualism* modes of EVOLUTION. The record is too incomplete to be definitive, but the overall pattern—multiple lineages in the earlier phases, with a single evolving lineage in the later phase—accords better with phyletic gradualism than with the punctuationist view.

**humanism,** philosophical and literary movement in which human values and capabilities are the central focus. The term originally referred to a point of view particularly associated with the RENAISSANCE, with its emphasis on secular studies (the humanities), a conscious return to classical ideals and forms, and a rejection of medieval religious authority. BOCCACCIO, ERASMUS, and PETRARCA were outstanding humanists. In modern usage, humanism often indicates a general emphasis on lasting human values, respect for scientific knowledge, and cultivation of the classics.

**Humason, Milton,** 1891–1972, American astronomer. He worked at Mt Wilson Observatory with Edwin HUBBLE, playing a key role in the investigations into the velocity of recession of the galaxies and the expansion of the universe.

**Humber,** estuary formed by the rivers TRENT and Ouse in E Midlands of England. It flows into the North Sea between Spurn Head in Humberside, and North Cotes Point in Lincolnshire. The ports of HULL and GRIMSBY are situated on the N and S banks respectively.

**Humberside,** county in NE England (1984 est. pop. 851,606), 3512 km² (1370 sq mi), situated around the Humber estuary, bordering on the North Sea in the E. It was formed in 1974 from parts of the East Riding of Yorkshire and N Lincolnshire. Most of the county is flat, except for the southern end of the Yorkshire Wolds on the north side of the estuary. Kingston upon Hull, GRIMSBY, and Goole are ports and Scunthorpe is an old iron and steel town. Iron ore was mined in the S of the county, in the area around Scunthorpe.

**Humboldt, Alexander, Freiherr von,** 1769–1859, German naturalist and traveller. From 1799 to 1804 he made his renowned expedition with A.J.A. Bonpland to Central and SOUTH AMERICA and CUBA, a journey that did much to lay the broad foundations for the sciences of physical geography and meteorology. Humboldt explored the ORINOCO R. and the sources of the AMAZON R., and conducted experiments. He wrote *Personal Narrative of Travels to the Equinoctial Regions of America* (1805–34, tr. 1851) and *Cosmos* (1845–62).

**Humboldt Current** or **Peru Current,** cold ocean current off the west coast of South America. Carrying cold water north from Antarctic regions, it brings cool temperatures and fogs to the coasts of Chile and Peru. Nutrients brought up by upwellings of this current off Peru support a large population of plankton and Peruvian anchovy, which has been the basis of a dramatic recent growth in the Peruvian fishing industry.

**Hume, David,** 1711–76, Scottish philosopher and historian. Developing the EMPIRICISM of LOCKE and George BERKELEY, Hume was an implacable opponent of DESCARTES' world-view. Often mistaken for an arch-sceptic, he argued that fundamental human beliefs—in the self, the physical world, causation, space, time—are not produced by observation or reason but by a species of animal instinct. He introduced a theory of moral values as socially projected, in a version of UTILITARIANISM, and exposed the defects of rational or natural theology. Besides his masterpiece, *A Treatise of Human Nature* (1739–40), he wrote *An Inquiry concerning Human Understanding* (1748), *An Inquiry concerning the Principles of Morals* (1752), *Political Discourses* (1752), and *Dialogues concerning Natural Religion* (1779). His *History of England* (1754–62) was the standard work until MACAULAY.

**humidity,** moisture content of the atmosphere, a major element of CLIMATE. Humidity measurements include *absolute humidity,* the mass of water vapour per unit volume of natural air; *relative humidity* (usually meant when the term *humidity* alone is used), the ratio of the actual water-vapour content of the air to its total capacity at a given temperature; and *specific humidity,* the mass of water vapour per unit mass of natural air. Relative humidity is usually measured by means of a HYGROMETER.

**Hummel, Johann Nepomuk,** 1778–1837, Austrian composer and pianist. He was a pupil of MOZART and Joseph HAYDN, and friend and rival of BEETHOVEN, and his music influenced composers such as CHOPIN, SCHUMANN, and MENDELSSOHN. He wrote piano sonatas and concertos, chamber music, church music, four *Singspiele*, ballets, incidental music, and a three-volume manual of piano technique.

**hummingbird,** small, colourful BIRD with a long, slender bill, of the New World family Trochilidae, found chiefly in the mountains of South America. Hummingbirds vary in size from the 6-cm (2¼-in) fairy hummingbird of Cuba, the smallest of all birds, to the 22-cm (8½-in) giant hummer of the Andes. They are usually seen hovering or darting (at speeds of up to 100 kph/60 mph in the air, beating their wings at 50 to 75 beats per sec. Constant feeding supplies their enormous energy needs. At night they lapse into a state of torpor similar to HIBERNATION.

Male broad-tailed **hummingbird** feeding on nectar

**Humperdinck, Engelbert,** 1854–1921, German composer and teacher, friend and associate of Richard WAGNER. He is known chiefly for his first opera, *Hänsel und Gretel* (1893), successful because of its fairy-tale subject and folk-based music.

**Humphrey, Doris,** 1895–1958, American dancer, teacher, and choreographer. After an early career with Denishawn (see Ruth ST DENIS) she entered important collaborations with Charles WEIDMAN, with whom she formed (1928) the Humphrey–Weidman company, and José LIMON. A leading figure in the development of MODERN DANCE, she developed her own dance technique, as well as choreographing numerous works, many of which she performed in. She wrote *The Art of Making Dances.* See also CHOREOGRAPHY.

**Humphrey, Hubert Horatio,** 1911–78, US vice president (1965–69). He served as mayor of Minneapolis (1945–48) and US senator from Minnesota (1949–64, 1971–78). A strong advocate of civil rights, he was vice president under L.B. JOHNSON. In 1968 he was the Democratic presidential candidate but lost a close election to Richard M. NIXON.

**Humphries, Barry,** 1934–, British–Australian comedian and satirist; b. Melbourne, which remains the source of his humour despite the increasingly international appeal of his Dame Edna Everage. He was the first to identify the distinctive cadences of Australian suburbia. He has also made films, most notably *The Adventures of Barry McKenzie* (1972).

**humus,** organic matter decayed to a relatively stable, amorphous state. An important component of fertile SOIL, it affects physical properties such as soil structure, water retention, and EROSION resistance. Humus is formed when soil microorganisms decompose animal and plant material into elements usable by plants (see FERTILIZER).

**Hunan,** province (1985 est. pop. 56,220,000), 210,000 km² (81,081 sq mi), central China, N of GUANGDONG prov. Major cities are CHANGSHA, the capital, and Xiangtan. The province includes much hill land, particularly to the W and S. Most of the area is the drainage basin of the Xiang R. as it flows N in Dongting lake, China's second-largest lake, and then into the Yangtze R. near the border with Hubei province. The basin and valley land is fertile, and the province is second only to SICHUAN as a producer of grain, particularly rice. Cotton and tea grown in the hills are significant cash crops. The hill lands are also important for forestry and wood products. Mineral resources are abundant, particularly of nonferrous metals including antimony, mercury, manganese, and tungsten. As yet industrial growth has been limited. Hunan was a frontier province into which Chinese settlers and culture moved from northern regions. By the Ming dynasty (1368–1644) it had become a major rice producer. Mao Zedong was born (1893) in the province at Shaoshan, a frequent site for political pilgrims in the 1960s and 70s.

**Hundred Days,** in French history, the period (20 Mar. to 28 June 1815) that began when NAPOLEON I reentered Paris after his exile on Elba. It ended when LOUIS XVIII was restored after Napoleon's defeat in the WATERLOO CAMPAIGN.

**Hundred Years War,** 1337–1453, conflict between England and France. Its basic theme was a dynastic quarrel between the kings of England, who held the duchy of Guienne, in France, and who resented paying homage to the kings of France. There were several immediate causes: a quarrel between EDWARD III of England and PHILIP IV of France over a part of Guienne held by France; English attempts to control the commercially important FLANDERS, a French possession; fishing disputes in the English Channel; and Philip's support of Scotland in its dispute with England. The war began in 1337 when Edward, assuming the title king of France, invaded France. The English won a sea battle at Sluis (1340) and land battles at Crécy (1346), Calais (1347), and Poitiers (1360), where King John II of France was captured. The Treaty of Brétigny (1360) awarded England Calais, Aquitaine, and a large ransom for the captured king. In return, England gave up its claim to the French crown. The war resumed in 1369 when nobles in Aquitaine rebelled over the oppressive tax policies of EDWARD THE BLACK PRINCE. By 1373 DU GUESCLIN had won back most of the English claims. The conflict then languished until 1415, when HENRY V of England defeated France's best knights at AGINCOURT. He allied himself with Burgundy and went on to subdue Normandy. In the Treaty of Troyes (1420) CHARLES VI of France was forced to recognize Henry as regent and heir to the throne of France, disinheriting his own son, the dauphin. By 1429 Henry and his Burgundian allies controlled practically all of France N of the Loire and had Orléans under siege. French fortunes were reversed that year, however. JOAN OF ARC lifted the siege of Orléans and saw the dauphin crowned as CHARLES VII at Rheims. Her capture and execution did not end the string of French victories. In 1435 Charles obtained an alliance with Burgundy, and by 1450 France had reconquered Normandy. By 1451 all of Guienne except Bordeaux was in French hands. Bordeaux fell in 1453, leaving the English only Calais (which they retained until 1558). Domestic difficulties, specifically the Wars of The ROSES, kept England from making any further attempts to conquer France. The Hundred Years War inflicted untold misery on the French people. Famine, the Black Death, and roving bands of marauders decimated the population. An entirely new France emerged. The virtual destruction of the feudal nobility allowed the monarchs to unite the country more solidly under the royal authority and to ally themselves with the newly rising middle class. England ceased thinking of itself as a continental power and began to develop as a sea power.

**Hungarian language,** member of the Ugrian group of the Finno-Ugric languages, which form a subdivision of the URALIC AND ALTAIC family of languages. See LANGUAGE (table).

**Hungary,** Hung. *Magyarország,* officially the Hungarian People's Republic, republic (1985 est. pop. 10,797,000), 93,030 km² (35,919 sq mi), central Europe; bordered by Czechoslovakia (N), the USSR (NE), Romania (E), Yugoslavia (S), and Austria (W). The capital is BUDAPEST. The DANUBE R. forms part of the border with Czechoslovakia, then turns S and bisects the country. E of the Danube lies the Great Hungarian Plain (Hung. *Alföld*); W of the river are the Little Alföld and the Transdanubian region. Lake BALATON, the largest lake in Europe, is a leading resort area. Traditionally agricultural, Hungary has become heavily industrialized since World War II, producing machinery, textiles, metal goods, chemicals, and motor vehicles. Major farm products are maize, wheat, rice, potatoes, turnips, grapes and other fruit, livestock, and poultry. Bauxite and manganese are the most important mineral resources. The GNP per capita is US$2150 (1983). About two-thirds of the population is Roman Catholic, but there is a large Calvinist minority. Hungarian is the official language. The country is governed under a 1949 constitution, amended in 1972, which provides for a 352-member national assembly. Political power resides in the Communist party (Hungarian Socialist Workers Party).

*History.* Most of the area that is now Hungary and TRANSYLVANIA was conquered in the late 9th cent. AD by the MAGYARS, a Finno-Ugric people from beyond the Urals; Christianization was completed by St STEPHEN (r.1001–1038), first king of Hungary. A feudal society developed, controlled by a few powerful nobles, the magnates. Hungary was ruled after 1307 by the Angevin dynasty and after 1386 by other foreign houses. In 1526 the Ottoman Turks defeated the Hungarians at the battle of Mohács. In the long wars that followed the Turks dominated most of Hungary, while Transylvania was ruled by noble families (see BÁTHORY and RÁKÓLCZY). By 1711, however, all Hungary had fallen under HABSBURG control. A short-lived independent Hungarian republic (1849) under Louis KOSSUTH was overthrown by Austrian and Russian troops, and in 1867 the AUSTRO-HUNGARIAN MONARCHY was established, in which Austria and Hungary were nearly equal partners. After the collapse of the Dual Monarchy in WORLD WAR I, Hungary was proclaimed (1918) an independent republic and drastically reduced in area and population by the Treaty of Trianon (1920). The soviet republic (1919) of Béla KUN was put down by Romanian intervention, and in 1920 Adm. Nicholas HORTHY DE NAGYBÁNYA became regent. In WORLD WAR II Hungary joined (1941) the AXIS and was invaded (1944) by the USSR. A republican constitution was adopted in 1946, but a communist coup d'etat in 1948 set up a people's republic in 1949, Hungary becoming a founder member of both the COUNCIL FOR MUTUAL ECONOMIC ASSISTANCE and the WARSAW TREATY ORGANIZATION. In 1956 a popular anti-communist revolution, led by former premier Imre NAGY, was suppressed by Soviet forces. However, the subsequent Soviet-supported government of János KÁDÁR brought increasing liberalization to the country's economic, political, and cultural life. Since 1988 the process has accelerated, and in 1989 Kádár lost his offices.

**hunger strike,** refusal to eat, as a form of protest. An ancient device, usually used by prisoners, the hunger strike was revived in the early 20th cent. by imprisoned suffragists (see WOMEN'S SUFFRAGE) in England and was a major weapon in Mahatma GANDHI's movement of passive resistance to British rule in India. More recently, it has been used by Soledad Prison (California) inmates (1970) to protest against prison conditions, and by US protesters against the VIETNAM WAR. In 1981 a protest by Irish nationalist prisoners in ULSTER resulted in the deaths by starvation of 10 men, including Bobby Sands who had been elected to the British Parliament.

**Hunkers,** conservative faction of the New York state Democratic party in the 1840s, so named because they were said to 'hanker' or 'hunker' after office. The Hunkers opposed the radical Democrats, or BARNBURNERS. They favoured internal improvements and liberal chartering of state banks, and opposed antislavery legislation.

**Huns,** nomadic people who originated in north-central Asia. Although in customs they resemble the MONGOLS and MAGYARS, they appear not to have

Hungary

been related ethnically to other groups. Short and somewhat Mongoloid in appearance, the Huns were organized into ravaging military hordes riding small, rapid horses. In the 3rd cent. BC they invaded China, where part of the GREAT WALL was built to exclude them. They appeared in the Volga valley c.372; the GOTHS were pushed west, where they destroyed the Roman Empire. Most of European Russia, Poland, and Germany paid tribute to ATTILA, the greatest Hun king. Defeated (451) in Gaul, the Huns ravaged Italy until Attila's death (453), after which little is known of them.

**Hunt, Holman:** see HUNT, WILLIAM HOLMAN.

**Hunt, (James Henry) Leigh,** 1784–1859, English writer. Hunt edited liberal weeklies, notably the *Examiner* (1808–21), and wrote critical articles, plays and narrative verse. He befriended the important writers of his time, among them KEATS and SHELLEY. His own fame rests on his essays, his lyrics 'Abou Ben Adhem' and 'Jenny Kissed Me', and his autobiography (1850).

**Hunt, William Holman,** 1827–1910, English painter. He was a founder of the PRE-RAPHAELITE brotherhood, and his sincere devotion to its principles can be seen in such paintings as *The Light of the World* (1853; Keble College, Oxford).

**hunter–gatherer,** name for a type of social group which does not cultivate food or domesticate animals but is wholly dependent for its livelihood on the gathering of wild, noncultivated food, such as nuts, berries, etc. (which among many hunter–gatherer groups constitutes some 80% of the diet) and small trapped or larger hunted animals. Such groups are almost always small and nomadic; social organization is characteristically flexible with few if any hierarchical or formalized political roles and little corporate or individual property.

**Hunter Valley,** region of New South Wales, E Australia. The Hunter Valley, 470 km (260 mi) long, has a drainage basin of 26,000 km² (10,000 sq mi), and lies between the EASTERN HIGHLANDS and the Pacific Ocean. The valley is important as a wine-producing area, with beef, wool, and coal as exports through the port of NEWCASTLE. The main urban centre is MAITLAND.

**Huntington's chorea:** see under CHOREA.

**Huntsville,** US city (1984 est. pop. 150,000), N Alabama; inc. 1811. A major space research centre, Huntsville is the site of the Redstone Arsenal, the US Army's missile and rocket centre; NASA's Marshall Space Flight Center; and the Alabama Space and Rocket Center, the world's largest space museum. Local industry also includes tyres, glass, and electrical equipment.

**Hunyadi, John** (ˌhoonyodee), c.1385–1456, Hungarian national hero. Chosen (1441) *voivode* [governor] of Transylvania, he won many victories over the Turks. He became (1446) regent for young King LADISLAUS V, but when Ladislaus assumed his rule (1453) Hunyadi resumed fighting the Turks, whom he defeated (1456) at Belgrade. His son was King MATTHIAS CORVINUS.

**Hupei** or **Hupeti:** see HUBEI.

**hurling,** the Irish national game. Two teams of 15 players each play the game with broad-bladed sticks (camans or hurleys) 1.07 m (3½ ft) long and a ball (sliothar). The pitch is 137 by 91.5 m (150 by 100 yd) with a goal at either end which measures 6.4 by 6.4m (21 by 21 ft) and has a crossbar 2.4 m (8 ft) from the ground. Three points are scored for hitting the ball under the crossbar and one point for over. The hurley is used to catch and balance the ball while running. Players may also catch and strike the ball with their feet and hands, but are not allowed to pick the ball up and throw it. Hurling was first mentioned in a description of the Battle of Moytura (13th cent.); it is the ancestor of SHINTY.

**Huron, Lake,** second largest (59,596 km²/23,010 sq mi) of the GREAT LAKES, on the US–Canada border. It is 332 km (206 mi) long and up to 295 km (183 mi) wide, with a surface elevation of 177 km (580 ft). It receives the waters of Lake Superior through the St Marys R. and of Lake Michigan through the Straits of Mackinac, and it drains S into Lake Erie through the St Clair R.–Lake St Clair–Detroit R. system.

**Huron Indians,** confederation of four NORTH AMERICAN INDIAN groups of the Eastern Woodlands who spoke Wyandot, (see AMERICAN INDIAN LANGUAGES). Numbering about 20,000 in the 17th cent., they lived in palisaded villages near Georgian Bay in Ontario and grew tobacco. In the mid-17th cent. the Iroquois (see IROQUOIS CONFEDERACY) hunted them down relentlessly. In 1750 they settled in Ohio; there they were known as the Wyandot to the British, with whom they sided in the AMERICAN REVOLUTION. In 1867 they were removed to NE Oklahoma, where some hundreds now live as citizens, the tribe having been terminated in 1959.

**hurricane,** tropical CYCLONE formed over the N Atlantic Ocean in which the winds attain speeds greater than 120 km/hr (75 mph). A tropical cyclone passes through two stages, tropical depression and tropical storm, before reaching hurricane force. An average of 3.5 tropical storms per year become hurricanes; one to three of these approach the US coast. Hurricanes usually develop between July and October. A hurricane is nearly circular in shape, and its winds cover an area about 800 km (500 mi) in diameter. As a result of the extremely low central air pressure (around 72 cm/28.35 in of mercury), air spirals inwards towards the hurricane's eye, an almost calm area about 30 km (20 mi) in diameter. Hurricanes, which may last from 1 to 30 days, usually move westwards in their early stages and then curve northwards towards the pole. Deriving their energy from warm tropical ocean water, hurricanes weaken after prolonged contact with colder northern ocean waters, becoming extratropical cyclones; they decay rapidly after moving over land areas. The high winds, coastal flooding, and torrential rains associated with a hurricane may cause enormous damage. Tropical cyclones that form over the Pacific Ocean are called typhoons.

**Hurston, Zora Neale,** 1901–60, black American writer. An anthropologist who sympathetically interpreted black folktales in such collections as *Mules and Men* (1935) and *Tell My Horse* (1938), Hurston also wrote two novels, *Jonah's Gourd Vine* (1934) and *Their Eyes Were Watching God* (1937).

**Husák, Gustav** (ˌhoohsahk), 1913–, Czechoslovakian Communist leader. After the Soviet-led invasion of 1968, he succeeded (1969) DUBČEK as Communist Party leader. He reestablished close ties with the Soviet Union and reinstituted tight party control over the government. After 1975 he was president of the country, but was obliged to relinquish the party leadership to Miklos JAKES in late 1987.

**Husayn** or **Hussein Ibn Ali,** 626–80, grandson of the Prophet MUHAMMAD and son of 'ALI IBN ABI TALIB. Having come into conflict with the Umayyads over succession to the CALIPHATE, his small contingent was routed and he was killed by an Umayyad force at Karbala in Iraq in 680. His death became a focal point of the sacred calendar of SHI'ISM with the annual celebration of ASHURA. His descendants are seen by Shi'ites as the legitimate line of IMAMS.

**Husayn ibn Ali,** 1856–1931, Arabian political and religious leader. He led the revolt against the Turks and made himself (1916) king of the Hejaz, but he was overthrown (1924) by IBN SAUD. His effort to claim the title of caliph was also unsuccessful. He was the father of ABDULLAH of Jordan and FAISAL I of Iraq.

**Hu Shih** (hooh shuh), 1891–1962, Chinese philosopher in Republican China. He promoted vernacular literature to replace writing in the

classical style. He was ambassador to the US (1938–42) and chancellor of Peking Univ. (1946–48).

**Huss, John** (hus), Czech *Jan Hus,* 1372?–1415, Czech religious reformer. A priest, he was influenced early by the writings of John WYCLIF. Huss attacked the abuses of the clergy and was supported by Holy Roman Emperor WENCESLAUS, who made him rector of the Univ. of Prague (1409). Huss, however, incurred the hostility of the archbishop of Prague, who had him excommunicated in 1411. He then wrote his chief works, including *De ecclesia,* in exile near Tabor. Because Huss denied the infallibility of an immoral pope and asserted the ultimate authority of Scripture over the church, he is generally considered a forerunner of the Protestant REFORMATION. The Emperor SIGISMUND invited him to defend his views at the Council of Constance (1414–18) and granted him a safe-conduct. In 1414 Huss presented himself at the council, which refused to recognize his safe-conduct, tried him as a heretic, and burned him at the stake.

**Hussein, Saddam,** 1937–, president of IRAQ (1979–). A leader of the socialist Baath Party, a fervently nationalist Arab group, he was the long-time strongman of Iraq before actually becoming president. In 1980 he escalated a long-standing border dispute with Iran into a full-scale war, which was to last until 1988.

**Hussein I,** 1935–, king of JORDAN (1953–). He has generally maintained a moderate course in his relations with the West and other Arab leaders. The loss of W Jordan to Israel in the 1967 ARAB–ISRAELI WAR led to hostility between Hussein and the Palestinian guerrilla movement and to a civil war (1970) in Jordan that Hussein won, achieving stronger control of the country. In 1974 he agreed to relinquish all Jordanian claims to the Jordanian WEST BANK to the PALESTINE LIBERATION ORGANIZATION (PLO). In 1978 Hussein married his fourth wife, an American, Elizabeth Halaby, who took the name Queen Noor al-Hussein.

**Husserl, Edmund,** 1859–1938, German philosopher, founder of PHENOMENOLOGY. A student of BRENTANO, Husserl offered a descriptive study of consciousness for the purpose of discovering the laws by which experiences are had, whether of the objective world or of pure imagination. He concluded that consciousness has no life apart from the objects it considers. In his later work he moved toward IDEALISM, denying that objects exist outside consciousness. His chief works were *Logical Investigations* (1900–01) and *Ideas for a Pure Phenomenology* (1907). His most prominent pupil was HEIDEGGER.

**Hussites,** 15th-cent. religious reformers in Bohemia and Moravia, followers of John HUSS. In the Four Articles of Prague (1420) they called for freedom of preaching, communion in both bread and wine, limits to church property holding, and civil punishment of mortal sin. Papal and imperial forces opposed the reformers in the Hussite Wars, during which the Hussites split into two factions, the moderate Utraquists and the radical Taborites. The Utraquists were reconciled to the church in 1436, but the Taborites remained obstinate and were finally defeated at Lipany (1434). During the REFORMATION, some Utraquists became Lutherans. The MORAVIAN CHURCH probably descended from the Taborites.

**Huston, John,** 1906–87, American film director. His films include *The Maltese Falcon* (1941); *The Treasure of the Sierra Madre* (1947), with his father, the actor Walter Huston (1884–1950); *The African Queen* (1951); *Moby Dick* (1956); *Wise Blood* (1979); and *Annie* (1982).

**Hutchinson, Lucy,** 1619–c.1675, English writer. Her biography of her husband, the regicide Colonel Hutchinson, *Memoirs of the Life of Colonel Hutchinson* (first published 1806) gives a vivid insight into the implications of the CIVIL WAR in rural England. She also wrote her autobiography.

**Hutchinson, Thomas,** 1711–80, colonial governor of MASSACHUSETTS, US (1771–74). As lieutenant governor (1758–71) and governor, he aroused the colonists' anger by supporting strict enforcement of unpopular British measures.

**Hutton, James,** 1726–97, Scottish geologist who formulated controversial theories of the origin of the earth (see UNIFORMITARIANISM) which paved the way to modern geology. His great work was *The Theory of the Earth* (2 vol., 1795). John Playfair, in his *Illustrations of the Huttonian Theory of the Earth* (1802), simplified Hutton's theories.

**Huxley, Aldous (Leonard),** 1894–1963, English author; grandson of T.H. HUXLEY. His early novels, *Crome Yellow* (1921), *Antic Hay* (1923), and *Point Counter Point* (1928) satirize the contemporary intelligentsia. His most influential work, *Brave New World* (1932), describes a nightmarish 25th-cent. utopia. His later novels of ideas include *Eyeless in Gaza* (1936) and *Ape and Essence* (1948). After World War II he became strongly interested in mysticism and Eastern philosophy. Huxley also published many short stories and essays.

**Huxley, Andrew Fielding,** 1917–, English physiologist; half brother of Aldous and grandson of Thomas HUXLEY. He and Alan HODGKIN shared with Sir John Eccles the 1963 Nobel Prize for physiology or medicine for their analysis of the electrical and chemical events in nerve-cell discharge.

**Huxley, Thomas Henry,** 1825–95, English biologist and educator. He gave up his own biological research to become an influential science publicist and was the principal exponent in England of Charles DARWIN's theory of EVOLUTION. An agnostic (see AGNOSTICISM), he doubted all things not immediately open to logical analysis and scientific verification. However, he placed human ethics outside the scope of materialistic evolutionary processes, and believed that progress was achieved by the human control of evolution. He was a prominent member of the London School Board, and an active protagonist for technical and science education.

**Hu Yaobang,** 1915–89, Chinese Communist leader. A prominent moderate and associate of DENG XIAOPING, he was named (1980) general secretary of the Chinese Communist Party. After the removal of HUA GUOFENG, Hu became (1981) party chairman until the post was abolished in 1982, when he again became general secretary. However, in early 1987 he was forced to resign after student demonstrations in favour of greater democracy had alarmed the still powerful conservative elements in the ruling hierarchy.

**Huygens, Christiaan** (ˌhoygəns), 1629–95, Dutch mathematician and physicist; son of Constantijn HUYGENS. He improved telescopic lenses and was the first person to interpret correctly the ring structure surrounding SATURN; he also discovered its satellite Titan. He was the first to use a pendulum in clocks. Huygens developed a wave theory of LIGHT opposed to Isaac NEWTON's corpuscular theory and formulated Huygens's principle of light waves, which holds that every point on a wave front is a source of new waves. He discovered that light could be polarized (see POLARIZED LIGHT) whilst experimenting with the mineral calcite.

**Huygens, Constantijn,** 1596–1687, Dutch humanist and poet. His poems, descriptive and satirical, were highly esteemed, and he was knighted by both the English and French monarchs. Love for his wife is expressed in the graceful ornamental verse of *Daghwerck* (1639).

**Hwang Ho:** see YELLOW RIVER.

**hyacinth,** bulbous herb (genus *Hyacinthus*) of the LILY family, native to the Mediterranean region and South Africa. The common hyacinth, cultivated primarily in Holland, has a single spike of fragrant flowers in shades of red, blue, white, or yellow. The smaller, related grape hyacinth (*Muscari*), mostly blue-flowered, is also commonly cultivated.

**hyaena,** chiefly nocturnal MAMMAL of the family Hyaenidae of Africa and SW Asia. Known for its cry, which sounds like maniacal laughter, it feeds mostly on carrion and can crush bones with its strong teeth and jaws. Three species are generally recognized: the 150-cm (5-ft) long spotted hyaena (*Crocuta crocuta*) of sub-Saharan Africa; the smaller striped hyaena (*Hyaena hyaena*) of Asia and N Africa; and the brown hyaena (*H. brunnea*) of S Africa.

**Hyatt, John Wesley,** 1837–1920, American inventor. He is known especially for his development of CELLULOID, which he manufactured with his brothers beginning in 1872. Among his other inventions were the Hyatt filter, a means of chemically purifying water while it is in motion, and a widely used type of roller bearing.

**hybrid,** term of plant and animal breeders for the offspring of a cross between two different subspecies or species. In genetics it is the term for the offspring of parents differing in any genetic characteristic.

**Hyde, Douglas,** 1860–1949, Irish scholar and political leader. He was largely responsible for the revival of the Irish language and literature through his founding of the Gaelic League in 1893. He was president of Eire (1938–45).

**Hyde, Edward:** see CLARENDON, EDWARD HYDE, 1st EARL OF.

**Hyde Park,** an open space in the centre of London, maintained by the crown. It stretches from Park Lane in the E to Kensington Gardens in the W. Within the park is the large ornamental lake known as the Serpentine. There is a large monumental gateway in the SE, at Hyde Park Corner, and just to the NE of the park is Marble Arch (a monumental arch originally erected at the entrance to Buckingham Palace), near which is 'Speakers' Corner' where members of the public make impromptu political speeches.

**Hyderabad,** former princely state (ruler, the Nizam), S central India, now divided among the states of Karnataka, Maharashtra, and Andhra Pradesh. Located almost entirely on the Deccan plateau, it has cotton, rice and other food grain crops, and deposits of iron and coal. The seat of an ancient Hindu civilization, it fell to the MOGULS in the 17th cent. Following the failure of protracted negotiations with the (Muslim) Nizam, it was occupied by India in 1949. In 1950 it was divided among neighbouring states. **Hyderabad,** city (1981 pop. 2,187,262), capital of Andhra Pradesh state, is an administrative, industrial and commercial centre. Its historic structures include the 16th-cent. Char Minar ('four minarets') and Old Bridge.

**Hyderabad,** city (1981 est. pop. 795,000), S Pakistan. The fifth largest city in Pakistan, it has chemical, engineering, and other industries. It was founded in 1768 and was the capital of the emirs of Sind. The British EAST INDIA COMPANY occupied it when the Sind became (1839) a British protectorate. The birthplace of the MOGUL emperor AKBAR is nearby.

**hydra,** freshwater organism (class Hydrozoa) widely distributed in lakes, ponds, and sluggish streams; a COELENTERATE. Hydras are small, cylindrical, solitary animals, about 2.5 cm (1 in) long, that attach themselves temporarily to submerged objects by means of a disc at the anal end. Tentacles equipped with stinging cells (nematocysts) surround the mouth; hydras use these to stun their prey.

The looping movement of a **hydra**

**Hydra,** Gr. *Ydra*, island off the Argolis peninsula, Greece. Served by ferries and hydrofoils, the rocky island, 14 km (9 mi) by 3 km (1.8 mi), has a population of c.2500. As part of the Venetian empire, it was a busy centre of shipbuilding in the 17th and 18th cent. and supported a population of almost 30,000.

**Hydra,** in Greek mythology, many-headed water serpent. When one of its heads was cut off, two new ones appeared. It was killed by HERCULES, who burned the neck after decapitation.

**hydrangea,** common and generic name for members of the family Hydrangeaceae, formerly classified in the family Saxifragaceae. These shrubs and climbers grow especially well in coastal areas. The common hydrangea (*H. macrophylla*) is a deciduous shrub with a dense mass of florets arranged in a large, globular head. Flower colour varies from blue to red according to soil type. Varieties of this species are generally divided into 'mop heads' (Hortensia group) with rounded floret clusters, and 'lace caps' (Normalis group) with flattened floret clusters.

**hydraulic machinery,** machines that derive their power from the motion or pressure of water or some other liquid. Water or oil under pressure is commonly used as a source of power for many types of machines. The hydraulic press, whose uses include forming three-dimensional objects from sheet metal or plastics and compressing large objects, consists of two cylinders of different size, each filled with liquid and fitted with a piston, and each connected to a pipe filled with the same liquid. According to Pascal's law, pressure exerted upon the smaller piston is transmitted undiminished through the liquid to the surface of the larger piston, which is forced upwards. A small pressure exerted on the smaller piston creates a stronger force on the larger piston because the area of the latter is larger and the distance it moves is less. The same principle is used to power the hydraulic jack, which is used to lift heavy loads. The hydraulic LIFT is also an application of Pascal's law.

**hydraulics,** branch of engineering that studies the mechanical properties of fluids. There are two subdivisions. *Hydrostatics,* the study of liquids at rest, involves the problems of buoyancy and flotation, pressures on dams and submerged devices, and hydraulic presses. *Hydrokinetics,* the study of liquids in motion, is concerned with such matters as friction and turbulence generated in pipes by flowing liquids, and the use of hydraulic pressure in machinery.

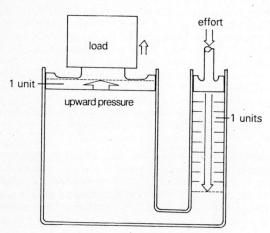

Hydraulics

**hydrocarbon,** any organic compound composed solely of CARBON and HYDROGEN. Hydrocarbons include aliphatic compounds, in which the carbon atoms form a chain, and AROMATIC COMPOUNDS, in which the carbon atoms form stable rings. The aliphatic group is divided into alkanes (e.g., METHANE and PROPANE), alkenes, and alkynes (e.g., ACETYLENE), depending on whether the molecules of the compounds contain, respectively, only single bonds, one or more carbon–carbon double bonds, or one or more carbon–carbon triple bonds. PETROLEUM distillation yields useful fractions that are hydrocarbon mixtures, e.g., diesel oil, PETROL, KEROSENE, home heating oil, lubricating oils, PARAFFIN WAX, and ASPHALT. Coal TAR is also a source of hydrocarbons. Hydrocarbon derivatives contain additional elements, e.g., oxygen, and include ALCOHOLS, aldehydes, ketones, carboxylic acids, and halocarbons.

**hydrochloric acid,** chemical compound formed by dissolving hydrogen chloride (HCl) in water. Most hydrochloric acid produced has a concentration of 30% to 35% hydrogen chloride by weight. Hydrochloric acid is a strong acid (see ACIDS AND BASES) and reacts with most common metals, releasing hydrogen and forming the metal chloride. The major use of hydrochloric acid is in the manufacture of other chemicals. It is also used in pickling (cleaning) metal surfaces, e.g., iron, before galvanizing.

**hydrodynamics:** see FLUID MECHANICS.

**hydroelectric power:** see POWER, ELECTRIC.

**hydrofoil,** finlike device, attached by struts to the hull of a watercraft, that lifts the moving craft above the water's surface. The term also designates the vessel itself. Like an aircraft wing, the foil develops lift as it passes through the water; the hull is raised above the surface, and the reduced water drag permits greater speed. Some hydrofoil vessels are capable of travelling faster than 113 km/hr (70 mph). Hydrofoil vessels are used as ferries in Europe and Asia. A type of hydrofoil called a stabilizer is used on oceangoing passenger ships to minimize the effect of wave action on the vessel.

**hydrogen** (H), gaseous element, discovered by Henry CAVENDISH in 1766. The first element in the PERIODIC TABLE, hydrogen is colourless, odourless, tasteless, slightly soluble in water, and highly explosive. The hot flame produced by a mixture of oxygen and hydrogen is used in welding, and in melting quartz and glass. Normal hydrogen has two atoms in the molecule ($H_2$). The most abundant element in the universe, hydrogen is the major fuel in fusion reactions of the SUN and other STARS. Atmospheric hydrogen has three isotopes: *protium* (nucleus: one proton), the most common; *deuterium,* or heavy hydrogen (nucleus: one proton and one neutron), used in particle accelerators and as a tracer for studying chemical-reaction mechanisms; and *tritium* (nucleus: one proton and two

neutrons), a radioactive gas used in the hydrogen bomb, in luminous paints, and as a tracer. Hydrogen's principal use is in the synthesis of AMMONIA; liquid hydrogen has been greatly used as a rocket fuel, in conjunction with oxygen or fluorine. Deuterium oxide, or heavy water, is used as a moderator in nuclear reactors. See ELEMENT (table); PERIODIC TABLE.

**hydrogen bomb,** weapon deriving a large portion of its energy from the nuclear fusion of hydrogen isotopes. In fusion, lighter elements are joined together to form heavier elements. To enable such light nuclei to fuse, they must approach each other at very high velocities. Since in a hydrogen bomb these velocities are generated by having very high temperatures the weapon is also referred to as a thermonuclear bomb. The presumable structure of a hydrogen bomb is as follows: an ATOMIC BOMB is surrounded by a layer of lithium deuteride (a compound of lithium and deuterium) and then by a tamper, or thick outer layer, frequently of fissionable material, that holds the contents together in order to obtain a larger explosion. The atomic explosion produces neutrons that fission the lithium into helium, tritium, and energy, and also produces the extremely high temperature needed for the subsequent fusion of deuterium with tritium, and tritium with tritium. The first thermonuclear bomb was exploded in 1952 at ENIWETOK by the US, the second in 1953 by the USSR. See also DISARMAMENT, NUCLEAR.

**hydrogen chloride:** see HYDROCHLORIC ACID.

**hydrogen cyanide:** see CYANIDE.

**hydrogen peroxide:** see PEROXIDE.

**hydrology,** study of water and its properties, including its distribution and movement in and through the land areas of the earth. The hydrologic cycle consists of the passage of water from the oceans into the atmosphere; onto, through, and under the lands; and back to the ocean. Hydrology is mainly concerned with the part of the cycle that follows the precipitation of water onto the land and precedes its return to the oceans. See also METEOROLOGY; OCEANOGRAPHY.

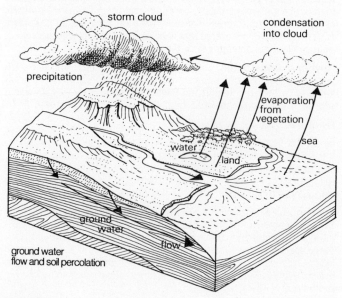

Hydrology

**hydrolysis,** chemical reaction of a compound with WATER, usually resulting in the formation of one or more new compounds. The most common hydrolysis occurs when a salt of a weak acid or weak base (or both) is dissolved in water. Water ionizes into negative hydroxyl ions ($OH^-$) and positive hydrogen ions ($H^+$), which become hydrated to form positive hydronium ions ($H_3O^+$). The salt also breaks up into positive and negative ions, and the formed ions recombine.

**hydrometer,** calibrated glass float used to determine the RELATIVE DENSITY of a liquid. It usually consists of a thin glass tube that is weighted at one end so that it will float upright in a liquid. The scale reading on the tube that is level with the surface of the liquid in which the hydrometer floats indicates the number of times heavier or lighter the liquid is than water, i.e., the specific gravity of the liquid. The hydrometer is based on ARCHIMEDES' PRINCIPLE.

**hydrophobia:** see RABIES.

**hydrophone,** device, used in SONAR apparatus and in certain underwater weapons, that receives underwater sound waves and converts them to electrical energy; the voltage generated can then be read on a meter or played through a loudspeaker. It is the marine equivalent of the MICROPHONE.

**hydrophyte,** plant which grows only in water or waterlogged soil. Frequently such plants are anatomically modified to suit their particular environment.

**hydroponics,** growing of plants without soil, in water (and sometimes a sterile medium, e.g., sand) containing balanced concentrations of essential nutrients. Hydroponics can increase yields of commercial crops because plants are grown closer together than in the field; it also almost eliminates weeds and some pests. The technique is limited by the support required to hold a given plant upright.

**hydroxide,** chemical compound that contains the hydroxyl (—OH) radical. The term refers especially to inorganic compounds. An organic compound that has the hydroxyl radical as a functional group is referred to as an ALCOHOL. Most metal hydroxides are bases. The hydroxides of ALKALI METALS, such as sodium hydroxide (NaOH), are strong bases and are very soluble in water. The hydroxides of ALKALINE-EARTH METALS are less basic, and magnesium hydroxide (MILK OF MAGNESIA) is only slightly basic. Some hydroxides, such as aluminum hydroxide $[Al(OH)_3]$, exhibit AMPHOTERISM. Others such as sodium hydroxide, emit light when crystallizing from the molten state.

**hygrometer,** instrument used to measure the moisture content of a gas, as in determining the relative HUMIDITY of the air. The most common type of hygrometer is the wet- and dry-bulb psychrometer. It consists of two identical mercury thermometers, one of which has a wet wick around its bulb. The sling type of psychrometer is swung around in the air. Water evaporating from the wick absorbs heat from the bulb, causing the thermometer reading to drop. The observer, after reading the dry-bulb temperature and the drop in the wet-bulb temperature, can determine the relative humidity from appropriate tables. Among other kinds of hygrometers are ones that use human hair or electrical resistance of a chemically treated wire, rather than thermometers, to determine moisture content.

**Hyksos** [Egyptian, = rulers of foreign lands], invaders of ancient EGYPT, now substantiated as the XV–XVII dynasties. A northwestern Semitic people, they entered Egypt c.1720–10 BC and subdued the Middle Kingdom pharaohs. The Hyksos established a peaceful, prosperous reign. Their introduction of Canaanite deities and Asian artifacts broke down the isolationism of Egypt.

**hymn,** song of praise, devotion, or thanksgiving, especially of a religious character. Early Christian hymns were mainly biblical texts chanted in unison (see PLAINCHANT). Metrical Latin hymnody, usually four-line stanzas in iambic pentameter, developed from the 4th cent. and was the basis of nearly all Christian hymns until the 16th cent. With the REFORMATION, Protestant hymnody developed; the first Lutheran hymnal was published in WITTENBERG in 1524. Calvinism contributed the Genevan Psalter, containing the familiar doxology tune *Old Hundredth.* Notable English hymn writers of the 18th cent. were Isaac Watts, Charles Wesley (see under WESLEY, JOHN), and William COWPER. In the 19th cent. there was a revived interest in plainchant. Early American settlers used hymn books brought from Europe, until the *Bay Psalm Book* (1640), the earliest American hymnal, was published in Cambridge, Mass. In the late 19th cent. the gospel hymn developed, with lively music and simple text. In the 20th cent. there have been radical variations in church music alongside a newly vital, more conservative hymnody.

**hyperbola:** see CONIC SECTION.

**hyperbolic function:** see article on e.

**hyperbolic geometry:** see NON-EUCLIDEAN GEOMETRY.

**hypergamy** (hie puhgэmi) and **hypogamy,** MARRIAGE systems (found particularly in India) in which partners have to come from groups of different social status. In *hypergamous* systems a woman should marry a man of higher social status than her father, although she can marry an equal, but a man should not marry a woman of higher rank than his.

Hypergamous systems tend to considerable instability. In *hypogamous* marriage systems men are supposed to marry women of higher status than their own.

**Hyperion,** in astronomy, natural satellite of SATURN.

**hypermetropia** or **hyperopia:** see LONGSIGHTEDNESS.

**hyperon:** see ELEMENTARY PARTICLES.

**hypertension,** high blood pressure resulting from an increase in the amount of blood pumped by the heart or from increased resistance to the flow of blood through the small arterial blood vessels (arterioles). When the cause is unknown, the condition is called primary, or essential, hypertension. When a cause can be identified (e.g., a disorder of the adrenal glands, kidneys, or arteries), the condition is known as secondary hypertension. Factors such as age, heredity, obesity, high salt intake, and emotional stress are thought to play a part in the development of essential hypertension. Known as the 'silent killer', hypertension produces few overt symptoms. Untreated, however, it can cause damage to the heart, eyes, kidneys, or brain and ultimately lead to HEART FAILURE or STROKE. Treatment of hypertension includes weight- and salt-control diets and various drugs, including DIURETICS and BETA BLOCKERS.

**hyphen:** see PUNCTUATION.

**hypnosis,** a term which can refer both to a procedure (once known as 'mesmerism', after its early exponent Franz Anton Mesmer (1733–1815); and to the mental state induced by this procedure. The hypnotic state superficially resembles SLEEP, but EEG patterns do not resemble any of the stages of sleep. Subjects under hypnosis display a narrowing of attention, a lack or loss of volition and heightened suggestibility; and may be induced to follow many (but not all) instructions, or to endure painful sensations. A 'post-hypnotic suggestion' is a suggestion or instruction, which the subject is instructed to erase from consciousness on 'awaking', which is subsequently 'activated' by a particular STIMULUS specified by the hypnotist. Hypnosis is sometimes employed therapeutically, as an aid to the recall of lost or repressed memories, and as an aid to eliminating unwanted habits such as smoking or over-eating.

**hypnotic,** drug that induces sleep by depressing brain function. Hypnotics, including the BARBITURATE drugs and nitrazepam, are used to treat insomnia. They can become habit-forming and they often leave hangover effects in the morning. **Sedatives** are used to relieve anxiety, tension, and restlessness without producing sleep. They also act by depressing the central nervous system and the distinction between the two types of drug is not sharply defined; the same drug may have either a sedative or hypnotic effect depending on the conditions of use and dosage.

**hypogamy:** see HYPERGAMY.

**hypoglycaemia,** abnormally low level of blood glucose, the body's chief energy source. It is most often caused by an oversecretion of INSULIN from the pancreas triggered by stress, exercise, fasting, or disorders of the adrenal or pituitary glands, liver, or pancreas; in people with DIABETES it may result from an overdose of insulin. Symptoms range from weakness, fatigue, shakiness, and anxiety to mental disturbances, convulsions, coma, and death if unrelieved by administration of glucose. Long-term treatment involves control of causative factors and diet regulation.

**hypothalamus,** important supervisory centre in the BRAIN. The hypothalamus regulates body temperature, water balance, thirst, hunger, and sexuality. It is also closely connected with emotional activity and sleep and the control of the autonomic NERVOUS SYSTEM and endocrine function (see ENDOCRINE SYSTEM).

**hysterectomy,** surgical removal of the uterus, sometimes including the removal of the cervix, Fallopian tubes, and ovaries (see REPRODUCTIVE SYSTEM). It is performed in cases of malignant tumours, or benign growths causing bleeding and pain. Hysterectomy does not interfere with sexual activity, but it eliminates the possibility of childbearing.

**hysteria,** a NEUROSIS whose symptoms may include paralysis, dissociation, anesthaesia, sensory loss (e.g., blindness), sleep-walking, and hallucination. The term hysteria derives from the Greek *hysteron* [uterus], but it was recognized in the late 19th cent. that hysteria may afflict both men and women. Since the work of Sigmund FREUD and BREUER it has generally been agreed that hysteria is caused by the conversion of a psychological conflict or source of anxiety into a physical symptom.

**I,** chemical symbol of the element IODINE.

**iambic pentameter:** see PENTAMETER.

**Iapetus,** in astronomy, natural satellite of SATURN.

**Iaşi** or **Jassy** (yash, ˌyasee), city (1983 pop. 265,176), E Romania, in Moldavia, near the USSR border. The centre of a farming region, it produces textiles, machinery, and other goods. It was (1565–1859) MOLDAVIA's capital. In World War II its large Jewish population was massacred by the Nazis.

**IATA:** see INTERNATIONAL AIR TRANSPORT ASSOCIATION.

**Ibadan,** city (1981 pop. 2,100,000), SW Nigeria. The chief town of Oyo state and the largest town in West Africa, it is a major commercial and industrial centre, producing canned goods, metal products, palm oil, and chemicals. The centre of a rich agricultural area, it is a market for cocoa beans, which, with cotton, are grown in the region. Founded in the 1830s, it developed into the most powerful Yoruba city-state before coming under British protection in 1893.

**Ibagué,** city (1979 est. pop. 272,625), central Colombia, capital of Tolima dept. It is situated on the principal route between the country's western and central highlands.

**Ibáñez del Campo, Carlos** (ee ˌbanyays dhel ˌkampoh), 1877–1960, president of CHILE (1927–31, 1952–58). An army major, he attained power (1927) as dictator and launched public works programmes and social reforms before being forced into exile. In 1952 he was elected president but proved ineffectual.

**Iberian Peninsula,** SW Europe, c.596,740 km² (230,400 sq mi). Occupied by Spain and Portugal, it is separated from the rest of Europe (NE) by the PYRENEES and from Africa (S) by the Strait of GIBRALTAR.

**Ibert, Jacques** (ee ˌbeə), 1890–1962, French composer. His colourful, tuneful works include *Ports of Call* (1924); and *Divertissement* (1930), for small orchestra.

**ibex,** wild goat (genus *Capra*) found in rugged, mountainous country from central Asia to the Himalayas, S Europe, and NE Africa. Sure-footed and agile, ibexes live in small herds and feed on vegetation. They are sturdily built, with brown to grey coats and heavy horns of varying size; the chin is bearded and the tail short. The adult ibex stands from 75 to 110 cm (2½ to 3½ ft) at the shoulder.

**ibis,** wading BIRD with long, slender, downcurved bill, found in warmer regions of the world. Its body is usually about 60 cm (2 ft) long; most feed on fish and other aquatic animals. The sacred ibis of ancient Egypt (*Threskiornis aethiopica*), a white and black bird, no longer frequents the NILE basin, although it inhabits other parts of Africa.

**Ibiza:** see BALEARIC ISLANDS.

**Ibn al-Haytham** or **Alhazen** (ˌibən el-hiethahm), 965–c.1040, Egyptian mathematician, physicist, and astronomer; b. Persia. His *Optics,* which influenced the work of Johannes KEPLER and René DESCARTES, introduced the important idea that light rays emanate in straight lines in all directions from every point on a luminous surface. In mathematics, al-Haytham elucidated and extended EUCLID's *Elements.*

**Ibn Arabi, Muhyiddin,** 1165–1240, Muslim SUFI. Born in Murcia Ibn Arabi travelled extensively and finally settled in Damascus, where he died. He was the author of the most elaborate theoretical edifice of pantheism in SUFISM.

**Ibn Batuta, Abu Abdallah Mohammed,** 1304–77, Arab traveller; b. Morocco. Between 1325 and 1354 he journeyed extensively throughout Asia and Africa before returning to his native Morocco. He subsequently wrote his *Travels* which has since remained a major source of information on the medieval, particularly Islamic, world.

**Ibn Ezra, Abraham ben Meir,** 1098–1164, Jewish grammarian, commentator, poet, philosopher, and astronomer; b. Spain. Best known as a critical bible commentator, he was the inspiration for Robert BROWNING's poem 'Rabbi Ben Ezra.'

**Ibn Gabirol, Solomon ben Judah,** c.1021–58, Jewish poet and philosopher, also known as Avicebron; b. Spain. He wrote hundreds of poems, both sacred and secular; much of his religious poetry has been incorporated into the Judaic liturgy. His great philosophical work *The Fountain of Life* greatly influenced Christian neo-Platonic thought.

**Ibn Hanbal, Ahmad,** 780–855, Muslim divine and HADITH scholar. A fierce opponent of MU'TAZILA, he endured the famous *mihna*, or inquisition, ordered by the Caliph al-Ma'mun (r.813–33) and his successor to enforce Mu'tazilism as official state doctrine. His piety, emphasis on faith rather than reason, and scripturalist impulse made him the paradigm of Sunnite Islam's longing for doctrinal simplicity and minimalism. See FIQH; KALAM.

**Ibn Khaldun, Abd al Rahman,** 1332–1406, Arab historian; b. Tunisia. After a frustrated political career he retired in 1387 to write his seminal work *Kitab Al Ibar.* One of the most important works of universal history, its introduction, or *Mugaddima*, develops the idea of history as both science and philosophy.

**Ibn Saud** (ˌibən sah-oohd), c.1888–1953, founder of SAUDI ARABIA and its first king. As leader of the Wahabi sect he claimed ancient rights in the area. By 1912 he had conquered the Nejd. In 1924 he triumphed over HUSAYN IBN ALI and became king of the Hejaz. In 1932 he combined the provinces into the kingdom of Saudi Arabia.

**Ibn Taimiyya,** 1263-1328, Hanbalite divine and fundamentalist reformer. A most accomplished scholar and polemicist, he agitated in Damascus against the cult of the saints, pantheistic theosophy, and many other matters, and was often imprisoned. In the 19th and 20th cent., he has exercised a considerable influence of Islamic radicalism and HANBALISM.

**Ibo,** ethnic group in Nigeria, chiefly from SE Nigeria and numbering about 7 million. Receptive to Christianity and education under British colonialism, they became heavily represented in professional, managerial, and technical occupations. They played a major role in securing (1963) Nigerian independence. Political conflict in the 1960s caused the Ibos to secede from Nigeria and form the Republic of BIAFRA. Civil war followed, and by 1970 Biafra had been defeated.

**Ibrahim, Hafiz,** 1870–1932, Egyptian neoclassical poet. A contemporary of Ahmad SHAWQI, he is remembered as the poet of the people, full of passionate concern for social and political issues. One of his best-known poems was written on the occasion of the Dinshaway atrocity (1906).

**Ibrahim Pasha,** 1789–1849, Egyptian general; b. Macedonia. He was the eldest son or stepson of Egyptian ruler MEHMET ALI. During much of his father's reign he commanded the Egyptian army in a series of remarkable victories. In 1824 he was made ruler of S Greece and largely succeeded in defeating the Greek independence movement. In 1827 Ibrahim's success led to the intervention of Britain, France, and Russia, whose combined naval forces destroyed the Turko-Egyptian fleet at Navarino. In 1831 Ibrahim turned on the Ottomans and wrested Syria and much of Anatolia from their control, threatening the Ottoman empire. Renewed intervention by Britain, France, and Russia in 1841 forced Ibrahim to withdraw to Egypt. In 1847 he took over the Egyptian government from his ailing father but finally predeceased him.

**Ibsen, Henrik,** 1828–1906, Norwegian dramatist, probably the most influential figure in modern theatre. He was stage manager and playwright of the National Stage in Bergen (1851–57) and director of the Norwegian Theatre in Oslo (1857–62). Because his early plays went unrecognized or were greeted with hostility, he went to Italy in 1864, and it was there and in Germany that he wrote the bulk of his dramas. Ibsen's work can be divided into three periods. The first phase, that of poetic drama, deals primarily with historical themes, folklore, and romantic pageantry, and includes the tragedy *Brand* (1866) and the existentialist *Peer Gynt* (1867). Then came the realistic social plays for which he is best known, e.g., *Pillars of Society* (1877), *A Doll's House* (1879), *Ghosts* (1881), *An Enemy of the People* (1882), *The Wild Duck* (1884), *Rosmersholm* (1886), and *Hedda Gabler* (1890), in which Ibsen rebelled against sterile and restrictive social conventions. The final period is characterized by a strong emphasis on symbolism, e.g., *The Master Builder* (1892) and *John Gabriel Borkman* (1896), which blend an introspective realism with folk poetry.

**Icarus:** see DAEDALUS.

**ICBM:** see MISSILE, GUIDED.

**iceberg,** mass of ice that has become detached from an ice sheet or GLACIER and is floating in the ocean. Only about one-ninth of its total mass projects above the water. Rocks dropped to the ocean floor by melting icebergs have been studied to determine the range of icebergs during glacial periods. Because of the 1912 collision of the ocean liner TITANIC with an iceberg, a constant census of icebergs is maintained and their locations reported to nearby ships.

**icebreaker,** ship of special hull design and wide beam, with a relatively flat bottom, designed to force its way through ice. When the icebreaker charges into the ice at full speed, its sharply inclined bow, meeting the edge of the ice, slides onto it, and the weight of the vessel causes the ice to collapse. Able to force their way through ice up to 11 m (35 ft) thick, icebreakers have been important in keeping northern waterways open.

**ice cream,** sweet frozen food, churned from milk or vegetable fat and milk solids, sugar, flavouring, a stabilizer (usually gelatin), and sometimes eggs, fruits, or nuts. Marco POLO brought back reports of flavoured, iced foods from the Far East. From Italy the confection spread to France and England, reaching as far as America by the early 18th cent. Commercial manufacture of ice cream began in the mid 19th cent. and has become an important industry.

**Iceland,** Icel. *Island,* officially the Republic of Iceland, republic (1987 pop. 240,443), 102,819 km² (39,698 sq mi), the westernmost state of Europe, occupying an island in the Atlantic Ocean just S of the Arctic Circle. REYKJAVÍK is the capital. Iceland, whose coasts are indented by deep fjords, is a plateau averaging 610 m (2000 ft) in height and culminating in vast icefields. There are about 200 volcanoes, many still active. Hot springs abound and are used for inexpensive heating. Only about one-quarter of the island is habitable, and most settlements are on the coast. The climate is relatively mild and humid in the W and S, and polar and tundralike in the N and E. Fishing is the most important industry, with codfish and herring the chief exports. Agriculture is limited (hay, potatoes, turnips), but sheep, horses, and cattle are grazed extensively. Aside from aluminum smelting there is little heavy industry, and imports provide most of the country's needs. The GNP is $2,469 million and the GNP per capita is $10,270 (1983). The Lutheran Church is established. Icelandic (Old Norse) is the official language; Old Norse literature reached its greatest flowering in Iceland.

*History.* Iceland was settled (c.850-75) by the Norse (see VIKINGS). A general assembly, the ALTHING, was established in 930 and Christianity

was introduced c.1000. Norwegian rule was imposed after 1261, and in 1380 Iceland, with Norway, passed to the Danish crown, inaugurating a national decline that lasted to 1550. The 17th and 18th cent. were disastrous: pirate raids destroyed trade; epidemics and volcanic eruptions killed a large part of the population; and a private trade monopoly, created in Copenhagen in 1602, caused economic ruin. The 19th cent. brought a rebirth of national culture and a strong independence movement led by Jón Sigurðsson. A constitution and limited home rule were granted in 1874, and Iceland became a sovereign state in personal union with DENMARK in 1918. In WORLD WAR II British and US forces defended the island. Icelanders voted in 1944 to end the union with Denmark, and an independent republic was proclaimed on 17 June 1944. Disputes with the UK over fishing rights in Iceland's waters resulted in a four-month break in diplomatic relations before a settlement was reached in 1976. In 1980 Vigdís Finnbogadóttir was elected president of Iceland and became the republic's first female head of state.

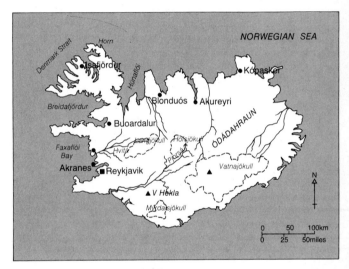

Iceland

**Icelandic language,** member of the North Germanic, or Scandinavian, group of the Germanic subfamily of the Indo-European family of languages. See LANGUAGE (table).

**Iceland spar,** colourless variety of crystallized CALCITE, known for its properties of transparency and double refraction, found primarily in Iceland. It is used chiefly in the manufacture of Nicol prisms.

**ice skating:** see SKATING.

**iconoclasm** [Gr., = image-breaking], opposition to the religious use of images. Religious pictures and statues were an early feature of Christian worship (see ICONOGRAPHY). Opponents of their use claimed that they led to idolatry. Iconoclasm flourished in Asia Minor in the 8th and 9th cent. and was favoured by several Byzantine emperors. Opponents of iconoclasm were Popes Gregory II and ADRIAN I and Empress IRENE, who restored the images. Iconoclasm was rejected at the Second Council of NICAEA (787).

**iconography,** in art history, the study and interpretation of figural representations and their symbolic meanings. Each epoch develops its own iconography, and the term is qualified to indicate specific study areas, e.g., the iconography of Egyptian deities, Buddhist or Hindu iconography, Byzantine iconography. The aim of iconography is to recover and express the thought from which a convention or representation has arisen, particularly in interpreting symbols. For example, the medieval reminder of the transitory quality of earthly pleasure was symbolized by a skull, candle, and hourglass. In Christian iconography, one of the richest and most varied in art, the symbolic code includes the use of the dove to signify the Holy Spirit and the fish to symbolize Christ (from an acrostic of the Greek *ichthus*). In every art the conventions and symbols change with time and can often be recovered only by intensive study. Among the foremost iconographic scholars are Émile Mâle, Aby Warburg, and Erwin Panofsky.

**Ictinus,** fl. 2nd half of 5th cent. BC, Greek architect. With CALLICRATES as his associate, he built the PARTHENON on the Acropolis at Athens (447–432 BC).

**Id,** in PSYCHOANALYSIS, one of the components of Sigmund FREUD's model of the psychic apparatus, together with the EGO and the SUPEREGO. The Id is the most primitive part of the psyche, the seat of unconscious desires governed by the 'pleasure principle'.

**Idaho,** state of the US (1984 est. pop. 1,001,00), area 216,413 km² (83,557 sq mi), located in the NW and bordered by Montana and Wyoming (E), Utah and Nevada (S), Oregon and Washington (W), and the Canadian province of British Columbia (N). BOISE is the capital, and Pocatello and Idaho Falls are the other large cities. Idaho lies within the ROCKY MTS and is heavily forested. In the southwest the SNAKE R. cuts deep gorges, one of which is the deepest in the US, Hell's Canyon (2408 m/7900 ft). Two-thirds of the state is controlled by the federal government, including Yellowstone National Park. Agriculture is the major economic sector, led by cattle ranching and dairying. The state is the chief producer of potatoes in the US, and wheat, barley, hay, timber, and wood products are also important. It is the largest silver producer, and in addition zinc, phosphate, lead, and gold are mined. Less than 18% of Idaho's population lives in metropolitan areas, and the state's population grew by one-third in the 1970s. The indigenous inhabitants were the Nez Percé and Shoshone tribes; the first Europeans to arrive were fur trappers in the first half of the 19th cent. Settlers poured in after gold and silver were discovered in the 1860s, and after them came the railways and cattle-ranchers. In recent years, the Snake R. projects have provided a huge hydroelectrical capacity and a greatly expanded water supply for irrigated agriculture.

**ideal gas:** see GAS LAWS.

**idealism,** in philosophy, the attempt to account for all objects in nature and experience as representations of the mind, and sometimes to assign to such representations a higher order of existence. It is opposed to MATERIALISM and NATURALISM. Early idealism (e.g., that of PLATO) conceived a world in which eternal ideas constituted reality; in modern times idealism (e.g., that of George BERKELEY in the 18th cent.) has come to refer the source of ideas to the individual's consciousness. In KANT's transcendental idealism, the phenomenal world of human understanding opposes a world of things-in-themselves, while the later German idealists (e.g., FICHTE, SCHELLING, and HEGEL) treated all reality as the creation of mind or spirit. More recent idealists include F.H. BRADLEY and CROCE.

**identikit,** system used by POLICE for reconstructing the facial appearance of suspects from witnesses' descriptions. Identikit was developed by Hugh D. MacDonald, and used artists' drawings of facial features, which were put together to make up a composite picture. It was first used by the Los Angeles police in 1959, and introduced to the UK by SCOTLAND YARD in 1961. It has now been replaced by a 'photofit' system, developed for Scotland Yard by Jacques Penry in 1970. Photofit is a similar system placing together photographs of various facial features (e.g., hair, mouth, nose) chosen by witnesses. With the advent of computer technology, even more sophisticated systems are now being developed.

**identity:** see EQUATION.

**ideology,** system of ideas, or world view, expressing the beliefs and values of a particular class or group and serving to rationalize their interests. First employed by the French philosopher De Tracy in about 1796 to mean 'the science of ideas', the word was used by MARX to mean a misleading or partial account of reality, particularly that associated with the dominant class. In so far as this ruling ideology was accepted by the dominated, it represented 'false consciousness' on their part. But the existence of an ideology need not entail a conscious attempt by one group to mislead others for their own advantage. An ideological view is usually experienced as the truth, and some writers cast doubt on the possibility of a non-ideological view when they define ideology simply as a framework of interpretation by means of which a particular group makes sense of the world. Nevertheless, the use of ideology in the sense of a distorted view capable of being contrasted with objective reality has become commonplace. There is also the important sense of ideology as a fighting creed; a set of ideals, formulas, and symbols of sufficient power and importance to be able to inspire a group to action. *Ideological warfare* means a struggle between opposing belief-systems, such as capitalism and communism, for the allegiance of third parties, or simply the attempt to influence the population of a rival power, especially by means of PROPAGANDA. In the 1960s the American sociologist Daniel Bell and others posited 'the end of ideology', by which they meant the inability of the great 19th cent. ideologies, particularly MARXISM, to explain the modern world and inspire people to action. They noted what appeared to be a growing consensus of values between political parties in the West, and suggested that growing affluence had taken the steam out of violently partisan disputes about the justice of the existing system. However, the world recession of the 1970s, the neo-liberalism and MONETARISM of the New Right in the 1980s, and the radical responses to these developments by the New Left indicate that the clash of ideologies is far from dead.

**Ides:** see CALENDAR.

**Ido** (ˌeedoh), short name of Esperandido, an artificial language that is a simplified version of Esperanto. See INTERNATIONAL LANGUAGE.

**Idrisi** or **Edrisi** (iˌdreesee, e-), c.1099–c.1165–86, Arab geographer. Under the protection of Roger II, king of Sicily, he drew on all available sources to produce a planisphere and 70 maps of the world as then known in a volume called the *Book of Roger*.

**Ieyasu** (eejeˌjahsooh), see TOKUGAWA IEYASU.

**Ife,** city (1987 est. pop. 176,000), SW Nigeria, at the intersection of the roads from IBADAN (64 km/40 mi to the west), ILESHA, and ONDO. It trades in agricultural products including cocoa, nuts, and palm products. Ife is one of the oldest towns of the Yoruba peoples and remains their chief religious centre. By the 11th cent. it was the capital of a well established kingdom. Artisans produced terracotta heads and bronze pieces made by the cire perdue process for which the Ife kingdom is famous. It became a university town in 1961.

Terracotta head from **Ife**

**Ignatius of Antioch, Saint,** d. c.107, bishop of Antioch (Turkey) and Christian martyr. He wrote letters to Christian communities in Rome and

Asia Minor to combat heresy. He stressed the virgin birth, the TRINITY, and the role of the bishop, and was the first Christian writer to use the word *Catholic*. Feast: 17 Oct.

**Ignatius of Constantinople, Saint**, c.800–77, Greek churchman, patriarch of CONSTANTINOPLE. A son of Byzantine Emperor MICHAEL I, he was castrated and imprisoned by Emperor LEO V to prevent his accession. In 846 or 847 he was made patriarch and opposed ICONOCLASM. In 858 Ignatius was replaced with PHOTIUS, but on the accession (867) of BASIL I, Ignatius again became patriarch and was confirmed by the Fourth Council of CONSTANTINOPLE. Feast: 23 Oct.

**Ignatius of Loyola, Saint**, 1491–1556, Spanish churchman, founder of the JESUITS. A soldier, he was converted in 1521 and began to study religion. In 1534, in Paris, he and six others took vows of poverty and chastity, and were later (1537) ordained. They were received (1538) by the pope, and in 1540 Ignatius won papal approval for his *Formula* for a new order. In 1541 he was elected general of the order, a post he held until his death. Ignatius was a leader in the COUNTER-REFORMATION, but he was more interested in education and missionary work than in converting Protestants. His *Spiritual Exercises* are a major devotional work. Feast: 31 July.

**igneous rock:** see ROCK.

**iguana,** large LIZARD (family Iguanidae) found in tropical America and the GALAPAGOS ISLANDS. The common iguana (*Iguana iguana*), a tree-living species found along streams from Mexico to N South America, is bright green with a crest of spines from the neck to the striped tail. Its tail accounts for two thirds of its length (90–180 cm/3–6 ft). The unique marine lizard, the marine iguana, is found only on the Galapagos islands. In the Old World, the niche filled by iguanas is occupied by AGAMAS.

Land **iguana** from the Galapagos Islands

**Iguazú Falls,** waterfalls 19 km (11 mi) upstream on the Iguazú R. from its confluence with the upper PARANÁ R. and situated on the boundary between Brazil and Argentina. Above the falls the river opens to a width of 4 km (2.5 mi) and 1750 m³ (2290 cu yd) of water fall each second over the 275 faces of the falls. These falls in conjunction with the recently completed ITAIPÚ hydroelectric dam have stimulated an active tourist industry in the region and the growth of local towns such as PUERTO IGUAÇU in Argentina, Foz Do Iguaçu in Brazil and Puerto Stroessner in Paraguay.

**Ihara Saikaku,** 1642–93, Japanese writer. He wrote poetry until the age of 40, then turned to prose fiction. His themes were love and sex, the samurai code, and the daily life of the merchant class into which he was born. His best-known stories are in *The Life of an Amorous Woman* (1686; tr. 1963), *Five Women Who Loved Love* (1686; tr. 1956), and *The Japanese Family Storehouse (1688; tr. 1959)*.

**IJsselmeer** (ˌiesəlˈmeə), shallow freshwater lake, NW Netherlands, created when much of the old Zuider Zee, an inlet of the North Sea, was enclosed in 1932 by two dams totalling 31 km (19 mi) in length. During

the next half century, more than 2200 km² (850 sq mi) of fertile farmland, in five polders (tracts), was reclaimed from the IJsselmeer.

**Ikeda Hayato** (eeˌkaydah), 1899–1965, Japanese prime minister (1960–64). A Liberal-Democrat, he was finance minister (1949–52, 1956–57). As prime minister he stressed economic progress.

**Ikhnaton** or **Akhenaton** (äˈkənäˌtən), d. c.1354 BC, Egyptian king (c.1372–54) of the XVIII dynasty; son of Amenhotep III. A religious innovator, he abandoned polytheism to embrace an absolute solar monotheism, holding that the sun alone was God and he the sun's physical son. A new school of artists abandoned convention and returned to nature (to glorify the sun). His fanaticism was his undoing; he defaced earlier monuments, arousing the anger of the priests and the people. Neglecting the provinces, he left to his successors only EGYPT and the upper NILE valley, not the empire he had inherited. Of the art works of his reign, the bust of his wife, NEFERTITI, is the most famous. He is the subject of the opera *Akhenaton* by Philip Glass.

**Îles Crozet:** see FRENCH SOUTHERN AND ANTARCTIC LANDS.

**Îles d'Hyères** (eeldee-ˌeə), group of islands off the coast of Provence, SE France. In the past the islands have been a stronghold of pirates and of others seeking a refuge from the law. They are noted for their maquis vegetation; Mediterranean flora of pine and evergreen oak, with heather, cistus, and many other flowering shrubs. The Île de Port Cros has been designated a national park on account of the richness of its flora and fauna.

**Ilesha,** city (1981 pop, 306,200), Oyo state, SW Nigeria. Its exports include cocoa, cotton, and palm oil.

**Îles Kerguelen:** see FRENCH SOUTHERN AND ANTARCTIC LANDS.

**Ilf, Ilya Arnoldovich** (eelf), pseud. of **Ilya Arnoldovich Fainzilberg** 1897–1937, Russian writer. He was joint author with Yevgeny PETROV of a hugely popular satirical novel, *The Twelve Chairs* (1928), whose anti-hero, the master crook Ostap Bender, was active during the New Economic Policy period (1921–28).

**Iliad:** see HOMER.

**Ilion** or **Ilium:** see TROY.

**Illia, Arturo,** 1900–, president of Argentina (1963–66). A physician, he was elected president with only 25% of the vote. He was unable to deal effectively with the country's deteriorating economy or with the Peronists. In addition, he cancelled Argentina's petroleum contracts with foreign countries. He was deposed by military leaders in 1966.

**Illinois,** state of the US Midwest (1984 est. pop. 11,511,000), area 146,076 km² (56,400 sq mi), bordered by Lake Michigan, Indiana, and Kentucky (E), Missouri and Iowa (W), and Wisconsin (N). The capital is SPRINGFIELD, and CHICAGO, the third largest city and metropolitan area in the US, is a major centre of communications, industry, commerce, and finance. Other important cities are Peoria and Rockford. Most of Illinois consists of broad, fertile, level plains drained by more than 275 rivers, including the MISSISSIPPI and OHIO, which border the state to the W and SE respectively. Illinois has one of the country's most productive economies, led by manufacturing, principally of machinery, electrical equipment, steel and other products, and chemicals. It is also the leading producer of soybeans, has the second largest output of pigs and corn, and earns income from cattle, hay, and wheat. There is also some coal, petroleum, and fluorspar. Illinois has an advantageous central location in the US, and the port of Chicago is linked to the Atlantic via the GREAT LAKES and SAINT LAWRENCE SEAWAY. In 1980 over 80% of the population lived in metropolitan areas, 78% was non-Hispanic white, 15% was black, and almost 6% was of Spanish origin. Indian tribes, including the Illinois, Sac, and Fox, lived in the area when French explorers arrived in the late 17th cent. After a brief period of British rule it passed to the US at the end of the American Revolution, and in 1842 the Black Hawk War ended Indian resistance. Abraham LINCOLN launched his political career from Illinois and in the late 19th cent. there was unrest both among farmers, in the Granger Movement, and labourers. New oilfields were discovered in 1937, and industrial growth continued until the present, although heavy industry suffered a serious decline in the 1980s. In 1980 the first US president born in Illinois, Ronald REAGAN, was elected.

**Illinois Indians,** confederation of NORTH AMERICAN INDIAN tribes of the Eastern Woodlands, who spoke an Algonquian language (see AMERICAN INDIAN LANGUAGES). In the mid-17th cent. 6500 Illinois lived in the N Illinois area, but by 1750 warfare had reduced them to 2000. They were all but exterminated in retaliation for the assassination of PONTIAC by a member of the Illinois tribe. In 1833 the survivors moved West. Descendants have lived on a reservation in NE Oklahoma, although few now remain.

**illumination,** in art, decoration of manuscripts and books with coloured and gilded pictures, decorated initials, and ornamental borders. Both ink outline and colour drawings were common, the colour medium usually being TEMPERA. Executed largely in monasteries, illuminations were commonly applied to religious books, including gospels, psalters, and BOOKS OF HOURS. The earliest known illustrated rolls are from ancient Egypt, e.g., BOOK OF THE DEAD. It is thought that by the 2nd cent. AD the papyrus roll was replaced by the parchment codex (leaved book), which produced a compact framework for illuminations. Outstanding examples of the art of illumination include the 7th- and 8th-cent. works of the Irish school, with their rich geometric designs and human and animal interlacing, e.g., *Book of Kells;* Romanesque illumination of the 12th cent., with its beautifully decorated initials and stylized figures, e.g., Winchester Bible; Gothic miniatures of the 13th cent., strikingly parallel to STAINED GLASS in colour and outline; and works of the early 15th cent., marked by realism, elegance, and a wealth of marginal ornament, e.g., *Très Riches Heures.* Illumination continued as a vigorous form until the end of the 15th cent., when it began to be replaced by woodblock printing. Illumination was also highly developed in the Middle East and the Orient. See ISLAMIC ART AND ARCHITECTURE; MUGHAL ART AND ARCHITECTURE; PERSIAN ART AND ARCHITECTURE.

**illustration,** picture or decoration used in a book to embellish or clarify the text. Modern illustration began in the 15th. cent. with the block book, after the decline of ILLUMINATION. During the 16th and 17th cent. copperplate ENGRAVING and ETCHING tended to replace the WOODCUT. At the end of the 18th cent. illustration was revolutionized by the invention of LITHOGRAPHY and by BEWICK's use of wood engraving, processes exploited by such masters as DAUMIER and DORÉ. In the late 19th cent. photomechanical processes made possible the mass reproduction of illustrations. While these methods were used to great effect by illustrators such as Aubrey BEARDSLEY and Howard Pyle, others, e.g., William MORRIS, MATTISSE, ROUAULT, PICASSO, and Rockwell KENT, turned to hand processes. Other artists famous for their illustrations are DÜRER, William HOGARTH, William BLAKE, CRUIKSHANK, MANET, and Winslow HOMER. Some of the finest illustrations have been executed for CHILDREN'S LITERATURE. Many, from Edward LEAR to Beatrix POTTER to Maurice Sendak, have illustrated their own writings. Other great children's book illustrators include TENNIEL, CALDECOTT, and GREENAWAY. The art of Oriental book illustration is very old. In both China and Japan woodblock printing was used to enhance volumes from the 9th cent., and in Japan *ukiyo-e* printing (see JAPANESE ART) was used in books into the 18th cent.

**Illyés, Gyula** (ˌeelyes), 1902–83, Hungarian populist writer, poet, and playwright concerned with national issues. Notwithstanding his intense public life for half a century under very different regimes, his authority and standing in the country were growing all the time. His best-known work is *The People of the Puszta.*

**Illyria** and **Illyricum,** ancient regions of the Balkan peninsula occupied by Indo-European-speaking tribes including the Dalmatians and Pannonians. Warlike and piratical, they withstood (6th cent. BC) Greeks attracted by their mines and later attacks by Macedonians. The Romans conquered them and set up (168–167 BC) the province of Illyricum. Today Illyria means the Adriatic coast N of central Albania.

**Ilorin,** city (1987 est. pop. 282,000), capital of Kwara state, N Nigeria, at the main junction of the Nigerian railway system linking the north and south. It is an agricultural centre and its industries include the manufacture of textiles, pottery, and sugar. It was the capital of Yoruba kingdom c.1800 and came under British control in 1900.

**imaginary number:** see NUMBER.

**imagists,** group of English and American poets (c.1909–c.1917) who rebelled against the exuberance and sentimentality of 19th-cent. verse. Influenced by CLASSICISM, Chinese and Japanese poetry, and the French SYMBOLISTS, they advocated a hard, clear, concentrated poetry, free of artificialities and replete with specific physical analogies. The group included Ezra POUND, Richard ALDINGTON, Amy LOWELL, and Hilda DOOLITTLE.

**imam** [Arab., = leader]. 1 In SUNNISM, a prayer leader, and a religious teacher recognized by peers and authorities. In these senses, a caliph (see CALIPHATE) was also called an imam. 2 In SHI'ISM, the imamate indicates a specific succession of designated descendants of 'ALI. These individuals are each endowed with a special esoteric knowledge of present, past, and future directly inspired by God, and are the sole fount of legitimacy for a political order which establishes itself according to divine intent. See also MAHDI.

**immigration,** entrance into a new country for the purpose of establishing permanent residence. The largest waves of global migration have resulted from a combination of the following factors: population growth, economic hardship, and political or religious persecution. However, these 'push' factors can also be affected by 'pull' factors from the country of destination. England has been host to numerous waves of immigrants: Protestant HUGUENOT weavers, fleeing religious persecution in France (17th cent.); the Irish, following the Great Famine (1845–50); after 1881, East European Jews fleeing the pogroms (the Jewish population in London's East End was 100,000 by 1914); finally Afro-Caribbean and Asian immigrants after World War II. The growth of the American economy was a magnet attracting labour and other poor or displaced peoples (38 million between 1801 and 1935)—mainly from Europe, subsequently from Asia (to the West coast), Latin America, and Puerto Rico. Some immigration began as seasonal (e.g., Turkish male workers going to Germany) or remains so (e.g., Southern Italian workers to Northern Europe). Increasingly, immigration flows are controlled. America restricted the influx by the Chinese Exclusion Act (1882) and the McCorran–Walter Act (1952). Britain restricted permanent settlement to voucher-holders (Commonwealth Immigration Act 1962); to only those immigrants with a parent or grandparent born in the UK (Immigration Act 1964); and defined all settlers who had not acquired citizenship as aliens (the British Nationality Act 1981). This legislation, which appears to discriminate against ex-colonial non-white ethnic groups, has proved controversial, as have efforts to prevent illegal entry and to restrict the rights of Asians to bring in their dependants as permanent settlers. A category of immigrant that has grown in importance during the 20th cent. is that of political refugees.

**Immingham,** town (1981 pop. 11,480), Humberside, NE England, at mouth of R. Humber, 11 km (7 mi) NW of Grimsby. Development of this seaport began with the opening of the docks in 1912; oil jetties were opened in 1963. There is deeper water here than at the neighbouring port of GRIMSBY. In 1984 Immingham and Grimsby together handled 26.9 million tonnes. Other industries in the town include oil-refining and chemical manufacture.

**immunity,** ability of an organism to resist disease by production of antibodies. The introduction into the body of a foreign substance, called an antigen, which may be a virus, bacterium, fungus, parasite, or some nonliving substance, triggers the production of antibodies by special white blood cells called lymphocytes, located chiefly in the spleen and lymph nodes (see LYMPHATIC SYSTEM). The process is highly specific, with different lymphocytes recognizing only certain antigens and producing antibodies against that particular antigen alone. The antibodies act to neutralize the effect of the antigen by removing the antigen from the body's circulation. This is done by coating the antigen or antigen-producing agent so that it can be more easily destroyed by the body's scavenger cells, or by combining with the antigen in such a way as to make it incapable of infecting body cells. The body also resists invading agents by phagocytosis, a process by which special white cells (macrophages and others) engulf and destroy the invading microorganism. Immunity has been found to be important not only in resisting infectious disease, but also in the defence against CANCER, in successful organ transplants (see TRANSPLANTATION, MEDICAL), in allergies, and in cases of AUTOIMMUNE DISEASE (the result of an organism producing antibodies against its own proteins and cell components). IMMUNOSUPPRESSIVE DRUGS (substances used to prevent the production of antibodies) are used to treat some autoimmune diseases and to prevent the body's rejection of organ transplants. See also IMMUNOLOGY.

**immunity, diplomatic:** see EXTRATERRITORIALITY.

**immunology,** study of the resistance of organisms to infection. Immunologists study the behaviour of pathogenic (disease-causing) organisms (see TOXIN), factors that enable the host to resist infection, and defensive measures used by organisms to fight invading pathogens. See IMMUNITY.

**immunosuppressive drug,** substance that suppresses the activity of lymphocytes, the white blood cells that form antibodies (the body's response to foreign substances; see IMMUNITY). Such drugs, including CORTISONE and other STEROID hormones, are administered to prevent rejection by a recipient's body of an organ transplanted from a donor (see TRANSPLANTATION, MEDICAL). Other immunosuppressives act by interfering with NUCLEIC ACID synthesis. These drugs, which are especially effective against rapidly proliferating cells, are used in the treatment of cancer (see CHEMOTHERAPY), particularly leukaemia.

**impala:** see GAZELLE.

**Impatiens,** generic name for groups of herbs and small shrubs of the family Balsaminaceae. They are sometimes called 'touch-me-not' because of the explosive release of seeds when the fruit is touched. *I. balsamina*, the 'Busy Lizzie', is a showy greenhouse and garden bedding plant, very easily multiplied from cuttings.

**impeachment,** formal accusation by a LEGISLATURE against a public official, to remove him or her from office. The term loosely includes both the bringing of charges and the trial that may follow. Impeachment developed in England in the 14th cent. In the UK, the use of impeachment receded as more offences were tried in the courts, and ministers became politically responsible to PARLIAMENT for their actions. In the US, impeachment is provided for in the CONSTITUTION and is conducted by the Senate (see CONGRESS). In 1868 Andrew JOHNSON became the only president to be impeached, though he was later acquitted. In 1974, Pres. NIXON resigned the presidency before impeachment proceedings could be brought.

**impedance,** in electricity, measure of the degree to which an electric circuit resists electric-current flow when a voltage (see POTENTIAL, ELECTRIC) is impressed across its terminal. Impedance, expressed in OHMS, is the ratio of the voltage impressed across a pair of terminals to the current flow between those terminals. In direct-current (DC) circuits, impedance corresponds to RESISTANCE. In alternating-current (AC) circuits, impedance is a function of resistance, INDUCTANCE, and CAPACITANCE. Inductors and CAPACITORS build up voltages that oppose the flow of current. This opposition, called reactance, must be combined with resistance to find the impedance. The reactance produced by inductance is proportional to the frequency of the alternating current, whereas the reactance produced by capacitance is inversely proportional to the frequency. In order to transfer maximum electrical power from one device to another, the two impedances must be matched. See also OHM'S LAW.

**imperative:** see MOOD.

**Imperial Conference,** assembly of representatives of the self-governing members of the BRITISH EMPIRE, held about every four years until WORLD WAR II. The assemblies were first called Colonial Conferences (1887–1902) and were concerned with defence problems. More formalized meetings were held later (1907–37) to discuss defence and economic problems. Since WORLD WAR II, Commonwealth policy has been coordinated through regular meetings of the prime ministers and other ministers of Commonwealth nations.

**imperialism,** broadly, the extension of rule or influence by one government, nation, or society over another. Evidence of the existence of empires dates back to the dawn of written history, when local rulers extended their realms by conquering other states. Ancient imperialism reached its climax under the Roman Empire, but it was an important force elsewhere, e.g., the Middle East, N Africa, and central Asia. In the West, imperialism was reborn with the emergence of the modern NATION-STATE and the age of exploration and discovery. European COLONIZATION of the Western Hemisphere and Africa from the 15th to 17th cent. was followed in the 18th cent. by attempts to regulate the trade of colonies in the interests of the mother country. Later, the growth of manufacturing after the INDUSTRIAL REVOLUTION introduced a new form of imperialism, as industrial nations scrambled for raw materials and new markets for manufactured products. The inequities of the system produced a growing opposition by the end of the 19th cent., when Marxists argued that imperialism was the ultimate state of capitalism. After WORLD WAR I, anti-imperialist feeling grew rapidly, and since WORLD WAR II most of the countries once subject to Western control have achieved independence. Contemporary debate centres on neo-imperialism, with many less-developed countries contending that their economic development is largely determined by the developed countries through unfair trading practices, control over capital, and the power of MULTINATIONAL CORPORATIONS. See also WORLD-SYSTEM THEORY.

**Imperial units:** see ENGLISH UNITS OF MEASUREMENT; WEIGHTS AND MEASURES.

**Imperial Valley,** low-lying depression in a desert area S of the Salton Sea, S California. Irrigated by water diverted from the Colorado R. by the All-American Canal, it is an important US source of cotton, citrus, dates, and winter vegetables. Completion of HOOVER DAM (1936) ended periodic inundation there.

**impetigo,** highly contagious skin infection affecting mainly infants and children, usually caused by staphylococci or streptococci bacteria. The rash consists of red spots or blisters that rupture, discharge, and become encrusted. It is readily spread by contact and via towels and flannels. ANTIBIOTIC ointment is usually effective.

**impotence,** inability of the male to perform sexual intercourse. Impotence can result from psychological factors or such physical causes as hormonal abnormalities, DIABETES, DRUGS, and ALCOHOLISM. Treatment depends on the underlying cause. Impotence should be distinguished from sterility (inability to produce sperm adequate for reproduction). See also SEX THERAPY.

**impressionism,** in music, a French movement of the late 19th and early 20th cent. It was begun by Claude DEBUSSY as a reaction to the emotionalism of romantic music. Using new chord combinations and exotic rhythms and scales, Debussy developed a style in which atmosphere and mood take the place of strong emotion or a story. The influence of impressionism is evident in the music of RAVEL, DELIUS, FALLA, and SATIE.

**impressionism,** in painting, late-19th-cent. French school. It was generally characterized by the attempt to depict transitory visual impressions, often painted directly from nature, and by the use of broken colour to achieve brilliance and luminosity. Subjects were drawn from modern life. The movement began with MONET, RENOIR, and SISLEY, who met regularly with CÉZANNE, PISSARRO, and MORISOT; associated with them were, DEGAS and MANET. They repudiated academic standards, the romantics' emphasis on emotion, and literary and anecdotal subject matter; they also rejected the role of the imagination. Dubbed 'impressionists' by hostile journalists after Monet's painting *Impression: Sunrise, 1872* (Musée Marmottan, Paris), they observed nature closely, with scientific interest. Impressionist objectivity proved to be limiting, but the movement produced an aesthetic revolution, influencing many later painters.

**Imru al-Kais,** fl. 6th cent., Arabic poet, long esteemed by Arabs as the model for erotic poetry. Like much pre-Islamic poetry, his verse is subjective and stylistically perfect.

**In,** chemical symbol of the element INDIUM.

**Inca,** pre-Columbian Indian empire in W South America (see SOUTH AMERICAN INDIANS) whose language was Quechua (see AMERICAN INDIAN LANGUAGES). From its centre at CUZCO (Peru), the empire at its height dominated the entire Andean region, extending 3200 km (2000 mi). It was a closely knit state ruled by an emperor who required total obedience, but who looked after his subjects' welfare. The state owned almost everything and could draft people to work in mines or on public projects. Priests, government servants, the aged, sick, and widowed were supplied from imperial storehouses. The large royal family formed the nobility; a privileged, Quechua-speaking 'Inca class' governed colonies. Lesser officials formed a minor nobility. The empire was administratively divided and subdivided down to local communities. Surveys and census reports were recorded on knotted strings called quipas. The Incas' pantheistic, ritualistic religion sometimes incorporated human sacrifice. By terracing and irrigation, Inca engineers made a difficult terrain fertile; the llama and alpaca were domesticated. Remarkable feats of construction were accomplished in such cities as MACHU PICCHU, using clay models, tools such as plumb bobs, and wooden rollers to transport huge stone blocks. A network of roads included bridges, ferries, and relay stations. The Inca also made elaborate tapestries, fine polished pottery, and complex metalwork. Inca history begins when the legendary MANCO CAPAC brought his people from mountain caves into the Cuzco valley. In their early period (c.1200–c.1440) the Inca subjugated neighbouring peoples. Their great conquests (1440–93) came under Pachacuti and his son Topa Inca.

The present Ecuador was won by Huayna Capac, the last of the great Inca emperors. At his death (1525), his sons fought over the empire; just as Atahualpa triumphed, Francisco PIZARRO arrived (1532) to begin the Spanish conquest. Pizarro executed Atahualpa and entered Cuzco. Despite resistance and the rebellion (1536–37) of the second Manco Capac, the Inca were subdued and their culture was eventually Hispanicized. Only in recent years have efforts been made to integrate Peruvian Indians (about 50% of the population) into the national life.

**incense-tree,** common name for deciduous shrubs and trees of the family Burseraceae, found chiefly in tropical America and NE Africa. The incenses frankincense and myrrh are prepared from the resin exuded by some species. Frankincense, or olibanum, derived mainly from *Boswellia carterii*, is used medicinally and for fumigation. Myrrh, prepared especially from *Commiphora erythraea* and common myrrh, *C. myrrha,* is used medicinally and in perfumes, and was used by the ancients in embalming. The Australian incense plant (*Humea elegans*) is a very decorative greenhouse biennial of the COMPOSITE family.

**incest,** the taboo on sexual relations between close kin, most frequently father and daughter, mother and son, brother and sister, as well as those who are culturally defined as in an equivalent relationship to the individual. Incest was encouraged in the royal houses of Ptolemaic and Roman Egypt and in the Hawaiian kingdoms to preserve power within one LINEAGE. There is considerable variation across societies as to the categories of kin with whom sexual relations are proscribed (not necessarily equivalent to those with whom marriage is proscribed). LÉVI-STRAUSS sees the incest taboo as embodying the universal rule: to marry out. As such it is one of the foundations of human society.

**Inchon,** city (1984 pop. 1,295,107), NW South Korea, on the Yellow Sea. The country's second largest port, Inchon is a major industrial centre, producing steel, coke, textiles, chemicals, and fertilizers. Fishing is an important industry, and the city is also the port and commercial center for SEOUL. During the KOREAN WAR, US troops landed (15 Sept. 1950) at Inchon to launch a UN counteroffensive against the North Koreans.

**inclination,** in astronomy: see ORBIT.

**inclined plane:** see MACHINE.

**inclosure** or **enclosure,** in British history, the process of inclosing (with fences, ditches, hedges, or other barriers) land formerly subject to common rights. In England the practice dated from the 12th cent. and accompanied the breakdown of the MANORIAL SYSTEM. Its great development came in the 14th cent. with the rapid expansion of the Flemish wool trade and the resulting monetary advantages of fenced sheep pastures. Inclosure reached its peak in the 17th cent. Though hard on the small farmer, it produced more efficient farming.

**income tax,** assessment levied on individual or corporate income. The first modern income tax was levied (1799–1816) in Britain to fund the Napoleonic Wars, but it did not become permanent until 1874. In the UK personal income tax is assessed on total income in a given year less specific deductions and allowances. Up to a certain level a basic rate of tax is payable and in 1987 there were five higher rate bands. From the late 1970s tax rates in the UK fell and in 1988 the basic rate was 28%. In the mid 1980s the annual total of income tax paid was about £35 billion. See also CORPORATION TAX; INLAND REVENUE; PAY-AS-YOU-EARN.

**incontinence,** involuntary passage of urine or faeces. Urinary incontinence is common in women after childbirth, in certain neurological conditions, such as MULTIPLE SCLEROSIS, and in old age, when double incontinence may exist.

**incunabula,** plural of **incunabulum** [late Lat., = cradle (books); i.e., books of the cradle days of printing], books printed in the 15th cent. The known incunabula represent about 40,000 editions, the products of more than 1000 presses, including such printers as CAXTON, GUTENBERG, JENSON, and ALDUS MANUTIUS. Incunabula show the development of typography in its formative period.

**Independence, American War of:** see AMERICAN REVOLUTION.

**Independence, Declaration of:** see DECLARATION OF INDEPENDENCE.

**Independence Day:** see FOURTH OF JULY.

**Independence Hall,** building in Philadelphia, US, in Independence National Historical Park. The DECLARATION OF INDEPENDENCE was proclaimed here, and it was the site of the CONTINENTAL CONGRESS and the FEDERAL CONSTITUTIONAL CONVENTION.

**index,** in books or periodicals, a list, usually alphabetical, of topics treated. It directs the reader to specific names and subjects. Periodical-index subject entries are less specific than those in books. Book indexes began before printing was invented but until the 17th cent. were rarely alphabetical. Periodical indexes have existed almost as long as periodicals themselves; the best known is the *Readers' Guide to Periodical Literature*. Special indexes exist in many fields, e.g., law, medicine, art; citation indexes (e.g., *Science Citation Index*) list articles which cite a given article, and are a further help in finding all relevant published material on a particular subject. Newspaper indexes include those to the London *Times* (1906–) and New York *Times* (1913–). COMPUTERS are increasingly used in indexing.

**Index,** in the Roman Catholic Church, list of publications forbidden to be read, called *Index librorum prohibitorum* [list of forbidden books]. Last published in 1948, it was declared inoperative in 1966 following the Second VATICAN COUNCIL.

**index number,** in statistics, a figure reflecting a change in value or quantity as compared with a standard or base. The base usually equals 100 and the index number is usually expressed as a percentage. For example, if a commodity cost twice as much in 1980 as it did in 1970, its index number would be 200 relative to 1970. The best-known example of an index is that relating to changes in prices paid by consumers for goods they typically buy. The retail price index, often known as the consumer price index, takes a selection of items and measures their fluctuating prices against a base period, usually a year.

**India,** officially the Republic of India, republic (1987 est. pop. 765,000,000), 3,287,263 km² (1,269,212 sq mi), S Asia, occupying most of the Indian subcontinent, bordered by Pakistan (W); Afghanistan, China, Nepal, and Bhutan (N); and Burma (E); Bangladesh forms an enclave in the NE. Jutting into the INDIAN OCEAN, southern India has a shoreline of about 5630 km (3500 mi) along the Bay of BENGAL in the east and the ARABIAN SEA in the west. The capital is NEW DELHI; other important cities include CALCUTTA, BOMBAY, DELHI, MADRAS, and BANGALORE.

*Land and People.* The land may be divided into three topographical zones: the towering HIMALAYAS in the north; the fertile, densely populated Indo-Gangetic alluvial plain in the north-central section; and the southern peninsula, dominated by the uplands of the DECCAN plateau. The GANGES R., sacred to the Hindus, flows through the heart of the country. About 70% of the work force is engaged in agriculture, growing rice, wheat, groundnuts, maize, and millet for subsistence; cash crops include sugarcane (India is the world's largest producer), tea, oilseeds, cotton, and jute. In recent years traditional agriculture has been modified by improved irrigation, the introduction of chemical fertilizers, and the use of high-yielding strains of rice and wheat. By the late 1970s India was said to be self-sufficient in grain, but there was much malnutrition. India has perhaps more cattle per capita than any other country, but their economic value is severely limited by the Hindu prohibition against the slaughter of cattle. Among the country's rich mineral resources are coal, zinc, iron, and lead. India has industrialized notably since independence. Although the long-standing textile industry is still important, the emphasis is on heavy industry, which produces iron and steel, machine tools and other engineering products, transport equipment, fertilizers, and chemicals. The GNP is $194,792 million and the GNP per capita $260 (1984). India is the world's second most populous country (after China). It is a multi-ethnic society. There are 14 major languages and some 1500 dialects; Hindi and English are the official languages, and 14 others are recognized by the constitution. The population is overwhelmingly Hindu, but there are significant numbers of Muslims, Christians, Buddhists, Sikhs, Jains, and Parsis. About 80% of the population is rural. The caste system, under which people are socially classified at birth, is an important facet of Hinduism and thus a dominant feature of Indian life; the 1950 constitution abolished untouchability, but the custom persists and caste conflicts have become a serious problem.

*History.* The INDUS VALLEY CIVILIZATION (c.2500–c.1500 BC) was the first to flourish on the Indian subcontinent (in present-day Pakistan). It fell c.1500 BC to Aryan invaders from the northwest, who dominated the area for 2000 years and developed HINDUISM, the socioreligious system that is the basis of India's institutions and culture. Under the MAURYA dynasty (c.325–c.183 BC) especially ASOKA (d. 323 BC), who accepted and patronized Buddhism, Indian culture had its first great flowering. A golden age of Hindu culture was achieved under the GUPTA dynasty, in the 4th–5th cent. AD, considered India's classical period. By the 10th cent. Turkish–Afghan armies from the northwest were raiding India, and in 1192 the DELHI SULTANATE, the first Turko–Afghan empire whose dynasts were Muslim by faith, was established in India. The small Muslim kingdoms that succeeded it were swept away by BABUR, a descendant of TAMERLANE based in Afghanistan, who established the MUGHAL empire in 1526. Portugal, which captured Goa in 1510, was the first European nation to gain a foothold in India, but the British, French, and Dutch were soon vying with the Portuguese for Indian trade. With the weakening of the Mughal empire in the 18th cent., the struggle was renewed, this time between France and Britain, with the English EAST INDIA COMPANY emerging dominant. In 1857, after the bloody INDIAN MUTINY against the British, the East India Company was abolished and control of India was transferred directly to the British crown. Discontent with British rule became intense during the early 20th cent., and the INDIAN NATIONAL CONGRESS (founded 1885), led by Mohandas GANDHI and Jawaharlal NEHRU, mounted a movement for independence. The British instituted a programme of power-sharing, but Congress leaders saw these reforms as instruments for continuing British control indefinitely, and organized movements of Non-co-operation and Civil Disobedience from 1920 onwards. The desire of the Congress to maintain a united front against Britain was frustrated, however, by the MUSLIM LEAGUE, which demanded the partition of India into separate Hindu and Muslim states. Finally, in 1947, British India was divided into two independent nations: India, with Nehru as prime minister, and PAKISTAN, with Muhammad Ali JINNAH as governor-general. More than one million people died in the disorder that ensued. Relations between the two new nations were hostile and led to the INDIA–PAKISTAN WARS (1947–48, 1965, 1971). A particular subject of dispute was jurisdiction over KASHMIR, which both countries claimed. India was also involved in a border conflict (1962) with China. A sovereign republic within the COMMONWEALTH from 1950, India became a leader of the nonaligned nations and in 1974 exploded its first atomic device. Indira GANDHI (Nehru's daughter), who became prime minister in 1966, precipitated a crisis in 1975 when, after being convicted of campaign fraud, she declared a state of emergency and suspended civil liberties. Her Congress I party was defeated in national elections in 1977, but the new ruling coalition, the Janata Party, was beset by factionalism and economic difficulties. Mrs Gandhi was reelected in 1980 but was assassinated by Sikh extremists in 1984 and succeeded by her son, Rajiv Gandhi, who then led the Congress I to a massive election victory. Thereafter, the country's cohesion was challenged in particular by a continuing campaign of terror by Sikh militants demanding an autonomous state.

### Presidents of India
Rajendra Prasad (Congress), 1950–62
Sarvepalli Radhakrishnan (non-party), 1962–67
Zakir Husain (non-party), 1967–69
Varahagiri Venkatagiri (Congress), 1969–74
Fakhruddin Ali Ahmed (Congress), 1974–77
Neelam Sanjiva Reddy (Janata), 1977–82
Giani Zail Singh (Congress I), 1982–87
Ramaswamy Venkataraman (Congress I), 1987–

### Prime ministers of India
Jawaharlal Nehru (Congress), 1947–64
Lal Bahadur Shastri (Congress), 1964–66
Indira Gandhi (Congress), 1966–77
Morarji Desai (Janata), 1977–79
Charan Singh (Janata), 1979–80
Indira Gandhi (Congress I), 1980–84
Rajiv Gandhi (Congress I), 1984–

**Indiana,** state of the US (1984 est. pop. 5,498,000), area 93,994 km² (36,291 sq mi), situated in the north–central US and bordered by Michigan (N), Ohio (E), Kentucky (S), and Illinois (W). The capital is INDIANAPOLIS, and other major cities include Fort Wayne, Gary, Evansville, and South Bend. The northern part of the state consists of lakeshore dunes and glaciated lakes, separated by the Wabash R. from the fertile lowlands in the south. The leading source of income is manufacturing, concentrated along Lake MICHIGAN and adjacent to CHICAGO, where steel is a chief product, along with electrical and transport equipment, machinery, chemicals, and primary metals. Agriculture covers three-

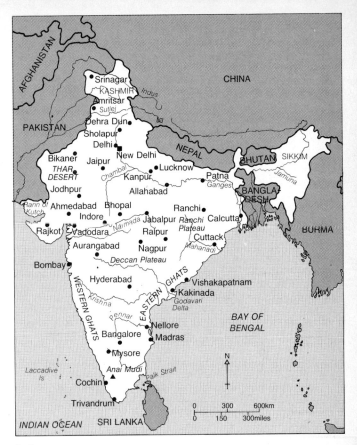

India

quarters of the state, producing corn, soya beans, pigs, cattle, hay, and wheat. There is also building limestone, coal, and some petroleum. More than 70% of the population lives in metropolitan areas. Indiana's earliest inhabitants were Mound Builders, and they were followed by Miami, Delaware, and Potawatomi Indians. The French and British held the area in the 18th cent. before it passed to the US at the end of the American Revolution. It was the site of major battles with the Indians before becoming a state in 1816. Canals and railways linked Indiana with the east in the 1840s, and industrial growth followed. In 1959 the opening of the St Lawrence Seaway gave the lake ports access to the Atlantic and increased the importance of shipping to the economy.

**Indian Affairs, Bureau of** (BIA), created in 1824 in the War Dept. with jurisdiction over the Indian trade, Indian protection, and removal and settlement of Indians on reservations. In 1849 the bureau was transferred to the Dept. of the INTERIOR, where it became primarily a land-administration agency. In the 1970s the AMERICAN INDIAN MOVEMENT and other Indian groups began actively to express dissatisfaction with the work of the bureau. Today, BIA's objectives include encouragement and training of Indians to manage their own affairs; improvement of their educational opportunities and social services; and the development and utilization of native skills for the economic advancement of native Americans.

**Indianapolis,** US city (1984 est. pop. 710,000), state capital of Indiana, on the White R. By far the state's largest city, it is the chief processing point in a large agricultural region, and an important grain and livestock market. Its manufactures include chemicals, pharmaceuticals, telephone and electronic equipment, processed foods, and vehicle and aircraft parts. An insurance centre, it has numerous educational and medical facilities. Indianapolis is a centre of transport and of the trucking industry. The Indianapolis Motor Speedway is the scene of the world-famous annual 800-km (500-mi) automobile race. Urban renewal projects in the 1970s and early 80s have produced many modern, multistorey buildings.

**Indian art and architecture,** is essentially traditional and religious. Each work of art is both a symbol and a manifestation of a god or his powers. In both Buddhist and Hindu art, symbolism in every gesture, posture, and attribute contains many levels of meaning (see BUDDHISM;

HINDUISM). The earliest Indian art emerged in the Indus R. valley during the 2nd half of the 3rd millennium BC. The Indus valley civilization (c.2500–c.1500 BC) produced early examples of city planning and drainage systems, as well as many statuettes and square seals with naturalistically rendered bulls as decorations. From the MAURYA dynasty the most famous architectural remains are the edict pillars, over 15 m (50 ft) high, surmounted by lotus flowers and animal figures. Also dating from this period are the stone ogival *chaitya* windows found at a sanctuary near Bodh Gaya. The early classic period of the Sunga dynasty (2nd–1st cent. BC) and early Andhra dynasty (1st cent. BC) has left the earliest extant STUPAS, mounds surrounded by railings and gateways covered with ornament. Between the 2nd and 5th cent. AD art from the Gandhara and Mathura regions developed. Gandhara art presents the first human images of the BUDDHA and was profoundly influenced by 2nd-cent. Hellenistic art (see HELLENISTIC CIVILIZATION). Ornate stupas and monasteries held colossal gilt figures and imported glassware. Mathura created a wholly Indian sculptural art, usually employing reddish limestone. Heavier symmetrical Buddhas smile benignly at worshippers. The GUPTA period (AD 320–600) was the golden age of Buddhist art. Smooth, elegant reliefs cover the facades and interiors of remaining chaitya halls. The murals in the caves at Ajanta depict the joys of secular life and the beauty of the spiritual. From the 6th cent. onwards, with the Hindu dynasties, temples were built that were so exuberantly embellished with sculpture that their style is called 'sculptural architecture'. The Dravidian-style temple is constructed in five pyramidal *raths* (temples). Skilled CIRE-PERDUE sculptures were produced until the late 19th cent. Most Indian wall paintings, except for fragments from the caves of Ajanta, were destroyed, but examples of manuscript ILLUMINATION remain. Jain manuscript illuminations are brightly coloured and have the characteristic protruding farther eye. Rajput painting is characterized by an interest in nature and sinuous grace in the human form. Little of the glorious tradition of Indian artistic achievement survived British rule. A revival of Indian themes in the 20th cent. has produced such artists as Abanindranath TAGORE, Nandalal Bose, and Ram Kinker.

**Indian Hemp:** see HEMP.

**Indian literature.** Oral literature in the vernacular languages of India is of great antiquity, but it was not until about the 16th cent. that an extensive written literature appeared. Its development was spurred by the emergence of Hindu pietistic movements that encouraged the popularizing of SANSKRIT LITERATURE, e.g., the RAMAYANA was put into popular verse form. Among Muslims, classical Persian poetry was the basis for Urdu verse written for the Mughal court. In the early 19th cent., with the establishment of vernacular schools and the importation of printing presses, a great impetus was given to popular prose. Today literature is written in all the important languages of India, Pakistan, and Bangladesh, and there is a large literature in English. Among the best-known writers of the 19th and 20th cent. are Rammohun ROY, Bankim Chandra CHATTERJEE, Rabindranath TAGORE, Mohandas GANDHI, Jawaharlal NEHRU, R.K. NARAYAN, Raja RAO, and Bhabhani BHATTACHARYA.

**Indian music,** the primarily monodic classical music systems of the Indian subcontinent as well as a rich diversity of light-classical, popular (mainly for commercial films), and folk musics. Two distinct classical systems exist: North Indian (Hindustani) and South Indian (Karnatak). Both share the concepts of *rāg* and *tal*: *rāg* relates both to the overall melodic system and to specific modes, and *tal* to the rhythmic system and specific metric cycles in which melodic compositions are set. Characteristically, a vocalist or an instrumentalist, accompanied by a drummer, intersperses statements of a fixed composition in a particular *rāg* with improvisations designed to display technical virtuosity and a profound knowledge of the *rāg*'s musical subleties. Karnatak and Hindustani musics differ firstly in performance structure and style, the former tending towards the highly systematic treatment of shorter forms and the latter towards the gradual unfolding of longer pieces lasting up to two hours, and secondly in instrumentation: the violin, *bin* (plucked lute), and *mridangam* (double-headed, barrel-shaped drum) predominate in the south, and the *sitar, sarod* (long- and short-necked plucked lutes), and *tabla* (two-piece drum set) in the north. Instruments have been developed mainly to imitate the quality and flexibility of the voice (in particular portamento), and melody and rhythm may also be orally transmitted by means of solmization (associating each note of the scale with a particular syllable) and mnemonic systems.

**Indian art and architecture:** Brother of Krishna, 19th-cent cire-perdue bronze sculpture

**Indian Mutiny,** 1857–58, also known as the Sepoy Rebellion, revolt of the Indian soldiers (sepoys) in the British army in BENGAL that developed into a widespread uprising against British rule in India. The N Indian soldiers resented British annexation (1856) of Oudh. They were also angered by the issuing of cartridges coated in beef and pork fat, taboo to Hindu and Muslims respectively. Fighting quickly spread all over N India and the civil population were involved in the rising; the rebels besieged Lucknow and conquered Cawnpore and Delhi. British reconquest was completed by Mar. 1858. Various reforms resulted, the most important being the transfer of rule from the East India Company to the British crown. Some Indian nationalists described the rising as the first Indian War of Independence. The atrocities committed by both sides embittered race relations.

**Indian National Congress,** Indian political party, founded in 1885 to promote economic reforms. It became the spearhead of the Indian movement for independence from Great Britain. Its membership became overwhelmingly Hindu, as most Muslim members left it for the MUSLIM LEAGUE. In 1919, led by Mohandas GANDHI, it adopted a policy of *satyagraha* (nonviolent resistance toward the British). The party was outlawed during WORLD WAR II for refusing to support the British war effort, and most of its leaders were jailed. After India achieved independence (1947), Jawaharlal NEHRU headed both the government and the party. Its dominance continued after Nehru's death (1964) under Shri Lal Bahadur SHASTRI and Nehru's daughter, Indira GANDHI. In 1969 the party split: the conservative wing became the Old Congress party, and Indira Gandhi's followers became the New Congress party, winning a landslide victory in 1971. But this party was also to split. After its electoral defeat in 1977, Mrs Gandhi withdrew and in 1978 formed a new faction, the Congress-I (for Indira) party, which brought her back into power in Jan. 1980. Following her assassination in 1984, her son Rajiv assumed the party leadership.

Indian music: sitar

**Indian Ocean,** world's third largest ocean, c.73,427,000 km² (28,350,000 sq mi), between S Asia, Antarctica, E Africa, and SW Australia. It is c.6400 km (4000 mi) wide at the equator and reaches a maximum depth of 7725 mi (25,344 ft) in the Java Trench S of Indonesia. Its major arms include the Arabian Sea, Red Sea, Gulf of Aden, Persian Gulf, Bay of Bengal, and Andaman Sea. A complex series of mid-oceanic submarine ridges intersect to enclose deep-sea basins, their summits rising to the surface in places to form the Andaman, Nicobar, Seychelles, and other island groups.

**Indian Ocean Commission,** intergovernmental organization for cooperation formed (1982) by Madagascar, Mauritius, and Seychelles, and joined later (1985) by the Comoros.

**Indian philosophy.** Systematized Indian philosophy begins in the period of the UPANIṢADS (900–500 BC). The rise of BUDDHISM (from the 5th cent. BC) led to the development of philosophical tenets presented in the form of sūtras, concise aphorisms intended to serve as a memory aid and as a basis for oral elaboration. There are six classical schools that accept the authority of the VEDA. The first, *Nyāya* (6th cent. BC), is a school of logic and epistemology. *Vaiśeṣika* (3rd cent. BC) posits a sixfold classification of reality (substance, quality, activity, generality, particularity, inherence). The *Sāmkhya* system (6th cent. BC) expounds two basic metaphysical principles: *puruṣa* (soul) and *prakṛti* (matter or nature). *Puruṣa* appears bound to *prakṛti*, but may become free through the realization that it is distinct from *prakṛti*. The YOGA system of Patañjali (2nd cent. BC), which accepts Sāmkhya metaphysics and the concept of a supreme soul, presents an eight-stage discipline of self-control and MEDITATION. The *Purva Mīmāṃsā* school (2nd cent. BC) sets forth principles of interpretation of the Vedic texts. The different schools of *Uttara Mīmāṃsā*, or VEDĀNTA, all based on the *Brahma-Sūtras* of Bādarāyana (early cent. AD), epitomize the teachings of the Upaniṣads. The three main heterodox schools not based on the Veda and Upaniṣads are BUDDHISM, JAINISM, and the materialist school called *Cārvāka* or *Lokāyata*. The latter, the only Indian school to reject the ideas of KARMA and spiritual liberation, held that only this world exists and that religious ideas are delusion.

**Indians, American:** see MIDDLE AMERICAN INDIANS; NORTH AMERICAN INDIANS; SOUTH AMERICAN INDIANS; and individual tribes. See also AMERICAN INDIAN LANGUAGES; AMERICAN INDIANS, PREHISTORY OF.

**Indian Territory,** in US history, name of land set aside for the Indians by the Indian Intercourse Act (1834). In the 1820s the US government began moving the CHEROKEE, Creek, Seminole, Choctaw, and Chickasaw Indians W of the Mississippi R. The act of 1834 designated the area of present-day Oklahoma, as well as Kansas and Nebraska, for the Indians. In 1854 the territory was delimited by the creation of the Kansas and Nebraska territories, and it was abolished in 1907 with the entrance of Oklahoma into the US Union.

**Indian wars,** in American history, term referring to the series of conflicts, beginning in colonial times, between white settlers and North American Indians. After 1815 the US government began removing Indians to reservations W of the Mississippi R., a policy that often triggered war. The Indian wars W of the Mississippi reached their height between 1869 and 1878. WOUNDED KNEE (1890) is often called the last battle of the Indian wars.

**India–Pakistan Wars,** the series of conflicts between INDIA and PAKISTAN since 1947, when the Indian subcontinent was partitioned as British rule there ended. More than one million people are believed to have died in the communal rioting that took place immediately after partition, and many millions more were forced to relocate. The Muslim majority state of Kashmir became a bone of contention. An uneasy peace was worked out and lasted until 1965, when fighting broke out in the Rann of Kutch, and spread to Kashmir and the Punjab, but a ceasefire mediated by the USSR went into effect in 1966. In 1971 East Pakistan, with the support of India, revolted against the rule of West Pakistan. Again, brutal fighting and massive relocations took place. East Pakistan declared itself independent as BANGLADESH, and in 1974 Pakistan recognized that status.

**India-rubber plant,** common name for *Ficus elastica*, of the fig family. It is an excellent houseplant of upright habit with large shiny, dark-green leaves with a prominent mid-rib, red on the underside. It grows about 2m (6 ft) according to the size of the pot, but reaches at least 30m (100 ft) in tropical Asia. Although it yields latex, most commercial rubber is obtained from *Hevea brasiliensis*, a tree of the spurge family.

**indicative:** see MOOD.

**indicators, acid–base,** organic compounds that in water solution exhibit colour changes that indicate the acidity or basicity of the solution (see ACIDS AND BASES). LITMUS, for example, is red in acidic solution and blue in basic. Other common indicators are phenolphthalein and methyl orange.

**Indic languages,** group of languages belonging to the Indo-Iranian subfamily of the Indo-European family of languages. See LANGUAGE (table).

**indictment,** in law, a written accusation against a person charging him or her with a crime triable by JURY. In England and Wales, it is served in the name of the sovereign, in Scotland, in the name of the Lord Advocate. In the UK, indictments are not necessary for summary offences (over 90% of all criminal offences) which are triable before a Magistrates' Court, following the issue of a summons ordering the defendant to attend. In the US, the use of an indictment is guaranteed by the US CONSTITUTION in all trials for capital or other serious crimes.

**indium** (In), metallic element, discovered spectroscopically in 1863 by Ferdinand Reich and H.T. Richter. Soft, malleable, ductile, lustrous, and silver-white, it remains liquid over a wide temperature range. Indium wets glass and can be used to form a mirror surface more corrosion-resistant than one of silver. See ELEMENT (table); PERIODIC TABLE.

**individual differences,** a term in psychology used to denote both variations between individuals in some dimension of behaviour, performance, competence, personality, or response; and the approach to a psychological phenomenon or field of study which focuses upon such differences between individuals. Strictly, the term should be inter-individual differences, to distinguish it from intra-individual differences (over time, situation, task, etc.).

**Indo-Aryan,** variant name for Indic languages. Broader uses referring to racial stocks are now obsolete. See LANGUAGE (table).

**Indochina,** term used in a wide sense for the entire SE Asian peninsula occupied by BURMA, MALAYSIA, THAILAND, LAOS, KAMPUCHEA, and VIETNAM, whose cultures reflect the long-term influence of neighbouring India (W) and China (N). The term was also commonly used in the recent past in a more restricted sense for the colonial empire developed by France in the eastern part of the peninsula after 1862. During World War II France offered greater self-government to the various states it ruled there, within a French federation of Indochina. Vietnamese nationalists rejected the offer (which Laos and Cambodia accepted), demanding (1945) the complete independence of the colony of COCHIN CHINA and of the TONKIN and ANNAM protectorates, or what is now Vietnam. After a long and bitter war, the French were defeated at DIENBIENPHU (1954) and subsequently lost control of all Indochina at the GENEVA CONFERENCE (1954). See also VIETNAM WAR.

**Indochina War:** see VIETNAM WAR.

**Indo-European,** family of languages to which English belongs. It includes more speakers than any other language family. See LANGUAGE (table).

**Indo-Iranian,** subfamily of the Indo-European family of languages. See LANGUAGE (table).

**Indonesia,** officially the Republic of Indonesia, republic (1986 est. pop. 165,000,000), c.1,916,600 km² (740,000 sq mi), SE Asia, comprising more than 3000 islands stretching along the equator from the Malaysian mainland to New Guinea; the main islands are JAVA, SUMATRA, Kalimantan (Indonesian BORNEO), CELEBES (Sulawesi), BALI, TIMOR, the MOLUCCAS (Maluku), and Irian Jaya (West New Guinea). The capital is DJAKARTA, on Java. The islands are mountainous and dotted with volcanoes, both active and dormant; the climate is tropical, with abundant rainfall. About 70% of the work force is engaged in agriculture, and fertile soil sustains a rich yield; principal crops are rice, sugarcane, fruit, cassava, and maize. Indonesia's natural resources are among the richest in the world; the nation is a leading producer of petroleum, its most valuable export; liquefied natural gas, tin, bauxite, and nickel are important. Products of the vast rain forests include hardwoods, rubber, palm oil, and cinchona. Primarily a supplier of raw materials, the country has little industry. The population is mainly Malayan and Papuan; there is an important Chinese minority. Islam is the predominant religion. The official language is Bahasa Indonesia, but more than 250 tongues are spoken.

*History.* Early in the Christian era Indonesia came under the influence of Indian civilization, and after the 7th cent. important Buddhist and Hindu kingdoms arose, notably the 13th-cent. Majapahit empire of Java. Arab traders first arrived in the 14th cent., and by the end of the 16th cent. Islam had become the dominant religion. Reduced by internal dissension to a number of small, weak states, the area was easy prey for Europeans (Portuguese, 1511; Dutch, 1596; British, 1600) lured by the rich spice trade. By the 17th cent. the Dutch EAST INDIA COMPANY emerged as the dominant power, and in 1799 the Netherlands assumed direct control of the area, thereafter known as the Netherlands (or Dutch) East Indies. Agitation for independence began early in the 20th cent. Following Japanese occupation of the islands in World War II, nationalist leader SUKARNO proclaimed (1945) an independent Indonesian republic; after four years of intermittent, sometimes heavy fighting, the Dutch finally

transferred sovereignty in 1949. Netherlands New Guinea became part of Indonesia in 1963 and was renamed Irian Jaya in 1973. Indonesia annexed Portuguese East Timor in 1976, a move not recognized by the UN. The dictatorial, Marxist-tending regime of Indonesia's first president, Sukarno, was inefficient, corrupt, and chaotic. An abortive Communist coup in 1965 led to an anti-Communist takeover by the military, under Gen. SUHARTO, who was elected president in 1968, and reelected in 1973 and 1978. Under Suharto, who has moved Indonesia closer to the West, top priority has been given to economic rehabilitation; a five-year economic plan (1979–83) stressed self-sufficiency. By 1982 Indonesia was enjoying an unprecedented degree of prosperity, although the slump in world oil prices of the mid-1980s caused new economic problems.

**Indore,** city (1981 pop. 829,327), Madhya Pradesh state, C India, at the confluence of two small streams, the Khan and the Saraswati. It is a district administrative, cultural and commercial centre with many markets and some industries, especially cotton textiles. In spite of the choice of BHOPAL as the capital of Madhya Pradesh in 1956, it remains larger than the latter and has grown rapidly to become the virtual metropolis of the Malwa plateau. It was founded only in the 18th cent., but in the following century became the capital of Holkar princely state, known also by the name of its capital. This, and the building of roads and railways, gave it a considerable fillip.

**inductance,** quantity that measures the electromagnetic INDUCTION of a component in an ELECTRIC CIRCUIT. The self-inductance $L$ of a circuit component determines the magnitude of the ELECTROMOTIVE FORCE (emf) induced in it as a result of a given rate of change of current through the component. The mutual inductance $M$ of two components, one in each of two separate but closely located circuits, determines the emf that each may induce in the other for a given current change. The unit of inductance is the HENRY (see ELECTRIC AND MAGNETIC UNITS). A device designed to produce an inductance, e.g., a wire coil, is called an inductor.

**induction,** in ELECTRICITY and MAGNETISM, common name for three distinct phenomena. **Electromagnetic induction** is the production of an ELECTROMOTIVE FORCE (emf) in a conductor as a result of a changing magnetic FIELD about the conductor. Such a variation may be produced by relative motion between the conductor and the source of the magnetic field, as in an electric GENERATOR, or by varying the strength of the entire field. Changing the current in a given circuit can also induce an emf in a nearby circuit unconnected with the original circuit; this is called mutual induction and is the basis of the TRANSFORMER. **Electrostatic induction** is the production of an unbalanced electric CHARGE on an uncharged metallic body as a result of a charged body being brought near it but without touching it. If the charged body is positively charged, electrons in the uncharged body will be attracted toward it; if the opposite end of the body is then earthed, electrons will flow into it to replace those drawn to the other end. The body thus acquires a negative charge after the earth

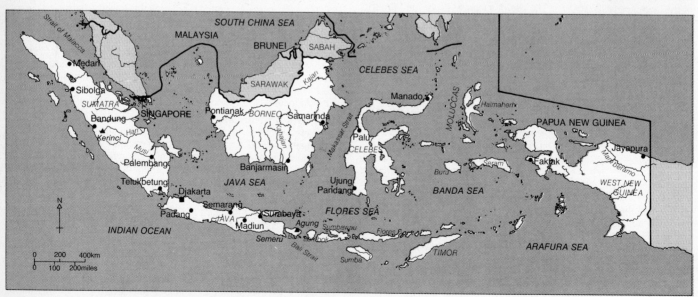

Indonesia

connection is broken. **Magnetic induction** is the production of a magnetic field in a piece of unmagnetized iron or other ferromagnetic substance when a magnet is brought near it. The magnet causes the individual particles of the iron, which act like tiny magnets, to line up so that the sample as a whole becomes magnetized. See also INDUCTANCE.

**induction,** in LOGIC, the process of reasoning from the particular to the general. Francis BACON proposed inductive logic as the logic of scientific discovery, holding DEDUCTION as the logic of argumentation. In fact, both processes are used together regularly in the empirical sciences: by the observation of particular events (induction) and from already known principles (deduction), new hypothetical principles are formulated and laws induced.

**induction motor:** see MOTOR, ELECTRIC.

**inductor:** see INDUCTANCE.

**indulgence,** in the Roman Catholic Church, the pardon of temporal punishment due for SIN. Indulgences are granted out of the Treasury of Merit won for the church by Christ and the saints. Until their sale was made unlawful by the Council of TRENT (1562), the abuse of indulgences was common, and it was this abuse that Martin LUTHER first denounced.

**Indus,** chief river of Pakistan, c.3000 km (1900 mi) long, site of the prehistoric INDUS VALLEY CIVILIZATION. It rises in the TIBET region of China, flows west across KASHMIR (disputed between India and Pakistan), then southwest through Pakistan, where it receives the 'five waters' of the PUNJAB (the Chenab, Jhelum, Ravi, Beas, and Sutlej rivers), to an infertile delta on the Arabian Sea SE of Karachi. The Indus, which is navigable only by small craft, is harnessed for irrigation and hydroelectricity by the Sukkur and Kotri dams. A treaty signed (1960) by India and Pakistan regulates withdrawals of water from the river and its tributaries.

**industrial archaeology,** the study of the industrial past, especially of western Europe since the beginning of the INDUSTRIAL REVOLUTION. Interest in recent and contemporary technology reflects the concern of modern archaeology with the way economic and technological developments influence society through the material world they create.

**industrial espionage:** see INTELLIGENCE GATHERING.

**industrialization,** the process of substituting machine power for human power within productive activity. In England, it depended on the commercialization of agriculture and the creation of a market economy. Originating in British workshops and factories, in the second half of the 18th cent., the process of industrialization went through many stages and is now a global phenomena. Social changes typically associated with industrialization are: (1) the movement of productive activity from the home into factories, which themselves tend to become larger and more technologically advanced over time; (2) the movement of factories and populations from country to town and cities (URBANIZATION); (3) the growth of major industrial classes (the owners and controllers of industry, the skilled and unskilled wage-workers, those who manage and supervise the labour process and service the distribution and sale of its products). There have been different routes to industrialization: by private ownership and capital, as in the UK and US, with significant state involvement, as in Prussia and Japan, or by state ownership and direction, as in the USSR. Third World countries often explain their relative economic underdevelopment in terms of the failure of, or blockages against, industrialization. Some manufacturing industries are now transferred to 'developing' nations because of cheap labour costs (e.g., in Taiwan, Korea) and other developing countries are attempting to industrialize (India, Brazil).

**industrial pollutants:** see POLLUTION; WASTE DISPOSAL.

**industrial relations,** the relationship between employers and employees in an industrial environment. The term came into being when the rise of the TRADE UNIONS enabled workers' interests to be represented. In modern CAPITALISM, styles of industrial relations range from at one end the Japanese style of paternalistic management under which workers have their welfare both inside and outside the company benevolently directed by the management, to the opposite end of the spectrum, with worker participation on the board of the company (as practised in West Germany). This latter was recommended in the UK by the Bullock Report (1977) but has not found favour with British management. In recent years British governments have introduced legislation to reduce the number of industrial disputes, and overall industrial relations have become more conciliatory.

**Industrial Revolution,** term usually applied to the social and economic changes that mark the transition from a stable agricultural and commercial society to a modern industrial society. Historically, it is used to refer primarily to the period in British history from c.1750 to c.1850. Dramatic changes in the social and economic structure took place as inventions and new technology created the factory system of large-scale machine production and greater economic specialization. The labouring population, formerly employed mainly in agriculture, increasingly gathered in great urban factory centres. The same process occurred at later times and in different degrees in other countries. The crucial development of the Industrial Revolution in Britain was the use of steam for power, made possible by the STEAM ENGINE (1769) of James WATT. Cotton textiles was the key industry early in this period. The presence of large quantities of coal and iron proved a decisive factor in Britain's rapid industrial growth. Canals and roads were built, and the advent of the railway and steamship widened the market for manufactured goods. New periods of development came with electricity and the petrol engine, but by 1850 the revolution was accomplished, with industry having become a dominant factor in British life. The effects of the Industrial Revolution were worldwide. France (after 1830), Germany (after 1850), and the US (after the Civil War) were transformed by industrialization. Europeans introduced the revolution to Asia about the turn of the 20th cent., but only Japan eventually grew into an industrial giant. The RUSSIAN REVOLUTION had as a basic aim the introduction of industrialism. The Industrial Revolution has changed the face of nations, providing the economic base for population expansion and improvement in living standards, and it remains a primary goal of less developed countries. But with it have also come a host of problems, including labour-management conflicts, worker boredom, and environmental pollution.

**Industrial Workers of the World** (IWW), revolutionary industrial union organized in Chicago in 1905 by 43 labour organizations. Its programme reflected the doctrines of SYNDICALISM. After 1908 the IWW became an organization largely of the unskilled, reaching its peak strength (60,000 to 100,000 members) on the eve of WORLD WAR I. Wartime strikes led to suppression by the federal government, including arrest of its entire leadership, and it declined rapidly thereafter.

**Indus valley civilization,** c.2500–c.1500 BC, ancient civilization that flourished along the Indus R. in present-day Pakistan. Its chief cities were Mohenjo-Daro and Harappa, where archaeologists have unearthed impressive public and private buildings that are evidence of a complex society based on a highly organized agriculture supplemented by active commerce. The arts flourished, and examples in copper, bronze, and pottery have been uncovered. Also found were examples of a pictograph script that long baffled archaeologists but was finally deciphered in 1969. The fate of the Indus valley civilization remains a mystery, but it is believed that it fell victim to invading Aryans.

**Indy, Vincent d':** see D'INDY, VINCENT.

**inequality,** in mathematics, statement that one expression is less than or greater than another. The symbols $<$ (less than), $>$ (greater than), $\leq$ (less than or equal to), and $\geq$ (greater than or equal to) are used to indicate inequalities, as in $3 < 5$ and $2x + 1 \geq 7$. As with an EQUATION, an inequality containing variables can be solved; the solution is also an inequality. For instance, $2x + 1 \geq 7$ has the solution $x \geq 3$, because any number greater than or equal to 3 can be substituted for $x$ to make the left side greater than or equal to 7.

**inert gas** or **noble gas,** any of the elements in group 0 of the PERIODIC TABLE. In order of increasing atomic number, they are HELIUM, NEON, ARGON, KRYPTON, XENON, and RADON. Sometimes called the rare gases (although argon makes up 1% of the atmosphere), they are colourless, odourless, and tasteless. Inert gases have very low chemical activity because their outermost, or valency, electron shell is complete, containing two electrons in the case of helium and eight in the remaining cases.

**inertia,** in physics, the resistance of a body to any alteration in its state of MOTION, i.e., the resistance of a body at rest to being set in motion or of a body in motion to any change of speed or of direction of motion. See MASS.

**Inez de Castro:** see CASTRO, INÉS DE.

**infallibility,** in Christian thought, the inability of the church to err, believed since early Christian times to be guaranteed by Scripture. As proclaimed at the First VATICAN COUNCIL (1870), Roman Catholics believe in the infallibility of the pope when he speaks *ex cathedra* on faith and morals. The Orthodox hold that ecumenical councils are infallible. Protestants largely reject the infallibility of the church.

**infanticide,** killing of the newborn. In many societies since ancient times a parent had the right to kill, sell, sacrifice, or otherwise dispose of offspring. The practice could arise for a number of reasons, e.g., shortage of food or the need to conserve property within the family (often leading to killing daughters). Although outlawed in the developed nations, infanticide still occurs, particularly in rural areas and amongst disadvantaged groups. However, due to the moral sanctions against such action it would be difficult to ascertain its exact frequency or social location. See also ABORTION; EUGENICS.

**infant mortality rate** (IMR), number of deaths of babies aged under one year old, expressed per 1000 live births in a given year. The IMR is regarded as one measure of a country's social affluence and well-being.

**infantry,** body of soldiers who fight on foot, as distinct from CAVALRY or other branches of an ARMY. In ancient times, the relative military value of infantry fluctuated. The Romans are believed to have made the most effective use of the foot soldier, but with the decline of Rome cavalry became dominant in war, remaining so until firearms were introduced in the mid-14th century. Armed with muskets, and then rifles, troops fought in mass formation until the early 20th cent., when trench warfare and automatic weapons affected deployment. Aircraft, TANKS, and ARTILLERY supported a massive use of infantry in WORLD WAR II. Despite the innovations in weaponry since then, strategists continue to regard the infantry as the indispensable factor in military victory.

**infectious mononucleosis** or **glandular fever,** acute infectious disease of older children and young adults, occurring sporadically or in epidemic form. The causative organism is thought to be an airborne herpes virus. Symptoms include fever, enlarged spleen (in about half the cases), sore throat, and extreme fatigue. HEPATITIS is common. Therapy includes bed rest and the treatment of symptoms. Convalescence may be prolonged.

**inferiority complex:** see COMPLEX.

**infertility,** inability to reproduce (see REPRODUCTIVE SYSTEM). In the male, malfunctioning of the sex glands, or testes, usually results in the production of defective sperm or a decreased number of sperm, causing infertility. In the female, malfunctioning of the sex glands, or ovaries, disturbs ovulation (production of the egg cell). Structural deformity (e.g., blockage of a tube), metabolic and infectious diseases, and psychological factors may also cause infertility. Voluntary sterilization is a form of CONTRACEPTION. See also ARTIFICIAL INSEMINATION; IN VITRO FERTILIZATION.

**infinitive:** see MOOD.

**infinity,** in mathematics, that which is not finite; it is often indicated by the symbol $\infty$. A SEQUENCE of numbers is said to approach or *diverge* to infinity if the numbers eventually become arbitrarily large, i.e., larger than any specified number (see LIMIT). Conversely, an infinite (never ending) sequence may converge to a finite limit, as in the sequence $1, 1\frac{1}{2}, 1\frac{3}{4}, 1\frac{7}{8}, 1\frac{15}{16}, \ldots$. The word *infinite* is also used to describe a SET with more than any finite number of elements, e.g., the set of points on a line or the set of all prime numbers (see NUMBER THEORY). Georg CANTOR showed that there are different orders of infinity, the infinity of points on a line being of a greater order than that of prime numbers, and developed the theory of transfinite numbers as a means of distinguishing them.

**inflation,** a sustained increase in general price levels. This usually occurs when demand for a range of goods or services, or even for a single commodity, exceeds supply, or when a group in society tries to increase its share of income. In centrally controlled economies suppressed inflation is frequently reflected in thriving black markets for goods and the national currency, while official prices remain stable. Excessive government borrowing is another cause of inflation, notably in Latin America. Moderate inflation rates may stimulate business activity and wages but all governments fear the adverse consequences which include falls in export earnings and a widening of income disparities. As a rule, annual price increases of less than 2% or 3% have not been considered inflationary. But the 1970s brought the onset of worldwide inflation (often occurring as STAGFLATION), commonly attributed to the soaring cost of petroleum.

Inflation of 10% or more became common in many countries and caused severe economic dislocations. In the early 1980s, however, recession and lower oil prices reduced the inflation rate and in most European countries it had ceased to be a problem by 1985. The opposite of inflation is **deflation,** a time of falling prices, curtailed business activity, and high unemployment (see DEPRESSION).

**inflection,** in grammar. In many languages, words or word parts are arranged in sets consisting of a root, or base, and various affixes. Thus *walking, walks, walked* have in common the root *walk* and an affix (e.g., *-ing, -s, -ed*). An inflectional affix carries grammatical restrictions with it, so that a plural inflection on a noun requires a change in verb form. Many languages, e.g., Latin and Eskimo, have far more extensive inflection than English. In Latin grammar, adjectives and nouns are inflected for CASE and number, adjectives for the gender of the noun, and verbs for MOOD, VOICE, TENSE, person, and number. Noun inflection is called declension, verb inflection conjugation. Derivation, as distinguished from inflection, is the process of forming words by adding affixes that themselves have meaning or denote word function, e.g., *de-press, work-er.* A root with its derivational affixes is a stem. Thus, in *racketeers, racket* is the root, *racketeer* the stem, and *-s* the inflection. Languages are classified according to the amount of derivation and inflection they use. Isolating languages such as Chinese use none. Agglutinative languages such as Turkish are highly inflected, employing readily identifiable roots and affixes.

**influenza,** acute, highly contagious disease caused by a number of different viruses. The disease usually begins abruptly with fever, muscular aches, and inflammation of the respiratory mucous membranes. Usually brief and self-limiting, it can be fatal to infants and the elderly and can be complicated by secondary lung infections, such as PNEUMONIA. Influenza epidemics have decimated large populations. An outbreak in 1918 killed over 15 million people. An injection with influenza virus vaccine can confer temporary immunity, but against a specific identified strain only.

**information processing,** an approach in COGNITIVE SCIENCE or psychology which views mental processes in terms of mechanisms and procedures for organizing, storing, transforming, and transmitting information. Typically, information processing theories address problem-solving and inference, which are analysed into a sequence of processing steps oriented to a specific goal. There is also a wider sense in which information processing, seen as synonymous with computation, is held by many psychologists to be the most powerful and fruitful available metaphor for understanding the human mind.

**information processing:** see DATA PROCESSING.

**information storage and retrieval,** the systematic process of collecting and cataloguing data so that it can be located and displayed upon request. DATA PROCESSING and the COMPUTER have made possible the high-speed, selective retrieval of large amounts of information in such fields as science and technology, banking, law enforcement, jurisprudence, and medicine. There are several basic types of information-storage-and-retrieval systems. *Document-retrieval systems* store entire documents; these are usually retrieved by title or through a series of key words that denote the category to which they belong. Full text searching, the capability of retrieving on the basis of any word in the document, is becoming increasingly common, particularly in legal research. DATABASE systems store the information as a series of discrete records, each of a specified type. For each type, each record is divided into discrete fields depending on that type (e.g., name, height, and weight); records can be searched and retrieved on the basis of the content of the fields (e.g., all people who weigh more than 68 kg/150 lb). The data is stored within the computer, either in main storage or auxiliary storage, for ready access. Upon retrieval it may be delivered on magnetic tape or microfilm, or it may be printed. *Reference-retrieval systems* store references to documents; references relevant to a particular request are retrieved and printed in a list. Such a system can therefore provide an index to literature from a wide variety of sources (e.g., books, periodicals, technical journals) on a particular subject (e.g., obesity).

**information theory,** mathematical theory that explains aspects and problems of information and communication. In information theory, the term *information* is a measure of the freedom of choice with which a message is selected from the set of all possible messages. Information is distinct from meaning, because a string of nonsense words and a meaningful sentence may be equivalent with respect to information content. Numerically, information is measured in bits (short for *binary digits*). One bit is equivalent to the choice between two equally likely choices. When several choices are equally likely, the number of bits is equal to the LOGARITHM of the number of choices taken to the base two. When the various choices are not equally probable, the situation is more complex. The mathematical expression for information content closely resembles the expression for ENTROPY in thermodynamics. The greater the information in a message, the lower its randomness, or 'noisiness', and hence the smaller its entropy. A message proceeds along some channel from the source to the receiver; information theory defines for any given channel a limiting capacity or rate at which it can carry information, expressed in bits per second. The theory succeeds remarkably in outlining the engineering requirements and limitations of communications systems.

**infrared radiation,** ELECTROMAGNETIC RADIATION having a wavelength in the range of 750 to 1,000,000 nanometres, thus occupying that part of the electromagnetic spectrum with a frequency less than that of red visible LIGHT and greater than that of MICROWAVES. Infrared radiation is normally thermal, or heat, radiation, and is produced by any body having a temperature above absolute zero. It has many of the same properties as visible light, such as being reflected or refracted.

**Ingres, Jean Auguste Dominique** (,anhgrə), 1780–1867, French painter. Ingres was an unparallelled draughtsman, who, as the leading neo-classical (see CLASSICISM) artist of his day, became the official opponent of DELACROIX's ROMANTICISM. A student of J.-L. DAVID, he also drew inspiration from Greek and Etruscan vases; in Rome (1806–24) he studied RAPHAEL and the art of the Renaissance. Ingres's highly individual, often erotic, classicism depended on the revelation of form through flowing line. He painted elegant portraits e.g., *Mme Moitessier* (1856; National Gall., London); ambitious historical and religious themes; voluptuous nudes in oriental settings, as *Le Bain turc* (1863; Louvre, Paris).

**inheritance tax,** tax imposed on chargeable transfers made during a person's lifetime and, following death, on his or her estate. In the UK the inheritance tax replaced what had been the capital transfer tax in changes introduced by the Finance Act 1986. Under the act lifetime gifts may be transferred between individuals and certain trusts provided death of the donor does not occur within seven years of the transfer. The *gift tax* remained retrospective on transfers made before 17 Mar. 1986. The tax is extremely complicated because of the number of rules which govern it, the exemptions, and the rates at which it is imposed.

**inhibition,** a term with a variety of meanings in psychology. These include: (1) generally, any restraint, prohibition, or diminution of a mental, organic, or behavioural process; (2) in PSYCHOANALYSIS, control of instinctual DRIVES by the SUPEREGO; (3) in neuropsychology, the counter-action of arousal or activation; (4) in LEARNING theory, the diminution of the frequency or intensity of a RESPONSE; (5) in COGNITIVE SCIENCE or psychology, the reduction in performance resulting from competing demands upon memory or other processing resources.

**initiation,** the process of learning about and entering into a new social status. The most important of these are those associated with key points in the life cycle; birth, the transition from childhood to adulthood, marriage, and death. Of these points of transition the most universally significant seems to be the transition from childhood to adulthood. In some societies young people are initiated collectively, almost invariably in segregated groups, in large and elaborate ceremonies, in others individuals are initiated on their own. It has been argued that initiation rituals are one major symbolic form in which male social control of women's natural reproductive power is demonstrated. See RITES DE PASSAGE.

**initiative, referendum, and recall,** processes by which voters can directly influence the making of laws and the removal of public officials. An **initiative** is the originating of a law or constitutional amendment by obtaining a prescribed number of signatures on a petition. It is then either voted on in a special election or the next general election, or taken up by the legislature. **Referendum** is a vote of the whole electorate on a specific law or policy. **Recall** is a petition method for removing an elected official, before his or her term has expired, by requiring a special election.

**injunction,** in law, formal court order directing a party to perform or refrain from performing a specified act. It is often used where monetary

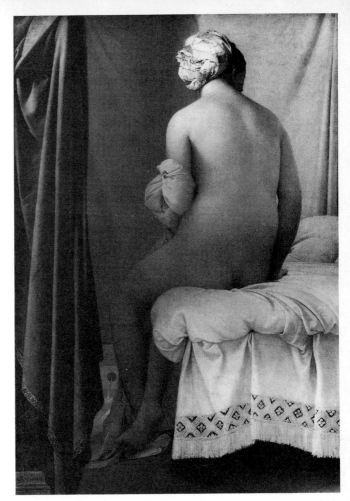

Jean **Ingres,** *Valpicon Baigneuse.* Louvre, Paris.

damages cannot satisfy a plaintiff's claim. Developed in EQUITY courts, injunctions were at first only prohibitory; but the practice of issuing positive orders in negative guise (e.g., 'Do not allow the wall to stand', meaning 'Tear down the wall') led to acceptance of the mandatory injunction. Where appropriate, the courts will also issue an interlocutory injunction, preserving the *status quo* until the full hearing. Injunctions are granted in many circumstances, usually by a judge sitting without a jury, and are enforced by CONTEMPT OF COURT proceedings.

**ink,** pigmented fluid used for writing or drawing, or viscous compound used for printing. The oldest known variety, India or China ink, is still used with brushes in the Far East. Plant dyes and other fluids have been used as ink. The black and blue-black inks used today date from as early as the 2nd cent. Soluble dyes allow modern inks to be filtered through writing instruments. Newsprint ink is absorbed into the paper; many other inks evaporate, leaving pigment on the surface.

**Inland Revenue,** UK government department responsible for administration of the country's direct taxes. These are usually charged on income and capital as distinct from indirect taxes which are paid in the price of goods or services (see CUSTOMS AND EXCISE; VALUE ADDED TAX). The department is also responsible for the collection of National Insurance contributions on behalf of the Department of Health and Social Security, and the department's Valuation Office also plays an important and extensive role in the valuation of land and buildings in the UK apart from Northern Ireland. The Board of the Inland Revenue was created in 1849. See also INCOME TAX. In 1986/87 the total tax collected in the UK was £100,825.9 million of which 56.7% was collected by the Inland Revenue (£57,168.3 million). This compared with a total of £59,672.6 milion in 1980/81 in which year the Inland Revenue collected 55.2% (£32,982.6 million).

**Inland Sea,** shallow arm of the Pacific Ocean, c.9510 km² (3670 sq mi), S Japan, between Honshu, Shikoku, and Kyushu islands. The shallow sea is dotted by islands and linked to the Sea of Japan by a narrow channel. Its shores are heavily populated and contain many of Japan's greatest ports, e.g., OSAKA, KOBE, and Mizushima. Known also for its natural beauty, the sea is the site of a national park.

**inlaying,** process of ornamenting a surface by setting into it material of a different colour or substance. Of ancient origin, inlaying of materials such as wood, stone, ivory, glass, metal, and mother-of-pearl has been used on a wide variety of architectural and decorative objects.

**Inn,** river, 510 km (320 mi) long, rising in the Engadine valley of Switzerland and flowing through the Austrian Tyrol and Bavaria, to join the Danube R. at Passau. Its valley in Austria forms an important routeway and the principal city is INNSBRUCK.

**innate,** those characteristics of an organism which are inborn, by virtue of genetic or hereditary factors; and which are not acquired or developed through experience or LEARNING. Both universal characteristics of a species, and individual differences between members of a species, may be innate. Rationalist theories postulate the existence of innate ideas or human mental capacities.

**Inner Mongolia,** officially Inner Mongolia Autonomous Region, Chinese *Nei Mongol Zizhiqu,* autonomous region (1985 est. pop. 20,070,000), 1,183,000 km² (456,756 sq mi), N China, bordered by the Mongolian Peoples Republic to the north. Major cities include the capital, Huhhot (Huhehot), and Baotou (Pao-t'ou). The Mongolia plateau occupies much of the province, with natural grassland degenerating to scrub and desert to the northwest. This is an important animal-rearing area, with extensive herds of cattle, sheep, and horses. There are limited but important arable crops including wheat. There is little industry, with the exception of iron and steel production at Batou. Historically, Inner Mongolia had closer contact with the Chinese state than did the neighbouring 'Outer Mongolia' (now the Mongolian Peoples Republic). Han Chinese immigration has long been a feature of the area, but since 1949 this has increased. Minority or non-Han Chinese now form only 15% of the province's population.

**Inner Temple:** see INNS OF COURT.

**Innocent I, Saint,** d. 417, pope (401–17), an Italian. He was champion of papal supremacy. In 410, he tried but failed to halt ALARIC's sack of Rome. Feast: 28 July.

**Innocent II,** d. 1143, pope (1130–43), a Roman named Gregorio Papareschi. Opposed by the antipope Anacletus II, Innocent won the support of BERNARD OF CLAIRVAUX and Holy Roman Emperor LOTHAR II and prevailed over Anacletus's successor, Victor IV. He convened the Second Lateran Council (1139) and condemned the teachings of Peter ABELARD and Arnold of Brescia.

**Innocent III,** 1160?–1216, pope (1198–1216), an Italian named Lotario di Segni, one of the most prominent figures of medieval history. A learned theologian, he was firmly convinced that the pope, as church ruler, should be superior to lay rulers of states, a theory not held in present Roman Catholic doctrine. He was the first to make current the title Vicar of Christ. To establish papal supremacy, Innocent was active in political affairs. In the Holy Roman Empire, he arbitrated the dispute of PHILIP OF SWABIA and OTTO IV in Otto's favour (1202); later favoured Philip (1207–08); crowned Otto (1209) after Philip's murder, only to excommunicate him (1210) and bring about the election of FREDERICK II, who was his ward. In England, Innocent, by naming Stephen Langton as archbishop of Canterbury, infuriated King JOHN; in the quarrel, Innocent put England under interdict and excommunicated (1209) the king. John submitted and received England and Ireland as a fief from the pope. Later, Innocent declared that MAGNA CARTA was not binding on John because it was extorted by force and without the knowledge of his overlord (Innocent). In France the pope could not establish political power over PHILIP II, but did force him to bow to canon law in the matter of a divorce. In Italy he reclaimed papal territories and was recognized as overlord of Tuscany. Thus in all Europe he went far to put his theory of papal monarchy into effect, though history was to make his victories hollow. He promoted the Fourth CRUSADE and protested when the Crusaders attacked the Byzantine Empire; nevertheless, he recognized the Latin Kingdom of Constantinople, which they set up, and tried to spread the Latin rite there, embittering relations between the Eastern and Western churches. Similarly, he protested when the crusade he had started against the ALBIGENSES was turned to political and economic ends; he later supported

St DOMINIC's mission. Innocent was vigorous in administering internal church affairs and dominated the Fourth Lateran Council (1215). He wrote extensively and his *De contemptu mundi* [on the contempt of this world] was popular in the Middle Ages.

**Innocent IV,** d. 1254, pope (1243–54), a Genoese named Sinibaldo Fieschi. His papacy was preoccupied by a contest with the HOHENSTAUFEN rulers. He opposed Holy Roman Emperor FREDERICK II and had to flee to Lyons, where he convened (1245) the First Council of Lyons, which declared Frederick deposed. Innocent supported pretenders to Frederick's throne and, after Frederick's death, continued the struggle against the emperors Conrad IV and MANFRED.

**Innocent VIII,** 1432–92, pope (1484–92), a Genoese named Giovanni Battista Cibò. His close friend Giuliano della Rovere (later Pope JULIUS II) largely directed papal affairs. Innocent failed to organize a crusade against the Turkish sultan BEYAZID II, but in 1490 wrung a peace agreement from Beyazid by threatening to recognize Beyazid's brother, Djem, as sultan.

**Innocent XI,** 1611–89, pope (1676–89), an Italian named Benedetto Odescalchi. Noted for his saintliness, he quarrelled with LOUIS XIV of France over papal authority and denounced Louis's Gallican Articles (1682), which claimed that kings are not subject to the pope. He also condemned the king's revocation of the Edict of NANTES (1685). He was beatified in 1956. Feast: 12 Aug.

**Innsbruck,** city (1981 pop. 117,287), capital of TYROL prov., SW Austria, on the Inn R. Established in the 12th cent., it became an important trans-alpine trading post. Today it is an industrial centre and a summer and winter resort. The winter Olympic games were held in Innsbruck in 1964 and 1976. The city's historic buildings include the Hofkirche, a 16th-cent. Franciscan church, and the 15th-cent. Fürstenburg castle.

**Inns of Court,** in England and Wales, term to describe the societies and buildings that house the barristers' branch of the LEGAL PROFESSION. All barristers must belong to one of the Inns of Court. Historically, they date back to the 13th cent. and arose through aspiring barristers coming to reside and work with established members of the profession. There are presently four inns: Gray's Inn, Lincoln's Inn, Middle Temple, and Inner Temple. The Inns now run the barristers' examinations through the Council of Legal Education (est. 1852) and control admission to the Bar. In 1966, the four Inns established the Senate of the Inns of Court in order to give them a collective voice on matters of common interest.

**inoculation:** see VACCINATION.

**inorganic chemistry:** see CHEMISTRY.

**inquiline,** in ENTOMOLOGY, an INSECT or other ARTHROPOD, living as a guest, in the nest of a social hymenopteran (see ANT, BEE, and WASP) or of a TERMITE. Some inquilines are simply scavengers, feeding on dead bodies and waste products, e.g., the larvae of *Volucella,* a hover-fly (Syrphidae), in the nests of bumble bees and social wasps. Ant colonies, even those of the nomadic Dorylinae, support many other insects. There are about 300 species of inquilines in Britain, of which 70 are beetles. Some are scavengers but will also feed on ant brood and are barely tolerated. Others, which include the diminutive CRICKETS (Myrmecophila), are tolerated and often exploit the ants' mutual feeding, imbibing some of the liquid being passed from one ant to another. Some insects are welcome guests, and are carefully looked after and fed because they produce secretions, from glands in various parts of their bodies, of which ants are very fond, e.g., the larvae of some blue butterflies (Lycaenidae). There are also some slave-making ants (e.g., *Formica sanguinea*) which supplement their workforce by stealing pupae from the nests of related species (e.g., *Formica fusca*), and others (e.g., *Anergates*) which no longer have workers of their own and have become social parasites.

**Inquisition,** tribunal of the Roman Catholic Church formed to suppress heresy. In 1233 Pope GREGORY IX established the papal Inquisition to combat the heresy of the ALBIGENSES. The Inquisition used judicial torture, but rarely condemned prisoners to burn; imprisonment was the norm. To deal with Protestantism, PAUL III assigned (1542) the Inquisition to the Holy Office. This was replaced (1965) by the Congregation for the Doctrine of the Faith, which governs vigilance in matters of faith. The **Spanish Inquisition,** independent of the papal Inquisition, was established (1479) by the Spanish monarchs to punish converted Jews and Muslims who were insincere. Headed by men such as Tomás de TORQUEMADA, it was notoriously harsher than the medieval Inquisition and much freer with the death penalty. Soon every Spaniard came to fear its power. It was finally abolished in 1820.

**insanity,** in law, term denoting a mental disorder so severe as to render its victim incapable of managing his or her affairs, e.g., incapable of entering into a CONTRACT. In CRIMINAL LAW, insanity may relieve a person from the legal consequences of his or her acts. In the UK (except Scotland), some Commonwealth countries, and parts of the US, insanity is decided according to the McNaughton Rules, first laid down in the House of Lords in 1843. The main rule states that for a person to be found not guilty by reason of insanity they must prove that as a result of a disease of the mind they did not know what they were doing, or if they did, that they did not know it was wrong. In the UK, 'irresistible impulse' is not a valid defence. In some jurisdictions a defendant can plead present insanity, i.e., that he or she is incapable of understanding the legal proceedings against them. A defendant found not guilty by reason of insanity is committed to a mental institution rather than a prison. Verdicts involving insanity are often controversial, and there has been criticism from the legal and medical professions of the assumptions behind the present rules.

**insect,** invertebrate animal of the class Insecta, an ARTHROPOD. There are more than one million known species. Insects have a chitinous exoskeleton and a segmented body composed of a head (with basically three pairs of mouthparts, compound and simple eyes, and sensory antennae), a three-segmented thorax (with three pairs of jointed legs and two pairs of wings), and an abdomen (with reproductive appendages). They breathe through a complex network of air tubes (tracheae) opening on the sides of the body. Reproduction is usually sexual, although PARTHENOGENESIS is also common. Some 80% of insect species undergo complete METAMORPHOSIS. Insects are both harmful to mankind as disease carriers and agricultural pests and beneficial as pollinating agents, as predators on harmful species, as providers of HONEY, WAX, and SILK, and as food (e.g., LOCUSTS and TERMITES) in some parts of the world. The class includes BEETLES; MOTHS and BUTTERFLIES; WASPS, ANTS, and BEES; FLIES; MOSQUITOES; true BUGS; APHIDS; COCKROACHES; and GRASSHOPPERS.

**insecticide,** chemical agent used to kill insect pests. Insecticides have helped increase the yield and improve the quality of crops, but there has been concern about the dangers of insecticide residues in the ecosystem (see ECOLOGY) and in foodstuffs. Such concerns have led in some countries to governmental regulation and the replacement of toxic insecticides that persist in the environment (e.g., DDT and other chlorinated hydrocarbons) by compounds that break down more quickly into nontoxic forms. In addition, partly because insects can become resistant to insecticides, there has been interest in comprehensive pest-management techniques, including the use of biological control agents (e.g., predator insects) that harm only certain pests.

**instinct,** in psychology and ethology, a term denoting a type of behaviour, a tendency to behave in a particular way, or a primary DRIVE which is characteristic of all members of a species and which is not acquired, but may be modulated, by LEARNING. Instincts and instinctual behaviour are therefore frequently said to be INNATE. However, the development of many types of instinctual behaviour depends upon both innate capacities or RESPONSE patterns, and specific types of experience. For example, in many species of songbird, there is an instinct to sing which is manifest even in the absence of a 'model' to learn from; but in natural conditions the developing bird will acquire the particular birdsong 'dialect' characteristic of its social community.

**Institut de France** (ənhstee,ty də frahnhs), cultural institution of the French state. Founded in 1795 by the DIRECTORY, it replaced five learned societies that had been suppressed in 1793 by the Convention. Today it is made up of five academies, the French Academy (Académie Française), the Académie des Inscriptions et Belles-Lettres (history and archaeology), the Académie des Sciences, the Académie des Beaux-Arts, and the Académie des Sciences morales et politiques. The awards and prizes given by these academies have encouraged endeavor in various fields.

**instructional television:** see AUDIOVISUAL AIDS.

**instrumental:** see CASE.

**insulation,** use of materials to inhibit or prevent the CONDUCTION of heat or of electricity. Common heat insulators are ASBESTOS, CELLULOSE fibres, FEATHERS, FIBRE GLASS, FUR, stone, WOOD, and WOOL; all are poor conductors of heat. In the conduction of electricity from point to point, the conductor acts as a guide for the electric current and must be insulated at every point of contact with its support to prevent escape, or leakage, of the current. Good electrical insulators, or DIELECTRIC materials, include dry air, dry COTTON, GLASS, PARAFFIN WAX, PORCELAIN, RESIN, RUBBER, and VARNISHES.

**insulin,** HORMONE secreted by the islets of Langerhans in the PANCREAS. Insulin is a PROTEIN consisting of 51 amino acids in two cross-linked chains. Its amino acid sequence was discovered by Frederick SANGER and its synthesis was reported by several groups in the mid 1960s. In general, insulin acts to reduce levels of glucose in the blood by interacting with cell membranes, provoking changes in METABOLISM within the cell. It also increases protein synthesis in muscle. Insufficient insulin in the body results in DIABETES, a condition treated by the administration of insulin.

**insurance** or **assurance,** system or business for indemnifying or guaranteeing an individual against loss. Reimbursement is made from a fund to which many individuals exposed to the same risk have contributed specified amounts, known as premiums, so that payment for the loss is divided among many, not falling heavily upon the actual loser. The essence of the contract of insurance, called a policy, is mutuality. The amount of the premium is determined by the operation of the law of averages, as calculated by actuaries. Re-insurance, whereby losses are distributed among many companies, was devised to meet the enormous claims resulting from disasters. Insurance may now be obtained against almost any conceivable risk. Fire insurance usually covers damage from lightning; other insurance against the elements includes hail, tornado, flood, and drought. Life insurance, known in the UK as assurance, was originally conceived to protect a wage-earner's family when he or she died, and has developed policies that provide the insured a lump sum at the end of a term of years. Annuity policies, which pay the insured a yearly income after a certain age, are also available. Motor-car insurance compensates not only for fire and theft but also for damage to the car and for injury to the victim of an accident. Under British law all motor cars on the road must be insured for third party risks. Bonding, or fidelity insurance, protects an employer against dishonesty or default by an employee. In group insurance, employees pay a lower premium than they would as individuals. By investing premium payments in a wide range of revenue-producing projects, insurance companies have become a major supplier of capital. Many forms of insurance today, such as SOCIAL SECURITY, workmen's compensation, and unemployment benefits, are government-sponsored. Bottomry contracts (under which a ship's owner borrowed money to finance a voyage, pledging the ship itself as security) are recorded from 4000 BC and were the forerunners of modern marine insurance which by the mid-14th cent. was widely practised by the maritime nations of Europe. The first life-insurance policy is believed to have been issued in England in 1583, and Lloyds, perhaps the world's best-known insurance firm, began issuing marine insurance in London in the 1600s. See also HEALTH INSURANCE.

**intaglio,** design cut into stone or other material, or etched or engraved in a metal plate, producing a concave effect that is the reverse of relief or CAMEO. Intaglio PRINTING techniques include engraving and etching.

**integer:** see NUMBER; NUMBER THEORY.

**integral calculus:** see CALCULUS.

**integrated circuit (IC),** an electronic circuit in which all the individual electronic components (for example, transistors) are fabricated onto a single chip of semiconducting material, commonly silicon (see SEMICONDUCTOR). A chip is classified in terms of the number of components it contains as follows; VLSI, Very Large Scale Integration (more than 100,000); LSI, Large Scale Integration (10,000 to 100,000), MSI, Medium Scale Integration (100 to 10,000) and SSI, Small Scale Integration (less than 100). The rate of technological progress and miniaturization is such that the number of components on a chip has doubled every two years and this process has revolutionized computing; for example, it is now cost-effective to provide individuals with personal workstations which may lie idle for considerable periods of time (see PERSONAL COMPUTER). A MICROPROCESSOR is an IC containing a computer processor unit and a limited amount of memory; a MICROCOMPUTER contains a microprocessor plus memory ICs and other ICs to interface with peripherals.

**integration,** the process whereby a distinctive racial, cultural, or religious minority group merges with and is accepted by, the dominant group within a society, without fundamentally changing its own way of

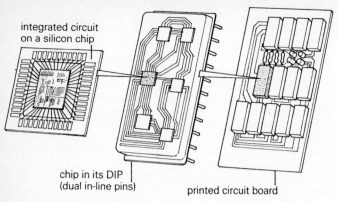

integrated circuit
on a silicon chip

chip in its DIP
(dual in-line pins)

printed circuit board

Integrated circuit

life giving rise to a 'multicultural' society. This process is contrasted to *assimilation*, where the minority group is expected to change its values to facilitate incorporation into the dominant group. In some places, distinct ethnic groups coexist without integration (plural societies), sometimes peacefully (e.g., Afro-Caribbean and Asian descendants in Trinidad), more often with tensions and violence (e.g., Protestants and Catholics in Ireland, Jews and Palestinians on the West Bank of the Jordan R. Sinhalese and Tamils in Sri Lanka). In South Africa black/white social integration is illegal (see APARTHEID). In the American South following the Civil War, blacks were often segregated in education, housing, transport, and other public facilities, a practice upheld by the Supreme Court (1896) and only effectively challenged by the Civil Rights movement from the 1950s and the campaigns associated with Martin Luther KING. Many areas of American life are still, however, subject to informal segregation. Apart from laws restricting immigration of particular ethnic groups, Britain has no legally enforced segregation though there is considerable, informal, residential, occupational and cultural segregation between Afro-Caribbean or Asian groups and the white population. Discrimination in terms of equal access to education, jobs, promotion, etc., continues to be a source of tension. The Commission for Racial Equality (founded 1976) and many voluntary community groups are dedicated to the full ethnic integration of the New Commonwealth immigrant settler groups, which has not yet been achieved. This aim is opposed by those who favour separate cultural development or by groups committed to theories of racial and cultural superiority (e.g., the National Front).

**intelligence,** in general, an attribute of cognition or of behaviour manifesting cognitive processes. Intelligent behaviour is that which involves reasoning, judgment, planning, inference and other generalized and complex mental or intellectual activities. Intelligence may also be seen as an attribute of an organism which behaves in an intelligent fashion, where it is characterised by flexible and general, as opposed to rigid and specific, modes of adaptation. This is the basis for PIAGET's approach to the development of intelligence. In a more limited sense, human intelligence is sometimes equated with Intelligence Quotient (IQ), a measure of performance based upon individual differences in test scores. IQ tests have been widely used as predictors of scholastic achievement, but have also been criticized for being socio-culturally biased, discriminating against individuals from disadvantaged ethnic and/or social class backgrounds. It is widely accepted that, within a given group, differences in IQ scores reflect an interaction between HEREDITY AND ENVIRONMENT. The suggestion by a minority of psychologists that measured IQ differences between, for example, ethnic groups also reflect genetic factors has led to fierce controversy, and is widely repudiated both on scientific grounds, and because of its racist connotations.

**intelligence gathering,** securing of military, political, or other information, usually about one nation for the benefit of another. It includes the analysis of diplomatic reports, publications, statistics, and broadcasts, as well as **espionage,** or spying, a clandestine activity. French revolutionary Joseph FOUCHÉ developed (1799–1802) the first modern political espionage system, and FREDERICK II of Prussia is considered the father of modern military espionage, which was to play an important role in WORLD WAR I. The efficient British system, particularly in CRYPTOGRAPHY, was the keystone of Allied intelligence in WORLD WAR II. The US CENTRAL INTELLIGENCE AGENCY (CIA) is of enormous influence worldwide, in that its activities go beyond the gathering of intelligence and extend to covert intervention in the affairs of foreign states. The UK's equivalent (though for less important) is MI6. Modern techniques include reconnaissance satellites, long-distance photography, sophisticated sensing and listening ('bugging') devices, and computer analysis and cryptanalysis. Defence against espionage is principally a function of counterintelligence specialists. In the business world, the massive task of information-gathering that is a normal part of marketing may occasionally include so-called industrial espionage; an attempt by one company to discover another's secrets.

**interaction,** term used in STATISTICS to indicate the change in a response to one experimental treatment as a result of the effects of other treatments in the same experiment. R.A. FISHER, working on the effects of fertilizers on agricultural crops, developed methods for the DESIGN OF EXPERIMENTS which enabled the effects of several experimental treatments and their interactions to be determined simultaneously. The term 'interaction' is now more widely used to show the joint effects of two or more factors in a complex situation. For example, there is an interaction between the effects of alcohol and tiredness on response times of drivers.

**interest,** charge for the use of money, usually calculated as a percentage of the principal and computed annually. Such charges have been made since ancient times, and they fell early into disrepute. The Jews and the Christian church forbade interest charges, or usury, as it was called, within their own groups. The early classical economists such as Adam SMITH regarded interest simply as income on capital but as theories developed, it became more a factor determined by supply and demand. Today, international and national factors combined with the element of risk are important determinants of interest rates. For example, the bank rate (see BANKING) may be heavily influenced by capital movements and the need to maintain the value of a national currency. In the UK, this rate influences loan rates of BUILDING SOCIETIES which provide a high proportion of all housing finance. At the same time the societies must balance their loan rates against their deposit rates in order to attract sufficient funds to maintain capital levels. High interest rates may have a dampening affect on a country's economy since they constrain business profits and expansion, and curbs consumer demand, particularly for housing. Low rates may lead to overborrowing and eventual disaster.

**interference,** in physics, the effect obtained when two WAVE systems reinforce, neutralize, or in other ways interfere with each other. Interference is observed in waves both in a material medium (such as SOUND) and in ELECTROMAGNETIC RADIATION. *Constructive interference* occurs when two waves in the same phase combine. The waves reinforce each other, and the amplitude of the resulting wave is equal to the sum of the amplitudes of the interfering waves. When the phases of the two waves differ by 180°, i.e., the maximum positive amplitude of one wave coincides with the maximum negative amplitude of the other wave, *destructive interference* occurs, which results in the cancelling of the waves when they have the same amplitude. See DIFFRACTION.

**interferon,** protein produced by cells in the body in response to viruses. Interferon impairs the growth and replication of the attacking virus and may have some antitumour properties. Its possible role in the treatment of disease is still in the early stages of investigation.

**interjection:** see PART OF SPEECH.

**Interlingua:** see INTERNATIONAL LANGUAGE.

**internal-combustion engine,** engine in which combustion of fuel takes place in a confined space, producing expanding gases that are used to provide mechanical powers there. The most common internal-combustion engine is the four-stroke reciprocating engine used in motor vehicles. Here, mechanical power is supplied by a piston fitting inside a cylinder. A downstroke of the piston, the first stroke, draws a mixture of fuel and air into the cylinder from the CARBURETTOR through an intake valve; the piston moves up to compress the mixture at the second stroke; at ignition, the third stroke, a spark from a spark plug ignites the mixture, forcing the piston down; in the exhaust stroke, an exhaust valve opens to vent the burned gas as the piston moves up. A rod connects the piston to a crankshaft. The reciprocating (up and down) movements of the piston rotate the crankshaft, which is connected by gearing to the drive wheels of the vehicle. The ignition spark is provided by an electrical system whose power comes from a battery, which also supplies power to the starting system, a small electric motor that turns the crankshaft until the

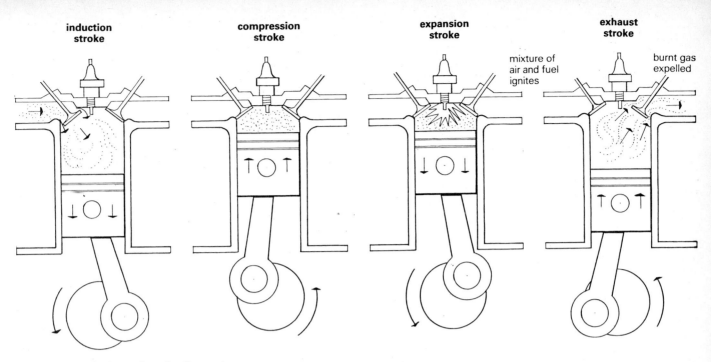

induction stroke   compression stroke   expansion stroke   exhaust stroke

mixture of air and fuel ignites

burnt gas expelled

Cycle of a four-stroke internal combustion engine

engine takes over. The engine is cooled by water circulating around the cylinders and is lubricated by motor oil driven around the moving engine parts by an oil pump. The two-stroke engine, which combines intake and compression in the first stroke and power and exhaust in the second, is used in lawn mowers and for small vehicles such as motorcycles. Other variations of the internal-combustion engine include the WANKEL ENGINE, which replaces the piston and cylinder with a triangular rotor moving inside an oval chamber, and the DIESEL engine. (For a description of an external-combustion engine, see STEAM ENGINE.)

**Internal Macedonian Revolutionary Organization,** (IMRO or, in Bulgarian, VMRO), a liberation movement founded in 1893 in Thessaloniki to fight for Macedonian Slav unity and autonomy, sometimes envisaged as occurring through union with BULGARIA and at other times through formation of a Balkan confederation. IMRO led the 1903 Ilinden Rising against the Turks which proclaimed a short-lived republic in W MACEDONIA, but after the partition of the region in the BALKAN WARS (1912–13) the main wing of the organization fell under Sofia's control. It became notorious for its bloody infighting and was more important for its destabilizing role in Bulgarian politics than for its terrorist provocations in Greek or Yugoslav-ruled Macedonia. The organization was forcibly disbanded by Czar BORIS in 1934.

**International Air Transport Association,** (IATA), body controlling cooperation between international airlines. The first IATA was founded in 1919, with British, Danish, Norwegian, Swedish, and German airlines as members. After World War II the present Association was formed (1945) on a wider basis, with permanent staff in Montreal and Geneva; its concerns are cooperation on safety measures, on inter-airline agreements, and on standardization of procedures, and it acts as a currency clearing house for members. By the late 1980s IATA had a membership of 131 international airlines and 29 associated airlines, whose combined operating revenue was about US$90,000 billion per year. See also AIR TRANSPORT.

**International Atomic Energy Agency:** see UNITED NATIONS (table 3).

**International Civil Aviation Organization:** see UNITED NATIONS (table 3).

**International Council for Bird Preservation (ICBP),** council founded in London in 1922 by ornithologists and conservationists to co-ordinate bird preservation throughout the world. It has worked to protect migrating wildfowl in Europe and instigated the setting up of the Advisory Committee for the Prevention of Pollution of the Sea, with a research project on the cleaning and rehabilitation of oiled sea birds. The ICBP

acquired Cousin Island in the Seychelles group in 1968 and set it up as an international reserve.

**International Court of Justice:** see UNITED NATIONS (table 2).

**International Criminal Police Organization:** see INTERPOL.

**international date line,** imaginary line on the earth's surface, generally following the 180° meridian of LONGITUDE, where, by international agreement, travellers change dates. Travelling eastward across the line, one subtracts one day; travelling westward, one adds a day. The date line is necessary to avoid confusion. For example, if an aeroplane were to travel westward with the sun, 24 hours would elapse as it circled the globe, but it would still be the same day for those in the aeroplane, while it would be one day later for those on the ground below. The date line and the time zones into which the world is by convention divided are devices by which local time everywhere on the globe is made to correspond with day and night: noon occurs approximately in the middle of the day and midnight about halfway through the hours of darkness.

**International Democrat Union** (IDU), international coordinating centre (est. 1983) of about 30 conservative and centre-right political parties. The IDU's regional organizations are the European Democrat Union (est. 1978), the Pacific Democrat Union (est. 1982), and the Caribbean Democrat Union (est. 1986).

**International Energy Agency** (IEA), intergovernmental organization set up in 1974 within the framework of the ORGANIZATION FOR ECONOMIC COOPERATION AND DEVELOPMENT to coordinate oil-consuming countries' response to the oil supply and price crisis of the 1970s. Initially including Austria, Belgium, Canada, Denmark, West Germany, Ireland, Italy, Japan, Luxembourg, the Netherlands, Spain, Sweden, Switzerland, Turkey, the UK, and the US, the IEA was later joined by Australia, Greece, New Zealand, Norway, and Portugal.

**International Finance Corporation:** see UNITED NATIONS (table 3).

**International Fund for Agricultural Development:** see UNITED NATIONS (table 3).

**International Labour Organization:** see UNITED NATIONS (table 3).

**international language,** sometimes called universal language, a language intended to be used by people of different linguistic backgrounds to facilitate communication. Latin was an international language during the Middle Ages and Renaissance. During the 18th cent., French was known as the language of diplomacy, and English is often said to fill such a role today in world commerce. Many artificial languages, i.e., languages constructed by human agents, have also been promoted as international languages. It has been estimated that since the 17th cent. several hundred efforts have been made to create such artificial tongues. Among the best known of these is Esperanto, invented by Dr Ludwig L. Zamenhoff of Poland and first presented to the public in 1887. It has enjoyed some recognition as an international language, being used, for example, at international meetings and conferences. The vocabulary of Esperanto is formed by adding various affixes to individual roots and is derived from Latin, Greek, the Romance languages, and the Germanic languages. The grammar is based on that of European languages but is regular and greatly simplified. The spelling is phonetic. A simplified form of Esperanto is Ido, short for Esperandido. Another well-known artificial language is Interlingua, created in 1951 by the International Auxiliary Language Association. It is derived from English and the Romance languages in both grammar and vocabulary, and has been used at medical and scientific meetings.

**international law,** body of laws considered legally binding among national states; also known as the law of nations. It is based both on customary usages and on provisions of multilateral or bilateral agreements. It is influenced, but not made, by the writings of jurists, unratified conventions, and decisions of the WORLD COURT, the INTERNATIONAL COURT OF JUSTICE, and other tribunals. Since it is not enforced by any supranational sovereign body, some theorists, including HOBBES, have denied it true legal status. But it is recognized in practice, and enforcement is by virtue of world opinion, third-state intervention, sanctions of international organizations like the UN, and, in the last resort, war. In some areas, such as WAR CRIMES, international law governs individuals as well as states. The development of international law coincides with the rise of national states after the Middle Ages, and the first comprehensive formulation of international law, *Concerning the Law of War and Peace,* by Hugo GROTIUS, appeared in 1625; among the principles that he enunciated as the basis of international law are the SOVEREIGNTY and legal equality of all states. International law thereafter grew largely through treaties among states. Following the Napoleonic period, the 1815 Congress of VIENNA re-established and expanded international law. The GENEVA CONVENTION (1864) and the HAGUE CONFERENCES (1899, 1907), dealing with the rules of war, are other landmarks in development of an international legal code. The 20th cent. presented new problems: two world wars led to the formation of the LEAGUE OF NATIONS, and then of the UNITED NATIONS, as a body capable of compelling obedience to international law; nuclear proliferation exacerbated the need for international arms treaties; and burgeoning space exploration has led to creation of the field of SPACE LAW.

**International Maritime Organization:** see UNITED NATIONS (table 3).

**International Monetary Fund:** see UNITED NATIONS (table 3).

**international monetary system,** rules and procedures by which different national currencies are exchanged for each other in world trade. The first formal international monetary system of modern times was the GOLD STANDARD, in effect during the late 19th and early 20th cent. Gold served as an instrument of exchange and the only standard of value. The international gold standard broke down in 1914, however, partly because of its inherent lack of liquidity. It was replaced by a gold-bullion standard, but that, too, was abandoned in the 1930s. In the decades following World War II, international trade was conducted under a gold-exchange standard. Under this system, nations fixed the value of their currencies not to gold but to some foreign currency, which was in turn fixed to and redeemable in gold. Most nations fixed their currencies to the US dollar. During the 1960s, however, a severe drain on US gold reserves led to the introduction (1968) of the so-called two-tier system. In the official tier, the value of gold was set at $35 per ounce; in the free-market tier, the price was free to fluctuate according to SUPPLY AND DEMAND. At the same time, the International Monetary Fund (IMF) created SPECIAL DRAWING RIGHTS as a new reserve currency. In the early 1970s new troubles plagued the international monetary system, resulting in the temporary adoption of 'floating' exchange rates based largely on supply and demand. Finally, under a 1976 agreement IMF members accepted a system of controlled floating rates and took steps to diminish the importance of gold in international transactions, including elimination of the official price. See FOREIGN EXCHANGE.

**International Physicians for the Prevention of Nuclear War** (IPPNW), international umbrella organization for many national groups of doctors (such as the Medical Campaign Against Nuclear Weapons in Britain) campaigning to prevent nuclear war. Established by Soviet and American physicians in 1980, it encourages discussion and research on the effects of nuclear war. It was awarded the 1986 Nobel Peace Prize.

**International style,** in architecture, form that originated in the 1920s and became the dominant mode of public architecture in the 1950s and 1960s. Structure was regularized, mass lightened, and ornament suppressed, often resulting in an austere framework and great expanses of glass. Outstanding examples of the International style are the BAUHAUS (1926) at Dessau, Germany by GROPIUS, and the Barcelona pavilion (1929), by MIÈS VAN DER ROHE.

**International Telecommunication Union:** see UNITED NATIONS (table 3).

**International Union for the Conservation of Nature and Natural Resources** (IUCN), organization founded in 1948 to co-ordinate conservation efforts by governments. First named the International Union for the Protection of Nature, the name was changed to the present one in 1956. In 1961 it gave rise to the WORLD WIDE FUND FOR NATURE, and it publishes the RED DATA BOOK.

**International Workingmen's Association:** see under SECOND INTERNATIONAL.

**Inter-Parliamentary Union** (IPU), forum for contact between the world's parliamentary assemblies. Established in 1889 by eight countries, the IPU now includes almost all parliaments throughout the world without distinction as to political system.

**Interpol,** acronym for the International Criminal Police Organization, a worldwide clearinghouse for POLICE information. Established in Vienna in 1923, it was reconstituted in Paris in 1946. Focusing on counterfeiting, forgery, smuggling, and the drugs trade, it serves more than 100 member nations, providing information about international criminals and helping to apprehend them.

**interstellar matter,** matter in a galaxy between the stars. About 1% is tiny interstellar grains, believed to be largely frozen water vapour and carbon dioxide. The grains may appear optically as bright reflection or dark NEBULAE. The bulk of the matter is gas, mostly hydrogen and helium, but many molecules have been detected by RADIO ASTRONOMY techniques.

**intestine,** muscular, hoselike portion of the DIGESTIVE SYSTEM extending from the lower end of the STOMACH to the anal opening. In humans, the small intestine is a narrow tubelike structure that winds compactly back and forth within the abdominal cavity. Its muscular walls contract rhythmically (peristalsis) propelling food onwards while digestion is completed. Innumerable small fingerlike projections (villi) in the intestinal lining absorb the nutrients for distribution by the BLOOD and LYMPHATIC SYSTEM to the rest of the body. In the lower right abdominal cavity the small intestine joins the large intestine (colon), where most of the water content of the remaining mass is absorbed.

**Intolerable Acts,** name given by American patriots to five laws (including the QUEBEC ACT) adopted by the British Parliament in 1774, limiting the geographical and political freedom of the colonists. Four of the laws were passed to punish Massachusetts for the BOSTON TEA PARTY.

**Intracoastal Waterway,** toll-free, sheltered water route, extending 3950 km (2455 mi) along the US Atlantic Coast (Trenton, New Jersey–Key West, Florida) and the Gulf Coast (NW Florida–Brownsville, Texas), with open-water extensions of 1038 km (645 mi) N to Boston and along the W Florida coast. Authorized by Congress in 1919 and maintained by the Army Corps of Engineers, the waterway has a minimum depth of 4 m (12 ft) for most of its length, and is used by commercial and pleasure boats.

**intrauterine device** (IUD), variously shaped contraceptive device, made of plastic or metal, which is inserted into the uterus by a doctor. The IUD is thought to create a hostile environment for the sperm or fertilized egg. Its efficacy is good but it poses health risks of infection and perforation of the uterus. See also CONTRACEPTION.

**introspection,** the mental act of examining one's own experiences and the contents of consciousness. Early experimental psychology frequently employed introspection, but this technique was virtually abandoned with the rise of BEHAVIOURISM. Although it remains an important method in theoretical linguistics, it is generally believed that many processes of COGNITION are not available to introspection.

**Inuit:** see ESKIMO.

**Inverness,** town (1981) pop. 38,204), Highland region, N Scotland, at mouth of R. Ness at entrance to Beauly Firth. It is an administrative and tourist centre, whose industries include distilling, manufacture of woollen goods, and sawmills. The Caledonian Canal passes to the W of the town.

**invertebrate,** any multicellular animal lacking a backbone. Invertebrates include all animals except the fishes, amphibians, reptiles, birds, and mammals, which are in the phylum Chordata (see CHORDATE). The major invertebrate groups are the segmented or ANNELID WORMS, ARTHROPODS, COELENTERATES, ECHINODERMS, FLATWORMS, MOLLUSCS, ROUNDWORMS, and SPONGES.

**investiture,** feudal ceremony by which a lord 'invested' a vassal with a fief, usually by giving him a symbolic stone or clod. In clerical investiture, the symbols were the pastoral ring and staff. Since bishops and abbots were both spiritual and temporal lords, kings and popes disputed the right of investiture in the Middle Ages. Lay investiture, the investiture of a cleric by a temporal lord, generated a bitter quarrel between Pope GREGORY VII and the Emperor HENRY IV when Gregory forbade (1075) it. After a long conflict, HENRY V and Pope CALIXTUS II resolved the issue in the Concordat of WORMS. In England, WILLIAM II began a long struggle over investiture that was settled (1107) by a compromise between HENRY I and St ANSELM by which the king gave up investiture but retained homage of the bishops.

**investment trust,** a company which exists solely to invest its capital in other companies. In order to raise capital it issues shares and may also issue fixed interest securities. Management expenses incurred by an investment trust are taken out of taxed income and not from the income of shareholders. See UNIT TRUSTS.

**in vitro fertilization,** technique for conception of a human embryo outside the mother's body. The ovum, or egg, is removed from the mother's body and placed in a special laboratory culture medium; sperm from the father are then added. If fertilization occurs, the fertilized ovum, after undergoing several cell divisions, is transferred to the mother's body for normal development in the uterus. First developed in Britain by Dr Patrick C. Steptoe and Dr Robert G. Edwards (the first 'test-tube baby' was born under their care in 1978), the technique was devised for use in cases of infertility where the woman's fallopian tubes are damaged and cannot be surgically repaired or the man's sperm count is low. See also ARTIFICIAL INSEMINATION; REPRODUCTIVE SYSTEM.

**Io,** in astronomy, natural satellite of JUPITER.

**Io,** in Greek mythology, princess of Argos. She was turned into a heifer by ZEUS to protect her from HERA's jealousy. Hera claimed the heifer and had the many-eyed monster ARGUS guard it. When HERMES killed Argus, Hera's gadfly drove Io until she came to rest in Egypt. There Zeus returned her to human form. She appears in AESCHYLUS's *Prometheus Bound.* Io has been identified with the Egyptian ISIS.

**iodine** (I), nonmetallic element, discovered in 1811 by Bernard Courtois. The least active of the HALOGEN elements, it is a dark-grey to purple-black solid that, when heated, sublimes directly to the vapour state. The violet-coloured vapour has a characteristic irritating odour. Tincture of iodine and iodoform have important medical uses. Silver iodide is used in photography. Starch turns deep-blue in the presence of iodine; this is a test for either substance. Thyroid-gland hormones contain iodine; inadequate dietary iodine results in goitre, a swelling of the thyroid. Thyroid defects are treated with iodine-131. See ELEMENT (table); PERIODIC TABLE.

**ion,** atom or group of atoms that carries a positive or negative electrical charge acquired by gaining or losing one or more electrons or protons. A simple ion consists of only one charged atom; a complex ion consists of an aggregate of atoms with a net charge. Because the electron and proton have equal but opposite unit charges, the charge of an ion is always expressed as a whole number of positive or negative unit charges. If an atom or group loses electrons or gains protons, it will have a net positive charge and is called a **cation.** If an atom or group gains electrons or loses protons, it will have a net negative charge and is called an **anion.** See also ACIDS AND BASES; COMPOUND; ELECTROLYTE.

**Iona,** island, 5.6 km (3.5 mi) long and 2.4 km (1.5 mi) wide, NW Scotland, one of the Inner HEBRIDES. Tourism is the main industry. The island is famous as the early centre of Celtic Christianity. In 563 St COLUMBA founded a monastery there and spread Christianity to Scotland.

**Ionesco, Eugène** (yo͵neskoh), 1912–, French playwright; b. Romania. His works express the absurdity of bourgeois values and the futility of human endeavour in a universe ruled by chance. *La cantatrice chauve* (1950; tr. The Bald Soprano), a classic of the theatre of the absurd, was followed by *Le leçon* (1951; tr. The Lesson), *Les chaises* (1952; tr. The Chairs), and *Rhinocéros* (1959).

**Ionia** (ie͵ohneeə), ancient Greek region of ASIA MINOR, on the E Mediterranean (in present-day TURKEY), and including the Aegean Islands. It was here that the Ionians, Greek colonists driven from the mainland by the Dorians, established colonies before 1000 BC There came to be 12 important cities among them MILETUS, SÁMOS, and EPHESUS. After invasions by Cimmeria and Lydia the cities came under Persian rule (546 BC). In 500 BC they revolted against DARIUS I; Athens and Eritrea came to their aid, and the PERSIAN WARS resulted. Ionia was conquered by ALEXANDER THE GREAT in 335 BC The cities remained rich and important during the Roman and Byzantine empires, but after the Turkish conquest (15th cent. AD) their culture was destroyed.

**Ionic order:** see ORDERS OF ARCHITECTURE.

**ionization chamber:** see PARTICLE DETECTOR.

**ionosphere:** see ATMOSPHERE.

**Iowa,** state of the US (1984 est. pop. 2,910,000), area 145,791 km² (56,290 sq mi), located in the north–central region, bordered by Wisconsin and Illinois (E), Missouri (S), Nebraska and south Dakota (W), and Minnesota (N). DES MOINES is the capital and Cedar Rapids and Davenport are the other major cities. Most of Iowa is composed of gently rolling prairies, covered with some of the world's most fertile soil, between the high bluffs of the MISSISSIPPI and MISSOURI rivers. With a greater area under cultivation than any other state, Iowa is one of the most prosperous agricultural economies in the US, producing corn, soyabeans, wheat, and barley, which also feed cattle and pigs. Manufacturing, however, provides more income, in the form of nonelectrical machinery, electronic equipment, processed foods, and chemicals. Only 37% of the population lives in metropolitan areas, 97% is non-Hispanic white. The earliest known inhabitants were Mound Builders, followed by Sac and Fox, Iowa and Sioux Indians, and then the French in the late 17th cent. The US obtained the area with the LOUISIANA PURCHASE (1803), and after the Indians lost their lands in the Black Hawk War the prairies were settled. Iowa's rural population supported many reform movements in the 19th cent., including the Granger Movement, Greenback Party, and Populist Party. Despite an increase in the urban population in the 20th cent. it is still essentially a rural state, and the fall in farm commodity prices in the 1980s has caused severe problems.

**Iphigenia** ('ifiji͵neeə), in Greek mythology, daughter of CLYTEMNESTRA and AGAMEMNON. When his ships were becalmed en route to the TROJAN WAR, Agamemnon sacrificed Iphigenia to ARTEMIS. In another version, Artemis saved her and made her a priestess at Taurus. Later, Iphigenia saved her brother, ORESTES, and the two fled to Greece. EURIPIDES dramatized both legends, later adapted as operas by GLUCK, and the story also inspired plays by RACINE and GOETHE.

**IPPNW:** see INTERNATIONAL PHYSICIANS FOR THE PREVENTION OF NUCLEAR WAR.

**Ipsambul:** see ABU-SIMBEL.

**Ipswich,** county town (1981 pop. 129,661), Suffolk, E England, on R. Orwell, 106 km (66 mi) NE of London. It is an industrial centre and port. In 1984 the port handled 4 million tonnes. The town is built on the site of the Saxon town of Gipeswic and has many old buildings. Cardinal WOLSEY was born here.

**Iqbal, Sir Mohammed,** (͵ikbahl), 1877–1938, Indian Muslim thinker. He played an important part in realizing the idea of Muslim separatism in India, and in his *Reconstruction of Religious Thought in Islam* (1934) he put forward a modernist interpretation of Islam which marks him off from fundamentalist supporters of the idea of Muslim separatism.

**Iquitos,** city (1981 pop. 173,629), E Peru, on the upper Amazon. Though situated 3750 km (2330 mi) from the Atlantic, it has been the principal river port of Peru since the 19th cent. Its original growth was associated with the late 19th-cent. rubber boom in the upper Amazon basin and the first government buildings were erected in the town in

1863. Its river connection with Brazil continues to give the city importance as a commercial centre for E Peru.

**Ir,** chemical symbol of the element IRIDIUM.

**Iran,** officially the Islamic Republic of Iran, known as Persia until 1935, republic (1985 est. pop. 45,190,000), 1,648,000 km² (636,290 sq mi), SW Asia, bordered by the USSR and the Caspian Sea (N), Afghanistan and Pakistan (E), the Persian Gulf and the Gulf of Oman (S), and Turkey and Iraq (W). TEHERAN is the capital; other major towns are ABADAN, ESFAHAN, TABRIZ and MASHHAD. Iran lies on a high plateau (alt. c.1200 m/4000 ft) surrounded by the ELBURZ and ZAGROS mountain ranges; there are great salt deserts in the interior; the climate is one of hot summers and cold winters; the wettest and most fertile areas are in the north and west. Iran is subject to numerous and often severe earthquakes. The country is one of the world's leading oil producers, and revenues from petroleum contribute 80% of the nation's wealth. However, agriculture supports 75% of the population. Textiles are Iran's second most important industrial product, and traditional handicrafts (such as carpet weaving) still play a role in the economy. The GNP is US$159,215 million and the GNP per capita is US$3670 (1983). Iran's culturally diverse population, with Persian, Kurdish, Turkic, Afghan, Baluchi, and Arab strains, is predominantly rural, with a sprinkling of nomadic pastoralists. The urban population is increasing rapidly. Islam is the official religion; about 98% of Iranians are Shi'ite Muslims, although most of the Kurds and Arabs are Sunnites. The principal language is Persian (Farsi).

*History.* Village life on the Iranian plateau as early as c.4000 BC. The Persian empire, founded (c.550 BC) by CYRUS THE GREAT, was succeeded, after Greek and Parthian occupation, by the SASSANID dynasty in AD 226 (see PERSIA). Iran's modern history may be said to have begun in 641, when the Arabs overthrew the Sassanids, introduced Islam, and incorporated Persia into the CALIPHATE. Persia was later invaded by the Turks (10th cent.), JENGHIZ KHAN (13th cent.), and TAMERLANE (14th cent.). The Safavid dynasty (1502–1736), which reached its height under ABBAS I, restored internal order and established the Shi'ite form of Islam as the state religion. Persia then entered into a long period of decline during which steadily lost territory and fell under the domination of the European powers. The discovery of oil in the early 1900s intensified European interest, and the Anglo-Russian Agreement of 1907 divided Persia into British and Russian spheres of influence until after World War I. In 1921 Reza Khan, an army officer, overthrew the decadent Kajar dynasty, and as REZA SHAH PAHLEVI established the Pahlevi dynasty in 1925; in 1941, when British and Russian forces occupied Iran for the duration of World War II, he abdicated in favour of his son MUHAMMAD REZA SHAH PAHLEVI. In the 1950s the power of the shah was challenged by Premier Muhammad MUSSADEGH, a militant nationalist who nationalized the oil industry and forced the shah to flee the country. However, with strong Western backing, monarchist elements ousted Mussadegh in 1953. In the 1960s the shah initiated a broad modernization programme, which was designed to improve economic and social conditions, including a big land reform, but which also brought widespread social and political unrest. The regime, supported by the US, became increasingly repressive, and in 1979 popular opposition forced the shah to leave the country. Ayatollah Ruhollah KHOMEINI, an Islamic leader exiled since 1964, returned and established an Islamic republic. Hundreds of the shah's supporters were tried and executed, and the Westernization of Iran was reversed. On 4 Nov. 1979, Iranian militants seized the US embassy in Teheran, held the occupants hostage, and demanded the return of the shah, who had entered the US. After the shah's death (1980) in Egypt, an agreement was finally negotiated that freed the hostages on 20 Jan. 1981. Meanwhile, a full-scale border war with Iraq erupted in Sept. 1980 over the disputed SHATT AL ARAB waterway and severely reduced Iran's oil production. The government was also plagued by increasing internal violence and unrest among ethnic minorities and political leftists, and assassination of high-level government officials became frequent. In the 1984 parliamentary elections the Islamic Republican Party won a further overwhelming victory, with its radical Marxist wing increasing its strength, but officially disolved in 1987. After huge losses of men and materials in the continuing war with Iraq, Iran in 1988 agreed to a ceasefire.

**Iranian languages,** group of languages belonging to the Indo-Iranian subfamily of the INDO-EUROPEAN family of languages. See LANGUAGE (table).

**Iraq,** officially the Republic of Iraq, republic (1987 est. pop. 16,000,000), 434,924 km² (167,924 sq mi), SW Asia, bordered by the

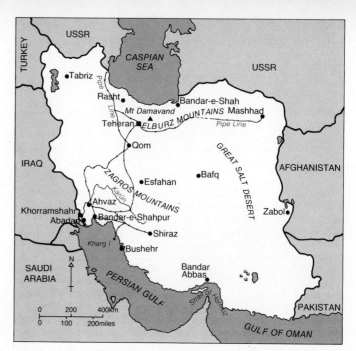

Iran

Persian Gulf, Kuwait, and Saudi Arabia (S), Jordan and Syria (W), Turkey (N), and Iran (E). Principal cities include BAGHDAD (the capital), BASRA, and MOSUL. Iraq is an almost landlocked country, its only outlet to the sea a short stretch of coast on the PERSIAN GULF. It is composed of a mountainous region in the northeast and the vast Syrian Desert, inhabited by a few nomadic shepherds, in the southwest; in between is the heart of the country, a fertile lowland region watered by the TIGRIS and EUPHRATES rivers. Although more than 50% of the labour force is engaged in agriculture, oil production, notably in the great fields of Mosul and Kirkuk, dominates the economy. Iraq is among the largest oil producers of the Middle East. All of its petroleum resources were nationalized in 1972 and oil revenues have been used to promote industrialization. The country has a small, diversified industrial sector. Iraq is the world's leading exporter of dates; other crops include cotton, cereals, and vegetables. Agriculture depends largely on irrigation. The GNP is US$42,713 million and the GNP per capita is US$2830 (1982). Most of the population (c.80%) are Muslim Arabs, divided almost equally between Sunni and Shia sects. The principal minority is the tribal Kurds, in the northeast, who have long demanded independence.

*History.* Modern Iraq is approximately coextensive with ancient MESOPOTAMIA, and prior to the Arab conquest in the 7th cent AD was the site of a number of flourishing civilizations, including SUMER, AKKAD, ASSYRIA, and BABYLONIA. In the 8th cent., as capital of the ABBASID caliphate, Baghdad became an important centre of learning and the arts. Mesopotamia fell to the Ottoman Turks in the 16th cent. The British invaded Iraq in World War I, and in 1920 the country became a LEAGUE OF NATIONS mandate under British administration. Iraq was made a kingdom under FAISAL I in 1921, and the British mandate was terminated in 1932, although British military bases remained. Meanwhile, the first oil concession had been granted in 1925, and in 1934 the export of oil began. Domestic politics were marked by turbulence, and the country experienced seven military coups between 1936 and 1941. Following an army coup in 1958, Iraq became a socialist republic under Gen. Abdul Karim Kassem, but he was overthrown and murdered in 1963, whereafter there followed the five-year dictatorship of the Aref brothers. The chronic Kurdish problem had flared up in 1962, when tribes demanding an autonomous KURDISTAN gained control of much of N Iraq; the rebellion collapsed (1975), but intermittent warfare has continued. Meanwhile, a further coup in 1968 had brought to power Gen. Ahmed Hassan Bakr, who was succeeded in 1979 by Saddam Hussein Takriti both as president and as leader of the Iraqi section of the dominant Baath Arab Socialist Party. Relations between Iran and Iraq were strained following Britain's withdrawal from the region in 1971, and full-scale war between the neighbours erupted in 1980, mainly over the disputed SHATT

Iraq

Ireland

AL ARAB waterway. Like other Arab states, Iraq remains strongly hostile to Israel. In 1981 Israeli planes destroyed a nearly completed nuclear reacto near Baghdad, which the Israelis claimed (and Iraq denied) was capable of producing nuclear weapons. Iraq suffered huge losses in men and materials in the continuing war with Iran but appeared to gain the upper hand in 1988, when a ceasefire was agreed.

**Ireland,** Irish *Eire,* second largest island (84,429 km²/32,598 sq mi) of the British Isles. It lies west of the island of GREAT BRITAIN, from which it is separated by the North Channel, the Irish Sea, and St George's Channel. It is divided politically into Northern Ireland and the Republic of Ireland; physically, it is composed of a large, fertile central plain roughly enclosed by a highland rim. Heavy rains (over 200 cm/80 in annually in some areas) account for the brilliant green grass that makes Ireland the 'emerald isle.' The interior is dotted with lakes and wide stretches of river called loughs. The longest river is the SHANNON.

*History.* Celtic tribes in ancient Ireland established a distinctive culture (see CELT) that, in its full flower after the introduction (5th cent. AD) of Christianity by St PATRICK, produced superb works of art and literature. Beginning in the 8th cent. Norsemen (see VIKINGS) invaded the area, remaining until the Irish king, BRIAN BORU, broke their strength in 1014; Ireland then remained free from foreign interference for 150 years. But in the 12th cent. Pope Adrian granted overlordship of Ireland to HENRY II of England, initiating an Anglo-Irish struggle that has lasted for nearly 800 years. The bitter religious contention between Irish Catholics and Protestants began in the 16th cent. after England tried to impose Protestantism on a largely Catholic Ireland. Irish rebellions flared up repeatedly under HENRY VIII, ELIZABETH I, and Oliver CROMWELL. The Act of Union (1800) united England and Ireland; the Irish parliament was abolished, and Ireland was represented in the British parliament. Agitation by the Irish leader Daniel O'CONNELL resulted in passage of the CATHOLIC EMANCIPATION Act in 1829. But political developments were dwarfed by the Great Potato Famine (1845–49), in which nearly a million Irish died of starvation and disease; another 1,600,000 emigrated (1847–54) to the US. Irish desire for domestic control persisted. The failure of the British government to implement HOME RULE, complicated by the fear in Protestant Ulster of Catholic domination, led to the Easter Rebellion of 1916. The militant SINN FEIN, founded (1905) among Irish Catholics, emerged as the dominant nationalist group, declaring themselves the Dáil Éireann (Irish Assembly) and proclaiming an Irish republic (1918). Outlawed by the British, the Sinn Fein went underground and waged guerrilla warfare. In 1920 a new Home Rule bill provided for partition of Ireland, with six counties of Protestant Ulster remaining part of the United Kingdom as Northern Ireland. In 1922 a

treaty gave the remainder of Ireland dominion status within the British Empire as the Irish Free State. See IRELAND, NORTHERN; IRELAND, REPUBLIC OF.

**Ireland, David,** 1927–, Australian novelist. His work includes *The Unknown Industrial Prisoner* (1971), *The Glass Canoe* (1976), *A Woman of the Future* (1979), *City of Women* (1981), and *Bloodfather* (1987), all characterized by intensely imagined, often fantastic visions of the pessimism, futility, and violence of contemporary industrial and urban life.

**Ireland, John,** 1879–1962, British composer and teacher. Like BAX, he was attracted to Celtic legend and history as a source of inspiration for works such as *Mai-dun* (1920-21) for orchestra, but he was also attached to the idiom of English folk song. He wrote choral works, chamber pieces, and songs, and works for piano, including a Sonata (1918–20) and a Concerto (1930).

**Ireland, Northern,** political division of the United Kingdom of Great Britain and Northern Ireland (1983 est. pop. 1,572,700), 14,147 km² (5642 sq mi), comprising six counties of Ulster in NE Ireland. It is now divided into 26 local authority districts for the purposes of local government. The capital is BELFAST, one of Britain's chief ports. Farming is the principal occupation. Shipbuilding, food processing, and the manufacture of textiles are the leading industries. About three-fifths of the population is Protestant and one-third is Catholic.

*History.* Northern Ireland's relatively distinct history began in the 17th cent. when the British crown, after suppressing an Irish rebellion, populated much of Ulster with Scottish and English settlers, giving the area a Protestant character in contrast to the rest of Ireland. The question of political separation did not arise, however, until proposals for HOME RULE for Ireland, first broached in 1886 by British prime minister William GLADSTONE, aroused fears in Protestant Ulster of domination by the Catholic majority in the south. The situation continued to deteriorate, and by World War I civil war was imminent. The Government of Ireland Act (1920) attempted to solve the problem by enacting Home Rule separately for the two parts of Ireland. Protestant Ulster thus became the province of Northern Ireland, but the Irish Free State (now the Republic of Ireland), established in the remainder of Ireland in 1922, refused to recognize the finality of the partition. The situation remained relatively stable until the late 1960s, when protest by the Catholic minority against economic and political discrimination led to widespread violence by the 'provisional' wing of the IRISH REPUBLICAN ARMY (IRA) on one side and the Ulster Defence Association, a Protestant group, on the other. In reply, the British government sent in British troops in 1969, suspended the Ulster parliament in 1972, and assumed direct rule of the province in 1973. Protestant and Catholic extremists rejected several efforts at power-sharing, and sectarian conflict marked by bloodshed continued into the 1980s. See IRELAND; IRELAND, REPUBLIC OF.

**Ireland, Republic of,** independent republic (1986 pop. 3,537,195), 70,282 km² (27,136 sq mi), occupying all but the northeastern corner of the island of Ireland in the British Isles; formerly the **Irish Free State** (1922–37) and **Eire** (1937–49). DUBLIN is the capital. Agriculture, primarily the raising of livestock and poultry, is the primary economic activity; crops include flax, oats, wheat, turnips, potatoes, sugar beets, and barley. Tourism is the second largest source of income. Industry produces linen and laces (for which Ireland is famous), food products, and textiles, particularly wool. Gaelic and English are the official languages, but English is more widely spoken. About 95% of the population is Roman Catholic, but there is no established church. The Dáil Éireann is the lower house of parliament, with 166 members elected (by proportional representation) for a five-year term; there is also an upper house or senate (Seanad Éireann) of nominated and appointed members.

*History.* The establishment by treaty with GREAT BRITAIN of the Irish Free State in 1922 completed the partition of Ireland into two states (Northern Ireland was created in 1920) and resulted in civil war between supporters of the treaty and opponents. The anti-treaty forces, embodied in the IRISH REPUBLICAN ARMY (IRA) and led by Eamon DE VALERA, were defeated, but the IRA continued as a secret terrorist organization. De Valera and his Fianna Fáil party finally entered the Dáil (parliament) in 1927 and De Valera became prime minister in 1932. Under his administration a new constitution was promulgated (1937), establishing the sovereign state of Ireland, or Eire, within the COMMONWEALTH. In World War II Eire, remaining neutral, denied the use of Irish ports to Britain, although many Irishmen served voluntarily in the British armed forces. In 1948 Ireland demanded total independence from Great Britain; the Republic of Ireland was proclaimed in 1949 and the country withdrew from the Commonwealth. In the late 1960s problems flared up with Northern Ireland, aggravated by the terrorist activities in Northern Ireland of the IRA, which was headquartered in the republic. In 1973 the country joined the EUROPEAN COMMUNITY, which has brought substantial benefits to the agricultural sector. In the 1980s political power has alternated between Fianna Fáil led by Charles Haughey and coalitions of Fine Gael and the Labour Party. See IRELAND; IRELAND, NORTHERN.

**Post-war Irish presidents**
Seán T. O'Kelly (Fianna Fáil), 1945–59
Éamon de Valera (Fianna Fáil), 1959–73
Erskine Childers (Fianna Fáil), 1973–74
Cearbhall Ó Dálaigh (Fianna Fáil), 1974–76
Patrick J. Hillery (Fianna Fáil), 1976–

**Post-war Irish prime ministers**
Éamon de Valera (Fianna Fáil), 1932–48
John A. Costello (Fine Gael), 1948–51
Éamon de Valera (Fianna Fáil), 1951–54
John A. Costello (Fine Gael), 1954–57
Éamon de Valera (Fianna Fáil), 1957–59
Seán F. Lemass (Fianna Fáil), 1959–66
John M. Lynch (Fianna Fáil), 1966–73
Liam Cosgrave (Fine Gael), 1973–77
John M. Lynch (Fianna Fáil), 1977–79
Charles J. Haughey (Fianna Fáil), 1979–81
Garret FitzGerald (Fine Gael), 1981–82
Charles J. Haughey (Fianna Fáil), 1982
Garret FitzGerald (Fine Gael), 1982–87
Charles J. Haughey (Fianna Fáil), 1987–

**Irene,** c.750–803, Byzantine empress (r.797–802). As regent for her son, CONSTANTINE VI, she neglected wars in her zeal to suppress ICONOCLASM. Her son's misconduct enabled her to depose him (797), have him blinded, and ascend the throne. Her accession gave CHARLEMAGNE a pretext for having himself crowned emperor (800). Irene was deposed (802) and died in exile.

**iridium** (Ir), metallic element, discovered by Smithson Tennant in 1804. Chemically very unreactive, iridium is a very hard, usually brittle, extremely corrosion-resistant, silver-white metal used in chemical crucibles, surgical tools, and pivot bearings. The international kilogram standard is an iridium-platinum alloy. See ELEMENT (table); PERIODIC TABLE.

**iris,** common name for members of the genus *Iris* of the Iridaceae, a family of perennial herbs that includes the CROCUS, freesia (genus *Freesia*), and gladiolus (genus *Gladiolus*). The family is typified by modified stems (corms and RHIZOMES) and by linear or sword-shaped leaves. Distributed worldwide except in the coldest regions, the family is closely related to the LILY and AMARYLLIS families. The cultivated irises, freesias, and gladioli show a wide variety of colours in their usually perfumed blossoms. The many species of wild iris are often called flags. Orrisroot, a violet-scented flavouring used in perfumes and other products, is made from the powdered rhizomes, especially of *I. germanica.*

**Irish Land Question,** name given in the 19th cent. to the problem of Irish land ownership, which went back many centuries. In the 12th cent. a feudal landholding system was imposed on Ireland. The TUDORS, CROMWELL, and WILLIAM III continued land confiscations; the result was the creation of an absentee landlord class and an impoverished Irish peasantry. The 18th-cent. penal laws increased the difficulty of landowning by Catholics; CATHOLIC EMANCIPATION did not help much, although it did bring Irish Catholics into the British Parliament. Irish hatred for England grew through the great famine of the 1840s and the influx of speculators after the Encumbered Estates Act of 1849. The violent FENIAN MOVEMENT alarmed British opinion, but GLADSTONE pinned his hopes in a new Land Act (1870). The National Land League, led by Michael Davitt and C.S. PARNELL, subsequently fought for passage of the Land Act of 1881, which gave the three 'Fs'—fair rent, fixity of tenure, and freedom from sale. Land purchase by the tenant now became the main issue, and agitation by the Irish Union League led to passage of the Wyndham Act (1903), which provided loans at reduced rates for tenants who wanted to buy land, and bonuses for landlords willing to sell. By 1921 Irish tenants owned two thirds of the land; the rest was confiscated by law and given to them.

**Irish language,** also called Irish Gaelic, member of the Goidelic group of the Celtic subfamily of the Indo-European family of languages. See LANGUAGE (table).

**Irish literary renaissance,** late 19th- and early 20th-cent. movement that aimed to revive ancient Irish folklore, legends, and traditions in new literary works. Essentially, it was a rebirth of literature in Ireland as Irish literature rather than as a pale reflection of English literature. Major figures in the movement were J.M. SYNGE, Sean O'CASEY, W.B. YEATS, and Lady Augusta GREGORY.

**Irish Republican Army** (IRA), nationalist organization dedicated to the unification of Ireland. It was organized by Michael COLLINS after the Easter Rebellion of 1916 (see IRELAND) and became the military wing of the SINN FÉIN Party. Despite the establishment of the Irish Free State (1922), the IRA refused to accept a separate Northern Ireland under British rule. With popular support lessened by its violent actions and pro-German agitation during WORLD WAR II, it was outlawed by both Irish governments and became a secret organization. Quiescent for many years, the IRA regained prominence with the onset of civil strife in Northern Ireland in the late 1960s. In 1971 it split into an 'official' wing, which disclaimed violence, and a terrorist 'provisional' wing (the 'Provos'), whose attacks on British troops in Northern Ireland, random bombings, and other acts of terror in England kept tensions high. In 1981 nine imprisoned IRA leaders, engaged in hunger strikes to death, thereby generating increased support for the organization among the minority Catholic community in Northern Ireland as well as international sympathy for its aims. In 1984 the provisional IRA claimed responsibility for a bomb explosion at a Brighton (England) hotel where Prime Min. Margaret THATCHER and other government ministers were staying for the annual CONSERVATIVE PARTY conference, five people being killed. See also IRELAND, NORTHERN.

**Irkutsk,** city (1985 pop. 597,000), E Siberian USSR, at the confluence of the Irkut R. and the Angara R., 65 km (40 mi) W of Lake BAYKAL. It is at the centre of a rapidly industrializing area, using power from the nearby Cheremkhovo coalfields and the hydroelectric station on the Angara R.

Chemical industries are based on local salt deposits and by-products from the oil refinery at Angarsk. Other industries include aluminium smelting, timber production, wood-working, food processing, and machinery and motor-vehicle production. There are eight research institutes of the Siberian Branch of the Soviet Academy of Sciences. The city was founded in 1652 as a fortress.

**iron** (Fe), metallic element. Iron is a lustrous, ductile, malleable, silver-grey metal. A good conductor of heat and electricity, it is attracted by a magnet and is itself easily magnetized (see MAGNETISM). Iron is abundant in the universe; it is found in many stars, including the sun. It is the fourth most common element in the earth's crust, of which it constitutes about 5% by weight, and is believed to be the main component of the earth's core. Iron is rarely found uncombined in nature except in METEORITES, and it rusts readily in moist air. LIMONITE and haematite are the chief iron ores; other ores include MAGNETITE, taconite, and siderite. Iron ores are refined in a BLAST FURNACE to produce pig iron, which can be remelted and poured into moulds to make CAST IRON, commercially purified to make WROUGHT IRON, or alloyed with carbon and other elements to make STEEL. Iron compounds are used as paint pigments, in dyeing, and in ink manufacture. A component of HAEMOGLOBIN, the oxygen-carrying pigment of red BLOOD cells in vertebrates, iron is important in NUTRITION; one cause of ANAEMIA is iron deficiency. See ELEMENT (table); IRON AGE; PERIODIC TABLE; VITAMINS AND MINERALS.

**Iron, Ralph:** see SCHREINER, OLIVE.

**Iron Age,** technological period from the first general use of iron to modern times. In Asia, Egypt, and Europe it followed the BRONZE AGE; Europeans brought it to the Americas. Hammered iron was known in Egypt before 1350 BC, and after the fall of the HITTITE empire (1200 BC) migrants carried iron technology through S Europe and the Middle East. Smelting was known in the ETRUSCAN CIVILIZATION. During the Early Iron Age (c.800–500 BC) migrating CELTS from central Europe, began to spread the use of iron into W Europe and the British Isles, where Late Iron Age peoples used it for tools, vehicles, and art objects (see LA TÈNE). Metal technology increasingly influenced CULTURE up to the INDUSTRIAL REVOLUTION and beyond.

Iron Age (La Tène) blacksmith's tools found at Waltham Abbey

**iron curtain,** boundary in Europe between the Soviet sphere of influence, containing communist regimes closely allied with Moscow, and the open democracies of Western Europe. The term was given wide currency by Winston Churchill after WORLD WAR II. In 1961 the abstract concept of an iron curtain obtained concrete reality with the construction of the BERLIN Wall. See also BAMBOO CURTAIN.

**Iron Gate,** gorge section of the Danube R. between Orşova and Turnu Severin, on the border of Romania and Yugoslavia. To assist navigation, a canal was made in the gorge in the 1890s. Since World War II the two countries have jointly built a dam incorporating navigation locks and a hydroelectric station.

**Iron Guard,** Romanian anti-Semitic terrorist organization founded under the name of 'The Legion of the Archangel Michael' by Corneliu Codreanu in 1927. Although officially banned in 1933, it continued under different names and was responsible for the murder of its opponents, including two prime ministers and prominent cultural figures. It was suppressed by ANTONESCU in 1941.

**iron pyrites:** see PYRITE.

**Iroquois Confederacy** or **Iroquois League,** NORTH AMERICAN INDIAN confederation of five nations, Mohawk, Oneida, Onondaga, Cayuga, and Seneca, founded c.1570. The Tuscarora joined c.1722. They spoke Iroquoian languages of the Hokan-Siouan stock (see AMERICAN INDIAN LANGUAGES), and in the early 17th cent. inhabited New York N and W of the Hudson R., numbering c.5,500. Materially, politically, and militarily their culture was the most advanced in the Eastern Woodlands. The Iroquois conceived of themselves as living in a metaphorical long house in which each nation had a role, e.g., the Mohawks guarded the eastern door. By absorbing neighbouring tribes in territorial wars, the League came to number 16,000 by the late 17th cent. Led by Cornplanter, Red Jacket, and Joseph BRANT, all but the Oneida sided with the British in the AMERICAN REVOLUTION. Today the Iroquois live mostly in Ontario and in New York, where in the 1970s and early 1980s they occupied disputed lands. Many, however, have become urban. Many Mohawks, for instance, have become structural steel workers.

**irrational number:** see NUMBER.

**Irrawaddy,** one of the great rivers of Asia and the chief river of Burma, c.1600 km (1000 mi) long, formed by the confluence in N Burma of the Mali and Nmai rivers. It flows S, receiving the Chindwin R. just below Mandalay, to form a vast delta c.320 km (200 mi) wide beginning at Henzada, c.290 km (180 mi) from the Andaman Sea. The river is navigable up to Myitkyina and serves as Burma's economic lifeline.

**irredentism,** originally, the nationalist movement for annexation to Italy of predominantly Italian areas *Italia irredenta* [unredeemed Italy] retained by Austria after 1866. It was a strong motive for Italy's entry into WORLD WAR I. The term is also applied to similar movements in other nations.

**irrigation,** in AGRICULTURE, artificial watering of the land, using water diverted from rivers and lakes or pumped from underground (see DAM). Modern large-scale irrigation is often part of a multipurpose project that may also produce hydroelectric power and provide systems for water supply and flood control. Surface irrigation delivers water to a field directly from a canal, well, or ditch. In surface-pipe irrigation, the water is piped to the field and distributed via sprinklers or smaller pipes. Drip irrigation, a recent development, delivers a small, measured amount of water to each plant through narrow plastic tubes and helps prevent the two major problems caused by irrigation: waterlogging, saturation of the soil as a result of inadequate drainage, and soil salinization, the accumulation of salts deposited by irrigation water. See also AQUEDUCT.

**Irtysh,** river, c.4260 km (2650 mi) long, W Siberia, USSR, chief tributary of the OB R. It rises as the Kara-Irtysh in NW China and flows through the Kazakh Republic and past Semipalatinsk, Omsk, and Tobolsk to join the Ob near Khanty-Mansiysk. A Soviet plan for a 2500-km (1400-mi) canal to divert water from the Irtysh to the SYR DARYA and AMU DARYA rivers was announced in the early 1980s.

**Irving, Sir Henry,** 1838–1905, English actor and manager; b. John Henry Brodribb. As the innovative manager (1878–1903) of the Lyceum Theatre, London, he reigned supreme on the English stage, appearing with his leading lady, Ellen TERRY, in numerous Shakespearean and contemporary productions. He was the first English actor to be knighted (1895).

**Irving, Washington,** 1783–1859, American author. His earliest works, *Letters of Jonathan Oldstyle, Gent.* (1802–03) and *Salmagundi* (1807–8; written with William Irving and J.K. Pauling), were collections of amusing essays. Under the pseudonym Diedrich Knickerbocker he wrote *A History of New York* (1809), perhaps America's first great book of comic literature. Irving's reputation at home and abroad was established with the essays in *The Sketch Book of Geoffrey Crayon, Gent.* (1820), including such tales as 'Rip Van Winkle' and 'The Legend of Sleepy Hollow'. While a diplomat in Madrid (1826–29) he wrote several works on Spanish subjects, among them the charming sketches in *The Alhambra* (1832). After returning to the US he wrote a number of books on the American West, e.g., *A Tour of the Prairies* (1835). Except for a term as US minister to Spain (1842–46), Irving spent most of his later years at his estate, Sunnyside, near Tarrytown, New York. There he completed several works, including his biography of George Washington (5 vol., 1855–59). A gentle satirist who was master of a graceful, sophisticated style, Irving created some of the most popular essays and tales in American literature.

**Isaac,** Byzantine emperors. **Isaac I,** c.1005–61 (r.1057–59), first of the COMNENUS dynasty, was proclaimed emperor by the army. He abdicated after losing popularity and failing in war. **Isaac II** (Angelus), d. 1204 (r.1185–95, 1203–04), was made emperor by the people. He repulsed the Normans but failed to suppress a Bulgar rebellion. He was deposed and blinded by his brother, ALEXIUS III, but the army of the Fourth CRUSADE restored him as co-ruler with his son, ALEXIUS IV. After their overthrow by ALEXIUS V the Crusaders sacked Constantinople.

**Isaac,** in the BIBLE, a patriarch, only son of ABRAHAM and SARAH. He married REBECCA, and their sons were ESAU and JACOB. ISHMAEL was his half-brother. As a supreme act of faith, Abraham offered Isaac at an early age as a sacrifice to God, a deed prevented by divine intervention. Gen. 21–27. In the NEW TESTAMENT Isaac is taken as a type of Christ and of the Church.

**Isabella,** Spanish queens. **Isabella I** (the Catholic), 1451–1504, queen of Castile and León (1474–1504) and queen of Aragón (1479–1504), with her husband, FERDINAND V, established the unified Spanish kingdom. She suppressed the lawless Castilian nobles by reviving the medieval HERMANDAD, administered the holdings of powerful religious military orders, and placed the INQUISITION under royal control. Isabella was a prime mover (1492) in the expulsion of the JEWS, the conquest of GRANADA from the MOORS, and discovery of the New World by COLUMBUS. Together she and Ferdinand advanced learning and the arts, especially architecture. The accession of **Isabella II,** 1830–1904, queen of Spain (1833–68), caused the CARLIST wars. Her marriage (1846) to Francisco de Asis, which contravened Anglo-French agreements regarding the choice of husbands for certain Spanish princesses, contributed to a rift between England and France. Frequent conflicts between moderates and liberals led to her deposition. In 1870 she abdicated her rights in favour of her son, ALFONSO XII.

**Isabella,** 1292–1358, queen consort of EDWARD II of England; daughter of PHILIP IV of France. Neglected and mistreated by her husband, she hated the royal favourites, the Despensers, who had seized her lands. While in France (1325), she formed a liaison with Roger de MORTIMER. They invaded England in 1326, forced Edward to abdicate, and caused his murder. They ruled corruptly until EDWARD III seized power in 1330.

**Isaiah** or **Isaias,** (īsā,yəs) book of the OLD TESTAMENT. It consists of a collection of prophecies attributed to Isaiah, apparently a nobleman in the kingdom of Judah (c.740 BC). The book falls into two sections of metrical prophecies (1–35; 40–66) divided by a prose section. The first set of poems deals with prophecies against the Assyrians and other nations; those affecting Israel and JUDAH announce destruction and subsequent redemption. The second poetic section is a prophecy of redemption of the state of Israel, delivered from captivity and from sin; it is nowadays held to be the work of another writer, or writers, than Isaiah, and to date from the 6th cent. BC or later. The book contains several prophecies thought by Christians to refer to Christ.

**Iscariot:** see JUDAS ISCARIOT.

**ischaemic heart disease** (is,keemik): see CORONARY HEART DISEASE.

**Ischia** (,iskiə), island 46 km² (18 sq mi), on the edge of the Gulf of NAPLES, S Italy. Vines and fishing support a dense population. A volcanic island, its hot springs have made it a popular health resort.

**Ise** (,eesay), city (1986 est. pop. 106,112), Mie prefecture, S Honshu, Japan. One of the foremost religious centres of SHINTO, it is the site of the shrines of Ise, for centuries a popular place of pilgrimage for the emperor's court and for the people. Said to have been built in 4 BC, the three shrines,

set deep in a forest, exhibit an archaic style of architecture, without Chinese or Buddhist influence. One houses the Sacred Mirror of the imperial regalia.

**Iseult:** see TRISTRAM AND ISOLDE.

**Isfahan:** see ESFAHAN.

**Isherwood, Christopher,** 1904–85, English author. His experiences in Germany gave him material for *Mr Norris Changes Trains* (1935) and *Goodbye to Berlin* (1939). These form the basis of John Van Druten's play *I Am a Camera* (1951) and the musical *Cabaret* (1966). Isherwood collaborated with AUDEN on three plays and on *Journey to a War* (1939), recording a trip to China. He moved to the US in 1939. His later writings include several novels, studies of Eastern religion, and a memoir of his life in the 1930s, *Christopher and His Kind* (1977).

**Ishmael** (,ishmayəl), in the BIBLE, son of ABRAHAM and Hagar, half brother to ISAAC, and ancestor of 12 tribes in N Arabia. Through SARAH's jealousy, he and his mother, who was Sarah's handmaid, were sent into the desert. Gen. 16. Hence the name Ishmael came to mean 'outcast'. The Muslims consider the Arabs the descendants of Ishmael.

**Ishtar,** ancient fertility deity, the most widely worshipped goddess in Babylonian and Assyrian religion. Ishtar was important as a mother goddess, goddess of love, and goddess of war. Her cult spread throughout W Asia, and she became identified with various other earth goddesses (see GREAT MOTHER OF THE GODS).

**Isis,** nature goddess whose worship, originating in ancient Egypt, gradually extended throughout the lands of the Mediterranean world and became one of the chief religions of the Roman Empire. The worship of Isis, together with that of her brother and husband OSIRIS and their son HORUS, resisted the rise of Christianity and lasted until the 6th cent. AD.

**Iskenderun,** city (1980 pop. 124,824), Hatay prov., S Turkey, on the Gulf of Iskenderun. It was known until the 7th cent. as Alexandretta after its founder, Alexander the Great. Since 1939 it has been a part of Turkey and is now a military base and centre of iron and steel manufacture.

**Islam** [Arab., = submission to God], the religion of which MUHAMMAD was the prophet. Muslims consider Muhammad's prophecy to be one in direct continuity with previous monotheistic prophecies which found their expression in the Old and the New Testaments. They also believe that Muhammad's prophecy was anticipated in these scriptures, and that Jews and Christians had altered their original texts, an action helped by the unreliability of scribes and the passage of time. Muhammad therefore delivered the same heavenly message as his predecessors, but is himself the Seal of prophecy and the scripture he received in revelation, the KORAN, is considered the most definitive expression of the divine word and will. All Muslims, Shi'ites (see SHI'ISM) Sunnites (see SUNNISM), and the marginal Kharijites (who still exist in Oman and in the Algerian Sahara), take the KORAN as their scripture, perform the canonical devotions, termed the five pillars of Islam, consisting of prayer, almsgiving, fasting during RAMADAN, pilgrimage or HAJJ, and the profession of the unicity of God and the theological prophecy of MUHAMMAD, and believe in the Angels and the Afterlife. All Muslim sects have developed distinct legal systems (FIQH), and different theological schools (KALAM). Islam started in Arabia as a local religion composed of various local traditions, pagan, Christian, and Jewish, the latter especially marked by SAMARITAN elements. The distinctive synthesis of Muhammad as embodied in his revelation, the Koran, and his words and actions as recorded in the HADITH, was a new religion that was instrumental in unifying Arabia and launching the early Arab conquests of Sassanian and BYZANTINE territories. The religion of Arab conquerors gradually became the name for an ecumenical, universal culture based in Baghdad, Cordoba, and elsewhere, and grounded in an international system of trade and of a common high culture, from the western borders of China to Spain. This universal culture was not dependent on universal Islamization, but was the work of what later became a Muslim majority and Christian and Jewish men of letters, scientists, administrators, and others. This high culture, reflected in distinctive architectural styles, artistic motifs, literary forms, theological concerns, legal systems, and natural-scientific achievements, incorporated elements of various ethnic, cultural, and religious provenances. Chief among those was the ARABIC language, the *lingua franca* of this ecumenical civilization, but also Hellenistic philosophy, Persian statecraft, Christian, Jewish, Sabean (see SABEANS), and other religious lore, Greek and Near Eastern scientific traditions, and much else. This universal civilization, like all others, was superimposed on a bewildering variety of social structures, local traditions, legal traditions, and other differences, which it incorporated or fought against in its own distinctive way. From the middle of the 10th cent., Islam began to acquire its classical form. It was adapted and readapted by the various states that claimed it for inspiration, the Ayyubid and Mamluk states that fought off the CRUSADES, and the OTTOMAN EMPIRE that pushed the limits of islamization into the Balkans and beyond. Varieties of Islam are now the predominant religion in the Near and Middle East, in North Africa, Malaysia, Indonesia, Pakistan, and Bangladesh. Very sizeable Muslim minorities live in India, the Soviet Union, China, and parts of east Africa, as well as along the river Niger.

**Islamabad**, city (1981 est. pop. 201,000), capital of Pakistan, NE Pakistan. Construction of Islamabad [city of Islam], which replaced nearby RAWALPINDI as the capital, began in 1960. Points of interest include the Grand National Mosque and the botanical gardens.

**Islamic art and architecture.** In the century after the death (AD 632) of the prophet MUHAMMAD, his Arab followers spread his teachings through Egypt and North Africa, as far west as Spain, and as far east as Sassanid Persia. Because of their rapid expansion and the paucity of their artistic heritage, the Muslims derived their unique style from a synthesis of the arts of the Byzantines, the Copts, the Romans, and the Sassanids. The great interior surface of the Mosque of Damascus (715) was covered with stone MOSAICS in the Byzantine technique. No figures of humans or animals were allowed, but there were crowns, fantastic plants, realistic trees, and empty towns. In AD 750 the ABBASID dynasty moved the capital to Baghdad, and immediately Persian influence became stronger. In the ruins of Samarra lustreware fragments have been found. The Great Mosque of Al Qayrawan (c.862) is decorated with square lustre tiling. The 9th cent. saw the development of metalwork in Egypt, and skilled craftsmanship can be seen in rock-crystal carving, a Sassanid art. From the 10th to the 13th cent. great strides were made in the minor arts in Egypt. CALLIGRAPHY, BOOKBINDING, papermaking, and ILLUMINATION were developed. The Kufic script was animated with floriated, interlaced, and anthropomorphic designs. Early in the 13th cent. a school of secular manuscript painting arose near Baghdad with pictures of two types: those that illustrate scientific works, descending from late Hellenistic models, and those that illustrate anecdotal tales and whose miniatures represent the true spirit of CARICATURE. After the Mongol invasions there was a revitalization of art through Chinese taste and artifacts. TEXTILES and CARPETS were again manufactured throughout Islam, and Turkish ceramics reached their peak in the 'Iznik' ware of the 16th and 17th cent. Early Islamic architecture used the Syrian cut-stone technique of building, as in the Mosque of Damascus, and popularized the DOME (see MOSQUE). Sassanid building techniques such as the squinch arch were combined with the mosque form. In the 10th cent. the FATIMIDS introduced into Egypt the decorative stalactite ceiling and placed emphasis on ornamental flat mouldings. The cruciform Mosque of Hasan, in Cairo (1536) reflects Persian influence, while the square Char Minar of Hyderabad (1591), with its large arches, arcades, and minarets, is characteristic of the Indian style of the Delhi Sultanate. The art of Islamic Spain used faïence and lacy, pierced-stone screen windows. Turkish architects were influenced by the Byzantine church of HAGIA SOPHIA. In general, all Islamic art and architecture is the result of synthesis rather than origination, with decoration of the surface the most important factor in every work. Interlaced lines and brilliant colour characterize the style. See also MUGHAL ART AND ARCHITECTURE.

**Islamic Conference Organization,** loose intergovernmental organization (est. 1971) for solidarity and cooperation between Islamic countries, based in Jeddah (Saudi Arabia). Member countries are Algeria, Bahrain, Bangladesh, Brunei, Burkina Faso, Cameroon, Chad, Comoros, Djibouti, Egypt, Gabon, Gambia, Guinea, Guinea–Bissau, Indonesia, Iran, Iraq, Jordan, Kuwait, Lebanon, Libya, Malaysia, Maldives, Mali, Mauritania, Morocco, Niger, Oman, Pakistan, Qatar, Saudi Arabia, Senegal, Sierra Leone, Somalia, Sudan, Syria, Tunisia, Turkey, Uganda, United Arab Emirates, North Yemen, and South Yemen; the PALESTINE LIBERATION ORGANIZATION is also a full member, while Nigeria and the TURKISH REPUBLIC OF NORTHERN CYPRUS have observer status.

**Islamic Jihad,** group or groups of extremist Islamic fundamentalists claiming responsibility for various actions against Western or pro-Western

**Islamic art and architecture:** Tower of the Great Mosque of Al Qayrawan, Tunisia, c.862

targets in the Middle East and elsewhere, including kidnappings of Westerners in Lebanon.

**island,** relatively small (compared to a CONTINENT) body of land completely surrounded by water. The largest, in descending order, are GREENLAND, NEW GUINEA, BORNEO, MADAGASCAR, BAFFIN ISLAND, SUMATRA, HONSHU, and GREAT BRITAIN. Islands are either *continental,* caused by partial submergence of coastal highlands or by the sea breaking through an isthmus or peninsula, or *oceanic,* originating from the ascension of the ocean floor above water through volcanic activity or other earth movements. Tropical oceanic islands sustained above sea level by coral growth are called atolls (see CORAL REEFS).

**Islington,** London borough (1981 pop. 157,522), inner NE London. It includes the districts of Holloway, Highbury, Canonbury, and Finsbury. Mainly a residential borough, it is also an important commercial and industrial zone. Arsenal football club is located within the borough, as is Sadler's Wells Theatre.

**Isma'il I,** 1487–1524, shah of PERSIA (1501–24), founder of the Safavid dynasty. He defeated the Aq-Qoyunlu rulers of Iraq and W Persia and the Uzbeks in the east, but was himself defeated by the Ottoman Turks at Chaldiran (1514). He imposed the Shi'i form of Islam on the Persian people.

**Ismâ'ilîa,** city (1987 pop. 145,930), NE Egypt, on Lake Timsah. It is a halfway station on the Suez Canal. Founded in 1863, the city was a major population centre before the ARAB–ISRAELI WAR in June 1967. It was evacuated during the war but is now under reconstruction and is rapidly being repopulated. The rail service to Cairo, which was suspended in 1967, was reopened in 1974.

**Isma'ilis,** a major branch of SHI'ISM, named after Isma'il, son of JA'FAR AL-SADIQ. They achieved political dominance in the Egyptian dynasty of the FATIMIDS (969–1171). Theologically they expound a doctrine of an utterly transcendent deity together with an interpretation of a hidden level of meaning in the KORAN based on an intricate cosmology and on notions of correspondence between the human microcosm and a transcendent macrocosm. Also important is their notion of the Imamate with its cyclical vision of history (see IMAM). Of their two principal sub-divisions, the Nizaris and the Musta'lians, the first are led by the Agha Khans.

**Ismail Pasha,** 1830–95, ruler of Egypt (1863–79), the first to bear the title khedive (viceroy); son of IBRAHIM PASHA. His grandiose schemes, including building the SUEZ CANAL, forced him to submit (1876) to joint Anglo-French management. He was deposed (1879) in favour of his son, Tewfik Pasha.

**Isocrates** (ie,sokrateez), 436–338 BC, Greek orator, pupil of SOCRATES. A great teacher, he taught every young orator of his time. His most celebrated oration is *Panegyricus,* in which he urges Hellenic unity against Persia.

**isolationism,** doctrine that a country's best interests are served by remaining outside any alliances with other states or involvement therein. Practitioners have included China under its emperors, the UK in the 19th cent. and the US under the MONROE DOCTRINE of 1823. Most commonly associated with the US, isolationist tendencies explained the American people's refusal to join the LEAGUE OF NATIONS after WORLD WAR I as advocated by Pres. Woodrow WILSON. In the later 20th-cent. US governments have abandoned isolationism.

**Isolde:** see TRISTRAM AND ISOLDE.

**isomer,** in chemistry, one of two or more compounds having the same molecular formula (i.e., the same number of atoms of each element in a molecule) but different structures (arrangements of atoms in the molecule). Isomers have the same number of atoms of each element in them and the same atomic weight but differ in other properties. **Structural isomers,** e.g., ETHANOL ($CH_3CH_2OH$) and dimethyl ether ($CH_3OCH_3$), differ in the way the atoms are joined together in their molecules. **Stereoisomers** have the same basic arrangement of atoms in their molecules but differ in the way the atoms are arranged in space. Geometric isomers, which are stereoisomers that differ in the positioning of groups about a double bond or some other feature that gives the molecule a certain amount of structural rigidity, differ in physical properties such as melting and boiling points. Optical isomers are stereoisomers in which the two molecules are mirror images of each other and, each being asymmetrical, cannot be superposed on each other; optical isomers differ in the direction in which they rotate light passed through the molecules.

ethanol          dimethyl ether

Isomers

**isomer,** in nuclear physics, name given to an excited state of a NUCLEUS which has an extremely long lifetime, possibly several years. Because of the long lifetime, an isomer can be regarded as a separate nuclear species with different radioactive properties from the nucleus of which it is an excited state, but having the same number of protons and neutrons (i.e., the same ATOMIC NUMBER and MASS NUMBER). The eventual GAMMA DECAY of an isomer is known as an *isomeric transition.*

**isotope,** either of two or more atoms having the same ATOMIC NUMBER but differing in ATOMIC WEIGHT and MASS NUMBER. The nuclei of isotopes of the same element have the same PROTON number (equal to the element's atomic number) but have different numbers of NEUTRONS. The isotopes of a given element have identical chemical properties but slightly different physical properties. A radioactive isotope, or radioisotope, is a natural or artificially created isotope having an unstable nucleus that decays, emitting alpha, beta, or gamma rays (see RADIOACTIVITY) until stability is reached. For most elements, both stable and radioactive isotopes are known.

**Israel,** officially the state of Israel, republic (1987 est. pop. 4,300,000), 20,700 km² (7992 sq mi) (excluding occupied Arab territories), SW Asia, bounded by Lebanon (N), Syria and Jordan (E), the Mediterranean Sea and Egypt (W), and the Gulf of Aqaba (S). The capital is JERUSALEM; other major cities are TEL AVIV-JAFFA and HAIFA. There are four geographical regions: the Mediterranean coastal plain; a mountain area in the northeast and centre; the semiarid NEGEV in the south; and, in the extreme east, a portion of the GREAT RIFT VALLEY, including the JORDAN valley and the DEAD SEA, which at 396 m (1300 ft) below sea level is the lowest point on earth. Despite adverse conditions, agriculture has flourished in Israel, with extensive irrigation compensating for the lack of rainfall. Citrus fruit is the major export crop. A wide variety of industrial goods is produced, including textiles, chemicals, and machinery; Israel is second only to Belgium in processing diamonds. Tourism is also important. The standard of living is high for a Middle Eastern nation, but in recent years a high trade deficit, heavy defence expenditure, and an inflation rate of over 100% (in the early 1980s) have put the economy under a great strain. The GNP is US$25,067 million and the GNP per capita is US$5970 (1984). About 85% of the population are Jews, about half of whom are immigrants from Europe, North America, Asia, and North Africa. The non-Jewish population consists mainly of Muslim and Christian Arabs. The official languages are Hebrew and Arabic, but English and many European languages are widely spoken. Israel is highly urbanized. About 7% of the people live on COLLECTIVE FARMS known as *kibbutzim*, and in co-operative farm villages known as *moshav ovdim* and *moshav shitufim*. Government is by a unicameral parliament (*Knesset*) of 120 members elected for a four-year term.

*History.* For the earlier history of the region, see PALESTINE. In November 1947 the United Nations proposed a division of Palestine, then under British mandate, into Jewish and Arab states. Six months later the British withdrew, and on 14 May 1948, the state of Israel was proclaimed. The neighbouring Arab states of Lebanon, Syria, Jordan, Egypt, and Iraq rejected both the partition of Palestine and the existence of the new nation. In the war that followed (1948–49), Israel emerged victorious and with its territory increased by one half. Arab opposition continued, however, and full-scale fighting broke out again in 1956 (the Sinai campaign), 1967 (the Six-Day War), and 1973 (the Yom Kippur War). Israel emerged from these conflicts (see ARAB–ISRAELI WARS) with large tracts of its neighbours' territories, which it refused to surrender without a firm peace settlement. In 1977 the hitherto dominant Labour Party was replaced as the main government party by the right-wing Likud alliance. The first real move toward permanent peace occurred in 1978, when Israeli Prime Min. Menachem BEGIN and Egyptian Pres. Anwar al-SADAT signed the so-called CAMP DAVID ACCORDS; a peace treaty between Egypt and Israel was signed (1979) in Washington, DC, and Israel began a phased withdrawal from the SINAI, completed in 1982. However, little progress was made in negotiations on autonomy for the GAZA STRIP and the WEST BANK of Jordan, and major questions about the continuation of the peace process were raised by the assassination of Sadat in 1981. Israel's relations with its other neighbours remained tense. In 1981 Israel effectively annexed the GOLAN HEIGHTS (captured from Syria in 1967), and Israeli bombers destroyed an Iraqi nuclear reactor, which the Israelis believed capable of producing nuclear weapons. Israel's fierce, intermittent fighting with the PALESTINE LIBERATION ORGANIZATION in Lebanon led to a devastating Israeli invasion in 1982. The 1984 elections brought Labour back to political dominance, with Shimon PERES becoming prime minister of a national unity coalition; under the coalition agreement, the Likud leader, Itzak SHAMIR, took over the premiership in 1986. After the inconclusive 1988 elections, a further national unity coalition was formed, with Shamir as prime minister and Peres as his deputy.

### Presidents of Israel
Chain Weizmann (Labour), 1948–52
Itzhak Ben-Zvi (Labour), 1952–63
Zalman Shazar (Labour), 1963–73
Ephraim Katzair (Labour), 1973–78
Itzhak Navon (Labour), 1978–83
Chaim Herzog (Labour), 1983–

### Prime ministers of Israel
David Ben-Gurion (Labour), 1948–53
Moshe Sharett (Labour), 1954–55
David Ben-Gurion (Labour), 1955–63
Levi Eshkol (Labour), 1963–69
Golda Meir (Labour), 1969–74
Itzhak Rabin (Labour), 1974–77
Menachem Begin (Likud), 1977–83
Itzhak Shamir (Likud), 1983–84
Shimon Peres (Labour), 1984–86
Itzhak Shamir (Likud), 1986–

**Israel** [as understood by Hebrews, = striven with God], in the Bible, name given JACOB. The Hebrews adopted the name as a national designation. Under REHOBOAM, in 931 BC, the Hebrew kingdom broke into a northern kingdom called Israel and a southern one called JUDAH.

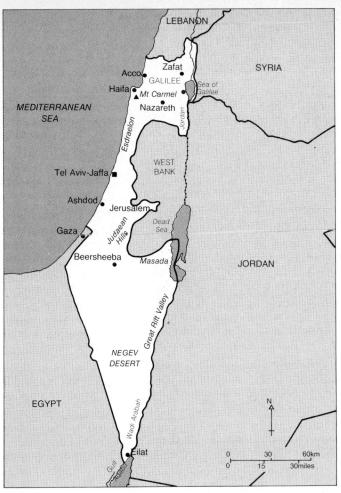

Israel

**Israel, Tribes of,** in the BIBLE, the 12 tribes of Hebrews named after 10 sons of JACOB (Reuben, Simeon, Judah, Zebulun, Issachar, Dan, Gad, Asher, Naphtali, and Benjamin) and the two sons of Jacob's son JOSEPH (Ephraim and Manasseh). The 13th tribe, Levi (the third of Jacob's sons), was set apart and had no one portion of its own. After the break in the Hebrew kingdom under REHOBOAM, the tribes of Judah, Benjamin, and some Levites formed a southern kingdom called Judah; the other 10 tribes formed a northern kingdom called Israel. These 10 were later (721 BC) conquered and transported to Assyria. They became known as the 10 lost tribes; numerous conjectures have been advanced as to their fate, and they have been identified with various peoples.

**Israëls, Jozef** (ˌeesrah-els), 1824–1911, Dutch GENRE painter. He used dramatic, silver-grey light to express the melancholy character of his themes, e.g., *Toilers of the Sea* (Amsterdam) and *Expectation* (Metropolitan Mus., New York).

**Issachar:** see ISRAEL, TRIBES OF.

**Isserles, Moses ben Israel,** c.1525–1572, Polish rabbi, annotator, and philosopher, known as *Remah.* He is best known for his works on Jewish law, notably his additions to the code of Joseph CARO, which made the code acceptable to Ashkenazic Jews (see under SHULHAN ARUKH).

**Issigonis, Sir Alec,** 1906–88, British engineer and inventor; b. Turkey. He pioneered the economy MOTOR CAR with his design of the Morris Minor (1948), followed in 1959 by the smaller, lower-capacity Mini Minor, innovative in that its engine was transversely mounted. Over 1 million of each were manufactured.

**Istanbul,** city (1980 pop. 2,772,708), capital of Istanbul prov., NW Turkey, on both sides of the Bosporus where it enters the Sea of Marmara. The city's name was changed from CONSTANTINOPLE in 1930; before AD 330 its site was occupied by BYZANTIUM. Turkey's largest city and chief seaport, it produces tobacco products, cement, and other manufactures. The part

of Istanbul corresponding to historic Constantinople is built on seven hills rising from both sides of the Golden Horn, an inlet of the BOSPORUS. Points of interest include the HAGIA SOPHIA, once a church and mosque; the Seraglio, the palace of the Ottoman sultans; and many museums. In 1973 the Bosporus Bridge united the city's European and Asian sections.

**Itaípu Dam,** on the PARANÁ R., on the boundary between Brazil and Paraguay. Started in 1973 and completed in 1984, it is the largest hydroelectric project in the world. A joint Brazilian–Paraguayan venture, the complex was engineered to generate, by 1990, 12,000 megawatts which is greater than the power generated by the ASWAN and Gran Coulée dams combined and is the equivalent of 100,000 barrels of oil daily. See IGUAZÚ FALLS.

**Italian East Africa,** former federation of Italian territories in E Africa that comprised the colonies of ERITREA and Italian Somaliland (see SOMALIA) and the kingdom of ETHIOPIA. Formed in 1936, when Italian forces conquered Ethiopia, it lasted until the territories were freed of Italian rule by the British in 1941.

**Italian language,** member of the Romance group of the Italic subfamily of the Indo-European family of languages. See LANGUAGE (table).

**Italian Wars,** 1494–1559, efforts by the great European powers, chiefly France and Spain, to control the small, independent states of Renaissance Italy. In 1494 CHARLES VIII of France invaded Italy and seized Naples (1495), only to be forced to retreat by a coalition of Spain, Holy Roman Emperor MAXIMILIAN I, the pope, Venice, and Milan. In the second phase (1499–1505), LOUIS XII of France occupied Milan, Genoa, and (jointly with Spain) Naples. In 1508 Pope JULIUS II formed an alliance with France, Spain, and Maximilian I against Venice. The pope and Louis soon fell out, and in 1511 the pope formed the HOLY LEAGUE, this time including the Swiss, for the purpose of expelling France from Italy. Julius died in 1513, and the league dissolved. In 1515 the great victory of FRANCIS I at the battle of Marignano reestablished French power in Italy. The wars between Francis and Emperor CHARLES V began in 1521. In 1526, after being defeated and captured, Francis was forced to renounce all claims in Italy. Once freed, however, he formed the League of Cognac with the pope, HENRY VIII of England, Venice, and Florence. In retaliation, Charles V's forces sacked Rome (May 1527). The pope capitulated, and the war ended (1529) with the Treaty of Cambrai. France again was forced to renounce its Italian claims. The death of Francis (1547) and the Treaty of Cateau-Cambrésis (1559) effectively ended France's exploits in Italy and left Spain supreme there.

**Italic languages,** subfamily of the Indo-European family of languages. See LANGUAGE (table).

**Italy,** Ital. *Italia,* officially the Italian Republic, republic (1985 est. pop. 56,874,000), 301,225 km² (116,303 sq mi), S Europe; bordered by France (NW), the Ligurian and Tyrrhenian seas (W), the Ionian Sea (S), the Adriatic Sea (E), Yugoslavia (NE), and Austria and Switzerland (N). It includes the large Mediterranean islands of SICILY and SARDINIA. VATICAN CITY and SAN MARINO are independent enclaves on the Italian mainland. ROME is the capital. About 75% of the country is mountainous or hilly, and 20% is forested. N Italy, made up of a vast plain contained by the ALPS in the north, is the richest region, with the best farmland, largest industrial centres, and a flourishing tourist trade; Gran Paradiso 4061 m (13,323 ft), the highest peak wholly within Italy, is located here. Central Italy has great historic and cultural centres, such as Rome and FLORENCE. S Italy is generally the poorest and least developed area. The GNP is $357,570 million and the GNP per capita is $6350 (1983). The Italian peninsula, bootlike in shape, is traversed for its entire length by the APENNINES. Italian is the major language, although there are small German-, French-, and Slavic-speaking minorities. Almost all Italians are Roman Catholic.

*Economy.* Largely agricultural until World War II, Italy industrialized rapidly after 1950. By the early 1970s industry contributed about 40% of the national product, compared with only 11% for agriculture. Chief manufactures include iron and steel, refined petroleum, chemicals, textiles, motor vehicles, and machinery. Principal farm products include wheat, maize, sugar beets, rice, tomatoes, citrus fruits, olives and olive oil, and livestock. Wine production is important. Tourism is a major source of foreign exchange. Mineral resources are limited, and 75% of energy needs must be imported.

*Government.* Under the 1948 constitution, legislative power is vested in a bicameral parliament, consisting of a 630-member chamber of deputies and a senate of 315 elected and 5 life members. The council of ministers, headed by the premier, is the country's executive.

*History.* After the expulsion of the Etruscans from what is now central Italy, ancient Italian history (5th cent. BC–5th cent. AD) is largely that of the Roman Empire, of which Italy was the core. Like the rest of the empire, Italy was overrun by barbarian tribes in the early 5th cent. AD. The Eastern emperors struggled over its remains, but Byzantine rule was soon displaced (569) by that of the LOMBARDS, except in Rome, where Pope GREGORY I (r.590–604) laid the foundation for the PAPAL STATES. The persisting Lombard threat against Rome brought the intervention of PEPIN THE SHORT (754, 756) and CHARLEMAGNE (800), who established Frankish hegemony over Italy. The German king OTTO I invaded (961) Italy and was crowned (962) emperor by the pope; this union of Italy and Germany marked the beginning of the HOLY ROMAN EMPIRE. Southern Italy, conquered (11th cent.) by the Normans, eventually passed to the Angevins of NAPLES and the Aragonese kings of Sicily. North and central Italy saw the rise of separate city-states; these, despite constant internecine warfare, built huge commercial empires, dominated European finance, and produced the great cultural flowering known as the RENAISSANCE. Beginning in the late 15th cent. Italy became the battleground of French, Spanish, and Austrian imperialism. By the 18th cent. Italian subjection to foreign rule, notably by the Spanish BOURBONS and the Austrian HABSBURG, was complete and remained so until the FRENCH REVOLUTIONARY WARS and NAPOLEON I redrew the map of Italy. After the Congress of VIENNA (1814–15) Austria, whose influence in Italy was now paramount, could not long suppress the burgeoning nationalist movement for unification (see RISORGIMENTO). Unification was ultimately achieved under the house of SAVOY, largely through the efforts of CAVOUR, GARIBALDI, and VICTOR EMMANUEL II, who became king of Italy in 1861. Italy later acquired Venetia (1866) and Rome and its environs (1870). Though a member of the TRIPLE ALLIANCE, Italy entered (1915) WORLD WAR I on the Allied side and in the peace treaty obtained additional territory, including S TYROL, TRIESTE, and Istria. After the war, political and social unrest encouraged the growth of fascism, and in 1922 MUSSOLINI seized power. He created a totalitarian corporative state, conquered Ethiopia (1936), seized Albania (1939), and entered (1940) WORLD WAR II as an ally of Germany. In 1943 Italy surrendered to the Allies. Italy became a republic in 1946, and the king was exiled. The 1947 peace treaty deprived Italy of its colonies and considerable territory. Trieste was regained in 1954. The postwar era has been marked by a succession of short-lived, pro-Western coalition governments dominated by the Christian Democrats; the Communists, although strong electorally, have been excluded from ministerial positions. In the late 1970s leftist guerrilla terrorism, led by the Red Brigade, plagued the country, most notably in the kidnapping and murder (1978) of former premier Aldo MORO. In 1981 Giovanni Spadolini became Italy's first non-Christian Democratic premier since the war; following their losses in the 1983 elections the Christian Democrats agreed to serve in a five-party coalition headed by the Socialist leader, Bettino Craxi. This was replaced in 1987 by a further centre-left coalition, with the Christian Democratic leader Ciriaco DE MITA becoming prime minister in 1988.

**Post-war Italian presidents**
Enrico de Nicola (non party), 1946–48
Luigi Einaudi (Liberal), 1948–55
Giovanni Gronchi (Christian Democrat), 1955–62
Antonio Segni (Christian Democrat), 1962–64
Giuseppe Saragat (Social Democrat), 1965–71
Giovanni Leone (Christian Democrat), 1971–78
Sandro Pertini (Socialist), 1978–85
Francesco Cossiga (Christian Democrat), 1985–

**Post-war Italian prime ministers**
Alcide de Gasperi (Christian Democrat), 1945–53
Giuseppe Pella (Christian Democrat), 1953–54
Amintore Fanfani (Christian Democrat), 1954
Mario Scelba (Christian Democrat), 1954–55
Antonio Segni (Christian Democrat), 1955–57
Adone Zoli (Christian Democrat), 1957–58
Amintore Fanfani (Christian Democrat), 1958–59
Antonio Segni (Christian Democrat), 1959–60
Fernando Tambroni (Christian Democrat), 1960

Italy

Amintore Fanfani (Christian Democrat), 1960–63
Giovanni Leone (Christian Democrat), 1963
Aldo Moro (Christian Democrat), 1963–68
Giovanni Leone (Christian Democrat), 1968
Mariano Rumor (Christian Democrat), 1968–70
Emilio Colombo (Christian Democrat), 1970–72
Giulio Andreotti (Christian Democrat), 1972–73
Mariano Rumor (Christian Democrat), 1973–74
Aldo Moro (Christian Democrat), 1974–76
Giulio Andreotti (Christian Democrat), 1976–79
Francesco Cossiga (Christian Democrat), 1979–80
Arnaldo Forlani (Christian Democrat), 1980–81
Giovanni Spadolini (Republican), 1981–82
Amintore Fanfani (Christian Democrat), 1982–83
Bettino Craxi (Socialist), 1983–87
Giovanni Goria (Christian Democrat), 1987–88
Ciriaco De Mita (Christian Democrat), 1988–

**Itard, Jean Marc,** 1774–1838, French physician, psychologist, and educator. Itard's work with Victor, the 'Wild Boy of Aveyron'—a child found wandering and abandoned in the forest, who had apparently lacked human contact for many years—laid the basis for many subsequent methods of instruction in educational psychology.

**Itháki** or **Ithaca,** island (1981 pop. 4,952), c.96 km² (37 sq mi), W Greece, one of the Ionian Islands. Olive oil, currants, and wine are produced there. It is traditionally celebrated as the home of ODYSSEUS.

**Itō Hirobumi,** 1841–1909, Japanese statesman and one of the architects of modern Japan. A visit to England in 1863 convinced him of the technical superiority of the West and he accordingly abandoned his anti-Western beliefs. After the MEIJI restoration he served in several ministries and in 1882 went abroad to study foreign systems of government. He established a cabinet system and a civil service in 1885 and a privy council in 1888, and he helped draft the constitution of 1889. He was prime minister three times (1892–96, 1898, 1900–01). He was assassinated while resident-general of Korea, and as a result Japan annexed Korea in 1910.

**Itten, Johannes,** 1888–1967, Swiss artist. He studied with Hoelzel at Stuttgart (1913–16) and opened his own school of art in Vienna. In 1919 he went to the BAUHAUS where he taught the preliminary course. Itten was interested in new teaching ideas, involving the students in free expression and their intuitive responses to colour, form, and materials. These expressionist ideas, combined with his eccentric lifestyle and left-wing politics, led to his leaving the Bauhaus in 1923. He was replaced by MOHOLY-NAGY. His work was of a geometrical abstract style, illustrating his researches into the psychology of colour perception.

**Iturbide, Agustín de** (eetooɔˌbeedhay), 1783–1824, Mexican revolutionary leader. In 1821, while commanding royalist troops, he agreed to the Plan of Iguala and the Treaty of Córdoba, assuring MEXICO's independence from Spain. He favoured a conservative state and had himself proclaimed emperor (1822), but radical rebels forced him to abdicate and go into exile (1823). When he returned illegally to Mexico, he was executed.

**IUD:** see INTRAUTERINE DEVICE.

**Ivan** (eeˌvahn), rulers of Russia. **Ivan III** (the Great), 1440–1505, grand duke of Moscow (1462–1505), was the creator of the consolidated Muscovite (Russian) state. He subjugated Great Novgorod and other territories and in 1480 freed Muscovy from allegiance to the GOLDEN HORDE. He married Sophia, niece of the last Byzantine emperor, and claimed Moscow as the successor to the Roman and Byzantine empires. **Ivan IV** (the Terrible), 1530–84, grand duke of Moscow (1533–84), had himself crowned czar in 1547. He began trade with England, engaged in an unsuccessful war with Poland and Sweden to improve his access to the Baltic Sea, and began Russia's eastward expansion; Siberia was conquered during his reign. In later years he grew tyrannical and paranoid. He formed a special corps, the *oprichniki,* with which he conducted a reign of terror against the BOYARS. In one of his rages he killed his son and heir, Ivan (1581). He married seven times, disposing of his wives by forcing them to take the veil or ordering their murder. His sons Feodor I and DMITRI survived him, but his favourite, Boris GODUNOV, took power. **Ivan V,** 1666–96, czar (1682–90), succeeded his brother, Feodor III, ruling with PETER I under the regency of his sister, Sophia Alekseyevna. Feebleminded, he was excluded from affairs of state. He was father of Czarina ANNA, who was succeeded by her infant grand-nephew, **Ivan VI,** 1740–64, a German by birth. Deposed (1741) by Czarina ELIZABETH, Ivan VI was murdered in 1764 by order of CATHERINE II.

**Ivanov, Lev,** 1834–1901, Russian choreographer. He worked with PETIPA in St Petersburg and was a major force in Russian Romanticism. He choreographed *Nutcracker* (1892), and with Petipa revived *Swan Lake.* He sought a closer relation of music to dance, and influenced FOKINE.

**Ives, Charles,** 1874–1954, American composer. An organist who entered the insurance business, Ives quietly composed music advanced in style, anticipating some of the innovations of SCHOENBERG and STRAVINSKY. Most of his music was written before he suffered a heart attack in 1918, and it is largely unpublished. In 1939 a performance of his second piano sonata, *Concord* (1909–15), won him recognition. His works, which include chamber, orchestral, and choral pieces and about 150 SONGS, draw often on American folk music and hymnody. His Second Quartet of 1907–13 is regarded by some as his finest work.

**Ives, James Merritt:** see CURRIER & IVES.

**ivory,** type of dentine present only in ELEPHANT tusks. Major sources are Africa and Asia. Ivory was long used for carvings and inlay work and as a surface for miniature painting. The ancient civilizations of Egypt, Assyria, Babylon, Greece, Rome, India, China, Japan, Byzantium, and early Christian Europe produced works in ivory. In modern times it has been used chiefly to make keys for pianos and other instruments, billiard balls, and handles. The diminishing elephant population (largely the result of their slaughter for ivory) and efforts to protect existing herds have led to greater use of substitutes, such as PLASTIC. In the past, teeth or tusks of such animals as the hippopotamus, walrus, narwhal, sperm whale, and wild boar were also called ivory.

**Ivory Coast:** see CÔTE D'IVOIRE.

**ivy,** name applied loosely to several trailing or climbing plants, particularly cultivated forms; more properly, the English ivy (*Hedera helix*) and some other members of the family Araliaceae. The evergreen English ivy has many named ornamental varieties, e.g., 'Jubilee', with a large, golden leaf blotch. The GRAPE family (Vitaceae) also includes some ivies, most notably the VIRGINIA CREEPER (*Parthenocissus*).

**Ivy League,** an informal grouping of the most prestigious universities in the US. They are: Brown (founded 1764), Columbia (1754), Cornell (1865), Dartmouth College (1769), Harvard (1636), Princeton (1746), Pennsylvania (1755), and Yale (1701).

**Iwo,** city (1981 pop, 292,500) Oya state, SW Nigeria. The town's principal exports are cocoa and palm oil. Its chief industries are the manufacture of textiles (weaving and dyeing) and glass.

**Iwo Jima,** volcanic island, c.12 km$^2$ (8 sq mi), W Pacific, largest and most important of the Volcano Islands. Annexed by Japan in 1891, the island, site of a Japanese air base, was captured (Feb.–Mar. 1945) by US marines at great cost. American administration ended in 1968. The island's Mt Suribachi is an extinct volcano.

**IWW:** see INDUSTRIAL WORKERS OF THE WORLD.

**Izmir,** formerly **Smyrna,** city (1980 pop. 757,854), capital of Izmir prov., W Turkey, on the Gulf of Izmir, an arm of the Aegean Sea. It is Turkey's second largest seaport and an industrial centre with such manufactures as paper and metal goods. Settled during the Bronze Age (c.3000 BC), it was colonized (c.1000 BC) by Ionians and destroyed (627 BC) by the Lydians. Under Macedon and Rome it prospered. It changed hands many times from the 7th to 15th cent. AD, when the Ottoman Turks conquered it. Greece contested the city after the collapse (1918) of the OTTOMAN EMPIRE; when the Treaty of Lausanne confirmed it as Turkey's, the two countries traded minorities, making Izmir mostly Turkish. Earthquakes in 1928 and 1939 caused severe damage.

**Izmit,** city (1980 pop. 190,423), capital of Izmit prov., NW Turkey, on the Sea of Marmara. It has grown rapidly as a port and centre of industries that include oil refining and chemical manufacture. Founded in the 8th cent. BC, it has little to show for its antiquity except a ruined Byzantine citadel.

# J

**Jabalpur** (formerly **Jubbulpore**), city (1981 pop. 649,085), Madhya Pradesh state, C India, near the source of the NARMADA R. It is a district administrative and communications centre at the convergence of many natural, rail, and road routes. It has railway shops, and factories making pottery, glass, furniture, and military and telecommunications equipment. There are two universities.

**Jabavu, John Tengo,** 1859–1921, South African politician, journalist, and educationalist. He founded (1883) the first independent African-language (Xhosa) newspaper in South Africa, *Imvo Zabantsundu* [the views of the Bantu People]. He was active in politics, supporting white moderate politicians, until 1913, and subsequently devoted his life to fostering African education.

**jackal,** carnivorous MAMMAL (genus *Canis*) related to the DOG and WOLF and similar in size and behaviour to the COYOTE. They are 56–74 cm (22–29 in) long, and they feed by both scavanging and hunting. Some authorities classify jackals in a separate genus (*Thos*). Jackals are found in Africa and S Asia, where they inhabit deserts, grasslands, and brush country. They forage by night and spend the day in holes or hidden in grass or brush.

**jackdaw,** small BIRD of the CROW family. The jackdaw (*Corvus monedula*) is a lively, intelligent bird ranging across Europe and Asia. It is the smallest crow, only 33 cm (13 in) long. It is very sociable, the birds forming a loose community in their roosts. Their behaviour was studied by Konrad LORENZ. Jackdaws are mainly carnivores but use their great aerobatic skills for courtship and play rather than hunting. The birds readily nest near humans and have a place in many legends and stories which credit jackdaws with wisdom and craftiness. Like MAGPIES they are thieves, as described in the long poem *The Jackdaw of Rheims* by R.H. Barham.

**Jackson,** US city (1984 est. pop. 209,000), state capital of Mississippi, on the Pearl R.; inc. 1833. The state's largest city, it has electrical machinery, food, stone, glass, and other industries, and is the centre of the state's oil industry. Jackson is also a major southern rail and distribution centre. It became capital in 1821 and was named after Andrew JACKSON. A centre for the VICKSBURG CAMPAIGN in the CIVIL WAR, it was largely destroyed by SHERMAN's forces. The old capitol (1839) survives and is now a museum. During the 1960s it was the site of many demonstrations for black civil rights.

**Jackson, Andrew,** 1767–1845, 7th president of the US (1829–37). Born in poverty, Jackson moved to Tennessee, where he became a successful lawyer, land speculator, and planter. He helped to draft the Tennessee Constitution and was elected (1796) to the US Congress. In the WAR OF 1812 he defeated the CREEK INDIANS at Horseshoe Bend (Mar. 1814), was made a major general, and decisively defeated seasoned British troops at New Orleans (8 Jan. 1815). In 1818 he led a reprisal against the Seminoles in Florida and captured Pensacola, involving the US in serious trouble with Spain and Britain. These exploits made Old Hickory, as he was called, the greatest hero of his time and came to symbolize the movement for increased popular participation in government. This so-called Jacksonian democracy almost won him the presidency in 1824, but the election ended in the House of Representatives, with a victory for J.Q. ADAMS. Jackson was elected president in 1828, greatly enlarged executive authority, made the presidency a more personal and effective office, and developed the Spoils System. Jackson and Vice Pres. J.C. CALHOUN differed on NULLIFICATION,

and Calhoun resigned (1832). Jackson's fight against the Bank of the United States was an important issue in the election of 1832, in which he defeated Henry CLAY. He then transferred federal assets from the bank to chosen state, or 'pet', banks. In 1836 he issued the Specie Circular, which said that all public lands must be paid for in specie and which hastened the Panic of 1837.

**Jackson, Glenda,** 1938–, English actress. She has starred as Charlotte CORDAY in Peter WEISS's play *Marat/Sade* (1965); won Academy Awards for the films *Women in Love* (1969) and *A Touch of Class* (1972); and portrayed ELIZABETH I in the television production *Elizabeth R* (1971). Her later productions include *Stevie* (1977), *Rose* (1980), *Great and Small* (1983), and *Phedre* (1984).

**Jackson, Mahalia,** 1911–72, black American singer. Living in Chicago from 1927, she sang in churches and revival meetings, and began to make recordings. By the 1950s her powerful, joyous GOSPEL MUSIC style had gained her an international reputation.

**Jackson, Stonewall** (Thomas Jonathan Jackson), 1824–63, Confederate general in the AMERICAN CIVIL WAR. At the first battle of BULL RUN he earned his sobriquet when he and his brigade stood 'like a stone wall'. He conducted the brilliant Shenandoah Valley campaign (May–June 1862) and joined Gen. R.E. LEE for the Seven Days Battles. Serving under Lee, Jackson outflanked the Union army to set up the Confederate victory at the second battle of Bull Run (Aug. 1862), and fought in the ANTIETAM CAMPAIGN and at Fredericksburg. At Chancellorsville (May 1863) Jackson again outflanked the Union army to make possible a resounding Confederate victory, but he was mortally wounded by fire from his own troops. He was Lee's ablest and most trusted lieutenant.

**Jacksonville,** US city (1984 est. pop. 578,000), NE Florida, on the St Johns R. near its mouth on the Atlantic; settled 1816, inc. 1832. The largest city in Florida, it is a major port and rail, air, and motorway hub, with extensive shipyards and freight-handling facilities. Timber, paper, processed food, computer components, and chemicals are leading products. Naval operations are important, as is tourism. The city's growth was interrupted by the Seminole War (see SEMINOLE INDIANS) and the CIVIL WAR, and the city was destroyed by fire in 1901 and rebuilt. Points of interest include the Gator Bowl sports stadium.

**Jacob,** in the BIBLE, ancestor of the Hebrews, the younger of the twin sons of ISAAC and REBECCA. By bargain and trickery, Jacob got the birthright and the blessing that was intended for his twin ESAU. Jacob had two wives, Leah and her younger sister, RACHEL. On the banks of the Jabbok, he wrestled with an angel and received the name of Israel. Gen. 25–50. He was the ancestor of the 12 tribes of Israel (see ISRAEL, TRIBES OF).

**Jacob, François,** 1920–, French microbiologist. By studying the genetic basis of lysogeny (integration and replication of the DNA of a BACTÉRIOPHAGE with that of a bacterial host), he and Elie Wollman discovered (1961) a new class of genetic elements, the episomes. Studies of the regulation of bacterial enzyme synthesis led Jacob and Jacques MONOD to propose (1961) the concepts of messenger RNA (see NUCLEIC ACID) and the operon (functional unit of a chromosome). For this work Jacob and Monod shared with André LWOFF the 1965 Nobel Prize for physiology or medicine.

**Jacobean style,** an early phase of English Renaissance architecture and decoration, a transition between the ELIZABETHAN STYLE and the pure

Renaissance style introduced by Inigo JONES. Under James I (r.1603–25) Renaissance motifs, communicated through German and Flemish carvers, were freely adopted, but some Gothic influence lingered. Columns and pilasters, round-arch arcades, and other classical elements mixed with characteristic English ornamental detail. The style influenced furniture design and other arts. Holland House, London, and Knole House, Kent, are noted Jacobean buildings.

**Jacobi, Carl Gustav Jacob**, 1804–51, German mathematician and professor of mathematics at Königsberg and Berlin. He worked in many branches of mathematics but chiefly on determinants, infinite series, differential equations, the theory of numbers, the calculus of variations, and elliptic functions. A functional determinant was named the Jacobian after him.

**Jacobins**, political club of the FRENCH REVOLUTION. Formed in 1789, the club was named after the monastery of the Jacobins (Parisian name of the Dominicans), where it met. The members were mainly bourgeois and at first included moderates such as Honoré de MIRABEAU. With the FEUILLANTS, the Jacobins were (1791–92) the chief parties in the Legislative Assembly. They sought to limit the power of the king, and many had republican tendencies. The group split on the issue of war in Europe, which the majority, the GIRONDISTS, sought. The minority, supported by the lower classes of Paris, opposed the war and grew more radical and republican. In the National Convention, which proclaimed the French republic, these Jacobins and other extremist opponents of the Girondists were called the MOUNTAIN. After contributing heavily to the fall (1793) of the Girondists, the Jacobins, under Maximilien ROBESPIERRE, instituted the REIGN OF TERROR, which they used not only against counterrevolutionaries, but also against their former allies, the CORDELIERS and Georges DANTON. The Jacobins lost power on the fall (1794) of Robespierre, but their spirit lived on in revolutionary doctrine.

**Jacobites**, adherents of the exiled branch of the house of STUART after the GLORIOUS REVOLUTION of 1688. They took their name from the Latin form (*Jacobus*) of the name James. The Jacobites sought the restoration of JAMES II, then advanced the claims of his descendants, until 1807 when the direct Stuart line ended. They included many Catholics, high churchmen, and extreme Tories. After the death of Queen ANNE (1714), Henry St John and the 6th earl of Mar attempted a rising known as 'the '15' (1715) to crown the Old Pretender, James Edward STUART; they were defeated in the disastrous battles of Preston and Sheriffmuir. The second major Jacobite rising, called 'the '45', occurred when the Young Pretender, Charles Edward Stuart, invaded (1745) England and was crushed at the battle of Culloden Moor (1746).

**Jacobs, Aletta**, 1851–1929, Dutch feminist and birth-control pioneer. She was the first qualified woman doctor in Holland and opened the world's first birth-control clinic (1882), in Amsterdam. A suffrage campaigner, she founded (1894) Holland's Association for Women's Suffrage, and was active in the international women's peace movement during World War I.

**Jacobs, Louis**, 1920–, British rabbi and theologian. He was the Founding-Minister (1964) of the first Conservative congregation in Britain, the New London Synagogue. Jacobs' new community comprised former members of the Orthodox United Synagogue, who had resigned as a token of support for him and the spirit of free inquiry into biblical tradition and Revelation which he was promoting. These views caused the Chief Rabbi, Israel Brodie, to veto Jacobs' appointment as principal of Jews' College, the leading Orthodox rabbinical seminary. The 'Jacobs Affair' split Anglo-Jewry and injected a spirit of polarization into a hitherto quite united Jewish community. Rabbi Dr Jacobs has written over 30 books on Jewish mysticism, philosophy, and Hasidism.

**Jacobs, W(illiam) W(ymark)**, 1863–1943, English author. He wrote humorous sea stories, e.g., *Many Cargoes,* 1896, and horror stories, including 'The Monkey's Paw'.

**Jacobsen, Jens Peter** (ˌyahkopsən), 1847–85, Danish writer, creator of a curt prose style that greatly influenced NATURALISM. His principal work is *Marie Grubbe* (1876), a historical romance dealing with spiritual degeneration.

**Jacobson, Dan**, 1929–, white South African novelist. He has lived permanently in England since the mid-1960s. His main concern in his novels, e.g., *The Trap* (1955), and in his short stories, e.g., *Through the Wilderness* (1968), is the manner in which human beings collaborate in their own degradation.

**Jacopone da Todi**, 1230?–1306, Italian poet and mystic. A Franciscan, he wrote many ardent religious poems and has been thought to be the author of the hymn *Stabat Mater Dolorosa.*

**Jacquard, Joseph Marie**, 1752–1834, French engineer and inventor of the Jacquard LOOM. The son of a weaver, he was apprenticed to a bookbinder and later a cutlery maker but returned to weaving when his parents died leaving him the family business. He invented a loom with multi-coloured bobbins which could be controlled from a plate with holes and feeders and which resulted in the ability to weave complicated coloured patterns. By 1812 there were 11,000 such looms in France. The Jacquard loom still forms the basis of computer-controlled weaving. Jacquard made many inventions and developments in textile machinery helped by his knowledge of leather and steel, and was highly honoured in France.

**Jacquerie** [Fr., = collection of *Jacques,* a nickname for the French peasant], 1358, a revolt of the French peasantry. The uprising stemmed from poor economic conditions, high taxation, and pillaging during the HUNDRED YEARS WAR. It was brutally crushed by CHARLES II of Navarre and other nobles.

**jade**, common name for either of two minerals, both white to green in colour, used as GEMS. Jadeite [NaAl(SiO$_3$)$_2$], rarer and costlier, is found in Burma, China, Japan, and Guatemala. Nephrite [Ca$_2$(Mg,Fe)$_5$Si$_8$O$_{22}$(OH,F)$_2$] occurs in New Zealand, Central Asia, Siberia, and parts of North America. Jade was much used by primitive peoples to make implements and has been prized by the Chinese and Japanese as the most precious of gems.

**Ja'far al-Sadiq**, c.700–765, Shi'ite IMAM and HADITH scholar. To him is attributed the FIQH of SHI'ISM, and he was the last Imam on whom agreement between the ISMA'ILIS and the Twelve Shi'ites obtains. He is also the object of many legends.

**Jaffa** or **Joppa**, ancient port on the Mediterranean coast of Palestine and now in Israel. In biblical times it was the nearest harbour to JERUSALEM and it remained important until the 19th cent. A poor and small harbour on a difficult and dangerous coast, it declined as ships became larger. Until 1948 it was a predominantly Arab town, but it has since been merged administratively with the adjoining new Jewish town of TEL AVIV. It has given its name to the variety of large seedless oranges grown in the district.

**Jaffna**, town (1981 pop. 118,215), Sri Lanka. It is a district administrative and commercial centre, and a cultural centre for the Sri Lanka Tamil community. It has a university, and small-scale tobacco and textile industries. Of recent years it and its district have been much disturbed by armed communal disturbances.

**jaguar**, large CAT (*Panthera onca*) found from the SW US to S central Argentina. It has a yellow or tawny coat with black rings and spots; some rings surround spots, a feature which distinguishes it from a LEOPARD. An adult male may be 1.5 m (4½ ft) long (excluding the long tail), stand 75 cm (2½ ft) high at the shoulder, and weigh 90 kg (200 lb). Mainly forest dwellers, jaguars are also found in rocky, semidesert areas and on the PAMPAS.

**jai alai**, also called pelota, handball-like game of Spanish Basque origin. It is played as either singles or doubles on a three-walled court (*fronton*) with a hard rubber ball (*pelota*) that is hurled with a wicker basket (*cesta*) attached to the player's arm. The sport is popular in Latin America and in some states of the US.

**Jainism** [the religion of Jina], religious system of India, practised by about 2 million followers. It arose in the 6th cent. BC in protest against the ritualism of HINDUISM and the authority of the VEDA, and was established by a succession of 24 saints, the last of whom was Vardhamāna (called Mahāvīra or Jina), apparently a historical figure. He preached asceticism and concern for all life as a means of escaping from the cycle of rebirths that results from one's past actions (see KARMA) and of achieving NIRVĀNA. Early Jainism spread from NE India, according to tradition converting the emperor CHANDRAGUPTA and other rulers.

**Jaipur**, city (1981 pop. 977,165), Rajasthan state, NW India. It is the capital of Rajasthan and an important district administrative, communications, and commercial centre. It has a university, and some industrial development. It is a tourist attraction because of its own interest and beauty, and because of the nearby abandoned hilltop fort and palace at Amber. Jaipur itself was founded by the Maharaja Jai Singh II in 1727, and is an example of a planned princely city built largely in rose-red stone. The Maharajas of Jaipur continued to rule their princely state in British times; and a latter-day Maharani has been active in post-independence politics.

**Jaja of Opobo,** 1821–91, founder and ruler of the state of Opobo in NIGERIA. Jaja rose from the status of a slave boy to found his own trading house on the R. Opobo after 1869. His wealth and power was based upon his control of the palm-oil trade with the delta. The British recognized his state in 1884 but a year later incorporated it into a British protectorate over the Niger delta. Jaja refused to cooperate with the British who deported him to the West Indies in 1887. He died on his way home from exile.

**Jakarta:** see DJAKARTA.

**Jakes, Milos,** 1922–, Czechoslovak political figure and Communist Party leader (1987–). A longserving member of the country's top ruling bodies, he acquired a reputation as a conservative pragmatist. Closely identified with President HUSÁK, he succeeded the latter as general secretary of the ruling party in Dec. 1987.

**Jakobovits, The Lord Immanuel,** 1921–, rabbi and writer; b. Konigsberg, Germany. His family fled to England from Nazi oppression. He served as rabbi to three London congregations before being called to Dublin as Chief Rabbi of Ireland in 1949. Between 1958 and 1967 he served as rabbi of the Fifth Avenue Synagogue in New York, before being elected Chief Rabbi of the United Hebrew Congregations of the British Commonwealth. He has written a number of books and learned articles, and is an acknowledged authority on the application of Jewish law in the sphere of medical ethics. He established the Jewish Educational Development Trust, which provides funds for the expansion of Jewish education in Britain. He was knighted in 1981, he was elevated to the peerage in 1988, and he has been the recipient of many honorary degrees from academic institutions in the US, Israel, and Britain.

**Jakobson, Roman Osipovich,** 1896–, American linguist; b. Russia. One of the founding members of the PRAGUE LINGUISTIC CIRCLE, he wrote on many areas of LINGUISTICS, but his most influential contribution has been in the area of PHONETICS where he proposes a systematic universal 'psychological system' of sounds underlying the sounds used in human languages (communication). He moved to the US in 1939 and has been influential in the rapid and radical development of linguistics over the past 30 years.

**Jalandhar** (formerly **Jullundur**), town (1981 pop. 408,196), Punjab state, N India. It is a district administrative and railway centre in the middle of the Bist Doab between the Beas and Sutlej Rs. Since independence it has developed industries, many of them started by refugees from what is now Pakistan: these make sports goods and light engineering products, mainly in small units. It became a district headquarters in British days.

**Jamaica,** island republic (1987 est. pop. 2,346,700), 10,962 km² (4232 sq mi), West Indies, S of Cuba and W of Haiti. The capital is KINGSTON. Most of Jamaica is an elevated plateau with a mountainous spine reaching 2256 m (7402 ft) in the Blue Mts., but there are low-lying plains along the north and south coasts. The economy is based on sugar (mainly in the form of molasses and rum), bauxite, and tourism. Jamaica is one of the world's largest suppliers of bauxite and alumina, which, though depressed, account for half of its export earnings. Tourism, stimulated by the island's mild, subtropical climate and excellent beaches, is the second-largest source of exchange, although the violent nature of Jamaican society has held back its expansion. Besides sugar, export crops are coffee, bananas, citrus fruits, and tobacco. The GDP is US$225 million and the GDP per capita is US$1034. A large majority of the people are of African descent. The chief religions are Protestant (increasingly US evangelical sects), and the official language is English, although most Jamaicans speak a 'Creole English' patois.

*History.* Discovered by COLUMBUS in 1494 and first settled (1509) by Spaniards, Jamaica was captured by England in 1655; formal cession was in 1670. A large black slave population was gathered to work sugar plantations during the 18th cent., when Jamaica was one of the world's leading sugar producers. The decline of sugar after the abolition of slavery

in 1838 produced economic hardship, civil unrest, and (from 1865 to 1884) British suppression of local autonomy. Black rioting, sparked by poverty and British racial policies, recurred periodically, reaching a peak in 1938. In 1944 universal adult suffrage was introduced. After a brief period (1958–62) as part of the WEST INDIES Federation, in 1962 Jamaica became a fully independent member of the COMMONWEALTH. After 1975 a move towards socialism under a People's National Party government headed by Michael Manley led to violence between the two main political parties and to US economical and political pressure, and produced a severe economic crisis. Edward Seaga, of the conservative Jamaica Labour Party, took office in 1980 and has restored some measure of economic stability with IMF support, but has not been able to attract the foreign investments his pro-US policy anticipated. In 1983 Jamaica participated in the US-led invasion of Grenada.

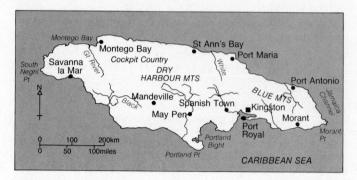

Jamaica

**James,** kings of England, Scotland, and Ireland. **James I,** 1566–1625 (r.1603–25), was the son of Lord DARNLEY and MARY QUEEN OF SCOTS. He succeeded to the Scottish throne on the forced abdication of his mother. During his minority, Scotland was ruled by a series of regents, and he was the creature of successive combinations of his mother's pro-French Catholic party and the Protestant faction, which favoured an alliance with England. He began his personal rule in 1583. Allying himself with ELIZABETH I, he accepted calmly his mother's execution in 1587. He succeeded Elizabeth in 1603. At the Hampton Court Conference of 1604 (which commissioned the translation that resulted in the Authorized or King James Version of the BIBLE), he displayed an uncompromising anti-Puritan attitude. His inconsistent policy toward English Catholics (which resulted in the GUNPOWDER PLOT) angered them as well as Protestants. After the death (1612) of his able minister Robert Cecil, earl of SALISBURY, he strongly asserted his divine right, battling with Sir Edward COKE and relying on incompetent favourites, e.g., George Villiers, 1st duke of BUCKINGHAM. These actions, his extravagance, and his refusal to recognize the importance of Parliament furthered discontent and led to the stormy parliamentary sessions. In 1611 he dissolved Parliament, ruling without it (except for the Addled Parliament, 1614) until 1621. In 1624 he acceded to its wish for war with SPAIN. His reign saw the beginnings of colonization in North America. He was succeeded by CHARLES I. **James II,** 1633–1701 (r.1685–88), was the second son of Charles I and the brother and successor of CHARLES II. He escaped to France (1648) in the ENGLISH CIVIL WAR. At the RESTORATION (1660) he returned to England and was made lord high admiral, serving (1665; 1672) in the DUTCH WARS. In 1669 he became a Roman Catholic. After his resignation as admiral because of the TEST ACT (1673) and his marriage to the staunchly Catholic Mary of Modena (1673), he became increasingly unpopular. His daughter MARY married the Protestant William of Orange (later WILLIAM III), and they became, after James, heirs presumptive to the English throne. Exiled after the false accusations of a Popish Plot (1678) by Titus OATES, James was recalled in 1680. After the failure of Parliament to exclude him from succession and the abortive RYE HOUSE PLOT, Charles II's death brought him to the throne in 1685. His unpopularity was increased by the Bloody Assizes of Baron JEFFREYS OF WEM, his attempts to fill important positions with Roman Catholics, and his autocratic dealings with a hostile Parliament. The birth of his son, James Edward STUART, as a possible Catholic heir led to the GLORIOUS REVOLUTION of 1688, in which William of Orange became king. James fled to France. In 1689 he attempted to restore himself in Ireland but was defeated (1690) at the battle of the Boyne. He died in exile.

**James,** kings of Scotland. **James I,** 1394–1437 (r.1406–37), was the son of ROBERT III. Fearful for his safety, because of the ambitions of the king's brother, Robert Stuart, duke of Albany, Robert III sent James to France in 1406. The prince was captured by the English and held captive until 1424. Treated as a royal guest, he was well educated. Ransomed by several Scottish nobles, he returned to Scotland and governed energetically. He brought peace by ruthless methods, exterminating members of the Albany family. James's popularity was lessened by his vindictiveness, cupidity, and quick temper; he was assassinated by a group of nobles. He is thought to be the author of a number of fine poems. His son, **James II,** 1430–60 (r.1437-60), had successive earls of Douglas as regents during his minority. Allying himself with William Douglas, the 6th earl, he was by 1450 ruling in his own right. When he discovered (1452) him in a conspiracy, William killed himself. After the ensuing revolt, he seized the Douglas lands. He invaded England in the Wars of the ROSES and was accidentally killed. His son, **James III,** 1452–88 (r.1460–88), was seized at his mother's death by the Boyd family, who ruled until 1469. A cultivated king, James lacked the force necessary in a turbulent period. He fought with his brother, Alexander STUART, who, aided by other nobles, rebelled in 1482. The nobles rebelled again in 1488 and murdered James at Sauchie Burn. His son, **James IV,** 1473–1513 (r.1488–1513), was a popular and able monarch who brought progress and stability to Scotland. In 1503 he married Margaret Tudor, daughter of HENRY VII of England. Scottish relations with England deteriorated with the accession of HENRY VIII. James invaded England in 1513 and was killed in the battle of Flodden, in which the Scottish aristocracy was almost annihilated. His son, **James V,** 1512–42 (r.1513–42), was the object of a struggle between his regents. Held captive, he escaped (1528) and allied himself with France against Henry VIII. He married MARY OF GUISE in 1538. War with England broke out in 1542. James's nobles gave him little support, and his army was routed at Solway Moss. He died shortly thereafter and was succeeded by his infant daughter, MARY QUEEN OF SCOTS. **James VI,** king of Scotland (r.1567–1625): see JAMES I, under JAMES, kings of England, Scotland, and Ireland.

**James,** EPISTLE of the NEW TESTAMENT. It is traditionally placed among the Catholic or General Epistles and ascribed to St James the Lord's brother. A practical work, it gives diverse admonitions in no special order, among them two general ethical principles: 'Be doers of the word, not hearers only' (1.19–27) and 'Faith without works is dead' (2.14–26).

**James, C(yril) L(ionel) R(obert),** 1901–, Trinidadian novelist, historian and critic. His writings on black political theory include *The Future in the Present* (1977), *Spheres of Existence* (1980), and *At the Rendezvous of Victory* (1984). He wrote an account of TOUSSAINT L'OUVERTURE's revolt in San Domingo—the only successful black slave revolt in the Caribbean—as *The Black Jacobins* (1938) which formed the basis of David Blake's opera *Toussaint l'Ouverture* (1974; revised 1982) novels, concerned with working-class aspirations, include *Minty Alley* (1936) and his critical writings include *Beyond a Boundary* (1963).

**James, Henry,** 1843–1916, American novelist; brother of William JAMES. He settled in London in 1876 and became a British citizen in 1915. In his early novels, such as *Daisy Miller* (1879) and *The Portrait of a Lady* (1881), he compared the sophisticated culture of Europeans with the naive quality of Americans. In his next period, James dealt with revolutionaries, as in *The Bostonians* (1886) and *The Princess Casamassima* (1886). He also wrote several powerful short novels, such as *The Aspern Papers* (1888) and *The Turn of the Screw* (1898). He returned to the international theme in his last novels, *The Wings of the Dove* (1902), *The Ambassadors* (1903), and *The Golden Bowl* (1904). He was also a fine short-story writer and a noted critic. Considered one of the great masters of the novel, James is particularly noted for his portrayals of the subtleties of character and for his complex style.

**James, Jesse,** 1847–82, American outlaw. From 1886 Jesse and his brother Frank headed a band of outlaws whose trail of robberies and murders led through many central states. He was killed by a gang member seeking a reward.

**James, Saint,** d. AD c.43, one of the Twelve Disciples; called St James the Greater. The son of Zebedee and brother of St JOHN, he is venerated widely, especially (as Santiago) in Spain.

**James, Saint** (the Less or Little), one of the Twelve Disciples. He was the son of Alphaeus and Mary.

**James, Saint,** the 'brother' of Jesus Christ, according to the Gospels. Since belief in the perpetual virginity of Mary precludes a blood relationship, many assume him to have been a stepbrother or cousin. The Roman Catholic Church identifies him with St James the Less. He apparently opposed the imposition of Jewish Law on Gentile Christians and is probably the author of the Epistle of James.

**James, William,** 1842–1910, American philosopher and psychologist, brother of the novelist Henry JAMES. He was a proponent of the philosophy of PRAGMATISM. His best-known books are *The Principles of Psychology* (1890) and *Pragmatism* (1907).

**Jameson, Sir Leander Starr,** 1853–1917, British colonial administrator in South Africa. In 1895 he led the unauthorized Jameson Raid into the Boer colony of the Transvaal, an act that helped to precipitate the SOUTH AFRICAN WAR. He was captured and turned over to the British, who imprisoned him briefly. He later returned to South Africa, where he was prime minister of the Cape Colony (1904–8).

**Jamestown,** former village, SE Virginia, US, first permanent English settlement in America; est. 14 May 1607, by the London Company on a peninsula (now an island) in the James R.; named after the reigning English king, JAMES I. Disease, starvation, and Indian attacks decimated the settlement, and the remaining colonists prepared to return; but new settlers and supplies were sent, and Lord DE LA WARR arrived in 1610. John SMITH was an early colonial leader. John ROLFE began the cultivation of tobacco there in 1612; in 1614 he married POCAHONTAS, assuring peace with the Indians. The first representative government in the colonies met there (1619); Jamestown was capital of VIRGINIA through most of the 17th cent. The village was almost entirely destroyed during Bacon's Rebellion (1676; see BACON, NATHANAEL).

**Jami, Nur ad-Din Abd ar-Rahman** (,jahmee), 1414–92, Persian poet and DERVISH. Among his works are *Seven Thrones,* a collection of poems including 'Salaman and Absal', and *Abode of Spring,* a collection of short stories.

**Jammu,** town (1981 pop. 214,737), Jammu and KASHMIR state, N India (Pakistan disputes sovereignty), on Tawi R. It is a district administrative and trading centre in a strategic position; and has a modern industrial estate. An ancient town, it was the original capital of the Dogras who became rulers of Kashmir as well.

**Jamnagar,** town (1981 pop. 294,344), Gujarat state, W India, near the northwest coast of the Kathiawad peninsula. It is a district administrative and commercial centre with handicrafts and some more modern industry, for example, textiles and ceramics. It was the capital of the former princely state of Navanagar, by which name Jamnagar is also sometimes known.

**Jamshedpur,** town (1981 pop. 457,061), Bihar state, NE India, on the Subarnekha R. The town owes its origins to the establishment by the Tata brothers in the first decade of the present century of a giant iron- and steelworks. It has since gained associated industries. It is also a railway centre, and has acquired trading and marketing functions in what is still largely a 'tribal' area.

**Janáček, Leoš** (,yanachek), 1854–1928, Czech composer, theorist, and collector of Slavic folk music. His works include the operas *Jenufa* (1904), *Katya Kabanova* (1921), *The Cunning Little Vixen* (1924), *The Makropulos Case* (1926) and *From the House of the Dead* (1930); a song cycle; a Sinfonietta (1926), two String Quartets (1923 and 1928) and the *Glagolitic Mass* (1926).

**Janissaries,** elite corps of war captives and Christian youths in the service of the OTTOMAN EMPIRE (Turkey). Converted to Islam and trained under the strictest discipline, they eventually became powerful enough to make and unmake sultans. By the 17th cent. membership was largely hereditary. Their power came to an abrupt end in 1826 when Sultan MAHMUD II had them massacred in their barracks.

**Jan Mayen,** a small volcanic island off the coast of Greenland. It was known to the Vikings but rediscovered by the Dutchman Jan May in 1614. Many sealers and whalers used it in subsequent centuries but attempts at wintering caused tragic deaths. It is a dependency of Norway, which maintains an administrative settlement and meteorological station there.

**Jansco, Miklos,** 1921–, Hungarian film director. He is notable for his shooting methods, which involve very long camera takes, and the elaborate integration of traditional Hungarian peasants with their rural landscape. His films include *Agnus Dei* (1971), *Red Psalm* (1972), and *Private Vices—Public Virtues* (1976).

**Jansen, Cornelius,** (,jansən), 1585–1638, Dutch Roman Catholic theologian, bishop of Ypres. He sought to reform Christian life by a return to St AUGUSTINE. From his posthumous *Augustinus* (1640) arose the movement called **Jansenism,** which stressed greater personal holiness. The movement, centred in France, caused great controversy within the Roman Catholic Church because of its advocacy of an extreme form of PREDESTINATION and its insistence on the need for special grace to fulfil God's commandments. It was attacked in papal bulls (1653, 1705, 1713), and the Jansenist convent of Port-Royal, near Paris, was closed. Jansenists are still found in the Netherlands.

**Jansky, Karl Guthe,** 1905–50, American radio engineer; While trying to determine the causes of radio communications static for Bell Telephone Laboratories, Jansky discovered (1931) radio waves from extraterrestrial sources; a discovery that led to the development of the science of RADIO ASTRONOMY; by 1932 he had concluded that the source of the interference was located in the direction of the centre of the Milky Way galaxy.

**Janson, Nicolas:** see JENSON, NICOLAS.

**January:** see MONTH.

**Janus,** in Roman mythology, custodian of the universe, god of beginnings. The guardian of gates and doors, he held sacred the first hour of the day, first day of the month, and first month of the year (which bears his name). He is represented with two bearded heads set back to back, often appearing on Roman coins.

**Japan,** Jap. *Nihon* or *Nippon,* country (1986 pop. 120,720,542), 369,881 km² (142,811 sq mi), occupying an archipelago off the coast of E Asia. The capital is TOKYO, the world's fourth most populous city. Japan proper has four main islands; these are, from north to south, HOKKAIDO, HONSHU (the largest island, where the capital and major cities are located), SHIKOKU, and KYUSHU. Many smaller islands lie in an arc between the Sea of Japan and the E China Sea, and the Pacific Ocean. Honshu, Shikoku, and Kyushu enclose the INLAND SEA. Mountains, including a number of volcanoes, cover two-thirds of Japan's surface; the most famous peak is Mt FUJI. The land is also marked by short, rushing rivers, forested slopes, irregular lakes, and small, rich plains. Rainfall is abundant, and typhoons and earthquakes are frequent.

*Economy.* Mineral resources are meagre, except for coal, which in the past was an important source of industrial energy. The rapid streams provide hydroelectric power, and nuclear energy is also produced. A high-speed train service, inaugurated between Tokyo and OSAKA in 1964, now extends to many parts of the country. Japan's farming population has been declining steadily and comprised only 10.9% of the total labour force in the late 1970s. Arable land (less than 14.7% of the country's area) is intensively cultivated; rice and other cereals are the main crops. Fishing is highly developed, and the annual catch is one of the largest in the world (14.7% of the world total in 1983). Since its defeat in World War II, Japan has developed into the third greatest economic power in the world, with an enormous foreign trade. The world's leading producer of ships and cars, it also ranks high in the production of steel, electronic equipment, and machine tools. Japan's industry depends heavily on imported raw materials, especially petroleum and iron ore.

*People.* The Japanese are primarily descended from various peoples who migrated from Asia in prehistoric times; the dominant strain is N Asian or Mongoloid. The principal religions are SHINTO and BUDDHISM, and Japanese thought has also been deeply affected by CONFUCIANISM. The present educational system, established after World War II, has created a highly educated and skilled population. The standard of living improved dramatically in the 1960s and 70s, and Japan is now one of the world's leading postindustrial societies.

*Government.* The constitution, adopted in 1946, calls for a democratic form of government. It declares the emperor to be the symbolic head of state and renounces Japan's right to declare war. The national diet (parliament), which has sole legislative power, is composed of the 512-member house of representatives and the 252-member house of councillors. Executive power rests with the prime minister, who is elected by the diet, and his appointed 21-member cabinet. Japan is divided into 47 prefectures, each governed by a governor elected by the people, and a legislature.

*History.* According to legend, Japan was founded in 660 BC, but reliable records date only to about AD 400. By the 5th cent. Japan was unified by the Yamato clan, and the foundations of a centralized imperial state were laid by the 8th cent. Court culture was influenced first by Chinese learning and institutions and then by a rebirth of native Japanese culture. By the 9th cent. the powerful FUJIWARA family ruled as regents, and imperial authority was undermined. The 12th cent. ushered in Japan's medieval period, with the development of feudalism, the rise of a warrior class called the SAMURAI, and the establishment of military rule under MINAMOTO NO YORITOMO, appointed the first SHOGUN. After civil war between rival warrior clans, the country was unified in 1600 under a new shogun, TOKUGAWA IEYASU. For more than 250 years the TOKUGAWA family ruled over a Japan internally at peace and cut off from the outside world. In 1854 the US naval officer Matthew C. PERRY forced the opening of trade with the West, and the shogunate soon collapsed. In 1868 the Meiji Restoration returned formal power to the Emperor MEIJI, and a new government was established under the control of able samurai leadership. Adopting the techniques of Western civilization, Japan modernized rapidly into an industrial state and military power. A constitutional monarchy and a diet were established by the Constitution of 1889. The success of Japan in the First Sino-Japanese War (1894–95) and the RUSSO-JAPANESE WAR (1904–5) brought the nation to international prominence. Japan annexed Korea in 1910, established a puppet-state in MANCHURIA in 1932, and began the Second SINO-JAPANESE WAR (1937–45) by invading N China. Japan formed a military alliance with Germany and Italy in WORLD WAR II and opened hostilities against the US with an attack on PEARL HARBOR in 1941. After rapid initial success, the Japanese were defeated by the Allies. Following the dropping of atomic bombs by the US on HIROSHIMA and NAGASAKI, Japan surrendered in Aug. 1945 and was occupied by US forces. The signing of a peace treaty in 1951 led to full Japanese sovereignty over the main islands in 1952. The US returned the BONIN and nearby islands to Japan in 1968 and the RYUKYU ISLANDS (Okinawa) in 1972. Since 1955 the Japanese diet has been controlled by the conservative Liberal Democratic Party (LDP). Elections in 1986 gave the LDP an absolute parliamentary majority and resulted in the continuation in office of Yasuhiro NAKASONE, although he was succeeded in 1987 by Noboru TAKESHITA. Japan's powerful economic surge after World War II produced huge foreign trade surpluses that created tension with the US and the EUROPEAN COMMUNITY by the late 1970s. In the 1980s Japan regularly agreed to take measures to correct its trade surplus, but with little concrete result.

**Post-war Japanese prime ministers**
Naruhiko Higashikuni (non-party), 1945
Kijuro Shidehara (non-party), 1945–46
Shigeru Yoshida (Liberal), 1946–47
Tetsu Katayama (Socialist), 1947–48
Hitoshi Ashida (Democrat), 1948
Shigeru Yoshida (Liberal), 1948–54
Ichiro Hatoyama (Liberal Democrat), 1954–56
Tanzan Ishibashi (Liberal Democrat), 1956–57
Nobusuke Kishi (Liberal Democrat), 1957–60
Hayato Ikeda (Liberal Democrat), 1960–64
Eisaku Sato (Liberal Democrat), 1964–72
Kakuei Tanaka (Liberal Democrat), 1972–74
Takeo Miki (Liberal Democrat), 1974–76
Takeo Fukuda (Liberal Democrat), 1976–78
Masayoshi Ohira (Liberal Democrat), 1978–80
Zenko Suzuki (Liberal Democrat), 1980–82
Yasuhiro Nakasone (Liberal Democrat), 1982–87
Noboru Takeshita (Liberal Democrat), 1987–89

**Japan, Sea of,** arm of the Pacific Ocean, c.1,048,950 km² (405,000 sq mi), located between Japan, Korea, and the Far East region of the USSR. A branch of the warm Japan Current flows northeast through the sea, modifying climatic conditions and keeping coastal ports ice-free as far north as VLADIVOSTOK, the USSR's only major all-year outlet to the Pacific Ocean sea lanes.

**Japanese,** language of uncertain origin that is spoken by more than 100 million people, most of whom live in Japan. Japanese appears to be unrelated to any other language; however, some scholars see a kinship to Korean, and others link Japanese and Korean to the ALTAIC languages (see URALIC AND ALTAIC LANGUAGES).

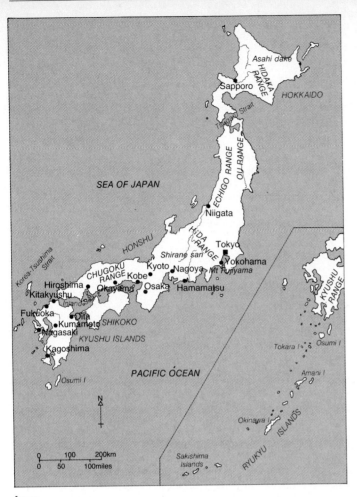

Japan

(*jomon*). This was replaced by bronze bells with simple designs, clay tomb figures (*haniwa*), and some painted burial chambers. With the introduction of BUDDHISM in the 6th cent., and throughout its history, Japanese art relied on Chinese forms and techniques. In the Nara period (710–784) traditional technical methods of Japanese painting were established. The work was executed on thin silk or soft paper with Chinese ink or watercolours. Mounted on silk brocade or paper, the paintings were of two types: hanging scrolls (*kakemono*) and horizontal scrolls (*emakimono*). The Jogan period (794–897) witnessed the beginning of an indigenous style of art. The Fujiwara period (898–1185) was marked by the crystallization of the *Yamato-e* tradition of painting, based on national rather than Chinese taste. The famous scroll *Tale of Genji* (see MURASAKI SHIKIBU) reflects the extreme sensitivity and overrefinement of the court of that period. The Kamakura period (late 12th–14th cent.) restored vigour and realism, as seen in scrolls like *Tales of the Heiji Insurrection* (13th cent.; Mus. of Fine Arts, Boston). Here, unlike in Chinese painting, man occupies the most important role. In the Momoyama period (1568–1615) architectural sculpture achieved unprecedented grandeur. The KANO family of artists succeeded in fusing Chinese ink-painting technique with Japanese decorative quality. During the Edo period (1615–1867) miniature sculptures called *netsuke* became popular, as did painted screens, often with finely studied animals, birds, and plants. In the 18th cent., influenced by Dutch engravers, a new type of art arose in the form of woodblock prints known as *ukiyo-e* [pictures of the fleeting or floating world]. *Ukiyo-e* colour-print designers won worldwide renown, the best known being HARUNOBU and HIROSHIGE. Mid-19th-cent. contacts with European culture enervated Japanese art, and in the 20th cent. the majority of painters and sculptors have been overwhelmingly influenced by Western styles.

**Japanese art:** Badger wrapped in lotus leaf, 19th-cent. netsuke in wood

**Japanese architecture.** Evidence of neolithic building in Japan remains. Chinese religious architecture came to Japan with BUDDHISM in the 6th cent. Parts of the monastery of Horyu-ji, near Nara, illustrate the first epoch of Japanese architecture (6th–8th cent.), characterized by gravity and simple, vital construction, sparsely ornamented. Wood has always been the favoured material, and wood construction was brought to a culmination as complete as that of any of the great masonry styles. Interior columns and thin woodwork and plaster walls were characteristic. Vitality and grace are communicated by the refined curvatures in columns and overhanging roofs. Emulation of the Chinese style is seen in the monastery of Todai-ji (begun 745), with its great hall housing the Daibutsu (colossal Buddha), fronted by twin pagodas. Distinctively Japanese architecture dates from the late Heian period (898–1185). The Phoenix Hall at Uji, near Kyoto, represents the apogee of Japanese design, with its airiness and beautiful situation near a lotus lake. In the 13th cent. a renewed interest in CHINESE ARCHITECTURE came with the emergence of ZEN BUDDHISM. Japanese temple design adhered to the Chinese symmetrical pattern. In front of the main building stood an impressive gateway. Accessory structures included the PAGODA. The Shinto temple was small and simple; greatest importance was attached to the landscape setting. Regard for the environment was seen also in secular building, as in the housing schemes called *shinden-zukuri*, in which buildings connected by corridors surrounded a garden and pond. The Japanese upper-class dwelling was unexcelled for refinement and simplicity. Exterior walls were usually movable panels; interiors were subdivided by screens. Important rooms contained a *tokonoma*, an alcove for display of flower arrangements. European architectural influence entered Japan after 1868. In the 20th cent. the Japanese began to influence the development of the INTERNATIONAL STYLE in MODERN ARCHITECTURE. Important Japanese architects include Tange Kenzo and Kurokawa Kisho.

**Japanese art.** The earliest Japanese art, probably dating from the 3rd and 2nd millennia BC, consisted of monochrome POTTERY in a cord pattern

**Japanese literature.** Although Japanese and Chinese are different languages, the Japanese borrowed and adapted Chinese ideographs early in the 8th cent. so that their spoken language could be written. This system was used in the writing of *Records of Ancient Matters* (712), the sacred book of SHINTO, but other works of the period were written in pure Chinese. The addition of two phonetic syllabaries (*katakana* and *hiragana*) during the Heian era (794–1185) opened a golden age in which Japanese literature, written in Japanese, reached its first peak of development. Much of the Heian literature was written by women, notably MURASAKI SHIKIBU, a noblewoman whose *Tale of Genji* (early 11th cent.) is ranked with the world's greatest novels. The four basic forms of Japanese drama were evolved (see ORIENTAL DRAMA) from the 12th to the 17th cent. Under the TOKUGAWA shogunate (17th–19th cent.), the written language was standardized and freer verse forms, e.g., the HAIKU, began to replace the *tanka*, the classical form. While Heian literature dealt mostly with the aristocracy, the Tokugawa era was concerned with the Samurai and the merchant class. CHIKAMATSU's plays are the first tragedies about the common man in world literature. Other important writers were the poet Matsuo BASHO, and the novelists IHARA SAIKAKU and UEDA AKINARI. Modern Japanese literature reflects the profound influence of the West, and many

20th-cent. writers have faced the problem of reconciling Japanese tradition with that influence. They include MORI OGAI, NATSUME SOSEKI, TANIZAKI JUNICHIRO, KAWABATA YASUNARI (who won the 1968 Nobel Prize for literature), MISHIMA YUKIO, ABE KOBO, OOKA SHOHEI, and ENDO SHUSAKU.

**Japanese music.** The Japanese borrowed instruments, scales, and styles from neighbouring cultures. Early songs and temple music employed only a few notes; importations, particularly from China, began in the 5th cent. *Gagaku*, which includes medieval Chinese courtly entertainment music using mouth organ, flute, oboe, lute, zither, and percussion, was preserved in Japan. Buddhist song came from China via Korea in the 6th cent. Many instruments, e.g., the zither *koto*, were introduced from China before the 9th cent. The accompanied RECITATIVE of the *No* drama dates from the 14th cent., and popular secular music, with the spiked lute *samisen*, from the 16th. The Japanese use two hemitonic pentatonic SCALES. RHYTHM is almost invariably in duple time. Western music, introduced into Japan in the late 19th cent., is now an integral part of the culture.

Japanese music: koto

**japanning:** see LACQUER.

**Japheth:** see NOAH.

**Jarrell, Randall,** 1914–65, American poet. His poetry, e.g., *Losses* (1948), *The Woman at the Washington Zoo* (1960), reflects a sensitive, tragic world view. Among his other works are children's books, a novel, and critical essays, which were collected in *Poetry and the Age* (1953).

**Jarrett, Keith,** 1945–, black American jazz pianist, saxophonist, drummer, and composer. From his early work with Art BLAKEY in the 1960s, through the Miles DAVIS electric band of the early 1970s, he then developed a rhapsodically complex and technically masterful improvised piano style, which pleased audiences beyond the jazz world, e.g., The Koln Concert albums. He has also written and performed a number of non-jazz compositions.

**Jarry, Alfred,** 1873–1907, French writer. He is mostly remembered as creator of the monstrous and farcical hero of *Ubu-Roi* (1896), a symbol of aggressive greed, tyranny and stupidity, and of 'pataphysics', the science of imaginary solutions, which has appealed to surrealists and absurdists ever since.

**Jaruzelski, Wojciech** (yarooh,zelskee), 1923–, Polish military and political leader. He fought in WORLD WAR II, became a general in 1956, and began his rise in the ruling Communist Party in 1960. During the grave crisis involving the free trade union SOLIDARITY, Jaruzelski in 1981 became both premier and party leader. Known as a moderate, he sought a compromise but finally ordered a military crackdown, placed Poland under martial law, and ordered the arrest of Solidarity leader Lech WALESA. Late in 1982 his government outlawed Solidarity, put down attendant protest demonstrations and strikes, and announced the gradual suspension of martial law. In 1984 Jaruzelski became head of state, surrendering the premiership but retaining the party leadership.

**jasmine** or **jessamine,** plant (genus *Jasminum*) of the OLIVE family, chiefly of Old World tropical and subtropical regions but cultivated in other mild areas and greenhouses. The blossoms, mostly yellow or white and usually fragrant, are used in scenting tea; the oil is used in perfumery.

**Jason,** one of the greatest heroes of Greek mythology. Raised by the centaur CHIRON, Jason claimed the kingdom of Iolcus, which his uncle, Pelias, had stolen from his father, Aeson. Pelias agreed to return it if Jason gathered the GOLDEN FLEECE, owned by King Aeëtes of Colchis. In quest of it, Jason assembled the Argonauts, sailed in the Argo, and had many adventures. In Colchis, they captured the fleece with the help of Aeëtes' daughter, MEDEA, who loved Jason. Medea returned with Jason, married him, and helped him to secure the throne. When he later tried to divorce her, she brutally destroyed his betrothed, Creusa; Creusa's father; and, in some versions, her own children. The gods then caused Jason to wander for many years. The story of Jason and Medea appears frequently in literature, notably in EURIPIDES.

**jasper,** opaque, impure CHALCEDONY, usually red but also yellow, green, and greyish-blue, used as a GEM. Ribbon jasper has colours in stripes.

**Jaspers, Karl,** 1883–1969, German philosopher. Generally placed within the orbit of EXISTENTIALISM, Jaspers believed that genuine philosophy must spring from the study of a person's individual existence, which he viewed as enclosed by an all-embracing, transcendental reality he called 'the encompassing'. Among his works are *Man in the Modern Age* (1931) and *Philosophy* (3 vol., 1932).

**jaundice,** yellowing of the skin and the whites of the eyes as a result of excess bilirubin in the blood. This substance is normally removed from the bloodstream by the LIVER and eliminated from the body in BILE. Causes of jaundice include excessive disintegration of red blood cells (as in some types of ANAEMIA); damage to liver cells by disease (e.g., CIRRHOSIS, HEPATITIS); and bile duct blockage (e.g., by gallstones or tumours). Jaundice in the newborn may indicate a RHESUS FACTOR reaction.

**Jaurès, Jean** (zhoh,res), 1859–1914, French socialist leader and historian. In 1885 he entered the Chamber of Deputies, where he promoted SOCIALISM and world peace. He supported Dreyfus (see DREYFUS AFFAIR), worked for the separation of church and state, and helped found (1905) the unified French Socialist Party. In 1914 he called for arbitration to avert WORLD WAR I; he was assassinated by a patriotic fanatic.

**Java,** island (1974 est. pop. 75,000,000), Indonesia, c.51,000 sq mi (132,090 sq km), one of the world's most densely populated regions. It constitutes only one seventh of Indonesia's area but contains two thirds of the population. A chain of volcanic, forested mountains traverses the island east to west, rising to 12,060 ft (3,676 m) at Mt. Semeru. The climate is warm and humid, and the volcanic soil is exceptionally productive, yielding two or three crops a year when irrigated. From the 10th to 15th cent. the island was the center of Hindu-Javanese culture, from which it derives today's highly developed art forms. It was under Dutch rule from 1619 to 1946.

**Java man:** see HOMO ERECTUS.

**Javanese music,** termed *karawitan*, includes vocal and instrumental genres. The word *gamelan* is used for the various kinds of tuned percussion ensembles found in Indonesia and Malaysia, and in Java their instrumentation can include suspended and mounted gongs, keyed metallophones, drums, xylophone, bowed spike-fiddle, zither and bamboo flute. Many *gamelan* also include a singer or small choir. There are regional differences between orchestras and compositions in East, Central, and West Java though all music has much the same basic structure: a nuclear melody (*balungan*) which is stressed at intervals by individual gongs and which is elaborated or improvised upon by various instruments including the gong-chimes, *gender* metallophones, spike-fiddle, and bamboo flute. There are two separate tonal systems: *pelog* (seven tones with unequal intervals) and *slendro* (five tones with intervals more equidistantly spaced). Each tuning system has three modes (*patet*), and different musical forms are determined by the relationship between the basic melody and the temporal structure. Besides classical *gamelan* music, which is performed primarily in elite circles at social and ritual gatherings, there is also much folk and popular music, ranging from Portuguese-influenced *kroncong* to modern Indonesian pop.

**javelin throwing,** athletics FIELD EVENT in which the competitor runs about 36 m (40 yd) and throws a pointed shaft weighing about 800 g (1 lb 12½ oz) for men and 600 g (1 lb 5 oz) for women as far as possible. It has been an Olympic sport since 1908.

**Jawlensky, Alexei von,** 1864–1941, Russian painter. He studied at the St Petersburg Academy but left for Munich in 1896. In 1905 he visited Brittany and met the Pont-Aven artists, and Paris where he worked for a short while with MATISSE. Here he developed a style similar to FAUVISM, using bright strong colours and a simplified and distorted drawing style. In 1909 he was a founder member with KANDINSKY of the Neue Künstlervereinigung [new artists' association] but did not leave with Kandinsky to become a member of the BLAUE REITER group.

**jay,** BIRD (family Corvidae) related to the CROW and found, in Europe, Asia, and the Americas. The common jay (*Garrulus glandarius*) is the most widely spread, ranging over Europe and Asia. It is 34 cm (13½ in) long, a noisy bird which can mimic other birds, mechanical sounds, and the human voice. Most species are American, including the beautiful blue jay (*Cyanocitta cristata*). They all eat soft fruits, nuts, and INVERTEBRATES.

**Jay, John,** 1745–1829, American statesman, 1st chief justice of the US SUPREME COURT (1789–95). A lawyer, he guided the drafting of the New York State constitution. He was president (1778–79) of the CONTINENTAL CONGRESS and one of the commissioners who negotiated (1781–83) peace with Great Britain (see PARIS, TREATY OF). As secretary of foreign affairs (1784–89), he advocated strong central government. During his tenure as chief justice, he was sent (1794) on a mission to England, where he negotiated what became known as JAY'S TREATY.

**Jayawardene, J(unius) R(ichard),** 1906–, prime minister (1977–78) and then president of SRI LANKA (1978–89). Having become leader of the National Party in 1973, he led the party to victory in the 1977 elections. Initially prime minister, he became executive president in 1978 under a constitutional amendment establishing a presidential system of government; he was reelected in 1982 and thereafter faced a major crisis arising from the insurgency of Tamil separatists.

**Jay's Treaty,** concluded in 1794 between the US and Britain to settle difficulties arising mainly out of violations of the Treaty of PARIS of 1783, and to regulate commerce and navigation. The treaty, signed in England by John JAY and Lord GRENVILLE, provided for British evacuation of posts in the Northwest, unrestricted navigation of the Mississippi, and equal privileges to American and British vessels in Great Britain and the East Indies. It placed severe restrictions on US trade in the West Indies, referred to joint commissions the payment of pre-Revolutionary American debts, and did not allow indemnity for Americans whose black slaves were carried off by Britain's evacuating armies. These and other provisions aroused indignation in the US, and appropriations to put the treaty into effect were delayed until 1796.

**Jazirah, Al:** see GEZIRA.

**Jazz,** American musical form, developed c.1890 from black work songs, SPIRITUALS, and other forms whose harmonic, melodic, and rhythmic elements were mainly African. It came to general notice in the 1920s when whites adapted or imitated it. Jazz began in the South and spread north and west. The *blues* has remained a vital part in all periods. Blues generally employs a 12-bar construction and a 'blue' SCALE thought to be African in origin. Vocal blues have earthy, direct lyrics. The tempo may vary, and the mood ranges from despair to cynicism to satire. Major early blues artists were Blind Lemon Jefferson, Ma Rainey, and Bessie SMITH. W.C. HANDY popularized blues. *Ragtime,* a syncopated, polyphonic genre (fl. 1890s–1910s), spread through sheet music and piano rolls (see POLYPHONY). Scott JOPLIN was its most famous exponent. *New Orleans* or *Dixieland* jazz developed from military music, blues, and the French tradition in New Orleans. Pioneer musicians like Buddy Bolden and Jelly Roll Morton performed at functions from funerals to dances. In World War I musicians went north up the Mississippi seeking work. In Chicago, King Oliver, Louis ARMSTRONG, and others introduced jazz to a wider audience, and young whites like the cornettist Bix Beiderbecke were drawn to it. At the end of the 1920s a new phenomenon, *swing,* emerged. The small New Orleans band had played polyphony, but swing involved larger groups (14–18) featuring soloists with arranged backgrounds. The bands of Count Basie, Duke ELLINGTON, and Benny GOODMAN were especially notable. *Bop* (bebop), a 1940s revolt against the

formulas of swing, was rhythmically complex and harmonic, rather than melodic, at base. Charlie PARKER and Dizzy GILLESPIE were the leaders. In the 1950s *progressive jazz,* with bop's harmonics but simpler melody and rhythm, flourished, chiefly on the West Coast, inspired largely by the swing giant Lester YOUNG. Stan Getz and Dave Brubeck were key figures. *Hard bop,* a second wave, was led by such musicians as Sonny ROLLINS and John COLTRANE. Jazz continues to evolve. An exploratory avant-garde of the 1960s coexisted with the efforts of Miles DAVIS and others to bring ROCK MUSIC into jazz, and in the 1970s reached into the past to create a music with elements of all jazz styles, epitomized in the work of the Art Ensemble of Chicago. Almost all jazz styles remain current today.

**Jeanneret, Charles Édouard:** see LE CORBUSIER.

**jeans,** trousers which originated in the later 19th cent. as work wear for men, now worn by both sexes, for leisure as well as work, all over the world and by all classes of people. They were originally made from jean or denim, strong, densely woven cotton fabrics, usually blue in colour, (dyed with hard-wearing indigo). Levis, one make of jeans, are called after Levi Strauss, who made the first pairs for miners in the San Francisco gold rush in the 1850s. He used copper rivets to strengthen the pockets and belt loops; the firm he founded is still one of the main manufacturers. Jeans first entered women's fashion in the 1930s in the US, and began to be generally worn in the 1950s.

**Jeans, Sir James Hopwood,** 1877–1946, English mathematical physicist and astronomer. He made numerous contributions to thermodynamics, cosmology, the theory of the origin of the solar system and of stars, the subject of the structure of the stars and to many other astronomical topics. His popular books were outstandingly successful.

**Jebel Akhdar,** [Arab, = green mountain], mountainous region of SE Arabia, c.36,000 km² (14,000 sq mi), between the Gulf of Oman and the RUB AL KHALI, extending in the northwest into the United Arab Emirates. The highest point is over 2740 m (9000 ft). It receives some rain from the summer monsoon, and there are some fertile valleys where irrigated cultivation is carried out.

**Jefferson, Thomas,** 1743–1826, 3rd president of the US (1801–9). A member (1769–75) of the Virginia house of burgesses, he was a leader of the patriot faction. At the Second CONTINENTAL CONGRESS he drafted the DECLARATION OF INDEPENDENCE, a historic document that reflects his debt to John LOCKE and other philosophers. In 1779 he became governor of Virginia, guiding that state through the troubled last years of the AMERICAN REVOLUTION. A member (1783–84) of the Continental Congress, Jefferson drew up an ordinance for the Northwest Territory that formed the basis for the ORDINANCE OF 1787. In 1785 he became minister to France. Appointed secretary of state (1790–93) in Pres. WASHINGTON's cabinet, Jefferson defended agrarian interests against the Federalist policies and broad constitutional interpretations of Alexander HAMILTON and, after resigning from the cabinet (1793), led a group called the Republicans who were ancestors of the present DEMOCRATIC PARTY. He served as vice president (1797–1801) and protested against the passage of the ALIEN AND SEDITION ACTS by writing the Kentucky Resolutions (see KENTUCKY AND VIRGINIA RESOLUTIONS). The Republicans triumphed at the polls in 1800, but Aaron BURR, who had been designated to become vice president, tied with Jefferson in the presidential vote. Jefferson was finally chosen as president by the House of Representatives, largely on the advice of Hamilton, who considered Jefferson less dangerous than Burr. Jefferson was the first president inaugurated in Washington, a city he had helped to plan. He cut federal expenditures, believing that the federal government should be concerned mainly with foreign affairs, leaving local matters to the states and local authorities. Usually strict in interpreting the Constitution, he pushed through the LOUISIANA PURCHASE of 1803, an action which it did not expressly authorize. He also planned the LEWIS AND CLARK EXPEDITION. During his second administration, difficulties arose from attacks on neutral US shipping by the warring powers of Britain and France. With such measures as the EMBARGO ACT of 1807 he tried to use economic pressure to gain a solution, but this aroused strong opposition in the US. In retirement after 1809 at his beloved home, Monticello, Jefferson brought about the founding of the Univ. of Virginia, and continued his lifelong interests in science, architecture, philosophy, and the arts.

**Jefferson City,** US city (1980 pop. 33,619), state capital of Missouri, on the Missouri R., near the mouth of the Osage R.; inc. 1825. State government is the major employer; the city is also the processing centre for an agricultural area. Printing and various manufactures are important.

**Jefferson Memorial,** monument in Washington, DC, US, honouring Thomas JEFFERSON. Dedicated in 1943, the domed white marble structure was designed by the American neoclassical architect John Russell Pope; it houses a 5.8-m (19-ft) statue of Jefferson by Rudulph Evans.

**Jeffreys of Wem, George Jeffreys,** 1st **Baron,** 1645?–89, English judge under CHARLES II and JAMES II; noted for his cruelty. In the Bloody Assizes following the rebellion (1685) of the duke of MONMOUTH, he caused nearly 200 persons to be hanged, some 800 transported, and many more imprisoned or whipped.

**Jehoshaphat** or **Josaphat,** king of Judah (r. c.873–849 BC), son and successor of King Asa. He was an ally of King AHAB of Israel and his successors, and was the first king of Judah to make a treaty with the kingdom of Israel. 1 Kings 22; 2 Kings 3; 2 Chron. 17–21. The **Valley of Jehoshaphat,** mentioned in Joel 3 as a place of judgment, has been identified by tradition with the northern extension of the vale of Kidron to the east of JERUSALEM.

**Jehovah:** see GOD.

**Jehovah's Witnesses,** an international sect founded in the US in the late 19th cent. by Charles Russell. They were called Russellites before 1931. Their doctrine centres on the second coming of Christ. Witnesses refuse to salute the flag, bear arms, or participate in government, nor will they give blood or receive blood transfusions. All members are considered ministers, and the group engages in zealous house-to-house canvassing. Its magazine, *Watchtower,* had a circulation of over 10 million, in some 80 languages, in the early 1980s.

**Jehu,** king of Israel (r. c.842–815 BC). Anointed king by ELISHA, Jehu murdered King Jehoram of Israel, King Ahaziah of Judah, and the rest of the house of AHAB. Jehu's rapid chariot driving has become proverbial. 2 Kings 9.

**Jellicoe, John Rushworth Jellicoe,** 1st **Earl,** 1859–1935, British admiral. As commander in chief of the Grand Fleet (1914–16) in WORLD WAR I, he was engaged in the inconclusive battle of JUTLAND (1916). He was later first sea lord (1916–17) and governor general of New Zealand (1920–24).

**jellyfish,** free-swimming stage (see POLYP AND MEDUSA) of invertebrate animals (COELENTERATES) of the classes Hydrozoa and Scyphozoa of the phylum Cnidaria. Many jellyfish are coloured and are considered to be among the most beautiful of animals. Most have bell- or umbrella-shaped bodies with a clear, jellylike material filling most of the space between the upper and lower surfaces. A mouth is located on the underside and tentacles dangle from the bell margin. Most catch their prey with stinging cells located in the tentacles and most are marine, living in the PLANKTON of the surface waters and along the coasts.

**Jena** (,yaynə), city (1984 pop. 107,062), Gera district, S East Germany, on the Saale R. Its industries include pharmaceuticals, and the precision and optical instruments of the Zeiss works. Known since the 9th cent., the city gained international repute in the 18th and 19th cent., when SCHILLER, HEGEL, FICHTE, and SCHELLING taught at its university (est. 1557). GOETHE also lived there.

**Jenghiz Khan** or **Genghis Khan** (,jenggis ,kahn), 1167?–1227, Mongol conqueror. After uniting the Mongol tribes, Jenghiz Khan conquered (1213–15) most of the Chin empire of N China. From 1218 to 1224 he subdued Turkistan, Transoxania, and Afghanistan and raided Persia and E Europe. A brilliant military leader, he ruled one of the greatest land empires of history from his capital at KARAKORUM. After his death his empire was divided among his sons and grandsons.

**Jenkins, Roy (Harris),** 1920–, British politician. He entered the House of Commons in 1948 as a Labour member and subsequently was minister of aviation (1964–65), home secretary (1965–67, 1974–76), and chancellor of the exchequer (1967–70). He served (1977–80) as president of the Commission of the EUROPEAN COMMUNITY. In 1982 he was elected to Parliament as a member of the new SOCIAL DEMOCRATIC PARTY, which he had helped to found. He lost his seat in 1987, becoming instead a life member of the House of Lords and joining (1988) the new SOCIAL AND LIBERAL DEMOCRATS formation.

**Jenkins's Ear, War of,** 1739–48, struggle between England and Spain. It was based on commercial rivalry and led into the larger war of the AUSTRIAN SUCCESSION. Captain Jenkins's alleged loss of his ear (1731) was but one of the atrocities used to stir up feeling against Spain in the late 1730s. Despite the opposition of Prime Min. Robert WALPOLE war was declared. Britain captured Porto Bello (1739), but, after the failure to take Cartagena (1741), the war became inconclusive, as both powers devoted their energies to European struggles.

**Jenner, Edward,** 1749–1823, English physician. His experiments, beginning in 1796 with the vaccination of James Phipps with matter from a cowpox vesicle on the hand of a milkmaid, proved that cowpox provided immunity against SMALLPOX, helped rid many areas of the disease, and laid the foundations of modern immunology as a science. He received £10,000 from Parliament for his discovery.

**Jensen, Johannes Vilhelm** (,yensən), 1873–1950, Danish author. He wrote essays, travel books, and lyric poems. His epic novel cycle, *The Long Journey* (1908–22), was based on Darwinian theory. Jensen developed a distinctive style of anecdotal writing based on local legends and folklore. He was awarded the 1944 Nobel Prize for literature.

**Jenson** or **Janson, Nicholas,** d. c.1480, Venetian printer; b. France. He studied with GUTENBERG and started publishing, using his own roman TYPE, in Venice in 1470. His roman type inspired GARAMOND, CASLON, William MORRIS, and others.

**Jeremiah** or **Jeremias,** book of the OLD TESTAMENT. It contains the career and teaching of Jeremiah, a prophet who preached (c.628–586 BC) in Jerusalem. His message was a summons to moral reform, personal and social, backed by threats of doom. Jeremiah was allowed to stay in Jerusalem after its fall to Babylon (586 BC), and continued prophesying in Egypt. The prophecies in the book were arranged by his secretary Baruch, and are not in strict chronological order. They include prophecies against Gentile nations and well-known Messianic passages (in 14, 23, 30, 32).

**Jerez de la Frontera** (khe,reths de la 'fron,teəra), city (1981 pop. 176,238), Andalusia, SW Spain. A centre of the wine trade, it is famous for its sherries (named after Jerez) which have been exported to England since the reign of Henry VII. The city has a reputation for its flamenco music.

**Jericho,** ancient city of Palestine, in the Jordan valley N of the Dead Sea, near modern Ariha, Jordan. According to the Bible, JOSHUA took Jericho from the Canaanites and destroyed it. It later fell to HEROD, the Muslims, and others. Excavations of the original site, begun early in the 20th cent., reveal the world's oldest known settlement, dating perhaps from c.8000 BC Nearby, a Hellenistic fortress and Herod's palace have been excavated.

**Jeroboam I,** first king of the northern kingdom of Israel (r. c.922–901 BC). When SOLOMON's son, REHOBOAM, became king, Jeroboam led the secession of the ten tribes who formed the northern kingdom of Israel. He was notorious for fostering idolatry. 1 Kings 11–14; 2 Chron. 10; 13.

**Jerome, Jerome Klapka,** 1859–1927, English writer. He is noted for his humorous novel *Three Men in a Boat* (1889) and his drama *The Passing of the Third Floor Back* (1907).

**Jerome, Saint,** c.347–420, Christian scholar, Father of the Church, Doctor of the Church. Following a vision (375) in Antioch (Turkey) he renounced his pagan learning and fled to the desert, where he undertook scriptural studies. He was ordained (378) and, after serving as secretary to Pope Damasus I, began a new version of the BIBLE at the pope's request. From 386 he lived in Bethlehem, revising his Latin translations of the Bible and translating some portions from the Hebrew. All this became the basis for the Vulgate. He also wrote exegetical works, tracts, and biographies of Christian writers. Feast: 30 Sept.

**Jersey:** see CHANNEL ISLANDS.

**Jersey City,** US city (1984 est. pop. 223,000), NE New Jersey, a port on a peninsula formed by the Hudson and Hackensack rivers and Upper New York Bay, opposite lower Manhattan; settled before 1650; inc. 1836. It is a great centre of shipping, commerce, and manufacturing. There are docks, oil refineries, railway workshops, warehouses, and hundreds of factories. Located on the site of a 17th-cent. Dutch trading post, it grew with the arrival (1840s) of the railway.

**Jerubbaal:** see GIDEON.

**Jerusalem,** city (1983 pop. 428,700), capital and largest city of Israel, on a high ridge of the Judaean Mts, W of the Dead Sea and the Jordan R. A holy city for Jews, Christians, and Muslims, Jerusalem is also an administrative and cultural centre. The Hebrew Univ. was founded in 1925. Manufactures include cut and polished diamonds, plastics, and shoes. The eastern part of Jerusalem is the Old City; the New City, to the south and southwest, has been largely developed since the 19th cent. and is the site of the Knesset, Israel's parliament. Archaeology indicates that Jerusalem was already settled in the 4th millennium BC. DAVID captured it (c.1000 BC) from the Jebusites (Canaanites), and after SOLOMON built the Temple there (10th cent. BC), Jerusalem became the spiritual and political capital of the Hebrews. The city fell to many conquerors, e.g., Babylonia (586 BC) and Rome (63 BC), and it was the scene of JESUS's last ministry. The Roman emperor TITUS destroyed the rebuilt (Second) Temple (AD 70) to punish rebellious Jews. The Muslims, who believe that MUHAMMAD ascended to heaven from the city, treated it well after they captured it in 637. It was conquered by the Crusaders in 1099 and was recaptured (1187) by the Muslims under SALADIN. It came under the sway of the Ottoman Turks from 1517 to 1917. The walls of the old city were rebuilt by SULAYMAN THE MAGNIFICENT in 1537. Jerusalem was the capital (1922–48) of the British mandate of PALESTINE. During the ARAB-ISRAELI WARS, the city was divided (1949–67); the Old City became part of Jordan and the New City became the capital of Israel. In 1967 Israel captured the Old City and formally annexed it. Israel reaffirmed its annexation of the Old City in 1980, an action not accepted by many nations. The Old City contains many holy places of Christianity, e.g., the Church of the Holy Sepulchre; of Islam, e.g., the Dome of the Rock (688–91); and of Judaism, e.g., the Western (or Wailing) Wall (part of the Second Temple compound).

The Wailing Wall, Jerusalem

**Jerusalem, Latin kingdom of,** feudal state founded by GODFREY OF BOUILLON after the conquest of Jerusalem in the First CRUSADE (1099). Antioch, Edessa, and Tripoli were the kingdom's great fiefs. Jerusalem comprised the counties of Jaffa and Ashqelon, the lordships of Kerak, Montreal, and Sidon, and the principality of Galilee. The nominally elective kingship and the law, as in the Assizes of Jerusalem, were ideally feudal. In practice, the great feudal lords rarely supported the king in his wars. The rise of the great military orders, e.g., KNIGHTS TEMPLARS, further weakened royal power. Edessa fell (1144), then Jerusalem (1187), and lastly Akko (Acre) (1291). Godfrey's brother BALDWIN I was Jerusalem's first king, followed by BALDWIN II, the Angevin kings Fulk, BALDWIN III, AMALRIC I, and BALDWIN IV, and, finally, BALDWIN V (d. 1186). Later kingship was nominal only.

**Jerusalem artichoke,** perennial (*Helianthus tuberosus*) of the COMPOSITE family; it is the only root plant of economic importance to have originated in North America. Its potatolike tubers, most favoured as a food in Europe and China, contain inulin, a valuable source of FRUCTOSE for diabetics. A species of SUNFLOWER, it has recently become important as a source of ALCOHOL.

**Jerusalem cherry:** see NIGHTSHADE.

**Jespersen, Otto Harry** (,yespəsən), 1860–1943, Danish linguist and philologist. His major work was *Modern English Grammar* (7 vol., 1909–49). His main concerns were the history and structure of English and syntactic analysis, although his emphasis was always on language in use and language teaching.

**jessamine:** see JASMINE.

**Jesuit,** a member of the Society of Jesus (see JESUS, SOCIETY OF), a Roman Catholic religious order of priests and brothers. Jesuits are noted as educators, theologians, and missionaries.

**Jesus** or **Jesus Christ,** in Christian belief, the Son of God, the second person of the TRINITY. The name Jesus is Greek for the Hebrew *Joshua,* a name meaning 'Saviour'; Christ is the Greek word for the Hebrew *Messiah,* meaning 'Anointed'. Traditional CHRISTIANITY says Jesus was God made man, wholly divine, wholly human; he was born to MARY, a virgin, and died to atone for mankind's sins; his resurrection from the dead provides man's hope for salvation. The principal sources for his life are the four Gospels of MATTHEW, MARK, LUKE, and JOHN. There are also several brief references to Jesus in non-Christian sources, e.g., TACITUS. According to the Gospels, Jesus was born a Jew in Bethlehem of Mary, wife of Joseph, a carpenter of Nazareth. His date of birth is now reckoned to be between 8 BC and 4 BC. When he was about 30, Jesus began a three-year mission as a preacher. His activity was centred around Galilee, and he gathered a small band of disciples. Jesus preached the coming of the Kingdom of God, often in PARABLES, and called on his hearers to repent. The Gospels also describe miracles he performed. His uncompromising moral demands on his hearers, his repeated attacks on the Pharisees (see JEWS) and scribes, and his sympathy for social outcasts and the oppressed kindled popular enthusiasm. In the third year of his mission, while in Jerusalem for Passover, he was betrayed to the authorities by one of his companions, JUDAS ISCARIOT. After sharing the Last Supper (a Passover 'seder') with his disciples, he was arrested. The Gospels indicate that he was interrogated by Jewish authorities and handed over to the Romans, who crucified him, perhaps as an agitator. On the third day, his tomb was found empty, and an angel (or a man) announced that he had risen from the dead. According to the Gospels, Jesus later appeared to several of his disciples, and after 40 days he ascended into heaven.

**Jesus, Society of,** religious order of the Roman Catholic Church founded (1534–39) by St IGNATIUS OF LOYOLA. Its members, called Jesuits, have a highly disciplined structure and are especially devoted to the pope. They were a major force in the COUNTER-REFORMATION and were leaders in European education. Their missionary work in China, Paraguay, and Canada was remarkable. In 1773, under pressure from the Bourbon monarchies, Pope CLEMENT XIV suppressed the order, but it was restored in 1814. Jesuits have a tradition of learning and science, e.g., St Robert Bellarmine and TEILHARD DE CHARDIN.

**jetlag,** see BIORHYTHM.

**jet propulsion,** movement of a body caused by the force created by the ejection of a high-speed jet of gas. The principle is shown by fireworks such as rockets. An ignited chemical mixture (the Chinese used saltpetre, sulphur, and charcoal in early fireworks) blows at high temperature causing high-speed expansion of hot gases. The propulsion force is essentially that of NEWTON's third law (every action produces an equal and opposite reaction). The jet of hot gas being emitted with some force reacts on the chamber from which it is contained. This occurs even in a vacuum or very low-pressure atmosphere, and is of great consequence in driving and steering vehicles in outer space. The jet engine used in aircraft, which has transformed civil and military flying since World War II, depends on compressing air to a high pressure and then burning fuel, causing the high temperature and high pressure needed to produce a gas stream of extremely high velocity. This has enabled aircraft to fly faster than the speed of sound. In the turbo jet engine the high-speed gases drive turbine blades on a shaft before being expelled through the exit nozzle. The shaft drives a turbine-type pump which pressurizes the intake air at the front opening and pushes it into the ignition chamber which is fed continuously with fuel. The ramjet engine designed for very high speeds relies entirely on its forward motion for the compression of the intake air before ignition. Both turbojets and ramjets rely on air; this sets an upper limit about 15,250 m (about 50,000 ft) on their efficient utilization. Above this height special rocket fuels are required which not only burn at high temperatures but produce large volumes of gas on combustion.

**jet stream,** narrow, swift air currents at altitudes of c.11 to nearly 13 km (7 to 8 mi). The two major jet streams, one in each hemisphere, circle the globe (although discontinuous at some points), varying between 30° and 40° in latitude. They flow in easterly directions in wavelike patterns, with speeds averaging 56 km/hr (35 mph) in summer and 120 km/hr (75 mph) in winter, although speeds as high as 320 km/hr (200 mph) have been recorded. Eastbound aircraft fly with the jet stream (a tail wind) to gain speed and save fuel; westbound aircraft avoid the jet stream (a head wind).

**jewellery,** decorative objects worn, usually on or near the head or hands, to signify status, ritual, wealth, fashion, and sentiment. An infinite variety of durable or ephemeral materials are used: bone, shell, teeth, horn, feathers, wood, stone and glass, traditional metals and gem stones, modern plastics, and new refractory metals, titanium, tantalum, and niobium. The intrinsic qualities of gold, silver, and platinum remain unsurpassed for colour, durability, and working properties, and cultures worldwide have applied techniques which include casting, beating, chasing, granulation, wirework, piercing, engraving and enamelling, and stone setting. The origins of jewellery are prehistoric, and pre-date clothing; associations with magic carry forward to the present day. The ancient cultures of the Middle East worked thin, beaten gold or electrum sheet, vibrant with stones, beads, and glass paste to make powerful, emblematic jewels. The MINOAN, PHOENICIAN and early Hellenic (see HELLENISTIC CIVILIZATION) craftsmen worked fragile gold sheet, pressed into delicate designs often based on natural forms, flowers, and seeds. The ETRUSCANS were unsurpassed for exquisite gold granulation and elegant metalwork. Later, the less refined Roman jewellery favoured cabochon stones and cut gems, cameos and heavy finger rings, and influenced the sumptuous Byzantine work, rich with enamels and Christian symbols, which, spreading across eastern and western Europe, remained popular into medieval times. Other traditions arising out of ancient cultures and the influence of trade persist in the Indian craft communities, notable for delicate designs of ancient origin, chisel-pierced, or in fine filigree wirework; similar techniques are found in the Far East. China developed its own traditions, particularly fine casting, although not rich in precious metals; gold hair ornaments were highly valued. In contrast, the PRE-COLUMBIAN civilizations used gold in abundance, cast, hammered, and cut sheet, formed into mysterious, symbolic designs, which still influence work in Mexico. During the Renaissance period, fantastic jewelled pendants were created using pearls and precious stones, sometimes designed by famous artists, and worn with gold chokers and chains of intricate design. Gold gave way to sprays of faceted gems by the 1700s, and diamonds dominated the next two centuries. Jewelled and enamelled buckles, buttons, watches and snuff boxes became popular, and with the Georgian paste, costume jewellery became established. Iron, steel, pinchbeck, glass, and jet became even more widely used as the Industrial Revolution promoted both the manufacturing techniques and a new middle-class market, aware of the rediscovery of Pompeii and the Classical revival. FABERGÉ exemplified the established forms of fine gold and jewellery of the 19th cent., across Europe. LALIQUE, the supreme innovator of the ART NOUVEAU, created new forms, carrying their impact over fallow years. Modern plastics and metals have revitalized design in

the mass market since 1960, accompanied by an increasing interest in the art of the goldsmith.

**Jewett, Sarah Orne,** 1849–1909, American author. She is noted for her perceptive, gently humorous studies of small-town New England life. The most memorable of her short-story collections is *The Country of the Pointed Firs* (1896); her best-known novel is *A Country Doctor* (1884).

**Jewish Agency,** body created in 1929 to promote the establishment of a Jewish national home in Palestine. It formed the nucleus of the government of the state of ISRAEL (est. 1948). Since then the agency has encouraged immigration to and investment in Israel.

**Jewish holidays.** There are seven major holidays in the Jewish calendar. **Rosh Hashanah,** the New Year, falls on the 1st and 2nd days of the Hebrew month Tishri (Sept.–Oct.). It is spent in solemn prayer, and a *shofar,* or ram's horn, is blown in the synagogue. Rosh Hashanah begins the Ten Days of Penitence, which end with **Yom Kippur,** on the 10th of Tishri. This is the Day of Atonement, a day of fasting and praying for forgiveness for the past year's sins. **Sukkoth,** or the Feast of Tabernacles, is the fall harvest festival; it begins on the 15th of Tishri and lasts eight days (seven in Israel). Meals are eaten in a *sukkah,* a booth with a roof of thatch, to recall the shelters of the Israelites when they wandered in the wilderness. The day after Sukkoth is Simhath Torah [Heb., = rejoicing of the law], celebrating the annual completion of the reading of the TORAH. Hanukkah recalls the victory of Judas Maccabeus (see MACCABEES) and the rededication of the Temple in Jerusalem. It lasts for eight days, beginning on the 25th of Kislev (Dec.). This festival of lights is marked by the lighting of candles in a *menorah,* an eight-branched candlestick, to commemorate the miracle of a small vial of oil that burned for eight days. **Purim,** the Feast of Lots, on the 14th of Adar (Feb.–Mar.), celebrates the deliverance of the Persian Jews from a general massacre (according to the Book of ESTHER, which is read in the synagogue on this holiday). The day is one of merrymaking, feasting, and wearing costumes. **Passover** or **Pesach,** from the 14th to the 22nd of Nisan (14th to 21st of Nisan in Israel; Mar.–Apr.), possibly a spring festival originally, recalls the exodus of the Jews, led by MOSES, from Egypt. Throughout the holiday, *matzah* (unleavened bread) is eaten. At the *seder,* a special Passover meal, the *Haggadah,* telling the story of the deliverance from Egypt, is read. **Shavuot,** on the 6th and 7th of Sivan (the 6th of Sivan in Israel; May–June), the Feast of Weeks, is an agricultural festival. The Book of RUTH, which is set against the background of a grain harvest, is read in the synagogue. Traditionally, Shavuot also commemorates the receiving of the TEN COMMANDMENTS. In most communities, *Yom Ha-Atzmaut,* Israel's Independence Day, and *Yom Yerushalayim,* anniversary of the reunificiation of Jerusalem, are marked by a special thanksgiving service, followed by an appropriate celebration.

**Jewish liturgical music.** Music was common among the ancient Jews on religious and secular occasions. Singing was responsorial and antiphonal. Early instruments were the lyre, flute, trumpet, and ram's- or goat's-horn *shofar.* Ritual cantillation, or recitative chanting, was evidently similar to ARABIAN and INDIAN MUSIC, i.e., melodies with improvisations. After the destruction of Jerusalem in AD 70 the instrumental music was lost, but 'Oriental' Jews preserved the chant. With the growth of the SYNAGOGUE came the rise of the cantor. The *maqām* system during the 16th cent., and Italian and German SONG, were all influential in Europe; traditionalists reintroduced 'Oriental' elements. Post-Renaissance cantors developed a coloratura style. New instruments, particularly the ORGAN, became important. Subsequent movements have tended back to or away from the ancient style, and in the 20th cent. several composers have contributed to synagogue music.

**Jews,** accepted designation of believers in JUDAISM; originally represented in the Bible as the descendants of Judah and the dominant group in Judea. In the Bible, Jewish history begins with the patriarchs ABRAHAM, ISAAC, and JACOB in CANAAN. Jewish agricultural tribes lived in Egypt until MOSES led them away from the persecutions of Ramses II and eventually back to Canaan. DAVID, an early Jewish king from the tribe of Judah, defeated the enemies of the Jews, expanded his territory, and brought peace and prosperity to his people. His son SOLOMON built the first TEMPLE and was famous for his wealth and wisdom. After Solomon's death the Jewish kingdom split into two smaller kingdoms, ISRAEL and JUDAH. In 722 BC the Assyrians conquered Israel, sending most Israelites into exile (see ISRAEL, TRIBES OF). Judah also was conquered. Under Babylonian rule the Temple was destroyed (586 BC), but it was rebuilt by 516 BC. The MACCABEES (2nd and 1st cent. BC) restored Jewish independence for a time, but Roman domination followed (see ROME), and Jerusalem was destroyed (AD 70). After the fall of the Roman Empire, Jews migrated to Western Europe. From the 9th to 12th cent. their conditions improved, particularly in Spain, but the period from the Crusades to the 18th cent. was one of intermittent persecution in Europe, where the Jews served as a convenient scapegoat in troubled times (see ANTI-SEMITISM; INQUISITION). The rise of capitalism improved their economic condition, and Jews gained political emancipation, in the 17th cent. in Holland and later in other countries. With the coming to power of the NAZIS in Germany, in 1933, persecution of the Jews became increasingly widespread and violent (see HOLOCAUST). The establishment of the state of Israel in 1948 restored the Jewish homeland after almost 2000 years but has remained a source of conflict with the Arabs (see ARAB-ISRAELI WARS). The population of Jews worldwide before WORLD WAR II was 16 million; 6 million died in the Holocaust. In 1980 the world Jewish population was estimated at 13 million: US, 5.7 million; Israel, 3.3 million; Europe, 3 million (including 1.7 million in the Soviet Union); the remainder in Africa and other parts of the Americas and Asia. See also HASIDIM; SEPHARDIM.

**Jex-Blake, Sophia Louisa,** 1840–1912, English physician and pioneer of the right of women to practise medicine. She studied under Elizabeth BLACKWELL in New York and founded the London School of Medicine for Women in 1874. She was not permitted to practise until 1877, by which time she had obtained her MD at Bern, Switzerland.

**Jezebel:** see AHAB.

**Jhansi** (j(ə),hənsee), town (1981 pop. 246,172), Uttar Pradesh state, N India near the Betwa R. It is a district administrative and communications centre. It has railway workshops and military establishments, and is a somewhat unattractive town, apart from its historic fort, which played a part in the wars of the Mogul period. The town owes its origin as a large settlement to a Maratha leader of the 18th cent. The princely state of Jhansi was annexed by the British in 1853. Four years later its high-spirited Rani was prominent in the INDIAN MUTINY, which shows that vigorous feminine leadership is no new thing in India.

**Jiang Qing** (jeeang ching), 1913–, Chinese Communist leader, widow of MAO ZEDONG. She was a radical figure in the CULTURAL REVOLUTION (1966–69) and was appointed (1969) to the politburo. After Mao's death, she was one of the GANG OF FOUR arrested (1976) for planning a coup. In 1981 she was convicted and received a death sentence, which was, however, commuted to life imprisonment in 1983.

**Jiangsu** or **Kiangsu,** province (1985 est. pop. 62,130,000), 102,600 km² (39,613 sq mi), E China, bordering the Yellow Sea and the provincial city of SHANGHAI to the east. Major cities are NANJING, the capital, and WUXI. The province's low-lying fertile plains and subtropical climate support wheat, rice, and cotton. Mineral resources are limited, but the area S of the Yangtze R is an important industrial area. Early cotton and silk manufacture has now been supplemented by a wide variety of industries including food processing and mineral working. Because of its proximity to major urban markets, this area has long been one of the most important agricultural and industrial regions of China. This is reflected in the contemporary tourist attractions of cities such as Suzhou (Soochow).

**Jiangxi** or **Kiangsi,** province (1985 est. pop. 34,600,000), 166,000 km² (64,092 sq mi), S China. It lies S of the YANGTZE R. and between the provinces of HUNAN (W) and FUJIAN (E). Major cities include NANCHANG, the capital, and Jingdezhen. The province is largely a massive drainage basin for the Yangtze. The Gan R. flows northwards through the Poyang lake, one of China's few large inland lakes, which serves as a natural flood reservoir for the Yangtze. Mountains fringe the province's western, southern, and eastern borders. Flat, fertile land and a subtropical climate enables intensive cultivation and the province is a significant grain producer and exporter. Crops include rice, winter wheat, cotton, rape seed, and oranges. Natural-resource-based industries include timber and bamboo production (based in the mountains) and freshwater fishing. The mountain regions also contain significant mineral deposits including copper, silver, and tungsten. Though its coal production is limited, Jiangxi and GUANGDONG provs. are the only significant coal producers S of the Yangtze. Much of Jiangxi's coal has been exported to the steel industry in WUHAN, Hubei province. Jiangxi is an important province in the history of the Chinese Communist Party. In 1927 the urban base of the

party was destroyed by the Nationalists in Shanghai. One group of the party, under Mao Zedong, retreated to the Jinggang Hills in W Jiangxi. There they developed their guerrilla tactics and policies of enlisting peasant support. In 1931 they created the Jiangxi Soviet, a provisional government with Mao as Chairman. Encirclement and attacks by Chiang Kai-Shek's Nationalist forces led the Red Army in 1934 to commence the LONG MARCH to Yan'an.

**Jidda** or **Jedda,** city (1981 est. pop. 900,000), W Saudi Arabia, on the Red Sea. It is the port of MECCA and annually receives a huge influx of pilgrims. It has an international airport and university. Present-day Jidda is not more than three centuries old, but Old Jidda, c.19 km (12 mi) south of the modern city, was founded c.646 by the caliph Uthman. Jidda was ruled by the Turks until 1916 and was conquered by IBN SAUD in 1925.

**jihad** (ji,hahd), [Arab., = struggle], the injunction of early ISLAM for expansion, entailing waging war against non-Muslim dominions with the aim of establishing rule by Muslims, without this necessarily entailing the conversion of DHIMMI communities.

**Jilin** or **Kirin,** province (1985 est. pop. 22,980,000), 187,400 km² (72,355 sq mi), NE China; bordered by Korea (SE), HEILONGJIANG prov. (N), and LIAONING prov. (S). The major cities are CHANGCHUN, the capital, and Jilin. The SE section is mountainous, with the rest of the province comprising a largely grassy plateau through which flows the SONGHUA R. Much of the mountainous area is forested and the plateau region has an important animal-rearing industry. Industrialization has benefited from important mineral deposits, including coal and iron ore, and a relatively well-developed transport system. Changchun is the centre of a variety of metalworking industries, including a car plant. Historically and economically the province's development has been linked to that of the other NE provinces (see LIAONING).

**Jiménez, Juan Ramón** (hi,meneth day thiz,neros), 1881–1958, Spanish poet. Early identified with MODERNISMO, as in his *Elel Pl68 as* (1908) and the distinctive prose poems of *Platero y yo* (1914–16), he later adopted a simpler, sparer style suffused with mysticism, as in *La estación total* (1946; tr. Total Season). Jiménez left Spain during the civil war to live first in the US, then in Puerto Rico. He was awarded the 1956 Nobel Prize for literature.

**Jiménez de Cisneros, Francisco** (hi,meneth day thiz,neros), 1436–1517, Spanish prelate and statesman. As archbishop of Toledo, he tried to convert the MOORS in Granada and provoked an uprising (1500–02). He twice acted as regent of CASTILE (1506–07, 1516) and was appointed inquisitor general and cardinal. In 1509 he led the Spanish expedition that captured Oran in Africa. Cardinal Jiménez enacted clerical reforms, promoted better education for churchmen, and had the Polyglot Bible compiled at his own expense.

**Jiménez de Quesada, Gonzalo** (hi,meneth day ke,sahdhah), c.1499–1579, Spanish CONQUISTADOR in Colombia. Commissioned to explore the Magdalena R. in search of EL DORADO, he set out in 1536. He defeated the Chibcha and founded (1538) BOGOTÁ as the capital of New Granada (now COLOMBIA). In 1550 he was made marshal of New Granada and councillor of Bogotá for life. His 1569 expedition in search of El Dorado was disastrous.

**Ji'nan** or **Tsinan** (jeenan), city (1984 pop. 3,436,000), capital of SHANDONG prov., E China, 4.8 km (3 mi) S of the Yellow R. Over 100 natural springs are located in Jinan, which is also a regional manufacturing centre producing metals, machinery, chemicals, textiles, and paper. It is a major communications centre, being the junction of the railways from Beijing to Shanghai, and Jinan to Qingdao. A historic walled city, its contemporary development dates from the completion (1904) of the Jinan–Qingdao rail link. This was a German concession and subsequently English and Japanese investment was central to the city's industrialization.

**jingoism,** name given to belligerent English chauvinism, following the Russo-Turkish War of 1877–78 when a popular song referred to the movement of the British Mediterranean fleet to Gallipoli, with the refrain 'We don't want to fight, yet by jingo, if we do, we've got the ships, we've got the men, and got the money too!'

**Jinnah, Muhammad Ali,** 1876–1948, founder of PAKISTAN. He at first supported the INDIAN NATIONAL CONGRESS and its advocacy of Hindu–Muslim unity, but after 1934 he led the MUSLIM LEAGUE in its agitation for a separate

Muslim nation. He gained power during World War II when the Congress was declared to be an illegal organization after it initiated the Quit India movement (1942). In the postwar independence negotiations he was successful in his insistence on the creation of Pakistan (1947) as the homeland for India's Muslims.

**jinni,** plural **jinn** (ji͵nee), in Arabic and Islamic folklore, spirit or demon with supernatural powers, especially of changing size and shape. Both good and evil, jinn are popular figures in Near Eastern literature, particularly in the *Thousand and One Nights. Genie* is the English form.

**Jívaro,** Indians of Ecuador (see SOUTH AMERICAN INDIANS). They engage in farming, hunting, fishing, and weaving. Each patrilineal family group lives in a large, isolated communal house. The Jívaro, who were once famous for the practice of ritual head shrinking, long resisted conquest.

**Joanna** (the Mad), 1479–1555, Spanish queen of CASTILE and LEÓN (r.1504–55). Because of her insanity the kingdoms were ruled by two regents, her husband PHILIP I (1504–06) and her father FERDINAND V (1506–16). Her son Charles (later Holy Roman Emperor CHARLES V) was proclaimed joint ruler of Castile in 1516, and Joanna was confined to a castle for her lifetime.

**Joan of Arc,** 1412–31, French saint and national heroine, called the Maid of Orléans. A farm girl, she began at a young age to hear the 'voices' those of St Michael, St Catherine, and St Margaret. When she was about 16, the voices exhorted her to bear aid to the DAUPHIN, later CHARLES VII of France, then kept from the throne by the English in the HUNDRED YEARS WAR. Joan journeyed in male attire to meet the dauphin and conquered his scepticism as to her divine mission. She was furnished with troops, but her leadership provided spirit and morale more than military prowess. In May 1429 she raised the siege of Orléans, and in June she defeated the English at Patay. After considerable persuasion the dauphin agreed to be crowned at Rheims, and Joan was at the pinnacle of her fortunes. In Sept. 1429 she unsuccessfully besieged Paris. The following spring she went to relieve Compiègne, but was captured by the Burgundians and sold to the English, who were eager to put her to death. In order to escape responsibility, the English turned her over to the ecclesiastical court at Rouen, where she was tried for heresy and witchcraft by French clerics who supported the English. Probably her most serious crime was the claim of direct inspiration from God; in the eyes of the court this refusal to accept the church hierarchy constituted heresy. Only at the end of the lengthy trial did she recant. She was condemned to life imprisonment, but shortly afterwards she retracted her abjuration. She was then turned over to the secular court as a relapsed heretic and was burned at the stake (30 May 1431) in Rouen. The proceedings of the original trial were annulled in 1456. Joan was canonized in 1920. Her career lent itself to numerous legends, and she has been represented in much art and literature. Feast: 30 May.

**João Pessoa** (͵choohow ͵pesohə), city (1980 pop. 290,247), NE Brazil, capital of Paraíba state. Established on the Atlantic coast as a port during the colonial period, it now serves primarily coastal traffic with oceangoing shipping handled at the outport of Cabedelo. The city contains a number of major colonial buildings of considerable architectural merit.

**Job** (johb), book of the OLD TESTAMENT. Based on a folktale, it may have been written between 600 and 400 BC. It discusses, in dialogue or dramatic form, the problem of good and evil in the world. In the prologue (1–2), Satan obtains God's permission to test the 'upright man' Job; accordingly, all Job has is destroyed, and he is physically afflicted. The main part of the book (3–31) consists of speeches by Job and three friends who come to 'comfort' him. A fourth speaker, Elihu (32–37), who accuses Job of arrogant pride, is followed by God himself (38–42), who rebukes Job and his friends. Job is restored to happiness. The ethical problem of the book is not explicitly resolved; rather, the author effectively criticizes the traditional view that suffering is the result of sin, and asserts the omnipotence of God.

**Jocasta:** see OEDIPUS.

**Jodhpur,** city (1981 pop. 506,345), Rajasthan state, NW India. It is a district administrative and commercial centre. It has craft industries, and modern factories making cotton and wool textiles and chemicals. Its fort played a part in the wars between the Moguls and Rajput princes. The Maharaja of Jodhpur made a treaty with the British in 1817 and he and

his successors continued to rule their princely state until after Indian independence.

**Joel,** book of the OLD TESTAMENT. Dated probably c.400 BC, it first calls the people to repentance to avert a plague of locusts, and then foretells the future outpouring of the Spirit on all flesh.

**Joffre, Joseph Jacques Césaire** (͵zhofrə), 1852–1931, marshal of France. French commander in chief from 1911, he deserves partial credit for the victory of the Marne (1914) in WORLD WAR I. After the Germans nearly captured Verdun (1916), Joffre was replaced by Robert Georges Nivelle.

**Joffrey, Robert:** see Robert Joffrey Ballet under DANCE (table).

**Johanan ben Zakkai,** fl. 1st cent. AD, leader of the Pharisees of Jerusalem before the destruction of the Temple (AD 70) and, later, founder of the academy at Jabneh. The academy became the new religious centre and the site of the SANHEDRIN, assuring the continuation of Judaism.

**Johannesburg,** largest city (1985 pop. 1,609,408) of South Africa, TRANSVAAL prov., on the southern slopes of the WITWATERSRAND. The sprawling city, situated in the nation's major gold-mining region, is a manufacturing and commercial centre and a transport hub. Founded (1886) as a gold-mining settlement, it grew rapidly and had c.100,000 people by 1900. Most of Johannesburg's large black population, which provides labour for the mines, lives in nearby SOWETO.

**John,** Byzantine emperors. **John I** (Tzimisces), c.925–76 (r.969–76), began his reign with the murder of NICEPHORUS II. He extended Byzantine power against the Russians and Arabs. **John II** (Comnenus), 1088–1143 (r.1118–43), succeeded his father, ALEXIUS I. He failed in efforts to cancel Venetian trade privileges but won military victories. **John III** (Ducas Vatatzes), d. 1254 (r.1222–54), succeeded his father-in-law, Theodore I. During his reign the empire thrived, and he almost reunited the Byzantine territories. **John IV** (Lascaris), b. c.1250, d. after 1273, succeeded his father, Theodore II, under a regent (1258–61). Michael Palaeologus became co-ruler (1259), had the boy emperor blinded and imprisoned (1261), and succeeded as MICHAEL VIII. **John V** (Palaeologus), 1332–91 (r.1341–76, 1379–91), had his throne usurped during his minority by **John VI** and later by his son Andronicus IV. He lost territory to the Ottoman Turks and recognized their suzerainty (1371). **John VI** (Cantacuzene), c.1292–1383 (r.1347–55), usurped the throne of John V, calling to the Ottoman Turks for aid. He later abdicated. **John VII** (Palaeologus), c.1370–1408, grandson of John V, briefly usurped (1390) the throne of John V with Turkish help and later became co-ruler (1394–1402) with his uncle MANUEL II. **John VIII** (Palaeologus), 1390–1448 (r.1423–48), son of Manuel II, ruled an empire reduced to the city of Constantinople. He sought in vain to secure Western aid against the Turks by agreeing at the Council of Florence (1439) to a union of the Eastern and Western churches. His brother and successor, CONSTANTINE XI, was the last of the Byzantine emperors.

**John,** 1167–1216, king of England (r.1199–1216); youngest son of HENRY II. After his brother RICHARD I left on the Third CRUSADE, John conspired unsuccessfully with PHILIP II of France to supplant Richard as king. On Richard's death, John ascended the throne to the exclusion of his nephew ARTHUR I of Brittany, who, with the aid of Philip II, began a revolt in France. Although Arthur was captured (1202), John lost many of his French possessions to Philip. John's refusal to accept a new archbishop of Canterbury led to his excommunication (1209). To regain papal favour, he was forced to surrender (1213) his kingdom to Pope INNOCENT III, and received it back as a papal fief. In England his abuse of feudal custom in raising money aroused intense opposition from the barons. They rebelled in 1215 and compelled John to accept MAGNA CARTA. He was succeeded by his son HENRY III.

**John,** kings of France. **John I** (the Posthumous), 1316, was the posthumous son of LOUIS X and lived only five days. He was succeeded by his uncle PHILIP V. **John II** (the Good), 1319–64 (r.1350–64), was the son of PHILIP VI. His reign was troubled by the HUNDRED YEARS WAR with England and by his quarrels with CHARLES II of Navarre. Captured (1356) by the English at Poitiers, John was released (1360) by the Treaty of Brétigny for a ransom and hostages. In 1364 one of the hostages escaped, and John, to save his honour, returned to England, where he died. He was succeeded by his son CHARLES V.

**John,** kings of France. **John I** (the Posthumous), 1316, was the posthumous son of LOUIS X and lived only five days. He was succeeded by his uncle PHILIP V. **John II** (the Good), 1319–64 (r. 1350–64), was the son of PHILIP VI. His reign was troubled by the HUNDRED YEARS WAR with England and by his quarrels with CHARLES II of Navarre. Captured (1356) by the English at Poitiers, John was released (1360) by the Treaty of Brétigny for a ransom and hostages. In 1364 one of the hostages escaped, and John, to save his honour, returned to England, where he died. He was succeeded by his son CHARLES V.

**John,** kings of HUNGARY. **John I** (John Zápolya), 1487–1540 (r. 1526–40), *voivode* [governor] of Transylvania (1511–26), was the son of Stephen ZÁPOLYA. He succeeded King Louis II, who was killed at the battle of Mohács (1526). The succession was challenged by Ferdinand of Austria (later Holy Roman Emperor FERDINAND I), but John prevailed and was confirmed as king by the Turkish sultan, who exercised real power. His son and successor, **John II** (John Sigismund Zápolya), 1540–71 (r. 1540–71), was crowned as an infant. Sultan SULAYMAN I invaded (1541) Hungary and made John prince of TRANSYLVANIA under Turkish suzerainty. Deposed (1551) by Austrian interests, John was restored (1556) by Turkish pressure. During his reign Transylvania adopted (1564) Calvinism as the state religion.

**John,** kings of POLAND. **John II** (John Casimir), 1609–72 (r. 1648–68), succeeded his brother, LADISLAUS IV. During John's reign, known as the Deluge, Poland lost the E Ukraine to Russia, and E Prussia to Brandenburg. Wars against Cossacks, Turks, Tatars, Russia, Transylvania, and Sweden occupied much of his time. He succeeded in reconquering Lithuania and W Ukraine from Russia. He abdicated in 1668 and retired to a monastery. **John III** (John Sobieski), 1624–96 (r. 1674–96), was the champion of Christian Europe against the Turks. In 1683 he relieved the Turkish siege of Vienna, and in 1684 he joined a Holy League with the Pope, the Holy Roman emperor, and Venice. He failed to wrest Moldavia and Walachia from Turkey. He was succeeded as king by the elector of Saxony, whose reign as AUGUSTUS II marked the virtual end of Poland's independence.

**John,** kings of PORTUGAL. **John I** (the Great), 1357?–1433 (r. 1385–1433), illegitimate son of PETER I, led a popular revolt in 1384 against the Portuguese regency and withstood a Castilian seige of Lisbon. Elected king the next year, he defeated the Castilians and assured Portugal's independence. His reign was one of the most glorious in Portuguese history. **John II** (the Perfect), 1455–95 (r. 1481–95), was an astute politician and a patron of Renaissance culture. He supported Portuguese exploration and in 1494 agreed to set bounds for Portuguese and Spanish colonization. **John III** (the Pious), 1502–57 (r. 1521–57), ruled at the height of the Portuguese empire, when the colonization of BRAZIL began and its Asian territories were extended. But the decline of agriculture and population portended Portugal's stagnation following his reign. **John IV,** 1604–56 (r. 1640–56), became king of independent Portugal upon the successful revolt from Spain (1640). He consolidated his position against Spain by concluding alliances with France and other nations. **John V** (the Magnanimous), 1689–1750 (r. 1706–50), maintained Portugal's alliance with England and kept the peace. Gold from Brazil permitted him to become a great patron of arts and letters and he beautified Lisbon. Wealth also made him independent of the CORTES, and he ruled with increasing absolutism. **John VI,** 1769–1826 (r. 1816–26), was regent for his mother, Maria I, who was insane. He lost a war to France (1801) and eventually fled (1807) to Brazil. He returned (1821) after a revolution and the proclamation of a liberal constitution, but he did everything he could to modify it. In 1825 he recognized Brazil's independence.

**John,** three epistles of the NEW TESTAMENT, ascribed to St JOHN, the disciple. First John was clearly written by the author of the GOSPEL or someone in his circle. Second and Third John are generally agreed to be by the same man. First John is a homily insisting that mystical experience needs to be complemented by practical religion. Second John, the Bible's shortest (13 verses) book, warns against false teachers who deny JESUS's historicity. Third John criticizes the failure of a church leader to receive teaching missionaries.

**John, Augustus** 1878–1961, British painter, brother of Gwen JOHN. John was a flamboyant personality famed for his self-consciously Bohemian way of life. He was a brilliant draughtsman, and his early pictures of figures in landscapes, where forms and colours are simplified, were indebted to the Fauves (see FAUVISM). Later he concentrated on portraits, and painted many of the leading figures of his day, including W.B. Yeats and Dylan Thomas.

**John, Barry,** 1945–, Welsh RUGBY UNION player. Widely regarded as the greatest figure in rugby of modern times, John played outside half for Llanelli, Cardiff, Wales, and the British Lions. His partnership with Gareth Edwards was the most profitable in the history of the game, John's kicking being noted for its pinpoint accuracy. For the British Lions in New Zealand in 1971 he scored a record 180 points. He retired in 1972.

**John, Gospel according to Saint,** book of the NEW TESTAMENT. It is clearly set off from the other three Synoptic GOSPELS, although John may have used both MARK and LUKE as sources. The evangelist seems to have two aims—to show that JESUS is the vital force in the world now and forever, and that he lived on earth to reveal himself in the flesh. In a philosophical prologue, Jesus is identified with the Word (Logos). The book recounts selected incidents from Jesus's ministry and (13–21) the Passion and RESURRECTION. The influence on CHRISTIANITY of the Gospel of John, particularly with reference to its enunciation of Christ's position in the TRINITY, has been enormous.

**John, Gwen,** 1876–1939, British painter, sister of Augustus JOHN. She trained at the Slade and with WHISTLER in Paris. Her works, often portraits of young girls, are painted in tones of grey and convey an intensely private, reticent vision.

**John, Saint,** one of the Twelve Disciples, traditional author of the fourth GOSPEL, three EPISTLES, and the REVELATION. He and St James the Great were sons of Zebedee; Jesus called them Boanerges, or Sons of Thunder. With PETER, they were closest to Jesus, witnessed the Transfiguration, and were at Gethsemane. Jesus, dying, committed the Virgin Mary to John's care. He may be the same as St John of Ephesus (d. AD c. 100). He is variously known as St John the Evangelist, St John the Divine, and the Beloved Disciple.

**John VIII,** d. 882, pope (872–82), a Roman. He strenuously opposed St Ignatius, patriarch of Constantinople, and when Ignatius died, he recognized PHOTIUS as patriarch, momentarily solving the differences between East and West. John crowned the emperors CHARLES II (the Bald; 875) and CHARLES III (the Fat; 881). He was murdered by members of his entourage.

**John XII,** c. 937–64, pope (955–64), a Roman named Octavian. Elected pope before age 20, John led a notoriously immoral life. He was allied with OTTO I and crowned him (962) the first German emperor, but later sided with Berengar II of Italy. Otto conquered Rome, deposed John, and elected Leo VIII as pope. John retook Rome (964), but soon had to flee, and died of a stroke.

**John XXIII,** antipope (1410–15): see COSSA, BALDASSARRE.

**John XXIII,** 1881–1963, pope (1958–63), an Italian named Angelo Giuseppe Roncalli. He was a papal diplomat in the Balkans and Near East (1925–44), papal nuncio to France (1944–53), and in 1953 was named cardinal and patriarch of Venice. As pope he showed great concern for church reform, the promotion of peace, world social welfare (expressed in his encyclical *Mater et magistra*), and for dialogue with other faiths. The convening (1962) of the Second VATICAN COUNCIL was the high point of his reign. His heartiness, his overflowing love of humanity, and his freshness of approach to ecclesiastical affairs made John one of the best-loved popes of modern times.

**John Birch Society,** right-wing, anti-Communist organization in the US. It was founded (1958) by Robert Welch. Among its objectives are the repeal of social security legislation and of the graduated income tax, and the impeachment of certain government officials.

**John Bull:** see ARBUTHNOT, JOHN.

**John Chrysostom, Saint** (ˌkrisəstəm), c. 347–407, Doctor of the Church, greatest of the Greek Fathers. Made (398) patriarch of CONSTANTINOPLE, he came to be admired for his eloquence, ascetic life, and charity. After attempting church reform and denouncing the ways of the imperial court, John was illegally deposed (403) by the Empress Eudoxia and Bishop Theophilus. Recalled briefly, he was again sent into exile, where he died. His writings, notable for their purity of Greek style, greatly influenced Christian thought. Feasts: 13 Nov. in the East; 13 Sept. in the West.

**John Damascene, Saint:** see JOHN OF DAMASCUS, SAINT.

**John of Austria,** 1545–78, Spanish admiral and general, illegitimate son of Holy Roman Emperor CHARLES V. In 1571 he won the famous naval victory of LEPANTO over the Turks. Appointed governor-general of the NETHERLANDS (1576–78), he tried to stamp out rebellion.

**John of Austria,** 1629–79, Spanish general, illegitimate son of Philip IV. He was viceroy of Sicily (1648–51) and fought (1656–58) in the SpanishNETHERLANDS, where he lost the battle of the Dunes (1658). His campaign (1661–64) to reconquer Portugal also failed. In 1677 he overthrew the Spanish regency of the queen-mother Mariana but ruled only briefly.

**John of Damascus, Saint,** or **Saint John Damascene,** c.675–c.749, Syrian theologian, Father of the Church, Doctor of the Church. He wrote against ICONOCLASM and defended orthodoxy. *The Fountain of Wisdom* is his theological masterpiece. Feast: 4 Dec.

**John of Gaunt,** 1340–99, duke of Lancaster, fourth son of EDWARD III of England. He acquired the Lancaster holdings (see LANCASTER, HOUSE OF) through marriage and became one of the most influential nobles in England. He served under his brother EDWARD THE BLACK PRINCE in the HUNDRED YEARS WAR and by his second marriage (1371) gained a claim on the throne of Castile. For a short time John, in effect, ruled England for his ageing father; he remained powerful under his nephew RICHARD II. From 1386 to 1388 he fought in vain to make good his Castilian claims. Returning (1389) to England, John helped to restore peace between Richard II and the barons. In 1396 he married Catherine Swynford; they were ancestors of the TUDORS. John was the patron of CHAUCER. His eldest son was HENRY IV.

**John of Lancaster, duke of Bedford:** see BEDFORD, JOHN OF LANCASTER, DUKE OF.

**John of Leiden,** c.1509–36, Dutch Anabaptist leader. In 1534, following a revolt in Münster by ANABAPTISTS, he set up a theocracy and led, as 'king', a communistic and polygamous state until expelled (1535) by the prince bishop. He and the other leaders were tortured and executed.

**John of Luxemburg,** 1296–1346, king of Bohemia (r.1310–46), son of the Emperor HENRY VII. He was elected king after the death of his father-in-law, Wenceslaus II. Although blind, he fought on the French side at Crécy in the HUNDRED YEARS WAR, where he was killed.

**John of the Cross, Saint,** 1542–91, Spanish mystic and poet, Doctor of the Church. He was a founder of the Discalced CARMELITES and a friend of St TERESA of Ávila. His reforming zeal antagonized the hierarchy, and he was imprisoned in 1577. In his cell he wrote *Spiritual Canticle* and began *Songs of the Soul*, which are among the finest creations of Spanish literature. After escaping (1578), he went to Andalusia, where he wrote masterly prose treatises on mystical theology, notably *The Dark Night of the Soul* and *The Ascent of Mount Carmel.* Feast: 14 Dec.

**John Paul I,** 1912–78, pope (1978), an Italian named Albino Luciani. He had been patriarch of Venice. He was elected pope in Aug. 1978 and reigned for only 34 days before his death, in which foul play was suspected.

**John Paul II,** 1920–, pope (1978–), a Pole named Karol Wojtyla. Archbishop of Kraków, he was elected pope in Oct. 1978. He was the first non-Italian pope in 450 years and the first Polish pope. Conservative on doctrine, John Paul has travelled widely throughout his reign, e.g., to Poland and the US in 1979. Following a trip to the Far East (1981), he was seriously wounded at the Vatican on 13 May 1981, by a Turkish terrorist. Since his recovery, John Paul has worked for ecumenism, e.g., his 1982 trip to Britain, where he held an ecumenical service in Canterbury Cathedral. He has also been an outspoken commentator on world events, and has been uncompromising in his condemnation of LIBERATION THEOLOGY and his defence of the traditional Catholic theology of marriage and sexuality.

**Johns, Jasper,** 1930–, American artist. Influenced by Marcel DUCHAMP, Johns tried to transform common objects into art by placing them in an art context, e.g., his bronze beer cans with painted labels (1961). His paintings of flags and targets (1954–59) heralded POP ART.

**Johnson, Amy,** 1901–41, British aviator. Trained as an economist, she learned to fly in 1929 and in 1930 became the first woman to fly solo to Australia. She made several more notable flights, including the fastest from London to Cape Town and back (1936). Her flights with her husband Jim Mollison as copilot were not so successful; they were both injured crash-landing after an east-to-west Atlantic crossing. She died serving with the Air Transport Auxiliary in World War II, when she baled out over the Thames estuary; her body was not recovered.

**Johnson, Andrew,** 1808–75, 17th president of the US (1865–69). A self-educated tailor, he rose in Tennessee politics to become congressman (1843–53), governor (1853–57), and US senator (1857–62). In Washington, Johnson voted with other Southern legislators on questions of slavery, but after Tennessee seceded (June 1861) he remained in the Senate and vigorously supported Pres. LINCOLN, who appointed him (1862) military governor of Tennessee. As a Southerner and a war Democrat, he was an ideal choice as the Union candidate for vice president, accompanying Lincoln in 1864, and he succeeded to the presidency after Lincoln's assassination. As president he was denounced by the radical Republicans for his RECONSTRUCTION programme, and in 1866 his political power began to decline sharply. When Johnson tried to oust Secy of War Edwin M. Stanton whom he rightly suspected of conspiring with congressional leaders, the radical Republicans sought to remove the president. On 24 Feb. 1868, the House passed a resolution of IMPEACHMENT against him. The most important of the charges, which were purely political, was that he had violated the TENURE OF OFFICE ACT in the Stanton affair. In spite of tremendous pressure brought to bear on several senators, the Senate failed to convict by one vote. After Johnson's presidency he was returned (1875) to the Senate from Tennessee, but died shortly afterwards.

**Johnson, Eyvind,** 1900–1976, Swedish novelist and short-story writer. He is probably best known for his cycle of four autobiographical novels, *The Novel about Olof* (1934–37), which is noted for its psychological penetration. Other novels include *Return to Ithaca* (1946) and *Steps into Silence* (1973). He shared the 1974 Nobel Prize for literature with his countryman Harry MARTINSON.

**Johnson, Linton Kwesi,** 1952–, Jamaican poet. He came to England when he was 11; his poetry articulates the feelings of black people in a British society in which they feel themselves to be marginalized. His best-known collections are *Voices of the Living and the Dead* (1974; 1983), *Dread Beat and Blood* (1975), and *Inglan is a Bitch* (1980).

**Johnson, Lyndon Baines,** 1908–73, 36th president of the US (1963–69). As a Democratic congressman from Texas (1937–49) he supported Pres. F.D. ROOSEVELT's New Deal. He was elected senator in 1948 and became majority leader following the 1954 elections. After losing the 1960 presidential nomination to J.F. KENNEDY, Johnson agreed to become Kennedy's running mate and was elected vice president. After Kennedy's assassination (22 Nov. 1963) Johnson was immediately sworn in as president. Announcing that he would carry out the late president's programmes, he skilfully prodded Congress into enacting (1964) an $11 billion tax cut and a sweeping Civil Rights Act. Elected (1964) to a full term, he launched a programme of social and economic welfare measures to create what he termed the Great Society. It included a Medicare bill (see HEALTH INSURANCE), federal aid for education, increased antipoverty programmes, and the 1965 Voting Rights Act. Johnson's domestic achievements, however, were soon obscured by foreign affairs. When North Vietnam allegedly attacked (Aug. 1964) US destroyers, Congress passed the TONKIN GULF RESOLUTION, which gave the president authority to take any action necessary to protect US troops. Johnson began (Feb. 1965) the bombing of North Vietnam and increased US forces in South Vietnam to nearly 550,000 men (1969). The VIETNAM WAR aroused widespread opposition in Congress and among the public, and rioting (1968) in the black ghettos of American cities further marred his presidency. In 1965 Johnson sent US troops into the DOMINICAN REPUBLIC. He announced (Mar. 1968) that he would not run for reelection and retired to his Texas ranch.

**Johnson, Philip Courtelyou,** 1906–, American architect and historian. He wrote *The International Style* (1932) with Henry-Russell Hitchcock and became a major advocate of the new architecture. His glass house in New Canaan, Connecticut (1949) reveals the influence of MIES VAN DER ROHE, with whom he collaborated on the Seagram Building (1958), New York City. He also designed the New York State Theater at Lincoln Center (1964) and the American Telephone and Telegraph Headquarters Building (1978), both in New York City.

**Johnson, Samuel**, 1709–84, English writer. The leading literary scholar and critic of his day, he has been used by writers to define the period of English literature known as the Augustan Age. He is as celebrated for his brilliant conversation as for his writing. He began writing for London magazines around 1737, on literary and political subjects. The anonymously published poem *London* (1738) won the praise of POPE, and his reputation was further enhanced by his poetic satire *The Vanity of Human Wishes* (1749) and his moral essays in *The Rambler* (1750–52). Johnson's place was permanently assured by his *Dictionary of the English Language* (1755), the first comprehensive English lexicography. *Rasselas,* a moral romance, appeared in 1759, and the *Idler* essays between 1758 and 1760. In 1763 Johnson met James BOSWELL, and his life thereafter is documented in Boswell's great biography (1791). With Joshua REYNOLDS he founded (1764) 'The Club', with such members as GOLDSMITH, BURKE, and GARRICK. In 1765 he published his edition of SHAKESPEARE, the model for later editions. His last works include an account (1775) of a trip with Boswell to the Hebrides and the 10-volume *Lives of the Poets* (1779–81).

**Johnson, Uwe** (‚yonzon), 1934–84, German novelist. He grew up in East Germany, but after publishing difficulties with his first manuscript, *Ingrid Babendererde. Growing up* (1953; pub. 1983), emigrated to West Berlin in 1959. After two years in New York (1966–68), he lived reclusively in England from 1974. His novels go beyond the clichés of 'the author of both Germanies', exploring experimentally the epistemological problems of constructing possible realities, in such characteristically-titled novels as *Mutmassungen über Jakob* (1959; tr. Speculations about Jacob), *Das dritte Buch über Achim* (1961; tr. The Third Book about Arnim), and *Zwei Ansichten* (1965; tr. Two Views). His greatest achievement is the tetralogy *Anniversaries* (1970–83), located in a woman's lifetime between East Berlin and New York.

**Johnson, Virginia E.:** see MASTERS AND JOHNSON.

**Johnston, Albert Sidney**, 1803–62, Confederate general in the AMERICAN CIVIL WAR. Confederate commander in the West, he attacked (6 Apr. 1862) Gen. GRANT at SHILOH. Johnston was killed in the battle, and the South lost one of its ablest generals.

**Johnston, Joseph Eggleston**, 1807–91, Confederate general in the AMERICAN CIVIL WAR. He took part in the first battle of BULL RUN and was commander in the PENINSULAR CAMPAIGN until May 1862. Given command in the West, he was unable to stem the Union success in the VICKSBURG CAMPAIGN and the Atlanta campaign, and he was relieved of command (July 1864). Later reinstated, he surrendered (26 Apr. 1865) to Gen. SHERMAN.

**John the Baptist, Saint**, d. AD c.28–30, Jewish prophet, the forerunner of JESUS; son of Zachariah and Elizabeth, a kinswoman of the Virgin MARY. He preached in the Jordan valley, baptizing many, including Jesus, whom he recognized as the Son of God. Herodias, wife of HEROD, and her daughter (traditionally called SALOME) had him beheaded. Feast: 24 June.

**John the Fearless**, 1371–1419, duke of Burgundy (1404–19), son of PHILIP THE BOLD. Continuing his father's feud, he had Louis, duc d'Orléans, assassinated (1407) and won control of the French government. In 1411 civil war broke out between the Orléanists, or Armagnacs, and the Burgundians. Forced to flee Paris (1413), John did not aid the now Armagnac-controlled government against HENRY V of England and in 1418 took advantage of French defeats to retake Paris and seize the king, CHARLES VI. John was assassinated at a meeting with the DAUPHIN (later CHARLES VII) and was succeeded by his son PHILIP THE GOOD.

**joint**, in anatomy, the juncture between two bones. Some joints are immovable, e.g., those connecting bones of the skull. Hinge joints provide a forward and backward motion, as at the elbow and knee. Pivot joints permit rotary movement, like the turning of the head from side to side. Ball-and-socket joints, like those at the hip and shoulder, allow the greatest range of movement. Ease of movement is aided by elastic cartilage, lubricating synovial fluid, and, in some joints, a cushioning, fluid-filled sac (bursa), which reduces friction.

**Joinville, Jean, sire de** (zhahnh‚veel), 1224?–1317?, French chronicler. His memoir of LOUIS IX (whom he served as a close adviser) is an invaluable record of the king, feudal France, and the Seventh CRUSADE, written in a simple, delightful style, with a sharp eye for graphic detail.

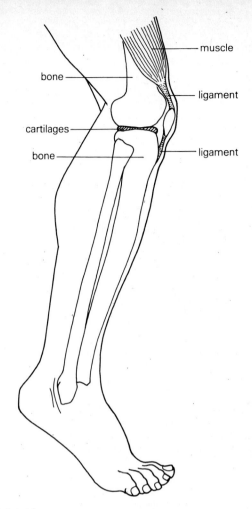

Hinge **joint** at knee

**Jókai, Mór** (‚yohkoy), 1825–1904, Hungarian novelist. Often compared to DICKENS and Sir Walter SCOTT, Jókai was a prolific and popular writer whose novels include *An Hungarian Nabob* (1853–54) and *Black Diamonds* (1870).

**joking relationship**, a relationship of joking or familiarity and sexual licence between certain categories of people, usually kin or affines (see KINSHIP). Such relationships can be between those of equal or those of unequal status, such as that between a mother's brother and sister's son, or son and father's sister. Joking relationships are seen as structurally similar to AVOIDANCE RELATIONSHIPS.

**Joliet, Louis:** see JOLLIET, LOUIS.

**Joliot-Curie, Frédéric** and **Irène:** see CURIE, family.

**Jolley, Elizabeth**, 1923–, Australian novelist; b. England. She has lived in Australia since 1959. Her writing has a sly and sometimes startling wit, and a recurring interest in eccentricity, particularly in the lives of her middle-aged, outwardly respectable heroines whose inner lives are full of surprises. She has published three short-story collections and her novels include *Palomino* (1980), *Miss Peabody's Inheritance* (1983), *Foxybaby* (1983), *The Well* (1986), and *The Sugar Mother* (1988).

**Jolliet** or **Joliet, Louis** (‚johlee-'et), 1645–1700, French explorer; b. Quebec province, Canada. He discovered, with Jacques MARQUETTE, the upper MISSISSIPPI R. in 1673.

**Jonah, Jonas** or **Jona**, book of the OLD TESTAMENT. It tells of a Hebrew PROPHET in the reign of Jeroboam II (c.793–753 BC) sent to reform NINEVEH. To avoid the command, he sails for Tarshish, but his disobedience brings a storm; the crew throw him overboard. Swallowed by a 'great fish', he is cast up after three days and fulfills his mission. Jonah's escape from the fish is seen as foreshadowing Christ's RESURRECTION.

**Jones, (Alfred) Ernest**, 1879–1958, Welsh psychoanalyst. He played a key role in British PSYCHOANALYSIS and was author of *The Life and Work of Sigmund Freud* (2 vol., 1953, 1955), the standard English biography.

**Jones, Allen**, 1937–, British painter. He was one of the most successful of British exponents of POP ART. From the 1960s he used imagery of women's legs, stockings, and shoes taken from women's magazines, giving them a sexual and fetishistic character.

**Jones, Bobby** (Robert Tyre Jones, Jr), 1902–71, American golfer. A laywer, he played golf as an amateur and won the US Open (1923, 1926, 1929, 1930), the US Amateur Championship (1924–25, 1927–28, 1930), and the British Open (1926–27, 1930). The first golfer to win the US Open and British Open in the same year (1926), he was the only player ever to score what was then the grand slam of golf, taking the open and amateur titles in both the US and Britain in 1930. Still an amateur, he retired that year with 13 major championships.

**Jones, Daniel**, 1881–1967, English linguist and one of the founders of the British school of phonetics. He invented a system of vowel classification and wrote an *English Pronouncing Dictionary* (1917) which adopted the educated speech of southern England (see RECEIVED PRONUNCIATION).

**Jones, Sir Edward Burne:** see BURNE-JONES.

**Jones, Inigo**, 1573–1652, one of England's first great architects. He studied Renaissance and Palladian buildings in Europe. He became in 1615 the king's surveyor of works, and began (1616) the Queen's House, Greenwich, the first English design to embody Palladian principles (see PALLADIO). He then built (1619–22) the royal banquet hall, Whitehall. In many houses in London and in the country he broke from the prevailing JACOBEAN STYLE, marking a starting point for the Renaissance and Georgian periods in England. He introduced the proscenium arch to English theatre, and is also thought to have been the first in his time to use revolving screens to denote changes of scene. He was famous for his spectacular settings and costumes for court masques.

**Jones, James**, 1921–77, American novelist. Written in the tradition of NATURALISM, his powerful novels include *From Here to Eternity* (1951), his best-known work; *Some Came Running* (1957); and *The Thin Red Line* (1962).

**Jones, John Paul**, 1747–92, American naval hero; b. Scotland. In the AMERICAN REVOLUTION he raided British shipping in the waters off Great Britain. He captured the British warship *Drake* (1778) and, whilst commanding the *Bon Homme Richard,* captured the *Serapis* (1779). When he was asked to surrender his badly damaged ship in the latter battle, Jones defiantly replied, 'Sir, I have not yet begun to fight.'

**Jones, Mary Harris**, 1830–1930, American labour leader, known as Mother Jones; b. Ireland. She won fame as an orator and labour organizer and for more than half a century after 1870 was active in every major strike.

**Jones, Sir William**, 1746–94, English philologist and jurist. Celebrated for his understanding of jurisprudence and of Oriental languages, he was for 11 years a supreme court judge in Calcutta. He was the first to suggest that SANSKRIT had the same source as Latin and Greek, thus laying the foundation for modern comparative philology.

**Jongkind, Johann Barthold** (ˌjongkint), 1819–91, Dutch landscape painter and etcher. His work forms a transition between the BARBIZON SCHOOL and IMPRESSIONISM. He is known for his etchings of marine scenes.

**jonquil:** see AMARYLLIS.

**Jonson, Ben**, 1572–1637, English dramatist and poet. At first an actor, he produced his first important play, *Every Man in His Humour,* in 1598 and *Every Man out of His Humour* in 1599. *The Poetaster* (1601) satirized fellow playwrights. After collaborating with CHAPMAN and MARSTON on *Eastward Ho!* (1604), he entered his great period, marked by the comic masterpieces *Volpone* (1606), *Epicoene* (1609), *The Alchemist* (1610), and *Bartholomew Fair* (1614) all characterized by biting satire and tightly structured plots involving intrigue and deceit. A moralist, he aimed to inspire virtue by exaggerating the foibles and passions (humours) of his characters. Jonson became a court dramatist of JAMES I and wrote court MASQUES, as well as two Roman tragedies, *Sejanus* (1603) and *Catiline* (1611). After *The Devil Is an Ass* (1616), his dramatic career declined. Jonson's nondramatic poetry includes the collections *Epigrams* (1616); *The Forest* (1616), notable for the songs 'Drink to me only with thine eyes' and 'Come, my Celia, let us prove'; and *The Underwood* (1640), Jonson presided over a literary coterie, including Shakespeare, which met at the Mermaid Tavern, and he had many followers, generally known as the 'sons of Ben'.

**Joos of Ghent:** see JUSTUS OF GHENT.

**Jooss, Kurt**, 1901–79, German choreographer. Trained by LABAN, he is best known for his expressionistic, anti-war *Green Table* (1932). In England with Ballet Jooss during the Hitler era, he returned to Germany after World War II and became a leading figure in the development of central European MODERN DANCE.

**Joplin, Scott**, 1868–1917, black American ragtime pianist and composer. The best-known ragtime composer (see JAZZ), he wrote such works as 'Maple Leaf Rag' (1899) and the ragtime opera *Treemonisha* (1911).

**Jordaens, Jacob** (yaw,dahns), 1593–1678, Flemish BAROQUE painter. His works include religious, allegorical, and mythological pictures, and designs for tapestry. His style derives from that of RUBENS, whom he often assisted. Yet his pictures are more robust and earthy, and he delighted in folklore and proverb, and in genre scenes of boisterous merrymaking, e.g., *The King Drinks* (c.1640–45; Musées Royaux des Beaux Arts, Brussels). In his last years his style became more classical, as in the rigidly composed *Christ and the Doctors* (Mainz).

**Jordan**, officially Hashemite Kingdom of Jordan, kingdom (1985 est. pop. 3,337,000), 36,800 km² (94,400 sq mi), SW Asia, bordered by Israel (W), Syria (N), Iraq (NE), and Saudi Arabia (E, S). AMMAN is the capital and largest city. Jordan falls into three main geographical regions: East Jordan, part of the Arabian desert which encompasses about 92% of the country's land area; the Jordanian Highlands (highest point, 1754 m/5755 ft); and West Jordan, part of historic Palestine. In the Arab-Israeli War of 1967, Israel captured and occupied all of the WEST BANK of Jordan in the area W of the JORDAN R. and the DEAD SEA. The inhabitants of Jordan are mostly of Arab descent (about half are Palestinian refugees), and Arabic is the official language. About 90% of the people are Sunni Muslims. Jordan's economy is largely agricultural, although only about 10% of the land is arable. The principal crops are wheat, barley, lentils, tomatoes, vegetables, and citrus fruits. Manufactures are limited to basic items such as foodstuffs, clothing, and cement. Phosphate rock and potash are the only minerals produced in quantity. The annual cost of Jordan's imports far exceeds its earnings from exports. The GNP is US$3966 million and the GNP per capita is US$1180 (1984). Aqaba, on the Gulf of AQABA, is the only seaport.

*History.* This section deals primarily with the region east of the Jordan River; for the history of the area to the west, see PALESTINE. The region of present-day Jordan was conquered successively by the Seleucids (4th cent. BC), Romans (mid-1st cent. AD), and Muslim Arabs (7th. cent.). After the Crusaders captured (1099) Jerusalem, it became part of the Latin Kingdom of Jerusalem. The Ottoman Turks gained control in 1516, and what is now Jordan remained in the OTTOMAN EMPIRE until World War I. In 1922 The Amirate of Transjordan (as it was then known) was made part of the British mandate of Palestine. The country gained independence in 1946, and the name was changed (1949) to Jordan, reflecting its acquisition of land W of the Jordan R. during the Arab-Israeli War of 1948. ABDULLAH ibn Husain, a member of the Hashemite dynasty that headed Jordan since 1921, was assassinated in 1951. His grandson, HUSSEIN I, became king the following year. Jordanian forces were routed by Israel in the 1967 war (see ARAB–ISRAELI WARS), and Jordan lost the West Bank. Growing hostility between Hussein and the Palestine guerilla organizations operating in Jordan reached a climax during a brief civil war in 1970, and the guerilla bases were finally destroyed the following year. Under pressure from Arab states, Hussein renounced (1974) Jordanian claims to the West Bank in order to allow the PALESTINE LIBERATION ORGANIZATION (PLO) eventually to organize a state in this territory. Jordan also joined other Arab countries in opposing the 1979 peace treaty between Egypt and Israel, although it later (1984) reestablished relations with Cairo. Under the 1952 constitution, the king is the most powerful figure in the country; he appoints a cabinet (headed by a prime minister). A bicameral parliament, dissolved by Hussein in 1974, was recalled in 1984, although party activity remained circumscribed.

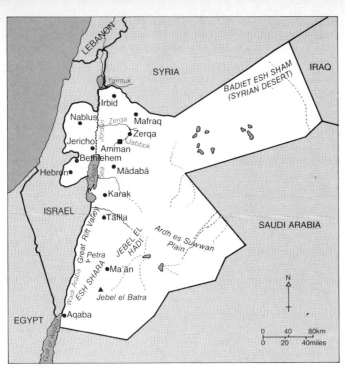

Jordan

**Jordan,** river, Israel and Jordan, c.320 km (200 mi) long. Its three major tributaries rise on the side of Mt Hermon in S Lebanon and N Israel. The united river flows south from near Dan to the DEAD SEA, rapidly falling below Mediterranean sea level. Its valley is part of the GREAT RIFT VALLEY. It flows through the sea of GALILEE (see GALILEE, SEA OF) at 209 m (686 ft) below sea level and then in a wide valley, the Ghor, where it forms the boundary between Israel and Jordan. Its major east bank tributary is the YARMUK R. and much of the combined waters are diverted for irrigation, some of it outside the Jordan valley, so that the level of the Dead Sea is now falling slowly. The reputed site of Christ's baptism is near JERICHO.

**Josaphat,** in the Bible: see JEHOSHAPHAT.

**Joseph,** rulers of the HOLY ROMAN EMPIRE. **Joseph I,** 1678–1711, emperor (r.1705–11) of Bohemia during the War of the SPANISH SUCCESSION and died before it ended. He vigorously supported the Spanish claims of his brother, who succeeded him as Emperor CHARLES VI. **Joseph II,** 1741–90, emperor (r.1765–90), king of Bohemia and Hungary (r.1780–90), was the son of MARIA THERESA and Emperor Francis I, whom he succeeded. Until his mother's death in 1780, he exerted little authority, but once in power he instituted far-reaching social, economic, and religious reforms, including the law (1781) abolishing serfdom. His aim was to abolish hereditary and ecclesiastical privileges by creating a centralized and unified state administered by a civil service based on merit. He liberalized the legal codes, reformed tax policies, and founded hospitals, orphanages, and asylums. His attacks on the church were unpopular and he was opposed by the nobles and the clergy. Most of his reforms did not outlive him. His foreign policy, focused on attempts to annexe Bavaria and his military adventures in Turkey, was generally not successful.

**Joseph,** kings of Bohemia and Hungary: see JOSEPH, rulers of the Holy Roman Empire.

**Joseph,** in the BIBLE, the favoured son of JACOB and RACHEL. He was sold into slavery by his brothers, who were jealous of his dreams and his coat of many colours. Taken to Egypt, Joseph rose to authority in the house of Potiphar, only to be imprisoned on the false accusations of Potiphar's wife. Released after interpreting Pharaoh's dream, Joseph rose in Pharaoh's favour. He was reunited with his family when, as governor of Egypt, he helped them during a famine. Gen. 30; 37; 39–50.

**Joseph, (Michael) Stephen,** 1921–67, English theatre producer. He founded the first two professional repertory theatres-in-the-round in England, the Victoria Theatre, Stoke-on-Trent and the Stephen Joseph

Theatre in Scarborough. The first became famous for its documentary dramas and the second for its director and playwright Alan AYCKBOURN.

**Joseph, Saint,** husband of the Virgin, a carpenter, a descendant of the house of DAVID. He is highly honoured in the orthodox Christian tradition as the chaste spouse of the Virgin MARY and the foster father of JESUS. Feast: 19 Mar.

**Josephine,** 1763–1814, empress of the French (1804–09) as the consort of NAPOLEON I. Born Marie Josèphe Rose Tascher de La Pagerie, in Martinique, she married (1779) Alexandre de BEAUHARNAIS, who was executed (1794) in the FRENCH REVOLUTION. In 1796 she married Napoleon, but he had the marriage annulled (1809) so that he might marry the Austrian princess MARIE LOUISE. Josephine thereafter lived in retirement.

**Josephus, Flavius** (joh‚seefəs), AD 37–95?, Jewish historian. A soldier, he took part in the war between the Romans and Jews and won the favour of the Roman general VESPASIAN. His works include *The Jewish War*, *Antiquities of the Jews*, and *Against Apion* (a defence of the Jews).

**Joshua** or **Josue,** book of the OLD TESTAMENT. It is a historical sequel to DEUTERONOMY, telling of the occupation of Palestine by the Hebrews. The chief figure is Joshua, MOSES' successor as leader of Israel. The book may be divided into three sections: the conquest of the Promised Land (1–12), the allotment of the land by tribes (13–22), and the farewell sermon and death of Joshua (23–24). The fall of Jericho (6) is a famous passage.

**Josquin Desprez** or **Des Prés,** c.1440–1521, Flemish composer, regarded as the greatest of his age. His earlier works were contrapuntal (see COUNTERPOINT); his later, more chordal. He composed 18 Masses, nearly 100 motets, and numerous chansons and secular pieces.

**joule** (J), unit of ENERGY and WORK, in the SI system of units (see METRIC SYSTEM). It is defined as the work done by a FORCE of one newton in moving its point of application through a distance of one metre.

**Joule, James Prescott,** 1818–89, English physicist. He established the mechanical theory of HEAT and was the first to determine the relationship between heat energy and mechanical energy (the mechanical equivalent of heat). Joule discovered the first law of THERMODYNAMICS, which is a form of the law of conservation of ENERGY. The mechanical unit of WORK, the joule, is named after him.

**journalism,** an industry devoted to the collection and periodic dissemination of news and information. Journalism begins with the age of print and extends and develops through radio and television broadcasting. In modern times it has become an international industry. News definition is not a matter of absolute values, as what is 'news' in one location might be of no interest elsewhere; consequently news definition and identity depends on the location, socioeconomic class, and political ideology of the consumer. From the very beginning of the industry the dissemination of news as a commodity has had very close connections with commerce. The first writers of newsletters were the financial correspondents employed by European finance houses whose task it was to keep their masters informed about commodity prices and currency exchange rates. Gradually court and political information became included and with the age of print the first newsheets appeared. Nathiel Butter (died 1664) was the first in London to print a regular weekly redactions of local and foreign news and half-yearly volumes of foreign news. Journalism is the trained and skilled professionalism which turns the raw information of such events into 'news' suitable for public consumption. The basic ingredients of news—catastrophes, births/marriages/deaths of the famous, crime, showbusiness, the unusual and human-interest stories—have changed very little since the 16th cent. Print journalism and commercial broadcasting depend considerably on advertising revenue for economic survival and this means that news selection and treatment is influenced by market factors; even public-service broadcasting, because it has to compete for ratings with the commercial channels, is not free from the market entirely. Journalism includes writing for, editing, and managing such media as the NEWSPAPER, the PERIODICAL, RADIO, and TELEVISION.

**Jouvet, Louis** (zhooh‚vay), 1887–1951, French actor and director. He was the first to produce and act in plays by GIRAUDOUX. He was also notable in *Dr Knock* (1923).

**Jove:** see JUPITER.

**Jovian,** c.331–64, Roman emperor (r.363–64). He made a humiliating peace with Persia and restored Christianity to the privileged position which it had held before JULIAN THE APOSTATE's reign.

**Joyce, James,** 1882–1941, Irish novelist. A major 20th-cent. writer in English, Joyce was a master of language, exploiting its total resources. Educated in Dublin Jesuit schools, he lived after 1904 on the continent, returning to Ireland only briefly. *Dubliners,* his short stories, was suppressed in Ireland because of topical references and published in London (1914). His autobiographical novel *A Portrait of the Artist as a Young Man* (1916) was followed by a play, *Exiles* (1918). *Ulysses,* his masterpiece of prose fiction, was published in Paris (1922), but banned in Britain and the United States for some years on grounds of obscenity. After 1922, Joyce worked on *Finnegans Wake* (1939); early instalments of this appeared under the title *Work in Progress.* With each major work, Joyce's profundity and complexity grew. *Dubliners* is indebted to French NATURALISM, but its indictment of Irish society and taut stylistic control are Joyce's own. In *A Portrait* the artist-hero, Stephen Dedalus, finds that his destiny requires him to free himself from the restrictions of his Irish upbringing. *Ulysses* recounts the events of 16 June 1904, in the actions and thoughts of the salesman Leopold Bloom, his wife, Molly, and Stephen Dedalus, now a homeless young poet. The book follows the design of HOMER's *Odyssey* in theme and image. With its shifts in consciousness, its rich allusion, and its play with language, it is a difficult but rewarding celebration of life. *Finnegans Wake* seems at times to present the dreams of a Dublin publican, at times to represent a universal consciousness. Its punning dream-language represents Joyce at his most experimental. His other works include two volumes of lyric verse, *Chamber Music* (1907) and *Pomes Penyeach* (1927), and *Stephen Hero* (1944), a fragmentary draft of *A Portrait.*

**József, Attila** (ˌyohzhef), 1905–37, Hungarian poet. Born in poverty, he published his first book at 17 and in 1930 joined the illegal Communist Party. After periods of schizophrenia he committed suicide. His compassionate poetry deals with political and existential themes.

**Juana Inés de la Cruz** (kroohs), 1651–95, Mexican poet and nun. Considered the greatest lyric poet of the colonial period, her long poem *Primero sueño* (1680; tr. First Dream) was her major achievement. She also wrote plays, both religious and worldly. Her last years were devoted to the spiritual life; she died aiding victims of an epidemic.

**Juan Carlos I** (hwahn ˌkahlos), 1938–, king of SPAIN (1975–). The grandson of ALFONSO VIII, he married (1962) Princess Sophia of Greece. Francisco FRANCO named him (1969) his successor as head of state. Upon Franco's death (1975), Juan Carlos became the first Spanish king since his grandfather was deposed in 1931. Personally popular, he proved to be a strong force for Spain's political stability and new democracy. In Feb. 1981 he successfully foiled an attempted right-wing military coup.

**Juan Fernández Islands,** archipelago in the Pacific belonging to Chile and situated 650 km (405 mi) W of Valparaiso. The islands were discovered by the Spanish in 1574; the Scottish sailor Alexander Selkirk was marooned on one of them from 1704 to 1709. Defoe's *Robinson Crusoe* was based on Selkirk's adventures and one of the islands has been renamed Robinson Crusoe; in 1984 a resolution to rename the other islands the Falklands was vetoed by the Chilean president. The islands currently have a permanent population of 550.

**Juan Manuel, Infante Don,** 1282–1348, Spanish prose writer. His works, which reflect his aristocratic upbringing and preoccupations, include the *Libro de los armas* (genealogy), *Libro de los estadas* (royal education), *Libro de la caza* (falconry), and *Libro de caballero y del escudero* (chivalry). The famous *Conde Lucanor* (1335), a collection of moral tales and fables, is a landmark in the development of Spanish prose-writing.

**Juárez** or **Ciudad Juárez,** city (1980 est. pop. 750,000), N Mexico, on the Río Grande, opposite El Paso, Texas. It is a cotton-processing centre and resort at the edge of a desert. First called El Paso del Norte, it was a base for Spanish colonial expansion northward and later served as the headquarters of Benito JUÁREZ, for whom it was renamed in 1888.

**Juárez, Benito** (ˌhwahrays), 1806–72, Mexican statesman. An Indian lawyer, he helped to overthrow (1855) SANTA ANNA's dictatorship and to limit the privileges of the church and army. He led the liberals to victory in the War of the Reform (1858–61) and, as president (1857–65, 1867–72), oversaw the transfer of political power in MEXICO from the creoles to the mestizos. Juárez defeated France's attempt (1864–67) to establish a Mexican empire and tried to implement reforms.

**Juda:** see JUDAH.

**Judaea** or **Judea** (joohˌdeeə), Greco-Roman name for S Palestine. At the time of Christ, it was both part of the province of Syria and a kingdom ruled by the HERODS.

**Judah** or **Juda,** in the BIBLE, fourth son of JACOB and Leah and the eponymous ancestor of one of the 12 tribes of Israel (see ISRAEL, TRIBES OF). Judah is a distinctive figure, a leader in the family counsels. His tribe gave its name to the Kingdom of Judah.

**Judah,** more southerly of two kingdoms created by the division of the kingdom of the JEWS under REHOBOAM. Judah, which lasted from 931 to 586 BC, had its capital in JERUSALEM and was ruled by the house of DAVID.

**Judah ha-Nasi** [prince] or **Judah I,** AD 135?–220?, religious and political leader of the Palestinian Jews and head of the SANHEDRIN. He collected and edited the Oral Law, which he compiled as the MISHNAH.

**Judaism,** the religious beliefs and practices and the way of life of the JEWS. Central to these is the notion of monotheism, adopted by the biblical Hebrews. In this early period there also developed a belief in the ultimate coming of God's kingdom on earth, a time of peace and justice. With the destruction (586 BC) of the First Temple and the consequent Babylonian captivity came the expectation of national restoration under the leadership of a MESSIAH. In Babylonia the Israelites were exposed to, and adopted, new ideas, e.g., the personification of evil (Satan) and the resurrection of the dead. In the post-exilic period (not later than the 5th cent. BC) began the practice of the public reading and exposition of the TORAH, or Pentateuch. These expositions—delivered in the Aramaic vernacular—were later collected in the Targumim. The conquests of Alexander the Great brought other new ideas, most significantly that of the immortality of the soul. Conflict over the acceptable level of Hellenization led to the revolt of the MACCABEES. As conditions of life deteriorated, apocalyptic beliefs grew: national catastrophe and the Messianic kingdom were seen as imminent events, particularly by sectarian groups, such as the Essenes whose theology is preserved in the Dead Sea Scrolls. Out of these beliefs grew both Christianity and classical, or rabbinic, Judaism. Rabbinic Judaism, which evolved over five centuries (until AD c.500), replaced the Temple with the SYNAGOGUE (the Second Temple was destroyed in AD 70), the priesthood with the RABBI, and sacrificial ceremony with the prayer service. Emphasis was placed on study of the Torah, on the growing need for national restoration in the Promised Land, and on the function of this world as preparatory for the World to Come. In the medieval period two new developments arose: the KABBALAH, influenced predominantly by NEOPLATONISM, and, opposed to it, rationalism, whose principal exponent was Maimonides (see MOSES MAIMONIDES). Although the Jewish Middle Ages extended into the 18th cent., the general European Renaissance had its Jewish counterpart, e.g., in the work of the poet Judah Ha-Levi. At the same time, the influence of the SEPHARDIM, particularly the Marranos, came to be felt, generally as a liberalizing force. The 18th cent. produced the great communal, rabbinic figure ELIJAH BEN SOLOMON (the Gaon of Vilna), the anti-establishment BAAL-SHEM-TOV, the founder of HASIDISM, and Moses MENDELSSOHN, spiritual progenitor of the later Reform movement. With the 19th cent. came the question of how Jews were to maintain tradition when the non-Jewish world demanded its abandonment. In Eastern Europe this problem was dealt with by the Haskalah, or Jewish enlightenment, movement, whose members, e.g., Nachman KROCHMAL, sought to revitalize Jewish life by recreating it along the lines of the best in European culture. Finally, in reaction to the needs of a persecuted people and to growing nationalistic desires ZIONISM arose, promising a return to the Holy Land. Ultimately, it was HALAKAH (the law) over which Jews divided; Orthodoxy regards halakah as derived from God and therefore authoritative, whereas Reform sees it as binding only in its ethical content. The Conservative movement assumes a middle position, maintaining most of the traditional rituals but recognizing a need for change in accordance with overriding contemporary considerations. Reconstructionist Judaism, a 20th-cent. movement, accepts all forms of Jewish practice, regarding Judaism as a culture rather than a theological system. See also JEWISH HOLIDAYS.

**Judas,** in the Bible. 1 See JUDE, SAINT. 2 Judas Maccabeus: see MACCABEES. 3 See JUDAS ISCARIOT.

**Judas Iscariot,** JESUS's betrayer, one of the Twelve Disciples. The chief priests paid him 30 pieces of silver for which he led soldiers to

Gethsemane and identified Jesus to them by kissing him. Later he repented and killed himself. The blood money bought a potter's field. The name Iscariot suggests he may have belonged to an anti-Roman sect, the Sicarii, and may have betrayed Jesus out of disappointment that Jesus was not the political Messiah he had looked for.

**Judas Maccabeus:** see MACCABEES.

**Judd, Donald,** 1928–, American sculptor. Associated with MINIMAL ART, he is known for geometric works in wood or steel painted with industrial pigments which stress the objective and nonexpressive elements of sculpture.

**Jude,** epistle of the NEW TESTAMENT. A Catholic, or General, EPISTLE, it warns against some heresy that led to immorality, and has a close literary relationship with Second PETER.

**Jude, Saint,** or **Saint Judas,** [Jude is an English form to distinguish him from JUDAS ISCARIOT], one of the Twelve Disciples; also called Lebbaeus and Thaddaeus.

**Judea:** see JUDAEA.

**Judges,** book of the OLD TESTAMENT. It tells of the Hebrews from Joshua's death until the time of SAMUEL. The religious interpretation, stated in an introduction, is that the book recounts Israel's successive apostasies and their consequences. The judges, primarily military leaders of the tribes, include Deborah, GIDEON, Jephthah, and SAMSON.

**judicial review,** the review by a court, of the decision of another body (e.g., a lower court or LEGISLATURE). In England and Wales, an individual with an interest in the matter can apply to the high court for review of the decision (or non-decision) of a lower court, TRIBUNAL, local authority or government department. Among the grounds for review are that the body has acted *ultra vires* (outside its powers), or has breached natural justice in taking the decision. If the court finds that one of the grounds exist, it may quash the decision; order a decision to be taken; or prohibit the decision from being implemented. In the US, judicial review is the name given to the doctrine developed by the US SUPREME COURT in MARBURY V. MADISON (1803), whereby the court can strike down a federal or state law that is contrary to the US CONSTITUTION.

**Judith,** book included in the OLD TESTAMENT of the Western canon and the Septuagint but not in the Hebrew Bible, and placed in the APOCRYPHA in the Authorized Version. It tells of an armed attack on the Jewish city of Bethulia and of how Judith, a beautiful widow, saved the city by killing Holofernes, the enemy leader. The book probably dates from before 100 BC.

**judo:** see MARTIAL ARTS.

**Judson, Adoniram,** 1788–1850, American Baptist missionary. He led the movement out of which grew the American Board of Commissioners for Foreign Missions. Sailing (1812) to India as a Congregational minister, he became a Baptist and went (1813) to Burma, where he remained for 30 years. Judson compiled an English–Burmese dictionary and translated the Bible into Burmese.

**Jugurtha,** d. 104 BC, king of Numidia (r.113–105 BC). His uncle left the kingdom jointly to Jugurtha and his own sons Hiempsal and Adherbal. When Jugurtha had Hiempsal murdered, the Roman senate intervened to divide Numidia between him and Adherbal. Jugurtha attacked and killed Adherbal in a savage massacre (112 BC); Rome, after several reverses, finally sent an army which under MARIUS defeated (106–105 BC) Jugurtha who was brought to Rome and executed.

**Juiz de Fora** (khwiz day ‚fawra), city (1980 pop. 299,432), central Brazil, in Minas Gerais state 150 km (93 mi) N of Rio de Janeiro. It is situated in the deep valley of the Paraibuna R. and provides an important routeway between Rio de Janeiro and Belo Horizonte. It has important industries including steel-making, textiles, and sugar-refining.

**jujitsu:** see MARTIAL ARTS.

**Julia,** feminine name in the Julian gens. **1** Died 54 BC, daughter of Julius CAESAR and wife of POMPEY. She maintained the bond between them, but after her death they became open enemies. **2** 39 BC–AD 14, daughter of AUGUSTUS and wife, in turn, of Marcus Claudius Marcellus (d. 23 BC), Marcus Vipsanius Agrippa, and TIBERIUS. Her infidelities caused her banishment by Augustus. Soon after Tiberius became emperor, she died of starvation.

**Juliana,** 1909–, queen of the NETHERLANDS (1948–80). She succeeded her mother, WILHELMINA, and abdicated in favour of her eldest daughter, BEATRIX.

**Julian of Norwich,** c.1343–after 1413, English mystic. In 1373, while seriously ill, she experienced a sequence of revelations, about which she wrote in her *Book of Showings*, a moving and original prose work, which is the earliest English text attributable to a woman.

**Julian the Apostate,** 331?–363, Roman emperor (r.361–63); nephew of CONSTANTINE I. A scholar, writer, and general, he was a just ruler who sponsored far-reaching legislation. He decreed religious toleration but tried unsuccessfully to restore paganism. Killed in battle, he was succeeded by JOVIAN.

**Julius I, Saint,** pope (337–52), a Roman. When asked for his opinion on ARIANISM, he summoned a council at Rome (340). The Arians did not come, and Julius wrote them a letter, chiding them for lack of sincerity; the letter was remarkable as an early claim to papal jurisdiction over the whole church. Feast: 12 Apr.

**Julius II,** 1443–1513, pope (1503–13), an Italian named Giuliano della Rovere. A warrior, he completed the work of his enemy, Cesare BORGIA, of restoring the Papal States to the church and took a vigorous part in the ITALIAN WARS. Julius assembled (1512) the Fifth Lateran Council, which declared papal elections tainted with simony null. An art patron, he favoured RAPHAEL (who painted his portrait), MICHELANGELO, and BRAMANTE. He laid the cornerstone of St Peter's, Rome. Worldly as Julius was, he was one of the first to try to break the hold of Renaissance corruption on Rome.

**Julius Caesar:** see CAESAR, JULIUS.

**July:** see MONTH.

**July Revolution,** revolt in France in July 1830 against CHARLES X. The attempt of the ultraroyalists under Charles to return to the *ancien régime* provoked opposition from the more liberal middle class. When Charles's minister, Jules Armand de Polignac, issued the July Ordinances, which controlled the press, dissolved the newly elected chamber of deputies, and reduced the electorate, insurrection followed. Charles fled and abdicated, and LOUIS PHILIPPE was proclaimed king.

**June:** see MONTH.

**Juneau** (jooh‚noh, ‚joohnoh), US city (1980 pop. 19,528), state capital of Alaska, in the Alaska Panhandle; settled by gold miners 1880, inc. 1900. Lying at the foot of two lofty peaks, it has an ice-free harbour. Government, fishing, timber, and tourism are important in the city's economy. It has been Alaska's capital since 1906. The city is the largest in area in the US (8050 km²/3108 sq mi).

**June Days,** insurrection of French workingmen in June 1848. After the FEBRUARY REVOLUTION of 1848, the workers sought economic and social reform, but the triumph of the bourgeoisie dashed their hopes. When a workshop experiment was abolished (21 June), workers in Paris rebelled and were harshly suppressed after four days (23–26 June) of street fighting. The events encouraged social analysis in CLASS terms.

**Jung, Carl Gustav** (yoong), 1875–1961, Swiss psychoanalyst. He was an early associate of Sigmund FREUD and first president of the International Psychoanalytical Association, but broke with Freud when he published his *Psychology of the Unconscious* (1912), which introduced the concept of the 'collective unconscious'. Jung intended this as a complementary dimension to the 'personal unconscious' of Freudian PSYCHOANALYSIS. The collective unconscious consists of 'archetypical' symbols, images, or narratives, common either to members of a culture or to humanity as a whole which may be manifested in dreams, fairy tales, or myths. Jung also introduced the EXTRAVERSION–INTROVERSION distinction in personality theory. His version of psychoanalysis is termed 'analytical psychology'. Jung's collected works were published in English (1951–79).

**Jungaria:** see DZUNGARIA.

**Jünger, Ernst** (‚yynga), 1895–, German writer, brother of the poet Friedrich Georg Jünger. He volunteered as an officer in World War I and won the *Pour le mérite* in 1918. His *Storm of Steel* (1920) fostered the mystique of militarism. Later his imagination was captured by the idea of the elitist technological state (*Total Mobilization*, 1931; *The Worker*, 1932), but he was as much a dandy as a conservative revolutionary, and after Hitler came to power he soon retreated, disillusioned, into the army. Stationed in Paris in World War II, he has maintained a high reputation among the French right, although his novels *On the Marble Cliffs* (1939) and *Heliopolis* (1949) have been read as coded resistance texts. His postwar writing ranges from war diaries (*Gardens and Highways*, 1942; *Radiances*, 1949–66), through Huxley-like drug experiments (*Visit to Gordenholm*, 1952) to his novel *The Sling* (1973) and the late journal *Seventy Passed* (1981).

**jungle fowl,** forest-dwelling member of the PHEASANT family, found in S Asia and W Indonesia. The red jungle fowl (*Gallus gallus*) is probably the ancestor of the domestic CHICKEN. It is an extremely wary bird, scratching the forest floor for seeds and insects during the day and roosting in the trees at night. In Australia the name is given to brush turkeys, but these are not true jungle fowl.

**juniper,** aromatic evergreen tree or shrub (genus *Juniperus*) of the CYPRESS family, widely distributed over the north temperate zone. Many are important sources of lumber and oil. The insect-repellent wood of the red cedar (*J. virginiana*) is especially valuable for furniture, such as wardrobes, and posts; the oil is used in medicine and perfumery. The common juniper (*J. communis*) in its many varieties, and other species showing a wide range of growth forms from prostrate, creeping, to tall, pyramidal, are grown ornamentally; its fruits are used to flavour GIN.

**Junius,** pseud. of an English political writer. His letters, sent to the London *Public Advertiser* (Nov. 1768–Jan. 1772), attacked GEORGE III and his ministers, and centred on the John WILKES controversy. His identity remains a mystery.

**Juno,** in Roman mythology, wife and sister of JUPITER; great goddess of the state. Like the Greek HERA, she was the protectress of women.

**Jupiter,** in astronomy, 5th PLANET from the Sun, at a mean distance of 778.3 million km (483.6 million mi), and largest planet in the solar system, with an equatorial diameter of 143,800 km (89,400 mi). It is a gaseous planet with an atmosphere composed mostly of hydrogen and helium, with traces of methane, ammonia, and other gases, and about five or six zones each of counterflowing eastward- and westward-flowing winds. The most prominent atmospheric features (all in the southern hemisphere) are the Great Red Spot, at least 300 years old and measuring c.48,000 by 16,000 km (30,000 by 10,000 mi), and three large white ovals that formed in 1939. Jupiter has 16 known natural satellites, 12 of which are of small diameter. The four larger Galilean satellites were discovered by GALILEO in 1610. **Callisto** (diameter: 4820 km/2995 mi), the most distant and the least active geologically of the four, has a heavily cratered surface. **Ganymede** (diameter: 5276 km/3279 mi), second most distant of the four and the largest satellite in the solar system, has heavily cratered regions, tens of kilometres across, that are surrounded by younger, grooved terrain. **Europa** (diameter: 3126 km/1942 mi) is a white, highly reflecting body whose smooth surface is entirely covered with dark streaks up to 70 km in width and from several hundred to several thousand kilometers in length. **Io** (diameter: 3632 km/2257 mi), the closest to Jupiter of the four, is the most active geologically, with eight active volcanoes that are probably energized by the tidal effects of Jupiter's enormous mass. The red colour of **Amalthea** (diameter: 240 km/150 mi), a small, elongated satellite interior to Io's orbit that was discovered (1892) by Edward BARNARD, probably results from a coating of sulphur particles ejected from Io. Four SPACE PROBES have encountered the Jovian system: *Pioneers 10* and *11* (1973 and 1974) and *Voyagers 1* and *2* (both 1979). The latter two discovered Io's volcanoes, a thin ring system surrounding Jupiter, and three of the smaller satellites. The US space probe *Galileo* will orbit Jupiter in the mid 1990s and send a probe into the planet's atmosphere.

**Jupiter,** in Roman mythology, supreme god; also called Jove; son of SATURN and Ops; brother and husband of JUNO. Originally an agricultural god, he developed into the prime protector of the state and was identified with the Greek ZEUS. His temple stood on the CAPITOL at Rome.

**Jura** (ˌjooərə), upland area of limestone hills and plateaux on the Swiss-French border, extending from the RHONE R. at GENEVA to the RHINE R. at BASEL. HUGUENOT refugees made use of the resources of minerals, forests and pastures to develop small-scale industries. Many of these survive in highly specialized forms and include cheese-making and the manufacture of clocks and watches, toys, jewellery, pipes, and spectacles.

**Jupiter** taken from *Voyager I* at a distance of 28.4 million kilometres, showing its great Red Spot (bottom left) and three of its four largest satellites.

**Jurassic period:** see GEOLOGICAL ERA (table).

**jurisprudence,** the study of law in the abstract, without reference to particular substantive areas. Jurisprudence has traditionally encompassed the examination of legal concepts (e.g., rights, justice, and authority) the SOCIOLOGY of law, and legal PHILOSOPHY. Sociological jurisprudence is concerned with the (changing) role of law in society. Its main contribution has come from sociologists, e.g., Emile DURKHEIM and Max WEBER. Legal philosophy is concerned with the definition of law, and has a history going back to ARISTOTLE. Early studies were dominated by the theory of natural law, which held that law was only valid if it accorded to certain universal moral principles, that could be established through reason. In modern times, natural law has been superseded by legal POSITIVISM, which holds that law is to be valid if passed by a sovereign body (e.g., PARLIAMENT), and that no question of morality enters into the definition of law. Influential positivists have included Jeremy BENTHAM, Hans KELSEN and H.L.A. HART.

**jury,** in common law, a group of laypersons, summoned to study the EVIDENCE, an determine the facts in a dispute tried in a court of law. The jury was probably brought to England by the NORMAN CONQUEST (11th cent.). Early juries consisted of people with personal knowledge of the dispute. In England, until the decision in BUSHELL'S CASE (1670), the jury were liable to be imprisoned for reaching a verdict the judge disagreed with. Since then an objective jury has reached its decision solely on the basis of the evidence heard. In criminal cases, the jury is available for indictable offences (see INDICTMENT), but not for summary offences, which are tried before a Magistrates' Court. It is rarely used in civil cases. The jury consists of 12 laypersons, chosen from the local community, though until 1969 only householders were qualified for jury service. Traditionally, jury verdicts were required to be unanimous, but since 1968 a majority of 10 has been sufficient to convict. In the US, a distinction is made between a grand jury, which considers whether sufficient evidence exists to bring a prosecution, and a petty jury, which sits at the full trial and delivers the verdict.

**justice of the peace:** see MAGISTRATE.

**Justin I,** c.450–527, Byzantine emperor (518–27). He strongly opposed MONOPHYSITISM and had close relations with the Western Church. Lacking education, he entrusted government to his nephew, who succeeded him as JUSTINIAN I.

**Justinian I,** 483–565, Byzantine emperor (527–65), nephew of JUSTIN I. His heavy taxes and the discontent of the Monophysites (see MONOPHYSITISM) involved internal political factions in the Nika riot, which was crushed (532) by Empress THEODORA. She was helped by two generals, BELISARIUS and NARSES, who had recovered Africa and Italy for the empire. Justinian advocated caesaro-papism, i.e., the supremacy of emperor even over church, and called the Second Council of Constantinople (553) in a fruitless effort to reconcile the Monophysites to the church. His chief accomplishment was the codification of ROMAN LAW. His many public works included the church of HAGIA SOPHIA.

**Justin Martyr, Saint,** c.100–c.165, Christian apologist. He opened a school of Christian philosophy at Rome, where he was martyred. Two undisputed works remain, both philosophic defences of Christian doctrine, the *Apology* and the *Dialogue*. Feast: 1 June.

**Justus of Ghent,** fl. c.1460–c.1480, Flemish religious and portrait painter, known as Jodocus or Joos of Ghent. His simple, quiet style provides a clear link between Flemish and Italian art, e.g., the *Adoration of the Magi* (late 1460s; Metropolitan Mus., New York).

**jute,** tropical annual (genus *Corchorus*) of the LINDEN family, and its fibre. Although the fibre, of comparatively low CELLULOSE content, is weak and deteriorates quickly, it is the principal coarse fibre in commercial production; chief sources are *C. capsularis* and *C. olitorius*. India is the unrivalled world producer and processor. Easily dyed and spun, jute is used for coarse fabrics, especially burlap and sacking, and for twine, rope, and insulation.

**Jutland,** peninsula, c.400 km (250 mi) long and up to 177 km (110 mi) wide, N Europe, occupied by parts of Denmark (N) and W Germany (S). Danish Jutland, which includes most of the peninsula, covers 29,632 km² (11,441 sq mi) with adjacent islands and contains about half of Denmark's population.

**Jutland, Battle of,** 31 May 1916, only major naval engagement between the British and German fleets in WORLD WAR I. They met off the coast of JUTLAND, in Denmark. The outnumbered German fleet performed brilliantly and escaped in the fog. The tactics of the British commander, Admiral JELLICOE, and the heavy British losses caused much controversy.

**Juvenal** (Decimus Junius Juvenalis) fl. 1st–2nd cent. AD, Roman satiric poet. His verse established a model for the SATIRE of indignation. Written from the stern viewpoint of older standards, his 16 satires denounce a lax and luxurious society, tyranny, affectations, and immorality; the form is terse, polished, and epigrammatic.

**juvenile court:** see COURT SYSTEM IN ENGLAND AND WALES.

**K,** chemical symbol of the element POTASSIUM.

**K2** or **Mount Godwin Austen,** world's second highest peak, 8611 m (28,250 ft) high, in the Karakoram range, N Kashmir, at the Chinese border. It was discovered and measured by the Survey of India in 1856 and first climbed in 1954 by an Italian team led by Ardito Desio.

**Kaaba,** the most sacred spot in ISLAM enclosed by a sanctuary, the Great Mosque at MECCA. It is a cubical object built to enclose the Black Stone, the most venerated object for Muslims. It is to the Kaaba that Muslims turn during their prayers, and walking round it is the high point of HAJJ, the Muslim pilgrimage. Non-Muslims are forbidden to approach it, and Muslims generally attribute its construction to Abraham.

**Kabalega** or **Kabarega,** c.1850–1923, last independent ruler of the Bunyoro kingdom, UGANDA, (r.1869–99). He successfully revived the authority of the state after the ruin wrought by a war with his brother for the succession. He fought off the aggression of the Baganda and the Egyptians during the 1870s and 80s but succumbed to British imperialism in the 1890s. He was deposed and exiled in 1899.

**Kabalevsky, Dmitri,** 1904–86, Soviet composer, originally destined for a career in mathematics and economics. His many works, melodic and harmonically conservative, include the opera *Colas Breugnon* (1938); the OPERETTA *The Sisters* (1967), three piano concertos (1928, 1936, and 1952) and chamber works. He was especially active as a writer on music and was a key figure in the Union of Soviet Composers, which was founded in 1932.

**kabbalah** [Heb., = traditional lore], mystical Jewish system of interpretation of the Scriptures. Kabbalah is based on the belief that every word, letter, number, and even accent of the Scriptures contains mysteries. Kabbalistic signs and writings were used as amulets and in magical practices. Kabbalah has two principal written sources. The first, *Sefer Yezirah* (tr. *Book of Creation*), probably written in the 3rd cent., is a series of monologues supposedly delivered by the patriarch Abraham. The second, *Zohar*, is a mystical commentary on the Pentateuch written by Moses de Leon (13th cent.) but attributed to Simon ben Yohai, a great scholar of the 2nd cent. The movement appears to have arisen in 11th-cent. France and spread from there, most notably to Spain. After the expulsion of the Jews from Spain in 1492, kabbalah became messianic in emphasis, especially as developed by Isaac Luria. This form of kabbalah had many adherents, including the pseudo-Messiah Sabbatai Zevi. It was also a major influence in the development of 18th-cent. HASIDISM.

**Kabuki:** see Japanese drama under ORIENTAL DRAMA.

**Kabul,** city (1979 pop. 913,164), capital of Afghanistan and its largest city and economic and cultural centre, E Afghanistan, on the Kabul R. Manufactures include textiles, beet sugar, ordnance, and machinery. Strategically located, the city, whose history dates back more than 3000 years, became Afghanistan's capital in 1773. It has been destroyed and rebuilt many times. It has an old quarter, with narrow, crooked streets, and a modern section. Kabul has a university (est. 1931), numerous colleges, and a fine museum. From 1979–89 the city was occupied by Soviet troops, the most recent in a series of foreign conquerors.

**Kádár, János** (ˌkahdah), 1912–, Hungarian Communist leader. He was imprisoned (1951–54) for alleged pro-Titoism. In the 1956 uprising (see HUNGARY) he first joined the cabinet of Imre NAGY but then formed a counter-government with support from the USSR, which crushed the revolt. He was premier (1956–58, 1961–65) and became first secretary of the party in 1956. Kádár instituted substantial economic liberalization from the early 1960s. In 1989 he lost all his offices.

**Kaduna,** city (1987 est. pop. 202,000), capital of Kaduna state, N Nigeria, at the main junction of the Nigerian railway system linking north and south. A city which has grown rapidly in recent years due to rural-urban migration, it is noted for its many cotton textile mills and has become a centre of the oil industry. In 1917 it became capital of the Northern Provinces at the instigation of Lord Lugard, first British Governor of N Nigeria. It was also capital of the Northern Region from 1954 to 1967.

**Kaendler, Johann Joachim** (ˌkendlə), 1706–75, German sculptor and porcelain figure modeller. Kaendler joined the MEISSEN porcelain factory in 1731 and was promoted Modelmeister (chief modeller) in 1733. During the 1730s and 40s he developed a European idiom for porcelain figures, previously heavily influenced by Oriental examples, exploiting a wide range of themes, such as the Commedia dell'Arte, aristocratic pastimes and low life. His animals are exceptionally lifelike and his human figures have bold gestures, witty characterization and superb modelling. They were copied and adapted by many European factories.

**Kafka, Franz,** 1883–1924, German novelist and short-story writer, of a Jewish family; b. Prague. In remarkably clear and precise prose, Kafka presents a world at once real and dreamlike, in which modern people, burdened with guilt, isolation, and anxiety, make a futile search for personal salvation. Among his symbolic novels are *Der Prozess* (1925; tr. The Trial), *Das Schloss* (1926; tr. The Castle), and *Amerika* (1927). Important stories include *The Metamorphosis* (1915), *The Judgment* (1916), 'A Country Doctor' (1919), and 'In the Penal Colony' (1919), all translated into English, as are his diaries (1948–49) and several volumes of correspondence.

**Kagoshima,** city (1986 est. pop. 524,638), capital of Kagoshima prefecture, on the southermost tip of Kyushu island, Japan. A port on Kagoshima Bay, the city is overlooked by the still active volcano of Mt Sakurajima. Kagoshima is the major economic and transport centre of S Kyushu with air links to the southern islands, SE Asia, and Nauru. The city was a prosperous castle town when St Francis Xavier, the Spanish Jesuit, arrived (1549) to be the first Christian missionary to Japan. For a while it was the most advanced industrial centre in Japan, when, just before the Meiji Restoration (1868), the lord Shimazu sent 17 young clansmen to learn about modern English industrial technology and to import modern machines. Kagoshima is developing as a centre of high-technology industries.

**Kagwa, Apolo,** c.1869–1927, prime minister (1885–1926) of Buganda (now part of UGANDA). From humble origins (he began his career as a page at the court of MUTESA I) he rose to become commander of the royal guards. He became prime minister after helping to restore MWANGA II to the throne. When Mwanga revolted against the British, Kagwa collaborated with the Europeans and was rewarded by being recognized as regent and leader of the Ganda after Mwanga's defeat in 1899. He wrote the first modern histories of the Ganda to be written by an E African.

**Kahn, Louis Isadore,** 1901–74, American architect; b. Estonia. From the 1920s he worked on many housing projects, e.g., Carver Court

(1944), Coatesville, Pennylvania. He also planned the Yale Univ. Art Gallery and the Kimbell Art Museum, Fort Worth, Texas, and exerted wide influence as a professor.

**Kaiser, Georg** (ˌkiezə), 1878–1945, German expressionist playwright. His early plays treat erotic and psychological themes. Later he explored social questions, attacking the brutality of the machine age in *From Morning to Midnight* (1916), and the trilogy *The Corals* (1917), *Gas* (1918) and *Gas II* (1920).

**Kakadu,** national park in Northern Territory, northern Australia. It lies to the E of Darwin in Arnhem Land and is drained by the East and South Alligator Rs. Natural rock galleries contain outstanding Aboriginal paintings, the best-known site being Ubirr (Obiri Rock). Large tropical wetlands provide rich breeding grounds for rare local and annually migrating birds; one-third of all Australian bird species are found here. The park is a sanctuary for large saltwater and smaller freshwater crocodiles. Feral buffaloes, descendants of Asian water buffalo brought from Timor in the early 19th cent. to early British settlements on the northern coast, have created a major environmental threat to the wetlands' ecology. The development of rich mineral deposits, including the controversial Ranger uranium mines at Jabiru, presents another threat.

**kakapo** or **owl parrot,** flightless PARROT living in the rainforests of New Zealand. The kakapo (*Strigops habroptilus*) is 50 cm (20 in) long, nocturnal, and rarely seen. It hides in crevices and tree cavities during the day, feeding at night on grasses and fruits. It climbs trees, like any parrot, with claws and bill, and can glide back to the ground with its small, soft wings.

**Kakiemon,** Japanese family of potters whose kilns were near Arita. Sakaida Kakiemon I, 1596–1666, was reputedly the first Japanese to paint porcelain on glaze in enamel colours. His immediate successors were probably responsible for developing the style of decoration named after them. In the late 17th and early 18th cent. much Kakiemon porcelain was exported to Europe and was imitated at MEISSEN, Chantilly, Chelsea, WORCESTER, and elsewhere. Its milky-white paste is sparsely decorated with asymmetrically placed motifs in blue, orange–red, yellow and green, sometimes with black outlines and a little gilding. Among the best-known designs are 'quail and millet', 'tiger and bamboo', and a figure subject known in England as 'Hob-in-the-Well'.

Late 17th-cent. **Kakiemon** dish

**Kakinada** (formerly **Cocanada**), town (1981 pop. 226,409), Andhra Pradesh state, E India, on the coast of the northern end of the GODAVARI delta. It is the administrative centre of East Godavari dist.; and is a minor port, hampered by siltation so that larger vessels have to stand off. It has developed a number of industries: salt evaporation and the processing of agricultural produce are of long standing, while more recently has come metallurgical manufactures. As with other places on India's east coast, Kakinada's use as a port goes back to medieval times or earlier; but with a long struggle against siltation.

**kala-azar:** see LEISHMANIASIS.

**Kalahari,** arid desert area, c.259,000 km² (100,000 sq mi), SW Africa, with a yearly rainfall ranging from 12.7 cm (5 in) in the southwest to 50.8 cm (20 in) in the northeast. The nomadic San (or Bushmen) and Khoikhoi are among the principal inhabitants.

**kalam** (kaˌlam), [Arab., = enunciation], Islamic dogmatic theology. From its beginnings in the late 8th–early 9th cent. as a dialectical weapon against Christian and Zoroastrian polemics to its peak in the 12th cent., kalam maintained positions stretching from the complete reliance on faith of some of the adherents of HANBALISM through the qualified mixture of faith and reasoning of Ashari and his school to the systematic philosophical rationalism of late Asharism (with Juwaini, GHAZALI, and Razi in the 11th–13th cent.) and the polemical rationalism of early Mu'tazilism, which had been proclaimed official state doctrine by some ABBASID caliphs in the 9th cent. The main preoccupations of kalam concerned divine attributes, the relative status of reason and revelation, and the theory of the imamate. For various reasons, Ash'arism became associated with the Shafi'i and Maliki schools of Sunni law, Mu'tazilism became associated with central Asian Hanafism. See FIQH; IMAM; MU'TAZILA.

**Kaldor, Nicholas,** 1908–86, British economist; b. Hungary. He graduated (1930) at the London School of Economics, where he remained as a lecturer for many years. He was Director of the Research and Planning Division of the Economic Commission of Europe (1947–49) and later served the Royal Commission on Taxation of Profits and Incomes. Kaldor was appointed professor of economics at Cambridge Univ. and served as special adviser to the UK chancellor of the exchequer on two occasions (1964–68 and 1974–76). He was a firm believer in the long-term capital-gains tax and selective employment tax. His macroeconomic theory on distribution explains the relative shares of the different factors of production in national income. One of its objectives was to explain the constancy of the relative shares of wages and profits in the national income, which could be observed over an historical period. His theory differs from the traditional microeconomic approach.

**kale,** and **collards,** common names for nonheading types of CABBAGE (mostly of the variety *acephala*), cool-weather crops of the MUSTARD family. They are grown for their edible greens and, in Europe, for fodder.

**Kalends:** see CALENDAR.

**Kalevala,** the title of Finland's national epic poem of ancient life in the far north, subtitled *The Land of Heroes*. It tells of Väinämöinen, the god of music and poetry, and Ilmarinen the smith, and how the north heroes of ancient myth fought with magic and sword against the powers of darkness. *Kalevala* was compiled from popular lays transmitted orally until the 19th cent., and constructed into coherent form by the Finnish physician and later professor of Finnish, Dr Elias Lönnrot (1802–84), in two versions: the shorter *Old Kalevala* in 1835, and the longer version of 23,000 lines in 1849. The metre is the alliterative eight-syllabled trochaic verse of *Hiawatha*. *Kalevala* was the inspiration for the independence movement in the 19th cent. for national culture and identity, and has been translated into more than 30 languages.

**Kalgoorlie,** town (1986 pop. 22,232), Western Australia. The state's fifth largest centre, the town was established in 1893 when gold was discovered; it is now the centre of gold and nickel mining and processing, and treats ore from nearby Boulder and Kambalda. Major new discoveries of ore were made in 1966.

**Kālī** [Hindi, = the Black One], important goddess in popular HINDUISM and TANTRA, associated with destructive forces. In popular HINDUISM, Kālī is regarded as the mother goddess who kills demons, the impersonations of evil.

**Kalidasa** (ˈkahliˌdahsə), fl. 5th cent.?, Indian dramatist and poet, the greatest figure in classical SANSKRIT LITERATURE. His three surviving plays *Shakuntala, Vikramorvasi,* and *Malavikagnimitra* are court dramas in verse and relate fanciful or mythological tales of romantic love ripened by adversity. He also wrote fine epic and lyric poetry.

**Kalimantan:** see BORNEO.

**Kaliningrad,** formerly Königsberg, city (1985 pop. 385,000), W European USSR, on the Pregolya R. An ice-free Baltic seaport and naval base, it produces ships and machinery. Königsberg, in E Prussia, was founded (1255) as a fortress of the TEUTONIC KNIGHTS and joined (1340) the HANSEATIC LEAGUE. The Univ. of Königsberg (founded 1544) reached its greatest fame when KANT taught there. The city became part of the USSR in 1945 and was renamed after the Soviet leader Mikhail KALININ. Most of the population is now Russian.

**Kalmar Union,** combination of the crowns of Denmark, Sweden, and Norway, effected at Kalmar, Sweden, by MARGARET I in 1397. Because all three crowns were elective, the union could not be maintained by inheritance. Margaret's successors controlled Sweden intermittently until GUSTAVUS I of Sweden dissolved the union (1523). Norway became independent in 1814.

**Kamakura,** city (1986 est. pop. 176,569), central Honshu, Japan, on Sagami Bay. A religious centre and resort, Kamakura is famous for its 12.8-m/42-ft-high bronze Buddha, cast in 1252. The city was the seat of Yoritomo, the first SHOGUN, and his descendants, the Hōjo family (1192–1333); under the Ashikaga Shogunate (1333–1573), it was the government headquarters of E Japan and a centre of Zen Buddhism.

**Kamakura period,** 1185–1333, period in Japanese history named after Kamakura, a town near modern Tokyo, which was the base of the shogunate established by MINAMOTO NO YORITOMO. It marked the beginning of the dominance of the SAMURAI class in Japanese history. See also SHOGUN.

**Kamchatka,** peninsula, c.1210 km (750 mi) long, NE USSR, projecting SW from the Asian mainland between the Sea of Okhotsk (W) and the Bering Sea and Pacific Ocean (E). It is traversed by two parallel volcanic ranges containing the only active volcanoes in the USSR, and has a cold and humid climate. Fishing (notably for crabs), seal hunting, fur-trapping, and tree-felling are the main occupations. The population is predominantly Russian, with large Koryak minorities.

**Kamehameha I** (kah͵mayhahmayhə), c.1738–1819, Hawaiian king. He was king of the island of Hawaii after 1790 and through conquest became (1810) ruler of all the Hawaiian islands.

**Kamenev, Lev Borisovich** (͵kahminyif), 1883–1936, Soviet Communist leader; b. L.B. Rosenfeld. After the RUSSIAN REVOLUTION (1917) he was a member of the first politburo of the Communist party. When LENIN died (1924), Kamenev, STALIN, and ZINOVIEV excluded TROTSKY from power, but in 1925 the Stalinist majority defeated Kamenev and Zinoviev, who joined Trotsky's opposition. In 1936 Kamenev, with Zinoviev and others, was tried for treason and executed.

**kamikaze** [Jap., = divine wind], term applied to the suicide tactics used by the Japanese at the end of WORLD WAR II and particularly the suicide pilots. The first kamikaze attack took place on 25 Oct. 1944 and more than 1000 planes and pilots had been lost by the time Japan surrendered. Originally, kamikaze was the name given to the storms that destroyed the Mongol fleets off the Japanese coast in 1274 and 1281.

**Kampala,** largest city (1983 pop. 454,974) and capital of Uganda, on VICTORIA NYANZA (Lake Victoria). It is linked by railway to SW Uganda and Mombasa, Kenya, and by ships crossing the lake to ports in Kenya and Tanzania. The city is built on and around six hills. An international airport is nearby, at ENTEBBE. Kampala, which grew up around a British fort constructed in 1890, replaced Entebbe as the capital in 1962.

**Kampuchea** or **Cambodia,** country (1987 est. pop. 7,000,000), 181,035 km² (69,898 sq mi), SE Asia. It is bordered by Thailand (N and W), Laos (N), Vietnam (E), and the Gulf of Siam (S). The capital is PHNOM PENH. The heart of the country consists of a large central alluvial plain, drained by the MEKONG R. and including the Tônlé Sap (Great Lake). Mountains flank the plain in the northwest and southwest. Kampuchea has a tropical monsoonal climate ideal for growing rice, the chief crop. Corn, vegetables, peanuts, tobacco, and sugar palm are also grown. The industrial sector centres on the processing of agricultural products. Mineral resources are limited to various kinds of stone and salt. Both the industrial and agricultural sectors were virtually destroyed during the war and civil strife of the 1970s. About 90% of the population is ethnic Khmer and speaks Khmer; minorities include Chinese, Vietnamese, Cham-Malays, and a number of hill tribes. Buddhism is practised, but is discouraged by the government.

*History.* The early history of Cambodia is that of the KHMER EMPIRE. After the empire's fall (15th cent.), Cambodia fell prey to Siam and later (17th cent.) to ANNAM. It was declared (1863) a French protectorate and became (1887) part of French-ruled INDOCHINA. Cambodia was occupied by the Japanese in World War II. It became self-governing (1946) and gained full independence (1953) as the Kingdom of Cambodia. NORODOM SIHANOUK led the country until he was deposed (1970) in a military coup led by Gen. LON NOL. Cambodia became (1970) the Khmer Republic and was a major battlefield of the VIETNAM WAR. The ousted Sihanouk formed a government in exile in Peking, and the Communist KHMER ROUGE waged a successful full-scale civil war that overthrew (1975) the Lon Nol government. Sihanouk was restored as head of state, and a new socialist constitution (1976) renamed the country Democratic Kampuchea. However, Sihanouk was soon succeeded by Khieu Samphan, and POL POT became prime minister. The economy deteriorated following a massive collectivization drive in which urban populations were evacuated to work in the countryside. Many Cambodians fled to Thailand, and perhaps as many as 3 million had been killed or had died from enforced hardships by 1978. Border conflicts (1977–78) with Vietnam led to a Vietnamese invasion and the installation (1979) of a rebel Communist government opposed to Pol Pot. The country was renamed the People's Republic of Kampuchea, and was headed by HENG SAMRIN. Khmer Rouge forces and other anti-Vietnamese groups continued to wage guerrilla warfare against the new regime, however, and in 1982 three factions headed by Sihanouk, Khieu Samphan, and former premier Son Sann formed a coalition government-in-exile to represent Democratic Kampuchea. The latter continued to be recognized by a majority of UN member states. Following an announcement (1988) that Vietnamese forces would be withdrawn progressively, talks on a political settlement were initiated between the government and Prince Sihanouk.

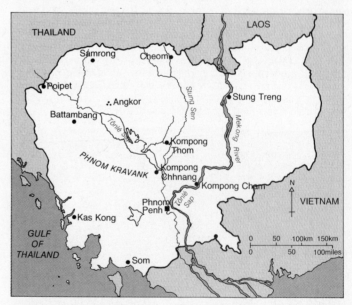

Kampuchea

**Kananga,** formerly Luluabourg, city (1976 est. pop. 704,211), S central Zaïre, on the Lulua R. It is the chief town of the Kasai Occidental prov., and is the commercial and transport centre for a cotton-growing region. Founded in 1884, the city developed rapidly in the early 20th cent. with the coming of the railway. Shortly after the nation's independence (1960), Kananga was the scene of violent clashes between the Luba and Lulua peoples.

**Kanarese** (͵kənəreez), Dravidian language of India. See LANGUAGE (table).

**Kandahar,** city (1979 pop. 178,409), capital of Kandahar prov., S Afghanistan. The country's second largest city, it is a market for sheep, cotton, grain, and dried fruit. Manufactures include woollen cloth, felt, and silk. Possibly founded by Alexander the Great, the city was the capital (1748–73) of the kingdom of Afghanistan and was occupied (1839–42,

1879–81) by the British in the Afghan wars. After the 1979 Soviet invasion of Afghanistan, the Soviets and Afghan rebels engaged (1981) in heavy fighting in Kandahar.

**Kandinsky, Wassily,** 1866–1944, Russian painter. After studying law at Moscow Univ. he went in 1897 to study art in Munich. He initially worked in the *Jugendstil* or Art Nouveau style, and became a founder member of the Neue Künstlervereinigung [new artists' association] in 1909. His disaffection with Western capitalism and materialism promoted an interest in children's art, local folk art, and spiritualism, especially THEOSOPHY, with which he sought to reintroduce a spiritual element into art. His book *Concerning the Spiritual in Art* (1912), develops these ideas and formulates an art in which abstract colours and forms can carry specific meanings and not just be reducible to decorative patterning. In 1911 he formed the BLAUE REITER group. He returned to Russia for the years 1914–21, and not fitting in with the post-Revolutionary constructionist ideas, took up a teaching post at the BAUHAUS in 1921. He continued his experiments with abstraction which he wrote up in *Point and Line to Plane* (1926).

Wassily **Kandinsky,** *Composition IV,* 1911. Oil on canvas 159.5 × 250.5 cm. Dusseldorf.

**Kandy,** town (1981 pop. 101,281), Sri Lanka on the Mahaweli Ganga R. It is a district administrative, commercial, cultural, and religious centre in a beautiful setting. Nearby is Peradeniya Univ. Kandy is a great attraction to tourists, as are its craft industries. It was the capital of the last king of Sri Lanka.

**Kanellopoulos, Panayotis,** 1902–86, prime minister of GREECE (1945, 1967). A professor of sociology, he was ousted at the end of his second term by a military junta.

**kangaroo,** hopping MARSUPIAL of the family Macropodidae, found in Australia and Tasmania. Kangaroos have powerful hind legs, long feet, short forelimbs, and long, muscular tails for maintaining balance. The female has a pouch in which she suckles the newborn kangaroo (joey). The chief grazers of Australian plains, kangaroos are diurnal and live in herds. Great red kangaroo males may attain a height of 210 cm (7 ft) and weigh over 90 kg (200 lb). Smaller members of the kangaroo family include the rabbit-sized wallabies and pademelons some of which live in New Guinea. Kangaroos have been extensively hunted as pests and for their valuable hides.

**Kangaroo Island,** island off the southern coast of South Australia. Australia's second largest offshore island, it was named by Matthew FLINDERS in 1802 and first settled by American sealers in 1803. Regular car ferry services have reduced the isolation from the mainland, but numerous shipwrecks along the rugged SW coast are grim relics of the early sailing days. Flinders Chase Conservation Park has thriving colonies of koalas which have been used to restock mainland parks.

**Kania, Stanislaw,** 1927–, Polish political leader. He joined the Communist Party in 1945, becoming a member of the Politburo in 1975. Soon after the SOLIDARITY free trade union was formed in 1980 he was named party leader, but as the crisis precipitated by the union's activities worsened he was replaced (1981) by Gen. JARUZELSKI.

Grey **kangaroo** with her 'joey'

**Kano** (ˌkahnoh), family or school of Japanese painters. **Kano Masanobu** c.1434–c.1530, the forerunner of the school, painted landscapes, birds, and figure pieces. Done chiefly in inks, his work is Japanese in spirit, with Chinese technical influence. His son, **Kano Motonobu,** c.1476–1559, was the actual founder of the school. He introduced heavily stressed outlines and bold decorative patterns into Chinese-style ink paintings that appealed to the warrior class. **Kano Eitoku,** 1543–90, grandson of Motonobu, painted screens with energy, ease, and inventiveness, using brilliant colours against gold-leaf backgrounds. **Kano Tanyu,** 1602–74, first known as Morinobu, was the grandson of Eitoku and was called the reviver of the Kano school. He was the official painter of the Tokugawa government (1621) and established a school of his own. His *Confucius and Disciples* is in the Museum of Fine Arts, Boston. See also JAPANESE ART.

**Kano,** city (1981 pop. 545,000), N Nigeria. The chief town of Kano state, it is the commercial centre for an agricultural region that produces cotton, cattle, and peanuts. A rapidly growing city, it is the chief industrial centre of N Nigeria, manufacturing textiles, leather goods, glass, chemicals, furniture, and soap. Kano is connected by rail with LAGOS and has an international airport. One of the seven HAUSA city-states, KANO reached the height of its power in the 17th and 18th cent. The British captured the city in 1903.

**Kanpur,** city (1981 pop. 1,486,522), Uttar Pradesh state, N central India, on the GANGES (Ganga) R. An industrial centre, it produces chemicals, textiles, and other manufactures. It was a village until the Nawab of Oudh ceded it to the British in 1801. During the INDIAN MUTINY (1857) the entire British garrison, including women and children, was killed.

**Kansas,** state of the US (1984 est. pop. 2,438,000), area 213,064 km² (82,264 sq mi), situated in the centre of coterminous US and bordered by Nebraska (N), Colorado (W), Oklahoma (S), and Missouri (E). The capital is TOPEKA, but Wichita and KANSAS CITY are the largest cities. Kansas is part of the GREAT PLAINS which stretch from eastern alluvial prairies to the semiarid high plains and foothills of the ROCKY MTS in the west. It has a continental climate of seasonal extremes. The state is a prosperous farming region and the leading producer of wheat in the US; much sorghum, corn, and hay are also grown. Cattle-ranching, meat-packing, and dairying constitute a major economic sector, but the production of transport equipment and nonelectrical machinery is a greater source of revenue. Kansas is the leading US producer of helium and also extracts petroleum, natural gas, and salt. The nomadic, buffalo-hunting lifestyles of the Kansas, Wichita, and Pawnee Indians were transformed when the Spanish introduced horses after the 16th cent. Kansas was obtained by the US in the LOUISIANA PURCHASE (1803), and in the 1850s became the focus of national controversy over slavery, with the abolitionist John Brown at the centre. The state suffered higher casualties than any other in the Union during the Civil War, after which the prairies were heavily settled by farmers. As part of the DUST BOWL, Kansas sustained serious land erosion during the drought of the 1930s. During World War II, aeroplane manufacturing became very important, and industry continued to grow in the early 1980s.

**Kansas City,** two adjacent US cities: one, (1984 est. pop. 160,000); seat of Wyandotte co., NE Kansas (inc. 1859); the other, (1984 est. pop. 443,000), in NW Missouri (inc. 1850). Ports at the junction of the Missouri and Kansas rivers, they form a commercial, industrial, cultural, and transport centre. The cities are a huge market for crops and livestock with stockyards, grain elevators, refineries, and mills. Motor vehicles, soap, farm machinery, and printed materials are leading products. The area was the starting place for many Western expeditions, and several early 19th-cent. settlements were the predecessors to today's cities.

**Kansas–Nebraska Act,** bill passed (1854) by the US Congress to establish the Kansas and Nebraska territories. Controversy over SLAVERY and conflict over the route of the proposed transcontinental railway had delayed territorial organization of the region. Finally, Sen. Stephen A. DOUGLAS presented a bill that made concessions to the South. It created two territories, Kansas and Nebraska, and called for 'popular sovereignty' (see SQUATTER SOVEREIGNTY). An amendment repealed the antislavery clause of the MISSOURI COMPROMISE. The squatter sovereignty provision caused both proslavery and antislavery forces to try to swing the popular decision in Kansas in their favour (see EMIGRANT AID COMPANY). The tragedy of 'bleeding Kansas' resulted, and sectional division reached a point that precluded reconciliation and culminated in the AMERICAN CIVIL WAR.

**Kansu:** see GANSU.

**Kant, Immanuel,** 1724–1804, German philosopher, one of the greatest figures in the history of METAPHYSICS. After 1755 he taught at the Univ. of Königsberg and achieved wide renown through his teachings and writings. According to Kant, his reading of HUME woke him from his dogmatic slumber and led him to become the 'critical philosopher', synthesizing the rationalism of LEIBNIZ and the SCEPTICISM of Hume. Kant proposed that objective reality is known only insofar as it conforms to the essential structure of the knowing mind. Only objects of experience, *phenomena*, may be known, whereas things lying beyond experience, *noumena*, are unknowable, even though in some cases we assume a priori knowledge of them. The existence of such unknowable 'things-in-themselves' can be neither confirmed nor denied, nor can they be scientifically demonstrated. Therefore, as Kant showed in the *Critique of Pure Reason* (1781), the great problems of metaphysics—the existence of God, freedom, and immortality are insoluble by scientific thought. Yet he went on to state in the *Critique of Practical Reason* (1788) that morality requires belief in their existence. Kant's ETHICS centres in his categorical imperative, or absolute moral law, 'Act as if the maxim from which you act were to become through your will a universal law.' His *Critique of Judgment* (1790) considered the concepts of beauty and purposiveness as a bridge between the sensible and the intelligible worlds. Kant's influence on modern philosophy has continued to the present day. His work fostered the development of German IDEALISM by FICHTE, SCHELLING, and HEGEL. The neo-Kantianism of the late 19th cent. applied his insights to the study of the physical sciences (Hermann Cohen, Ernst CASSIRER), and to the historical and cultural sciences (Heinrich Rickert); his influence is also seen in the thought of DILTHEY; in the pragmatism of John DEWEY and William JAMES; in the theology of SCHLEIERMACHER; and in GESTALT psychology.

**Kaohsiung** (gowshyoong), city (1985 pop. 1,876,761), S Taiwan. It is the second largest city of TAIWAN, the leading port in S Taiwan, and an important heavy industrial centre. It produces steel, ships, and chemicals. The city was developed by the Japanese, who occupied Taiwan in 1895.

**Kapitza, Peter Leonidovich,** 1894–1986, Soviet physicist. He worked in Cambridge under Lord RUTHERFORD; and was elected fellow of the ROYAL SOCIETY in 1929. He returned to the USSR in 1934, and was made director of the Institute of Physical Problems of the Academy of Science, USSR. He was a joint winner of the 1978 Nobel Prize for physics for basic work in low temperature physics.

**Kaplan, Mordecai Menahem,** 1881–1983, American rabbi, educator, and philosopher; b. Lithuania. He is the originator of Reconstructionist JUDAISM and the founder of its Society for the Advancement of Judaism.

**kapok,** tropical tree of the BOMBAX family, and the resilient fibre obtained from its seeds. The water- and decay-resistant fibre, obtained chiefly from the genus *Ceiba* is used as a stuffing, especially for life preservers, and for insulation against sound and heat.

**Karachi,** largest city (1981 est. pop. 5,103,000), and former capital of Pakistan, capital of Sind prov., on the Arabian Sea near the Indus R. delta. It is Pakistan's chief seaport and industrial centre, with such manufactures as road vehicles, petroleum products, textiles, and steel. Developed (18th cent.) as a port and trade centre by Hindu merchants, it passed (1843) to the British, who made it the seat of the Sind government, a military outpost, and a major seaport. It was Pakistan's capital from independence (1947) until 1959, when RAWALPINDI became the interim capital pending completion of ISLAMABAD. Points of interest include the tomb of Muhammad Ali JINNAH, Pakistan's founder.

**Karadjordje** ('kara,jawjə), 1768?–1817, b. Djordje Petrović; livestock merchant, leader of the first Serbian uprising against the Turks (1804–13), and founder of the KARADJORDJEVIĆ dynasty. After liberating the Belgrade Pashalik, he was proclaimed the Serbs' hereditary chief (1808), but fled to Hungary when Ottoman forces returned to crush the rebellion. He was murdered at the instigation of MILOŠ Obrenović, leader of the less ambitious second uprising (1815), when he sought to re-enter Serbia.

**Karadjordjević** or **Karageorgevich,** Serbian dynasty descended from KARADJORDJE that reigned from 1842 to 1858 and from 1903 to 1945, alternating with the rival OBRENOVIĆ dynasty.

**Karadžić, Vuk Stefanović,** 1787–1864, Serbian folklorist, lexicographer, and linguistic reformer. His collections of Serbian folk poetry, dictionaries and grammars, published in numerous editions between 1814 and 1866, as well as his polemics on linguistic and national questions, were influential both in introducing the South Slav oral tradition to a wide European audience and in fostering Serb nationalism. His reformed Cyrillic orthography became the Serbian norm (making the language almost perfectly phonetic).

**Karaganda,** city (1985 pop. 617,000), Soviet Central Asia, on the SE edge of the steppe in the KAZAKH SOVIET SOCIALIST REPUBLIC. It is an important coal-mining city and centre of heavy industry. Industrial products include constructional and mining machinery, chemicals, cement, and foodstuffs. Founded in 1926, initial industrial development was hampered by inadequate water supplies, but this was overcome with the construction of the 480-km (300-mi) Irtysh–Karaganda Canal bringing water from the IRTYSH R.

**Karageorge:** see KARADJORDJE.

**Karageorgevich:** see KARADJORDJEVIĆ.

**Karajan, Herbert von** (,kahrayan), 1908–, Austrian conductor. Since 1955 he has been musical director of the Berlin Philharmonic. He is especially noted for his voluminous recording activity.

**Karakorum,** site of ancient capital of the Mongol empire, W of present capital of Mongolian People's Republic ULAN BATOR. Situated on the Orhon R., it was established as the capital by Jenghiz Khan between 1206 and 1219, 40 km (25 mi) from the site of the 8th-cent. capital of the Uighur Kingdom, which was also called Karakorum. It was the base from which the conquests of the Old World, from China to eastern Europe, were launched; but as the Mongol empire split into several khanates, Kublai, grandson of Jenghiz, moved the capital in 1267 to Cambaluc (the modern Beijing).

**Kara-Kum** [Turkmen = black sands] desert, c.360,000 km² (140,000 sq mi), Soviet Central Asia, in the Turkmen SSR. It borders on the Caspian Sea (W); the AMU DARYA R. (E); the Kopet Dag Mts (S); and the Ust-Urt Plateau (N). It is an area of many shifting dunes, supporting seminomadic tribes with some irrigated agriculture in oasis settlements. Agriculture in Ashkhabad, capital of the Turkmen SSR, is irrigated by the 800 km (500 mi) **Kara-Kum Canal** that flows from the Amu Darya R. and was constructed in the period 1954–62.

**Karamanlis, Constantine,** 1907–, prime minister of GREECE (1955–63, 1974–80) and president (1980–85). A conservative, he was ousted as premier (1963) but returned to power (1974) when the post-1967 military junta fell after a disastrous war in Cyprus. Principal architect of the 1975 constitution, he took Greece into the EUROPEAN COMMUNITY (1981), having become president in 1980. He resigned the presidency in 1985, however, in protest against the Socialist government's reduction of presidential powers.

**Karamzin, Nikolai Mikhailovich** (kərəm,zeen), 1766–1826, Russian writer. Karamzin made the Russian literary language more polished and rhythmic. His sentimental story, 'Poor Liza' (1792), forecast the novel of social protest. His greatest work was an 11-volume *History of the Russian State* (1818–24).

**karate:** see MARTIAL ARTS.

**Kardelj, Edward** (kar,dely), 1910–79, Yugoslav politician and ideologist. Kardelj was picked by TITO to join the leadership of the illegal Yugoslav Communist Party in 1937. He was noted before World War II for his work on the national question and afterwards for his theoretical justification of the 1948 split with STALIN. He was the principal architect of workers' self-management and of Yugoslavia's successive constitutions and party programmes. He also held high government offices and was long considered Tito's most likely successor, but predeceased him.

**Kariba Dam,** one of the world's largest dams, S central Africa, impounding the ZAMBEZI R. to form **Kariba Lake** (c.280 km/175 mi long and 32 km/20 mi wide), on the Zambia–Zimbabwe border. The dam is 128 m (420 ft) high and 579 m (1900 ft) long. It was built (1955–59) to provide hydroelectricity.

**Karlfeldt, Erik Axel** (,kahlfelt), 1864–1931, Swedish lyric poet who wrote of nature, love, and peasant life. He was posthumously awarded the 1931 Nobel Prize for literature, which he had refused in his lifetime.

**Karl-Marx-Stadt,** formerly **Chemnitz,** city (1984 pop. 317,210), S East Germany. Chartered in 1143, it has been a textile centre since medieval times, and is now an industrial centre with such manufactures as machine tools, chemicals, and optical instruments. Notable buildings include a late-Gothic church. Heavily damaged in WORLD WAR II, the city has been rebuilt since 1945. It was renamed in 1953.

**Karloff, Boris,** 1887–1969, American actor; b. England as William Henry Pratt. A fine actor with a superb speaking voice, he won fame as the monster in such horror films as *Frankenstein* (1931) and *The Bride of Frankenstein* (1935).

**Karlskrona,** city (1984 pop. 59,660), S Sweden. A Baltic port, it has been the headquarters of the Swedish navy since 1680.

**Karlsruhe,** city (1984 pop. 268,700), Baden-Württemberg, West Germany. A port on the RHINE, it has important oil-refinery, petrochemical, and electrical engineering industries. It was founded in 1715 to serve as royal capital of the margrave of Baden and continued to act as such until 1945. It is laid out to a semicircular plan with the palace at the hub of its radial avenues, and is a cultural centre, with galleries and theatres.

**Karlstadt:** see CARLSTADT.

**karma,** [Skt., = action, work, or ritual], an Indian religious concept common to HINDUISM, BUDDHISM, and JAINISM. The doctrine holds that one's state in this life is the result of physical and mental actions in past incarnations and that present action can determine one's destiny in future incarnations. Karma also stands for a natural, impersonal law of moral cause and effect: our past actions even in this life determine our later state. Only those who have attained NIRVĀNA, or liberation from rebirth, can transcend karma.

**Karnak,** village, central Egypt, on the Nile R., 1 mi (1.6 km) E of LUXOR. Remains of the pharaohs abound at Karnak. Most notable is the Great Temple of AMON; its huge hypostyle hall (118 m by 52 m/388 ft by 170 ft) has 134 columns arranged in 16 rows. The temple was largely conceived and built, on an older foundation, in the XVIII dynasty.

**Károlyi, Count Michael** (,kahrolyi), 1875–1955, Hungarian politician. He became (1919) provisional president of Hungary but surrendered the government to the Communists under Béla KUN. After serving as Hungarian ambassador to France (1947–49) he resigned and lived in exile in France. He was a fervent supporter of European Union.

**Karpov, Anatoly,** 1951–, Soviet chess master. In 1970 he became the world's youngest international grand master. Karpov won (1975) the world championship by default when Bobby FISCHER, the title-holder, refused to agree to terms for a match. In 1978 and 1981 he successfully defended his title against Viktor KORCHNOI.

**Karsavina, Tamara,** 1885–1978, Russian ballet dancer. Her debut was at Maryinsky, St Petersburg in 1902. She joined DIAGHILEV in Paris (1909) and created principal roles in *Firebird*, *Petrouchka*, and other works, with NIJINSKY as partner.

**Karsh, Yousouf,** 1908–, Canadian photographer. Born in Armenia, he came to the US and studied in Boston. He is famous for his portrait photographs and has taken most of the best-known political and cultural figures of the mid 20th cent., from statesmen such as Winston CHURCHILL and Jawarharlal NEHRU to writers and artists such as Thomas MANN and Pablo PICASSO.

**Karst,** barren limestone plateau, NW Yugoslavia, extending c.80 km (50 mi) SE from the lower Isonzo Valley. Characterized by underground drainage, caves, pot-holes, deep gullies, and other features associated with dissolution and collapse of carbonate rocks, the name has become a generic term used to describe any area where similar landforms occur.

**Karun,** river, SW Iran, 500 km (300 mi) long. With its major tributary, the Dez, it drains a large area in the central ZAGROS MOUNTAINS before flowing across the plains of Khuzistan to enter the SHATT AL ARAB at Khorramshahr. A number of large dams on the river system have been built recently to irrigate the Khuzistan plain.

**Kasavubu, Joseph,** c.1917–69, 1st president (1960–65) of the Republic of the Congo (now ZAÏRE). Under his leadership the Congo gained independence from Belgium. Kasavubu won a struggle for power with Premier LUMUMBA but was ousted by Gen. MOBUTU in 1965.

**kasher** or **kosher,** [Heb., = proper], term applied to food that is in accordance with Jewish dietary laws. Animals that chew their cud and have cloven hooves (e.g., cows and sheep) are kasher; rules governing their slaughter and preparation also apply to fowl. Proper preparation of kasher meat includes complete drainage of blood by means of salting and rinsing. Kasher fish are those with scales and fins. Milk products may not be cooked or eaten with, or immediately after, meat or poultry. The origins of and motivations for Jewish dietary laws and customs have been variously explained as hygienic, aesthetic, folkloric, ethical, and psychological.

**Kashmir,** disputed territory, former princely state, S Asia, administered since 1972 as the Indian state of **Jammu and Kashmir** (1981 pop. 5,987,389; c.139,900 km²/54,000 sq mi; capital Srinagar) and the Pakistani Azad Kashmir (1977 est. pop. 1,700,000; c.82,900 km²/ 32,000 sq mi; capital, Muzaffarabad). Known for its beauty, Kashmir is traversed by lofty, rugged mountains, including sections of the HIMALAYAS and the Karakoram ranges. The heart of the region is the Vale of Kashmir, where wheat and rice are grown. After years of Buddhist and Hindu rule, Kashmir was converted to Islam in the late 14th cent., and became part of the MOGUL empire in 1586. The British installed a Hindu prince as ruler in 1846. Since the partition of India in 1947, control of the territory has been contested by India and Pakistan (see INDIA-PAKISTAN WARS). The present division of the territory was drawn up in 1972.

**Kashmiri,** language belonging to the Dardic group of the Indo-Iranian subfamily of the Indo-European family of languages. See LANGUAGE (table).

**Kasparov, Garik Weinstein,** 1953–, Soviet chess master. He became the youngest player to win the world championship when he defeated Anatoly KARPOV in Moscow in 1985. He successfully defended his title against Karpov in 1986.

**Kassel,** city (1984 pop. 186,100), HESSE, West Germany, on the Fulda R. Railway and motor-vehicle engineering are amongst its most important industries. It was favoured as the seat of the rulers (electors) of Hesse who, in the 18th cent., adorned the city with their Baroque mansions. Very severe damage was suffered in World War II.

**Katanga:** see SHABA.

**Katayev, Valentin Petrovich** (kə,tie-əf), 1897–1986, Russian novelist, playwright, poet, and short-story writer; brother of Yevgeny Petrov (see under ILF, ILYA). In *The Embezzlers* (1926), a novel, and *Squaring the Circle* (1928), a play, he satirized Soviet economic conditions. His four-part novel, *Black Sea Waves* (1936–61), portrays Russian life from 1905 to World War II. *The Holy Well* (1966) and *Broken Life* (1972) are memoirs.

**Katharine of Aragón,** 1485–1536, first queen of HENRY VIII of England; daughter of Ferdinand V of Castile and León and ISABELLA I of Castile. In 1501 she married Arthur, eldest son of HENRY VII. He died in 1502; a papal dispensation allowed Henry VIII, his brother, to marry Katharine in 1509. Only one of her six children (MARY I) survived infancy, and Henry became impatient for a male heir. Also, with the collapse of the English–Spanish alliance in 1525, Katharine's political influence waned. In 1527 Henry tried to have the marriage annulled, a move that led to the English REFORMATION. After his secret marriage (1533) to Anne BOLEYN, Henry had a court declare his first marriage invalid. Katharine was confined at various estates; she refused to recognize the break with Rome.

**Katherine,** town (1986 pop. 5691), Northern Territory, northern Australia. Located 354 km (250 mi) S of *Darwin* on the Stuart Highway, it is a tourist centre for the nearby Katherine Gorge National Park, 1820 km² (7000 sq mi). Aboriginal rock paintings and freshwater crocodiles can be seen in the gorge.

**Katmandu,** city (1981 pop. 393,494), capital of Nepal, central Nepal, c.1370 m (4500 ft) above sea level, in a fertile Himalayan valley. Nepal's administrative and commercial centre, it lies on an ancient route from India to China. The Buddha was reputedly born nearby. Ruled by the Newars, it became independent (15th cent.), but fell (1768) to the GURKHAS. Landmarks include the royal palace, temples, and Sanskrit libraries.

**Katowice** ('kato,veetsee), city (1984 pop. 361,000), capital of Upper Silesia, S Poland. It is the commercial and administrative centre of an important mining and metallurgical region. Ulice Armii Czerwonej [Red Army street] is a wide avenue designed as a socialist showplace.

**Katsina,** city (1969 pop. 104,996), N Nigeria, c.137 km (85 mi) NW of KANO. Modern Katsina is a commercial centre exporting leather, cotton, and peanuts. It also has a steel-rolling mill, a product of government priority attached to the development of the iron and steel industry. An ancient seat of learning, Katsina is estimated to have had a population of about 100,000 in the 17th and 18th cent. Seized by Fulahs in the early 19th cent., it was taken over by the British in 1904.

**Katsushika Hokusai:** see HOKUSAI.

**Kattegat,** body of water between Denmark and Sweden, one of the straits linking the North and Baltic seas. It is c.230 km (140 mi) long and from 60 to 160 km (40 to 100 mi) wide.

**katydid:** see CRICKET.

**Katyn Forest** (kə,tin), near Smolensk, in W Russia, the site of a massacre of some 4500 Polish officers whose bodies were discovered by occupying German forces in 1943. The Katyn victims formed part of a larger group of 15,000 Polish officers taken prisoner by the Red Army in Sept. 1939, and missing since early 1940. Although the Soviet government claimed that the massacre was a Nazi war crime, there seems no reason to contest the overwhelming circumstantial evidence of Soviet guilt. It is one of the 'blank spots' in Polish–Soviet history which Mikhail GORBACHEV suggested in 1987 should cease to be taboo. (Not to be confused with KHATYN).

**Kauffmann, Angelica,** 1741–1807, Swiss neo-classical painter and graphic artist. A protégée of Sir Joshua REYNOLDS and one of the original members of the Royal Academy, she was a success in England as a fashionable portraitist and decorator. After her marriage in 1781 she lived in Italy. Her works include the portrait of *Winkelmann* (1764; Kunsthaus, Zürich) and the etching *La Pensierosa*.

**Kaufman, George S.,** 1889–1961, American playwright. He collaborated on over 40 plays, including *Beggar on Horseback* (1924; with Marc Connelly), *Dinner at Eight* (1932; with Edna Ferber), and *Of Thee I Sing* (1932; with Morrie Ryskind and George GERSHWIN). Many of his most famous plays were written with Moss Hart, e.g., *You Can't Take It with You* (1936), *The Man Who Came to Dinner* (1939).

**Kaunda, Kenneth** (kah,-oondə), 1924–, African political leader, president of ZAMBIA (1964–). He led the nationalist movement in Northern Rhodesia, and when it became independent (1964) as Zambia he became its first president.

**Kaveri** (formerly **Cauvery**), river of India flowing c.760 km (470 mi) E from the Western GHATS across the southern DECCAN to enter the Bay of Bengal through a large and fertile delta at whose head stands the town of TIRUCHIRAPALLI and in whose heart is the town of Thanjavur (Tanjore). The town of MYSORE is near its southern bank. The Kaveri is very sacred to Hindus.

**Kawabata Yasunari** (kah,wahbahtah), 1899-1972, Japanese novelist. Written in a lyrical, impressionistic style, his novels are distinguished by a masterful use of imagery. Often they treat, in a delicate, oblique fashion, the relationship of men to women, of man to nature. His novels include *Snow Country* (1934–47; tr. 1956) and *The Sound of the Mountain* (1954; tr. 1970). In 1968 Kawabata became the first Japanese author to receive the Nobel Prize for literature.

**Kawasaki,** city (1986 est. pop. 1,077,817), Kanagawa prefecture, central Honshu, Japan, on Tokyo Bay. Located in the Tokyo–Yokohama industrial area, it has steel mills, shipyards, oil refineries, factories producing electrical machinery and motors, and petrochemical plants. Heigenji Temple, dedicated to the Buddhist priest Kukai, is in Kawasaki.

**Kay, James Phillips,** (later Sir James Kay-Shuttleworth), 1804-77, English doctor and education administrator. As a physician in Manchester in the late 1820s and 30s he developed an interest in the condition of the poor and the social institutions needed in the new urban conditions. He was appointed secretary of the newly created (1839) Committee of Privy Council on Education, which supervised the use of the parliamentary grants for education first made available in 1833, and appointed the first of *Her Majesty's Inspectors* of schools. He attempted unsuccessfully in 1839 to establish a state normal school (teacher-training institution), but in 1846 inaugurated a pupil-teacher scheme. He had a particular interest in workhouse schools, and contributed widely to debates about education. He is considered the most important pioneer educational administrator in Britain in the 19th cent. His educational writings include *Public Education* (1853) and *Four Periods of Public Education* (1862).

**Kayseri,** city (1980 pop. 281,320), capital of Kayseri prov., E central Anatolia, Turkey. It acts as the market centre of an agricultural region and has cotton textile and engineering industries. Known as Caesarea of Cappadocia in Roman times, it flourished under Byzantine and Seljuk rule. The 13th-cent. Seljuk citadel was built on Roman foundations.

**Kazakh Soviet Socialist Republic** or **Kazakhstan** (kah,zahk), constituent republic (1985 pop. 15,858,000), c.2,719,500 km² (1,050,000 sq mi), S USSR. It borders on Siberia (N); China (E); the Kirghiz, Uzbek, and Turkmen republics (S); and the Russian Soviet Federated Socialist Republic and Caspian Sea (W). The capital is ALMA-ATA. It is the second-largest republic in size and the third largest in population. There is a transition from vast areas of semi arid steppe in the N and central parts to desert in the southern regions. In the SE rise the mountains of the Altai and Tien Shan ranges. The main rivers are the Irtysh, Ural, Syr Darya, and Ili. The Kazakh SSR is well-endowed with rich mineral reserves, including coal, oil, tungsten, copper, lead, and zinc. Based on these resources, it is one of the most important industrial republics in the USSR. The opening up of virgin lands in this region and in W Siberia by KHRUSHCHEV in the 1950s caused massive soil losses as the steppe was stripped of vegetation and ploughed. Agricultural products include grain and cotton, and stock-raising is also important. The Turkic-speaking Muslim Kazakhs comprise a third of the population; other groups include Russians (two-fifths), Ukrainians, and Uzbeks. The region was ruled by the MONGOLS from the 13th to 18th cent. and then by Russia; it became part of the USSR in 1920, and a constituent republic in 1936.

**Kazan,** city (1985 pop. 1,047,000), capital of the Tatar Autonomous Soviet Socialist Republic, E European USSR, on the Volga R. A major port, its industries include shipbuilding and aircraft manufacture. Founded in 1401, it became (1445) the capital of a powerful TATAR khanate that was conquered (1552) by IVAN IV of Russia. TOLSTOY and LENIN studied at the Univ. of Kazan (founded 1804).

**Kazan, Elia,** 1909–, American stage and film director, producer, and writer; b. Turkey as Elia Kazanioglous. A founding member of the Actors' Studio (see STRASBERG, LEE), he directed *A Streetcar Named Desire* (1947), *Death of a Salesman* (1949), and the film *On the Waterfront* (1954). He has also written several novels, e.g., *The Anatolian* (1982).

# British Isles

## 1

Conical Orthomorphic Projection

©Oxford University Press

**2**

# Europe

0  100  200  300  400 km

Boundaries — International ————  (in sea) ————

Roads — Motorways ════  Other roads ————

Railways ————

Airports — International ✈  Domestic ○

Canals ············

Marsh ═ ═ ═

Sand Desert limits ·····

Seasonal rivers, lakes

---

Metres
5000
3000
2000
1000
500
300
200
100
Sea level
Land depression

Spot heights in metres

---

Shetland Is.

Bergen
Haugesund
Stavanger
Kristiansand
Skagerrak
Esbjerg
Flen

Hebrides    Orkney Is.

200 metres

**SCOTLAND**
Inverness
Aberdeen
Dundee
Glasgow  Edinburgh
Londonderry
**NORTHERN IRELAND**  Belfast
Newcastle
**UNITED**
Teesside
**KINGDOM**
**IRISH**
Irish Sea
pool  Leeds  Hull
Manchester
**REPUBLIC**  Stoke  Sheffield
Dublin
Limerick  Nottingham
Waterford  **Birmingham**  Norwich  Amsterdam
Cork  Stoke
**WALES**  **ENGLAND**  The Hague
Swansea  Rotterdam
Cardiff  **London**  **NETHERLANDS**  Arnhem
Bristol  Ostend  Antwerp  Essen  Düsseldorf
Southampton  Dover  Gent  **Brussels**  Cologne  Dortr
Land's End  Calais  **LUX**  Bonn  **GERM**
Plymouth  **English Channel**  Lille  Wiesbaden
Cherbourg  Le Havre  Luxembourg  Mannheim
Brest  Seine  **Paris**  Reims  Saarbrück
Rennes  Marne  Nancy
Le Mans  Meuse
Loire  Dijon  Belfort
Nantes  **FRANCE**  Bern  **SWIT**

North Sea

Hebrides

**ATLANTIC**

**OCEAN**

Bay of Biscay

La Coruña
C. Finisterre
Gijón
San Sebastián  Bayonne  Toulouse
Vigo  Cantabrian Mts.  Bilbao  **Pyrenees**  Nîmes
León  **ANDORRA**  Marseille
Oporto  Duero  Valladolid  Zaragoza  Sabadell
**PORTUGAL**  Duero  **Barcelona**
Coimbra  **SPAIN**
Tagus  **Madrid**  C. Tortosa
**Lisbon**  Badajoz
Setúbal  Évora  Ciudad Real  Valencia  Balearic Islands
Guadiana  Júcar  Palma  Majorca
C. St. Vincent  Sierra  Morena  1325  Alicante
Faro  Guadalquivir  Córdoba  Murcia
Gulf of Cadiz  **Seville**  Cartagena
Cádiz  Jérez  Sierra Nevada  3481
C. Trafalgar  Málaga  Almería
Tangier  **GIBRALTAR** (Br.)
Ceuta (Sp.)
Tetuán

Limoges  Clermont  Geneva
Ferrand  **Lyons**
Bordeaux  Massif Central  **Milan**
Dordogne  **Turin**
Lot  Po
Tarn  Rhône
Toulouse  Nice  **MONACO**
Gulf of Lions  Ligurian Sea
**Corsica** (Fr.)
Ajaccio
(Sp.) Minorca
Sassari
**Sardinia** (It.)
Cagliari

Algiers  Bejaia  Annaba
El Aspam  Chéliff  **ALGERIA**  Constantine
Oran  Sidi-bel-Abbès  1729
Melilla (Sp.)  Oujda
**MOROCCO**  Tlemcen  Atlas
El Rif  Moulouya
El Dar el Beida  Rabat  Fès  **ALGERIA**
(Casablanca)  Mèknes  Béchar  Djelfa
Safi  Méchéria
Essaouira  Ksabi  Atlas  Saharan Atlas
Marrakesh  High  Atlas  Touggourt
Béchar

**Mediterranean**

50°N

45°N

40°N

35°N

30°N

10°W   5°W   0°   5°E

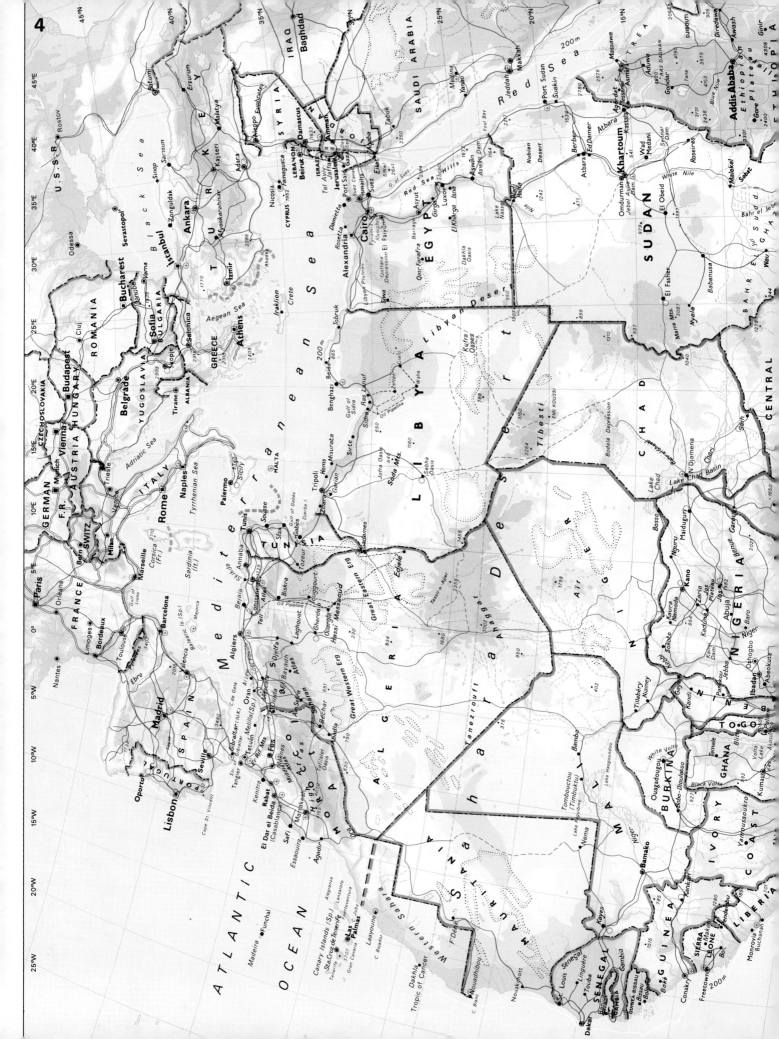

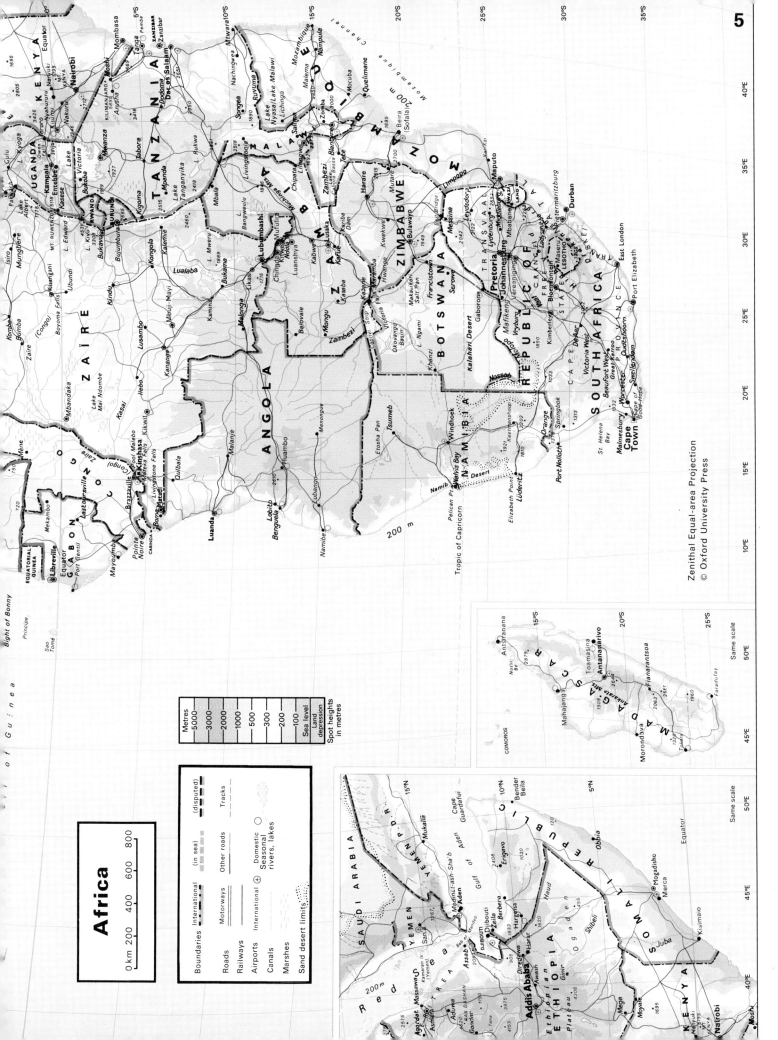

**5**

## Africa

0 km  200  400  600  800

**Boundaries**
International ▬▬▬▬  (in sea) ▦▦▦▦  (disputed) ▬▬▬▬
**Roads**
Motorways ▬▬▬  Other roads ▬▬▬  Tracks ▬▬▬
Railways ▬▬▬
**Airports** ⊕ International  ○ Domestic
Canals ▬▬▬  Seasonal rivers, lakes
Marshes
Sand desert limits

**Metres**
5000
3000
2000
1000
500
300
200
100
Sea level
Land
depression
Spot heights
in metres

Zenithal Equal-area Projection
© Oxford University Press

Same scale

Same scale

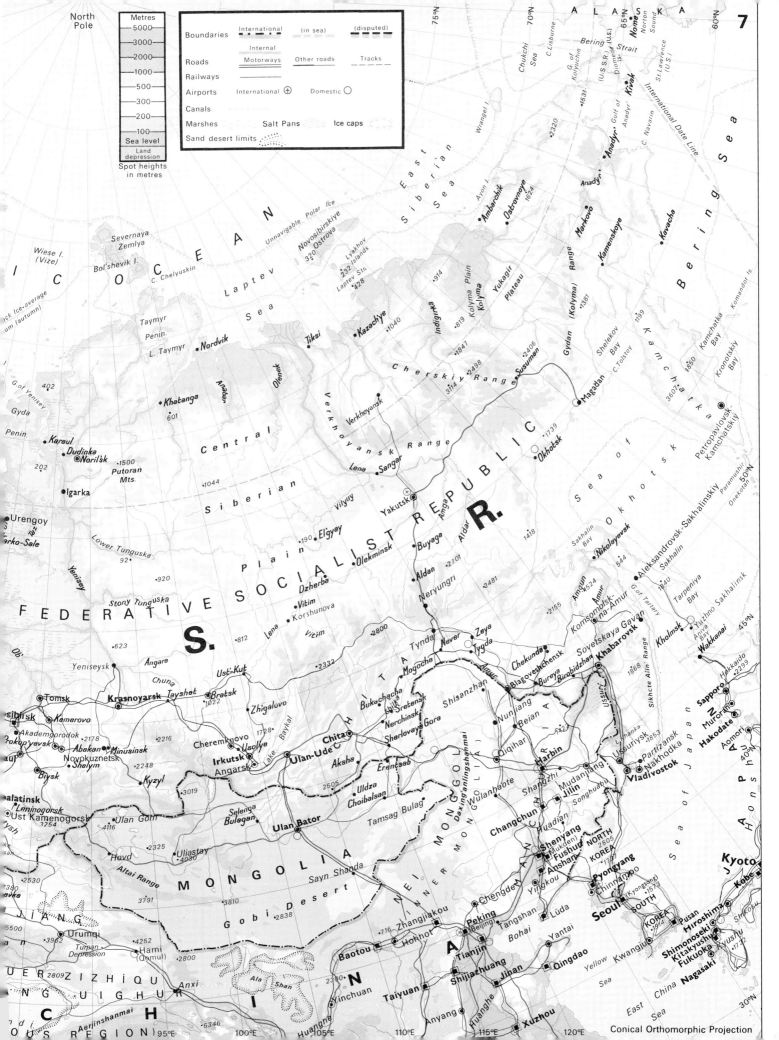

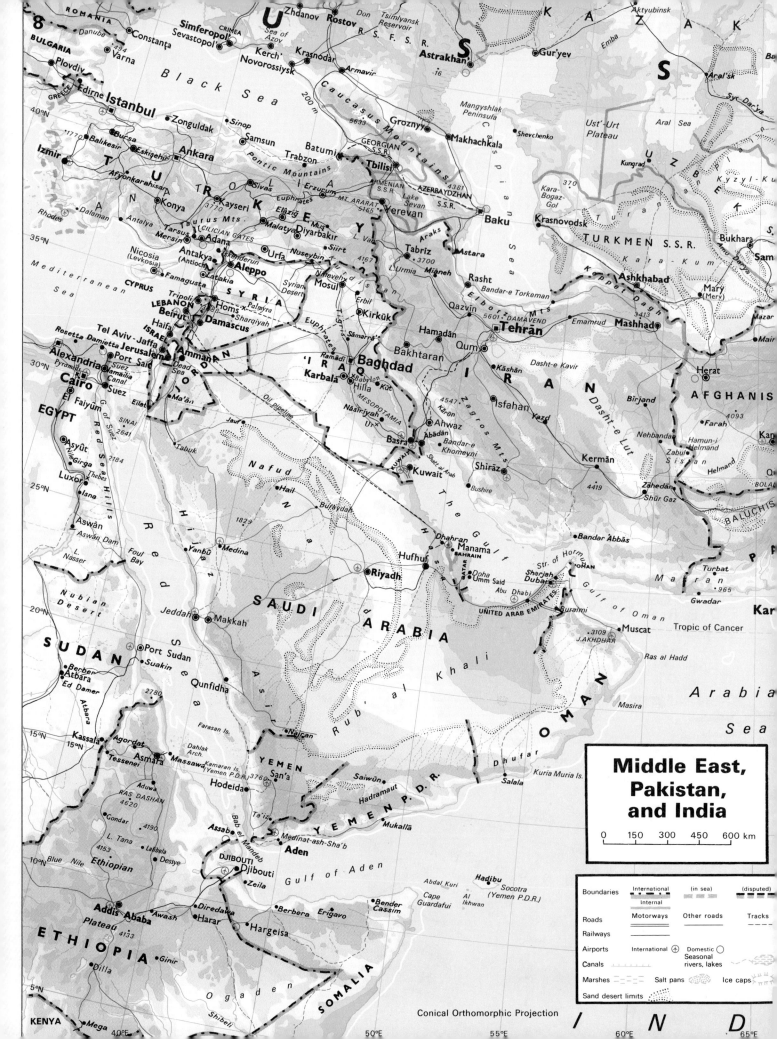

## Middle East, Pakistan, and India

0 150 300 450 600 km

| Boundaries | International | (in sea) | (disputed) |
|---|---|---|---|
| | Internal | | |
| Roads | Motorways | Other roads | Tracks |
| Railways | | | |
| Airports | International ⊕ | Domestic ○ | |
| Canals | | Seasonal rivers, lakes | |
| Marshes | | Salt pans | Ice caps |
| Sand desert limits | | | |

Conical Orthomorphic Projection

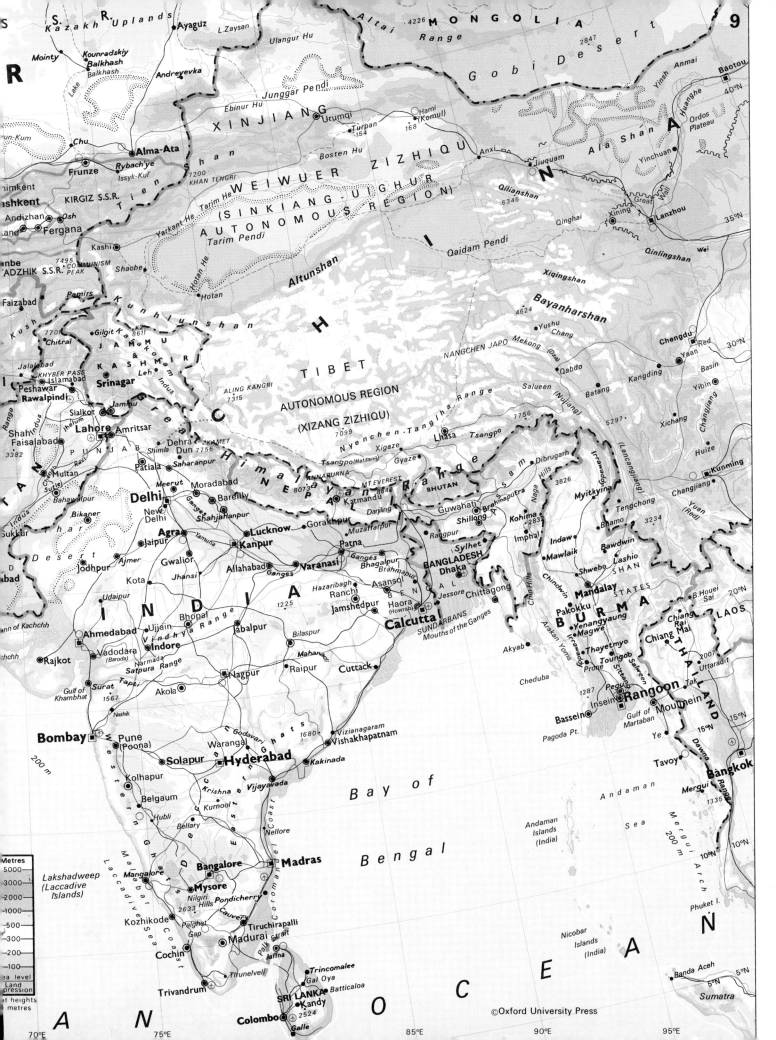

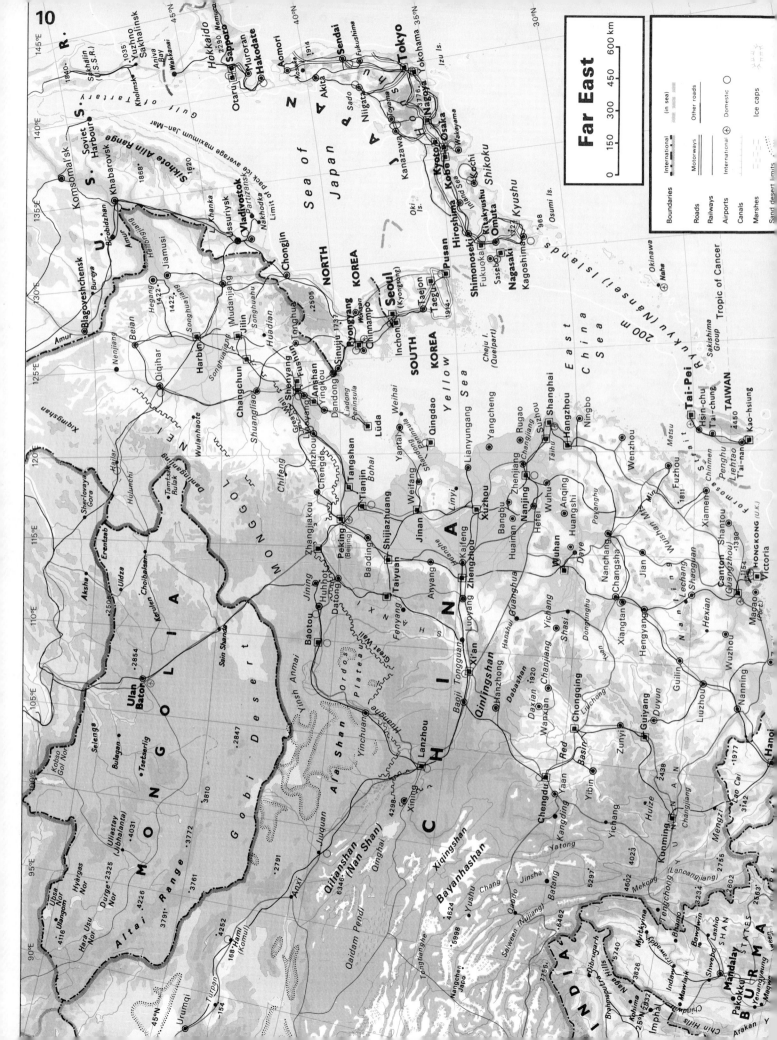

# Far East

**Far East**

| | 0 | 150 | 300 | 450 | 600 km |

| Boundaries | International | |
| | | (in sea) |
| Roads | Motorways | |
| | Other roads | |
| Railways | | |
| Airports | International | ⊕ |
| | Domestic | ○ |
| Canals | | |
| Marshes | | |
| Ice caps | | |
| Sand desert limits | | |

S.S.R.

U. S. S. R.

Sakhalin (U.S.S.R.)
Yuzhno Sakhalinsk
Kholmsk
Soviet Harbour
Komsomolsk
Khabarovsk
Blagoveshchensk
Birobidzhan
Amur
Hegang
Jiamusi
Mudanjiang
Ussuriysk
Vladivostok
Nakhodka
Partizansk

Wakkanai
HOKKAIDO
Sapporo
Otaru
Muroran
Hakodate
Aomori
Akita
Sado
Niigata
Toyama
Kanazawa

Sea of Japan

Chongjin

NORTH KOREA
Pyongyang
Chinnampo
Wonsan
Sinuiju
Dandong
Liaoyang
Fushun
Shenyang
Anshan
Yingkou

Seoul (Kyongsong)
Inchon
Taejon
SOUTH KOREA
Taegu
Pusan

Shimonoseki
Kitakyushu
Fukuoka
Saseo
Nagasaki
Kagoshima
Kumamoto
Omuta

KYUSHU
Osumi Is.

Tokyo
Yokohama
Nagoya
Kyoto
Kobe
Osaka
Wakayama
SHIKOKU
Kochi
Hiroshima
Inland Sea

Harbin
Qiqihar
Changchun
Jilin
Huadian

MONGOLIA
Ulan Bator

Peking (Beijing)
Tianjin
Baoding
Shijiazhuang
Taiyuan
Datong
Huhhot
Baotou
Yinchuan
Lanzhou
Xining
Qinghai

C H I N A

Jinan
Qingdao
Weihai
Yantai
Lianyungang
Xuzhou
Zhengzhou
Kaifeng
Luoyang
Xian
Nanjing
Shanghai
Hangzhou
Ningbo
Wenzhou
Wuhan
Nanchang
Changsha
Chongqing
Chengdu
Guiyang
Kunming
Guilin
Liuzhou
Nanning
Canton (Guangzhou)
HONG KONG (U.K.)
Victoria
Macao (Port.)

TAIWAN
Tai-Pei
Tai-chung
Kao-hsiung

East China Sea

Yellow Sea

Ryukyu Is. (Nansei Shoto)
Okinawa
Naha

Tropic of Cancer

BURMA
Mandalay

INDIA

Hanoi

Gobi Desert

Altai Range

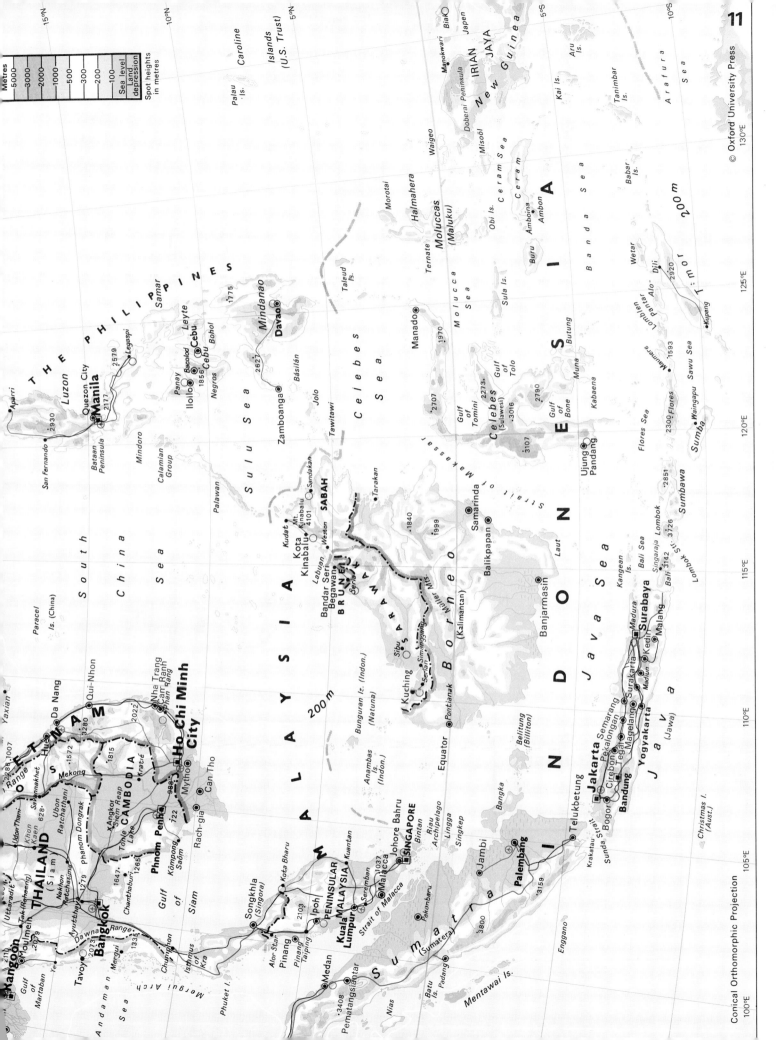

Conical Orthomorphic Projection

**Metres**
5000
3000
2000
1000
500
300
200
100
Sea level
Land
depression

Spot heights
in metres

100°E  105°E  110°E  115°E  120°E  125°E  130°E

*Caroline*

*Palau Is.*

*Islands (U.S. Trust)*

IRIAN JAYA

*New Guinea*

•Biak

*Japen*

*Manokwari*

*Doberai Peninsula*

*Waigeo*

*Misoöl*

*Aru Is.*

*Arafura Sea*

*Tanimbar Is.*

*Kai Is.*

*Babar Is.*

*Wetar*

*Alor*  •Dili

*Timor*  •2920

*Kupang*

200 m

THE PHILIPPINES

•Aparri

*Luzon*

Quezon City
**Manila**  •2179
•2930  •2177

*Bataan Peninsula*

San Fernando•

*Mindoro*

*Calamian Group*

*Panay*

Iloilo•  *Bacolod*  •1856
•2579
Legaspi•

*Samar*

*Leyte*
**Cebu**  *Cebu*
•2627  *Bohol*

**Mindanao**  •1775
**Davao**

*Negros*

*Básilán*

*Jolo*

*Tawitawi*

*Sulu Sea*

*Talaud Is.*

Manado•

*Morotai*

*Halmahera*

*Ternate*

*Moluccas (Maluku)*

*Obi Is.*  *Ceram Sea*  *Ceram*

*Buru*  *Amboina*  Ambon•

•1970

*Molucca Sea*

*Sula Is.*

*Banda Sea*

*Butung*

*Muna*

*Kabaena*

CELEBES

*Celebes Sea*

Gulf of Tomini  •2273

*Celebes (Sulawesi)*

•3016

Gulf of Bone

•2790

•2707

•3107

Ujung Pandang

*Flores Sea*

*Singaraja Lombok*  •2851

*Flores*  •2300

*Sumba*

*Waingapu*

*Sumbawa*

*Maumere*

•1593

*Lombok*

South China Sea

*Paracel Is. (China)*

VIETNAM

•Qui-Nhon

•Da Nang

•Hué  •2088, 1007

Nha Trang•
Cam Ranh•  •2022

•1280

**Ho Chi Minh City**

•1815

•1572

CAMBODIA

•Kratié

×Angkor  ×Siem Reap

*Tonlé Sap Lake*  •1265

**Phnom Penh**

•988

*Mekong*

•722

Mytho•

Can Tho•

Rach-gia•

*Kômpông Saôm*

•628

*phnom Dongrak*

Ubon Ratchathani•

Sakon Nakhon•  •2079

•2028

Khon Kaen•

Udor Thani•

THAILAND (Siam)

Nakhon Ratchasima•

•1279

*phnom Dongrak*

Chanthaburi•  •1647

Ayutthaya•

**Bangkok**

*Dawna Range*  •2073

Chumphon•

*Isthmus of Kra*

Alor Star•

*Pinang*
Pinang•  •2103

Taiping•

Ipoh•

PENINSULAR MALAYSIA

**Kuala Lumpur**

Seremban•  •1037

Kuantan•

Kota Bharu•

Songkhla (Singora)•

Medan•  •3408

Pematangsiantar•

*Nias*

*Batu Is.*  Padang•

*Mentawai Is.*

Phuket I.

*Andaman Sea*

*Mergui Arch.*

*Gulf of Siam*

Yaxian•

•2211

•Moulmein

•Tavoy

•Ye

Mergui•

*Gulf of Martaban*

**Rangoon**

•2079

•1335

MALAYSIA

*Anambas Is. (Indon.)*

*Bunguran Is. (Indon.) (Natuna)*

200 m

*I. Kuching*  •Pontianak

*Serian*  •Simanggang

Sibu•

SARAWAK

BRUNEI

**Bandar Seri Begawan**

*Seria*

Mt. Kinabalu
•4101

Kudat•

Kota Kinabalu

*Labuan*  •Weston

SABAH

Sandakan•

Tarakan•

•1840

•1999

Samarinda•

Balikpapan•

BORNEO (Kalimantan)

*Muller Mts.*

*Laut*

Banjarmasin•

Johore Bahru•

**SINGAPORE**

*Bintan*

*Riau Archipelago*

*Lingga*

*Singkep*

*Malacca*
*Strait of Malacca*

Pekanbaru•  •3800

Jambi•

*Bangka*

*Belitung (Billiton)*

*Sumatra (Sumatera)*

•3159

Telukbetung•

Palembang

*Krakatau*  *Sunda Strait*

Jakarta  Cirebon•  *Bogor*
Pekalongan•  Semarang•  Surakarta•  Kedin•
**Bandung**  Tegal•  Magelang•  Yogyakarta  Madiun•  Malang•  **Surabaya**

*Java (Jawa)*

*Madura*

*Bali*  •3142

*Bali Strait*

*Kangean Is.*

*Christmas I. (Aust.)*

*Java Sea*

INDONESIA

Equator

Strait of Makassar

*Enggano*

Gulf of Bone

•3726

*Lombok Strait*

•Kinabalu

*Laut*

145°E  150°E  155°E  160°E  165°E  170°E  175°E

Equator

P

A

C

I

F

I

C

Tarawa  *Gilbert*

Nauru

Ocean I.
(Br.)

*Islands*
(Br.)

0°

Pura
Aitape
Newak •
Manus
Admiralty
Is.
Kavieng

Madang •

**PAPUA - NEW GUINEA**

New
Ireland
Rabaul
New Britain

Bismarck
Archipelago

Central Ra.

NEW

GUINEA

• Lae  • Finschhafen

Owen Stanley Ra.

•3993

Gulf of
Papua

Port
Moresby

3422

Str.
C. York

714•

•3106

*Solomon Islands*

Bougainville

Shortland Is.
Ganongga
New
Georgia
Vangunu

Choiseul

Santa
Isabel

Stewart Is.

Honiara
Guadalcanal 2440
Ulawa

Malaita

San Cristobal

5°S

D'Entrecasteaux Is.

Louisiade Arch.

Rennell I.

Santa Cruz Is.

Cherry I.

Mitre I.

*Tuvalu*

Funafuti

10°S

C.
York
Cape
595.

586•

*Coral*

*Sea*

Espiritu
Santo

Malekula

**VANUATU**

Vila •
Efate
Erromanga

15°S

*Vanua Levu*

*Fiji Is.*

Viti Levu

• Suva

Lau Group

Peninsula
Cooktown
1387•
Cairns

Innisfail
Great

Mitchell

Gilbert

•714

Forsayth
Norman

Flinders

Townsville

Charters
Towers

•1055

Hughenden

Barrier

Reef

Chesterfield Is.
(Fr.)

*Loyalty Is. (Fr.)*

New
Caledonia
(Fr.)

• Nouméa

Tropic of Capricorn

20°S

O

C

E

A

Winton

Longreach
Barcaldine

Barcoo

Yaraka

Quilpie

•628
Mt. Morgan
Rockhampton
Gladstone

•738

Bundaberg

QUEENSLAND

Dividing  Range

Maryborough

Gympie

Nambour

Charleville
•394
Cunnamulla

Goondiwindi

Darling
Toowoomba
Downs

**Brisbane**
**Gold Coast**

Murwillumbah
Lismore

•1555

Grafton

Coffs Harbour

Norfolk I.
(Austl.)

25°S

Creek

Bourke

Cobar

Tamworth

•1615

Port Macquarie

Taree

Broken Hill

**NEW**

**SOUTH**

Darling

Dubbo

•520

Orange
Lachlan

Maitland
•1274
Lithgow
Katoomba

**Newcastle**

**Sydney**

Dividing  Range

30°S

N

Mildura

Murray

Murrumbidgee

Swan Hill

**WALES**

Wagga Wagga

Albury
Shepparton

Goulburn

**Canberra**
A.C.T.

Australian Alps

Wollongong

*Tasman*

North Cape

•771  • Kaikohe

35°S

Adelaide

Murray

Bendigo

**VICTORIA**

Ballarat

Geelong

**Melbourne**

Warrnambool

MT. KOSCIUSKO
2230

1167•

Gippsland
Orbost

Cape Howe

*Sea*

NORTH ISLAND

**Auckland**

Hamilton

•819

New Plymouth

•1754

2517•

Gisborne

Napier

King I.

Bass
Strait

Furneaux
Group

•1213
Nelson

1439•

Burnie
Mt. Lyell
Launceston

•1573
• St. Marys

**Hobart**

**TASMANIA**

SOUTH ISLAND

Westport
Greymouth

•2338

Cook

Strait

Palmerston N.

2751•

**Wellington**

**NEW**

**ZEALAND**

40°S

MT. COOK
3764
Southern Alps

3035•

**Christchurch**

2027•
Invercargill

Stewart I.

170°E

• Dunedin

45°S

© Oxford University Press

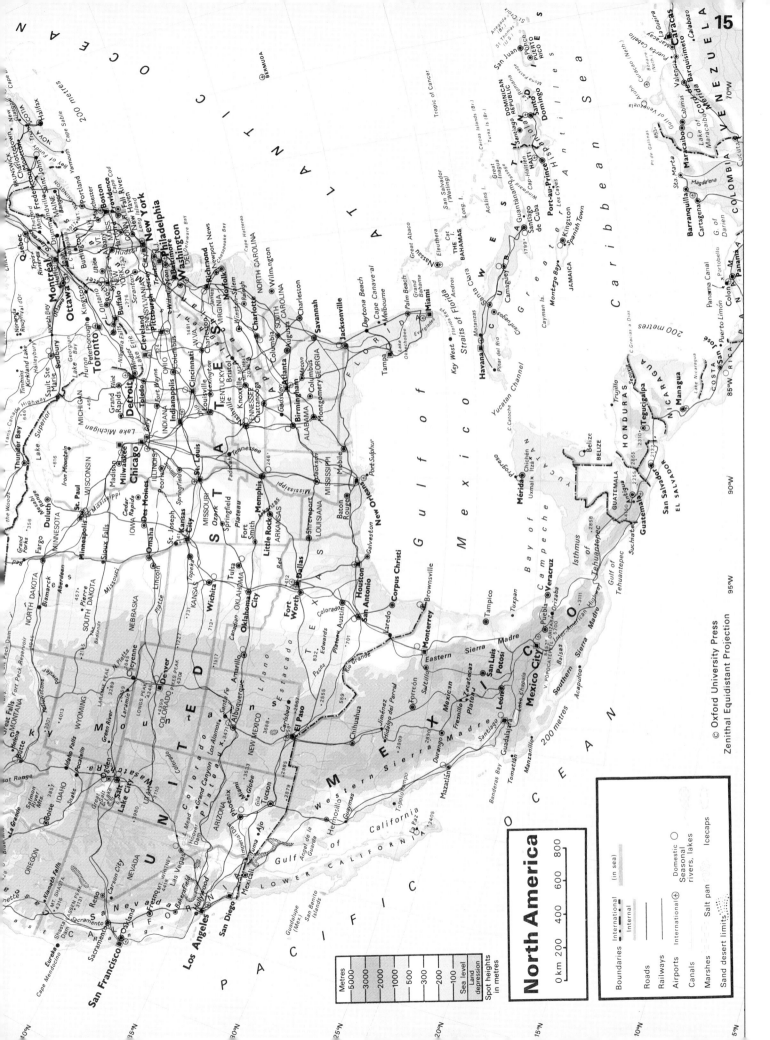

**South America**

0    300    600 km

| Boundaries | International |
| --- | --- |
| Roads | Roads    Tracks |
| Railways | |
| Airports | International ⊕    Domestic ○ |
| Canals | Seasonal rivers, lakes |
| Marshes | Salt pan    Icecaps |
| Sand desert limits | |

Metres
5000
3000
2000
1000
500
300
200
100
Sea level
Land depression
Spot heights in metres

Transverse Mercator Projection
© Oxford University Press

**Kazantzakis, Nikos** ('kazan,dzakis), 1883–1957, Greek writer; b. Crete. Of an intensely poetic and religious nature, he produced his most ambitious work in *The Odyssey, a Modern Sequel* (1938), a verse tale that explores the world views of BUDDHA, JESUS, NIETZSCHE, LENIN, and others. He is, however, better known for two earthy, realistic novels, *The Greek Passion* (1938) and *Zorba the Greek* (1946), both of which were filmed.

**Kazimierez.** For Polish rulers thus named, see CASIMIR.

**Kean, Edmund,** 1787?–1833, English actor. His violent acting style expressed the romantic ideal. Popular in England and the US, he was famous for Shakespearean roles, notably Richard III, Macbeth, Iago in *Othello,* and Shylock in *The Merchant of Venice,* the last a landmark in theatre history. His son, **Charles John Kean,** 1811?–1868, was best known for his spectacular and historically accurate productions. Charles's wife, **Ellen Tree Kean,** 1806–80, was a noted comedienne.

**Kearny, Stephen Watts,** 1794–1848, American general in the MEXICAN WAR. Made (1846) commander in the West, Kearny captured Santa Fe and Los Angeles and was military governor of California until 1847.

**Keaton, Buster,** 1895–1966, American film actor and director. A comic genius, he made such silent films as *Sherlock Junior* (1924), *The Navigator* (1924), and *The General* (1927).

**Keats, John,** 1795–1821, English poet, considered one of the greatest English poets. Apprenticed to a surgeon in 1810, he soon came to know Leigh HUNT and in 1816 gave up surgery for poetry. His first volume of poems appeared in 1817; it included 'On First Looking into Chapman's Homer'. The long poem *Endymion,* published in 1818, was vigorously attacked by the critics. Keats's passionate love for Fanny Brawne began in 1818, but he had contracted tuberculosis and they did not marry. Shortly after the publication of *Lamia, Isabella, The Eve of St Agnes, and Other Poems* (1820), Keats went to Italy for his health and died in Rome at the age of 25. Keats's poems are unequalled for dignity, melody, and richness of imagery. They include 'Ode to a Nightingale', 'Ode on a Grecian Urn', 'To Autumn', 'Ode on Melancholy', and the unfinished epic 'Hyperion'. 'The Eve of St Agnes' and 'La Belle Dame sans Merci' are examples of romantic medievalism at its best. His sonnets include 'When I have fears that I may cease to be' and 'Bright star, would I were stedfast as thou art'. His superb letters are now as much valued as his poetry.

**Kebalai:** see BUREH BAI.

**Keble, John,** 1792–1866, English clergyman and poet. His popular poetical work *The Christian Year* (1827), based on the BOOK OF COMMON PRAYER, won him a professorship of poetry at Oxford (1831–41). J. H. NEWMAN called his sermon 'National Apostasy' (1833) the start of the OXFORD MOVEMENT, in which he took a leading part for the rest of his life. He is widely recognized as an Anglican saint, being assigned a holy day (29 Mar.) in the calendar of The Alternative Service Book (1980) of the Church of England.

**Kecskemét,** city (1985 pop. 102,000), central Hungary. It grew up to serve an agricultural population, handling grain and fruit. Industries have been added under the socialist regime.

**Kekkonen, Urho Kaleva** (,kekohnən), 1900–86, president of FINLAND (1956–81). Leader of the Agrarian Party (from 1965 the Centre Party), he held various cabinet posts from 1936 and was prime minister (1950–56). He resigned the presidency for reasons of health and was succeeded (1982) by Mauno KOIVISTO.

**Kekulé von Stradonitz, Friedrich August** (,kekoohlay), 1829–96, German organic chemist. A professor at Bonn, he is most noted for his representation of the molecular structure of BENZENE as a ring. Such a ring is the basic structural feature of an AROMATIC COMPOUND.

**Keller, Gottfried,** 1819–90, Swiss novelist, poet, and short-story writer. He is esteemed for his vital, realistic, and purposeful fiction, especially the outstanding autobiographical novel *Der grüne Heinrich* (1854–55; tr. Green Henry) and his collections of novellas, *The People of Seldwyla* (1856 and 1874), located in a typical small Swiss town.

**Keller, Helen Adams,** 1880–1968, American writer and lecturer. Blind and deaf from the age of two, she was put (1887) in the care of Anne Sullivan (see MACY, ANNE SULLIVAN), who became her teacher and lifelong companion. Keller made rapid progress and in 1904 was graduated from Radcliffe College with honours. She published and lectured widely to raise funds for the training of the blind and for other social causes.

**Kellogg–Briand Pact,** or Pact of Paris, agreement reached in 1928 by 15 nations (and eventually ratified by 62 nations) who agreed to settle all conflicts by peaceful means and who renounced war as an instrument of national policy. US Secy of State Frank Billings KELLOGG and French Foreign Minister Aristide BRIAND were its sponsors. Its effectiveness was vitiated by its failure to provide measures of enforcement. Ultimately, the pact proved to be meaningless, especially as nations adopted the practice of waging undeclared wars.

**Kelly, Ellsworth,** 1923–, American painter. He paints flat colour areas, usually with sharp, geometric contours, e.g., *Atlantic* (1956; Whitney Mus., New York City), and is one of the main exponents of hard-edge painting in the school of post-painterly abstractions.

**Kelly, Grace,** 1929–82, American film actress and princess consort of Monaco. She was a major film star until 1956, when she married RAINIER III, the ruling prince of Monaco. She won the 1954 Academy Award for her performance in *The Country Girl* but is best remembered for her role opposite Gary COOPER in *High Noon* (1952).

**Kelly, Ned (Edward),** 1855–80, Australian BUSHRANGER and folk hero. From an impoverished rural background, he and his associates enjoyed considerable local support in conflict with the police that led in 1878 to the death of three of his pursuers. From then until 1880 his depredations were so audacious as to engender a political crisis. He was captured and hanged in 1880: his last words were 'Such is life'.

**Kelsen, Hans,** 1881–1973, Austrian jurist. He was professor of Law at Vienna and author of the Austrian Constitution (1920). One of the most influential writers on JURISPRUDENCE in the 20th cent., his works include *General Theory of Law and State* (1945). A believer in legal POSITIVISM, he has been criticized for glorifying state power and preferring order to justice.

**kelvin:** see METRIC SYSTEM; TEMPERATURE.

**Kelvin, William Thomson,** 1st **Baron,** 1824–1907, British mathematician and physicist; b. Ireland. He was professor (1846–99) of natural philosophy at the Univ. of Glasgow. His work in THERMODYNAMICS, coordinating the various existing theories of heat, established the law of the conservation of ENERGY as proposed by James JOULE. He discovered the Thomson effect in thermoelectricity and introduced the Kelvin scale, or absolute scale, of TEMPERATURE. His work on the transmission of messages by undersea cables made him a leading authority in this field.

**Kelvin temperature scale:** see TEMPERATURE.

**Kemal Pasha, Mustafa:** see ATATÜRK, KEMAL.

**Kemble, Roger,** 1721–1802, English actor and manager. The father of 12 children (with his wife, Sarah Wood), he founded one of England's most distinguished stage families. Best known was Sarah Kemble SIDDONS. **John Philip Kemble,** 1757–1823, the eldest son, managed (1788–1803) the Drury Lane Theatre and COVENT GARDEN (1803–17). He was a tragedian, and his best role was Coriolanus. His brother **George Stephen Kemble,** 1758–1822, managed companies in Edinburgh and Ireland, achieving success as Falstaff. Another brother, **Charles Kemble,** 1775–1854, excelling in romantic roles, managed (1822–32) Covent Garden. His sister, **Elizabeth Kemble,** 1761–1836, as Mrs Whitlock, was popular in the US. Charles's daughter **Fanny Kemble** (Frances Anne Kemble), 1809–93, gained fame in both comedy and tragedy and won extravagant praise when she toured (1832–34) the US with her father. Her sister, **Adelaide Kemble,** 1814–79, was an opera singer.

**Kemény, Zsigmond,** 1814–75, Hungarian novelist. He used the framework of the historical novel to elaborate his pessimistic determinist views of society and the individual. The strongest passages in his works are detailed, almost obsessive, analyses of the psychological motivations of his characters, often in the form of interior monologues. Frequent among his themes are frustrated love and religious fanaticism, set against the background of his native Transylvania. His chief works are *A Widow and her Daughter* (1855–57), *The Fanatics* (1858), and *Grim Times* (1862).

**Kemerovo,** formerly Shcheglovsk, city (1985 pop. 507,000), S Siberian USSR, on the Tom R., a tributary of the Ob R. Situated in the Kuznetsk coal basin, it is principally concerned with coal-mining and associated chemical industries, as well as a wide variety of metal-working and food industries.

**Kemp, Lindsay,** 1939–, English mime, actor, dancer, and director. He studied at Bradford art school and Rambert ballet school. He now has his own internationally acclaimed company, based in Barcelona, which performs his works.

**Kempe, Margery,** c.1373–c.1439, English writer. Her *Book*, describing her troubled spiritual life and wide travels in England and abroad, is an extraordinary human document, and the earliest autobiography in English.

**Kempis, Thomas à:** see THOMAS À KEMPIS.

**Kendall, Edward Calvin,** 1886–1972, American biochemist. For his work on the treatment of rheumatoid ARTHRITIS with cortisone, Kendall received, with HENCH and Reichstein, the 1950 Nobel prize for physiology or medicine.

**kendo:** see MARTIAL ARTS.

**Keneally, Thomas,** 1935–, Australian novelist. A self-styled 'middlebrow' writer, he combines popularity with serious concerns in his historical and often violent novels. His work includes *Bring Larks and Heroes* (1967), *The Chant of Jimmie Blacksmith* (1972), *The Cut-Rate Kingdom* (1980), *Schindler's Ark* (1982), which won the Booker Prize in the UK, and *Playmaker* (1987).

**Kennan, George Frost,** 1904–, US diplomat and historian. A formulator of the policy of 'containment' towards the USSR, he was ambassador to Moscow (1952) until the Russians demanded his removal. He later served (1961–63) as ambassador to Yugoslavia. His works include *American Diplomacy, 1900–1950* (1951) and his memoirs (2 vol., 1967–72).

**Kennedy,** American family, active in US government and politics. **Joseph Patrick Kennedy,** 1888–1969, engaged in banking, shipbuilding, and motion-picture distribution before serving as chairman of the Securities and Exchange Commission (1934–35) and head of the US Maritime Commission (1936–37). He was US ambassador to Great Britain (1937–40). His son **John Fitzgerald Kennedy** was president of the US (see separate article). His son **Robert Francis Kennedy,** 1925–68, served (1961–64) as US attorney general. He resigned after Pres. Kennedy's death and was elected (1964) US senator from New York. In 1968 he sought the Democratic presidential nomination, but after winning the California primary he was mortally wounded by a gunman, Sirhan B. Sirhan. Joseph Kennedy's youngest son, **Edward Moore Kennedy,** 1932–, has served as US senator from Massachusetts since 1962. A spokesman for liberal causes, he has advocated such reforms as national health insurance and tax reform. His political career was marred somewhat by the Chappaquiddick incident (July 1969) in which Mary Jo Kopechne, a passenger in a car he was driving on an island near Martha's Vineyard, Massachusetts, was drowned when the car ran off a bridge. Kennedy unsuccessfully challenged Pres. Jimmy CARTER for the 1980 Democratic presidential nomination.

**Kennedy, John Fitzgerald,** 1917–63, 35th president of the US (1961–63); son of Joseph P. Kennedy; brother of Robert Francis Kennedy and Edward Moore Kennedy (see KENNEDY, family). After enlisting in the US navy in World War II, he served with distinction in the Pacific. He was a Democratic congressman from Massachusetts (1947–53) and in 1952 won a seat in the US Senate. The next year he married Jacqueline Lee Bouvier. Kennedy narrowly lost the Democratic vice presidential nomination in 1956 and in 1960 won the party's presidential nomination. He defeated Republican Richard NIXON, becoming at 43 the youngest man to be elected president. His domestic programme, the New Frontier, called for tax reform, federal aid for education, medical care for the aged under Social Security, and the extension of civil rights. Many of his reforms, however, stalled in Congress, and foreign-affairs crises occupied much of his time. He was much criticized for his approval for the abortive BAY OF PIGS INVASION (1961) of Cuba. In Oct. 1962 US reconnaissance planes discovered Soviet missile bases there. In the ensuing CUBAN MISSILE CRISIS, Kennedy ordered a blockade of Cuba and demanded the removal of the missiles. After a brief and tense interval, the USSR complied with his demands. The next year the US and the Soviet Union signed a limited treaty banning nuclear tests. Kennedy also increased the number of US military advisers in South Vietnam to about 16,000 (see VIETNAM WAR). He established the Alliance for Progress to give economic aid to Latin America and created the PEACE CORPS. He also pressed hard to achieve racial INTEGRATION in the South. On 22 Nov. 1963,

Kennedy was shot and killed in Dallas, Texas. Vice Pres. Lyndon JOHNSON succeeded him as president. The WARREN COMMISSION, appointed to investigate the assassination, concluded that it was the work of a single gunman, Lee Harvey Oswald. In 1979, however, the House Select Committee on Assassinations, relying in part on acoustical evidence, concluded that a conspiracy was 'likely' and that it may have involved organized crime.

**Kenneth I,** d. 858, traditional founder of the kingdom of Scotland. He united (c.843) the thrones of Dalriada and the Picts.

**Kenney, Annie,** 1879–1953, English trade unionist and suffragette. Already an organizer in the Lancashire mills, she joined the WOMEN'S SOCIAL AND POLITICAL UNION, becoming one of its leading speakers and activists throughout the militant suffragette campaign. In 1914 she joined Emmeline PANKHURST in her World War I recruiting drive.

**Kensington and Chelsea,** London borough (1981 pop. 125,892), in central London N of the R. Thames. It is a royal borough, containing many important public buildings. Kensington Palace is situated in gardens here. Just S of Kensington Gardens are the Albert Hall and Albert Memorial. South Kensington is a centre of museums and colleges, including the Science Museum, the British Museum (Natural History), Imperial College, the Royal College of Art, the Royal College of Music, and the Royal Geographical Society.

**Kent,** county in S England (1984 est. pop. 1,491,700), 3731 km² (1455 sq mi), bordering the Thames estuary in the N and the English Channel in the SE. The county town is MAIDSTONE. The North Downs cross the county from the NW to the E where they form the white Cliffs of DOVER. Most of the county is flat and low-lying, including the fertile Romney Marsh in the S, where sheep are farmed. The Isle of Thanet, Isle of Grain, and Isle of Sheppey are situated on the coast of Kent, separated from the mainland by narrow channels. Much of the county is on rich agricultural land, producing fruit, hops, cereals, and market-garden crops. There is a small coalfield E of Deal, and sand, gravel and chalk are quarried. Dover and Folkestone are ports with cross-Channel ferry services and Chatham has a naval dockyard. Margate is one of several resort towns on the coast and CANTERBURY thrives on tourism.

**Kent, kingdom of,** one of the kingdoms of Anglo-Saxon England. Kent was settled (mid-5th cent.) by the Jutes, who overcame the British inhabitants. Their kingdom comprised essentially the area of the present county of Kent. King ÆTHELBERT of Kent established hegemony over England south of the Humber R. and became a Christian. Kent was later subject to King OFFA of MERCIA and in 825 became part of WESSEX. The kingdom remained an advanced area of pre-Norman England because of the archbishopric of CANTERBURY and because of steady intercourse with the Continent.

**Kent, Rockwell,** 1882–1971, American artist and writer. Kent is known for his stark, powerful graphic art and paintings. His major works include *Toilers of the Sea* (Art Inst., Chicago) and *Winter* (Metropolitan Mus.). Among his books are *Wilderness* (1921) and *Salamina* (1935).

**Kent, William,** 1685–1748, English architect, landscape designer, and furniture designer. He designed furniture in a grand and exuberant style as part of unified schemes for the great English houses, built under the stylistic influence of PALLADIO in the 1720s and 30s. Much of his furniture was of massive proportions and richly carved and gilded.

**Kentucky,** state of the US (1984 est. pop. 3,723,000), area 104,623 km² (40,395 sq mi), located in south–central US and bordered by West Virginia (E), Tennessee (S), Missouri and Illinois (W), and Indiana and Ohio (N). The capital is FRANKFORT and Louisville is the largest city, followed by Lexington. The state stretches from the APPALACHIAN MTS in the east to the low flatlands of the MISSISSIPPI R. in the west, between which lie the agricultural plains and rocky hillsides of the bluegrass region. Manufacturing accounts for most of Kentucky's income, with nonelectrical machinery, chemicals, and electrical equipment being chief products. Tobacco has long been the main agricultural crop, and cattle, soybeans, dairy products, corn, and hay are also significant. The state has the largest deposits of bituminous and lignite coal in the US; stone, petroleum, and natural gas are mined. Tourism is attracted by the Mammoth Cave National Park and the annual Kentucky Derby horse races. In 1980 92% of the population was non-Hispanic white and 45% lived in metropolitan areas. Kentucky was an early frontier state, the first west of the Appalachians to join the Union (1792), prospering from trade along the Mississippi and Ohio rivers. Although it remained in the Union in the Civil War, residents fought on both sides. Coal-mining began on a large scale in the 1870s, and continued into the 20th cent. despite a postwar decline. Harlan Co. was the location of violent labour strife in the coalfields in the 1930s. After the national energy crisis in the 1970s strip-mining succeeded underground extraction.

Mahogany and parcel-gilt serving table designed by William **Kent** (c.1740)

**Kentucky and Virginia Resolutions,** in US history, resolutions passed in 1798 and 1799 by the Kentucky and Virginia legislatures in opposition to the ALIEN AND SEDITION ACTS. The Kentucky Resolutions, written by Thomas JEFFERSON, stated that the federal government had no right to exercise powers not delegated to it by the Constitution. A further resolution declared that the states could nullify objectionable federal laws. The Virginia Resolutions, written by James MADISON, were milder. Both were later considered the first notable statements of the STATES' RIGHTS doctrine.

**Kenya** (ˌkenyə, ˌkeen-), officially Republic of Kenya, republic (1987 est. pop. 20,333,000), 582,646 km² (224,960 sq mi), E Africa, bordered by Somalia (E), the Indian Ocean (SE), Tanzania (S), Victoria Nyanza (Lake Victoria, SW), Uganda (W), the Sudan (NW), and Ethiopia (N). Principal cities are NAIROBI, the capital, and MOMBASA, the chief port. Kenya, which lies astride the equator, has five main regions: a narrow, dry coastal strip; bush-covered plains in the interior; high-lying scrublands in the northwest; fertile grasslands and highland forests in the southwest; and the GREAT RIFT VALLEY in the west, location of some of the country's highest mountains, including Mt KENYA (5199 m/17,058 ft). Except for the temperate highlands, the climate is hot and dry. Black Africans, of about 40 ethnic groups, make up 97% of the population. Most of the people follow traditional beliefs, but about 30% are Christian and about 6% Muslim. Swahili is the official language. The great majority of Kenyans engage in subsistence farming. Coffee, tea, sisal, and pyrethrum are the chief exports; coconuts, cashew nuts, cotton, and sugarcane are also grown, and large numbers of cattle are pastured in the grasslands. Industry, which is expanding, includes petroleum-refining, food-processing, and the manufacture of cement and textiles. Tourists,

attracted by Kenya's protected wildlife in Tsavo National Park and by the coastal resorts, e.g., Mombasa, are an important source of income. The GNP is US$5665 million, and the GNP per capita is US$290 (1985).

*History.* Anthropological discoveries indicate that humans, perhaps the first on earth, probably inhabited S Kenya some 2 million years ago. In the Kenya highlands farming and domestic herds can be dated to 1000 BC. Arab traders settled on the coast by the 8th cent. AD, establishing several autonomous city-states. The Portuguese, who first visited the Kenya coast in 1498, gained control of much of it but were expelled by Arabs in 1729. In 1886, under a British-German agreement on spheres of influence in E Africa, most of present-day Kenya passed to Britain, and in 1903, after a railway opened up the interior, the first European settlers moved in. Under Britain, Europeans controlled the government, and Indians, who had arrived earlier, were active in commerce, while black Africans were largely confined to subsistence farming or to work as labourers. Protests by blacks over their inferior status reached a peak in the so-called MAU MAU emergency (1952–56), an armed revolt against British rule. After the rebellion Britain increased black African representation in the legislative council, and in 1963 Kenya gained independence within the COMMONWEALTH. The country became a republic in 1964, with Jomo KENYATTA as president. The first decade of independence was marked by disputes among ethnic groups (especially the Kikuyu and the Luo), by the exodus of many Europeans and Asians, and by sporadic fighting with Somalia over boundary issues. Daniel arap MOI, candidate of the Kenya African National Union (the only legal party), succeeded to the presidency after Kenyatta's death in 1978.

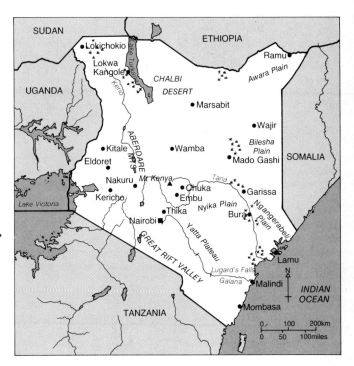

Kenya

**Kenya, Mount,** or **Mount Kirinyaga,** extinct volcano, 5199 m (17,058 ft) high, in Kenya. The snow-capped peak, located near the equator, is the second-highest mountain in Africa, after KILIMANJARO.

**Kenyatta, Jomo,** c.1893–1978, 1st president of KENYA (1964–78). One of the best-known African leaders, he founded various pan-African nationalist movements. He was imprisoned by the British in 1953 following the MAU MAU uprising and was exiled in 1959. He was released in 1961 to negotiate Kenya's independence (1963).

**Kepler, Johannes,** 1571–1630, German astronomer. He was professor of mathematics at Graz (1593–98) and court mathematician to Holy Roman Emperor Rudolf II. In 1596 he wrote *Mysterium cosmographicum,* which led to exchanges with GALILEO and Tycho BRAHE. His *Astronomia nova* (1609) contained the first two of what became

KEPLER'S LAWS; the third law appeared in 1619 in his *Harmonice mundi*. These laws were the result of calculations based on Brahe's accurate observations, which Kepler published in the *Tabulae Rudolphinae* (1627).

**Kepler's laws,** three mathematical statements made by Johannes KEPLER that accurately describe the revolutions of the planets around the Sun. The first law states that the shape of each planet's orbit is an ellipse (see CONIC SECTION) with the Sun at one focus. The second law states that if an imaginary line is drawn from the Sun to the planet, the line will sweep out equal areas in space in equal periods of time throughout the orbit. The third law states that the ratio of the cube of the semimajor axis of the ellipse (i.e., the average distance of the planet from the Sun) to the square of the planet's period (the time it needs to complete one revolution around the Sun) is the same for all the planets. Newton gave a physical explanation of Kepler's laws with his laws of MOTION and law of GRAVITATION. See also CELESTIAL MECHANICS.

**Kerensky, Aleksandr Feodorovich,** 1881–1970, Russian revolutionary. He was prime minister in the provisional government that followed the Feb. 1917 RUSSIAN REVOLUTION, but his failure to withdraw Russia from WORLD WAR I or to deal with economic problems enabled the Bolsheviks (see BOLSHEVISM) to overthrow him in Nov. 1917. He fled to Paris and then (1940) to the US.

**Kérkira** or **Corfu,** island (1981 pop. 99,477), 593 km² (229 sq mi), NW Greece, in the Ionian Sea. Its industries include agriculture, fishing, and tourism. Settled c.730 BC by Corinthians, it later concluded a rebellious alliance with Athens that helped to precipitate (431 BC) the PELOPONNESIAN WAR.

**Kern, Jerome,** 1885–1945, American composer. Among his numerous successful MUSICALS were *Show Boat* (1927; with Oscar HAMMERSTEIN 2nd) and *Roberta* (1933). He wrote many famous songs, including 'Smoke Gets in Your Eyes'.

**kerosene** or **kerosine** a colourless, thin oil that is less dense than water; also called paraffin or paraffin oil in Britain. It is a mixture of HYDROCARBONS commonly obtained in the fractional DISTILLATION of PETROLEUM, but also from coal, oil shale, and wood. Once the most important refinery product because of its use in lamps, kerosene is now used chiefly as a carrier in insecticide sprays and as a fuel in jet engines.

**Kerouac, Jack** (ˌkeroohak), 1922–69, American writer. A leader of the BEAT GENERATION, he wrote of the frenetic pursuit of new experience. His best-known work is the novel *On the Road* (1957). He also wrote other novels and poetry.

**Kerry,** county in the SW of Republic of Ireland (1986 pop. 123,922), 4654 km² (1815 sq mi), bordering on the Atlantic Ocean in the S and E. It is situated in Munster province. The county town is TRALEE. It has a very indented coastline and much of the inland portion of the county is mountainous. The Slieve Mish Mts are in the NW, MACGILLYCUDDY'S REEKS in the W and the Derrynasaggart Mts in the SE. The highest point in Ireland is Carrauntoohil in Macgillycuddy's Reeks at 1041 m (3414 ft). The main rivers are the Feale, Maine, and Laune. Agriculture is important in the lowland areas. The Lakes of Killarney (including the largest, Lough Leane) are popular tourist spots and the town of KILLARNEY is a tourist centre. Much of the county is picturesque.

**Kesselring, Albert,** 1885–1960, German field marshal. During WORLD WAR II he served in virtually every theatre, becoming commander in chief in the West (1945). He was convicted (1947) of WAR CRIMES and imprisoned, but was freed in 1952.

**kestrel** or **windhover,** small BIRD of prey in the FALCON family, distributed over Europe, Asia, and Africa. The common kestrel (*Falco tinnunculus*) is 34 cm (13½ in) long. It earns the name windhover by hanging in the air, scanning the ground below for any movement, gliding along with a few wing flaps to scan a new section in the same way. Kestrels normally eat small rodents, but will also take birds. They have adapted to town life, nesting in tall buildings and often being seen hunting along motorways.

**kettledrum:** see DRUM.

**Kew Gardens,** BOTANICAL GARDEN and research institute on the Thames just W of London; officially, Royal Botanic Gardens. It was founded in 1761 and officially established as a National Institute in Britain in 1841. Its 300 acres of gardens, park, and glasshouses contain one of the most comprehensive collections of living plants, while its HERBARIUM is an international standard for plant identification. Its laboratories research into all aspects of plant science.

**Kew Gardens:** The Princess of Wales Conservatory, which houses plants from 10 different climatic zones, was opened in 1987.

**key,** in music, is used to indicate the scale from which the tonal material of a composition is derived. To say that a composition is in the key of C major means that it uses as its basic tonal material the tones of the C-major scale and that its harmony employs the chords built on the tones of that scale. MODULATION to another key may be utilized within the composition. A term usually used synonymously with *key* is TONALITY; absence of a feeling of key is ATONALITY.

**Key Largo:** island: see FLORIDA KEYS.

**Keynes, John Maynard, Baron Keynes of Tilton** (kaynz), 1883–1946, English economist and monetary expert. His theories, known as Keynesian economics, stand as the most influential economic formulation of the 20th cent. In 1919 he represented the British treasury at the peace conference ending WORLD WAR I, but he resigned in protest over the VERSAILLES Treaty's economic provisions. He gained world fame with *Economic Consequences of the Peace* (1919). His departure from the classical concepts of a free economy dates from 1929, when he endorsed a government public-works programme to promote employment. In the 1930s his theories prompted several nations to adopt spending programmes, such as those of the NEW DEAL, to maintain high national income. His main work, *The General Theory of Employment, Interest, and Money* (1936), sums up his advocacy of active government intervention in the market and, during recessionary times, deficit spending and easier monetary policies to stimulate business activity. At the Bretton Woods Conference (1944) he helped to win support for the creation of a world bank. He was raised to the peerage in 1942.

**Khabarovsk,** city (1985 pop. 576,000), Soviet Far East, on the Amur R. near the border with Manchuria. It occupies a strategic position on the TRANS-SIBERIAN RAILWAY and is the centre for all air traffic for the Far East. Its varied industries serve the Far Eastern market and include machine-building, metal-working, oil refining, chemicals, shipbuilding, timber production, textiles, and food-processing. The city was founded in 1652 as a fortress by the Russian explorer of the same name.

**Khachaturian, Aram Ilyich,** 1903–78, Soviet composer of Armenian parentage. His colourful music uses Armenian and Oriental folk elements. He is best known for the ballets *Gayane* (1942, including the popular *Sabre Dance*) and *Spartacus* (1954), and his Piano Concerto (1936).

**Khalid ibn Abd al-Aziz al-Saud,** 1913–82, king of SAUDI ARABIA (1975–82). He became king after the assassination of his half-brother FAISAL. A son of IBN SAUD, the founder of Saudi Arabia, he was the third of Ibn Saud's sons to become king. He continued the widespread economic and social reforms begun by Faisal and was succeeded by his half-brother FAHD.

**Khama, Tshekedi,** 1905–59, regent of Bangwato (r.1926–49), largest of BOTSWANA's eight principal ethnic groups. He championed the struggle of the Batswana not to be incorporated into the Union of South Africa. He was deposed from the regency by the British when he refused to consent to the marriage of his nephew, and heir to the chieftainship, Seretse Khama, to a European.

**Khama III,** c.1835–1923, king of the Bangwato (r.1875–1923), one of the eight principal ethnic groups of BOTSWANA. In 1895 he visited England with two other Tswana kings, SEBELE I and BATHOENG I, to protest the annexation of their territories by Cecil RHODES's British South Africa Company. The following year however, his territory secured by British protection, he helped Rhodes defeat the Ndebele. A progressive ruler, he abolished many traditional practices, and, with the help of the London Missionary Society, tried to impose Christianity on his people.

**Kharg,** island, S Iran, in the PERSIAN GULF, c.20 km² (8 sq mi), lying 40 km (25 mi) from the Iranian coast and 200 km (120 mi) from the SHATT AL ARAB. It is connected to the mainland by an oil pipeline and has a terminal where large oil tankers unable to enter the Shatt Al Arab can load Iranian oil. Its importance grew after the outbreak of the Iran-Iraq war (1980) and it became a regular target for Iraqi air attacks.

**Kharkov** (ˌkhahkəf), city (1985 pop. 1,554,000), S European USSR, in the UKRAINE, at the confluence of the Kharkov, Lopan, and Udy rivers in the upper Donets valley. It is the sixth-largest Soviet city and a main rail junction. Products include metals and chemicals. Founded in 1656 as a military outpost, it became a centre of commerce and culture. From 1919 to 1934 it was the capital of the Ukraine, until superseded by KIEV.

**Khartoum,** city (1983 pop. 476,218), capital of Sudan, a port at the confluence of the Blue Nile and White Nile rivers. Food, beverages, cotton, gum, and oil seeds are processed. Khartoum is a rail centre, with road connections to the adjacent cotton-growing region and an international airport. Founded in 1821 as an Egyptian army camp, it developed as a trade centre and slave market. British forces resisted a long siege here in which Gen. Charles GORDON was killed (1885). The city was retaken in 1898 by a joint British and Egyptian force under Lord KITCHENER.

**Khartoum North,** city (1983 pop. 341,146), Sudan, on the Blue Nile opposite Khartoum. The town's economy is based on tanning, weaving, and food processing industries and on the export of cotton and cereals.

**Khatyn,** village in Byelorussia, USSR, destroyed by the invading German army in 1941, now the site of the Byelorussian national war memorial. See also KATYN FOREST.

**Khayyam, Omar:** see OMAR KHAYYAM.

**Khazars,** ancient Turkic people who appeared in Transcaucasia in the 2nd cent. AD and subsequently settled in the lower Volga region. They rose to great power; the Khazar empire at its height (8th–10th cent. AD) extended from the northern shores of the Black Sea and the Caspian Sea as far west as Kiev. The Khazars maintained friendly relations with the Byzantine Empire. Their empire came to an end in 965 when they were defeated by the duke of Kiev. In the 8th cent. the Khazar nobility embraced Judaism and thus are believed by some to be the ancestors of many East European Jews.

**Khíos** or **Chios,** island (1981 pop. 49,865), c.910 km² (350 sq mi), E Greece, in the Aegean Sea. Its main industries are agriculture and marble quarrying. Colonized by Ionians, the island was independent by 479 BC. It claims to be the birthplace of HOMER and is famed for its scenic beauty.

**Khmer Empire,** ancient kingdom of SE Asia, roughly corresponding to modern CAMBODIA and LAOS; fl. 6th–15th cent. It reached its greatest extent in the ANGKOR period (AD 889–1434), which produced exquisite architecture and sculpture. Khmer civilization was formed largely by Indian influences. The Khmers fought repeated wars against CHAMPA and the Annamese. The empire declined after invasions from Thailand.

**Khmer Rouge,** Kampuchean Communist guerrilla force. Aided by Vietnamese Communists, it waged a war (1970–75) that toppled the LON NOL regime. Under POL POT, it then undertook a ruthless collectivization drive in which an estimated 3 million people died. Disputes with Vietnam led to a Vietnamese invasion (1978–79), the ousting of the Khmer Rouge, and installation of the Vietnamese-backed HENG SAMRIN regime. The Khmer Rouge, however, continued to field an army of about 30,000 men near the Thai border and retained UN recognition as the official Kampuchean government. In 1982 it formed a coalition with former premier NORODOM SIHANOUK and the non-Communist leader Son Sann to oppose the Heng Samrin government.

**Khoikhoi,** people of Namibia and the Cape prov. of the Republic of South Africa. Formerly called Hottentots by whites, they speak a Khoisan language close to that of the San (Bushmen). A pastoral, nomadic people, they were decimated as Dutch colonialists took over their lands beginning in the 17th cent.; most of the c.40,000 survivors live in villages in Namibia.

**Khomeini, Ayatollah Ruhollah** (ˌkomayˌnee), 1900–89, religious leader of IRAN; b. Ruhollah Hendi. A SHI'ITE Muslim, he adopted the name Khomeini in 1930. After teaching at a theological school in Qom, he was arrested (1963) and exiled to Turkey and Iraq before moving to Paris in 1978. Following the revolution that deposed MUHAMMAD REZA SHAH PAHLEVI, Khomeini returned in triumph to Iran in 1979, declared an Islamic republic, and began to exercise ultimate authority in the nation. His rule was marked by the holding of US hostages (1979–81) and by war with Iraq (1980–88).

**Khorezm** or **Khwarazm** (khəˌrezəm), ancient Central Asian state; now in the NW Uzbek Soviet Socialist Republic, USSR. Part of the empire of CYRUS THE GREAT (6th cent. BC), Khorezm was conquered by the Arabs and converted to Islam in the 7th cent. AD. Briefly independent (late 12th cent.), it ruled from the Caspian Sea to Bukhara and Samarkand, but fell to JENGHIZ KHAN (1221), to TAMERLANE (late 14th cent.), and then to the Uzbeks (early 16th cent.), who called it the khanate of Khiva.

**Khosru,** kings of PERSIA. **Khosru I,** d. 579 (r.531–79), was the greatest of the Sassanid monarchs and extended Persian rule E to the Indus River and W across Arabia, and N and NW by taking part of Armenia and Caucasia from the Byzantines. **Khosru II,** d. 628 (r.590–628), of the Sassanid dynasty, conquered much Byzantine territory before being assassinated by his son and successor, Kauadh II Shiruya.

**Khrennikov, Tikhon** (ˌkrenikov), 1913–, Soviet composer and president of the Union of Soviet Composers, whose secretary he became in 1948. Amongst his orchestral works are three symphonies and a Violin Concerto (1958–59), two Piano Concertos (1932–33 and 1971), a Cello Concerto (1964), and several operas, especially *Into the Storm (V buryu,* 1939), which was noted for its socialist realism and for being the first opera to feature LENIN as a character.

**Khrushchev, Nikita Sergeyevich** (ˌkroos-chof), 1894–1971, Soviet leader. Of Russian origin from the Ukraine, he joined the Communist Party in 1918, becoming a member of its central committee in 1934. As first secretary of the Ukrainian party (from 1938) he carried out Joseph STALIN's purge of its ranks, and as a full member of the politburo (after 1939) he was a close associate of Stalin. In the power struggle after Stalin's death (1953) he emerged as first secretary of the party. At the 1956 party congress he delivered a 'secret' report denouncing Stalin's policies and personality, and signalling the acceleration of destalinization. The new atmosphere of freedom, however, encouraged uprisings in Poland and Hungary that year. In 1957 he replaced BULGANIN as premier, becoming head of both state and party. As part of his policy of 'peaceful coexistence' in the COLD WAR he toured the US in 1959 and met Pres. EISENHOWER; but in 1960 he cancelled the Paris summit conference after a US reconaissance plane was shot down over the USSR (see U2 INCIDENT). Repeated crop failures, his retreat in the CUBAN MISSILE CRISIS (1962), and the ideological rift with China led to his removal from power in Oct. 1964.

**Khufu** or **Cheops** (ˌkoohfooh, ˌkee-ops), (kēˌōps), fl. c.2680 BC, Egyptian king, founder of the IV dynasty. He ruled for 23 years and built the greatest PYRAMID at Gizeh.

**Khwarazm:** see KHOREZM.

**Khyber Pass,** narrow, steep-sided mountain pass, c.1070 m (3500 ft) high and 45 km (28 mi) long, on the Pakistan–Afghanistan border. For centuries the main western land approach to India, it was used by ALEXANDER THE GREAT, TAMERLANE, and other conquerors. A modern highway and a railway (built 1920–25) with 34 tunnels link Peshawar, Pakistan, with the Afghan capital, Kabul.

**Kiangsi:** see JIANGXI.

**Kiangsu:** see JIANGSU.

**kibbutz,** most important type of Israeli COLLECTIVE FARM or industrial settlement. The land is held by the Jewish National Fund and rented at a nominal fee; all other property (except certain personal possessions) is collectively owned. Planning and work is communal, and collective living is the rule for children although adults have private quarters. Elected officials administer social and economic affairs. About 5% of Israel's population live on kibbutzim.

**Kickapoo Indians:** see NORTH AMERICAN INDIANS.

**Kid, Thomas:** see KYD, THOMAS.

**Kidd, William** (Captain Kidd), 1645?–1701, English pirate. Commissioned (1695) as a privateer to guard English ships in the Red Sea and Indian Ocean, he turned pirate. He was tried for piracy and murder and hanged in England. Legends of his barbaric cruelty and buried treasure are unsubstantiated.

**kiddush** [Heb., = sanctification], Jewish ceremonial blessing over a goblet of wine; it highlights the sanctity of the Sabbath or a Hebrew festival. In the evenings it is recited both in synagogue as well as in the home before the commencement of the festive meal. During the daytime, it is not recited during the service, but is reserved for the refreshment served afterwards, in the synagogue hall, as well as at home before the midday meal.

**kidnapping,** unlawful taking away of someone by force, threat, or deceit, to detain the person against his or her will. Kidnapping is usually carried out by criminal gangs, in order to extort ransom payments from relatives, or by political extremists, as a means of forcing concessions from governments (e.g., release of prisoners). Kidnapping is considered a serious offence and is punishable in most countries by death or life imprisonment.

**kidney,** either of a pair of small, bean-shaped organs of the URINARY SYSTEM, located near the spine at the small of the back. The kidneys extract water and urea, mineral salts, toxins, and other nitrogenous waste products from the blood with filtering units called nephrons. From the nephrons the collected waste (URINE) is sent to the bladder for excretion. One kidney must function properly for life to be maintained. Kidney diseases include nephritis, inflammation of the kidneys, and the nephrotic syndrome, a condition characterized by general oedema and by the excretion of protein in the urine. See also DIALYSIS; TRANSPLANTATION, MEDICAL.

**kidney machine:** see DIALYSIS.

**Kiel** (keel), city (1984 pop. 246,900), N West Germany, on Kiel Bay, capital of SCHLESWIG-HOLSTEIN. Germany's chief naval base from 1871 to 1945, it is now a shipping and industrial centre producing ships, textiles, processed foods, and printed materials. Kiel was chartered in 1242 and joined the HANSEATIC LEAGUE in 1284. It passed to Denmark in 1773 and to Prussia in 1866. A naval mutiny at Kiel touched off a socialist revolution in Germany in 1918.

**Kiel Canal,** waterway almost 100km (62 mi) long built (1887–95) to permit the German navy to pass safely between the Baltic and the North Sea. Originally 9 m in depth and subsequently deepened, it links Kiel with Brunsbuttel on the ELBE R. and now ranks as one of the world's most important ship canals.

**Kielce** (ˌkaylitse), city (1984 pop. 197,000), S Poland. It is the administrative centre of Kielce voivodship. Engineering and chemical industries established in the area have boosted its population since World War II.

**Kielland, Alexander Lange** (ˌkhellahn), 1849–1906, Norwegian author of the realistic school, a follower of George BRANDES. His witty novels of social reform include *Garman and Worse* (1880) and *Skipper Worse* (1882). He also wrote short stories and plays.

**Kierkegaard, Sören Aaby,** 1813–55, Danish philosopher and writer. He is regarded as the progenitor of modern existentialism, expounded in *Concluding Unscientific Postscript* (1846). He championed the cause of subjective commitment based on personal choice and belief, in *Either/Or* (1845–47). His theory of the three stages of intellectual development (the aesthetic, ethical, and religious) was expressed in *Stations on Life's Way* (1845), which contained his best-known short story, 'In Vino Veritas'. His writings are marked by trenchant social criticism and denunciation of the vapidness of established religion in Denmark.

**Kiev** (ˌkee-ef), city (1985 pop. 2,448,000), capital of the UKRAINE, SW European USSR, on the Dnepr R. It is the USSR's third-largest city and a major port. Industries include food processing, metallurgy, and chemicals. One of the oldest European cities, it was a commercial centre as early as the 5th cent. and became the capital of KIEVAN RUSSIA in the 9th cent. Invaded (1240) by the Mongols, it paid tribute to the GOLDEN HORDE until it passed (14th cent.) under the control of LITHUANIA. It became (17th cent.) part of the Russian Empire and later (1920) of the USSR. During the German occupation (1941–44) thousands of Kiev's residents, including 50,000 Jews, were massacred. Reconstruction of the city ended c.1960. Its architectural treasures include the 11th-cent. Cathedral of St Sophia.

**Kievan Russia,** the medieval state of the Eastern Slavs, who at that period were not yet differentiated into Great Russians and Ruthenes (Belorussians and Ukrainians). It included most of the present-day UKRAINE and BELORUSSIA, and parts of RUSSIA. In about 862 Rurik, a Varangian (Scandinavian) warrior, founded a dynasty at NOVGOROD. His successor, Oleg (d. 912), seized Kiev, establishing the Kievan state, and freed the Eastern Slavs from the sway of the KHAZARS. Under Sviatoslav (d. 972) Kievan power reached the lower Volga and N Caucasus. VLADIMIR I (r.980–1015) introduced Christianity. Under his son, YAROSLAV (r.1019–54), the state reached its cultural and political apex, but after Yaroslav's death it was weakened by internal strife and ultimately fell to the Mongols (1237–40). In the subsequent period, the western and southern parts of Kievan Russia were overrun by the Lithuanians, and passed in due course into the Commonwealth of Poland-Lithuania. The north-eastern part formed the basis of the Grand Duchy of Moscow, which set itself the long-term goal of reuniting all the lands of Kievan Russia under the name of 'RUSSIA'.

**Kigali,** town (1981 est. pop. 156,650), capital of Rwanda. Founded by Germany in 1907, it is the country's main administrative and economic centre, and has an international airport. A new tin-smelting plant was built in the early 1980s to process cassiterite (tin ore), which is mined in the vicinity.

**Kikuyu,** Bantu-speaking agricultural people of northern Kenya, inhabiting highlands NE of Nairobi; they number around 2 million. The most influential of Kenya's peoples, they fought the British during the 1950s MAU MAU rebellion. Dwelling traditionally in family homesteads, more recently in villages, they have a patrilineal social organization with much emphasis on age groups. Kikuyu tribal customs are described in Jomo KENYATTA's *Facing Mount Kenya* (1938).

**Kilauea** (ˌkeelahˌwayə), volcanic crater, Hawaii island, on the southeastern slope of MAUNA LOA in Hawaii Volcanoes National Park. It is c.13 km (8 mi) in circumference and 1111 m (3646 ft) deep, with a lake of molten lava c.230 m (740 ft) below its rim.

**Kildare,** inland county in E of Republic of Ireland (1986 pop. 116,015), 1677 km² (654 sq mi), bordering on Co. Dublin in the E. The county town is NAAS. It is situated in Leinster province. Most of the county is low-lying and fertile. The Bog of Allen is in the N and the Curragh in the centre. The SE of the county is more hilly, rising towards the Wicklow Mts. The main rivers are the LIFFEY and the BARROW. The Curragh is well-known for racehorse breeding. Root crops and cereals are grown, and there is some manufacturing industry in Naas.

**Kilimanjaro,** highest mountain of Africa, NE Tanzania. An extinct volcano, it rises in two snow-capped peaks, Kibo (5895 m/19,340 ft) and Mawenzi (5354 m/17,564 ft).

**Kilkenny,** county in SE of Republic of Ireland (1986 pop. 73,094), 2041 km², (796 sq mi), bordering on Co. Tipperary in the W. It is situated in the province of Leinster. The county town is KILKENNY. The R. BARROW forms much of the eastern border and the R. SUIR forms the SW border. The R. Nore crosses the centre of the county from N to S. Most of the county is hilly, including the Slieve Ardagh Hills in the W. Mixed agriculture is an important economic activity in the fertile valleys.

The southwest face of **Kilimanjaro**

**Killarney,** urban district (1986 pop. 7859), Co. Kerry, SW Republic of Ireland. The town, which has some light industry, is a tourist centre for the three nearby Lakes of Killarney.

**killer whale:** see DOLPHIN.

**kiln,** furnace for firing pottery and enamels; for making brick, charcoal, lime, and cement; for roasting ores; and for drying various substances. A kiln may be fired intermittently or continuously. Pottery kilns vary in size and shape, and in the temperature they attain: c.500–1150°C for earthenware, c.1200–1400°C for stoneware, and c.1280–1450°C for porcelain. Early kilns were wood-fired, but by the 18th cent. English potters were already using coal-fired ovens. In the late 19th and 20th cent. the downdraught bottle oven was developed to use heat more efficiently. Today, pottery and porcelain factories use tunnel kilns, fired continuously by gas or electricity. Bricks are fired in continuous kilns or in tunnel kilns. Rotary kilns, much used in continuous processes, e.g., cement manufacturing, consist of long tubes, lying almost horizontally, that are rotated slowly as heat is applied to the material being treated inside the tubes.

**kilogram:** see METRIC SYSTEM; WEIGHTS AND MEASURES, table.

**kilowatt:** see POWER.

**kilt,** a skirt arranged in narrow regular pleats. Originally associated with the traditional dress worn by men in the Highlands of Scotland, where it formed the lower part of the belted PLAID. It is still worn by men as part of the Highland dress and is part of the uniform of some Scottish regiments, but is also worn by women in a general fashionable context. A short kilted skirt is still worn by the Evzone soldiers of the Greek National Guard.

**Kilvert, Francis,** 1840–79, English diarist and clergyman. His diary, describing the landscape and people of the Welsh border with delicate insight, was not published till 1938–40, but has since become a classic.

**Kimbangu, Simon,** 1887–1951, W African independent church leader; b. Zaire. He was converted to Christianity in 1915 and soon after founded his own independent church which placed special emphasis on faith healing. He was arrested in 1921 by the colonial authorities and found guilty of subversion. He spent the rest of his life in Elizabethville (now Lubumbashi) prison. His church is reputed to have the second largest following in Zaïre after the Roman Catholic church.

**Kimberley,** region of northern Western Australia. This rugged, dissected plateau is bounded on the E by the Ord R., on the S by the Fitzroy R. and covers about 3% of Australia. Isolated by land and sea, Hall's Creek saw the first gold strike in Western Australia in 1885. Today the inland area is largely occupied by cattle stations. The main settlements, along the coast, are BROOME, Derby and Wyndham. Commercial development of diamond mines has commenced at Argyle, producing industrial and gem-quality stones. Iron ore is mined at Yampi Sound and Cockatoo Island. Construction of dams on the Ord R. provides

irrigation water for experimental agriculture and research into the development of tropical crops. The Wandjina figures are important examples of Aboriginal rock paintings in this area.

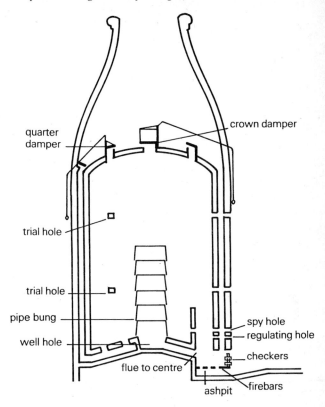

Kiln: The downdraught bottle oven

**Kimhi** or **Kimchi** (ˌkimkhee), family of Jewish scholars and grammarians in Spain and France. **Joseph ben Isaac Kimhi,** 1105?–1170?, wrote a biblical commentary, translations from Arabic, and poetry, and made grammatical reforms. His *Sefer ha-Berit* is an anti-Christian polemic. His son **Moses Kimhi,** d. 1190?, wrote *Paths of Knowledge,* a grammatical text used by 16th-cent. Christian Hebraists for its philological information. Another son, **David Kimhi,** known as Redak, 1160?–1235?, was the author of a noted Hebrew grammar, a biblical dictionary, and learned commentaries that were included in standard editions of the Hebrew Bible.

**Kim Il Sung,** 1912–, North Korean political leader. Trained as a Communist in Moscow, he was North KOREA's first premier (1948–72) and led his nation in the KOREAN WAR. In 1972 he became president under a revised constitution.

**kindergarten,** system of infant education designed (1837) by Friedrich FROEBEL. In an educational situation less formal than elementary school, children's play instincts are organized constructively through songs, stories, games, simple materials, and group activities, to develop habits of cooperation and application. Froebel's approach was one of the first applications of child-centred theory to the infant classroom. The first kindergarten in Britain was established by two refugees from Germany, Johannes and Bertha Ronge, in 1851, and a kindergarten movement spread in Britain and internationally from the 1850s.

**Kindi, al-,** ?–c.872, Islamic philosopher, full name Abu-Yusuf Ya'qub ibn Ishaq al-Kindi. Known as the father of Islamic philosophy, he was a major figure of NEOPLATONISM, who tried to combine Greek philosophy with Muslim theology, although most of his views were rejected by his successors Al-Farabi and AVICENNA.

**kinematics:** see DYNAMICS.

**kinetic art,** term referring to sculpture in which motion is a significant feature. Developed in response to technology, it was pioneered by Marcel DUCHAMP, Naum GABO, and Alexander CALDER. The art can be either mechanical or nonmechanical.

**kinetic energy:** see ENERGY.

**kinetics:** see DYNAMICS.

**kinetic theory of gases,** physical theory that explains the behaviour of gases by assuming that any gas is composed of a very large number of very small particles, called molecules, that are very far apart compared to their sizes. The molecules are assumed to exert no forces on one another, except during the rare collisions. A gas corresponding to these assumptions is called an ideal gas. The analysis of the behaviour of an ideal gas according to the laws of mechanics leads to the GAS LAWS. The theory also shows that the absolute TEMPERATURE is directly proportional to the average kinetic energy of the molecules, the constant of proportionality being BOLTZMANN's constant $k = 1.381 \times 10 - 23$ joule/K. Pressure is seen to be the result of large numbers of collisions between molecules and the walls of the container in which the gas is held. See THERMODYNAMICS.

**King, Billie Jean,** 1943–, American tennis player; b. Billie Jean Moffitt. Outstanding in both singles and doubles play, she won six singles and 10 doubles championships at WIMBLEDON by 1979, and took the US Open singles crown four times between 1967 and 1974. King has been instrumental in improving the status of women's professional tennis.

**King, Martin Luther, Jr.,** 1929–68, black American clergyman and civil rights leader. An active Baptist minister and a moving orator, he first gained national prominence by advocating passive resistance to segregation and leading a year-long boycott (1955–56) against the segregated bus lines in Montgomery, Alabama. He subsequently set up the Southern Christian Leadership Conference as a base for nonviolent marches, protests, and demonstrations for black rights, such as the 1963 March on Washington and the 1965 voter-registration drive in Selma, Alabama. King was awarded the 1964 Nobel Peace Prize, but his leadership was challenged as civil-rights activists became more militant. In the late 1960s he intensified his opposition to the war in Vietnam and to economic discrimination. While planning a multiracial Poor People's March for antipoverty legislation, he was shot and killed in Memphis, Tennessee. James Earl Ray was convicted of the murder.

**King, William Lyon Mackenzie,** 1874–1950, prime minister of CANADA (1921–30, 1935–48). He was editor (1900–1908) of the *Labour Gazette* and minister of labour (1909–11) in the Liberal government before he succeeded (1919) Wilfred LAURIER as the Liberals' leader. As prime minister during World War II, King directed the Canadian war effort and signed agreements with the United States providing for joint defence.

**King Arthur:** see ARTHURIAN LEGEND.

**king crab** or **horseshoe crab,** large marine invertebrate animal (class Merostomata), an ARTHROPOD living in coastal waters off America and Asia. It has a heavy, dark brown, domed exoskeleton divided into a broad horseshoe-shaped front part (prosoma), a tapered middle region (opisthosoma), and a spiky, taillike part (telson). King crabs swim or burrow using five pairs of walking legs. The largest reach 60 cm (2 ft) in length. They are not true crabs, but living fossils, surviving virtually unchanged for nearly 200 million years.

**kingfisher** or **halcyon,** widespread group of small carnivorous BIRDS of the family Alcedinidae. Many hunt in fresh waters, diving in to catch fishes, amphibians, and insects, while other species hunt on land, taking lizards and small invertebrates. These brightly coloured birds live everywhere in the world except deserts and cold regions. The beautiful common kingfisher (*Alcedo atthis*) is found across Europe and southern Asia. The bird digs burrows in river banks by flying at one spot until it has loosened enough soil to make a ledge on which to stand and finish excavating its nest. The Australian kookaburras (*Dacelo sp.*) are kingfishers.

**King George's War:** see FRENCH AND INDIAN WARS.

**Kingis Quair,** poem attributed to King JAMES I of Scotland (1394–1437). It was written in the Chaucerian style while he was a prisoner in England, and probably relates to his marriage to Joan Beaufort.

**King Philip's War,** 1675–76, the most devastating Indian war in NEW ENGLAND, US. Named after King Philip, chief of the Wampanoag Indians, the war began when the English executed three Indians for murder. It involved several Indian tribes and all the New England colonies before the Indians were subdued.

**Kings,** books of the OLD TESTAMENT, called First and Second Kings in the Authorized Version. They continue the history of 1 and 2 SAMUEL from the death of DAVID to the destruction of the southern kingdom of Judah (i.e., from 1000 to 560 BC). They include the reign of SOLOMON (1 Kings 1–11); a parallel account of the two Hebrew kingdoms (1 Kings 12–2 Kings 17), including the stories of the house of AHAB and the prophets ELIJAH and ELISHA; and the end of the southern kingdom (2 Kings 18–25).

**Kingsley, Charles,** 1819–75, English author and clergyman. His views on CHRISTIAN SOCIALISM were expressed in the novels *Alton Locke* (1850), *Yeast* (1850) and *Two Years Ago* (1857). A remark by Kingsley denigrating the Roman Catholic clergy produced a controversy with J.H. NEWMAN and led to Newman's *Apologia.* Kingsley's historical novels include *Westward Ho!* (1855). *The Water Babies* (1863) is a children's classic, and some of his songs and ballads became popular traditions.

**King's Lynn,** town (1981 pop. 37,323) in Norfolk, E England, on R. Ouse, just S of The Wash. It is a port, market town and industrial centre. In 1984 the port handled 1.1 million tonnes. Industries found within the town include canning and sugar-beet refining. It has been an important town since Saxon times, and was a leading port in the Middle Ages. Several old buildings remain, including a 17th-cent. customs house. It is the birthplace of George VANCOUVER.

**Kingston,** city (1986 est. pop. 750,000), SE Jamaica, capital of Jamaica. It is the island's commercial hub, chief port, and largest city. Founded in 1692 on one of the Caribbean's best-protected harbours, near the early capital of Port Royal, Kingston replaced Spanish Town as Jamaica's capital in 1872. Tourism, oil-refining, and food-processing are major industries. The city's botanical gardens are famous.

**Kingston upon Thames,** London borough (1981 pop. 131,236), in SW of London on right bank of R. Thames upstream from central London. It is a royal borough and includes Malden, Coombe, and Surbiton. A residential and industrial borough, it is a place of ancient foundation, where Saxon kings were crowned.

**Kingstown,** city (1980 pop. 23,959), capital of SAINT VINCENT AND THE GRENADINES.

**King William's War:** see FRENCH AND INDIAN WARS.

**Kinneret:** see GALILEE, SEA OF.

**Kinnock, Neil,** 1942–, British politician, leader of the LABOUR PARTY (1983–). Having entered Parliament in 1970 for a Welsh constituency, Kinnock identified himself with the Labour Party's left wing at a time when it was in the ascendancy. After Labour's election defeat in 1983 he succeeded his mentor Michael FOOT as party leader, despite having had no ministerial experience, becoming the youngest-ever person to hold the post. As leader he sought to curb extremist elements in the party, taking a prominent role in the expulsion of leading members of the MILITANT TENDENCY in 1986. He also committed the party to a non-nuclear defence strategy and the removal of US nuclear bases from British territory, although revisions of this and other aspects of Labour policy were initiated in 1988 following the party's third successive election defeat in 1987, and accepted in 1989 after a policy review.

**Kinsey, Alfred Charles,** 1894–1956, American biologist and behavioural scientist. He is most widely known for his studies of sexual behaviour, based upon interviews with over 10,000 American informants. This work was summarized in *Sexual Behaviour in the Human Male* (1948) and *Sexual Behaviour in the Human Female* (1953). Kinsey founded and was first director (1942–56) of the Institute for Sex Research at the Univ. of Indiana.

**Kinshasa,** largest city (1981 pop. 2,338,246) and capital of Zaïre, W Zaïre, a port on the Zaïre R. It is the country's communications and commercial centre, with rail links upriver to Matadi, motorboat service to BRAZZAVILLE, Congo Republic, and an international airport. Its industries include textiles and footwear manufacture. Founded in 1881 by Henry M. STANLEY, who named it Leopoldville (after Leopold II of Belgium), the city became the capital of the Belgian Congo in 1926. A rebellion there in 1959 launched the country's drive for independence. Modern Kinshasa (so named in 1966) is an educational and cultural centre.

**kinship,** the method of establishing basic relationships with others through assigning parenthood, tracing DESCENT, classifying relatives, transmitting rights across generations, and regulating mating. Such relationships are modelled on those which supposedly exist between mother and father and child. Major disagreement exists between the approaches of STRUCTURAL FUNCTIONALISM and STRUCTURALISM to kinship; the former argues the primacy of mother–child relations and of descent, using psychological universals to support their claims, the latter argues that EXCHANGE, thus the exchange of women, is basic to kinship. See also LINEAGE.

**kinship terminology,** a system of terms, specific to a given society, which are used to denote kin of different categories. Known kinship terminologies have been classified into five main groups: (1) the Crow, which distinguishes maternal and paternal lines but uses the same term for siblings and the children of parallel cousins, while cross cousins are addressed by the same term as those of their father's generation; (2) Eskimo, in which both cross and parallel cousins are grouped together but distinguished from siblings; (3) Hawaiian, in which all same-sex relatives of the same generation are grouped under the same term; (4) Iroquois, in which cross cousins are differentiated from parallel cousins and siblings who are equated with each other; (5) Omaha, the mirror image of the Crow system. Kinship terminologies do not necessarily reflect the actual operation of the KINSHIP system.

**Kintu,** the 1st king (14th–15th cent.) of the Ganda state (UGANDA), according to oral tradition. His history is shrouded in legend and myth, and he may represent many rulers or possibly a time of great political and cultural change marked by centralization of the state and major migrations.

**Kiowa Indians,** NORTH AMERICAN INDIANS of the Plains. They had a pictographic calendar and worshipped a stone image, the *taimay*. Nomads, they acquired horses c.1710. Forced from the Black Hills by the CHEYENNE and SIOUX, they joined the COMANCHE in raids as far south as Mexico. In the 19th cent. they opposed white settlers and migrating eastern Indians until subdued (1874) by the US Army. About 4000 Kiowa live in Oklahoma today.

**Kipling, Rudyard,** 1865–1936, English author; b. India. Kipling's popular works interpret India in all its heat, strife, and ennui. His romantic view of English imperialism is reflected in such well-known poems as 'Mandalay', 'Gunga Din', and *Recessional* (1897). His works include poems, in *Departmental Ditties* (1886) and *Barrack-Room Ballads* (1892); stories, in *Plain Tales from the Hills* and *Soldiers Three* (both 1888), and several later collections; a novel, *The Light That Failed* (1890); and children's stories, such as *The Jungle Book* (1894) and *Captains Courageous* (1897). His masterpiece is *Kim* (1901), in which Indian life is portrayed through the experiences of an abandoned child who becomes a British secret agent. He received the 1907 Nobel Prize for literature.

**Kirby, William,** 1817–1906, Canadian author; b. England. He is noted for *The Golden Dog* (1877), also published as *Le Chien d'or* (1884), a popular romance of 17th-cent. Quebec.

**Kirchhoff, Gustav Robert** (kiəkhhof), 1824–87, German physicist. He was professor of physics at the universities of Breslau, Heidelberg, and Berlin. He and Robert BUNSEN, working with the spectroscope, discovered the elements CAESIUM and RUBIDIUM. Kirchhoff explained the Fraunhofer lines in the solar spectrum (see SUN) and formulated KIRCHHOFF'S LAWS describing current and voltage in an electric circuit.

**Kirchhoff's laws,** pair of laws stating general restrictions on the current and voltage (see POTENTIAL, ELECTRIC) in an ELECTRIC CIRCUIT or network. The first states that at any given instant the sum of the voltages around any closed path, or loop, in the network is zero. The second states that at any junction of paths in a network the sum of the currents arriving at any instant is equal to the sum of the currents flowing away.

**Kirchner, Ernst Ludwig** (kiəkhnə), 1880–1938, German expressionist painter and graphic artist. Inspired by primitive sculpture; late Gothic WOODCUTS; and the art of MUNCH, VAN GOGH, and the Fauves (see FAUVISM), he cofounded (1905) the BRÜCKE group in Dresden. The theme of his work sought to undermine the traditional bourgeois values and conventions, especially attitudes to sexual behaviour and decorum. In 1911 he went to Berlin and painted a series of street scenes in a more expressive and frenzied style. By 1913 he had quarrelled with the other die Brücke members and the group split up.

**Kirghiz Soviet Socialist Republic, Kirghizia** or **Kirghizstan** (kiə‚geez), constituent republic (1985 pop. 3,976,000), c.198,400 km² (76,600 sq mi) Soviet Central Asia. It borders China (SE) and the Kazakh, Uzbek, and Tadzhik republics (N, W, and SW, respectively). The capital is FRUNZE. A mountainous state on the Tien Shan Mts, agriculture is centred on the plains in the N, where wheat, grains, and other fodder are grown. Livestock are important, particularly sheep and cattle, but also yaks for meat and milk in the more mountainous parts. Industry is being developed. There are sugar refineries, tanneries, and cotton and wool-cleaning works, as well as food-processing and metallurgy industries. The Kirghiz, a nomadic, Turkic-speaking, Muslim people with Mongol strains, comprise half the population; Russians, Uzbeks, and others make up the rest. The Kirghiz emigrated in the 17th cent. from the region of the upper Yenisei R., where they had lived since the 7th cent. Kirghizia was annexed (1855–76) by Russia and became part of the USSR in 1924. In 1936 it became a constituent republic.

**Kiribati,** officially the Republic of Kiribati, independent nation (1987 est. pop. 65,000), 886 km² (342 sq mi), consisting of 33 islands scattered across 3860 km (2400 mi) of the Pacific Ocean near the equator. It includes islands in the Gilbert, Phoenix, and Line groups and Banaba (formerly Ocean) Island. The population is nearly all Micronesian, with about 30% concentrated on TARAWA, site of the capital, Bairiki. Languages spoken are English (official) and Gilbertese. Fishing and the growing of taro and bananas form the basis of the mainly subsistence economy. Copra became the chief export after mining of Banaba's once thick phosphate deposits ended in 1979. The islands were administered (1892–1916) with the Gilbert Islands as a British protectorate that became (1916) the British Gilbert and Ellice Islands colony. They gained self-rule in 1971, and, after the Ellice Islands gained (1978) independence as TUVALU, the remaining islands were granted independence (1979) as Kiribati. A member of the COMMONWEALTH, the country is a republic with a president (who is head of state and head of government), a cabinet, and a unicameral legislature. US claims to several islands, including Kanton (formerly Canton) and Enderbury, were abandoned in 1979.

**Kirin:** see JILIN.

**Kirinyaga, Mount:** see KENYA, MOUNT.

**Kirke, Sir David,** 1597–1655?, English adventurer. With his brothers, Lewis and Thomas, he seized (1627) a French fleet off Newfoundland and raided French stations in Nova Scotia. In 1629 he forced CHAMPLAIN to surrender Quebec, but peace between Britain and France restored the city to France. In 1638 he went to Newfoundland as governor and colonizer.

**Kirov Ballet:** see DANCE (table).

**Kirstein, Lincoln,** 1907–, American dance and theatre executive and writer. He was responsible for bringing to the US George BALANCHINE with whom he was co-founder (1934) of the American Ballet Co. From 1948 he has been general director of the New York City Ballet; he has written many books on dance. See also DANCE (Table).

**Kisangani,** formerly Stanleyville, city (1987 pop. 339,210), capital of Haut-Zaïre prov., NE Zaïre, on the Congo (Zaïre) R. A port and commercial centre for the surrounding region, it produces palm oil products, rubber, coffee, cotton, rice, and gold. The city was founded in 1898.

**Kishinev,** city (1985 pop. 624,000), capital of the MOLDAVIAN SOVIET SOCIALIST REPUBLIC, SW European USSR, on a tributary of the Dnestr R. It has administrative and cultural functions, with some light industry, including food, wine, leather, and tobacco processing, chemicals and textiles, and machine construction. Severely damaged in World War II, at least half of the city's suburbs have since been rebuilt.

**Kissinger, Henry Alfred,** 1923–, US secretary of state (1973–77); b. Germany. An expert in international affairs and nuclear defence, he was national-security adviser (1969–75) to Presidents NIXON and FORD, and played a major role in the formulation of US foreign policy. He arranged Nixon's visit (1972) to mainland China, shared (1973) the Nobel Peace Prize for negotiating a cease-fire with North Vietnam, and helped arrange a cease-fire in the 1973 ARAB–ISRAELI WAR.

**Kisumu,** formerly Port Florence, city (1987 est. pop. 167,100), capital of Nyanza prov., W Kenya. It is located on the northeastern shores of Victoria Nyanza (Lake Victoria).

**Kitagawa Utamaro:** see UTAMARO.

**Kitaj, R.B.** (ki‚tie), 1932–, American painter. He trained and then taught in Britain (1958–67), meeting Allen JONES and David HOCKNEY at the Royal College of Art. Although not a pop artist himelf he was influential for the development of British POP ART. His pictures used multiple sources taken from 20th-cent. art, demanding an informed viewer to decode them and postulate possible meanings.

**Kitakyushu** (kee,tahkyoohshooh), city (1986 est. pop. 1,047,355), Fukuoka prefecture, N Kyushu, Japan, on the Shimonoseki Strait between the Inland Sea and the Korea Strait. A port and one of Japan's major manufacturing and rail centres, it has a great variety of industries producing iron and steel, textiles, chemicals, machinery, ships, and porcelain. It is also the base for a deep-sea fishing fleet. Kitakyushu is connected with Shimonoseki on Honshu by rail and road tunnels, and by one of the longest suspension bridge in Asia (built 1973). The city was formed in 1963 by the amalgamation of five existing cities: Kokura, Moji, Wakamatsu, Yahata, and Tobata.

**Kitasato Shibasaburo,** 1852–1931, Japanese physician. With Emil BEHRING he studied the tetanus bacillus and developed (1890) an antitoxin for diphtheria. He discovered (1894) the infectious agent of bubonic plague, which he described simultaneously with Alexandre Yersin.

**Kitchen Cabinet,** in US history, popular name for the close advisers of Pres. JACKSON. This unofficial cabinet, which formed the policies of Jackson's early administration, included journalists F.P. Blair and Amos Kendall. J.H. Eaton, a regular cabinet member, met with the group, as did Martin VAN BUREN. Following the cabinet reorganization of 1831, the Kitchen Cabinet became less important.

**Kitchener,** city (1980 est. pop. 138,271), S Ontario, Canada, in the Grand R. valley, adjoining the smaller city of Waterloo. Major manufactures include hardware, tools, and rubber goods. Called Berlin until 1916, Kitchener was settled in 1806 by MENNONITES from Pennsylvania. It is renowned in Canada for its annual Oktoberfest.

**Kitchener, Horatio Herbert Kitchener, 1st Earl,** 1850–1916, British field marshal and statesman. In 1896 he began the Anglo-Egyptian reconquest of the Sudan that culminated in a victory at Omdurman (1898). He served under F.S. Roberts in the SOUTH AFRICAN WAR and, when Roberts returned (1900) to England, was left to face continued guerrilla warfare. By extending blockhouses, interning civilians, and denuding the land, methods that received much criticism, he secured Boer submission (1902). In WORLD WAR I he was secretary for war and, despite weaknesses as a politician and strained relations with the cabinet, carried out a vast expansion of the British army. He was drowned on a mission to Russia when his ship was sunk by a German mine.

**kite,** BIRD of prey whose soaring, gliding flight gave its name to the flying toy. There are two groups of birds called kites, one the scavenging group of true kites living in S Europe and the warmer regions of Africa and Asia, the other a hunting group of black-shouldered kites of Australia, S Asia, Africa, and America, which are not true kites. The black kite (*Milvus migrans*) is a common sight in towns and cities, where it performs a useful cleaning function. The lammergeier (*Gyptaetus barbatus*), a scavenger which cracks large bones by dropping them from high in the air on to flat rocks, belongs to the kite group.

**kite,** a lightweight frame for flying in the air, controlled from the ground by a string. Kites seem to have been invented in Asia, having long been popular in China, Japan, Korea, and Malaysia, where they are used for sport and to ward off evil spirits. The Greek scientist Archytas of Tarentum (4th cent. BC) knew of kites but was not, as is sometimes claimed, their inventor. Benjamin FRANKLIN's famous experiment with a kite to show that lightning is electrical took place in 1752. Kites have been used for signalling, weather observations, and aerial photography. The first man-lifting kites for military observations were developed in the late 19th cent., but were soon superseded by balloons and aeroplanes.

**Kitt Peak National Observatory,** important astronomical institution in Arizona including a considerable number of major telescopes.

**Kitwe,** city (1980 pop. 314,794), Copperbelt prov., N central Zambia, near Zaïre; founded 1936. It is the main commercial and industrial centre of a rich mining region. Industries include the manufacture of batteries, paint, plastic goods, and electrical equipment. Founded in 1937, the city expanded in 1970 to include the neighbouring townships of Chambesi, Chibulma, Itimpi, and Kalulushi.

**kiva,** large, underground chamber used by PUEBLO INDIAN men for secret ceremonies. A modern kiva is a rectangular or circular structure, with a fire pit in the centre and a timbered roof; it is accessible by ladder. An opening in the floor represents the entrance to the lower world and the place through which life emerged into this world.

**Kivi, Aleksis (Stenvall),** 1834–72, Finnish writer and dramatist, who wrote in Finnish, not Swedish. His only novel, *Seven Brothers* (1870), is considered the first and best 'classic' Finnish novel. As a playwright he wrote both comedies, e.g., *The Cobblers on the Heath* (1864), and a tragedy, *Kullervo* (1864), based on one of the central figures in Kalavela. His poems have come to be regarded as classics in their own right, too, especially *Kanervala* (1866).

**kiwi** or **apteryx,** flightless BIRD (genus *Apteryx*) of New Zealand related to the OSTRICH and EMU. The size of a large chicken, the kiwi has short legs and coarse, dark plumage that hides rudimentary wings. There are three living species, all protected.

Brown **kiwi** (*Apteryx Australis*)

**Kizil-Kum:** see KYZYL-KUM.

**Klagenfurt,** city (1981 pop. 87,321), capital of Carinthia, S Austria, on the Glan R. It serves as administrative, ecclesiastical and market centre for its region. A convergence of international routeways adds to its importance, and it is a winter sports resort.

**Klee, Paul** (klay), 1879–1940, Swiss painter, graphic artist, and art theorist. His sophisticated theories of abstraction, combined with his personal inventiveness, give his works the appearance of great innocence. Associated with the BLAUE REITER, he became aware of new theories of colour use, and thereafter his whimsical and fantastic images show a luminous, subtle colour sense. Characteristic works are the witty *Twittering Machine* (1922; Mus. of Mod. Art, New York City) and the disturbing *Revolutions of the Viaducts* (1937; Hamburg). His *Pedagogical Sketchbooks* (tr. 1944) define his approach to art.

**Klein, (Christian) Felix,** 1849–1925, German mathematician, noted for his work in geometry and on the theory of functions. His 'Erlangen Programm' (1872) for unifying the diverse forms of geometry through the study of equivalence in transformation groups was influential for over 50 years. Klein was a prolific writer and lecturer on the theory, history, and teaching of mathematics.

**Klein, Melanie,** 1882–1960, Austrian psychoanalyst. She fled to England in the 1930s and subsequently practised at the Tavistock Clinic in London. Klein was a pioneer in the field of child PSYCHOANALYSIS, but her unorthodox theories led to disagreements with Anna FREUD and provoked a long-standing split in British psychoanalytic circles. Kleinian psychoanalysis, also known as the 'object relations' school, emphasizes the importance of the developmental processes involved in working through innate impulses of aggression and hostility. Klein's publications include *Envy and Gratitude: a Study of Unconscious Sources* (1957).

**Klein, Yves,** 1928–62, French artist. He was a member of the European neo-DADA movement. In 1958 he exhibited 'an exhibition of emptiness' which consisted of an empty gallery painted white. Klein's interests were more in making statements about art than with a concern with the art-object itself, causing the public to reassess the meaning and function of art.

**Klein bottle,** in mathematics, one-sided surface formed by taking a tapering tube, pulling the small end through the side of the tube, then enlarging this end and smoothly joining it to the other end. The resulting surface has no edges and no inside or outside.

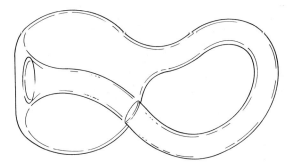

Klein bottle

**Kleist, Heinrich von** (kliest), 1777–1811, German dramatic poet. His unhappy life ended in suicide. His dominant theme of the ultimate insecurity of knowledge and self-knowledge can be seen in his ambivalent comedies, *The Broken Pitcher* (1806) and *Amphitryon* (1807) and in his tragedies *Penthesilea* (1808), *Das Käthchen von Heilbronn* (1810), and *Prinz Friedrich von Homburg* (1821). Kleist's labyrinthine style and sense of his epistemological uncertainty are also evident in his novellas, e.g., *Die Marquise von O.* and *The Earthquake in Chile* (both 1810).

**Klemperer, Otto,** 1885–1973, German conductor. Working in Prague, in Berlin, and later in Los Angeles and Pittsburgh, he was celebrated for his interpretations of Beethoven, Mahler, and Richard Strauss.

**Klimt, Gustav** , 1862–1918, Austrian painter, the foremost exponent of ART NOUVEAU in Vienna. His greatest works were portraits and landscapes of exotic and erotic sensibility, replete with symbolic themes and extravagant rhythms.

**Kline, Franz,** 1910–62, American painter. In the 1950s he developed an original style of expressive abstraction using calligraphic black strokes on a white ground. Sometimes in his later works he used notes of bright colour.

**Klondike,** region in the YUKON TERRITORY, NW Canada, near the Alaska border, the scene of a great gold rush in the late 1890s. The area is crossed by the Klondike R., which enters the YUKON R. at DAWSON, the principal town. Rich placer-gold deposits were discovered in Rabbit (now Bonanza) Creek, a tributary of the Klondike, in 1896. When news of the find reached the US in July 1897, thousands rushed to the virtually uninhabited region by a variety of difficult overland and river routes, swelling its population to c.25,000 in 1898 and causing near-famine conditions during winter months. Some $100 million in gold was mined there in about 10 years. The area still produces small amounts of gold, together with some silver, lead, and other minerals.

**Klopstock, Friedrich Gottlieb,** 1724–1803, German poet, important for his influence on GOETHE and the STURM UND DRANG. A major work is *Messias* (1748–73). His lyrical *Odes* (1747–80) influenced German song composition.

**knight,** in medieval history, an armed and mounted warrior of the nobility or, under FEUDALISM, of the landholding class. Knighthood was conferred by the overlord by a blow on the neck or shoulder with the flat of a sword. A class of landless knights, created by the fact that under primogeniture only the eldest son could inherit estates, formed in the CRUSADES such great military religious orders as the KNIGHTS TEMPLARS and KNIGHTS HOSPITALLERS. Secular orders of knights also appeared, e.g., the

Order of the Garter in Britain and the Golden Fleece in Burgundy. As feudalism waned, knightly service was often commuted into the cash payment known as SCUTAGE. Feudal knighthood ended in Germany in the early 16th cent., and in Britain in the mid-17th cent. In modern Britain, knighthood is conferred by the sovereign on commoners or nobles for civil or military achievements. A knight is addressed as Sir; a woman, knighted in her own right, as Dame.

**Knights Hospitallers,** members of the military religious order of the Hospital of St John of Jerusalem, called also the Knights of St John, of Jerusalem, of Rhodes, or of Malta. The order grew out of an 11th-cent. pilgrims' hospital in the Holy Land (see PALESTINE). As a military order it grew rich and powerful. After the Saracen conquest (1291) of Akko, the Knights took RHODES (1310), which they defended (1480) against the Ottoman sultan MUHAMMAD II but yielded (1522) to SULAYMAN I. Emperor CHARLES V gave them Malta (1530), which they defended against the Turks. After the Turkish defeat (1571) at LEPANTO, the Hospitallers engaged peacefully in hospital work until Napoleon seized Malta (1798). The order as constituted in the 19th cent. bears little relation to the old order.

**Knights of Jerusalem:** see KNIGHTS HOSPITALLERS.

**Knights of Labor,** American labour organization started in Philadelphia in 1869. Becoming a national body in 1878, it was organized on an industrial basis, welcoming female and black workers, and even employers. Among its aims were an 8-hr day, abolition of child and convict labour, and equal pay for equal work. The Knights of Labor attained its peak membership of 702,000 in 1886, but unjust blame for the HAYMARKET SQUARE RIOT of that year, together with factional disputes and weak management, resulted in its virtual extinction by 1900.

**Knights of Malta and Knights of Rhodes:** see KNIGHTS HOSPITALLERS.

**Knights of St John of Jerusalem:** see KNIGHTS HOSPITALLERS.

**Knights Templars,** members of the military religious order of the Poor Knights of Christ, also called Knights of the Temple of Solomon. Like the KNIGHTS HOSPITALLERS and the TEUTONIC KNIGHTS, they rose during the CRUSADES. From a band of nine knights united (c.1118) to protect pilgrims, the order grew large and rich, and lodged beside Solomon's temple. They were famous for dashing military exploits. After the city of Akko (Acre) fell (1291), they went to Cyprus. Their wealth made them the bankers of Europe and led to persecution (1308–14) by PHILIP IV of France. The last grand master and their other leaders were burned as heretics (1314), after the order had been abolished by Clement V at the Council of Vienne (1312).

**knitting,** construction of fabric by interlocking loops of yarn or thread with needles or hooks. Hand knitting uses needles, upon one of which a row of loops is cast on. Successive rows of stitches are looped through these moving the fabric from one needle to the other. The direction in which the thread is looped determines whether knit or purl stitches are formed. Most forms of hand knitting use two needles but with more a circular fabric can be made. All stitches and patterns are derived from these two basic stitches. Needles were originally made from wood, bone, ivory, and horn, but now are made from wood, metal, or plastic in varying thicknesses. Hand knitting is believed to have evolved from sprang, an ancient form of knotting. The earliest pieces of true knitted fabric were found in the Middle East. The Egyptian Copts, an early Christian sect, were famous for their knitting and the craft spread through Europe with Christianity. By the 16th cent. there was a considerable trade in fine silk brocade knitting from Spain and Italy. The first knitting machine was invented in England in 1589 by William Lee, and later developments included LACE and warp knitting machines. In warp knitting the fabric is constructed of vertical chains of loops held together by the yarn zig-zagging from one chain of loops to another. Weft knitting (which includes hand knitting) uses one continuous thread to produce a horizontally constructed fabric. Warp-knit fabric is stable and run-resist; weft-knit fabric is more elastic. Wool or similar synthetics are the most widely used yarns but any textile can be used to further the decorative effect. Patterns using two or more colours are popular; one, based on repeated geometric forms, is called Fair Isle after its place of origin, in the Hebridean Islands, Scotland.

**Knopf, Alfred A.,** 1892–1984, American publisher. In 1915 he founded his own firm, Alfred A. Knopf, Inc., emphasizing translations of great contemporary European literature, and specializing in producing books outstanding for fine printing, binding, and design. Random House, Inc. acquired the company in 1960, but the Knopf imprint remains.

**Knossos** (ˌnosəs), ancient city on the N coast of CRETE. Occupied long before 3000 BC, it was the centre of MINOAN CIVILIZATION, known mainly from the study of the great palace of Knossos. In Greek legend, Knossos was the capital of King MINOS and the site of the labyrinth. The palace was destroyed by fire c.1375 BC and the region fell under the influence of the MYCENAEAN CIVILIZATION.

**knot,** an interlacing of string, rope, etc. Knots fall into several groups according to their form and purpose: those used for joining one piece of rope, etc., to another are generally called bends, those for attaching a rope to an object (anchor, pole, etc.) are hitches. A knot may be formally analysed using the discipline of TOPOLOGY. The knots in use today have been known for centuries, the only novel one being Hunter's bend, discovered by a British doctor in 1978. See also SPLICE.

**Know-Nothing movement,** US political movement in the mid 19th cent. The increased immigration of the 1840s had resulted in concentrations of Roman Catholic immigrants in the Eastern cities, where secret nativist societies were formed to combat 'foreign' influences and uphold the 'American' view. When outsiders made inquiries of supposed members, they were met with a statement that the person knew nothing; hence members were called Know-Nothings. The Know-Nothings sought to elect only native Americans to office and to require 25 years of residence for citizenship. In 1854 they had widespread striking successes in local and state elections. In 1855 they adopted the name American party and dropped much of their secrecy. The issue of slavery, however, split the party, and many antislavery members joined the new REPUBLICAN PARTY. Millard FILLMORE, the American party's presidential candidate in 1856, won only Maryland, and the party's national strength was broken.

**Knox, John,** 1514?–72, Scottish religious reformer, founder of Scottish PRESBYTERIANISM. A Catholic priest, he had attached himself by 1545 to the reformer George Wishart and soon became a Protestant. In England (1549–53), Knox preached, was a royal chaplain briefly, and helped prepare the second Book of Common Prayer. After the accession (1553) of MARY I, he went into exile, chiefly in Geneva, where he consulted with John CALVIN. In 1557 the Scottish Protestant nobles made their first covenant (see SCOTLAND, CHURCH OF) and invited (1559) Knox to return to lead their fight against the regent, MARY OF GUISE. After a civil war, the reformers forced the withdrawal of Mary's French forces and won their freedom as well as dominance for the new religion. They tried (1560) to abolish the pope's authority and condemn the practices of the old church. Knox verbally attacked the Roman Catholic MARY QUEEN OF SCOTS, and, after her abdication (1567), the acts of 1560 were confirmed and Presbyterianism was established in Scotland. Knox's single-minded zeal made him the outstanding leader of the Scottish Reformation and an important influence in Protestant movements elsewhere.

**Knoxville,** US city (1984 est. pop. 174,000), E Tennessee, on the Tennessee R.; settled c.1785, inc. 1876. Trade centre for a farm, coal, and marble area, it manufactures aluminium sheeting and textiles. It was territorial capital (1792–96) and twice (1796–1812, 1817–18) served as state capital. Knoxville was occupied by federal troops during the CIVIL WAR. The city is a tourist centre; Great Smoky Mts National Park is nearby, and the 1982 Worlds Fair was held there.

**Koacen, Mohammed,** 1880–1919, Tuareg anticolonial resistance leader; b. Niger. He fought the French in CHAD and NIGER between 1909 and 1917. In 1917 he was forced, by the joint Anglo-French 'pacification', to flee to Libya where he was betrayed, arrested, and hanged.

**koala,** arboreal, nocturnal MARSUPIAL (*Phascolarctos cinereus*) native to Australia. Bearlike in appearance, it has thick, grey fur, a tailless body 60 to 75 cm (2 to 2½ ft) long, a black nose, and large, furry ears. Its diet consists of only one species of eucalyptus (see MYRTLE) at a particular stage of maturation. The koala has been hunted for food and fur and is now endangered.

**Kobe** (ˌkohbay), city (1986 est. pop. 1,404,172), capital of Hyogo prefecture, S Honshu, Japan. The second largest Japanese port, and an industrial and trade centre, it has shipbuilding yards and iron and steel mills. It is also noted for its high-quality sake. Originally an outer port of Kyoto, it was redeveloped as an international trade port in 1868. Kobe

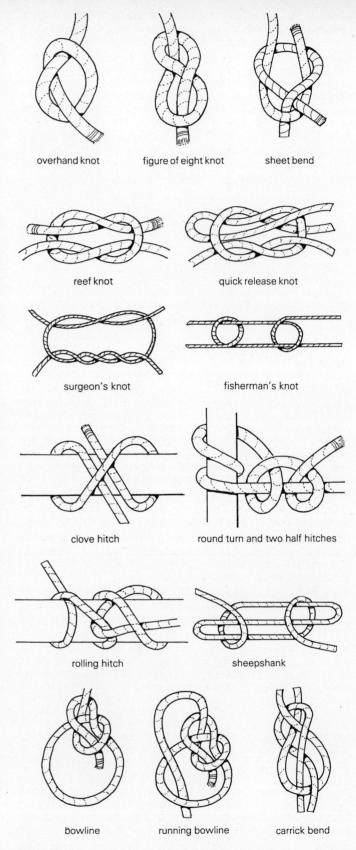

overhand knot     figure of eight knot     sheet bend

reef knot     quick release knot

surgeon's knot     fisherman's knot

clove hitch     round turn and two half hitches

rolling hitch     sheepshank

bowline     running bowline     carrick bend

Knots

was heavily bombed during World War II but has since been rebuilt and enlarged, and is now one of the leading cities in urban renewal in Japan.

**Koblenz,** city (1984 pop. 111,500), Rhineland-Palatinate, West Germany. Situated at the confluence of the MOSEL R. and the RHINE, its name is derived from that of the Roman settlement, Confluentes. It is essentially a commercial and administrative centre, handling some of the Rhine wine trade. From the 11th cent. to 1794, it was ruled by the archbishops of TRIER whose great palace was erected in 1780. As capital of a Prussian province it was refortified between 1815 and 1825. Famous buildings include the 9th-cent. Church of St Castor.

**Koch, Robert** (kok), 1843–1910, German bacteriologist. He devised a method of staining bacteria with aniline dyes and developed bacteriological culture techniques which are still used. He established the bacterial cause of many infectious diseases, including anthrax (1876), tuberculosis (1882), conjunctivitis (1883), and cholera (1884), and studied sleeping sickness, malaria, bubonic plague, rinderpest, and other diseases. For developing tuberculin as a test of tuberculosis he received the 1905 Nobel Prize for physiology or medicine.

**Kochanowski, Jan,** ('kokha,novskee), 1530–84, Polish poet. His most original work was his cycle of laments, *Treny* (1580), on the death of his daughter. He also did a version of *The Psalms of David* (1579) and represents Polish humanism with, for example, his *Lyricorum libellus* (1580).

**Kocher, Emil Theodor,** 1841–1917, Swiss surgeon. He was awarded the 1909 Nobel Prize for physiology or medicine for his work on surgical treatment of thyroid disease.

**Kodály, Zoltán** (,kohdie), 1882–1967, Hungarian composer, music educator, and collector of folk music. With BARTÓK he collected thousands of Hungarian FOLK SONGS and dances. His best-known works are the opera *Háry János* (1926; orchestral suite, 1927); the *Psalmus Hungaricus* (1923); *Dances of Galánta* (1933) and *'Peacock' Variations* (1939), and *Missa Brevis* (1945). He devoted much time and energy during the latter part of his life to problems of music education, especially in Hungary. The Kodály method for teaching music to children has been adopted in many countries.

**Koestler, Arthur,** 1905–83, English writer; b. Hungary. A communist in the 1930s, he left the party over the Stalin purge trials. His best-known novel, *Darkness at Noon* (tr.1940), describes the purge of a Bolshevik 'deviationist'. He is also known for his essay 'The Yogi and the Commissar', in *The God That Failed* (ed. by R.H. Crossman, 1950), for philosophical studies like *The Ghost in the Machine* (1967), and for his interest in parapsychology.

**Koffka, Kurt:** see GESTALT PSYCHOLOGY.

**Kohl, Helmut,** 1930–, German politician, chancellor of West GERMANY (1982–). A member of the Christian Democratic Union, Kohl led (1976–82) the opposition in the Bundestag (federal diet). He replaced Social Democrat Helmut SCHMIDT (1982) as chancellor during a period of economic difficulty and retained power in the 1987 elections.

**Köhler, Wolfgang:** see GESTALT PSYCHOLOGY.

**Koivisto, Mauno,** 1923–, president of FINLAND (1982–). Originally a manual worker, he later pursued a banking and political career, serving as finance minister and governor of the Bank of Finland in the 1960s and 1970s. He was Social Democratic prime minister in 1968–70 and again from 1979 until in 1982 he was elected to the presidency for a six-year term in succession to Urho KEKKONEN; he was reelected in 1988.

**Kokoschka, Oskar** (koh,koshkah), 1886–1980, Austrian expressionist painter and writer. Influenced by KLIMT's elegant work, he developed an expressionist style that emphasizes psychological tension, e.g., the portrait of Hans Tietze and his wife (1909; Mus. Mod. Art, New York City). His striking landscapes include *Jerusalem* (Detroit Inst. Arts). He remained unaffected by later developments in 20th cent. art and continued to paint in his personal version of pre-1914 expressionism.

**kola:** see COLA.

**Kolarovgrad** or **Shumen,** city (1983 pop. 104,089), NE Bulgaria. It is a rail junction and commercial centre. Founded in AD 927, it has architecture dating from the period of Turkish rule.

**Kolhapur,** town (1981 pop. 340,625), Maharashtra state, W India, on the Panchganga R. It is a district administrative, cultural, and commercial centre with some industry. It has a fort at its core, and a former royal palace and temple complex within the walls. It became the capital of the Mahrattas in the 18th cent. and survived as a princely state of the same name during the British period.

**kollel,** institute of higher rabbinical studies. After a five-year period in a YESHIBAH, the leading students, who wish to pursue a rabbinical career, proceed to a kollel, for a more intensive research programme. The kollel prepares them to become *dayyanim* (see under BET DIN), rabbis or lecturers.

**Kollwitz, Käthe Schmidt** (,kolvits), 1867–1945, German graphic artist and sculptor. She is best known for her superb WOODCUTS and lithographs. An ardent socialist and pacifist, she produced anguished portrayals of misery and hunger, e.g., *Death and the Mother* (1934; Philadelphia Mus. Art).

**Kolonia,** town (1980 pop. 5,549), capital of the Federated States of MICRONESIA, on the island of Ponape.

**Kolwezi,** city (1977 pop. 297,318), SHABA prov., S Zaïre. It is a centre of the copper-mining industry.

**komodo dragon,** LIZARD of the MONITOR family. It is the largest lizard living today and one of the largest ever to have lived on earth. Males grow up to 3 m (10 ft) long and weigh up to 136 kg (300 lb). Komodo dragons are found on a few Indonesian islands, the largest being Komodo. They are carnivorous, feeding on carrion and probably also killing pigs and deer. They are diurnal, spending their nights among rocks and emerging to sunbathe in the mornings before hunting. Despite its large size, the Komodo dragon was not discovered by scientists until 1912.

**Kongo,** kingdom in W Central Africa that flourished from the 14th to 17th cent. in the region that is now ANGOLA and ZAÏRE. It was ruled by a *manikongo,* or king, and its capital was Mbanza (later São Salvador). After 1491 Kongo was increasingly under the influence of the Portuguese, who attempted to Christianize the kingdom. Their rapaciousness, particularly that of the slave traders, played a major part in weakening the kingdom. After 1665 the *manikongo* was little more than a Portuguese vassal.

**Kongsberg,** [Nor., = king's hill], an historic mining centre, SW of OSLO, Norway. Silver mining began in 1624 and Kongsberg is still the site of the royal mint.

**Königsberg:** see KALININGRAD.

**Konoye Fumimaro, Prince,** 1891–1945, Japanese prime minister (1937–39, 1940–41). He favoured the use of military force against China to support Japanese expansionist aims and to counter the spread of Western influence in Asia. In 1938 he proclaimed that Japan's goal was a 'new order in East Asia'. In 1940 he concluded an alliance with the AXIS powers but resigned his office in October 1941 after Hitler's attack on the Soviet Union and following his own inability to reduce rising tensions between the US and Japan. He killed himself just before his expected arrest as a war criminal.

**Konya,** city (1980 pop. 329,139), capital of Konya prov., central Anatolia, Turkey. Set in a prosperous agricultural area, it has food-processing industries. Known as Iconium in Roman times, it flourished as a route centre, and became an administrative centre in the OTTOMAN EMPIRE from the 15th cent. It was the religious headquarters of the Mevlevi (whirling) Dervish sect, and retains old city walls and medieval mosques.

**Kook, Abraham Isaac,** 1864–1935, Jewish scholar, mystic, poet, and philosopher; b. Latvia. In his view, PALESTINE and ZIONISM were necessary to Judaism. A chief rabbi of the Ashkenazic community of Palestine from 1921, he was one of the first rabbis to apply Jewish law to the current problems of new and developing pioneering settlements.

**kookaburra:** see KINGFISHER.

**Köprülü,** family of humble Albanian origin, several members of which served as grand viziers in the OTTOMAN EMPIRE (Turkey) in the 17th and 18th cent. The name is also spelled Kiuprilu, Koprili, and Kuprili. The most eminent member of the family was **Mehmed Köprülü,** c.1578–1661, who became grand vizier to Sultan MEHMED IV in 1656 and gained complete authority. He regained some of the former Ottoman prestige by restoring internal order, reforming finances, and rebuilding the Ottoman military forces.

**Koran** or **Qur'an** [Arab., = recitation], the corpus of MUHAMMAD's revelations in MECCA and Medina. It constitutes a manual of legislative, theological, ethical, sociological, and prophetic material. It is divided into 114 chapters (*suras*) of unequal length and arranged with the longest coming first. The Koran is Islam's most sacred source of doctrine though that source has been variously interpreted throughout the ages by scholars. Their professional interpretation (*tafsir*) is enshrined in encyclopedic volumes which combine literary, linguistic, philological, and historical scholarship. Islamic tradition teaches that the final text of the Koran was put together in the caliphate of the 3rd caliph 'Uthman (644-56); some Western scholars have disputed this and believe that the present version of the Koran was the product of a somewhat later age.

**Korchnoi, Viktor,** 1931–, Swiss chess master; b. USSR. One of the USSR's leading players, he was barred from chess tournaments for six months for criticizing Anatoly KARPOV after losing (1974) to him. In 1976 Korchnoi defected to Switzerland. An innovative but erratic tactician, he lost to Karpov in world championship matches in 1978 and 1981.

**Korda, Sir Alexander,** 1893–1956, Hungarian film director and producer; b. Sandor Laszlo Korda. He settled in England in 1930, began the London Films company, and injected much-needed energy and creativity into the British film industry. His films as producer include *The Scarlet Pimpernel* (1934), *Things To Come* (1937), and *The Thief of Baghdad* (1940).

**Korea,** Korean *Choson,* historic country, 220,277 km² (85,049 sq mi), E Asia. A peninsula 966 km (600 mi) long, Korea separates the Yellow Sea (W) from the Sea of Japan (E). It is bounded by the Korea Strait (S), and its land boundaries with China and the USSR (N) are marked by the great YALU and Tumen rivers. The land is largely mountainous, rising in the northeast to its highest point at Mt Paektu, 2744 m (9003 ft). Some 3420 islands, mostly uninhabited, lie off the coast. Korea has great mineral wealth, with 80% to 90% of it concentrated in the north. Of the peninsula's five major minerals: gold, iron ore, coal, tungsten, and graphite, only the last two are found principally in the south. North Korea, which has some 300 different kinds of minerals, is especially rich in iron and coal. It ranks among the world leaders in production of graphite, gold, tungsten, magnesite, zinc, molybdenum, and other minerals. Only about 20% of Korean land is arable; rice (the chief crop), barley, wheat, corn, soya, and grain sorghums are extensively cultivated. The fishing waters off Korea are among the best in the world, and fish remains the chief source of protein in the Korean diet. The economy was shattered by the war of 1950–53, but huge amounts of foreign aid and intensive government programmes in both north and south speeded postwar reconstruction. Important industrial advances were made in the 1960s and 70s, and South Korea now has one of the most rapidly growing economies in Asia. Major North Korean products include iron, steel, machinery, textiles, and chemicals. South Korean manufactures include textiles, electrical and electronic equipment, chemicals, ceramic goods, plywood, and a variety of consumer products. Most Koreans are Confucians or Buddhists; there are many Christians in the south.

*History.* Documented Korean history begins in the 2nd cent. BC, when the Chinese founded a colony at Pyongyang. The first native Korean state, the kingdom of Koguryo, arose in the north in the 1st cent. AD. The kingdom of Silla emerged AD c.350 and unified the peninsula in the 7th cent. The Koryo dynasty ruled a united Korea from 935 until Mongol invasions from China in the 13th cent. forced an alliance under Mongol control. The Yi dynasty (1392–1910) built a new capital at Hanyang (now SEOUL) and established CONFUCIANISM as the official state doctrine. Japanese troops moved into Korea during the First Sino-Japanese War (1894–95) and the RUSSO-JAPANESE WAR (1904–05), and Japan formally annexed (1910) the country, which remained under Japanese colonial rule until 1945. During World War II the Allies promised Korea independence, and after the war the country was divided into two zones of occupation, with Soviet troops north and Americans south of the line of lat. 38°N. In 1948 two separate regimes were established, the Republic of Korea in the south, and the Democratic People's Republic under Communist rule in the north.

*Government.* Since the KOREAN WAR (1950–53) the peninsula has remained two independent nations divided roughly at the 38th parallel. **North Korea,** or Democratic People's Republic of Korea (1987 est. pop. 20,400,000), 120,538 km² (46,540 sq mi), has its capital at PYONGYANG, the largest city. After the Korean War the Communist government launched an ambitious programme of industrialization. The GNP is US$14,089 million and GNP per capita is US$762 (1984). North Korea has maintained close relations with the USSR and the People's Republic of China, both of which have provided aid for reconstruction. Postwar

politics have been dominated by KIM IL SUNG and his Workers' Party of Korea. **South Korea,** or Republic of Korea (1987 est. pop. 41,500,000), 98,477 km² (38,022 sq mi), has its capital at SEOUL, the largest city; PUSAN is the chief port. The GNP is US$84,860 million (1984), with GNP per capita US$1998 (1984). Syngman RHEE, elected the first president in 1948, was forced to resign in 1960 by a popular uprising against his authoritarian rule. A military junta under Gen. PARK CHUNG HEE seized power in 1961 and had by 1975 assumed near-dictatorial powers. In the 1960s foreign trade, especially with Japan, replaced American aid. Ties with the US were temporarily strained by alleged Korean influence peddling in the US. Congress and by Pres. CARTER's decision (later suspended) to withdraw US troops from South Korea. In 1979 Pres. Park was assassinated in an apparent coup attempt; soon after, Lt Gen. CHUN DOO HWAN led a military coup and took effective control. Despite widespread opposition to the new government's repressive measures, Chun was elected president and reelected in 1981 (as candidate of the dominant Democratic Justice Party). He was succeeded by ROH TAE WOO, elected in a controversial poll in 1987.

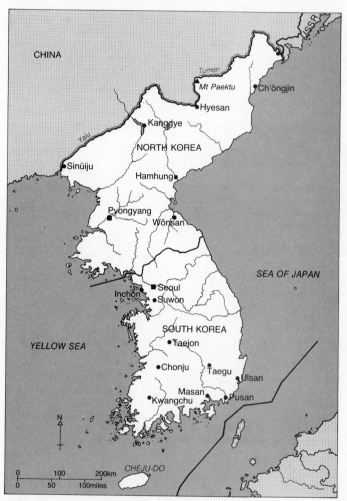

Korea

**Korean,** language of uncertain relationship that is spoken by about 36 million people, most of whom live in Korea. It is thought by some scholars to be akin to JAPANESE, by others to be a member of the Altaic subfamily of the URALIC AND ALTAIC family of languages (see LANGUAGE [table]), and by still others to be unrelated to any known language.

**Korean music** is a mixture of Chinese and indigenous elements. It is broadly divided into *minsogak* (folk music), and *chongak* or *aak* (correct music, Confucian ritual music). The traditional court repertory was divided into *tangak* (music borrowed from Tang China) and *hyangak* (secular pieces of Korean origin). The music is heterophonic in form and two pentatonic modes have been used since at least the 15th cent. Korean music is distinguished from Chinese and Japanese music by its characteristic triple metre, duple metre being common only in folk music. There is a variety of genres and ensembles, for which the basic instruments are oboe, flute, fiddle, and hourglass drum. The most popular amateur instrument is the large 12-string zither (*kayagum*).

**Korean War,** conflict between Communist and non-Communist forces in KOREA from 25 June 1950, to 27 July 1953. At the end of WORLD WAR II, Korea was divided at the 38th parallel into Soviet (North Korean) and US (South Korean) zones of occupation. In 1948 rival governments were established. When North Korean forces invaded South Korea, the UN authorized member nations to aid South Korea. Gen. Douglas MACARTHUR commanded the UN forces until 1951, when he was replaced by Gen. Matthew B. Ridgway. In Oct. 1950 Chinese Communist forces joined the North Korean army. Fighting centred around the 38th parallel. In 1951 negotiations for a cease-fire were begun at Panmunjom; it was achieved on 27 July 1953.

**Kornberg, Arthur,** 1918–, American biochemist. For his discovery of the mechanisms in the biological synthesis of DNA, he shared with Severo OCHOA the 1959 Nobel Prize for physiology or medicine.

**Korolev, Sergei Pavlovich,** 1907–66, Soviet rocket designer. Korolev's role as the chief designer of the Soviet space programme was not revealed until after his death. After he successfully launched two intercontinental ballistic missiles in Aug. 1957, Soviet premier Nikita Khrushchev allowed him to attempt the orbiting of a test satellite; as a result, *Sputnik 1,* the first artificial earth satellite, was orbited successfully on 4 Oct. 1957. Korolev also directed the launching of the USSR's first unmanned space probes and manned space missions.

**Koror,** island (1973 pop. 7,669), capital of BELAU.

**Kosciusko, Mount** ('kosee,uskoh), 2,230 m (7316 ft) high, in SE New South Wales, Australia. It is the highest point in Australia. In 1840 the Polish-born Count Paul de Strzelecki was the first European to climb the mountain.

**Kościuszko, Tadeusz,** 1746–1817, Polish general and patriot. He fought for the colonists in the AMERICAN REVOLUTION and then returned to Poland, where he became a champion of independence. In 1794 he led an unsuccessful insurrection against Russian and Prussian control of Poland (see POLISH RISINGS).

**Košice** (ko,sheetsə), Hung. *Kassa,* city (1984 pop. 214,000), E Slovakia, Czechoslovakia. Situated on a routeway across the Carpathian Mts that has been important since medieval times, it has varied industries including an iron and steel works built in the 1960s which draws its ore from the USSR. Important buildings include its 14th-cent. Gothic cathedral and the town houses of the former Hungarian notables.

**Kosovo** (kos,ovə), Albanian *Kosova,* socialist autonomous province of SERBIA in SE Yugoslavia (1981 pop. 1,677,000), 10,636 km² (4126 sq mi). Priština (Albanian *Prishtinë*) is the capital. A region of mountains and upland plains, it is the least developed of Yugoslavia's constituent units, despite abundant mineral deposits and extensive industrial investments since the 1960s. The centre of the medieval Serb empire, the area became predominantly Albanian in population under Ottoman rule and a focus of periodic nationalist conflict between Slavs and Albanians in this century Serbs and Montenegrins now comprise a small and declining minority. At Kosovo Polje [field] in 1389 the Ottomans defeated a Serb-led Christian army, the symbolic inauguration of four centuries of Turkish rule over the W Balkans and the subject of numerous cycles of popular epic verse. A second battle of Kosovo was fought in 1448 when the Turks defeated an army led by John HUNYADI. The Serbs' conquest of the region in the BALKAN WARS (1912–13) was regarded by them as avenging the cataclysm of 1389.

**Kossel, (Karl Ludwig Martin Leonhard) Albrecht,** 1853–1927, German biochemist. He was awarded the 1910 Nobel Prize for physiology or medicine for his discovery of the bases of NUCLEIC ACIDS.

**Kossuth, Louis,** Hung. *Kossuth Lajos,* 1802–94, Hungarian revolutionary hero. A fiery orator, Kossuth was one of the leaders of the Hungarian revolution of 1848 (see HUNGARY). His principles were liberal and nationalistic. When Austria prepared to move against the Hungarians, he became head of the government of national defence.

He served as president of the newly formed Hungarian republic from Apr. to Aug. 1849 but was forced to resign after Russian troops intervened in favour of Austria. Thereafter he lived in exile.

**Kosygin, Aleksei Nikolayevich** (kə,seegin), 1904–81, Soviet leader. Appointed to the central committee of the Communist Party in 1939, he became first deputy chairman of the USSR council of ministers in 1960 and succeeded Nikita KHRUSHCHEV as premier in 1964, sharing power with Leonid BREZHNEV.

**Kosztolányi, Dezsö,** 1885–1936, Hungarian poet and prose writer. He is the pre-eminent stylist of the 20th cent. His poetry is formally brilliant, his essays incisive. He is considered to be one of the best Hungarian short-story writers. Kosztolányi excelled in all verse forms and his fiction is psychologically analytical, frequently with symbolist and decadent overtones. His chief works are *Esti Kornél* (1936), *Nero, Poet of Blood* (1936), and *Collected Poems* (1936).

**Kota,** town (1981 pop. 358,241), Rajasthan state, NW India, on the Chambal River. It is a district administrative and commercial centre set in a region that has benefited greatly from recent irrigation schemes. It has grown to be a considerable industrial centre making a variety of engineering and other goods. In British days it was the capital of a princely state of the same name.

**Kōtoku Shūsui,** 1871–1911, Japanese socialist and anarchist. An activist in the popular rights movement in his teens, he later became a pioneer socialist and was a pacifist during the RUSSO-JAPANESE WAR. With a colleague he published (1904) the first Japanese translation of the *Communist Manifesto.* In 1906 he abandoned parliamentary means and advocated direct action. Accused of plotting to assassinate emperor MEIJI, he was executed in 1911 with 11 other alleged conspirators.

**Kountché, Seyni,** 1931–87, president of NIGER (1974–87). He was army chief of staff when he ousted Hamani Diori, Niger's first president, in a military coup. He suspended the constitution, dissolved parliament, and suppressed all political activities. In the early years of his rule, he was forced to cope with a catastrophic drought and famine.

**Koussevitzky, Serge,** 1874–1951, American conductor, composer, and double-bass player; b. Russia. In 1909 he set up Editions Russes de Musique, to help publicize new Russian music. He came to the US in 1924 and conducted (1924–49) the Boston Symphony Orchestra. He directed (from 1936) the Berkshire Symphonic Festivals. A champion of modern music, he commissioned and performed new works by COPLAND, BARBER, William SCHUMAN, and others.

**Kovalevsky, Sonya** or **Sophie,** 1850–91, Russian mathematician. A student of Karl WEIERSTRASS, she received (1874) a Ph.D. from the Univ. of Göttingen for a remarkable thesis on partial differential equations. She won (1888) a French Academy of Sciences prize for a memoir on the rotation of a solid body about a fixed point.

**Kozhikode** (formerly **Calicut**), town (1981 pop. 394,447), Kerala state, S India. It is a district administrative centre and minor port on India's SW coast. Large ships have to anchor offshore. It has fish-processing and pottery industries. It was off Kozhikode, an ancient entrepot, that Vasco da GAMA dropped anchor in 1498 and so initiated the modern period of European maritime contact with S Asia.

**Kr,** chemical symbol of the element KRYPTON.

**Krafft-Ebbing, Richard von,** 1840–1902, German psychiatrist and sexologist, recognized as an authority on deviant sexual behaviour. He wrote *Psychopathia sexualis* (1886).

**Krag, Jens Otto** (krahkh), 1914–78, prime minister of DENMARK (1962–68, 1971–72). A Social Democrat, he helped shape economic policy in various cabinet posts (1947–67). After his goal of EUROPEAN COMMUNITY membership for Denmark was realized (1973), he resigned the prime ministership for personal reasons.

**Krakatoa** or **Krakatau,** active volcano, W Indonesia, forming an island (c.13 km²/5 sq mi) in Sunda Strait, between Java and Sumatra. The volcano, which rises to 813 m (2667 ft), is famous for its 1883 eruption, one of the most violent of modern times, which darkened skies over vast areas and scattered debris as far as Madagascar. The associated TSUNAMI swept over nearby coastal areas, causing great loss of life.

**Kraków** or **Cracow**, city (1984 pop. 735,000), S Poland, on the Vistula R. It is a river port and industrial centre with one of E Europe's largest iron and steel plants. Founded c.700, the city was (1320–1596) the residence of Poland's kings. Its university was founded in 1364. Annexed by Austria in 1795, it was an independent City Republic (1815–46), and reverted to Poland in 1918. It was the capital of the Nazi general-government (1939–45). On a hill, the Wawel, are the royal castle (rebuilt 16th cent.) and a Gothic cathedral (rebuilt 14th cent.).

**Král', Janko**, 1822–76, leading Slovak romantic poet. His verse manifests not only standard restlessness, dissatisfaction, and patriotism, but also social alienation and obsessive eroticism. He had a strong influence on the Slovak and Czech avant-gardes of the 1920s and 30s.

**Krasnodar**, formerly Yekaterinodar, city (1985 pop. 609,000), SE European USSR, on the Kuban R., 225 km (140 mi) from the Black Sea. It is the chief administrative, commercial, and industrial centre of the rich Kuban agricultural area. Industries include flour-milling, the processing of fats and other foodstuffs, petroleum-refining, and engineering. The city was founded in 1794 as a fortress.

**Krasnoyarsk**, city (1985 pop. 872,000), S Siberian USSR, at the point where the TRANS-SIBERIAN RAILWAY crosses the Yenisei R. Power from the nearby 6,000,000-kW hydroelectric station on the Yenisei supplies the varied industries. These include aluminium smelting, wood-based industries, construction of agricultural and mining machinery, railway repair works, machine tools industries, oil-refining, petrochemicals, and food-processing. Krasnoyarsk also has a steelworks and is a centre for gold production and refining. It was founded in 1628 as a Russian fortress.

**Kraus, Karl**, 1874–1936, Austrian satirist. He is best known for the essays, aphorisms, epigrams, and glosses which he published in his own journal *The Torch* (1899–1936). Regarding literary style as coterminous with morality, he waged war on newspaper jargon and newspaper lies, on officialese and official economy on the truth alike. His touchstone of true language was SHAKESPEARE, and he translated the *Sonnets* (1933) and selected dramas (1934, 1935). His public readings from Shakespeare and from his own work were famous, as testified by Elias CANETTI's *The Torch in my Ear*. His vast drama *Die letzten Tage der Menschheit* (1922; tr. The Last days of Mankind) is a savage polemic against the multiple stupidities of World War I; but Hitler, he admitted, defeated his invention. His work lends itself to ad-hoc collections: among his own are *Morality and Criminality* (1908), *Heine and the Consequences* (1910), and *Literature and Lie* (1929); among those of his translators *In These Great Times* (1984) and *Half-truths and One-and-a-half Truths* (1986).

**Krebs, Sir Hans Adolf**, 1900–82, English biochemist; b. Germany; emigrated to England, 1933. For his studies of intermediary metabolism he shared with Fritz Lipmann the 1953 Nobel Prize for physiology or medicine. These studies included the elucidation of the cycle of chemical reactions by which pyruvic acid is oxidized to carbon dioxide (KREBS CYCLE), the major source of energy in living organisms, and the cyclical process of UREA formation.

**Krebs cycle, citric acid cycle** or **tricarboxylic acid cycle**, series of chemical reactions occurring in the cells of higher plants, animals, and many microorganisms. Discovered by Sir Hans KREBS, the cycle is essential for the metabolism of GLUCOSE and other simple sugars in the presence of oxygen. Pyruvic acid (originating from glucose) is converted to citric acid which passes through several intermediate products before being regenerated. Each cycle releases carbon dioxide, hydrogen ions, and electrons which are necessary for the next stage of the metabolic process to generate chemical energy (in the form of molecules of ADENOSINE TRIPHOSPHATE) for the organism.

**Krefeld**, city (1984 pop. 219,700), North Rhine–Westphalia, W West Germany. Its silk industry dates from the 17th cent. when it was introduced by refugee HUGUENOTS. Silks and velvets are still a speciality, using both natural and man-made fibres. Other industries include soap and fertilizer manufacture and the making of special steels.

**Kreisky, Bruno** (ˌkrieskee), 1911–, Austrian Socialist politician and chancellor of AUSTRIA (1970–83). Foreign minister (1959–66) and Socialist Party chairman from 1967, he became (1970) chancellor in AUSTRIA's first single-party government since World War II. He vacated the

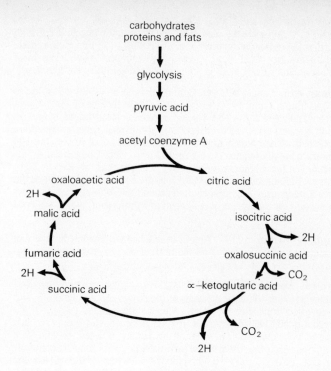

Krebs cycle

chancellorship in 1983 and in 1987 resigned as honorary chairman of the Socialist Party in protest against its decision to form a coalition with the conservative People's Party.

**Kreisler, Fritz** (ˌkrielə), 1875–1962, American violinist and composer; b. Austria. He composed the operetta *Apple Blossoms* (1919) and some charming violin pieces, e.g., *Tambourin Chinois*. In 1939 he settled in the US.

**kremlin**, Russian *kreml*, citadel or walled centre of a city. A medieval kremlin protected against attack and was a city in itself. Those of MOSCOW and several other cities still stand. Moscow's, called simply the **Kremlin**, occupies 36 hectares (90 acres). Along its crenellated walls, built in the 15th cent., are palaces; one houses the czars' crown jewels, another the parliament of the USSR. Inside the Kremlin are three cathedrals and a bell tower. The czars' residence until St Petersburg became the capital (1712), the Kremlin has since 1918 been the political and administrative centre of the USSR.

**Křenek, Ernst**, 1900–, Austrian-American composer. In the 1920s he composed in a neoclassical style. His jazz opera *Johnny Strikes Up* (1926) was a great success. After a neo-Romantic period, e.g., the opera *Leben des Orest* (1930), he adopted the TWELVE-TONE system, as in his opera *Karl V* (1933). In 1937 he moved to the US. The operas *Dark Waters* (1950) and *Sardakai* (1969), and *Eleven Transparencies* (1956) for orchestra and ELECTRONIC MUSIC, are among later pieces. He has also written several books.

**Krige, Uys**, 1910–87, white South African poet, playwright, novelist, and translator. His experiences as a war poet as well as a prisoner-of-war in Italy inform *Oorlogsgedigte* [war poems] (1942) and the novel *The Way Out* (1946), while *Die Ballade van die Groot Begeer* [the ballad of the grand desire] (1960) is about the aspirations of the 'Cape Coloured' community. He translated Lorca into Afrikaans: *Vir die Luit en die Kitaar* [for the lute and the guitar] (1950).

**Krishna** (formerly **Kistna**), river of India flowing c.1300 km (800 mi) from the Western GHATS eastward across the DECCAN to enter the Bay of Bengal through a large and fertile delta at whose head stands VIJAYAWADA. Its tributaries include the Malaprabha and Tungabhadra. On or near its banks stand the towns of Raichur and GUNTUR. The Krishna and its tributaries supply many irrigation works.

**Krishna Menon, Vengalil Krishnan**, 1897–1974, Indian diplomat. As a lawyer practising in England he was a long-time propagandist for Indian nationalism. After independence he represented India in Britain

(1947–52) and in the United Nations (1952–62). As defence minister (1957–62), he was forced from office because of the army's poor showing in the Chinese border invasion of N India.

**Krivoi Rog**, city (1985 pop. 684,000), S European USSR, in the Dnepr Bend territorial production complex. The area surrounding the city has rich deposits of coal, iron ore, rock salt, and limestone that is used as a flux in the steel-making process. It is an expanding iron and steel and engineering centre, with a well-developed metallurgical industry.

**Krleža, Miroslav**, 1893–1981, Yugoslavian novelist, playwright, and poet; b. Croatia. He captured the concerns of a revolutionary era in Yugoslavia in his trilogy of social dramas about the Glembaj family (1928–32) and in novels like *The Return of Philip Latinovicz* (1932) and *Balade Petrice Kerempuha* (1936), a collection of poems showing the Croatian peasant as the victim of history.

**Krochmal, Nachman Kohen** (͵krokhmahl), 1785–1840, Jewish secular historian and writer; b. Galicia. He was a leader of the Haskalah, or Jewish enlightenment, and a founder of Conservative JUDAISM.

**Kroeber, Alfred Louis**, 1876–1960, American anthropologist. A major figure in the founding of modern anthropology and an associate of F. BOAS, he clearly set forth the relationship between cultural patterns and the individual. He held, with DURKHEIM, that cultural factors should only be explained in terms of cultural or social theories, not reduced to other levels of explanation, e.g., psychological or ecological. His major works include *The Nature of Culture* (1952) and *Style and Civilization* (1957).

**Kroetz, Franz Xaver** (kruhts), 1946–, German dramatist. Predominantly Naturalistic in mode, Kroetz's dramas represent the constricted and brutalized lives of the farmers of Upper Bavaria (*Stallerhof, Wildwechsel*, both 1972) or the Munich petty bourgeoisie (*Münchener Kindl*, 1974). He has revived the 'Volksstück' to find a stunted language for his inarticulate figures: indeed, *Wunschkonzert* (1972; tr. *Request Programme*) is a scenario for solo performance with no speech at all. Use of dialect and close rendering of distinctive local life-styles present problems of cultural transposition, but he has been widely translated and performed. His most recent work is the 2-vol. novel *The Moonlight Labourer* (1980–82). Socially committed, he joined the Communist Party in 1972, but left in 1980.

**Krogh, (Schack) August Steenberg**, 1874–1949, Danish physiologist. He received the Nobel Prize for physiology or medicine in 1920 for his research into the physiology of capillaries.

**Kronecker, Leopold**, 1823–91, German mathematician. After making a fortune in business, he became a noted algebraist. He was a pioneer in the field of algebraic numbers (see NUMBER) and formulated the relation between number theory, the theory of equations, and elliptic functions.

**Kronos:** see CRONUS.

**Kropotkin, Piotr Alekseyevich**, Prince, 1842–1921, Russian anarchist. A noted geographer, he was imprisoned (1874–76) for political activities and fled Russia. Kropotkin settled in England, but after the February 1917 RUSSIAN REVOLUTION returned to Russia. When the Bolsheviks took power, he retired from political life. His writings include *Mutual Aid* (1902), which holds that cooperation rather than competition is the norm in both animal and human life, and *Memoirs of a Revolutionist* (1899).

**Kṛṣṇa** or **Krishna**, [Skt., = black], a very popular deity in HINDUISM, the eighth avatāra, or incarnation, of Viṣṇu. He is the main character in the epic *Mahābhārata*. Both in the *Mahābhārata* and the *Bhāgavata Purāṇa*, he is said to be the Ultimate Lord (Iśvara, Bhagavān).

**Kruger, Paul**, 1825–1904, South African Transvaal statesman, known as Oom Paul. He was a founder (1852) of the Transvaal, and after its annexation by Britain (1877) he was a leader of the Boer settlers there. He led the Boer Rebellion (1880) that forced Britain to restore independence and was president (1883–1900) of the Transvaal. In the SOUTH AFRICAN WAR (1899–1902) he went to Europe, where he made vain attempts to enlist aid for his country.

**Krupp**, family of German armament manufacturers who flourished in the 19th and 20th cent. **Friedrich Krupp**, 1787–1826, built a small steel plant at Essen c.1810. His son, **Alfred Krupp**, 1812–87, the 'cannon king,' specialized in armaments and acquired mines all over Germany. Under Alfred's son, **Friedrich Alfred Krupp**, 1854–1902, the family

vastly extended its operations. The husband of his daughter, Bertha Krupp (after whom the 'Big Bertha' guns were named), took the name **Gustav Krupp von Bohlen und Halbach**, 1870–1950. He took over what was then a public company and made it the centre of Nazi rearmament in the 1930s. In 1943, HITLER converted the company back into a family holding, and **Alfred Krupp von Bohlen und Halbach**, 1907–67, son of Gustav and Bertha, ran the company until the end of World War II. He was convicted (1948) as a war criminal but was released from prison (1951) and allowed to resume control of the firm. After his death, Krupp became a public corporation and the Krupp family ceased (1968) to control it.

**Krylov, Ivan Andreyevich**, 1769–1844, Russian writer. In over 200 fables (some adapted from AESOP and LA FONTAINE) he satirized human weaknesses and social customs.

**krypton** (Kr), gaseous element, discovered by William RAMSAY and M.W. Travers in 1898. It is a rare INERT GAS used to fill electric light bulbs and various electronic devices, and to detect heart defects. The definition of a metre is based on the emission spectrum of the krypton-86 isotope. See ELEMENT (table); PERIODIC TABLE.

**Kuala Lumpur**, largest city (1980 pop. 997,100) and capital of the Federation of Malaysia, S Malay Peninsula, at the confluence of the Klang and Gombak rivers. It is the trade centre of a tin-mining and rubber-growing district. Founded (1857) by Chinese miners, it became the capital of the Federated Malay States (see MALAYSIA) in 1896.

**Kubitschek, Juscelino** (͵koohbichek), 1902–76, president of BRAZIL (1956–61). His administration launched a huge public-works programme and built the new capital city, BRASÍLIA. The large deficit spending spurred runaway inflation, however.

**Kublai Khan** (͵koohblie kahn), 1215?–94, Mongol emperor, founder of the YÜAN dynasty of China. He succeeded (1260) his brother Mangu as khan of the empire founded by their grandfather JENGHIZ KHAN. Kublai Khan defeated (1279) the Song dynasty of China, but his campaigns against Japan, Southeast Asia, and Indonesia failed. His rule was nominal except in Mongolia and China. He improved public works and established a magnificent capital at Cambuluc (now Beijing), where Marco POLO visited him.

**Kubrick, Stanley**, 1928–, American film director. He is a meticulous film maker, who treats large-scale themes, such as warfare, with a pessimistic slant. His films include *Paths of Glory* (1957), *2001: A Space Odyssey* (1968), and *Full Metal Jacket* (1987).

**Kudrun:** see GUDRUN.

**Kuhn, Richard**, 1900–67, Austrian chemist. Awarded the 1938 Nobel Prize for chemistry for his work on the carotenoids (plant and animal pigments) and on vitamins, he was unable, because of the Nazis, to accept the award until after World War II. He isolated vitamins $B_2$ (riboflavin) and $B_6$.

**Kuhn, Walt**, 1880–1949, American painter. He is known for his boldly interpretive studies of backstage and circus life, e.g., *Blue Clown* (Whitney Mus., New York City). Kuhn was one of the organizers of the famed ARMORY SHOW.

**Kūkai**, 774–835, Japanese Buddhist priest, otherwise known as Kōbō Daishi. After studying esoteric Buddhism in China (804–806), he established a monastic centre on Mt Kōya (819) to the south of Nara. He was known as an accomplished lexicographer, poet, and calligrapher.

**Ku Klux Klan**, designation mainly given to two distinct American secret societies. The first, founded in the South in 1866, opposed RECONSTRUCTION and sought to maintain 'white supremacy'. Organized by ex-Confederates and led by Nathan B. Forrest, it used elaborate disguises and rituals, augmented by whippings and lynchings, to terrorize blacks and their supporters. The second Klan, organized in 1915, had a wider scope: embracing anti-Catholic, anti-Semitic, nativist, and fundamentalist impulses, it spread to the North, fuelled by the militant patriotism of World War I. In the mid-1920s it had 4 to 5 million members; it declined rapidly thereafter but contributed to the 1928 presidential election defeat of Alfred E. SMITH, a Catholic. The Klan revived in reaction to civil-rights activism in the 1960s, using violence against both black and white civil-rights workers in the South. Despite its split into a number of competing factions, the Klan became involved in racial confrontations late in the 1970s and was actively recruiting new members, largely in response to growing AFFIRMATIVE ACTION, unstable economic conditions, and other factors.

**kula,** a system of ceremonial exchange operating between the Trobriand Islands in the Pacific, first described and analysed by B. MALINOWSKI. In the kula system ceremonial necklaces flow one way round a system which is composed of regular high-status exchange partners on the different islands. These are exchanged for armbands which flow the opposite way round the system. The kula is central to the system of rank and hierarchy as well as the economic exchange system in the area within which goods circulate. See also GIFT.

**Kulayni, Muhammad Ibn Ya'qub,** d. c.940, Shi'ite Muslim scholar. His works, controversial after his death, later became and have remained one of the most authoritative statements of doctrine and tradition in Twelver SHI'ISM.

**Kulkulcán:** see QUETZALCOATL.

**Kumamoto,** city (1986 est. pop. 544,766), capital of Kumamoto prefecture, central Kyushu, Japan. It is one of the most important high-technology centres in Kyushu, as the result of the construction (1985) of Kumamoto Technopolis Research Park. The city is also a tourist centre for visitors to Mt Aso, an active volcano with the largest crater in the world. Kumamoto castle was constructed by Kyomasa Kato, loyal retainer of Toyotomi Hideyoshi, the ruler of Japan in the late 16th cent. Suizenji Garden, built in the 17th cent., is notable for its delightful landscapes and fountains.

**Kumasi,** city (1982 pop. 439,717), capital of the ASHANTI region, central Ghana. The nation's second largest city, it is a commercial and transport centre in a cocoa-producing region. Industries include food processing, metal work, and textile manufacture. It was founded c.1700 as the capital of the ASHANTI confederation. The town's importance grew following British occupation in the 1890s and the development of railways to the south coast.

**kumquat,** evergreen shrub (genus *Fortunella*) of the RUE family, cultivated for its small, orange-yellow CITRUS FRUITS, eaten fresh or in preserves. Kumquats, with their sweet-scented white flowers, are also sometimes grown as ornamentals.

**Kun, Béla** (koohn), 1886–1939?, Hungarian Communist leader. In 1919, when Count KAROLYI's government resigned, the Communists and Social Democrats formed a coalition government under Kun. He set up a socialist government and raised a Red Army that overran SLOVAKIA. The Allies forced him to evacuate Slovakia, and a counterrevolution broke out. Kun was defeated by a Romanian army of intervention. He went (1920) to the USSR and probably died in prison or Siberia.

**Kundera, Milan,** 1929–, Czech writer. He wrote sober but refreshing verse in the 1950s, and the successful socialist-realist drama, *The Keepers of the Keys* (1963) and the absurdist drama, *Cock-up* (1969). His short stories, *Laughable Loves* (3 vol., 1963–68), manifest great craftsmanship; but since his first two, *The Joke* (1967) and *Life is Elsewhere* (in French 1973, in Czech 1979), his novels have moved ever closer to philosophizing journalism. The authorities deprived him of his nationality while he was working in France. His best known work is probably *The Unbearable Lightness of Being*, which was filmed in 1988.

**Kunene, (Raymond) Mazisi,** 1930–, black South African poet. Steeped in oral tradition, he writes in Zulu, then makes his own translations. *Zulu Poems* (1970) was followed by the historical and political epic *Emperor Shaka the Great* (1979) and the further exploration of Zulu cosmology and creation myth, *Anthem of the Decades* (1981). He has lived in exile in England and the US since the early 1960s.

**Küng, Hans,** 1928–, Swiss Roman Catholic theologian. A professor at Tübingen Univ. and an adviser (1962–65) to the Second VATICAN COUNCIL, he has consistently criticized papal authority. His *Infallible? An Inquiry* (1971) rejects papal infallibility. In 1979 Küng was stripped of his right to teach as an official Roman Catholic theologian.

**Kunming,** city (1984 pop. 2,725,000), capital of YUNNAN prov., SW China. It comprises an old walled city, a modern commercial suburb, and a residential and university section. Home to more than a dozen of China's minority nationalities and noted for its scenery, Kunming is an industrial, administrative, commercial, cultural, and transport hub of SW China. The city's handicrafts are known throughout China. On its outskirts is a famed Ming dynasty temple.

**Kunsthistorisches Museum** ('koonsthis,tawrish'esmoos), Vienna, one of the world's greatest art collections. Formerly the Imperial collection, begun by the Habsburg emperors in the early 16th cent., it was opened to the public in 1783 in the Upper Belvedere Palace. It moved to its present home on Vienna's fashionable Ringstrasse in 1891, and became the property of the Austrian state on the abdication of the last emperor in 1918. The collections include paintings, sculpture, Egyptian, Greek and Roman antiquities, and coins and medals. Amongst the world-famous paintings are works by GIORGIONE (*Three Philosophers*), TITIAN, DÜRER, BREUGEL (many of whose works were bought by the Habsburgs), RUBENS, and REMBRANDT.

**Kuomintang** or **Chinese Nationalist Party,** ruling party of CHINA 1928–49, and subsequently of TAIWAN. Founded by SUN YAT-SEN, it was taken over shortly after his death (1925) by CHIANG KAI-SHEK.

**Kupka, Frank, (Francois),** 1871–1957, Czech painter. His interest in the occult and THEOSOPHY, led him to attempt to express a quasi-religious notion of a spiritual inner-life by means of abstract colour and form; he exhibited the first European abstract paintings at the 1912 salon d'automne. His *Newton-Disques* (1912), were similar to DELAUNAY's experiments with contrasting colours.

**Kuprin, Aleksandr Ivanovich** (,koohprin), 1870–1938, Russian novelist and short-story writer. His best-known novels are *The Duel* (1905), an attack on Russian military life, and *The Pit* (1924), a sensational exposé of prostitution.

**Kurashiki,** city (1986, est. pop. 414,271), Okayama prefecture, Honshu, Japan, on the INLAND SEA. A large heavy industrial complex has developed to the south of the city, round the port and coastal area of Mizushima. Steel, vehicles, and chemicals are the chief products. During the Edo (or Tokugawa) period (1601-1867), Kurashiki was important as a trading centre under the direct control of the Shogunate. Many of the old machiya (town houses) and kura (store houses) of the wealthy merchants still exist, built in traditional style with white walls and black tiles.

**kurchatovium:** see UNNILQUADIUM.

**Kurdistan,** extensive plateau and mountain region in SW Asia, c.191,660 km² (74,000 sq mi), inhabited mainly by Kurds and including parts of E Turkey, NE Iraq, NW Iran, and smaller sections of NE Syria and Soviet Armenia. There are an estimated 7.6 million Kurds; including 2.5 million in Turkey, 2.0 million in Iran, and 2.2 million in Iraq. Ethnically and linguistically close to the Iranians, the Kurds were traditionally nomadic herdsmen who are now mostly seminomadic or sedentary. The majority are devout SUNNI Muslims. The Kurds have traditionally resisted subjugation by other nations. Kurdistan was conquered by the Arabs and converted to Islam in the 7th cent. The region was held by the Seljuk Turks in the 11th cent., by the Mongols from the 13th to 15th cent., and then by the Ottoman Empire. Since World War I the Kurds have struggled unsuccessfully in the various countries in which they live, notably Iraq and Iran, for self-determination and independence.

**Kuril Islands** or **Kuriles,** island chain, NE Asia, stretching for c.1250 km (775 mi) S from the Kamchatka Peninsula to near HOKKAIDO, Japan. Long disputed between Russia and Japan, they were re-annexed by Soviet forces in 1945, together with four other adjoining islands still claimed by Japan.

**Kurnool** (,kuhnoohl), town (1981 pop. 206,362), Andhra Pradesh state, E India, on the KRISHNA R. It is a district administrative and marketing centre set in a generally poor area. It has, however, grown markedly in population since independence, partly because of the fillip it received when, for three years (1953–56), it was the capital of the nascent Andhra state.

**Kurosawa Akira** (koohrə,sahwə ə,kiərə), 1910–, Japanese film director. His *Rashomon* (1950) brought Japanese cinema to world attention. His other films include *Ikiru* (1952), *Seven Samurai* (1954), *Yojimbo* (1961), *Dersu Uzala* (1976), and *Kagemusha* (1980).

**kuru,** fatal disease affecting members of the Fore tribe of New Guinea only and causing degeneration of nerve cells in the brain. The disease is unique in that it is transmitted by ritual cannibalism, the eating of brains of dead relatives.

**Kuwait,** officially the State of Kuwait, independent sheikhdom (1985 pop. 1,695,128), 17,818 km² (6877 sq mi), NE Arabian peninsula, at the head of the Persian Gulf, bounded by Saudi Arabia (S) and Iraq (N and W). The capital is KUWAIT city. It is a sandy and generally barren country. With about one fifth of the world's estimated oil reserves, Kuwait is a leading exporter of petroleum. A great part of the oil profit has been devoted to social improvements. In the 1960s the government launched a programme of industrial diversification, successfully introducing oil refining and production of natural gas and fertilizers. The GNP is US$21,706 million and the GNP per capita is US$12,130 (1984). The population is predominantly Arab and Sunni Muslim, although only half the inhabitants are native-born.

*History.* Kuwait, settled by Arab tribes in the early 18th cent., has been ruled since its inception by the al-Sabah dynasty. Nominally an Ottoman province, the sheikhdom became a British protectorate in 1897, remaining so until independence in 1961. Oil production began in the 1940s and was controlled by a joint British–American firm until 1974, when Kuwait nationalized most of the operations. Kuwait took part in the Arab oil embargo against nations that supported Israel in the 1973 Arab–Israeli war, and is a leading member of the ORGANIZATION OF THE PETROLEUM EXPORTING COUNTRIES (OPEC). Following a five-year suspension, elections for the 50-member national assembly were easily won (1981) by conservatives supporting the government. In the early 1980s Kuwait moved towards closer cooperation with its neighbours within the framework of the GULF COOPERATION COUNCIL.

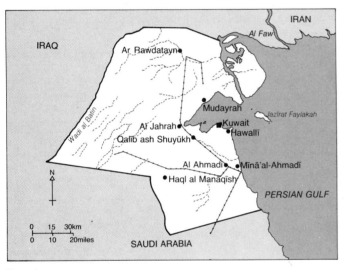

**Kuwait**

**Kuwait** or **Al-Kuwait**, city (1985 pop. 167,750), capital of Kuwait, situated on a Persian Gulf inlet. It was an important trading fishing, pearling and boat-building town. The city was modernized and greatly enlarged after oil was discovered in 1938. Its port, Mina al-Ahmad, has refineries and shipyards. The country's first university (est. 1966) is there.

**Kuybyshev**, formerly Samara, city (1985 pop. 1,257,000), E central European USSR, on the left bank of the Volga and at the mouth of the Samara R. A port and rail centre, located near a hydroelectric plant, it manufactures cars, aircraft, and many other industrial products. Grain and livestock are the chief exports. Founded in 1586, Samara was the Volga's grain centre. Industry grew as rail links to Siberia and central Asia were built (early 20th cent.). The city was renamed in 1935. During World War II the USSR's central government was moved (1941–43) from Moscow to Kuybyshev.

**Kuyp**, family of Dutch painters: see CUYP.

**Kuznets, Simon (Smith)**, 1901–85, American economist; b. Russia. After emigrating (1922) to the US, he worked for the National Bureau of Standards (1927–63) and taught at the Univ. of Pennsylvania (1930–54),

Johns Hopkins (1954–60), and Harvard (1960–71). Generally credited with having developed GROSS NATIONAL PRODUCT as a measure of economic output, he received the 1971 Nobel Prize for economics. *National Income and Its Composition, 1919 to 1938* (1941) is considered his major work.

**Kwajalein:** see MARSHALL ISLANDS.

**Kwakiutl Indians,** NORTH AMERICAN INDIANS of the Northwest Coast who live in Vancouver Island and adjacent British Columbia, Canada. They speak a Wakashan language (see AMERICAN INDIAN LANGUAGES). In the 19th cent. they conducted elaborate POTLATCH ceremonies. Numbering c.15,000 before white contact, they are now reduced to a few thousand, mostly fishermen and farmers.

**Kwangchu**, city (1984 pop. 869,874), capital of South Cholla prov., SW South Korea. A regional agricultural and commercial centre, Kwangchu has rice mills and produces textiles and beer. There are several ancient tombs and temples in the area. In 1980 Kwangchu was seized for several days by rebels protesting against martial law in South Korea; government troops eventually suppressed the uprising.

**Kwangsi Chuang:** see GUANGXI ZHUANG.

**Kwantung:** see GUANGDONG.

**kwashiorkor** ('kwaʃeeˌawkə), protein deficiency disorder of children, prevalent in overpopulated parts of the world where the diet consists mainly of starchy vegetables, particularly Africa, Central and South America, and S Asia. Such a diet makes it impossible for the child to consume the required quantity to obtain sufficient protein. Depending on the extent, onset, and duration of the deficiency, symptoms include skin and hair changes, oedema, severely bloated abdomen, diarrhoea, and apathy. The child fails to thrive.

**Kweichow:** see GUIZHOU.

**Kweiyang:** see GUIYANG.

**Kyd, Thomas,** 1558–94, English dramatist. He was a friend of MARLOWE, and author of the highly successful Senecan revenge play *The Spanish Tragedy* (1592), which was to influence SHAKESPEARE's *Hamlet* and T.S. ELIOT's *The Waste Land.*

**Kylian, Jiri,** 1947–, Czech choreographer. After choreographing for Netherlands Dance Theatre he became (1975) their artistic director, raising standards and gaining international status. Combining classical and modern techniques, he is one of the most important European choreographers. See also BALLET; CHOREOGRAPHY.

**Kyoto,** city (1986 pop. 1,469,270), capital of Kyoto prefecture, S Honshu, Japan. Founded in the 8th cent., it was Japan's capital from 794 to 1868. The cultural heart of Japan, the city has magnificent art treasures and is the seat of Kyoto Univ. (est. 1897) and other institutions of higher education. Kyoto is a religious centre, noted especially for its ancient Buddhist temples. Rich in historic interest, its buildings include the old imperial palace and Nijo Castle, built in 1603 by Tokugawa IEYASU and the former palace of the Ashikaga SHOGUNS. Industries include electronics, copper rolling, and the manufacture of tools and cameras. The city is famous for its silk, cloisonné, bronzes, damascene work, and porcelain.

**Kyprianou, Spyros** ('kipreeˌahnooh), 1932–, president of CYPRUS (1977–88). He served (1960–72) as foreign minister and in 1976 was a founder of the Cypriot Democratic Party. He succeeded Archbishop MAKARIOS as president on the latter's death.

**Kyushu,** island (1986 pop. 13,265,143), c.35,640 km² (13,760 sq mi), southernmost and 3rd largest of the main islands of Japan. NAGASAKI is one of the chief ports. The island is mainly of volcanic origin, with a scenic, mountainous interior rising to 1794 m (5886 ft) at Kuju-san. There are many hot springs. Coal, mined in the north, contributed to the early development of the principal industrial cities (KITAKYUSHU, and Omuta).

**Kyzyl-Kum** or **Kizil-Kum**, desert, Soviet Central Asia, in the Kazakh and Uzbek republics, SE of the ARAL SEA. Seminomadic tribes inhabit most of the region, which has important gold deposits and supports limited agricultural settlements in the river valleys and irrigated oases.

**La**, chemical symbol of the element LANTHANUM.

**Laban, Rodolf Von**, 1879–1958, Hungarian dancer, choreographer, and dance theoretician. Considered one of the most influential thinkers of dance in the 20th cent., Laban attacked the rarification of dance (especially classical ballet) arguing that dance was for everyone. Forced to move to England in 1938, Laban taught first at Dartington College, then Manchester (1946), where with Lisa Ullman he established The Art of Movement Studio which continues today under the name of the Laban Centre. He trained most of the dancers of the central European movement, WIGMAN, JOOSS, and LEEDER among them. Laban is also remembered for his development of *Kinetographie Laban*, or **Labanotation**, a system created by him and his pupils to facilitate the recording of movement and dance. See DANCE NOTATION; MODERN DANCE.

**Labour Force Survey**, Britain's contribution (established 1973) to a general SURVEY of the workforce in the EUROPEAN COMMUNITY. The main emphasis of the survey is to obtain information on the employment situation of the respondent. However, information is also collected on the following: the education, training, and qualifications of the respondent; his/her nationality and ethnic origin; the nature of the housing and the number of dependent children of school age in his/her household. The sample size is 100,000 which, with a response rate of around 85%, produces data on roughly 85,000 households. It is a valuable source of data on the ethnic and gender composition of both the UK and EEC labour force.

**labour law**, legislation affecting workers and their conditions of employment. It consists of individual labour laws relating to unfair dismissal, equal pay, redundancy, working conditions etc., and collective labour law relating to strikes, PICKETING, and the CLOSED SHOP. The earliest UK law (1802) dealt with the health, safety, and morals of child textile workers. Trade unions were legalized in Britain in 1825, but agreements among their members to seek better hours and wages were punishable as conspiracy until 1871. Since then legislation has protected the right to STRIKE, by granting trade unions and the members immunity from civil action for certain torts (e.g., conspiracy) committed during strike action. See also COLLECTIVE BARGAINING; EQUAL PAY ACT; SEX DISCRIMINATION ACT.

**Labour Party**, major British political party, the other being the CONSERVATIVE PARTY. Spurred by the increased enfranchisement of the working class (1867, 1884) and with the help of the FABIAN SOCIETY and the TRADES UNION CONGRESS, the Labour Representation Committee was founded in 1900; it was renamed the Labour Party in 1906 and adopted a democatic socialist constitution in 1918. Labour rose to official opposition status by 1922 and formed minority governments in 1924 and 1929-31, both under the premiership of Ramsay MACDONALD. After serving in the all-party wartime coalition, Labour won an overwhelming victory in the 1945 elections under the leadership of Clement ATTLEE; his government instituted extensive nationalization and welfare state measures, including the creation of a national health service. In opposition from 1951, Labour returned to power in 1964 under Harold WILSON, but faced serious economic crises and lost power in 1970. Back in office as a minority government from March 1974, the party achieved a narrow overall majority in the second 1974 general election. Wilson was succeeded (1976) as party leader and prime minister by James CALLAGHAN, who was obliged to enter a pact with the small LIBERAL PARTY to maintain a parliamentary majority. After disruptive public-sector strikes

during the winter of 1978-79, Labour was decisively defeated in the 1979 general election. Michael FOOT replaced Callaghan as leader in 1980 and the Labour left wing gained ascendancy, this development contributing to the formation by dissident right-wing elements of the SOCIAL DEMOCRATIC PARTY. Labour suffered a further heavy election defeat in 1983, following which Neil KINNOCK, then 41, was elected as the party's youngest-ever leader. A third successive election defeat followed in 1987, in light of which the party initiated a revision of its ideological and policy programmes completed for party approval in 1989.

**labour union:** see TRADE UNION.

**Labov, William**, 1927–, American linguist. He is regarded as a founder of sociolinguistics. He used methods employed in SOCIOLOGY to systematically analyse speech variation in language communities, correlating his findings with such social factors as sex, age, class, and ethnicity. His work also had a major impact on the theories of how languages change over time.

**Labrador:** see NEWFOUNDLAND.

**La Brea**, formerly Rancho La Brea, area, S California, known for its asphalt (tar) pits. Now within the boundaries of Hancock Park, Los Angeles, the pits are an extensive source of Pleistocene plant and animal fossils.

**Lacan, Jacques**, 1901–82, French psychoanalyst. Lacan's interpretation of Sigmund FREUD is based upon an analogy between the UNCONSCIOUS and the structure of language, and is characterized by an insistence both that PSYCHOANALYSIS is a human, rather than biological science; and that the majority of 'culturalist' interpretations distort Freud's original theory. His theory of the pre-Oedipal (see COMPLEX) 'mirror stage' influenced the work of Donald WINNICOTT. Lacan and his colleagues broke with the International Psychoanalytic Association in 1953. Lacan's writings—*Écrits* (1966)—are extremely arduous to read; despite or because of this, he became something of a cult figure in the Parisian intellectual milieu of the 1960s and after.

**lace**, patterned openwork fabric made by plaiting, knotting, looping, or twisting threads. Needlepoint lace, done with a needle in variations of the buttonhole stitch, arose in Italy during the Renaissance. The art later passed to France, Belgium, England, and Ireland. Bobbin or pillow lace (so named because the threads are wound onto bobbins resting on a pillow and are then twisted around pins) reached Flanders from Italy in the 15th cent. Laces are often named after their places of origin, e.g. Alençon, Honiton, and Maltese. Linen and, less frequently, silk, gold, or silver thread was used. KNITTING, MACRAME, tatting, and CROCHET can also be used to produce lace. The finest crochet lace was made in Ireland. Machine-made lace appeared c.1760, but it was improvements in cotton spinning c.1830, with subsequent substitution of linen by cotton, that enabled machine-made lace to replace hand-made lace almost completely, so that it is no longer a luxury item. Today almost all lace is machine-made, much of it using man-made fibres.

**Laclos, Pierre, Ambroise, François Choderlos de** (la‚kloh), 1741–1803, French novelist. An officer who also wrote on the education of women, he is famous for his epistolary novel *Les liaisons dangereuses* (1782), one of the outstanding creative masterpieces of French literature although perhaps based on real-life models. It is remarkable by its stylistic variety, its relentless plot, its picture of 18th-cent. society, its erotic explicitness, and above all the acute analysis of the two main characters, who manipulate the others with a cynicism which may hide some wistfulness at the Rousseauesque realization that happiness is impossible in society for the virtuous and the sincere.

Honiton **lace** border and collar

**lacquer,** solution of film-forming materials, natural or synthetic, usually applied as an ornamental or protective coating. Quick-drying synthetic lacquers are used to coat such products as motor cars, furniture, and textiles. Lacquer-work was one of the earliest industrial arts of the Orient. It was highly developed in India; the Chinese inlaid lacquer-ware with ivory, jade, coral, or abalone. The art spread to Korea, then to Japan, where it took new forms. The ware, which is often given more than 40 coats of lacquer, may be decorated in colour, gold, or silver and enhanced by relief, engraving, or carving. In the 17th cent. the technique known as japanning was used to make Western European imitations of lacquer-ware. Commercial production of lacquer-ware in the 19th cent. resulted in a decline in quality.

**lacrosse,** soccerlike ball and goal game, played by two teams of 10 players each on a field 55 to 64 m (60–70 yd) wide and 100 m (110 yd) long. The hard rubber ball is received, carried, and passed in the pocketlike head of the stick (crosse). Teams attempt to advance the ball until it can be hurled with the crosse or kicked into the opponent's goal (counting for one point). Only the goalkeeper may touch the ball with the hands. Lacrosse can be a game of rough physical contact; fouls are penalized by disqualification or temporary suspension (as in ice HOCKEY) that leave the penalized team with a player handicap. Of North American Indian origin, the game was developed in Canada.

**lactose** (empirical formula: $C_{12}H_{22}O_{11}$), white crystalline SUGAR formed in the mammary glands of all lactating animals and present in their milk, hence its common name of milk sugar. A disaccharide (see CARBOHYDRATE), lactose can be broken down by HYDROLYSIS into GLUCOSE and galactose. When milk sours, the lactose in it is converted by bacteria to lactic acid. Lactose is less sweet-tasting than SUCROSE and, unlike sucrose, is not found in plants and is not fermented by the action of ordinary yeast. Lactose intolerance is caused by deficiency of the ENZYME lactase.

**Ladin:** see RHAETO-ROMANIC.

**Ladino:** see SEPHARDIM.

**Ladislaus,** Polish rulers. **Ladislaus I,** 1260–1333, duke (1306–20) and king of POLAND (1320–33), unified the kingdom after 82 years of division. **Ladislaus II** or **Ladislaus Jagiello,** 1350?–1434, king of Poland (1386–1434) and grand duke of Lithuania (1378–1401), acceded to the Polish crown by marrying Queen Jadwiga, at which time he was baptized and agreed to convert Lithuania to Christianity. He defeated (1410) the TEUTONIC KNIGHTS. **Ladislaus III,** 1424–44, king of Poland (1434–44) and, as Ladislaus I, king of Hungary (1442–44). He led two crusades against the Turks (1443, 1447); the first was successful, the second ended with

his defeat and death at the battle of VARNA. **Ladislaus IV,** 1595–1648, king of Poland (1632–48), and sometime Czar-elect of Russia ruled over Poland's last period of relative peace of prosperity.

**Ladislaus I,** king of Bohemia: see LADISLAUS V, king of Hungary.

**Ladislaus II,** king of Bohemia: see ULADISLAUS II, king of Hungary.

**Ladislaus V** or **Ladislaus Posthumous,** 1440–57, king of HUNGARY (r.1444–57) and, as Ladislaus I, king of Bohemia (r.1453–57). The posthumous son of the German king Albert II, he was duke of Austria by birth. His guardian, Holy Roman Emperor FREDERICK III, refused to let him leave his custody until 1452. Ladislaus was crowned (1453) king of Bohemia but governed none of his realms. George of Podebrad was regent in Bohemia; John HUNYADI and later Ulrich, count of Cilli, were regents in Hungary.

**ladybird,** small, brightly coloured BEETLE, generally under 8 mm (⅓ in) long, with an hemispherical body and relatively short legs. Ladybirds are usually red or yellow with black spots, or black with red or yellow spots. Most adults and larvae feed on APHIDS and related, soft-bodied BUGS. Consequently they are very useful in regulating numbers in pest species and have been employed in biological control programmes (e.g., the Australian *Rodolia cardinalis* against cottony-cushion scale, *Icerya purchasi*, in California). Some ladybirds feed on plants, e.g., the black-spotted yellow *Thea 22-punctata*, which, in France, is a carnation pest. Most of the genus *Epilachna* are also crop pests: *E. chrysomelina* attacks melons in Mediterranean countries and *E. sparsa* aubergines and other crops in India.

**Lady Day,** popular name in England for the feast of the Annunciation of the Blessed Virgin MARY (i.e., the announcement to her by the archangel Gabriel that she was to be the mother of JESUS), which falls on 25 Mar. Until 1752, when it was replaced by 1 Jan., Lady Day marked the start of the civil year in England. It still counts as a QUARTER DAY, and Old Lady Day (6 Apr.) still begins the new tax year.

**lady's-slipper:** see ORCHID.

**Laetoli,** district in Tanzania, site of early hominid fossils SW of OLDUVAI GORGE excavated by M.D. LEAKEY. It has yielded teeth and jaws of *Australopithecus afarensis* (see AUSTRALOPITHECUS), and there are preserved hominid footprints dated to 3.6 million years ago, showing that bipedalism was established early in HUMAN EVOLUTION.

**laetrile,** drug consisting chiefly of the chemical amygdalin, found in the kernels of many fruits, notably apricots, bitter almonds, and peaches. The subject of controversy for many years, laetrile has been purported by some to be a cure for CANCER. In 1981 the US National Cancer Institute reported laetrile to be ineffective against cancer.

**laevulose:** see FRUCTOSE.

**La Farge, John,** 1835–1910, American artist and writer. He was primarily engaged in mural painting and the design and manufacture of STAINED GLASS, e.g., his works in Trinity Church, Boston. La Farge also created notable oils, watercolours, and drawings. A man of the widest culture, he did much to establish a tradition of American fine arts and is known for his many urbane pieces of art criticism.

**Lafayette** or **La Fayette, Marie Joseph Paul Yves Roch Gilbert du Motier, marquis de,** 1757–1834, French general and statesman. Enthusiastic about the AMERICAN REVOLUTION, he sailed (1777) to America and was made a major general by the CONTINENTAL CONGRESS. A close friend of Gen. WASHINGTON, he served at Brandywine, VALLEY FORGE, and in the YORKTOWN CAMPAIGN. In the FRENCH REVOLUTION, Lafayette became (1789) commander of the militia (later the National Guard) and tried unsuccessfully to mediate between the contending factions. Given command (1792) of the army of the centre, he was relieved of command after he had spoken in favour of the monarchy. He fled from France and was imprisoned in Austria. Freed in 1797, he later made a triumphal tour (1824–25) of the US. He led the moderates in France during the JULY REVOLUTION of 1830. The modern French flag was created by Lafayette in 1789.

**La Fayette, Marie Madeleine Pioche de La Vergne, comtesse de,** 1634–93, French novelist of the classical period. Her chief work, *La Princesse de Clèves* (1678), analyzing a woman's renunciation of an illicit love, is the first great French novel.

**La Follette, Robert Marion,** 1855–1925, US senator from Wisconsin (1906–25). A Republican, he was a member of the House of Representatives (1885–91) and later, as governor of Wisconsin (1901–06), he introduced reforms that became known as the Wisconsin Idea. As senator he was at odds with the Republican leadership and generally supported Pres. WILSON's reforms, but he voted against the US entry into World War I and opposed the League of Nations. In 1924 he ran for president as a PROGRESSIVE PARTY candidate and polled 5 million votes.

**La Fontaine, Jean de,** 1621–95, French poet. His *Selected Fables* (1668–94), 12 books of some 230 fables drawn largely from AESOP, place him among the masters of world literature. Told with wit and acumen, in brilliant verse and narrative, the fables have achieved worldwide success. Although their charm and simple facade have made them popular with children, most are sophisticated satires and serious commentaries on French society. Other works include *Tales and Novels in Verse* (1664–74), humorous tales drawn largely from BOCCACCIO and ARIOSTO; comedies and librettos for opera; and poems on classical themes.

**Lagerkvist, Pär Fabian** (ˌlahgəkvist), 1891–1974, Swedish writer, winner of the 1951 Nobel Prize for literature. His concern with good and evil and with man's search for God is expressed in such novels as *The Hangman* (1933), *The Dwarf* (1944), and *Barabbas* (1950), and the play *Man Without a Soul* (1936). His verse collections include *Evening Land* (1953).

**Lagerlöf, Selma** (ˌlahgəˈløːv), 1858–1940, Swedish novelist. Her novels, often set in her native Värmland and based on legends and sagas, include *The Story of Gösta Berling* (1891) and *The Ring of the Lowenskolds* (1925–28). She also wrote the children's classic, *The Wonderful Adventures of Nils* (1906). She received the 1909 Nobel Prize for literature, the first woman to be thus honoured.

**Lagos,** largest city (1975 est. pop. 1,060,848) and capital of Nigeria, on the Gulf of Guinea. It comprises four islands and four mainland sections, interconnected by bridges and causeways. Lagos is Nigeria's chief port and industrial centre, a road and rail terminus, and site of an international airport. Its economy is based on sawmilling, fishing, brewing, and gas and chemical production. An old Yoruba town, Lagos grew as a trade centre and seaport from the 15th cent. It was a centre of the slave trade until Britain annexed the city in 1861. The colony of Lagos was created in 1862 and administered from FREETOWN, Sierra Leone. It became the capital of Nigeria in 1960. Because of severe congestion in the modern city and its peripheral location, a new federal capital for Nigeria was designated at ABUJA in 1976.

**Lagrange, Joseph Louis, Comte** (laˌgranhzh), 1736–1813, French mathematician and astronomer; b. Italy. He was director of mathematics (1766–87) at the Berlin Academy of Sciences. After moving to Paris, he became (1793) chairman of the French commission on weights and measures and was influential in the adoption of the decimal system as the basis for the metric system. Under Napoleon, Lagrange was made senator and count. His contributions to mathematics included work on the calculus, the calculus of variations, number theory, the solutions of equations, and the application of calculus to probability theory. In astronomy, he made theoretical calculations on the libration of the moon and on the motions of the planets and the satellites of Jupiter. He also did research on the nature and propagation of sound and on the vibration of strings. His chief work was the *Mécanique analytique* (1788).

**LaGuardia, Fiorello Henry,** 1882–1947, American politician and mayor of NEW YORK CITY (1934–45); A Republican, he was a US congressman (1917–19, 1923–33) and was elected mayor in 1933. Known as 'the Little Flower' (from his first name), he achieved numerous municipal reforms, including setting up slum clearance and housing projects, building various public facilities, and fighting racketeering and official corruption.

**La Guma, Alex,** 1925–86, black South African writer and revolutionary. He suffered several periods of imprisonment, house arrest, and banning, before living in exile in England and Cuba, where he was the permanent representative of the AFRICAN NATIONAL CONGRESS of South Africa. His fiction celebrates and charts the lives of ordinary victims of APARTHEID, e.g., *A Walk in the Night and Other Stories* (1962) and *And a Threefold Cord* (1964), and charts the gradual growth of militancy and resistance, e.g., *The Stone Country* (1967), *In the Fog of the Seasons' End* (1973), and *Time of the Butcherbird* (1979).

**Lahore,** city (1981 est. pop. 2,922,000), capital of Punjab prov., E central Pakistan, on the Ravi R. Pakistan's second largest city, it is the commercial centre of an agricultural region and has such industries as railway workshops, textiles and steel-making. In 1206 India's first Muslim emperor was crowned in Lahore. The city flourished (16th cent.) as a capital of the MOGUL empire, was annexed by the Sikhs in 1767, and passed to the British in 1849. The palace and mausoleum of Emperor Jehangir and the Shalimar gardens are among the splendid remains of the Mogul period.

**Laing, Ronald David,** 1927–, Scottish psychiatrist, psychoanalyst, and existential philosopher. Laing's clinical work with patients and families at the Tavistock Institute during the 1960s focused upon communication and interaction from a PHENOMENOLOGICAL perspective. His attempt to understand the experience of patients diagnosed as suffering from SCHIZOPHRENIA led him to criticize conventional psychiatry for failing to help, and in many cases harming, the individuals concerned, because of its failure to grasp the social and personal intelligibility of madness. Laing was a key figure in the development of the ANTI-PSYCHIATRY movement. His books *The Divided Self* (1965) and *The Politics of Experience* (1967) achieved wide readership within the post-1968 'New Left'.

**laissez-faire,** [Fr., = leave alone], in economics and politics, a doctrine holding that an economic system functions best when there is no interference by government. It is based on the belief that the natural economic order tends, when undisturbed by artificial stimulus or regulation, to secure the maximum well-being for the individual and therefore for the community as a whole. The principles of laissez-faire were formulated by the French PHYSIOCRATS in the 18th cent. in opposition to MERCANTILISM. In Britain, Adam SMITH, Jeremy BENTHAM, and J.S. MILL developed laissez-faire into a tenet of classical economics and a philosophy of individualism. During the 19th cent. the so-called MANCHESTER SCHOOL of economics popularized the doctrine of free trade and brought laissez-faire into politics (e.g., by securing repeal of the CORN LAWS). In time, laissez-faire came to be perceived as promoting monopoly rather than competition and as contributing to 'boom-and-bust' economic cycles, and by the mid-20th cent. the principle of state noninterference in economic affairs had generally been discarded. Nevertheless, laissez-faire, with its emphasis shifted from the value of competition to that of profit and individual initiative, remains a bulwark of conservative political thought, influential in the early 1980s in such government administrations as that of Ronald REAGAN in the US and Margaret THATCHER in the UK.

**Laius:** see OEDIPUS.

**lake,** body of standing water occupying a depression in the earth. Most lakes are freshwater bodies; a few (e.g., the GREAT SALT LAKE, the DEAD SEA), however, are more salty than the oceans. The GREAT LAKES of the US and Canada are the world's largest system of freshwater lakes. The CASPIAN SEA is the world's largest lake. Most lake basins were formed by the erosive action of GLACIERS on bedrock. Other sources include volcanic calderas and natural and human-made dams in streams and RIVERS. Lakes are transient geological features, eventually disappearing because of several factors, e.g., climatic changes, erosion of an outlet, and EUTROPHICATION.

**Lake District,** scenic mountain region, c.50 km (30 mi) wide, NW England. It includes 15 lakes, among them Ullswater, Derwentwater, and Windermere, and reaches a high point of 978 m (3210 ft) in Scafell Pike. Many writers and artists have lived there, including William WORDSWORTH, Samuel Taylor COLERIDGE, and Robert SOUTHEY, who are known as the Lake Poets.

**lake dwelling,** prehistoric habitation built over waters of a lake shore or marsh, usually on a pile-supported platform, probably for access to fish, marsh fowl, and good crop land. Remains are found worldwide and dating from all recent periods. Small artificial islands, called *crannogs*, were built in the late BRONZE AGE and early IRON AGE in Scotland and during the Early Christian period in Ireland, and in England, a large IRON AGE lake village is located at GLASTONBURY.

**Lake Mungo,** dry lake forming part of the Willandara Lakes system in western New South Wales, SE Australia. In 1969 remains of a woman who died 26,000 years ago, and had undergone cremation before burial, were unearthed: this is the oldest such cremation site yet found in the world. Fossil remains of large animals and fish indicate abundant food supplies could have supported a large population of Aborigines in wetter climatic periods. A large eroded crescent-shaped dune, or lunette, 28 km (18 mi) long and 40 m (120 ft) high along the edge of the lake was called by early settlers the 'Wall of China'.

**Lalique, René,** 1860–1945, French jewellery designer and goldsmith. He was an influential innovator and manufacturer, well known c.1900 for exquisite work in the ART NOUVEAU style, using horn, glass, and enamel with precious materials. After 1920, he turned to the design and manufacture of decorative items and costume jewellery in glass.

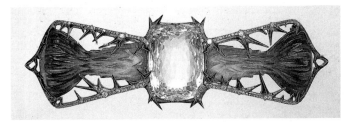

Brooch by René **Lalique**

**Lalo, Édouard Victor Antoine** (lah‚loh), 1823–92, French composer. His opera *Le Roi d'Ys* (1888) and *Symphonie espagnole* (1875) gained him renown in his day.

**Lama** [spiritual teacher], a term reserved for a Tibetan or Mongolian monk. The most famous Lama is Dalai Lama, the leader of TIBETAN BUDDHISM (a form of Mahāyāna Buddhism).

**Lamarck, Jean Baptiste Pierre Antoine de Monet, chevalier de,** 1744–1829, French naturalist. Regarded as the founder of invertebrate palaeontology, he is noted for his study and classification of invertebrates and for his evolutionary theories; the latter were first made public in his *Système des animaux sans vertèbres* (1801). **Lamarck's theory of evolution,** or **Lamarckism,** asserts that all life forms have arisen by a continual process of gradual modification throughout geological history. It was based on the theory of ACQUIRED CHARACTERISTICS, which held that new traits in an organism develop because of a need created by the environment and that they are transmitted to its offspring. Although the latter hypothesis was rejected as the principles of heredity were established, Lamarck's theory was an important forerunner of Charles DARWIN's theory of EVOLUTION, and influenced agricultural policy in the USSR until 1964, see LYSENKO.

**Lamartine, Alphonse Marie Louis de** (lamah‚teen), 1790–1869, French romantic poet, novelist, and statesman. Drawing on traditional and contemporary sources, his best-known work *Méditations poétiques* (1820; tr. Poetic Meditations), including the well-known poem 'Le lac', is noted for its musical lyricism and affinity for nature. Other poetic volumes include *Harmonies poétiques et religieuses* (1830) and the narrative *Jocelyn* (1836). Lamartine wrote *Histoire des Girondins* (1847; tr. The History of the Girondists), in praise of the GIRONDISTS, and after the FEBRUARY REVOLUTION of 1848 he briefly headed the provisional government. Among his later works is the novel *Graziella* (1849).

**Lamb, Charles,** 1775–1834, English essayist. A friend from boyhood of COLERIDGE, he worked as a clerk in East India House (1792–1825). He lived with his sister, **Mary Ann Lamb,** who was subject to violent fits of insanity, in one of which she killed her mother. With her he wrote *Tales from Shakespeare* (1807). Lamb established his reputation as a critic with *Specimens of English Dramatic Poets* (1808) and as an essayist with *Essays of Elia* (collected 1823, 1833). A humorous and familiar tone of great charm distinguishes both his essays and his admirable letters.

**Lambert, Constant,** 1905–51, British composer, conductor, and writer. His nostalgic style and his interests in jazz and musical exoticism first flowered in the popular *Rio Grande* (1928) for chorus, piano, and orchestra. From 1930 he was musical director of the Sadler's Wells Ballet, and thereafter he devoted so much energy to conducting and arranging music that he had little time for original composition. Amongst his major scores are the cantata *Summer's Last Will and Testament* (1935), and the ballets *Pomona* (1926), *Horoscope* (1937), and *Tiresias* (1951).

**Lambeth,** London borough (1981 pop. 244,143), on S side of R. Thames, in inner London. The Thames here is crossed by the Vauxhall, Lambeth, Westminster, and Waterloo road bridges, and the Charing Cross railway bridge. The railway terminus of Waterloo is in the borough, as is the South Bank complex, which includes the Royal Festival Hall, and the National Theatre, the National Film Theatre, and the Hayward Art Gallery. Upstream of this is Lambeth Palace, residence of the Archbishop of Canterbury.

**Lambeth Conferences,** meetings of the bishops of the ANGLICAN COMMUNION, held approximately every 10 years under the presidency of the Archbishop of Canterbury, originally at his London residence, Lambeth Palace, but in 1978 and 1988 at the Univ. of Kent, Canterbury. The first Conference met in 1867 and was attended by 76 of the 144 bishops holding office at the time; the 1988 Conference, the 12th, was attended by around 500 bishops. The conferences are consultative, not legislative; they discuss matters of practical as well as of theological interest, and their decisions have considerable moral weight.

**Lambing Flat riots,** a series of violent racial affrays on the Lambing Flat goldfield of New South Wales in 1860 and 1861. Inflamed by racial prejudice and competition for the best gold deposits, 3000 Australian miners attacked Chinese miners and destroyed their dwellings.

**Lamennais** or **La Mennais, Félicité Robert de** (lama‚nay), 1782–1854, French Roman Catholic apologist and liberal. In the journal *L'Avenir* (founded 1830), he opposed Gallicanism and the royalist clergy and championed the role of the pope. However, his doctrines on the separation of church and state were condemned by Pope Gregory XVI. Lamennais died excommunicated.

**Lamentations,** book of the OLD TESTAMENT. It is a series of poems mourning the destruction of JERUSALEM by Babylon, and has been ascribed to JEREMIAH since ancient times.

**Lamm, Norman,** 1927–, American rabbi, theologian, and writer. He founded the prestigious journal, *Tradition,* and was its first editor. Currently, he is president of Yeshivah Univ.

**lammergeier** (‚lamə'gieə): see KITE.

**Lamming, George Eric,** 1927–, Barbadian writer. His imaginative insights as well as radical political vision have inspired many younger writers; he is best known for his celebrated study of adolescence in the Caribbean, *In the Castle of My Skin* (1953), but his highly allegorical and allusive fiction also deals with themes such as displacement and the search for Caribbean identity. In his collection of critical essays *The Pleasures of Exile* (1960), he writes about Shakespeare's *The Tempest* and the colonial encounter generally.

**Lampedusa, Giuseppe Tomasi di,** 1896–1957, Italian novelist. A Sicilian prince, he drew on his own family history for his acclaimed novel *Il gattopardo* (1958; tr. The Leopard), which describes the effects of Sicily's annexation to Italy (1860) on an aristocratic family.

**lamprey,** primitive marine and freshwater FISH (family Petromyzontidae) lacking a sympathetic nervous system, spleen, and scales. Although unrelated, the lamprey resembles the HAGFISH and EEL. Most lampreys are parasitic bloodsuckers, attaching themselves to other fish by means of horny teeth set in a circular, jawless mouth; an anticoagulant in the saliva keeps the blood of the host fluid. Some freshwater lampreys eat flesh as well. They are found in temperate regions worldwide. The sea lamprey, (*Petromyzon marinus*) of the North Atlantic is the best known example. Lampreys were once considered to be a great delicacy: the English King Henry I is said to have died from eating too many lampreys.

**lamp shell,** marine invertebrate animal (phylum Brachiopoda) with a bivalve shell. In appearance it resembles a mollusc, but is not related. Found in shallow seas, lamp shells attach themselves to objects by means of a short stalk (pedicel) and feed by means of a characteristic tentacled organ (lophophore) surrounding the mouth. The lophophore creates currents that draw water, with food and oxygen, into the shell. Lamp shells are usually from 2.5 to 5 cm (1 to 2 in) across. They are living fossils; the earliest known animal fossil was a lamp shell. *Lingula* has remained unchanged for about 450 million years.

**Lancashire,** county in NW England (1984 est. pop. 1,379,100), 3063 km² (1195 sq mi), bordering on the Irish Sea in the W. The county town is LANCASTER. It is hilly in the E in the Pennines and low-lying in the W. The main river is the Ribble. In the boundary changes of 1974 Lancashire lost much of the industrial area in the S. Agriculture is important in the more fertile lowlands with cultivation of oats and potatoes and dairy farming undertaken. BLACKPOOL, on the W coast, is an important holiday resort and conference centre. BURNLEY and Blackburn in the S of the county are old industrial towns whose prosperity was based upon the textile industries and nearby coal deposits.

**Lancaster,** county town (1981 pop. 43,902), in Lancashire, NW England, on R. Lune 32 km (20 mi) N of Preston. Industries found within the town include the manufacture of linoleum and rayon. There are several old buildings, including a Norman castle and a Georgian Old Town Hall. Lancaster Univ. (1964) is at Bailrigg, 3 km (2 mi) to the S. The town is the birthplace of Richard OWEN.

**Lancaster, Burt,** 1913–, American film actor. A former trapeze artist, his films include *All My Sons* (1948), *From Here to Eternity* (1953), *Elmer Gantry* (1960; Academy Award), *The Leopard* (1963), *The Swimmer* (1968), and *Atlantic City* (1981).

**Lancaster, house of,** royal family of England. The line was founded by the second son of HENRY III, **Edmund Crouchback,** 1245–96, who became earl of Lancaster in 1267. His nickname 'Crouchback',or crossed back, refers to the fact that he went on crusade and was entitled to wear the cross. His son **Thomas, earl of Lancaster,** 1278?–1322, led the barons against his cousin EDWARD II and was (1314–18) the virtual ruler of England. Defeated at the battle of Boroughbridge, he was beheaded for treason. Thomas's brother, **Henry, earl of Lancaster,** 1281?–1345, was chief adviser to the young EDWARD III. His son, **Henry, duke of Lancaster,** 1300?–61, was made duke in 1351 for excellent service in the HUNDRED YEARS WAR. When he died without male heirs, JOHN OF GAUNT inherited the Lancastrian lands by marrying Henry's daughter Blanche. John's son Henry deposed (1399) RICHARD II and became king as HENRY IV. Other Lancastrian kings were HENRY V and HENRY VI. Claims by the rival house of YORK led to the Wars of the ROSES; the Lancastrian claims passed to the house of TUDOR.

**Lancaster, Joseph,** 1778–1838, English pioneer of popular education. In 1798 he founded an elementary school for poor children using the MONITORIAL SYSTEM. A Royal Lancasterian society was formed in 1808, and six years later it became the British and Foreign School Society —an undenominational school system in opposition to Andrew BELL's Anglican National Society. Having failed financially and quarrelled with his supporters, he lectured and tried to promote schools in the US from 1818. He and Bell are the founding fathers of British mass elementary education.

**lancelet** or **amphioxus,** small, fishlike lower chordate (see CHORDATE), related to the VERTEBRATES. Usually about 2.5 cm (1 in) long, with a transparent body tapering at both ends, the lancelet has no distinct head and no paired fins. A filter-feeder that lives in shallow marine waters, it is usually found buried in the sand with only the mouth end projecting. The lancelet has a nerve cord but no heart, no brain, and no eyes. LAMPREY larvae resemble the lancelet and so do TUNICATES. The relationship between the lancelet and vertebrate and invertebrate animals is very interesting as it has features from both groups.

**Lancelot:** see ARTHURIAN LEGEND.

**Lanchow:** see LANZHOU.

**Land, Edwin Herbert,** 1909–, American inventor and industrialist. As a student at Harvard, he became interested in POLARIZED LIGHT and invented (1932) a material to eliminate glare, now known by the trademark Polaroid. In 1937, Land established the Polaroid Corp. to manufacture such products as sunglasses, camera filters, and headlights. He also developed a process for three-dimensional pictures (1941); invented the POLAROID CAMERA (1947), which takes and prints photos in one step; and introduced 'instant' colour photographs (1963) and motion pictures (1977).

**Landes,** a largely flat, forested area, SW France. The sandy heaths and marshes were once the home of shepherds who used stilts to follow their flocks over the swampy ground. Pine trees were planted in the 19th cent. and gave rise to a new economy based on pit props, railway sleepers, and the collection of turpentine. The pine forests support timber industries and paper-making, and there are large maize-growing farms in the clearings. Sand dunes and lagoons add to the attraction of the coastal belt for holiday-making. The capital of Landes dept. is Mont-de-Marsan.

**landlord and tenant,** terms used to describe the relationship between the owner of a residence and its occupier. The relationship is usually defined by a type of LEASE, or tenancy agreement, granted by the landlord in favour of the tenant, under which the landlord will grant the tenant exclusive possession of the residence, in return for rent, paid by the tenant. In the 19th and early 20th cent., the relationship between landlord and tenant was governed by whatever terms were contained in the tenancy agreement. However, because of the inequality of bargaining power between the parties, tenants were often charged excessive rents and were offered no protection from eviction. As a result, in the UK acts of parliament have been passed placing restrictions on the rent that can be charged and giving tenants security of tenure. In recent years landlords have been able to avoid these provisions by using LICENCE agreements.

**Landor, Walter Savage,** 1775–1864, English poet and essayist. He spent much of his life in Italy, where he wrote *Imaginary Conversations* (1824–9, 1853), a series of imaginary dialogues between ancient and modern notables. His poetry, ranging from the epic to the epigrammatic, includes 'Rose Aylmer' and 'I Strove with None'.

**Landowska, Wanda** (lan͵dofskah), 1877–1959, French harpsichordist and pianist; b. Poland. She founded the École de Musique Ancienne, near Paris, giving many concerts between 1919 and 1940. She went to the US in 1940 and is largely responsible for the revival of interest in the harpsichord. She is known for her interpretation of J.S. BACH.

**landscape gardening** or **landscape architecture,** art of laying out gardens and open spaces and relating them to buildings. In most periods water and its control has played an important part in such schemes. The art was practised in antiquity and by the Romans whose villas were introduced to Britain. The main tradition however stems from the gardens of the Italian Renaissance and from the French formal gardens, influenced by Italy, that reached a climax at Vaux le Vicomte and Versailles designed by LENÔTRE. In England the formal gardens of the Tudor period were transformed by the great landscape movement started by William Kent (1684–1748) who 'leapt the fence and found all nature was a garden', and by Lancelot Brown (1716–83). Brown, better known as Capability Brown, was a master at creating apparently natural parkland, including great lakes, around country houses, e.g., Blenheim in Oxfordshire. He influenced landscape design in most parts of the world.

**landscape painting.** Although paintings from the Hellenistic era onwards contained landscape backgrounds, landscape painting as an independent art form was a late development in the West. Originally used as a background for religious subject matter, landscape became a genre in its own right when, during and after the Reformation, the use of religious subjects was restricted. Artists of the 16th cent., such as Pieter Bruegel the Elder (see BRUEGEL, family), became landscape specialists; Venetian artists GIORGIONE and TITIAN used landscape to convey a mood. The ideal landscape was perfected in the serene pastoral scenes of the 17th-cent. painter CLAUDE LORRAIN. His works and those of POUSSIN contrasted with the concurrent realism of such Dutch artists as van GOYEN, HOBBEMA, and RUISDAEL. The ROCOCO revived idealized pastoral tableaus in the work of WATTEAU, GAINSBOROUGH, and others. The great landscape painting of the 19th cent. may be regarded as beginning in England with the naturalistic views of CONSTABLE and the visionary panoramas of J.M.W. TURNER. The direct study of nature was continued by the French BARBIZON SCHOOL; and the poetic tradition was sustained by FRIEDRICH in Germany, and the HUDSON RIVER SCHOOL in the US. Elevated to its most exalted position in the late 19th cent. in IMPRESSIONISM, landscape remained a source for realistic and abstract painters in the 20th cent. In the Far East, the landscape tradition has been important for centuries. In China, landscape painting was perfected by the 8th cent. and continued through the T'ang, Sung, and Ming dynasties (see CHINESE ART).

**Landseer, Sir Edwin Henry,** 1802–73, British painter. Specializing in animals, he is best known for his painting *The Monarch of the Glen* (1859; Dewar House, London).

**Land's End,** headland in Cornwall, SW England. It is famous as the most westerly point on the English mainland.

**landslide,** rapid slipping of a mass of earth or rock from a higher elevation to a lower level owing to gravity and water lubrication. In humid climates, slow-moving earthflows can block roads and cause property damage. The more spectacular mudflows that pour down canyons in areas subject to erosion cause severe damage as well as loss of life.

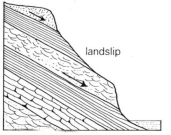 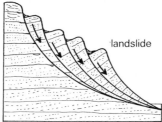

Two types of **landslide**

**landsmål:** see NORWEGIAN LANGUAGE.

**Landsteiner, Karl,** 1868–1943, Austrian pathologist; came to US, 1922. For demonstrating human BLOOD GROUPS he was awarded the 1930 Nobel Prize for physiology or medicine. He continued his research in immunology and the chemistry of antigens and serological reactions. With Alexander Wiener and Philip Levine he identified the RHESUS FACTOR (1940).

**Lane, William,** 1861–1917, Australian socialist; b. England. He was an early leader of the Australian labour movement who, after the defeat of the trade unions in the national strike of 1890, led 220 followers to establish a utopian settlement in Paraguay. His temperence, sexual puritanism, and autocratic manner caused internal divisions and Lane left for New Zealand in 1899. Those who remained merged into the Paraguayan society.

**Lanfranc,** 1005–89, Italian churchman, monk, and theologian, archbishop of Canterbury (1070–89). He became prior of the famous school at Bec in Normandy (c.1045) and wrote (c.1070) *Concerning the Body and Blood of the Lord* (c.1060), a treatise on the Eucharist (see COMMUNION) that became a medieval classic. An associate of WILLIAM I of England, he reluctantly became archbishop of Canterbury. In England his reforms included establishing ecclesiastical courts, strengthening the monasteries, and shifting bishoprics from small towns to important cities.

**Lang, Andrew,** 1844–1912, Scottish scholar and poet. He applied anthropological theory to the study of myth in *Myth, Ritual and Religion* (1887). In addition to poetry and criticism, he published (with others) translations of HOMER's *Odyssey* (1879) and *Iliad* (1883). His story for children, *Prince Prigio* (1889) and his collections of fairy tales, each volume named for a different colour, remain popular.

**Lang, Fritz,** 1890–1976, German-American film director; b. Austria. Among his German films are *Metropolis* (1926), a science-fiction classic, and *M* (1930), a study of a child-murderer. His Hollywood work includes *Fury* (1936), *You Only Live Once* (1937), *Ministry of Fear* (1944), and *The Big Heat* (1953).

**Lang, John Dunmore,** 1799–1878, Australian clergyman and politician; b. Scotland. He established the first Presbyterian church in Australia in 1823, and promoted Scottish migration. A sectarian zealot and frequent litigant, he was a leading reformer during the campaign for colonial self-government.

**Lang, John Thomas,** 1876–1975, Australian politician. As premier of New South Wales (1925–27, 1930–32) during the financial crisis of 1931, he proposed the suspension of interest payments to British bondholders. He was dismissed from office by the state governor in 1932.

**Lange, David Russell,** 1942–, NEW ZEALAND Labour politician and prime minister (1984–). Elected Labour leader in 1983, he led the party to victory in the 1984 elections. His government's anti-nuclear policy caused a crisis in relations with the US, leading to New Zealand's suspension from the ANZUS PACT.

**Lange, Dorothea,** 1895–1965, American photographer. Lange's *Migrant Mother* (1936) is typical of her powerful documentary portraits of rural America in the Depression years. She also recorded the Japanese-American internment (1941).

Migrant Mother, Nipomo, California (1936) by Dorothea **Lange**

**Langland, William,** born c.1330, English poet. He was the author of *The Vision of William concerning Piers the Plowman* (*Piers Plowman*), a widely read Middle English allegorical poem in unrhymed alliterative verse. Consisting of a series of dream visions, it begins as a social satire but becomes a personal quest for the means to salvation.

**Langley, Samuel Pierpont,** 1834–1906, American scientist. He invented the bolometer, an instrument for recording variations in heat radiation, and with it he measured the distribution of heat in the solar and lunar spectra and made other contributions to astronomy.

**Langtry, Lillie,** 1853–1929, English actress; b. Jersey, Channel Islands as Emilie Charlotte Le Breton. Called the Jersey Lily, she was noted for her great beauty and her liaison with EDWARD VII. *Lady Windermere's Fan* was written for her by Oscar WILDE.

**language,** systematic communication by vocal symbols. It is a universal characteristic of the human species. The earliest forms of language known are no more 'primitive' than modern forms. Because language is a cultural system, individual languages classify objects and ideas differently. There are between 3000 and 4000 speech communities (groups speaking the same language). The smallest have only a few members; the largest, in approximate descending order, are North Chinese vernacular (Mandarin), English, Hindustani, Spanish, Russian, and German. Differences within speech communities are DIALECTS. Languages change continuously, but various factors, especially literacy, and more recently the expansion of radio and television broadcasting, lead to the development of a community's standard language, usually one dialect, e.g., standard southern British English. Literary and colloquial standards may differ, and a group jargon may be unintelligible to outsiders; the differences are primarily in vocabulary. Groups of related languages are called families and stocks. For a survey of the important languages by family, see table overleaf. See also AFRICAN LANGUAGES (table); ALPHABET; AMERICAN INDIAN LANGUAGES (table).

**Languedoc** (lanhg,dok), region and former prov. of Mediterranean France, extending from CARCASSONNE in the west to the RHÔNE valley in the east. Its name is derived from the *langue d'oc* (see separate entry), the form of French that was once spoken in the south. It has the most extensive area of vineyards in France although much of the wine produced is *vin ordinaire*, and an ambitious irrigation scheme has been introduced in order to diversify farming and encourage the production of fruit and vegetables. MONTPELLIER is the leading city. New resorts have been built along what used to be an undeveloped, mosquito-ridden coast, some, like La Grande Motte, with spectacular modern architecture.

**Langue d'oc,** language spoken in medieval France. It is now a group of closely related Romance dialects spoken in the S of France characterized by empty subject positions (viz. Italian, Spanish, and Portuguese) and a rich verbal morphology.

**L'Anse aux Meadows,** site on the N coast of Newfoundland of a Viking settlement, the only direct evidence of any pre-Columbian Old World contact in the New World. The turf houses, iron artifacts and slag from the forging of bog iron, metal-cut wood, and a soapstone spindle whorl clearly indicate Norse origin. Radiocarbon dates covering the 10th cent. AD support the testimony of the sagas, which describe the Norse discovery of a land west of Greenland which they called Vinland.

**Lansing,** US city (1984 est. pop. 128,000), state capital of Michigan, at the confluence of the Grand and Red Cedar rivers; inc. 1859. It was made state capital in 1847. The arrival of the railway in the 1870s and of the motor vehicle industry in 1897 spurred its growth. Motor vehicles and parts are the main manufactures. Michigan State Univ. is in East Lansing, a suburb.

**lanthanide series,** RARE-EARTH METALS with atomic numbers 58 to 71 in group IIIb of the PERIODIC TABLE. They are, in order of increasing atomic number, CERIUM, PRASEODYMIUM, NEODYMIUM, PROMETHIUM, SAMARIUM, EUROPIUM, GADOLINIUM, TERBIUM, DYSPROSIUM, HOLMIUM, ERBIUM, THULIUM, YTTERBIUM, and LUTETIUM. Although they closely resemble LANTHANUM and each other in their chemical and physical properties, lanthanum (atomic number 57) is not always considered a member of the series.

**lanthanum** (La), metallic element, discovered in 1839 by C.G. Mosander. One of the RARE-EARTH METALS, it is silver-white, soft, malleable, ductile, and chemically active. Lanthanum is used in making ductile cast IRON and as an alloy in cigarette-lighter flints. It occurs in MONAZITE. See ELEMENT (table); PERIODIC TABLE.

**Lanzhou** or **Lanchow** (lan-joh), city (1984 pop. 2,436,000), capital of GANSU prov., NW China, on the Yellow R. The transport and industrial centre of NW China, it has a large oil refinery and a gas-diffusion plant. Its products include petrochemicals, copper, and machinery. The city is a centre for China's Muslims. Lanzhou was a link on the Silk Road which at one time connected China with the Roman Empire. In World War II Lanzhou was an important supply depot in the struggle against Japan.

**Laocoön** (lay,okohon), in Greek mythology, priest of APOLLO who warned the Trojans not to touch the wooden horse made by the Greeks during the TROJAN WAR. He and his two sons were crushed by sea serpents

---

## MAJOR LANGUAGES OF EUROPE, ASIA, AND SOME ISLANDS OF THE PACIFIC AND INDIAN OCEANS
*(*Asterisk indicates a dead language)*

**Caucasian Languages** (*spoken in the Caucasus region of the USSR and in Turkey and Iran*)

| | |
|---|---|
| NORTHERN | Abkhaz, Adyghe (including Circassian and Kabardin), Chechen |
| SOUTHERN | Georgian |

**Dravidian Languages** (*spoken in S India and N Sri Lanka*)

Brahui, Kanarese, Malayalam, Tamil, Telugu

**Hamito-Semitic** or **Afroasiatic Languages** (*spoken in W Asia; for languages of this family spoken in Africa, see the Hamito-Semitic classification in the table of AFRICAN LANGUAGES*)

SEMITIC

| | | |
|---|---|---|
| North Semitic | | |
| | Akkadian | Old Akkadian,* Assyrian,* Babylonian* |
| | Canaanite | Hebrew,* Israeli Hebrew, Moabite,* Phoenician,* Punic* |
| | Ugaritic | Ugaritic* |
| | Aramaic | Biblical Aramaic,* Nabataean,* Palestinian,* Palmyrene,* Samaritan,* Syriac |
| South Semitic | | Classical Arabic,* Modern Arabic, South Arabic (or Himyaritic, including Sabaean* and Minaean*) |

**Indo-European Languages** (*spoken originally in an area between and including India and Europe, but now spoken on every continent and on a number of islands*)

| | |
|---|---|
| ANATOLIAN | Hieroglyphic Hittite,* Hittite (Kanesian),* Luwian,* Lycian,* Lydian,* Palaic* |
| BALTIC | Lettish (or Latvian), Lithuanian, Old Prussian* |

CELTIC

| | |
|---|---|
| Brythonic | Breton, Cornish,* Welsh |
| Continental | Gaulish* |
| Goidelic (or Gaelic) | Irish (or Irish Gaelic), Manx, Scottish Gaelic |

GERMANIC

| | |
|---|---|
| East Germanic | Burgundian,* Gothic,* Vandalic* |
| North Germanic (or Norse or Scandinavian) | Old Norse,* Danish, Faeroese, Icelandic, Norwegian, Swedish |
| West Germanic | |
| High German | German, Yiddish |
| Low German | Afrikaans, Dutch, English, Flemish, Frisian, Plattdeutsch |
| GREEK | Aeolic,* Arcadian,* Attic,* Byzantine Greek,* Cyprian,* Doric,* Ionic,* Koine,* Modern Greek |

INDO-IRANIAN

| | |
|---|---|
| Dardic | Kafiri, Kashmiri, Khowar, Kohistani, Romany (or Gypsy), Shina |
| Indic (or Indo-Aryan) | Pali,* Prakrit,* Sanskrit,* Vedic* |
| Central Indic | Hindi, Hindustani, Urdu |
| East Indic | Assamese, Bengali, Bihari, Oriya |
| NW Indic | Punjabi, Sindhi |
| Pahari | Central Pahari, Eastern Pahari (or Nepali), Western Pahari |
| South Indic | Marathi (including the major dialect Konkani), Sinhalese |
| West Indic | Bhili, Gujarati, Rajasthani (has many dialects) |
| Iranian | Avestan,* Old Persian* |
| East Iranian | Baluchi, Khwarazmian,* Ossetic, Pamir dialects, Pushtu (or Afghan), Saka (or Khotanese),* Sogdian,* Yaghnobi |
| West Iranian | Kurdish, Pahlavi (Middle Persian),* Parthian,* Persian (or Farsi), Tadzhiki |

ITALIC

| | |
|---|---|
| Non-Romance | Faliscan,* Latin,* Oscan,* Umbrian* |
| Romance (or Romanic) | |
| Eastern Romance | Italian, Rhaeto-Romanic (including Romansh, Ladin and Friulian), Romanian, Sardinian |
| Western Romance | Catalan, French, Ladino, Portuguese, Provençal, Spanish |

---

**MAJOR LANGUAGES OF EUROPE, ASIA, AND SOME ISLANDS OF THE PACIFIC AND INDIAN OCEANS** *(Continued)*
(*Asterisk indicates a dead language)*

| | |
|---|---|
| SLAVIC (or SLAVONIC) | |
| East Slavic | Belorussian (or White Russian), Russian, Ukrainian |
| South Slavic | Bulgarian, Church Slavonic,* Macedonian, Serbo-Croatian, Slovenian |
| West Slavic | Czech, Kashubian, Lusatian (or Sorbian or Wendish), Polabian,* Polish, Slovak |
| THRACO-ILLYRIAN | Albanian, Illyrian,* Thracian* |
| THRACO-PHRYGIAN | Armenian, Grabar (Classical Armenian),* Phrygian* |
| TOKHARIAN (was spoken in W China) | Tokharian A (or Agnean),* Tokharian B (or Kuchean)* |

**Luorawetlan Languages** *(spoken in E Siberia)*

Chukchi, Kamchadal, Koryak

**Malayo-Polynesian** or **Austronesian Languages** *(spoken in the Malay Peninsula; Madagascar; Taiwan; Indonesia; New Guinea; the Melanesian, Micronesian, and Polynesian islands; the Philippine Islands; and New Zealand)*

| | |
|---|---|
| WESTERN | Balinese, Batak, Bikol, Bugi, Dayak, Ilocano, Indonesian (or Bahasa Indonesian), Javanese, Madurese, Malagasy, Malay, Sundanese, Tagalog, Visayan |
| EASTERN | |
| Melanesian | Fijian, Malo, Marovo, Mono |
| Micronesian | Chomorro, Caroline, Gilbertese, Marianas, Marshallese |
| POLYNESIAN | Hawaiian, Maori, Samoan, Tahitian, Tongan |

**Sino-Tibetan Languages** *(spoken in central and SE Asia)*

| | |
|---|---|
| CHINESE | Amoy-Swatow, Cantonese, Hakka, Fukienese, Mandarin Chinese, Wu |

| | |
|---|---|
| THAI (or TAI) | Lao, Shan, Thai (or Siamese) |
| TIBETO-BURMAN | Burmese, Bodo, Garo, Kachin, Karen, Lolo, Lushai, Tibetan |

**Southeast Asian** or **Austroasiatic Languages** *(spoken in SE Asia)*

| | |
|---|---|
| ANNAMESE-MUONG | Muong, Vietnamese (or Annamese) |
| MON-KHMER | Cambodian (or Khmer), Cham, Khasi, Mon (or Talaing), Nicobarese, Sakai, Samang |
| MUNDA | Santali |

**Uralic and Altaic Languages** *(spoken discontinuously in a vast area that reaches from E Europe across the USSR and Asia to the Pacific Ocean)*

| | | |
|---|---|---|
| ALTAIC | | |
| Turkic | | |
| Eastern | Uigur, Uzbek | |
| Southern | Azeri (or Azerbaijani), Chuvash, Turkish, Turkoman | |
| Western | Kazakh, Kazar, Kirghiz, Noghay, Tatar | |
| Mongolian | Buryat, Kalmuck, Khalkha (or Mongol proper) | |
| Tungusic | Manchu, Tungus | |
| URALIC | | |
| Finno-Ugric | | |
| Finnic | Cheremiss, Estonian, Finnish (or Suomi), Karelian, Lapp, Mordvinian, Permian tongues | |
| Ugrian (or Ugric) | Hungarian (or Magyar), Ostyak, Vogul | |
| Samoyedic | Samoyed | |

Note: The numerous aboriginal languages of Australia and the numerous Papuan languages have not as yet been studied sufficiently to be classified with any certainty as far as relationships with each other are concerned. They are, however, unrelated to the other languages of the world.
  The nonrelated languages of the world include Ainu, Basque, Elamite,* Etruscan,* Hurrian,* Japanese, Korean, Meroitic,* and Sumerian.*

---

as they sacrificed to POSEIDON, and the Trojans brought the horse into the city. The death struggle of the family is portrayed in a famous Greek sculpture by Agesander, Athenodorus, and Polydorus, now in the Vatican.

**Laois,** inland county in central Republic of Ireland (1986 pop. 53,270), 1703 km² (664 sq mi), bordering on Co. Tipperary in the W. It is situated in the province of Leinster and was formerly known as Queen's County. The county town is Port Laoise. There are hills in the S and NW and the land rises to 528 m (1732 ft) in the Slieve Bloom Mts in the NW. The main rivers are the R BARROW and the Nore. Much of the NE part of the county is low-lying, with boggy areas. Agriculture is the major economic activity.

**Laos** (lows), officially the Lao People's Democratic Republic, republic (1987 est. pop. 4,120,000), 236,800 km² (91,428 sq mi), SE Asia, bordered by China (N), Vietnam (E), Cambodia (S), and Thailand and Burma (W). The capital is VIENTIANE. Except for lowlands along the MEKONG R., where most of the people live, and three sparsely populated plateaus, the terrain is mountainous and thickly forested. The climate is monsoonal. Economically, the country is one of the least developed in Asia; there are no railways, few roads, and practically no mining or industry. The predominantly rural population is engaged primarily in fishing and subsistence agriculture; rice, corn, vegetables, coffee, tobacco, sugarcane, and cotton are the chief crops. The GNP is US$296

million, and GNP per capita is US$80 (1981). Ethnic Lao, a Thai people, make up about half the population; minorities include Vietnamese and Chinese as well as a number of tribal mountain groups. Lao is the official language, and Buddhism is the most widely practised religion.

*History.* Part of the KHMER EMPIRE, Laos was infiltrated in the 13th cent. by Lao people from Yunnan, China, and by the 17th cent. a powerful Lao kingdom called Lan Xang held sway over much of SE Asia. After 1707 internal dissension split the kingdom, which passed to Siam (early 18th cent.) and then became (1893) a protectorate in the French-ruled union of INDOCHINA. After occupation by Japanese forces in World War II Laos became (1949) a semiautonomous state within the French Union. It received independence in 1953. By that time the Pathet Lao, a Communist nationalist movement aided by the Vietminh (Vietnamese Communists), had gained control of N Laos, and a rival government headed by Prince Souphanouvong. A protracted civil war followed, and after 1965 the VIETNAM WAR increasingly spilled over into Laos. A cease-fire was finally signed in 1973, and a coalition government was formed under Premier Souvanna Phouma. It soon collapsed, however, and the Pathet Lao took over the government in 1975, abolished the monarchy, and established the Lao People's Revolutionary Party led by Kaysone Phomvihane as the ruling party. A flood of refugees, including most of the professional and commercial classes, fled the country; many who remained were confined in 'political reeducation' centres. In recent years Laos has become increasingly dependent on Vietnam for military and economic assistance, the two countries having

Laos

signed a 25-year treaty of friendship in 1977. Relations with neighbouring Thailand worsened in the mid-1980s over a border dispute.

**Lao She**, pseud. of **Shu Qingchun**, 1899–1966, Chinese novelist and playwright. Born into an impoverished Manchu family in Peking, Lao She worked as a teacher before going to England to teach Chinese (1924–29). His first novels were written there; his greatest fictional success was *Luo tuo xiangzi* [lit. Xiang zi the camel; tr. as Rickshaw Boy] (1936–37), a tragic story of the corruption and fate of a kindhearted rickshaw-puller. In 1943, he began to publish plays, including *Long xu gou* [dragon beard ditch] (1951) and *Cha guan* [teahouse] (1957). Lao She died after being beaten up by Red Guards in the Cultural Revolution; his reputation has recently been enhanced by the television serialization of *Si shi tong tang* [four generations under one roof], saga of the Japanese occupation of Peking.

**Lao Zi**, b. c.604 BC, legendary Chinese philosopher. According to legend and to sources from the 1st cent. BC, he was a royal librarian and keeper of the lacquer grove. He is traditionally cited as the author of the *Dao de jing*, the central text of TAOISM, but modern scholars date that work as a whole from the 4th cent. BC.

**La Paz**, city (1982 est. pop. 881,400), W Bolivia, administrative capital of Bolivia since 1898. (The constitutional capital is SUCRE.) It is the nation's largest city and its commercial centre. Manufactures include clothing and processed food. Situated in a narrow Andean river valley at an elevation of c.3600 m (12,000 ft), it is the highest capital city in the world. It was founded in 1548 and was a key point on colonial trade routes. Tourist attractions in the area include Lake TITICACA.

**lapis lazuli**, GEM composed of lazurite and other minerals in shades of blue, usually flecked with PYRITE. Most often found in massive form in metamorphosed limestones, it has been used since ancient times for beads and small ornaments. Lapis lazuli was the original pigment for ultramarine and was the 'sapphire' of the ancients.

**Laplace, Pierre Simon, marquis de** (la‚pläs), 1749–1827, French astronomer and mathematician. On the basis of Isaac NEWTON's gravitational theory, he made mathematical studies of the motions of comets, the Moon, Saturn, Jupiter, and Jupiter's satellites, as well as of the theory of tides. His research results, which together with those of Joseph LAGRANGE and earlier mathematicians established Newton's theory beyond a doubt, were published in his famous *Mécanique céleste* (5 vol., 1799–1825). His more popular *Exposition du système du monde* (1796) gave scientific form to the nebular hypothesis of the origin of the solar system. Laplace also made a great contribution to the theory of PROBABILITY.

**Lapland**, vast region of N Europe, largely within the Arctic Circle, occupying N Norway, N Sweden, N Finland, and the Kola Peninsula of the USSR. The climate is severe, and the vegetation cover a sparse tundra except in the forested southern zone. Reindeer are essential to the economy. There are important high-grade iron ore deposits at Gällivare and Kiruna (Sweden), copper deposits at Sulitjelma (Norway), and nickel and apatite deposits in the USSR. The **Lapps** or **Laplanders,** who constitute the indigenous population, number less than 40,000 and are concentrated mainly in Norway, where they are called Samme or Finns. They speak a Finno-Ugric language, and are believed to have originated in central Asia and to have been pushed into the northern extremities of Europe by the later migrations of Finns, Goths, and Slavs.

**La Plata**, city (1980 pop. 473,233), central Argentina, capital of Buenos Aires prov. Founded in 1882 on the Plate R, 58 km (36 mi) SE of Buenos Aires, its port is accessible to ships of the largest tonnage. It is the main national outlet for the produce of the Pampas. Previously a noted centre of meat-processing and packing, its major industrial activity now consists of oil-refining.

**larch**, deciduous CONIFER (genus *Larix*) of the PINE family, found in the Northern Hemisphere. The needles of the larch are borne in characteristic radiating clusters. The common larch (*L. decidua*) produces good quality timber in N Europe. The Western larch (*L. occidentalis*), of N America, achieves great height; its wood is used for interior construction and cabinetmaking. The American larch, or tamarack (*L. laricina*), also a source of timber, is often cultivated for its beauty.

**Lardner, Ring(gold) Wilmer,** 1885–1933, American writer. A sports reporter (1907–19), he became known for short stories in a racy sports idiom, e.g., *You Know Me, Al* (1916). His later stories, cynical and pessimistic, yet humorous, include *What of It?* (1925) and *First and Last* (1934).

**lares and penates** (‚leəreez pə‚nayteez), in Roman mythology, household gods. The lares were considered guardian spirits, often of a family's ancestors. The penates were primarily guardians of the storeroom and, with VESTA, of the hearth.

**Larisa**, Gr. *Lárissa*, city (1981 pop. 102,048), capital of Thessaly, N Greece. It serves as market, administrative and route centre. Annexed by Macedonians in the 4th cent. BC, it later became a Roman capital.

**lark**, perching BIRD of the mainly Old World Alaudidae family. Skylarks (*Alauda arvensis*), the best known of the larks, are about 18 cm (7¼ in) long and similar in coloration (greys and browns above and light underneath) and nesting habits (meadows, plains, and other open areas). Although larks are usually associated with meadows there are species of desert larks which have adapted to the arid centre of Arabia, where a dark race is found in rocks and a sand-coloured race adjacent to it in the sandy desert.

**Larkin, Philip,** 1922–85, English poet. A meticulous stylist whose spare, self-deprecating verse summed up the mood of retrenchment in England after World War II. His subtle wit and vivid evocation of the commonplace enliven a basically sombre outlook. His collections include *The Less Deceived* (1955), *The Whitsun Weddings* (1964) and *High Windows* (1974). A professional librarian, he also wrote the novels *Jill* (1945) and *A Girl in Winter* (1946), and published a collection of jazz reviews.

**larkspur** or **delphinium,** north temperate, herbaceous plant (genus *Delphinium*) of the BUTTERCUP family, many popular as garden plants. The annuals are commonly called larkspur; the perennials, delphinium. The spurred flowers, usually shades of blue, rise in a spire above the leaves.

**La Rochefoucauld, François, duc de** (roshfooh‚koh), 1613–80, French author. As head of an ancient family, he opposed RICHELIEU and was later active in both FRONDES, which gives his *Mémoires* (1662) historical interest. However, his place in French literature rests on the *Maxims* (1665), a collection of several hundred lucid and polished moral maxims expressing his pessimistic view that selfishness is the source of all human behavior.

**La Rochelle** (laro‚shel), city (1982 pop. 78,231, agglomeration 102,143), capital of Charente-Maritime dept., W France. It serves the surrounding countryside of Aunis, exporting the brandies of Cognac, and has some engineering industries. A centre of Protestant control after the Edict of Nantes (1598) (see NANTES, EDICT OF), it capitulated to RICHELIEU after a long siege in 1628. A deep-water outport of La Pallice was opened in 1890 and the old port is now used mainly by fishing and pleasure crafts. The picturesque old town attracts many visitors.

**larva,** immature form of an animal, hatched from a relatively small egg. These eggs do not contain enough food to allow the animal to reach its mature form inside the egg, and they hatch into a non-breeding form which may be quite unlike the adult. This larva feeds until it has ingested enough material to allow development to continue. In animals that undergo complete METAMORPHOSIS the egg hatches into a larva, which feeds until it becomes a pupa. This is frequently an overwinter stage that will develop into an adult form. In insects that undergo partial metamorphosis the egg hatches to produce a NYMPH. Crustaceans may have several types of larvae. Crabs' eggs hatch first into a zoea larva which becomes a megalopa larva before growing into an adult crab. Some fishes and amphibians have larval stages. The familiar TADPOLE is the larva of the FROG and NEWT.

**larynx,** organ responsible for the production of vocal sounds in mammals. The human larynx is a small, boxlike chamber with walls of cartilage bound by muscles and membranes, situated in the front of the neck above the trachea (windpipe). Air passes through it to the lungs. The vocal cords, a pair of elastic folds in the mucous-membrane lining, lie across the larynx. During speech the cords are stretched and outgoing breath, forced between them, causes vibrations and produces sound. The sound varies with the tension of the cords and the space between them.

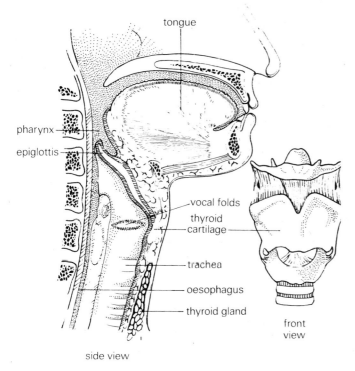

Larynx

**La Salle, René Robert Cavelier, sieur de** (la͵sal), 1643–87, traveller and explorer of Canada; b. Rouen, France. He commanded Fort Frontenac, developed trade, and built many forts. In 1682 he and his lieutenant, Henri de Tonti, descended the MISSISSIPPI to its mouth. La Salle took possession of the whole valley, naming it LOUISIANA. After three futile attempts to find the mouth of the Mississippi by sea, he was murdered by his own men.

**Las Casas, Bartolomé de** (lahs ͵kahsahs), 1474–1566, Spanish missionary in Latin America. Ordained a priest (1510), he worked to improve the condition of Indians and to abolish Indian slavery and forced labour. He converted uncivilized tribes, tried but failed to establish (1520–21) a model Indian colony, and visited Spain to urge government action. Chiefly through his efforts, a humanitarian code known as the

New Laws was adopted (1542) to protect the Indians in Spanish colonies. The New Laws were later so altered as to be ineffective, however.

**Lascaux,** a painted cave of the Upper PALAEOLITHIC period in the Dordogne, SW France. The paintings reveal the sophistication of artists 15,000 years ago: colour and line were used to great effect in large, dynamic images of animals, many of them enhanced with different shades of ochre and manganese pigment and often using the humps and hollows of the cave's surface. Discovered in 1940, the cave was closed in 1961 because of the spread of algae; a full-sized replica of the cave has been developed on the site to provide the many tourists and students with a substitute for the original.

Rhino, dead man, and bison from the painted caves at **Lascaux**

**laser** [acronym for *l*ight *a*mplification by *s*timulated *e*mission of *r*adiation], device for the creation and amplification of a narrow, intense beam of monochromatic (of one wavelength) and coherent (having waves in phase) LIGHT. In a laser, the atoms or molecules are excited so that more of them are at higher energy levels than are at lower energy levels. If a PHOTON whose frequency corresponds to the energy difference between the excited and ground states strikes an excited atom, the atom is stimulated, as it falls back to a lower energy state, to emit a second photon of the same frequency, in phase with and in the same direction as the bombarding photon. This process is called stimulated emission. The bombarding photon and the emitted photon may then each strike other excited atoms, stimulating further emission of photons, all of the same frequency and phase. This process produces a sudden burst of coherent radiation as all the atoms discharge in a rapid chain reaction. First built in 1960, lasers are widely used in industry, medicine, communications, scientific research, and HOLOGRAPHY. See also MASER.

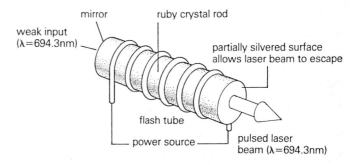

The first **laser,** built in 1960, used a ruby rod with polished ends; the chromium atoms embedded in the ruby's aluminium oxide crystal lattice were pumped to an exited state and saturated the rod with light of a frequency higher than that of the laser frequency.

**Lashley, Karl Spencer,** 1890–1958, American neuropsychologist. Lashley's work on the neurophysiological foundations of PERCEPTION, MEMORY, and skilled action emphasized the importance of 'mass' rather than 'local' action or organization; and had many affinities with GESTALT PSYCHOLOGY.

**Laski, Harold Joseph,** 1893–1950, English political scientist. He taught (1920–50) at the London School of Economics and served on the executive committee of the FABIAN SOCIETY (1922–36) and of the Labour Party (from 1936). He was chairman of the party (1945–46) when under ATTLEE it won its famous postwar victory over the Conservatives, but was excluded from power by its leaders, whom he subsequently criticized for failing to adopt socialist policies. His many works include *A Grammar of Politics* (1925), *The State in Theory and Practice* (1935), *The Rise of European Liberalism* (1936), and *Reflections on the Revolutions of Our Time* (1943).

**Las Marismas,** salt marshes in the estuary of the GUADALQUIVIR R., ANDALUSIA, SW Spain. This swampy area is similar to the CAMARGUE at the mouth of the RHÔNE in France and has a rich bird life, including flamingoes. A curiosity of the area were the wild camels, descendents of ones brought from the Canary Islands as beasts of burden in the 19th cent.

**La Spezia** (las̩petsee·ə), city (1984 pop. 111,353), N Italy, on the Ligurian coast. As a seaport it grew rapidly after the establishment of a naval base in 1857. To employment in the naval arsenal and dockyards has been added the oil and petrochemical industry.

**Lassa fever,** serious viral illness occurring in West Africa. Believed to be caused by contact with the excreta of an infected rat, the disease is fatal in up to 50% of cases. Strict security in handling the virus must be observed.

**Lassalle, Ferdinand,** 1825–64, German socialist. Although partially influenced by MARXISM, Lassalle's theory of state socialism differed from it in contending that once universal suffrage was achieved, the state could be forced to establish workers' cooperatives. He played a key role in founding (1863) the first workers' political party in Germany, the forerunner of the Social Democratic party.

**Lasso, Orlando di,** 1532–94, Franco-Flemish composer, also Orlande Lassus or Roland de Lassus. He represents the culmination of Renaissance music. A famous singer and choirmaster, he published his first books of MADRIGALS in Antwerp in 1555 and subsequently held positions in other cities. Lasso brought Flemish POLYPHONY to its highest development. His more than 2000 works are in every form known in his day MASSES, MOTETS, chansons, madrigals, and others.

**Last Supper,** repast taken by JESUS and his disciples on the eve of the passion (Mat. 26.17–29; Mark 14.12–25; Luke 22.7–38; John 13–17; 1 Cor. 11.23–25). At that time Jesus instituted the SACRAMENT called COMMUNION.

**Las Vegas,** US city (1984 est. pop. 183,000), S Nevada; inc. 1911. The largest city in Nevada, it is one of the fastest-growing urban areas in the US. Revenue from gambling, entertainment, and other tourist industries forms the backbone of its economy, although in the 1970s diversified industry began to play a more important role.

**László V,** king of Hungary: see LADISLAUS V.

**La Tène,** a phase of the IRON AGE in western and central Europe named after a site on Lake Neuchatel, Switzerland. Known largely from burials, early La Tène material culture revealed influences from Greece and Italy. It included an art style in which representational and abstract forms were fused together in stylized fluid compositions almost prefiguring the style of Art Nouveau; this developed in the 5th cent.BC and spread widely, especially in the decoration of weapons and ornaments. La Tène art reached its height in Britain in the 1st cent. BC, appearing at sites such as the lake village at GLASTONBURY.

**latent heat:** see BOILING POINT; MELTING POINT.

**laterality,** a preference or favouring of one of a left-right pair of limbs or sense organs (such as hands or eyes) over the other, caused by the asymmetry of the distribution of cognitive functions (see COGNITION) in the two cerebral (brain) hemispheres. In most individuals, the left hemisphere is 'dominant', which leads to their being right-handed, right-eyed, etc. Not all left-handed individuals, however, are right-hemisphere dominant. In the majority of both right- and left-handed individuals, the left cerebral hemisphere is 'specialized' for INFORMATION PROCESSING involving speech and language, while the right cerebral hemisphere appears to be relatively more efficient in visual and spatial

perception and manipulation. Cerebral dominance is to some extent innate, but becomes more pronounced and established in development.

**Lateran,** group of buildings, SE Rome, on land presented to the church by CONSTANTINE I. The Lateran basilica is the cathedral of Rome, the pope's church, the first-ranking church of the Roman Catholic Church. Officially it is the Basilica of the Saviour, familiarly St John Lateran. Built perhaps before 311, it has been often rebuilt or restored. Much of the decoration, including the mosaics of the apse, is medieval. The Lateran baptistery (c. 4th cent.) was much restored. The Lateran palace, the papal residence until the 14th cent., was demolished in the 16th cent. to make way for the smaller present palace.

**Lateran Treaty,** 1929, concordat between the Holy See and Italy. In 1871 the unity of Italy was perfected by limiting papal sovereignty to a few buildings. The papacy objected to the loss of Rome and the Papal States, creating the dilemma called the Roman Question. The Lateran Treaty resolved the matter by creating the new sovereign state of VATICAN CITY. It also recognized Roman Catholicism as the only state religion of Italy. The treaty was signed for the pope by Cardinal Pietro Gasparri, and for Italy by Benito MUSSOLINI.

**Lateur, Frank:** see STREUVELS, STIJN.

**latex:** see RUBBER.

**Latimer, Hugh,** 1485?–1555, English Protestant martyr. Bishop of Worcester under HENRY VIII, he refused to recant his Protestantism when the Roman Catholic MARY I became queen. With Nicholas RIDLEY, he was burned at the stake.

**Latin,** the language of ancient Rome and its empire, a member of the Italic sub-family of the Indo-European family of languages. It is the basis of all the ROMANCE languages. As the official and literary language of the Roman empire, it remained the major language of communication and scholarship in Western Europe during the Middle Ages and, in the cases of law, science, medicine, and religion, until much later. The liturgy and the official language of the ROMAN CATHOLIC CHURCH was Latin until the mid 20th cent. The term Vulgar Latin is applied to the popular and provincial varieties which gave rise to the Romance languages. See also ALPHABET (illustration).

**Latin America,** collective term for the 20 republics of South and Middle America where Romance languages are generally spoken. It includes Portuguese-speaking BRAZIL, French-speaking HAITI, and Spanish-speaking ARGENTINA, BOLIVIA, CHILE, COLOMBIA, COSTA RICA, CUBA, DOMINICAN REPUBLIC, ECUADOR, EL SALVADOR, GUATEMALA, HONDURAS, MEXICO, NICARAGUA, PANAMA, PARAGUAY, PERU, URUGUAY, and VENEZUELA. It is also sometimes extended to include PUERTO RICO and the French WEST INDIES and, less frequently, BELIZE, GUYANA, FRENCH GUIANA, and SURINAME.

**Latin American Economic System** (SELA), intergovernmental organization formed in 1975 to promote economic cooperation. Its members are Argentina, Barbados, Bolivia, Brazil, Chile, Colombia, Costa Rica, Cuba, Dominican Republic, Ecuador, El Salvador, Grenada, Guatemala, Guyana, Haiti, Honduras, Jamaica, Mexico, Nicaragua, Panama, Paraguay, Peru, Spain, Suriname, Trinidad and Tobago, Uruguay, and Venezuela. Based in Caracas (Venezuela), SELA's supreme organ is the Latin American Council.

**Latin American Integration Association** (ALADI), intergovernmental organization formed (1981) as successor to the Latin American Free Trade Association. ALADI's members are Argentina, Bolivia, Brazil, Chile, Colombia, Ecuador, Mexico, Paraguay, Peru, Uruguay, and Venezuela. Its headquarters are in Montevideo (Uruguay).

**Latin Empire of Constantinople:** see CONSTANTINOPLE, LATIN EMPIRE OF.

**Latin Empire of Jerusalem:** see JERUSALEM, LATIN KINGDOM OF.

**Latins,** in ancient times, inhabitants of Latium. Rome early became a dominant city in Latium, and Roman hegemony was definitely established by 338 BC. The Latins were admitted to Roman citizenship in 90 BC.

**latitude,** angular distance from the EQUATOR of any point on the earth's surface. The equator is latitude 0°, and the poles are 90° N and S respectively. One degree of latitude is about 110 km (69 mi), increasing slightly poleward as a result of the earth's polar flattening. See also LONGITUDE.

**La Tour, Georges de,** 1593–1652, French painter. Influenced by CARAVAGGIO, he specialized in religious and GENRE subjects. His early works

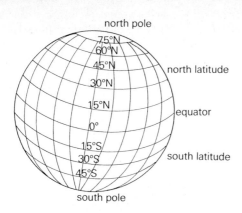

Latitude

are detailed genre scenes of card-players, musicians, fortune-tellers; his later religious works are often night-time scenes, tender in feeling, and dramatically lit by a single candle or hidden light source. Outstanding examples are the *Magdalene with Two Flames* (Metropolitan Mus., New York) and *St Sebastian* (Louvre, Paris).

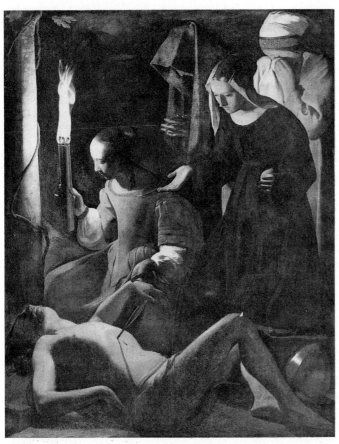

George de **La Tour**, *St Sebastian Tended by St Irene*. Louvre, Paris.

**Lattakia** (lataˌkeeə), city and port (1981 pop. 196,791), N Syria, on the Mediterranean coast. Before the modern harbour was constructed (1950) most of Syria's foreign trade passed through BEIRUT and TRIPOLI (Lebanon). It is developing as an industrial town and is connected by railway to ALEPPO. The principal exports are raw cotton, cotton textiles, and cereals. It imports a wide range of goods, particularly metals and machinery. Its port is sometimes used by the Soviet navy.

**Latter-Day Saints, Church of Jesus Christ of:** see MORMONS.

**Latvia** or **Latvian Soviet Socialist Republic,** constituent republic (1985 pop. 2,604,000), 63,688 km² (24,590 sq mi), NW European USSR. It borders on Estonia (N); Lithuania (S); the Baltic Sea and Gulf of Riga (W), the Russian Soviet Federated Socialist Republic (E); and

Belorussia (SE). The capital is RIGA. Generally low-lying level land, about one-fifth of which is forest, supports dairying and timber as the chief occupations. Industry is well-developed. Latvia is the USSR's main producer of electric-railway passenger cars and long-distance telephone exchanges. Shipbuilding, engineering, chemicals, and textiles are also important. The majority of the people are Letts and Latgalians; minorities include Russians and Belorussians. The region was conquered and Christianized by the Livonian Knights (13th cent.) and later fell to Poland (1561), Sweden (1629), and Russia (1721–95). German merchants and landowners had reduced the population to servitude, but in 1819 serfdom was abolished. Russian replaced German as the official language in 1885. Latvia became independent in 1920 but was absorbed into the USSR in 1940. It was occupied (1941–44) by the Germans in World War II. Nationalization of the economy took place after the war. Latvia's incorporation into the USSR is still not recognized in international law, and there is a Latvian chargé d'affaires in Washington DC.

**Latvian language:** see LETTISH.

**Laud, William,** 1573–1645, English prelate. Laud was hostile to the Puritans and worked with CHARLES I to eliminate them from important positions in the church. Named (1633) archbishop of Canterbury, he tried to standardize Anglican ritual along High Church lines. He persecuted and imprisoned many nonconformists and supported Charles to the end. He was impeached (1640) by the Long Parliament, condemned (1644) to death by the Commons, and executed on Tower Hill.

**laughing gas:** see NITROUS OXIDE.

**Laughton, Charles,** 1899–1962, American actor; b. England. A versatile character actor, he appeared in such films as *The Private Life of Henry VIII* (1933), *Mutiny on the Bounty* (1935), and *Advise and Consent* (1962).

**Launceston,** city (1986 pop. 66,286), Tasmania, southern Australia. Tasmania's second largest city, it is located at the head of the R. Tamar estuary and is noted for its tranquil setting and its parks. Founded in 1806, it was never a penal settlement. The first hydroelectric power station was built near here in 1895 to harness the South Esk R. and Launceston was one of the first cities in the Southern Hemisphere to be electrically lit. At Bell Bay, some 50 km (35 mi) away, alumina is converted to aluminium using hydropower. Cataract Gorge is a local tourist attraction.

**Laura,** subject of the love poems of PETRARCA, possibly Laure de Noves (1308?–48), wife of Hugues de Sade.

**Laurasia:** see CONTINENTAL DRIFT.

**laurel,** common name for the family Lauraceae, trees and shrubs found chiefly in tropical SE Asia and America; most are evergreen. The true laurel (*Laurus nobilis*), also called bay or sweet bay, is native to the Mediterranean, and is the source of bay leaf, a seasoning. Laurel symbolized victory and merit to the ancients. Other members of the family include the sassafras (*Sassafras albidum*), the aromatic bark of which is used for tea, and the avocado of Central America, now widely grown in the tropics and sub-tropics for its nutritious fruits, which have a high protein content. Members of the Asiatic genus *Cinnamomum* are cultivated largely for their aromatic bark, yielding the spice cinnamon, from *C. zeylanicum*, and camphor oil from the wood of *C. camphora*.

**Laurel and Hardy,** American film comedy team. Its members were Stan Laurel, 1890–1965, b. England as Arthur Stanley Jefferson, and Oliver Hardy, 1892–1957. Their zany comic routines often involved pantomime. Among their films are *Sons of the Desert* (1933), *Babes in Toyland* (1934), and *A Chump at Oxford* (1940).

**Laurence, (Jean) Margaret,** 1926–87, Canadian author. Her novels of character include *This Side Jordan* (1960), *A Jest of God* (1966), and *The Diviners* (1974). She has also written stories, essays, and works on African literature.

**Laurencin, Marie** (lohranhˌsanh), 1885–1956, French painter and printmaker. Her elegant, highly personal style consists of simplification of form, flat and decorative surface, and delicate pastel colours, e.g., *The Assembly* (1910). She was introduced to APOLLINAIRE and PICASSO in 1907 and exhibited with the cubist group (see CUBISM).

**Laurens, Henri,** 1885–1954, French sculptor. His early work was in the style of RODIN but developed a more structured style. In 1911 he met BRAQUE, and borrowed ideas from CUBISM, e.g., geometrical analysis of forms and multiple viewpoints. In the 1920s he reintroduced curvilinear forms as well as mythological subjects.

**Laurentian Plateau:** see CANADIAN SHIELD.

**Laurier, Sir Wilfrid** (ˌloreeay), 1841–1919, prime minister of CANADA (1896–1911), the first French Canadian to hold the office. He worked for French–English political cooperation and became (1887) the Liberal opposition leader. As prime minister he advanced Western development, the railways, preferential tariffs, and Canada's defences.

**Lausanne,** city (1984 pop. 126,200, agglomeration 255,000), capital of Vaud canton, SW Switzerland, on Lake Geneva. It is a university city and tourist centre, with metallurgical and food-processing industries. Ruled by its bishops from 590 to 1536, it passed under the control of Bern and adopted Protestantism. It became capital of the new canton of Vaud in 1803. The Gothic cathedral was completed in the 13th cent. and restored in the 19th cent.

**Lautréamont,** pseud. of **Isidore Ducasse,** 1846–70, French author. He wrote *Les chants de Maldoror* (1868), a prose-poem where a Byronesque hero sadistically expresses his contempt for humanity through irony and violent images which made him a hero for Surrealists.

**Lautrec, Henri de Toulouse:** see TOULOUSE-LAUTREC, HENRI DE.

**lava,** molten ROCK erupted on the earth's surface by a VOLCANO or through a fissure in the earth. It solidifies into igneous rock that is also called lava. Before reaching the surface, lava is known as magma. See also PUMICE.

**Laval,** city (1980 est. pop. 268,754), coextensive with Île-Jésus, a 243-km² (94-sq-mi) island, S Quebec, E Canada. A mainly residential suburb of MONTREAL, the city was created in 1966 through amalgamation of 14 small communities on the island.

**Laval, Pierre,** 1883–1945, French politician. Entering politics as a Socialist, Laval later became an independent and was premier (1931–32, 1935–36). In 1935 he proposed a plan to halt Italy's conquest of Ethiopia by appeasing MUSSOLINI. After the fall of France in WORLD WAR II, Laval was vice premier (1940) in the VICHY government, but he was dismissed on suspicion of trying to overthrow Marshal PÉTAIN. Outspoken in favour of collaboration with Nazi Germany, Laval was reinstated (1942) with dictatorial powers. He agreed to draft labour for Germany and began a reign of terror. In 1945 he surrendered to the Allies and was executed for treason. His poorly conducted trial was denounced by many.

**Lavalleja, Juan Antonio,** c.1786–1853, Uruguayan revolutionary leader. He led the small group the Thirty-three Immortals that declared (1825) Uruguay's independence from Brazil. After being denied the presidency of the new nation, he revolted twice (1832, 1834) against Pres. Fructuoso Rivera and joined in the civil war (1843–51). From the war two dominant political parties emerged: the Blancos (whites), which he led; and the Colorados (reds), under Rivera.

**Laver, Rod(ney George),** 1938–, Australian tennis player. He won the grand slam of tennis (Australian, US, British, and French titles) in 1962 and 1969, the only person to do so twice. In 1971 he became the first professional tennis player to earn over $1 million. His many national championships included four at WIMBLEDON.

**Laveran, Charles Louis Alphonse,** 1845–1922, French physician. While an army surgeon in Algiers, he discovered (1880) the parasite that causes MALARIA. For his work on protozoa in the causation of disease he received the 1907 Nobel Prize for physiology or medicine.

**Lavoisier, Antoine Laurent** (lavwah,zyay), 1743–94, French chemist and physicist. A founder of modern chemistry, he was one of the first to use effective quantitative methods in the study of reactions. His classification of substances is the basis of the modern distinction between chemical elements and compounds and of the system of chemical nomenclature. He proposed the oxygen theory of combustion, thereby discrediting the PHLOGISTON theory, and described oxygen's role in respiration. Concerned with improving social and economic conditions in France, he held various government posts; he was guillotined during the Reign of Terror. Count RUMFORD married his widow, but the marriage was brief.

**law,** rules of conduct of organized society, enforced by threat of punishment. Early examples from Babylonia (the code of HAMMURABI), India (laws of MANU), and Palestine (Mosaic code) suggest a universal tendency of religious and ethical systems to produce a legal order. ROMAN

LAW developed the distinction between public law, in which the state is directly involved, and private law, concerned with disputes between persons. Roman influence survived in the CANON LAW of the Catholic Church and in the laws of FEUDALISM, and it is the basis of modern CIVIL LAW. In England, law made by royal judges became COMMON LAW, later modified by the laws of EQUITY. See also CRIMINAL LAW.

**law centre,** publicly funded centre offering free legal advice and representation to (usually poorer) members of society. First developed in the US in the 1960s, the first British law centre opened in North Kensington, London in 1970; there are now over 50 law centres in the UK. Law centres tend to concentrate on the legal problems of the poor, that the LEGAL PROFESSION has traditionally ignored, e.g., housing, social security, and immigration law. They employ both barristers and solicitors as well as general advice workers. In addition to dealing with individual legal problems, law centres also mount campaigns on issues affecting a large number of people, e.g., a lack of repairs on a large housing estate. See also CITIZEN'S ADVICE BUREAU.

**Law Commission,** in the UK, two permanent bodies, one for England and Wales, the other for Scotland, established in 1965, whose task it is to review the whole of the law with a view to repeal, codification and reform. Initially the English Law Commission set out a programme aiming to codify CONTRACT, LANDLORD AND TENANT, and family law into a set of principles along CIVIL LAW lines. Though they have been unsuccessful in this task, they have brought about the repeal of many out-of-date statutes, and the introduction of much new (especially family) law. However, in recent years an increasing number of Law Commission reports have not been implemented, either because of government unwillingness, or lack of parliamentary time.

**Lawes, Sir John Bennet,** 1814–1900, English agriculturist. He founded the internationally- famous experimental farm at Rothamsted, where, with chemist Sir J.H. Gilbert, he experimented on plant and animal production. His development of superphosphate marked the beginning of the chemical fertilizer industry.

**Lawler, Ray,** 1921–, Australian playwright. His *Summer of the Seventeenth Doll* (1955), in 1977 made the concluding play of a trilogy, is a slightly sentimentalized view of traditional Australia which holds its ground by the vigour of its writing.

**Law Lord,** popular term to describe the LORD CHANCELLOR, lords of appeal, and other peers who have held high judicial office. As the Appellate committee of the House of Lords, five Law Lords make up the highest court in the English court structure, and will sit to hear appeals from lower courts. See also COURT SYSTEM IN ENGLAND AND WALES; PRECEDENT.

**Lawrence, Charles,** 1709–60, British soldier and governor of NOVA SCOTIA (1756–60). During his regime the Acadians were deported (see ACADIA) and the colony's first elected assembly met (1758), though not with his approval.

**Lawrence, D(avid) H(erbert),** 1885–1930, English author. The son of a coal-miner, his works express his hatred of industrialism and lifelong search for a more natural and emotionally fulfilling way of life. His great novels are *Sons and Lovers* (1913), *The Rainbow* (1915), and *Women in Love* (1920). After World War I, he travelled widely and lived in Italy, France, and New Mexico. *The Plumed Serpent* (1926), considered a failure, reflects his interest in ancient religions and his fascination with the idea of a superhuman leader. *Lady Chatterley's Lover* (1928), with its gospel of sexual fulfilment, was banned in Britain until 1960, when it was the subject of a famous obscenity trial. Lawrence wrote in a sensuous, lyrical style, brilliantly conveying the specific, and greatly influenced 20th-cent. fiction. He was a prolific short-story writer and essayist, and published poetry, plays, travel books, and criticism. The first collection of his *Letters* (1932) was edited by his friend Aldous HUXLEY.

**Lawrence, Gertrude,** 1898–1952, English actress; b. Alexandre Dagmar Lawrence-Klasen. On the musical stage from childhood, she charmed audiences in shows such as *Private Lives* (1931), *Lady in the Dark* (1941), and *The King and I* (1951).

**Lawrence, Sir Thomas,** 1769–1830, English portrait painter. He succeeded Sir Joshua REYNOLDS as Painter in Ordinary to the king, became an Academician, and was knighted in 1815. After doing portraits of state and church officials in Austria and Italy, he became president of the Royal Academy. Among his best portraits are the *Calmady Children*

(Metropolitan Mus., New York), and *Queen Charlotte* (National Gall., London).

**Lawrence, T(homas) E(dward),** 1888–1935, British adventurer, soldier, and author, known as Lawrence of Arabia. After the outbreak of World War I, he was attached to the intelligence section of the British army in Egypt. In 1916 he joined the Arab forces under Faisal al Husein (see FAISAL I) and took part in their revolt against Turkish domination. After the war he was a delegate to the Paris Peace Conference. By now a legendary figure, he was regarded as a champion of Arab independence. Seeking anonymity, he later served in the ranks of the Royal Air Force, changing his name to do so. His works include *Seven Pillars of Wisdom* (1935; abr. ed., *Revolt in the Desert*, 1927), his account of his Arabian adventures, and *The Mint* (1955, published pseudonymously).

**lawrencium** (Lr), radioactive element, first prepared in 1961 by A. Ghiorso and co-workers by boron nuclei bombardment of californium. It is an ACTINIDE-SERIES element. In 1965 a Soviet group prepared a different isotope by the reaction of oxygen-18 with americium-243. See ELEMENT (table); PERIODIC TABLE.

**Law Society,** in England and Wales, controlling body of the solicitor's branch of the LEGAL PROFESSION, formed in 1825. Every practising solicitor must belong to the Law Society. It is responsible for the legal education of solicitors, representing solicitors interests to the outside world, and dealing with complaints from the public about solicitors (e.g., NEGLIGENCE or misconduct). It has been argued that its dual role can lead to a conflict of interest. A separate but similar body operates in Scotland (see SCOTLAND, LEGAL SYSTEM IN).

**Lawson, Henry,** 1867–1922, Australia's best-loved poet and short-story writer. He wrote sympathetically, humorously and ironically of the hardships of pioneering life in the bush, and of the mateship which sustained men isolated from civilized comforts. His best-known prose collections were *While the Billy Boils* (1896), *On The Track* (1900), *Over the Sliprails* (1900), and *Joe Wilson and His Mates* (1901).

**laxative,** agent which promotes emptying of the bowel. Laxatives, also known as aperients or purgatives, are grouped as bowel stimulants (such as senna), bulking agents (such as bran), faecal softeners (such as liquid paraffin), and rectally administered suppositories and enemas. Simple constipation is prevented by a diet sufficiently high in fibre.

**Laxdœla Saga,** Old Icelandic SAGA (c.1245), named after the inhabitants of Laxárdalur (Salmon River Dale) on the west coast of Iceland. At its heart is the tragic romance of Guðrún Ósvífursdóttir, the imperious beauty who married her lover's best friend against her will and then forced her reluctant husband to kill her former lover, the hero Kjartan Ólafsson, and forfeit his own life thereby. It has always been the most widely popular of the Icelandic sagas.

**Laxness, Halldór Kiljan** (ˌlakhsnes), 1902–, Icelandic novelist. He set a new style for Icelandic literature in such epic novels of rural life as *Salka Valka* (1931–32), *Independent People* (1934–35), and *World Light* (1937–40). Later important works are *Iceland's Bell* (1943–46). *The Atom Station* (1948), *The Fish Can Sing* (1958), *Paradise Reclaimed* (1960), and *Christianity at Glacier* (1968), some of which reflect a growing interest in Taoism. He has also written a number of highly successful plays, and adapted some of his novels to the stage. He was awarded the Nobel Prize for literature in 1955.

**Layamon,** fl. c.1225, first major Middle English poet. His *Brut* gives a history of Britain from the fall of Troy to Brutus's arrival in Britain through the death of Cadwaladr (a semi-legendary Welsh king, d. 664?). Important in the development of the ARTHURIAN LEGEND, it contains the first mention of LEAR and CYMBELINE.

**lay reader,** in the ANGLICAN COMMUNION a lay person, male or (since 1969 in England) female, who is licensed by the bishop to conduct religious services and preach. Lay readers are usually licensed for a particular parish, of which they assist the incumbent.

**Lazarus,** 1 Brother of MARY and Martha of Bethany; he was brought back to life by JESUS. John 11. 2 Beggar in a parable who was spurned in life by a rich man. After death, the rich man, parching in hell, pleads in vain that Lazarus, now in heaven, be permitted to give him a drink. Luke 16.

**L-dopa** or **laevodopa,** drug used to alleviate symptoms of PARKINSON'S DISEASE, particularly rigidity, slow movements, and trembling, resulting from a deficiency of dopamine (chemical that transmits nerve impulses) in

the brain. Patients vary in response and side effects include nausea and involuntary facial movements. Introduced into the bloodstream, L-dopa is probably converted to dopamine by neurones in the brain.

**Leach, Bernard Howell,** 1887–1977, English studio potter and writer. Leach went to Japan (1909) intending to teach etching, but was attracted by Japanese raku pottery and decided to become a potter (1911). He studied in Tokyo, and visited kilns in various parts of Japan. He returned to England (1920), and with the help of Hamada Shoji set up a pottery at St Ives, Cornwall. Leach's work and his philosophy had a profound effect on the development of studio pottery. He wrote several influential books, including *A Potter's Book* (1940) and *A Potter's Work* (1967).

Stoneware, pagoda-lidded pot by Bernard **Leach** (c.1950–60)

**Leach, Sir Edmund R,** 1910–, British anthropologist. A pioneer of STRUCTURALISM, he introduced the work of LÉVI-STRAUSS to Britain. His early work *The Political Systems of Highland Burma* (1954) explored the political structures of peoples whose unstable political institutions fluctuated between egalitarian and hierarchical models, showing the complex interaction between ideal models and political action. He taught at Cambridge Univ., becoming professor in 1972.

**lead** (Pb), metallic element, one of the earliest known metals, used by the ancient Egyptians and Babylonians. A poor conductor of heat and electricity, lead is silver-blue, dense, relatively soft, and malleable, with low tensile strength. It is used in lead-acid storage batteries (see CELL, in electricity), SOLDER, and plumbing, and as protective shielding against X-rays and radiation from nuclear reactors. The principal lead ores are GALENA, cerussite, and anglesite. Lead compounds (all poisonous) include tetraethyl lead (an antiknock additive in petrol) and oxides used in mordants and pigments. Continued exposure to lead through inhalation of fumes or sprays and ingestion of food containing lead can result in a cumulative chronic disease called **lead poisoning.** It was once a serious occupational hazard, but protective equipment and other precautionary measures have reduced the incidence in industry. A frequent cause of lead poisoning in children, especially in poor areas, is ingestion of paint chips from peeling walls or pipes. See ELEMENT, table; PERIODIC TABLE.

**lead glance:** see GALENA.

**lead poisoning:** see under LEAD.

**leaf,** the chief food-manufacturing organ of higher plants, a lateral outgrowth of the STEM. The typical leaf consists of a stalk, or petiole, and a thin, flat, expanded portion (needlelike in most CONIFERS), or blade. The blade, veined with sap-conducting tubes (xylem and phloem), consists of upper and lower layers of epidermal cells, including cells that control the size of tiny pores (stomata) that are used in gas exchange and TRANSPIRATION. Between the two layers are cells, rich in CHLOROPHYLL, that conduct PHOTOSYNTHESIS.

## structure of a generalised leaf

leaf margin
blade
mid rib
vein

upper epidermis
palisade cell
spongy cell
air space
lower epidermis
stoma   guard cell

petiole or stalk

### types of leaf

Cordate   Deltoid   Elliptic   Hastate   Linear

Palmate   Pinnate   Sagittate   Serrate   Trifoliate

Leaf structures and types

**leaf insect,** tropical herbivorous INSECT, of the same order as STICK INSECT (Phasmida). Adults are about 100 mm (4 in) long, and their flattened, green, irregularly-shaped bodies have a remarkably leaf-like appearance.

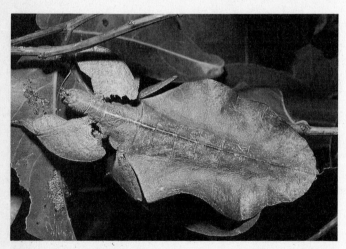

Adult leaf insect (*Phyllum sp.*)

**League** or **Holy League,** during the Wars of Religion (see RELIGION, WARS OF), organization of French Catholics aimed at the suppression of Protestantism. Founded (1576) by Henri, 3rd duc de Guise, it was dissolved (1577) by King HENRY III. Although revived (1585), it failed to survive HENRY IV's military successes.

**League of Nations,** a former international organization, formed after WORLD WAR I to promote international peace and security. The basis of the League, the Covenant, was written into the Treaty of VERSAILLES and other peace treaties and provided for an assembly, a council, and a secretariat. A system of colonial mandates was also set up. The US, which failed to ratify the Treaty of Versailles, never became a member. Based in Geneva, the League proved useful in settling minor international disputes, but was unable to stop aggression by major powers, e.g., Japan's occupation of Manchuria (1931), Italy's conquest of Ethiopia (1935–36), and

Germany's seizure of Austria (1938). It collapsed early in World War II and dissolved itself in 1946. The League established the first pattern of permanent international organization and served as a model for its successor, the UNITED NATIONS.

**Leakey,** family of anthropologists and archaeologists working in East Africa (mainly Kenya and Tanzania) whose discoveries have provided major evidence of HUMAN EVOLUTION. **Louis Seymour Bazett Leakey,** 1903–72, b. Kenya, began excavating at OLDUVAI GORGE in 1931. There he and his wife, **Mary Leakey,** 1913–, b. England, discovered stone tools and fossils that both extended back the hominid record and indicated that early human evolution centred on Africa rather than Asia. Notable finds were *Australopithecus boisei* 'Zinjanthropus' (1959) (see AUSTRALOPITHECUS) and HOMO HABILIS (1961). Mary Leakey recovered much archaeological evidence for early hominid behaviour at Olduvai. She later excavated the older site of LAETOLI discovering remains of *A. afarensis* and early hominid footprints indicating bipedalism 3.6 million years ago. Their son, **Richard Leakey,** 1944–; b. Kenya, began excavating at Lake TURKANA in 1968. There he and associates recovered further archaeological evidence and highly variable hominid fossils indicating that the pattern of early human evolution was a complex one, with several species. He is Director of the Kenya National Museums. See also HOMO ERECTUS.

**Leander:** see HERO.

**leap year:** see CALENDAR.

**Lear,** legendary English king. GEOFFREY OF MONMOUTH claimed to have translated Lear's story from Old English records, but it probably had its origins in Celtic mythology. It is the subject of SHAKESPEARE's tragedy *King Lear.*

**Lear, Edward,** 1812–88, English humorist and artist. His illustrated limericks and nonsense verse, collected in *A Book of Nonsense* (1846) and in several later volumes in the 1870's, include 'The Owl and the Pussy Cat' and 'The Jumblies'. He recorded his wide travels in the Mediterranean and Middle East in masterly water-colours and admirable letters. He was an epileptic, and never married.

**learning,** generally, the process of acquiring new knowledge, skills, or patterns of behaviour. In psychology, learning theory concerns the mechanisms underlying relatively permanent changes in response potentiality which occur as a result of reinforced practice. Learning theory has usually been interpreted as referring to the variants and successors of either classical (see PAVLOV) or operant (see SKINNER) conditioning models. Learned behaviours are distinguished from INNATE behaviours and those which are a result of maturation by virtue of being acquired, rather than inherited, and are generally susceptible to being 'unlearned' by extinction or reversal. Many contemporary psychological theories, especially those addressing the acquisition of complex skills or abilities (such as those underlying language use), depart significantly from traditional learning theory, being based upon notions of rule and system learning. Furthermore, the distinction between innate and learned behaviour is far from absolute (see INSTINCT; PIAGET).

**learning disabilities,** in education, any of various disorders involved in understanding or using spoken or written language, including difficulties in listening, thinking, talking, READING, writing, spelling, or ARITHMETIC. They may affect people of average or above-average intelligence. Learning disabilities include conditions referred to as perceptual handicaps, minimal brain dysfunction (MBD), DYSLEXIA, developmental aphasia, and attentional deficit disorder (ADD); they do not include learning problems due to physical handicaps (e.g., impaired sight or hearing, or orthopedic disabilities), mental retardation, emotional disturbance, or cultural or environmental disadvantage. Techniques for remediation are highly individualized, including the simultaneous use of several senses (sight, hearing, touch), slow-paced instruction, and repetitive exercises to help make perceptual distinctions. Pupils are also assisted in compensating for their disabilities; for example, one with a writing disability may use a tape recorder for taking notes or answering essay questions. Behaviour often associated with learning disabilities includes hyperactivity (hyperkinesis), short attention span, and impulsiveness. School programmes for learning-disabled students range from a modified or supplemental programme in regular classes to placement in a special school, depending upon the severity of the disability. The field of learning disabilities is considered to have emerged as a separate discipline in 1947 with the publication of the book *Psychopathology and Education of the Brain-Injured Child* by neuropsychiatrist Alfred A. Strauss and Laura E. Lehtinen. Famous people considered to have had a learning disability include Winston Churchill, Thomas Edison, Albert Einstein, and Nelson Rockefeller.

**leasehold,** in law, an interest (see ESTATE) in land, allowing exclusive possession of it for a fixed number of years. It is contrasted with freehold, where the land may be held for unlimited duration. The granter of the lease is called the 'lessor', the holder the 'lessee'. In the UK, leases are classed as personal PROPERTY. Since 1967, the holders of long leases have had the right to buy their leases and become freeholders.

**leather,** skin or hide of animals, cured by TANNING to prevent decay and to impart flexibility and toughness. Early peoples used pelts preserved with grease or smoke for garments, tents, and containers. Since the 18th cent. machines have been used to split the tanned leather into the desired thicknesses of flesh layers and grain (hair-side) layers. Pelts are prepared by dehairing, cleaning, tanning, and treating with fats to ensure pliability. Finishes include glazing, staining or dye colouring, enamelling or lacquering (as for patent leather), and sueding (buffing to raise a nap). Artificial leather, made since c.1850, is now mainly manufactured from vinyl PLASTIC. The flexible and waterproof qualities of leather made it useful for industrial purposes (e.g., washers), for which it has now been replaced by synthetics. It has always been used for horse harness and riding equipment, and still is. In modern FASHION, leather is used to make coats, jackets, trousers, and skirts, and for accessories; it is also used for furniture upholstery.

**Leavis, F(rank) R(aymond),** 1895–1978, English literary critic and teacher. His books include *New Bearings in English Poetry* (1932) and *The Great Tradition* (1948). An early champion of T.S. ELIOT and D.H. LAWRENCE, his influence was exerted through the journal *Scrutiny* (1932–53), which he edited. His wife, **Q(ueenie) D(orothy) Leavis,** 1900–82, was a noted critic of 19th-cent. fiction.

**Lebanon,** officially the Republic of Lebanon, republic (1984 est. pop. 3,500,000), 10,400 km² (4015 sq mi), SW Asia, bounded by the Mediterranean Sea (W), Syria (N, E), and Israel (S). The capital is BEIRUT. Much of the terrain is mountainous, with two main ranges the Lebanon in the west and the Anti-Lebanon in the east paralleling the coast; the fertile Al BIQA valley lies between them. It is one of the wetter parts of the Middle East with winter rain and snow on the mountains. Until the disruption caused by the civil war of 1975–76, Lebanon had a service-oriented economy, and Beirut, a free port, was the financial and commercial centre of the Middle East. Today about half the labour force is engaged in agriculture, and the principal crops are grains, olives, and citrus fruits. Remittances from Lebanese working abroad are an important source of foreign exchange. The GNP is US$2656 million and the GNP per capita is US$620 (1982). Most Lebanese are Arabs, and Arabic is the official language, but French and English are also widely spoken. The population is about equally divided between Christians (mainly Maronites) and Muslims of both Sunni and Shia sects together with Druse and Alawites.

*History.* The site of the ancient maritime empire of PHOENICIA, the area later fell to successive Middle Eastern powers. Christianity was introduced under the Roman Empire and persisted even after the coming of Islam with the Arab conquest (7th cent.). In the late 11th cent. Lebanese Christians aided the Crusaders (see CRUSADES) in the region. The area came under the Ottoman Turks in the 16th cent., and after the Turkish defeat in WORLD WAR I it became part of a French mandate known as Greater Lebanon. Since independence in 1943, Lebanon has been plagued by civil strife, involving different religious sects and Palestinians, and problems with its neighbours. Although a member of the ARAB LEAGUE, it took little part in the ARAB–ISRAELI WARS that followed Israel's independence in 1948, but the stage was set for future problems when many Palestinians fled Israel and settled in Lebanon. Meanwhile, Lebanon's internal equilibrium was shaken (1958) by a rebellion against pro-Western policies, and US forces were called in briefly. In 1975 full-scale civil war erupted between leftist Muslims, aided by the PALESTINE LIBERATION ORGANIZATION (PLO), and conservative Christians. In 1976 Syrian troops intervened, and a cease-fire was declared, but Israel and the PLO engaged in a sporadic border war in S Lebanon. In 1978, following a limited Israeli invasion, a UN peacekeeping force was placed in S Lebanon. Fighting continued, however, and in 1982 Israel invaded

Lebanon, forcing many of the PLO from the country and causing widespread devastation in S Lebanon. A massacre of Palestinians by Lebanese Christians during the Israeli occupation of Beirut led to worldwide criticism of Israel and the establishment of a multinational peacekeeping force in Beirut. In the same year (1982) newly elected President Bashir GEMAYEL of the (Christian) Phalangist Party was assassinated and succeeded by his brother Amin. Israeli forces finally withdrew in 1985, leaving the (Christian) Southern Lebanon Army in control of the sensitive border area. Fierce conflict continued between Lebanon's contending religious, ethnic and ideological factions, reducing the country to economic chaos.

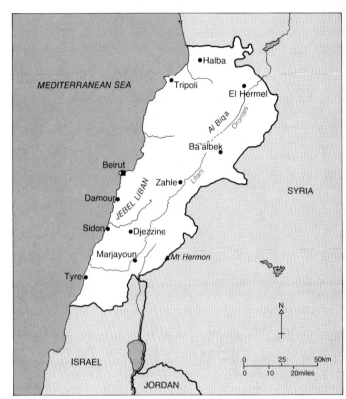

Lebanon

**Le Brun, Charles,** 1619–90, French painter, decorator, and architect. Influenced by POUSSIN, he developed a more decorative form of CLASSICISM. His first royal commission, *The Family of Darius before Alexander* (1661), gained him the favour of LOUIS XIV. He became painter to the king (1662), controlling artistic theory and production in France for two decades. Head of the GOBELINS works, he designed royal furnishings and was director of the Académie royale. The atmosphere of richness and splendour he created can be seen at VERSAILLES.

**Lebrun, Élisabeth Vigée:** see VIGÉE-LEBRUN.

**LeCarré, John,** pseud. of **David John Moore Cornwell,** 1931–, English novelist. His bleak, complex studies of international espionage are highly popular and have influenced the language of contemporary politics. His novels include *The Spy Who Came In From the Cold* (1963), *Tinker, Tailor, Soldier, Spy* (1974), and *Smiley's People* (1980).

**Lecce,** city (1984 est. pop. 84,000), Apulia, S Italy. It serves as market centre of the Salentine peninsula. The soft local limestone is easily worked and has been employed in the richly-sculptured Baroque buildings for which Lecce is principally renowned.

**Leck, Bart van der,** 1876–1958, Dutch painter. A founder member at the de STIJL group in 1917, he worked in a highly simplified and stylized manner, reducing figurative elements to flat geometric planes of colour. In 1917 he began to paint abstract compositions which were influential in MONDRIAN'S development of neo-plasticism.

**Leconte de Lisle, Charles Marie** (lə‚conht də leel), 1818–94, French poet, the leading PARNASSIAN. Anti-Christian and a pessimist, he saw death as the only reality and drew his inspiration from antiquity, Indian mythology, Northern or exotic countries, as in *Poèmes antiques* (1852), *Poèmes barbares* (1872), and *Poèmes tragiques* (1884).

**Le Corbusier,** pseud. of **Charles Édouard Janneret** (lə kawbyˌzyay), 1887–1965, French architect; b. Switzerland. His buildings and writings had a revolutionary effect on the international development of MODERN ARCHITECTURE. After 1915 he began to produce radical schemes for houses and flats, drawing inspiration from industrial forms. In 1923, at Vaucresson, near Paris, the first building (a villa) was constructed according to his principles. His book *Towards a New Architecture* (1923) gained wide circulation. His plan for a 'vertical city' was partially realized in the Unité d'Habitation, Marseilles (1946–52). His most ambitious work was the main buildings for the capital of the Punjab, Chandigarh (begun 1951). Other famous buildings include a chapel at Ronchamp (1950–55) and the Visual Arts Centre, Harvard Univ., Massachusetts (1961–62).

Le Corbusier: Notre Dame du Haut, Ronchamp (1950–55)

**Lecouvreur, Adrienne** (ləkoovˌruh), 1692–1730, French actress. After her 1717 debut, her natural style made her the idol of France. Her mysterious death, ascribed to poison administered by her rival for the love of Maurice de SAXE, became the subject of a play (by SCRIBE) and an opera.

**LED** (light-emitting diode): see DIODE.

**Leda,** in Greek mythology, wife of Tyndareus, king of SPARTA, mother by him of CLYTEMNESTRA. In most legends Leda was seduced by ZEUS, who appeared as a swan. She bore two eggs: from one issued CASTOR AND POLLUX, from the other HELEN.

**Lederberg, Joshua,** 1925–, American geneticist. For their studies establishing that sexual recombination occurs in bacteria, he and Edward TATUM shared the 1958 Nobel Prize for physiology or medicine with George BEADLE. Lederberg and his student Norman Zinder discovered the process called transduction, by which certain VIRUSES transfer a chromosome from one bacterial cell to another. In 1978 he was named president of Rockefeller Univ.

**Le Duan** (lay dwahn), 1908–86, Vietnamese Communist leader. Imprisoned by the French colonial regime, he later rose rapidly in North VIETNAM's Communist Party to become (1959) first secretary. In 1976, after Vietnam's reunification, he was renamed party leader with the title of secretary general.

**Lee, Christopher,** 1922–, British film actor. A tall, distinguished actor, he first came to fame playing Dracula in Hammer horror films. His films include *Dracula* (1958), *The Three Musketeers* (1974), and *The Man with the Golden Gun* (1974).

**Lee, Robert E(dward),** 1807–70, Confederate general in the AMERICAN CIVIL WAR. He served with distinction in the MEXICAN WAR, was superintendent at West Point (1852–55), and led (1859) the US marines who captured John BROWN. After the secession of the lower South, he declined the field command of US forces. After Virginia's secession, however, he assumed command of Virginia's military and naval forces. When Gen. J.E. Johnston was wounded, Lee succeeded him (June 1862) as commander of the Army of Northern Virginia and immediately took the

offensive in the Seven Days Battles. He crushed the Union army at the second battle of BULL RUN, but Gen. G.B. McClellan halted Lee's first invasion of the North in the Antietam Campaign. Lee repulsed Union advances at the battles of Fredericksburg (1862) and Chancellorsville (1863), where he lost his ablest lieutenant, Stonewall JACKSON. His second invasion of the North ended in defeat in the GETTYSBURG CAMPAIGN (1863). He repulsed Gen. U.S. GRANT's direct assaults in the Wilderness Campaign (May–June 1864), but in July Grant laid siege to Petersburg. Lee became (Feb. 1865) general in chief of all Confederate armies, but the South was near collapse. He surrendered (9 Apr. 1865) to Grant at APPOMATTOX Courthouse. After the war he was president of Washington College (now Washington and Lee Univ.). Lee was idolized by his soldiers, and many historians consider him to be the greatest general of the Civil War.

**leech,** segmented or ANNELID WORM with a cylindrical or slightly flattened body having suckers at both ends; it usually feeds on blood, which it stores in pouches large enough to hold several months' supply. Most are aquatic. Leeches were once used to bleed patients suffering from almost any ailment; they are still used in some regions to treat bruises.

**Leeder, Sigurd,** 1902–81, German dancer. After studying with LABAN, he collaborated with Kurt JOOSS becoming the co-director of Ballet Jooss (1934–53). He and Jooss together developed the MODERN DANCE technique that bears their names.

**Leeds,** city (1981 pop. 445,242), W Yorkshire, N central England, on the Aire R. Lying between manufacturing and agricultural regions, Leeds is a centre of communications, transport, and regional government. Manufactures include woollens, locomotives, and farm implements. Triennial music festivals, including an international piano competition, are held in the classical town hall (1858).

**leek:** see ONION.

**Leeuwenhoek, Antony van** (ˌlayvənˌhoohk), 1632–1723, Dutch student of natural history. He made over 247 MICROSCOPES, some of which magnified objects 270 times. He examined microorganisms and tissue samples and gave the first complete descriptions of bacteria, protozoa (which he called animalcules), spermatozoa, and striped muscle. He also studied capillary circulation and observed red blood cells.

**Leeward Islands:** see WEST INDIES.

**Lefanu, Sheridan,** 1814–73, Irish novelist. His chilling novels of mystery and suspense, of which *Wylder's Hand* (1864) and *Uncle Silas* (1864) are the best known, bridge the gap between the Gothic tales of terror and the modern suspense story, and his short stories of the supernatural, some of them collected in *In A Glass Darkly* (1872) are memorably terrifying.

**left-handedness,** preferential use of the left hand (sinistrality). About 7–10% of populations of white European descent are left-handed. The condition appears to be partly genetically determined, though the pattern of inheritance is complex. It does not always coincide with preferential use of the left foot or left eye. Enforcement of right-handedness in naturally left-handed children (because of social bias against sinistrality) has been associated with various conditions such as stammering and reading difficulties but not proven to be a causal factor.

**legal aid,** system of payment to people who are unable to pay the costs of civil litigation or criminal defence. Introduced in Britain in 1949, it was designed to allow access to the law by poorer members of society, by paying for the costs of legal action. To receive legal aid, the applicant, as well as having a sufficiently low income, must also, in civil cases, establish that the action has a reasonable chance of success, and in criminal cases (available for criminal defence only), show that the payment is necessary in the interests of justice. Legal aid is not available for a case held before a TRIBUNAL (except the lands tribunal). Many countries now have a legal aid system; some follow the US pattern of having lawyers paid a salary by the state to represent poor defendants.

**legal profession,** body of persons who are professionally trained to assist people with legal problems. They offer both general legal advice, and represent people in courts whether in a civil dispute (e.g., NEGLIGENCE) or a criminal trial. In most countries, the legal profession consists of a single group of people, called lawyers, who will deal with both the preparatory work and act as advocates in court. In England and Wales, the legal profession is divided into two branches, with separate training, organization, and work. **Barristers** are the branch that represent people in court. They are prohibited from dealing with the public directly (their clients are passed on by solicitors) but have exclusive rights of 'audience' in all courts except the Magistrates' Court. They work from offices called 'chambers' and must be a member of one of the INNS OF COURT; the profession as a whole is known as 'the Bar', and a new entrant is said to be 'called to the Bar'. Senior barristers are known as Queen's (or King's) Counsel (or 'silks'). All barristers tend to specialize in one or two areas of law. **Solicitors** offer a general legal service to the public, often working in partnerships. Traditionally their work has involved PROPERTY matters, especially the admininistration of wills and conveyancing (the law relating to the buying and selling of houses). However, the solicitors' MONOPOLY on conveyancing was abolished in 1985. Solicitors are barred from most courts; but they offer legal advice to people who need to go to court and undertake all the preparatory work before passing the case (known as a 'brief') to a barrister. Most solicitors employ **Legal Executives**, who are not legally qualified but who assist the solicitor with less specialist aspects of a case. Solicitors are also employed by local authorities, companies, and government departments. Both solicitors and barristers are employed by LAW CENTRES.

**Legendre, Adrien Marie** (lə‚zhanhdrə), 1752–1833, French mathematician, noted especially for his work on number theory and elliptic integrals. He invented, independently of Carl GAUSS, and was the first to state in print (1806), the method of least squares.

**Léger, Alexis Saint-Léger** (le‚zhay), see PERSE, SAINT-JOHN.

**Léger, Fernand**, 1881–1955, French painter. He met PICASSO and BRAQUE in 1910 and developed a modified CUBISM, based on the curvilinear and geometrical shapes of machinery. This machine aesthetic was developed after the war in the 1920s with his involvement with LE CORBUSIER and Ozenfant's PURISM.

**Leghorn**, Ital. *Livorno*, city (1984 pop. 175,803), Tuscany, N central Italy, on the Ligurian coast. It has a naval academy and is a busy oil and container port with chemical and agricultural processing industries. Created between 1571 and 1618 by the MEDICI family of FLORENCE to a planned design, it replaced the silted port of PISA as the principal outlet of the ARNO basin. Growth was encouraged by its free-port status.

**legion**, large unit of the Roman army. It varied in number from 3,000 to 6,000 men in Caesar's time. The legion was composed of 10 cohorts, which were in turn divided into centuries. Its principal elements were heavy infantry. The legions accomplished the Roman conquests, but were vulnerable to their enemies' cavalry and guerrilla warfare.

**Legionnaire's disease**, infectious, sometimes fatal form of PNEUMONIA. The disease affected over 180 people attending an American Legion convention in Philadelphia in July 1976, hence the name. The causative bacterium, later identified as *Legionella pneumophilia*, is thought to spread through air conditioning and ventilation systems and thus infect many people simultaneously. The disease is treated with the ANTIBIOTIC erythromycin.

**legislature**, representative assembly empowered to enact statute law and to levy taxes. In a DEMOCRACY its members are elected by the general populace. One of the oldest is the English PARLIAMENT, a bicameral legislature whose lower (House of Commons) and upper (House of Lords) chambers derive from class divisions. In the US CONGRESS, which is also bicameral, the House of Representatives and the Senate were established on federal principles. The Israeli Knesset is an example of a unicameral legislature. Most democracies accept the doctrine of the separation of powers, whereby members of the legislature, cannot also be members of the EXECUTIVE or the judiciary. In the UK, this is not the case, as members of the government are drawn from both Houses of PARLIAMENT.

**Leguía, Augusto Bernardino** (lay‚gee-ah), 1863–1932, president of PERU (1908–12, 1919–30). He modernized the country and settled (1929) a territorial dispute with Chile, but a depression and his harsh rule led to his overthrow (1930). He was charged with misappropriating funds and was imprisoned.

**legume**, name for any plant of the PULSE family; more generally, any vegetable. Botanically, a legume is a pod that splits along two sides, with the seeds attached to one of the sutures. It is the characteristic FRUIT of the pulse family.

**Lehár, Franz** (‚layhah), 1870–1948, Austrian composer of OPERETTAS. He is best known for *The Merry Widow* (1905), *The Count of*

*Luxembourg* (1909), and *Gypsy Love* (1910), works filled with gaiety and engaging melodies.

**Le Havre**, city (1982 pop. 200,411), N France, on the English CHANNEL coast, one of the country's leading ports. Founded in 1517, it remained principally a fortified naval port until the early 19th cent. when a regular passenger service to New York was started. It is now France's leading container port, and handles 40% of French imports of crude oil, much of which is processed in several large refineries along the lower Seine. It also has important passenger links with England.

**Lehmann, Lilli** (‚layman), 1848–1929, German operatic soprano. She began as a coloratura, but became a great Wagnerian singer (see WAGNER, RICHARD) with a repertory of 170 roles. She also interpreted LIEDER and was a teacher.

**Lehmann, Lotte**, 1888–1976, American soprano; b. Germany. After singing in Berlin and Vienna, she made her American debut in Chicago (1930) and sang with the METROPOLITAN OPERA, New York City (1934–45). She was noted for her performances in operas by Richard STRAUSS.

**Lehmann, Rosamond**, 1901–, English novelist. Her novels *Dusty Answer* (1927) and *Invitation to the Waltz* (1932) are sensitive portrayals of young girls on the threshold of adulthood. Her later work includes an autobiography, *The Swan in the Evening* (1967). Her brother, **John Lehmann** (1907–87), was a poet and editor of *New Writing* (1936–46).

**Lehmbruck, Wilhelm** (‚laymbrook), 1881–1919, German sculptor. Influenced by RODIN, BRANCUSI, and MAILLOL, he executed large, elongated figures that express dramatic poignancy, e.g., *Woman Kneeling* (Mus. Mod. Art, New York City), that has a Gothic expressiveness.

**Leibniz** or **Leibnitz, Gottfried Wilhelm, Baron von**, 1646–1716, German philosopher and mathematician. His career as a scholar embraced the physical sciences, law, history, diplomacy, and logic, and he held diplomatic posts (from 1666) under various German princes. Leibniz also invented the CALCULUS, concurrently with but independently of NEWTON. His philosophical writings, including *Theodicy* (1710) and *Monadology* (1714), popularized by the philosopher Christian von Wolff, were orthodox and optimistic, claiming that a divine plan made this the best of all possible worlds (a view satirized by VOLTAIRE in *Candide*). According to Leibniz, the basic constituents of the universe are simple substances he called monads, infinite in number, nonmaterial, and hierarchically arranged. His major work, *New Essays on Human Understanding,* a treatise on John LOCKE's *Essay concerning Human Understanding,* was written in 1704 but because of Locke's death published only in 1765. A critique of Locke's theory that the mind is a blank at birth, it exerted great influence on KANT and the German ENLIGHTENMENT. Modern studies have tended to focus on Leibniz's contributions to mathematics and logic; manuscripts published in the 20th cent. show him to be the founder of symbolic logic (see LOGIC). He devised Leibniz's rule for differentiating a product $n$ times. The extension of the binomial theorem to multinomials is attributed to him and he also anticipated determinants (see MATRIX).

**Leicester**, city (1981 pop. 324,394), county town of Leicestershire, central England. Of industrial importance as early as the 14th cent., it now manufactures shoes, hosiery, machinery, and other products. It was, in turn, a town of the Romans, the early Britons, and the Danes. Extensive Roman and medieval remains are found there.

**Leicester, Robert Dudley, earl of**, 1532?–88, English courtier and favourite of Queen ELIZABETH I. He aided (1553) the plot to place Lady Jane GREY on the throne, but was pardoned. After the accession (1558) of Elizabeth, he became a privy councillor, and was rumoured to be Elizabeth's most likely choice for a husband. Though his wife Amy Robsart's suspicious death (1560) darkened his reputation and his remarriage (1578) temporarily estranged the queen, he retained Elizabeth's confidence. Later he led (1585–87) an unsuccessful expedition against the Spanish in the Netherlands.

**Leicestershire**, inland county in the Midlands of England (1984 est. pop. 866,100), 2553 km² (996 sq mi). The county town is LEICESTER. In the local government reorganization of 1974 Leicestershire absorbed the county of Rutland. Much of the county is low-lying and gently undulating. The chief river is the Soar which crosses the centre of the county flowing S to N. Dairy farming is the most important agricultural activity, although, cereals are cultivated in the W. The county is famous for cheeses:

Leicester (hard) and Stilton (blue), produced near Melton Mowbray. The main industrial and urban centres are Leicester and Loughborough.

**Leiden** or **Leyden,** city (1985 pop. 104,668), W Netherlands. Among its various manufactures, the textile industry has flourished since the 16th cent. It is famous for its university (est. 1575), the nation's oldest, a centre (17th–18th cent.) of science, medicine, and Protestant theology. Leiden took part in the Dutch revolt against the Spanish and was saved (1574) by WILLIAM THE SILENT. It is the birthplace of REMBRANDT.

**Leif Ericsson** or **Eriksson,** fl. 999–1000, Norse discoverer of America; b. probably in Iceland; son of ERIC THE RED. Information about his travels is taken from Norse SAGAS. One states that he was blown off course on a trip to GREENLAND c.1000 and landed in an area that he named Vinland (probably in either NOVA SCOTIA or NEW ENGLAND).

**Leigh, Vivien,** 1913–67, English actress; b. Vivien Hartley. As Cleopatra in both Shakespeare's *Antony and Cleopatra* and Shaw's *Caesar and Cleopatra*, she played opposite her then husband, Sir Laurence Olivier. She is perhaps best known for her portrayal of Scarlett O'Hara in the film *Gone With The Wind* (1939) and of Blanche du Bois in both stage and screen versions of Tennessee Williams's *A Streetcar Named Desire* (1949).

**Leino, Eino,** 1878–1926, Finnish neo-romantic poet and novelist. He developed the KALEVALA metre into a distinctive style of his own. His best known work is *Whitsongs* (1903–16), sensitive, lyrical poetry which gives expression to a 'tragic optimism' with overtones of Nietzsche. He was also a notable translator into Finnish of world classics such as Dante, Racine, Corneille, Goethe, and Schiller.

**Leinster,** province in E and SE of Republic of Ireland (1986 pop. 1,851,134), 19633 km² (7657 sq mi). It includes the counties of Carlow, Dublin, Kildare, Kilkenny, Laoighis, Longford, Louth, Meath, Offaly, Westmeath, Wexford, Wicklow, and Dublin city. Agriculture is the most important economic activity. About 30% of the total population lives in DUBLIN city.

**Leipzig,** city (1984 pop. 555,764), S central East Germany. The second largest city in East Germany, it manufactures textiles, steel, chemicals, toys, and other goods. It has been a commercial centre since medieval times and became a cultural centre in the 17th and 18th cent. LEIBNIZ and WAGNER were born there; J.S. BACH (buried in the 15th-cent. Church of St Thomas), SCHUMANN, MENDELSSOHN, and the young GOETHE worked there. Its university (est. 1409) is the largest in East Germany. A monument commemorates the victory over NAPOLEON I in the Battle of Leipzig (1813).

**leishmaniasis** ('leeshmə‚nieəsis), infection with microscopic parasitic PROTOZOA (genus *Leishmania*). Common in tropical countries, infection can cause diseases affecting the skin or internal organs. Visceral leishmaniasis, or kala-azar, is transmitted by the bite of sandflies and causes enlargement of the spleen and liver, fever, blood disorders, and death if untreated.

**Leitrim,** county in N of Republic of Ireland (1986 pop. 27,000), 1510 km² (589 sq mi), bordering on Co. Sligo in the W and Co. Cavan in the N. It is situated in the province of Connacht. The county town is CARRICK-ON-SHANNON. It has a short northern coastline in Donegal Bay. The northern half of the county is hilly, rising to 643 m (2109 ft) in Truskmore in the N. It contains Lough Allen and many other smaller lakes. Agriculture is an important economic activity in the southern part of the county.

**Lekain** (lə‚kanh), 1728–78, French actor; b. Henri Louis Cain. A protégé of VOLTAIRE, he introduced realistic acting and historically accurate costuming to the French theatre.

**Lely, Sir Peter,** 1618–80, Dutch portrait painter in England; b. Pieter van der Faes. He painted the great figures of the court of CHARLES I, the Protectorate under Oliver CROMWELL, and the RESTORATION. His luscious portraits, e.g., *The Windsor Beauties* (Hampton Court, London), perfectly capture the atmosphere of voluptuous pleasure associated with the Restoration court.

**Lem, Stanislaw,** 1921–, Polish writer. Lem's writings, including many widely translated works of SCIENCE FICTION, reflect his serious philosophical concern over the moral implications of modern science and technology, and also reflect his acute sense of comedy and irony. Among his works are the novels *Solaris* (tr. 1970), *The Invincible* (tr. 1973), and *Tales of Pirx the Pilot* (tr. 1979).

**Lemaître, Georges, Abbé,** 1894–1966, Belgian astronomer. He is chiefly known for his seminal work on the big bang theory (see COSMOLOGY).

**Le Mans,** city (1982 pop. 150,331, agglomeration 191,080), capital of Sarthe dept., NW France. It is an agricultural centre and its industries include food-processing. Growth followed the arrival of the railway in mid-19th cent.; later vehicle manufacture developed. Le Mans is internationally known for its 24-hr car race for touring cars which has taken place annually since 1923 round the town's roads. The circuit is 13.64 km (8½ mi) and the record distance covered stands at 5047.934 km (3137 mi), achieved in 1983. Crowds of 400,000 are not unusual.

**Lemercier, Jacques** (ləmeə‚syay), c.1585–1654, French architect, a major contributor to classical French style. He became noted as a designer of Jesuit churches, and his chief remaining work is the church of the Sorbonne, Paris (1635). He also designed Cardinal RICHELIEU's Paris residence, later transformed into the Palais-Royal, and the town of Richelieu.

**lemma:** see THEOREM.

**lemming,** mouselike RODENT of arctic or northern regions, inhabiting tundra or open meadows. All are about 12 cm (5 in) long, with stout bodies, thick fur, and short tails. Two or three times per decade, Norway lemmings (*Lemmus lemmus*) undergo a population explosion that forces them to set out in search of food. Crossing bodies of water by swimming, some reach the sea and drown giving rise to folklore about lemmings committing mass suicide.

**lemon,** yellow-skinned CITRUS FRUIT of a small tree (*Citrus limon*) of the RUE family. High in VITAMIN C, they are historically associated with preventing scurvy. Products include CITRIC ACID, juice, oil, polish, pectin, and flavourings. Lemons grow best in a mild climate, e.g., the Mediterranean, California, and Florida.

**lemur,** prosimian, or lower PRIMATE, of the related families Lemuridae and Indriidae, found only on Madagascar and adjacent islands. Lemurs have monkeylike bodies, long, bushy tails, pointed muzzles, large eyes, and flat nails, except the second toe, which has a stout claw. Most are arboreal. Best known is the ring-tailed lemur (*Lemur catta*), which is atypically terrestrial.

**Lena,** river, easternmost of the great rivers of Siberia, USSR, c.4300 km (2670 mi) long. It flows generally N, then NE, from a source near Lake BAYKAL to empty into the ARCTIC OCEAN through a delta c.400 km (250 mi) wide. The river, which is navigable for 3436 km (2135 mi) in summer, is frozen at its mouth from Oct. to June.

**Le Nain** (lə ‚nanh), family of French painters consisting of three brothers. **Antoine Le Nain,** c.1600/10–1648, painted small pictures on copper of figures around a table or making music. **Mathieu Le Nain,** c.1607–77, was painter to the city of Paris, specializing in portraiture and depicting the city militia. **Louis Le Nain,** c.1600/10–1648, conceived the famous GENRE scenes in which peasant life is treated sympathetically and realistically, e.g., *The Peasant's Meal* (1642; Louvre, Paris).

**lend-lease,** WORLD WAR II arrangement whereby the US furnished necessary supplies, including food, machinery, and services, to its allies. The Lend-Lease Act (1941) empowered the president to sell, lend, lease, and transfer such material under whatever terms he deemed proper. Originally intended to aid Britain and the Commonwealth countries, and China, by the war's end virtually all the Allies (including the USSR) were part of it. Total lend-lease aid exceeded $50 thousand million. By 1972 the US had reached settlements with all the nations that had received lend-lease aid.

**Lenin, Vladimir Ilyich,** 1870–1924, Russian revolutionary, founder of Bolshevism, and major force behind the founding of the USSR; b. Vladimir Ilyich Ulyanov. Born in the Volga region, the son of a school inspector, he was deeply influenced by his brother Aleksandr, who was executed in 1887 for plotting to kill the Czar. Lenin, after graduating with distinction in law, devoted himself to Marxist study and agitation among workers, and was arrested and exiled to Siberia in 1895. There he married Nadezhda K. Krupskaya. In 1900 they left Russia for W Europe; about this time he took the name Lenin (after the Siberian river Lena). Lenin's insistence that only a disciplined party of professional revolutionaries could bring socialism to Russia (expressed in his 1902 pamphlet *What Is to Be Done?*) led the Russian Social-Democratic

Le Nain, *The Peasant's Meal*, 1642. Louvre, Paris.

Workers' Party, meeting in London in 1903, to split into two factions: the Bolsheviks, led by Lenin, and the Mensheviks (see BOLSHEVISM AND MENSHEVISM). Lenin returned to Russia on the outbreak of the 1905 Revolution but left in 1907. He continued to write and to engage in Social-Democratic party politics in W Europe. When WORLD WAR I began he saw it as an opportunity for worldwide socialist revolution. In March 1917 (February according to the Old Style calendar) the RUSSIAN REVOLUTION broke out and the Czar abdicated. Lenin returned to Petrograd (later renamed Leningrad), where in November (October OS) he led the Bolsheviks in overthrowing KERENSKY's provisional government. As chairman of the Council of People's Commissars he became virtual dictator; his associates included STALIN and TROTSKY. The Soviet government's first two acts were the signing of the Treaty of BREST-LITOVSK with Germany and the distribution of land to the peasants. The Bolsheviks (who became the Communist party) asserted that the October Revolution had created a proletarian dictatorship; in fact, it was the party that ruled. Political opposition was suppressed, but civil war, complicated by foreign invasion and war with Poland, continued until late 1920. In 1919 Lenin established the Third International, or COMINTERN, to further world revolution. The policy of 'war Communism', brought extensive nationalization, food rationing, and detailed control over industry. However, widespread economic dislocation, famine, and a mutiny of sailors at Kronstadt, previously loyal to the Bolsheviks, led to its collapse in 1921. In an attempt to boost the economy, he launched the NEW ECONOMIC POLICY (NEP), which allowed some private enterprise. Lenin's death in 1924 precipitated a power struggle in which Joseph Stalin was victorious. Lenin's main contributions to Marxism were his book *Imperialism: the Highest stage of Capitalism*, which predicted capitalism's imminent collapse, and his concept of a revolutionary party as a highly disciplined unit, capable of carrying out a revolution even in circumstances quite unlike those envisaged by Marx himself.

**Leningrad,** formerly St Petersburg and Petrograd, city (1985 pop. 4,867,000), NW European USSR, at the head of the Gulf of Finlan on both banks of the Neva R. and on the islands of its delta. The second-largest Soviet city, it is a major sea and river port and rail junction; canals also carry cargo. Principal industries include the production of electric and electronic equipment, machinery, nuclear equipment, chemicals, and refined oil. The city is also a centre for education and scientific research. Construction of St Petersburg began (1703) under PETER I, who employed Italian and French architects. The city's landmarks include the Winter Palace, HERMITAGE museum, Alexander Nevsky monastery, the Cathedral of St Isaac, and a university. From 1712 to 1918 it replaced MOSCOW as the capital of the USSR. A brilliant cultural centre, the city was immortalized by such writers as PUSHKIN and TOLSTOY. In 1914 it was renamed Petrograd. The city was in the forefront of the RUSSIAN REVOLUTION. On LENIN's death in 1924, it was renamed Leningrad. Many thousands of its citizens died during World War II when the people heroically withstood the prolonged German siege (1941–44).

Little Hermitage, **Leningrad,** built 1771–84

**Lenôtre** (lə‚nohtrə),or **Le Nôtre, André,** 1613–1700, French landscape architect. Working for LOUIS XIV, he brought to full development the spacious formal French garden, at the palace of VERSAILLES, the TUILERIES, and other sites.

**lens,** a device for forming an image of an object by the REFRACTION, or bending, of light. In its simplest form it is a disc of transparent material, commonly glass, with its two surfaces curved or with one surface plane and the other curved. Generally, each curved surface (called *convex* if curved outwards and *concave* if curved inwards) of a lens is made as a portion of a spherical surface; the centre of the sphere is called the centre of curvature (C) of the surface. All rays of light passing through a lens are refracted except those that pass directly through a point called the optical centre. A divergent lens (concave–thicker at the edges than at the centre) bends parallel light rays passing through it away from each other. The image formed by a diverging lens is always erect (upright), smaller than

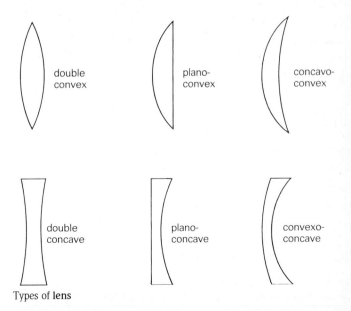

double convex          plano-convex          concavo-convex

double concave          plano-concave          convexo-concave

Types of **lens**

the object, and virtual (located on the same side of the lens as the object). A converging lens (convex–thicker at the centre than at the edges) bends parallel light rays towards one another; if they are parallel to the principal axis of the lens, they converge to a common point, or focus (F), behind the lens. The image formed by a converging lens depends on the position of the object relative to the lens' focal length (distance between the focus and the optical centre) and its centre of curvature. See ABERRATION, in optics; CAMERA; MICROSCOPE; TELESCOPE.

**Lent** [from Old Eng. *lencten,* = spring], Christian period of fasting and penitence preparatory to EASTER. Lent begins on Ash Wednesday, the 40th weekday before Easter Sunday. Of the Sundays of Lent, the fifth is Passion Sunday, and the last is Palm Sunday. The week preceding Easter is Holy Week and includes GOOD FRIDAY. Lent ends at midnight on Holy Saturday.

**lentil,** Old World annual (*Lens culinaris*) of the PULSE family. Its pods contain two dark seeds. Lentils are unusually high in PROTEIN content and can therefore be useful in a strict vegetarian diet. In cookery, they make excellent purées and soups. They were one of the first food plants cultivated in Europe.

**Lenya, Lotte,** 1900–1981, Austrian actress; b. Caroline Blamauer. She was married to the composer Kurt WEILL and was the foremost interpreter of his songs, appearing in *The Threepenny Opera* and *Mahagonny.*

**Leo,** Byzantine emperors. **Leo I** (the Great or the Thracian), d. 474 (r.457–74), enlisted Isaurians to break the power of Germans in his army. His naval attack on the Vandals failed (468). **Leo III** (the Isaurian or the Syrian), c.680–741 (r.717–41), deposed Theodosius III. He checked the Arab threat, ended anarchy in the empire, and issued a civil code, the *Ecloga.* His ICONOCLASM alienated Popes Gregory II and Gregory III, who ended Byzantine suzerainty over Rome. **Leo IV** (the Khazar), d. 780 (r.775–80), succeeded his father, CONSTANTINE V. Leo's widow, IRENE, became regent for their son, CONSTANTINE VI. **Leo V** (the Armenian), d. 820 (r.813–20), made a 30-year truce with the BULGARS. Reviving iconoclasm, he deposed the patriarch Nicephorus (815) and persecuted St Theodore of Studium. **Leo VI** (the Wise or the Philosopher), 862?–912 (r.886–912), modernized the code of JUSTINIAN I in his *Basilica* (887–93). By renewing (906) the schism with the patriarch PHOTIUS he forced Photius's resignation.

**Leo I, Saint** (Leo the Great), c.400–61, pope (440–61), an Italian. One of the greatest pontiffs and a Doctor of the Church, Leo waged a campaign against schism and heresy. He attacked MANICHAEISM in Italy and, in a conflict with St Hilary of Arles, asserted his authority over all bishops. He defended church teaching against NESTORIANISM and MONOPHYSITISM. In 452 he persuaded ATTILA not to attack Rome. Feast: 10 Nov.

**Leo III, Saint,** d. 816, pope (795–816), a Roman. After being physically attacked by the family of his predecessor, ADRIAN I, Leo escaped to CHARLEMAGNE and won his support. Leo crowned (800) Charlemagne emperor at Rome, thus initiating the Holy Roman Empire. In the interests of East–West unity, he rejected the emperor's request to include the *Filioque* clause in the Nicene CREED. Feast: 12 June.

**Leo IX, Saint,** 1002–54, pope (1049–54), a German named Bruno. A relative of Holy Roman Emperor CONRAD II, Leo, aided by Hildebrand (later Pope GREGORY VII), launched a programme of clerical reform. Leo was also concerned with the heresy of Berengar of Tours and was defeated (1053) by the Normans in S Italy. Michael Cerularius, patriarch of Constantinople, attacked (1053) the pope, and Leo excommunicated him in 1054, beginning the formal schism between East and West. Feast: 19 Apr.

**León,** region and former kingdom, NW Spain, E of Portugal and Galicia. It includes the provinces of León, Salamanca, and Zamora. The climate is harsh; the sparse population engages in coal mining, stock-raising, agriculture, and linen manufacturing. The kings of ASTURIAS took the region (8th–9th cent.) from the MOORS, and the city of León became (10th cent.) their capital. The kingdom of León was permanently joined (1230) with CASTILE.

**León,** city (1979 est. pop. 624,816), central Mexico. Founded in the 1570s, it is in a fertile river valley c.1700 m (5600 ft) high. It is a commercial, agricultural, and mining centre and is noted for its shoe manufactures.

**León,** city (1980 est. pop. 121,104), W Nicaragua, W of Lake Managua. The nation's second largest city, it is a major commercial hub. Founded in 1524, it was colonial Nicaragua's political centre and, after independence (1821), a stronghold of liberal forces. Its bitter rivalry with conservative Granada led to the founding (1855) of a 'neutral' capital, MANAGUA. It is the seat of the Univ. of Nicaragua and is noted for its 18th-cent. cathedral, which houses the tomb of Rubén DARIO.

**León,** city (1981 pop. 131,134), capital of León prov., NW Spain. On the edge of the MESETA, it commands the route through the CANTABRIAN MTS to OVIEDO and the coast. It is a market and commercial centre, with chemical and pharmaceutical industries. Founded by the Romans, it succeeded Oviedo in the 10th cent. as capital of the kingdom of León and Asturias. It has a renowned 13th to 14th-cent. Gothic cathedral.

**Léon, Juan Ponce de:** see PONCE DE LEÓN, JUAN.

**Leonard, Hugh,** 1926–, Irish playwright; b. John Keyes Byrne. His first full-length play *The Big Birthday* was produced by the Abbey Theatre in 1956. A prolific writer, he spent over 10 years in England, from 1959, writing for television as well as the stage before returning to Ireland in the early 1970s. His works include adaptations, such as *Stephen D* (1962); farce, such as *The Patrick Pearse Motel* (1971); and more serious work, such as *The Au Pair Man* (1966). His best-known piece which has received many productions over the years is *Da.*

**Leonardo da Vinci** (də ˌvinchee), 1452–1519, Italian painter, sculptor, architect, musician, engineer, and scientist, probably the supreme example of RENAISSANCE genius. Born in Vinci, Tuscany, he was the illegitimate son of a Florentine notary and a peasant girl. His precocious artistic talent brought him to VERROCCHIO's workshop in 1466, where he met BOTTICELLI and GHIRLANDAIO. The culmination of his art in this first period in Florence is seen in the magnificent, unfinished *Adoration of the Magi* (Uffizi), with its characteristic dramatic movement and chiaroscuro. In c.1482 Leonardo went to the court of Ludovico Sforza in Milan and there composed most of his *Trattato della pittura* and the notebooks that demonstrate his versatile genius. The severe plagues in 1484 and 1485 drew his attention to town planning, and his drawings and plans for domed churches reflect his concern with architectural problems. In 1483, Leonardo and his pupil Ambrogio de Predis were commissioned to execute the famous *Madonna of the Rocks* (two versions: 1483–c.1486, Louvre; 1483–1508, National Gall., London). The now badly damaged *Last Supper* (c.1495–1498; Milan) was executed during the period when he was experimenting with the FRESCO medium, and this partly accounts for its damage. Despite this, a sublime spiritual content and power of invention mark it as one of the world's masterpieces. Leonardo's model for an equestrian monument to Francesco Sforza was never cast, and in 1500 he returned to Florence, where he did much theoretical work in mathematics and pursued his anatomical studies in the hospital of Santa Maria Nuova. As a military engineer for Cesare Borgia he studied swamp reclamation and met Niccolò MACHIAVELLI. In c.1503 he executed the celebrated *Mona Lisa* (Louvre). Then, as architect and engineer in Milan to the French king LOUIS XII, he continued his scientific investigations into geology, botany, hydraulics, and mechanics. In 1510–11 he painted *St Anne, Mary, and the Child* (Louvre), a work that exemplifies his handling of *sfumato* misty, subtle transitions in tone. His enigmatic *St John the Baptist* (c.1513; Louvre) was executed for Pope LEO X and his brother Giuliano de' Medici in Rome. Shortly after 1515, Leonardo accepted an invitation from FRANCIS I of France to settle in the castle of Cloux. Here he pursued his own researches until his death. His versatility and creative power, as well as the richness and originality expressed in his notebooks, drawings, and paintings, mark him as one of the great minds of all time.

**Leoncavallo, Ruggiero,** 1858–1919, Italian composer. His one great success was the opera *I Pagliacci* (1892), a classic example of Italian *verismo,* opera based on a realistic plot. It is almost always performed as a double-bill with *Cavalleria Rusticana* (see MASCAGNI).

**Leone, Sergio** (lay ˌohni), 1921–, Italian film director. He made his name by inventing the operatic 'spaghetti' westerns of the 1960s, and has since moved into large-scale epic historical films. His films include *A Fistful of Dollars* (1964), *The Good, the Bad, and the Ugly* (1966), *Once Upon a Time in the West* (1968), and *Once Upon a time in America* (1984).

**Leonov, Aleksei Arkhipovich** (lyay ˌonəf), 1934–, Soviet cosmonaut. While serving as copilot of *Voskhod 2* (18–19 Mar. 1965), he became the first person to perform extravehicular activity. Leonov was also command pilot for *Soyuz 19* in the *Apollo-Soyuz Test Project* (15–21 July 1975).

Example of **Leonardo da Vinci's** anatomical sketches

**Leonov, Leonid Maksimovich,** 1899–, Soviet novelist and playwright. The novels *The Thief* (1927) and *The Russian Forest* (1953), and the drama *The Orchards of Polovchansk* (1938), are among his best works. His complex style, insight, and compassion owe much to DOSTOYEVSKY.

**Leontief, Wassily** (‚lee-onteef), 1906–, American economist; b. Russia. He served on the faculty of Harvard from 1931 to 1975. He is best known for developing the input–output method of economic analysis, used by most industrialized nations, for which he won (1973) the Nobel Prize for economics.

**leopard,** large carnivore (*Panthera pardus*) of the CAT family, found in Africa and Asia. Its yellowish fur is patterned with black spots and rings. Black leopards, a colour variant, are called PANTHERS. The largest male leopards are about 2.4 m (8 ft) long, including the tail. They live mainly near trees and are solitary and nocturnal, preying on small animals and livestock. Leopards often take their prey up into a tree, to store it more safely.

**Leopardi, Giacomo, Count,** 1798–1837, Italian poet and scholar. His fame rests mainly on his *Canti* (songs), written between 1816 and 1836. Based on a deeply pessimistic philosophy, they are by turns lofty and lyrical, patriotic and private, satirical and wistfully evocative. He is regarded as the outstanding 19th-cent. Italian poet.

**Leopold,** rulers of the HOLY ROMAN EMPIRE. **Leopold I,** 1640–1705, emperor (r.1658–1705), king of Bohemia (r.1656–1705) and of Hungary (r.1655–1705), fared badly against Louis XIV of France in the third (1672–78) of the DUTCH WARS and in the War of the GRAND ALLIANCE (1688–97). He was more successful against the Ottomans, and the Treaty of Karlowitz (1699) greatly increased his domains. He made VIENNA a cultural centre. **Leopold II,** 1747–92, emperor (r.1790–92), was the younger son of MARIA THERESA and Emperor Francis I, and the brother of Emperor JOSEPH II, whom he succeeded. His defence (1791) of his brother-in-law, Louis XVI of France, helped to precipitate the FRENCH REVOLUTIONARY WARS, which spelt the end of the Holy Roman Empire.

**Leopold,** kings of the Belgians. **Leopold I,** 1790–1865 (r.1831–65), was the youngest son of Francis Frederick, duke of Saxe-Coburg-Saalfeld. After the death (1817) of his wife, Princess Charlotte, daughter of the English prince regent, Leopold lived in England until elected king of newly formed Belgium. In 1832 he married a daughter of LOUIS PHILIPPE of

France; their daughter became the wife of MAXIMILIAN, emperor of Mexico. Leopold introduced ministerial responsibility, electoral reform, and a national bank. He had strong opinions on European issues and was a regular correspondent of Queen VICTORIA. **Leopold II,** 1835–1909 (r.1865–1909), was the son of Leopold I. With the aid of H.M. STANLEY he founded (1884–85) the Congo Free State (see ZAÏRE) under his personal rule. Using slave labour he amassed a huge fortune, until scandal forced him to turn the Congo over to the Belgian government. In Belgium, labour unrest forced the granting (1893) of universal male suffrage. His nephew, ALBERT I, succeeded him. **Leopold III,** 1901– (r.1934–51), was the son of Albert I. He led the Belgian army in resisting the German invasion in May 1940, but surrendered on 28 May over cabinet opposition. Held by the Germans until 1945, he was accused of collaboration on his return to Belgium and forced into exile in Switzerland while his brother, Prince Charles, acted as regent. He was allowed to return in 1950 but soon abdicated in favour of his son, BAUDOUIN.

**Leopold,** kings of Bohemia and Hungary: see LEOPOLD, rulers of the Holy Roman Empire.

**Leo X,** 1475–1521, pope (1513–21), a Florentine named Giovanni de' Medici. Son of Lorenzo de' MEDICI, he was famous for his patronage of RAPHAEL, the continuation of St Peter's by BRAMANTE, and his literary circle. The Fifth Lateran Council, which he resumed, failed to effect the desired reforms, and the Protestant REFORMATION began when Martin LUTHER posted (1517) his 95 theses. Leo excommunicated the reformers, notably with the bull, *Exsurge Domine* (1520), but failed to deal effectively with the crisis.

**Leo XIII,** 1810–1903, pope (1878–1903), an Italian named Gioacchino Pecci. He devoted himself to forming Catholic attitudes appropriate to the modern world and issued encyclicals to that end. *Immortale Dei* (1885) charted the course for Catholics as responsible citizens in modern democratic states. *Rerum novarum* (1891), a most important encyclical, outlined Catholic social ideals, pointing to the abuses of capitalism and the deficiencies of Marxism. To meet intellectual attacks on the Church, he wrote *Aeterni Patris* (1879), which declared the philosophy of St THOMAS AQUINAS official, and he founded the Inst. of Thomistic Philosophy at Louvain. In his reign, the conflict in Germany between the government and the church (the Kulturkampf) was ended (1887) with a victory for the church.

**Lepanto, battle of,** 7 Oct. 1571, naval battle between the Christians and Turks fought in the Gulf of Patras, off Lepanto, Greece. The fleet of the Holy League, commanded by JOHN OF AUSTRIA, virtually destroyed the fleet of the OTTOMAN EMPIRE (Turkey), ending the threat of Turkish naval supremacy in the Mediterranean.

**Lepidus,** family of the ancient Roman patrician gens Aemilia. **Marcus Aemilius Lepidus,** d. 77 BC, was given a proconsulship in Gaul, but raised an army in N Italy. He was defeated, and fled from Italy. His son, **Marcus Aemilius Lepidus,** d. 13 BC, supported ANTONY and, with Antony and Octavian (AUGUSTUS), formed the Second TRIUMVIRATE. Octavian became suspicious of Lepidus and curbed his powers.

**leprosy** or **Hansen's disease,** chronic infectious disease, caused by the bacillus *Mycobacterium leprae,* affecting the skin and superficial nerves. It is found mainly, but not exclusively, in tropical regions and is transmitted by direct contact. It has an incubation period of 1 to 30 years. The disease produces numerous skin and nerve lesions, which, if left untreated, enlarge and may result in severe disfigurement. Leprosy is controlled by dapsone and other drugs, which halt the progress of the disease and make it noninfectious.

**lepton:** see ELEMENTARY PARTICLES.

**Lerdo de Tejada, Miguel** (leədhoh day tayhahdah), d. 1861, Mexican public official. He initiated (1856) the Ley Lerdo, providing for the forced sale of church property, and helped to draft the liberal constitution of 1857. His brother, **Sebastián Lerdo de Tejada,** 1827–1889, succeeded JUÁREZ as president (1872–76) and incorporated the new reform laws in the constitution of 1874. He was overthrown by Gen. DÍAZ.

**Lérida** (‚ler'eedə), city (1981 pop. 109,573), capital of Lérida prov., NE Spain, on the Segre R. It is surrounded by extensive irrigated gardens which produce a wide range of fruits and vegetables for its food-processing factories. A Roman settlement (Ilerda), it witnessed Caesar's victory over the army of Pompey in 49 BC. It has a cathedral in the Romanesque style and a medieval castle.

**Lermontov, Mikhail Yurevich** (ˌlyeəməntəf), 1814–41, Russian romantic poet and novelist. His poem 'Death of a Poet' (1837), protesting at the death of PUSHKIN in a duel, led to his banishment to the Caucasus, whose stirring landscape became a vital element in his work. The Byronic poem 'The Angel' (1832), the narrative *The Demon* (1841), and *Mtsyri* (1840) are among the works on which his poetic reputation, second only to Pushkin's, rests. His novel *A Hero of Our Time* (1840), about a disenchanted nobleman, is a classic of psychological realism. Lermontov was killed in a duel.

**Le Sage, Alain René** (lə ˌsahzh), 1668–1747, French novelist and dramatist. His masterpiece, *Gil Blas* (1715–35), a rambling picaresque romance, was unusual for its realism and attention to detail. It was a major influence on the development of the realistic NOVEL. The satirical comedy *Turcaret* (1709) is his best dramatic work.

**lesbianism:** see SEXUAL ORIENTATION.

**Lesbos** or **Lésvos,** island (1981 pop. 104,620), c.1630 km² (630 sq mi) E Greece, in the Aegean Sea, near Turkey. It has vast olive groves and also produces wine, wheat, and citrus fruits. A centre of BRONZE AGE civilization, it was settled c.1000 BC by the Aeolians and became a brilliant cultural centre of ancient Greece. It was the home of SAPPHO, ARISTOTLE, and EPICURUS.

**Leskov, Nikolai Semyonovich,** 1831–95, Russian writer, whose stories and novels give a rich picture of 19th-cent. Russian life outside the big cities. His best-known novel, *Cathedral Folk* (1872), is a study of the provincial clergy. His novella *The Left-handed Craftsman* (1881) reflects his patriotic pride in the prowess of the Russian workman. His short story *Lady Macbeth of Mtsensk District* (1865) was later the subject of a much-criticised opera (1934) by SHOSTAKOVICH.

**Lesotho** (ləˌsohtoh), officially Kingdom of Lesotho, formerly Basutoland, kingdom (1987 est. pop. 1,585,000), 30,355 km² (11,720 sq mi), S Africa, enclave within the Republic of SOUTH AFRICA. The capital is MASERU. The eastern two-thirds of Lesotho is dominated by the Drakensberg mountain range, with elevations of more than 3353 m (11,000 ft) the rest of the country is a narrow, rocky tableland. Only a small percentage of the land is arable, but maize, sorghum, and wheat are extensively cultivated. Sheep, cattle, and Angora goats are raised. Diamonds are the only mineral resource and an important export. Industry is limited to light manufacturing. Lesotho is heavily dependent on South Africa for economic support, and more than 100,000 Basotho work in South African mines. The GNP is US$696 million, and the GNP per capita is US$470 (1985). The population is homogeneous, with over 90% belonging to the black African Basuto tribal group, and more than 80% of these being Christian. The non-Basuto minority are barred from owning land. English and Sesotho, a Bantu tongue, are official languages.

*History.* The region that is now Lesotho was originally inhabited by the San (Bushmen). In the 17th and 18th cent. refugees from various tribal wars entered the area, and in the early 19th cent. they were welded together into the Basuto nation by the paramount chief, Moshoeshoe. Threatened by Boer incursions, in 1868 Moshoeshoe placed his people under British protection. Basutoland, as the territory was known, resisted plans for its incorporation into the newly created Union of South Africa (1910) and ultimately gained independence as Lesotho (1966), becoming a member of the COMMONWEALTH. Chief Leabua Jonathan, prime minister following independence, suspended the constitution in 1970. Parliamentary democracy was restored in 1985, but in a military coup in 1986 Chief Jonathan was overthrown by Maj-Gen. Justin Lekhanya.

**Lesseps, Ferdinand Marie, vicomte de,** 1805–94, French diplomat and engineer. After retiring from consular service, he organized a company and supervised (1859–69) the building of the SUEZ CANAL. In 1878 he headed another company formed to build the PANAMA CANAL. Its bankruptcy (1888) led to his conviction for misappropriation of funds. Later observers have felt he was guilty only of negligence.

**Lesser Antilles:** see WEST INDIES.

**Lessing, Doris,** 1919–, British novelist; b. Iran. Brought up in Southern Rhodesia (now Zimbabwe), she moved to England in 1949. Her *Children of Violence* series of five novels (1952–69) traces the experiences of a broadly autobiographical heroine, Martha Quest. *The Golden Notebook* (1962) is celebrated for its experimental form and its topical concerns with communism, psychic experience, and the position of women. Her later novels include a space-fiction sequence, *Canopus in Argos: Archives*

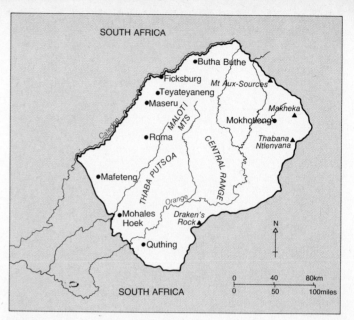

Lesotho

(1979–83) and a story of global catastrophe, *The Memoirs of a Survivor* (1974). She has also written short stories and essays. Two novels, collected as *The Diaries of Jane Somers* (1984), were originally published pseudonymously.

**Lessing, Gotthold Ephraim,** 1729–81, German dramatist and critic. The first dramatist of quality to write for the new middle-class audience, Lessing virtually founded the German repertoire with its first comedy *Minna von Barnhelm* (1767), its first tragedy *Emilia Galotti* (1771), and the great Utopian play on the theme of religious toleration, *Nathan the Wise* (1779). His most important works on aesthetic and dramatic theory respectively are *Laokoon, or, On the Limits of Painting and Poetry* (1766) and the *Hamburg Dramaturgy* (1767–68). His last years produced the theological polemic *Anti-Goeze* (1778) in defence of the free-thinker Samuel Reimarus, and the great ENLIGHTENMENT treatise on human progress, *Erziehung des Menschengeschlechts* (1780; tr. On the Education of the Human Race).

**letter:** see ALPHABET.

**letterpress:** see PRINTING.

**Lettish** or **Latvian,** language belonging to the Baltic subfamily of the Indo-European family of languages. See LANGUAGE (table).

**Lettow-Vorbeck, Paul Emil von,** 1870–1964, German commander in E Africa during World War I. He tied up British forces totalling ten times his own in a campaign which was fought in what are now Tanzania, Kenya, Mozambique, and Zambia, and which lasted the duration of the war.

**lettuce,** garden annual (*Lactuca sativa* and varieties) of the COMPOSITE family. Long cultivated as a salad plant and unknown in the wild state, lettuce is possibly derived from the weed called wild lettuce (*L. scariola*). Three types of lettuce are grown: head, leaf, and Cos, or romaine (the most heat-tolerant).

**Leucippus,** c.450–420 BC, pre-Socratic Greek philosopher. He was the first to hold that all matter is composed of atoms. His ideas were developed by his pupil DEMOCRITUS.

**leucotomy** or **lobotomy,** surgical operation interrupting the pathways of white nerve fibres in the brain with the aim of reducing severe emotional disturbance unrelieved by other treatments. In a prefrontal leucotomy, the nerve fibres between the frontal lobes and the thalamus of the brain are cut. Since the introduction of tranquillizers, the operation has been rarely used.

**leukaemia,** term for any of a variety of cancerous disorders characterized by the abnormal proliferation of white blood cells. The disease may be chronic or acute. The cause of leukaemia is unknown, but genetics, certain viruses, and exposure to radiation may play a role.

Symptoms include weakness, fever, bleeding, and susceptibility to infection. CHEMOTHERAPY and RADIOTHERAPY are effective against some forms of leukaemia, especially those occurring in children. See also CANCER.

**Le Vau, Louis** (lə‿voh), 1612–70, French architect, involved in most of the important building projects for LOUIS XIV. He worked (after 1655) on the LOUVRE, and designed the palace of VERSAILLES and the chateau of Vaux-le-Vicomte.

**lever:** see MACHINE.

**leveret:** see HARE.

**Leverkusen,** city (1984 pop. 156,500), North Rhine–Westphalia, W West Germany, at the confluence of the Wupper R. and the RHINE. It is a major centre of the German chemical industry: the wide range of products manufactured also includes photographic materials.

**Leverrier, Urbain Jean Joseph** (ləve‿ryay), 1811–77, French astronomer. On the basis of calculations derived from the perturbations of the motions of the planet Uranus, he and John Couch ADAMS independently and accurately predicted the presence of a transuranian planet; Leverrier's prediction, published first, led directly to the discovery (1846) of the planet NEPTUNE.

**Lévesque, René** (lay‿vek), 1922–87, French-Canadian separatist leader, premier of QUEBEC (1976–85). Originally a member of the Liberal Party, he helped form (1968) the Parti Québécois, which advocated the secession of Quebec from the rest of Canada. In 1980 Quebec voters rejected a sovereignty-association scheme in a provincial referendum. Lévesque resigned as premier in 1985, and later the same year the Parti Québécois was defeated at the polls.

**Levi:** see LEVITES.

**Levi, Primo,** 1919–87, Italian writer. Trained as a chemist, he survived deportation to Auschwitz. His wartime experiences were the starting-point (in *If This is a Man*, 1956, and *The Truce*, 1963) for his literary work, which he combined with a career in industry and which culminated in *The Periodic Table* (1975) and *If not now, when?* (1982).

**levirate,** a system in which a dead man's brother (or an equivalent male kinsman, i.e., one who stands in the KINSHIP system in the same classificatory position) must marry his widow. Children born of such a marriage are the children of the dead man.

**Lévi-Strauss, Claude,** 1908– , French anthropologist and leading exponent of STRUCTURALISM; (b. Belgium.) For Lévi-Strauss different cultural manifestations are the surface manifestations of the underlying universal tendency of the human mind to classify and order perceived phenomena and experience. Structuralism compares the formal relationships among the elements in each system, revealing the structural similarities underlying all cultures, and the cross-cultural patterns of human logic. Lévi-Strauss's central contributions have been in the fields of myth analysis, primitive classification, and kinship. His works include *Structural Anthropology* (1958), *The Savage Mind* (1962), *Totemism* (1962), and *Mythologiques* (4 vol., 1964–71).

**Levites,** among the ancient Hebrews, a religious caste of priests, descended from Levi, son of JACOB. They alone of the tribes received no allotment of land in CANAAN. With the unification of worship at JERUSALEM, the Levites became temple servants with hereditary assignments. LEVITICUS is named after them.

**Leviticus** (liˌvitikəs), book of the OLD TESTAMENT ascribed by tradition to MOSES. It is essentially a collection of liturgical legislation, including laws on the installation of priests (8–10) and on purity and impurity, e.g., dietary laws (11–16).

**Lewes,** county town (1981 pop. 14,449) of E Sussex, SE England, 13 km (8 mi) NE of Brighton, on R. Ouse within the South Downs. It is a market town containing the remains of a Norman castle and several old houses. In 1264 Simon de MONTFORT and the rebel barons defeated Henry II in the Battle of Lewes.

**Lewes, George Henry** (ˌlooh-is), 1817–78, English author. As the editor of the *Fortnightly Review,* he gained fame as a critic. His most noted work is his *Life of Goethe* (1855). He also published many studies on science and philosophy. In 1854 he began living with George ELIOT, whose work he encouraged.

**Lewin, Kurt:** see GESTALT PSYCHOLOGY.

**Lewis.** For rulers thus named, see LOUIS.

**Lewis, Cecil Day:** see DAY LEWIS, CECIL.

**Lewis, C(live) S(taples),** 1898–1963, English author, noted for literary scholarship and for his exposition of Christian tenets. His works include *The Allegory of Love* (1936), on medieval romantic love, and the ironic *Screwtape Letters* (1942). He also wrote criticism, children's fiction, and a Christian science-fiction trilogy beginning with *Out of the Silent Planet* (1938).

**Lewis, Matthew Gregory,** 1775–1818, English writer, called 'Monk' Lewis after his thriller *The Monk* (1796), inspired by Ann RADCLIFFE's GOTHIC ROMANCES. His melodramatic plays and ballads influenced Sir Walter SCOTT.

**Lewis, Meriwether,** 1774–1809, American explorer. Friend and secretary to Pres. JEFFERSON, Lewis headed (1803–6) the LEWIS AND CLARK EXPEDITION. In 1807 he was made governor of the Louisiana Territory.

**Lewis, Oscar,** 1914–70, American anthropologist. Theorizing that poverty creates an identifiable culture that transcends national differences, he wrote *Five Families* (1959), *The Children of Sánchez* (1961), *La Vida* (1966), and *Anthropological Essays* (1970). See POVERTY, CULTURE OF.

**Lewis, (Percy) Wyndham,** 1882–1957, English author and painter; b. US. The inventor of VORTICISM and editor of *Blast* (1914–15), he was a leader of the early 20th-cent. avant-garde in England. His novels include *Tarr* (1918) and a philosophical trilogy, *The Human Age* (1928–55). He also wrote social satires like *The Apes of God* (1930), and was an iconoclastic critic and essayist, notably in *Time and Western Man* (1927). His paintings range from vorticist abstractions to noted portraits of such literary contemporaries as Edith SITWELL and Rebecca WEST.

**Lewis, Sinclair,** 1885–1951, American novelist. A brilliant satirist, he presented a devastating picture of middle-class American life. He achieved notice with *Main Street* (1920), a satire on small-town midwestern life. *Babbitt* (1922), a portrait of an average American destroyed by conformity, is widely considered his greatest book. Lewis satirized the medical profession in *Arrowsmith* (1925) and attacked hypocritical religiosity in *Elmer Gantry* (1927). Among his 22 novels are *Dodsworth* (1929), *It Can't Happen Here* (1935), and *Cass Timberlane* (1945). In 1930 Lewis became the first American to win the Nobel Prize for literature.

**Lewis, Sir (William) Arthur,** 1915– , British economist; b. St Lucia, West Indies. After teaching at the London School of Economics and the Univ. of Manchester, he was (1959–63) an administrator at the Univ. of the West Indies and (from 1963) a professor at Princeton Univ. A specialist in the economy of developing nations, he was a co-winner of the 1979 Nobel Prize for economics, becoming the first black Nobel laureate in a category other than peace.

**Lewis and Clark Expedition,** 1803–06, US expedition that explored the LOUISIANA PURCHASE and the land beyond to the Pacific Ocean. Led by Meriwether LEWIS and William Clark, it was dispatched to find a land route to the Pacific, strengthen US claims to the OREGON territory, and gather information on the Indians and the country. Their well-documented expedition opened vast new territories to the US.

**Lewisham,** London borough (1981 pop. 230,488), S of R. Thames. It is mainly residential, and includes the districts of Catford, Forest Hill, and Deptford.

**Lewitt, Sol,** 1928– , American sculptor. An exponent of minimalism and SERIALISM, Lewitt bases his open-frame structures made of enamelled aluminum girders upon a system of logic and attempts to exclude individual personality factors from artistic creativity. These interests led Lewitt to experiment with conceptual art in the 1970s.

**Lexington,** US city (1984 est. pop. 210,000), north-central Kentucky, in the bluegrass region; inc. 1832. It is the major US centre for the breeding of thoroughbred horses, and a tobacco and bluegrass seed market. Shipping of Kentucky's coal and other products is important, and there are diversified manufactures. The Univ. of Kentucky is in Lexington.

**Lexington and Concord, battles of,** 19 Apr. 1775, opening battles of the AMERICAN REVOLUTION. To seize colonial military stores at CONCORD, the

British marched from Boston and were met at Lexington by colonial militia. After a brief engagement, the colonials withdrew. The British marched to Concord, where they fought another battle and began a harried retreat to Boston that cost them over 200 casualties.

**Leyden, Lucas van:** see LUCAS VAN LEYDEN.

**Lhasa** (ˌlahsə), city (1977 est. pop. 140,000), capital and chief trade centre of TIBET, SW China. The centre of TIBETAN BUDDHISM before the Chinese occupied Tibet in 1951, Lhasa was known as the Forbidden City because of its remoteness and the hostility of the Lamaist clergy to foreigners. Located here are the magnificent Potala, former palace of the Dalai Lama; the Drepung monastery, one of the largest in the world; and the outwardly unimpressive, but extremely holy, Jokang temple. It has recently been opened to Western tourists.

**Li,** chemical symbol of the element LITHIUM.

**Lianyungang,** city (1984 pop. 2,962,500), JIANGSU prov., E China, on the Yellow Sea. A developing industrial port with rail connections to the interior, its industries include chemicals, machinery, food-procesing, and mining of phosphates and coal.

**Liaoning,** province (1985 est. pop. 36,860,000), 145,740 km² (56,270 sq mi). NE China, bordering the Yellow Sea (S) and Korea (SE). Major cities include SHENYANG, the capital, and ANSHAN. The area contains a mixture of plains, mountains, and basins. The Liao R., running NE to SW, provides a relatively fertile plain. Here millet, corn, tobacco, and cotton are grown; there are extensive coal and iron ore deposits, and a relatively well-developed railway network. Anshan is still China's major iron- and steel-producing centre, and the province has a wide range of metalworking industries. Historically, Liaoning and the two other NE provinces of HEILONGJIANG and JILIN were somewhat separate from the rest of China. They were the homeland of the Manchu people whose leaders prohibited Chinese immigration until the 19th cent. There was extensive Chinese migration in the early 20th cent. but the area became a prize sought by the USSR and Japan for its extensive mineral resources. From 1932 to 1945 the three NE provinces formed the Japanese puppet state of Manchukuo and extensive industrialization occurred. Since 1949 the area has been central to the development policies of China.

**Liaquat Ali Khan** (lee-ˌahkət aˌlee kahn), 1895–1951, 1st prime minister of PAKISTAN (1947–51). He was the chief lieutenant of Muhammad Ali JINNAH and a leader of the Muslim League. After Pakistan was created in 1947, he served as prime minister until he was assassinated in 1951.

**Li Bai,** or **Li Bo,** c.700–62, Chinese poet. He is known for his unconcern for worldly preferment and love of retirement and wandering. Extremely fecund and facile, he wrote of the grief of lovers parted by duty, the beauty of the countryside, and the solace and wisdom found in wine.

**libel and slander,** in TORT law, two forms of defamation (unjustified disparagement of the good name and reputation of an individual). Defamation is classed as libel when it is in some permanent form, such as writing or a picture; when it is oral, it is classed as slander. In both cases, it must be revealed to a third party. A statement is generally not defamatory if it is true, but under some statutes a defendant must prove good motives in the utterance. Certain privileged situations (e.g., proceedings in PARLIAMENT) shield a defamer from liability. The usual remedy for defamation is monetary damages.

**Liberal International,** coordinating body (est. 1947) of about 40 liberal parties around the world. Liberal parties within the EUROPEAN COMMUNITY are linked within the Federation of Liberal, Democratic, and Reformist Parties of the European Community.

**Liberalism,** a set of political ideas, developed and amended over three centuries, of which the central values are freedom and individualism. It arose in the 17th and 18th cent. as the IDEOLOGY of the BOURGEOISIE, the rising industrial and commercial middle class, and is inseparably connected with the birth of the modern capitalist society. In an age of faith, liberalism urged open-mindedness, rational scientific enquiry, and religious tolerance, and helped to erode the traditional social hierarchy and the economic controls of the medieval world. It advocated freedom of thought, freedom of expression, freedom of association, free enterprise, free trade, and the free market. In the 17th cent. John LOCKE, in his account of the original SOCIAL CONTRACT, argued that the arbitrary personal power of monarchs should be replaced by a legally defined state controlled by representatives of the people, and that in order to prevent excessive concentrations of power, there should be a balanced constitution, with a separation of power between the legislative, executive, and judicial branches. The CONSTITUTION OF THE UNITED STATES is a famous example of these principles. In the 18th cent., the economist Adam SMITH argued that the role of the state should be limited to providing law and order at home, and protection from enemies abroad; this would guarantee political stability, security of property, and the enforcement of contracts. Smith believed that, given this framework, progress in wealth, intellect, and humanity would proceed simply from the free and open competition of individuals, ideas and goods, as if guided by 'a hidden hand'; any further state intervention in society, and any additional taxation to finance it, were likely to prove inefficient at best, oppressive at worst. Central to *classical liberalism* was a commitment to LAISSEZ-FAIRE economics and free trade. In the 19th cent., these ideas were triumphant: in England the Utilitarians (see UTILITARIANISM) and the Liberal Party under GLADSTONE brought about electoral, administrative, and economic reforms which produced the outline of a recognizably modern liberal society. John Stuart MILL's 'On Liberty' (1859) was a sustained argument for protecting the rights of minorities from the tyranny of majority opinion, and for creating the optimum conditions for the full personal development of each individual. But as the century progressed, the misery and inequality produced by unregulated industrial capitalism made clear that laissez-faire and the minimal liberal state had not produced for the mass of individuals the kinds of freedom that mattered most: freedom from want, freedom from disease, and freedom from ignorance. A new generation of liberal thinkers such as L. T. Hobhouse and T. H. GREEN came to the view that in pursuit of these positive freedoms it would be necessary for the state, representing the common good, to enact social reforms. This *new liberalism* marked a decisive shift in liberal thinking, which found expression in the welfare reforms of the last great Liberal government in England under ASQUITH and LLOYD GEORGE (1906–18). With the rise of SOCIALISM and SOCIAL DEMOCRACY however, the torch of political reform was passed on to more radical parties. At the same time, the experience of FASCISM and world war undermined the distinctively liberal faith in man's rationality and the inevitability of progress. In Western Europe liberal parties went into a long decline, their historic mission perhaps achieved with the implementation of *liberal democracy* itself. 20th cent. liberal thinkers such as F. A. HAYEK and Robert Nozick have concentrated on the threats to individual freedom and civilization posed by the size and range of activity of the modern state, and in the 1970s and 80s there has been a significant revival of classical liberal ideas on the economy (*neo-liberalism*) amongst modern conservative parties (see CONSERVATISM). In the social sphere, the emphasis of contemporary liberalism remains on civil liberties and the rights of minorities: this has been shown in Britain by liberal pressure for the relaxation of official CENSORSHIP and the reform of the laws regulating birth control and homosexuality.

**Liberal Party,** former independent British political party, now part of a broader centrist formation called the SOCIAL AND LIBERAL DEMOCRATS. An outgrowth of the WHIG PARTY, it was supported by the bulk of the industrial and business classes enfranchised by the REFORM BILL of 1832. Lord John Russell, a leading Liberal, became prime minister in 1846. The party advocated LAISSEZ FAIRE and initially opposed social legislation. Under William GLADSTONE, however, it accepted electoral and social reforms and, in 1884, took up the cause of Irish HOME RULE. Herbert Asquith (see OXFORD AND ASQUITH, 1ST EARL OF), a Liberal imperialist, became prime minister in 1908. He was followed by David LLOYD GEORGE, who led a coalition government during WORLD WAR I. Thereafter, the Liberal Party became divided and went into decline, a process accelerated by the rise of the LABOUR PARTY on the strength of universal adult suffrage. By the 1930s the Liberals had become a small third party, a status which endured in the postwar era. Under the leadership of David STEEL (from 1976), the party entered into a parliamentary pact with the then ruling Labour Party. After 1979 the Liberals sought to present a centrist alternative to both Labour and the ruling CONSERVATIVE PARTY, to which end they formed (1981) an alliance with the new SOCIAL DEMOCRATIC PARTY. In the 1983 elections this alliance secured substantial popular support (25% of the vote), but only 23 seats (17 for the Liberals). In the 1987 elections the Liberals retained 17 seats but the alliance slipped to 22 (23% of the vote) whereupon Steel proposed a full merger with the Social Democrats. This resulted, eventually (1988), in the creation of the SOCIAL AND LIBERAL DEMOCRATS (although anti-merger Social Democrats maintained their party in being under the leadership of David OWEN). Paddy ASHDOWN was elected leader of the new party.

**Liberal Republican Party,** US political party formed in 1872 by a heterogeneous group of liberals and reformers with the corruption and policies of Pres. Grant's administration. Among its leaders were Carl SCHURZ, Horace GREELEY, and Charles SUMNER. The party nominated Greeley for president, a choice reluctantly endorsed by the Democrats. Its platform, adopted only after much wrangling, called for withdrawal of troops from the South and civil-service reform. Grant easily won reelection and the Liberal Republican Party came to an end.

**liberation theology,** a trend in contemporary Christian theology which, envisaging Christ as the liberator whose message is one of freedom for the oppressed (e.g., Luke 4.18–21), identifies the evil from which men and women need deliverance as economic, social, and political deprivation. Arguing that Christ, himself the personification of poverty, was the champion of the poor, it conceives of the role of his church as cooperation with the oppressed majority against the oppressing minority. Without being formally Marxist, it employs the Marxist concept of the class struggle, and allows or condones the use of violence by the underprivileged in their efforts to recover their human dignity. One of its Protestant manifestations is the 'black theology' which in the US claims that the gospel speaks with unique concern to the black victims of former slavery or actual racial discrimination. In its Roman Catholic form it has been widely influential in Latin America, where the church has tended to ally itself with revolutionary movements against the rich and politically corrupt dominant class. In 1984 Pope JOHN PAUL II condemned liberation theology for what he considered its largely material, this-world understanding of salvation.

**Liberec** (libeə͵raych), city (1984 pop. 100,000), Bohemia, W Czechoslovakia, on the Neisse R. It is an established centre of the textile industry, and also manufactures clothing.

**Liberia,** officially Republic of Liberia, republic (1986 est. pop. 2,190,000), 113,370 km² (43,000 sq mi), W Africa, bordered by the Atlantic Ocean (SW), Sierra Leone (NW), Guinea (N), and Côte d'Ivoire (E). MONROVIA is the capital. Liberia has three geographic regions: a flat coastal plain, a dominant interior area of densely forested foothills, and a northern mountain area with elevations of over 1370 m (4500 ft). Liberia's economy, formerly dependent on subsistence farming and rubber production, is now based primarily on exports of iron ore. Other exports are rubber, diamonds, timber, coffee, and cocoa. The government derives a sizable income from registration of foreign ships under very flexible rules, a practice that has made the Liberian merchant marine appear to be one of the world's largest. The GNP is US$991 million, and the GNP per capita is US$470 (1985). The indigenous African population has diverse tribal origins and practices traditional religions or Islam. The descendants of American settlers, though not numerous, wield considerable political influence. English is the official language, but tribal tongues are widely spoken.

*History.* Liberia was founded in 1821 as a haven for freed American slaves by the AMERICAN COLONIZATION SOCIETY. The first American Negroes arrived in 1822, and some 15,000 were eventually settled. The colony became independent in 1847. Constitutional issues, mounting foreign debts (the government was bankrupt by 1909), and the loss of disputed territory threatened the stability of the new nation, but with US help, independence was preserved. In 1930 revelations of government connivance in a slave trade from Liberia resulted in the downfall of the regime and proposals for international control. Such action was averted, however, by the leadership of presidents Edwin Barclay (1930–44) and William V.S. Tubman (1944–71); the latter opened Liberia to international investment, gave tribal peoples a greater voice in the country's affairs, and improved living standards. In 1979, after years of political stability, a government proposal to increase the price of rice (the main staple) produced widespread violence. A year later a coup led by soldiers of African origin ended 100 years of rule by Americo-Liberians; Pres. William R. Tolbert (who had succeeded Tubman in 1971) was assassinated, and the country was placed under a military government headed by Master Sergeant (later Gen.) Samuel K. Doe. The latter was elected president in 1985 in Liberia's first multi-party elections.

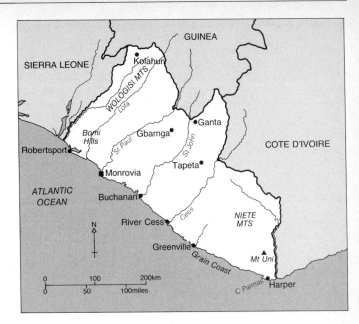

Liberia

**Liberty, Statue of,** colossal (46-m/152-ft) statue on Liberty Island, in New York harbour, US. Designed by F.A. BARTHOLDI, it was presented to the US by the Franco-American Union to commemorate the AMERICAN REVOLUTION. Dedicated in 1886, it became a national monument in 1924.

Statue of **Liberty**

**Liberty Bell,** historic relic housed near Independence Hall, Philadelphia, US. Hung in 1753, it was rung in July 1776 to proclaim the DECLARATION OF INDEPENDENCE. It was hidden (1777–78) from the British in Allentown, Pennsylvania, and later returned. The bell was cracked in 1835 and again in 1846.

**Liberty's,** department store in London founded in 1875 by Sir Arthur Lasenby Liberty (1843–1917), to retail goods imported from the Near and Far East. To compete with the growing popularity of William MORRIS designs he commissioned work from members of the Aesthetic Movement and Art Workers' Guild such as C.F.A. Voysey, Linsey Butterfield, and Walter CRANE. Liberty's style is strongly associated with ART NOUVEAU (known as Stile Liberty in Italy) mixed with classic English historic chintz and brocade designs.

**Li Bo:** see LI BAI.

**library.** The earliest known library was a collection of clay tablets in Babylonia in the 21st cent. BC. Other early libraries were the Babylonian library at Nineveh of King ASSURBANIPAL (d. 626? BC) and the sacred library in the Temple at JERUSALEM. In 330 BC the first public library in Greece was established in order to preserve accurate examples of the works of the great dramatists. The most famous libraries of antiquity were those at ALEXANDRIA, in Egypt, and PERGAMON. Roman libraries were brought from Greece, Asia Minor, and Syria as the result of conquests (1st and 2nd cent. BC). The great Roman public libraries were the Octavian (destroyed AD 80) and the Ulpian, founded in the reign of TRAJAN. Early Christian libraries were attached to churches; the one at Caesarea was the largest, often mentioned by St JEROME. The Anglo-Saxon monastery libraries produced fine manuscript ILLUMINATION. The Arabs (9th–15th cent.) collected many fine libraries, e.g., at Baghdad and Córdoba. In medieval Europe libraries were kept by monasteries; ALCUIN was a notable librarian. In the RENAISSANCE, nobles like Lorenzo de' Medici (see MEDICI, family) had great libraries, and many of the major university libraries, e.g., Bologna and Oxford, were created. The Vatican Library, the oldest public library in Europe, was founded in the 15th cent. In the US, the Boston Public Library opened in 1653; the BRITISH MUSEUM opened as a library in 1759. Libraries in the US and Britain benefited greatly from the philanthropy of Andrew CARNEGIE, who strengthened local interest in libraries by making his grants contingent upon public support. Among the innovations of the late 19th cent. were free public access to books and branch libraries. In the early 20th cent. travelling libraries began to take books to readers in rural areas. Modern innovations include readers' advisory services, interlibrary loans, lecture series, public book reviews, and the maintenance of special recording and juvenile collections. Two widely used systems of classification are the Dewey decimal system of Melvil DEWEY and the Library of Congress system. Since the 1930s libraries have had several technological tools at their disposal: microphotographic techniques for text preservation (microfilm); photocopiers; and COMPUTER data banks that enable them to store vast amounts of information (see INFORMATION STORAGE AND RETRIEVAL) and produce comprehensive INDEXES and CATALOGUES. See also BIBLIOGRAPHY.

**libretto** [Ital., = little book], the text of an OPERA or an ORATORIO; usually a loose plot connecting a series of episodes. Outstanding librettists include Pietro METASTASIO, Lorenzo DA PONTE, W.S. GILBERT, and Hugo von HOFMANNSTHAL. Many composers, e.g., Richard WAGNER and Michael TIPPETT, have written their own librettos.

**Libreville,** city (1985 est. pop. 350,000), capital of Gabon, a port on the Gabon R. estuary, near the Gulf of Guinea. It is an administrative centre and has petroleum and plywood industries. Founded in 1843 as a settlement for slaves freed by the French it was named Libreville [Fr., = freetown] in 1848. It was the chief port of FRENCH EQUATORIAL AFRICA until the development of Pointe-Noire in the 1930s.

**Libya,** officially Socialist People's Libyan Arab Jamahirya ('State of the Masses'), republic (1984 est. pop. 3,624,000), 1,759,540 km² (67,358 sq mi), N Africa, bordered by Algeria and Tunisia (W), the Mediterranean Sea (N), Egypt and Sudan (E), and Chad and Niger (S). The principal cities are TRIPOLI (the capital) and TOBRUK. Most of Libya is part of the SAHARA desert; the population is restricted to a coastal strip along the Mediterranean and a few widely scattered oases in the Libyan desert, in the east, and the Fazzan region, in the south. The discovery of oil in 1958 transformed Libya from a poor agricultural country into one of the world's leading petroleum producers, with vast sums to spend on social, agricultural, and military development. It is also an important producer of natural gas. However, although petroleum accounts for 95% of export earnings and more than 50% of national income, agriculture occupies almost half of the labour force; major crops include cereals, olives, fruits, dates, and vegetables. The GNP is US$25,984 million, and the GNP per capita is US$7170 (1985). The majority of the inhabitants are of Arab descent, but there are scattered communities of Berbers and, in the southwest, many people of mixed Berber and black African descent. Islam is the official religion, and Arabic is the language.

*History.* At various times in its history the territory that is now Libya was occupied by Carthage, Rome, Arabia, Morocco, Egypt, and Spain. It was part of the Ottoman Empire from 1551 to 1911, serving in the 18th cent. as a base for pirates who, in return for immunity, provided large revenues to the local ruler. Libya was seized by Italy in 1911, but Libyan resistance continued until the 1930s. During WORLD WAR II, as an Italian colony, it was one of the main battlegrounds of N Africa (see NORTH AFRICA, CAMPAIGNS IN), passing under an Anglo-French military government when the Axis was defeated in the area in 1943. In accordance with a UN decision, in 1951 the country became independent as the United Kingdom of Libya, with King Idris I as ruler. Idris was ousted in 1969 in a coup d'etat led by Col. Muammar al-QADAFFI, who established an anti-Western dictatorship. British and American bases were closed in 1970, and unification was sought, unsuccessfully, with several other Arab countries. An implacable foe of Israel, Qadaffi used Libya's vast oil wealth to help support the Palestinian guerrilla movement; he has also taken action against opponents of his regime at home and abroad. In recent years Qadaffi has become increasingly concerned with African affairs; in 1979 he intervened in Uganda to help keep Idi AMIN in power, and in 1981 and again in 1983 he dispatched troops into neighbouring CHAD. As a member of OPEC (see ORGANIZATION OF THE PETROLEUM EXPORTING COUNTRIES), Libya under Qadaffi became a leading exponent of limiting production and increasing prices of petroleum. In the mid-1980s Libya's relations were particularly bad with neighbouring Tunisia and with the US, which accused Qadaffi of sponsoring international terrorism and also opposed his claim to territorial rights over the Gulf of Sirte; a series of confrontations culminated in a major US air strike on Libya in April 1986. After a series of military reverses in 1987–88, Libya effectively abandoned the aspirations in Chad.

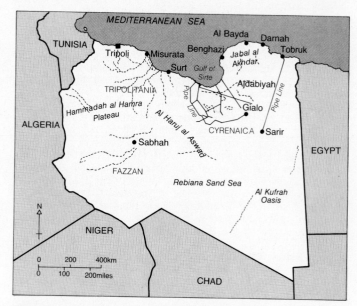

Libya

**licence,** in law, the granting of permission to do something which would otherwise be unlawful, e.g., permission to enter land that would usually be a trespass. A licence passes no interest (see ESTATE) in the land. A bare licence (e.g., an invitation to dinner) can be revoked at any time; a contractual licence (granted by way of a CONTRACT) can be revoked only at the end of the contractual period. In recent years, landlords have used the licence to avoid the statutory protections given to their tenants (see LANDLORD AND TENANT).

**lichen,** simple plant consisting of blue-green or green ALGAE living symbiotically with FUNGI, usually sac fungi. Lichens commonly grow on rocks or trees. The body, or thallus, is composed of fungal filament, or hyphae. The fungi obtain food from the algae and, in turn, absorb and retain the water that is used by the algae for PHOTOSYNTHESIS. Reproduction of the algae and fungi is usually simultaneous. Lichens can withstand great extremes in temperature and can be found in deserts and the polar regions.

**Lichfield,** town (1981 pop. 25,408), Staffordshire, W Midlands of England, 24 km (15 mi) N of Birmingham. It is a market town, with industries which include light engineering and iron-founding. There is a cathedral which was built between the 12th cent. and 15th cent. The town is the birthplace of Samuel JOHNSON.

**Lichtenstein, Roy,** 1923–, American painter. Linked to the POP ART movement, he derives his subject matter from sources such as comic strips, e.g., *Whaam* (1963; Tate Gall., London). His technique suggests the cheap screen-printing process of newspaper printing, which reduces the simple subject matter to large, strongly stylized patterns of great graphic inventiveness.

**Licinius,** 250–325, Roman emperor. Co-emperor (308) with Galerius, he allied himself with CONSTANTINE I and defeated Maximin in 313, thus becoming sole ruler in the East. He was later defeated and put to death by Constantine.

**Licinius** (Caius Licinius Calvus Stolo), fl. 375 BC, tribune to whom the Licinian Rogations are attributed. They strictly limited the amount of public land that one person might hold, limited grazing rights, regulated debts, and ordained that one consul must be a plebeian. See also AGRARIAN LAWS.

**Liddell Hart, Sir Basil Henry** (ˌlidəl ˌhaht), 1895–1970, English author and military strategist; b. Paris. He was an advocate of mechanized warfare, and his thinking had a profound effect on the German high command prior to WORLD WAR II. He also developed infantry tactics and training methods adopted by the British army. His works include *The Future of Infantry* (1933).

**Lidice** (ˌliditse), village near Prague, Czechoslovakia. It was the site in June 1942 of a massacre perpetrated by the Nazis in reprisal for the assassination of the deputy protector of Bohemia and Moravia, Reinhard Heidrich. The men of the village were shot; the women and children deported to the concentration camp at Ravensbrueck. The Lidice Massacre, which had many parallels in occupied Poland and the USSR, scandalized western opinion partly because Heydrich's killers had originally been sent from London.

**Lie, Trygve Halvdan** (lee), 1896–1968, Norwegian statesman, first secretary general (1946–53) of the UNITED NATIONS. He served in ministerial posts and was foreign minister of his government in exile during World War II before being elected to the UN. His support of UN action during the KOREAN WAR earned him the enmity of the USSR. On leaving the UN he resumed an active role in Norwegian politics.

**Liebermann, Max,** 1847–1935, German GENRE painter and etcher. Influenced by the BARBIZON painters, and by Jozef ISRAËLS, he developed a style close to IMPRESSIONISM. He depicted the working classes, scenes of peasant rural life, landscapes, and outdoor groups. Among his works is *The Parrot Keeper* (1902; Museum Folkwang, Essen).

**Liebig, Justus, Baron von** (ˌleebikh), 1803–73, German chemist. As professor (1824–52) at Giessen, he was among the first to establish a chemical teaching laboratory, where some of the leading 19th-cent. chemists were trained. A professor (1852–73) at Munich, he improved methods of organic analysis and discovered chloral; he was also one of the discoverers of chloroform. His work in agricultural chemistry aided in the development of artificial fertilizers.

**Liechtenstein,** principality (1984 est. pop. 26,680), 157 km² (61 sq mi), W central Europe, in the Alps between Austria and Switzerland; the Rhine R. forms its western boundary. Vaduz is the capital. Increasingly industrial in recent years, Liechtenstein produces machinery and other metal goods, precision instruments, ceramics, and textiles. Most of the firms are owned and operated by Swiss. Tourism and the sale of postage stamps, as well as revenues from some 25,000 foreign corporations nominally headquartered in Vaduz because of low taxes and bank secrecy, are important sources of income. The GNP is $438 million and the GNP per capita is $16,440 (1980). Roman Catholicism is the state religion; German is the national language.

*History.* The principality was created in 1719 as a fief of the HOLY ROMAN EMPIRE. A member of the GERMAN CONFEDERATION from 1815, it became independent in 1866. It is closely linked with SWITZERLAND and is represented abroad by the Swiss government. Since 1938 Leichtenstein's government has been a coalition of the Patriotic Union and the Progressive Citizens' Party. In a national referendum in 1984 the electorate (only males under the 1921 constitution) voted narrowly in favour of female suffrage at national level; in 1986 female suffrage was also extended to those local communes where it had not previously been operative.

**lieder** [Ger., = songs], songs written in the German vernacular. Although the term encompasses centuries of musical history, it is popularly used to denote German art songs of the 19th cent. These songs, usually for a single voice, have as lyrics poems by such authors as GOETHE. The most noted composers of lieder are SCHUBERT, SCHUMANN, BRAHMS, WOLF, MAHLER, and Richard STRAUSS.

**lie detector,** instrument designed to determine whether a subject is lying or telling the truth, generally by detecting evidence of the slight increase in body tension believed to occur when a person knowingly lies. Various devices developed in the 20th cent. and used mainly in US POLICE work measure blood pressure, respiration, pulse, electrical changes on the skin, and voice frequencies. In the UK lie detectors are rarely used by the police, and test results are not accepted as evidence in court. The use of lie detectors to screen employees and job applicants is highly controversial.

**Liège,** city (1985 pop. 202,314), E Belgium, at the confluence of the Meuse and Ourthe rivers. The cultural centre of French-speaking Belgium, it is a transportation hub and an industrial city whose manufactures include metal goods, armaments, and textiles. It was largely rebuilt after considerable damage in World War II.

**Lifar, Serge,** 1905–87, Russian dancer. He worked with DIAGHILEV (1923–29) and created the title role in BALANCHINE's *Prodigal Son* (1929). As principal dancer, then ballet master of the Paris Grand Opera (1930–44) he revolutionized French BALLET.

**lifeboat,** shore-based boat designed for rescuing mariners in distress and saving life at sea; also, small boat carried by a larger ship for use when abandoning ship in an emergency. A typical modern rescue-service lifeboat is about 16 m (52 ft) long and self-righting, making it virtually unsinkable. Inflatable lifeboats are often used for inshore operations. Increasingly, lifeboat services are supported by the use of HELICOPTERS in air–sea rescue work. In Britain the service is administered by the RNLI (ROYAL NATIONAL LIFEBOAT INSTITUTION).

**life cycle:** see CYCLES.

**Liffey,** river in Republic of Ireland, c.80 km (50 mi) long. It rises in the Wicklow Mts, Co. Wicklow, and flows W and then N into Co. Kildare, then E past DUBLIN, entering the Irish Sea in Dublin Bay. At Poulaphouca Falls there is a hydroelectric power station.

**Lifford,** county town (1986 pop. 1461) of Co. Donegal, Republic of Ireland, on R. Foyle, near the border with Northern Ireland. It is a small market town.

**lift,** mechanical device for transporting people or goods from one level to another; called elevator in America. The American inventor Elisha G. Otis demonstrated (1853) a safety device designed to prevent the fall of a lift if its supporting cable should break; in 1861 he patented a steam-powered lift. Steam was gradually replaced, first in the early 1870s by hydraulic power (see HYDRAULIC MACHINERY) and then toward the end of the 19th cent. by electricity. Safety devices were improved and automatic controls introduced as lift speeds increased.

**ligament,** strong band of white fibrous CONNECTIVE TISSUE that joins a BONE to other bones or to cartilage in the JOINT areas. Ligaments tend to be pliable but not elastic, permitting limited movement while holding attached bones in place. Fibrous sheets supporting internal organs are also ligaments.

**Ligeti, György,** 1923–, Hungarian composer, who settled in Cologne after 1956. He has developed a distinctive world of sound masses with dense polyphony, which is epitomized in orchestral works such as *Apparitions* (1960), *Atmosphères* (1961), and the Requiem (1963–65). Other characteristic compositions are *Lux aeterna* (1966) and *Clocks and Clouds* (1972–73).

**light,** that part of ELECTROMAGNETIC RADIATION to which the human eye is sensitive. The wavelengths of visible light range from c.400 to c.750 nanometres ($10^{-9}$ metres). If white light, which contains all wavelengths, is separated into a SPECTRUM, each wavelength is seen to correspond to a different COLOUR. The scientific study of the behaviour of light is called OPTICS; it covers REFLECTION of light by a MIRROR or other object, REFRACTION of light by a LENS or PRISM, and DIFFRACTION of light as it passes by an opaque object. Christiaan HUYGENS proposed (1690) a theory that explained light as a WAVE phenomenon. Isaac NEWTON, however, held (1704) that light is composed of tiny particles, or corpuscules, emitted by luminous bodies. By combining his corpuscular theory with his laws of mechanics, he was able to explain many optical phenomena. Newton's corpuscular theory of light was favoured over the wave theory until important experiments, which could be interpreted only in terms of the wave theory, were done on the diffraction and INTERFERENCE of light by Thomas YOUNG (1801) and A.J. FRESNEL (1814–15). In the 19th cent. the wave theory became the dominant theory of the nature of light. The electromagnetic theory of James Clerk MAXWELL (1864) supported the view that visible light is a form of ELECTROMAGNETIC RADIATION. With the acceptance of the electromagnetic theory of light, only two general problems remained. It was assumed that a massless medium, the ETHER, was the carrier of light waves, just as air or water carries sound waves. The famous experiments (1881–87) by A.A. MICHELSON and Edward Morley, in which they tried unsuccessfully to measure the velocity of the earth with respect to this medium, failed to support the ether hypothesis. With his special theory of RELATIVITY, Albert EINSTEIN showed (1905) that the ether was unnecessary to the electromagnetic theory. Also in 1905, Einstein, in order to explain the PHOTOELECTRIC EFFECT, suggested that light, and other forms of electromagnetic radiation, travel as minute bundles of energy, called light quanta, or photons, that behave as particles (see PHOTON; QUANTUM THEORY). Light thus behaves as a wave, as in diffraction and interference phenomena, or as a stream of particles, as in the photoelectric effect. The theory of relativity predicts that the speed of light in a vacuum 299,792.458 km/sec = 186,282 mi/sec is the limiting velocity for material particles.

**light-emitting diode:** see DIODE.

**lighthouse,** tower or other building emitting a bright light to guide shipping or aircraft. Among the most famous lighthouses are the Pharos of Alexandria (c.280 BC), one of the ancient Seven Wonders of the World, and the Eddystone lighthouse, off the Plymouth coast, built in 1698. Originally, fibres or candles were used as the light source. In the modern lighthouse an electric or acetylene light is magnified and beamed out to the horizon (or upwards for aircraft) using mirrors or optical lenses. Signals are either flashing (the dark intervals exceeding the light) or occulting (equal or longer light intervals). In conditions of fog or poor visibility sirens, horns, and sometimes explosives are employed. Some lighthouses are remote-controlled. LIGHTSHIPS are used instead of lighthouses where conditions dictate. The British lighthouse service is administered by TRINITY HOUSE and the Commissioners for Northern Lighthouses.

**lightning,** electrical discharge accompanied by THUNDER, commonly occurring during a THUNDERSTORM. The discharge may take place between two parts of the same cloud, between two clouds, or between a cloud and the earth. Lightning may appear as a jagged streak (forked lightning), as a vast flash in the sky (sheet lightning), or, rarely, as a brilliant ball (ball lightning). The electrical nature of lightning was proved by Benjamin FRANKLIN in his famous kite experiment of 1752.

**lightship,** a specialized vessel having the same function as a LIGHTHOUSE. Lightships are used where reefs, sandbanks, or other conditions such as accessibility make the building or maintenance of a lighthouse impossible. Supplementary to lightships are lightbuoys, which operate unattended for up to one year and emit sound signals activated by the waves in foggy weather.

**light-year,** in astronomy, the distance $(9.46 \times 10^{12}$km$/5.87 \times 10^{12}$mi$)$ that LIGHT travels in one sidereal YEAR.

**lignite** or **brown coal,** carbon-containing fuel intermediate between COAL and PEAT, brown or yellowish in colour and woody in texture. Lignite contains more moisture than coal and tends to dry and crumble when exposed to air. It burns with a long, smoky flame but little heat.

**lignum vitae,** tropical American evergreen tree (genus *Guaiacum*). Its dense, durable wood, chiefly from *G. sanctum* and *G. officinale,* is used where strength and hardness are required, e.g., in turning. It produces a fragrant resin known as gum guaiacum, used medicinally.

**lilac,** Old World shrub or small tree (genus *Syringa*) of the OLIVE family, noted for its fragrant, cone-shaped masses of lavender or white flowers. Many variations in form, e.g., double flowers, and colour, e.g., rosy pink, have been hybridized from the familiar common lilac (*S. vulgaris*).

**Lilienthal, Otto** (ˌleelyəntahl), 1848–96, German aeronautical engineer. A pioneer in experiments with gliders, he based his developments largely on observations of birds. He died shortly after the crash landing of the last of his more than 2000 glider flights.

**Lilith,** Jewish female demon, probably originally the Assyrian storm demon Lilitu. In Jewish folklore she is a vampire-like child-killer and the symbol of lust.

**Liliuokalani** (leelee'ooh ohkah ˌlahnee), 1838–1917, last reigning queen of the Hawaiian islands (1891–93). Her rule caused a revolt of sugar planters (mostly Americans), who deposed her. She wrote many songs, including the popular 'Aloha Oe' or 'Farewell to Thee'. Much of her later life was spent in the US.

**Lille,** city (1982 pop. 174,039, agglomeration (incl. Roubaix and Tourcoing) 936,295), capital of Nord dept., N France. Long known for its textiles, it is the heart of a large, industrially developed metropolitan area. Once chief city of the county of Flanders and home of the 16th-cent. dukes of Burgundy, Lille was captured by the duke of Marlborough (1708) and restored to France by the Treaty of Utrecht (1713).

**Lillie, Beatrice,** 1898–, English comedienne; b. Canada. She won an international reputation for sophisticated wit in revues, radio and television shows, and films.

**Lilly, John:** see LYLY, JOHN.

**Lilongwe** (leeˌlonggway), city (1985 est. pop. 186,800), capital of Malawi. Located in a fertile agricultural area, it became Malawi's capital in 1966. New government buildings were completed in the 1980s and a new international airport and a railway link were also built.

**lily,** common name for the family Liliaceae, perennial plants having showy flowers and erect clusters of narrow, grasslike leaves. The lily family is distributed worldwide but is particularly abundant in warm temperate and tropical regions. Most species grow from BULBS or enlarged underground STEMS. Common wildflowers in the family are ASPHODEL, DOGTOOTH VIOLET, LILY OF THE VALLEY, and TRILLIUM. Ornamentals of commercial importance include lilies, HYACINTHS, MEADOW SAFFRON, SQUILL, and TULIPS; food plants of commercial importance are ASPARAGUS and plants of the ONION genus. YUCCA and ALOE species are popular SUCCULENTS. True lilies include the Madonna lily (*Lilium candidum*) of Europe; the white trumpet lily (*L. longiflorum*) of Japan, which includes the Easter, or Bermuda, lily (var. *eximium*); the tiger lily (*L. tigrinum*) of China; and the Turk's-cap lily (*L. martagon*) and panther lily (*L. pardalinum*), both of North America.

**lily of the valley,** fragrant, spring-blooming, woodland perennial (genus *Convallaria*) of the LILY family. It has dainty, bell-shaped white flowers on a stalk between two shiny leaves and grows in the shade. The widely cultivated *C. majalis* is native to Europe, and there are several cultivated varieties with rose-coloured flowers or variegated leaves.

**Lima,** city (1981 pop. 3,968,972), W Peru, capital of Peru. Its port is CALLAO. Lima is Peru's largest city, and its urban area is the nation's economic centre, with oil-refining and diversified manufacturing industries. Founded by Francisco PIZARRO in 1535, Lima was the magnificent capital of Spain's New World empire until its surrender by Spanish troops in 1825 marked the final removal of Spanish colonial rule on the American mainland. Rebuilt several times, it retains the architectural styles of several periods but is dominated by modern buildings erected since World War II. Its focal point is the central Plaza de las Armas, with its huge palace and cathedral. The Univ. of San Marcos (est. 1551) is one of the finest in South America.

**Lima, Jorge de,** 1893–1953, Brazilian poet and novelist. Converted to Catholicism in middle life, he became interested in the connection between religious and poetic experience. His *Invenção de Orfeu* (1952) was highly influential in Brazilian poetry. His novels range from SURREALISM to autobiography in subject-matter.

**Limann, Hilla,** 1934–, president of GHANA (1979–81). In 1979, after seven years of military rule, Ghana's new military leader, Jerry RAWLINGS, handed over power to Limann, who had been elected to head a civilian government. Limann's People's National Party, which he founded, was moderately socialist but enjoyed the support of business. In 1981, however, he was deposed by Rawlings in a military coup.

**limbic system:** see BRAIN.

**Limbourg brothers** (lanhbooə), fl. 1380–1416, Pol, Jan, and Herman, Franco-Flemish manuscript illuminators. In 1411 they became court painters to Jean, duc de Berry for whom they did their Gothic masterpiece, the *Très riches heures* (c.1415; Musée Condé, Chantilly). This exquisite BOOK OF HOURS shows scenes of daily life, and profoundly influenced Flemish painting.

**Limburg,** southermost region of the Netherlands, extending into Belgium. The sandy heathlands of the N contrast sharply with the fertile and picturesque hills and valleys of the S. Arable and fruit farming has always supported a dense rural population in the S and this grew rapidly following the opening up of the Limburg coalfield after 1900. Coal production has been phased out in modern times, but chemical and other industries survive. MAASTRICHT is the leading urban centre. The division into Dutch and Belgian provs. of Limburg dates from 1839.

**lime:** see CALCIUM OXIDE.

**lime. 1** Small, shrublike tree (*Citrus aurantifolia*) of the RUE family. Its bright-green fruit, smaller and more acid than the LEMON, has long been used to prevent scurvy. The plant grows well in rocky or sandy soils. It is the most frost-sensitive of the CITRUS FRUITS, and chief production areas are in tropical regions. **2** A deciduous tree of the genus *Tilia*, common in temperate zones. About 30 m (100 ft) tall, its attractive habit has made it popular for parks and avenues.

**Limerick,** county in SW of Republic of Ireland (1986 pop. 164, 204), 2659 km² (1037 sq mi), bordering on the Shannon estuary in the N. It is situated in the province of Munster. The county town is LIMERICK. Most of the county is low-lying, but there are hills in the S. The Galty Mts are in the extreme SE, and here the land rises to 827 m (2713 ft). The main rivers are the Deel, Maigue, and Mulkear. The lowlands are fertile and agriculture predominates. There is much manufacturing industry in the town of Limerick.

**Limerick,** county town (1986 pop. 56,241), of Co. Limerick, Republic of Ireland, at the head of the Shannon estuary. It is a seaport and industrial town, whose major industries are various forms of food processing. In 1979 the port handled 1.7 million tonnes. There are several historic buildings, including the 12th-cent. Protestant cathedral and the 19th-cent. Roman Catholic cathedral. There are also the remains of a Norman castle. There is an important hydroelectric power station nearby at Ardnacrusha.

**limestone,** sedimentary rock composed of calcium carbonate. It is ordinarily white but may be coloured brown, yellow, or red by iron oxide and blue, black, or grey by carbon impurities. Most limestones are formed from the skeletons of marine invertebrates; a few are chemically precipitated from solution. Organic acids acting on underground deposits lead to formations such as those in the caves at Cheddar Gorge, Somerset, UK. Limestone is used in iron extraction, in cements and building stones, and as a source of lime (see CALCIUM OXIDE). Limestone varieties include CHALK, DOLOMITE, MARBLE, OOLITE, and travertine.

**lime-tree** or **linden,** tall deciduous tree (genus *Tilia*) of the family Tiliaceae, which includes the tropical genus *Corchorus* from which JUTE is obtained. The name most often refers to *T. vulgaris*, a park and avenue tree, thought to be a hybrid between *T. cordata*, the only native British lime, and *T. platyphyllos*, of continental Europe. It is the tallest broad–leaved tree in Britain. The light, strong wood of *Tilia* species is useful for specialist, high-grade items such as musical-instrument parts. Fibre from the tough, inner bark is used in wickerwork, canework, mats, and in making footwear. Their flowers are a high-grade source of honey, and important in BEE culture.

**limit,** in mathematics, value approached by a SEQUENCE or a FUNCTION under certain specified conditions. For example, the terms of the sequence $\frac{1}{2}$, $\frac{1}{4}$, $\frac{1}{8}$, $\frac{1}{16}$, . . . are obviously getting smaller and smaller. Because one can, if enough terms are taken, make the last term as small, i.e., as close to zero, as one pleases, the limit of this sequence is said to be zero. If $s_n$ denotes the $n$th term of a sequence, the equation $\lim_{n \to \infty} s_n = s$ (read 'the limit of $s_n$ as $n$ approaches infinity is $s$') expresses the fact that $s$ is the limit of the sequence; in the example, $s_n = \frac{1}{2}^n$ and $\lim_{n \to \infty} \frac{1}{2}n = 0$. Similarly, although the function $f(x) = (x - 1)/(x^2 - 1)$ is not defined

for $x = 1$ (where the denominator would be zero), values of $x$ increasingly close to 1 yield values of $f(x)$ increasingly close to $\frac{1}{2}$. Thus, the limit of $f(x)$ as $x$ approaches 1 is $\frac{1}{2}$, which is symbolized as $\lim_{x \to 1} f(x) = \frac{1}{2}$. Limits are the basis of differential and integral CALCULUS.

**limited liability,** limitaton on the liability of a limited company for the company's debts. The company may be limited by share, where the shareholder is liable for the value of his or her investment; or it may be limited by guarantee, where the shareholder is liable for a predetermined sum. Limited liability developed in the 19th cent., in order to encourage people to invest in companies without risking their personal assets. It is usually confined to companies, though limited partnerships may be created, as long as one of the partners remains fully liable for the partnership's debts.

**limner,** the work of untrained, generally anonymous artists in the American colonies. Their work often showed flat, awkward figures in richly detailed costumes and landscape settings. The limner tradition extended into the 19th cent.

**Limoges,** city (1982 pop. 144,082, agglomeration 171,689), capital of Haute-Vienne dept., W central France, on the Vienne R. A Roman town, it was famous for its enamel-making by the 12th cent. Local supplies of kaolin provided a basis for the later porcelain industry established in the 18th cent. A new university was opened in 1968 and engineering industries have been set up as a result of government decentralization policies. There is a fine 13th–16th-cent. Gothic cathedral and museums of chinaware and enamels.

Limoges porcelain dish

**Limon, José,** 1908–72, American dancer, teacher and choreographer; b. Mexico. After an early career with the Humphrey, Wiedman Company he founded his own company in 1947, one of the leaders of its time. He was responsible for the development of many of Doris HUMPHREY's ideas and movement theories, and was considered one of the greatest dramatic male dancers. See also MODERN DANCE.

**limonite,** yellowish to dark brown mineral [FeO(OH) · $n$H$_2$O] ocurring worldwide in deposits formed by the alteration of other minerals containing iron. It is used as a pigment (in ochre) and as an ore of IRON. Both iron rust and bog iron ore are limonite.

**Limousin** (leemooh‚zanh, leemaw‚aanh), region and former prov., central France, in the NW of the MASSIF CENTRAL. A tableland of old crystalline rocks, it rises to over 800m in the Plateau de Millevaches. Upland pastures support livestock and the Limousin breed of cattle is exported throughout France and abroad. A long history of temporary migration has been succeeded by permanent migration and the uplands are amongst the most sparsely-populated parts of France. The viscounty of LIMOGES, the historic capital, passed under English rule in 1152 and Limousin thereafter was a scene of struggles between English and French for possession. Recovered for France by Du Guesclin, it finally passed to the French crown in 1589.

**limpet,** GASTROPOD mollusc with a flattened conical shell and a muscular foot with which it clings tightly to rocks. Several similar unrelated species of mollusc are called limpets. They are found mainly in cooler waters of the Atlantic and Pacific oceans. They are edible, and piles of shells of the common limpet (*Patella vulgata*) have been found in very early settlements.

**Lincoln,** US city (1984 est. pop. 180,000), state capital of Nebraska; inc. 1869. It is the rail, trade, and industrial centre for a large grain and livestock area. Many insurance companies have home offices there.

**Lincoln,** cathedral city and county town (1981 pop. 79,980) in Lincolnshire, E England, on R. Witham. Industries found within the town include engineering and the manufacture of agricultural equipment. The town is built on the site of the Roman town of Lindum. The cathedral was built mainly in the 13th cent. Among the many other historic buildings within the town are the Norman Castle (begun by William the Conqueror) and the Jew's House. In World War I the first British tanks were made in Lincoln.

**Lincoln, Abraham,** 1809–65, 16th president of the US (1861–65). Born in a log cabin in the backwoods of Kentucky, Lincoln was almost entirely self-educated. In 1831 he settled in New Salem, Illinois, and worked as a shopkeeper, surveyor, and postmaster while studying law. In 1834 he was elected to the state legislature, and in 1836 he became a lawyer. He served one term (1847–49) in Congress as a Whig. In 1856 he joined the new REPUBLICAN PARTY. He ran (1858) for the Senate against Stephen A. DOUGLAS, and in a spirited campaign he and Douglas engaged in seven debates. Lincoln was not an ABOLITIONIST, but he regarded slavery as an evil and opposed its extension. Although he lost the election, he had by now made a name for himself, and in 1860 he was nominated by the Republicans for president. He ran against a divided Democratic party and was elected with a minority of the popular vote. To the South, Lincoln's election was a signal for secession. By Inauguration Day seven states had seceded, and four more seceded after he issued a summons to the militia. It is generally agreed that Lincoln handled the vast problems of the AMERICAN CIVIL WAR with skill and vigour. Besides conducting the war, he faced opposition in the North from radical abolitionists, who considered him too mild, and from conservatives, who were gloomy over the prospects of success in the war. His cabinet was rent by internal rivalries, and the progress of the war went against the North at first. In 1863 he moved to free the slaves by issuing the EMANCIPATION PROCLAMATION, but preserving the Union remained his main war aim. His thoughts on the war were beautifully expressed in the GETTYSBURG ADDRESS (1863). In 1864 Lincoln ran for reelection against George B. McClellan and won, partly because of the favourable turn of military affairs after his appointment of Gen. U.S. GRANT to command all the Union armies. Lincoln saw the end of the war but did not live to implement his plan for RECONSTRUCTION. On 14 Apr. 1865, while attending a play at Ford's Theatre in Washington, District of Columbia, he was shot by the actor John Wilkes Booth (see under BOOTH, JUNIUS BRUTUS). He died the next morning. As time passed a full-blown 'Lincoln legend' grew, and he became the object of adulation and a symbol of democracy.

**Lincoln Memorial,** monument in Washington, DC, US, built 1914–17. Designed by the American architect Henry Bacon and styled after a Greek temple, it houses a heroic statue of Abraham LINCOLN by Daniel Chester FRENCH and two murals by the American painter Jules Guérin.

**Lincolnshire,** county in E England (1984 est. pop. 556,600), 5915 km² (2307 sq mi), bordering on the North Sea in the E. The county town is LINCOLN. The Lincoln Wolds form an upland area in the E of the county, but most of the land is relatively flat and low-lying. In the SE the county borders on The Wash and there is a large area of fenland. The major rivers in the county are the Witham, Welland, and Nene. Mixed agriculture is an important economic activity in much of the county. Boston is a port town, and Lincoln and Grantham are the other main urban areas.

**Lincoln's Inn:** see INNS OF COURT.

**Lind, Jenny,** 1820–87, Swedish soprano. She became a noted operatic singer in Europe before 1849, when she abandoned opera for concert and oratorio until 1870. Known as the 'Swedish nightingale', she was one of the great coloraturas of her period.

**Lindbergh, Charles Augustus,** 1902–74, American aviator. While serving as a pilot in the US Air Mail service, he specified and bought the monoplane Spirit of St Louis, in which he flew from New York to Paris on 20–21 May 1927—the first nonstop solo flight across the Atlantic (it took 33 hrs 30 mins). He returned home to unprecedented acclaim, which led to an upsurge of development of air transport in the US. With his wife, Anne Spencer Morrow, a writer and also a pilot, he surveyed the Great Circle air route from New York to Europe via Greenland and Iceland. After the kidnapping and murder of their son in 1932, the Lindberghs went to live in England, then France. Convinced of the power of the German air force, Lindbergh opposed US entry into the war he foresaw as inevitable. He did, however, serve in the US air force in the Pacific in World War II. After the war he was a director of Pan-American World Airways.

**linden:** see LIME TREE.

**Lindisfarne,** England: see HOLY ISLAND.

**Lindow Man,** an extremely well-preserved IRON AGE body found in a Cheshire peat bog in 1984. Because of its recent recovery, it has been the most intensively studied of all the bog burials of Europe. Lindow Man was intentionally killed, possibly in the course of a ritual.

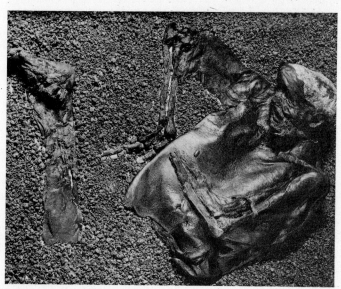

Lindow Man

**Lindsay, Norman,** 1879–1969, Australian artist and writer. A member of a large and influential family of prominent artists, he was radical in his views on creative sexual and aesthetic freedom. His novels include the originally banned *Redheap* (1930), *Saturdee* (1933), and one of Australia's favourite children's books, *The Magic Pudding* (1918).

**lineage,** a unilineal DESCENT group based on patrilineal or matrilineal descent from an apical ancestor/ancestress. The lineage is a key concept in the work of the British structural functionalist anthropologists who stressed the central importance of such groups in social organization, particularly in African tribal societies. They defined lineage groups as localized, corporate, exogamous descent groups and argued that the most important political, jural, and religious processes were undertaken by groups recruited through lineage ties. Further, it was argued that it was only on the basis of unilineal principles that corporate groups could be constructed in KINSHIP-based societies. Through unilineal descent, groups of fixed and unambiguous membership and of very different sizes could be created according to the generation of the ancestor from whom common descent was traced. Such groups would range from the very small, usually co-residential DOMESTIC GROUP to huge groups recruited on the basis of a shared ancestor several generations back. The principles of unilineal descent were also seen as central to the value system in such societies. It has subsequently been argued that these explanations both ignored the importance of other kinds of kinship ties, and represented idealized models rather than the empirical reality they claimed to represent. Marxist anthropologists working in similar ethnographic areas have argued for a lineage mode of production—a subsistence-based system of production in which the primary producing units are domestic groups headed by elders who crucially control the system of marriage exchanges and through this control the labour of the younger men and of women; such systems are thus seen as class systems, the elders controlling access to the means of production and reproduction and exploiting the labour of junior men and women.

**Linear B,** a syllabic script found on clay tablets at Knossos, Pylos, and other sites on Crete dating from the Mycenean supremacy (c.1400–1100 BC). It was deciphered by the English architect Michael Ventris (1922–56) who realized that it represented an early form of Greek. Another syllabic script found on clay tablets in Crete but from earlier, Minoan sites (c.1700–1400 BC) is Linear A, which has not been deciphered.

**linear motor,** an electric motor used to generate a thrust on one body moving parallel to another body. In transport, typically a linear motor consists of an array of coils mounted on a vehicle body carrying currents which generate a travelling electromagnetic field. This field generates a thrust when it interacts (a) with a conductor mounted on the track in which currents are induced (the linear induction motor) or (b) with a set of coils energized separately, such that their field is locked onto the travelling wave (the linear synchronous motor). Linear motors are used for propulsion in vehicles supported by MAGNETIC LEVITATION.

**linen,** fabric or yarn made from FLAX, probably the first vegetable FIBRE known. Linen fabric dating from 5000 BC has been found in Egyptian tombs. Egyptian, Greek, and Jewish priests wore linen to symbolize purity. Brought to N Europe by the Romans, it became the chief European textile of the Middle Ages. French HUGUENOTS carried the art of working flax to Ireland, still a major producer of fine linen. Power LOOMS were first used to weave linen in 1812, but many textile inventions were not applicable to linen thread because its inelasticity made it break readily. Thus the expense of linen weaving relative to that of cotton limits its use. It is woven into fabrics ranging from heavy canvas to sheer handkerchief linen.

**lingua franca,** an auxiliary language, usually hybrid, that is used over an extensive area by people speaking different and mutually unintelligible tongues, in order to communicate with one another. Such a language is used primarily for commercial purposes. Examples are PIDGIN English, Swahili, and Chinook jargon. The original Lingua Franca was employed in Mediterranean commerce in the Middle Ages; its name, meaning 'language of the Franks', came about because Arabs used to call Western Europeans 'Franks'. See also INTERNATIONAL LANGUAGE.

**linguistics,** systematic and objective study of LANGUAGE, covering structure (GRAMMAR, PHONETICS, SEMANTICS, morphology) as well as the role of language in human behaviour and the history of relations between one language and another. Interest in language led independently to linguistic enquiry in many earlier civilizations. By the 4th cent. BC a strong discipline of linguistic study had developed in India and continued, unknown in the West until the 19th cent. Philosophical debate on the nature of language is first recorded in Greece in the 5th–4th cent. BC and was closely followed by linguistic analysis to provide a consistent descriptive grammar for Greek. This was adapted and developed by the Romans for LATIN and so spread throughout Western Europe. During the 13th and 14th cent. *speculative grammar* attempted to provide a comprehensive synthesis of language, thought, and objective reality. The RENAISSANCE witnessed the discovery of many previously unknown languages and their analysis was prompted by the need for translations of the Bible during the Reformation. In the 17th and 18th cent. the philosophical debate between language and thought, and linguistics and logic, was a predominant area of study in Western Europe. The *Grammaire générale et raisonnée* of PORT ROYALE was an attempt at such a synthesis. By the 19th cent. the areas of historical and comparative linguistics had become prominent with the discovery of SANSKRIT, the establishment of the INDO-EUROPEAN language family, and attempts to classify and compare other language groups. During the 20th cent. the emphasis changed to descriptive and theoretical linguistics. The recognition of the AMERICAN INDIAN LANGUAGES in the US led to the development of anthropological linguistics (see SAPIR) and, coupled with behavioural psychology, to the school of linguistics known as American Structuralism. STRUCTURALISM used in a slightly different sense was pioneered by Ferdinand de SAUSSURE who believed in language as a systematic structure linking thought and language output. Throughout Europe various schools of linguistic thought developed, perhaps the most influential being the PRAGUE LINGUISTIC CIRCLE which continued to influence

linguistics in both Europe and the US well after World War II. A radical change in the direction of linguistics is linked with CHOMSKY who developed a model of language known as TRANSFORMATIONAL–GENERATIVE GRAMMAR. His concept of an innate predisposition to acquire language and the universality of underlying structures common to all languages set the trend towards a cognitive approach to linguistic research which still pertains today. As the subject has developed it has diversified into specialized fields, notably sociolinguistics, psycholinguistics, and child language development.

**Linna, Väinö,** 1920–, Finnish novelist. His best-known works are *The Unknown Soldier* (1954), a highly controversial novel about the Russo-Finnish War, and his trilogy *Here Under The North Star* (1959–62) about Finnish independence in 1918.

**Linnaeus, Carolus,** 1707–78, Swedish botanist and taxonomist. He is considered the founder of the binomial system of nomenclature and the originator of modern scientific CLASSIFICATION of plants and animals. In *Systema naturae* (1735) and *Genera plantarum* (1737) he presented and explained his classification system, which remains the basis for modern taxonomy. His more than 180 works also include *Species plantarum* (1753), books on the flora of Lapland and Sweden, and the *Genera morborum* (1763), a classification of diseases.

**Linnell, John,** d. 1796, English furniture designer and cabinetmaker. Many of his designs were in the ROCOCO style but most of his furniture is neo-classical, many pieces being made to the designs of Robert ADAM; much of the furniture at Osterley Park is attributed to him. He had a large and fashionable clientele.

Gilt wood armchair, designed by John **Linnell**, from the state bedchamber at Osterley

**Linotype:** see PRINTING.

**linseed oil,** amber-coloured oil extracted from linseed, the seed of the FLAX plant. The oil obtained from hydraulically pressed seeds is pale in colour and practically odourless and tasteless. Oil that has been boiled or extracted by application of heat and pressure is darker, with a bitter taste and unpleasant odour. Linseed oil is used as a drying oil in paints and VARNISHES and in making linoleum, oilcloth, and certain inks. See also FATS AND OILS.

**Linz,** city (1981 pop. 199, 910), capital of Upper Austria, NW Austria, a major port on the Danube R. Manufactures include iron and steel, machinery, and textiles. A Roman settlement, it became (15th cent.) a provincial capital of the Holy Roman Empire. Anton BRUCKNER was organist at the 17th-cent. baroque cathedral. Other historic buildings include the Romanesque Church of St Martin (8th cent.).

**lion,** large carnivore (*Panthera leo*) of the CAT family, found in open country in Africa, with a few surviving in India. The tawny-coated male lion usually has a long, thick mane and may reach 2.7 m (9 ft) in length and 180 kg (400 lb) in weight. Lions live in prides of up to 30 individuals. Females do most of the hunting, often as a team, preying on zebra, antelope, and occasionally domestic livestock.

**Lipari Islands** or **Aeolian Islands,** group of inhabited volcanic islands, 177 km² (44 sq mi), pop. c.12,000, off the N coast of Sicily, Italy. The principal islands are Lipari, Vulcano, Salina, and Stromboli. The latter is the most active of the group, rising to over 900 m (3000 ft). Pumice is quarried and grapes are grown on terraced hillsides.

**Lipchitz, Jacques** (‚lipshits), 1891–1973, French sculptor; b. Lithuania. Associated with the cubists (see CUBISM), he originated vibrant skeletal constructions, and then transparent sculptures. During the late 1930s allegories of the political struggle of Europe preoccupied him, e.g., *The Rape of Europa.* His later sculpture includes *The Spirit of Enterprise* (Fairmont Park, Philadelphia) and his celebrated semi-automatics masses of clay or plasticine moulded underwater.

**Li Peng,** 1928–, premier of China (1988–). He is the adopted son of Zhou Enlai and Deng Yingchao. Educated in Moscow, he has served as minister of power, minister of the state education commission, and vice-premier. He has a reputation for being a technocrat and reformer.

**lipids,** natural substances present in living systems; also known as fats. Lipids are insoluble in water but soluble in organic solvents, e.g., alcohol and ether. Major classes of lipids include simple lipids (animal and vegetable FATS AND OILS, and waxes); compound lipids (including glycolipids, phospholipids, and lipoproteins); and derived lipids (especially STEROIDS). The fat-soluble vitamins (see VITAMINS AND MINERALS) can also be classified as lipids.

**Lippi,** two 15th-cent. Italian painters. **Fra Filippo Lippi,** c.1406–69, called Lippo Lippi, was one of the foremost Florentine painters of the early RENAISSANCE. He may have studied under MASACCIO, and his graceful narrative style influenced northern Italian painters. He is known for his many easel paintings, e.g., *Virgin Adoring the Christ Child* (1452; Uffizi, Florence) and *Madonna with Saints* (1437; Louvre, Paris). His most important works are the FRESCO paintings of the lives of St Stephen and St John the Baptist (1452–65; Prato cathedral). His son, **Filippino Lippi,** c.1457–1504, studied under BOTTICELLI. He completed Masaccio's frescoes in the Brancacci Chapel, Florence in 1484. His later works, such as the dramatic frescoes of St John and St Philip (1495–1502; Santa Maria Novella, Florence), were greatly influenced by Botticelli and echo the expressive line and emotional power of his late works.

**liqueur,** strong alcoholic beverage made of nearly neutral spirits flavoured with herbs, fruits, or other materials, and usually sweetened. The alcoholic content ranges from c.27% to 80%. Cordials are prepared by steeping fruit pulps or juices in sweetened alcohol. Well-known liqueurs include Benedictine, Chartreuse, cherry brandy, Cointreau, crème de menthe, Grand Marnier, kirsch, and kümmel.

**liquid:** see STATES OF MATTER.

**liquid crystal,** liquid whose component particles—atoms or molecules —tend to arrange themselves with a degree of order far exceeding that of ordinary liquids and approaching that of solid crystals. As a result, liquid crystals have many of the optical properties of solid crystals. Moreover, because its atomic or molecular order is not as firmly fixed as that of a solid crystal, a liquid crystal can be easily modified by electromagnetic radiation, mechanical stress, or temperature, with corresponding changes in its optical properties. This characteristic has made possible

Fra Filippo **Lippi,** *Virgin Adoring the Christ Child,* 1452. Galleria Uffizi, Florence.

liquid crystal displays (LCD) such as those used on some digital clocks and watches, electronic calculators, and personal computers.

**liquorice,** European, blue-flowered perennial (*Glycyrrhiza glabra*) of the PULSE family; also, the sweet, black substance obtained from its roots, used medicinally and as a flavouring mainly in sweets. It is cultivated chiefly in the Near East.

**Lisbon,** Port. *Lisboa,* city (1984 pop. 807,937, Greater Lisbon, 1,707, 500), W Portugal, capital of Portugal on the Tagus R. near the Atlantic Ocean. Lisbon is Portugal's largest city and its cultural, administrative, commercial, and industrial centre. It is set on seven terraced hills and has one of the best harbours in Europe. Its manufactures include textiles, chemicals, and steel. Held by Rome from 205 BC, it fell (714) to the MOORS, who were expelled in 1147. It became the capital c.1260 and reached its height in the 16th cent. with the establishment of Portugal's empire. Earthquakes, notably in 1755, have destroyed many of the city's old buildings, but some remain, e.g., the Castelo de São Jorge, the Church of St Roque, and the monastery at Belém. The old quarter, the picturesque Alfama, surrounds the 12th-cent. cathedral (rebuilt later).

**Lisburn,** town (1981 pop. 40,391) in district of Lisburn, N Ireland, 13 km (8 mi) SW of BELFAST, on R. Lagan. It is an industrial town, with varied manufacturing industry. The linen industry was established here in the late 17th cent. by the Huguenots.

**Lismore,** city (1986 pop. 24,896), New South Wales, E Australia. The centre is a rich dairy industry in the fertile North Arm of the Richmond R.; the area is prone to extensive flooding.

**LISP:** see PROGRAMMING LANGUAGE.

**Lissitzky, El (Eliezer Markowich),** 1890–1947, Russian painter and sculptor. A friend of CHAGALL, he worked in a style that combined CUBISM and FUTURISM with the Russian folk-art tradition. In 1918 he joined Chagall at Vitebsk art school as professor of architecture and graphic art. He met

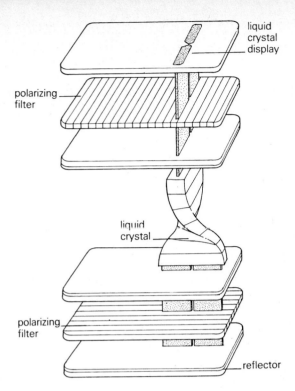

Liquid crystal display

MALEVICH there in 1919 and became a leading figure in Russian CONSTRUCTIVISM. He produced a book *The Story of Two Squares* which was influential in the development of modern typography. After organizing an exhibition of Russian art in Berlin in 1922, he met and collaborated with Van Doesburg, MOHOLY-NAGY, and GABO, and returned to Russia in 1928.

**Lister, Joseph,** 1st **Baron Lister of Lyme Regis,** 1827–1912, English surgeon. He introduced to surgery the principle of antisepsis, an outgrowth of Louis PASTEUR's theory that bacteria cause infection, and he carried out (1865) the first modern surgical operation. Using carbolic acid as an antiseptic agent in conjunction with heat sterilization of instruments, he went on to decrease dramatically post-operative fatalities. He also developed absorbable ligatures and the drainage tube, both now in general use for wounds and incisions.

**Liszt, Franz,** 1811–86, Hungarian composer. A revolutionary figure of romantic music, acknowledged as the greatest pianist of his time, he studied with CZERNY and lived in Parisian artistic circles (1823–25), enthralling audiences with his expressive, dramatic playing. Liszt taught most of the major pianists of the next generation. In his compositions he favoured programme music, originating the SYMPHONIC POEM, e.g., *Les Préludes* and *Mazeppa* (both: 1856). In his Sonata in B Minor (1853) he developed the technique of transformation of themes and thereby changed the concept of the SONATA form. He influenced Richard WAGNER and Richard STRAUSS. His piano works include six Paganini Études (1851); concertos; and 20 Hungarian Rhapsodies. The music of his last years looked forward to many characteristics and techniques of 20th-cent. composers. As well as being a bold innovator, Liszt was a most generous and cosmopolitan person.

**literacy,** the ability to read and write. These abilities are measured and defined differently across time and place, and the distribution of literacy has varied by country and locality. For Britain evidence is scanty before the mid-19th cent., before then relying on marriage registers to show how many brides and grooms could sign their names. Early industrial England had a literacy rate of under two-thirds for men, and nearly a half for women. The trend was upwards for men and women through the late 19th and 20th cent. Estimates now relate to adult literacy, functional literacy, reading age, and similar concepts. Variations have depended on the extent of schooling, occupational changes, the position of women in the family and the labour market, and a number of economic and cultural factors. Intensive literacy campaigns have been waged by many governments, e.g., Cuba, Tanzania, and Nicaragua, particularly since

World War II. Adult education and adult literacy have been a specific responsibility of UNESCO, which conducted an Experimental World Literacy Programme from 1967 to 1974. An adult literacy campaign in the UK gave tuition to some 200,000 people in the decade from 1975.

**lithium** (Li), metallic element, discovered in 1817 by J.A. Arfvedson. A soft, silver-white, corrosive member of the ALKALI METALS, lithium is the least dense metal. Lithium compounds are used in lubricating greases, special glasses, and ceramic glazes; as brazing and welding fluxes; and in the preparation of plastics and synthetic rubber. Lithium is also a medical antidepressant used to treat manic depressive psychosis and control mania. It can prove dangerously toxic in high doses and blood tests are taken to monitor lithium levels during long-term therapy. See ELEMENT (table); PERIODIC TABLE.

**lithography,** type of planographic or surface printing used as an art process and in commercial PRINTING, where the term is synonymous with offset printing. Lithography was invented c.1796 by Aloys SENEFELDER, and the Bavarian limestone he used is still considered the best material for art printing. Lithography is based on the immiscibility of oil and water. A drawing is made in reverse on the ground (flat) surface of the stone with a crayon or ink that contains soap or grease. The image produced on the stone will accept printing ink and reject water. Once the grease in the ink has penetrated the stone, the drawing is washed off and the stone kept moist. It is then inked with a roller and printed on a lithographic press. As a process, lithography is probably the least restricted in its applications, allowing a wide range of tones and effects. Several hundred fine prints can be taken from a single stone. The medium was employed by many 19th-cent. artists, including DELACROIX, DAUMIER, DEGAS, WHISTLER, REDON, and TOULOUSE-LAUTREC. The medium remains popular with contemporary artists. **Photolithography** is frequently used in the commercial reproduction of art works. In this process, a photographic negative is exposed to light over a gelatin-covered paper, and those portions of the gelatin that are exposed become insoluble. The soluble portions are washed away, and the pattern to be printed is transferred to a stone or metal plate. In colour lithography or colour photolithography, a stone or plate is required for each colour used.

**Lithuania,** constituent republic (1985 pop. 3,572,000), 65,201 km² (25,174 sq mi), W European USSR. It borders on the Baltic Sea (W); Latvia (N); Belorussia (E); and Kaliningrad oblast (SW). The capital is VILNIUS. Lithuania is a plain, with numerous lakes and swamps drained by the Nemen R. and its tributaries. Chief agricultural products include meat, eggs, sugar beet, and flax. Forests cover about one-sixth of its area, and the timber industry is important. Among the other industries are heavy engineering, shipbuilding, textiles, chemicals, and food-processing. Vilnius has one of the largest airports in the USSR, and the Baltic Sea port of Klaipeda is of national importance as a nonfreezing harbour and fishery base. The majority of the population is Lithuanian; minorities include Russians and Poles. The Lithuanians may have settled along the Nemen as early as 1500 BC. In the 13th cent., to protect themselves against the Livonian and Teutonic knights, they formed a strong, unified state which, by absorbing neighbouring Ruthenian principalities, became one of the largest in medieval Europe, stretching from the Baltic to the Black Sea. Between 1386 and 1569, Lithuania was joined to Poland under the personal union of the Jagiellonian dynasty, and from 1569 to 1793 became part of the constitutional Commonwealth of Poland–Lithuania. During the four centuries of union with Poland, most of the upper classes were polonized. From 1793 to 1918, Lithuania passed under Czarist rule. Indpendence from 1918 to 1940 was declared in the NW area, centred on Kaunas, whereas Vilnius remained under Polish control. During WORLD WAR II, Lithuania was twice occupied by the Soviets, 1940–44 and 1944, and once by the Nazis (1941–44). During the German occupation, Lithuania's large Jewish community was virtually exterminated. Lithuania's incorporation into the USSR is not recognized in international law. There has been an upsurge of nationalism there and in other Baltic states since 1988.

**Lithuanian,** a language belonging to the Baltic subfamily of the Indo-European family of languages. See LANGUAGE (table).

**litmus,** organic dye usually used as an indicator of acidity or alkalinity (see ACIDS AND BASES). Naturally pink in colour, it turns blue in alkaline solutions and red in acids. Litmus paper is paper treated with the dye.

**litre:** see WEIGHTS AND MEASURES, tables.

**Little Entente,** loose alliance formed in 1920–21 by Czechoslovakia, Romania, and Yugoslavia and supported by France. Its aims were to contain Hungary and to prevent the restoration of the HABSBURGS. Romania and Yugoslavia were also members of the Balkan Entente (1934). The general purposes of both ententes were to preserve the territorial status quo and to encourage closer economic ties. The Little Entente was successful until the rise of HITLER in Germany and was ended by the MUNICH PACT (1938).

**Little Rock,** US city (1984 est. pop. 170,000), state capital of Arkansas, a port on the Arkansas R.; inc. 1831. It is the administrative, commercial, industrial, and cultural centre of the state. Agricultural processing, and bauxite and timber industries are important. A river crossing before 1819, Little Rock became territorial capital in 1821. It was a centre of world attention in 1957, when federal troops enforced a school desegregation order.

**Littlewood, Joan,** 1914–, English theatre director. She founded the socialist Theatre of Action in Manchester with the folk-singer Ewan MacColl, but is best known for founding the Theatre Workshop which was eventually based at the Theatre Royal, Stratford East, London. Productions included *The Quare Fellow* (1956) and *The Hostage* (1958) with writer Brendan BEHAN. Probably her most notable production was *Oh What A Lovely War* (1963), devised with and for the company, and later filmed.

**liturgy,** form of public worship, particularly the form of rite or services prescribed by the various Christian churches. The liturgy of the Roman Catholic and Orthodox Eastern churches focuses on the Mass. The Orthodox Eastern Church has several liturgies (e.g., in Greek, Old Slavonic, and Coptic). In the West the Roman liturgy became dominant in the 8th cent. and used the Latin language until vernacular liturgy was introduced after the Second VATICAN COUNCIL (1962–65). In the ANGLICAN COMMUNION the BOOK OF COMMON PRAYER has been normative.

**Litvinov, Maxim Maximovich** (lyit͵veenəf), 1876–1951, Russian revolutionary and diplomat; b. M.M. Wallach. He left Russia after the abortive 1905 Revolution, returning in 1917. As commissar for foreign affairs (1930–39) he obtained US recognition of the USSR and urged joint action by the great powers against fascism. He was ambassador to the US (1941–43).

**Liu Shao-Ch'i:** see LIU SHAOQI.

**Liu Shaoqi** (lyoh show-chee), 1898?–1969, Chinese Communist leader. An expert on organization and party structure, he was chairman and head of state of the People's Republic of China (1959–68). Liu was criticized during the Cultural Revolution (1966–69) and was removed from power in 1968. He was posthumously rehabilitated (1980) and a collection of his writings was published in 1982.

**Liutprand** (lee͵oohtprand), d. 744, king of the LOMBARDS (r.712–44). The first Christian Lombard ruler, Liutprand favoured Roman law and institutions, and centralized power in his kingdom. Under his rule the Lombard kingdom reached its zenith.

**liver,** largest glandular organ of the body. It lies on the right side of the abdominal cavity, beneath the diaphragm, and is made up of four unequal lobes. Liver tissue consists of thousands of tiny lobules, in turn made up of hepatic cells, the basic metabolic cells. The liver is thought to perform over 500 functions involving the DIGESTIVE SYSTEM, EXCRETION, blood chemistry and detoxification, and the storage of vitamins and minerals. Of the liver's many digestive system functions, the production of BILE (for fat digestion) and storage of glucose (see GLYCOGEN) are particularly important.

**Liverpool,** city (1981 pop. 538,809), Merseyside, NW England, on the Mersey R. It is one of Britain's greatest ports and largest cities and a major outlet for industrial exports. Food-processing and the manufacture of glass and chemicals are major industries. Chartered in 1207, the city was once famous for its pottery and its textile industry. It enjoyed world-wide celebrity in the 1960s as the home of the BEATLES.

**liverwort,** small, flowerless, primitive, green land plant (division Bryophyta), characterized by horizontal encrusting growth and related to the MOSSES. Usually growing in moist places, liverworts are considered intermediate between the aquatic ALGAE and the terrestrial mosses and FERNS. It was believed that liverworts could cure diseases of the liver, hence their name.

**Livingstone, David,** 1813–73, Scottish explorer in Africa. While a medical missionary in what is now BOTSWANA (1841–52), he crossed the KALAHARI desert and discovered the ZAMBEZI R. In 1855 he discovered VICTORIA FALLS. He set out to seek the source of the NILE in 1866. H.M. STANLEY went in search of him, finding him in 1871. Stanley then joined him on a journey (1871–72) to the north end of Lake TANGANYIKA. Livingstone died in an African village; his body is buried in Westminster Abbey.

**living will:** see EUTHANASIA.

**Livy** (Titus Livius), 59 BC–AD 17, Roman historian; b. Patavium (Padua). His life work was a beautifully written history of Rome (entitled *Books from the Founding of Rome*) from its founding in 753 BC to DRUSUS (9 BC). Of the original 142 books, 35 are extant.

**Li Xiannian,** 1907?–, Chinese Communist leader. Born of peasant background, he is a survivor of the LONG MARCH. Since the mid 1950s he has held a succession of high posts related to economic and financial matters. He served as president of the People's Republic of China from 1983 to 1988.

**lizard,** REPTILE of the order Squamata, which also includes the SNAKE, distributed worldwide (except for the Arctic and Antarctic) but most common in warm climates. Lizards typically have four legs with five toes on each foot, although a few are limbless, retaining internal vestiges of legs. They also differ from snakes in having ear openings, movable eyelids, and less flexible jaws. Several, most notably CHAMELEONS, undergo colour changes under the influence of environmental and emotional stimuli. Lizards range in size from species under 7.5 cm (3 in) long to the 3-m (10-ft) KOMODO DRAGON, and include IGUANAS, SKINKS, GECKOS, and AGAMAS.

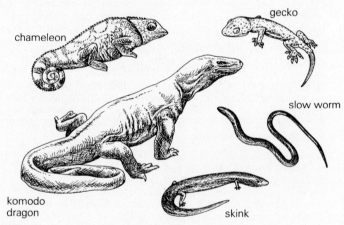

Lizard

**Ljubljana** (͵lyoobliy'ənə), city (1981 pop. 305,211), capital of Slovenia, NW Yugoslavia, on a tributary of the Sava R. It is an important route centre with engineering, electrical and other industries. Originating as a Roman fort, it retains interesting buildings in the Baroque style, and has had a university since 1919.

**llama,** South American domesticated hoofed MAMMAL (*Lama peruana*) of the CAMEL family. It resembles a large, long-eared, long-necked sheep and provides Andes Indians with wool, milk, and meat. Its usefulness as a pack animal is enhanced by its ability to work at exceptionally high altitudes.

**llanos,** extensive areas of lowland savanna grasslands at the eastern and southern edges of the northern Andes. The most extensive area is the llanos of the Orinoco, constituting an area of 1000 by 320 km (621 by 200 mi) between the central highlands of Venezuela and the Orinoco R. In Venezuela this great grassland area traditionally has been ranching country with the migrations of cattle corresponding with the seasonal rains. From these activities has originated the cowboy traditions of the *llaneros* similar to those of the *gauchos* on the Argentine PAMPAS.

**Lleras Camargo, Alberto** (ˌlyeərahs kaˌmahgoh), 1906–, president of COLOMBIA (1945–46, 1958–62). After his first brief term as Liberal president, he became (1948) the first secretary general of the Organization of American States. In 1957 he helped to depose dictator Rojas Pinilla and to institute bipartisan Liberal–Conservative rule, ending 10 years of bloody political strife in the nation.

**Lleras Restrepo, Carlos** (ˌlyeəras resˌtraypoh), 1908–, president of COLOMBIA (1966–70). He was Liberal party leader during Colombia's bloody civil war (1948) and became so again in 1961. His government reduced inflation, diversified the economy, and instituted land reform.

**Llewlyn ap Gruffydd** (loohˌelin ap groohfidh), d. 1282, Welsh prince; last independent ruler of Wales. By 1263 he had recovered much of Wales from the English. He sided with Simon de MONTFORT in the BARONS' WAR and was recognized (1267) by HENRY III as prince of Wales. In 1277 he submitted to EDWARD I, but was killed in a subsequent revolt.

**Lloyd, Harold,** 1893–1971, American film actor. A bespectacled innocent, he blundered into hair-raising situations in such silent comedies as *Safety Last* (1923) and *The Freshman* (1925).

**Lloyd George, David,** 1st **Earl Lloyd-George of Dwyfor,** 1863–1945, British statesman, proud of his Welsh origins. Elected as a Liberal to Parliament in 1890, he served until 1945. He gained a reputation as an anti-imperialist and as the author of far-reaching social reforms, while chancellor of the exchequer (1908–15) under Herbert ASQUITH. They included all age pensions and national insurance. His 1909 budget, which proclaimed a war on poverty, led to the protracted dispute between the COMMONS and the LORDS. Replacing (1916) Asquith as prime minister during WORLD WAR I after serving as Minister of Munitions, he formed a strong war cabinet, waged war aggressively, and played a moderating role in shaping the Treaty of VERSAILLES. His coalition fell (1922) when the Conservatives withdrew. He later (1926–31) led a section of the LIBERAL PARTY while encouraging policy-orientated research on unemployment and other issues, and played a somewhat quixotic part in politics between the formation of the National Government in 1931 and the early months of WORLD WAR II.

**Lloyd's of London,** an association of some 23,000 individual insurance underwriters who provide insurance services. The corporation of Lloyd's itself does not accept insurance liability but sets the regulations by which its members, usually organized into syndicates, may operate. All types of insurance are transacted but the emphasis is on high risk, particularly marine, aviation, and motor insurance. Lloyd's was started by Edward Lloyd in 1688 when merchants, bankers, and underwriters informally carried out their business in a London coffee house. In its early years Lloyd's dealt exclusively with marine insurance and providing shipping information; the daily *Lloyd's List*, which provides shipping news and data, was first published in 1734. At the end of the 1970s, Lloyd's was implicated in a number of financial scandals. Because of this, the Lloyd's Act 1982 more tightly regulated the operations of the company.

**Lloyd Webber, Andrew,** 1948–, English composer and impresario, who, with Tim Rice as lyricist, had an early success with the musicals *Joseph and the Amazing Technicolour Dreamcoat* (1968) and *Jesus Christ Superstar* (1970). Lloyd Webber is a master of the genre, and compositions such as his *Requiem Mass* (1985) are less impressive. The quality of the music and record sales have played an important part in ensuring the phenomenal success of shows such as *Evita* (1976), *Cats* (1981), *Starlight Express* (1984), and *The Phantom of the Opera* (1986).

**Lobachevsky, Nikolai Ivanovich,** 1793–1856, Russian mathematician. Independently of János BOLYAI, he developed (1826) hyperbolic geometry, one type of NON-EUCLIDEAN GEOMETRY.

**Lobatse,** town (1987 pop. 19,034), South-East District, Botswana. On the Cape Town–Bulawayo railway line, it is an industrial centre with a large abbatoir.

**lobbying,** practice of influencing government decisions by agents who serve special interests. The term originated in the US in the 1830s, when agents gathered in the lobbies of Congress and state legislatures to press their causes. Today all major interests in modern democracies, such as business, organized labour, and farmers, maintain permanent lobbies with their national governments. Consumer and pressure-groups also lobby in the public interest or on particular issues. Theorists of democracy hold that such groups offer a means of representation to citizens between elections, and are likely to prove a more effective way of achieving particular aims than attempting to work through one of the political parties.

**lobefin:** see COELACANTH.

**Lobengula,** 1836–94, king (r.1868–94) of the Ndebele, who occupied a region of what is now S ZIMBABWE. The son of MZILIKAZI, he managed to preserve his inheritance for 20 years, until 1888 he unwisely signed the Rudd concession which allowed the occupation of his land by RHODES's British South Africa Company. In 1893 the Ndebele and the Company fought a one-sided war which resulted in the destruction of the Ndebele kingdom and the death of Lobengula.

**Lobito,** city (1970 pop. 59,258), W central Angola, on the Atlantic Ocean. It is Angola's chief port, with such exports as ores, grains, and coffee. Industries include shipbuilding and food processing. Founded (1843) by the Portuguese and built mainly on reclaimed land, the city became a commercial centre after the completion (1929) of the Benguela RR, but declined in the 1970s due to damage of port facilities during the war of independence from Portugal.

**lobster,** large marine CRUSTACEAN with five pairs of jointed legs, the first pair bearing large pincerlike claws of unequal size adapted to crushing the shells of its prey. The dark blue European common lobster (*Homarus gammarus*) and the Norway lobster or Dublin Bay prawn (*Nephrops norvegicus*) range along the European coast from the Arctic circle to the Mediterranean. Both are delicious to eat, the common lobster turning red when it is cooked. Norway lobster becomes scampi.

**local area network** (LAN), a computer network covering a restricted geographic area and usually owned by a single private company, educational establishment, or laboratory. The transmission bandwidth is high compared with wide area networks, typically 10 Mbps (megabits or million bits per sec), with research networks operating at around 100 Mbps. The medium is virtually error free, allowing a simple COMMUNICATIONS PROTOCOL to be used. Since the network is confined to a single geographic site there is no requirement to lease lines from the local PTT (post, telephone, and telegraph service provider), nor do any of the restrictions of PTTs apply. *Distributed computer systems* are built on LANs. These typically consist of PERSONAL COMPUTERS, or more powerful workstations, networked to allow access to shared data storage and expensive high-quality printers, and to allow services such as computer mail to be used within the LAN and across connected wide area networks.

**Local Education Authorities,** the 104 education authorities in England and Wales responsible, within limits laid down by the Secretary of State of the DEPARTMENT OF EDUCATION AND SCIENCE, for the provision of education in their area. Each local authority establishes an education committee for the exercise of its educational responsibilities. LEAs are required to provide primary, secondary, and further education, administer a system of mandatory and discretionary grants for students, provide careers and youth services, and carry out other community obligations. LEAs in the UK employ over half a million full-time teachers in schools and further and higher education, and maintain over 30,000 schools. Their finance derives from the local rates and from the Rate Support Grant, which, since 1966, has replaced other earmarked grants to local authorities from central government.

**Local Group of galaxies:** see GALAXY.

**Locarno Pact,** 1925, agreement reached at Locarno, Switzerland by the UK, France, Germany, Italy, Belgium, Poland, and Czechoslovakia. It guaranteed the demilitarization of the Rhineland and the permanence of Germany's western, though not its eastern, frontiers. The 'spirit of Locarno' was hailed in the West as the start of an era of peace and goodwill, but is often regarded in Eastern Europe as the starting point of the western powers' appeasement of German ambitions.

**Lochner, Stephan** (ˌlokhnə), d.1451, German religious painter of the school of Cologne. His combination of Gothic tradition with a new naturalism, bright colour, and tender sentiment is seen in his best-known work, the Cologne Cathedral altarpiece called the *Dombild* (c.1445), that shows *The Adoration of the Magi*.

**Loch Ness,** lake, 35 km (22 mi) long, N central Scotland, part of the Caledonian Canal. It is ice-free all year and more than 200 m (700 ft) deep.

Stephan **Lochner**, *Dombild*, c.1445. Cologne Cathedral.

**Loch Ness Monster,** name given to supposed large animal inhabitant of Scottish loch, not seeming to fit the description of any known mammal, fish, or reptile. Since the 1930s many sightings, some with photographic evidence, have been claimed. Some types of evidence presented, e.g., footprints and bones, have been proved to be hoaxes. In 1982 sonar equipment gave strong signals of an object, moving deep within the loch, larger than echoes obtained from fish. Since Loch Ness is of geological and hydrological interest, an elaborate expedition titled 'Operation Deepscan' was mounted in 1987 to survey the loch bottom in a detailed manner. Although not primarily aimed to investigate the supposed monster, the equipment used in the survey should have been able to detect such an animal, but no monster was discovered.

**lock, canal:** see CANAL.

**Locke, John,** 1632–1704, English philosopher, founder of British EMPIRICISM. Locke's two most important works, *Essay concerning Human Understanding* and *Two Treatises on Civil Government,* both published in 1690, quickly established him as the leading philosopher of freedom. In the *Essay* he opposed the rationalist belief in innate ideas, holding that the mind is born a blank upon which all knowledge is inscribed in the form of human experience. He distinguished the primary qualities of things (e.g., extension, solidity, number) from the secondary qualities (e.g., colour, smell, sound), which he held to be produced by the direct impact of the world on the sense organs. The primary qualities affect the sense organs mechanically, providing ideas that faithfully reflect reality; thus science is possible. Later empiricists such as HUME and George BERKELEY based their systems largely on Locke's theory of knowledge. In political theory he was equally influential. Contradicting HOBBES, Locke maintained that the original state of nature was happy and characterized by reason and tolerance; all human beings were equal and free to pursue 'life, health, liberty, and possessions'. The state formed by the SOCIAL CONTRACT was guided by the natural law, which guaranteed those inalienable rights. He set down the policy of checks and balances later followed in the US CONSTITUTION; formulated the doctrine that revolution in some circumstances is not only a right but an obligation; and argued for broad religious freedom. Much of the liberal social, economic, and ethical theory of the 18th cent. was rooted in Locke's social-contract theories. In *Some Thoughts Concerning Education* (1693) Locke outlined a practically-oriented education, with respect for children and a curriculum of useful learning based on activity and discovery rather than rules; the book widely influenced 18th-cent. educational thought if not practice. One of the major influences on modern philosophical and political thought, he epitomized the ENLIGHTENMENT's faith in the middle class, in the new science, and in human goodness.

**Lockhart, John Gibson,** 1794–1854, Scottish critic and novelist; son-in-law of Sir Walter SCOTT. As a contributor to *Blackwood*'s he fiercely criticized KEATS, Leigh HUNT and HAZLITT as 'the Cockney School'. Later he was editor of the *Quarterly Review* (1825–53). His *Memoirs of the Life of Sir Walter Scott* (7 vol., 1837–38) is a classic.

**lockjaw:** see TETANUS.

**Lockyer, Sir Joseph Norman,** 1836–1920, English astronomer. One of the first to make a spectroscopic study of the Sun and stars, he devised (1868) a way of observing solar prominences in daylight; he also identified helium in the Sun and applied the name *chromosphere* to the layer of gas around the Sun. He was director (1890–1913) of the Solar Physics Observatory and was the founder and first editor (1896–1919) of *Nature,* considered the world's leading general scientific periodical.

**locomotive,** vehicle used to a pull or push a train of unpowered RAILWAY cars, coaches, or wagons. The earliest railway vehicles were hauled by humans or horses. In the late 18th cent. Richard TREVITHICK used high-pressure steam in an engine sufficiently light and compact to be portable, and then built the first railway locomotive which ran in 1804. The principal features of the steam locomotive were developed over the next quarter century, the major contribution being made by George STEPHENSON and his son Robert. For example, *Rocket* in 1825 had most of the technical features of the modern steam locomotive such as the

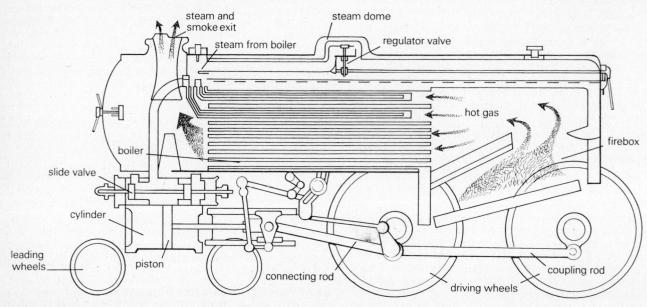

Steam locomotive

multi-tubular boiler and direct mechanical connection between pistons and wheels. As railways developed, train weights and speeds increased, and locomotives grew in size until about 1940 when weights of freight locomotives reached over 500 tonnes and speeds of passenger trains of 200 kph (125 mph) were achieved. Steam locomotives survive in large-scale commercial service only in countries such as China where both labour and coal are cheap. The more efficient electric locomotive, introduced in 1879 by Werner SIEMENS, obtains its power from overhead wires or from a third rail by means of a sliding contact. Because the generation of power is carried out at the power station, electric locomotives have a high power/weight ratio and are therefore ideally suited for high speed trains, or steeply graded lines. However, track electrification is only economic where there is heavy traffic and so on many railways diesel-electric traction, introduced during the 1920s, is used. Here DIESEL engines generate electrical power on board and the wheels are driven by electric motors. Other prime-movers such as gas TURBINES have also been used.

**locust,** in zoology, 11 species of fairly large to large (50–110 mm/2–4½ in), subtropical and tropical species of GRASSHOPPER having, in addition to the normal solitary and usually sedentary phase, a gregarious migratory phase. Under unusually favourable environmental conditions so large a proportion of young nymphs survive that changes both in behaviour and colour occur, through frequent physical contact. Instead of being an inconspicuous green or straw-colour and leading an independent life, the conspicuous (often black and yellow or orange) 'hoppers' aggregate, forming active bands often exceeding 10,000 m² (11,960 sq yd) in area and containing 100–1000 individuals per m² (84–840 per sq yd). Adult swarms can be much larger covering more than 30 km² (11½ sq mi) and numbering in excess of 1000 million locusts, with a total weight of around 1500 tonnes (1476 tons). With the onset of less favourable conditions the population reverts to the solitary phase. Because of the size of swarms and the distance and speed with which they can travel (about 1000 km/625 mi) from southern Morocco to Portugal in October 1945), it was not until the development in the 1950s of air-spraying synthetic INSECTICIDES such as DDT and dieldrin that effective control became possible. Locusts are however still a problem, often because of a lack of international cooperation as much as a shortage of funds for control operations. In many parts of Africa, barbecued locusts are a popular dish.

Locust

**locust,** in botany, deciduous tree or shrub (genus *Robinia* of the PULSE family, native to the US and Mexico. The black locust or false acacia (*R. pseudoacacia*), a popular ornamental, has elongated, pendulous clusters of fragrant white flowers; its durable wood is used for treenails in shipbuilding, for fenceposts, and for turning. The CAROB (genus *Ceratonia*), thought to be the biblical locust tree, and the HONEY LOCUST (genus *Gleditschia*) occur in the same family.

**lodestone:** see MAGNETITE.

**Lodge, Henry Cabot,** 1850–1924, US senator from Massachusetts (1893–1924). He wrote several historical and biographical works and was a member of the House of Representatives from 1887 to 1893. A conservative Republican senator, he welcomed war with Spain in 1898, bitterly criticized Pres. WILSON's peace policy, and opposed US entry into the LEAGUE OF NATIONS. His grandson, **Henry Cabot Lodge, Junior** 1902–85, was also a Republican senator from Massachusetts (1937–44, 1947–53). In 1952 he lost a bid for reelection to John F. KENNEDY. Later he served as US representative to the UN (1953–60). He was ambassador to South Vietnam (1963–64, 1965–67) and West Germany (1968–69), and chief US representative (1969) at the Paris peace talks on Vietnam.

**Lodge, Thomas,** 1558–1625, English writer. His pastoral romance *Rosalynde* (1590) was used by SHAKESPEARE as the basis of his *As You Like It*. Other works include a sonnet sequence, *Phillis* (1593), moral pamphlets, plays, and translations of SENECA and JOSEPHUS.

**Lłódz** (wooch), city (1984 pop. 849,000), central Poland. Lłódź is Poland's second largest city and the centre of its textile industry. Other manufactures include machinery and chemicals. The city was founded in 1820, and quickly grew into the largest textile centre of Eastern Europe.

**Loewi, Otto,** 1873–1961, American pharmacologist; b. Germany. For his discovery of the chemical transmission of nerve impulses he shared with Sir Henry DALE the 1936 Nobel Prize for physiology or medicine. Loewi investigated the physiology and pharmacology of metabolism, the kidneys, the heart, and the nervous system. He was professor of pharmacology at the Univ. of Graz, Austria from 1909 to 1938 (leaving Austria after the Nazi occupation), and at New York Univ. from 1940 to 1961.

**Logan, Mount,** 6050 m (19,850 ft), highest mountain in Canada and second highest in North America, in SW Yukon Territory, at the centre of a vast glacial expanse. Named after Sir William Logan, a Canadian geologist, it was first climbed in 1925.

**logarithm,** the power to which a number, called the base, must be raised in order to obtain a given positive number. For example, the logarithm of 100 to the base 10 is 2, because $10^2 = 100$. Common logarithms use 10 as the base; natural, or Napierian, logarithms (after John NAPIER) use the number e (see separate article) as the base.

**logic,** systematic study of valid inference. Classical, or Aristotelian, logic is concerned with the formal properties of an argument, not its factual accuracy. Aristotle, in his *Organon,* held that any logical argument could be reduced to a sequence of three propositions (two premises and a conclusion), known as a SYLLOGISM, and posited three laws as basic to all logical thought: the law of identity (*A is A*); the law of contradiction (*A cannot be both A and not A*); and the law of the excluded middle (*A must be either A or not A*). Aristotle assumed a correspondence linking the structures of reality, the mind, and language, a position known in the Middle Ages as REALISM. The opposing school of thought, NOMINALISM, represented by WILLIAM OF OCCAM, maintains that language and logic correspond to the structure of the mind only, not to that of reality. John Stuart MILL in the 19th cent. helped to formulate the scientific method of INDUCTION, i.e., movement from specific perceptions to generalizations. Aristotelian logic basically held sway in the Western world for 2000 years, but since the 19th cent. it has been largely supplanted as a field of study by symbolic logic, which replaces ordinary language with mathematical symbols. Symbolic logic draws on the concepts and techniques of mathematics, notably SET theory, and in turn has contributed to the development of the foundations of mathematics. Bertrand RUSSELL, Gottlob FREGE, and Alfred North WHITEHEAD attempted to develop logical theory as the basis for mathematics. See also DEDUCTION.

**logical positivism,** also known as scientific EMPIRICISM, modern school of philosophy that in the 1920s attempted to introduce the methodology and precision of mathematics to the study of philosophy, much as had been done in symbolic logic (see LOGIC). Led by the Vienna Circle, a group including the philosophers Rudolf CARNAP and Moritz Schlick and the mathematician Kurt GÖDEL, the logical positivists held that metaphysical speculation is nonsensical; that logical and mathematical propositions are tautological; and that moral and value statements are merely emotive. The function of philosophy, they maintained, is to clarify concepts in both everyday and scientific language. The movement received its inspiration from the work of FREGE, Bertrand RUSSELL, WITTGENSTEIN, and G.E. MOORE. The Vienna Circle disintegrated in the late 1930s after the Nazis took Austria, but its influence spread throughout Europe and America, and its concept, particularly its emphasis on the analysis of language as the function of philosophy, has been carried on throughout the West.

**logic circuit,** ELECTRIC CIRCUIT whose output depends upon the input in a way that can be expressed as a function in symbolic LOGIC; it has one or more binary inputs (capable of assuming either of two states, e.g., 'on' or 'off') and a single binary output. Logic circuits that perform particular functions are called gates. Basic logic circuits include the AND gate, the OR gate, and the NOT gate, which perform the logical functions *AND, OR,* and *NOT.* A logic circuit, which is mainly used in a digital COMPUTER, can be built from any binary electric or electronic device, including a SWITCH, RELAY, ELECTRON TUBE, solid-state DIODE, or TRANSISTOR.

**Logroño,** city (1981 pop. 110,980), capital of Logroño prov., N Spain. The market centre of a rich fruit- and vine-growing area, the Rioja, it has food and wine-making industries.

**Lohengrin** (ˌlohən-grin), in medieval German story, knight of the Holy Grail, son of Parzival. He rescues and marries Princess Elsa but is doomed to leave her. An epic poem (c.1285–90), ascribed to WOLFRAM VON ESCHENBACH, tells the story. Richard WAGNER based his libretto for the opera *Lohengrin* (1850) on this source.

**Loire** (lwah), longest river of France, flowing c.1015 km (630 mi) in a wide arc N and W to the Atlantic from the Cévennes Mts of SE France. It crosses the MASSIF CENTRAL through deep gorges and, at Orléans, enters a broad valley in the nation's agricultural heartland. It widens at Nantes into an estuary c.55 km (35 mi) long. Important in French history, the Loire is noted for its elegant châteaus.

Chambord Château, the **Loire**

**Loki** (ˌlohkee), in Norse mythology, the personification of evil. He constantly sought to overthrow the gods of ASGARD. His worst exploit was the murder of BALDER.

**Lollardy** or **Lollardry,** medieval English movement for church reform, led by John WYCLIF, whose 'poor priests' spread his ideas in the late 14th cent. Opposed to the great wealth of the church, Lollards taught that the clergy should be poor, that believers could interpret the Bible for themselves, that the doctrine of TRANSUBSTANTIATION was false, and that clerical and monastic celibacy was unnatural. In the early 15th cent. the movement gained momentum and was put down by statute (1401) and by force (1414). The Lollards then went underground and survived until the 16th cent. Many Lollard ideas were reflected by the HUSSITES.

**Lombard, Carole,** 1908–42, American film actress; b. Jane Alice Peters. A sophisticated comedian, she was both glamorous and warm. Her films include *Twentieth Century* (1934), *Nothing Sacred* (1937), and *To Be or Not To Be* (1942).

**Lombard League,** alliance formed in 1167 by the communes of Lombardy against the Emperor FREDERICK I when he tried to assert his authority in Lombardy. Previously, some communes had favoured the emperor, others had favoured Pope ALEXANDER III. The league, which was supported by the pope, defeated (1176) Frederick at Legnano, but after the peace (1183) it tended to split into rival factions. The league was revived in 1226 against the Emperor FREDERICK II, who in 1237 defeated it at Cortenuova. The Lombard communes then took opposing sides, favouring either the popes or the HOHENSTAUFEN.

**Lombards,** an eastern Germanic people. The Byzantines allowed the Lombards to settle (547) in the area of modern Hungary and E Austria. In 568 they invaded N Italy and established a kingdom, with Pavia as its capital. Soon they spread into central and S Italy, where the Lombard duchies of Spoleto and Benevento were set up independently. However, the Byzantines still held much of the Adriatic coast, and the PAPACY kept Rome and the PAPAL STATES. The Lombard kingdom reached its height in the 7th and 8th cent., and paganism and ARIANISM gave way to Catholicism. King LIUTPRAND consolidated the kingdom and reduced Spoleto and Benevento to vassalage. His successors took RAVENNA (751) and threatened Rome (772). CHARLEMAGNE then intervened to defeat the Lombards; he was crowned (774) with the Lombard crown at Pavia. Of the Lombard kingdom only Benevento remained; it was conquered by the Normans in the 11th cent.

**Lombardy,** region (1984 est pop. 8,885,224), c.23,830 km² (9,200 sq mi), N Italy. MILAN is the capital. Lombardy has Alpine peaks and glaciers, and upland pastures that slope to the rich Po valley. Agriculture is important, but Lombardy is also Italy's industrial heart, with such manufactures as steel, textiles, and machinery. In 569 the area became the centre of the kingdom of the LOMBARDS, after whom the region is named. In the 11th cent. autonomous communes arose, and Lombard merchants did business throughout Europe. Spanish rule (1535–1713) was followed by Austrian (1713–96) and French (1796–1814). In 1815 the Lombardo-Venetian kingdom was established under Austrian rule. Lombardy passed to Sardinia in 1859 and in 1861 became part of the new kingdom of Italy.

**Lomé,** city (1983 pop. 366,476), capital of Togo, on the Gulf of Guinea. It is the country's administrative, communications, and economic centre, and the chief port, shipping such commodities as phosphates, coffee, cocoa, and cotton. Its industries include the manufacture of plastics and metal products. Lomé is linked by road, rail, and air to other towns in Togo, and it has an international airport. It was a small village until it became (1897) the capital of the German colony of Togo.

**Lomé Conventions,** trade, economic cooperation, and financial aid agreements between the EUROPEAN COMMUNITY and developing African, Caribbean, and Pacific (ACP) states. The first convention was signed in the Togolese capital in 1975, the second in 1980 and a third in 1984. By 1986 the number of ACP countries involved had reached 66.

**London,** capital city (1981 pop. 6,756,000) of Great Britain and chief city of the COMMONWEALTH, SE England, on both sides of the Thames R. The city is made up of 32 boroughs and the Corporation of London (The City). Under a 1963 Act the boroughs were administered by the Greater London Council until its abolition in April 1986. The City, sometimes known as 'the square mile' (2.6 km²), the historical and commercial core of London, has its own constitution and elects its own lord mayor. London is one of the world's foremost financial, commercial, industrial, and cultural centres, and one of its greatest ports. Little is known of the city prior to Queen BOUDICCA's revolt against the Romans in AD 61. The Roman legions withdrew in the 5th cent. Celts, Saxons, and Danes contested the area, but it was not until 886 that London emerged as an important town under King ALFRED. Under the Normans and Plantagenets the city became self-governing and grew commercially and politically. By the 14th cent. it had become the political capital of England. The reign of ELIZABETH I brought London great wealth, power, and influence as the centre of England's RENAISSANCE in the age of SHAKESPEARE. A plague (1665) was followed by a fire (1666) that virtually destroyed the city. Sir Christopher WREN played a large role in rebuilding London, designing over 50 churches, notably SAINT PAUL'S CATHEDRAL. London grew enormously in the 19th cent., acquiring great prestige in the Victorian era as the capital of the BRITISH EMPIRE. The city was heavily bombed during WORLD WAR II in raids that killed thousands of civilians. Many of the bombed areas were subsequently rebuilt with tall, modern buildings. London's cultural institutions include the BRITISH MUSEUM, NATIONAL GALLERY, TATE GALLERY, and VICTORIA AND ALBERT MUSEUM. Among its landmarks are the remains of the city's Roman walls, BUCKINGHAM PALACE, the Houses of PARLIAMENT, the TOWER OF LONDON, Trafalgar Square, and WESTMINSTER ABBEY.

**London,** city (1980 est. pop. 256,789), SE Ontario, Canada, on the Thames R. An important industrial and commercial centre, with manufactures including electrical goods and automotive parts, the city has streets and bridges named after those of London, England. London was settled in 1826. Earlier (1792), Governor John Simcoe had tried unsuccessfully to have the capital of Upper Canada (now Ontario) located at the site.

**London, Declaration of,** international code of MARITIME LAW, especially as related to war, proposed in 1909. At Britain's invitation, the leading European powers, the US, and Japan assembled in London in 1908. The declaration they issued comprised 71 articles dealing with such controversial points as blockade and contraband. It was primarily a restatement of existing law, but in its high regard for neutrals it represented an advance. The code never went into effect officially.

**London, Jack** (John Griffith London), 1876–1916, American author. A sailor, gold-seeker in the Klondike, and war correspondent, he drew from his own life when creating his romantic yet realistic and often brutal fiction. Among his many popular novels are *The Call of the Wild* (1903), *The Sea-Wolf* (1904), *White Fang* (1905), and the partially autobiographical *Martin Eden* (1909). A socialist, London expressed his views in many tracts and in several novels, e.g., *The Iron Heel* (1907). In later years he was beset by alcoholism and financial problems, and he committed suicide at 40.

**London borough,** London borough, (1981 pop. 230,488), S of R. Thames. It is mainly residential, and includes the districts of Catford, Forest Hill, and Deptford.

**London Bridge,** granite bridge formerly over the Thames in London. It replaced (1831) earlier wood (10th cent.) and stone (12th cent.) bridges. In 1968 it was dismantled and moved to Lake Havasu City, Arizona, US. A new concrete bridge replaced it.

**London Conference,** any of numerous international meetings held in London, England, only some of which are listed here. **1** 1830–31, at which the chief powers of Europe discussed the status of GREECE and later the Belgian revolt against the Dutch king. Greece was recognized as a fully independent nation, and the conference ordered the separation of BELGIUM and the NETHERLANDS. **2** 1838–39, followed up on the 1830–31 conference by preparing the final Dutch–Belgian separation treaty. Luxembourg and Limburg were divided between the Dutch and Belgian crowns. **3** 1908, see LONDON, DECLARATION OF. **4** 1933, also known as the World Monetary and Economic Conference. Its purpose was to check the world depression by stabilizing the world's currencies. It was a total failure. **5** 1954, see PARIS PACTS.

**Londonderry,** city (1981 pop. 86,148), NW Northern Ireland, on the Foyle R. Northern Ireland's second largest city, it is a naval base and seaport and is known for its linen manufactures. It grew up around an abbey founded (546) by St COLUMBA. When it was turned over (1613) to the corporations of the City of LONDON, its name was changed from Derry. The city underwent a 105-day siege by JAMES II in 1689.

**Londonderry,** former county in the N of N Ireland, 2087 km² (814 sq mi), bordering on the Atlantic in the N and Co. Donegal in the W. The county town is LONDONDERRY (Derry City). It is mainly hilly rising to over 2000 m (610 ft) in the Sperrin Mountains. It is drained by the BANN, Foyle and Roe rivers. The coast is deeply indented into Lough Foyle. Textile and metal manufacture and engineering are important industries. Coleraine is the home of the New Univ. of Ulster, situated in the NE of the county.

**London Group,** a group of young artists, formed in 1913. The group had no particular aesthetic doctrine or style; its main function was to organize alternative exhibitions, which it has continued to do up to the 1980s. GILMAN was the first president (1913), SICKERT joined in 1916, Roger FRY in 1917, and Vanessa Bell in 1919.

**London University,** the first university to be created in England after the medieval foundations of Oxford and Cambridge. It was originally created out of University College (est. 1826) and King's College (est. 1831). The University, incorporated in 1836, became a broadly based federal body, bringing in other affiliated COLLEGES (later known as 'schools'). The University created, in 1858, a system of external examinations which enabled students all over the country to obtain its degrees (see DISTANCE LEARNING). In the second half of the 19th cent. it acted as the examining body for affiliated 'university colleges', which became independent UNIVERSITIES in the late 19th and 20th cent. By the 1980s the University had 29 non-medical schools and institutes, 12 undergraduate medical and dental schools, and 15 postgraduate medical schools or institutes; these numbers were considerably reduced in the late 1980s by amalgamations. The University's headquarters are at Senate House in central London, but its component institutions are scattered throughout London and district.

**Londrina,** city (1980 pop. 257,899), S Brazil, in NW of Paraná state. Originally developed in the 1930s by a British company, the small original settlement has grown rapidly into a modern city with skyscrapers and modern steel and concrete public buildings, including a cathedral. Its rapid growth has been due to its proximity to São Paulo and to the regional boom in agriculture, originally coffee and now increasingly soya beans.

**Long, Huey Pierce,** 1893–1935, American politician. As LOUISIANA governor (1928–31), the 'Kingfish' used ruthless and demagogic methods to establish dictatorial power and achieve his programme of social and economic reform. Elected to the US Senate in 1930, he continued to control the Louisiana government from Washington through his hand-picked successor as governor. A presidential aspirant, he gained national support for his 'Share the Wealth' programme. He was assassinated in Baton Rouge, Louisiana, in Sept. 1935. His son, **Russell Billiu Long,** 1918–, served as US senator from Louisiana (1948–87).

**Long, Stephen Harriman,** 1784–1864, American explorer. An army engineer, he explored the upper MISSISSIPPI R. (1817), the ROCKY MTS (1819–20), and the regions of the Platte and Arkansas rivers.

**Long Beach,** US city (1984 est. pop. 379,000), S California, on San Pedro Bay, S of Los Angeles; inc. 1888. Having an excellent harbour, it is a port and tourist centre. Oil (discovered 1921) is found both underground and offshore. Diverse manufactures include aircraft, missiles, and electronics equipment, and there is a large shipyard and dry dock. Points of interest in the city include the ocean liner *Queen Mary*, purchased in 1967 and converted into a museum, hotel, and tourist centre, and Howard HUGHES's wooden aeroplane, the 'Spruce Goose', installed nearby in 1982.

**Longfellow, Henry Wadsworth,** 1807–82, American poet. A professor of modern languages, he taught at Bowdoin College (1829–35) and Harvard Univ. (1836–54). One of the most popular poets of his time, Longfellow created a body of romantic American legends in such long narrative poems as *Evangeline* (1847), *The Song of Hiawatha* (1855), *The Courtship of Miles Standish* (1858), and *Paul Revere's Ride* (1861). Among his best-known shorter poems are 'The Village Blacksmith', 'Excelsior', and 'A Psalm of Life'. His often sentimental and moralizing verse has a unique metrical quality produced by his use of unorthodox, 'antique' rhythms.

**Longford,** inland county in N of Republic of Ireland (1986 pop. 31,491), 1033 km² (403 sq mi), bordering on Co. Roscommon in the W. It is situated in the province of Leinster. The county town is LONGFORD. It is generally low-lying, apart from an area of hills in the N. It is crossed by the Royal Canal and drained in the north by the R. SHANNON. Lough Ree forms the SW border and there are several smaller lakes within the county. There are several boggy areas. Agriculture is the main economic activity, including dairy farming.

**Longford,** county town (1986 pop. 6510) of Co. Longford, Republic of Ireland, on R. Camlin. It is a small market town, whose historic buildings include a 17th-cent. castle and a 19th-cent. Roman Catholic cathedral.

**Longinus,** fl. 1st cent.? AD, Greek writer of *On the Sublime,* a monument of literary criticism defining the qualities that would now be called 'loftiness of style.' It is the source for SAPPHO's second ode.

**Long Island,** in SE New York, largest island of the coterminous US (4463 km²/1723 sq mi). It is 190 km (118 mi) long and 19–32 km (12–20 mi) wide. Its eastern end, site of the American defeat in the **Battle of Long Island** (27 Aug. 1776), is part of New York City. The southern shore, fringed by sandy barrier beaches, is a popular recreation area.

**longitude,** angular distance on the earth's surface measured along the EQUATOR east or west of the PRIME MERIDIAN, which is at 0°. All other points have longitudes from 0° to 180° east or west. Meridians of longitude (imaginary lines drawn from pole to pole) and parallels of LATITUDE form a grid by which any position on the earth's surface can be specified.

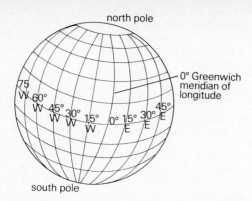

north pole

0° Greenwich
meridian of
longitude

south pole

Longitude

**Long March,** the journey of c.9660 km (6000 mi) undertaken by the Red Army of China in 1934–35. Escaping from Nationalist forces in Jiangxi prov., some 90,000 men and women marched W to Guizhou prov. Led by MAO ZEDONG, they then pushed on to Shaanxi prov. in the north, despite natural obstacles and harassment by Nationalist troops. More than half the marchers were lost in this almost incredible one-year trek.

**Longo, Luigi,** 1900–80, Italian politician. A founder (1921) of the Italian Communist Party, he organized partisan units to fight against the Germans in WORLD WAR II. He was elected to the constituent assembly (1946) and to parliament (1948), and was secretary general of the party (1964–72).

**Long Parliament:** see CHARLES, kings of England; ENGLISH CIVIL WAR.

**longsightedness, hypermetropia** or **hyperopia,** defect of vision in which distant objects are clearly seen but close objects appear blurred. The eyeball is too short or the eye's refractive power is too weak to focus the image of the object on the retina, and the image occurs behind the retina instead (see EYE). The condition, which commonly develops in middle age, can be corrected by spectacles with convex lenses.

**Longstreet, James,** 1821–1904, Confederate general in the AMERICAN CIVIL WAR. His delay in taking the offensive at Gettysburg (see GETTYSBURG CAMPAIGN) is said to have cost Gen. R.E. LEE the battle. He participated in the defence of Richmond and surrendered at APPOMATTOX.

**Longueuil,** city (1980 est. pop. 131,900), S Quebec, E Canada, on the St Lawrence R. The city, now a residential suburb of MONTREAL, is at the eastern end of the Jacques Cartier Bridge. It was originally settled as a seigniory in 1657.

**Longus,** fl. 3rd cent. AD, Greek writer. The popular PASTORAL romance *Daphnis and Chloë,* about the love of a goatherd and shepherdess, is attributed to him.

**Lon Nol,** 1913–85, Kampuchean general and political leader. As premier, he led (1970) a coup that deposed NORODOM SIHANOUK and assumed control of the government. His government was overthrown (1975) by communist guerrillas in a bloody civil war. Lon Nol fled and died in the US 10 years later.

**Lonsdale, Michel** (Michael), 1931–, French film actor. A lugubrious, amused character actor with a distinctive voice, he also acts in English-language films. His films include *The Bride Wore Black* (1968), *The Day of the Jackal* (1973), and *Mr Klein* (1976).

**Lonsdale belt,** boxing award for British champions. First awarded by Lord Lonsdale, the president of the National Sporting Club, to Freddie Welsh after he had won the British lightweight title at the NSC in 1909. Thereafter winners of all British title fights at the NSC were awarded the belt. After the NSC was dissolved, the British Boxing Board of Control maintained the tradition.

**loofah:** see GOURD.

**loom,** frame or machine used for WEAVING; used since 4400 BC. Looms on which the warp threads are stretched horizontally have several fundamental parts: a warp beam, on which the warp threads are wound; heddles, each with an eye through which a warp thread is drawn; harnesses, frames that contain the heddles and that, when raised or

lowered, form a shed between the warp threads for insertion of the weft, or woof; a comblike reed, which separates the warp threads; a beater, which pushes the weft against the cloth after each row of weaving; a breast beam, over which the cloth is wound before being rolled onto the cloth beam; and a brake, which maintains the tension of the warp threads. The shuttle is a tool that carries the weft through the shed. The foot loom operates the harnesses by treadles. Looms on which the warp threads are stretched vertically, e.g., TAPESTRY and NAVAHO INDIAN looms, are more simply constructed. Edmund CARTWRIGHT patented (1785) the first practical power loom, and Joseph Marie JACQUARD perfected (1804) a device using punched cards to weave complicated designs on a power loom.

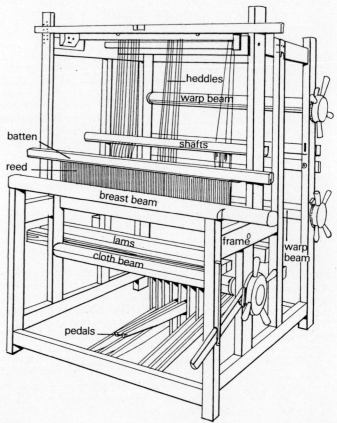

Loom

**loon,** migratory aquatic BIRD, found in fresh and salt water in the colder parts of the Northern Hemisphere. Its strange, laughing call carries for great distances. Expert swimmers and divers, loons walk on the land with difficulty. Their long, sharp beaks are well adapted for catching fish.

**Lope de Rueda** (ˌlohpay day roohˌaydhah), 1510?–65, Spanish dramatist. He is best known for his *pasos* (short farces), based on popular language and themes, e.g., *Las aceitunas* (1548; tr. Incident of the Olives). His work was published posthumously.

**Lope de Vega Carpio, Félix** (ˌlohpay day ˌvaygah ˌkahpyoh), 1562–1635, Spanish dramatist, poet, and novelist, founder of modern drama, one of the great figures of Spain's GOLDEN AGE. As a peasant boy of 12 he wrote the first of some 1800 plays, of which almost 500 are extant. His turbulent life included countless love affairs, scandals, and service in the Spanish ARMADA. His masterworks are such *comedias* as *Peribáñez* (c.1607) and *Fuenteovejuna* (c.1613), which combine the serious and the comic in treating themes of honour, justice, and the conflict between peasant and nobleman. He expounded his dramatic precepts in *El arte nuevo de hacer comedias* (1609; tr. The New Art of Writing Plays): he kept his plays fairly short to hold the audience's attention, invented startling turns of plot, and wrote so as to be understood by ordinary people. In 1614 Lope took religious orders. He completed *La Dorotea* (1632), a novel partly based on his life and amorous adventures, in his last years.

**López, Francisco Solano,** 1826–70, president of PARAGUAY (1862–70). He succeeded his father, Carlos Antonio López (1790?–1862), as *Caudillo* [leader]. A cruel megalomaniac who sought to increase Paraguay's prestige, he waged and lost the War of the TRIPLE ALLIANCE (1865–70). He was killed at the end of the war.

**López de Mendoza, Íñigo, marqués de Santillana:** see SANTILLANA.

**López Portillo y Pacheco, José** (ˌlohpez pawˌteeyoh ee pahˌchaykoh), 1920–, president of MEXICO (1976–82). A lawyer and university professor, he wrote novels and works on political theory. He served (1973–75) as finance minister under Pres. ECHEVERRÍA, whom he succeeded. As president, López Portillo developed Mexico's oil reserves, but faced a national financial crisis at the end of his term. He also served as a mediator in pan-American disputes.

**loran** [*long-range navigation*], long-range, accurate radio navigational system used by a ship or aircraft to determine its geographical position. The measured time-of-arrival difference between signals transmitted from two geographically separated ground stations determines the hyperbolic curve on which the receiver is situated. By taking a similar time-difference reading from a second pair of stations whose curve intersects that of the first pair, a definite geographical fix may be obtained.

**Lorca, Federico García:** see GARCÍA LORCA.

**Lord Chancellor,** a political appointment combining the roles of head of the English legal system, Speaker of the House of Lords, and member of the CABINET. The office originated in the 12th cent., the original holders being ecclesiastics who acted as the king's secretary. The office became the province of a lawyer in the 15th cent. with the rise of the Court of Chancery and the development of EQUITY. The office in modern times involves a number of tasks. The head of the English legal system is responsible for the appointment of magistrates, circuit judges, and High Court judges (except the LORD CHIEF JUSTICE), as well as occasionally sitting as a judge. As Speaker of the House of Lords, he or she plays a legislative role in the Upper House of PARLIAMENT, and as a member of the cabinet is responsible for law reform and changes in the LEGAL PROFESSION. In Scotland, the judicial role of the Lord Chancellor is performed by the Lord Advocate (see SCOTLAND, LEGAL SYSTEM IN).

**Lord Chief Justice,** in England and Wales, a high-ranking judge, president of the Queen's Bench Division of the High Court and ex officio member of the Court of Appeal. The old COMMON LAW courts had chief justices from the earliest times, and the head of the King's Bench adopted the title Lord Chief Justice. However, the position was not officially recognized until 1859. The holder is appointed by the sovereign on the advice of the prime minister and is second only to the LORD CHANCELLOR in the judicial hierarchy. See COURT SYSTEM IN ENGLAND AND WALES.

**Lord Howe Island,** island in the South Pacific Ocean 700 km (450 mi) NE of Sydney, Australia. First settled in 1834, it was proclaimed a botanic reserve in 1883. The island, of outstanding natural beauty, supports a wide diversity of plant and animal species, many of which are extinct elsewhere.

**Lord's,** cricket ground in London, named after Thomas Lord, which is the headquarters of cricket. Lord's and the MARYLEBONE CRICKET CLUB (MCC) were founded in 1787. Three grounds have been known as Lord's: Dorset Square (1787–1810); North Bank (1809–13); and, since 1814, the present site in St John's Wood, which is owned by MCC. The pavilion was built in 1890; A.E. Trott, batting for MCC v. the Australians in 1809, remains the only player to have hit a ball over the top.

**lords-and-ladies:** see ARUM.

**Lord's Prayer** or **Our Father,** principal Christian prayer taught by Jesus to his disciples (Mat. 6.9–13; Luke 11.2–4). English translations used to vary but since the 1970s there has been broad agreement with the versions proposed by the interdenominational International Consultation on English Texts.

**Lord's Supper:** see COMMUNION.

**Lorelei,** rock overlooking the RHINE gorge in the section between KOBLENZ and Bingen, West Germany. This narrow portion of the river was dangerous for navigation before improvements were made in 1834 and shipwrecks were common. HEINE's poem 'Die Lorelei' tells of the fairy who entranced sailors by her singing, causing wrecks.

**Loren, Sophia,** 1934–, Italian film actress; b. Sophia Scicoloni. A beautiful leading lady, she has appeared in such films as *Two Women* (1961; Academy Award), *Yesterday, Today, and Tomorrow* (1963), and *A Very Special Day* (1977).

**Lorentz, Hendrik Antoon,** 1853–1928, Dutch physicist. For his explanation of the Zeeman effect (a change in spectral lines in a magnetic field), which was based on his postulating the existence of the ELECTRON, he shared with Pieter Zeeman the 1902 Nobel Prize for physics. He extended the hypothesis of George Fitzgerald, an Irish physicist, that a body's length contracts as its speed increases (the Lorentz–Fitzgerald contraction) and formulated the Lorentz transformation, by which space and time coordinates of one moving system can be correlated with the known space and time coordinates of any other system. This work influenced, and was confirmed by, Albert EINSTEIN's special theory of RELATIVITY.

**Lorenz, Konrad,** 1903–, Austrian zoologist and ethologist. For his work in ETHOLOGY, particularly his studies of the organization of individual and group behaviour patterns, he shared the 1973 Nobel Prize in physiology or medicine with Karl von FRISCH and Nikolaas TINBERGEN. With Oscar Heinroth, Lorenz discovered imprinting, a rapid and nearly irreversible learning process occurring early in life. His popular book *King Solomon's Ring* (1952) is a very readable account of animal behaviour. His controversial book *On Aggression* (1966) maintains that aggressive impulses are to a degree innate, and draws analogies between human and animal behaviour.

**Lorenzetti,** two brothers who were major Italian painters of the Sienese school. **Pietro Lorenzetti,** c.1280–c.1348, was influenced by Giovanni Pisano (see under PISANO, NICOLA) and by GIOTTO's profound emotion and simple grandeur of form. His works include the magnificent *Birth of the Virgin* (1342; Cathedral Mus., Siena). **Ambrogio Lorenzetti,** d. 1348?, was the more inventive brother. Also influenced by Pisano and Giotto, he had a remarkable ability to depict spatial depth. His greatest work is the cycle of FRESCOES (1337–39) in the Palazzo Pubblico, Siena, which consists of allegories of good and bad government and is a revealing portrait of 14th-cent. Italian life; it contains one of the earliest naturalistic landscapes in Italian art.

One of Ambrogio **Lorenzetti's** frescos from the Palazzo Pubblico, Siena (1337–39)

**Lorenzo de' Medici:** see under MEDICI, family.

**Lorenzo Monaco,** c.1370–1425?, a leading early 15th-cent. Italian painter; b. Piero di Giovanni. His *Adoration of the Magi* (c.1423; Uffizi, Florence), with its elongated figures and rich pageantry, reflects the international Gothic style.

**Loria, Isaac ben Solomon:** see LURIA, ISAAC BEN SOLOMON.

**Lorient,** city (1982 pop. of agglomeration 104,125), port on southern coast of Brittany, NW France. It was founded by Colbert in the 1660s to serve the newly-established French East India Company (see EAST INDIA COMPANY, FRENCH), hence its name (*L'orient* = the east). The naval port was established in 1690 and the naval arsenal continues to be the main employer. There is some fishing from the sheltered estuary.

**Lorrain, Claude:** see CLAUDE LORRAIN.

**Los Alamos,** town (1980 pop. 11,039), north-central New Mexico, US, on a long mesa extending from the Jemez Mts. The site of childhood holidays of J.R. OPPENHEIMER, it was chosen by him in 1942 to be the top-secret location for building the atomic bomb. Government control ended in 1962. The Los Alamos Scientific Laboratory is now operated by the Univ. of California and is a US national historic landmark.

**Los Angeles,** US city (1984 est. pop. 3,097,000), S California, on the Pacific Ocean, with a harbour at San Pedro Bay. The second largest city in the US, it is the shipping, communications, and financial hub of a rich agricultural area. The Spanish visited the site in 1769 and founded a town in 1781. At times the capital of Alta California, it was captured by the US from Mexico in 1846 and incorporated in 1850. Late-19th-cent. railway development and the discovery of oil in the 1890s spurred growth. In the 20th cent., the film industry and, later, the radio and television industry have been important. Today Los Angeles is a major industrial, technological, and research centre, and is particularly important in the area of electronic and aerospace products. Other manufactures include clothing, textiles, machinery, and chemicals. Its metropolitan area, which ranks second only to New York in size, covers five counties and 88,000 km² (34,000 sq mi). Los Angeles is the second most popular metropolitan destination for immigrants to the US, and over half of its population is other than non-Hispanic white. It is the only major US city without a public transport system, (although construction of a metro system has begun after lengthy delays); vehicle density is high, and SMOG has been a major problem. Los Angeles grew by absorbing neighbouring communities; it now surrounds the independent municipalities of Santa Monica, Beverly Hills, and San Fernando. The city, which attracts thousands of tourists yearly, is noted for its parks; for many and varied museums; for its enormous Music Center and Convention Center; for the fossil-rich La Brea Tar Pits; for its ethnic communities; for its climate and beaches; and for its educational institutions, including the Univ. of Southern California and the Univ. of California at Los Angeles. The 1984 Summer Olympics were held in the city.

**Losey, Joseph,** 1909–84, American film director. Originally a theatre director, he drew inspiration from BRECHT. Some of his best films were made after he came to Europe, especially those with Harold PINTER as scriptwriter: *The Servant* (1963), *King and Country* (1964), and *The Go-Between* (1971).

**Losonczi, Pál** (lo‚shontsee), 1919–, Hungarian Communist politician. He was president of Hungary from 1967 until 1987.

**lost tribes:** see ISRAEL, TRIBES OF.

**lost-wax casting:** see CIRE PERDUE.

**Lot,** nephew of ABRAHAM. Warned of Sodom's coming destruction (see SODOM AND GOMORRAH), Lot fled with his family. His wife, disobeying God's orders, looked back at the city and was turned into a pillar of salt. Gen. 11–14; 19.

**Lothair,** Frankish and German emperors. **Lothair I,** 795–855, emperor of the West (r.840–55), was the son and successor of LOUIS I, with whom he served as coemperor after 817. A grandson of CHARLEMAGNE, he was in almost constant territorial wars with his father and his three brothers, Pepin, CHARLES II (Charles the Bald), and LOUIS THE GERMAN. Eventually, the Treaty of Verdun (843) subdivided Charlemagne's empire among the brothers. **Lothair II,** c.1060–1137, of Supplinburg, emperor (r.1133–37) and German king (r.1125–37), was elected monarch against the will of his predecessor, Henry V. With the help of his son-in-law, Henry the Proud, he defeated his rival Frederick of HOHENSTAUFEN and Frederick's brother Conrad (who was elected as anti-king in 1127 as CONRAD III), thereby clearing the way to being crowned emperor. He Christianized NE Germany.

**Lotharingia** (lothə‚rinjeeə), name given to the northern portion of the lands assigned (843) to Emperor of the West LOTHAIR I in the first division of the CAROLINGIAN empire. It comprised roughly the present Netherlands, Belgium, Luxembourg, Lorraine, Alsace, and NW Germany, including Aachen and Cologne. Lothair I, in turn, gave the land to his son King Lothair (d. 869), after whom the kingdom was named. After King Lothair died, Lotharingia was divided between the East Frankish and West Frankish kingdoms (i.e., Germany and France). Throughout history the territories composing Lotharingia have been contested between Germany

and France. Only one part of it, the duchy of Lorraine (the modern form of Lotharingia), has remained a consistent political entity.

**Lothian,** region in SE Scotland (1985 est. pop. 749,591), 1755 km² (684 sq mi), bordering on the Firth of Forth in the N and the North Sea in the E. The administrative centre is EDINBURGH. It was formed in 1975 from E Lothian, W Lothian and Middle Lothian. It is generally low-lying in the N and hilly in the S, where it rises to the Lammermuir Hills. The main rivers are the N and S Esk. Much of the area is cultivated and coal and oil shale is mined.

**Loti, Pierre,** pseud. of **Julien Viaud** (law‚tee), 1850–1923, French novelist. Famous for his descriptions of sensuous and melancholy tropical countries he had known as a naval officer, his most enduring novels, however, are *Pêcheur d'Islande* (1886; tr. An Iceland Fisherman), a tale of Breton fishermen, and *Ramuntcho* (1897), a story of French Basque peasant life.

**Lotophagi:** see LOTUS-EATERS.

**lottery,** scheme for distributing money or other prizes by lot or other method of chance selection to persons who have paid for the opportunity to win. Lotteries were started in Europe in the 15th cent. as a means of raising money in towns to aid the poor or for defence purposes. Most European countries hold state lotteries but they are illegal in the UK. They are widespread throughout the world and are particularly important in Australia where they are used to finance public works.

**Lotto, Lorenzo,** c.1480–1556, Venetian painter. He was an unconventional painter, whose religious works, e.g., *The Annunciation* (1508; Pinacoteca, Recanati) are often highly individual and dramatic. He was a great portrait painter, and his best works, often melancholy in feeling, include the *Andrea Odoni* (1527; Hampton Court Palace, London) and the *Young Man in a Striped Coat* (1526; Castello Sforzesco, Milan).

**lotus:** see WATER LILY.

**lotus-eaters** or **Lotophagi** (lə‚tofə'jie), in Greek mythology, fabulous people from N Africa who lived on the lotus, which brought forgetfulness and happy indolence. They appear in HOMER's *Odyssey* and in TENNYSON's poem 'The Lotus-Eaters'.

**loudspeaker** or **speaker,** device used to convert electrical energy into sound. It consists essentially of a thin flexible sheet called a diaphragm that is made to vibrate by an electric signal from an AMPLIFIER. The vibrations passed on to the air around the speaker produce sound waves. In a common dynamic speaker, the diaphragm has a cone shape and is attached to a wire coil suspended in a magnetic field. A signal current in the suspended coil creates another magnetic field that interacts with the already existing field, causing the coil and the diaphragm attached to it to vibrate. Quality sound systems often employ three different-sized speakers. The largest one, the woofer, reproduces low frequencies; the medium-sized one, called a mid-range speaker, reproduces middle frequencies; the smallest one, called a tweeter, reproduces high frequencies. See also STEREOPHONIC SOUND.

**Louis,** Frankish and German emperors. **Louis I** or **Louis the Pious,** 778-840, emperor of the West (r.814–40), son and successor of CHARLEMAGNE, tried to create a kingdom for Charles (later Emperor CHARLES II), his son by a second marriage, and thereby caused several revolts by his elder sons, Pepin I, LOTHAIR I, and LOUIS THE GERMAN. Eventually he partitioned his empire between Lothair and Charles. **Louis II,** d. 875, emperor of the West (r.855–75) and king of Italy (r.844–75), was the son of Emperor Lothair I. His title as emperor had little meaning since he ruled only in Italy, and even there his reign was constantly challenged by independent Lombard dukes and by Arab invaders of S Italy. He supported his brother Lothair, king of LOTHARINGIA, in a dispute with the pope and briefly (864) occupied Rome; but he subsequently submitted to the pope. He unsuccessfully tried to claim Lotharingia after Lothair's death. **Louis IV** or **Louis the Bavarian,** 1287?–1347, Holy Roman emperor (1328–47) and German king (1314–47), was in constant struggle with the papacy. When he was elected German king, a minority faction elected Frederick the Fair of Habsburg. Louis defeated Frederick in 1322, but the pope refused to recognize or crown him, so Louis had himself crowned emperor by 'representatives of the Roman people'. In 1346 Pope Clement VI declared him deposed and secured the election of CHARLES IV. Louis was successfully resisting his rival when he died in a hunting accident.

**Louis,** Frankish kings and kings of France of the Carolingian, Capetian, Valois, and Bourbon dynasties.

*Carolingian dynasty.* **Louis I:** see LOUIS I under LOUIS, Frankish and German emperors. **Louis II** (the Stammerer), 846–79, son of CHARLES II, emperor of the West, was the king of France (r.877–79). His succession was shared by his sons Carloman and **Louis III,** c.863–82, (r.879–82), who defeated the Normans at Saucourt (881). **Louis IV** or **Louis d'Outremer** [Fr., = Louis from overseas], 921?–54, (r.936–54), was the son of King CHARLES III. He spent his youth in exile in England and was recalled by the nobles under the duke Hugh the Great at the death of King Raoul. His energy and independence displeased Hugh, who waged war on the king but was forced to submit in 950. Louis was succeeded by his son Lothair, whose own son **Louis V** (the Sluggard), c.967–87, (r.986–87), was the last French king of the CAROLINGIAN dynasty. He died childless and was succeeded by HUGH CAPET.

*Capetian dynasty.* **Louis VI** (the Fat), c.1081–1137 (r.1108–37), succeeded his father, PHILIP I. He was almost continuously at war with HENRY I of England in Normandy, and in 1124 resisted an invasion by the Emperor HENRY V. Louis strengthened royal authority by suppressing robber barons, favouring the church, and issuing royal charters to towns to gain their support. His son and successor, **Louis VII** (the Young), c.1120–80 (r.1137–80), married ELEANOR OF AQUITAINE before his accession. He quarrelled with the papacy over an appointee to the archbishopric of Bourges but capitulated in 1144. Louis left (1147) on the Second CRUSADE but returned (1149) when the enterprise failed. In 1152 he had his marriage annulled, and Eleanor's subsequent marriage to Henry Plantagenet (later HENRY II of England) resulted in Henry's claim to Aquitaine and recurrent warfare between Louis and Henry. Louis's son PHILIP II succeeded him. Philip II's son **Louis VIII,** 1187–1226 (r.1223–26), was invited by English lords in rebellion against their king, JOHN, to become king of England. He invaded (1216) England, but was defeated in 1217 and withdrew. He seized (1224) Poitou from the English and resumed (1226) the crusade against the ALBIGENSES. His son and successor, **Louis IX** or **Saint Louis,** 1214–70 (r.1226–70), began his reign under the regency of his mother, Blanche of Castile. In 1240–43 he secured the submission of Poitou and Toulouse, and repulsed a weak invasion by HENRY III of England. Louis left on the Seventh Crusade against Egypt in 1248, but was captured in 1250. Ransomed, he remained in the Holy Land until 1254 to strengthen Christian defences. Returning to France, he reached peaceful agreements with England's HENRY III and with James I of Aragón. In 1270 he undertook the Eighth Crusade, but he died after landing in Tunis. He was succeeded by his son, PHILIP III. Under Louis IX, France enjoyed unprecedented prosperity and peace. He curbed private warfare, simplified administration, improved tax distribution, and encouraged the use of ROMAN LAW. Louis was an ideal Christian monarch, pious and ascetic, yet a good administrator and diplomat. He was canonized in 1297. Feast: 25 Aug. **Louis X,** Fr. **Louis le Hutin** [the quarrelsome], 1289–1316 (r.1314–16), was the son and successor of PHILIP IV. Dominated by his uncle, Charles of Valois, Louis made concessions to the barons in the form of charters. The death soon after birth of his posthumous son, John I, opened the succession to PHILIP V.

*Valois dynasty.* **Louis XI,** 1423–83 (r.1461–83), was the son and successor of CHARLES VII. As DAUPHIN, he was involved in a revolt against his father called the Praguerie (1440), and his constant intrigues led to his exile from court. His measures as king to curb the power of the great nobles aroused (1465) the League of the Public Weal, headed by CHARLES THE BOLD, Francis II of Brittany, and others, against the crown. Louis successfully defended Paris but in Oct. 1465 granted the demands of the rebels. Soon he ignored the settlement, and in 1467 a new coalition against the king was formed by Charles the Bold, now duke of Burgundy, and Francis II, with the support of EDWARD IV of England. Louis forced Francis to sign (1468) a peace, but fell prisoner to Charles, who exacted important concessions from him. After his release, Louis involved himself in English affairs against Edward IV. He aided the restoration of HENRY VI and, after Edward regained the throne, halted Edward's invasion (1475) of France by buying him off. Louis also united the enemies of Charles the Bold and, after Charles's death (1477), took Burgundy, Picardy, Boulogne, Artois, and Franche-Comté from Charles's daughter, MARY OF BURGUNDY. Despite his revocation (1461) of his father's PRAGMATIC SANCTION of Bourges, he intervened freely in church affairs. A born diplomat, Louis checked his foreign and domestic enemies and set up an efficient central administration. He also encouraged industry and expanded trade. Fearing

assassination, he spent his last years in virtual self-imprisonment near Tours. He was succeeded by his son, CHARLES VIII. **Louis XII,** 1462–1515 (r.1498–1515), succeeded his cousin Charles VIII and ensured the continuation of the personal union of France and Brittany by having his first marriage annulled and marrying ANNE OF BRITTANY, Charles VIII's widow. Thereafter Louis tried to assert his claims in Italy (see ITALIAN WARS). He conquered Milan and Genoa, but failed to secure Naples, which he had conquered with the Spanish king FERDINAND II. His Italian territories were attacked (1511) by the HOLY LEAGUE of Pope JULIUS II. Louis abandoned Milan, and in 1513 his armies were defeated at Novara and Guinegate. In 1514 he made a truce with all his enemies save Holy Roman Emperor MAXIMILIAN I. Louis tried to rule France with justice and moderation, and was known as the Father of the People. He was succeeded by his cousin and son-in-law, FRANCIS I.

*Bourbon dynasty.* **Louis XIII,** 1601–43 (r.1610–43), succeeded his father, HENRY IV, under the regency of his mother, MARIE DE' MEDICI, and married (1615) ANNE OF AUSTRIA. Even after being declared of age in 1614, he was excluded from state affairs by his mother. In 1617 he caused the assassination of her minister, Concino Concini, with the help of his own favourite, the duc de LUYNES. Marie was forced into retirement, but was temporarily reconciled with Louis when he entrusted the government to her protégé, Cardinal RICHELIEU. Melancholy and retiring by nature, Louis gave full support to Richelieu and to his successor, Cardinal MAZARIN. His son and successor, **Louis XIV,** 1638–1715 (r.1643–1715), began his reign under the regency of his mother, Anne of Austria, but real power was in the hands of Cardinal Mazarin. Although Louis's majority was declared (1651), he did not take control of the government until the cardinal's death (1661). The centralizing policies of Richelieu and Mazarin had prepared the ground for Louis, under whom absolute monarchy, based on the theory of divine right, reached its height. Seeking to gather power into his own hands, he forced the nobility into financial dependence on the crown, attempted to curtail local authorities, and sought to increase his domestic authority. Under his minister, Jean Baptiste COLBERT, industry and commerce were expanded according to MERCANTILISM. Under the war minister, the marquis de LOUVOIS, the foundations of French military greatness were laid. In foreign policy Louis strove for supremacy. His marriage (1660) to the Spanish princess Marie Thérèse served as a pretext for the War of DEVOLUTION (1667–68), which netted him part of Flanders. In the Dutch War (1672–78), Louis gained Franche-Comté, but depleted his treasury. Over the next 10 years he seized, on various pretexts, a number of cities, notably Strasbourg (1681). Fear of Louis's rapacity resulted in two great European wars, the War of the GRAND ALLIANCE and the War of the SPANISH SUCCESSION. These left France in debt and weakened it militarily. In religion, Louis resorted in the 1680s to the persecution of French Protestants, or HUGUENOTS, which culminated (1685) in the revocation of the Edict of NANTES, after which many Huguenots fled France. Despite his orthodoxy, Louis resisted papal interference in France, and his quarrels with the papacy neared schism (1673–93). He had many mistresses, among them Mlle de La Vallière and Mme de MONTESPAN. In 1684 he married Mme de MAINTENON, who was a great influence on him in later years. Louis was a supporter of the arts and a patron of writers and artists such as MOLIÈRE and LE BRUN. The architect Jules MANSART supervised the building of Louis's lavish palace at VERSAILLES. Because of the brilliance of his court, Louis is often called the Sun King. His great-grandson **Louis XV,** 1710–74 (r.1715–74), succeeded him under the regency of Philippe II d'ORLÉANS. André Hercule de FLEURY was the young king's chief adviser from 1726. After Fleury's death (1743), Louis was influenced by a succession of favourites, such as Mme de POMPADOUR. As a result of the king's marriage (1725) to the Polish princess Marie Leszcynska, France took part in the War of the POLISH SUCCESSION (1733–35), and eventually obtained the duchy of Lorraine. Louis was also involved in the War of the AUSTRIAN SUCCESSION (1740–48) and in the SEVEN YEARS WAR (1756–63). In the latter, France lost most of its colonial empire and reached a low point in its prestige on the continent. The expense of the wars and Louis's extravagant court left the government nearly bankrupt. The failure by the monarchy to solve its fiscal problems and to effect needed reforms led directly to the French Revolution. The saying 'Après moi le déluge' [after me, the flood], though wrongly attributed to Louis, aptly sums up his reign. His grandson and successor, **Louis XVI,** 1754–93 (r.1774–92), was unsuited to provide the leadership needed to control the situation he inherited. Shy, dull, and corpulent, he preferred hunting and working in his locksmith's workshop to council chambers.

Reforms begun by his minister A.R.J. TURGOT were opposed by the court faction and by the PARLEMENT of Paris, which had been revived by Louis to pacify the privileged classes. Louis was forced to dismiss (1776) Turgot and replaced him with Jacques NECKER, but the costly French involvement in the AMERICAN REVOLUTION increased the debt greatly and led to Necker's resignation (1781). His successors were unable to ward off bankruptcy, and Louis recalled Necker in 1788. In 1789 the king called the STATES-GENERAL, an act which led to the FRENCH REVOLUTION. Louis's mismanagement of this assembly caused the third, or lowest, estate to demand increased representation and declare itself the National Assembly, and when the king sent troops to Paris, rumours began that he intended to suppress it. After the dismissal of Necker, violence erupted as Parisians stormed (July 1789) the BASTILLE. Although outwardly accepting the revolution, Louis refused to approve the abolition of feudal rights and allowed the reactionary plotting of his queen, MARIE ANTOINETTE. In Oct. 1789 a mob marched on Versailles and forced the royal family to move to the TUILERIES palace in Paris. Louis's position was definitely ruined when the royal family attempted to escape (June 1791) and was caught at Varennes. Its flight was considered proof of treasonable action. Louis was forced to accept the constitution of 1791, which reduced him to a figurehead. Early French losses in the war with Austria and Prussia increased suspicion of the king. The royal family was imprisoned in the Temple (Aug. 1792), and the monarchy was abolished (Sept.). Incriminating evidence against Louis was discovered, and he was tried by the Convention, which had replaced the National Assembly. Condemned to death as a traitor to the nation, he was guillotined on 21 Jan. 1793, facing death with steadfast courage. His son **Louis XVII,** 1785–1795?, was titular king of France (1793–95) and is known in popular legend as the 'lost dauphin'. In 1792 revolutionaries imprisoned him with the royal family in the Temple. After the execution of Louis XVI, the comte de Provence (later Louis XVIII) proclaimed Louis king, but he remained imprisoned until his death. Various stories of his escape and fate opened the way to a series of impostors who claimed to be the lost DAUPHIN. Most historians disregard their claims because evidence indicates that the boy died in prison. **Louis XVIII,** 1755–1824 (r.1814–24), was the brother of Louis XVI. Known as the comte de Provence, he fled (1791) from the French Revolution and intrigued against the revolutionaries from abroad. After the death of Louis XVII (1795), he was proclaimed king by French émigrés. With the assistance of Charles de TALLEYRAND, he was restored (1814) to the French throne by the allies after their entry into Paris, and he granted a constitutional charter. Forced to flee on the return of NAPOLEON I from Elba, Louis returned with the allies after Napoleon's defeat at Waterloo. His chief ministers were at first moderates, but he later relied on ultraroyalists. This reactionary trend was continued by his successor, CHARLES X.

**Louis, Joe,** 1914–81, American boxer; world heavyweight champion (1937–49); b. Joseph Louis Barrow. He turned professional in 1934 and in 1937 won the world heavyweight championship over James J. Braddock. He avenged (1938) his only early defeat with a first-round knockout of Max Schmeling. The 'Brown Bomber' defended his title a record 25 times, scoring 21 knockouts. After a brief retirement he returned to the ring in 1950 but lost to Ezzard Charles and Rocky MARCIANO. He lost only three of 71 professional bouts.

**Louis, Morris,** 1912–62, American painter. Associated with COLOUR FIELD PAINTING, Louis is noted for soaking poured paint through unsized canvas, often in transparently coloured columns or muted organic patterns.

**Louisburg,** town (1980 est. pop. 1519), Nova Scotia, E Canada, on CAPE BRETON ISLAND. Its ice-free port, guarded by the great fortress of Louisbourg (built 1720–40), served as headquarters for the French fleet in ACADIA. The stonghold played a major role in the struggle for control of North America between France and England until it was captured and destroyed by the British in 1758. The restored fort is a popular tourist attraction.

**Louis I** or **Louis the Great,** 1326–82, king of HUNGARY (1342–82) and of POLAND (1370–82). He succeeded his father, CHARLES I, in Hungary and his uncle, CASIMIR III, in Poland. Two successful wars (1357–58, 1378–81) against Venice gained him Dalmatia and Ragusa, and the rulers of Serbia, Walachia, Moldavia, and Bulgaria became his vassals. Louis brought Hungarian power to its peak, and fostered art and learning. In Poland, however, he was unable to prevent revolts. His daughter Mary succeeded him in Hungary, his daughter Jadwiga in Poland.

**Louis I,** 1838–89, king of Portugal (1861–89). His reign was marked by political turmoil over a growing republican movement, but Portugal progressed considerably in its commercial and industrial development.

**Louisiana,** state of the US (1984 est. pop. 4,462,000), area 125,675 km² (48,524 sq mi), located in the S, bordered by the Gulf of Mexico (S), Texas (W), Arkansas (N), and Mississippi (N). BATON ROUGE is the capital, and the biggest city is NEW ORLEANS, a leading US port. The southern part of the state consists of coastal lowlands threaded by creeks, and the MISSISSIPPI R. delta plains. Inland are rolling prairies and pine-covered hills, and the climate is hot with only brief, cool winters. The alluvial soils make Louisiana a leading producer of rice, cotton, and sugarcane. The state is the third largest producer of petroleum and the leading producer of natural gas, most of it extracted off-shore. Industry is dominated by petroleum refining and chemicals. Tourism centres on the annual Mardi Gras carnival in New Orleans. The population is diverse, including French-speaking Cajuns expelled from Nova Scotia (1755), French- and Spanish-descent Creoles, and the second largest black population in the US (29% in 1980). The area was claimed for France in the late 17th cent., and New Orleans had become a thriving port when the land was acquired by the US in the LOUISIANA PURCHASE (1803). Huge sugar and cotton plantations based on slavery were developed, and the state seceded from the Union in the Civil War. In the 20th cent. the poverty of the state was partly relieved by the discovery of oil and natural gas, while the Mississippi R. was contained by a flood-control system built after the disastrous floods of 1927.

**Louisiana Purchase,** 1803, US acquisition from France of the region of LOUISIANA. Uneasy at news that Spain had secretly returned Louisiana to aggressive Napoleonic France, Pres. JEFFERSON in 1802 dispatched Robert R. Livingston and James MONROE to purchase NEW ORLEANS and W FLORIDA for $2 million. The French, to whom Louisiana was of diminishing importance, offered to sell the entire territory to the surprised envoys for $15 million. The treaty of cession was dated 30 Apr. 1803, and the US flag was raised over New Orleans on 20 Dec. 1803. The Louisiana Purchase, extending from the Mississippi R. to the Rocky Mts and from the Gulf of Mexico to British North America, doubled the area of the US.

**Louis Napoleon:** see NAPOLEON III.

**Louis period styles,** 1610–1793, series of modes of interior decoration and architecture in France. The Louis XIII (1610–43) style was a transition from the Italian-influenced BAROQUE to the classical dignity of the Louis XIV [*Louis Quatorze*] (1643–1715) style. Colbert, Louis's chief minister, set up manufactories of textiles, furniture, and ornaments, and chose Charles LE BRUN to direct the GOBELINS tapestry works and to decorate the palace of Versailles. Le Brun and J.H. Mansart (see under MANSART, FRANÇOIS) created splendid interiors filled with massive furniture. The Régence style, named after the regency of Philippe II, duc d'Orléans (1715–23), used delicate, curved lines and bronze reliefs. The Louis XV [*Louis Quinze*] period (1723–74) was noted for ROCOCO ornament and CHINOISERIE. In the Louix XVI [*Louis Seize*] period (1774–93) the CLASSIC REVIVAL replaced excess with simplicity.

**Louis Philippe,** 1773–1850, king of the French (1830–48), the son of Philippe Égalité (see Louis Philippe Joseph, duc d'Orléans, under ORLÉANS, family). Known as the duc d'Orléans before his accession, he joined the army of the FRENCH REVOLUTION, but deserted (1793) and remained in exile until the Bourbon restoration (1814). He figured in the liberal opposition to LOUIS XVIII and CHARLES X, and after the JULY REVOLUTION of 1830 he was chosen king. Although a constitutional monarch, Louis Philippe gained considerable personal power by splitting the liberals, and eventually a conservative ministry to his liking came to power. It was dominated (1840–48) by François GUIZOT. The king promoted friendship with Britain by supporting (1831) Belgian independence, but the Spanish marriages (1846) of ISABELLA II and her sister violated an earlier Franco-British agreement. In France, Louis Philippe became increasingly unpopular with both the right and the left. His opponents began a banquet campaign against the government that led to the FEBRUARY REVOLUTION of 1848. The king abdicated in favour of his grandson, but a republic was declared. Louis Philippe fled to England, where he died. He was known as the 'citizen king' because of his bourgeois manner and dress.

**Louis the German,** c.804–876, king of the East Franks (r.817–76), son of Emperor LOUIS I, who gave him BAVARIA in 817. In the shifting conflict among his father and his brothers, LOTHAIR I, Pepin I, and CHARLES II, he sided first with one, then with the other. Eventually the Treaty of Verdun

(843) gave him the kingdom of the East Franks (roughly modern Germany). Later, part of Lothair's territory of LOTHARINGIA came to him. He survived several revolts by his sons, Louis the Younger, Carloman, and Charles the Fat (later Emperor CHARLES III).

**Louis the Great:** see LOUIS I, king of Hungary.

**Louisville,** US city (1984 est. pop. 290,000), NW Kentucky, at the falls of the Ohio; settled 1778, inc. 1828. Named after LOUIS XVI of France, Louisville developed as a fort, portage place, river port, and commercial centre. During the CIVIL WAR it was a base for federal forces. It is the largest city in Kentucky, and one of the South's most important industrial, financial, marketing, and shipping centres, with distilleries and cigarette factories as well as electrical appliance, chemical, motor vehicle, tyre, and other plants. Churchill Downs, scene of the Kentucky Derby horse race, is there.

**Lourdes,** town (1982 pop. 17,619), SW France. Each year, millions visit the Roman Catholic shrine where the Virgin Mary is said to have appeared (1858) to St Bernadette.

**louse,** very small (0.5–10 mm/¹⁄₅₀–²⁄₅ in), rather flat, wingless INSECT with well-developed claws, living as an ectoparasite on the body of a mammal or bird. The majority of those infesting mammals are blood-suckers (order Siphunculata). Two species are cosmopolitan human parasites, the pubic or crab louse (from its shape) *Phthirus pubis* and the human louse *Pediculus humanus*. The former, in addition to infesting the pubic region, also occurs under the arms, in beards and eyebrows, but very rarely on the head. One of the two forms of the human louse (often referred to as *corporis*), occurs in the same places, but the smaller (*capitis*) lives on the head. 'Nits' are the eggs, of both species, firmly glued to hairs. In addition to the discomfort these lice cause, the human louse is also the vector of two major diseases, TYPHUS and relapsing fever caused by the spirochaete *Borrelia recurrentis*. Two economically important lice infest domestic animals, the pig louse *Haematopotinus suis* and the cattle louse *H. eurysternus*. The first reference to the use of an insecticide (naturally-occurring arsenic sulphide) for human body-louse control appears in the Chinese *Pharmacopoeia of the Heavenly Husbandman* written between AD 100 and 200.

**Louth,** county in NE of Republic of Ireland (1986 pop. 91,698), 813 km² (317 sq mi), bordering on the Irish Sea in the E. It is situated in the province of Leinster and is the smallest county in Ireland. The county town is DUNDALK. It is mostly low-lying, but there are hills in the N where the land rises to 590 m (1935 ft) in Carlingford Mt. It is crossed from W to E by the Castletown, Glyde, Fane, and Dee rivers. Much of the land is occupied with agriculture, but there is manufacturing industry in Dundalk and Drogheda, including linen manufacture.

**Louvois, François Michel Le Tellier, marquis de** (looh‚vwah), 1641–91, French statesman under LOUIS XIV. With his father, **Michel Le Tellier,** 1603–85, whom he replaced (1677) as war minister, Louvois shared in the reforms that made France the most powerful military force in Europe. They closely coordinated the infantry, artillery, and corps of engineers, and introduced the bayonet and the flintlock rifle. After the death (1683) of J.B. COLBERT, Louvois became Louis's chief adviser and helped to shape France's aggressive policies.

**Louvre** (‚loohvrə), Paris, foremost French museum of art. The building was a royal fortress built by PHILIP II in the late 12th cent. In 1546 a new building was erected on the site by FRANCIS I, designed by Pierre Lescot. LEONARDO's *Mona Lisa* and other works by Italian artists came into the royal collections. In 1606, under HENRY IV, the Grande Galerie was completed. Art was collected with state funds, and more buildings were constructed, including the colonnade, completed in 1670 by Louis Le Vau and Claude Perrault. In 1793 the Grande Galerie was officially opened, with the area beneath serving as artists' studios and workshops. The museum is famous for its collection of Greek, Roman, and Egyptian antiquities, and old masters such as REMBRANDT, RUBENS, TITIAN, and LEONARDO. Its famous sculptures include the NIKE, or *Victory of Samothrace,* and the *Venus de Milo.* See also MUSÉE D'ORSAY.

**Lovelace, Richard,** 1618–57?, English Cavalier poet. An ardent royalist, he was imprisoned under Oliver CROMWELL and died in extreme poverty. He is remembered chiefly for two much-quoted lyrics, 'To Althea, from Prison' and 'To Lucasta, Going to the Wars'. His poems were published in 1649 and 1660.

**Lovell, Sir (Alfred Charles) Bernard,** 1913–, English radio astronomer. He was the leader of the team that built at Jodrell Bank, near Manchester, England, what was the largest steerable radio telescope (completed 1957). The telescope (which has since been surpassed in size) is now a part of the Nuffield Radio Astronomy Laboratories, which Lovell directed from 1951 until his retirement in 1981.

**Low Countries,** region of NW Europe, comprising the former FLANDERS and the present-day NETHERLANDS, BELGIUM, and LUXEMBOURG. One of the wealthiest areas of medieval and modern Europe, it has been the scene of chronic warfare.

**Lowell, James Russell,** 1819–91, American man of letters. His poetry ranges from the didactic *The Vision of Sir Launfal* (1848) to the satiric *The Bigelow Papers* (1848; 2nd series, 1867) to the critical *A Fable for Critics* (1848). A professor of modern languages at Harvard (1855–76), he was also the editor of the *Atlantic Monthly* (1857–61) and the *North American Review* (1864–72). He later turned to scholarship and criticism. As US minister to London (1877–85), Lowell did much to increase European respect for American letters and institutions, and his speeches in England, published as *Democracy and Other Addresses* (1887), are among his best work.

**Lowell, Percival,** 1855–1916, American astronomer; brother of Abbott Lawrence LOWELL and Amy LOWELL. His contention that there was a planet beyond Neptune was confirmed (1930) by the discovery of Pluto. The observations that he and his assistants made at the Lowell Observatory (Flagstaff, Arizona.), which he founded in 1894, led him to interpret visually apparent linear features seen on the planet Mars as artificial waterways, or canals, and thus to believe that Mars was inhabited.

**Lowell, Robert,** 1917–77, American poet. His poetry is intense, richly symbolic, and often autobiographical. Volumes include *Life Studies* (1959), *Lord Weary's Castle* (1946), *The Dolphin* (1973), and *Day by Day* (1977). His other works include translations, e.g., Racine's *Phèdre* (1969), and plays.

**Lower Saxony,** state (1984 pop. 7,216,304), 47,384 km² (18,295 sq mi), N West Germany. HANOVER is the capital. Lower Saxony was formed (1946) by the merger of the former Prussian province of Hanover and the former states of Brunswick, Oldenburg, and Schaumburg-Lippe. The state is drained by the Weser, Ems, Aller, Leine, and Elbe rivers and has several North Sea ports. Farming and cattle-raising are important occupations. Manufactures include iron and steel, textiles, and machinery. The region, although still considered a geographic entity, has had no historic unity since the dissolution of the duchy of HENRY THE LION of Saxony in 1180.

**Lowry, (Clarence) Malcolm,** 1909–57, English novelist. He is famous for *Under the Volcano* (1947), a subtle, complex, highly autobiographical study of dissolution, set in Mexico. After his death, a reworking of his first novel, *Ultramarine* (1933), poetry, and short stories appeared.

**low temperature physics** or **cryogenics,** science concerned with the production and maintenance of very low temperatures, and with the effects that occur under such conditions. Although it is impossible to reach absolute zero, a temperature as low as about one millionth of a degree above absolute zero on the Kelvin scale can be attained. Low temperatures are achieved by removing energy from a substance. By using a succession of liquified gases, a substance may be cooled to as low as 4.2 K, the boiling point of liquid helium. Still lower temperatures may be reached by successive magnetization and demagnetization. Some unusual conditions, notably SUPERCONDUCTIVITY and SUPERFLUIDITY, occur in some substances at cryogenic temperatures.

**Loyang:** see LUOYANG.

**Loyola, Ignatius of:** see IGNATIUS OF LOYOLA, SAINT.

**Lr,** chemical symbol of the element LAWRENCIUM.

**LSD** or **lysergic acid diethylamide,** an extremely potent HALLUCINOGENIC DRUG, causing physiological and behavioural changes. Reactions to LSD, such as heightened sense perceptions, anxiety, and hallucinations, are influenced by the amount of the drug taken and the user's personality and expectations. Prolonged psychic disturbances have been reported with LSD use, and there is some evidence linking it with chromosome damage.

**Lu,** chemical symbol of the element LUTETIUM.

**Luanda,** formerly São Paulo de Loanda, city (1982 est. pop. 700,000), capital of Angola, a port on the Atlantic Ocean. Angola's largest city, Luanda is an administrative and manufacturing centre producing such goods as cotton, timber, sugar, and tobacco. A refinery processes petroleum from nearby wells. Founded (1576) by Paulo Dias de Novais, it was the centre (16th–19th cent.) of a slave trade to Brazil. A modern city, it is the seat of the Univ. of Angola. The 17th-cent. Fort of São Miguel is among its points of interest.

**Lubbock,** US city (1984 est. pop. 179,000), NW Texas; settled 1879, inc. 1909. On a branch of the Brazos R., it is a trade centre for a grain and cotton region of W Texas and E New Mexico. Lubbock has growing industry, including the manufacture of electronic and oilfield equipment.

**Lübeck,** city (1984 pop. 213,400), Schleswig-Holstein, N West Germany, on the Trave R. near its mouth on the Baltic Sea. It is a major port and has such industries as shipbuilding and confectionery. Chartered c.1158, it headed (13th–17th cent.) the HANSEATIC LEAGUE. Its medieval Gothic architecture, damaged during WORLD WAR II, has been restored. The writers Thomas and Heinrich MANN were born in Lübeck.

**Lublin,** city (1984 pop. 320,000), E central Poland. An important industrial centre, commercial vehicles are manufactured and there is brown-coal working in the vicinity. In 1569 the parliament (diet) which joined Poland and Lithuania was established here. A provisional Polish government was installed in Lublin after Soviet liberation in 1944. The royal castle and houses of the 16th and 17th cent. survive. The city has both Catholic (1918) and state universities.

**Lubumbashi,** formerly Elizabethville, city (1976 est. pop. 451,332), capital of Shaba region, SE Zaïre, near the Zambian border. It is a commercial and industrial centre, situated on a transcontinental railway. Founded in 1910, it prospered from the region's copper-mining industry. As capital of the secessionist state of Katanga (now SHABA), it was the scene of heavy fighting in the early 1960s.

**Luca Giordano:** see GIORDANO, LUCA.

**Lucan** (Marcus Annaeus Lucanus), AD 39–65, Latin poet, nephew of SENECA. Ten books of his EPIC *Bellum civile* (on the civil war between POMPEY and CAESAR), wrongly called *Pharsalia,* survive; they were esteemed by later writers.

**Lucas, George,** 1945–, American film director and producer. After showing initial promise as a director, he had enormous box-office success with *Star Wars* (1977), and now acts as producer to both the rest of the *Star Wars* series and other films. His films as director include *THX-1138* (1971) and *American Graffiti* (1973).

**Lucas van Leyden** (van ˌliedən), 1494–1533, Dutch historical and GENRE painter and engraver. Dutch paintings of daily life begin with Lucas. His art is noted for its realism, dramatic power, and careful execution. His paintings include the *Last Judgment* triptych (1526–27; Stedelyk Mus., Leyden).

**Luce, Henry Robinson,** 1898–1967, American publisher; b. China. In 1923, with Briton Hadden, he founded *Time,* a weekly news magazine featuring capsulated news accounts written in a brisk, adjective-laden style. His other periodicals included *Fortune* (1930), *Life* (1936), and *Sports Illustrated* (1954). His wife, **Clare Booth Luce,** 1903–, is a playwright and diplomat. She is best known for her witty, satirical play *The Women* (1936). She was US ambassador to Italy (1953–56).

**Lucerne:** see LUZERN.

**Lucian** (Lucianus), b. AD c.125, d. after 180, Greek prose writer. Most characteristic of his vigorous and witty satire are his dialogues (*Dialogues of the Gods, Dialogues of the Dead, The Sale of Lives*) dealing with ancient mythology and contemporary philosophy. His fantastic *True History* influenced SWIFT and RABELAIS.

**Luciani, Sebastiano:** see SEBASTIANO DEL PIOMBO.

**Lucifer:** see SATAN.

**Lucilius, Gaius,** c.180–102? BC, the father of Latin SATIRE. He influenced HORACE, PERSIUS, and JUVENAL.

**Lucknow,** city (1981 pop. 916,954), Uttar Pradesh state, N India, on the Gomati (Gumti) R. It is a district and divisional administrative and commercial centre, and the state capital. There is considerable industry, including cotton and paper mills, sugar refineries, and railway workshops. Lucknow (sometimes spelt Lakhnau) is also an army

headquarters. It became important only in the 18th cent., when it was the capital of the Nawabs of Awadh (Oudh), whose territory was annexed by the British in 1856. The siege and relief of the residency at Lucknow was a critical event in the INDIAN MUTINY. Lucknow retains many interesting buildings from the days of the Nawabs, and the residency is preserved as an historic ruin.

**Lucretius** (Titus Lucretius Carus), c.99–c.55 BC, Roman poet and philosopher. His poetry consists of one great didactic work in six books, *De rerum natura* [on the nature of things]. In powerful and dignified hexameter verse, full of striking imagery and vigorous language, he set forth arguments based on the philosophy of DEMOCRITUS and EPICURUS. Using the so-called atomic theory of the ancients, he argued that man need not fear the gods or death because everything, even the soul, is made up of atoms controlled by natural laws; thus there is no immortality, consciousness ending with death. Though not the same as modern atomic theory, Lucretius' teachings have been upheld in many respects by later investigation.

**Lucullus** (Lucius Licinius Lucullus Ponticus), c.110–56 BC, Roman general. He served in the Social War (90–88 BC) under Sulla, who made him his favourite. Lucullus defeated MITHRIDATES VI of Pontus. He then provoked great unpopularity in Rome by reforming the provincial finances. In 66 BC POMPEY replaced Lucullus, who retired to Rome and became known for showy elegance; hence the term 'Lucullan'.

**Lüda** or **Lüta** (ly-dah), city (1980 pop. 4,400,000), S Liaoning prov., NE China, at the tip of the Liaodong peninsula. It comprises Lüshun (the former Port Arthur) and Dalian (Dairen). The city is centred on the harbour, which employs 13% of its population, is China's third largest foreign trade port, and is an important naval centre. Lüda produces ships, diesel engines, machine tools, chemicals, and textiles, and is a major fishing centre.

**Luda:** see DALIAN.

**Luddites,** bands of labourers who rioted (1811–16) in the industrial areas of England; named after the mythical Ned Ludd or King Ludd. Starting in Nottinghamshire, rioters destroyed textile machines, to which they attributed high unemployment and low wages. The riots were harshly suppressed.

**Ludendorff, Erich,** 1865–1937, German general. As chief of staff to Field Marshal Hindenberg in WORLD WAR I, he was largely responsible for German military strategy. After 1916 he also intervened in civilian matters. He supported the Nazis in the 1920s and wrote pamphlets idealizing the 'Aryan' race and attacking the pope, Jews, Jesuits, and Freemasons.

**Ludhiana** ('loodee-ˌahnə), city (1981 pop. 607,052), Punjab state, N India, on the Beas R. It is a district administrative and railway centre, and has become the most important location of industry in the remarkable Punjab industrial belt, helped by the activities of refugees from what is now Pakistan. From the base provided by the 19th-cent. hosiery industry, production has expanded to include engineering and other goods. It became a district headquarters and nascent industrial centre in British days.

**Ludwig:** for German rulers thus named, see LOUIS.

**Ludwig, Christa,** 1928–, German mezzo-soprano. She starred at the Vienna State Opera (from 1955) and the METROPOLITAN OPERA (from 1959). Possessing an expressive voice of considerable range, she is a noted interpreter of MAHLER.

**Ludwigshafen,** city (1984 pop. 156,000), Rhineland–Palatinate, West Germany, on the RHINE opposite MANNHEIM. It is a major centre of the chemical industry.

**luffa:** see GOURD.

**luge,** type of small sleigh in which one or two persons race down snowy hillsides or steeply banked, curving chutes. Steering is accomplished by shifting weight, pulling straps attached to the runners, and use of the feet. Lugeing is an Olympic event for both men and women.

**Lugones, Leopoldo** (looh,gohnays), 1874–1938, Argentine poet. He expressed his adherence to MODERNISMO in *Las montañas de oro* (1897; tr. The Golden Mountains) and *Los crepúsculos del jardín* (1905; tr. Twilight in the Garden). His prose includes history and short stories.

**Lu Hsun:** see LU XUN.

**Lukács, Georg** (‚loohkach), 1885–1971, Hungarian literary critic and social theorist. A lifelong Marxist, he explored the links between creativity and social struggle in such books as *History and Class Consciousness* (1923), *Studies in European Realism* (1946), and *The Destruction of Reason* (1954).

**Luke, Gospel according to Saint,** book of the NEW TESTAMENT. It was composed late in the 1st cent. AD, ascribed since the 2nd cent. to St LUKE. A literary composition, it shows the thoughtful use of several sources, including MARK. Luke contains a unique account of the birth and boyhood of JESUS. The GOSPEL shows Pauline influences, e.g., with regard to the equality of men and the universality of salvation.

**Luke, Saint,** early Christian, traditional author of the third GOSPEL and of the ACTS OF THE APOSTLES. A Gentile called by St PAUL 'the beloved physician', he accompanied Paul to Rome.

**Lully, Jean Baptiste** (ly‚lee), 1632–87, French violinist and composer; b. Italy. From 1653 he was a chamber composer and conductor for LOUIS XIV. He wrote BALLETS and in 1672 obtained a patent for the production of OPERA. Among his operas are *Cadmus et Hermione* (1673), *Alceste* (1674), and *Amadis* (1684). He established the form of the French OVERTURE and set French operatic style until GLUCK.

**lumbar puncture,** the extraction of cerebrospinal fluid (fluid round brain and spinal cord) from the spine for diagnostic examination. A needle is inserted into one of the intervertebral spaces and the procedure also allows for the injection of anaesthetic agents or other drugs.

**Lumière, Louis Jean** (ly‚myeə), 1864–1948, and **Auguste,** 1862–1954, French inventors, brothers. In 1895 they patented and demonstrated the Cinématographe, the first documented device for photographing, printing, and projecting films.

**luminescence,** the emission of light by sources other than a hot, incandescent body. It is caused by the movement of electrons within a substance from more energetic states to less energetic states. Among several types are chemiluminescence, electroluminescence, and triboluminescence, which are produced, respectively, by chemical reactions, electric discharges, and the rubbing or crushing of crystals. See also BIOLUMINESCENCE; FLUORESCENCE; PHOSPHORESCENCE.

**luminism,** American art movement of the 19th cent., related to IMPRESSIONISM, that sought to render the mystical effect of diffused light on the landscape. Luminists included J.F. Kensett, FitzHugh Lane, and Frederick E. CHURCH.

**luminosity,** the rate at which energy of all types is radiated by a STAR in all directions. A star's luminosity varies approximately as the square of its radius and the fourth power of its absolute surface temperature. Apparent luminosity is the rate at which the energy of its radiation is received on the Earth, and must be corrected for the star's distance to infer its (absolute) luminosity. See MAGNITUDE; SPECTRAL CLASS.

**Lumumba, Patrice Emergy,** 1925–61, 1st prime minister of the Republic of the Congo (now ZAÏRE). Shortly after becoming (1960) prime minister, he clashed with KASAVUBU and MOBUTU. He was arrested and died under mysterious circumstances.

**Luna, Pedro de,** 1324?–1423, Spanish cardinal, antipope (1394–1417) as Benedict XIII. He supported the election of URBAN VI, but deserted him for Robert of Geneva, who as Antipope Clement VII, launched the Great SCHISM. On Robert's death, De Luna was elected to succeed him. He refused to abdicate at the Council of Pisa (1409), but was deposed by the Council of Constance (1417). To his death he continued to claim he was the rightful pope.

**lungfish,** lung-bearing FISH, often resembling an EEL, found in rivers in South America, Africa, and Australia. Like the COELACANTH, it is ancestrally related to the four-footed land animals. The most primitive living lungfish is a stout-bodied Australian species *Neoceratodus*, 150 cm (5 ft) long with paired fins set on short stumps. African species, which AESTIVATE in hard clay during the dry season, breathe through gills in water. Other species will drown if held under water.

**lungs,** pair of elastic organs used for breathing in vertebrate animals. In humans, they are located on either side of the heart, filling much of the chest cavity. Air enters each lung through a large tube, or bronchus, which divides and subdivides into a network of bronchioles. These tiny tubules lead to cup-shaped air sacs known as alveoli, each of which is surrounded by a net of capillaries. As blood flows through the capillary net, there is an exchange of gases: oxygen diffuses into the bloodstream and carbon dioxide is passed back into the lungs. Covered by a thin membrane, the pleura, which allows them to move freely during breathing, the lungs are expanded (inhalation) and contracted (exhalation) by the combined movement of the diaphragm and the rib cage. Diseases of the lungs include cancer, bronchitis, pleurisy, and pneumonia. See RESPIRATION.

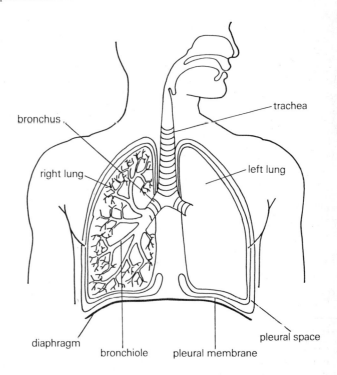

Lungs

**Luoyang** or **Loyang,** city (1984 est. pop. 2,559,100), NW HENAN prov., central China, on the Luo R. Since 1949 it has become an important industrial city, its products including mining machinery, tractors, and ball bearings. A major cultural centre, it was the capital of several ancient dynasties, e.g., the Eastern Zhou (Chou) kingdom (770–256 BC) and the Tang (T'ang) dynasty (AD 618–906). The famous Buddhist caves of Longmen (6th cent. AD), with their colossal carvings, are nearby.

Rock carvings in the Lung Mei Gorge, near **Luoyang**

**lupus erythematosus:** see AUTOIMMUNE DISEASE.

**Lurçat, Jean** (lyə͵sah), 1892–1966, French artist. A painter and lithographer who illustrated many books, he is best known as a TAPESTRY designer. His bright, gay tapestries hang in many palaces; a major example is in the Musée national d'art moderne (Paris). *Designing Tapestry* (tr. 1950) is among his books.

**Luria** or **Loria, Isaac ben Solomon**, 1534–72, Jewish kabbalist, surnamed Ashkenazi, called *Ari* [lion]; b. Jerusalem. He settled (c.1570) at Safed, Palestine, where he led an important school of mysticism that combined Messianism with older kabbalistic doctrines (see KABBALAH). Luria was concerned with the nature of, and the connection between, earthly redemption and cosmic restoration.

**Luria, Alexander Romanovitch**, 1902–77, Russian psychologist and neurologist. He was a colleague of VYGOTSKY and a central figure in the development of Soviet neuropsychology and cross-cultural psychology. Luria rejected both the view that the functions of COGNITION are strictly localized in specific brain regions, and the view that they are uniformly distributed throughout the brain. Instead, he proposed the theory of 'functional systems', incorporating elements of both these other positions. Luria's autobiography *The Making of Mind* was published in English in 1979.

**Lusaka**, largest city (1980 pop. 538,469) and capital of Zambia, S central Zambia. Located in a productive farm area, it is a commercial centre and a transport hub, at the junction of major roads to Tanzania and Malawi and on the Tanzania–Zambia railway, which opened in 1975. Founded in 1905, the city developed after 1935, when it became the capital of Northern Rhodesia.

**Lushun:** see DALIAN.

**Lusitania**, British liner sunk off the Irish coast by a German submarine on 7 May 1915. Of the 1195 lives lost, 128 were US citizens. Even though the Germans had warned Americans not to take passage on British ships, the incident contributed to the rise of American sentiment in favour of entering WORLD WAR I on the side of the Allies.

**Lüta:** see LÜDA.

**lute:** see STRINGED INSTRUMENT.

**lutetium** (Lu), metallic element, discovered independently by Georges Urbain in 1907 and by Carl Auer von Welsbach in 1908. Silver-white, one of the RARE-EARTH METALS, and a member of the LANTHANIDE SERIES, lutetium has few commercial uses. It is found in MONAZITE. See ELEMENT (table); PERIODIC TABLE.

**Luther, Martin**, 1483–1546, German leader of the Protestant REFORMATION. In 1505, Luther completed his master's examination and began the study of law. Several months later, after what seems to have been a sudden religious experience, he entered an Augustinian monastery at Erfurt, was ordained (1507) a priest, and was assigned (1508) to the Univ. of Wittenberg. In 1510, on a mission to Rome, he was shocked by the spiritual laxity in high ecclesiastical places. Returning to Wittenberg, he developed a great spiritual anxiety about his salvation, but in his study (1513) of the Scriptures, especially St Paul, he found a loving God who bestowed upon sinful humans the free gift of salvation, received by faith alone, and not by works. This resolved his turmoil. From 1516 he denounced the dispensation of INDULGENCES, then being preached by John Tetzel, whose arrival in Saxony in 1517 prompted Luther to post his historic 95 theses on the door of the castle church. While these were appreciated by many within Germany, they were a threat to the church. Several attempts at reconciliation failed, and Luther broadened his position to include widespread reforms. He supported the new nationalism by advocating German control of the German church. When a bull of condemnation (*Exsurge Domine*) was issued, he burned it publicly and was excommunicated in 1521. Summoned before the Diet of Worms (1521), Luther was forced to take refuge in the Wartburg after the diet ordered his seizure. There, under the protection of Elector Frederick III of Saxony, Luther translated the New Testament into German and began a translation of the entire Bible. He then returned to Wittenberg, where he stayed for most of the remainder of his life. His opposition to the Peasants' War (1524–25) cost him some popular support. Nevertheless, through his forceful writings and preaching, his doctrines spread. He married (1525) a former nun, Katharina von Bora, and raised six children. Luther worked to build a competent educational system and wrote extensively on church matters, including a liturgy, hymns, and two catechisms, but his uncompromising attitude in doctrinal matters helped break the unity of the Reformation. Controversies with Huldreich ZWINGLI and John CALVIN eventually divided the Protestants into the Lutheran and the Reformed churches. Under his sanction, Philip MELANCHTHON wrote a Lutheran confession of faith, the Augsburg Confession, at the Diet of Augsburg in 1530. About this time control of the Lutheran Church passed further into the hands of the Protestant princes, and Luther's last years were troubled with ill health and the plagues of political and religious disunion. He left behind an evangelical doctrine that spread throughout the Western world. In Germany his socio-religious concepts laid a new basis for German society, and his writings helped to fix the standards of the modern German language.

**Lutheranism,** branch of Protestantism that arose as a result of the REFORMATION, whose religious faith is based on the principles of Martin LUTHER, although he opposed such a designation. Luther's conservative attitudes, as distinguished from those of Calvinists, held that the Scriptures contained all that was necessary for salvation, which came by faith alone. His two catechisms contain the principal statements of faith. Baptism is necessary for spiritual regeneration, and the sacrament of the Lord's Supper (see COMMUNION) was also retained, although transubstantiation was replaced by consubstantiation. Some churches are episcopal, e.g., in Sweden, and others have a synodal form of organization, but unity is based on doctrine rather than structure. In Germany, Lutheranism has had close associations with political life, and it is the established church of the Scandinavian countries. Lutherans in America first formed (1638) a congregation at Fort Christina (Wilmington, Delaware). World membership in the Lutheran church is more than 70 million, and the Lutheran churches in most countries belong to the Lutheran World Federation, which has its office at Geneva.

**Luthuli, Albert John,** c.1898–1967, South African political leader. A ZULU chief and a Christian, he opposed racial discrimination in South Africa and advocated nonviolence and passive resistance against APARTHEID. He was banished by the white government, but he retained the loyalty of black South Africans. He won the 1960 Nobel Peace Prize.

**Luton,** town (1981 pop. 163,209), in Bedfordshire, S Midlands of England, 45 km (28 mi) NW of London. Industries found within the town include motor-vehicle manufacture, brewing, and the manufacture of precision instruments. Straw-plaiting was introduced as an industry here in the reign of James I, and the town was famous for hat-making. 3 km (2 mi) to the E is Luton Airport which is an international airport. In 1984 it handled 1.8 million passengers.

**Lutoslawski, Witold,** 1913–, Polish composer, teacher, and conductor. During the German occupation he played the piano daily in Warsaw cafes. After the performance in 1948 and the subsequent banning of his First Symphony, he continued to write a series of works based on Polish folk music (1945–55) but was obliged by the government of the time to avoid the dense atonal counterpoint towards which his style was moving. His popular Concerto for Orchestra (1950–54) was also written during this period. Conditions eased and he returned to his earlier style in *Musique Funèbre* for string orchestra (1954–58), *Jeux vénitiens* (1961), the Second and Third Symphonies (1965–67, and 1983) and other works which have been recorded and performed in many countries.

**Lutyens, Sir Edwin,** 1869–1944, English architect. The most successful English architect of the 20th cent. Lutyens designed more than 100 COUNTRY HOUSES as well as major public buildings. Munstead Wood in Godalming, Surrey (1896), designed for the landscape gardener Gertrude Jekyll, made his reputation as a brilliant exponent of the ARTS AND CRAFTS style. The Deanery Garden at Sonning-on-Thames, Berkshire (1899–1902) is a brilliant exercise in informal composition. After c.1905 Lutyens's design became more formal. Examples of his work include banks, e.g., the Midland Bank headquarters, London (1924–39); the British Embassy in Washington (1925–28); the plan for New Delhi, India (1912); and the biggest commission ever handled by a single architect, the Viceroy's house, New Delhi (1912–30).

**Lutyens, Elizabeth,** 1906–83, British composer. Her first major works, such as the Chamber Concerto No. 1 (1939) pioneered the composition of SERIAL MUSIC in England. Her interest in literature from all parts of the world inspired and sometimes provided the texts for a large number of compositions.

**Luxembourg** or **Luxemburg,** officially the Grand Duchy of Luxembourg, constitutional monarchy (1985 est. pop. 365,900), 2586

The Viceroy's house, New Delhi (1912–30) by Sir Edwin **Lutyens**

km² (998 sq mi), W Europe; bordered by Belgium (W and N), West Germany (E), and France (S). The city of LUXEMBOURG is the capital. The grand duchy is drained by tributaries of the MOSEL R. The ARDENNES Mts extend into N Luxembourg. Part of the Luxembourg–Lorraine iron-mining basin is in the SW, and Luxembourg is a major iron and steel producer, although the industry suffered from a recession in the 1970s. Other manufactures include food products, leather goods, textiles, and chemicals. Grains and potatoes are grown and livestock, especially cattle, are raised. Luxembourg is an important banking centre. The GNP is $4470 million and the GNP per capita is $12,190 (1983). The people, chiefly Roman Catholic, speak French (the official language), Letzeburgesch (a Low German dialect), and German. The present ruling house of NASSAU came to the throne in 1890.

*History.* The medieval county of Luxembourg (originally Lützelburg), which lay between the Meuse and Moselle rivers and included parts of present-day BELGIUM, was one of the largest fiefs of the HOLY ROMAN EMPIRE. It rose to prominence when its ruler was elected emperor as Henry VII in 1308, and it was raised to the status of duchy in 1354. Conquered by PHILIP THE GOOD of Burgundy in 1443, the duchy passed in 1482 to the Habsburgs and in 1797 to the French. The Congress of Vienna (1814–15) made Luxembourg a grand duchy under the king of the Netherlands. Luxembourg joined Belgium in revolt (1830) against the Netherlands, and after Belgian independence the greater part of the grand duchy became (1839) part of Belgium (the present Belgian Luxembourg prov.). The remainder became autonomous in 1848. Although neutral, Luxembourg was occupied by the Germans in both world wars. Since WORLD WAR II Luxembourg has played an active role in fostering Western European integration, joining the BENELUX ECONOMIC UNION and the EUROPEAN COMMUNITY; it is also a member of the NORTH ATLANTIC TREATY ORGANIZATION. Since 1947 there has been a series of coalition governments, each formed by two of the three main parties (the Christian Social, Socialist Workers' and Democratic parties).

**Luxembourg** or **Luxemburg,** capital (1985 pop. 76,050) of the Grand Duchy of Luxembourg. A commercial, industrial, administrative, and cultural centre, the picturesque city developed around a 10th-cent. castle. Of note are the Cathedral of Notre Dame and the city hall (both 16th cent.).

**Luxemburg, Rosa,** 1871–1919, German revolutionary; b. Russian Poland. While a student, she helped to found (1892) the Polish Socialist party. After 1898 she was a leader in the German Social Democratic party. A brilliant writer and orator, she and Karl Liebknecht founded (c.1916) the Marxist SPARTACUS LEAGUE, forerunner to the German Communist party. Arrested in the Spartacist uprising of 1919, she and Liebknecht were murdered by soldiers.

**Luxor,** city (1970 est. pop. 84,600), central Egypt, on the Nile R., 1.6 km (1 mi) E of KARNAK. The temple of Luxor (190 m/623 ft long), the city's greatest monument of antiquity, was built under Amenhotep III and altered by later pharaohs. Many temples and burial grounds, including the Valley of the Tombs of the Kings, are nearby.

Luxembourg

**Lu Xun,** pseud. of **Zhou Shuren,** 1881–1936, Chinese writer. Lu Xun sought to awaken the Chinese to the values of Western science and philosophy. His gift for satire and his use of the vernacular made him popular. At first attacked as bourgeois by the Communists, he was later called the GORKY of China. A prolific essayist, polemicist, critic, and short-story writer, his influence was wide, ranging from progressive circles to MAO ZEDONG.

**Luynes, Charles d'Albert, duc de** (ly͵een), 1578–1621, constable of France (1621) and minister of LOUIS XIII. With Louis's aid he caused (1617) the assassination of the minister Concino Concini, seized the government, and exiled MARIE DE' MEDICI.

**Luzern,** city (1984 pop. 62,000, agglomeration 158,000), capital of Luzern canton, central Switzerland, on Lake Luzern. It lies on the international route between BASEL and MILAN via the ST GOTTHARD pass. A major tourist centre, its industries include the manufacture of jewellery. It joined the original three Forest Cantons of the Swiss Confederation in 1332, and was prominent in the formation of the League of Catholic Cantons (Sonderbund) in the 1840s. Notable structures include the remains of city walls, the 8th-cent. church (Hof Kirche, rebuilt 17th cent.), 14th to 15th-cent. covered bridges, and the Renaissance town hall (16th cent.).

The Old Bridge, **Luzern**

**Luzon**, island (1970 pop. 16,669,724), Philippines, largest (104,688 km²/40,420 sq mi) and most populous of the Philippine Islands. Much of it is mountainous, rising to a high point of 2928 m (9606 ft) at Mt Pulog. Most of the population is concentrated in the MANILA metropolitan area and between the mountains in the low-lying central Luzon Plain, c.160 km (100 mi) long and 65 km (40 mi) wide, along the Pampanga and Agno Rs. Rice, sugarcane, hemp, tobacco, and corn are important crops. Manufacturing is centred around Manila, where the major industries produce textiles, chemicals, metal products, and cars. During WORLD WAR II Japan invaded Luzon in 1941, and in early 1942 the Allied forces made their last stand there on BATAAN peninsula and the offshore island of CORREGIDOR.

**Luzzatto, Moses Hayyim** (looh¸tsattoh), 1707–46, Italian Jewish writer and mystic who wrote in Hebrew and Italian. He was a leader of the renaissance of Hebrew literature. A student of the CABALA, he claimed divine revelation for his mystical writings. He is best known for the ethical work *The Path of the Upright* (1740).

**Lvov** (lyə¸vof), city (1985 pop. 742,000), SW European USSR, chief city of the UKRAINE, at the watershed of the W Bug and Dnestr rivers and in the northern foothills of the Carpathian Mts. The city has such industries as oil refining and car manufacturing. Founded c.1256, it became a commercial centre on the trade route from Vienna to Kiev. It developed as a largely Polish–Jewish city within the Kingdom of Poland (1340–1773). Its famous university was established in 1661. In 1772 it passed to Austria and, as Lemberg, became the capital of the region of GALICIA. Held by Poland after 1919 and by the USSR after 1939, it was occupied for much of World War II by the Germans, who exterminated most of the Jewish population. In 1945 Poland formally ceded the city to the USSR. In 1944 it was re-annexed by the USSR.

**Lvov, Prince Georgi Yevgenyevich**, 1861–1925, Russian public official. He headed the provisional government formed after the Feb. 1917 RUSSIAN REVOLUTION but resigned in favour of KERENSKY in July. Lvov later emigrated to Paris.

**Lwoff, André**, 1902–, French microbiologist. For his contributions to the genetic control of synthesis of viruses and enzymes, Lwoff shared with François JACOB and Jacques MONOD the 1965 Nobel Prize for physiology or medicine.

**Lyallpur:** see FAISALABAD.

**lycanthropy**, in folklore, assumption by a human, through witchcraft or magic, of the form and nature of an animal. Belief in lycanthropy has been widespread since ancient times. One of the best-known superstitions is a belief in werewolves, persons who consume human flesh or blood and change to and from wolves. The term *lycanthropy* [Gr., = wolfman] also applies to a psychosis in which victims believe themselves to be animals.

**lychee**, Chinese tree (*Litchi chinensis*), also cultivated in other warm countries. It has a small, aromatic pulpy fruit in a thin, rough shell. The best-known Chinese fruit, it is eaten fresh, dried, preserved, or canned.

**Lycopsida**, division of the plant kingdom consisting of the CLUB MOSSES and quillworts.

**Lydgate, John**, c.1370–c.1450, English poet, one of the most versatile and prolific medieval writers. He wrote Chaucerian poems, e.g., *Complaint of the Black Knight;* long translations; and fables and other short poems.

**lye:** see SOAP.

**Lyell, Sir Charles**, 1797–1875, English geologist. He helped win acceptance of James HUTTON's theory of UNIFORMITARIANISM and of Charles DARWIN's theory of EVOLUTION. Lyell's *Principles of Geology* (3 vol., 1830–33) went into 12 editions in his lifetime. His research led him to divide the Tertiary period into the Eocene, Miocene, and Pliocene epochs.

**Lyly** or **Lilly, John**, 1554?–1606, English dramatist and prose writer, best known for his novel *Euphues*, published in two parts (*The Anatomy of Wit*, 1578; *Euphues and His England*, 1580), in which he tried to establish an ideal prose style, actually artificial and convoluted (see EUPHUISM). Lyly's plays introduced prose as a vehicle for comic dialogue. He also wrote elegant, semi-allegorical plays for performance by boys, including *Campaspe* (1584) and *Endimion* (1591).

**lymphatic system**, network of vessels carrying lymph from the tissues into the bloodstream. The cells of the tissues are bathed in tissue fluid, a colourless fluid derived from BLOOD but containing no red blood cells or platelets and considerably less protein, which is continuously passing through the walls of the capillaries. It transports nutrients and oxygen to the cells and collects waste products. Most of the tissue fluid passes back into the bloodstream via the venous capillaries; however, a small amount enters the lymphatic system as lymph before being returned to the blood. The lymphatic system is composed of fine lymph capillaries lying adjacent to the blood capillaries. These merge first into larger tributaries called trunks, and then into two still larger vessels called ducts. Ducts feed into the circulatory system in the region of the collarbone, returning the lymph to the bloodstream there. The walls of the lymph vessels are permeable to substances of much greater size than those of the blood capillaries, so lymph can transport large molecules, such as proteins, and bacteria which are unable to enter the circulatory system. Along the lymphatic network, in the neck, armpit, groin, abdomen, and chest, are small reservoirs, the lymph nodes. These filter out bacteria and other deleterious agents, thus acting as a barrier against the entrance of these substances into the blood, and add white blood cells (lymphocytes) and antibodies. In addition, the lymphatic system, like the circulatory system, absorbs nutrients, particularly LIPIDS, from the small intestine.

**lynching**, unlawful killing (especially hanging) of a person by a mob. N American pioneers, sometimes organized as vigilantes to suppress crime, often lynched known or suspected offenders. During and after RECONSTRUCTION, the KU KLUX KLAN lynched blacks they accused of crimes. More than 3000 US blacks were lynched in the South and elsewhere from the 1880s to the 1960s.

**Lynd, Robert Staughton**, 1892–1970, American sociologist. A teacher at Columbia Univ. (1931–61). Together with his wife **Helen Merrell Lynd** (1894–), he produced two influential studies of 'middle America': *Middletown* (1929), and *Middletown in Transition* (1937), largely based on Muncie, Indiana, at two different periods (1890–1914 and 1924–35). Those studies, of a community undergoing secularization and modernization, contain data on work, leisure, family life, schooling, and relations with central government. In the second study, the emphasis is on how the community deals with the conflicts and antagonisms engendered by economic depression at home, and fascism and socialism abroad.

**lynx**, tail-less members of the CAT family, the Felidae. Lynxes include the American bobcat and the caracal. They are found from Europe across Asia to the Pacific coast of Siberia. The European lynx (*Lynx lynx*) lives in the forests of Scandinavia, with pockets of the Spanish lynx surviving in Spain and the Alps. They grow to about 1 m (3½ ft) long. The lynx is a solitary animal, hunting by tracking its prey at walking pace for most of the time or by dropping on it from an ambush on an overhead branch. They are good swimmers and their wide paws help them to cross snow. Each lynx has its own territory, which it marks with urine on prominent boundary features. They were once common all over Europe, and now survive in Norway and Sweden because they are protected.

**Lyons** (ly¸awnh), city (1982 pop. 418,476, agglomeration 1,220,844), capital of Rhône dept., E central France. A leading city in French silk and rayon production, it has many industries, e.g., metal and machine, and is a leader in banking and education. There, during Roman rule, Christianity was introduced into Gaul. Lyons was ruled by its archbishops until c.1307, when it passed to the French crown. In the 12th cent. the WALDENSES were organized there. During World War II the resistance was based (1940–44) in Lyons.

**Lyons, Councils of:** see COUNCIL, ECUMENICAL.

**Lyons, Joseph Aloysius**, 1879–1939, Australian prime minister (1932–39). In 1931 he broke with the Labor Party and helped form the United Australia Party.

**lyre:** see STRINGED INSTRUMENT.

**lyric**, in ancient Greece, a poem accompanied by music, usually a lyre. The term now refers to any short poem expressing personal emotion: SONNET, ODE, song, or ELEGY. The Greek monody or individual song was developed by SAPPHO and ALCAEUS, the choral lyric by PINDAR, the Latin lyric

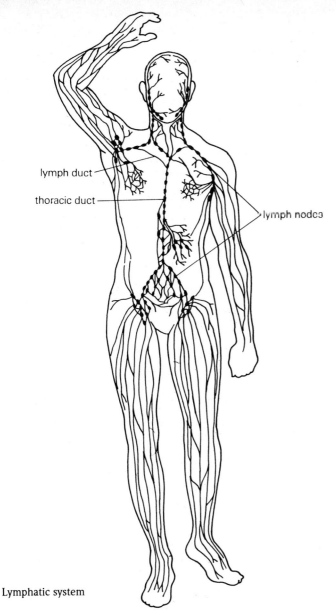

lymph duct

thoracic duct

lymph nodes

Lymphatic system

by CATULLUS and HORACE. The lyric became common in Christian HYMNS, in FOLK SONGS, and in TROUBADOR songs. Renaissance lyric reached a peak in the sonnets of PETRARCA and SHAKESPEARE, and the short poems of RONSARD and DONNE. Poets of all subsequent periods have written innumerable lyrics.

**Lyric Players Theatre, The,** the only producing theatre in Belfast. It was privately founded in 1951 by Mary and Pearse O'Malley in their own house. As well as presenting all of Yeats's plays plus selections from world drama and Irish writers such as Shaw, Synge, O'Casey, and Beckett, the O'Malleys' group raised the funds to build a 300-seat theatre which opened in 1968 and continues its promotion of local writers.

**Lysander** (lie,sandə), d. 395 BC, Spartan naval commander. He was responsible for the capture of the Athenian fleet (405 BC) and the final submission (404) of ATHENS to SPARTA that ended the PELOPONNESIAN WAR.

**Lysenko, Trofim Denisovich,** 1898–1976, Soviet agronomist. As president (1938–56, 1961–62) of the Lenin Academy of Agricultural Science, he was the scientific and administrative head of Soviet agriculture; he also directed (1940–65) the Institute of Genetics of the

Soviet Academy of Sciences. He rejected Mendelian genetics in favour of the doctrine of ACQUIRED CHARACTERISTICS. His ideas were presented and accepted as Marxist orthodoxy until after the death of Joseph STALIN, when they were severely criticized. Under the protection of Nikita KHRUSHCHEV he nevertheless continued to influence agricultural policy in the USSR until 1964. See also VAVILOV, NIKOLAI IVANOVICH.

**lysergic acid diethylamide:** see LSD.

**Lysippos** (lie,sipəs), fl. late 4th cent. BC, Greek sculptor, head of the Sicyon school. He modified the proportions for the human figure set by POLYKLEITOS, and Hellenistic sculpture was based on this more slender form with its new sense of movement. Many copies were made of the 1500 works he was said to have produced, which included many portraits of Alexander the Great, but none of the originals remains.

Apoxyomenos by **Lysippos**, Vatican Museum, Rome.

**Lyttleton, Humphrey,** 1921–, English jazz trumpeter and bandleader. Since the late 1940s 'Humph' has been the leading British champion of traditional and mainstream jazz. From his roots as a New Orleans revivalist, through the controversial move of introducing saxophones into his 1950s and later bands, his integrity as a forcefully inventive trumpet lead and soloist and charismatic bandleader has remained intact. He has also contributed invaluably to the health of jazz in Britain as a broadcaster.

**Lytton, Edward George Earle Lytton Bulwer-Lytton,** 1st **Baron:** see under BULWER-LYTTON.

# M

**Maas,** river, Europe: see MEUSE.

**Maastricht,** city (1985 pop. 114,008), capital of Limburg prov., S Netherlands. Old, established industries include glass-working and paper-making. Founded by the Romans at a bridging point of the Maas (Meuse), it is the most ancient city in the Netherlands. Fine churches and town walls are a legacy of its early ecclesiastical and strategic importance. The 6th-cent. cathedral of St Servatius is the oldest church in the Netherlands.

The cathedral of St Servatius, **Maastricht**

**Mabinogion,** collective title given medieval Welsh stories found in two manuscripts, the *White Book of Rhydderch* (c.1300–25) and the *Red Book of Hergest* (c.1375–1425). *The Four Branches of the Mabinogi* tells the tale of Prince Gwri (Pryderi), and includes three Arthurian romances —*Geraint, The Lady of the Fountain,* and *Peredur*—and other material making it an invaluable source of ARTHURIAN LEGEND.

**Mabuse, Jan de** (məˌbyoohz), c.1478–1533, Flemish painter; b. Jan Gossaert, or Gossart. He was among the first Flemish painters to represent the nude and classical mythology in the Italian manner. *A Donor and His Wife* (Brussels) and *Neptune and Amphitrite* (Berlin) are characteristic paintings.

**MAC** or **multiplex analogue components,** form of coding used for the transmission of colour TELEVISION signals from satellites. The black and white information (the luminance component) and the colour information (the chrominance component) are sent at different times so that there can be no mutual interference between them. The two components are then recombined to provide an accurate representation of the original colour picture. This avoids the cross luminance/colour interference defects of various systems used terrestrially and also results in significantly less noise in saturated colour signals. In the MAC signal the sound is carried as bursts of digital data between each line of the picture.

**Mac, Mc** or **M',** element in names derived from Irish and Scottish Gaelic patronymics. In most of these names the second element was a forename (e.g., *Macdonald,* in various spellings). Notions that some forms of the prefix are more typically Scottish or Irish are fallacious.

**McAdam, John Loudon,** 1756–1836, Scottish inventor. He went to New York in 1770, and returned to Scotland with a fortune 13 years later. Appalled at the condition of the roads in Britain, he experimented with road-building techniques and devised the system known as 'macadamizing', which uses broken stones. The use of tar was a later development ('tar-macadamizing' or 'tarmac').

**macadamia,** edible fruit of an evergreen tree (*Macadamia ternifolia*) native to Australia but also grown in other tropical regions. The small, edible kernel of the nut is white and crisp.

**Macao** or **Macau** (məˌkow), Mandarin *Aomen,* Portuguese overseas prov. (1985 pop. 350,000), 15.5 km² (6 sq mi), adjoining GUANGDONG prov., SE China; on the estuary of the Pearl R., (see XI JIANG), 64 km (40 mi) W of HONG KONG and 105 km (65 mi) S of GUANGZHOU (Canton). It consists of a rocky, hilly peninsula (c.5 km²/2 sq mi), connected by a 214-m (700-ft) wide isthmus to China, and two small islands. Macao is a free port and a leading trade, tourist, and gambling centre. Fishing and textiles are also important. The oldest permanent European settlement in Asia, it became a Portuguese trading post in 1557. In 1849 Portugal proclaimed it a free port. Macao has been swelled with refugees from China since 1949. Many historic structures, including fine examples of Italian and Portuguese architecture, dot the city. In March 1987 Portugal and China made a joint declaration by which Macao is to return to Chinese sovereignty as of 20 Dec. 1999.

**macaroni:** see PASTA.

**MacArthur, Douglas,** 1880–1964, American five-star general. He fought in France in WORLD WAR I and was army chief of staff (1930–35). During WORLD WAR II he commanded the Allied forces in the Southwest Pacific and directed the postwar occupation of Japan. In the KOREAN WAR, as commander of the UN military forces, he became involved in a policy dispute with Pres. TRUMAN, who removed him from command in April 1951.

**Macaulay, Herbert,** 1864–1946, Nigerian politician. He founded NIGERIA's first political party, the Nigerian National Democratic Party, in 1922. Campaigning for self-determination and against racial discrimination, his party won and retained the three Lagos seats in the Legco between 1923 and 1948. He became the first president of the National Council for Nigeria and the Cameroon (Nigeria branch) in 1944. He is popularly regarded as the father of Nigerian nationalism.

**Macaulay, Thomas Babington,** 1800–59, English historian. He sat in Parliament (1830–34, 1839–47, 1852–56) as a Whig, served in India with the EAST INDIA CO. (1834–38), and was secretary of war (1839–41). His greatest work is his *History of England from the Accession of James the Second* (5 vol., 1849–61), a vivid recreation of the political and social world of the 17th cent. An unprecedented business success, it was and has been criticized for its bias. Macaulay was elevated to the peerage in 1857.

**Macbeth,** d. 1057, king of Scotland (r.1040–57). Macbeth seized the Scottish throne by killing Duncan I in battle, but was himself defeated and killed by Duncan's son, who reigned as MALCOLM III. He is the subject of Shakespeare's *Macbeth.*

**Maccabees,** also called **Hasmoneans** and **Asmoneans,** Jewish family (in Palestine) of the 2nd and 1st cent. BC who brought about a restoration of Jewish political and religious life. When the Syrian ruler

Antiochus IV stripped and desecrated the Temple of Jerusalem and began a religious persecution, **Mattathias of Modin** and his five sons, together with many HASIDIM, began a guerrilla war. On Mattathias's death (166 BC), leadership passed to his son **Judas Maccabeus** (from whose surname, from Heb. *Makkevet* [hammer], the family name derives), who occupied Jerusalem and cleansed and rededicated the Temple; the feast of Hanukkah (see JEWISH HOLIDAYS) celebrates this event (165 BC). Judas was defeated by DEMETRIUS I of Syria and killed (161? BC), but he has gone down in Jewish history as the epitome of courage and the symbol of religious defiance. The Maccabees remained in power mostly peacefully until 63 BC, when Pompey conquered Palestine for Rome.

**Maccabees**, two books included in the OLD TESTAMENT of the Western canon, but not in the Hebrew Bible, and placed in the APOCRYPHA in the Authorized Version. First Maccabees is an account of the struggles of the house of MACCABEES against Antiochus IV of Syria. Second Maccabees is a devout history of the persecutions of Antiochus and the career of Judas Maccabeus.

**McCarrison, Sir Robert**, 1878–1960, Irish physician and nutritionist. Renowned for his work on nutritional deficiency diseases (see DEFICIENCY DISEASE), he was knighted in 1933.

**McCarthy, Joseph Raymond**, 1908–57, US senator from Wisconsin (1947–57). He achieved national prominence and power with his sensational and unsubstantiated accusations against those US officials (frequently in high positions) he termed 'Communists'. After the Senate 'condemned' him (1954), his influence steadily declined.

**McClellan, George Brinton**, 1826–1885, Union general in the AMERICAN CIVIL WAR. Appointed general in chief (1861), he was criticized for overcaution in the unsuccessful PENINSULAR CAMPAIGN and removed from command. Called on again (1862), he checked Robert E. LEE in the Antietam Campaign, but he allowed the Confederates to withdraw across the Potomac and was again removed. He ran against Abraham LINCOLN for president in 1864 but was soundly defeated.

**McClure, Sir Robert John Le Mesurier**, 1807–73, English Arctic explorer. As commander (1850–53) of one of two ships searching the Arctic Archipelago for the lost party of Sir John FRANKLIN, he discovered McClure Strait and proved the existence of the NORTHWEST PASSAGE.

**McCormack, John**, 1884–1945, American tenor; b. Ireland. Moving to the US in 1909, he sang with the Boston and Chicago operas, appeared in concerts, and made many famous recordings, often of simple, sentimental songs.

**McCormick, Cyrus Hall** 1809–84, American inventor. The reaper that he invented in 1831 marked the beginning of mechanized farming.

**McCrae, John**, 1872–1918, Canadian physician and poet. His famous war poem 'In Flanders Fields' appeared in *Punch* in 1915 and in a posthumous volume, *In Flanders Fields* (1919).

**McCullers, Carson**, 1917–67, American author. She often explored spiritual isolation in her fiction, using outcasts and misfits as main characters. Her works include the novels *The Heart Is a Lonely Hunter* (1940) and *The Member of the Wedding* (1946; dramatized, 1950), and the short-story collection *The Ballad of the Sad Cafe* (1951; dramatized by Edward ALBEE, 1963).

**MacDiarmid, Hugh**, pseud. of **Christopher Murray Grieve**, 1892–1978, Scottish poet and critic. A communist and Scottish nationalist, he wrote both in English and in the Scots vernacular. His early collections of lyrics, *Sangschaw* (1925) and *Penny Wheep* (1926), were the most influential in Scottish poetry since BURNS. *A Drunk Man Looks at the Thistle* (1926) and *In Memoriam James Joyce* (1955) are longer works. His later verse amounts to an uncompleted epic of the Celtic consciousness.

**Macdonald, Sir John Alexander**, 1815–91, Conservative leader of Upper Canada and 1st prime minister of the Dominion of Canada. In this role (1867–73, 1878–91) he established strong links with Britain and facilitated western development. Although he resigned (1873) over the Pacific Scandal, he was returned (1878) to office.

**Macdonald, Ramsay**, 1866–1937, British statesman. An organizer of the LABOUR PARTY, he was elected (1906) to the House of Commons, where he was party leader (1911–14). Discredited for his pacifism during World

War I, he was defeated (1918), but returned to Parliament in 1922. In Jan. 1924 he became prime minister in the country's first Labour government, but in December Labour was defeated amid charges that it was pro-Communist. In 1929 Macdonald again became prime minister in a Labour government, but in 1931 formed the coalition National government, which leaned on Conservative support. He resigned the premiership to Stanley BALDWIN in 1935.

**Macdonald, Ross**, pseud. of **Kenneth Millar**, 1915–, American author. Featuring the tough but compassionate private detective Lew Archer, his novels include *The Galton Case* (1959), *The Chill* (1964), *The Good-bye Look* (1969), *The Underground Man* (1971), and *Sleeping Beauty* (1973).

**Macdonald-Wright, Stanton**, 1890–1973, American painter. With the artist Morgan Russell, he founded synchronism (1912), an American abstract movement related to ORPHISM that employed harmonizing colours and geometric forms.

**mace:** see NUTMEG.

**Macedon** (ˌmasədon), ancient country of N GREECE, the modern MACEDONIA. The first known population included Anatolian and Hellenic peoples. By the 7th cent. BC a Greek-speaking family had set themselves up as rulers of a state in W Macedon. Hellenic influences grew, and the state became stronger until, with the great victory of PHILIP II at Chaeronea (338 BC), Macedon became master of Greece. Expanding upon Philip's conquests, his son, ALEXANDER THE GREAT, forged his fabulous empire, at the same time spreading Hellenistic civilization. When Alexander died (323 BC) his successors, the DIADOCHI, engaged in incessant warfare that split the empire and drained Macedon. Finally Antigonus II (r.277–239 BC) restored Macedon economically, and Antigonus III (r.229–221 BC) reestablished Macedonian hegemony. But PHILIP V and PERSEUS were defeated in the Macedonian Wars (215–168 BC) by Rome, which divided Macedon into four republics. After a pretender, Andriscus, tried to revive a Macedonian kingdom, Macedon was made the first Roman province (146 BC). It never again had political importance in ancient times.

**Macedonia**, region, SE Europe, on the BALKAN PENINSULA, divided among Greece, Yugoslavia, and Bulgaria. It extends N from the Aegean Sea between Epirus and the Pindus mountains (W) and Thrace and the Rhodope range (E) as far as the Šar Mts, comprising approximately 40,000 km² (25,000 sq mi). Largely mountainous on either side of the Vardar-Axios valley, its climate is continental in the N and Mediterranean in the S. Tobacco-growing, stock-raising, and mining are the main economic pursuits. THESSALONIKI is the major city and port. With Rome's division (AD 395) Macedonia came under Byzantium. Slav tribes settled the region in the 6th cent. and were converted to Christianity by Sts Clement and Naum, disciples of Sts CYRIL and METHODIUS. Control was contested (9th–14th cent.) by the Byzantine, Bulgarian, Serbian, and other empires before Macedonia fell to the Ottomans. In the 19th cent. all or part of the region was claimed by the expanding Greek, Serbian, and Bulgarian states, as well as by indigenous Slavs who advocated its unity and autonomy. Each side backed terrorist bands that aimed to provoke great power intervention against the Turks (see INTERNAL MACEDONIAN REVOLUTIONARY ORGANIZATION). The BALKAN WARS (1912–13) established roughly the present boundaries, to the fury of Bulgaria, which allied with Germany in both World Wars in order to reverse the verdict. Greek Macedonia was effectively Hellenized by refugees from Asia Minor after 1922; whereas the Slavs of Serbian (later Yugoslav) Macedonia were recognized as a separate Macedonian nation in the post-1945 Yugoslav federation, an innovation still disputed by Bulgaria.

**Macedonia**, constituent republic of Yugoslavia (1981 pop. 1,909,136), 25,713 km² (9928 sq mi), SE Yugoslavia. SKOPJE is the capital. A less developed republic, industrialization has proceeded since 1945. The population is composed of Macedonians (67%), Albanians (20%), Turks (4.5%) and other lesser groups. The bulk of the territory of the present republic was incorporated in Serbia in the BALKAN WARS (1912–13) and reincorporated in its Yugoslav successor following Bulgarian occupation during World War I. The populace was regarded as Serb by the interwar Yugoslav regime, which stimulated violence and pro-Bulgarian sentiment. Recognition and promotion of a distinct Macedonian national identity and status by the Yugoslav Communists led, after Bulgaria's occupation in World War II, to the establishment of the Macedonian republic and the affirmation of its language, literature, and Orthodox Church.

**Maceió** (masie,yooh), city and port (1980 pop. 375,711), NE Brazil, capital of Alagôas state. It was founded in 1815 and has been the provincial capital since 1839. Situated on the Atlantic coast it is the regional port for the export of sugar, cotton, rum, and tobacco.

**McEnroe, John (Patrick, Jr.),** 1959–, American tennis player; b. West Germany. With three straight US Open victories by 1981 and a Wimbledon title that year, he gained top world ranking, and at the same time became known for his on-court temper displays.

**McGillivray, Alexander,** 1759–93, CREEK INDIAN chief, son of a Scots trader and French-Creek mother. Educated in Charleston, South Carolina, he returned to Creek country as a British agent during the AMERICAN REVOLUTION. He signed (1784) a treaty with Spain to gain an annuity and arms, which he used against American settlers until Pres. Washington made him a brigadier general by the Treaty of New York (1790). A skilled diplomat, he acknowledged US sovereignty and promised peace, but in 1792 he resumed Spanish-subsidized attacks.

**Macgillycuddy's Reeks,** mountain range, in SW of Republic of Ireland. They are situated in the S of Co. Kerry, to the W of Killarney. The highest point is Carrantuohill, which at 1041 m (3414 ft) is the highest peak in Ireland.

**McGovern, George Stanley,** 1922–, US senator (1963–81). He was among the first senators to oppose the VIETNAM WAR. He ran for president on the Democratic ticket in 1972, on a platform promising to end the war, cut defence spending, and provide a guaranteed annual income for all Americans, but he was defeated by Richard M. NIXON.

**MacGregor, Robert:** see ROB ROY.

**Mach, Ernst** (makh), 1838–1916, Austrian physicist and philosopher. He did his major work in the philosophy of science, striving to rid science of metaphysical assumptions, and is regarded as the father of LOGICAL POSITIVISM. He also did work in ballistics; the MACH NUMBER is named after him.

**Mácha, Karel Hynek** (,mahkhah), 1810–36, Czech writer. The romantic EPIC *May* (1836), considered the finest lyric work in Czech, reveals his determinism and ironic conception of nature and woman.

**Machado, Antonio** (mah,chahdhoh), 1875–1939, Spanish poet, essayist, and dramatist. His poetry, including *Soledades* (1902; tr. Solitudes), *Campos de Castilla* (1912; tr. Castilian Fields), and *Complete Poems* (1917, 1928), was influenced by Castilian life and landscape and the death of his young wife. He also wrote philosophical and literary essays, and, with his brother, the poet and dramatist **Manuel Machado,** 1874–1947, several plays. In the SPANISH CIVIL WAR, however, they were on opposing sides; in 1939 Antonio, a Loyalist, fled to France, where he died.

**Machado, Gerardo,** 1871–1939, Cuban president (1925–33). He tried to free CUBA from political and economic dependence on the US by taxing US investments and developing Cuba's economy. When he resorted to terrorism to crush opposition, the US intervened (1933), and he fled.

**Machado de Assis, Joaquim Maria,** 1839–1908, Brazilian novelist, considered Brazil's greatest writer. In his subtly ironic novels he displayed his keen psychological insight and his pessimistic vision. His novels include *Epitaph of a Small Winner* (1881), *Philosopher or Dog* (1891), and *Dom Casmurro* (1900).

**Machaut, Guillaume de** (ma,shoh), c.1300–1377, French poet and composer. His chivalric experience is seen in *Le livre du voir dit* (1361–65), a long poem of courtly love with musical interpolations. He wrote lais, ballads, rondeaux, and virelais, and used COURTLY LOVE texts for his secularized MOTETS. His innovative, polyphonic MASS led to the great masses of JOSQUIN DESPREZ and PALESTRINA.

**Machel, Samora Moïsés,** 1933–86, president of MOZAMBIQUE (1975–86). He was army commander (1966–74) and president (1970–86) of Frelimo, a revolutionary group that fought to free Mozambique from Portuguese rule. In 1975 he became the first president of independent Mozambique and worked to convert the nation into a Marxist society. He was killed in 1986 when the airliner in which he was returning from Zambia crashed just inside South African territory.

**Machiavelli, Niccolò,** 1469–1527, Italian political philosopher and statesman. As defence secretary of the Florentine republic he substituted a citizens' militia for the mercenary system. Through diplomatic missions he became acquainted with power politics, meeting such leaders as Cesare BORGIA. When the MEDICI family returned to power (1512) he was dismissed, and briefly imprisoned and tortured. He then retired to his country estate, where he wrote on politics. His most famous work, *The Prince* (1532), describes the means by which a leader may gain and maintain power. His 'ideal' prince is an amoral and calculating tyrant capable of unifying Italy. Despite the ruthless connotation of the term *Machiavellian,* such works as the *Discourses* (1531) and the *History of Florence* (1532) express republican principles. Machiavelli also wrote poems and plays, notably the comedy *Mandragola* (1524).

**machine,** any arrangement of stationary and moving mechanical parts used to perform some useful WORK or a specialized task. By means of a machine, a small force can be applied to move a much greater resistance or load; the force, however, must be applied through a much greater distance than it would if it could move the load directly. The mechanical advantage of a machine is the factor by which it multiplies any applied force. The simplest machines are (1) the *lever,* consisting of a bar supported at some stationary point (the fulcrum) along its length, and used to overcome resistance at a second point by application of force at a third point; (2) the *pulley,* consisting of a wheel over which a rope, belt, chain, or cable runs; (3) the *inclined plane,* consisting of a sloping surface, whose purpose is to reduce the force that must be applied to raise a load; (4) the *screw,* consisting essentially of a solid cylinder around which an inclined plane winds spirally, whose purpose is to fasten one object to another, to lift a heavy object, or to move an object by a precise amount; and (5) the *wheel and axle,* consisting of a wheel mounted rigidly upon an axle or drum of smaller diameter, the wheel and axle having the same axis. The more complicated machines are merely combinations of these simple machines. Machines used to transform other forms of energy (as heat) into mechanical energy are known as engines, e.g., the STEAM ENGINE or the INTERNAL COMBUSTION ENGINE. The electric MOTOR transforms electrical energy into mechanical energy; its operation is the reverse of that of the electric GENERATOR. In the past, the first machines, e.g., the catapult, were built to improve war-making capacity. The first manufacturing machines, powered by steam engines, appeared during the 18th cent., causing the onset of the INDUSTRIAL REVOLUTION.

**machine gun:** see SMALL ARMS.

**machine tool,** power-operated tool used for shaping or finishing metal parts by removing chips, shavings, large pieces, or extremely small particles. Machine tools vary in size from hand-held devices used for drilling and grinding to large stationary machines that perform a number of different operations. The lathe, for example, can turn, face, thread, and drill. The working surfaces of a machine tool are made of such substances as high-speed steels, sintered carbides, and diamonds, substances that can withstand the great heat generated by the action of the working surface against the workpiece. Numerical-control machine tools (NCM) are machine tools operated and controlled from a digital computer. The operator is a computer software programmer working straight from engineering drawings. Such tools offer tremendous flexibility in manufacturing capability. See also AUTOMATIC CONTROL.

**Mach number,** measure of air speed, being the ratio between the air speed of an aircraft to the local velocity of sound under specific conditions of temperature and height. It is named after Dr Ernst Mach of Vienna, who built a wind tunnel in Germany in 1893. Mach 1 in international standard atmosphere is 1124 kph (761 mph) at sea level, falling to 1062 kph (660 mph) at a height of 11,000 m (36,000 ft), above which it remains constant. Subsonic speeds are those below Mach 1, supersonic are those at Mach 1 and above, and hypersonic speeds are Mach 5 and above. See also FLIGHT, POWERED.

**Machu Picchu,** fortress city of the ancient INCAS, in a high saddle between two peaks 80 km (50 mi) NW of Cuzco, Peru. The extraordinary pre-Columbian ruin, about 13 km² (5 sq mi) of terraced stonework linked by 3000 steps, was probably the last Inca stronghold after the Spanish Conquest; it was virtually intact when discovered by the American Hiram Bingham in 1911.

**Mackay,** city (1986 pop. 38,603), Queensland, NE Australia. As a tourist centre this is the southern base for visitors to the GREAT BARRIER REEF, particularly Hayman Island and the Whitsunday group of islands. An important sugar-producing area, it also exports coal. Hay Point, the port, ranks as fourth largest in Australia by tonnage of cargo handled.

Machu Picchu

**Macke, August** (ˌmakə), 1887–1914, German painter. A brilliant colourist, he met KANDINSKY and MARC in Munich in 1909–10 and joined and exhibited with the BLAUE REITER group. In 1914 (before being killed in the war) he went to Tunisia with Paul KLEE, doing watercolours of prismatic patterns derived from DELAUNAY's ORPHISM, which he saw on a visit to Paris in 1912.

**Mackendrick, Alexander**, 1912–, British film director. Despite a limited output, he proved a distinctive director of both British Ealing studio films and American features. His films include *The Ladykillers* (1955), *Sweet Smell of Success* (1957), and *A High Wind in Jamaica* (1965).

**Mackenzie**, one of the world's great rivers, NW Canada, flowing c.1800 km (1120 mi) generally NW from Great Slave Lake to enter the Arctic Ocean through a vast delta. Navigable only in summer (June–October), it drains the northern portion of the GREAT PLAINS and is the main channel of the c.4180 km (2600 mi) Finlay–Peace–Mackenzie river system. Oil, discovered at Norman Wells in the 1930s, and natural gas, found in the delta region in the 1970s, are major resources.

**Mackenzie, Sir Alexander**, 1764?–1820, Scottish explorer in Canada. A fur trader, he followed (1789) an unknown river (later named after him) to the Arctic Ocean. He discovered (1793) the Fraser River while pioneering the first overland route through the Canadian Rockies to the Pacific.

**Mackenzie, William Lyon**, 1795–1861, Canadian insurgent leader. A Scottish immigrant (1820), he published (1824–34) the *Colonial Advocate,* which attacked the FAMILY COMPACT clique. As leader of the Reform party he became (1834) the first mayor of TORONTO. After the Reform party's defeat he led (1837) an armed rebellion in Toronto that was quickly put down. He fled to the US but was imprisoned for violating the neutrality laws. After a general amnesty (1849) he returned to Canada and served in the assembly.

**Mackenzie King, William Lyon:** see KING, WILLIAM LYON MACKENZIE.

**mackerel,** open-sea FISH of the family Scombridae, which includes the albacore, bonito, and tuna. Mackerel have deeply forked tails, narrowed where they join the body, finlets behind the dorsal and anal fins, and streamlined bodies. They are superb, swift swimmers of generally large size and are important commercially as food. They travel in schools feeding on fish, especially HERRING, and SQUID, and migrate between deep and shallow waters. The largest mackerel is the tuna (700 kg/¾ ton); among the smallest (700 g/1½ lb) is the common mackerel (*Scomber scombrus*) of the Atlantic. Many members of the family, especially tuna and mackerel, are important food-fishes.

**Mackerras, Sir Charles**, 1925–, Australian conductor. He was principal conductor of the English National Opera 1970–77. He arranged Sir Arthur SULLIVAN's music for the ballet *Pineapple Poll.*

**Mackinder, Sir Halford John**, 1861–1947, English geographer. Mackinder, appointed in 1887 as reader at Oxford University, established geography as an academic subject, was a director (1903–08) of the London School of Economics, and was a member of Parliament (1909–22). In *Democratic Ideals and Reality* (1904) he put forth the view of Eurasia as the geographical pivot and 'heartland' of history, a theory that received little attention until it was adopted in Germany to support Nazi GEOPOLITICS.

**McKinley, Mount** or **Denali**, 6194 m (20,320 ft), S central Alaska, US, the highest point in North America. It was first climbed in 1913 by American explorer Hudson Stuck.

The South face of **Mount McKinley**, Alaska

**McKinley, William**, 1843–1901, 25th president of the US (1897–1901). As Republican congressman from Ohio (1877–91), he strongly advocated a protective tariff, and the McKinley Tariff Act of 1890 cost him his congressional seat. With the support of Ohio political boss Marcus A. Hanna, McKinley was elected governor of Ohio in 1891 and 1893. Again with Hanna's help, he won the Republican nomination for president in 1896. Running against William Jennings BRYAN on a platform advocating a protective tariff and endorsing the gold standard, McKinley was elected. His administration was marked by adoption of the highest tariff rate in US history, annexation of Hawaii, the OPEN DOOR policy in China, and the Currency Act of 1900, which consolidated the gold standard. Foreign affairs were dominated by the brief SPANISH-AMERICAN WAR, from which the US emerged a world power. McKinley was reelected in 1900. He was shot in Buffalo, New York State, by Leon Czolgosz, an anarchist, on 6 Sept. 1901, and died on 14 Sept.

**Mackintosh, Charles Rennie**, 1868–1928, Scottish architect, artist, and furniture designer. His decorative and graphic works epitomize the imagination and elegance of ART NOUVEAU. His few buildings display Scottish simplicity, subtlety, and a mastery of spatial design; outstanding is the Glasgow School of Art (1897–1909).

Charles Rennie **Mackintosh**: Library in Glasgow School of Art (1897–1909)

**MacLennan, Hugh,** 1907– , Canadian writer. His novels, including *Two Solitudes* (1945), *The Watch That Ends the Night* (1959), and *Return of the Sphinx* (1967), use Canadian life as a paradigm of the human condition.

**Macleod, John James Rickard,** 1876–1935, Scottish physiologist. For their discovery of INSULIN (together with Charles BEST and James COLLIP) and studies of its use in treating diabetes, he and Sir Frederick BANTING shared the 1923 Nobel Prize for physiology or medicine.

**MacLiammoir, Michael,** 1899–1978, Irish actor and playwright; b. Alfred Williams. Appearing as a child actor in *Peter Pan* with the great Beerbohm TREE in London, he was well-known for 60 years on the Dublin stage. In 1928 he founded the Dublin Gate Theatre with the Englishman Hilton Edwards.

**McLuhan, (Herbert) Marshall,** 1911–80, Canadian communications theorist and educator. He taught at universities in Canada and the US, gaining fame in the 1960s with his proposal that electronic media, especially television, were creating a 'global village' in which 'the medium is the message', i.e., the means of communications has a greater influence on people than the information itself. His books include *The Gutenberg Galaxy* (1962) and *Understanding Media* (1964).

**MacMahon, Marie Edmé Patrice de** (makma-ˌonh), 1808–93, president of the French republic (1873–79). Of Irish descent, he won a victory at Magenta in the Italian war of 1859, served in the FRANCO-PRUSSIAN WAR, and aided the suppression of the COMMUNE OF PARIS. A monarchist, he was chosen by the royalists in the National Assembly as president, but did not restore the monarchy. Under the new constitution, MacMahon caused a crisis by dismissing (May 1877) a republican cabinet that had the support of the new chamber of deputies. In December he was finally forced to accept a ministry that had the approval of the chamber, thus establishing the principle of ministerial responsibility to the chamber rather than to the president.

**MacMillan, Kenneth,** 1929– , Scottish dancer and choreographer. After an early career with Sadlers Wells Ballet, he went to the Royal Ballet: he was resident choreographer (1965), director (1970–77), and from 1977 on, principal choreographer. He was director of German Opera (1966–69). He developed the full-length ballet as an instrument of intense dramatic expression, e.g., *Anastasia* (1971), *Manon* (1974), *Mayerling* (1978), and *Isadora* (1981).

**Macmillan, (Maurice) Harold (Earl of Stockton),** 1894–86, British statesman. A Conservative, he entered Parliament in 1924 and later served as minister of housing and local government (1951–54), minister of defence (1954–55), foreign secretary (1955), and chancellor of the exchequer (1955–57). As prime minister (1957–63) he strove to improve East–West relations and (unsuccessfully at that stage) to gain Britain's entry into the EUROPEAN COMMUNITY. In 1963 his government's prestige was damaged by a scandal linking his minister of war, John Profumo, to a call girl and a Soviet official; his resignation that year was, however, occasioned by ill-health. He accepted an earldom in 1984.

"I TOLD YOU THIS SORT OF STUFF WILL FETCH 'EM BACK INTO THE OLD CINEMA . . ."

**Macmillan** as 'Supermac', Vicky's most successful cartoon characterization which first appeared in the *Evening Standard* in 1958

**McNamara, Robert Strange,** 1916– , US secretary of defence (1961–68). He was president (1960–61) of the Ford Motor Co. At the Defence Dept. he modernized management techniques and deemphasized nuclear weapons. His doubts about the VIETNAM WAR led him to resign (1968) from the cabinet. He later served (1968–81) as president of the World Bank.

**McNaughton, Andrew George Latta,** 1887–1966, Canadian general. He was Canadian chief of staff (1929–35) and commander of Canadian forces in Britain during WORLD WAR II. He served as defence minister (1944–46) and in other posts.

**MacNeice, Louis,** 1907–63, Irish poet. Educated in England, he became a leading exponent of the 1930s style in poetry. He collaborated with W.H. AUDEN in *Letters from Iceland* (1937). His *Autumn Journal* (1939), a long poem, is a wry, frank record of personal and political dilemmas. His later books of poetry include *Springboard* (1954), *Autumn Sequel* (1954), and *Solstices* (1961). A classical scholar and professional broadcaster, his works include radio dramas and a translation of AESCHYLUS.

**McPherson, Aimee Semple,** 1890–1944, US evangelist. She opened (1923) the Angelus Temple in Los Angeles and was a founder (1927) of the International Church of Foursquare Gospel. In 1926 her disappearance and reappearance, with a bizarre tale of kidnapping, led to a trial for fraud. Although she was acquitted, her business dealings resulted in numerous other legal actions. She died from an accidental overdose of sleeping pills.

**Macpherson, James,** 1736–96, Scottish writer. He wrote *Fragments of Ancient Poetry Collected in the Highlands of Scotland* (1760), supposedly translations from Gaelic, and two epic poems, *Fingal* (1761) and *Temora* (1763), represented as the work of OSSIAN, a 3rd-cent. bard. The works were mainly Macpherson's own, and they strongly influenced ROMANTICISM.

**Macquarie Island**, small isolated island in the Southern Ocean, S of Tasmania, of which it is a dependency. Discovered in 1810 (although a shipwreck found then indicated earlier visitors), it was the site of sealing and penguin-oil industries until 1919. A permanent meteorological station was established in 1948.

**macramé**, decorative knotting technique. Named after an Arabic word for knotted fringe, it arose in the 13th cent. and reached Europe during the next hundred years. A traditional sailors' pastime, after decades of obscurity it was revived in the 1960s for wall hangings, jewellery, and other objects.

**Macready, William Charles**, 1793–1873, English actor and manager. His portrayal of Richard III (1819) established him as a major tragedian. His 1849 US tour was marred by a riot by supporters of his rival Edwin FORREST.

**macroeconomics:** see under ECONOMICS.

**McTaggart, John McTaggart Ellis**, 1866–1925, British philosopher. He wrote three studies on HEGEL, but his major work is *The Nature of Existence* (2 vol., 1921, 1927), which expounds a highly idiosyncratic version of HEGEL's idealism. Space, time, and matter are unreal; ultimate reality comprises only immortal minds and their contents, and the apparent physical universe is merely a systematic 'misperception' of parts of these minds.

**Macy, Anne Sullivan**, 1866–1936, American educator. Partially blinded by a childhood infection, she attended Perkins Institution for the Blind, learned the manual alphabet, and was chosen (1887) to teach Helen KELLER. Macy based her instruction on a system of touch teaching, pioneering in techniques of education for the handicapped, and helped promote the newly founded (1921) American Foundation for the Blind.

**Madagascar**, officially Democratic Republic of Madagascar, formerly Malagasy Republic, republic (1987 est. pop. 9,985,000), 587,045 km² (226,658 sq mi) in the Indian Ocean, separated from E Africa by the Mozambique Channel. The nation comprises Madagascar, the world's fourth largest island, and several small islands. ANTANANARIVO (Tananarive) is the capital. The island of Madagascar is a largely deforested highland plateau fringed by a lowland coastal strip; mountains in the north rise to more than 2745 m (9000 ft). The economy is predominantly agricultural, producing rice (the staple crop), coffee, sugarcane, cloves, and vanilla. Large numbers of livestock and poultry are raised. Manufacturing, mostly confined to food-processing and textiles, is becoming more diversified. Chromite, graphite, and phosphates are extracted, and petroleum was found offshore in 1980. The GNP is US$2378 million, and the GNP per capita is US$240 (1985). The two main population groups are of Indonesian and black African descent. French and Malagasy, an Indonesian language spoken by all the people, are the official languages. About 40% of the population is Christian, 5% is Muslim, and the rest follow traditional beliefs.

*History.* Black Africans and Indonesians first reached Madagascar about 2000 years ago; they were joined in the 9th cent. AD by Muslim traders from E Africa and the COMOROS. The first Europeans to visit the island were the Portuguese (1500), but it was the French who established footholds, beginning in 1642. In the 19th cent. the rulers of the Merina kingdom, one of several that had developed on the island, opened the island to European traders and Christian missionaries who, in return, helped spread Merina control and culture; by the end of the century the Merina kingdom included almost the entire island. In 1885 France established a protectorate over Madagascar, but the Merina resisted fiercely, and it was not until 1904 that the French fully controlled the island. In WORLD WAR II Madagascar was aligned with Vichy France until taken (1942) by the British and turned over to a Free French regime (1943). A major uprising against the French in 1947–48 was crushed, but the independence movement gained momentum in the 1950s, and in 1958 the country, renamed the Malagasy Republic, gained autonomy. Full independence came in 1960, with Philibert Tsiranana as president. In 1972 widespread protests over economic failures prompted the autocratic president to step aside. Political strife continued, however, and in 1975 power was seized by a military directorate, a Marxist regime was installed, and the country was renamed the Democratic Republic of Madagascar. In Assembly elections in 1983, Pres. Didier Ratsiraka's Vanguard of the Malagasy Revolution confirmed its dominance within the National Front for the Defence of the Revolution (the umbrella body for legal parties).

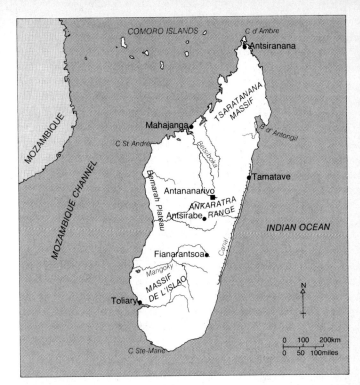

Madagascar

**Madariaga, Salvador de** (mahdhah,ryahgah), 1886–1978, Spanish writer and diplomat. He headed the disarmament section of the League of Nations (1922–27); later he was the Spanish Republic's ambassador to the US (1931) and France (1932–34) and chief delegate to the League of Nations (1931–36). After the SPANISH CIVIL WAR he exiled himself to England. His many books include *The Genius of Spain* (1923), *Don Quixote* (1934), *Bolívar* (1951), *Anatomy of the Cold War* (1955), novels, poetry, plays, historical and psychological studies, and memoirs (1974).

**madder**, common name for the family Rubiaceae, chiefly tropical and subtropical trees, shrubs, and herbs. The family is important economically for several tropical crops, e.g., COFFEE and QUININE (from CINCHONA), and for many ornamentals, e.g., the madder, GARDENIA and bedstraw. True madder, called dyer's madder (*Rubia tinctorum*), is a dye plant native to S Europe. The herb's long, fleshy root was the principal source of various brilliant red dye pigments until artificial production of alizarin, the pigment chemical in madder. The bedstraws (genus *Galium*), formerly used for mattress filling because of their pleasing odour, have clusters of tiny white or yellow flowers.

**Madeira Islands**, archipelago (1984 est. pop. 264,787), 798 km² (308 sq mi), coextensive with Funchal dist., Portugal, in the Atlantic Ocean c.560 km (350 mi) off Morocco. Madeira, the largest island, and Porto Santo are inhabited; the Desertas and Selvagens are not. Madeira is a scenic, year-round resort. The islands produce sugarcane and Madeira wine. Known to the Romans, they were rediscovered (15th cent.) under HENRY THE NAVIGATOR.

**Maderna, Bruno**, 1920–73, Italian composer. He played a major role in the postwar development of Italian music; e.g., in 1955 he assisted Luciano BERIO in founding the electronic music studio in Milan. His *Musica su due dimensioni* for flute, percussion, and tape (1952) was the first to combine live and electronic instruments.

**Madero, Francisco Indalecio**, 1873–1913, president of MEXICO (1911–13). A champion of democracy and social reform, he led (1910) the revolution that swept through Mexico and overthrew (1911) the DIAZ regime, but he failed to implement notable reforms. Revolts broke out, and Gen. HUERTA treacherously assassinated Madero's brother, seized power, and arrested and imprisoned Madero. He was killed while allegedly attempting to escape.

**Madison,** US city (1984 est. pop. 171,000), state capital of Wisconsin, on an isthmus between Lakes Monona and Mendota; inc. 1856. It is a trading centre in a rich agricultural area, and produces meat products, machinery, medical equipment, and other goods.

**Madison, James,** 1751–1836, 4th president of the US (1809–17). An early opponent of British colonial measures, he helped draft the Constitution for the new state of VIRGINIA (1776), served in the CONTINENTAL CONGRESS (1780–83, 1787), and was a member of the Virginia legislature (1784–86). He was active in the call for the ANNAPOLIS CONVENTION (1786), and his contributions at the FEDERAL CONSTITUTIONAL CONVENTION (1787) earned him the title 'master builder of the Constitution'. A principal contributor to the *Federalist Papers,* he was largely responsible for securing ratification of the Constitution in Virginia. As a congressman from Virginia (1789–97), he was a strong advocate of the Bill of Rights. A steadfast enemy of the financial measures of Alexander HAMILTON, he was a leading supporter of Thomas JEFFERSON and drew up the Virginia resolutions opposing the Alien and Sedition Acts (see KENTUCKY AND VIRGINIA RESOLUTIONS). After Jefferson triumphed in the presidential election of 1800, Madison became (1801) his secretary of state. He succeeded Jefferson as president in 1809. The unpopular and unsuccessful WAR OF 1812, known disparagingly as 'Mr Madison's War', was the chief event of his administration.

**Madras,** city (1981 pop. 3,276,622), capital of Tamil Nadu state, SE India, on the Bay of Bengal. A port and industrial centre, it has chemical and motor vehicle plants, tanneries, and textile mills. It was largely built around a 17th-cent. British outpost and became a trade centre. The city's cultural institutions include the Univ. of Madras (est. 1857).

**madrasa,** Islamic institution of higher learning. From the 11th cent. these colleges spread from Khurasan westwards and within two centuries had become the major educational institutions throughout the lands of Islam, the most illustrious being the Nizamiyya at Baghdad, founded in 1067 by the Seljuq vizier Nizam al-Mulk. The normal curriculum comprised advanced studies of the KORAN, HADITH, and FIQH, along with ancillary linguistic, historical, and occasionally natural-scientific subjects. The ULAMA were graduates of these institutions, which were the major factor in the crystallization of SUNNISM.

**Madrid,** city (1981 pop. 3,188,297), capital of Spain and of Madrid prov., central Spain, on the Manzanares R. A modern city of broad, tree-lined avenues, Madrid also has old quarters with picturesque winding streets. The city is Spain's chief transportation and administrative centre and the focus of modern industrial development. It became the capital of Spain in 1561 under PHILIP II but remained small until expanded in the 18th cent. under the Bourbons (especially CHARLES III). Two of the city's most famous landmarks, the royal palace and the PRADO, date from that period. Madrid's resistance against the French in the PENINSULAR WAR in 1808 was immortalized in two of GOYA'S best-known paintings (now in the Prado), and the city again played an heroic role in the SPANISH CIVIL WAR (1936–39) by holding out against an Insurgent siege for 29 months.

**madrigal,** name for two different forms of Italian music. The poetic madrigal of the 14th cent. consisted of one to four strophes of three lines each, followed by a two-line strophe (ritornello). These early examples were emotionally restrained and featured three or four voices in homophony, i.e., with one voice carrying the melody. The 16th-cent. madrigal was a musically unrelated, free poetic imitation of the earlier form. The classic madrigals of Andrea Gabrieli, Luca Marenzio and others were polyphonic and usually written for five voices, with their musical expression closely allied to the text. A final phase, exemplified by Carlo Gesualdo and Claudio MONTEVERDI, featured use of the chromatic scale of twelve tones and special effects (such as multiple choirs) devised to intensify the expression of the text. The polyphonic madrigal also flourished in Elizabethan England with the work of Thomas MORLEY, Thomas Weelkes, and others.

**Madurai,** city (1981 pop. 820,891), Tamil Nadu state, S India, on the Vaigai R. It is a district administrative, commercial, and communications centre, and holds a dominant position in the economic, social, and cultural life of the southernmost part of India. It has traditional craft industries, especially silk, and modern cotton textile factories. It is an ancient city dating from the 9th cent. and has been an important place almost ever since, though subject to many vicissitudes. Its famous temple dates from the period of the Nayak dynasty (16th–18th cent.). Madurai became a British district headquarters.

**Maecenas** (mee͵seenas), (Caius Maecenas), d. 8 BC, Roman statesman and patron of letters under AUGUSTUS. His famous literary circle included HORACE, VIRGIL, and PROPERTIUS. His name is the symbol of the wealthy benefactor of the arts.

**maenads** ͵(meenadz), in Greek and Roman mythology, female devotees of DIONYSUS or BACCHUS. Waving the thyrsus, they roamed the mountains and forests, and performed frenzied, ecstatic dances. They are also known as Bacchae.

**Maerlant, Jacob van** ͵(mahlant), c.1235–c.1300, Flemish poet, the earliest important figure of Dutch literature. He wrote lyric poems and chivalric verse romances as well as long didactic poems, chief of which is *The Mirror of History.*

**Maeterlinck, Maurice** (͵maytə'lingk), 1862–1949, Belgian author who wrote in French. His 60-odd volumes, with their suggestion of universal mystery and sense of impending doom, can be read as a SYMBOLIST manifesto. Major works include the plays *Pelléas et Mélisande* (1892) and *Monna Vanna* (1902); the allegorical fantasy *The Blue Bird* (1909); and the essay *The Life of the Bee* (1901). He was awarded the Nobel Prize in literature in 1911.

**Mafia,** name given, probably in the 1800s, to organized, independent groups of brigands in Sicily. Following a feudal tradition, the Mafia disdained all legal authorities, sought justice through direct action (as in the vendetta), and observed a rigid code of secrecy, practices that enabled Mafiosi to rise in ORGANIZED CRIME after coming to the US as Italian immigrants in the late 19th and early 20th cent. The Mafia survived MUSSOLINI's attempt to stamp it out in Italy before World War II. In the US, the Mafia was reputedly active in both illegal and legal (or 'front') operations in the early 1980s.

**Mafikeng,** formerly Mafeking, town (1970 pop. 6,900), N central South Africa. It is the market for a cattle-raising and dairy-farming area and is an important railway depot. In the SOUTH AFRICAN WAR (1899–1902), a British garrison here withstood a 217-day Boer siege. Formerly in Cape Province, Mafikeng was incorporated into BOPHUTHATSWANA in 1980.

**Magdalen:** see MARY, in the Bible, 2.

**Magdalena,** one of the major rivers of South America situated totally within the boundaries of Colombia. It rises in the high plateau of the Andes on the frontier with Ecuador and its 1600 km (1000 mi) course traverses Colombia from N to S passing through 9° of latitude. About 320 km (200 mi) from its mouth on the Caribbean it is joined by its major tributary, the Cauca R., Colombia's second most important river.

**Magdalenian industry,** a manufacturing technology of the Upper PALAEOLITHIC period in W Europe, named after the site of La Madeleine in the Dordogne, France. The tool kit includes a wide variety of stone tools, including tanged points and scrapers, and bone and antler points, needles, and awls. The great flowering of Palaeolithic art—cave paintings (see ALTAMIRA; LASCAUX), engravings, and carved antler and bone—is linked to this period, about 16,000–10,000 BC.

Magdalenian industry: bover, point burin, and scraper (left to right)

**Magdeburg,** city (1984 pop. 288,934), W East Germany, on the Elbe R. It is a large inland port and an industrial centre producing steel, paper, and other goods. Founded by the 9th cent., it accepted the REFORMATION in 1524. During the THIRTY YEARS WAR it was sacked and burned by imperial forces; 85% of the population perished. Rebuilt under the electorate of BRANDENBURG, it became a Prussian fortress in the 17th cent. During WORLD WAR II it was badly damaged. Landmarks include an 11th-cent. Romanesque church.

**Magellan, Ferdinand,** c.1480–1521, Portuguese navigator, leader of the first expedition to circumnavigate the globe. Of noble birth, he was backed by CHARLES I of Spain to reach the MOLUCCAS by sailing west. He began in 1519 with five ships and explored the Río de la Plata, wintering in PATAGONIA. He then sailed through the straits which bear his name and headed NW across the Pacific, reaching the Marianas and the PHILIPPINES, where he was killed by natives. His voyage proved the roundness of the earth and revealed the Americas as a new world.

**Magellan, Strait of,** c.530 km (330 mi) long and 4–24 km (2½–15 mi) wide, N of Cape HORN. Separating TIERRA DEL FUEGO from mainland South America, it was important in the days of sailing ships. The strait was discovered (1520) by Ferdinand MAGELLAN.

**Magellanic Clouds,** two irregular GALAXIES that are the nearest extragalactic objects (nearly 200,000 LIGHT-YEARS distant). They are visible to the naked eye in the southern skies. The Large Magellanic Cloud, about 7° in angular diameter, is located mostly in the constellation Dorado; the Small Magellanic Cloud, about 4° in diameter, is almost completely in the constellation Tucana.

The Small **Magellanic Cloud**

**Maghreb** or **Magrib,** Arabic term for NW Africa. It is generally applied to all of MOROCCO, ALGERIA, and TUNISIA, but more specifically it pertains only to the area of the three countries that lies between the Atlas Mts and the Mediterranean Sea.

**Magi** (ˌmaygie), priestly caste of ancient Persia. Magian priests headed ZOROASTRIANISM. The Magi were revered by classic authors as wise men, and their reputed power over demons gave rise to the word *magic.* For the Magi of Mat. 2, see WISE MEN OF THE EAST.

**magic,** the attempt to influence the natural or supernatural world by supernatural, ritualized means in such a way as to gain specific effects. Sympathetic magic treats an image (e.g., sticking pins in a doll representing one's enemy), while contiguous magic deals with things that have touched a person (clothing, hair, or even a footprint); the two can be used together. Magic has been seen by anthropologists as a primitive version of science, offering as it does some means of explaining phenomena in the natural and social world.

**Maginot Line** (ˌmazhinoh), fortifications on the eastern border of France, running from the Swiss border to the Belgian. Named after André Maginot, minister of war (1929–32), who directed its construction, it was considered impregnable. The Germans, however, flanked it in 1940 during WORLD WAR II.

**magistrate,** in England and Wales, part-time judge, who sits in Magistrates' Courts to deal with matters of a criminal, quasi-criminal, and civil nature, also known as Justice of the Peace. Magistrates are unpaid volunteers and not legally qualified, the idea being that people are tried by their peers. They are assisted in court by a legally qualified clerk, who advises on matters of law and procedure, though not with the actual decision. Some magistrates, known as stipendiary magistrates, are paid, full-time and legally qualified; they are entitled to hear cases alone. In criminal matters, magistrates hear and decide upon less serious and summary offences. As regards more serious or indictable offences, magistrates hear commital proceedings, where they will decide if sufficient EVIDENCE exists to send the accused for trial at the Crown Court. Over 90% of all criminal cases take place before magistrates. See COURT SYSTEM IN ENGLAND AND WALES.

**magma:** see LAVA.

**Magna Carta** [Lat., = great charter], the most famous document of British constitutional history, issued (1215) by King JOHN at Runnymede under compulsion by the barons. The purpose of the original charter was to ensure feudal rights and to guarantee that the king could not encroach on baronial privileges. The document also guaranteed the freedom of the church and the customs of the towns; implied laws protecting the rights of subjects and communities, which the king could be compelled to observe; and vaguely suggested at least to later generations guarantees of trial by jury and HABEAS CORPUS. After John's death (1216) the charter was reissued with significant omissions. In later centuries, particularly in the 17th cent., parliamentarians portrayed it as a document guaranteeing rights, but in the 19th cent. some scholars maintained that it was reactionary in that it merely guaranteed feudal privileges. It is now generally recognized that the charter showed the viability of opposition to the excessive use of royal power. There are four extant copies of the original.

**Magna Graecia** (ˌmagnə ˌgreeshə) [Lat., = great Greece], Greek colonies in S Italy, founded in the 8th cent. BC, on both coasts, S of the Bay of Naples and the Gulf of Taranto. They included Tarentum, Cumae, and Heraclea, and brought the Etruscans and Romans into early contact with Greek civilization. Magna Graecia did not thrive to the same degree as the related cities of Greek Sicily, and by 500 BC had begun a steady decline.

**Magnasco, Allessandro** (magˌnaskoh), 1667–1749, Italian painter. He painted gloomy, storm-torn landscapes and ruins with small figures and flickering light, scenes of torture, magic, and witchcraft, and scenes with saints and monks.

**magnesia,** common name for the chemical compound magnesium oxide (MgO). The fine powder is used in soaps, cosmetics, pharmaceuticals, and as a filler for rubber goods. Because of its refractory properties (it melts at c.2800° C), it is used in crucibles and ceramics. Crude magnesia is prepared by roasting DOLOMITE or MAGNESITE. Magnesia is also extracted from seawater.

**magnesite,** white, yellow, or grey magnesium carbonate mineral ($MgCO_3$). It is formed by the alteration of olivine or SERPENTINE by waters carrying carbon dioxide; by the replacement of calcium with magnesium in DOLOMITE or LIMESTONE; and by precipitation from magnesium-rich water that has reacted with sodium chloride. It is used for floorings, as a stucco, and to make firebrick, Epsom salts, face powder, boiler wrappings, and disinfectants.

**magnesium** (Mg), metallic element, discovered as an oxide by Sir Humphry DAVY in 1808. One of the ALKALINE-EARTH METALS it is ductile, silver-white, and chemically active, and it is the eighth most abundant element in the earth's crust. Its commercial uses include lightweight alloys in aircraft fuselages, jet-engine parts, rockets and missiles, cameras, and optical instruments. The metal is used in pyrotechnics. Magnesium is found in plant chlorophyll and is necessary in the diet of animals and humans. See ELEMENT (table); PERIODIC TABLE.

**magnesium hydroxide:** see MILK OF MAGNESIA.

**magnesium oxide:** see MAGNESIA.

**magnetic levitation,** suspension system for moving vehicles. In transport, motion without contact with the track reduces costs and improves the ride. A vehicle can be levitated by using a magnetic suspension in which an electromagnet mounted on the vehicle is attracted upwards to a reaction rail mounted on the track. By measuring the gap between vehicle and track, the current in the magnet can be controlled so that stable levitation can be achieved. An alternative technique is to generate an electromagnetic lifting force by the interaction of vehicle-borne electromagnets with eddy currents generated in a conducting strip in the track. The first regular magnetically levitated passenger service was inaugurated at Birmingham airport in 1984. Vehicles supported by magnetic levitation are usually driven by LINEAR MOTORS.

Magnetic levitation: Birmingham City Airport maglev vehicle

**magnetic pole,** either of two points on the earth, one in the Northern Hemisphere and one in the Southern; each point attracts one end of a compass needle and repels the opposite end. Studies of magnetism in rocks indicate that in the geological past the earth's magnetic field has reversed its polarity often and that rock movement (due to CONTINENTAL DRIFT and PLATE TECTONICS) relative to the magnetic poles has occurred.

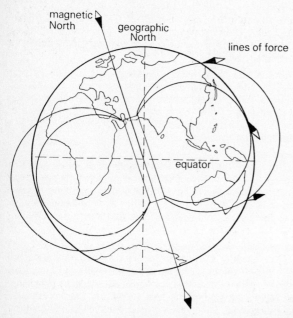

Magnetic pole

**magnetic resonance,** in physics and chemistry, phenomenon produced by simultaneously applying a steady magnetic field and ELECTROMAGNETIC RADIATION (usually radio waves) to a sample of some material and then adjusting the frequency of the radiation and the strength of the magnetic field to produce absorption of the radiation. The resonance refers to the enhancement of the absorption that occurs when the correct combination of field and frequency is reached. Most magnetic resonance phenomena depend on the fact that both the proton and the electron behave like microscopic magnets, a property that can be ascribed to an intrinsic rotation, or SPIN. Types of magnetic resonance include electron paramagnetic resonance (EPR), involving the magnetic effect of electrons, and nuclear magnetic resonance (NMR), involving the magnetic effects in the nuclei of atoms. The NMR resonant frequency provides information about the molecular material in which the nuclei reside. For the use of NMR in medicine, see NUCLEAR MAGNETIC RESONANCE.

**magnetic suspension,** the ability to suspend magnetic and conducting material, e.g., a copper plate, in air, using a controlled magnetic field. The technique requires measuring devices to measure the air gap and ensure uniformity, and computer analysis of the measurements in determining and controlling the strength of the magnetic field. The advent of the THYRISTOR has made possible the use of alternating magnetic fields from alternating current, inducing forces in conducting material in such a way as to cause the material to float above the inducing coils. Electromagnets using controlled direct current may be used either in attraction, when the floating body is supported magnetically below the magnets, or in repulsion which takes more power, when the floating object is above the excitation magnets. In conjunction with linear induction motor drives, magnetic suspension forms a friction free smooth 'ride' in linear track motion.

**magnetism,** FORCE of attraction or repulsion between various substances, especially those containing iron and certain other metals, such as nickel and cobalt; ultimately it is due to the motion of electric charges, or to the intrinsic magnetic moment (qv) of the electron. Any object that exhibits magnetic properties is called a magnet. An ordinary magnet has two poles where the magnetic forces are the strongest; these poles are designated as a north (north-seeking) pole and a south (south-seeking) pole, because a magnet freely rotating in the Earth's magnetic field tends to orient itself along a north–south line. The like poles of different magnets repel each other, and the unlike poles attract each other. Whenever a magnet is broken, a north pole appears at one of the broken faces and a south pole at the other, such that each piece has its own north and south poles. In the 18th cent. Charles COULOMB found that the magnetic forces of attraction and repulsion are directly proportional to the product of the strengths of the poles and inversely proportional to the square of the distances between them. The strength of a magnet is expressed in terms of its magnetic moment which is the product of its pole strength (both poles have the same strength) and the length of the magnet. As with electric charges, the effect of this magnetic force acting at a distance is expressed in terms of a FIELD of force. A picture of the magnetic field lines can be obtained by placing a piece of paper over a magnet and sprinkling iron filings on it. The individual pieces of iron become magnetized by entering a magnetic field, i.e., they act like tiny magnets, lining themselves up along the magnetic field lines. The connection between magnetism and ELECTRICITY was discovered in the early 19th cent. Hans OERSTED found (1820) that a wire carrying an electrical current deflects the needle of a magnetic compass because a magnetic field is created by the moving electric charges constituting the current. A small loop of current behaves like a magnet, and its corresponding magnetic moment has a value equal to the product of the current flowing in the loop and the area of the loop. André AMPÈRE showed (1825) that magnets exert forces on current-carrying conductors. In 1831 Michael FARADAY and Joseph HENRY independently discovered electromagnetic INDUCTION, the production of a current in a conductor by a change in the magnetic field around it. The magnetic properties of matter are explained by the magnetic fields due to the motion of charges and the intrinsic magnetic moments of electrons associated with their SPINS. In many atoms, all the electrons are paired within energy levels, so that the electrons in each pair have opposite (antiparallel) spins, and their magnetic fields cancel one another. In some atoms there are more electrons with spins in one direction than the other, resulting in a net magnetic moment for the atom as a whole. Placed in an external field, the individual atoms will tend to align their moments with the external field.

Because of thermal vibrations the alignment is not complete, and materials (called *paramagnetic* materials) that contain such atoms react only weakly to a magnetic field. Materials such as iron, nickel, or cobalt that respond strongly to a magnetic field are called *ferromagnetic*. In a ferromagnetic substance there are more electrons with spin in one direction than in the other. The individual magnetic fields of the atoms in a given region, called a domain, tend to line up in one direction, so that they reinforce each other. Materials such as bismuth and antimony that are repelled by a magnetic field are called *diamagnetic*. In a diamagnetic substance, an external magnetic field accelerates the electrons rotating in one direction and retards those rotating in the opposite direction; this situation produces an induced magnetization opposite in direction to the external field. See also ELECTROMAGNET; ELECTROMAGNETIC RADIATION.

**magnetite**, lustrous, black, magnetic iron mineral ($Fe_3O_4$), occurring as crystals, masses, and sand in Sweden, South Africa, Italy, and parts of the US. It is an important ore of IRON. Lodestone is a naturally magnetic variety that exhibits polarity. It has recently been discovered that certain bacteria are magnetotactic owing to the presence of magnetite inside them. Magnetite can form in the body of some humans suffering from certain genetic faults.

**magnetohydrodynamics** (MHD), study of the motions of electrically conducting fluids and their interactions with magnetic fields. The principles of magnetohydrodynamics are of particular importance in PLASMA physics.

**magnetosphere:** see ATMOSPHERE; VAN ALLEN RADIATION BELTS.

**magnitude**, measure of the brightness of a celestial object. Apparent magnitude is that determined on the basis of an object's relative brightness as seen from the earth. Objects differing by one magnitude differ in brightness by a factor of 2.512 (the 5th root of 100). The brightest stars have an apparent magnitude of about + 1; the sun's magnitude is −26.8. Absolute magnitude, a measure of the intrinsic luminosity, or true brightness, of an object, is the apparent magnitude an object would have if located at a standard distance of 10 PARSECS.

**magnolia**, common and generic name for members of the family Magnoliaceae, deciduous and evergreen trees and shrubs. Many bear magnificent, highly-scented flowers and are especially prized as specimen trees. *M. grandiflora*, an evergreen tree from the southern US, is not very hardy in Britain and is usually grown as a wall shrub. *M. sieboldii*, from Japan, is deciduous and bears large white flowers with red centres and decorative orange SEEDS. *M. soulangeana* is a hybrid between the Chinese yulan and 'lily' magnolia trees. It is deciduous and bears huge flowers, reddish-purple outside and white inside, which open on the bare tree in spring. The tulip tree (*Liriodendron tulipifera*) is a member of the same family.

**Magnus**, Norwegian kings. **Magnus I** (the Good), 1024 47, king of Norway (r.1035–47) and Denmark (r.1042–47), was the son of OLAF II. He succeeded CANUTE's sons Sweyn of Norway and Harthacnut of Denmark. In 1046 he was forced to share the Norwegian crown with his uncle, HAROLD III, who became sole king on his death. **Magnus VI** (the Law Mender), 1238–80, king of Norway (r.1263–80), was the son of HAAKON IV. He made peace with ALEXANDER III of Scotland by ceding (1266) the Hebrides and the Isle of Man for a large sum. His legal reforms introduced the concept of crime as an offence against the state rather than the individual, thus discouraging personal vengeance and making the king the source of justice; defined the limits of church and state power; and created a new royal council and nobility. His sons, Eric II (r.1280–99) and Haakon V (r.1299–1319), succeeded him. **Magnus VII** (Magnus Ericsson), 1316–73?, king of Norway (r.1319–43) and Sweden (r.1319–65), succeeded his grandfather, Haakon V of Norway, and was elected by the Swedish nobles to succeed his exiled uncle, King Birger of Sweden. He was declared of age in 1332. Educated in Sweden, he neglected Norway and was forced to recognize (1343) his son, later Haakon VI, as his successor as king of Norway. He lost part of Sweden (1356) to his son Eric but regained it on Eric's death (1359). After Haakon married MARGARET I, daughter of WALDEMAR IV of Denmark, the Swedish nobles deposed Haakon and Magnus, choosing Albert of Mecklenburg as king (1363). Magnus was imprisoned until 1371.

**magpie**, name for certain BIRDS of the CROW and JAY family. The common magpie (*Pica pica*) ranges right across temperate Europe and Asia to W North America. It has iridescent black plumage and white wing patches and abdomen. Other species are found in Europe, Asia, and Africa. Magpies are scavengers and often collect small, bright objects earning the title of 'thieving magpies'. In captivity they can learn to imitate some words.

**Magrib:** see MAGHREB.

**Magritte, René** (ma,greet), 1898–1967, Belgian surrealist painter. Influenced by CHIRICO, he developed a style in which a misleading realism is combined with mocking irony. He moved to Paris in 1927 and was associated with the French surrealists (see SURREALISM) until 1930.

René **Magritte**, *Time Transfixed*, 1938. Oil on canvas, 147 × 98.7 cm. The Art Institute of Chicago.

**Magsaysay, Ramón** (mag,siesie), 1907–57, president (1953–57) of the PHILIPPINES. As secretary of national defence (1950–53) he suppressed the Communist-led Hukbalahap guerrillas; he was then elected president. He died in a plane crash.

**Maguiguana**, c.1850–97, general and leader of an anti-Portuguese rebellion in Gaza, in present-day S Mozambique. The Portuguese forces invaded Gaza in 1895 and easily overwhelmed its army and deposed the king. Maguiguana became the leading Gaza spokesman and in 1897, frustrated by Portuguese indifference, he led a brave but futile rebellion in which he met his death.

**Magyars**, the dominant people of Hungary, who speak a Finno-Ugric language. The nomadic Magyars migrated c.460 from the Ural Mts to the N Caucasus, where they remained until forced into present-day Rumania late in the 9th cent. by the Pechenegs, a Turkic group. Under their leader Arpad, the Magyars defeated the Bulgars but were pushed northwards (c.895) into Hungary. They conquered Moravia and penetrated Italy and Germany until checked (955) by the Emperor OTTO I. In the 11th cent. they adopted Christianity.

**Mahabharata** (mə'hah,bahrətə), classical Sanskrit epic, probably composed between 200 BC and AD 200. Traditionally ascribed to the sage Vyasa, the 18-book work is the longest poem in world literature and the foremost source on classical Indian civilization. Although there are many subplots and irrelevant tales, the *Mahabharata* is primarily the fabulous account of a dynastic struggle and great civil war in the kingdom of Kurukshetra. The BHAGAVAD-GITA, a religious classic of Hinduism, is contained within the epic.

**Mahalla el-kubra,** city (1987 pop. 259,387), N Egypt, in the Nile delta. It is a major centre of the Egyptian textile industry and also has rice and flour mills.

**Mahan, Alfred Thayer,** 1840–1914, American naval officer and historian. In works like *The Influence of Sea Power upon History, 1660–1873* (1890), he argued that naval power was the key to success in international politics. His books had a major influence on policy.

**Mahanadi,** river of India flowing c.900 km (560 mi) E from the hills of C India across the Ne Deccan to enter the Bay of Bengal through a large and fertile delta at whose head stands the town of CUTTACK. On or near its banks are the towns of Raipur and Sambalpur. A few miles upstream from the latter is the massive Hirakud reservoir, which feeds irrigation works and a hydroelectric power station, and helps to control the floods for which the Mahanadi is notorious.

**Mahdi** [Arab., = rightly-guided], a figure who plays the role of Messiah in Muslim eschatology. On the basis of prophetic HADITH, Sunni Muslims (see SUNNISM) believe that, at the end of time, the Mahdi will deliver the world from horrendous calamities and cataclysms and restore the rectitude of the Adamic order. The Mahdi will be a member of the tribe of Quraish, from which MUHAMMAD came, but his precise line of descent depends on the political circumstances surrounding particular apocalyptic traditions. Among Shi'ite Muslims (see SHI'ISM), the figure of the Mahdi is intermeshed with the Imamate (see IMAM). In all cases, the Mahdi is descended from ALI, most usually through his son HUSAYN. Twelver Shi'ites consider that the Mahdi is an apocalyptic figure who will appear at the end of the world, but many other Shi'ite sects believe that his coming will usher in a period of godly rule on earth. The states of the FATIMIDS and ALMOHADS arose under leaders who claimed messianic status and gave rise to millenarian hopes, and many rebellions in Islamic history were accompanied by similar expectations. There have also been millenarian movements in Sunnite Islam, one of which was Mahdism in the SUDAN of the late 19th cent.

**'Mahdi', Mohammed Ahmed,** 1848–85, militant Sudanese religious leader who took the title *Mahdi* [guided one]. After a long period of religious training he emerged believing he had been divinely ordained to redeem injustice during his time through holy war. In 1881 he led a revolt against Egyptian rule in his country and in 1885 his forces succeeded in taking Khartoum after a siege in which the British Gen. GORDON was killed; thus he brought most of Sudan under his theocratic control. He died the same year but his state survived until 1898 when it fell to British invaders.

**Maherero, Samuel,** c.1854–1923, paramount chief of the Herero of NAMIBIA (r.1890–1904). He led a Herero revolt against German occupation in 1904 but suffered overwhelming defeat and was forced to flee to Bechuanaland (now BOTSWANA). As many as 70% of the Herero were killed in the course of the rebellion.

**Mahfuz, Nagib** or **Mahfouz, Naguib,** , 1911–, Egyptian novelist and short-story writer. One of Egypt's major contemporary writers, he depicts urban life in such novels as *Midaq Alley* (tr. 1975), *Miramar* (tr. 1978), and *Children of Gabelawi* (tr. 1981). Among his volumes of short stories is *God's World* (tr. 1973).

**Mahican Indians,** a confederacy of NORTH AMERICAN INDIANS of the Eastern Woodlands with an Algonquian language (see AMERICAN INDIAN LANGUAGES). They occupied both banks of the Hudson R., almost to Lake Champlain. The MOHEGANS were a tribe of the Mahican group; both have been called Mohicans. By 1664 the Mohawk had driven the Mahicans E to Massachusetts. Their complete dispersal was hastened when their enemies were armed by the Dutch.

**mah jongg,** four-handed game, played in many variations throughout China, where it probably originated. It became popular in the 1920s, after an American, Joseph P. Babcock, patented a standardized Western version played with 152 tiles, 108 of which are 'suit tiles' (there being three suits), the remainder representing other symbols, usually of greater value. As in RUMMY, the object is to build sets, but the rules governing the distribution and accumulation of tiles are extremely complex.

**Mahler, Gustav** (,mahlə), 1860–1911, Austrian composer and conductor; b. Austrian Bohemia. In Budapest, Hamburg, Vienna, and in New York (1908–11) he set CONDUCTING standards that have become legendary. He wrote 10 symphonies; songs; and song cycles, mostly with orchestral accompaniment. Of the cycles, *Songs of a Wayfarer* (1883–85), *Kindertotenlieder* [songs of dead children] (1901–4), and *Das Lied von der Erde* [song of the earth] (1907–10) are most notable. Following BRUCKNER in the Viennese symphonic tradition, he added folk elements and expanded the form in length, emotional contrast, and orchestral size.

**Mahmud II,** 1784–1839, Ottoman sultan (1808–39). An able ruler, he was nonetheless unable to halt the disintegration of the OTTOMAN EMPIRE (Turkey). During his reign the EASTERN QUESTION assumed increasing importance. He was a vigorous reformer who began the Westernization of Turkey and ruthlessly destroyed (1826) the JANISSARIES. He was unable to defeat the Greek rebels in their War of Independence or to prevent Egypt from attaining virtual independence.

**mahogany,** common name for the Meliaceae, a family of chiefly tropical shrubs and trees, from which the valuable hardwood called mahogany is obtained. Principal sources of the hardwood, often used for furniture, are trees of the American and W Indian genus *Swietenia*. Varying in colour from golden to deep red-brown, the woods are usually scented, close-grained, and resistant to insect attack.

**Mahrattas** or **Marathas,** Marathi-speaking people of W central India. From their homeland in Maharashtra (see INDIA) these Hindu warriors rose to power in the 17th cent. Led by SIVAJI they resisted the MUGHALS under AURANGZEB. Expanding into the DECCAN and S India, they became the strongest rival to British supremacy but then split into several warring groups. The British subdued them in 1818.

**Mahzor** [Heb., = cycle], Heb. festival prayer book. There is a special Mahzor for each of the major JEWISH HOLIDAYS. While the basic structure of the festival services is the same as for Sabbath, extra psalms, as well as compositions dealing with themes related to the particular festival, are recited on these occasions.

**Maiden Castle,** a HILLFORT located in Dorset, S England. The hill was first a NEOLITHIC enclosure and then the site of an earthen BARROW before the first IRON AGE fortifications were begun. By the 2nd cent. BC the heavily fortified hilltop enclosed a permanent settlement; it fell to the Roman army in AD 44 and was abandoned.

Maiden Castle

**maidenhair tree:** see GINKGO.

**Maidstone,** county town (1981 pop. 86,067) of Kent, S England, on R. Medway. Industries found within the town include brewing, engineering, and paper manufacture. There are several historic buildings here, including the 14th-cent. All Saints' Church. It is the birthplace of William HAZLITT.

**Maiduguri,** city (1987 est. pop. 189,000), capital of Bornu state, NE Nigeria. It is on the seasonal Ngadda R. swamps 112 km (70 mi) SW of Lake Chad, and lies at the northeast terminus of the railway network from Lagos and Port Harcourt in the south. The town is an important commercial centre, trading in leather, bricks, and ground nuts. Maiduguri was selected by the British as their military headquarters in 1908, after which it became the capital of British BORNU.

**Mailer, Norman,** 1923–, American writer. He won early renown with his World War II novel *The Naked and the Dead* (1948). His sharp views of American society are reflected not only in such semi-autobiographical novels as *An American Dream* (1966) but also in *The Armies of the Night* (1968) a journalistic account of the 1967 peace march on Washington, and *The Executioner's Song* (1979), a novelistic treatment of the convicted killer Gary Gilmore.

**Maillol, Aristide,** 1861–1944, French sculptor. He met GAUGUIN in 1883 and produced tapestry designs based on his ideas. It was not until the early 1900s that he started to sculpt, restricting himself to the female nude. His style was based upon a classical attitude to form and composition, and moved away from the expressive romanticism of RODIN.

**mail order,** type of retail organization. Mail-order houses issue catalogues and use agents to generate sales among friends and family. In the UK mail-order purchase traditionally appealed to the lower-paid members of society since it provided extra income, by taking on an agency (commission), offered attractive credit terms, armchair shopping, and free delivery of goods. Mail-order business prospered in the 1960s and 1970s, after which it declined to account for only 3.3% of retail sales in 1985. Since then the five big mail-order houses have changed their image and provide better quality goods. The use of mail order without agencies has spread, and catalogue selling was being adopted by other organizations such as CREDIT CARD companies. It is still potentially a highly lucrative business for operators; in Japan motor cars are sold by this method.

**Main,** river, 490 km (307 mi) long, in West Germany. It rises in the Fichtel-Gebirge [Fir Mts] of BAVARIA and follows a highly irregular course, with several sharp changes in direction, before joining the RHINE above MAINZ. It is navigable below Bamberg where there is a canal link with the DANUBE. WÜRZBURG and FRANKFURT are the principal cities along its course.

**Mainbocher:** see FASHION (table).

**Maine,** state of the US (1984 est. pop. 1,156,000), area 86,027 km² (33,215 sq mi), situated in the NE, bordered by New Hampshire (W), the Canadian provinces of Quebec (NW) and New Brunswick (NE), and the Atlantic Ocean (S). The capital is AUGUSTA and the largest city is PORTLAND. Maine consists of a forested and glacially smoothed plateau sloping from the N and W towards the S and E, which is covered by lakes and rivers, relics of the Pleistocene ice age. Maine's economy is mainly industrial, with wood products, textiles, leather goods, canned foods, and transport and electrical equipment being the main manufactures. Despite a short growing season, major farm products are dairy products, eggs, broiler chickens, and apples. Lobster and sardine fishing is also important. In 1980 98% of the population was non-Hispanic white. The state was settled by the French and the British in the 17th cent., before becoming a centre for fishing, timber, and shipbuilding in the late 18th cent. Maine became a centre for commerce and industry, achieving statehood in 1820, but growth slowed down after the Civil War. In the 1970s the state was opened up by highway construction and began to attract residents to the coastal region and industry from the nearby crowded BOSTON area.

**mainstreaming,** in education, practice of teaching handicapped children in regular classrooms with nonhandicapped children to the fullest extent possible; handicaps may be orthopaedic, intellectual, emotional, or visual, or associated with hearing or learning. Mainstreaming has been of increasing interest since the late 1960s in response to a number of factors including research showing that many handicapped pupils learned better in regular than in special classes. In the US there were charges that racial imbalances existed in special education classes. In Britain, the Warnock report on *Special Educational Needs* (1978), considered the US and European experience of educating handicapped children in ordinary schools, and made a series of recommendations, including that severely handicapped pupils should be educated in ordinary schools wherever this was 'reasonable and practicable'.

**Maintenon, Françoise d'Aubigné, marquise de** (manhtɔ̃‚nawnh), 1635–1719, second wife of LOUIS XIV of France. Educated as a Protestant, she later became a devout Roman Catholic and at 16 married the poet Paul Scarron. After his death (1660) she was the governess of the children of Louis XIV and Mme de MONTESPAN. She gained considerable influence over Louis, and in 1684 she was morganatically married to the king.

**Mainz** (mients), (1984 pop. 187,100), capital of Rhineland-Palatinate, W central West Germany, on the Rhine R., opposite the mouth of the Main R. It is an industrial centre with such manufactures as chemicals and motor vehicles, and a trade centre for Rhine wines. The site (1st cent. BC) of a Roman camp, it became (746) the seat of the first German archbishop, St BONIFACE. Johann GUTENBERG made it (15th cent.) the first printing centre of Europe. It was (1873–1918) a fortress of the German Empire. Badly damaged during WORLD WAR II, it has been rebuilt since 1945. Historic buildings include the 10th-cent. Romanesque cathedral.

**maiolica,** tin-glazed earthenware associated with Italy. A glaze containing tin oxide is applied to a fired piece of earthenware forming a white, opaque, porous surface on which a design is painted. The piece is then fired again, sometimes after application of a transparent lead glaze. The technique was in use in Mesopotamia by the 9th cent. AD and well established in Spain and Italy by the 13th cent. The term *maiolica* originally denoted lustred Hispano-Moresque pottery imported into Italy, but was soon applied to all Italian tin-glazed earthenware. Elsewhere the technique is known by different names, e.g., faience in France. Maiolica is still made today for everyday use and for the tourist trade.

Maiolica dish, painted in blue and lustred silver-yellow (Deruta, c.1500–30; Fitzwilliam Museum)

**Mairet, Ethel,** 1872–1953, British weaver. She believed that the movement led by William MORRIS had isolated the craftsperson from industrial developments and thus had inhibited the creativity and flexibility required to produce truly contemporary designs; her book *Handweaving Today* attempted to re-establish the relationship between the artist/craftsperson and the machine.

**Mais, Roger,** 1905–55, Jamaican novelist, photographer, painter, journalist and dramatist. He was one of a group of middle-class intellectuals who sought to give leadership to trades union and political movements during the 1940s and 50s. He describes in sometimes awkward, yet passionate, prose the lives of ordinary people in such novels as *The Hills Were Joyful Together* (1953).

**Maisonneuve, Paul de Chomedey, sieur de** (mayzawnh̩nøv), 1612–76, founder and first French governor of MONTREAL (1642–63). Commanding a detachment of French soldiers, he landed (1642) on Montreal Island and founded the city of Ville Marie, later Montreal.

**Maitland,** city (1986 pop. 43,247), New South Wales, E Australia. As regional centre for the HUNTER VALLEY, it was formerly a centre for wool brought from inland by bullock dray. Its growth to become the second largest urban centre in New South Wales, outside of Sydney, is partly due to the coalfield which is linked to the coast by a private railway. The city was extensively damaged by disastrous floods in 1955, although much of the low-lying land is protected by an extensive system of levees.

**Maitland, Frederick William,** 1824–97, English historian and jurist. Maitland was called to the Bar in 1876, and in 1888 he became Downing professor of law at Cambridge. A thorough and vigorous historian, Maitland opened up many subjects for further examination. His books include *Domesday Book and Beyond* (1897), and he wrote many stimulating essays.

**maize,** cereal plant (*Zea mays*) grown mainly in the tropics and subtropics. It has a higher yield per hectare than either WHEAT or RICE, and the main producers are the US, Brazil, and Mexico, in which country it is assumed to have originated. As grown today, maize is a man-made crop, having been subjected to more intensive study and breeding than any other GRAIN, and would probably be unable to survive outside cultivation. The main crop consists of dent maize, so called because the hard kernel is capped by soft starch which shrinks on drying, and is used for stock feed. Flour corn (so-called Indian corn), with a soft starch, is suitable for grinding into a flour. Sweet corn consists of varieties which have a high sugar content before full maturity of the grains, and is eaten as a delicacy. Flint corn has a very hard layer all around the kernel, and popcorn was selected by early American Indians for its property of exploding upon heating due to the entrapped water turning to steam, making it easier to grind into a meal. The young, green maize crop is used as a forage for stock feeding, and for making silage. Maize is important commercially in the manufacture of vegetable oil (corn oil), starch, adhesives, plastics, sizing, paints, and breakfast cereals. The Inca, Maya, and Aztec civilizations were built upon the culture of maize, and the plant appeared in their religious rites.

**Maji Maji,** rebellion in colonial Tanganyika (now TANZANIA) against colonial rule (1905–07). The rising was sparked by an apocalyptic message spread by Kinjitkile Ngwale, a religious cult leader who promised the defeat of the Germans by his followers if they received sacred water (*maji*) from a special pool. The rebellion was ruthlessly suppressed and many Africans were executed, including Ngwale.

**Majlis,** name of the representative assembly in many Muslim countries, notably Iran.

**majolica,** type of earthenware decorated with brightly coloured glazes, developed by MINTON in the mid 19th cent. The term was also used in the 19th and early 20th cent. to denote the Italian tin-glazed earthenware correctly described as MAIOLICA.

**Majorca,** Span. *Mallorca,* island (1981 pop. 561,215), 3639 km² (1405 sq mi), Spain, largest of the BALEARIC ISLANDS, in the W Mediterranean. Palma is the chief city. A separate kingdom (1276–1343), the island is now a popular resort noted for its fine scenery and architecture.

**Majorian,** d. 461, Roman emperor of the West (457–61). He tried to protect the people from unfair taxation. His expedition (461) against GAISERIC failed, and his general RICIMER, who had enthroned him as puppet emperor, became jealous of his power and murdered him. This began the decline of the empire.

**Majuro,** atoll (1973 pop. 10,290), c.9 km² (3.5 sq mi), capital (comprising c.64 islets) of the MARSHALL ISLANDS.

**Makarios III,** 1913–77, Orthodox Eastern archbishop and first president of CYPRUS (1960–77). As archbishop of Cyprus he led the movement that culminated in the island's independence in 1960. As president he maintained a policy aimed at reducing conflict between the Greek and Turkish populations on the island. He survived four assassination attempts and was turned out of office briefly in 1974.

**Makarova, Natalia,** 1940–, Russian ballet dancer. She studied at Leningrad with the Kirov Ballet (1959–70). She danced classic roles, e.g., *Giselle* and Odette/Odile in *Swan Lake* with the American Ballet Theatre (1970–72), then made guest appearances in London. She has also written and presented a television series about ballet.

**Malabo,** formerly Santa Isabel, city (1983 pop. 15,253), capital of Equatorial Guinea, on Bioko Island (formerly Fernando Po), in the Gulf of Guinea. The island's chief port and commercial centre, Malabo exports cocoa, coffee, and other agricultural products. The city was founded in 1827 by the British as a base for the suppression of the slave trade and was called Port Clarence, or Clarencetown.

**Malacca, Strait of,** c.800 km (500 mi) long and c.50 to 320 km (30 to 200 mi) wide, between Sumatra and the Malay Peninsula. SINGAPORE is the chief port. The strait, one of the world's most important sea passages, links the INDIAN OCEAN and the SOUTH CHINA SEA.

**Malachi** or **Malachias** (maləkie, -ke, ˌmaləˈkieəs, ˌmaləkee), book of the OLD TESTAMENT. Written in early 5th cent. BC, it denounces insincere worship, mixed marriages, and divorce, and announces a day of judgment. Malachi means in Hebrew 'my messenger'; the prophecy in 3.1 about the messenger who will prepare the Lord's way is applied in the GOSPELS to JOHN THE BAPTIST.

**malachite,** green copper carbonate mineral $[Cu_2CO_3(OH)_2]$, found in crystals and, more commonly, massive form. It is used as a GEM, a COPPER ore, and, when ground, a pigment. It occurs associated with other copper ores in the US, Chile, the USSR, Zimbabwe, Zaïre, and Australia.

**Málaga,** city (1981 pop. 503,251), capital of Málaga prov., S Spain, on the Mediterranean coast. It handles locally grown grapes, wine, citrus fruit, and nuts, and has sugar-refining, cotton textile, and chemical industries. A Phoenician foundation, it became a Roman colony and was principal port of the Moorish kingdom of Granada before its fall to Ferdinand and Isabella in 1487. The city prospered on trade with Africa in the 19th cent. when it also became a winter resort. Moorish remains include the Alcázaba citadel and the Gibralfaro castle. It is the birthplace of PICASSO.

**Malagaon,** town (1981 pop. 245,883), Maharashtra state, W India, on the Girna R. It is an administrative and service centre that has grown rapidly and has a sizable cotton weaving industry.

**Malamud, Bernard,** 1914–86, American author. Often reflecting a concern with Jewish tradition, his works include the novels *The Assistant* (1957), *The Fixer* (1966), *Dubin's Lives* (1979), and *God's Grace* (1982) and such short-story collections as *The Magic Barrel* (1958).

**malaria,** infectious parasitic disease characterized by high fever, severe chills, enlargement of the spleen, and sometimes ANAEMIA and JAUNDICE. It can be acute or chronic and is frequently recurrent. Widespread throughout tropical and subtropical areas of the world, malaria is transmitted by the *Anopheles* mosquito, which picks up the causative *Plasmodium* parasite from the blood of an infected person and transfers it to that of a healthy person. Quinine, the traditional treatment, has largely been replaced by modern antimalarial drugs, including chloroquine, mepacrine, and proguanil.

**Malatesta,** Italian family that ruled Rimini and neighbouring cities from the 13th to 16th cent. Among its members was the hunchback Gianciotto Malatesta, who killed his wife, Francesca da Rimini, when he learned of her love affair with his brother, Paolo. Their story was immortalized in DANTE's *Divine Comedy*. **Sigismondo Pandolfo Malatesta** (1417–68) was a patron of the arts and a bitter enemy of the papacy.

**Malatya,** city (1980 pop. 179,074), capital of Malatya prov., E Anatolia, Turkey. Centre of a fertile, irrigated plain, it is a commercial and administrative centre and manufactures cotton textiles. The city, established in 1838, is successor to more ancient foundations nearby (Melitene).

**Malawi** (məˈlahwee), officially Republic of Malawi, formerly Nyasaland, republic (1987 est. pop. 7,280,000), 117,068 km² (45,200 sq mi), E central Africa, bordered by Zambia (W), Tanzania (N), and Mozambique (E, S, and SW). Principal cities are LILONGWE (the capital) and BLANTYRE. About one-fifth of the country is occupied by Lake Malawi (Lake Nyasa), in the Great Rift Valley; the remainder is largely a high plateau. The economy is overwhelmingly agricultural, and per capita income is very low. Most of the farmland is given to subsistence crops, but large estates produce tea, tobacco, peanuts, sugar, cotton, and maize for export. Large numbers of poultry, goats, cattle, and pigs are raised. Malawi's extensive mineral resources are largely unexploited. The GNP is US$1162 million, and the GNP per capita is US$170 (1985). Nearly all the people are Bantu-speaking black Africans, and most follow traditional beliefs. There are large Christian, Muslim, and Hindu minorities. English is the official language.

*History.* The Malawi kingdom, established in the Shire R. valley in the 15th cent., conquered much of modern Rhodesia and Mozambique in the 18th cent. It declined shortly thereafter, and a flourishing slave trade developed. Missionary activity and the threat of Portuguese annexation led Britain in 1889 to proclaim a protectorate in the area (known from 1907 to 1964 as Nyasaland). The British ended the slave trade and established large coffee-growing estates. In 1915 a small-scale revolt against British rule was easily suppressed, but it was an inspiration to other Africans intent on ending foreign domination. In 1953 the Federation of Rhodesia and Nyasaland (linking Nyasaland, Northern Rhodesia, and Southern Rhodesia) was formed despite the protests of Nyasaland's blacks, who feared the white-dominated policies of Southern Rhodesia (now ZIMBABWE). The Federation was dissolved in 1963, and Nyasaland became independent as Malawi in 1964. It became a republic within the COMMONWEALTH in 1966. Under Dr Hastings Kamuzu BANDA, president for life and autocratic ruler of a state in which the Malawi Congress Party is the only legal party, Malawi has alienated its black neighbours by maintaining friendly relations with white-run governments in South Africa.

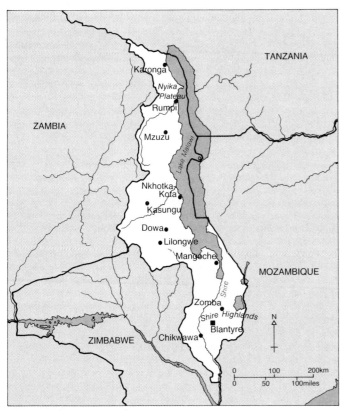

Malawi

**Malawi, Lake** or **Lake Nyasa**, freshwater lake, c.580 km (360 mi) long, bounded by steep mountains, in the GREAT RIFT VALLEY of E Africa. It is drained in the south by the Shire R., a tributary of the Zambezi.

**Malayalam,** Dravidian language of India. See LANGUAGE (table).

**Malay language:** see MALAYO-POLYNESIAN LANGUAGES.

**Malayo-Polynesian languages,** family of languages spoken in the Malay Peninsula; Madagascar; Taiwan; Indonesia; New Guinea; the

Melanesian, Micronesian, and Polynesian Islands; the Philippine Islands; and New Zealand. See LANGUAGE (table).

**Malay Peninsula,** southern extremity, c.181,300 km² (70,000 sq mi), of the continent of Asia, between the Andaman Sea of the Indian Ocean and the Strait of Malacca (W), and the Gulf of Siam and the South China Sea (E). It forms part of Thailand (N) and part of Malaysia (S); at its southern tip is the island of Singapore. A mountain range 2190 km (7186 ft) at its highest point, from which many swift rivers flow east and west, forms the backbone of the peninsula. More than half its area is covered by tropical rainforest. It is a major rubber and tin producer; other products include timber, rice, and coconut oil. Malays, who probably came from S China c.2000 BC, form a majority of the population. Chinese are almost as numerous. Indians and Thais are important minorities, and aborigines are found in the hills and jungles. Thais, Indians, and Indonesians invaded the peninsula periodically from the 8th cent. until the primacy of a Malay state was established c.1400. Later in the 15th cent. the Malays were converted to Islam. European contacts began in the 16th cent. In 1511 the Portuguese seized the prime Malay state of Malacca, which fell to the Dutch in 1641. The British dominated the southern part of the peninsula from 1826 and wrested the north from Siam in 1909. In 1948 the Malay Peninsula became part of the Federation of Malaya (see MALAYSIA, FEDERATION OF).

**Malaysia,** independent federation (1987 est. pop. 15,600,000), 332,633 km² (128,430 sq mi), SE Asia, consisting of **Peninsular Malaysia** (also called West Malaysia or Malaya), on the Malay Peninsula; and, about 640 km (400 mi) across the SOUTH CHINA SEA, **East Malaysia** (made up of the states of SABAH and SARAWAK), on the island of BORNEO. Peninsular Malaysia is bordered by Thailand (N), the South China Sea (E), Singapore (S), and the Strait of Malacca and the Andaman Sea (W); East Malaysia is bordered by the South China and Sulu seas (N), Brunei (NE), the Celebes Sea (E), and Indonesia (S and W). The capital of Malaysia is KUALA LUMPUR. Both Peninsular and East Malaysia have densely forested, mountainous interiors flanked by coastal plains; the climate is tropical. Malaysia has a high standard of living by SE Asian standards. The economy is primarily agricultural, with a small but expanding industrial sector. The country is a major world producer of rubber and tin; palm oil, timber, and petroleum are other major exports. The GNP is US$30,280 million (1984), and GNP per capita is US$1990 (1984). Although it has only 31% of the country's area, Peninsular Malaysia has more than 80% of its people. The majority of the polyglot population are ethnic Malays and Chinese; there is a sizeable Indian (mainly Tamil) minority. The official language is Bahasa Malaysia (Malay), but Chinese, English, Tamil, Hindi, and tribal dialects are widely spoken. Islam, practised by the Malays, is the established religion.

*History.* Part of the Buddhist Sri Vijaya kingdom (8th–13th cent.), converted (15th cent.) to Islam as part of a Muslim Malay state, the Malayan Peninsula was first visited by Europeans in the 16th cent. Malacca, on the west coast, was occupied by Portugal (1511) and the Dutch (1641). The British acquired Pinang island in 1786, uniting it in 1826 with Malacca and Singapore as the STRAITS SETTLEMENT. By the beginning of the 20th cent. Britain had established many protectorates on the Malayan Peninsula, as well as in North Borneo (Sabah) and Sarawak. After the Japanese occupation during World War II, Britain united all its territories on the peninsula in the Union of Malaya (1946); Sabah and Sarawak became crown colonies. In 1948, in response to pressure from the ethnic Malays, who feared the reorganization would bring increased Chinese and Indian influence, Britain created the Federation of Malaya. A largely Chinese-led Communist insurrection was not fully suppressed until 1960. Meanwhile, the Federation of Malaya became an independent state within the COMMONWEALTH in 1957. In 1963 it emerged with SINGAPORE, Sarawak, and Sabah to form the Federation of Malaysia; Singapore withdrew in 1965. The country continued to be torn by the struggle between the Muslim Malays and the ethnic Chinese, and bloody race riots in 1969 led to a 22-month suspension of parliament. Since then, the ruling Front multiracial coalition, headed by the United Malays National Organization (UMNO), has sought to advance the economic status of ethnic Malays, although the party has itself experienced divisions. In 1984 Sultan Mahmood Iskandar of Johore was installed as Malaysia's eighth supreme head of state.

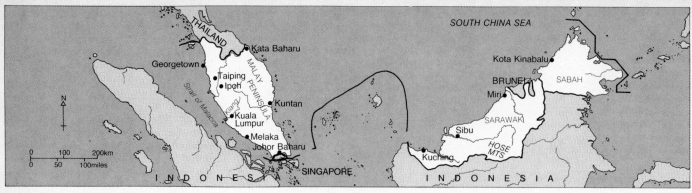

Malaysia

**Malaysian prime ministers**
Tunku Abdul Rahman (UMNO), 1957–59
Tun Haji Abdul Razak (UMNO), 1959
Tunku Abdul Rahman (UMNO), 1959–70
Tun Haji Abdul Razak (UMNO), 1970–76
Datuk Hussein bin Onn (UMNO), 1976–81
Datuk Seri Mahathir bin Mohamed (UMNO), 1981–

**Malcolm III** (Malcolm Canmore), d. 1093, king of Scotland (r.1058–93); son of Duncan I; successor to MACBETH. In aid of Edgar Atheling, pretender to the English throne, Malcolm waged wars against England that helped to ensure Scottish independence and made possible church reorganization by his wife, Margaret, daughter of Edward the Atheling.

**Malcolm X,** 1925–65, American black militant leader, also known as El-Hajj Malik El-Shabazz; b. Malcolm Little. Convicted of burglary (1946), he adopted the BLACK MUSLIM faith while in prison, and on his release (1952) became a Muslim minister and charismatic advocate of black separatism. Following a split (1963) with Black Muslim leader Elijah MUHAMMAD and a pilgrimage to Mecca, he converted to orthodox Islam and founded (1964) the Organization of Afro-American Unity, which promoted black nationalism but admitted the possibility of interracial brotherhood. In Feb. 1965 he was assassinated in Harlem, New York City, purportedly by Black Muslims. The *Autobiography of Malcolm X* (1964) is a classic of the 1960s black power movement.

**Maldives** (ˌmaldievz), officially Republic of Maldives, formerly Maldive Islands, republic (1986 est. pop. 190,000), 298 km² (115 sq mi), 19 atolls in the N Indian Ocean, about 675 km (420 mi) SW of Sri Lanka. They comprise nearly 2000 coral islands, of which about 200 are inhabited. Malé is the capital. The islands are covered with tropical vegetation, particularly coconut palms. Although some fruit, corn, and other grains are cultivated, most food staples must be imported. The chief sources of revenue are fishing, coconut products, shipping, and a growing tourist industry. A fish processing plant began operation on Malé in 1978. The GNP is $59 million and the GNP per capita is $373. The inhabitants are of mixed Indian, Sinhalese, and Arab stock.ISLAM is the official religion, and Dhivehi (a Sinhalese tongue) is spoken.

*History.* The Maldives were originally settled by peoples from S Asia; Islam was introduced in the 12th cent. From the arrival of the Portuguese in the 16th cent., the islands were intermittently under European influence. In 1887 they became a British protectorate and military base but retained internal self-government. The Maldives achieved full independence within the COMMONWEALTH as a sultanate in 1965, but in 1968 the ad-Din dynasty, which had ruled since the 14th cent., was ended, and a republic was declared. In 1976 Britain closed its air force base on the island of Gan, dealing a blow to the country's economy; however, a Soviet offer to lease the facility was rejected. In 1983 Pres. Maumoun Abdul Gayoom was reelected for a second five-year term. An attempted coup in 1988 was put down by Indian troops.

**Malé,** city (1978 pop. 29,555), capital of MALDIVES.

**Malebranche, Nicolas** (mahlˌbrahnsh), 1638–1715, French philosopher and theologian. He expounded and developed the views of DESCARTES, but differed from him on central issues. *In Search of Truth* (1674–75) offers an occasionalist account of causation—on which God is the real cause of all changes—and propounds the doctrine of vision in God ('In God we see all things'), according to which all our ideas and perceptions are archetypes of objects in God's mind. His denial that we can make sense of causal agency in objects inspired HUME. Other works include the *Treatise of Nature and Grace* (1680) and the *Dialogues on Metaphysics and Religion* (1688).

**Malenkov, Georgi Maksimilianovich,** 1902–88, Soviet leader. An aide of STALIN, he became a full member of the politburo and a deputy premier in 1946. As premier (1953–55) he pursued a conciliatory foreign policy and curtailed the power of the secret police. He was forced to resign as premier (1955) in favour of BULGANIN; removed from other posts in 1957; and expelled from the party in 1961.

**Malevich, Casimir,** or **Kasimir** (maˌlyayvich), 1878–1935, Russian painter, the founder (1913, but more probably 1915) of SUPREMATISM. His nonobjective paintings are geometric forms on a flatly painted surface, e.g., *White on White* (Mus. Mod. Art, New York City). His theoretical ideas were influenced by KANDINSKY, and were likewise based upon the ideas of THEOSOPHY. This idealist element in his work and theory came into conflict with other post-revolutionary artists in Russia who held Constructivist views.

**Mali,** officially Republic of Mali, republic (1985 est. pop. 8,206,000), 1,240,000 km² (478,764 sq mi), the largest country in W Africa, bordered by Algeria (N), Niger (E and SE), Burkina Faso and Côte d'Ivoire (S), and Guinea, Senegal, and Mauritania (W). BAMAKO is the capital. With the SAHARA desert in the north, much of the country is arid and barely supports grazing (mainly cattle, sheep, and goats). The south, watered by the NIGER and Senegal rivers (both important transport arteries), contains fertile areas where peanuts and cotton, the chief cash crops, are grown. Subsistence crops include rice, maize, sorghum, and millet. Fish from the Niger and livestock are exported. Industry is limited mainly to food processing, cotton ginning, and textile production. Salt, gold, and phosphates are mined on a small scale, but extensive mineral resources remain unexploited. The GNP is US$1231 million, and the GNP per capita is US$150 (1985). Six tribal groups make up most of the population. About 65% of the people are Muslims; most of the remainder are animists. French is the official language, but several indigenous tongues are spoken.

*History.* Several extensive empires and kingdoms dominated the early history of the region. The medieval empire of Mali (see separate article), a powerful state and one of the world's chief gold suppliers, reached its peak in the early 14th cent. Such cities as TIMBUKTU and Djenné became important centres of trade and culture. The Songhai empire of Gao rose to prominence in the late 15th cent. but was shattered by a Moroccan army in 1590, after which the vast region broke up into petty states. Despite a resurgence of Islam and the opposition of Muslim emperors, French conquest of the Mali area was virtually complete by 1898, and Mali, then called French Sudan, became part of FRENCH WEST AFRICA. Between the two World Wars a nationalist movement developed, and the militant Sudanese Union, led by Modibo Keita, emerged as the leading political force. A 1958 referendum created the autonomous Sudanese Republic, which joined (1959) with Senegal in the Mali Federation. The union ended in 1960, when the new Republic of Mali obtained full independence and broke with the FRENCH COMMUNITY. With Keita as president, Mali became a one-party, socialist state. It withdrew from the franc zone in 1962 but was forced by financial problems to return to the

French bloc in 1967. Keita was overthrown by junior army officers in 1968, and Lt Moussa Traoré assumed power as head of a military regime. In the early 1970s Mali's agrarian economy was devastated by a severe drought that struck the SAHEL region of Africa, destroying livestock herds and croplands. The resulting famine contributed to the deaths of thousands of people. In 1979 a new constitution restored civilian rule, and Traoré was reelected president, as candidate of the ruling Mali People's Democratic Union, in 1979 and again in 1985. In late 1985 Mali fought a brief war with Burkina over a disputed border area.

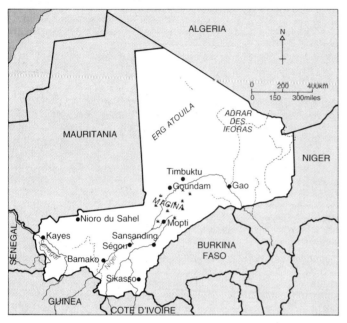

Mali

**Mali,** medieval Muslim empire in W Africa, in the region that is now the Republic of MALI. One of the world's chief gold suppliers, it reached its peak in the early 14th cent. under Emperor Mansa Musa (r.c.1312–37). During his reign TIMBUKTU and Djenné became important centres of trade and culture. In the 15th cent. the Mali empire was weakened by attacks from the Mossi and Tuareg, and the area was slowly taken over by the SONGHAI empire.

**Malik Ibn Anas,** d. 795, HADITH scholar of Medina and founder of the Malikite school of FIQH.

**Malindi,** town (1962 pop. 5818), SE Kenya. A seaport on the Indian Ocean, it was the early capital of Portuguese E Africa. Vasco da GAMA, who reached the site in 1498, erected a monument which still stands. Nearby are ruins of ancient Gede with a mosque, tombs, a palace, and an encircling wall.

**Malinowski, Bronislaw** (mali͵nofskee), 1884–1942, British anthropologist; b. Poland. He was the founder of FUNCTIONALISM, the theory which saw cultural and social structure as being organized in ways that would enable the satisfaction of fundamental biological and psychological needs. After studying (1914–18) Trobriand Islanders he did research in Africa and the Americas. He established at the London School of Economics the first department of anthropology in the UK (1924). His writings include *Argonauts of the Western Pacific* (1922), *Crime and Custom in Savage Society* (1926), and *Magic, Science and Religion* (1948).

**Mallarmé, Stéphane** (malah͵may), 1842–98, French poet. The chief forebear of the SYMBOLISTS, he held that poetry should be transcendental, a fit medium for the expresion of pure essences. Thus, his language defies traditional syntax and is exceedingly obscure, and he even later turned to an experimental case of typography. Major works include *Hérodiade* (1869) and *L'après-midi d'un faune* (1876; tr. The Afternoon of a Faun). Mallarmé was the centre of a literary group that gathered every Tuesday, and his theories had a major influence on modern French writing.

**Mallea, Eduardo** (ma͵yayah), 1903–, Argentine writer. His novels, many dealing with alienation, include *La bahia de silencio* (1940; tr. The

Bay of Silence), *All Green Shall Perish* (1941), *Posesión* (1958), and *Gabriel Andaral* (1971). Also of note are the partly autobiographical study *Historia de una pasión argentina* (1935; tr. History of an Argentine Passion) and the stories in *La ciudad junto al río inmóvil* (1936; tr. City on the Motionless River).

**mallow,** common name for the Malvaceae, a family of widely distributed shrubs and herbs, most abundant in the American tropics and typified by mucilaginous sap and showy flowers with a prominent column of fused stamens. The family includes the true mallows (genus *Malva*) of the Old World, and the false mallows (genus *Malvastrum*), and rose, or swamp, mallows (genus *Hibiscus*) of North America. Introduced *Hibiscus* species include the rose of Sharon (*H. syriacus*), a popular ornamental, and okra, or gumbo (*H. esculentus*), whose mucilaginous pods are used as a vegetable. The most popular ornamental of the family, the hollyhock (*Althea rosea*), originally a Chinese perennial, is widely cultivated in many varieties and colours. The European marsh mallow (*A. officinalis*) is used medicinally and was formerly used in the confection marshmallow, now usually made from syrup, gelatin, and other ingredients. Economically the most important plant of the family is COTTON.

**Mallowan, Sir Max Edgar Lucien,** 1904–78, British archaeologist known for excavations at UR (1925–30), NINEVEH (1931–32), and Nimrud (1949–58), all in present-day Iraq. His books include *Twenty-five Years of Mesopotamian Discovery* (1956). Married to Dame Agatha CHRISTIE, he was knighted in 1968.

**Malmö,** city (1984 pop. 229,107), capital of Malmöhus co., S Sweden, on the Øresund. It is a major naval and commercial port. Founded in the 12th cent., it was an important trade centre in Danish hands until it passed to Sweden in the mid-17th cent. Its castle is now a museum.

**malnutrition,** insufficiency of one or more nutrients necessary for health. Primary malnutrition is caused by a lack of essential foodstuffs in the diet, particularly vitamins, minerals (see VITAMINS AND MINERALS), or PROTEINS. Such a lack can be caused by regional conditions such as drought and famine or by poor eating habits. Secondary malnutrition is caused by failure to absorb or utilize nutrients, as in disease of the gastrointestinal tract, KIDNEY, or LIVER; by failure to satisfy increased nutritional requirements, as during PREGNANCY; or by excessive excretion, as in diarrhoea. Malnutrition can cause such conditions as ANAEMIA and KWASHIORKOR. One form of malnutrition is *overnutrition*, caused by an excessive intake of one or more nutrients. In richer countries the classic deficiency diseases (e.g., scurvy and rickets) are being replaced by diseases caused by eating too much fat and sugar (e.g., coronary heart disease and late-onset diabetes).

**Malory, Sir Thomas,** d.1471, English author of *Morte d'Arthur*, originally called *The Book of King Arthur and His Knights of the Round Table* and consisting of eight loosely connected romances. The printer William CAXTON gave it the misleading title in 1485. The first masterpiece of English secular prose, it became the standard source for later versions of the ARTHURIAN LEGEND.

**Malouf, David,** 1934–, Australian poet and novelist who has divided his time between Europe and Australia. His subtly poetic and intensely evocative novels include *Johnno* (1975), *An Imaginary Life* (1978), *12 Edmonstone Street* (1985), and *Harland's Half Acre* (1984). He has also written the libretto for the opera *Voss*, based on Patrick WHITE's novel, the music written by Richard Meale.

**Malpighi, Marcello,** 1628–94, Italian physician. A pioneer in the use of the MICROSCOPE, he made many valuable observations on the structure of plants and animals. He completed William HARVEY's theory of circulation by his observation of the movement of blood through capillaries; this and his study of lung structure appeared in *De pulmonibus observationes anatomicae* (1661). He is noted also for studies of the brain and other organs, and of the embryo.

**Malraux, André,** 1901–76, French man of letters and statesman. He published an anti-colonialist paper in Indochina (now Vietnam), followed closely the fortunes of the Communists in the Chinese civil war (1925–27), and fought with the Loyalists in the Spanish civil war (1936–39); these experiences are the source for his outstanding social novels, *La condition humaine* (1933; tr. Man's Fate) and *L'espoire* (1937; tr. Man's Hope). An intellectual with a broad knowledge of archaeology, art history, and anthropology, he wrote extensively on art and civilization in such works as *Les voix du silence* (1951; tr. The Voices of Silence) and *La métamorphose des dieux* (1957; tr. The Metamorphosis of the Gods). Malraux was a resistance leader during World War II, and he served under Charles DE GAULLE as minister of information (1945) and minister of cultural affairs (1958–68).

**malt,** a grain (usually BARLEY) steeped in water, partially germinated, then dried and cured. It is used in brewing to convert cereal starches to sugars by means of the ENZYMES (chiefly diastase) produced during germination.

**Malta,** officially the Republic of Malta, republic (1985 est. pop. 382,000), 316 km² (122 sq mi), in the Mediterranean Sea S of Sicily, comprising the islands of Malta, Gozo, and Comino. Valletta is the capital. The economy is supported by light industry, agriculture, tourism, and shipbuilding. The GNP is $1310 million and the GNP per capita is $3710 (1983). English and Maltese (a Semitic language) are the official languages, but Italian is widely spoken. Roman Catholicism is the state religion. Under the 1964 constitution, amended in 1974, Malta is governed by a unicameral legislature, a president, and a cabinet. In ancient times Malta belonged successively to the Phoenicians, Greeks, Carthaginians, Romans, and Saracens. The Normans of SICILY occupied it c.1090, and in 1530 Holy Roman Emperor CHARLES V granted Malta to the KNIGHTS HOSPITALLERS, who held it until it was surrendered (1798) to NAPOLEON I. Taken (1800) by the British, the island became of great strategic importance as a military and naval base after the opening (1869) of the SUEZ CANAL. In WORLD WAR II Malta sustained heavy Axis bombing but was never subdued. Limited self-government began in 1921, and Malta became fully independent in 1964 as a member of the COMMONWEALTH. The Labour government of Dom Mintoff which came to office in 1971 followed a policy of neutrality and nonalignment, the last British forces being withdrawn in 1979 and Malta's neutrality being formally declared in 1980. Mintoff was succeeded as prime minister by Carmelo Mifsud Bonnici (also Labour) in 1984, but elections in 1987 brought the Nationalist Party led by Edward Fenech Adami back to power.

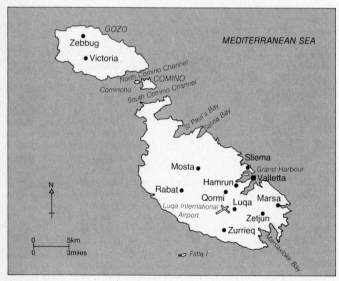

Malta

**Malthus, Thomas Robert** (ˌmalthəs), 1766–1834, English economist, sociologist, and pioneer in modern population study. In *An Essay on the Principle of Population* (1798; rev. ed. 1803) he contended that poverty and distress are unavoidable because population increases faster than the means of subsistence. As checks on population growth, he accepted only war, famine, and disease but later added 'moral restraint' as well. His controversial theory was adapted by neo-Malthusians and influenced such classical economists as David RICARDO.

**maltose** or **malt sugar** (empirical formula: $C_{12}H_{22}O_{11}$), crystalline SUGAR involved in brewing beer. Maltose can be produced from STARCH by HYDROLYSIS in the presence of diastase, an enzyme found in MALT. A disaccharide (see CARBOHYDRATE), maltose is hydrolysed to GLUCOSE by maltase, an enzyme present in YEAST. The glucose thus formed can be fermented by another enzyme in yeast to produce ETHANOL.

**Malvinas, Islas:** see FALKLAND ISLANDS.

**mamba,** African SNAKE of the family Elapidae, related to the COBRA. There are two species of mambas, the retiring green mamba (*Dendroaspis angusticeps*), which is usually about 180 cm (6 ft) long, and the black mamba (*D. polylepis*), which is 240–270 cm (8–9 ft) long and the fastest snake. The green mamba lives in trees and the black mamba mostly on the ground. Both are very poisonous, but the green mamba is much less aggressive than the black mamba. Both eat birds and small mammals. The speed of the black mamba travelling across the ground has been estimated at 16, 32, and 48 kph (10, 20, and 30 mph) at various times. These speeds are impossible for a POIKILOTHERM, but the black mamba has been accurately timed at 11 kph (7 mph) and can probably do short bursts at 24 kph (15 mph).

**Mambo,** title used by the rulers of the states of CHANGAMIRE, MWENE MUTAPA, and other Shona states in pre-colonial Zimbabwe. A *Mambo* performed the duties of a high priest as well as a political leader.

**Mamelukes,** Egyptian warrior caste dominant for over 700 years. They were originally slaves brought to Egypt by Fatimid caliphs in the 10th cent. Many were freed and rose to high rank. Aybak was the first Mameluke actually to become ruler (1250). For 250 years after that, Egypt was ruled by Mameluke sultans chosen from the caste of warriors. In 1517 the Ottoman Turks captured Cairo and put an end to the Mameluke sultanate. The Mamelukes maintained their vast landholdings and their private armies, however, and remained provincial governors. As Turkish rule weakened, they reasserted their power, and by the 18th cent. they were virtual rulers again. NAPOLEON I defeated them in 1798, but their final defeat came in 1811 when they were massacred by MUHAMMAD ALI.

**mammal,** warm-blooded animal of the class Mammalia, the highest class of VERTEBRATES, found in terrestrial and aquatic habitats. The female has mammary glands, which secrete milk for the nourishment of the young after birth. The body is partially or wholly covered with hair, the heart has four chambers, and a muscular diaphragm separates the chest from the abdominal cavity. Except for the egg-laying MONOTREMES (e.g., the DUCK-BILLED PLATYPUS), mammals give birth to live young. In some MARSUPIALS and higher mammals the young receive prenatal nourishment through a placenta. Terrestrial mammals include carnivores (e.g., CAT, DOG, BEAR); rodents (e.g., BEAVER, SQUIRREL); hoofed animals (e.g., HORSE, RHINOCEROS, DEER, PIG, CATTLE); primates (e.g., human being, MONKEY, LEMUR); and others, such as the BAT and ELEPHANT. Aquatic mammals include the carnivorous SEAL and WALRUS and the omnivorous WHALE and DOLPHIN.

**mammary gland** or **breast,** organ of the female mammal that produces milk for nourishment of the young. Breasts develop during puberty and distend during pregnancy in preparation for nursing.

**mammoth,** name for several prehistoric ELEPHANTS of the extinct genus *Mammuthus,* found in Eurasia and North America in the Pleistocene epoch. The imperial mammoth of North America was about 4 m (13½ ft) high at the shoulder. As depicted in Palaeolithic cave paintings in S France, the mammoth had a shaggy coat, complex molar teeth, slender tusks, and a long trunk.

**Man, Isle of,** a dependency of the British crown in the Irish Sea (1986 pop. 65,000), 518 km² (221 sq mi), capital Douglas. Ceded by Norway to Scotland in 1266, the island came under British crown administration in 1765. It retains its own government and laws, with a Court of Tynwald (parliament) consisting of a crown-appointed lieutenant-governor, a legislative council (executive) and a popularly-elected assembly called the House of Keys. Laws enacted by the Westminster parliament in London only apply to the island if this is specified in the legislation. The economy is based on tourism and offshore UK banking and insurance. The annual motor-cycle race round the island's roads is the most prestigious in the world.

**management,** the technique or practice of managing or controlling. In business, systems of management vary widely according to the type of organizational structure, enterprise, and business objectives. Traditional economists assumed that maximizing profit was the prime objective of most companies but this raises a number of issues and any strategies adopted must measure short-term gains against longer-term objectives. For example, quick profits may be made by cutting costs and neglecting to make desirable investment, but such a course of action is likely to jeopardize longer-term profitability. Other factors, such as maintaining a committed and cooperative workforce and satisfying shareholders, also complicate the management process. In the UK and much of Western Europe, there has been a growing trend toward management by consensus and 'team spirit' is encouraged. The individualism which was a characteristic of many entrepreneurs has diminished in modern business. In the 1970s and 1980s there was increased demand for professional management skills such as those acquired at Harvard Business School (US) and at the London and Manchester business schools in the UK. This is in contrast to the Japanese system of management where skills are commonly gained by a lifetime spent with the same company; only toward the end of his long career would the Japanese worker be rewarded with managerial status. This resulted in a paternalistic style of management for which Japan has become famous. See INDUSTRIAL RELATIONS.

**Managua,** city (1980 est. pop. 661,976), W Nicaragua, capital of Nicaragua, on the southern shore of Lake Managua. The nation's largest city and commercial and industrial centre, it became the capital in 1855 to end a feud between the cities of LEÓN and Granada. There has been some rebuilding since 1972, when earthquakes almost levelled the city and took some 10,000 lives.

**Manasseh** or **Manasses, 1** First son of Joseph and eponymous ancestor of one of the 12 tribes of ISRAEL. **2** King of Judah (r. c.696–c.642 BC). He fostered foreign cults. 2 Kings 21. The **Prayer of Manasses,** one of the pseudepigrapha, placed in the APOCRYPHA in the Authorized Version, is given as his penitential prayer.

**Manasseh ben Israel,** 1604–57, Jewish scholar and communal leader; b. Portugal. A Marrano (see SEPHARDIM), he returned to Judaism in Holland, where he served as a rabbi and started (1627) the first Hebrew press. He obtained Oliver CROMWELL's unofficial assent for Jews to settle in London, where they had been forbidden to live since 1290.

**manatee, sea cow** or **sirenian,** aquatic MAMMAL of the family Trichechidae, related to the dugong. Sea cows are completely adapted to life in water, giving birth and suckling at sea. They live on the Atlantic coasts of Central and northern S America, and the west coast of West Africa. Manatees are HERBIVORES, feeding on seaweeds and any other plants that they can reach. They grow to 4.5 m (15 ft) and are very slow, inquisitive, inoffensive animals.

**Manaus,** city (1980 pop. 613,068), NW Brazil, capital of Amazonas state, on the Rio Negro. Surrounded by jungle, it is the westernmost of Brazil's major cities, the commercial centre of the upper AMAZON region, and a major river port accommodating oceangoing vessels. Founded in 1669, it grew rapidly during the rubber boom of the late 19th cent when its renowned opera house was built and performed in by many famous European artistes of the day. The recent increased interest in development of the Amazon basin has brought Manaus new importance.

**Manchester,** city (1981 pop. 437,612), Greater Manchester, NW England, on the Irwell, Medlock, Irk, and Tib rivers. The MANCHESTER SHIP CANAL provides access to oceangoing vessels. The centre of England's most densely populated area, Manchester has long been the nation's leading textile city and is a key distribution point for nearby cotton mills. Machinery, chemicals, printing, and publishing are also important. A Celtic and Roman town, it was chartered in 1301. Parliamentary representation was achieved in 1832. Important in liberal thought, the city was the centre of the MANCHESTER SCHOOL of economics in the 19th cent. and the site of the founding (1821) of the influential daily newspaper the *Guardian (Manchester Guardian* until 1959). It is the birthplace of David LLOYD GEORGE.

**Manchester school,** group of 19th-cent. English economists, led by Richard COBDEN and John BRIGHT, who advocated free trade and held that the state should interfere as little as possible in economic matters (see LAISSEZ-FAIRE).

**Manchester Ship Canal,** artificial waterway in NW England, approximately 56 km (35 mi) long. It runs from Manchester to the Mersey estuary at Eastham, and is navigable to oceangoing ships. Originally built to save Manchester cotton manufacturers the cost of land transport to and from Liverpool for their goods and raw materials, it was started in 1887 and completed in 1894.

**Manchu,** inhabitants of Manchuria descended from the Jurchen, a tribe known in Asia since the 7th cent. Originally pastoral nomads, they swept into N China in the 12th cent., but were driven out in the 13th cent. by the MONGOLS. They settled in the Sungari valley, developing an agrarian civilization and increasing their territory. In 1644 they conquered China and founded the Ch'ing dynasty. When the dynasty ended (1912), they merged with the Chinese.

**Manchuria,** Mandarin *Dongbei* [northeast], region (1980 est. pop. 90,000,000), c.1,554,000 km² (600,000 sq mi), NE China. Comprising the provinces of Heilongjiang, Jilin, and Liaoning and part of INNER MONGOLIA, Manchuria is bordered by the USSR, North Korea, and Mongolia. It has vast timber resources and mineral deposits, including oil, coal, gold, magnesium, and uranium. A major manufacturing and agricultural centre, Manchuria has huge coal mines and produces steel, heavy machinery, motor vehicles, chemicals, and aircraft in the highly industrialized cities, and wheat, beans, corn, soya beans, and sweet potatoes in the fertile Manchurian plain. It is the traditional home of peoples that have invaded and sometimes ruled N China, notably the MANCHU. Controlled successively by Russia, Chinese warlords, Japan, and the Soviet Union in the 20th cent., Manchuria was occupied by the Communists in 1948 and is now an important strategic region.

**Manco Capac,** legendary founder of the INCA dynasty of Peru; one of four brothers who, with their four sisters, conquered the peoples of the Cuzco valley. Manco Capac's son may be the Sinchi Roca whom authorities accept as the first historical Inca chief (c.1105–c.1140). **Manco Capac** was also the name of the last Inca ruler. A puppet emperor crowned in 1534 by the Spanish conqueror Francisco PIZARRO, he raised a huge army and in 1536 besieged Spanish-occupied CUZCO. Abandoning the siege after 10 months, he fought a bloody guerrilla war against the Spanish until he was murdered in 1544.

**Mandalay,** city (1977 est. pop. 458,000), central Burma, on the Irrawaddy R. Burma's second largest city, it is a major transportation hub. It dates from c.1850 and was the capital of the Burman kingdom from 1860 until Britain annexed Burma in 1885. Mandalay is a centre of Burmese Buddhism. Much of the city was destroyed by British bombing

The Arakan pagoda, **Mandalay**

in World War II, but numerous Buddhist monuments, notably the Arakan pagoda, remain.

**Mandan Indians:** see NORTH AMERICAN INDIANS.

**Mandarin,** a high official of imperial China. Mandarin Chinese, the language spoken by the official class, was based on the Beijing dialect. It is now the official language of China.

**mandates,** system of national trusteeships established (1920) under the LEAGUE OF NATIONS to administer former territorial possessions of Germany and Turkey after WORLD WAR I. Its long-term goal was self-government in the administered territories, which included Iraq, Syria, Lebanon, Palestine, several African countries, and various Pacific islands. The mandates system was superseded by the TRUSTEESHIP system of the UNITED NATIONS.

**Mandela, Nelson,** 1918–, South African black leader, former organizer of the banned AFRICAN NATIONAL CONGRESS. He was sentenced to life imprisonment in 1964 on subversion and sabotage charges, but from prison has continued to be a focus for black political aspirations. In 1988 his conditions of detention were relaxed for health reasons. His wife, **Winnie Mandela,** has become a leading opponent of the government in her own right, but ran into difficulties in 1988/89.

**Mandelstam, Osip Emilyevich** (‚mandəlshtəm), 1891–1938?, Russian poet. A leader of the ACMEISTS, he wrote fatalistic, meticulously constructed lyrics, collected in *Stone* (1913) and *Tristia* (1922). Arrested in 1934 for an anti-Stalin poem, he wrote three *Voronezh Notebooks* (1934) while in exile. He was released, but later was re-arrested, and died as a political prisoner.

**Mandeville, Bernard,** 1670–1733, English writer; b. Holland. A physician, he wrote on medical and ethical subjects. His most important work is *The Fable of the Bees* (1714), whose ironic presentation of virtue and vice in the structure of society was widely misunderstood and criticized.

**mandolin:** see STRINGED INSTRUMENT.

**mandrake,** herbaceous perennial plant (genus *Mandragora*) of the NIGHTSHADE family, native to the Mediterranean and Himalayan regions. True mandrakes contain several ALKALOIDS of medicinal value, and they have been used as pain-killers. Magical powers have often been attributed to the root, which crudely resembles the human form.

**mandrill,** large MONKEY (*Mandrillus sphinx*) found in the forests of central W Africa, related to the BABOON. The fur of the mandrill is mostly dark brown, but the bare face and buttocks are patterned in colours particularly spectacular in the adult male—bright red, blue, black, purple, and pale yellow.

**maneater shark:** see SHARK.

**Manet, Édouard** (ma‚nay), 1832–83, French painter. He was influenced by VELÁZQUEZ and GOYA, and later by Japanese printmakers. In 1861 the Salon accepted his *Guitarist.* Two years later, with the exhibition of *Luncheon on the Grass* (Musée d'Orsay, Paris), he was violently attacked; the painting depicts a nude woman enjoying a picnic in the woods with two fully clothed men. Manet's *Olympia* (1863; Musée d'Orsay, Paris), an arresting portrait of a courtesan, elicited outrage and abuse from critics and public. This hostility from the art establishment attended his work throughout his life. His subject matter and technical innovations were considered heresy, but he profoundly influenced IMPRESSIONISM. Although often called an impressionist, he remaind an urban artist; he did not employ broken colour, and was only briefly attracted by outdoor painting. All his work was a successful attempt to describe the natural immediacy of the eye's perception, and he worked in broad, flat areas of colour abolishing half-tones. His major works include *The Balcony* (1869) and *The Fife Player* (1866; both: Musée d'Orsay, Paris).

**Manfred,** c.1232–1266, last HOHENSTAUFEN king of Sicily (r.1258–66); illegitimate son of Emperor FREDERICK II. He was regent in Sicily for his brother, CONRAD IV, and for his nephew, Conradin. In 1254 he was forced to restore the kingdom to the papacy, but he soon rebelled. Assuming the leadership of antipapal forces, Manfred reconquered Sicily and S Italy, and had himself crowned (1258) at Palermo. Pope Urban IV reacted by investing Charles of Anjou with Sicily as CHARLES I. Manfred was defeated

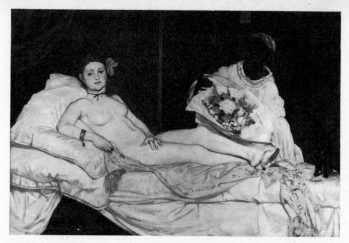

Edouard **Manet**, *L'Olympia*, 1863. Oil on canvas, 130 × 187 cm. Musée d'Orsay, Paris.

by Charles and killed at Benevento (1266), and Conradin was later captured and executed (1268).

**manganese** (Mn), metallic element, first isolated by J.G. Gahn in 1774. It is pinkish-grey and chemically active, and resembles iron. It is a unique deoxidizing and desulphurizing agent in the manufacture of steel and is widely used in making alloys. See ELEMENT (table); PERIODIC TABLE.

**mange,** contagious skin disease of animals, caused by parasitic MITES, invisible to the naked eye, that burrow into the skin, HAIR follicles, or sweat glands. This leads to itching, inflammation, hair loss, and secondary bacterial infection producing small abscesses. The disease is also called scabies.

**mango,** evergreen tree of the SUMAC family, native to tropical E Asia but now grown in both hemispheres. The trees grow rapidly and can attain heights of up to 27 m (90 ft); they are densely covered with glossy leaves and bear small, fragrant yellow or red flowers. The aromatic, slightly acid fruit, a fleshy drupe with a thick, greenish to yellow-red skin, is an important food in the tropics.

**mangrove,** large, tropical evergreen tree (genus *Rhizophora*) found on muddy tidal flats and along shorelines, most abundant in tropical Asia, Africa, and the SW Pacific. Aerial roots, produced from the trunk, become embedded in the mud and form a tangled network that serves as a prop for the tree and a means of aerating the roots. The fruit is a conical, reddish-brown berry with a single seed; it germinates inside the fruit while it is still on the tree, forming a primary root that quickly anchors the seedling in the shifting tidal mud on falling from the tree.

**Manhattan:** see NEW YORK CITY.

**Manhattan Project,** the US wartime programme to design and build the first nuclear weapons (see ATOMIC BOMB). A $2-billion effort, centred at Oak Ridge, Tennessee, and Hanford, Washington, was required to obtain sufficient amounts of two necessary isotopes, uranium-235 and plutonium-239. The design and building of the bombs took place at Los Alamos, New Mexico, where J. Robert OPPENHEIMER directed a large group of US, British, and European-refugee scientists. Following the test explosion of a plutonium device on 16 July, 1945, near Alamogordo, New Mexico, a uranium bomb and a plutonium bomb were dropped on, respectively, HIROSHIMA (6 Aug.) and NAGASAKI (9 Aug.).

**manic-depressive:** see PSYCHOSIS.

**Manichaeism** or **Manichaeanism,** religion founded by Mani (AD c.216–c.276), a visionary prophet, probably of Persian origin. After his martyrdom, his religion spread rapidly throughout the Roman Empire and Asia. Manichaeism synthesized elements from earlier religions such as GNOSTICISM, ZOROASTRIANISM, and Christianity; it taught dualism between good and evil, the transmigration of souls, and the possibility of salvation. St AUGUSTINE was a Manichee until his conversion. The religion survived in the West until the 6th cent. and in the East (Chinese Turkistan) until at least the 14th cent.

**Manifest Destiny,** 19th-cent. doctrine that the US was intended by Providence to expand its territory and influence throughout North America. First gaining currency in the 1840s, when it was cited in support of the annexation of Texas and of American claims to Oregon, the concept was revived as justification for the SPANISH–AMERICAN WAR (1898).

**Manila,** city (1980 pop. 1,626,249), capital of the Philippines, SW Luzon, on Manila Bay. The Philippine capital before 1948 and after 1976, it is the country's largest city, its chief port and transport centre, and the focus of its commercial, industrial, and cultural activities. Manufactures include cars, textiles, and chemicals. Founded in 1571 and developed by Spanish missionaries, Manila was taken (1898) by the US in the SPANISH-AMERICAN WAR. During WORLD WAR II it was occupied (1942) by the Japanese; many 17th-cent. buildings were destroyed in the Allied assault (1945); only the Church of San Augustin (1606) survived. Among the city's outstanding modern buildings is the Philippine Cultural Centre complex.

**Manila hemp,** plant (*Musa textilis*) of the BANANA family, native to the Philippines, and the cordage fibre obtained chiefly from it. Manila hemp, or abaca, yields exceptionally strong, durable, saltwater-resistant fibres, useful for cordage and fabrics. It is unrelated to true HEMP.

**Manitoba,** province of Canada (1984 est. pop. 1,058,100), area 651,900 km² (251,699 sq mi), situated in west–central region, bordered by Northwest Territories (N), Hudson Bay and Ontario (E), Minnesota and North Dakota, US (S), and Saskatchewan (W). Winnipeg is the capital and contains half the population. Manitoba is the easternmost of the Prairie Provinces. While the N consists of the treeless tundra of the Canadian Shield, and the centre is dominated by the remnants of the glacial Lake Agassiz (such as Lakes Winnipeg, Manitoba and Winnipegosis), 95% of the population lives in the southern plains. These are marginal for agriculture, except in the Red River lowlands. Grain farming led the economy after the 1880s, but now manufacturing is the main economic sector, producing foods, electrical items, clothing, and chemicals. Timber and mining (chiefly nickel, copper, and zinc) are also important. In 1670 the area was given to the Hudson's Bay Company, which established fur trading posts. The French contested control, but British claims were confirmed (1763), although the North West Company also fought for the area. Settlement began after the two companies merged (1821) and the region was sold to the confederation of Canada, becoming a province in the process (1870). The indigenous buffalo-hunting peoples of the plains were confined to reservations and the confederation encouraged homesteading and the ploughing up of the grasslands. The immigrant population contained many Germans and Mennonites. Since 1940 the economy has diversified towards manufacturing although the population has not increased significantly.

**Maniu, Iuliu,** 1873–1953, Romanian politician. A Transylvanian by birth, Maniu was elected in 1909 to the Hungarian parliament where he was a powerful advocate of Romanian aspirations. He was one of the principal architects of the union (1918) of Transylvania with Romania. In 1919 he was elected president of the National Party, and was prime minister on several occasions (1928–30, 1930, 1932–33) but his distaste for CAROL II's liaison with Madame Lupescu led him to break with the king. He returned to head the democratic opposition first to Carol's royal dictatorship (1938), and then to ANTONESCU's regime (1940). A consistent opponent of the Soviet-inspired suppression of the democratic process in Romania after the war, he was arrested in 1947 on charges of plotting to overthrow the state and sentenced to life imprisonment. He died in prison.

**Manizales** (manee,sahles), city (1979 est. pop. 247,280), W Colombia, capital of Caldas dept. Founded in 1848 by settlers from Antioquía dept. to the S, it is the centre of the region which today produces one-third of Colombia's coffee. Overlooking the city is the Nevada El Ruíz volcano, which erupted in November 1985 causing great destruction and loss of life.

**Manley, Norman,** 1893–1969, prime minister of Jamaica (1959–62). An internationally known lawyer, of Irish and black descent, he, with his cousin Alexander BUSTAMANTE, dominated Jamaican politics for many years. Manley was chief minister (1955–59) before being designated prime minister. His son, **Michael Norman Manley,** 1923–, prime minister from 1972 to 1980, partially nationalized foreign-owned

industry and established close ties with Cuba and the USSR. He was re-elected in 1989.

**Mann,** family of German writers. **Heinrich Mann,** 1871–1950, wrote novels of sharp social criticism such as *Professor Unrat* (1905; tr. *The Blue Angel*) and the trilogy *The Patrioteer* (1921), *The Poor* (1917), and *The Chief* (1925). A vigorous political activist and left-wing essayist (*Intellect and Action*, 1931; *The Day Will Come*, 1936), he left Germany in 1933 first for France, where he wrote his masterpiece, the historical novel *Henri IV* (1935, 1938); and thence to the US, where he died. His last major work was his autobiography *An Age is Viewed* (1946). His brother, **Thomas Mann,** 1875–1955, is an outstanding literary figure of the 20th cent. whose novels developed themes relating inner problems to changing European cultural values. His first novel, *Buddenbrooks, Decline of a Family* (1901), brought him fame. Translations of his shorter fiction, collected in *Stories of Three Decades* (1936), including *Tonio Kröger* (1903) and the classic *Death in Venice* (1912), reflect Mann's preoccupation with the proximity of creative art to neurosis and disease, and with the problem of artistic values in bourgeois society. These themes feature in his major work, *Der Zauberberg* (1924; tr. The Magic Mountain). His tetralogy *Joseph und seine Brüder* (1933–43; tr. Joseph and his Brothers) is a modern psychologization of the Biblical story. Later works include *Doctor Faustus* (1947), a paradigmatic reckoning with his nation's history, *Der Erwählte* (1951; tr. The Holy Sinner), and *Bekenntnisse des Hochstaplers Felix Krull* (1954; tr. Confessions of Felix Krull). Translations of Mann's political writings include *Betrachtungen eines Unpolitischen* (1919, tr. Observations of a Non-Political Man), his conservative polemic of World War I which provoked a great quarrel with his brother, and *Order of the Day* (1930), a selection of his humanist, anti-fascist essays; his major literary essays are collected in *Essays of Three Decades* (1947). He left Hitler's Germany in 1933 and lived in the US after 1938, moving to Switzerland in 1953. He received the Nobel Prize for literature in 1929. Mann's daughter, **Erika Mann** (1905–69), was an actress and author and was married to the poet W.H. AUDEN. Mann's son, **Klaus Mann,** 1906–49, was a novelist, essayist, and playwright. His works include *Alexander* (1929), *Mephisto* (1936), and the autobiographical *Turning Point* (1942). Mann's younger son **Golo Mann,** 1909–, the historian, is the influential author of *German History in the 19th and 20th Centuries* (1958) and *Wallenstein* (1971).

**Mann, Horace,** 1796–1859, American educator. While serving as secretary of the Massachusetts state board of education, he started a movement for better teaching and better-paid teachers, established state normal schools, and improved schoolhouses and equipment. After serving (1848–53) in the US House of Representatives, he became (1853) the first president of Antioch College, where he demonstrated the practicability of coeducation and set high academic standards.

**Mannerheim, Baron Carl Gustav Emil,** 1867–1951, Finnish field marshal and president (1944–46). He fought the Bolsheviks in 1918 and was briefly regent (1919). In 1939–40 and 1941 44 he headed the Finnish forces against the USSR. The **Mannerheim Line** of defence, across the Karelian Isthmus, was planned by him; Soviet forces broke through it in 1940.

**mannerism,** style in art and architecture (c.1520–1600), originating in Italy. It developed the technical virtuosity and grace of late RAPHAEL and MICHELANGELO, and in some cases reacted against the equilibrium of form and proportion characteristic of the High Renaissance. Artists such as PONTORMO, BRONZINO, ROSSO, and PARMIGIANO created elongated, elegant figures, and explored improbable, often expressively distorted poses, e.g., Parmigiano's *The Madonna of the Long Neck* (c.1535; Uffizi, Florence). Light was unreal and often harsh, colour complex and sometimes acrimonious. Mannerists confused scale and spatial relationships and created strange tunnel-like spaces, as in the works of TINTORETTO and El GRECO. Sculptors such as Giovanni BOLOGNA, CELLINI, and Jean GOUJON created figures of extraordinary stylish grace; their compositions emphasize the serpentine line, and spiralling poses demand multiple viewpoints, e.g., Giovanni Bologna's *The Rape of the Sabines* (1579–83; Loggia dei Lanzi, Florence). In architecture, the style used unbalanced proportions and arbitrary arrangements of the decorations, as in the Laurentian Library, designed c.1525 by Michelangelo, and the Uffizi, planned by VASARI (1560–80). In France, the style developed at Fontainebleau, where Rosso and PRIMATICCIO decorated (1530–40) the Gallery of Francis I. In N Europe, as with the Antwerp mannerists, the style sometimes degenerated into extravagant contrasts of elaborate poses and expressions. The ZUCCARO brothers gave mannerism an academic formalism, but by the end of the 16th cent. it yielded to the naturalism of the early baroque.

**Mannheim,** city (1984 pop. 297,200), Baden–Württemberg, West Germany, at the confluence of the Neckar R. and the RHINE. A route centre and an active river port, its industries include electrical engineering and vehicle-building. Originally founded in 1606 as a Rhineland frontier town, it suffered destruction by the French, but was rebuilt in the early 18th cent. to a formal plan focusing on the electoral palace. It served as capital of the Rhineland Palatinate (1720–88). The Mannheim orchestra achieved great prominence in the 18th cent.

**Manning, Henry Edward,** 1808–92, English Roman Catholic churchman. An Anglican priest, he became an adherent of the OXFORD MOVEMENT and in 1851 followed John Henry NEWMAN into the Roman Catholic Church; he was later ordained. Made archbishop of Westminster (1865) and a cardinal (1875), he disagreed violently with Newman over the promulgation of papal infallibility, which Manning favoured. A strong advocate of social reform, he was influential in the labour movement, and in 1889 he supported the London dock strike and then single-handedly settled it.

**manorial system** or **seignorial system,** a socio-economic system of medieval Europe (fl. 11th–15th cent.), which regulated the landholding and production of peasants. It was based on the holding of lands from a lord *(seigneur)* in return for fixed dues in kind, money, and services. Unlike FEUDALISM, the manorial system lacked the military or political concept of the fief, and it declined with the emergence of towns, a money economy, and centralized monarchies. In its simplest form the system consisted of the division of land into self-sufficient estates, each held by a lay or ecclesiastical lord, who lent it to peasants for cultivation. The peasant might be personally free although his land was not (see VILLEIN), or servile (see SERF). The manor was an administrative and political unit, with a court presided over by the lord and systems of taxation and public works. In the UK lordships of the manor persist but the title carries only nominal rights.

**Manpower Services Commission,** British body (est. 1974) intended to promote the efficient working of the labour market, and provide services in the employment and traning fields. It operated schemes for the young unemployed (Youth Opportunities Programme) and school-leavers entering employment with little opportunity for traning (Unified Vocational Preparation). A more comprehensive Youth Training Scheme, initially a one-year training course, later extended to two years, was introduced in 1983. The MSC also became involved in school curricula through the Technical and Vocational Initiative (TVEI), which began with pilot schemes in 1983. The aim is to provide 'integrated courses of technical and vocational education' between the ages of 14 and 18. Both YOP and YTS have been strongly criticized by trades unionists, who see in them merely a means of keepimg wages low and of making the unemployment figure appear less bad than they really are.

**Mansard:** see MANSART.

**mansard roof,** type of roof so named because it was frequently used by François MANSART, but used earlier, e.g., at the LOUVRE (early 16th cent.). It was characteristic of French Renaissance and, later, of European and American Victorian architecture. The roof's two-section slope, with the lower slope almost vertical, allows a higher, more useful, interior space.

Mansard roof

**Mansart** or **Mansard, François** (mahnh,sah), 1598–1666, French classical architect. His Hôtel de la Vrillière (1635) was long a model for the elegant Paris house. Surviving works include the château of Maisons and, in Paris, the alterations to the Hôtel Carnavalet. His pupil and grand-nephew **Jules Hardouin Mansart,** 1646–1708, was also an architect. In 1699 he was named chief architect for the royal buildings for LOUIS XIV. At VERSAILLES he built the Galérie des Glaces, the Grand Trianon, the palace chapel, and the vast orangery. As a town planner he designed the Place des Victoires (1684–86) and the Place Vendôme (1699), both in Paris. The Dôme des Invalides (1706) in Paris is regarded as his greatest achievement.

**Mansfeld, Peter Ernst von,** 1580?–1626, commander in the THIRTY YEARS' WAR. In the service of FREDERICK THE WINTER KING he defeated TILLY (1622). He became a Dutch mercenary in 1623. With an English subsidy (1625) he recruited a force to fight on the Protestant side but was defeated by WALLENSTEIN.

**Mansfield,** town (1981 pop. 71,325) in Nottinghamshire, E Midlands of England, 22 km (14 mi) N of Nottingham, on R. Maun. It is an industrial town in the middle of an important coal-mining district, Industries include engineering and the manufacture of hosiery.

**Mansfield, Katherine,** 1888–1923, English author; b. New Zealand as Kathleen Beauchamp. A master of the modern impressionistic short story, her best work evokes the settings of her New Zealand upbringing. Collections include *Bliss* (1920), *The Garden Party* (1922), *The Dove's Nest* (1923), and *Something Childish* (1924). She was married to J.M. MURRY.

**manslaughter:** see HOMICIDE.

**Mansur, al-** (Muhammad ibn Abi-Amir al-Mansur billah) [Arab., = the victorious], 914–1002, Moorish regent of CÓRDOBA. Known in Spanish as Almanzor, he became royal chamberlain (978) and controlled the caliphate. He campaigned against the Christian states of N Spain, sacking BARCELONA (985) and razing the city of LEÓN (988).

**Mansûra,** city (1987 pop. 259,387), N Egypt, in the Nile delta. A commercial and industrial city, its economy is based on textiles. Founded in 1221, it was the scene of battle in 1250 when the Crusaders (Sixth Crusade) under Louis IX of France were defeated and Louis was captured.

**manta:** see DEVIL FISH.

**Mantegna, Andrea** (man,tenyah), c.1431–1506, Italian painter of the Paduan school. Married to the daughter of Jacopo Bellini (see BELLINI, family), he was the greatest artist in N Italy outside of Venice. His passion for the antique is evidenced in all his work, and he was one of the first artists to collect Greek and Roman works. A rigorous draughtsman and anatomist, and a perfectionist in perspective, he nevertheless gave his statuesque forms intense life. Among his celebrated early works is the St Luke altarpiece (Milan). He became court painter to the Gonzaga: for them he painted his famous frescoes in the Camera degli Sposi [bridal chamber] of the Gonzaga palace, Mantua. His illusion of a dome opening to the sky was widely imitated in the BAROQUE period. About 1497 he painted *Parnassus* and *Triumph of Virtue* (Louvre, Paris) for Isabella d'Este. Among his late works are nine large canvases of *The Triumph of Caesar* (1486–94; Royal Coll., Hampton Court Palace, Richmond, London).

**mantra. 1** In HINDUISM and BUDDHISM, mystic word used in ritual and MEDITATION. It is believed to have power to bring into being the reality it represents. The *bīja-mantra* [seed-sounds] used in TANTRA are syllables having occult affinity for particular deities; use of such mantras usually requires initiation by a guru, or spiritual teacher. **2** The Hymn section in the Vedic scriptures (see BRĀHMAṆA).

**Manu,** in Hindu legend, a divinely inspired lawgiver. With the help of a big fish, he saved mankind and other living creatures in a large boat during the Great Flood (comparable to Noah's Ark). Traditionally ascribed to him are the *Laws of Manu,* compiled (probably between 200 BC and AD 200) from diverse ancient sources and providing detailed rules, presumably for the four castes, the priests, Kṣatriya, Vaiśya and Śūdra. See also HINDUISM.

**Manuel,** Byzantine emperors. **Manuel I** (Comnenus), c.1120–80 (r.1143–80) was the son of John II. In the Second CRUSADE (1147–49) he made a truce with the Turks to protect his western provinces. Later he made peace (1158) with William I of Sicily. Manuel supported Pope

Andrea **Mantegna**, *Triumph of Virtue*. Louvre, Paris.

ALEXANDER III against Holy Roman Emperor FREDERICK I, and tried to reunite the empires and churches of the East and West. His neglect of Asia Minor brought a crushing defeat (1176) by the Turks. Manuel encouraged Western merchants in Constantinople. His son, ALEXIUS II, succeeded him. **Manuel II** (Palaeologus), 1348?–1425, (r.1391–1425), reigned over an empire reduced by the Turks to CONSTANTINOPLE and its environs. TAMERLANE's victory over the Ottoman sultan BAYEZID I (1402) temporarily saved Constantinople. Manuel's son, JOHN VIII, ruled during his father's last years.

**Manuel**, kings of Portugal. **Manuel I**, 1469–1521 (r.1495–1521), had a reign notable for Portugal's advances in overseas exploration, especially Vasco da GAMA's epochal voyage (1497–99) to India. Wealth from the Indies made Portugal the West's leading commercial nation. In order to marry the Spanish princess Isabel, Manuel agreed (1496) to expel the JEWS, but he first attempted their forcible conversion. He was unable to prevent the departure of some Jews and their massacre in Lisbon (1506). **Manuel II**, 1889–1932, (r.1908–10), became king after the assassination of his father and brother. He was the last king of Portugal: in 1910 a republican revolution deposed him.

**Manx**, virtually extinct language belonging to the Goidelic or Gaelic group of the Celtic subfamily of the Indo-European family of languages. See LANGUAGE (table).

**Manyōshū** [Jap., = Collection of a myriad leaves], (tr. 1929, 1965), a Japanese late-8th-cent. anthology of around 4500 poems by over 250 poets from all social classes, covering the period from the 4th to 8th cent., based on 31-syllable form (lines of 5, 7, 5, 7, 7 syllables), known as *tanka* [short poem] or *waka* [Japanese poem].

**Manzoni, Alessandro**, 1785–1873, Italian novelist and poet. His most famous work, *I promessi sposi* (1825–27; tr. The Betrothed), a historical novel set in 17th-cent. Lombardy, and suggested by the example of Sir Walter SCOTT, had gone through 118 editions by 1875, and greatly influenced the development of Italian prose. He also wrote tragedies and poetry, including the celebrated *Cinque maggio* (1821; tr. Fifth of May), on the death of Napoleon, translated into English by GLADSTONE and others. VERDI's *Requiem* commemorates the poet's death.

**Manzù Giacomo**, 1908–, Italian sculptor. His first works were religious subjects, many in relief-sculpture. His series of female busts showed his skill as a portraitist, exemplified in his bust of Pope John XXIII (1983). He often reworked subjects and themes over many years, as in his *Girl with a Chair*. His work stands outside the mainstream avant-garde movements and continues the classical Western traditions of sculpture.

**Mao Dun**, pseud. of **Shen Yanbing**, 1896–1985, Chinese writer. Founder and editor of *Xiaoshuo yuebao* [short story monthly] (1921–23), an influential journal introducing foreign fiction and the new Chinese fiction Mao Dun entered politics early but turned to fiction after the purge of left-wingers in Chiang Kai-shek's KUOMINTANG in 1927. His most famous novel, *Zi ye* [midnight] (1933), is a study of the industrial life of Shanghai in a period of depression. He wrote little after 1949 but served as Minister of Culture (1949–65), dismissed at the outbreak of the CULTURAL REVOLUTION.

**Maori**, Polynesian people of New Zealand, making up about 8% of the nation's population. They speak a language related to Tahitian and Hawaiian. Believed to have migrated from POLYNESIA in canoes in early times, the Maori established an agricultural society. In the 19th cent., after wars against European encroachment, they were reduced to 100,000 and later even fewer. Their population has since increased to 225,000; today, they are economically self-sufficient while maintaining their cultural identity.

Maori

**Maori language**, spoken by the MAORI people of New Zealand, belonging to the Polynesian subfamily of the Malayo-Polynesian family of languages. See LANGUAGE (table).

**Mao Tse-tung**: see MAO ZEDONG.

**Mao Zedong** or **Mao Tse-tung** (‚mow tsay ‚toong), 1893–1976, founder of the People's Republic of CHINA. Born in Hunan prov., he was one of the original members of the Chinese Communist Party. Mao organized unions for the KUOMINTANG, but after the Communist–Kuomintang split (1927) he worked to establish rural soviets and to build the Red Army. In the course of the LONG MARCH (1934–35) from Jiangxi N to Yan'an in Shaanxi prov., he gained control of the Chinese Communist Party. In 1949, when the Communists had seized most of the mainland, Mao became the first chairman of the People's Republic of China. In 1958 he launched the Great Leap Forward, a programme for industrial growth; after it failed he was replaced (1959) as chairman by LIU SHAOQI, but still retained his party leadership. Mao launched the CULTURAL REVOLUTION (1966–69), a period of widespread upheaval in which Liu and other leaders were purged. In the 1970s he consolidated his position as China's most powerful figure, but as his health deteriorated he was subject to the influence of JIANG QING and the GANG OF FOUR. Mao's policies often strained relations with the USSR, but his ideas on revolutionary struggle became very influential in the Third World. In 1972 he developed closer ties with the West by meeting US Pres. NIXON in Beijing. His reputation in China is now equivocal.

**maple**, common name for the genus *Acer* of the Aceraceae, a family of deciduous trees and shrubs of the Northern Hemisphere, characterized by winged seeds. Maples are popular as shade trees and many are prized for their brilliant spring and autumn colours. Most of the highly ornamental species are from Japan and China. The timber is close-grained and hard. The sugar maple (*A. saccharum*) and the black maple (*A. nigrum*), of N America, are the main source of maple syrup. *Acer pseudoplatanus* (the 'false plane', native to mainland Europe) is called the sycamore in Britain, where it has become naturalized. It is very resistant to adverse climate, and produces a valuable timber used in furniture-making.

**maple sugar**: see SUCROSE.

**Mapondera, Kadungire,** 18??–1904, anticolonial resistance leader who operated along the Zimbabwe–Mozambique border. The Mapondera movement was founded in 1894 as a protest against Portuguese taxation. For the next 10 years Mapondera led a guerrilla campaign against the colonialists, burning warehouses, stores, and fields owned by Portuguese concessionaires. Regarded as a bandit by the authorities, he was a hero in the eyes of the peasants. He was eventually captured and killed.

**map projection,** transfer of the features of the earth's surface or those of another spherical body onto a flat sheet of paper. Only a globe can represent surface features correctly with reference to area, shape, scale, and direction. Projection from a globe to a flat map always causes some distortion. A grid or net of two intersecting systems of lines corresponding to parallels and meridians must be drawn on a plane surface. Some projections (equidistant) aim to keep correct distances in all directions from the centre of the map. Others show areas (equal-area) or shapes (conformal) equal to those on the globe of the same scale. Projections are cylindrical, conical, or azimuthal in geometric origin. See also MERCATOR MAP PROJECTION.

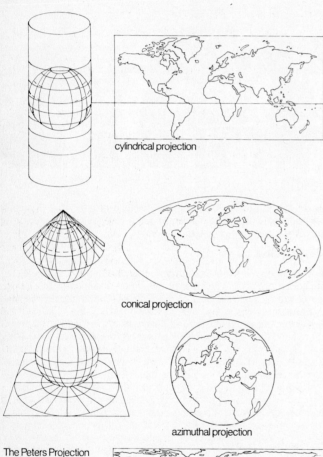

cylindrical projection

conical projection

azimuthal projection

The Peters Projection is mathematically constructed to produce a map with zero area distortion.

Examples of **map projections**

**Maputo** formerly Lourenço Marques, city (1980 pop. 755,300), capital of Mozambique kand a port on the Indian Ocean. The country's largest city and economic centre, it is linked by rail with South Africa and Zimbabwe. Manufactures include food products, cement, and furniture; the chief

exports are cotton, sugar, coal, and chrome. The city's excellent beaches are a tourist attraction. Founded in the late 18th cent., it became the capital of Portuguese East Africa in 1907 and was renamed (1976) after independence.

**Maracaibo** ('marə,kieboh), city (1980 est. pop. 900,000), NW Venezuela, capital of Zulia state, at Lake MARACAIBO's outlet to the Caribbean Sea. It is the nation's oil capital and a major commercial and industrial centre, exporting shrimp and crab as well as coffee and other inland products. Founded in 1571, Maracaibo developed slowly until 1918, when foreign interests began to exploit the vast petroleum resources of the area. Lake Maracaibo bridge, one of the world's longest bridges, is S of the city.

Maracaibo bridge

**Maracaibo, Lake,** large, brackish lake, c.13,210 km² (5100 sq mi), NW Venezuela, extending c.180 km (110 mi) inland from the Caribbean. It is one of the world's richest oil-producing regions. The city of Maracaibo is at the lake's outlet to the sea.

**Maracay** (marə,kie), city (1980 est. pop. 344,000), N central Venezuela, capital of Aragua state. It is the focus for an important agricultural region. The city was favoured by the 20th-cent. Venezuelan dictator, General GÓMEZ, who added a number of exotic follies to the city, including zoos, an unfinished opera house, and an exact replica of the Seville bullring.

**marasmus,** syndrome of protein-deficiency malnutrition in children, causing loss of growth and emaciation but continued alertness. See MALNUTRITION.

**Marat, Jean Paul** (mah,rah), 1743–93, French revolutionary. A doctor, he turned to politics when the FRENCH REVOLUTION began (1789) and founded the journal *L'Ami du peuple,* in which he bitterly attacked all who were in power. Outlawed, he fled to England (1790, 1791) and also hid in the Paris sewers, thereby worsening a skin disease; it required treatments in warm baths. He continued to publish in secret and helped to inflame the public. Elected (1792) to the Convention, he supported the JACOBINS against the GIRONDISTS. Marat was murdered in his bath by a Girondist admirer, Charlotte CORDAY.

**Marathi** (mə,rahtee), language belonging to the Indic group of the Indo-Iranian subfamily of the Indo-European family of languages. See LANGUAGE (table).

**Marathon,** village and plain of ancient Greece, NE of ATHENS, site of an Athenian victory (490 BC) over the first Persian expedition sent against Greece (see PERSIAN WARS). In legend, the plain was the scene of the victory of THESEUS over a great bull.

**marathon race,** long-distance endurance race, named after Marathon, Greece, from where, in 490 BC, the runner Pheidippides carried news to Athens of a Greek victory over the Persians. Included in the first modern Olympic Games (1896), the marathon was standardized at 42.2 km (26 mi, 385 yd) in 1908. Today, annual marathon races in leading cities of the world attract thousands of distance runners.

**marble,** a ROCK formed by the METAMORPHISM of LIMESTONE. The term is loosely applied to any limestone or DOLOMITE that takes a good polish and is otherwise suitable as a building or ornamental stone. Its colour varies depending on the types of impurities present. It has been used since ancient times for statuary, monuments, and facing stones. Like all limestones, it is corroded by water and acid fumes and is therefore ultimately uneconomical for use in exposed places.

**Marbury v. Madison,** case decided in 1803 by the US SUPREME COURT. In a dispute over federal appointments, Chief Justice MARSHALL held that the statute that was the basis for the remedy sought gave the Court authority denied it by Article III of the US CONSTITUTION. This decision, the first to invalidate an act of Congress, established the doctrine of JUDICIAL REVIEW, vastly expanding the judiciary's power.

**Marc, Franz,** 1880–1916, German expressionist painter. A member of the BLAUE REITER group, he developed a rich chromatic symbolism to depict a mystical world of animals. *Blue Horses* (Walker Art Center, Minneapolis) is representative. He met DELAUNAY in Paris in 1912 and his late works are more abstract and cubist (see CUBISM).

**marcasite** or **white iron pyrites,** mineral closely resembling and having the same chemical composition ($FeS_2$) as PYRITE; paler in colour, it becomes darker upon oxidation. Marcasite occurs worldwide in marls, clays, and limestones.

**Marceau, Marcel** (mah‚soh), 1923–, French mime. Famed for his sad-faced clown character, Bip, he has performed frequently with his company in the US since 1955.

**Marcellus, Marcus Claudius,** c.268–208 BC, Roman consul. He besieged Syracuse in the Second PUNIC WAR and took the city in 212 BC. He also captured (211 BC) Capua. Earlier (222 BC), he had killed the king of the Insubrian Gauls in single combat.

**March:** see MONTH.

**March, earl of:** see MORTIMER, ROGER DE, EARL OF MARCH.

**Marcian,** 396–457, the last Theodosian to be East Roman emperor (450–57). He called the Council of CHALCEDON (451). By refusing tribute to ATTILA he brought on the HUN invasion.

**Marciano, Rocky,** 1924–69, American boxer; b. Rocco Francis Marchegiano. He turned professional in 1947 and won the world heavyweight championship in 1952 by knocking out Jersey Joe Walcott. Noted as a powerful puncher, he won 43 of his 49 professional bouts by knockouts. He retired in 1956 as the only heavyweight champion who never lost a professional bout. He died in a plane crash.

**Marcion,** fl. AD 140, controversial Christian teacher, founder of the Marcionites, the first great Christian heresy to rival Catholic Christianity. He taught that there were two gods, the stern creator God of the OLD TESTAMENT and the superior merciful God of the NEW TESTAMENT, and he rejected the Old Testament entirely. Excommunicated by the Christian community at Rome in 144, he founded a church of his own which was efficiently organized and was later absorbed by MANICHAEISM.

**Marcomanni:** see GERMANS.

**Marconi, Guglielmo,** 1874–1937, Italian engineer and inventor. In 1896 he came to England and filed the first patent for the use of Hertzian waves for telegraphic communication. A year later he formed the world's first radio company: it was first called the Wireless Telegraph and Signal Co. and later became the Marconi Co. In 1897 he succeeded in communicating some 13 km (8 mi) across the Bristol Channel and in 1901 he demonstrated for the first time radio communication across the Atlantic, from Poldhu in Cornwall to St John's in Newfoundland. Marconi held many patents including one for coupled tuned circuits, the magnetic detector, the radio valve, and a directional aerial. He shared the 1909 Nobel Prize for physics for his contribution to wireless telegraphy.

**Marco Polo:** see POLO, MARCO.

**Marcos, Ferdinand Edralin,** 1917–, president of the PHILIPPINES (1965–86). He maintained close ties with the US and attempted to suppress Muslim rebels and Communist and liberal opposition to his rule. Marcos proclaimed martial law in 1972, and the next year he assumed virtual dictatorial rule under a new constitution. He was eventually overthrown by a military-popular revolt and forced into exile, together with his wife, Ismelda.

**Marcus Aurelius** (Marcus Aelius Aurelius Antoninus), 121–180, Roman emperor and philosopher. He was adopted by the emperor Antoninus Pius and succeeded him in 161, ruling jointly with his adoptive brother, Lucius Verus. Sole emperor after 169, he spent most of his reign repressing rebellions and attacks by the Parthians, Germans, and Britons. He was a humanitarian ruler who nevertheless accepted the then-prevalent view of the Christians as the empire's chief enemies. His spiritual reflections, the *Meditations,* are considered a classic work of STOICISM. They were strongly influenced by the thought of EPICTETUS.

**Marcuse, Herbert,** 1898–1979, American political philosopher; b. Germany. A founder of the Frankfurt Institute of Social Research, he fled from the Nazis (1934) and became a US citizen. He taught at Harvard and other universities before becoming (1965) professor of philosophy at the Univ. of California at San Diego. He is known for his synthesis of Marxist and Freudian theory, expounded in *Eros and Civilization* (1954), *One Dimensional Man* (1964), and other books. Marcuse was a hero to American radicals of the 1960s.

**Mar del Plata,** city (1980 pop. 423,989) on the Atlantic coast 400 km (250 mi) S of Buenos Aires in central Argentina. It is a celebrated national seaside resort and international conference location which attracts an estimated two million summer visitors each year.

**Mardi Gras,** last day before the fasting season of Lent. It is the French name for Shrove Tuesday. Carnivals are held in some countries, usually lasting a week or more before Mardi Gras itself. Among the most celebrated carnivals are those of New Orleans, Rio de Janeiro, Nice, and Cologne.

**Marechera, Dambudzo,** 1952–87, Zimbabwean novelist. He wrote superbly about cultural and personal deprivation, both before and after independence, in, e.g., *The House of Hunger* (1979) and *Black Sunlight* (1980). His excessive life-style led to an early death.

**Margai, Sir Milton,** 1895–1964, prime minister of SIERRA LEONE (1961–64). He was a prominent doctor who turned to politics and led his country to independence (1961). His brother, **Sir Albert Margai,** 1910–, succeeded him as prime minister (1964–67).

**Margaret,** Danish queens. **Margaret I,** 1353–1412, queen of Denmark, Norway, and Sweden, was the daughter of WALDEMAR IV of Denmark. Married (1363) to Haakon VI of Norway (d. 1380), the son of MAGNUS VII, she was regent for her son OLAF V in Denmark (r. 1375–87) and Norway (r. 1380–87). After he died (1387), she defeated and captured (1389) the Swedish king, Albert, and persuaded the Danish, Norwegian, and Swedish diets to accept her grandnephew, Eric of Pomerania, as king. He was crowned (1397), and the KALMAR UNION was established. Margaret remained the actual ruler of all three kingdoms until her death. **Margaret II** (Margrethe), 1940–, queen of Denmark (r. 1972–), is the daughter of King FREDERICK IX and Queen Ingrid (daughter of GUSTAVUS VI of Sweden). She became queen under a new constitution (1953) allowing female succession. She and her husband, Comte Henri de Laborde de Monpezat, have two sons.

**Margaret,** 1930–, British princess; sister of ELIZABETH II. Her 1960 marriage to Antony Armstrong-Jones (later earl of Snowden) produced two children: Viscount Linley (b. 1961) and Sarah (b. 1964). It ended in divorce in 1978.

**Margaret Maid of Norway,** 1283–90, infant queen of Scotland (r. 1286–90); daughter of Eric II of Norway; granddaughter of ALEXANDER III of Scotland, whom she succeeded. Her early death led to an English attempt to subjugate Scotland.

**Margaret Maultasch** (‚mowltash) [Ger., = pocket mouth], 1318–69, countess of Tyrol, called the Ugly Duchess. She expelled her first husband from Tyrol, received a secular annulment, and married (1342) Lewis of Bavaria, son of the emperor Lewis IV. The act offended the nobles, who rebelled. Margaret eventually abdicated (1363), and Tyrol passed to the HABSBURGS. Lion FEUCHTWANGER used her story in his novel *The Ugly Duchess.*

**Margaret of Angoulême:** see MARGARET OF NAVARRE.

**Margaret of Anjou,** 1430?–1482, queen consort of HENRY VI of England. She married Henry in 1445 and was very influential at court. In the first 16 years of the Wars of the ROSES, she defended the cause of her husband and her son Edward against the house of YORK. Captured (1471) by the Yorkist EDWARD IV, she returned (1476) to France, and died in poverty.

**Margaret of Austria**, 1480–1530, Habsburg princess, regent of the NETHERLANDS; daughter of MAXIMILIAN I. First betrothed to the future CHARLES VIII of France, she was married (1497) to John of Spain (d. 1497) and (1501) to Philibert of Savoy (d. 1504). In 1507 she became guardian of her nephew, the future Emperor CHARLES V, and regent of the Netherlands, mediating between her father and his Dutch subjects.

**Margaret of Navarre** or **Margaret of Angoulême** (ahnhgooh,laym), 1492–1549, sister of FRANCIS I of France. Married (1527) to Henri d'Albret, king of Navarre, she was a patron of writers such as François RABELAIS. She wrote the *Heptaméron,* an original collection of 72 stories in the manner of Boccaccio.

**Margaret of Parma**, 1522–86, Spanish regent of the NETHERLANDS; illegitimate daughter of Holy Roman Emperor CHARLES V. She was married (1536) to Alessandro de' Medici (d. 1537) and (1538) to Ottavio Farnese (see FARNESE, family), duke of Parma. In 1559 she became regent of the Netherlands under her half brother, PHILIP II. She resigned in 1567, opposing the duke of ALBA's harsh suppression of the revolt led by WILLIAM THE SILENT.

**Margaret of Valois** (val,wah), 1553–1615, queen of France and Navarre; daughter of HENRY II. Her marriage (1572) to the Protestant Henry of Navarre (later HENRY IV of France) was a prelude to the massacre of Protestants on SAINT BARTHOLOMEW'S DAY. She became estranged from her husband and her brother, HENRY III, and took up arms against them. Captured (1586) by royal troops, she was confined (1587–1605) at Usson, where she assembled a literary circle. In 1599 Margaret agreed to have her marriage annulled, and she spent her last years in Paris. Her own writings show much literary ability.

**Margaret Tudor**, 1489–1541, queen consort of JAMES IV of Scotland; sister of HENRY VIII of England. She married James in 1503, and after his death (1513) their infant son, JAMES V, became king. Margaret remarried twice and played a large part in Scottish politics, her affiliation varying with her personal interest. JAMES I of England was her descendant.

**Mari**, ancient city of Mesopotamia, on the middle Euphrates R. Discovered in the 1930s, the site has since been excavated. Evidence of habitation dates to the 3rd millennium BC. Mari was the commercial and political focus (c.1800 BC) of W Asia, and the inhabitants were referred to as Amorites in the Old Testament. HAMMURABI conquered (c.1700 BC) Mari, which never regained its former status.

**Maria**, queens of PORTUGAL. **Maria I**, 1734–1816 (r.1777–1816), was married (1760) for political reasons to her uncle, PETER III, who ruled jointly with her. Together they brought about the fall of the powerful minister POMBAL and freed his enemies from jail or exile. The deaths of Peter (1786) and her eldest son, Joseph (1788), contributed to unhinging her mind, and her second son, later JOHN VI, assumed power (1792) and became regent (1799). **Maria II**, 1819–53 (r.1834–53), was designated queen by her father, PEDRO I of Brazil, on condition that she marry her uncle, Dom Miguel, but he usurped the throne (1828) before she could return to Portugal. Her father led an invading army into Portugal and deposed Miguel in the Miguelist Wars (1832–34), restoring Maria as queen. Her reign was torn by dissent and revolutions.

**Mariam, Mengistu Haile:** see MENGISTU HAILE MARIAM.

**Marianas trench, Marianas trough** or **Marianas deep**, depression in the Pacific Ocean, 338 km (210 mi) SW of Guam. The deepest (11,033 m/36,198 ft) part of any ocean, it was reached (1960) by two men in a US navy bathyscaphe.

**Maria Theresa**, 1717–80, Austrian archduchess, queen of Bohemia and Hungary (r.1740–80); consort of Holy Roman Emperor FRANCIS I. The daughter of Emperor CHARLES VI, she succeeded (1740) to the HABSBURG lands by the PRAGMATIC SANCTION of 1713. Her succession was contested in the War of the AUSTRIAN SUCCESSION, in which she lost Silesia to Prussia but secured (1745) the election of her husband as emperor. Aided by her chancellor, Wenzel Anton Kaunitz, she allied Austria with France in the SEVEN YEARS' WAR (1756–63) and joined in the partition (1772) of Poland. With her son, JOSEPH II (with whom she jointly ruled her lands after 1765), Maria Theresa carried out agrarian reforms and centralized the administration. During her reign Vienna developed as a centre for music and the arts. Among her 16 children were Emperors JOSEPH II and LEOPOLD II, and MARIE ANTOINETTE of France.

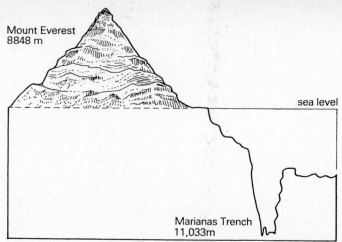

Marianas trench

**Maribor**, city (1981 pop. 185,699) in Slovenia, N Yugoslavia, on the Drava R. A commercial centre, it has textile, chemical, electrical, and vehicle industries. Founded in the 11th cent., it resisted the Turks and was Austrian until 1919. Its buildings include the 12th-cent. cathedral and the 15th-cent. town hall.

**Marie Antoinette**, 1755–93, queen of France, wife of LOUIS XVI; daughter of Holy Roman Emperor FRANCIS I. In 1770 she married the DAUPHIN, who became king in 1774. The marriage, made to strengthen France's ties with Austria, was not popular and was unconsummated for seven years. Unhappy, the queen surrounded herself with an unpopular clique and threw herself into a life of pleasure and extravagance. Her notorious reputation led to several scandals. The famous solution to the bread famine, 'Let them eat cake', is unjustly attributed to the queen. Although she contributed to the downfall of A.R.J. TURGOT in 1776, her influence on Louis in the first two years of the FRENCH REVOLUTION has been exaggerated. She was brought (Oct. 1789) to Paris with the king from VERSAILLES and was seized at Varennes when the royal family tried to escape (1791). The king's apathy led her to negotiate first with the comte de MIRABEAU and later with Antoine Barnave, and she secretly urged Austrian intervention in France. After the TUILERIES palace was stormed (Aug. 1792), the king and queen were imprisoned and charged with treason. The king was executed in Jan. 1793, and Marie Antoinette's son (see LOUIS XVII) was taken from her. In October she was tried by a revolutionary tribunal and guillotined (16 Oct.).

**Marie de' Medici**, 1573–1642, queen of France; daughter of Francesco de' MEDICI, grand duke of Tuscany. She became the second wife of HENRY IV in 1600 and after his assassination (1610) became regent for her son LOUIS XIII. She chose as minister her favourite, Concino Concini, who dissipated the treasury by extravagance. Exiled after Concini's murder (1617), Marie was reconciled with her son in 1622. She tried (1630) to gain the dismissal of her former protégé and the king's minister, Cardinal RICHELIEU, but Louis exiled her again. Her daughter, HENRIETTA MARIA, married CHARLES I of England.

**Marie Louise**, 1791–1847, empress of the French (1810–15), as consort of NAPOLEON I; daughter of Holy Roman Emperor FRANCIS II. She married Napoleon in 1810 and was the mother of NAPOLEON II. After her husband's defeat the Congress of VIENNA awarded her the duchies of Parma, Piacenza, and Guastalla, which she ruled (1816–47) ineptly. She remarried twice.

**marigold**, plant (genus *Tagetes*) of the COMPOSITE family, mostly Central and S American herbs cultivated as garden flowers. Two common annuals are the large-flowered, strong-scented, yellow or orange African marigold (*T. erecta*) and the smaller, yellow or orange and red French marigold (*T. patula*). Both are native to Mexico and Guatemala.

**marijuana** or **marihuana**, relatively mild, nonaddictive drug with hallucinogenic properties, obtained from the flowering tops, stems, and leaves of the HEMP plant. Resins found on the surface of the female plant are used to prepare the most potent form of marijuana, hashish. The primary active substance is tetrahydrocannabinol. Marijuana produces a dreamy, euphoric state of altered consciousness, with feelings of detachment and gaiety. The appetite is usually enhanced, whilst the sex drive may increase or decrease. Adverse reactions are relatively rare, and most can be attributed to adulterants frequently found in marijuana preparations. Marijuana has been used experimentally to reduce nausea from cancer CHEMOTHERAPY and in the treatment of GLAUCOMA. In some parts of the world the drug is freely available whilst in others it is proscribed. Efforts have been made in Britain and in the US to reduce criminal penalties for possession and use of marijuana.

**Marimba:** see XYLOPHONE.

**marine biology,** study of ocean plants and animals and their ecological relationships. Marine organisms are classified according to their mode of life as nektonic (free-swimming), planktonic (floating), or benthic (bottom-dwelling). Their distribution depends on the chemical and physical properties of seawater (e.g., temperature, salinity, and dissolved nutrients), ocean current, and penetration of light. See also OCEANOGRAPHY.

**marines,** troops that serve on board ships of war or in conjunction with naval operations. A British marine corps was established in 1664, reflecting the need for skilled riflemen aboard military vessels. The most famous marine corps is the US Marines, created by Congress in 1798. It has been prominent in all US wars, and has also been used between wars to quell disturbances abroad and to serve as a temporary occupying force, notably in the Caribbean and Central America.

**Marinetti, Filippo Tommaso,** 1876–1944, Italian avant-garde poet, novelist, playwright, and critic. He was the founder (1909) of FUTURISM and an early Fascist. His iconoclastic works include *The Bleeding Mummy* (1904) and *Mafarka il futurista* (1910).

**Marini, Marino,** 1901–80, Italian sculptor and painter. He is best known for his equestrian statues of horse and rider, which as a subject dominated his work. Marini remained isolated from the tradition of FUTURISM in Italy and other later European avant-garde movements. His riders have been interpreted as having a complex and obscure meaning, acting as a symbol for 20th-cent. humanity.

**Marino, Giambattista,** 1569–1625, Italian poet; b. Naples. He served ecclesiastical dignitaries, then became a courtier at Turin and in France. His major work, the mythological narrative *Adonis* (1623), was dedicated to King LOUIS XIII, when he was already famous for his lyric poetry, collected in *The Lyre* (1614) and *The Gallery* (1619). His flamboyant style, with its verbal ingenuity and metaphorical extravagance, was widely imitated and represents the chief manifestation of the BAROQUE in Italian letters.

**maritime law,** body of law governing navigation and overseas commerce. It was first compiled in the late Middle Ages and was based on the customs developed between trading nations. Since then it has developed according to both the principles of CIVIL LAW, and decisions of the English and foreign courts. It is part of INTERNATIONAL LAW only in so far as it governs relations between nations. See also SEA, LAW OF THE.

**Maritime Provinces,** Canada, term applied to NOVA SCOTIA, NEW BRUNSWICK, and PRINCE EDWARD ISLAND, which, before the formation of the Canadian confederation (1867), were politically distinct from Canada proper.

**Maritsa,** river in SE Europe, c.480 km (300 mi) long, rising in western Bulgaria, flowing across the Thracian Plain of central Bulgaria and forming the Greek–Turkish border before reaching the AEGEAN SEA. Its principal cities are PLOVDIV (Bulgaria) and Edirne (Turkey).

**Marius, Caius,** 155–86 BC, Roman general. He was seven times consul and won a reputation in wars against the Germans. The rival of SULLA, he fled Rome when Sulla got the command against MITHRIDATES VI. With the help of CINNA, Marius returned to Rome and fought Sulla in a bloody civil war that Sulla won after Marius' death.

**Marivaux, Pierre Carlet de Chamblain de,** 1688–1763, French novelist and playwright. He was a member of the French Academy (1742). In his novels, e.g., *La vie de Marianne* (1731–41) and *La paysan parvenu* (1734–35), he anticipates Proust by his acute psychological and social analysis. In his plays, which include *Le jeu de l'amour et du hasard* (1730), the same percipience, and its delicate expression, especially when applied to love, have given rise to the term *marivaudage*.

**marjoram** or **sweet marjoram,** Old World perennial aromatic herb (*Marjorana hortensis*) of the MINT family, cultivated for flavouring and for origanum oil, used in perfumed soaps. The closely related European wild marjoram (*Origanum vulgare*) is the herb usually sold as OREGANO.

**Mark, Gospel according to Saint,** book of the NEW TESTAMENT. It is the simplest and earliest of the GOSPELS (probably AD 60–70), and is used as a source by MATTHEW and LUKE. It may be divided into the beginning of the ministry of JESUS (1.1–13), his first two years of preaching (1.14–6.56), his third year (7–13), and the Passion and RESURRECTION (14–16).

**Mark, Saint,** Christian apostle, traditional author of the 2nd GOSPEL. Christians in Jerusalem met at his mother's house. He accompanied St PAUL and St BARNABAS to Cyprus. Traditionally, he was an associate of St PETER, who is thought to have provided him with many of his facts. The Alexandrian church claims Mark as its founder; he is patron saint of Venice. Feast: 25 Apr.

**Mark Antony:** see ANTONY.

**market gardening,** production of crops, mainly vegetables, for the domestic market by highly intensive methods, usually on very fertile land. Originally sited near large towns and cities for convenience of marketing, with the expansion of air-freight facilities it has become an international trade. It is one of the more labour-intensive aspects of farming.

**market research,** organized use of sample surveys, POLLS, and other techniques to study market characteristics (e.g., ages and incomes of consumers; consumer attitudes) and improve the efficiency of sales and distribution. Development of new products, opening of new markets, measurement of advertising effectiveness, and knowledge of business competitors are among its basic aims. Developed in the US in the early 20th cent., the practice expanded rapidly after World War II, spreading to Europe and Japan.

**Markievicz, Constance (Gore-Booth), Countess Markievicz** (mahr‚kyayvits), 1868–1927, first woman to be elected (1918) a Member of Parliament in the UK. Born into an Irish landowning family, she married Count Casimir Markievicz, a Polish painter. A supporter of the radical suffrage movement, in which her sister Eva Gore-Booth, the poet and trade unionist, was active, her foremost commitment was to Irish Republicanism. She was condemned to death for her part in the 1916 Dublin Easter Rising, but a reprieve commuted the sentence to imprisonment. Her refusal as a Republican to take the Oath of Allegiance meant that she never entered Parliament. She is remembered as a heroine of Irish Independence.

**Markova, Dame Alicia,** 1910–, English ballet dancer. She joined DIAGHILEV, (1925), then the Vic-Wells ballet, London (1932). She formed a company with Sir Anton DOLIN (1935), and appeared with many other companies, displaying precision and ethereal grace in classical roles, e.g., *Giselle*.

**Marks and Spencer,** British chain of shops. Founded in Leeds market in 1884 by Michael Marks and Tom Spencer, as a penny bazaar, it expanded between the two wars. During the 1950s it increasingly promoted quality clothing and other products, including food, for a mass market, mainly of British manufacture. From 1928 it has used the brand name St Michael. Since the 1970s, there has been increased diversification and its business has greatly expanded.

**Marlborough,** town (1981 pop. 5330), in Wiltshire, SW England, on R. Kennet, 16 km (10 mi) S of Swindon at the foot of the Marlborough Downs. It is a market town surrounded by good agricultural land. The famous public school, Marlborough College, was founded in 1843.

**Marlborough, John Churchill, 1st duke of,** 1650–1722, English general and statesman, one of the greatest military commanders in history. Under JAMES II he crushed the rebellion (1685) of the duke of MONMOUTH. During the GLORIOUS REVOLUTION he supported WILLIAM III against JAMES II but later (1692–98) fell into William's disfavour. Marlborough's power reached its peak in the reign of Queen ANNE. Created duke (1702), he was involved in many victories in the War of the SPANISH SUCCESSION, including Blenheim (1704), Ramillies (1706), Oudenarde (1708), and Malplaquet (1709). Politically he favoured the WHIGS during the war; when they fell he was dismissed (1711). On the accession of GEORGE I in 1714, Marlborough resumed chief command of the army. His wife, **Sarah Churchill, duchess of Marlborough,** 1660–1744, was a favourite of Queen Anne. Born Sarah Jennings, she married John Churchill in 1677. She wielded great influence at Anne's court until they quarrelled in 1705. After her husband's death she supervised the building of Blenheim Palace.

**Marley, Bob,** 1945–81, black West Indian singer and songwriter; b. Jamaica. With his group The Wailers and having adopted the doctrine of Rastafarianism, he became a national hero and, more than any other musician, developed and spread the popularity of REGGAE music beyond the West Indies to a truly international audience. A mesmeric and charismatic performer, his music frequently carried a social and political message.

**marlin,** group of powerful oceanic FISH which include the spearfish, recognized by the extension of the upper jaw into a spike. Marlins are found worldwide. They are probably the fastest of all swimmers, reaching speeds of 65–80 kph (40–50 mph). They are popular game fishes.

**Marlowe, Christopher,** 1564–93, English dramatist and poet. A major Elizabethan figure, he broke with TRAGEDY modelled on SENECA. His dramas have heroic themes, usually that of a great character destroyed by his own passions and ambition. Marlowe introduced blank verse as the medium for drama, paving the way for SHAKESPEARE. His most important plays are *Tamburlaine the Great* (c.1587), *Dr Faustus* (c.1588), *The Jew of Malta* (1589), and *Edward II* (c.1592). His best-known nondramatic works are the long poem *Hero and Leander* (1598, finished by George CHAPMAN) and the lyric 'Come live with me and be my love'.

**marmot,** GROUND SQUIRREL of the family Sciuridae. Marmots are about 80 cm (30 in) long, weighing up to 8 kg (18 lb). They live in mountains ranging from the European Alps across Asia to China. The Asian marmot is called a bobak. Feeding on grasses, sedges, and roots and making warm sleeping nests of dried grass, they are diurnal and hibernate through the winters.

**Marne, battle of the,** two WORLD WAR I battles that took place at the Marne R., in France. In the first one (6–9 Sept. 1914), the German advance on Paris was halted by the Allies, thus ending the German plan named after Alfred, Graf von Schlieffen. In the second (July 1918), the last great German advance of the war was decisively repulsed by the Allies.

**Marprelate controversy,** a 16th-cent. English religious argument. Under the pseudonym Martin Marprelate, several Puritan pamphlets appeared (1588–89), satirizing the Church of England's episcopal structure and starting a flood of literature from both Martinist and anti-Martinist factions.

**marquetry,** the decorative use in furniture-making of small pieces of VENEER of different coloured woods. Designs most often make use of floral forms or classical motifs; small pieces of ivory or bone are sometimes introduced into the designs. Developed in France and Holland in the mid 17th cent., it was quickly copied elsewhere. Where geometrical designs are used it is properly referred to as parquetry.

**Marquette, Jacques,** 1637–75, French missionary and explorer in NORTH AMERICA, a Jesuit priest. He accompanied (1673) Louis JOLLIET on a journey down the MISSISSIPPI R., proving the existence of a water highway from the ST LAWRENCE to the GULF OF MEXICO.

**Marrakesh** or **Marrakech,** city (1982 pop. 482,605), W central Morocco. A principal commercial centre of Morocco, the city's economy is based on tourism and the manufacture of carpets and leather goods. It was founded (1062) by the ALMORAVIDS. The French captured the city in 1912. Beautifully situated near the ATLAS MOUNTAINS, Marrakesh has extensive gardens, a 14th-cent. palace, and a former palace of the sultan, now a museum of Moroccan art. The minaret of the famous Koutoubya mosque dominates the city.

**marriage,** socially sanctioned union of one or more men with one or more women. Some form of marriage has been claimed to be universal, true for all societies at all time. It is difficult to produce a comprehensive definition of this relationship, but it is generally agreed that there are certain key social functions that marriage, almost always, although not inevitably, undertakes. One of the most important is the assignation of children to membership of particular groups, another the assignation of rights over a woman's sexuality. Two of the most famous kinds of marriage which have posed definitional problems are found among the Nuer of the Sudan: ghost marriage, in which a marriage takes place between the widow and a kinsman of a childless man, in the name of the latter, the children resulting from this relationship are considered to be the children of the dead man; and marriages which occur between a woman and an older barren woman, children subsequently born to the younger woman then become the legitimate children of the older woman. For ALLIANCE theorists in particular the importance of marriage

has been seen as the creation of an EXCHANGE relationship between groups. In the West, the Christian churches supervised marriage, declaring it a SACRAMENT. Civil unions are now permitted in most societies. In Anglo-American LAW, marriage differs from other CONTRACTS in that it may be terminated by a court (through DIVORCE), but not by the partners agreeing between themselves. All states establish age and other requirements for marriage, as well as conditions for legal dissolution of a marriage that detail certain rights and obligations of the partners, particularly with regard to PROPERTY. Anglo-American law was formerly characterized by the view that husband and wife were one legal personality, in effect, that of the husband. During the last century, the rights of married women to own property, enter into contracts, bring legal suits, and otherwise act independently of their husbands have gradually been expanded. See also KINSHIP.

**Marryat, Frederick** (ˌmareeət), 1792–1848, English novelist. His 24 years of service in the British navy provided background for his thrilling tales of sea adventure, e.g., *Peter Simple* (1834) and *Mr Midshipman Easy* (1836). His children's tales, including *Masterman Ready* (1841) and *Children of the New Forest* (1847) remain popular.

**Mars,** in astronomy, 4th PLANET from the Sun, at a mean distance of 227.9 million km (141.6 million mi). It has a diameter of 6796 km (4223 mi) and a thin atmosphere composed largely of carbon dioxide. The surface of Mars is highly diverse: the younger, lower terrain of the northern hemisphere is sparsely cratered, whereas the older, higher terrain of the southern hemisphere is often densely cratered and contains numerous channels tens of miles wide and hundreds of miles long. It also has numerous volcano-like mountains including Olympus Mons (c.600 km/370 mi in diameter and 26 km/16 mi tall, the largest in the solar system, and plains. Dust storms, often local sometimes global in extent, have been observed moving across the Martian surface. Mars has two known satellites, **Phobos** and **Deimos,** both discovered by the American astronomer Asaph Hall in 1877; both are very small, irregular ellipsoids. SPACE PROBES that have encountered Mars include *Mariners 4, 6* and *7*, and *9* (1965, 1969, 1971); *Vikings 1* and *2* (1976); and several Soviet Mars spacecraft. Experiments on the Viking landing craft detected no definite evidence of life.

Mars taken from *Viking*

**Mars,** in Roman mythology, god of war and of the state; originally an agricultural god; father of ROMULUS and husband of Bellona. The martial Romans considered him second in importance only to JUPITER. His love for VENUS is a favourite subject of Italian Renaissance painters, e.g., BOTTICELLI (*Mars and Venus*; Nat. Gall., London). His festivals were held in March (named after him) and October. Mars was identified with the Greek ARES.

**Marseilles** (mah,say), city (1982 pop. 878,689, agglomeration 1,110,511), capital of Bouches-du-Rhône dept., SE France. France's second city and a major seaport, it is an important industrial centre and produces many food products. It is the oldest French town, settled (c.600 BC) by Phocaean Greeks and annexed by Rome in 49 BC. During the CRUSADES (11th–14th cent.), Marseilles was a commercial centre and transit port for the Holy Land. Taken by Charles I of Anjou (13th cent.), it was absorbed by PROVENCE and bequeathed to the French crown in 1481. It grew as a port in the 19th cent., with the opening of the SUEZ

CANAL and the conquest of Algeria. It is known for its great avenue, the Canebière, and for the Chateau d'If (1524), a castle in its harbour.

**Marsh, Dame Ngaio,** 1899–1982, New Zealand detective novelist. Her many books, acute in characterization and literary in style, include *A Man Lay Dead* (1934), *Artists in Crime* (1938), *False Scent* (1959), and *Photo Finish* (1980).

**Marsh, George Perkins,** 1801–82, American diplomat, geographer, and linguist. He was United States minister resident in Turkey (1849–54) and the first US minister to the Kingdom of Italy from 1861 until his death. He published many works on language and the role of man in nature, amongst other subjects, and contributed to many academic fields, but he is best known as a founding father of the conservation movement.

**Marshall, Alfred,** 1842–1924, English economist. While a professor (1885–1908) at Cambridge Univ., he systematized the classical economic theories and made new analyses of his own, thus laying the foundation of the neoclassical school of economics. He was concerned with theories of cost, value, and distribution, and developed a concept of marginal utility. His *Principles of Economics* (1890) became a standard work.

**Marshall, George Catlett,** 1880–1959, American army officer and statesman. He was a staff officer in WORLD WAR I, an aide to Gen. Pershing (1919–24), and army chief of staff (1939–45). He helped direct Allied strategy in WORLD WAR II and was named general of the army (five-star general) in 1944. As secretary of state (1947–49), he organized and directed the European Recovery Program (the MARSHALL PLAN) to promote postwar recovery in Europe, for which he received the 1953 Nobel Peace Prize.

**Marshall, John,** 1755–1835, 4th chief justice of the US SUPREME COURT (1801–35). A noted lawyer, Marshall defended the new US CONSTITUTION. As a chief justice, he established the modern prestige and independence of the Supreme Court and formulated basic principles of constitutional law. In MARBURY V. MADISON he established irrevocably the Court's power to determine the constitutionality of legislation. In this and many other cases, the breadth and wisdom of his interpretations earned him the appellation the Great Chief Justice.

**Marshall Islands,** self-governing island group (1987 pop. 34,000), c.181 km² (70 sq mi), consisting of c.1225 atolls and reefs, in the central Pacific; part of the US Trust Territory of the PACIFIC ISLANDS. The main atolls are MAJURO, the capital; Arno; Ailinglaplap; Jaluit; and Kwajalein, site of a US military missile range. The predominantly Micronesian population depends for the most part on US aid and subsistence farming and fishing. The islands were named after a British captain who visited them in 1788. They were annexed (1885) by Germany and were seized (1914) by Japan, which received (1920) a League of Nations mandate over them. In WORLD WAR II, US forces occupied (1943–44) the islands and they were included (1947) in the trust territory placed under US administration by the UNITED NATIONS. After the war both ENEWETAK and BIKINI atolls were used as sites for US nuclear-weapons tests, and Kwajalein is presently the site of American intercontinental ballistic missiles testing. The Marshalls became (1979) self-governing under US military protection. A compact signed in 1982 moved them towards 'free association' status with the US, this arrangement being confirmed by plebiscite in 1983, when Amata Kabua was reelected president.

**Marshall Plan** or **European Recovery Programme,** a coordinated effort by the US and many nations of Europe to foster European economic recovery after WORLD WAR II. First urged (5 June 1947) by US Secy of State George C. MARSHALL, the programme was administered by the Economic Cooperation Administration (ECA) and from 1948 to 1951 dispensed more than $12 billion in American aid. Sixteen European countries, led by the UK and France, set up the Committee of European Economic Cooperation to coordinate the European participation. It later became the Organization for European Economic Cooperation (OEEC).

**marsh mallow:** see MALLOW.

**Marston, John,** 1576–1634, English satirist and dramatist. After his early verse satires were suppressed (1599), he turned to drama, writing *Antonio and Mellida* (1599); *Antonio's Revenge* (1599); *The Malcontent* (1604), his masterpiece; and *The Dutch Courtezan* (1605). He collaborated (1605) with JONSON and CHAPMAN on *Eastward Ho!*

**marsupial,** member of the order Marsupialia, or pouched MAMMALS. All but the New World OPOSSUMS and an obscure South American family are found only in Australia, Tasmania, and New Guinea, and on a few nearby islands. Unlike that of higher mammals, the marsupial embryo is generally not connected to its mother by a placenta. The young are born in an undeveloped state and crawl to the mother's nipples which are in a pouch, or marsupium, formed by a fold of abdominal skin. The order includes the KANGAROO, KOALA, TASMANIAN DEVIL, and WOMBAT.

**Martello towers,** fortifications containing cannon, erected against the threat of invasion by Napoleon in parts of Britain, Ireland, and Guernsey from 1804 to 1812. The name was derived from a tower at Martella Point, Corsica.

**Martens, Conrad,** 1801–78, Australian artist. He studied painting in London, with Copley Fielding (c.1816), before sailing to Montevideo where he was commissioned as ship's artist on board the *HMS Beagle*. He arrived in Sydney, New South Wales, in 1835, to establish himself as a professional landscape painter and art teacher. Although he travelled widely, he is best known for his views of Sydney Harbour and its environs. During 1850–51, he published a set of lithographs, *Sketches of Sydney.*

**Martha:** see MARY, in the Bible, 3.

**Martha's Vineyard,** island (1980 pop. 8942), c.260 km² (100 sq mi), SE Massachusetts, US, off the southern coast of CAPE COD. Settled in 1642, it was an important whaling and fishing centre in the 18th and early 19th cent. before developing as a summer resort in the late 1800s.

**Martí, José** (mahtee), 1853–95, Cuban poet and patriot. He achieved fame with his modernist poetry, e.g., *Ismaelillo* (1882) and *Versos sencillos* (1891; tr. Plain Verses). A lifelong advocate of Cuban independence, he lived in other Latin American countries and in the US (1881–95), where he founded the Cuban Revolutionary Party. He was killed at the start (1895) of the final Cuban insurrection against Spain.

**Martial** (Marcus Valerius Martialis), AD c.40–c.104, Roman poet; b. Spain. His verses, characterized by a twist of wit at the end of each and by clever use of metre and form, became models for the modern EPIGRAM.

**martial arts,** any of various forms of self-defence, usually weaponless, based on techniques developed in ancient China, India, Tibet, and by the Samurai in Japan. In modern times they have come into wide use for self-protection and as competitive sports. The basic system, **jujitsu,** teaches skills that enable one to overcome a physically superior opponent. **Judo,** a Japanese sport created in 1882, makes use of jujitsu principles. Other popular forms include **karate,** which emphasizes blows with the side of the hand, and **kendo,** in which bamboo 'swords' covered with leather are used.

**martial law,** law administered by domestic military forces when war or serious internal dissension prevents civil authorities from governing. The army may take over administrative and judicial functions, and civil safeguards (e.g., freedom of speech and HABEAS CORPUS) are suspended. Martial law is to be distinguished from military law, rules governing those in the military forces.

**Martin, Kenneth,** 1905–, British painter and sculptor. In the 1930s, influenced by the Euston Road School, he painted in a naturalistic style. In 1948/9 he painted his first abstract work and with Victor PASMORE became the leader of British CONSTRUCTIVISM, developing geometric abstractions in the form of paintings, mobiles, and constructions.

**Martin, Saint,** c.316–397, bishop of Tours. Born a heathen, he was converted as a boy and was a hermit until acclaimed (371) bishop against his will. The first great leader of MONASTICISM in the West, Martin is patron saint of France. Feast: 11 Nov.

**Martin I, Saint,** d. 655, pope (649–53), an Italian. Defying Byzantine Emperor Constans II, he called a council that condemned MONOTHELETISM. The emperor banished him to Crimea, where he died. He was acclaimed a martyr. Feast: 13 Apr.

**Martin du Gard, Roger** (mah,tanh də gah), 1881–1958, French novelist. His fame rests on *Les Thibaults* (1922–40), an eight-part novel cycle that explores the conflicts of French society in the early 20th cent. He was awarded the Nobel Prize in literature in 1937.

**Martineau, Harriet,** (,mahtinoh), 1802–76, English political economist and novelist. She embodied her theories of social reform in her very influential *Illustrations of Political Economy* (1832–34), supported the American abolitionists, and throughout her life, though handicapped by ill health and deafness, wrote prolifically on social and economic topics, as well as children's stories and novels, the best known of which is *Deerbrook* (1839).

**Martínez de la Rosa, Francisco** (mah,teeneth day lah,rohsah), 1787–1862, Spanish dramatist, poet, statesman, and historian. His play *La conjuración de Venecia* (1834; tr. The Conspiracy of Venice) is a landmark of romantic drama in Spain.

**Martínez Ruiz, José,** pseud. **Azorín** (mah,teeneth rooh,eeth), 1873?–1967, Spanish writer. Collections of his descriptive essays include *España* (1909) and *Castilla* (1912). Among his other works are the autobiographical novel *Antonio Azorín* (1903), plays, and short stories.

**Martini, Simone** or **Simone di Martino,** c.1283–1344, major Italian painter of the Sienese school. His work is admired for its Gothic spirituality combined with a vibrancy and a great elegance of line. His earliest known work (1315) is the *Maestà (Madonna and Child Enthroned with Saints and Angels)*, in the Palazzo Pubblico, Siena. One of the first commemorative portraits, the impressive image of the soldier Guidoriccio da Fogliano (1328; Palazzo Pubblico, Siena), is usually attributed to him. His *Annunciation* (1333; Uffizi, Florence) is famous for its graceful line. His FRESCOES at Assisi (probably 1320s) include elegant scenes from the life of St Martin.

Simone **Martini**, *Maesta*, 1315. Palazzo Pubblico, Siena.

**Martinique,** overseas department of France (1982 pop. 327,000), 1101 km² (425 sq mi), in the Windward Islands. Sugar and rum are exported. This rugged volcanic island, discovered (c.1502) by Columbus, was settled (from 1635) by the French, who eliminated the native Caribs and introduced African slaves. It became a French department in 1946. Sporadic, violent agitation for independence developed in the late 1970s; recent local elections have been won by the Progressive Party, which favours independence in the longer term.

**Martín-Santos, Luis,** 1924–64, Spanish novelist and psychiatrist; b. Morocco. His brilliantly inventive *Tiempo de silencio* (1962; tr. Time of Silence), owing much to James JOYCE, is perhaps the most influential post-war Spanish novel.

**Martinson, Harry,** 1904–78, Swedish writer. He is best known for his long narrative poem *Aniara* (1956), about a journey in space, and his novel *The Road* (1948). He shared the 1974 Nobel Prize for literature with Eyvind JOHNSON.

**Martinů, Bohuslav,** 1890–1959, Czech composer. Outstanding among his numerous works are six symphonies, *Julietta* (1938), an opera; a *Concerto Grosso* (1938); *Memorial to Lidice* (1943) for orchestra and *The Epic of Gilgamesh* (1955).

**Martin V,** 1368–1431, pope (1417–31), a Roman named Oddone Colonna. His election at the Council of Constance ended the Great SCHISM. Martin rebuilt Rome, pacified the papal states, and restored church unity. He rejected the view that councils are supreme in the church, but at the request of the Council of Constance he did call a

council at Pavia (1423–24). Later, he summoned another council that began (1431) at Basel. Martin received ineffectual opposition from the Spanish antipope Benedict XIII (Pedro de LUNA) and his successor.

**Marvell, Andrew,** 1621–78, English METAPHYSICAL POET. Marvell, who served as MILTON's assistant in the Latin secretaryship and was a member of Parliament, was one of the chief wits and satirists of his time. Today he is known for his brilliant lyric poetry, including 'The Garden', 'Bermudas', and 'To His Coy Mistress', and for his 'Horatian Ode' on CROMWELL.

**Marvin, Lee,** 1924–87, American film actor. After playing a decade of brutal heavies in the 1950s, he won an Oscar for his dual role in *Cat Ballou* (1965) and became a leading man who often specialized in violent roles. His films include *Bad Day at Black Rock* (1957), *The Dirty Dozen* (1967), *Point Blank* (1967), and *The Big Red One* (1979).

**Marx, Karl,** 1818–83, German social philosopher and revolutionary; with Friedrich ENGELS, a founder of modern SOCIALISM and COMMUNISM. The son of a lawyer, he studied law and philosophy; he rejected the idealism of G.W.F. HEGEL but was influenced by Ludwig FEUERBACH and Moses HESS. His editorship (1842–43) of the *Rheinische Zeitung* ended when the paper was suppressed. In 1844 he met Engels in Paris, beginning a lifelong collaboration. With Engels he wrote the *Communist Manifesto* (1848) and other works that broke with the tradition of appealing to natural rights to justify social reform, invoking instead the laws of history leading inevitably to the triumph of the working class. Exiled from Europe after the REVOLUTIONS OF 1848, Marx lived in London, earning some money as a correspondent for the New York *Tribune* but dependent on Engels's financial help while working on his monumental work *Das Kapital* (3 vol., 1867–94). In this he combined elements of British political economy, socialist theory, and Hegelian philosophy to analyse economic and social history, predicting the collapse of capitalism and the inevitability of socialism. Engels edited vol. 2 and 3 after Marx's death. With Engels, Marx helped found (1864) the International Workingmen's Association, but his disputes with the anarchist Mikhail BAKUNIN eventually led to its breakup. MARXISM has profoundly influenced the development of modern thinking, especially socialist thought; and many scholars consider Marx not only a great economic theoretician but also a founder of economic history and sociology.

**Marx Brothers,** American comedy team. The major members were Groucho (Julius), 1895–1977; Harpo (Arthur), 1893–1964; and Chico (Leonard), 1891–1961. Their anarchic brand of humour depended on slapstick, sight gags, and outrageous puns and wisecracks. They starred in such films as *Horse Feathers* (1932), *Duck Soup* (1933), and *A Night at the Opera* (1935). Zeppo (Herbert), 1901–79, left the team in 1935; Gummo (Milton), 1893–1977, left after their vaudeville days.

**Marxism,** economic and political philosophy originated by Karl MARX and Friedrich ENGELS. The *Communist Manifesto* (1848) by Marx and Engels suggests many of the themes rigorously developed in Marx's *Das Kapital* (3 vol., 1867–94), in which Engels claimed Marx had laid bare the laws of capitalist development. Marx was influenced by the German philosophers HEGEL and FEURBACH, by the English classical economists, e.g., RICARDO, and by the knowledge of English industrialization he shared with Engels. His philosophical method is known as DIALECTICAL MATERIALISM. Marxism holds that in the analysis of societies the economic structure is fundamental. All history is the history of class struggle, and CLASS, for Marx, is defined in terms of a group's relation to the means of economic production. The ruling ideas of every era are the ideas of the ruling class. Historical eras succeed one another as ruling classes, with their associated ideas and forms of production, are challenged by new classes, new ideas, and new forms. Just as the BOURGEOISIE, or capitalist class, replaced the feudal nobility, so they in turn are doomed by inexorable laws to be overthrown by the working class, the historical bearers of socialism. The capitalist class flourishes by extracting surplus value, or profit, from the wealth produced by the workers, who themselves are alienated from their labour and its products. Although CAPITALISM provided an immense stimulus to production, Marx predicted that its internal contradictions and weaknesses would cause increasingly severe economic crises and deepening improverishment of the working class, who would ultimately revolt and seize the instruments of production. The 'dictatorship of the proletariat' would lead, after an interim phase of socialism, to a classless communist society, in which ALIENATION would be overcome, the coercive apparatus of the bourgeois state would wither away, and rational economic cooperation would usher in the era of plenty and individual fulfilment. Historically, Marx's predictions have proved somewhat inaccurate. Socialist revolutions have not occurred in the advanced industrial nations, but in undeveloped and Third World nations such as Russia and China. The proletariat have become better, not worse, off under capitalism. Capitalism itself has its economic cycles of boom and recession, but its imminent collapse, predicted by Marx over 100 years ago, does not yet appear to be at hand. But Marx's method of enquiry, his materialist conception of history, his insight into the fundamentals of capitalist society, and his moral protest against systematic inequality have had an extraordinary influence on subsequent political, social, and economic thought. The richness and subtlety of his writings have enabled a host of scholars to revise and reformulate his ideas to encompass changed historical circumstances, and to apply his methods to new fields of enquiry, such as literary criticism, aesthetics, and psychoanalysis. In the political field, LENIN, STALIN, and MAO ZEDONG are only the best known of those who have adapted Marx's work for their own times and situations (see MARXISM–LENINISM). Marxism in some form has become the official ideology of almost half of mankind.

**Marxism–Leninism,** the central tenets of COMMUNISM, the official ideology of the Soviet Union and of other countries which have followed the Soviet model. It shows important differences from classical MARXISM, and stresses LENIN's ideas on political methods and organization, including Democratic Centralism (see COMMUNIST PARTY). Variants of Marxism–Leninism, condemned by Soviet ideologists, would include the political ideas of TROTSKY, TITO, and MAO ZEDONG.

**Mary,** queens of England. **Mary I** (Mary Tudor), 1516–58 (r. 1553–58), was the daughter of HENRY VIII and KATHARINE OF ARAGÓN. Following her parents' divorce, Mary was forced to acknowledge herself illegitimate and to renounce the Roman Catholic Church. The pope later absolved her from these statements, and she remained loyal to Rome. Mary succeeded her half-brother, EDWARD VI, after the unsuccessful attempt to put Lady Jane GREY on the throne. Her marriage (1554) to Philip of Spain (later PHILIP II), a consequent Spanish alliance, and the reestablishment of papal authority followed. All this, together with the religious persecution of Protestants, which earned her the name 'Bloody Mary', and the loss (1558) of Calais to France, gained her a measure of unpopularity. **Mary II,** 1662–94, queen of England, Scotland, and Ireland (r. 1689–94), was the daughter of JAMES II and Anne Hyde. Reared as a Protestant, she married (1667) William of Orange and became joint sovereign with him (see WILLIAM III) after the GLORIOUS REVOLUTION. She actually ruled only during William's absences.

**Mary,** 1867–1953, queen consort of GEORGE V of England. Of Württemburger royal blood and great-granddaughter of GEORGE III, she was first engaged to Albert, duke of Clarence, upon whose death in 1892 she married (1893) his brother George, the younger son of EDWARD VII, then Prince of Wales. She was the mother of EDWARD VIII and GEORGE VI.

**Mary,** in the Bible, **1 The Virgin,** mother of JESUS, the principal saint, called Our Lady. Her name is the Hebrew *Miriam.* The events of her life mentioned in the NEW TESTAMENT include the archangel GABRIEL's annunciation to her of Jesus's birth; her visitation to Elizabeth, mother of JOHN THE BAPTIST; Jesus's nativity; and her station at the Cross upon which Jesus was crucified. According to Scripture she was first betrothed, then married, to St JOSEPH and was the cousin of Elizabeth. Tradition has it that Mary was the daughter of Sts Joachim and Anne. From ancient times she has been highly honoured by Christians. The Orthodox, Roman Catholic, and Anglican churches all teach the perpetual virginity of Mary, placing a nonliteral interpretation on New Testament references to Jesus' 'brothers'. The Roman Catholic Church has also proclaimed (1854) the dogmas of the Immaculate Conception, i.e., that Mary was conceived and born without original sin, and (1950) of the Assumption, i.e., that she was taken up into heaven on her death. From earliest times her intercession was believed to be efficacious, and she is called upon to meet every kind of need. Her principal feasts are the Assumption (15 Aug.), the Nativity of Our Lady (8 Sept.), the Immaculate Conception (8 Dec.), the Purification (2 Feb.), and the Annunciation or Lady Day (25 Mar.). Apparitions of the Virgin have been reported at Guadalupe Hidalgo, Mexico (1531), Paris (1830), LOURDES, France (1858), and FATIMA, Portugal (1917). **2 Mary Magdalene,** a woman whom, according to the Gospels, Jesus healed of evil spirits, who was present at his crucifixion, and who was the first witness of the Risen Lord.

**Maryborough,** city (1986 pop. 20,177), Queensland, NE Australia. A centre for the sugar industry and forestry, this city was the centre of a major controversy over the mining of the titanium sands on nearby Fraser Island. The island has been declared a national park, causing a cessation of the extractive industries which threatened the island's freshwater lakes with their rare flora and fauna.

**Maryland,** state of the US (1984 est. pop. 4,349,000), area 27,394 km² (10,577 sq mi), located on the mid-Atlantic coast, bordered by Delaware and the Atlantic Ocean (E), the District of Columbia (S), Virginia and West Virginia (S,W), and Pennsylvania (N). ANNAPOLIS is the capital and almost 85% of the population lives in the Greater BALTIMORE area. Maryland is divided by the CHESAPEAKE BAY which separates the rural Eastern Shore from the Piedmont plateau and the BLUE RIDGE hills in the W. Most of the state consists of low coastal plains. Government dominates employment, but industry is the principal source of income, with processed foods, electronic equipment, and primary metals the leading products. Its chief farm product is broiler chickens, and dairy products, corn, and soybeans are important; fishing in the bay has declined because of water pollution. Baltimore is a major port and coal is mined in the W. In 1980 74% of the population was non-Hispanic white and 22% was black. Persecuted Catholics formed a colony in the area in the mid-17th cent. and the Algonquin-speaking Indians withdrew gradually. Maryland was one of the 13 colonies to sign the Declaration of Independence and contributed land to the new national capital in the District of Columbia after the American Revolution. Owing to strong divisions over the slavery issue the state was under military rule during the Civil War, but afterwards industry flourished. The opening (1952) of the Chesapeake Bay Bridge spurred industrial development on the Eastern Shore, and in recent years federal- and government-related employment has created a high-income population adjacent to WASHINGTON, DC.

**Marylebone Cricket Club,** a private club, founded in 1787, with LORD'S cricket ground as its headquarters. It dominated the administration of the game until 1968, when it yielded much of its power to the Cricket Council, the governing body; the Test and Country Cricket Board, which controls what its name implies; and the National Cricket Association, which fosters the game below county level. Until 1968, MCC organized all foreign tours; and the England side on tour still wears the MCC colours of red and yellow. The club owns a memorial gallery, a library, and an indoor cricket school at Lord's, all of them open to the public. The Laws of Cricket remain the copyright of MCC.

**Mary of Burgundy,** 1457–82, daughter and heiress of CHARLES THE BOLD of Burgundy. Her marriage (1477) to Maximilian of Austria (later Holy Roman Emperor MAXIMILIAN I) established the HABSBURGS in the Low Countries. On her father's death (Jan. 1477) LOUIS XI of France seized Burgundy and Picardy, and prepared to annex the Low Countries and the rest of Mary's inheritance. In May she married Maximilian, who came to her aid with an army. Mary's premature death left her young son, Philip (later PHILIP I of Castile), her heir. In 1493 Maximilian regained control of the Low Countries, but Burgundy and Picardy remained French.

**Mary of Guise,** 1515–60, queen consort of JAMES V of Scotland; mother of MARY QUEEN OF SCOTS. She was regent for her daughter from 1554. Earlier she had aligned herself with France by arranging Mary's marriage to the DAUPHIN. As regent, she began suppressing Protestantism in Scotland, backed by the French. Civil war ensued (1559), and the Protestants, with English support, prevailed.

**Mary Queen of Scots** (Mary Stuart), 1542–87, daughter of JAMES V of Scotland and MARY OF GUISE. She became queen of Scotland on the death (1542) of her father, just six days after her birth. Mary was sent by her mother to France, where she grew up and married (1558) the French DAUPHIN (later FRANCIS II). After his death in 1560, she returned to Scotland as queen in 1561. Despite harsh attacks from JOHN KNOX, she refused to abandon her Roman Catholicism, and her charm and intelligence won many over. To reinforce her claim to succeed ELIZABETH I on the English throne, she married (1565) her English cousin Lord DARNLEY. Soon despised by Mary, he joined a conspiracy of Protestant nobles who murdered her trusted counsellor, David RIZZIO. Mary was temporarily reconciled to Darnley. Their son, James, was born soon after. At this period she fell in love with the earl of BOTHWELL. Darnley, widely disliked, was murdered in 1567; Bothwell, widely suspected of the murder, was acquitted and married Mary. Outraged Scots flew to arms, and Mary surrendered and abdicated (1567) in favour of her son, James VI (later

JAMES I of England), naming the earl of Murray as regent. She escaped (1568) and gathered a large force, but was defeated by Murray and fled to England. There she became a prisoner and was involved in several ill-fated plots against Elizabeth with English Catholics, the Spanish, and others. In 1586 a plot to murder Elizabeth was reported. Charged with being an accomplice, Mary was brought to trial; she defended herself with eloquence, although there was little doubt of her complicity. Elizabeth reluctantly signed the death warrant, and Mary was beheaded at Fotheringay Castle on 8 Feb. 1587. Mary's reported beauty and her undoubted courage have made her a particularly romantic figure in history. She is the subject of much literature.

**Mary Rose,** a Tudor warship, the flagship of Henry VIII's fleet, which sank in Portsmouth harbour on its maiden voyage, 19 July 1545. A sonar scanning device located the wreck, completely buried in silt, in 1967. Excavation was begun in 1969 and in 1982 the vessel was raised from its grave of four centuries. The recovery of the *Mary Rose* provided a glimpse of the life of a ship in the Tudor period. Problems of conservation of the chests of longbows, bundles of arrows, and other fragile wood and leather artifacts within her provided fresh technical challenges and gave new impetus to UNDERWATER ARCHAEOLOGY.

The hull of the **Mary Rose** breaking surface on 11 Oct. 1982, suspended by cables beneath the 67 tonne underwater lifting frame

**Mary Tudor,** queen of England: see under MARY, queens of England.

**Masaccio** (ma‚zatchoh), 1401–1428?, Italian painter, one of the foremost figures of the Florentine RENAISSANCE; b. Tommaso Guidi. Most of Masaccio's works have perished, but three major works remain: a polyptych (1426) for the Church of the Carmine, Pisa (now dismembered with parts in London and Naples); the great *Trinity* fresco (1428) in Santa Maria Novella, Florence, which revolutionized the understanding of perspective in painting; and his masterpiece, the FRESCO paintings (c.1425–28) in the Brancacci Chapel of Santa Maria del Carmine (Florence), a major monument in the history of art. These frescoes were a training school and inspiration to generations of painters such as MICHELANGELO and RAPHAEL. Masaccio imparted a new sense of grandeur and austerity to the human figure. He used light to create space and volume and achieved a classic sense of proportion. He also created a diversity of character within a unified group.

**Masada,** ancient mountaintop fortress in the Judaean Desert, Israel. Ornately renovated (37–31 BC) by Herod the Great, it was seized (AD 66) by Jewish Zealots in their revolt against Rome. When 1000 Zealots were overcome (AD 73) by 15,000 Roman soldiers, all but two women and five children killed themselves to escape capture. Masada was excavated (1963–65) by Israeli-led international archaeologists.

**Masai** (‚mahsie), nomadic pastoral people of E Africa, chiefly in Kenya and Tanzania. Cattle and sheep form the basis of the economy they have maintained in resistance to cultural change. Masai society is patrilineal; polygyny is practiced. Boys are initiated into a warrior age-group responsible for herding and other tribal labours; only after serving as a

Masaccio, *Trinity* fresco, 1428. Florence.

warrior may a man marry. The Masai, who are characteristically tall and slender, live traditionally in the kraal, a compound within which are mud houses.

The site of **Masada** in Israel's Judaean Desert

**Masan,** city (1984 pop. 440,773), SE South Korea. An industrial city based on the Japanese-built port, its manufactures include iron and pipe works, synthetic fibres and ceramics; light industries include optical, medical, and musical instruments. The city was South Korea's first Free Trade Zone (est. early 1970s).

**Masaryk, Thomas Garrigue,** 1850–1937, principal founder and first president of Czechoslovakia (1918–35). A philosophy professor at the Univ. of Prague, he led the Czech independence movement from 1907 and became the first president of the new republic after WORLD WAR I. An ardent liberal and democrat, he was revered by the Czech people, although he was always faced with strong opposition from extremist groups. Edward BENEŠ succeeded him as president. Among Masaryk's writings is *The Making of a State* (1927). His son, **Jan Masaryk**, 1886–1948, became foreign minister of the Czech government-in-exile in London during WORLD WAR II. He kept that post after his government's return to Prague in 1945. His death, shortly after the Communist coup in 1948, was officially described as suicide by leaping from a window, although the exact circumstances have been subject to speculation ever since.

**Mascagni, Pietro** (mas‚kahnyee), 1863–1945, Italian operatic composer. He is known for *Cavalleria rusticana* (1890), a classic example of Italian *verismo*, or realism of plot. It is almost always performed as a double-bill with *I Pagliacci* (see LEONCAVALLO).

**Masefield, John**, 1878–1967, English poet. A seaman and journalist, he gained fame with the poetry collections *Salt-Water Ballads* (1902) and *Ballads* (1903). His longer narrative poems include *The Everlasting Mercy* (1911), *Dauber* (1913), and *Reynard the Fox* (1919). Masefield also wrote plays, in both verse and prose; novels; literary studies; war sketches; and adventure stories for boys. He was POET LAUREATE from 1930 to 1967.

**maser** [acronymn for *m*icrowave *a*mplification by *s*timulated *e*mission of *r*adiation], device, first operated in 1954, for the creation and amplification of high-frequency radio waves. The waves produced by the maser are coherent, i.e., all of the same frequency, direction, and phase relationship. Used as an oscillator, the maser provides a very sharp, constant signal and thus serves as a time standard for atomic clocks. The maser can also serve as a relatively noise-free amplifier. The optical maser is now called a LASER.

**Maseru**, city (1981 est. pop. 60,000), capital of Lesotho, on the Caledon R. It is a trade and transport centre linked with South Africa's rail network. Manufactures include candles and carpets. Maseru was a small trading town when Moshesh I, paramount chief of the Basuto people, chose it for his capital in 1868 and placed the kingdom under British protection.

**Mashhad**, city (1982 est. pop. 1,119,700), NE Iran. It is an industrial and trade centre and a transport hub. Formerly known as Sanabadh, the city was attacked by the Oghuz Turks (12th cent.) and by the Mongols (13th cent.). It recovered by the 14th cent. and prospered under the Safavids. Shah ABBAS I embellished Mashhad with many fine buildings, and NADIR SHAH made it the capital of Persia in the 18th cent. It is a centre of pilgrimage for Shia Muslims.

**Mashonaland**, region (1982 pop. 2,918,353), Zimbabwe. Settled by the Shona peoples, it was occupied by the British South Africa Company in 1890. Despite risings (1896–97) by the Shona and Matabele peoples, the region was incorporated into Southern Rhodesia. Since political independence in 1980 Mashonaland Central, East, and West have formed three of Zimbabwe's eight provinces.

**Masinissa** or **Massinissa** (masi‚nisə), c.238–148 BC, king of NUMIDIA. He fought with the Romans in the Second PUNIC WAR and led a cavalry to victory at the battle of ZAMA. His goading of CARTHAGE brought on the Third Punic War.

**mask,** face or head covering used for disguise or protection. Masks have been worn by primitive peoples since ancient times in MAGIC and religious ceremonies. Notable are those of W and central Africa, of the Iroquois Indians and tribes of the Pacific Northwest, and of the AZTECS. Masks have been integral to drama in East and West, particularly ORIENTAL DRAMA and the COMMEDIA DELL'ARTE. Protective masks are worn by warriors, athletes, and surgeons. See also AFRICAN ART; NORTH AMERICAN INDIAN ART; MASQUE.

**Maslow, Abraham:** see HIERARCHY OF NEEDS.

**Masolino da Panicale** (panee‚kahlay), 1383–c.1447, Florentine painter of the early RENAISSANCE; b. Tommaso di Cristoforo Fini. He worked with MASACCIO on the frescoes in the Brancacci chapel, Florence, and was influenced by Masaccio's interest in perspective and volume. His later works, e.g., the frescoes in the Baptistery and Collegiata of Castiglione d'Olona (1435), are more graceful and decorative.

**Mason, George,** 1725–92, American statesman at the time of the AMERICAN REVOLUTION. He wrote the Virginia declaration of rights (1776), the model for the first part of Jefferson's DECLARATION OF INDEPENDENCE. He was active in drafting the US Constitution (1787), but, unhappy with several provisions, he campaigned against its ratification. The bill of rights he advocated was the basis for some of the first 10 amendments to the Constitution.

**Mason, James,** 1909–86, English film actor. A handsome, sardonic leading man, he turned to Hollywood in the 1950s for lack of suitable British roles. His films include *Odd Man Out* (1947), *A Star Is Born* (1954), and *North by Northwest* (1959).

**Mason–Dixon Line,** boundary between Pennsylvania and Maryland, US, surveyed (1763–67) by the English astronomers Charles Mason and Jeremiah Dixon and extended (1779) to present-day West Virginia. Before the Civil War it was the popular term for the boundary between the 'slave states' and the 'free states', and it is still used on occasion to distinguish the South from the North.

**masque,** courtly form of dramatic spectacle popular in 17th-cent. England. Characterized by the use of masks and the mingling of actors and spectators, it employed pastoral and mythological themes, with an emphasis on music and dance. The foremost writer of masques was Ben JONSON.

**Mass,** the name commonly given by Roman Catholics (and others) to the celebration of the SACRAMENT of the Eucharist (see COMMUNION). The Mass was traditionally based on the Latin rite of Rome, which became the official rite of most Roman Catholic churches. Since the Second VATICAN COUNCIL (1962–65) the Roman Mass liturgy has undergone extensive revision, including the use of vernacular languages in place of Latin. Mass is usually said in a church at an altar containing relics, and two lighted candles are essential. Among the types of Masses are High Mass, celebrated in its full form by a priest, assisted by a deacon and choir; Low Mass, much commoner, said by one priest; and a REQUIEM, a proper Mass said for the dead. Some of the sung portions of the Mass are chanted solo at the altar with choral response. There are also nine hymns for the choir; four of these change with the occasion and are related in theme, with texts usually from the PSALMS; there are also five invariable choral pieces: Kyrie eleison, Gloria in excelsis, Credo, Sanctus, and Agnus Dei. PLAINSONG is permitted for all texts, but latitude is granted the choir. A musical setting for the five ordinary hymns, called a Mass, has been an important musical form. Among the composers who have produced masses are PALESTRINA, J.S. BACH, HAYDN, MOZART, VERDI, and STRAVINSKY.

**mass,** in physics, the quantity of matter in a body regardless of its volume or of any forces acting on it. There are two ways of referring to mass, depending on the laws of physics defining it. The *gravitational* mass of a body may be determined by comparing the body on a beam balance with a set of standard masses; in this way the gravitational factor is eliminated (see GRAVITATION; WEIGHT). The *inertial* mass of a body is a measure of the body's resistance to acceleration by some external force. All evidence seems to indicate that the gravitational and inertial masses are equal. According to the special theory of RELATIVITY, mass increases with speed according to the formula $m = m_0/\sqrt{(1 - v^2/c^2)}$, where $m_0$ is the rest mass (mass at zero velocity) of the body, v its speed, and c the speed of light in vacuum. The theory also leads to the Einstein mass–energy relation $E = mc^2$, where $E$ is the energy and $m$ the relativistic mass.

**Massachusetts,** state of the US (1984 est. pop. 5,798,000), area 21,386 km² (8257 sq mi), located in the NE and bordered by Vermont and New Hampshire (N), New York (W), Connecticut and Rhode Island (S), and the Atlantic Ocean (E). BOSTON is the capital and largest city; Worcester and SPRINGFIELD are also important. The coast is heavily indented with many natural harbours, and offshore lie the resort islands of NANTUCKET and MARTHA'S VINEYARD. Inland the Connecticut R. valley divides two areas of gently rolling uplands. Massachusetts is an overwhelmingly industrial state, with electrical and electronic equipment, leather goods, clothing and textiles, shipping, and printing and publishing being important manufactures. The leading agricultural products are dairy products, greenhouse vegetables, cranberries, and eggs, while fishing is also of significance. The Atlantic coast attracts many visitors. It is the third most densely populated state in the US and in 1980 90% of the population was non-Hispanic white. The Pilgrims landed in 1620, and their Plymouth Colony was followed by the Massachusetts Bay Colony and Puritan settlers. By the mid-18th cent. the colony was thriving on trade in molasses, rum, and black slaves. It suffered from British trade restrictions in the 1760s and, following the Boston Massacre and the Boston Tea Party, the American Revolution started in 1775. After independence textiles led an industrial expansion, later drawing upon huge numbers of immigrants who arrived after the Civil War from Ireland and elsewhere. Massachusetts was the centre of religious, philosophical, and social movements in the 19th cent., and of labour strife in the early 20th cent. The decline of the state's shoe and textiles industries since World War II has been offset by the continued growth of defence- and computer-related industries, especially around Boston's Route 128. These have close links to the state's higher educational institutions, including Harvard Univ. and the Massachusetts Institute of Technology.

**Massachusetts Bay Company,** English chartered company (1628) that established the Massachusetts Bay colony on a grant of land between the Charles and Merrimack rivers in Massachusetts, US. Puritan colonists sailed for New England in 1630 and founded their chief settlement at Boston as a religious and political refuge. The company and colony were synonymous until 1684, when the company was dissolved.

**Massasoit,** c.1580–1661, powerful chief of the Wampanoag Indians of New England, US. Faithful to his treaty (1621) with the PILGRIMS, he befriended Roger WILLIAMS. Massasoit's son, Metacomet, was the leader of KING PHILIP'S WAR.

**Masséna, André** (masay,nah), 1758–1817, marshal of France. He won the battle of Rivoli (1797) in NAPOLEON I's Italian campaign and defeated (1799) the Russians at Zürich. He was later defeated in the PENINSULAR WAR (1808–14). Napoleon made him duke of Rivoli and prince of Essling. After Napoleon's fall, Massena supported LOUIS XVIII. He was neutral during the HUNDRED DAYS.

**Massenet, Jules** (masə,nay), 1842–1912, French composer. Among his 20 OPERAS, *Manon* (1884) exemplifies his sensuous style and contains accompanied spoken dialogue instead of traditional recitative. Others are *Werther* (1892) and *Thaïs* (1894).

**Massif Central** (ma,seef sanh,trahl), diverse mountainous plateau, c.85,470 km² (33,000 sq mi), occupying almost one-sixth of France. It rises to a high point of 1866 m (6187 ft) in the Puy de Sancy of the once-volcanic Auvergne Mts. and also includes the rugged Cévennes Mts (SE) and the plateaus of the Causses (SW). CLERMONT-FERRAND and ST-ÉTIENNE are major cities.

**Massine, Léonide,** 1896–1979, American ballet dancer; b. Russia. He was principal dancer and choreographer with DIAGHILEV (1914–20), and worked with The Ballet Russe de Monte Carlo (1932–42). He was a noted character dancer. His works include *Parade* (1917) and *The Red Shoes* (1948).

**Massinger, Philip,** 1583–1640, English dramatist. Many of his plays, largely collaborations, are lost. He is best known for two realistic domestic comedies, *A New Way to Pay Old Debts* (1625) and *The City Madam* (1632). A harsh moralist, he attacked the evils of a frivolous society.

**mass number,** represented by the symbol $A$, the total number of nucleons (NEUTRONS and PROTONS) in the nucleus of an ATOM. All atoms of a chemical ELEMENT have the same ATOMIC NUMBER (number of protons) but may have different mass numbers (from having different numbers of neutrons in the nucleus). Atoms of an element having the same atomic number but different mass numbers are referred to as ISOTOPES of that element. Isotopes of different elements may have the same mass number but will have a different atomic number.

**Masson, André** (ma,sawnh), 1896–, French painter and graphic artist. A member of the French surrealist (see SURREALISM) group (1924–28), he was strongly interested by AUTOMATISM as a means of investigating the power of the unconscious. He developed 'automatic painting', by directly applying adhesive to the canvas and then spreading on coloured sand. He was in America from 1940 to 1946 and influenced the work of GORKY.

**mass spectrometer** or **mass spectrograph,** device for measuring the mass of ISOTOPES. First devised by the English physicist F.W. Aston in 1919, it consists basically of an ION source whose ions pass through a combination of electric and magnetic fields and are then detected electronically (see PARTICLE DETECTOR). Since the precise motion of the ions depends on their mass as well as their charge, different isotopes will be detected at different positions at the end of their trajectories thus enabling their masses to be determined.

**Massys, Matsys** or **Metsys, Quentin** (mə,sies, matsies, me-, met-), c.1466–1530, Flemish painter. He was the leading painter of his time at

Antwerp. Influenced by Italian art, he developed from an older Flemish tradition a calm, measured style with solid figures and soft textures. He developed the portrait-type of a scholar in his study, e.g., in the portrait of *Erasmus* (1517; Museo Nazionale, Rome).

**mastaba,** in EGYPTIAN ARCHITECTURE, a sepulchral structure built above ground. Mastabas of the early dynastic period (3200–2680 BC), evidently modelled on contemporary houses, were elaborate and had many compartments. Better known are those of the Old Kingdom (2680–2181 BC), which elaborated on the predynastic burial-pit and mound form. The typical mastaba was rectangular and flat-roofed, with inward sloping walls. The superstructure was solid except for the offering chamber—a decorated chapel, and the serdab—a smaller chamber containing a portrait statue of the deceased.

**mastectomy,** surgical removal of all or part of the breast. For small tumours, a partial mastectomy may be performed, removing only the affected breast tissue. To combat CANCER, a modified radical mastectomy may be performed, excising the breast and lymph nodes of the adjacent armpit.

**Master of the Queen's (King's) Musick,** a title created in the first half of the 17th cent. for the musician in charge of the British sovereign's private band of musicians. Today the duties include only the occasional composition of music for royal or state occasions. Amongst holders of the office have been William BOYCE (1755–79), John Stanley (1779–86), Walter Parratt (1893–1924), Edward ELGAR (1924–34), Walford Davies (1934–41), Arnold BAX (1942–52), Arthur BLISS (1953–75), and Malcolm Williamson (1975–).

**Master of the Rolls,** in England and Wales, a high-ranking judge who sits as president of the Court of Appeal. The office originated with the chancery clerk, who was the keeper of the king's records and assistant to the LORD CHANCELLOR. As the role of the Court of Chancery increased he became a regular judge, and later a member of the Court of Appeal. Until 1958, he was responsible for keeping the public records. The most famous recent holder of the office was Lord DENNING.

**Masters, Edgar Lee,** 1869–1950, American poet. He is best known for *The Spoon River Anthology* (1915), a group of free-verse epitaphs revealing the secret lives of small-town Americans. He also wrote such biographies as *Lincoln the Man* (1931) and *Whitman* (1937).

**Masters and Johnson,** pioneering American research team in the field of human sexuality and sex therapy, consisting of the gynaecologist **William H. Masters** (1915–), and the psychologist **Virginia E. Johnson** (1925–). Their best-known work is *Human Sexual Response* (1966).

**mastodon,** name for several prehistoric MAMMALS of the extinct genus *Mammut*, from which ELEPHANTS are believed to have evolved. Long-jawed mastodons about 135 cm (4½ ft) high, with four tusks, lived in Africa during the Oligocene epoch. Later forms were larger, with long flexible trunks and two tusks. Forest dwellers, mastodons fed by browsing.

**Mastroianni, Marcello,** 1923–, Italian film actor. He is a handsome leading man, who has enjoyed international fame, largely because of *La Dolce Vita* (1960), as an archetype of the modern Italian male. His many other films include *8½* (1963) and *Leo the Last* (1970).

**Masudi** (ma,soohdee), d. 956, Arab historian, geographer, and philosopher; b. Baghdad. He travelled in many lands and wrote the comprehensive *Muruj adh-Dhahab* [meadows of gold], a history of the world from the creation to AD 947.

**Matabele** ('matə,beelee): see NDEBELE.

**Matabeleland,** region (1982 pop. 1,404,975), S Zimbabwe. BULAWAYO is the chief town. In 1837, as a result of conflict with settlers of the Transvaal Republic, the NDEBELE peoples moved across the Limpopo R. into present Matabeleland. The establishment of the British South Africa Company led to further conflict with colonists. In 1893 the Ndebele were defeated in war and the area became administered by the Company as a number of separate districts. Since political independence in 1980 Matabeleland North and South have formed two of Zimbabwe's eight provinces.

**Mata Hari,** 1876–1917, Dutch dancer and spy for Germany in WORLD WAR I; b. Margaretha Geertruida Zelle. A member of the German secret service in Paris, she obtained military secrets from high Allied officers. The French tried and executed her.

**match,** small piece of wood paraffin, cardboard, or combustible material with a special chemical tip which ignites into flame by friction. Before matches were invented, fire for lighting candles and oil lamps was obtained by the use of a tinder box. In 1781 a phosphoric taper came on the market which when dipped into acid burst into flame. Chancel of Paris perfected a less dangerous match in 1805 made of wood with a head of potassium chlorate and sugar. This was ignited by dipping into a bottle of sulphuric acid. The friction match was devised in 1827 by the English apothecary John Walker but was only partially successful. The 'strike anywhere' phosphorus match was developed by Dr Charles Sauria of France and was quickly copied all over the world. In 1855, J.E. Lundström of Sweden perfected the safety match, which contained potassium chlorate in the match head and ignited only when struck on a specially prepared surface. Because of the poisonous nature of phosphorus, white or yellow phosphorus was prohibited internationally at a treaty at Berne in 1906. All matches today use nontoxic phosphorus sesquisulphide as the igniting agent.

**maté, yerba maté** or **Paraguay tea,** name for a South American evergreen tree (*Ilex paraguensis* and related species) of the HOLLY family and for a tea brewed from the young leaves and tender shoots. Less astringent than genuine TEA, maté is a stimulant containing considerable caffeine. It is the most popular beverage in much of South America.

**materialism,** in philosophy, a widely held system of thought that explains the nature of the world as entirely dependent on matter, the final reality. Early Greek teaching, e.g., that of DEMOCRITUS, EPICURUS, and the proponents of STOICISM, conceived of reality as material in nature. The theory was renewed and developed beginning in the 17th cent., especially by HOBBES, and in the 18th cent. LOCKE's investigations were adapted to the materialist position. The system was developed further from the middle of the 19th cent., particularly in the form of DIALECTICAL MATERIALISM and in the formulations of LOGICAL POSITIVISM.

**mathematics,** deductive study of numbers, geometry, and various abstract constructs.

*Branches.* Mathematics is very broadly divided into foundations, algebra, analysis, geometry, and applied mathematics. The term *foundations* is used to refer to the formulation and analysis of the language, AXIOMS, and logical methods on which all of mathematics rests (see LOGIC); SET theory, originated by Georg CANTOR, now constitutes a universal mathematical language. ALGEBRA, historically, is the study of solutions of one or several algebraic equations, involving POLYNOMIAL functions of one or several variables; ARITHMETIC and NUMBER THEORY are areas of algebra concerned with special properties of the integers. ANALYSIS applies the concepts and methods of the CALCULUS to various mathematical entities. GEOMETRY is concerned with the spatial side of mathematics, i.e., the properties of and relationships between points, lines, planes, figures, solids, and surfaces; TOPOLOGY studies the structures of geometric objects in a very general way. The term *applied mathematics* loosely designates a wide range of studies with significant current use in the empirical sciences. It includes COMPUTER science, mathematical physics, PROBABILITY theory, and mathematical STATISTICS.

*History.* The earliest records indicate that mathematics arose in response to the practical needs of agriculture, business, and industry in the 3rd and 2nd millennia BC in Egypt and Mesopotamia and, possibly, India and China. Between the 6th and 3rd cent. BC, the Greeks THALES, PYTHAGORAS, PLATO, ARISTOTLE, EUCLID, ARCHIMEDES, and Zeno of Elea profoundly changed the nature of mathematics, introducing abstract notions such as INFINITY and irrational numbers (see NUMBER) and a deductive system of proof. Their work was carried on in the 2nd and 3rd cent. AD by HERO OF ALEXANDRIA, PTOLEMY, and Diophantus. With the decline of learning in the West, the development of mathematics was continued in the East by the Chinese, the Indians (who invented the NUMERAL system now used throughout the civilized world), and the Arabs. Their writings began to reach the West in the 12th cent., and by the end of the 16th cent. Europeans had made advances in algebra, TRIGONOMETRY, and such areas of applied mathematics as mapmaking. In the 17th cent. decimal fractions (see DECIMAL SYSTEM) and LOGARITHMS were invented, and the studies of projective geometry and probability were begun. Blaise PASCAL, Pierre de FERMAT, GALILEO, and Johannes KEPLER made fundamental contributions. The greatest advances of the century, however, were the invention of ANALYTICAL GEOMETRY by René DESCARTES and of the calculus by Sir Isaac NEWTON and, independently, G.W. LEIBNIZ. The history of mathematics in the 18th cent. is dominated by the development of the methods of the calculus and their application to physical problems, both terrestrial and celestial, with leading roles being played by the BERNOULLI family, Leonhard EULER, Joseph LAGRANGE, and Pierre de LAPLACE. The modern period of mathematics dates from the beginning of the 19th cent., and its dominant figure is Carl GAUSS, who made fundamental contributions to algebra, arithmetic, geometry, number theory, and analysis. In that century NON-EUCLIDEAN GEOMETRY was invented independently by Nikolai LOBACHEVSKY, János BOLYAI, and, in another form, G.F.B. RIEMANN, whose work was of great importance in the development of the general theory of relativity. Number theory and abstract algebra received significant contributions from Sir William Rowan HAMILTON, M.S. Lie, Georg Cantor, Julius DEDEKIND, and Karl WEIERSTRASS. Weierstrass and Augustin CAUCHY brought new rigour to the foundations of the calculus and of analysis. In the 20th cent. there have been two main trends. One is towards increasing generalization and abstraction, exemplified by investigations into the foundations of mathematics by David HILBERT, Bertrand RUSSELL and Alfred North WHITEHEAD, and Kurt GÖDEL. The other trend is towards concrete applications to such areas as linguistics and the social sciences, as well as computer science, made possible by the work of John VON NEUMANN, Norbert WIENER, and others.

**Matilda** or **Maud,** 1102–67, queen of England, daughter of HENRY I. In 1114 she married Emperor HENRY V. After his death she married (1128) Geoffrey IV of Anjou. At her father's death (1135) her cousin Stephen seized the English throne. In 1139 Matilda and her half brother Robert, earl of Gloucester, challenged Stephen, and she was elected 'Lady of the English' in 1141. Unable to establish her rule, she withdrew from England in 1148 in effect giving up her claim to her son Henry (later HENRY II).

**Matisse, Henri,** 1869–1954, French painter, sculptor, and lithographer. He explored IMPRESSIONISM, e.g., *The Dinner Table* (1897; Niarchos Coll., Athens); neo-impressionism, e.g., *Luxe, calme et volupté* (1905, private coll.) (see POSTIMPRESSIONISM); and made variations on the old masters in the Louvre. In 1905 he began using pure primary colour as a significant structural element, e.g., *The Green Line* (1905; State Mus., Copenhagen). A leader of FAUVISM, he always used colour in bold patterns and different sorts of expressive abstraction, e.g., *The Blue Nude* (1907; Baltimore Mus. of Art). In his last years he made brilliant paper cutouts, e.g., *Jazz* (Philadelphia Mus. of Art), and decorated the Dominican chapel at Vence, France with fresh, joyous windows and murals.

Henri **Matisse,** *Luxe, calme et volupté.*

**matriarchs,** Four Jewish heroines in the Old Testament especially famed for their virtues as mothers. They are Leah, RACHEL, REBECCA, and SARAH.

**matriarchy,** a form of society in which positions of power and authority are held by women. Although 19th-cent. anthropologists argued that such social forms predated patriarchal forms, and were characterized by MATRILINEAL DESCENT, there is no empirical evidence to support the existence of such a form of social organization. However it is clearly a highly significant cultural myth, for matriarchal societies figure in mythological accounts of the past or are claimed to exist among other peoples (e.g., the Amazons) in a range of very different cultures. Matrilineal descent indeed has little to do with the distribution of power to women, although there is a far greater degree of potential space available to women in matrilineal than PATRILINEAL societies.

**matrifocal,** a descriptive term for mother-centred forms of family organization, in which the father is peripheral (either absent or not significant within family organization). Such family forms have frequently been related to particular kinds of economic circumstances, e.g., high male unemployment.

**matrilineal descent,** a principle of DESCENT from an ancestress through her female children to their daughters, etc. Societies organized in this way are found far less frequently than those organized around patrilineal principles. Forms of inheritance based on matrilineal descent are not the mirror image of patrilineal descent systems. In most matrilineal descent systems although links are traced through the female line it is males who inherit land and property or occupy the positions of power associated with their matrilineal groups. Thus inheritance in fact passes from mother's brother to sister's son. Hence the 'matrilineal puzzle': if it is indeed the men of the group who form a corporate exogamous group (see EXOGAMY) it is the women who have to move and yet it is their children who will inherit, therefore some means of ensuring the return of these children has to be devised. Post-marital forms of residence are very significant in matrilineal systems, and matrilineages tend to be associated with large corporation territories (in which marriage does not entail moving any great distance), highly intensive agricultural production, and a division of labour in which women undertake key agricultural tasks. Women tend to have some power and autonomy in such systems, and marriage tends to be fragile.

**matrix,** in mathematics, a rectangular array of elements that can be used to represent certain sets of information more concisely. For example the equations $a_{11}x_1 + a_{12}x_2 = b_1$ and $a_{21}x_1 + a_{22}x_2 = b_2$ could be represented by the matrix

$$\begin{bmatrix} a_{11} & a_{12} & b_1 \\ a_{21} & a_{22} & b_2 \end{bmatrix}$$

The solution of the equations can then be found by manipulating the matrix according to specific rules. Matrices can also be used as an aid in the solution of other types of problem, e.g., finding the frequencies and normal modes of vibration of an oscillating system. No single numerical value is attached to a matrix but, in the case of a square matrix (one with an equal number of rows and columns), there is defined the determinant of the matrix whose value can be calculated according to specific rules. In the case of the matrix

$$\begin{bmatrix} a_{11} & a_{12} & a_{13} \\ a_{21} & a_{22} & a_{23} \\ a_{31} & a_{32} & a_{33} \end{bmatrix}$$

the determinant is

$$\begin{vmatrix} a_{11} & a_{12} & a_{13} \\ a_{21} & a_{22} & a_{23} \\ a_{31} & a_{32} & a_{33} \end{vmatrix}$$

and has the value

$$a_{11}\begin{vmatrix} a_{22} & a_{23} \\ a_{32} & a_{33} \end{vmatrix} - a_{12}\begin{vmatrix} a_{21} & a_{23} \\ a_{31} & a_{33} \end{vmatrix} + a_{13}\begin{vmatrix} a_{21} & a_{22} \\ a_{31} & a_{32} \end{vmatrix}$$

where

$$\begin{vmatrix} a_{22} & a_{23} \\ a_{32} & a_{33} \end{vmatrix} = a_{22}a_{33} - a_{23}a_{32}, \text{ etc.}$$

**Matsu:** see MAZU DAO AND JINMEN DAO.

**Matsuo Bashō:** see BASHO.

**Matswa, André,** 1889–1942, W African anticolonial agitator; b. Congo Republic (then French Congo). After enlisting in the French army and serving in Morocco between 1924 and 1925 he lived in Paris where he founded a welfare organization, 'Amicale', to help people from Equatorial Africa living in France. In 1930 after Amicale opened up branches in the Congo and made loud protests against colonialist policies in W Africa, Matswa was arrested and deported to the Congo. He spent much of the rest of his life in prison and died in confinement in Chad.

**Matsys, Quentin:** see MASSYS, QUENTIN.

**Matta, Roberto Sebastian Matta Echaurren,** 1911–, Chilean–French painter. He worked (1933) as a draughtsman in the Paris studio of LE CORBUSIER. In 1936 he met DALI and BRETON and joined the surrealist group (see SURREALISM). He developed automatic composition techniques in his *Psychological Morphologies.* In the 1940s his compositions became more dynamic and included both organic and mechanistic elements; and after meeting DUCHAMP in 1944, he changed his style to include floating geometrical planes. His interest in the problems of humans confronted by a modern machine age led him to reintroduce the human figure into his work in the 50s, and in the 60s his work became more political, treating themes such as the Vietnam War.

**Mattathias,** the elderly priest, father of JUDAS MACCABEUS and his brothers, who started the Jewish revolt against the attempts of Antiochus Epiphanes to impose Hellenism on Judaea in 167 BC.

**matter,** anything that has MASS. Because of its mass, all matter has WEIGHT, if it is in a gravitational field, and INERTIA. The three common STATES OF MATTER are solid, liquid, and gas; scientists also recognize a fourth, PLASMA. Ordinary matter consists of ATOMS and MOLECULES. See also ELEMENT; ELEMENTARY PARTICLES.

**Matterhorn,** distinctive pyramidal peak, 4478 m (14,690 ft) high, in the Alps, on the Swiss–Italian border, near ZERMATT. It was first climbed in 1865 by Edward Whymper.

The **Matterhorn**

**Matthew, Gospel according to Saint,** book of the NEW TESTAMENT. It is now generally accepted as postdating MARK. Containing more allusions to the OLD TESTAMENT than the other GOSPELS, it was clearly written for Jewish Christians, to prove that JESUS was the promised Messiah.

**Matthew, Saint,** one of the Twelve Disciples, also called Levi, a publican (tax collector) from Capernaum. The attribution to him of the first GOSPEL is most likely incorrect.

**Matthews, Sir Stanley,** 1915–, English professional footballer. He played in his first football league match in 1931 and for England in 1934, after which he won 55 caps. He played for Blackpool FC 1947–61 and for Stoke City 1961–65. He was knighted in 1965.

**Matthias,** 1557–1619, Holy Roman emperor (r.1612–19), king of Bohemia (r.1611–17) and of Hungary (r.1608–18); son of Emperor MAXIMILIAN II. The ill health of his brother Emperor Rudolf II gave Matthias the opportunity to increase his political authority, and he was recognized as head of the house of HABSBURG in 1606 and as emperor in 1617. His conciliatory policy toward the Protestants under his rule gave rise to an opposing Catholic faction led by his brother the Archduke Maximilian and by the Archduke Ferdinand (later Emperor FERDINAND II). Old and ailing, Matthias was unable to prevent their takeover, and he was succeeded by Ferdinand.

**Matthias, Saint,** apostle chosen by lot to replace JUDAS ISCARIOT by the remaining disciples. See Acts 1.23–26.

**Matthias Corvinus,** 1443?–1490, king of Hungary (r.1458–90) and Bohemia (r.1478–90), son of John HUNYADI. After succeeding LADISLAUS V in Hungary, he took up arms against the Hussite George of Podebrad, king of Bohemia, and the latter's successor, Ladislaus II. Matthias had himself crowned (1469) king of Bohemia, but the Bohemian diet did not recognize him. In 1478 a compromise allowed both Matthias and Ladislaus to keep the title of king whilst dividing the lands. Matthias made war (1477, 1479, 1482) on Holy Roman Emperor FREDERICK III, but most of his conquests were lost after his death.

**Maugham, W(illiam) Somerset,** 1874–1965, English author. An expert storyteller, he wrote with irony and, frequently, cynicism. His novels include the partly autobiographical *Of Human Bondage* (1915) and the satirical *Cakes and Ale* (1930). He was a prolific dramatist, his first stage success being *Lady Frederick* (1907), and his collections of short stories included *The Trembling of a Leaf* (1921) and *Ashenden* (1928).

**Mau Mau,** secret terrorist organization in KENYA, comprising chiefly members of the Kikuyu tribe. In 1952 the Mau Mau began bloody reprisals against the Europeans. By 1956 British troops had driven the Mau Mau into the hills, and later the entire Kikuyu tribe was relocated.

**Mauna Kea,** dormant volcano, Hawaii island, 4205 m (13,796 ft) high, highest point in the Hawaiian Islands. It has many cinder cones on its flanks and a great crater at the summit. Near the peak of Mauna Kea, where the dry air is ideal for optical and especially infrared astronomical observations, are several major telescopes, including the 3.8-m (150-in) United Kingdom Infrared Telescope, the largest in the world designed particularly for infrared observations, and the 3.6-m (142-in) Canada–France–Hawaii reflector.

**Mauna Loa,** intermittently active volcano, Hawaii island, 4170 km (13,680 ft) high, in Hawaii Volcanoes National Park. One of its many craters is KILAUEA.

**Maundy Thursday,** the Thursday in Holy Week preceding Easter Sunday; it commemorates the Institution of the Last Supper. The liturgy of the day in the Roman Catholic and Eastern Orthodox churches includes the ceremonial washing of the feet of 12 persons in memory of Christ's washing of the feet of his disciples recorded in John 13. In England it is customary for the sovereign to distribute specially minted silver coins (the Royal Maundy) to selected persons (the number determined by the monarch's age) in Westminster Abbey or some other chosen church. The term Maundy is a corruption of the Latin *mandatum* [commandment], and recalls Christ's words before the Last Supper: 'A new commandment I give you, that you love one another' (John 13.34).

**Maupassant, Guy de** (mohpa,sahnh), 1850–93, French author. He poured out a prodigious number of short stories, novels, plays, and travel sketches until 1891, when he was the victim of insanity due to syphilis. Writing in a simple, objective style reminiscent of FLAUBERT, Maupassant is an exemplar of French psychological realism. His influence on all European literature was enormous. His best works are some 300 short stories, many unsurpassed in their genre. Among his masterpieces are 'Boule de suif' (Tallow Ball), 'La parure' (The Necklace), and 'La ficelle' (The Piece of String). His novels include *Une vie* (1883; tr. A Life), *Bel-Ami* (1885), and *Pierre et Jean* (1888).

**Mauretania,** ancient district of Africa in Roman times, usually including most of present-day N Morocco and W Algeria. In the 2nd cent. BC

Mauna Kea

Bocchus, father-in-law of Jugurtha of Numidia, established the kingdom of Mauretania. The Roman emperor AUGUSTUS put Juba II on the throne in 25 BC, and the Emperor CLAUDIUS I made the region into two Roman provinces, but the native chiefs were never wholly subdued. By the end of the 5th cent. AD Roman control over Mauretania had disappeared.

**Mauriac, François** (moh,ryak), 1885–1970, French novelist and playwright. He was one of the best exponents of the Catholic novel, as in *Le noeud de vipères* (1932; tr. Vipers' Nest), *Genitrix* (1923), or *Thérèse Desqueyroux* (1927), often set in or near his native Bordeaux. He explores the darker side of erotic or maternal love or of bourgeois institutions like marriage or the family, as battlefields where the victory of divine Grace can shine. He won the Nobel Prize in 1952, and expressed his Gaullist sympathies in his polemical journalism during the Algerian war.

**Maurice, Frederick Denison,** 1805–72, English clergyman and social reformer. Brought up a Unitarian, he became an Anglican, studied law, and took holy orders in 1834. Because of the views contained in his *Theological Essays* (1853), he lost the post of professor of divinity at King's College, London. He was a leader of the CHRISTIAN SOCIALISM movement and founded two colleges in London.

**Maurice of Nassau,** 1567–1625, prince of Orange (r.1618–25); son of WILLIAM THE SILENT. In the independence struggle of the NETHERLANDS he took the offensive against the Spanish under Alessandro Farnese (see FARNESE, family). His victories led (1609) to a 12-year truce, making the United Provinces virtually independent. He broke with his chief adviser, OLDENBARNEVELDT, over the split between the Calvinists and the more liberal Remonstrants; Oldenbarneveldt, a leader of the Remonstrants, was executed in 1619. Maurice's campaigns against Spain after hostilities resumed (1621) had little success. His brother FREDERICK HENRY succeeded him.

**Mauritania,** officially Islamic Republic of Mauritania, republic (1985 est. pop. 1,874,000), 1,030,700 km² (397,953 sq mi), NW Africa. It is bordered by the Atlantic Ocean (W), Morocco (N), Algeria (NE), Mali (E and SE), and Senegal (SW). NOUAKCHOTT is the capital. Most of the country is low-lying desert, forming part of the SAHARA, but some fertile soil is found in the semiarid SAHEL of the southwest, along the Senegal R. The economy is divided between a traditional agriculture sector and a modern mining industry developed in the 1960s. Irrigated crops include millet, dates, rice, and sorghum. Stock-raising (cattle, sheep, goats, and camels) was sharply reduced by the great drought of the early 1970s. The fishing industry, based in the Atlantic, is growing rapidly, and fish-processing is now an important industry. Shipments of iron ore account for 75% of export earnings. The GNP is US$787 million, and the GNP per capita is US$420 (1985). The majority of the population are nomadic MOORS, of Berber and Arab background; the rest are mostly black Africans, who live as agriculturalists near the Senegal R. Islam is the state religion; French and Arabic are official languages.

*History.* Settled by Berbers in the 1st millennium AD, the region was the centre of the ancient empire of GHANA (700–1200) and later became part of the empire of MALI (14th–15th cent.). By this time the Sahara had encroached on much of Mauritania, limiting agriculture and reducing the population. In the 1440s Portuguese navigators established a fishing base, and from the 17th cent. European traders dealt in gum arabic along the southern coast. France gained control of S Mauritania in the mid-19th cent., declared a protectorate over the region in 1903, and made it a separate colony in FRENCH WEST AFRICA in 1920, but did little to develop the economy. Nationalist political activity began after World War II, and Mauritania gained full independence in 1960. A Muslim state was created in 1961 under Makhtar Ould Daddah as president, and Mauritania joined the ARAB LEAGUE in 1973. His rule was troubled by ethnic tensions between black Africans and the Arab–Berber group, by economic problems aggravated by the severe drought in the Sahel, and by worker–student protests. A military clique deposed Ould Daddah in 1978, power passing first to Lt.Col. Ahmed Ould Bousseif and then, following Bousseif's death in a plane crash in 1979, to Lt.Col. Khouna Ould Haydalla; in 1985, however, Haydalla was himself deposed by his former prime minister, Col. Moaouia Ould Sidi Mohamed Taya. A 1975 agreement with Spain and Morocco giving Mauritania control over the southern third of the Spanish (Western) Sahara ignited a conflict in the former colony. The Polisario Front, a pro-independence guerrilla group backed by Algeria, waged war against Mauritanian and Moroccan troops until 1979, when Mauritania renounced its claims to the area and signed a peace treaty with Polisario leaders.

Madagascar. The capital is PORT LOUIS. The island of Rodrigues and two groups of small islands are dependencies of Mauritius. Surrounded by coral reefs, the principal island consists of a central plateau and volcanic mountains that rise to c.820 m (2700 ft). The one-crop economy is based on sugarcane, which represents about 80% of export earnings and employs nearly a third of the workers. Tea production, light industry, and tourism are being developed in a government programme to diversify the economy. The fishing industry is also being expanded. The GNP is US$1092 million, and the GNP per capita is US$1090 (1985). About 60% of the population are of Indian descent; the rest are of either Creole (mixed French and African) or French descent. More than half the people are Hindu, about 30% are Christian, and about 14% are Muslim. French and English are the official languages. Overpopulation, resulting from the eradication of malaria after World War II, is a serious problem, but a programme to lower the birth rate has proved successful.

*History.* Originally uninhabited, Mauritius was occupied by the Dutch (1598–1710), who named it after Prince Maurice of Nassau. It was settled (1715) by the French, who established a colony called Île de France. The French imported large numbers of African slaves to work the sugarcane plantations. In 1810 the British captured the island and restored the Dutch name. After slavery was abolished in 1833 the British imported indentured labourers from India, whose descendants constitute a majority of the population today. Extension of the franchise in 1947 gave political rights to the Indians, who favoured independence. They were opposed by the French and Creoles, who feared domination by the Hindu Indian majority. Sir Seewoosagur Ramgoolam's pro-independence Labour Party won control of the assembly in 1967, and independence within the COMMONWEALTH was achieved the following year. In 1976 the left-wing Mauritian Militant Movement (MMM) became the largest party in the assembly, but Ramgoolam retained office by forming a new coalition government. The coalition ended when the MMM was overwhelmingly elected in 1982 and Anerood Jugnauth became prime minister. A year later Jugnauth broke with the MMM and in further elections his newly formed Mauritian Socialist Movement, allied with the Labour and Social Democratic parties, secured a parliamentary majority, which it retained in 1987.

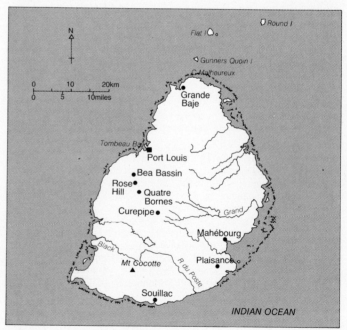

Mauritius

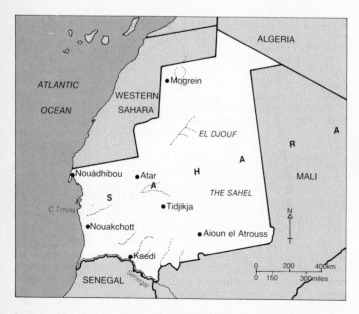

Mauritania

**Mauritius** (mə,rishəs), island country (1983 pop. 1,002,178), 2046 km² (790 sq mi), in the SW Indian Ocean, c.800 km (500 mi) E of

**Maurois, André** (mo,rwah), 1885–1967, French author; b. Émile Herzog. He is noted for his biographies of Shelley, Byron, Disraeli, Chateaubriand, Washington, and others. His novel, *Les silences du Colonel Bramble* (1918), about British military life, was also highly successful.

**Maury, Matthew Fontaine,** 1806–73, American hydrographer and naval officer. His wind and current charts of the Atlantic cut sailing time on many routes, and his *Physical Geography of the Sea* (1855) was the first classic work of modern oceanography.

**Maurya,** ancient Indian dynasty, c.325–c.183 BC, founded by CHANDRAGUPTA. His grandson, ASOKA, brought nearly all of India, along with Afghanistan, under one rule. The accounts of the Greek ambassador, at Chandragupta's court, Megasthenes, describe a centralized administration and a high civilization. Architecture and sculpture flourished under the Mauryas. Asoka's pillars are fine examples of these.

**mausoleum,** sepulchral structure or tomb, especially one of some size and architectural pretension; named after the sepulchre of Mausolus at Halicarnassus, Asia Minor (c.352 BC). One of the SEVEN WONDERS OF THE WORLD, this was a magnificent white marble structure; some of its sculpture survives in the British Museum, London. A notable Roman mausoleum is that of HADRIAN (AD 135–39) in Rome, originally a great drum, now called the Castel Sant' Angelo. Under the Mogul emperors of India great domed mausoleums were built, many used as pleasure palaces during the owner's lifetime. The most celebrated is the TAJ MAHAL. Notable modern mausoleums include; the mausoleum at Castle Howard, England; NAPOLEON I's, in the Invalides, Paris; and LENIN's, in Red Square, Moscow.

**Mauss, Marcel,** 1872–1950, French anthropologist, nephew of DURKHEIM. A forerunner of STRUCTURALISM, Mauss is known for his highly influential book *The Gift* (1923–24; tr. 1954) in which he proposed the principle of RECIPROCITY as the fundamental moral force in society. He was editor of the important journal *L'Année sociologique.*

**Mavrokordatos** or **Mavrocordatos, Alexander,** 1791–1865, Greek statesman and premier (1833–34, 1841, 1843–44, 1854–55). He was a leading patriot in the Greek War of Independence (1821–29) against Turkey and wrote the Greek declaration of independence.

**Mawardi, Abul-Hasan,** d. 1056, Muslim jurist from Baghdad. His treatise on *Governmental Institutes* (*Al-Ahkam al-Sultaniyya*) contains the most classical expression of the juristic theory of the CALIPHATE.

**Mawdudi, Abul-A'la,** 1903–79, Pakistani Muslim fundamentalist. His notion of *hakimiyya,* that sovereignty which is not exclusively God's is a usurpation of sovereignty, and that the only legitimate order is one regulated by the SHARI'A, was profoundly to influence radical Muslim political thinkers like Sayyid QUTB, and the Jamaati Islami, the Pakistani counterparts to the MUSLIM BRETHREN.

**Maxim,** family of American inventors and munitions makers. **Sir Hiram Stevens Maxim,** 1840–1916, invented the Maxim machine gun (1884; see SMALL ARMS), a smokeless powder, and a delayed-action fuse. He became a British citizen in 1900. His brother **Hudson Maxim,** 1853–1927, developed a high explosive, smokeless powder, and a propellant for torpedoes. Sir Hiram's son **Hiram Percy Maxim,** 1869–1936, created (1908) the Maxim silencer for explosive weapons.

**Maximian** (Marcus Aurelius Valerius Maximianus), d. 310, Roman emperor, with DIOCLETIAN (286–305). Both emperors abdicated in 305 in favour of Constantius I and Galerius, but the death (306) of Constantius caused a complicated struggle for power. Maximian at first aided his son Maxentius in this struggle. He later revolted against CONSTANTINE I and in 310 was forced to commit suicide.

**Maximilian,** rulers of the HOLY ROMAN EMPIRE. **Maximilian I,** 1459–1519, emperor (r.1493–1519), son and successor of Emperor FREDERICK III, attempted to aggrandize his Habsburg lands, chiefly through marriage diplomacy, thus involving himself in wars through most of his reign. His marriage (1477) to MARY OF BURGUNDY led to war with Louis XI of France over her vast holdings (Burgundy, the Low Countries, and Luxembourg) and with Louis's successor, Charles VIII. A later marriage involved him in the ITALIAN WARS. He arranged the marriage of his son Philip, later PHILIP I of Castile, into the Spanish royal family. That marriage later gave his grandson, Emperor CHARLES V, one of the largest territorial inheritances in history. He also arranged the marriages that assured HABSBURG succession to the Bohemian and Hungarian thrones. **Maximilian II,** 1527–76, emperor (r.1564–76), king of Bohemia (r.1562–76) and of Hungary (r.1563–76), was the son and successor of FERDINAND I. He was sympathetic to Lutheranism and allowed considerable religious freedom, while at the same time encouraging Catholic reform. In 1568 he made a truce with Turkey whereby he agreed to pay tribute to the sultan for his share of Hungary. He died while preparing to invade Poland, where he had been elected rival king to STEPHEN BÁTHORY.

**Maximilian,** 1832–67, emperor of Mexico (1864–67). An Austrian archduke, he was escorted (1864) to MEXICO by French soldiers to establish an empire for NAPOLEON III, but the Mexicans were hostile to him and loyal to Pres. JUÁREZ. Although the French drove Juárez's army from the capital, the flimsy fabric of the empire disintegrated when French troops withdrew (1866–67). Maximilian's wife, Carlotta (1840–1927), went to Europe seeking help from Napoleon III. Her pleas were in vain, and Maximilian was captured and executed.

**Maxwell, James Clerk,** 1831–79, Scottish physicist. In 1871 he became the first professor of experimental physics at Cambridge, where he organized the Cavendish Laboratory. Maxwell's outstanding work in ELECTRICITY and MAGNETISM was summarized in his *A Treatise on Electricity and Magnetism* (1873). He developed the theory of the electromagnetic field on a mathematical basis and concluded that electric and magnetic energy travel in transverse waves that propagate at a speed equal to that of light; light is thus only one type of ELECTROMAGNETIC RADIATION. Maxwell's theoretical study (1859) of Saturn's rings foreshadowed his later investigations of heat and the kinetic theory of gases.

**Maxwell, Robert Ian,** 1923–, British publisher and newspaper proprietor; b. Czechoslovakia. A self-educated man, he served in World War II in the British Army and the German Section of the Foreign Office (Head of Press Section, Berlin), 1945–47. He became a successful publisher and entrepreneur and was active in politics. He was chairman of Pergamon Press, Oxford 1949–69 and director of Gauthier-Villars in Paris 1961–69. He was Labour MP for Buckingham 1964–70. Since 1984 he has been chairman of the *Daily Mirror* group newspapers, and with fierce competition in the tabloid market, particularly from the *Sun* (run by Rupert MURDOCH) the *Daily Mirror's* circulation has remained at about 3 million, against the *Sun's* daily sale of about 4 million.

**May:** see MONTH.

**Maya,** related tribes of CENTRAL AMERICA (see MIDDLE AMERICAN INDIANS) occupying the YUCATÁN and E Chiapas in Mexico, much of Guatemala, and W Honduras, and speaking Mayan languages (see AMERICAN INDIAN LANGUAGES). They may derive from the OLMEC, or they may have originated c.1000 BC among nomadic tribes in N central Petén, Guatemala, where there are evidences of a once-flourishing agricultural people. Among American Indian cultures the Maya emerge as undisputed masters of abstract knowledge, the only people to develop an original system of writing (ideographic), with which they recorded chronology, astronomy, history, and religion. Their system of mathematics was an achievement not equalled for centuries in Europe. The 365-day Mayan year was so divided as to be more accurate than that of the Gregorian CALENDAR. Sculpture, used in architecture, reached a beauty and dignity unequalled in aboriginal America. Most of the population, estimated at 14 million in the 8th cent., lived in suburban agricultural communities. Mayan history is divided into three periods. From early in the Pre-Classic period (1500 BC?–AD 300), maize was cultivated. Late in that period the calendar, chronology, and hieroglyphic writing developed. In the Early Classic (300–600), Maya culture spread throughout the area. The greatest Maya accomplishments in art and science occurred in the Late Classic (600–900) at such centres as Copán, Honduras; Palenque, in Chiapas; and Uxmal, in the Yucatán, all abandoned in the following century. Probably in two migrations ending in 889, the Maya went north into the Yucatán, and founded CHICHÉN ITZÁ. At the beginning of the Post-Classic period (900–1697) an invasion by Kulkulcán (see QUETZALCOATL) brought TOLTEC elements into Mayan culture. The Toltec took Chichén Itzá, but were absorbed c.1200 by the Maya. In 1283 Mayapán became the civil capital. The century preceding the Spanish conquest (1546) was dominated by civil wars and a series of calamities. Today more than 2 million Maya in Mexico, Guatemala, and Honduras retain many elements of their culture combined with that of the CONQUISTADORS. Numerous Mayan-derived dialects are spoken, and agriculture and religious practices owe much to Mayan tradition.

**Mayakovsky, Vladimir Vladimirovich,** 1893–1930, Soviet poet and dramatist. *A Cloud in Trousers* (1915), a poem written almost entirely in metaphors, typifies his early style. With the drama *Mystery-Bouffe* (1918) he welcomed the RUSSIAN REVOLUTION (1917), but his satirical plays *The Bedbug* (1928) and *The Bathhouse* (1929) express the disillusionment with Soviet life that contributed to his suicide.

**May Day,** first day of May. Its celebration probably originated in the spring fertility festivals of India and Egypt. The festival of Flora, Roman goddess of spring, ran from 28 Apr. to 3 May. In medieval England, May Day's chief feature was the Maypole, which dancers circled. The Second Socialist International designated (1889) May Day as the holiday for radical labour; it is an important holiday in the USSR.

**Mayer, Johann Tobias,** 1723–62, German mathematician and astronomer. His highly accurate lunar tables (1752) were used to compute the lunar ephemerides in the early editions of the *Nautical Almanac,* enabling navigators to determine precisely longitude at sea. He also made improvements in mapmaking and invented the repeating circle, later used in measuring the arc of the meridian.

**Mayer, Julius Robert von,** 1814–78, German physician and physicist. From a consideration of the generation of animal heat, he was led to determine the relationship between HEAT and WORK. As a result he announced (1842), independently of James JOULE, the mechanical equivalence of heat, a foundation of the law of conservation of ENERGY.

**Mayflower,** ship that in 1620 brought the PILGRIMS from England to New England, America. Under Capt. Christopher Jones, she sailed from Southampton on 16 Sept. 1620, sighted land (Cape Cod) on 19 Nov., and landed at Plymouth on 26 Dec. Before disembarking, the colonists drew up the **Mayflower Compact,** an agreement providing for the temporary government of the colony by the will of the majority.

**May Fourth Movement,** student protest at Beijing on 4 May 1919 against the decision at Versailles to assign Germany's rights in Shandong Prov. to Japan (TWENTY-ONE DEMANDS). The incident sparked a political and cultural revolt against Chinese traditions and inspired a new generation of leaders.

**Mayo,** county in W of Republic of Ireland (1986 pop. 115,016), 5344 km² (2084 sq mi), bordering on the Atlantic Ocean in the N and W. It is situated in the province of Connacht. The county town is CASTLEBAR. The E of the county is mainly low-lying and fertile. In the W there are mountains, including the Nephin Beg Range, the Sheeffry Hills, and the Partry Mts. The highest point in the county is Croagh Patrick which reaches 765 m (2509 ft). There are several lakes in the county, the largest of which is Lough Conn. The coastline is highly indented and there are several offshore islands including Achill Island and Clare Island. Mixed agriculture is common in the lowlands.

**Mayo Clinic,** world-famous medical and philanthropic institution in Rochester, Minnesota, US, offering high standards of patient care, teaching, and research. It was founded at the turn of the century by William Worrall Mayo and developed by his two sons, William James Mayo and Charles Horace Mayo.

**Mayotte,** island (1985 est. pop. 57,400), 374 km² (144 sq mi), French territorial collectivity, Indian Ocean, in the Comoro chain. It exports perfume oils, vanilla, coffee, and copra. When the largely Muslim COMOROS republic became independent (1975), Mayotte, mostly Roman Catholic, decided to remain French, but is claimed by the Comoros' government as its sovereign territory.

**Mayr, Ernst Walter,** 1904–, American zoologist; b. Germany. After field work (1928–30) in New Guinea, he settled (1931) in the US. He worked at the American Museum of Natural History from 1931 to 1953, becoming curator in 1944. Later (1953–75) he was professor of zoology at Harvard Univ. His books include *Animal Species and Evolution* (1963) and *Evolution and the Diversity of Life* (1976).

**Mazarin, Jules** (maza,ranh), 1602–61, French statesman. An Italian, born Giulio Mazarini, he was a papal nuncio to France (1634–36) and entered French service under Cardinal RICHELIEU. Although never ordained a priest, Mazarin was made a Roman Catholic cardinal. After the death (1643) of LOUIS XIII, he was the chief minister of the regent, ANNE OF AUSTRIA, to whom he may have been secretly married. He gained favourable terms at the Peace of WESTPHALIA (1648), but his centralizing policy in France provoked the uprisings of the FRONDE. In 1659 he ended the war with Spain by negotiating the Peace of the Pyrenees.

**Mazarin Bible,** considered the first important work printed by Johann GUTENBERG and the earliest European book printed from movable TYPE. It was completed at Mainz, Germany, not later than 1455. The text was in Latin, in a Gothic type related to Old English, illuminated by hand, on vellum and paper. The first copy to recapture attention was in the library of Cardinal MAZARIN. The book is popularly known as the Gutenberg Bible.

**Mazepa, Ivan,** 1645–1709, Ukrainian ruler. Elected *Hetman* (see ZAPOROZHIAN COSSACKS) in 1687, he ruled for 22 years, and as a skilful statesman and consummate diplomatist won for Ukraine a considerable degree of autonomy and political stability. While remaining aligned with Moscow during the great Northern war he entered in 1705 into secret negotiations with the Poles and later with Charles XII of Sweden hoping for a Swedish victory. However, the Muscovite victory at Poltava (1709) forced Mazepa to flee to Turkey, where he died.

**Mazu dao and Jinmen dao** or **Matsu and Quemoy,** islands off the coast of China, c.160–240 km (100–150 mi) W of TAIWAN. Mazu dao is a single island, while Jinmen dao is a group including 12 islets in Xiamen Bay. The islands remained Chinese Nationalist outposts after the Communist takeover of mainland China in 1949 and were bombarded several times from the mainland.

**Mazzini, Giuseppe** (ma,tseenee), 1805–72, Italian patriot and revolutionary, a leading figure in the RISORGIMENTO. A proponent of Italian unity under a republican government, he wrote eloquent revolutionary propaganda from exile, chiefly in London after 1837. He believed that unity should be achieved by revolution and war, based on direct popular action. His influence on Italian liberals and on some liberals abroad was enormous. Mazzini returned to Italy during the REVOLUTIONS OF 1848 and took part in the Roman republic of 1849. He organized unsuccessful uprisings in Milan (1853) and in S Italy (1857). Mazzini supported GARIBALDI's expedition to Sicily (1860), but unlike Garibaldi he remained a resolute republican.

**Mazzola, Francesco:** see PARMIGIANO.

**Mbabane** (əmbah,bahnay), town (1982 pop. 38,636), administrative capital of Swaziland, in the Mdimba Mts. The city serves as the commercial centre for an agricultural region.

**Mbandzeni,** c.1850–89, king of SWAZILAND (r.1874–89). He signed away his kingdom by granting mining, trading, and farming concessions to white settlers in return for bribes. As a result Swaziland became an appendage of the South African Republic until the SOUTH AFRICAN WAR.

**Mboya, Thomas Joseph,** 1930–69, Kenyan political leader. After KENYA gained (1963) its independence, he held a number of high posts. He was widely regarded as a likely successor to Jomo KENYATTA, but he was assassinated in 1969.

**Mbuji Mayi,** formerly Bakwanga, city (1987 pop. 382,632), capital of Kasai Oriental prov., S Zaïre, on the Bushimaie R. Its economy is based on diamond mining.

**Mc-.** Names beginning thus are entered as if spelt Mac-. See MAC.

**Md,** chemical symbol of the element MENDELEVIUM.

**Mdbuli, Gwamile,** c.1850–1925, principal wife of MBANDZENI, king of Swaziland. After the death of her husband she acted as queen regent of Swaziland until the installation of her grandson SOBHUZA II in 1921. She actively encouraged her people to work in South African mines in order to be able to buy back their land which had been stolen by the Boers.

**Mead, George Herbert,** 1863–1931, American psychologist and social theorist. Mead's general philosophy was based upon American PRAGMATISM, but his theories emphasized the crucial role of language and social interaction in the development of mind, and his developmental psychology has frequently been compared to that of VYGOTSKY. His particular contribution was the proposal that the self grows out of interactions with 'significant others'. A collection of his University of Chicago lectures was published as *Mind, Self and Society* (1934).

**Mead, Lake,** reservoir, 640 km² (247 sq mi), on the Colorado R. in Arizona and Nevada, the largest in the US. Impounded by HOOVER DAM, it is 185 km (115 mi) long, 1.6–13 km (1–8 mi) wide, and up to 180 m (c.550 ft) deep, and has a shoreline of 885 km (550 mi).

**Mead, Margaret,** 1901–78, American anthropologist. A student of F. BOAS, she won world fame through studies of child-rearing, personality, and culture. Her primary fieldwork was among peoples of OCEANIA. In comparing the turbulence and repressed sexuality of adolescence in the US with the apparently trouble-free and unrestricted sexual development of young girls in Samoa, she challenged the notion that the patterns of sexual roles were innate and biologically determined. Affiliated with the American Museum of Natural History from 1926 until her death, after 1954 she was also adjunct professor of anthropology at Columbia Univ. Some of her widely-read books are *Coming of Age in Samoa* (1928), *Growing Up in New Guinea* (1930), *Male and Female* (1949), and *Culture and Commitment* (1970).

**Meade, George Gordon,** 1815–72, Union general in the AMERICAN CIVIL WAR; b. Spain. He distinguished himself in 1862 at the Seven Days battles, Bull Run, and Antietam, and later at Fredericksburg and Chancellorsville. In command of the Army of the Potomac from 1863, he won the important battle of Gettysburg (see GETTYSBURG CAMPAIGN), although he was criticized for not following up his victory.

**Meade, James Edward,** 1907–, British economist. An expert on theories of international trade, he taught (1947–57) at the London School of Economics and thereafter at Cambridge Univ. For his pioneering work in the early 1950s on foreign-trade and balance-of-payments problems, he was a co-recipient, with Bertil OHLIN, of the 1977 Nobel Prize for economics.

**meadow saffron** or **autumn crocus,** perennial garden ornamental (*Colchicum autumnale*) of the LILY family, native to Europe and N Africa. Its highly poisonous corms and seeds yield the drug colchicine. The purplish flowers resemble those of the unrelated true CROCUS and true SAFFRON (of the IRIS family) and appear in the autumn, before the leaves.

**mealybug:** see SCALE INSECT.

**mean free path,** average distance travelled by a molecule in a gas between collisions with other molecules. See KINETIC THEORY.

**means test** the practice of assessing a person's present financial position in order to decide whether he or she is eligible for some benefit (e.g., a scholarship, or unemployment benefit). The idea is probably as old as charity relief itself. In modern times it has often been applied both with private and public benefits (notoriously with the unemployment benefit in the UK during the depression in the 1930s). Means testing sits somewhat uneasily with the notion of the WELFARE STATE, and in the Britain of the 1980s is applied only here and there throughout the gamut of benefits available. The best-known examples are the tests for SUPPLEMENTARY BENEFIT (with 4½ million claimants in the mid 1980s) and for student grants (500,000 claimants). Trends in the 1980s are to replace such benefits with loans where possible, in which case means testing becomes less relevant as no one can be thought of as 'getting something for nothing'.

**measles** or **rubeola,** highly contagious viral disease of young children spread by droplet spray from the mouth, nose, and throat during the infectious stage (beginning two to four days before the rash appears and lasting two to five days thereafter). Early symptoms (fever, redness of eyes) are followed by characteristic white spots in the mouth and a facial rash that spreads to the rest of the body. Although one attack confers lifelong immunity, immunization is advisable because of the possibility of serious secondary infection. See also RUBELLA.

**Meath,** county in NE of Republic of Ireland (1986 pop. 103,762), 2315 km² (903 sq mi), bordering on the Irish Sea in the E. It is situated in the province of Leinster. The county town is TRIM. Most of the county is gently undulating and fertile, but there are some hills in the NW. The main rivers are the Boyne and the Blackwater. Cattle and horses are bred, and potatoes produced. Trim is a market town, and Drogheda has a range of industries including engineering and cotton milling. Zinc is mined near Navan.

**Mecca,** city (1981 est. pop. 400,000), W Saudi Arabia. The birthplace (AD c.570) of MUHAMMAD, it is the holiest city of ISLAM. Called Macoraba by Ptolemy, it was an ancient centre of commerce. Muhammad's flight (the hegira) from Mecca in 622 is the beginning of the Muslim era. Mecca was taken by the Ottoman Turks in 1517 and fell to IBN SAUD in 1924. At the city's centre is the Great Mosque, the Haram, which encloses the KAABA, the most sacred Islamic sanctuary and the goal of Muslim pilgrimage (see HAJJ). The commerce of the city, which non-Muslims may not enter, depends almost wholly on the pilgrims. In 1979, Muslim fundamentalists seized the Great Mosque; the government retook it after suppressing the rebels. As a multifaceted symbol, Mecca has remained powerful; but because of its marginal political position there has not been any lasting assertion of central authority based in the city.

**mechanics,** branch of PHYSICS concerned with MOTION and the FORCES causing it. The field includes the study of the mechanical properties of matter, such as DENSITY, elasticity (see STRENGTH OF MATERIALS), and VISCOSITY. Mechanics is divided into STATICS, which deals with bodies at rest or in equilibrium, and DYNAMICS, which deals with bodies in motion. Isaac NEWTON, who derived three laws of motion and the law of universal GRAVITATION, was the founder of modern mechanics. For bodies moving at speeds close to that of light, Newtonian mechanics is superseded by the theory of RELATIVITY, and for the study of very small objects, such as ELEMENTARY PARTICLES, quantum mechanics (see QUANTUM THEORY) is used.

**mechanized warfare,** employment of modern mobile attack-and-defence tactics that depend upon machines, particularly armoured motor vehicles, TANKS, and, increasingly, aircraft. Mechanized warfare was first used in WORLD WAR I. It was of great importance in WORLD WAR II, e.g., in the German blitzkrieg against Poland and France. Gen. Erwin ROMMEL was a leading proponent and practitioner of mechanized warfare, and the Allies' success with it (1944–45) in Europe under Gen. George PATTON and others helped to end the war. Israeli offensives in 1956, 1967, and 1982 (see ARAB–ISRAELI WARS) involved close coordination of motorized infantry with air forces. Helicopters proved to be a new and effective component of mechanized warfare during the KOREAN WAR and VIETNAM WAR. See also MILITARY SCIENCE.

**Medan** (ma͵dahn), city (1980 pop. 1,373,000), capital of North Sumatra prov., Indonesia, 25 km (15 mi) from the mouth of the Deli R., site of its port. The largest city in SUMATRA, it is the marketing, commercial, and transport centre of a rich agricultural area with great tobacco, rubber, and palm oil estates. Manufactures include machinery and tile production.

**Medawar, Peter Brian,** 1915–87, British zoologist; b. Brazil. During World War II he developed a method for joining the ends of severed nerves; later he did notable experimental work in transplanting living tissue from one body to another. Working on a theory of Sir Macfarlane BURNET, he proved that under certain circumstances an organism can be made to overcome its normal tendency to reject foreign tissue or organs. For this work he and Burnet shared the 1960 Nobel Prize in physiology or medicine. He made outstanding contributions to the understanding of immunity.

**Medea,** in Greek mythology, princess of Colchis; famed for her skill in sorcery. She fell in love with JASON and helped him obtain the GOLDEN FLEECE. After marrying Jason she returned with him to Iolcus and bore him two children. Years later, when Jason wished to marry Creusa, the vengeful Medea sent her an enchanted gown, which burned her to death. Then she killed her own children. Her story was dramatized by EURIPIDES and SENECA, and has since been the inspiration of an eponymous play by CORNEILLE (1635), an opera by CHERUBINI (1797), and a film by PASOLINI (1969).

**Medellín,** city (1979 est. pop. 1,506,661), W central Colombia, capital of Antioquia dept. Virtually isolated in its remote mountain valley until the mid-19th-cent. local development of coffee, it is now one of Colombia's chief cities and manufacturing centres. Its leading products include textiles, clothing, tobacco, and metal goods. Coal, gold, and silver are mined in the surrounding region. Medellín has three universities and a world-famous orchid garden.

**Media,** ancient country of W Asia, in a region now in W Iran and S Azerbaijan. Its inhabitants were the Medes, an Indo-European people, who extended their rule over PERSIA in the time of Sargon of Assyria (d. 705 BC) and captured NINEVEH in 612 BC. Their capital was Ecbatana. Media was forcibly annexed (c.550 BC) to Persia by CYRUS THE GREAT.

**median,** one type of AVERAGE used in STATISTICS as an alternative to the ARITHMETIC MEAN. It is obtained by arranging all of the values, usually of a sample from the whole population, in ascending or descending order, and identifying the value which lies at the centre of the range, i.e., so that there are equal numbers of larger or smaller values. The median is often a more appropriate average when the DISTRIBUTION of values is asymmetric; for example, the median income would more nearly represent an average income than the arithmetic mean.

**Medicaid:** see HEALTH INSURANCE.

**Medical Campaign for the Prevention of Nuclear War:** see INTERNATIONAL PHYSICIANS FOR THE PREVENTION OF NUCLEAR WAR.

**Medical Register:** see GENERAL MEDICAL COUNCIL.

**Medical Research Council,** body providing grants from British government funds to support medical research in universities, research institutions, and hospitals in Britain, and to some institutions in developing countries. Established in 1920, it is responsible to the Department of Education and Science.

**Medicare:** see HEALTH INSURANCE.

**Medici** (͵medichee, mə͵deechee), Italian family that directed the destinies of Florence from the 15th cent. until 1737. Of obscure origin, they gained immense wealth as merchants and bankers, became affiliated through marriage to the major houses of Europe, and produced three popes (LEO X, CLEMENT VII, and LEO XI) and two queens of France (CATHERINE DE' MEDICI and MARIE DE' MEDICI). Until 1532 the democratic constitution of Florence was outwardly upheld, but the Medici exerted actual control over the government without holding any permanent official position. They were exiled from Florence in 1433–34, 1494–1512, and 1527–30. Through their patronage of the arts they helped to make the city a great repository of European culture. The first important member of the family was **Giovanni di Bicci de' Medici**, 1360–1429, whose sons founded the two branches of the family.

*Senior Line.* His elder son, **Cosimo de' Medici** (Cosimo the Elder), 1389–1464, was the first Medici to rule Florence. Exiled from Florence in 1433, he returned in 1434 and doubled his wealth through banking. He ended Florence's traditional alliance with Venice and supported the SFORZA family in Milan. His chief fame is as a patron to such artists as BRUNELLESCHI, DONATELLO, and GHIBERTI, and as the founder of the Medici Library. He was succeeded as head of the family by his son, **Piero de' Medici**, 1414–69, nicknamed Il Gottoso [the gouty] because of ill health. In 1466 Piero put down a conspiracy against him by the Pitti family. His son and successor, **Lorenzo de' Medici** (Lorenzo the Magnificent), 1449–92, was one of the towering figures of the Italian RENAISSANCE. He had little success in business, however, and his lavish entertainments depleted his funds. In 1478 Pope SIXTUS IV helped to foment the Pazzi conspiracy against him. Lorenzo's brother Giuliano was murdered, but Lorenzo escaped with only a wound, and the plot collapsed. In spite of the attacks of Girolamo SAVONAROLA, Lorenzo allowed him to continue preaching. Lorenzo was a patron of BOTTICELLI and MICHELANGELO. His second son later became pope as Leo X. His successor was his eldest son, **Piero de' Medici**, 1471–1503. Piero was driven (1494) from Florence by the democratic party led by Savonarola during the invasion of Italy by CHARLES VIII of France. Piero's brother, **Giuliano de' Medici**, 1479–1516, duke of Nemours (1515–16), entered Florence in 1512 when the HOLY LEAGUE restored the Medici as rulers. After his death, control over Florence was exercised by Pope Leo X through Piero's son **Lorenzo de' Medici**, 1492–1519, duke of Urbino (1515). Lorenzo was the father of Catherine de' Medici. Giuliano's and Lorenzo's statues by Michelangelo adorn their tombs in the Church of San Lorenzo in Florence. After 1523 Pope Clement VII headed the Medici family and controlled Florence through **Ippolito de' Medici**, 1511–35, Giuliano's illegitimate son, and **Alessandro de' Medici**, 1510?–37, probably the illegitimate son of Lorenzo de' Medici (d. 1519). The Medici were banished (1527) from Florence as a result of the invasion of Italy by Holy Roman Emperor CHARLES V, but Pope Clement restored them to power in 1530. Clement soon favoured Alessandro, who became head of the republic (1531) and hereditary duke (1532). In 1535 Ippolito was sent by the Florentines to present their grievances to the emperor, but he died on the way, possibly poisoned at Alessandro's command. Alessandro, who had married Margaret of Austria (see MARGARET OF PARMA), was assassinated by a relative, **Lorenzino de' Medici**, 1515–47, and the leadership of the family passed to Cosimo I de' Medici, of the younger branch.

*Younger Line and Grand dukes of Tuscany.* This line descended from **Lorenzo de' Medici**, d. 1440, younger son of Giovanni di Bicci de' Medici. Lorenzo's great-grandson **Giovanni de' Medici**, 1498–1526, called Giovanni delle Bande Nere [of the black bands], was a famous *condottiere* [mercenary]. He fought for Pope Leo X in the ITALIAN WARS, but later changed sides and fought for FRANCIS I of France. His nickname probably derives from the black bands of mourning he put on his banners after Leo's death. His older son, **Cosimo I de' Medici**, 1519–74, succeeded Alessandro de' Medici as duke of Florence in 1537. He acquired (1555) SIENA and was made (1569) grand duke of Tuscany. His son, **Francesco de' Medici**, 1541–87, grand duke 1574–87, devoted himself to alchemy and allowed the HABSBURGS of Spain and Austria to establish a virtual protectorate over his kingdom. He was the father of Marie de' Medici. His brother, **Ferdinand I de' Medici**, 1549–1609, grand duke 1587–1609, built the famous Villa Medici at Rome and created a free port at Leghorn. His son, **Cosimo II de' Medici**, 1590–1621, grand duke 1609–21, was a patron of GALILEO. Cosimo's grandson, **Cosimo III de' Medici**, 1642–1723, grand duke 1670–1723, headed a corrupt and bigoted regime. His son, **Gian Gastone de' Medici**, 1671–1737, grand duke 1723–37, was the last male member of the family. He ruled a Tuscany that had fallen from glory into decadence and impoverishment. In 1735 his succession was settled on Francis of Lorraine (later the Emperor FRANCIS I).

**Medici, Giovanni de'** (1475–1521): see LEO X.

**Medici, Giulio de':** see CLEMENT VII.

**medicine,** science and art of diagnosing, treating, and preventing disease. For centuries, because the origin of disease was unknown, its treatment was coupled with magic and superstition. The more scientific practice of medicine, however, began in ancient Asian civilizations. In Sumer, the Laws of HAMMURABI established the first known code of medical ethics. In China, the ancient practice of ACUPUNCTURE and ideas about the circulation of blood presuppose familiarity with anatomy, vascular systems, and the nervous system. The Greeks advanced medical knowledge in anatomy and physiology, diet, exercise, and other areas, and provided the Hippocratic oath, still used today (see HIPPOCRATES). The Romans improved public health through their sophisticated sanitation facilities, and GALEN provided a final synthesis of the medicine of the ancient world. After a period of decline during the Middle Ages, when medical knowledge was kept alive mainly by Arab and Jewish physicians, VESALIUS proved that there were errors in Galen's work and again opened medicine to discovery. In the 17th cent., William HARVEY demonstrated the circulation of blood and the role of the heart as a pump. With the introduction of the compound microscope, minute forms of life were discovered and a major step was made towards diagnosing disease. In the 18th cent., Edward JENNER introduced the concept of VACCINATION, and surgery was transformed into an experimental science. The beginnings of modern medicine date from the 19th cent., with the development of the germ theory of disease; the use of antiseptics and ANAESTHESIA in surgery; and a revival of public-health measures and better sanitation. Medicine in the 20th cent. has been characterized by the introduction (in the UK) of the NATIONAL HEALTH SERVICE; an increased understanding of IMMUNITY, the ENDOCRINE SYSTEM, and the importance of nutrition; advances in SURGERY, organ transplants (see TRANSPLANTATION, MEDICAL), and diagnostic techniques (see COMPUTERIZED AXIAL TOMOGRAPHY; ULTRASOUND; X-RAY); and the use of DRUGS, especially ANTIBIOTICS. Advances have also been notable in the treatment of mental illness through both PSYCHOTHERAPY and the administration of drugs (see ANTIDEPRESSANT; PSYCHIATRY; TRANQUILLIZER). With growing specialization and complex diagnostic and therapeutic technology alongside a growing population of old people with chronic and degenerative diseases untouched by the achievements of medicine, modern health care is at a crossroads in the allocation of both personnel and capital.

**Medina,** city (1981 est. pop. 200,000), W Saudi Arabia. It is situated in an oasis c.180 km (110 mi) inland from the Red Sea. Before the flight (the hegira) of MUHAMMAD from MECCA to Medina in 622, the city was called Yathrib. Muhammad used it as a base for converting and conquering Arabia. It came under the sway of the Ottoman Turks in 1517 and was held by them until 1918. In 1924 it fell to IBN SAUD. Medina's large mosque contains the tombs of Muhammad and his daughter Fatima. The city's holy sites are forbidden to non-Muslims.

**meditation,** religious discipline in which the mind is led to focus on a single point of reference. It may be a means of invoking divine GRACE, as in the contemplation by Christian mystics of a spiritual theme, question, or problem; or it may be a means of attaining conscious union with the divine, e.g., through visualization of a deity or inward repetition of a prayer or MANTRA (sacred sound). Employed since ancient times in various forms by all religions, the practice of meditation gained popular interest in reaction to high-technical culture in the 20th cent., when ZEN BUDDHISM rose in the West after World War II. In the 1960s and 70s the Indian Maharishi Mahesh Yogi taught a mantra system called Transcendental Meditation (TM), which is now also used by many nonreligious adherents as a method for achieving a relaxed physical and mental state.

**Mediterranean Sea,** strategically important sea between Europe, Africa, and Asia, c.2,499,350 km² (965,000 sq mi), opening to the Atlantic Ocean through the Strait of GIBRALTAR; to the BLACK SEA through the DARDANELLES, Sea of Marmara, and the BOSPORUS; and to the RED SEA through the SUEZ CANAL. It is c.3900 km (2400 mi) long, up to 1600 km (1000 mi) wide, and reaches a maximum depth of c.4400 m (14,450 ft) off Greece. The sea has little variation in tides. It was the focus of Western civilization from earliest times (see AEGEAN CIVILIZATION) until the 15th cent. when open-ocean shipping around Africa became common. It was revitalized as a trade route in 1869 by the opening of the Suez Canal and, more recently, by its proximity to Middle East and North African oil fields.

**Medusa:** see GORGON.

**medusa,** in zoology: see POLYP AND MEDUSA.

**Medway,** river in SE England, approximately 112 km (70 mi) long. It rises near E Grinstead in W Sussex, flows E into Kent, past Tonbridge and MAIDSTONE, then N to Rochester and Chatham, where it widens into an estuary which flows E, joining the R. THAMES at Sheerness. It is tidal up as far as Allington, which is between Maidstone and Aylesford.

**meerschaum** or **sepiolite** (ˌmiəshəm), hydrous magnesium silicate mineral [ideally, $Mg_8(H_2O)_4(OH)_4Si_{12}O_{30}$] resembling white clay. It is found in many parts of the world and is used primarily to make pipes and cigar and cigarette holders. Meerschaum pipes, often carved into ornate forms, become dark brown with use.

**Meerut,** town (1981 pop. 417,395), Uttar Pradesh state, N India, on the Kali Nadi R. It is a district administrative and commercial centre, and at the northern end of an industrialized belt stretching to Delhi. Meerut has cotton mills and a variety of other industries. Cities on the site of Meerut go back at least to the time of ASOKA (3rd cent. BC). Meerut was important in Mogul times; modern growth started with the establishment of a military cantonment by the British. It was there that the INDIAN MUTINY erupted in 1857.

**megalithic monuments** [Gk., = great stone], ancient structures made of one or more huge stone slabs. Megalithic forms of art and architecture are found throughout the world and have undoubtedly served many different purposes. In Europe, the term is applied to the various types of chambered tombs which began to appear during the mid 5th millennium BC (see, e.g., NEW GRANGE) and solitary standing stones (*Menhirs*), alignments (see CARNAC), and the massive stone circles typified by STONEHENGE and AVEBURY. A chamber tomb was usually covered with earth to form a BARROW. Some monuments are marked by engravings, from seemingly random cup and ring marks and spirals to the elaborate geometric patterns which decorate NEW GRANGE and many sites in Malta. As the erection of megaliths required a considerable investment in time and labour, current interest in these sites concerns their potential as evidence of the development of social differentiation and social inequality.

**Megiddo** (məˌgidoh), ancient city in Palestine, on the S edge of the plain of Esdraelon. Inhabited since the 4th millennium BC, it has been the scene of many battles throughout history, from the victory of THUTMOSE III (c.1468 BC) to that of Gen. Edmund ALLENBY in World War I. The plain is called the valley of **Megiddon** in the Bible.

**Mehmed,** sultans of the OTTOMAN EMPIRE (Turkey). **Mehmed I,** 1389?–1421 (r.1413–21), was the son of BEYAZID I. He renewed Ottoman power by defeating his brothers and reuniting most of his father's empire. **Mehmed II** (the Conqueror), 1429–81 (r.1451–81), is considered the true founder of the Ottoman Empire. He destroyed the remains of the Byzantine Empire by capturing (1453) Constantinople, which he made his capital. He conquered the Balkan Peninsula, including Greece, Bosnia, and several Aegean islands, and annexed the Crimea, Trebizond, and Karamania. The reign of **Mehmed IV,** 1641–92 (r.1648–87), was

Meissen, covered cream bowl and stand painted in enamel colours, purple lustre, and gold chinoiserie decoration (1726; Fitzwilliam Museum, Cambridge)

marked by disorder and corruption, although Grand Vizier KÖPRÜLÜ restored (1656) some order. Mehmed suffered military defeats and was deposed. **Mehmed V,** 1844–1918, sultan (1909–18), succeeded to the throne after the Young Turks had toppled his brother, ABD AL-HAMID II. He exercised no power, the government being dominated by Enver Pasha, and during his reign Turkey lost most of its remaining European possessions in the BALKAN WARS (1912–13); it also lost Tripoli to Italy (1911–12). Germany was the dominant influence in his reign, and he sided with the Central Powers in World War I. He was succeeded by his brother, **Mehmed VI,** 1861–1926, the last sultan (r.1918–22). He was under the control of the victorious Allies and was forced to submit to a harsh peace treaty. Meanwhile, Kemal ATATÜRK established a rival government, declared the sultanate abolished (1922), and proclaimed Turkey a republic. Mehmed VI fled and died in exile.

**Mehmet Ali,** 1769–1849, ruler of Egypt; b. Albania or Macedonia of Albanian stock. As a Turkish officer he overcame internal and external opposition to establish a strong centralized state in Egypt under his leadership. Although theoretically acting on behalf of the Ottoman sultan, after 1805 he governed with de facto independence. Under him the Egyptian economy was modernized through state intervention, and a powerful military established which conquered Sudan and, under his son IBRAHIM PASHA, much of the Middle East. In 1841 the Europeans forced him to abandon his non-African possessions as well as possible ambitions to supplant the power of the Ottoman sultan. After his death his descendants continued to rule Egypt until the 1952 antimonarchist revolt.

**Meiji** (ˌmayjee), 1852–1912, reign name of the emperor of Japan whose given name was Mutsuhito and who ruled 1867–1912. The period of his reign is known as the **Meiji period.** In 1868, just after his accession, a revolution known as the **Meiji restoration** occurred, that brought the TOKUGAWA shogunate to an end. The shogunate was facing an internal economic crisis and demands from the US and Europe that the country be opened to foreign trade. The opinions of the DAIMYO were divided and opponents of the shogunate and of ABE MASAHIRO's policy of Westernization congregated in the city of Kyoto around the emperor. In 1867 the last shogun surrendered to the emperor and power nominally returned to the imperial house. In 1868 the emperor moved to Edo, which was renamed Tokyo and designated the national capital.

**Meinecke, Friedrich** (ˌmieɪnɪkə), 1862–1954, German historian. A nationalist and a liberal, he believed that the state must serve cultural needs and promote individualism. His works include *Machiavellism* (1924) and *The German Catastrophe* (1946).

**Meinong, Alexius,** 1853–1920, Austrian psychologist and philosopher. A student of Franz BRENTANO, he developed theories of evidence, value, and the emotions, but his major work was *The Theory of Objects* (1904) where he distinguished the act of thought, its content, and its object. He argued that there are objects which do not exist but merely 'subsist', a view which influenced the early work of Bertrand RUSSELL.

**meiosis,** process of nuclear division in a cell by which the CHROMOSOMES (genetic material) are reduced to half their original number. Meiosis occurs only during formation of sex cells (OVUM and SPERM). An ordinary body cell contains two of each type of chromosome (diploid). Meiosis produces cells with one chromosome of each pair (haploid). In FERTILIZATION, two haploid cells are united; the resulting zygote then contains a diploid number of chromosomes.

**Meir, Golda** (mayˌeeə), 1898–1978, prime minister of ISRAEL (1969–74); b. Russia as Golda Mabovitch. After a teaching career in the US, she settled in Palestine (1921), where she became active in the labour movement and later served as Israel's minister of labour (1949–56) and of foreign affairs (1956–66). As Labour prime minister she sought peace for Israel and resigned in 1974 after she and Moshe DAYAN were criticized for the country's lack of preparation for the 1973 ARAB–ISRAELI WAR.

**Meissen,** the Royal Saxon Porcelain Manufacture, near Dresden, Saxony (now in E Germany). Its foundation in 1710 by Augustus the Strong, Elector of Saxony and King of Poland, followed the discovery of the secret of PORCELAIN manufacture by J.F. BÖTTGER. Until the early 1750s it was the most influential factory in Europe. During this great period, Meissen employed two exceptionally gifted ceramic artists working in the baroque and rococo styles: J.G. Herold (1696–1775) who perfected the paste and introduced various colours, chinoiserie and other types of decoration; and the modeller J.J. KAENDLER (1706–1775) who established

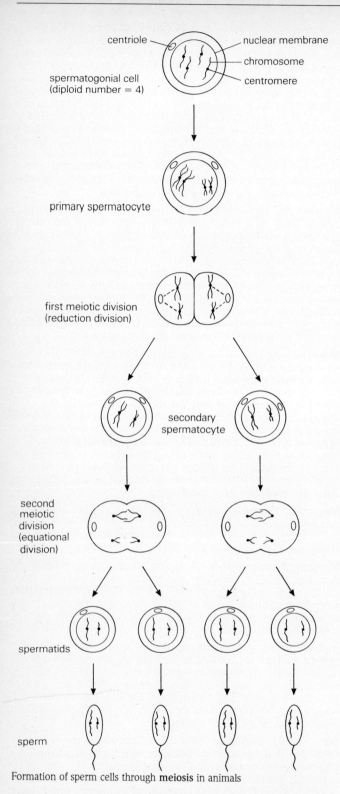

centriole · nuclear membrane

chromosome

centromere

spermatogonial cell
(diploid number = 4)

primary spermatocyte

first meiotic division
(reduction division)

secondary
spermatocyte

second
meiotic
division
(equational
division)

spermatids

sperm

Formation of sperm cells through **meiosis** in animals

the factory's reputation for porcelain figures. During the 1750s the factory's stylistic leadership passed to SÈVRES, and although it was extremely prolific during the 19th cent., its output was dominated by 18th-cent. revivals.

**Meissonier, Jean Louis Ernest** (mayson,yay), 1815–91, French GENRE and military painter. His meticulous genre works include *The Lute Player* (Metropolitan Mus., New York), and his battle scenes include *Napoleon I with His Staff* (Louvre, Paris).

**Meissonier, Juste Aurèle**, 1695–1750, French designer. A goldsmith, he was designer to Louis XV from 1724 to his death. He specialized in interiors. His engravings helped spread the ROCOCO style throughout Europe.

**meistersinger** [Ger., = mastersinger], member of a 15th-16th cent. German musical and poetical guild. Candidates for the rank of *Meister* were judged in public contests. Richard WAGNER's opera *Die Meistersinger von Nürnberg* faithfully represents guild practices.

**Meitner, Lise**, 1878–1968, Austrian physicist and mathematician. She escaped to Sweden in 1938 after the German occupation of Austria to avoid persecution under the Nazi anti-Jewish laws. Later that year she and her nephew Otto Frisch correctly interpreted the experimental results of Otto HAHN and Fritz Strassmann on the bombardment of uranium by neutrons as evidence for nuclear fission. This discovery offered the first clue that the large amounts of energy known to exist in nuclear transmutations might be available for exploitation. Meitner also discovered the protactinium-231 isotope and did extensive work on the radioactive decay products of the elements radium, thorium, and actinium. See NUCLEAR ENERGY.

**Meknès** (mek,nes), city (1982 pop. 386,085), N central Morocco. It has a noted carpet-weaving industry as well as woollen mills, cement and metal works, oil distilleries, and food-processing plants. Meknès was founded c.1672 by Sultan Ismail, who built many palatial buildings, of which little survives. The city declined when the capital moved to FEZ in 1728. A European town is laid out beside the old one.

**Mekong** (mee,kong), one of the great rivers of Southeast Asia, c.4180 km (2600 mi) long. It rises as the Za Qu in Tibet and flows generally south through SW China, then circuitously across or along the borders of Burma, Laos, Thailand, and Kampuchea (Cambodia). It enters the SOUTH CHINA SEA through several mouths across a vast, fertile delta, c.194,250 km² (75,000 sq mi), near HO CHI MINH CITY (Saigon), in S Vietnam. Its densely populated lower valley, in Kampuchea and Vietnam, is one of the world's great rice-growing regions. PHNOM PENH is a major port.

**Melanchthon, Philipp** (mə,langkthən), 1497–1560, German scholar, humanist, and religious reformer. His name is the Greek rendering of the German Schwarzerd ('black earth'). A man of great intellect and wide learning, he was professor of Greek at the Univ. of Wittenberg when he met Martin LUTHER, and they soon became associates. His *Loci communes* (1521) was the first systematic presentation of the principles of the REFORMATION and clarified the new gospel to those outside the movement. A mediator between Luther and the humanists, he also represented him at many conferences and wrote the Augsburg Confession (1530). Melanchthon was more conciliatory than Luther, as evidenced by his friendship with John CALVIN and his willingness to compromise on doctrinal issues. For his role in creating the German schools, he is known as preceptor of Germany.

**Melanesia**, one of the three main divisions of OCEANIA, in the SW Pacific Ocean, NE of Australia and S of the equator. It includes the SOLOMON ISLANDS, VANUATU, TUVALU, NEW CALEDONIA, the Bismarck Archipelago, FIJI, and the Admiralty Islands. The Melanesians are largely of Australoid stock and speak languages of Malayo-Polynesian origin.

**melanin**, dark brown pigment found in human skin, hair, and eyes. Contained in special cells of the skin, melanin production is stimulated by the action of the sun (tanning) to protect underlying tissues from the sun's radiation. An inherited lack of the enzyme tyrosinase, required for melanin synthesis, results in one form of albinism (see ALBINO).

**Melba, Dame Nellie**, 1861–1931, Australian soprano; b. Helen Porter Mitchell. She sang throughout Europe and America but based herself in Covent Garden. Her technical accomplishment and imperious personality enabled her to epitomize the golden age of opera before World War I. In fact her repertory was small and her acting ability limited, but she was the first major singer to take to the gramophone.

**Melbourne**, city (1986 pop. 2,645,484), capital of Victoria, SE Australia, on Port Phillip Bay, at the mouth of the Yarra R. Australia's second largest city, it is a commercial and industrial centre with such manufactures as ships, motor vehicles, farm machinery, textiles, and electrical equipment. The city was settled in 1835 and named (1837) after the British Prime Minister, Lord MELBOURNE. It was the seat of the Australian federal government from 1901 to 1927. The population, once primarily British in origin, has changed since World War II with immigration from E and S Europe. Melbourne was the site of the 1956 Olympic Games. The Melbourne Cup horse race is run annually. There are three universities in the city: Melbourne, Monash, and La Trobe.

**Melbourne, William Lamb, 2nd Viscount,** 1779–1848, British statesman. He was home secretary under Earl GREY (1830–32) and his successor as prime minister (1834, 1835–39, 1839–41). A Whig with aristocratic views, he was responsible for the new Poor Law (1834) and the Municipal Corporations Act (1835). He had no sympathy with radicals, CHARTISTS or the ANTI-CORN LAW LEAGUE. A favourite of the young Queen VICTORIA, he taught her important lessons in statecraft. His wife, **Lady Caroline Lamb,** 1785–1828, wrote several minor novels, but is best known for her love affair with Lord BYRON.

**Melchior** (ˌmelkeeaw), see WISE MEN OF THE EAST.

**Meleager** ('melee,aygə), hero of Greek mythology. At his birth a prophecy said that he would die when a certain log in the fire burned. His mother hid the log, and Meleager grew to be a famous warrior. When ARTEMIS sent a huge boar to ravage his land, Meleager led a band of heroes, including CASTOR AND POLLUX, THESEUS, and JASON, in the Calydonian hunt, and killed the boar. Meleager gave its pelt to the huntress ATALANTA, and when his uncles tried to take it he killed them. In revenge his mother burned the hidden log, and Meleager died.

**Melilla** (may,leelyah), city (1982 pop. 54,571), Spanish possession, on the Mediterranean coast of Morocco, NW Africa. It is a fishing port and an export point for iron ore. Held by Spain since 1496, it was the site of the army revolt that began (1936) the SPANISH CIVIL WAR.

**melodrama,** originally a spoken text with musical background, as in Greek drama. Popular in the 18th cent., it was varied to include drama interspersed with music, e.g., *The Beggar's Opera* by John GAY. The term now applies to all plays with overdrawn characterizations, smashing climaxes, and sentimental appeal.

**melon,** fruit of *Cucumis melo,* a plant of the GOURD family, native to Asia but now widely cultivated in warm regions. Many varieties exist, differing in taste, colour, and skin texture e.g., Persian, honeydew, casaba, muskmelon, and cantaloupe. The true cantaloupe (var. *cantalupensis*) is a hard-shelled melon grown in Mediterranean countries.

**melting point,** temperature at which a substance changes its state from solid to liquid (see STATES OF MATTER). Under standard atmospheric pressure, different pure crystalline solids will each melt at a different specific temperature; thus the melting point is a characteristic of a substance and can be used to identify it. The quantity of heat necessary to change 1 gram of any substance from solid to liquid at its melting point is known as its latent heat of fusion.

**Melville, Andrew,** 1545–1622, Scottish religious reformer and scholar. An academic, he became (1590) rector of St Andrews and reorganized the Scottish universities. More importantly, as successor to John KNOX, he was largely responsible for the introduction of a presbyterian system into the Scottish church. A foe of prelacy and royal supremacy, he struggled to assert church independence.

**Melville, Herman,** 1819–91, one of the greatest American writers. His experiences on a whaler (1841–42) and ashore in the Marquesas (where he was captured by cannibals) and other South Sea islands led to the writing of *Typee* (1846), *Omoo* (1847), and other widely popular romances. Melville's masterpiece, *Moby-Dick; or, The Whale* (1851), the tale of a whaling captain's obsessive search for the white whale that had ripped off his leg, is at once an exciting sea story, a heavily symbolic inquiry into good and evil, and one of the greatest novels ever written. Both *Moby-Dick* and the psychological novel *Pierre; or, The Ambiguities* (1852) were misunderstood at the time of their publication and badly received. Although disheartened by his failure to win an audience, by ill health, and by debts, Melville continued to produce such important works as *The Piazza Tales* (1856), a collection including the stories 'Benito Cereno' and 'Bartleby the Scrivener', *The Confidence Man* (1857), and the novella *Billy Budd, Foretopman* (1924). After holding the position of customs inspector in New York City for 19 years, Melville died in poverty and obscurity. Neglected for many years, his work was rediscovered c.1920.

**Melville, Jean-Pierre,** 1917–73, French film director; b. Jean-Pierre Grumbach. He began making fast, economical films on criminal or spiritual themes after the war, and served as a model to the French 'new wave' of the 1960s. His films include *Le silence de la mer* (1949), *Bob le flambeur* (1955), and *Le Samourai* (1967).

**Melville Island,** island 80 km (50 mi) north of DARWIN, Northern Territory; Australia's largest offshore island. Together with adjacent Bathurst Island the population in 1986 was 1806, consisting mainly of Aborigines. In 1824 a convict settlement was established at Fort Dundas but abandoned in 1829. A small timber industry using cypress pines has been developed.

**Memling** or **Memlinc, Hans,** c.1430–1494, Flemish religious and portrait painter; b. Germany. His religious works are rather bland, reflecting Roger van der WEYDEN's figure types without their intensity. They include *The Mystic Marriage of St Catherine* (1479) and the 1489 *St Ursula Shrine* panels (both: Memling Mus., Bruges). Memling's portraits are more original, showing bust-length, single figures against landscape backgrounds.

**memory,** the retention or storage of information by a biological or other physical system; the medium in which an organism or other physical system stores or retains information. Memory is a key research topic in COGNITIVE SCIENCE, and psychologists and other scientists have proposed many different distinctions between types of memory and memory process; recall v. recognition, short-term v. long-term, episodic v. semantic, storage v. working, being some examples. Memory is also used as a technical term in computer science.

**Memphis,** ancient city of EGYPT, capital of the Old Kingdom (c.3100–c.2258 BC), at the apex of the NILE delta, 18 km (12 mi) from Cairo. The PYRAMIDS and other monuments are nearby. Memphis declined and fell into ruin under the Arabs.

**Memphis,** US city (1984 est. pop. 648,000), SW Tennessee, on a bluff above the Mississippi R., at the mouth of the Wolf R.; est. (by Andrew JACKSON and others) 1819, inc. 1826. The largest city in the state, it is a major river port, rail centre, and market for timber, cotton, and livestock. Textiles, furniture, flooring, heating equipment, and motor vehicle parts are among its manufactures. Strategically important in the CIVIL WAR, it was an object of fighting and fell to Union forces in 1862. The city has numerous medical, educational, and cultural institutions. The site of the famous Beale St, it is associated with such musicians as W.C. HANDY and Elvis PRESLEY.

**Menam Chao Phraya:** see CHAO PHRAYA.

**Menander,** 342?–291? BC, Greek poet, most famous writer of New COMEDY. His ingenious plays, based on love plots, have highly developed characters. Through imitations by PLAUTUS and TERENCE he influenced 17th- and 18th-cent. COMEDY.

**Mencken, H(enry) L(ouis),** 1880–1956, American author. He was a journalist, notably on Baltimore's *Sun* papers (1906–56). He and George Jean NATHAN edited the *Smart Set* (1914–23) and started (1924) the *American Mercury,* which Mencken alone edited (1925–33). His pungent critical essays, aimed mainly at the complacent bourgeoisie, were collected in *Prejudices* (6 vol., 1919–27). He also wrote many other critical and autobiographical works. In philology, he compiled the monumental *The American Language* (1919; 4th edn, 1936; supplements).

**Mendel, Gregor Johann,** 1822–84, Austrian monk noted for his experimental work on heredity. At the Augustinian monastery in Brno (1843–68) he conducted experiments, chiefly on garden peas and involving a controlled pollination technique and a careful statistical analysis of his results, that produced the first accurate and scientific explanation for hybridization. His findings, published in 1866, were ignored during his lifetime, but were rediscovered by three separate investigators in 1900. Mendel's conclusions have become the basic tenets of GENETICS and a notable influence in plant and animal breeding. **Mendelism** is a system of heredity based on his conclusions. Briefly summarized, the Mendelian system states that an inherited characteristic is determined by the combination of two hereditary units (now called genes), one from each of the parental reproductive cells, or gametes; and that these two units are in no way blended together but maintain their separate identities and are thus transmitted unchanged (although in different combinations) over infinite numbers of generations.

**Mendeleev, Dmitri Ivanovich** (mendə,layəf), 1834–1907, Russian chemist. He formulated (1869) the periodic law and invented the PERIODIC TABLE, a system of classifying the elements that allowed him to predict properties of then-unknown elements. He was a professor (1868–90) at the Univ. of St Petersburg, a government adviser on the development of the petroleum industry, and the director of the bureau of weights and measures.

**Mendele mocher sforim** (ˌmendələ ˌmohkhə ˌsfawrim), pseud. of **Sholem Yakob Abramovich**, 1836–1917, Russian Yiddish novelist who also wrote in Hebrew. He is considered the father of modern Hebrew literature, and his Yiddish style was influential. His novels include *The Travels of Benjamin the Third* (1878).

**mendelevium** (Md), artificial radioactive element, detected in 1955 by A. Ghiorso and colleagues, who produced it one atom at a time by alpha-particle bombardment of einsteinium-253. Little is known about its properties. See ELEMENT (table); PERIODIC TABLE.

**Mendelssohn, Felix**, 1809–47, German composer, a major figure in 19th-cent. music; grandson of Moses MENDELSSOHN. A prodigy, he composed his first mature work, the Overture to *A Midsummer Night's Dream*, at 17. In 1829 he conducted a performance of the *St Matthew Passion* that revived interest in J.S. BACH. Mendelssohn's music is characterized by emotional restraint, refinement, and sensitivity, and by adherence to classical forms. Of his five symphonies, the *Scottish* (1830–42), *Italian* (1833), and *Reformation* (1830–32) are best known. His Violin Concerto in E Minor (1844) is popular, as are his ORATORIOS and various piano pieces.

**Mendelssohn, Moses**, 1729–86, German Jewish philosopher, leader in the movement for cultural assimilation; grandfather of Felix MENDELSSOHN. He was a close friend of the playwright G.E. LESSING. His works on aesthetics were highly regarded in his time, and several of his ideas were adopted by KANT.

**Menderes, Adnan**, 1899–1961, prime minister of TURKEY (1950–60). A founder of the Democratic Party, he was premier under its aegis. He was executed for violating the constitution after an army coup toppled (1960) his government.

**Mendoza, Antonio de** (menˌdohthah), 1490?–1552, first Spanish viceroy of New Spain (1535–50). He improved the condition of the Indians, fostered religion, and encouraged education. By quelling Indian revolts, sponsoring northward explorations, and developing agriculture, he extended and consolidated the Spanish conquest of MEXICO. He later served (1551–52) as viceroy of PERU.

**Menelaus** (menəˌlayəs), in Greek mythology, king of SPARTA; husband of HELEN; brother of AGAMEMNON. When PARIS abducted Helen to Troy, Menelaus asked the Greek kings to join him in the TROJAN WAR. At its end he returned to Sparta with Helen.

**Menelik II**, c.1844–1913, emperor of ETHIOPIA, (r.1889–1913). He was *ras* [duke] of Shoa in central Ethiopia after 1865 and proclaimed himself emperor after the death of Emperor Yohannes IV. He is best remembered for his crushing defeat of the Italians at the battle of Adowa (1886), which preserved Ethiopian independence until 1935. During his reign he also did much to modernize the economy; he founded the present capital, ADDIS ABABA, and doubled the size of the Ethiopian state.

**Mengistu Haile Mariam**, 1937–, Ethiopian army officer and political leader (1977–). He took a leading part in the 1974 coup that deposed Emperor HAILE SELASSIE and by 1977 had ruthlessly consolidated his power as chairman of the ruling military council. He has established close ties with the USSR and Cuba, which have given him military aid, but his regime has been plagued by uprisings in ERITREA, famine, and military clashes with Somalia.

**meningitis** or **cerebrospinal meningitis**, acute inflammation of the membranes covering the BRAIN or SPINAL CORD, or both. It can be caused by bacteria, viruses, protozoa, yeasts, or fungi, usually introduced from elsewhere in the body. Symptoms include fever, headache, vomiting, neck and back rigidity, delirium, and convulsions. Examination of the cerebrospinal fluid by means of a spinal tap permits a specific diagnosis. ANTIBIOTIC drugs have reduced mortality and decreased the incidence of such complications as brain damage and paralysis.

**Mennonites,** Protestant sect arising among Swiss ANABAPTISTS and for a time called Swiss Brethren. They derive their name from MENNO SIMONS, a Dutch reformer. The group seceded (1523–25) from the state church in Zürich after rejecting its authority and infant baptism. They believed in nonresistance, refused to take oaths, and held the Bible as their sole rule of faith. Their distinctive beliefs were embodied in the Dordrecht Confession of Faith (1632). Mennonites have two sacraments, baptism (for adults only) and the Lord's Supper. The sect spread to Russia, France, and Holland. In America Mennonites first settled (1683) at Germantown,

Pennsylvania, and it is in the US that they have the largest number of adherents: in 1980 some 230,000 out of a world total of about 650,000.

**Menno Simons**, 1496–1561, Dutch religious reformer. In 1536 he left the Roman Catholic priesthood because of his disbelief in infant baptism and other Catholic teachings. He organized and led the less aggressive division of ANABAPTISTS in Germany and Holland. The name MENNONITES is derived from his name, although he did not actually found the sect.

**menopause:** see MENSTRUATION.

**menorah** [Heb., = candelabrum], Temple candelabrum comprising seven branches. It was the task of the Temple priests to ensure that it was kept perpetually burning by being replenished daily with pure olive oil. In addition to their utilitarian purpose, as a source of Temple illumination, the lights also symbolized the (presence of the) divinity: 'Light dwelleth with Him' (Dan. 2:22). The original menorah was wrought in solid gold, for the desert sanctuary, by the divinely-inspired artist and craftsman, Bezalel. Rabbinic tradition has it that Bezalel's menorah survived the Babylonian exile (see under BABYLONIAN CAPTIVITY), which would add credence to the theory that it is that menorah which is depicted on the Arch of Titus in Rome. The miracle of the oil, associated with the festival of Hanukkah (see under JEWISH HOLIDAYS), enabled the menorah (now called *Hanukkiah*) to remain an important ritual object even after the destruction of the second Temple. The miraculous burning of the menorah for eight days, at the rededication of the Temple by the Hasmoneans (165 BC), was perpetuated in the selection of an eight-branched menorah for use during that festival (see also MACCABEES). The menorah is the motif of the State of Israel.

**Menotti, Gian-Carlo** (məˌnotee), 1911–, Italian operatic composer. In 1946 his melodrama *The Medium* was tremendously popular in New York City. His major works include *The Old Maid and the Thief* (1939) and *Amahl and the Night Visitors* (1951), both written for radio broadcast; *The Saint of Bleecker Street* (1954); *Tamu-Tamu* (1973); and other operas with dramatic impact and skilful use of music to heighten effects. In 1958 he founded the Festival of Two Worlds at Spoleto, Italy.

**Menshevism:** see BOLSHEVISM AND MENSHEVISM.

**Menshikov, Aleksandr Danilovich, Prince** (ˌmenshikəf), 1672?–1729, Russian field marshal and statesman. Friend and chief advisor to PETER I, he held various governorships, becoming notorious for his financial misdeeds. On Peter's death (1725) he helped CATHERINE I (who had been his mistress before marrying Peter) to accede to the throne; he, however, became the real ruler. After the accession of PETER II (1727) he was removed from power and exiled to Siberia.

**menstruation,** periodic discharge of blood and fragments of the lining of the uterus from the vagina at intervals of about one month in women of childbearing age. In this cycle (menstrual cycle), the hormone OESTROGEN, secreted by the ovaries (egg-producing organs), first acts to thicken the lining (endometrium) of the uterus, or womb (the muscular organ that carries developing young). After 8 to 10 days the ovary releases an egg and begins to secrete the hormone PROGESTERONE. If the egg is fertilized, it will embed itself in the thick uterine lining. If the egg is not fertilized, the secretion of progesterone declines, and the lowered level of progesterone causes the uterine lining to be sloughed off. The menstrual cycle is the result of complex interactions between ovarian and pituitary hormones and the nervous system. Menstruation, which endures for about three to seven days, commences at puberty (about age 12 to 14) and ceases at the menopause (about age 45 to 50). In many societies considerable importance is attached to menstruation and menstrual fluids. Frequently contact with menstrual blood is seen as highly dangerous and polluting, particularly for men, and women during their periods are confined to special areas, not allowed to prepare food, etc. The time of first menstruation is in many societies the occasion for female initiation rites, the RITES DE PASSAGE which symbolize her entry to adult social life.

**mental handicap,** subnormal mental development, manifested from birth or early childhood, that may be caused by a variety of conditions. Although mental handicap can be diagnosed by significantly lower than normal scores on INTELLIGENCE tests, other characteristics such as social maturity and ability to sustain personal and social independence are now used to evaluate mental competence. Many mentally handicapped people achieve some language development, can be taught to perform manual

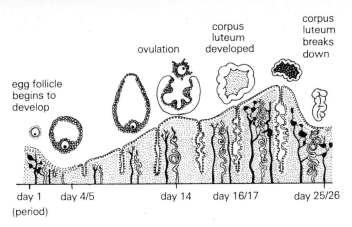

corpus luteum developed

ovulation

corpus luteum breaks down

egg follicle begins to develop

day 1 (period)  day 4/5  day 14  day 16/17  day 25/26

Menstruation

tasks of moderate complexity, and appear to lead fulfilled lives at home or in hospital. See also AUTISM; DOWN'S SYNDROME.

**mental illness:** see PSYCHIATRY.

**Menuhin, Sir Yehudi,** 1916–, British violinist; b. US. He made his debut in San Francisco at the age of 7 and has appeared around the world. In 1957 he initiated his own music festival at Gstaad, Switzerland, and in 1963 founded the Yehudi Menuhin School of Music in Surrey, England. Menuhin is an active promoter of Asian music and little-known works.

**Menzies, Sir Robert Gordon,** 1894–1978, Australian prime minister. In 1939 he succeeded Joseph Aloysius LYONS as leader of the United Australian Party and prime minister (1939–41) but resigned because of mounting criticism of his wartime leadership. In 1944 he established the Liberal Party and led it to victory in 1949. He subsequently held office as prime minister (1949–66) for a record term. He was knighted in 1963.

**Mephistopheles:** see FAUST.

**mercantilism,** an economic policy of the major trading nations during the 16th, 17th, and 18th cent., based on the premise that national wealth and power were best served by increasing exports and collecting precious metals in return. State action, an essential feature of the mercantile system, was used to accomplish its purposes to sell more than it bought in order to accumulate bullion and raw materials. Under a mercantilist policy, a government exercised much control over economic life by regulating production, encouraging foreign trade, levying duties on imports to gain revenue, making treaties to obtain exclusive trading privileges, and generally furthering business interests in the colonies. In England, HENRY VIII, ELIZABETH I, and Oliver CROMWELL pursued mercantilist policies; in France, J.B. COLBERT was the chief exponent. Superseding the medieval feudal organization in Western Europe, mercantilism did not decline until the coming of the INDUSTRIAL REVOLUTION and the doctrine of LAISSEZ-FAIRE.

**Mercator, Gerardus** (muh‚kaytə),Latin form of his real name, **Gerhard Kremer,** 1512–94, Flemish geographer, mathematician, and cartographer. He surveyed Flanders and made terrestrial and celestial globes. He was named (1552) to the chair of cosmography of Duisburg, Germany, where he subsequently lived. In 1568 his first map using the projection that bears his name appeared (see MAP PROJECTION). He began (1585) a great atlas, published (1594) by his son.

**Mercator map projection,** a cylindrical MAP PROJECTION of the features of the surface of the earth that can be constructed only mathematically. The parallels of LATITUDE, which on the globe are equal distances apart, are drawn with increasing separation as their distance from the EQUATOR increases in order to preserve shapes. However, the price paid for this is that areas are exaggerated with increasing distance from the equator. For instance, Greenland is shown with enormously exaggerated size, although its shape is preserved. The poles themselves cannot be shown on a Mercator projection. This type of projection gives an incorrect impression of the relative sizes of the world's countries.

**mercerization,** chemical treatment of cotton yarn to improve its characteristics for textile use. The process was discovered and developed by John Mercer in 1840. Yarn is run through a bath of concentrated caustic soda (sodium hydroxide) which contracts the fibre lengths and expands their diameters making them more circular in cross-section. The space between the fibres, the lumen, is also reduced. The shrinking in length also removes kinks so that the mercerized cotton pulls smoothly through needle eyes without snagging. If the cotton is under tension whilst being treated this enhances the process and gives lustre to the finished yarn. The action of sodium hydroxide on cotton also improves its ability to take dyes.

**merchant bank,** institution which owes its foundations to the business developed by merchants involved in overseas trade. The merchants' knowledge of trade enabled them to deal by means of bills of exchange which facilitated trade at a distance without the need to ship actual coin. Such transactions may be traced back to the 13th cent. Today merchant banks issue loans, provide risk capital, manage portfolios, and offer some of the services associated with commercial banks. They are also important as advisers to companies on MERGERS and takeovers.

**merchant navy,** commercial shipping, including general cargo vessels, bulk carriers, container ships and light carriers, tankers, ferries, and passenger vessels. Merchant ships are generally owned by companies or corporations, except in the USSR and other Communist countries where they are state-owned and allied to the navy. Merchant-navy vessels are registered by country of ownership, or often under a 'flag of convenience', e.g. to avoid stricter safety regulations or union rules governing crew pay. Consequently, Liberian and Panamanian registered ships together account for about a quarter of the tonnage of the world's merchant fleets. Japan, the next largest owner by flag, and the world's leading shipbuilder, has a 10% share. The total tonnage now stands at over 400 million tonnes, an increase of nearly a quarter over the previous decade. During that same period the tonnage on order has declined by one-third to less than 40 million tonnes, in recent years falling by as much as 1 million tonnes per quarter and resulting in the closures of shipyards in Europe and the UK. Japan, South Korea, China, Brazil, Yugoslavia, and Taiwan together make up the 'big six' of the world's shipbuilders, and account for three-quarters (by weight) of the ships being built, with the largest share, 20%, going to Japan. Japan also has the largest tonnage on order by flag ownership, over 100 ships weighing some 7 million tonnes and consisting mainly of dry-cargo ships, tankers, and bulk carriers.

**Mercia,** kingdom of Anglo-Saxon England, consisting generally of the area of the Midlands. An initial settlement (c.500) by the Angles in the Trent valley was extended by Penda (d.654).This hegemony was strengthened under OFFA (r.757–96), but declined after his death. The eastern part became (886) part of the DANELAW; the western part fell under the control of ALFRED of Wessex.

**mercury** (Hg), metallic element, known to the ancient Chinese, Hindus, and Egyptians; also called quicksilver. Silver-white and mirrorlike, it is the only common metal existing as a liquid at ordinary temperatures. Mercury is used in barometers, thermometers, electric switches, mercury-vapour lamps, and certain batteries; a mercury alloy, called an amalgam, is employed in dentistry. Mercury compounds have been used as insecticides, in rat poisons, and as disinfectants. Not easily discharged from the body, the metal is a cumulative poison; its inhalation or its ingestion in more than trace amounts in contaminated food or its absorption by the skin or mucous membranes results in **mercury poisoning**, which can cause damage to the nervous system, skin disorders, haemorrhage, liver and kidney damage, and gastrointestinal disturbances. Workers in many industries have been affected, and mercury POLLUTION of rivers, lakes, and oceans, usually through the discharge of industrial wastes, has become a serious environmental problem. In the early 1970s Minemata, Japan, suffered disaster when mercury-contaminated fish caused poisoning and deformities. In 1972 more than 90 nations approved an international ban on the dumping of mercury in the ocean, where the metal has tended to work its way into the food cycle of aquatic life and to reach dangerous levels in certain food fish, e.g., tuna. See ELEMENT (table); PERIODIC TABLE.

**Mercury,** in astronomy, nearest PLANET to the Sun, at a mean distance of 57.9 million km (36.0 million mi). It has a diameter of 4878 km (3031 mi), a cratered, lunarlike surface, and almost no atmosphere. Because its greatest ELONGATION is 28°, it can never be seen more than 2 hr after sunset or 2 hr before sunrise. The observed motion of Mercury's perihelion (closest point to the sun) is more, by 43″ each cent., than can be explained by planetary perturbations (see CELESTIAL MECHANICS) but is in nearly exact agreement with the prediction of the general theory of RELATIVITY. Mercury has no known satellites. The only SPACE PROBE to study Mercury was *Mariner 10,* which made three encounters in 1974–75.

Mercury photographed near greatest elongation (when the planet is at its furthest distance from the Sun as seen from Earth)

**Mercury,** in Roman mythology, god of commerce and messenger of the gods; identified with the Greek HERMES.

**mercury poisoning:** see under MERCURY.

**Meredith, George,** 1828–1909, English novelist and poet. His first distinguished novel, *The Ordeal of Richard Feverel* (1859), was followed by *Evan Harrington* (1860), *The Adventures of Harry Richmond,* (1871), *The Egoist* (1879), *Diana of the Crossways* (1885), and others. *Modern Love* (1862), a series of 50 poems, traces the dissolution of a marriage, and was followed by *Poems and Lyrics* (1883) which contained his 'Love in a Valley'. Written in a witty, oblique style, his works contain penetrating analyses of individual character and social institutions.

**Merezhkovsky, Dmitri Sergeyevich** (merish,kofskee), 1865–1941, Russian writer. Enormously influential in pre-Revolutionary Russia, he is best known for his study of TOLSTOY and DOSTOYEVSKY (1901–02) and for the philosophical novel trilogy *Christ and Antichrist* (1896–1905). With his wife, the poet Zinaida Gippius, he emigrated to Paris in 1918.

**merger,** the fusion of two or more companies either by creating a new organization through consolidation of the old companies, or by absorption by one of the others. Essentially a merger is by agreement as distinct from a takeover which may be against the wishes of one company. It may be a purchase or a pooling of interests. Where it is a purchase the larger company normally absorbs the smaller one and remains in managerial control. In the UK there were a large number of mergers in the 1960s and again in the run up to the 'BIG BANG' in 1986. Where a planned merger may result in a company taking more than one-third of the market, it may be referred to the MONOPOLIES AND MERGERS COMMISSION.

**Mérida,** city (1979 est. pop. 269,582), SE Mexico, capital of Yucatán state. Founded in 1542 on the site of Mayan city of Tihoo, it is the centre of an important agricultural region and the hub of the tourism attracted by the many famous surrounding Mayan archaeological sites, such as CHICHÉN-ITZÁ.

**meridian circle:** see TRANSIT INSTRUMENT.

**Mérimée, Prosper** (mayree,may), 1803–70, French author. His concise, understated style was most fully realized in such short novels as *Carmen* (1846, the basis for BIZET's opera) and *Colomba* (1852). His short story 'Mateo Falcone' (1829) is a masterpiece of the genre.

**meristem,** in plant anatomy, a zone of undifferentiated CELLS retained in the plant body and undergoing repeated divisions to produce new tissues.

**Merleau-Ponty, Maurice,** 1908–61, French philosopher. Influenced by Edmund HUSSERL, he advocated a form of PHENOMENOLOGY but, unlike most phenomenologists, affirmed the material reality of a world that transcends one's consciousness of it. In the 1940s and 50s he was sympathetic to the historical materialism of Karl MARX, but later he turned his attention to the study of language and meaning. His major works are *The Structure of Behavior* (1942) and *Phenomenology of Perception* (1945).

**mermaid,** in folklore, sea-dwelling creature commonly represented with the head and body of a woman, and a fishtail instead of legs. Beautiful, charming, and treacherous, they and their counterparts, mermen, have figured in legend from earliest times. Some regard the dugong (see SIRENIAN) as the original mermaid.

**Merman, Ethel,** 1909–84, American musical comedy star, noted for her booming voice; b. Ethel Zimmerman. Her greatest successes were *Annie Get Your Gun* (1946), *Call Me Madam* (1950), and *Gypsy* (1958).

**Merovingian art and architecture** ('merə,vinjeeən). Named after Merovech, founder of the first Germanic–Frankish dynasty (AD c.500–751), the Merovingian period was marked by a decline of classical tradition, and the absorption of a radically new element into the artistic mainstream—the abstract and brilliantly ornamental style of the nomadic barbarian tribes. Their art was confined to small, portable objects. The Central European and Eastern settlers introduced CLOISONNÉ and excelled at enamelwork and metalwork. Merovingian architecture, monumental sculpture, and painting, by contrast, were based on classical and Early Christian traditions. Little remains of the structures, but larger churches were said to be based on the basilican plan, with characteristic Merovingian timber roofs. Their most original device was the use of a bell TOWER. Merovingian stone sculpture simplified antique forms. Animal motifs were common, and manuscript ILLUMINATION elaborated initial letters based on animal forms, e.g., birds and fish. The human figure became an abstract sign.

**Merovingians,** dynasty of Frankish kings that flourished from the 5th cent. to 751. They traced their descent from the semilegendary Merovech, or Meroveus, chief of the Salian Franks. His grandson, CLOVIS I, founded the Frankish monarchy in 481. His descendants divided his domains into Austrasia, Neustria, AQUITAINE, BURGUNDY, Paris, and Orléans. These territories were often combined and sometimes reunited under a single Merovingian ruler. Dagobert I (c.612–c.639) was the last Merovingian to exercise personal power. His successors, the 'idle kings', left governing to the mayors of the palace, the CAROLINGIANS. In 751 PEPIN the Short deposed Childeric III, the last Merovingian king.

**Merrimack:** see MONITOR AND MERRIMACK.

**Mersey,** river in NW England, approximately 112 km (70 mi) long. Formed by the confluence of the rivers Goyt and Tame at Stockport, it flows W into the Irish Sea at LIVERPOOL, Merseyside. Its tributaries are the Irwell and Weaver rivers, and it is also joined by the MANCHESTER SHIP CANAL at Eastham. The estuary is approximately 26 km (16 mi) long, and an important shipping lane. The river is tidal up as far as WARRINGTON.

**Merseyside,** former metropolitan county in NW England (1984 est. pop. 1,460,700), 652 km² (254 sq mi), bordering on the Irish Sea in the W. It was formed in the local government reorganization of 1974 around LIVERPOOL and the Mersey estuary. It is mainly low-lying and heavily industrialized. It includes ST HELENS, BIRKENHEAD and Southport, and the Wirral peninsula. There are large dockland areas and much heavy industry, including chemical manufacture. The county council was abolished in April 1986 and the area is now administered by the borough and city councils.

**Mersin,** city (1980 pop. 216,306), capital of Mersin prov., S Turkey. As a port, Mersin succeeded TARSUS when the latter became silted in the Middle Ages. It handles the agricultural products of the plains around ADANA, exports metallic ores, and imports crude oil for its own oil refinery and related chemical industries.

**Merton,** London borough (1981 pop. 165,102), outer SW London. It comprises the districts of Merton and Morden and the former boroughs of Mitcham and Wimbledon. It is mainly residential, and contains the remains of a 12th-cent. Augustinian priory.

**mesa,** name given in the SW US to a small, isolated, flat-topped hill with two or more steep, usually perpendicular sides. Mesas are thought to have formed when a relatively hard rock layer protected those beneath it from the regional erosion that wore away the surrounding rock. The rock layers composing mesas are more or less horizontal. See also BUTTE.

**Meseta,** plateau, averaging over 600 m (1900 ft) which occupies the whole of central Spain. The northern and southern parts largely correspond with Old and New CASTILE and are separated by the Central Sierras. It is a dry region, traditionally given over to grain production, but has several ancient cities including VALLADOLID, SALAMANCA and TOLEDO.

**Mesolithic period,** or Middle Stone Age, phase of human cultural development beginning at the end of the last glacial era, over 10,000 years ago. It was a transitional period in which the PALAEOLITHIC form of hunting and gathering adaptation gave way to features that anticipated the NEOLITHIC several thousand years later, including gradual domestication of plants and animals, formation of settled communities, use of the bow, development of delicate stone microliths, and pottery. Many Mesolithic artifacts have been recovered from the North Sea, which was at that time a tract of marshy land.

**meson:** see ELEMENTARY PARTICLES.

**Mesopotamia** [Gr., = between rivers], ancient region of W Asia around the Tigris and Euphrates rivers, now in Iraq. Called the 'cradle of civilization,' the heart of the area was a plain rendered fertile in ancient times by canals. Settlements have been found in N Mesopotamia, which probably date from 5000 BC, and urban civilization later arose in S Mesopotamia in city states such as Erech and Ur (see SUMER). AKKAD emerged (c.2340 BC) as the region's first empire and was followed by BABYLONIA and ASSYRIA. Mesopotamia was still important in the Byzantine Empire and in the Abbasid caliphate, but the Mongols devastated the area in AD 1258. Today it is largely arid and barren, but its rich oil fields have international importance.

**Mesopotamian art and architecture.** The artistic traditions of ancient MESOPOTAMIA exerted a considerable influence on the culture of neighbouring regions. With few natural resources other than an abundance of clay, precious metals, stone, and wood had all to be imported; trade and conquest thus facilitated the diffusion of Mesopotamian art and culture, including the use of CUNEIFORM writing invented by the Sumerians before 3000 BC. In the first half of the third millenium BC, the models on which the foundations of classical Mesopotamian art were based were created by the Sumerians and the Semitic-speaking Akkadians. In turn, their essentially urban culture and its art was strongly influenced by the themes and styles of an earlier age (or, prehistoric and protoliterate art). This is well illustrated by a gypsum model of a cattle trough from Warka (ancient Erech) c.3000 BC. It shows sheep returning to the fold where their lambs are waiting; carved in low relief, it contains a representation of a reed-hut similar to those of the present-day Marsh Arabs. The sculpture, which is in the British Museum, is vigorously executed and may have come from the temple complex. A marble head of a woman, sculpted in the round, from the same site and now in the Iraq Museum, Baghdad, represents a major peak of Sumerian artistic achievement. Sumerian art and architecture is known to us from excavations at Warka, Kish, Lagash, Tell Asmar, Ur, Mari and elsewhere. From Ur a number of objects reveal the skill of Sumerian craftsmanship in the working of metal, semiprecious stones, and inlay. A fine example of Sumerian mosaic, 'The Standard of Ur', probably a sounding box, is decorated on four sides with shell, lapis lazuli, and red limestone, inlaid in bitumen; the two main sides depict scenes of war and peace, the end panels show rustic senes and mythical beasts. The whole is an animated execution of Sumerian life (British Museum). Votive sculptures from Tell Asmar representing tall, bearded figures with large, staring eyes and wearing pleated skirts, are splendid examples of the sculpture of these people. In architecture, the ZIGGURAT or temple tower was their most striking achievement. At Warka, the ziggurat extended over 50,000 m² (500,000 sq ft). The best-preserved ziggurat, at Ur, was built by Ur-Nammu (2112–2095 BC); the structure, which measures 60 × 40 m (190 × 130 ft), was cased with baked brick. The outer face was decorated with buttresses and the centre of the tower was a mass of

brickwork with layers of reed matting. The ziggurat stood on a high terrace, dominating the city, and originally it probably had three stages. It was dedicated to Nanna, the moon god and tutelary deity of the city. The miniature art of the cylinder seal is one of the most typical and commonly found objects in Mesopotamia and neighbouring regions. The engraver's technique varied greatly during the 3000 years in which the seal was in use, and there were some periods of superb engraving. The subject matter is varied, but typical are the scenes of contests, of heroic figures, deities and mythological figures. Under Sargon, king of Akkad, Mesopotamian rule extended beyond the bounds of Sumer and Akkad (southern Mesopotamia), and from this period comes a beautiful bronze head from Nineveh, thought to be his portrait (c.2300 BC; Iraq Museum, Baghdad). Following the destruction of Sargon's empire by invaders from the east, the city of Lagash survived; from this site several superb statues of its governor Gudea give an idea of the quality of the sculpture of this period, when Sumerian art underwent a renaissance (construction of Ur-Nammu ziggurat dates from this time). This last Sumerian era was brought to an end by Elamite and Amorite invasions. At the palace at Mari, on the Euphrates near the Syrian border, excavation has revealed the architecture, painting, and sculpture of an Amorite kingdom strongly influenced by the art and culture of its eastern Sumerian neighbours. In the 18th century BC Mesopotamia was dominated by Babylonia under Hammurapi; a carved diorite head in the Louvre (1792–1750 BC) is thought to be his portrait. From Mari, a sculpture of a fertility goddess (Aleppo Museum), holding a vase from which water flows down her skirt, attests to the genius of the Babylonian sculptor. Following the death of Hammurapi and the demise of his empire under his successors, Mesopotamia suffered a number of invasions. Generally known as a 'Dark Age', this period is gradually becoming better known. For more than four centuries Kassites ruled Babylonia. Though of non-Mesopotamian origin, they adopted the age-old conventions of the region, including the rebuilding of ancient temples. The outer wall of the Inanna temple of Kara-indash at Uruk is decorated in relief with deities holding the traditional flowing vase. The figures are, however, made of moulded baked brick, a characteristic feature of architectural ornament of the Kassite period. This moulded brick ornament was later perfected by the neo-Babylonian craftsmen into one of their most striking arts: polychrome-glazed brick walls modelled in relief. The great building works carried out at Babylon under the neo-Babylonian ruler Nebuchadrezzar made it the most magnificent city of its time. The great Ishtar gate and the Processional way were decorated with reliefs of lions, dragons, and bulls of superb workmanship (Berlin Museum). Less than a century later, Babylonia was invaded by the Persians, who were succeeded by Greeks and Romans. It was not until the 19th cent. that excavation brought to light the artistic achievements of the ancient Mesopotamians.

**Mesopotamian art and architecture:** One end of an early Sumerian limestone drinking trough, c.3000 BC, from Warka (ancient Erech).

**mesosphere:** see ATMOSPHERE.

**Mesozoic era:** see GEOLOGICAL ERA (table).

**mesquite,** spiny tree or shrub (genus *Prosopis*) of the PULSE family, native to tropical and subtropical regions. The seed pods of *P. juliflora*, the

Algaroba bean, contain an edible, sweet pulp that is used as forage and to make bread and a fermented drink; the durable wood is used for fence posts. Mesquite roots may penetrate 15m (50 ft) into the ground for water, enabling the plant to grow in sites unsuited to most crops.

**Messalina** (Valeria Messalina), d. AD 48, Roman empress, wife of CLAUDIUS I, who had her killed after a serious scandal in which she publicly married her lover.

**Messenia** (me,seeneeə), ancient region of SW GREECE, in the PELOPONNESUS, corresponding to modern Messinia. From the 8th cent. BC Messenia was engaged in a series of revolts against Spartan domination, and it was finally freed when THEBES defeated Sparta at the battle of Leuctra (371 BC). Excavation has revealed an important centre of MYCENAEAN CIVILIZATION at the Messenian city of PYLOS.

**Messiaen, Olivier** (mes,yahnh), 1908–, French composer and organist. He is a noted teacher and theorist. His works, all reflecting his religious mysticism, include *L'Ascension* (1935) and *Des canyons aux étoiles* (1974) for orchestra; *Le Banquet celeste* (1936), for organ; *Oiseaux exotiques*(1956); and *Turangalila* (1949), a symphony in 10 movements.

**Messiah** or **Messias** [Heb., = anointed], in Judaism, a man who is to be sent by God to restore Israel and reign righteously over all humanity. The idea developed among the Jews especially in adversity; self-proclaimed messiahs, e.g., SABBATAI ZEVI and Jacob FRANK, always attracted some followers. Jewish Messianic expectations generally focused on a kingly figure of the house of DAVID who would be born in Bethlehem. JESUS may have considered himself, and is generally considered by Christians, to be the Messiah promised by the Bible; the name *Christ* is Greek for 'Messiah.' Expectation of a redeemer is also found in some ancient Middle Eastern texts and among Buddhists, Zoroastrians, Confucians, and Muslims (see MAHDI).

**Messier catalogue,** systematic list of 103 nebulous celestial objects published (1771, 1780, 1781) by the French astronomer Charles Messier. Of these, 33 were identified by later observers as galaxies, 55 as star clusters, and 11 as true nebulae within our galaxy; the 4 others are a double star; an asterism, or small group of stars; a patch of the Milky Way; and a duplicate observation. Objects on the list include the CRAB NEBULA (M1) and the ANDROMEDA GALAXY (M31).

**Messina,** city (1984 pop. 265,772), Sicily, Italy, on the Strait of Messina. It has a protected harbour and acts as ferry port to the mainland. Citrus fruits grown in the area are exported. Founded by Greeks (as Zankle) in the 8th cent. BC, it passed to Rome in 264 BC when it flourished as a trading port. The earthquake of 28 Dec. 1908, one of the worst ever recorded, devastated the city. Severe damage also took place during World War II.

**Messina, Straits of,** channel separating the island of Sicily from mainland Italy. 32 km (20 mi) long and varying in width from 3.2 km (2 mi) to 16 km (10 mi), it connects the Tyrrhenian and Ionian Seas. Coastal rocks and whirlpools in the Straits gave rise to the Greek legends of Scylla and Charybdis.

**metabolism,** sum of all living processes in living systems. Two subcategories of metabolism are anabolism, the building up of organic molecules from simpler ones, and catabolism, the breaking down of complex substances, often accompanied by the release of energy. Thus the energy required for anabolism is obtained from catabolic reactions. Basal metabolism, the heat produced by an organism at rest, represents the minimum amount of energy required to maintain life at normal body temperature.

**metal,** chemical ELEMENT displaying certain properties, notably metallic lustre, the capacity to lose electrons and form a positive ION, and the ability to conduct heat and electricity (see CONDUCTION), by which it is normally distinguished from a nonmetal. The metals comprise about two thirds of the known elements (such as iron, aluminium, gold, silver). Some elements, e.g., arsenic and antimony, exhibit both metallic and nonmetallic properties, and are called metalloids. Metals fall into groups in the PERIODIC TABLE determined by similar arrangements of the orbital electrons and a consequent similarity in chemical properties. Such groups include the ALKALI METALS (Group Ia in the periodic table), the ALKALINE-EARTH METALS (Group IIa), and the RARE-EARTH METALS (LANTHANIDE SERIES and ACTINIDE SERIES). Most metals other than the alkali metals and the alkaline-earth metals are called transition metals (see TRANSITION ELEMENTS). The oxidation states, or valencies (see VALENCY), of the metal ions vary from +1 for the alkali metals to +7 for some transition metals. Chemically, the metals differ from the nonmetals in that they form positive ions and basic oxides and hydroxides. Upon exposure to moist air, a great many metals undergo corrosion, i.e., enter into a chemical reaction, the oxygen of the atmosphere uniting with the metal to form the oxide of the metal, e.g., rust on exposed iron. See also ALLOY; METALLURGY.

**metalloid:** see METAL; PERIODIC TABLE.

**metallurgy,** science of extracting metals from their ores. The processes employed depend upon the chemical nature of the ORE to be treated and upon the properties of the METAL to be extracted. When an ore has a low percentage of the desired metal, a method of physical concentration, e.g., the FLOTATION PROCESS, must be used before the extraction process begins. Because almost all metals are found combined with other elements in nature, chemical reactions are required to set them free. These chemical processes are classified as *pyrometallurgy,* the use of heat for the treatment of an ore, e.g., in SMELTING and roasting; *electrometallurgy,* the preparation of certain active metals by ELECTROLYSIS; and *hydrometallurgy,* or leaching, the selective dissolution of metals from their ores. Modern metallurgical research is concerned with preparing radioactive metals, with obtaining metals economically from low-grade ores, with obtaining and refining rare metals hitherto not used, and with formulating ALLOYS.

**metamorphic rock:** see METAMORPHISM; ROCK.

**metamorphism,** in geology, process of change in the structure, texture, or composition of ROCKS caused by heat, deforming pressure, and/or hot, chemically active fluids. In general, metamorphic rock is coarser, denser, and less porous than the rock from which it was formed. The change in texture commonly results in a rearrangement of MINERAL particles into a parallel alignment called foliation, probably the most characteristic property of metamorphic rocks; it is seen in SLATE, SCHIST, and GNEISS. Local metamorphism is usually caused by the intrusion of a mass of igneous rock into older rock. Regional metamorphism accompanies mountain-building activity associated with large-scale crustal movements.

**metamorphosis,** in zoology, a term used for the changes in body form during development from egg to adult. For example, in the BUTTERFLY an active grub-like caterpillar (larva) hatches from the egg (ovum) and then passes through a series of growth stages (instars), each ending in a moult (ecdysis). At the end of the last larval instar, when fully grown, it changes into a chrysalis (pupa) which is outwardly inactive but undergoes major changes in internal organization. Thus when the insect emerges it has become transformed into its adult stage (imago), a butterfly. Metamorphosis is called complete when, as in the butterfly, the larva is very different from the adult and the two are separated by a distinct pupal stage. In incomplete metamorphosis, the larval (nymphal) stages generally resemble the adult (e.g., GRASSHOPPER) and there is no true pupal stage. Insects having complete metamorphosis include the ANT, BEETLE, and FLY; incomplete metamorphosis occurs in the APHID, COCKROACH, and CRICKET.

**metaphysical poets,** name first used by Samuel JOHNSON (1744) for a group of 17th-cent. English lyric poets. Their hallmark is the metaphysical conceit (employing unusual and paradoxical images), wit, learned imagery, and subtle argument. Most important were John DONNE, George HERBERT, Henry VAUGHAN, Abraham COWLEY, Richard CRASHAW, and Andrew MARVELL. They influenced 20th-cent. modernist poetry.

**metaphysics,** branch of philosophy concerned with the ultimate nature of existence. Ontology (the study of the nature of being), cosmology, and philosophical theology are usually considered its main branches. The term comes from the metaphysical treatises of ARISTOTLE, who presented the First Philosophy (as he called it) after the *Physics* [Gk. *meta-physica* = after physics]. Metaphysical systems in the history of philosophy have included Aristotelian SCHOLASTICISM and the rationalistic systems of the 17th cent. (e.g., those of DESCARTES, SPINOZA, and LEIBNIZ). KANT, in the 18th cent., held scientific metaphysical speculation to be an impossibility but considered metaphysical questions a moral necessity. His work influenced that of FICHTE, SCHELLING, and HEGEL.

**Metastasio, Pietro,** 1698–1782, Italian poet and librettist. He became court poet at Vienna in 1729 and continued the efforts of his predecessor, Apostolo Zeno, to reform the *melodramma* or heroic opera (see OPERA). The most celebrated Italian dramatist of his time, his *Attilio Regolo* (1750)

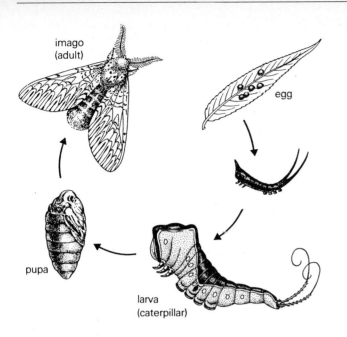

imago
(adult)

egg

pupa

larva
(caterpillar)

Metamorphosis

is usually held to the most dramatically valid of his librettos. The innumerable settings of his works include MOZART's *Clemenza di Tito* (1791).

**Metaxas, Joannis,** 1871–1941, Greek general and dictator. A longtime royalist, he became premier in 1935 when the monarchy was restored under GEORGE II. He dissolved (1936) parliament, declared (1938) himself premier for life, and instituted a reactionary dictatorship. At his death he was defending Greece against an Italian invasion.

**Metchnikoff, Élie,** 1845–1916, Russian microbiologist. He introduced the theory of phagocytosis, i.e., that certain white blood cells can engulf and destroy harmful substances such as bacteria. For his work on immunity he shared with Paul EHRLICH the 1908 Nobel Prize for physiology or medicine. He also developed a theory that lactic-acid bacteria in the digestive tract could prolong life. He conducted his research at the Univ. of Odessa, the Italian seaport of Messina, and the Pasteur Inst., Paris.

**Metellus,** ancient Roman family of the plebeian gens Caecilia. It was one of the families that controlled the senate. **Quintus Caecilius Metellus Macedonicus,** d. 115 BC, conquered (148 BC) Macedonia and pacified (146 BC) Greece. **Quintus Caecilius Metellus Numidicus,** d. 91? BC, a leader of the senatorial party and consul (109 BC), conducted the Numidian War against Jugurtha. He antagonized Marius and was exiled (100 BC). His son, **Quintus Caecilius Metellus Pius,** d. c.63 BC, continued his father's opposition to Marius. In 89 BC he fought in the Social War and in the civil war that followed defended Rome against Marius and Lucius Cornelius CINNA. In 83 BC Metellus joined SULLA and defeated the Marians in Umbria and Cisalpine Gaul. He warred unsuccessfully (79–72 BC) against Sertorius in Spain.

**meteor,** small piece of extraterrestrial matter that becomes visible as a 'shooting star' or 'falling star' when it enters the Earth's atmosphere. While still outside the atmosphere, it is called a meteoroid. As a meteor it is heated to incandescence through friction (due to collisions with air molecules) and usually disintegrates completely before reaching the earth; those meteors large enough to reach the ground are called METEORITES. A meteor of considerable duration and brightness is known as a fireball; a fireball that explodes in the air is called a bolide. The frequency of meteors increases when the Earth, in its orbit, passes through a swarm of particles generated from the breakup of a comet. The meteors of such a **meteor shower** all appear to originate at a single point, or radiant, in the sky. Some of the better-known showers (named after the constellations in which their radiants are located) and their approximate dates are: Lyrids, 21 Apr.; Perseids, 12 Aug.; Orinoids, 20 Oct.; Taurids, 4 Nov.; Leonids, 16 Nov.; Geminids, 13 Dec.

**meteorite,** large METEOR that survives the intense heat of atmospheric friction and reaches the earth's surface. Meteorites may have originated as fragments of asteroids. They are classified in three general categories. The siderites, or irons, are composed entirely of metal (chiefly nickel and iron). The aerolites, or stony meteorites, show a diversity of mineral elements including large percentages of silicon and magnesium oxides; the most abundant type of aerolite is the chondrite, so called because the metal embedded in it is in the form of grainlike lumps, or chondrules. The siderolites, or stony irons, which are rarer than the other types, are of both metal and stone in varying proportions. It is difficult to find fallen meteorites, unless they differ greatly from their surroundings (e.g., siderites on rocky ground, or any meteorite in the icy wastes of Antarctica). When a meteorite reaches the Earth, the tremendous force of impact with the Earth's surface causes great compression, heating, and partial vaporization of the outer part of the meteorite and of the materials in the ground; expansion of the gases thus formed and of steam produced from groundwater causes an explosion that shatters the meteorite and carves out a **meteorite crater** in the ground. One of the best-preserved craters is Meteor, or Barringer, Crater, near Winslow, Arizona, c.1½ km (¾ mi) in diameter and 180 m (600 ft) deep. The largest meteorite discovered, the 60-ton Hoba West, rests where it was found (in 1920), near Grootfontein, Namibia.

**meteorology,** branch of science that deals with the ATMOSPHERE of a planet, particularly that of the earth. Meteorology is based on the accurate scientific measurement of various atmospheric conditions with a wide assortment of instruments. Air temperature is measured with the THERMOMETER; air pressure with the BAROMETER; wind direction with the weather vane; wind speed with the anemometer; high-altitude air-pressure and wind information with the WEATHER BALLOON; relative humidity with the HYGROMETER; precipitation with the rain gauge; and cloud formations and weather fronts with both radar and high-altitude WEATHER SATELLITES. The meteorologist combines the data collected from many geographical locations into a weather map. On a typical map the various weather elements are shown by figures and symbols. Isobars are drawn to show areas of equal pressure, and FRONTS and areas of precipitation are also indicated. Meteorologists analyse the data collected and illustrated on the weather map in order to predict, or forecast, the WEATHER for the next few hours and the next few days. Long-range weather forecasts, which are more general and less accurate, are also made for future periods of several months.

**methadone,** synthetic NARCOTIC, similar in effect to MORPHINE, used primarily in the treatment of drug addiction. Given to addicts, as a substitute for HEROIN, it causes the same problems of dependence as heroin. Methadone is also used an an ANALGESIC, especially in patients who are terminally ill.

**methanal:** see FORMALDEHYDE.

**methane** ($CH_4$), colourless, odourless, gaseous HYDROCARBON formed by the decay of plant and animal matter. It occurs naturally as the chief component of NATURAL GAS, as the firedamp of coal mines, and as the marsh gas released in swamps and marshes. Methane can also be made synthetically by various means. It is combustible and can form explosive mixtures with air. Used for fuel in the form of natural gas, methane is also an important starting material for making solvents and certain fluorocarbons (see FREON). In New Zealand, methane from large reserves of natural gas is burnt to a mixture of carbon monoxide and hydrogen which is then catalytically converted to METHANOL. This is in turn converted to petrol.

**methanol, methyl alcohol** or **wood alcohol** ($CH_3OH$), a colourless, flammable liquid and the simplest ALCOHOL. Methanol is a fatal poison. Small internal doses, prolonged exposure of the skin to the liquid, or continued inhalation of the vapour may cause blindness. It can be obtained from wood, but now is made synthetically from the direct combination of hydrogen and carbon monoxide gases. Methanol is used to make FORMALDEHYDE, as a solvent, and as an ANTIFREEZE, and can be converted to petrol over a zeolitic catalyst, a process carried out commercially in New Zealand.

**Methodism,** the doctrines, polity, and worship of those Protestant denominations that have developed from the movement started in England by the teaching of John WESLEY. He, with his brother Charles, George WHITEFIELD, and others, formed (1729) a group at Oxford that met for religious exercises. From their resolution to conduct their lives and study by 'rule and method', they were given the name Methodists.

Influenced by the Moravians, the Wesleys began (1738) evangelistic preaching, often in barns, houses, and open fields. The moving of preachers from one appointment to another was the beginning of the system of itinerancy. John Wesley was essentially a follower of Jacobus ARMINIUS, but Whitefield was unable to accept Arminian doctrine and broke away (1741) to form the Calvinistic Methodists. The first annual conference (1744) drew up the Articles of Religion, which stressed repentance, faith, sanctification, and full, free salvation for all. The group adopted a constitution in 1784 and withdrew from the Church of England in 1791 to become the Wesleyan Methodist Church. In America Methodism began after 1766 in New York with the preaching of Philip Embury and spread rapidly under Francis ASBURY. The first conference was held in 1773, and the Methodist Episcopal Church in America was formed in 1784. In both England and the US, Methodists splintered into many groups, but significant progress toward unity has been made in the 20th cent. In the early 1980s there were about 500,000 Methodists in the UK, over 11 million in the US (the second-largest Protestant denomination), and over 20 million worldwide.

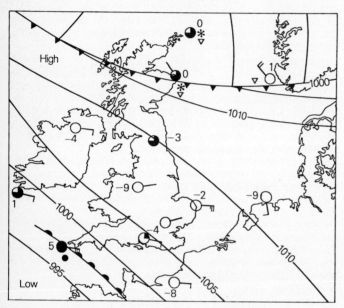

**Methodius, Saint:** see CYRIL AND METHODIUS, SAINTS.

**Methuselah** (mi,thyoohzələ), descendant of Seth; son of ENOCH. The BIBLE says he lived 969 years. Gen. 5.21–27.

**methyl orange:** see INDICATORS, ACID–BASE.

**metre:** see METRIC SYSTEM; WEIGHTS AND MEASURES (table).

**metric system,** system of weights and measured planned in France and adopted there in 1799. Now used by most of the technologically developed countries of the world, it is based on a unit of length called the metre (m) and a unit of mass called the kilogram (kg). The metre is now defined in terms of a reproducible, universally available atomic standard, being equal to 1,650,763.73 wavelengths of the red-orange light given off by the krypton-86 isotope under certain conditions. The kilogram is defined as the mass of the International Prototype Kilogram, a platinum-iridium cylinder kept at Sèvres, France, near Paris. Other metric units can be defined in terms of the metre and the kilogram (see WEIGHTS AND MEASURES, table). Fractions and multiples of the metric units are related to each other by powers of 10, allowing conversion from one unit to a multiple of it simply by shifting a decimal point. This avoids the lengthy arithmetical operations required by other systems, such as the foot-pound-second system or imperial units (ENGLISH UNITS OF MEASUREMENT). Prefixes have been accepted for designating multiples and fractions of the metre, the gram ($= \frac{1}{1000}$ kilogram), and other units. Several other systems of units based on the metric system have been in wide use. The cgs system (now very rarely used) has the centimetre ($= \frac{1}{100}$ metre) of length, the gram of mass, and the SECOND of time as its fundamental units; other cgs units are the dyne of FORCE and the erg of WORK or energy. The mks system uses the metre of length, the kilogram of mass, and the second of time as its fundamental units; other mks units include the newton of force, the joule of work or energy, and the watt of POWER. The units of the mks system are generally much larger and of a more practical size than the comparable units of the cgs system. ELECTRIC AND MAGNETIC UNITS have been defined for both of these systems. The International System of Units (officially called the Système International d'Unités, or SI) is a system of units adopted by the 11th General Conference on Weights and Measures (1960) and now used internationally for practically all scientific and technical purposes. Its basic units of length, mass, and time are those of the mks system; the other basic units are the AMPERE of electric current, the kelvin of temperature (a degree of temperature measured on the Kelvin TEMPERATURE scale), the candela (see PHOTOMETRY) of luminous intensity, and the MOLE, used to measure the amount of a substance present. All other units are derived from these basic units and from two supplementary geometrical units, the radian, used to measure plane angle, and the steradian, used to measure solid angle.

**Metropolitan Museum of Art,** New York City, the foremost art museum in the US; founded 1870, opened 1880. Owned by the city, it is largely supported by private endowment. The museum's most outstanding collections include European paintings and sculpture of the Renaissance, Baroque, and modern periods. It has extensive Egyptian holdings, e.g., the Temple of Dendur, and a vast collection of Oriental works. Much of its collection of medieval art is housed at the CLOISTERS. Its American Wing contains a comprehensive array of US arts and crafts of all periods, its Costume Institute includes thousands of authentic costumes and accessories, and its Michael C. Rockefeller Wing houses a large collection of primitive art. The museum is also known for its collections of Greek pottery, Greek and Roman sculpture, and graphic arts.

**Metropolitan Opera Company,** The original opera house was on West 39th Street, where the first presentation (22 Oct. 1883) was a performance of GOUNOD's *Faust*. In 1966 the Met moved to Lincoln Centre for the Performing Arts, opening with a performance of Samuel BARBER's *Antony and Cleopatra*. A galaxy of great stars has sung at the Met, e.g., Enrico CARUSO, Kirsten FLAGSTAD, Feodor CHALIAPIN, Maria CALLAS, Joan SUTHERLAND, and Luciano PAVAROTTI. Conductors of the opera orchestra have included Gustav MAHLER and Arturo TOSCANINI. The Met features weekly live radio broadcasts and a yearly national tour.

**Metsu** or **Metzu, Gabriel** (,metsy), 1629?–67, Dutch GENRE painter. He is best known for his charming bourgeois interiors. His fine draftsmanship

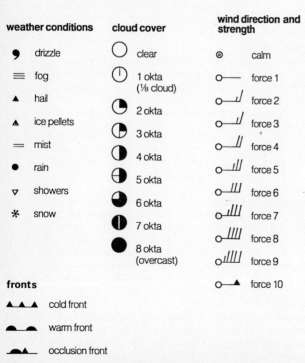

**weather conditions**

🌢 drizzle
≡ fog
▲ hail
▲ ice pellets
= mist
● rain
▽ showers
✳ snow

**cloud cover**

○ clear
◔ 1 okta (⅛ cloud)
◔ 2 okta
◑ 3 okta
◑ 4 okta
◕ 5 okta
◕ 6 okta
◕ 7 okta
● 8 okta (overcast)

**wind direction and strength**

◎ calm
force 1
force 2
force 3
force 4
force 5
force 6
force 7
force 8
force 9
force 10

**fronts**

▲▲▲ cold front
●●● warm front
▲●▲ occlusion front

Meteorology: A typical weather map showing a very frosty day (temperatures are in degrees Celsius) and exquisite handling of light and texture can be seen in *Music Lesson* (The Hague) and *The Letter Reader* (c.1665; Bert Coll., Blessington, Ireland).

**Metsys, Quentin:** see MASSYS, QUENTIN.

**Metternich, Clemens Wenzel Nepomuk Lothar, Fürst von** (ˌmetənikh), 1773–1859, Austrian statesman. He became foreign minister in 1809 and secured (1812) a temporary alliance with France. Later he developed a policy of substituting Austrian for French supremacy, and Austria joined the QUADRUPLE ALLIANCE (1814). Staunchly conservative, he was one of the guiding spirits at the Congress of VIENNA (1814–15) and succeeding European congresses. Indeed, the period 1815–48 has been called the Age of Metternich. He sought to maintain a balance of power in Europe, and to make Austria supreme in Italy and in the newly formed GERMAN CONFEDERATION. His system depended on censorship, a supply of information through espionage, and the suppression of liberal revolutionary and nationalist movements in Austria and abroad. He was forced from office by the REVOLUTIONS OF 1848.

**Metz,** city (1982 pop. 118,502, agglomeration 186,437), capital of Moselle dept., E France, on the Moselle R. It is principally a centre of administration, trade and other services. Originally a large Roman settlement, it became one of the three bishoprics of Lorraine in the Middle Ages. Strong fortifications were erected in 1728 when it became a military headquarters. The city was a part of the German Empire (1871–1918). It retains medieval buildings including the Gothic cathedral with its famous stained-glass windows.

**Metzinger, Jean,** 1883–1956, French painter and writer. His paintings employ cubist faceting that is never wholly abstract. He was a founding member of the SECTION D'OR. With GLEIZES he wrote *Du cubisme* (1912) (see CUBISM).

**Metzu, Gabriel:** see METSU, GABRIEL.

**Meunier, Constantin** (mønˌyay), 1831–1905, Belgian sculptor and painter. His works express the dignity of labour. He is best known for his bronze reliefs and monuments, e.g., the unfinished *Monument of Labour* (1901; Brussels), which includes reliefs, statues, and a group, *Maternity*.

**Meuse** or **Maas,** river, one of the chief waterways of N Europe, c.900 km (560 mi) long. It rises in NE France, flows through an important mining and industrial region of Belgium, and into the S Netherlands, where it branches out to form a common delta with the RHINE R.

**Mexicali,** city (1979 est. pop. 348,528), NW Mexico, capital of Baja California state. It is the centre of an agricultural area and a resort town located across the US border from Calexico, California.

**Mexican art and architecture,** were highly developed before the Spanish Conquest. The tenets of art introduced by the 'Conquistadors' were initially strictly upheld in an attempt to eradicate signs of pagan worship. However, as native artisans became proficient in newly introduced techniques such as oil on canvas, wax working and sculpting Christian themes in wood and stone, they began to produce a unique blend of European and indigenous styles. Baltasar de Echave the elder (1548–1620) might be considered the foremost Hispanic painter of the era and had great influence on later indigenous painters. Contemporary architects working in the Renaissance style include Fransisco Becerra and Juan de Vtrera. The purist style of early cathedrals coexisted with the more decorative expression of the PLATERESQUE style, which was often Indian in character. In the 17th cent. a degeneration of the Classical style can be seen. Mexican Baroque was free from the purist repression evident in contemporary Spain. It displays a particular exuberance and richness of colour, especially in the gilded wood and stucco interiors of the churches. The iconography and depiction of saints is often distinctly Indian. The term Churriqueresque (named after José CHURRIGUERA) describes the exaggerated ornamental style found in 18th-cent. Mexico, which reflected the brilliance and prosperity of the times. José Ibarra and Miguel Cabrera were renowned 18th-cent. painters, whose work avoids the sentimentality of many of their contemporaries. In the 19th cent. José Maria VELASCO was a celebrated landscape artist. The satirical prints of José Guadalupe POSADA reflect the growing social discord. In 1864 with the arrival of the French under MAXIMILIAN, the heavy splendour of French Second Empire architecture became dominant, remaining so until 1876 when Porfirio Diaz came to power. After the 1910 revolution, it is this spirit which manifests itself in art, the most famous examples being the murals of Diego RIVERA and José Clemente OROZCO. Rufino Tamayo is an outstanding abstract artist. In recent times a resurrection of pre-Columbian iconography and a growing respect for indigenous arts is reflected both in nationalistic murals such as those in the University of Mexico City and also in the government policy to support the production of traditional crafts such as pottery, textiles, metal-working, and stone carving.

**Mexican art and architecture:** Insurgentes Theatre – Murals of Diego de Rivera, Mexico City.

**Mexican War,** 1846–48, armed conflict between the US and Mexico. The immediate cause of the war was the US annexation of TEXAS (Dec. 1845); other factors included the existence of long-standing claims by US citizens against MEXICO and the American ambition to acquire CALIFORNIA. In 1845 Pres. Polk sent John Slidell to Mexico to purchase California and New Mexico. When the mission failed, Polk prepared for war, and in Mar. 1846 Gen. Zachary TAYLOR occupied Point Isabel, on the Rio Grande. This was viewed as an act of aggression by the Mexicans, who claimed the Nueces R. as the boundary, and Mexican troops crossed the Rio Grande and shelled (3 May) Fort Brown. Polk pronounced these actions an invasion of American soil, and the US declared war on 13 May 1846. In the final campaign of the war, Gen. Winfield SCOTT captured Veracruz (Mar. 1847), defeated Gen. SANTA ANNA at Cerro Gordo (April), and stormed CHAPULTEPEC. On 14 Sept. 1847, American troops entered Mexico City, where they remained until peace was restored. The Treaty of GUADALUPE HIDALGO (2 Feb. 1848) ended the war. Mexico ceded two-fifths of its territory to the US and received an indemnity of $15 million.

**Mexico,** officially United Mexican States, republic (1985 est. pop. 79,100,000), 1,972,544 km² (761,600 sq mi), S North America; bordered by the US (N), the Gulf of Mexico and the Caribbean Sea (E), Belize and Guatemala (SE), and the Pacific Ocean (W). Principal cities include MEXICO CITY (the capital), GUADALAJARA, and MONTEREY. The country is predominantly mountainous, and no more than 15% of the land is considered arable. There is lowland in the SE and along the coasts, but the heart of the country is the extensive Mexican plateau, with elevations generally above 1220 m (4000 ft). Fringed by the ranges of the SIERRA MADRE, the plateau (except for the arid north) is a region of broad, shallow lakes where more than half of the country's population is concentrated. To the S is a chain of extinct volcanoes, including POPOCATÉPETL, Ixtacihuatl, and ORIZABA, which at 5700 m (18,700 ft) is Mexico's highest point. Since World War II Mexico has enjoyed considerable economic growth, and industry and commerce now account for more than 50% of the national product. Agriculture, however, continues to engage more than half the work force, which, despite major irrigation projects that have increased yields, often farms by old, inefficient methods. Cotton, coffee, sugar, and tomatoes are the major agricultural export crops, and much maize, wheat, beans, and citrus fruits are grown. Mexico has considerable mineral resources (including vast petroleum reserves, discovered in the mid-1970s); recently crude petroleum and natural gas have accounted for two-thirds of total exports. Other mineral exports include zinc, sulphur, silver, antimony, copper, and manganese. Tourism is important. Industries, usually in or near the larger cities, produce iron and steel, motor vehicles, processed foods, refined petroleum and petrochemicals, chemical fertilizers, and many other products. By 1983 the total value of exports was three times greater than the cost of a much reduced volume of imports, but by mid-1985 servicing an external debt of US$96,000 million presented severe problems for Mexico's balance of payments. In 1984 GDP was US$175 thousand million or US$2231 per capita. The population has grown rapidly in the 20th cent., more than tripling between 1940 and 1980. The great majority of the people are of mixed Spanish and Indian descent, but a sizable minority are pure Indian. The official language is Spanish, but many Indians still speak only Indian tongues. Over 95% of the people are Roman Catholic.

*History.* Before the arrival of the Spanish in the early 16th cent., great Indian civilizations (the AZTEC, MAYA, TOLTEC, MIXTEC, Zapotec, and OLMEC) flourished in Mexico. Arriving in 1519, Hernán CORTÉS overthrew the Aztec empire (1521) and captured its ruler, MONTEZUMA. The territory became the viceroyalty of New Spain in 1535. The Spanish conquerors exploited the mineral wealth of the land, using as labourers the Indians and a growing mestizo class; at the same time they extended Spanish rule to the remainder of Mexico and to what is now the southwestern US. A rebellion led (1810–15) by Miguel HIDALGO Y COSTILLA failed, but in 1821 Spain accepted Mexican independence, and an 'empire', headed by Augustín de ITURBIDE, was established in 1822. In 1823 army officers overthrew the empire and established a federal republic. The early years were marked by turmoil and corruption. Texas broke free of Mexican rule in 1836, and in the ensuing MEXICAN WAR (1846–48) with the US, Mexico lost much territory. Internally, the republic was torn by strife among contending political leaders, and in 1855 a democratic reform movement, led by Benito JUÁREZ, overthrew the dictatorship of Antonio López de SANTA ANNA and drafted a liberal constitution. Civil war followed, and in 1864 NAPOLEON III of France, who had colonial ambitions, established another ill-starred Mexican empire, under the Habsburg prince MAXIMILIAN; it collapsed in 1867, and Maximilian was killed. Then followed the long reformist dictatorship of Porfirio DÍAZ, who ruled Mexico with a firm hand for most of the 35 years after 1876. Díaz promoted economic growth and provided a degree of stability, but his encouragement of the concentration of wealth in the hands of a few spawned a new generation of revolutionaries. Among these were Emiliano ZAPATA, Francisco 'Pancho' VILLA (whose raid into the US in 1916 resulted in a brief retaliatory US invasion of Mexico), and Francisco I. MADERO, who toppled Díaz in 1911 but was himself overthrown and murdered in 1913. A foundation for reform was laid by Venustiano CARRANZA's constitution of 1917. In 1929 Plutarco Elías CALLES founded the National Revolutionary Party (renamed the Institutional Revolutionary Party, or PRI, in 1946), which has governed Mexico ever since. During the presidency of Lázaro CÁRDENAS (1934–40), land was redistributed, illiteracy reduced, power projects initiated, and some industries nationalized. Cárdenas's successors have tended to stress industrial development, which has benefited the middle and upper classes but has left most of Mexico's rapidly growing population at or below the subsistence level. In 1982 the faltering economy caused the government to devalue the peso and nationalize the banks. In inter-American affairs, Mexico had by the early 1980s become a major moderating influence, having long maintained good relations with both the US and Cuba. The 1982 presidential election was won by Miguel DE LA MADRID HURTADO and congressional elections in 1985 resulted in a further overwhelming large majority for the ruling party. In 1988 Carlos SALINAS DE GORTARI (also of the PRI) was elected president, although by a much smaller margin than his predecessors. In the 1980s insurgent activities of extreme left and right declined considerably as compared with the 1970s.

## Post-war Mexican presidents
Miguel Alemán (PRI), 1946–52
Adolfo Ruíz Cortines (RPI), 1952–58
Adolfo López Mateos (PRI), 1958–64
Gustavo Díaz Ordaz (PRI), 1964–70
Luis Echeverría Alvarez (PRI), 1970–76
José López Portillo (PRI), 1976–82
Miguel de la Madrid Hurtado (PRI), 1982–88
Carlos Salinas de Gortari (PRI), 1988–

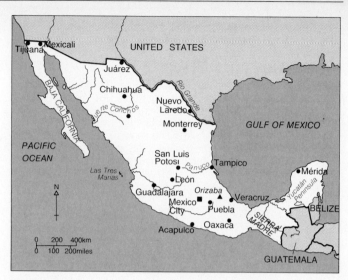

Mexico

**Mexico, Gulf of,** arm of the Atlantic Ocean, c.1,813,000 km² (700,000 sq mi), off SE North America. Oil and natural gas occur along the coast and offshore on the continental shelf. TAMPA, Pensacola, Mobile, NEW ORLEANS, Galveston, and CORPUS CHRISTI are major US ports; TAMPICO and VERACRUZ are important Mexican ports.

**Mexico City,** city (1979 est. pop. 9,191,295), central Mexico, capital and largest city of Mexico. Since 1940 Mexico City has grown more rapidly than any other urban region in the world, creating suburbs such as NETZAHUALCÓ YOTL (1979 est. pop. 2,331,351) which have become major towns in their own right. In 1985 it was estimated that 18 million lived in the urban area of Mexico City, making it second only to Tokyo–Yokohama among the world's most populous conurbations. Mexico City is on the Mexican plateau, in the Valley of Mexico, at an elevation of c.2400 m (7800 ft), and is ringed by mountains. It is the nation's political, cultural, and commercial hub and its main centre of both light and heavy industry. The oldest part of the city surrounds a large central plaza from which wide avenues radiate to the environs. Structures such as a 16th-cent. cathedral and the colonial-baroque National Palace (both on the plaza), 19th-cent. public buildings, skyscrapers, and the boldly modern University City reflect a rich, 400-year architectural heritage. Mexico City was founded soon after the conquest of Mexico (1521) at the site of the AZTEC capital, Tenochtitlán, and was the capital of New Spain before Mexico's independence (1821). The city was captured (1847) by US troops during the MEXICAN WAR, was conquered (1863) by the French army, and was occupied (1914–15) by rebel forces during the Mexican Revolution. In 1957 an earthquake caused extensive damage to the capital. Mexico City was host to the 1968 OLYMPIC GAMES. Large-scale destruction of central districts of the city was caused by the 1985 earthquake.

**Meyer, Conrad Ferdinand,** 1825–98, Swiss poet and novelist. His historical novellas, e.g., *Die Hochzeit des Mönchs* (1884; tr. The Monk's Wedding), deal mainly with RENAISSANCE themes and show psychological insight and a concern for ethical problems.

**Meyerbeer, Giacomo,** 1791–1864, German operatic composer, noted for his spectacular French grand operas *Robert le Diable* (1831) and *Les Huguenots* (1836). Two *opéras comiques*, *North Star* (1854) and *Dinorah* (1859), are noteworthy. Meyerbeer made a fortune and was famous for his brilliant orchestration and great scenic effects.

**Meyerhold, Vsevolod** (ˌmeeəholt), 1874–1940?, Russian theatrical producer and director. He led the revolt against NATURALISM in the Russian theatre and, after the RUSSIAN REVOLUTION (1917), as head of the state's theatrical activities opposed SOCIALIST REALISM. His avant-garde productions, emphasizing the visual and nonverbal, made use of PANTOMIME, acrobatics, constructivist sets (see CONSTRUCTIVISM), and formalized scenery. The first to specialize in Soviet plays, he later fell victim to the Stalinist purges.

**mezzo-soprano:** see VOICE.

**mezzotint,** method of copper or steel engraving that gives tone or shades. The mezzotint plate is given an overall, even grain by uniformly roughening the surface with a curved, sawtoothed tool. The picture is then developed in light and shade with a scraper and a burnisher. The resulting print is softly tonal, with no sharp lines. Said to have been invented by Ludwig von Siegen c.1640, the process became prominent in 18th-cent. England, where it was often used to reproduce paintings.

**Mfecane,** [Nguni, = the forced wanderings], term used to describe the wars and disturbances which accompanied the rise of the ZULU kingdom under SHAKA and which affected virtually all of southern Africa during the 1820s and 30s. To a certain extent the result of population pressure on scarce resources, the Mfecane introduced new patterns of settlement and authority, which largely remain intact to this day.

**Mg,** chemical symbol of the element MAGNESIUM.

**Miami,** US city (1984 est. pop. 373,000), SE Florida, on Biscayne Bay; inc. 1896. Tourism is its main industry, and there are extensive recreational and convention facilities. A famous resort and cruise-ship port, it is also the processing and shipping centre for an agricultural region. Aircraft rebuilding and textiles are among its growing industries. First settled in the 1870s, it was developed into a recreational centre after 1896. Miami's first boom occurred during the Florida land speculation in the 1920s. In the 1960s the city became a focus for immigration from the Caribbean, and in the late 1970s and early 1980s many Cuban and Haitian refugees arrived, taxing the city's facilities. Today over half of the population is Hispanic, and the distinctive Cuban influence resulted in the election of a Cuban-born mayor in 1985. Miami has also become a major centre of trade, narcotics smuggling, and finance with Latin America. The city has a major international airport.

**Miami Indians:** see NORTH AMERICAN INDIANS.

**mica,** general term for a large group of hydrous aluminium and potassium silicate minerals, usually occurring in scales and sheets. The most important commercial micas are muscovite and phlogopite. Muscovite, the commoner variety, is usually colourless but may be red, yellow, green, brown, or grey; it is found most often in pegmatite dykes. Phlogopite ranges in colour from yellow to brown and occurs in crystalline limestones, dolomites, and serpentines. Sheet mica is used as an insulating material and in certain acoustic devices. Scrap and ground mica is used in wallpaper, fancy paint, ornamental tile, roofing, lubricating oil, and Christmas-tree snow.

**Micah** or **Micheas,** book of the OLD TESTAMENT. It contains the prophecy of Micah, a contemporary of ISAIAH (fl. 730 BC), on the doom and redemption of JUDAH and ISRAEL.

**Michael,** archangel prominent in Jewish, Christian, and Muslim traditions. In the BIBLE he is mentioned as the guardian angel of Israel. In Christian tradition he is the conqueror of SATAN. His feast (jointly with the other archangels) is Michaelmas, 29 Sept.

**Michael,** Byzantine emperors. **Michael I** (Rhangabe), d. c.845 (r.811–13), was the son-in-law of NICEPHORUS I. Orthodox in religion, he restored the monastic reformer St Theodore of Studium. He was deposed after a defeat by the BULGARS. **Michael II** (the Stammerer), d. 829 (r.820–29), helped LEO V to succeed Michael I, and himself succeeded after Leo's murder. Tolerant in religion, he himself favoured ICONOCLASM. He lost (825) Crete to the Arabs. **Michael III** (the Drunkard), 836–67 (r.842–67), was the grandson of Michael II. Early in his reign iconoclasm was punished and the heretic Paulicians persecuted. The administration of government by the debauched Michael's uncle, Bardas, was marked by the missions of Sts CYRIL AND METHODIUS. Michael's favourite, Basil, ordered the murders of Bardas (866) and Michael himself (867), and succeeded as BASIL I. **Michael VIII,** c.1225–82 (r.1261–82), was the first of the Palaeologus dynasty. He became emperor of Nicaea (1259) by usurping the throne of JOHN IV after blinding him. In 1261 he recovered Constantinople from the Latin emperor Baldwin II and was crowned Byzantine emperor by the patriarch. For the rest of his reign he struggled with CHARLES I of Naples and with the despotate of Epirus, which Charles invaded. Michael negotiated with Pope Gregory X for a union of Eastern and Western churches (see COUNCIL, ECUMENICAL), but failed. To defeat Charles he financed the SICILIAN VESPERS (1282).

**Michael,** 1921–, last king of ROMANIA (1927–30, 1940–47). He became king under a regency after his father, CAROL II, renounced the throne. In 1930, however, Carol returned and was proclaimed king. On Carol's abdication in 1940 Michael again became king although he was largely a figurehead under the rule of ANTONESCU. Michael's pro-Allied sentiments and dislike of Antonescu prompted him to order the latter's arrest on 23 Aug. 1944 after Soviet forces had crossed into Romania. Despite strong resistance to Communist pressure, he was forced to abdicate at the end of 1947.

**Michaelmas,** the popular term for the feast of St Michael the Archangel and All Angels, observed in the West on 29 Sept. and in the East on 8 Nov. In the Middle Ages it was a popular religious and social festival, the traditional dish served being goose. In England the university and law terms which start shortly after it are designated Michaelmas terms. A QUARTER DAY, it was traditionally the date on which the ownership or tenancy of farms changed hands, when the harvest was in and the work for the following year had not yet begun.

**Michael the Brave,** d.1601, prince of Walachia (1593–1601), of Transylvania (1599–1600), and of Moldavia (1600). His unification, albeit brief, of the three major Romanian-inhabited provinces in 1600 has acquired him the status of a Romanian national hero.

**Michelangelo,** 1475–1564, Italian sculptor, painter, architect, and poet; full name Michelangelo Buonarroti. He was a towering figure of RENAISSANCE art. From 1490 to 1492 he lived in Lorenzo de' MEDICI's house, where he was influenced by Neoplatonic thought. His early drawings show the influence of GIOTTO and MASACCIO, whereas the marble reliefs of the *Madonna of the Stairs* and *Battle of the Centaurs* (c.1492; both: Casa Buonarroti, Florence) show the influence of DONATELLO and Roman sarcophagi. In 1494 he executed statuettes for San Petronio (Bologna). Between 1496 and 1501, Michelangelo worked in Rome, doing the marble *Bacchus* (Bargello, Florence) and the exquisitely balanced *Pietà* (St Peter's, Rome). He returned to Florence in 1501, where he was commissioned to do the magnificent *David* (Academy, Florence). From these years date the *Bruges Madonna* (Notre Dame, Bruges) and the painted tondo of the *Holy Family* (Uffizi, Florence). In 1505 he was ordered back to Rome by Pope JULIUS II to do his sepulchral monument. This was the most frustrating project of his life. Michelangelo spent a year on the gigantic bronze, which was melted for cannon shortly after its completion. Shortly after awarding the contract for the tomb, Julius commissioned the decoration of the ceiling of the SISTINE CHAPEL, which Michelangelo worked on from 1508 to 1512. The ceiling is divided into three zones, the highest showing scenes from Genesis. Below are prophets and sibyls. In the lunettes and spandrels are figures identified as ancestors of Christ or the Virgin, which seem to suggest a vision of primordial humanity. After the death of Julius II, his heirs again contracted for the execution of his monument and 30 years of litigation ensued. Michelangelo had to abandon his plan for a vast mausoleum for Julius II in St Peter's. His colossal *Moses* (1513–16; San Pietro in Vincoli, Rome) and the statues known as *Slaves* (Academy, Florence; Louvre, Paris) were to have been included. From 1520 to 1534 he worked on the Medici Chapel (San Lorenzo, Florence) and designed the elegant,

Michelangelo, ceiling of the sistine chapel, 1508–12.

mannerist (see MANNERISM) Laurentian Library of this church. In the chapel, a forceful contrast between contemplation and action is seen in his statues of Giuliano and Lorenzo de' Medici, and his allegorical figures of *Dawn, Evening, Night,* and *Day.* In 1529 he assisted as engineer in the defence of Florence. After working on the *Last Judgment* (1536–41) of the Sistine Chapel and the *Conversion of Paul* and *Martyrdom of Peter* in the Pauline Chapel (1542–50; Vatican), he devoted himself to architecture as chief architect of ST PETER'S CHURCH. In his last years Michelangelo's work shows a more spiritualized and abstract form, e.g., two unfinished *Pietà* groups (Academy and Cathedral Mus., Florence) and the Rondanini *Pietà* (Castello Sforzesco, Milan). He thought of himself primarily as a sculptor, and a feeling for the expressive potentialities of sculptural form manifests itself in all his work. Many of his designs have survived only through his drawings, which used vigorous cross-hatching. Great collections of his drawings are in the Louvre and Uffizi.

**Michelet, Jules** (meeshə‚lay), 1798–1874, French historian of the romantic school. His *History of France* (many volumes, 1833–67) is a masterpiece of French literature, in terms of its style, its emotional strength, and its powerful evocation, but it has weaknesses as a history, in its use of evidence and its emotional bias.

**Michelozzo Michelozzi,** 1396–1472, Italian sculptor and architect. He shared leadership with BRUNELLESCHI and ALBERTI in establishing the Renaissance style. His best work includes the Medici-Riccardi palace at Florence, one of the finest city houses ever built, and the Medici villa at Fiesole (1458–61), noted for its terraced gardens.

**Michels, Robert,** 1876–1936, German sociologist and economist. Michels is best known for his *Political Parties* (1911), in which he formulated 'the iron law of oligarchy': as organizations grow larger and more complex, rank and file participation becomes impractical; a privileged organizational elite establishes itself, and gradually comes to value the preservation of its own power above the original aims of the organization or the general interest of the ordinary members. This analysis, originally arrived at by a study of the German Social Democratic Party, has been extended, notably by Milovan DJILAS, to the bureaucratization of trade unions and to the state bureaucracy of communist countries.

**Michelson, Albert Abraham,** 1852–1931, American physicist; b. Prussia. He was head (1892–1931) of the physics department at the Univ. of Chicago. Michelson designed the modern interferometer, with which he measured the speed of light to an unequalled degree of accuracy. His measurement of the length of the standard metre in Paris in terms of the wavelength of the red line of the cadmium spectrum, using the interferometer method, provided an absolute and exactly reproducible standard of length. With Edward Morley he conducted the Michelson–Morley experiment (see LIGHT), which led to the refutation of the ETHER hypothesis and was eventually explained by Einstein's theory of RELATIVITY. Michelson became (1907) the first American to win the Nobel Prize for physics.

**Michigan,** state of the US (1985 est. pop. 9,075,000), area 150,779 km² (58,216 sq mi), located in the Midwest, consisting of two peninsulas projecting into the GREAT LAKES, bordered by Ohio and Indiana (S), Wisconsin (NW), and the Canadian province of Ontario (E). The capital is LANSING and the biggest city is DETROIT, the sixth largest in the country; Grand Rapids, Flint, and ANN ARBOR are also important. The Lower Peninsula is separated from Canada (E) by Lakes HURON and ERIE, and by Lake MICHIGAN from the sparsely populated Upper Peninsula (NE), which is separated from Canada (N) by Lake SUPERIOR. Michigan is an industrial state, led by the Detroit region, the centre of US car manufacturing, and also a major producer of nonelectrical machinery and fabricated metals. Dairy products and cattle are the leading sources of agricultural income. Michigan is the leading state in the production of calcium chloride, gypsum, magnesium, and peat; it is second to Minnesota in the extraction of iron ore. In 1980 84% of the population was non-Hispanic white, 13% was black and over 80% lived in metropolitan areas. The original inhabitants were Ojibwa, Ottawa, and Potawatomi Indians. First the French and then the British (1763) took control of the area, which passed to the US in 1796. Timber helped the state economy in the late 19th cent., and in 1903 Henry Ford established his automated car assembly line in Detroit. The industry declined in the 1970s, but oil discovered in Lake Michigan promises development in the 1980s.

**Michigan, Lake,** third largest (57,441 km²/22,178 sq mi) of the GREAT LAKES and the largest freshwater lake entirely within the US. It is 494 km (307 mi) long and 48–193 km (30–120 ml) wide, with a surface elevation of 177 m (581 ft) and a maximum depth of 280 m (923 ft), and it is joined to Lake Huron by the Straits of Mackinac. Chicago and Milwaukee are major lakeshore cities, and Indiana Dunes National Lakeshore (est. 1966) borders the southern shore. Discovered in 1634 by the French explorer Jean Nicolet, the lake passed to England in 1763 as part of the NORTHWEST TERRITORY and to the US in 1796.

**Mickiewicz, Adam** (meets‚kyevich), 1798–1855, Polish poet. In 1823 he was arrested for nationalist activities and deported to Russia. After 1829 he lived in W Europe but devoted himself to the cause of Polish independence. His masterpiece is the epic poem *Pan Tadeusz* (1834), depicting the life of the Polish gentry. His other major works are *Forefathers' Eve* (1923), a drama; *Crimean Sonnets* (1825); and the narrative poems *Grazyna* (1823) and *Konrad Wallenrod* (1828).

**Micmac Indians:** see NORTH AMERICAN INDIANS.

**microcomputer:** see MICROPROCESSOR.

**microeconomics:** see under ECONOMICS.

**microelectronics,** branch of ELECTRONICS devoted to the design and development of extremely small electronic devices that consume very little electric power. The simplest, but least effective, approach used is to make circuit elements, such as resistors (see RESISTANCE), CAPACITORS, and SEMICONDUCTOR devices, extremely small but discrete. In another approach, circuit elements fabricated as thin films of conductive, semiconductive, and insulating materials are deposited in sandwich form on an insulating substrate. The most advanced method is to form circuits within and upon single semiconductor crystals (see INTEGRATED CIRCUIT). See also TRANSISTOR.

**microfiche,** sheet of film containing numerous pages of printed or graphic material that have been greatly reduced by microphotography. Unlike microfilm, in which individual frames are reproduced consecutively on a roll of film, a single 10 × 15-cm (4 × 6-in) microfiche card may contain hundreds of pages, in rows and columns, providing faster access to a desired item. The image is magnified to approximately full size by a viewing machine or reader. Microfiche became popular as an inexpensive way of storing bulky information (e.g., library catalogues), but the more sophisticated searching techniques that can be used with databases or compact discs meant that the technique was in decline by the mid 1980s.

**micrometer,** instrument used for measuring extremely small distances. In the micrometer caliper, the object to be measured is held between the two jaws of the instrument; the distance between the jaws is measured on a scale calibrated to the rotation of the finely threaded screw that moves one of the jaws. In astronomical and microscopic micrometers, the distance that a filament moves from one end to the other of the image of an object is read on a calibrated scale.

**Micronesia,** one of the three main divisions of OCEANIA, in the W Pacific Ocean, N of the equator. The principal island groups include the Caroline Islands (see MICRONESIA, FEDERATED STATES OF), NAURU, the Gilbert Islands (see KIRIBATI), the NORTHERN MARIANA ISLANDS, and the MARSHALL ISLANDS. The inhabitants are of Australoid and Polynesian stock and speak Malayo-Polynesian languages.

**Micronesia, Federated States of,** self-governing island group (1987 est. pop. 80,000), c.702 km² (271 sq mi), in the W Pacific Ocean, part of the US Trust Territory of the PACIFIC ISLANDS. It comprises four states Kosrae, Pohnpei, Truk, and Yap and the capital, Kolonia, is on the island of Pohnpei. The population is predominantly Micronesian. Mainstays of the economy are subsistence farming and fishing. Germany purchased the islands from Spain in 1898. They were occupied (1914) by Japan, which received them (1920) as a League of Nations mandate. During WORLD WAR II US forces captured the islands and in 1947 they became part of the trust territory placed under US administration by the UNITED NATIONS. In 1979, as negotiations for termination of the trusteeship continued, they became self-governing as the Federated States of Micronesia. A 1982 compact moved them toward 'free association' status with the US.

**microphone,** device (invented c.1877) used in radio broadcasting, recording, and sound-amplifying systems to convert sound into electrical energy. Its basic component is a flexible diaphragm that responds to the pressure of sound waves. In a CAPACITOR, or condenser, microphone, used in high-quality sound systems, two parallel metal plates are given opposite electrical charges. One of the plates is attached to the diaphragm and moves in response to its vibrations, generating a varying voltage. See also TELEPHONE.

**microprocessor,** INTEGRATED CIRCUIT that interprets and executes instructions from a COMPUTER PROGRAM. When combined with other integrated circuits that provide storage for data and programs, often on a single SEMICONDUCTOR base to form a CHIP, the microprocessor becomes the heart of a small COMPUTER, or microcomputer. The evolution of the microprocessor has made possible the inexpensive hand-held electronic CALCULATOR, the digital wristwatch, and the ELECTRONIC GAME. The microprocessor is also used to control consumer appliances, to regulate petrol consumption in cars and to monitor home and industrial alarm systems.

**microscope,** optical instrument used to increase the apparent size of an object. A magnifying glass, an ordinary double convex LENS having a short focal length, is a simple microscope. When an object is placed nearer such a lens than its principal focus, i.e., within its focal length, an image is produced that is erect and larger than the object. The compound microscope, invented in the early 17th cent., consists essentially of two or more such lenses fixed in the two extremities of a hollow metal cylinder. This cylinder is mounted upright on a screw device, which permits it to be raised or lowered above the object until a clear image is formed. The lower lens (nearer to the object) is called the objective; the upper lens (nearer to the eye of the observer), the eyepiece. When an object is in focus, a real (formed by the convergence of light rays), inverted image is formed by the lower lens at a point inside the principal focus of the upper lens. This image serves as an 'object' for the upper lens, which produces another image, larger still, but virtual (formed by the apparent rather than actual convergence of light rays), and visible to the eye of the observer. The compound microscope is widely used in bacteriology, biology, and medicine in the examination of such extremely minute objects as bacteria and other unicellular organisms, and plant and animal cells and tissues. Technical advances making use of different forms of light and other forms of radiation (see ELECTRON MICROSCOPE) have increased enormously the magnification and resolution of microscopes.

**microwave,** ELECTROMAGNETIC RADIATION having a frequency range from 1000 to 300,000 megahertz, corresponding to a wavelength range from 300 to 1 mm (about 12 to about 0.04 in.). Microwaves are used in MICROWAVE OVENS, RADAR, and communications links spanning moderate distances.

**microwave oven,** cooking device that uses MICROWAVES to penetrate foods and rapidly cook them. The microwaves cause water molecules in the food to vibrate, a process that produces heat. Once used almost exclusively in fast-food restaurants, microwave ovens have become increasingly popular in home kitchens. Some microwave radiation has been found to leak from the ovens, however, and it is not yet known whether such low exposures might be harmful. See RADIATION.

**Midas,** in Greek mythology, king of Phrygia. Because he befriended SILENUS, DIONYSUS granted him the power to turn everything he touched into gold. When even his food became gold, he washed away his power in the Pactolus, a river which ever since has had golden sands.

**Middle Ages,** period in W European history roughly from the fall of the West Roman Empire in the 5th cent. to the 15th cent., once called the Dark Ages. Christianity became the unifying force of culture. FEUDALISM and the MANORIAL SYSTEM, the HOLY ROMAN EMPIRE, the CRUSADES, and CHIVALRY fused Christian ideals with economic, political, and military institutions. Guilds in rising towns maintained the Christian spirit in economic life. Universities developed under the auspices of the church. The philosophy of SCHOLASTICISM, expounded by St THOMAS AQUINAS, combined new learning with Christian faith. GOTHIC ARCHITECTURE and the writings of DANTE and CHAUCER show the vitality and spirit of the age. Transition to the modern age came with a money economy, political centralization, exploration, secularization, and the humanism of the RENAISSANCE. The Protestant REFORMATION shattered the medieval unity of Christianity and the Scientific Revolution of the 17th cent. produced a new world view.

**Middle American Indians,** aboriginal peoples of the area between the present-day US and South America. The MAYA of the YUCATÁN, with their highly advanced culture, had links with the Chorotega of Nicaragua and

Honduras, and these in turn had contacts with the Chibcha of Colombia. High civilizations flourished in Mexico after the domestication of maize, e.g., beside the Maya, the OLMEC, TOLTEC, MIXTEC, Zapotec, and AZTEC. They developed architecture, agriculture, and stonework and metalwork to a remarkable degree (see PRE-COLUMBIAN ART AND ARCHITECTURE). Following the Spanish conquest in the 16th cent., Mexico's Indians were used as labourers, first under the ENCOMIENDA system of tributary labour, then under PEONAGE. Indian artisans did, however, continue to make notable contributions to painting and architecture. Not until the Mexican revolution of 1910 and the *indianismo* movement of ZAPATA were efforts made to advance the Indian socially and economically. Today descendants of the Mexican civilizations, along with Huastecs, TARASCANS, Yaquis, Tarahumaras, and members of other tribes, constitute a major element of the population of Middle America. Both full-blooded Indians and mixed bloods (mestizos) are found in all levels of society, and millions still speak AMERICAN INDIAN LANGUAGES.

**Middle East,** term applied to a region that includes SW Asia and part of NE Africa, lying W of Afghanistan, Pakistan, and India. It includes the Asian part of TURKEY; SYRIA; CYPRUS; ISRAEL; JORDAN; IRAQ; IRAN; LEBANON; the countries of the Arabian peninsula, that is, SAUDI ARABIA, YEMEN, SOUTH YEMEN, OMAN, UNITED ARAB EMIRATES, QATAR, BAHRAIN, KUWAIT; EGYPT; and LIBYA. The region was the site of great ancient civilizations, e.g., MESOPOTAMIA and Egypt, and it was the birthplace of JUDAISM, CHRISTIANITY, and ISLAM. It contains much of the world's oil reserves and has many strategic trade routes, e.g., the SUEZ CANAL. In the 20th cent. the area has been the scene of political turmoil and major warfare, e.g., in WORLD WAR I, WORLD WAR II, and the ARAB-ISRAELI WARS. The term *Middle East* is also sometimes used in a cultural sense for that part of the world predominantly Islamic in culture, in which case Afghanistan, Pakistan, and the remaining countries of North Africa are included. Before 1939 British use of the term often limited it to Arabia, Iraq, and Iran; maintaining the name Near East for Egypt and the countries of the E Mediterranean including Greece, Turkey, and Cyprus. American use of the term usually implies this extended sense of the area.

**Middlesbrough,** town (1981 pop. 158,516) in Cleveland, NE England, on right bank of R. Tees. It is an industrial and port town, which forms part of the Teesside urban complex. The major industries within the town are iron and steel, engineering, and the manufacture of chemicals. The town developed rapidly in the 19th cent. with the discovery of iron ore in the nearby Cleveland Hills, and the opening of the Stockton-to-Darlington railway. Captain COOK was born in Marton, which is 5 km (3 mi) to the SW.

**middle schools,** schools in Britain teaching children aged 8–12 or 8–13 (sometimes 10–13). The first middle school opened in 1968 and by the 1980s there were nearly 400 such schools. As part of a three-tier system, they take children from first schools and the pupils go on to 'high schools'.

**Middle Temple:** see INNS OF COURT.

**Middleton, Thomas,** 1580–1627, English dramatist. He collaborated with DEKKER, DRAYTON, and others, and wrote (1604–11) realistic, satiric comedies, including *Michaelmas Term, A Trick to Catch the Old One,* and *A Mad World, My Masters.* Later (1621–27) he wrote two powerful tragedies, *The Changeling* (with William Rowley) and *Women Beware Women.*

**Middle West** or **Midwest,** US region usually defined as including the N central states of OHIO, INDIANA, ILLINOIS, MICHIGAN, WISCONSIN, MINNESOTA, IOWA, MISSOURI, KANSAS, and NEBRASKA. It is a rich farm area, noted for its corn and pig farming, as well as an important industrial region, home of the nation's vehicle and rubber industries.

**midge,** name used for any small, delicate, long-legged FLY, having many-segmented antennae (suborder Nematocera), but correctly applied, in Britain, only to the true midges (Chironomidae), owl midges (Psychodidae), biting midges (Ceratopogonidae) and gall midges (Cecidomyidae). Adult true midges or chironomids closely resemble mosquitoes but are nonbiting; indeed they are so short-lived they do not feed at all. Their larvae are aquatic, usually living in still or slow-moving water, even that with quite a high level of organic pollution. To help them respire in such conditions some larvae, unlike almost all other insects, have haemoglobin in their blood. Lake Victoria in E Africa, supports an enormous population of chironomids and the adults form a useful addition to the diet of people living on the Uganda shore.

**Mid Glamorgan,** county in SE Wales (1984 est. pop. 533, 900), 1018 km² (397 sq mi), bordering on Gwent in the E and West Glamorgan in the W. It was formed in 1974 from the central part of Glamorganshire and a small part of S Breconshire. It is mountainous in the north. It contains some of the major valleys of the South Wales coalfield. Coalmining and metal industries were the most important economic activities, but have now declined. The main towns are Bridgend and Merthyr Tydfil.

**Midgley, Albert,** 1881–1961, English inventor and electrical engineer. He is credited with more than 212 successful patents. Many of his original patent drawings and inventions are held at the Watford Museum. He was the pioneer inventor of motor-vehicle electricity and the first person to create (1907) a dynamo small enough to function from a motor car. His inventions ranged over a wide area, covering motor-car lighting and starting motors, automatic transmission, magnetos for aircraft, automatic gun firing (used in aircraft in World War I), gyroscopes, signalling lamps, range-finding, radio, loudspeakers, amplifiers, sound recording equipment, pipe and electronic organs, bombs and fuses, automatic time switches for domestic appliances, and traffic indicators for motor cars.

**Midian** or **Midianites** (ˌmideeən, ˌmideeəniets), in the BIBLE a nomadic tribe of N Arabia said to be descended from ABRAHAM (Gen. 25.2). JOSEPH fell into the hands of Midianite merchants, and MOSES married the daughter of a Midianite, who advised him on the administration of justice and may have influenced his religious ideas (Ex. 18).

**midnight sun,** phenomenon in which the sun remains visible in the sky continuously for 24 hr or longer. It occurs in the polar regions because of the tilt of the equatorial plane to the plane of the ecliptic (the sun's apparent path through the sky). It occurs at the polar circles only at the SOLSTICE (summer for Arctic, winter for Antarctic), but as one approaches the pole it increases in occurrence up to a continuous six months (from vernal to autumnal equinox for the North Pole; the reverse for the South Pole).

**mid-ocean ridge:** see OCEAN; PLATE TECTONICS.

**midrash,** verse-by-verse interpretation of Hebrew Scriptures, consisting of homily and exegesis, by Jewish teachers of the talmudic era. The *Midrash Rabbah* is the most authoritative of the collections of commentaries on the TORAH and the Five Scrolls (the books Song of Solomon, Ruth, Lamentations, Ecclesiastes, and Esther in the Hebrew Bible).

**midsummer day and midsummer night,** feast of the nativity of St JOHN THE BAPTIST (24 June) and the preceding night (23 June). Close to the summer SOLSTICE, midsummer has been associated with solar ceremonies since before Christianity. Supernatural beings were thought to roam on midsummer night.

**Midway,** island group (5.2 km²/2 sq mi), central Pacific, c.1850 km (1150 mi) NW of Honolulu. Annexed by the US in 1867, it is a naval base with no indigenous population. On 3–6 June, 1942, the Japanese navy was crippled in the battle of Midway, fought nearby with carrier-based aircraft.

**midwifery,** art of assisting at childbirth. The term *midwife* for centuries referred to a woman who was an overseer during the process of delivery. Professional schools of midwifery were established in Europe in the 16th cent. Midwives are still used widely in Europe and are experiencing an upsurge of popularity in the US.

**Mielziner, Jo** (meelˌzeenə), 1900–76, American theatrical designer; b. France. Among the more than 200 productions for which he designed sets are *Strange Interlude* (1928), *A Streetcar Named Desire* (1947), and *Death of a Salesman* (1949).

**Miës van der Rohe, Ludwig** (ˌmeez van de ˌrohə), 1886–1969, American architect; b. Germany, a founder of MODERN ARCHITECTURE. His work in Germany was rewarded by his appointment (1930) as director of the BAUHAUS. But in 1937 he left Germany to teach at the Armour Inst., Chicago (now Illinois Inst. of Technology), where he also planned a new campus. His combination of the glass skyscraper concept with surface expression of structural members is seen in the Seagram Building, New York City (1956–58).

Ludwig **Miës van der Rohe's** Seagram Building, New York

**Mifune Toshiro,** 1920–, Japanese film actor. He is best known for his roles in films directed by KUROSAWA AKIRA, including *Rashomon* (1950), *Seven Samurai* (1954), *Throne of Blood* (1957), and *Yojimbo* (1961).

**migraine,** headache characterized by recurrent attacks of severe pain, usually on one side of the head. The pain is believed to be associated with intense vasoconstriction, followed by prolonged dilation of blood vessels leading to and within the brain. Attacks vary in duration and frequency but frequently cause prostration. In classic migraines the pain is preceded by visual disturbances (e.g., flashes before the eyes), sensitivity to light, nausea, and dizziness. ERGOT derivatives can alleviate the headache; the BETA BLOCKER propranolol is used to prevent the condition.

**migration of animals,** regular, periodic movements of animals in large numbers, usually away from and back to a place of origin. A round trip may take an entire lifetime or may be made more frequently, as on a seasonal basis. Seasonal migrations occur among many insects, fishes, reptiles, birds, marine mammals, and large herbivorous mammals. Such migrations provide more favourable conditions of temperature, food, or water and may involve a change of latitude, altitude, or both. The chief function is to supply a suitable breeding place. Migration may be initiated by physiological stimuli such as reproductive changes, external pressures such as drought, or a combination of both. Studies show that salmon depend on the olfactory sense to locate and return to the stream of their origin. Bats, whales, and seals use echo location to navigate in the dark. Experiments in planetariums indicate that night-flying birds navigate at least in part by the stars. Day-flying birds orient themselves by the sun. A one-time, one-way wholesale migration out of an area prompted by explosive population increase is called an irruption. It is common among small rodents, notably LEMMINGS, and some species of birds and insects, e.g., the so-called migratory locusts of North Africa and Australia. See BUTTERFLY; EEL; GNU; PETREL; TURTLE; WHALE.

**Mihailović** or **Mihailovich, Dragoljub-Draža** (miˌhielohˈvich), 1893–1946, Yugoslav general. During World War II he organized and led the Četniks, a traditionally-minded Serb resistance movement loyal to the exiled King PETER II which, because of its hostility to the Communist-led Partisans of Marshal TITO and disbelief in the efficacy of immediate armed struggle, entered into collaboration with the Axis occupiers in order to extirpate the Communists. He was captured, tried, and executed by Tito's victorious forces after the war.

**Mikoyan, Anastas Ivanovich**, 1895–1978, Soviet leader. A member of the Communist Party's central committee in 1923 and of the politburo in 1935, he later became first deputy premier (1955–57, 1958–64) and chairman of the presidium of the Supreme Soviet, i.e., head of state (1964–65). In 1974 he was dropped from the Supreme Soviet and retired from public office.

**Mikszáth, Kálmán**, 1847–1910, Hungarian prose writer. He portrays Hungarian society with gentle irony. Tragicomic in tone, he was the first Hungarian writer to master the surprise ending. His chief works are *The Good People of Palóc* (1882), *The Siege of Bystrica* (1896), *The Gentry* (1897), and *Strange Marriage* (1900).

**mikveh**, ritual bath, primarily used for purification rite by women on completion of their monthly menstrual period. Immersion in mikveh is a pre-requisite for resumption of marital relations.

**Milan**, Ital. *Milano,* city (1984 pop. 1,535,722), capital of LOMBARDY, N Italy, in the Po basin. It is the economic heart of modern Italy, with such manufactures as textiles, machinery, chemicals, and motor vehicles. Capital of Rome's Western Empire and a Christian centre, it was damaged by barbarian invasions. It became a free commune (12th cent.) and rose to leadership in Lombardy. Losing its republican liberties, it was ruled by the VISCONTIS (1277–1447) and the SFORZAS (1447–1535). Later it passed to Spain, Austria, and Napoleon I before union (1861) with Italy. Milan was severely damaged in World War II. Dominated by its white marble cathedral (1386–1813), it is also known for the renowned opera house, the Church of Santa Maria delle Grazie (housing LEONARDO's *Last Supper*), the Brera Palace, and the Ambrosian Library.

The white marble cathedral, **Milan**

**Milankovitch hypothesis**, theory that changes in the shape and position of the Earth's orbit around the Sun cause changes in the amount of heat received at the Earth's surface, thereby being of great importance in the interpretation of climatic fluctuations during the Pleistocene, especially the advance and retreat of ice.

**mildew**, name for certain FUNGI and the plant diseases they cause, and for the discoloration and disintegration of materials (e.g., leather, fabrics, and paper) caused by related fungi. The powdery mildews (class Ascomycetes) form a grey-white coating on plant tissues, e.g., the rose and pea mildews. The downy mildews (class Phycomycetes) form white, purplish, or grey patches. A downy mildew was the potato BLIGHT that caused the Great Potato Famine (1845–49) in Ireland, and is still a disease of economic importance.

**Mildura**, town (1986 pop. 20,512), Victoria, SE Australia. Located on the MURRAY R. it is the provincial centre of the Sunraysia District. Since irrigation was first established here in 1886, the area has been important for its production of fruit, vegetables, and wines; food-processing and tourism are the main industries. A restored paddle-wheel steamer provides river trips and the Workingman's Club boasts the longest bar in Australia, 89 m (296 ft) in length.

**Milesian school**, group of pre-Socratic Greek philosophers. Most came from the city of Miletus in Ionia (part of modern Turkey), which can be regarded as the birthplace of Western philosophy. The known members are ANAXAGORAS, ANAXIMANDER, ANAXIMENES, and THALES, the founder of the school. It is also known as the Ionian school.

**Miletus** (mi͜leetəs), ancient seaport of W ASIA MINOR, in Caria, near Samos. Occupied by the Greeks (c.1000 BC), it became a leading IONIAN city. The pre-Socratic philosophers THALES, ANAXIMANDER, and ANAXIMENES all came from Miletus (6th cent.). It led the revolt (499 BC) against the Persians, who sacked the city (494).

**Milford Haven** or **Aberdaugleddau**, town and port (1981 pop. 13,883), in Dyfed, SW Wales, on N bank of Milford Haven estuary. It is a fishing and oil port, which in 1984 handled 32 million tonnes. There are oil refineries situated nearby on the N and S banks of the estuary.

**Milhaud, Darius**, 1892–1974, French composer. His music incorporates polytonality, JAZZ, and Brazilian elements. He wrote 12 symphonies, several concertos and orchestral pieces, and a great deal of chamber music, including 18 quartets. One of the Parisian group 'les SIX', he is noted for his operas *Le Pauvre Matelot* (1927; LIBRETTO by COCTEAU) and *Christophe Colombe* (1930; libretto by CLAUDEL) and for his ballets, e.g., *The Creation of the World* (1923).

**Militant Tendency**, British Trotskyist faction associated with the *Militant* newspaper, active from the mid-1970s as an extreme left-wing pressure group within the LABOUR PARTY. Accused of being a 'party within a party', the tendency was proscribed by the Labour leadership (1982) and several prominent members were expelled from the party (1986).

**military band**, ensemble of brass, woodwind, and percussion instruments attached to military units. The military band appeared in Europe after the Crusades made Westerners aware of the Turkish *janissaries*, the first professional armies, with their *mehter music*—duval (bass drum), borozan (trumpet), zil (finger cymbals), timbal (big kettle drums), nakkare (small kettle drums), and zurna (ancestor of the oboe.) Henry VIII and James I lavished great sums on providing impressive bands at court. Frederick the Great encouraged the flamboyant dressy military band and by the time of Napoleon bands were an essential part of military ceremonial and routine. British military bands in their modern form date from the foundation of the academy of military music in Kneller Hall in 1857, and continue to play a significant part in the military presence and are enjoyed by the public at various tattoos and ceremonies, e.g., the Trooping of the Colour. Bands comprise a full complement of brass and woodwind and sometimes have string sections as well. See also BRASS BAND.

**military science**, study and application of the rules and principles of warfare, designed to achieve success in military operations. It comprises the two basic elements of military strategy and tactics, as adapted to utilize the latest developments in weapons and communications technology. Strategy and tactics are relative terms referring, respectively, to large-scale and small-scale military operations. Strategy may be defined as the general scheme of the conduct of a war, often referred to as 'grand strategy'. On the highest level it has come to mean national strategy, involving complex assessments of technological resources, national priorities, and geopolitical factors. Tactics, on the other hand, refers to the planning and execution of means to achieve strategic objectives.

*Historical Development.* Military science evolved in ancient times under such leaders as CYRUS THE GREAT, known as the first accomplished strategist; ALEXANDER THE GREAT, who pioneered in the use of reserves, stockpiles of supplies, and military intelligence; HANNIBAL, the outstanding field commander and tactician of the Punic Wars; and Julius CAESAR. After a period of decline in the West during the Middle Ages, the use of strategy and tactics was revived in the 15th cent. by John ZIZKA, who became the first to combine cavalry, infantry, and artillery. NAPOLEON I transformed existing military principles with his powerful shock attacks, inspiring Karl von CLAUSEWITZ's classic treatise *On War* (1832). The American CIVIL WAR, fought with mass ARMIES and improved firearms, marked the beginning of modern total warfare, employing almost the entire resources of both sides. WORLD WAR I saw the introduction of rapid-fire SMALL ARMS and ARTILLERY, trench warfare, and the advent of aerial warfare (see AIR FORCE), which reached its height in the massive strategic bombardments of WORLD WAR II. Naval strategy and tactics (see NAVY) have evolved along lines parallel to those of land- and air-warfare principles. With the introduction of artillery, the early method of closing with an enemy vessel and boarding it was replaced by that of forcing enemy vessels into submission by gunfire. In the 1890s Alfred MAHAN defined the central theme of naval strategy as 'command of the sea', i.e., the ability to deny an enemy use of the sea as a means of transport and at the same time protect one's own merchant shipping from attack. Another important naval strategy is 'overseas presence', i.e., the visible display of sea power as a deterrent to intervention by opposing powers in key areas of international tension. All types of warfare have undergone revolutionary changes since the development of guided MISSILES and strategic and tactical nuclear weapons (see ATOMIC BOMB; HYDROGEN BOMB). Even in the nuclear age, however, the periodic outbreak of 'limited wars' has obliged the leading powers to maintain large conventional forces, whose conduct is governed by traditional battle techniques modified to exploit their unprecedented mobility and firepower. See also AMPHIBIOUS WARFARE; FORTIFICATION; GUERRILLA WARFARE; MECHANIZED WARFARE; SIEGE.

**militia,** military organization composed of citizens enrolled by enlistment or CONSCRIPTION and trained for service in times of national emergency. When the emergency is over, militia members traditionally resume civilian status. An early prototype of the militia was developed by PHILIP II of Macedon, and the concept still persists in Europe. In Switzerland, which has no regular army, every adult male must possess a rifle and be ready if called upon in an emergency. In Britain, the World War II Local Defence Volunteers, or Home Guard, have been replaced by the Territorial Army, composed of civilian volunteers who do occasional training and represent a second line of defence. This is the more common pattern.

**milk,** liquid secreted by the mammary glands of female mammals to feed their young. Cow's milk is most widely used by humans, but milk of such animals as the mare, goat, ewe, buffalo, camel, and yak is also consumed. An almost complete food, milk contains fats; proteins (mainly casein); salts; sugar (lactose); vitamins A, C, and D; some B vitamins; and minerals, chiefly calcium and phosphorus. The composition of milk varies with the species, breed, feed, and condition of the animal. Commercially-produced milk commonly undergoes PASTEURIZATION to check bacterial growth and homogenization for uniformity. Dried (powdered) milk and concentrated milk have been in use since the mid 19th cent. Concentrated milk may be condensed (sweetened) or evaporated (unsweetened). Skimmed milk, valuable in fat-free diets, is low in vitamin A. See BUTTER; CHEESE; DAIRYING; YOGURT.

**milk of magnesia,** common name for the chemical compound magnesium hydroxide $[Mg(OH)_2]$. The viscous, white, mildly alkaline mixture used as a medicinal antacid and laxative is a suspension of about 8% magnesium hydroxide in water.

**Milky Way,** large spiral GALAXY containing about 100,000 million stars, including the Sun. It is characterized by a central nucleus of closely packed stars, lying in the direction of the constellation Sagittarius, and a flat disc marked by spiral arms. Seen edgewise as a broad band of light arching across the night sky from horizon to horizon, the Milky Way passes through the constellations Sagittarius, Aquila, Cygnus, Perseus, Auriga, Orion, and Crux. The disc is c.100,000 LIGHT-YEARS in diameter and on the average 10,000 light-years thick (increasing up to 30,000 light-years at the nucleus). A thin halo of star CLUSTERS surround the galaxy. The Sun is c.30,000 light-years from the nucleus and takes 200 million years to revolve once around the galaxy.

**Mill, John Stuart,** 1806-73, British philosopher and economist. He received a rigorous education under his father, James Mill (1773-1836), and Jeremy BENTHAM (1748-1832), who were close friends and together had founded UTILITARIANISM. John Stuart Mill's own philosophy, influenced by his wife, Harriet Taylor, developed into a more humanitarian doctrine than that of utilitarianism's founders: he was sympathetic to socialism, and was a strong advocate of women's rights and such political and social reforms as proportional representation, trade unions, and farm cooperatives. In his *System of Logic* (1843) he formulated rules for the process of induction, and he stressed the method of EMPIRICISM as the source of all knowledge. *On Liberty* (1859), probably

his most famous work, argues that the prevention of harm to others provides the only justification for restrictions on the freedom of individuals. Among his other books are *Principles of Political Economy* (1848), *Utilitarianism* (1863), and his celebrated *Autobiography* (1873). One of the most important liberal thinkers of the 19th cent., Mill strongly influenced modern economics, politics, and philosophy.

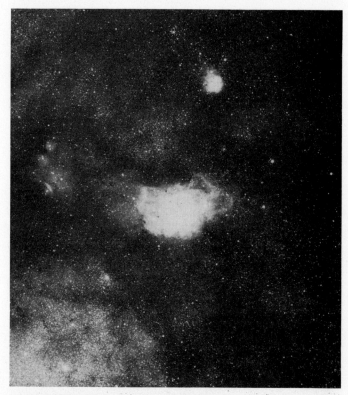

The **Milky Way** in Sagittarius taken in red light

**Millais, Sir John Everett** (mi,lay), 1829-96, English painter. He was one of the founders of the PRE-RAPHAELITE movement. His early work shows a painstaking rendering of detail, e.g., *Christ in the Carpenter's Shop* (1850; Tate Gall., London). A friend of RUSKIN, he was (1896) president of the Royal Academy.

**millenarianism,** any religious movement which believes in the imminence or final arrival on earth of a new world which will overthrow the established order, and inaugurate paradise on earth. Millenarian beliefs have been identified with the religious movements of the oppressed and the dispossessed peasantry, and have frequently occurred in colonial contexts.

**Miller, Arthur,** 1915-, American dramatist. His masterpiece, *Death of a Salesman* (1949), is the story of an ordinary American destroyed by hollow values. Miller's other works, all dealing with political or moral issues, include *All My Sons* (1947), *The Crucible* (1953), *A View from the Bridge* (1955), *After the Fall* (1964), *The Price* (1968), and *Playing for Time* (1980, a television film).

**Miller, George,** 1945-, Australian film director. He enjoyed considerable success as the director of the fast, violent *Mad Max* films, and has since moved to America to make films. His films include *Mad Max* (1978), *Mad Max II—the Road Warrior* (1982), and *The Witches of Eastwick* (1987).

**Miller, George Armitage,** 1920-, American psychologist. He is best known for his espousal of cognitive theories and his work in the field of MEMORY and psycholinguistics.

**Miller, Glenn,** 1904-44, American popular composer, bandleader and trombonist. After playing jazz trombone in his early years, he formed his own band in 1937 which reached phenomenal heights of popularity during World War II, with a series of hits, e.g., 'Moonlight Serenade', 'Little Brown Jug', and 'In The Mood'. A key factor in his success was 'the Miller Sound'—the unison voicing of clarinet over four saxophones.

He was lost, presumed killed, in an aeroplane flying over the English Channel in 1944.

**Miller, Godfrey,** 1893–1964, New Zealand painter. In the 1920s in Melbourne he painted small landscapes and in 1929 he went to London where he was taught by TONKS. Here the work of SEURAT and the post-impressionists were influential. In the 1930s he studied CUBISM and abstract art but by 1940 had turned his attention to the study of the nude. In 1952 he exhibited with the Sydney Group.

**Miller, Henry,** 1891–1980, American author. He lived in Paris in the 1930s and later settled in Big Sur, California. His controversial novels, mixing frank sexual description, autobiographical incident, and speculation on philosophy, literature, and society, include *Tropic of Cancer* (1934) and *Tropic of Capricorn* (1939), both banned in the US until 1961, and the trilogy *The Rosy Crucifixion* (1949–60). He also wrote a travel book, *The Colossus of Maroussi* (1941); essays; and the autobiography *My Life and Times* (1972).

**Miller, Jonathan,** 1934 , English director, actor, and writer. He was coauthor of and actor in the zany satirical revue *Beyond the Fringe* (London, 1961; New York, 1962). A physician, Miller has also directed plays for the National Theatre and television, e.g., *The Shakespeare Plays,* and operas, and has written television series, including *The Body in Question* (1978).

**Miller, Perry,** 1905–63, American historian. A towering figure in the field of American intellectual history, he taught at Harvard (1931–63). In *The New England Mind* (1939) he argued that religion, rather than economics, was the prime motive behind the settling of New England. His work stimulated renewed interest in American Puritanism.

**Millerand, Alexandre** (meel‚rahnh), 1859–1943, president of France (1920–24). Expelled from the Socialist Party, he moved to the right politically and was minister of war (1912–13, 1914–15). In 1920 he was premier before becoming president.

**millet,** common name for several plants of the GRASS family cultivated mainly for cereals in India, Africa, and the USSR, and for forage and hay in N America. The main varieties are foxtail, pearl, barnyard, and proso millets.

**Millet, Jean François** (mee‚lay), 1814–75, French painter. He studied with Hippolyte Delaroche and was associated with the BARBIZON SCHOOL. Millet introduced a new realism to scenes from rural life: he produced works noted for their power and simplicity, e.g., *The Gleaners* (1857) and *The Angelus* (1859; both: Louvre, Paris).

**Millikan, Robert Andrews,** 1868–1953, American physicist and educator. He taught (1896–1921) physics at the Univ. of Chicago and later (1921–45) was chairman of the executive council of the California Institute of Technology and director of the Norman Bridge Laboratory there. He received the 1923 Nobel Prize for physics for his measurement of the ELECTRON's charge and his work on the PHOTOELECTRIC EFFECT. He also studied COSMIC RAYS (which he named), X-rays, and physical and electric constants.

**Millin, Sara Gertrude,** 1889–1968, white South African historian and novelist. As a historian, she celebrates the white society in *The South Africans* (1926) as in her highly selective biographies of Cecil John RHODES and Jan Christiaan SMUTS. She is best remembered for tendentious and racist portrayals of black people and their history in her novels *God's Stepchildren* (1924) and *The King of the Bastards* (1949).

**millipede,** wormlike segmented ARTHROPOD with two pairs of legs on each body segment except the first few and last. Most temperate species are small and dull in appearance, but tropical millipedes are often brightly coloured, may be 20 cm (8 in) long, and poisonous. In contrast to the carnivorous CENTIPEDES, which they resemble, millipedes feed mostly on vegetation. They can be pests, damaging potatoes and beet.

**Milne, A(lan) A(lexander),** 1882–1956, English author. He is known for his verse collections for children, *When We Were Very Young* (1924) and *Now We Are Six* (1927), and for the classic children's stories *Winnie-the-Pooh* (1926) and *The House at Pooh Corner* (1928).

**Milnes, Richard Monckton** (later Baron Houghton), 1809–85, English poet and Member of Parliament. He published several volumes of verse, including *Palm Leaves* (1844) but is best known for his *Life and Letters of Keats* (1848), which first brought general public recognition of KEATS's génius.

**Miloš** or **Milosh** (Obrenović), 1780–1860, prince of Serbia (1817–39, 1858–60), founder of the OBRENOVIĆ dynasty and of modern SERBIA. In 1815 he led the second uprising against the Turks and, after having his rival, KARA DJORDJE murdered, was named (1817) prince of Serbia under the suzerainty of the sultan. He ruled Serbia as a personal possession and abdicated in favour of his sons Milan and Michael rather than abide the Turkish-imposed constitution of 1839. He was recalled to power in his dotage.

**Mílos** or **Milo,** island (1981 pop. 3,771), c.150 km² (58 sq mi), SE Greece, in the Aegean Sea; one of the CYCLADES. It was a centre of early AEGEAN CIVILIZATION because of its strategic location between the Greek mainland and Crete, and much excavation has been done there. The Venus of Milo (now in the Louvre, Paris) was discovered there in 1820.

**Milosz, Czeslaw** (‚meewosh), 1911–, Polish poet, novelist, and essayist; b. Lithuania. He has lived in the US since 1960. The main source of his early poetry was the Lithuanian countryside of his youth, which also figures prominently in his autobiographical novel, *The Issa Valley* (tr. 1981). His classically styled verse appears in English translation in *Selected Poems* (tr. 1973) and *Bells in Winter* (tr. 1978). Milosz is also well known for the sociopolitical essays in *The Captive Mind* (1953) and for the novel *The Seizure of Power* (1955). He was awarded the 1980 Nobel Prize for literature.

**Miltiades** (mil‚tieədeez), d. 489 BC, Athenian general in the PERSIAN WARS. In 490 BC he defeated the Persians at MARATHON and then marched his exhausted army 20 mi (32 km) to Athens, which he defended from the Persian fleet.

**Milton, John,** 1608–74, English poet. As a Cambridge undergraduate he wrote poems in Latin and English, including 'Ode on the Morning of Christ's Nativity' (1629). 'L'Allegro' and 'Il Penseroso' were probably written soon after. Continuing his studies at home, he produced the MASQUE *Comus* (1634) and the great ELEGY 'Lycidas' (1638). After a year in Italy, Milton supported the struggle to reform the Church of England with pamphlets attacking the episcopal form of church government. *Areopagitica* (1644), an important argument for freedom of the press, grew out of dissatisfaction with Parliament's strict censorship. Milton gradually broke with the Presbyterians and in 1649 wrote *The Tenure of Kings and Magistrates,* supporting the Independents, who had imprisoned Charles I, and arguing that subjects may depose and put to death an unworthy king. The pamphlet earned him a Latin secretaryship in CROMWELL's Commonwealth government. During this period Milton went blind and had to work through secretaries, one of them MARVELL. He had long planned to write an epic, and in retirement after the RESTORATION (1660), he worked on *Paradise Lost* (published in 1667). The story of Satan's rebellion against God and of the expulsion of Adam and Eve from the Garden of Eden, it is generally considered the greatest epic in the English language. *Paradise Regained* (1671) tells how Christ overcame Satan's temptations. *Samson Agonistes* (also 1671) is a poetic drama modelled on Greek tragedy but with biblical subject matter. Milton also wrote some of the most famous English sonnets. His use of blank verse, of sonorous proper names, and of intricate classical syntax have been profoundly influential on English poetry, an influence deplored by some 20th-cent. critics.

**Milton Keynes,** town (1981 pop. 93,305), Buckinghamshire, S Midlands of England. It is a New Town, designated in 1967. It includes Bletchley in the S, Stony Stratford and Wolverton in the NW, and the original village of Milton Keynes in the E. It is the site of the headquarters of the Open University, established in 1969.

**Milwaukee,** US city (1984 est. pop. 621,000), SE Wisconsin, on Lake Michigan; inc. 1848. The largest city in the state, it is a major GREAT LAKES port, shipping cargo from the Midwest to world ports via the SAINT LAWRENCE SEAWAY. Heavy machinery and electrical equipment, diesel and petrol engines, and vehicles are produced; the city's beer industry is famous. Throughout the early 19th cent. it grew as a fur trading and shipping site. Heavy 19th-cent. immigration, especially from Germany, made it a great industrial city.

**Mimas,** in astronomy, natural satellite of SATURN.

**mime:** see PANTOMIME.

**mimicry,** in biology, the advantageous resemblance of one species to another, often unrelated, species, or to a feature of its own habitat (see PROTECTIVE COLORATION). Mimicry serves to protect the mimic from predators or to deceive its prey (e.g. in ant-eating spiders that themselves resemble ants). Although most common among insects, mimicry occurs in both plants and animals.

**mimosa,** tree, shrub, or herb (genus *Mimosa*) of the PULSE family, found mainly in the tropics. Mimosas usually have feathery foliage and rounded clusters of fragrant pink to purple flowers atop the branches; they are grown as ornamentals. Best known is the sensitive plant (*M. pudica*), whose leaves fold up and collapse under stimuli such as touch, darkness, or drought. The similar and related yellow-flowered ACACIA is often sold as mimosa.

**Minamoto no Yoritomo,** 1147–99, Japanese SAMURAI leader and founder of the Kamakura shogunate (see KAMAKURA PERIOD). Following the defeat of his rivals, the Taira, at the battle of Dannoura (1185), he was made SHOGUN (1192) and established Japan's first hereditary line of shoguns.

**minaret,** in Islamic architecture, TOWER from which the faithful are called to prayer by a muezzin. Most MOSQUES have one or more minarets, usually at the corners. The earliest minarets were at the Mosque of Amr (AD 673) in Egypt. At first, minarets were generally square; free-standing conical minarets, probably derived from the Babylonian ZIGGURAT, appeared in the 9th cent. The mosque of El-Azhar (15th cent.) in Cairo is an example of the octagonal Egyptian style.

**Mindanao,** island (1970 pop. 7,292,691), Philippines, southernmost and second largest (c.94,640 km²/36,540 sq mi) of the main Philippine islands. The terrain is generally mountainous and heavily forested, with a high point of 2954 m (9690 ft) at Mt Apo. Pineapples, hemp, coffee, rice, coconut, and rubber are grown. Heavy industry includes steel, chemical, and fertilizer plants powered by hydroelectricity from the Maria Christina Falls, on the Agus R. The population is about one third Muslim, with small pagan minorities surviving in isolated areas. Muslim demands for autonomy have led to guerrilla warfare. Davao and Zamboanga are the principal cities.

**Mindszenty, Jozsef** (mind͵sentee), 1892–1975, Hungarian primate, Roman Catholic cardinal. An opponent of Communism, Mindszenty was arrested (1948) by the Hungarian government and at his trial pleaded guilty to most of the charges. It was widely believed that he had been drugged to obtain a confession. Sentenced to life imprisonment, he found refuge in the US legation during the Hungarian uprising of 1956. In 1971 the Vatican arranged his departure from Hungary, and in 1974 he was removed as primate.

**mine,** in warfare, a bomb placed in a fixed position, to be detonated by contact, magnetic proximity, or electrical impulse. Land mines, both antitank and antipersonnel, came into wide use in World War II; they were normally equipped with pressure sensors placed slightly above or below ground. Naval mines, known since the 16th cent., were first widely employed in World War I. The modern naval mine is often equipped with sonar or magnetic sensors and is laid on the bottom of the sea or anchored just below the surface of the sea.

**mineral,** natural inorganic substance having a characteristic and homogeneous chemical composition, definite physical properties, and, usually, a definite crystalline form. A few (e.g., carbon, gold, iron, and silver) are elements, but most are chemical compounds. ROCKS are combinations of minerals. Important physical properties of minerals include hardness, specific gravity, cleavage, fracture, lustre, colour, transparency, heat conductivity, feel, magnetism, and optical and electrical properties. Minerals originate by precipitation from solution, by the cooling and hardening of magmas, by the condensation of gases or gaseous action on rock, and by METAMORPHISM. They are of great economic importance in manufacturing; many are valued as GEMS. Minerals are essential to the human body, and must be obtained from food. (see IRON, CALCIUM, PHOSPHORUS, POTASSIUM, MAGNESIUM, SODIUM, CHLORINE, SULPHUR, FLOURINE, ZINC, COPPER, IODINE, MANGANESE, CHROMIUM, and COBALT).

**Minerva,** in Roman mythology, goddess of handicrafts and the arts; identified with the Olympian ATHENA.

**Ming,** dynasty: see CHINA.

**Ming tombs,** tombs of 13 of China's 16 Ming emperors (1398–1644), located c.50 km (c.31 mi) N of Beijing. Only two of the tombs have been excavated, the Chang Ling (1403–24) and the Ding Ling (1562–1620). The road to the tombs, once a sacred way forbidden to all but the

emperor's funeral cortege, is marked by statues of animals (including the tortoise as a symbol of longevity), and military and court officials. The tombs are now a popular excursion for citizens of Beijing and Western tourists.

One of the many temples and shrines at the **Ming Tombs**

**Mingus, Charles,** 1922-79, black American jazz bassist, pianist, cellist, composer, arranger, and bandleader. As a virtuoso bassist, he played with a number of jazz greats in the 1940s and 50s, including Louis ARMSTRONG, Duke ELLINGTON, and Charlie PARKER. By the mid 1950s he began to mature as a creative composer, extending the horizons of jazz by experimenting with atonality and dissonant effects, whilst retaining strong blues and gospel elements, e.g., his 'Blues and Roots' album. His 1971 autobiography *Beneath the Underdog* is required reading for anyone interested in jazz.

**minimal art,** movement in American painting and sculpture that originated in New York City in the early 1960s. Arising from a reaction against the subjectivity and romanticism of ABSTRACT EXPRESSIONISM, minimalism stressed impersonality and anonymity in precise, often monumental, geometric forms and pure colours intended to have no references beyond the works themselves. Minimal art is typified by the primary structures of such sculptors as Carl ANDRE, Donald JUDD, and Tony Smith, and by the hard-edge paintings of such artists as Ellsworth KELLY, Kenneth NOLAND, and Frank STELLA.

**minimum wage,** lowest wage legally permitted in an industry, or in a government or other organization. Minimum wages are intended to ensure that workers have a standard of living above the lowest permitted by health and decency. The minimum has been set by labour unions (through COLLECTIVE BARGAINING), through arbitration, and by legislation. Introduced (1894) in New Zealand, it was adopted by several other countries, but not by the UK.

**mining,** extraction of solid MINERAL resources from the earth, including ORES (which contain commercially valuable amounts of METAL), precious stones (see GEM), building stones, and solid fuels. OPEN-CAST MINING and QUARRYING are the most common mining methods that start from the earth's surface and maintain exposure to it. Under certain circumstances surface mining can become prohibitive, and underground mining is then considered. The objective of underground mining is to extract the ore below the surface of the earth safely and economically. Entry is through a tunnel or shaft, and the ore is mined in stopes, or rooms. Material left in place to support the ceiling is called a pillar and can sometimes be recovered afterwards. A modern underground mine is a highly mechanized operation, using vehicles, rail haulage, and multiple drill units. To protect miners and their equipment, much attention is paid to mine safety, including proper ventilation and roof support. There are a number of other mining methods, including *solution mining,* in which the ore is brought into a liquid solution by a chemical or by bacteria and pumped to the surface, and *placer mining,* in which gravel, sand, or talus is removed from deposits by hand, hydraulic nozzles, or dredging. See also COAL MINING.

**mink,** semiaquatic carnivorous MAMMAL (genus *Mustela*), related to the WEASEL and highly prized for its thick, lustrous, rich brown fur. Found in Europe and North America, it has a slender, arched body about 50 cm (20 in) long and a bushy tail. Minks live near water, where they feed on rodents, fishes, frogs, and birds. The mink is widely bred on farms for the fur trade.

**Minkowski, Hermann** (min͵kofskee), 1864–1909, Russian mathematician. He evolved a four-dimensional geometry of space and time that represented special relativity most clearly.

**Minneapolis,** US city (1984 est. pop. 358,000), E Minnesota, at the head of navigation on the Mississippi R., at St Anthony Falls; inc. 1856. Minneapolis and adjacent SAINT PAUL are called the Twin Cities. The largest city in the state and a major port, it is an industrial and rail centre. Flour milling and computer and electronic industries are particularly important. In the 19th cent. it was the nation's leading timber centre.

**Minnesota,** state of the US (1984 est. pop. 4,162,000), area 217,736 km² (84,068 sq mi), situated in the upper Midwest, bordered by Lake SUPERIOR and Wisconsin (E), Iowa (S), North Dakota and South Dakota (W), and the Canadian provinces of Ontario and Manitoba (N). The capital is SAINT PAUL, its twin city MINNEAPOLIS is the largest centre, and Duluth is a major port. Minnesota is covered in many lakes, stretching from the boulder-strewn hills of the glaciated north to the broad prairies of the south. In the NE there are iron-rich mountains. The MISSISSIPPI R. originates in the state and flows SE. Minnesota has cold winters and hot summers typical of continental interiors. Manufacturing leads the economy, based on nonelectrical machinery, food processing, and electronic equipment. It is a major dairying state; beef cattle, corn, soybeans, hay, and wheat are also of importance. Minnesota is the leading state in the mining of iron ore. In 1980 96% of the population was non-Hispanic white and more than 64% lived in metropolitan areas. The original inhabitants were Ojibwa and Sioux Indians. After the French arrived in the mid-17th cent. the area was acquired by the US in the LOUISIANA PURCHASE (1803). Many Scandinavians were among the first settlers in the 1820s, and the large rural population was receptive to late 19th cent. reform movements; the Granger Movement, the Populist Party, and the Farmer–Labour Party were formed there. In the 20th cent. the tradition continued, producing national figures in the Democratic Party, such as presidential nominees Hubert HUMPHREY and Walter MONDALE.

**minnow,** small European freshwater FISH (*Phoxinus phoxinus*) in the family Cyprinidae. The name has since been given to a number of related fishes in the carp family and small carp, bream, chub, dace, and shiners are now included. Most minnows are small and drab, but a few species are brightly coloured. Minnows are important in freshwater aquatic life, feeding on insects, larvae, and CRUSTACEANS and in turn serving as food for larger fishes. Studies have shown that if a minnow's skin is broken, it gives out a substance which causes other minnows to bunch together and swim away.

**Minoan civilization** (mi͵nohən), a Bronze Age AEGEAN CIVILIZATION that flourished in CRETE. The Cretans were generally similar to other agricultural groups in the S Aegean until about 2000 BC, when palaces were built at KNOSSOS, Phaistos, and Mallia and a linear writing (see LINEAR B) emerged to replace earlier hieroglyphics. Cretan influence was strong in the Aegean until about 1450 BC when all the palaces with the exception of Knossos were destroyed, possibly as the result of a volcanic eruption or invasion. Knossos itself succumbed to fire some 80 years later under similarly obscure circumstances. The late Minoan period faded out in poverty, and the cultural centre passed to the Greek mainland.

**Minorca:** see BALEARIC ISLANDS.

**minor planet:** see ASTEROID.

**Minos** (͵mienos, -nəs), in Greek mythology, king of CRETE, son of ZEUS and Europa. His legends appear to have some basis in historical fact since the MINOAN CIVILIZATION, rich and powerful, was named after Minos or his dynasty. In legend, he was the husband of Pasiphaë and the father of Androgeus, Glaucus, ARIADNE, and PHAEDRA; he imprisoned DAEDALUS and Icarus on Crete.

**Minotaur** (mienətaw), in Greek mythology, monster with a bull's head and man's body. When King MINOS of CRETE failed to sacrifice a bull to POSEIDON, the god caused Queen Pasiphaë to lust after the animal. By it, she conceived the Minotaur, which was confined in the labyrinth built by DAEDALUS. There it devoured human beings until it was killed by THESEUS. It has often been represented in art, e.g., by PICASSO (*Vollard Suite;* 1930-37).

**Minseito** ('meen͵saytoh), Japanese political party, usually called the Liberal party in English. A successor of the Kaishinto (founded 1882) of Shigenobuo KUMA, it merged (1955) with the Democrats to form the Liberal-Democratic party.

**Minsk,** city (1985 pop. 1,472,000), capital of BELORUSSIA, W European USSR, on a tributary of the Berezina R. An industrial centre and rail junction, it produces machinery and tractors among other products. Founded c.1067, it became the capital of the Minsk principality in 1101, and a major trade and craft centre by c.1500. Annexed by Lithuania (1326) and Poland (1569), it passed to Russia in 1793 and developed industrially in the 1870s. During World War II Minsk was heavily damaged and most of its large Jewish population was exterminated by occupying Nazi forces. The city was rebuilt and industry reestablished after the war.

**minstrel,** professional secular musician of the Middle Ages. They were particularly skilled itinerant entertainers who became attached to a court to perform the songs of the TROUBADOURS or TROUVÈRES who employed them. The term has also been applied to the semiprofessional musicians of West Africa, especially the hereditary castes of *griots.*

**mint,** place where legal coinage is manufactured. The name is derived from the temple of Juno Moneta [Latin, = *mint*] in Rome, where silver coins were made as early as 269 BC. Mints existed earlier elsewhere, as in Lydia and Greece. The UK is unusual in having two mints. Most coinage is produced in the Llantrisant mint in Wales while the London mint at Tower Hill is used mainly for administration. In the UK coins have been struck for other countries since the 16th cent. See also COIN; NUMISMATICS.

**mint,** in botany, common name for the Labiatae, or the Lamiaceae, a large family of chiefly annual or perennial herbs, distributed worldwide but most common in the Mediterranean region. The family is typified by square stems, paired opposite leaves, and white, red, blue, or purple flowers. The aromatic ESSENTIAL OILS in the plants' foliage are used in perfumes, flavourings, and medicines. The true mints (genus *Mentha*), SAGE, lavender, and ROSEMARY are important sources of essential oils; these and BASIL, THYME, MARJORAM, and OREGANO are common kitchen herbs. Other well-known members of the family are CATNIP and horehound. The most commercially important true mints are peppermint (*M. piperita*), a source of menthol, and the milder spearmint (*M. spicata*). Mints are also grown as ornamentals.

**Minton,** English family of potters. **Thomas Minton,** 1765–1836, founded a pottery firm at Stoke-on-Trent in 1793 and reputedly created the famous willow-pattern ware. His son **Herbert Minton,** 1793–1858, developed the firm and made it famous.

**minuet,** French dance from Poitou, introduced at Louis XIV's court in 1650. In 3/4 time and moderate tempo, it was danced by open couples with graceful, gliding steps. Many composers, e.g., HAYDN and W.A. MOZART, used its musical form in sonatas and symphonies.

**Minuit, Peter** (͵minyoohit), c.1580–1638, first director general of NEW NETHERLAND. Sent to America by the Dutch West India Company, he purchased (1626) Manhattan from the Indians for trinkets valued at $24. He later headed the group that established (1638) NEW SWEDEN.

**Miocene epoch:** see GEOLOGICAL ERA (table).

**mir,** Russian peasant community. Among free peasants the mir owned the land; among SERFS it allocated land reserved for serf use. When serfdom ended (1861; see EMANCIPATION, EDICT OF) land was allotted to the mir rather than to individuals, but this proved impractical. The 1908 reforms of STOLYPIN broke many mirs into individual holdings. After the RUSSIAN REVOLUTION of 1917 the COLLECTIVE FARM replaced the mir.

**Minton,** maiolica ewer and stand (1856; Fitzwilliam Museum, Cambridge)

**Mir,** Soviet manned space station, developed from the earlier Salyut series, and launched in Feb. 1986 by a Proton launch vehicle. The core module is 13.1 m (43 ft) long, 4.2 m (13½ ft) in diameter, and has a mass of 21 tonnes. It is similar in size to Salyut, but provides more comfortable crew accommodation to cater for up to six male or female cosmonauts. Six docking ports allow the station to be extended by the addition of further modules. The first extra module, *Kvant*, was added in Apr. 1987 and is devoted to astrophysical research. Further modules may be concerned with geophysics, biology, and materials processing.

The **Mir** orbital space station, designed as the basic component of a multi-purpose, permanently-manned space laboratory with specialized modules for scientific and economic purposes.

**Mirabeau, Honoré Gabriel Riquetti** or **Riqueti, comte de** (meerah,boh), 1749–91, politician of the FRENCH REVOLUTION. After a life of wild excess and repeated imprisonment, he was elected (1789) to the STATES-GENERAL. With his fiery eloquence, he became the spokesman of the third estate and tried to create a constitutional monarchy that would permit him to become prime minister. As a member of the Constituent Assembly, however, he was thwarted when the Assembly barred its members from the cabinet. Mirabeau then began secret dealings with the king and queen, but the couple did not heed his advice. He died just before his dealings with the court were discovered.

**mirage,** atmospheric optical illusion in which an observer sees a nonexistent body of water or an image of some object. Examples of mirages are pools of water seen over hot desert sands or hot pavements, and, at sea, an inverted image of a ship seen in the sky. These phenomena can be explained by the facts (1) that light rays undergo REFRACTION, i.e., are bent, in passing between media of differing densities, and (2) that the boundary between two such media acts as a mirror for rays of light coming in at certain angles. Mirages can be photographed.

**Mirambo,** c.1840–84, empire-builder in 19th-cent. TANZANIA. He succeeded to a minor Nyamwezi chiefdom NW of Tabora in 1858 and by the late 1860s had gained control of the surrounding chiefdoms. Leading a formidable standing army of RUGA-RUGA warriors, he exacted tribute in the form of ivory and slaves and sold them for guns and gunpowder, so gaining control of profitable trade routes. His empire fragmented after his death.

**Miranda,** in astronomy, natural satellite of URANUS.

**Miranda, Francisco de** (mee,randah), 1750–1816, Venezuelan revolutionary. A Spanish army officer, he fought in both the American Revolution and the French Revolutionary Wars, was in the service of Catherine the Great, then joined (1810) the revolution against Spanish rule in VENEZUELA. He commanded rebel forces and served briefly as dictator, but military reverses forced his surrender (1812) and imprisonment. He is known as the Precursor, to distinguish him from Simon BOLÍVAR, who completed the task of liberation.

**Miranda, Francisco de Sá de,** 1481–1558, Portuguese poet. He travelled to Italy (1521–26) and brought back to Portugal the literary and humanistic ideas of the RENAISSANCE. He wrote poetry and prose plays, e.g., *Os Estrangeiros* (1559), and some of his best works are his verse epistles embodying his idealistic moral outlook.

**Miranda v. Arizona,** case decided in 1966 by the US SUPREME COURT, reversing an Arizona conviction. Miranda had been questioned and had confessed without being told that he had the right to a lawyer. Chief Justice WARREN ruled that EVIDENCE such as Miranda's confession could not be introduced unless the defendant had, before questioning, been told of his rights through what came to be called 'Miranda warnings'.

**Miró, Joan** (mee,roh), 1893–1983, Spanish surrealist painter. In his abstract surrealist images he attempted a kind of psychic automatism, an expression of the subconscious in free form. By 1930 he had developed a lyrical style distinguished by the use of brilliant colour and the playful juxtaposition of delicate lines with abstract, often amoebic shapes, e.g., *Dog Barking at the Moon* (1926). The explicit social and political critiques of SURREALISM find little expression in Miró's work, except for a brief period during the SPANISH CIVIL WAR.

**mirror,** in OPTICS, a reflecting surface that forms an image of an object when light rays coming from that object fall upon it (see REFLECTION). A plane mirror, which has a flat reflecting surface, reflects a beam of light without changing its character. In a convex spherical mirror, the vertex, or midpoint, of the mirror is nearer to the object than the edges, and parallel rays from a light source diverge after reflection. In a concave mirror, the vertex is farther away from the object than the edges, and rays parallel to the principal axis are reflected to a single point, or principal focus. A concave parabolic mirror is the principal element of a reflecting TELESCOPE.

**Mirror for Magistrates,** a collection of English poems on the falls of great men, first published in 1555 and reprinted in enlarged and extended editions throughout the 16th cent. It was generally popular, influencing many Elizabethan writers, including SPENSER, SHAKESPEARE, and DANIEL.

**MIRV:** see MISSILE, GUIDED.

**miscarriage:** see ABORTION; PREGNANCY AND BIRTH.

**Mishima Yukio,** 1925–70, Japanese short-story writer, novelist, and playwright; b. Hiraoka Kimitake. A brilliant stylist, Mishima was obsessed by what he saw as the materialist contentment of modern Japan, by sexual perversion, and death by disembowelment (*seppuku*). His *Confessions of a Mask* (1949; tr. 1958) is a semi-autobiographical account of the hero's discovery of his homosexuality; *The Temple of the Golden Pavilion* (1956; tr. 1959), describes the burning down of the Kinkakuji Temple in Kyoto by a crazed student, and the four novels of *The Sea of Fertility* (1965–70; tr. 1972–74) evoke the reappearance of a dead hero under various forms, a lover in the early years of the century, a young officer in the 1936 rebellion, a Thai princess in post-war Bangkok, and finally a beautiful sadistic boy in the Japan of the 1960s. Mishima committed ritual suicide after an unsuccessful attempt to rouse the Japanese Self-Defence Forces to join in a *coup d'état* in 1970.

**Mishnah,** first systemization and codification of Jewish law. The Mishnah and the Gemara, a commentary on the Mishnah, constitute the TALMUD. Next to the Scriptures, the Mishnah is the basic textbook of Jewish life and thought, covering, e.g., agriculture, Sabbath and festivals, marriage and divorce, and civil and criminal matters. The final compilation of the Mishnah was made under the direction of JUDAH HA-NASI from the work of the Tannaim, a group of sages of the 1st and 2nd cent. AD, including AKIBA BEN JOSEPH, and particularly Rabbi Meir. The Mishnah has been widely translated and has had a considerable influence beyond the confines of Judaism.

**Miskolc** (‚mishkolts), city (1985 pop. 212,000), NE Hungary, on the Sajó R. Hungary's second largest city, it is an industrial centre producing iron and steel, cement, machinery, and other manufactures. Frequent invasions, e.g., by the Mongols (13th cent.), have marked its history. Landmarks include the Avas Reformed Church (15th cent.).

**Misratah:** see MISURATA.

**missile, guided,** self-propelled, unmanned space or air vehicle carrying a high-explosive warhead (short-range missiles) or a nuclear warhead (long-range missiles). Its path can be adjusted during flight, either by automatic self-contained controls or by distant human control. Guided missiles are powered either by ROCKET engines or by JET PROPULSION. They were first developed in modern form by the Germans, who in WORLD WAR II employed V–1 and V–2 guided missiles against Great Britain and the Low Countries. Missiles may be aerodynamic, i.e., controlled by aerodynamic surfaces and following a straight-line trajectory to the target, or ballistic, i.e., powered during flight and following a parabolic trajectory. Aerodynamic missiles are of four types. Air-to-air missiles supplement antiaircraft guns and are often guided by self-contained controls that detect and target the missile toward heat sources. Air-to-surface missiles, launched by aircraft against ground positions, are generally radio-controlled. Surface-to-air missiles (SAM) operate against aircraft or other missiles. Surface-to-surface missiles include antitank and naval missiles. The intermediate-range ballistic missile (IRBM) can reach targets up to 2800 km (1750 mi) away. The intercontinental ballistic missile (ICBM), and the submarine-launched ballistic missile (SLBM) have ranges of many thousands of kilometres. A multiple independently-targeted reentry vehicle (MIRV) permits one booster to carry several warheads, each guided to a separate target. An antiballistic missile (ABM) is designed to detect and intercept enemy missiles. Technological advances, together with the development of nuclear warheads, have made guided missiles the key strategic weapon of modern warfare.

**missions,** name of organizations that extend religious teaching and of efforts to disseminate the Christian religion. CHRISTIANITY was spread through the Roman Empire by missions, and in later centuries it was extended by missionary labours in Ireland, Germany, Russia, and Scandinavia. In the 16th cent. missions were formed in the New World, especially by the FRANCISCANS and the Jesuits (see JESUS, SOCIETY OF). In Colonial America, Roger WILLIAMS and John ELIOT did notable work among the Indians, as did the Moravian Church. Mission activity became intense in Africa and Asia in the 19th and 20th cent. and was greatly furthered by the work of David LIVINGSTONE and Albert SCHWEITZER.

**Mississippi,** state of the US (1984 est. pop. 2,598,000), area 123,584 km² (47,716 sq mi), located in the Deep South, bordered by Alabama (E), the Gulf of Mexico (S), Arkansas and Louisiana (W), and Tennessee (N). The capital and largest city is JACKSON. The state consists of the flat alluvial delta of the MISSISSIPPI R. to the W and hilly land to the E. Along the lowlands of the coast the climate is subtropical. Industry has dominated the economy since 1965, led by transport equipment, timber products, processed foods, and clothing. Soya beans is the main agricultural product, followed by cotton, cattle, broiler chickens, rice, and hay. Petroleum and natural gas are found extensively, and fishing and forestry are also important. Almost 75% of the population lives outside metropolitan areas, and the black population (35%) forms a higher percentage than in any other state. The Chocktaw, Chickasaw, and Natchez Indians were the first inhabitants, before the area came under French, then Spanish control in the 18th cent. Acquired by the US (1795), Mississippi produced cotton on plantations with slave labour and

provided the president of the Confederacy during the Civil War, Jefferson DAVIS. Even after readmittance to the Union, the state effectively disenfranchised blacks by means of the so-called 'Jim Crow' laws. The federal government built an extensive flood-control programme after the disastrous 1927 flood. After the war poverty and racial division persisted, and the state was a centre of the civil rights movement. In recent years both problems have been ameliorated.

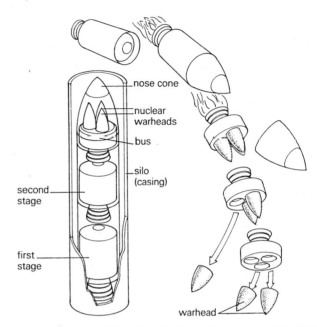

Guided missile: A multiple independently targeted reentry vehicle (MIRV)

**Mississippi,** principal river of the US and of North America, flowing generally south c.3780 km (2350 mi) from Lake Itasca (alt. 446 m/1463 ft) in N Minnesota to enter the Gulf of Mexico through a vast, birdsfoot-type delta in Louisiana. It forms, with the MISSOURI R., its chief tributary, the world's third longest (c.6020 km/3740 mi) river system. The Mississippi is navigable by ocean-going vessels to Baton Rouge, Louisiana, and by barges and towboats through a 2.7–m (9–ft) channel as far as Minneapolis, Minnesota, with canals circumventing rapids near Rock Island, Illinois, and Keokuk, Iowa. There are 41 dams above Minneapolis and c.2580 km (over 1600 mi) of levees below Cape Girardeau, Missouri, to regulate and restrain the river's flow. Normally, the Mississippi is c.1070 m (3500 ft) wide near St Louis and c.1370 m (4500 ft) wide at Cairo, Illinois, but it reached a width of nearly 130 km (80 mi) in places during a disastrous flood in 1927 and inundated large areas during the rainy spring of 1973. Probably seen by De Soto in 1541, the river was claimed by France after LA SALLE descended it to reach the Gulf of Mexico in 1682. It was ceded to Spain in 1763 and was regained by France in 1800, before it passed to the US in 1803 as part of the LOUISIANA PURCHASE. Mark TWAIN's *Life on the Mississippi* (1883) describes vividly the end of the river's steamboat era, which began in 1811.

**Missouri,** state of the US (1984 est. pop. 5,008,000), area 180,487 km² (69,686 sq mi), located in the Midwest and bordered by Illinois, Kentucky, and Tennessee (E), Arkansas (S), Oklahoma, Kansas, and Nebraska (W), and Iowa (N). The capital is JEFFERSON CITY, while the largest cities are KANSAS CITY, SPRINGFIELD, and the great inland port of SAINT LOUIS. Two great rivers have shaped the state: the MISSISSIPPI, which forms its eastern border, and the MISSOURI, which flows W to E across the state to join the Mississippi above St Louis. North of the Missouri R. the state consists of plains, and the elevation rises in the S to the Ozark plateau, a tourist centre. Missouri is a heavily industrialized state, with transport equipment, processed foods, and chemicals the leading products. Agriculture produces cattle, soya beans, pigs, dairy commodities, hay, and sorghum. Missouri is the leading producer of lead, and also extracts barite, lime, zinc, coal, and iron. In 1980 88% of the population was non-Hispanic white and 10% black, and over 60% lived in large metropolitan areas. The inhabitants of the area when the French arrived in the 17th cent. were Osage and Missouri Indians. Passing to the US with the LOUISIANA PURCHASE (1803), Missouri was admitted to the Union as a slave state after much controversy, in the Missouri Compromise (1821). It became the starting point for the wagon trains travelling west, attracting many German immigrants before the Civil War. The state stayed in the Union, but was the location for much guerilla warfare, which persisted after the war in the form of lawlessness on the part of Jesse James and other outlaws. Industry increased, especially after World War II, when Missouri became the country's second largest manufacturer of motor vehicles.

**Missouri,** longest river of the US, flowing c.4130 km (2565 mi) from its source in the Rocky Mts to join the MISSISSIPPI R. 27 km (17 mi) N of St Louis, Missouri, forming the world's third longest (c.6020 km/3740 mi) river system. Its principal headwaters are the Jefferson, Madison, and Gallatin rivers, which unite to form the main stream at Three Forks, Montana. The river is navigable for 1225 km (760 mi) to Sioux City, Iowa. Above Sioux City, its fluctuating flow is regulated by seven major dams—Gavins Point, Fort Randall, Big Bend, Oahe, Garrison, Fort Peck, and Canyon Ferry—that are part of the coordinated Missouri River Basin Project authorized by the US Congress in 1944. MARQUETTE and JOLLIET passed the mouth of the river in 1683, and Vérendrye explored its upper reaches in 1738. Other early explorers were David Thompson (1797), and Meriwether Lewis and William Clark (see LEWIS AND CLARK EXPEDITION) on their journey (1803–06) to the Pacific Ocean. River traffic, begun when the first steamboat reached Fort Benton in 1819, declined with the loss of freight to the railways after the Civil War but was revitalized in the early 20th cent. through navigational improvements below Sioux City.

**Missouri Compromise,** 1820–21, measures passed by the US Congress to end the first of a series of crises concerning the extension of SLAVERY. By the terms of the compromise, Maine was admitted as a free state and Missouri as a slave state, and slavery was prohibited in the rest of the LOUISIANA PURCHASE north of 36°30′. This proviso held until 1854, when the KANSAS–NEBRASKA ACT repealed the Missouri Compromise.

**mistletoe,** common name for the Loranthaceae, a family of chiefly tropical parasitic herbs and shrubs with leathery leaves and waxy white berries. Mistletoes, aerial hemiparasites with green leaves that carry out PHOTOSYNTHESIS, attach themselves to their hosts by modified roots called haustoria. They are widely associated with folklore and are used as Christmas decorations. The mistletoe most commonly sold is the 'true' mistletoe (*Viscum album*).

**Mistral, Frédéric** (mees,trahl), 1830–1914, French Provençal poet. He led the Félibrige movement to promote Provençal as a literary language and was its greatest poet. His best-known work is the verse romance *Mirèio* (1859). He shared the 1904 Nobel Prize in literature with José ECHEGARAY.

**Mistral, Gabriela,** pseud. of **Lucila Godoy Alcayaga,** 1889–1957, Chilean poet. An educator and diplomat, she was the first Latin American to receive the Nobel Prize for literature (1945). Her lyric works include *Sonetos de la muerte* (1914; tr. Sonnets of Death), *Desolación* (1922), *Tala* [havoc] (1938), and *Lagar* [wine press] (1954).

**Misurata** or **Misratah,** city and port (1982 est. pop. 285,000), N Libya, on the Mediterranean coast. Its economy is based on fishing and iron and steel industries.

**Mitchell, Margaret,** 1900–49, American novelist. Her one novel, *Gone with the Wind* (1936), is set in Georgia during the CIVIL WAR and RECONSTRUCTION. It and the film adaptation (1939) were enormously successful.

**Mitchell, Wesley Clair,** 1874–1948, American economist. He held teaching posts at several institutions, including the Univ. of California and Columbia, and helped found the National Bureau of Economic Research. One of the most eminent US economists, he focused much of his research on statistical investigation of the business cycle. His major work is *Business Cycles* (1913; 2nd ed. 1927).

**Mitchell, William** ('Billy'), 1879–1936, American general, commander of the American expeditionary air force in World War I; b. France. He advocated a large, independent air force, but his public criticism of the military for neglecting air power led to his court martial (1925) and resignation.

**Mitchum, Robert,** 1917–, American film actor. A nonchalant heavyweight with sleepy eyes, he is yet one of the subtlest actors that cinema has produced. His films include *Out of the Past* (1947), *The Night of the Hunter* (1955), *El Dorado* (1967), and *The Friends of Eddie Coyle* (1973).

**mite,** small, often microscopic ARACHNID. Mites are often parasites of animals and plants and infest stored foodstuffs. Some burrow into the skin of mammals, causing MANGE and scabies. Chiggers, which are the larvae of harvest mites, transmit the organism that causes scrub typhus. There are many free-living mites, such as the red water mites found in fresh waters and the Antarctic mites that live on fungi and decaying plants. Some have adapted to humans, the cheese mite living in and feeding on cheese.

**Mitford, Nancy,** 1904–73, English writer. She satirized the aristocracy she was born into in novels like *The Pursuit of Love* (1945) and *Love in a Cold Climate* (1949). Her sister **Jessica Mitford,** 1917–, is a writer best known for her exposé of the funeral business, *The American Way of Death* (1963), and an autobiography, *Hons and Rebels* (1960).

**Mithra:** see MITRA.

**Mithridates VI,** c.131–63 BC, king of ancient PONTUS, called Mithridates the Great. The extension of his empire brought him into war with Rome. In the First Mithridatic War (88–84BC) he conquered (88 BC) most of Asia Minor, but in 85 BC he was defeated there and in Greece. The Second Mithridatic War (83–81 BC) ended in a Roman defeat. In the Third Mithridatic War (76–63 BC) LUCULLUS defeated Mithridates, and POMPEY drove the king into the Crimea, where he had himself killed by a slave. He is the hero of Mozart's early opera *Mithridate Re di Ponto* (1770).

**mitosis,** process of nuclear division in a living cell by which the hereditary carriers, or CHROMOSOMES, are exactly replicated, the two parts being distributed to identical daughter nuclei. In mitosis each cell formed receives chromosomes that are alike in composition and equal in number to the chromosomes of the parent cell. Mitotic division occurs in somatic (body) cells; in sex cells (OVUM and SPERM) MEIOSIS (halving of the number of chromosomes) also takes place.

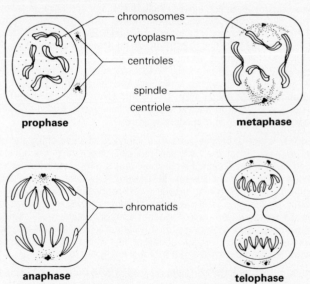

Mitosis: The four phases of nuclear division in an animal cell. In the prophase the chromosomes become visible by thickening and contracting, and split into paired chromatids; in the metaphase the chromosomes become arranged in the equatorial plane of the spindle; in the anaphase the chromosomes move towards the ends of the spindle; and the telophase is characterized by the appearance of two new nuclei, each with the same number of chromosomes as the original cell, and that is subsequently followed by the division of the original cell.

**Mitra,** god of ancient India and Persia (where he is known as **Mithra**). In the 5th cent. BC he appears as the principal Persian deity, god of light and wisdom. His cult expanded to become a worldwide religion, called **Mithraism.** In the 2nd cent. AD it was more general in the Roman empire than Christianity, to which it bore many similarities. Mithraism taught the dualistic struggle between the forces of good and evil and offered hope of immortality through the practice of rites and a system of rigorous ethics. It declined rapidly in the late 3rd cent. In India (in Ṛg-Vedic Hymns) Mitra is usually associated with another deity, Varuṇa (later called rain-god).

**Mittelholzer, Edgar Austin,** 1909–65, Guyanese novelist. His prolific output is best represented in the account of a family and its history in the *Kaywana* trilogy. Other works include *A Morning at the Office* (1950), *The Adding Machine: A Fable for Capitalists and Commercialists* (1954), and *My Bones and My Flute: A Ghost Story in the Old-Fashioned Manner* (1955).

**Mitterrand, François Maurice** (meetə̩rahnn), 1916–, French Socialist leader and president (1981–). During WORLD WAR II he fought in the Resistance. Elected a deputy in 1946, he held several cabinet posts in the 1950s. He joined the weak Socialist Party, in 1971 became first secretary, and led it to increasing success at the polls. After losing to Valéry GISCARD D'ESTAING in 1974, Mitterrand defeated him in 1981 to become the first Socialist president of the French Fifth Republic. He continued in office despite the election of a centre-right government in 1986, but since his reelection as president in 1988, he once more had a Socialist-led government under Rocard.

**mitzvah** [Heb., = command], term applied to each of the 613 positive and negative laws found in the Pentateuch. It is also applied, more generally, to 'a good deed'; 'a kindly act'.

**Mixtec,** MIDDLE AMERICAN INDIANS of SW Mexico, who speak a language of the Otomian stock (see AMERICAN INDIAN LANGUAGES). Important from ancient times, the Mixtec seem to have had an advanced culture before the coming of the TOLTEC. They began spreading southwards about 900 and by the 14th cent. overshadowed their rivals the Zapotec. Excelling in stonework and metalwork, wood carving, and pottery decoration, the Mixtec strongly influenced other Mexican cultures. They resisted the Spanish in the 16th cent., but were subjugated with the aid of the Zapotec. There are about 300,000 Mixtec-speaking people in Mexico today.

**mixture:** see COMPOUND.

**mks system:** see METRIC SYSTEM.

**Mkwawa,** c.1860–98, ruler of the Hehe of late 19th-cent. S TANZANIA, and anticolonial resistance leader. He defeated a German column in 1891 but three years later lost his capital. Mkwawa carried on a guerrilla campaign until 1898 when he committed suicide rather than be taken prisoner.

**Mn,** chemical symbol of the element MANGANESE.

**Mnemosyne:** see MUSES.

**Mnesicles** (‚nesikleez), Greek architect, 5th cent. BC. He designed the Propylaea, and the ERECHTHEUM is sometimes ascribed to him. Both are on the Acropolis, Athens.

**Mo,** chemical symbol of the element MOLYBDENUM.

**Moab,** ancient nation in the uplands E of the Dead Sea, now part of Jordan. The Moabites were close kin to the Hebrews, and the language of the Moabite stone (dating to 850 BC) is practically the same as biblical Hebrew. Moab is continually mentioned in the Bible. Its people were later absorbed by the Nabataeans.

**Moberg, Vilhelm** (‚moohberyə), 1898–1973, Swedish novelist who often wrote of farm life. His works include *The Earth Is Ours* (1935–39) and the antitotalitarian *Ride This Night!* (1941). Two films (1973), *The Emigrants* and *The New Land*, were based on his epic about Swedish emigration to the US.

**mobile,** type of moving sculpture developed by Alexander CALDER in 1932 and named by Marcel DUCHAMP. Often constructed of coloured metal pieces connected by wires, mobiles have moving parts that are sensitive to a breeze or light touch.

**Möbius strip,** in mathematics, a one-sided surface formed by taking a strip of material, e.g., paper, twisting one end through 180° about the strip's longitudinal axis and then joining this end to the other end.

**Mobutu Sese Seko,** 1930–, president of ZAÏRE (1967–); b. Joseph Désiré Mobutu. He became prime minister of the Belgian Congo in 1966 after staging a coup that toppled the government of Joseph KASAVUBU. In

1967 he established a presidential form of government headed by himself, and in 1971 he changed the Congo's name to Zaïre.

**mockingbird,** American BIRD of the Mimidae family, related to the European WREN. It is an excellent mimic, copying other birds, human sounds, and machines.

**mock orange:** see SAXIFRAGE.

**mode,** in music. 1 Any pattern or arrangement of the intervals of a SCALE. In the Middle Ages eight modes each in the range of an octave (derived from ancient Greek theory), developed as the basis of PLAINCHANT composition. They were grouped in four pairs, each pair containing an authentic mode and (at the interval of a fourth below that) a plagal mode. These modes were the basis of musical composition for 11 centuries. In the late 16th and early 17th cent. the series was limited to the major and minor modes in use today. The use of medieval modes by later composers such as VAUGHAN WILLIAMS is called modality in contrast to TONALITY. 2 In the 13th cent., six rhythmical patterns in ternary meter that governed composition. 3 In 20th-cent. music, any of four forms of the tone row, an arbitrary arrangement of the 12 equal chromatic tones of the diatonic scale of Western music (see SERIAL MUSIC). 4 Modes are used in different ways in folk music and in Asian classical music. The Arabic *maqām* and Indian *Rāg* systems, for instance, use numerous different modes, each with its own characteristic motifs and intervals.

**mode,** one type of AVERAGE used in STATISTICS as an alternative to the ARITHMETIC MEAN. It is the value which actually occurs more frequently than any other and is sometimes a more appropriate average when the DISTRIBUTION of values contains many extreme values. The mode, for example, would be a better representation of the average length of life of a medieval peasant than the arithmetic mean.

**mode,** in grammar: see MOOD.

**modelling,** used in STATISTICS to indicate the use of mathematical descriptions of ecological, social, or economic systems. Whereas a good SIMULATION should include as much detail as possible, a good model should include as little as possible. Thus, models attempt to provide the simplest possible description of a system that nevertheless captures the essential features and behaviour of that system. Models of the relationships between the numbers of predators and their prey, for example, often enable effective control measures to be planned for the conservation of threatened animals in wildlife parks.

**Model Parliament:** see PARLIAMENT.

**Modena,** city (1984 pop. 178,328), Emilia-Romagna, N Italy. Racing-cars and tractors are the principal products of its vehicle-building industries. Originating as an Etruscan settlement, it developed under Roman domination and later had a long association with the ESTE family. Famous buildings include its cathedral (1099–1184) in the Romanesque style and the Torre Ghirlandina tower.

**moderator:** see NUCLEAR REACTOR.

**modern architecture,** homogeneous architectural style appearing in most Western countries after World War I and continuing to develop through the mid-20th cent. It possesses no appellation more precise than modern, although other labels, e.g., INTERNATIONAL STYLE and functionalism, have also been applied. A conscious attempt to assimilate modern technology is one characteristic. Technical progress in the development of materials was evident in the construction of the CRYSTAL PALACE in 1851. In the ensuing years iron, steel, and glass determined the

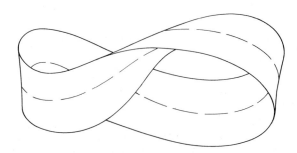

Möbius strip

form of many buildings, but irrelevant ornament persisted. As late as 1889 the EIFFEL TOWER found a public not yet ready to accept pure structure as beautiful. The use of a steel skeleton for a tall building began with the first SKYSCRAPER, by William Jenney, in Chicago (1883). Industrial architecture in Europe was pioneered by Peter BEHRENS, Auguste PERRET, and others. At the end of the 19th cent. a revolution occurred in the buildings and writings of Louis H. SULLIVAN and Frank Lloyd WRIGHT. Wright in the US and the exponents of ART NOUVEAU in Europe introduced the concept of rhythmic flow of interior space, eliminating rigid room divisions. Conversely, the architects of De STIJL returned to more disciplined structural form. By 1920 the interrelation of building type with materials and function was widely accepted. The concept of buildings as volumes enclosed by massive materials had given way to a concentration on space supported or enclosed by light, thin materials. The idea of enclosure was de-emphasized, so that structural elements themselves came into focus. Major exponents of this view were LE CORBUSIER and Walter GROPIUS. Abstract painting and sculpture were looked to for new ideas, and did much to condition the public to recognize abstract structural beauty, free from past associations. By the mid-century, modern architecture and town planning, influenced by new technology and mass production, were dealing with increasingly complex social needs. Important characteristics of modern architectural works are expanses of glass and the use of reinforced concrete. Advances in lift technology, air conditioning, and electric lighting have all had important effects. The use of an unvarying module, or basic dimensional unit, characteristic of the works of Buckminster FULLER and Moshe Safdie, among others, echoes machine-tool precision. Pioneers of the 1920s were MIES VAN DER ROHE and Gropius. Important contributors to modern design include Marcel BREUER, Richard NEUTRA, and I.M. PEI. Criticism in the 1950s attacking modern architecture's 'sterility' and 'institutional' anonymity produced a tendency toward individual expression typified by Louis KAHN, E.D. STONE, Philip JOHNSON, and the architects of the 'new brutalism' movement in England and the US. A dynamic sculptural unity characterizes the work of Le Corbusier and Eero SAARINEN. Other major modern architects include Alvar AALTO, P.L. NERVI, Paolo SOLERI, and Oscar NIEMEYER.

**modern art:** see ABSTRACT EXPRESSIONISM; BLAUE REITER, DER; BRÜCKE, DIE; CONSTRUCTIVISM; CUBISM; DADA; EIGHT, THE; EXPRESSIONISM; FAUVISM; FUTURISM; IMPRESSIONISM; MINIMAL ART; NABIS; NAZARENES; PHOTOREALISM; POSTIMPRESSIONISM; POSTMODERNISM; STIJL, DE; SUPREMATISM; SURREALISM.

**modern dance,** theatrical dance forms that are distinct from BALLET and from the show dancing of the musical comedy or variety stage. Developed in the 20th cent., both in America and Europe, it resembles modern art and music in being experimental and iconoclastic. It is founded on theories first advanced by the French music teacher François Delsarte (1811–71), who influenced such modern-dance pioneers, as Emile Jaques DALCROZE, Rudolf von LABAN, and Ted Shawn. In the US modern dance began with the work of Isadora DUNCAN, Loie Fuller, and Ruth ST DENIS in the early 20th cent. Duncan emphasized freedom of movement, Fuller made great use of lighting, and St Denis improvised on ethnic sources, and with her husband Ted Shawn founded Denishawn, their influential dance company and schools, which increased the popularity of dance in the US. In Europe, the generation of modern dancers including Mary WIGMAN, Kurt JOOSS, Sigurd LEEDER and Harald Kreutzberg either had their work restricted by the Nazi movement, or moved abroad. In the US the second generation of modern dance innovators, led by the Americans Martha GRAHAM, Doris HUMPHREY, and Charles WEIDMAN and the German Hanya HOLM led the development of the new trends through their teaching, choreography, and performance. These figures dominated dance until the late 1940s, when more surreal and abstract forms were developed by Merce CUNNINGHAM who, working with the composer John CAGE, appeared to dispense with formal organization or any relationship between music and movement. In the 1960s, a further development took place through the work of the postmodernist Judson Dance Theatre, whose members included Steve PAXTON and Twyla THARP and whose emphasis was largely based on non-dance movement (e.g., acrobatics or marching). The development of modern dance continues today, drawing on the work of its forebears, either advancing, rejecting or combining differing styles and in some instances incorporating that which it initially rejected, the vocabulary of the classical ballet.

**modernism,** in religion, movement to reconcile developments of 19th- and 20th-cent. science and philosophy with historical Christianity. It

arose from the application of modern critical methods to the study of the Bible and the history of dogma and stressed the humanistic aspects of religion. Its ideas permeated many Protestant churches and called forth a reaction in FUNDAMENTALISM. A similar movement in Roman Catholicism was condemned (1907) as heretical.

**modernismo,** movement in Spanish literature, c.1890–1920. It arose in Latin America, derived in part from the French SYMBOLISTS and PARNASSIANS. *Azul* [blue] (1888), by the Nicaraguan poet Rubén DARÍO, typified the new aesthetic, with its elegant form, exotic images, and subtle word music. Other major Latin American *modernistas* were CHOCANO, LUGONES, RODÓ, and SILVA. *Modernismo* spread to Spain, influencing JIMÉNEZ, UNAMUNO, and VALLE-INCLÁN. After World War I, a new generation of writers rejected the mannerism and hollow elegance of *modernismo*.

**Modersohn-Becker, Paula** (,mohdeǝrsohn'bekǝ), 1876–1907, German artist. She was an important woman artist of the period. She trained in Berlin and then worked in the artists' colony at Worpswede. After several visits to Paris in the early 1900s she became influenced by GAUGUIN and by FAUVISM, and simplified her form and colour. She was important for the development of German EXPRESSIONISM.

**Modigliani, Amedeo** ('modi,lyahnee), 1884–1920, Italian painter and sculptor. He went to Paris in 1906 and remained there for the rest of his life. Influenced at first by TOULOUSE-LAUTREC and then by CÉZANNE and PICASSO and by primitive sculpture. In 1909 he met BRANCUSI who encouraged his interest in sculpture. His work was eclectic as well as individualistic, and does not really relate to mainstream French avant-garde art of the period. His lifestyle was almost a parody of the romantic artist, and he suffered from drink and drug abuse.

**Modoc Indians:** see NORTH AMERICAN INDIANS.

**modulation,** in communications, process in which some characteristic of a WAVE (the carrier wave) is made to vary in accordance with an information-bearing signal wave (the modulating wave) superimposed on it; demodulation is the process by which the original signal is recovered from the wave produced by modulation. In modulation the carrier wave is generated or processed in such a way that its amplitude, frequency, or some other property varies. In *amplitude modulation* (AM), widely used in radio, the frequency is constant and the intensity, or amplitude, of the carrier wave varies in accordance with the modulating signal. In *frequency modulation* (FM) the amplitude is constant and the frequency of the carrier wave varies in such a way that the change in frequency at any instant is proportional to another time-varying signal. The principal application of FM is also in radio, where it offers increased noise immunity and greater sound fidelity at the expense of greatly increased bandwidth. FM broadcasts can also be transmitted in stereo with an audio frequency range of up to 15 kHz resulting in a much improved quality compared with AM on medium waves which is limited to a maximum audio frequency of 5 kHz. In *pulse modulation* the carrier wave is a series of pulses that are all of the same amplitude and width and are all equally spaced. By controlling one of these three variables, a modulating wave may impress its information on the pulses. In *pulse code modulation* (PCM) it is the presence or absence of particular pulses in the carrier stream that constitutes the modulation.

amplitude modulation (am)

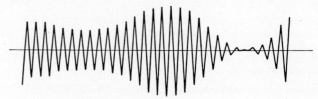

frequency modulation (fm)

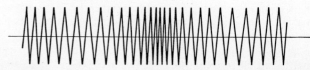

Modulation

**modulation,** in music, shift in the KEY centre of a composition, a means of achieving variety in use since the late 15th cent. In modulating from one key to another, a chord common to both keys is used as a pivot chord. If there is no chord common to the two keys, the passage may move through several keys before the desired modulation is effected.

**Moerae:** see FATES.

**Mofaddaliyat:** see MUFADDALIYAT.

**Mofolo, Thomas Mopoku,** 1876–1948, Sotho novelist; b. Lesotho. A schoolteacher and journalist, he wrote three novels, *Moetioa Bochaela* (1907), *Pitseng* (1910), and *Chaka* (1910). The last novel was Mofolo's masterpiece and though its publication was delayed until 1926 because of missionary opposition, it was eventually translated into both English (1931) and French (1940).

**Mogadishu** or **Muqdisho** (mogǝˌdishooh), city (1983 est. pop. 600,000), capital of the Somali Democratic Republic, a port on the Banaadir coast of the Indian Ocean. It is the country's largest city and chief commercial centre. Its principal industries are oil refining, food processing, and uranium mining. Mogadishu was settled by Arabs c.900 and became an important trade centre for E Africa. Occupied by the sultan of Zanzibar in 1871, the city was leased in the following year to the Italians who eventually purchased the site in 1905.

**Mogul:** see MUGHAL.

**mohair** see FIBRE.

**Mohawk Indians:** see IROQUOIS CONFEDERACY.

**Mohegan Indians,** NORTH AMERICAN INDIAN tribe of the Eastern Woodlands, speaking an Algonquian language (see AMERICAN INDIAN LANGUAGES). Sometimes called Mohicans, they were a branch of the MAHICAN INDIANS, occupying SW Connecticut. United with the Pequot Indians in the early 1630s, they became a powerful force that had British support. Sale of their land to the whites led to decline. They became widely known through J.F. COOPER's *The Last of the Mohicans.* Today a few Mohegan and Pequot live on a small Connecticut reservation.

**Mohican Indians:** see MAHICAN INDIANS; MOHEGAN INDIANS.

**Moholy-Nagy, László,** (ˌmohoy ˌnodyǝ), 1895–1946, Hungarian painter and sculptor. In 1919 he went from Budapest to Vienna and was influenced by MALEVICH, LISSITZKY, and GABO. In Berlin (1921–23) he experimented with collage and photomontage. Moholy-Nagy replaced ITTEN at the BAUHAUS in 1923, where he taught until 1928. His constructivist ideas are summed up in his book *The New Vision from Material to Architecture* (1929). In 1935 he moved to London and was involved in the Circle group, and in 1937 emigrated to the US.

**Mohorovičić discontinuity** or **Moho** (ˈmohhǝˌrohvichich), boundary layer between the crust and the mantle of the EARTH. It is marked by a sharp alteration in the velocity of earthquakes passing through that region.

**Moi, Daniel arap,** 1924–, president of KENYA (1978–). He was vice president (1967–78) under Jomo KENYATTA and succeeded to the presidency in 1978. In 1980 he concluded a military and economic accord with the US. An attempt by the military to oust Moi in 1982 was thwarted by troops loyal to the president.

**moiety** (ˌmoyǝti), the division of society into two halves. This is characteristic of Australian Aboriginal forms of social organization; see SECTION SYSTEMS.

**Moirai:** see FATES.

**Moiseyev Dance Company:** see DANCE (table).

**Mojave** or **Mohave Desert,** arid area, SE California, US part of the Sonoran section of the western Basin and Range physiographic division. It is warm throughout the year, but with marked diurnal temperature changes, and receives an average annual rainfall of 13 cm (5 in), mostly in winter. Joshua Tree National Monument preserves the region's unique ecosystem.

**molasses:** see SUCROSE.

**Moldavia,** historic province (c.38,100 km/14,700 sq mi), E Romania, separated in the east from the MOLDAVIAN SOVIET SOCIALIST REPUBLIC by the Prut R. and in the west from Transylvania by the Carpathian Mts. Suceava and IAŞI, its historic capitals, and *Galaţi*, its port on the Danube R., are its chief cities. Moldavia is a fertile plain on which grains, fruits, and other crops are grown. Timber and oil-drilling are the major industries. Part of the Roman province of Dacia, the area became (14th cent.) a principality under native rulers, notably Stephen the Great (r.1457–1504). It came under Turkish suzerainty in the 16th cent. and later lost Bukovina (1775) to Austria and Bessarabia (1812) to Russia. In 1856 Moldavia and WALACHIA became independent under nominal Turkish suzerainty. The accession (1859) of Alexander John CUZA as prince of both areas began the history of modern ROMANIA.

**Moldavian Soviet Socialist Republic** or **Moldavia,** constituent republic (1985 pop. 4,105,000), c.33,670 km² (13,000 sq mi), SW European USSR. It borders on Romania (W) and the Ukraine (E, N, and S). The capital is KISHINEV. Moldavia consists of steppes and hilly plains. The area of Bessarabia has very fertile soils and contains one-quarter of all vineyards in the USSR. Fruit-growing and market gardening are also important. Industry is largely based on processing agricultural products and includes food-canning, wine making, and timber processing. The majority of the population is Moldavian; minorities include Ukrainians and Russians. An independent principality in the 14th cent., the region fell to the Ottoman Turks in the 16th cent. Some portions, including Bessarabia, passed to Russia between 1791 and 1812; others later became part of Romania. The Moldovian SSR was created in 1924. These territories have been disputed between Romania and the Soviet Union, Bessarabia being in Romanian possession from 1918 to 1940; Romania also occupied the Moldavian republic beween 1941 and 1944.

**mole,** any of the small, burrowing, insectivorous MAMMALS of the family Talpidae of the Northern Hemisphere. About 15 cm (6 in) long, moles have pointed muzzles and powerful, clawed front feet for tunnelling. Their eyes are covered with fur and they have no external ears, but their senses of hearing, smell, and touch are acute. They eat half their weight daily in worms, insects, and small animals. Moles are trapped as pests and for their fur.

**mole,** in chemistry, a quantity of particles of any type equal to Avogadro's number ($6.02252 \times 10^{23}$). One gram-atomic weight (or one gram-molecular weight)—the amount of an atomic (or molecular) substance whose weight in grams is numerically equal to the ATOMIC WEIGHT (or MOLECULAR WEIGHT) of that substance—contains exactly one mole of atoms (or molecules). For example, one mole, or 12.011 grams, of carbon contains $6.02252 \times 10^{23}$ carbon atoms, and one mole, or 180.16 grams, of glucose ($C_6H_{12}O_6$) contains the same number of glucose molecules.

**Molech Moloch** (ˌmohlek, ˌmohlok), Canaanite god of fire to whom children were offered in sacrifice. He is also known as an Assyrian god. His worship was contrary to Hebrew law, and the prophets strongly condemned it.

**molecular weight,** weight of a MOLECULE of a substance expressed in atomic mass units (see ATOMIC WEIGHT). The molecular weight is the sum of the atomic weights of the atoms making up the molecule.

**molecule,** smallest particle of a COMPOUND that has all the chemical properties of that compound. Molecules are made up of two or more ATOMS, either of the same ELEMENT or of two or more different elements. Ionic compounds, such as common salt, are made up not of molecules but of ions arranged in a crystalline structure (see CRYSTAL). Unlike ions, molecules carry no electrical charge. Molecules differ in size and MOLECULAR WEIGHT as well as in structure (see ISOMER).

**Molière, Jean Baptiste Poquelin** (moˌlyeǝ), 1622–73, French playwright and actor, the creator of high French COMEDY; b. Jean Baptiste Poquelin. The son of a merchant, Molière early joined the Béjart troupe of actors. After touring the provinces for 13 years, the company, now headed by Molière, returned to Paris under the patronage of Louis XIV. It performed with continuous success at the Palais Royal and was the forerunner of the Comédie Française. At once actor, director, stage manager, and writer, Molière produced farces, comedies, masques, and ballets for the entertainment of the court. Best known are the comedies of character that ridicule a vice or a type of excess by caricaturing a person who incarnates it. Among these satires are *Tartuffe* (1664) the religious hypocrite; *Le Misanthrope* (1666) the antisocial man; *L'avare* (1668; tr. The Miser); *Le bourgeois gentilhomme* (1670; tr. The Would-be Gentleman) the parvenu; *Les femmes savantes* (1672; tr. The Learned Women) affected intellectuals; *La malade imaginaire* (1673; tr. The Imaginary Invalid) the hypochondriac. Molière's genius is equally apparent in his broad farces: *Le médecin malgré lui* (1666; tr. The Doctor in Spite of Himself), and *George Dandin* (1668). Other works include the poetic *Amphitryon* (1668), after Plautus, and *Le mariage forcé* (1664; tr. The Forced Marriage). Translations of Molière's comedies abound.

**mollusc,** animal in the phylum Mollusca, the second largest invertebrate phylum. Mostly aquatic, molluscs have usually soft, unsegmented bodies enclosed in a shell; in some forms the shell is internal, and in a few it is absent. An organ called the mantle secretes the substance that forms the shell. A muscular foot under the body is used for locomotion. Some molluscs, such as SLUGS and SNAILS are garden pests. Certain molluscs, such as COCKLES, mussels, OYSTERS, and SCALLOPS, are important food sources, and mollusc shells are highly valued by collectors. Molluscs include GASTROPODS, or univalves, BIVALVES, CEPHALOPODS (OCTOPUSES and SQUIDS), and CHITONS.

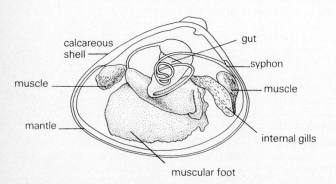

Internal anatomy of a bivalve **mollusc**

**Molly Maguires,** secret organization of Irish-Americans in the coal districts of Scranton, Pennsylvania (c.1865–1875). Organized to combat oppressive mining conditions, the Mollies often resorted to murdering or intimidating the owner-controlled police. They succeeded in calling a strike in 1875, but the organization was finally broken by Pinkerton detectives hired by management. Twenty Molly Maguires were hanged.

**Molnár, Ferenc** (ˌmolnah), 1878–1952, Hungarian dramatist and novelist. His best-known plays are *Liliom* (1909), made into the musical *Carousel; The Guardsman* (1910); and *The Swan* (1920). His novels include *The Paul Street Boys* (1907).

**Moloch:** see MOLECH.

Thorny devil (*Moloch horridus*) of Australia

**moloch** or **thorny devil,** Australian lizard of the family Agamidae. The moloch is an extraordinary looking animal, being covered by thorn-shaped scales. These 15-cm (6-in) AGAMAS live in deserts and dry regions, feeding on ants which they flick into their mouths one at a time. As a meal can consist of between 1000 and 5000 ants, they take a long time to eat. Despite their appearance, they are harmless. They are not related to the IGUANA called the horned toad, which has similar appearance and habits but lives in North America.

**Molotov, Vyacheslav Mikhailovich** (ˌmolətof), 1890–1986, Soviet leader. Rising rapidly through the Communist Party, he became premier of the USSR in 1930. In 1941 STALIN assumed the post and Molotov became vice premier. As commissar of foreign affairs (a title later changed to foreign minister) he negotiated the 1939 Russo-German nonaggression

pact. After the 1941 German invasion he worked to strengthen ties with the West, later sharing in the founding of the UN. In 1949 VISHINSKY became foreign minister; Molotov remained vice premier. After Stalin's death he was again foreign minister (1953–56). He was expelled from the central committee of the party for opposing KHRUSHCHEV in 1957, held minor posts for some years, and was expelled from the party in 1964; he was readmitted to the party in 1984 on his 94th birthday.

**Moltke, Helmuth Karl Bernard, Graf von,** 1800–91, Prussian field marshal. Moltke was made chief of the general staff in 1858 and moulded the Prussian army into a formidable war machine. His strategy was responsible for the Prussian triumphs in the Danish War (1864), the AUSTRO-PRUSSIAN WAR (1866), and the FRANCO-PRUSSIAN WAR (1870–71). He was named count after the Prussian victory at Metz (1870).

**Moluccas** or **Spice Islands,** island group and province (1980 pop. 1,411,000), c.32,300 sq mi (83,660 sq km), E Indonesia, between Celebes and New Guinea. The capital is Ambon. Of volcanic origin, the Moluccas are mountainous, fertile, and humid. They are the original home of nutmeg and cloves; other spices and copra are produced. Explored by MAGELLAN (1511–12), the islands were taken by the Dutch, who secured a monopoly in the clove trade, in the 17th cent.

**molybdenum** (Mo), metallic element, recognized as a distinct element by Karl SCHEELE in 1778. Hard, malleable, ductile, silver-white, and high-melting, it is used in X-ray and electronic tubes, electric furnaces, and certain rocket and missile parts. It is a hardening agent in STEEL alloys. Molybdenum disulphide is used as a lubricant in spacecraft and cars. It is also the catalyst used for removing sulphur from petroleum products. See ELEMENT (table); PERIODIC TABLE.

**Mombasa,** city (1984 pop. 341,148), SE Kenya, on the Indian Ocean. It is Kenya's chief port and a major commercial and industrial centre. Industries include oil refining, cement processing, and motor vehicle assembly. Most of the city is on an island connected with the mainland by a causeway. From the 8th to 16th cent. Mombasa was a centre of Arab trade in ivory and slaves. Later held by the Portuguese, the Arabs, and Zanzibar, the city passed (1887) to the British, who made it the capital of their E Africa protectorate.

**moment of force:** see TORQUE.

**moment of inertia,** measure of the resistance of a body to accelerated rotation due to some external TORQUE or moment of a force. A particle of mass at a perpendicular distance from the axis of rotation contributes to an amount $mn^2$ to the resistance to changes in the speed of rotation.

**momentum,** in mechanics, the quantity of MOTION of a body. The linear momentum of a body is the product of its mass and velocity. The angular momentum of a body rotating about an axis is the product of its MOMENT OF INERTIA about that axis and its ANGULAR VELOCITY. Both linear and angular momentum of a body or system of bodies are conserved (see CONSERVATION LAWS, in physics) if no external force is acting.

**Mommsen, Theodor** (ˌmomzən), 1817–1903, German historian. His *History of Rome* (1854–56, 1885) is an unmatched recreation of Roman society and culture based on his study of ancient coins, inscriptions, and literature. He won the 1902 Nobel Prize for literature.

**Monaco,** independent principality (1986 est. pop. 30,000), c.150 hectares (370 acres), on the Mediterranean Sea, an enclave in SE France, near the Italian border. Monaco-Ville is the capital. Its beautiful location, natural harbour, mild climate, and world-famous gambling casino at Monte Carlo make Monaco a leading tourist resort. Shipping and perfume manufacture also contribute to the economy. Monaco has no income or corporation taxes; disagreement with the French government in the 1960s led to the severe curtailment of the use of Monaco as a tax haven by French citizens. Under the 1962 constitution Monaco is governed by the ruling prince (currently RAINIER III), assisted by a minister of state, a cabinet, and an elected national council.

*History.* Monaco was ruled by the Genovese Grimaldi family from the 13th cent. In 1731 the French Goyon-Matignon family succeeded to the principality by marriage and assumed the name Grimaldi. Monaco passed under the protection of Spain (1542), France (1641), and Sardinia (1815), returning to French protection in 1861. Until Monaco's first constitution in 1911, the prince was an absolute ruler. A treaty of 1918 provides that succession to the throne must be approved by the French government.

**Monaco, Lorenzo:** see LORENZO MONACO.

**Monaghan,** county in NE of Republic of Ireland (1986 pop. 52,332), 1277 km² (498 sq mi), bordering on Northern Ireland in the N and E. It is in the province of Ulster. The county town is MONAGHAN. Much of the county is gently undulating or hilly, and the land rises to 366 m (1200 ft) in Slieve Beagh in the NW. The main rivers are the Blackwater and the Finn, and there are several small loughs and bogs. The major economic activity is agriculture, especially the cultivation of oats and potatoes.

**Monaghan,** county town (1986 pop. 6047) of Co. Monaghan, Republic of Ireland, on the Ulster Canal, on the border with Northern Ireland. A small market town, it has a 19th-cent. Roman Catholic cathedral.

**monarchy,** form of government in which sovereignty is vested in a single person whose right to rule is generally hereditary and lifelong. In ancient societies divine descent of the monarch was often claimed. Medieval Christian monarchs were considered the appointed agents of divine will and as such were crowned by the church; their power, however, was often dependent on the nobles. The power of later monarchs, e.g., HENRY VIII of England and LOUIS XIV of France, became increasingly absolute and there developed (16th–17th cent.) the theory of **divine right,** which claimed that the monarch was responsible not to the governed but to God alone. The GLORIOUS REVOLUTION (1688) in England and the FRENCH REVOLUTION (1789) ended these pretensions, and while monarchs remained symbols of national unity, real power gradually passed to constitutional assemblies, as in the UK and Sweden. Saudi Arabia is one of the few remaining functional monarchies.

**monasticism,** organized life in common in a retreat from worldly life, for religious purposes. Men who belong to such communities are monks and their houses are monasteries; communities of women are commonly called convents, and their inhabitants are nuns. Vows of poverty, chastity, and obedience are typical of monastic life, which is known to most great religions: Buddhism, Jainism, Islam, and Christianity. In Christianity monasticism arose from the movement toward the extreme asceticism of a hermit's life. In the Orthodox Eastern Church monks still lead a hermit-like life, but live in common, usually following the rules prescribed by St Basil the Great. Western monasticism was shaped by St BENEDICT. The Benedictine abbeys under his rule preserved Roman civilization and became centres of learning in the Middle Ages. There are many Roman Catholic monastic orders, including the FRANCISCANS, the DOMINICANS, the CARMELITES, and the Jesuits (see JESUS, SOCIETY OF). Some orders are entirely secluded (enclosed), but most are devoted to teaching, charity, or missionary work. Generally Protestantism has not adopted monasticism.

**monazite,** phosphate mineral [(Ce,La,Y,Th)PO$_4$], found in the form of sand in the US, Madagascar, Brazil, India, Sri Lanka, and Australia. Monazite is an important source of CERIUM, THORIUM, YTTRIUM, and other RARE-EARTH METALS.

**Mönchen-Gladbach,** city (1984 pop. 256,300), North Rhine–Westphalia, W West Germany. A leading centre of the cotton textile industry, its factories also make hosiery, embroidery, and clothing as well as various forms of machinery.

**Monck** or **Monk, George, 1st duke of Albemarle,** 1608–70, English soldier and politician. Under Oliver CROMWELL, he served in Scotland and in the first DUTCH WAR. In 1659, when the Protectorate of Richard Cromwell fell, Monck marched on London, called for a new Parliament, and declared openly for the RESTORATION of CHARLES II. Charles later heaped honours upon him. Monck also served in the Second Dutch War.

**Monck, Charles Stanley, 4th Viscount,** 1819–94, 1st governor-general of the Dominion of CANADA (1867–68). As governor-general of British North America (1861–67) he had worked for confederation and formation (1867) of the dominion.

**Mondale, Walter,** 1928–, vice president of the US (1977–81). A liberal Democrat, he was a political protégé of Hubert H. HUMPHREY and was US senator from Minnesota (1964–77). In 1976 he was chosen by Jimmy CARTER as his running mate and was elected vice president. Carter and Mondale ran for reelection in 1980 but lost to the Republican ticket of Ronald REAGAN and George BUSH. Mondale was the Democratic candidate for president in 1984 but was heavily defeated by Pres. Reagan.

**Monday:** see WEEK.

**Mondrian, Piet** (ˌmondreeʼahn), 1872–1944, Dutch painter. Influenced by CUBISM, he developed a geometric, nonobjective style that he called neoplasticism. Cofounder of the STIJL group and the magazine *De Stijl,* he published (1920) a book on his theories: *Le Neo-Plasticisme.* His theories were strongly influenced by idealist philosophy and THEOSOPHY. These gave his writing and works a quasi-spiritual content, where the use of only vertical and horizontal lines and primary colours on a white canvas reduced the artist's subjective input to decisions concerning composition only. This Mondrian considered to be the highest achievement of art before man attained a purely spiritual existence. In 1924 he ceased collaboration with De Stijl due to Van Doesburg's use of diagonal lines. In 1940 he went to America; there he painted his *Boogie-Woogie* compositions, inspired by jazz and New York City life.

Piet **Mondrian,** *Composition with Red, Yellow, and Blue,* 1920. Oil on canvas, 100.5 × 101 cm. Tate Gallery, London.

**Monet, Claude** (moˌnay), 1840–1926, French painter. A founder of IMPRESSIONISM, he is considered one of the foremost figures in the history

Claude **Monet,** *The Beach at Trouville,* 1870. Oil on canvas, 38 × 45.5 cm. National Gallery, London.

of LANDSCAPE PAINTING. He laid emphasis on working out of doors, to capture fleeting effects of light; he eliminated black and grey from his palette, breaking down light into its colour components as a prism does; his comma-like, variegated brushstrokes capture light's vibration. Through the early 1870s the Impressionists worked closely together, and characteristics of this period are Monet's many pictures of modern subjects at Argenteuil—snow scenes, sun-drenched meadows and gardens, pleasure craft on the river. Later Monet settled at Giverny, and increasingly painted series of pictures of the same subject under changing conditions of light and weather, e.g., *Haystacks*. Amongst his last works are a series of *Waterlilies* (1899–1926) painted in his garden at Giverny.

**monetarism,** economic theory that monetary policy, or control of the money supply, is the primary if not sole determinant of a nation's economy. Monetarists believe that management of the money supply to produce credit ease or restraint is the chief factor influencing inflation or deflation, recession or growth; they dismiss fiscal policy (government spending and taxation) as ineffective in regulating economic performance. Milton FRIEDMAN has been the leading modern spokesman for monetarism.

**monetary system, international:** see INTERNATIONAL MONETARY SYSTEM.

**money,** abstract unit of account in terms of which the value of goods, services, and obligations can be measured. By extension, the term may designate anything that is generally accepted as a means of payment. Almost all economic activity is concerned with the making and spending of money incomes. Historically, a great variety of objects have served as money, among them stones, shells, ivory, wampum beads, tobacco, furs, and dried fish, but from the earliest times precious metals have been favoured because of ease of handling, durability, divisibility, and high intrinsic value. Money has four principal functions: as a medium of exchange, as which it has many advantages over the less sophisticated barter system; as a unit of account, which facilitates a pricing system; as a store of value, because its durable qualities (unlike butter, for example) allow it to represent savings; and as a standard of deferred payment, whereby goods may be purchased against a fixed amount payable back over a term and to which an interest charge is added (see HIRE PURCHASE). In Great Britain, the Anglo-saxons (5th cent. onwards) introduced the pound of silver which was minted into 240 pence and this was the main coin until the 14th cent. Gold had not been used because of its higher intrinsic value. In 1489 the first gold sovereign worth £15 was minted after which silver and gold coin were in common circulation. In the early 17th cent. banknotes were introduced and although they were primarily receipts, being more convenient than money, they gradually became acceptable as legal tender. Until 1914 the UK monetary system was based on the the GOLD STANDARD whereby Bank of England notes were fully redeemable for gold, but the outbreak of World War I brought an end to this practice.

**money-market fund,** type of MUTUAL FUND that invests in high-yielding, short-term money-market instruments, such as UK government securities, COMMERCIAL PAPER, and CERTIFICATES OF DEPOSIT. Returns of money-market funds usually parallel the movement of short-term interest rates. Some funds buy only UK government securities, such as Treasury bills, while general-purpose funds invest in various types of short-term paper. They became enormously popular with investors in the early 1980s because of their high yields, relative safety, and high liquidity.

**money supply,** the measure of MONEY in the economy at a specific time. Definitions of such money differ according to what is included; in some countries the most narrow definition, usually M1, includes only notes and coin. In the UK there are six definitions. MO is notes and coin plus bankers' operational deposits with the Bank of England; M1 is notes and coin plus interest- and non-interest-bearing bank sight deposits; M2 is notes and coin, non-interest-bearing bank sight deposits plus real deposits with the bank, building societies and ordinary accounts of the National Savings Bank; M3 is M1 plus bank time deposits; M4 is M3 plus building society shares and deposits (net of their holdings of M3 instruments); M5 is M4 plus quasi money. M3 is a widely used measure but by 1988 the increasing role of building societies as bankers made the use of M4 seem more appropriate. Growth of the money supply is believed by many monetarists to have a direct bearing on the rate of INFLATION, and the high inflation rates experienced in the UK in the 1970s would appear to support this theory. At that time both narrowly and broadly defined money supply expanded rapidly, however, and there were many inflationary pressures at work. In fact, a rapid expansion of money supply does not necessarily provoke high inflation rates, as many cases show. To assess the likely impact on prices of an increase in money supply it is necessary to interpret the components. In the UK, for example, M4 expanded fast in 1982–87 but inflation rates were modest. Private borrowing increased rapidly during the period but public borrowing was declining, stifling the potential inflationary impact. Similarly wages and salaries were a stimulant to the money supply but not to prices because of corresponding productivity increases.

**Monge, Gaspard, comte de Péluse** (mawnhzh), 1746–1818, French mathematician, physicist, and public official; a founder of the École polytechnique. He laid the foundations of descriptive geometry, a field essential to mechanical and architectural drawing, and made important contributions to differential geometry.

**Mongolia,** officially Mongolian People's Republic, unofficially Mongolia or Outer Mongolia, country (1986 pop. 1,914,700), 1,565,000 km² (604,247 sq mi), N central Asia. Bordered by the USSR (N) and China (S), it occupies more than half of the region historically known as Mongolia. The capital is ULAN BATOR. The average elevation exceeds 1554 m (5100 ft); mountain ranges and high plateaus cover most of the northwest and the central south, and the GOBI desert lies in the south and east. Wide seasonal variations in temperature, rugged terrain, and an arid climate limit agriculture; nomadic year-round grazing of sheep, goats, cattle, horses, yaks, and camels has been the major occupation for centuries. Under the Communist government the herders have been organized into state cooperatives. A small industrial sector, supported by the USSR, is based primarily on livestock processing and the manufacture of textiles and consumer goods. Some timber is cut in the north, and coal, copper, molybdenum, iron ore, and tungsten are mined. The GNP is US$1786 million and the GNP per capita is US$940 (1978). The population is composed primarily of Khalkha Mongols, who speak Khalkha Mongolian; there are also minorities of Oirat Mongols, Kazakhs, Tuvinians, Chinese, and Russians. Lamaist Buddhism, once widely practised, has been discouraged by the Communist government.

*History.* Mongolia's early history is that of the MONGOLS. It was under Chinese suzerainty from 1691 until the collapse of the Qing dynasty in 1911, when a group of Mongol princes proclaimed an autonomous republic under Jebtsun Damba Khutukhtu (the Living Buddha of Urga). The new state was reoccupied by the Chinese in 1919, taken by the White Russians in 1921, and occupied the same year by Mongolian Communists. Mongolia was proclaimed an independent state, and remained a monarchy until 1924, when the Mongolian People's Republic was established. Rural collectivization and the persecution of Lama priests led to a mass exodus (1932) of people with their livestock into China's Inner Mongolia. In the ideological dispute between the USSR and Communist China, Mongolia has maintained its traditional alliance with the USSR, which has given the Mongolians considerable economic aid. The ruling Mongolian People's Revolutionary Party was led since 1952 by Yumjaagiyn Tsedenbal, until 1984, when he was succeeded as party leader and head of state by Jambyn Batmounkh.

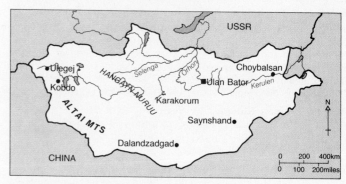

Mongolia

**Mongolian languages,** group of languages forming a subdivision of the Altaic subfamily of the URALIC AND ALTAIC family of languages. See ALPHABET; LANGUAGE (table).

**mongolism:** see DOWN'S SYNDROME.

**Mongoloid:** see RACE.

**Mongols,** Asiatic people, numbering nearly 3 million, who today live mainly in the Mongolian People's Republic (formerly Outer Mongolia), Inner Mongolia (part of China), and the Soviet Union. A nomadic pastoral people, they merged their traditional shamanism with Buddhism in the 16th cent., creating Lamaism (see TIBETAN BUDDHISM). Early in the 13th cent. JENGHIZ KHAN united the many feuding Mongol tribes into a powerful nation. From their capital at KARAKORUM the Mongols swept into Europe and China, by 1260 ruling a huge empire: the Great Khanate (see KUBLAI KHAN), comprising all of China; the Jagatai khanate, in Turkistan; the Kipchak khanate, in Russia (see GOLDEN HORDE, EMPIRE OF THE); and a khanate in Persia. The Mongol hordes with prominent Turkic elements came to be called TATARS. TAMERLANE, who founded a new empire in the 14th cent., claimed descent from Jenghiz Khan, as did BABUR, founder of the MOGUL empire. After their expulsion from China in 1382, the Mongols declined.

**mongoose,** small, carnivorous MAMMAL of the civet family, found in S Asia and Africa, with one species extending into S Spain. Typical mongooses (genus *Herpestes*) are weasel-like in appearance, with long, slender bodies and pointed faces. They range in length from 45 to 110 cm (1½ to 3½ ft). The Indian grey mongoose (*H. edwardsi*) is known for its ability to kill snakes, including COBRAS. Mongooses are fierce hunters but make good pets in their native lands. They become pests if introduced into new territory. The mongoose was immortalised by Rudyard KIPLING with his tale of Rikki-tikki-tavi.

Banded **mongooses** eating eggs they smashed on rocks

**monism,** in METAPHYSICS, term applied from the 18th cent. to any theory that explains phenomena by one unifying principle or as the manifestation of a single substance, variously identified as spirit or mind (e.g., HEGEL), energy, or an all-pervasive deity (e.g., SPINOZA). The opposites of monism are pluralism, the explanation of the universe in terms of many principles or substances, and DUALISM.

**monitor** or **goanna,** any of various dragonlike, mostly tropical LIZARDS (genus *Varanus*), found in the Eastern Hemisphere. The carnivorous monitor lizard has a long head and neck, long tail, and strong legs with sharp claws. Monitors range in size from the 20-cm (8-in) species of W Australia to the 3-m, 136-kg (10-ft, 300-lb) KOMODO DRAGON. The Nile monitor (*V. niloticus*) is aquatic and there are tree-living species.

**Monitor and Merrimack,** American ships that fought the first battle between ironclad warships, in the AMERICAN CIVIL WAR. On 9 Mar. 1862, the Confederate frigate *Merrimack,* converted into an ironclad and renamed the *Virginia,* engaged in battle at Hampton Roads with the Union ironclad *Monitor.* The combat, which ended in a draw, revolutionized naval warfare.

**monitorial system,** method of elementary education devised (19th cent.) by the British educators Joseph LANCASTER and Andrew BELL to school the underprivileged despite severely limited facilities. It was sometimes called the mutual or Lancasterian system. All pupils met in one room, with about 10 students and a monitor to each bench. Monitors, older and better students, were instructed by the teacher and, in turn, instructed the other pupils. There were elaborate systems of rewards for behaviour and scholarship, and punishment by 'shame rather than pain'.

**Moniz, António Caetano de Abreu Freire Egas,** 1874–1955, Portuguese neurosurgeon. He was the first to carry out cerebral examination of the blood vessels and frontal LEUCOTOMY (lobotomy). He received the Nobel prize for physiology or medicine in 1949.

**Monk, George:** see MONCK, GEORGE, 1st DUKE OF ALBEMARLE.

**Monk, Thelonious (Sphere),** 1917–82, black American pianist and composer. Considered one of the most important, and eccentric, modern JAZZ figures, Monk played in a dissonant, often humorous style characterized by subtle rhythmic irregularities. His many compositions include ''Round Midnight' and 'Straight No Chaser'.

**monkey,** PRIMATE, belonging to either of the two superfamilies Cercopithecoidea (Old World) and Ceboidea (New World). Monkeys are excellent climbers, and most are primarily arboreal. Unlike APES, they cannot swing arm-over-arm but run on branches on all fours. Nearly all live in tropical or subtropical climates. Monkeys have flat, rather human faces and highly developed hands and feet, with opposable big toes and, where present, thumbs. Old World monkeys, more closely related to apes and humans than New World monkeys, include the macaque, the BABOON, and the MANDRILL; New World monkeys include the marmoset, tamarin, spider monkey, and capuchin.

Monkey

**monkey-puzzle tree,** evergreen tree (*Araucaria araucana*) of the PINE family native to Chile, widely cultivated as an ornamental. The symmetrical branches have an unusual angularity and are completely covered by stiff, overlapping leaves. The monkey-puzzle tree, the related Norfolk Island pine (*A. excelsa*), and the bunya-bunya (*A. bidwillii*) of Australia are good timber trees. Species of *Araucaria* form the dominant vegetation of the coniferous forests of Chile and S Brazil.

**monkfish,** marine FISH related to the SHARK. Found in tropical and temperate waters the monkfish (*Squatina squatina*) is an important food-fish both in its own right and because its boneless flesh can be passed off as scampi.

**Mon–Khmer languages** ('mon-kə‚meə), group of languages frequently considered as a subfamily of the Southeast Asian family of languages. Included in the subfamily are Kampuchean (or Khmer); Mon (or Talaing), spoken in Burma; and a number of other languages, such as Cham of Kampuchea and southern Vietnam, and Khasi of Assam, in India. See LANGUAGE (table).

**Monmouth, James Scott, duke of,** 1649–85, pretender to the English throne, illegitimate son of CHARLES II. Supporters of a Protestant succession championed Monmouth as heir to Charles II. After the accession (1685) of the Roman Catholic JAMES II, Monmouth landed in Dorset and was proclaimed king, but forces loyal to James soon routed his army. Monmouth was captured and beheaded.

**Monnet, Jean** (mo͵nay), 1888–1979, French economist and public official, leading proponent of European unity after World War II. He served (1919–23) as deputy general of the LEAGUE OF NATIONS. In 1947 he drew up the Monnet Plan for French economic revival, which led to French participation in the MARSHALL PLAN. Following a proposal by Robert SCHUMAN, he drafted the Schuman Plan, which established (1952) the European Coal and Steel Community (ECSC). Monnet, its first president (1952–55), conceived the ECSC as the initial step toward European economic and political integration (see EUROPEAN COMMUNITY). His ideas also contributed to the development of the COMMON MARKET.

**monoclonal antibodies,** antibodies specific to a single antigen (see IMMUNITY) produced by a single clone of cells grown in culture medium in the laboratory. Enormous quantities of identical and pure antibodies can be produced by this technique. They have great potential for use in diagnosing and treating disease, such as cancers, and in organ transplants (see TRANSPLANTATION, MEDICAL).

**monocoque,** type of construction for the wings, the fuselage, or the nacelles of aircraft in which the skin-covering is designed to absorb all, or most of, the stresses from the flight, or ground, loadings of the structure. First developed in 1917 by Dr Adolf K. Rohrbach, it is also known generically as a 'stressed skin' structure.

**monocotyledon:** see ANGIOSPERM.

**Monod, Jacques** (mo͵noh), 1910–76, French biologist and author. He and François JACOB proposed (1961) the concepts of messenger RNA (see RNA) and the operon. For their work they shared with André LWOFF the 1965 Nobel Prize for physiology or medicine. In *Chance and Necessity* (1970) Monod argued that humans are products of chance genetic mutations.

**Monomotopa:** see MWENE MUTAPA.

**Monophysitism** [Gr., = belief in one nature], a heresy of the 5th and 6th cent., a reaction against NESTORIANISM. It challenged the orthodox creed of the Council of Chalcedon (451) by saying Jesus Christ had only a divine nature. When the East temporarily repudiated Chalcedon, there was a split between it and the West which lasted until 519. In Syria, Egypt, and Armenia, monophysitism dominated, and a permanent schism set in by 600, resulting in the creation of the Jacobite, Coptic, and Armenian churches.

**monoplane,** AEROPLANE with a single pair of wings, one on each side of the fuselage. There are four types: low wing, middle wing, high wing, and parasol, each named according to the position of the wings in relation to the fuselage. The first successful monoplane was a hang-glider made in Germany by Otto LILIENTHAL in 1891; the first powered one was built in France by Louis BLÉRIOT in 1908 (see FLIGHT, POWERED). The earliest monoplanes were more dangerous and unstable than contemporary biplanes. Low-wing cantilever monoplanes of metal construction were developed from 1915 by Hugo Junkers, and from the 1940s this type of aeroplane has dominated the aviation scene.

**Monopolies and Mergers Commission,** in the UK, an independent body, established 1948, which on referral investigates proposed mergers to see whether they would be in the public interest. Mergers will be investigated if they may lead to a monopoly in the supply of goods, services, exports, and newspapers. The Commission makes recommendations to the government, which is under no obligation to follow them. The Commission also publishes general reports on monopoly practice in industry and commerce. Its powers are more restricted than those under the ANTITRUST LAWS in the US.

**Monopoly,** board game for as many as eight players, using counters, dice, special cards, imitation money, and small blocks representing buildings. The object is to accumulate wealth and property and to bankrupt opponents. Invented and trademarked in 1933, the game won instant and enduring popularity in Britain and the US.

**monopoly,** market condition in which strictly speaking there is only one seller of a commodity. By virtue of control over supply, the seller is able to exert nearly total control over prices. By adopting laws excluding competition from an industry, governments have often created public service monopolies. These may be public monopolies or publicly regulated private monopolies. Control of a supply by a few producers, who often act to restrain price competition, is known as an oligopoly. In the UK, most forms of monopoly and, to a lesser extent, oligopoly are illegal. A Monopolies Commission was established in 1948. A company which controls, or may control more than a fair share, usually defined as one-third, of the market may be brought under the scrutiny of the Commission on referral by the Dept. of Trade and Industry.

Junkers F.13 all-metal, six-seat, low-wing **monoplane** (1923)

**monorail,** RAILWAY system whose vehicles run on a single rail, thus reducing track cost. In a true monorail vehicles are either suspended beneath the rail which is elevated (as at Wuppertal, West Germany, opened in 1901 and still in use) or run erect upon the rail stabilized by gyroscopes (as demonstrated by L. Brennan, 1910). The more common monorail is one in which the rail is large enough to support both vertical and horizontal wheels, thus stabilizing the vehicle vertically. About 20 examples of this type of monorail have been built, for example at Disneyland, California, US (1959); the longest (13.1 km/8 mi) is at Tokyo, connecting the city to the Haneda airport, built in 1964.

Tokyo **monorail** connecting Haneda airport to the city

**monotheism,** in religion, belief in one GOD. The term is applied particularly to JUDAISM, CHRISTIANITY, and ISLAM, but early ZOROASTRIANISM and Greek religion in its later stages were monotheistic as well. See also POLYTHEISM.

**Monotheletism** or **Monothelitism,** [Gr., = belief in one will], 7th-cent. heresy condemned by the Third Council of Constantinople

(680). First proposed in 622, it said that Christ had two natures, but operated with one will. It was adopted by Emperor HERACLIUS I as a compromise between MONOPHYSITISM and orthodoxy and was vehemently opposed by Rome.

**monotreme,** name for members of the primitive mammalian order Monotremata, found in Australia, Tasmania, and New Guinea. The only members are the DUCK-BILLED PLATYPUS and several species of ECHIDNA. They are unique among MAMMALS in laying eggs instead of bearing live young. Certain skeletal features resemble those of REPTILES, from which the monotremes evolved. Adults are toothless; males have spurs connected to poison glands on their hind feet.

**Monroe, James,** 1758–1831, 5th president of the US (1817–25). He fought in several campaigns in the AMERICAN REVOLUTION. He served in the Virginia legislature (1782) and the CONTINENTAL CONGRESS (1783–86), where he opposed the Constitution for creating an overly centralized government. In the US Senate (1790–94), he was a staunch supporter of Thomas JEFFERSON and a violent opponent of the FEDERALIST PARTY. Governor of VIRGINIA from 1799 to 1802, and again in 1811, he undertook diplomatic missions to England, Spain, and France, and helped negotiate (1803) the LOUISIANA PURCHASE. He served as James MADISON's secretary of state (1811–17), doubling briefly as secretary of war (1814–15). Monroe was easily elected president in 1816 and again in 1820. His administration was characterized as an 'era of good feeling'. He signed the MISSOURI COMPROMISE, settled boundaries with Canada, and acquired Florida (1819). In 1823 he issued the MONROE DOCTRINE, one of the most important principles of US foreign policy.

**Monroe, Marilyn,** 1926–62, American film actress; b. Norma Jean Baker. A famed sex symbol, she showed innocence and vulnerability in such films as *Bus Stop* (1956), *Some Like It Hot* (1959), and *The Misfits* (1960).

**Monroe Doctrine,** dual principle of US foreign policy enunciated 2 Dec. 1823, in Pres. James MONROE's message to Congress. Formulated with the help of his secretary of state, John Quincy ADAMS, it stated that the American continents were no longer open for colonization by European powers and that the US would view with displeasure any European intervention in the Americas. Although the doctrine was never formally recognized in international law, it was invoked successfully several times and became important in US foreign policy. As imperialistic tendencies grew, the Monroe Doctrine came to be viewed with suspicion by Latin American countries, who associated it with the possible extension of US hegemony. Pres. Theodore ROOSEVELT's corollary stated (1904) that a disturbance in Latin America might force the US to intervene to prevent European intervention. This interpretation was invoked extensively by presidents Taft and Wilson to justify US intervention in the Caribbean region. By the end of the 1920s the doctrine had become less important, and under Pres. F.D. ROOSEVELT the emphasis was on Pan-Americanism. Despite the reemergence of the spectre of unilateral intervention in Latin America in recent decades, for the most part the US has continued to support cooperation within the framework of the ORGANIZATION OF AMERICAN STATES.

**Monrovia,** city and port (1981 pop. 306,460), capital of Liberia, on the Atlantic coast at the mouth of the St Paul R. Monrovia is Liberia's largest city and its administrative and commercial centre. The city's economy revolves around its harbour, which was improved by US forces under LEND-LEASE during World War II. It is a free port, and some 150 shipping companies are registered there under the Liberian flag. Manufactures include cement and refined petroleum. Monrovia was founded in 1822 by the American Colonization Society as a settlement for repatriated American slaves and was named after US Pres. James MONROE.

**monsoon,** wind that changes direction with the seasons. Monsoons are the result of differing air pressures caused by the varied heating and cooling rates of continental land masses and oceans. Winter monsoons associated with India and Southeast Asia are generally dry; summer monsoons in those regions are extremely wet.

**montage,** the art and technique of motion-picture editing in which contrasting shots or sequences are used impressionistically to affect emotional or intellectual responses. It was developed creatively after 1925 by Sergei EISENSTEIN. See also CINEMATOGRAPHY.

**Montagnards:** see MOUNTAIN, THE.

**Montagu, John:** see SANDWICH, JOHN MONTAGU, 4th EARL OF.

**Montagu, Lady Mary Wortley,** 1689–1762, English author, noted primarily for her highly descriptive *Turkish Letters* written in 1724 (publ. in 1763) from the British Embassy in Constantinople. On her return to England she introduced inoculation against smallpox. *Town Eclogues* (1747) and her lively letters give an entertaining picture of contemporary manners. She had a notorious quarrel with POPE who attacked her in his poetry.

**Montaigne, Michel Eyquem, seigneur de** (mawnh̩tenyə), 1533–92, French essayist. Initiator and greatest master of the ESSAY as a modern literary form, he was a magistrate (1557–70) and mayor of Bordeaux (1581–85). He produced his first two books of *Essays* while living in retirement between 1571 and 1580, and the third after 1586. The essays show the development of Montaigne's thinking, from a study of himself into a more general study of mankind and nature. The early works reflect his concern with pain and death. A middle period is characterized by his skepticism regarding all knowledge. Montaigne's last essays reflect his acceptance of life as good and his conviction that people must discover their own nature in order to live in peace and dignity. The *Essays,* models of the familiar, digressive style, treat a wide variety of subjects of universal concern and have greatly influenced both later French writing and English literature.

**Montale, Eugenio,** 1896–1981, Italian poet and critic. His poetry, complex and often pessimistic, has appeared in such volumes as *Cuttlefish Bones* (1925), *Occasions* (1939), *The Storm and Other Things* (1956), and *The Four-year Notebook* (1977). Prose collections include *The Butterfly of Dinard* (1956) and *On Poetry* (1976). Awarded the 1975 Nobel Prize for Literature, he is regarded as the greatest Italian poet of the century.

**Montana,** state of the US (1984 est. pop. 824,000), area 381,087 km² (147,138 sq mi), situated in the NW, bordered by Idaho (W), Wyoming (S), South Dakota and North Dakota (E), and the Canadian provinces of British Columbia, Alberta, and Saskatchewan (N). HELENA is the capital and Billings is the largest city, followed by Great Falls and Butte. The eastern part of the state lies in the GREAT PLAINS, and the west is part of the ROCKY MTS. The climate is cold and continental, with short summers. The economy is dominated by mining and agriculture. Petroleum, coal, copper, antimony, vermiculite, and other minerals are extracted. Cattle are raised in the E, and wheat, corn, dairy products, barley, and sugar beets, some grown on irrigated land, are also important. Most industries are based on local raw materials: timber milling, food processing, and oil refining. Less than 25% of the population lives in metropolitan areas, and in 1980 93% was non-Hispanic white. The Great Plains originally supported buffalo and the Indians who hunted them, including Blackfoot, Sioux, Arapaho, Cheyenne, and Flathead, some of whose descendants still live on reservations. After Montana was acquired by the US in the LOUISIANA PURCHASE (1803), trappers arrived, then gold-diggers, and finally ranchers in the 1860s. Despite defeating Gen. George Custer at the Little Big Horn (1876), the Indians were vanquished. Cattle-ranchers, sheep-ranchers, and then farmers competed for the land, until it was fenced in (1909–18). Copper companies struggled for control of the mines and the state in the 1880s, and are still powerful. Since World War II the economy has grown, especially after the national energy crisis of the 1970s encouraged coal mining.

**Montand, Yves,** 1921–, French film actor; b. Italy. Originally a singer with Edith PIAF, he later achieved popularity as a world-weary leading man, particularly in thrillers. His films include *The Wages of Fear* (1953), *Let's Make Love* (1960), and *Z* (1969).

**Montbéliard,** city (1982 pop. of agglomeration 128,194), E France. Using local water power and a strong HUGUENOT tradition it developed textile and watch- and clock-making industries. Montbéliard-Sochaux has since emerged as a major centre of the French motor-vehicle industry; hardware and various kinds of machinery are also manufactured.

**Mont Blanc** (mawnh ̩blanh), highest peak 4807 m (15,771 ft) in Europe outside the USSR, located in the Alps near Chamonix, SE France. It was first climbed in 1786.

**Montcalm, Louis Joseph de** (mont̩kahm), 1712–59, French general. During the FRENCH AND INDIAN WARS he captured (1756–57) Fort Ontario and Fort Henry, and beat off (1758) a British attack on Fort Ticonderoga. He defended Quebec against Gen. WOLFE's army until he lost (1759) the open battle on the Plains of Abraham, in which both Montcalm and Wolfe were killed; as a result, Quebec fell to the British.

**Monte Carlo:** see MONACO.

**Montego Bay,** city (1980 pop. 70,000), NW Jamaica. A port, railway terminus, and commercial centre, it is one of the most popular resorts in the Caribbean. There is an active trade in sugar, bananas, coffee, and rum.

**Montenegro,** Serbo-Croatian *Crna Gora,* smallest republic of Yugoslavia (1981 pop. 584,000), 13,810 km² (5332 sq mi), SW Yugoslavia. TITOGRAD is the capital. Only 4.2% of the largely mountainous region is arable. Stock-raising was the dominant way of life before industrialization began after 1945. As Zeta a constituent principality of the Serbian empire, parts of Montenegro continued to defy the Ottomans after Serbia's defeat at Kossovo Polje (1389) (see KOSOVO). Most Montenegrin territory eventually fell either to the Turks or, on the coast, to Venice (later Austria), but an unsubdued tribal kernel remained, the independence of which was recognized by the Porte in 1799 and by the European powers in 1878. From 1696 the unique office of prince–bishop (*vladika*) became hereditary in the Petrović-Njegoš clan (nephew succeeding uncle) until the dynasty was secularized (1852). The last monarch, NICHOLAS, was deposed when Montenegro united with Serbia in 1918. Annexed by Italy in 1941, Montenegro became a Yugoslav republic after World War II and Montenegrins were regarded as a nation distinct from Serbs. Despite its small size and primitive society, Montenegro played a disproportionate role in the rise of South Slav nationalism.

**Monterey,** US city (1980 pop. 27,558), W California, on the northern side of the Monterey Peninsula, on Monterey Bay; inc. 1850. A famous resort, it is one of the oldest cities in the state and is rich in history. A presidio was built in 1770, and Monterey was capital of the Spanish territory of Alta California for much of the period 1775–1846. The US Navy took the city in 1846; California's constitution was written there (1849). It became a fishing and whaling centre.

**Monterrey,** city (1980 est. pop. 1,300,000), NE Mexico, capital of Nuevo León state, c.240 km (150 mi) S of Laredo, Texas. Mexico's second-ranking industrial centre, Monterrey has the country's largest iron and steel foundries. It is in a mountain valley where a moderate, dry climate and hot springs have made it a popular resort. Founded in 1579, it was captured (1846) by US forces during the MEXICAN WAR.

**Montespan, Françoise Athénaïs, marquise de** (mawnhtə,spanh), 1641–1707, mistress of LOUIS XIV of France. She replaced (1667) Mlle de La Vallière as the king's mistress and bore him several children. She was supplanted by Mme de MAINTENON.

**Montesquieu, Charles Louis de Secondat, baron de la** 1689–1755, French jurist and political philosopher. His satire on French institutions, *Persian Letters* (1721), brought him fame. *The Spirit of Laws* (1748), his greatest work, compares the republican, despotic, and monarchical forms of government, revealing the influence of John LOCKE. Montesquieu advocated the separation and balance of powers within government as a means of guaranteeing the freedom of the individual; this doctrine helped form the philosophical basis for the US CONSTITUTION.

**Montessori, Maria,** 1870–1952, Italian educator and physician. She was the originator of the **Montessori method** of educating small children and the first woman to receive (1894) a medical degree in Italy. At the Orthophrenic School in Rome she worked as a psychiatrist with retarded children, using an environment rich in manipulative materials. In 1907 she started her first day-care centre, utilizing the same methods with normal preschool children on the theory that a child will learn naturally if placed in an environment consisting of 'learning games' suited to its abilities and interests. Relying on self-motivation and auto-education, the teacher intervenes only when a child needs help. Montessori also developed child-sized furniture. Her writings include *The Montessori Method* (1912) and *The Secret of Childhood* (1936).

**Monteverdi, Claudio,** 1567–1643, Italian composer, the first great figure in the history of OPERA and one of the supreme musical dramatists. His first opera, *Orfeo* (1607), was revolutionary in its combination of dramatic power and orchestral expressiveness. His *Vespers* of 1610 used similar technical advances to express the depths of religious feeling. After settling in Venice (1613) he wrote mostly church music, but continued to produce operas and MADRIGALS. He set the style for Venetian opera. His late works include *The Coronation of Poppaea* (1642) and *Il Ritorno d'Ulisse in patria* (1641), revived successfully since 1945.

**Montevideo,** city (1980 pop. 1,298,546), S Uruguay, capital of Uruguay, on the Río de la Plata. One of the continent's major ports, it is Uruguay's only large city, with nearly half its population; handles virtually all its foreign trade; has diverse manufactures; and is the base for much of the South Atlantic fishing fleet. It is a spacious, attractive city with outstanding architecture and popular beaches. Settled by the Spanish after 1724, it became Uruguay's capital in 1828.

**Montez, Lola,** 1818?–1861, Irish dancer who became the mistress of King Louis I of Bavaria. He made her a countess, and her influence over Bavarian political affairs before the REVOLUTIONS OF 1848 was considerable. She was subsequently banished and eventually settled in the US, where she died in poverty.

**Montezuma** or **Moctezuma,** 1480?–1520, AZTEC emperor (c.1502–20), sometimes called Montezuma II. Believing the Spanish conquerors to be descendants of the god QUETZALCOATL, he gave them gifts to persuade them to leave, but Hernán CORTÉS captured him and attempted to govern through him. Montezuma was killed by stoning by his own people. His name is linked with fabulous treasures that the Spanish took and presumably lost at sea.

**Montfort, Simon de, earl of Leicester,** 1208?–65, leader of the baronial revolt against HENRY III of England. Simon was active in forcing Henry to accept (1258) the PROVISIONS OF OXFORD. After the king's annulment (1261) of the provisions, Simon became a leader in the BARONS' WAR, and won a great victory over the king at Lewes (1264). He was then master of England. His famous Parliament of 1265, to which he summoned not only knights from each shire but also, for the first time, representatives from the boroughs, was an attempt to rally national support. Opposition to Montfort grew. It was rallied in the Welsh Marches by the king's son Edward (later EDWARD I); the war was resumed, and Montfort was defeated and killed at Evesham.

**Montgolfier, Joseph Michel** (mawnhgol,fyay), 1704–1810, and Jacques Etienne Montgolfier, 1745–99, French aviators, inventors of the hot-air BALLOON. After a successful demonstration of a paper balloon on 19 Sept. 1783 to an audience including King Louis XVI, Queen Marie Antoinette, and Benjamin Franklin, the brothers achieved the first manned flight on 21 Nov. 1783 with a balloon that flew for 20 mins over Paris.

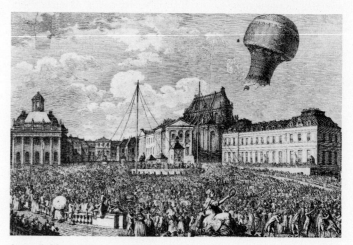

An early **Montgolfier** ascent with a hot air balloon from Versailles on 19 Sept. 1783, carrying a sheep, a duck, and a cock.

**Montgomery,** US city (1984 est. pop. 185,000), state capital of Alabama, on the Alabama R.; inc. 1819. A major agricultural market centre, it is in the cotton-rich Black Belt. Glass and furniture are among its important manufactures. Named state capital in 1847, it boomed as a port and cotton market. The Confederate States of America were formed (Feb. 1861) in the old capitol (built 1857), where Jefferson DAVIS was inaugurated, and Montgomery served as Confederate capital throughout 1861. In 1955 the black community began a bus boycott which brought both civil rights and Rev. Martin Luther KING, Jr to national prominence.

**Montgomery, Bernard Law, 1st Viscount Montgomery of Alamein** 1887–1976, British field marshal. In WORLD WAR II, he became the idol of the British public after his victory (1942) at El Alamein (see NORTH AFRICA,

CAMPAIGNS IN), and served in Sicily and Italy until Dec. 1943. In Normandy he was field commander of all ground forces until Aug. 1944, then led the 21st Army Group across N Germany to the Baltic. He headed (1945–46) British occupation forces in Germany and served (1951–58) as deputy commander of the Allied powers in Europe.

**month,** time required for the MOON to orbit once around the Earth. The *sidereal month,* or time needed for the Moon to return to the same position relative to the fixed stars, averages 27 days 7 hr 43 min 12 sec; the *synodic month,* or time needed for the Moon to go through its complete cycle of PHASES, averages 29 days 12 hr 44 min 3 sec. For the month's harmony with the solar calendar, see CALENDAR.

**Montherlant, Henri de** (mawnhteə‚lanh), 1896–1972, French author. His novels, such as *Les bestiaires* (1926; tr. The Bullfighters) and *Les célibataires* (1934; tr. The Bachelors), give voice to a conflict between sensuality and ascetic pride. His plays, all very successful, include *Le maître de Santiago* (1947), *Port-Royal* (1954), *Don Juan* (1958), and *La reine morte* (1942), probably his masterpiece.

**Monticello,** estate near Charlottesville, Virginia, US, home and burial place of Thomas JEFFERSON, who designed it. Begun in 1770, the mansion is one of the earliest examples of the American CLASSIC REVIVAL. Today it is a national shrine.

**Montpelier,** US city (1980 pop. 8241), state capital (since 1805) of Vermont, on the Winooski and North Branch rivers; inc. 1855. State government and insurance offices are the chief employers; timber and granite are produced in the area. A tourist centre, the city is surrounded by the Green Mountains, with Mt Mansfield nearby.

**Montpellier,** city (1982 pop. 201,067), capital of Hérault dept., S France. A centre of the wine trade of Languedoc, it has an old-established university (1289) with a renowned medical faculty. Bought by France from the kings of Majorca in 1349, it became a centre of Protestantism. The city has grown rapidly since 1960 with the arrival of repatriate settlers from Algeria and the establishment of electronics industries.

**Montpensier, Anne Marie Louise d'Orléans, duchesse de** (monhpanh‚syay), 1627–93, French princess, called La Grande Mademoiselle, daughter of Gaston d'Orléans. A rebel leader in the FRONDE, she relieved (1652) Orléans with her troops and opened the gates of Paris to the prince of CONDÉ's army. She later married the duc de Lauzun, a soldier, but they soon separated.

**Montreal,** officially Montréal, city (1983 est. pop. 1,005,000), S Quebec, E Canada, part of Montreal urban community on Montréal Island, in the St Lawrence R. at the entrance to the SAINT LAWRENCE SEAWAY. Canada's largest city, it is second only to Paris as the largest primarily French-speaking city in the world (although it has a large English-speaking minority). It is also the nation's chief east-coast seaport and rivals TORONTO as the principal industrial, financial, and commercial centre. Landmarks include 233-m (764-ft) Mt Royal, the hill after which the city is named; historic Old Montreal (*Vieux Montréal*), along the waterfront; Place Ville Marie (built 1960s), first of several underground urban complexes that have transformed life in the centre of the city; a modern underground railway (opened 1966); and *Man and His World,* a permanent mini-version of the international exposition *EXPO '67,* on an island in the St Lawrence. Montreal was founded in 1642 by French settlers as Ville Marie de Montréal, on the site of the Indian village of Hochelaga. Vaudreuil de Cavagnal surrendered the city to the British in 1760, and Americans under Richard Montgomery briefly held it (1775–76) during the AMERICAN REVOLUTION. Montreal's importance as a transshipment port for Great Lakes–Atlantic commerce increased rapidly after construction of the Lachine Canal (1825), which allowed ships to bypass the Lachine Rapids, and its volume of trade took another leap forward after the opening (1957) of the St Lawrence Seaway.

**Monts, Pierre du Gua, sieur de** (mohnh), c.1560–c.1630, French colonizer in Canada. After he and Samuel de CHAMPLAIN explored (1604–05) the coasts of New Brunswick and New England, he founded (1605) the first French colony in Canada at Port Royal (see ANNAPOLIS ROYAL).

**Mont-Saint-Michel,** rocky isle (1982 pop. c.80), in the Gulf of St-Malo, NW France. Access to this major tourist attraction is by causeway or by land at low tide. The Benedictine abbey was founded (708) by St Aubert. Three-storey buildings and the rock summit provide a base for the abbey church, a superb achievement of Gothic architecture.

**Montserrat,** island (1984 est. pop. 11,800), 102 km² (39.5 sq mi), British dependency, West Indies, one of the Leeward Islands. Plymouth is the capital. It was discovered (1493) by Columbus and colonized (1632) by the English. After years of Anglo-French rivalry it became a British possession in 1783. It has had internal self-government as a British Dependent Territory since 1960. Political power has alternated between the People's Liberation Movement (in office since 1978) and the Progressive Democratic Party, neither of which favours independence.

**Monument, The,** a column in E central London, built to commemorate the Great Fire of London in 1666. The monument is situated in Monument Street, near to the point where the fire broke out (Pudding Lane). The Monument was built from designs by Christopher WREN and consists of a Doric column standing on a plinth. There is a gallery at the top of the column, from which an excellent view of London can still be obtained, though The Monument is overshadowed by taller modern buildings.

**Monza,** city (1984 pop. 122,421), Lombardy, N Italy. Its proximity to Milan has made it a dormitory and industrial suburb of that city. Mulberries are grown in the area and support the raising of silkworms. The town is noted for the circuit on which international motor races are held. In the altar of its 13th-cent. cathedral is the Iron Crown used in the coronation of Italian kings.

**mood** or **mode,** in verb INFLECTION, the forms of a verb that indicate its manner of doing or being. In English the forms are called indicative (for direct statement or question, or to express an uncertain condition), imperative (for commands), and subjunctive (for sentences suggesting doubt, condition, or a situation contrary to fact). The infinitive is sometimes considered an example of mood, as are phrases formed with *may, might, can, could, should, would, must,* and *ought.*

**Moody, Dwight Lyman,** 1837–99, American evangelist. In 1870 he met Ira Sankey, who became associated with him in evangelistic campaigns in the US and in Britain. They became famous for their hymns. In Massachusetts, Moody founded Northfield Seminary (1879) and Mt Hermon School (1881), which were merged (1971) as the Northfield Mt Hermon School. He also opened (1889) a Bible institute (now the Moody Bible Inst.) in Chicago.

**Moody, Helen Wills:** see WILLS, HELEN NEWINGTON.

**Moon,** the single natural SATELLITE of the Earth. The lunar orbit is elliptical, and the average distance of the Moon from the Earth is about 385,000 km (240,000 mi). The Moon's orbital period around the Earth, and also its rotation period, is 27.322 days. The average angular size of the Moon's diameter is about ½°, which also happens to be the Sun's apparent diameter. This coincidence coupled with the ellipticity of the Moon's orbit permits both total and annular solar ECLIPSES to occur. The moon's radius is about 1740 km (1080 mi); it has about 1/81 the mass of the Earth and is as dense. The Moon completely lacks both water and atmosphere. Instruments landed by the Apollo missions and other efforts

Mont-Saint-Michel

are gradually giving us knowledge about the interior of the Moon. The lunar surface is divided into the densely cratered, mountainous highlands and the large, roughly circular, smooth-floored plains called maria. See also SPACE EXPLORATION; SPACE PROBE.

Moon

**Moon, Sun Myung**, 1920–, Korean religious leader. He was an engineering student and dock worker before founding (1954) the Unification Church with a doctrine loosely based on Christianity as interpreted by Moon, who has suggested that he may be the 'real Messiah'. By the early 1980s Moon claimed 40,000 followers in the US (his headquarters are at Tarrytown, New York State) and 3 million worldwide. Accused of brainwashing converts and of various illegal activities, he was convicted (1982) of conspiracy to evade taxes. See also CULT.

**moonstone**, type of FELDSPAR, found in Sri Lanka, Burma, and Madagascar, used as a GEM. The refraction of light by its thin, paired internal layers causes its milky, bluish sheen.

**Moor, Antonis:** see MORO, ANTONIO.

**Moore, George**, 1852–1933, English author; b. Ireland. He introduced NATURALISM into the Victorian novel with *A Mummer's Wife* (1885). *Esther Waters* (1894) is his best-known novel. His association with the IRISH LITERARY RENAISSANCE is described in *Hail and Farewell* (3 vol., 1911–14), an autobiography.

**Moore, G(eorge) E(dward)**, 1873–1958, English philosopher. He taught (1898–1939) at Cambridge Univ. and edited (1921–47) the journal *Mind*. First influenced by F.H. BRADLEY and KANT, Moore later became more interested in critical EPISTEMOLOGY, and particularly in distinguishing between acts of consciousness and their possible objects. He also became concerned (with Bertrand RUSSELL and WITTGENSTEIN) with the philosophical implications of linguistic analysis and questioned the definition of 'reality'. Although Moore provided no systematic set of philosophical doctrines, he is acknowledged as an important influence on contemporary British and American philosophy, especially through his work on commonsense beliefs; his interest in the use of signs (see SEMIOTICS); his representation of REALISM; and his works on ETHICS, *Principia ethica* (1903) and *Ethics* (1912).

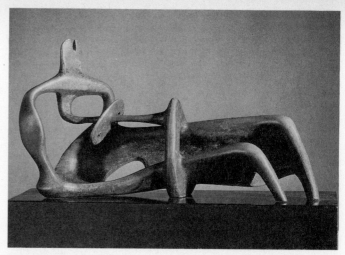

Reclining Figure by Henry **Moore**, 1939. Tate Gallery, London.

**Moore, Henry**, 1898–1986, English sculptor. His early sculpture was rough and angular, influenced by PRE-COLUMBIAN ART. Around 1928 he developed a more personal style that gained him international repute. His works in bronze, wood, stone, and cement are characterized by smooth organic shapes that include empty hollows. His favourite subjects were mother and child and the reclining figure. Moore, as an official war artist (1940–42) produced a series of images of the London Underground shelters that are a powerful record of life during the Blitz.

**Moore, Marianne**, 1887–1972, American poet. Her poetry is witty, crisp, intellectual, and often satirical. Volumes of her verse include *Poems* (1921), *Observations* (1924), *Collected Poems* (1951), and *Complete Poems* (1967). Among her other works are translations and essays.

**Moore, Thomas**, 1779–1852, Irish poet. His *Irish Melodies* (1808–34) include 'Believe Me If All Those Endearing Young Charms' and 'The Harp That Once Through Tara's Halls'. *Lalla Rookh* (1817), a long poem on Oriental themes, was very popular. Moore was a friend and biographer of BYRON.

**moorhen:** see COOT.

**Moorhouse, Frank**, 1938–, Australian writer of short fiction. A fine stylist, he is a chronicler of contemporary urban society, employing the narrative method of discontinuous narrative obliquely connecting his characters and tales. His collections include *The Americans, Baby* (1972), *The Electrical Experience* (1974), *Days of Wine and Rage* (1980), and *Forty-Seventeen* (1988).

**Moors**, nomadic people of N Africa, originally inhabitants of Mauretania. They became militant Muslims in the 8th cent. and crossed over to Spain (711), where they easily overran the Visigoths. They spread northwards across the Pyrenees into France but were turned back by CHARLES MARTEL in 732. In S Spain, however, they established the Umayyad emirate (later caliphate) at Córdoba. The court there grew in wealth, splendour, and culture. Other great centres of Moorish culture were Toledo, Granada, and Seville. The Moors never established a stable central government. In the 11th cent. the caliphate fell, and Moorish Spain fell to the ALMORAVIDS and (in 1174) to the ALMOHADS. Throughout this period, efforts by Christian rulers in N Spain to extend their power occurred. In 1085 ALFONSO VI of León and Castile recovered Toledo. Córdoba fell in 1236, and one by one the Moorish strongholds surrendered. The last Moorish city, Granada, fell to FERDINAND V and ISABELLA I in 1492. Most of the Moors were driven from Spain, but two groups, the Mudejares and MORISCOS, remained.

**moose**, largest member (genus *Alces*) of the DEER family, found in N Eurasia and N North America. It stands 2.4 m (7¾ ft) at the shoulder and is 2.9 m (9½ ft) long. The Eurasian species (*A. alces*) is known in Europe as the ELK. The larger American moose is sometimes classed as a separate species (*A. americana*); it has a heavy, brown body with humped shoulders, long, lighter-coloured legs, a thick, almost trunklike muzzle, and broad, flattened antlers in the male. Moose spend part of their time in water, feeding on water plants, browsing on shoots and bark in the winter.

**Mor, Antonis:** see MORO, ANTONIO.

**Moradabad,** town (1981 pop. 330,051), Uttar Pradesh state, N India, on the Ramganga R. It is a district administrative, railway, and commercial centre with some industry, producing cotton textiles, fertilizers, and iron, steel, brass, and copper goods. Moradabad was a centre of the Wahabi (Islamic puritanism) movement of the 19th cent.

**moraine,** rock and soil debris carried and finally deposited by a GLACIER. A lateral moraine is the material that falls onto a glacier's edges from valley cliffs. A ground moraine is the debris deposited by a melting glacier. A terminal moraine is the debris left at the edge of a glacier's extreme forward movement. The great ice sheets of the Pleistocene epoch left terminal moraines stretching across North America and Europe. See also DRIFT.

**Moral Re-Armament:** see BUCHMAN, FRANK NATHAN DANIEL.

**Morant, Robert Laurie,** 1863–1920, British civil servant. He played a major part in framing the Education Act 1902 (see EDUCATION ACTS), and became permanent secretary of the newly created Board of Education (1903–11). His 1904 Regulations helped to model the new grammar schools largely on the traditional curriculum. He was instrumental in developing school health and medical services. He chaired the National Health Insurance Commission (1911–19), and was first secretary of the new Ministry of Health from 1919. He was knighted in 1907.

**Morava,** river, 360 km (225 mi) long, in Czechoslovakia. It rises in the Sudeten Mts and flows through Olomouc in a southerly direction to join the Danube just above Bratislava.

**Moravia,** region, central Czechoslovakia, bordered by Bohemia (W), the Little and White Carpathian Mts (E), and the Sudeten Mts (N). BRNO is the chief city and the former Moravian capital. A fertile agricultural area, Moravia is also highly industrialized, with such manufactures as machinery, armaments, and motor vehicles, and has lignite, coal, and other resources. In the 9th cent. Moravia became a great empire, ruling Bohemia, Silesia, Slovakia, and S Poland. From the early 11th cent. it was in effect a crown land of BOHEMIA, with which it passed (1526) to the HABSBURGS of Austria. Moravia, however, retained its own diet and suffered less than Bohemia in the civil and religious strife of the 16th cent. It became an Austrian crown land in 1849. After WORLD WAR I Moravia was incorporated into the new republic of Czechoslovakia. The MUNICH PACT (1938) transferred NW and S Moravia to Germany, which occupied (1939–45) all of Moravia during WORLD WAR II. Since 1960 the region has comprised two administrative regions, North and South Moravia.

**Moravia, Alberto,** pseud. of **Alberto Pincherle,** 1907–, Italian novelist. His first novel, *Time of Indifference* (1929), is a powerful study of moral inertia in a middle-class Roman milieu. Other novels include *The Woman of Rome* (1947), *The Conformist* (1951), *Two Women* (1957), *The Empty Canvas* (1960), and *Time of Desecration* (tr. 1980). He has also written short stories and essays.

**Moravian Church, Renewed Church of the Brethren,** or **Unitas Fratrum,** an evangelical Christian communion. It originated in Bohemia among some of John HUSS's followers, who broke with Rome in 1467. Persecution reduced their numbers, but a renewal took place after 1722 at Herrnhut, on the Saxon estate of Graf von ZINZENDORF. They take Scripture as the rule of faith and morals and have a simple liturgy and a modified episcopacy. The Moravian Church has some 17 provinces linked together by a general synod.

**Mordecai:** see ESTHER.

**More, Sir Anthony:** see MORO, ANTONIO.

**More, Sir Thomas** (Saint Thomas More) 1478–1535, English statesman, author of *Utopia,* and martyr of the Roman Catholic Church. He received a Latin education and became a humanist through contact with John Colet, John LYLY, and ERASMUS. As a lawyer he attracted the attention of HENRY VIII, whom he served as a diplomat; More was lord chancellor (1529–32). His refusal to subscribe to the Act of Supremacy led to his imprisonment and execution. More wrote works in Latin (*Utopia,* 1516, is a picture of an ideal state founded on reason) and in English, including devotions, tracts, poems, prayers, and meditations. His English works were published in 1557.

**Moreau, Gustave,** 1826–98, French painter. Moreau painted sumptuously rich allegorical and mythological scenes that evoke a distant and fabulous world. He was fascinated by the destructive power of

women, as in *Salome dancing* and *Helen at the Gates of Troy* (both: Musée Gustave Moreau, Paris). Moreau was admired by the SYMBOLISTS in the 1880s and 1890s and by the Surrealists (see SURREALISM) in the 1920s.

**Moreau, Jeanne,** 1928–, French film actress and director. In such films as *The Lovers* (1959), *Les liaisons dangereuses* (1960), *Jules and Jim* (1961), and *The Bride Wore Black* (1967) she has portrayed amoral romantic heroines. She has directed *Lumière* (1977) and *The Adolescent* (1979).

**Morelia,** city (1979 est. pop. 251,011), central Mexico, capital of Michoacán state. Founded in 1541 it remains strongly colonial in atmosphere and is noted for the local reddish stone used in the construction of its central buildings. The Mexican revolutionary leader, José Maria MORELOS Y PAVÓN, and the Mexican emperors Augustín de ITURBIDE and MAXIMILIAN of Austria were residents.

**Morelos y Pavón, José María** (moh͵raylos ee pa͵von), 1765–1815, Mexican revolutionary leader. A liberal priest, he led (1810–13) rebel forces to initial victories over the Spanish army, becoming generalissimo. But he was defeated (1813) by Gen. ITURBIDE at Valladolid and later captured, defrocked, and executed.

**Moreto y Cabaña, Agustín** (moh͵raytoh ee ka͵banyah), 1618–69, Spanish dramatist of the GOLDEN AGE. His greatest play, of more than 100, is *El desdén por el desdén* (Disdain for Disdain).

**Morgan, Sir Henry,** 1635?–88, Welsh buccaneer. He led West Indian privateers who were commissioned by the British government to raid Spanish possessions. Despite their ruthlessness, his operations earned him a knighthood in 1673.

**Morgan, Lewis Henry,** 1818–81, American anthropologist. A lawyer by training, Morgan was the first anthropologist to undertake fieldwork (see PARTICIPANT OBSERVATION). Derived from his unexcelled studies of the Iroquois, *Systems of Consanguinity and Affinity of the Human Family* (1870) describes his theory correlating KINSHIP terminology with forms of marriage and rules of descent. *Ancient Society* (1877), which classifies world cultures by progressive stages of savagery, barbarism, or civilization, influenced MARX and ENGELS, who interpreted its evolutionary doctrine as support for their theory of history. (See EVOLUTION, SOCIOCULTURAL).

**Morgan, Thomas Hunt,** 1866–1945, American geneticist. He made important contributions to the understanding of the function of chromosomes, developed in work on the fruit fly (genus *Drosophila*), for which he was awarded the 1933 Nobel prize for physiology or medicine.

**Mörike, Eduard** (͵møːrikə), 1804–75, German poet and clergyman. Many of his rich lyrics were set to music by Hugo WOLF. He also wrote a novel, *Maler Nolten* (1832), and a novella, *Mozart's Journey from Vienna to Prague* (1856).

**Mori Ōgai,** 1862–1922, Japanese writer and army surgeon. He studied medicine in Germany, where he acquired a great love for German literature and translated GOETHE and SCHILLER (and IBSEN). He was very influential in introducing modern European literature to Japan. He combines confessional style with realist description; his fiction includes *The Wild Geese* (1911–13; tr. 1951); *Sanshō dayū* (1914; tr. 1952, 1977); *Takasebune* (tr. 1918), and 'The girl who danced' (1890; tr. 1964, 1975).

**Moriscos** (mə͵riskohz), MOORS converted to Christianity after the Christian reconquest (11th–15th cent.) of Spain. The religion and customs of Muslims in the Christian parts of Spain were generally respected until the fall of Granada (1492), after which Moors who refused conversion were coerced. They rebelled (1499–1502), but were defeated. Although most Moors accepted conversion, others were persecuted by the INQUISITION. Philip II's determination to force the Moriscos to accept Spanish customs and language led them to rebel in Granada (1568–70), but they were defeated. They prospered in spite of persecution, but Philip III decreed (1609) their expulsion for both religious and political reasons.

**Morison, Samuel Eliot,** 1887–1976, American historian. He taught at Harvard (1915–55). In 1926 he was appointed the official historian of Harvard and 10 years later completed his history in three volumes. Commissioned by Pres F.D. ROOSEVELT, he wrote a *History of Naval Operations in World War II* (15 vol., 1947–62). His other works include *The European Discovery of America* (2 vol., 1971–74).

**Morisot, Berthe** (moree‚zoh), 1841–95, French painter. She was the first woman member of the Impressionist group (see IMPRESSIONISM). Morisot often painted scenes of women and children, sitting in the garden, picking fruit or chasing butterflies; her brilliantly free, dashing brushstrokes suggest the effects of dazzling sunlight. Among her works are *The Cradle* (1873; Musée d'Orsay, Paris) and *Woman and Child in the Garden at Bougival* (1882; National Mus. of Wales, Cardiff).

**Morley, Thomas,** c.1577–1603, English composer, pupil of William BYRD. His works include MOTETS, music for Anglican services, and charming MADRIGALS, as well as a guide to 16th-cent. English music practice.

**Mormons,** name commonly used for the members of the Church of Jesus Christ of Latter-Day Saints. The religion was founded by Joseph SMITH after he claimed that golden tablets containing the Book of Mormon were revealed to him at Palmyra, New York State. He and his followers established (1831) a headquarters at Kirtland, Ohio. The group grew rapidly, and Smith planned to make W Missouri its permanent home until conflict with neighbours caused their expulsion (1838–39). The Mormons soon moved west and founded (1847) SALT LAKE CITY in Utah, where, under Brigham YOUNG, they weathered hardships and built a communal economy. Plural marriages within the group prevented Utah's admission to the US until 1896, but in 1890 the church withdrew its sanction of polygamy. The church is led by a three-member First Presidency and by the Council of Twelve (the Apostles). In the 1980s world membership was over 5 million, the majority living in the US. Mormonism is marked by the importance that it attaches to revelation, by stress on the interdependence of spiritual and temporal life, and by vigorous proselytizing. Mormon beliefs are based on the Bible, the Book of Mormon, revelations to Smith (*Doctrine and Covenants*), and *The Pearl of Great Price* (sayings attributed to Moses and Abraham).

**morning glory,** common name for the family Convolvulaceae, herbs, shrubs, and small trees (many of them climbing forms) of warm regions. The tropical morning glory genus (*Ipomoea*), which includes the SWEET POTATO, and the temperate bindweed genus (*Convolvulus*) are chiefly herbaceous vines of prolific growth with colourful funnel-shaped blossoms that often open only in the morning.

**Moro, Aldo,** 1916–78, Italian politician. A Christian Democrat, he was minister of justice (1955–57), prime minister (1963–68, 1974–76), and foreign minister (1970–72). In 1978 he was kidnapped and murdered by the terrorist RED BRIGADES.

**Moro, Antonio,** c.1519–c.1575, Flemish portrait painter, known as Antonis Mor or Moor and Sir Anthony More. Court painter to the house of Habsburg, he was influenced by TITIAN. His portraits, e.g., of Mary Tudor (1554; Prado, Madrid) influenced international court portraiture.

**Morocco,** officially Kingdom of Morocco, kingdom (1987 pop. 23,500,000), 445,050 km² (171,834 sq mi), NW Africa, bordered by the Mediterranean Sea (N), the Atlantic Ocean (W), Mauritania (which lies beyond the disputed territory of Western Sahara (S), and Algeria (E). Principal cities include RABAT (the capital), CASABLANCA, MARRAKESH, and FEZ. The ATLAS MOUNTAINS, rising to 4167 m (13,671 ft) in Jebel Toubkal in the southwest, dominate most of the country. In the south lie the sandy wastes of the SAHARA desert, but in the north is a fertile coastal plain, home of most of the population. Agriculture and mining are the mainstays of the economy. Morocco is the world's leading producer and exporter of phosphates; other important minerals include iron ore, copper, lead, zinc, cobalt, molybdenum, and coal. Half the labour force is employed in agriculture, growing cereals, citrus fruits, and vegetables. Tourism and fishing also contribute to the economy. The GNP is US$11,434 million, and the GNP per capita is US$560 (1985). Most Moroccans are Muslim Arabs, but there are Berber, Christian, and Jewish minorities. Arabic is the official language; Berber, French, and Spanish are also spoken.

*History.* Originally inhabited by Berbers, Morocco became a province of the Roman Empire in the 1st cent. AD. After a period of successive invasions by barbarian tribes, Islam was brought by the Arabs, who swept into Morocco c.685. An independent Moroccan kingdom was established in 788; its dissolution in the 10th cent. began a period of political anarchy. The country was finally united in the 11th cent. by the ALMORAVIDS, a Berber-Muslim dynasty, who established a kingdom stretching from Spain to Senegal. Unity was never complete, however, and conflict between Arabs and Berbers was incessant. European

encroachment, particularly by Portugal and Spain, began in 1415, when Portugal captured Ceuta, and did not end until the Portuguese defeat at the battle of Alcazarquivir in 1578. In the 19th and early 20th cent. the strategic importance and economic potential of Morocco once again excited the interest of the European powers, sparking an intense, often violent, rivalry among France, Spain, and Germany. Finally, in 1912, most of Morocco became a French protectorate; a small area became a Spanish protectorate. Nationalist feelings first began to surface in the 1930s, becoming more militant after World War II, and in 1956 Morocco gained its independence. In 1957 the sultan became King Muhammad V. He was succeeded in 1961 by his son, HASSAN II, whose early reign, plagued by internal unrest, coups, and assassination attempts, was maintained by repressive measures. Hassan's position was strengthened in 1976, when Spain responded to his pressure and relinquished the WESTERN SAHARA to joint Moroccan-Mauritanian control. Challenged by the Polisario Front, a local liberation movement backed by Algeria and engaged in guerrilla warfare to achieve independence for the area (which they named the Saharan Arab Democratic Republic), Mauritania withdrew in 1979, but Morocco maintained its presence. In 1981 it agreed to a referendum for the area but disagreed with the Polisario Front over who should vote. In 1984 Morocco signed a 'treaty of federation' with Libya. In general elections that year the conservative Constitutional Union won the most seats and a centre-right coalition was formed. In 1988 Morocco and the Polisario Front signed a ceasefire agreement.

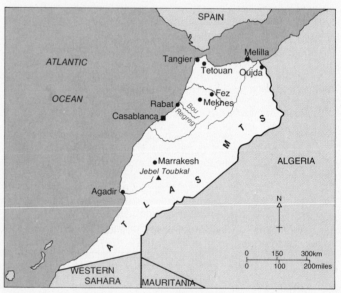

Morocco

**Moroni,** city (1980 est pop. 20,112), capital of COMOROS.

**Moronobu** (Hishikawa Moronobu), c.1618–c.1694, Japanese painter and colour-print designer of the *ukiyo-e* school (see JAPANESE ART). One of his few surviving works is a screen painting, a typical GENRE scene, in the Museum of Fine Arts, Boston.

**morphine,** powerful NARCOTIC derivative of OPIUM used for the relief of pain. Morphine suppresses anxiety and alleviates pain. Side effects include euphoria, constipation, confusion, and apathy. Addiction develops rapidly. Its use is strictly controlled (see DRUG ADDICTION AND DRUG ABUSE).

**Morris, Gouverneur,** 1752–1816, American statesman. An early supporter of the AMERICAN REVOLUTION, he helped handle the finances of the new government (1781–85) and was active in the writing of the Constitution.

**Morris, Robert,** 1734–1806, American merchant, signer of the DECLARATION OF INDEPENDENCE; b. England. His role in raising money for George WASHINGTON's army earned him the title 'financier of the Revolution'.

**Morris, William,** 1834–96, English artist, craftsman, designer, writer, social reformer, and printer. He became interested in medieval philosophy and principles of chivalrous life as well as its art, design, and decoration, and his political and social views were influenced by Thomas CARLYLE and Charles KINGSLEY. He became associated with the PRE-RAPHAELITES and, influenced by D.G. ROSSETTI, began to paint and write poetry, e.g., *The Earthly Paradise* (3 vol., 1868–70). His talent for and interest in the design and manufacture of decorative artefacts and his antipathy to the shoddy work produced by contemporary industrial methods led him to establish the firm of Morris, Marshall, Faulkner & Co. (1861) which later became Morris and Co. (1875–1940). He initially designed, made, and sold murals, carvings, STAINED GLASS, metal work, furniture, and later added CERAMICS, wallpaper, and TEXTILES (in PRINT, WEAVE, TAPESTRY, and EMBROIDERY). His immense decorative talent, his insistence on perfection, and his conviction that craftmanship in the production of an article was essential revitalized British design. By the time of his death, the firm had established a style of textiles and interior design which was so strong that the designs and their imitators are still in production for printed furnishings and wallpapers. In the 1880s Morris became preoccupied by politics turning to revolutionary socialism, and was influenced by MARX. In 1884 he formed the Socialist League. In his *News from Nowhere* (1891) he states his philosophy that art is an expression of joy in labour rather than a luxury. His final important venture was the Kelmscott Press (1890) at Hammersmith, where he designed type, page borders, and bindings of fine books.

Vine pattern designed by William **Morris** and worked by Mary Morris

**Morris, William Richard, Viscount Nuffield**, 1877–1963, British industrialist and philanthropist. Beginning in 1910 he founded Morris Motors at Cowley, Oxford, to produce low-cost cars for the general public (see ISSIGONIS). He endowed Nuffield College, Oxford, in 1937 and the Nuffield Foundation in 1943.

**Morrison, Herbert Stanley, Baron**, 1888–1965, British Labour politician. Of London working-class origins, he was elected to Parliament and was Minister of Transport (Mar.–Aug. 1931) in the second government headed by Ramsay MACDONALD. Under Morrison's leadership the Labour Party won control of the London County Council in 1934. In Churchill's wartime coalition government, Morrison was home secretary, and under Clement ATTLEE he held the posts of lord president of the council (1945–51) and foreign secretary (1951). He was elevated to the House of Lords as Lord Morrison of Lambeth in 1959.

**Morse, Samuel Finley Breese**, 1791–1872, American inventor and noted portraitist. After spending 12 years perfecting his own version of André AMPÈRE's idea for an electric TELEGRAPH, Morse demonstrated the practicability of his device to Congress in 1844. Because many phases of the invention had been anticipated by others, his originality as the inventor of telegraphy has been questioned. Morse later experimented with submarine cable telegraphy.

**Morse code** [after Samuel MORSE], a method of transmitting alphabetical and numerical information together with some simple punctuation, using 'dots' and 'dashes'. These may be realized as electrical pulses (in telegraphy) or as flashes of light (in visual signalling). The *dot* is a very brief pulse or flash while the *dash* is three times as long. Distinct combinations of dots and dashes code each symbol that can be transmitted. The International Morse Code differs considerably from the version adopted in America.

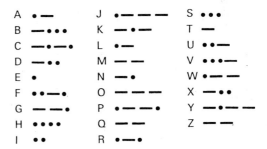

International Morse code

**mortar**, in warfare, a short-range weapon that fires a shell on a high trajectory. The name once applied to a heavy ARTILLERY piece but lately has designated a much lighter, muzzle-loaded, smooth-bore INFANTRY weapon consisting principally of a tube and a supporting bipod that fires a fairly heavy projectile in a high arc.

**mortgage**, in law, a pledge of PROPERTY as security for payment of a debt. If the borrower (the mortgagor) fails to pay the debt, the lender (the mortgagee) has the right to seek foreclosure, a procedure through which the property is sold to satisfy the lender's claims. Almost any kind of property may be mortgaged; probably the most familiar mortgage is that on a home.

**Mortimer, Roger de, 1st earl of March**, 1287?–1330, English nobleman. He opposed EDWARD II in the wars of 1321–22 and escaped to France, where Edward's queen, ISABELLA, became his lover. Together they invaded (1326) England, deposed and murdered Edward, and had young EDWARD III crowned. Mortimer, with Isabella, then virtually ruled England until 1330, when Edward III had him tried and executed.

**mortuary rites**, the rituals associated with death and burial, the final rituals in the life cycle, the last RITES DE PASSAGE. These rites can last for some time after the actual death has occurred, and in some societies 'secondary burial' takes place years later. In many societies funerary rites are highly significant in that they are the occasion for the disposal of property, titles to office, and position in the social order. Funerary rites have been identified by some archaeologists as one of the earliest signs of human culture.

**mosaic**, art of producing surface design by closely inlaying coloured pieces of marble, glass, tile, or semiprecious stone. In the Roman Empire, floors were decorated with mosaics made up of large marble slabs in contrasting colours or of small marble cubes (tesserae). Tessera floors varied from black-and-white geometrical patterns to large pictorial scenes. Glass mosaics were used in early Christian basilicas. The craft reached its height in the 6th cent. at Byzantium (later Constantinople), where the HAGIA SOPHIA was decorated with gold mosaics. The use of gold and of colours produced by metallic oxides later reached the West. In the 5th and 6th cent. RAVENNA, NE Italy, became the centre of Western mosaic art. A revival in Italy (11th–13th cent.) produced such mosaics as those in St. Mark's Church, Venice. Mosaic was also used in Russia, particularly in Kiev. The advent of FRESCO decoration in 14th-cent. Italy caused mosaic art to decline. In the 19th cent., the Gothic revival produced modern attempts at mosaics, e.g., those in WESTMINSTER ABBEY. Mosaics are important in 20th-cent. Mexico, where they continue a pre-Columbian tradition. Contemporary examples are also found in Europe, South America, and Israel.

**Mosca, Gaetano,** 1858–1941, Italian political scientist and politician. A senator and professor of constitutional law, Mosca's most famous work, *The Ruling Class* (1896), elaborated on the theme that every society, whatever its character or IDEOLOGY, is in fact composed of a small elite class which rules, and a much larger mass which is ruled. Later contributions to this elite theory have discussed the origins, character, and 'circulation' of elites; a principal theme has been the necessity of a degree of openness on the part of elites to merit and new blood, based upon the historical instability of states ruled by closed aristocratic elites when they run out of energy and ideas.

**Moscow,** Russian *Moskva,* city (1985 pop. 8,642,000), capital of the UNION OF SOVIET SOCIALIST REPUBLICS and of the RUSSIAN SOVIET FEDERATED SOCIALIST REPUBLIC, W central European USSR, on the Moskva R. The largest city in the USSR, Moscow is the hub of its rail network, an inland port, and the site of civil and military airports. Its many industrial products include machinery and machine tools, cars, chemicals, and textiles. First mentioned by chroniclers in 1147, it became (c.1271) the seat of the grand dukes of Vladimir-Suzdal and (by the 15th cent.) capital of the Russian state. From the 14th cent. it was the seat of the metropolitan (later patriarch) of the Russian Orthodox Church. The capital was transferred (1712) to the new city of St Petersburg (now LENINGRAD). Built largely of wood until the 19th cent., Moscow burned many times, notably after NAPOLEON's invasion (1812). In the 19th and early 20th cent. it was the focus in Russia of social democracy and other political movements. It became the capital of the USSR in 1918. Economic growth doubled the population between 1926 and 1939. In World War II the German offensive against Moscow (1941) was stopped about 32 km (20 mi) from the city's centre, but damage was minimal. The city's major sectors form concentric circles around the KREMLIN. Red Square, the Lenin Mausoleum, and St Basil's Cathedral (now an antireligious museum) are major landmarks. Among Moscow's cultural institutions are the Univ. of Moscow (est. 1755), Lenin Library, Tretyakov Gallery, and Bolshoi Theatre.

**Moscow Art Theatre:** see THEATRE (table).

**Mosel,** Fr. *Moselle,* river 510 km (320 mi) long, rising in the VOSGES Mts of E France and flowing through METZ, along the border between Luxembourg and West Germany, and then joining the RHINE at KOBLENZ. Its German section is deeply cut and winding, with famous vineyards on its slopes and many castles.

**Moseley, Henry Gwyn Jeffreys,** 1887–1915, English physicist. Studying the relations among bright-line spectra of different chemical elements, he derived the atomic numbers from the frequencies of vibration of X-rays emitted by each element. Moseley concluded that the ATOMIC NUMBER is equal to the charge on the nucleus. This work explained discrepancies in the Mendeleev system (see PERIODIC TABLE). He was killed in action in World War I.

**Moses,** Hebrew lawgiver; b. probably Egypt. The prototype of the prophets, in the 13th cent. BC he led his people out of bondage in Egypt to the edge of Canaan. According to the Bible (EXODUS; LEVITICUS; NUMBERS; DEUTERONOMY), he lived in constant touch with God, who promulgated the Law (often called Mosaic law) through Moses' mouth. Moses never entered the Promised Land with his people but only saw it from Mt Pisgah before he died. Authorship of the first five books of the Bible, the Pentateuch or TORAH, has traditionally been ascribed to him; hence they are called the Books of Moses.

**Moses ben Maimon:** see MOSES MAIMONIDES.

St Basil's Cathedral in Red Square, **Moscow**

**Moses Maimonides,** 1135–1204, Jewish philosopher and jurist. He wrote a commentary to the MISHNAH, as well as a major Code of Law, entitled *Mishneh Torah* or *Yad Ha-Hazakah,* which has figured in subsequent discussions on all matters of Jewish law. He also wrote hundreds of responses, applying the fruits of talmudic law to a wide variety of social and religious issues. His philosophic work, *Moreh Nevukim* ('Guide for the Perplexed') sets out to achieve a synthesis between Jewish theology and the Greek Aristotelian system.

**Moshoeshoe I,** c.1785–1870, founder of the Basotho nation (see LESOTHO). During the 1820s and 30s he gathered together refugees from the MFECANE in a mountain stronghold called Thabu Bosui. With the help of French missionaries he extended his rule to include the Caledon Valley and spent the remainder of his reign defending his fledgling state against the Boers of the Orange Free State. In 1868, at Moshoeshoe's request, the British intervened and established the British colony of Basutoland.

**Moskito Coast,** section of the Caribbean coast of the isthmus of Central America named after the local Moskito or Miskito Indian tribes. That part of the Moskito coast which now forms Zelaya dept. on the W coast of Nicaragua was held as a British protectorate from 1665 to 1860; the present inhabitants are of Afro-Indian descent and continue to be English-speaking. In 1860 Britain ceded all the coastal territory from the present Honduras–Nicaragua border in the N to the mouth of the San Juan R. to the S to Nicaragua but the region was not formally incorporated into the Republic of Nicaragua until 1894. Since 1979 the region has been a principal conflict zone between the Nicaraguan government forces and insurgents.

**Moslem:** form of Muslim: see ISLAM.

**Mosley, Sir Oswald,** 1896-1980, British politician. Elected to Parliament (as a Conservative 1918–22, and Labour 1926–31), he resigned from Ramsay MACDONALD's cabinet in 1930 and from the Labour Party in 1931. He launched in 1932 the British Union of Fascists, which was influenced by the ideas of MUSSOLINI and of HITLER. Mosley enjoyed some public support during the 1930s. During WORLD WAR II he was imprisoned as a risk to national security.

**mosque,** Muslim worship building. ISLAM is little dependent on ritual, and the house and courtyard of MUHAMMAD at Medina were the first worship site. As Islam spread, almost any edifice was used, including Christian and Zoroastrian temples. The mosque's basic elements are space to assemble and some orientation so that the faithful may pray toward MECCA. This direction is marked by a *mihrab,* usually a decorated niche. The elaborate mihrabs of later mosques are covered with intricate woodwork, carved marble, or tiles. A mosque may also contain a pulpit; a *maqsura,* or enclosed space around the *mihrab,* often with lacy screenwork; MINARETS; a courtyard surrounded by colonnaded or arcaded porticos with wells or fountains for ablutions; and space for a school. Decoration is abstract or geometrical. Early Egyptian and Syrian mosques adhered to the primitive pattern. The mosque of Omar (AD 691) at Jerusalem, called the Dome of the Rock, follows an octagonal Byzantine plan and has a wooden dome, but domed mosques were not common for another six centuries. In the 14th cent. a cruciform mosque with pointed vaults around a central court appeared; the arm toward Mecca was wider and deeper. The finest example of the cruciform mosque is the great mosque of Sultan Hasan (1356) at Cairo. Mosques of N Africa and Spain tended to be simple, but that at Córdoba (begun AD 780) was larger than any Christian church. It became the Cathedral of Córdoba in 1238. In the 15th and 16th cent., colonnaded halls were replaced by large, square, domed interiors, as in the Blue Mosque of Tabriz (1437–68) and the imperial mosque at Isfahan (1585–1612). After 1453, the converted HAGIA SOPHIA became a model for Islamic religious structures. The pointed, bulbous domes and polychrome tile decoration of Persian mosques are distinctive. Indian mosques, following the Persian style, employed stone and marble exteriors that gave them a more solid monumentality.

**mosquito,** fairly small (12–25 mm/½–1 in), slender, long-legged, FLY (family Culicidae). The males have conspicuously feathery antennae and both sexes have a long, forward-projecting proboscis, adapted for feeding on nectar and other plant juices and, in most females, on the blood of mammals and birds. Eggs are laid in still water and both larvae and pupae (which are surprisingly active) are aquatic. Many human diseases, especially in the tropics, are transmitted by mosquitoes, including MALARIA (exclusively by *Anopheles* species), YELLOW FEVER, and ENCEPHALITIS (by *Anopheles* as well as by *Culex, Aedes,* and other species of mosquitoes).

Mosquito on a human

**moss,** small primitive plant (division Bryophyta) typified by tufted growth that is usually vertical. Although limited to moist habitats because they require water for FERTILIZATION and lack a vascular system for conducting water, mosses are extremely hardy and grow nearly everywhere. The green moss plant visible to the naked eye, seldom over 15.2 cm (6 in) in height, is the GAMETOPHYTE generation, which gives rise to the sporophyte generation. Mosses are important in soil formation, filling in surfaces lacking other vegetation, and providing food for certain animals. SPHAGNUM, or peat moss, is commercially valuable as the main constituent of PEAT. CLUB MOSS and SPANISH MOSS are unrelated to true moss.

**Mössbauer effect,** effect reported in 1958 by the German physicist, R.L. Mössbauer, in which a nucleus emitting or absorbing a GAMMA ray does not recoil when embedded in an appropriate crystal. This enables gamma rays of very precise wavelength to be emitted and detected so that small changes (as small as a few parts in $10^{11}$) in the wavelength due to external effects can be measured. The effect has been used, for example, to study magnetic fields in solids and to verify the RED SHIFT predicted by RELATIVITY theory in the wavelength of radiation emitted in a gravitational field. Mössbauer, with R. Hofstadter, was awarded the Nobel Prize for physics in 1961.

**most-favoured-nation clause,** provision in trade agreements between nations that extends to the signatories the automatic right to any tariff reduction or other trade advantage negotiated with a third country. Nations belonging to the General Agreement on Tariffs and Trade (see UNITED NATIONS) accept this principle, which is intended to promote free trade (see TRADE). Today there are efforts to relax this principle to accommodate developing countries seeking preferential treatment for their exports. Regional trading groups such as the COMMON MARKET, which abolish tariffs within the group while maintaining them for trade with nonmembers, pose another challenge to the principle.

**Mosul,** city (1976 est. pop. 857,000), N Iraq, on the Tigris R. Trade in agricultural goods and exploitation of oil are the two main occupations of the inhabitants, who are mostly Arabs. Recently it has developed many manufacturing industries, notably in textiles, bitumen and cement. The surrounding area, however, is peopled by Kurds. Mosul was devastated (13th cent.) by the MONGOLS and was part (1534–1918) of the OTTOMAN EMPIRE. Its possession by Iraq was disputed (1923–25) by Turkey but was confirmed (1926) by the League of Nations.

**motet,** a type of musical composition outstanding in the 13th cent., and a different type in the Renaissance. The 13th-cent. motet, originating in Paris, was a polyphonic piece for three voices: a tenor (a fragment of PLAINSONG or other melody arranged in a pattern) and two accompanying voices, sometimes based on secular French songs. The Renaissance motet, originating in Flanders, was polyphonic and unaccompanied, with a single, Latin text for four to six voices. JOSQUIN DESPREZ, LASSO, PALESTRINA, TALLIS, and BYRD were important motet composers. Since BACH's time the term has referred to various kinds of sacred choral POLYPHONY.

**moth,** any INSECT of the order Lepidoptera other than a BUTTERFLY or a skipper. Of the order's 21 superfamilies, 19 are moths. In most moths there is a bristle-like projection (frenlum) from the base of the hind wing which engages in a clip (retinaculum) on the underside of the fore wing, linking the two wings together in flight (frenlar coupling); this is in contrast to butterflies, whose wings join by overlapping. Moths undergo complete METAMORPHOSIS. The larvae are mostly terrestrial, and feed on living or dead plant material; many are serious pests of growing crops and stored produce. Many moth larvae spin cocoons of silk in which to pupate, usually rather flimsy but very substantial in some species (e.g., the SILKWORM). Adults range in size from 2.5 to 270 mm (¹⁄₁₀ to 10½ in) in wingspan. A few (e.g., the SILKMOTH) do not feed as adults, but the majority of those that do have a proboscis for drinking liquids.

**mother-of-pearl** or **nacre,** iridescent substance that lines the shells of some molluscs, notably the pearl OYSTER, pearl MUSSEL, and ABALONE. Valued for its delicate beauty, it is used for buttons, knife handles, and inlay work.

**Motherwell, Robert,** 1915–, American painter and writer. A painter, teacher, and theoretician of ABSTRACT EXPRESSIONISM, he paints canvases characterized by large, amorphous shapes painted in strong, austere colours, e.g., his best-known series, *Elegy for the Spanish Republic.*

**motion,** in MECHANICS, the change in position of one body with respect to another. The study of the motion of bodies is called DYNAMICS. The time rate of linear motion in a given direction by a body is its *velocity;* this rate is called the *speed* if the direction is unspecified. If during a time *t* a body travels over a distance *s,* then the *average speed* of that body is $s/t$. Correspondingly, the time rate of angular motion of a body about an axis is its *angular velocity.* The change in velocity (in magnitude and/or direction) of a body with respect to time is its acceleration. The relationship between FORCE and motion was expressed by Isaac NEWTON in his three laws of motion: (1) a body at rest tends to remain at rest, or a body in motion tends to remain in motion at a constant speed in a straight line, unless acted on by an outside force; (2) the acceleration *a* of a mass *m* by a force *F* is directly proportional to the force and inversely proportional to the mass, or $a = F/m$; (3) for every action there is an equal and opposite reaction. The second law implies that the total MOMENTUM of a system of bodies not acted on by an external force remains constant (see CONSERVATION LAWS, in physics). Motion at speeds approaching that of light must be described by the theory of RELATIVITY, and the motions of extremely small objects (atoms and elementary particles) are described by quantum mechanics (see QUANTUM THEORY).

**motion sickness** or **travel sickness**, malaise, nausea, and vomiting by susceptible individuals when travelling by car, train, boat, or aeroplane. This common condition is thought to be caused by overstimulation of the balance organs in the inner ear (see EAR) and aggravated by movements of the horizon.

**motor, electric,** machine that produces mechanical motion and energy directly from electrical energy. Operating principle is the reverse of that of a GENERATOR. If a current is caused to flow in a conductor from an external source of electricity and the conductor is in a magnetic field then a mechanical force is induced in the conductor. The size of the force is dependent on the magnitude of the current, the strength of the magnetic field, and the effective length of the conductor in the field. There are many types of machines all having different characteristics. In any motor the stationary parts constitute the stator and the conducting coil-carrying assembly is the rotor, or armature. The synchronous motor is the opposite of the alternating-current (AC) generator, or alternator, and many machines can be used either as generator or motor. It rotates at a fixed speed proportional to the cycles per second of the alternating current fed to it. Direct-current (DC) machines have commutators similar to DC generators. Different characteristics are obtained by having the magnetic field coils either totally separately excited, or connected in parallel with the armature (shunt-wound), or in series with the armature (series-wound). The last (series motor) is used in traction applications where a large torque at low speeds for starting is required. Between 1930 and 1960 many sophisticated machines were developed, such as AC machines with commutators which enabled variable speed drives with different characteristics. The induction motor is a type of AC motor requiring no electrical connections to the moving parts. In this machine the stator has an arrangement of coils displaced geometrically one from another and fed by alternating currents to create a rotating magnetic field. The rotor, a combination of magnetic material and conducting material, e.g., a thin hollow copper tube filled with iron, is dragged round by the rotating field. There is slip between the speed of rotation of the magnetic field, which is determined by the supply frequency, and the rotor speed, which depends on the mechanical loading. Above a certain value of peak load the machine stalls. A development of the rotary induction motor is the linear induction motor in which the coils are laid in a track overlapping each other and fed with currents of different phases.

**motor car,** self-propelled vehicle used for travel on land. The fundamental structure of the motor car consists of seven basic systems: the engine, usually mounted in front and driving either the two front or the two back wheels; the fuel system, using a CARBURETTOR to produce the optimal combustible mixture of fuel and air; the electrical system, including a battery that provides a power source to the ignition; the cooling, steering and suspension, and brake systems; and the TRANSMISSION, which transmits power from the engine crankshaft to the wheels by means of a series of gears. Evolving from earlier experiments with steam-powered vehicles, models using the petrol-fuelled INTERNAL-COMBUSTION ENGINE were first developed by the German engineers Karl BENZ (1885) and Gottlieb DAIMLER. US leadership in motor-car production began with Henry FORD's founding (1903) of the Ford Motor Co., its production (1908) of the inexpensive Model T, and its development of assembly-line techniques. General Motors, Ford's principal competitor, became the world's largest motor-vehicle manufacturer in the 1920s, and US dominance of the field continued until the 1970s, when it was challenged by growing sales of Japanese and German cars. Motor-vehicle ownership worldwide is increasing. Between 1976 it rose by 23% in the USA and the UK, and by more than 30% in France. In the US, there are about 136 million private motor cars, owned by more than half the country's population. By the 1980s between 35 and 40% of the adult population of Western Europe and the UK were motor-car owners, while in Japan the corresponding figure more than doubled since the early 1970s to well over 20%. Third World countries such as Chile now have between about 60 and 80 motor cars per thousand population. Correspondingly, an increasing proportion of the individual consumer's expenditure is now taken up by the motor car. In the UK, for example, where about 63% of households own one or more cars, private travel, including motor-car purchases, accounts for more than three-quarters of the average consumer's transport expenditure. More than 80% of all road traffic in an advanced country such as the UK is accounted for by the motor car, with a further projected rise of up to half the present volume again by the year 2000. Despite the greater volume of traffic on the roads, in most advanced countries the number of fatal road accidents fell between the 1970s and mid 1980s, in France and the UK by around 25%. Air pollution too, caused by the release of toxic fumes from motor-car exhausts, has also been reduced. In the UK lead emissions fell by 12% over about 15 years, and the permissible lead content of petrol has also been steadily reduced. Unleaded petrol has long been available in the US, and is now on sale in Europe and the UK. Road construction and repair costs in Britain have risen by more than 80% over 10 years, but after some fluctuation have now stabilized.

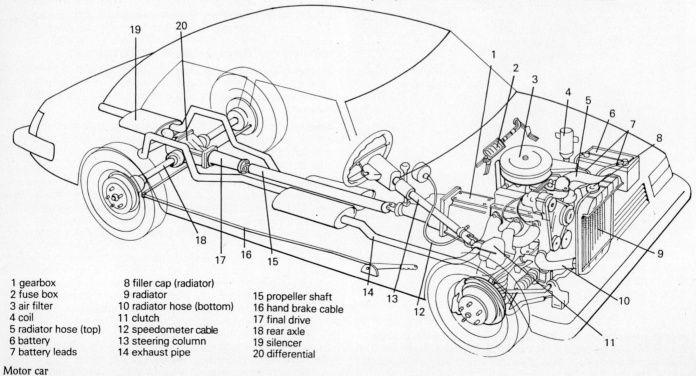

| | | |
|---|---|---|
| 1 gearbox | 8 filler cap (radiator) | |
| 2 fuse box | 9 radiator | 15 propeller shaft |
| 3 air filter | 10 radiator hose (bottom) | 16 hand brake cable |
| 4 coil | 11 clutch | 17 final drive |
| 5 radiator hose (top) | 12 speedometer cable | 18 rear axle |
| 6 battery | 13 steering column | 19 silencer |
| 7 battery leads | 14 exhaust pipe | 20 differential |

Motor car

**motorcycle**, a form of transport consisting of a BICYCLE (or tricycle) powered by an INTERNAL-COMBUSTION ENGINE. The first was a tricycle built in England in 1884, but the development of motorcycles was mostly carried out in France and Belgium, the first commercial model being a de Dion of 1895. Much use was made of motorcycles in World War I, and they were extremely popular for a decade after that, but they began to be gradually displaced by motor cars in the 1930s as cheap models came within the reach of more people. After World War II British motorcycle manufacturers were still making fine machines, to be again displaced by small cars, and also by smaller-engined Japanese motorcycles. Mopeds (with engines of under 50 c.c. capacity) became extremely popular in continental Europe in the 1950s, and have remained so. Motor scooters (with slightly larger engines, about 125 c.c., and with an enclosed style of bodywork) became immensely popular in Britain in the 1960s, over 400,000 being in use, nearly all owned by young people. Since the 1960s the motorcycle has been revived as a sports item (see MOTORCYCLE RACING) and as a cult item of collectable engineering. On a modern motorcycle (or 'motorbike') a one to four cylinder engine fires on a two or four stroke cycle. Transmission of power is by means of a gearbox, usually having between two and six speeds, and chain or shaft drive to the rear wheel. Wheels are of steel or aluminium, with heavy-treaded tyres providing extra traction for turning. Suspension on the front forks and a sprung rear wheel allow a more comfortable and controlled ride. Many motorcycles 'kick-start', the traditional method, but electric starters are more common on the models with larger engines. Clutch, throttle, and front brake are operated from the handlebars, and gear change is by pedal. Today's leading motorcycle manufacturer is Japan, commanding around 80% of the world market. In countries such as the UK the popularity of the motorcycle has fluctuated since the 1970s, the number of licensed motorcycles in Britain having fallen by about 15%.

1895 de Dion **motorcycle**

**motorcycle racing**, competitive sport employing purpose-built vehicles. Three kinds dominate the international scene: scrambling, road racing, and speedway. Scrambling takes place over rough terrain on 125-, 250-, or 500-cc bikes. Road racing takes place over tarred roads on low-slung 350–750-cc bikes whose speeds may reach 290 km (180 mph). The best-known road race is the Isle of Man Tourist Trophy. Speedway takes place on an oval track of shale or cinders, usually on 500-cc bikes specially designed to be ridden with a sideways tilt. Races in which a sidecar is attached to the motorcycle are known as 'combination' or 'passenger' races.

**motor racing**, sport in which high-speed, specially constructed motor cars are raced on outdoor or indoor courses. The five basic types of competition are the grand prix, a series of races in several countries that leads to the designation of a world-champion driver; stock car, using standard cars with special equipment; midget car; sports car; and drag racing, involving acceleration tests over 402.5m (¼-mi) tracks. The sport originated in France in 1894. The best-known European race is the LE MANS Grand Prix.

**motorway**, a road specially built for the use of fast motor traffic, linking major centres of population. The need for better, faster roads to cope with the increasing volume of motor traffic was generally recognized between the wars but acted upon first by Germany and Italy. By 1942 Germany had built 2107 km (1310 mi) of motorway (*Autobahn*). The first American motorway (superhighway) was unveiled in 1940, a 254-km (159-mi) stretch between Harrisbury and Pittsburgh. Britain followed in 1959, with the opening of the M1 motorway between London and Birmingham, and Japan in 1965. Today Japan's network has expanded to 3640 km (2275 mi), with 2250 km (1400 mi) under construction, while now Britain has over 27,000 km (17,000 mi) of motorway, completing the 312-km (195-mi) M25 London orbital in 1986. All the advanced countries of Europe have motorways, and the need for better roads worldwide is increasing with the increase in motor-vehicle traffic and numbers of privately-owned MOTOR CARS. *Motorway design and construction.* Motorway building represents a considerable feat of modern engineering and design. Planners must continuously monitor volumes of traffic to assess motorway needs, taking account of types and weights of vehicles using a route, vehicle ownership patterns, future projections of demand, as well as landscape and environment. An important part in modern motorway planning is played by aerial photography. Choice of road-building materials must sometimes provide for extremes of climate. Of the motorways built in 1986, one, from the Saudi capital Riyadh, had to be able to resist melting at very high temperatures while another, the 160-km (100-mi) stretch of road linking Norway and Sweden inside the Arctic Circle, had to be built to withstand temperatures as low as -45°C (-49°F).

**Mott, Lucretia Coffin**, 1793–1880, American feminist and reformer. A well-known Quaker lecturer for temperance, peace, labour rights, and abolition, she aided fugitive slaves and helped form the Philadelphia Female Anti-Slavery Society. When the World Anti-Slavery Convention in London (1840) refused to recognize women delegates, she joined Elizabeth Cady STANTON in organizing (1848) the first women's rights convention, in Seneca Falls, New York.

**Mott, Sir Nevill Francis**, 1905–, English physicist. Head of the Cavendish Laboratory, Cambridge (1953–72), he shared the 1977 Nobel Prize for physics for research into noncrystalline semiconductors.

**mouflon**, European wild SHEEP originally found in Sardinia and Corsica and introduced into mountainous areas north of the Mediterranean. Some scientists believe that the same species is found right across Asia, to include the urial of southern Asia. These species do interbreed in zoos. The mouflon stands 68 cm (27 in) high at the shoulder, the males particularly having long spirally curved horns. It is the only wild sheep with a woolly undercoat in its winter fur, and, with the urial, is a likely ancestor of the domestic sheep.

**mould**, multicellular organism of the division FUNGI, typified by plant bodies composed of a network of cottony filaments. The colours of moulds are due to spores borne on the filaments. Most moulds are SAPROPHYTES. Some species (e.g., *Penicillium*) are used in making cheese and ANTIBIOTICS. See also SLIME MOULD.

**moulting**, periodic shedding and renewal of the outer skin, exoskeleton, fur, or feathers of any animal. Most birds moult annually; development in young birds is marked by a succession of moults during the first year. Arthropods (e.g., insects and crustaceans) moult their exoskeletons in order to grow; the process involves partial digestion of the old cuticle, emergence of the animal from the old covering, and hardening of the new cuticle. Amphibians and snakes moult a few times a year. Mammals change from heavy winter to light summer coats.

**mound builders**, peoples who built mounds in E central North America, in particular the Mississippi and Ohio river valleys, from 1000 BC until historic times. Undoubtedly ancestors of the Indians found in that region by Europeans, they were politically diverse and developed distinct cultures. Artifacts indicate fine stone carving, pottery-making, and weaving, as well as widespread trade in copper, mica, and obsidian. The mounds varied in size, up to a massive 40 hectares (100 acres) in area, and shape, with many representing animal effigies, and they were used for burial, defence, and religious purposes.

**mountain**, high land mass projecting above its surroundings, usually of limited width at its summit. Some are isolated, but they usually occur in ranges. A group of ranges closely related in form, origin, and alignment is a mountain system; an elongated group of systems is a chain; and a complex of ranges, systems, and chains continental in extent is a cordillera, zone, or belt. Some mountains are remains of PLATEAUS dissected by erosion (see BUTTE; MESA). Others are cones of VOLCANOES or intrusions of igneous rock that form domes. Fault-block mountains occur where huge blocks of the earth's surface are raised relative to neighbouring blocks. All the great mountain chains are either FOLD mountains or complex structures in which folding, faulting, and igneous activity have taken part. The ultimate cause of mountain building has been a source of controversy. The concept of PLATE TECTONICS, however, is the first reasonable unifying theory, hypothesizing that the earth's crust is broken into several plates that sideswipe each other or collide. Where they collide (see CONTINENTAL DRIFT), compressional stresses are generated along the margin of the plate containing a continent, causing deformation and uplift of the continental shelf and continental rise, where accumulated sediments become complex folded and faulted mountain chains. Mountains have important effects on the climate, population, economics, and civilization of the regions where they occur. Major mountain ranges include the ALPS, the ANDES, the CAUCASUS, the HIMALAYAS, the PYRENEES, and the ROCKY MOUNTAINS. The highest elevation on earth above sea level is the peak of Mt EVEREST.

**Mountain, the,** in the FRENCH REVOLUTION, nickname for the deputies of the extreme left who occupied the raised seats in the National Convention. The Montagnards [men of the Mountain] included the JACOBINS and the CORDELIERS; they ruled France in the REIGN OF TERROR (1793–94). See also PLAIN, THE.

**mountain climbing,** the practice of climbing to elevated points for sport, pleasure, or research. It is also called mountaineering. The three principal types are (1) trail climbing, or hiking through trails to the top of small mountains; (2) rock climbing, the ascent of steeper mountains requiring the use of rope and steel spikes (pitons) that are driven into the rock; and (3) ice climbing, on very high mountains with peaks above the timber line. The 'golden age' of mountain climbing began in the 1850s and ended with the conquest (1865) of the last of the great Alpine peaks, the Matterhorn. Mt Everest, the world's tallest mountain, was first climbed (1953) by Edmund HILLARY and TENZING NORGAY.

**mountain laurel,** evergreen shrub (*Kalmia latifolia*) of the HEATH family, native to E North America. It is planted as a hardy ornamental shrub in both Northern and Southern Hemispheres. Poisonous to livestock, mountain laurel has leathery leaves and large clusters of spring-blooming pink or white flowers borne at the ends of the branches. True LAUREL is in a separate family.

**mountain lion:** see PUMA.

**mountain men,** trappers and traders in the 1820s and 30s who opened the Rocky Mountain region. They lived in the wilderness, gathering furs, and guided the first wagon trains to OREGON. The arrival of settlers and the waning popularity of the beaver hat ended their activities by the early 1840s.

**Mountbatten:** see BATTENBERG, family.

**Mountbatten, Louis Francis Albert Victor Nicholas, Earl Mountbatten of Burma,** 1900–1979, British admiral; great-grandson of Queen VICTORIA. In WORLD WAR II he directed commando raids in Europe and commanded Allied operations in Burma from 1943. As viceroy of India (1947) Mountbatten concluded the negotiations for the independence of India and Pakistan. He was (1959–65) chief of the British defense staff. In 1979 he was killed when a bomb planted by Irish Republican Army members exploded aboard his fishing boat off the Irish coast.

**Mount Communism,** 7495 m (24,590 ft), highest point in the USSR, in the Pamir Mts in Tadzhik SSR. Originally called Garmo Peak, it was renamed Stalin Peak (1933) and Mount Communism (1962).

**Mount Gambier,** city (1986 pop. 20,813), South Australia. Situated 460 km (290 mi) SE of Adelaide, it is the regional centre for the Lower South-east. Agricultural activities include beef, sheep, vines, and vegetables with associated food-processing industries. Surrounding softwood pine plantations support a major timber industry, which was seriously threatened by a disastrous bushfire on Ash Wednesday in Feb. 1983. Thousands of hectares of forest were destroyed and 70 people died. The city is built around the base of an extinct volcano, within whose

crater lies the Blue Lake, which changes its water from a grey to a strong blue colour in early summer, for no known cause. Mount Gambier is the birthplace of the late Sir Robert HELPMANN, international ballet performer and choreographer.

**Mounties:** see ROYAL CANADIAN MOUNTED POLICE.

**Mount of Olives:** see OLIVES, MOUNT OF.

**Mount Rushmore National Memorial,** near Keystone, South Dakota, US, with the monumental heads of four US presidents—Washington, Jefferson, Lincoln, and Theodore Roosevelt—carved on the face of a mountain. Visible for 97 km (over 60 mi), the heads were sculpted (1927–41) by Gutzon Borglum with the help of his son.

Mount Rusmore National Memorial

**Mount Vernon,** NE Virginia, US, overlooking the Potomac R. near Alexandria, S of Washington, DC; home of George WASHINGTON from 1747 until his death in 1799. The land was patented in 1674, and the house was built (1743) by his half-brother Lawrence Washington. George Washington inherited it in 1754. A wooden structure of Georgian design, the mansion has wide lawns, fine gardens, and subsidiary structures, all restored with attention to Washington's detailed notes.

**mouse,** any of numerous species of small RODENTS. The house mouse (*Mus musculus*), found worldwide, usually measures about 15 cm (6 in) in length including the tail and weighs under 28 g (1 oz). It has grey to brown fur, large, rounded ears, and a naked, scaly tail. It causes great destruction and contamination of food supplies, and may carry human diseases, e.g., typhoid. House mice are used in scientific experiments and sometimes kept as pets. The Old World field mouse (genus *Apodemus*) is closely related to the house mouse. In North America the name *field mouse* is applied to the VOLE.

**Moussorgsky** or **Mussorgsky, Modest Petrovich,** 1839–81, Russian composer. A member of the FIVE, he was one of the first to promote a national Russian style. His finest work is the opera *Boris Godunov* (produced 1874). Other major pieces include the piano SUITE *Pictures at an Exhibition* (1874), later orchestrated by RAVEL; and *A Night on the Bare Mountain* (1860–66), for orchestra. Moussorgsky made much use of folk songs. His rejection of European traditions influenced other Russian composers and also Debussy.

**Mousterian industry,** a stone-tool technology of the Middle PALAEOLITHIC, named after the site of Le Moustier in the Dordogne, France and widespread in Europe, the Middle East, and North Africa. The characteristic tool was a flake struck from a core. Users of this technology (most often identified as NEANDERTHAL MAN) had a larger range of tool types than the people of the earlier ACHEULIAN industries; and they appear to have specialized in the hunting of herd animals. The sites date from c.80,000 BP to c.35,000 BP.

**mowing machine,** machine for cutting grass, especially for lawns. Gardens are as old as civilization with famous ones like the 'Hanging Gardens of Babylon' being one of the Ancient Wonders of the World. Gardens for ordinary citizens owning houses became popular in Britain from the 15th cent. James I was especially fond of laid-out gardens in his palaces but none of these had lawns. It was not until the end of the 18th cent. when landscape architecture had become important for the rich that lawns became an important feature. They were labour-intensive in their maintenance, requiring special dwarf grasses to be cut frequently by hand shears and rolled, to be weed free, and also to be pest free. Edwin Beard Budding invented and developed a horse drawn rotary barrel close-cutting grass cutter in 1830, and had it manufactured by Robert Ransome who ran a large business making agricultural implements. This was a boon to those estates with extensive lawns. The first motorized lawnmower was made by Robert Ransome's son, James Edward. This gave 1.067-m (42-in) cut, or swathe, and was powered by a six horsepower, four-stroke petrol engine. Competition came from the Leyland Steam Motor Company (now part of British Leyland) who developed a similar cutter powered by a small steam engine. The petrol engine had many advantages, and when King Edward VII ordered two Ransome machines in 1905 for Buckingham Palace, the steam engine machine died. The advent of the small portable petrol cutter made the development of lawns within the reach of a much wider section of the population. Lawns became popular and a 'must' for all English gardens.

Mousterian industry: double continous scraper, transverse scraper, scraper, and piercer (left to right)

**Mozambique,** officially People's Republic of Mozambique, republic (1985 pop. 13,527,000), 783,030 km² (302,328 sq mi), SE Africa, bordered by the Indian Ocean (E), South Africa and Swaziland (S), Zimbabwe, Zambia, and Malawi (W), and Tanzania (N). Major cities include MAPUTO (the capital; formerly Lourenço Marques) and SOFALA (formerly Beira). The Mozambique Channel, an arm of the Indian Ocean, separates the country from Madagascar. The c.2575-km (1600-mi) coastline is indented by numerous rivers, notably the ZAMBEZI, which is navigable for c.465 km (290 mi) within the country. The northern and central interior is mountainous, rising to a high point at Monte Binga 2436 m/7992 ft). About one-third of Lake NYASA falls within Mozambique's borders. Much of the country is covered with savanna, and there are extensive hardwood forests. Mozambique's economy is based almost entirely on agriculture, which engages about 90% of the workforce, mostly in subsistence farming. The main cash crops are cotton, cashew nuts, sugarcane, tea, and sisal. Coal, diamonds, and bauxite are mined on a small scale, but extensive mineral reserves remain unexploited. Industry is limited to the processing of raw materials (notably food and cotton) and the manufacture of fertilizers and cement. The GNP is US$2164 million, and the GNP per capita is US$160 (1985). More than 95% of the people are Bantu-speaking black Africans, most of whom follow traditional beliefs. There are large Christian and Muslim minorities. Tribal dialects are spoken, but Portuguese is the official language.

*History.* From the first visit of the Portuguese explorer Vasco da GAMA in 1498 until independence in 1975, the history of the region has been one of suppression and exploitation of black African peoples by a European colonial power. The first traders were intent on gold and ivory shipped from the coast, but attempts to penetrate the interior met strong resistance. By the late 16th cent. black Africans were forced to work on large feudal estates operated by private Portuguese adventurers with little government control, and an extensive slave trade developed in the mid-18th cent. In the 1890s Portugal launched a military campaign to crush African resistance, and after 1926 it assumed direct control of the economic exploitation of blacks. The Mozambique Liberation Front (Frelimo) opened guerrilla warfare against white rule in 1964 and, after heavy fighting against a Portuguese army of about 60,000, controlled much of the country by the early 1970s. Following the 1974 military coup in Portugal a ceasefire was arranged, and Mozambique gained independence in 1975. Samora MACHEL, leader of Frelimo, became president of a Marxist regime that nationalized the land. Most of the country's 220,000 whites fled, and its relations with Portugal and the US became strained. In the late 1970s, Mozambique served as a base for guerrillas fighting the white government of Rhodesia (now ZIMBABWE) and suffered severe damage from incursions by Rhodesian army troops. Faced in the early 1980s with a serious insurgent threat from South African-backed guerrillas, Mozambique in 1984 concluded the Nkomati nonaggression accord with South Africa under which each side pledged not to support antigovernment movements against the other. In 1986 Pres. Machel was killed in a plane crash just inside South African territory and was succeeded as Frelimo leader and head of state by Joaquim Chissano.

Mozambique

**Mozart, Wolfgang Amadeus,** 1756–91, Austrian composer. His works, written in every genre, combine beauty of sound with classical grace and technical perfection. He learned to play harpsichord, violin, and organ from his father, **Leopold Mozart,** 1719–87, a composer and violinist. A remarkable prodigy, the young Mozart was composing by the age of five, presenting concerts throughout Europe as a child, and by the age of 13 had written concertos, Sonatas, Symphonies, and OPERETTAS. In Italy (1768–71) he absorbed Italian style, and in 1771 he was appointed concertmaster to the archbishop of Salzburg, a position in which he was restless. *Idomeneo* (1781), one of the best examples of 18th-cent. OPERA *seria*, was the first opera of his maturity. He moved to Vienna (1781), married, and met Joseph HAYDN, to whom he dedicated six string quartets

(1782–85), testimony to the two composers' influence on each other. *The Abduction from the Seraglio* (1782), a *singspiel* combining songs and German dialogue, brought some success. He turned to the Italian *opera buffa*, creating the comic masterpiece *The Marriage of Figaro* (1786). *Don Giovanni*, considered 'difficult' in its day but now recognized as one of the most brilliant operas ever written, followed in 1787. In the same year Mozart succeeded GLUCK as court composer to Joseph II; *Eine kleine Nachtmusik* (1787) is an example of the elegant occasional music he wrote in this role. In 1788 he wrote his last three symphonies, Nos. 39–41, which display his complete mastery of classical symphonic form and intense personal emotion. In Vienna he produced his last *opera buffa, Cosi fan tutte* (1790). In *The Magic Flute* (1791) he returned to the *singspiel*, bringing the form to a lyrical height. He then worked feverishly on a requiem commissioned by a nobleman; it proved to be Mozart's own, and the work was completed by his pupil Franz Süssmayr. The composer died at 35 and was buried in a pauper's grave. A catalogue of Mozart's works was made in 1862 by Ludwig von Köchel; they are usually identified accordingly, e.g., the Piano Concerto in B Flat, K. 595.

**Mphahlele, Es'kia (Ezekiel)**, 1919–, black South African writer. He is best known for his autobiography, *Down Second Avenue* (1959), presented in the style of a novel; *The African Image* (1962; revised 1974), in which he links his personal experience of exile and literary criticism; and a collection of essays, *The Unbroken Song* (1981).

**Mrożek Slawomir** (,mrohzhek), 1930–, Polish prose writer and dramatist. He is best known for his absurdist parables satirizing bureaucracy and social conformism. His main concerns are power, the degeneracy of consumer society, and the alienation of the individual. Among his best-known plays are *The Elephant* (1957), *Tango* (1965), and *Emigrés* (1975). He lives in Paris.

**Msiri**, c.1830–91, founder of the Garenganze (Yeke) empire in 19th-cent. Katanga, S ZAIRE. He began his career as a trader in copper and ivory but turned to guns and politics in the mid 1860s to establish control over the sources of production. By the 1880s his empire was the most powerful state in S Zaïre. However, incipient revolt among his subject peoples and pressures exerted by European imperialism fragmented the empire following his death at the hands of an agent of the Congo Free State in 1891.

**Mswati**, c.1820–65, king of SWAZILAND (1845–65). He preserved and consolidated the state founded by his father, Sobhuza I (c.1780–1839). Zulu invasions were beaten off with the help of the Boers, and Swazi influence extended as far as Lourenço Marques (now MAPUTO) in Mozambique. The Swazi people and Swaziland are named after him.

**Mtshali, Oswald Mbuyiseni** 1940–, black South African poet. His work is especially concerned with urban township life, e.g., *Song of a Cowhide Drum* (1971). *Fireflames* (1980) is dedicated to the children of SOWETO, written in vibrant, often highly innovative style, and aimed primarily at a black readership.

**Muallaqat** (mooh'alah,kaht), Arabic anthology consisting of seven (in some versions, nine or ten) odes by 6th- or early 7th-cent. poets. Esteemed as the finest Arabic odes, they present an unsurpassed picture of pre-Islamic Bedouin life.

**Mubarak, Muhammad Hosni**, 1929–, president of EGYPT (1981–). Air force commander (1972–75) and vice president (1975–81), he was chosen to succeed Pres. SADAT after the latter was assassinated. Mubarak pledged to continue Sadat's policies, particularly the CAMP DAVID ACCORDS with Israel. But he has criticized Israeli policies and moved with success to mend Egypt's strained relations with other Arab states.

**Mucha, Alphonse** (,mookhah), 1860–1939, Czech artist. His ART NOUVEAU style, characterized by twisting, swirling, flower and hair motifs, is best seen in his POSTERS for Sarah BERNHARDT. His academic paintings glorify the Slavic peoples.

**muckrakers**, name applied to American journalists, novelists, and critics in the first decade of the 20th cent. who tried to expose the abuses of business and corruption in politics. The word derives from the term *muckrake* (derived from John BUNYAN's *Pilgrim's Progress*), used by Pres. Theodore ROOSEVELT in a 1906 speech in which he agreed with some of the muckrakers' aims but said that their methods were sensational and irresponsible. In effect muckraking is only a perjorative term for investigative journalism—which is always distrusted by those in power.

**mudskipper**, FISH in the family Gobiidae. Mudskippers live on mudflats and in mangrove swamps from W Africa to SE Asia and round the SW Pacific. They are unusual among fishes because they spend considerable time out of water, feeding on the diatoms and algae on the surface of the mud exposed at low tide. Mudskippers must keep moist, but they are able to breathe air through their mouths and throats. The Malayan mudskipper (*Periophthalmus chrysopilos*) has its fins adapted to form a sucker, so that it can climb mangroves.

Mudskippers in mangrove swamp

**Mufaddaliyat** or **Mofaddaliyat** (mooh'fadəlee,aht, moh-), great anthology of Arabic poetry, compiled by the philologist Al- Mufaddal ad-Dabbi. The best collection of poems by authors from the Golden Age of Arabic poetry (500–650), it is also a valuable source of information on pre-Islamic Arab life.

**mufti**, in both classical and modern SUNNISM, the officer occupying the pinnacle of such legislative authority as was derived from islamic law (see FIQH). In this capacity the mufti issues an authoritative statement (*fatwa*) in response to questions of legality brought forward by lay individuals or political authorities. The OTTOMAN mufti was a particularly powerful personality.

**Mugabe, Robert Gabriel** (moo,gahbee), 1924–, prime minister of ZIMBABWE (1980–87) and executive president (1988–). He was a founder of the Zimbabwe African National Union (ZANU) in 1963 and, after being imprisoned (1964–74) by the white regime, became co-leader, with Joshua Nkomo, of the Patriotic Front in 1976. A Marxist, Mugabe led ZANU guerrilla forces until independence, and following elections in 1980 became prime minister. He ousted Nkomo from the cabinet in 1982 but reappointed him early in 1988 following the merger of ZANU with Nkomo's party. Shortly before, Mugabe had been elected Zimbabwe's first executive president.

**Mughal** or **Mogul**, empire of India (1526–1857). It was founded by BABUR, a descendant of TAMERLANE, and flourished until the 18th cent., when the emperor virtually lost all power and the SIKHS and MAHRATTAS among others triumphed over it. The British kept a puppet Mughal emperor on the throne until 1857. The flowering of Indo-Muslim art and architecture was the most lasting achievement of the Mughals. Many features of their administration were adopted by the British in India.

**Mughal art and architecture.** A characteristic Indo-Islamic art style, evolved from PERSIAN ART AND ARCHITECTURE, developed in India under the Mughal emperors. The school of Mughal painting began in 1549 when Emperor Humayun invited two Persian painters to direct the illustration of the *Amir Hamza,* a fantastic narrative of which some 1400 large paintings were executed on cloth. The first Mughal monument was the mausoleum to Humayun erected by AKBAR (r.1556–1605), who went on to build an entire city, FATEHPUR SIKRI, making use of the low arches and bulbous DOMES that characterize the Mughal style. Modelling and PERSPECTIVE were also adapted from Western painting. Emperor Jahangir (r.1605–27) encouraged portraiture and scientific studies of birds, flowers, and animals, which were collected in albums. SHAH JAHAN (r.1628–58) perfected Mughal architecture and erected, at Agra, the TAJ MAHAL with its symmetrical Persian plan, in memory of his favourite wife. This period saw the amalgamation of influences into a true Mughal style. Portraiture was most highly developed and ink drawings were of high quality at the court of Shah Jahan. Under the puritanical Emperor AURANGZEB (r.1658–1710) the decline of the arts began, although the ornate Pearl Mosque (1662) at Delhi is impressive. During his reign the Mughal academy was dispersed, and the artists joined RAJPUT courts.

**mugwumps,** in US history, slang term for the Republicans who, in 1884, deserted their party nominee, James G. BLAINE, to vote for the Democratic candidate, Grover CLEVELAND.

**Muhammad,** c.570–632, the founder prophet of ISLAM. Born in MECCA into the Hashim clan of the Quraish tribe, he was orphaned early. He began to receive his revelations, later recorded in the KORAN, in about 610 and tried to win followers in MECCA. The hostility engendered caused him to make his famous HIJRA to Medina (622) where he was able to establish an embryo Islamic community in a more favourable environment. In a virtually bloodless coup, after three significant clashes between Mecca and Medina (624, 625, and 627), Muhammad conquered and re-entered his native city (630). In spite of Muhammad's success both as a warrior and a prophet, Arabia was by no means wholly Islamic or subservient to Mecca at the time of his death. Muhammad's success must be attributed as much to the qualities of the man as the circumstances of his times. His significance has naturally been interpreted in a host of different ways: for Muslims he is simply The Prophet; and for those of a mystical orientation he is also the Perfect Man. For the historian he is a focus of particular interest since he succeeded where many contemporary prophets in the Arabian peninsula failed.

**Muhammad, Elijah,** 1897–1975, American black nationalist leader; b. Elijah Poole. On the disappearance of Wali Farad in 1934, he assumed leadership of the Temple of Islam in Detroit, the sect that became the BLACK MUSLIMS. Preaching black separatism, Muhammad called himself 'the messenger of Allah' and exercised autocratic control over his followers through a moralistic doctrine of social reform. On his death his son **Wallace D. Muhammad,** 1933–, became the movement's leader. He has moved the sect closer to orthodox Islam and lifted restrictions on political activity and military service.

**Muhammad Ali,** 1769?–1849, pasha of Egypt (after 1805). He was a common soldier who rose through the ranks. As pasha he was virtually independent of his nominal overlord, the Ottoman sultan. In 1811 he exterminated the MAMELUKES, who had ruled Egypt for c.700 years. He won great victories for the Turks in Arabia and the Sudan. He fought the rebels in Greece, but his fleet was destroyed (1827) at Navarino by the British, French, and Russians. In the 1830s he turned against the sultan and made inroads in Syria and Asia Minor, but he was forced to give up his gains by the European powers.

**Muhammad Reza Shah Pahlevi,** 1919–80, shah of IRAN (1941–79). He ascended the throne after the British and Russians deposed his father, REZA SHAH PAHLEVI, suspecting him of German sympathies. He fled the country briefly in 1953 during the rule of Muhammad MUSSADEGH but was reinstated, due in part to the support of the US. Iran's great petroleum wealth allowed the shah to institute economic and social reforms. He was bitterly opposed, however, by orthodox Muslims, who resented his modernizing policies, and by liberals and leftists, who accused him of maintaining a brutal police state. Revolution broke out in the autumn of 1978, and on 5 Jan. 1979, the shah fled the country. He died in exile in Egypt.

**Muhammad V,** 1910–61, king of MOROCCO (1957–61). He became sultan in 1927. An ardent nationalist, he was deposed and exiled (1953–55) by the French, but they were forced to recall him. He obtained (1956) full sovereignty from France and Spain, and took (1957) the title of king of Morocco.

**Muir, Edwin,** 1887–1959, Scottish poet and critic. His childhood in Orkney was reflected in volumes of poems such as *The Labyrinth* (1949) and in an autobiography, *The Story and the Fable* (1940). He also wrote novels and critical studies, and translated the works of KAFKA (1930–49).

**Mujaheddin,** lit. 'holy warriors', guerrilla groups which opposed the USSR-backed regime and Soviet military presence in AFGHANISTAN. They were externally based in NW Pakistan and received US-financed arms supplies.

**Mukden:** see SHENYANG.

**Muktar, Omar Sayyid,** c.1880–1932, Libyan anticolonial resistance leader. During the 1920s he led SANUSSI forces in a guerrilla campaign aginst the imposition of Italian rule in his country. His victories led the Italians to employ increasingly brutal tactics to defeat him. By 1931 as many as 12,000 Libyans had been executed while many more were placed in concentration camps. In 1931 Mautar was himself captured and executed bringing the campaign of resistance to a close.

**Mulambwa,** 1770?–1835, ruler (r.c.1790–1835) of the Lozi kingdom in precolonial W ZAMBIA. He wrested control of the Lozi from his brother in 1790 and proceeded to centralize and reform the administration of the state. At his death the Lozi kingdom was at its greatest extent – but his sons divided the country in civil war and his legacy was destroyed.

**Mulay Ismail, Adu Al Nasir,** c.1655–1727, sultan of Morocco from 1672. During his long reign he reestablished central authority over his country and preserved its sovereignty from the interventions of European powers. He also promoted normal diplomatic and trade relations with Europe. Internally he used African and captive Christian slave labour for public works on a massive scale. His achievements helped to entrench the Alawi dynasty which continues to rule Morocco.

**mulberry,** common name for the Moraceae, a family of deciduous or evergreen trees and shrubs, often climbing, mostly of pantropical distribution and typified by milky sap. Several genera bear edible fruit, e.g., *Morus* (mulberries), *Ficus* (FIGS), and *Artocarpus,* which includes the breadfruit. Both the white (*M. alba*) and the red (*M. rubra*) mulberries are cultivated. Mulberry fruits are tender and juicy and resemble blackberries; the fruit of *M. rubra* is used to make wine. SILKWORMS feed on mulberry leaves. The Osage orange (*Maclura pomifera*) is a hardy tree native to the south central US and is a source of a durable wood and a dye. The breadfruit (*A. ultilis*) is a cultivated, staple food plant in the Pacific tropics and West Indies; its wood, fibre, and latex are also utilized.

**Muldoon, Sir Robert David,** 1921–, NEW ZEALAND political leader and prime minister (1975–84). In 1960 he entered Parliament and served (1967–72) as finance minister. After his National Party defeated the Labour government in the 1975 elections, Muldoon became prime minister and finance minister. He and his party were defeated in the 1984 general elections, following which he was replaced as party leader.

**mule,** sterile, hybrid offspring of a male donkey (see ASS) and a female HORSE, bred as a work animal. Mules are slower but more surefooted than horses and have great powers of endurance. They have been used as pack and draught animals since prehistoric times.

**mule,** in manufacturing: see SPINNING.

**Mülheim,** city (1984 pop. 174,800), North Rhine–Westphalia, W West Germany. A centre of RUHR industry, its manufactures include steel, electrical, and leather products. It is linked by deep-water canal to the RHINE.

**Mulhouse,** city (1982 pop. 113,794, agglomeration 220,613), E France, on the Ill R. It has a strategic site, commanding routeways along the RHINE rift valley and through the Belfort gap between the VOSGES and the JURA. Mulhouse was a free imperial city from the 13th cent. and an allied member of the Swiss Confederation from 1515. The city chose to become a part of France in 1798. Population grew rapidly in the 19th cent. with the rise of the cotton textile industry and, later, with the development of the nearby potash deposits. More recently it has become a centre of motor-vehicle manufacture. It serves as regional centre of upper Alsace and has close economic links with BASEL in Switzerland.

**Müller, Friedrich Maximilian:** see MÜLLER, MAX.

**Muller, Hermann Joseph,** 1890–1967, American geneticist and educator. He was awarded the 1946 Nobel Prize for physiology or medicine for discovering a technique of artificially inducing MUTATIONS by means of X-rays. He also proposed and developed the theory that genes, because of their unique ability to self-replicate themselves and any alterations arising in them, are the basis of life; his theory was later supported by the discovery of the structure of DNA.

**Müller, Max, (Friedrich Maximilian Müller),** 1823–1900, German philologist and Orientalist. An authority on Sanskrit and Eastern religions, he taught at Oxford Univ. He did more than any other scholar to popularize philology and mythology, e.g., his lectures *Science of Language* (1861, 1863).

**Mullingar,** county town (1981 pop. 7854) of Co. Westmeath, Republic of Ireland, on R. Brosna and the Royal Canal, 72 km (45 mi) W of Dublin. It is a small market town with a modern Roman Catholic cathedral, and is well known for the trout fishing in the near-by loughs.

**Mulroney, Brian,** 1939–, prime minister of CANADA (1984–). A lawyer by profession, he became leader of the Progressive Conservative Party in 1983 and the following year won a landslide general-election victory, thus ending over two decades of Liberal dominance.

**Multan,** city (1981 est. pop. 730,000), E central Pakistan, in the Punjab. It is the commercial centre of a farming region and has such industries as metal-working, oil-milling, and carpet-weaving. One of the South Asian subcontinent's oldest cities, it fell to such conquerors as Alexander the Great (326 BC), the Arabs (8th cent.), Tamerlane (1398), and the Sikhs (1818). The British ruled it from 1848 to 1947.

**multicultural education,** in Britain, an education designed to take account of and promote respect for the diversity of racial and ethnic origins of the population. Since the major period of immigration from the West Indies, the Indian subcontinent, and Africa in the late 1950s and 1960s there have been various policies to develop education for a multicultural or multiracial society, including an emphasis on 'antiracism'. The programmes developed have concerned the teaching of English and the mother tongue, an understanding of the historical and other aspects of racial and cultural differences, compensatory programmes for children at a disadvantage in specific curriculum areas, and educational support services of various kinds. A major report on the education of children from ethnic minority groups was the Swann report on *Education for All* (1985). See also ETHNIC STUDIES.

**multinational corporation,** business enterprise with manufacturing, sales, or service subsidiaries in a number of foreign countries. Such corporations originated early in the 20th cent. and proliferated after World War II. Typically, a multinational company develops new products in its native country and manufactures them abroad, thus gaining trade advantages and economies of labour and materials. Although most of the largest multinational firms are US-owned, many are European and Japanese.

**multiple personality,** also known as 'split personality', a relatively rare mental disorder. It is characterized by the loss of subjective integrity, or sense of self; and the differentiation of the self into two or more independent personalities or identities, which may appear to have no 'knowledge' of each other. The term should not be confused with SCHIZOPHRENIA.

**multiple sclerosis,** chronic degenerative disease of the central NERVOUS SYSTEM in which patches of the myelin sheath around nerve fibres are lost. The cause is thought to arise from a combination of immunogenetic and infective influences. Symptoms include multiple disturbances in vision, speech, balance, and coordination, as well as numbness and tremors. The onset of the disease generally occurs between ages 20 and 40. Although it usually results in severe disability, its course varies widely, with symptoms appearing at irregular intervals for years. There is no specific treatment.

**multiplex analogue components:** see MAC.

**Mumford, Lewis,** 1895–, American social philosopher and educator. A critic of architecture and city planning, Mumford argues that people must turn from dehumanizing technology back to human feelings and moral values. His books include *The Culture of Cities* (1938), *The Condition of Man* (1944), and *The City in History* (1961).

**Mumia,** c. 1850–1949, last independent ruler of the Wanga kingdom, W KENYA (r. 1882–1926). He collaborated with the British in their E African conquests, lending aid in the form of troops and allowing his capital to be used as the imperialists' headquarters. He was rewarded with the title of paramount chief of the region but his authority was never recognized by non-Luyia peoples and in 1926 he was deposed by the British.

**mummy,** human or animal body preserved by embalming or by natural conditions. The word refers primarily to ancient burials found in Egypt. Mummies, embalmed and tightly wrapped, were preserved for over 5000 years in the dry air of Upper Egypt, making it possible to determine fairly accurately how the great pharaohs appeared in life. Mummification seems to have been performed to prepare the body for reunification with the soul in an afterlife; royal figures, their retinue, and even food were preserved.

Similar practices occurred in other parts of the world, e.g., among the Incas. Natural mummification, caused by certain soil and climatic conditions, is seen in bodies found in Danish peat bogs dating from 300 BC to AD 300 and in the LINDOW MAN, a bog burial from Cheshire, England.

**mumps** or **epidemic parotitis,** acute contagious viral disease whose symptoms include pain and swelling of the salivary glands, pain on swallowing, and fever. Mumps usually affects children between ages 5 and 15 and rarely lasts more than three days. In adults it is often more severe, especially in males, who may experience such complications as pain and swelling of the testes and, infrequently, sterility. A childhood attack of mumps confers lifelong immunity.

**Munch, Edvard** (moongk), 1863–1944, Norwegian painter and graphic artist. His exciting, violent, and emotionally charged style expressed his sense of isolation in themes of fear, death, and anxiety. Among his strongest and best-known works are *The Scream* (1893; National Gall., Oslo), *The Kiss* (1895; drypoint and aquatint), and *Vampire* (1893; Mus. of Art, Göteborg). Munch's work was of primary importance in the birth of German EXPRESSIONISM. He also made powerful and shocking WOODCUTS.

Edvard **Munch,** *The Scream*, 1893. Pastel and crayon on cardboard, 91 × 76.2 cm. National Gallery, London.

**Munda languages** (,moondə), group of languages spoken in parts of N and central India, and generally regarded as a subfamily of the Southeast Asian family of languages. See LANGUAGE (table).

**Munich,** Ger. *München,* city (1984 pop. 1,277,000), capital of Bavaria, S West Germany, on the Isar R. It is an industrial centre with such manufactures as machinery and chemicals. Founded in 1158 by HENRY THE LION, it became (1255) the residence of the WITTELSBACH family. It was the capital of the kingdom of BAVARIA after 1806 and became a cultural centre in the 19th cent. NATIONAL SOCIALISM (Nazism) was founded in Munich and had its party headquarters there. The MUNICH PACT (1938) was signed in the city. Badly damaged during WORLD WAR II, it was rebuilt after 1945. Its many points of interest include the 15th-cent. Frauenkirche and the Old Pinakothek museum.

**Munich Pact,** 1938, agreement signed at Munich, Germany, by Germany, the UK, France, and Italy, which surrendered the SUDETENLAND, Czechoslovakia, to Germany. CZECHOSLOVAKIA, not invited to the talks, was forced to give in to the pact's terms, and President BENEŠ, realizing that he had been abandoned by his allies, resigned. British Prime Min. Neville CHAMBERLAIN, upon his return to London, announced that he had achieved 'peace in our time', but the pact was widely regarded as an abject surrender to HITLER. The Munich Pact became a symbol of appeasement, and WORLD WAR II began barely one year after its signing.

**Munk, Kaj** (moongk), 1898–1944, Danish playwright, a clergyman. His ethical plays, *Cant* (1931) and *The Word* (1932), led the Danish dramatic revival of the 1930s. An opponent of National Socialism, he wrote the patriotic drama *Niels Ebbesen* in 1943 and was shot by the Nazis.

**Muñoz Rivera, Luis** (mooh͵nyos reevayrah), 1859–1916, Puerto Rican journalist and nationalist. A leader of PUERTO RICO's independence movement, he headed (1901) the first cabinet under US occupation. He published the *Puerto Rico Herald* in New York City, and he obtained American citizenship for Puerto Ricans.

**Munro, Hector Hugh,** pseud. **Saki,** 1870–1916, English author; b. Burma. He is known for his witty, often bizarre stories, collected in *Reginald* (1904), *The Chronicles of Clovis* (1911), and other volumes. He also wrote novels.

**Munster,** province in Irish Republic (1986 pop. 1,019,694), 24,127 km² (9409 sq mi). It is the largest of the four Irish provinces and contains the counties of Clare, Cork, Kerry, Limerick, Tipperary, Waterford, and Cork, and Limerick and Waterford cities. It was one of the ancient kingdoms of Ireland.

**Münster,** city (1984 pop. 273,500), North Rhine–Westphalia, NW West Germany, on the Dortmund–Ems Canal. As a market for the surrounding agricultural region, it handles grain, cattle and wood products. Founded as a see in the time of Charlemagne, the district of Münsterland was a prince–bishopric until secularized in 1803. The university dates from 1773, occupying the bishop's palace. Many medieval buildings were destroyed in World War II but have been rebuilt in traditional style.

**Münzer, Thomas** (͵myntsə), c.1489–1525, German Protestant reformer, generally linked with the ANABAPTISTS, although he rejected baptism altogether. He was an associate of LUTHER in 1519, but his position soon diverged from Luther's as he became increasingly iconoclastic in theology and radical in political and social beliefs. During the Peasants' War (1524–26) he set up a communistic theocracy at Mühlhausen. He was later overthrown and beheaded.

**muon:** see ELEMENTARY PARTICLES.

**Muqdisho:** see MOGADISHU.

**Murad,** sultans of the OTTOMAN EMPIRE (Turkey). **Murad I,** 1326?–89 (r.1362?–89), widened Ottoman holdings by conquering Macedonia and Serbia, forced the Byzantine emperor to pay him tribute, and founded the JANISSERIES. He was assassinated. **Murad II,** 1403–51 (r.1421–51), put down Mustafa, a pretender, and established Ottoman naval power by seizing (1430) Salonica from the Venetians. In 1444 he won a great victory over the crusading LADISLAUS IV of Poland and Hungary. **Murad IV,** 1612?–1640 (r.1623–40), the last of the warrior–sultans recovered Baghdad. **Murad V,** 1840–1904 (r.1876), was declared insane and was succeeded by his brother ABD AL-HAMID II.

**Murasaki Shikibu** ('myooərə͵sahkee ͵sheekee'booh), c.978-1031?, Japanese novelist and diarist. She was a lady of the Imperial court in Kyoto. Her *Tale of Genji* (tr. 1925–33 by Arthur Waley; tr. 1976 by Edward Seidensticker) is a long and complex novel about the loves of Prince Genji and the refined manners and customs of the court in the Heian period (10th and 11th cent.).

**Murat, Joachim** (my͵rah), 1767–1815, marshal of France, king of Naples (1808–15). A brilliant cavalry leader, he served in many of NAPOLEON I's campaigns, helped him to overthrow (1799) the DIRECTORY, married (1800) Napoleon's sister Caroline Bonaparte, and succeeded (1808) Joseph Bonaparte (see BONAPARTE, family) as king of Naples. He reached an agreement (1814) with Austria to keep his throne, but turned against Austria during the HUNDRED DAYS and met defeat. He was executed after trying to regain Naples.

**Muratori, Lodovico Antonio,** 1672–1750, Italian scholar. Ducal Librarian at Modena from 1700 to 1750, and convinced of the importance to the historian of primary sources, he left vast and still invaluable compilations, most notably the *Rerum italicarum scriptores* (1723–50), and based his *Annals of Italy* (21 vol., 1744–49) on the chronicles and documents contained in them. His influential treatise *On Perfect Italian Poetry* (1703) formulates the reaction against BAROQUE extravagance in the name of reason, good taste, and the classical tradition.

**Murcia,** city (1981 pop. 288,631), capital of Murcia prov., SE Spain, on the Segura R. Melons, citrus and other fruits, vegetables including tomatoes and peppers, are grown intensively and support food-processing industries. Silk-worms are raised on locally-grown mulberries. Rebuilt by the Moors in the 8th cent., it was for a time in the 13th cent. the capital of a small kingdom.

**murder:** see HOMICIDE.

**Murdoch, (Jean) Iris,** 1919–, English author. A philosopher by training, her novels are subtle, witty, and highly melodramatic. They include *The Flight from the Enchanter* (1955), *A Severed Head* (1961), *An Accidental Man* (1971), and *Nuns and Soldiers* (1980).

**Murdoch, (Keith) Rupert,** 1931–, Australian publishing magnate. Combining sensationalist journalism with aggressive promotional techniques, he established a worldwide communications empire that by 1987 included powerful holdings in Australia; three of London's largest newspapers, the *News of the World*, the *Sun*, and *The Times*, and, in the US, a new weekly tabloid, the *Star*, the *New York Post*, the *Village Voice*, and *New York* and *New West* magazines. He obtained US citizenship in 1985 so as to purchase substantial holdings in American broadcasting industries. Murdoch was one of the first British newspaper owners to initiate production with new compositing technology. In 1985 he removed production of *The Times* from London WC1 to Wapping in east London and replaced the print-union workers with unqualified electricians; in the resulting labour dispute there were violent episodes as police clashed with pickets and local residents.

**Mureş,** river, 880 km (550 mi) long, which rises in the Carpathian Mts, flows across the central plateau of Transylvania and eventually joins the Tisza R. at Szeged in Hungary. The largest city is Tîrgu Mureş (146,322 in 1983), an industrial centre in Transylvania.

**Murillo, Bartolomé Estéban** (mooh͵reelyoh), 1617/18–82, Spanish religious and portrait painter. His early works, e.g., *Birth of the Virgin* (Louvre, Paris), show the influence of ZURBARÁN in the dramatic use of light and shadow. He was instrumental in founding (1660) the Seville Academy. Murillo became famous for devotional pictures, painted softly and sweetly, with fluttering draperies and delicate colour; many show *The Immaculate Conception*. He also painted elegant and simple portraits e.g., *Knight of the Collar* (Prado, Madrid) and sentimental GENRE scenes of peasant children.

**Murmansk,** city (1985 pop. 419,000), NW European USSR, on the Kola Gulf of the Barents Sea. The terminus of the NORTHEAST PASSAGE, it is a major ice-free port, a base for naval and fishing vessels, and the world's largest city N of the Arctic Circle. Industries include shipbuilding and timber production. The city was a village before World War I. The port and the rail line from Petrograd (now Leningrad) were built in 1915–16. Allied forces occupied Murmansk in 1918–20. In World War II it was a major supply base and port for Anglo-American convoys.

**Murnau, F(riedrich) W(ilhelm)** (͵mooənow), 1889–1931, German film director. His films, including *Nosferatu* (1922), *The Last Laugh* (1924), and *Sunrise* (1927), are noted for the use of a constantly moving camera to depict states of mind.

**Murray,** chief river of Australia, 2589 km (1609 mi) long. It rises in SE New South Wales, flows westwards to form the *New South Wales–Victoria* boundary, and empties into the Southern Ocean in *South Australia*. Its waters, combined with those of the DARLING and MURRUMBIDGEE rivers, are used for irrigation and hydroelectricity and domestic supplies for urban areas.

**Murray, (George) Gilbert Aimé,** 1866–1957, British classical scholar; b. Australia. He taught at Oxford Univ. and translated many Greek plays. Active in the cause of world peace, he worked for the League of Nations and the UN.

**Murray, James,** 1721?–94, British general, first civil governor of CANADA (1764–68). After his distinguished service in the FRENCH AND INDIAN WARS he was named governor. His protection of French Canadians led to charges that he had betrayed England, but he was exonerated (1766).

**Murray, Sir James Augustus Henry,** 1837–1915, English lexicographer. From 1879 he was editor of the *New English Dictionary* (the *Oxford English Dictionary*), the major work of his career; it was published in 1928.

**Murray, Les,** 1938–, Australian poet. His work celebrates the unique value of Australian rural life and landscapes; his many volumes of poetry include *The Ilex Tree* (1965), *The Weatherboard Cathedral* (1969), a novel in verse, *The Boys Who Stole the Funeral* (1980), and *The People's Otherworld* (1983).

**Murrow, Edward R(oscoe),** 1908–65, American newscaster. He was noted for his dramatic and accurate broadcasts from London during World War II. He later produced the popular television programmes *See It Now* and *Person to Person.*

**Murrumbidgee,** river, SE Australia, flowing generally W 1690 km (c.1050 mi) through New South Wales to join the MURRAY R. on the Victoria border. Its irrigated valley is Australia's most productive farming area.

**Murry, John Middleton,** 1889–1957, English critic and editor. His criticism includes *The Problem of Style* (1922) and *Keats and Shakespeare* (1925). He wrote *The Necessity of Pacifism* (1937); edited his wife Katherine MANSFIELD'S papers; and wrote *God* (1929) and other mystical philosophical works.

**Muscat** or **Maskat,** city (1986 est. pop. 80,000), capital of Oman, SE Arabia, on the Gulf of Oman. It has a fine harbour, dominated by two 15th–16th-cent. Portuguese forts, and exports dates, fish, and mother-of-pearl. Since the discovery and production of petroleum in Oman in 1967 the town has been extended and modernized. As a port it has lost trade to the nearby harbour of Mutrah and the oil terminal at Mina al Fahal. Portugal held it from 1508 to 1648, and Persian princes until 1741, when it became Oman's capital.

**muscle,** contractile tissue that effects the movement of the body. Muscle tissue is classified according to its structure and function. Skeletal muscle, sometimes known as voluntary muscle, is under conscious control, effecting purposeful movements of limbs and other body parts. It is also called striated muscle, because microscopic examination reveals alternating bands of light and dark. Smooth muscle, which lines most hollow organs, is involuntary, i.e., regulated by the autonomic NERVOUS SYSTEM. It produces movement within internal organs such as those of the DIGESTIVE SYSTEM. Cardiac muscle is striated like skeletal muscle but, like smooth muscle, is controlled involuntarily. It is found only in the HEART, where it forms that organ's thick walls. Contraction, thought to be a similar process in all types of muscle, involves two proteins, actin and myosin, lengthening and shortening muscle fibres.

**muscovite:** see MICA.

**Muscovy Company** or **Russia Company,** first major English joint-stock trading company; chartered in 1555. It financed trading expeditions to Russia and Asia. In 1698 its monopoly was lost, but the company continued to exist until 1917.

**muscular dystrophy,** any of several inherited diseases characterized by progressive weakness and wasting of muscles, believed to be due to an abnormality in the muscle tissue itself. The most common form, Duchenne dystrophy, affects boys, beginning with leg weakness before the age of 3 and progressing rapidly, with death often occurring before the age of 30. Another form involves primarily facial and shoulder muscles and affects both sexes, usually from adolescence. There is no known cure, although physiotherapy can relieve some of the disability.

**Musée d'Orsay** (mooh,zaydaw'say), Paris, opened in 1986 in the disused former railway terminal, the Gare d'Orsay, which was restored to house the art of the second half of the 19th and early 20th cent., including the Impressionist and Post-impressionist paintings formerly in the Jeu de Paume. See IMPRESSIONISM and POST-IMPRESSIONISM. The collection also includes decorative arts, sculpture, and ART NOUVEAU.

**Muses,** in Greek mythology, the nine patron goddesses of the arts; daughters of ZEUS and Mnemosyne, a TITAN who personified memory. They were: Calliope (epic poetry and eloquence), Euterpe (music and

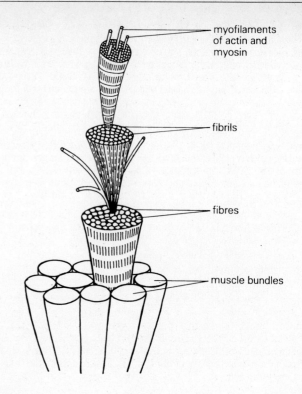

Muscle

lyric poetry), Erato (love poetry), Polyhymnia (oratory or sacred poetry), Clio (history), Melpomene (tragedy), Thalia (comedy), Terpsichore (choral song and dance), and Urania (astronomy).

**Museum of Modern Art,** New York City; incorporated in 1929 and privately supported. Among the museum's founders were Mrs John D. ROCKEFELLER and Lillie P. Bliss, whose bequest of modern paintings began its permanent collection. In addition to one of the world's finest collections of modern art, the museum has outstanding photography and film departments. It has specialized in loan exhibitions of contemporary European and American art.

**Musgrave, Thea,** 1928–, British composer. She studied with Nadia BOULANGER (1950–54), and has used modern techniques within conventional frameworks. She has written many chamber and orchestral works, as well as the operas *The Decision* (1964–65), *Mary, Queen of Scots* (1977), and *A Christmas Carol* (1979).

**mushroom,** fungus characterized by spore-bearing gills on the underside of an umbrella- or cone-shaped cap. The term *mushroom* is properly restricted to the plant's above-ground portion, which is the reproductive organ. Once a delicacy for the elite, edible mushrooms are now grown commercially, especially strains of the meadow mushroom (*Agaricus campestris*). Although mushrooms contain some protein and minerals, they are largely water and hence of limited nutritive value. Inedible, or poisonous, species are often popularly referred to as toadstools; one of the best-known poisonous mushrooms is the death cap (genus *Amanita*).

**musical comedy:** see MUSICALS.

**musical notation,** symbols used to make a written record of musical sounds. In Europe, BOETHIUS applied the first 15 letters of the alphabet to notes in use at the end of the Roman period. By the 8th cent. notation of Gregorian chant was by means of neumes, thought to derive from accentual signs once used in the Latin language (see PLAINSONG); they indicated groupings of sounds to remind a singer of a melody already learned by ear. By the end of the 12th cent. the Benedictine monk Guido d'Arezzo had perfected the staff, placing letters on certain lines to indicate their pitch. These letters evolved into the clef signs used today. In the 15th cent. the shape of notes became round and time signatures replaced coloration to indicate note value. The key signature developed early, although sharps were not used until the 17th cent. The five-line staff (with ledger lines used to extend the range) became standard in the 16th cent.

Expression signs and Italian phrases to indicate tempo and dynamics came into use in the 17th cent. Notation for ELECTRONIC MUSIC is still not standardized but generally combines traditional symbols with specially adapted rhythm and pitch notation. On notation of lute and keyboard music, see TABLATURE. In Asia, different systems of notation were devised, in many cases before European notation, and are still used in India, China, Japan, Korea, Thailand, Tibet, Indonesia, etc.

**musicals,** form of stage entertainment originating in late-19th-cent. England as musical comedy. Incorporating music, chorus dancing, and topical numbers, it has flourished primarily in the US. The best-known composers of musicals include Irving BERLIN, Jerome KERN, Cole PORTER, Noel COWARD, George GERSHWIN, Richard RODGERS, Lorenz HART, Oscar HAMMERSTEIN 2ND, and Stephen SONDHEIM. Innovations came with Rodgers and Hammerstein's *Oklahoma!* (1943), which integrated music, song, and dance with a detailed plot, and *West Side Story* (1957), which introduced serious themes, causing the genre to be called simply 'musicals'. In the 1960s the 'ROCK musical' came into prominence with the production of *Hair* (1967). Film musicals attained their greatest popularity in the 1930s, 40s, and 50s.

**music festivals,** series of performances separate from the normal concert season, and often organized around an idea or theme (e.g., the work of a single composer). They are usually held in the summer, often in open air, and have been traced back as far as the 6th-cent. BC Pythian Games at Delphi. Medieval guilds sponsored competitive festivals; the EISTEDDFOD in Wales is a descendant. In the 1950s and 1960s, JAZZ, folk, and ROCK MUSIC began to be presented at festivals. Notable festivals include Bayreuth (featuring the music of Richard WAGNER, Salzburg (featuring MOZART), and Aldeburgh (founded by Benjamin BRITTEN and featuring contemporary music).

**music-hall,** in England, a form of entertainment featuring song, dance, acrobatics, PANTOMIME, and comic sketches, catering to the lower and middle classes. Originally offered in inns and taverns, the music-hall as a separate establishment first appeared in the mid 1800s. Following a rapid rise, the music-hall went into a decline with the coming of radio and cinema.

**Musil, Robert** (‚moohzil), 1880–1942, Austrian novelist. Musil's first novel, *Young Törless* (1906; tr. 1955) is a subtle account of boarding-school bullying, seen through the ambivalent perceptions of the participant observer. His major work is the unfinished novel *Der Mann ohne Eigenschaften* (1931–43; tr. The Man without Qualities), a witty pathology of Kakanian (= Austrian) high bourgeois culture in transition to a mass society, as experienced by the intelligent opter-out of the title, who ultimately seeks his own salvation in a mystical eroticism.

**musk,** odorous substance secreted by an abdominal gland in the male musk DEER, used in PERFUME as a scent and fixative. Its odour comes from an organic compound called muscone. Musklike substances are also obtained from the muskrat and the civet; some plants yield oils that resemble musk.

**muskeg,** a Canadian Indian name for subarctic areas of N America of essentially flat, marshy land, with scattered lakes and very slow, meandering rivers. The waterlogged depressions are usually covered with sphagnum moss while higher ground may be colonized by groups of tamarack and fir.

**musket:** see SMALL ARMS.

**muskmelon:** see MELON.

**musk ox,** hoofed animal (*Ovibos moschatus*) of the CATTLE family, found in arctic North America and Greenland. The musk ox is covered with shaggy fur and has a musky odour. It has splayed hooves and broad, flat horns that curve down along the sides of the head; it stands 1.5 m (5 ft) at the shoulder. Hunted to near extinction in the 19th cent., it is now restored.

**muskrat:** see VOLE.

**Muslim:** see ISLAM.

**Muslim art and architecture:** see ISLAMIC ART AND ARCHITECTURE; MUGHAL ART AND ARCHITECTURE.

**Muslim Brethren, Society of,** political–religious society founded in 1928 by the Egyptian Hassan al-Banna. The Society has spread throughout islamic lands, sometimes organizationally and sometimes as

an ideological model, and has come to embody modern Islamist politics for Sunni Muslims (see SUNNISM). It is culturally anti-Western and calls for the restoration of a romanticized conservative social order, while its ideological fundamentalism calls for the restitution of a political utopia modelled on a pattern of social and political authority which the Society derives from the early CALIPHATE at Medina. Largely under the influence of Sayyid QUTB, who was executed in Egypt in 1966, many small radical groups have formed on the margins of the Society. These have opted for a radical separatism from society, which they consider infidel, and some have resorted to direct military action, such as the assassination of Anwar SADAT.

**Muslim League,** political organization of the Muslims of the Indian subcontinent. Founded (1906) by AGA KHAN III, it grew into an independent party under Muhammad IQBAL and, later, Muhammad Ali JINNAH. In 1947 it became the ruling party of newly formed Pakistan. It split into several factions by 1953 and declined thereafter.

**Mussadegh, Muhammad** (‚moohsahdayg), 1880–1967, prime minister of IRAN (1951–53). He led the militant nationalists who succeeded in nationalizing (1951) the British-owned oil industry. The shah openly opposed him and, after trying (1952) to oust Mussadegh, was forced into temporary exile. Upon the shah's return to power (1953), Mussadegh was imprisoned until 1956; after that he lived under house arrest.

**mussel,** edible BIVALVE mollusc, abundant in cooler seas. Mussels form extensive, crowded beds, anchoring themselves to pilings or rocks by a secretion of strong threads known as the byssus. The dark-shelled burrowing freshwater mussel is a source of PEARLS and MOTHER-OF-PEARL.

**Musset, (Louis Charles) Alfred de** (my‚say), 1810–57, French Romantic poet. In his exquisite love lyrics, e.g., *Les Nuits* (1835–37), and his narrative poems, e.g., *Rolla* (1833), he combined classic clarity with the passionate subjectivity of ROMANTICISM. He also wrote short novels and plays, including the Shakespearian *Lorenzaccio* (1834) probably the masterpiece of French Romantic theatre. An autobiographical novel, *La confession d'un enfant du siècle* (1836; tr. Confession of a Child of the Century), gives an account of his unhappy love affair with George SAND.

**Mussolini, Benito,** 1883–1945, Italian Fascist leader and dictator. He edited Socialist newspapers but broke with the Socialists to support Italy's entry into World War I. In 1919 Mussolini organized his staunchly nationalistic followers, who wore black shirts as uniforms and practiced terrorism in armed groups. In 1921 he was elected to Parliament and founded the National Fascist Party (see FASCISM). His Fascists marched (Oct. 1922) on Rome, and King VICTOR EMMANUEL III called on Mussolini to form a government. Called *Duce* [leader], the new premier gradually created a dictatorship and ended parliamentary government (1928). In 1929 he concluded the LATERAN TREATY with the Vatican. His imperialistic designs led to the conquest of Ethiopia (1935–36) and the occupation of Albania (1939). He signed (1939) an alliance with Nazi Germany, but Italy's involvement in WORLD WAR II was a military failure in Greece and N Africa. The imminent Allied invasion of the Italian mainland led to a rebellion within the Fascist Party. The king dismissed Mussolini and had him imprisoned (July 1943), but the Germans snatched him from imprisonment and made him a puppet ruler in N Italy. On the German collapse (1945) Mussolini was captured by Italian partisans, summarily tried, and executed.

**Mussorgsky, Modest Petrovich:** see MOUSSORGSKY.

**mustard,** common name for the Cruciferae, a large family chiefly of herbs of north temperate regions, typified by flowers with four petals arranged diagonally ('cruciform') and alternating with the four sepals. The Cruciferae, often rich in SULPHUR compounds and VITAMIN C, include many important food and condiment plants, e.g., RAPE, swede, TURNIP, mustard, numerous CABBAGE varieties, WATERCRESS, HORSERADISH, and RADISH. The herbs called mustard are species of *Brassica* native to Europe and W Asia. Black (*B. nigra*) and white (*B. alba*) mustard are cultivated for their seeds, which are ground and used as a condiment, usually mixed to a paste with vinegar or oil. Mustards are also grown as salad plants and for greens.

**mustard gas:** see POISON GAS.

**mutagens,** physical or chemical agencies which increase the frequency of changes to the genetic material inherited by the descendants of the cell affected. If the cells are sex cells which produce eggs or sperms, then the change will be passed on to the offspring of that organism. If the altered cells are body cells, then the change is termed a somatic mutation, and is seen only in the tissues produced from that cell and not handed on to the offspring. Mutagens are also frequently carcinogenic in their action, and often occur in an industrial environment. As with CARCINOGENS, direct testing for the mutagenicity of substances is difficult and long-term, and animals vary widely in their reactions and degree of susceptibility. Confusion exists because of the activation to mutagenicity of otherwise harmless materials by human metabolism, or the detoxification in the body of substances known to cause mutations in lower organisms such as bacteria and fungi used as test objects. It is of course not possible to test for effects on humans, and for the safe use of chemicals or processes in industry substances may be designated as being of 'mutagenic potential' either because of their chemical structure or their known effects on micro-organisms or test animals such as rats. Methods of testing persons already exposed to potential mutagens include examination for observable changes in certain cells of blood, the production of abnormal sperm in males, and an increase in the number of spontaneous abortions by their partners (due to fertilization of eggs by abnormal sperm) or by females exposed to the same risk. Physical agencies such as ULTRAVIOLET RADIATION are strongly mutagenic and more is known about their mode of action. This involves chemical changes in the DNA (genetic material) of the cell due to preferential absorption of UV light, or energy transfer from radiation, both of which can be measured with some degree of accuracy. The mutagenic effects of the ATOMIC BOMBS dropped on Japan in 1945 were the most long-lasting damage inflicted. Similar effects are feared in relation to NUCLEAR ENERGY, where workers or the general population may be exposed to high doses of radiation in an accident.

**Mutanabbi, al-**, 915–65, Arab poet, considered the greatest classical Arabic poet; b. Iraq. His early involvement with a religious cult earned him the sobriquet 'the would-be prophet'. He was part of the brilliant court of the Hamdanid ruler Sayf al-Dawlah in Aleppo, where he wrote many of the elaborate panegyrics upon which much of his fame rests.

**mutation,** in biology, a sudden change in a GENE, or unit of hereditary material, that results in a new inheritable characteristic. In higher animals and many higher plants a mutation may be transmitted to future generations only if it occurs in germ, or sex cell, tissue; body cell mutations cannot be inherited. Changes within the chemical structure of single genes (see NUCLEIC ACID) may be induced by exposure to radiation, temperature extremes, and certain chemicals. The term *mutation* may also be used to include losses or rearrangements of segments of CHROMOSOMES, the long strands of genes. Drugs such as colchicine double the normal number of chromosomes in a cell by interfering with cell division (see MITOSIS). Mutation, which is the source of new traits which may become established in a population, is important in EVOLUTION.

**Mu'tazila,** school of Muslim theology or KALAM. Flourishing at various times in BAGHDAD and elsewhere, it emphasized the neccessity for an allegorical interpretation of scriptural pronouncements about God and about heaven, judgment, and the afterlife. It also developed a notion of divine justice which it applied to its own elaboration of the principles of Islamic law (see FIQH). Though generally marginal as a school, its unacknowledged impact on all areas of islamic thought, including that of its Ash'arite enemies, was very considerable. Its main themes and ethos were also of considerable influence on modern reformist Muslim thinkers such as Muhammad ABDUH and SYED AHMAD KHAN.

**Mutesa I,** c.1838–84, *kabaka* [King] of Buganda (now part of UGANDA) from 1856 to 1884. During his reign Buganda was regarded as one of the most powerful states in E Africa. Mutesa's armies constantly raided neighbouring states for ivory and slaves which were then exchanged for guns. His reign also saw the opening up of Buganda to Christian missionaries, though he himself never converted.

**Mutsuhito:** see MEIJI.

**mutton bird:** see SHEARWATER.

**mutual fund,** in finance, investment company or trust that has a very fluid capital stock. It is unique in that at any time it can sell, or redeem, any of its outstanding shares at net asset value (i.e., total assets minus liabilities, divided by the total number of shares). A mutual fund, also called an open-end investment company, owns the securities of several corporations and receives dividends on the shares held. A closed-end investment company differs from an open-end company in that the number of shares sold to investors is limited and the price of the shares may fluctuate above and below the net asset value. Mutual funds provide skilled management and diversification, thereby lessening risk. Earnings are distributed to shareholders in the form of income and capital-gains dividends. Common-stock funds invest mainly in common shares, while more conservative funds invest in preferred stocks and bonds as well. See also MONEY-MARKET FUND.

**Muybridge, Eadweard** (ˌmiebrij), 1830–1904, English photographer. A specialist in animal locomotion, he recorded motion with sequential still cameras. He invented (1881) the zoöpraxiscope to project animated images. Much of his work appeared in *Animals in Motion* (1899).

One of Eadweard **Muybridge's** many studies of animal locomotion

**Mwanga II,** c.1866–1903, last independent ruler (r.1884–99) of Buganda (now part of UGANDA). An alliance of Christian factions forced Mwanga out of Buganda in 1888. A bloody, four-year civil war followed in which he was restored as *kabaka* [king] but only after ceding real power to the Christians. When the British declared a protectorate over Buganda in 1894, Mwanga rebelled but was captured in 1899 and exiled to the Seychelles.

**Mwanza,** city (1987 pop. 170,823), NW Tanzania, on the southern shore of Victoria Nyanza (Lake Victoria). At a height of 1135 m (3724 ft), it is the administrative centre of the densely populated Mwanza region where cotton is the main crop. Steamship services on Victoria Nyanza use Mwanza regularly as a port of call.

**Mwene Mutapa, Mwanamutapa,** or **Monomotapa,** title taken by the rulers of a 15th–17th cent. Shona kingdom in what is now ZIMBABWE. The state fragmented after the CHANGAMIRE state was established in S Zimbabwe, though Mwene Mutapa continued to rule until 1902.

**Myall Creek massacre,** infamous slaughter of 28 Australian Aborigines on 9 June 1838. Seven white men were executed for the murder; they were the first white to be convicted and executed for murdering Aborigines.

**myasthenia gravis,** chronic disorder of the muscles, characterized by weakness and abnormal fatigue. Most commonly found in young adults, the disease is caused by impaired ability to induce muscle contraction. The muscles of the head and neck are most frequently involved, those of the trunk and extremities less frequently. Symptoms typically advance irregularly, with varying intensity and severity, but there is a gradual worsening over a period of years, with the major danger resulting from respiratory paralysis or infection. Drugs that improve neuromuscular function are used to treat the symptoms of the disease.

**Mycenaean civilization** (miesineeən), an ancient AEGEAN CIVILIZATION known from excavations at Mycenae. Undertaken by Heinrich SCHLIEMANN and others after 1876, they helped revise early Greek history. The Mycenaeans were Indo-European, Greek-speaking people who entered GREECE from the north c.2000 BC, bringing with them advanced techniques in art and architecture. Mercantile contact with the Minoans on Crete advanced their culture, and by 1600 BC Mycenae had become a major centre of the ancient world, competing with CRETE for maritime control of the Mediterranean. After the destruction of KNOSSOS (c.1400 BC) Mycenae achieved supremacy, and much of the Minoan cultural tradition was transferred to the mainland. The invasion by the Dorians (c.1100 BC) ushered in a period of decline, and by 900 BC the centres of culture and wealth had shifted elsewhere.

**Mýkonos** (ˌmeekə'nos), island (pop. c.4000), of c.25 km² (9 sq mi), SE Greece, in the AEGEAN SEA, one of the CYCLADES. Its white-painted houses, its many small churches, and its windmills, have helped to make this one of the most popular of the Greek island resorts.

**My Lai incident** (ˌmie ˌlie, ˌmee-), massacre of civilians in the VIETNAM WAR. On Mar. 16, 1968, US soldiers, led by Lt. William L. Calley, invaded the South Vietnamese hamlet of My Lai, an alleged Viet Cong stronghold, and shot to death 347 unarmed civilians, including women and children. The incident was not made public until 1969. Special army and congressional investigations followed. Five soldiers were court-martialed, and one, Lt Calley, was convicted (Mar. 29, 1971) and sentenced to life imprisonment. In Sept. 1974 a federal court overturned the conviction, and Calley was released.

**mynah** or **myna, grackle**, an Asiatic STARLING, a bird found chiefly in India and Sri Lanka and known for its power of mimicry. The hill mynah (*Gracula religiosa*), c. 30–38 cm (12–15 in), is the best known. Glossy black with yellow head wattles, it is a forest dweller and lives mostly on fruit. When trained, it is a better mimic than the PARROT. The common or Indian mynah *Acrido theres tristis* is a popular cage-bird.

**myopia:** see SHORTSIGHTEDNESS.

**Myrdal, Gunnar** (ˌmeeədahl), 1898–1987, Swedish economist, sociologist, and public official. Winner, with F.A. von Hayek, of the 1974 Nobel Prize for economics, Myrdal taught at the Univ. of Stockholm (1933–50, 1960–67), held several government posts, and was executive secretary (1947–57) of the UN Economic Commission for Europe. As head of a Carnegie Corp. study (1938–42) of American blacks, he collaborated on *An American Dilemma* (1944; new ed. 1962), maintaining that the US racial problem was inextricably entwined with the democratic functioning of American society. Other works include *Crisis in the Population Question* (1934), written with his wife, and *Challenge of World Poverty* (1970).

**Myron**, fl. 5th cent. BC, Greek sculptor, noted for animals and athletes in action. His works are known through description and Roman copies, the best copies being the Lancelotti *Discobolus* (Terme Mus., Rome) and *Athena and Marsyas*.

**myrrh:** see INCENSE-TREE.

**myrtle,** common name for the family Myrtaceae, trees and shrubs mostly native to tropical regions, especially in America and Australia. The family is characterized by usually evergreen leaves containing aromatic volatile oils; many have showy blossoms. Myrtles are of economic importance for their timber, gums and resins, oils, spices, and edible fruits. The true myrtle genus (*Myrtus*) is chiefly of the American tropics, but the classical myrtle (*M. communis*) is native to the Mediterranean area. Its glossy leaves were made into wreaths for victors in the ancient OLYMPIC GAMES. Other trees in the myrtle family include the CLOVE, EUCALYPTUS, GUAVA, and PIMENTO, or allspice.

**Mysore,** city (1981 pop. 441,754), Karnataka state, S India, near the KAVERI R. It is a district administrative and commercial centre and railway junction with a number of varied industries. It is the former capital of the princely state of Mysore and still contains palaces and other marks of its former importance; it is now overshadowed by the Maharaja's later capital, BANGALORE. It was under the walls of the nearby fort of Srirangapatnam (formerly Seringapatam), on the Kaveri river, that the British under Cornwallis were able to dictate peace terms to Tipu Sultan; while later, for some fifty years from 1831, the territory of Mysore was ruled directly by the British, until the Maharajas were reinstated and in due course won a reputation for progressive rule.

**mysteries,** important secret cults in Greek and Roman religion. Possibly based on primitive fertility rites, their elaborate, mystic ritual appealed to individuals who had tired of the formalistic, state-centred rites of traditional Greek and Roman religion, and who sought a promise of personal salvation and immortality. Some mysteries were survivals of indigenous rites, while others (e.g., the cult of CYBELE) were of foreign origin. Especially important in Greece were the Eleusinian and ORPHIC MYSTERIES.

Discobolus by **Myron**. Terme Museum, Rome.

**Mystery Plays,** medieval English religious plays in verse, dating from the late 14th cent. onwards and forming cycles covering the whole of sacred history from Creation to Doomsday. Sponsored by local craft guilds, they were performed in many towns, usually on Corpus Christi day. Four complete cycles (from York, Wakefield, 'N-Town', and Chester) and some fragments survive.

**mystery story:** see DETECTIVE STORY.

**mysticism** [Gr., = the practice of those who are initiated into the mysteries], the practice of putting oneself into direct relation with GOD, the Absolute, or any unifying principle of life. There are two general tendencies in the speculation of mystics: to regard God as outside the soul, which rises to God by successive stages, or to regard God as dwelling within the soul, to be found by delving deeper into one's own reality. The contemplative path to union conventionally requires a series of steps involving purgation, illumination, and increase of spiritual love. Various rituals may assist the process. The language of mysticism is difficult and usually symbolic; biographies and autobiographies of mystics are the major sources for direct study (for example, those of such mystics as St TERESA of Ávila; St JOHN OF THE CROSS; Jakob BOEHME; and Aurobindo GHOSE). Although mysticism is inseparably linked with religion, the term itself is used very broadly in English, being extended to magic, occultism, or the esoteric. Mysticism is encountered in Greek NEOPLATONISM, CHRISTIANITY, JUDAISM, BUDDHISM, HINDUISM, ISLAM, and TAOISM.

**myth,** sacred or religious accounts (which are believed to be true) of how the world came to be the way it is and of the supernatural worlds that underlie or precede the natural world. There is often a close connection established between myth and rituals: the latter may enact myths, while myths explain ritual practices. For MALINOWSKI myths were a 'social charter', which represented and justified the fundamental features and relationships of a given society. For LÉVI-STRAUSS myth is a cultural form which represents a way of thinking about the structural principles which underlie social relations, and which mediates some of the basic contradictions inherent in all social systems; myths are the means of conceptualizing and resolving all possible, unliveable social relationships and thus represent the free play of the human imagination and reveal the fundamental structures of human thought.

**mythology,** collective myths of a people and scientific study of such myths. Myths are traditional stories occurring in a timeless past and involving supernatural elements. Products of prerational cultures, myths express and explain such serious concerns as the creation of the universe and of humanity, the evolution of society, and the cycle of agricultural fertility. Myths are differentiated from folktales (e.g., CINDERELLA and tales from *The Arabian Nights*) by being more serious, less entertaining, more supernatural, and less rational and logical. Legends and sagas, by contrast with myths, are historical or quasi-historical in nature. Many theories have been advanced to explain myths. The Greeks' explanation of their own mythology was most fully developed in STOICISM, which reduced the gods to moral principles and natural elements. Such allegorical interpretations continued into the 18th cent. Theologians have tended to view myths (e.g., the blood myth or the myth of a golden age) as foreshadowings or corruptions of Scripture. Modern investigations of mythology began with the 19th-cent. philologist Max MÜLLER, who saw myths as having evolved from linguistic corruptions. Anthropological explanations have also abounded. Sir James FRAZER in his *Golden Bough* (1890) proposed that all myths were originally connected with the idea of fertility in nature, with the birth, death, and resurrection of vegetation as a constantly recurring motif. Bronislaw MALINOWSKI considered myths to be validations of established social patterns. Among influential psychologists, Sigmund FREUD related the unconscious myth and dream, while Carl JUNG believed that all peoples unconsciously formed the same mythic symbols. In the 20th cent. Mircea Eliade believes that myths serve to return their adherents to the time of the original creative act, and Claude LÉVI-STRAUSS contends that myths should be interpreted structurally. Important mythologies include the Greek, largely codified and preserved in the works of HOMER and HESIOD; the Roman, primarily derived from the Greek, and, with it, the best known; the Norse, which is less anthropomorphic; the Indian (Vedic), which tends to be abstract and otherworldly; the Egyptian, which is closely related to religious ritual; and the Mesopotamian, which exhibits a strong concern with the relationship between life and death. Mythology has enriched literature since the time of AESCHYLUS and has been used by some of the major English poets, e.g., MILTON, SHELLEY, KEATS. Some great literary figures, e.g., William BLAKE, James JOYCE, Franz KAFKA, W.B. YEATS, and T.S. ELIOT, have constructed symbolic personal myths by reshaping old mythological materials.

**Mzilikazi,** c.1795–1868, first king and founder of the Ndebele kingdom in what is now S ZIMBABWE. His early life was spent in Zululand where he was chief of the Kumalo. Under SHAKA he became a successful general but in 1821 he left Zululand for the Transvaal where he built up his own predatory state. In 1837 this state was broken up by successive defeats inflicted by the Zulu and the Boers. Mzilikazi fled north across the Limpopo R. and settled in present-day MATABELELAND, where BULAWAYO became the capital of the Ndebele kingdom.

**N,** chemical symbol of the element NITROGEN.

**Na,** chemical symbol of the element SODIUM.

**NAACP:** see NATIONAL ASSOCIATION FOR THE ADVANCEMENT OF COLORED PEOPLE.

**NAAFI,** the network of canteens and shops provided for serving members of the British armed forces, both in the UK and overseas. The name comes from the initials of **Navy, Army,** and **Air Force** (Institutions).

**Naas,** county town (1986 pop. 9972), of Co. Kildare, Republic of Ireland, 29 km (18 mi) SW of Dublin. It is known as a racing and hunting centre; the Punchestown racecourse is nearby.

**Nabis** (na‚bee), [from Heb., = prophets], a group of artists in France active during the 1890s. The principal theorists were Paul Sérusier and Maurice DENIS, and the members included VUILLARD, BONNARD, MAILLOL, and Félix Valloton. Influenced by GAUGUIN, they developed a style characterized by flat areas of bold colour and heavily outlined surface patterns. They were unified by their dislike of IMPRESSIONISM.

**Nablus,** city (1971 est. pop. 64,000), Jordan, on the WEST BANK. It is the market centre for a region where wheat and olives are grown and sheep and goats are grazed. Soap–making is a local industry. Nablus has remains dating from c.2000 BC The Samaritans (see SAMARIA) made it their capital, and under Rome it was named Neapolis, from which the present name derives. The city came under Israeli occupation after the 1967 ARAB-ISRAELI WAR. It has an Arab university and is a centre of Palestinian-Arab nationalism.

**Nabokov, Vladimir** (‚nabəkof), 1899–1977, Russian-American novelist; b. St Petersburg; one of the most original masters of 20th-cent. fiction. After the Russian Revolution of 1917 he lived in England and Germany, went to the US (1940), taught at Cornell (1948–59), and settled in Switzerland (1959). Nabokov's novels are frequently experimental and obscure but are always erudite, witty, and intriguing. His early fiction, in Russian, includes *Despair* (1936) and *Invitation to a Beheading* (1938). His most famous work in English, *Lolita* (1958), the story of a middle-aged European intellectual's infatuation with a 12-year-old American 'nymphet', brought him overnight fame and became a modern classic. Among his other novels are *Pnin* (1957), *Pale Fire* (1962), and *Ada* (1969). Nabokov also wrote poetry, criticism, stories, and autobiographies, and was an internationally recognized lepidopterist.

**Nadar:** see TOURNACHON, GASPARD FÉLIX.

**Nader, Ralph,** 1934–, American lawyer. From the time that his book *Unsafe at Any Speed* (1965) influenced the American Congress to bring MOTOR CAR design under control of the federal government, Nader was the most prominent leader of the American consumer-protection movement. His Center for the Study of Responsive Law (est. 1969) investigated government regulatory agencies; other Nader groups lobby, organize citizen action on various fronts, and finance legal proceedings.

**Nadir Shah** or **Nader Shah,** 1688–1747, shah of IRAN (1736–47), founder of the Afshar dynasty. After victories over the Afghans and the Turks, he became shah by deposing (1736) the last of the Safavid dynasty. He successfully invaded India in 1739; the great treasures he carried off included the Peacock Throne and the Koh-i-noor diamond. He greatly, though only temporarily, extended Iran's territory.

**Nagasaki,** city (1986 est. pop. 446,739), capital of Nagasaki prefecture, W Kyushu, Japan. The port was the first to receive Western trade with the arrival of Portuguese traders in 1570 and was the only international trade port during Japan's long period of national isolation (1641–1854). Shipbuilding is the major industry. Nagasaki was the second city to be hit (9 Aug. 1945) by an atomic bomb, following Hiroshima. Prayers for peace are said every year at Oura Catholic church, built in Gothic style by French missionaries and completed in 1865.

**Nagoya,** city (1986 est. pop. 2,077,439), capital of Aichi prefecture, central Honshu, Japan. It is the fourth largest Japanese port, and a major centre of transportation and industry, producing steel, textiles, ceramics, aircraft, and cars. The city was founded as a castle town in 1604 by the Tokugawa shogunate. It was heavily bombed in World War II and is famous for its reconstruction plan. Nagoya has one of the most famous shrines, the Atsuta (founded 2nd cent.), where the sacred imperial sword is housed.

**Nagpur,** city (1981 pop. 1,219,461), Maharashtra state, C India, on a tributary of the Wainganga R. It is an important district administrative, commercial, and railway centre in the heart of India, and it dominates eastern Maharashtra. It has cotton mills and other industries of more recent growth. Nagpur was founded in the 18th cent. by Gond kings; became the capital of the Mahratta Bhonslas; and was the capital also of the Central Provinces in British days.

**Nagy, Imre** (‚nodyə), 1895?–1958, Hungarian Communist leader. As premier (1953–55), he loosened government controls and was critical of Soviet influence. Denounced and removed from office, he was recalled as premier during the 1956 uprising (see HUNGARY). After the revolt was crushed, he was tried and executed by KÁDÁR's regime.

**Nahum,** book of the OLD TESTAMENT. It is a prophecy of doom against NINEVEH, the Assyrian capital, by Nahum the Elkoshite, who is otherwise unknown.

**naiads,** in Greek mythology: see NYMPH.

**Naipaul, V(idiadhar) S(urajprasad)** (‚niepawl), 1932–, British writer; b. Trinidad. An elegant prose stylist, with superb comic skills, his earliest works chart the lives of ordinary people in Trinidad, e.g., the classic, *A House for Mr Biswas* (1961). These have been followed by an increasingly alienated reaction (in novel as well as in travel documentary forms) to events in the THIRD WORLD: e.g., *In a Free State* (1971) and *A Congo Diary* (1984); to contemporary issues, e.g., *Among the Believers* (1981); and with his own ambivalence towards India, e.g., *An Area of Darkness: an Experience of India* (1964) and *India: A Wounded Civilisation* (1977).

**Nairobi,** city (1984 est. pop. 1,161,000), capital of Kenya, in the E African highlands. A modern metropolis with broad boulevards, it is Kenya's largest city; its administrative, communications, and economic centre; and the distribution centre for such agricultural products as coffee and cattle. Manufactures include food products, chemicals, soap, and paper. Nairobi is linked by rail with the port of MOMBASA. Nairobi National Park, a large wildlife sanctuary, attracts many tourists. Founded in 1899 on the Mombasa–Uganda railway, Nairobi became (1905) the capital of a British protectorate (later Kenya Colony). Rebuilt on drained land in the 1920s, it achieved city status in 1950.

**Nakasone, Yasuhiro,** 1918–, prime minister of JAPAN (1982–87). He served in the Diet after 1946. A political ally of Kakuei TANAKA, Nakasone succeeded Zenko SUZUKI as prime minister. A member of the (conservative) Liberal–Democratic Party, he adopted an overtly nationalist stance on major international policy issues.

**Namibia** or **South West Africa,** country (1984 est. pop. 1,507,000), c.823,620 km² (318,000 sq mi), SW Africa, bordered by Angola (N), Zambia (NE), Botswana (E), South Africa (SE), and the Atlantic Ocean (W). Namibia, which is administered by the Republic of South Africa, includes the CAPRIVI STRIP in the northeast and the South African enclave of WALVIS BAY in the west. WINDHOEK is the capital. The country consists of four main geographical regions: the barren Namib Desert, along the entire Atlantic coast; a large central plateau that rises to 2561 m (8402 ft) at Brandberg Mt; the western edge of the KALAHARI desert; and an alluvial plain in the north. The agricultural sector of the economy is based on stock raising (cattle, goats, and sheep), with income derived mainly from Karakul pelts, meat and livestock, and dairy goods. Namibia has rich deposits of diamonds, copper, lead, uranium, manganese, zinc, tin, silver, vanadium, and tungsten; its extensive mining industry is run chiefly by foreign companies. Fishing fleets operate in the Atlantic. Manufacturing is on a small scale. The population includes Bantu-speaking ethnic groups and whites of South African, German, and British descent. English and Afrikaans are the official languages. About half the people are Christian; the rest follow traditional beliefs.

*History.* The coastal regions of present-day Namibia were explored by Portuguese and Dutch expeditions beginning in the early 15th cent. They were followed by English missionaries in the 18th cent. and by German missionaries in the 1840s. The German government proclaimed (1884) a protectorate over what is now Lüderitz and soon extended it to all of South West Africa. An uprising of the Nama and the Herero was crushed by German forces in 1908, resulting in the deaths of some 84,000 black Africans. In World War I the country was occupied by SOUTH AFRICA, which afterwards administered it under a League of Nations mandate. In 1945 South Africa refused to surrender its mandate and place South West Africa under the UN trusteeship system, and it has since rejected demands by the UN General Assembly, backed (1971) by the International Court of Justice, that it withdraw from the territory. The UN adopted the name Namibia. In the 1970s South Africa proceeded with plans for independence on its own terms, holding elections and forming (1979) a national assembly, while a nationalist group, the South West Africa People's Organization (SWAPO), based largely in Angola, waged a campaign of guerrilla warfare. Five Western nations (Canada, France, West Germany, the UK, and the US) offered (1977) a plan for independence that would permit both blacks and whites to participate in the new government, but the plan failed to gain acceptance by South Africa. A UN Security Council plan for Namibian independence (adopted in 1978) also remained stalled, over S Africa's insistence on a prior withdrawal of Cuban forces from Angola. Namibia's national assembly was dissolved in 1983 amid disputes between the local parties and the S African-appointed administrator-general, who took over the government of the territory pending agreement on an independence plan. In 1985, however, S Africa installed a 'transitional government of national unity' (not including SWAPO, which nevertheless had UN recognition as representing the Namibian people) and in 1986 repeated its willingness to implement the UN independence plan on condition that Cuban forces left Angola. In 1988 an international UN-sponsored agreement was signed on these lines, providing for Namibian independence by mid-1991.

**Namier, Sir Lewis Bernstein,** 1888–1960, British historian. Born in Poland of Jewish parents, he became a naturalized British citizen in 1913. He established his reputation as a historian while professor of modern history at Manchester Univ. (1931–53). His meticulous work on 18th-cent. English politics, sometimes called 'namierizing', was based on a detailed study of individual biographies and parliamentary groupings; an example is *The Structure of Politics at the Accession of George III* (1929). During the last nine years of his life, Namier played a crucial role in the shaping of the multivolume *History of Parliament.* His stimulating essays on 19th- and 20th-cent. European political and diplomatic history commanded an appreciative general audience.

**Namur,** city (1985 pop. 102,022), capital of Namur prov., S Belgium. It occupies a strategic site at the confluence of the Sambre and Meuse rivers and as a result of its position, the city has suffered heavily in time

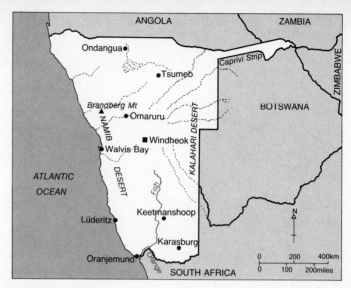

Namibia

of war. It serves an area of profitable market gardens and has a diverse industrial structure.

**Nanak, Baba,** 1469–1539, the first human guru of the SIKHS, founder of Sikhism. He wrote many hymns, some of which are part of the ADI GRANTH.

**Nanchang** or **Nanch'ang,** city (1984 pop. 3,316,400), capital of JIANGXI prov., S China, on the Gan R. Noted for the porcelain produced in the town of Jingdezhen, it is an important industrial city with products that include iron and steel, electronic equipment, machinery, textiles, and cars. An old walled city, it dates from the Song (Sung) dynasty (12th cent.). Important in the Chinese revolution, it was the site of the Nanchang Uprising (1927), led by Zhou Enlai and Zhu De.

**Nancy,** city (1982 pop. 99,307, agglomeration 306,982), capital of Meurthe-et-Moselle dept., E France, on the Meurthe R. Capital of the former Duchy of Lorraine, the city enjoyed a golden age under the last duke, Stanislas (1736–66), who carried out an ambitious programme of building and town planning. Place Stanislas, Place de la Carrière, and the cathedral are the outstanding products of this 18th-cent. scheme of beautification.

**Nanjing** or **Nanking,** [Chin., = southern capital], city (1984 pop. 4,607,500), capital of JIANGSU prov., E China, on the Yangtze R. One of China's largest cities, it is dominated by the Yangtze R. bridge, a crucial link in China's transport network. Nanjing's products include iron and steel, coal, metals, petroleum, chemicals, textiles, machine tools, and motor vehicles, as well as grain, tea, and vegetables. It served (3rd–6th cent., 14th–15th cent.) as capital of China and played an important role in the Taiping Rebellion (1850–64), the second Sino-Japanese War (1937–45), and the Chinese Revolution. A celebrated literary centre, it is known for its educational institutions, its large library, and its astronomical observatory.

**Nanking:** see NANJING.

**nanometer:** see ANGSTROM (unit).

**Nansen, Fridtjof,** 1861–1930, Norwegian Arctic explorer, statesman, scientist, and humanitarian. From 1893 to 1896 he tried to reach the NORTH POLE by drifting in ice across the polar basin in a special crush-resistant ship. Though he failed, his information on oceanography, meteorology, and diet laid the basis for future Arctic work. He was professor of zoology and oceanography at the University of Kristiania (now Oslo); Norway's first minister to England (1906–08); and the LEAGUE OF NATIONS high commissioner for refugees, for which he received the 1922 Nobel Peace Prize.

**Nantes** (nahnht), city (1982 pop. 247,727, agglomeration 464,857), capital of Loire-Atlantique dept., W France. It is a major ocean port with such manufactures as food products and naval and farm equipment. A Roman administrative centre, it was held by Norsemen (843–936) and

Breton dukes (10th cent.) before union with France (1524). It has a 10th-cent. castle and a 15th-cent. cathedral.

**Nantes, Edict of,** 1598, decree issued at Nantes by HENRY IV of France at the end of the Wars of Religion (see RELIGION, WARS OF); the edict defined the rights of French Protestants (see HUGUENOTS). These included liberty of conscience and public worship wherever it had been previously granted, full civil rights including the right to hold public office, and Protestant control of some 200 cities. The last condition gave French Protestants a virtual state within a state and was incompatible with the centralizing policies of RICHELIEU and MAZARIN, and of LOUIS XIV. The Peace of Alais (1629) ended Protestant political privileges and persecution began after 1665 under Louis XIV. Finally, in 1685, Louis revoked the edict. Thousands of Protestants fled abroad. The edict's revocation weakened the French economy by driving out a skilled and industrious segment of the nation, though possibly less so than certain historians have argued.

**Nantong,** city (1984 pop. 7,426,900), JIANGSU prov., E China, on the N bank of the Changjiang (Yangtze) R., inland from Shanghai. From the late 19th cent. it developed as an industrial town based on textile manufacture but now including engineering, chemical, and electronics industries. It is a major river port.

**Nantucket,** island, SE Massachusetts, US, 40 km (25 mi) S of CAPE COD. First settled in 1659, it was a major whaling centre until the mid-19th cent. and is now one of the most popular summer resorts in the US. It is c.23 km (14 mi) long.

**Naomi:** see RUTH.

**Naoroji, Dadabhai** (nah͵rohjee), 1825–1917, Indian nationalist leader. He wrote on the economic effects of British rule in India. A founder of the INDIAN NATIONAL CONGRESS, he was the first Indian elected (1892) to the British Parliament. Originally an enthusiast for British rule, he later moved the resolution demanding *swaraj* [self-rule].

**napalm,** incendiary material used in bombs and flame throwers. Developed during World War II, napalm is a mixture of petrol and a thickening agent. The thickener turns the mixture into a dense jelly that flows under pressure, as when shot from a flame thrower, and sticks to a target as it burns. Earlier SOAP thickeners have been replaced by polystyrene and similar polymers. Its use by the US against civilians in the VIETNAM WAR caused unanimous international outrage.

**Naphtali:** see ISRAEL, TRIBES OF.

**Napier, John,** 1550–1617, Scottish mathematician, the inventor of logarithms and compiler of the first set of LOGARITHM tables. He also introduced the decimal point in writing numbers. His *Rabdologiae* (1617) gives various methods for abbreviating arithmetical calculations, including a method of multiplication using a system of numbered rods called Napier's rods or Napier's bones. Napier was also known as an outspoken exponent of the Protestant cause.

**Naples,** Ital. *Napoli,* city (1984 pop. 1,206,955), capital of Campania, S central Italy, on the Bay of Naples. A crowded, noisy city, it is a major seaport, and a commercial and industrial centre. Naples has long been known for its music. A Greek colony, it was taken by Rome (4th cent. BC) and the Byzantines (6th cent. AD). It was an independent duchy from the 8th cent., later becoming (1139) part of the kingdom of Sicily. From 1282 it was the capital of the kingdom of Naples (see separate article). It fell (1860) to GARIBALDI and joined united Italy. Historic buildings include the Cathedral of St Januarius (14th cent. and later), the Castel Nuovo (1282), and the Royal Palace (17th cent.).

**Naples, kingdom of,** former state in S Italy, with Naples as its capital. In the 11th and 12th cent. the Normans under ROBERT GUISCARD and his successors conquered S Italy from the Byzantines. The pope invested (1139) Roger II, Guiscard's nephew, with the kingdom of Sicily, which included lands in S Italy. The kingdom passed to the house of HOHENSTAUFEN and was ruled successively by FREDERICK II, CONRAD IV, MANFRED, and Conradin. Under them S Italy flowered. In 1266 CHARLES I (Charles of Anjou), founder of the Angevin dynasty, became king. He lost Sicily because of an armed revolt (1282) but retained his mainland possessions, which became known as the kingdom of Naples. The Angevins fought the house of Aragón for Sicily until 1373. After 1380 a struggle for succession in Naples began between Charles of Durazzo (see CHARLES III of Naples) and Louis of Anjou (later Louis I of Naples). In 1442 Naples was seized by ALFONSO V of Aragón. Meanwhile, the Angevin

claims had passed to the French crown, and CHARLES VIII of France briefly seized Naples in 1495, thus starting the ITALIAN WARS. The Treaties of Blois (1504–5) gave Naples and Sicily to Spain, and heavy Spanish taxes impoverished the land. In the War of the SPANISH SUCCESSION the kingdom was seized (1707) by Austria, but it was returned (1738) to Spain and ruled by a cadet line of the Spanish BOURBONS. In 1806 the French took Naples, and Joseph Bonaparte (see BONAPARTE, family) was made king. He was succeeded (1808) by Joachim MURAT. In 1815 the Bourbons were restored, and Naples became (1816) part of the kingdom of the TWO SICILIES.

**Napoleon I,** 1769–1821, emperor of the French; b. Ajaccio, Corsica, son of Carlo and Letizia Bonaparte. Young Napoleon was sent to military schools in France and received a commission in the French artillery in 1785. After the start of the FRENCH REVOLUTION, he took part in the Corsican rebellion against Pasquale PAOLI and was forced to leave the island. Returning to France, Bonaparte was associated with the JACOBINS and gained notice by dislodging (1793) the British from Toulon. He was briefly imprisoned in 1794, but his career was reopened when the Convention was assailed (Oct. 1795) by a Parisian mob, and Napoleon was called on to disperse it. Made commander of the army in Italy, Bonaparte conducted the brilliant Italian campaign (1796–97) against Austria, and concluded it with the favourable Treaty of Campo Formio. Bonaparte then drew up a plan to strike at Britain's colonial empire by attacking Egypt. His victory over the Mamelukes in the battle of the Pyramids (July 1798) was made useless when the French fleet was destroyed in Aboukir Bay (1–2 Aug.) by Adm. NELSON. Leaving a hopeless situation in Egypt, Bonaparte returned to France and joined a conspiracy already hatched by Emmanuel SIEYÈS.

*The Consulate.* The French DIRECTORY was overthrown by the coup of 18 Brumaire (9–10 Nov. 1799), and the Consulate was set up with Bonaparte as first consul. He centralized the administration, stabilized the currency, reformed the tax system, and promulgated the Napolenic Code, the basis of a new legal system. He also made peace with the Roman Catholic Church by the CONCORDAT OF 1801. In 1800 Napoleon defeated the Austrians at Marengo, Italy (14 June), and the treaties of Lunéville (1801) and AMIENS (1802) made peace with Austria and Britain respectively. This phase is generally considered to divide the FRENCH REVOLUTIONARY WARS from the Napoleonic Wars. In 1802 Napoleon became first consul for life, and in 1803 Britain again declared war on France. Napoleon had himself crowned emperor in 1804 and was proclaimed king of Italy in 1805, but a third Coalition was formed against him by Britain, Austria, Russia, and Sweden. On land Napoleon crushed the Austrians at Ulm, won (2 Dec. 1805) his most brilliant victory at Austerlitz, over the Austrians and Russians, and defeated Prussia, which joined the coalition in 1806, at Jena (14 Oct.). At sea, however, his navy was defeated at TRAFALGAR at the hands of Nelson and although he then instituted the Continental System to try to halt British trade with France and her allies, he failed to close the seas. On land, war with Russia continued. The indecisive battle of Eylau (8 Feb. 1807) was made good by Napoleon at Friedland (14 June), and the treaties of Tilsit (July 1807) with Russia and Prussia left him master of the Continent. In consequence, the whole map of Europe was rearranged. The HOLY ROMAN EMPIRE was dissolved (1806), and the kingdoms of Holland and Westphalia were created, with Napoleon's brothers Louis and Jérôme Bonaparte (see BONAPARTE, family) as kings. A third brother, Joseph, became (1806) king of Naples and was made (1808) king of Spain. In 1809 Austria's attempt to reopen warfare was defeated at Wagram (6 July), and Napoleon annexed the Papal States to France despite the objections of Pope PIUS VII. In 1809 Napoleon had his marriage to the Empress JOSEPHINE, whom he had married in 1796, annulled and with dynastic ambitions in mind married (1810) MARIE LOUISE of Austria, who bore him a son (see NAPOLEON II). Britain remained a formidable opponent, however, and in the PENINSULAR WAR (1808–14), French armies suffered defeats in Spain and Portugal where WELLINGTON established his reputation. Meanwhile, his alliance with Russia was tenuous, and when Czar ALEXANDER I rejected the Continental System, Napoleon invaded (1812) Russia with the 500,000-man *Grande Armée*. After the indecisive battle of Borodino (7 Sept.), Napoleon entered Moscow, but the winter and lack of supplies forced him to begin a disastrous retreat that became a rout after his troops crossed the Berezina R. in late November. Napoleon left his army and hastened to Paris to prepare French defences. Prussia quickly turned against France and was joined in a coalition by Britain, Sweden, and

Austria. The allies defeated the emperor at Leipzig (Oct. 1813), pursued him into France, and took Paris (Mar. 1814). Napoleon abdicated (11 Apr. 1814) and was exiled to the island of Elba, which the allies gave him as a sovereign principality. His victors were still deliberating at the Congress of VIENNA when Napoleon landed at Cannes and marched on Paris. King LOUIS XVIII fled, and Napoleon ruled during the HUNDRED DAYS. He was defeated, however, by Wellington in the WATERLOO CAMPAIGN (12–18 June 1815) and abdicated again. Sent as a prisoner of war to the lonely British island of SAINT HELENA, he died there of cancer or poison on 5 May 1821. His remains were returned to Paris in 1840. Estimates of Napoleon's place in history differ widely. Beyond doubt one of the greatest conquerors of all time, he also promoted the growth of liberalism and of nationalism through his lasting administrative and legal reforms. His Empire gave its name to a style—in art, furniture and clothes—and his nephew NAPOLEON III, profiting from a Napoleonic legend, proclaimed a Second Empire in 1851.

**Napoleon II,** 1811–32, son of NAPOLEON I and MARIE LOUISE; known as the king of Rome (1811–14), as the prince of Parma (1814–18), and after that as the duke of Reichstadt. Although Napoleon I abdicated (1815) in his favour, he never ruled. After 1815 he was a virtual prisoner in Austria, where he died.

**Napoleon III** (Louis Napoleon Bonaparte), 1808–73, emperor of the French (1852–70); son of Louis BONAPARTE, king of Holland; and nephew of NAPOLEON I. He spent his youth in exile and attempted (1836, 1840) two coups against the French government. Sentenced to life imprisonment, he escaped (1846) to England, returning to France after the FEBRUARY REVOLUTION of 1848. Elected to the National Assembly, he defeated (Dec. 1848) Gen. L.E. Cavaignac in the presidential election by a wide margin. Louis Napoleon's success was due largely to his name, which evoked French nostalgia for past Napoleonic glory. As president of the Second Republic, he consolidated powerful conservative support and instigated the coup of 3 Dec. 1851; the legislative assembly was dissolved, and an attempted workers' uprising was suppressed. Louis Napoleon gained dictatorial powers in the new constitution of Jan. 1852, and after a plebiscite in November overwhelmingly approved the establishment of the Second Empire, he became emperor as Napoleon III. For eight years he exercised authoritarian rule, tempered by material progress. Railway building was encouraged, and Paris was planned with new boulevards and vistas. He was also interested in social reforms. The CRIMEAN WAR (1854–56) and the Congress of PARIS restored French leadership on the Continent. A supporter of Italian nationalism, Napoleon III met with Sardinian premier Camillo CAVOUR and planned a joint campaign with Sardinia to expel Austria from Italy (see RISORGIMENTO). After his costly victory at Solferino (1859), however, Napoleon III made a separate peace with Austria. Having lost popularity, the emperor now began a more liberal domestic policy. Opposition leaders such as Jules Favre and Adolphe THIERS became prominent, although by no means all of his opponents were reconciled. His foreign policy remained ambitious. Cochin China was acquired, and Napoleon supported the building of the SUEZ CANAL. Less fortunate was his intervention (1861–67) in Mexico; US opposition forced a French withdrawal. The FRANCO-PRUSSIAN WAR (1870–71) brought about his downfall. Napoleon took the field himself and was captured at Sedan. He was deposed (4 Sept. 1870) by a bloodless revolution in Paris. After peace was restored, he lived in exile in England with his wife, EUGÉNIE. His only son was killed in Africa while serving in the British army.

**Napoleonic Wars:** see NAPOLEON I.

**Nara,** city (1986 est. pop. 327,356) capital of Nara prefecture, S Honshu, Japan. Founded in 706 by imperial decree, it was an ancient cultural and religious centre having the greatest image of Buddha (Daibutsu). Nara was (710–84) the first permanent capital of Japan. Nara Park, constructed in 1880 and Japan's largest park (506 hectares/1250 acres), includes the celebrated Imperial Museum. Near the city is wooded Mt Kasuga, the traditional home of the gods.

**Nara period,** 710–794, period in Japanese history when Nara was the capital. Close contacts with China were maintained and the influence of China was pervasive. Japan's first chronicles were written, the *Kojiki* (712) and *Nihon Shoki* (720), and a Chinese-style system of government was established. To escape the political influence of the Buddhist clergy, the capital was moved to Kyoto in the years 784–94 and the HEIAN PERIOD followed.

**Narayan, R(asipuram) K(rishnaswamy),** 1906–, Indian novelist. He writes in English. His witty, perceptive novels of Indian life include *The Financial Expert* (1952), *The Vendor of Sweets* (1967), and *Malgudi Days* (1982).

**Narayanganj,** town (1981 pop. 405,562), Bangladesh, on the Lakhya R. some 16 km (10 mi) SE of DHAKA. It is essentially an industrial satellite of that city, engaged in jute baling and milling and in boat-building for shallow-water navigation, for it is also a river port.

**Narcissus,** in Greek mythology, beautiful youth who refused all love, including ECHO's. As punishment for his indifference, he was made to fall in love with his own image in a pool, whereupon he pined away, and turned into a flower. His story occurs prominently in OVID's *Metamorphoses*, and has inspired many painters, e.g., POUSSIN.

**narcissus,** showy-blossomed plant (genus *Narcissus*) of the AMARYLLIS family, native chiefly to the Orient and the Mediterranean region but now widely distributed. The genus includes the yellow daffodil (*N. pseudo-narcissus*), with a long, trumpet-shaped central corona; the yellow jonquil (*N. jonquilla*), with a short corona; and the narcissus, any of several usually white-flowered species, e.g., the poet's narcissus (*N. poetica*), with a red rim on the corona. The biblical ROSE OF SHARON may have been a narcissus.

**narcotic,** any of a group of drugs with potent ANALGESIC effects, associated with alteration of mood and behaviour. The chief narcotic drugs are OPIUM, CODEINE, MORPHINE, and the morphine derivative HEROIN. Narcotics are thought to act by mimicking and/or enhancing the activity of ENDORPHINS, proteins produced by the brain and believed to modulate pain and other nervous system functions. Narcotics are valuable in numbing the senses, alleviating pain, inducing sleep, and relieving diarrhoea. Common side effects include nausea, vomiting, and allergic reactions. In large doses, narcotics can cause respiratory depression, COMA, and death. All narcotics are addictive, including synthetic narcotics, such as METHADONE, which have fewer side effects and are less potent. See DRUG ADDICTION AND DRUG ABUSE.

**Nariño, Antonio** (nah‚reenyoh), 1765–1823, Colombian revolutionary. One of the first to foment revolution against Spanish rule in South America, he suffered imprisonment and exile before becoming president (1811) of a small, newly independent state. He then engaged in civil war to unite the small states, but was defeated (1814) and imprisoned. He served briefly (1821) as vice president of Greater Colombia.

**Narmada** (formerly **Narbada**), river flowing c.1280 km (800 mi) from C India westward to the Arabian Sea, which it enters through an estuary at whose head stands the historic town of Broach. On or near its banks stand the town of JABALPUR and Hoshangabad.

**Narragansett Indians,** NORTH AMERICAN INDIANS of the Eastern Woodlands, speaking an Algonquian language (see AMERICAN INDIAN LANGUAGES). They occupied most of Rhode Island. Survivors of the plague of 1617 in other tribes joined the Narragansett, making them powerful. Their chief Canonicus sold land (1636) to Roger Williams and supported the colonists in the war against the Pequot Indians. They numbered 5000 in 1674, but KING PHILIP'S WAR destroyed Indian power in the region. A few survive today.

**Narses,** c.478–c.573, Roman general under JUSTINIAN I, rival and successor of BELISARIUS in Italy. After defeating TOTILA (552) and an army of Franks and Alemanni (554) he became exarch of Italy, but his administration was unpopular.

**Narutowicz, Gabriel,** 1865–1922, Polish engineer and politician. A hydroelectrical engineer, he was outlawed because of suspected nationalist activities, and went to Switzerland. In 1920–21 he became minister of public works in Poland, and in 1922, foreign minister. His election as president of the Republic in 1922 was unexpected and controversial, being brought about by a grouping of centre, left-wing and minority parties united in opposition to the right-wing National Democrats. Five days after his election he was assassinated by a nationalist extremist.

**Narváez, Pánfilo de** (nah‚vah-eth), c.1470–1528, Spanish CONQUISTADOR. In CUBA he served Diego de VELÁZQUEZ, who in 1520 sent him to MEXICO to recall CORTÉS; he failed. Commissioned to conquer FLORIDA, he arrived there in 1528, sent his ships to Mexico, and led his men inland in search of gold. Disappointed and harassed by Indians, they returned to the coast, built crude vessels, and set sail for Mexico. All save CABEZA DE VACA and three others were lost.

**NASA:** see NATIONAL AERONAUTICS AND SPACE ADMINISTRATION.

**Nash, Beau** (Richard Nash), 1674–1761, English dandy. A leader of society in Bath, he gambled for a living until gaming was outlawed in 1745. He died a poor pensioner.

**Nash, John,** 1752–1835, English architect, best known for his town plans, as in the Marylebone section of London, including Regent's Park (1818). He initiated the REGENCY STYLE and the extensive use of stucco for city building facades.

**Nash, Ogden,** 1902–71, American poet. His humorous verses with their cleverly outrageous rhymes appeared in such volumes as *I'm a Stranger Here Myself* (1938), *You Can't Get There from Here* (1957), and *Bed Riddance* (1970).

**Nash, Paul,** 1889–1946, British painter. After training with B. NICHOLSON (1910–12), he concentrated on landscape painting and became a war artist in 1917, depicting the horrors of World War I. During the 1920s Nash became influenced by the ideas of SURREALISM, including the use of images derived from OBJET TROUVÉ, e.g., *Landscape with Megaliths* (1937). His late landscapes took on a visionary quality, e.g., *Landscape of the Vernal Equinox* (1943–44) and *Eclipse of the Sunflower* (1945). He was unaffected by POST-IMPRESSIONISM and produced works that were influential for the development of 20th-cent. British landscape art.

Paul **Nash**, *Landscape of the Vernal Equinox*, 1943–44. Oil on canvas, 63.5 × 76.2 cm. Edinburgh Museum of Modern Art.

**Nashe, Thomas,** 1567–1601, English satirist and pamphleteer. He was involved in the MARPRELATE CONTROVERSY, and also wrote an imaginative burlesque of the picaresque tale, *The Unfortunate Traveller* (1594); a mock encomium of the red herring, or kipper, *Nashes Lenten Stuffe* (1599); and several plays, some of which were suppressed because of their satirical content. His attack on Gabriel HARVEY, *Have with you to Saffron-Walden* (1596) initiated a vigorous controversy between the two writers.

**Nashik** (formerly Nasik), town (1981 pop. 262,428), Maharashtra state, W India, on a tributary of the Darna R. It is a district administrative centre. It has been a Hindu religious centre since ancient times, and more recently has acquired some industry.

**Nashville,** US city (1984 est. pop. 462,000), state capital of Tennessee; inc. 1806. A Cumberland R. port, cotton centre, and hub of a rail network, it developed from a 1779 settlement. It was named state capital in 1843 and became (1862) an important Union base during the CIVIL WAR. A major agricultural market and important regional centre of finance and industry, it has diversified industries, including insurance, printing, and chemicals. Nashville is famous as a country-music centre and is the site of

the 'Opryland' entertainment complex. The city has many notable buildings of classical design, including a replica (1897) of the PARTHENON.

**Nassau,** city (1970 pop. 3233; met. area 101,503), capital of the BAHAMA ISLANDS. A port on New Providence island, it is the cultural, commercial, and financial heart of the Bahamas and is a famous winter resort. First known as Charles Towne, it was renamed in 1695. Nassau was a rendezvous for pirates in the 18th cent. and was held briefly by American revolutionaries in 1776. It has three old forts.

**Nassau,** former duchy, central West Germany. Most of it is now included in the state of HESSE; a smaller part is in the state of Rhineland-Palatinate. Wiesbaden was the capital. In 1255 the ruling dynasty split into two main lines. Under the Walramian line Nassau became (1806) a duchy and was absorbed (1866) by PRUSSIA. The Walramians succeeded (1890) to the grand duchy of LUXEMBOURG. The Ottonian line of Nassau settled in the Netherlands and became prominent with WILLIAM THE SILENT. Members of the Dutch line, called the house of Orange, became rulers of the Netherlands.

**Nasser, Gamal Abdal,** 1918–70, Egyptian army officer and political leader, first president of the republic of EGYPT (1956–70). In 1952 he led the coup that deposed King FAROUK. He became premier (1954) and president (1956). He nationalized the Suez Canal in 1956, precipitating the short-lived invasion by Britain, France, and Israel. Nasser suffered a disastrous defeat in the 1967 Six-Day War (see ARAB–ISRAELI WARS), but his political support remained strong. He instituted far-reaching land reforms and economic and social development programmes, the most spectacular being the building of the ASWAN HIGH DAM. A pan-Arabist, he was president (1958–61) of the United Arab Republic, a short-lived merger of Egypt and Syria.

**nasturtium** (nəˌstuhsh(ə)m), herb (genus *Tropaeolum*) native to mountainous areas of the American tropics. The common nasturtiums (*T. majus* and *T. minus*) are cultivated for their red or yellow flowers. The plants are also used for food, e.g., the seeds are pickled as capers and the leaves and flowers are used in salads. *Nasturtium* is also the botanical name for the genus that includes the unrelated WATERCRESSES of the MUSTARD family.

**Natal,** city and port (1980 pop. 376,446), NE Brazil, capital of Rio Grande do Norte dept. It was founded in 1597 and was briefly occupied by the Dutch between 1633 and 1654. It lies a short distance from the Atlantic coast on the Potengi R. and has an important commercial port and naval base. It is the commercial and adminstrative centre for the sugar plantations in its hinterland.

**Nathan,** prophet in the time of DAVID and SOLOMON. With his parable of the ewe lamb he denounced David for his abduction of BATH-SHEBA. Later his advice saved the kingdom for Solomon.

**Nathanael,** disciple mentioned only in the Gospel of St JOHN, plausibly identified with St BARTHOLOMEW.

**National Aeronautics and Space Administration** (NASA), US federal civilian agency with the mission of conducting research and developing operational programmes in the areas of manned spaceflight (see SPACE EXPLORATION); lunar, planetary, and interplanetary SPACE PROBES; artificial Earth-orbital satellites (see SATELLITE, ARTIFICIAL.); rocketry; and aeronautics. Its creation on 1 Oct. 1958, was spurred by American unpreparedness at the time the USSR launched (4 Oct. 1957) *Sputnik 1,* the first artificial satellite. NASA's major installations include the Kennedy Space Center, on Merritt Island, north of Cape Canaveral, Florida, where most launchings occur; the Johnson Space Center, Houston, Texas, where US manned spaceflights are controlled; and the Jet Propulsion Laboratory (operated under contract by the California Institute of Technology), Pasadena, California, where the US Viking and Voyager deep-space probes are controlled.

**National Association for the Advancement of Colored People** (NAACP), organization of American blacks, with many white members, dedicated to ending racial inequality and segregation; est. 1910 with the merging of the Niagara Movement of W.E.B. DU BOIS and a group of concerned whites. The organization grew quickly, at first directing its efforts to eradicating lynching; by the 1950s this goal was achieved. The 1954 Supreme Court school-desegregation decision (see INTEGRATION) followed a long effort by the independent NAACP Legal Defense and Education Fund. A consistent advocate of nonviolent protest, the NAACP has at times been accused of passivity by more militant groups. In 1982 its membership was over 500,000.

**National Ballet of Canada:** see DANCE (table).

**National Council for Civil Liberties,** independent British organization (est. 1934) seeking to defend and extend the liberties and rights of individual citizens.

**national debt:** see DEBT, PUBLIC.

**National Front** (NF), extreme right-wing British political formation created (1967) from a merger of the British National Party, the League of Empire Loyalists and the Racial Preservation Society. It campaigns for the repatriation, voluntary or otherwise, of black immigrants. Particularly active in centres of heavy immigrant population, the NF has periodically been banned from staging marches; several prominent members have been prosecuted for incitement to racial hatred. NF parliamentary candidates have made only marginal impact at the polls.

**National Gallery,** London, one of the permanent national art collections of Great Britain, established in 1824. Its Greek-style building was designed (1832–38) by William Wilkins, subsequently much enlarged and was shared for 30 years with the Royal Academy of Arts until the latter was moved to Burlington House, Piccadilly. The nucleus of the collection was formed with 38 pictures from the Angerstein collection. It has fine collections of 15th-, 16th- and 17th- cent. Italian paintings, and French, Flemish, and Dutch masters. The National Portrait Gallery was adjoined to it in 1896.

**National Gallery of Art,** Washington, DC, a branch of the Smithsonian Institution, est. by act of Congress, 1937; opened 1941. Its building and a collection of American portraits were donated by Andrew W. Mellon. The gallery received many important bequests. Its outstanding collections include Italian masterpieces, American naive paintings, French art, prints and drawings, and the Index of American Design. Its East Building, designed by I.M. PEI, opened in 1978.

**National Health Service** (NHS), comprehensive health service established in Britain in 1948, following the BEVERIDGE report (1942), to diagnose and treat physical and mental health free of charge. It consisted of hospital and specialist services, GENERAL PRACTICE, and the public health service (responsible for infectious disease control, maternity and child welfare, and environmental health). The UK was divided into 14 regions in England, and 4 in Scotland, Wales, and Northern Ireland, each Regional Health Authority (RHA) having at least one medical school and teaching hospital. In 1974 a reorganization took place establishing 90 Area Health Authorities (AHAs) in England accountable to the RHA and to the DEPARTMENT OF HEALTH AND SOCIAL SECURITY (DHSS). The NHS was reorganized again in 1982 when the AHAs and that whole tier of management was abolished and replaced by 192 District Health Authorities (DHAs) in England accountable to the RHA and to the DHSS. The NHS is financed by general taxation and resources are allocated by RHAs. The system of management introduced in the 1980s review adapts business methods to the management of the health service at every level and places pressure on the NHS in the search for value for money and increased productivity.

**nationalism,** political philosophy holding that the welfare of the NATION–STATE is paramount, an attitude often strengthened when people share a common history, religion, language, or ethnic background. The term also refers to a group state of mind in which patriotism, or loyalty to one's country, is regarded as an individual's principal duty. Nationalism, which in its modern sense can be traced to the time of the FRENCH REVOLUTION, has played an important part in supplementing the formal institutions of society, providing much of the cohesiveness necessary for the orderly conduct of affairs in modern nations. Although it has contributed to excesses of militarism and IMPERIALISM, as in Europe under NAPOLEON I or under German Nazism (see NATIONAL SOCIALISM), it has also inspired movements against such abuses. It remains a powerful force in world politics despite the spread of trade and communications and the growing interdependence of nations.

**nationalization,** acquisition and operation by a government of businesses formerly owned and operated by private individuals or corporations. In socialist countries it is perceived as a means to social and economic equality. After World War II Communist Eastern Europe nationalized all industry and agriculture; in the UK the Labour government (1945–50) nationalized the electricity, gas, coal, transport, iron and steel industries, and the BANK OF ENGLAND. In many countries transport is controlled by the state. In the UK, however, a policy of PRIVATIZATION was actively being pursued in the 1980s and the practice spread to many other countries throughout the world. Non-Communist countries usually compensate the owners, whereas most Communist nations do not. Nationalization of foreign-owned property, e.g., the Suez Canal Co. by Egypt (1958) and the copper-mining industry by Chile (1971), often occurs in countries where foreign control of industry is resented and poses complex problems for INTERNATIONAL LAW.

**National Organization for Women** (NOW), group est. 1966 to support full equality for women in America; its founder and first president was Betty FRIEDAN. Through legislative lobbying, litigation, and demonstrations it seeks to end discrimination against women. The largest US women's rights group, NOW has over 200,000 members, both women and men. See also FEMINISM.

**National Republican Party,** a short-lived US political party originating in the split in the Republican party after the presidential election of 1824. While supporters of Andrew JACKSON took the name of Democratic Republicans, the conservative Adams–Clay wing became known as National Republicans. Favouring high tariffs and a national bank, the party nominated Henry CLAY in the 1832 presidential election. Clay was badly defeated, and by 1836 the National Republicans had joined with other anti-Jackson forces to form the WHIG PARTY.

**National Savings Bank** (NSB), established in the UK in 1861 as the Post Office Savings Bank. It is the largest organization of its kind in the world with over 20 million active accounts with savings deposits being accepted from the public through the 20,000 or so post offices throughout the UK. Accounts are of two types, ordinary and investment. NSB funds are passed to the National Debt Commissioners which invest them in government Securities. Because the money raised by the NSB contributes toward government spending, tax benefits are offered to savers.

**National Security Council,** US federal executive council established (1947) to coordinate the defence and foreign policy of the US. Its members are the president, vice president, and secretaries of state and defence. Their special advisers are the chairman of the Joint Chiefs of Staff (part of the Defence Dept.) and the director of the CENTRAL INTELLIGENCE AGENCY. The national security adviser heads the council's staff.

**National Socialism** or **Nazism,** doctrines and policies of the National Socialist German Workers' party, which ruled Germany under Adolf HITLER from 1933 until Germany's defeat (1945) in WORLD WAR II, at which time it was outlawed. Members were first called Nazis as a derisive abbreviation. National Socialism appealed to the masses through nationalism, especially by playing on the humiliation suffered by Germany after its defeat in WORLD WAR I, and to activists by a particularly virulent anti-Semitism. It attracted the bankers and industrialists by its hostility to trade unions, to social democracy, and to communism, and by its promise to rebuild the German economy. The party was founded by Anton Drexler as the German Workers Party in 1919, changing its name a year later when Hitler became leader. Amongst the earliest members were GOERING, GOEBBELS, and HIMMLER. Its bible was Hitler's *Mein Kampf* (1923), and its official philosopher was Alfred ROSENBERG. Among the principles of the party were the superiority of the Aryan 'master race' led by an infallible *Führer* (leader); the establishment of a pan-Germanic 'Third Reich', which would last a thousand years; and the annihilation of Germany's 'greatest enemies', the Jews and Communists. After Hitler took power, the Nazis became the sole legal party. Its policy was enforced by the Gestapo (secret police), the SA (storm troops), and the SS (the Führer's elite bodyguard) which later ran the CONCENTRATION CAMPS. During World War II, the Germans imposed their system and dogma on Europe by force. Millions of Jews, Poles, Russians, and others such as homosexuals or communists were interned in concentration camps and executed. Millions more were used for forced labour.

**National Space Development Agency** (NASDA), the Japanese space agency responsible for the development and operation of launch vehicles (such as the N- and H- series; see ROCKET), satellites, space probes, and a manned module for the international SPACE STATION. Its major facilities are the Tsukuba Space Research Centre and the Tanegashima launch site.

**National Theatre of Great Britain,** London, established after many years of planning in 1963, with Laurence OLIVIER, director, at OLD VIC. Peter Hall succeeded Olivier in 1973, and in 1976 it moved to the SOUTH BANK. The company has a repertoire of classics (*Hamlet, Saint Joan*) and new plays like *Equus* (1974) and goes on tour.

**National Trust**, British organization founded in 1895 as a voluntary body able to acquire land of natural beauty and houses of historic and architectural interest to ensure their preservation. The National Trust is now the largest land and property owner in Great Britain. Most of its properties are given or bequeathed by owners, who may continue to live in all or part of the house. Properties are only accepted if they are self-supporting or endowed with sufficient funds to ensure their maintenance. Among the outstanding properties are Knole in Kent, Hardwick Hall in Derbyshire, Nostell priory in Yorkshire, Castle Drogo near Dartmoor, Fountains Abbey and Studley Royal in Yorkshire, and Penrhyn in N Wales. A parallel body is the National Trust for Scotland which owns such properties as Culzean Castle and Crathes Castle as well as small vernacular houses and spectacular mountain scenery. Most of the properties are open to the public as is membership of the Trusts.

**National Union of Women's Suffrage Societies**, umbrella organization formed (1897) to unite women's suffrage societies all over Britain. See WOMEN'S SUFFRAGE.

**National Youth Orchestra of Great Britain**, a training school for young people between the ages of 13 and 18, founded in 1947 by Ruth Railton (created DBE in 1966). The players are selected by audition, and they rehearse and study during the school holiday under a professional conductor. The standards have been very high, and those entering the profession have won scholarships to universities and colleges, and have become established performers and conductors.

**nation–state** or **state**, association of relatively homogeneous people on a defined territory, ruled by a sovereign power (see SOVEREIGNTY), which is recognized for the purposes of diplomacy as an equal member of the international community. Where the population of such a unit exhibits a common history, language, and culture, it is proper to speak of a nation–state. A nation, however, may overlap several states, as Germany now does, and a state may contain more than one nation, as the USSR does. The emergence of the modern nation–state in Europe from the 16th cent. involved a number of processes including the decline of FEUDALISM, the break-up of empires, religious challenges to the universalism of the ROMAN CATHOLIC CHURCH, the unification of smaller principalities, and the concentration and centralization of political power within each state. The growing consciousness of national identity was accelerated by the belief, expressed by the FRENCH REVOLUTION, that every people had a right to self-determination; the aspiration of every nation became to find expression as a sovereign state. Since the 18th cent. the nation–state has become the principal form of political association in the world, and in 1987, 157 nations were represented at the UNITED NATIONS. Speculation that the era of the nation–state might be nearing its end, due to erosion from below (by separatist groups such as the Basques in Spain, the nationalists in Scotland, and the French in Canada) and from above (by suprastate institutions such as the EUROPEAN COMMUNITY) appears to be premature.

**NATO:** see NORTH ATLANTIC TREATY ORGANIZATION.

**Natsume Sōseki**, 1867–1916, Japanese writer. He is considered the greatest novelist of the Meiji and Taishō periods (early 20th cent.), and was also a poet and literary critic. Imbued with the Chinese classics, he lived in London (1900–04) and later became professor of English Literature at Tokyo Univ. One of his main themes is the spiritual stress of modernization and Westernization. His novels include *Botchan* (1906; tr. 1963, 1968), *I am a Cat* (1905; tr. 1906, 1961), *Kokoro* (1914; tr. 1957), and *The Three-Cornered World* (1906; tr. 1965).

**natterjack** or **running toad**, European TOAD of the family Bufonidae. The natterjack (*Bufo calamita*) has very short legs and cannot jump, but it covers the ground very quickly by running. Natterjacks are mainly terrestrial, living in dry, sandy areas, where they can burrow easily. They feed on worms and snails as well as insects and spiders which they catch by running them down, before shooting out their sticky tongues. Natterjacks return to water to breed, those living in sand dunes breeding in brackish water, most unusually for an amphibian. They lay eggs embedded in short strings of jelly. Adult natterjacks are about 8 cm (3½ in) long and can blow themselves up until they are almost spherical when they are alarmed. If they are handled natterjacks exude an unpleasant-smelling white fluid. They are becoming rare in Britain.

**natural childbirth:** see under PREGNANCY AND BIRTH.

**natural gas,** natural mixture of flammable gases found issuing from the ground or obtained from specially driven wells. Largely a mixture of hydrocarbons, natural gas is usually 80–95% METHANE. The composition varies in different localities, and minor components may include carbon dioxide, nitrogen, hydrogen, carbon monoxide, and helium. Often found with petroleum, natural gas also occurs apart from it in sand, sandstone, and limestone deposits. In the late 19th cent. in Britain, plants for the generation of gas from coal were developed and gas was stored under constant pressure in large variable-volume gasometers. Pipelines were laid underground to distribute the gas to houses and industry in most towns and cities to be used for fuel and as an illuminant (a flame heating an incandescent mantle). Natural gas is found widely, especially in the USSR and US, and its discovery in the North Sea (1965) has transformed the gas scene. A huge national grid has been built, delivering 'North Sea' gas all over the UK and making the old gas plants and gasometers redundant. Liquified natural gas (LNG) is natural gas cooled under pressure until it liquifies with considerably reduced volume. In high-pressure containers it is convenient for shipping and storage.

**naturalism,** in literature, an approach to reality grounded in a belief in the determining power of natural forces like heredity and environment. Émile ZOLA, the founder and chief exemplar of the school, theorized in *The Experimental Novel* (1880) that the novelist should observe and record dispassionately, like the scientist. Besides Zola and Guy de MAUPASSANT in France, naturalism included the American novelists Stephen CRANE, Theodore DREISER, and James T. FARRELL, and such modern dramatists as Henrik IBSEN, Gerhart HAUPTMANN, and Maxim GORKY.

**naturalism,** in philosophy, a position that attempts to explain phenomena by means of strictly natural (as opposed to supernatural) categories. Generally considered the opposite of IDEALISM, naturalism looks for causes and takes little account of reasons. It is often (mistakenly) equated with MATERIALISM, POSITIVISM, and EMPIRICISM. Some naturalists (e.g., COMTE, NIETZSCHE, and MARX) have professed ATHEISM, while others (e.g., ARISTOTLE, SPINOZA, and William JAMES) have accepted some form of a deity. Later thinkers such as WHITEHEAD have sought to unify the scientific viewpoint with the concept of an all-encompassing reality.

**naturalization,** official act by which a person is made a national of a country other than his or her native one. In the UK, a naturalized person acquires all the rights, privileges and obligations of native citizens. Under UK law naturalization conditions include a set period of residence, good character, a knowledge of the English language, and an oath of allegiance to the CROWN. Naturalization conditions vary widely. In Switzerland a long residence period is required, whereas any Jew may become an Israeli citizen without having been resident. It is also possible to acquire the citizenship of another country by marriage. See also ALIEN; PARTIAL.

**natural law,** theory that some laws are fundamental to human nature and discoverable by human reason without reference to man-made, or positive, law, which is conditioned by history and subject to continuous change. ROMAN LAW, drawing on theories of Greek STOICISM, recognized a common cause regulating human conduct; this was the basis for the later development by GROTIUS of the theory of international law. St THOMAS AQUINAS, SPINOZA, and LEIBNIZ all interpreted natural law as the basis of ethics and morality. J.J. ROUSSEAU regarded it as the basis of democratic principles. The influence of natural law declined greatly in the 19th cent. under the impact of POSITIVISM, EMPIRICISM, and MATERIALISM, but regained importance in the 20th cent. as a necessary opposition to totalitarian theory.

**natural selection,** important mechanism in Charles DARWIN's theory of EVOLUTION. As a result of various factors in the environment (e.g., temperature and the quantity of food and water available) and the geometrically increasing overproduction of plants and animals that results from the process of reproduction, a struggle for existence arises. In this struggle, according to Darwin, those organisms better adapted to the environment (that is, those having favourable differences or variations) survive and reproduce, while those least fitted do not. Favourable variations among members of the same species are thus transmitted to the survivors' offspring and spread to the entire species over successive generations. Natural selection suggests that the origin and diversification of species results from the gradual accumulation of individual modifications. Artificial selection, the selection by humans of individuals best suited for a specific purpose, is common in plant and animal breeding.

**nature reserve** or **wildlife refuge,** haven or sanctuary for animals and plants in an area of land or land and water set aside and maintained for their preservation and protection. The hunting of pheasants and partridges without the owner's permission was prohibited in Henry VII's time. Closed seasons on certain species of game were in force in 12 of the 13 states of the US by the time of the American Revolution. Yellowstone in the US (see NATIONAL PARKS) was the world's first national park (1872). Sanctuaries have proliferated since the mid-19th cent., together with preserves in America and Africa for big game, larger predators, and nesting birds and, in the US, migratory waterfowl, which supply areas for breeding, wintering, resting, and feeding along major flight paths during MIGRATION. British nature reserves differ from those elsewhere in being generally smaller, more frequented, and further from the primitive state; most are open to the public. In the UK, the National Parks and Access to the Countryside Act (1949) laid down legislation for the creation of national parks and nature reserves, and the Wildlife and Countryside Act (1981) aimed to provide for the protection of individual species, the preservation of habitats, and access to the countryside. The Nature Conservancy Council is the government's wildlife conservation agency. International cooperation began in the latter part of the 19th cent., with the realization that wildlife knows no national boundaries and that legislation and the possibility of prosecution are futile if offenders can avoid penalties by slipping into a neighbouring state. An International Conference for the Protection of the Fauna and Flora of Africa, called by the British government, became binding in 1936 and was not only the foundation for the preservation of wildlife in Africa but also provided the pattern for Asian refuges and for other regions where laws were being formulated. In the Americas, protection of nature became a matter of recognized policy with the signing in Washington, DC, of the Convention on Nature Protection and Wildlife Preservation in the American Republics (1940), which defined the different categories of reserve and set out criteria for their administration. The International Union for the Conservation of Nature and Natural Resources monitors wildlife conditions worldwide. See also CONSERVATION; ENDANGERED SPECIES.

**Nauplia** (now plee·ə), Gr. *Náfplio,* town (pop. c.10,000), Peloponnesus, Greece, on the Argolis peninsula. It has been a port since ancient times, and was briefly the capital of Greece (1829–34). Evidence of its occupation by Venetians, which ended in 1715, it to be seen in its distinctive houses and in the huge Palamidi fortress.

**Nauru,** officially the Republic of Nauru, independent nation (1987 est. pop. 8500), c.20 km² (8 sq mi), atoll in the Pacific Ocean near the equator. One of the world's smallest nations, it has an economy almost entirely dependent on phosphate mining. Nauruans are predominantly Polynesian with heavy intermixtures of Micronesian and Melanesian strains. The official language is Nauruan. Nauru was discovered and named Pleasant Island by the British in 1798. It was annexed by Germany in 1888 and returned to its original name of Nauru. Occupied by Australia in World War I, Nauru was administered by Australia until granted independence in 1968 as a special member of the COMMONWEALTH. It is a parliamentary republic with a president, elected by a legislative council, and a small cabinet. In 1983 Pres. Hammer De Roburt announced that negotiations were in progress with the Philippines for the acquisition of a 'home island' to which Nauru's population could move on the likely exhaustion of phosphate deposits in the 1990s.

**nautilus,** mollusc with a spirally coiled shell consisting of a series of chambers; as the nautilus grows, it builds larger chambers, sealing off the old ones. A CEPHALOPOD, the animal lives in the largest and newest chamber, breathing by means of gills and feeding on crabs and other animals it catches with long, slender tentacles. Nautiluses are found in deep waters of the S Pacific and Indian oceans. The paper nautilus, which is not a true nautilus, is related to the OCTOPUS.

**Navaho Indians** or **Navajo Indians** ( navəhoh), NORTH AMERICAN INDIANS of the SW of the US with an Athabascan language (see AMERICAN INDIAN LANGUAGES). Thought to have migrated from the north, the nomadic Navaho assimilated with the Shoshone and Yuma, but remained a distinct social group with over 50 clans. They farmed, hunted, and gathered plants, but became primarily pastoral after sheep were introduced in the 17th cent. Matrilineal, they have elaborate ceremonies and myths; many practise peyotism. Navaho metalworking, as in silver jewellery, and weaving are famous. The Navaho raided the PUEBLO INDIANS and Spanish settlements in New Mexico until Kit CARSON subdued them (1863–64)

by killing their sheep. In 1868, c.9000 Navaho were given a reservation that has since grown to 16 million acres in Arizona, New Mexico, and Utah, today sustaining such enterprises as timber, mining, and farming. With a population estimated in 1981 at about 160,000, the Navaho constitute the largest tribe in the US.

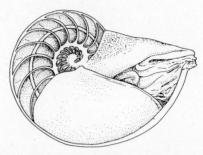

Cross section of a **nautilus** showing successive chambers

**naval conferences,** series of international assemblies that met to consider the limitation of naval armaments, the rules of naval war, and other matters relating to peace. **1 London Naval Conference** (1908–09), see LONDON, DECLARATION OF. **2 Washington Conference** (1921–22), called by Pres. HARDING after WORLD WAR I, resulted in several treaties. The Five-Power Treaty (US, Great Britain, France, Italy, Japan) called for the scrapping of a number of ships so that an agreed-upon ratio could be reached. With the Four-Power Treaty (US, France, Japan, Great Britain) the signatories agreed to respect each others' possessions in the Pacific. Another treaty outlawed the use of poison gas in warfare. **3 Geneva Conference** (1927) failed to reach agreement on more comprehensive limitations on warships. **4 London Conference** (1930) saw Japan succeed in raising its ratios of warships, although France and Italy objected. Also agreed upon was an escalator clause allowing the powers to raise the number of their ships where national security was threatened. **5 London Conference** (1935) was called after Japan announced (1934) that it was withdrawing from the Washington Conference treaties. Despite this, the other powers continued to limit their warships until the outbreak of WORLD WAR II in 1939.

**Navarino, battle of,** Oct. 1827, naval engagement in the Greek War of Independence. It resulted from the refusal of the OTTOMAN EMPIRE (Turkey) to accept the armistice demanded by the European powers (Britain, France, and Russia). Turkey's ally Egypt had a fleet anchored at Pylos (then Navarino); it was attacked and destroyed by the fleet of the European powers. The defeat led Egypt to leave (1828) the war.

**Navarre,** province, N Spain, bordered by France, between the W Pyrenees and the Ebro R. Pamplona is the capital. Navarre's mountain slopes provide cattle pastures and yield hardwoods, and its fertile valleys produce sugar beets, grains, vegetables, and grapes. The population is mainly of BASQUE stock. The kingdom of Navarre reached its zenith under Sancho III (r.1000–35), who ruled most of Christian Spain. Much reduced in area, it came under French rule (1305–28) and regained importance in the HUNDRED YEARS WAR under CHARLES II (r.1349–87). Most of Navarre was annexed (1515) by Spanish king FERDINAND V. Lower Navarre, N of the Pyrenees, remained an independent kingdom until annexed (1589) by France.

**nave,** in general, all that part of a church that extends from the atrium to the altar and is intended for the laity. In a strictly architectural sense, however, the term indicates only the central aisle, excluding side aisles. In Gothic churches, the nave became the main body of the structure. See also BASILICA; CATHEDRAL.

**navigation,** science and technology of finding the position, and directing the course, of vessels and aircraft. In ancient times navigation was based on observing landmarks along the coast and the positions of the sun and the stars. A tremendous advance took place with the introduction (c.12th cent.) of the COMPASS into Europe. Instruments used to find latitude in medieval times included the ASTROLABE, the cross-staff, and the quadrant. The problem of finding the longitude, however, was not satisfactorily solved until the 18th-cent. inventions of the CHRONOMETER and the SEXTANT and the appearance (1765) of the British *Nautical Almanac.* The next great revolution in navigation occurred in the 20th cent., when radio signals came into wide use. The development of RADAR, LORAN, and radio direction-finding during World War II and, subsequently, of NAVIGATION SATELLITES caused fundamental changes in navigational practice.

**Navigation Acts,** in English history, name given to the British Acts of Trade. An outgrowth of MERCANTILISM, the acts were designed to expand the English carrying trade, to provide England with raw materials, and to develop colonial markets for English manufactures. The threat to English shipping posed by the Dutch led to the Navigation Act of 1651. This legislation was substantially reenacted in the First Navigation Act of 1660, which gave England monopolies of certain colonial produce. In 1663 shipment from English ports was required of all foreign goods bound for the American colonies. The Molasses Act of 1733 forced colonists to buy more expensive British West Indian sugar and led to an increase in smuggling. The acts also caused colonial unrest prior to the AMERICAN REVOLUTION. Their adverse effects were felt in Ireland, in Scotland (before 1707), and in the Channel Islands, which did not share England's favoured position. The acts were repealed in 1849.

**navigation satellite,** artificial SATELLITE designed expressly to aid navigation at sea and in the air. Two major navigational satellite systems have been launched into orbit, both by the U.S. In the Transit system (first launch, 1960), a navigator determines a ship's position by measuring the Doppler shift (see DOPPLER EFFECT) in radio signals from a Transit satellite passing overhead. In the NAVSTAR Global Positioning System (GPS), which will eventually replace the Transit system, each satellite will broadcast time and position messages continuously.

**navy,** originally, all ships of a nation, whether for war or commerce; the term now designates only such vessels as are built and maintained specifically for war. The ancient Greeks and Romans had navies, and the famous VIKING ships were organized into small but effective fleets. It was to meet their attacks that ALFRED the Great, in the 9th cent., organized a royal fleet and became the first to realize that a navy was essential to England. Soon after its defeat (1588) of the Spanish ARMADA, the British royal navy became the strongest in the world, ruling the seas for 300 years. British naval power rested not so much on numbers or superior ship construction as on its professional class of officers. During the two world wars naval warfare was revolutionized by such weapons as the torpedo and the rifled naval gun, and even more so by the increasing dominance of the SUBMARINE and the aeroplane (see AIRCRAFT CARRIER). With Germany, Italy, and Japan stripped of their navies and Britain economically weakened, the US emerged with the strongest navy in the world at the end of WORLD WAR II. By the 1980s the Soviet navy, with its huge submarine fleet, was challenging America's naval lead. Nuclear power and weapons have drastically altered naval strategy and tactics.

**Nazarenes,** group of early 19th-cent. German artists who attempted to revive Christian art. Known as the Brotherhood of St Luke, they worked in an unused monastery in Rome. They used early Italian and medieval German pictures as models, working within the limits of religious dogma. They influenced German art and the PRE-RAPHAELITES in England.

**Nazareth,** town (1981 pop. 63,800), N Israel, in GALILEE, the home of JESUS. It is a place of pilgrimage and the trade centre of a farming area. Although first mentioned in the New Testament, it predates historic times. Part of the Ottoman Empire (1517–1918), and of Britain's Palestine mandate (1922–48), Nazareth has been held by Israel since 1948. Many of the Arab population are Christian, but there are now new Jewish quarters.

**Nazarite** or **Nazirite,** in the OLD TESTAMENT, a man dedicated to God. After taking a special vow, he abstained from intoxicating beverages, never cut his hair, and avoided corpses. SAMUEL, the prophet, and SAMSON were Nazarites.

**Nazca** or **Nasca,** ancient Indian culture of S Peru, fl. before AD 1000. The Nazca are known for their polychrome pottery and skilful weaving and dyeing. Aerial exploration of the arid tableland surrounding their valley has revealed a network of lines interspersed with giant animal forms probably related to Nazca astronomy and religion.

**Nazca Lines,** large-scale man-made markings on the ground of parallels, geometrical shapes and the outlines of animals situated 20 km (12 mi) N of the town of Nazca in S Peru. The lines are located in the region where the Nazca civilization reached its highest point of developement at about

**Nazca Lines,** Peru: Part of the Great Rectangle and bird 'condor' figure on Pampa de San Jose

AD 800. A bewildering variety of theories have been advanced concerning the purpose and significance of the Nazca Lines.

**Nazi,** term for member of the National Socialist German Workers' Party. Led by Adolf HITLER after 1920, the Nazis advocated rabid NATIONALISM, ANTI-SEMITISM, and anti-Communism. In the 1933 German election the Nazis were easily the largest party with 43.9% of the votes cast, but they were never to receive an absolute majority from the German people. Their rule (1933–45) in GERMANY ended in defeat during WORLD WAR II. See NATIONAL SOCIALISM; see also CONCENTRATION CAMPS; WAR CRIMES.

**Nazianzen:** see GREGORY NAZIANZEN, SAINT.

**Nb,** chemical symbol of the element NIOBIUM.

**Nd,** chemical symbol of the element NEODYMIUM.

**Ndebele** Bantu-speaking people inhabiting Ndebeleland, W ZIMBABWE. The Ndebele originated as a tribal following in 1823 when Mzilikazi, a general under the ZULU King Shaka, fled with a number of warriors into the Transvaal; they were driven north into their present homeland by the BOERS and the Zulu. After the British suppressed an 1896 revolt, the Ndebele abandoned warfare, becoming herdsmen and farmers.

**N'Djamena,** city (1984 est. pop. 402,000), capital of Chad, on the Chari R. Founded by the French as Fort-Lamy in 1900, it was renamed in 1973. The city is a central African transportation hub, Chad's main administrative centre, and a market for livestock, salt, dates, and grains.

**Ndola,** city (1980 pop. 282,439), N central Zambia, near the border with Zaïre. It is a commercial, manufacturing, and mining centre located in the rich Copperbelt, where copper was mined long before the coming of the Europeans (c.1900). Industries include the production of cement, footwear and soap, and motor-vehicle assembly. Built at the crossroads of trading routes, Ndola was an important slave trade centre.

**Ne,** chemical symbol of the element NEON.

**Neagh, Lough** (nay), largest lake in the British Isles, in E of Northern Ireland. It is approximately 29 km (18 mi) long and 18 km (11 mi) wide. It is fed by the Upper Bann and Blackwater rivers, and drained by the

Lower Bann. The shores of the lake are mainly low-lying, with bogs in places.

**Neanderthal man,** subspecies of HOMO SAPIENS known from finds dating from the last interglacial/early last glacial (30,000–120,000 years ago) in Europe, S Russia, the Middle East, and possibly N Africa. Characteristic features are a long skull with large brain (as big or bigger than that of many modern individuals), sloping frontal, prominent brow ridges and projecting face. Neanderthal people were of short to moderate stature and powerfully muscled. Specimens from W Europe show more extreme development of these features than finds elsewhere. Neanderthals occupied caves or rock shelters, and used fire. Their tools include finely flaked flints (e.g. Mousterian, see STONE AGE) and some bonework; they had rituals concerned with hunting, and with burial (the dead were buried in crouched position). The latest Neanderthal, from St Cesaire, France, is dated c.30,000 BP (Before the Present); the earliest anatomically modern man (Cromagnon) is known by 25,000 BP suggesting that *H. sapiens sapiens*' appearance in Europe results from migration and interbreeding with, rather than *in situ* evolution from, Neanderthals. See also HUMAN EVOLUTION.

**Nebraska,** state of the US (1984 est. pop. 1,606,000), area 200,018 km² (77,227 sq mi), located in the Midwest, bordered by Iowa and Missouri (E), Kansas (S), Colorado (SW), Wyoming (NW), and South Dakota (N). The capital is LINCOLN and the largest city is OMAHA. The land gradually rises from the GREAT PLAINS in the E to the ROCKY MTS in the W, and the shallow, braided Platte R. crosses the state from W to E. The climate is continental. Agriculture is by far the leading source of income, with cattle, corn, pigs, soyabeans, hay, wheat, and sorghum. Food processing is the major industry, and petroleum and natural gas extraction dominate mining. Both Omaha and Lincoln are centres of the insurance industry. In 1980 94% of the population was non-Hispanic white, and nearly 45% lived in metropolitan areas. The Pawnee, Cheyenne, and Arapaho Indians lived by hunting buffalo when first the Spanish (1541) and then the French arrived. Obtained by the US in the LOUISIANA PURCHASE (1803), Nebraska saw many wagon trains pass through in the 19th cent. before the Homestead Act (1862) and the arrival of the railway brought settlers. Farming was severely affected by the drought during the Great Depression, but subsequent federal projects on the MISSOURI R. basin helped extend crop irrigation. The state's agricultural economy remains strong in the 1980s.

**Nebuchadnezzar,** d. 562 BC, king of BABYLONIA (r. c.605–562 BC). In 597 BC he quelled a revolt by Judaea and set ZEDEKIAH on the throne. Putting down a new revolt, he destroyed Jerusalem (586 BC) and took the king and many nobles captive, thus beginning the BABYLONIAN CAPTIVITY. Under Nebuchadnezzar Babylonia flourished, and BABYLON became magnificent. His palace and temples have been excavated. The Old Testament book of Daniel depicts Nebuchadnezzar as a conceited and domineering king, and tells of his going mad and eating grass.

**nebula,** immense body of highly rarified gas and dust in the interstellar spaces of galaxies. A diffuse nebula, such as the CRAB NEBULA, is irregular in shape and ranges up to 100 light-years in diameter. A bright emission nebula, composed primarily of hydrogen gas ionized by nearby hot blue-white stars, radiates its own light; a bright reflection nebula, located near cooler stars, reflects the starlight. A dark nebula, which neither emits nor reflects light because it is too distant from any star, appears as an empty patch in a field of stars or as a dark cloud obscuring part of a bright nebula in the background. A planetary nebula consists of a well-defined shell of gaseous material that glows from the radiation emitted by the central hot star it surrounds. The shell, measuring about 20,000 ASTRONOMICAL UNITS in diameter, is slowly expanding, indicating that it was expelled in a nova or SUPERNOVA explosion. For a long time the diffuse patches of light which we now know to be GALAXIES were also called nebulae (or spiral nebulae for the common spiral galaxies), but this usage has ended.

**Necho** (ˌneekoh), pharaoh (609–593 BC) of EGYPT, of the XXVI dynasty. In the first part of his reign he invaded PALESTINE and SYRIA; his aim was to aid the Assyrians, who were besieged by NEBUCHADNEZZAR and the Babylonians. Defeated on the Euphrates in 605, he returned to Egypt. He later tried to reexcavate the Nile–Red Sea canal and sent Phoenicians on an expedition that may have circumnavigated Africa.

**Neckar,** river, 365 km (228 mi) long, rising in the BLACK FOREST of West Germany and and flowing N through TÜBINGEN, STUTTGART and HEIDELBERG to join the RHINE at MANNHEIM. It is navigable below Stuttgart and the scenery of its basin is renowned.

**Necker, Jacques** (neˌkeə), 1732–1804, French financier and statesman; b. Switzerland. In 1750 he went to Paris and became a banker. He opposed the free trade policies of A.R.J. TURGOT, was named director of the treasury (1776) by LOUIS XVI, and later became director general of finances (1777). By reform and retrenchment measures, and by borrowing at high interest to finance French involvement in the AMERICAN REVOLUTION, he sought to restore the nation's finances. In 1781 he demanded greater reform powers, and resigned when the king refused to widen his powers. Louis XVI recalled him (1788) as director general of finances and minister of state. Acclaimed by the populace, he supported the summoning of the STATES-GENERAL to effect reforms. His dismissal (1789) was followed by the storming of the BASTILLE. Necker was once more recalled to office, but he resigned in 1790.

**nectarine,** name for a tree (*Prunus persica nectarina*) of the ROSE family and for its fruit, a smooth-skinned variety of the PEACH. In appearance, culture, and care the nectarine tree is almost identical to the peach tree. Occasionally a nectarine tree will produce peaches, and a peach tree, nectarines.

**Nedreaas, Torborg,** 1906–, Norwegian novelist. She began writing late in life, after World War II. She is a left-wing writer of feminist novels highlighting social life and struggle in Norwegian urban society, especially *Music from a Blue Well* (1960) and *At the Next New Moon* (1971), about a girl called Herdis growing up in Bergen between the wars.

**Needham, Joseph,** 1900–, English zoologist and historian. A distinguished biochemist, first elected as a fellow of Gonville and Caius College, Cambridge in 1924. Needham's reputation as a historian rests on his multivolume project, *Science and Civilisation in China* (1954–), five volumes of which have appeared. His interest in the subject was awakened while serving in Chongqing as head of a British scientific mission in 1942. He was a strong supporter of the Chinese Communist Revolution and was founder-president of Britain's Society for Anglo-Chinese Understanding. His historical work seeks to identify what was unique in Chinese scientific history and why the history diverged from that of Europe.

**needlepoint,** type of embroidery worked on a cotton or linen mesh with a blunt needle. The mesh, called a canvas, may be printed with a pattern, or original patterns may be created. Wool, cotton, or silk yarns are used, their weight varying with the fineness of the canvas. Among the many needlepoint stitches are tent stitch, Florentine stitch (also called bargello or flame stitch), and cross stitch. Needlepoint worked on a canvas with more than 16 holes per inch is called petit point; with 8 to 16 holes, gros point; and with fewer than 8, quick point. Needlepoint was also known as canvas work; after wool yarn and patterns from Berlin became popular in the 19th cent. it was called Berlin wool work.

**Needles, The,** rocky headland, Isle of Wight, S England, on the English Channel coast. The headland extends from the westernmost extremity of the island, and ends in a group of isolated jagged rocks, which have a needle-like appearance.

The **Needles**

**needlework:** see CROCHET; EMBROIDERY; KNITTING; LACE; QUILTING.

**Nefertiti** or **Nefretete** ('nefə‚teetee, 'nefrə‚teetee), fl. c.1372–1350 BC, queen of Egypt; wife of IKHNATON and aunt of TUTANKHAMEN. The famous and exquisite limestone bust of Nefertiti is in the Berlin Museum.

**Negev** or **Negeb**, hilly desert region of S Israel, c.13,310 km² (5140 sq mi), bordered by the Judaean Hills, and the coastal plain (including the GAZA STRIP) to the north, the Wadi Arabah and the border with Jordan to the east, and the border with the Egyptian province of SINAI to the west; it comprises more than one half of Israel's land area. In the NW Negev, irrigation by the Israelis has reclaimed some fertile land which produces early fruits and vegetables. The region also has a good mineral potential and already produces copper, phosphates, and natural gas. BEERSHEBA, Arad, and ELAT are the Negev's principal cities.

**negligence,** a TORT involving failure to act without the care required by law to protect the rights and PROPERTY of others. Unless more specifically defined by the terms of a CONTRACT, the duty of care is that of the 'reasonable man'. In the UK, negligence, involving duties imposed outside of a contractual action, did not exist until the case of DONOGHUE V. STEVENSON (1932). Negligence is now the most common tort, and takes innumerable forms (e.g., vehicular or industrial accidents). Negligence is usually remedied by the award of damages, though these may be reduced if the injured person has contributed to his or her injuries (e.g., by not wearing a seat belt in a car accident).

**negotiable instrument,** bill of exchange, check, promissory note, or other written contract for payment that may serve as a substitute for money. Transfer of negotiable instruments is easily accomplished and gives the new holder of the contract the right to enforce fulfillment. Like COMMERCIAL PAPER, they were developed to meet the needs of trade.

**Negroid:** see RACE.

**Nehemiah,** book of the Bible: see EZRA.

**Nehemiah,** cup-bearer of the Persian monarch, Artaxerxes I. He was appointed governor of Judah in 445 BC, and continued the organization of religious life already begun by EZRA. By a series of radical economic and social reforms, he helped to alleviate the situation of impending bankruptcy confronting the peasants and small landowners of the country. Like Ezra, his name forms the title of the biblical book covering this period.

**Nehru, Jawaharlal,** 1889–1964, Indian statesman, 1st prime minister of INDIA (1947–64). He was educated at Harrow and Cambridge, and practised as a barrister. After the British massacre of Indians at Amritsar (1919) he became an ardent nationalist. A leader of the INDIAN NATIONAL CONGRESS and an associate of Mohandas GANDHI, he suffered long prison sentences. Unlike Gandhi he favoured industrialization and socialism. He participated in the negotiations that created an independent India in 1947 and served as its prime minister until his death. Although an advocate of nonviolence and neutralism in foreign affairs, he did not hesitate to employ force in opposing Pakistan in Kashmir, in seizing (1961) Goa from the Portuguese, and in resisting (1962) Chinese border incursions. He was the father of Indira GANDHI.

**Neill, A(lexander) S(utherland),** 1883–1973, Scottish educationist. He was most famous for Summerhill, the school he founded in 1921 'to make the school fit the child'. In his writings and at the school he advocated total respect for the child as an individual and Summerhill became the 20th cent.'s best-known 'free activity' school with pupil self-government. He was somewhat outside the main stream of PROGRESSIVE EDUCATION, being more individualistic and libertarian than most of his contemporaries. The school still exists, at Leiston, Suffolk, and takes up to 50 pupils aged 5–16, from many countries. A resurgence of interest in Neill took place in the US in the 1960s, and schools in the image of Summerhill were founded. His writings include *A Dominie's Log* (1915), *That Dreadful School* (1937), *Summerhill's Radical Approach to Education* (1960), and '*Neill! Neill! Orange Peel!*' (1972).

**Nei Mongol Zizhiqu:** see INNER MONGOLIA.

**Nekhtnebf I** ('nekt‚nebəf), king of Egypt (379–361 BC), founder of the XXX dynasty. He saved his country from a Persian invasion in 374, and built splendid temples at Bubastis, MEMPHIS, Abydos, Al Karnak, and Edfu.

**Nekrasov, Nikolai Alekseyevich** (nyi‚krahsəf), 1821–77, Russian poet, editor, and publisher. In his literary journal *The Contemporary* he published early works by DOSTOYEVSKY and TOLSTOY. His poems, notably *The Red-Nosed Frost* (1863), *Russian Women* (1867), and the satirical epic *Who Is Happy in Russia?* (1873), express his compassionate social views.

**nekton,** aquatic animals that swim as opposed to those in the PLANKTON that drift in the currents. Fishes, dolphins, and squid are nektonic animals.

**Nellore,** town (1981 pop. 237,065), Andhra Pradesh state, E India on the Pennar R. It is a district administrative and commercial centre set in a rather poor district. It has pottery and ceramic industries.

**Nelson, Horatio Nelson, Viscount,** 1758–1805, English naval hero of the FRENCH REVOLUTIONARY WARS. His destruction of the French fleet at Aboukir crippled NAPOLEON I's Egyptian expedition. Later stationed at Naples, Nelson fell in love with Emma, Lady HAMILTON, who became his mistress; he was suspected of prolonging his stay there on her account. In 1801, Nelson defeated the Danes at Copenhagen, and in 1805 he achieved his greatest victory, defeating the combined fleets of France and Spain at TRAFALGAR. He was mortally wounded in the action. His statue now stands on a column in London's Trafalgar Square.

**Nelson's Column,** monument in central London. A large column, 58 m (170 ft) high, with a statue of Lord NELSON on the top, it is situated in the middle of Trafalgar Square. The column is surrounded by statues of lions by LANDSEER. These were cast from guns recovered from the wreck of the Royal George.

Nelson's Column

**nematode,** any of a large class of the unsegmented ROUNDWORMS. Nematodes live in the water or soil. Many species, such as roundworms and hookworms, are parasites of plants and animals, including humans.

**Nemery, Mohammed Jaafar al-,** 1930–, army officer and political leader in SUDAN (1969–85). In 1969 he led the leftist military coup that toppled the civilian government. He was elected president (1971) and also became prime minister (1977). An ally of Egypt, he contended with several attempted coups and severe economic problems. In 1985 he was deposed by a military coup while visiting Egypt.

**Nemesis,** in Greek mythology, the avenger; personification of the gods' retribution for violation of sacred law.

**Németh, Károly,** 1924–, Hungarian Communist politician. He was elected president of the country in 1987.

**Nemirovich-Danchenko, Vladimir** (naymi‚rohvich ‚danchengkoh), 1859–1943, Russian stage director. With STANISLAVSKY he founded (1897) the Moscow Art Theatre (see THEATRE, table).

**Nene,** river in E England, approximately 144 km (90 mi) long. It rises just to the SW of Daventry, Northamptonshire, flows E past NORTHAMPTON and Wellingborough, then generally NE past Oundle and PETERBOROUGH, and across the FENS to Wisbech. It enters The Wash near Sutton Bridge. Below PETERBOROUGH it flows in an artificial, straightened channel.

**neocatastrophism,** a term originally used in palaeontology (the study of fossil remains) to refer to the sudden, massive changes in the natural system causing the extinction of all species in one or more major groups of organisms. An example would be the demise of the dinosaurs at the end of the Cretaceous period. The term is now widely used in geology and geomorphology to describe a theory in which processes are episodic in nature, changing from long periods of relative stability to short periods of instability. See also EVOLUTION.

**neoclassicism:** see CLASSICISM.

**neodymium** ('neeoh,dimiəm), (Nd), metallic element, discovered in 1885 by C.A. von Welsbach. A lustrous, silver-yellow member of the LANTHANIDE SERIES of RARE-EARTH METALS, it is present in MONAZITE and bastnasite. Neodymium is used in the manufacture of certain solid-state (glass) lasers. Its oxide is used in colouring spectacles and in an alloy in cigarette-lighter flints. See ELEMENT (table); PERIODIC TABLE.

**neoexpressionism**, international art movement that originated in the late 1970s and early 1980s. Drawing on the traditions of 20th-cent. EXPRESSIONISM and rejecting a sleek modernism and the depersonalization of such movements as MINIMAL ART, neoexpressionism is characterized by violent and often erotic subject matter, an ironic use of kitsch imagery, drawing that is often crude and childlike, and a vigorous painting style. Among the many artists in this varied and individualistic movement are: in the US, Julian Schnabel and David Salle; in Italy, Francesco Clemente and Sandro Chia; and in Germany, A.R. Penck and Georg Baselitz.

**neo-impressionism:** see POSTIMPRESSIONISM.

**Neolithic period,** or New Stone Age, phase in human cultural development identified by the appearance of permanent villages, cultivated grains and domesticated animals, organized pottery and weaving industries. The construction of MEGALITHIC MONUMENTS and tombs provide clear evidence of social differentiation. A wide variation exists in the onset and cultural features of this period in different parts of the world and consequently, the term is best seen as a description of economic adaptation at a regional level. The earliest known Neolithic culture, based on the cultivation of RYE and a primitive WHEAT, developed from the Natufian in SW Asia before 8000 BC. In SE Asia a distinct type of Neolithic culture cultivated rice before 2000 BC. New World peoples independently domesticated plants and animals, and by 1500 BC Neolithic cultures existed in Mexico and South America that led to the AZTEC and INCA civilizations.

**neon** (Ne), gaseous element, discovered in 1898 by William RAMSAY and M.W. Travers. A colourless, odourless, and tasteless INERT GAS, it emits a bright-red glow when conducting electricity in a tube. Neon is used in advertising signs (see LIGHTING), LASERS, Geiger counters, PARTICLE DETECTORS, and high-intensity beacons. Liquid neon is a cryogenic refrigerant. See ELEMENT (table); PERIODIC TABLE.

**neoplasm:** see TUMOUR.

**Neoplatonism,** ancient mystical philosophy based on the later doctrines of PLATO, especially those in the *Timaeus*. Considered the last of the great pagan philosophies, it was developed in the 3rd cent. AD by PLOTINUS. Rejecting DUALISM, he saw reality as one vast hierarchical order containing all the various levels and kinds of existence. At the centre is the One, an incomprehensible, all-sufficient unity that flows out in a radiating process called emanation, giving rise to the Divine Mind, or Logos. The Logos contains all intelligent forms of all individuals. This in turn generates the World Soul, which links the intellectual and material worlds. Despite his mysticism, Plotinus's method was thoroughly rational, based on the logical traditions of the Greeks. Later Neoplatonists grafted onto its body such disparate elements as Eastern mysticism, divination, demonology, and astrology. Neoplatonism, widespread until the 7th cent., was an influence on early Christian thinkers (e.g., ORIGEN) and medieval Jewish and Arab philosophers. It was firmly joined with Christianity by St AUGUSTINE, who was a Neoplatonist before his conversion. Neoplatonism has had a lasting influence on Western metaphysics and MYSTICISM. Philosophers whose works contain elements of Neoplatonism include St THOMAS AQUINAS, BOETHIUS, and HEGEL.

**Nepal,** officially the Kingdom of Nepal, independent kingdom (1987 est. pop. 17,000,000), 132,442 km² (51,136 sq mi), Asia, bordered by China (N) and India (W, S, E). Nepal comprises three major areas: forests and cultivatable land in the south; the towering HIMALAYAS, including Mt EVEREST, in the north; and moderately high mountains, much subject to soil erosion, in the central region, which contains the Katmandu valley and most of the population. The capital is KATMANDU. The economy is overwhelmingly agricultural. Rice, maize, wheat, millet, jute, timber, and potatoes are the principal products. Livestock raising is also important, and manufactures include textiles and rice and sugar mills. Tourism is a major source of foreign income. The GNP is $2576 million and the GNP per capita $160, one of the lowest in the world. The population is mostly very poor, tending to emigrate. About 90% of the people are Hindus.

*History.* A Hindu–Buddhist culture flourished in the Katmandu valley by the 4th cent. AD. In the Middle Ages many small principalities were established. One of these, the GURKHAS, became dominant in 1768. In 1816, after defeat by the British army, Nepal became a protectorate of Britain. Internal power struggles led in 1846 to the dominance of the Rana family, which controlled the country until 1951. Under the Ranas, Nepal was isolated from foreign influence, and there was little economic modernization. Nepal became fully sovereign in 1923, and a limited constitutional monarchy was established in 1951. After a brief period of democracy (1959–60), political activity was banned. A form of partyless government, the panchayat system, was set up (1962), with executive power resting in the king. This system was narrowly approved (1980) in a national referendum, but the opposition Nepali Congress Party continued to have a significant following. King Birendra has occupied the throne since 1972. Long influenced by India, Nepal has developed closer ties with China since the 1960s.

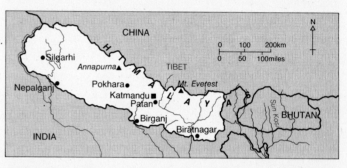

Nepal

**nephrite:** see JADE.

**nephritis:** see KIDNEY.

**Nepos, Cornelius,** b. c.109 BC, in the Po valley, Latin biographer. A friend of CATULLUS and CICERO, but a writer inferior to either, his *Lives of Famous Men* are important because they are the earliest surviving Latin biographies, and the first to compare Romans with foreigners. His aim was popular entertainment and moral uplift, not historical accuracy, but the *Life* of his and Cicero's friend Atticus has some interest and value.

**Neptune,** in astronomy, 8th PLANET from the Sun, at a mean distance of 4496.6 million km (2794.1 million mi). It has an equatorial diameter of c.49,500 km (c.30,760 mi) and an atmosphere composed of hydrogen, helium, methane, and ammonia. Neptune was the first planet to be discovered on the basis of theoretical calculations; such calculations, based on the observed irregularities in the motion of the planet URANUS, were made independently by John Couch ADAMS and Urbain LEVERRIER. The German astronomer Johann Galle discovered Neptune on 23 Sept. 1846, within 1° of the position predicted and sent to him by Leverrier. Neptune has two known natural satellites: Triton (discovered 1846) has an estimated diameter of 1800 to 2600 km (1100 to 1600 mi) and travels in an unusual retrograde orbit; Nereid (discovered 1949) has an estimated diameter of 235 to 470 km (145 to 290 mi). The *Voyager 2* SPACE PROBE is expected to encounter Neptune in 1989.

**Neptune,** in Roman mythology, god of water. Probably an indigenous fertility god, he was later identified with POSEIDON, the Greek god of the sea. He is often represented as an ornamental figure on a fountain, e.g., BERNINI's Trevi fountain at Rome.

**neptunium** (Np), radioactive element, discovered in 1940 by E.M. McMillan and P.H. Abelson by neutron bombardment of uranium. It is a silvery metal in the ACTINIDE SERIES and is the first TRANSURANIC ELEMENT. Neptunium is found in very small quantities in nature in association with uranium ores. The neptunium-237 isotope has a half-life of 2 million years. See ELEMENT (table); PERIODIC TABLE.

**Nereid,** in astronomy, natural satellite of NEPTUNE.

**nereids:** see NYMPH.

**Nernst, Walther Hermann,** 1864–1941, German physicist and chemist. A founder of modern physical chemistry, he won the 1920 Nobel Prize for chemistry for his work in THERMODYNAMICS. He established what is often called the third law of thermodynamics, which deals with the behaviour of matter at temperatures approaching absolute zero. He also did work in electrochemistry, electroacoustics, and astrophysics.

**Nero** (Nero Claudius Caesar), AD 37–68, Roman emperor (r.54–68), the son of Lucius Domitius Ahenobarbus and Agrippina II, who was the great-grandaughter of AUGUSTUS. Agrippina married (AD 49) CLAUDIUS I and persuaded him to adopt Nero. In AD 55, Agrippina saw that she was losing control of Nero and intrigued in favour of Claudius's son, Britannicus, but Nero poisoned the boy. Poppaea Sabina became Nero's mistress, and according to rumour she was to blame for the worst of his behaviour. In AD 59 he murdered his mother and in AD 62 divorced his wife OCTAVIA so as to marry Poppaea (this is recounted in Monteverdi's opera *The Coronation of Poppaea*). When half of Rome was burned in a fire (AD 64), Nero accused the Christians of starting it and began the first Roman persecution. In AD 65 there was a plot to make Caius Calpurnius Piso emperor. The detection of this plot began a string of violent deaths, e.g., of SENECA, LUCAN, and Thrasea Paetus. Nero had ambitions to be a poet and artist. Revolts in AD 68 caused him to commit suicide. Among his last words were, 'What an artist the world is losing in me!'

**Neruda, Jan** (ne͵roodah), 1834–91, Czech writer. His verse ranges from iconoclastic lyric, *Graveyard Flowers* (1858), to the rhapsodic *Ballads and Romances* (1883), to the nationalistically liturgical *Friday Hymns* (1896). He is best known for his *Tales of the Lesser Town* (1878), stories which combine irony with sentimentalization to depict typical Czech petit-bourgeois life.

**Neruda, Pablo,** pseud. of Neftalí Ricardo Reyes Basualto, 1904–73, Chilean poet, diplomat, and Communist leader. From the publication of the early *Veinte poemas de amor y una canción deserperada* (1924; tr. Twenty Love Poems and One Song of Despair) his highly personal poetry brought him enormous acclaim. His evocative poems, filled with grief and despair, proclaim the dramatic Chilean landscape and rage against the exploitation of the Indian. Subsequent volumes include the surrealistic *Residencia en la tierra* (1933; tr. Residence on Earth), the famous *Canto general* (1950) celebrating all of Latin America, and *A New Decade: 1958–1967* (tr. 1969). Neruda received the 1971 Nobel Prize for literature while serving as ambassador to France.

**Nerval, Gérard de,** pseud. of **Gérard Labrunie,** 1808–55, French poet and prose-writer. A contemporary of the Romantics, he has increasingly been recognized as one of the most modern, as well as one of the greatest, French poets thanks to his fusion of mythical and affective elements in the hauntingly beautiful though obscure sonnets of *Les Chimères* (1854) and his plea for a recognition of the visionary and spiritual power of madness in *Aurélia* (1855), which recounts his psychotic episodes and appeared after his suicide.

**nerve:** see NERVOUS SYSTEM.

**nerve gas:** see POISON GAS.

**Nervi, Pier Luigi,** 1891–1979, Italian architectural engineer. In the mid-1940s he developed *ferro-cemento,* a strong, light material consisting of steel mesh and concrete that enabled him to achieve complicated building units for vast, complex structures. His innovations made possible such intricate, beautiful buildings as the exposition halls in Turin (1949–50) and the Olympic buildings in Rome (1956–59).

**nervous system,** network of specialized tissue that controls actions and reactions of the body, enabling it to adjust to its environment. In general the system functions by receiving signals from all parts of the body, relaying them to the BRAIN and SPINAL CORD, and then sending appropriate return signals to muscles and body organs. Virtually all multicellular animals have at least a rudimentary nervous system; the system is most complex in vertebrates. The basic unit of the nervous system is the nerve cell (neurone). Of the billions of neurones in humans, half are in the brain. The neuron consists of a cell body, containing the cell nucleus; dendrites, branchlike extensions that receive incoming signals; and the axon, the long cell extension that carries signals long distances. A neurone works by receiving chemical signals, some excitatory, some

inhibitory, through its dendrites and sending electrical impulses along its axon. Chemical transmitters (neurotransmitters) released at the terminal fibres of the axon diffuse across a junction called the synapse and bind to dendrites of recipient neurones (see ACETYLCHOLINE; NORADRENALINE). Dendrites and axons are called nerve fibres; a nerve is a bundle of nerve fibres. The nervous system has two major divisions: the central nervous system and the peripheral nervous system. The central nervous system, consisting of the brain and spinal cord, receives impulses from sensory (afferent) nerve fibres delivering impulses from receptors in the skin and organs; it returns impulses via motor (efferent) fibres to terminals in muscles and glands. Peripheral nerves mediate these pathways. The peripheral nervous system comprises cranial nerves, controlling face and neck; spinal nerves, radiating to other parts of the body; and autonomic nerves. The latter form a subsidiary system, the autonomic nervous system, which is itself divided into the sympathetic and parasympathetic nervous systems, regulating the iris of the eye and muscles of heart, glands, genitals, lungs, stomach, and other organs. The sympathetic and parasympathetic nervous systems act in opposition in certain organs, with the sympathetic system increasing the rate and strength of heartbeat, causing contraction of blood vessels, depressing secretion of digestive juices, and decreasing the tension and contractility of smooth muscle (see MUSCLE), and with the parasympathetic system having the opposite effects.

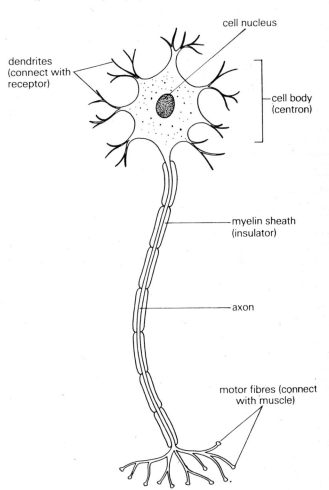

**Nervous system:** Structure of a neurone

**Nestorianism,** 5th-cent. heresy advanced by Nestorius (d. 451?), patriarch of Constantinople. It declared that Jesus was two distinct persons, one human, one divine. Nestorius opposed the title of Mother of God for the Virgin, contending that she bore Jesus only as a man. The councils of Ephesus (431) and Chalcedon (451) set out the orthodox Catholic view that Jesus's two natures are inseparably joined in one person and partake of the one divine substance. The Nestorian Church that was formed in Persia has few connections today with Nestorianism.

**Netherlands,** Dutch *Nederland,* officially the Kingdom of the Netherlands, constitutional monarchy (1985 est. pop. 14,506,000), 41,344 km² (15,963 sq mi), NW Europe, popularly known as Holland; bordered by the North Sea (N and W), Belgium (S), and West Germany (E). Major cities include AMSTERDAM, the legal and administrative capital; The HAGUE, seat of government; and ROTTERDAM. About 40% of the land is situated below sea level and is guarded by dunes and dykes. The country is crossed by drainage canals, and the main rivers are interconnected with artificial waterways. Despite one of the world's highest population densities, the Netherlands maintains a high standard of living. Industry provides 40% of national income, primarily from textiles, machinery, electrical equipment, iron and steel, refined petroleum, processed foods, ships, and chemicals. Agricultural commodities include dairy products (especially cheese), poultry, and horticultural goods (especially bulbs). Foreign trade, the financial industry, and tourism are very important. Large natural gas reserves supply over half of the country's energy needs; natural gas is a major export. The GNP is $142,420 million and the GNP per capita is $9910 (1983). The population has nearly equal numbers of Protestants (mostly Calvinists) and Roman Catholics. Dutch is the almost universal language. The Kingdom of the Netherlands also incorporates the NETHERLANDS ANTILLES and ARUBA.

*History.* Settled in Roman times by Germanic tribes, the LOW COUNTRIES (the Netherlands, Belgium, Luxembourg) passed successively to the Franks (4th–8th cent.), the Holy Roman Empire (10th cent.), and the dukes of BURGUNDY (14th–15th cent.); they came under HABSBURG rule after 1477 (see NETHERLANDS, AUSTRIAN AND SPANISH). In 1579 the northern provinces under WILLIAM THE SILENT broke away from Spain and formed the Union of Utrecht. Independence was declared in 1581, but the new nation the United Provinces was not formally recognized until 1648, after the THIRTY YEARS' WAR. The 17th cent., the Netherlands' golden age, was a time of commercial prosperity, colonial expansion, religious tolerance, and cultural achievement (see DUTCH WARS; DUTCH WEST INDIA COMPANY; EAST INDIA COMPANY, DUTCH; REMBRANDT; SPINOZA; VERMEER). In the 18th cent. this supremacy was lost to England and France. Conquered by the French during the FRENCH REVOLUTIONARY WARS, the United Provinces were reconstituted (1795) as the BATAVIAN REPUBLIC; transformed (1806) by NAPOLEON I into the kingdom of Holland under Louis Bonaparte (see BONAPARTE, family); and finally, at the Congress of VIENNA (1814–15), united with present-day Belgium as the kingdom of the Netherlands. Belgium seceded in 1830. Neutral in WORLD WAR I, the Netherlands suffered severely during the German occupation (1940–45) in WORLD WAR II. Postwar recovery was rapid, despite the loss of the eastern empire (the Netherlands gave INDONESIA independence in 1949 and relinquished Netherlands NEW GUINEA in 1962) and disastrous floods in 1953. Under a series of coalition governments, the Dutch economy (especially the industrial sector) expanded greatly and the country took a leading role in Western European integration, joining the BENELUX ECONOMIC UNION and the EUROPEAN COMMUNITY; the Netherlands was also a founder member of the NORTH ATLANTIC TREATY ORGANIZATION. Queen BEATRIX ascended the nation's throne in 1980. In the 1986 elections nine parties secured representation in the 150-seat second chamber, the outcome being the formation of a further centre-right coalition.

**Post-war prime ministers of the Netherlands**
Willem Schermerhorn (non-party), 1945–46
Louis Beel (Christian Democrat), 1946–48
Willem Drees (Labour), 1948–58
Louis Beel (Christian Democrat), 1958–59
Jan de Quay (Christian Democrat), 1959–63
Victor Marijnen (Christian Democrat), 1963–65
Joseph Cals (Christian Democrat), 1965–66
Jelle Zijlstra (Christian Democrat), 1966–67
Piet de Jong (Christian Democrat), 1967–71
Barend Biesheuvel (Christian Democrat), 1971–73
Joop den Uyl (Labour), 1973–77
Andreas van Agt (Christian Democrat), 1977–82
Ruud Lubbers (Christian Democrat), 1982–

**Netherlands, Austrian and Spanish,** that part of the Low countries controlled from 1482 to 1794 by the HABSBURG dynasty. The harsh rule of the Spanish Habsburgs led to a revolt (16th–17th cent.) by which the northern provinces gained independence as the United Provinces of the NETHERLANDS. The Peace of Utrecht transferred (1714) the remaining

Netherlands

Spanish lands to the Austrian branch of the Habsburgs. French armies seized the area in 1794. For its later history, see BELGIUM and LUXEMBOURG.

**Netherlands Antilles,** islands (1984 est. pop. 200,000) 882 km (302 sq mi), West Indies, an autonomous part of the Kingdom of the Netherlands. They are in two groups. The Leewards (including CURACAO) lie off Venezuela and the Windwards (including SAINT MARTIN) are east of PUERTO RICO. Autonomy was granted in 1954. Formerly part of the Netherlands Antilles, the island of ARUBA achieved separate autonomous status in 1984.

**nettle,** common name for the family Urticaceae, fibrous herbs, small shrubs, and trees found chiefly in the tropics and subtropics. Several species are covered with small stinging hairs that on contact emit a skin irritant. Stinging nettles include species of *Urtica,* widely distributed, and species of *Laportea,* a group of tropical and subtropical herbs, shrubs, and trees.

**Netzahualcóyotl** (netsahwahl,koyohtəl), city (1979 est. pop. 2,331,351), S central Mexico. It is a rapidly growing communications centre and residential community near Mexico City.

**Neuchâtel** (,nuhsha'tel), city (1984 pop. 33,700), capital of Neuchâtel canton in NW Switzerland, on Lake Neuchâtel. A university city, it is a centre of the wine trade and of the watch and clock-making industry. The 'new castle' which gives the city its name was built in the 5th cent. It was a county of the HOLY ROMAN EMPIRE, and later passed into the possession of the French house of Orléans–Longueville and (1707) of the Kings of Prussia. It became a Swiss canton in 1815.

**Neue Sachlichkeit** ('noyes,ahklikiet), [Ger., = new objectivity], a term used in art in 1923 to describe the growing interest in a new realistic representation. This was both in terms of technique, as a reaction against IMPRESSIONISM and EXPRESSIONISM, and in terms of subject, as a reaction against the excesses of the emotional and spiritual content of pre-World War I expressionist art. An exhibition in Mannheim in 1925 used the label and included the work of GROSZ and DIX.

**neuralgia,** acute, throbbing pain along a peripheral sensory nerve (see NERVOUS SYSTEM), commonly in the area of the facial, or trigeminal, nerve.

Its causes include SHINGLES, infections, and extreme cold. Unlike NEURITIS, neuralgia does not involve degeneration of the nerve tissue.

**neural tube defect,** congenital defect of the brain or spinal cord (see CONGENITAL ABNORMALITIES) resulting from defective development of the neural tube (embryonic central nervous system) and usually accompanied by malformation of the skull or backbone. In the relatively common case of spina bifida (which can be diagnosed with AMNIOCENTESIS), the bony arches of the spine that protect the SPINAL CORD fail to develop or close properly, often allowing the membranes surrounding the spinal cord to protrude. Neural tube defects cause varying degrees of neurological conditions and mental and physical handicap.

**neuritis,** inflammation of a peripheral nerve (see NERVOUS SYSTEM), often accompanied by degenerative changes in nerve tissue. Sensory nerve involvement causes a tingling sensation or loss of sensation, while symptoms of motor nerve involvement range from slight loss of muscle tone to paralysis. Neuritis commonly occurs in DIABETES, SHINGLES, rheumatoid ARTHRITIS, and other disorders. Treatment varies, depending on the cause.

**neurosis,** a mental disturbance or disorder, not attributable to neurological or other organic impairment, involving one or more of: excessive and inappropriate ANXIETY, PHOBIA, HYSTERIA, compulsive or obsessive behaviour, psychosomatic symptoms. Generally, any enduring non-organic mental disorder in which the individual experiences distress, but does not, unlike in PSYCHOSIS, experience loss of touch with reality, is classified as neurotic. Treatment of the neuroses forms the basis of the therapeutic practice of PSYCHOANALYSIS.

**Neuss** (noys), city (1984 pop. 144,800), North Rhine–Westphalia, W West Germany. Of Roman origin, its early prosperity was based on the trade route which followed the west bank of the RHINE. When that river changed its course, Neuss declined in favour of DÜSSELDORF. It has revived with modern industries which include soap and margarine manufacture and the making of farm machinery.

**Neutra, Richard Joseph,** 1892–1970, American architect; b. Austria. He worked in Los Angeles after 1926, adhering to a functionalist approach (see MODERN ARCHITECTURE), e.g., the Lovell House (1929) and Northridge Medical Arts Building (1968).

**Neutrality Act,** 1935, law designed to keep the US out of a possible European war by banning shipment of war material to belligerents and forbidding US citizens to travel on belligerent vessels except at their own risk. A second Neutrality Act (1936) forbade loans or credits to belligerents and a third (1937) made travel on belligerent ships unlawful. Later revisions and the LEND-LEASE Act of 1941 made the laws practically inoperable even before American neutrality ended with the PEARL HARBOR attack.

**neutralization:** see ACIDS AND BASES; TITRATION.

**neutrino,** ELEMENTARY PARTICLE emitted during the decay of certain other particles. It was first postulated in 1930 by Wolfgang PAULI in order to maintain the law of conservation of energy during BETA-DECAY. Further studies showed that the neutrino was also necessary to maintain the conservation laws of momentum and angular momentum. The neutrino was not detected directly until 1956. The neutrinos associated with the electron, muon and tauon are distinct; each has its own antiparticle. Neutrinos are stable; they are created and destroyed only by particle decays involving the weak nuclear force or interaction (see FORCE). Neutrinos have SPIN½ and little or no mass.

**neutron,** uncharged ELEMENTARY PARTICLE, discovered by James CHADWICK in 1932, of slightly greater mass than the PROTON. The stable isotopes of all elements except hydrogen contain within the nucleus a number of neutrons equal to or greater than the number of protons. The preponderance of neutrons becomes more marked for very heavy nuclei. A free neutron is unstable and converts by BETA DECAY into a proton, an electron and an antineutrino (see RADIOACTIVITY). However, when bound within a nucleus, because of energy conservation reasons, the neutron is in general stable except when the excess of neutrons in the nucleus is too large; the nucleus then beta decays. The neutron and the proton are regarded by physicists as two aspects, or states, of a single entity, the nucleon. The antineutron, the neutron's antiparticle (see ANTIMATTER), was discovered in 1956.

**neutron bomb:** see HYDROGEN BOMB.

**neutron star,** extremely small, extremely dense star comparable to the Sun in mass but only a few miles in radius. At these enormous densities, matter is largely in the form of NEUTRONS, their resistance to yet tighter packing being sufficient, for a range of mass, to support the star against collapse under its own immense gravitational force. Though the existence of neutron stars had long been anticipated theoretically, it was only the discovery of pulsars by HEWISH and Bell and their identification with rotating neutron stars by GOLD that confirmed their existence observationally. Neutron stars are believed to be the dead stellar corpses remaining after the SUPERNOVA explosion of an intermediate-mass star. See GRAVITATIONAL COLLAPSE; PULSAR; STELLAR EVOLUTION.

**Nevada,** state of the US (1984 est. pop. 911,000), area 286,299 km² (110,540 sq mi), located in the W, bordered by Oregon and Idaho (N), Utah and Arizona (E), and California (SW,W). CARSON CITY is the capital, and LAS VEGAS and Reno are the largest cities. The state lies mostly within the GREAT BASIN, and mountain ranges and plateaus alternate with valleys. The COLORADO R. flows along the southwestern border where HOOVER DAM forms Lake MEAD, the largest of many water projects in this arid state. Over 85% of the land is controlled by the federal government. Tourism is the largest source of income, attracted to the legalized gambling and nightlife of Las Vegas, and to the resort at Lake Tahoe. Nevada is the leading producer of mercury and barite; fluorspar, pumice, tungsten, gold, copper, and silver are also mined. Industry is dominated by food processing, building materials, and nonelectrical equipment. Agriculture is of little significance. Between 1970 and 1980 Nevada had the fastest rate of population growth of any state (63.5%). After Nevada was ceded by Mexico to the US in 1846, population growth began with the discovery of silver (1858), and thereafter the economy depended upon the silver market. During the 20th cent. the federal government invested in water projects and military installations, despite local opposition to federal land ownership in the 1970s. A huge expansion of high-technology industries since the 1970s has helped make Nevada the fastest growing state in the SUN BELT.

**Nevins, Allan,** 1890–1971, American historian. A prolific writer in many areas of history, including business history, he taught at Columbia Univ. (1928–58). His biographies include *Grover Cleveland* (1932) and *Hamilton Fish* (1936). *The Ordeal of the Union* (8 vol., 1947–71) is a comprehensive history of the CIVIL WAR era. Nevins established the nation's first oral-history programme at Columbia.

**Newark,** US city (1984 est. pop. 314,000), NE New Jersey, on the Passaic R. and Newark Bay; settled 1666, inc. as a city 1836. Only 13 km (8 mi) from New York City, it is the largest city in New Jersey, and a major port. Among its diversified industries, leather, jewellery manufacture, and insurance have long histories. Newark is also a financial centre and has many state government offices. The city has lost industry since the 1930s, and its population has declined since the 1950s, dipping by nearly 14% between 1970 and 1980.

**Newbery, John,** 1713–67, English publisher who established CHILDREN'S LITERATURE as an important branch of the field. Among his publications is *Little Goody Two Shoes* (1766). The Newbery Medal (est. 1922) is named after him.

**New Brunswick,** province of Canada (1984 est. pop. 714,200), area 73,436 km² (28,354 sq mi), situated in the E, bordered by Quebec (N), the Gulf of St Lawrence and Nova Scotia (E), the Bay of Fundy (S), and Maine, US (W). Fredericton is the capital, and St John is the principal city; 53% of the population is urban. One of the Maritime Provinces, New Brunswick has a rolling countryside, dissected by tributaries of the St John R., where exceptionally high tides cause the famous 'reversing falls', and by the Miramichi R. The irregular coastline provides many harbours and supports an extensive fishing industry. Timber is the major industry, agriculture is important, and, since the 1940s, manufacturing and mining (chiefly of zinc) have expanded. One-third of the population speak French as a mother-tongue, and New Brunswick is the only officially bilingual province. The original inhabitants were Micmac Indians when the area became part of the French region of Acadia (1604). In 1713 the British gained control and expelled many of the Acadians (1755, 1758), some of whom moved to Louisiana, US. After the American Revolution many United Empire Loyalists settled in the area, making it a separate colony (1784). New Brunswick was one of the four original provinces of the dominion of Canada (1867). In the late 19th cent. the leadership of the economy moved to central Canada, and a long period of poverty and stagnation followed. Since the 1960s a small industrial base and government aid have revived the fortunes of New Brunswick.

**New Caledonia,** French overseas territory (1979 est. pop. 137,000), 18,342 km² (7082 sq mi), land area in the South Pacific. It comprises New Caledonia, the Isle of Pines, the Loyalty Islands, and smaller islands; Nouméa is the capital. Industries include iron and nickel mining, and coffee and copra production. Captain COOK sighted (1774) the main island; France annexed it in 1853. A strong and often violent pro-independence movement developed in the 1970s among the Melanesian (Kanak) population (constituting just under half the total) but has been fiercely resisted by the French settlers and other groups, whose political parties have dominated recent elections.

**Newcastle,** city (1986 pop. 255,787), urban agglomeration, New South Wales, SE Australia, on the Pacific Ocean. It is a major port, Australia's second largest by cargo handled, and the centre of the country's largest coal-mining area. Manufactures include steel, chemicals, and ships. The city was settled in 1804, and has one university.

**Newcastle upon Tyne,** city (1981 pop. 199,064), in Tyne and Wear, NE England, on R. Tyne 17 km (10 mi) upstream of the river mouth. It is a commercial and industrial centre, and a port town. Industries found in the town include shipbuilding, coal-mining and the manufacture of chemicals. There are the remains of a 12th-cent. castle and the 13th-cent. town walls. The cathedral of St Nicholas dates mainly from the 14th cent.

**Newcomb, Simon,** 1835–1909, American astronomer. He was director (1877–97) of the *American Nautical Almanac*. Newcomb's investigations and computations of the orbits of six planets enabled him to construct tables of their predicted motions, which were almost universally adopted by the world's observatories. In addition, his long study of the Moon's motion allowed him to establish formulae that made possible the compilation of accurate lunar tables.

**Newcomen, Thomas,** 1663–1729, English inventor of an early atmospheric STEAM ENGINE (c.1711) used to pump water. It was an improvement over Thomas Savery's engine (patented 1698).

**New Deal,** in US history, term for the domestic reform programme of Pres. F.D. ROOSEVELT. It had two phases. The first (1933–34) attempted to provide recovery and relief from the GREAT DEPRESSION through programmes of agricultural and business regulation, inflation, price stabilization, and public works; numerous emergency organizations, e.g., the National Recovery Administration, were established. The second (1935–41) while continuing with relief and recovery measures, provided for social and economic legislation, e.g., SOCIAL SECURITY, to benefit the mass of working people. Neither phase succeeded completely in restoring prosperity. A number of New Deal measures were invalidated by the SUPREME COURT, and the programme, which had been enthusiastically endorsed by agrarian, liberal, and labour groups, was increasingly criticized by conservatives. Nonetheless, at the end of World War II most New Deal legislation was still intact.

**New Delhi,** city (1981 pop. 273,636), capital of India, DELHI union territory, N central India. Built (1912–29) to replace CALCUTTA as the capital, it was inaugurated in 1931. It has textile mills, printing plants, and light industry. New Delhi's broad streets provide vistas of historic monuments. GANDHI was assassinated (1948) at a prayer ground in the city.

**New Economic Policy** (NEP), official economic programme of the USSR, 1921–28. Initiated by LENIN, the NEP replaced the 'war Communism' of the 1918–21 civil war period, which had caused scarcity and popular unrest. Under the NEP peasants could sell some of their produce for a profit and small businesses could operate privately. The first FIVE-YEAR PLAN supplanted the NEP.

**New England,** region in New South Wales, SE Australia. As part of the GREAT DIVIDING RANGE, the tableland runs 320 km (200 mi) N–S and 130 km (80 mi) E–W, rising to an elevation of 1200 to 1500 m (4000 to 5000 ft), and extends from the Granite Belt of Queensland to the Darling Downs of New South Wales. The main activity is wool production and beef-cattle raising. The main centre is ARMIDALE.

**New England,** region of the NE US, comprising MAINE, NEW HAMPSHIRE, VERMONT, MASSACHUSETTS, RHODE ISLAND, and CONNECTICUT. Agriculture was never important owing to the poor, rocky soil, but excellent harbours and fisheries made it a commercial centre. Manufacturing grew rapidly in the 19th cent. and has since dominated the economy. Traditional industries, e.g., shoes and textiles, have largely been superseded by electronics and tourism. New England was the centre of many of the historical events that led to the AMERICAN REVOLUTION.

**New England Confederation,** 1643–1684, union for 'mutual safety and welfare' formed by the English colonies in America of Massachusetts Bay, Plymouth, Connecticut, and New Haven. It was weakened by rivalry among the colonies and its inability to do more than advise. Its most important action was to break the power of the Indians in KING PHILIP'S WAR.

**New Forest,** area of heath and woodland in Hampshire, S England, extending W from Southampton. It covers an area of approximately 390 sq km (150 sq mi), about two-thirds of which are crown lands. It was newly forested in the 11th cent. for William 1. The famous New Forest wild ponies roam at large.

**Newfoundland,** province of Canada (1984 est. pop. 579,000), area 404,517 km² (156,184 sq mi), located in the E, consisting of the island of Newfoundland, lying at the mouth of the Gulf of St Lawrence and bounded by the Atlantic Ocean, and the mainland area of Labrador, bordered by the Atlantic Ocean (E) and Quebec (W). St John's, the capital and Corner Brook are the principal cities, both on the island; 50% of the population lives in urban areas. Labrador's terrain is barren, rocky and covered in lakes, with a heavily indented coastline and forested river valleys which are suitable for hydroelectric power. Newfoundland is also rugged, the interior drainage was disrupted by glaciation, and the coast is indented; there is a strip of lowland along the NE coast. The province's economy depends upon primary industry. Although cold and isolated, Labrador is rich in mineral resources, notably iron, and mining is the main industry; timber is also important. The fishing area of the Grand Banks, where the cold Labrador current meets the Atlantic, is probably the best in the world for catching cod, lobster, herring, and salmon. There is a small Inuit population, and pockets of Francophones on the island; 50% of the population lives in urban areas. Vikings briefly established a settlement in the area (c. 1000), and in the late 16th cent. both France and England contested control. Awarded to Britain at the Treaty of Paris (1763), the area was run dictatorially by English merchants until responsible government (1855). Voters rejected union with Canada (1869) and possession of Labrador was contested between Newfoundland and Quebec until 1927. In the 1930s Newfoundland was bankrupted and became governed by joint commission with Britain. In World War II the opening of many military bases revived the economy, enabling Newfoundland to become the 10th and last province (1949). Subsequent prosperity was based on primary industry rather than manufacturing, although the prospect of offshore oil and natural gas promises a degree of wealth.

**New General Catalogue,** (NGC), standard reference list of 7840 nebulous celestial objects published by the Danish astronomer J.L.E. Dreyer in 1888, basing his work on that of John HERSCHEL. Two supplements (1895, 1908), called Index Catalogues (IC), brought the list to over 13,000 objects, more than 12,000 of which are galaxies.

**New Granada,** former Spanish colony, N South America, that included at its greatest extent modern Colombia, Ecuador, Panama, and Venezuela. Colonized by Spain in the 16th cent., the area was called 'the new realm of Granada' by the explorer JIMÉNEZ DE QUESADA. Civil government was established in 1549 and the area was made a viceroyalty in 1717. After independence (1819) it became the state of Greater Colombia, but by 1830 Ecuador and Venezuela had seceded. The remainder (Colombia and Panama) became the Republic of New Granada and later (1886) the Republic of Colombia, from which Panama seceded in 1903.

**New Grange,** an elaborately constructed and decorated passage grave (see MEGALITHIC MONUMENTS), one of a group located near the bank of the river Boyne in Ireland. Dating from the late 4th millennium BC, the very long tomb passage (19 m/60 ft) leads to a cruciform burial chamber with a corbelled roof. The interior is decorated with a variety of pecked geometric designs. The tomb has an astronomical orientation: the chamber is illuminated at sunrise on the winter solstice through an opening above the door (see ARCHAEOASTRONOMY).

New Grange grave entrance

**New Guinea,** world's second largest island (after Greenland), c.885,780 km² (342,000 sq mi), in the SW Pacific Ocean N of Australia. It is c.2410 km (1500 mi) long and c.640 km (400 mi) wide. Djaja Peak (5030 m/16,503 ft) is the highest point in the mountainous interior. The island is politically divided between Indonesia (W) and Papua New Guinea (E). Headhunting and cannibalism are still practised in some inaccessible regions. The inhabitants include Melanesians, Papuans, and Negritos.

**Newham,** London borough (1981 pop. 209,128), on N side of R. Thames, bounded by R. Lea in the W and R. Roding in the E. It contains the towns of East and West Ham and the Royal Victoria, Royal Albert, and King George V docks.

**New Hampshire,** state of the US (1984 est. pop. 977,000), area 24,097 km² (9304 sq mi), situated in New England, NE US, bordered by Massachusetts (S), Vermont (W), Maine and the Atlantic Ocean (E), and the Canadian province of Quebec (NW). CONCORD is the capital, and Manchester the largest city; only c.36% of the population lived in metropolitan areas in 1980. The state is hilly or mountainous, except for the Connecticut R. valley along the W border and the coastal plain in the E. The winters are severe and the summers are cool. Manufacturing dominates the economy; electrical equipment, nonelectrical machinery, paper, leather goods, and textiles are important. The leading farm products are dairy products, eggs, greenhouse products, apples, hay, and maple syrup. Forestry and tourism add to the state's revenue. In 1980 98% of the population was non-Hispanic white. Settlement by the Puritans began in the 1620s, and New Hampshire was the first state to declare its independence from Great Britain (1776). In the 19th cent. the state thrived on water-powered textile manufacture, which declined in the 1930s. In recent years a low tax rate has helped to attract electronics industries, leading to rapid population growth and economic prosperity. New Hampshire is traditionally the first state to hold primary elections in the campaign for the presidency of the US.

**Newhaven,** US city (1984 est. pop. 124,000), S Connecticut, a port where the Quinnipiac and other rivers enter Long Island Sound; inc. 1784. An educational centre, the city is the seat of Yale Univ. (chartered 1701, moved to New Haven 1716) and several other institutions. Its manufactures include firearms, prestressed concrete, hardware, clothing, and chemicals. Founded (1637–38) by Puritans, it was a planned theocratic community joined (1665) with the Connecticut Colony.

**Newhaven,** town (1981 pop. 10,697), E Sussex, S England, on the English Channel at the mouth of the R. Ouse. It is a port town, which has facilities for container traffic and a passenger ferry service to Europe. In 1984 the port handled 1.6 million tonnes.

**New Hebrides,** former Anglo-French condominium granted independence in 1980 as VANUATU.

**Ne Win, U** (ˌooh ˌnay ˌwin), 1911–, army general and political leader in BURMA. He became prime minister by twice deposing (1958, 1962) U NU in military coups. Ne Win's 'Burmese way to socialism' made Burma a police state and failed to improve the economy. In 1974 he became president under a new constitution. He resigned the presidency in 1981, but remained chairman of Burma's ruling party until 1988, when he resigned amidst serious political unrest.

**New Jersey,** state of the US (1984 est. pop. 7,515,000), area 20,295 km² (7836 sq mi), situated on the mid-Atlantic, bordered by the Atlantic Ocean (E), Delaware (S), Pennsylvania (W), and New York (N). The capital is TRENTON and the largest city is NEWARK, followed by Jersey City and Paterson; many communities are suburbs of NEW YORK CITY. More than half of the state is covered by coastal plains that give way to the Piedmont plains inland and to the ridges of the APPALACHIAN MTS in the NW. Although nicknamed the 'Garden State', New Jersey has an economy dominated by manufacturing; chemicals and pharmaceuticals are the most valuable products. Farms produce a wide range of dairy products, vegetables, and fruit. The resorts of the Atlantic coast are major tourist attractions, while ports across the Hudson R. from New York City have revived in recent years. New Jersey is a small state, but is the most densely populated and highly urbanized (89%) in the country, and among the most ethnically diverse. In 1980 79% of the population was non-Hispanic white, 12% was black, c.7% of Spanish origin, and c.2% Asian. The area was inhabited by Delaware Indians when first the Dutch and then the British (1664) controlled it. New Jersey was one of the thirteen colonies to sign the Declaration of Independence (1776), and many of the battles of the American Revolution were fought there. In the 19th cent. there was expansion of the economy based on water-powered textile manufacture, accompanied by political corruption until it was ended in the 1910s. After World War II the industrial economy expanded, but faltered in the 1970s. More recently Atlantic City has revived as a gambling and seaside resort, and the depressed urban areas have benefited from the construction of sports arenas, the expansion of transatlantic air traffic, and the decentralization of offices from New York City.

**New Jerusalem, Church of the** or **New Church,** religious body instituted by followers of Emanuel SWEDENBORG, who are generally called Swedenborgians. It was first organized (1787) in London. It was introduced to the US in 1784, and New Church bodies exist in the UK, Europe, and Australia. Its polity is modified episcopacy, with each society enjoying great freedom.

**Newlands, John Alexander Reina,** 1838–98, British chemist. He prepared the first PERIODIC TABLE of the elements arranged in the order of atomic weights. His observation that every eighth element has similar properties (the 'Law of Octaves') was accepted only after Dmitri MENDELEEV's work five years later.

**New Laws:** see LAS CASAS, BARTOLOMÉ DE.

**Newman, Barnett,** 1905–71, American artist. Forming a link between ABSTRACT EXPRESSIONISM and COLOUR FIELD PAINTING, his influential canvases are frequently monumental planes of flat colour cut by slender vertical bands.

**Newman, John Henry,** 1801–90, English churchman, Roman Catholic cardinal, a founder of the OXFORD MOVEMENT. Ordained (1824) in the Church of England, he began (1833) his series *Tracts for the Times* and helped guide the Oxford Movement. *Tract 90* (1841), which demonstrated that the THIRTY-NINE ARTICLES were consistent with Catholicism, outraged Anglicans, and Newman converted to Catholicism in 1845. He was one of the most influential English Catholics of all time, and his *Apologia pro vita sua* (1864) is a masterpiece of religious autobiography. Newman, unlike H.E. MANNING, disapproved of the promulgation of papal infallibility in 1870; though he did not oppose the dogma itself, he lost favour with the papacy until 1879, when he was made a cardinal.

**Newman, Paul,** 1925–, American film actor. His films include *The Hustler* (1961), *Hud* (1963), *Butch Cassidy and the Sundance Kid* (1969), *The Verdict* (1982), and *The Colour of Money* (1986) in which he reprised the role of Fast Eddie, from *The Hustler*, for which he won an Academy Award. He has directed such films as *Rachel, Rachel* (1968).

**New Mexico,** state of the US (1984 est. pop. 1,424,000), area 3,135,115 km² (121,666 sq mi), in the SW US, bordered by Colorado (N), Oklahoma (NE), Texas (E,S), and the Mexican state of Chihuahua (S). The capital is SANTA FE and Albuquerque is the largest city. Much of the northern and western parts of the state consist of the ROCKY MTS, bisected by the RIO GRANDE running N to S; broad semiarid plains cover the S. The climate has exceptionally hot summers and freezing winters. Almost one-third of the land is federally owned, including the famous Carlsbad Caverns. Mining is the source of much of the wealth of New Mexico, which leads the US in the production of uranium, potash, and perlite, and also in output of mineral fuels. Agriculture is restricted to cattle and sheep grazing, while industry is dominated by the manufacture of electrical equipment and building materials. Tourism and forestry also bring revenue. In 1980 37% of the population was of Spanish origin, many being descended from the early Spanish settlers; 8% was native American. Prehistoric cultures long preceded the civilization of the Pueblo Indians, who were subdued by the Spanish missions in the 16th cent. US settlers began arriving via the Santa Fe Trail even before the area was ceded by Mexico to the US at the end of the Mexican–American War (1848). The arrival of the railway and the defeat of the Apache Indian chief GERONIMO opened up the area to settlement and ranching. In the 20th cent. New Mexico's growth has benefited from government and military expenditure, notably on Los Alamos National Laboratory, where the first atomic bomb was built in 1945.

Carlsbad Caverns, **New Mexico**

**New Netherland,** American territory granted by Holland to the DUTCH WEST INDIA COMPANY in 1621. The first permanent settlement was at Fort Orange (now Albany, New York State), in 1624. New Amsterdam (later New York City) was bought from the Indians in 1626 by Peter MINUIT. In 1664 the territory was taken by the English, who divided it into the colonies of New York and New Jersey.

**New Orleans,** US city (1984 est. pop. 559,000), SE Louisiana, between the Mississippi R. and Lake Pontchartrain, 172 km (107 mi) from the river mouth; founded 1718, inc. 1805. Built on a bend in the river, it is protected by levees. A major international port and a centre of business and banking, it is one of the largest and most important cities in the South. Its imports include coffee, sugar, iron and steel, and ores; its exports, machinery, chemicals, paper, and grains. Food processing is a major enterprise. The city has oil, aerospace, and chemical industries; shipyards; and diverse manufacturing plants. The capital (from 1722) of the French colony, it became a cosmopolitan city; French influence (Creole culture) and the city's reputation for glamour and gaiety have lasted to the present. The French Quarter (Vieux Carré), around Jackson Square, retains much of its early elegance. Two manifestations of the city's heterogeneous culture are its famous MARDI GRAS festival and the development of JAZZ. Today its history and continuing beauty draw many tourists.

**Newport,** US city (1980 pop. 29,259), SE Rhode Island, on Aquidneck (or Rhode) Island; settled 1639, inc. 1784. A refuge for Quakers, Jews, and other religious groups in its early history, the city became in the 19th cent. one of the world's most famous resorts. Its palatial mansions are now a tourist attraction. Newport is also noted for yachting (the America's Cup races were long held there). Its many points of interest include the old colony house (1739) and the Touro Synagogue (1763), the oldest in the US.

**Newport,** county town (1981 pop. 115,896), of Gwent, SE Wales, on R. USK, near its entry into the Severn estuary. It is an industrial and port town, whose major industries include engineering, the manufacture of iron, steel, brass, and aluminium, and the production of electrical goods. In 1984 the port handled 2.5 million tonnes. The town developed rapidly in the late 19th cent. owing to its favourable position on a tidal river. The parish church of St Woollos became the cathedral in 1921. There are the remains of a 12th-cent. castle.

**Newport News,** US city (1984 est. pop. 155,000), SE Virginia, on the Virginia peninsula, at the mouth of the James R., off Hampton Roads; inc. 1896. It is one of the world's major shipbuilding and repair centres, and a port handling raw materials in great volume. Settled c.1620, it did not grow appreciably until 1880, when the railway arrived. In 1862 the *Monitor* and the *Merrimack* fought off Newport News.

**news agency,** local, national, international, or technical organization that gathers and distributes news, selling its services to NEWSPAPERS, PERIODICALS, and broadcasters; also called press agency, press association, and wire service. The major international news organizations are: (1) Agence France-Presse, founded in 1835 as Agence Havas of Paris; (2) Associated Press (AP), founded in 1892 as the Associated Press of Illinois, which adopted its present name in 1900; (3) Reuter Telegram Company of London, founded in 1851 and known simply as Reuters; (4) United Press International (UPI), formed in 1958 from the merger of the United Press (formed 1892) and the International News Service (founded 1906 by W.R. HEARST). Some countries have government-owned and -controlled agencies, like the Soviet Union's Telegraphnoye Agentstvo Sovyetskovo Soyuza (TASS); founded in 1918, it serves many Communist-bloc nations. News agencies transmit copy through the use of the TELEGRAPH, TELEPHONE wires, underwater cables, and satellites (see SATELLITE, ARTIFICIAL). Many offer their clients photographs, news analyses, and special features.

**New South Wales,** state (1986 pop. 5,531,500), 801,457 km² (309,443 sq mi), SE Australia, bounded by the Pacific Ocean (E). The capital is SYDNEY; NEWCASTLE and WOLLONGONG are among the other urban centres. New South Wales produces most of Australia's steel; other manufactures include machinery, electrical products, clothing, textiles, and chemicals. The state mines much of Australia's coal and has one of the world's richest silver, zinc and lead deposits, at BROKEN HILL. Agricultural products include beef, cattle, wool, dairy products, wheat, sugar, and fruits. New South Wales was settled in 1788 as a penal colony and until 1825 included all of Australia E of long. 135°E. It became a British colony in 1846 and was federated as a state of the Commonwealth of Australia in 1901. The AUSTRALIAN CAPITAL TERRITORY, site of CANBERRA, Australia's capital, was ceded (1911, 1915) by New South Wales to the federal government.

**newspaper,** publication issued periodically, usually daily or weekly, to convey information about current events. The Roman *Acta diurna* (c.59 BC), posted daily in public places, was the first recorded newspaper effort. The invention and spread of PRINTING in the 15th cent. was the major factor in the early development of the newspaper. One of the oldest continental newspapers, *Avisa Relation oder Zeitung*, appeared in Germany in 1609; the *Nieuwe Tijdingen* was published in Antwerp in 1616; and the first French newspaper, the *Gazette*, was founded in 1631. The first newspaper to appear in the American colonies was a newssheet, *Publick Occurrences*, which was issued in Boston in 1690. The first daily paper in England was the *Daily Courant* (1702). Thereafter many journals of opinion set a high literary standard, e.g., Daniel DEFOE's *Review* (1704–13) and the SPECTATOR (1711–12). After John WILKES's successful battle for greater freedom of the press (see PRESS, FREEDOM OF THE), English newspapers began to reach the masses in the 19th cent. In the 20th cent. great newspaper empires were built by Lords ROTHERMERE, NORTHCLIFFE, and BEAVERBROOK in England, and Joseph PULITZER, W.R. HEARST and E.W. Scripps in the US. Important British newspapers of today are *The Times* of London (founded in 1785) and the *Guardian* (originally the *Manchester Guardian*), the *Daily Telegraph*, *The Independent*, and the *Scotsman*, all for serious readers; popular daily newspapers include the *Sun* and the *Daily Mirror*. Important newspapers of the world today include *Frankfurter Allgemeine Zeitung* (Germany), *Washington Post* (US), *Wall Street Journal* (US), *Figaro* (France), *Osservatore romano* (Vatican), *Pravda* and *Izvestia* (USSR), *Asahi Shinbum* (Japan), and the *Times of India* (Delhi). In the late 1950s cheap colour photography introduced the coloured supplement, especially for weekly papers, which brought in considerable advertising revenue. By 1980 the Australian magnate Rupert MURDOCH was publishing newspapers in Australia, Great Britain, and the US. Since the invention of the TELEGRAPH, which facilitated the rapid gathering of news, the great NEWS AGENCIES have sold their services to many newspapers. Improvements in typesetting and printing (especially the web press) have made possible the publication of huge editions at great speed. Newspapers are able to print in colour. During the 1970s such technological developments as photocomposition and the use of satellites (see SATELLITE, ARTIFICIAL) to deliver news and photographs were revolutionizing the newspaper industry. See also COMPUTER; PERIODICAL; TYPE.

**New Style dates:** see CALENDAR.

**New Sweden,** Swedish colony on the Delaware R., in parts of present-day Pennsylvania, New Jersey, and Delaware, US. It was founded in 1638 by the New Sweden Company, led by Peter MINUIT, with the capital at Tinicum Island. It was captured by the Dutch under Peter STUYVESANT in 1655.

**newt,** AMPHIBIAN in the SALAMANDER family. Newts spend their summers in fresh waters, returning to land in winter to hibernate. They live in Europe, Asia, North Africa and North America. True newts belong to the genus *Triturus*. The smooth newt (*Triturus vulgaris*) is the most common, found all over Europe. It is about 10 cm (4 in) long and feeds on worms, snails, and insects on land and crustaceans, insect larvae, and tadpoles in water. All newts lay eggs that hatch into TADPOLES. The largest newt is the crested newt (*Triturus cristatus*), about 15 cm (6 in) long. It will eat smooth newts, and it exudes venom through its skin if it is handled.

**New Testament,** the distinctively Christian portion of the BIBLE, 27 books dating from the earliest Christian period, transmitted in *koiné,* a popular form of Greek spoken in the biblical regions from the 4th cent. BC. The conventional order is: four narrative accounts of JESUS, namely the GOSPELS, Matthew, Mark, Luke, and John; a history of missionary activity, the ACTS OF THE APOSTLES; 21 letters written in apostolic times, called epistles, named (first 14) after their addressees or (last 7) after their supposed author—ROMANS, First and Second CORINTHIANS, GALATIANS, EPHESIANS, PHILIPPIANS, COLOSSIANS, First and Second THESSALONIANS, First and Second TIMOTHY, TITUS, PHILEMON, HEBREWS, JAMES, First and Second PETER, First, Second, and Third JOHN, and JUDE; and finally a prophecy, the REVELATION or Apocalypse. There are many more than these 27 early Christian works. Selection of New Testament books as canonical was slow, the present canon appearing for the first time in the Festal Epistle of St Athanasius (AD 367). All major Christian churches use the same canon.

**newton:** see FORCE.

**Newton, Sir Isaac,** 1642–1727, English mathematician and natural philosopher (physicist); considered by many to be the greatest scientist of all time. He was Lucasian professor of mathematics (1669–1701) at Cambridge Univ. Between 1664 and 1666 he discovered the law of universal GRAVITATION, began to develop the CALCULUS, and discovered that white light is composed of every colour in the SPECTRUM. In his monumental *Philosophiae naturalis principia mathematica* [mathematical principles of natural philosophy] (1687), he showed how his principle of universal gravitation explained both the motions of heavenly bodies and the falling of bodies on earth. The *Principia* covers DYNAMICS (including Newton's three laws of MOTION), FLUID MECHANICS, the motions of the planets and their satellites, the motions of the comets, and the phenomena of TIDES. Newton's theory that LIGHT is composed of particles, elaborated in his *Opticks* (1704), dominated the field of optics until the 19th cent., when it was replaced by the wave theory of light; the two theories were combined in the modern QUANTUM THEORY. Newton also built (1668) the first reflecting TELESCOPE, anticipated the calculus of variations, and devoted much energy towards alchemy, theology, and history, particularly problems of chronology. He was president of the Royal Society from 1703 until his death.

**new town,** town planned as a complete and autonomous unit, to provide all housing, employment, and leisure needs. New towns have been built at almost every period of history: notable examples were Greek and Roman towns on the Aegean and in Sicily, the 13th- and 14th-cent. English and French bastide towns which were laid out geometrically, and the 16th-cent. neoclassic 'ideal' towns in Italy. The most comprehensive scheme for building new towns followed World War II in Great Britain. As part of postwar reconstruction, it was decided that the big cities, particularly London, were too large and overcrowded and that population and employment should be dispersed beyond the GREEN BELT planned to contain the city. The report of the New Towns Committee chaired by Lord Reith was quickly followed by the New Towns Act 1946 which provided for the creation of new towns where that was in the national interest. They were expected to develop a 'balanced community enjoying a full social, industrial and commercial life'. They were planned for populations between 50,000 and 70,000, though most were smaller. The majority of new towns were created beyond the green belt surrounding London; others were created in Scotland, the Midlands, and Wales. Altogether 32 new town development corporations were set up. Most have now been disbanded as the new towns have been absorbed by existing local authorities. The first group to be built had relatively low population densities, the second had higher densities in an attempt to achieve urban character, and the third (and last) group were planned for motor cars and were spread widely.

**New World,** zoological term used to describe several families of animals in North and South America which are, in many cases, exclusive to the Americas. The New World monkeys, the Cebidae, are recognized by their prehensile tails. Garpikes, boas, pit vipers, iguanas, hummingbirds, toucans, rheas, anteaters, and sloths are examples of New World animals.

**New Year's Day,** the first day of the year. Christians usually celebrated New Year's Day on 25 Mar. until the Gregorian CALENDAR (1582) moved it to 1 Jan. The Jewish New Year (1 Tishri) falls sometime in September or early October. The Chinese New Year falls between 10 Jan. and 19 Feb.

**New York,** state of the US, second most populous (1984 est. pop. 17,735,000), area 128,402 km² (49,576 sq mi), located on the mid-Atlantic coast, bordered by the Atlantic Ocean (SE), New Jersey and Pennsylvania (S), Lakes ONTARIO and ERIE, and the Canadian province of Ontario (NW), and the province of Quebec (N). The capital is ALBANY and the dominant city is New York, the largest in the US and an international financial and cultural centre; BUFFALO, Syracuse, and Rochester are other large cities. The state is divided N to S by the HUDSON R. and Lake CHAMPLAIN valleys. Lying to the W are the ADIRONDACK MTS and the Catskill Mts, and to the E the APPALACHIAN MTS. Long Island extends eastwards into the Atlantic Ocean from the SE corner. New York's industrial output is second only to California's; printing and publishing, the production of instruments, nonelectrical machinery, processed foods, clothing, and electrical equipment are the main manufactures. A wide range of agricultural commodities are produced, including apples, dairy products, grapes (for wine-making), and greenhouse vegetables. Mineral resources include emery, garnet, salt, talc, and silver. Tourism is a major year-round industry, focused on New York City, NIAGARA FALLS and the northern mountains. Nearly 90% of the population lived in metropolitan areas in 1980, and 13% was black, 9% of Spanish origin, and c.2% Asian. The Indians of the Iroquois Confederacy lived in the area when Dutch traders founded New Amsterdam on the lower tip of Manhattan Island in 1624. Britain captured the region after the Second Dutch War (1664–67), and shipping, farming, and fishing thrived. About one-third of the fighting in the American Revolution (1776–82) occurred in New York. After the war commerce thrived, especially after the ERIE CANAL linked the Atlantic Ocean to the GREAT LAKES (1825). In the 1840s mass immigration from Europe began, with many immigrants settling in New York City and assisting the expansion of the industrial economy. Many state governors gained national political prominence, including Thomas E. DEWEY, Nelson A. ROCKEFELLER, and Franklin D. ROOSEVELT, who became president. In the 20th cent. New York state has continued to be one of the two most popular destinations for new immigrants (California being the other).

**New York City** US city (1984 est. pop. 7,165,000; metropolitan area 9,119,737), SE New York, on New York Bay, at the mouth of the Hudson R.; chartered 1898. Each of its five boroughs is a county: Manhattan (New York co.), an island; the Bronx (Bronx co.), on the mainland, NE of Manhattan across the Harlem River; Queens (Queens co.), on Long Island, E of Manhattan across the East River; BROOKLYN (Kings co.), also on Long Island, on the East River adjoining Queens and on New York Bay; and Richmond (Richmond co.), on Staten Island, SW of Manhattan across the Upper Bay. The nation's largest city, New York is the largest US port, the country's trade centre, and, with its banks and stock exchanges, the financial centre of the world. Manufacturing accounts for a large but declining proportion of employment; clothing, chemicals, and processed foods are major products. Publishing, television and radio, advertising, and tourism are major industries. Theatres, nightclubs, shops, and restaurants draw millions of visitors.

*History.* Giovanni da Verrazano may have been the first European to explore the region, and Henry HUDSON visited it, but Dutch settlements truly began the city. In 1624 the town of New Amsterdam was established on lower Manhattan; Peter MINUIT supposedly bought the island from its Indian inhabitants for about $24 worth of trinkets. In 1664 the English seized the colony and renamed it; during the AMERICAN REVOLUTION they held it from 1776 to 1781. New York was briefly (1789–90) the US capital and was state capital until 1797. By 1790 it was the largest city in the US and the opening (1825) of the ERIE CANAL, linking New York with the GREAT LAKES, led to even greater expansion. In 1898 a new charter was adopted, making the city Greater New York, a metropolis of five boroughs. Massive IMMIGRATION, mainly from Europe, swelled the city's population in the late 19th and early 20th cent. and produced a chequerboard of ethnic neighbourhoods. After World War II, shifts in population brought to the city many blacks from the South and many Hispanics from Puerto Rico and other parts of Latin America. The metropolitan area is the most popular destination for immigrants to the US, and almost half of its population is other than non-Hispanic white. The Flatiron building (1902) ushered in the SKYSCRAPER era that brought New York its famous skyline. The first subway (1904) was the forerunner of today's huge transit system. In the late 1970s and early 80s the city faced enormous financial problems, and stringent budget-cutting was imposed.

*Points of Interest.* Noted sights include the EMPIRE STATE BUILDING, the WORLD TRADE CENTER, the Statue of LIBERTY, BROADWAY and Fifth Avenue, GREENWICH VILLAGE, and Central Park. Among New York's bridges are the BROOKLYN BRIDGE (opened 1883), the George Washington Bridge (1931), and the VERRAZANO-NARROWS BRIDGE (1964). ELLIS ISLAND and Castle Garden (at the Battery) were entry points for many immigrants. The UNITED NATIONS has its headquarters in New York. Cultural institutions include Lincoln Center for the Performing Arts and Carnegie Hall; the METROPOLITAN MUSEUM OF ART, MUSEUM OF MODERN ART, and the Whitney Museum of American Art.

**New York City Ballet:** see DANCE (table).

**New Zealand,** country (1987 est. pop. 3,307,100), 268,676 km² (103,736 sq mi), in the South Pacific Ocean, 1600 km (1000 mi) SE of Australia. The major cities are WELLINGTON (the capital), AUCKLAND, and CHRISTCHURCH. New Zealand comprises two main islands, North Island and South Island, separated by Cook Strait; Stewart Island; the Chatham Islands; and several small outlying islands, of which only Raoul, in the Kermadec group, and Campbell Island are inhabited. Also part of New Zealand are the Ross Dependency, in Antarctica, and the TOKELAU Islands. Residents of the self-governing COOK ISLANDS and NIUE share New Zealand citizenship. North Island, with its active volcanoes and hot springs around Lake Taupo, is subtropical in the north and temperate in the south. It contains New Zealand's major river, the Waikato. On South Island are the massive Southern Alps, with many peaks over 3048 m (10,000 ft) high; the productive Canterbury Plains, the country's chief lowland area; acres of virgin forest; and many fjords. Among the unusual animals native to New Zealand are the takahé and KIWI. Most of the people are of British descent. The MAORI, native New Zealanders of Polynesian descent, numbered 385,210 in 1981; most live on North Island. Sheep and cattle, the mainstays of the economy, provide New Zealand with exports of frozen meat (especially lamb), dairy products (especially butter), and wool. Food processing dominates the industrial sector. Tourism is of increasing importance.

*History.* The Maori are thought to have migrated to the islands prior to AD 1400. Abel TASMAN was the first European to visit (1642) the islands, which were named after the Dutch province of Zeeland, but they attracted little interest until described in detail by Capt. James COOK, who visited them four times between 1769 and 1777. Whalers, missionaries, and traders followed, and in 1840 the first permanent European settlement was established at Wellington by E.G. WAKEFIELD. The same year the Maori signed the Treaty of Waitangi, by which they recognized British sovereignty in exchange for guaranteed possession of their land. Nevertheless, wars over land between the Maori and white settlers were waged until 1870. Originally part of the Australian colony of New South Wales, New Zealand became a separate colony in 1841 and was made self-governing in 1852. Dominion status was attained in 1907, and full independence within the COMMONWEALTH was conferred by the Statute of Westminster (1931), which was confirmed by New Zealand in 1947. New Zealand was a leader in passing social legislation, e.g., woman suffrage (1893) and social security (1898), and it aided Britain in both world wars. Legislative power rests with a unicameral parliament; executive power is vested in a governor general, representing the crown, and a cabinet and prime minister. Political power has alternated between the National and Labour parties, the latter being elected to office in 1984 under David LANGE. Implementation of Labour's antinuclear policies led in 1985 to the suspension of New Zealand's participation in the ANZUS PACT with Australia and the US.

Post-war New Zealand prime ministers
Peter Fraser (Labour), 1940–49
Sidney Holland (National), 1949–57
Keith Holyoake (National), 1957
Walter Nash (Labour), 1957–60
Keith Holyoake (National), 1960–72
John Marshall (National), 1972
Norman Kirk (Labour), 1972–74
Wallace (Bill) Rowling (Labour), 1974–75
Robert Muldoon (National), 1975–84
David Lange (Labour), 1984–

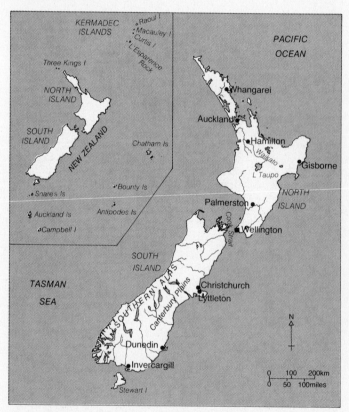

New Zealand

**Nexø, Martin Andersen:** see ANDERSEN NEXØ, MARTIN.

**Ney, Michel** (nay), 1769–1815, marshal of France. Called 'the bravest of the brave' by NAPOLEON I, he rose to glory rapidly in the FRENCH REVOLUTIONARY WARS. He gave decisive aid to Napoleon at Friedland (1807) and brilliantly defended the rear during Napoleon's retreat (1812) from Moscow. After Napoleon's abdication (1814) he was raised to the peerage by LOUIS XVIII, but rejoined Napoleon for the HUNDRED DAYS and fought in the WATERLOO CAMPAIGN (1815). After Napoleon's defeat, Ney was condemned for treason by the house of peers and was shot.

**Nez Percé Indians,** NORTH AMERICAN INDIANS of the Plateau, speaking a Sahaptin-Chinook language (see AMERICAN INDIAN LANGUAGES). They lived in W Idaho, NE Oregon, and SE Washington, subsisting typically on salmon and plant roots. After acquiring the horse, they became noted breeders and adopted other Plains traits, including the buffalo hunt. A fraudulent land cession extracted from them (1863) during the GOLD RUSH led to an uprising (1877) under Chief JOSEPH. Today those living on the Idaho reservation are mostly farmers.

**Ngo Dinh Diem,** 1901–63, president (1955–63) of South VIETNAM. Named (1954) premier, he ousted (1955) BAO DAI as head of state and emerged as president. His rule grew authoritarian, and he was murdered in a military coup that was apparently backed by the US.

**Ngugi wa Thiong'o,** 1938–, Kenyan novelist and dramatist. His first novels about the impact of British colonialism and resistance to it, e.g., *The River Between* (1965), were published under the name of James Ngugi. His opposition to post-independence Kenyan governments has led to several periods of imprisonment, culminating in exile, but it also led to a range of works about that resistance, including the highly-acclaimed works *Petals of Blood* (1977) and *Devil on the Cross* (1982). His plays include *The Black Hermit* (1968) and *This Time Tomorrow* (1970). Among his critical writings is *Decolonising the Mind: the Politics of Language in African Literature* (1986), a justification for his decision to abandon writing in English in favour of Gikuyu.

**Nguyen Van Linh,** 1916–, Vietnamese political figure and Communist Party leader (1986–). A longserving member of the country's top ruling bodies, he acquired a reputation as a reformist. On succeeding to the leadership of the ruling party (1986), he brought in more moderate internal and external policies than his predecessors.

**Nguyen Van Theiu,** 1923–, president (1967–75) of South VIETNAM. In 1963 he helped lead the coup that overthrew Pres. NGO DINH DIEM. He was elected president in 1967 and continually opposed negotiations with North Vietnam to end the VIETNAM WAR. Thieu fled (1975) from South Vietnam when it fell to the Communists.

**NHS:** see NATIONAL HEALTH SERVICE.

**Ni,** chemical symbol of the element NICKEL.

**niacin:** see VITAMINS AND MINERALS (table).

**Niagara Falls,** internationally famous waterfall, on the US–Canada border between Niagara Falls, New York, and Niagara Falls, Ontario, formed where the Niagara R. drops from Lake ERIE to Lake ONTARIO. Goat Island splits the cataract into the American Falls (51 m/167 ft high; 323 m/1060 ft wide) and the Horseshoe, or Canadian, Falls (48 m/158 ft high; 792 m/2600 ft wide), and overlooks the Niagara Gorge (c.11 km/7 mi long) with its Whirlpool Rapids and Whirlpool. Under terms of the Niagara Diversion Treaty (1950), water is diverted in New York to power the 13 generators of the Robert Moses Niagara Power Plant (1,950,000-kW capacity; opened 1961) and in Ontario into the Sir Adam Beck Generating Stations (1,775,000 kW; opened 1954). The falls were formed c.10,000 years ago and are retreating upstream faster in the Horseshoe Falls because of the greater volume of water that they carry.

**Niagara-on-the-Lake,** town (1980 est. pop. 12,307), S Ontario, Canada, part of the regional municipality of Niagara (1980 est. pop. 367,665), on Lake ONTARIO. Located near NIAGARA FALLS, it is a popular tourist centre known for its 19th-cent. atmosphere and architecture and for the annual Shaw Festival, held during the summer. Niagara-on-the-Lake was originally settled as Butlersburg in 1784. Renamed Newark, it served (1792–96) as the first capital of Upper Canada (now Ontario). The city was destroyed, along with Fort George (built 1796–99 to defend it), by the Americans in the WAR OF 1812. Subsequently rebuilt, it took its present name in 1906.

**Niamey** (nyah͵may), largest city (1980 est. pop. 230,000) and capital of Niger, SW Niger, a port on the Niger R. At the crossroads of two main highways, the city handles trade for an agricultural region specializing in peanuts. Manufactures include bricks, food products, and cement. A small town when the French colonized the area (late 19th cent.), Niamey grew after it became the capital of Niger in 1926.

**Nibelungen** or **Nibelungs** (͵neebə͵loongən), in Germanic myth, an evil family possessing a magic hoard of gold. The *Nibelungenlied* (–lēt') is a Middle High German epic by a south German poet of the early 13th cent., recounting the story of Siegfried, who wins the hoard, marries Kriemhild, and captures Queen Brunhild for Kriemhild's brother Gunther. Brunhild contrives Siegfried's death, and Kriemhild wreaks vengeance on Gunther's court. *The Ring of the Nibelungs* is an operatic tetralogy by Richard WAGNER, comprising *Das Rheingold, Die Walküre, Siegfried,* and *Götterdämmerung.*

**Nicaea, Councils of,** two ecumenical councils of the Christian Church. The first council (325), convened by the Emperor CONSTANTINE I, rejected ARIANISM and established the divinity and equality of the Son in the Trinity. The second council (787), called to refute ICONOCLASM, declared that religious images ought to be venerated (but not worshipped).

**Nicaea, empire of,** 1204–61, one of the Greek states that arose after the Fourth CRUSADE set up the Latin empire of Constantinople. Founded by Theodore I, Nicaea continued the institutions of Byzantium, including emperors and patriarchs. Theodore and his successors became supreme in Asia Minor. The Nicaean emperor MICHAEL VIII captured Constantinople (1261) and restored the Byzantine Empire.

**Nicaragua,** officially Republic of Nicaragua, republic (1986 est. pop. 3,300,000), 128,410 km² (49,579 sq mi), Central America; bordered by Honduras (N), the Caribbean Sea (E), Costa Rica (S), and the Pacific Ocean (SW). The capital is MANAGUA. Mountainous in the NE, Nicaragua is the least densely populated Central American nation; the people live mainly on a narrow, volcanic belt between the Pacific and Lakes Managua and Nicaragua. There are gold and salt mines, and some manufacturing,

The Horseshoe, **Niagara Falls**

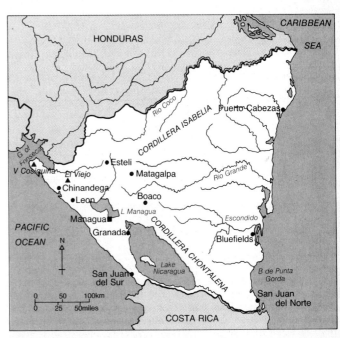

Nicaragua

but the country is primarily agricultural, exporting coffee, cotton, sugarcane, and meat. In 1983 GDP was US$3600 million or US$1200 per capita. The population is Spanish-speaking, Roman Catholic, and predominantly mestizo.

*History.* The first Spanish colonial cities in the area, LEÓN and Granada, were founded in 1524. Ruled as part of GUATEMALA, Nicaragua achieved independence in 1821. After brief periods as part of the Mexican Empire and the CENTRAL AMERICAN FEDERATION, Nicaragua became a separate republic in 1838. Marked by extreme liberal–conservative antagonism, the country has had an unusually violent history. Foreign interference was frequent, especially by the US, which from the early 19th cent. expressed interest in a possible inter-ocean waterway in Nicaragua. US marines intervened in a civil war in 1912, remaining in the country until 1933. In 1937 Anastasio SOMOZA García became president and ruled the country as his private domain until being assassinated in 1956. He was succeeded by his son Luis, then by a family nominee (to conform with the constitution) and from 1967 by another son, Gen. Anastasio Somoza Debayle. In 1979, however, the Somoza regime was overthrown, after prolonged fighting by the SANDINISTAS—members of the Sandinist National Liberation Front (FSLN), named after an early guerrilla hero, August César Sandino. Having at first included moderate conservatives, the FSLN moved to the left in the early 1980s and faced vigorous opposition from the US administration and from US-backed counterrevolutionary guerrilla groups (the Contras). Elections in 1984 resulted in a susbtantial victory for the FSLN and its presidential candidate, Daniel Ortega Saavedra.

**Nice** (nees), city (1982 pop. 338,486, agglomeration 449,496), capital of Alpes-Maritimes dept., SE France, on the Mediterranean Sea. This famous French Riviera resort relies mostly on tourists, but electronics and other manufactures are important. Nice probably originated as a Greek colony in the 5th cent. BC. Sardinia held it from 1814 to 1860, when a plebiscite gave it to France.

**Nicephorus** (ni,sefərəs), Byzantine emperors. **Nicephorus I,** d. 811 (r.803–11), deposed Empress IRENE. He reformed the treasury and taxation, and asserted the supremacy of emperor over church, a doctrine opposed by the monastic reformer St Theodore of Studium. **Nicephorus II** (Phocas), c.912–69, a general under ROMANUS II, married the emperor's widow and usurped the throne (r.963–69). Disliked for taking land from monasteries and imposing heavy taxes to finance his wars, he was murdered by his wife's lover, who succeeded to the throne as JOHN I.

**niche,** in ecology, the particular position occupied by a species within its HABITAT, considered in relation to other species. No two species may occupy the same niche for any length of time since competition for the same food supply will ensure the extinction of one or other species. The number of niches available and therefore the number of species present in any one habitat depends on the characteristics of that habitat: habitats that are warm and wet tend to contain the largest number of niches.

**Nicholas,** czars of Russia. **Nicholas I,** 1796–1855 (r.1825–55), was the third son of PAUL I. On his first day as czar he crushed the uprising of the DECEMBRISTS. During his reign laws were codified, the first Russian railway was completed and the condition of SERFS belonging to the state somewhat improved, but political progress was stifled and minorities were persecuted under the slogan 'autocracy, orthodoxy, and nationality'. Intellectual ferment generated the SLAVOPHILES AND WESTERNIZERS, and GOGOL, LERMONTOV, and PUSHKIN began a golden age in literature. Nicholas brutally suppressed the uprising in POLAND (1830–31) and in 1849 helped Austria crush the revolution in HUNGARY. He died during the disastrous CRIMEAN WAR and was succeeded by his son ALEXANDER II. **Nicholas II,** 1868–1918 (r.1894–1917), was the son of ALEXANDER III. As a youth he received little training in affairs of state. His reign continued the suppression of political opposition and persecution of minorities. Revolutionary groups proliferated, while liberals demanded constitutional government. An aggressive policy in the Far East led to defeat in the RUSSO-JAPANESE WAR (1904–05). In Jan. 1905 a peaceful crowd of petitioners was fired upon in front of the Winter Palace; this 'Bloody Sunday' began the 1905 Revolution. In October Count WITTE induced Nicholas to sign a manifesto promising constitutional government and basic civil liberties, but the czar dissolved the DUMA shortly after it began to sit, and Witte was replaced as premier by STOLYPIN in 1906. WORLD WAR I began in 1914; in 1915 Nicholas took command of the army, leaving Czarina ALEXANDRA FEODOROVNA and her adviser, RASPUTIN, in control of the government. Discontent spread, the army tired of war, food shortages

worsened, the government tottered, and in Mar. 1917 Nicholas was forced to abdicate (see RUSSIAN REVOLUTION). He and his family were shot in Ekaterinburg (now Sverdlovsk) on 16 July 1918.

**Nicholas, Saint,** patron of children and sailors, of Greece, Sicily, and Russia, and of many other persons and places. Traditionally he is identified with a 4th-cent. bishop of Myra in Asia Minor. His legend was combined in Germany with local folklore to make him the bringer of secret presents to children, and in Dutch- and English-speaking countries his name was corrupted into Santa Claus.

**Nicholas I, Saint** (Nicholas the Great), c.820–67, pope (858–67), a Roman. He established the right of a bishop to appeal to Rome against his superior and blocked the divorce of LOTHAR of Lorraine. He supported St IGNATIUS OF CONSTANTINOPLE over PHOTIUS as patriarch of Constantinople and sought Roman ecclesiastical jurisdiction over Bulgaria. Feast: 13 Nov.

**Nicholas (Nikola Petrović-Njegoš),** 1841–1921, prince (1860–1910) and king (1910–18) of MONTENEGRO. Famous in his lifetime as a poet and provider of marriageable daughters to greater European dynasties, Nicholas brought Montenegro to full independence (1878) and expanded its frontiers, but failed to retain Montenegrin leadership of the Serb and South Slav causes. He was deposed when a national assembly voted for union with Serbia in the new Yugoslav state.

**Nicholson, Ben,** 1894–1982, English painter. Developing the purism of de STIJL with great elegance, he produced geometric abstractions of landscapes and still lifes. He visited PICASSO, BRAQUE, BRANCUSI, and ARP in Paris in 1932 with HEPWORTH, and joined the Abstraction-Création group. His first all-white relief was shown in 1934. In 1937 he was coeditor of *Circle,* the British constructivist manifesto.

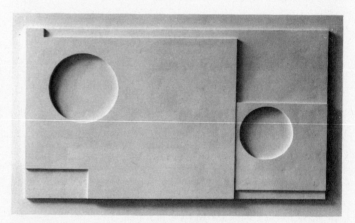

White Relief by Ben **Nicholson** (Tate Gallery, London)

**Nicias** (,nisheeəs), d. 413 BC, Athenian statesman and general. An opponent of CLEON and his war party, he favoured peace with SPARTA during the PELOPONNESIAN WAR, and in 421 BC he arranged the truce known as the Peace of Nicias. Although he had opposed the project, he was placed in command of an expedition to SYRACUSE. His vacillation led to an Athenian defeat; Nicias was captured and executed.

**nickel** (Ni), metallic element, discovered in 1751 by A.F. Cronstedt. It is a silver-white, hard, malleable, ductile, and lustrous metal whose chief use is in the preparation of alloys, to which it brings strength, ductility, and resistance to corrosion and heat. Many stainless STEELS contain nickel. Nickel's chief ores are garnierite, pentlandite and pyrrhotite. Nickel is present in most METEORITES. Trace amounts are found in plants and animals. See ELEMENT (table); PERIODIC TABLE.

**Nicklaus, Jack (William),** 1940– , American golfer. Generally considered the greatest golfer of all time, he was a master of every kind of shot. Nicknamed the 'Golden Bear', he won two national amateur titles (1959, 1961) while a student at Ohio State Univ. By winning the US Masters title in 1986, he raised his total of major championships to 18, far more than any other player. These included the Masters (six), the PGA (five), the US Open (four), and the British Open (three).

**Nicolà da Urbino,** fl. 1520–38, Italian painter of Renaissance MAIOLICA. Little is known of his life. In the 1520s he was working at Urbino, where in 1528, he signed and dated a dish, inscribing it as having been painted in the workshop of Guido Durantino, one of the city's leading potters. Nicola decorated several services for members of noble families, including Isabella d'Este, widow of Francesco Gonzaga of Mantua. The subjects of his designs were drawn from classical mythology and history, or from the Bible.

**Nicomedia,** ancient city (modern Izmit, Turkey), NW Asia Minor. It was the residence of the kings of BITHYNIA from 264 BC. Diocletian chose it as the eastern imperial capital, but it was soon superseded by Byzantium.

**Nicosia,** city (1982 est. pop. 161,100), capital of Cyprus. An agricultural trade centre, it manufactures textiles, brandy, and other goods. It was the residence of the Lusignan kings of CYPRUS from 1192 and a Venetian possession (15th cent.) before it fell (1571) to the Turks. Since Cypriot independence (1960) it has been the scene of conflict between Greeks and Turks. Its museums house notable antiquities.

**nicotine,** an ALKALOID produced by the TOBACCO plant. Its main pharmacological action is transient stimulation followed by more persistent depression of the autonomic NERVOUS SYSTEM. Nicotine is addictive and toxic, playing a role, along with other components in tobacco smoke, particularly tar and carbon monoxide, in the causation of lung CANCER, other cancers, pulmonary disease, CORONARY HEART DISEASE, and fetal growth retardation.

**Niebuhr, Barthold Georg** (ˌneebooə), 1776–1831, German historian; b. Denmark. His history of Rome (3 vol., 1811–32) may be said to have inaugurated modern scientific historical method. In it he related individual events to the political and social institutions of ancient Rome.

**Niebuhr, Reinhold,** 1892–1971, American theologian and social thinker. He taught (1928–60) at Union Theological Seminary, New York City, and became interested in social problems. In the early 1930s he shed his liberal Protestant hopes for the church's moral role in society and became a political activist and a socialist. His writings include *Moral Man and Immoral Society* (1932), *Christianity and Power Politics* (1940), and *The Nature and Destiny of Man* (2 vol., 1941–43). His brother, **Helmut Richard Niebuhr,** 1894–1962, was a professor at Yale Divinity School (1931–62). His thought was early influenced by KIERKEGAARD and BARTH; later, however, he turned his attention to the personal nature of mankind's relationship to God and advocated a reworking of Christianity in light of the developments of the 20th cent.

**nielsbohrium:** see UNNILPENTIUM.

**Nielsen, Carl August,** 1865–1931, Danish composer. He is known for his six symphonies. His orchestral writing frequently features POLYPHONY, and his use of contrasting KEYS has been described as 'progressive tonality'.

**Niemeyer (Soares), Oscar,** 1907–, Brazilian architect. Influenced by LE CORBUSIER, he is noted for projects like the Ministry of Education, Rio de Janeiro (1937–43), and, especially, for his direction of the creation of the new Brazilian federal capital, Brasília (1950–60).

**Niemoeller** or **Niemöller, Martin** ('neemølə), 1892–1984, German Protestant churchman. A submarine commander in World War I, he later led the CONFESSING CHURCH and opposed the religious policies of HITLER's regime. He was imprisoned from 1938 to 1945. He later became (1947) president of the Evangelical Church in Hesse-Nassau and was also a president (1961–68) of the World Council of Churches.

**Niepce, Joseph Nicéphore** (nyeps), 1765–1833, French chemist. He originated a process of photography (see PHOTOGRAPHY, STILL) that was later perfected by Louis Daguerre. A nephew, **Claude Félix Abel Niepce de Saint-Victor,** 1805–70, also a chemist, introduced the use of albumen in photography and produced photographic engravings on steel.

**Nietzsche, Friedrich Wilhelm,** 1844–1900, German philosopher. An individualistic moralist rather than a systematic philosopher, influenced by SCHOPENHAUER and by his early friendship with Richard WAGNER he passionately rejected the 'slave morality' of Christianity for a new, heroic morality that would affirm life. Leading this new society would be a breed of supermen whose 'will to power' would set them off from the 'herd' of inferior humanity. His works include *Thus Spake Zarathustra* (1883–92), *Beyond Good and Evil* (1886), *The Genealogy of Morals* (1887), and *The Antichrist* (1895). Some were later used as a philosophical justification for NAZI doctrines of racial and national superiority; most scholars, however, regard this as a perversion of Nietzsche's thought.

**Niger,** officially Republic of Niger, republic (1986 est. pop. 6,475,000), 1,267,000 km² (489,189 sq mi), W Africa, bordered by Burkina Faso and Mali (W), Algeria and Libya (N), Chad (E), Nigeria and Benin (S). NIAMEY is the capital. The landlocked country is largely semidesert or part of the SAHARA, except along the NIGER R. and near the southern border. The Aïr Mts, in N central Niger, rise to c.1800 m (5900 ft). The economy is increasingly supported by high-grade uranium ore deposits, which have been worked since the early 1970s. By 1980 Niger had become one of the world's leading producers, and shipments of uranium provided 75% of export earnings. Other minerals extracted include cassiterite (tin ore), phosphates, and coal. About 90% of the work force is engaged in farming, largely of a subsistence type; major crops include millet, sorghum, cassava, and peanuts. Stock-raising (cattle, sheep, goats) is also important. Manufacturing is limited mainly to basic consumer goods. A small but growing fishing industry operates in the Niger R. and Lake Chad. The GNP is US$1450 million, and the GNP per capita is US$250 (1985). The population is black African, with the Hausa making up about 55% of the total. About 85% of the people are Muslim; most of the rest follow traditional beliefs. French is the official language.

*History.* About 1300 the Tuareg established a state centred at Agadès (Agadez), situated on a major trans-Saharan caravan route, and in the 14th cent. the Hausa founded several city-states in S Niger. Parts of the region came under the SONGHAI empire in the early 16th cent., the state of Bornu in the late 16th cent., and the Fulani people in the early 19th cent. After the Conference of BERLIN (1884–85) placed the territory of Niger within the French sphere of influence, France established military posts in the south but for a time met concerted Tuareg resistance. In 1922 Niger became a separate colony within FRENCH WEST AFRICA. Nationalist political activity, which began in 1946, was led at first by the Niger Progressive party (PPN) and in the mid-1950s by a leftist party (later called Sawaba). The PPN, which favoured autonomy within the FRENCH COMMUNITY, regained power in 1958, when a referendum supported that course. Niger became fully independent in 1960, with PPN leader Hamani Diori as president (he was reelected in 1965 and 1970). Niger enjoyed political stability and maintained close ties with France. The severe Sahelian drought (1968–75) caused economic disruption and civil unrest, however, leading to an army coup (1974), suspension of the constitution, and military rule under a regime led by Lt.-Col. Seyni KOUNTCHÉ. The new government curtailed French influence in the rich uranium industry, concluded a more favourable economic agreement with France, and later brought civilians into the administration. In 1983 the advisory National Development Council was reconstituted as the highest tier of a representative structure for Niger's 'development society'. Col. Kountché died in late 1987 and was succeeded by Col. Ali Saibou.

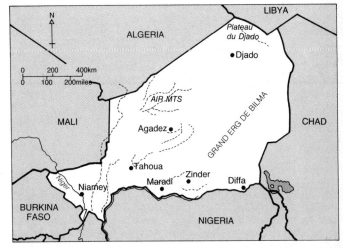

Niger

**Niger,** chief river of W Africa, flowing c.4180 km (2600 mi) in a circuitous, generally eastward course from SW Guinea to a vast delta on the Gulf of Guinea, in Nigeria. An inland delta, in central Mali, is irrigated by a large dam at Sansanding. The chief tributary of the Niger is the Benue R.

**Nigeria,** officially Federal Republic of Nigeria, independent state, (1986 est. pop. 95,200,000), 923,768 km² (356,667 sq mi), W Africa, bordered by the Gulf of Guinea (S), Benin (W), Niger (NW and N), Chad (NE), and Cameroon (E). Nigeria is the most populous country on the continent, and its oil wealth supports the strongest economy in black Africa. The nation is divided into 19 states. Major cities include LAGOS (the capital), IBADAN, OGBOMOSHO, and KANO; a new capital is under construction at ABUJA. Nigeria's main geographical regions include a 800-km (500-mi) coastline of sandy beaches, behind which lies a belt of mangrove swamps and lagoons; a broad, hilly region north of the coastal lowlands, with rain forests in the south and savanna in the north; and the great plateau, a region of plains covered largely with savanna. The highest point (c.2040 m/6700 ft) is in the Adamawa Massif, in the east. Most of the country is drained by the NIGER R. and its tributaries. Petroleum production, which began in the late 1950s, has become the mainstay of the economy. By 1980 average daily production was 2.2 million barrels per day, making Nigeria the world's sixth leading producer, and three refineries were in operation. Other minerals include tin, coal, columbite, iron ore, lead, zinc, and uranium. Agriculture employs about 70% of the work force. The chief crops grown in the north include sorghum, millet, soya beans, peanuts, and cotton; those in the south include maize, rice, palm products, cocoa, and rubber. Livestock raising, forestry, and fishing are also important. The manufacturing sector is growing rapidly; major industries include oil-refining, food-processing, brewing, cement, aluminium, motor vehicles, and textiles. The GNP is US$73,629 million, and the GNP per capita is US$800 (1985). The inhabitants of Nigeria are black Africans, divided into about 250 ethnic groups, of which the Hausa, Fulani, Yoruba, and Ibo together make up two-thirds of the population. Nearly half the people are Muslim, living mostly in the north, and about 35% are Christian, almost all in the south; the rest follow traditional beliefs. English and Hausa are the official languages.

*History.* Before the coming of the British in the late 19th cent., a series of states and city-states were established by various ethnic groups. These included the state of Kanem-Bornu, which expanded into present-day Nigeria in the 11th cent., followed by seven independent Hausa city-states (11th cent.), the Yoruba states of Oyo and BENIN (14th cent.), and the SONGHAI empire (16th cent.). Portuguese navigators, arriving in the late 15th cent. were joined by British, French, and Dutch traders, and a lucrative slave trade developed that continued until about 1875. In the 19th cent. Muslim culture flourished in the Fulani empire, while both Bornu and the Oyo empire were rent by civil wars. Sir George Goldie's commercial activities in the region enabled Britain to claim S Nigeria at the Conference of BERLIN (1884–85). By 1906 Britain controlled all of Nigeria and had established a protectorate over it. Under British rule, the economy grew and the country became more urbanized. In the 1950s new constitutions led to the emergence of political parties and elected representation, and Nigeria was divided (1954) into three regions: Eastern, Western, and Northern, plus Lagos. By 1959 the regions had gained internal autonomy; in 1960 Nigeria attained full independence as a member of the COMMONWEALTH. It became a republic in 1963, with B.N. Azikiwe as president. Severe conflicts within and between regions marked the early years of independence, climaxed by an Ibo-led coup in 1966 that resulted in the deaths of Prime Min. A.T. Balewa and two regional prime ministers, and ended civil government. A second coup that year by Hausa army officers installed a new military regime headed by Lt.-Col. Yakubu Gowon. The Ibos of the Eastern Region proclaimed the independent republic of BIAFRA in 1967, precipitating a disastrous civil war that continued until Biafra's surrender in 1970. Gowon was overthrown in a military coup in 1975, but the new regime restored civilian rule in 1979, when a democratic constitution took effect and Alhaji Shehu SHAGARI became president in free elections. He was reelected in 1983 but was overthrown at the end of the year by another military coup which brought Maj.-Gen. Muhammad Buhari to power. The latter was in turn overthrown in 1985 by fellow army officers, who installed Maj.-Gen. Ibrahim Babangida as president. In the mid-1980s Nigeria faced chronic economic difficulties arising principally from the fall in world oil prices.

**Nigerian heads of government**
*Abubakar Tafawa Balewa (Northern People's Congress), 1960–66
Johnson Aguiyi-Ironsi (military), 1966
Yakubu Gowon (military), 1966–75
Murtala Mohammed (military), 1975–76
Olusegun Obasanjo (military), 1976–79

Shehu Shagari (National Party), 1979–83
Muhammad Buhari (military), 1983–85
Ibrahim Babangida (military), 1985–
*prime minister*

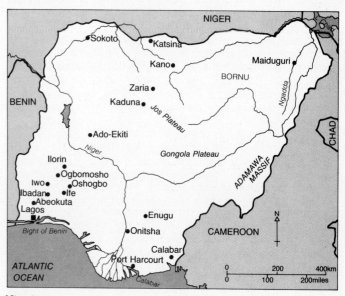

Nigeria

**nightingale,** migratory Old World BIRD of the THRUSH family, celebrated for the song the male sings at night during the breeding season. The 17-cm (6½-in) common nightingale of England and W Europe (*Luscinia megarhynchos*), reddish-brown above and greyish-white below, is shy and rarely seen. It winters in Africa.

**Nightingale, Florence,** 1820–1910, English nurse, the founder of modern NURSING; b. Italy. Her life was dedicated to the care of the sick and war-wounded. In spite of considerable opposition from officialdom, she organized (1854) a unit of 38 women nurses for the Crimean War, and by war's end she had become a legend. The death rate at her hospital in Scutari fell from 42% to 2% in the year of her arrival. In 1860 Nightingale established a nursing school at St Thomas's Hospital, London. In 1907 she became the first woman to be given the British Order of Merit.

**nightjar** or **night hawk, goatsucker, brain-fever bird, poorwill,** secretive members of the BIRD family Caprimulgidae found in both the Old World and New World. The European nightjar (*Caprimulgus europaeus*), 26 cm (10½ in) long, is superbly camouflaged and almost invisible when its rests on the ground during the day. Nightjars are rarely seen, resting by day and hunting moths and other insects at night, but their calls are frequently heard on clear nights. The American whippoorwill (*C. vociferus*) is a nightjar and the related poorwill was the first bird proved to hibernate.

**nightshade,** common name for the family Solanaceae, herbs, shrubs, and trees of warm regions. Many are climbing or creeping types. Rank-smelling foliage typifies many species; the odour is due to the presence of various ALKALOIDS, e.g., scopolamine, nicotine, and atropine. The chief drug plants of the family are BELLADONNA, MANDRAKE, thorn apple, and TOBACCO. The family also includes important food plants, e.g., POTATO, TOMATO, red PEPPER, and AUBERGINE, and ornamentals, e.g., PETUNIA. The name *nightshade* is commonly restricted to members of the genus *Solanum,* typified by white or purplish star-shaped flowers and orange berries. Among the better-known species are Jerusalem cherry (*S. pseudocapsicum*), a house plant popular for its scarlet berries, and the BITTERSWEET, or woody nightshade (*S. dulcamara*).

**Niigata,** city (1986 est. pop. 464,757), capital of Niigata prefecture, N Honshu, Japan, on the Sea of Japan. It is the main international trade port for W Honshu, and exports oil, machinery, and textiles. Niigata had an important chemical industry based on the area's oil and natural gas deposits. The city suffered badly from earthquake damage in 1964.

**Nijinsky, Vaslav,** 1890–1950, Russian ballet dancer. He was trained and made his debut (1907) at St Petersburg. As DIAGHILEV's *premier danseur* he created many of the greatest ballet roles, e.g., *Petrouchka*

(1911; music by STRAVINSKY), *L'Aprés-midi d'un faune* (1912; music by DEBUSSY), and *Le Sacre du printemps* (1913; music by Stravinsky, Nijinsky's own choreography). His career was cut short (1919) by insanity.

**Nijmegen** (‚niemaygən), city (1985 pop. 146,452, agglomeration 235,739), Gelderland prov., central Netherlands, on the Waal R. Its varied industries include representatives of several American companies. The Treaty of Nijmegen (1678-79) ended the Dutch Wars. Notable buildings include the 13th-cent. Groote Kerk and 16th-cent. city hall (Raadhuis). There are ruins of a palace built by Charlemagne in AD 777.

**Nike** (‚niekee), in Greek mythology, goddess of victory. The daughter of Pallas and Styx, she presided over all contests. Representations of her winged form include the *Victory (Nike) of Samothrace* (LOUVRE), one of the greatest Greek sculptures.

**Nikko,** city (1986 est. pop. 21,789), central Honshu, Japan, in Nikko National Park. It is a tourist resort and religious centre famous for its ornate temples and shrines dating from the Edo period (1600–1868); particularly noteworthy is the great shrine (*Toshogu*), constructed in 1617 and housing the tomb of IEYASU.

**Nile,** great river of Africa. The longest river in the world, it flows generally north c.6695 km (4160 mi) from its remotest headstream, the Luvironza R. (in Burundi), to enter the Mediterranean Sea through a vast, triangular delta in N Egypt. Its trunk stream is formed at Khartoum, Sudan by the convergence of the Blue Nile (c.1610 km/1000 mi) and the White Nile (c.3700 km/2300 mi). The Blue Nile, rising in Lake Tana in a region of summer rains, was the source of Egypt's soil-replenishing annual floods prior to construction of the ASWAN HIGH DAM. The White Nile, rising in VICTORIA NYANZA (Lake Victoria), has a more constant flow. Waters from the Nile, which nourished the most long-lived of the great ancient civilizations (see EGYPT), now supply hydroelectricity and support irrigated agriculture in Egypt and in the Sudan's GEZIRA region.

**Nilotes,** people of E Africa, including the Nuer and MASAI, who speak Nilotic languages. Originally from E Sudan, they now inhabit S SUDAN, N UGANDA, and N KENYA. Noted for their tall stature, they are primarily pastoralists. The best ethnographic account of a Nilotic people is E. EVANS-PRITCHARD's *The Nuer.*

**Nilsson, Birgit** (‚nilsən), 1918–, Swedish soprano. Possessed of a powerful voice, she is noted primarily for her Wagnerian roles (see WAGNER, Richard).

**nimbus,** in art, the luminous disc, circle, or other indication of light around the head of a sacred person. Employed in Buddhist and other Oriental art, it was used by the ancient Greeks and Romans to designate gods and heroes. The device appeared in Christian art in the 5th cent. In Christian ICONOGRAPHY, the nimbus may have a number of geometric shapes. *Halo* is a nontechnical term for *nimbus.*

**Nîmes,** city (1982 pop. 129,924), capital of Gard dept., S France. A centre of the wine trade, it handles the fruit and vegetables grown under irrigation to the south. It was a centre of Roman administration and culture. Textile and other industries flourished under later Protestant domination. There are spectacular Roman remains, including the amphitheatre, Maison Carrée (temple of the 1st–2nd cent. AD), Tour Magne, and the nearby aqueduct of Pont-du-Gard.

**Nin, Anaïs** (neen), 1903–77, American writer; b. Paris. Although she wrote several novels, including *A Spy in the House of Love* (1954), Nin is best known for six volumes of diaries (1966–76), recording her psychological and artistic development. She also wrote criticism and essays.

**Nineveh** (‚ninəvə), ancient city, capital of the Assyrian empire, on the Tigris R. opposite modern Mosul, Iraq. Nineveh reached its full glory under SENNACHERIB and ASSURBANIPAL. Excavations have revealed palaces and a CUNEIFORM library. The city fell in 612 BC to a coalition of Babylonians, Medes, and Scythians. It is mentioned often in the Bible.

**Ningbo** or **Ningpo,** city (1984 pop. 4,841,900), ZHEJIANG prov., E China. It is a port and industrial city, with chemical, textile, and engineering industries. In 1984 it was designated as one of 14 coastal cities to receive further foreign investment, and a canal is being built to the GRAND CANAL which will accentuate its role as a communications centre. It has historic importance as a trading port, trading particularly with Japan and with towns along the China coast. Following the Opium War, when Ningbo was blockaded by British forces, it was made a treaty port.

**Ningxia Hui Autonomous Region** or **Ningsia Hui Autonomous Region,** autonomous region, (1985 est. pop. 4,150,000), c.78,000 km² (30,115 sq mi), N central China. A narrow strip separating GANSU and INNER MONGOLIA, during the last 50 years its status and borders have varied considerably. The capital is Yinchuan. The YELLOW RIVER flows through Ningxia and its valley is the main agricultural area with spring wheat, millet, and kaoliang (a type of sorghum) the principal crops. The more mountainous south has extensive pasture lands and forests. Mineral resources are extensive and varied and include major deposits of gypsum. Coal is mined and exported to LANZHOU in Gansu prov. and Baotou in Inner Mongolia. As yet only limited industry has developed.

**niobium** (Nb), metallic element, discovered in 1801 by Charles Hatchett. Formerly called columbium, it is a rare, soft, malleable, ductile, grey-white metal that is used in high-temperature-resistant alloys and special stainless steels. See ELEMENT (table); PERIODIC TABLE.

**Nirvāna,** in BUDDHISM, JAINISM, and HINDUISM, liberation from suffering and from *samsāra,* one's bondage to the repeating cycle of death and rebirth, which is brought about by desire. According to some, it is a state of supreme bliss; according to others, it is simply cessation of suffering. Nirvāna is attainable in life through moral discipline and the practice of YOGA, leading to the extinction of all attachment and ignorance. See also KARMA.

**Niš,** city (1981 pop. 230,711), Serbia, SE Yugoslavia, in the valley of the Nišava R. It is on important N–S rail routes through the Balkans and has railway-engineering industries. A Roman settlement (Naïssus), it was the birthplace of the Emperor CONSTANTINE. It was mainly under Turkish rule from the late 14th cent. to 1877.

**Nishida Kitarō,** 1870–1945, Japanese philosopher. The first Japanese philosopher to join the mainstream of Western philosophical thought, he attempted to combine Western philosophy with Buddhist traditions of thought.

**Niterói,** city (1980 pop. 382,736), in central Brazil. Previously it was the capital of the state of Rio de Janeiro. It is situated across the bay from Rio de Janeiro to which it is connected by bridge and ferry.

**nitric acid,** chemical compound (HNO₃), colourless, highly corrosive, poisonous liquid that gives off choking fumes in moist air. It is miscible with water in all proportions. Commercially, it is usually available in solutions of 52% to 68% nitric acid in water. Solutions containing over 86% nitric acid are commonly called fuming nitric acid. Nitric acid is a strong oxidizing agent (see OXIDATION AND REDUCTION). It reacts with metals, oxides, and hydroxides, forming nitrate salts. See also AQUA REGIA; Wilhelm OSTWALD.

**nitrogen** (N), gaseous element, discovered by Daniel Rutherford in 1772. Nitrogen is a colourless, odourless, tasteless, diatomic gas that is relatively inactive chemically; it occupies about 78% (by volume) of dry air. Its chief importance lies in its compounds, which include NITROUS OXIDE, NITRIC ACID, AMMONIA, many EXPLOSIVES, CYANIDE compounds, FERTILIZERS, and PROTEINS. Nitrogen is present in the PROTOPLASM of all living matter; it and its compounds are necessary for the continuation of life (see NITROGEN CYCLE). See ELEMENT (table); PERIODIC TABLE.

**nitrogen cycle,** the continuous flow of nitrogen from the atmosphere, which is about 78% nitrogen, through the BIOSPHERE by the processes of nitrogen fixation, ammonification (decay), nitrification, and denitrification back to the atmosphere. Nitrogen is an essential constituent of all protoplasm. To enter living systems, however, it must first be 'fixed' (combined with oxygen or hydrogen) into compounds that plants can utilize, such as nitrates or ammonia. Most fixation is performed by certain bacteria living in the soil or in nodules in the roots of leguminous plants (see PULSE, in botany). Plants elaborate the fixed nitrogen into plant protein; then animals consume the plants and convert plant protein into animal protein. Organic nitrogen is returned to the soil as ammonia when animal remains and wastes decay. Then nitrifying bacteria oxidize the ammonia to nitrites and the nitrites to nitrates, which can, like ammonia, be taken up by plants. Still other soil micro-organisms can reduce ammonia nitrates to molecular nitrogen. See also ECOLOGY.

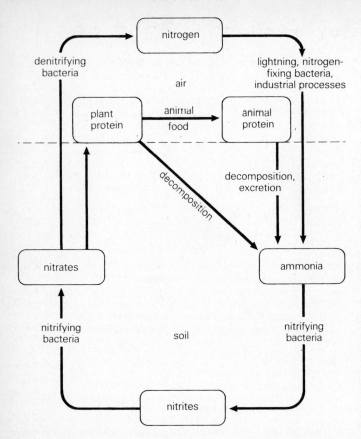

Nitrogen cycle

**nitroglycerine** (C₃H₅N₃O₉), colourless, oily, liquid EXPLOSIVE. An unstable compound that decomposes violently when heated or jarred, nitroglycerine is made less sensitive to shock when mixed with an absorbent material to form DYNAMITE. Nitroglycerine is also a component of smokeless powder and is used in medicine for relief from the symptoms of ANGINA pectoris. It was first produced commercially by Alfred NOBEL.

**nitrous oxide,** colourless gas (N₂O), with a sweetish taste and odour. Although it does not burn, it supports combustion because it decomposes into oxygen and nitrogen when heated. A major use is in dental anaesthetics. It is often called laughing gas because it produces euphoria and mirth when inhaled in small amounts. It is also used in making certain canned pressurized foods, e.g., instant whipped cream.

**Niue,** coral island and self-governing dependency of New Zealand (1979 est. pop. 4000), 260 km² (100 sq mi), in the South Pacific Ocean. The island has fertile soil and exports copra and bananas. It became internally self-governing in 1974, with New Zealand retaining responsibility for defence and external affairs.

**Nixon, Richard Milhous,** 1913–, 37th president of the US (1969–74). As a Republican US representative from California (1947–51) he gained national prominence for his investigation of Alger HISS. In the Senate (1951–53), he attacked the Democratic administration as favourable to socialism. He was elected to the vice presidency on the Republican ticket with Dwight D. EISENHOWER in 1952; they were reelected in 1956. Kept closely informed, Nixon played an important role in government affairs. He ran for president in 1960 but was defeated by John F. KENNEDY, and in 1962 he was defeated in the race for governor of California. In 1968 he again won the Republican presidential nomination and, with his running mate, Spiro T. AGNEW, defeated Hubert H. HUMPHREY and George C. WALLACE. As president, Nixon achieved a cease-fire in the VIETNAM WAR, but only after he had ordered invasions of Kampuchea (1970) and Laos (1971) and the saturation bombing of North Vietnam. In other areas of foreign affairs, he initiated strategic arms limitation talks with the Soviet Union (1959) and visited (1972) the People's Republic of China. At home, he reversed many of the social and economic welfare programmes of Pres. JOHNSON's administration and, hoping to woo the South into the

Republican Party, weakened the federal government's commitment to racial equality. His administration was plagued by economic difficulties that led to the imposition (1971) of wage and price controls. Despite these problems, he and Agnew were easily reelected in 1972, winning a landslide victory over George S. MCGOVERN. (Agnew was forced to resign in 1973 and was replaced by Gerald R. FORD.) Investigations into the WATERGATE AFFAIR and studies by the Internal Revenue Service revealed pervasive corruption in Nixon's administration, and in 1974 the US House of Representatives initiated impeachment proceedings. After completing its investigations, the House judiciary committee recommended (27–30 July) three articles of impeachment: obstruction of justice, abuse of power, and failure to comply with congressional subpoenas. On 5 Aug. Nixon admitted that he had ordered the FBI to halt its investigation of the Watergate burglary. On 9 Aug. he resigned, becoming the first president to do so. A month after succeeding Nixon, Pres. Ford granted him a full pardon, thus quashing the possibility of criminal proceedings against the former president.

**Nizami, al-bin Ilyas ibn-Yusof,** 1140–1202, Persian poet. He was the author of the famous *Five Treasures*, consisting of five short epics; the fourth of these is the *Book of Alexander*, a superb treatment of the medieval legend of ALEXANDER THE GREAT and his quest for the Fountain of Life.

**Njál's Saga,** Old Icelandic SAGA (c.1280), mightiest and most famous of all the sagas. The action of this epic masterpiece takes place in the south of Iceland at the end of the 10th cent. At its core is the drama of the sage farmer, Njál Thorgeirsson, who is burned alive in his home with his violent sons by a confederacy of enemies, and his young friend and protégé, the peerless hero Gunnar of Hlíðarendi, who is also done to death by a band of enemies after a heroic lone defence.

**Njegoš, Petar II Petrović,** 1813–51, last *vladika* (prince–bishop) of MONTENEGRO (r.1830–51) and one of the foremost South Slav poets. A reforming and centralizing ruler, Njegoš is best remembered for three long dramatic poems: *The Ray of the Microcosm* (1845), *The False Czar Stephen the Little* (1851), and *The Mountain Wreath* (1847). The last, an account of a 17th-cent. massacre of Slav converts to Islam, is a lyric–epic meditation on national freedom and the sanctity of life which is a masterpiece of 19th-cent. South Slav literature.

**Njoya, Ibrahim,** 1875–1933, sultan of Bamoun in CAMEROON (r.1890–1923). He tried to blend elements of Islam, Christianity, and Bamoun traditional religion to create a new religion which would unite his people. In 1923 the French dismantled his kingdom into 17 small chiefdoms. He was deported to Yaoundé in 1931.

**Nkrumah, Kwame** (əng̱kroohmah), 1909–72, prime minister (1957–60) and president (1960–66) of GHANA. He was a leader in the struggle to gain independence for the British Gold Coast (now Ghana). His leadership of the new nation grew increasingly dictatorial and autocratic, and he was ousted in 1966.

**No,** chemical symbol of the element NOBELIUM.

**Noah** or **Noe,** in the BIBLE the upright patriarch who, alone with his family, was saved when all his wicked contemporaries perished in the flood. Warned in advance by God, he built the ark, and took on board specimens of every kind of animal. When the flood subsided, he emerged to become the ancestor of subsequent generations. He is also credited with the discovery of agriculture and the growing of vines. Gen. 6–9.

**Nobel, Alfred Bernhard,** 1833–96, Swedish chemist and inventor. He was involved, with his family, in the development and manufacture of explosives, and his invention of DYNAMITE, a mixture of nitroglycerine and inert filler, greatly improved the safety of explosives. Inclined towards pacifism and concerned about the potential uses of the explosives he had invented, he established a fund to provide annual awards, called NOBEL PRIZES, in the sciences, literature, and the promotion of international peace.

**nobelium** (No), radioactive element, first produced artificially in 1958 by A. Ghiorso, T. Sikkeland, J.R. Walton, and Glenn T. Seaborg by carbon-ion bombardment of curium. It is a TRANSURANIC ELEMENT in the ACTINIDE SERIES. Seven isotopes are known. See ELEMENT (table); PERIODIC TABLE.

**Nobel Prize,** award, established and endowed by the will of Alfred NOBEL, given annually for outstanding achievement in one of five fields. By the terms of Nobel's will, the physics and chemistry prizes are judged by the Royal Swedish Academy of Sciences; the physiology or medicine prize, by Sweden's Royal Caroline Medico-Chirurgical Institute; the literature prize, by the Swedish Academy; and the peace prize, by a committee of the Norwegian parliament. Each recipient is presented a gold medal and a sum from the £1.75 million he left as prize money. These five awards were first given in 1901. A sixth, related award, the **Nobel Memorial Prize in Economic Science,** was established and endowed in 1968 by Sveriges Riksbank, the Swedish national bank, and first awarded in 1969. It is judged by the Royal Swedish Academy of Sciences.

**noble gas:** see INERT GAS.

**node,** the name given to each of two points at which the ORBIT of a celestial body crosses a reference plane (usually the ECLIPTIC). The south-to-north crossing occurs at the ascending node; the north-to-south crossing at the descending node. Perturbations due to other bodies cause the nodes to move along the reference plane.

**Noel-Baker, Philip John Noel-Baker, Baron,** 1889–1982, British statesman. After helping to draft (1919) the Covenant of the LEAGUE OF NATIONS, he served (1929–31, 1936–70) as a Labour member of Parliament. After World War II he helped draft the UNITED NATIONS Charter and worked actively for world disarmament. He was awarded the Nobel Peace Prize in 1959.

**Noether, (Amalie) Emmy** (ˌnoːtə), 1882–1935, German mathematician. She made important contributions to the development of abstract algebra, which studies the formal properties, e.g., ASSOCIATIVE LAW, COMMUTATIVE LAW, and DISTRIBUTIVE LAW, of algebraic operations. After finally gaining an official appointment at Göttingen Univ. in 1919, she developed the theories of ideals and of noncommutative algebras. After the Nazis dismissed her and other Jewish professors in 1933, she worked in the US at Bryn Mawr College and at the Institute for Advanced Study, Princeton.

**no-fault insurance:** see INSURANCE.

**Noguchi, Hideyo** (noˌgoohchee), 1876–1928, American bacteriologist; b. Japan; went to the US, 1900. He made important studies of snake venoms and of smallpox and yellow-fever vaccines. In 1913 Noguchi isolated the bacterium *Treponema pallidum* from a syphilis patient, proving that this organism was the cause of syphilis; he also developed a skin test for this disease.

**Noh drama:** see Japanese drama under ORIENTAL DRAMA.

**noise pollution,** sounds produced by human commercial and industrial activities at levels and/or frequencies harmful to health or welfare. Transport vehicles (e.g., trains) and construction equipment (e.g., pneumatic drills) are particular offenders in this regard. Apart from hearing loss, excessive noise can cause lack of sleep, irritability, indigestion, ulcers, and high blood pressure. Noise-induced stress can create severe tension in daily living and may contribute to mental illness. Environmental interests are concerned to determine the noise limits required to protect health and to see the introduction of noise emission standards. See also ENVIRONMENTALISM; POLLUTION.

**Nolan, Sir Sidney Robert,** 1917–, Australian artist. Virtually self-taught, from Melbourne, he achieved his first success in the late 1940s with a series of paintings based on the life of bushranger, Ned KELLY. Subsequent paintings reflect his fascination with Australian explorers, convicts, and the desolate outback. By the 1960s he was based in London, where a retrospective exhibition of his work had been organized by the Whitechapel Gallery (1957). Knighted in 1981, he has recently designed sets for ballets, operas, and plays.

**Noland, Kenneth,** 1924–, American painter. Associated with COLOUR FIELD PAINTING, Noland is best known for stained canvases in target or chevron designs.

**Nolde, Emil,** 1867–1956, German expressionist painter and graphic artist. He was briefly a member of the BRÜCKE group. Influenced by VAN GOGH and German Gothic art, Nolde produced a series of Expressionistic religious pictures. Despite claiming to represent the new Nazi ideology in his work, he was, with the other Expressionists denounced as degenerate (1941) and forbidden to paint.

**nomadism,** a way of life which involves moving from place to place. It is characteristic of HUNTER-GATHERERS but is most frequently applied to pastoralists who move to ensure regular supplies of pasture and water for themselves and above all for their livestock. See EVOLUTION, SOCIOCULTURAL; PASTORALISM.

**Nomenklatura,** an important feature of COMMUNIST PARTY organization which permits a ruling party to control all offices and appointments throughout the country. It consists on the one hand of a list of leading offices to be filled, and on the other a list of people approved by the party to fill them. In effect, the individuals whose names are included in the Nomenklatura form the political elite which runs the collective dictatorship of the communist system.

**nominalism,** in philosophy, theory holding that universal words (*nomina*) or concepts have no objective reality outside the mind, and that only individual things and events exist objectively. The theory, contrasted to Platonic IDEALISM and, in the Middle Ages, to REALISM, is appropriate to MATERIALISM and EMPIRICISM and was strongly held by Hobbes.

**nominative:** see CASE.

**Non-Aligned Movement,** grouping of over 100 THIRD WORLD countries and liberation movements rejecting alignment with either the communist or the Western blocs. Inspired by Jawaharlal NEHRU of India and Josip Broz TITO of Yugoslavia, the movement dates from the 29-nation Bandung (Indonesia) conference of 1955 and was formally established in 1961. Seeking to build closer Third World cooperation in the political, economic, and cultural fields, the movement has been particularly opposed to colonialism and in favour of coexistence. A non-aligned coordinating bureau was set up in 1973 and the movement holds triennial summit conferences.

**nonconformists,** in religion, those who refuse to conform to the requirements (in doctrine or discipline) of an established church. The term is especially applied to Protestant dissenters from the Church of England, who arose soon after the REFORMATION. As the Act of Uniformity (1662) required all clergy to be episcopally ordained, a split became unavoidable.

**non-Euclidean geometry,** branch of GEOMETRY in which the fifth postulate of EUCLIDEAN GEOMETRY is replaced by one of two alternative postulates. From EUCLID's fifth postulate it can be concluded that one and only one line parallel to a given line can be drawn through a point external to the line. The first alternative, which allows two parallels through any external point, leads to the *hyperbolic geometry* developed independently by Nikolai LOBACHEVSKY (1826) and János BOLYAI (1832). The second, which allows no parallels through any external point, leads to the *elliptic geometry* developed by G.F.B. RIEMANN (1854). The results of these two types of non-Euclidean geometry are similar to those of Euclidean geometry in every respect except for the propositions involving parallel lines, either explicitly or implicitly.

**Nonintercourse Act:** see EMBARGO ACT OF 1807.

**Nono, Luigi,** 1924–, Italian composer and teacher. A committed Communist, he also became involved with Pierre BOULEZ and Karlheinz STOCKHAUSEN as a leader of the musical avant-garde. The complexities and esotericism of his serial procedures are made more accessible by the rhetoric and verbal content of his works, such as the cantata *Il canto sospeso* (1955–56), the opera *Intolleranza* (1960–61, rev. 1970), and *Non consumiamo Marx* (1969).

**Nonpartisan League,** organization of Western US farmers and workers formed by Arthur C. Townley in 1915. Its greatest strength was in Minnesota and the Dakotas. Demanding state-owned grain elevators, flour mills, and packing houses, as well as low-cost public housing, it endorsed and even nominated candidates of the major parties. Its influence declined sharply after World War I.

**noradrenaline** ('nawəˌdrenəlin), a CATECHOLAMINE, one of the major neurotransmitters of the sympathetic NERVOUS SYSTEM. An impulse reaching the end of a nerve cell stimulates the cell to secrete noradrenaline, which diffuses to a receptor site on a target organ; this role parallels that of ACETYLCHOLINE in the rest of the nervous system. Noradrenaline also acts as a HORMONE, with effects sometimes opposite to those of ADRENALINE.

**Nordenskiöld, Nils Adolf Erik,** 1832–1901, Swedish explorer; b. Finland. He voyaged to the Arctic, discovering the NORTHEAST PASSAGE in 1878–79.

**Nordic Council,** a five-nation (Denmark, Finland, Iceland, Norway and Sweden) parliamentary assembly. Formed in 1953, it meets annually to discuss Nordic matters and to issue advisory opinions. The Nordic Council of Ministers (est. 1971) implements cooperative measures on the basis of the Treaty of Nordic Cooperation (the Helsinki Convention) signed in 1962.

**Norfolk,** US city (1984 est. pop. 280,000), SE Virginia, on the Elizabeth R. and the southern side of Hampton Roads; founded 1682, inc. 1845. The world's largest naval base is located in its port. Virginia's largest city, Norfolk is also a major coal and grain exporter. Shipbuilding is the leading industry. The city was the object of fighting in the AMERICAN REVOLUTION and in the CIVIL WAR.

**Norfolk,** county in E England (1984 est. pop. 714,500), 5368 km² (2094 sq mi), bordering on the Wash in the NW and the North Sea in the N and E. The county town is NORWICH. It is mainly flat and low-lying with the FENS in the W. The major rivers are the Yare, Bure, Waveney, and Great OUSE, and the famous Norfolk Broads are situated in the E of the county. Agriculture is the most economic activity, with cereal and root crops grown over large areas. GREAT YARMOUTH and Lowestoft are fishing ports, and the coastal area is a popular holiday resort.

**Norfolk Island,** island in the South Pacific Ocean 1700 km (1000 mi) NE of Sydney, Australia. Of volcanic origin, the island, 8 km by 5 km (5 mi by 4 mi), with an area of 40 km² (13 sq mi), was discovered by Captain Cook in 1774 and used as a convict penal settlement (1788–1814; also 1825–55). In 1856 descendants of the *Bounty* mutiny were granted landownership by Queen Victoria and were resettled from the Pitcairn Islands. In 1913 Norfolk Island became a territory of Australia and in 1979 was granted responsible legislative and executive government.

**normal distribution,** of fundamental importance in STATISTICS and defined as a continuous DISTRIBUTION with a relative frequency density defined by $\phi(x) = \dfrac{1}{s\sqrt{(2\pi)}} \exp\left(-\dfrac{x^2}{2s^2}\right)$. In this distribution, originally associated with GAUSS, $x$ is a continuous variate with an ARITHMETIC MEAN of zero and a STANDARD DEVIATION $s$. The distribution is symmetrical about the mean, and the probability corresponding to any interval in the range of the variate can be read from specially prepared tables. In general, as the size of a SAMPLE from any POPULATION increases, the distribution of the sample values approaches that of the normal distribution. For example, measurements of the size of people's feet are nearly normally-distributed, and the distribution can be used to plan the production of the right number of pairs of shoes of each size.

**Norman architecture,** term applied to buildings erected in lands conquered by the Normans: N France, England, S Italy, and Sicily. In France and England, Norman buildings were based on the ROMANESQUE ARCHITECTURE of Lombardy. Churches, abbeys, and castles were massive and sparsely decorated, and featured round arches. The style was developed from 1066 to 1154. The great French works include the beginnings of MONT-SAINT MICHEL and two abbeys at Caen. In England the Normans began nearly all the great cathedrals, including Durham and Westminster Abbey, where only foundations remain. The earliest intact design is the small St John's Chapel (c.1087) at the TOWER OF LONDON. English and French churches were cruciform and square-towered. Blind arcades, carved mouldings, and grotesque sculptured animal forms were common. The ribbed vault at Durham Cathedral (begun 1093) indicated a shift from Norman to GOTHIC ARCHITECTURE. In Italy and Sicily, Byzantine and Arabic elements modified the massive Norman style.

**Norman Conquest,** period in English history following the defeat (1066) of King HAROLD of England by William, duke of Normandy (see WILLIAM I). The conquest was formerly thought to have brought about broad changes in English life. More recently historians have stressed the continuity of English law, institutions, and customs, but the subject remains controversial. The initial military conquest was quick and brutal. By 1070 most of the Anglo-Saxon nobles were dead or had been deprived of their land, and a Norman aristocracy was superimposed on the English. William used the existing Anglo-Saxon administrative system, and the English church gained closer ties with Europe. Norman French was spoken at the court and had a great impact on the English language. NORMAN ARCHITECTURE was also introduced into England.

**Normandy,** region and former province, NW France, bordering on the English Channel. Its economy is based on cattle, fishing, and tourism. Rouen, Le Havre, and Cherbourg have heavy industry. Conquered by the Romans and later (5th cent.) by the FRANKS, the area was repeatedly raided (9th cent.) by the NORSEMEN, or Normans, after whom the region is named. Normandy was ceded (991) by CHARLES III of France to their chief, Rollo, the 1st duke of Normandy. In 1066 Duke William invaded England, where he became king as WILLIAM I. During the HUNDRED YEARS WAR Normandy was permanently restored (1450) to France. The region was the scene of an Allied invasion (1944) during WORLD WAR II.

**Normandy campaign:** see WORLD WAR II.

**Norns,** Norse FATES, who spun and wove the web of life. They were usually three: Urth (Wyrd), past; Verthandi, present; and Skuld, future. The three weird sisters in Shakespeare's *Macbeth* are probably Scottish equivalents of the Norns.

**Norodom Sihanouk** ('nɔrə,dom ,seeənook), 1922–, king (1941–55) of KAMPUCHEA. In 1955 he abdicated the throne in favour of his father and became premier. After his father's death (1960) Sihanouk again became head of state, but not king. He was deposed (1970) in a military coup led by LON NOL. After Lon Nol was overthrown (1975) by Communist forces, Sihanouk returned briefly to Kampuchea as head of state (1975–76). In 1981–82, Sihanouk, in exile, forged a coalition with former POL POT supporters and others to oppose the Vietnamese-dominated HENG SAMRIN government in Kampuchea. In early 1988, however, he entered into negotiations with the Heng Samrin regime.

**Norris, Frank** (Benjamin Franklin Norris), 1870–1902, American novelist. Influenced by the NATURALISM of ZOLA, he wrote the novel *McTeague* (1899), on greed, and two powerful novels attacking the American railroad and wheat industries, *The Octopus* (1901) and *The Pit* (1903).

**Norrköping,** city (1984 pop. 118, 451), Östergötland prov., SE Sweden. It has been a centre of textile manufacture since the early 17th cent. The 16th-cent. castle survived Russian attack in 1719.

**Norse,** another name for the North Germanic, or Scandinavian, group of the Germanic subfamily of the Indo-European family of languages. Norse is the language of Norway and Iceland at any period. Old Norse was the language of the EDDAS and SAGAS. See LANGUAGE (table).

**Norsemen,** Scandinavian VIKINGS who raided and settled on the coasts of NW Germany, the Low Countries, France, and Spain in the 9th and 10th cent. Among the causes of the influx were the desire for wealth, power, and adventure and the attempt of HAROLD I of Norway to subjugate the independent Norwegian nobles, forcing them to look to foreign conquests. The Norsemen's impact was especially lasting in N France, where they began (c.843) to sail up the French rivers, repeatedly attacking, looting, and burning such cities as Rouen and Paris and ruining commerce and navigation. In 911 one of their leaders, Rollo, was given the duchy of NORMANDY by CHARLES III. Rollo's successors expanded their lands and were only nominal vassals of the French kings. The Norsemen accepted Christianity, adopted French law and speech, and continued in history as Normans.

**North, Frederick, 2nd earl of Guilford,** 1732–92, British statesman, known as Lord North. As prime minister (1770–82) under GEORGE III, he pursued colonial policies that led to the AMERICAN REVOLUTION. North later formed (1783) a coalition ministry with Charles James FOX.

**North Africa, campaigns in,** fighting in WORLD WAR II for control of the southern coast of the Mediterranean. It began in Sept. 1940, after the swift Italian conquest of British Somaliland in East Africa. The Italian army in Libya was routed, but the German Afrika Korps, commanded by Field-Marshal ROMMEL, came to their aid. In May 1941 Rommel drove the British back to the Egyptian border, but the British mounted (Nov. 1941) a successful counterattack. On 26 May 1942, the British suffered a major defeat but dug in around Alamein. Commanded by Gen. MONTGOMERY, they withstood German attacks until reinforcements arrived. Montgomery's thrust began on 23 Oct. 1942, and was a brilliant success. The Germans were forced to retreat all the way to Tunisia, where they were bottled up. Meanwhile, US and British troops were occupying territories west of Rommel, around Algiers, Oran, and Casablanca. In May 1943, Rommel's troops were attacked from the W by US troops under Gen. EISENHOWER, from the S by Montgomery's troops, and from the SW by a Free French army. On 12 May about 250,000 Axis soldiers capitulated. Earlier, the British had reconquered most of East Africa.

**North America,** third largest continent, 24,346,000 km² (c.9,400,00 sq mi), usually considered to include all the lands and adjacent islands in the Western Hemisphere located N of the Isthmus of Panama (which connects it with South America). The countries of the continent are the US and Canada, known as Anglo-America; Mexico; the nations S of Mexico, known as CENTRAL AMERICA; and the countries of the WEST INDIES or Caribbean islands (the many islands located in and around the CARIBBEAN SEA off the SE mainland coast). HAWAII (formerly part of Oceania), the French islands of ST PIERRE AND MIQUELON, and GREENLAND are all categorized as part of North America. The principal topographical feature is the North American Cordillera, a complex mountain region in the west that includes the ROCKY MTS. Mt MCKINLEY (6194 m/20,320 ft), in Alaska, is the highest point; the lowest point is 86 m (282 ft) below sea level, in DEATH VALLEY. The climate ranges from polar to tropical, with arid and semiarid conditions predominating over much of the interior. See map in separate section.

**North American Indian art,** diverse traditional arts of native North Americans. These arts were a significant part of the everyday lives of their creators. In each region at least one art form was developed in response to the environment, the ideology and way of life, and the availability of materials. In all regions animal skins were worked. The cultures of the Eastern woodlands, e.g., the Iroquois, made pottery, baskets, and quill- and bead-work as well as carved wooden MASKS. The Plains Indians, e.g., the SIOUX, used beads and quills to paint or decorate their hides, which were used for clothing, containers, and teepees. Using stone, ivory, and bones, the ESKIMO of the Arctic carved fine sculptures of animal life. The Indians of the Northwest Coast, e.g., the KWAKIUTL, used elaborate wood-carving techniques to fabricate houses, huge CANOES, and TOTEM poles. In this work human and animal figures were stylized to abstraction. The Southwest tribes had a highly developed art whose tradition went back to pre-Columbian times. An art of strong, graphic, geometric design developed for pottery decoration. The PUEBLO INDIANS, e.g., the NAVAHO, developed sophisticated silver-working techniques, used largely for jewelry. In recent years, works of the ever-diminishing number of North American Indian craftsmen have come into vogue, e.g., jewelry, ESKIMO ART, textiles, and KACHINA dolls.

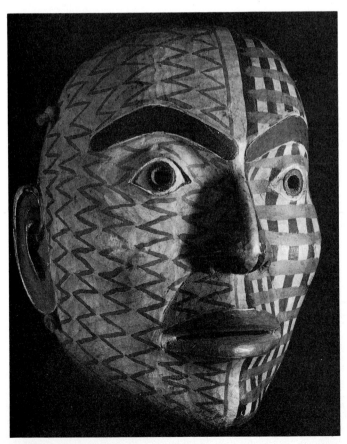

North American Indian mask

**North American Indians,** peoples inhabiting North America before the arrival of the Europeans; now also known as native Americans. They were called Indians because it was incorrectly believed that COLUMBUS had reached the East Indies. Migrating in waves from Asia (see AMERICAN INDIANS, PREHISTORY OF), these peoples spoke widely varying AMERICAN INDIAN LANGUAGES, but all had Mongoloid straight black hair, dark eyes, and yellow- to red-brown skin. In 1492 they numbered 1 to 2 million N of Mexico, in six major cultural areas: Northwest Coast, Plains, Plateau, Eastern Woodlands, Northern, and Southwest.

*Northwest Coast.* Peoples of the Northwest Coast (e.g., KWAKIUTL, Haida, Modoc, Tsimshian) lived along the Pacific from S Alaska to N California and spoke Nadene, Wakashan, and Tsimshian languages. They subsisted chiefly on salmon, sea and land mammals, and wild fruits, and built wooden houses and boats. Their arts included weaving, basketry, masks, and TOTEM poles. Their generally stratified societies, whose ceremonial displays of wealth included the POTLATCH, were not affected by whites until the late 18th cent.

*Plains.* Plains peoples lived in the grasslands from the Mississippi R. to the Rocky Mts. and from S Canada to Texas, speaking mainly Algonquian–Wakashan, Aztec–Tanoan, and Hokan–Siouan languages. Sedentary tribes (e.g., Omaha, Mandan, PAWNEE) farmed the river valleys and lived in walled villages of domed earth lodges. The nomadic tribes (e.g., BLACKFOOT, CHEYENNE, COMANCHE) hunted buffalo on foot until they acquired horses in the 18th cent. for food, clothing, and TEPEES. Their culture was characterized by warrior clans, the coup (a war honour awarded for striking an enemy with conspicuous bravery), the SUN DANCE, and bead-and-feather artwork. A mutually intelligible sign language developed among the nomadic Plains Indians, who were the last to submit to white encroachments.

*Plateau.* Peoples of the Plateau (e.g., Kootenai, NEZ PERCÉ, Paiute), from S Canada to California and the Southwest, were diverse in language and culture. Sedentary California native Americans, living in brush shelters or lean-tos, gathered edible plants, made acorn bread, and hunted small game. Their basketry was highly developed. Indians in the harsh environment between the Cascades and the Rockies lived in partly buried lodges and hunted small game, fished with nets and spears, and gathered insects. Their social, religious, and political institutions were simple. The adoption (c.1730) from the Plains Indians of the horse and tepee changed the plateau culture markedly.

*Eastern Woodlands.* In the Eastern Woodlands, Algonquian–Wakashan and Hokan–Siouan speakers predominated. Peoples from the Atlantic to the Mississippi (e.g., DELAWARE, HURON, IROQUOIS CONFEDERACY, MOHEGAN) were deer hunters; the women also grew corn, squash, and beans. Their houses included the dome-shaped wigwam and the longhouse; they used the birchbark canoe. Males wore deerskin clothing, face and body paint, and scalp locks. Peoples in the area from the Ohio R. to the Gulf of Mexico (e.g., CHEROKEE, Choctaw, Natchez, SEMINOLE) developed a farming and trading economy featuring a high technology and excellent pottery. A stratified society observed elaborate rites including sun worship; burial mounds (see MOUND BUILDERS) were unique to these groups.

*Northern Tribes.* In the semiarctic Northern area, covering most of Canada, Algonquian–Wakashan and Nadene tongues predominated. Nomadic hunters (e.g., Kutchin, Montagnais, and Naskapi) followed caribou migrations for food, clothing, and shelter; the snowshoe was important to their material culture. Religion centred on the SHAMAN.

*Southwest.* Peoples of the Southwest (e.g., APACHE, NAVAHO, PUEBLO INDIANS), spoke mainly Aztec–Tanoan languages and reflected the advanced culture of the AZTECS to the south. By 700 BC the basketmakers had mastered intensive agriculture and pottery making. The 'cliff dwellers' later built terraced community houses and ceremonial KIVAS on cliff ledges. The Pueblo tribes further developed farming, pottery, textiles, and a complex mythology and religion.

*Contemporary Indian Life.* After the long struggle (see INDIAN WARS) between whites and Indians came to an end in the 1890s, Indians settled into a life dominated by poverty, poor education, unemployment, and gradual dispersal. US government policy, administered by the Bureau of INDIAN AFFAIRS, encouraged converting tribal lands into individual holdings, many of which were sold to whites. The Indian Reorganization Act of 1934 aimed at revitalization of Indian economic life, but also at assimilation into white society; the policy of the 1950s to terminate tribes aggravated the situation. In the 1970s the AMERICAN INDIAN MOVEMENT was organized, and various Indian tribes filed suits to reclaim formerly seized lands from the US government. Of approximately 1.5 million Indians in the US today, most live in the Southwest and mountain states. Survivors of many eastern tribes live among whites in OKLAHOMA, while unassimilated native culture is strongest among the Pueblos of Arizona and New Mexico and among some tribes of the Pacific Northwest. See also articles on individual tribes.

**Northampton,** county town (1981 pop. 154,172) of Northamptonshire, Midlands of England, on R. Nene, 97 km (60 mi) NW of London. It has a variety of industries, including the manufacture of footwear, for which the town is famous. It was designated as a New Town in 1968. There are two churches within the town which date back to the 12th cent.

**Northamptonshire,** inland county in E Midlands of England (1984 est. pop. 539,800), 2367 km² (923 sq mi), bordering on Leicestershire in the N. The county town is NORTHAMPTON. The land is generally undulating with low hills and broad valleys. The main rivers are the Welland and the NENE which drain into The Wash. Agriculture is the main economic activity over much of the county, including wheat production and cattle and sheep raising. Iron ore was formerly mined within the county and there were large iron works at Corby.

**North Atlantic Drift,** warm ocean current in the N Atlantic Ocean. It is a continuation of the GULF STREAM, the merging point being at lat. 40°N and long. 60°W. Off the British Isles, it splits into two branches, one north and one south. It is responsible for the warm climate of W Europe.

**North Atlantic Treaty Organization** (NATO), military alliance established (1949) by Belgium, Canada, Denmark, France, Iceland, Italy, Luxembourg, the Netherlands, Norway, Portugal, the UK, and the US, and later joined by Greece and Turkey (1952), West Germany (1955), and Spain (1982). Its aim is to safeguard the Atlantic community, particularly against the Soviet bloc. NATO's policies are determined and coordinated by the North Atlantic Council, which has headquarters in Brussels (Belgium) and is under the chairmanship of NATO's secretary general. The strategic area covered by NATO is divided into three commands: Allied Command Europe (ACE) with its headquarters (SHAPE) in Mons (Belgium) and under the command of the Supreme Allied Commander Europe (SACEUR); Allied Command Atlantic (ACLANT) with headquarters in Norfolk (Virginia, US); and Allied Command Channel (ACCHAN) with headquarters at Northwood (UK). NATO's highest military authority is its Military Committee, located in Washington (US). France withdrew from NATO's integrated military command in 1966; Spain does not participate; and Greece has participated only intermittently because of tensions with fellow member Turkey.

**North Carolina,** state of the US (1984 est. pop. 6,165,000), area 136,198 km² (52,586 sq mi), situated in the SE US, bordered by the Atlantic Ocean (E), South Carolina and Georgia (S), Tennessee (W), and Virginia (N). RALEIGH is the capital, and Charlotte is the largest city, followed by Greensboro and Winston-Salem. The low-lying coastal tidewater country, marked by Cape Hatteras and off-shore islands, is separated by the rolling hills of the Piedmont plateau from the BLUE RIDGE and GREAT SMOKY MTS, both parts of the APPALACHIAN range, in the W. North Carolina's prosperous economy is led by the production of tobacco and related products, textiles, chemicals, and furniture. Broiler chickens, pigs, soybeans, and peanuts are the other main agricultural commodities. The state is a major source of feldspar, mica, phosphate, and other minerals; forestry and fishing are also important. In 1980 75% of the population was non-Hispanic white and 22% was black; c.1% was native American, mostly Cherokee. During the 1580s Sir Walter Raleigh tried but failed to establish a colony on Roanoke Island. In the 18th cent. settlement was slow because of conflicts with the Indians and quarrels with the proprietors of the colony. The Cherokees were forcibly removed in the 19th cent., and North Carolina sided with the confederacy in the Civil War. During Reconstruction manufacturing and farm tenancy replaced the plantations, and industrial expansion has continued until the present. Despite considerable poverty in the 1930s, in recent years North Carolina's economy has grown faster than that of any other southern state.

**Northcliffe, Alfred Charles William Harmsworth, Viscount,** 1865–1922, English journalist, one of the most spectacular of popular journalists and publishers in the history of the British press; b. Ireland; brother of Harold, Viscount ROTHERMERE. He launched *Answers to Correspondents,* a weekly, in 1888 and in five years increased circulation to more than a million copies. In 1894 he bought the London *Evening News,* later founding the *Daily Mail* (1896) and the *Daily Mirror* (1903). Gaining control of the dying *Times* (1908), he put it back on its feet. His newspaper campaigns in WORLD WAR I influenced England's conduct of the war.

**North Dakota,** state of the US (1984 est. pop. 686,000), area 183,022 km² (70,665 sq mi), located in north–central US, bordered by Minnesota (E), South Dakota (S), Montana (W), and the Canadian provinces of Saskatchewan and Manitoba (N). The capital is BISMARCK; the largest city, Fargo, had only 60,000 residents in 1980. Low-lying plains to the E give way to the rolling hills of the drift prairie, and, across the MISSOURI R. in the SW, are found the wind- and rain-eroded clay and sand formations known as the Badlands. The W is semiarid but the E has enough rainfall to support crops on rich chernozem soils. The state produces one-tenth of the US wheat crop, and its economy is largely agricultural; cattle and grain are also significant. Oil, natural gas, and the country's largest reserves of lignite are found in North Dakota. Most industries are based on the processing of these mineral and agricultural products. It is one of the most sparsely populated states and in 1980 97% of the population was non-Hispanic white. The area was obtained by the US in the LOUISIANA PURCHASE (1803) and from the British (1818), but it was not until 1851 that the first farming community was established. In the 1860s the Indians were subdued, and subsequently thousands of European immigrants arrived. Agrarian discontent fuelled support for the Populist Party. Oil was discovered in 1951, and in the 1970s the national energy crisis encouraged the exploitation of North Dakota's mineral resources.

**Northeast Passage,** sea route along the northern coast of Europe and Asia, between the Atlantic and Pacific Oceans. The British, seeking a shorter route to India, made (1550s) the first attempts to find the passage. The Dutch explorer Willem BARENTZ and the Englishman Henry HUDSON continued the search, as did the Russians. In 1878–79 N.A.E. Nordenskjöld of Sweden first traversed the passage. Soviet icebreakers now keep the route open for most of the year.

**Northern Ireland:** see IRELAND.

**northern lights:** see AURORA.

**Northern Mariana Islands,** commonwealth of the US (1980 est. pop. 16,758), c.479 km² (185 sq mi), comprising 16 islands (6 inhabited) of the Marianas (all except GUAM), in the W Pacific Ocean; formerly part of the US Trust Territory of the PACIFIC ISLANDS. The three main islands are SAIPAN, the capital of the Northern Marianas and administrative centre of the trust territory; Rota; and Tinian. US aid, tourism, and the production of small amounts of copra, beef, and sugar are mainstays of the economy. Most of the people are Chamorros (i.e., of mixed Spanish, Filipino, and Micronesian descent). The islands were discovered (1521) and named the Ladrones (Thieves) Islands by MAGELLAN, and renamed (1668) by Spanish Jesuits. Germany purchased them from Spain in 1899. In 1914 they were captured by Japan and were made a Japanese mandate by the League of Nations in 1920. US forces occupied the Marianas in 1944 during WORLD WAR II, and in 1947 they became part of the US Trust Territory. Voters approved separate status for the islands as a US commonwealth in 1975; they became internally self-governing under US military protection in 1978.

**Northern Territory,** territory (1986 pop. 154,400), 1,347,525 km² (520,280 sq mi), north central Australia. DARWIN is the capital, largest city, and chief port. ALICE SPRINGS is a major tourist centre for AYERS ROCK. The Aboriginal population of the Northern Territory accounts for almost one-quarter of the total, a large proportion living in a traditionally oriented style on land to which they secured title under the Aboriginal Land Rights (Northern Territory) Act 1976. Mining is the principal industry; uranium, bauxite, manganese, copper, gold, and bismuth are the most valuable mineral resources. Beef cattle, grazed in the hot, semiarid plains of the interior, are the leading agricultural product. The Northern Territory was transferred to direct rule by the Commonwealth in 1911 after being part of NEW SOUTH WALES (1825–63) and SOUTH AUSTRALIA (1863–1911). It became self-governing in 1978, in preparation for eventual statehood.

**Northern War,** 1700–21, European conflict, the main purpose of which was to break the power of the Swedish empire, then the major Baltic power. Sweden's chief antagonists were Russia, under PETER I, and Saxony–Poland. Russia was anxious to seize some of Sweden's territories in order to gain a Baltic coastline. CHARLES XII, the young Swedish king, met with initial success. After forcing Denmark out of the war he turned eastward, where he defeated a superior Russian force at Narva (1700). He invaded Poland, took Warsaw and Cracow (1702), and forced the election of STANISLAUS I as king of Poland. He was less successful in Russia. After invading the Ukraine (1708) with the help of MAZEPA, he was cut off and utterly defeated by Peter at Poltava (1709). Forced into exile in Bessarabia, he induced the sultan to declare war on Russia (see RUSSO-TURKISH WARS). Meanwhile, the Swedish possessions in the north were being taken over by Russia and its allies: Denmark and Poland (which had expelled Stanislaus and again switched sides), Saxony, Hanover, and Prussia. Charles returned north in 1714 but was killed (1718) while fighting in Norway. His successors sued for peace. By the Treaty of Nystad (1721) Russia gained Estonia, Ingria, and Livonia. The war marked the end of Swedish power and the emergence of Russia as a great European power.

**North Pole,** northern end of the earth's axis, lat. 90°N, distinguished from the north MAGNETIC POLE. See ARCTIC, THE.

**North Rhine–Westphalia,** state (1986 pop. 16,674,000), 34,054 km² (13,148 sq mi), capital of Düsseldorf, NW Germany. Formed in 1947, in the British zone of occupation, it includes the former province of Westphalia and the districts of Aachen, Cologne, Düsseldorf, and Lippe. It includes the RUHR and is a heavily industrialized and urbanized region, producing coal and steel and a wide range of metal manufactures and textiles. It joined the Federal Republic in 1949.

**North Sea,** arm of the Atlantic Ocean, c.574,980 km² (222,000 sq mi), NW Europe, separating Great Britain from Norway and central Europe. Long known for its rich cod and herring fisheries, it is now more important for the substantial oil and gas deposits discovered (1970) under its floor.

**Northumberland,** county in NE England (1984 est. pop. 300,700), 5031 km² (1962 sq mi), bordering on the North Sea in the E. In the 1974 local government reorganization it lost the SE industrial area to the newly formed county of Tyne and Wear. It is the most northerly county in England, bordering on Scotland. The land is hilly in the N in the Cheviot Hills and in the W in the PENNINES. The R. TWEED forms the N border and the county is drained by the Coquet and Blyth rivers. Sheep-rearing is common and coal is mined in the extreme S. LINDISFARNE (Holy Island) and the Farne Islands are situated a short distance offshore towards the N.

**Northumbria, kingdom of,** one of the Anglo-Saxon kingdoms in England. It was originally formed by the union (early 7th cent.) of the kingdoms of Bernicia and Deria, which had been settled (c.500) by invading Angles. At the Synod of Whitby (663) King Osiu established the Roman Church over the Celtic Church. The late 7th and 8th cent. were Northumbria's cultural golden age. In the 9th cent. much of the kingdom fell to invading Danes, but in 920 all Northumbria recognized Edward the Elder of WESSEX as overlord.

**North West Cape,** region in NW Western Australia on the Indian Ocean. The first evidence of a European landing on Australian shores, a pewter plate dated 1616, nailed to a wooden post by Dirk Hartog, was found at Cape Inscription. The Monte Bello Islands were used for British atomic tests in 1952. Exmouth Gulf was the site of Australia's first oil flow followed in 1964 by Barrow Island; Learmonth is the mainland service point for current offshore oil exploration and development on the North-West Shelf. At the northern tip of the Cape is a US naval communications base.

**North West Company,** fur-trading organization (1784–1821) which explored western Canada. Organized by Montreal trading companies, it established new trading routes and posts in the Pacific Northwest. The company's aggressive rivalry with the HUDSON'S BAY COMPANY led to ruinous warfare over the RED RIVER SETTLEMENT and to amalgamation of the two companies in 1821.

**Northwest Ordinance:** see ORDINANCE OF 1787.

**Northwest Passage,** sea ways along the northern coast of North America, between the Atlantic and Pacific Oceans. The idea of a short route from Europe to India and China prompted many expeditions to find the passage. The English explorer Sir Martin FROBISHER explored (1576–78) the eastern approaches to the region. Subsequent explorations were made by John Davis, Henry HUDSON, William BAFFIN, William Parry, and Sir John FRANKLIN, whose mission, although it proved the passage existed, ended in tragedy. The expedition (1850–54) of Robert J. Le M. McCLURE first brought news of the existence of the passage to England, but it was not traversed by ship until 1903–06, when Roald AMUNDSEN of Norway accomplished the feat. In the 1960s the discovery of oil on Alaska's North Slope (see PRUDHOE BAY) renewed commercial interest in the route.

**Northwest Territories,** region of Canada (1984 est. pop. 49,500), over one-third of the country's area (3,379,684 km²/1,304,896 sq mi), situated in the NW, including all W of Hudson Bay, E of the Yukon, and N. of lat. 60° N. It lies only 800 km (500 mi) from the North Pole, making it the most northern landmass. The area is divided into three administrative units: Keewatin, W of Hudson Bay; Mackenzie, E of the Yukon; and Franklin, in the N, which includes the Arctic Archipelago. YELLOWKNIFE is the territorial capital and largest settlement. Northwest Territories slopes from the Mackenzie Mts in the W towards Hudson Bay in the E and to the Arctic Archipelago in the NE. The treeline runs from the Mackenzie R. delta in the NW to Hudson Bay, and beyond it lies treeless tundra, with lakes, swamps and muskeg. The southern half is dominated by lakes, including the Great Bear Lake and the Great Slave Lake, both of which are drained into the Beaufort Sea by the Mackenzie R. Parts of the archipelago are mountainous, and the climate is moderated by the sea, which is nonetheless iced over for most of the year. Mining is the major industry in this sparsely populated region, extracting zinc, lead, gold, tungsten, and fossil fuels. White Canadians comprise only 42% of the population, and they are concentrated in the relatively fertile Mackenzie R. valley. The 15,000 indigenous Inuit of the northern coast and archipelago make a living from fishing and fur trapping. The 11,000 Indian or Dene live S of the treeline hunting caribou and fur trapping. Most of the area is impassable by road or railway. Between 1610 and 1870 the area was owned and exploited for its furs by the Hudson's Bay Company. Sold to the Canadian confederation, the boundaries were established in 1912. Not until the 20th cent. was the N exploited for its minerals, despite the problems of the climate and permafrost. The federal government has financed much of the development. There are competing claims for the land rights between white Canadians and indigenous peoples.

**Northwest Territory,** first national territory of the US, including present-day states of Ohio, Indiana, Illinois, Michigan, Wisconsin, and part of Minnesota. Explored by the French in the 1600s, it was ceded to Britain (1763) after the FRENCH AND INDIAN WARS, and to the US (1783) after the AMERICAN REVOLUTION. The ORDINANCE OF 1787 set up the machinery for organization of the territory. British–American rivalry for control of the area continued, however, until the Treaty of GHENT (1814), ending the WAR OF 1812, gave the region irrevocably to the US.

**North Yorkshire,** county in NE England (1984 est. pop. 691,100), 8309 km² (3241 sq mi), bordering on Lancashire in the W and the North Sea in the E. The county was formed in 1974 from the North Riding of Yorkshire. In the W there is the upland area of the PENNINES with peaks such as Ingleborough at 723 m (2371 ft). The central part is occupied by the Vale of York with the North York moors to the E. The Cleveland Hills are in the N and the Yorkshire Wolds are in the SE. The Vale of York contains much fertile agricultural land where cereals, potatoes, and other crops are grown. YORK is the main town, and Scarborough and Whitby are coastal resorts. Harrogate is a famous spa town.

**Norway,** Nor. *Norge,* officially the Kingdom of Norway, constitutional monarchy (1985 pop. 4,150,00), 324,219 km² (125,181 sq mi), N Europe, on the W Scandinavian peninsula; bordered by the North Sea (SW), the Skagerrak (S), Sweden (E), Finland and the USSR (NE), the Barents Sea (N), and the Atlantic Ocean (W). Major cities include OSLO (the capital), BERGEN, and TRONDHEIM. Norway is a rugged, mountainous country. Its 2740-km (1700-mi) coastline is fringed with islands and deeply indented by FJORDS; from the coast the land rises precipitously to high plateaus, reaching 2468 m (8098 ft) in the Jotunheimen range and including Jostedalsbreen, the largest glacier field in Europe. Norway's economy was transformed in the late 1960s by discovery of large oil and gas reserves in the NORTH SEA; by 1978 petroleum accounted for 20% of export earnings. Forestry, fishing, and the shipping and trading carried on by Norway's great merchant fleet are mainstays of the economy. The production of aluminium, pulp and paper, and electrochemicals is also important. Less than 4% of the land is cultivated; cattle, sheep, and reindeer are raised. The many rapid rivers furnish hydroelectric power. The GNP is $57,090 million and the GNP per capita is $13,820 (1983). The majority of the people are of Scandinavian stock, but there are many Lapps and Finns in the north. Two forms of Norwegian, Bokmål and Nynorsk, are official languages. The Lutheran Church is established. The parliament (*Storting*) has a lower house of 116 and an upper house of 39 members, elected for a four-year term.

*History.* In the 9th cent. Norway was still divided into numerous petty kingdoms. The move toward political unity began c.900 under its first king, HAROLD I, and Christianity was established by OLAF II (r.1015–28). Dynastic feuds wracked the country until the 12th cent., when King Sverre consolidated royal power, and Norway enjoyed peace and prosperity under HAAKON IV and MAGNUS VI in the 13th cent. In 1397 the KALMAR UNION united Norway, Denmark, and Sweden; Sweden broke away in 1523, but Norway was ruled by Danish governors until 1814, when Denmark ceded it to Sweden. In the 19th cent. Norwegian nationalism emerged as a potent force, and in 1905 the union with Sweden was dissolved and Norway became an independent constitutional monarchy under HAAKON VII. Norway was neutral in World War I but was occupied (1940–45) by German forces in WORLD WAR II; the Norwegian merchant fleet, however, was placed in Allied service. Postwar recovery was rapid. Economic policy included a degree of socialization under the Labour Party, which dominated the government until 1965. Norway broke from its traditional neutrality by joining the NORTH ATLANTIC TREATY ORGANIZATION in 1949. King Haakon, who had reigned for 52 years, died in 1957 and was succeeded by his son, OLAF V. In 1972 Norway voted in a referendum against joining the EUROPEAN COMMUNITY, following which minority Labour governments were in power until 1981 and again from 1986, under Gro Harlem Brundland.

**Post-war Norwegian prime ministers**
Einar Gerhardsen (Labour), 1945–51
Oscar Torp (Labour), 1951–55
Einar Gerhardsen (Labour), 1955–63
John Lyng (Conservative), 1963
Einar Gerhardsen (Labour), 1963–65
Per Borten (Centre), 1965–71
Trygve Bratteli (Labour), 1971–72
Lars Korvald (Christian Democrat), 1972–73
Trygve Bratteli (Labour), 1973–76
Odvar Nordli (Labour), 1976–81
Gro Harlem Brundtland (Labour), 1981
Kåre Willoch (Conservative), 1981–86
Gro Harlem Brundtland (Labour), 1986–

**Norwegian language,** member of the North Germanic, or Scandinavian, group of the Germanic subfamily of the Indo-European family of languages. Today there are two official forms of Norwegian: *bokmål* [book language] (also called *riksmål* [national language] and Dano-Norwegian), which is the language of the cities, the official and professional classes, and literature; and *nynorsk* [new Norwegian] (also called *landsmål* [country language]), which is a standardization of rural dialects and is spoken primarily in rural areas. See LANGUAGE (table).

**Norwich,** county town (1981 pop. 169,814) of NORFOLK, E England, at confluence of R. Wensum and R. Yare, 158 km (98 mi) NE of London. Industries found in the town include engineering, printing and the manufacture of footwear and mustard. There is a cathedral which is partly Norman. Other historic buildings within the town include the Norman castle and a 15th-cent. guildhall. The Univ. of East Anglia is situated 4 km (2 mi) to the W of the city centre. It admitted its first students in 1963.

**Norwid Cyprian,** 1821–83, Polish poet. He wrote experimental verse; his *Promethidion* (1851) and *Vademecum* (1863) have had a far greater impact since his death than during his lifetime.

**nose,** organ of breathing and smell. The external nose consists of bone and cartilage. The hollow internal nose, above the roof of the mouth, is divided by the septum (wall) into two nasal cavities extending from the nostrils to the PHARYNX. The cavities are lined with a mucous membrane, which is covered with fine hairs that help to filter dust and impurities from the air before it reaches the lungs; the air is also moistened and warmed.

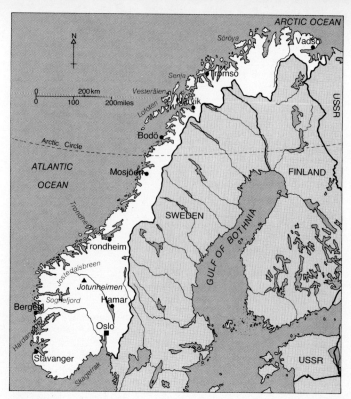

Norway

High in each nasal cavity is a small tract of mucous membrane containing olfactory cells. Hairlike fibres in these nerve cells, responding to various odours, send impulses along the olfactory nerve to the brain and thus produce the sense of smell. The back of the nasal cavity is connected to the EAR by the eustachian tube.

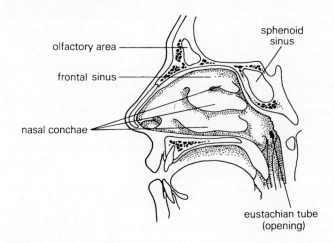

Nose

**Notre-Dame de Paris,** cathedral of Paris, a major achievement of early GOTHIC ARCHITECTURE, on the Île de la Cité, in the Seine R. The cornerstone was laid in 1163, the high altar consecrated in 1183, and the nave completed except for roofing in 1196. In 1230 the nave was reconstructed and flying BUTTRESSES added. Chapels were soon added between the buttresses, altering the building's plan and aesthetic. The cathedral was not completed until the 14th cent. Its majestic west front is famous for its portals, sculptures, and huge ROSE WINDOW.

**Nottingham,** city and county town (1981 pop. 273,300), Nottinghamshire, E Midlands of England, on R. Trent 72 km (45 mi) NE of Birmingham. It was once famous for lace-making, but the major industries now are bicycles, hosiery, and light engineering. There is a

17th-cent. castle which was restored in the 19th cent. Nottingham Univ. was created in 1948 from the former University College (established 1881). The city is the birthplace of William BOOTH.

**Nottinghamshire,** inland county in E Midlands of England (1984 est. pop. 1,000,100), 2164 km² (844 sq mi), bordering on Derbyshire in the W and Lincolnshire in the E. The county town is NOTTINGHAM. Most of the county is low-lying, apart from a hilly area in the SW between Nottingham and Mansfield. There are remnants of Sherwood Forest. The major river is the TRENT. Mixed farming is common in rural areas and coal is mined in the W. Mansfield, Worksop, and Nottingham are all important industrial towns. There are several large coal-fired power stations situated along the R. Trent.

**Nouakchott** (nwahk͵shot), city (1984 pop. 350,000), capital of Mauritania, on the Atlantic Ocean. A small village in 1957, when it became Mauritania's capital, Nouakchott has grown into the country's largest city. Its ocean port, c.6.5 km (4 mi) from the city proper, has modern storage facilities, especially for petroleum, and a deepwater harbour was built in the 1980s. The city is situated on a major road and has an international airport.

**noun:** see PART OF SPEECH.

**Novalis,** pseud. of **Friedrich von Hardenberg** (noh͵vahlis), 1772–1801, German poet. Influenced by FICHTE, he was one of the great German romantics. His major work, the novel *Heinrich von Ofterdingen* (1802), describes symbolically the artist's search for the 'blue flower' of Romantic poetry which will transform the world. *Hymns to the Night* (1800) is a collection of erotic religious lyrics composed after the death of his young love, Sophie von Kühn. His fragments and aphorisms are an important contribution to Romantic aesthetic theory, while his early essay, *Christendom, Or Europe* was an influential conservative perspective on European religious and cultural history.

**Nova Scotia,** province of Canada (1984 est. pop. 872,000), area 55,491 km² (21,425 sq mi), located in the eastern Maritime provinces, bordered by the Gulf of St Lawrence (N), the Atlantic Ocean (E,S), and New Brunswick and the Bay of Fundy (E). HALIFAX is the capital and largest city, followed by Sydney on the island; 56% of the population is urban in residence. The mainland peninsula is separated from Cape Breton Island by a narrow channel. It consists of NW highlands and a SE lowland coast, which is rocky and indented. Considerable mining (of coal, gypsum, barite, and salt) occurs in Nova Scotia and fishing (for cod, lobster, and haddock) is next in importance. Most of the industry involves fish- and food-processing, while there is some dairying and orchard farming in the NW. The Micmac Indians were the original inhabitants, and present-day Annapolis Royal was settled by the French in 1605, in part of the region called Acadia. Although Britain gained control of the mainland (1713), France still held Cape Breton Island until losing it in the FRENCH AND INDIAN WARS. The French Acadians were expelled and many United Empire Loyalists settled after the American Revolution. In 1820 the two parts became a single province, and Nova Scotia was the first colony to achieve responsible government (1848) before joining the Canadian federation (1867). Many British immigrants arrived in the first half of the 19th cent., but in the 20th cent. development was thwarted by high freight rates to the rest of Canada. Since 1950 the federal government has tried to bring prosperity, but has not been entirely successful.

**novel,** sustained work of prose fiction, as distinguished from the SHORT STORY. The term derives from the Italian Renaissance *novella,* a compact, realistic tale exemplified in BOCCACCIO's *Decameron* (14th cent.). The novel also descended from the often supernatural medieval romance. A realistic precursor of the novel is PETRONIUS' *Satyricon* (1st cent.); the *Metamorphoses* (2nd cent.) of APULEIUS is a fantastic prototype. The two strains converge in CERVANTES's *Don Quixote* (17th cent.). The novel established itself in England in the 18th cent. through the realistic works of Daniel DEFOE, Samuel RICHARDSON, and Henry FIELDING. During the 19th cent. it became the dominant form of literature, and many nations produced great novelists: England, Jane AUSTEN, W.M. THACKERAY, Charles DICKENS, George ELIOT, and Thomas HARDY; France, Victor HUGO, Honoré de BALZAC, and Gustave FLAUBERT; Russia, Leo TOLSTOY and Fyodor DOSTOYEVSKY; and the US, Nathaniel HAWTHORNE, Herman MELVILLE, Mark TWAIN, and Henry JAMES. In the 20th cent. novelists strove for greater freedom of form and expression. In superb associative novels James JOYCE, Marcel PROUST, and William FAULKNER represented their characters' thoughts and feelings. Thomas Mann (see MANN, family) wrote

philosophical novels; and Franz KAFKA produced influential symbolic novels treating the anxiety-ridden condition of modern man. The French nouveau roman abandoned plot and character, and the South Americans and others introduced magical realism.

**novella** see NOVEL.

**Novello, Ivor,** pseud. of **Davies, David Ifor,** 1893–1951, British composer, actor, and playwright, whose first great success was the song 'Keep the Home Fires Burning' (1914). By the mid 1930s he had developed an individual style which he maintained in a series of well written, popular operettas, ranging from *Glamorous Night* (1935), and *The Dancing Years* (1939), to *Perchance to Dream* (1945) and *King's Rhapsody* (1949).

**November:** see MONTH.

**Novembergruppe,** a group of Berlin artists formed in 1918 with the aim of bringing progressive art closer to the public and everday life. The group covered a wide range of ideas, from pre-War EXPRESSIONISM to DADA. In 1919 the founders created the Workers' Council for Art. By 1924 the group had broken up due to internal disagreements and to the public's political shift to the right and lack of interest in avant-garde art.

**Novgorod,** city (1985 pop. 220,000), NW European USSR, on the Volkhov R. Its products include china, bricks, and furniture. Among the old Russian cities, it was a medieval centre of trade and culture, and the capital of the Russian state founded by Rurik (AD 862). Although KIEV became the capital in 886, Novgorod remained the centre of foreign trade. In 1136 it became the capital of an independent republic comprising all of N Russia to the Urals. One of the four chief trade centres of the HANSEATIC LEAGUE, Novgorod levied tribute, founded colonies, and repulsed Teutonic, Livonian, and Swedish invasions. In 1478 it came under the control of MOSCOW. Its commercial importance waned after St Petersburg (now LENINGRAD) was built (1703). Many of its medieval architectural treasures were damaged during the German occupation (1941–44) in World War II.

**Novi Sad,** city (1981 pop. 257,685), capital of the Vojvodina Autonomous Region, NE Yugoslavia, on the Danube R. It is a river port and has food-processing industries. Successor to the fortress town of Petrovaradin, it was founded in 1690 and was a centre of Serbian cultural revival in the 18th and early 19th cent. during the resistance against the Turks.

**Novokuznetsk** (͵nohvoh'kyoohznetsk), formerly Stalinsk, city (1985 pop. 577,000), W Siberian USSR, on the Tom R. It is a centre of heavy industry, being in the Kuzbass coalfield. There are two integrated iron and steel works, and plants producing aluminium and chemicals. Other industries include heavy and light metallurgy, machine construction, and metal-working. It was founded during the first Five-Year Plan as a new steel centre across the Tom R. from the old town of Kuznetsk.

**Novosibirsk,** city (1985 pop. 1,393,000), S Siberian USSR, on the Ob R. and the TRANS-SIBERIAN RAILWAY. A hub of river, rail, and air transport, it is SIBERIA's major industrial centre producing textiles, chemicals, and metals. Founded as Novonikolayevsk in 1893, during construction of the railway, it grew as a trade centre and was renamed in 1925.

**Novotný, Antonín,** 1904–75, Czechoslovakian Communist leader. He participated in the Communist coup of 1948 and after 1953 headed both the government and the party. His regime was characterized by repression and economic stagnation. In 1968 he was removed from power by a liberal majority headed by DUBČEK.

**NOW:** see NATIONAL ORGANIZATION FOR WOMEN.

**Nowra, Louis,** 1950–, playwright and novelist. He was the first Australian dramatist to address himself primarily to international themes. *Inner Voices* (1977), *Visions* (1978), and *The Precious Woman* (1980), range from the court of Ivan VI to 19th-cent. Paraguay and 20th-cent. China.

**Np,** chemical symbol of the element NEPTUNIUM.

**Nu, U,** 1907–, premier of BURMA (1948–56, 1957–58, 1960–62). He helped to secure (1948) Burma's independence from Britain and was its first premier. In 1962 he was deposed in a military coup led by NE WIN.

**Nubia** (͵nyoohbeeə), ancient state of NE Africa, which extended from Khartoum in the Sudan almost to Aswan in Egypt. In the 8th and 7th cent. BC, Egypt was ruled by a Nubian dynasty. Later, in the 3rd cent. AD, a

Negro tribe, the Nobatae, settled in Nubia and formed a powerful kingdom. Converted to Christianity in the 6th cent., it succumbed to the Muslims in 1366. MUHAMMAD ALI of Egypt conquered it in the 19th cent.

**nuclear disarmament:** see DISARMAMENT, NUCLEAR.

**nuclear energy,** the energy stored in the nucleus of an atom. Following the discovery of the radioactivity of uranium by BECQUEREL in 1896, it was quickly realized that the energies involved were vastly greater than anything ever before observed. In 1901 RUTHERFORD and Soddy observed the decay of thorium-232 into radium-228 by alpha particle emission, the first transmutation of an element. In 1903 they discovered that the Th$^{232}$–Ra$^{228}$ transition involved a release of 4.2 million eV of energy for each reaction. This was a million times the energy available in a typical chemical reaction (the explosive burning of hydrogen gas as in the spectacular conflagration of the dirigible Hindenberg in 1937 in New Jersey released only 4.86 eV for each hydrogen molecule involved in the reaction). Soddy, an experienced lecturer and popularizer, began to publicize the discovery: his book *The Interpretation of Radium* (1909) outlined the vast reserves of energy available from the atomic nucleus —a beaker of uranium could drive a steamship across the Atlantic—and it warned against the explosive use of nuclear power where a single mistake could reduce the human race to the stone age, or even worse. H.G. WELLS followed with his best-seller *The World Set Free: A Story for Mankind* (1913) which described a nuclear war initiated by the dropping of bombs the size of bowling balls with a massive release of energy. These books were not exceptional: the subject of radium occupied the same percentage of space in the press in the period 1903–1913 as did the subject of nuclear power in the 1960s, and by the 1920s the promise of nuclear power was a commonplace idea. In 1934, Hungarian physicist Leo SZILARD realized that a nuclear reaction induced by neutrons that released still more neutrons could produce a chain reaction that would release energy on a massive scale. It was then only a matter of time until the right reaction was discovered. The discovery of the neutron by CHADWICK in 1932 stimulated researchers in Britain, Germany, France, Italy, and the US to begin bombarding elements with neutrons. Numerous nuclear reactions were discovered and in 1938 experiments by HAHN and Fritz Strassmann showed that neutrons were capable of actually splitting a uranium nucleus into smaller fragments. MEITNER and Otto Frisch quickly interpreted the reaction as a fission of the uranium nucleus. Shortly afterwards groups in France and the US found that extra neutrons were produced in the fission reaction. It was immediately clear that once the fission process was begun the extra neutrons could then split other uranium nuclei releasing more energy and more neutrons. If a sufficient amount of fissionable material is present (the *critical mass*) then a self sustaining chain reaction ensues. Only a relatively rare (0.7%) isotope of uranium, U-235, is fissionable, and for many purposes uranium enriched in the isotope is required. Enrichment, which means separating two chemically-identical substances differing by only just over 1% in mass (235 compared with the common 238 isotope), is always a difficult and energy-consuming process now carried out in a few large plants in the US, UK, France, Japan, USSR, etc. Nuclear reactions can, however, be sustained in natural uranium piles. In any such reaction a considerable amount of uranium 238 is converted into plutonium which is itself fissionable. Nuclear explosives (for atomic and hydrogen warheads) consist of plutonium or of highly enriched uranium, or of a combination of the two. For the generation of electricity in nuclear power stations nuclear reactors of various types have been developed using natural or more often slightly enriched uranium. See ATOMIC BOMB; HYDROGEN BOMB; MANHATTAN PROJECT; NUCLEAR REACTOR; RADIOACTIVITY.

**nuclear magnetic resonance** (NMR), in medicine, a diagnostic technique using radio waves and magnets. Used for many years in chemistry and physics to analyse samples of solids and liquids, as well as tissues removed from the body, nuclear magnetic resonance became a diagnostic tool early in the 1980s for detecting and analysing changes in body structure and function. The patient is placed in the field of an electromagnet, which causes the nuclei of certain atoms in the body (especially those of hydrogen) to align magnetically. The patient is then subjected to radio waves, which cause the aligned nuclei to 'flip'; when the radio waves are withdrawn the nuclei return to their original positions, emitting radio waves that are then detected by a receiver and analysed by computer. Able to pass through bones and record changes in blood and body tissues, NMR is expected to aid in the early diagnosis of

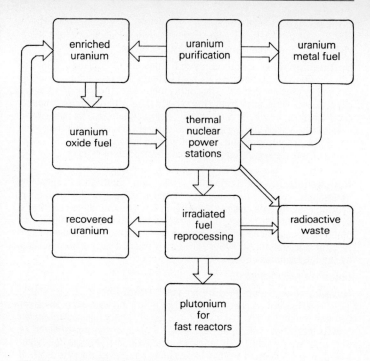

**Nuclear energy:** Nuclear fuel cycle

brain abnormalities and such diseases as cancer, multiple sclerosis, and heart disease. From its early use as a diagnostic tool, NMR has been considered to be without risk to the patient.

**nuclear physics,** study of the components, structure, and behaviour of the nucleus of the ATOM. It is especially concerned with the nature of matter and with NUCLEAR ENERGY. The subject is commonly divided into three fields: low-energy nuclear physics, the study of RADIOACTIVITY; medium-energy nuclear physics, the study of the force between nuclear particles; and high-energy, or particle, physics, the study of the transformations among subatomic particles in reactions produced in a PARTICLE ACCELERATOR or by cosmic rays. See also ELEMENTARY PARTICLES.

**nuclear reaction,** process in which usually a light atomic NUCLEUS (typically a PROTON or an ALPHA particle) from a PARTICLE ACCELERATOR strikes a heavier target nucleus leading, through a reorganization of the component neutrons and protons, to the formation of different product nuclei. For example, an alpha particle striking the nitrogen nucleus can lead to the formation of an oxygen ISOTOPE and a proton.

**nuclear reactor,** a device for generating a controlled chain reaction of the fission of uranium or plutonium nuclei (see NUCLEAR ENERGY). The first nuclear reactor was achieved by Enrico FERMI and colleagues in 1942 in Chicago. They piled 200 tons of graphite and 6 tons of spherical uranium lumps layer by layer into an egg-like shape approximately 3 m long and 4 m high. Graphite was used as a moderator to slow down the neutrons produced from the fission of the uranium so that they could more effectively produce another fission. They also nailed thin sheets of cadmium, an element that strongly absorbs neutrons, to wooden rods and inserted the rods into the pile to control the number of neutrons in the pile at any one time. When the 57th layer was reached the neutron flux in the pile became self-sustaining—as many neutrons were being produced as were being lost either through escape from the pile, through fission, or through being absorbed by the cadmium-covered control rods. The power output of the pile was 0.5W. Modern reactors operate on the same principles. They all have: a URANIUM or PLUTONIUM core, manufactured into long fuel rods; a moderator of either water, heavy water, or graphite; control rods, generally of cadmium; and in addition, a coolant to extract the heat from the pile. The coolant drives a turbine to generate electricity and keeps the pile from overheating and suffering a meltdown as happened at THREE MILE ISLAND and CHERNOBYL. A loss-of-coolant accident (LOCA) is the most serious nuclear reactor accident. In the worst case a LOCA can result in the dispersal of billions of curies of the extremely dangerous radioactive isotopes formed in the core by the fission process (see RADIOACTIVITY). Reactor design is highly controversial, with each type of reactor having its supporters and opponents. Some common designs are the *pressurized water reactor* (PWR), used at Three Mile Island, which uses uranium oxide as a fuel and circulates water under a pressure of 150 atmospheres as a moderator and as a coolant. The British *advanced gas-cooled reactor* (AGR) uses carbon dioxide gas as a coolant and graphite as a moderator. The Soviet RMBK reactor used at Chernobyl uses boiling water as a coolant and graphite as a moderator. Nuclear reactors generate not only power but also a variety of radioactive materials. The plutonium amongst them can produce further power, but some of it might also be used in nuclear weapons. The remainder is waste difficult to dispose of (see WASTE DISPOSAL). The extremely high power densities in a nuclear reactor along with the immense inventory of hazardous radioactive isotopes stored in the core make nuclear reactor technology an unforgiving technology. A relatively minor error can quickly lead to tragic consequences affecting millions of people. At Three Mile Island a power-operated relief valve stuck open allowing coolant water to escape but the operators ignored the instruments showing the escape. At Chernobyl the operators similarly ignored the instruments that indicated that the reactor was in trouble. Accident reviews at both Three Mile Island and Chernobyl found serious defects in the operating procedures at each plant. The difficulties with nuclear reactors have produced widespread public demands that since the technology is out of control it should be stopped.

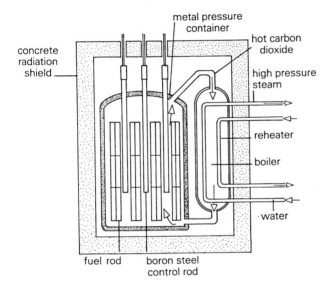

Advanced gas-cooled **nuclear reactor**

**nuclear waste disposal:** see WASTE DISPOSAL.

**nucleic acid,** organic substance, found in all living cells, in which the hereditary information is stored and from which it can be transferred. Nucleic acid molecules are long chains that generally occur in combination with proteins. The two chief types are DNA (deoxyribonucleic acid), found mainly in cell nuclei as a double helical structure containing two separate molcules, and RNA (ribonucleic acid), found mostly in cytoplasm (see CELL). Each nucleic acid chain is composed of subunits called nucleotides, each containing a sugar, a phosphate group, and one of four bases: adenine (A), guanine (G), cytosine (C), and thymine (T). RNA contains the sugar ribose instead of deoxyribose and the base uracil (U) instead of thymine. The specific order of bases determines the cell's genetic code; each sequence (triplet) of three bases specifies one particular AMINO ACID. The long sequences of DNA nucleotides in one of the strands of the molecule thus correspond to the sequences of amino acids in the cell's proteins. In order to be expressed as protein, the genetic information is carried to the protein-synthesizing machinery (which involves various forms of RNA) of the cell, usually in the cell cytoplasm, by messenger RNA. DNA not only provides information but also specifies its own exact replication. The cell replicates both strands of its DNA by making a complementary copy of the exact nucleotide sequence of each: T for every A, C for every G, G for every C, A for every T. Although the triplet nucleotide code seems to be universal, the actual sequences of the nucleotides vary according to the species and individual. See GENE; GENETIC ENGINEERING; MUTATION.

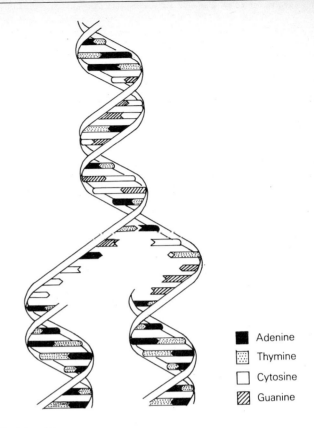

- ■ Adenine
- ▦ Thymine
- □ Cytosine
- ▨ Guanine

Nucleic acid

**nucleogenesis,** theory in astronomy. The elements hydrogen and helium comprise the bulk of all material known to us in the universe. Helium is synthesized from hydrogen in the nuclear reactions that power the Sun and almost all stars. Since the 1920s it has therefore been suspected that all elements other than helium are built up from hydrogen in nuclear processes which, it used to be thought, could only occur at the extraordinary densities and temperatures supposed to have occurred in the Big Bang of cosmology. The incompatibility of this with steady state cosmology led HOYLE to suspect a stellar origin. E.M. BURBIDGE, G. Burbidge, W.A. Fowler and Hoyle showed in 1956, in a theory since further developed, that the particular types of star known to exist account perfectly for the existence and abundance of all elements and their isotopes through synthesizing them in known nuclear reactions from hydrogen, which is thus shown to be the original material of the universe.

**nucleus,** in biology, see CELL.

**nucleus,** in physics, the central core of an ATOM. It is an assembly of PROTONS and NEUTRONS bound together by the powerful nuclear force, a manifestation of the strong interaction (see ELEMENTARY PARTICLES). A nucleus is characterized by its ATOMIC NUMBER Z, equal to the number of protons and the MASS NUMBER A, equal to the total number of protons and neutrons it contains. Nuclei are spherical or nearly spherical with radii in the region $10^{-15}$ to $10^{-14}$ metres.

**Nuevo Laredo,** city (1979 est. pop. 223,606) NE Mexico, across the Río Grande from Laredo, Texas. Founded in 1755, it is a major trade and transport centre and the chief point of entry for US tourists driving into Mexico.

**nuisance,** in law, act without legal justification interfering with safety, comfort, or use of PROPERTY. A nuisance may be private (affecting only a few persons) or public (affecting many persons). Nuisances, usually treated as TORTS, may be restrained by INJUNCTION or remedied by the award of damages. Public nuisances, injurious to the community, may be prosecuted as crimes.

**Nukualofa,** town (1976 pop. 18,312), capital and chief port of TONGA, in the S Pacific Ocean.

**Nullarbor Plains,** region along the southern coast of Australia in South Australia and Western Australia. The name comes from Latin, meaning 'no trees', and well describes the flat, treeless plain extending 182,000 km² (70,000 sq mi) along the head of the Great Australian Bight. Limestone caves contain relics of ancient Aboriginal occupation. Cocklebiddy Cave, with its lake 80 m (250 feet) below the surface, and Mullamullong Cave, with its 8 km (5 mi) of tunnels, attract local and overseas cave exploration groups. The Indian-Pacific railway traverses the plain with straight sections of line up to 530 km (330 mi) in length. After rain the land is covered with a mass of spectacular flowers.

**nullification,** in US history, an extremist doctrine of STATES' RIGHTS holding that a state can declare null and void any federal law it deems unconstitutional. The KENTUCKY AND VIRGINIA RESOLUTIONS (1799) were the first notable expressions of the doctrine. Nullification was a forerunner of the doctrine of secession that brought about the CIVIL WAR.

**number,** entity describing the magnitude or position of a mathematical object, or extensions of these concepts. Cardinal numbers (one, two, three, etc.) describe the size of a collection of objects; ordinal numbers (first, second, third, etc.) refer to position relative to an ordering. Both types can be generalized to infinite collections (see INFINITY). The finite cardinal and ordinal numbers, represented by the NUMERALS 1, 2, 3, . . . , are called the *natural numbers*. The *integers* are the natural numbers together with their negatives and zero. The ratios $a/b$, where $a$ and $b$ are integers and $b \neq 0$, constitute the *rational numbers,* which may also be represented by repeating decimals (see DECIMAL SYSTEM), e.g., $\frac{1}{2} = 0.500$ . . . , $\frac{2}{3} = 0.666$ . . . . The *real numbers* are all numbers representable by an infinite decimal expansion, which may be repeating or nonrepeating; they are in a one-to-one correspondence with the points on a straight line. Real numbers that have nonrepeating decimal expansions, i.e., that cannot be represented by any ratio of integers, are called *irrational*. The Pythagoreans knew in the 6th cent. BC that $\sqrt{2}$ was irrational. The number $\sqrt{2}$ is also an example of an algebraic number, i.e., it is the ROOT of a POLYNOMIAL equation, in this case $x^2 - 2 = 0$. Numbers that are not algebraic are called *transcendental;* e (see separate article) and $\pi$ (PI) are examples. The *imaginary numbers* were invented to deal with equations, such as $x^2 + 2 = 0$, that have no real roots. The basic imaginary unit is $i = \sqrt{-1}$. Imaginary numbers take the form $yi$, where $y$ is a real number, e.g., $\sqrt{-2} = (\sqrt{2})i$. Numbers of the form $x + yi$, where $x$ and $y$ are real (e.g., $8 + 7i$), are called *complex numbers*. The complex numbers are in a one-to-one correspondence with the points on a plane, with one axis defining the real parts of the numbers and another axis defining the imaginary parts.

**Numbers,** book of the OLD TESTAMENT ascribed by tradition to MOSES. It continues the narrative of EXODUS, beginning at Sinai and ending at Moab on the eve of the entry into Palestine. Bare in geographical detail, it includes accounts of the curse of Balaam and other events.

**number theory,** branch of mathematics concerned with the properties of the integers (the NUMBERS 0, 1, −1, 2, −2, . . . ). Modern number theory made its first great advances through the work of Leonhard EULER, Carl GAUSS, and Pierre de FERMAT. Much of the focus is on the analysis of prime numbers, i.e., those integers, $p$, greater than 1 that are divisible only by 1 and $p$; the first few primes are 2, 3, 5, 7, 11, 13, 17, and 19. The fundamental theorem of arithmetic asserts that any positive integer, $a$, is a product of primes that are unique except for the order in which they are listed. For example, the number 20 is uniquely the product $2 \cdot 2 \cdot 5$. This theorem was known to the Greek mathematician EUCLID, who also proved that there is an infinite number of primes.

**numeral,** symbol denoting NUMBER. The Arabic numerals (which apparently originated in India) are 1, 2, 3, 4, . . . ; the Roman numerals are I, II, III, IV, . . . . Both types probably derive from counting on the fingers. The word *digit*, used for the ten numerals 0, 1, 2, . . . , 9, is from the Latin for *finger*. Some languages show traces of reckoning by units of 20, using the toes as well as the fingers. The numeral for zero in the Arabic system is much more recent than the other numerals. See also DECIMAL SYSTEM; NUMERATION. The hexadecimal system, also used in computing, has a base of 16 and uses the decimal numbers 0–9 and the letters A, B, C, D, E, and F.

**numeration,** in mathematics, process of designating NUMBERS according to a particular system. In any system of numeration a base number is specified, and groupings are then made by powers of the base number.

The most widely used system of numeration is the DECIMAL SYSTEM, which uses base 10. In the decimal system the NUMERAL 302 means $(3 \times 10^2) + (0 \times 10^1) + (2 \times 10^0)$, or $300 + 0 + 2$. The binary system, used in most computers, has a base of 2 and only two digits, 0 and 1. The binary numeral 1110 means $(1 \times 2^3) + (1 \times 2^2) + (1 \times 2^1) + (0 \times 2^0)$, i.e., $8 + 4 + 2$, or 14, in the decimal system. The decimal numeral 14 and the binary numeral 1110 thus represent the same number. The ancient Babylonians used a system of base 60, which survives in our smaller divisions of time and angle, i.e., minutes and seconds.

**Numidia** (nyooh͵mideeə), ancient country of NW Africa, roughly equivalent to modern Algeria. In the PUNIC WARS, its king MASINISSA sided with Rome and won freedom from CARTHAGE. JUGURTHA fought a fatal war with Rome, but Juba II was restored as a prince subject to Rome (1st cent. AD). Numidia declined after the Arabs came (8th cent.).

**numismatics,** collection and study of coins, medals, and related objects as works of art and as sources of information. The COIN and the medal preserve old forms of writing, portraits of eminent persons, and clues to the history of the region where they were minted or struck.

**nun:** see MONASTICISM.

**Nuremberg,** city (1984 pop. 471,700), Bavaria, S West Germany, on the Pegnitz R. It is an industrial centre with such manufactures as electrical equipment and machinery. Founded by 1050 and chartered in 1219, it became a free imperial city and a trade centre on the route from Italy. Humanism, science, and art flourished there during the German RENAISSANCE (15th–16th cent.), with such artists as DÜRER in residence. The city declined after the THIRTY YEARS WAR but became a centre of industry during the 19th cent. A shrine of NATIONAL SOCIALISM (Nazism) and a site of armaments factories, Nuremberg was heavily bombed during WORLD WAR II; it was rebuilt after 1945. Its historic structures include the city walls (14th–17th cent.) and the Church of St Sebald (13th cent.). Nuremberg was the site (1945–56) of a WAR CRIMES tribunal.

**Nuremberg Trials:** see WAR CRIMES.

**Nureyev, Rudolf,** 1938–, Austrian ballet dancer; b. USSR. A soloist with the Kirov ballet (1958), he left the USSR in 1961. He is held by many to be the leading classical dancer of his generation, especially in partnership with FONTEYN. He took the title role in the film *Valentino* (1977), and has been director of the Paris Opera Ballet since 1980.

**nursery schools,** schools—or often 'nursery classes'—for children below the age of five. In the 1980s more than 40% of children aged between 3 and 5 attended such schools, the total for the UK being 676,000 in 1985. The schools are either part of local authority school provision or private. The nursery school movement in Britain is associated with the work of Margaret McMillan in the early decades of the 20th cent., and the writings of Susan Isaacs, such as *The Nursery Years* (1929).

**nursing,** profession dealing with prevention of illness and the care and rehabilitation of the sick, encompassing the physical and emotional well-being of the patient as a whole. Nursing includes individualized care on a continuing basis, the carrying out of medical regimens, coordination of necessary interdisciplinary services, and health counselling. Until the middle of the 19th cent. nurses were trained in hospitals to provide bedside care. The first school designed primarily to train nurses rather than provide nursing service for the hospital was established (1860) in London by Florence NIGHTINGALE. The profession in recent years has expanded and includes the specialized services of nurse practitioners (who assume some medical responsibility), midwives (see MIDWIFERY), and health visitors. Although traditionally most nurses have been women, the number of males in the profession has increased.

**Nusayriyya** or **'Alawites,** esoteric branch of SHI'ISM whose name perhaps derives from that of their first theologian Muhammad b. Nusayr (d. 883). They have flourished mainly in Syria and their theology shares certain principles with the ISMA'ILIS, such as a hiearchy of orders of creation and a cyclical theory of history. The figure of the 4th caliph 'ALI IBN ABI TALIB is of cardinal significance for the Nusayriyya. Persons of Nusayri origin have played an important part in contemporary Syrian politics.

**nut,** in botany, a dry, one-seeded, usually oily FRUIT. True nuts include the acorn, chestnut, and hazelnut. The term *nut* also refers to any seed or fruit with a hard, brittle covering around an edible kernel, e.g., the peanut pod (a LEGUME), and almond (a drupe fruit). Others that are not

## NUTRITION

| Nutrient | Important sources | Function | Result of excess/deficiency |
|---|---|---|---|
| **Protein**<br>animal<br><br>plant | meat, fish, cheese, eggs<br><br>cereals, pulses, yams | The growth, repair, and renewal of the body | Excess animal proteins result in a diet high in saturated fat. Kwashiorkor is the result of a serious deficiency particularly in children – dry, scaly skin, reddish hair and swollen belly. |
| **Fat**<br>saturated<br><br>polyunsaturated | butter, meat, cheese, hard margarine<br><br>safflower, sunflower and corn oil, fish, soft margarine | A reserve and concentrated source of energy. Fat also forms part of the structure of all cell membranes and is important in the production of some hormones. | There is a clear correlation between a high fat intake, coronary heart disease, and obesity. A diet exceptionally low in fat might be lacking the essential fatty acids and the fat-soluble vitamins. |
| **Carbohydrate**<br>sugar<br><br>starch | sweets, cakes, jams, biscuits, drinks<br><br>bread, potatoes, pasta, cereals, cassava, yams | Sugar is only a source of energy and is not a necessary nutrient. Unrefined carbohydrates should provide the bulk of our energy. These economical, staple foods are the major part of peoples' diets all over the world. | Excess sugar results in obesity and dental caries and contributes towards diabetes. A deficiency of unrefined carbohydrates can result in a diet too high in fat and deficient in dietary fibre and vitamin B. |
| **Dietary Fibre**<br>cellulose<br>lignin<br>pectin | whole cereal products, fresh and dried fruit, vegetables, and nuts | The healthy working of the colon and the prevention of constipation. Also important in controlling calorie intake and may be vital in the prevention of late-onset diabetes. | A lack of fibre is thought to be the cause of diverticular disease and one cause of cancer of the colon. |
| **Water** | drinks, soups, fruit, and vegetables | Is the major component in all cells, transports nutrients around the body, transports waste out in faeces and urine, provides sweat for body temperature control. | A shortage of water in the body, perhaps caused by vomiting and diarrhoea, can result in serious dehydration particularly in babies and young children |

true nuts are the CASHEW, COCONUT, LYCHEE, PISTACHIO, and WALNUT. Nuts are a valuable food and are often cultivated in nut orchards.

**nutation,** slight wobbling motion of the Earth's axis, superimposed on that which produces the PRECESSION OF THE EQUINOXES. Caused by the combination of the gravitational attractions exerted by the Sun and the Moon, it has an 18.6-yr period. A small spontaneous wobble of the Earth is called the free nutation.

**nutmeg,** evergreen tree (*Myristica fragrans*) native to the Moluccas. Its fruit is the source of two spices: whole or ground nutmeg, from the seed; and mace, from the fibrous seed covering that separates the seed from the husk.

**nutritional science,** the study of food and the part it plays in the processes of growth, maintenance, and repair of the human body. It is a complex science with particular ethical difficulties in obtaining evidence. Whole-population comparisons, volunteer trials, studies of sick people, and knowledge gained from extreme situations such as explorers have been the methods used to back up laboratory work (see ANIMAL EXPERIMENTATION). Social aspects of food are also studied, e.g., ethnic differences in eating habits. See accompanying table for essential nutrients.

**Nyabingi,** a spirit-possession cult that exercised a powerful hold on African societies in late 19th-cent. Rwanda, Ndorwa, and the Congo. By 1909 the cult was dominated by Muhumusa, a widow of a former ruler of Rwanda who hoped to use her position to put her son on the throne. She was captured and imprisoned by the Germans in 1911 and by the 1920s the influence of the cult had begun to wane.

**Nyasa, Lake:** see MALAWI, LAKE.

**Nyasaland:** see MALAWI.

**Nyerere, Julius Kambarage** (nyə‚reəree, ni-), 1921–, first president of TANZANIA (1964–85). He was the leading nationalist of Tanganyika and became prime minister upon independence (1961). He was the architect of the union (1964) of Tanganyika and Zanzibar as the republic of Tanzania. After retiring as president, the following year (1986) he accepted the chairmanship of an Independent Commission of the South on Development Issues.

**nylon:** see SYNTHETIC TEXTILE FIBRES.

**nymph,** in Greek mythology, female divinity, immortal or long-lived, associated with various natural objects or places. Some represented specific localities, e.g., the acheloids of the River Achelous; others were identified with more general physiographic features, e.g., oreads with mountains, naiads with bodies of fresh water, nereids with the Mediterranean, oceanids with the ocean, dryads with trees; and some were associated with a function of nature, e.g., hamadryads, who lived and died with a particular tree. Nymphs were regarded as young, beautiful, musical, and amorous

**nymph,** immature form of an INSECT that undergoes partial metamorphosis. The egg hatches into a nymph, which looks similar to the adult but has very small wings. At each successive moult the small wings increase in size until the insect reaches the adult stage, with full-sized wings. There are many aquatic nymphs. The DRAGONFLY, mayfly, GRASSHOPPER, and COCKROACH are among those insects that lay eggs which hatch into nymphs.

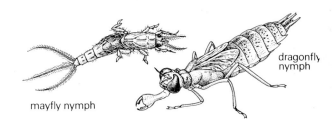

mayfly nymph

dragonfly nymph

**Nymph**

**O,** chemical symbol of the element OXYGEN.

**oak,** tree or shrub (genus *Quercus*) of the BEECH family. About 230 species are found in north temperate zones and POLYNESIA; the more southerly species are usually evergreen. Oaks are cultivated for ornament and are a major source of hardwood of great economic value. Their durable, attractively grained WOOD is valued for shipbuilding, construction, flooring, furniture, barrels, and veneer. However, because of its slow growth to maturity, little is planted at the present time except for amenity purposes. Luckily, it readily seeds itself. *Q. robur,* the common European oak, and *Q. alba,* the American white oak, are the most valuable timber trees of the genus; the cork oak (*Q. suber*) supplies CORK. The bark of many species is a source of tannin for leather-making, and acorns, the fruit of oak trees, are a source of food, tannin, oil, and forage.

**Oakland,** US city (1984 est. pop. 352,000), W California, on the eastern side of San Francisco Bay; inc. 1852. It is a leading container port and railhead with shipyards, chemical plants, glassworks, and food processing plants. It is connected by the Bay Bridge (1936), tunnels, and the Bay Area Rapid Transit system with SAN FRANCISCO and other nearby cities. There are major military supply facilities in the city.

**Oakley, Annie,** 1860–1926, American markswoman; b. Darke co., Ohio, as Phoebe Anne Oakley Mozee. She was a star attraction (1885–1902) of BUFFALO BILL's Wild West Show.

**OAS:** see ORGANIZATION OF AMERICAN STATES.

**oasis,** fertile area in a desert where there is enough moisture for vegetation. The water may originate in springs or collect in mountain hollows. Oases vary considerably in size, ranging from a pond with a group of date palms to oasis cities with extended agricultural cultivation.

**Oates, Joyce Carol,** 1938–, American writer. In realistic novels, tinged with surrealism, she has often explored the connection between violence and love in American life. Extraordinarily prolific, she has written such novels as *A Garden of Earthly Delights* (1967), *them* (1969), *Childwold* (1976), *Bellefleur* (1980), and *A Bloodsmoor Romance* (1982), as well as short stories, poems, and literary criticism.

**Oates, Lawrence Edward Grace,** 1880–1912, British cavalry officer and member of Capt. R.F. SCOTT's expedition to the SOUTH POLE. Aware that exhaustion and gangrene made him a burden to the others, the 'very gallant gentleman' went out to meet his death in a blizzard.

**Oates, Titus,** 1649–1705, English conspirator. He invented (1678) the story of the Popish Plot, describing it as a Jesuit plan to assassinate CHARLES II. In the ensuing frenzy several innocent Roman Catholics were persecuted and killed.

**oats,** cereal plants (genus *Avena*) of the GRASS family. Most species are annuals growing in moist temperate regions. Oats are valued chiefly as a pasturage and hay crop, for animal feed as grain, and for crop rotation; less than 10% of the oats grown commercially are for human consumption. The common cultivated species, *A. sativa,* is thought to be native to Eurasia.

**OAU:** see ORGANIZATION OF AFRICAN UNITY.

**Oaxaca** (wah,hahkah), city (1978 est. pop. 131,200), S Mexico, capital of Oaxaca state. A commercial and tourist centre famed for its pre-Colombian ruins such as those at Monte Albán, its gardens and colonial churches. It is the chief city of S Mexico and one of the nation's most historic cities. It was founded (c.1500) by the AZTECS and was taken (1522) by the Spaniards. Benito JUÁREZ and Porfirio DÍAZ were born in Oaxaca.

**Ob,** one of the great rivers of Siberia, USSR, flowing generally N c.3700 km (2300 mi) into an estuary on the ARCTIC OCEAN. With its chief tributary, the IRTYSH R., it forms the world's fourth-longest river (c.5600 km/3460 mi). Although frozen for almost half the year and subject to flooding in its middle course, the Ob is a major trade and transport route. NOVOSIBIRSK and BARNAUL are the chief ports.

**Obadiah** or **Abdias,** book of the OLD TESTAMENT. Dated from the 6th to 5th cent. BC, it calls down doom on Edom and says Israel will triumph.

**obbligato** [It., = obligatory], in music, originally a term by which a composer indicated that a certain part was indispensable to the music. Misunderstanding of the term, however, resulted in a reversal of its meaning, so that if a part added to a song is today designated 'obbligato', the part may be omitted if desired.

**obelisk,** slender, four-sided, tapering monument, usually a monolith, terminating in a pointed or pyramidal top. The ancient Egyptians dedicated them to the sun god and placed them in pairs at the sides of temple portals. A line of incised hieroglyphs, giving the names and titles of the Pharaoh, commonly ran down each of their sides. Many obelisks were taken from Egypt, notably those called CLEOPATRA'S NEEDLES in London (Thames embankment) and New York City (Central Park).

**Oberammergau,** village on the edge of the Bavarian Alps, near GARMISCH-PARTENKIRCHEN, West Germany. It is noted for its Passion Play, performed every tenth year, 1970, 1980, etc., by local residents.

**Oberhausen,** city (1984 pop. 224,100), North Rhine–Westphalia, W West Germany, on the Rhine–Herne Canal. In the 19th cent. it was a centre of RUHR coal-mining; iron and steel and engineering are now its major industries.

**Oberon,** in astronomy, natural satellite of URANUS.

**Oberth, Hermann Julius,** 1894–, German astronautical pioneer; b. Romania. Beginning his studies in astronautics before World War I, he proposed a liquid-propellant ROCKET in 1917 and in 1923 published his unsuccessful Ph.D. dissertation, *The Rocket into Interplanetary Space,* which discussed many aspects of rocket travel. He expanded this small pamphlet into a larger work, *The Road to Space Travel* (1929), which won wide recognition.

**obesity,** condition of excess body fat defined as exceeding 120% of ideal body weight. It is very common in Western society and is an important risk to health contributing to the development of CORONARY HEART DISEASE, HYPERTENSION, DIABETES, CANCER, and many other diseases. Varicose veins and respiratory disorders are more likely to occur in an obese individual, who also undergoes a greater than normal risk with surgery.

**object permanence,** a crucial stage or attainment in the child's cognitive development in PIAGET's developmental psychology. Object permanence is achieved at the end of the sensorimotor period (18–24 months), and involves the recognition that objects exist independently of the child's own actions upon them, and continue to exist outside the field of immediate perception.

**objet trouvé** (ob͵jay ͵troohvay), [Fr., = found object], technique in 20th-cent. art. The use of 'found' objects was first deployed by SCHWITTER in his construction of rubbish. DUCHAMP's ready-mades used a similar strategy, in which anti-art shock tactics were the main intention. The surrealists (see SURREALISM) used to more positive effect found or non-art objects; Paul NASH, by placing pebbles, branches, etc., on pedestals made the natural object one for aesthetic consideration, and used their forms in his finished landscapes.

**oboe,** a WOODWIND instrument with a double reed and a conical bore. It has a range of over two and a half octaves upwards from the B♭ below middle C. The oboe has been a member of the orchestra since the 18th cent., and has a fair amount of solo and chamber repertoire. The cor anglais (English horn) is an alto oboe with a range of two and a half octaves from the E below middle C upwards.

**Obote, (Apollo) Milton,** 1925–, president of UGANDA (1966–71, 1980–85). He became (1962) prime minister after Uganda's independence and staged (1965) a revolution to make himself president. He was overthrown (1971) by Idi AMIN but returned to power after Amin's downfall (1979), but was again overthrown by the military six years later.

**Obradović, Dositej-Dimitrije** (ob͵rahdovich), 1742-1811, Serbian writer. An itinerant scholar and teacher after abandoning his monastic vocation in 1757, Obradović travelled throughout Europe before returning to Serbia to introduce his countrymen to the ideas of the ENLIGHTENMENT. Writing in the demotic, his popularizations of European works promoted reason, religious tolerance, and anti-clericalism, and attacked superstition and the oppression of women. He helped to reintegrate the Serbs in European culture and to found a secular national literature. His autobiography, *Life and Adventures* (1788), is his most lasting work.

**Obregón, Álvaro,** 1880–1928, president of MEXICO (1920–24). A successful general in the Mexican revolution (1910–17), he rose (1920) against Pres. CARRANZA and became president. His administration enacted agrarian, labour, and educational reforms. Chosen president again, the anticlerical Obregón was assassinated by a fanatical Roman Catholic before he could take office.

**Obrenović** or **Obrenovich,** Serbian dynasty founded by MILOŠ Obrenović that ruled 1817–42 and 1858–1903, alternating with the rival KARADJORDJEVIĆ dynasty. Prince Michael (r.1839–42 and 1860–68) was the most successful Obrenović ruler and King ALEXANDER the worst and last.

**O'Brien, Flann,** pseud. of **Brian O'Nolan,** 1911–1966, Irish novelist, journalist and Gaelic scholar. His comic, surrealistic novels include *At Swim-Two-Birds* (1939) and *The Third Policeman* (1967). His humour and linguistic extravagance are reminiscent of BECKETT and JOYCE. Under the pseudonym Myles na Gopaleen he contributed a famous satirical column to the *Irish Times.*

**O'Brien, James Bronterre** 1805–64, Irish socialist. He edited the *Poor Man's Guardian* (1832–35) and was an active Chartist with a strong historical sense, who became known as 'the Chartist schoolmaster', (see CHARTISM).

**obscenity,** legal concept allowing the banning or restricting of printed materials and other forms of expression offensive to public morals; it has been applied only to materials treating sexual subjects. The obscenity lies in the impression left on the mind of the reader, rather than in the content of the material itself. In the UK, the COMMON LAW recognized obscenity as an offence as early as 1727, though the first statute was not passed until 1857. Definitions of obscenity tend to change with time, and from country to country. See also CENSORSHIP.

**observatory, astronomical,** scientific facility especially equipped to detect and record astronomical phenomena. Early civilizations established primitive observatories to regulate the calendar and predict the changes of season. Later observatories were established to compile accurate star charts and an annual ephemeris that would be of use to navigators in determining longitude at sea. Early instruments used included the armillary sphere, the ASTROLABE, the quadrant, and the SEXTANT. The 17th-cent. invention of the TELESCOPE permitted not only more accurate measurement of the positions and motions of celestial bodies, but also analysis of the physical nature of the bodies. The 19th-cent. development of dry-plate photography, which permitted long exposure times, offered a much more sensitive method of recording images than the drawings made from visual observations by earlier observers. The spectroscopic study of starlight by various instruments has provided information on the temperature and chemical composition of stars, stellar motions, and magnetic fields. Celestial objects may send out ELECTROMAGNETIC RADIATION of any or all frequencies, but only optical and radio wavelengths penetrate the Earth's atmosphere. Thus ground-based astronomy uses either optical frequencies, as is old established, or radio frequencies (see RADIO ASTRONOMY OBSERVATORY). Optical observatories are nowadays normally located well away from population centres, so as to avoid disturbance from their intense illumination, and at high altitudes to minimize the effects on visibility due to the atmosphere, and to permit observations in frequencies of the infrared close to visible ones. Modern telescopes are large both to gather more light from faint sources and to improve accuracy. For other frequencies (gamma rays, X-rays, ultraviolet, general infrared) observations must be made from outside the atmosphere through instruments carried on artificial SATELLITES or on SOUNDING ROCKETS. Major optical observatories are listed under TELESCOPE.

**obsidian,** volcanic glass, commonly black, but also red or brown, formed by LAVA that has cooled too quickly for crystals to form. Chemically it is rich in silica and similar to GRANITE. Obsidian was used extensively by pre-industrialized peoples to make knives, arrowheads, and other weapons and tools.

**obstetrics:** see under GYNAECOLOGY.

**O'Casey, Sean,** 1880–1964, Irish dramatist, important in the IRISH LITERARY RENAISSANCE. His great early plays, *The Shadow of a Gunman* (1923), *Juno and the Paycock* (1924), and *The Plough and the Stars* (1926), are grim, satirical, and not always kind to the Irish people. After the last one set off a riot in the Abbey Theatre, he moved to England. His later plays, e.g., *The Silver Tassie* (1929), are more experimental. *Mirror in My House* (1956) is a collection of his six earlier autobiographical volumes.

**occupational disease,** any illness resulting from the conditions or environment of employment. Environmental causes include unusual dampness, causing diseases of the respiratory tract, skin, or muscles and joints; changes in atmospheric pressure, causing DECOMPRESSION SICKNESS; and exposure to infrared or ultraviolet rays or radioactive substances (see RADIATION SICKNESS). The most common of the industrial dust-related disorders are the lung diseases caused by SILICA, ASBESTOS, iron ore, and other metals to which workers are exposed (see PNEUMOCONIOSIS). Other causes include poisonous fumes and metals in factories and infectious diseases on farms. Additional health risks are posed by mechanical hazards.

**ocean,** interconnected mass of water covering about 71% of the surface of the earth. It is subdivided into the PACIFIC, INDIAN, ATLANTIC, and ARCTIC OCEANS. The world ocean has an area of about 361,000,000 km² (139,400,000 sq mi), an average depth of about 3730 m (12,230 ft), and a total volume of about 1,347,000,000 km³ (322,280,000 cu mi). Its salinity averages about 3.5% by weight. The best-known regions of the oceans, where virtually all petroleum and fishery reserves are found, are the relatively shallow waters above the continental shelves surrounding the CONTINENTS. The deep ocean floor consists mainly of vast abyssal plains. One of the most significant features of the ocean basins is the mid-ocean ridge system, where, it is believed, new oceanic crust has been forming continuously for at least 200 million years in a process of volcanic activity called seafloor spreading (see CONTINENTAL DRIFT; PLATE TECTONICS). Current theory holds that ocean water also originated through this activity. The ocean's deepest parts are the trenches, located near the margins of continents. Ocean water retains heat, and ocean currents, vitally important in dispersing heat energy, are intimately tied to planetary wind systems. The marine environment of the ocean is divided into two major realms, the benthic (ocean floor) and the pelagic (all waters above the benthic). See also DEEP SEA DRILLING PROJECT; OCEANOGRAPHY.

**Oceania** or **Oceanica,** collective name for the approximately 25,000 small islands scattered across the Pacific Ocean away from the Asian mainland. It is generally considered synonymous with the term South Seas and is divided ethnologically into MELANESIA, MICRONESIA, and POLYNESIA. Only a few thousand of the islands are inhabited, and many of these are little more than coral atolls.

**Oceanian languages,** aboriginal languages spoken in the region known as OCEANIA. If Oceania is restricted to the Melanesian, Micronesian, and Polynesian islands, the indigenous tongues spoken on these islands belong for the most part to the Malayo-Polynesian family of languages. If it is extended to include Australia and Malaysia, the indigenous languages of the Australian group spoken in Australia may be added as tongues of this region. In fact, the term 'Oceanian languages' amounts to a geographical rather than a linguistic classification. See LANGUAGE (table).

**Oceanic art,** works produced in the Continent of Australia and by the island peoples of the S and NW Pacific, including MELANESIA (Bismarck archipelago, the Solomons, Vanuatu, New Caledonia, and Fiji), MICRONESIA (the Marianas, Caroline, Marshall, and Kiribati islands), and POLYNESIA (Hawaii, the Marquesas, Samoa, Tonga, Easter Island, and often New Zealand). Melanesian artifacts, ancestor figures and human heads, woodcarvings, and ritual MASKS, are brilliantly coloured and dramatically sexual in nature. They were decorated with reference to a complex mythology and influenced 20th-cent. European artists, e.g., Henry MOORE. Micronesian art objects are functional, streamlined, and highly finished, e.g., graceful CANOES. Rows of figures placed on Mortlock Atoll illustrate mythological events and were thought to protect the islanders from typhoons. Very little Polynesian art survived the influx of Western missionaries, who, thinking it idolatrous and pornographic, destroyed it. The greenish pottery of Fiji and examples of Hawaiian featherwork remain. The Marquesa islanders developed the tattoo into a fine art. On EASTER ISLAND, the abundant reddish stone, tufa, was carved into gargantuan human figures weighing as much as 20 tons. The ritual significance of most Polynesian art has been lost. Aborigine art in Australia stood apart. Drawings, on rocks, in caves, or on the ground use complex, flat patterns and symbolic images of people and animals.

Oceanic art: Two tortoiseshell masks from Darnley Island in the Torres Straits

**oceanids:** see NYMPH.

**oceanography,** study of the sea integrating marine applications of geography, geology, physics, chemistry, marine biology, and meteorology. Comprehensive study of the sea dates from the 1872–76 *Challenger* expedition. Today there are about 250 oceanographic institutions, notably the Scripps Institution of Oceanography in California, the Woods Hole Oceanographic Institution in Massachusetts, and the Lamont–Doherty Geological Observatory of Columbia Univ. Oceanography is important to shipping, fisheries, the laying of telegraph cables, and climatological studies.

**ocelot,** medium-sized CAT (*Felis pardalis*) of Central and South America, sometimes found as far north as Texas. About 75 cm (30 in) long, excluding the tail, and weighing up to 18 kg (35 lb), it has a yellow-brown coat with black spots, rings, and stripes. It is closely related to the margay cat, which is very like it. Ocelots live in forests, preying on small animals. They are hunted for their fur

**Ochoa, Severo** (oh͵choh ah), 1905–, American biochemist; b. Spain; went to the US, 1940. For his synthesis of ribonucleic acid (see NUCLEIC ACID; RNA) Ochoa shared with Arthur KORNBERG the 1959 Nobel Prize for physiology or medicine.

**O'Connell, Daniel,** 1775–1847, Irish political leader. He founded (1823) the Catholic Association, and led an agitation which culminated in the CATHOLIC EMANCIPATION Act of 1829. Afterwards he sat in the British Parliament, where he worked for repeal of the union of Great Britain and Ireland, for the reform of the government of Ireland, for the disestablishment of the Church of Ireland, and for a solution to the IRISH LAND QUESTION. His willingness to work with the WHIGS after 1834 estranged him from some of his radical allies. Yet he is remembered as 'the Liberator'.

**O'Connor, Feargus Edward,** 1796–1855, Irish political leader. He turned to radical agitation in England in 1835, when be broke with Daniel O'CONNELL and became the main personality in the mass movement of CHARTISM. He was a persuasive speaker and his journal the *Northern Star* (started 1837) had a wide circulation. He was elected to Parliament in 1847, but after the failure of the Chartist petition of 1848 lost influence. He was declared insane in 1852.

**O'Connor, Frank,** 1903–66, Irish short-story writer; b. Michael O'Donovan. A director of the Abbey Theatre (1936–39), a poet, and a critic, he is primarily known for his stories, which are tender, penetrating studies of Irish life.

**O'Connor, (Mary) Flannery,** 1925–64, American author. In the novels *Wise Blood* (1952) and *The Violent Bear It Away* (1960), and the short stories in *A Good Man Is Hard to Find* (1955) and *Everything That Rises Must Converge* (1965), she portrays contemporary Southern life as a grotesque and gothic combination of brutal comedy and violent tragedy.

**octane number,** quality rating for PETROL indicating the ability of the fuel to resist premature detonation and to burn evenly when exposed to heat and pressure in an INTERNAL-COMBUSTION ENGINE. Premature detonation, indicated by knocking and pinging noises, wastes fuel and may cause engine damage. The octane number can be increased by varying the relative amounts of the different HYDROCARBONS that make up the petrol or by additives, e.g., tetraethyl lead. Since the early 1970s in the US, and the 1980s in Europe, many cars have been built to operate on low octane petrol with little or no lead added, because the lead, which is exhausted into the atmosphere, constitutes an environmental pollutant and health hazard, especially to young children.

**Octavia,** Roman matrons. **1** d. 11 BC, sister of Emperor AUGUSTUS and wife of Mark ANTONY. She helped to maintain peace between her brother and her husband until Antony deserted her for CLEOPATRA. **2** AD 42–62, daughter of Emperor CLAUDIUS I and MESSALINA, and wife of NERO, who deserted her for Poppaea. She was falsely accused of adultery, banished, and put to death.

**Octavian** and **Octavius:** see AUGUSTUS.

**October:** see MONTH.

**October Revolution,** in Russian history: see RUSSIAN REVOLUTION.

**octopus,** marine mollusc, with a pouch-shaped body and eight muscular arms or tentacles; a CEPHALOPOD. It seizes its prey with the sucker-bearing arms and paralyses it with a poisonous secretion. Octopus species range in size from only 5 cm (2 in) in the North Atlantic to 10 m (33 ft) in the Pacific. Octopuses can change colour, from pinkish to brown, and eject a dark 'ink' from a special sac when disturbed. They are used for food in many parts of the world.

**ode,** elaborate and stately poem of some length, dating back to Greek choral songs. PINDAR's odes were poems of praise or glorification in stanzas patterned in sets of three strophe, antistrophe, and the differently structured epode. The odes of HORACE and CATULLUS used a simpler LYRIC form. Later Europeans wrote in both Pindaric and Horatian form. Pierre de RONSARD in France and Ben JONSON, Robert HERRICK, and Andrew MARVELL in England were major RENAISSANCE odists. In general, the odes of such 19th-cent. poets as KEATS, P.B. SHELLEY, SWINBURNE, G.M. HOPKINS, and others tended to be freer in form and subject matter than the classical ode.

**Odense,** city (1985 pop. 171,468) a port on the island of Funen, Denmark. It serves as market and ecclesiastical centre for a densely-populated rural area. It has shipyards and industries relating to its prosperous agricultural hinterland. It has a 14th-cent. cathedral and was the birthplace of Hans Christian ANDERSEN.

**Oder,** river, 904 km (562 mi) long, the second longest river of Poland. It rises in N central Czechoslovakia and flows generally NW through Poland, then N along the Polish–East German border to the Baltic Sea. Navigable from Racibórz, Poland, the Oder connects the industrial region of SILESIA with the sea. WROCLAW, FRANKFURT AN DER ODER, and SZCZECIN are the chief cities on the river.

**Oder–Neisse line,** post–World War II frontier between Germany and Poland along the Oder and W Neisse rivers from the Baltic Sea to the Czechoslovak border. Proposed (1945) by the Allies at the Yalta and Potsdam conferences, the border was recognized as permanent by East Germany and Poland in 1950, but not accepted by West Germany until 1971.

**Odessa,** city (1985 pop. 1,126,000), SW European USSR, in the UKRAINE, a port on Odessa Bay of the BLACK SEA. It is a rail junction, the major Soviet Black Sea port, a naval base, and the home port of fishing fleets. Shipbuilding and oil-refining are among its industries. Nearby are large health resorts. The city is said to occupy the site of an ancient Miletian Greek colony that disappeared in the 3rd or 4th cent. AD. Between the 14th and 18th cent. Odessa was held by the Lithuanians, Crimean Tatars, and Turks; in 1792 it passed to Russia. In the 19th and early 20th cent. it was a centre of Ukrainian and Jewish culture and of various political movements. It was the scene of a 1905 revolt led by sailors from the battleship *Potemkin*. Contested by opposing forces in the Russian civil war, it fell to the Red Army in 1920. During World War II it was held by the Romanians and Germans (1941–44), who massacred or deported c.280,000 civilians, mostly Jews.

**Odets, Clifford,** 1906–63, American dramatist. Regarded as the most gifted of the American social-protest playwrights of the 1930s, he is known for such works as *Waiting for Lefty* (1935); *Awake and Sing* (1935), considered his finest play; and *Golden Boy* (1937). His later plays include *Clash by Night* (1942) and *The Country Girl* (1950).

**Odin,** Norse god: see WODEN.

**Odoacer** or **Odovacar** (odə‚aysə), c.435–493, Germanic chieftain. He and his soldiers were mercenaries for Rome when, in 476, the Heruli, a Germanic tribe, revolted and named Odoacer king. He seized RAVENNA and deposed ROMULUS AUGUSTULUS, last Roman emperor of the West. The date 476 is often accepted as the end of the West Roman Empire. Odoacer's authority was recognized by ZENO, emperor of the East, but in 488 Zeno sent THEODORIC THE GREAT to expel Odoacer, and Theodoric treacherously assassinated Odoacer.

**Odysseus** (ə‚diseəs), Lat. *Ulysses,* in Greek mythology, king of Ithaca; husband of PENELOPE. A Greek leader in the TROJAN WAR, he is depicted by HOMER as wise and cunning. In later legends he is wily, lying, and evil. His wanderings are described in the *Odyssey,* and have inspired many different works of literature including TENNYSON's 'Ulysses', James JOYCE's *Ulysses* (1914-21), and KAZANTZAKIS' *The Odyssey, a Modern Sequel* (1938). He is also the hero of operas by MONTEVERDI (1641) and DALLAPICCOLA (1968).

**Odyssey:** see HOMER.

**Oeben, Jean-François,** d. 1763, French cabinetmaker. Noted for his MARQUETRY decoration in floral and geometrical forms, he also specialized in mechanisms such as those whereby drawers opened by the movement of another section. He invented the roll-top desk.

**Oedipus** (‚eedipəs), in Greek mythology, son of King Laius of THEBES and Queen Jocasta. Warned by an oracle that Oedipus would kill his father and marry his mother, his parents left the baby on a mountainside. However, he was adopted by the king of CORINTH. When grown, Oedipus heard the prophecy and, ignorant of his real parentage, fled to Thebes. On the way he met, quarrelled with, and killed Laius, without recognizing him. At Thebes he solved the SPHINX's riddle and married Jocasta. After many years he learned the truth and, in horror, blinded himself. Jocasta committed suicide. Oedipus was exiled, looked after by his daughter ANTIGONE, and Jocasta's brother, Creon, became king. Later, Oedipus' sons battled for the throne (see SEVEN AGAINST THEBES). The story of Oedipus is brilliantly dramatized in SOPHOCLES' *Oedipus Rex;* his later life is described in the same playwright's *Oedipus at Colonus.* The Oedipus

Roll-top desk by Jean-François **Oeben**

myth has been given new interest since its interpretation by FREUD, inspiring such works as STRAVINSKY's oratorio *Oedipus Rex* (1927; libretto by COCTEAU) and PASOLINI's film (1967) of the same title.

**Oedipus complex:** see COMPLEX.

**Oehlenschläger, Adam Gottlob,** 1779–1850, Danish poet and dramatist, the 'father of Danish romanticism' and its most important representative. He wrote 24 tragedies and was made professor of Aesthetics at Copenhagen Univ., but is best remembered for his early works: *Poems* (1803), and the elaborate closet-drama *Aladdin or the Miraculous Lamp* (1805), as well as his first tragedies, *Hakon Jarl* (1807) and *Correggio* (1809).

**Oersted, Hans Christian** (‚uhsted), 1777–1851, Danish physicist and chemist. His discovery that a magnetic needle is deflected by a conductor carrying an electric current showed a relation between ELECTRICITY and MAGNETISM and initiated the study of electromagnetism. The unit of magnetic field strength, the oersted, is named after him. Oersted was the first to isolate ALUMINIUM.

**oestrogen,** any of a group of hormones synthesized by the reproductive organs and ADRENAL GLANDS. Oestrogens are important in the regulation of the female menstrual cycle (see MENSTRUATION) and in the development of female secondary sexual characteristics. Excessive production in men gives rise to feminization. Oestrogens are used to treat menopausal symptoms and OSTEOPOROSIS, and they are a major constituent of ORAL CONTRACEPTIVES.

**O'Faoláin, Seán** (oh‚falən), 1900–, Irish writer. He is best known for his stories about Ireland, collected in *Midsummer Night Madness* (1932), *The Heat of the Sun* (1966), *The Talking Trees* (1971), and other volumes. He has also written novels and biographies of DE VALERA (1933) and O'CONNELL (1938).

**Offa,** d. 796, king of MERCIA (r.757–96). Gradually he extended Mercian power to most of S England and gained the rulers of WESSEX and NORTHUMBRIA as sons-in-law. In 796 he and CHARLEMAGNE signed the first recorded English commercial treaty. He also built the earthwork called Offa's Dyke.

**Offaly,** inland county in centre of Republic of Ireland (1986 pop. 59,806), 1977 km² (771 sq mi), bordering on Westmeath in the N. It is situated in the province of Leinster. The county town is TULLAMORE. Much of the county is low-lying, including a part of the Bog of Allen in the NE. The Slieve Bloom Mts are situated in the S. The county is crossed by the Grand Canal from W to E. The main rivers are the SHANNON, BARROW, Nore, and Brosna. Mixed agriculture is important.

**Offenbach, Jacques Levy,** 1819–80, French composer; b. Germany. He is famous for his OPERETTAS, of which he wrote over 100. His masterpiece was the opera *Tales of Hoffmann* (1881), after E.T.A. HOFFMANN.

**Offenbach am Main,** city (1984 pop. 107,600), HESSE, central West Germany, on the MAIN R. It is noted for its leatherware, including boots and shoes, and an international fair in leather goods is held each year.

**offset printing:** see PRINTING.

**O'Flaherty, Liam,** 1897–1984, Irish novelist. He wrote realistic stories of the common man, including *The Informer* (1925) and *The Assassin* (1928). *Famine* (1937) and *Land* (1946) are among his novels of 19th-cent. Ireland.

**Ogaden** ('ogə,den), region, Harar prov., SE Ethiopia, bordering the Somali Democratic Republic. It is an arid region inhabited mainly by Somali pastoral nomads. Since the 1960s it has been the focus of a secessionist movement by Somali nationalists demanding union of the Ogaden with Somalia. Somali troops invaded the region in 1977 but were repulsed a year later by Ethiopian forces with Soviet support. Guerrilla warfare continued into the 1980s.

**Ogbomosho,** city (1975 est. pop. 432,000), SW Nigeria. It is the trade centre for an agricultural region, and cotton textiles are woven. Founded in the 17th cent., the city resisted invasions by the Fulani people in the early 19th cent. and grew by absorbing refugees from Fulani attacks.

**Oglethorpe, James Edward,** 1696–1785, English general and philanthropist. In 1733 he founded the American colony of GEORGIA partly as an asylum for debtors. He assured the colony's survival by defeating a Spanish force in 1742.

**Ogot, Grace,** 1930–, Kenyan writer. In her short stories, she celebrates traditional African culture, e.g., *The Promised Land* (1966) and *Land Without Thunder* (1968), but her chief strength lies in her delineation of women in her society, e.g., *The Other Women and Other Stories* (1976) and *The Graduate* (1980).

**O'Higgins, Bernardo,** 1778–1842, South American revolutionary ruler (1817–23) of Chile. The illegitimate son of Ambrosio O'Higgins, governor of Chile (1789–96), he and SAN MARTÍN liberated (1817) Chile from Spanish rule. He became supreme director, but his reforms aroused so much opposition that he was deposed (1823). He died in exile in Peru.

**Ohio,** state of the US (1984 est. pop. 10,752,000), area 106,765 km² (41,222 sq mi), located in the Midwest, bordered by Pennsylvania and West Virginia (E), Kentucky (S), Indiana (W), and Michigan and Lake Erie (N). The capital is COLUMBUS and the largest city is CLEVELAND; CINCINNATI, Toledo, AKRON, and DAYTON are also important. The state is mostly flat, bordered by the Ohio R. on the S, and has a continental climate. Its manufacturing output is the third largest in the US, led by transport equipment, nonelectrical machinery, primary and fabricated metals, and rubber. The rich farmlands produce soybeans, corn, dairy products, cattle, hay, and wheat. Ohio's mineral resource include lime, stone, clay, and coal. The Lake ERIE ports of Toledo and Cleveland make use of the SAINT LAWRENCE SEAWAY as access to the Atlantic Ocean. Almost 80% of the population lives in metropolitan areas, and in 1980 88% was non-Hispanic white and 10% was black. The early inhabitants were Mound Builders, and later the area was home for the Erie, Miami, Shawnee, and Ottawa Indians. In the 18th cent. the British fought the French and the Indians for control of the land, finally being defeated by the US in 1812. Canals, railways, and the discovery of oil opened Ohio up after the Civil War. After the disastrous floods of 1913 the federal and state governments built water projects along the Ohio R. The Great Depression afflicted the state but heavy industry brought prosperity until the recession of the 1970s. In recent years chemical and electronics industries have begun to transform some depressed local economies, such as Columbus.

**Ohio,** major US river, flowing 1580 km (980 mi) from the confluence of the Allegheny and Monongahela rivers at Pittsburgh, Pennsylvania, W to the Mississippi R. at Cairo, Illinois. It is regulated by a modern system of locks and dams, built since 1955 to replace older structures, and is navigable by barges and pleasure craft for its entire length. Reportedly seen by LA SALLE in 1669, the river passed to British control in 1763 and to the US in 1783. From then until the opening of the ERIE CANAL (1825), it was the principal route to the West.

**Ohio Company,** organization formed (1747) by American land speculators to settle 80,940 hectares (200,000 acres) at the forks of the Ohio R. Its activities challenged the French in the region and helped to bring on the final conflict of the FRENCH AND INDIAN WARS (1754–63).

**Ōhira Masayoshi,** 1910–80, Japanese political leader, prime minister (1978–80). After serving in the house of representatives, he became foreign minister (1962–64, 1972–74) and minister of finance (1974–76). A Liberal-Democrat, he was elected prime minister in 1978 but died in office.

**Ohlin, Bertil** (,oolin), 1889–1979, Swedish economist and political leader. He taught (1924–29) at the Univ. of Copenhagen and later at the Stockholm School of Economics. Ohlin also led Sweden's Liberal party (1944–67) and was minister of commerce (1944–45). He shared the 1977 Nobel Prize for economics for his pioneering studies of international trade.

**ohm** (ohm), symbol $\Omega$, unit of electrical RESISTANCE, equal to the resistance between two points of an electrical conductor, when a constant potential difference of 1V applied to these points produces a current of 1 amp in the conductor. See OHM'S LAW.

**ohmmeter,** device used to measure, in OHMS, the electric RESISTANCE of a conductor. It is usually included in a single instrument with a VOLTMETER and often an AMMETER. In normal usage, the ohmmeter operates by using the voltmeter to measure a voltage drop, then converting this reading into a corresponding resistance reading through OHM'S LAW.

**Ohm's law,** law stating that the electric current I flowing through a given RESISTANCE R is equal to the applied voltage V divided by the resistance, or $I = V/R$. In alternating-current (AC) circuits, where INDUCTANCE and CAPACITANCE may also need to be taken account of, the law must be amended to $I = V/Z$, where Z is the IMPEDANCE. The law was formulated by the German physicist **Georg Simon Ohm,** 1787–1854.

**oils:** see ESSENTIAL OILS; FATS AND OILS; PETROLEUM.

**oil tanker,** specialized vessel for the transport of liquid petroleum. The world's first oil tanker, the Glückauf, built in Britain for a German company to carry oil from the US, measured 91 m (300 ft) from bow to stern and had a top speed of 9 knots. It carried 2090 tonnes of oil. Today's supertankers, designed for long hauls between Europe or Japan and the oil-rich countries of the Middle East, can measure up to 400 m (1300 ft) with a cargo of oil on board weighing 450,000 tonnes or more. Because of their size and weight supertankers are not easily manoeuvrable and can have docking problems, requiring harbours 30 m (100 ft) deep for unloading. They can also be a hazard to other shipping particularly in foggy and narrow waterways, and collisions can result in fires and serious pollution through oil spills. Since its peak in 1977 the world's tanker fleet has declined and now numbers around 2000, representing a fall of about 25–30% in tanker tonnage over the last decade.

**Oisin:** see OSSIAN.

**Oita,** city (1986 est. pop. 385,046), capital of Oita prefecture, NE Kyushu, Japan, on the INLAND SEA. In the latter half of the 16th cent., the castle town and port (then known as Funai) flourished through international trade with the Portuguese, but then declined. In recent years the city has grown rapidly as an industrial centre, with modern steel, engineering, and shipbuilding factories, and a new technology park. To the north of Oita is the coastal resort of Beppu, famous for its hot springs, and to the south is Usuki, the site of a former temple containing many statues of Buddha carved out of the stone cliffs.

**Ojibwa Indians** or **Chippewa Indians** (oh,jibway), NORTH AMERICAN INDIANS of the Eastern Woodlands and Plains, speaking an Algonquian language (see AMERICAN INDIAN LANGUAGES). In the 17th cent. they occupied the shores of Lake Superior, and drove the SIOUX across the Mississippi R. in a contest for the wild rice lands of their region. Some Ojibwa continued west to North Dakota and became the Plains Ojibwa. The sedentary Woodlands Ojibwa subsisted on fish, deer, corn, squash, and wild rice. One of the largest tribes north of Mexico, c.60,000 in Canada alone, the Ojibwa pursue various occupations in Canada and in Michigan, Minnesota, and other states.

Buddha carved out of the stone cliffs at Usuki, **Oita**

**okapi**, nocturnal, ruminant MAMMAL (*Okapi johnstoni*) of the rain forests of the upper Congo R., unknown to zoologists until the early 20th cent. In shape it resembles the related GIRAFFE, but is smaller and has a shorter neck. It is red-brown with zebra-striped hindquarters.

**Okapi** in San Diego Zoo

**Okayama**, city (1986 est. pop. 565,481), capital of Okayama prefecture, W Honshu, Japan. A former castle town, Okayama is the commercial centre for the surrounding rich agricultural areas which produce rushes for the traditional floor mats (tatami) and fruit. Manufacturing products include rubber goods, fibres and textiles, and machinery. Korakuen Park, one of Japan's most famous traditional gardens, was laid out in 1700 by the lord Tiikeda.

**O'Keeffe, Georgia**, 1887–1986, American painter. Her works are marked by organic abstract forms painted in clear, strong colours. They are often strongly sexual in symbolism, particularly her flower paintings. O'Keeffe lived much of her life in New Mexico and frequently employed motifs from the Southwest in her works, e.g., *Cow's Skull, Red, White, and Blue* (1931; Metropolitan Mus.).

**Okefenokee Swamp**, large (c.1550 km²/600 sq mi) swamp, SE Georgia, US, extending into N Florida, noted for its varied and abundant

wildlife. It is a saucer-shaped depression, with small islands rising above the water and its thick cover of vegetation.

**Okhotsk, Sea of**, c.1,528,100 km² (590,000 sq mi), NW arm of the Pacific Ocean, between the KAMCHATKA Peninsula and the KURIL ISLANDS, USSR. Ice-bound from Nov. to June and subject to heavy fogs, it connects with the Sea of Japan through the Tatar and La Pérouse straits. Magadan and Korsakov are the chief ports.

**Okigbo, Christopher** 1932–67, Nigerian poet. A superb stylist, he combined academic knowledge of European classical and English literary forms with Igbo myth and oral traditions in three immensely influential collections, *Heavensgate* (1962), *Limits* (1964), and *Labyrinths, with Paths of Thunder* (1971). He was killed in the Biafran War.

**Okinawa**, island (1986 est. pop. 1,199,290), 1176 km² (454 sq mi), W Pacific Ocean, SW of Kyushu; part of Okinawa prefecture, Japan. Okinawa is the largest of the RYUKYU ISLANDS and the only area of Japan allowed to develop free trade zones; Naha, the capital of Okinawa prefecture, is the largest city and chief port. Sugarcane and rice are grown, and fishing is important. In a bloody campaign during WORLD WAR II, US forces seized (Apr.–June 1945) the island from Japan. The Japanese lost 103,000 men; US casualties were 48,000. Okinawa was returned to Japan in 1972, but the US retained its military bases.

**Oklahoma**, state of the US (1984, est. pop. 3,298,000), area 181,090 km² (69,919 sq mi), situated in the SW bordered by Kansas and Colorado (N), Missouri and Arkansas (E), Texas (S,W), and New Mexico (W). OKLAHOMA CITY is the capital and largest urban centre, followed by Tulsa. A panhandle extends the state into the high prairies of the GREAT PLAINS, and the elevation declines eastwards until the OZARKS and the Ouachita Mts in the far E. The climate is continental, and the Great Plains experience seasonal extremes of temperature. Mining is the principal source of income and the base of the industrial sector; natural gas and petroleum are the chief extractions. The leading industries manufacture nonelectrical machinery, fabricated metals, and refined petroleum. Cattle, wheat, cotton, dairy products, hay, and peanuts are the main sources of farm income. More than 55% of the population lives in metropolitan areas, and 169,464 (6%) of the population is native American, a community second in size only to that of California. The Plains Indian tribes, including the Osage, Kiowa, Comanche, and Apache, lived in the area when it was acquired by the US in the LOUISIANA PURCHASE (1803). The federal government forced the five so-called civilized tribes (Cherokee, Chocktaw, Chickasaw, Creek, and Seminole) to move there from the E, naming it the Indian Territory. Throughout the 19th cent. the land assigned to the Indians was gradually diminished by the demands of ranching, oil production, and settlement. In the 1930s NW Oklahoma became part of the DUST BOWL; the crisis forced thousands of farmers to leave their lands and become migrant labourers in California and elsewhere. Since World War II the extraction of minerals has revived the economy, making Oklahoma one of the most prosperous states of the SUN BELT.

**Oklahoma City**, US (1984 pop. 443,000), state capital on the North Canadian R.; inc. 1890. Settled overnight (1889) in a land rush, it became state capital in 1910. Oil, cattle, grain, and cotton were the major industries in its development. Today it has diversified manufactures and is the commercial centre of the region. Vast in area, the city has many parks and tourist attractions.

**okra**, annual plant (*Hibiscus esculentus*) of the hollyhock family. Okra is sometimes known as 'ladies' fingers'. These slim, green, octagonal seed pods are boiled and served as a vegetable. Related to the COTTON plant and originally from Africa, Okra features a great deal in CREOLE cookery.

**Ōkuma Shigenobu** (ˌohkoohmah), 1838–1922, Japanese statesman. As a member of government in the early MEIJI period he opposed the conservatives led by ITŌ HIROBUMI and in 1882 founded a reformist party, the Kaishintō, a forerunner of the MINSEITŌ. As foreign minister (1888–89, 1896–97) he succeeded in revising Japan's unequal treaties with the West. While he was prime minister (1914–16) Japan entered WORLD WAR I on the Allied side and presented the TWENTY-ONE DEMANDS to China.

**Olaf,** kings of Norway. **Olaf I** (Olaf Tryggvason), c.963–1000 (r.995–1000), was the great grandson of HAROLD I. A Christian convert, he overthrew Haakon (995) and undertook the conversion of Norway. After his death in battle, Sweyn of Denmark and Olaf of Sweden divided Norway. His nephew **Olaf II** (Saint Olaf), c.995–1030 (r.1015–28), continued to Christianize Norway. An uprising of nobles (1028) supporting CANUTE of England and Denmark forced him to flee. In 1030 he tried to wrest the crown from Canute's son Sweyn but died in battle. His son MAGNUS I later ruled Norway. **Olaf V,** 1903– (r.1957–), is the son of HAAKON VII. After the Germans invaded Norway (1940), he led the Norwegian struggle for liberation. His son Harald (Harold) is his heir.

**Olbers, Heinrich Wilhelm Matthäus,** 1758–1840, German physician and astronomer. Inventor (1797) of the first successful method for calculating the orbits of comets, he discovered the comet of 1815, now known as Olbers' comet, and two asteroids, Pallas (1802) and Vesta (1807). His analysis of the background light of the universe to be expected for a uniform static cosmos is known as 'Olbers' paradox'.

**old-age pension** an income provided by the state for old people. This forms part of the services provided by a comprehensive WELFARE STATE. The old-age pension in Britain was introduced in 1908 by Lloyd George. The value of the pension has always been a matter of political controversy. Although the real value of the pension actually rose throughout the 1980s it was not perceived as doing so, because average earnings at the time were rising even faster. If the old-age pension is considered as a proportion of average earnings, British pensioners received in the 1980s about half of what their French or German counterparts did.

**Old Bailey:** see COURT SYSTEM IN ENGLAND AND WALES.

**Old Catholics,** Christian denomination, established by German clergy and laymen who separated from the Roman Catholic Church when they rejected the dogma of papal infallibility issued (1870) by the First VATICAN COUNCIL. By 1874 a new church had been established with a bishop consecrated by a Dutch Jansenist bishop. It retained Roman ritual (in the vernacular), allowed priests to marry, and made confession optional.

**Old Church Slavonic:** see CHURCH SLAVONIC.

**Oldenbarneveldt, Johan van,** 1547–1619, Dutch statesman. He aided WILLIAM THE SILENT and MAURICE OF NASSAU in the struggle for independence from Spain. With Oldenbarneveldt as permanent advocate of Holland (from 1586) commerce expanded greatly and the Dutch EAST INDIA COMPANY was formed. His negotiation (1609) of a 12-year truce with Spain gave the Dutch virtual independence. As leader of those favouring control of state affairs by the States-General he clashed with the party of the nobles and the house of Orange, which used his affiliation with the Remonstrants, a sect at odds with the strict Calvinists, as a pretext for his execution.

**Oldenburg,** city (1984 pop. 138,700), LOWER SAXONY, northern West Germany, on the Hunte R. Its major industry is food-processing, and the locality is noted for horse-breeding. The district around Oldenburg has enjoyed a considerable measure of independence since the 12th cent. and was a grand duchy from 1815 to 1918. It became part of Lower Saxony in 1946.

**Oldenburg, Claes,** 1929–, American sculptor; b. Sweden. A leader in POP ART, he is noted for his soft or giant sculptures of common objects, e.g., *Lipstick* (1969; Yale Univ.).

**Old English:** see ANGLO-SAXON LITERATURE; ENGLISH LITERATURE; TYPE.

**Oldham,** town (1981 pop. 107,095), Greater Manchester, NW England, 12 km (7 mi) NE of Manchester. It is an industrial town, which was an important centre of the English cotton industry, especially for spinning. Industries found in the town now include textiles, engineering, and the manufacture of paper.

**Old Testament,** Christian name for the Hebrew Bible, the first portion of the Christian Bible (see NEW TESTAMENT). It consists of a varying number of books, in varying order. The canon of the JEWS, adopted AD c.100, is drawn from one Hebrew source, the Massorah, whose origin is unknown. The contemporary Jewish reckoning of the Old Testament is as follows: (1) the five books of the Law (TORAH or PENTATEUCH), i.e., GENESIS, EXODUS, LEVITICUS, NUMBERS, and DEUTERONOMY; (2) the Prophets (e.g., JOSHUA, ISAIAH) and the 12 Minor Prophets; (3) the Writings (Hagiographa), including such books as PSALMS and JOB; the Rolls (*Megilloth*), e.g., SONG OF SOLOMON and RUTH; and others. The Old

Claes **Oldenburg,** *Giant Hamburger,* 1962. Painted sail cloth stuffed with foam, 132 × 213 cm. Art Gallery of Ontario.

Testament long used in the Christian church was based on a different text, the Septuagint, a Hellenistic Jewish translation into Greek about the 3rd cent. BC. The Latin Bible's official form was the VULGATE of St JEROME, based on the Hebrew original; the Vulgate's list and order were the canon of the Western Church. At the REFORMATION, the English Protestants considered only those books appearing in the Massorah canonical; the others, regarded as suitable for instruction but not necessarily inspired, were placed by translators of the Authorized Version (AV) in an appendix to the Old Testament, the APOCRYPHA (see BIBLE). Thus the Reformed canon became the Massoretic text, but in Western order. The AV compares with the Douai Version (published by Roman Catholic scholars in France in 1610), representing the Western canon, as follows, the names in parentheses being the usual Douai names when different from AV, those in italics not appearing in AV: Genesis, Exodus, Leviticus, Numbers, Deuteronomy, Joshua (Josue), Judges, Ruth, First and Second Samuel (First and Second Kings), First and Second Kings (Third and Fourth Kings), First and Second Chronicles (First and Second Paralipomenon), Ezra (First Esdras), Nehemiah (Second Esdras), *Tobias, Judith,* Esther, Job, Psalms, Proverbs, Ecclesiastes, Song of Solomon (Canticle of Canticles), *Wisdom, Ecclesiasticus,* Isaiah (Isaias), Jeremiah (Jeremias), Lamentations, *Baruch,* Ezekiel (Ezechiel), Daniel, Hosea (Osee), Joel, Amos, Obadiah (Abdias), Jonah (Jonas), Micah (Micheas), Nahum, Habakkuk (Habacuc), Zephaniah (Sophonias), Haggai (Aggeus), Zechariah (Zacharias), Malachi (Malachias), *First* and *Second Maccabees.* Dating of the Bible is difficult; before 1000 BC there are few outside sources against which to check. From the time of DAVID, a chronology with checks is possible; no single system, however, is widely accepted. Authorship is known from tradition or from internal evidence. Scholarship of the 19th cent. questioned traditions about the Bible, particularly in regard to the 'historical' books; but 20th-cent. archaeology has occasionally supported, rather than contradicted, the narratives. Generally modern critics hold that about 1000 BC the first of a series of editors began to collect folkloric and historical material. Two dominant compilations can be traced. These were combined by a Judaean of the southern kingdom of Judah some time after the fall of the northern kingdom (Israel).

**Olduvai Gorge,** Tanzania, on edge of Serengeti Plain, site excavated by L.S.B. and M.D. LEAKEY between the 1930s and 70s, providing important evidence for HUMAN EVOLUTION. Deposits cover the period 1.9 million years ago to recent times, but attention has focused on the remains from earlier than 0.7 million years ago. The gorge contains many sites which have yielded major hominid finds, including the first specimen of *Australopithecus boisei* (see AUSTRALOPITHECUS) and HOMO HABILIS, and HOMO ERECTUS. A recent important discovery by D.C. Johanson and T.D. White is of a *H. habilis* partial skeleton. There is also much archaeological material which has provided evidence for the ecology of early hominids and, indirectly, insight of their mental capabilities.

**Old Vic,** London theatre opened 1914 by Lilian Baylis to present Shakespearean repertoire. It was famous for classic revivals featuring Sir Alec GUINNESS, Sir John GIELGUD, and others. It became the temporary (1963–76) home of the NATIONAL THEATRE OF GREAT BRITAIN but was closed in 1981.

**Old World,** zoological term used to describe several families of animals which originated in Eurasia, Africa, Indonesia, and Australia and may be exclusive to those areas. The Old World monkeys, the Cercopithecidae, do not have tails which can grasp and may be tail-less. Pythons, vipers, agamas, hornbills, ostriches, aardvarks, and pangolins are examples of Old World animals.

**Oligocene epoch:** see GEOLOGICAL ERA (table).

**oligopoly:** see MONOPOLY.

**Olinda,** city (1980 pop. 266,751), NE Brazil, Pernambuco state. Founded in 1536 it served as a departmental capital for several centuries and is situated 6 km (4 mi) N of the present state capital of Recife. Restoration of this old colonial city and its proximity to major coastal beaches have combined to enhance the city's reputation as a national and international tourist resort.

**olive,** common name for the family Oleaceae, trees and shrubs of warm temperature climates and the Old World tropics, and for the true olive tree (*Olea europaea*), the most important member of the family commercially. Native to Asia Minor, the true olive is a small evergreen that bears a fruit (also called olive), which is pressed to obtain olive oil or is eaten. Green olives for eating are picked when full grown but unripe; purplish-black olives are usually ripe and richer in oil (see FATS AND OILS). The Mediterranean region is the chief area of olive production. Olive wood and ASH, also of the olive family, are hardwoods used in furniture. Popular ornamentals in the family include the LILAC, true JASMINE, and FORSYTHIA. The olive branch has been a symbol of peace since ancient times.

**Olives, Mount of** or **Olivet,** ridge E of Jerusalem. In the OLD TESTAMENT it is associated with DAVID, Ezekiel, and Zechariah. According to the NEW TESTAMENT, it was a frequent resort of JESUS and the scene of his Ascension.

**Olivier, Laurence Kerr** (Baron Olivier of Brighton), 1907–, English actor, director, and producer, often called the greatest actor of the 20th cent. Olivier has been successful both in the classics, e.g., as Oedipus Rex, Richard III, and Othello, and in modern dramas, e.g., John OSBORNE's *The Entertainer* (1957) and Eugene O'NEILL's *Long Day's Journey into Night* (1971). He has made several outstanding films, including *Wuthering Heights* (1939), *Henry V* (1944), and *Hamlet* (1948; Academy Award). After appearing with the Old Vic, he was the first director (1962–73) of the National Theatre of Great Britain. Knighted in 1947, he was the first actor to be created (1970) a life peer.

**Ollivier, Émile,** 1825–1913, French statesman in the 'Liberal Empire' of NAPOLEON III. He became premier in Jan. 1870 and transformed the empire into a parliamentary regime, but his government fell in August during the FRANCO-PRUSSIAN WAR.

**Olmec,** culture of ancient MIDDLE AMERICAN INDIAN peoples (c.1250 BC–400 BC) of the E Mexico lowlands. A highly developed agricultural society, they left sculptured stone heads weighing over 20 tonnes. The Olmec seem to have been the earliest users (from 31 BC) of the bar and dot system of recording time. They influenced the cultures of the Zapotec, MIXTEC, and TOLTEC.

**Olomouc,** Ger. *Olmütz*, city (1984 pop. 104,000), Moravia, Czechoslovakia, on the Morava R. It lies on a route between the Sudeten Mts and the Carpathian Mts. Manufactures include engineering and brewing. Its historic buildings include a 12th-cent. cathedral and a 13th-cent. city hall.

**Olson, Charles,** 1910–70, American writer. He made his reputation with *Call Me Ishmael* (1947), a critical study of MELVILLE's *Moby-Dick*. His 'projective' (open) poetry was particularly influential in the 1950s.

**Olympia,** ancient Greek sanctuary in the W PELOPONNESUS, near the Alpheus River. It was an important centre of the worship of ZEUS and the

A giant **Olmec** head

site of the OLYMPIC GAMES. Excavation revealed the great temple, which housed a gold-adorned statue of Zeus by PHIDIAS, one of the SEVEN WONDERS OF THE WORLD.

**Olympiad,** a four-year time unit in ancient GREECE, each beginning with the OLYMPIC GAMES. The first Olympiad was reckoned to have begun in 776 BC.

**Olympian,** in Greek mythology, one of the 12 gods who ruled the universe from their home on Mt Olympus. Led by ZEUS, they were: HERA, his sister and wife; POSEIDON and PLUTO (HADES), his brothers; HESTIA, his sister; and his children, ARES, HERMES, APOLLO, HEPHAESTUS, ATHENA, APHRODITE, and ARTEMIS. Similar to humans in appearance and character, the Olympians are known to us mainly from the works of HOMER and HESIOD.

**Olympias,** d. 316 BC, wife of PHILIP II of Macedon and mother of ALEXANDER THE GREAT. She reputedly had great influence in moulding her son. After his death she tried to seize power, but CASSANDER had her executed.

**Olympic games,** series of international amateur sports contests that originated in ancient Greece. The Greek games were held once every four years, reaching their height in the 5th and 4th cent. BC. Later they fell into disfavour because of professionalism, and were discontinued at the end of the 4th cent. AD. The first Olympics were confined to running, but many events were added in ancient times. The modern revival of the games began in Athens in 1896. They have since been staged at four-year intervals (except during the world wars) in cities around the world. The number of entrants, of competing nations, and of athletic events has steadily increased. Women were first allowed to compete in 1912, and a separate series of winter games was begun in 1924. The International Olympic Committee is the governing body.

## OLYMPIC GAMES, 1896–1988

### Summer Games

| | | | |
|---|---|---|---|
| 1896 | Athens, Greece | 1952 | Helsinki, Finland |
| 1900 | Paris, France | 1956 | Melbourne, |
| 1904 | St Louis, US | | Australia |
| 1908 | London, UK | 1960 | Rome, Italy |
| 1912 | Stockholm, Sweden | 1964 | Tokyo, Japan |
| 1920 | Antwerp, Belgium | 1968 | Mexico City, Mexico |
| 1924 | Paris, France | 1972 | Munich, |
| 1928 | Amsterdam, The | | West Germany |
| | Netherlands | 1976 | Montreal, Canada |
| 1932 | Los Angeles, US | 1980 | Moscow, USSR |
| 1936 | Berlin, Germany | 1984 | Los Angeles, US |
| 1948 | London, UK | 1988 | Seoul, South Korea |

### Winter Games

| | | | |
|---|---|---|---|
| 1924 | Chamonix, France | | |
| 1928 | St Moritz, | | |
| | Switzerland | 1960 | Squaw Valley, US |
| 1932 | Lake Placid, US | 1964 | Innsbruck, Austria |
| 1936 | Garmisch-Partenkirch- | 1968 | Grenoble, France |
| | en, Germany | 1972 | Sapporo, Japan |
| 1948 | St Moritz, | 1976 | Innsbruck, Austria |
| | Switzerland | 1980 | Lake Placid, US |
| 1952 | Oslo, Norway | 1984 | Sarajevo, Yugoslavia |
| 1956 | Cortina, Italy | 1988 | Calgary, Canada |

**Olympus,** mountain range, c.40 km (25 mi) long, N Greece. It rises to c.2920 m (9570 ft) at Mount Olympus, described in Greek mythology as the home of the OLYMPIAN gods.

**Olynthus** (oh‚linthəs), ancient city of GREECE, on the Chalcidice peninsula. It headed the Chalcidian League, and opposed ATHENS and SPARTA. Originally allied with PHILIP II of Macedon against Athens, it later sought Athens's aid against Philip. DEMOSTHENES' *Olynthiac* orations urged Athens to help. Athens complied, but Philip razed the city (348 BC).

**Omaha,** US city (1984 pop. 334,000), E Nebraska, on the Missouri R.; inc. 1857. Settled in 1854, it grew as a supply point for westward migration. The largest city in the state, located in the heart of the country's farm region, it is a busy port and one of the world's great livestock markets and meat-processing centres. The city has diversified manufactures, and insurance, banking, and medical treatment and research are major enterprises. Offut Air Force Base, headquarters of the Strategic Air Command, is south of the city.

**Omaha Indians:** see NORTH AMERICAN INDIANS.

**Oman,** officially the Sultanate of Oman, formerly Muscat and Oman, independent sultanate (1987 est. pop. 2,000,000), c.272,000 km² (105,000 sq mi), SE Arabian peninsula, bounded by the Gulf of Oman (E), the Arabian Sea (S), Southern Yemen and Saudi Arabia (W), and the United Arab Emirates (N), which separate the main portion of the country from an enclave jutting into the Strait of HORMUZ. The capital is MUSCAT. Oman comprises a coastal plain and an interior region which is largely sandy desert but includes the JEBEL AKHDAR Mts. Some summer rain occurs on Jebel Akhdar and in the Southwest. Dates are cultivated in the north and there is an abundance of sugarcane and cattle in the southwest, but the major product is oil, with an annual production of over 150 million barrels. The GNP is US$8826 million and the GNP per capita is US$7480 (1984). The population is predominantly Muslim Arab, with Indian and Baluchi minorities. Occupied by Portugal in 1508 and Turkey in 1659, Oman came under Ahmad ibn Said of Yemen, founder of the present royal line, in 1741. It has had close ties with Britain since the 19th cent. In 1970 Qabus bin Said overthrew the strict regime of his father, Sultan Said bin Timur, and instituted a programme of liberalization and modernization. In recent years the government has been opposed by guerrilla forces in Dhofar prov., in the south and has received military assistance from the UK in this context. In 1980 the US, following the

Oman

example of Britain, obtained the use of ports and airfields in Oman in exchange for economic and military aid. In the early 1980s Oman established closer ties with neighbouring states within the framework of the GULF COOPERATION COUNCIL.

**Omar Khayyam,** fl. 11th cent., Persian poet and mathematician. He wrote several mathematical studies and participated in a calendar reform, but he is best known for his *Rubaiyat* (epigrammatic quatrains), which express a hedonistic philosophy. A paraphrased English translation (1859) by Edward FITZGERALD popularized his work in the West.

**ombudsman,** popular name for the Parliamentary Commissioner for Administration, the name originating from Sweden, where the office first was established in 1809–10. In the UK, the first ombudsman was appointed by PARLIAMENT in 1967 to investigate complaints from the public of maladministration in government departments. Investigations can only be carried out at the request of a Member of Parliament, acting on behalf of a constituent. The ombudsman acts independently of both the government and the individual; on completing his or her investigations a report is published which the government may or may not implement. Separate ombudsmen have been appointed for both local government (1974) and the National Health Service (1973).

**Omdurman,** city (1983 pop. 526,287), central Sudan, on the White Nile opposite KHARTOUM. It is the country's chief commercial centre and part of a tri-city metropolitan area (with Khartoum and Khartoum North). The MAHDI, who is buried in the city, based his forces here for the attack on Khartoum (1885), and his successor, Khalifa Addallah, made it his capital. The battle of Karari (1898), near Omdurman, marked the defeat of the Mahdist state by an Anglo-Egyptian army under Lord KITCHENER.

**omnivore,** an animal which eats both plant and animal food. Many are animals with extremely adaptable diets, able to eat whatever food is available. Omnivorous mammals' teeth are fairly unspecialized, able both to cut flesh and grind plant materials. Their digestive tracts produce enzymes which will digest starches and sugars as well as animal fats and proteins. Humans are omnivores.

**Omsk,** city (1985 pop. 1,108,000), W Siberian USSR, at the confluence of the Irtysh and Om rivers, and on the Trans-Siberian railway. It is a major river port and has plants producing railway equipment and farm machinery, oil refineries, and grain mills. Founded in 1716 as a fortress, it became a transportation and administrative centre in the 19th cent.

**Onassis, Aristotle Socrates,** 1906?–1975, Greek shipowner and financier; b. Turkey. After reviving the family tobacco business in Argentina, he received (1925) Argentinian and Greek citizenship. He bought his first ships in the early 1930s and later entered the tanker business. Onassis was related by marriage to the Greek shipowners Stavros Livanos and Stavros Niarchos; together the three men formed the most powerful shipping clan in the world. He also founded (1957) Olympic Airways of Greece. In 1968 Onassis married Jacqueline Bouvier Kennedy, widow of US Pres. J.F. Kennedy.

**Oñate, Juan de** (oh‚nyahtay), fl. 1595–1614, Spanish explorer; probably b. New Spain. He took possession of NEW MEXICO for Spain in 1598. Searching for Quivira in 1601, he explored as far east as Kansas and went down the Colorado R. to the Gulf of California. He was governor of New Mexico until 1609.

**onchocerciasis** ('ongkohsuh‚kie·əseez), infestation with the parasitic worm *Onchocerca volvulus*. A common condition in parts of Africa and tropical America, it is transmitted to humans by the blackfly (genus *Simulium*) which breeds near fast-flowing water. It causes lesions under the skin, particularly in the head region, and may migrate to the eyes causing blindness, a condition known as river blindness.

**oncology:** see CANCER.

**Oneida Indians:** see IROQUOIS CONFEDERACY.

**O'Neill, Eugene (Gladstone),** 1888–1953, American playwright. The son of an actor, he was a prospector, seaman, derelict, and newspaper reporter, experiences he later used in his plays. He created many one-act plays before writing *Beyond the Horizon* (1920), the first of his full-length plays to be performed. The dramas that followed included *The Emperor Jones* (1920); *Anna Christie* (1921); *The Hairy Ape* (1922); *Desire under the Elms* (1924), considered his first great play; *The Great God Brown* (1926); *Strange Interlude* (1928); the mighty trilogy *Mourning Becomes Electra* (1931); *Ah, Wilderness!* (1933), his only comedy; *The Iceman Cometh* (1946), often regarded as his finest work; and *A Moon for the Misbegotten* (1947). His last years were filled with family tragedy and ill health. At his death he left several important plays in manuscript, including the autobiographical masterpiece *Long Day's Journey into Night* (produced 1956). Although uneven and often clumsily experimental, O'Neill's powerful work is filled with poetry and genius. He was awarded the Nobel Prize for literature in 1936.

**Onetti, Juan Carlos,** 1909–, Uruguayan novelist and short-story writer. His major themes of loneliness, frustration, and disillusion are all present in his best novel, *El astillero* (1961; tr. The Shipyard).

**Onganía, Juan Carlos** (ongah‚neeah), 1914–, president of Argentina (1966–70). A former commander in chief of the army (1963–65), he was established as president by a military junta. His integration of the armed forces and the government and his attempts to force moral and educational reform aroused opposition, and the junta deposed him in 1970.

**onion,** plant (genus *Allium*) of the LILY family, of the same genus as the chive (*A. schoenoprasum*), garlic (*A. sativum*), leek (*A. porrum*), and shallot (*A. ascalonium*). Believed native to SW Asia, these plants are typified by an edible bulb composed of sugar-rich food-storage leaves that are also the source of a pungent oil. Their long, tubular, above-ground leaves are also eaten. The onion (*A. cepa*) is a cultivated biennial with many varieties; it is no longer found in the wild form. Common varieties include the red onion, the yellow onion, the white onion, and the large, delicately-flavoured Bermuda and Spanish onions. The more pungent garlic, a perennial, has a bulb consisting of small bulbils called cloves. The perennial shallot has clusters of small, onionlike bulbs; the biennial leek has a single small bulb. The chive, found wild in Italy and Greece, is a perennial whose leaves are the desirable portion. *Scallion* is a popular term for any edible *Allium* species with a reduced bulb, especially the leek and shallot.

**Onitsha,** city (1981 pop. 300,700), Anambra state, S Nigeria on the Niger R. Metal work, brewing, and textiles are the basis of the town's economy. It is occupied largely by people of the Ibo tribe. Onitsha was established as a British trading post in the 19th cent.

**Onondaga Indians:** see IROQUOIS CONFEDERACY.

**Ontario,** province of Canada, most populous (1984 est. pop. 8,946,900), area 1,068,582 km² (412,580 sq mi), located in the east-central region, bordered by Hudson and James Bays (N), Quebec (E), the St Lawrence R., Lakes Ontario, Erie, Huron, and Superior, and Minnesota (US) (S), and Manitoba (W). The capital is TORONTO, the largest metropolitan area in Canada (1984 est. 2,998,947); other major cities include HAMILTON, WINDSOR, LONDON, and Thunder Bay; the national capital, OTTAWA, is situated in the province. Ontario is divided between the rugged and mostly impassable area of the Canadian Shield in the W and centre; the Hudson Bay lowlands in the N; and the lowlands of the St Lawrence R. and the Great Lakes, which are covered in glacial landforms and deposits, including fertile soils. Ontario has half of Canada's manufacturing industry, led by transport equipment, food-processing, metals, electrical goods, machinery, and chemicals. The province also has the highest agricultural income, mostly from livestock and livestock products, tobacco, and vegetables. Its mining income, largely from nickel, copper, uranium, precious metals, and iron ore, is the second greatest in Canada. Over one-third of Canada's population lives in Ontario, 90% of it in the southern lowlands; 5% speaks French as the mother-tongue, and the population contains many European nationality groups. Although the French were the first to explore the area, it was obtained by the British at the Treaty of Paris (1763). Many United Empire Loyalists migrated there after the American Revolution, and the Algonquian and Iroquoian Indians were subdued. In 1791 it split from Quebec, becoming Upper Canada. After a period of unsuccessful reunion Ontario and Quebec joined the newly founded Canadian confederation as separate provinces. In the first half of the 19th cent. British immigrants began farming, while in the second half European immigrants helped develop a thriving industrial base. Ontario is so diverse that it contains pockets of both prosperity and poverty, and the economy has remained buoyant in recent years.

**Ontario, Lake,** smallest (19,529 km²/7,540 sq mi), lowest (elevation 75 m/246 ft), and easternmost of the GREAT LAKES, between the US and Canada. It is 311 km (193 mi) long and up to 85 km (53 mi) wide and 237 m (778 ft) deep. The lake is part of the St Lawrence & Great Lakes Waterway and opens to the SAINT LAWRENCE SEAWAY and W to Lake Erie via the WELLAND SHIP CANAL. Toronto is the principal port.

**ontogenesis:** see DEVELOPMENT.

**onychophore** ('oni‚kofor), wormlike animal with unsegmented, stumpy legs; member of the phylum Onychophora. Because onychophores possess characteristics of both ANNELID WORMS and ARTHROPODS, they are considered to be the 'missing links' between them.

**onyx,** variety of CHALCEDONY, similar to AGATE but with parallel, regular bands. Black-and-white specimens are used for cameos. Sardonyx has alternate layers of onyx and carnelian, or sard.

**Ōoka Shōhei,** 1909–, Japanese writer. A student of French literature, he translated STENDHAL. He was taken prisoner in the Philippines in World War II, and became obsessed by the horrors of war, which form the basis of his best-known books: *Furyoki* (1948; tr. Prisoners of War, 1967), *Nobi* (tr. 1957 as *Fires on the Plain*), and *Reite senki* [The Battle for the Philippines].

**oolite,** sedimentary rock composed of small concretions, usually of calcium carbonate, containing a nucleus and clearly defined concentric shells. In Britain, oolitic LIMESTONE is characteristic of the Jurassic geological period.

**Oort, Jan Hendrik,** 1900–, Dutch astronomer. He confirmed (1927) Bertil Lindblad's theory of the Milky Way galaxy's rotation. In the 1950s he and his colleagues used radio astronomical means to map the spiral-arm structure of the galaxy. Oort proposed (1950) that comets originate in a cloud of material orbiting the sun at great distance and that they are occasionally deflected into the inner solar system by gravitational perturbation from the passing of nearby stars.

**opal,** hydrous silica mineral ($SiO_2 \cdot nH_2O$), formed at low temperatures from silica-bearing water, that can occur in cavities and fissures of any rock type. GEM opal has rich iridescence and a remarkable play of colours, usually in red, green, and blue. Most precious opals come from South Australia; other sources include Mexico (fire opal) and parts of the US.

**op art,** movement in the US and Europe in the mid-1960s that sought to produce a purely optical art stripped of perceptual associations. Vibrating colours and pulsating moiré patterns characterized op works by such practitioners as Victor VASARELY, Richard Anusziewicz, and Bridget RILEY.

**OPEC:** see ORGANIZATION OF THE PETROLEUM EXPORTING COUNTRIES.

**open-cast mining,** process of extracting coal (or certain metallic ores) in which the surface material is removed to expose a coal seam or bed (see COAL MINING). The coal is then usually removed in a separate operation.

The environment can be protected by respreading soil and by seeding or planting grass or trees on the fertilized, restored surface. Sometimes the terms *strip* or *surface mining* are used in the same sense as open-cast mining. The Chuquicamata copper mines in N Chile are all open-cast mines and yield the world's largest amount of copper.

**open classroom,** informal educational system featuring decentralized learning areas, group and individual activities, freedom of movement, and unstructured periods of study. In eliminating formalized student–teacher roles, the system focuses on children wanting to learn and taking the initiative to do so. The open classroom was a development largely in British primary schools after World War II, and became popular in the US in the late 1960s.

**open cluster:** see CLUSTER, STAR.

**Open Door,** maintenance in a certain territory of equal commercial and industrial rights for all countries. It is generally associated with CHINA, which in the 19th cent. was divided into spheres of influence by the major world powers. The US, as a lesser power, feared that an actual partition of China would damage American trade and sought to preserve equal privileges. US Secy of State John HAY advanced the Open Door policy in two diplomatic notes (1899, 1900), asking the major powers to uphold the free use by all nations of the TREATY PORTS within their spheres of influence and to respect Chinese territorial and administrative integrity. Disregard for the Open Door policy, especially by Japan (see TWENTY-ONE DEMANDS), led to the Nine-Power treaty (1922), which reaffirmed the policy but failed to stop Japanese aggression against China. After World War II China's full sovereignty was recognized, and the Open Door policy ceased to exist.

**open-end investment company:** see MUTUAL FUND.

**open shop:** see TRADE UNION.

**Open University,** British non-residential university using television, radio, correspondence with tutors, summer schools, and a network of study centres (see DISTANCE LEARNING). Its foundation was supported by the Labour government of Harold Wilson from 1964. The first intake of students was in 1971, with initial provision for over 20,000 student places, rising to 120,000 in 1986. Courses are prepared by teams of tutors, students earn credits, the University provides texts and publishes books in association with commercial publishers, and prepares radio and television material in collaboration with the BBC. These materials have been widely used by other students and institutions, in Britain and internationally. The University offers short courses, a BA, diplomas, and higher degrees. Its headquarters are at Milton Keynes, Bucks.

**opera,** drama set to music. There may be spoken dialogue, but more often the music is continuous, with set pieces (solos, duets, etc.) designed to dramatize the action and display the vocal skills of the singers. Opera began in Florence, Italy, where a group of scholars and musicians promoted the principle of simple melodic declamation, emulating ancient Greek drama. Jacopo Peri and Guilio Caccini both composed operas on the Orpheus legend. Peri's *Euridice* was performed in 1600 and Caccini's in 1602. BAROQUE opera developed in Rome and Venice, reaching its peak with the work of Claudio MONTEVERDI. In 1637 the first public opera house in the world opened in Venice. The *opera seria* of the 17th and 18th cent. featured mythological themes and great pageantry. In the mid 17th cent. an international style emerged, emphasizing individual virtuosity, and interest in antiquities was superseded by a trend toward comedy. French opera from 1669 was led by J.B. LULLY and J.P. RAMEAU. The Neapolitans favoured the *opera seria* of Alessandro SCARLATTI, but now added *opera buffa*, or comic opera. After the death of Henry PURCELL, opera in England was dominated by the Italian style championed by G.F. HANDEL. By the 18th cent. German opera had developed the *singspiel,* comic opera with spoken dialogue, which reached its culmination in the works of W.A. MOZART. Yet Italian *opera seria* dominated through the 18th cent., until the compositions of C.W. von GLUCK served to emphasize the dramatic over the musical aspects of opera. Romantic elements entered 19th cent. opera, as in Ludwig van BEETHOVEN's *Fidelio* (1805) and Carl Maria von WEBER's *Der Freischütz* (1821). These paved the way for the grandiose music dramas of Richard WAGNER. Spectacular opera became popular in France and Italy after the French Revolution, and grand opera was founded in Paris, exemplified by the works of Giacomo MEYERBEER, featuring historical themes and violent passions. Opera with spoken dialogue, or *opéra comique,* led towards OPERETTA, but also towards the serious, lyrical works of Georges BIZET and Charles GOUNOD. The works of G.A. ROSSINI, Gaetano DONIZETTI, and Vincenzo BELLINI continued to feature melody and voice (see BEL CANTO), and the lyric-dramatic Italian style was exemplified by Giuseppe VERDI and, later, Giacomo PUCCINI. The 19th cent. also saw the birth of Russian opera (M. GLINKA, P.I. TCHAIKOVSKY, Modest MOUSSORGSKY, Nicolai RIMSKY-KORSAKOV). Foremost in the early 20th cent. were the romantic, richly orchestrated works of Richard STRAUSS and the atonal operas of Alban BERG and Arnold SCHOENBERG. The music-dramas of Kurt WEILL draw on the operatic tradition. Contemporary operas tend to be either traditional in idiom, as the works of Benjamin BRITTEN, Gian-Carlo MENOTTI, and Michael TIPPETT or atonal and experimental, as the compositions of H.W. HENZE, and Karlheinz STOCKHAUSEN.

**operant conditioning:** see B.F. SKINNER.

**operational calculus:** see TRANSFORM METHODS.

**operational research,** development and implementation of mathematical techniques to analyse and solve problems, e.g., business, management, or the waging of war, that involve complex systems. These techniques include matrix-based methods, networks, statistics, and simulation.

**operetta,** type of light OPERA with a frivolous, sentimental story, often employing parody and satire, and containing spoken dialogue and much light, pleasant music. It developed from 19th-century *opéra comique*. Noted operetta composers include OFFENBACH, J. STRAUSS the younger, LEHÁR, A. SULLIVAN (with librettist W.S. GILBERT), and Victor Herbert.

**Ophir** (ˌohfə), seaport or region, mentioned in the BIBLE, from which the ships of SOLOMON brought great treasures, including gold, jewels, and ivory. The location of Ophir is unknown, although it has been variously identified.

**ophthalmology,** branch of medicine specializing in the function and diseases of the eye. It is concerned with prevention of BLINDNESS; treatment of disorders, e.g., GLAUCOMA; surgery, including CATARACT removal and corneal transplants; and errors of refraction, e.g., SHORTSIGHTEDNESS, and the prescription of corrective lenses, including CONTACT LENSES.

**Ophüls, Max,** 1902–57, German film director. He is famed for filming his melodramas with a constantly moving, fluid camera, adding to the lush romanticism of his subjects. He became a naturalized Frenchman in 1938. His films include *Letter From an Unknown Woman* (1948), *La Ronde* (1950), *Madame de . . . (1953), and Lola Montès* (1955).

**Opitz, Martin** (ˌohpits), 1597–1639, leader of the Silesian school of German poetry. He was influential as a poet, critic, and metrical reformer. His *Buch von der deutschen Poeterey* (1624; tr. Book on German Poetry) was his greatest literary contribution.

**opium,** dried milky juice of unripe seedpods of the opium poppy (*Papaver somniferum*). The chief constituents of opium are the ALKALOIDS CODEINE, papaverine, noscapine, and MORPHINE, from which HEROIN is synthesized. Opium is grown worldwide; despite international laws and agreements to control its use, an illicit opium traffic persists. See NARCOTIC.

**Opium War,** 1839–42, conflict between Great Britain and China. Britain, seeking to end restrictions made by China on foreign trade, found a pretext for war when China prohibited the import of opium and British opium was destroyed at Guangzhou. The British were easy victors, and by the Treaty of Nanking (1842) China ceded Hong Kong to Britain and opened five ports to British trade. A second war (1856–58) ended with the treaties of Tientsin (1858), to which France, Russia, and the US were party. These treaties opened 11 more ports.

**Oporto,** Port. *Pôrto,* city (1984 pop. 327,368), capital of Pôrto dist., NW Portugal, near the mouth of the Douro R. Portugal's second largest city and an Atlantic port, it is known for its wine (port), named after the city. Other exports include cork, fruits, and olive oil. The ancient settlement, probably of pre-Roman origin, became known as Portus Cale (the source of the name Portugal). It was held (716–1092) by the MOORS and was later and for some time the chief city of Portugal. Its landmarks include the Dom Luis bridge (1881–87) and the Torre dos Clérigos, a baroque tower.

**opossum,** name for several MARSUPIALS of the family Didelphidae, native to Central and South America, with one species in the US. Mostly arboreal and nocturnal animals, opossums have long noses, naked ears, prehensile tails, and black-and-white fur. They eat small animals, eggs, insects, and fruit. When frightened they collapse as if dead, giving rise to the expression 'playing possum'. Opossums are hunted as pests as well as for food and sport.

**Oppenheimer, J. Robert,** 1904–67, American physicist. He taught at the Univ. of California and the California Institute of Technology and was from 1947 director of the Institute for Advanced Study at Princeton. Director (1942–45) of the laboratory at Los Alamos, New Mexico, that designed and built the first ATOMIC BOMBS (see MANHATTAN PROJECT), Oppenheimer later became a main proponent of the civilian and international control of atomic energy. He was chairman (1946–52) of the general advisory committee of the US Atomic Energy Commission. In 1953 the AEC suspended him as an alleged security risk, which inspired international protest.

**opposition,** in astronomy: see SYZYGY.

**optical sensing,** in general, any method by which information that occurs as variations in the intensity, or some other property, of light is translated into an electrical signal. This is usually accomplished by the use of various photoelectric devices. Optical sensing is used in various pattern-recognition systems, e.g., in military reconnaissance and astronomical observation, and in photographic development, to enhance detail and contrast.

**optics,** scientific study of LIGHT. Physical optics is concerned with the origin, nature, and properties of light; physiological optics with the part light plays in vision (see EYE); and geometrical optics with the geometry involved in the REFLECTION and REFRACTION of light as encountered in the study of the MIRROR and the LENS.

**Opus Dei,** a Roman Catholic organization, conservative and activist, consisting mainly of lay persons who strive after personal perfection and the fulfilment of Christian ideals in their chosen walks of life. Founded in Madrid in 1928 and approved by the pope in 1950, it has adherents in some 80 countries, maintains numerous educational institutions, and exerts a powerful, usually unseen influence on the Church's behalf.

**oracle,** in Greek religion, priest or priestess who imparted a god's response to a human questioner; also the response itself and the shrine. Methods of divination included interpretation of dreams, observation of signs, and interpretation of the actions of entranced persons. Among the famous oracles were those of ZEUS at Dodona and of APOLLO at DELPHI.

**Oradea,** city (1983 pop. 197,968), W Romania. Situated on the Criş R., it commands an important W–E routeway from BUDAPEST to TRANSYLVANIA. It is a market centre, with vine-growing and varied industries. The old city suffered under the Turks in the 16th cent. It was ceded by Hungary to Romania after World War I.

**oral contraceptive** preparation of one or more synthetic hormones taken by women to prevent conception; commonly known as 'the pill'. It works by preventing ovulation. The combination of OESTROGEN and a progestogen (e.g., PROGESTERONE) is taken every day for three weeks with MENSTRUATION occurring during the fourth week. Side-effects can include weight gain, nausea, depression, and loss of libido, and there is an increased risk of thrombosis and infertility after prolonged use. Debate about whether oral contraceptives contribute to the development of cancer in women is growing. Oral contraceptives, despite these drawbacks, provided women with an unprecedentedly reliable form of CONTRACEPTION.

**oral history,** compilation of historical data through interviews, usually tape-recorded, with participants in, or observers of, significant events or times. Primitive societies have long relied on oral tradition to preserve a record of the past in the absence of written histories, but the modern concept of oral history was developed in the US in the 1940s by Allan NEVINS and his associates at Columbia Univ., and in the UK by Paul Thompson and the Oral History Society, founded in 1973.

**oral rehydration,** method of counteracting severe and often fatal dehydration. Thousands of young children die every day in the Third World from diarrhoeal diseases, because severe and prolonged diarrhoea leads to dehydration and loss of essential salts. This threat to life can be removed by frequent application of rice water, water in which salt and sugar have been dissolved, or water containing specially prepared oral rehydration salts.

**Oran,** city (1983 est. pop. 663,504), NW Algeria, on the Gulf of Oran of the Mediterranean Sea. Algeria's second largest city, Oran is a major port exporting wheat, wine, and other goods, and a commercial, industrial, and financial centre. Nearby are important petrochemical installations. The site of modern Oran has been inhabited since prehistoric times, but the city's founding (10th cent.) is generally attributed to Moorish traders from Andalusia. Held alternately (1509–1791) by the Spanish and the Ottoman Turks, Oran fell to the French in 1831 and was developed as a naval base. During WORLD WAR II the city was held (1940–42) by Vichy forces. It played an important role in the Algerian independence struggle (1954–62).

**Orange,** major river of S Africa, flowing generally west c.2090 km (1300 mi) from Lesotho through parts of the Namib and KALAHARI deserts to the Atlantic Ocean. As part of a 30-year project (begun in the early 1960s), much of its water is being diverted through two long tunnels to provide hydroelectricity and to irrigate c.305,000 hectares (750,000 acres) in South Africa.

**orange,** tree (genus *Citrus*) of the RUE family, native to China and Indochina, and its fruit. A CITRUS FRUIT, the orange is rich in VITAMIN C. Among the commercially important species are the sweet, or common, orange (*C. sinensis*), which furnishes varieties such as the navel and Valencia; the sour, or Seville, orange (*C. aurantium*), used as an understock on which to bud sweet orange varieties and in marmalade; and *C. reticulata,* which includes the mandarin orange, the tangerine, and the hardy Satsuma varieties. Oranges hybridize readily. The citrange is a cross between two varieties of orange; the tangelo is produced by crossing a tangerine and a grapefruit. Oranges may be artificially coloured before marketing. They are eaten fresh, made into juice, or used in preserves and confections. Essential oils from orange rind, flowers, and leaves are used in perfumes and cookery.

**Orangemen,** members of the Loyal Orange Institution, a society in Northern Ireland, est. 1795 to maintain Protestant ascendancy. Its name was taken from the family name of WILLIAM III of England, who defeated (1690) the Catholic JAMES II.

**orang utan,** APE (*Pongo pygmaeus*) found in swampy coastal forests of Borneo and Sumatra. Their name means 'old man of the woods'. With their extremely long arms and short, bowed legs, orang utans are highly specialized for arboreal life and rarely descend to the ground. An adult male is about 1.5 m (4½ ft) tall and weighs about 70 kg (150 lb); the body is covered with long reddish fur.

**oratorio,** musical composition employing chorus, orchestra, and soloists and usually, but not necessarily, a setting of a sacred LIBRETTO without stage action or scenery; originally performed in an oratory of the Church of San Filippo Neri at Rome. Outstanding oratorios are by METASTASIO, SCHÜTZ, J.S. BACH, HANDEL, F.J. HAYDN, and MENDELSSOHN.

**oratory,** the art of persuasion by eloquent speech. In Greece and Rome it was part of *rhetoric,* the composition as well as delivery of a speech. As analysed by ARISTOTLE and QUINTILIAN, the study of oratory and rhetoric remained an important part of the medieval liberal arts curriculum. Among the great orators of the ancient world were DEMOSTHENES, CATO THE ELDER, and CICERO. The religious struggles of the REFORMATION (15th–16th cent.) produced the fiery sermons of SAVONAROLA, LUTHER, CALVIN, and KNOX. With the growth of parliaments, great political oratory returned. Edmund BURKE, Daniel O'CONNELL, Patrick HENRY, and Georges Jacques DANTON were unrivalled in the 18th cent. Abraham LINCOLN, in the 19th. cent., and Woodrow WILSON and Winston CHURCHILL in the 20th cent. continued the tradition of great oratory, and Adolf HITLER possessed an extraordinary power to excite an audience. The advent of radio, however, encouraged the adoption of a more intimate approach, as in Franklin D. ROOSEVELT's 'fireside chats', and party political broadcasts on television owe more to advertising techniques than to great oratory. A 19th-cent. evangelical style was used most effectively by Martin Luther KING in his 1963 speech 'I have a dream'.

**orbit,** path in space described by a body under the influence of gravitational forces (see CELESTIAL MECHANICS; GRAVITATION; KEPLER'S LAWS). The size and shape of the elliptical orbit followed in a two body system are specified by (1) the semimajor axis (a length equal to half the greatest diameter of the orbit) and (2) the eccentricity (the distance of the larger body from the centre of the orbit divided by the length of the orbit's semimajor axis). The position of the orbit in space is determined by three factors: (3) the inclination, or tilt, of the orbital plane to the reference plane (the ECLIPTIC for Sun-orbiting bodies; a planet's EQUATOR for natural and artificial satellites); (4) the longitude of the ascending NODE (measured from the vernal EQUINOX to the point where the smaller body cuts the reference plane moving south to north); and (5) the argument of pericentre (measured from the ascending node in the direction of motion to the point at which the two bodies are closest). These five quantities, plus the time of pericentre passage, are called orbital elements. The gravitational attractions of other bodies causes perturbations in a two body system making the parameters of the orbits vary in time. Precession of the orbits and wobbles of the bodies are the most common effects.

**Orcagna** or **Arcagnolo**, c.1308–1368, Florentine painter, sculptor, and architect; b. Andrea di Cione. The figures in his famous altarpiece *Christ in Glory with Saints Thomas and Peter* (1354–57; Santa Maria Novella, Florence) represent a reversion to the hieratic quality of Byzantine art. He was chief architect of the cathedral at Orvieto.

**orchestra and orchestration.** An orchestra is a musical ensemble, under the direction of a conductor (see CONDUCTING), generally employing four classes of instruments: the STRINGED INSTRUMENTS, which convey the melody and the expressive qualities of the music; the WOODWIND, adding colour and, in some passages, the melody; the brass, adding dynamic sound (see BRASS INSTRUMENTS); and the PERCUSSION INSTRUMENTS, those used to emphasize rhythm. The strings, except the harp, have several players for each part, the others usually only one or two. The orchestra in the modern sense did not exist before the 17th cent. Earlier instrumental music was CHAMBER MUSIC, and parts were not assigned to specific instruments. The first known example of specific orchestration occurs in the *Sacrae symphoniae* (1597) of Giovanni Gabrieli (see under GABRIELI, ANDREA). MONTEVERDI's *Orfeo* (1607), one of the first OPERAS, demands a large, varied group of instruments. Throughout the BAROQUE period, orchestras were small, and the basso continuo was an integral part of the scoring, requiring that a harpsichord or other chord-playing instrument fill in the harmonies above the FIGURED BASS. In the latter half of the 18th cent. the continuo fell out of use, and by the time of the late works of F.J. HAYDN and W.A. MOZART the classical orchestra was standardized. The 19th cent. saw major mechanical improvements in instruments, and the size of the orchestra expanded greatly. The 20th cent. has been interested in diverse instrumental combinations and original exploitation of instruments' capabilities.

**orchid,** name for the Orchidaceae, a large family (16,000 species in over 600 genera) of perennial herbs distributed worldwide, but most abundant in tropical and subtropical forests. The family is the most highly advanced of the monocotyledon division of the flowering plants. Orchid flowers have three petals and three sepals, the central one modified and specialized to secrete insect-attracting nectar. The diverse flower forms are apparently complicated adaptations for POLLINATION by specific insects. Orchids are highly prized ornamentals. Most tropical species are EPIPHYTES, while those of the temperate regions are terrestrial, growing in moist woods and meadows. Most of the European species are tuberous, e.g., the lady's slipper (*Cypripedium acaule*), a striking wild orchid with maroon and yellow flowers with dark veining and red spots. A few species are SAPROPHYTES. Orchid culture is largely devoted to the production of hybrids, e.g., *Cattleya* crosses. A species of the tropical American genus *Vanilla* is the source of natural VANILLA flavouring.

**orders in council:** see DELEGATED LEGISLATION.

**orders of architecture.** In classical styles of architecture, columnar types fall in general into five so-called classical orders: Doric, Ionic, Corinthian, Composite, and Tuscan. Each comprises the column and the entablature, and each has a distinctive character as to proportions and detail. The Roman writer Vitruvius attempted to formulate the proportioning of the three Greek orders. Doric, the earliest, was used for the PARTHENON and most Greek temples. The Doric column, thought to have developed from earlier wood construction, was massive, fluted, without a base, and topped with a simple capital; the entablature was also fairly plain. The Ionic order, largely Asian in origin, had a scroll-shaped capital above a more slender, fluted column; the entablature was more intricate than that of the Doric. In Greece, the only major example of the Ionic is the ERECHTHEUM. The third Greek order, the Corinthian, was little used until the Romans adopted it. It was the latest (fully developed in the 4th cent. BC) and the most ornate. The delicate, foliated details of the capital are its distinctive feature. The Romans used it widely in monumental architecture and developed a variant, or Composite, order that combined the Corinthian foliate pattern with a moulding similar to

Orchid (*Calypso bulbosa*)

the Ionic. The 16th-cent. Italians established a simplified form of Doric, or Tuscan, order, with unfluted columns and unadorned capital and entablature. The Renaissance saw variations of the orders, but during the CLASSIC REVIVAL strict adherence to the Greek and Roman originals was the rule.

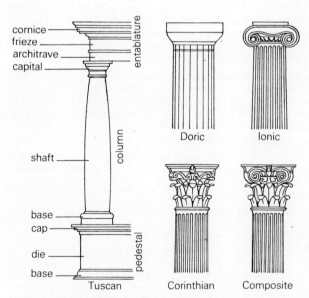

Orders of architecture

**Ordinance of 1787,** in US history, ordinance adopted by the Congress of the Confederation to create and govern the NORTHWEST TERRITORY. It marked the beginning of Western expansion in the US and prescribed the political procedures by which territories were established and later became states. It provided for an elected legislature when the population totalled 5000 voting citizens, and for statehood when the population reached 60,000.

**Ordnance Survey,** UK government agency responsible for surveying the country and publishing detailed topographical maps at various scales, including route-planning maps and town plans, and a number of thematic maps. The Ordnance Survey was established when there was a fear of invasion by Napoleon and it was realized that there were no adequate maps of Britain.

**Ordovician period:** see GEOLOGICAL ERA (table).

**ore,** metal-bearing MINERAL mass that can be profitably mined. Nearly all rocks contain some metallic minerals, but often the concentration of metal is too low to justify MINING. Ores often occur in veins in rock, varying in thickness from less than a centimetre to 100 m or more. Minerals with no commercial value, called gangue minerals, are usually found mixed with the ore in the vein. Recovering minerals from their ores is one area in the field of METALLURGY.

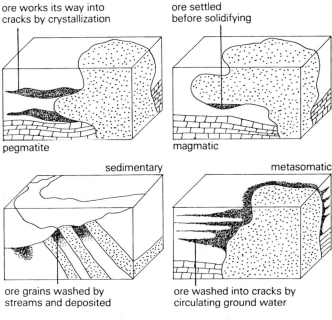

ore works its way into cracks by crystallization

pegmatite

ore settled before solidifying

magmatic

sedimentary

metasomatic

ore grains washed by streams and deposited

ore washed into cracks by circulating ground water

Ore

**oregano** (ori,gahnoh, ɔ,regɔnoh), name for several herbs used in cooking. *Origanum vulgare*, of the MINT family, is the usual source of the herb sold as oregano in Western countries. Its flavour is similar to that of MARJORAM but slightly less sweet. Other *Origanum* species are also sold as oregano. A related herb, *Coleus amboinicius*, is known as oregano in Mexico and the Philippines.

**Oregon**, state of the US (1984 est. pop. 2,674,000), area 251,181 km² (96,981 sq mi) located in the NW bordered by the Pacific Ocean (W), Washington (N), Idaho (E), and California and Nevada (S). The capital is SALEM, and the largest city is PORTLAND. The COAST RANGES, the CASCADE RANGE, and the COLUMBIA PLATEAU cover the most of the state; the most extensive lowlands are along the COLUMBIA R. and its tributary, the Willamette, in the north. Half the land is covered by pine forest, and timber and paper manufacturing are the industries. The farms are famous for their apples and other fruits, and the salmon-fishing industry is one of the world's largest. Oregon's beaches, lakes, mountains, and scenic sites, such as Crater Lake, attract tourists year-round. About 60% of the population lives in metropolitan areas and 93% was non-Hispanic white in 1980. The coast was explored by Capt. James Cook (1778) in his search for the Northwest Passage, when the inhabitants were Nez Percé and other Indians. In the early 19th cent. fur trading began, and settlers arrived over the Oregon Trail in 1842–43. The area became part of the US after the US–Canadian border was fixed at the 49th parallel (1846), after which the railways helped the exploitation of the natural resources. In the 20th cent. prosperity has depended on the national demand for timber for construction, although the Bonneville Dam (1943) on the Columbia R. provided abundant hydroelectricity. Oregon has been in the forefront of environmental protection, providing for public ownership of river land and ocean beaches, and banning disposable beverage containers and aerosol spray cans.

**Oregon Trail**, route used (1840s to 1870s) by Western settlers in the US to reach the Oregon Territory. Their wagon trains generally started at Independence or Westport, Missouri, traveled NW along the Platte and N Platte rivers to Fort Laramie, Wyoming, and crossed the Rocky Mts. by the South Pass to the Colorado R. basin. The Oregon Trail continued SW to Fort Bridger, where the Mormon Trail diverged to the southwest, and then ran NW, via the Snake R., Blue Mts, and Columbia R., to the Willamette valley, Oregon. It totalled c.3200 km (2000 mi) in length and required about six months for the average wagon train to traverse it.

**Orenburg** (,orən'buhg), formerly (1938–57) Chkalov, city (1985 pop. 519,000), Central Asian USSR, on the Ural R. Founded (1735) as a fortress, it resisted a siege (1773–74) by PUGACHEV. Today it is a junction on the Trans-Caspian railway and a major food-processing and agricultural machine centre.

**Orestes**, in Greek mythology, son of AGAMEMNON and CLYTEMNESTRA, brother of ELECTRA and IPHIGENIA. The young Orestes was exiled after the slaying of Agamemnon by Clytemnestra and AEGISTHUS. Later he returned and, helped by Electra, killed his mother and her lover. He was pursued by the FURIES until he reached Athens, where he was tried and acquitted by the prime council, the Areopagus. To complete his purification, he took the image of ARTEMIS from Taurus (where he was reunited with Iphigenia) to Greece. His vengeance and expiation are dramatized in AESCHYLUS' *Oresteia*. SOPHOCLES and EURIPIDES also used the story.

**Orff, Carl**, 1895–1982, German composer and educator. His best-known work is *Carmina Burana* (1937), a secular ORATORIO derived from medieval German and Latin poems. His system for teaching music to children, based on rhythmic and verbal patterns and the pentatonic scale, is widely used.

**organ**, musical wind instrument in which sound is produced by one or more sets of pipes, each producing a single pitch by means of a mechanically or electrically controlled wind supply. Several keyboards (manuals) are played with the hands. Projecting knobs (stops) to the sides of the keyboard operate wooden sliders that pass under the mouths of a rank of pipes to 'stop' a particular rank. The pedals of the organ are like another keyboard, played with the feet. The prevailing organ for several centuries from the 3rd cent. BC was the Greek *hydraulos*. Organs in the Middle Ages already had several ranks of *diapason* pipes, their timbre characteristic only of the organ. The 15th cent. added stops, including those imitative of other instruments, e.g., flute. Organ building reached a peak in the German BAROQUE, then declined. The 19th cent. obscured diapason tone by adding stops imitative of orchestral sound and by the use of crescendo. While the early 20th cent. developed electrification of the mechanical parts of the organ, Albert SCHWEITZER and others led a movement back to baroque ideals.

**organic chemistry**, branch of CHEMISTRY dealing with CARBON compounds. Of all the elements, carbon forms the greatest number of different compounds; indeed, compounds that contain carbon are about 100 times more numerous than those that do not. Compounds containing only carbon and HYDROGEN are called HYDROCARBONS. Organic compounds containing NITROGEN are of great importance to BIOCHEMISTRY. Organic chemistry is of importance to the petrochemical, pharmaceutical, and textile industries; in textiles a prime concern is the synthesis of new organic molecules and POLYMERS.

**organic farming**, farming practices that exclude or avoid synthetic PESTICIDES, FERTILIZERS, growth regulators, and feed additives. Organic farmers prefer biological pest control, manure, and practices such as ROTATION OF CROPS to supply plant nutrients and control pests. Interest in organic farming has been fostered partly by awareness of the dangers caused by PESTICIDES and the excessive use of chemical fertilizers, and partly by the higher prices obtainable by farmers for organic-farmed produce. See also ENVIRONMENTALISM.

**Organization for Economic Cooperation and Development** (OECD), intergovernmental organization of developed countries. Formed in 1961, it superseded the Organization for European Economic Cooperation. The 24 full members are Australia, Austria, Belgium, Canada, Denmark, Finland, France, West Germany, Greece, Iceland, Ireland, Italy, Japan, Luxembourg, the Netherlands, New Zealand, Norway, Portugal, Spain, Sweden, Switzerland, Turkey, the UK, and the US. Yugoslavia has associate membership status. Members are pledged to work together to promote economic growth, aid developing countries (through the Development Assistance Committee) and expand world trade. The headquarters are in Paris. An important OECD subsidiary body is the INTERNATIONAL ENERGY AGENCY.

**Organization of African Unity** (OAU), organization (est. 1963) to promote unity, development, and defence of African states; eradicate colonialism; and coordinate economic, health, and other policies. In 1988 there were 50 independent member states. Morocco withdrew in 1984 after the OAU had admitted the Saharan Arab Democratic Republic (see WESTERN SAHARA). The headquarters of the OAU are in Addis Ababa

(Ethiopia). The organization's heads of government hold annual conferences and the OAU chairmanship rotates between these conferences. An important OAU body is its liberation committee, which provides financial and military aid to African liberation movements.

**Organization of American States** (OAS), regional agency (est. 1948) to promote peace and development in the Americas, with 31 member states. It succeeded the Pan-American Union, which became the OAS secretariat, currently based in Washington (US). The inter-American programme of economic assistance called the Alliance for Progress, proposed by Pres. John KENNEDY, was created within the OAS framework in 1961, but was formally terminated in 1980. The OAS has sought to settle disputes between member nations and has discouraged foreign intervention in their internal affairs. In 1962 it expelled Cuba, charging attempted subversion of other OAS countries. The OAS charter, as amended in 1967, specifies that member states should take joint action in the event of extra continental aggression against any member.

**Organization of the Petroleum Exporting Countries** (OPEC), intergovernmental organization (est. 1960) coordinating petroleum policies of THIRD WORLD oil-producing nations. Its members are Algeria, Ecuador, Gabon, Indonesia, Iran, Iraq, Kuwait, Libya, Nigeria, Qatar, Saudi Arabia, the United Arab Emirates, and Venezuela. During the 1970s its members, acting as a CARTEL, raised oil prices sharply, causing inflation, recession, and other problems in the oil-importing nations. In the 1980s, however, increasing non-OPEC oil production, notably from British and Norwegian fields in the NORTH SEA, forced down world and thus OPEC prices, creating serious economic difficulties for most member countries. The headquarters of OPEC are located in Vienna.

**organized crime,** nationally (sometimes internationally) coordinated criminal activities. Most common in the US, the term was first applied during PROHIBITION to the activities of local gang leaders, such as Al CAPONE in Chicago, who built criminal organizations on the profits of BOOTLEGGING. Organized crime has usually centred around activities such as gambling and drug trafficking although it also includes corporate fraud and other illegal business practices. It continues to flourish in the US, often concealed behind 'front' organizations. The MAFIA has played an important role in the development of organized crime both in the US and Italy. In the UK, organized crime has been less common, although in the 1960s the activities of gangs like that of the Kray twins in East London gained notoriety. Successful organized crime usually requires internal security and the development of trustworthy contacts with local officials, such as POLICE officers and judges.

**orgone therapy:** see Wilhelm REICH.

**Oriental drama.** Of the three major Oriental dramas Sanskrit, Chinese, Japanese, the oldest is Sanskrit. (fl. 1500 BC–AD 1100).

*Sanskrit drama.* Sanskrit plays were written for the aristocracy, and involve music, dance, and highly stylized gesture and costume. They are full of religious and supernatural elements. Love and heroism are the most common sources of emotion, with a frequent infusion of awe produced by the supernatural. Indeed, some plays centre on the supernatural, while others treat political and historical topics and ordinary people. The language of Sanskrit drama alternates between prose and lyric poetry, and Sanskrit, a literary language, is used only by important characters; inferior characters speak Prakrit, the vernacular. Few Sanskrit plays survive. The earliest known playwright was Bhasa (c.3rd cent. AD); among the most renowned were KALIDASA, Bhavabhuti (c.8th cent.), and Harsha (7th cent.).

*Chinese drama.* Written for a popular audience, Chinese drama developed in the Yüan dynasty (1260–1328) from the story cycles of professional storytellers. Acting style, character types, stage properties, and other features are highly conventionalized; until the 19th cent. lines were sung or declaimed. There is, however, great narrative freedom in the plays. Although Chinese drama avoids TRAGEDY, it is frequently infused with pathos. Chinese drama is more social and less concerned with romantic love than Sanskrit, and it often propounds Confucian ethics (see CONFUCIANISM). Among the masterpieces of Chinese drama are *The Western Chamber* by Wang Shi-fu (13th cent.), *The Peony Pavilion* by T'ang Hsien-tsu (16th cent.), and *The Palace of Long Life* by Hung Sheng (17th cent.). After World War I a realistic, spoken drama developed, but under the People's Republic of China the theatre (except in Taiwan) has usually devoted itself to propaganda.

*Japanese drama.* Traditional Japanese theatre has three major forms, Nō (Noh), Kabuki, and Jōruri. The Nō drama is about 600 years old, a non-realist symbolic form, employing archaic literary language, male actors, stylized gestures, and a small orchestra of flute and drums. There are over 2000 Nō plays, of which around 200 form the stock repertory. The main actor (*shite*) is masked, as are the secondary actors (*tsure*) when playing female parts. The *waki*, who sets the scene and is the foil to the *shite*, wears no mask. The plays are acted out on a stage open on two sides to the audience, and their subject is frequently a supernatural event, the appearance of a dissatisfied ghost, etc. Performances often include a comic interlude known as *kyōgen*, which guys the theme of the main play. Zeami Motokiyo (1363–1443) is the best known of the Nō playwrights, author of *The Well-Curb*, *The Lady Aoi*, and *Prince Genji's Exile in Suma*. He is also the theoretician of the aesthetics of Nō. Originally songs and dances performed by groups of women to attract men to the brothel quarters in Kyoto, **Kabuki** grew into a complex art after women were banned from the stage and all parts were taken by male actors. By the early 18th cent., Kabuki was a luxuriously costumed, sophisticated drama, combining dialogue, recitative, songs, dances, and orchestral accompaniment. The best known Kabuki is perhaps the revenge tragedy, *The Treasury of Loyal Retainers* (Chūshingura, 1748). Kabuki has many themes in common with **Jōruri**, the puppet plays also known as Bunraku from the Bunraku Theatre in Osaka where they were performed. The puppet theatre is a late-16th-cent. creation using chanted play-texts, with shamisen accompaniment, and puppets; some of which are nearly two-thirds life-size and require two or three puppeteers to manipulate them. CHIKAMATSU wrote his greatest plays for the puppet theatre.

**Origen** (Origines Adamantius), 185?–254?, Christian philosopher; b. Egypt. Origen taught in Alexandria for 28 years and became famed for his profound interpretations of the Scriptures. He attempted to synthesize the principles of Greek philosophy, particularly NEOPLATONISM and STOICISM, with those of Christianity. The most influential theologian of the early church, he is said to have written 800 works, of which few survive. His system of philosophy is contained in *On First Principles*.

**Orinoco,** river, Venezuela, flowing south c.2600 km (1600 mi) from Mt Délgado Chalbaud, in the Guiana Highlands, to a very large, marshy delta in the northeast. The volume of flow varies markedly with the seasons. Ciudad Guayana is the principal city and the focus of the industrialization of the Orinoco region since the 1960s. The river is connected to the AMAZON R. system by the Casiquiare, a natural canal.

**oriole,** name for various perching BIRDS of the Old World (family Oriolidae) and New World (family Icteridae). The European oriole is allied to the CROW, while the small American oriole is related to the American blackbird. Swift fliers with clear calls, orioles feed on fruit, mainly berries, or insects. Both Old World and New World orioles have orange and black (or brown) markings.

**Orion** (ə‚rieən), in Greek mythology, Boeotian hunter. While drunk he violated his betrothed, Merope, and was then blinded by her father. His vision was restored by the rays of the sun. At his death ARTEMIS turned him into a constellation.

**Orissa,** state (1981 est. pop. 26,300,000), 155,782 km² (60,132 sq mi), E India, on the Bay of Bengal. Its capital is Bhubaneswar and its official language is Oriya.

**Orizaba** ('ohri‚zahbə), snow-capped, inactive volcano, highest peak (5700 m/18,700 ft) in Mexico and third highest in N America. Called Citlaltépetl in Aztec times, it last erupted in 1687.

**Orkney Islands,** region off the N of Scotland (1985 est. pop. 19,182), 976 km² (381 sq mi), separated from the mainland by the Pentland Firth. The administrative centre is Kirkwall. It contains about 90 islands and islets, of which one-third are inhabited. Fishing, farming, and the exploitation and processing of nearby North Sea oil deposits are the principal industries. Ruled by Viking, then Scottish, earls, the Orkneys passed to the Scottish crown in 1472. The islands include Mainland, Hoy, Stronsay, Westray, and Sanday. Scapa Flow separates Mainland from Hoy and was the war station of the Grand Fleet between 1914 and 1919. Many of the islands contain Pictish and Scandinavian remains.

**Orlando, Vittorio Emanuele,** 1860–1952, Italian statesman. As Italian premier (1917–19), he was one of the 'Big Four' leaders at the Paris Peace Conference (1919), where he demanded territorial compensation for Italy in Dalmatia. Meeting stiff opposition from US Pres. WILSON, he temporarily left the conference. When his demand was still not met, he resigned as premier. Opposed to Fascism, he gave up (1925) his seat in the Italian parliament. After World War II he served as a senator (1948–52).

**Orléans,** family name of two branches of the French royal line. The house of Valois-Orléans was founded by **Louis, duc d'Orléans,** 1372–1407, brother of CHARLES VI of France. Louis's assassination, ordered by JOHN THE FEARLESS, duke of Burgundy, caused a civil war between the Orléanists, or Armagnacs, and the Burgundians. Louis's son **Charles, duc d'Orléans,** 1391–1465, became the titular head of the Armagnacs. He was captured (1415) by the English at Agincourt and remained a captive until 1440. Charles's son ascended the French throne (1498) as LOUIS XII, but he died without a male heir. The modern house of Bourbon-Orléans (see BOURBON) was founded by **Philippe I, duc d'Orléans,** 1640–1701, a brother of LOUIS XIV. A notorious libertine, he was excluded from state affairs. His son, **Philippe II, duc d'Orléans,** 1674–1723, regent of France (1715–23) in the minority of LOUIS XV, distinguished himself in the wars of the GRAND ALLIANCE and the SPANISH SUCCESSION. To solve the financial crisis, Orléans called on John LAW, but Law's schemes collapsed in 1720. Social life during his regency reached an apex of licentiousness. The ambitions of the regent and of his descendants brought the house of Orléans into open opposition to the ruling house. The regent's great-grandson, **Louis Philippe, Joseph, duc d'Orléans,** 1747–93, known as Philippe Égalité, supported the FRENCH REVOLUTION, voted to execute Louis XVI, and was himself guillotined during the REIGN OF TERROR. His adherents, the Orleanists, who sought a compromise between monarchical and revolutionary principles, came to power in the JULY REVOLUTION of 1830 and put Philippe Égalité's son LOUIS PHILIPPE on the French throne. After his fall (1848), they continued to support the claims of his descendants, the Orleanist pretenders. Their prospects, high under the presidency of Marshal MACMAHON, dwindled steadily, especially after the Third Republic exiled all pretenders in 1886. Louis Philippe's grandson **Louis Philippe Albert d'Orléans, comte de Paris,** 1838–94, fought on the Union side in the US Civil War. He relinquished his claims to the legitimist pretender, Henri de Chambord (1873), but on Chambord's death (1883) he became head of the entire house of Bourbon. His son **Louis Philippe Robert, duc d'Orléans,** 1869–1926, succeeded his father as pretender in 1894. Born in England, he served briefly in the Indian army and travelled widely. He died childless, and his pretensions to the French throne passed to a cousin and his heirs.

**Orléans,** city (1982 pop. 105,589, agglomeration 220,478), capital of Loiret dept., N central France, an industrial and transportation centre. First inhabited by the Celtic Carnutes, the city revolted against Julius CAESAR (52 BC) and was burned. It repelled (451) Attila but fell (498) to CLOVIS I. In the 10th cent. it became an important part of the royal domain. In 1429, during the HUNDRED YEARS WAR, JOAN OF ARC lifted the English siege of Orléans. Many historic buildings were destroyed in World War II, and the city has been extensively rebuilt, utilizing traditional architectural styles.

**Ormandy, Eugene,** 1899–1985, American conductor; b. Hungary. He went to the US in 1921, joined the Philadelphia Orchestra in 1936, and became its music director (1938–80). Ormandy was noted for his romantic interpretations.

**ormer:** see EAR SHELL.

**ormolu,** gilded bronze or brass, particularly that applied as gilded mounts to furniture. Widely used in France from the late 17th cent. but uncommon in England before the mid-18th cent. See also GILDING.

**orogeny,** a process, resulting from the phenomenon of PLATE TECTONICS, of construction of mountain chains on continents. Orogenies are produced in one of two ways: the collision of two continental plates, e.g., the Himalayas, or the overriding of an oceanic plate by a continental one, e.g., the Andes. Characteristically, orogeny produces crustal thickening and deformation, and volcanic activity. The Caledonian orogeny of Silurian and Devonian times produced the mountain chain whose remnants may be seen in northern Scotland.

**Orontes,** Arab. *Nahr al Asi,* river, c.500 km (300 mi) long, rising in N Lebanon, flowing northwards through Syria and entering the Mediterranean near ANTAKYA, Turkey. Much of its course is in Lebanon and Syria is through the GREAT RIFT VALLEY. It is important for irrigation in Syria.

**Orozco, José Clemente** (oh,rohskoh), 1883–1949, Mexican painter, working in an Expressionist style. His boldly painted works often deal with social themes, and, like RIVERA, he carried out commissions for several revolutionary governments. He was noted for his FRESCOES, e.g., the mural *Mankind's Struggle* (1930; New School for Social Research, New York City).

**Orpheus** (,awfeeəs), in Greek mythology, Thracian musician; son of the MUSE Calliope by APOLLO or by Oeagrus, a king of Thrace. He is said to have played the lyre so beautifully that he charmed the beasts, trees, and rivers. He married the nymph Eurydice, and when she died he descended to HADES to search for her. He was allowed to return with her on condition that he not look back at her, but he disobeyed and lost her forever. Grief-stricken, he wandered for years. In one legend, he worshipped Apollo above DIONYSUS, who caused the Thracians to tear him to pieces. Orpheus was celebrated in the ORPHIC MYSTERIES. As a musician his story has often been set to music, most notably by MONTEVERDI (1607) and GLUCK (1762).

**Orphic Mysteries** or **Orphism,** religious cult of ancient Greece, ascribed to Orpheus. The Orphics affirmed the divine origin of the soul, but also the dual aspect of human nature as good and evil. They believed that through initiation into the Orphic MYSTERIES and through the process of transmigration, the soul could be liberated from its inheritance of evil and achieve eternal blessedness. Orphism followed a strict ethical and moral code and adopted practices such as VEGETARIANISM for purification.

**orphism,** a short-lived movement in art founded in 1912 by Robert DELAUNAY, Frank KUPKA, the DUCHAMP brothers, and Roger de la Fresnaye. APOLLINAIRE coined the term to describe the lyrical, shimmering, chromatic effects these painters sought to introduce into the drier aesthetic of CUBISM. This included a move away from figurative art towards a 'pure art', e.g., Delaunay's series *Simultaneous Discs* (1912). The movement influenced the German BLAUE REITER group and the American artists Stanton MACDONALD-WRIGHT and Morgan Russell.

**Ortega y Gasset, José** (aw,taygah ee ga,set), 1883–1955, Spanish essayist and philosopher. A professor of metaphysics at the Univ. of Madrid, he sought to establish the ultimate reality in which all else was rooted. He gained world fame with *The Revolt of the Masses* (1929), which contends that the masses must be directed by an intellectual minority, or chaos will result.

**Ortelius, Abraham,** 1527–98, Flemish geographer, of German origin. He travelled with MERCATOR, who inspired him to begin *Theatrum orbis terrarum* (1570), the first modern world atlas. In 1575 he was made geographer to PHILIP II of Spain.

**orthodontics:** see DENTISTRY.

**Orthodox Judaism:** see JUDAISM.

**orthopaedics,** medical specialty concerned with deformities, injuries, and diseases of the bones, joints, ligaments, tendons, and muscles. It includes surgical treatment for fractures, bone grafting, joint and limb replacement, manipulation and traction, and the fitting of corrective appliances.

**Orton, Joe,** 1933–67, English dramatist. He was a writer of black comedies such as *Entertaining Mr Sloane* (1964), *Loot* (1966), and *What The Butler Saw*, which was not produced until 1969, two years after Orton, a homosexual, had been murdered by his lover.

**Orwell, George,** pseud. of **Eric Arthur Blair,** 1903–50, English writer. He served as a colonial policeman in Burma, and later fought on the Republican side in the Spanish Civil War. Many of his works, like *Down and Out in Paris and London* (1933), *The Road to Wigan Pier* (1937), and *Homage to Catalonia* (1938), are autobiographical and sociopolitical. His grimly humorous realistic novels include *Burmese Days* (1934) and *Coming Up for Air* (1939). Later he published *Animal Farm* (1945), a satirical fable about Soviet communism, and *Nineteen Eighty-Four* (1949), a prophetic novel depicting a totalitarian world. A controversial socialist and trenchant critic and essayist, his greatest influence was exerted posthumously.

**oryx:** see ANTELOPE.

**Os,** chemical symbol of the element OSMIUM.

**Osage Indians:** see NORTH AMERICAN INDIANS.

**Osaka,** city (1986 est. pop. 2,541,163), capital of Osaka prefecture, S Honshu, Japan. The third largest city and the sixth largest port in Japan, Osaka is the focal point of a chain of industrial cities (called the *Hanshin* or *Kinki*), with food processing, printing, and manufacturing the chief industries. An educational and cultural centre, Osaka is known for its puppet and other theatres and for its universities. The city was one of the historical castle towns constructed by Japan's ruler Toyotomi Hideyoshi in 1583. Landmarks include the Buddhist temple of Shitennoji, founded 593, and Temmangu, a Shinto shrine founded in 949. Kansai International Airport is under construction, due for completion by 1992.

**Osborne, John,** 1929–, English dramatist. His *Look Back in Anger* (1956), about a restless young working-class man at war with himself and society, became the seminal work of the so-called angry young men, a group of rebellious English writers of the 1950s. Later plays include *The Entertainer* (1957), *Luther* (1961), *Inadmissable Evidence* (1964), and *Time Present* (1968).

**Oscan** (ˌoskən), extinct language belonging to the Italic subfamily of the Indo-European family of languages. See LANGUAGE (table).

**Osceola,** c.1800–38, leader of the SEMINOLE INDIANS who denounced 1832 and 1833 treaties requiring Indians to move west. During the Seminole Wars (1835–42) he skilfully used guerrilla tactics in the Florida Everglades to elude the US army. Duped into agreeing to peace talks under a flag of truce he was seized (1837) and imprisoned at Fort Moultrie, South Carolina, where he died.

**oscilloscope,** device based on a CATHODE-RAY TUBE used to produce a visual display of electrical signals. Typically the horizontal position of the illuminated point is controlled by the value of the independent variable (often time), while the vertical position is controlled by the dependent variable. A third signal is often used to control the brightness of the point.

**Oshawa** (ˌoshəwə), city (1980 est. pop. 115,486), SE Ontario, on Lake Ontario, part of the regional municipality of Durham (1978 est. pop. 265,538). The production of automobiles, begun by the McLaughlin family in 1907 and taken over by General Motors in 1918, dominates the local economy. Oshawa was founded (1795) at the site of a French fur-trading post.

**Oshogbo,** city (1987 est. pop. 344,500), Oyo state, SW Nigeria, on the Niger R. It is a trading centre for the area. Industries include dyeing, weaving, cotton ginning, and brewing.

**Osiris,** in EGYPTIAN RELIGION, legendary ruler of predynastic Egypt and god of the underworld. Osiris symbolized the creative forces of nature and the imperishability of life. Called the great benefactor of humanity, he brought to the people knowledge of agriculture and civilization. In a famous myth he was slain by his evil brother Set, but his death was avenged by his son HORUS. The worship of Osiris, one of the great cults of ancient Egypt, gradually spread throughout the Mediterranean world and, with that of ISIS and Horus, was especially vital during the Roman Empire.

**Osler, Sir William,** 1849–1919, Canadian physician. A renowned medical historian, he was also the most brilliant teacher of medicine in his day, at McGill Univ. (1875–84), the Univ. of Pennsylvania (1884–89), Johns Hopkins Univ. Hospital, Baltimore (1889–1904), and Oxford Univ. (from 1905). His many observations include those on blood platelets and on the abnormally high red blood cell count in polycythaemia. He wrote *Principles and Practice of Medicine* (1892), one of the most prestigious medical texts of modern times.

**Oslo,** city (1985 pop. 447,351), capital of Norway, SE Norway, at the head of a fjord of the Skagerrak. It is Norway's largest city; main port; and chief commercial, industrial, and transportation centre. Founded c.1050 by HAROLD III, it became the national capital in 1299. It was rebuilt after being razed by fire in 1624. It came under HANSEATIC LEAGUE domination in the 14th cent. Oslo's modern growth dates from the 19th cent. During WORLD WAR II it was occupied (1940–45) by Germany. In the modern city, government-sponsored modern art shares attention with the medieval Akerskirke and Akershus fortress and the royal palace (1848). The city was the site of the 1952 Olympic winter games.

**osmium** (Os), metallic element, discovered by Smithson Tennant in 1804. It is a very hard and dense, brittle, lustrous, bluish-white metal found in platinum ores. Its tetroxide is used as a stain in microscopy, in fingerprint detection, and as a catalyst. Osmium alloys are used in fountain-pen points, gramophone needles, and instrument bearings. See ELEMENT (table); PERIODIC TABLE.

**osmosis,** spontaneous transfer of a liquid solvent through a semipermeable membrane that does not allow dissolved solids (solutes) to pass. Osmosis refers only to the transfer of solvent; transfer of solute is called DIALYSIS. In osmosis, the direction of transfer of the solvent is from a solution of lower CONCENTRATION to a solution of higher concentration, until both solutions are of equal concentration. Thus, if a vessel is separated into two compartments by a semipermeable membrane, both compartments filled to the same level with a solvent, and if solute is added to one side, thus making it more concentrated, then osmosis will occur and the level of the liquid on the side containing the solute will rise. If an external pressure is exerted on the side containing the solute, the transfer of solvent can be stopped. The minimum pressure to stop solvent transfer is called the osmotic pressure. Osmosis plays an important role in the control of the flow of liquids in and out of a living CELL.

**Osnabrück,** city (1984 pop. 154,700), LOWER SAXONY, West Germany. A major rail junction, its industries include iron, textile, and paper manufacture. The Treaty of Westphalia, ending the THIRTY YEARS' WAR, was signed here in 1648. Postwar restoration of its Gothic buildings has taken place.

**osprey,** BIRD of prey related to the HAWK and the New World VULTURE, found near water in much of the world. The osprey, or fish hawk, (*Pandion haliaetus*) has a wingspan of 150–180 cm (5–6 ft) and feeds solely on live fish. They were exterminated in the British Isles by gamekeepers and egg-collectors, but have returned in recent years, and are breeding again in well-protected sites.

**Ossian** or **Oisin** (ˌoshən, əˌsheen), legendary Gaelic poet, supposed son of FINN MAC CUMHAIL. One cycle of Ossianic poetry treats Finn and his 3rd-cent. exploits, a second tells of the hero Cuchulain. In the 1760s the Scottish poet James MACPHERSON represented his own work as Ossian's.

**Ossietzky, Carl von,** 1889–1938, German pacifist. Arrested (1932) for exposing the secret rearmament of Germany in his antimilitarist weekly, *Weltbühne,* he was moved to a concentration camp after Hitler's rise to power in 1933. When he was awarded the 1935 Nobel Peace Prize, the German government protested and barred all Germans from future acceptance of any Nobel Prize. Ossietzky died in prison.

**Ostade, Adriaen van** (van ˌawstahdə), 1610–85, Dutch GENRE painter. Trained in Frans HALS's studio, he created good-humoured depictions of village and peasant life. Among his many works is *An Alchemist* (1661; National Gall., London). His brother and pupil, **Isaak van Ostade,** 1621–49, created many fine winter landscapes and peasant genre scenes.

**Ostend Manifesto,** document drawn up (1854) by three US diplomats at Ostend, Belgium, suggesting that the US should take Cuba by force if Spain refused to sell it. The three Americans—James BUCHANAN, John Y. Mason, and Pierre Soulé—were pro-slavery Democrats acting at the behest of Secy. of State William L. Marcy. When the secret manifesto was made public and denounced in the press as a plot to extend slavery, Marcy repudiated it.

**osteoarthritis:** see ARTHRITIS.

**osteomyelitis** (ˌostiohmieˑəˌlietəs), acute or chronic infection of the bone and bone marrow characterized by pain, high fever, and an ABSCESS at the site of infection. The infection may be caused by a variety of microorganisms and reaches the bone through an open wound or fracture, or through the bloodstream. Treatment includes ANTIBIOTIC drugs and sometimes surgery.

**osteopathy** (ˌostiˌopəthi), system of treatment of disease based on manipulation of bones and muscles. Osteopaths maintain that the normal body produces forces necessary to fight disease and that most ailments are due to the misalignment of bones and other faulty conditions of the muscle tissue and cartilage. Osteopathy was founded (1828–1917) by an American, Andrew Taylor Still.

**osteoporosis,** deficiency of bone tissue caused by insufficient production of bone matrix or excessive loss of calcium, resulting in brittle porous bones liable to fracture. Associated with aging and hormonal changes, the condition occurs particularly in old age and in women after the menopause. Prolonged malnutrition and certain diseases can also contribute to its development. Oestrogen therapy may prevent osteoporosis in post-menopausal women and regular, but not excessive, exercise may also prevent its development.

**Ostia,** ancient city of Italy, at the mouth of the Tiber. Founded (4th cent. BC) as a protection for Rome, it became a Roman port. From the 3rd cent. AD it declined.

**ostracism,** a method of banishing public figures in ancient GREECE, particularly ATHENS. No accusation was made, but a popular vote was taken, and the person with the most votes was exiled, usually for 10 years.

**Ostrava,** city (1984 pop. 324,000), N central Czechoslovakia, near the junction of the Oder and Ostravice rivers. In the heart of Czechoslovakia's major industrial area, Ostrava produces coal, iron, steel, machinery, and chemicals. It is the site of several hydroelectric stations.

**ostrich,** large, flightless BIRD (*Struthio camelus*) of Africa and parts of SW Asia, resembling the South American RHEA and the Australian EMU; the largest living bird. Some males reach 2.5 m (8 ft) in height and weigh from 90 to 135 kg (200 to 300 lb). The male is black, with long white plumes on wings and tail; the female is greyish brown. Ostriches can run at great speeds.

**Ostrogoths** or **East Goths,** a division of the Goths, one of the chief groups of the east GERMANS. In the 3rd cent. the Goths split into VISIGOTHS, or West Goths, and Ostrogoths, who were subjects of the HUNS until 453. The Ostrogoths then settled in Pannonia (modern Hungary) as allies of the Byzantine Empire. Their ruler, Theodoric the Great, defeated ODOACER (493) and set up the Ostrogothic kingdom of Italy. After the murder (535) of Theodoric's daughter, Amalasuntha, who as regent for her son was under Byzantine protection, JUSTINIAN I reconquered Italy through his generals BELISARIUS and NARSES. When Narses defeated (552) an Ostrogothic revolt under TOTILA, the Ostrogothic kingdom was crushed.

**Ostrovsky, Aleksandr Nikolayevich** (əs,trofskee), 1823–86, Russian dramatist. Most of his many plays depict patriarchal family life; all but eight are in blank verse. His masterpiece is the tragedy *The Storm* (1860). The composers JANÁČEK, RIMSKY-KORSAKOV, and TCHAIKOVSKY drew upon Ostrovsky's work.

**Ostwald, Wilhelm** (,ostvalt), 1853–1932, German physical chemist and natural philosopher; b. Latvia. He won the 1909 Nobel Prize for chemistry for his work on catalysis, equilibrium, and rates of reaction. He also studied colour and originated the **Ostwald process** for preparing nitric acid. In this process, ammonia mixed with air is heated and led over a catalyst (platinum). It reacts with oxygen to form nitric oxide, which is then oxidized to nitrogen dioxide; this in turn reacts with water to form nitric acid.

**Otis, Elisha Graves,** 1811–61, American inventor. From his invention (1852) of an automatic safety device to prevent the fall of hoisting machinery he developed the first passenger LIFT (1857), a basic step in the development of the SKYSCRAPER.

**Otis, James,** 1725–83, American colonial political leader. As leader of the radical wing of the American opposition to Britain, he defended colonial rights. Otis helped Samuel ADAMS draft the circular letter to other colonies denouncing the TOWNSHEND ACTS (1767).

**Ottawa,** city (1982 est. pop. 303,144), capital of Canada, SE Ontario, part of the regional municipality of Ottawa–Carleton, at the confluence of the Ottawa and Rideau rivers. It functions as a government centre and as a major location of high-technology industry. Of special interest are the Parliament Buildings, on Parliament Hill; the National Gallery; and the National Arts Center. Ottawa was founded as Bytown in 1825 and acquired its present name in 1854. The city was selected by Queen Victoria in 1858 as the capital of the newly formed United Provinces of Canada, and began to function as such in 1865. It became the capital of modern Canada in 1867.

**Ottawa Indians:** see NORTH AMERICAN INDIANS.

**otter,** several aquatic, carnivorous MAMMALS of the WEASEL family, found on all continents except Australia. Common river otters of Eurasia and the Americas (genus *Lutra*) are slender, streamlined, and agile, with thick, brown fur. They are about 120 cm (4 ft) long. Otters are social and playful, sliding down mudbanks and snowbanks. They feed on fish,

amphibians, and molluscs. The South American giant otter which is 2 m (6½ ft) long and the sea otter of the Pacific, hunted to near extinction, are now protected.

**Otto,** rulers of the HOLY ROMAN EMPIRE. **Otto I** or **Otto the Great,** 912–73, emperor (r.962–73) and German king (r.936–73), son and successor of Henry I of Germany, is often regarded as the founder of the Empire. He brought Italy, BURGUNDY, and LOTHARINGIA under German control and broke the independence of the duchies. In 955 at the battle of the Lech he defeated the Magyars. He married Adelaide, the widowed Italian queen, and crowned himself king of the LOMBARDS in 951. Pope JOHN XII, who crowned Otto emperor in 962, soon found Otto too powerful and allied himself with Otto's enemies; he was unsuccessful but established the long tradition of enmity between pope and emperor. **Otto II,** 955–83, emperor (r.973–83) and German king (r.961–83), was forced to defend the great empire left him by his father. He put down a revolt by his cousin, the duke of Bavaria; repulsed Danish attacks from the north; and resisted French efforts to annex Lorraine. He was defeated by the Arabs in S Italy, and his failure to expel them greatly diminished the prestige of his empire. His son, **Otto III,** 980–1002, emperor (r.996–1002) and German king (r.983–1002), was elected king shortly before his father's death; his mother and then his grandmother acted as regent for him. He installed (996) his cousin as Pope Gregory V, and later made his tutor pope (999) as SYLVESTER II. He attempted to establish his imperial headquarters in Rome, but a Roman mob forced him to flee (1001). He died while trying to regain the city. **Otto IV,** 1175?–1218, emperor (r.1209–15) and German king, was the son of HENRY THE LION, duke of Saxony. His uncle, RICHARD I of England, had him named anti-king to Philip of Swabia in 1198. Philip's murder (1208) was not of Otto's doing, but it revived his cause. He won over the princes and was elected emperor. He had made important concessions to the papacy regarding its Italian territories, but he quickly reverted to the HOHENSTAUFEN policy of dominance. He seized church lands and invaded Sicily, whereupon Pope INNOCENT III excommunicated him (1210). With the help of France and some German nobles, the pope succeeded in deposing him in 1215, having declared this at the Fourth Lateran Council.

**Otto,** German kings: see OTTO, rulers of the Holy Roman Empire.

**Otto, Nikolaus August,** 1832–91, German engineer. Co-inventor (1867) of an INTERNAL-COMBUSTION ENGINE, he developed (1876) the four-stroke Otto cycle, widely used for car, aeroplane, and other motors.

**Otto I,** 1815–67, first king (1833–62) of the Hellenes (Greece). The second son of Louis I of Bavaria, he was chosen by the European powers to rule over newly independent Greece. Highly unpopular, he was finally forced (1862) to abdicate.

**Ottoman Empire,** vast state founded in the 13th cent. by the Ottoman or Osmanli TURKS and ruled by the descendants of Osman I, the empire's first sultan, until its dissolution after World War I. It was the largest of the modern states, extending into Asia, Europe, and Africa; modern TURKEY formed only a part of the empire, but the terms 'Turkey' and 'Ottoman Empire' are often used interchangeably. The Ottoman state began as one of the many small Turkish states that emerged in Asia Minor as the power of the Seljuk Turks declined. The Ottomans began absorbing those small states as later (14th cent.) they absorbed territory belonging to the BYZANTINE EMPIRE. The great Balkan conquests of the late 14th cent. awoke Europe to the Ottoman threat. In spite of opposition from TAMERLANE, the Turks, under MEHMED II, conquered Constantinople in 1453 and established it as the Ottoman capital. The Ottoman Empire reached its height in the 16th cent. under SELIM I, who assumed the CALIPHATE after his victories in Syria and Egypt (1516–17), and under SULAYMAN I (the Magnificent), who brought much of the Balkan peninsula, Hungary, and Arabia under Turkish rule. The Turkish fleet, under BARBAROSSA, became the scourge of the Mediterranean. Despite Sulayman's reforms Turkey remained a medieval state, and decline set in at his death. The Turkish fleet was destroyed (1571) at Lepanto, and other military defeats followed. Succession to the throne was a continuing problem; fratricide was common within the royal family, and later heirs were protected in luxurious isolation until they assumed the throne. Actual rule fell to the grand viziers, often hereditary, like the KÖPRÜLÜ family, and to the elite JANISSARIES. Corruption and bribery were rampant. Serious disintegration began in the 18th cent. with the RUSSO-TURKISH WARS and continued with the loss of Greece and Egypt in the early 19th cent., when Turkey became known as the Sick Man of Europe. The Western powers feared Russian expansion (see EASTERN QUESTION) and loss of their commercial arrangements. Those arrangements had, in fact, gradually caused the Ottoman Empire to lose its economic independence and to rely almost wholly on foreign capital and loans. An attempt to reform the Turkish government was made with a new constitution in 1876, but this failed when the sultan abolished the constitution. After 1908 the Young Turks, a reformist and nationalist group, were increasingly important. Turkey lost most of its remaining European territories in the BALKAN WARS (1912–13), and World War I confirmed its disintegration. Turkey sided with the losing Central Powers, and in 1918 the peace treaties ending the war formally dissolved the Ottoman Empire. In 1922 Kemal ATATÜRK overthrew the last sultan, and the history of modern Turkey began.

**Otto the Great** (Otto I): see under OTTO, rulers of the Holy Roman Empire.

**Otway, Thomas,** 1652–85, English dramatist. His plays *The Orphan* (1680) and *Venice Preserved* (1682) are noted for their simple power and for the romantic beauty Otway brought to the formal manner of Restoration heroic TRAGEDY.

**Ouagadougou** or **Wagadugu** (wahgə‚doohgooh), city (1985 est. pop. 375,000), capital of Burkina Faso. It is a communications and economic centre, as well as the market for an agricultural region, trading in millet, ground nuts, and livestock. The city has rail connections with the Côte d'Ivoire and road links with Niger. Founded in the late 11th cent. as the capital of the black African Mossi empire, it was a centre of Mossi power until captured (1896) by the French.

**Oudh,** historic region of India: see INDIAN MUTINY.

**Oujda,** city (1982 pop. 478,919), NE Morocco, close to the Algerian border. The chief town of the Oujda prov., its economy is based on trade in wool, grain, wine, and fruit. The city was founded in the 10th cent. and was occupied by the French in 1844, 1859, and after 1907.

**Ouologuem, Yambo,** 1940–, controversial novelist from Mali. He was the first African to receive a major French literary award, the Prix Renaudot, for his first novel, *Le devoir de violence* (1968; tr. *Bound to Violence,* 1971).

**Ouse** or **Great Ouse,** river in E England, approximately 250 km (156 mi) long. It rises to the SW of Towcester, Northamptonshire, and follows a circuitous route past Buckingham, Newport Pagnell, BEDFORD, Huntingdon, St Ives, ELY, Downham Market, and KING'S LYNN, ending up in the WASH. As it crosses the FENS it follows two artificial straight channels called 'the Bedford Rivers' as well as its natural course.

**Ousmane, Sembene,** 1923–, Senegalese writer and film-maker. The themes of Ousmane's novels and short stories are partly autobiographical, e.g., *Le Docker noir* (1956), and partly actualizations of historical events, e.g. *Les Bouts de bois de Dieu* (1960; tr. *God's Bits of Wood*). *Xala* (1973; tr. 1976, filmed 1974) is a satire on the Senegalese privileged classes.

**Ouwe, Hartmann von:** see HARTMANN VON AUE.

**ovary:** see REPRODUCTIVE SYSTEM.

**overpopulation,** an excess of population in an area in relation to resources or to other broader social or economic goals. It may exist at local, regional, or national levels, but is most frequently seen in underdeveloped rural areas where the outstripping of resources by population growth may be evident in underemployment or undernourishment. Governments typically take action to limit population growth by promoting BIRTH CONTROL programmes or by offering tax incentives to parents who limit their families. However, some economists believe that the right response to apparent overpopulation in developing countries is to increase resources rather than limit the number of people.

**over-the-counter,** method of buying and selling securities outside the standard STOCK EXCHANGE. The over-the-counter (OTC) market in the UK in 1987 was composed of 40 licensed securities dealers who conducted business in the shares of about 160 companies.

**over-the-counter drugs:** see PATENT MEDICINE.

**overture,** instrumental musical composition written as an introduction to an OPERA, BALLET, ORATORIO, MUSICAL, or play. Early examples were simply symphonic pieces, but by C.W. von GLUCK's time the overture began to foreshadow what was to come in the opera. In many 19th-cent.

operas and 20th-cent. musicals, the overture is a potpourri of the work's tunes. The concert overture is a composition in one movement.

**Ovid** (Publius Ovidius Naso) 43 BC–AD 17 or 18, Latin poet. His highly perfected elegiacs (see ELEGY) fall into three groups— erotic poems, mythological poems, and, after he was banished to the Black Sea for unknown reasons in AD 8, poems of exile. The love poems include *Amores, Epistulae heroidum* (Letters from Heroines), and *Ars amatoria* (The Art of Love). His masterpiece *Metamorphoses,* in hexameters, is his major mythological work. *Fasti* is on myths connected with days of the year; *Tristia* is on the sorrows of exile. Ovid was a major source of inspiration for the RENAISSANCE.

**Oviedo** (ovee‚aydo), city (1981 pop. 190,123), capital of Oviedo prov., N Spain. Close to Spain's largest coalfield, it manufactures equipment for the mines, armaments, and chemicals. It was capital of the kingdom of the Asturias in the 9th cent. The cathedral dates from the late 14th cent. and its university was founded in 1598.

**oviparous,** description of any animal that lays eggs which contain all the food needed to allow the developing embryo to reach the hatching stage. In cases where the food supply is small, as in some insects, fishes, and amphibians, the egg hatches into a LARVA, which continues to feed. Where there is a sufficient supply of food as in birds and reptiles, the egg will hatch into a small, immature version of the adult. Most invertebrates, fishes, amphibians, and reptiles lay eggs and all birds and monotremes do so.

**ovoviviparous,** description of those animals which produce eggs, but keep them inside their bodies until they hatch, so that they give birth to live young. Any invertebrate, fish, amphibian, or reptile that produces live young is ovoviviparous.

**ovum,** in biology, specialized female plant or animal sex cell, also called the egg. In higher animals the ovum differs from the SPERM (male sex cell) in that it is larger and nonmotile. Its nucleus contains the CHROMOSOMES, which bear the hereditary material of the parent. Ova are produced in the ovary of the female; they undergo a maturation process that includes MEIOSIS, by which the number of their chromosomes is reduced by half. The union of mature sperm and ovum (see FERTILIZATION), with each bearing half the normal number of chromosomes, results in a single cell (the zygote) with a full number of chromosomes. The zygote eventually becomes a mature individual. The pattern is similar in plants that reproduce sexually. The term *egg* also refers to a complex structure, such as a bird's egg, in which the ovum is swollen with yolk (food material) and the rest of the egg is secreted around the ovum. Development from an unfertilized ovum is called PARTHENOGENESIS. See also REPRODUCTION; REPRODUCTIVE SYSTEM.

**Owen, David,** 1938–, British politician, leader of the SOCIAL DEMOCRATIC PARTY (SDP) (1983–87, 1988–). A doctor of medicine, he entered parliament in 1966 as a Labour member, rising rapidly to become Foreign and Commonwealth Secretary (1977–79) in the CALLAGHAN government. Opposed to what he regarded as the Labour Party's leftward swing in opposition, he participated in the formation of the SDP in 1981 and became its leader in 1983. After a majority of the SDP had opted for full merger with the LIBERAL PARTY, Owen resigned as leader (1987), but the following year was elected leader of an SDP rump which declined membership of the new SOCIAL AND LIBERAL DEMOCRATS.

**Owen, Robert,** 1771–1858, Welsh social reformer, a pioneer in the cooperative movement. In 1800 he began to convert old mills in New Lanark, Scotland, into a model industrial town, instigating reforms later reflected in the Factory Act of 1819. Believing that individual character is moulded by environment and can be improved in a society based on cooperation, he founded several self-sufficient cooperative agricultural–industrial communities, including New Lanark in Scotland, and New Harmony in the US.

**Owen, Wilfred,** 1893–1918, English poet. Owen, who died on the French front in World War I, wrote of the horror and pity of war in verse that transfigured traditional metre and diction. Siegfried SASSOON published 24 of Owen's poems posthumously (1920). His *Collected Poems,* ed. DAY LEWIS (1963), reflected the steady growth of his reputation.

**Owen Glendower,** 1359?–1416?, Welsh leader. In 1400 he rebelled against HENRY IV of England, taking the title of Prince of Wales. Allying himself with the Percy family and with France, he had some military success and summoned (1405) his own parliament, but by 1409 the English had rendered him powerless.

**Owens, Jesse,** 1913–81, American track star. While at Ohio State Univ. he broke (1935–36) several world records. At the 1936 Olympics in Berlin, Owens, a black, upset Hitler's 'Aryan' theories by setting world records in the long jump and the 200-m long race and equalling the record in the 100-m long race. His fourth gold medal came in the 400-m long relays.

**owl,** nocturnal BIRD of prey found worldwide, belonging to the families Tytonidae and Strigidae. Owls resemble short-necked HAWKS, except that their eyes are directed forwards and surrounded by discs of radiating feathers. Their eyes are specially adapted to seeing in partial darkness, and most sleep during the day. Owls' soft, fluffy plumage makes them almost noiseless in flight. They feed on rodents, frogs, insects and small birds. Many usurp the deserted nests of other birds; others live in burrows.

Barn **owl** (*Tyto alba*) with prey

**owl parrot:** see KAKAPO.

**ox:** see CATTLE.

**oxalis** or **wood sorrel,** plant (genus *Oxalis*), usually with cloverlike leaves that respond to darkness by folding back their leaflets. Most cultivated forms are tropical herbs. Temperate zone species include the white wood sorrel (*O. acetosella*), a plant identified as the SHAMROCK, along with the white clover.

**Oxenstierna, Count Axel Gustaffson,** 1583–1654, Swedish statesman. Named chancellor in 1612, he was Sweden's real administrator because GUSTAVUS II was occupied with foreign wars. After Gustavus II died in battle (1632) he unified the German Protestant princes and secured France's entry into the war. As leader of the council of regency (1632–44) in the minority of CHRISTINA, Gustavus's daughter, he was virtual ruler of Sweden. He wrote the constitution of 1634, centralizing administration, and directed the war with Denmark (1643–45), in which Sweden gained several Danish provinces. Clashes with Christina diminished his power. After her abdication (1654), which he had opposed, he served her successor, CHARLES X.

**Oxfam,** officially the Oxford Committee for Famine Relief (est. 1942), a non-governmental British disaster relief and food aid organization particularly active in poorer developing countries.

**Oxford,** city (1981 pop. 113,847), Oxfordshire, S central England. It is famous as the seat of Oxford Univ. (est. 12th cent.). In its suburbs vehicles and steel products are manufactured. During the civil wars (17th cent.) Oxford was the royalist headquarters. It has many historic buildings, including the Ashmolean Museum, the Bodleian Library, Christ Church Cathedral, and the various colleges.

**Oxford, Provisions of:** see PROVISIONS OF OXFORD.

**Oxford and Asquith, Herbert Henry Asquith, 1st earl of,** 1852–1928, British statesman. Entering Parliament as a Liberal in 1886, he was a 'Liberal imperialist' who supported (1899) the South African War. His main interest was in domestic politics, and he became prime minister (1908–16). His government put through a social welfare programme, including old age pensions (1908) and unemployment insurance (1911), and began a naval buildup. Asquith also secured passage of the parliamentary Reform Act of 1911, which stripped the House of Lords of its veto power. Dissatisfaction with his leadership in World War I led to his resignation and to a split in the Liberal Party from which it did not recover. His second wife, **Margot (Tennant) Asquith,** 1864–1945, was a prominent socialite whose frank autobiography (1920–22) created a sensation.

**Oxford Group:** see BUCHMAN, FRANK NATHAN DANIEL.

**Oxford Movement,** religious movement begun in 1833 by Anglican clergy at Oxford Univ. to revitalize the Church of England by reviving certain traditional Catholic doctrines and rituals. Among its leaders were J.H. NEWMAN, John KEBLE, and R.H. Froude. Under Newman a series of pamphlets, *Tracts for the Times* (1833–41), were issued that preached Anglicanism as a middle way between Catholicism and evangelicalism. The group then became known as Tractarians. Newman's *Tract 90* on the Thirty-nine Articles aroused a storm of controversy and brought the series to an end. The movement began to lose valuable supporters to Roman Catholicism, including Newman and H.E. MANNING. Its leadership passed to E.B. PUSEY, and opponents dubbed the movement 'Puseyism'. Its clergy, known as Anglo-Catholics, adopted innovations, such as chanting prayers, wearing vestments, and using elaborate ritual within the services. For these actions they were often labelled ritualists. This revival of ceremonial customs caused much public agitation, but the movement exerted a great influence on doctrine, spirituality, and liturgy in the ANGLICAN COMMUNION. It was responsible for the revival of Anglican religious communities and, through an emphasis on social concern, was an antecedent of CHRISTIAN SOCIALISM.

**Oxfordshire,** inland county in S Midlands of England (1984 est. pop. 555,700), 2608 km² (1017 sq mi), bordering on Gloucestershire in the W and Buckinghamshire in the E. The county town is OXFORD. The COTSWOLD HILLS are situated in the W and the Chiltern Hills in the SE. Much of the central part of the county is occupied by the broad vale of Oxfordshire. Cereal crops are grown and sheep and cattle raised. The Vale of the White Horse in the S is a fertile agricultural area. The principal towns are Oxford, Witney, Banbury, and Abingdon.

**Oxford University,** at Oxford, England. One of the world's most prestigious universities, it had its beginnings in the early 12th cent. Its system of residential colleges dates from the mid-13th cent., when University, Balliol, and Merton colleges were founded. Oxford was a leading centre of learning in the Middle Ages. There are 40 colleges, 28 of which admit undergraduates, and only a small proportion of which

The Old Ashmolean Building, **Oxford**

have remained for men only or women only. Its Ashmolean Museum and Bodleian Library are known world-wide. Oxford's Rhodes scholarships for foreign students were initially financed by a gift from Cecil RHODES.

**oxidation and reduction,** complementary chemical reactions characterized by the loss or gain, respectively, of one or more electrons by an atom or molecule. When an atom or a molecule combines, or forms a chemical bond, with oxygen, it tends to give up electrons to the oxygen. Similarly, when it loses oxygen, it tends to gain electrons. Oxidation is defined as any reaction involving a loss of electrons, and reduction as any reaction involving the gain of electrons. The two processes, oxidation and reduction, occur simultaneously and in chemically equivalent quantities; the number of electrons lost by one substance is equalled by the number of electrons gained by another substance. The substance losing electrons (undergoing oxidation) is said to be an electron donor, or a reducing agent (or reductant). Conversely, the substance gaining electrons (undergoing reduction) is said to be an electron acceptor, or an oxidizing agent (or oxidant). Common reducing agents (substances readily oxidized) are the active METALS, CARBON, CARBON MONOXIDE, HYDROGEN, hydrogen sulphide, and sulphurous acid. Common oxidizing agents (substances readily reduced) include the HALOGENS, NITRIC ACID, OXYGEN, OZONE, potassium permanganate, potassium dichromate, and concentrated SULPHURIC ACID.

**oxidation state:** see VALENCY.

**oxygen** (O), gaseous element, first isolated (c.1773–74) independently by Joseph PRIESTLEY and Karl SCHEELE. A colourless, odourless, tasteless gas, it is the most abundant element on earth, constituting about half of the surface material. It makes up about 90% of water, two-thirds of the human body, and 20% by volume of air. Normal atmospheric oxygen is diatomic, i.e., it contains two atoms in the molecule ($O_2$). OZONE is a highly reactive triatomic ($O_3$) allotrope of oxygen (see ALLOTROPY). Oxygen forms compounds with almost all of the elements except the inert gases. The common reaction in which it unites with another substance is called oxidation (see OXIDATION AND REDUCTION). The burning of substances in air is rapid oxidation, or combustion. The RESPIRATION of plants and animals is a form of oxidation essential to the liberation of the energy stored in such food materials as carbohydrates and fats. Chief industrial uses are in STEEL production (e.g., in the BESSEMER PROCESS) and the oxyacetylene torch (see ACETYLENE); in medicine it is used to treat respiratory diseases. Liquid oxygen is used in rocket fuel systems. See ELEMENT (table); PERIODIC TABLE.

**Oxyrhynchus,** excavation site in Upper Egypt, now Behnesa. Important papyrus finds there (1896–97, 1906–07, and from excavations still continuing) have retrieved lost Greek literary classics, chiefly in Roman and Byzantine scrolls dating from the 1st cent. BC to the 10th cent. AD.

**Oyo,** city (1987 est. pop. 152,000), capital of Oyo state, SW Nigeria. The economy is based chiefly on agriculture and handicrafts. The city became the seat of the *alafin* of Oyo (the political leader of the Yoruba people) in the 1830s, after the capital of the Oyo empire was destroyed by the Muslim Fulani conquerers from ILORIN.

**Oyono, Ferdinand,** 1929–, Cameroon writer. He is arguably the most incisive satirist of French colonialism with *Une vie de boy* (1956; tr. *Houseboy,* 1966), *Le vieux nègre et la medaille* (1956; tr. *The Old Man and the Medal,* 1969), and *Chemin d'Europe* (1960).

**oyster,** BIVALVE mollusc found in beds in the shallow, warm waters of all oceans. Except in the free-swimming larval stage, oysters spend their lives attached to substrates of rocks, shells, or roots by means of a cementlike secretion. The pearl oyster, from which the PEARL is obtained, is a large (30-cm/12-in) tropical species. The edible oyster (*Ostrea edulis*) was once abundant in Britain, exported to Rome in Roman times and poor people's food in the 1800s and early 1900s. A combination of neglect of oyster beds, the arrival of the American oyster drill and pollution has greatly reduced the British oyster and it is now an expensive rarity. The American, Japanese, and Portuguese oysters (*Crassostrea* species) are still plentiful, but they are not as sweet as the edible oyster.

**oysterwork,** a decorative VENEER used on furniture, formed of transverse cuts from small branches of walnut, laburnum, or other trees, in which the growth rings somewhat resemble oyster shells. The technique originated in Holland in the second half of the 17th cent. and was soon adopted elsewhere.

**Oz, Amos,** 1939–, Israeli novelist. He writes in Hebrew and often assists in the translation of his novels into English. Richly atmospheric and often incorporating elements of fantasy, his novels usually treat contemporary Israeli life. They include *Elsewhere Perhaps* (1966), *My Michael* (1968), and *Touch the Water, Touch the Wind* (1974).

An example of **oysterwork** veneer

**Ozarks, the** or **Ozark Plateau,** forested upland region, c.130,000 km² (over 50,000 sq mi) mostly in Missouri and Arkansas, US. Referred to locally as mountains, the Ozarks rise prominently from surrounding plains to more than 600 m (2000 ft) in the rugged Boston Mts. The economy is based on agriculture, lead and zinc mining, and tourism, with subsistence farming and household crafts remaining as features of life in the more isolated areas.

**ozone,** form of OXYGEN having three atoms in the molecule ($O_3$). Pure ozone is an unstable, faintly bluish gas with a characteristic fresh, penetrating odour. It is the most chemically active form of oxygen. Ozone is formed in the ozone layer of the stratosphere (see ATMOSPHERE) by the action of solar ultraviolet light on oxygen; this layer plays an important role in preventing most ultraviolet and other high-energy radiation, which is harmful to life, from penetrating to the earth's surface. Some environmentalists fear that certain man-made pollutants, e.g., nitric oxide (NO), may cause a drastic depletion of stratospheric ozone. Ozone is also formed when an electric discharge passes through air; it is produced commercially by passing dry air between two electrodes connected to an alternating high voltage. Ozone is used as a disinfectant and decontaminant for air and water.

**Ozu Yasujiro,** 1903–63, Japanese film director. His many studies of character development within family relationships include *The Story of Floating Weeds* (1934), *There Was a Father* (1942), *Tokyo Story* (1953), and *Late Autumn* (1960).

**P**, chemical symbol of the element PHOSPHORUS.

**Pa**, chemical symbol of the element PROTACTINIUM.

**Pabst, G(eorg) W(ilhelm),** 1885–1967, German film director; b. Austria. He used MONTAGE in such works of social realism as *The Joyless Street* (1925), *The Love of Jeanne Ney* (1927), *Pandora's Box* (1929), *Westfront 1918* (1930), and *The Threepenny Opera* (1931).

**pacemaker,** device used to stimulate a rhythmic heartbeat by means of electrical impulses. Implanted in the body when the heart's own electrical conduction system does not function normally, the battery-powered device emits electrical pulses that trigger heart-muscle contraction at a rate preset or controlled by an external remote switch.

**Pacific, War of the,** 1879–84, fought between CHILE and the allied nations, PERU and BOLIVIA. It began when Bolivia rescinded (1879) a contract with a Chilean company to mine nitrates in its territory and Chile, in reprisal, seized the Bolivian port of Antofagasta. Peru was drawn into the war by a defensive alliance with Bolivia. Chilean forces conquered (1879) a Peruvian border province, gained control of the sea, and entered (1881) Lima in triumph. As a result Bolivia's only coastal territory, Atacama (now Antofagasta), was assigned to Chile. By the truce at VALPARAISO (1884) Peru ceded Tarapacá and control of Tacna and Arica provinces to Chile; eventually, Chile returned (1929) Tacna to Peru.

**Pacific Islands,** trust territory (1980 pop. 116,974), administered by the US since 1947, consisting of c.2180 islands and islets with a combined land area of 1375 km² (531 sq mi). The territory is spread out over c.7,770,000 km² (3,000,000 sq mi) of the W Pacific Ocean in the area generally known as MICRONESIA. The islands were seized by Japan from Germany in 1914, occupied by the US in 1944 during WORLD WAR II, and made a trusteeship in 1947. As the result of negotiations for termination of the trusteeship, the NORTHERN MARIANA ISLANDS gained US commonwealth status in 1978, and three other self-governing units, under the military protection of the US, were established: the Republic of BELAU, the Federated States of MICRONESIA, and the MARSHALL ISLANDS.

**Pacific Ocean,** world's largest ocean, c.181,300,000 km² (70,000,000 sq mi), occupying about one third of the Earth's surface between the west coasts of North and South America and the east coasts of Australia and Asia. It has a maximum length of c.14,500 km² (9000 mi), a maximum width of c.17,700 km (11,000 mi), and a maximum depth of 11,033 m (36,198 ft) in the Challenger Deep, in the Marianas Trench c.400 km (250 mi) SW of Guam. A series of volcanoes, the Circum-Pacific Ring of Fire, rims the ocean. Along the eastern shore there is a narrow continental shelf, and high mountains rise abruptly from a deep sea floor. The Asian coast is generally low and fringed with islands rising from a wide continental shelf.

**pacifism,** opposition to war through individual or collective action. Motivated by religious or humanitarian impulses, pacifism is often connected with international cooperation toward the goal of disarmament. Local peace societies were founded in the US (1815) and Britain (1816), and the first international peace congress met (1843) in London. The movement was advanced during the late 1800s by the work of the Frenchman Frédéric PASSY and others and was publicized through the establishment (1901) of the NOBEL PRIZE for peace. The horrors of World War I gave it new vigour after 1920, when it was influenced by both the LEAGUE OF NATIONS and GANDHI's effective practice of nonviolent (or passive) resistance. The number of British and American CONSCIENTIOUS OBJECTORS grew in World War II. In the 1960s and 70s, US pacifists were in the forefront of the opposition to the VIETNAM WAR. See also CAMPAIGN FOR NUCLEAR DISARMAMENT; DISARMAMENT, NUCLEAR.

**paddle tennis,** form of lawn TENNIS but played on a smaller court 15.2 by 6.1 m (50 by 20 ft) with a short-handled paddle and a soft (punctured) tennis ball. Unlike tennis, only one underhand serve is allowed. Originally a children's game, invented in 1898, it gained an adult following in the 1960s after the court was enlarged and the rules were revised.

**pademelon:** see KANGAROO.

**Paderewski, Ignace Jan** ('padǝ,refskee), 1860–1941, Polish pianist, composer, and statesman. His playing won him a reputation exceeding that of any performer since LISZT. An ardent patriot, he was the first prime minister of the new Poland for 10 months in 1919 and again in 1940–41 (in exile). He died while in the US to plead Poland's cause. The Minuet in G for piano is his best-known work, but he wrote more substantial compositions, such as a Piano Concerto (1888), a Symphony (1907) and the opero *Manru* (1901).

**Padua,** city (1984 pop. 229,156), in Venetia, NE Italy. A major Roman city, it was an important free commune (12th–14th cent.), then passed to the Carrara family (1318) and to Venice (1405). Its Capella degli Scrovegni has magnificent frescoes (1304–06) by GIOTTO. Among its other treasures are sculptures by DONATELLO and paintings by MANTEGNA, who was born there.

**paediatrics,** branch of medicine specializing in the care of children and the treatment of childhood diseases. It includes treatment of such diseases as MEASLES, CHICKEN POX, and MUMPS; immunization against serious childhood infections such as DIPHTHERIA and WHOOPING COUGH; and recognition and treatment of disorders due to MALNUTRITION, poor hygiene, and child abuse. Other specialties include paediatric SURGERY and **perinatology** (the care of the fetus and newborn, and the study of diseases of infancy and SUDDEN INFANT DEATH SYNDROME).

**Paestum** (,pestǝm), ancient city of S Italy. Originally a Greek colony called Posidonia, it was taken by the Romans in 273 BC and renamed Paestum. The ruins include some of the finest and best-preserved Doric temples in existence.

**Páez, José Antonio** (,pah-ays), 1790–1873, first president of VENEZUELA (1831–35, 1839–43). He boldly led (1810–19) a guerrilla band and drove the Spanish from their last Venezuelan stronghold. A leader of separatism from Colombia, he headed the new state of Venezuela, but was exiled (1850–58), served briefly as dictator (1861–63), and was exiled again.

**Paganini, Niccolò,** 1782–1840, Italian violin virtuoso. He extended the violin's compass by employing harmonics, perfected the use of double and triple stopping, and revived *scordatura,* diverse tuning of strings. His 24 caprices for violin were adapted for piano by SCHUMANN and LISZT.

**Pagnol, Marcel** (pan,yohl), 1895–1974, French playwright and film-maker. He was a member of the Académie française and was famous mostly for his trilogy of Marseilles life *Marius* (1929), *Fanny* (1931), and *César* (1937) and many other plays and screenplays where realism and satire can sometimes be flawed by sentimentality. His two-part novel

*L'eau des collines* (1963) and several volumes of autobiography have since revealed a skilful and moving *conteur*.

**pagoda,** name given in the East to a variety of buildings in tower form, usually part of a temple or monastery, and serving as shrines. The Indian masonry STUPA, chiefly pyramidal, is elaborately decorated with carvings or sculpture. The Chinese pagoda, of Indian origin, is hexagonal, octagonal, or square in plan. It is built in as many as 15 superimposed storeys. From each storey an upward-curving tile roof projects. Brick, faced with tiles, is the most common material. Japanese pagodas, usually square and five-storeyed, are made of wood and exhibit superb carpentry craftsmanship. See also CHINESE ARCHITECTURE; JAPANESE ARCHITECTURE.

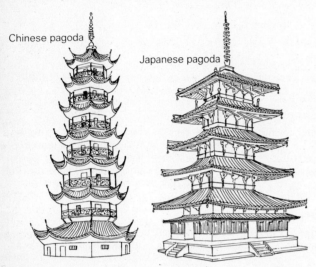

Chinese pagoda

Japanese pagoda

Pagoda

**Pago Pago,** (1980 pop. 3058), capital of AMERICAN SAMOA.

**Pahari** (pə,hahree), languages or dialects of the Indic group of the Indo-Iranian subfamily of the Indo-European family of languages. See LANGUAGE (table).

**Pahlavi language** or **Pehlevi language** (,pahlə'vee, ,paylə'vee), member of the Iranian group of the Indo-Iranian subfamily of the Indo-European family of languages. It is also called Middle Persian. See LANGUAGE (table).

**Paine, Thomas,** 1737–1809, American political theorist and writer; b. England. In 1774 he emigrated to America, where he wrote (1776) the hugely successful pamphlet *Common Sense*. During the AMERICAN REVOLUTION he began a series of 16 pamphlets, *The Crisis* (1776–83). In *The Rights of Man* (two parts, 1791, 1792), written in England, he defended the FRENCH REVOLUTION in reply to Edmund BURKE, arguing that only democratic institutions can guarantee natural rights. To escape prosecution for treason in England, he fled to Paris, where he became a member of the National Convention and was imprisoned (1793–94) during the Reign of Terror. He wrote his deistic work *The Age of Reason* (2 parts, 1794, 1795) at this time. He returned to the US in 1802 living there in ostracism and poverty until his death.

**pair production,** in physics, the conversion of a photon into an ELECTRON and a POSITRON. This is an excellent example of the conversion of electromagnetic energy into rest mass energy. To take place the photon must have an energy greater than $2mc^2 (= 1.02$ MeV) where $m$ is the mass of the electron (positron) and $c$ is the velocity of light. See MASS.

**paisley:** see SHAWL.

**Paisley, Rev. Ian,** 1926–, Irish Protestant political leader, Presbyterian minister and founder of the anti-Catholic Democratic Unionist Party (1969). Elected to the House of Commons in 1970 and to the European Parliament in 1979, he has strongly opposed any loosening of Northern Ireland's status as an integral part of the UK. See also IRELAND, NORTHERN.

**Paiute Indians:** see NORTH AMERICAN INDIANS.

**Pakistan,** officially the Islamic Republic of Pakistan, republic (1987 est. pop. 100,000,000), 796,095 km² (307,372 sq mi), Asia, on the NW corner of the South Asian subcontinent, bordered by India (E), the Arabian Sea (S), Iran (SW), Afghanistan (W and N), and Jammu and Kashmir (NE). The capital is ISLAMABAD; other important cities are KARACHI, LAHORE, and RAWALPINDI. Pakistan may be divided into four geographic regions: an arid plateau in the west; alluvial plains in the east; hills and semiarid valleys in the northwest; and high mountains of the HINDU KUSH, the HIMALAYAS, and KARAKORUM ranges in the north. The INDUS R. runs the length of the country. Agriculture is the mainstay of the economy, with wheat, rice, maize, cotton, and sugarcane the principal crops. The country inherited vast British irrigation works. These new works, high yielding crop varieties, and fertilizer have increased output in recent years. Pakistan has a rapidly expanding industrial base, including metal processing and the production of textiles, cement, and fertilizers. The GNP is $35,112 million and the GNP per capita is $380. The people are a mixture of many ethnic and linguistic groups, with the Punjabis the most numerous; Pathan tribesmen in the northwest and Baluchis in the west have pressed for autonomous states. Islam is by far the dominant religion, and Urdu is the official language, although English is widely used.

*History.* The area that is now Pakistan was the site of the INDUS VALLEY CIVILIZATION, the earliest known culture on the Indian subcontinent. The territory's location placed it on the historic route from central Asia to India, and for thousands of years invaders, including Aryans, Persians, Alexander the Great, Seleucids, and Parthians, swept down on the settlements there. Arriving in force in AD 712, Muslim Arabs controlled most of Sindh and Baluchistan for more than a century. They were followed by Turks, who established an important Muslim centre in Bengal after 1200. In the 18th and 19th cent., NW India was invaded by the Persians and Afghans before becoming part of British India. The Sikhs established a short-lived kingdom based on Lahore. The separate political aspirations of Indian Muslims led to the founding of the MUSLIM LEAGUE, in 1906. Led by Muhammad Ali JINNAH the League demanded establishment of a separate Muslim state in 1940. Finally, in 1947, under the provisions of the Indian Independence Act, Pakistan consisting of East Bengal (renamed East Pakistan in 1955) and West Pakistan, separated by 1600 km (1000 mi) of Indian territory became a separate, independent dominion, with Jinnah as governor-general. The new state faced precarious economic conditions. In addition, dissension with India, particularly over KASHMIR, was immediate and violent (see INDIA–PAKISTAN WARS), and strife between Hindus and Muslims was widespread. In 1956 Pakistan formally became a republic, but in 1958 the constitution was abrogated and martial law imposed under Gen. Muhammad AYUB KHAN, who was elected president in 1960. Under his dictatorship, a vigorous land reform and economic development programme was begun, but after disastrous riots in 1968 and 1969 he resigned in favour of Gen. Agha Muhammad YAHYA KHAN. Almost from its inception, Pakistan was plagued by tension between East Pakistan, which had the majority of the population, and West Pakistan, which dominated the army and federal government. In May 1971, after the government's refusal to recognize the election victory of Sheikh Mujibur Rahman's Awami League, which advocated autonomy for East Pakistan, East Pakistan declared independence as Bangladesh. In the ensuing civil war, West Pakistan was quickly defeated with the aid of Indian troops. In 1972 Pakistan left the COMMONWEALTH in protest against the recognition of Bangladesh by the UK and other members. Political turmoil continued in West Pakistan, and opposition to Zulfiqar Ali BHUTTO, who had become president (later prime minister) after the war, became intense. In 1977 an army coup placed Gen. Muhammad ZIA UL-HAQ in the office of president; Bhutto was arrested on charge of abetting a murder and later (1979) hanged. Since 1980 more than 1.7 million refugees, fleeing from the Soviet invasion of Afghanistan, have poured into Pakistan, creating serious economic problems. In 1982 Pres. Zia inaugurated a Federal Advisory Council but has refused demands for democratic multi-party elections despite increasing internal opposition, notably from the People's Party now led by Bhutto's daughter Benazir. Following Zia's death in an air crash (1988), multi-party elections were held and resulted in Benazir Bhutto becoming prime minister.

### Presidents of Pakistan
Iskander Mirza (Republican), 1956–58
Muhammed Ayub Khan (military), 1958–69
Agha Muhammad Yahya Khan (military), 1969–71
*Zulfiqar Ali Bhutto (People's Party), 1971–73
Chaudhri Fazal Elahi (People's Party), 1973–77

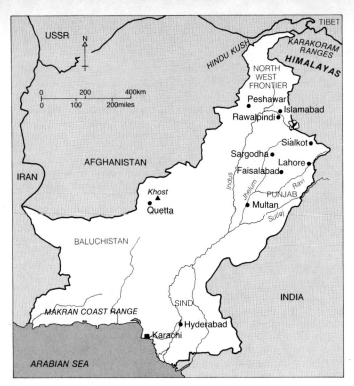

Pakistan

Muhammad Zia ul-Haq (military), 1977–88
Ghulam Ishaq Khan (acting), 1988–
*Prime minister 1973–77

**Palaeocene epoch:** see GEOLOGICAL ERAS (table).

**Palaeozoic era:** see GEOLOGICAL ERAS (table).

**Palaeolithic art,** art from the later part of last glaciation. The art is concentrated in southern France, the Pyrenees and Cantabria with rarer examples from other parts of Europe. There is a general unity of style and method over some 20,000 years; the earliest art was engraved sometime after 30,000 years ago, but with most of the classic sites dating to between 15,000 and 10,000 years ago. The artists illustrated a variety of animals, but tended to concentrate on horse, bison, mammoth, and deer. Occasionally humans, vulvae and other more schematic designs were drawn. Various techniques were used, such as painting with red, black, and yellow ochres, which have usually survived in caves like LASCAUX and ALTAMIRA. Engraving and sculpting with flint tools was also used both on the walls of caves and rock shelters, one of the finest examples being the 'Venuses' from Laussel (see VENUS FIGURINES), but also on pieces of bone, antler, and ivory, such as the 'swimming reindeer' from Montastruc. The ritual of religious significance of the art is not well understood, but it is clear that they form the masterpieces of prehistoric Europe.

**Palaeolithic period,** the earliest and longest phase of human history, from the first appearance of stone tools, more than 2 million years ago, to the end of the Pleistocene GEOLOGIC ERAS (see table); also known as the Old Stone Age (see THREE-AGE SYSTEM). Palaeolithic peoples were generally nomadic HUNTERS–GATHERERS who fashioned stone tools. The Palaeolithic is traditionally divided into three sub-phases: the Lower Palaeolithic, associated with HOMO ERECTUS and other small-brained hominids and typified by the ACHEULIAN stone tool industry; the Middle Palaeolithic, with NEANDERTHAL MAN (*Homo sapiens neanderthalensis*) and the MOUSTERIAN industry; and the Upper Palaeolithic, with *Homo sapiens sapiens* (anatomically modern man) and the Aurignacian, Solutrean, and MAGDALENIAN industries and later cultures. It is no longer presumed that these technological changes are equal to stages in human intellectual development; in recent years the traditional scheme of biological and social progress implemented by invasions of advanced peoples has been replaced by the idea that cultural change may be motivated by social and environmental adaptation. In addition, the wide variation in tool assemblages over time and space during the Lower and Middle

Palaeolithic has reduced the value of the distinction as a chronological marker. Only during the Upper Palaeolithic, when new evidence of human expression—burials, ornamentation, and the appearance of cave art (see ALTAMIRA; LASCAUX) and ritual activity—does a significant developmental shift appear. As a result, research interest has turned from the isolated analysis of individual sites and the stylistic position of their tool assemblages to regionally-based studies of human social interaction and adaptation in the late Pleistocene landscape.

**Palaeologus,** ruling Greek dynasty of the Byzantine Empire, 1261–1453. Its emperors included MICHAEL VIII, Andronicus II, JOHN V, JOHN VII, JOHN VIII, and CONSTANTINE XI. Noted for learning, the family helped the Greeks to retain their culture under Turkish rule.

**palaeontology:** see FOSSIL.

**Palamas, Kostis,** 1859–1943, Greek poet. He produced epics, lyrics, plays, and short stories in demotic (vernacular) Greek. They include *Royal Blossom* (1903), a lyric drama; *Life Immovable* (1904), poems; and *The King's Flute* (1910), a historical epic.

**Palatinate** (pəˌlatinət), two regions of West Germany. The Rhenish or Lower Palatinate is a district of the state of Rhineland-Palatinate. The Upper Palatinate is a district in NE Bavaria. Holy Roman Emperor FREDERICK I bestowed (1156) the title count palatine on his half-brother Conrad, who held lands E and W of the Rhine. In 1214 the Palatine passed to the Bavarian WITTELSBACH dynasty, whose holdings near Bohemia were constituted as the Upper Palatinate. In 1356 the palatine were confirmed as electors. The Rhenish Palatine became a centre of the German REFORMATION, and the choice of Elector Frederick V (see FREDERICK THE WINTER KING) as king of Bohemia precipitated the THIRTY YEARS WAR. Both the Rhenish Palatinate and the Upper Palatinate eventually became parts of Bavaria. In 1946 the Rhenish Palatinate became part of the new state of Rhineland-Palatinate.

**Palau:** see BELAU.

**Pale,** in Irish history, the area around Dublin under English rule. The term was first used in the 14th cent., and disappeared as England extended its control over all Ireland. Another English pale existed around CALAIS in France until 1558. In Russia the pale designated areas where Jews could live, created from land gained (1792) from the partition of Poland.

**Palembang,** city (1980 pop. 786,000), capital of South Sumatra Province, on SE Sumatra, Indonesia. A deepwater port, it is one of the island's largest cities, and the trade and shipping centre for the S SUMATRA oil fields. There are large oil refineries, textile mills, fertilizer factories, and food-processing plants. The Dutch began trading there in 1617, and abolished its sultanate in 1825.

**Palermo,** city (1984 pop. 716,149), capital, largest city, and chief port of Sicily, Italy. Manufactures include textiles and ships. A Phoenician town founded between the 8th and 6th cent. BC, and a Carthaginian base, it was taken by Rome (153 BC). Later rulers included Byzantines (535–831), Arabs (831–1072), and Normans (1072–1194), whose legacies are visible in its art and architecture.

**Palestine,** historic region on the eastern shore of the Mediterranean Sea, comprising parts of modern Israel, Jordan, and a small portion of southern Syria; also known as the Holy Land. This article discusses the physical geography and history of Palestine until the UN took up the Palestine problem in 1947; for the economy and later history, see ISRAEL and JORDAN. Palestine is the Holy Land of the Jews, having been promised to them by God; of the Christians because it was the scene of Jesus' life; and of the Muslims because Jerusalem is the traditional site of Muhammad's ascent to heaven. Palestine comprises four physical or geographical regions: the coastal plain from Tyre to El Arish, the hill regions of GALILEE, SAMARIA and JUDAEA, a portion of the GREAT RIFT VALLEY including the Jordan R. and the DEAD SEA, and in the E the hill districts of the GOLAN HEIGHTS, Gilead, Moab, and Edom. The earliest known settlements in Palestine, e.g., JERICHO, may date from c.8000 BC An independent Hebrew kingdom was established c.1000 BC. After c.950 BC this kingdom broke up into two states, Israel and Judah. Assyrians, Babylonians, Persians, Greeks, and Romans in turn conquered Palestine, which fell to the Muslim Arabs by AD 640. The area was the focus of the CRUSADES and was conquered by the Ottoman Turks in 1516. By the late 19th cent., ZIONISM arose with the aim of establishing a Jewish homeland in Palestine, and during World War I the British, who captured the area, appeared to support this goal, as evidenced by the Balfour Declaration made in 1917. After the League of Nations approved (1922) the British mandate of Palestine, Jews immigrated there in large numbers despite Arab opposition. There was tension and violence between Jews and Arabs, and the British, unable to resolve the problem, turned (1947) the Palestine question over to the UN.

**Palestine Liberation Organization** (PLO), coordinating council for PALESTINE refugee groups, recognized (1974) by the UN and the Arab states as the government of the Palestinians. Founded in 1964, it has been dominated by the Al Fatah guerrilla group of Yasir ARAFAT. The PLO regards ISRAEL as an illegal country and is committed to establishing a Palestinian state. It has committed many acts of TERRORISM. In 1982 the PLO was weakened when, after the Israeli siege of BEIRUT, Lebanon (see ARAB–ISRAELI WARS), some 8500 PLO guerrillas in W Beirut were dispersed to other Arab countries, notably Syria and Tunisia. In the mid-1980s the PLO experienced a serious split between its 'moderate' wing led by Arafat and the more extreme factions. The former was in the ascendant by 1988, when the PLO indicated its willingness to recognize Israel on the basis of a corresponding commitment to a Palestinian state.

**Palestrina, Giovanni Pierluigi da,** c.1525–1594, Italian composer. He was undisputed master of the MASS, of which he wrote 105, for four, five, six, and eight parts. His other works included MOTETS, MADRIGALS, magnificats, offertories, litanies, and settings of the Song of Songs.

**Palgrave, Francis Turner,** 1824–97, English poet and anthologist. His fame rests on *The Golden Treasury of the Best Songs and Lyrical Poems in the English Language* (1861), a pioneer in anthologies for the general reader, although it omitted DONNE and BLAKE.

**Pali** (,pahlee), language belonging to the Indic group of the Indo-Iranian subfamily of the Indo-European family of languages. See LANGUAGE (table).

**Palissy, Bernard** (pahlee,see), c.1510–c.1590, French potter. Palissy created a widely imitated earthenware, admired for its richly coloured lead-glazes. He is noted for pieces reproducing scriptural and mythological subjects and for rustic pieces with forms copied from nature, reptiles, insects, plants. Few pieces can be firmly associated with him.

**Palladio, Andrea** (pal,lahdeeoh), 1508–80, Italian Renaissance architect. His measured drawings of ROMAN ARCHITECTURE, with plans of his own and a treatise based on Vitruvius, the Roman writer, were published in *The Four Books of Architecture* (1570). Palladio's formally classic buildings were mainly palaces and villas in or near Vicenza. The country houses displayed a classic temple front, and the ground plan had a central hall surrounded by rooms in absolute symmetry. Noted examples (1550s–60s) are the Villa Rotunda, Chiericati Palace, and Villa Barbaro. At Venice, Palladio adapted the classical motif to three famous church facades—San Francesco della Vigna, San Giorgio Maggiore, and Il Redentore. Palladio's works greatly influenced English architecture, through Inigo JONES and others. The term **Palladian** is used to describe works in or reminiscent of his style.

Andrea **Palladio's** Villa Rotunda

**palladium,** (Pd), metallic element, discovered in 1803 by William WOLLASTON. It is a lustrous, corrosion-resistant, silver-white metal with a great ability to absorb hydrogen. Major uses are in alloys used in low-current electrical contacts, jewellery, dentistry, and increasingly, along with platinum and rhodium, in car-exhaust catalysts for emission control. See ELEMENT (table); PERIODIC TABLE.

**palm,** common name for the Palmae, or the Arecaceae, a large family of chiefly tropical trees, shrubs, and vines. Most species are trees, typified by a crown of compound leaves (fronds) terminating a tall, woody, unbranched stem. The fruits, covered with a tough, fleshy, fibrous, or leathery outer layer, usually contain a large amount of stored food. Important economically, especially in the tropics, palms, e.g., COCONUT and DATE palms, provide food and other products. Important palm fibres are raffia and RATTAN. **Palm oil** is fat pressed from the fruit, principally that of the coconut palm, African oil palm (genus *Elaeis*), and some other species. The oils are widely used in soap, candles, lubricants, margarine, fuel, and other products.

**Palma:** see MAJORCA.

**Palma Nova,** town (1984 pop. c.6000) Venezia, NE Italy. It is a perfect example of the 16th-cent. search for the ideal city layout. Palma Nova was begun in 1593 to a design that is usually attributed to Vincenzo Scamozzi. It is radial-concentric in plan with star-shaped fortifications.

**Palme, Olof** (,palmə), 1927–86, prime minister of SWEDEN (1969–76, 1982–86). Head of the Social Democratic Party, he led Sweden's rejection (1971) of EUROPEAN COMMUNITY membership and was sharply critical of US policy in Vietnam. In 1982 Palme again became prime minister after his party won the parliamentary elections. He was shot dead in a Stockholm street (1986) by an assailant whose identity and motivation became the subject of protracted police inquiries.

**Palmer, Arnold,** 1929–, American golfer. Winner of seven major championships, he popularized modern golf with his stirring victories in the 1960s. Cheered on by 'Arnie's army', as his fans were known, he was the first golfer to win four Masters titles (1958, 1960, 1962, 1964). He also captured the US Open (1960) and British Open (1961–62) while becoming the first golfer to reach $1 million in earnings.

**Palmer, Samuel,** 1805–81, English painter and etcher. His pastoral landscapes, as *A Hilly Scene* (c.1826–28; Tate Gall., London), evoke an intensely personal visionary world. Palmer is best known for works painted at Shoreham, Kent (1827–35), when he became the leader of the ancients, a group of artists inspired by William BLAKE. His work influenced many 20th-cent. British painters, especially the Neo-Romantics (see ROMANTICISM) of the 1940s.

**Palmerston, Henry John Temple,** 3rd **Viscount,** 1784–1865, British statesman. He first took office under CANNING, but established his reputation as foreign secretary (1830–34; 1835–41; 1846–51), in Whig governments. He had a remarkable grasp of foreign affairs, and while supporting liberal constitutionalism at home and abroad, he was at pains to identify and to defend what he took to be national interests. Twice prime minister (1855–58; 1859–65), he vigorously prosecuted the CRIMEAN WAR, facilitated the unification of Italy, and suppressed the INDIAN MUTINY. He had many critics, including Queen VICTORIA and ALBERT, but his style of diplomacy, however controversial, advanced British prestige. He held back parliamentary reform, and his death opened up a new phase in Britain's politics.

**Palm Sunday:** see LENT.

**Palmyra,** ancient city of central Syria, NE of Damascus, traditionally founded by SOLOMON. A trade centre, it gradually expanded and became a powerful state after the Romans established control (AD c.30). Its ambitious queen, Zenobia, provoked a Roman expedition (AD 272), which partly destroyed Palmyra. The city declined, and after being sacked by TAMERLANE, it fell into ruins.

**Palomar Observatory,** astronomical observatory located at an altitude of 1680 m (5500 ft) on Palomar Mt, NE of San Diego, California, and operated by the California Institute of Technology. Its primary instrument is the 200-in. (500-cm) Hale reflector, which was the largest in the world at the time of its completion (1948). Its 48-in (120-cm) Schmidt camera telescope was used to prepare a monumental photographic atlas of about three-quarters of the entire sky.

**Pampas,** c.777,000 km² (300,000 sq mi), grassy plains of temperate S South America, extending from the **Pampa** (c.647,500 km²/250,000 sq mi) of central and N Argentina into Uruguay. Livestock and wheat are produced in the drier west, while corn and more intensive forms of agriculture predominate in the more populous and humid east. BUENOS AIRES is the main shipping point. The Pampa is associated with the gaucho, the Argentine cowboy.

**Pamplona,** city (1981 pop. 183,126), capital of Navarre prov., N Spain, and of the former Pyrenean kingdom of NAVARRE. It is a market centre, with confectionery and furniture-making industries. Many visitors are drawn to the city on the feast of San Fermin (7 July) when bulls are let loose to pursue young men through the streets to the bull-ring.

**Pan,** in Greek mythology, pastoral god of fertility; worshipped principally in ARCADIA. He was depicted as a merry, ugly man with a goat's horns, ears, and legs. All his myths deal with his amorous affairs. He came to be associated with the Greek DIONYSUS and the Roman FAUNUS, both fertility gods.

**Panama,** Span. *Panamá,* officially Republic of Panama, republic (1987 est. pop. 2,250,000), 75,650 km² (29,209 sq mi), on the Isthmus of Panama, which connects Central and South America; bordered by Costa Rica (E), the Caribbean Sea (N), Colombia (W), and the Pacific Ocean (S). The capital is PANAMA CITY. There are mountains in the E and W, and lowlands along both coasts. The PANAMA CANAL, which cuts through low hills in the central area, bisects the country. The nation has varied industries and promising mineral deposits, but its exports (bananas, shrimp, sugar, and petroleum derivatives) lag far behind its imports. The canal provides 25% of national income and much employment. In 1983 GDP was US$4310 million or US$2155 per capita. Panama is a Spanish-speaking, Roman Catholic country with a mestizo majority.

*History.* Spaniards founded settlements on the north coast before 1513, when Vasco Núñez de BALBOA crossed the isthmus and discovered the Pacific. This discovery of the short distance from sea to sea has dominated Panama's history ever since. Soon the isthmus became the route by which silver from PERU reached the Atlantic in colonial times; later it was crossed by US gold prospectors travelling to California after 1849. Long a part of COLOMBIA, in 1903 Panama supported by the US, which wanted to build a canal across the isthmus, revolted and became a separate republic. The Panama Canal was completed in 1914. Internal politics have been stormy, with many changes of administration. Following a military coup in 1968 a left-leaning regime was established, dominated by Gen. Omar TORRIJOS HERRERA (commander of the National Guard) until his death in 1981 and later by his successor, Gen. Manuel Antonio NORIEGA. After much agitation and prolonged negotiations, the US turned over the Canal Zone to Panama in 1979 and agreed to eventual (in the year 2000) Panamanian control of the canal itself. In the 1980s the National Guard has continued to exert political power, bringing about several changes of president. Elections in 1984 were won by Ardito Barletta of the Revolutionary Democratic Party, but he was obliged to resign in 1985 in favour of his vice president, Eric Arturo del Valle (Republican Party). The latter was in turn dismissed in early 1988, amid a major political crisis centring on internal and US attempts to depose Gen. Noriega (because of his alleged involvement in drug-trafficking), who nevertheless remained in effective power.

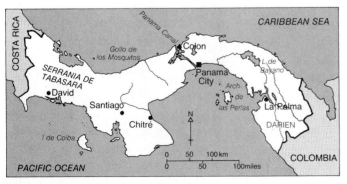

Panama

**Panama Canal,** waterway across the Isthmus of Panama, connecting the Atlantic (by way of the CARIBBEAN SEA) and Pacific Oceans. It was built by US military engineers in 1904–14 across land leased from the Republic

of PANAMA. The eradication of malaria and yellow fever in the area was a vital accomplishment. The canal is 51 mi (82 km) long, has six locks, and traverses two natural lakes, one of which is 26 m (85 ft) above sea level. With the development after 1950 of supertankers and other ships too large to navigate the canal, it lost some of its earlier strategic importance. The **Panama Canal Zone** (1432 km²/553 sq mi), which extends 8 km (5 mi) on either side of the canal, was administered by the US until 1979, when it was turned over to Panama under the terms of two US–Panamanian treaties narrowly ratified (1978) by the US Senate. In the year 2000, control of the canal itself is to pass to Panama, with that nation guaranteeing the neutral operation of the canal.

**Panama City,** city (1980 pop. 388,638), central Panama, capital of Panama, on the Gulf of Panama, at the Pacific entrance to the PANAMA CANAL. Panama's largest city and an industrial hub, it was in Spanish colonial days the Pacific port for the export of Andean silver. Panama City prospered with the building of the canal (1904–14) and grew rapidly after World War II.

**Pan-American Union:** see ORGANIZATION OF AMERICAN STATES.

**Panathenaea:** see ATHENA.

**Panchatantra,** anonymous collection of Sanskrit animal fables, probably compiled before AD 500. Derived from Buddhist sources and intended for the instruction of sons of royalty, the prose fables are interspersed with aphoristic verse.

**pancreas,** glandular organ of the DIGESTIVE SYSTEM that secretes digestive enzymes and hormones. In humans, the pancreas is a yellowish organ that lies crosswise beneath the stomach and is connected to the small intestine at the duodenum. It produces trypsin, amylase, and lipase enzymes essential to the digestion of proteins, carbohydrates, and fats, respectively. Small groups of cells in the pancreas, called islets of Langerhans, secrete two hormones, INSULIN and glucagon, which regulate blood-sugar levels.

**panda,** two nocturnal Asian MAMMALs, the red panda (*Ailurus fulgens*) and giant panda (*Ailuropoda melanoleuca*). The red panda, or lesser panda, resembles a RACCOON and is found in the Himalayas and the mountains of W China and N Burma. The giant panda resembles a BEAR, although it is anatomically more like a raccoon; it lives in the high bamboo forests of central China. Its body is mostly white, with black limbs, ears, and eye patches; adults weigh from 90 to 140 kg (200 to 300 lb). The destruction of its habitat is endangering the giant panda, and zoos all over the world are trying to set up a breeding programme, only China having had much success.

**Pandora,** in Greek mythology, first woman on earth. ZEUS ordered her creation as vengeance on man and his benefactor, PROMETHEUS, to whose brother Epimetheus he sent her. Zeus gave her a box that he forbade her to open. She disobeyed and let out all the world's evils. Only Hope remained in the box.

**Panduro, Leif,** 1923–77, Danish writer and dramatist, a dentist by profession. He was an innovator in Danish drama of the 1960s and 1970s, especially with his plays for television, which were refreshingly iconoclastic. His best-known novel is *Screw Traditions!* (1958), and his best-known play is *Adam's World* (1973).

**Pangaea:** see CONTINENTAL DRIFT; PLATE TECTONICS.

**panic,** financial and economic crisis, marked by public loss of confidence in the financial structure. Panics are characterized by runs on banks and a rapid fall of the securities market. Bank failures and bankruptcies ensue. Perhaps the earliest panic of modern capitalism occurred in France and England in 1720, touched off by wild speculation in the stock of John LAW's colonizing company. Panics occurred in the US in 1819, 1837, 1857, 1869, 1873, 1907, and 1929, when the stockmarket crash precipitated a worldwide financial crisis and led to the GREAT DEPRESSION. A more recent example occurred in Oct. 1987, when stockmarkets all round the world experienced disastrous falls.

**Panini,** fl.500 BC, Indian grammarian. He wrote probably the earliest existing grammatical treatise and scientific work on an Indo-European language, SANSKRIT. Many of the features of present-day descriptive linguistics can be traced back to his work, the *Astadhyayi.*

**Panizzi, Sir Anthony** (pa‚neetsee), 1797–1879, English librarian; b. Italy. He was chief librarian at the BRITISH MUSEUM (1856–67). His 91 rules (1839) became the basis of the museum's CATALOGUE. Panizzi enforced the act requiring deposition at the museum of all books copyrighted in Great Britain (see COPYRIGHT LIBRARY).

**Pankhurst, Emmeline Goulden,** 1858–1928, English suffragette. She founded (1903) the Women's Social and Political Union and urged extreme militancy in the furtherance of women's rights. In 1912–13 she was repeatedly arrested and imprisoned under the 'CAT AND MOUSE ACT'. During World War I she turned her energies from the women's movement to the patriotic war effort, along with other leading members of the WSPU, although some sections of the movement continued to agitate for the vote and for pacifism. See WOMEN'S SUFFRAGE. Her daughter **Sylvia Pankhurst,** 1882–1960, was a suffragette and prominent activist in the WOMEN'S SOCIAL AND POLITICAL UNION, until a political split with her mother and sister Christabel. A socialist, she set up the East London Federation of Suffragettes, which worked in cooperation with the Labour Party. It established community restaurants, a baby clinic, and small-scale factories and day nurseries for working mothers. During World War I she was a pacifist and joined with other anti-war feminists in Europe and the US to organize a Women's International Congress for Peace (1915) in The Hague, which attempted to persuade heads of governments to end the war.

**Panmunjom,** village, in the demilitarized zone between North and South Korea. In the KOREAN WAR negotiations were moved to Panmunjom in Oct. 1951 and the truce was signed on 27 July 1953. In 1976, after two US soldiers were killed there by North Koreans, the joint security area at Panmunjom was partitioned by North Korea and the UN command.

**pansy:** see VIOLET.

**pantanal,** vast swampland area in W Brazil along its border with Bolivia. It remains one of the world's largest wildlife preserves that is still only partially accessible to the visitor. Within these open and seasonally flooded plains are 600 species of birds, 350 varieties of fish and a rich range of animal life. Over large areas this wild fauna has been able to coexist with extensive cattle grazing.

**pantheism** [Gr. *pan* = all, *theos* = God], any system of belief or speculation that identifies the universe with GOD. Some pantheists view God as primary and the universe as a finite and temporal emanation from Him; others see nature as the great, inclusive unity. The various types of pantheism have religious, philosophical, scientific, and poetic bases. HINDUISM is a noteworthy form of religious pantheism; philosophical pantheism is most completely represented in the monistic system of SPINOZA.

**pantheon,** term applied originally to a temple to all the gods. The **Pantheon,** Rome (built 27 BC, destroyed, and rebuilt in the 2nd cent AD by HADRIAN), is of brick with a great hemispherical dome. In 609 it became a Christian church. The term is now applied to a monument in which the illustrious dead are buried. The **Panthéon,** Paris, designed by J.G. Soufflot, was built between 1764 and 1781. Several times secularized and reconsecrated, it became finally a national mausoleum.

Interior of the **Pantheon,** Rome

**panther,** name commonly applied to black LEOPARDS, a colour variant of the leopard, not a distinct species. The generic name *Panthera* refers to all big roaring cats.

**pantomime** or **mime,** silent drama using movement, gesture, and facial expression to develop a story. Although pantomime dates from ancient times, its traditional characters (e.g., Columbine and Harlequin) have their origin in the 16th-cent. Italian COMMEDIA DELL' ARTE. Popular modern pantomimists include Charlie CHAPLIN and Marcel MARCEAU.

**Paoli, Pasquale** (‚pahohlee), 1725–1807, Corsican patriot. In 1755 he led a revolt against Genoese rule and was chosen president of CORSICA under a republican constitution. Genoa sold its rights to Corsica to the French, who defeated Paoli in 1769. He then fled to England. During the FRENCH REVOLUTION he was named (1791) governor of Corsica, but he opposed the radical turn of the revolution and with British aid drove (1794) the French from the island. A British protectorate was proclaimed, but Paoli was disappointed in his hope of becoming viceroy. In 1795 he went to England, where he died. The Corsicans, with help from the French, expelled the British in 1796.

**Paolozzi, Eduardo,** 1924–, British sculptor and painter. Influenced by DADA and SURREALISM in the late 1940s, he produced collages of juxtaposed images taken from popular sources and regarded them as ready-made metaphors of the popular dream of the masses. With these works he became one of the first exponents of English POP ART. His sculptures of the 50s and 60s were large figures made up of casts of machinery and later works of the 70s were large machine-like masses.

*Cyclops* by Eduard **Paolozzi** (Tate Gallery, London)

**papacy,** office of the pope, head of the ROMAN CATHOLIC CHURCH. The pope is bishop of Rome and thus, according to Roman Catholic belief, the successor of St PETER, the first bishop of the see of Rome (the Holy See). The pope claims to be head of all Christianity and the representative of Christ, a claim not accepted by the ORTHODOX EASTERN CHURCH and

## CHRONOLOGY OF POPES

*In the following list, the date of election, rather than of consecration, is given. Before St Victor I (189), dates may err by one year. Anitpopes—i.e., those men whose elections have been declared uncanonical—are indicated.*

St Peter, d. 64? or 67?
St Linus, 67?–76?
St Cletus, or Anacletus, 76?–88?
St Clement I, 88?–97?
St Evaristus, 97?–105?
St Alexander I, 105?–115?
St Sixtus I, 115?–125?
St Telesphorus, 125?–136?
St Hyginus, 136?–140?
St Pius I, 140?–155?
St Anicetus, 155?–166?
St Soter, 166?–175?
St Eleutherius, 175?–189?
St Victor I, 189–99
St Zephyrinus, 199–217
St Calixtus I, 217–22
*antipope:* St Hippolytus, 217–35
St Urban I, 222–30
St Pontian, 230–35
St Anterus, 235–36
St Fabian, 236–50
St Cornelius, 251–53
*antipope:* Novatian, 251
St Lucius I, 253–54
St Stephen I, 254–57
St Sixtus II, 257–58
St Dionysius, 259–68
St Felix I, 269–74
St Eutychian, 275–83
St Caius, 283–96
St Marcellinus, 296–304
St Marcellus I, c.308–309
St Eusebius, 309–c.310
St Miltiades, or Melchiades, 311–14
St Sylvester I, 314–35
St Marcus, 336
St Julius I, 337–52
Liberius, 352–66
*antipope:* Felix, 355–65
St Damasus I, 366–84
*antipope:* Ursinus, 366–67
St Siricius, 384–99
St Anastasius I, 399–401
St Innocent I, 401–17
St Zosimus, 417–18
St Boniface I, 418–22
*antipope:* Eulalius, 418–19
St Celestine I, 422–32
St Sixtus III, 432–40
St Leo I, 440–61
St Hilary, 461–68
St Simplicius, 468–83
St Felix III (or II), 483–92
St Gelasius I, 492–96
Anastasius II, 496–98
St Symmachus, 498–514
*antipope:* Lawrence, 498–505
St Hormisdas, 514–23
St John I, 523–26

St Felix IV (or III), 526–30
Boniface II, 530–32
*pope or antipope:* Dioscurus, 530
John II, 533–35
St Agapetus I, 535–36
St Silverius, 536–37
Vigilius, 537–55
Pelagius I, 556–61
John III, 561–74
Benedict I, 575–79
Pelagius II, 579–90
St Gregory I, 590–604
Sabinian, 604–06
Boniface III, 607
St Boniface IV, 608–15
St Deusdedit, or Adeodatus I, 615–18
Boniface V, 619–25
Honorius I, 625–38
Severinus, 640
John IV, 640–42
Theodore I, 642–49
St Martin I, 649–55
St Eugene I, 654–57
St Vitalian, 657–72
Adeodatus II, 672–76
Donus, 676–78
St Agatho, 678–81
St Leo II, 682–83
St Benedict II, 684–85
John V, 685–86
Conon, 686–87
*antipope:* Theodore, 687
*antipope:* Paschal, 687
St Sergius I, 687–701
John VI, 701–05
John VII, 705–07
Sisinnius, 708
Constantine, 708–15
St Gregory II, 715–31
St Gregory III, 731–41
St Zacharias, 741–52
Stephen II, 752 (never consecrated)
Stephen II (or III), 752–57
St Paul I, 757–67
*antipope:* Constantine, 767–69
*antipope:* Philip, 768
Stephen III (or IV), 768–72
Adrian I, 772–95
St Leo III, 795–816
Stephen IV (or V), 816–17
St Paschal I, 817–24
Eugene II, 824–27
Valentine, 827
Gregory IV, 827–44
*antipope:* John, 844
Sergius II, 844–47
St Leo IV, 847–55
Benedict III, 855–58
*antipope:* Anastasius, 855

St Nicholas I, 858–67
Adrian II, 867–72
John VIII, 872–82
Marinus I, 882–84
St Adrian III, 884–85
Stephen V (or VI), 885–91
Formosus, 891–96
Boniface VI, 896
Stephen VI (or VII), 896–97
Romanus, 897
Theodore II, 897
John IX, 898–900
Benedict IV, 900–03
Leo V, 903
*antipope:* Christopher, 903–04
Sergius III, 904–11
Anastasius III, 911–13
Lando, 913–14
John X, 914–28
Leo VI, 928
Stephen VII (or VIII), 928–31
John XI, 931–35
Leo VII, 936–39
Stephen VIII (or IX), 939–42
Marinus II, 942–46
Agapetus II, 946–55
John XII, 955–64
Leo VIII, 963–65, or Benedict V,
   964–66 (*one of these was an
   antipope*)
John XIII, 965–72
Benedict VI, 973–74
*antipope:* Boniface VII, 974, 984–85
Benedict VII, 974–83
John XIV, 983–84
John XV, 985–96
Gregory V, 996–99
*antipope:* John XVI, 997–98
Sylvester II, 999–1003
John XVII, 1003
John XVIII, 1004–09
Sergius IV, 1009–12
Benedict VIII, 1012–24
*antipope:* Gregory, 1012
John XIX, 1024–32
Benedict IX, 1032–44
Sylvester III, 1045
Benedict IX, 1045
Gregory VI, 1045–46
Clement II, 1046–47
Benedict IX, 1047–48
Damasus II, 1048
St Leo IX, 1049–54
Victor II, 1055–57
Stephen IX (or X), 1057–58
*antipope:* Benedict X, 1058–59
Nicholas II, 1059–61
Alexander II, 1061–73
*antipope:* Honorius II, 1061–72

St Gregory VII, 1073–85
*antipope:* Clement III, 1080–1100
Victor III, 1086–87
Urban II, 1088–99
Paschal II, 1099–1118
*antipope:* Theodoric, 1100
*antipope:* Albert, 1102
*antipope:* Sylvester IV, 1105–11
Gelasius II, 1118–19
*antipope:* Gregory VIII, 1118–21
Calixtus II, 1119–24
Honorius II, 1124–30
*antipope:* Celestine II, 1124
Innocent II, 1130–43
*antipope:* Anacletus II, 1130–38
*antipope:* Victor IV, 1138
Celestine II, 1143–44
Lucius II, 1144–45
Eugene III, 1145–53
Anastasius IV, 1153–54
Adrian IV, 1154–59
Alexander III, 1159–81
*antipope:* Victor IV, 1159–64
*antipope:* Paschal III, 1164–68
*antipope:* Calixtus III, 1168–78
*antipope:* Innocent III, 1179–80
Lucius III, 1181–85
Urban III, 1185–87
Gregory VIII, 1187
Clement III, 1187–91
Celestine III, 1191–98
Innocent III, 1198–1216
Honorius III, 1216–27
Gregory IX, 1227–41
Celestine IV, 1241
Innocent IV, 1243–54
Alexander IV, 1254–61
Urban IV, 1261–64
Clement IV, 1265–68
Gregory X, 1271–76
Innocent V, 1276
Adrian V, 1276
John XXI, 1276–77
Nicholas III, 1277–80
Martin IV, 1281–85
Honorius IV, 1285–87
Nicholas IV, 1288–92
St Celestine V, 1294
Boniface VIII, 1294–1303
Benedict XI, 1303–04
Clement V, 1304–14
John XXII, 1316–34
*antipope:* Nicholas V, 1328–30
Benedict XII, 1334–42
Clement VI, 1342–52
Innocent VI, 1352–62
Urban V, 1362–70
Gregory XI, 1370–78

## The Great Schism, 1378–1417

Roman Line
 Urban VI, 1378–89
 Boniface IX, 1389–1404
 Innocent VII, 1404–06
 Gregory XII, 1406–15
Avignon Line
 *antipope:* Clement VII, 1378–94
 *antipope:* Benedict XIII,
  · 1394–1423
 *antipope:* Clement VII, 1423–29
 *antipope:* Benedict XIV, 1425–30
Pisan Line
 *antipope:* Alexander V, 1409–10
 *antipope:* John XXIII, 1410–15
Martin V, 1417–31
Eugene IV, 1431–47
*antipope:* Felix V, 1439–49
Nicholas V, 1447–55
Calixtus III, 1455–58

Pius II, 1458–64
Paul II, 1464–71
Sixtus IV, 1471–84
Innocent VIII, 1484–92
Alexander VI, 1492–1503
Pius III, 1503
Julius II, 1503–13
Leo X, 1513–21
Adrian VI, 1522–23
Clement VII, 1523–34
Paul III, 1534–49
Julius III, 1550–55
Marcellus II, 1555
Paul IV, 1555–59
Pius IV, 1559–65
St Pius V, 1566–72
Gregory XIII, 1572–85
Sixtus V, 1585–90
Urban VII, 1590

Gregory XIV, 1590–91
Innocent IX, 1591
Clement VIII, 1592–1605
Leo XI, 1605
Paul V, 1605–21
Gregory XV, 1621–23
Urban VIII, 1623–44
Innocent X, 1644–55
Alexander VII, 1655–67
Clement IX, 1667–69
Clement X, 1670–76
Innocent XI, 1676–89
Alexander VIII, 1689–91
Innocent XII, 1691–1700
Clement XI, 1700–21
Innocent XIII, 1721–24
Benedict XIII, 1724–30
Clement XII, 1730–40
Benedict XIV, 1740–58

Clement XIII, 1758–69
Clement XIV, 1769–74
Pius VI, 1775–99
Pius VII, 1800–23
Leo XII, 1823–29
Pius VIII, 1829–30
Gregory XVI, 1831–46
Pius IX, 1846–78
Leo XIII, 1878–1903
St Pius X, 1903–14
Benedict XV, 1914–22
Pius XI, 1922–39
Pius XII, 1939–58
John XXIII, 1958–63
Paul VI, 1963–78
John Paul I, 1978
John Paul II, 1978–

Protestant churches. Roman Catholics believe in papal INFALLIBILITY. On the death of a pope, a new pope is elected by the college of CARDINALS in a secret conclave. Election requires a two-thirds vote plus one. Early popes, including (some claim) CLEMENT I, asserted their right to guide the church, and with the decline of the Roman Empire in the West, the pope became an important political leader. With the founding (756) of the Papal States, the pope became a secular ruler as well. The papacy was surrounded by corruption in the 10th cent., but after the reforms of GREGORY VII in the 11th cent., the popes had great prestige. By the end of the 12th cent. INNOCENT III attempted with some success to assert his claims as arbiter of all temporal affairs. In the 14th cent. the papal see was moved by CLEMENT V to Avignon and came under French control (the Babylonian captivity) from 1309 to 1377. The papacy's return to Rome was followed by the Great SCHISM (1378–1417), in which there were two or three rival popes at one time, a contest ended by the Council of CONSTANCE. In the 15th cent. the popes were characterized by worldly rule in Italy, patronizing Renaissance art, and forwarding family fortunes. This spiritual apathy led to the Protestant REFORMATION. Reform within the church followed the election of PAUL III (see COUNTER-REFORMATION). The loss (1870) of the Papal States proved in the end to be a boon (see LATERAN TREATY) since it made the pope perforce a purely ecclesiastical ruler with great spiritual and moral influence. He now governs only the tiny state of VATICAN CITY. The election of JOHN PAUL II of Poland in 1978 broke the long line of Italian popes that dated from the 16th cent.

**Papadopoulos, George,** 1919–, colonel and political leader in GREECE. He headed the military junta that overthrew the government in 1967. He became premier and ruled over an authoritarian government. In 1973 he abolished the monarchy and became president. Following the return to democracy (1974), Papadopoulos was (1975) sentenced to life imprisonment for high treason in having initiated the 1967 coup.

**Papago Indians:** see NORTH AMERICAN INDIANS.

**Papal States,** from 754 to 1870 the territory under temporal rule of the popes. In 1859 the area included c. 41,440 km² (16,000 sq mi). In 754 the papacy received extensive lands in central Italy, including RAVENNA, from PEPIN THE SHORT. Papal rule in these areas was often negligible, but in the 16th cent. Pope JULIUS II consolidated papal power. NAPOLEON I conquered the Papal States in 1796, but they were restored to the pope in 1815. During the RISORGIMENTO most of the Papal States joined (1860) Sardinia and became part of the new kingdom of Italy. The rest of the area came under French protection. The fall of NAPOLEON III in France allowed Italy to seize (1870) the remaining territory, including Rome. The status of Rome was not settled until the LATERAN TREATY (1929) created VATICAN CITY.

**Papandreou, Andreas,** 1919–, prime minister of GREECE (1981–), son of **George Papandreou** (1888–1968), himself a former premier of Greece (1964–65) and founder of the Centre Union Party (1961). Having held US citizenship for a time (1944–64), Andreas Papandreou gave it up to serve in the Greek parliament and as an aide to his father. He was imprisoned after the 1967 coup and later exiled. While in exile he formed what later became the Panhellenic Socialist Movement (Pasok). He returned to Greece after the fall (1974) of the junta. In 1981 he became premier and began a widespread reform programme, while abandoning his party's commitment to withdrawal from the NORTH ATLANTIC TREATY ORGANIZATION and the EUROPEAN COMMUNITY. In 1988 he announced his intention to divorce his wife in order to marry his 33-year-old mistress, Dimitra Liani.

**Papen, Franz von,** 1879–1969, German diplomat and politician. In 1932 he was named chancellor, but he was unable to assemble enough support and Kurt von Schleicher quickly succeeded him. His manipulations behind the scenes brought HITLER to power (1933). He served briefly as vice chancellor in Hitler's cabinet and as his ambassador to Turkey (1939–44). In 1946 the Nuremburg tribunal acquitted him of WAR CRIMES; he was convicted (1947) by a German 'denazification court', although the sentence was later rescinded.

**paper,** thin, flat sheet usually made from plant fibre. It was probably invented c.105 in China, where it was made from a mixture of bark and hemp. The Moors introduced the papermaking process into Spain c.1150, and by the 15th-cent., when PRINTING developed in Europe, paper mills had spread throughout the Continent. The basic papermaking process exploits the ability of plant cell fibres to bond together when a pulp made from the fibres is spread on a screen and dried. Today, paper

is made principally from wood pulp combined with pulps from waste paper or, for fine grades of paper, with fibres from cotton rags. For newsprint, tissue, and other inexpensive papers, the pulp is prepared mechanically, by grinding the wood. Chemical pulp is made by boiling a mixture of wood chips with either soda, sulphite, or sulphate, a process that removes lignin. The pulp is poured onto a wire screen, where the water drains away and the fibres begin to mat. The paper layer then passes through a series of rollers that dry, press, and smooth it, and add various finishes. Writing papers contain a water-resistant substance such as rosin to prevent the spreading of ink.

**Papineau, Louis Joseph** (papee͵noh), 1786–1871, French Canadian insurgent leader. As speaker (1815–37) of Lower CANADA's assembly, he headed the Reform Party, and though inactive in the revolt of 1837, he fled to the US after it was put down. He later returned (1845) to Canada and served again (1848–54) in the assembly.

**Papinian (Aemilius Papinianus),** d. 212, Roman jurist. A stern moralist, he became known through his writings, chiefly *Quaestiones* (37 books) and *Responsa* (19 books), as the pre-eminent figure in ROMAN LAW.

**Papp, Joseph,** 1921–, American director and producer; b. Joseph Papirofsky. A theatrical innovator, he has made fine plays available to large and varied audiences through his New York Shakespeare Festival and the Public Theater in New York City. His major productions include *Hair* (1967), *Sticks and Bones* (1971), *A Chorus Line* (1975), and *The Pirates of Penzance* (1980).

**paprika:** see PEPPER.

**Papua New Guinea,** independent nation (1986 est. pop. 3,625,000), 475,369 km² (183,540 sq mi), SW Pacific Ocean, north of Australia. It includes the eastern half of the mountainous island of NEW GUINEA; the Bismarck Archipelago, including New Britain and New Ireland; Bougainville and Buka, which are part of the W SOLOMON ISLANDS; and other adjacent islands. PORT MORESBY is the capital and chief port. The native population is Melanesian but is divided into many distinct cultures. Pidgin English has become a *lingua franca*. The climate is monsoonal. Mainstays of Papua New Guinea's developing economy include copper and gold mining; timber and plywood; and the cultivation of cocoa, coffee, and copra. Papua, the southern region of the country, became a British protectorate in 1884 and in 1905 passed to Australian control as the Territory of Papua. In 1884 Germany took possession of the northern region as Kaiser-Wilhelmsland; the area fell to Australia in World War I and was mandated to that nation in 1920 as the Territory of New Guinea. The two territories were combined in 1949 as the Territory of Papua and New Guinea, and became self-governing in 1973 and independent in 1975 as a member of the COMMONWEALTH. The nation has a parliamentary government with a governor general, representing the British crown; a prime minister and cabinet; and a unicameral, popularly elected parliament. In 1985 the government of Michael Somare (of the Pangu Pati Party) was replaced by a five-party coalition headed by Paias Wingti.

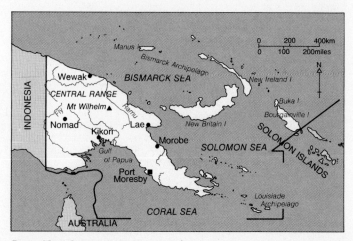

Papua New Guinea

**papyrus,** plant (*Cyperus papyrus*) of the sedge family, now almost extinct in Egypt but universally used there in antiquity. The roots were used as fuel; the pith was eaten. The stem was used for sandals, boats, twine, mats, and cloth, and, most notably, the pith from the flowering stems was used in a paperlike writing material.

**parable,** in the BIBLE, term used in the GOSPELS for short illustrative narratives with an underlying message. OLD TESTAMENT parables include the unproductive vineyard (Isa. 5.1–7). Among well-known parables of JESUS are the Good Samaritan (Luke 10.29–37); the hidden treasure (Mat. 13.44); the prodigal son (Luke 15.11–32); the rich man and LAZARUS (Luke 16.19–31); the tares (Mat. 13.24–30, 36–43); and the labourers in the vineyard (Mat. 20.1–16). Parables are also common in the TALMUD.

**parabola:** see CONIC SECTION.

**Paracel Islands** or **Xi sha qun dao,** group of low coral islands and reefs in the potentially oil-rich South China Sea, c.280 km (175 mi) SE of HAINAN Island. Also claimed by Vietnam, the islands were part of French Indochina prior to World War II, when they were occupied by the Japanese. They passed to China in 1945.

**Paracelsus, Philippus Aureolus,** 1493–1541, Swiss physician and alchemist, originally named Theophrastus Bombastus von Hohenheim. He rejected the authority of Avicenna and GALEN's humoral theory of disease; advocated the use of specific remedies for specific diseases (introducing many chemicals, e.g., laudanum, mercury, sulphur, iron, and lead); and noted relationships, such as the hereditary pattern in syphilis, the association of cretinism with endemic goitre, and the association of paralysis with head injuries. He so outraged his colleagues in Basle that he was forced to wander through Europe preaching medicine based on clinical experience.

**paracetamol,** important ANALGESIC. It has the pain-relieving properties of ASPIRIN and is less irritant to the stomach, but has no anti-inflammatory action. Overdosage can cause liver damage, which can be fatal.

**parachute,** umbrellalike device designed to retard the descent of a falling body by creating drag as it passes through air. A parachute is usually constructed from a flexible material; when extended, it takes the form of an umbrella from which a series of cords converge downward to a harness strapped to the user. It can be folded into a small package and thus can be easily carried aboard an aircraft or strapped onto a person's body. The rate of descent for a human-carrying parachute is about 5.5 m/sec (18 ft/sec). The first successful parachute descent from a great height was made in 1797 by the French aeronaut Jacques Garnerin, who dropped 920 m (3000 ft) from a balloon. Parachutes are used as escape systems for persons aboard aircraft unable to land safely, as braking devices for rockets, space vehicles, aeroplanes, and high speed surface vehicles, and as a means to land airborne military units and their equipment from transport planes. Parachute jumping for sport is known as skydiving.

**paraffin.** 1 see KEROSENE. 2 see PARAFFIN WAX.

**paraffin wax** or **paraffin,** white, semitranslucent, odourless, tasteless, water-insoluble, waxy solid. Though relatively inert, it burns readily in air. A mixture of HYDROCARBONS obtained from PETROLEUM during refining, paraffin is used in candles and for coating paper.

**Paraguay,** officially Republic of Paraguay, republic (1987 est. pop. 3,800,000), 406,752 km² (157,047 sq mi), S central South America, one of two landlocked nations on the continent, enclosed by Bolivia (N, E), Brazil (W), and Argentina (S, E). The most populous region, between the Paraguay and PARANÁ rivers, is a lowland, rising to a plateau region in the E and N. To the W is a dry plain, part of the GRAN CHACO. Important cities include ASUNCIÓN (the capital), Villarrica, and Concepción. Agriculture and forestry occupy more than half of the work force. Meat-packing, processing of vegetable oil and forest products, and textile manufacturing are the main industries. Completion of the Itaipú dam in 1982, which eventually will have a higher generating capacity, at 12,600 megawatts, than any other hydroelectric power plant in the world, make its hydroelectric potential the country's most valuable resource. In 1983 GDP was US$6400 million or US$2133 per capita. The population is largely mestizo, a mixture of Spanish and GUARANÍ INDIAN strains. Spanish is the official language, but Guaraní is widely spoken. Roman Catholicism is the established religion.

*History.* European influence in Paraguay was introduced with the early explorations of the Río de la PLATA, beginning with Juan Diaz de Solís (1516). A colony founded at Asunción (1536 or 1537) became the centre of the La Plata region. The strong rule of Hernando Arias de Saavedra,

in the early 1600s, established Paraguay's virtual independence from Spanish administrators in Buenos Aires and Peru; it was also during his tenure that the Jesuit missions, so important in 16th- to 18th-cent. Paraguayan culture, were founded. Full independence from Spain came in 1811, when Paraguay's colonial officials were quietly overthrown. Then followed three great dictators who moulded the future of the country: José Gaspar Rodríguez de FRANCIA, incorruptible, harsh, autocratic, known as *El Supremo,* kept Paraguay in the palm of his hand from 1814 to 1840; Carlos Antonio López held absolute power from 1844 to 1862; and his son, Francisco Solano LÓPEZ, who ruled from 1862 to 1870, involved Paraguay in a disastrous war (1865–70) with Brazil, Argentina, and Uruguay (see TRIPLE ALLIANCE, WAR OF THE) that cost the nation more than half its population. Recovery was slow, and just as conditions were beginning to improve, Paraguay was plunged into another major war, the Chaco War (1932–35), with Bolivia from which it emerged victorious but exhausted. A rapid succession of governments followed, ending with the oppressive dictatorship (1940–48) of Higinio Morínigo, finally overthrown in 1948. After another round of short-lived regimes, Gen. Alfredo STROESSNER came to power in 1954 and, by suppressing opposition and maintaining a 'state of siege', had by the mid-1980s become S America's longest surviving dictator. In the 1988 elections Stroessner and his National Republican Association–Colorado Party secured a further overwhelming majority over the Liberals. In 1989, however, Stroessner was overthrown by a military coup.

Paraguay

**Paraguay,** river, South America, chief tributary of the PARANÁ R. It flows generally S c.2090 km (1300 mi) from central Brazil along parts of the Brazil, Paraguay, and Argentine borders. It is a major artery in the Río de la PLATA system and is navigable for most of its length. ASUNCIÓN, Paraguay, is the chief port.

**Paralipomenon:** see CHRONICLES.

**parallax,** any alteration in the relative apparent positions of objects produced by a shift in the position of the observer. Stellar parallax is the apparent displacement of a nearby star against the background of more distant stars resulting from the motion of the Earth in its orbit around the Sun; formally, the parallax of a star is the angle at the star that is subtended by the mean distance (1 ASTRONOMICAL UNIT) between the Earth and the Sun. A star's distance $d$ in PARSECS is thus the reciprocal of its parallax $p$ in seconds of arc (or $d = 1/p$). Friedrich BESSEL measured (1838) the first stellar parallax (0.3 seconds of arc for the star 61 Cygni). The stars are so far from us that even the nearest ones have only a parallax of less than one second of arc, and only a few hundred of the myriads of stars have a parallax large enough to be measured. Geocentric parallax, used to determine the distances of solar-system objects, is measured similarly; the diameter of the Earth, rather than that of its orbit, however, is used as the baseline.

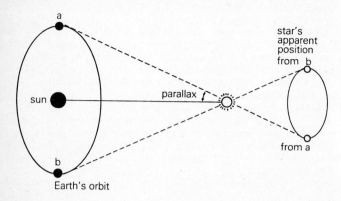

Parallax

**paramagnetism:** see MAGNETISM.

**Paramaribo,** city (1980 pop. 67,905), capital of Suriname, on the Suriname R., 27 km (17 mi) from the Atlantic Ocean. It exports bauxite, sugarcane, rice, shrimp, and hardwoods. Settled in the 1630s by British from Barbados, Paramaribo came under Dutch rule in 1815. Canals give the modern city a Dutch aspect.

**paramecium** or **slipper animalcule** ('parə‚meesyəm), microscopic, one-celled, slipper-shaped animal (genus *Paramecium*), in the phylum PROTOZOA. Paramecia are among the most complex single-celled organisms. Found in fresh water, they swim rapidly, usually in a corkscrew fashion, by means of coordinated, wavelike beats of their many short, hairlike CILIA. Paramecia feed on smaller organisms, such as bacteria.

**Paraná,** river, SE South America. Formed by the confluence of the Paranaíba and Rio Grande rivers in SE Brazil, it flows generally SSW c.3200 km (2000 mi) to meet the Uruguay R. at the head of the Río de la PLATA estuary, in Argentina. Its major tributary is the PARAGUAY R. It is a major transport artery and has the continent's second largest drainage system.

**Paraná,** city (1980 pop. 215,700), NE Argentina, capital of Entre Ríos. It was founded in 1588 on the Paraná R. and was the capital of the Argentine Republic from 1853 to 1862.

**paranoia,** a disturbed mental state, or condition, characterized by excessive and delusional fears and beliefs involving persecution, jealousy and grandiosity. See also SCHIZOPHRENIA.

**parapraxis,** a slip of the tongue, minor loss of memory, or accident of execution which, according to psychoanalytic theory, betrays an UNCONSCIOUS wish or DEFENCE MECHANISM. It is popularly known as a 'Freudian slip'.

**parapsychology,** the study of the paranormal; that is, phenomena inexplicable by reference to known natural laws, otherwise known as psychic phenomena or psi-phenomena. Such phenomena include extrasensory perception (ESP), pyschokinesis (mental influence on physical objects), clairvoyance or precognition, and telepathy. Though a considerable research effort has been devoted to parapsychology, the results of experiments are inconclusive.

**Pará rubber tree,** large tree (*Hevea brasiliensis*) of the SPURGE family, native to tropical South America and the source of the greatest amount and finest quality of natural RUBBER. The yellow or white latex from which rubber is made occurs in vessels in the bark layers. Trees, which may grow over 30 m (100 ft) high, are tapped for the latex.

**parasite,** organism that obtains nourishment from another living organism (the host). The host, which may or may not be harmed, never benefits from the parasite. Many parasites have more than one host and most cannot survive apart from their host; they are carried from one host to another by VECTORS. Parasites include bacteria (e.g., those causing TUBERCULOSIS), invertebrates such as worms (e.g., TAPEWORM), and vertebrates (e.g., the CUCKOO, which lays its eggs in the nests of other birds).

**parasympathetic nervous system:** see NERVOUS SYSTEM.

**parathyroid glands,** two pairs of small yellowish endocrine bodies (see ENDOCRINE SYSTEM) behind the THYROID GLAND that govern calcium and phosphorus metabolism. A low calcium ion concentration in the blood causes these glands to produce parathyroid hormone, or parathormone, which increases calcium absorption in the intestines and kidneys and takes calcium salts from the bones. The hormone also decreases the concentration of phosphate ions, which form a relatively insoluble salt with calcium. High parathormone levels can lead to bone degeneration; low levels lead to calcium deficiency (typified by muscle spasms and, eventually, convulsions and psychiatric symptoms).

**Parcae:** see FATES.

**parchment,** untanned animal skins, especially of sheep, calf, or goat, prepared for use as a writing material. The skins are soaked, scraped, and stretched, then rubbed with chalk and pumice. More durable than the PAPYRUS used in ancient times, parchment was the chief writing material in Europe until the advent of printing brought PAPER into wide use. It is still used for drum skins. Vellum is a fine grade of parchment.

**Pardo Bazán, Emilia, condesa de** (pahdhoh ba‚thahn), 1852–1921, Spanish novelist and critic. In such novels as *Los Pazos de Ulloa* (1886; tr. The Mayor of Ulloa) and *La madre naturaleza* (1887; tr. Mother Nature) she introduced NATURALISM into Spanish literature.

**pardon:** see SENTENCE.

**parenthesis:** see PUNCTUATION.

**Parini, Giuseppe,** 1719–99, Italian poet. The foremost representative of the ENLIGHTENMENT in Italian poetry, he achieved celebrity with *Morning* (1763) and *Noon* (1765), the first two parts of *The Day*, an unfinished satire of the Milanese aristocracy giving a young peer ironic instruction in the day's round of frivolities. In 1771 he wrote a drama, *Ascanio in Alba*, which the young MOZART set to music. The finest of his 19 *Odes* are quietly philosophic or elegantly erotic in theme and manner.

**Paris,** city (1982 pop. 2,188,918; met. area pop. 8,706,963), N central France, the French capital. It is the commercial and industrial focus of France, a major transport hub, and a cultural and intellectual centre of international renown. A beautiful city in which tourism is the main industry, Paris is cut by the Seine River. On its stately, formal right (northern) bank are many of the most fashionable streets and shops, and such landmarks as the ARC DE TRIOMPHE, Place de la Concorde, LOUVRE, and Sacré Coeur. The left bank houses governmental offices and is the site of much of the city's intellectual life. It is known for its old Latin Quarter and for such landmarks as the Sorbonne, the Luxembourg Palace, and the Panthéon. The historic core of Paris is the Île de la Cité, a small island occupied in part by the Palais de Justice and the Cathedral of NOTRE DAME DE PARIS. Above the city rises the EIFFEL TOWER. Paris is divided into 20 *arrondissements* (boroughs) and governed by a mayor. A fishing village when it was conquered (52 BC) by CAESAR, it became an important Roman town. It was a Merovingian capital in the 5th cent. and became the national capital with the accession (987) of Hugh Capet, count of Paris. It flowered as the centre of medieval commerce and SCHOLASTICISM but suffered severely during the HUNDRED YEARS WAR. Paris consistently displayed a rebellious and independent spirit, as in its resistance to Henry IV (1589–93); the first FRONDE (1648–49); the revolutions of 1789, 1830, and 1848; and the COMMUNE OF PARIS (1871). During WORLD WAR II it was occupied (1940–44) by the Germans, but was relatively undamaged.

**Paris** or **Alexander,** in Greek mythology, son of Priam and HECUBA. Because of a prophecy that he would destroy Troy, he was abandoned on Mt Ida, but shepherds rescued him. Later he returned to Troy and was chosen as judge in a dispute among HERA, ATHENA, and APHRODITE. Spurning Hera, who offered him greatness, and Athena, who promised success in war, he awarded the golden apple of discord to Aphrodite, who offered the most beautiful woman in the world. His abduction of that woman, HELEN, caused the TROJAN WAR.

**Paris, Congress of,** 1856, conference held by Great Britain, France, the Ottoman Empire (Turkey), Sardinia, Russia, Austria, and Prussia to negotiate the peace after the CRIMEAN WAR. In the Treaty of Paris that resulted, Russia was forced back to its prewar borders and was made to accept the neutralization of the Black Sea and the placing of the lower Danube R. under international control. Moldavia and Walachia (later Romania) were given quasi-independence under the suzerainty of

Turkey. Turkish integrity was guaranteed, and in return the sultan promised to improve the status of his Christian subjects. The congress also adopted the **Declaration of Paris,** which was the first major effort to codify the international law of the sea. Privateering was banned, contraband was defined and codified, and a blockade was to be legal only when it prevented access to the enemy's coastline. The US, which at first rejected the provisions of the declaration, finally accepted them during the Civil War. Technological advances in the 20th cent. (e.g., submarine warfare) made many of the declaration's provisions inapplicable.

**Paris, Matthew** or **Matthew of Paris,** d. 1259, English historian, a monk of St Albans. He wrote *Chronica majora* [great chronicle], a history of the world (containing a hostile portrait of King JOHN), and *Historia Anglorum,* a history of England.

**Paris, Treaty of,** any of several important treaties signed at or near Paris, France. 1 The Treaty of 1763 was signed by Great Britain, France, and Spain. Together with the Treaty of Hubertusburg it ended the SEVEN YEARS WAR. France lost Canada to Britain, Cuba and the Philippines were restored to Spain, and India in effect passed to Britain. From this treaty dated the colonial and maritime supremacy of Britain. 2 In the Treaty of 1783 Great Britain formally acknowledged the independence of the Thirteen Colonies as the US. The treaty also fixed the boundaries of the new nation. In addition, the warring European powers, Britain against France and Spain, with the Dutch as armed neutrals effected a large-scale peace settlement. Spain reacquired the Floridas and Minorca from Britain, and Britain relinquished its restrictions on the French port of DUNKIRK. Otherwise, the territorial dispositions of the 1763 Treaty of Paris were reaffirmed. 3 The Treaty of 1814, concluded between France on the one hand and Britain, Russia, Austria, and Prussia on the other after the first abdication of NAPOLEON I. Its provisions never went into effect owing to the return of Napoleon from Elba and the resumption of the war. 4 The Treaty of 1815 was signed after Napoleon's final surrender. Many provisions of the treaty of 1814 and the Final Act of the Congress of VIENNA remained binding. France was reduced to its 1790 borders and was forced to pay 700 million francs in reparations plus the costs of an army of occupation for five years. 5 For the Treaty of 1856, see PARIS, CONGRESS OF. 6 For the Treaty of 1898, see SPANISH-AMERICAN WAR. After WORLD WAR I several treaties were signed (1919–20) in or near Paris, the most important of which was the Treaty of VERSAILLES. After WORLD WAR II separate treaties were signed (1947) by the Allies at or near Paris with Italy, Romania, Hungary, Bulgaria, and Finland.

**Paris, University of,** at Paris, France; founded 12th cent. Its first endowed college, opened in 1253 and later called the **Sorbonne,** gained academic and theological distinction during the late Middle Ages and early modern times, the name Sorbonne often being used to designate the university itself. The university was suppressed during the French Revolution and replaced (1808) by a school of the centralized Univ. of France. Reestablished as the Univ. of Paris in 1890, it was divided (1970) into 13 separate, state-supported universities, each with academic autonomy.

**Paris Pacts,** 1954, four international agreements that recognized the full sovereignty of the Federal Republic of GERMANY (West Germany) and brought to an official end the post-WORLD WAR II occupation of that country. Participants were the former Western Allies. West Germany was permitted to rearm within certain limitations and was accepted into the NORTH ATLANTIC TREATY ORGANIZATION; it also became a member of the newly created WESTERN EUROPEAN UNION. A bilateral agreement between France and West Germany giving 'European status' to the SAARLAND was later rejected by the Saarlanders.

**Paris Peace Conference,** 1919: see VERSAILLES, TREATY OF.

**parity,** behaviour of a wavefunction in QUANTUM THEORY when its spatial coordinates are reflected. It is said to have *even* parity if it remains the same and *odd* parity if it changes sign. Up until 1956 it was believed that the parity of the wavefunction describing the evolution of any physical process remained constant (parity conservation). This belief was based on the assumption that the laws of physics are the same in a left-handed coordinate system as in a right-handed system. In 1956 the Chinese-American physicists T.D. Lee and C.N. Yang proposed that this symmetry did not hold for the weak interaction. The first of many experiments confirming this was carried out at Columbia Univ. in 1957 by C.S. Wu and her collaborators on the BETA DECAY of radioactive

cobalt-60. Lee and Yang were awarded the Nobel Prize for physics in 1957. See ELEMENTARY PARTICLES.

**Park, Mungo,** 1771–1806, Scottish explorer. Employed by the African Association to explore the NIGER R., he wrote *Travels in the Interior Districts of Africa* (1799). He was drowned when his party was attacked on the Niger.

**Park Chung Hee,** 1917–79, president (1963–79) of South KOREA. Park took part in the military coup of 1961 and was three times elected president. His rule became increasingly dictatorial, and in 1972 he declared martial law. He was assassinated (1979) by Kim Jae Kyu, head of the Korean Central Intelligence Agency.

**Parker, Charlie 'Bird'** (Charles Christopher Parker, Jr), 1920–55, black American musician and composer. A brilliant improvising saxophonist, he was with Dizzy GILLESPIE the leader of the bop movement in JAZZ.

**Parker, Dorothy (Rothschild),** 1893–1967, American writer and wit. Her light, ironic verse is contained in such volumes as *Enough Rope* (1926) and *Death and Taxes* (1931). She also wrote satirical, often poignant short stories, e.g., 'Big Blonde', collected in *Laments for the Living* (1930) and *Here Lies* (1939).

**Parker, Sir Gilbert,** 1862–1932, Canadian novelist. His works include *Pierre and His People* (1892), *The Seats of the Mighty* (1896), and *The Promised Land* (1928).

**Parker, Matthew,** 1504–75, English prelate, archbishop of Canterbury (1559–75). He was called by Elizabeth I to the see of Canterbury and maintained a distinctly Anglican position between Roman Catholicism and extreme Protestantism. In 1562 he revised the Thirty-nine Articles and later supervised (1563–68) the preparation of the Bishops' Bible.

**Parkes, Sir Henry,** 1815–96, Australian politician; b. England. He arrived in Sydney in 1839 and established a newspaper, the *Empire.* At first an advanced liberal, Parkes became the dominant figure in 19th-cent. colonial politics, and was five times premier of New South Wales (1872-75, 1877, 1878-83, 1887-89, 1889-91). He became known as the 'Father of Federation' for early leadership of the movement that culminated in the creation of a Commonwealth of Australia.

**Parkinson's disease** or **Parkinsonism,** degenerative brain disorder initially characterized by trembling lips and hands and muscular rigidity, later producing body tremors, a shuffling gait, and eventually possible incapacity. The disease may occur as a late result of ENCEPHALITIS, carbon monoxide poisoning, or as a side effect of certain drugs, especially the phenothiazines (see TRANQUILLIZER), but in most cases the cause is unknown. Symptoms, which usually appear after the age of 40, may respond to the drugs L-DOPA (combined with carbidopa to reduce the side effects) and amantadine (an antiviral drug). Emotions may be affected and mental capacity impaired, but assessment of these is difficult because depression often accompanies the disease. Parkinsonism is named after the English surgeon James Parkinson, who first described it in 1817.

**Parkman, Francis,** 1823–93, American historian. He overcame nervous affliction and near-blindness to become a prolific historian. His *Oregon Trail* (1849) is a fascinating, popular account of his journey west in 1846.

**parlement,** chief judicial body in France until 1789. The Parlement of Paris grew out of the Curia Regis [king's court] in the reign (1226–70) of LOUIS IX, and provincial parlements were established from the 15th cent. onward. At first strictly judicial, the parlement gradually gained political power by its function of registering royal edicts before they became law. The parlements joined in the FRONDE (1648–53), an abortive aristocratic revolt against Cardinal MAZARIN. LOUIS XV abolished (1771) them to centralize his political control, but after his death (1774) LOUIS XVI restored the parlements to pacify the privileged classes. In 1787–88 they successfully opposed fiscal reforms and forced Louis XVI to summon the STATES-GENERAL to consider the reforms. As bastions of reaction and privilege, the parlements were abolished early in the FRENCH REVOLUTION.

**Parliament,** legislative assembly of GREAT BRITAIN. It has evolved into the nation's sovereign power, while the monarchy remains sovereign in name only. Technically, it consists of the monarch, the House of Commons, and the House of Lords, but the term usually refers only to the Commons, a democratically elected body of 635 members. The House of Lords is composed of hereditary peers, Anglican prelates, and life members elevated to the peerage for services to the community. Since 1911 it has been able only to revise and delay bills, having lost the power of veto. The House of Commons is presided over by a nonpartisan speaker elected by the Commons. The governing party elects the PRIME MINISTER, the executive head of government, who by modern tradition must be a member of the Commons. The rest of the government's ministers, the CABINET, may be selected from either house. Thus, the executive branch is in effect a committee of the legislature. Elections must be held every five years; the prime minister may call elections earlier, although no more frequently than once a year. If the party in power fails to obtain a parliamentary majority on an important issue, it may be subject to a vote of no confidence: if it loses that it must call a general election. The major parties in Parliament are Conservative, Labour, and the Social and Liberal Democrats. The origins of Parliament go back to the medieval Curia Regis, or great council, a body of noble and ecclesiastical advisers to the monarch that evolved into the House of Lords. In the 13th cent. representatives of the knights and burgesses were also assembled to approve royal acts. Parliamentary power grew slowly in relation to that of the monarchy. During the ENGLISH CIVIL WAR (1642–48) and its aftermath, Parliament gained legislative supremacy over taxation and expenditures. Parliamentary sovereignty was finally affirmed by the GLORIOUS REVOLUTION (1688). Parliamentary constituencies were of grossly unequal size, and many 'rotten boroughs' were in the gift of members of the Lords, who thus exerted a considerable control over the Commons. The need to reform this system, and demands for representation by the new classes created by the INDUSTRIAL REVOLUTION, led in the 19th cent. to passage of REFORM BILLS that greatly extended male suffrage; universal male and female suffrage was granted in the 20th cent. (see REPRESENTATION OF THE PEOPLE ACTS; WOMEN'S SUFFRAGE). In the modern era increased party discipline has led to the demise of the independent member, and although the Commons is still capable of acting as 'the grand inquest of the nation', the balance of power has passed to the prime minister and cabinet, and to extraparliamentary pressure groups, lobbying the state directly.

**Parliamentary Commissioner for Administration:** see OMBUDSMAN.

**parliamentary law,** rules that govern the conduct and operations of law-making assemblies. Clubs, corporate boards, and other private organizations also follow the rules of parliamentary law in their deliberations. In English-speaking countries these rules are based on the practices and traditions of the British Parliament, particularly the House of Commons. In the UK, parliamentary law has been codified in *May's Parliamentary Practice*, first published in 1844 by Thomas Erskine MAY. Parliamentary law in the House of Commons is interpreted by the Speaker of the House. Bristish parliamentary law has been very influential in Commonwealth countries, who have established Constitutional systems on British lines following independence.

**Parma,** city (1984 pop. 177,136) Emilia-Romagna, N Italy. One of the settlements along the VIA EMILIA, it has industries related to the varied agriculture of its surrounding region, including the making of Parmesan cheese and Parma ham. It was established as a colony by the Romans in the 2nd cent. BC. Parma was later in the possession of the Farnese family (1545–1731). Its university dates from the early 16th cent. and the city is rich in church architecture and in paintings by the Italian masters.

**Parmenides,** b. c.515 BC, pre-Socratic Greek philosopher. The founder of the Eleatic school, he held that unchanging being is the material substance of which the universe is composed, and that generation, change, destruction, and motion are all illusions of the senses. His major contribution to philosophy was the method of reasoned proof for assertions. As Europe's first metaphysician he is often known as Father Parmenides.

**Parmigiano** or **Parmigianino** (pahmee͵jahnoh,  -jah͵neenoh), 1503–40, Italian painter and etcher; b. Francesco Mazzola. A mannerist (see MANNERISM) he became noted for the grace and sensuality of his style and for his elongated figures. Representative paintings are the *Vision of St Jerome* (National Gall., London) and *The Marriage of St Catherine* (Parma Gall.). An unusual work is a self-portrait seen in a convex mirror (Vienna). He was among the first to use etching.

**Parnassians** (pah͵naseeənz), group of 19th-cent. French poets, named after their journal the *Parnasse contemporain* (1866–76). It included LECONTE DE LISLE, SULLY-PRUDHOMME, VERLAINE, and HEREDIA. Influenced by GAUTIER and reacting against ROMANTICISM, they strove for faultless workmanship, precise form, and emotional detachment.

Parmigiano, *Vision of St Jerome*. National Gallery, London.

**Parnassós** or **Parnassus,** mountain, c.2430 m (8060 ft) high, Phocis, central Greece. In ancient Greece it was believed sacred to APOLLO and DIONYSUS, and to the MUSES.

**Parnell, Charles Stewart,** 1846–91, Irish nationalist leader. The son of a Protestant landowner, he attached himself to the HOME RULE movement and in 1875 entered the British Parliament. He used filibusters there to stress the gravity of Irish problems, and in Ireland itself his agitation on the IRISH LAND QUESTION led to violence against landlords. Imprisoned (1881–82), he was released after he promised to help check the violence. After flirting with the Conservatives in 1886 he formed an alliance with the Liberal William GLADSTONE, who attempted unsuccessfully to pass the first Home Rule Bill. One of Ireland's most effective and popular leaders, Parnell lost his political influence after being named (1889) a co-respondent in a divorce suit, and died a broken man.

**parole:** see SENTENCE.

**Parr, Catherine,** 1512–48, sixth queen of HENRY VIII of England. She marrried Henry in 1543 and had a beneficial influence on the ageing king. After his death, she married (1547) Thomas SEYMOUR, but died in childbirth.

**parrakeet** or **parakeet,** name for a widespread group of small PARROTS, with generally green plumage, native to Australasia and tropical America and popular as cage birds. The BUDGERIGAR, also called the shell, zebra, or grass, parakeet, is the best known of the true parakeets. The only parrot native to North America was the Carolina parrakeet (*Conuropsis carolinensis*), now extinct.

**parrot,** common name for brilliantly coloured BIRDS of the pantropical order Psittaciformes. Parrots have large heads, short necks, and strong feet with two front and two back toes (for climbing and grasping). Parrots range from the 9-cm (3½-in) pygmy parrot of the South Pacific to the 100-cm (40-in) Amazon parrot of South America. Species include the

PARRAKEETS, COCKATOOS, cockatiels, KAKAPO, and macaws. Parrots are long-lived, and many are popular as cage-birds; some species can learn to mimic speech.

**Parry, Sir (Charles) Hubert (Hastings)**, 1848–1918, British composer, teacher, and writer. He played a major role in the revival of English musical life in the last quarter of the 19th cent. and wrote several important books as well as many compositions. He was director of the Royal College of Music from 1894 and Professor of Music at Oxford University from 1900–08, and one of his pupils was Ralph VAUGHAN WILLIAMS. His five symphonies and finely crafted choral works are rarely performed, with the exception of the Coronation anthem *I was glad* (1902), *Blest Pair of Sirens* (1887), and the magnificent setting of Blake's *Jerusalem* (1916).

**Parry, Sir William Edward**, 1790–1855, British Arctic explorer and rear admiral. In 1818 he accompanied Sir John ROSS on an expedition to find the NORTHWEST PASSAGE, and later he led other attempts (1819–20, 1821–23, 1824–25). The Parry Islands bear his name.

**parsec**, unit of length equal to the distance (206,265 ASTRONOMICAL UNITS; 3.26 LIGHT-YEARS; $1.917 \times 10^{13}$ mi; or $3.086 \times 10^{16}$ m) at which a hypothetical star's PARALLAX would be one second of arc. The distance in parsecs of an object from the earth is thus the reciprocal of the parallax in seconds of the object.

**Parsifal** or **Percivale, Sir**: see ARTHURIAN LEGEND.

**Parsis** or **Parsees**, religious community of India, numbering about 120,000 followers of ZOROASTRIANISM, whose ancestors migrated from Iran in the 7th cent. to escape Muslim persecution. They revere fire and other aspects of nature as manifestation of Ahura Mazdah, the divinity. They have an elaborate fire-ritual as part of their religious practice, for which they are sometimes referred to as 'fire-worshippers'. To avoid contaminating fire, earth, or water, they dispose of their dead by exposing the bodies in circular towers, where vultures devour them.

**parsley**, Mediterranean aromatic herb (*Petroselinum crispum*) of the CARROT family. It has been cultivated since Roman antiquity for its foliage, used as a seasoning and garnish.

**parsnip**, garden plant (*Pastinaca sativa*) of the CARROT family native to the Old World and cultivated since ancient times for its long fleshy, edible root.

**Parsons, Sir Charles Algernon**, 1854–1931, English mechanical engineer. Parsons, son of the Earl of Rosse, was educated at Trinity College, Dublin and St John's College, Cambridge, and in 1877 entered apprenticeship in an engineering company near Newcastle-upon-Tyne. In 1884 he designed and built the first steam TURBINE and in 1889 formed his own company producing turbines that were used to drive electric generators. His love, however, was the sea and he turned his attention to steam turbines for marine propulsion. In 1897 he constructed the first turbine-driven ship, the *Turbinia*, which achieved 20 knots but was limited by the propeller design which was intended for a piston engine. He spent some years redesigning and experimenting with screw propellers. Parsons engines fitted in the *Lusitania* and *Mauritania* developed some 70,000 horsepower.

**Parsons, Talcott**, 1902–79, American sociologist. Parsons's STRUCTURAL FUNCTIONALISM was the dominant school of American postwar sociology until the mid 1970s. Parsons held that all societies can be understood as functional wholes, in which each part performs a role vital to the continuation of the social system. He identified a number of major institutional sites for this process: the family, the educational system, the military, the political, etc. He assumed that all of these institutions share common goals and together work for the maintenance of the status quo; his views are to be found in the work he edited with E.A. Shils, *Towards a General Theory of Action* (1967).

**Parsons, William**: see ROSSE, WILLIAM PARSONS, 3rd EARL OF.

**parthenogenesis** (pahthinoh,jenəsis), in zoology, reproduction in which an unfertilized egg develops into a new individual. It is common in lower animals, especially insects, e.g., the APHID. In many social insects, e.g., the honey-bee, unfertilized eggs produce male drones and fertilized eggs produce female workers and queens. Artificial parthenogenesis has been achieved by scientists for most major groups of animals, although it usually results in abnormal development. In plants, the phenomenon (called parthenocarpy) is rare.

**Parthenon**, [Gr., = the virgin's place], temple to ATHENA on the Acropolis, Athens, built 447–432 BC, the masterpiece of Greek architecture. ICTINUS and CALLICRATES were the architects; PHIDIAS supervised the sculpture. Surrounded by 46 Doric columns, the temple stands on a three-step stylobate. The body comprised a main hall, with an inner chamber (the Parthenon proper) behind it. Within the hall a Doric colonnade divided the space into a broad nave and side aisles. Toward the west end stood the colossal gold and ivory *Athena Parthenos* of Phidias, destroyed in antiquity. Sculpture groups on the east and west pediments depicted the birth of Athena and her contest with POSEIDON. Of 160 m (525 ft), of sculpture on the interior frieze, 102 m (335 ft) still exist, the western portion in place and most of the rest in the British Museum (see ELGIN MARBLES). In the 6th cent. the temple became a Christian church and later a MOSQUE (with the addition of a MINARET). Used for storing gunpowder in 1687, the centre section was destroyed by an explosion, but has been reconstructed.

Parthenon

**Parthia**, ancient country of Asia, SE of the Caspian Sea. It was included in the Assyrian and Persian empires, the Macedonian empire of Alexander the Great, and the Syrian empire. In 250 BC the Parthians, led by ARSACES, founded the Parthian empire. They defeated the Romans in 53 BC but were in turned vanquished by them in 39–38 BC. The empire declined and in AD 226 was conquered by ARDASHIR I, the founder of the Persian Sassanid dynasty. The chief Parthian cities were Ecbatana, Seleucia, Ctesiphon, and Hecatompylos.

**participant observation**, the research methodology which is one of the defining characteristics of anthropology, as opposed to sociology, and which was formulated by B. MALINOWSKI. Long periods were to be spent by the anthropologists in the field, living among the people studied, learning the language, immersing themselves in, and as far as possible participating in their everyday lives, while at the same time observing and noting what was occurring. Inevitably such a method involves a far more detailed knowledge than is available to those undertaking large-scale survey work, but this knowledge is only of a small number of people and generalizations are thus problematic. There is also inevitably some impact of the observer upon the people studied.

**particle accelerator**, device used to produce beams of energetic charged particles (see ELEMENTARY PARTICLES) and to direct them against various targets for studies of the structure of the atomic nucleus and the interactions between elementary particles. Accelerators also have applications in medicine and industry, most notably in the production of radioisotopes. The first stage of any accelerator is an ION source to produce the charged particles from a neutral gas. The charged particles are accelerated by electric fields. In linear accelerators, which are the most powerful and efficient electron accelerators, the particle path is a straight line. The early linear accelerators used large static electric charges, which produced an electric field along the length of an evacuated tube to accelerate the particles. Still in use today for the acceleration of protons (and heavier nuclei) to energies of the order 10 MeV (see ELECTRON VOLT) is the Van de Graaff electrostatic generator in which charge is transferred by a moving belt to build up the required electric field. Higher energy electron linear accelerators use electromagnetic waves to accomplish the acceleration. To reach high energies without prohibitively long paths, E.O. LAWRENCE designed the cyclotron, in which a cylindrical magnet bends the particle beam into a circular path in a hollow circular metal box that is split in half to form two *D*-shaped sections. A radio-frequency electric field is applied across the gap, accelerating the particle each time it crosses the gap. In the synchrocyclotron, used to accelerate protons, the frequency of the accelerating electric field steadily decreases to match the decreasing angular velocity of the proton caused by the increase of its mass at relativistic velocities, i.e., those close to the speed of light. In the synchrotron, a ring of magnets surrounding a doughnut-shaped vacuum tank produces a magnetic field that rises in step with the proton velocities, thus keeping the radius of their paths constant; this design eliminates the need for a centre section of the magnet, allowing construction of rings with diameters measured in kilometres. Machines in use at the present time (e.g., at CERN) can accelerate protons to energies of many 100 GeV. By means of storage rings it is possible to carry out experiments in which protons of these energies collide with antiprotons of the same energy moving in the opposite direction. This has enabled the creation of very heavy new elementary particles.

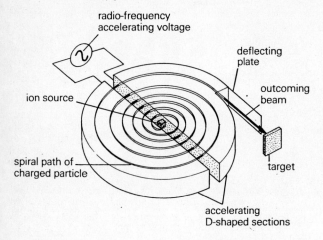

Particle accelerator: In a cyclotron, as the charged particles move faster, they spiral out to the edge of the D-shaped sections (Ds)

**particle detector,** in physics, one of several devices for detecting, measuring, and analysing particles and other forms of radiation entering it. For example, in the *ionization chamber* (consisting basically of a sealed chamber containing a gas and two electrodes between which a voltage is maintained by an external circuit) and the *Geiger Counter* (consisting commonly of a gas-filled metal cylinder that acts as one electrode, and a needle or thin, taut wire along the axis of the cylinder that acts as the other electrode), the ionizing radiation is measured by changes in the external circuit; these changes are caused by a current resulting from the motion of charged ions, produced by the radiation, moving under the influence of the electric field in the chamber. In other devices, ionization (see ION) is used to make visible the track of the charged particle causing the ionization: the *bubble chamber* is filled with liquid hydrogen or some other liquefied gas; the *cloud chamber* is filled with a supersaturated vapour; and the *spark chamber* contains a high-pressure gas that fills the gaps between a stack of metal plates or wire grids that are maintained with high voltage between alternate layers. In the *scintillation counter*, radiation is detected and measured by means of small, visible flashes produced by the radiation when it strikes a sensitive substance known as a phosphor (see PHOSPHORESCENCE).

**particles, elementary:** see ELEMENTARY PARTICLES.

**part of speech,** in traditional English GRAMMAR, any of about eight major classes of words, based on the parts of speech of ancient Greek and Latin. The parts of speech are: noun, verb, adjective, adverb, interjection, preposition, conjunction, and pronoun. A noun can be used to name a person, place, thing, idea, or time. It generally functions as the subject, object, or indirect object of the verb in a sentence. A noun may be recognized by INFLECTION (e.g., *'s* and *-s*) or by derivation (*-ness, -ity,* and *-ion*). The words *woman, country, flower, death,* and *goodness* are

nouns. A verb is typically used to indicate an action, e.g., *run, smile, sing.* English verbs are inflected for person, number, and TENSE, and partially for MOOD. Adjectives and adverbs refer typically to attributes. They are functionally different in that adjectives modify nouns or pronouns (e.g., *fat* dog, *beautiful* tree), while adverbs modify verbs, adjectives, or other adverbs (e.g., walked *quickly, very* tall). Many adverbs belong to the form class of words ending in *-ly.* An interjection is an exclamatory word, such as *oh, alas,* and *ouch;* it is usually marked by a feature of intonation shown in writing by an exclamation mark, e.g., *alas!* (see PUNCTUATION). Prepositions are used before nouns and pronouns to connect them to the preceding material, e.g., *in, about.* In English, conjunctions serve to connect words or constructions, e.g., *and, but.* Pronouns are used as substitutes for antecedent nouns that are clearly understood and with which the pronouns agree in number. In English, pronouns are classified as personal (*I, we, you*), demonstrative (*this, these, that*), relative (*who, which, that*), indefinite (*each, all, everyone*), possessive (*my, your, his*), and reflexive (*myself, herself*).

**partridge,** name for henlike BIRDS of various families. The true partridges of the Old World belong to the PHEASANT family. The grey partridge (*Perdix perdix*) of Europe and Asia, about 30 cm (1 ft) long, is famous as a game bird. It lives on open land, but related species of wood partridge, tree partridge, and bamboo partridge live where their names suggest.

**Partridge, Eric (Honeybrook),** 1894–1979, English lexicographer; b. New Zealand. He studied in Australia and at Oxford Univ., taught briefly in England, and founded a small publishing company. For the next half century he devoted himself to the study of English and its correct usage, compiling 16 lexicons on such subjects as slang, clichés, catch phrases, and etymology. His works were acclaimed for their scholarship.

**Pasadena. 1** US city (1984 est. pop. 125,000), S California, at the base of the San Gabriel Mts; inc. 1866. Its manufactures include electronic and aerospace components; the California Inst. of Technology, with its NASA Jet Propulsion Laboratory, is in the city. **2** US city (1980 pop. 112,560), S Texas, on the Houston ship channel, an industrial suburb of HOUSTON; inc. 1929. The port of Houston, and oil and related industries provide much employment. NASA's manned space centre (on Clear Lake) and the San Jacinto battlefield (1836) are nearby.

**PASCAL:** see PROGRAMMING LANGUAGE.

**Pascal, Blaise,** 1623–62, French scientist and religious philosopher. A mathematical prodigy, Pascal founded the modern theory of PROBABILITY, discovered the properties of the cycloid (the curve traced by a point on the circumference of a circle rolling along a straight line), and contributed to the advance of differential CALCULUS. In physics his experiments in the equilibrium of fluids led to the invention of the hydraulic press (see HYDRAULIC MACHINERY). As a young man Pascal came under Jansenist influence (see under JANSEN, CORNELIUS), and after a profound religious experience in 1654 he entered the convent at Port-Royal, thereafter devoting his attention primarily to religious writing. His best-known works are *Provincial Letters* (1656), a defence of the Jansenists; and the posthumously published *Pensées* (1670), which preach the necessity of mystic faith in understanding the universe.

**Pascal's law:** see HYDRAULIC MACHINERY.

**Paschal II** (or Pascal II), d. 1118, pope (1099–1118), an Italian named Raniero. A Cluniac monk, he succeeded URBAN II. During his reign, PHILIP I of France was reconciled with the church, St ANSELM triumphed in England, and the first Crusade was successful. In 1110 Holy Roman Emperor HENRY V invaded Italy and forced Paschal to surrender the papal position on INVESTITURE. Paschal later repudiated this surrender.

**Pascoli, Giovanni,** 1855–1912, Italian poet. After a tragic childhood and early socialist activism, he pursued a successful career in teaching, which he concluded (1906–12) as CARDUCCI's successor at Bologna. The best of his poetry is contained in *Tamarisks* (1891) and *Songs of Castelvecchio* (1903). It typically dwells upon the phenomena of nature and country life, on the mystery of the universe, and on the interdependence and parity of all creatures. Overshadowed by D'ANNUNZIO in his day, he surpasses him in importance as an innovator in language and metre. He is also noted for his Latin verse and his Dante criticism.

**Pashto:** see PUSHTU.

**Pašić, Nikola** (ˌpaseech), 1845–1926, Yugoslav politician. A founder of SERBIA's first modern political party, the National Radicals, Pašić shed his youthful populism and socialism to become the embodiment of the Serb nationalist political establishment. From 1904 to his death he held high office almost continuously, presiding over Serbia's transformation from a small Balkan state into the dominating element in the Kingdom of Serbs, Croats, and Slovenes.

**Pasiphaë,** in Greek mythology, wife of King MINOS.

**Pasmore, (Edwin John) Victor,** 1908–, British painter. In 1934 he joined the LONDON GROUP and contributed to the objective abstraction exhibition. By 1937 he had returned to a naturalistic style; in 1947 he again experimented with abstraction and by the 1950s was working consistently in a geometrical abstract style. His reliefs, influenced by Ben NICHOLSON, led him to be regarded as one of the main exponents of the British CONSTRUCTIVISM.

**Pasolini, Pier Paolo,** 1922–75, Italian writer and film director. A Marxist, he brought to his novels, poetry, and films a combination of religious and social consciousness. His films include *The Gospel according to St Matthew* (1964), *Theorem* (1968), *Medea* (1969), and *Salò or the 120 Days of Sodom* (1975).

**Passion play,** surviving genre of the medieval miracle play. First given in Latin, then evolving into German by the 15th cent., it has as its subject the suffering, death, and resurrection of JESUS. The Passion play given every 10 years at Oberammergau, Bavaria, dates from 1633.

**passive:** see VOICE.

**Passover:** see under JEWISH HOLIDAYS and OLDER.

**Passy, Frédéric** (pa͵see), 1822–1912, French economist who shared with J.H. DUNANT the first Nobel Peace Prize (1901). He founded the International League for Permanent Peace (1867) and, with Sir William R. Cremer, the Inter-Parliamentary Union of Arbitration (1889).

**pasta,** shaped and dried dough prepared from strong WHEAT flour and water, associated especially with Italian cuisine. Often mixed with eggs or egg solids, the dough is cut into many shapes, such as shells and tubes (macaroni) and ribbons (e.g., spaghetti). Long known in Asia, similar flour and rice pastes are believed to have been introduced into Europe during the 13th-cent. Mongol invasions.

**pastel,** artists' medium of chalk and pigment, tempered with gum water and usually moulded into sticks; also, a work in the medium. Pastel has been very popular in France, where it was introduced in the 18th cent. It was used by such 19th-cent. masters as DEGAS, TOULOUSE-LAUTREC, WHISTLER, and CASSATT. In the 20th cent. MATISSE created superb pastels.

**Pasternak, Boris Leonidovich,** 1890–1960, Russian poet, novelist, and translator. His first book of poems was *The Twin in the Clouds* (1914). *Over the Barriers* (1916) and *My Sister, Life* (1922) established him as a major poet with a fresh, lyrical, passionate voice. In the repressive intellectual climate of the 1930s he ceased publishing his own work, devoting himself to translating works of SHAKESPEARE, GOETHE, and other major Western poets. Two World War II collections brought only censure. His masterpiece, the novel *Doctor Zhivago,* an epic treatment of the tragic upheavals of 20th-cent. Russia, was finished by 1955. Denied publication in the USSR, it was first published (1957) in Italy, and soon acclaimed worldwide. Though Pasternak was awarded the 1958 Nobel Prize for literature, official Soviet pressure compelled him to refuse it. He spent his last years at an artists' colony near Moscow, where he remained an international symbol of artistic incorruptibility.

**Pasteur, Louis** (pas͵tuh), 1822–95, French chemist and microbiologist. Renowned for his studies of fermentation and BACTERIA, he disproved the theory of spontaneous generation and advanced the germ theory of infection. Of enormous economic and social importance are the process of PASTEURIZATION, which he developed; his studies of silkworm disease and chicken cholera; and his discovery of ANTHRAX and RABIES vaccines. In 1888 the Pasteur Inst. was founded in Paris, with Pasteur as director, providing a distinguished clinical research centre on virulent and contagious diseases.

**pasteurization,** treatment of food with heat to destroy disease-causing and other undesirable organisms. The process was developed (but not discovered) by Louis PASTEUR in the 1860s. Modern pasteurization standards for milk require temperatures of about 63°C (145°F) for 30 min followed by rapid cooling. The harmless lactic acid bacteria survive the process and can sour warm milk.

**pastoral,** literary work based on a conventionalized portrait of shepherd or rural life, whose purity and simplicity are contrasted with the corruption and artificiality of court and city. The pastoral, found in poetry, drama, and fiction, may embrace love, death, religion, and politics as themes. The idyls of THEOCRITUS (3rd cent. BC) introduced Daphnis, Amaryllis, and other figures who became standard fixtures of the genre. VERGIL's *Bucolics,* or eclogues, describe an imaginary Arcadia yet glorify Rome. *Daphnis and Chloë,* by LONGUS (3rd cent. AD), was the first pastoral romance. The pastoral revived during the RENAISSANCE in the work of DANTE, PETRARCA, BOCCACCIO, and Angelo Poliziano, and it has enriched English literature from Edmund SPENSER, Sir Philip SIDNEY, and SHAKESPEARE to John MILTON's 'Lycidas,' P.B. SHELLEY's 'Adonais,' and Matthew ARNOLD's 'Thyrsis.' Its conventions had faded by the 20th cent.

**pastoralism,** a way of life in which dependence on livestock is the major means of subsistence. Pastoral nomadism involves herding with considerable mobility, in order to find the best environment for the livestock. Most pastoralists also have some involvement with agriculture.

**Patagonia,** semiarid, windswept plateau, c.777,000 km² (300,000 sq mi), S Argentina. The sparsely populated plateau has large coal, oil, and iron ore deposits, and vast untapped mineral wealth. The origins of Patagonia's original inhabitants, such as the Tehuelches ('Patagonian giants'), and of its unusual wildlife have greatly interested palaeontologists and zoologists.

**Patel, Vallabhbhai,** 1875–1950, Indian political leader. A long-time leader in the INDIAN NATIONAL CONGRESS, he helped negotiate India's independence in 1947 and served as deputy prime minister until his death. He played a crucial role in securing the accession of the princely states to India.

**Patenier, Joachim de:** see PATINIR, JOACHIM DE.

**patent,** in law, governmental grant of exclusive privilege of making, using, selling and authorizing others to make, use and sell an invention. The term derives from the medieval letters patent, public letters granting monopolistic control of useful goods to an individual. In the UK, a patent is granted on application to the Patent Office, providing the product is new, inventive and capable of industrial adaptation; the patent is valid for 16 years. The UK courts have jurisdiction over breach of British patents, and EUROPEAN COMMUNITY patents granted in Munich. Breach of patent may be remedied by damages, or an account of the profits derived from its use. See also COPYRIGHT.

**patent medicine** or **proprietary medicine,** packaged DRUGS that can be obtained without a prescription; also called over-the-counter drugs. Sale of these drugs is regulated by the COMMITTEE ON SAFETY OF MEDICINES. Analgesics, antiseptics, laxatives, antacids, some cough medicines, and skin preparations are examples of common patent medicines.

**Pater, Walter Horatio,** 1839–94, English essayist and critic. He believed that the ideal life consisted of cultivating an appreciation for the beautiful and profound. *Studies in the History of the Renaissance* (1873), *Marius the Epicurean* (1885), *Imaginary Portraits* (1887), and other works exhibit his precise, subtle, and refined style.

**Pathé, Charles** (pa͵tay), 1863–1957, French film mogul. Pathé Frères dominated (c.1901–14) world production, world distribution, and European manufacture of film stock and equipment. The *Pathé Gazette* newsreel was among the firm's many films.

**pathology,** study of the nature of disease and of the changes produced in an organ or part of the body by disease. Diagnostic techniques include microscopic examination of tissue for detecting tissue changes (see BIOPSY), RADIOGRAPHY, NUCLEAR MAGNETIC RESONANCE imaging, and the analysis (assay) of body fluids (e.g., BLOOD and URINE) from the living patient and after death (autopsy).

**Patiala,** town (1981 pop. 206,254), Punjab state, N India, on the Patiala R. It is a district administrative and railway centre that has developed a number of industries, notably steel-forging, and the manufacture of biscuits and electrical goods. In British days it was the capital of a princely state of the same name ruled by a Sikh maharaja.

**Patinir, Patenier,** or **Patiner, Joachim de,** d. 1524, Flemish landscape and religious painter. He was the first Flemish painter to regard himself primarily as a landscape painter. The small figures in his vistas were sometimes painted by other artists. A characteristic painting is *Flight into Egypt* (Antwerp).

**Patmore, Coventry**, 1823–96, English poet. His major works are *The Angel in the House* (1854–62), a sequence of poems on married love, and *The Unknown Eros* (1877) which contains some of his best-known lyrics such as 'The Toys', and odes inspired by his Catholic mysticism.

**Patna**, city (1981 pop. 813,963), Bihar state, NE India. It is the capital of Bihar, and also a divisional and district administrative centre, on the south bank of the GANGES (Ganga) R. It retains its historic functions as a scene of trade (especially in grain and spice) and has craft industries and a few modern mills; it also has a university. Patna is the site of one of the most important capital cities of ancient India, Pataliputra, particularly prominent in the Mauryan and Gupta periods.

**Paton, Alan**, 1903–88, white South African writer. He is best known for *Cry, the Beloved Country* (1958). Other works include the novel *Too Late the Phalarope* (1953), the polemics *South Africa in Transition* (1956) and *Hope for South Africa* (1958), and the memoir about his wife *Kontakion for You Departed* (1969).

**Patras**, city (1981 pop. 141,529), N Peloponnesus, Greece, on the Gulf of Patras. It is a market centre for trade in currants, and as a port has passenger ferry links with CORFU and the Italian port of BRINDISI. Held by Venice before 1715, it was destroyed during the Greek War of Independence in 1821, but later rebuilt.

**patrial**, legal term to describe a person who has the right of abode in the UK: it means British citizens born in the UK or having a parent or grandparent born in the UK. Patrials are permitted to enter and leave the UK without hindrance, compared with the non-patrial, who can only work or settle in the UK with the permission of, and subject to the control of, the British government.

**patrician** [Lat., = of the fathers], member of the privileged class of ancient Rome. From the 6th cent. BC the PLEBS struggled constantly for political equality with the patricians. The patricians wore a distinctive tunic and shoe. Later the term became a title of honour.

**Patrick, Saint**, c.390–c.461, Christian missionary, the Apostle of Ireland. Though obscured by legend, a few points in his life seem certain. He was born in Roman Britain, and taken to Ireland by Irish raiders. Escaping, he fled to Britain, suffering many privations, and may have briefly visited Gaul. Moved by a dream, he returned to Ireland as a missionary, and made numerous converts. It is probable that c.444 he set up his episcopal see at Armagh. By the time he died Ireland was Christianized. The prime sources of his life are his *Confession* and his *Letter*, written during his last years. Feast: 17 Mar.

**patrilineal descent**, a principle of descent in which the significant ties are those established through the male line. See LINEAGE; MATRILINEAL DESCENT.

**Patroclus**, in Greek mythology, friend of ACHILLES.

**patron/client**, the relationship that is established between individuals with very different positions in the political and economic system, both local and national. Clients attach themselves, ostensibly on a voluntary basis—although there is seldom any viable alternative—to a more powerful individual, who will supposedly negotiate and mediate on behalf of his clients with the institutions of the wider society. In return the client will be expected to perform all kinds of services and above all give support (usually political) for his patron; in some contexts the relationship is essentially one of debt slavery. This relationship of individual ties established across the class divide has been seen as a way in which in a class-divided society the formation of any inter-class solidarity is prevented or inhibited.

**Patti, Adelina**, 1843–1919, Spanish coloratura soprano of Italian parentage. She made her debut in New York City in 1859 and became the most popular singer of her day.

**Patton, George Smith, Jr.**, 1885–1945, American general. During WORLD WAR II he commanded (1942–43) a corps in North Africa, the 7th Army in Sicily and the 3rd Army, which spearheaded the liberation of France (1944) and the defeat of Germany (1945).

**Pau**, city (1982 pop. of agglomeration 131,265), capital of Pyrénées-Atlantiques dept., SW France. The former capital of the old territory of Béarn, it was the residence of the kings of NAVARRE and the birthplace of Henry IV. Its early fame rested on the reputation of its university and its textile industries but this was extended in the late 19th cent. when the city became a popular winter resort. Recent growth followed the development of the nearby natural gas field of Lacq in the 1950s.

**Paul**, 1901–64, king (1947–64) of the Hellenes (Greece), brother and successor of GEORGE II. His reign was pro-Western, and he was succeeded by his son, CONSTANTINE II.

**Paul, Jean:** see RICHTER, JOHANN PAUL FRIEDRICH.

**Paul, Saint**, d. AD 64? or 67?, the apostle to the Gentiles; b. Saul of Tarsus, Asia Minor. A Jew, son of a Roman citizen, he was a tentmaker. Educated in Jerusalem, he became a zealous nationalist and probably a Pharisee. Sources for his life are the ACTS OF THE APOSTLES and the Pauline Epistles. Of the epistles, ROMANS, CORINTHIANS, GALATIANS, PHILIPPIANS, COLOSSIANS, First THESSALONIANS, and PHILEMON are indisputably Paul's work. EPHESIANS and Second Thessalonians are generally accepted. First and Second TIMOTHY and TITUS are thought in their present form to be later; HEBREWS was not written by Paul himself. Paul assisted approvingly at the martyrdom of St STEPHEN and shortly thereafter was commissioned by the chief priest to help suppress Christianity in Damascus (AD c.32). On his way there a light blinded him, and he heard Jesus asking, 'Why persecutest thou me?'. In Damascus he was found by the disciple Ananias. On regaining his sight he was baptized and began preaching. He spent 13 years, some of them in the Arabian desert, learning the faith. In AD 47 Paul set out with St BARNABAS and St MARK on his first missionary journey, establishing churches in Cyprus and Asia Minor. About AD 50 he was at the council of the apostles in Jerusalem, opposing the Judaistic group's support for circumcision, which would have made Christianity a Jewish sect. On his second mission (AD 50–53) Paul was accompanied by Silas and visited Galatia, Troas, Philippi, Thessaloniki, Athens, and Corinth, where he remained for some time. On his third journey (AD 53–57) he remained two and a half years in Ephesus. On what proved to be his last visit to the Holy Land (AD 57–59), he was arrested in Jerusalem for provoking a riot; after two years of imprisonment and hearings, he claimed his Roman citizen's right and was taken to Rome, where he was imprisoned (AD 60) but allowed to conduct his ministry among his visitors. His final fate is uncertain. His tomb and shrine are at the basilica of St Paul's Without the Walls, Rome. St Paul dominated the apostolic age. The first Christian theological writing is found in his epistles, and he became a fountainhead of Christian doctrine.

**Paul I**, 1754–1801, czar of Russia (1796–1801); son of CATHERINE II. Reversing his mother's policies, he limited the power of the nobility and did not continue her expansionism. He briefly joined (1798) the second coalition against France and, with Denmark, Sweden, and Prussia, formed an armed league to counter English interference in neutral shipping. He prohibited foreign travel and importation of Western books and music. A conspiracy of nobles and officers led to Paul's murder and the accession of his son, ALEXANDER I.

**Paul III**, 1468–1549, pope (1534–49) a Roman named Alessandro Farnese. An astute diplomat, he favoured reform and began the COUNTER-REFORMATION. To achieve Catholic reform, he convened (1545) the Council of TRENT and supported the newly founded Jesuits (see JESUS, SOCIETY OF). A patron of the arts, he had Michelangelo continue to decorate the SISTINE CHAPEL, and he founded the Farnese Palace. He excommunicated HENRY VIII of England.

**Paul VI**, 1897–1978, pope (1963–78), an Italian named Giovanni Battista Montini. He reconvened the Second VATICAN COUNCIL, which had been called (1962) by his predecessor, JOHN XXIII, and carried out many of its reforms, such as vernacularization and reform of the liturgy. Rules of fasting and abstinence were relaxed, and some restrictions on intermarriage were lifted. In 1964, Paul undertook a pilgrimage to the Holy Land and became the first pope to leave Italy in over 150 years. That journey was followed by visits to India (1964), the US (1965), Africa (1969), and Southeast Asia (1970). Paul brought a new ecumenism to the church; limited doctrinal agreements were reached with the Anglicans and the Lutherans. A strong defender of papal primacy and infallibility, Paul sparked dissent from liberal church factions with his encyclical *Humanae vitae* (1968), which reaffirmed the church's long-standing ban on contraception. He also faced challenges from Catholic traditionalists, who wished to return to the old liturgy. Although criticized, Paul was universally respected for his intellect and spirituality, his humility and compassion.

**Pauli, Wolfgang**, 1900–58, American physicist; b. Austria. A professor at the Federal Institute of Technology, Zürich, and a member (1935–36, 1940–46) of the Institute for Advanced Study, Princeton, New Jersey, he won the 1945 Nobel Prize for physics for his exclusion principle, according to which no two electrons in an atom may be in the same quantum state (see QUANTUM THEORY). He also suggested the existence of the NEUTRINO before it was directly observed, and put forward the accepted theory of paramagnetism (see MAGNETISM) of metals.

**Pauling, Linus Carl**, 1901–, American chemist. The recipient of two Nobel prizes, he won the chemistry award in 1954 and the peace prize in 1962. His long career at the California Inst. of Technology began in 1931. He wrote a classic study of the chemical bond, and did important work in molecular biology. He became a champion of disarmament, the use of large doses of vitamin C for treating the common cold, and of the use of chemotherapy for mental diseases.

**Paul Knutson**, fl. 1354–64, Norse leader, alleged explorer of America. In 1354 or 1355 King MAGNUS of Norway directed him to conduct an expedition to GREENLAND to ensure the continuity of Christianity there. He is said to have set out in 1355 and returned in 1363 or 1364.

**Pausanias**, fl. 2nd cent. AD, Greek writer. His work *Periegesis* [guided tour] is a comprehensive guide-book to the topography of Greece, and to the buildings and sculpture which survived in his time. It was written from his own observation and reading.

**Pavarotti, Luciano**, 1935–, Italian tenor. He made his debut in Italy in 1961, in London in 1963, and in the US in 1965. He is noted for his brilliance and style, notably in works by BELLINI, DONIZETTI, PUCCINI, and VERDI.

**Pavese, Cesare** (pa͵vesay), 1908–50, Italian poet, novelist, and translator. He progressed, under American influences, from Whitmanesque quasi-narrative poetry (*Work Wearies*, 1936) to the poetic narrative of *Il compagno* (1941; tr. The Harvesters), *The House on the Hill* (1949), and *La luna é i falò* (1950; tr. The Moon and the Bonfires), which treat man's search for stability and release from isolation. His many translations from English and American writers include a memorable version of MELVILLE's *Moby-Dick*.

**Pavlov, Ivan Petrovich**, 1849–1936, Russian physiologist and experimental psychologist. Using dogs as experimental animals, he obtained secretions of the salivary glands, pancreas, and liver without disturbing the nerve and blood supply; for this work on the physiology of the DIGESTIVE SYSTEM he received the 1904 Nobel Prize for physiology or medicine. He also experimented on nervous stimulation of gastric secretions and thus demonstrated the conditioned reflex, a physiological reaction to environmental stimuli, which influenced the development of BEHAVIOURISM. His chief work was *Conditioned Reflexes* (1926).

**Pavlova, Anna Matveyevna**, 1881–1931, Russian ballet dancer. She made her debut (1899) at St Petersburg. After working with DIAGHILEV (1909) she made her London debut in 1910. She formed her own company and embarked on many world tours. She is considered to have been the greatest ballerina of all time. Noted for her classical technique, she is particularly remembered in the role *The Dying Swan*.

**Pawnee Indians**, NORTH AMERICAN INDIANS speaking a Caddoan language (see AMERICAN INDIAN LANGUAGES). Their material culture was typical of the Plains, but they had elaborate myths and rituals, including a supreme god and, until the 18th cent., the custom of human sacrifice to their god of vegetation. In 1541 the Pawnee were living in S Nebraska. By the early 18th cent. they numbered 10,000, but epidemics and wars with the SIOUX greatly reduced their numbers. Fierce fighters, they never warred against the US, but instead provided protection in the INDIAN WARS. In 1876 they moved to a reservation in Oklahoma. In the early 1980s they numbered about 2000, but few were still living on the reservation.

**Pawsey, Joseph L.**, 1908–1962, Australian astronomer, who established and contributed to the great Australian school of RADIO ASTRONOMY.

**Paxton, Sir Joseph**, 1803–65, English gardener, architect, and hero of SELF-HELP. He is best known for his Crystal Palace (1851).

**Paxton, Steve**, 1939–, American dancer and choreographer. After an early career with the CUNNINGHAM company he became a founder member of the Judson Dance Theatre in 1962. He is important in the founding and development of the dance/movement technique known as 'contact improvisation'. See also MODERN DANCE; THARP, TWYLA.

**pay-as-you-earn (PAYE)**, widely used system of collecting INCOME TAX by employers from employees on a regular weekly or monthly basis. The system was introduced in 1944 on the recommendation of J.M. KEYNES and it covers both basic-rate and higher-rate income tax. The use of code numbers given to the employer by the tax authorities ensure that the personal circumstances of taxpayers remain confidential. Under PAYE, wages whether cash or cheque are paid net of income tax and national insurance contribution and reflect any change in the tax liability of the employee.

**Paz, Octavio** (pahs), 1914–, Mexican poet and critic, distinguished for his insight, elegance, and erudition. His poetry includes *La estación violenta* (1958; tr. The Violent Season) and *Configurations* (1971). Among his prose works are *El laberinto de la soledad* (1950; tr. The Labyrinth of Solitude), *El arco y la lira* (1956; tr. The Bow and the Lyre), *Los hijos del limo: Modern Poetry from Romanticism to the Avant-Garde* (1974), and *El mono gramático* (1974; tr. The Monkey Grammarian) is a collection of Paz's translations of other poets.

**Paz Estenssoro, Victor** (pahs aystayn͵sohroh), 1907–, president of BOLIVIA (1952–56, 1960–64). He founded (1941) and helped to bring the National Revolutionary Movement (MNR) to power (1943). Elected (1951) president while in exile, he took office by means of an MNR-led revolt and instituted social reforms. He amended the constitution to permit himself a third term, and though reelected, he was ousted (1964) by a military coup. He returned, however, as constitutional president in 1985.

**Pb**, chemical symbol of the element LEAD.

**p'Bitek, Okot**, 1931–, Ugandan poet. He utilizes oral form as a basis for sharp satire on an emergent society's new materialism. His best works include translations from his mother-tongue, Acoli, in *The Song of Lawino* (1966) and *Song of a Prisoner* (1970).

**PCB**, or **polychlorinated biphenyl**, any of a group of organic compounds that were once widely used as liquid coolants and insulators in industrial equipment, e.g., power transformers. They were later found to be dangerous pollutants, the more so since they are very stable substances which persist in the environment. PCB effluents are cumulative poisons for vertebrates, especially fish, concentrations having first been detected in the eggs of British auks, shags, and terns and subsequently in other pelagic seabirds. Animal reproduction is thought also to be adversely affected by the chemical. Certain PCBs are carcinogenic to mice and rats and possibly to man. Human deaths attributed to PCB poisoning have been associated with fatty degeneration, necrosis, and cirrhosis of the liver. As a result of a PCB leak in Japan in 1968 which contaminated rice oil, 1000 people developed a skin disease and babies showed signs of poisoning. The US Congress banned the manufacture of PCB compounds after 1978. In the UK concern about incineration (some toxic substances arise from the combustion of PCBs) led to the closure of an incineration plant in Scotland.

**Pd**, chemical symbol of the element PALLADIUM.

**pea**, hardy, annual, climbing plant (*Pisum sativum*) of the PULSE family, long grown for food and no longer found in the wild form. The round seeds, borne in a pod, are highly nutritious, having a high PROTEIN content. Split peas are obtained from the field pea (var. *arvense*), grown also for forage and as a green manure. The pods of sugar peas, or mange-touts, are also eaten. The CHICK-PEA and SWEET PEA belong to different genera.

**Peace**, river, W central Canada, flowing 1520 km (945 mi) N and E from the confluence of the Finlay and Parsnip rivers at Williston Lake to join the Slave R. at Lake Athabasca.

**Peace Corps**, US agency established (1961) to assist developing countries to train manpower for their needs. In 1971 it was transferred to ACTION, an agency that coordinates several federal volunteer programmes. The programme now tries to attract people with technical vocational training or special skills, particularly in agriculture; volunteers serve two-year tours in foreign countries.

**peach**, tree (*Prunus persica*) of the ROSE family having decorative pink blossoms and a juicy, sweet, drupe fruit. Peach fruits have a characteristically fuzzy skin; the NECTARINE is the smooth-skinned variety. The numerous kinds of peaches are generally distinguished as clingstone (in which the fruit's ripe flesh does not readily separate from the seed) and freestone (flesh readily separates from the seed). Purple-leaved and double-flowering peach trees are often cultivated as ornamentals.

**peacock** or **peafowl,** large BIRD of the PHEASANT family, native to E Asia. During courtship, the crested male common peacock (*Pavo cristatus*) displays his magnificent green-and-gold upper tail coverts before the drabber peahen. When the term *peafowl* is used, *peacock* refers to the male and *peahen* to the female.

**Peacock, Thomas Love,** 1785–1866, English novelist and poet. His satires on the intellectual modes of the day include *Headlong Hall* (1816), *Nightmare Abbey* (1818), and *Crotchet Castle* (1831). His best poems are interspersed in the novels.

**Peak District,** hilly area and national park, N Derbyshire, northern Midlands of England. It also covers part of NE Staffordshire and a corner of Cheshire, and forms the southern part of the PENNINES. The northern part is known as the High Peak, whose summit is Kinder Scout (636 m/2088 ft). The High peak consists of millstone grit hills, and there is also a larger area of lower limestone hills, with many caves.

**Peake, Mervyn,** 1911–68, English writer and artist. He is best known for his trilogy of Gothic fantasy novels. *Titus Groan* (1946), *Gormenghast* (1950), and *Titus Alone* (1959). He also wrote verse and children's books, and was a commissioned war artist in World War II.

**Peale, Charles Willson,** 1741–1827, American painter, naturalist, and inventor. Peale studied under J.S. COPLEY and Benjamin WEST and later served as a captain in the American Revolution. Succeeding Copley as the most popular US portraitist, he painted such figures as Franklin, Jefferson, Hamilton, and John Adams. His many paintings of George Washington include the earliest-known portrait (1772; Washington and Lee Univ.).

**peanut,** low plant (*Arachis hypogaea*) of the PULSE family, and its protein-rich, edible seeds. Native to South America, it is now widely cultivated. The seeds (peanuts) are eaten fresh or roasted and used in cooking and confection. They are ground to make peanut butter and yield an oil used for margarine, cooking oil, soap manufacture, and industrial purposes. The peanut plant is unusual for its geocarpy: when the pod begins to form, it is pushed into the ground by elongation of the stalk and matures underground.

**pear,** name for a tree (genus *Pyrus*) of the ROSE family and for its fruit. Most of the pear strains grown for fruit are varieties of the common pear *(P. communis)* or of its hybrids. The sweet and juicy fruit, broad at the base, generally narrows toward the stem; common varieties include Comice, Williams, and Conference. Pears are sold fresh, canned, or dried. Several pear species are cultivated as ornamentals for their blossoms, and pear wood is used in cabinetmaking. The pear is closely related to the APPLE.

**pearl,** hard, rounded gem formed by certain BIVALVE molluscs, particularly the pearl OYSTER and the freshwater pearl MUSSEL. In response to an irritation caused by a foreign object such as a parasite or a grain of sand within the shell, the mantle (specialized layer of tissue between the shell and body mass) secretes layers of calcium carbonate, identical in composition to MOTHER-OF-PEARL, around the object. In several years, a pearl is formed. Pearls vary in shape (from round to irregular) and colour (white to black). Cultured pearls, mainly from Japan, are produced by placing a small bead in the mantle of an oyster.

**Pearl, The,** one of four Middle English alliterative poems, presumably by the same author, in a manuscript of c.1400. It is an allegorical vision of singular beauty, in which a dead child is encountered as a saved soul. Two of the other poems are the homiletic *Cleanness* (or *Purity*) and *Patience.* The fourth, *Sir Gawain and the Green Knight,* is perhaps the most brilliantly conceived of all Arthurian romances (see ARTHURIAN LEGEND).

**Pearl Harbor,** landlocked harbour on Oahu island, Hawaii, site of important US military installations. It is best known as the scene of the devastating Japanese surprise air attack on 7 Dec. 1941, which catapulted the US into WORLD WAR II. It is now a national historic landmark.

**Pearl River:** see XI JIANG.

**Pearlstein, Philip,** 1924–, American painter. He is known for his large, stark, and carefully composed nudes painted in a harsh light without idealization.

**Pearson, Lester Bowles,** 1897–1972, prime minister of CANADA (1963–68). He helped to found (1944) the UNITED NATIONS and became (1947) chairman of the UN political and security committee. As Liberal minister of external affairs (1948–57), he helped to form the NORTH ATLANTIC TREATY ORGANIZATION and was a mediator in the wake of the 1956 ARAB–ISRAELI WAR, for which he received the 1957 Nobel Peace Prize. He led the Liberal Party to victory in the 1962 elections and took office as prime minister.

**Peary, Robert Edwin,** 1856–1920, American Arctic explorer, discoverer of the NORTH POLE. He made several expeditions to the Arctic, including GREENLAND and Peary Land, which bears his name. He reached the North Pole on 6 April 1909. Although challenged by the prior claim of Frederick Albert Cook, his accomplishment was recognized by the US Congress in 1911.

**peasant,** primary agricultural producer living in a socially differentiated, state society. Peasants produce for themselves but, crucially, their product also supports the dominant urban classes. Peasant communities are thus subordinated to a wider society, to economic and political relations structured outside their local environment. There is no means of identifying the peasantry according to any other universal characteristics since their relationship to the elite is dependent on the form of social relationships characteristic of the society as a whole, on the dominant mode of production. It has been increasingly recognized that the peasantry is not a homogeneous class and that considerable economic and social differentiation exists within given peasant communities.

**peat,** soil material consisting of partially decomposed organic matter, formed by the slow decay of aquatic and semiaquatic plants in SWAMPS and bogs. Principal types include moss peat, derived chiefly from SPHAGNUM and used as mulch and stable litter, and fuel peat, used where wood and coal are scarce. Peat is the first stage of transition from compressed plant growth to the formation of COAL.

**peat moss:** see SPHAGNU.

**pecan:** see HICKORY.

**Pechstein, Max,** 1881–1955, German painter. He studied at Dresden and joined the Die BRÜCKE group in 1906. In 1908 he went to Berlin and was involved with the Neue Sezession. He was strongly influenced by FAUVISM and by primitive art, visiting the Palan Islands in the Pacific in 1913–14. He was a founder member of the NOVEMBERGRUPPE in 1918 and taught in the Berlin Academy from 1923 until 1933 when he was dismissed by the National Socialists.

**Peckinpah, Sam,** 1925–84, American film director. His films attained notoriety for their violence, particularly the blood-letting of *The Wild Bunch* (1969), which many saw as a response to Vietnam, but in fact the habitual tone of his films include *Ride the High Country* (1962), *Pat Garrett and Billy the Kid* (1973), and *Bring Me the Head of Alfredo Garcia* (1974).

**Pécs,** city (1985 pop. 175,000), S Hungary. Local coal provided the impetus to industries which include the manufacture of leather goods and glazed earthenware. Of Roman or even earlier origin, it acquired Hungary's first university in 1367. It was under Turkish rule 1543 to 1686 and mosques survive from that time.

**Pedro** (‚paydroh), for Spanish and Portuguese rulers thus named, see PETER.

**Pedro,** emperors of BRAZIL. **Pedro I,** 1798–1834 (r.1822–31), fled as a child with the Portuguese royal family to Brazil and became regent of Brazil (1821) when his father, JOHN VI, returned to Portugal. Heeding his Brazilian advisers, he declared Brazil a separate empire (1822) and granted its first constitution (1824). Upon his father's death (1826), he conceded the Portuguese crown to his daughter, MARIA II. His inability to cope with Brazil's problems led him to abdicate (1831) in favour of his son, **Pedro II,** 1825–91 (r.1831–89). Pedro II was extremely popular, and his long reign was marked by internal peace and great material progress. Opposition to a law freeing the slaves brought about his downfall, however, and he was deposed in 1889.

**Peel, Sir Robert,** 1788–1850, British statesman, prime minister (1834–35, 1841–56). As home secretary in 1829, he established the London police force, whose members were called Bobbies after him. A close ally of WELLINGTON and a powerful figure in the House of Commons, he opposed the REFORM BILL of 1832, but in 1834, in the Tamworth manifesto, he accepted the new system and tried to ensure that the Conservative Party would have an active role within it. He supported pragmatic reforms and created a party prepared under his first prime-ministership to reintroduce an income tax, to liberalize trade, and to reform banking. Yet, as a result of his decision to secure passage of a bill for CATHOLIC EMANCIPATION, which he had formerly opposed, and to repeal (1846) the CORN LAWS he had built up, the party forced his resignation. His followers, known as Peelites, remained an important force after his death, many of them, including GLADSTONE, becoming liberals.

**Peele, George,** 1556–96, English poet and dramatist. He specialized in patriotic themes and accounts of court events, celebrating the Queen in his play *The Arraignment of Paris* (1584) and in such poems as *Polyhymnia* (1590) and *The Honour of the Garter* (1593). Other plays include *The Battle of Alcazar* (1594), based on actual events in Arabia in 1578.

**Pegasus,** in Greek mythology, winged horse that sprang from the neck of the dying GORGON Medusa. Associated with the arts, he was captured by the hero BELLEROPHON, who rode him.

**pegmatite:** see GRANITE.

**Pehlevi language:** see PAHLAVI LANGUAGE.

**Pei, I(eoh) M(ing)** (pay), 1917–, American architect; b. China. His designs integrate structure and environment. Among his works are Place Ville Marie, in Montreal; Government Center, in Boston; the East Wing of the National Gallery of Art, in Washington, DC, which opened in 1978; and the West Wing of the Museum of Fine Arts, in Boston, which opened in 1981.

**Peierls, Sir Rudolf Ernst,** 1907–, English theoretical physicist; b. Germany. He worked with Wolfgang PAULI in Zurich (1929–32) on the theory of electrons in metals, before coming to England in 1932. With O.R. FRISCH, he produced the memorandum which showed that the critical size of a uranium bomb was small enough for the bomb project to be practical. From 1943 he worked at Los Alamos Atomic Research Laboratory, New Mexico, US. After the war he was professor of theoretical physics in Birmingham, then in Oxford, making contributions both to solid-state and nuclear physics.

**Peirce, Charles Sanders,** 1838–1914, American philosopher. Viewing logic as the beginning of all philosophic study, he held that the meaning of an idea was to be found in an examination of the consequences to which the idea would lead; he coined the term PRAGMATISM to describe this principle. His followers included William JAMES, John DEWEY, and more recently QUINE. Peirce was virtually unknown during his lifetime; his major essays appeared posthumously as *Chance, Love, and Logic* (1923), and his collected papers were published between 1931 and 1958.

**Peisistratus:** see PISISTRATUS.

**Peking:** see BEIJING.

**Peking man:** see HOMO ERECTUS.

**pelagic** (pe,layjik), description of plants and animals that live on or swim in the surface waters of the seas, as opposed to those that are part of the BENTHOS.

**Pelé** (,pelay), 1940–, Brazilian soccer (football) player. His real name was Edson Arantes do Nascimento. Perhaps the greatest soccer player ever, he joined the Santos team at 16 and led Brazil's national team to world titles in 1958, 1962, and 1970. Pelé scored over 1000 goals, and in international matches he averaged one goal per game. In 1975 he signed a multimillion-dollar contract with the New York Cosmos, popularizing the sport in the US before retiring in 1977.

**Pelée** (pə,lay), volcano, 1397 m (4583 ft), on N Martinique, in the West Indies. Its great eruption of 1902 caused the death of more than 30,000 people and engulfed Saint-Pierre, the city at its base.

**Peleus,** in Greek mythology, father of ACHILLES.

**pelican,** large aquatic BIRD of warm regions, related to the CORMORANTS and gannets. Pelicans are long-necked birds with large, flat bills; they store fish in a deep, expandable pouch below the lower mandible. There are eight Old World species and two American. The birds are colonial, building untidy tree-top nests. White pelicans (*Pelecanus onocrotalus*)

White **pelicans** (*Pelecanus onocrotalus*)

feed in the shallows but the American brown pelican (*P. occidentalis*) dives into the sea like a BOOBY.

**pellagra** (pə,laygrə, -,la-), deficiency disease due to a lack of nicotinic acid, vitamin B$_3$. See table under VITAMINS AND MINERALS.

**Peloponnesian League:** see SPARTA.

**Peloponnesian War,** 431–404 BC, a struggle in ancient GREECE between ATHENS and SPARTA, long-standing rivals. The war began after a contest between Athens and Corinth (Sparta's ally) over dependencies. The first important action was the invasion of Attica (Athenian home territory) by a Spartan army in 431 BC. The Athenians retired behind the walls of their city, and the Athenian fleet began raids, winning victories off Naupactus (429). A plague (430–428) wiped out a quarter of Athens's population. After PERICLES died, his successor, CLEON, won a great victory at Sphacteria (425) and rejected a Spartan bid for peace. The tide began to turn, and the Spartan leader Brasidas surprised Athens with a campaign in NE Greece that ended in a decisive Spartan victory at Amphipolis (422), in which both Brasidas and Cleon were killed. The new Athenian leader, NICIAS, arranged a peace (421), but his rival ALCIBIADES persuaded the Athenians to invade SYRACUSE. Alcibiades was accused of sacrilege, and the expedition, led by Nicias, ended in disaster (413). Alcibiades, who had fled to Sparta, sailed the Spartan fleet across the Aegean, inciting revolt in Athens's colonies. Recalled to Athens (410), he destroyed the Spartan fleet at Cyzicus, but Sparta, with a new fleet led by LYSANDER, defeated the Athenians at Notium (407), and Alcibiades was driven from Athens for good. After a last Athenian victory at Arginusae (406), Lysander crushed the Athenian navy at Aegospotamoi (405) and sailed to Piraeus. Athens, besieged by land and sea, capitulated in 404. It never again regained its former importance, and for about 30 years afterward Sparta was the main power in Greece.

**Peloponnesus** or **Pelopónnisos,** formerly Morea, peninsula, S Greece, linked to the northern mainland by the Isthmus of Corinth. It is mainly mountainous, with fertile coastal strips in the N and W. Among its ancient Greek cities were SPARTA, CORINTH, Argos, and Megalopolis.

**Pelops,** in Greek mythology, son of TANTALUS. Murdered by his father, he was served at a banquet for the gods, who realized the trick, punished Tantalus, and restored Pelops, giving him an ivory shoulder for the one DEMETER had eaten. To win his wife, Hippodamia, he cheated in a chariot race and killed the charioteer Myrtilus, who cursed him before dying. Thus Pelops caused the many misfortunes visited upon his sons, ATREUS and Thyestes. The PELOPONNESUS was named after Pelops.

**Pemba:** see ZANZIBAR, region.

**Pembroke,** town (1981 pop. 7049) in Dyfed, SW Wales, on R. Pembroke. A market town, it has several industries including engineering. There are several historic buildings in the town, including the remains of the 11th-cent. castle. A government dockyard was established in 1814 and closed in 1926, around which the town of Pembroke Dock developed. Pembroke is the birthplace of HENRY VII.

**pen,** pointed implement used in writing or drawing to apply INK or a similar coloured fluid to any surface, such as paper. Various pens have been used since ancient times, including reeds, styluses, quills, metal fountain pens, ballpoint pens, and felt- and fibre-tipped pens.

**penance,** SACRAMENT used in the Roman Catholic and Eastern Orthodox churches, restored in the ANGLICAN COMMUNION in the 19th cent., in which a penitent confesses his or her SINS to a priest. A penance, usually of prayers, is then fixed by the priest. The penitent must have contrition for sin and make restitution for injuries to others.

**penates:** see LARES AND PENATES.

**pencil,** pointed implement used in writing or drawing to apply graphite or a similar coloured solid to any surface, especially paper. The lead pencil, a rod of graphite encased in wood, first came into use in the 16th cent.

**Penderecki, Krzysztof** ('pende‚retskee), 1933–, Polish composer. His music is characterized by unusual sonorities, and he has devised his own system of MUSICAL NOTATION to convey the effects desired. His works include the *St. Luke Passion* (1963–65), a concerto for five-stringed violin (1967–68), two operas (1968, 1975–78) and two symphonies (1973, 1980).

**Pendragon, Uther:** see ARTHURIAN LEGEND.

**pendulum,** a mass suspended from a fixed point so that it can swing in an arc. The length of a pendulum is the distance from the point of suspension to the centre of gravity of the mass. The period $T$, or time for one complete swing, depends on the length $l$ of the pendulum and on the acceleration $g$ of gravity at the pendulum's location, according to a formula derived by Christiaan HUYGENS: $T = 2\pi\sqrt{l/g}$. Huygens introduced (1673) the use of the pendulum to regulate the speed of clocks. See also HARMONIC MOTION.

**Penelope,** in Greek mythology, wife of ODYSSEUS, mother of Telemachus; in HOMER's *Odyssey,* a model of fidelity. Pursued by suitors during Odysseus' absence, she agreed to marry after weaving her father-in-law's shroud but unravelled her work each night. She finally promised to marry the man who could bend Odysseus' bow, but none could. Odysseus returned disguised as a beggar, bent the bow, and slew the suitors.

**Penghu dao** or **Pescadores,** group of 64 small islands in the Formosa Strait between S China and Taiwan c.130 km² (50 sq mi); administratively part of Taiwan. The islands, which were ceded to Japan by China in 1895 and returned after World War II, came under Chinese Nationalist rule after the Communist takeover of mainland China in 1949.

**penguin,** originally the common name for the extinct great AUK and now used, starting in the 19th cent., for unrelated, flightless Antarctic diving birds. Penguins swim by means of their flipperlike wings, using their webbed feet as rudders; they waddle awkwardly on land. Species range from the largest, the emperor (90–120 cm/3–4 ft in height), to the smallest, the fairy or little blue (32 cm/13 in). Penguins are highly gregarious and nest in colonies of up to half a million birds in 200 hectares (500 acres).

**penicillin,** any of a group of ANTIBIOTIC drugs obtained from moulds of the genus *Penicillium,* and the first to be used successfully to treat bacterial infections in man. Penicillin acts to inhibit cell wall formation in most gram-positive bacteria (see GRAM'S STAIN) and some gram-negative bacteria (meningococci, gonococci). Penicillin remains extremely important in antibiotic therapy, although it can induce allergic reactions (see ALLERGY) and resistant microorganisms can develop. Synthetic derivatives of penicillin include ampicillin and cloxacillin. Erythromycin and other antibiotics have become important in treating infections that are resistant to penicillin and in the treatment of hypersensitive patients.

**Peninsular campaign,** in the AMERICAN CIVIL WAR, failed attempt (April–July 1862) by the Union army to capture RICHMOND, Virginia, by invading the Virginia peninsula between the York and James rivers. A Union force of 100,000 men under Gen. George B. MCCLELLAN invaded the tip of the peninsula by sea and forced the Confederate general Joseph E. JOHNSTON to evacuate Yorktown and abandon Norfolk. The Union army drew near Richmond and beat off a Confederate attack at Fair Oaks, where Gen. Johnston was wounded. He was succeeded by Gen. Robert E. LEE, who withdrew the Confederate army to Richmond and subsequently forced McClellan to retreat from the peninsula by a brilliant counteroffensive in the Seven Days battles.

**Peninsular War,** 1808–14, conflict between France and Great Britain on the Iberian Peninsula, growing out of the efforts of NAPOLEON I to control

Spain and Portugal. When a palace revolt in Madrid (Mar. 1808) deposed the pro-French CHARLES IV, Napoleon invaded Spain and made his brother Joseph Bonaparte (see BONAPARTE, family) king of Spain (June). Both Spain and Portugal then revolted, and the British sent a force, under the future duke of WELLINGTON, to aid the rebels. Portugal was quickly won, but the fighting in Spain went on for years. By the time Napoleon abdicated, however, the British had won all of the peninsula and had penetrated France as far as Toulouse.

**penis:** see REPRODUCTIVE SYSTEM.

**penitential psalms:** see PSALMS.

**Penn, William,** 1644–1718, English Quaker leader and founder (1681) of PENNSYLVANIA colony in America as a religious and political haven for Quakers to enjoy (see FRIENDS, RELIGIOUS SOCIETY OF). During his first visit there (1682–84), Penn drew up a liberal Frame of Government and established friendly relations with the Indians.

**Pennines,** mountain range and hill system in England extending approximately 240 km (150 mi) from the Cheviot Hills in the N to The Peak in the S. It forms the watershed for the main rivers of England, and is sometimes called 'the backbone of England'. The highest peak is Cross Fell, which reaches 893 m (2930 ft). The upper parts are mainly rough moorland and sheep pasture, with beautiful scenery which attracts many tourists. The Pennine Way footpath, opened in 1965, stretches for 400 km (250 mi) from Kirk Yetholm in the Borders region, Scotland, to Edale in Derbyshire in the S.

**Pennsylvania,** state of the US (1984 est. pop. 11,901,000), area 117,412 km² (45,333 sq mi), located in the mid-Atlantic region, bordered by lake Erie and New York (N), New Jersey (E), Delaware, Maryland, and West Virginia (SW), and Ohio (W). HARRISBURG is the capital and the dominant city is PHILADELPHIA, fourth largest in the US; PITTSBURGH, Erie and Allentown are also important. Most of Pennsylvania's terrain consists of mountains extending diagonally across the state, with ridges and mountains in the W and the Allegheny plateau in the N. Lowland is found in the SE and NW corners. Pennsylvania produces about one-quarter of the country's steel, and it also has extensive deposits of coal. Chief manufactures are primary metals, nonelectrical machinery, and processed foods. Extensive farmlands provide dairy products, cattle, corn, eggs, mushrooms, and apples. More than 80% of the population lives in metropolitan areas; in 1980 89% was non-Hispanic white, and almost 9% black. The original inhabitants of the area were Delaware, Shawnee and Susquehanna Indians. In the 17th cent. the Swedes, Dutch, and then British controlled the region, the latter granting proprietary rights to the [Baker William PENN, who viewed the colony as a haven for persecuted groups. Pennsylvania was one of the centres of the independence movement, and saw much fighting in both the American Revolution and the Civil War. In the late 19th cent. oil, coal, and steel caused the state's industry to expand. In the 1980s Pennsylvania's heavy industries, especially steel mills, were severely affected by the national economic slowdown; however, there was increased national demand for the state's coal.

**pension,** regular payments by the state to people over a certain age to enable them to subsist without work, or by an employer to an employee who has retired. Pensions schemes in the UK started in 1812 with the Civil Service. Today private pension plans (organized by local authorities, trade unions, corporations, professional associations, and others) supplement benefits due under the national insurance scheme which took effect in 1948.

**Pentagon, the,** structure housing the US Dept of Defense, in Arlington, Virginia. Completed in 1943, it comprises five concentric buildings, connected by corridors, and covers an area of 13.8 hectares (34 acres).

**pentameter** [Gr., = measure of five feet], in VERSIFICATION, a line to be scanned in five feet, as in Thomas NASHE's 'Cold doth/not sting,/the pret/ty birds/do sing.' Iambic pentameter, with short-long feet, is the most common English meter, appearing first in CHAUCER's poetry. In the *Canterbury Tales* he used rhymed pentameter couplets; since he pronounced a final *e,* the lines often had eleven syllables. Later, with the final *e* dropped, this form became the heroic couplet, used notably by John DRYDEN and Alexander POPE. Blank verse, a succession of unrhymed iambic pentameters, is primarily an English form; it has been used in the loftiest epic and dramatic verse from SHAKESPEARE and John MILTON to the

The **Pentagon**

present. The SONNET is one of the most successful uses of iambic pentameter in English poetry.

**Pentateuch** (‚pentətyoohk), [Gr., = five books], first five books of the OLD TESTAMENT, the TORAH of MOSES.

**pentathlon,** composite athletic event. In ancient Greece it comprised jumping, running, wrestling, discus, and javelin. The modern pentathlon, an Olympic event since 1912, involves a cross-country horseback ride, a cross-country run, swimming, épée fencing, and pistol shooting.

**Pentecost** [Gr., = fiftieth], important Jewish and Christian feasts. In Judaism it is called *Shavuot* and marks the end of the Palestinian spring grain harvest (see JEWISH HOLIDAYS). In Christianity it commemorates the coming of the HOLY GHOST to the disciples of Jesus, 50 days after the Passover in which Jesus died. In England it is called Whitsunday.

**Pentecostalism,** fundamentalist Protestant religious movement which began both in the US (1906) and in Britain (1907) in the first decade of the 20th cent. Pentecostalists believe in baptism with the Holy Ghost, 'Speaking in tongues', faith healing, and the impending Second Coming of Christ. Since the 1960s Pentecostalism has had a widespread impact in the traditional churches, e.g., the Roman Catholic and the Anglican.

**penumbra:** see ECLIPSE; SUNSPOTS.

**Penza,** city (1985 pop. 527,000), SE European USSR, on the Volga Heights, W of the Volga R. It is a rail junction and adminstrative centre, with light industries including engineering and food- and wood-processing. It was founded as a military centre in 1666.

**peonage,** system of involuntary servitude based on the indebtedness of the labourer (peon) to his creditor. It arose in Spanish America to supply labour for European settlers and was instituted in the West Indies with the ENCOMIENDA. Despite attempted reforms by Bartolomé de LAS CASAS in the 16th cent., it persisted in some form well into the 20th cent.

**peony,** popular flowering plant (genus *Paeonia*) from Siberia, belonging to the buttercup family. Herbaceous peonies (most are varieties of *P. lactiflora*) are hardy, bushy perennials that die back each year. The large, usually spring-blooming, single or double flowers are generally shades of red, pink, or white. Tree peonies (*P. suffruticosa*) have a somewhat brittle woody base and are usually taller, with more abundant and larger blossoms but are very subject to wind damage.

**People's Liberation Army,** Chinese national army. The People's Liberation Army includes all branches of the military. It occupies a special place in Chinese society. This is due to its historical legacy of the LONG MARCH, second SINO-JAPANESE WAR, and the civil war, and because it performs ideological, political, and economic as well as military functions. Since 1978 it has been undergoing a difficult transformaton towards modernization, professionalization, and curtailment of its political activities. In 1985 it was decided to reduce its strength from 4 million to 3 million.

**People's party:** see POPULIST PARTY.

**Peoria,** US city (1984 est. pop. 117,000), central Illinois, on the Illinois R.; inc. 1845. A busy port, it is the trade and transport centre for a region producing grain, livestock, and coal. Although it is an industrial city with distilleries and factories producing heavy machinery, steel, and chemicals, Peoria is known for its scenic beauty. Lasalle established a fort in the region in 1680. The first permanent American settlement was in 1819.

**Pepin** (‚pepin), rulers of the FRANKS. **Pepin of Landan** (Pepin I), d. 639?, mayor of the palace of the Frankish kingdom of Austrasia, forced the succession (629) of Dagobert I as king and established the foundation for the CAROLINGIAN dynasty. His grandson, **Pepin of Heristal** (Pepin II), d. 714, mayor of the palace (680–714) of Austrasia and Neustria, established Carolingian power over the MEROVINGIAN kings by making himself the actual ruler of the Franks. He was the father of CHARLES MARTEL and the grandfather of **Pepin the Short** (Pepin III), c.714–768, the first Carolingian king of the Franks (r.751–68). He overthrew the Merovingian dynasty and had himself crowned king with the support of Pope Zacharias. Pepin defended papal interests and in 754 turned over to the pope what became the foundation of the PAPAL STATES. He was the father of CHARLEMAGNE.

**pepper,** name for the fruits of several plants used as condiments or in medicine. **Black pepper** (*Piper nigrum*), the true pepper, is economically the most important species of the pantropical pepper family (Piperaceae). A perennial climbing shrub native to Java, it bears pea-sized berries, the 'peppercorns' of commerce. Black pepper, sold whole or ground, is the whole fruit; white pepper, made by removing the dark, outer hull, has a milder, less pungent flavour. Other *Piper* species of value include the betel pepper (*P. betle*), whose leaves are a principal ingredient in BETEL. The **red peppers,** native to warm temperate and tropical regions of the Americas, are various species of *Capsicum* (of the NIGHTSHADE family). The hot varieties include cayenne pepper, whose dried, ground fruit is sold as a spice, and chilli pepper, sold similarly as a powder or in a chilli sauce. Paprika (the Hungarian word for red pepper) is a ground spice from a less pungent variety. The pimiento, or Spanish pepper, is a mild type; its small fruit is used as a condiment and for stuffing olives. The common garden, or bell, pepper has larger, also mild fruits; they are used as vegetables and in salads. Bell peppers are also seen as yellow and green peppers because they are most often marketed while still unripe.

**peppermint:** see MINT.

**Pepple, William Dappa,** 1817–64, king of Bonny, in the Niger delta, NIGERIA (r.1835–54). He organized and led a guerrilla war against British traders who in turn engineered his deposition and deportation in 1854. He returned to Bonny after seven years in exile, part of which time was spent in London.

**pepsin,** digestive enzyme secreted by the STOMACH that degrades protein. Most active in the acidic medium normally present in the stomach, pepsin breaks down proteins into short PEPTIDE chains and AMINO ACID molecules which are readily absorbed.

**peptide,** biochemical formed by the linkage of two or more AMINO ACID molecules. The amino acids are coupled by a peptide bond, a special linkage in which the nitrogen atom of one amino acid binds to the carboxyl atom of another. Peptides are classified according to the number of amino acid residues (e.g., dipeptides or polypeptides).

**Pepys, Samuel,** 1633-1703, English public official and author of the most famous English DIARY. He was an admiralty official, sat in Parliament (1679), and in 1684 was named president of the ROYAL SOCIETY. Forced into retirement on the accession of William III, he wrote *Memoirs . . . of the Royal Navy* (1690). Pepys's diary, in cipher, was partially deciphered and published in 1825, and almost all the text appeared from 1893 to 1899. An intimate record of his private life from 1 Jan. 1660, to 31 May 1669, the diary gives a vivid picture of social life and conditions in the early RESTORATION period.

**Pequot Indians:** see NORTH AMERICAN INDIANS.

**perception,** in psychology, those processes underlying the selection, organization, and processing of sensory input in one or more modality (e.g., vision, hearing). Perceptual processes are difficult in principle to separate from purely sensory stimulation on the one hand, and processes of COGNITION, on the other. Contemporary theories of perception are frequently of an INFORMATION PROCESSING or computational nature.

**perch,** symmetrical freshwater FISH of the family Percidae, related to sunfishes and sea BASSES. The European perch (*Perca fluviatilis*) gave the family its name. It is a freshwater fish, usually weighing about 500 g (1 lb). They feed on smaller fishes as adults, the fry feeding on small invertebrates. Perch are familiar to fishermen, and can be very large, 4.5 kg (10 lb) being the record catch.

**Percier, Charles** (peə‚syay), 1764–1838, French architect. With Pierre FONTAINE he developed the Empire style under NAPOLEON I in Paris, Antwerp, Brussels, and Rome. They worked (1802–12) on the palaces of the LOUVRE and the TUILERIES, designed the Arc de Triomphe du Carrousel, and altered and decorated imperial châteaux at VERSAILLES and elsewhere. Their furniture and fabric designs also conformed to Empire motifs.

**percussion instrument,** any instrument that produces a musical sound when struck with an implement such as a mallet, a stick, a disc, or with the hand. They are used in ORCHESTRAS and BANDS most often to emphasize rhythm. The most common type is the DRUM, technically known as a membranophone, which consists of a membrane stretched over a frame to be struck with sticks or with the hand. Idiophones are percussion instruments in which the vibrating agent is the solid substance of the instrument itself. These include the triangle, a steel rod bent into an angle and struck with a straight rod; sticks clicked against each other; castanets, commonly consisting of two joined pieces of wood or ivory snapped together between the palm and the fingers; cymbals, a pair of concave metal plates that are struck together; the gong, a metal disc struck with a mallet or drumstick; the celesta, a high-pitched instrument consisting of steel bars fastened over wood resonators and struck by hammers operated from a keyboard; the glockenspiel, a curved frame enclosing metal bars that are struck with a hammer; the XYLOPHONE; and the BELL. In general, percussion instruments are not tuned by construction; pitch, tone, and volume depend on the skill of the player.

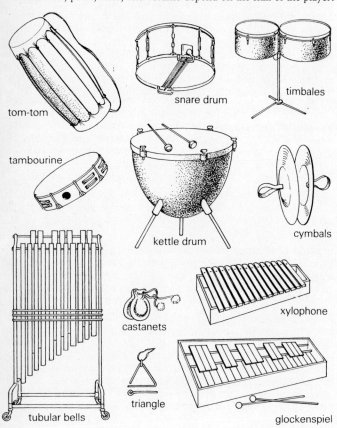

tom-tom

snare drum

timbales

tambourine

kettle drum

cymbals

castanets

xylophone

tubular bells

triangle

glockenspiel

Percussion instruments

**Percy, Sir Henry,** 1366–1403, English nobleman, called Hotspur; son of Henry Percy, 1st earl of Northumberland. He fought against the Scots at Otterburn (1388) and Hamildon (1402). Although he had earlier supported the Lancastrian cause, in 1403 Hotspur and his father planned with Thomas Percy, OWEN GLENDOWER, and Sir Edmund de Mortimer to dethrone HENRY IV. Henry triumphed at Shrewsbury, and Hotspur was slain.

**peregrine,** BIRD of prey in the FALCON family distributed worldwide, except for Antarctica. The peregrine (*Falco peregrinus*) is probably the most famous of all birds of prey, widely used in falconry. Another claim to fame is the speed with which it dives, or stoops, on its prey: it can dive out of the sky at more than 320 kph (200 mph). It takes birds such as PIGEON and DUCK, but will also eat small mammals and amphibians. This beautiful bird with its large, bright black eyes and black-barred underparts ranges in size from 38 to 48 cm (15 to 19 in). The peregrine population has been declining in recent years as pesticides such as DDT (see INSECTICIDE) cause infertile eggs to be laid. Despite the care of conservationists, young peregrine are taken illegally for falconry.

**Pereira** (pə‚rayrə), city (1979 est. pop. 257,039), capital of Risaraldas dept. in the fertile Cauca Valley of W Colombia. Founded in 1863 its own growth has paralleled the development of the surrounding region as an important area of coffee and cattle farming.

**Perelman, S(idney) J(oseph),** 1904–79, American comic writer. The titles of some of his best-known books suggest his screwball type of humour *Strictly from Hunger* (1937), *The Road to Miltown; or, Under the Spreading Atrophy* (1957), and *The Rising Gorge* (1961). Perelman wrote the scripts for several MARX BROTHERS films.

**perennial,** in botany, plant that normally lives for more than two growing seasons, as contrasted to an ANNUAL or BIENNIAL. In horticulture the term is usually restricted to hardy herbaceous plants, such as IRIS, PEONY, and TULIP, which die down to the ground each year and survive the winter on food stored in specialized underground stems.

**Peres, Shimon,** 1923–, prime minister of ISRAEL (1984–86), b. Poland. A Labour politician, he was first appointed to the cabinet in 1969, subsequently becoming defence minister (1974–77) and acting prime minister (1977). After the 1984 elections he became prime minister of a national unity coalition including the Labour and Likud parties; in accordance with the coalition agreement, he handed over the premiership to the Likud leader, Itzhak SHAMIR, in 1986, becoming foreign minister and deputy premier. Following the 1988 elections he took the finance portfolio and deputy premiership in a further Labour-Likud coalition.

**perestroika,** (Rus., = restructuring), term denoting the wideranging economic, political, and social reforms pursued by Soviet leader Mikhail GORBACHEV since he came to power in 1985. Central aims of the perestroika process are to make the Soviet economy more efficient and productive by reducing central state controls in favour of market forces, and to make the political hierarchy more accountable to the people. See also GLASNOST.

**Peretz** or **Perez, Isaac Loeb,** 1852–1915, Polish Jewish poet, novelist, playwright, and lawyer. A voice of the renaissance of progressive culture among the Jews (*Haskalah*), he wrote in Hebrew and Yiddish of the material poverty and spiritual riches of European Jews. His finest work is contained in his Hasidic sketches, e.g., *Stories and Pictures* (1900–01).

**Pérez, Antonio** (‚payreth), 1534?–1611, Spanish politician. The ambitious, unscrupulous secretary of PHILIP II, he and the princesa de Eboli were implicated in the assassination (1578) of Juan de Escobedo, secretary to the governor of the NETHERLANDS, probably because Escobedo had threatened to reveal Pérez's intrigues to the king. One theory is that Pérez told Philip that Escobedo was plotting treason and that the king ordered the murder. Pérez was prosecuted and in 1590 fled to his native Aragón, where he openly accused Philip of ordering the assassination. The people of Aragón sided with Pérez and started a revolt (1591), which was ruthlessly suppressed. Pérez then fled the country.

**Pérez de Ayala, Ramón** (‚payreth day əh‚yahlah), 1880?–1962, Spanish writer. His work includes such novels of ideas as *Belarmino y Apolonio* (1921), *Tigre Juan* (1926), and *El curandero de su honra* (1926; tr. The Healer of His Honour); essays; and poetry.

**Pérez de Cuéllar, Javier,** 1920–, Peruvian diplomat, secretary general of the UNITED NATIONS. He entered the Peruvian foreign service in 1940 and served in several important posts, including ambassador to the USSR (1969–71) and to the UN (1971–75). He represented the UN on the CYPRUS problem (1975–78) and in 1982 succeeded Kurt Waldheim as secretary general, being reelected for a further five-year term from 1987.

**Pérez Galdós, Benito** (pay‚reth gal‚dohs), 1843–1920, Spanish novelist and dramatist. He is considered the finest Spanish exponent of

REALISM. For his panoramic and psychologically acute treatment of Spanish society he has been called the greatest Spanish novelist since CERVANTES. His works include a cycle of 46 historical novels, *Episodios nacionales,* covering 1805 to 1874; 21 *novelas españolas contemporáneas,* including *Fortunata y Jacinta* (1886–87); and 6 *novelas españolas de la primera época,* notably *Doña Perfecta* (1876) and *La familia de León Roch* (1878). His plays include dramatizations of some of his novels.

**perfume,** aroma produced by essential oils of plants and by synthetic aromatics. The burning of incense in religious rites of ancient China, Palestine, and Egypt led gradually to the personal use of perfume, widespread in ancient Greece and Rome. During the Middle Ages Crusaders brought knowledge of perfumery to Europe from the East. After 1500 Paris was the major centre of perfume-making. Since the early 19th cent. chemists have produced thousands of synthetic scents. In the 20th cent. perfumes for men and women, most a blend of natural and synthetic scents, were produced by prominent fashion designers (see FASHION).

**Pergamon,** ancient city of Asia Minor on the Caicus R., now in Turkey. An independent kingdom, it flourished as a brilliant centre of Hellenistic culture in the 3rd and 2nd cent. BC. It was particularly notable for its sculptures and for a large library of books on PARCHMENT (which takes its name from the city). King Attalus III (d. 133 BC) bequeathed Pergamon to Rome.

**Pergolesi, Giovanni Battista,** 1710–36, Italian composer. In his very short life, he wrote two masterpieces, the short comic opera *The Maid as Mistress* (1733) and a *Stabat Mater* (1736) for treble voices and strings, as well as two operas.

**Peri-Antarctic Islands,** islands and island groups in the far southern oceans around and related to the Antarctic continent; from 0° going E they are BOUVETOYA, PRINCE EDWARD ISLANDS, ÎLES CROZET, ÎLES KERGUELEN, HEARD AND McDONALD ISLANDS, Îles Saint-Paul et Amsterdam, MACQUARIE ISLAND, Islands, Auckland Islands, Campbell Island, Scott Island, Peter I Øy, SOUTH SHETLAND ISLANDS, SOUTH ORKNEY ISLANDS, Shag Rocks, SOUTH GEORGIA, SOUTH SANDWICH ISLANDS, and GOUGH ISLAND. About half have permanent meteorological and scientific stations.

**Pericles,** c.495–429 BC, Athenian statesman. In 461 BC he secured the exile of Cimon, whom he replaced as leader of ATHENS. Under his tutelage Athens reached its zenith. The DELIAN LEAGUE was powerful, a truce was arranged (445) with Sparta that brought 14 years of peace, and democratic reforms were introduced. Pericles became a great patron of the arts, encouraging music and drama, and was responsible for the building of such great monuments as the PARTHENON and Propylaea on the Acropolis. In 430 BC, during the PELOPONNESIAN WAR, he made a strong appeal to the pride and patriotism of the Athenians but was driven from office. Reinstated (429), he died in the plague six months later.

**perigee** and **perihelion:** see APSIS.

**periglacial,** nonglacial tundra regions. Today the term is used to describe a large variety of cold nonglacial conditions at either high latitude or high altitude in temperate latitudes, regardless of proximity to glaciers. Periglacial regions are characterized by a unique set of geomorphological processes and are often underlain by PERMAFROST.

**Perim,** island (13 km²/5 sq mi) of Southern Yemen, in the Strait of BAB EL MANDEB. Formerly a coaling station and British naval base, it is now used by the Soviet navy.

**perinatology:** see under PAEDIATRICS.

**period,** in physics: see HARMONIC MOTION; WAVE.

**periodical,** publication issued regularly, distinguished from the NEWSPAPER in format in that its pages are smaller and usually bound, and in that it is published weekly, monthly, or quarterly, rather than daily. Periodicals range from technical and scholarly journals to illustrated magazines for mass circulation. The French *Journal des scavans* (1665–1791) is considered the first periodical, whereas the English monthly *Gentleman's Magazine* (1731–1868) was the first to use the word *magazine* in the sense of a periodical for entertainment. English period journalism may be said to have begun with Richard STEELE's the *Tatler,* which appeard between Apr. 1709 and Jan. 1711 and was published three times a week, and *The Spectator,* which Steele ran in collaboration with Joseph ADDISON and was published between 1 Mar. 1711 and 6 Dec. 1712. Both these publications may be classed as periodicals as they aimed to improve public taste by discussion rather than to convey news. Neither of them survived the imposition of the Stamp Act which made such publications expensive to produce. In 1731 Edward Cave started the immensely successful *Gentleman's Magazine* which continued in publication until 1907. The *Scots Magazine* followed, 1739–1817, and the 18th cent. also saw the publication of the *Monthly Review* (1749–1845), Samuel Johnson's the *Rambler* (1750–52) and in the next century the celebrated through briefly published *London Magazine* (1820–29) and the formidable *Blackwood's Magazine* (founded 1817) and *Edinburgh Review* which was founded in 1802 and lasted until 1929. Both these publications profoundly affected periodic journalism in the UK, raising its standard and tone considerably. At that time periodicals published fiction, either as short stories or serialized novels: many of the greatest novels of the era appeared in this way, e.g., those of Dickens, Eliot, and Trollope. Other Victorian periodicals for the gentlemanly and middle classes were *Fraser's Magazine,* the *Cornhill, Review of Reviews,* the *Strand Magazine,* and—above all—*Punch, or the London Charivari* which first appeared in 1841 and today still has a circulation of 65,000. The end of the 19th cent. brought new titles aimed at the lower end of the market, such as *Answers* and *Titbits,* and the 20th cent. has witnessed an explosion of periodic journalism. These include general magazines, trade and technical journals, political journals, magazines on hobbies and pastimes and a considerable number of journals aimed at female readership. To give some idea of scope and readership —of those aimed at general interests *Readers Digest* has a circulation of 1½ milllion, *Motor Cycle News* has 143,364 readers a week, *The Economist* has 290,000 a week, *Shoot Magazine* (football) has 158,000 readers a week and *Woman's Own* has 1,065,367 readers a week. Periodic journalism has benefitted from the new printing and photographic technologies. Many of these magazines have a very high ADVERTISING content (50% is not unusual), and can be seen as at least as an important medium in stimulating consumer demand as television.

**periodic table,** chart that reflects the periodic recurrence of chemical and physical properties of the chemical elements (see ELEMENT) when the elements are arranged in order of increasing ATOMIC NUMBER. The periodic table was devised by Dmitri MENDELEEV and revised by Henry MOSELEY. It is divided into vertical columns, or groups, numbered from I to VIII, with a final column numbered 0. Each group is divided into two categories, or families, one called the a series (the representative, or main group, elements) the other the b series (the TRANSITION ELEMENTS, or subgroup elements). All the elements in a group have similar configurations of electrons and the same number of VALENCY electrons, and have similar chemical properties. The horizontal rows of the table are called periods. The elements of a particular period have the same number of electron shells; the number of electrons in these shells, which equals the element's atomic number, increases from left to right within each period. In each period the lighter METALS appear on the left, the heavier metals in the centre, and the nonmetals on the right. Elements on the borderline between metals and nonmetals are called metalloids. Elements in group Ia are called the ALKALI METALS; in group IIa, the ALKALINE-EARTH METALS; in group VIIa, the HALOGENS; and in group 0, the INERT GASES.

**periodontitis** or **pyorrhoea,** inflammation and degeneration of the gums and other tissues surrounding the teeth. Symptoms are bleeding gums, followed by the receding of gums from the TEETH, loosening of the teeth, and resorption of the bone supporting the teeth. Causes include poor nutrition, plaque, and poor oral hygiene.

**periscope,** instrument to permit the viewing of an object either out of one's direct line of vision or concealed by some intervening body. The image is received in a mirror and reflected through a tube with lenses to a mirror visible to the viewer. Submarine periscopes, with tubes up to 9 m (30 ft) long, can be rotated to permit a scan of the entire horizon.

**peristyle:** see ATRIUM.

**peritoneum:** see ABDOMEN.

**peritonitis,** acute or chronic inflammation of the peritoneum, the membrane lining the abdomen and surrounding the internal organs. It is caused by invasion of bacteria or foreign matter following rupture of an internal organ, by infection from elsewhere in the body, by penetrating injury to the abdominal wall, or by accidental pollution during surgery. Treatment includes ANTIBIOTIC therapy.

## Periodic Table

**Legend (sample):**
- atomic number — 89
- atomic symbol — Ac
- name of element — Actinium
- atomic weight — (227)
- (parentheses indicate most stable isotope)

| 1 | 2 | 3 | 4 | 5 | 6 | 7 | 8 | 9 | 10 | 11 | 12 | 13 | 14 | 15 | 16 | 17 | 18 |
|---|---|---|---|---|---|---|---|---|---|---|---|---|---|---|---|---|---|
| 1 **H** Hydrogen 1.00794 | | | | | | | | | | | | | | | | | 2 **He** Helium 4.00260 |
| 3 **Li** Lithium 6.941 | 4 **Be** Beryllium 9.01218 | | | | | | | | | | | 5 **B** Boron 10.81 | 6 **C** Carbon 12.011 | 7 **N** Nitrogen 14.0067 | 8 **O** Oxygen 15.9994 | 9 **F** Fluorine 18.998403 | 10 **Ne** Neon 20.179 |
| 11 **Na** Sodium 22.98977 | 12 **Mg** Magnesium 24.305 | | | | | | | | | | | 13 **Al** Aluminium 26.98154 | 14 **Si** Silicon 28.0855 | 15 **P** Phosphorus 30.97376 | 16 **S** Sulphur 32.06 | 17 **Cl** Chlorine 35.453 | 18 **Ar** Argon 39.948 |
| 19 **K** Potassium 39.0983 | 20 **Ca** Calcium 40.08 | 21 **Sc** Scandium 44.9559 | 22 **Ti** Titanium 47.88 | 23 **V** Vanadium 50.9415 | 24 **Cr** Chromium 51.996 | 25 **Mn** Manganese 54.9380 | 26 **Fe** Iron 55.847 | 27 **Co** Cobalt 58.9332 | 28 **Ni** Nickel 58.69 | 29 **Cu** Copper 63.546 | 30 **Zn** Zinc 65.38 | 31 **Ga** Gallium 69.72 | 32 **Ge** Germanium 72.59 | 33 **As** Arsenic 74.9216 | 34 **Se** Selenium 78.96 | 35 **Br** Bromine 79.904 | 36 **Kr** Krypton 83.80 |
| 37 **Rb** Rubidium 85.4678 | 38 **Sr** Strontium 87.62 | 39 **Y** Yttrium 88.9059 | 40 **Zr** Zirconium 91.22 | 41 **Nb** Niobium 92.9064 | 42 **Mo** Molybdenum 95.94 | 43 **Tc** Technetium (98) | 44 **Ru** Ruthenium 101.07 | 45 **Rh** Rhodium 102.9055 | 46 **Pd** Palladium 106.42 | 47 **Ag** Silver 107.8682 | 48 **Cd** Cadmium 112.41 | 49 **In** Indium 114.82 | 50 **Sn** Tin 118.69 | 51 **Sb** Antimony 121.75 | 52 **Te** Tellurium 127.60 | 53 **I** Iodine 126.9045 | 54 **Xe** Xenon 131.29 |
| 55 **Cs** Caesium 132.9054 | 56 **Ba** Barium 137.33 | 57 **La** Lanthanum 138.9055 | 72 **Hf** Hafnium 178.49 | 73 **Ta** Tantalum 180.7479 | 74 **W** Tungsten 183.85 | 75 **Re** Rhenium 186.207 | 76 **Os** Osmium 190.2 | 77 **Ir** Iridium 192.2 | 78 **Pt** Platinum 195.08 | 79 **Au** Gold 196.9665 | 80 **Hg** Mercury 200.59 | 81 **Tl** Thallium 204.383 | 82 **Pb** Lead 207.2 | 83 **Bi** Bismuth 208.9804 | 84 **Po** Polonium (209) | 85 **At** Astatine (210) | 86 **Rn** Radon (222) |
| 87 **Fr** Francium (223) | 88 **Ra** Radium 226.0254 | 89 **Ac** Actinium 227.0278 | 104 **Unq†** Unnilquadium (261) | 105 **Unp*** Unnilpentium (262) | 106 **Unh** Unnilhexium (263) | 107 **Uns** Unnilseptium (262) | | 109 **Une** Unnilennium (266) | | | | | | | | | |

**Lanthanide series** (*Rare Earth Elements*)

| 58 **Ce** Cerium 140.12 | 59 **Pr** Praseodymium 140.9077 | 60 **Nd** Neodymium 144.24 | 61 **Pm** Promethium (145) | 62 **Sm** Samarium 150.36 | 63 **Eu** Europium 151.96 | 64 **Gd** Gadolinium 157.25 | 65 **Tb** Terbium 158.9254 | 66 **Dy** Dysprosium 162.50 | 67 **Ho** Holmium 164.9304 | 68 **Er** Erbium 167.26 | 69 **Tm** Thulium 168.9342 | 70 **Yb** Ytterbium 173.04 | 71 **Lu** Lutetium 174.967 |
|---|---|---|---|---|---|---|---|---|---|---|---|---|---|

**Actinide series** (*Radioactive Rare Earth Elements*)

| 90 **Th** Thorium 232.0381 | 91 **Pa** Protactinium 231.0359 | 92 **U** Uranium 238.0289 | 93 **Np** Neptunium 237.0482 | 94 **Pu** Plutonium (244) | 95 **Am** Americium (243) | 96 **Cm** Curium (247) | 97 **Bk** Berkelium (247) | 98 **Cf** Californium (252) | 99 **Es** Einsteinium (254) | 100 **Fm** Fermium (257) | 101 **Md** Mendelevium (258) | 102 **No** Nobelium (259) | 103 **Lr** Lawrencium (260) |
|---|---|---|---|---|---|---|---|---|---|---|---|---|---|

† Other proposed names are kurchatovium (USSR) and hahnium (US).
\* Other proposed names are nielsbohrium (USSR) and rutherfordium (US).

**periwinkle,** mollusc with a conical spiral shell, a variety of SNAIL. Periwinkles are marine GASTROPODS that feed on algae and seaweed and are found at the water's edge. They are often brightly coloured in yellows and tans. The edible winkle is a periwinkle.

**perjury,** in law, the offence of making a false statement in court, while on oath as a witness. The witness must know the statement to be false, and possess an intent to commit the offence. Perjury is not the same as CONTEMPT OF COURT, though it may result in an obstruction of justice. Perjury is largely an offence against the oath itself; thus a second perjury while still on oath will be tried as one charge. If another person is aware of the perjury and does not tell the court, he or she may be guilty of subordindination of perjury.

**Perkins, Frances,** 1882–1965, US secretary of labour (1933–45). The first woman appointed to the cabinet, she promoted and administered liberal trade union legislation during Pres. F.D. ROOSEVELT's NEW DEAL administration.

**Perm** (pyeəm), city (1985 pop. 1,056,000), NE European USSR, on the Kama R. A transfer centre for rail and river cargo, it is a major producer of machinery in the Urals industrial and mining region and has oil refineries and chemical plants. Founded in 1780, it was named Molotov from 1940 to 1958.

**permafrost,** a condition existing below the ground surface in either soil or rock where the ground temperature has remained below 0°C (32°F) for at least two consecutive years. Moisture need not be present within the ground for permafrost to be present. The word is a shortened form of 'permanently frozen ground'; however, mineralization of ground waters may depress their freezing point such that temperatures below 0°C (32°F) do not produce 'frozen ground'. Permafrost is usually overlain by an 'active layer' of ground that is subject to seasonal thawing.

**Permian period:** see GEOLOGICAL ERA (table).

**permutations and combinations,** the study of techniques for counting arrangements and choices of objects; such techniques are often used in PROBABILITY problems. A *permutation* of a SET is a way in which the elements of the set can be arranged or ordered. In general, the number of permutations of $n$ things taken $r$ at a time is given by $^nP_r = n!/(n-r)!$, where the symbol $n!$, denoting the product of the integers from 1 to $n$, is called $n$ factorial. A *combination* is a choice of different elements from a larger set, without regard to order. In general, the number of combinations of $n$ things taken $r$ at a time is $^nC_r = n!/r!(n-r)!$ *Combinatorics* considers the arrangements of the elements of a set into patterns.

**Perón, Juan Domingo** (pe͟ˌrohn), 1895–1974, president of Argentina (1946–55, 1973–74). An army officer, he rose to prominence when Ramón Castillo was overthrown in 1943. He developed a following among workers, churchmen, landowners, and industrialists. In 1946 he was elected president by a huge majority. He set up a dictatorship and instituted a programme of revolutionary, nationalistic measures (known as *peronismo*), which were supposed to lead to economic self-sufficiency. By the early 1950s, however, the economy had deteriorated and Perón had broken with the church. After the death in 1952 of his enormously popular wife, Eva, his support weakened, and in 1955 he was overthrown by a military coup. *Peronismo* nevertheless remained a potent political force and contributed to governmental chaos. In 1971 Perón returned to Argentina, and in 1973 he was elected president. His wife, María Estela ('Isabelita') Martínez de Perón (see below), was elected vice president, and she succeeded to the presidency when he died in 1974. Perón's second wife, **Eva Duarte de Perón** (dooh͟ˌahtay), 1919–52, had been a minor actress before her marriage to Perón in 1945. After he became president, she virtually ran the ministries of health and labour, and she commanded a huge political following. She died of cancer at the age of 33. Perón's third wife, **María Estela (Isabel) Martínez de Perón,** 1931–, was a dancer before she married the exiled Perón in 1961. Upon her husband's death in 1974 she became president of Argentina, but her complete inability to govern led to economic and political chaos, and the armed forces deposed her in 1976. She was placed under house arrest, but on being freed in 1981 went into exile in Spain. In 1989 the Peronista Party, led by Carlos Menem, won the presidential elections.

**peroxide,** chemical compound containing two oxygen atoms, each of which is bonded to the other and to a radical or some element other than oxygen; e.g., in hydrogen peroxide ($H_2O_2$) the atoms are joined together in the chainlike structure H O O H. Peroxides are unstable, releasing oxygen when heated, and are powerful oxidizing agents. Peroxides may sometimes be formed directly by the reaction of an element or compound with oxygen.

**Perpendicular:** see GOTHIC ARCHITECTURE AND ART.

**perpetual-motion machine,** a machine, considered impossible to build, that would be able to operate continuously and supply useful work without needing a continuous supply of heat or fuel. A perpetual-motion machine of the first kind, which would produce more ENERGY in the form of work than is supplied to it in the form of heat, violates the first law of THERMODYNAMICS. A perpetual-motion machine of the second kind, which would continuously supply work without a flow of heat from a warmer body to a cooler body, violates the second law of thermodynamics.

**Perpignan** (ˌpeəpin'yon), city (1982 pop. 113,646, agglomeration 137,915), capital of Pyrénées-Orientales dept., S. France, on the Tet R. It is a trading centre for the rich wine, fruit, and market-garden region of Roussillon. Formerly capital of the Spanish kingdom of Majorca, Perpignan became a part of France in 1642. Notable buildings include the castle and merchants' exchange of the 14th cent. and the 14th–15th-cent. Gothic cathedral.

**Perrault, Charles** (pe͟ˌroh), 1628–1703, French poet famed for his *Contes de ma mère l'oye* (1697; tr. Mother Goose Tales) for children. One of his poems (1687) touched off the celebrated 'quarrel of the ancients and the moderns'; Boileau-Despréaux, the chief defender of the ancients, bandied insults with Perrault until 1694.

**Perret, Auguste** (pe͟ˌray), 1874–1954, French architect. He was a pioneer in the use of reinforced concrete, notably in the church of Le Raincy, near Paris (1922–23). He also built warehouses, factories, residences, and theatres in the new material.

**Perrot, Jules,** 1810–92, French dancer and choreographer. He studied with Auguste VESTRIS, and was famous as a dancer. As a choreographer, he worked at the Imperial Theatre, St Petersburg (1948–59), where his ballets included *Esmerelda*, *Ondine*, and part of original *Giselle*. He is generally considered the greatest choreographer of Romantic ballet.

**Perry, Frederick John,** 1909–, English lawn tennis player. Starting as a table tennis champion, Fred Perry became the most successful British lawn tennis player of recent times. He was the mainstay of the British team that won the Davis Cup in 1933; won the US singles title in the same year; and, a unique achievement for his era, won the men's singles title at WIMBLEDON three years running (1934-36).

**Perry, Matthew Calbraith,** 1794–1858, US naval officer. Commodore Perry opened up isolationist JAPAN to Western trade and influence. In 1853 he anchored his squadron of four US navy ships in lower Tokyo Bay. A skilled diplomat, Perry negotiated a treaty (1854) that permitted American ships to use two Japanese ports. His brother, **Oliver Hazard Perry,** 1785-1819, was also a US naval officer. He commanded the US fleet that defeated a British force in the Battle of Lake Erie (1813) during the WAR OF 1812.

**Perse, Saint-John,** pseud. of **Alexis Saint-Léger Léger,** 1887–1975, French poet and diplomat; b. Guadeloupe. He was the permanent head of the foreign affairs ministry from 1933 to 1940. His reputation as a poet of great lyric power grew after his self-imposed exile to the US in 1940. His works include *Éloges* (1911), *Anabase* (1924), *Exil* (1942), and *Amers* (1957; tr. Seamarks). He received the 1960 Nobel Prize in literature.

**Persephone or Proserpine,** (pə͟ˌsefənee, proh͟ˌsuhpinə), in Greek and Roman mythology, goddess of fertility, queen of the underworld; daughter of ZEUS and DEMETER. She was abducted by PLUTO, who held her captive in HADES. Demeter persuaded the gods to let her return to earth for eight months a year. Her story, celebrated in the ELEUSINIAN MYSTERIES, symbolized the vegetative cycle. When she left the earth, life withered; when she returned, it blossomed anew.

**Persepolis** (pə͟ˌsepəlis), ancient city of Persia, NE of present-day Shiraz. It was the ceremonial (but not administrative) capital of the Persian empire under DARIUS I and his successors. The ruins contain several palaces as well as a citadel.

**Perseus,** c.212–166 BC, last king of MACEDON (r.179–168 BC), son and successor of PHILIP V. His anti-Roman policy caused the Third Macedonian

War (171–168); he was defeated (168) by the Romans at Pydna and died in captivity.

**Perseus,** in Greek mythology, son of ZEUS and Danaë. Told by an oracle that Perseus would kill him, his grandfather Acrisius set him and Danaë afloat in a chest, from which they were rescued by King Polydectes. Later, seeing Perseus as an obstacle to his love for Danaë, the king sent him to fetch the head of the GORGON Medusa. The gods aided Perseus, and he slew Medusa. Fleeing from the other Gorgons, Perseus was refused aid by ATLAS, who was turned into a stone mountain by Medusa's head. On his way home, Perseus rescued ANDROMEDA and married her. Later, while competing in a discus contest, Perseus accidently killed Acrisius, thus fulfilling the prophecy. Benvenuto CELLINI's famous statue of Perseus is in FLORENCE, Italy. The subject of Perseus and Andromeda was popular with painters from the Renaissance to the 19th cent.

**Persia,** old name for the Asian country of IRAN, in which the ancient Persian empire had its core. The early Persians were presumably a nomadic tribe that filtered through the Caucasus to the Iranian plateau. By the 7th cent. BC they were established in the present region of Fars, which then belonged to the Assyrian empire. Persian rulers were early associated with the Medes, who created a strong state in the 7th cent. BC. CYRUS THE GREAT, the first of the ACHAEMENIDS, made himself ruler of MEDIA in the mid-6th cent. BC and by rapid conquest established the great Persian empire. From the beginning the Persians built on the foundations of earlier states, borrowing the political structure of Assyria and the arts of Babylonia and Egypt. The country was beset by dynastic troubles, concerning first the claims of Cambyses and later those of DARIUS I. Darius organized a highly efficient centralized system of administration and extended Persian rule east into modern Afghanistan and NW India and as far north as the Danube. The Greeks revolted successfully in the PERSIAN WARS, and after the mid-5th cent. BC Persia was weakened by dynastic troubles, e.g., the rebellion of CYRUS THE YOUNGER against ARTAXERXES II and the successful revolt of Egypt. Finally, ALEXANDER THE GREAT destroyed the Achaemenid empire. After Alexander's death most of Persia fell to the Seleucids, who, though they introduced a fruitful Hellenistic culture, were unable to maintain control. PARTHIA, which broke away in the mid-3rd cent. BC, became a kind of successor to the old Persian empire and came to rival Rome. Its decline was followed by the establishment of a new Persian empire in AD c.226 under the Sasanids. This magnificent state flourished until AD 637, when invading Arabs took the capital, Ctesiphon. Islam replaced ZOROASTRIANISM, and the caliphate made Persia part of a larger pattern, from which modern Iran eventually emerged.

**Persian art and architecture.** Vase painting as represented by the superb ceramics of Susa and Persepolis, c.3500 BC was practised throughout Iran in prehistoric times. Stylized abstractions of birds and animals form an integral part of the design of bowls and goblets. Much Iranian art of the 4th to 2nd millenia BC is strongly influenced by that of Mesopotamia, particularly in the SW region of Elam. A lifesize statue of Queen Napir-Asu (c.1266–1246 BC), whilst Mesopotamian in style, is a truimph of the Elamite metal-worker. It was cast in bronze in two parts and although the head is missing it is more than 1.2 m (4 ft) high. (Louvre). The controversial Luristan bronzes (fl. 9th–7th cent. BC) are further witness to the skill of the Iranian metal-worker. Though some would link these bronzes to the Cimmerians, or to even earlier Kassites, as yet, the identity of these people is unknown. Little is known of events in Iran at the beginning of the 1st millenium, when Indo-European speaking groups moved into the region. Medes, Persians, Cimmerians, Scythians and Assyrians and others have left their traces in the art of Iran prior to the Achaemenid period. The Ziwiye Treasure, a hoard of ivory, gold and silver objects (from Sakiz in Kermanshah) illuminates the diversity of artistic styles and themes in the 7th cent. BC. Almost certainly a burial, possibly of a Scythian prince, it contains objects of Assyrian, Scythian, proto-Achaemenid and native workmanship. In the Achaemenid period a unified style emerges (c.550–330 BC). Monumental relief sculpture is used as an adjunct to massive architectural complexes, such as the tribute-bearing scenes at Persepolis and the famous *Frieze of the Archers*, from the palace of Darius I at Susa. After the death of ALEXANDER THE GREAT (323 BC) there was internal turmoil until the rise of the Parthians (c.230 BC), whose art synthesized Hellenistic motifs with Iranian forms. Of greater artistic importance was the work of the SASSANIDS (AD 226–7th cent.). Their architecture is decorated with carved stone and stucco reliefs, and makes use of colourful stone MOSAICS. Beautiful gold and silver dishes are decorated with hunting scenes and animals in high

relief. Little remains of the early centuries of Islam in Iran, but a significant innovation by the Persians was the raising of a DOME over a square hall by means of squinches. During this early period ceramics became an art form. Under the Seljuk Turks in the 11th and 12th cent., lustre and 'minai' ceramics with intricate scenes of court life were produced. The most famous work of the Mongol school of the 14th cent. is an illustrated book, the Demotte *Shah Namah* (The History of Kings), which is free and lively in execution. Chinese influence is seen in 15th-cent. Timurid painting. Under the Safavids illustration became decoratively patterned, as in the 16th-cent. *Shah Namah* of Shah Tamasp, which incorporates the great developments in painting of the period; it was published in facsimile as *The King's Book of Kings* in 1972. In the 17th cent. Persian art fell under the influence of Europe and India, and it rapidly degenerated.

Persian art and architecture: Luristan bronze, 9th cent. BC, 15.3 × 7 cm. Metropolitan Museum of Art, New York.

**Persian Gulf,** called the Arabian Gulf by Arabs, arm of the ARABIAN SEA, extending c.970 km (600 mi) from the mouth of the SHATT AL ARAB (N) to the Strait of HORMUZ (S), through which it connects with the Gulf of Oman. It is of great strategic importance as the chief maritime outlet for the bordering oil-rich states of Saudi Arabia, Bahrain, the United Arab Emirates, Kuwait, Iran, and Iraq.

**Persian language,** member of the Iranian group of the Indo-Iranian subfamily of the Indo–European family of languages. See LANGUAGE (table).

**Persian literature.** The oldest extant Persian writing is found in ancient inscriptions, but it is only of historical interest. The first major literary works are the scriptures of ZOROASTRIANISM and the Pahlavi writing of SASSANID Persia. The Arab invasion (7th cent. AD) made Arabic the literary language and ISLAM the dominant literary theme. Many notable works of ARABIC LITERATURE are by Persians. Persian reemerged as the literary language in the 9th cent., and in the following centuries classical Persian literature flowered. The first great poet was RUDAKI (9th–10th cent.); after him FIRDAUSI (10th cent.) wrote the *Book of Kings,* the national epic, and OMAR KHAYYAM (11th cent.) crafted his well-known *Rubaiyat.* Also among the great writers are the poets of SUFISM. FARID AD-DIN ATTAR, Jalal ed-Din RUMI, and SADI (12th–13th cent.) all wrote mystical poetry of the highest order, full of finely wrought symbols; NIZAMI in the same period is remembered for his epics. In the 14th cent. HAFIZ was the author of a number of exquisite lyrics. Prose tales, fables, allegories, and philosophical and scientific works also flourished. The most outstanding prose works were the histories; many of these surpassed their Arabic models. After the 15th cent. Persian literature went into a decline that lasted until the rise of BABISM and BAHA'ISM in the 19th cent. brought about a religious literary revival. In the 20th cent. Western influence and the struggle for independence and social justice in Iran made political and social themes paramount, and literary language became simple and direct. Modern poets include Iradj Mirza, Adibe-Pishawari, Parwin Etesami, and Nima Yushig; S. Hedayet, M.M. Hejazi, M.A. Jamalzadeh and B. Alavi are celebrated novelists.

**Persian music,** the musical tradition of Iran (Persia) dating back to pre-Islamic times. It was developed to a high art form during the Islamic period, particularly from the 9th to the 13th cent. It employs diverse intervals and is organized in a system of twelve *dastgāhs*, each of which represents a main mode and a series of secondary modes. Improvisation within established melodic principles is of paramount importance. Compositions in fixed forms have also come into usage in the 20th cent., employing the traditional modes of the twelve *dastgāhs*. The main instruments are the *tār* (6-stringed lute), the *setār* (4-stringed lute), the *santur* (dulcimer), *kamānché* (fiddle), *nāy* (flute), and the *tombak* (drum).

**Persian Wars,** 500–449 BC, conflict between the Greek city-states and the Persian Empire. It began in 500 BC, when the Ionian Greek cities, aided by ATHENS and Eretria, revolted against the despotic rule of DARIUS I. They were subdued by the Persians (494), and Darius decided to punish Athens and Eretria, and annex all of Greece. His first expedition (492) ended ignominiously when his fleet was crippled by a storm. A second expedition destroyed (490) Eretria and then proceeded against Athens, which, under MILTIADES, expelled the invaders at MARATHON. (The Spartans, whose aid had been sought, arrived the day after the battle.) A third expedition, under preparation when Darius died (486), was completed by his son XERXES I, who reached Greece in 480. His huge land force was delayed at the narrow pass of THERMOPYLAE by a small but gallant force of Spartans, who fought until their last man died. The Athenians, under THEMISTOCLES, put trust in their navy and made little effort to defend their city, which was taken (480) by the Persians. Shortly afterward the Persian fleet was crushed off Salamis by the Greeks. Xerxes returned to Persia, leaving behind a military force, which was defeated (479) at Plataea by a Greek force under the Spartan Pausanias. The Greeks also won a naval victory at Mycale. Although the wars dragged on for many years, these two victories marked the end of the Persian threat to Europe and the beginning of the period of Greek greatness.

**Persius** (Aulus Persius Flaccus), AD 34–62, Roman satirical poet. He wrote in the manner of HORACE and LUCILIUS, preaching Stoic moral doctrine (see STOICISM). He was often harsh in exposing the corruption and folly of contemporary Rome.

**personal computer (PC),** small but powerful single-user COMPUTER system primarily used in an office or at home. Personal computers are designed to operate autonomously but it is increasingly likely that a COMPUTER NETWORK connection will be provided for office and business systems to allow access to shared resources. Personal computers evolved after the development of the MICROPROCESSOR made possible the hobby computer movement of the late 1970s, when computers could be built from components or kits. They became popular in the early 1980s when the first low-cost, fully assembled units were mass-marketed. The typical PC consists of a video display (possibly in colour or with high resolution), a keyboard, processor, memory, and external storage in the form of cassette, floppy disc or high-capacity 'hard' disc. Small inexpensive printers may also be purchased. Some systems have taken advantage of increases in processing power and memory sizes and have provided sophisticated graphical interfaces with multiple windows, icons to supplement textual commands and a 'mouse' pointing device as well as a keyboard. A wide range of software is available for PCs including computer games, word-processing systems, DATABASE management

systems, and packages to support the running of small businesses. As well as running games and packages, the PC user may write programs in a PROGRAMMING LANGUAGE. Originally assembler and BASIC were most often used but a wide range of modern languages may now be purchased for PCs.

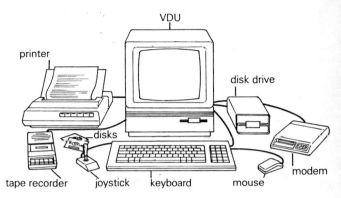

Personal computer

**personal equity plan (PEP),** scheme introduced in the UK in 1987 to encourage investment in UK companies. Limited sums may be invested through a PEP manager for investment in ordinary shares of public companies listed on a UK stock exchange, or for dealing on the unlisted securities market. Provided the shares are held for at least a complete calendar year, capital gains and reinvested dividends will be free of tax.

**personality,** the set of enduring psychological characteristics of a person, relatively independent of particular situations or circumstances, which differentiates them from other persons. Theories of personality often involve notions such as 'type' and 'trait'.

**perspective,** in art, any method employed to represent three-dimensional space on a flat or relief surface. Linear perspective, in the modern sense, was probably first formulated in 15th-cent. Florence by the architects BRUNELLESCHI and ALBERTI. It depends on a system in which objects are foreshortened as they recede into the distance, with lines converging to a vanishing point that corresponds to the spectator's viewpoint. Used by such RENAISSANCE artists as DONATELLO, MASACCIO, and PIERO DELLA FRANCESCA, the technique of linear perspective exerted an enormous influence on subsequent Western art. Its use declined in the 20th cent. Aerial (atmospheric) perspective, which is based on the perception that contrasts of colour and shade appear greater in near objects than in far, and that warm colours appear to advance and cool colours to recede, was developed primarily by LEONARDO DA VINCI, in the West, and was often used in Far Eastern art, where zones of mist were often used to separate near and far space.

**Perth,** city (1986 pop. 895,710), capital of Western Australia, SW Australia, on the Swan R. The suburbs of Kwinana, Welshpool, and FREMANTLE, a port, have heavy industry. Perth is the most isolated capital in Australia; ADELAIDE, the nearest city, is 2250 km (c.1400 mi) away. Settled in 1829, Perth received about 10,000 convict labourers in the 1850s, and the Coolgardie gold rush of the 1890s brought an influx of settlers. The Univ. of Western Australia and Murdoch Univ. are in the city.

**Perth,** town (1981 pop. 41,916), Tayside, central Scotland, on the Tay R. It is famous for its dye works and cattle markets, and has linen and wool factories. The capital of Scotland (11th–15th cent.), it played a role in the civil wars and in the JACOBITE rebellions.

**perturbation:** see CELESTIAL MECHANICS.

**pertussis:** see WHOOPING COUGH.

**Peru,** Span. *Perú,* officially Republic of Peru, republic (1987 est. pop. 20,800,000), 1,285,210 km² (496,220 sq mi), W South America, bordered by the Pacific Ocean (W), Ecuador and Colombia (N), Brazil and Bolivia (E), and Chile (S). Major cities include LIMA (the capital), AREQUIPA, and CALLAO. Peru has three main geographical regions. A narrow strip along the coast is mostly desert, but fertile where irrigated by streams flowing from the mountains; Peru's leading ports, as well as the centres of its commercial agriculture, are located here. A central region, with

35% of the population, consists of three ranges of the ANDES Mts, with Huascarán as the highest peak (6768 m/22,205 ft). The largest region, in the E, is composed of forested mountains and low-lying tropical plains drained by the AMAZON R. system. The coast and mountain regions are frequently shaken by severe earthquakes; the last major earthquake, in 1970, killed 50,000 people. Peru ranks among the world leaders in copper and silver production, and its petroleum industry is being expanded. Chief commercial crops are sugarcane and cotton. Fishing is important. Manufactures include processed food (notably fish), iron and steel, refined minerals, and textiles. In 1984 GDP was US$17,700 million or US$899 per capita. The population is chiefly Indian (50%), mestizo (37%), and white (13%). Spanish and Quechua are the official languages, and most of the whites and mestizos are Roman Catholic.

*History.* Inhabited since at least the 9th millennium BC, Peru was later the centre of several advanced Indian cultures. The Spanish conquest of the area began in 1532, when Francisco PIZARRO and a small band of adventurers overthrew the great INCA empire, capturing and treacherously executing its ruler, Atahualpa. Lima (founded 1535) became the centre of Spanish rule in South America, and the viceroyalty of Peru eventually included all Spanish-ruled lands on the continent except Venezuela. Independence, proclaimed in 1821, was achieved through the efforts of José de SAN MARTÍN and Simón BOLÍVAR and assured by the defeat (1824) of Spain at the battles of Junín and AYACUCHO. Following independence, Peruvian society remained sharply divided between the wealthy oligarchy (mostly Creoles) and the poverty-ridden majority (mostly Indians). Political life was chaotic, alternating between revolts and dictatorships. A disastrous war with Chile (see PACIFIC, WAR OF THE) in 1879 further slowed the country's progress. The first third of the 20th cent. was dominated by Pres. Augusto B. LEGUÍA (1908–12, 1919–30), a virtual dictator who promoted economic development in the interest of the wealthy minority. The American Popular Revolutionary Alliance (APRA), a radical reform party, founded in 1924 and dedicated especially to improving the conditions of the Indians, gained influence in the 1940s. Fernando BELAÚNDE TERRY, a moderate reformer, won election as president in 1963, but was deposed (1968) by a military junta which assumed dictatorial powers, instituted a programme of social reform, and seized US-owned companies. Constitutional government returned in 1980 with elections that returned Belaúnde to the presidency. He was succeeded in 1985 by Alán García (APRA), who had to confront a severe economic crisis and rising guerilla activity, neither of which had been resolved by late 1980s. However, the 1985 elections produced a clear majority for APRA. Meanwhile, the (Maoist) Sendero Luminoso in ('Shining Path') guerrilla movement had launched an armed insurgency centred on the Ayacucho region (SE).

### Post-war Peruvian presidents
José Luís Bustamente (Reformist), 1945–48
Manuel Odría (military), 1948–56
Manuel Pradoy y Ugartache (Conservative), 1956–62
Ricardo Pérez Godoy (military), 1962–63
Fernando Belaúnde Terry (Popular Action), 1963–68
Juan Velasco Alvarado (military), 1968–75
Francisco Morales Bermúdez (military), 1975–80
Fernando Belaúnde Terry (Popular Action), 1980–85
Alan García Pérez (APRA), 1985–

**Perugia,** city (1984 pop. 144,946), Umbria, central Italy. It is a university town (13th cent.) and seat of an archbishop, with industries that include the manufacture of chocolate confectionery. It was an Etruscan foundation and has remains of Etruscan fortifications. During the 15th cent. it was a leading centre of Italian art.

**Perugino** ('perooh,jeenoh), c.1445–1523, Italian painter of the Umbrian school; b. Pietro di Cristofero Vannucci. He probably trained with VERROCCHIO. In 1481 he helped decorate the SISTINE CHAPEL, where his *Christ Giving the Keys to St Peter* is famous. His many altarpieces, e.g., *The Virgin and Child Enthroned* (1491–92; Louvre, Paris) are characterized by their harmonious compositions, their lucid space, and the sweet grace of his figures. He was the teacher of RAPHAEL.

**Pesaro,** city (1984 est. pop. 86,000), Marche, E central Italy, on the Adriatic coast. It is a holiday resort with some industry, including the manufacture of motor cycles. Its life was dominated by prominent families, including the SFORZAS, until 1631 when it came under the control

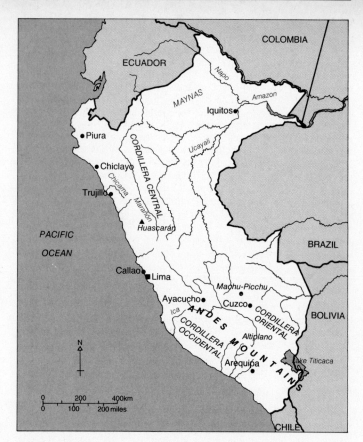

Peru

of the Papal States. A planned layout was imposed on the city in the 18th cent. It is noted for its ceramics and was the birthplace of ROSSINI.

**Pescadores:** see PENGHU DAO.

**Pescara,** city (1984 pop. 131,921), capital of Abruzzi, E central Italy. It has oil and metallurgical industries as well as traditional fishing and food-processing. Severe damage was suffered in World War II.

**Peshawar,** city (1981 pop. 555,000), North West Frontier province, Pakistan. It is the provincial capital and a district administrative centre; and a strategically important military base controlling the route to the Khyber Pass and Afghanistan. It also now has some industry, mainly textiles, and a notable university. Peshawar is an ancient city going back to the 2nd cent., when, under the name of Purushupura, it was the capital of the Buddhist king Kanishka. Its strategic position ensured that it played an important role in succeeding centuries, often as a fortified city; and it was a vital base, in due course, to the British.

**Pessoa, Fernando António Nogueira,** 1888–1935, Portuguese poet. The four distinct poetic personas he claimed for himself, the messianic, the rationalist, the stoic, and the Nietzschean, reflect his disbelief in the idea of an integrated personality. His highly original verse collections, some written in English, include *Sonnets* (1918), *Mensagem* (1934), and *English Poems* (1922).

**Pestalozzi, Johann Heinrich** ('pestah,lotsee), 1746–1827, Swiss educational reformer. His theories laid the foundation of modern elementary education. He was director (from 1805) of an experimental institute established at Yverdon on his principle that choice of pedagogical method should be based on the individual's development and concrete experience. He opposed rote-learning and strict discipline, and pioneered the use of tactile objects in the teaching of natural science. He also promoted broad liberal education followed by professional training for teachers. His works include *Leonard and Gertrude* (1781–87) and *How Gertrude Teaches Her Children* (1801).

**pesticide,** biological, physical, or chemical agent used to kill plants or animals considered harmful to human beings; see FUNGICIDE; HERBICIDE; INSECTICIDE.

**Pétain, Henri Philippe** (pay͵tanh), 1856–1951, marshal of France, head of the VICHY government (1940–44). In WORLD WAR I he halted the Germans at Verdun (1916) and became (1917) French commander in chief. Named ambassador to Spain (1939), he succeeded (June 1940) Paul REYNAUD as premier when France was on the brink of collapse in WORLD WAR II. He soon arranged an armistice with Germany. On 10 July the French constitution was suspended, and Pétain became 'chief of state' at Vichy. Pétain's fascist government collaborated with Nazi Germany and grew unpopular as it yielded to harsh German demands. In 1942 Pierre LAVAL took power, and Pétain remained chiefly a figurehead. After the Allied victory, he was convicted of treason (1945) and was sentenced to death; the sentence was commuted by Charles DE GAULLE to life imprisonment.

**Peter,** czars of Russia. **Peter I** or **Peter the Great,** 1672–1725 (r.1682–1725), was the youngest child of Czar Alexis by his second wife, Natalya Naryshkin. Alexis was succeeded by Feodor III, a son by his first wife, Maria Miloslavsky. On Feodor's death a bloody struggle erupted between the Naryshkins and Miloslavskys. Peter was made joint czar with IVAN V, Feodor's feebleminded brother, under the regency of Sophia Alekseyevna, Feodor's sister. In 1689 Sophia Alekseyevna attempted a coup against Peter; she was overthrown, and for some years the Naryshkins ruled, until Peter took personal control. In 1697–98 he toured Europe, where he tried but failed to form an alliance against Turkey; laid the basis for a coalition against Sweden; studied industrial techniques; and hired craftsmen to work in Russia. He returned on news of an attempt to restore Sophia Alekseyevna; he forced her into a nunnery and took brutal revenge on her followers. The ruthless reforms that marked his reign began on the day after his return, when he personally cut off the beards of his nobles and ordered them to wear Western dress henceforth. To pursue his almost continuous wars, particularly the NORTHERN WAR (1700–21) with Sweden under CHARLES XII, he introduced territorial conscription, enlarged and modernized the army, founded a navy, and set up military–technical schools. Financing was provided by state monopolies, poll taxes, and levies on many items. Private industry was subsidized, and state mines and factories were established to supply war materials. Peter increased the number of nobles owing service to the state; forced nobles' sons to attend military–technical schools; and created a bureaucratic hierarchy in which promotion depended on merit rather than birth. The serfs, who paid the bulk of taxes and comprised most of the soldiery, were bound more securely to their masters and to the land. The Academy of Sciences was founded, the calendar reformed, and the alphabet simplified. On the swamps of Ingermanland (ceded by Sweden in 1721) Peter had St Petersburg built to replace the capital at Moscow. The discontented looked to his son, Alexis, who was tried for treason and tortured to death in 1718. Peter proclaimed himself 'emperor of all Russia' in 1721. His second wife, crowned as CATHERINE I in 1724, succeeded him. **Peter II,** 1715–30 (r.1727–30), was the grandson of Peter I. He succeeded Catherine I under a regency. During his reign his grandfather's great minister MENSHIKOV fell from power. He was succeeded by his cousin ANNA. **Peter III,** 1728–62 (r.1762), was the son of Charles Frederick, dispossessed duke of Holstein–Gottorp, and of Anna Petrovna, daughter of Peter the Great. He succeeded his aunt, Czarina ELIZABETH. One of his first acts was to withdraw Russia from the SEVEN YEARS' WAR and make an alliance with FREDERICK II of Prussia. His domestic policy included the abolition of the secret police and the extension of religious freedom. Forced to abdicate in favour of his wife, CATHERINE II, he was later murdered.

**Peter,** kings of ARAGÓN. **Peter III** (the Great), 1239?–85 (r.1276–85), was also king of Sicily (r.1282–85). He obtained from his marriage (1262) to Constance, daughter of MANFRED of SICILY, claims to the island, which he seized in 1282. Pope Martin IV excommunicated him and organized with the French a crusade against Catalonia, but Peter repulsed the French invasion. He left Aragón to his eldest son, ALFONSO III, and Sicily to his second son, James II. **Peter IV** (the Ceremonious), 1319?–87 (r.1336–87), recovered Majorca for Aragón and fought an indecisive naval war against Genoa and Pisa over SARDINIA. Although he was forced to confirm privileges granted earlier to the nobles, he defeated (1348) them in battle and withdrew their charter. He was succeeded by his son, John I.

**Peter,** kings of Portugal. **Peter I,** 1320–67 (r.1357–67), was the son of ALFONSO IV. Although married (1340) to Constance Manuel, he fell in love with Inés de CASTRO. When his father allowed Inés to be murdered (1355),

Peter led a rebellion against him. Although peace was made and Peter formally pardoned the murderers, he had two of them executed after he became king. This act and his concern for legal reform earned him the names Peter the Severe and Peter the Justiciar. **Peter II,** 1648–1706 (r.1683–1706), ruled Portugal from 1667 as regent for his incompetent brother, ALFONSO VI. His reign was one of prosperity and peace until 1703, when he was reluctantly drawn into the War of the SPANISH SUCCESSION. **Peter III,** 1717–86, married his niece, MARIA I and was joint ruler with her from 1777 until his death.

**Peter,** two EPISTLES of the NEW TESTAMENT. Both state that they are by the apostle St PETER. First Peter, addressed from Rome to the Christians of Asia Minor, stresses the duties of Christians and offers them consolation under persecution. Second Peter, one of the last books accepted in the New Testament canon, urges virtue and warns against false teachers.

**Peter,** kings of Serbia and Yugoslavia. **Peter I,** 1844–1921, king of Serbia (1903–18) and of the Serbs, Croats, and Slovenes (1918–21), was head of the KARADJORDJEVIĆ dynasty in exile while the OBRENOVIĆS were in power. The assassination (1903) of King ALEXANDER brought him to the throne. He proved a democratic-minded ruler and Serbia under him became a point of attraction to the South Slaves of Austria–Hungary, especially after doubling in size in the BALKAN WARS (1912–13). PETER II, 1923–70, king of Yugoslavia (1934–45), reigned as a minor through a regency led by his uncle, Prince Paul Karadjordjević, until the latter was deposed in an anti-AXIS *coup d'état* in Mar. 1941. The German invasion that followed sent him into exile, where he remained after TITO's assumption of power at the end of the war.

**Peter, Saint,** d. 64?, most prominent of the Twelve Disciples, traditionally the first bishop of Rome. His name was Simon, but Jesus called him Cephas (Aramaic, = rock), or, in Greek, Petros. A native of Bethsaida in Galilee, he was the brother of St ANDREW. Fishermen, they were called by Jesus at the same time as James (James the Great) and John. Peter appears in the gospels as leader and spokesman of the disciples, and Jesus most often addressed him when speaking to them. When Peter confessed Jesus to be the Christ, he was told, 'Upon this rock I will build my church.' With James and John, he was chosen to see the Transfiguration and after the Last Supper witnessed the agony at Gethsemane. When Jesus was betrayed, Peter denied him, as Jesus had predicted he would. After the Resurrection Jesus appeared and charged Peter to 'feed my sheep'. The ACTS OF THE APOSTLES describes Peter's role as leader in the early apostolic period. According to 2nd-cent. sources, he apparently left Antioch for Rome c.55 and there died as head of the local church, a martyr under NERO, traditionally crucified on the Vatican Hill. Over his supposed burial place stands ST PETER'S CHURCH, the principal shrine of Europe. Peter is said to have helped St MARK write his Gospel, but the epistles of PETER are regarded as mistakenly attributed. His successors as bishop of Rome based their claim to be leaders of the church on Christ's promises to him (see PAPACY). Feast: 29 June.

**Peterborough,** town (1981 pop. 113,404), Cambridgeshire, Midlands of England, on R. Nene, 117 km (73 mi) N of London. It is a railway junction, industrial centre, and cathedral city on the W edge of the FENS. The major industries are brick manufacture, engineering, and the refining of agricultural products. The cathedral was begun in the 12th cent.

**Peter Damian, Saint,** 1007–72, Italian reformer, Doctor of the Church. A Camaldolese monk, he was strong in the reform party of Hildebrand (later Pope GREGORY VII). In 1057 he was made cardinal. His *Gomorrhianus* is a violent denunciation of clerical abuses. Feast: 21 Feb.

**Peterhead,** town (1981 pop. 16,804), Grampian region, NE Scotland, 44 km (27 mi) N of Aberdeen. The most easterly town on the Scottish mainland, it is a fishing port and supply base for the North Sea oilfield. Industries include engineering, food-processing, and petrochemicals. It was the landing place in 1715 of the Old Pretender (see STUART, JAMES FRANCIS EDWARD).

**Peter Lombard,** c.1100–c.1160, Italian theologian, archbishop of Paris. His *Sentences,* a compilation of the often conflicting opinions of theologians, was the standard work on theology until the 16th cent. His doctrine of the SACRAMENTS was made official by the Council of TRENT.

**Peter Martyr,** 1500–62, Italian Protestant reformer, originally Pietro Martire Vermigli. An honoured Augustinian scholar and preacher, he became a Protestant and fled to Switzerland, Strasbourg, and, at the invitation of Archbishop Cranmer, to England, where he taught at Oxford

(1547–53). Under Mary I he left England and returned to Strasbourg and then went to Zürich as a professor. There is dispute as to the extent of his influence on the Forty-two Articles of 1553 and on the revision of the BOOK OF COMMON PRAYER.

**Peterson, Oscar,** 1925–. black Canadian jazz pianist and organist. Blessed with a stunning technique, he was originally inspired by Art Tatum. Since the mid 1940s, with his own trios and supporting a galaxy of jazz greats from Dizzy GILLESPIE to Coleman HAWKINS, he has contributed a constant flow of inventive and frequently blues-tinged piano-playing rarely emulated in jazz.

**Peter the Cruel,** 1334–69, Spanish king of CASTILE and LEÓN (1350–69). His desertion of his wife, Blanche of Bourbon, for María Padilla and his favours to the Padilla family offended the nobles and caused rebellions fomented by his half brother, later Henry II. With the help of ARAGÓN and France, Henry conquered Castile and was crowned king in 1366. Peter retaliated by defeating Henry's army with the help of England in 1367. But Henry raised a new army, which was victorious at Montiel (1369), and he killed Peter in a duel after the battle. Despite his reputation for cruelty, Peter is regarded by many historians as a defender of the rights of the commoners against the nobles.

**Peter the Great:** (Peter I) PETER, CZARS OF RUSSIA.

**Petipa, Marius,** 1822–1910, French choreographer. Regarded as the principal creator of modern classical BALLET, he brought European technique to the Imperial Theatre, St Petersburg, and expanded the male role in dance. His major works include *La Bayardère* (1875) and *Sleeping Beauty* (1890).

**Petition of Right,** 1628, statement sent by the English PARLIAMENT to CHARLES I. It laid down four principles: no taxes without the consent of Parliament; no imprisonment without cause; no quartering of soldiers on the citizenry; and no martial law in peacetime. Charles was constrained to give it the royal assent, but soon violated it.

**Petlyura, Symon,** 1879–1926, Ukrainian politician and national leader. Originally a writer and journalist, from Feb. 1919 he was head of the government called the Ukrainian Directory and commander-in-chief of the national army engaged in a prolonged war against the Red Army. Many 'pogroms' of Jews took place in the Ukraine at this time, although it seems that Petlyura was not himself anti-Semitic. In Apr. 1920 Petlyura signed a treaty with Poland headed by Marshal PILSUDSKI and led Ukrainian and Polish allied forces in a campaign to liberate Ukraine from Soviet domination. After a peace treaty was concluded (1921) between the emerging Soviet Union and Poland Petlyura maintained his government and the remnants of his military forces in exile, and was assassinated in Paris.

**Petöfi, Sándor** ('petø:fee), 1822–49, Hungarian poet. His epic *Janos the Hero* (1845) relates the fantastic adventures of a peasant-soldier. 'Rise, Magyar' (1848) voices the ideals of the Hungarian revolution, in which Petöfi died.

**Petra,** ancient ruined city, S JORDAN, 32 km (20 mi) W of Ma'an on the HEJAZ RAILWAY. The capital of the Nabataeans from the 4th cent. BC to the Roman occupation in AD 106, it remained a religious centre of Arabia. An early seat of Christianity, the Muslims (see ISLAM) conquered it in the 7th cent. and the Crusaders (see CRUSADES) built a citadel there in the 12th cent. Its ruins were found in 1812 by the Swiss traveller John Burckhardt. Famous for its public buildings and houses carved out of the face of the red sandstone cliffs, it is now a major tourist attraction.

**Petrarca, Francesco** or **Petrarch** (,petrahk), 1304–74, Italian poet and humanist. He played a pioneering role in the recovery of classical texts and himself wrote prolifically in Latin, which he valued above Italian. A 'citizen of the world' and the literary arbiter of the time, until 1353 his life was centred on Provence, where (at Avignon in 1327) he first saw LAURA, the inspiration of most of his vernacular lyrics. In 1341 he was crowned laureate in Rome in recognition of his Latin poetry, and later found patriotic inspiration in his enthusiasm for ancient Rome. His complex personality was marked by a tension between the classical and the Christian evident in the restless introspection of the *Canzoniere* (lyric-collection). The perfecter of the SONNET and Italy's greatest lyric poet, he exerted a unique influence on European love poetry throughout the RENAISSANCE and down to the 19th cent.

**petrel** or **tubenose, Mother Carey's chicken, Jesus bird,** name given to many sea BIRDS in the order Procellariformes which includes ALBATROSSES, SHEARWATERS, and FULMARS. Petrels are recognized by the tubular nostrils along their upper bills, which are hooked. The birds spend most of their lives at sea, feeding on fish and other marine life. They return to coasts to breed, nesting in burrows or rocky crevices, in colonies. Most live in the Pacific, where some, like Wilson's petrel (*Oceanites oceanicus*) 'walk' on water, flying low with their legs dangling, searching for food. The British storm petrel (*Hydrobates pelagicus*) is limited to the North Atlantic and the Mediterranean.

**Petrie, Sir William Matthew Flinders,** 1853–1942, British archaeologist and Egyptologist, best known for excavations at MEMPHIS and THEBES; founder (1894) of the British School of Archaeology in Egypt. He also dug in Britain (1875–80) and Palestine (1927–38), made notable discoveries at ancient Greek sites, and found ruins of 10 cities at Tel-el-Hesy (S of Jerusalem). His works include *Methods and Aims in Archaeology* (1904) and *Seventy Years in Archaeology* (1931).

**Petrograd:** see LENINGRAD.

**petrol,** light, volatile fuel oil; called gasoline in America. A mixture of HYDROCARBONS obtained in the fractional DISTILLATION and 'cracking' of PETROLEUM, it is used chiefly as a fuel for INTERNAL-COMBUSTION ENGINES. The quality of petrol used in engines is rated by OCTANE NUMBER. To increase octane rating, lead additives have been widely used. Because of the health hazard of lead as an environmental pollutant and the harmful effect it has on pollution-control devices, however, there have been moves, begun in the US in the 1970s, to change car design and petrol composition, so that lead additives can be eliminated.

**petrol engine:** see INTERNAL-COMBUSTION ENGINE.

**petroleum** or **crude oil,** oily, flammable liquid that occurs naturally in deposits, usually beneath the surface of the earth. The exact composition varies according to locality, but it is chiefly a mixture of HYDROCARBONS. Petroleum is a fossil fuel thought to have been formed over millions of years from incompletely decayed plant and animal remains buried under thick layers of rock. Drilling for oil is a complex, often risky process. Scientific methods are used to locate promising sites for wells, some of which must be dug several miles deep to reach the deposit. Many wells are now drilled offshore from platforms standing on the ocean bed. Usually the crude oil in a new well comes to the surface under its own pressure. Later it has to be pumped or forced up with injected water, gas, or air. Pipelines or tankers transport it to refineries, where it is separated into fractions, i.e., the portions of the crude oil that vaporize between certain defined limits of temperature. Fractions are obtained by a refining process called fractional DISTILLATION, in which crude oil is heated and sent into a tower. The vapours of the different fractions condense on collectors at different heights in the tower. The separated fractions are then drawn from the collectors and further processed into various petroleum products. Generally the fractions are vaporized in the following order: dissolved NATURAL GAS, PETROL, naphtha, KEROSENE, diesel fuel, heating oils, and finally tars (see TAR AND PITCH). Lighter fractions, especially petrol, are in greatest demand and their yield can be increased by breaking down heavier hydrocarbons in a process called cracking. The leading producers of petroleum in 1980 were the USSR, Saudi Arabia, the US, Iraq, Venezuela, China, Nigeria, Mexico, Libya, and the United Arab Emirates. The largest reserves are in the Middle East. Modern industrial civilization depends heavily on petroleum for motive power, fuel, lubrication, and a variety of synthetic products, e.g., dyes, drugs, and plastics. The widespread burning of petroleum as fuel has resulted in problems of air POLLUTION, and oil spilled from tankers and offshore wells has temporarily damaged coastlines. See also ENERGY, SOURCES OF.

**petrology,** branch of GEOLOGY concerned with the origin, composition, structure, and properties of ROCKS, as well as the laboratory simulation of rock-forming processes.

**Petronius,** d. AD 66, Roman satirist, known as Petronius Arbiter because he is identified with Caius Petronius, whom TACITUS calls the *arbiter elegantiae* in NERO's court. He is remembered as a luxurious profligate. Arrested in an intrigue, he slashed his veins and died in a leisurely fashion, attended by friends. He is credited with the *Petronii arbitri satyricon,* a prose and verse romance that preserves, often in colloquial language, a portrayal of the life and manners of his time.

**Petrov, Yevgeny Petrovich**, pseud. of **Yevgeny Petrovich Katayev**, 1903–42, Russian satirical writer. He was joint author for the very popular novel *The Twelve Chairs* (1928); see under ILF, Ilya.

**Petrov affair**, incident which began in Apr. 1954 with the defection of Vladimir Petrov, third secretary of the Soviet embassy in Australia. His wife Evdokia was allegedly forced by the Soviet ambassador to board an aircraft bound for the USSR, but Australian authorities took her from the aircraft. A royal commission (1954–55) investigated allegations made by the Petrovs about Soviet espionage.

**petunia**, annual or perennial Brazilian herb (genus *Petunia*) of the NIGHTSHADE family. Valued as garden ornamentals, petunias have a straggling habit but produce an abundance of large, colourful, funnel-shaped blossoms. They are widely used for summer bedding, modern petunias being crosses between *P. integrifolia* and *P. nyctaginiflora.*

**Pétursson, Hallgrímur**, 1614–74, Icelandic poet and hymnist. He was a poor parson who became the greatest religious poet that Iceland has produced, and died of leprosy. His masterpiece, a series of 50 *Passion Hymns* (1666), retell the last events in the life of Christ from the Garden of Gethsemane to the Cross, and each event is used for a profound religious meditation.

**Pevsner, Antoine**, 1886–1962, Russian sculptor and painter. He visited Paris in 1911 and was influenced by CUBISM. He and his brother Naum GABO worked together in 1920 on the Realistic Manifesto (see CONSTRUCTIVISM).

**Pevsner, Sir Nikolaus,** 1902–83, British art historian; b. Germany. He was editor of the multi-volume *The Buildings of England* and was the founder of the Victorian Society.

**pewter**, silver-white ALLOY consisting mainly of tin. The addition of lead imparts a bluish tinge and increased malleability. Other metals such as antimony, copper, bismuth, and zinc may also be added. Pewter is shaped by casting, hammering, or lathe-spinning on a mould. Ornamentation is usually simple. Pewter was used early on in the Far East, and Roman pieces still exist. In England during the Middle Ages pewter was the chief tableware, later being supplanted by china. It was made in America from c.1700. The craft had virtually died out by 1850 but was revived in the 20th cent.

**pH**, range of numbers expressing the relative acidity or alkalinity of a solution. The *p*H value is the negative common LOGARITHM of the hydrogen-ion CONCENTRATION in a solution, expressed in MOLES per litre of solution. A neutral solution, i.e., one that is neither acidic nor alkaline, such as pure water, has a concentration of $10^{-7}$ moles per litre; its *p*H is thus 7. Acidic solutions have *p*H values ranging with decreasing acidity from 0 to nearly 7; alkaline or basic solutions have a *p*H ranging with increasing alkalinity from just beyond 7 to 14. See also ACIDS AND BASES.

**Phaedra** (ˌfeedrə), in Greek mythology, daughter of MINOS and Pasiphaë, wife of THESEUS. When her stepson, Hippolytus, rejected her love, she accused him of rape, then hanged herself. The legend was dramatized by EURIPIDES, SENECA, and RACINE.

**Phaedrus** (ˌfaydrus), c.18 BC–AD 50, a Thracian slave freed by AUGUSTUS, he wrote FABLES (see also AESOP) in Latin verse. He aimed to entertain and instruct, and some of his stories are effective. But his attempt to turn the fable into an independent literary form was not entirely successful: James Thurber did it with more vigour and style.

**Phaeophyceae**, division of the plant kingdom consisting of brown ALGAE; almost all are SEAWEEDS.

**Phaëthon** or **Phaëton** (ˌfayəthən, ˌfayətən), in Greek mythology, son of HELIOS. He lost control of his father's golden chariot, which in falling dried the Libyan Desert. ZEUS avoided the universe's destruction only by killing Phaëthon.

**phage** (fayzh): see BACTERIOPHAGE.

**phallocentrism**, a term first introduced by Ernest JONES to characterize the male or masculinist bias of PSYCHOANALYSIS; in particular the Freudian notion that femininity is governed by the lack of a PHALLUS, and that neuroses in women derive from 'penis envy'.

**phallus**, the symbolic object corresponding to the penis. In PSYCHOANALYSIS, notably in the work of LACAN, the phallus represents the law of the father, power, and authority.

**Pham Van Dong**, 1906–, premier (1976–87) of the Socialist Republic of VIETNAM. A close associate of HO CHI MINH, he was premier of North Vietnam (1954–76) during the VIETNAM WAR which led to the reunification of the country.

**pharaoh** (ˌfeəroh), title of the kings of ancient EGYPT over a period of over 2000 years. The Pharaoh was an absolute, hereditary ruler who was seen as the incarnation of the god Horus, and presided over a centralized government sustained by the priesthood.

**pharmacology**, study of the changes produced in living animals by DRUGS, chemical substances used to treat and diagnose disease. It is closely related to other scientific disciplines, particularly BIOCHEMISTRY and PHYSIOLOGY. Areas of pharmacological research include the mechanisms of drug action, the use of drugs in treating disease, and drug-induced side-effects. See also PHARMACY.

**pharmacopoeia** (ˈfahməkəˌpee·ə), authoritative publication designating the properties, actions, uses, dosages, and standards of strength and purity of DRUGS. The Nuremberg pharmacopoeia, published in Germany in 1546, was the first work of its kind. In Britain, the Pharmacopoeia Commission is responsible for preparing new editions of the *British Pharmacopoeia* (*BP*), first compiled as a result of the Medical Act 1858. *The British Pharmaceutical Codex* supplements the *BP* by providing extra data on the undesirable side-effects of drugs and covering an additional range of substances. *The Extra Pharmacopoeia (Martindale)* is a further invaluable reference book. *The British National Formulary* is a handbook revised every six months for prescribers.

**pharmacy**, science of compounding and dispensing medication; also, an establishment used for such purposes. Modern pharmaceutical practice includes the dispensing, identification, selection, and analysis of DRUGS. Pharmacy has its origins in the movement of the apothecaries in the 17th and 18th cent.; they sought to practise medicine in addition to preparing and selling drugs. See also APOTHECARY; PHARMACOLOGY.

**pharynx**, section of the DIGESTIVE SYSTEM between the mouth and oesophagus. In humans the pharynx is a muscular cone-shaped tube, lined with mucous membrane, continuous with the mouth and nasal passages at its upper end and oesophagus at its lower end. It connects with the ears via the eustachian tubes (see EAR) and with the LARYNX by an opening covered by the epiglottis during swallowing.

**phase**, in astronomy, the measure of how much of the illuminated surface of a planet or natural satellite can be seen from a point at a distance from that body. The phase depends on the overlap of the half of the surface that is seen by the observer and the half that is illuminated by the Sun. An inferior planet, whose orbit lies inside the Earth's, shows all the phases that the Moon shows; a superior planet, whose orbit lies outside Earth's, is always gibbous or full, or nearly so.

**phases of matter:** see STATES OF MATTER.

**pheasant**, name for some henlike birds of the family Phasianidae, related to the GROUSE and including the Old World PARTRIDGES, the PEACOCK, some domestic and jungle fowl, and the true pheasants (genus *Phasianus*). Pheasants are typified by wattled heads and long tails, and by the brilliant plumage and elaborate courtship displays of the male. All are indigenous to Asia. The game pheasant *P. colchicus),* is one of the two true pheasants from E Asia, but it has been introduced as a game bird into Europe and North America. The group now includes birds such as the golden pheasant (*Chrysolophus pictus*) and the argus pheasant (*Argusianus argus*).

**Pheidias:** see PHIDIAS.

**phenomenology**, the method of philosophical enquiry proposed by Franz BRENTANO and developed by his pupil HUSSERL. It advocates a careful examination of one's conscious processes, elucidating their meaning through intuition. Anything that cannot be perceived, and thus is not immediately given to the consciousness, is excluded. The influence of phenomenology was strong, especially on EXISTENTIALISM.

**pheromone**, any chemical substance secreted by members of an animal species that alters the behaviour of other members of the same species. Sex-attractant pheromones are widespread, particularly among insects.

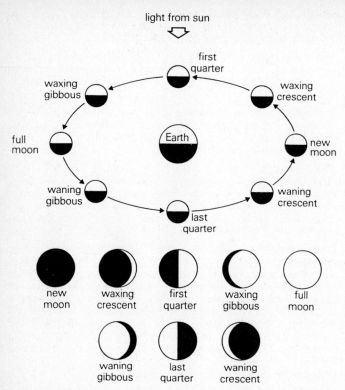

Phases of the Moon as seen from Earth

The reconstruction of the gold and ivory statue of Parthenos by **Phidias**, Royal Ontario Museum, Toronto, Canada.

Other pheromones act as signals for alarm and defence, territory and trail-marking, and social regulation and recognition.

**Phidias** or **Pheidias** c.500–c.432 BC, one of the greatest ancient Greek sculptors. Though numerous Roman copies of his works exist, no originals can be definitely attributed to him. His fame rests on the descriptions and estimates of ancient writers. His greatest works were the colossal chryselephantine (ivory and gold) *Athena Parthenos* at Athens (destroyed in ancient times) and *Zeus* at Olympia (destroyed), one of the SEVEN WONDERS OF THE WORLD. He is said to have been in charge of the PARTHENON and ACROPOLIS sculptures.

**Philadelphia,** US city (1984 est. pop. 1,647,000; metropolitan area 4.7 million), SE Pennsylvania, on the Delaware and Schuylkill rivers; chartered 1701. Founded in 1681 on the site of earlier settlements by William PENN as a Quaker colony, the city has played a prominent role in American history. By 1774 it was second only to London as the largest English-speaking city in the world. The CONTINENTAL CONGRESS met there, and it was the national capital during most of the period 1777–1800. The DECLARATION OF INDEPENDENCE was signed in Independence Hall. Benjamin FRANKLIN was one of the most famous of Philadelphia residents. A commercial, banking, insurance, and transport centre, Philadelphia is the fourth largest US city. It has one of the world's largest freshwater ports and is a major oil-refining centre. Leading manufactures include textiles, chemicals, metal products, and printed materials. A cultural nucleus since colonial times, the city is home to many artistic, dramatic, musical, and scientific societies, and has over 30 universities and institutions of higher learning. Cultural institutions include the Pennsylvania Academy of the Fine Arts, the Philadelphia Museum of Art, and an outstanding symphony orchestra.

**Philadelphia,** name of several ancient cities. One was in Lydia, W Asia Minor, near modern Alasehir, Turkey. It was founded in the 2nd cent. BC by Attalus II Philadelphus of Pergamum. AMMAN (capital of present-day Jordan) was renamed Philadelphia by PTOLEMY II in the 3nd cent. BC.

**Philemon,** epistle of the NEW TESTAMENT. It was written by St PAUL (probably AD c.60) to a Colossian named Philemon, asking him to forgive his fugitive slave Onesimus, who was carrying the epistle to him.

**Philip,** kings of France. **Philip I,** 1052–1108 (r.1060–1108), enlarged his small royal domain and quarrelled with the papacy over his marriages. He was succeeded by his son, LOUIS VI. **Philip II** or **Philip Augustus,** 1165–1223 (r.1180–1223), succeeded his father, LOUIS VII. During his reign the royal domains were more than doubled, and royal power was consolidated. He seized territory from the count of Flanders and from HENRY II of England. In 1190 he left on the Third CRUSADE with Henry's successor, RICHARD I of England, but they soon quarrelled, and Philip returned (1191) to France. He forced Richard's successor, King JOHN of England, to cede (1204) Normandy, Brittany, Anjou, Maine, and Touraine. In 1214, at Bouvines, he defeated the combined forces of John, Emperor Otto IV, and the count of Flanders. Philip condoned the crusade against the ALBIGENSES, which paved the way to the eventual annexation of S France by King LOUIS IX. The latter's son, **Philip III** (the Bold), 1245–85 (r.1270–85), took peaceful possession of Poitou, Auvergne, and Toulouse by a small cession of the Agenais and Southern Saintonge (1279) to England. He died during an unsuccessful invasion of Aragón. His son, **Philip IV** (the Fair), 1268–1314 (r.1285–1314), arrested (1301) Bishop Saisset and caused a quarrel with Pope BONIFACE VIII, who denounced the king. Philip retaliated by convoking the first STATES-GENERAL (1302–03) to hear a justification of his actions. Threatened with excommunication, Philip had Boniface seized and later gained control of the PAPACY with the election of CLEMENT V, who transferred (1309) the papacy to Avignon. Beginning in 1294, Philip tried to conquer Guienne from EDWARD I of England, but was forced to concede (1303) the duchy to Edward. His attempts to subdue the Flemish led to the disastrous French defeat (1302) at Courtrai. His son, LOUIS X, succeeded him. **Philip V** (the Tall), c.1294–1322 (r.1316–22), was regent for his infant nephew, JOHN I. When John died (1316), Philip had himself crowned despite the claims of John's sister. This helped to establish the SALIC LAW in France, which excluded females from the royal succession. Philip made notable administrative, judiciary, and military reforms and was succeeded by his brother CHARLES IV. Charles IV's successor, **Philip VI,** 1293–1350 (r.1328–50), grandson of Philip III, invoked the Salic law to set aside the claims of Charles's daughter and Charles's nephew, Edward III of

England. He was the first VALOIS king of France. After 1337 his reign was dominated by the HUNDRED YEARS WAR. In 1340 the French fleet was destroyed at Sluis, and in 1346 Edward III defeated Philip at Crécy. Philip was succeeded by his son, JOHN II.

**Philip,** kings of Macedon. **Philip II,** 382–336 BC (r.359–336), was the son of Amyntas II. He seized the throne while serving as regent for his nephew Amyntas. He reorganized the army and followed a policy of expansion, annexing Amphipolis (357), the gold mines of THRACE (356), and the Chalcidice (348). When his continued threats roused ATHENS and THEBES to war against him, he crushed them at Chaeronea (338) and became master of GREECE. He was preparing an attack on Persia when he was killed. His wife, OLYMPIAS, was accused, probably falsely, of the murder. Philip's consolidation of his kingdom and creation of a powerful army paved the way for the campaigns of his son, ALEXANDER THE GREAT. **Philip V,** 238–179 BC (r.221–179), was the son of Demetrius II. Successful in a war in Greece (220–217), he tried to take the Roman holdings in Illyria, precipitating the First Macedonian War with Rome (215–205). It ended favorably for Philip, but in the Second Macedonian War he was decisively defeated at Cynoscephalae (197). He was succeeded by his son PERSEUS.

**Philip,** Spanish kings. **Philip I** (the Handsome), 1478–1506, king of CASTILE (r.1506), was the son of Holy Roman Emperor MAXIMILIAN I and MARY OF BURGUNDY. He inherited Burgundy and the Low Countries from his mother and was titular joint ruler of Castile with his wife, JOANNA. But her father ruled these lands as his regent, so he contested (1504) Ferdinand's regency and assumed (1506) joint rule of Castile with his wife. Philip's early death, however, and his wife's deteriorating mental condition allowed Ferdinand to resume joint control of Castile. The Low Countries passed to Philip's son, who later became Holy Roman Emperor CHARLES V. **Philip II,** 1527–98, king of Spain (r.1556–98), king of NAPLES and SICILY (r.1554–98) and, as Philip I, king of Portugal (r.1580–98), centralized authority under his absolute monarchy and extended Spanish colonization to the present S United States and the Philippines (which were named after him). From his father, Holy Roman Emperor Charles V, he inherited NAPLES, SICILY, the Low Countries, and other territories. After the death of his first wife, Maria of Portugal, he married (1554) Queen MARY I of England and drew that nation into his father's war with France. Following Mary's death (1558), he married Elizabeth of Valois and concluded the war with France in 1559. Philip used the INQUISITION to repress the MORISCOS and assure Spanish religious unity. He dealt with the Dutch revolt in his Low Countries domain by reconquering the southern half of the country. English support of the rebels and their persistent attacks on Spanish ships led him to plan an invasion of England by the Spanish ARMADA (1588), which was ignominiously defeated. Earlier, he succeeded in conquering Portugal (1580). Despite his conquests and the influx of gold from America, the cumulative effects of depopulation, war, and burdensome taxation debilitated Spain by the end of his reign (1598). Philip was a hardworking bureaucrat with a capacity for infinite detail, and his administration was generally just. The French Wars of Religion (see RELIGION, WARS OF) allowed him to act as the most powerful ruler in western Europe. His court was at the ESCORIAL. **Philip III,** r.1578–1621, king of Spain, Naples, and Sicily, and, as Philip II, king of Portugal (r.1598–1621), lacked the determination and capacity for work of his father, Philip II, and left the actual government to the duque de Lerma. Shortly before his reign began, Spain had ended the war with France (1598) and then made peace with England (1604) and the Netherlands (1609). But the nation fought in Italy (1615–17) and entered the THIRTY YEARS' WAR. Although the church prospered and the grandees accumulated vast estates, the Spanish economy declined, partly as a result of Philip's expulsion (1609–14) of the Moriscos and partly due to a general European depression. During Philip's reign, Spanish culture flourished and gave to the world great artists such as the author CERVANTES and the painter El GRECO. **Philip IV,** r.1605–65, king of Spain, Naples, and Sicily (r.1621–65) and, as Philip III, king of Portugal (r.1621–40), intelligent but lacking energy, was unable to prevent Spain's political and economic decline. The war with the Dutch continued until 1648, and the war with France (1635–59) ended with Spain's humiliation. Portugal and Catalonia revolted (1640), and Spain had to recognize the independence of the Netherlands (1648). Philip was a patron of the arts and, thanks to VELÁZQUEZ, was perhaps the most frequently portrayed king in history. The accession of **Philip V,** 1683–1746, the first Bourbon king of Spain (r.1700–46), precipitated the War of the SPANISH SUCCESSION (1701–14)

because his grandfather, LOUIS XIV of France, had accepted the Spanish throne for Philip. By the Peace of Utrecht, Spain lost much territory, including the Spanish Netherlands, Naples, and Sicily. Philip was forced to introduce the SALIC LAW of succession, which forbade female monarchs, and was debarred from the French succession. The indolent and melancholy Philip was dominated by women, particularly after his marriage (1714) to Elizabeth Farnese (see FARNESE, family). Under her influence, he attempted to reconquer the Italian territories, causing the formation of the QUADRUPLE ALLIANCE of 1718, to which Spain had to submit. The latter years of his reign were plagued by wars, in which Naples and Sicily were conquered for Philip's son CHARLES III. Under Philip, however, Spain began to recover from economic stagnation and political weakness.

**Philip, Prince,** 1921–, Duke of Edinburgh, consort of ELIZABETH II of Great Britain etc.; b. Greece. The son of Prince Andrew of Greece and Princess Alice, daughter of Prince Louis of BATTENBERG, he is a great-great-grandson of Queen VICTORIA. In 1947, the year he married Elizabeth, he took his mother's name, Mountbatten; became a British citizen; and was created duke of Edinburgh. In 1957 Elizabeth conferred upon him the title of Prince.

**Philip, Saint,** one of the Twelve Disciples, from Bethsaida in Galilee. He is said to have been martyred in Phrygia.

**Philip Augustus** (Philip II): see under PHILIP, kings of France.

**Philip of Hesse,** 1504–67, German ruler, landgrave of Hesse (1509–67), champion of the REFORMATION. He was converted to Lutheranism in 1524 and founded (1531) the Schmalkaldic League to uphold Protestantism against Holy Roman Emperor CHARLES V. In 1547 Charles crushed the league and imprisoned Philip. At his death his lands were divided among his four sons (see HESSE).

**Philip of Swabia,** 1176?–1208, German king (r.1198–1208), son of Emperor FREDERICK I and brother of Emperor Henry VI. When he was elected king in 1198, a minority faction chose OTTO IV, his son-in-law, as antiking. The resulting war ended in 1206 in Philip's favour, but his murder by a personal enemy eventually placed Otto on the throne. Philip's role in diverting the Fourth CRUSADE (1202–04) to Constantinople for dynastic reasons has long been disputed.

**Philippe Égalité:** see Louis Philippe Joseph, Duc D'Orléans, under ORLÉANS, family.

**Philippians,** EPISTLE of the NEW TESTAMENT. It was written (AD c.60) by St PAUL to the Christians of Philippi (MACEDONIA), the first European city he evangelized. The book is noted for its intimate tone and stress on Christ's pre-existence.

**Philippics,** series of three denunciations of PHILIP II of Macedon by DEMOSTHENES. CICERO's polemics against Mark ANTONY are also called philippics.

**Philippines,** officially Republic of the Philippines (1987 est. pop 56,000,000), 300,000 km² (115,830 sq mi), SW Pacific Ocean, off the mainland of Southeast Asia, comprising over 7000 tropical islands; the two largest are LUZON and MINDANAO. The capital is MANILA, on Luzon. The islands are mountainous and volcanic; earthquakes are common. The economy is predominantly agricultural; rice, corn, and coconuts are the principal crops. Among the mineral resources are copper, gold, iron, and chromite. Manufactures include processed foods, textiles, chemicals, and refined metals. The islands have one of the world's greatest stands of commercial timber, a major export. The great majority of the population are ethnic Malays (known as Filipinos), but there are groups of Negritos (negroid PYGMIES), Dumugats (similar to the Papuans of New Guinea), and Chinese. Roman Catholicism is the predominant religion, with a Muslim minority in the south. Pilipino, based on Tagalog, is the national language, but English, Spanish, and some 70 native tongues are also spoken.

*History.* Europeans, led by Ferdinand MAGELLAN, first visited the islands in 1521. They were named after the future Philip II of Spain in 1542, and the Spanish conquest began in earnest in the 1560s. Manila, founded in 1571, was soon a leading commercial centre of the Far East. Spanish control of the region remained secure until the 19th cent., when resentment against Spanish injustice, bigotry, and oppression brought about a movement for independence, inspired by the writings of José RIZAL and led by Emilio AGUINALDO. The SPANISH–AMERICAN WAR, which broke out in 1898, ended Spanish rule, but, to the nationalists' bitter disappointment, control of the islands was transferred to the US. An armed revolt (1899–1901) against US rule was effectively crushed, but the question of Philippine independence remained a burning political issue until 1934, when the internally self-governing Commonwealth of the Philippines was established. Preparations for full independence, led by the first president, Manuel L. QUEZON, were interrupted by WORLD WAR II, in which, after bitter fighting, the Philippines were occupied by Japan. Liberated (1944–45) by US forces under Gen. Douglas MACARTHUR, the Philippines gained full independence in 1946. The combined tasks of reconstructing the war-torn country and building the new republic were complicated by the activities of Communist-led Hukbalahap (Huk) guerrillas, tensions over US military installations, inflation, the need for land reform, and government corruption. A succession of presidents did little to help the peasant majority or to curb political violence. Ferdinand E. MARCOS, elected president in 1965 and reelected in 1969, reacted to increasing civil disorder by declaring martial law in 1972; a new constitution (1973) gave Marcos near-dictatorial powers. Although martial law was nominally lifted in 1981, critics accused Marcos, who was again elected president (under a revised constitution permitting an unlimited number of six-year terms), of in fact retaining most of his former powers. Following disputed presidential elections in early 1986, Marcos was forced to flee the country and was succeeded by the opposition presidential candidate, Corazon AQUINO (widow of opposition leader Benigno S. Aquino Jr, assassinated on his return to the Philippines in 1983). As president, Mrs Aquino released political prisoners and offered to negotiate with the communist and Moslem guerrilla movements active in many parts of the country.

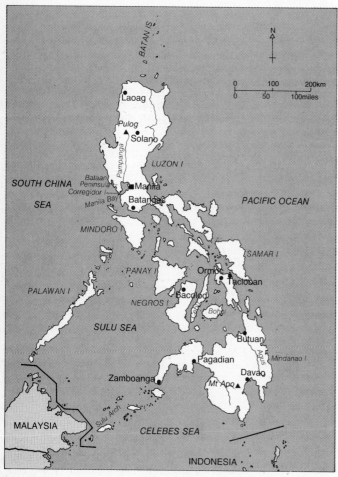

Philippines

**Philip the Bold** (Philip III): see under PHILIP, kings of France.

**Philip the Bold,** 1342–1404, duke of Burgundy (1363–1404); a younger son of JOHN II of France. In 1382 he helped to defeat Flemish

rebels, and he inherited Flanders in 1384. During the minority (1380–88) of CHARLES VI, Philip was virtual ruler of France. When the king became insane (1392), Philip fought with the king's brother, Louis d'ORLÉANS, for power. His son, JOHN THE FEARLESS, carried on the quarrel.

**Philip the Fair** (Philip IV): see under PHILIP, kings of France.

**Philip the Good,** 1396–1467, duke of Burgundy (r.1419–67), son of JOHN THE FEARLESS. By the Treaty of Troyes (1420) he supported the English cause in France until he made peace with CHARLES VII by the Treaty of Arras (1435). He later supported (1440) the Pragurie, a revolt against Charles, and gave asylum to the rebellious DAUPHIN (later LOUIS XI). By various means, Philip acquired Hainaut, Holland, Zeeland, and other possessions. He was succeeded by his son, CHARLES THE BOLD.

**Philip the Tall** (Philip V): see under PHILIP, kings of France.

**Phillip, Arthur,** 1738–1814, British admiral and colonial governor. He led the expedition that established British settlement in Sydney, Australia in 1788. The first governor of New South Wales, he guided the settlement through the hardships of its first four years.

**Phillips, Wendell,** 1811–84, American reformer. Ranked with Edward Everett and Daniel Webster as an orator, Phillips was a delegate to the World Anti-Slavery Convention in London (1840), opposed the Mexican War and annexation of Texas, advocated dissolution of the Union, and vehemently denounced slaveholding. He held that the government owed to the black slave not only freedom but land, education, and full civil rights. After the 15th Amendment to the US CONSTITUTION enfranchised blacks, Phillips continued his agitation for social reforms, including PROHIBITION, WOMAN SUFFRAGE, abolition of capital punishment, currency reform (see GREENBACK), and labour rights.

**philosophy** [Gk., = love of wisdom], study of the principles underlying being and thinking. Western philosophy, dating from c.600 BC, when the Greeks established inquiry independent of theological creeds, is traditionally divided into five major branches. METAPHYSICS inquires into the nature and ultimate significance of the universe, holding reality to subsist in thought (IDEALISM), in matter (MATERIALISM), or in both (DUALISM). LOGIC is concerned with the laws of valid reasoning. EPISTEMOLOGY investigates the nature of knowledge and the process of knowing. ETHICS deals with the problems of right conduct. AESTHETICS attempts to determine the nature of beauty and the criteria of artistic judgment. Historically, philosophy falls into three major periods. Classical (Greek and Roman) philosophy emphasized a concern with the ultimate nature of reality and the problem of virtue in a political context; in fact, virtually all of the problems of philosophy were defined by the Greeks. SOCRATES, PLATO, and ARISTOTLE were the towering figures of classical philosophy. Medieval philosophy in the West was virtually inseparable from Christian thought. SCHOLASTICISM, the high achievement of medieval philosophy, was based on Aristotelian principles as preserved by Arab philosophers, notably AVICENNA and AVERROËS. St THOMAS AQUINAS was the most prominent of the scholastics. The main concern of modern philosophy, beginning with the Renaissance, has been epistemology. DESCARTES, SPINOZA, LEIBNIZ, and other great rationalists of the 17th cent. attempted to give the new science a philosophical basis and thus paved the way for EMPIRICISM. (See articles on HOBBES; HUME; LOCKE.) KANT, representing a bridge between empirical and rationalist views, influenced the idealism of FICHTE, SCHELLING, and HEGEL; MARX, drawing from Hegel's system, developed DIALECTICAL MATERIALISM. Late in the 19th cent. philosophy and religious thinking diverged. Europe developed the schools of PHENOMENOLOGY and EXISTENTIALISM, while Britain and the US focused on the philosophy of science, epistemology, and logic. The many rigorous systems of Eastern philosophy are founded in religion (see BUDDHISM; CONFUCIANISM; HINDUISM; ISLAM; JAINISM; SHINTO; TAOISM; VEDANTA).

**philosophers' stone:** see ALCHEMY.

**phlebitis** (fli‚bietəs), inflammation of a vein, often accompanied by a blood clot, or THROMBOSIS, in the affected vein. When a blood clot is present, the condition is known as thrombophlebitis. Blood clot formation may follow injury, surgery, childbirth, or prolonged bedrest, or may be associated with infection. The chief danger is that the clot may dislodge and travel to a vital organ, causing serious damage (see STROKE). Phlebitis is treated with an ANTICOAGULANT.

**phloem:** see BARK; STEM.

**phlogiston theory** (flo,jist(ə)n), hypothesis regarding combustion. The theory, advanced by Johann Becher late in the 17th cent., postulates the presence in all flammable material of phlogiston, a substance that is without colour, odour, taste, or weight and that is given off in burning. The ash of the burnt material is held to be the true material. The theory was popular until the late 18th cent., when it was refuted by the work of Antoine LAVOISIER.

**phlogopite:** see MICA.

**phlox,** name for plants (genus *Phlox*) of the family Polemoniaceae, especially the perennial border phlox developed by crossing and selection of *P. paniculata* from North America. The family includes many popular wild and garden flowers, especially the genera *Phlox, Polemonium* (called Jacob's ladder), and *Gilia*. Most phlox are perennial, but some common garden varieties are annual hybrids e.g., *P. drummondii*.

**Phnom Penh,** capital of Kampuchea (formerly Cambodia) (1983 est. pop. 500,000), at the confluence of the MEKONG and Tônlé Sap rivers, S Kampuchea. The country's chief port and commercial centre, it became (c.1432) the capital of the KHMER EMPIRE and (1867) of Cambodia. The city was captured (1975) when Cambodia fell to the Communist KHMER ROUGE, and most of its population (then est. at over 700,000) was evacuated and put to work in the countryside. In 1979 it fell to a Vietnamese invasion and became the seat of the Vietnamese-backed government.

**phobia,** an intense, persistent, and irrational fear or dread of an object or a situation: Phobias are usually seen as kinds of NEUROSIS. Examples are arachnophobia (fear of spiders); agoraphobia (fear of open or public spaces); claustrophobia (fear of enclosed spaces); nyctophobia (fear of darkness).

**Phobos,** in astronomy, natural satellite of MARS.

**Phoebe,** in astronomy, natural satellite of SATURN.

**Phoebus** or **Phoebus Apollo:** see APOLLO.

**Phoenicia** (fi,neeshə), ancient territory occupied by Phoenicians. The name Phoenicia usually refers to the heart of the territory where the great Phoenician cities, notably TYRE and SIDON, stood (corresponding roughly to the coast of present-day Lebanon). By 1250 BC the Phoenicians, a Semitic people, were well established as navigators and traders. Organized into city-states, they later established outposts, notably UTICA and CARTHAGE, and travelled to the edges of the known world. The Phoenicians were also fine artisans, but their greatest contribution was the ALPHABET, an idea adopted by the Greeks; the use of symbols for sounds in place of clumsier CUNEIFORM and HIEROGLYPHIC was a tremendous advance. The rise of the Greeks in the 5th cent. BC challenged Phoenician maritime power, and Hellenistic culture gradually absorbed the last traces of Phoenician civilization.

**Phoenician art.** The art of the Phoenician city-states which flourished on trade and commerce, reflects the influences of neighbouring regions, particularly Egypt. There has been little excavation of the major Phoenician sites (e.g., Tyre and Sidon), so that it must be borne in mind that most of the art characterized as 'Phoenician' comes from Assyria, Cyprus, Asia Minor, and elsewhere in the Mediterranean and the Near East. The skill of the Phoenician metalworker and ivory-carver is exemplified by objects found at the Assyrian site of Nimrud and now in the British Museum. A deep metal bowl bearing an embossed and chased scene of a lion hunt is worked in the partly Egyptizing manner of the coastal cities of the Levant. Carved ivory panels, once attached to furniture, carry Phoenician letters on the reverse as a guide to the cabinet maker. A superb panel, one of a pair, shows a negro being attacked by lioness in a field of lotus and papyrus. The flowers are inlaid with blue frit and red carnelian, part of the gilding is still intact. The 'woman at the window' was another popular Phoenician representation: the goddess Astarte, in the guise of a sacred harlot, looks out from a window supported on small columns. Such a window has been found during

**Phoenician art:** Carved ivory panel found at the Assyrian site of Nimrud and now in the British Museum.

excavations at the site of Ramat Rahel. According to the Old Testament, Solomon's Temple and palace at Jerusalem were built by Phoenician craftsmen; excavations of Canaanite shrines suggests a close relationship between the Temple and Phoenician shrines of the period. Phoenician glass, faience, and jewellery is widely attested in the Mediterranean lands and the Near East.

**Phoenix,** US city (1984 est. pop. 853,000; metropolitan area 1.5 million), state capital of Arizona, on the Salt R.; inc. 1881. The largest city in Arizona and one of the fastest-growing cities in the US, it produces electronic, computer, and aerospace equipment, as well as citrus and other food products. Phoenix boomed after World War II. The dry, sunny climate makes it a popular resort centre.

**phoenix,** fabulous bird of ancient legend. When it reached 500 years of age it burned itself on a pyre from whose ashes another phoenix arose. It commonly appears in literature as a symbol of death and resurrection.

**phonetics** and **phonology,** system of sounds of language, studied from two basic points of view. 1 Phonetics is the study of the sounds of language according to their production in the vocal organs (articulatory phonetics) or their effect on the ear (acoustic phonetics). All phonetics are interrelated because human articulatory and auditory mechanisms are uniform. Systems of phonetic writing are aimed at transcribing accurately any sequence of speech sounds; the best known is the International Phonetic Alphabet. 2 Each language uses a limited number of all the possible sounds, called phonemes, and the hearer–speaker is trained from childhood to classify them into groups of like sounds, rejecting as nonsignificant all sorts of features actually phonetically present. Thus the speaker of English ignores sounds that are very important in another language, e.g., French or Spanish. Phonemes include all significant differences of sound, among them features of voicing, place and manner of articulation, accent, and secondary features of nasalization, glottalization, labialization, and the like. The study of the phonemes and their systematic arrangement, together with features of intonation such as stress and pitch, constitutes the phonology of a language.

**phosphorescence,** LUMINESCENCE produced by certain substances after absorbing radiant energy or other types of energy. Phosphorescence is distinguished from FLUORESCENCE in that it continues even after the radiation causing it has ceased. The luminescence is caused by electrons that are excited by the radiation and trapped in potential troughs, from which they are freed by the thermal motion within the crystal. As they fall back to a lower energy level, they emit energy in the form of light.

**phosphorus** (P), nonmetallic element, discovered c.1674 by Hennig Brand. It is an extremely poisonous, yellow to white, waxy, solid substance. Because phosphorus ignites spontaneously when exposed to air, it is stored underwater. Its major source is the mineral APATITE found in phosphate rocks. The principal use of phosphorus is in compounds in fertilizers, detergents, insecticides, soft drinks, toxic nerve gases, pharmaceuticals, and dentifrices. Phosphorus compounds are essential in the diet. Phosphorus is a component of ADENOSINE TRIPHOSPHATE (ATP), a fundamental energy source in living things, and of calcium phosphate, the principal material in bones and teeth. See ELEMENT (table); PERIODIC TABLE.

**Photius,** c.820–892?, Greek churchman and theologian, patriarch of CONSTANTINOPLE. In favour of treating repentant iconoclasts leniently (see ICONOCLASM), he replaced (858) St IGNATIUS OF CONSTANTINOPLE as patriarch, but Pope St NICHOLAS I refused to recognize him. When Photius called (867) a synod that challenged the pope, he was replaced as patriarch and condemned. Photius was again patriarch (877–86) and was recognized by Pope JOHN VIII, but he died in exile. The schism of Photius pointed out the growing differences between East and West.

**photocell:** see PHOTOELECTRIC CELL.

**photocopying,** processes that use various chemical, electrical, or photographic techniques to copy printed or pictorial matter. Most familiar is *xerography,* an electrostatic process that utilizes the attractive force of electric charges to transfer an image to a charged plate. Light, reflecting off the white areas of the object to be copied, erases the charge on the corresponding areas of the plate. A plastic ink powder, called toner, sticks to the charged areas of the plate and transfers an image of the original to paper. *Thermography* uses infrared rays on heat-sensitive paper to transfer an image. Several processes use cameras to make copies of an original. The *Photostat* can reduce or enlarge copied material photographically. *Microfilming* generates copies from $\frac{1}{12}$ to $\frac{1}{100}$ the size of the original, and advances in microphotography allow even greater miniaturization in the *microfiche,* where extremely small microphotographs are printed side by side on a card made of film. In the *transfer process,* chemically coated paper is placed in contact with the original, exposed to light, and developed. The blueprint and the whiteprint, used to reproduce the drawings of architects and engineers, are both examples of transfer processes.

**photoelectric cell** or **photocell,** device whose electrical characteristics (e.g., current, voltage, or resistance) vary when light is incident upon it. Common photoelectric cells consist of two electrodes separated by a light-sensitive SEMICONDUCTOR material. A battery or other voltage source connected to the two electrodes sets up a current even in the absence of light; when light strikes the semiconductor section of the photocell, the current increases in proportion to the light intensity. Photocells can be used to operate a SWITCH, RELAY, door opener, or burglar alarm. See also PHOTOVOLTAIC CELL.

**photoelectric effect,** the emission of electrons by substances, especially metals, when light falls on their surfaces. The effect was discovered by Heinrich HERTZ in 1887 and explained by Albert EINSTEIN in 1905. According to Einstein's theory, light is composed of discrete particles of energy, or quanta, called PHOTONS. When the photons with enough energy strike the material, they liberate electrons that have a maximum kinetic energy equal to the energy of the photons less the work function (the energy required to free the electrons from a particular material). See also QUANTUM THEORY.

**photofit:** see IDENTIKIT.

**photography, still,** science and art of making permanent images on light-sensitive materials. Photography's basic principles, processes, and materials were discovered independently and virtually simultaneously by a diverse group of individuals early in the 19th cent. Johann Heinrich Schulze had discovered in 1727 that silver nitrate darkens upon exposure to light. Using Schulze's research, Thomas Wedgwood and Sir Humphry DAVY created the first photogram. The French physicist Joseph Nicéphore

NIÉPCE made the first paper negative (1816) and the first known photograph, on metal (1827). He formed a partnership with a painter, Louis Jacques DAGUERRE, who in 1839 announced his method for making a direct positive image on a silver plate the daguerreotype. The English scientist William Henry Fox TALBOT developed a paper negative (the calotype) from which an infinite number of paper positives could be printed. Sir John Herschel (see HERSCHEL, family) discovered (1819) a suitable photographic fixing agent for paper images and is credited with giving the new medium its name. In 1851 Frederick Scott Archer developed the collodion process, or 'set plate' technique, which resulted in a negative image with the fine detail of the daguerreotype and was infinitely reproducible. Soon the photograph was considered incontestable proof of an event, experience, or state of being. Among the chief photographers of the 19th cent. were the explorer W.H. JACKSON; Roger FENTON, who documented the Crimean War; Mathew B. Brady and his photographic corps, who photographed the American Civil War; the painter Thomas EAKINS; and Eadweard MUYBRIDGE, who devised a means of making stop-action photographs. As accessory lenses were perfected, the moon and the microcosm became accessible. The development of the halftone process (see PRINTING) in 1881 made photographic reproduction possible in books and newspapers. In 1888 George EASTMAN introduced roll film and the simple Kodak box CAMERA, and photography became available to all. The notion that the fleeting images of nature and humanity could now be swiftly immortalized by a mechanical process instead of the artist's painstaking skills was a radical one; the 19th-cent. painter Paul Delaroche proclaimed, 'From today painting is dead'. Yet it at once became apparent that artists and photographers needed each other. Painters learned new ways of seeing from photography's studies of motion and perspective, while photographers sought to validate their process as an art by imitating paintings. Painters such as the PRE-RAPHAELITES used photographs as an aid to their art, while photographers like Julia Margaret CAMERON were influenced by the work of old masters such as REMBRANDT in creating superb portrait photographs. The American Alfred STIEGLITZ, founder of the Photo-Secession movement, upheld photography as an art in its own right, moving away from dependence on traditional art. As techniques grew more sophisticated the unique documentary ability of the camera to record a 'real' image of the social and historical scene grew in importance and PHOTOJOURNALISM emerged with the growth of the mass media. In the 20th cent. photography shared in the development of MODERNISM in the arts, becoming a central subject at the BAUHAUS, the new German school of design, and forming an integral part of the work of Dadaist and Surrealist followers like Man RAY. In the US Paul Strand and the European-educated Laszlo Moholy-Nagy continued avant-garde experiments with the medium. Since World War II the main influence of photography world-wide has been felt through the mass media, not only in photojournalism but in international advertising and fashion as well as specialized areas such as industry, medicine and science. The visual language of photography has become universal and indispensable to the modern world.

**Photojournalism,** use of the still photograph to record and comment upon news events. From the mid-19th cent. the camera had illustrated great occasions such as the jubilees of Queen VICTORIA, and photographers such as Roger FENTON and Mathew Brady took famous series of the Crimean War and the American CIVIL WAR respectively. However most of such photographs were published well after the event, as in the case of many of the vivid shots of the Western Front in World War I. Even so these helped to establish the powerful impact of the single image in the public consciousness, and the inter-war period saw the growth of a mass audience for photojournalism with journals such as *Life* magazine in America, and *Picture Post* in Britain edited by Tom Hopkinson. With the development of new equipment and techniques as well as the impetus of World War II and government demands for propaganda shots the photograph became increasingly important to the newspaper as a factor in the recording—and the making—of the news event. Although the photojournals declined after 1950, the emergence in Britain of Sunday newspaper magazines containing colour pictures revivified photojournalism and made famous news photographers such as Don McCullin during the 1960s and 70s and Eammon McCabe in the 1980s. The rise of television news coverage has affected but not displaced the power of the single image. Photojournalism was really born not with the news picture but with its immediate publication in mass circulation newspapers and periodicals. It contradicted received notions of

19th-cent. art in its ability to capture the momentary and ephemeral rather than the permanent and transcendent, and to endow it with significance. For the first time in history the sensation of being present at momentous happenings could be shared by millions, and therefore the news content of the photograph is paramount, although this may be enhanced or even created by the photographer's aesthetic skills. The capacity of the single image to affect the viewer profoundly is the essence of photojournalism: one of the most well-remembered press shots of recent times was Eddie Adam's picture in 1968 of a Vietnam police chief shooting a Vietcong prisoner in the head. There is always the possibility that the image may be manipulated to achieve particular effects for propaganda or other purposes. For a mass audience this faculty for isolating and making forever accessible a moment in time—the celebrated raising of the flag on Iwo Jima by the US marines in 1945, or the brief kiss of a prince and his bride on Buckingham Palace balcony in 1981—is the vital element. Both the great event and the everyday occurrence can be symbolized by the single photographic image, and it is this that makes photojournalism unique.

**photolithography:** see LITHOGRAPHY.

**photometry,** branch of physics dealing with the measurement of the intensity of light sources. Instruments used for such measurements are called photometers; most types are based on the comparison of the light source to be measured with a light source of known intensity. The modern unit, adopted in 1948, for the measurement of light intensity is the candela (cd); it is equal to the intensity of BLACK BODY radiation from a surface of $1/600,000$ m$^2$ at the temperature at which platinum freezes and solidifies (2046 K) and at a pressure of 101,325 newtons/m$^2$.

**photomontage,** a technique developed c.1917 by DADA artists, especially HAUSMANN, HEARTFIELD, Hoch, and GROSZ. By cutting up photographs and collaging on new sections, new images are created in which the original meaning and context of the images are transformed. The Berlin Dadavists used the technique specifically for political and social critique. It was also used and developed in SURREALISM, especially by ERNST, as well as by LISSITZKY and RODCHENKO in Russia. See also COLLAGE.

**photon,** or **light quantum,** the particle composing light and other forms of electromagnetic radiation. The PHOTOELECTRIC EFFECT and BLACK BODY radiation can be explained only by assuming that light energy is transferred in discrete packets, or photons, and that the energy of each photon is equal to the frequency of the light multiplied by Planck's constant $h$. Light gives energy to a charged particle when one of its photons collides with the particle. See also QUANTUM THEORY.

**photoperiodism,** sensitivity to the duration of light and dark periods, in plants controlling and resulting in a change of growth habit, e.g., to the flowering stage.

**photorealism,** international art movement of the late 1960s and 1970s that stressed the precise rendering of subject matter, often taken from actual photographs or painted with the aid of slides. Also known as superrealism, the style stressed objectivity and technical proficiency in producing images of photographic clarity, often street scenes or portraits. Well-known photorealists include the American painters Chuck Close and Richard Estes, the sculptor Duane HANSON, and the British painter Malcolm Morley.

**photosphere:** see SUN.

**photosynthesis,** process in which green plants use the energy of sunlight to manufacture carbohydrates from carbon dioxide and water in the presence of CHLOROPHYLL. The chlorophyll molecule is uniquely capable of converting active light energy into a chemical form (glucose) that is stored in food . The initial phase of the process requires direct light; water is broken down into oxygen (which is released as a gas) and hydrogen. Hydrogen and the carbon and oxygen of carbon dioxide are then converted into a series of increasingly complex compounds that result finally in a stable organic compound—glucose—and water. The oxygen released as a byproduct is atmospheric oxygen, vital to respiration in both plants and animals. Photosynthesis, in general, is the reverse of RESPIRATION, in which carbohydrates are broken down to release energy.

**photovoltaic cell,** SEMICONDUCTOR diode that converts light to electric current. When light strikes the exposed active surface, it knocks electrons loose from their sites in the crystal. Some of the electrons have sufficient energy to cross the DIODE junction and pass through an external circuit. Because the current and voltage obtained from these devices are small,

they are usually connected in large series-parallel arrays. Practical photovoltaic cells are currently about 10 to 15% efficient. Although cells constructed from indium phosphide and gallium arsenide are, in principle, more efficient, silicon-based cells are generally less costly. Solar photovoltaic cells have long been used to provide electric power for spacecraft. Recent developments, still in progress, have reduced costs to the point where these cells are being used more and more as terrestrial energy sources.

**phrenology:** see GALL, FRANZ JOSPEH.

**Phrygia,** ancient region, central Asia Minor (now central Turkey). The Phrygians, apparently Indo-Europeans, entered (c.1200 BC) the area from the Balkans. The kingdom of Phrygia (fl. 8th–6th cent. BC) is associated in Greek legend with MIDAS and GORDIUS. Phrygia was later dominated in turn by Lydia, the Gauls, Pergamon, and Rome.

**Phrynichus** (ˌfrinikəs), fl. c.512–476 BC, Athenian tragedian. Called by PLATO the founder of TRAGEDY, he was noted for his lyrics, choreography, and for introducing female characters. His *Taking of Miletus* moved the audience to tears, and he was fined for 'reminding the Athenians of their own misfortunes'.

**physical chemistry,** branch of science that combines the principles and methods of PHYSICS and CHEMISTRY. It provides a fundamental theoretical and experimental basis for all of chemistry, including organic, inorganic, and analytical chemistry. It first emerged as a distinct subject in Germany in the late 19th cent., but its foundations were laid by BOYLE, DAVY, FARADAY, GIBBS, and others. Important topics are chemical equilibrium, ELECTROCHEMISTRY, molecular structure, MOLECULAR WEIGHT, reaction rates, SOLUTIONS, and STATES OF MATTER.

**physics,** branch of science traditionally defined as the study of MATTER, ENERGY, and the relation between them. Physics today may be loosely divided into classical physics and modern physics. Classical physics includes the traditional branches that were recognized and fairly well developed before the beginning of the 20th cent.: MECHANICS (the study of MOTION and the forces that cause it), ACOUSTICS (the study of SOUND), OPTICS (the study of LIGHT), THERMODYNAMICS (the study of the relationships between HEAT and other forms of energy), and ELECTRICITY and MAGNETISM. Most of classical physics is concerned with matter and energy on the normal scale of observation. By contrast, much of modern physics is concerned with the behaviour of matter and energy under extreme conditions (see LOW-TEMPERATURE PHYSICS) or on the very small scale (see ATOM; ELEMENTARY PARTICLES; NUCLEAR PHYSICS; PARTICLE ACCELERATOR). On the very small scale, and for rapidly-moving objects, ordinary, commonsense notions of space, time, matter, and energy are no longer valid, and two chief theories of modern physics present a different picture of these concepts from that presented by classical physics. The QUANTUM THEORY is concerned with the discrete, rather than the continuous, nature of many phenomena at the atomic and subatomic level, and with the complementary aspects of particles and waves in the description of such phenomena. Quantum mechanics, developed from the quantum theory, deals with the quantitative explanation of the laws of chemistry, and with the behaviour of matter under ordinary and extreme conditions. The theory of RELATIVITY is concerned with the description of phenomena that take place in a frame of reference that is in motion with respect to an observer and its predictions differ from those of Newtonian mechanics for high velocities and densities. See also ASTRONOMY; SOLID-STATE PHYSICS.

**physiocrats,** school of 18th-cent. French thinkers who evolved the first complete system of ECONOMICS. Physiocracy's founder, François QUESNAY, argued that the source of all wealth was the land and that only the abundance and high prices of agricultural goods could create prosperity. His followers stressed that absolute freedom of trade was essential to guarantee the most beneficial operation of 'economic law,' which they considered immutable. The physiocrats influenced later advocates of LAISSEZ-FAIRE and contributed to the economic thinking of Adam SMITH.

**physiology,** study of the normal functioning of animals and plants, and of activities that maintain and transmit life. It is usually accompanied by the study of structure (see ANATOMY), the two being intimately related. Physiology considers basic activities such as METABOLISM and special functions within cells, tissues, and organs.

**physiotherapy,** treatment of disorders of the muscles, bones, or joints resulting from injury or disease of the muscles or nerves. Treatment, by a trained physiotherapist, includes remedial exercise, massage, manipulation, heat, electrical stimulation, and infrared and ultraviolet rays to promote healing. See also SPORTS MEDICINE.

**pi,** in mathematics, the ratio of the circumference of a CIRCLE to its diameter; its symbol is π. The ratio is the same for all circles and is approximately 3.1416. The NUMBER π is irrational and transcendental. An early value was the Greek approximation 3⅐; by the mid-20th cent. a computer had calculated π to 100,000 decimal places.

**Piacenza** (pee·ə‚chensə), city (1984 pop. 107,006), Emilia-Romagna, N Italy. It is a commercial administrative and ecclesiastical centre, with modern light industries. A Roman foundation (218 BC), it is situated where routes, including the VIA EMILIA, converge on a crossing of the PO R. Because of the danger from flooding, Piacenza is the last major city on that river.

**Piaf, Edith** (pyaf), 1915–63, French cabaret singer; b. Edith Giovanna Gassion. She began singing in cafes and in the streets at 15, and went on to fame in cabaret, concert, and movie appearances with her powerful emotional style.

**Piaget, Jean** (pya‚zhay), 1896–1980, Swiss developmental psychologist. He is best known for his investigations of children's thinking using the 'clinical method' he developed, which involves carefully questioning the subject during the course of an experimental procedure. Piaget's theory of cognitive development postulates that children move through a series of stages; the 'sensori-motor' stage, culminating in the establishment of OBJECT PERMANENCE; the 'pre-operational' stage, in which the child's thought remains egocentric (see EGOCENTRISM); the 'concrete operational' stage, marked by the attainment of CONSERVATION; and the 'formal operational' stage characteristic of adult logical and hypothetical reasoning. Each stage is characterized by certain formal and structural properties. Piaget was also concerned with general questions of the evolution and development of mind, and the nature of scientific thought. He coined the term 'genetic epistemology' to denote this interdisciplinary field of study.

**Pialat, Maurice,** 1925–, French film director. He has directed such films as *La gueule ouverte* (1974), *To Our Loves* (1984), and *Police* (1985), which often combine a startling *cinéma-vérité* style with occasional use of nonprofessional actors.

**piano** or **pianoforte,** musical STRINGED INSTRUMENT whose sound is produced by vibrating strings struck by felt hammers that are controlled from a keyboard. Its earliest predecessor was the medieval dulcimer. The 14th to 16th cent. saw the rise of the harpsichord and virginal, keyboard instruments whose strings were plucked by quills or jacks. The square harpsichord, often called the spinet, was common by the 16th cent. In c.1709 Bartolomeo Cristofori (1655–1731), a Florentine maker of harpsichords, constructed the first piano, calling it *gravicembalo con piano e forte.* It differed from the harpsichord in that by varying the touch one could vary the volume and duration of tone. This expressive quality was shared to some extent by the clavichord, a delicate instrument important in the 16th to 18th cent., but musical taste gradually favoured the piano's greater volume and expressiveness, and it largely supplanted both the harpsichord and clavichord by 1800. C.P.E. BACH, MOZART, and HAYDN were the first major composers to write for the piano. The main body of its literature is from the 19th cent., including the works of BEETHOVEN, SCHUBERT, CHOPIN, Robert SCHUMANN, MENDELSSOHN, BRAHMS, FRANCK, LISZT, DEBUSSY, and RAVEL. The piano was originally built in the shape of a harpsichord, and this style (the grand piano) has always been the standard form. Innovations in the 19th cent. included an iron framework, a double-action striking mechanism permitting rapid repetition of tone, the upright piano (in which the strings are perpendicular to, rather than parallel to, the keys), and the player piano, which incorporates a mechanical system that automatically plays the encoded contents of a perforated paper strip. An electric piano has also been developed.

**Piast,** 1st dynasty of Polish dukes and kings dating from the 9th cent. Duke Mieszko I (r. c.962–92) introduced Christianity to Poland. His son, BOLESLAUS I, was crowned king in 1025; not all of his successors, however, styled themselves king. During the reign (1102–38) of BOLESLAUS III, four hereditary duchies were created for his four sons; a fifth son, CASIMIR II (probably a posthumous child), carved out a fifth duchy for himself and secured the hereditary right to the kingship for his descendants. Dynastic

struggles continued, however, until the dynasty ended with the death (1370) of CASIMIR III. The Jagiellonian dynasty followed (1386–1572).

**Picabia, Francis,** 1878–1953, French painter. He was associated with IMPRESSIONISM, CUBISM, and SURREALISM, and was one of the first exponents of DADA in Europe, publishing his Dada review 391 in 1916 in Barcelona. In 1918 he joined the Zurich Dada group and later the Paris Dadaists.

**Picard, Jean,** 1620–82, French astronomer. His measurements led to a much improved determination of the length of a degree of meridian and consequently of the circumference of the Earth. Isaac NEWTON used Picard's figures to verify the accuracy of his principle of gravitation.

**Picardy,** former prov. and rich farming region of NE France. Its chief city is AMIENS. It has been the scene of many notable battles, including those of the Somme in 1916 and 1917. A prosperous agricultural region, its large farms yield heavy crops of cereals, sugar-beet, and animal fodder.

**Picasso, Pablo** (Pablo Ruiz y Picasso), 1881–1973, Spanish painter, sculptor, graphic artist, and ceramicist who worked in France. Leader of the SCHOOL OF PARIS, he was remarkable for his technical virtuosity, and ability to adapt his formal and technical interests to the changing artistic environment. Admitted to the Royal Academy of Barcelona at 15, he later moved to Paris, where he remained until 1947, then moving to the South of France. His early works, e.g., *Old Woman* (1901; Philadelphia Mus. Art), show the influence of TOULOUSE-LAUTREC. His production is usually described in series of overlapping periods. In his melancholy 'blue period' such works as *The Old Guitarist* (1903; Art Inst., Chicago) depicted, in blue tones, the world of the poor. His 'rose period' is characterized by a lighter palette and subjects from the circus. In 1907, Picasso painted *Les Demoiselles d'Avignon* (Mus. Mod. Art, New York City), a significant work in the development of CUBISM. It took formal ideas from CÉZANNE and from Iberian and Negro sculpture in a large and complex composition that was intended as an allegory on prostitution. It was not completed or publicly shown until 1937; however BRAQUE, introduced to Picasso by APOLLINAIRE, saw it and was greatly influenced by it. From 1909 to 1916 Picasso worked in close contact with Braque, first developing analytical cubism where figures and still lifes were reduced to interlocking facets and multiple viewpoints. In the synthetic phase of cubism, after 1912, his forms became larger and more representational, e.g., *The Three Musicians* (1921; Mus. Mod. Art, New York City). His second landmark work was *Guernica* (1936), an impassioned condemnation of war and fascism. In his later years, Picasso turned to creations of fantasy and comic invention, working in sculpture, ceramics, and the graphic arts.

Pablo **Picasso,** *Les Demoiselles d'Avignon,* 1907. Oil on canvas, 243.9 × 233 cm. Museum of Modern Art, New York.

**Piccard, Auguste** (pee,kah), 1884–1962, Belgian physicist, known for his balloon ascents into the stratosphere; b. Switzerland. In 1932 he reached an altitude of 16,700 m (54,800 ft). After 1946 he made ocean dives in a bathyscaphe of his own design. In 1960 his son, **Jacques Piccard**, 1922–, and Lt Don Walsh of the US Navy reached a depth of 10,920 m (35,800 ft) in the MARIANAS TRENCH.

**Piccoli, Michael,** 1925–, French film actor. A solid, sardonic leading man, he has starred in such films as *Contempt* (1963), *Belle du jour* (1967), and *La grande bouffe* (1973).

**piccolo:** see FLUTE.

**Piccolomini, Enea Silvio:** see PIUS II.

**picketing,** the practice of workers gathering at their place of work during industrial action, to persuade fellow workers to support them in the dispute. Picketing has always been an integral part of the right to strike. Under UK law, picketing is now only lawful at or near the workers' place of employment, to peacefully communicate information, and pickets have no right to stop people in vehicles to talk to them; formerly workers also had the right to picket the premises of companies indirectly concerned with the dispute, e.g., suppliers. Anti-trade union legislation in the 1980s also limited the number of workers who may legally picket in one place. If picketing is unlawful both trade unions and their members can be sued in TORT (e.g., NUISANCE), and the pickets themselves may be guilty of certain criminal offences (e.g., obstruction).

**Pickett, George Edward,** 1825–75, Confederate general in the AMERICAN CIVIL WAR. He is best remembered for 'Pickett's charge', the unsuccessful assault (1863) on Union forces during the GETTYSBURG CAMPAIGN that virtually annihilated his division.

**Pickford, Mary,** 1893–1979, American film actress; b. Canada as Gladys Smith. Called 'America's Sweetheart', she played plucky heroines in such films as *The Poor Little Rich Girl* (1917) and *Tess of the Storm Country* (1922).

**Picts,** ancient inhabitants of N and central SCOTLAND. First mentioned in AD 297, the Picts formed a unified kingdom by the 7th cent. The union (c.843) of the Picts and the Scottish kingdom of Dalriada became the kingdom of Scotland.

**pidgin,** a marginal language which is created to cater for a particular situation among people who have no common language. If adopted and developed as the mother-tongue of a community, it becomes a CREOLE. See also LINGUA FRANCA.

**Piedmont,** region (1984 est. pop. 4,411,921), 25,400 km (9,807 sq mi), NW Italy. The Piedmont is mostly mountainous, with the ALPS in the N and W, and the APENNINES in the S. TURIN, the capital, is a major industrial centre. Wheat, maize, rice, and grapes are grown in the upper Po valley. From the 11th cent. the counts (later dukes) of SAVOY were powerful in the area. They became kings of SARDINIA in 1720 and had acquired all of modern Piedmont by 1748. France greatly influenced Piedmontese culture and ruled the area from 1798 to 1814. The region was the centre of the RISORGIMENTO, and Turin was the first capital of the kingdom of Italy.

**Pied Piper of Hamelin,** legendary 13th-cent. figure who rid Hamelin, Germany, of its rats by charming them away with his flute-playing. When he was refused payment, he charmed away the town's children in revenge. Among those who retold the tale are GOETHE and Robert BROWNING.

**Pierce, Franklin,** 1804–69, 14th president of the US (1853–57). After an undistinguished career in New Hampshire state politics and in both houses of Congress, he served in the MEXICAN WAR as a brigadier general of volunteers. In 1852, as the compromise presidential candidate of the badly divided Democratic party, he defeated the Whig candidate, Gen. Winfield SCOTT. Pierce's readiness to defer to the strong personalities in his cabinet and in Congress, and to yield to Southern pressure over slavery and expansion showed him to be weak and vacillating. Although he had favoured the COMPROMISE OF 1850 on the slavery issue, he backed the Kansas–Nebraska Act of 1854 that precipitated virtual civil war between the pro- and antislavery forces in Kansas. The act enraged many Northerners and caused Pierce to be so unpopular that the Democrats passed him over for renomination and he returned to obscurity.

**Piero della Francesca,** c.1420–1492, major Italian RENAISSANCE painter. Early contact with the art of Florence gave him the basics of PERSPECTIVE, to which he added his own acute perception of nature, e.g., in the *Baptism of Christ* (c.1445; National Gall., London). He delighted in the play of mathematical ratios and painted *The Flagellation of Christ* (c.1456; Palazzo Ducale, Urbino) in a perfect, geometric framework. His most famous cycle, *The Story of the True Cross* (1452–66; Church of San Francesco, Arezzo), depicts scenes from the *Golden Legend*. He also painted court portraits, e.g., of the Duke and Duchess of Urbino (c.1472; Uffizi, Florence).

Piero della Francesca, 'L'Invenzione della Santa Croce e sua verificazione', from *The Story of the True Cross* cycle, 1452–66. Church of San Francesco, Arezzo.

**Piero di Cosimo,** 1462–1521, Florentine painter; b. Piero di Lorenzo. His scenes depicting mythology and the life of primitive man, e.g., *Hunting Scene* (Metropolitan Mus., New York) and *Vulcan and Aeolus* (National Art Gall. of Canada, Ottawa), are famous.

**Pierre,** US city (1980 pop. 11,973), state capital (since 1889) of South Dakota, on the Missouri R.; inc. 1883. Its economy is centred on agriculture (grains and cattle) and state government. Located on the site of an Aricara Indian settlement, it was a river trade centre from c.1822. The huge Oahe Dam and Lake Oahe are nearby.

**Piers Plowman:** see LANGLAND, WILLIAM.

**piezoelectric effect** (pie'eezoh·i,lektrik), generation of a small voltage or difference in electric POTENTIAL between surfaces of a solid DIELECTRIC when a mechanical stress is applied to it. This effect is exhibited by certain crystals, e.g., quartz and Rochelle salt, and ceramic materials. Conversely, when a voltage is applied across certain surfaces of a solid exhibiting the piezoelectric effect, the solid undergoes a mechanical distortion. Piezoelectric materials are used in TRANSDUCERS, e.g., record-player cartridges, microphones, and strain gauges, which produce an electrical output from a mechanical input, and in earphones and ultrasonic radiators, which produce a mechanical output from an electrical input.

**pig,** or **hog, swine,** cloven-hoofed MAMMAL of the genus *Sus*, family Suidae. Pigs were probably first domesticated in the Far East, but the modern Western farm pig is descended from the forest-dwelling European wild boar (*S. scrofa*), with occasional outcrossing to Asian species derived from the Chinese wild pig (*S. vittatus*). Many species exist, some having reverted to the wild condition, as in parts of Africa and New Guinea; most are between 120 and 180 cm (4 to 6 ft) long, although there is also a pygmy species (*S. salvanius*) in Nepal. Pigs are more akin to dogs in their general intelligence than to other cloven-hoofed animals; they are sometimes trained, e.g., to find truffles or sniff out drugs. They can exist as scavengers on almost any type of food (see OMNIVORE). The male (boar) is solitary except in the breeding season, when he will gather and aggressively defend a group of females (sows). In the wild, or when materials are available, the female builds an elaborate roofed nest, which behaviour is related to the helplessness of the piglets for some time after birth. This again shows a great difference from other members of their order, whose young are able to run with the herd within a few hours of being born. Modern domestic pigs are bred for their meat and their skins produce fine quality leather. Famous breeds include the Berkshire, the Yorkshire, the Duroc (developed in the US), and the Hampshire. The Landrace, from Denmark, and the Tamworth, from Staffordshire, are examples of pigs bred especially for bacon production. The pig has a short production cycle, and breeders are able to follow consumer requirements fairly closely. The use of vegetable oils for cooking, and the adverse publicity for animal fat has tended to produce modern pigs of large size, but with lean carcasses. In order to maintain profit pigs are usually kept in restricted housing with controlled environments and feeding programmes, and this has attracted strong criticism from the animal-rights movements. Under these conditions diseases such as swine fever and parasitic infections were originally severe problems, and it is obviously in the best interests of the pig farmer to ensure a healthy environment. Although the pig is an essential part of the economy in some parts of the world, e.g., China and the Pacific area, and is widely kept elsewhere, it is nevertheless abhorred in certain cultures, e.g., by Muslims and Jews. Anthropologists have not been able to discover the origins of such taboos.

**pigeon,** land BIRD of the family Columbidae, cosmopolitan in temperate and tropical regions, characterized by a stout body, small head, and thick plumage. The names *dove* and *pigeon* are interchangeable, although the former generally refers to smaller birds. The rock dove (*Columba livia*) of temperate W Eurasia is the wild progenitor of the common street and domestic pigeons. The fruit-eating green pigeons of Africa and Asia and the imperial pigeons of Australasia have brightly-coloured plumage. The once-abundant American passenger pigeon, became extinct in 1914.

**Piggott, Lester,** 1935–, English jockey. He won the DERBY nine times and the St Leger eight times. He was champion jockey 11 times and won the Arc de Triomphe three times. He rode his 4000th winner in Britain on 14 Aug. 1982. After retiring as a jockey he became a successful racehorse trainer (1985). Two years later he was imprisoned for tax evasion.

**pig iron,** IRON refined in a blast furnace, containing about 4% carbon and small amounts of manganese, silicon, phosphorus, and sulphur. About 95% of it is processed to make STEEL, and the balance is cast in sand moulds into blocks called pigs and further processed in foundries (see CASTING).

**pigment,** substance that imparts colour to other materials. Most paint pigments are metallic compounds, but organic compounds are also used. Some metallic pigments occur naturally, e.g., the oxides that produce the brilliant colouring of rocks and soil in the W US. Plants and animals also contain pigments. CHLOROPHYLL (green) and carotene (yellow) produce bright colours in plants. Blood receives its red colour from HAEMOGLOBIN, and various pigments colour human skin. Scientific techniques, such as MASS SPECTROMETRY, can readily distinguish old from modern pigments, thereby enabling fake art to be distinguished from genuine masterpieces. Trace elements, e.g., certain sulphur isotopes in ultramarine, quickly reveal provenance of the pigment.

**pike,** freshwater FISHes of the family Esocidae, found in Europe, Asia, and North America. The pike, muskellunge, and pickerel are long, thin fishes with spineless dorsal fins, large anal fins, and long, narrow jaws with formidable teeth. The 140-cm (4½-ft) pike (*Esox lucius*) is also called the freshwater shark, because it is the fiercest hunting fish in the fresh waters of the northern hemisphere. Found in both still and running waters, pike wait in water weeds for their prey, usually feeding on fishes in the carp and trout families. They will also take frogs, voles, and water fowl. Pike are thought to consume one fifth of their weight (5–15 kg/10–35 lb) daily. The pickerels are smaller members of the family. Pikes are strong fighters and valued as game and food. The walleyed pike is a PERCH.

**Pilate:** see PONTIUS PILATE.

**Pilbara,** region in NW Western Australia. The scene of gold rushes in 19th cent., this area now includes one of the largest and richest iron ore deposits in the world at Mt Newman, Mt Goldsworthy, and Mt Tom Price in the Hamersley Ranges; though discovered in 1952 the ore was not developed until 1962. Railways link the mines to the coast at Dampier and Port Hedland.

**piles:** see HAEMORRHOIDS.

**pilgrim,** one who out of religious motives travels to a shrine. Pilgrimages are a feature of many cultures. Jews made an annual pilgrimage to Jerusalem at Passover. Muslims try to visit MECCA once in their lives. In Christianity the Holy Land was early a place of pilgrimage. Modern Roman Catholic shrines include SANTIAGO DE COMPOSTELA, LOURDES, and FÁTIMA.

**Pilgrims,** the 102 English Puritan separatists and others who founded the PLYMOUTH COLONY in America. While crossing the Atlantic Ocean on the *Mayflower,* they signed the Mayflower Compact (see under MAYFLOWER) providing for majority rule. The Pilgrims landed at Plymouth in Dec. 1620.

**Pilinszky, János,** 1921–81. Hungarian poet. A Catholic whose experience of World War II dominated his life and work, Pilinszky wrote short, spare, intense poems, e.g., *Requiem* (1964) and *Icons of the Metropolis* (1970), and ritualistic pieces for the stage, which can be seen as a response to T.W. Adorno's dictum 'no poetry after Auschwitz'.

**pill, the:** see ORAL CONTRACEPTIVE.

**Pilnyak, Boris** (peeln,yahk),pseud. of **Boris Andreyevich Vogau,** 1894–1941, Soviet novelist and short-story writer. He first attracted attention with his novel *The Naked Year* (1921), depicting the chaos of the revolutionary period. *Mahogany* (1929) and *The Volga Falls to the Caspian Sea* (1930) were denounced by the Soviet regime. Arrested in 1937, Pilnyak either died in prison or was executed.

**pilot fish,** member of the FISH family Carangidae, noted for its habit of swimming with larger fishes such as SHARKS and WHALES. They will also follow boats; the Kon Tiki raft had a following of pilot fish. They are found throughout temperate and tropical seas and occasionally appear in the waters round the British Isles. Pilot fishes grow up to 560 cm (2 ft) long and have distinctive vertical stripes along their bodies. They were believed to guide lone swimmers and lost boats back to shore, which is how they got their name. The young of pilot fishes also shelter beneath a larger animal, in their case a JELLYFISH, the Portuguese man-of-war. They live amid the tentacles, apparently unharmed by the stings.

**pilot whale,** squid-eating MAMMAL of the DOLPHIN family, ranging the North Atlantic from Greenland to the Mediterranean and in the Caribbean and the Pacific. Pilot whales live in large schools which all seem to follow one leader. Sometimes large numbers of these 8.5-m (28-ft) dolphins become stranded on a beach, presumably from following a misguided leader. If a pilot whale is refloated, it will return to the beach apparently in answer to distress calls from those still stranded. These dolphins are slaughtered in large numbers in the Faeroes when they approach the shores, the practice still continuing despite a ban on the killing of all whales which came into force in 1986.

**Pilsudski, Marshal Józef,** 1867–1935, Polish soldier and statesman. Imprisoned during his early years for his revolutionary activities, he formed (1914) the POLISH LEGIONS which fought alongside the Central Powers during WORLD WAR I. In 1918, Pilsudski assumed control alongside the newly independent republic and remained head of state until 1922. He commanded Polish forces to victory during the Polish-Soviet War of 1919–20. His political views, initially socialist, were increasingly dominated by an authoritarian nationalism. In May 1926, impatient with the continuing crises of Polish democratic government, he reassumed control of a government which quickly took on all the elements of a military dictatorship. This repressive rule, carried out in the name of strong government, was continued by his followers after his death in 1935.

**Piltdown man,** name given to fossil remains found (1908) at Piltdown, Sussex, England, thought to be human and 200,000 to 1 million years old. Some anatomists were puzzled by the fossil's inconsistent features, and in 1950 fluorine tests and X-ray analysis proved that parts were modern and Piltdown man was a forgery.

**Pima Indians,** NORTH AMERICAN INDIANS of the Southwest, speaking a Uto-Aztecan language (see AMERICAN INDIAN LANGUAGES). Descendants of the Hohokam peoples, who built a network of irrigation canals, the Pima were sedentary farmers, noted for fine basketry. Warlike towards the APACHE INDIANS, they befriended both Spaniards and American pioneers. The Maricopa joined them in the 19th cent. Today, in central Arizona, they live on income from agriculture, crafts, and leasing land for mineral development.

**pimento** or **allspice,** tree (*Pimenta officinalis*) of the MYRTLE family. Its dried, unripe berries are used medicinally and as a spice. The spice supposedly combines the flavours of several other spices; it is used in pickles and relishes. Pimento (more correctly, *pimiento*) is also the name of a large, sweet Spanish PEPPER.

**pimpernel:** see PRIMROSE.

**Pindar,** 518?–c.438 BC, generally regarded as the greatest Greek LYRIC poet. He wrote choral lyrics and established a standard for the triumphal ode or epinicion. Celebrating an athletic victory, each ode contains a narrative myth, connected with the winner, that sets an elevated moral and religious tone. Pindar's diction and complex word order do not translate easily. The 17th–18th cent. **Pindaric ode** of Abraham COWLEY, John DRYDEN, and Thomas GRAY is based loosely on Pindar's form.

**Pindling, Sir Lynden Oscar,** 1930–, prime minister of the BAHAMAS (1967–). As leader of the Progressive Liberal Party, he represented the large black majority in the Bahamas and was the colony's first black prime minister. In 1973 he led the Bahamas to independence within the COMMONWEALTH. He has developed international banking and investment management as a major industry but has come under criticism in the US and elsewhere for the alleged involvement of his government in organized criminal activities such as drug trafficking.

**pine,** common name for the family Pinaceae, resinous woody trees chiefly of north temperate regions, with needlelike, usually evergreen leaves. The Pinaceae reproduce by means of cones rather than flowers, and have winged seeds suitable for wind distribution. The family is the largest and most important of the CONIFERS, providing pitch, turpentine, rosin, paper pulp, and more general-purpose timber than any other family. Their timber is the most important of all the softwoods, and is used for all construction work, joinery, telephone poles, pit props, sleepers, etc. The family's genera include the FIR, LARCH, SPRUCE, HEMLOCK, CEDAR, DOUGLAS FIR, and true pines. True pines (genus *Pinus*) can be identified by the leaf arrangement. The ponderosa, or Western yellow, pine (*P. ponderosa*) is second only to the Douglas fir as a commercial timber tree in N America; the Scots pine (*P. sylvestris*), ranging from Scotland to Siberia, is one of the most valuable European timber trees. Several Mediterranean and American pines yield edible seeds, called pine nuts.

**pineal body** or **pineal gland** (ˌpini·əl), pea-sized organ situated in the BRAIN. Generally regarded as an endocrine gland (see ENDOCRINE SYSTEM) even though no pineal HORMONE has been isolated in humans, it exerts some influence on sexual development in animals by secreting a substance called melatonin.

**pineapple,** fruit of a spiny herbaceous plant (*Ananas comosus*) of the BROMELIAD family. Native to South America, the pineapple plant is widely cultivated in tropical regions; Hawaii supplies the major portion of the world's canned pineapple. The fruit, whose spiny skin is yellowish brown when ripe, is sweet and juicy; it is topped by a distinctive rosette of green leaves.

**Pinero, Sir Arthur Wing,** 1855–1934, English dramatist. His early successes were farces and sentimental comedies, but plays like *The Profligate* (1889) and *The Second Mrs Tanqueray* (1893) brought him fame as a serious social dramatist.

**Pines, Isle of,** 3056 km² (1180 sq mi), off the coast of SW Cuba. It was discovered by COLUMBUS in 1494 and passed to US control in 1898, after the SPANISH–AMERICAN WAR. Because its name was omitted from the PLATT AMENDMENT, defining Cuba's boundaries, it was claimed by both the US and Cuba until a treaty signed in 1925 confirmed Cuba's possession. Near Nueva Gerona, the capital, is a prison in which political dissidents have been detained by several regimes.

**ping-pong:** see TABLE TENNIS.

**pink,** common name for some members of Caryophyllaceae, a family of small herbs chiefly of north temperate zones, typified by swollen stem nodes and notched, or 'pinked', petals ranging in colour from white to red and purple. The family includes several ornamentals and many wildflowers and weeds. Ornamental pinks include the fragrant flowers of the genus *Dianthus,* among which are the many varieties of carnation and sweet William. BABY'S BREATH (*Gypsophila paniculata*) is an unusual pink in being a bushy plant; it is often used by florists as a bouquet filler.

**Pinkerton, Allan,** 1819–84, American detective; b. Scotland. In Chicago he founded (1850) what was to become the Pinkerton National Detective Agency, and during the Civil War he directed an espionage system behind the Confederate lines. His agency, which solved numerous railway robberies, also gathered the evidence that broke up the MOLLY MAGUIRES in the 1870s. It subsequently became notorious as a private police force for hire to management as strikebreakers.

**pink eye:** see CONJUNCTIVITIS.

**Pinochet Ugarte, Augusto** (ˌpeenə'shay oohˌgahtay), 1915–, president of Chile (1973–). A professional military man, he led the coup

which overthrew socialist Pres. ALLENDE and soon assumed the dominant position in the military government which ensued. He put politics on ice and pursued a free-enterprise economic policy, improving the economy but at immense social cost. He also alienated Chile from international goodwill by his internal repressive policies. In 1988 he was defeated in a national plebiscite on whether he should continue in office until 1996; he was thus constitutionally required to vacate the presidency by early 1990.

**pinochle** (ˌpee'nukl), card game played by two to four players, with a pack of 48 cards made up of two of each from the 9 to the ace in all four suits, developed in the US in the 19th cent. Auction pinochle, probably the most popular form of the game, is based on a complicated system of bidding. Four-hand, or partnership, pinochle, and bottom card–trump opening pinochle are popular. In all of these, an arbitrary point goal, not simply game, is often set.

**Pinpri-Chindwad,** town (1981 pop. 220,966), Maharashtra state, W India. It is essentially a twin satellite town of PUNE, strung along the Pune–Bombay road some 16 km (10 mi) NW of the former. It has commercial, service, and industrial functions.

**Pinter, Harold,** 1930–, English dramatist. In his 'comedies of menace', the commonplace is invested with tension and mystery, often through the use of silence. *The Dumbwaiter* (1957), *The Birthday Party* (1958), *The Caretaker* (1960), and *The Homecoming* (1965), and *No Man's Land* (1975) are among his best-known plays. His screenplays include *The Servant* (1963) and *The French Lieutenant's Woman* (1981).

**Pinturicchio** or **Pintoricchio** ('pintoohˌrikkyoh, 'pintoh-), c.1454–1513, Umbrian painter; b. Bernardino di Betto. He painted the cathedral library in Siena and did mythological scenes for the Palazzo del Magnifico in Siena (Metropolitan Mus.).

**pinyin** [Chin. *pinyin zimu* = phonetic alphabet], system of romanization of Chinese written characters, approved in 1958 by the government of the People's Republic and officially adopted by it in 1979. Its use replaces that of the more complex Wade–Giles system (1859; modified 1912), among others. Objectives of pinyin include promoting a national language, establishing a means for writing non-Chinese (minority) languages in China, and encouraging foreigners to learn Chinese. Pinyin is not used in Taiwan or in Hong Kong.

**Pinzón, Martín Alonzo** (peenˌthohn), d. 1493, Spanish navigator. Commander of the *Pinta* on COLUMBUS's first voyage (1492), he deserted Columbus in the Antilles for six weeks and upon his return was censured for treasonable conduct. His younger brother, **Francisco Martín Pinzón,** fl. 1492, was master of the *Pinta*. Another brother, **Vicente Yáñez Pinzón,** fl. 1492–1509, commanded the *Niña*. When the *Santa María* was wrecked, he took Columbus aboard. He discovered the mouth of the AMAZON (1500), was governor of PUERTO RICO from 1505, and explored the coasts of YUCATÁN, HONDURAS, and VENEZUELA (1508–09).

**pion:** see ELEMENTARY PARTICLES.

**Piper, John,** 1903–, British painter. He began as an abstract painter in the circle of B. NICHOLSON and HEPWORTH, visiting Paris in 1933 where he met BRAQUE, BRANCUSI, and LÉGER. In the later 1930s he reverted to a representational landscape style and produced paintings of bombed buildings during World War II. He has also designed for the stage, as well as designing textiles and stained glass, e.g., at Eton Coll. and Coventry Cathedral.

**pipit:** see WAGTAIL.

**Pippin:** for Frankish rulers thus named, see PEPIN.

**piracy,** robbery by force of arms on the high seas. The pirate usually attacks ships of all nations; he holds no commission and receives the protection of no nation; he is thus distinguished from the privateer, whose actions are licensed by some government. Piracy has existed from the earliest times, and ancient Egyptian, Greek, Phoenician, and Roman commerce was plagued by it. In more modern times the Barbary pirates (see BARBARY STATES) flourished in the Mediterranean, the VIKINGS harassed the commerce of the Baltic Sea and the English Channel, and the English buccaneers pillaged the SPANISH MAIN. With the growth of national navies piracy declined, and the last pirate stronghold, along the Straits of Malacca and the China seas, was wiped out in the late 19th cent. Famous names in the history of piracy include BLACKBEARD, Sir Francis DRAKE, Capt. KIDD, and Jean Lafitte.

**Piraiévs** or **Piraeus**, city (1981 pop. 196,389), E central Greece, on the Saronic Gulf. Part of Greater Athens, it is the chief port of Greece and a commercial centre. It was built in 450 BC and was connected to Athens by the famed Long Walls, which were destroyed (404 BC) by Sparta.

**Pirandello, Luigi**, 1867–1936, Italian author; b. Sicily. A major figure in 20th-cent. theatre, he was awarded the 1934 Nobel Prize for literature. In the 1890s he began to write poetry and short stories, then produced a succession of novels, including *Il fu Mattia Pascal* (1904; tr. *The Late Mattia Pascal*). His fame, however, rests on his grimly humorous plays, exploring the problematic relationship between reality and illusion, which he began writing during World War I. They include *Così è, se vi pare* (1917; tr. *Right You Are If You Think You Are*), *Sei personaggi in cerca d'autore* (1921; tr. *Six Characters in Search of an Author*), *Henry IV* (1922), and *Tonight We Improvise* (1930).

**Piranesi, Giovanni Battista**, 1720–78, Italian etcher and architect. In Rome he made etchings, notable for their accuracy and grandeur, of the city's buildings and monuments. His fantastic and imaginary *Carceri* [prisons] (1745) fascinated the Romantic poets.

**piranha** or **caribe**, predatory freshwater FISH of the family Characidae, found in E and central South America, especially in the AMAZON. The piranha (genus *Serrasalmus*) has powerful jaws and razor-sharp triangular teeth and is capable of killing cattle and human beings. The largest piranha is about 60 cm (2 ft) long.

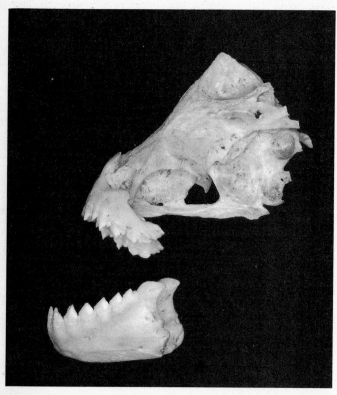

Upper and lower jaw of **piranha**

**Pirenne, Henri** (pee̱,ren), 1862–1935, Belgian historian. He skilfully related economic to general history. In *Mohammed and Charlemagne* (1935), he attributed the collapse of Western civilization to the spread of Islam, a thesis that aroused much controversy. He also wrote a *History of Belgium* (7 vol., 1899–1932) and *Medieval Cities* (1927).

**Pisa**, city (1984 pop. 104,213), in TUSCANY, N central Italy, on the Arno R. It is a centre of commerce and industry, producing glass, textiles, and drugs. An Etruscan town, it prospered under Rome. It was a strong maritime republic from the 9th to 11th cent. A Ghibelline centre, 13th–14th cent. (see GUELPHS AND GHIBELLINES), Pisa fell to FLORENCE in 1406. GALILEO was born and taught there. The school of sculpture founded by Nicola PISANO flourished in the city. Its Romanesque cathedral and Leaning Tower are famous.

The Campanile and the Cathedral, **Pisa**

**Pisa, Council of:** see SCHISM, GREAT.

**Pisanello** (peeza̱,nelloh), c.1395–1455?, N Italian RENAISSANCE medallist, painter, and draughtsman; b. Antonio Pisano. He painted in the highly detailed decorative style of international Gothic, as in his fresco of *St George and the Princess* (c.1435; Sant' Anastasia, Verona). Frescoes of scenes of medieval chivalry, in the Ducal Palace, Mantua, have recently been discovered and attributed to him. He revived the antique medal form of portraiture and there are good examples in the Victoria and Albert Mus., London.

**Pisano, Andrea** (pee̱,zahnoh), c.1290–c.1348, Italian sculptor, also called Andrea da Pontedera. His most important work is the first bronze doors (1330–37) for the BAPTISTERY in Florence, depicting the life of John the Baptist. His Gothic style was influenced by GIOTTO, whom he succeeded as head of the work on the Florence cathedral.

**Pisano, Antonio:** see PISANELLO.

**Pisano, Nicola**, fl. from 1258, d. between 1278 and 1284, major Italian sculptor. He founded a new school of sculpture in Italy. His first great work was the hexagonal pulpit (1260) decorated with scenes from the life of Christ, for the Baptistery in Pisa; the figure style of these reliefs was deeply influenced by classical art and brought a new realism and dignity to Italian sculpture. Later, as with the pulpit for Siena cathedral (1265–68), and the fountain at Perugia (c.1270), where he worked with his son, Giovanni, his style became more Gothic. His son, **Giovanni Pisano**, fl. c.1265–c.1314, was a major sculptor and architect. He worked on the facade of Siena cathedral (1285–97); his series of 14 life-size, intensely dramatic figures is now in the Cathedral Museum, Siena. His outstanding work is the pulpit (1301) in the church of San Andrea at Pistoia, where his style is Gothic and highly expressive.

**Piscator, Erwin**, 1893–1966, German theatrical director and producer. With Bertolt BRECHT he was the chief exponent of epic theatre, in which narrative, montage, self-contained scenes, and direct argument were used to create a shock of recognition in the spectator. His experimental productions in Berlin and New York City greatly influenced Western theatre methods. His theoretical essays were collected as *The Political Theatre* (1929, tr. 1980).

**Pisistratus** or **Peisistratus** (pie̱,sistratas), 605?–527 BC, tyrant of ATHENS. Having achieved popularity with liberal land laws, he seized power c.560 BC. Under his rule Athens established hegemony in the

Nicola **Pisano**, pulpit of the Baptistery in Pisa, 1260.

Dardanelles. Exiled twice by his rivals, he nevertheless ruled until his death, and was succeeded by his sons Hippias and Hipparchus.

**Pissarro, Camille** (peesah,roh), 1830–1903, French painter; b. Virgin Islands. Pissarro was a leading member of the Impressionist group (see IMPRESSIONISM), the only artist to exhibit at all of the eight Impressionist exhibitions. He was a rural painter, who worked at Pontoise and Louveciennes; his landscapes of the 1860s and 1870s, of village streets, orchards, vegetable gardens, are fresh and spontaneous in their observation of the weather and light of varying seasons, e.g., *Orchard with Flowering Fruit Trees, Springtime, Pontoise* (1877; Musée d'Orsay, Paris). In the 1880s and 1890s, after a brief period experimenting with Seurat's colour theories, his pictures of peasants became increasingly ambitious and monumental. In the 1890s Pissarro painted a series of townscapes in Paris and Rouen.

**pistachio**, tree or shrub (genus *Pistacia*) of the SUMAC family. The pistachio nut of commerce is obtained from *P. vera,* native to Turkey, Syria, and Palestine; the trade supply comes primarily from Iran, Syria, Turkey, Greece, Italy, and California. The nut is a greenish seed that is eaten salted or used in confections.

**pistil:** see FLOWER.

**Piston, Walter**, 1894–1976, American composer and teacher. A neoclassicist, he composed in traditional forms, e.g., SYMPHONIES, CONCERTOS, and string quartets, and wrote important textbooks on HARMONY, COUNTERPOINT, and orchestration.

**Pitcairn Island**, volcanic island (1980 est. pop. 61), 6.5 km² (2.5 sq mi), South Pacific, near the Tropic of Capricorn. The only inhabited island in the Pitcairn Islands group, it was discovered (1767) by the British and colonized (1790) by mutineers from the British naval vessel BOUNTY and Tahitian women. Their descendents, who speak English, still inhabit the island. It has been a British possession since 1839.

**pitch**, in music, the position of a tone in the musical scale, today designated by a letter name and determined by the frequency of vibration of the source of the tone. An international conference held in 1939 set a standard for A above middle C of 440 cycles per second. The word is also used to refer to the relative pitch of different tones.

**pitch:** see TAR AND PITCH.

**pitchblende**, dark, lustrous mineral composed chiefly of a massive variety of the mineral uraninite ($UO_2$); a source of RADIUM and URANIUM. Pitchblende and uraninite occur as primary constituents of quartz veins and with other metals, chiefly in the Great Lakes region in Canada, the Colorado Plateau in the US, Australia, Czechoslovakia, South Africa, and Zaïre.

**pitcher plant**, any of several insectivorous plants with leaves adapted as 'pitchers' for trapping insects. Lured by nectar and the plant's coloration, the insects drown in the rainwater solution contained in the pitcher and are digested by plant ENZYMES and, perhaps, BACTERIA. There are three families: the American family, Sarraceniaceae, including the common pitcher plant (*Sarracenia purpurea*), found in the bogs of E North America; the tropical family, consisting of the genus *Nepenthes,* found chiefly in BORNEO; and the Australasian genus *Dischidia*.

Pitcher plant (*Nepenthes pervillei*) found on Mahé, Seychelles

**Pithecanthropus:** see HOMO ERECTUS.

**Pitt, William**, 1st **earl of Chatham**, 1708–78, British statesman. A prominent opposition figure in the 1740s, Pitt benefited from British defeats in the early stages of the SEVEN YEARS' WAR and took a leading role in the Newcastle–Pitt ministry of 1757-61. He played a major role in securing the defeat of the French and, in particular, the conquest of Canada. He formed another ministry in 1766, but mental illness forced him to retire (1768). During the AMERICAN REVOLUTION he urged conciliation, and then, breaking with the WHIGS, favoured any settlement short of independence. He was known as the Great Commoner for his insistence on constitutional rights. His son **William Pitt**, 1759–1806, entered Parliament in 1781 and became prime minister in 1783 at age 24. He pursued liberal policies, including the reform of finance through the levying of new taxes to cut the national debt, constitutional reforms in India and Canada, and the signing of a commercial treaty with France, but he did not succeed in advancing the cause of parliamentary reform in which he believed. His liberal policies ended with the FRENCH REVOLUTIONARY WARS which he entered reluctantly but which forced his government into repressive measures against radicals. His costly military coalitions against France failed to achieve victory on land, but he became known as 'the pilot who weathered the storm'. In 1800 he secured the union of Great Britain and Ireland, but he failed to win CATHOLIC EMANCIPATION and resigned in 1801. Recalled to office in 1804, he died soon after hearing of Napoleon's victory at AUSTERLITZ. He was supported throughout by devoted Pittites and eloquently but ineffectively opposed by Charles James FOX.

**Pitt-Rivers, Augustus Lane-Fox,** 1827–1900, British soldier, collector, and scholar who made important contributions to both ethnology and archaeology. He used the biological concept of evolution to explain how manufactured objects changed in form over time, thereby advancing the development of systematic methods of collecting, analysing, and classifying cultural things. The idea that the form of common everyday objects reflected a larger process of development encouraged Gen. Pitt-Rivers to improve the precision of excavation techniques, which he demonstrated at Cranborne Chase, his estate in Dorset, with careful recording of the location of artifacts and the sequence of stratigraphic levels.

**Pittsburgh,** US city (1984 est. pop. 403,000), SW Pennsylvania, at the meeting of the Allegheny and Monongahela rivers, which there form the Ohio R.; settled 1760, inc. 1816. One of the world's largest inland ports, it is a centre for corporate headquarters, research, and commerce. Steel manufacturing is its major heavy industry; glass, machinery, chemicals, and oil are also produced. Located on the site of the 18th-cent. Fort Duquesne (later Fort Pitt), the city is hilly, with diverse industrial and residential neighbourhoods. Pittsburgh's huge and innovative urban renewal programme began in 1950 and has continued into the 1980s. The city's educational and cultural institutions include the Univ. of Pittsburgh and the Carnegie Institute.

**pituitary gland,** small, oval endocrine gland (see ENDOCRINE SYSTEM) that lies at the base of the BRAIN. It is called the master gland because the other endocrine glands depend on its secretions for stimulation. The pituitary has two distinct lobes, anterior and posterior. The anterior lobe secretes at least seven hormones: growth hormone, which stimulates overall body growth; ACTH (adrenocorticotrophic hormone), which controls steroid hormone secretion by the adrenal cortex (see ADRENAL GLANDS; CORTICOSTEROID); prolactin, which regulates the secretion of milk; thyrotrophic hormone, which stimulates the activity of the THYROID GLAND; two gonadotrophic hormones, which control growth and reproductive activity of the gonads; and melanocyte-stimulating hormone, which controls the skin pigmentation. The posterior lobe secretes antidiuretic hormone, which causes water retention by the kidneys, and oxytocin, which stimulates the mammary glands to release milk and also causes uterine contractions. An overactive pituitary during childhood can cause gigantism; during adulthood, it can cause acromegaly (enlargement of the hands, feet, and face). DWARFISM results from pituitary deficiency in childhood.

**pit viper,** poisonous SNAKE of the family Crotalidae. Like the Old World true VIPERS, pit vipers have long, hollow, erectile fangs. In addition, they have special heat-receiving organs, or pits, that help them sense warm-blooded animals, an ability especially useful at night, when many of them hunt. Pit vipers include the RATTLESNAKE, copperhead, and water moccasin, as well as the notorious fer-de-lance, a very poisonous snake of tropical America and the West Indies.

**Pius II,** 1405–64, pope (1458–64), an Italian named Enea Silvio Piccolomini. He became (1439) secretary to Antipope Felix V (Amadeus VII of Savoy) and gained a reputation as a humanist scholar. He became a priest in 1446. As pope he issued (1460) a bull (*Execrabilis*) condemning the doctrine that ultimate authority in the church rested in the general councils rather than with the pope. He tried in vain to unite Christian rulers in Europe against the Turks and quarrelled with LOUIS XI of France and the Bohemian king George of Podebrad. Among his literary works is an autobiography.

**Pius V, Saint,** 1504–72, pope (1566–72), an Italian named Michele Ghislieri, a Dominican. A leading figure in the COUNTER-REFORMATION, he put the decrees of the Council of TRENT into vigorous effect. He excommunicated Elizabeth I of England and united Spain and Venice

against the Turks, thus helping to bring about the Christian victory at the battle of LEPANTO. Feast: 30 Apr.

**Pius VII,** 1742–1823, pope (1800–23), an Italian named Barnabà Chiaramonti. He and NAPOLEON I signed the CONCORDAT OF 1801, but much of it was vitiated by Napoleon's Organic Articles, which Pius would not accept. In 1804, Napoleon made Pius come to Paris to consecrate him as emperor, and the French took Rome (1808) and the Papal States (1809). When Pius excommunicated the assailants of the Holy See, he was taken to France as a prisoner and forced to sign a new concordat. This humiliation Pius bore with stolid dignity. After Napoleon's downfall, Pius disavowed the enforced contract, recovered the Papal States at the Congress of VIENNA, and set about restoring the church. He reconstituted the JESUITS in 1814.

**Pius IX,** 1792–1878, pope (1846–78), an Italian named Giovanni M. Mastai-Ferretti. Driven from Rome by revolution in 1848, he returned (1850) and ruled with the aid of NAPOLEON III's troops. Opposed to the unification of Italy, he refused to deal with the Italians after they seized (1870) Rome. The resulting Roman Question was not resolved until the LATERAN TREATY of 1929. Pius also had difficulties in Germany with the Kulturkampf. In 1869 he convened the first VATICAN COUNCIL, which promulgated the doctrine of papal infallibility. His pontificate of 32 years was the longest in history.

**Pius X, Saint,** 1835–1914, pope (1903–14), an Italian named Guiseppe Sarto. In the decree *Lamentabili* (1907) and the encyclical *Pascendi* (1907), Pius condemned religious MODERNISM. He opposed anticlerical laws in France, set up commissions to recodify canon law and translate the Bible anew, and encouraged the use of PLAINSONG. Concerned with the poor, he was widely venerated during his life and subsequently (1954) was canonized by Pius XII. Feast: 21 Aug.

**Pius XI,** 1857–1939, pope (1922–39), an Italian named Achille Ratti. Before his election he was a papal nuncio to Poland and archbishop of Milan. His papacy was marked by great diplomatic activity and many important statements. The LATERAN TREATY (1929) ended the quarrel between the church and the Italian state, but Pius expressed his strong disapproval of Fascist methods in a letter, *Non abbiamo bisogno* (1931). A concordat with Germany (1933) was flouted by the Nazis, and the pope in a powerful encyclical (*Mit brennender Sorge,* 1937) branded Nazism criticized LAISSEZ-FAIRE capitalism in the encyclical *Quadragesimo anno* (1931) and renewed the plea for social reform made 40 years before by Leo XIII. Pius called for greater lay participation in all things religious; this he called Catholic Action. He was also concerned with the rights of Eastern Catholics and native cultures. In *Casti connubii* (1930) he condemned contraception and defined Christian marriage.

**Pius XII,** 1876–1958, pope (1939–58), an Italian named Eugenio Pacelli. Appointed papal secretary of state in 1930 by PIUS XI, he gained great diplomatic experience and negotiated (1933) the concordat with Nazi Germany. As pope during World War II, he believed that the Vatican could best work to achieve peace by maintaining formal relations with all the belligerents. He tried to alleviate the suffering of prisoners of war and displaced persons, but was later much criticized for not speaking out against Nazi persecution of the Jews and for not doing enough to protect them in Italy. After the war, Pius asked Catholics to oppose communism and excommunicated (1949) Italian Catholics who joined the Communist party. In the papal bull *Munificentissimus Deus* (1950), he defined the dogma of the Assumption of the Virgin Mary. He also reformed (1956) the Holy Week liturgy, relaxed the rules for fasting, permitted evening Mass, and favoured the appointment of native hierarchies in overseas dioceses.

**Pizarro, Francisco,** c. 1476–1541, Spanish CONQUISTADOR, conqueror of PERU. The illegitimate son of a gentleman, he accompanied Ojeda to COLOMBIA in 1510 and was with BALBOA when he discovered the PACIFIC. In 1524, with Diego de ALMAGRO, he began searching the coasts of Ecuador and Peru for the fabled INCA empire. In 1532 he met the Inca emperor Atahualpa. Professing friendship, he took the emperor prisoner, exacted ransom, and executed him. The conquest of Peru was completed with the capture of CUZCO, later successfully defended against a counterattack by MANCO CAPAC, the new Inca emperor. Pizarro founded Lima as Peru's capital. He sent Almagro to conquer CHILE, but cheated him of promised territory. Almagro rebelled, seized Cuzco, but was defeated and executed. Pizarro was later assassinated by Almagro's followers. Francisco's greed and ambition, extreme even in a conquistador, had offset his resourcefulness, courage, and cunning. His brother **Gonzalo Pizarro**, 1506–48, was a lieutenant in the conquest. He aided in the defence of Cuzco (1536–37), conquered Bolivia, and fought against Almagro. Governor of Quito from 1539, he led a revolt against the liberalized laws of the Spanish viceroy and was executed. A half-brother, **Hernando Pizarro**, fl. 1530–60, fought in the conquest and defended Cuzco. He defeated and executed Almagro in 1538. Because of his standing at the Spanish court, he was sent to Spain to argue the Pizarros' cause, but was held in partial confinement for 20 years. Another brother, **Juan Pizarro**, d. 1536, aided Francisco in the conquest of Peru. He fought valiantly in the defence of Cuzco against the forces of Manco Capac in 1536 and was killed leading an attack against the Indian fortress Sacsahuamán.

**PL/1:** see PROGRAMMING LANGUAGE.

**placebo,** inert chemical substance believed by the patient to be pharmacologically active. Placebo preparations contain no medicine but may be given for their positive psychological effects. They are also used as controls in clinical trials of new drugs to assure unbiased, statistically reliable results. In double-blind experiments, neither the doctor nor the patient knows whether a placebo or medication has been administered.

**placenta,** organ developed from interlocking embryonic and maternal tissues, attaching the foetus to the wall of the uterus. It is supplied with a network of blood vessels through which oxygen and nutrients pass from the mother to nourish the developing foetus and waste matter is removed from the foetus. The placenta is expelled after birth.

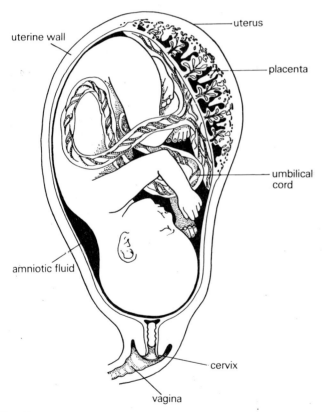

Placenta

**plague,** a general term used for any contagious epidemic disease, but usually used to refer specifically to bubonic plague, or the Black Death, an acute infectious disease caused by the bacterium *Yersinia pestis* (formerly known as *Pasteurella pestis*), transmitted to humans by fleas from infected rats. Symptoms include high fever; chills; prostration; enlarged painful lymph nodes (buboes), particularly in the groin, which burst and release pus; and bleeding under the skin producing black ulcers. Invasion of the lungs by the bacteria causes a rapidly fatal form of the disease (pneumonic plague), which can be transmitted from one person to another via droplets. Bacteria can also enter the bloodstream (septicaemic plague). Epidemics have occurred throughout history, the best known being the Black Death that swept Europe and parts of Asia in the 14th and 17th cent., killing as much as three-quarters of the population in less than 20 years. The disease is still prevalent in some areas of the world, but such ANTIBIOTIC drugs as tetracycline and streptomycin have greatly reduced the mortality rate.

**plaice:** see FLATFISH.

**plaid,** a long shawl or blanketlike outer wrap of woollen cloth, usually patterned in checks or tartan figures. Now a feature of the Scottish Highland costume, as a form of wrap worn over the shoulder. It was once worn in Scotland and Ireland as an enveloping garment belted at the waist to form a tunic skirt (see KILT) with the end used as a cloak. A tartan plaid has crossbars of three or more colours in designs which since the mid 19th cent. have been codified to signify particular Highland clans. *Plaid* may also refer to any fabric patterned like the traditional plaid.

**Plaid Cymru,** [Welsh = Party of Wales], Welsh nationalist formation (est. 1925) seeking full self-government for WALES and the restoration of the Welsh language and culture. It has established some strength at local government level and since 1974 has regularly returned two or three members to the House of Commons in London.

**Plain, the,** in the FRENCH REVOLUTION, the independent members of the National Convention. The name was applied because they sat on the lower benches in contrast to the raised seats of the radical MOUNTAIN. The Plain was a leaderless mass, but it aided in the overthrow (1794) of Maximilien ROBESPIERRE.

**Plains Indians:** see NORTH AMERICAN INDIANS.

**plainsong** or **plainchant,** all early unharmonized melody in free rhythm, but usually synonymous with Gregorian chant, the liturgical music of the ROMAN CATHOLIC CHURCH. Texts are taken from the MASS, the BIBLE, and HYMNS. Four main dialects of plainsong developed in the Western church: Ambrosian, Roman, Mozarabic, and Gallican. Gregorian chant derives originally from Jewish and Greek music, but is named after Pope GREGORY I, under whose reign church music was codified. In the Middle Ages polyphony largely supplanted plainsong, and distortions crept into its performance. In the 19th cent., the Benedictine monks of Solesmes, France, through years of research, established the original form and rhythm of the chant. The tonality of Gregorian chant is based on the system of eight MODES; the system of neumes developed for chant notation (see MUSICAL NOTATION) is still used.

**planarian,** any of several groups of turbellarians—free-living, primarily carnivorous FLATWORMS—with a three-branched digestive cavity. Most are freshwater forms, but marine and terrestrial planarians exist. White, grey, brown, black, or sometimes transparent, planarians range in size from 0.3 to 2.5 cm (⅛ to 1 in), although some tropical forms are as big as 60 cm (2 ft). Some species can regenerate severed parts of the body, in some cases even producing entire individuals from small pieces.

**Planck, Max,** 1858–1947, German physicist. From his hypothesis (1900) that atoms emit and absorb energy only in discrete bundles (quanta) instead of continuously, as assumed in classical physics, the QUANTUM THEORY was developed. Planck received the 1918 Nobel Prize for physics for his work on BLACK BODY radiation, which depended on this hypothesis. He was professor (1889–1928) at the Univ. of Berlin and president (1930–35) of the Kaiser Wilhelm Society for the Advancement of Science, Berlin. Planck's constant $h$ is named after him.

**plane,** in mathematics, flat surface of infinite extent but no thickness. A plane is determined by (1) three points not in a straight line; (2) a straight line and a point not on the line; (3) two intersecting lines; or (4) two parallel lines.

**planet,** any of the nine relatively large, nonluminous bodies MERCURY, VENUS, EARTH, MARS, JUPITER, SATURN, URANUS, NEPTUNE, and PLUTO that revolve around the Sun (see SOLAR SYSTEM). By extension, any similar body discovered revolving around another star would be called a planet. The ASTEROIDS are sometimes called minor planets. The major planets are classified either as inferior, with an orbit between the Sun and the orbit of the Earth (Mercury and Venus), or as superior, with an orbit beyond that of the Earth (Mars, Jupiter, Saturn, Uranus, Neptune, and Pluto). The terrestrial planets Mercury, Venus, and Mars resemble the Earth in size, chemical composition, and density. The Jovian planets Jupiter,

## MAJOR PLANETS OF THE SOLAR SYSTEM

| Planet | Distance from the Sun (AU)* | Period of revolution | Period of rotation | Mass (Earth = 1) | Diameter (Earth = 1) | Known satellites |
|--------|------|------|------|------|------|------|
| Mercury | 0.39 | 88 days | 59 days | 0.06 | 0.38 | 0 |
| Venus | 0.72 | 225 days | 243 days | 0.82 | 0.95 | 0 |
| Earth | 1 | 365 days | 24 hours | 1 | 1 | 1 |
| Mars | 1.52 | 687 days | 25 hours | 0.11 | 0.53 | 2 |
| Jupiter | 5.20 | 12 years | 10 hours | 317.89 | 11.27 | 16 |
| Saturn | 9.54 | 29 years | 10 hours | 95.15 | 9.44 | 17 |
| Uranus | 19.18 | 84 years | 16 hours | 14.54 | 4.10 | 5 |
| Neptune | 30.06 | 165 years | 18 hours | 17.23 | 3.88 | 2 |
| Pluto | 39.44 | 248 years | 6.4 days | .002? | 0.12–0.30 | 1 |

\* AU = Astronomical Unit (Earth = 1)

Saturn, Uranus, and Neptune are much larger in size and have thick, gaseous atmospheres and low densities. The rapid rotation of the latter planets results in polar flattening of 2–10%, giving them an elliptical appearance.

**planetarium,** optical device used to project a representation of the heavens onto a domed ceiling; the term also designates the building that houses such a device. As the axis of the device moves, beams of light emitted through lenses travel in predetermined paths on the ceiling. The juxtaposition of lights reproduces a panorama of the sky at a particular time as it might be seen under optimum conditions. The motions of the celestial bodies typically the fixed stars, the Sun, Moon, and planets, and various nebulae are accurately represented, although they can be compressed into much shorter time periods.

**planetoid:** see ASTEROID.

**plane tree,** deciduous tree (genus *Platanus*) indigenous to northern temperate regions. The dry, seedlike fruits are compressed into a hard, brown ball, which, when ripe, separates into windborne, downy tufts. The genus includes the American species (*P. occidentalis*) called buttonwood or sycamore and the Oriental plane (*P. orientalis*), both used for their wood. The London plane (*P. acerifolia*) is a hybrid between *P. occidentalis* and *P. orientalis*, and is frequently used as an ornamental shade tree in cities, where it is able to withstand pollution.

**plankton,** very small to microscopic plants and animals that have little or no power of locomotion and drift or float in surface waters. All aquatic life is either in the plankton or the NEKTON. Plankton is found worldwide in fresh and salt water. The plant forms, or phytoplankton, include DIATOMS and dinoflagellates (see PYRROPHYTA); planktonic animals, or zooplankton, include protozoans (see PROTOZOA), small CRUSTACEANS, JELLYFISH, COMB JELLIES, and FISH eggs and larvae. In the ocean, phytoplankton is the source of food, either directly or indirectly through the food chain, for all marine animals. It also produces a major part of the planet's oxygen.

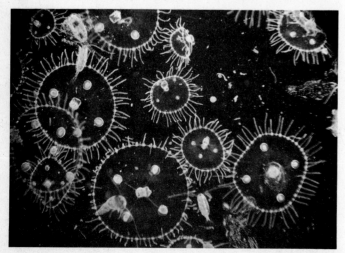

Living marine **plankton** with many medusae of *Obelia sp.* (approximately × 22 magnification)

**plant,** an organism of the plant kingdom (Planta) as opposed to one of the ANIMAL kingdom (Animalia). A plant may be microscopic in size and simple in structure (e.g., ALGAE) or a many-celled, complex system (e.g., a TREE). Plants differ from animals in that, with few exceptions, they possess CHLOROPHYLL, are fixed in one place, have no nervous system or sensory organs, and have rigid, supporting cell walls containing CELLULOSE. In addition, most plants grow continually and have no maximum size or characteristic form in the adult stage. Green plants, i.e., those with chlorophyll, manufacture their own food (GLUCOSE, a sugar) and give off oxygen in the process of PHOTOSYNTHESIS, thus representing the primary source of food for animals and providing oxygen for the earth's atmosphere. Some plants (e.g., FUNGI) do not make their own food, and certain unicellular forms (e.g., *Euglena*) are motile and can either make or ingest food. The scientific study of plants is BOTANY.

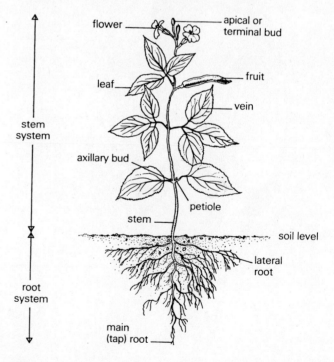

Plant

**Plantagenet,** royal family of England. Name adopted by Geoffrey V count of Anjou, husband of MATILDA, daughter of HENRY I king of England, who took the broom (planta genista) as his emblem. HENRY II, son of Geoffrey and Matilda, was the first member of the house to be king of England (1154–89), and RICHARD II (1377–99) the last in the main line. The houses of LANCASTER and YORK which followed were both related to the Plantagenets.

**plantain,** annual or perennial weed (genus *Plantago*), of wide distribution. Many species are lawn pests, and the pollen is often a hay fever irritant. Several species have medicinal uses. *P. major* and

*P. lanceolata* are used in the treatment of sores and wounds, having antiseptic properties. *P. psyllium,* or fleawort, is cultivated in Spain and France for its mucilaginous seed coats, which are used as a laxative. A tropical plant (*Musa rosaceae*) related to the BANANA is also called plantain.

**plant louse:** see APHID.

**Planudes Maximus** or **Maximus Planudes,** c.1260–c.1330, Byzantine monk and classical scholar whose edition of the GREEK ANTHOLOGY was standard until the 17th cent. His prose version of AESOP's fables is outstanding.

**plasma,** in physics, a fully ionized gas containing approximately equal numbers of positive and negative IONS. A plasma is an electric conductor and is affected by magnetic fields. The study of plasmas, called plasma physics, is important in efforts to produce a controlled thermonuclear reaction (see NUCLEAR ENERGY). In nature, plasmas occur in the interior of stars and in interstellar gas, making plasma a form of matter in the universe (see STATES OF MATTER).

**plaster of Paris:** see GYPSUM.

**plastic,** any synthetic organic material that can be moulded under heat and pressure into a shape that is retained after the heat and pressure are removed. There are two basic types of plastic: thermosetting, which cannot be resoftened after being subjected to heat and pressure; and thermoplastic, which can be repeatedly softened and reshaped by heat and pressure. Plastics are made up chiefly of a binder consisting of long chainlike molecules called POLYMERS. Binders can be natural materials, e.g., CELLULOSE, or (more commonly) synthetic RESINS, e.g., BAKELITE. The permanence of thermosetting plastics is due to the heat- and pressure-induced cross-linking reactions the polymers undergo. Thermoplastics can be reshaped because their linear or branched polymers can slide past one another when heat and pressure are applied. Adding plasticizers and fillers to the binder improves a wide range of properties, e.g., hardness, elasticity, and resistance to heat, cold, or acid. Adding PIGMENT imparts colour. Plastic products are commonly made from plastic powders. In *compression moulding,* heat and pressure are applied directly to the powder in the mould cavity. Alternatively, the powder can be plasticized by outside heating and then poured into moulds to harden (*transfer moulding*); be dissolved in a heating chamber and then forced by a plunger into cold moulds to set (*injection moulding*); or be extruded through a die in continuous form to be cut into lengths or coiled (*extrusion moulding*). The first important plastic, CELLULOID, has been largely replaced by a wide variety of plastics known by such trade names as Plexiglas, Lucite, Polaroid, and CELLOPHANE. New uses continue to be found and include contact lenses, machine gears, and artificial body parts. The widespread use of plastics has led to environmental problems. Because plastic products do not decay, large amounts accumulate as waste. Disposal is difficult because they melt when burned, clogging incinerators and often emitting harmful fumes, e.g., the hydrogen chloride gas given off by POLYVINYL CHLORIDE. See also POLYPROPYLENE, POLYURETHANES; TEFLON.

**plastic surgery,** surgical repair of congenital or acquired deformities and the restoration of contour to improve the appearance of tissue defects, e.g., disfigurements resulting from accidents such as severe burns or from removal of extensive skin cancers. It is also used to restore vital movement and function of destroyed tissues. The technique was first developed after World War I and is now also used for cosmetic purposes, e.g., to eliminate wrinkles. Microsurgery has refined many reconstructive operations.

**Plata, Río de la,** estuary, c.270 km (170 mi) long and up to 190 km (120 mi) wide, in SE South America, between Uruguay and Argentina. It is formed by the PARANÁ and Uruguay rivers and is part of a major system of inland navigation. Two capital cities, BUENOS AIRES and MONTEVIDEO, are on the estuary.

**plateau,** elevated, more or less level portion of the earth's surface bounded on at least one side by steep slopes. Plateaus are formed by successive lava flows, upward-folding earth movements, or the erosion of adjacent lands. Notable plateaus include the COLORADO and COLUMBIA PLATEAUS in the US and the DECCAN in India.

**Plateau Indians:** see NORTH AMERICAN INDIANS.

**plateresque** [Span., *platero* = silversmith], earliest phase (early 16th cent.) of Spanish Renaissance architecture and decoration. It drew richness from a mixture of Italian Renaissance, Moorish, and late Gothic design. Structure received little emphasis, while ornament was prominently displayed. Columns in candelabrum form and other fanciful motifs were common, as was ornate wrought iron. The town hall of Seville is a notable example.

**plate tectonics,** modern theory of CONTINENTAL DRIFT that has revolutionized geologists' understanding of EARTH history. It holds that the earth's crust is divided into contiguous, moving plates that carry the embedded CONTINENTS. Plate boundaries are marked by lines of EARTHQUAKE and volcanic activity (see VOLCANO). One kind of boundary is at the mid-ocean ridges, where tensional forces open rifts, allowing new crustal material to well up from the earth's mantle and become welded to the trailing edges of the plates (see OCEAN). When a continent straddles such a rift it is split apart, forming a new ocean area (e.g., the RED SEA and the Gulf of California). The ocean trenches mark subduction zones, where plate edges dive steeply into the mantle and are reabsorbed. A third boundary type occurs where two plates slide past each other in a shearing manner along great transform FAULTS (e.g., the SAN ANDREAS FAULT in California). MOUNTAIN ranges form where two plates carrying continents collide (e.g., the HIMALAYAS), or where ocean crust is subducted along a continental margin (e.g., the ANDES). Geologists believe that c.200 million years ago there was a supercontinent, Pangaea, which subsequent plate movements have split and resplit into the continents and islands we recognize today. See map overleaf.

**Plath, Sylvia,** 1932–63, American poet. Her finely crafted, intensely personal poems, known for their sharp, often violent imagery, appear in such volumes as *The Colossus* (1960), *Ariel* (1965), and *Collected Poems* (1981). She also wrote an autobiographical novel, *The Bell Jar* (1962). Plath committed suicide in London.

**platinum** (Pt), metallic element, known in natural alloy form since antiquity. It is a malleable, ductile, lustrous, silver-white, chemically inactive metal. Platinum and its alloys are used in surgical tools, laboratory utensils, electrical-resistance wires, contact points, standard masses, jewellery, dentistry, and very powerful magnets. Platinum is a CATALYST in many commercial processes. See ELEMENT (table); PERIODIC TABLE.

**Plato,** 427–348 BC, Greek philosopher. In 407 BC he became a pupil and friend of SOCRATES. After living for a time at the Syracuse court, Plato founded (c.387 BC) near Athens the most influential school of the ancient world, the Academy, where he taught until his death. His most famous pupil there was ARISTOTLE. Plato's extant work is in the form of some (mainly spurious) epistles, and many dialogues, divided according to the probable order of composition. The early, or Socratic, dialogues, e.g., the *Apology, Meno,* and *Gorgias,* present Socrates in conversations that illustrate his major ideas—the unity of virtue and knowledge and of virtue and happiness. They also contain Plato's moving account of the last days and death of Socrates. Plato's goal in dialogues of the middle years, e.g., the *Republic, Phaedo, Symposium,* and *Timaeus,* was to show the rational relationship between the soul, the state, and the cosmos. The later dialogues, e.g., the *Laws* and *Parmenides,* contain treatises on law, mathematics, technical philosophic problems, and natural science. Plato regarded the rational soul as immortal, and he believed in a world soul and a Demiurge, the creator of the physical world. He argued for the independent reality of Ideas, or Forms, as the immutable archetypes of all temporal phenomena and as the only guarantee of ethical standards and of objective scientific knowledge. Virtue consists in the harmony of the human soul with the universe of Ideas, which assure order, intelligence, and pattern to a world in constant flux. Supreme among them is the Idea of the Good, analogous to the Sun in the physical world. Only the philosopher, who understands the harmony of all parts of the universe with the Idea of the Good, is capable of ruling the just state. In Plato's various dialogues he touched upon virtually every problem that has occupied subsequent philosophers; his teachings have been among the most influential in the history of Western civilization, and his works are counted among the world's finest literature: they show imaginative, narrative, and dramatic power, and a sensitive use of language. See also NEOPLATONISM.

**Platonic solid:** see POLYHEDRON.

**Platt Amendment,** a rider attached to the Army Appropriations bill of 1901. It stipulated the conditions for US intervention in CUBA that virtually made the island a US protectorate. Proposed by Sen. Orville H. Platt of

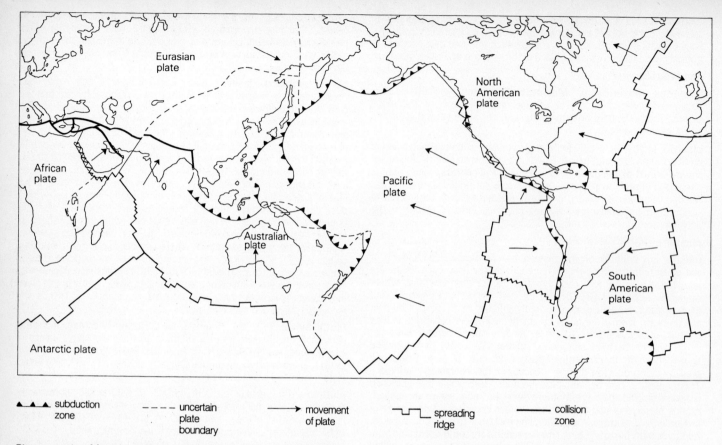

| ▲▲▲ subduction zone | - - - uncertain plate boundary | → movement of plate | ⎍⎍ spreading ridge | ── collision zone |

Plate tectonics: Map of the world showing major plates and plate boundaries

Connecticut, it was part of a Cuban–US treaty until abrogated in 1934. Under its terms the US established and has retained a naval base on Guantánamo Bay.

**Plattdeutsch** (ˌplatdoych), Low German, spoken mainly in N Germany, a region of lowlands. See LANGUAGE (table).

**Plautus** (Titus Maccius Plautus), c.254–184 BC, Roman comic poet. His plays, adapted from Greek New COMEDY, are popular and vigorous representations of middle-class and lower-class life. Writing in idiomatic Latin and with a genius for situation and coarse humour, Plautus is famous for his stock comic figures, e.g., the knavish, resourceful slave or the braggart soldier. His works were freely adapted by JONSON, SHAKESPEARE, MOLIÈRE, and others.

**playing cards,** parts of a pack or deck, used in playing various games of chance or skill. The origin of playing cards is lost in antiquity. The present-day variety of suits, hearts, diamonds, clubs, and spades, was adopted in France in the 16th cent. The modern standard pack consists of 52 cards. Each suit contains a king, queen, knave (or jack), and 10 cards bearing pips from 1 (the ace, the highest card in most games) to 10. See also TAROTS.

**Plaza Lasso, Galo** (ˌplahsah ˌlahsoh), 1906–, president of ECUADOR (1948–52). An experienced diplomat and liberal democrat, he permitted unprecedented political freedoms and brought a measure of economic prosperity to the country. He later served as a UN mediator.

**plea bargaining,** negotiation in which a defendant agrees to plead guilty to a criminal charge in exchange for concessions by the prosecution. The defendant waives the right to trial, losing any chance for acquittal, but avoids conviction on a more serious charge. The prosecution, on the other hand, is not required to go through a long, costly trial. Issues negotiated in plea bargaining include a reduction of the charge, a specific recommendation for sentence, or agreement by the prosecutor not to oppose a request for probation. In rare cases the police will offer the defendant immunity from prosecution in return for naming accomplices.

**plebiscite,** vote by the people of an entire country or district on a proposal submitted to them, as in a referendum. See INITIATIVE, REFERENDUM, AND RECALL.

**plebs** or **plebeians** (plebz, pliˌbee·ən), [Lat., *plebs* = people], general body of Roman citizens, as distinct from the PATRICIAN class. They lacked, at first, most of the patrician rights, but gradually achieved political equality by 300 BC.

**Pleiad** (ˌplie·əd), (from Pleiades), group of seven tragic poets of ALEXANDRIA who flourished c.280 BC. Only some of the work of Lycophron survives. A group of seven 16th-cent. French poets took the name **Pléiade.** They included Pierre de RONSARD (the leader) and Joachim DU BELLAY. Their purpose was to encourage the writing of French as against Latin so as to establish a vigorous literary language. They cultivated the use of classical and Italian forms, e.g., the SONNET.

**Pleiades** (ˌplie·əˈdeez), a galactic CLUSTER in the constellation Taurus.

**Pleiades,** in Greek mythology, seven daughters of ATLAS, attendants of ARTEMIS. Pursued by ORION, they were turned into stars. They gave their name to PLEIAD, a group of poets.

**Pleistocene epoch:** see GEOLOGICAL ERAS (table).

**Plekhanov, Georgi Valentinovich,** 1857–1918, Russian revolutionary and social philosopher, often called the father of Russian Marxism. Opposed to political terror, he broke (1879) with the populist movement and left Russia (1880). Turning to MARXISM, he helped to found the group that became the Russian Social Democratic Labour Party and with V.I. LENIN, published the newspaper *Iskra* [spark]. Plekhanov's view that socialist revolution could not occur in Russia until CAPITALISM and industrialization developed further became the basis for the anti-Leninist Menshevik position after the party split (1903) into BOLSHEVISM AND MENSHEVISM. After the February 1917 RUSSIAN REVOLUTION he returned from exile and opposed the Bolsheviks; after their victory he retired from political life. Among his works are *Socialism and Anarchism* (tr. 1895) and *Fundamental Problems of Marxism* (tr. 1929).

**pleurisy,** inflammation of the pleura, the membrane that covers the LUNGS and lines the chest cavity. It is sometimes accompanied by fluid (effusion) that fills the chest cavity; when the fluid is infected, the condition is known as empyema. Dry pleurisy (when the normally slippery surfaces become sticky) usually occurs with bacterial infections, whereas pleurisy with effusion is associated with chronic lung conditions, such as TUBERCULOSIS. Treatment is directed at the underlying cause.

**Pliny the Elder,** AD c.23–79, Roman polymath; b. Cisalpine Gaul. His one surviving work, *Historia naturalis,* consists of 37 books that deal with the nature of the physical universe, geography, anthropology, zoology, botany, and mineralogy. Although impressive in scope, this encyclopedic work, mostly secondhand information, is useless as science. His nephew, **Pliny the Younger,** AD 62?–c.113, was an orator and statesman who is remembered for his letters, which are an excellent mirror of Roman life in his time.

**Pliocene epoch:** see GEOLOGICAL ERA (table).

**PLO:** see PALESTINE LIBERATION ORGANIZATION.

**Ploieşti** (ploy₁eshtee), city (1983 pop. 215,500), S Romania. The oil industry dates from the late 19th cent. and Ploieşti is its centre in Romania, with refinery, petrochemical and related oil-equipment industries.

**Plomer, William Charles Franklyn,** 1903–73, white South African novelist and poet. Following the outcry after the publication of *Turbott Wolfe* (1925), which was interpreted as proposing miscegenation as a solution to the issue of race, Plomer settled in England. A versatile and humane scholar, Plomer was an editor of great skill (*Kilvert's Diary,* 1938–40); a perceptive novelist, especially in *Museum Pieces* (1952); and a poet of considerable subtlety, e.g., *Collected Poems* (1960; 1973). He also collaborated with Benjamin BRITTEN on, e.g., *Curlew River*

**Plotinus,** 205–270 AD, Greek philosopher, founder of NEOPLATONISM; b. Egypt. He went to Alexandria c.232 to devote himself to philosophy. After 244 he lived in Rome, where his school gained a wide following. In addition to Plato, Plotinus drew on other Greek philosophers, and on Zoroastrianism and possibly Hinduism. He explained the deity by developing the idea of emanation, and his teachings are infused with MYSTICISM. Although he rejected Christianity, Plotinus's influence on the early Christian thinkers, particularly St AUGUSTINE, was profound. Plotinus's writings were collected by his pupil Porphyry under the title *The Enneads.*

**Plovdiv,** city (1983 pop. 373,235), S central Bulgaria, on the Maritsa R. Bulgaria's second largest city, it is the chief market for a fertile area and has such industries as lead and zinc smelting, textiles, and brewing. Built by the Thracians, it was held (4th cent. BC–8th cent. AD) by Macedon, Rome, and Byzantium. It fell to Turkey c.1360 and passed to Russia in 1877. In 1885 it became part of Bulgaria. It has several Bulgarian Orthodox churches and Turkish mosques.

**plover,** common name for some shore BIRDS of the family Charadriidae, small to medium in size, found worldwide in ice-free lands. Plovers are wading birds with markings of black or brown above and white below. The best known plovers are the golden plovers and the ringed plovers. The plovers are migratory birds, the ringed plover recently colonizing Greenland and Baffin Island. The American golden plover migrates furthest, travelling from the Arctic to Australia. The wrybill migrates from South Island, New Zealand to North Island.

**plum,** name for many species of trees (genus *Prunus*) of the ROSE family, and their fruits. Numerous varieties and hybrids exist. The name *damson* is applied to several varieties of the common garden plum (*P. domestica*) having small leaves and small, oval, usually tart fruits. Greengage and prune plums are also varieties of *P. domestica.* Sloes (*P. spinosa*) are not cultivated; they have small, round blackish fruits and are used for making sloe gin. Many varieties are used as ornamentals; these usually have red or purple foliage and double pink, white, or lilac flowers. Prunes are dried plums.

**plumbago:** see GRAPHITE.

**Plunket, Saint Oliver,** 1629–81, Irish ecclesiastic and Roman Catholic martyr. He was educated and ordained priest in Rome. Appointed Catholic archbishop of Armagh (1669), he devoted himself energetically to his diocese, but had to go into hiding when anti-Catholic persecutions broke out (1673). He was betrayed (1679), tried for treason in London, and executed at Tyburn on 1 July 1681. The last man to suffer death for the Roman Catholic faith in England, he was canonized in 1975. Feast: 11 July.

**pluralism,** term used to describe a society in which power is divided in such a way that no single group, institution, or set of beliefs is dominant;

multiple interests and pressure-groups are free to compete with one another to influence public opinion and government policy. This influential picture of modern Western industrial democracies, presented in the 1950s and 60s by writers such as Robert DAHL and others, countered the Marxist assertion that in the analysis of societies class was the fundamental, determining factor. The freedom exhibited by pluralism was contrasted strongly with the character of totalitarian, state-dominated regimes such as that of the USSR. This pluralist analysis has received much criticism, not least for its assumption that all groups of citizens with an interest in common have equally effective organizing and bargaining power, and for its unreal account of the state as a sort of neutral referee above the clash of interests. Nevertheless it is an account of the operation of liberal democracy which is widely accepted and indeed regarded as desirable. Pluralist analyses of international relations point out that nation–states are not the only actors on the world stage; their relations are supplemented and compromised by a host of other international forces and organizations, including multinational corporations and financial institutions such as the International Monetary Fund.

**Plutarch,** AD 46?–c.120, Greek essayist and biographer. After travelling widely, he settled as a priest in his native BOEOTIA. His great work is *The Parallel Lives,* paired biographies of Greeks and Romans. Sir Thomas North's translation (1579) profoundly affected English literature, e.g., supplying the material for Shakespeare's *Julius Caesar* and *Antony and Cleopatra.* Plutarch's pride in Greece does not prejudice his treatment of Roman subjects. Concerned primarily with character and morality, he employed much anecdotal material.

**Pluto,** in astronomy, 9th and usually most distant PLANET from the Sun, at a mean distance of 5900 million km (3670 million mi). Because of the high eccentricity (0.250) of its elliptical orbit, Pluto occasionally (e.g., between 1979 and 1999) comes closer than the planet NEPTUNE to the Sun. Discovered in 1930 by Clyde Tombaugh, Pluto has an estimated diameter of 2400 to 3800 km (1500 to 2400 mi) and is thought to have a rocky, silicate core and a thin atmosphere containing methane. Its one known satellite, **Charon,** was discovered on 22 June 1978, by the American astronomer James Christy. It has a diameter estimated to be about one-third that of Pluto.

**Pluto,** in Greek mythology, god of the underworld, son of CRONUS and RHEA; also called HADES and, by the Romans, Dis. He ruled Hades with his wife, PERSEPHONE.

**plutonium** (Pu), radioactive element, first produced artificially by Glenn Seaborg and colleagues in 1940 by deuteron bombardment of uranium oxide. It is a silver-grey TRANSURANIC ELEMENT in the ACTINIDE SERIES. Plutonium-239 is a fuel for NUCLEAR REACTORs and weapons (see ATOMIC BOMB; NUCLEAR ENERGY). Plutonium is highly toxic if inhaled, since very small quantities can cause lung cancer. World production of plutonium is about 20,000 kg per year. By 1982 300,000 kg had been accumulated worldwide. See ELEMENT (table); PERIODIC TABLE.

**pluvial,** a period of moister conditions created by higher rain or snowfall and/or lower rates of evaporation and transpiration. Pluvials such as the Altantic period (5500–2500 BC) are responsible for higher lake levels (particularly at low latitudes), recharging groundwater reserves, and the integration of river systems. They may span hundreds or thousands of years.

**Plymouth,** city (1981 pop. 238,583), Devon, SW England, on Plymouth Sound. The Three Towns that Plymouth has comprised since 1914 are Plymouth, Stonehouse, and Devonport. Plymouth is an important port and naval base. It was the last port touched by the MAYFLOWER before its voyage to America in 1620.

**Plymouth,** US town (1980 pop. 35,913), SE Massachusetts, on Plymouth Bay; founded 1620. Plymouth is the oldest settlement in New England and a major tourist attraction. It is growing rapidly and has light industries but is primarily known for its historical sights, including Plymouth Rock, near which is moored the replica *Mayflower II;* several 17th-cent. houses; and the Pilgrim Village re-creation of the settlement.

**Plymouth Brethren,** a fundamentalist Christian body whose first English congregation was founded by John Nelson Darby, a former Anglican priest, at Plymouth in 1831. Emphasizing the speedy Second Coming of Christ and practising COMMUNION every Sunday, the Brethren have no ordained ministry and renounce many secular occupations as inconsistent with the New Testament. Since 1848 they have been divided into Exclusive and Open (i.e., less rigorous) Brethren. Numerically few, they are to be found in many countries (e.g., France, Switzerland, India, the US) as well as in Britain.

**Plymouth Colony,** founded by the PILGRIMS in MASSACHUSETTS in 1620. The settlers had difficulty surviving early hardships, although a treaty with neighbouring Indians assured peace for 50 years. Under the Mayflower Compact (see under MAYFLOWER) the colony developed into a quasi-theocracy, ruled by a governor (see BRADFORD, WILLIAM) and a council; a representative body, the General Court, was introduced in 1638. The colony expanded to include 10 towns and in 1643 joined the New England Confederation, which gave it critical aid during KING PHILIP'S WAR (1675–76). Plymouth Colony was incorporated into the royal colony of Massachusetts in 1691.

**Plzeň,** Ger., *Pilsen,* city (1984 pop. 174,000), Bohemia, W Czechoslovakia. Situated at a convergence of rivers and routeways, it is a manufacturing centre, famous for its beers and for its heavy engineering (Škoda). It was a Catholic stronghold in the HUSSITE wars of the 15th cent.

**Pm,** chemical symbol of the element PROMETHIUM.

**PMT:** see PREMENSTRUAL TENSION.

**pneumoconiosis** (nyoohmoh'koni,ohsis), any of a group of chronic diseases of the LUNGS caused by the inhalation of dust particles. Commonly known as black lung and primarily found among coal miners, sandblasters, and metal grinders, it may be caused by the inhalation of SILICA (silicosis), ASBESTOS (asbestosis), iron filings (siderosis), COAL dust, or other mineral or metal dust. Particles collect in the lungs and become sites for the development of fibrous tissue that replaces elastic lung tissue, often resulting in decreased lung function. Symptoms include shortness of breath, wheezing, cough, and susceptibility to PNEUMONIA, TUBERCULOSIS, and other respiratory infections. See also OCCUPATIONAL DISEASE.

**pneumonia,** acute infection of one or both lungs that can be caused by a bacterium, usually the pneumococcus bacterium, by a virus, or by another microorganism. Symptoms include high fever, pain in the chest difficulty in breathing, coughing, and sputum. Viral pneumonia is generally milder than the bacterial form. ANTIBIOTIC drugs are used to treat bacterial pneumonia and have greatly reduced the mortality rate of the disease.

**Po,** chemical symbol of the element POLONIUM.

**Po,** river, the chief waterway of N Italy, c.670 km (405 mi) long. It rises on the slopes of Monte Viso in the Cotian Alps and flows for much of its length across the North Italian Plain. Embankments have been built along its lower course to control flooding. The sediment which it carries is gradually extending its delta into the Adriatic Sea.

**Pocahontas,** c.1595–1617, daughter of Chief Powhatan of the Powhatan Indians of Virginia, US. She is said to have saved the life of Capt. John SMITH as Powhatan was about to execute him. Later, held hostage at Jamestown for the return of her father's English prisoners, she became a Christian and married (1614) a settler, John ROLFE. The union brought peace for eight years. Rolfe took her to England (1616), where she was received as a princess. She died during the trip home and was buried at Gravesend, England.

**Poe, Edgar Allan,** 1809–49, one of the most brilliant and original writers in American literature. Orphaned in 1811, he was raised by Mr and Mrs John Allan of Richmond, Virginia. He attended the Univ. of Virginia and West Point briefly but was forced to leave both because of various infractions. After publishing three volumes of poems (1827, 1829, 1831) Poe was an editor, critic, and short-story writer for magazines and newspapers in Richmond, Philadelphia, and New York City. His compelling short stories, such as 'The Masque of the Red Death' and 'The Fall of the House of Usher', create a universe that is beautiful and grotesque, real and fantastic. Poe is also considered the father of the modern detective story, e.g., 'The Murders in the Rue Morgue' (1841). His poems (including 'The Bells', 'The Raven', and 'Annabel Lee') are rich with musical phrases and sensuous images. Poe was also an intelligent and witty critic who often theorized about the art of writing, as in his essay 'The Poetic Principle'. His most important works include *The Narrative of Arthur Gordon Pym* (1838), *Tales of the Grotesque and Arabesque* (1840), and *The Raven and Other Poems* (1845). A complex, tormented figure, Poe died of alcoholism.

**poet laureate,** English title conferred by the crown on a poet whose duty it is to write commemorative verse. It is an outgrowth of medieval custom and later royal patronage of poets. Ben JONSON had what amounted to a laureateship, but DRYDEN, in 1670, was the first given the title. Among later laureates have been WORDSWORTH (1843–50), TENNYSON (1850–92), John MASEFIELD (1930–67), and John BETJEMAN (1972–).

**poetry.** For LYRIC poetry, see BALLAD; ELEGY; ODE; PASTORAL; SONNET. For narrative poetry, see EPIC; ROMANCE. Dramatic poetry is treated incidentally in the article TRAGEDY. See also technical discussions of FREE VERSE; PENTAMETER; RHYME; VERSIFICATION.

**pogrom,** a Russian term, meaning 'round-up' or 'lynching' and used in reference to violent attacks on Jews in Russia, especially between 1880 and 1920. They provoked large-scale Jewish emigation, especially to the US. Pogroms also occurred elsewhere in Central and Eastern Europe.

**poikilothermic,** scientific description of cold-blooded animals. Poikilothermic animals cannot maintain their body heat without using the warmth of the sun. By means of basking, they bring their bodies to the temperature at which it will work efficiently. Amphibians and reptiles are poikilothermic, and cannot live in extreme cold or heat. They are more limited than HOMOTHERMIC animals in the habitats available to them.

**Poincaré, (Jules) Henri** (pwahnhkah,ray), 1854–1912, French mathematician, physicist, and author; cousin of Raymond POINCARÉ. One of the greatest mathematicians of his age, Poincaré, by research in the theory of functions, expanded the field of mathematical physics. He also did notable work in differential equations and celestial mechanics, and wrote extensively on the philosophy of science.

**Poincaré, Raymond,** 1860–1934, French statesman; cousin of Henri POINCARÉ. He served as president (1913–20) and premier (1912–13, 1922–23, 1926–29). A conservative and a nationalist, he called for harsh punishment of Germany after World War I and sent (1923) French troops into the RUHR to force Germany to pay REPARATIONS. In 1928 he stabilized the franc.

**poinsettia:** see SPURGE.

**Pointe-Noire** (pwanh nwah), city (1980 est. pop. 185,105), chief seaport of the People's Republic of the Congo, on the Atlantic Ocean. Major exports include petroleum, timber, potash, and sugar. The city is also a centre for sport fishing. Founded in 1883, Pointe-Noire became important after construction of the harbour and completion (1948) of the railway to BRAZZAVILLE. It was (1950–58) the capital of the French Congo.

**pointillism:** see POSTIMPRESSIONISM.

**point-to-point,** steeplechase races for members of local fox hunts. Horses must have a certificate to show that they have been hunted during the year. There are about 200 point-to-points between February and May each year in Britain. The races were once held across country, from 'point' to 'point' (e.g., a church steeple), but are now held on temporary race courses, often on farming land. The first British hunt to organize races for its members was the Atherstone c.1870.

**poison,** any chemical that produces a harmful effect on a living organism. Almost any substance can act as a poison if it enters the body in sufficiently large quantities or in an abnormal way; e.g., water inhaled into the lungs becomes an asphyxial poison. The severity of a poison is determined by the nature of the poison itself, the concentration and amount ingested, the route of entry, the length of exposure, and the age, size, and health of the victim. Common poisonous substances include ARSENIC, CYANIDE, STRYCHNINE, LEAD, MERCURY, acids, venoms, HERBICIDES, and CURARE and other drugs. See also FIRST AID.

**poison gas,** any of various gases sometimes used in CHEMICAL WARFARE or riot control because of their poisonous or corrosive nature. These gases may be roughly grouped according to the portal of entry into the body and their physiological effects. Vesicants (blister gases, e.g., mustard gas) produce blisters on all body surfaces; lacrimators (tear gas) cause severe eye irritation; sternutators (vomiting gases) cause nausea; nerve gases inhibit proper nerve function; and lung irritants cause pulmonary oedema. World War I marked the first effective use of poison gas and the introduction of gas masks. The use of poison gas has been limited since World War I by fear of retribution, although the military powers have continued to develop new gases.

**poison hemlock,** lethally poisonous herb (*Conium maculatum*) of the CARROT family. It has clusters of small white flowers and a purple-mottled stem. The poisonous principle (the ALKALOID coniine) causes paralysis, convulsions, and eventual death. The plant was used in ancient Greece as a means of execution; a famous victim was SOCRATES.

**poison ivy, poison oak,** and **poison sumac,** woody vines and trailing or erect shrubs (genus *Toxicodendron,* although sometimes considered genus *Rhus*) of the SUMAC family, native to North America but naturalized in Europe. The names poison ivy and poison oak, often used interchangeably, describe several species, the most common being *T. radicans,* which has three smooth leaflets. Poison sumac (*T. vernix*) is a larger plant. Both species have whitish, berrylike fruits and red autumn foliage. Urushiol, an irritant present in almost all parts of the plant, causes a skin eruption that may vary from itching inflammations to watery blisters.

**Poisson distribution,** used in STATISTICS to calculate the relative frequencies of events occurring when the number of trials in a series becomes very large, but the probability of a particular outcome in a trial is very small. In the limiting form of the distribution, the probability of $r$ successes in an infinite series of trials is $\dfrac{m^r e^{-m}}{r!}$ where $m$ is the ARITHMETIC MEAN number of success. The VARIANCE of the Poisson distribution is also $m$. One classical application of the distribution, cited by R.A. FISHER, is the number of men killed by horse-kick on any one day in the Prussian army, but the distribution is also widely used in games of chance and in epidemiology. The incidence of relatively rare diseases like leukaemia is often closely approximated by this distribution.

**Poitier, Sidney,** 1927–, black American film actor and director. He has starred in such films as *The Defiant Ones* (1958); *Lilies of the Field* (1963; Academy Award); *In the Heat of the Night* (1967); and *A Patch of Blue* (1973) and *A Piece of the Action* (1977), both of which he directed.

**Poitiers** (pwah̩tyay), city (1982 pop. 82,884), capital of Vienne dept., W Central France. It is an industrial, agricultural, and communications centre. Before Roman rule it was the capital of the Pictons, a Gallic people. Later, its Christian orthodoxy and its monasteries made it a religious centre. The Visigoths, Franks, Muslims, Normans, and English held it or sacked it in turn. In 1356 EDWARD THE BLACK PRINCE defeated JOHN II of France there. Historic architecture includes Roman amphitheatres and churches, and homes dating from the 4th cent. to the Renaissance.

**Poitiers, Diane de:** see DIANE DE POITIERS.

**poker,** card game, traditionally a cutthroat gambling game, now an internationally popular social game. It remains basically a gambling game played for either money or chips. During betting intervals, each player must fold (leave the game), call (equal the bet made), or raise (increase the bet made). All bets are placed together to form a pot. The game's object is to win the pot either by holding the best hand or by bluffing (inducing opponents to drop out). The two basic forms are draw poker, in which all cards remain hidden, and stud poker, in which some are dealt face-up.

**Poland,** Pol. *Polska,* officially the Polish People's Republic, republic (1985 est. pop. 37,556,000), 312,677 km² (120,725 sq mi), central Europe; bordered by East Germany (W), the Baltic Sea (N), the USSR (E), and Czechoslovakia (S). Major cities include WARSAW (the capital), LLÓDŹ, KRAKÓW, WROCLAW, POZNAŃ, and GDAŃSK. The country is generally low-lying, except in the S, where the CARPATHIAN and Sudeten mountains form a natural barrier between Poland and Czechoslovakia. Poland's main rivers, including the Vistula and the Oder, are important routes to the BALTIC SEA. Industry, which has expanded rapidly since World War II, contributes more than half the national product. Leading manufactures include iron and steel, machinery, cement, chemicals, textiles, and processed food. Agricultural products include potatoes, sugar beets, rye, and wheat. Poland is an important producer of coal, sulphur, and copper. Industry is largely controlled by the state, but most farms are privately run. The GNP per capita (1980) is US$3900. Nearly all the homogeneous population speaks Polish, and Roman Catholicism is the dominant religion.

*History.* The Slavic groups that occupied the area of present-day Poland were first united under the Piast dynasty and Christianized in the 10th cent. The crown eventually passed to the Jagiello dynasty (r. 1386–1572), under whom Poland enjoyed its golden age. The arts and sciences flourished, and a Polish-Lithuanian state, created in 1569, maintained an empire that reached from the Baltic to the Black Sea. In the 16th and 17th cent. much territory was lost to Sweden and Russia, and with the accession (1697) of the electors of Saxony as kings of Poland, national

independence was virtually lost (see NORTHERN WAR; POLISH SUCCESSION, WAR OF THE). Three successive partitions (1772, 1793, 1795) among Prussia, Austria, and Russia resulted in the disappearance of Poland from the map of Europe. Polish nationalism persisted, and in 1918, following World War I, an independent Poland was proclaimed, with Joseph PILSUDSKI as chief of state. The Treaty of VERSAILLES (1919) redrew Poland's boundaries, but a dispute over the eastern border led to war with Russia (1920–21); the Treaty of Riga awarded Poland parts of its claims. A republican constitution was adopted in 1921, but in 1926 Pilsudski assumed dictatorial power, which passed to a military junta after his death (1935). On 1 Sept. 1939, citing as cause Poland's alleged maltreatment of Germans living in Polish territory, Germany invaded Poland, thus precipitating WORLD WAR II. On 17 Sept. Russia (then allied with Germany) invaded from the east, and the country was divided between Germany and Russia. When Germany attacked the USSR in 1941, all of Poland came under German rule. Massacres, starvation, and CONCENTRATION CAMPS such as that at Óświęcim (Auschwitz) decimated the population; about 6 million Poles, including some 3 million Jews, were killed. The Germans were expelled from Poland in 1945, and a provisional government was set up under Soviet auspices. Government-controlled elections in 1947 gave the communists full control. Poland became (1952) a people's republic on the Soviet model, with power residing in the Polish United Workers' Party (PUWP), and was a founder member of both the COUNCIL FOR MUTUAL ECONOMIC ASSISTANCE and of the WARSAW TREATY ORGANIZATION. In 1956 widespread riots against Soviet control brought to power 'rightist deviationist' Wladyslaw Gomulka. A period of increased freedom followed, but by the 1960s Gomulka had reverted to the more rigid policies of his predecessors; in 1968 Polish forces participated in the Soviet-led invasion of Czechoslovakia. Rapidly increasing food prices led to riots in 1970, and Gomulka was replaced by Edward Gierek, who instituted many reforms and controlled inflation. Poland's gravest postwar crisis began in 1980 (and removed Gierek from power), when strikes by factory workers, miners, and farmers spread throughout the country. An independent trade union, known as SOLIDARITY and led by Lech WALESA, demanded greater workers' control in industry and political democratization. The nation's economy deteriorated, bringing severe shortages of food and other goods. Gierek was replaced as PUWP leader by Stanislaw Kania (1980), but he was quickly replaced (1981) by Gen. Wojciech JARUZELSKI. Strict martial law was imposed, work stoppages were prohibited, and Solidarity leaders were arrested, and in 1982 Solidarity itself was banned. Late that year the government announced a gradual suspension of martial law, which was finally lifted in mid-1983. The underlying social and political situation remained tense, however, and continuing widespread support for Solidarity was periodically demonstrated in subsequent years amid worsening economic conditions. The ban was lifted from the union in 1989.

Poland

**Poland, Partitions of,** three successive efforts (1772, 1793, 1795) by Austria, Russia, and Prussia to weaken Poland by dividing its territories amongst themselves. In 1772 large parts of the country were divided among FREDERICK II of Prussia, CATHERINE II of Russia, and MARIA THERESA of Austria. In 1793, after it had become apparent that the remaining portion of independent Poland was showing signs of regeneration, Russia and Prussia invaded the country and took more land. Only the central section of Poland remained independent, and the three powers took that in 1795. Poland's partition was confirmed by the Congress of VIENNA (1814–15), but Russia received a much larger share.

**Polanski, Roman,** 1933–, Polish film director; b. France. After his first films in Poland, his films have always been made in English since the mid 1960s. They usually deal with mental aberration and violence. His films include *Knife in the Water* (1962), *Repulsion* (1965), *Rosemary's Baby* (1968), and *Chinatown* (1974).

**Polanyi, Karl,** 1886–1964, American economist. He proposed that economic systems could be classified according to their dominant form of distribution: (1) RECIPROCITY. (2) redistribution, and (3) the market. Polanyi supported this with extensive empirical detail, e.g., in *Dahomey and the Slave Trade* (1966).

**Polaris** or **Pole Star,** star nearest the north celestial pole (see ASTRONOMICAL COORDINATE SYSTEMS). It is in the constellation Ursa Minor (see URSA MAJOR). Polaris's location less than 1° from the pole makes it a very important navigational star in the northern hemisphere. See PRECESSION OF THE EQUINOXES.

**polarized light,** light in which the vibration of the electric or magnetic field is confined to one direction which may be fixed (plane polarization) or rotating (circular or elliptical polarization). Ordinary light consists of a mixture of waves vibrating in all directions perpendicular to the line of propagation. Polarized light can be obtained to a varying extent (depending on the angle of incidence) by reflection. It can also be obtained by double refraction, or birefringence, in certain crystals, such as calcite. These crystals have the property of refracting unpolarized light in two different directions to produce two beams, the ordinary ray and the extraordinary ray; both are polarized in directions perpendicular to each other. Some crystals have the property of dichroism and strongly absorb one of the polarized components; they are therefore natural polarizers. The commercial material Polaroid is formed from such crystals.

**Polaroid camera,** trade name for a single-step camera invented (1947 for black and white; 1963 for colour) by Edwin H. LAND. In the Land process, the camera holds both negative film and printing paper, as well as a pod of developer that is spread between film and paper when the film is exposed. A finished print is produced within seconds.

**Polders,** areas of reclaimed land created by enclosure of the former Zuider Zee in N Netherlands. The five polders have been progressively drained and deep-ploughed to yield rich farmland. Farms situated alongside the access roads are surrounded by a regular landscape of square or rectangular fields. Services are provided from planned new towns which include Lelystad and Emmeloord.

**pole, magnetic:** see MAGNETIC POLE.

**pole vault,** athletics FIELD EVENT in which the competitor runs with a flexible pole and uses it to vault over a crossbar. The use of fibreglass poles took the record over 5.48 m (18 ft) in 1970, and by 1984 it was up to 5.90 m (19⅓ ft).

**police,** public and private agents concerned with public protection and enforcement of law and order. Some of the police forces in Europe are of very ancient origin: the French gendarmes and the Italian carabinieri, for example, have their roots in medieval institutions. The first modern metropolitan police force was set up in London by Sir Robert PEEL (1829). As in the US, the British police force is decentralized, each local force being the joint responsibility of the chief constable (for police policy) and a local police authority consisting of two-thirds councillors and one-third magistrates (for maintaining police equipment and efficiency), rather than with a government minister. The British police force is almost unique in that it does not routinely carry firearms: these are only issued to officers in pursuit of individuals who are themselves suspected to be armed and dangerous. About 10% of the British force are plain-clothes detectives. Specialist agencies include a rapid deployment force (the Flying Squad), a group specializing in financial crime (the Fraud Squad), and an antiterrorist section (the Special Branch). Most European forces are

subject to centralized control, with the regular police responsible to the minister of the interior, and detectives to the minister of justice. Some (e.g., France) have a separate specialist force for dealing with public disorder. The manning of border posts, and in some cases fire brigades, are also police responsibilities. In some countries local police chiefs can make bye-laws and impose fines on the spot. Interpol is an international organization to pool data and, if necessary, coordinate action amongst European police forces. The powers of the police in every state are a subject of concern: there is a conflict between their need to collect information and interrogate suspected criminals, and the civil liberties of the individual. SECRET POLICE forces, where they exist, serve as political enforcement arms of national governments.

**poliomyelitis** or **polio,** acute viral infection which, in its severe form, invades the nervous system and causes paralysis. In its mild form the disease produces mild symptoms (e.g., low-grade fever, malaise), or none. Also known as infantile paralysis, it is found worldwide, occurring mainly in children. The Salk vaccine (killed-virus vaccine by injection) and the Sabin vaccine (live-virus vaccine taken orally) have greatly reduced the incidence of polio, nearly eradicating it from developed nations.

**Polish Corridor,** popular German name for a strip of territory, awarded to Poland in 1919, which separated East Prussia from the rest of Germany. In Polish eyes, this was the historic province of Royal Prussia which was inhabited by a Polish majority and which had formed part of the kingdom of Poland, 1454–1793. Disputes over the 'corridor', despite Germany's right of free transit, and over the adjacent city of Danzig (GDANSK), provided Hitler's pretext for the invasion of Poland in Sept. 1939 and the outbreak of WORLD WAR II.

**Polish language,** member of the West Slavic group of the Slavic subfamily of the Indo-European family of languages. See LANGUAGE (table).

**Polish Legions,** military units formed to further the cause of Polish independence after the partitions (late 18th cent.). With the intention either of aiding foreign statesmen or monarchs who would sympathise with and support the Polish cause, or of gaining military experience useful in organizing armed resistance on Polish soil, the Polish legionary tradition was established soon after the third partition, when Poles joined Napoleon's forces fighting in Italy and Germany (1797–1802). Polish service in Bonaparte's cause became more widespread when conscription was introduced in the Duchy of Warsaw in 1807. The tradition was revived during WORLD WAR I by PILSUDSKI's legions (1914–17), which fought for the Central Powers against Russia.

**Polish risings,** efforts to regain independence and statehood following the partitions of Poland at the end of the 18th cent. A tradition of armed rebellion developed which was one arm of a three-pronged policy; this included attempts to form armed Polish units abroad (see POLISH LEGIONS) and moves to solicit political and diplomatic support from western statesmen (see CZARTORYSKI). The most notable risings during the partition period were those against Russian rule—in 1794, 1830, 1863, and 1905 —and the 1848 revolt against Prussian rule in Posen (Poznań). The risings failed for various reasons but the most telling factor was the overwhelming military force that the occupying powers were able to bring to bear. The Polish rising became a symbol of a tragic, romantic gesture—heroic, but doomed to failure. However its role in reviving and prolonging national sentiment, as well as keeping the Polish Question in the forefront of European politics, should not be underestimated. The tradition of Polish risings has lasted into the 20th cent., the most vivid example of recent history being the Warsaw Rising of 1944.

**Polish–Soviet War,** war arising out of border disputes between the renascent Polish state and Soviet Russia following the withdrawal of German armies from Byelorussia in Feb. 1919. First the Poles fought for Wilno and Minsk; in 1920 however, Russian forces pressed the Poles back to the gates of Warsaw. Despite the failure of the Western powers to provide the Poles with material assistance, a brilliant encircling manoeuvre by the Polish forces under PILSUDSKI led to a reversal of fortunes. The Soviet forces were defeated and routed; Lenin sued for peace, and terms were agreed at the Treaty of Riga (Mar. 1921).

**Polish Succession, War of the,** 1733–35, European conflict arising out of rival claims to the Polish throne. France supported STANISLAUS I, while the Holy Roman emperor and Russia supported AUGUSTUS III. In 1734 Stanislaus was forced to flee to France, but the war continued along the

## PARTIES WITH PARLIAMENTARY REPRESENTATION IN MAJOR DEMOCRACIES

| country | extreme left/communist | democratic socialist | ecologist/anti-nuclear | liberal/centrist | conservative | extreme right | regional/communal |
|---|---|---|---|---|---|---|---|
| Argentina | | | | Radical Civic Union<br>Intransigent Party | Union of the Democratic Centre | Justicialist (Peronist) Party | |
| Australia | | Labour Party | Nuclear Disarmament Party | Democrats Party | Liberal Party<br>National Party | | |
| Austria | | Socialist Party | Green Alternative | | People's Party | Freedom Party | |
| Belgium | | Socialist Party (Wall.)<br>Socialist Party (Flem.) | Ecologist Party<br>Live Differently | Freedom and Progress Party (Flem.)<br>Liberal Reform Party (Wall.) | Christian People's Party (Flem.)<br>Christian Social Party (Wall.) | | People's Union (Flem.)<br>Flemish Bloc<br>Francophone Democratic Front<br>Walloon Party |
| Brazil | Workers' Party<br>Communist Party<br>Socialist Party | Democratic Labour Party | | Democratic Movement<br>Liberal Front Party<br>Labour Party<br>Liberal Party | Social Democratic Party<br>Christian Democratic Party | | |
| Canada | | New Democratic Party | | Liberal Party | Progressive Conservative Party | | Parti Québécois |
| Denmark | Socialist People's Party<br>Common Cause | Social Democratic Party | | Liberal Party<br>Radical Liberal Party<br>Centre Democrats<br>Christian People's Party | Conservative People's Party | Progress Party | People's Party (Faroes)<br>Siumut (Greenland)<br>Atassut (Greenland) |
| Finland | People's Democratic League<br>Democratic Alternative | Social Democratic Party | Green Party | Centre Party<br>Rural Party<br>Christian Union | National Coalition Party | | Swedish People's Party |
| France | Communist Party<br>Unified Socialist Party | Socialist Party<br>Left Radical Movement | | Union for French Democracy | Rally for the Republic | National Front | |
| Germany, West | | Social Democratic Party | Green Party | Free Democratic Party | Christian Democratic Union<br>Christian Social Union | | |
| Greece | Communist Party (Ext.)<br>Communist Party (Int.) | Pan-Hellenic Socialist Movement | | | New Democracy | National Political Society | |
| India | Communist Party<br>Communist Party (Marxist)<br>Revolutionary Socialist Party | Janata Party<br>Congress (Socialist) | | Congress (Indira) | Jan Sangh | | Moslem League<br>Anna Dravida Munnetra<br>Kazhagan (Tamil Nadu)<br>Land of Telugu (Andhra Pradesh) |
| Ireland | Workers' Party | Labour Party | | Fine Gael<br>Progressive Democrats | Fianna Fail | | |
| Italy | Communist Party<br>Proletarian Democracy | Socialist Party<br>Democratic Socialist Party | Green Party | Republican Party<br>Radical Party<br>Liberal Party | Christian Democratic Party | Social Movement | South Tirol People's Party<br>Sardinian Action Party<br>Val d'Aosta Union<br>Lombardy List |
| Japan | Communist Party | Socialist Party<br>Democratic Socialist Party | | Clean Government Party | Liberal-Democratic Party | | |
| Netherlands | Pacifist Socialist Party<br>Radical Political Party | Labour Party | | Freedom and Democracy Party<br>Democrats '66 | Christian Democratic Appeal<br>Reformational Political Federation<br>Reformed Political Association | | |
| New Zealand | | Labour Party | | Democratic Party | National Party | | |
| Norway | Socialist Left Party | Labour Party | | Christian People's Party<br>Centre Party | Conservative Party | Progressive Party | |
| Portugal | Communist Party | Socialist Party | | Social Democratic Party<br>Democratic Renewal Party | Christian Social Centre | | |
| Spain | Communist Party | Socialist Workers' Party | | Democratic Social Centre | Popular Coalition | | Convergence and Union (Catalonia)<br>Basque National Party<br>Basque Left<br>United People (Basque) |
| Sweden | Communist Left Party | Social Democratic Party | | Centre Party<br>Liberal Party | Moderate Party | | |
| Switzerland | Autonomous Socialist Party<br>Progressive Organizations<br>Party of Labour | Social Democratic Party | Green Federation | Radical Democratic Party<br>People's Party<br>Independents' Party<br>Liberal Party<br>Evangelical People's Party | Christian Democratic Party | National Action<br>Republican Movement | |
| United Kingdom | | Labour Party | | Social and Liberal Democrats<br>Social Democratic Party | Conservative Party | | Scottish National Party<br>Plaid Cymru (Wales)<br>Unionist Parties (NI)<br>Social Democratic and Labour Party (NI)<br>Sinn Fein (NI) |
| United States | | | | Democratic Party | Republican Party | | |

Rhine and in Italy. There Spain and Sardinia allied themselves with France, hoping to gain Italian territories then in the control of the emperor. The Treaty of Vienna (1735) called for a complicated dynastic reshuffling. Stanislaus (and France) got the duchies of Lorraine and Bar; Spain got Naples and Sicily; and the emperor retained Parma.

**politburo,** the central policy-making and governing body of the Communist party of the Soviet Union and of other Communist parties. Created in the USSR in 1917, it is normally elected by the party's central committee to direct party affairs between central committee plenary sessions; in reality, it governs the country. Although its size varies, it usually consists of 11 to 14 voting members and 6 to 9 nonvoting members. It was called the presidium from 1952 to 1966.

**political parties,** associations of likeminded individuals and/or interest groups seeking to achieve or retain governmental power for specific policy ends. Political parties in the modern sense of the term developed in the 19th cent. in countries with parliamentary systems, where loose factions of politicians gradually evolved into structured organizations seeking electoral support and active membership from the public at large. In the 20th cent. parties have become an almost universal feature of political life, existing in virtually every country, although in some they are officially banned by regimes which regard them as a threat to their exercise of power. Broadly they now fall into two main categories: (1) those operating in countries where one party has a legal monopoly of power; and (2) those operating in pluralist democracies in competition with other parties. Parties in the first category include ruling Communist parties (see COMMUNISM), which regard inter-party competition as having been superseded by their advent to power, and the ruling parties of many developing countries, notably in Africa, where multi-party democracy is regarded as likely to undermine national unity. Such parties do not permit any real challenge to their 'leading role' in the state, although for electoral purposes they may participate in broader fronts of 'popular' organizations and may also tolerate the nominal existence of other parties. Table 1 lists ruling Communist parties by country as well as other ruling parties in one-party states. Parties in the second category encompass a wide array of ideologies and credos, but are all subject to the requirement of obtaining popular support in competitive elections before they can influence the political process. Customarily categorized by their location on a left-to-right political spectrum, such parties range from those on the left advocating communism and SOCIALISM, to those with a specific interest in ECOLOGY (the so-called green parties), to liberal and centrist formations (which eschew what they regard as political extremes), to those embracing variants of CONSERVATISM and, on the far right of spectrum, to ultra-nationalist formations and those influenced by the doctrines of FASCISM. Table 2 shows parties currently represented in the parliaments of major countries with competitive electoral systems, classified according to their political orientation. It should be noted that, particularly in non-European countries, such labels are often not easily applicable, given that several ideological strands may coexist within the same party. Moreover, parties representing regional or communal interests vary greatly as regards their economic and social policies, which may be radical socialist in one country and strongly conservative in another. A further problem of classification is that, as the table shows, the name of a party does not always correspond with its political orientation.

**political science,** study of the processes, institutions, and activities of government. Although the study of politics dates back to ARISTOTLE and PLATO, political science only emerged as a separate discipline toward the end of the 19th cent. It generally includes the fields of political theory, the institutions and processes of national government, comparative government, and international relations.

**Polk, James Knox,** 1795–1849, 11th president of the US (1845–49). He served in the Tennessee state legislature (1823–25) and the US House of Representatives (1825–39), where he was Speaker (from 1835) and a leading Jacksonian Democrat (see JACKSON, ANDREW). He was elected (1839) governor of TENNESSEE but was defeated for reelection. When the 1844 Democratic convention reached deadlock, Polk, a 'dark horse', was advanced as a compromise candidate for president and won the nomination. He narrowly defeated Henry CLAY in the 1844 election. As president, Polk proved to be his own man. His promises to achieve 'four great measures'—reduction of the tariff, reestablishment of an independent treasury, settlement of the Oregon boundary dispute, and acquisition of California—were kept. Despite the aggressive Democratic slogan of '54°40¸ or fight', Polk resolved the dispute with Britain over OREGON by adopting the 49th parallel as the territory's northern boundary. His ordering of US troops to the Rio Grande brought about the MEXICAN WAR, which resulted in the US acquisition not only of California but of the entire Southwest. Few presidents have equalled Polk's record of attaining his stated aims.

**poll,** technique for determining popular attitudes or opinions on given questions. Preelection polling by US newspapers dates from 1824, and polling at voting places to report election returns dates from 1883; magazines conducted national polls in the early 20th cent. A scientific method called sampling was developed in the 1930s. Using a small percentage of voters, a pollster could predict election outcomes more accurately than with the old straw-ballot technique. George GALLUP's

## SOLE RULING PARTIES

| | | | |
|---|---|---|---|
| Afghanistan | People's Democratic Party *(Khalq)* | Kampuchea | People's Revolutionary Party |
| Albania | Party of Labour | Kenya | African National Union |
| Algeria | National Liberation Front | North Korea | Workers' Party |
| Angola | Popular Liberation Movement—Party of Labour | Laos | People's Revolutionary Party |
| | | Malawi | Congress Party |
| Benin | People's Revolutionary Party | Mali | People's Democratic Union |
| Bulgaria | Communist Party | Mongolia | People's Revolutionary Party |
| Burma | Socialist Programme party | Mozambique | Front for the Liberation of Mozambique |
| Burundi | Union for National Progress | Poland | United Workers' Party |
| Cameroon | National Union | Romania | Communist Party |
| Cape Verde | African Party for the Independence of Cape Verde | Rwanda | National Revolutionary Movement for Development |
| China | Communist Party | São Tomé and Príncipe | Movement for the Liberation of São Tomé and Príncipe |
| Comoros | Union for Comorian Progress | Seychelles | People's Progressive Front |
| Congo | Party of Labour | Sierra Leone | All-People's Congress |
| Côte d'Ivoire | Democratic Party | Somalia | Revolutionary Socialist Party |
| Cuba | Communist Party | Tanzania | Revolutionary Party |
| Czechoslovakia | Communist Party | Togo | Rally of the Togolese People |
| Djibouti | People's Party | USSR | Communist Party |
| Ethiopia | Workers' Party | Vietnam | Communist Party |
| East Germany | Socialist Unity Party | South Yemen | Socialist Party |
| Gabon | Democratic Party | Yugoslavia | League of Communists |
| Guinea-Bissau | African Party for the Independence of Guinea and Cape Verde | Zaïre | Popular Movement of the Revolution |
| Hungary | Socialist Workers' Party | Zambia | United National Independence Party |

correct prediction in the 1936 presidential election brought wide recognition of the sampling method. Polling technique has grown increasingly sophisticated and is an important part of social science methodology; it is also widely used in MARKET RESEARCH and in ADVERTISING. The movement of public opinion provoked by the publication of poll results themselves, the 'bandwagon effect', has attracted criticism, and some states, such as Australia, have banned political polls in the period shortly before an election.

**Pollaiuolo** (pohl-lahyooh-,awloh), family of Florentine artists. **Jacopo Pollaiuolo** was a noted 15th-cent. goldsmith. His son and pupil, **Antonio Pollaiuolo**, 1429?–1498, goldsmith, painter, sculptor, and engraver, headed one of Florence's foremost workshops. He is said to have been the first artist to study anatomy by dissection. His mastery of figures in action can be seen in the painting *Dancing Nudes* (Arcetri, Italy) and in a painting and a bronze statuette of *Hercules and Antaeus* (both: Uffizi). In Rome he executed the bronze tomb of Sixtus IV. His brother, **Piero Pollaiuolo**, 1443–96, was associated with him. Piero is generally considered an inferior artist, as seen in his independent works, e.g., the *Virtues* (Uffizi). Their nephew **Simone del Pollaiuolo**, 1457–1508, nicknamed Il Cronaca, was an architect, responsible for the noble Strozzi palace. He also worked on the Great Hall of the Palazzo Vecchio (1495) and the Church of San Salvatore al Monte (1504).

**pollen,** minute, usually yellow grains, borne in the anther sac at the tip of the stamen (the male reproductive organ of the FLOWER) or in the male cone of a CONIFER. Pollen grains are the male GAMETOPHYTE generation of seed plants. They are formed by the division, or MEIOSIS, of pollen mother cells and contain half the number of chromosomes of the parent plant, the full number typical of the species being restored at FERTILIZATION by fusion with the EGG cell. See also POLLINATION.

**pollination,** transfer of POLLEN from the male reproductive organ (the stamen of a FLOWER or staminate cone of a CONIFER) to the female reproductive organ (pistil or pistillate cone) of the same or another flower or cone. The most common agents of pollination are flying insects (for most flowering plants) and wind (for most trees and all GRASSes and conifers). The devices that operate to ensure cross-pollination and prevent self-pollination are highly varied and intricate. They include different maturation times for the pollen and eggs of the same plant; separate staminate and pistillate flowers on the same or separate plants; chemical properties that make the pollen and eggs of the same plant incompatible with each other; and special mechanisms and arrangements that prevent the pollinating agent from transferring a flower's pollen to its stigma. Pollination should not be confused with FERTILIZATION, which it may precede by some time—a full season in some conifers.

**Pollock, Jackson,** 1912–56, American painter, pioneer of ABSTRACT EXPRESSIONISM. In his attempt to express, rather than illustrate, feeling, Pollock developed an abstract art in which he vigorously drew or 'dripped' complicated linear rhythms onto enormous canvases. His attack on the canvas and his devotion to the act of painting led to the term 'action painting'.

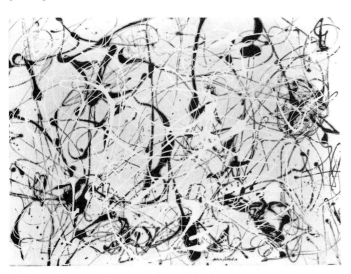

*Number 23* by Jackson **Pollock** (Tate Gallery, London)

**poll tax,** uniform tax levied on every adult in the community. Poll taxes are traceable to ancient tax systems and have long been criticized as an unfair burden on the poor. In the UK poll taxes levied in 1380 were a major cause of a revolt by peasants, led by Wat Tyler in 1381. Historically, in the US, they were enacted in the South as a prerequisite for voting, disfranchising many blacks and poor whites. The 24th Amendment to the US CONSTITUTION (1964) forbidding a poll tax, was extended to all elections. In Britain the term was revived in politics to describe the community tax (1988).

**pollution,** contamination of the environment as a result of human activities. During the 20th cent. pollution problems have arisen in all industrialized areas as well as in various inland and coastal waters and stretches of ocean. The capacity of the BIOSPHERE to disperse, degrade, and assimilate human wastes is in question (see ECOLOGY). Human activity now outweighs natural forces in putting toxic elements into the atmosphere; further, the microorganisms which in an undisturbed ecosystem disperse waste matter are unable to break down these alien toxic substances. Pollution of the atmosphere can also occur when the balance of its constituents is altered, as when an increase in levels of carbon dioxide, not biologically toxic itself, causes the 'greenhouse effect' (with consequent rises in temperature) and the ozone layer, which filters harmful rays from the sun, is damaged. An early sign of environmental limits was the air pollution of the INDUSTRIAL REVOLUTION, brought on by the burning of coal to run mills and machinery. It was not until after World War II, however, that pollution came to be viewed by many as a threat to the health of the planet. By the 1960s, population increases, industrial expansion, and far greater road vehicle use were producing wastes in such quantity that natural dispersing and recycling processes could not always keep pace. Exacerbating the problem was the appearance of synthetic substances which degraded with extreme slowness or not at all: plastics, fibres, organic pesticides such as DDT (which is still present in some fertilizer compounds and whose overall use is rising, though it is banned in most industrialized countries), industrial chemicals such as PCBs (polychlorinated biphenyls), and the wastes from their manufacture. There are some 35,000 different commercial products used to control insects, weeds, fungi, and other crop destroyers. Refuse, fertilizers, and other toxic chemicals have polluted the land and infiltrated ground and surface waters. Oil spills in oceans (e.g., *Torrey Canyon*, English Channel, 1967) may cause the death of thousands of seabirds and fish. Pesticides have poisoned wildlife, and industrial waste products have contaminated drinking water and, in more severe cases, in the US, caused evacuation of homes. Effects of industrial wastes have spread over larger areas as well, e.g., when toxic MERCURY reached high concentrations in widely distributed species of food fish in the early 1970s. In the UK the government in 1961 passed the Rivers (Control of Pollution) Act but its efficacy is impaired by a refusal to implement the provisions for prosecution of offenders. Airborne industrial wastes create ACID RAIN and, with vehicle exhaust emissions, produce severe air-pollution problems, including SMOG and fog (partly alleviated in the UK by the Clean Air Act of 1956). Excessive noise, excessive heating of rivers and lakes by industrial effluents, the glare of electric lighting, and radiation are also usually considered forms of pollution. Current evidence strongly implicates various pollutants in numerous health problems, such as CANCER; BIRTH DEFECTS; genetic changes; chronic headaches, fatigue, and irritability; and digestive disorders. By the 1970s many organizations and governments were seeking means of controlling pollution, sometimes in the face of opposition from agro-chemical manufacturers. In 1979, 31 of the 34 member governments of the United Nations Economic Commission for Europe signed the Convention on Long-Range Transboundary Air Pollution, eliciting a moral commitment from each nation to respect the environment of others. See also ENVIRONMENTALISM

**pollution,** in anthropology, a belief that some state, substance, or person is unclean and socially or ritually able to contaminate. Some castes for example, are seen as permanently polluting to those outside their caste, and frequently life crises, e.g., birth or death, can render those close to the event unclean in some way and force their exclusion from the social group for a period of time. Menstruating women are frequently thought of as particularly polluting (see MENSTRUATION). Pollution beliefs have been analysed in various ways. Mary DOUGLAS has argued that in many societies power and danger is seen as residing in the margins of society, areas that are anomalous and therefore threatening and that it is the marginal areas of the body (which so often symbolizes the body politic), the orifices and bodily substances, that threaten and pollute. It has been argued that the reason why so many cultures regard women as intrinsically polluting is precisely because their generative powers are never really controlled fully by culture, essentially a creation of men, and that they are never as tightly inserted into and controlled by the social world as men are. They are closer to nature and therefore on the margins of the social and in this way dangerous.

**Pollux,** Greek hero: see CASTOR AND POLLUX.

**polo,** ball and goal game played on horseback. Outdoor polo is played by two teams of four on a grass field with goal posts at either end. An indoor match is played with teams of three. In both versions, play is directed towards striking a ball (wooden in outdoor polo, rubber in indoor) with a long, flexible mallet into the goal. Because of the frequent collisions between horses (called polo ponies), each player must change mounts several times during a match. The origin of polo is uncertain, but it was played by British officers in India in the 19th cent. and then spread to England, Latin America, Australia, and the US.

**Polo, Marco,** 1254?–1324?, Venetian traveller in CHINA. He left Venice in 1271 with his father and uncle, who had previously journeyed as far east as Kaifeng, in China (1266). The party reached the court of KUBLAI KHAN, in Cambaluc (or Khan-balek, present-day BEIJING), in 1275. Marco Polo became the khan's favourite and served him in China, India, and SE Asia. He returned to Venice in 1295. His account of his travels has been of great value to historians.

**polonium** (Po), radioactive element, discovered in PITCHBLENDE by Marie CURIE in 1898. Extremely rare, it has 34 isotopes, more than any other element. Polonium is used in small, portable radiation sources, and in the control of static electricity. See ELEMENT (table); PERIODIC TABLE.

**Pol Pot,** 1928?–, Kampuchean Communist leader; b. Saloth Sar. After the KHMER ROUGE victory in Cambodia (KAMPUCHEA) in 1975, he became (1976) prime minister of the new Communist government. Under his regime, widespread executions, forced labour, and famine killed an estimated 3 million people. In 1979 a Vietnamese invasion ousted him from the capital, Phnom Penh, and established a rival government under HENG SAMRIN. Pol Pot continued to lead the Khmer Rouge regime in the countryside for some years, although by the mid-1980s he was less prominent in the coalition opposed to the Heng Samrin regime.

**poltergeist** [Ger., = knocking ghost], in SPIRITUALISM, cause of inexplicable phenomena such as rapping, movement of furniture, and breaking of crockery. These phenomena, common at seances, are taken as evidence of the presence of supernatural forces.

**polyandry,** the MARRIAGE of a woman to more than one man at the same time. This form of marriage is found infrequently and in most known instances the woman is married to a group of brothers, paternity being assigned, on the presentation of a recognized ritual object or 'payment', to the man it is agreed will be the father of a given child.

**Polybius** (poh,libeeəs), b. c.200 BC, d. after 118 BC, Greek historian; b. Megalopolis. In Rome, under the patronage of the Scipio family, he wrote a great universal history. Of the 40 books written, only the first five survive intact. Polybius tried to explain the sudden rise of Rome; his history covers the Mediterranean world from before c.220 to 146 BC.

**polychlorinated biphenyl:** see PCB.

**Polydorus,** Greek sculptor: see LAOCOÖN.

**polyester:** see SYNTHETIC TEXTILE FIBRES.

**polygon,** closed plane figure bounded by straight-line segments (sides) intersecting at points called vertices. Polygons of 3, 4, 5, 6, 7, 8, 10, and 12 sides are called, respectively, triangles, quadrilaterals, pentagons, hexagons, heptagons, octagons, decagons, and dodecagons. In a regular polygon, e.g., an equilateral triangle or a *square* (four sides), the sides are of equal length and meet at equal angles. A triangle is *isosceles* if two sides are equal and *scalene* if all sides differ in length; a *right-angled triangle* has one right angle (90°). A quadrilateral is a *rhombus* if its four sides are equal, a *trapezium* if it has one pair of parallel sides, and a *parallelogram* if it has two pairs of parallel sides. A *rectangle* is a parallelogram with four right angles.

**polygyny,** MARRIAGE of one man to more than one woman. This form of marriage is far more widespread than POLYANDRY or than monogamy and is often only practised by older and more powerful men. Through plural marriages such men gain a wide range of ALLIANCE contacts and a large labour force, since they have control over the labour of their wives and children.

**polyhedron** ('poli,heedrən), closed solid bounded by plane faces, each of which is a POLYGON. There are only five possible regular polyhedrons, having congruent faces, each the same regular polygon and meeting at equal angles. These are the Platonic solids: the tetrahedron (bounded by four equilateral triangles); the hexahedron, or cube (six squares); the octahedron (eight equilateral triangles); the dodecahedron (12 regular pentagons); and the icosahedron (20 equilateral triangles).

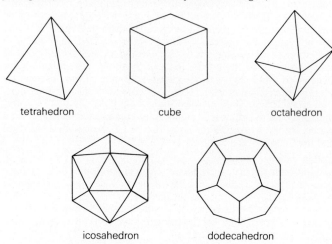

tetrahedron    cube    octahedron

icosahedron    dodecahedron

The five regular **polyhedrons**

**Polyhymnia:** see MUSES.

**Polykleitos, Polycletus** or **Polyclitus** (poli,klietəs, -klee-, -klie-), two Greek sculptors of the school of Argos. Polykleitos, the elder, fl. c.450–c.420 BC, made many bronze statues of athletes. His ideal of physical perfection, the 'canon of Polykleitos', became the standard for sculptors. It is seen in his statues the *Doryphorus,* or *Spear-Bearer* (Naples), the *Diadoumenos* (National Mus., Athens), and an *Amazon,* all known through copies. **Polykleitos,** the younger, fl. 4th. cent. BC, a sculptor and architect, designed the great theatre at EPIDAURUS.

**polymer,** chemical compound with high molecular weight consisting of a number of structural units linked together by covalent bonds. A structural unit is a group of molecules having two or more bonding sites. The simple molecules that may become structural units are called monomers. In a linear polymer, the monomers are connected in a chain arrangement and thus need only have two bonding sites. When the monomers have three bonding sites, a nonlinear, or branched, polymer results. Naturally occurring polymers include CELLULOSE, PROTEINS, natural RUBBER, and SILK; those synthesized in the laboratory have led to such commercially important products as PLASTIC, synthetic fibres, and synthetic rubber.

**Polynesia,** one of the three main divisions of Oceania, in the central and S Pacific Ocean. The principal island groups include the Hawaiian islands (see HAWAII), TONGA, Samoa (see AMERICAN SAMOA; WESTERN SAMOA), and the islands of FRENCH POLYNESIA. Languages spoken are of Malayo-Polynesian origin.

**Polynesian languages:** see MALAYO-POLYNESIAN LANGUAGES.

**Polynices:** see SEVEN AGAINST THEBES.

**polynomial,** mathematical expression containing terms of one or more variables or constants that are connected by addition or subtraction. No variable can appear as a divisor or have a fractional exponent. In one unknown, the general form of a polynomial is $a_0 x^n + a_1 x^{n-1} + a_2 x^{n-2} + \ldots + a_n^{-1} x + a_n$ *where* $n$ is a positive integer and $a_0$, $a_1$, $a_2$, . . . , $a_n$ are any numbers. The *degree* of a polynomial in one variable is the highest power of the variable. A polynomial of degree 2, i.e., $ax^2 + bx + c$ (where $a$, $b$, and $c$ are any numbers), is called a *quadratic.*

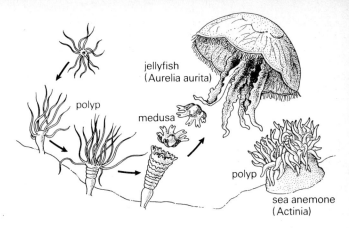

Two types of Cnidaria: one taking both the **polyp and medusa** forms during its life cycle (left), and the other (right) which remains a stationary polyp throughout its adult life.

Marble Roman copy of *Doryphoros* by **Polykleitos**, National Museum, Naples.

**polyp and medusa,** names for the two body forms of animals (COELENTERATES) of the phylum Cnidaria. One, the polyp or hydroid, is stationary; the other, the medusa, is free-swimming. Both consist of a cylindrical body with a mouth surrounded by stinging tentacles at one end. The polyp is elongated and attaches to a solid surface with the mouth and tentacles pointing upward; the medusa is rounded and swims with the mouth down and tentacles dangling. Some cnidarians are always polyps, some are always medusae, and some take both medusa and polyp forms during their life CYCLES. Common polyps are the SEA ANEMONE and HYDRA; a common medusa is the JELLYFISH. In many species, such as CORAL, the polyps form colonies. The Portuguese man-of-war is an elaborate floating colony of polyplike and medusalike individuals.

**polypeptide:** see AMINO ACID; PEPTIDE.

**Polyphemus** (poli‚feeməs), in Greek mythology, a CYCLOPS, son of POSEIDON. In the *Odyssey*, ODYSSEUS and his men were imprisoned in his cave, but they escaped by making him drunk and blinding him. *Ulysses Diriding Polyphemus* is the subject of a famous painting by J.W.M. TURNER (1829).

**polyphony** (pə‚lifəni), music whose texture is formed by the harmonic interweaving of several independent melodic lines through the use of COUNTERPOINT. Contrasting terms are *homophony,* wherein one part dominates while the others form a chordal accompaniment; and *monophony,* wherein there is a single melodic line (as in PLAINSONG). Polyphony developed in Europe by the late 9th cent. and culminated in the great age of polyphony in the 15th and 16th cent. Although polyphony was overshadowed by HARMONY in the BAROQUE period and by homophony in the classical and romantic periods, in the 20th cent. there has been renewed interest in polyphonic aspects of musical texture and structure. Ethnomusicological research has revealed that forms of polyphony are much more widespread and ancient than was originally thought. It is found in the traditional music of the San of the Kalahari and the Babinga of Central Africa.

**polypropylene** ('poli‚prohpileen), lightweight PLASTIC, a POLYMER of propylene ($C_3H_6$). It is less dense than water and resists moisture, oils, and solvents. It is used to make packaging material, textiles, luggage, ropes that float, and, because of its high melting point (121°C/250°F), objects that must be sterilized.

**polytechnics,** in Britain, institutions of higher education parallel with universities, offering a wide range of vocationally-orientated and other full- and part-time courses. They teach at undergraduate and postgraduate levels and conduct research. The polytechnics were created (1966) out of former technical colleges (sometimes merging with colleges of art, commerce, or education): 29 polytechnics were designated in England, plus the Polytechnic of Wales and the Ulster Polytechnic (which has since merged with the New University of Ulster). Degrees and diplomas of the polytechnics have been validated by the COUNCIL FOR NATIONAL ACADEMIC AWARDS, which from 1987 began to delegate greater autonomy to them under a scheme of 'accreditation'. Polytechnics have from 4000 to 11,000 students; the majority are in urban areas and have strong relations with employers in their regions, as well as with the professional bodies relating to the courses offered. They also provide courses at non-advanced level. Admission is adminstered by the Polytechnics Central Admissions System, set up in 1984 on the model of the UNIVERSITIES' CENTRAL COUNCIL ON ADMISSIONS; applicants apply simultaneously for up to four courses. This 1960s generation of polytechnics should not be confused with a first generation that was created in the 1880s and 1890s on the model of Quintin HOGG's Regent Street Polytechnic. Those London polytechnics developed in the 20th cent. providing courses of many kinds, some under the aegis of LONDON UNIVERSITY's degree system, and many of them became Colleges of Advanced Technology and were given university status in the 1960s (e.g., Battersea Polytechnic became the University of Surrey, and Northampton Polytechnic became City University).

**polytheism** ('polee‚thee-izəm), belief in a plurality of gods, not necessarily equal in importance, each of which is distinguished by a special function. The Indian VEDAS, for example, feature Agni the fire god, Vayu the wind god, and Indra the storm god. Dynastic Egypt had hundreds of deities, but worship (as in Greek Olympianism) was city-centred. The gods of polytheistic systems are organized into a cosmic family, featured in legend and myth and expressing beliefs about the individual's relationship to the universe. The lesser deities of polytheism tend to diminish with time until the religion exhibits monotheistic tendencies. Thus the Olympian sky god ZEUS became the head of all Olympian deities; the Egyptian RA became the supreme god; and the several thousand Vedic gods were gradually displaced by the trinity of VIṢṆU, ŚIVA, and BRAHMĀ. See MONOTHEISM.

**polyunsaturated fats:** see FATS AND OILS.

**polyurethanes** (poli‚yooəri'thayns), large group of PLASTICS that occur in a wide variety of forms. As a flexible foam, it is used for cushions and carpet backings. As a rigid foam, it can be moulded into furniture or used as insulation. Some polyurethanes are highly elastic, e.g., Lycra, a fibre used in stretch clothing; others form hard protective coatings.

**polyvinyl chloride** (PVC), thermoplastic that is a POLYMER of vinyl chloride. By adding plasticizers, hard PVC RESINS can be made into a flexible, elastic PLASTIC, used as an electrical insulator and as a coating for paper and for cloth in making fabric for upholstery and raincoats.

**Pombal, Sebastião José de Carvalho e Melo, marquês de** (poom͵bahl), 1699–1782, Portuguese chief minister (1756–77) under King Joseph. An anticlerical absolutist, he curbed the INQUISITION and expelled the Jesuits from PORTUGAL. He built up Brazil and strengthened commerce. Pombal ruthlessly put down all opposition, imprisoning thousands. He was deposed after Joseph's death (1777) and was banished.

**pomegranate,** deciduous, thorny shrub or small tree (*Punica granatum*) native to semitropical Asia and grown in the Mediterranean region. It has long been cultivated as an ornamental and for its fruit. The roughly apple-sized fruit contains many seeds, each within a fleshy red seed coat, enclosed in a tough yellowish-to-deep-red rind. It is eaten fresh or used for grenadine syrup.

**Pomerania,** region of N central Europe in Poland and East Germany, bordering the Baltic Sea. It is largely agricultural lowland, with such crops as grains, sugar beets, and potatoes. Stock-raising and forestry are important occupations. Industries include shipbuilding, metallurgy, and paper making. W Pomerania became (1181) a duchy of the HOLY ROMAN EMPIRE, while E Pomerania, or Pomerelia, came (1466) under Polish rule and passed (1772) to PRUSSIA, becoming known as West Prussia. Parts of W Pomerania were ruled (1648–1814) by Sweden, and from 1815 to 1919 all of Pomerania was held by Prussia. From 1919 to 1939 Pomerania was divided among Germany, Poland, and the free city of Danzig (GDAŃSK). During WORLD WAR II Germany held all of Pomerania. In 1945 Poland was awarded most of the region; the rest became part of East Germany.

**Pompadour, Jeanne Antoinette Poisson Le Normant Étioles, marquise de,** 1721–64, mistress of LOUIS XV of France for about five years after 1745. She was his confidante until her death. She urged the appointment of certain ministers, and fostered French ties with Austria, but her influence on state policy has been exaggerated.

**Pompeii,** ancient city of S Italy, a port near Naples and at the foot of Mt. Vesuvius. It was a Samnite city before it became Roman (1st cent. BC). Pompeii was a flourishing port and a prosperous resort. An earthquake in AD 63 damaged the city, and the eruption of Mt VESUVIUS in AD 79 buried Pompeii and the nearby city of Herculaneum under cinders and ashes that preserved their ruins. Pompeii was rediscovered in 1748, and excavations have revealed in great detail the habits and manners of life in Roman times.

A gate to the forum, **Pompeii**

**Pompeius Magnus:** see POMPEY.

**Pompey** (Cnaeus Pompeius Magnus), 106–48 BC, Roman general and statesman. He first achieved prominence through his support for SULLA, becoming one of his most successful commanders before he was 25. After Sulla's death, further commands were awarded to him by the senate, against Sertorius in Spain, the Mediterranean pirates, and MITHRIDATES VI of Pontus. After further successes in W Asia, he returned to Italy in 62 BC, in a position of apparently unrivalled strength. But he lacked political skills to match his military ability, allowed himself to be slighted by the senate, and entered into close alliance with CAESAR and CRASSUS, marrying Caesar's daughter Julia. The years that followed saw Caesar's rise to fame and the death of Crassus in Parthia; by 52 BC, the imminent threat of civil war with Caesar led the senate to appoint Pompey as their champion and sole consul. In the great struggle that ensued, Pompey was eventually defeated by Caesar at Pharsalia in 48 BC; fleeing to Egypt, he was murdered as he landed there on the orders of the ministers of PTOLEMY XII.

**Pompidou, Georges** (pawnhpee͵dooh), 1911–74, president of FRANCE (1969–74). From 1944 he was an aide to Charles DE GAULLE, who named him premier in 1962. Elected president after De Gaulle resigned, Pompidou worked to improve France's economy and foreign relations. He died in office.

**Pompidou (Georges) Centre,** Paris, the Musée de l'Art Moderne, also known as the Beaubourg, designed by the English architect Richard ROGERS and opened in 1975. It contains works by 20th-cent. artists, including PICASSO, GIACOMETTI, Jackson POLLOCK, Andy WARHOL and Salvador DALI. BRANCUSI's studio has been re-constructed there.

Pompidou Centre

**Ponce** (͵pohsay), city (1980 pop. 161,739), S Puerto Rico. It is an industrial centre and the island's chief Caribbean port. Tourism, sugar refining, and distilling are important. Founded in the early 16th cent., it is one of the oldest cities in the Americas.

**Ponce de León, Juan** (pons də ͵leeon), c.1460–1521, Spanish explorer, discoverer of FLORIDA. He conquered PUERTO RICO in 1508 and was governor from 1509 to 1512. In 1513 he landed in Florida. According to legend, he was seeking a 'fountain of youth'. He returned in 1521 to settle near Tampa Bay but was wounded by Indians. He died soon after in CUBA.

**Ponchielli, Amilcare** (pong,kyellee), 1834–86, Italian composer. He wrote *La Gioconda* (1876) and several other operas.

**pond lily:** see WATER LILY.

**Pons, Lily,** 1904–76, American coloratura soprano; b. France. After 1931 she sang with the METROPOLITAN OPERA and was particularly noted for her performances in DELIBES's *Lakmé* and DONIZETTI's *Daughter of the Regiment.*

**Ponte, Jacopo da:** see BASSANO, JACOPO.

**Pontiac,** fl. 1760–66, chief of the OTTAWA INDIANS. He encouraged opposition to the British, but PONTIAC'S REBELLION was probably the work of other leaders. When the uprising failed (1766), he is said to have gone west and been murdered by ILLINOIS INDIANS, but this account is not generally accepted.

**Pontiac's Rebellion** or **Pontiac's Conspiracy,** 1763–66, Indian uprising against the British at the end of the FRENCH AND INDIAN WARS; named after PONTIAC, chief of the Ottawa Indians. Angry at the British for fortifying and settling Indian lands, the Ottawa and allied tribes terrorized white settlers in W Pennsylvania, Maryland, and Virginia but failed to seize British forts at Detroit and Fort Pitt (now Pittsburgh). After some of his strongest allies sued for peace, Pontiac signed a peace treaty and was pardoned.

**Pontine Marshes,** former marsh and fen of c.50,000 hectares (125,000 acres), near Rome, S central Italy. Unsuccessful attempts were made over many centuries to drain this malarial lowland. After World War I a plan was evolved which brought about reclamation and the settlement of peasant farmers on planned holdings. A new town Littoria, now called Latina, was built to serve the area.

**Pontius Pilate** (ponshəs pielət), fl. AD 26, Roman procurator of JUDAEA (AD 26–36). He was supposedly a ruthless governor. His attempt to evade responsibility in the trial of JESUS was caused by his fear of the chief priests' power and his difficult responsibility for the peace of Palestine. Tradition says he committed suicide at Rome. Mat. 27; John 18; 19.

**Pontoppidan, Henrik** (pawn,tawpidahn), 1857–1943, Danish novelist. His major work, *Lucky Peter* (5 vol., 1898–1904), attacked bourgeois life in Copenhagen. He shared the 1917 Nobel Prize for literature.

**Pontormo, Jacopo da,** 1494–1556, Florentine painter; b. Jacopo Carrucci. One of the creators of MANNERISM, he painted in a nervous, contorted style. His *Deposition* (c.1526; St Felicita, Florence) is famous. He also painted many excellent portraits, including one of Cosimo the Elder (Uffizi, Florence).

**Pontus,** ancient country, NE Asia Minor (now Turkey), on the Black Sea coast. Pontus flourished from the 4th cent. BC. In the 1st cent. BC King MITHRIDATES VI conquered Asia Minor and the Crimea and threatened Greece, but the Romans under POMPEY defeated him in 65 BC. Rome later joined Pontus to the province of Galatia–Cappadocia.

**pony,** small breeds of HORSE, up to approximately 140 cm (56 in) high, noted for hardiness and endurance. They are considered highly intelligent. The various breeds include the Welsh pony, the Welsh cob, the Dales, the Quantock, the Fell, the New Forest, the Exmoor, Dartmoor, and Highland ponies, the Asian desert ponies, the Norwegian, the Connemara, the Australian, and the Shetland pony. The most widely popular is probably the Welsh Mountain pony, about 116 cm (46 in) high, a very old breed of beautiful form, which has been used for breeding crosses all over the world, producing e.g., the Australian pony. The Dartmoor is used for riding, and the Exmoor was used as a chariot pony in Roman times. These two breeds have been used in the production of polo ponies. The Dales, the Fell, the Highlands, and the Welsh cob are examples of small work horses, the Welsh cob having long been used by the army for pack work and hauling gun-carriages. The Shetland pony is one of the purest breeds and is also the smallest, being less than 106 cm (42 in) high. Used as a child's mount, it was bred as a pack animal, and was used extensively as a pit pony after it became illegal for women and children to work underground in mines. There are many crosses between breeds, and also between pony and horse breeds, e.g., the so-called 'riding pony' is the children's version of the hack, obtained by crossing throughbred stallions with pony mares.

**pool:** see BILLIARDS.

**Poole,** town (1981 pop. 122,815), Dorset, SW England, on Poole Harbour, 6 km (4 mi) W of Bournemouth. It is a resort and yachting centre, with industries including boat building and the manufacture of pottery. The port handled 1.5 million tonnes in 1984.

**Poona:** see PUNE.

**poor law:** see SOCIAL WELFARE.

**pop art,** movement that emerged at the end of the 1950s as a reaction againt the seriousness of ABSTRACT EXPRESSIONISM. Pop artists used the imagery of comic strips, soup cans, Coke bottles, and other common images to express abstract formal relationships. Artists such as Roy LICHTENSTEIN and Andy WARHOL attempted to fuse elements of popular and high culture and to erase the boundaries between the two.

**Pope, Alexander,** 1688–1744, English poet. He suffered physical disabilities and was largely self-taught. By age 17 he was regarded as a prodigy. Known for his literary quarrels, Pope nevertheless had many close friends. His interest in Tory politics was strengthened by friendship with SWIFT and by involvement in the SCRIBLERUS CLUB. Pope's poetry falls into three periods. In the first he wrote descriptive poetry, e.g., the *Pastorals* (1709) and *Windsor Forest* (1713); the famous *Essay on Criticism* (1711), defining the doctrine of CLASSICISM; the mock-heroic *Rape of the Lock* (1714), ridiculing fashionable life; and two poems on love, 'Elegy to the Memory of an Unfortunate Lady' and 'Eloise to Abelard'. After 1717, during the second period, his translations of the *Iliad* (1720) and *Odyssey* (1725–26), and his edition of Shakespeare (1725), made him rich. In the last period, living outside London at Twickenham, he wrote moral poems and SATIRES, including *The Dunciad* (1728–43), a mock epic attacking hack writers; *Imitations of Horace* (1733–38), including the 'Epistle to Arbuthnot' (1735), his personal apologia; and the famous *Essay on Man* (1734), summarizing current philosophical speculation. A master craftsman, Pope is now generally regarded as the leading 18th-cent. English poet and as the greatest of all English verse satirists.

**Popish Plot:** see OATES, TITUS.

**poplar,** trees of the genus *Populus.* Members of the WILLOW family with about 30 species in the temperate Northern Hemisphere. They are very fast-growing, and tolerate heavy, damp soils. The seeds are coated with a white, fluffy down, giving them the name of cottonwoods in N America. They are usually grouped as black, white, and balsam poplars, the first two with dark and light grey bark respectively, and the third producing a fragrant resin. The aspen, which is a large tree (*P. tremula*) in N Europe, yields a soft timber which is used for plywood, matches, and box-making. The 'Lombardy poplar', one of the black poplars, is the familiar tall narrow tree often planted as a windbreak or along roadsides in Europe.

**Popocatépetl** (pohpə,katəpetəl, poh'pohkah,taypətəl), [Aztec, = 'smoking mountain'], snow-capped volcano, 5452 m (17,887 ft) high, second highest peak in Mexico. Quiescent since colonial times, the volcano occasionally emits vast clouds of smoke and sulphur fumes.

**Popper, Sir Karl Raimund,** 1902–. British Philosopher; b. Vienna. Professor at the London School of Economics (1949–69), Popper made outstanding contributions to the philosophy of science and politics. He views science as the field where creatively invented hypotheses must offer themselves for empirical disproof by experiment and observation. He powerfully defends the values of liberal democracy against the philosophies based on the thoughts of Plato and of Marx, and particularly criticizes historicism (the view that history unfolds according to fixed and ascertainable laws). His most influential works are *The Logic of Scientific Discovery* (1931), *The Open Society and Its Enemies* (1945), *Objective Knowledge* (1972), and *The Self and its Brain* (with J.C. Eccles, 1977).

**poppy,** name for some members of Papaveraceae, a family composed chiefly of herbs of the Northern Hemisphere, typified by a milky or coloured sap. Many are cultivated for their brilliantly coloured but short-lived blossoms. The true poppy genus, *Papaver,* includes the Oriental poppy (*P. orientale*), bearing a large scarlet flower with a purplish-black base; the corn poppy (*P. rhoeas*); and the Iceland poppy *(P. nudicaule)*. The opium poppy (*P. somniferum*) is the most important species economically. The sap of its unripe seed pods is the source of the narcotics OPIUM, MORPHINE, CODEINE, and HEROIN. Its seed (poppyseed) is not narcotic and is used as birdseed and in baking; oil from the seed is also used in cooking and for paints, soaps, and varnishes. Other genera in the family are also called poppies, e.g., the celandine poppy (*Stylophorum diphyllum*) and the California poppy (*Eschscholtzia californica*).

**popular front,** name given in the 1930s to an alliance of all or most left-wing and centre parties in a European democracy. This policy was adopted by the COMINTERN in 1935, in response to the rise of NAZI Germany. Popular front governments held power intermittently in Spain and in France between 1936 and 1939. The British Labour Party expelled Sir Stafford CRIPPS from membership (temporarily) in Apr. 1939, for advocating a popular front in Britain.

**popular music:** see COUNTRY AND WESTERN MUSIC; FOLK SONG; JAZZ; REGGAE; ROCK MUSIC; SALSA.

**popular sovereignty:** see SQUATTER SOVEREIGNTY.

**population,** in demography, the total number of people within a given area. The world's population was due to pass five billion on 11 July 1987 (United Nations estimate). It has risen to that figure from 2.5 billion in 1950, 3.7 billion in 1970, and 4.4 billion in 1980. However, this growth in population is not evenly distributed. During the period 1980–85, the population of the globe grew at an average rate of 1.7%., that of Africa at 3%, America 1.7%, Asia 1.7%, Europe 0.3%, Oceania 1.5%, and the USSR 1%. World population grew slowly until the middle years of the 17th cent., when a number of factors (decrease in the mean age of marriage, advances in sanitation, ease of transport of food) brought about both increasing birth rates and declining death rates. The resulting surge of population caused MALTHUS to make the gloomy prediction of persistent near-starvation, due to the natural propensity of population growth rates (unless controlled) to increase faster than food supply. Modern opinion is divided as to whether to attribute world famine to overpopulation or to other factors such as mismatch of people and food, lack of conservation and efficient farming methods, system of land tenure, rural poverty and economic underdevelopment in agrarian-based Third World countries. Some demographers predict an end to world population growth in the next 100 years, though the majority believe that such forecasts are unreliable.

**population,** in STATISTICS, the assembly of all possible units or individuals relevant to a particular study. Thus, a population might consist of all the farms in Britain, all of the blood cells on a microscope slide, or all of the individuals in a village, according to the context. The aim of statistical theory is to find an efficient way of determining the characteristics of a population from a SAMPLE of the whole population.

**populations, stellar,** two distributions of star types. Population I stars are recently formed stars (see STELLAR EVOLUTION) that lie mostly on the main sequence of the HERTZSPRUNG–RUSSELL DIAGRAM. They are located in the interstellar dust of the spiral arms of galaxies and in galactic, or open, star CLUSTERS. The older and highly evolved population II stars are formed early in the history of a galaxy from pure hydrogen with a possible admixture of primordial helium. Population II stars are found in the central bulges of galaxies and in globular clusters in the halo surrounding galaxies.

**Populist Party,** American political party expressing the agrarian protest of the late 19th cent., when farmers suffered badly because agricultural prices were declining. Many believed that the federal government's currency policy favoured Eastern banks and industrialists at the expense of farmers and workers. Delegates from farm and labour groups met at Omaha in 1892 and formed the Populist Party. Its platform called for the free coinage of silver, a gradual income tax, public ownership of railways and telegraphs, an 8-hr day for labour, among other reforms. The Populist presidential candidate, James B. WEAVER, won more than 1 million votes in the 1892 election. But after the Democrats adopted free coinage of silver and ran William J. BRYAN for president in 1896, the Populists joined forces with them, thus jeopardizing their independence. After Bryan's defeat agrarian insurgency declined, in part as the result of rising farm prices, and the Populist Party dissolved.

**porcelain,** hard, non-porous, usually white and translucent pottery. First made by the Chinese during the Tang period (AD 618–907), true porcelain was hard-paste (a combination of kaolin, a white clay, and petuntse or chinastone, a feldspathic rock, fired at a high temperature of c.1280–1400°C). It was exported to the Islamic world and highly prized. During the Yuan period (1276–1368) underglaze blue decoration was introduced using cobalt from Iran. From the 15th cent. onwards, on glaze

enamel colours were used as well. In Europe, the earliest porcelain, made at the Medici factory in Florence (1575–87), was soft-paste (clay combined with an artificial compound, e.g., ground glass), which is not so strong as true porcelain. Soft-paste was made by 18th-cent. French factories, notably at SÈVRES; at Capodimonte in Italy; and by most 18th-cent. English factories. True porcelain was first produced in 1709 at MEISSEN, Saxony, and from there the secret of its manufacture spread to elsewhere in Europe. The English strengthened soft-paste with bone ash or with Cornish steatite (soapstone) from c.1749.

**porcupine,** member of either of two RODENT families, characterized by having some of its hairs modified as bristles, spines, or quills. Loosely attached, the quills pull out easily, remaining imbedded in predators that come in contact with them. The OLD WORLD porcupines, found in Africa and Eurasia, are terrestrial. The North American, or Canadian, tree porcupine (*Erethizon dorsatum*) is found in wooded areas over most of North America, excluding the SE US.

**porphyry,** igneous ROCK of large crystals (phenocrysts) embedded in a groundmass. The term refers only to the rock's texture, not to its chemical or mineral composition.

**porpoise,** small WHALE of the family Phocaenidae, distinguished from the DOLPHIN by its smaller size (120–80 cm/4–6 ft) and rounded, beakless head. Black above and white below, porpoises are found in all oceans and prey on fish. The common porpoise (*Phocaena phocaena*) is often seen in British waters. Traditionally it is a 'royal fish' and was offered to the crown if caught. Porpoises and dolphins are often confused, dolphins being called porpoises in N America.

**port:** see WINE.

**Porta, Carlo,** 1775–1821, Italian poet. Unsurpassed in the rich dialect literature of Milan, his work is a humorously realistic portrayal of the city's everyday life under NAPOLEON and, later, the Austrians. It reflects the anticlassical current represented after 1815 by Milan's self-styled Romantics, with whom he was associated. His best-known poem is 'The Appointment of the Chaplain'.

**Port Arthur,** historic ruin 50 km (30 mi) SW of Hobart, Tasmania, Australia. Australia's principal convict settlement (1833–77), it was isolated from the rest of the colony by a narrow sandspit, Eaglehawk Neck, once guarded by savage dogs to prevent the escape of convicts. The settlement was considered the most humanitarian of the penal colonies: floggings were early replaced by solitary confinement, and no executions were recorded as having taken place there. Nearby, spectacular coastal scenery is an added tourist attraction.

**Port Augusta,** city (1986 pop. 15,291), South Australia. Located 320 km (200 mi) N of Adelaide, at the head of Spencer Gulf, the city has become an important railway junction for both passenger and freight services. It is the regional centre for its pastoral hinterland and a major producer of electricity for the state, using brown coal from the Leigh Creek coalfields.

**Port-au-Prince,** city (1982 est. pop. 720,000), SW Haiti, capital of Haiti. The country's largest city, commercial centre, and chief seaport, it is laid out like an amphitheatre around a bay. Founded in 1749 by French sugar planters, it became the colonial capital in 1770, replacing Cap-Haitien. Although it has some manufactures, e.g., cement, food processing, shoes, and textiles, it has remained economically backward and has suffered frequent damage from earthquakes, fires, and civil warfare.

**Port Elizabeth,** city (1987 pop. 510,764), Cape prov., on the southern coast of South Africa. It is the country's main wool-exporting centre and the second major oil-exporting port. An industrial city, its main industries are motor-vehicle assembly, fruit and vegetable canning, and the production of tyres and motor-vehicle components. The town was founded in 1820 by British settlers. It developed on completion of the railway to the Kimberley mining area in 1873.

**porter:** see BEER.

**Porter, Cole,** 1893–1964, American composer and lyricist. He is noted for his witty, sophisticated lyrics and affecting melodies. His MUSICALS include *Kiss Me, Kate* (1948) and *Can-Can* (1953). 'Night and Day', 'Begin the Beguine', and 'Let's Do It' are among his best-known songs.

**Porter, Katherine Anne,** 1890–1980, American author. Her masterful short stories, accomplished in style, form, and language, are included in such volumes as *Flowering Judas* (1930), *Pale Horse, Pale Rider* (1939), and her collected short stories (1965). Her one novel, *Ship of Fools* (1962), is a moral allegory set aboard a German ship in 1931.

**Port Harcourt,** city (1987 est. pop. 296,200), capital of Rivers state, SW Nigeria, on the Bonny R. At the southern end of the Nigerian railway line to KANO, it is a major port and industrial centre. Its economy is based on oil refining, fishing, and the manufacture of glass, petrochemicals, and liquid propane gas. The city was established in 1912 and is named after Sir William Harcourt.

**Port Hedland,** town (1986 pop. 13,069), Western Australia. Located on the Indian Ocean coast, this is one of the major ports handling iron ore from the PILBARA region. It is the third largest port in Australia by tonnage of cargo handled.

**Portland,** US city (1984 est. pop. 366,000), NW Oregon, on the Willamette R.; inc. 1851. Founded in 1845, it grew rapidly as a supply point for western gold fields. The largest city in Oregon and the leading exporting port on the West Coast, it manufactures paper and wood products, electronic instruments, and machinery. The city grew rapidly after 1850, serving as a supply point for the California and Alaska gold fields. The region is noted for its dramatic scenery; Mt Hood is nearby.

**Portland, Isle of,** a limestone peninsula on English Channel coast, in Dorset, SW England, just S of Weymouth. It is connected to the mainland by Chesil Bank (Beach) which is a long ridge of shingle. The southernmost tip is called Portland Bill, where there is a lighthouse. There is a prison on the island, and quarries for the Portland limestone which has been used for many famous buildings, including ST PAUL'S CATHEDRAL, London.

**Port Laois,** county town (1986 pop. 4049), of Co. Laois, Republic of Ireland. Formerly called Maryborough, it is a small industrial town. Industries found here include flour milling, and the manufacture of woollen goods.

**Port Lincoln,** city (1986 pop. 11,552), South Australia. On the W coast of Spencer Gulf, at the S end of Eyre Pensula, the city is a regional centre for sheep and cereal-crop production. The port has large silos for bulk handling of wheat, and is also the base for a major tuna-fishing fleet. It was named in 1802 by Matthew FLINDERS, after his native English county. Considered as a possible site for the capital of the new colony of South Australia in 1836, it was rejected because of its lack of water. A whaling station was set up near here in 1837.

**Port Louis,** city (1983 pop. 148,040), capital of Mauritius, on the Indian Ocean. It is the country's largest city and its economic centre. Its economy is based on its well-sheltered port, which handles the country's international trade. A new terminal was opened in 1980 to facilitate the shipment of sugar, the leading export. Manufactures include cigarettes and rum. Founded by the French in 1735, Port Louis became an important naval base. It is largely populated by descendants of labourers who came from India in the 19th cent. Points of interest include the hilltop citadel (1838).

**Port Moresby,** town (1981 est. pop. 130,000), capital of Papua New Guinea, on the SE coast of the island of NEW GUINEA. It is the nation's largest city and chief port. Port Moresby was founded by Capt. John Moresby, who landed there in 1873. It was the chief Allied base on New Guinea during WORLD WAR II. A new capital centre is being constructed in the suburb of Waigani.

**Pôrto Alegre,** city (1980 pop. 1,114,867), SE Brazil, capital of Rio Grande do Sul state, at the mouth of the Guaíba R. A major commercial centre and the nation's chief river port, it exports agricultural products and has a shipyard and processing industries. It is noted as a cultural and literary centre. Founded c.1742, it is a handsome, modern city, with many colonial and baroque buildings preserved.

**Port of Spain,** city (1987 est. pop. 500,000), capital of Trinidad and Tobago, on the island of Trinidad. The nation's industrial hub and one of the major shipping centres in the Caribbean, it also has fine botanical gardens. It was the capital (1958–62) of the Federation of the WEST INDIES.

**Portolá, Gaspar de** (pawtoh͵lah), fl. 1734–84, Spanish explorer in the Far West. He was sent in 1767 to be governor of the CALIFORNIAS and to expel the Jesuits (see JESUS, SOCIETY OF). He founded SAN DIEGO in 1769 and the mission of San Carlos, in Monterey Bay, in 1770. He was governor of Puebla, Mexico, from 1776 to 1784.

**Porto-Novo,** city (1981 est. pop. 144,000), capital of Benin, a port on the Gulf of Guinea. It is the shipping centre for an agricultural region whose chief product is palm oil (the leading export). The capital of an ancient kingdom in the 16th cent., Porto-Novo became (17th cent.) a Portuguese trading post and a centre of slave trafficking to the Americas. It was taken by the French in 1883 and became the capital of Dahomey (now BENIN) in 1900.

**Port Pirie,** city (1986 pop. 13,960). On the eastern coast of Spencer Gulf, this industrial city forms part of the 'Iron Triangle' with PORT AUGUSTA and WHYALLA. It processes silver, lead, and zinc ore from BROKEN HILL and has the largest lead smelter in the world. The mines and the port were linked in 1880 by tramway to transport the ore. Important as a railway junction with lines of three different gauges, the conversion of interstate lines to one standard gauge has reduced this function. Wheat silos store and ship grain from the surrounding rural areas.

**Port Royal Logic,** a logic manual written by Antoine ARNAULD and Pierre Nicole which was extremely influential throughout the 18th and 19th cent. Published as *Logic, or the Art of Thinking* (1662), it is named after Port Royal, the base of the Jansenists.

**Port Said,** Arab. *Bûr Sa'îd,* city and port (1987 pop. 262,760), N Egypt, on the Mediterranean coast at the northern end of the Suez Canal. It was founded in 1859 with the construction of the Suez Canal. Before the ARAB–ISRAELI WAR in June 1967 it was a major population centre. Although evacuated during the war it is being repopulated.

**Portsmouth,** town (1981 pop. 174,218), Hampshire, S England, on English Channel coast. It is a port town and naval base, with a range of industries. In 1984 the port handled 1.6 million tonnes. The 12th-cent. church of St Thomas became a cathedral in 1927. Charles DICKENS and Isambard BRUNEL were born here.

**Port Sudan,** city (1987 pop. 206,727), NE Sudan on the Red Sea coast. Founded in 1908, it is the country's main port with a major road and oil import pipeline to KHARTOUM. It is the terminus of the railway from the Nile Valley.

**Port Talbot,** town (1981 pop. 40,078) W Glamorgan, S Wales, at mouth of R. Afan on Swansea Bay. It was formed in 1921 from Aberavon and Margam. It is a port and industrial town, whose industries include the manufacture of iron and steel and oil-refining.

**Portugal,** officially the Portuguese Republic, republic (1987 est. pop. 10,400,000), 92,082 km² (35,553 sq mi), SW Europe, on the W Iberian Peninsula; bordered by Spain (E and N) and the Atlantic Ocean (W and S). It includes the MADEIRA ISLANDS and the AZORES in the Atlantic Ocean. Principal cities are LISBON (the capital), OPORTO, COIMBRA, and Setúbal. N Portugal is dominated by mountains and high plateaus, while the south is mostly rolling countryside and plains. The country is crossed by the TAGUS and DOURO rivers. Portuguese agriculture, although noted for its vineyards, olive groves, and almond trees, is backward and inefficient, and half of the country's food is imported. Fishing (tuna and sardines) is important, as are food-processing and the manufacture of textiles, clothing, footwear, and chemicals. There are large forests, and Portugal supplies a major portion of the world's cork. The GNP is $22,490 million and the GNP per capita is $2190 (1983). The great majority of the people are Roman Catholic, and Portuguese is the official language.

*History.* The area that is now Portugal (see LUSITANIA) was conquered (AD c.5) by the Romans, overrun (from the 5th cent.) by Germanic tribes, and taken (711) by the MOORS. Portugal became an independent kingdom in 1139 under ALFONSO I, and with the conquest of Algarve in 1249 by ALFONSO III the last of the Moors were driven out and the kingdom consolidated. The reign of JOHN I (r.1385–1433), founder of the Aviz dynasty, introduced Portugal's glorious period of colonial and maritime expansion; by the 15th cent. the Portuguese empire extended across the world to Asia, Africa, and America. But decline was rapid. In 1580 PHILIP II of Spain seized Portugal, which remained under Spanish rule until a revolt in 1640 established the Braganzas, Portugal's last royal line. In the Napoleonic Wars, French forces occupied Portugal from 1807 to 1811 (see PENINSULAR WAR) and the royal family fled to the Portuguese colony of BRAZIL. In 1822 JOHN VI was forced to accept a liberal constitution, but opposition to the monarchy remained strong and in 1910 a revolution overthrew Manuel II and established a Portuguese republic. A period of great instability ensued. In 1926 a military coup overthrew the government, and in 1932 Antonio de Oliveira SALAZAR became prime minister and virtual dictator of a right-wing corporative state, a position he held until ill health forced his replacement by Marcello Caetano in 1968. Meanwhile, Portugal had become (1949) a founder member of the NORTH ATLANTIC TREATY ORGANIZATION. In 1974 a bloodless military coup led eventually to the restoration of full parliamentary democracy, with the Socialist Party led by Mário SOARES having a pivotal role, although a centre-right coalition came to power in 1985. Soares was elected president in 1986, when Portugal became a member of the EUROPEAN COMMUNITY. Almost all Portuguese overseas territories have become independent, Brazil in 1822, GUINEA-BISSAU in 1974, and ANGOLA, CAPE VERDE, MOZAMBIQUE, and SÃO TOMÉ AND PRINCIPE in 1975. MACAO, on the coast of China, is due to revert to the People's Republic of China in 1999.

Portugal

**Portuguese language,** member of the Romance group of the Italic subfamily of the Indo-European family of languages. See LANGUAGE (table).

**portulaca:** see PURSLANE.

**Posada, José Guadalupe** (poh,sahdhah), 1852–1913, Mexican artist. An enormously popular artist, he strongly influenced the generation of OROZCO and RIVERA. Posada's work is characterized by violent imagery, distortion, caricature, and vigorous lines and contrasts. An ardent opponent of the Porfirio DÍAZ dictatorship, he produced thousands of prints attacking it, which were sold cheaply to the masses.

**Poseidon** (pə,siedən), in Greek mythology, god of the sea, protector of all waters. Powerful, violent, and vengeful, he carried the trident, with which he caused earthquakes. He was the husband of Amphitrite and the father of many sons, most either brutal men (e.g., ORION) or monsters (e.g., POLYPHEMUS). He was also important as Hippios, god of horses, and was the father of PEGASUS. The Romans identified him with NEPTUNE.

**positivism,** in philosophy, a system of thought opposed to METAPHYSICS and maintaining that the goal of knowledge is simply to describe the phenomena experienced. Its basic tenets are contained in the works of Francis BACON, George BERKELEY, and HUME. The term itself was coined by COMTE, whose doctrines influenced the development of much of 19th- and 20th-cent. thinking, especially that of LOGICAL POSITIVISM.

**positron:** see ANTIMATTER; ELECTRON.

**poster,** placard designed to be posted in a public place, often for advertising or propaganda. The invention of printing, particularly LITHOGRAPHY, was of paramount importance to poster art. Poster design requires a clear expression of the idea or product being advanced. The poster must be visible at a distance and comprehensible at a glance. Thus, lines are generally simple, colours few and bold, and lettering kept to a minimum. The advertising poster originated in the 1870s. The poster as art was exploited by many 19th- and 20th-cent. painters, including DAUMIER, MANET, MUCHA, TOULOUSE-LAUTREC and PICASSO. Political posters were important during both world wars, and posters as decoration have been enormously popular since the 1960s.

**Postimpressionism,** term coined by Roger FRY, referring to the work of some late 19-cent. painters who, although they developed their varied styles quite independently, were united in their rejection of IMPRESSIONISM. The four painters who dominated this change of direction were CÉZANNE, SEURAT, VAN GOGH and GAUGUIN; Fry associated with them some of the Fauve (see FAUVISM) and Cubist (see CUBISM) artists. The term is now used widely, to embrace artists in France and elsewhere in Europe who strove to move beyond Impressionism.

**postmodernism,** in architecture, international movement that emerged in the 1960s and became prominent in the late 1970s and early 1980s. A reaction to the orthodoxy and austerity of the INTERNATIONAL STYLE, it is characterized by the incorporation of historical details, use of decorative structural elements, a more personal and exaggerated style, and some reference to popular modes of building. Postmodernism was greatly affected by the writings of Robert VENTURI. The style is evident in his buildings and in those of such architects as Denise Scott Brown and Robert Stern, and in the later work of Philip Johnson.

**Post Office,** a government department or authority in many countries responsible for postal services and often telecommunications. In England a Master of Post was first appointed in 1516 to operate postal services out of London, but the first genuinely public service was not established until 1635 under a royal proclamation 'for the settling of the letter-office in England and Scotland'. The post office developed almost without competition as a state monopoly. By the 18th cent. financial services were also being provided and in 1861 the Post Office Savings Bank (see NATIONAL SAVINGS BANK) was founded; two decades later postal orders were introduced. By the 20th cent. the role of the post office had increased markedly and when they were introduced, it was charged with responsibility for paying out social-security benefits and collecting revenue for state insurance schemes. In 1968 the financial services offered by the Post Office took on a new importance with the introduction of the National Girobank which facilitated the transmission of money through post offices. In 1969 the Post Office became a public corporation, having previously been a government department. In 1981 the activities of the Post Office were divided into two with telecommunications being administered separately from postal and banking services. In 1984 the privatization of the telecommunications part of the business, including telephone services, led to the creation of British Telecom.

**postulate:** see AXIOM.

**potassium** (K), metallic element, discovered in 1807 by Sir Humphry DAVY, who decomposed potash with an electric current. One of the ALKALI METALS, it is soft, silver-white, and extremely reactive. Potassium is the seventh most abundant element in the earth's crust and the sixth most abundant of the elements in solution in the oceans. It is an essential nutrient for plants and animals. Potassium compounds are used in fertilizers, soaps, explosives, glass, and baking powder, and in tanning and water purification. See ELEMENT (table); PERIODIC TABLE.

**potassium nitrate:** see SALTPETRE.

**potato,** tuber-bearing herb, *Solanum tuberosum*, of the family Solanaceae, of great importance as a staple crop in many parts of the world. Related species of the potato were first cultivated in the Andes and the common species has its origin in Peru and Bolivia near Lake Titicaca. It was brought to Europe at the end of the 16th cent. The aerial stems are hollow in the older parts, and triangular in cross-section, and the mature leaves are compound. What is normally considered as the root system is actually part of the stem below ground which produces branches from the axils of scale-leaves, terminating in the tuber as a swelling. The true, fibrous roots arise from these branches. The tuber is a means of vegetative reproduction, storing food for the new growth. Some varieties do not flower. A potato variety, e.g., King Edward, Wilja, is a CLONE, every plant bearing the varietal name being vegetatively produced from a single original plant. Varieties are grouped as *early*, *second early*, and as *early* and *late maincrop*, according to the time of maturation of the tubers. This is controlled by the length of day, which acts as an environmental signal causing the initiation of tubers underground. Breeding material is obtained from S America, where many wild species exist.

**potato blight:** see BLIGHT; MILDEW.

**Potemkin, Grigori Aleksandrovich,** 1729–91, Russian field marshal and favourite of CATHERINE II. He took part in the coup that made Catherine czarina (1762) and was created count for serving in her first war with Turkey (1768–74). Her lover for a time, he remained one of her chief advisers, encouraging her in an unsuccessful plan to break up the OTTOMAN EMPIRE and reestablish a Christian empire in the conquered region. For his part in annexing the Crimea (1783) he was created prince and appointed governor of the new province, which he administered ably.

**potential, electric,** work per unit electric charge expended in moving a charged body from a reference point to any given point in an electric field. The potential at the reference point is considered to be zero, while the reference point itself is usually chosen to be at infinity. The change in potential associated with moving a charged body is independent of the actual path taken and depends only on the initial and final points. Potential is measured in VOLTS and is sometimes called voltage. See also ELECTRIC CIRCUIT; ELECTROMOTIVE FORCE.

**potential energy:** see ENERGY.

**potentiometer** or **voltage divider,** manually adjustable variable electrical resistor that has a RESISTANCE element attached to an ELECTRIC CIRCUIT by three contacts, or terminals. The ends of the resistance element are attached to the two input voltage conductors of the circuit, and the third contact, attached to the output of the circuit, is usually a movable terminal that slides across the resistance element, dividing it into two resistors. Because the position of the movable terminal determines what percentage of the input voltage (see POTENTIAL, ELECTRIC) is applied to the circuit, a potentiometer can be used to vary the magnitude of the voltage, e.g., in radio-volume and television-brightness controls.

**Potiphar:** see JOSEPH.

**potlatch,** lavish ceremonial feast among Northwest Coast tribes (see NORTH AMERICAN INDIANS), at which the host distributed valuable gifts to guests to earn prestige. Recipients were obliged to reciprocate with more lavish gifts at a future potlatch. It is the most famous example of the form of prestige EXCHANGE characteristic of many CHIEFDOMS. See also RECIPROCITY.

**Potomac,** scenic river of the E US, flowing 459 km (285 mi) SE from the vicinity of Cumberland, Maryland, to the Chesapeake Bay. Washington, DC, just below the Great Falls, is the head of navigation.

**Potosí,** city (1982 est. pop. 103,100) S Bolivia, capital of Potosí dept. Built at an altitude of c.4200 m (13,780 ft) in the ANDES Mts, it is one of the highest cities in the world. It was founded in 1545 at the foot of one of the richest ore mountains ever discovered. By the late 16th cent., with a population of over 100,000, it was the largest city in the western hemisphere. Its silver mines were eclipsed by more accessible ones in Peru and Mexico after 1600, but modern technology has again made the area a source of silver, as well as of tin, lead, zinc, and copper.

**Potsdam,** city (1984 pop. 137,666), central East Germany. An industrial centre producing processed foods, textiles, pharmaceuticals, and other goods, it is also the centre of the East German film industry. It was the chief residence of FREDERICK II of Prussia, who built (1745–47) the palace and park of Sans Souci. The city was badly damaged in WORLD WAR II. The Potsdam Conference (1945) was held there by the Allies.

**Potsdam Conference,** meeting (17 July–2 Aug 1945), of the principal Allies of WORLD WAR II (the US, the USSR, the UK) to clarify and implement agreements previously reached at the YALTA CONFERENCE. The chief participants were Pres. TRUMAN, Premier STALIN, and Prime Min. CHURCHILL (who was replaced by ATTLEE after Churchill's Conservative Party lost the British election). The resulting Potsdam Agreement established four-power (American, British, Russian, French) occupation zones for postwar Germany. A comprehensive reordering of the German economy and German institutions was part of the agreement. The Council of FOREIGN MINISTERS was established to consider peace settlements. The conference issued an ultimatum to Japan either to surrender or risk total destruction. The rift between the USSR and the Western Allies caused the Potsdam Agreement to be consistently breached, which was an early manifestation of the COLD WAR.

**Potter, Beatrix,** 1866–1943, English author and illustrator. Her unsentimental, humorous animal stories, with her own drawings and watercolours, include *The Tale of Peter Rabbit* (1901) and *The Tailor of Gloucester* (1902).

**Potteries, The,** district in N Staffordshire, W Midlands of England, in the upper TRENT valley, famous for its manufacture of pottery. It contains the towns of STOKE-ON-TRENT and Newcastle-under-Lyme. The pottery industry here dates from the late 18th cent. when Josiah WEDGWOOD established a factory at Etruria. The industry was based upon the local reserves of coal and clays.

**pottery,** utensils made of clay hardened by heat. It is of three main types: earthenware, stoneware, and porcelain. When heated above 500°C raw clay becomes porous earthenware. Unlike sun-dried clay, it retains a permanent shape and does not disintegrate in water. STONEWARE is made by raising the temperature to c.1200–1400°C, and PORCELAIN is fired at still higher temperature of c.1280–1450°C which makes the clay glassy (vitrified) and adds strength. Pottery is shaped while the clay is in its plastic form. It can be hand-built, either by pinching the clay into shape, or by coiling rolls of clay. Alternatively, it can be thrown on a potter's wheel (adopted in Mesopotamia by c.3000 BC and in Ancient Egypt by c.2500 BC). It can also be formed by pressing the clay into or over a mould, or by pouring liquid slip into a plaster of Paris mould, a process adopted in England c.1740–45. After drying to a leather-like hardness, the piece is fired in a KILN. The desired finish or glaze, and the type of decoration, determine the number of firings. All three types of pottery may be left unglazed, in which case earthenware and porcelain are described as biscuit, and stoneware as dry-bodied. Earthenware is usually lead-glazed or tin-glazed; stoneware is salt-glazed; and porcelain can have either lead-glaze or feldspathic glaze, depending on whether it is soft-paste or hard-paste. Lead is injurious to health and since the early 19th cent. various glazes have been developed which do not use it. In most parts of the world pottery was one of the earliest crafts. Prehistoric remains of pottery are therefore of great importance in ARCHAEOLOGY. Notable pottery of the ancient civilizations includes Greek vases of c.800–350 BC; Roman Arretine and Samian ware of the late 1st cent. BC to early 4th cent. AD; Chinese pottery and porcelain of the Tang period, AD 618–906; and pre-Columbian pottery of South America, e.g., Mochica wares of the 7th cent. AD. The Islamic Middle East produced outstanding pottery from the 9th to 14th cent. AD. Earthenware (lead-glazed or tin-glazed) and stoneware were the main types of European pottery until the 18th cent. when porcelain factories became widespread. Medieval pottery was utilitarian, e.g., culinary vessels, jugs, and floor tiles. Plates and dishes did not come into general use until the 15th and 16th cent. when services of MAIOLICA began to be made for the upper classes. Imports of Oriental porcelain increased during the 17th cent., creating a mania for porcelain and stimulating efforts to emulate it. However, even after the establishment of European factories, porcelain remained a luxury far beyond the pockets of the masses. Tin-glazed imitations were widely available, e.g., from Delft. In the mid 18th cent. English potters developed white salt-glazed stoneware and cream-coloured earthenware which were attractive alternatives and introduced transfer-printed decoration. During the 19th and 20th cent. pottery manufacture has gradually become mechanized or machine-assisted. Transfers have largely replaced hand-painting, but traditional methods have been retained for high-quality tableware, ornaments and figures. Manufacturers have had to adapt their goods to changing economic and social conditions, e.g., informal meals and the use of dishwashers. New products include oven-to-table, and microwave oven ware, which have glazes and decoration able to withstand high temperatures and detergents. Industralization has been countered by the studio pottery movement (see Bernard LEACH) which has encouraged the revival of traditional techniques in Europe, America, Australia, and elsewhere.

**Poujadism,** populist, but essentially conservative political tendency, espoused by the petit bourgeoisie in some W European countries since the 1950s, encompassing opposition to state power and taxation and to large-scale economic development. The tendency takes its name from Pierre Poujade, whose Union for the Defence of Small Shopkeepers and Artisans obtained over 12% of the vote in the 1956 French parliamentary elections. Although Poujadism declined as an organized force in France, similarly oriented parties have since made an impact in other countries, notably in Scandinavia.

**Poulenc, Francis** (poo,lanhk), 1899–1963, French composer and pianist, one of 'les SIX'. His lyrical, spontaneous works include piano pieces, e.g., *Mouvements perpetuels* (1918); songs; the ballet *Les Biches* (1923); chamber music; the Mass in G (1937); and operas, e.g., *Dialogue des Carmélites* (1957).

**poultry,** domestic BIRDS generally raised for food as eggs or meat. The group comprises the comb-bearers (e.g., CHICKEN, TURKEY, PHEASANT, and PEACOCK), the swimmers (e.g., DUCK, GOOSE, and SWAN), and the doves (see PIGEON).

**pound:** see ENGLISH UNITS OF MEASUREMENT; WEIGHTS AND MEASURES (table).

**Pound, Ezra Loomis,** 1885–1972, American poet, one of the most influential and controversial figures in 20th-cent. poetry. In 1907 he left the US for Europe, eventually settling in England. There he led the IMAGISTS before founding VORTICISM, and there he encouraged and influenced other writers such as T. S. ELIOT and James JOYCE. In 1920 he moved to Paris; by 1925 he was settled in Italy, where he developed many of the economic theories that led him to broadcast Fascist propaganda during World War II. Indicted for treason after the war, he was confined to a US mental hospital (1946–58). On his release he returned to Italy. Pound's major poems are 'Homage to Sextus Propertius' (1918); *Hugh Selwyn Mauberley* (1920); and the *Cantos* (1925–60), a brilliant, often obscure, epic that weaves together many diversified cultural threads in an attempt to reconstruct the history of civilization. He is also noted for his varied translations from many languages.

**Poussin, Nicolas** (pooh,sanh), 1594–1665, French painter. Although he spent most of his life in Italy, his painting became the standard for French classical art. He travelled to Italy in 1624, where he settled in Rome and studied the Antique. For a brief period the style of contemporary baroque painters influenced Poussin, e.g., *Martyrdom of St Erasmus* (1629; Vatican). The works of TITIAN and VERONESE influenced his choice of mythological and bacchic subjects: his preoccupation with the works of antiquity and of RAPHAEL resulted in a new clarity of composition, e.g., *Adoration of the Magi* (1633; Dresden). He also became interested in the philosophical possibilities of painting, and this intellectualization influenced painting far into the 19th cent. As first painter to LOUIS XIII, he administered the decoration of the Great Gallery of the LOUVRE. In his later works he emphasized the contemplative aspects of his subject. In such works as the *Death of Phocion* (1648) he constructed a classical landscape ordered with mathematical precision. Of his last works, the four paintings in the series *The Four Seasons* (1660–64; Louvre, Paris) are the most imposing.

**poverty, culture of,** concept developed by O. LEWIS, and very influential in the US in the 1960s and 70s, that poverty generates its own way of life, characterized by fragile sexual relations, psychological stress, apathy, weak family structure, etc. This way of life is passed on through families over generations. Poverty in this perspective is thus seen as self-perpetuating, a question of attitudes, not of structures of inequality.

**Powell, Anthony,** 1905–, English novelist. In his 12-volume series *A Dance to the Music of Time,* which begins with *A Question of Upbringing* (1951) and ends with *Hearing Secret Harmonies* (1975), he provides a panoramic look at English upper- and middle-class life over a 60-year period.

**Powell, Enoch,** 1912–, British politician. In 1950 he won a seat in parliament and later (1960–63) became minister of health. However, following a controversial speech on immigration in 1968, he was ejected from Edward HEATH's shadow cabinet.

**Powell, John Wesley,** 1834–1902, American geologist and ethnologist. Noted for his explorations of the western US, he made a survey of the Colorado R. in 1869, passing through the Grand Canyon by boat, a hazardous feat described in his *Explorations of the Colorado River* (1875). His efforts helped establish the US Geological Survey, which he headed from 1881 to 1894.

Nicolas **Poussin,** *The Ashes of Phocion Collected by his Widow.* Walker Art Gallery, Liverpool.

**Powell, Michael,** 1905–, British film director. His conservative, romantic films all demonstrate a perfect use of cinematic expression in colour, movement, framing, and editing. Between 1942 and 1956 his films were co-directed, co-produced and co-written with Emeric Pressburger. His films include *The Life and Death of Colonel Blimp* (1943), *I Know Where I'm Going* (1945), *Black Narcissus* (1947), and *Peeping Tom* (1960).

**power,** in physics, the time rate of doing WORK or of producing or expending ENERGY. The SI unit of power (see METRIC SYSTEM) is the watt (W), which equals 1 joule per second. It is also the amount of power that is delivered to a component of an electric circuit when a current of 1 ampere flows through the component and a voltage of 1 volt exists across it. The imperial unit is the horsepower, which equals 745.7 watts.

**power, electric,** rate, per unit of time, at which electric ENERGY is consumed or produced. Electric POWER is usually measured in watts or kilowatts (1000 watts). The energy supplied by a current to an appliance enables it to work or to provide other forms of energy such as light or heat. The amount of electric energy an appliance uses is found by multiplying its power rating by the operating time. Units of electric energy are usually watt-seconds (joules), watt-hours, or kilowatt-hours (the choice for commercial applications). Generally, practical electric-power-generating systems convert mechanical energy into electric energy (see GENERATOR). Whereas some electric plants obtain mechanical energy from moving water (water power or hydroelectric power), the vast majority derive it from heat engines in which the working substance is steam generated by heat from combustion of fossil fuels or nuclear reactions (see NUCLEAR ENERGY; NUCLEAR REACTOR). Although the conversion of mechanical energy to electric energy may approach 100% efficiency, the conversion of heat to mechanical energy is about 41% efficient for a fossil-fuel plant and about 30% for a nuclear plant. It is thought that a magnetohydrodynamic generator, which operates by using directly the kinetic energy of gases produced by combustion, would have an efficiency of about 50%. Although FUEL CELLS develop electricity by direct conversion of hydrogen, hydrocarbons, alcohol, or other fuels, with an efficiency of 50 to 60%, their high cost has restricted their use to space programmes. SOLAR ENERGY has been recognized as a feasible power source. It can be exploited by using wind TURBINES, PHOTOVOLTAIC CELLS, and heat engines, as well as by using hydroelectric power plants. Research and development is bringing down the costs. An important problem in utilizing solar energy is related to the variable nature of sunlight and wind. To minimize energy losses from heating of conductors and to economize on the material needed for conductors, electricity is usually transmitted at the highest voltages possible. As the modern TRANSFORMER is virtually loss free, the necessary steps upwards or downwards in voltage are easily accomplished. Electricity is distributed from the major power stations to substations in each area, and from there to small substations which supply houses and industry, although some large factories will take their supply directly from the larger substations. The main power stations are tied together by transmission lines into a country-wide network (the national grid). They are thus able to exchange power, so that an area with low power demand can assist another with a high demand. See also ENERGY, SOURCES OF.

**Powhatan Confederacy,** group of 30 NORTH AMERICAN INDIAN tribes of Algonquian stock (see AMERICAN INDIAN LANGUAGES). The Powhatan lived in 200 palisaded settlements along coastal Virginia and Chesapeake Bay, hunting, fishing, and raising corn. Chief Powhatan, or Wahunsonacock, was head of the confederacy when JAMESTOWN was settled in 1607. The English seized his best land, but secured peace through John ROLFE's marriage (1614) to Powhatan's daughter POCAHONTAS. In 1622 Powhatan's successor, Opechancanough, attacked the English, killing 350; he was murdered after leading a last uprising (1644). After 1722 the tribes mixed with the settlers, and the confederacy disappeared. Their descendants include the Chickahominy and other small tribes of the Virginia and Chesapeake area.

**Powys,** county in E central Wales (1983 est. pop. 110,600), 5077 km² (1960 sq mi), situated on the English border. It was formed in 1974 in the reorganization of local government from the counties of Breconshire, Montgomeryshire, and Radnorshire. In the S are the Brecon Beacons and the Black Mts. The principal rivers of the county are the Wye, the USK, and the Vyrnwy (a tributary of the SEVERN). Agricultural, dairy cattle, and sheep farming are important, as well as afforestation and tourism. The major towns of the county are service and light industry centres. Llandrindod Wells is the administrative centre.

**Powys, John Cowper,** 1872–1963, English lecturer and author. A romantic and visionary writer, his novels include *Wolf Solent* (1929), and *A Glastonbury Romance* (1932). He was also a poet and critic. His brother Theodore Francis Powys, 1875–1953, wrote novels of Dorsetshire life, among them *Mr. Weston's Good Wine* (1927). Another brother, Llewellyn Powys, 1884–1939, expressed a rational yet poetic outlook in such writings as *Earth Memories* (1934).

**Poznań** (ˌpoznanyə), Ger. *Posen,* city (1984 pop. 571,000), W central Poland, on the Warta R. It is a port and producer of machinery and chemicals. Founded by the 10th cent., it passed to Prussia (1793, 1815) before reverting (1919) to Poland. In 1956 labour unrest in Poznań spread to other cities, leading to major political changes in Poland. The city possesses a Gothic cathedral and a 16th-cent. city hall.

**Pr,** chemical symbol of the element PRASEODYMIUM.

**Prado,** Madrid, national Spanish museum of painting and sculpture, one of the finest in Europe. Situated on the Paseo del Prado, it was begun by the architect Juan de Villanueva in 1785 for Charles III, as a museum of natural history, and finished under Ferdinand VII. It was maintained by the royal family and called the Royal Museum until 1868, when it became national property. The Prado has priceless masterpieces from the Spanish, Flemish, and Venetian schools, e.g., works by El GRECO, GOYA, RUBENS, and TITIAN.

**praetor** or **pretor,** in ancient Rome, a magistrate. In 242 BC two praetors were appointed; the urban praetor decided cases in which citizens were parties, and the peregrine praetor decided cases between foreigners.

**Praetorians,** bodyguard of the ancient Roman emperors, formally organized in the time of AUGUSTUS from the troop that had guarded the general commanding in Rome. They attended the emperor wherever he went, had special privileges, and in times of trouble chose many of the emperors. CONSTANTINE I disbanded them in 312.

**pragmatic sanction,** decision of state dealing with a matter of great importance. The **Pragmatic Sanction of Bourges,** issued by CHARLES VII of France in 1438, sharply limited papal power over the church in France. It began a long period of tense relations between church and state in France. There have been many pragmatic sanctions, but, when used alone, the term always refers to the **Pragmatic Sanction,** 1713, issued by Holy Roman Emperor CHARLES VI, whereby all the HAPSBURG lands would be inherited by his daughter, MARIA THERESA (but not the imperial dignity, which was elective). Owing to a long campaign by the emperor, most of the European powers accepted the sanction; the major exception was the Bavarian elector (later Emperor CHARLES VII), who was married to one of the Hapsburg princesses passed over in favor of Maria Theresa. In spite of the guarantees her father had obtained, when Maria Theresa acceded to the Hapsburg succession in 1740, she had to defend her rights in a long and bitter struggle, the war of the AUSTRIAN SUCCESSION. (1740–48). The treaty of Aix-la-Chapelle (1748) confirmed the Pragmatic Sanction.

**pragmatism,** method of philosophy in which the truth of a proposition is measured by its correspondence with experimental results and by its practical outcome. Thus pragmatists hold that truth is modified as

discoveries are made and that it is relative to time and place and purpose of inquiry. C.S. PEIRCE and William JAMES were the originators of the system, which influenced John DEWEY and more recently QUINE.

**Prague,** Czech *Praha,* city (1984 pop. 1,186,000), capital and largest city of Czechoslovakia, on both banks of the Vltava R. It is a port, an industrial centre producing cars, machinery, and other manufactures, and one of Europe's great historic cities. A trading centre by the 10th cent., it became the capital of BOHEMIA and was later (14th–17th cent.) one of the residences of the emperors of the HOLY ROMAN EMPIRE. The religious reformer Jan HUSS taught at its university (est. 1348). HABSBURG rule began in 1526. Prague figured prominently in the THIRTY YEARS WAR (1618–48), the War of the AUSTRIAN SUCCESSION (1740–48), the SEVEN YEARS WAR (1756–63), and the REVOLUTIONS OF 1848. In 1918 it became the capital of the new Czechoslovak republic. It was occupied (1939–45) by the Germans during World War II. In 1968 Prague was the centre of Czech resistance to the Soviet invasion. The old section is an architectural treasure, the site of such buildings as Hradčany Castle (14th cent.) and the Gothic Cathedral of St Vitus. The city's cultural tradition is typified by such figures as KEPLER, SMETANA, DVOŘÁK, KAFKA, and ČAPEK.

**Prague Linguistic Circle,** also known as the 'Prague School', a group of linguists who met regularly from 1926 until the beginning of World War II. They developed a particular view of linguistics which centred around the function of units of language and their relations within the overall system. Their influence on the development of postwar linguistics has been profound both in Europe and the US. Notable members of this group were Nikolaj TRUBETZKOY and Roman JAKOBSON.

**Praia,** city and port (1986 est. pop. 49,500), capital of CAPE VERDE.

**prairie dog:** see GROUND SQUIRREL.

**prairies,** generally level, originally grass-covered and treeless plains of N America, stretching from Ohio to the Great Plains. They correspond to the PAMPAS and LLANOS of South America, the STEPPE of Eurasia, and the high VELD of South Africa. Often called the vanishing grasslands, prairies are among the most productive agricultural regions.

**Prakrit** (ˌprahkrit), any number of languages belonging to the Indic group of the Indo-Iranian subfamily of the Indo-European family of languages. See LANGUAGE (table).

**Pram Factory, the,** location of the Australian Performing Group in Melbourne, 1970–80. This collective was successful in laying the foundations for a theatre built upon the Australian idiom. Radical in politics and practice, it ran as a cooperative with writers, actors, and directors changing roles. The playwrights Jack HIBBERD, John ROMERIL, David WILLIAMSON, and the comic Max Gillies, were among those associated with it.

**praseodymium** ('prayzi·oh,dimi·əm) (Pr), metallic element, discovered in 1855 by C.A. von Welsbach. One of the RARE-EARTH METALS in the LANTHANIDE SERIES, it is soft, silver-yellow, malleable, and ductile. Its compounds are used in carbon electrodes for arc lighting and to colour enamel and glass. See ELEMENT (table); PERIODIC TABLE.

**prawn,** name originally given to a CRUSTACEAN in the family Palaemonidae, about 6 cm (2½ in) long, found round European coasts, but now applied to several similar marine crustaceans. The original prawn (*Palaemon (Leander) serratus*) is a scavenger, walking on the sea bed or swimming through the sea backwards, using its flapped tail for propulsion. It is a popular food both with aquatic animals and with humans. It is fished commercially, and frozen for marketing. The 'Dublin Bay prawn' is a LOBSTER.

**Praxiteles** (prakˌsitəleez), fl. c.370–330 BC, famous Attic sculptor. His *Hermes with the Infant Dionysus* (museum; Olympia) is the only undisputed extant original by any of the ancient masters. Copies of his most renowned statues, e.g., the *Aphrodite of Cnidus* (Vatican), *Apollo Sauroctonus* (Vatican), and *Apollino* (Florence), illustrate his choice of youthful gods and other beings in which joy of life finds expression. In its delicate, perfect modelling and strength of conception, his treatment of marble is unsurpassed.

**prayer,** in Judaism, spiritual communion with God. While the early biblical patriarchs offered up prayers, these took the form of pleas for the fulfilment of purely personal wishes. Communal prayer only developed during the period of the first Temple as part of the sacrificial ritual. It was with the rise of the institution of the SYNAGOGUE that daily prayer became widespread. It was ultimately made statutory in the early rabbinic period (1st cent. AD). The central prayer of all services is the *Amidah* (Standing Prayer) which is a succession of 19 blessings incorporating praise and thanksgiving, as well as petition for a variety of personal and national needs. The basic services comprise: *shahrit* (the morning service), *Minhah* (the afternoon service) and *Ma'ariv* (the evening service). On Sabbaths and Holydays a *musaf* (additional service) is added. Public worship in a synagogue requires a quorum of 10 males over the age of BAR MITZVAH. Where this cannot be achieved, those present pray silently and individually, omitting the congregational responses.

The **praying mantis** (*Mantis religiosa*) guages its distance and prepares to seize the fly.

**Precambrian time** or **Precambrian era**: see GEOLOGICAL ERAS (table).

**precedent,** in COMMON LAW, a past decision of a superior court, which must be followed by a lower court in future cases of similar facts. Precedent is used to achieve certainty in the law. In order to operate, there must exist a hierarchal court system (see COURT SYSTEM IN ENGLAND AND WALES) and a system of law reporting, so that past cases can be read and followed. In the 19th cent. precedent was rigidly adhered to by the English courts. However, it was increasingly felt that this led to both injustice for individuals and to the law becoming out of touch with society. As a result, the judges are now more willing to depart from previous decisions.

**precession,** in mechanics, the motion of the axis of rotation of a spinning object (e.g., a GYROSCOPE) under the influence of an external force in which it sweeps out a conical shape.

**precession of the equinoxes,** westward motion of the EQUINOXES along the ECLIPTIC. The precession, first noted (c. 120 BC) by HIPPARCHUS and explained (1687) by Isaac NEWTON, is primarily due to the gravitational attraction of the Moon and Sun on the Earth's equatorial bulge, which causes the Earth's axis to describe a cone in somewhat the same fashion as a spinning top. As a result, the equinoxes, which lie at the intersections of the celestial equator and the ecliptic, move on the celestial sphere (see ASTRONOMICAL COORDINATE SYSTEMS). Similarly, the celestial poles move in circles on the celestial sphere, so that at various times different stars occupy positions at or near one of these poles (see POLARIS). After about 26,000 years the equinoxes and poles lie again at nearly the same points on the celestial sphere. The gravitational influences of the other planets cause a much smaller amount of precession.

*Hermes with the Infant Dionyses* by **Praxiteles**, Museum, Olympia, Greece.

**praying mantis** or **mantis,** fairly small to large (18–105 mm/¾–4 in), rather elongate carnivorous INSECT, so called because of the habit of standing in wait for prey with its front legs folded and held together, in an attitude of prayer. Mantids have widely spaced eyes to help them accurately judge their distance from their prey. When a suitably-sized insect comes within range, the substantial spiny front legs are shot out and the prey is trapped as they are snapped shut. It is then eaten voraciously; males of some species suffer the same fate, immediately after mating. Most mantids are an inconspicuous green or mottled brown, but some tropical species are brightly coloured, with extensions to legs and body, giving them a flower-like appearance. Some of the camouflaged mantids have distinctively coloured hind wings, often with a conspicuous 'eye-spot', to distract larger predators.

**prazo,** estate owned by a Portuguese merchant, trader or farmer in colonial Mozambique from the mid 16th cent. The owner of a prazo was a *prazero* and by the 19th cent. had become virtually an independent ruler dependent largely upon slavery and slave-trading for his existence. Prazeros fought among themselves and with other African rulers for supremacy and were only made subject to the authority of Lisbon in the 20th cent.

**precipitate,** a solid obtained by precipitation, i.e., the separation of a substance from a SUSPENSION, sol (see COLLOID), or SOLUTION. In a suspension, such as sand in water, the solid spontaneously precipitates (settles out) on standing. In a sol the particles are precipitated by coagulation. A solute may be precipitated by evaporation or by the addition of a compound that reacts with the solute to form an insoluble precipitate. In each case, the precipitate formed may settle out spontaneously or may be collected by filtration or centrifugation.

**pre-Columbian art and architecture.** The remarkable cultural achievement of the pre-Columbian civilizations of Latin America was first recognized in Europe in the early 16th cent., when the Spanish conquerors arrived on American shores. In Mexico, the AZTEC state was at the height of its power and still expanding. The Spanish accounts mention the dramatic architecture of Tenochtitlan, the Aztec capital, where stepped temples formed a backdrop to religious ceremony, such as human sacrifice. Altars were adorned with sculpted stone images of the gods and representations of animals of astounding detail. Many of the beautiful examples of worked gold, cut stones, featherwork and intricate weaving in the Aztec centre were tribute payments from subjugated peoples. Artistic techniques and iconographic traditions of the era represented the culmination of the influence of previous civilizations. The

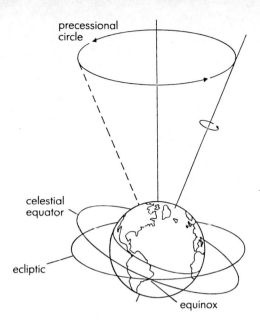

**Precession of the equinoxes** (the points at which the Earth's celestial equator intersects its ecliptic) is due to the slow rotation of the Earth's axis around a perpendicular to the ecliptic.

OLMEC of the Gulf coast were one of the earliest cultural groups to have widespread impact in Central America. Archaeological evidence shows that from about 800 to 400 BC the Olmec were building their ceremonial centres with features such as pyramids, plazas, and ball courts. Monumental sculpted heads of basalt were erected at such sites as La Venta and San Lorenzo. Glyphic inscriptions also appear at this time, the earliest possibly from Monte Alban, Oaxaca, apparently under Olmec influence. It may have been from these roots that the MAYA developed their complex writing and arithmetical system. In the Maya Classic era (300–900 AD), stone stelae were inscribed with the dates of the long count, a calendrical system which could compute thousands of years into the past and future. From the magnificent centres of Palenque, Yaxchilan, and Tikal, caches of beautifully carved jades and painted polychrome vessels have been excavated. Walls are decorated with stucco or painted fresco and facades adorned with limestone sculptures. Evidence of cultural exchange through trade and influence is found as far away as Teotihuacan in Central Mexico. This centre, with its huge pyramids and ceremonial roadways, flourished until about 600 AD. Later the TOLTEC of Tula were to dominate the central region. In the 10th cent. they infiltrated the post-Classic Maya area of Yucatan. At Chichen Itza depictions of Toltec warriors are moulded in stucco on the temple walls. Distinctive artistic and architectural styles were also found among other cultural groups, for example, the dramatic Zapotec centre of Monte Alban, Oaxaca or the MIXTEC centre of Mitla where exquisite gold and jade jewellery was buried with the dead. From the western stages of Nayarit and Colima, ceramic animals and human figures have been excavated. These often have humorous expressions and poses although they also have supernatural connotations. Further south in Latin America, local cultures produced a multitude of different textiles and crafts. Goldworking dates as far back as the 1st millenium BC with the Chavin culture of Peru. In Columbia, complicated techniques of CIRE PERDUE casting and working with copper and gold alloy were developed. The beautiful figurative vessels of the Darien culture or the pectorals from Calima attest to the craftsmen's skill. Dominant iconographic traditions reappear in a variety of mediums. In southern Peru, beautiful woven textiles were found wrapped around the bodies buried in the tombs of Paracas, over 2000 years ago. The dramatic pottery of NAZCA culture (100–800 AD) in this region depicts the same stylized animal forms as the famous Nazca lines drawn in the desert sand. In the North, the Mochica people produced ceramic effigy vessels with representations of men, birds, animals, and plants. They were also accomplished builders and the Mochica Pyramid of the Sun is the largest in South America. Of the numerous impressive centres, the stonework of the INCA fortresses such as Sacshisaman, Ollantaytambo, and Machu Picchu is unsurpassed. Inca

goldwork was also of the finest, although most of the delicate representations of birds, butterflies, animals, and plants were removed and smelted down by the Spanish conquerors in the 16th cent.

**predator,** an animal that hunts and kills other animals for food. Predators may be as small as a dragonfly larva or a shrew or as large as a killer whale or a tiger. Predators play an important role in controlling the population size of their prey, and the number of predators in an area is controlled by the numbers of prey animals, shown by cyclic increases and decreases in predator populations, echoing similar changes in the prey.

**predestination,** in theology, doctrine that asserts that God predestines from eternity the salvation of certain souls. So-called double predestination, as in Calvinism, is the added assertion that God also fore-ordains certain souls to damnation. Based on the omniscience and omnipotence of God, predestination is closely related to the doctrines of divine providence and grace. The traditional churches teach that predestination is consistent with FREE WILL since God moves the soul according to its nature. Calvinism rejects the role of free will, maintaining that grace is irresistible.

**preeclampsia:** see TOXAEMIA.

**Preemption Act,** US statute (1841) permitting squatters to preempt public lands, passed by Congress at the behest of Western states to encourage settlement. The law allowed a settler to buy 65 hectares (160 acres) for a minimum payment of $1.25 per acre after about 14 months' residence. The act was largely superseded by the Homestead Act (1862) and was repealed in 1891.

**prefabrication,** in architectural construction, a technique whereby large building units are produced in factories to be assembled on the building site. It has been applied in various ways to urban housing for more than a century. In Britain the best known examples were the

Pre-Columbian art and architecture: Example of Aztec art.

'prefab' house, designed after World War II, and the schools erected in the 1960s. Major architects, including Walter GROPIUS and Buckminster FULLER, have had important roles in the development of prefabrication.

**pregnancy and birth.** *Pregnancy,* the process in which the female mammal carries and nurtures within it the developing young, is the period between fertilization of an egg (conception) and delivery of a developed fetus (birth). Once fertilized, an egg divides into a tiny ball of cells and embeds itself in the wall of the uterus (or womb), a muscular, expandable organ. At this early stage of development, the growing organism is called the embryo. Some cells of the embryo develop into the PLACENTA (a disc of tissue that brings nourishment from the mother and accepts waste substances from the fetus); the umbilical cord (the cord between embryo and placenta, carrying nutrients and waste); and the protective amniotic sac and fluid surrounding the embryo. During the course of human pregnancy, changes take place in the mother's body to meet the fetal demands on it: the uterus and breasts enlarge, and blood composition and volume change. It takes about 280 days for the embryo (in later stages called the fetus) to develop the structures and organs of a fully formed human. *Birth* is the process by which the fetus is expelled from the uterus. Rhythmic contractions of the uterus, called labour, dilate the neck (cervix) of the uterus and expel the baby and later the placenta. *Natural childbirth* is birth with little or no use of painkilling drugs. Mothers are taught physical and mental techniques for reducing pain and discomfort and participating more fully in the birth process. Birth by the Leboyer method emphasizes extremely gentle handling of the newborn. CAESAREAN SECTION is delivery of an infant by removing it from the uterus surgically. See also AMNIOCENTESIS; GYNAECOLOGY; MIDWIFERY.

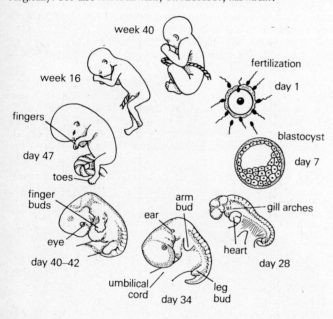

Pregnancy

**premenstrual tension** (PMT), set of symptoms including depression, tension, irritation, and tiredness affecting many women for a period extending up to about 10 days prior to MENSTRUATION. The condition is associated with the hormonal fluctuations and the accumulation of salt and water in tissues which causes the sensation of bloatedness. Treatments found helpful include vitamin $B_6$ (see table under VITAMINS AND MINERALS) and evening-primrose oil. A good diet can minimize symptoms.

**premier:** see PRIME MINISTER.

**Prendergast, Maurice Brazil,** 1859–1924, American painter; b. Canada. A member of the EIGHT, Prendergast travelled to Europe many times and evolved a style akin to POSTIMPRESSIONISM but executed with freer brushstrokes. His landscapes and figure compositions evoke the quality of a gay tapestry, e.g., *Promenade, Gloucester* (1913; Whitney Mus., New York City).

**preparatory schools,** in Britain, private schools which mainly prepare pupils for entry to independent PUBLIC SCHOOLS. Their origins date back to medieval song schools, 16–17th cent. 'petty' schools for the poor, and

private and illegal Roman Catholic schools in the 17th cent. With the expansion of the public schools the 'prep schools' also grew, and by the early 20th cent. there were some 500 of them. They take children at age 7–8 (4–5 if they have a 'pre-prep.' department), and keep them until 11-plus or 13-plus. A typical school is single-sex and has 100–250 pupils, either boarding or day.

**preposition:** see PART OF SPEECH.

**Pre-Raphaelites,** brotherhood of English painters and poets, formed in 1848 to protest against low standards in British art. The principal founders were D.G. ROSSETTI, W. Holman HUNT, and John MILLAIS; from 1851 they were supported by RUSKIN. They turned from the materialism of industrialized England, seeking refuge through literary symbolism and imagery in the beauty and simplicity of the medieval world. Influenced by the NAZARENES, they imitated the innocence of style of Italian painters prior to RAPHAEL. They attracted numerous followers, e.g., Edward BURNE-JONES and William MORRIS, before the movement disbanded after 1853. Their works are nostalgic in tone, painted on a white ground, and brightly coloured, with meticulous detail.

**Presbyterianism,** form of Christian church organization based upon administration by a hierarchy of courts composed of clerical and lay presbyters. In polity it stands between episcopacy and CONGREGATIONALISM. Presbyters (or elders) manage the spiritual conduct of the church; deacons and trustees may handle temporal affairs. The church courts, from lowest to highest, are the court of the congregation or session; the presbytery or colloquy; the synod; and the general assembly, presided over by a moderator. Presbyterianism is the main branch of the Reformed churches and embodies the principles of CALVINISM. It holds the Bible as the sole rule of faith and has two sacraments, BAPTISM and the Lord's Supper. Calvinism first influenced the churches of Geneva and of the HUGUENOTS, and John KNOX founded (1557) a Presbyterian church in Scotland. Francis Makemie, an Irish missionary, set up the first presbytery in America at Philadelphia in 1706. In 1982 the two largest US Presbyterian bodies, the 2.4-million-member United Presbyterian Church in the United States of America and the 838,000-member Presbyterian Church in the US, tentatively approved a merger plan, which was sent to the local presbyteries for ratification. In Europe the Church of Scotland, the Calvinistic Methodist Church in Wales, the Presbyterian Church of England (since 1972 merged into The United Reform Church), and the Presbyterian Church of Ireland are major Presbyterian bodies.

**preschool education:** see HEAD START; KINDERGARTEN; NURSERY SCHOOL.

**Prescott, William Hickling,** 1796–1859, American historian. He is famous for two colourful, vivid accounts of the exploits of the CONQUISTADORS, *History of the Conquest of Mexico* (1843) and *The Conquest of Peru* (1847).

**Prešeren, France,** 1800–49, Slovene poet (from what is now Yugoslavia). He wrote love verse and contemplative verse in which he affirms life and rejects political and physical violence. Among his chief collections are *Ghazels* (1833) and *Sonnets of Unhappiness* (1834).

**preserving:** see CANNING; FOOD PRESERVATION.

**president,** head of state and often head of government in modern republics. Presidential powers vary widely. In parliamentary republics, such as Italy and India, the office is largely ceremonial, with executive power exercised by the prime minister or premier. In France the president has considerable power but shares some executive functions with the premier. In the US the president is the head of state and commander in chief of the armed forces, as well as the chief executive officer. In some countries presidents have assumed dictatorial powers or installed themselves as 'president for life'.

**Presidential Medal of Freedom:** see DECORATIONS, CIVIL AND MILITARY.

**Presley, Elvis,** 1935–77, American singer. Influenced by rhythm and blues and COUNTRY AND WESTERN MUSIC, he played guitar and rose to stardom in 1956, dominating ROCK MUSIC until 1963. In performance he had a pleasant baritone voice and an aggressive, sexual delivery. His hits include 'Heartbreak Hotel' and 'Don't Be Cruel', and he appeared in a number of films.

**pre-Socratics,** the Greek speculative thinkers before SOCRATES. Only fragments of their work remain. PARMENIDES is the major figure, but references in later writings show that ANAXAGORAS, ANAXIMANDER,

ANAXIMENES, DEMOCRITUS, DIOGENES, EMPEDOCLES, HERACLITUS, LEUCIPPUS, Melissus, PYTHAGORAS, THALES, and Xenophanes were also important.

**Press, Freedom of the,** the liberty to print information and opinions without the prior permission of government. The publisher is legally responsible for what is printed and can be sued for LIBEL and other infringements of the law. The struggle against CENSORSHIP began in Britain during the 17th cent. and economic and political freedom of the press was achieved by 1855. The idea of a free press is fundamental in the concept of liberal democracy and implies that the press enjoys full liberty of expression and discussion in much the same way as the individual does. The concept needs severely to be qualified by considerations of ownership and legislation. In the 1980s three men controlled two-thirds of the UK national daily and Sunday newspapers. The first Royal Commission on the Press (1949) declared that 'Free enterprise is a prerequisite of a free press' and inclined to the belief that the press as a whole 'gives an opportunity for all important points of view to be effectively presented in terms of the varying standards of taste, political opinion and education' among the various groups making up pluralist society. Although it was technically possible for anyone to start up a newspaper, the economics of production and distribution rendered this ideal a theory rather than a practical reality. Press freedom is further restricted by the laws of libel and by the Official Secrets Act. Matters were pushed to crisis point in 1987 with the publication in Australia of the book *Spycatcher*, critical of the UK security forces. The British government attempted, and failed, in court action against the publication in Australia; several papers in Britain published excerpts from the book which could not be published in the UK and were restrained by court injunctions sought by the government. The case demonstrated to what lengths a government may go to restrict the 'freedom' of the press.

**Press Council,** watchdog body of the press in the UK. It was set up as a result of the recommendations of the Ross Report on the Press (1949); in 1963 it was reconstituted to include 20% lay membership. It is supposed to uphold good professional and ethical standards in the British press, and to deal with complaints which are referred to it. It has minimal powers and is severely handicapped by having been set up and financed by the press itself. In the period 1977–80 1566 complaints were referred to the Council: 1061 were withdrawn or delayed or disallowed: the remaining 155 were adjudicated upon and of this total a mere 73 were upheld. That represents a success rate for those who complained of 4.66%. The matter is long overdue for review, as it had become clear by the late 1980s that cheque-book journalism (the practice of paying large sums to people involved in illegal activities for their stories) was getting out of hand in the UK press.

**press stud** or **fastener** (US 'popper'), used for clothes or accessories. It consists of two small circular discs, on one of which is a shank, which fits into a corresponding hollow in the other. It was invented in the late 19th cent.

**pressure,** ratio of the force acting on a surface to the area of the surface. A fluid (liquid or gas) exerts a pressure on all bodies immersed in it. For a fluid at rest, the difference in pressure between two points in it depends upon only the density of the fluid and the difference in depth or altitude between the two points. Atmospheric pressure is measured with a BAROMETER. Other instruments for measuring pressure are commonly termed pressure gauges; they include the Bourdon gauge and the manometer. See also ARCHIMEDES' PRINCIPLE; GAS LAWS; HYDRAULIC MACHINERY.

**Prestel,** British Telecom computer-based information system that can be accessed over the public telephone network. A visual display unit terminal (VDU) or a home computer with an appropriate modem are needed to connect to the system via the telephone line and display information. Prestel contains some hundreds of thousands of 'pages', any one of which can be accessed within seconds. The index is arranged so that by answering a few questions about the information needed, the user is quickly led to the appropriate section and to the particular page required. Apart from the cost of the local telephone call, charges are made according to the value of the information that the pages called up contain. Some pages are free, some cost as little as a few pence, and some cost a few pounds. A postbox facility enables messages to be sent to other contributers to the system.

**Prester John,** legendary Christian priest and king who ruled over a vast, wealthy empire in either Asia or Africa. Dating from the 12th cent., his legend was fuelled in the Middle Ages by widely circulated letters purporting to be his.

**Preston,** town (1981 pop. 166,675), Lancashire, NW England, on N bank of R. Ribble, 45 km (27 mi) NW of Manchester. It is an industrial town, concentrating upon engineering and textile manufacture. It is the birthplace of Richard ARKWRIGHT.

**Preston, Margaret Rose,** 1875–1963, Australian artist; b. Margaret McPherson. She studied at the Adelaide School of Design and the Melbourne National Gallery School before travelling to Munich and Paris. She settled in Sydney after World War I, where she contributed much to the development of the local modernist art movement. Ardently patriotic, much of her work reflects the influence of Aboriginal bark painting. She is best known for her paintings and woodcut and lino-cut prints of native flowers.

**pretor:** see PRAETOR.

**Pretoria,** city (1985 pop. 822,925), administrative capital of South Africa and of TRANSVAAL prov. The city has important industries, especially iron and steel, as well as motor-vehicle assembly plants, railway and machine engineering, and flour mills. Founded in 1855 and named after the Boer leader Andries Pretorius, it became the capital of the South African Republic (the Transvaal) in 1860. During the SOUTH AFRICAN WAR (1899–1902), Winston CHURCHILL was imprisoned here before he escaped to Mozambique. Modern Pretoria is an educational and cultural centre.

**Pretorius, Andries Wilhelmus Jacobus,** 1799–1853, Boer leader. His defeat (1838) of the ZULUS led to the founding of the Boer Republic of Natal. In 1848 he created the nucleus of what became the Transvaal. The city of PRETORIA is named after him. His son, **Martinus Wessel Pretorius,** 1818?–1901, became the first president (1857–77) of the Transvaal; concurrently he was president (1859–63) of the Orange Free State. After Britain annexed the Transvaal in 1877, he served with Paul KRUGER in a government opposed to British rule. See also SOUTH AFRICA.

**Previn, André,** 1929–, American conductor, composer, and pianist; b. Germany as Andreas Ludwig Priwin. He has recorded classical music since 1946, and in the 1950s he made a number of highly successful JAZZ piano albums. He has also composed film scores. Previn has conducted the London Symphony Orchestra (1968–79) and the Pittsburgh Symphony (1976–84); since 1984 he has been musical director of the Los Angeles Philharmonic.

**Prévost d'Exiles, Antoine François,** known as **Abbé Prévost,** 1697–1763, French author. He entered a Benedictine abbey (1720), but fled (1728) to lead an adventurous life in England, Holland, and Germany. Returning to France, he was named head of a priory (1754) by the pope. Of his writings, only the brilliant psychological novel *Manon Lescaut* is still widely read.

**Priam,** in Greek mythology, king of Troy, husband of HECUBA. See TROJAN WAR.

**Price, (Mary) Leontyne,** 1927–, American soprano. She has sung at the METROPOLITAN OPERA (New York City) since 1961, and is known for the range and power of her voice, e.g., in the title roles of VERDI's *Aïda* and PUCCINI's *Madame Butterfly*.

**Pride, Thomas,** d. 1658, parliamentary soldier in the ENGLISH CIVIL WAR. Acting on orders of the army council, he undertook (Dec. 1648) **Pride's Purge,** expelling 143 members (mostly Presbyterians) from Parliament on the grounds that they were royalists.

**Priestley, J(ohn) B(oynton),** 1894–1984, versatile English writer and broadcaster. He took a broad, comic view of English life in novels such as *The Good Companions* (1929). His many plays include *Dangerous Corner* (1932) and *Time and the Conways* (1937). His other works include literary and social criticism and the travelogue *English Journey* (1934). He was noted for his radio talks during World War II.

**primary health care,** first line of medical care encountered by the patient. In Britain this means GENERAL PRACTICE or the accident and emergency ward of a general hospital, but in the developing world primary health care may be provided by a semitrained nurse or health-care attendant (formerly called barefoot doctor in China) responsible for contraception, antenatal care, immunization, and health education.

**primary schools,** in Britain, schools providing for children aged 5–11, often divided into infant (5–7) and junior (7–11) schools or departments.

In those areas with MIDDLE SCHOOLS the primary school is replaced by a 'first school' for children aged 5–8, 9, or 10. Primary schools may be maintained by local authorities or they may be private. The term 'primary school' was adopted by the Hadow report on *The Education of the Adolescent* (1926) in its proposal to replace separate 'elementary' and grammar schools tracks by a two-stage system of primary and SECONDARY schools; this was implemented in the Education Act 1944. Numbers of primary schools have fluctuated; the postwar baby boom was followed by a falling birth rate, causing schools to amalgamate or close. There are over 20,000 maintained primary schools in England and Wales, over half of which take the full range of infants and juniors. Primary schools normally take both boys and girls.

**primate,** member of the mammalian order Primates, which includes human beings, APES, MONKEYS, and prosimians, or lower primates (e.g., TREE SHREWS, LEMURS). Nearly all inhabit warm climates and are arboreal, although a few are terrestrial. Unspecialized anatomically, primates are distinguished by social organization and evolutionary trends within the order tending towards increased dexterity and intelligence.

**Primaticcio, Francesco** (preemah‚teetchoh), 1504–70, Italian mannerist painter (see MANNERISM), called Le Primatice by the French. He was influenced by GIULIO ROMANO's methods of illusionism. Invited (1532) by FRANCIS I of France to help decorate the castle at Fontainebleau, he became director of the project in 1540. Only a few of his works there survive. He decorated other châteaus, designed tomb monuments for Francis I and Henry II, and extended the influence of Italian art in France.

**prime meridian,** meridian designated 0° LONGITUDE, from which all other longitudes are measured. By international convention, it passes through the original site of the Royal Observatory in GREENWICH, UK. For this reason it is often called the Greenwich meridian.

**prime minister** or **premier,** in parliamentary systems, the head of government, but not of state, and chief member of the CABINET. Under the procedure evolved in the UK and followed by most parliamentary systems, the office holder is the leader of the party with or commanding a majority of members in the legislature and is himself or herself a member of that body. If support is lost in the legislature, the prime minister is expected to resign. In France the premier, appointed by the president, has fewer powers than the premiers of many other countries.

**prime number:** see NUMBER THEORY.

**prime rate:** see INTEREST.

**primitivism,** in art, fresh and fanciful style of works by untrained artists such as Henri ROUSSEAU and Grandma MOSES; also, the style of early American naive painters such as Edward HICKS.

**Primo de Rivera, Miguel** (‚preemoh dhay ree‚vayrah), 1870–1930, Spanish dictator (1923–30). Seizing power in a coup (1923), he dissolved the CORTES and established a military directory. Although his military government was replaced (1925) by a civil one, he continued to rule with an iron hand. After a liberal uprising failed (1929), he was forced to resign (1930) because of his government's economic failures.

**primrose,** name for the genus *Primula* of the family Primulaceae, low perennial herbs found on all continents. The family includes the primroses and cowslip, cyclamens (genus *Cyclamen*), and pimpernels (genus *Anagallis*). Species of all these genera are cultivated as rock-garden, border, and pot plants. The primroses hybridize easily and have given rise to a range of colourful garden plants. The EVENING PRIMROSE is not a true primrose. Cyclamens are chiefly native to the Alps; *C. indicum* is a common florists' pot plant. The scarlet pimpernel (*A. arvensis*), native to Eurasia has flowers that close on the approach of bad weather, giving it the common name of poorman's weatherglass. Although once used as a herb it is known to be poisonous.

**Prince Edward Island,** province of Canada (1984 est. pop. 125,600), the smallest in area (5657 km²/2184 sq mi), situated in the Maritime Provinces, lying in the Gulf of St Lawrence, separated from New Brunswick (SW) and Nova Scotia (SE) by the Northumberland Strait. CHARLOTTETOWN is the capital and largest city; two-thirds of the population is non-urban. Prince Edward Island is a low, level island, c.225 km (140 mi) long by up to 56 km (35 mi) wide. The original forest has been cleared and the red–brown soils are fertile. About 70% of the land is cultivated, producing mixed grain crops, fruits, and vegetables (especially potatoes). Fishing is an important industry, particularly for lobster and cod.

Manufacturing is minor and largely limited to food-processing. Although French explorers landed there in the 16th and 17th cents. the first permanent settlement was not until 1719. Acquired by Britain (1763), it was first annexed to Nova Scotia before becoming a separate colony (1769). Lord Selkirk established (1803) a large colony of Scots there, and their descendants still form a large part of the population. It joined the confederation in 1873, leading to a long period of economic domination by central Canada. In recent years Prince Edward Island has become heavily dependent on government assistance.

**Prince Edward Islands,** two small close islands (Marion Island and Prince Edward Island) in the far southern Indian Ocean S of Natal. Discovered by a Dutch expedition in 1663, they became the site of a sealing industry until early this century; British sovereignty was transferred to South Africa in 1950. The volcanoes that gave rise to the islands are still active. Marion Island has a permanent South African station.

**Princeton,** US borough (1980 pop. 12,035) and adjacent township (1980 pop. 13,683), W New Jersey; settled late 1600s, borough inc. 1813. It is the seat of Princeton Univ., the Inst. for Advanced Study, other educational institutions, and many corporate headquarters and research centres. Princeton was the scene of a Revolutionary War victory by WASHINGTON's army (3 Jan. 1777), and the university's administration building, Nassau Hall, was the seat of the CONTINENTAL CONGRESS from June to Nov. 1783.

**printed circuit,** thin board of insulating material on which are mounted the components of an electrical circuit interconnected by thin narrow strips of conductor that have been formed on the surface of the board by a photographic process. Initially the top surface of the board is covered with a thin coating of copper. After the conductor layout has been photographed onto this copper surface the space between the conductors is etched away leaving conducting strips. Holes are drilled through the conductor ends and the board to take the component wires which are then soldered to the conducting strips. Large complex circuits make use of multilayered boards. The system is compact, lends itself to automatic manufacture and assembly, and eliminates wiring errors.

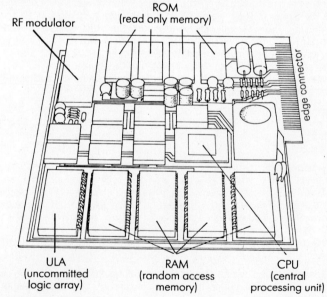

Printed circuit board

**printing,** the reproduction of lettered or illustrated matter through the use of mechanical, photographic, or electrostatic devices. (For the invention of printing and the development of the earliest forms of type, see TYPE.) In addition to the letters themselves, the elements involved in printing include the press and various methods for setting type and for making the reproducing printing surface, or plate. The press used by Johannes GUTENBERG in 15th-cent. Germany was a hand press, in which ink was rolled over the raised surfaces of hand-set letters held within a form and the form was then pressed against a sheet of paper. The hand press remained in use for all forms of printing until the early 19th cent. A steam-powered press with a flat type-bed was used by *The Times* of

London beginning in 1814. In 1847 the American Richard Hoe developed a high-speed rotary press in which the printing surface was wrapped around a cylinder. Later presses used continuous rolls of PAPER and incorporated folding, cutting, and paper-moving devices that vastly increased printing speed. The first mechanical typesetter, the Linotype machine, was invented by Ottmar Mergenthaler in 1884. Operated by a typewriter-keyboard, it assembles brass matrices into a line and casts the line as a single metal slug. Other machine-set type systems were developed, notably the Monotype (first used in 1897), which casts individual characters from a punched tape produced by a keyboard operator. The recent development of photocomposed 'cold type' (as distinguished from 'hot', or cast-metal, type) has further increased typesetting speeds. Electronic typewriters and computers project the type images onto a film that is then used to make a plate. **Letterpress** is printing from a raised, inked surface. Various inventions have improved the letterpress printing surface, especially the stereotype, which can produce a large metal plate of a newspaper page from a mould made of pulp; and the later electrotype, which uses an electrolytic process to create a curved metal plate. In **intaglio**, the design to be produced is cut below the surface of the plate, and the incised lines are filled with ink that is then transferred to paper. Photogravure is an intaglio process in which the plate is produced photographically. **Offset**, or **planographic**, **printing**, derived from LITHOGRAPHY, uses a plate treated so that ink will adhere only to the areas that will print the design. The plate transfers its ink to a rubber cylinder, which in turn offsets it onto paper. Colour printing is achieved by photographically separating four basic colours (black; magenta; yellow; and cyan, a blue-green) from the original picture, making a plate for each colour, then using the plates to print the colours consecutively over one another. See also BOOKBINDING; PHOTOCOPYING.

**Priscian**, 5th-cent. LATIN grammarian. His major work *Institutiones grammaticae* helped to establish a formal grammatical description of Latin, using the categories and terminology of earlier Greek grammarians.

**prism**, in optics, a piece of translucent glass or crystal with a triangular cross section, used to form a SPECTRUM of light by separating it according to colours. Prisms are also used in optical instruments for changing the direction of light beams by total internal reflection (complete reflection of a light ray at the boundary of two media rather than some reflection and some refraction as is usual).

**prison**, place of confinement for the punishment and rehabilitation of criminals. By the late 18th cent. in Europe, prison had emerged as the main form of punishment for all but capital crimes. Early prison conditions were appalling, and efforts to reform inhumane prisons were made by John Howard and later by Elizabeth FRY and Dorothy DIX in the 19th cent. Early prison regimes were aimed purely at punishment, but during the 20th cent. the trend has been towards prisoners' rehabilitation. This was particularly pronounced in the 1960s with the use of psychiatric aid, vocational training, and work programmes. Prisons are also used for people awaiting trial, and for aliens seeking to immigrate. In the UK the lack of new prisons and the increasing prison population have led to the courts handing out alternative punishments such as PROBATION and COMMUNITY SERVICE. Despite this the prisons have continued to be overcrowded and this has led to rising tension and riots in British prisons during the 1980s.

**Pritchard, Katharine Susannah**, 1883–1969, Australian novelist. A founding member of the Communist Party of Australia, she wrote novels that are rich in literary merit as well as politically committed. They include *Working Bullocks* (1926), *Coonardoo* (1928), the first realistic and sympathetic portrait of an Aboriginal, and the 'goldfields trilogy': *The Roaring Nineties* (1946), *Golden Miles* (1948), and *Winged Seeds* (1950), a historical account of the gold-mining industry in West Australia.

**Pritchett, Sir V(ictor) S(awdon)**, 1905–, English writer. A distinguished short-story writer, he is also a well-known reviewer and critic. His works include *Collected Stories* (1982); *The Spanish Temper* (1954), a travel book; *A Cab at the Door* (1968) and *Midnight Oil* (1972), memoirs; and *The Tale Bearers* (1980), literary essays.

**privatization**, the selling of state-owned assets to the private sector. The popularity of NATIONALIZATION which was extensively carried out after World War II in Western Europe gave way to disenchantment as subsidies mounted. In the 1980s there was an enormous shift of resources from government to the public. The trend was led by Mrs Thatcher's

Conservative government in the UK which sold many of its interests, notably in aerospace, telecommunications, and gas. These moves were followed elsewhere in Europe as well as in Japan, Southeast Asia and in many developing countries, including communist ones, where governments lacked the resources to support subsidies for often inefficient state enterprises. Opponents of the practice argue that the wealth of the people should not be transferred to a small shareholding minority. Its proponents argue that the public benefits from the improved efficiency of the enterprise concerned and from the more appropriate use by government of the resources which have been released.

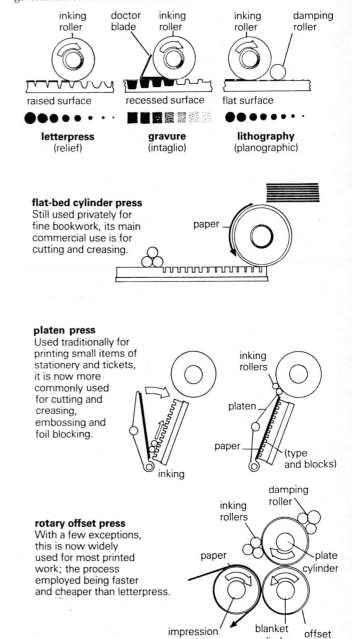

Printing

**privy council**, in British government, the principal council of the sovereign. In modern times it exercises only nominal powers. The privy council descends from the *Curia Regis* [king's council], a body of officials exercising the functions of government on behalf of the king. However, in the 17th cent., as the sovereign's authority was superseded by PARLIAMENT, the privy council decreased in importance and its political functions were taken over by the CABINET. In the 20th cent. though it consists of members of the cabinet, and high-ranking politicians and judges, its role has been limited to the issuing of Orders in Council (see DELEGATED LEGISLATION), and royal charters to charities and public bodies (e.g., universities). Its only remaining importance lies in the Judicial Committee of the Privy Council. This consists of the LAW LORDS, who sit as a final APPEAL court for many COMMONWEALTH jurisdictions (see COMMONWEALTH, LEGAL SYSTEMS IN THE). Its decisions are binding on the particular country involved, but do not act as a PRECEDENT in English courts.

**Prizren**, city (1981 pop. 134,526), S Yugoslavia. An important Serbian settlement in the Middle Ages, it was under Turkish rule from 1454 to 1912. Gold and filigree work is a speciality and its fortress, old streets, mosques, and fountains make it a picturesque sight.

**probability**, branch of MATHEMATICS that measures the likelihood that an event will occur. The theory of probability was first developed by Blaise PASCAL in the 17th cent. as a means of solving gambling problems; it was advanced by Pierre de LAPLACE in the early 19th cent. Given an experiment (e.g., tossing a coin), each possible outcome is assigned a number, called a probability measure, that corresponds to its chance of occurring. Probabilities must be between 0 and 1 inclusive (0 corresponding to impossibility, 1 to certainty), and the sum of all probabilities of simple outcomes of an experiment must be 1. For example, if a symmetrical coin is to be tossed, both possible outcomes, heads and tails, have probabilities of ½, because they have equal chances of occurring. Probabilities are often assigned on the basis of relative frequency of occurrence. For example, if weather records for 40 years show that the sun shone 32 times on July 1, then one would assign a probability of $^{32}/_{40}$, or $^4/_5$, to the event that the sun shines on July 1. Similar probability computations are used in insurance calculations. By adding or multiplying the probabilities of simple events, one can determine the probabilities of compound events, e.g., the probability that a husband and wife will both live to be 70. Sometimes sophisticated counting techniques, such as PERMUTATIONS AND COMBINATIONS, must be used. The analysis of data collected from samples is the province of STATISTICS.

**probate**, in law, the formal proof of the validity of a WILL by a court, applied for on the death of its maker. In the UK, the application is made to the Family Division of the High Court, who will issue a probate certificate, guaranteeing the validity of the will, and placing it in the hands of the executors to implement. In most cases, where the will is uncontested, 'common' probate will be granted. If another party disputes the will, the court, if satisfied of its validity, grants 'solemn' probate.

**probation**, in law, the binding over of a convicted offender, under the supervision of a probation officer, granted by a court as an alternative to imprisonment. Probation developed in both the US and the UK in the 1880s, when public-spirited citizens agreed to act as sureties for certain offenders. It was not until 1907 that probation was officially recognized in the UK, and prior to World War II, probation orders were rare. However, following the Criminal Justice Act 1948, probation grew rapidly, and during the 1960s, it became the main alternative to imprisonment used by the courts. Offenders were placed in the hands of probation officers whose duty it was to 'advise, assist and befriend' the offender. In recent years the use of probation has dropped as other alternatives (e.g., a suspended SENTENCE, or COMMUNITY SERVICE) have become available to the courts.

**Procopius** (proh₁kohpeeəs), d. 565?, Byzantine historian. His high connections and public offices give his histories great value as firsthand accounts. His chief works are *Procopius's History of His Own Time* and the largely scandalous and often scurrilous court chronicle *Secret History of Procopius*.

**procurator-fiscal:** see SCOTLAND, LEGAL SYSTEM IN.

**prodigal son**, parable of JESUS about a young man who leaves home and becomes a wastrel; repentant, he returns and is received with joyful welcome. Luke 15.11–32.

**profit**, in economics, the amount of money remaining from a business enterprise after all expenses, including taxes, have been paid. The economic concept of profit differs from that of the accountant. For example, an economist might deduct imputed costs from the outgoings (e.g., rent which would be due on land and property if not already owned); an accountant would include these in the profit. It is therefore possible to make an accounting profit but a loss in an economic sense. It is also called return on capital, or earnings. The various kinds of profit include that of the entrepreneur, as payment for management or risk-taking; that of the capitalist, in the form of interest; and that of the landlord, in the form of rent. Profit is the major incentive for production in a capitalist country, but with the rise of a salaried managerial class it has become less personal and more institutional in character.

**progeria**, syndrome of unknown aetiology causing premature aging in children; also known as Hutchinson-Gilford syndrome. Affected children appear normal up to the first year of life. Gradually, characteristics of the disorder become apparent: retarded growth and physical development, loss of body fat, absence of body hair, and baldness. Eventually the child develops dry, wrinkled skin, atherosclerosis (see ARTERIOSCLEROSIS), and other conditions, e.g., arthritis, diabetes, and cataracts, associated with old age. There is no treatment, and death occurs by the second decade.

**progesterone**, female sex hormone (see STEROID), secreted by the ovaries, the cortex of the ADRENAL GLANDS, and the placenta, that induces changes in the lining of the uterus essential for implantation of a fertilized egg (see MENSTRUATION). In a pregnant woman, progesterone prevents spontaneous abortion (miscarriage) and prepares the MAMMARY GLANDS for milk production. Because it inhibits ovulation, the hormone is widely used in ORAL CONTRACEPTIVES.

**programmed learning**, self-teaching method whereby material to be learned is arranged in a graded sequence of controlled steps (programmed), so that individual learners, working at their own speed, may instruct themselves, test their comprehension, and, if necessary, make corrections after each step. The programme may be delivered through a variety of instruments ranging from workbooks to COMPUTERS. Much of the programmed instruction in use today is based on B.F. SKINNER's theory of the nature of learning, introduced in the 1950s.

**programming language**, syntax, grammar, and symbols or words by means of which instructions are given to a COMPUTER. All *software* consists of COMPUTER PROGRAMS written in programming languages. Because computers work with binary patterns (see NUMERATION), the most primitive means of instructing the computer is through machine language. This is usually a direct representation of the binary codes for operations such as 'move data' or 'compare data' or some coded version of them. Because it is difficult to write machine code programs reliably, many languages have been designed to make programming easier and faster. The earliest of these, called assembly languages, are written using mnemonics such as 'SUB' for subtract, which are then translated into machine language by a computer program called an *assembler*. An extension used in such languages is the macro instruction, for example a mnemonic such as 'READ', for which the assembler substitutes a series of simple mnemonics to save the programmer time. The next advance was the development of 'high-level' languages which, unlike machine and assembly languages, vary little between computers. These languages, which are algorithmic or procedural, must be translated into machine code by a computer program called a *compiler* or *interpreter*. The first of these languages was FORTRAN (FORmula TRANslation), which was developed by John Backus in about 1956, and is most often used for scientific calculation. The first commercial language COBOL (COmmon Business Oriented Language) was developed in about 1959 under the leadership of Grace Hopper. ALGOL 60 (ALGOrithmic Language), developed in Europe, was used primarily in mathematics and science, and its structure influenced subsequent language design. Programming languages are now classified as imperative or declarative. Programming language development was originally of the *imperative* type, including Algol 68, PL/1, BASIC (developed by John Kemeny and Thomas Kurtz at Dartmouth College, US, in about 1967, now most often associated with PERSONAL COMPUTERS), Pascal (which was designed as a teaching language by Niklaus Wirth) and C (closely associated with the UNIX operating system). The most recent imperative languages, following Simula, are modular (therefore allowing a large software system to be programmed as many small components) and object orientated. Examples include Modula 2 (also by Niklaus Wirth; 1982), Ada (named after Ada Augusta, countess of Lovelace, the biographer of Charles BABBAGE, and developed under the direction of the US Department of Defense in 1981 with a requirement for real time as well as general purpose use), and SMALLTALK. *Declarative*, or applicative, language design has aimed for a direct mathematical basis for programming languages. LISP (LISt Processing) and ML are functional languages and PROLOG (PROgramming in LOGic) is a rule-based language. This style of language is associated with artificial intelligence or 'fifth generation' applications and parallel computers. SNOBOL (StriNg Oriented symBOLic language) was an early language designed for string processing and with a mathematical basis in Markov algorithms. The term 'fourth generation language' is used for high-level commands which drive applications packages such as GPSS (General Purpose System Simulator, used for simulation and modelling of physical and environmental events) and SPSS (Statistical Package for Social Sciences).

**progression,** in mathematics, SEQUENCE of quantities, called terms, with a fixed relationship between consecutive terms. In an *arithmetic progression* each term is derived from the preceding one by adding a given number $d$, called the common difference. An example is 3, 7, 11, 15, ..., where $d = 4$. The $n$th, or general, term is $a + (n-1)d$, where $a$ is the first term. In a *geometric progression* each term is derived by multiplying the preceding term by a given number $r$, called the common ratio. In the sequence 1, 3, 9, 27, ..., for example, $r = 3$. The $n$th term is $ar^{n-1}$. In a *harmonic progression* the terms are the reciprocals of the terms of an arithmetic progression, e.g., $\frac{1}{3}, \frac{1}{7}, \frac{1}{11}, \frac{1}{15}, \ldots$.

**progressive education,** worldwide educational movement in reaction against formal school structures and teaching methods. The movement developed at the end of the 19th cent., using the traditions of such educational thinkers as Jean Jacques ROUSSEAU, Johann PESTALOZZI, and Friedrich FROEBEL. Leading international figures included John DEWEY and Maria MONTESSORI. The movement embraced a range of different and often conflicting ideas, mostly child-centred, but also looking to social regeneration through forms of vocational or citizenship training. In the US and Europe a child study movement developed from the 1890s, and in 1921 a New Education Fellowship was created, originating with the US and a group of European countries, but extending world-wide. Dewey's writings, including *Democracy and Education* (1931), and his Laboratory School in Chicago (1896–1904) were influential in Britain and internationally, as were other American progressive educational concepts, including the Dalton Plan to encourage children's self-paced learning. The term 'progressive school' began to be applied to some British independent schools from the creation of Abbotsholme school in 1889; one of the best known of such schools is A.S. NEILL's Summerhill founded in 1921. The progressive education movement permeated the educational system, particularly primary schools, in a variety of ways, and it continues to be a movement for more open and less authoritarian styles of schooling.

**Progressive Party,** three separate political organizations that were active in the presidential elections of 1912, 1924, and 1948. The first Progressive party (the Bull Moose party) was formed by dissident Republicans who supported former Pres. Theodore ROOSEVELT against Pres. William H. TAFT. Its platform called for the direct election of US senators, WOMEN'S SUFFRAGE, and many social reforms. The party drew over 4 million votes, more than Taft received, and resulted in the election of the Democratic candidate, Woodrow WILSON The second Progressive party nominated Sen. Robert M. LA FOLLETTE for president and advocated public control of natural resources and recognition of trade unions, among other reforms. La Follette polled nearly 5 million votes in 1924 but carried only his home state of Wisconsin. The party remained active in the state until 1946. The third Progressive party accused Pres. Harry S. TRUMAN of fomenting the COLD WAR and ran the former vice president, Henry A. WALLACE, against him in 1948. Wallace polled only slightly more than 1 million votes as Truman won reelection.

**progressivism,** in US history, a broadly based reform movement that reached its height early in the 20th cent. It arose as a response to the social evils that inevitably accompanied the spectacular economic advances of the 19th cent. The progressive movement began in the cities, where reform was most needed. Educated middle-class women like Jane ADDAMS of Chicago and Lillian D. Wald of New York City moved into the slums and established settlement houses to offer social services and recreational facilities to the poor; other reformers attacked boss rule and machine politics, often by changing the structure of city government. During the 1890s reform mayors like Samuel M. JONES of Toledo and Hazen Pingree of Detroit introduced municipal ownership of public utilities, improved city services, and provided better housing. But municipal reformers were frequently obstructed by corporation-dominated state legislatures and were forced therefore to turn to state politics, where progressivism reached its fullest expression. In all parts of the country Progressive state

governors carried thorugh sweeping programmes of reform. The outstanding figure was Robert M. LA FOLLETTE who, as governor of Wisconsin (1901–06), secured from the legislature laws regulating railways and business corporations, restricting lobbying, limiting hours of work for women and children, and establishing income taxes and death duties. In an effort to diminish the influence of political bosses and pressure groups, state governments introduced such devices as secret ballots, direct primaries, the initiative, the referendum, and the direct election of senators. In national politics the adminstrations of Theodore ROOSEVELT, William Howard TAFT and Woodrow WILSON saw significant progressive gains. America's entry into the war in 1917 diverted the energies of reformers and after the war progressivism virtually died. It had tackled some of the worst evils of industrialization and made some improvements to the machinery of government. But it had neither solved the problem of monopoly nor stamped out political corruption. Moreover, most of the social reform measures the progressives had advocated were not adopted until the NEW DEAL.

**prohibition,** laws preventing the manufacture and distribution of alcoholic beverages. In the 19th cent., US TEMPERANCE MOVEMENTS urged prohibition, and the Prohibition party made it (1869) a national issue. It gained impetus in World War I, when conservation policies limited output from distilleries. In 1919 the 18th amendment to the CONSTITUTION established prohibition, but enforcement, through the VOLSTEAD ACT, failed to abolish BOOTLEGGING and the widespread lawbreaking associated with it. The 21st amendment (1933) repealed prohibition.

**projective test,** a psychological instrument used in the clinical assessment of personality, in which the responses of the subject to the test are interpreted as indicating unconscious feelings or conflicts. The Rorschach test, requiring the subject to interpret a series of ink-blot patterns, is a well-known test of this type.

**Prokofiev, Sergei Sergeyevich** (prə‚kofee-ef), 1891–1953, Russian composer. A student of GLIÈRE and RIMSKY-KORSAKOV, he toured the world as a pianist and conductor until 1938, when he returned to the USSR. His early works are often harsh and strident; later pieces are lyrical, simplified, and popular in style. Prokofiev's important works include seven symphonies, e.g., the *Classical Symphony* (1916–17); eight piano sonatas and five piano concertos; chamber music; operas, e.g., *The Love for Three Oranges* (1921); ballets, including *Romeo and Juliet* (1935–36; 1940); the symphonic fairy tale *Peter and the Wolf* (1936); and orchestral suites, e.g., *Lieutenant Kijé* (1934).

**proletariat,** in Marxian theory, the class of workers who depend for their means of existence on the sale of their labour for purposes of industrial production. Karl MARX believed that this class, formed by the rise of CAPITALISM, would become the overwhelming majority, revolt against their exploitation, seize power from the BOURGEOISIE, or capitalist class, and create a classless society.

**promenade concerts,** series of concerts inaugurated by (Sir) Henry Wood (1869–1944) in the summer of 1895 at Queen's Hall, London. Although they were intentionally popular, Henry Wood saw to it that audiences had a chance to hear the finest works in the orchestral repertoire as well as lighter pieces. He also introduced works by contemporary composers such as Schoenberg, Richard Strauss, and Shostakovich. They were immensely successful, and after Sir Henry's death (Sir) Malcolm Sargent (1895–1967) carried on the tradition with as much panache as his predecessor. After Queen's Hall was bombed during World War II, the concerts were transferred to the Royal Albert Hall, where they have since been held. After the death of Sir Malcolm Sargent, there developed a tradition in which several different orchestras and conductors were hired for each summer season. The concerts are so called because there was and is standing space directly in front of the orchestra and in the gallery, allowing people to walk in and out.

**Prometheus,** in Greek mythology, TITAN benefactor of man, whom, in one legend, he created. He stole fire from the gods, gave it to man, and taught him many arts and sciences. In retaliation, ZEUS plagued man with PANDORA and her box of evils, and chained Prometheus to a mountain, where an eagle preyed on his liver. In some myths HERCULES released him. Prometheus is the subject of many literary works, including AESCHYLUS' *Prometheus Bound* and SHELLEY's *Prometheus Unbound*.

**promethium** (Pm), artificially produced radioactive element, first identified definitely by J.A. Marinsky and colleagues in 1945 by ion-exchange chromatography. It is a RARE-EARTH METAL in the LANTHANIDE SERIES. The promethium-147 isotope is used in the making of phosphorescent materials, in nuclear-powered batteries for spacecraft, and as a radioactive tracer. See ELEMENT (table); PERIODIC TABLE.

**pronghorn** or **prongbuck,** hoofed herbivorous MAMMAL (*Antilocapra americana*) of the W US and N Mexico. Related to the ANTELOPES, it is the size of a goat, with a light brown coat and pronged horns. It lives in small bands on open plains, browsing on shrubs and grasses. The pronghorn is the swiftest of North American mammals. Nearly exterminated by hunting, it is now protected.

**pronoun:** see PART OF SPEECH.

**propaganda,** the manipulation and dissemination of information, usually on controversial issues or in situations of conflict, in order to attempt to influence the attitudes and behaviour of a target group. The term *propaganda* refers not only to the technique of putting across a message but to the content of the message itself. A common assumption is that the message is likely to be a partial truth at best, involving distortion or fabrication, and transmitted with the intent to mislead. In times of war, propaganda may be used to intimidate, confuse, or discourage rival troops and populations by dropping leaflets from the air, broadcasting by radio, and so forth, but a good deal of propaganda is directed inwards by the state or government towards its own citizens, to promote patriotism or encourage compliance with government plans and values. Technical improvements in the means of communication have increased the scope and range of propaganda. Ideological conflict between the great powers leads them to put out a constant stream of 'information' which puts their values and policies in a good light. COLD WAR propaganda is transmitted by radio from the USSR to Western Europe, by the West to Eastern Europe, on stations such as Radio Free Europe, and by both sides to the Third World. In the 20th cent. the use of propaganda has been very marked on the part of totalitarian powers which have abolished freedom of speech and publication. The Nazis were skilled in inciting nationalist fervour and hatred against selected enemies by the suppression of rival views, tight control of the press, dramatically staged mass rallies, and the use of emotive symbols, such as the swastika.

**propane** ($CH_3CH_2CH_3$), colourless gaseous HYDROCARBON that occurs in NATURAL GAS and PETROLEUM. It is used as a liquid fuel in lamps, portable stoves, and certain cigarette lighters, and sold compressed in cylinders, often mixed with other hydrocarbons.

**proper motion,** apparent motion of some stars across the celestial sphere, shifting their relative positions over the centuries. Proper motion is due to the transverse velocity of a star across the line of sight and is typically of the order of tens of kilometres per second. For the nearer stars such velocities can lead to proper motions of some seconds of arc per year; for the numerous very distant ones the proper motion is usually unobservably small.

**Propertius, Sextus,** c.50 BC–before AD 2. Roman elegiac poet, a member of the circle of MAECENAS. A master of the Latin ELEGY, he wrote with vigour and passion.

**property,** in law, the right of ownership, i.e., the exclusive right to possess, enjoy, and dispose of an object of value; also, the object of value possessed, enjoyed, and disposed of by right of ownership. Modern Anglo-American property law provides for the ownership of nearly all things of economic value; there are exceptions, such as the high seas or outer space, which are not subject to ownership. The law divides property into realty (real property) and personalty (personal property). Realty is chiefly land and improvements built thereon; personalty is chiefly movable objects whose distribution the owner can determine by sale, WILL, or gift. Realty, in medieval times, was the basis of wealth and the keystone of the social structure; its ownership was controlled to protect society. The ownership of personalty, being of minor importance, was almost unfettered. With the rise of commerce and a large landless middle class, personalty became the dominant form of property, and the law of realty gradually became assimilated in most respects into that of personalty. For special types of property, see COPYRIGHT, PATENT.

**prophet,** in the BIBLE, religious leader of Israel, especially in the period of the kingdoms and the Babylonian captivity. In Israel the prophet was believed to have been inspired by God to guide the chosen people. The Major Prophets are ISAIAH, JEREMIAH, EZEKIEL, and DANIEL. The Minor Prophets are HOSEA, JOEL, AMOS, OBADIAH, JONAH, MICAH, NAHUM, HABAKKUK, ZEPHANIAH, HAGGAI, ZECHARIAH, and MALACHI. The title is also given to other men, e.g., MOSES and ELIJAH. A Christian belief is that the HOLY GHOST 'spoke through the prophets' (Nicene CREED), who foretold the life and passion of Christ. Some varieties of Protestantism (e.g., ANABAPTISTS) have emphasized 'inspired' utterance or behavior. Islam knows MUHAMMAD as the last and greatest of the prophets.

**proportion,** in mathematics, the equality of two ratios. Two pairs of quantities *a*, *b* and *c*, *d* are in proportion if $\frac{a}{b} = \frac{c}{d}$. The lengths of two sides of any triangle and the lengths of the corresponding two sides of any similar (i.e., same-shaped) triangle are in proportion.

**proprietary medicine:** see PATENT MEDICINE.

**Proserpine:** see PERSEPHONE.

**prosimian:** see PRIMATE.

**prostate,** gland in the male REPRODUCTIVE SYSTEM situated below the neck of the bladder, encircling the urethra. The prostate produces a thin, milky, alkaline fluid that is secreted into the urethra at the time of emission of semen, providing an added medium for the life and motility of sperm. Prostatic enlargement, common in men over 50, can interfere with urination.

**prostitution,** granting of sexual access for payment. An epidemic of VENEREAL DISEASE in 16th-cent. Europe led to the first serious efforts to control prostitution, and public-health considerations motivated much subsequent regulatory legislation. In Britain the Contagious Diseases Acts were repealed (1886) after a lengthy public campaign exposed the inhumane double standard such regulations operated against women. International cooperation to control the traffic in prostitutes began in 1899. The trade in sex still operates on an international scale, despite illegal status in many of its centres. Prostitution is illegal in most of SE Asia and the Middle East. Today houses of prostitution are illegal in all US states but Nevada. In Britain a parliamentary act of 1959 forbids open solicitation but permits the practice of prostitution at home. Some European nations regulate prostitution as a public health measure.

**protactinium** ('prohtak,tini·əm), (Pa), radioactive element, discovered as a decay product of uranium-238 by K. Fajans and O. Göhring in 1913. A shiny, silver-grey metal with 14 isotopes, it is found in uranium ores. Alpha decay of protactinium leads to formation of ACTINIUM. See ELEMENT (table); PERIODIC TABLE.

**Protagoras,** c.490–421 BC, Greek philosopher. One of the leading SOPHISTS, he is most famous for the saying 'Man is the measure of all things'. He held that all truth is relative to the individual who holds it. Protagoras denied the possibility of objective knowledge and refused to differentiate between sense and reason. None of his works has survived, but his views are presented in the Platonic dialogue that bears his name.

**Proteaceae** (,prohti·'seeay), a family of over 1000 species of trees and shrubs in the Southern Hemisphere, especially Australia and South Africa, e.g., GREVILLEA and *Protea*, the latter genus producing magnificent flowers of great complexity and diversity of form in the various species.

**protection:** see TRADE.

**protective coloration,** in animals, coloration or colour pattern that facilitates escape from observation by predators or prey or serves as a warning device to predators or others of the same species. The most widespread form of protective coloration is called cryptic coloration in which the coloration and patterns on the skin of the animal enable it to blend in with its habitat. In some animals (e.g., the CHAMELEON), the pigmentation changes to resemble the surrounding environment. Some animals undergo a seasonal variation (e.g., the STOAT, which is usually brown with white underparts, but in snowy regions acquires a white coat in winter and is known as an ERMINE). See also MIMICRY.

**protectorate,** in international law, state which, while retaining nominal independence, surrenders part of its SOVEREIGNTY, such as control over foreign affairs, in return for protection by a stronger state. (The relationship between the two states may also be termed a *protectorate*.) The territory of the protected state remains distinct from, and its nationals are not citizens of, the protecting state. Protectorates appear in ancient Greek and Roman history; in modern times, European colonies were often governed as protectorates, but this form of political relationship is disappearing from today's world. See also TRUSTEESHIP, TERRITORIAL.

**proteins,** class of highly complex organic compounds found in all living cells. Proteins are the most abundant of all biological molecules, comprising about 50% of a cell's dry weight. Classified by biological function, proteins include ENZYMES, which catalyse cellular reactions; collagen, keratin, and elastin, which are structural, or support, proteins; HAEMOGLOBIN and other transport proteins; casein, ovalbumin, and other nutrient proteins; antibodies, which are necessary for IMMUNITY; protein HORMONES, which regulate METABOLISM; and proteins such as actin and myosin, the contractile muscle proteins, that perform mechanical work. Structurally, proteins are large molecules, linked by PEPTIDE bonds. Each protein is characterized by a unique and invariant amino acid sequence. Protein chains may contain hundreds of amino acids; some proteins incorporate phosphorus or such metals as iron, zinc, and copper. They also combine with other substances, such as nucleic acids, carbohydrates, and fats. The amino acid sequence determines the molecule's three-dimensional structure; this so-called native state is required for proper biological function. The information for the syntheses of the specific amino acid sequences from free amino acids is carried by the cell's NUCLEIC ACIDS. The human body needs proteins supplying these 22 amino acids, along with enough energy-giving food so that amino acids are not metabolized into energy. Eight amino acids must be provided ready-made in food (these are the essential amino acids).

**Protestantism,** form of Christian faith and practice that originated with the principles of the REFORMATION. The term, used in many senses, applies to Christians not belonging to the Roman Catholic Church or to an Eastern Orthodox church. Two distinct branches of Protestantism grew out of the Reformation. The evangelical churches of Scandinavia and Germany were followers of Martin LUTHER, and the reformed churches in other countries were followers of John CALVIN and Huldreich ZWINGLI. In England, neither Lutheran or Calvinist, some Anglicans, particularly since the OXFORD MOVEMENT in the 19th cent, have rejected the term.

**Protestant Union,** 1608–21, also known as the Evangelical League, an alliance of German Protestant rulers of cities and states for the avowed purpose of a mutual defence of their lands, persons, and rights. It was formed to block attempts by the Holy Roman emperor and the Catholic princes of Germany to restore all church lands that had been appropriated by the Protestant princes. Never very effective, the union went out of existence three years after the outbreak of the THIRTY YEARS' WAR.

**Protogenes** (proh,tojəneez), fl. c.300 BC, Greek painter, considered second only to APELLES in antiquity. His best-known work, the *Ialysus,* was removed by VESPASIAN to Rome, where it was destroyed when the Temple of Peace was burnt.

**proton,** ELEMENTARY PARTICLE having a single positive electrical charge and constituting the nucleus of the ordinary hydrogen ATOM. Every atomic nucleus contains one or more protons. The mass of the proton is about 1840 times the mass of the ELECTRON and slightly less than the mass of the neutron. In 1919 Ernest RUTHERFORD showed that the proton is a product of the disintegration of certain atomic nuclei. The proton and the neutron are regarded as two aspects, or states, of a single entity, the nucleon. The antiproton, the proton's antiparticle (see ANTIMATTER), was discovered in 1955.

**protoplasm,** fundamental material composing all living things. Protoplasm, which exists in all plants and animals in the small units called CELLS, is mainly water (85%–90%) and also contains proteins, fatty substances, and inorganic salts. It is always enclosed by a thin surface membrane that controls the passage of materials into and out of the cell. It displays the general properties associated with life—the capacity to respond to stimuli and the ability to perform the essential physiological functions.

**Protozoa,** large phylum of microsopic one-celled organisms. Most are solitary, but a few live in simple colonies. The majority are aquatic, living in fresh or salt water; some live in soil. Despite their small size and lack of multicellular organization, protozoans carry on all the metabolic functions of higher animals: digestion, excretion, respiration, and coordination of movement. Many species are parasitic, often causing diseases in humans and other animals. The phylum is usually divided into four classes: flagellates, AMOEBAS, sporozoans, and ciliates.

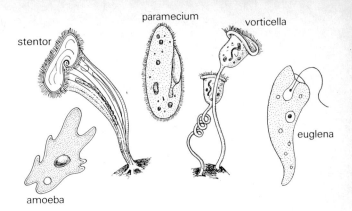

Protozoa

**Proudhon, Pierre Joseph** (prooh,dawnh), 1809–65, French social theorist. He achieved notice with the repetition of an 18th-cent. phrase that 'property is theft' in his pamphlet *What Is Property?* (1840). After the REVOLUTIONS OF 1848 he became a member of the constituent assembly. He advocated 'mutualism', in which small groups would interact economically and politically within a framework of agreement on basic principles, and the public issue of interest-free loans so that everyone might have access to private property in the means of production. Opposed to force, he believed that ethical progress would make government superfluous. His works include *System of Economic Contradictions; or, The Philosophy of Poverty* (1846).

**Proust, Joseph Louis,** 1754–1826, French chemist. He discovered dextrose (grape sugar) and established the law of definite proportions (also known as Proust's law), which states that elements in a compound are present in a fixed proportion by weight.

**Proust, Marcel,** 1871–1922, French novelist. He was one of the great literary figures of modern times. As a youth, he mingled ambitiously in Parisian society, but later he became increasingly withdrawn. After 1907, he lived mainly in a cork-lined room, working at night on his monumental cyclic novel, *A la recherche du temps perdu* (1913–27; tr. Remembrance of Things Past, 1922–32, in seven vol.). Discursive, but alive with brilliant metaphor and sense imagery, the work is rich in psychological, philosophical, and sociological understanding, a vital theme being the link between external and internal reality found in time and memory. In Proust's scheme, the individual is isolated, society is false and ruled by snobbery, and artistic endeavour is raised to a religion.

**Provençal** (provahnh,sahl), member of the Romance group of the Italic subfamily of the Indo-European family of languages. Although spoken by several million people in France, it has no official status in that country. Also called LANGUE D'OC, Provençal became important in the Middle Ages as the medium of the great literature of the TROUBADOURS. See LANGUAGE (table).

**Provence** (pro,vahns), region and former province, SE France. NICE and MARSEILLES are the chief cities. Fruits, vegetables, and tourism are economic mainstays. The coast was settled (c.600 BC) by the Greeks and later colonized (2nd cent. BC) by the Romans. Christianity was implanted early. In 933 Provence became part of the kingdom of ARLES. It later passed to the Angevin dynasty of Naples (1246) and to France (1486).

**Proverbs,** book of the OLD TESTAMENT. It consists of a collection of moral and other maxims. The practical teachings are individual and universal rather than nationalistic. Ascribed to SOLOMON, the book was compiled at various dates between c.700 BC and the 4th cent. BC.

**Providence,** US city (1984 est. pop. 154,000), state capital of Rhode Island, a port on Providence Bay; founded 1636 by Roger WILLIAMS, inc. 1832. The largest city in the state, it is a major shipping centre famous for its silverware and jewellery industries. Other manufactures include textiles and electronic equipment. An early refuge for religious dissenters, Providence industrialized after the Revolution.

**Provisions of Oxford,** 1258, a scheme of governmental reform forced upon HENRY III of England by his barons. Drawn up by Simon de MONTFORT, it provided for an advisory council, and tried to limit the king's power to tax. Henry's repudiation (1261) of the agreement led to the BARONS' WAR (1263–67), in which the king triumphed.

**Prudhoe Bay,** inlet of the Arctic Ocean, N Alaska, US. Oil from large deposits (discovered in 1968) is transported S to the port of Valdez via the Alaskan Pipeline (completed in 1977). Prudhoe Bay oil makes Alaska the leading petroleum-producing state in the US.

**prune:** see PLUM.

**Prussia,** originally the homeland of the ancient Prussians, a Baltic people living between the Vistula and the Niemen in the province known as 'East Prussia'. It was later the site of the Teutonic state (1226–1525), a principality created by the crusading Order of Teutonic Knights, who forcibly christianized and germanized the native inhabitants; also of the duchy of Prussia (1525–1660), capital Koenigsberg (KALININGRAD), which under Polish suzerainty but in the possession of the Hohenzollern dynasty, provided the eastern section of the Hohenzollerns' possessions, jointly known as 'Brandenburg–Prussia'. In the 18th and 19th cent., the name of 'Prussia' was retained by the Hohenzollerns for their enlarged kingdom (capital BERLIN), whose constituent parts were scattered right across northern Germany from the Rhineland to Lithuania. The union of the duchy of Prussia with the Hohenzollern's electorate of Brandenburg first occurred in 1618. In 1660 full independence from Polish suzerainty was obtained by FREDERICK WILLIAM, the Great Elector. The electors of Brandenburg gradually acquired other lands, and in 1701 Elector Frederick III had himself crowned king of Prussia as Frederick I. He remained a prince of the Holy Roman Empire as elector of Brandenburg, but not as king of Prussia, which lay outside imperial boundaries. This technically gave the kings of Prussia some independence from the emperor. King FREDERICK WILLIAM I (r.1713–40) worked to unify the state and built an efficient army. His son FREDERICK II (r.1740–86) won most of SILESIA from Austria in the War of the AUSTRIAN SUCCESSION and entered the SEVEN YEARS WAR. Prussia gained further territory in the partitions of POLAND (1772–95). The kingdom was eclipsed by the rise of France under NAPOLEON I but had a major part in the defeat (1813–15) of the French. In 1862 Otto von BISMARCK became Prussian premier; he sought to unify Germany under Prussian leadership. After territorial gains in the AUSTRO-PRUSSIAN WAR and the FRANCO-PRUSSIAN WAR, the Prussian king was proclaimed (1871) emperor of Germany as WILLIAM I. Thereafter, the history of Prussia is essentially that of GERMANY. Prussia remained a kingdom in the German Empire until Germany became a republic in 1918. Prussia was abolished as a state in 1947 and divided among West Germany, East Germany, the USSR, and Poland.

**Przybyszewski, Stanislaw** ('shibi‚shevskee), 1868–1927, Prussian and Polish writer. He was one of the earliest exponents of EXPRESSIONISM, but was also a seminal Satanist. He moved in the circles of Dehmel, MUNCH, and STRINDBERG. Works like *Mass of the Dead* (1893) and *Children of Satan* (1897) influenced Austrian–German and Czech as well as Polish literary development.

**Psalms** or **Psalter,** book of the OLD TESTAMENT. A collection of 150 poetic pieces which since the last centuries BC has been the chief hymnal of the Jews and subsequently of Christians. Many are attributed to DAVID, SOLOMON, and others. Most took their present form between c.537 BC and c.100 BC. Bible versions vary in dividing them, and numbering is therefore confusing. According to the text, the psalms are in five groups (numbering according to the Authorized Version): 1–41; 42–72; 73–89; 90–106; 107–150. They vary in tone and subject. Psalms of contrition, or penitential psalms, include 6, 32, 38, 51 (Miserere), and 130 (De profundis). Some are imprecatory, e.g., 52, 64, 137. Some, e.g., 78, 105–107, emphasize Israel's history. Didactic psalms include 37, 49, and 50. Some seem especially adapted to public worship, e.g., 95 (Venite). Others have been regarded as Messianic, e.g., 2, 8, 16. There are psalms elsewhere in the BIBLE, e.g., 1 Sam. 2.1–10. The history of translation of the psalms is more extensive than that of any other part of the Old Testament.

**Psalter:** see PSALMS.

**psaltery:** see STRINGED INSTRUMENT.

**Psilopsida,** division of the PTERIDOPHYTA characterized by the lack of roots; one species also lacks leaves. The green stem carries out PHOTOSYNTHESIS, and the life cycle is very much like that of FERNS.

**Psyche,** in Greek mythology, personification of the human soul. Loved by EROS, she was forbidden to look at him. When she disobeyed he left her, but after a series of trials she became immortal and was reunited with him forever. The story is related in APULEIUS' *The Golden Ass* and features prominently in literature and painting.

**psychedelic drug:** see HALLUCINOGENIC DRUG.

**psychiatry,** branch of the medical profession concerned with mental disorders. Psychiatrists may work in a general hospital or in a mental hospital. Psychiatric disorders are usually divided into varieties of NEUROSIS (e.g., anxiety and depression) and PSYCHOSIS (e.g., SCHIZOPHRENIA). Environment, genetic factors, family background, and stressful life all seem to play a part in their development. In old people, degenerative changes also occur in the brain. Treatments for psychiatric conditions include antipsychotic, ANTIDEPRESSANT, and TRANQUILLIZER drugs, and ELECTROCONVULSIVE THERAPY. Techniques such as PSYCHOTHERAPY and PSYCHOANALYSIS can be traced to the pioneering work of Sigmund FREUD; BEHAVIOUR MODIFICATION therapy is derived from the ideas of B.F. SKINNER. A critical reassessment of psychiatry took place in the 1960s, with such writers as Gregory BATESON and R.D. LAING pointing out the ambiguous role of the psychiatrist as both healer and reinforcer of social norms.

**psychoactive:** see PSYCHOTROPIC.

**psychoanalysis,** strictly, the theory and practice of PSYCHOTHERAPY according to the principles first elucidated by Sigmund FREUD; more generally used to refer to all 'psychodynamic' therapies, including those based on the theories of ADLER, JUNG, and others, which depend upon a distinction between conscious and UNCONSCIOUS processes. Psychoanalytic practice emphasizes the interpretation of the analysand's 'free associations' by the analyst, in terms of the discovery and working through of repressed (often infantile) wishes, conflicts, and memories. The interpretation of dreams and of neurotic symptoms as signs of, and masks for, repressed unconscious material was central to Freud's early theoretical and clinical work, in which he elaborated the tripartite classification of the human mind into the ID, the EGO, and the SUPEREGO. The later development of the theory (sometimes called the 'metapsychology') was based upon the postulation of two fundamental instincts: Eros, the life instinct, and Thanatos, the death instinct. Freud's work has been compared to that of Marx and Darwin in its impact on modern thought, and psychoanalytic interpretations have been extended into many areas of the human and social sciences, as well as literary and aesthetic theory.

**psychobiology,** study of anatomical and biochemical structures and processes and their effect on behaviour. It is closely related to physiological psychology. Areas of investigation include hormonal and biochemical changes in nerves, glands, and muscles, and how these changes influence development, emotions, and learning.

**psychology,** the study of the human mind and mental processes, of human behaviour, and of human interpersonal relationships. The boundaries of the discipline are fluid, bordering upon biology, sociology, anthropology, philosophy, neurology, linguistics, and other disciplines. There are consequently many subdisciplines of and in psychology. Cognitive psychology (now a part of COGNITIVE SCIENCE) is largely concerned with modelling mental processes; developmental psychology is concerned with all aspects of human psychological development; neuropsychology is concerned with the neurophysiological and neuroanatomical bases of psychological processes; social psychology is concerned with interpersonal and intergroup influences, interactions, and attitudes; cross-cultural psychology studies variations in psychological processes in different cultures, etc. This variety of subject matter is also reflected in the variety of methods employed in psychological research, including experimentation, observation, survey, and interview. The wide range of applications of psychology is reflected in the specializations of clinical psychology, educational psychology, occupational and organizational psychology, etc.

**psychoneurosis:** see NEUROSIS.

**psychopathology,** the study and classification of mental disorders, by psychologists and others. See PSYCHIATRY.

**psychopathy,** otherwise known as 'personality disorder'. The term refers to a condition in which the individual appears to lack normal affective responses, with a diminished or absent sense of guilt and remorse for wrongdoing. Psychopathy is not a coherent clinical entity, and is in some ways merely a label for medical and psychological ignorance regarding the psychology and PSYCHOPATHOLOGY of seriously disturbed, dangerous individuals.

**psychopharmacology,** science of the relationship between drugs and behaviour, usually applied to the study of four basic categories of drugs used in the treatment of psychiatric illness: antipsychotic drugs (see TRANQUILLIZER), ANTIANXIETY drugs, ANTIDEPRESSANTS, and psychotomimetics (see HALLUCINOGENIC DRUG).

**psychophysics,** in psychology, the study of the quantitative relationship between a physical STIMULUS and its perception by humans.

**psychosis,** a severe mental disturbance or disorder of either an organic or non-organic ('functional', psychological) origin. Psychotic disorders are characterized by a lack of conformity between the subject's experiences and the real world, a failure to distinguish fantasy from reality, and a distortion of perception and processes of COGNITION. Symptoms include delusions, hallucinations, dramatic mood-swings, and seriously inappropriate or regressive behaviour. The most commonly listed psychoses are SCHIZOPHRENIA (including paranoid schizophrenia) and manic depression; but there are wide variations in diagnostic classifications, as well as in forms of treatment, which may include drug therapy, PSYCHOTHERAPY, electro-shock therapy, and surgery, although the last two have been widely criticized (see ANTI-PSYCHIATRY).

**psychosomatic disorder,** emotional disturbance that is manifested as a physical disorder such as childhood ASTHMA, ULCERS, HYPERTENSION, endocrine disturbances, and possibly even HEART disease. In most cases the illness occurs only when there is both a physiological predisposition and psychological stress. Treatment may involve a medical regimen as well as some form of PSYCHOTHERAPY.

**psychotherapy,** the practice of treatment of mental, behavioural, or emotional illnesses and disorders, or of unwished-for mental or emotional states. Psychotherapeutic theories and techniques include behaviour therapy (see BEHAVIOUR MODIFICATION), client-centred therapy (see Carl ROGERS), GESTALT THERAPY, psychoanalytic psychotherapy (see PSYCHOANALYSIS), etc. Besides individual psychotherapy, there are also techniques of group psychotherapy, whose object is to change behaviours or feelings through the experience of interpersonal relations within a small-scale social setting, whose members jointly participate in observing and evaluating personal motivations and styles of interaction. Individual psychotherapy is also complemented by family therapy and marital therapy, which attempt to alter long-standing patterns of interpersonal relationship perceived by participants as unsatisfactory, unhappy, or destructive.

**psychotomimetic drug:** see HALLUCINOGENIC DRUG.

**psychotropic,** mind-altering or mood-altering. Drugs with such effects are used in the treatment of psychiatric symptoms and disorders. A general term which covers tranquillizing, anti-depressant, and anti-psychotic drugs, as well as psychedelic or hallucinogenic drugs.

**Pt,** chemical symbol of the element PLATINUM.

**Pteridophyta** (ˌteridohˈfeetə), division of flowerless plants consisting of the FERNS, HORSETAILS, and CLUB MOSSES. They possess true VASCULAR TISSUE.

**Pteropsida** (ˌteropseedə): see FERN.

**Ptolemaic system,** historically the most influential of the geocentric cosmological theories, i.e., theories that placed the earth motionless at the centre of the universe with all celestial bodies revolving around it. The system is named after the astronomer PTOLEMY (Claudius Ptolemaeus), who in the 2nd cent. AD combined simple circular motions to explain the complicated wanderings of the planets. Ptolemy explained RETROGRADE MOTION by assuming that each planet moved in a circle called an epicycle, whose centre was in turn carried around the earth in a circular orbit called a deferent. The Ptolemaic system dominated astronomy until the advent of the heliocentric COPERNICAN SYSTEM in the 16th cent.

**Ptolemy** (ˌtoləmee), rulers of the Macedonian dynasty of EGYPT (323–30 BC). **Ptolemy I,** d. 284 BC, a leading general of ALEXANDER THE GREAT, became one of the DIADOCHI. After Alexander's death he received Egypt, declared himself king (305 BC), and laid the basis for Ptolemaic administration. He sought to make ALEXANDRIA the cultural centre of the Greek world, especially by founding its library. His son, **Ptolemy II,** c.308–246 BC (r.285–246), continued his father's work, completing the Pharos (see SEVEN WONDERS OF THE WORLD). He encouraged the translation of

the PENTATEUCH into the Greek Septuagint and had a canal built from the Nile to the Red Sea. Ptolemy ended the war with Syria and increased his prestige by siding with Rome in the first PUNIC WAR. His son, **Ptolemy III,** d. 221 BC (r.246–221), renewed war with Syria. During his reign Egyptian fleets controlled most of the coast of Asia Minor, and the kingdom was enlarged. **Ptolemy V,** d. 180 BC (r.205–180), came to the throne as a small boy. Civil war characterized his reign; Syrian and Macedonian invasions cost Egypt all of Palestine and much of Asia Minor. **Ptolemy VI,** d. 145 BC (r.180–145), became king as an infant; the Syrians forced him to share the throne with his brother (later Ptolemy VII). Trouble between the brothers brought about intervention by Rome. Ptolemy VI was killed while fighting over the Syrian throne. **Ptolemy VII,** d. 116 BC (r.145–116), put his brother's young son to death and succeeded to the throne. He survived a revolt (130–127) by his brother's widow, Cleopatra, and ruled peacefully though despotically. He drove the scholars from Alexandria, causing the spread of Alexandrian culture. **Ptolemy XI,** d. 51 BC (r.80–58, 55–51), was unseated by the Alexandrians because of his misrule but was restored with the aid of POMPEY. He made the Roman senate executor of his will and named Pompey guardian of his son, Ptolemy XII. **Ptolemy XII,** 61?–47 BC (r.51–47), was from the start overshadowed by his sister, CLEOPATRA, who became his wife and ruled with him. She revolted (48) against the power of his advisers. At this juncture the defeated Pompey arrived in Egypt and was killed by Ptolemy's adviser Pothinus. Julius CAESAR followed immediately, fell under Cleopatra's influence, and forced Ptolemy to share the throne again.

**Ptolemy** (Claudius Ptolemaeus), fl. 2nd cent. AD, Greek–Egyptian mathematician and geographer, the last great astronomer of ancient times. He systematized and recorded the knowledge of Alexandrian men of science. In his famous treatise, of 13 volumes, later called the *Almagest,* which remained influential until the time of COPERNICUS, he presented the geocentric cosmological theory known as the PTOLEMAIC SYSTEM; the treatise also contained a catalogue of more than 1020 stars, as well as a table of chords and other mathematical information. His *Geography,* despite its many errors, remained in use until the 16th cent. Ptolemy discovered the irregularity in the Moon's motion known as the evection and wrote the *Tetrabiblos,* a study of astrology.

**Pu,** chemical symbol of the element PLUTONIUM.

**Public Lending Right,** a means of securing a fair payment for authors from the use of their books in libraries. The Public Lending Right Act 1979 in the UK was the result of campaigning by various writers' organizations, individual writers, politicians, and political parties. The Act required the appointment of a Registrar of Public Lending Right (1981) who after consultation laid the final draft scheme before Parliament in Mar. 1982. The scheme involves the registration by authors of all published titles with The Registrar of Public Lending Right. Annually authors then receive a payment based on the number of borrowings of their titles based on an agreed scheme of library loan sampling. First payments were made under PLR in 1984. There is an upper limit on the amount that a single author can receive, so that the money available is not all used up on a handful of the most popular writers. In 1986 £2,402,000 was paid to 11,010 authors, half of this amount being in payments of less than £1000.

**public schools,** in Britain, independent, fee-paying schools, normally boarding and at the secondary level, and often associated with high social status. In the US the term is used for tax-supported elementary or high schools open to anyone—what in Britain are referred to as state or local-authority schools. Some English public schools are of ancient lineage (e.g., Eton and Winchester), some developed from grammar schools in the 19th cent. (e.g., Rugby and Shrewsbury), and others were new 19th cent. foundations (e.g., Wellington). Most public schools admit pupils at 13, and the vast majority are single-sex schools. There are about 270 public schools, and 6% of British children attend the range (some 1500 altogether) of private, independent, and public schools.

**publishing:** see BOOK PUBLISHING.

**Pucci, Emilio:** see FASHION (table).

**Puccini, Giacomo** (poohtˌcheenee), 1858–1924, Italian composer. One of the preeminent composers of Italian opera, he is noted for his lyric style, masterful orchestration, and his powerful dramatic effects, as in

*Manon Lescaut* (1893), *La Bohème* (1896), *Tosca* (1900), *Madam Butterfly* (1904), and *Turandot* (produced, 1926).

**Pudovkin, Vsevolod Ilarionovich** (poo‚dawfkin), 1893–1953, Russian film director. Ranked with EISENSTEIN and DOVZHENKO, he used MONTAGE in such films as *Mother* (1926), *The End of St Petersburg* (1927), and *Heir to Genghis Khan* (1928).

**Puebla,** city (1979 est. pop. 710,833), E central Mexico, capital of Puebla state. It is a major agricultural and industrial centre and a tourist resort noted for the coloured tiles that decorate its buildings. It has one of the finest cathedrals in Mexico. Founded in the mid-16th cent., it long was a vital link between Mexico City and the coast.

**Pueblo Indians,** Spanish name for NORTH AMERICAN INDIANS who occupied stone or adobe community houses in more than 80 villages (pueblos) in the Southwestern culture area. They are the descendants of the prehistoric Anasazi culture of Utah, Colorado, Arizona, New Mexico, and N Mexico. By 2000 BC the earliest agriculturalists, known as the Cochise culture, were raising corn. The Mogollon people, with the first bows and arrows and true pottery in North America, built the first village settlements in the 1st cent. AD, while their contemporaries, the basketmakers, were living in caves. Irrigation and surface houses with KIVAS developed between 400 and 700, but multi-storey cliff houses on MESAS marked the Great Pueblo Period, from 1050 to the end of the 13th cent. By 1630, 90 years after CORONADO had explored the Pueblo villages, Spanish missionaries had converted 60,000 Pueblo Indians to Christianity. In 1680 Popé led the pueblos in a revolt that drove the Spanish out for 12 years; those in New Mexico were recaptured in 1692, but the Western Pueblos remained free. The contemporary Pueblos are quite diverse linguistically (see AMERICAN INDIAN LANGUAGES) and culturally. Their culture is the oldest N of Mexico, dating back 700 years for the still-occupied HOPI, ZUÑI, and ACOMA pueblos. Several of the two dozen surviving pueblos have retained pre-Spanish social systems and community organization to a surprising degree. They are sedentary farmers; men are weavers and women potters. The position of women remains high; there are important secret societies.

**Puente del Inca,** natural bridge situated at a height of 2178 m (7145 ft) in the Andes of W Argentina. The natural arch crosses the Mendoza R. at a height of 19 m (62 ft), has a span of 21 m (68 ft) and a width of 27 m (88 ft). Its formation is attributed to the effect of sulphur-bearing hotsprings. The nearby tourist resort of the same name is a centre for excursions into the high Andes and to the nearby peak of Aconcagua.

**Puerto Rico** [Span., = rich port], formerly Porto Rico, island (1987 est. pop. 3,400,000), 8860 km² (3421 sq mi), West Indies, 1610 km (1000 mi) SE of Miami. Officially it is the Commonwealth of Puerto Rico, a self-governing entity in association with the US. The capital is SAN JUAN; other urban centres include BAYAMÓN and PONCE. Easternmost of the Greater Antilles, it is bounded by the Atlantic (N), the Caribbean (S), the Dominican Republic (W), and the Virgin Islands (E). Puerto Rico is crossed by mountain ranges, notably the Cordillera Central, which rises to 1388 m (4389 ft). The climate is tropical. Sugarcane is the chief product, followed by livestock and dairy production. Coffee and tobacco are other leading crops. The dense population, however, depends chiefly on industrial employment encouraged since World War II by tax incentives; metallurgical and chemical industries, oil refineries, and manufactures of textiles, electronic equipment, and plastics are important. Tourism is also a major source of revenue. The GDP is US$17,352 million and the GDP per capita is US$5300. Population growth and social problems have led to much emigration, and one third of all Puerto Ricans live in the US. Puerto Ricans share the rights and duties of US citizens, except that they do not pay federal income taxes and do not vote in national elections (unless living on the mainland). The Puerto Ricans are descended from Spanish colonists, with admixed Indian and African strains. Spanish is the official language; English is taught in all schools. Roman Catholicism is the predominant religion.

*History.* When COLUMBUS arrived in 1493, Arawak Indians lived on Puerto Rico, which they called Boriquén or Borinquén. PONCE DE LEÓN began the conquest in 1508. Sugar culture was introduced, strategic San Juan was fortified, and African slaves replaced the annihilated Arawaks as plantation workers, though sugar output remained of minor significance by British Caribbean standards. In the 19th cent. popular unrest led finally to Spain's granting of some autonomy in 1898. After the SPANISH–AMERICAN WAR, Puerto Rico was ceded (1898) to the US, which set up (1900) an

administration under an American governor. Meanwhile an independence movement grew. In 1917 Puerto Ricans were granted US citizenship. As US holdings in the one-crop sugar economy increased, large corporations encroached on land that had been used to grow subsistence crops, and the subsequent economic distress was not relieved until World War II. After the war, 'Operation Bootstrap', encouraging American industrial investment with tax incentives, began to change the nature of the economy. In 1952 the Commonwealth of Puerto Rico was proclaimed. Nationalist agitation continued, however. By the 1960s statehood advocates and supporters of continued commonwealth status held power alternately, while advocates of independence eschewed the electoral process. The debate over the island's status continued into the 1980s. The 1984 legislative and gubernatorial elections were won by the Popular Democratic Party, which supports the island's existing status.

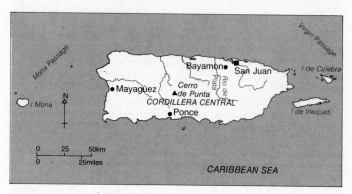

Puerto Rico

**Pueyrredón, Juan Martín de** (pwayiray‚dohn), 1776–1850, Argentine general, supreme director of the United Provinces of La Plata (1816–19). He resisted the invasion of Buenos Aires by the British (1806). He held several posts in the revolutionary government, including that of commander of the patriot Army of the North (1811–12).

**puffin,** migratory diving BIRD of the AUK family. Puffins have dumpy bodies, short legs set far back, small wings, and a large, brilliantly coloured bill adapted for carrying several fish at once. Clumsy on land and in flight, they are expert swimmers. Puffins nest in colonies in burrows or rock cavities on northern islands.

**Pugachev, Emelian Ivanovich** (poohgə‚chof), d. 1775, leader of the 1773–74 Russian peasant uprising. A Don COSSACK, he claimed to be PETER III, announced the end of serfdom, and gathered an army of Cossacks, serfs, and TATARS. After seizing towns in the Volga and Ural regions he was caught and executed. The revolt led CATHERINE II to strengthen serfdom.

**Puget Sound,** island-studded inlet of the Pacific Ocean, NW Washington, US, extending S c.160 km (100 mi) to Olympia and navigable by large ships. Seattle and Tacoma are important shoreline cities. Discovered in 1787, the sound was explored and named in 1792 by Capt. George Vancouver after his aide, Peter Puget.

**Pugin, Augustus Welby Northmore,** 1812–52, English architect. A key figure in the revival and development of Gothic architecture (see GOTHIC REVIVAL) in Britain and Ireland and thus of the world, he designed five cathedrals, several hundred churches, various great houses, and fittings and furniture, and died insane at the age of 40. He was responsible for all the detailed design of the Palace of Westminster (the Houses of Parliament) for Sir Charles Barry, who had won the competition to do the designs but was unfamiliar with Gothic work. His greatest influence however was through his books, including *Contrasts* (1836), which compared the architecture of the 14th and 15th cent. with that of the 19th to the detriment of the latter, and *The True Principles of Pointed or Christian Architecture* (1841) in which he announced the two principles upon which he believed architecture should depend, firstly, that there should be no features about a building which are not necessary for convenience, construction, or propriety, and, secondly, that ornament should be limited to the essential structure of the building. He can thus be seen as a prophet of MODERN ARCHITECTURE as well as a brilliant apologist for Gothic design.

Puffin (*Fratercula arctica*)

**Puig, Manuel,** 1932–, Argentinian novelist. Cultural and sexual margination and confusion are the themes of *La traición de Rita Hayworth* (1969) and *The Buenos Aires Affair* (1973).

**Pulitzer, Joseph,** 1847–1911, American newspaper publisher; b. Hungary. He left funds to endow what is now the graduate school of journalism at Columbia Univ., and he endowed the Pulitzer Prizes. Eight are given each year for journalism, and one each for fiction, drama, poetry, history, biography (or autobiography), nonfiction, and music; works with American themes are preferred.

**pulley:** see MACHINE.

**Pullman, George Mortimer,** 1831–97, American industrialist and developer of the railway sleeping car. He began in Chicago (1859) converting railway coaches into sleeping cars, whose success enabled him to found (1867) the Pullman Palace Car Company. Gaining great wealth from his invention he established (1880) the company-owned town of Pullman, now part of Chicago. Wage-cuts and the dismissal of union representatives precipitated (1894) the memorable Pullman strike which spread to the railway and for a time paralysed rail traffic in the Mid-West.

**pulsar,** in astronomy, a celestial object that emits brief, sharp pulses of radio waves. The pulses recur at precise intervals; the time between pulses ranges from milliseconds to some seconds. Pulsars are believed to be rotating NEUTRON STARS that emit radio waves in a narrow beam. Because of the rotation of the star, the beam will sweep across the line of sight, causing the observed pulses.

**pulse,** alternate expansion and contraction of artery walls as HEART action varies blood volume within them. Artery walls are elastic and become distended by the increase in blood volume when the heart contracts. When the heart relaxes, this volume decreases and the walls contract, propelling the blood through the arteries. The result is a pressure wave, with a pulsation for each heartbeat. See also BLOOD PRESSURE.

**pulse,** in botany, common name for Leguminosae or Fabaceae, a large family of herbs, shrubs, and trees, also called the pea, or legume, family. The family is typified by usually compound leaves, a fruit that is a LEGUME (a type of pod), and FLOWERS with an irregular butterflylike shape. Many species have thorny branches. The seeds of the family are rich in PROTEIN; in many areas where meat is scarce, legumes, e.g., BEANS, PEAS, LENTILS, PEANUTS, SOYA BEANS, and CAROB, are staples. Some species are fodder and forage plants, e.g., CLOVER, ALFALFA, soya beans, and vetch. The root

nodules of these food and forage plants have BACTERIA that fix NITROGEN (see NITROGEN CYCLE), making them valuable as COVER CROPS and green manure (see FERTILIZER). The family also provides gums and RESINS, dyes and tannins, timber, medications, oils, flavourings, fibres, and insecticides, and some legumes are ornamentals, e.g., ACACIA, LOCUST, MIMOSA, and WISTERIA.

**pulse code modulation:** see MODULATION.

**puma** or **cougar,** New World member (*Felis concolor*) of the CAT family. Also called mountain lion, catamount, and panther, it ranges from S British Columbia to southernmost South America. Pumas vary in size (up to 2.1 m/7 ft) and colour according to locale and live in many kinds of country, preying on animals as large as deer. Hunted as pests, they are nearly extinct in the US.

**pumice,** volcanic glass formed by the solidification of LAVA permeated with gas bubbles. It has the chemical composition of GRANITE, but is of low enough density to float on water. Pumice is used primarily as an ABRASIVE.

**pump,** device to lift, transfer, or increase the pressure of a fluid (liquid or gas) or to create a VACUUM. In a simple *reciprocating pump* used to lift water, a piston moves back and forth in a cylinder equipped with intake and outflow valves. On the piston's upstroke, atmospheric pressure forces water into the empty space beneath the piston. On the downstroke, the water in the cylinder is forced to flow above the piston. Reversing direction, the piston moves up, allowing more water to come up under it into the cylinder and lifting the water held above it to an outlet pipe. The *rotary pump* is like the reciprocating pump in that it allows a fluid to fill a space that then decreases in volume. The rotary pump, however, has no valves and uses rotating components in place of a piston.

**pumpkin,** common name for the genus *Cucurbita* of the GOURD family, including the pumpkins and squashes. Although the names are often used interchangeably, pumpkin, in the UK, usually refers to *C. maxima* and its varieties; in the US it means *C. pepo*. The most popular of these is a vine bearing orange fruits, or pumpkins, used as pie filling and also carved into jack-o'-lanterns at Halloween. Squash usually refers to *C. pepo* (*C. maxima* in the US) or *C. moschata*.

**Punch and Judy,** traditional English puppet play, deriving from COMMEDIA DELL' ARTE. Punch is cruel and boastful; his wife, Judy, whom he beats, is a loud, faithless nag.

**punctuation,** device of WRITING supplementing the use of letters. In English, stress, pauses, and tonal changes interlock in a set of patterns often called intonations, and such features are represented by punctuation. The intonations of declaration are classified as three types, symbolized by the comma (,), used to separate words or phrases for clarity; the semicolon (;), used to mark separation between elements in a series of related phrases, generally in a long sentence; and the full stop, or period (.), used to mark the end of a sentence. Other intonations are shown by the exclamation mark (!); the question mark (?); the parenthesis or bracket (), used to set off a word or phrase from a sentence that is complete without it; and the colon (:), typically used to introduce material that elaborates on what has already been said. Either single (' ') or double ('' '') quotation marks are used to indicate direct quotation. Punctuation of material intended to be read silently rather than aloud has introduced refinements to help the reader: square brackets ([]), a secondary parenthesis; ellipsis (. . .), used to indicate the place where material has been omitted; the long dash (—), for incomplete intonation patterns. Two more frequent signs are the apostrophe ('), marking an omission of one or two letters, or a possessive case; and the hyphen (-), marking a line division or an intimate joining, as in compound words. Each written language has a tradition of punctuation, often very different from that of English.

**Pune** (formerly **Poona**), city (1981 pop. 1,203,351), Maharashtra state, W India, at the confluence of the Mutha and Mula Rs. It is an important administrative, cultural, and communications centre, commanding the Bhor Ghat leading to BOMBAY. It has a number of famous Hindu temples and a university. It is the commercial capital of the surrounding agricultural area, which also has craft industries. Pune itself has growing industries, manufacturing textiles, paper, and metal goods, many of them located in trading estates (notably along the Pune–Bombay road). If Bombay is the commercial and principal administrative capital of Maharashtra, Pune is its cultural and educational capital, owing to its history. Two of its temples date from the 13th cent. It grew to importance in the 17th cent. and was the capital of the Mahrattas from 1735 until their overthrow by the British at nearby Kirkee in 1817. The British in their turn made Pune and Kirkee important military bases; and they remain the headquarters of independent India's Southern Command.

**Punic Wars,** three distinct conflicts between Carthage and Rome. When they began, Rome had nearly completed the conquest of Italy, while CARTHAGE controlled NW Africa and the islands and the commerce of the W Mediterranean. When they ended, Carthage was ruined, and Rome was the greatest power W of China. The **First Punic War,** 264–241 BC, grew immediately out of a quarrel between the Sicilian cities of Messana (now Messina) and Syracuse that involved Rome and Carthage. The Romans won naval victories at Mylae (260 BC) and Cape Ecnomus (256 BC), but a Roman excursion to Africa failed (255 BC). Although HAMILCAR BARCA blocked the Romans in Sicily, a Roman victory at sea off the Aegadian Isles (241 BC) caused Carthage to sue for peace. The treaty gave Sicily to Rome, but the Romans, contrary to the treaty, invaded Sardinia and Corsica. When the Carthaginians under HANNIBAL took (219 BC) the Spanish city of Saguntum (present-day Sagunto), a Roman ally, Rome declared war. This **Second Punic War,** or Hannibalic War, 218–201 BC, was one of the titanic struggles of history. It was marked by Hannibal's invasion of Italy and his initial victories there, but Hannibal's ultimate failure came at the battle of ZAMA (202 BC) in Africa. Carthage surrendered its Spanish province and its war fleet to Rome and never recovered. The **Third Punic War,** 149–146 BC, originated when Rome charged Carthage with a breach of treaty. Rome declared war, blockaded the city, and razed it. On 5 Feb. 1985 the mayors of Rome and Carthage signed a peace treaty, thus officially ending hostilities 2132 years after the fighting ceased.

**Punjab** [Sanskrit, = five rivers], historic region, bounded by the Indus R. (W) and Jamuna (Jumna) R. (E), in Pakistan and NW India. A centre of the ancient INDUS VALLEY CIVILIZATION, it is a semiarid but productive and progressive rice- and wheat-growing region, irrigated by the Jhelum, Chenab, Ravi, Sutlej, and Beas rivers, which unite to join the INDUS R. The Punjab was a province of British India from 1849 until 1947, when it was partitioned. The western areas (c.150,000 km²/58,000 sq mi) became the province of West Punjab (now Punjab) in Pakistan, and the eastern areas (c.235,000 km²/c.91,000 sq mi) became part of India, where they now form, after several reorganizations, the states of Haryana, Punjab, and part of Himachal Pradesh. The population of Punjab state (1981) was 16,788,915. The state is troubled by the demand of some Sikhs for independence.

**Punjabi,** language belonging to the Indic group of the Indo-Iranian subfamily of the Indo-European family of languages. See LANGUAGE (table).

**punk rock:** see ROCK MUSIC.

**Purcell, Henry,** c.1659–1695, English composer. He was the organist at Westminster Abbey (1679–95). In 1682 he was appointed one of the organists to the Chapel Royal. Combining lyrical melody, harmonic invention, and mastery of COUNTERPOINT to create an English BAROQUE style, he wrote the opera *Dido and Aeneas* (1689); *The Fairy Queen* (1692), a MASQUE and *The Indian Queen* (1695); songs for public occasions, e.g., odes for St Cecilia's Day; instrumental works; and church music.

**purgatory,** in the teaching of the Roman Catholic Church, the state after death in which the soul destined for heaven is purged of all unpunished or unrepented minor SINS. Souls in purgatory may be aided by the prayers of the living. The Orthodox and Protestants reject the Roman concept of purgatory, but the former believe in a middle state in which the dead may be helped by the prayers of the faithful.

**Purim:** see under JEWISH HOLIDAYS.

**purine,** organic compound found in the NUCLEIC ACID molecules of plant and animal tissue. The two major purines distributed almost universally in living systems are the bases adenine and guanine, present in DNA and RNA.

**Purism,** a style in art developed by LE CORBUSIER and Amedee Ozenfant in the early 1920s as a reaction against the decorative qualities of synthetic CUBISM. It was a style based upon a machine aesthetic where each object in their still life was a kind of 'object-type', where form and decoration were reduced to a functional minimum.

**Puritanism,** in the 16th and 17th cent., a movement for reform in the Church of England that had a profound influence on the social, political, ethical, and theological ideas in England and America. Originating in the reign of ELIZABETH I, the movement opposed the ecclesiastical establishment and aimed at purifying the church—hence the name Puritan. Many Puritans sided with the parliamentary party in the ENGLISH CIVIL WAR and held great power between 1640 and 1660. They were cast out of the Church of England after the RESTORATION, but their ideas were given a new lease of life in America, where the early New England settlements were Puritan in origin and theocratic in nature. The spirit of Puritanism has persisted in both countries, and its idea of congregational democratic government made a valuable contribution in both to the development of modern democracy.

**purslane,** common name for some plants of Portulaceae, a family of chiefly New World herbs and shrubs. The common purslane (*Portulaca oleracea*), is a common trailing weed of wide distribution used as a potherb and as a cooked vegetable. It was at one time a very important cure for scurvy. Some species, e.g., the showy-blossomed rose moss, or garden purslane (*P. grandiflora*), from Brazil, are cultivated in gardens.

**Pusan,** city (1984 pop. 3,495,289), extreme SE South Korea. It is the nation's second largest city and largest port, with an excellent natural harbour. It has served as a main southern gateway to Korea from Japan and is also the southern terminus of the main railway line from SEOUL. A leading industrial, commercial, and shipbuilding centre, Pusan is also a popular resort city. During the KOREAN WAR it was (Aug.–Sept. 1950) the site of a UN beachhead. Historic landmarks include several medieval palaces.

**Pusey, Edward Bouverie,** 1800–82, English scholar–priest, leader in the OXFORD MOVEMENT. In 1828 he was made regius professor of Hebrew at Oxford and canon of Christ Church. He formally aligned himself with the Oxford Movement in late 1833 and wrote the tracts on fasting (1834) and baptism (1836) in the series *Tracts for the Times*. When John Henry NEWMAN withdrew from the Oxford Movement in 1841, Pusey became its leader. He strongly defended High Church views and advocated the doctrine of the Real Presence, holding that the body and blood of Christ were actually present in the Eucharist. He assisted (1845) in the establishment of the first Anglican sisterhood, and his sermon 'The Entire Absolution of the Penitent' (1846) established the Anglican practice of private confession. Personally humble, he devoted himself to the sick and dying during the cholera epidemic of 1866.

**Pushkin, Aleksandr Sergeyevich** (‚pooshkin), 1799–1837, Russian poet and prose writer. Born to a noble family, he published his first major poem, *Russlan and Ludmilla,* in 1820. In that year both his *Ode to Liberty* and some satirical verses offended the court, and he was exiled to S Russia. There he composed such Byronic poems as *The Prisoner of the Caucasus* (1821). He was ordered to his family's estate in 1824 but was pardoned in 1826, settling first in Moscow and then in St Petersburg. He died of wounds received in a duel. The first to use the vernacular and to draw heavily on Russian history and folklore, Pushkin is revered as the founder of modern Russian poetry. His masterpiece is the verse-novel *Eugene Onegin* (1825–31), adapted as an opera by TCHAIKOVSKY. Among his other works are the verse-drama *Boris Godunov* (1831), the basis of a MOUSSORGSKY opera; the historical poem *The Bronze Horseman* (1833); the story *The Queen of Spades* (1834), also adapted as an opera by Tchaikovsky; *The Captain's Daughter* (1836), a short novel of the 1773–75 PUGACHEV uprising; and *The Negro of Peter the Great* (1837), an unfinished novel about Pushkin's maternal great-grandfather.

**Pushtu** (‚pushtooh), language belonging to the Iranian group of the Indo-Iranian subfamily of the Indo-European family of languages. It is also called Pashto and Afghan. See LANGUAGE (table).

**Puszta,** grazing lands on the great plain of E Hungary. Sandy or salt-encrusted, the least fertile portions of the plain were given over to grazing by horses, cattle, and sheep. Reclamation and irrigation has reduced the areas of steppe, the largest surviving portion being the Hortobágy puszta west of DEBRECEN.

**Puttenham, George,** 1529?–91, literary theorist, was probably the author of one of the most detailed theoretical accounts of Elizabethan rhetoric and poetry, *The Arte of English Poesie* (1589).

**Puvis de Chavannes, Pierre** (py͵vee də sha͵van), 1824–98, French mural painter. After studying with DELACROIX, he secured his reputation with the painting *War* (Amiens). His chaste murals with allegorical figures are in the Sorbonne and the Boston Public Library.

**Pu Yi, Henry,** 1906–67, last emperor (1908–12) of China, under the name Hsuan T'ung. In 1934 he became Emperor Kang De of the Japanese puppet state of Manchukuo, or Manchuria. Captured (1945) by the Russians, he was returned (1950) to China and imprisoned until 1959.

**PVC:** see POLYVINYL CHLORIDE.

**Pygmalion,** in Greek mythology, king of Cyprus, sculptor of a beautiful statue of a woman. When he prayed to APHRODITE for a wife like it, she brought the statue (Galatea) to life, and Pygmalion married her. The story is told in OVID's *Metamorphoses*, and retold by G.B. SHAW in his play *Pygmalion* (1913), popularized as the musical *My Fair Lady* (1956).

**Pygmies** or **Pigmies,** nomadic hunting and gathering peoples of equatorial Africa whose adult males average under 1.5 m (5 ft) in height. They were probably the sole inhabitants of the Congo valley before farming was developed. Numbering c.35,000, they live in small bands, dependent largely on the forest for their food, although they trade with the settled agriculturalists around them. Pygmy groups include the Akkas, in the upper Nile R. valley; the Batwas, in the great bend of the Congo R.; and the Mbuti, in the Ituri forest of NE Zaïre. They have been described by the British anthropologist Colin Turnball in: *The Forest People* (1961).

Pygmy settlement in the Huiri Rain Forest, Zaïre

**Pylos** (͵pielos), harbour of ancient MESSENIA, Greece, site of a 13th-cent.-BC Mycenaean palace, possible dwelling of King Nestor, in Greek mythology. The Bay of Pylos was the scene of an Athenian victory over SPARTA (425 BC) and, in modern times, of the battle of Navarino (1827) in the Greek war of independence.

**Pym, John,** 1583?–1643, English statesman. He was a leading Puritan opponent of the royalist party of CHARLES I in both the Short and Long Parliaments. Charles tried to remove him from the Commons by military arrest. After the outbreak of the ENGLISH CIVIL WAR Pym arranged an alliance (1643) with Scotland based on English acceptance of the Solemn League and Covenant (see COVENANTERS).

**Pynchon, Thomas,** 1937–, American novelist. Considered a major writer, he is noted for his extravagant sense of humour and imagination. He creates a wild, dark, and labyrinthine world in novels that include *V.* (1963), *The Crying of Lot 49* (1966), and *Gravity's Rainbow* (1973).

**Pyongyang** (͵pyong ͵yang), city (1981 pop. 1,280,000), capital of North Korea, NW Korea. Near large iron and coal deposits, it is a major industrial centre, producing steel, machinery, and armaments. Korea's oldest city, Pyongyang was founded, according to legend, in 1122 BC and served as the capital of several Korean kingdoms. It became the capital of North Korea in 1948 and was captured (1950) by UN forces during the KOREAN WAR. The city was later retaken by the North Koreans and rebuilt along modern lines. Only six gates remain of Pyongyang's great walls. Other landmarks include tombs (1st cent. BC) with notable murals.

**pyorrhoea** (ˈpie·ə͵riə): see PERIODONTITIS.

**pyramid.** The true pyramid exists only in Egypt. Usually of stone, it is square in plan, with triangular sides facing the compass points, sloping at an angle of about 50° and meeting at an apex. The oldest Egyptian tombs are MASTABAS. The true pyramid evolved about the IV dynasty (2680–2565 BC) and was favoured throughout the VI dynasty (2420–2258 BC). Later pyramid tombs were archaisms. Each monarch built his own pyramid, in which his mummified body might be preserved for eternity. Entrance was through an opening in the north wall. A small passage, traversing lesser chambers, led to the sepulchral chamber, excavated from the bedrock deep beneath the immense pile. Usually of stone blocks laid in horizontal courses, pyramids were sometimes of mud brick with stone casing. Most notable are the three pyramids of Gizeh (IV dynasty). The Great Pyramid of Khufu or Cheops (2680 BC), one of the SEVEN WONDERS OF THE WORLD, is the largest ever built, 5.3 hectares (13 acres) in area and 147 m (482 ft) high. Pyramidal structures are found also in Mesopotamia (the ZIGGURAT) and in Central America and Mexico. The Mayan pyramids, built in steep, receding blocks, were topped by ritual chambers. Some had interior tomb crypts.

The Great **Pyramid** and Sphinx at Giza

**Pyramus and Thisbe** (͵pirəməs, ͵thizbee), in classical myth, Babylonian lovers. Arriving at their trysting place, Thisbe fled from a lion and dropped her mantle. Pyramus found the garment bloodied and, thinking Thisbe dead, killed himself. On returning, Thisbe killed herself. The white fruit of the mulberry tree, which stood on the spot, was bloodied and remained red. Shakespeare derives much amusement from this legend by dramatizing it in *A Midsummer-Night's Dream*.

**Pyrenees,** mountain range, SW Europe, separating Spain from France. Rich in timber, pasturage, and hydroelectric-power resources, the range extends 435 km (270 mi) from E to W and reaches a high point of 3404 m (11,168 ft) in the Pico de Aneto in Spain. Along the steep slopes on the French side are many resorts and the noted place of pilgrimage, LOURDES.

**pyrimidine** (pie͵rimideen, -din), type of organic compound based on a six-membered carbon–nitrogen ring. Virtually all animal and plant tissue contains the pyrimidines thymine, cytosine, and uracil as part of certain COENZYMES and in the NUCLEIC ACIDS.

**pyrite** or **iron pyrites,** the most common sulphide mineral ($FeS_2$), brass yellow in colour, found in crystals and massive, granular, and stalactite forms. In spite of its nickname, 'fool's gold', it is often associated with gold. Pyrite, widely distributed in rocks of all ages, is used chiefly as a source of SULPHUR for sulphuric acid. See also MARCASITE.

**pyroxene,** name for a group of widespread magnesium, iron, and calcium silicate minerals. They are commonly white, black, and brown, but other varieties occur. Found chiefly in igneous and metamorphic rocks, they are abundant in lunar rocks.

**Pyrrho,** c.360–c.270 BC, Greek philosopher. The first great sceptic, he taught SCEPTICISM as an *agoge*, or way of life, rather than a philosophical tool. Some authorities claim that the 'suspension of judgment' he advocated entailed a heroic indifference to the dangers of the physical world, but a more likely interpretation, due to his disciple Timon of Phlius, is that he advised us to acknowledge our lack of comprehension of the universe in order to achieve peace of mind.

**Pyrrhus** (ˌpirəs), c.318–272 BC, king of EPIRUS. He invaded MACEDON (291) but was driven out (c.286). To aid the Tarentines, he went to Italy (280), where he defeated the Romans at Heraclea and Asculum, but with such heavy losses that he said: 'One more such victory and I am lost'; hence the term 'Pyrrhic victory'. Defeated by the Romans at Beneventum (275), he turned again to Macedon, defeating Antigonus II (273). He was later killed in Argos.

**Pyrrophyta,** division of the plant kingdom consisting of mostly unicellular, often flagellated, and usually photosynthetic organisms; the division includes the dinoflagellates, which are in some classification systems placed in a separate kingdom from plants and animals. They are extremely abundant in tropical oceans, where they are important in the food chain and largely responsible for the phosphorescence visible at night.

**Pythagoras,** c.582–c.507 BC, pre-Socratic Greek philosopher. We know little of his life and nothing of his writings; all of our knowledge comes from his followers, the **Pythagoreans,** a mystical brotherhood he founded at Crotona. Members of the order regarded Pythagoras as a demigod and attributed all their doctrines to him. They believed in the transmigration of souls, and followed moral and dietary practices in order to purify the soul for its next embodiment. Skilled mathematicians, they influenced early Euclidian geometry, e.g., through the Pythagorean theorem (which states that the square of the length of the hypotenuse of a right-angled triangle equals the sum of the squares of the lengths of the other two sides). They were also among the first to teach that the Earth is a spherical planet revolving about a fixed point. Beginning with the discovery of numerical relations between musical notes, they taught that the essence of all things was number and that all relationships even abstract concepts like justice could be expressed numerically.

**Pythian games,** in ancient GREECE, games held at DELPHI every four years to honour APOLLO. They included musical, literary, and athletic contests.

**python,** nonvenomous constrictor SNAKE of the BOA family, found in tropical regions of the Old World and the South Pacific islands. It kills its prey by squeezing them in its coils so that they suffocate. The reticulated, or royal, python (*Python reticulatus*), one of the largest snakes in the world, may reach a length of 9 m (30 ft) or more. The North Queensland python (*P. amethystinus*) is the largest Australian snake at 6 m (20 ft).

**Qaddafi, Muammar al-,** 1942–, army officer and chief of state of LIBYA (1969–). He led the 1969 army coup that deposed King Idris I. As chief of state he has blended Arab nationalism, revolutionary socialism, and Islamic orthodoxy into a stridently anti-Western and anti-Israeli dictatorship, financed by Libya's vast oil resources.

**qadi** or **kadi,** a senior judge presiding over legal procedures conducted according to Islamic law (see FIQH). In the contemporary Arab World, the same term indicates a judge in civil courts.

**Qatar** (ka͵tah), officially the State of Qatar, independent sheikhdom (1987 est. pop. 300,000), c.11,400 km² (4400 sq mi), on a largely barren peninsula in the PERSIAN GULF, bordering Saudi Arabia and the United Arab Emirates (S). The capital is DOHA. The climate is hot and dry but humid on the coast. The economy of Qatar is dominated by oil, which accounts for over 99% of exports and over 90% of government income. Oil revenues are being used to develop a programme of industrial diversification. The GNP is US$6468 million and the GNP per capita US$22,300 (1983). Most of the population are Arabs of the Wahabi sect of Islam; only about 25% of the population are native born Qataris. Qatar was closely tied to Great Britain until 1971, when it became independent. Since 1972 it has followed a policy of wide-ranging social and economic reform under Sheikh Khalifa bin Hamad al Thani (the Amir of Qatar). In the early 1980s Qatar established closer ties with neighbouring states within the framework of the GULF COOPERATION COUNCIL, although relations with Bahrain have been aggravated by a long-running territorial dispute.

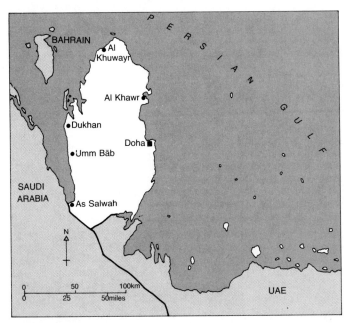

Qatar

**Qin,** dynasty: see CHINA.

**Qing** or **Manchu,** dynasty: see CHINA.

**Qingdao** or **Tsingtao** (͵ching ͵dow), city (1984 pop. 6,239,100), SE SHANDONG prov., E China, on the Yellow Sea. Famous for its beaches, Qingdao is one of China's tourist centres and the leading industrial city in Shandong prov. It makes textiles, machinery, and motor vehicles, and processes food and tobacco. Leased to Germany in 1898, the city retains German influences in architecture and in the beer from its well-known brewery. It was a US naval base from 1945 to 1949. In 1984 it was one of the 14 coastal cities given special incentives to attract foreign investment.

**Qinghai** or **Tsinghai,** province (1985 est. pop. 4,070,000), 720,000 km² (277,992 sq mi), W China, NE of TIBET. The capital is Xining (Sining). The province is a mixture of high plateaus, basins, and mountain ranges. The climate is harsh and dry. The sources of the Mekong and Yangtze rivers are in the western mountains, and Qinghai Lake, in the NE of the province, is the source of the Yellow R. Though one of China's largest administrative units, it is also one of the least densely populated. Much of the land is barren or at best pasture. Only in the few river valleys is there much cultivable land, and barley and spring wheat are major staple crops. There is little industry, though in the NW of the province the Qaidam Basin is being developed as an important petroleum producer. There is much potential hydroelectric power.

**Qiqihar** or **Tsitsihar** (chee chee hah), city (1984 pop. 5,651,100), S central HEILONGJIANG prov., NE China. It is an industrial city producing locomotive engines, machine tools, and other heavy industrial goods. One of the oldest Chinese communities in NE China, it is in winter one of the coldest of all Chinese urban areas. 35 km (c.21½ mi) to the southeast is the Zhalong nature reserve, established in 1979. The reserve is on a bird migration route from the Soviet Arctic to Southeast Asia, and among its many species are six species of crane.

**Qom** (kawm), city (1982 est. pop. 424,000), W central Iran. Located in a semiarid region, it is an industrial and transport centre. Important to Shiite Muslims since early Islamic times, Qom contains the lavish tomb of Fatima al-Masuma (d. 816) and became a place of pilgrimage in the 17th cent. After 1979 the city was the home of Ayatollah KHOMEINI.

**quadraphonic sound:** see STEREOPHONIC SOUND.

**quadrature,** in astronomy: see ELONGATION; SYZYGY.

**Quadruple Alliance,** name given to three European alliances. 1 The Quadruple Alliance of 1718 was formed by Great Britain, France, the Holy Roman emperor, and the Netherlands, in opposition to PHILIP V of Spain and his efforts to nullify the results of the War of the SPANISH SUCCESSION by taking over Sicily. It was generally successful. 2 The Quadruple Alliance of 1814 consisted of Great Britain, Austria, Prussia, and Russia and aimed at strengthening the coalition against NAPOLEON I. It is sometimes confused with the HOLY ALLIANCE (to which Britain did not belong). 3 The Quadruple Alliance of 1834 consisted of Great Britain, France, Spain, and Portugal. Its purpose was to strengthen the government of ISABELLA II of Spain against the pretensions of the CARLISTS. The alliance broke up after the Spanish marriages (of Isabella and her sister) in 1846, which Britain opposed.

**quail,** name for small, extremely popular game BIRDS of the PHEASANT family, including the New World quails, the Old World quails and PARTRIDGES, and the true pheasants. The migratory quail (*Coturnix coturnix*) is distributed across Europe, Asia, and North Africa. It is 17 cm

(7 in) long, a plump bird similar to species living in Australia and New Zealand, but not as brightly coloured. Quails have great reproductive potential, laying 12 to 15 eggs per clutch. They eat small invertebrates and seeds and travel in groups called bevies.

**Quakers:** see FRIENDS, RELIGIOUS SOCIETY OF.

**Quant, Mary,** 1934–, English FASHION designer. Her ingenue-style smock dresses were influential in the early 1960s, but she did not (as is often stated) invent the miniskirt. She was adept at picking up the street fashions of London's 'swinging sixties' though herself of an older age-group than the trend-setters. In the 1970s and 80s she marketed very successful ranges of COSMETICS and accessories under her name.

Mary **Quant** modelling one of her early-Sixties designs

**quantum electrodynamics,** name given to the QUANTUM THEORY of the electromagnetic interaction. See ELEMENTARY PARTICLES.

**quantum theory,** modern physical theory that holds that energy and some other physical properties can often only exist in very small, discrete amounts. The older theories of classical physics assumed that these properties could vary continuously. Quantum theory and the theory of RELATIVITY together form the theoretical basis of modern physics. The first contribution to quantum theory was the explanation of BLACK BODY radiation in 1900 by Max PLANCK, who proposed that the energies of any harmonic oscillator are restricted to certain values, each of which is an integral multiple of a basic minimum value. The energy $E$ of this basic quantum is directly proportional to the frequency $f$ of the oscillator; thus $E = hf$, where Planck's constant $h$ is equal to $6.63 \times 10^{-34}$ J-sec. The theory was applied to the normal modes of radiation in an enclosed space. In 1905 Albert EINSTEIN, in order to explain the PHOTOELECTRIC EFFECT, proposed that radiation is always quantized and consists of light quanta, or PHOTONS, that behave like particles. Niels BOHR used the quantum theory in 1913 to explain both atomic structure and atomic spectra. The light or other radiation emitted and absorbed by atoms is found to have only certain frequencies (or wavelengths), which correspond to the absorption or emission lines seen in atomic spectra (see SPECTRUM). These frequencies correspond to definite energies of the photons and result from the fact that the electrons of the atoms can have only certain allowed energy values, or levels. When an electron changes from one allowed level to another, a quantum of energy is emitted or absorbed whose frequency is directly proportional to the energy difference between the two energy levels $E_1$ and $E_2$; thus $E_2 - E_1 = hf$. Quantum mechanics, the application of a new set of laws to the motions of material particles, was developed during the 1920s. In 1924 Louis de BROGLIE proposed that not only does light exhibit particle-like properties but also particles may exhibit wavelike properties. The observation, by Clinton Davisson and Lester Germer in an 1927 experiment in the US, and also G.P. Thomson in Scotland, of the diffraction of a beam of electrons analogous to the diffraction of a beam of light confirmed this hypothesis. The associated theory involving the development of a wave equation whose solutions (wave functions) described the behaviour of the particles was carried out by Erwin SCHRÖDINGER. A particularly important consequence of quantum mechanics is the uncertainty principle, enunciated by Werner HEISENBERG in 1927; it places an absolute, theoretical limit on the combined accuracy of certain pairs of simultaneous, related measurements, such as position and velocity of a particle.

**quark,** any of a group of hypothetical entities, believed to be the basic constituents of all hadrons (see ELEMENTARY PARTICLES). Quarks and leptons are thought to be the most elementary classes of particles. Quarks have fractional charges of $\frac{1}{3}$ or $\frac{2}{3}$ of the basic charge of the electron or proton. The baryons, a subgroup of the hadrons, are assumed to consist of three quarks. Three antiquarks make up the antibaryons. Mesons, the other subgroup, are believed to consist of one quark and one antiquark. There is strong evidence for five kinds, or flavours, of quarks: up, down, strange, charm, and bottom, and a sixth, labelled top, is predicted. Each flavour of quark is believed to come in three varieties, differing in a property called colour.

**quarrying,** open, or surface, excavation of rock used for various purposes, including construction, ornamentation, and road building. The methods of excavation depend on the desired shape of the stone and its physical characteristics. Sometimes the rock is shattered by the use of explosives (e.g., for roadbeds). For building stones, a process called broaching, or channelling, is used, whereby holes are drilled and wedges inserted and hammered until the stone splits off. This method was probably used by the ancient Egyptians and the Incas.

**quarter days,** the days which begin the four quarters of the year. They are Lady Day (25 Mar.), Midsummer Day (24 June), Michaelmas Day (29 Sept.), and Christmas Day (25 Dec.). In COMMON LAW they are important as the days upon which rent is due.

**Quarter Sessions:** see COURT SYSTEM IN ENGLAND AND WALES.

**quartz,** one of the commonest rock-forming minerals ($SiO_2$), and one of the most important constituents of the earth's crust. It occurs in crystals, often distorted and commonly twinned. Varieties are classified as crystalline (e.g., AMETHYST) and cryptocrystalline (having crystals of microscopic size, e.g., CHALCEDONY and CHERT). Clastic quartzes are SAND and SANDSTONE.

**quartzite,** ROCK composed of firmly cemented QUARTZ grains, commonly resulting from the METAMORPHISM of sandstone and distinguished from the latter by fracturing across, rather than along the line of cementing material between, its constituent grains of sand.

**quasar** or **quasistellar object** (ˌkwaysah), one of a class of peculiar celestial objects first identified by RADIO ASTRONOMY, showing an unusual blue character in the optical. Quasar spectra show very large RED SHIFTS (reducing the frequency of emission by factors that can exceed two or more). If the distance is inferred from this red shift through HUBBLE'S LAW, it comes out in billions of light-years. Combining this estimate with the intensity of light received, the LUMINOSITY of such a pointlike object is calculated to exceed that of (extended) galaxies by a large factor.

**Quasimodo, Salvatore,** 1901–68, Italian poet and translator; b. Sicily. Five volumes of verse (1930–38) established him as a leading representative of 'hermeticism', with a poetry of evocation and private allusion that assimilated the example of the French SYMBOLISTS. His later, more accessible poetry of social conscience includes *Day after Day* (1947) and *Dare e avere* (1966; tr. To Give and To Have). Quasimodo was awarded the 1959 Nobel Prize for literature.

**quasi-stellar object:** see QUASAR.

**Quebec,** province of Canada (1984 est. pop. 6,541,000), largest in area (1,540,680 km²/594,855 sq mi), situated in the E, bordered by Hudson Strait (N), Labrador and the Gulf of St Lawrence (E), New Brunswick and

New England, US (S), and Ontario and Hudson Bay (W). QUEBEC city is the capital and MONTREAL is the largest city; 80% of the population is urban. Quebec has three major geographical regions; the plateau highlands and rugged, lake-filled terrain of the Canadian Shield in the northern nine-tenths, which includes the Hudson Bay lowlands; a projection of the Appalachian Mts in the SE; and the St Lawrence R. lowlands in the far S. The province has one-quarter of Canada's manufacturing industry, led by textiles and clothing, food-processing, pulp and paper, chemicals, and metal products. The main agricultural products are livestock, sugar beets, and tobacco. The forests of the N yield valuable timber, and also copper, zinc, iron, and precious metals; Quebec is a leading world producer of asbestos. It is the second most populous province and the centre of French Canadian culture; c.80% of the population is French-speaking. French explorers, traders, and missionaries began arriving in the area from 1534 onwards, and in 1663 it became a colony. The region came under British rule after the FRENCH AND INDIAN WARS, but the Quebec Act (1774) permitted it to retain French language and institutions. In 1791 English-dominated Ontario split from French Quebec, and they became separate provinces (1867). In the 20th cent. Quebec increasingly sought to maintain a separate political and cultural identity, as birth rates fell and the economy failed to free itself from Ontario's domination. Despite the Parti Québécois winning a large majority in the provincial assembly (1976), the voters turned down the sovereignty/association referendum (1980). Since 1977 French has been the sole official language.

**Quebec** officially Québec, city (1983 est. pop. 163,800), provincial capital of Quebec, part of the Québec urban community on the St Lawrence R. The population is largely French-speaking, and the city is a focus of French Canadian nationalism. Features of special interest include the historic Old Lower Town, centred in restored Place Royale at river level; the old Upper Town, dominated by the huge Château Frontenac hotel (1892), at the top of Cape Diamond, a 90-m high (300-ft) bluff; the Citadel fortress (1832); and the Parliament Building or National Assembly (1877–86). Quebec was founded by CHAMPLAIN in 1608 and, after a brief period of English rule (1629–32), was made the capital of New France in 1663. In 1759 English forces under James Wolfe defeated the French under Gen. MONTCALM on the Plains of Abraham and captured the city. It became the capital of Lower Canada (now Quebec province) in 1791 and was twice the capital of the United Provinces of Canada (1851–55, 1859–65).

**Quebec Act,** 1774, act passed by the British Parliament creating a permanent British government in CANADA, and granting religious freedom to Roman Catholics. The THIRTEEN COLONIES considered it one of the INTOLERABLE ACTS because it extended the boundaries of Quebec southwards, so nullifying many of their claims to Western lands; thus it helped to start the AMERICAN REVOLUTION.

**Queen Anne,** in architecture, style of English building first manifested during the reign of Queen Anne (1702–14). In this version, as the relatively short-lived precursor of Georgian architecture, it was an English form of Renaissance domestic architecture influenced by Inigo JONES and Sir Christopher WREN, and was a reaction against Jacobean decorative exuberance. More popular however was the revival of the style in the last 30 years of the 19th cent. when it was found to be ideal for both town and country houses. It combined Renaissance motifs with local vernacular characteristics in brick and stone, and resulted in irregular compositions which allowed for flexible planning. Typical details were stone mullioned windows in brick facades, pedimented doors, and majestic tall grouped chimneys. Being practical, the style was used for the London Board schools of the 1870s. On a less economical scale it was employed by architects such as R. Norman Shaw for great mansions such as Bryanston in Dorset (1890).

**Queen Anne's lace** or **wild carrot,** herb (*Daucus carota*) of the CARROT family, native to Europe and Asia but naturalized widely. Similar in appearance to the cultivated carrot, from which it was developed in Germany, it has feathery foliage but a woody root. The tiny white flowers bloom in a lacy, flat-topped cluster or umbel.

**Queen Anne's War:** see FRENCH AND INDIAN WARS.

**Queensberry, John Sholto Douglas,** 8th **marquess of:** see BOXING.

**Queen's Counsel:** see LEGAL PROFESSION.

**Queensland,** state (1986 pop. 2,624,600), 1,727,530 km² (667,000 sq mi), NE Australia. Almost half of Queensland's residents live in

Château Frontenac hotel, **Quebec**

metropolitan BRISBANE, the capital. Sugar is the main export crop; pineapples, papaws, bananas, and other fruits, peanuts, sorghum, and tropical grains are grown in the half of the state located in the tropics. Beef cattle and sheep predominate in drier areas W of the EASTERN HIGHLANDS, where the Great Artesian Basin (973,840 km²/376,000 sq mi) is a valuable water source. Queensland is also an important mining state with deposits of bauxite (near Weipa); copper, silver-lead, zinc, and phosphate (near Mt Isa); nickel (near TOWNSVILLE); and coal, oil, and natural gas. Originally a penal colony (1824–43) at Moreton Bay in NEW SOUTH WALES, Queensland became a separate colony in 1859 and a federated state of the Commonwealth of Australia in 1901. The GREAT BARRIER REEF is a major tourist attraction.

**Queirós, José Maria de Eça de** (ˌaysə di kayˌrooz), 1845–1900, Portuguese novelist. He travelled widely as a diplomat; his *Letters from England* (1903) give a wry view of Victorian values. A fine stylist, he used satire and elements of NATURALISM in such works as *The Maias* (1880) and *The City and the Mountains* (1901).

**Quemoy:** see MAZU DAO AND JINMEN DAO.

**Quental, Antero Tarquínio de** (keenˌtahl), 1842–91, Portuguese poet. The intellectual leader of his day, he abandoned Catholicism and became a socialist. He wrote some 150 sonnets describing his spiritual progress (e.g., *Sonetos*, 1881). He also helped organize the Portuguese Socialist Party. Ill health led to his suicide. He is considered a principal modern Portuguese poet.

**Querétaro,** city (1979 est. pop. 185,821), capital of the state of the same name in central Mexico. The original Indian town, thought to have been founded in AD 1400, was captured by the Spanish in 1535. The city is now an important industrial centre but its ancient and beautiful central buildings are rich with historical associations. In 1848 the Mexican Congress met here to ratify the peace treaty with the US. Following the French invasion of Mexico, Emperor MAXIMILIAN surrendered here and was shot outside the city in 1867. The city was the seat of the convention which met after the Mexican Revolution to adopt the 1917 Constitution.

**Quesnay, François** (keˌnay), 1694–1774, French economist, founder of the physiocratic school. A physician to Louis XV, he began his economic studies in 1756, when he wrote for the *Encyclopédie*. His chief work is *The Economical Table* (1758), which he and his followers believed summed up the natural law of economy. Quesnay and other PHYSIOCRATS greatly influenced the thought of Adam SMITH.

**question mark:** see PUNCTUATION.

**Quetta** (‚kwaytə), town (1981 pop. 285,000), Baluchistan province, Pakistan. It is the provincial capital and a district administrative centre; and a strategically important military base, controlling entry via the Bolan and Harnai passes to the Indus plains. It has acquired some industry, notably cotton textiles. Britain secured Quetta in 1876. The town was virtually destroyed by an earthquake in 1935.

**Quetzalcoatl** [Nahuatl, = feathered serpent], ancient deity and legendary ruler of the TOLTEC in Mexico. An early Toltec ruler credited with the discovery of maize, the arts, and science is also called Quetzelcoatl. As god of civilization, identified with the wind and the planet Venus, Quetzalcoatl represented the forces of good and light. The name was adopted by the AZTEC and linked to their chief god; their emperor MONTEZUMA mistook the invading Spanish for the hosts of Quetzalcoatl returning (as promised in legend) from travels over the sea. The MAYA Kulkulcán, also represented by a feathered serpent, probably derived from the same historical figure as Quetzalcoatl.

**Quevedo y Villegas, Francisco Gómez de** (kəy‚vaydhoh ee vee‚lyaygahs), 1580–1645, Spanish writer. A major figure of the GOLDEN AGE, he wrote brilliant moral satires such as *Sueños* (1627; tr. Visions); the picaresque novel *La vida del Buscón* (1626; tr. The Life of the Buscón); much verse; and political and religious works.

**Quezon, Manuel Luis** (‚kaysohn), 1878–1944, first president (1935–44) of the Commonwealth of the PHILIPPINES. He crusaded tirelessly for Philippine independence from the US. During WORLD WAR II he led a government-in-exile in the US.

**Quezon City**, city (1980 pop. 1,165,990), central Luzon, Philippines, adjacent to MANILA. The nation's second largest city, it was the Philippine capital from 1948 to 1976, when Manila replaced it. It is the seat of the Univ. of the Philippines.

**quicklime:** see CALCIUM OXIDE.

**quicksilver:** see MERCURY.

**quill:** see PEN.

**quilting,** process of stitching together two layers of fabric usually separated by an interlining of cotton, wool, or synthetic fabric. It is a traditional means of providing insulation against the cold or to provide defensive covering. Examples include Chinese jackets, tunics of ancient Egyptian and Aztec warriors, and coverlets of the Roman and Asian peoples. In Europe, bedcover quilts have been the most popular form of quilting and it is a tradition which has been utilized in North America since c.1750, in conjunction with appliqué and patchwork. Both in the US and Britain, quilting has been revived by textile artists and quilting groups alike.

**quince,** shrub or small tree (genera *Chaenomeles* and *Cydonia*) of the ROSE family. The common quince (*Cydonia oblonga*) is a spineless tree. Its edible fruit is similar to the related APPLE and PEAR but is very astringent and is used mainly in preserves; marmalade is said to have first been made from quince. Flowering quinces (genus *Chaenomeles*) are cultivated for their profuse, usually thorny branches and scarlet, pink, or white flowers.

**Quine, Willard Van Orman,** 1908–, American philosopher and mathematical logician. He studied under WHITEHEAD and CARNAP and taught at Harvard Univ. after 1936. Much of his work deals with the implications of viewing language as a logical system. He argued that empiricism cannot accept KANT's distinction between analytic and synthetic statements, claiming instead that any statement can be held to be true once a language's system of reference is adjusted. Influenced by DUHEM and PEIRCE, he argued that a study of translation shows that meanings are radically indeterminate and therefore not empirically respectable. In the field of logic he made important contributions to SET theory. His works include *A System of Logic* (1934), *From a Logical Point of View* (1953), *Word and Object* (1960), *Ontological Relativity and other Essays* (1969), and *Methods of Logic* (3rd ed., 1972).

**quinine,** ALKALOID isolated from the bark of several species of *Cinchona* trees. Prior to the development of synthetic agents (especially chloroquine), quinine was the specific drug treatment for MALARIA. It is administered by mouth. Excessive use may cause cinchonism, a condition characterized by ringing in the ears, dizziness, and blurring of the vision.

**Quintilian** (Marcus Fabius Quintilianus), AD c.35–c.95, Roman rhetorician and teacher. His influential *Institutio oratoria,* a survey of education, literature, the principles of rhetoric, and the life and training of the orator, demonstrates the necessity of moderation and good taste.

**Quiroga, Horacio** (kee‚rohgah), 1878–1937, Uruguayan short-story writer. Among his collections are *Cuentos de amor, de locura y de muerte* (1917; tr. Stories of Love, Madness, and Death), *Cuentos de la selva para niños* (1918; tr. Stories of the Forest for Children), *Anaconda* (1921), *El desierto* (1924; tr. The Desert), echoing KIPLING, and the sophisticated *Más allá* (1935; tr. Beyond).

**Quiroga, Juan Facundo,** 1790–1835, Argentine leader. As overlord of the Andean provinces he was a zealous and ruthless advocate of federalism. He rejected the unitarian constitution of 1826 and participated in the civil strife that followed. He was assassinated.

**Quisling, Vidkun,** 1887–1945, Norwegian fascist leader. Minister of defence (1931–33), he founded the fascist Nasjonal Samling [national unity] party. He helped the Germans prepare the conquest of Norway (1940), and they installed him as premier (1942–45). After the war he was tried for high treason and shot. From his name came the word *quisling* [traitor].

**Quito** (‚keetoh), city (1982 pop. 1,110,248), N central Ecuador, capital of Ecuador and of Pichincha prov. Though unimportant economically, it is Ecuador's political and cultural centre and second largest city. It is famous for its splendid setting, lying at an elevation of 2850 m (9350 ft) in a fertile Andean valley at the foot of a volcano. The colonial city was built at the site of the capital of the INCA kingdom of Quito, captured for Spain in 1534. In 1822 it was liberated from Spain by Antonio José de SUCRE. Although the city has often been damaged by earthquakes, many fine examples of Spanish colonial architecture remain, including the great Church of San Francisco.

**Qum:** see QOM.

**Qumran** (‚koomrahn), ancient village on the northwest shore of the Dead Sea, presently on the West Bank of Jordan. It is famous for its caves, in some of which the DEAD SEA SCROLLS were found.

**Qutb, Sayyid:** see MUSLIM BRETHREN.

**Qu Yuan,** ?340–278 BC, Chinese folk hero and writer. He is reputed to be author of the major poems in the *Chu ci* [songs of the South]. An upright but critical official, he was banished by his ruler and committed suicide in protest. This heroic sacrifice is still commemorated in the dragon boat races of South China.

# R

**Ra** or **Re**, in EGYPTIAN RELIGION, sun god, one of the most important gods of ancient Egypt. Called the creator and father of all things, he was chief of the cosmic deities. Early Egyptian kings alleged descent from him. Various other Egyptian gods, e.g., AMON, were identified with him. His symbol is the PYRAMID.

**Ra**, chemical symbol of the element RADIUM.

**Raabe, Wilhelm** (ˌrahbə), 1831–1910, German novelist. His ironical novels of provincial life, e.g., *Die Chronik der Sperlingsgasse* (1856), are characteristic of German Realism. Other novels are *Der Hungerpastor* (1864), *Abu Telfan* (1868), *Stopfkuchen* (1891) and *The Vogelsang Papers* (1895).

**Rabat,** city (1982 pop. 893,042), capital of Morocco, on the Atlantic coast at the mouth of the Bou Regreg estuary. The city is a minor port and has textile industries. There have been settlements there since ancient times. It became a Muslim fortress AD c.700 and was a stronghold of corsairs in the 17th and 18th cent. Prior to independence (1956), Rabat was the capital of the French protectorate of Morocco. Landmarks include the old city walls and the ruins of the Tour Hassan (12th cent.), a large, unfinished mosque.

Tour Hassan, **Rabat**

**rabbi** [Heb., = my teacher], the title of a Jewish religious leader. The term first came into common use among Palestinian Jews in the late 1st cent. AD. During the Middle Ages the rabbi, in addition to being a legal scholar, began to assume the roles of teacher, preacher, and communal leader. In the 1970s the Reform and Conservative rabbinical seminaries began to admit female students, and the acceptance of women rabbis has made slow but steady progress. Orthodox Judaism has maintained its traditional position against women rabbis. The title 'Rabbi' is conferred at an ordination ceremony following the successful completion of a lengthy course of study. Rabbinic expertise, called *hatarat hora'ah* [permission to decide on matters of Jewish law], is usually examined orally by a distinguished sage or panel of experts. A synagogue rabbi is employed by his congregation. Others are active in Jewish schools or as teachers in rabbinical colleges.

**rabbit** or **cony**, MAMMAL of the family Leporidae, which includes the HARE. Rabbits have large front teeth, short tails, and hind legs and feet adapted for running and jumping. Rabbits live in underground burrows, called warrens and give birth to blind, naked young. They feed on vegetation at dawn and dusk. Wild rabbits are up to 40 cm (16 in) long and have greyish-brown fur. The European common rabbit (*Oryctolagus cuniculus*), native to S Europe and Africa, is now found worldwide. It has flourished in those places where there were no natural enemies to the extent of becoming a pest, particularly in Australia. Rabbit populations have been controlled recently by myxomatosis, a lethal disease of rabbits. All domestic rabbits have been bred from the common rabbit.

**Rabelais, François** (rabˌlay), c.1490–1553, French humanist, one of the great comic geniuses of literature. Joining the Franciscan order, Rabelais studied Greek and Latin as well as science, law, philology, and letters. He later left the Franciscans to become a Benedictine monk. He received (1530) a degree in medicine from the Univ. of Montpellier, where he later taught (1537–38). He went to Lyons (1532) to practice medicine, and it was there that he published his satirical masterpiece, *Gargantua and Pantagruel* (1532–62). The work, in five books, is as gigantic in scope as the physical size of its heroes. Beneath its broad, often ribald humour are serious discussions of education, politics, philosophy, and religion. The breadth of Rabelais's learning and his zest for life are evident. The work was condemned by the Sorbonne, however, and Rabelais was saved from persecution for heresy only by the protection of his friend Cardinal Jean du Bellay. He spent his last years as curate at Meudon (1550–52).

**rabies** or **hydrophobia**, acute, usually fatal, disease of mammals. Caused by a virus, it is transmitted from animal to human through infected saliva, usually through a bite (commonly of a dog). After an incubation period of one week to several years, rabies produces fever, headache, nausea, and pain at the site of the bite, followed by convulsions, inability to drink fluids (the mere sight of water causes convulsions, hence hydrophobia), apathy, and death in four to five days. A VACCINATION of antirabies vaccine is administered to the bite victim in the hope of preventing the disease from developing.

**raccoon**, nocturnal New World MAMMAL (genus *Procyon*) with a heavily furred body, pointed face, and handlike forepaws. It has mixed grey, brown, and black hair, a black face mask, and black rings on the tail. Highly omnivorous, it is adaptable to civilization and will feed from dustbins. Its fur is commercially valuable.

**race,** a folk classification, found in many societies, of ethnic groups. The term as used makes various claims to biological status, through arguing that specific ethnic groups share common physical and, as a result, psychological and moral characteristics, and that these are inherited and therefore fixed and unchangeable. These arguments however bear no relation to what is known about genetics, evolutionary pressures, adaptive and historical population movements, etc. The concept of race has been and still is used to justify many discriminatory practices on the gounds that the natural characteristics of such groups makes them unsuitable, or particularly approriate, for certain activities.

**Rachel,** wife of JACOB and mother of JOSEPH and Benjamin. She is one of the four Jewish MATRIARCHS. Gen. 29–33; 35.

**Rachel,** 1828–58, French actress; b. Switzerland as Elisa Félix. The great tragic actress of her day, she excelled in the works of RACINE (*Phèdre*) and CORNEILLE.

**Rachmaninoff, Sergei Vasilyevich** (rak͵mani'nof), 1873–1943, Russian composer, conductor, and pianist. His romantic, dramatic music was strongly influenced by his friend TCHAIKOVSKY. His notable works include four piano CONCERTOS, Prelude in C Sharp Minor (1892), Rhapsody on a Theme by Paganini (1934), three SYMPHONIES, and many songs.

**Racine, Jean** (ra͵seen), 1639–99, French dramatist. He is the prime exemplar of French CLASSICISM. His third play, *Andromaque* (1667), established him as France's leading tragic dramatist, displacing CORNEILLE and earning him the patronage of Louis XIV as well as the enmity of Corneille's friends (including MOLIÈRE). His next six tragedies were all masterpieces, unsurpassed in nobility of verse, simplicity of diction, psychological realism, and dramatic construction: *Britannicus* (1669), *Bérénice* (1670), *Bajazet* (1672), *Mithridate* (1673), *Iphigénie en Aulide* (1674), and *Phèdre* (1677). His only comedy was *Les plaideurs* (1668; tr. The Litigants), satirizing the law courts. A concerted attack on *Phèdre* led Racine to give up the theatre, but Mme de MAINTENON persuaded him to write *Esther* (1689) and *Athalie* (1691) for performance at her school in Saint-Cyr. These differ from the earlier plays in their biblical subjects and use of a chorus.

**Rackham, Arthur,** 1867–1939, English illustrator and watercolourist. He is best known for his delicately coloured, imaginative children's book illustrations, e.g., for *Peter Pan* (1906) and *Alice in Wonderland* (1907).

**rack railway,** rail system for climbing steep gradients. Railway operation in which wheels are driven or braked is limited to inclines of about 7%. The first rack railway was the Mount Washington Railroad in New Hampshire, US which was opened in 1869. In this the gradient is up to 32% and cog wheels on the locomotive engage a toothed track, the rack, to climb or descend. Subsequently, many rack railways have been built in mountainous areas, such as Switzerland, where their insensitivity to snow and ice is particularly valuable.

**radar** [*ra*dio *d*etection *a*nd *ranging*], system or technique for detecting the position, motion, and nature of a remote object by means of radio waves reflected from its surface. Radar systems transmit pulses of electromagnetic waves by means of directional AERIALS; some of the pulses are reflected by objects in the path of the beam. Reflections are received by the radar unit, processed electronically, and converted into spots of light on a CATHODE-RAY TUBE. The distance of the object from the radar source is determined by measuring the time required for the radar signal to reach the target and return. The direction of the object with respect to the radar unit is determined from the direction in which the pulses were transmitted. In most units, the beam of pulses is continuously rotated at a constant speed, or it is scanned (swung back and forth) over a sector at a constant rate. The velocity of the object is sometimes determined by the DOPPLER EFFECT: if the object is approaching the radar unit, the frequency of the returned signal is greater than the frequency of the transmitted signal; if the object is receding, the returned frequency is less; and if the object is not moving relative to the radar unit, the frequency of the returned signal is the same as the frequency of the transmitted signal. These frequency changes are detected to determine the speed. Most radar units operate on microwave frequencies.

**Radcliffe, Ann (Ward),** 1764–1823, English novelist. Her *Romance of the Forest* (1791), *Mysteries of Udolpho* (1794), and *The Italian* (1797), characterized by brooding landscapes, terror, and suspense, were among the first GOTHIC ROMANCES.

**Radcliffe-Brown, Alfred Reginald,** 1881–1955, British anthropologist. With B. MALINOWSKI, he was of foremost importance in 20th-cent. British anthropology. Influenced by E. DURKHEIM, Radcliffe-Brown adopted a positivist view of anthropology as the natural science of culture: its business was to demonstrate the functional interrelationships of social institutions which guaranteed their persistence. He also contributed to the study of KINSHIP. His best-known work is *The Andaman Islanders* (1922).

**radial velocity,** the speed with which a star moves towards or away from the Sun. It is measured from the RED SHIFT or blue shift in the star's spectrum. See also PROPER MOTION.

**radiation,** the emission or transmission of energy in the form of WAVES through space or through a material medium; the term also applies to the radiated energy itself. The term includes electromagnetic, acoustic, and particle radiation, and all forms of ionizing radiation. According to QUANTUM THEORY, ELECTROMAGNETIC RADIATION may be viewed as made up of PHOTONS. Acoustic radiation is propagated as sound waves. Examples of particle radiation are alpha and beta rays in RADIOACTIVITY, and COSMIC RAYS.

**radiation sickness,** illness caused by the effects of ionizing radiation on body tissues. It may be acute, delayed, or chronic and may occur after repeated (cumulative) exposure to small doses of radiation (as in a plant, a laboratory, or the environment); or exposure to a nuclear detonation. Symptoms may be mild and transitory, or severe, depending on the type of radiation, the dose, and the rate at which exposure is experienced. Very high doses cause death within hours from destruction of the nervous system. Lower doses may still prove fatal and cause symptoms of nausea, vomiting, and diarrhoea, and, after a symptom-free interval, loss of hair, a tendency to bleed, anaemia, and susceptibility to infection (symptoms of bone marrow damage). Death may occur one to six weeks after exposure. Mild radiation sickness is a common side effect of radiotherapy for CANCER. Exposure to radiation is of concern even in small doses because of possible long-term genetic effects and increased incidence of cancer, especially LEUKAEMIA (see CARCINOGENS; MUTAGENS).

**Radić, Stjepan** (͵radeech), 1871–1928, nationalist politician of Croatia (now part of Yugoslavia). A founder of the Croatian Peasant Party (1904), Radić became the most popular and ardent spokesman for the Croats' discontent in the Serb-dominated Kingdom of Serbs, Croats, and Slovenes after 1918. His erratic leadership from abroad, from prison, and from inside a coalition government led by Nikola PAŠIĆ failed to wrest constitutional concessions from King ALEXANDER or the Serb politicians. He was shot and mortally wounded on the floor of parliament in 1928, in what proved to be the signal for the King's introduction of a personal dictatorship.

**radio,** transmission or reception of ELECTROMAGNETIC RADIATION in the radio frequency range from one place to another without wires. For the propagation and interception of radio waves, a transmitter and receiver are employed. A radio wave carries information-bearing signals; the information may be encoded directly on the wave by periodically interrupting its transmission (e.g., when transmitting MORSE CODE) or impressed on the carrier frequency by a process called MODULATION, e.g., amplitude modulation (AM) or frequency modulation (FM). In its most common form, radio transmits sounds (e.g., voice, music) which are converted into electrical signals by a MICROPHONE, amplified (see AMPLIFIER) and used to modulate a carrier wave that has been generated by a transmitter. The modulated carrier is also amplified, then applied to an AERIAL that radiates electromagnetic waves into space at the speed of light. Receiving aerials intercept part of this radiation and feed it to a receiver where it is amplified and detected to recover the modulating signal. Once these have been separated from the carrier wave, they are fed to a LOUDSPEAKER, where they are converted into sound. Radio is the senior of the electronic media: as a provider and source of broadcast news, information, education, and entertainment radio became for a period overshadowed (in technique) and outshone (in service offered to the public) by television. However, the invention of the TRANSISTOR, followed by world-wide marketing of small, lightweight, inexpensive transistor-radio sets, much helped radio's revival as a popular utility. In most of the developed countries, despite the sharply increased competition from other media and from the new technologies in communication, radio remains a prime source of news and information, especially at times of national or local emergency. A wide range of music —popular, specialist or classical—continues to attract a loyal audience (payments for the copyright on music is a major expense for radio, a medium otherwise much less costly to run than television). In the Third World the time-lag often involved in introducing a complex and expensive colour-television system has allowed radio a longer dominance than in the more prosperous economies. Even within the richer nations, radio has readjusted to the changing societies around it; 'localness' has again become a focus for radio programming in countries such as Australia, Canada, much of Europe (e.g., Spain, Sweden, and Yugoslavia) as well as in the US and UK. Illegal or pirate radio, operating from offshore ships or clandestine bases inland has also been a marked feature. Lively scheduling by some of these pirate stations attracted wide audiences and influenced the styles adopted by the legal radio services. Radio has been financed in various ways in different countries, not least in Britain where there is a licence fee, but increasingly broadcasters are also expected to finance themselves either through advertisement revenue or, as with the smaller 'community' stations (called in Australia 'flea-bite radio'), through donations and subscriptions. This has put pressure on the concept of 'public service broadcasting' as pioneered by Lord Reith, and new legislation has been proposed to open up the radio system, which is still subject in part to statutes and charters.

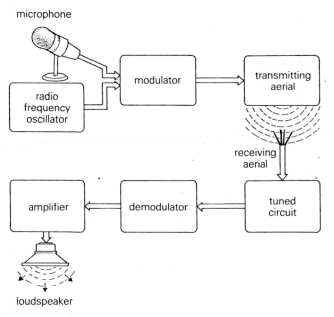

Radio

**radioactive dating:** see DATING.

**radioactive nuclear waste:** see WASTE DISPOSAL.

**radioactivity,** the spontaneous emission of a high-energy particle from an atomic nucleus. The vast majority of atomic nuclei are unstable. These instabilities lead to the emission of a succession of various kinds of particles until the nucleus reaches a stable state. In nuclei with too many neutrons, one of the neutrons undergoes a transition to a proton with the emission of an electron and an antineutrino to the environment. Such a process is called (negative) beta decay. An unstable nucleus such as strontium-90 will undergo two successive beta decays until it reaches the stable nucleus zirconium-90. Similarly, in nuclei with too many protons, one of the protons undergoes a transition to a neutron with the emission of a positive electron (positron) and a neutrino to the environment. Heavy nuclei can expel an alpha particle, a nucleus consisting of two protons and two neutrons, to the environment. The uranium-238 nucleus undergoes successive alpha particle emissions until it reaches the stable lead-206 nucleus. Other radioactive transitions include K-capture (the capture by a proton-rich nucleus of an inner orbital electron with the emission of a neutrino to the environment), direct proton emission to the environment, and spontaneous fission. The transitions frequently are accompanied by high-energy gamma rays as in the case of the decay of cesium-137 to barium-137. An activity of one becquerel is the emission of one particle per second to the environment. One curie is the emission of $3.7 \times 10^{10}$ particles per second to the environment. All radioactivity is harmful to a certain degree (see CARCINOGENS; MUTAGENS).

**radio astronomy,** study of celestial bodies by means of the radio waves they emit and absorb naturally. The atmosphere of the Earth being opaque to most of the electromagnetic spectrum, ground-based astronomy is confined to using one of the two portions to which it is transparent: visible light (optical astronomy) and the much longer wavelengths (exceeding a few mm) of the radio region exploited in radio astronomy. The much longer wavelength means that a radio telescope must involve very large dimensions for the beam of sensitivity to be narrow enough to identify the direction of the source of radiation with high accuracy (see RADIO ASTRONOMY OBSERVATORY). Radio emission by celestial objects was first noted by Karl JANSKY in 1931, but the subject started to be actively pursued only after 1945, initially especially in the UK and Australia. The sources of radio radiation are varied. Clouds of hot ionized gases are a major type of source, the heat being often due to powerful stars. In another type of source the radiation is emitted by fast electrons whose orbits are curved by strong magnetic fields emanating from, e.g., SUPERNOVA remnants. In cooler clouds of interstellar matter, ordinary atomic or molecular transitions radiate at distinct frequencies that allow the material to be identified. Whole galaxies are major emitters, as are QUASARS, making radio astronomy important for the study of cosmology. Indeed this subject was decisively influenced by the discovery of a uniform weak radio radiation coming equally from all parts of the sky. This radiation is thought to be the flash of the original big bang (see COSMOLOGY) with its frequencies enormously reduced by the cosmological red shift. PULSARS were also a major discovery of radio astronomy. Within the solar system radio astronomy has studied the radiation emanating from the Sun and from major planets, while in the RADAR mode (i.e., sending out a powerful signal and observing the radiation scattered by the target) major contributions have been made to the knowledge especially of the inner planets.

**radio astronomy observatory,** installation to study the (often weak) radio frequency radiation from celestial objects. In order to receive enough power for detection, the area of a radio telescope must be sufficiently large. To permit this detection without undue interference, several selected narrow bands of wavelengths (from millimetres to several metres) are by international agreement reserved for radio astronomy. To gain the greatest possible angular definition, the observatory needs to extend over very many wavelengths and thus over large distances. One type of observatory consists of a single large steerable parabolic bowl; the first major one of this type was built at Jodrell Bank, Cheshire, UK, under the leadership of Bernard LOVELL. Later ones are at Parkes, New South Wales, Australia, and now at sites in the US and many other countries, the largest (100-m diameter) being near Bonn, W Germany, while a much larger but fixed one is at Arecibo, Puerto Rico. In another type many smaller well separated telescopes are combined to give great angular accuracy through INTERFERENCE. By moving the 'discs' a vast area may be successively covered, giving a large synthetic aperture; this technique was invented by Martin RYLE and is exemplified by the Mullard Observatory outside Cambridge, UK. Through linking widely separated telescopes an angular accuracy can now be obtained exceeding that of optical telescopes.

**Radio Free Europe,** broadcasting complex headquartered in Munich, West Germany, that provides daily programmes to the peoples of Poland, Czechoslovakia, Hungary, Romania, and Bulgaria in their own languages. Founded in 1950, it is privately operated, although mainly financed by the US government. Its broadcasts include news and political commentaries, as well as music, sports coverage, and other entertainment. (See also PROPAGANDA.)

**radiography,** formation of images of the internal structures of the body on photographic plates or fluorescent screens by short-wave radiation, such as X-RAYS. See RADIOLOGY.

**radioimmunoassay,** highly sensitive technique used to measure the concentration of antigens (substances to which antibodies can be produced) in the body, including hormones and drugs present in very low concentrations. Radioactive tracers determine the levels of particular antibodies in the blood so that the amount of antigen present can be measured. The technique was developed by Solomon Berson and Rosalyn Yalow. Yalow was awarded the 1977 Nobel Prize for physiology or medicine for her work.

**radioisotope:** see ISOTOPE.

**radiology,** the use of radiation in the diagnosis and treatment of disease. Different aspects of the body can be visualized using X-RAY images, e.g., of the chest, of teeth, or of the colon (RADIOGRAPHY). An important development has been COMPUTERIZED AXIAL TOMOGRAPHY which has allowed improved visualization of organs and tumours deep within the body. NUCLEAR MAGNETIC RESONANCE is another new method of producing images of sections of the head and body. All these diagnostic images permit noninvasive exploration of the extent of disease and the planning of RADIOTHERAPY.

**radiometer,** instrument for the detection or measurement of ELECTROMAGNETIC RADIATION, particularly INFRARED RADIATION. Radiometers that function by increasing the temperature of the device are called thermal detectors; examples include the Bolometer and the THERMOCOUPLE.

**radiosonde,** group of instruments for simultaneous measurement and radio transmission of meteorological data. The instrument package is usually carried into the atmosphere by a WEATHER BALLOON; it may, however, also be carried by a rocket (rocketsonde) or dropped by parachute (dropsonde).

**radio telescope:** see RADIO ASTRONOMY.

**radiotherapy,** branch of medicine concerned with applying ionizing radiation, including X-RAYS, beta-rays, and gamma-rays, to the body for the treatment of disease, particularly CANCER. Beams of radiation are directed at diseased parts of the body. Successful treatment of a TUMOUR depends on the ability of healthy tissue to recover from the doses of radiation which will kill off malignant, rapidly proliferating cells. Improved treatment of many cancers has developed from combining radiotherapy with CHEMOTHERAPY, but the side-effects of both are extremely distressing for the patient (see RADIATION SICKNESS).

**radish,** herb (*Raphanus sativus*) of the MUSTARD family, with an edible, pungent root used as a relish. There are many varieties, with red, white, or black roots of different shapes and sizes, some quite large. HORSERADISH is not a radish but a related plant of the mustard family.

**Radishchev, Aleksandr Nikolayevich,** 1749–1802, Russian writer. He was author of the first open criticism of Czarism, *Journey from St Petersburg to Moscow* (1790). He was exiled to Siberia, was later pardoned, but finally committed suicide: he is regarded as the first martyr of Russian literature.

**radium** (Ra), radioactive metallic element, discovered in PITCHBLENDE in 1898 by Pierre and Marie CURIE. It is a rare, lustrous, white member of the ALKALINE-EARTH METALS that resembles barium in its chemical properties. Radium compounds are found in uranium ores. The RADIOACTIVITY of radium and its compounds is used in the treatment of cancer. Radium compounds are mixed with a phosphor in luminous paints. In its radioactive decay, radium emits alpha, beta, and gamma rays and produces heat. See ELEMENT (table); PERIODIC TABLE.

**Radom,** city (1984 pop. 199,000), at a hub of communications south of WARSAW, central Poland. The convergence of routeways ensured its importance in the Middle Ages. Engineering and other industries have been developed since World War II. It was a meeting place of Polish diets (parliaments) between the 14th and 16th cent.

**radon** (Rn), gaseous radioactive element, discovered by Ernest RUTHERFORD in 1899. A colourless, chemically unreactive INERT GAS, it is the densest gas known. Highly radioactive (emitting alpha rays), it is used chiefly in the treatment of cancer by radiotherapy. See ELEMENT (table); PERIODIC TABLE.

**Raeburn, Sir Henry,** 1756–1823, Scottish portrait painter. He was influenced by Sir Joshua REYNOLDS. His forceful work displays his virtuoso brush technique. He painted over 700 portraits, mostly of notable Scots; many are in the National Gall. of Scotland, Edinburgh.

**Raffles, Sir Thomas Stamford Bingley,** 1781–1826, British East Indian administrator. As lieutenant governor of Java (1811–15) and of Bencooleen, in SUMATRA (1818–23), he launched many reforms. In 1819 he secured the transfer of SINGAPORE to the English EAST INDIA COMPANY.

**Ragnarok** (ˌrahgnəˈrok), in Norse mythology, doomsday, on which the gods of ASGARD, led by Odin (see WODEN), would fight the forces of evil, led by LOKI. After the battle, the universe would be destroyed by fire and a new golden age would appear. A version of this legend was dramatized by WAGNER in his opera *Götterdämmerung* (1874).

**ragtime:** see JAZZ.

**ragweed,** weedy herb (genus *Ambrosia*) of the COMPOSITE family, mostly native to America but widely naturalized elsewhere. They have greenish flowers and subdivided leaves. Their POLLEN is one of the primary hay fever irritants, especially that of the common ragweed (*A. artemisiifolia*), also called American wormwood, and great ragweed (*A. trifida*).

**rail,** name for some marsh BIRDS of the family Rallidae, cosmopolitan in distribution, except in polar regions. Their extremely slender bodies are protectively coloured in drab browns and reds. There are two major types: the long-billed rails, which include the king and water rails; and those with short, conical bills, including the black rails. Rails, including the gallinule and COOT, are probably the most widely distributed bird family.

Water **rail** (*Rallus aquaticus*)

**railway,** form of transport in which vehicles run along, and are guided by, tracks. Crude railways with wagons pulled by horses along wooden rails were used for mining purposes in Central Europe in the 16th cent. and their use spread to England at the beginning of the 17th cent. The advent of the LOCOMOTIVE led to the first scheduled passenger service on the Stockton and Darlington railway in 1825, whilst the Liverpool and Manchester railway in 1829 was the first to use mechanical haulage exclusively, to operate a scheduled service according to a timetable, and to use a railway STATION. It demonstrated on a public and commercial scale the essential features of a railway: the provision of a dedicated right of way, the ability of vehicles to be guided by the track, and to be coupled together to form high-capacity trains. Railways provided the principal means of transport which supported and stimulated industrialization by making it possible for raw materials and manufactured goods to reach markets which formerly could not be tapped. They connected towns, and by providing mobility for a wide range of the population they enabled seaside resorts to develop. The railways made the growth of large cities possible, and encouraged people to live at a distance from their work thus stimulating the development of suburbs. Railways made it possible to open up undeveloped areas of the world for economic exploitation; for example, the American Mid-West became a principal provider of cheap grain for Europe towards the end of the last century after access had been provided by railways. Towards the end of the 19th cent. there was a trend towards luxury in passenger trains, exemplified by the invention of the sleeping car by G.M. Pullman in 1856, whose name lives on in connection with a superior standard of comfort in railway carriages. Specialized forms of railway were developed in order to provide service where conventional railways were not feasible; in mountainous areas the CABLE RAILWAY and RACK RAILWAY became established, and the MONORAIL originated as an attempt to reduce track costs. In some countries such as Britain and the US railways were promoted by private companies, whilst in other countries such as Belgium and Bavaria railways were developed by government as instruments of national policy. At the height of railway construction in Britain there was intense financial speculation and many lines were built which had an insecure economic basis. In the US land grants were given to encourage the development of railways, and the dishonesty and cavalier attitude to the public of some railway companies led to rigorous government regulation in later years, much to the disadvantage of the railways. In most countries there has been a definite trend towards state ownership of the railway system formed by successive amalgamations over the years of the various original constituent companies, on the basis that railways provide a service which should not be measured solely in financial terms. However, there are wide differences in the level of state support - for example in 1978 British Railways received 0.35% of Gross Domestic Product in financial support from government whilst the corresponding figure for the railways in Austria, Belgium, France, Italy, and West Germany ranged from 0.57% to 1.83%. The development of road transport and later air transport provided the railways with competition so that they were no longer the ubiquitous common carrier. This has led to a re-appraisal of the role of railways in developed countries, in Britain associated with Lord BEECHING. Railways are fully competitive with other modes of transport in the haulage of bulk freight such as coal, in HIGH SPEED TRAIN service between cities up to 400 km (250 mi) apart, and in providing mass transport into and within large cities. Urban railways take many forms such as high frequency suburban services, UNDERGROUND RAILWAYS, TRAMS, MONORAILS, and people-movers consisting of smaller vehicles automatically driven and operating at short intervals. Whilst in developed countries the length of railway open for operation has stabilized or even declined, world-wide there is vigorous growth. The emergence of many extremely large cities has stimulated much construction of new urban railways such as the Mexico City metro. The development of mineral resources is dependent on railways operating with trains weighing as much as 20,000 tonnes or more such as the VITORIA A MINAS RAILWAY in Brazil, and new railways for HIGH SPEED TRAINS are being constructed in several developed countries in order to cope with the growth of demand for transport.

**rain,** liquid form of precipitation. It consists of drops of water falling from CLOUDS; if the drops are very small, they are collectively termed *drizzle.* Clouds contain huge amounts of tiny water droplets. Raindrops are formed as additional water vapour from the air condenses on the droplets. When the raindrops become too heavy to be supported by the air currents in the cloud, they slowly fall. Collisions with other raindrops continue to increase their size until they hit the ground. Under warm, dry conditions, raindrops can evaporate completely before they land; such raindrops are called *virga.* Rainfall is one of the primary factors of CLIMATE. Average annual rainfall can vary from less than 2.5 cm (1 in) in an arid DESERT to over 1000 cm (400 in) in some rainforests. Factors that control rainfall include the belts of converging–ascending air flow (see DOLDRUMS), air temperature, moisture-bearing winds, ocean currents, location and elevation of mountains, and the proximity of large bodies of water. See also HAIL; SLEET; SNOW.

**rainbow,** arc showing the colours of the spectrum, which appears when sunlight shines through water droplets. It often appears after a brief shower late in the afternoon. The sun, the observer's eye, and the centre of the arc must be aligned—the rainbow appears in the part of the sky opposite the sun. It is caused by the refraction and reflection of light rays from the sun: a ray is refracted as it enters the raindrop, reflected from the drop's opposite side, and refracted again as it leaves the drop and passes to the observer.

**rainforest,** forest growth typical of tropical regions where high rainfall, high humidity, and low seasonal variation promote luxuriant growth throughout the year. Rainforests also occur along wet western coasts in temperate latitudes (e.g., in Canada and New Zealand). Rainforests are characteristically composed of a layer of tall trees forming a continuous canopy beneath which a wide variety of lesser trees, bushes, ferns, and other plants thrives. There is no seasonal change in the vegetation and leaves are shed all the year round. Rainforests are particularly notable for their vast range of different species and the rapid decomposition of leaf litter due to high bacterial activity.

**Rainier III,** 1923–, prince of MONACO (1949–). He succeeded his grandfather, Louis II, as prince and married (1956) the American film actress Grace Kelly (see GRACE, princess of Monaco).

**Raipur,** town (1981 pop. 338,245), Madhya Pradesh state, E India. It is a district administrative and commercial town, the centre of the region known as Chhattisgarh, which has profited from its position as a railway junction near the Bhilai steel-works (see BHILAINAGAR) and grown quite rapidly. It has rice mills and some other industries. It was the scene of princely rule as early as the 11th cent. but passed to the British in 1853.

**raisin:** see GRAPE.

**Rajagopalachari, Chakravarti** ('rahjegoh‚pahlə'chahree), 1878–1972, Indian political leader and first Indian governor-general of independent India. He was a prominent member of the INDIAN NATIONAL CONGRESS but supported the creation of the separate state of PAKISTAN. Increasingly opposed to the Socialist policies of the Congress Party, he founded (1959) the conservative Swatantra [freedom] Party.

**Rajahmundry,** town (1981 pop. 216,851), East Godavari dist., Andhra Pradesh state, E India, at the head of the GODAVARI delta. It processes agricultural produce such as rice and tobacco, and has paper mills and engineering industries. It has developed into an important trading centre. It is an ancient town, and was the capital of the Chalukya kings during the 10th and 11th cent.

**Rajkot,** town (1981 pop. 445,076), Gujarat state, W India, in the north-centre of the Kathiawad peninsula. It is a district administrative centre of some importance, and trades partly through an outport (Bedi) on the silt-laden Rann of Cutch. It has cotton-textile and ceramics factories. It was the capital of a former princely state.

**Rajputs,** dominant people of Rajputana, an historic region of NW India coextensive with present-day Rajasthan. Mainly Hindus of the warrior CASTE, but including some Muslims, their many clans claim divine origin. They were powerful in the 7th cent., but by 1616 had submitted to the MUGHALS. In the 18th cent. they expanded their territory, but they were driven back by the British in the 19th cent. Many Rajput princes maintained states under the British, but they gradually lost power after India gained independence (1947).

**Rákóczy** (‚rahkawtsee), noble Hungarian family. **Sigismund Rákóczy,** 1544–1608, was elected (1607) prince of Transylvania to succeed Stephen BOCSKAY. His son, **George I Rákóczy,** 1591–1648, became prince of Transylvania in 1630. In 1644 he attacked Holy Roman Emperor FERDINAND III, overran Hungary, and obtained (1645) religious freedom for Hungarians. He was succeeded as prince by his son, **George II Rákóczy,** 1621–60, who was deposed in 1657 and died in a Turkish invasion of Transylvania. His grandson, **Francis II Rákóczy,** 1676–1735, led a Hungarian uprising (1703) against Austrian rule. He was elected (1704) 'ruling prince' by the diet, and the Hungarian nobles proclaimed (1707) the HABSBURG dynasty deposed in Hungary. Rákóczy, however, suffered (1708, 1710) severe defeats, and the Austrians and Hungarians negotiated a peace at Szatmar in 1711. Rákóczy refused to accept it and thereafter lived in exile. He is a national hero in Hungary.

**Rákosi, Mátyás,** 1892–1971, Hungarian Communist dictator. As secretary-general of the Hungarian Communist Party, Rákosi picked off opponents one at a time and established a reign of terror in Hungary until the Russians removed him shortly before the 1956 revolution. He died in exile in the USSR.

**Raleigh** or **Ralegh, Sir Walter,** 1554?–1618, English soldier, explorer, courtier, and man of letters. A favourite of ELIZABETH I, and a rival of Robert Devereux, earl of ESSEX, Raleigh was given vast estates in Ireland. He conceived and organized the colonizing expeditions to America that ended tragically with the 'lost colony' on ROANOKE ISLAND. With Christopher MARLOWE and George CHAPMAN, he was associated with the poetic group known as the 'school of night', which won a reputation for atheism. In 1595 he embarked on an expedition up the Orinoco R. in Guiana in search of EL DORADO. His fortunes fell with the accession of JAMES I, who was convinced of his enmity. He was convicted of treason and imprisoned in the Tower. Released in 1616, he made another expedition to Orinoco in search of gold. It failed, and he returned to England where he was executed under the original sentence of treason. Raleigh wrote poetry, political essays, and philosophical treatises: the small body of authentic poems includes some sonnets and translations, an elegy of Sir Philip SIDNEY and a powerful but fragmentary appeal to Queen ELIZABETH I, surviving in his own handwriting and not published until the 19th cent. Prose writings include reflective essays, travel narratives such as *The Discoverie of Guiana* (1596), letters, and the weighty but unfinished *History of the World* (1614), written during his long imprisonment in the Tower.

**Raleigh,** US city (1984 est. pop. 169,000), state capital of North Carolina. A government, cultural, trade, and industrial centre, it manufactures food, textile, and electrical products. With Durham and Chapel Hill, it is part of North Carolina's Research Triangle complex. Selected as capital in 1788, it was laid out and incorporated in 1792.

Points of interest include the birthplace of Andrew JOHNSON and several 18th-cent. houses.

**Rallis, George John,** 1918–, prime minister of GREECE (1980–81). A conservative, he served in the legislature from 1950 and held cabinet posts before being imprisoned and exiled (1967–68) by the military regime then in power. Named foreign minister in 1978, Rallis became prime minister in 1980 but lost the 1981 election to Andreas PAPANDREOU.

**Rama,** hero: see RAMAYANA.

**Ramadan,** the ninth month of the Muslim lunar year, during which Muslims are obliged to abstain from food, drink, and sexual activity from sunrise to sunset. In pre-Islamic western Arabia, Ramadan was the month during which tribal warfare was suspended; it was also the month during which MUHAMMAD first received his revelation of the KORAN.

**Ramakrishna** or **Sri Ramakrishna Paramahansa,** 1836–86, Hindu mystic. He became a devotee of the goddess KĀLĪ c.1855 and lived for the rest of his life at her temple in Dakshineswar, outside Calcutta. He taught that all religions are valid means of approaching God. His saintliness attracted a large following, and after his death his teachings were spread by disciples, in the West notably by Swami Vivekananda, a major exponent of modern VEDĀNTA philosophy.

**Ramanujan, Srinivasa** (rah,mahnoojən), 1889–1920, Indian mathematician. A self-taught genius in pure mathematics, he made original contributions to function theory, power series, and number theory.

**Rāmāyaṇa** [story of Rāma], classical Sanskrit epic of India, probably composed in the 3rd cent. BC. Based on legend, it is traditionally the work of Vālmīki, a minor character. The *Rāmāyaṇa* relates the adventures of Rāma, who is deprived of his throne by guile and exiled with his wife, Sītā. When Sītā is abducted by a demon king, he allies himself with Sugrīva, the monkey king, and Hanumān, a monkey general. After a great battle in Lankā (Sri Lanka), Rāma frees Sītā and regains his kingdom.

**Rambert, Dame Marie,** 1888–1982, English dancer and teacher; b. Poland. She studied with Jaques DALCROZE, and assisted NIJINSKY with the rhythmic realization of the first performance of *Le Sacre du printemps*. She undertook further study under Checchetti. One of the greatest influences in the development of English ballet, she founded (1926) the **Ballet Rambert,** the oldest of existing English ballet companies. It began to give weekly performances in 1930, and developed such British talents as Sir Frederick ASHTON and Antony TUDOR. A highly successful, classically-based modern dance company, it changed its name to **Rambert Dance Company** in 1987.

**Rameau, Jean Philippe** (ra,moh), 1683–1764, French composer and theorist. His two treatises on HARMONY introduced the important theory of chord inversion. He wrote elegant harpsichord and chamber works, and more than 30 stage works, e.g., the opera *Castor et Pollux* (1737).

**Rameses:** or **Ramesses** see RAMSES.

**Rammohan Ray, Haja,** 1774?–1833, pioneer of modernization in India. He established a universalist theistic society (Brahmo Sabha), based on the Upanishadic doctrines, and fought for the abolition of suttee (immolation of Hindu widows). Also a pioneer of Western education and modern journalism in India, he went to England in 1830 as a representative of the Mughal emperor and gave valuable evidence before the Select Committee of Parliament on Indian affairs. A political liberal, he was in sympathy with the nationalist movements in Europe and Latin America. He died in Bristol.

**Rampur,** town (1981 pop. 204,610), Uttar Pradesh state, N India, on the Kosi R. It is a district administrative centre which, unlike many other towns in the state, has grown rather slowly. It does, however, have some industries, including textiles, engineering, chemicals, and sugar-refining. In British days it was the capital of a princely state of the same name.

**Ramsay, Allan,** 1685?–1758, Scottish poet. A pastoral comedy, *The Gentle Shepherd* (1725), is his most famous work. Ramsay compiled several collections of Scottish poems and songs, contributing greatly to the vernacular revival which culminated in the work of Robert BURNS.

**Ramsay, Allan,** 1713–84, Scottish portrait painter. Ramsay studied and travelled in Italy. He became a successful portrait painter in London from the early 1740s, when his style anticipated the grandeur of REYNOLDS. His late works, especially his portraits of women, brought to British

portraiture a new delicacy and soft naturalism, e.g., *The Artist's Wife* (c.1755; National Gall., Edinburgh).

**Ramsay, Sir William,** 1852–1916, Scottish chemist. He synthesized (1876) pyridine from acetylene and prussic acid. Ramsay discovered helium and was codiscoverer (with Lord RAYLEIGH) of argon and (with Morris Travers) of krypton, neon, and xenon. Knighted in 1902, he won the 1904 Nobel Prize for chemistry for his work on gases.

**Ramses, Rameses** or **Ramesses** (,ramseez, ,raməseez), the name of numerous Egyptian pharaohs. Most prominent were **Ramses II** (c.1304–1237 BC), the greatest ruler of the XIX dynasty and the longest-reigning of all pharaohs. After an inconclusive battle against the Hittite king at Kadesh (c.1290), he established a balance of power with the other great power of the day, the HITTITES, and set the limit of Egyptian control at the R. Orontes in Syria. Among the monuments of his reign is the larger temple at Abu Simbel. **Ramses III** (c.1197–1165 BC, XX dynasty), the last really powerful ruler of the New Kingdom, repelled successive attacks on Egypt by the Libyans and the SEA PEOPLES. Swift decline for Egypt followed his death.

**Ramsey, (Arthur) Michael,** 1904–88, English theologian, archbishop of Canterbury (1961–74). Ordained priest in 1928, he was professor of divinity at Durham Univ. (1940–50) and Cambridge Univ. (1951–61). In March 1966 he led a small delegation to Rome and held discussions with Pope PAUL VI (the first official meeting between heads of the Roman Catholic and Anglican Churches since the REFORMATION). He also developed relations with the EASTERN ORTHODOX CHURCH. His writings combine acute theological expertise with profound spiritual insight. On retirement (1974) he was created a life peer.

**Ramuz, Charles Ferdinand** (ra,myz), 1878–1947, Swiss novelist. His works deal with the simple people of his native canton of Vaud. Among them are *Présence de la mort* (1922; tr. The End of All Men) and *Derborence* (1935; tr. When the Mountain Fell). His *Soldier's Tale* (1918) provided the text for STRAVINSKY'S dance–drama.

**Ranchi,** city (1981 pop. 489,626), Bihar state, NE India, on the Ranchi plateau. It is a divisional and district administrative centre. In terms of industry it is chiefly remarkable for the heavy machinery plant established after independence, but it also has porcelain and other factories, and craft industries. It is the site of a university.

**Rand, the:** see WITWATERSRAND.

**Randolph, Edmund,** 1753–1813, American statesman. A founding father of the United States, he proposed (1787) the Virginia plan, favouring the large states, which considerably influenced the CONSTITUTION OF THE UNITED STATES. He was the nation's first attorney general (1789–93) and its second secretary of state (1794–95). His cousin, **John Randolph,** 1773–1833, served five terms (between 1799 and 1829) in the US Congress and vigorously opposed FEDERALIST PARTY policies.

**randomization,** one of the essential requirements of the theory of STATISTICS for the DESIGN OF EXPERIMENTS, through which the experimental treatments are assigned to replicated plots by an explicit device for allocating them at random so that no treatment can be favoured by position or selection of the experimental material. The randomization is usually done by consulting tables of random numbers, or by generating pseudo-random numbers on a computer. Randomization is also important in sample surveys if any estimate is to be made of the precision achieved by the survey.

**Randstad,** [Dutch, = rim-city], name in use since the 1930s to describe the ring of towns and cities in the W Netherlands that includes UTRECHT, AMSTERDAM, HAARLEM, LEIDEN, the HAGUE, ROTTERDAM and DORDRECHT, together accounting for some 37% of the country's population. The 'greenheart' of the Randstad is still mainly agricultural and every effort is made to prevent urban encroachment on to this valuable open space.

**Rangabe** or **Rhangavis, Alexandros Rizos** (rahnhgah,bay, 'rahng,gahvees), 1810–92, Greek scholar, dramatist, and diplomat; b. Constantinople. Prominent in the Greek classical revival, he was a leading representative of the classical trend in modern Greek literature, as in his successful comedy *The Marriage of Koutroulis* (1845).

**Rangoon,** largest city (1983 pop. 2,458,712) and capital of Burma, near the mouth of the Rangoon R. A major port, it is the country's foremost industrial, commercial, and transport centre. Its products include rice, teak, oil, and ships. Dominated by the ancient golden-spired Shwe Dagon

Pagoda, it was a fishing village until it was made the capital (1753) by Alaungapaya, founder of the last line of Burman kings. Modernized under British colonial rule (1852–1937), it was severely damaged by an earthquake (1930) and by bombing in World War II.

Shwe Dagon Pagoda, **Rangoon:** The largest Bhuddist place of worship in the world, it is surrounded by 64 smaller pagodas

**Rank, Otto,** 1884–1937, Austrian psychoanalyst. He was one of Sigmund FREUD's first and most valued followers, but unlike most early psychoanalysts, was not a physician, and contributed to the theory of PSYCHOANALYSIS by the analysis and interpretation of myths. He later diverged from Freud, emphasizing the 'birth trauma' as the most significant infantile experience and source of later NEUROSIS.

**Ranke, Leopold von** (ˌrangkə), 1795–1886, German historian, generally recognized as the father of the modern objective historical school. An outstanding teacher, he inaugurated at the Univ. of Berlin the seminar system of teaching history. His *Universal History* (9 vol., 1881–88) and his studies of aspects of the 16th, 17th, and 18th cent., particularly its statecraft, reveal both his methods and his purposes.

**Ransom, John Crowe,** 1888–1974, American poet and critic. A great stylist, he wrote elegant, impersonal verse in such collections as *Poems about God* (1919) and *Two Gentlemen in Bonds* (1926). He taught at Vanderbilt Univ. (1914–37), where he was a founder of the *Fugitive* (1922–25), and at Kenyon College (1937–58), where he founded the influential *Kenyon Review*. A 'new critic', he voiced his literary theories in such works as *The World's Body* (1938) and *The New Criticism* (1941).

**Ransome, Arthur (Mitchell),** 1884–1967, English writer. He is remembered for his novels for children beginning with *Swallows and Amazons* (1930), which reflect his keen interest in sailing and the countryside.

**Rao, Raja** (row), 1909–, Indian novelist. Among his works, written in English, are the novels *Kanthapura* (1938), *The Serpent and the Rope* (1960), and *Comrade Kirillov* (1976), and *The Cow of the Barricades and*

*Other Stories* (1947). From 1965 to 1980 he was professor of philosophy at the Univ. of Texas.

**Rapacki Plan,** Polish proposal first advanced in 1957 for the creation of a nuclear-weapons-free zone in central Europe covering the territories of East and West Germany, Poland, and Czechoslovakia. The plan envisaged that such a denuclearized zone would be jointly supervised by the WARSAW TREATY ORGANIZATION and the NORTH ATLANTIC TREATY ORGANIZATION and would lead to other measures of East–West DÉTENTE. The plan was rejected by the US and UK governments on the grounds that it would favour the Warsaw Treaty countries with their superiority in conventional forces, and also because it appeared to place the possibility of a neutral unified Germany on the international agenda.

**Rapallo Pact,** treaty unexpectedly signed in 1922 by Soviet Russia and Germany resolving differences outstanding from WORLD WAR I. The treaty's significance lay in its symbolism in ending the diplomatic isolation of the two signatories and demonstrating their desire for cooperation notwithstanding their contrasting political systems. Viewed with much suspicion by France and the UK, the treaty was a forerunner of the Soviet-German non-aggression pact signed in 1939 shortly before Hitler's invasion of Poland, but was annulled by the German invasion of the USSR in 1941.

**rape,** in law, the crime of performing sexual intercourse without the subject's consent. The victim may be legally incapable of consent if incapacitated (e.g., drugged or intoxicated) or below an age specified by statute (statutory rape). In recent years statutory definitions of rape have been in flux. For example, by some definitions the rapist may be of either sex; in actuality, however, almost all instances of prosecuted rape involve an assault by a man on a women. There are increasing protests in the wake of rape cases that highlight the discrepancy between public attitudes and the widely varying judicial viewpoints expressed in sentencing. In Britain the first of many Rape Crisis Centres offering raped women support and counselling was opened in 1976. In some countries, and in several US states, a wife may charge her husband with rape.

**Raphael,** 1483–1520, major Italian RENAISSANCE painter; full name Raphael Santi or Sanzio. Raphael's work is the clearest expression of the harmony and balance of High Renaissance composition. His father, Giovanni Santi, court poet and painter to the duke of Urbino, taught him the elements of art. After his father's death, Raphael entered the workshop of PERUGINO, whose influence is seen in *The Crucifixion* (1503) and *The Knight's Dream* (1500; both: National Gall., London). His style was already distinguished by its grace and harmonious compositions. In Florence (1504–08) he produced his self-portrait (Uffizi, Florence) and the numerous Madonnas, influenced by LEONARDO DA VINCI and renowned for their sweetness of expression. At Rome, his style matured, benefiting from MICHELANGELO's influence. He was wholly responsible for the Stanza della Segnatura (1511) in the Vatican (see VATICAN CITY), the two largest walls representing the *School of Athens* and the *Triumph of Religion*. In

**Raphael,** 'School of Athens' from the *Stanza della Segnatura*, 1511, in the Vatican

the Stanza d'Eliodoro he painted (1514), among others, *The Miracle of Bolsena* and *The Deliverance of St Peter*. The *Sistine Madonna* (Dresden) is from his Roman period. In 1514 he succeeded BRAMANTE as chief architect of the Vatican, and he designed ten tapestries for the SISTINE CHAPEL. Raphael was deeply indebted to the sculpture of antiquity, and he achieved a harmony and monumentality of interpretation that were emulated far into the 19th cent.

**rare-earth metals,** group of chemical elements including those in the LANTHANIDE SERIES, usually YTTRIUM, and sometimes SCANDIUM and THORIUM. Promethium, which is not found in nature, is often not considered a rare-earth metal. The metals occur together in minerals as their oxides (RARE EARTHS) and are difficult to separate because of their chemical similarity. The cerium metals are a subgroup, consisting of the elements with atomic numbers between 57 and 63 and ytterbium.

**rare earths,** oxides of the RARE-EARTH METALS. The name of an earth is formed from the name of its element by replacing *-um* with *-a*. Once thought to be very scarce, they are widely distributed and fairly abundant in the earth's crust. Rare-earth minerals include bastnasite, cerite, euxenite, gadolinite, MONAZITE, and samarskite. Mixed rare earths are used in glassmaking, ceramic glazes, and glass-polishing abrasives, and as catalysts for petroleum refining. Individual purified rare earths are used in lasers and as colour-television picture-tube phosphors.

**rare gas:** see INERT GAS.

**Ras al Khaimah,** small state on the coast of PERSIAN GULF. See UNITED ARAB EMIRATES.

**Rashi** pseud. of **Rabbi Solomon bar Isaac** (‚rahshee), 1040–1105, Jewish exegete, grammarian, and legal authority; b. France. His thorough and authoritative commentaries on the BIBLE and TALMUD are regarded as indispensable, particularly for the elucidation of the difficult style, vocabulary, and methodology of the Talmud. His inclusion of French words transliterated into Hebrew also makes his books useful to students of medieval French.

**Rask, Rasmus Christian,** 1787–1832, Danish philologist, a major linguistic pioneer. He published the first usable Anglo-Saxon and Icelandic grammars (translated into English), and much other valuable work on the relationship of the Indo-European languages.

**Rasmussen, Knud Johan Victor,** 1879–1933, Danish explorer and ethnologist; b. Greenland. Of Eskimo ancestry through his mother, he began in 1902 a lifelong study of the ESKIMO and in 1910 established Thule station as a base for exploration. Seeking proof that the Eskimo originated in Asia, he was the first to traverse (1921–24) the NORTHWEST PASSAGE. His translated works include *Across Arctic America* (1927).

**raspberry,** name for several thorny shrubs (genus *Rubus*) of the ROSE family and for their fruit (see BRAMBLE).

**Rasputin, Grigori Yefimovich,** 1872–1916, Russian holy man and courtier. A semiliterate peasant, he mixed religious fervour with sexual indulgence. His ability to check the bleeding of the czarevich, a haemophiliac, gave him power over Czarina ALEXANDRA FEODOROVNA and, through her, over Czar NICHOLAS II. In 1911 Rasputin's unscrupulous appointees began to fill high posts. After 1915, with the czar at the front in WORLD WAR I, the government was increasingly undermined. Amid suspicions that Rasputin and the czarina were plotting to make peace with Germany, a group of nobles murdered him.

**Rasputin, Valentin Grigorievich,** 1937–, Soviet writer, leading light of the 'village prose' school. His stories are set in his native Siberia, and express his concern over the disappearance of the old village way of life, particularly the old standards of moral behaviour. His best-known works are *Farewell to Matyora* (1976), about the impending drowning of an island village to make possible a hydroelectric scheme, and *The Fire* (1985), about moral degradation culminating in looting, in a northern Russian logging settlement.

**rat,** any of various stout-bodied RODENTS, usually having a pointed muzzle and long, scaly tail. The name refers particularly to the two species of house rat, the brown, or Norway, rat (*Rattus norvegicus*) and the black, or Alexandrine, rat (*R. rattus*). The brown rat is the larger of the two, growing up to 25 cm (10 in) long, excluding the tail, and sometimes weighing more than 500 g (1 lb). Rats spread human diseases and destroy food supplies; efforts to exterminate them have been relatively unsuccessful. Many other rodents are also called rats, e.g., the water rat (see VOLE).

**rates,** a direct tax on property levied in the UK by local authorities (district or borough councils). The tax is payable annually by the occupiers of non-agricultural land and buildings in a local-authority area as a contribution to the cost of local services. The amount paid depends upon the rateable value of the property (related to its notional annual rental value) and upon the rate poundage fixed by the rating authority. The rate poundage, which is the number of pence in the pound which occupiers have to pay on the rateable value of their property, is calculated by dividing the total sum to be raised by the estimated yield of a penny rate in the area of the rating authority. Thus, if expenditure to be met from the rates were to be £500,000 and the yield of a penny rate were £10,000, the rate poundage would be 50p. Rateable values are determined periodically by valuation officers of the Board of the INLAND REVENUE which is independent of the local authorities. Rates are a constant subject of controversy but finding an alternative tax which is acceptable to local and central government and to the general public is difficult. See also POLL TAX.

**ratio,** the quotient of two numbers, often used for comparison. For example, in a school with 500 children and 25 teachers, the teacher–pupil ratio is $^{25}/_{500} = ^1/_{20}$.

**rational number:** see NUMBER.

**rattan,** climbing PALM with bamboo-like stems (genera *Calamus* and *Daemonorops*) of tropical Asia. Rattan leaves, unlike those of most palms, are not clustered in a crown, and they have long barbed tips by which the plant climbs to treetops. Commercial rattan, a tough, flexible CANE of uniform diameter used for wickerwork, is obtained from the plant's long stem.

**rattlesnake,** poisonous New World SNAKE of the PIT VIPER family, distinguished by a rattle at the end of the tail. The rattle, a series of dried, hollow segments of skin, makes a whirring sound when shaken, serving to warn attackers. Most species are classified in the genus *Crotalus*. The sidewinder is a North American desert species.

**Ratzel, Friedrich,** 1844–1904, German geographer. A major influence on other geographers, he pioneered in developing anthropogeography and helped found modern political geography. In *Anthropogeography* (2 vol., 1882–91) and *Political Geography* (1897), he emphasized the importance of *Lebensraum*—the physical space occupied by a population as a factor determining human activity.

**Rauschenberg, Robert** (‚rowshənbuhg), 1925–, American artist. He was associated with the development of POP ART in New York in the 1960s with his friend Jasper Johns. Executed with great spontaneity, his paintings use images and objects from everyday life. *Gloria* (1956) is typical of his collages known as 'combines'.

**Rauschenbusch, Walter** (‚rowshən'boosh), 1861–1918, American clergyman. After working among German immigrants as a Baptist pastor in New York City, he became acquainted with the FABIAN SOCIETY in England. Appointed (1902) professor of church history at Rochester Theological Seminary, he was a leading figure in the SOCIAL GOSPEL movement.

**Ravel, Maurice** (ra‚vel), 1875–1937, French composer. With DEBUSSY he became a leading exponent of IMPRESSIONISM, composing highly original, fluid music within classical forms. His works for the piano include *Valses Nobles et Sentimentales* (1911) and *Le Tombeau de Couperin* (1917). Among his orchestral works are *Rapsodie Espagnole* (1908) and *Boléro* (1928) and two dazzling piano concertos (1931).

**raven,** the largest member of the CROW family, found in arctic and temperate regions of the Northern Hemisphere. The raven (*Corvus corax*) is a glossy, black scavenging bird about 65 cm (26 in) long with a call resembling a guttural croak; it can be taught to mimic human speech.

**Ravenna,** city (1984 pop. 136,569), in Emilia-Romagna, N central Italy, connected to the Adriatic by a canal. It is a farm-market and industrial centre based on oil, natural gas and petrochemicals. A Roman naval port, it was in turn the capital of the Western Empire (402–76), of the Ostrogoths (5th-6th cent.), and of the Byzantine exarchs (6th cent.–751). PEPIN THE SHORT took it from the LOMBARDS and gave it to the pope (754). Ruled by the Da Polenta family (13th–15th cent.), it returned to papal control in 1509. Ravenna is famous for its 5th- and 6th-cent. mosaics, as in the Church of San Vitale (547), and for its Roman and Byzantine buildings.

**Rawalpindi,** city (1981 est. pop. 806,000), NE Pakistan. It is an industrial centre producing refined petroleum and gas, textiles, steel, chemicals, and other manufactures. Sikhs settled the area in 1765. When the British occupied the PUNJAB in 1849 Rawalpindi became a major military outpost; it remains the Pakistani army's headquarters. It was Pakistan's interim capital from 1959 to 1970.

**Rawlings, Jerry,** 1947–, military and political leader in GHANA. He led a coup that ousted another military junta in 1979, but stepped aside to allow a civilian president, Hilla LIMANN, to govern. On 31 Dec. 1981, however, Rawlings deposed Limann and resumed power, suspending the constitution and banning all political parties.

**Rawls, John,** 1921–, American philosopher. His most famous work, *A Theory of Justice* (1971), is one of the most original and widely discussed contributions to 20th-cent. political theory. Rawls argues for a system of simple rules governing the distribution of wealth and position in a community, which provide justice by balancing considerations of both freedom and equality. These rules include the principle that an individual has a right to the maximum degree of liberty compatible with a like liberty for all, and that inequality can be justified if it works to everyone's advantage.

**Ray** or **Wray, John,** 1627–1705, English naturalist. He was extremely influential in laying the foundations of systematic biology. Together with his pupil Francis Willoughby, he planned a complete classification of the animal and vegetable kingdoms. His work—the botanical part of the project—includes the important *Historia plantarum* (3 vol., 1686–1704). Ray was the first to name and make the distinction between monocotyledons and dicotyledons and the first to define and explain the term *species* in the modern sense of the word.

**ray,** flat-bodied cartilaginous marine FISH (order Batoidea), related to the SHARK. Most rays have broad, flat, winglike pectoral fins along the sides of the head, whiplike tails, eyes and spiracles on top of the head, and mouth and GILL slits underneath. Many rays, such as the skates, lie on the sea floor and feed on smaller animals, e.g., snails. Fertilization is internal, and the eggs are often laid in horny cases called 'mermaids' purses'. The young develop inside the cases and hatch out from them. Rays include the DEVIL FISH, stingray, and sawfish. The common skate (*Raia batis*) and MONKFISH are important as food-fishes in this family.

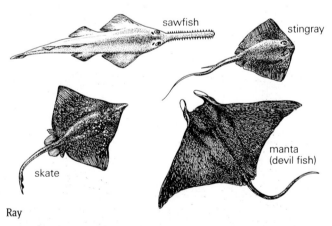

Ray

**Ray, Man,** 1890–1976, American artist and photographer. He helped to found the New York DADA movement. In 1921 he travelled to Paris where he participated in European Dadaism and the SURREALIST movement. His surrealist photographs are his best known and his work was exhibited in 1922 in the international Dada exhibition and also published. He invented the rayograph, a photograph made by direct application of objects to a light-sensitive plate. He eventually returned to the US after World War II and remained active until his death.

**Ray, Nicholas,** 1911–79, American film director; b. Raymond Nicholas Kienzle. His films such as *The Lusty Men* (1952), *Johnny Guitar* (1954), and *Rebel Without a Cause* (1955) show disquieted heroes caught in an uncaring society, filmed in a tight, restless style.

**Ray, Satyajit,** 1912–, Indian film director. His trilogy *The Song of the Road* (1955), *The Unvanquished* (1957), and *The World of Apu* (1958)

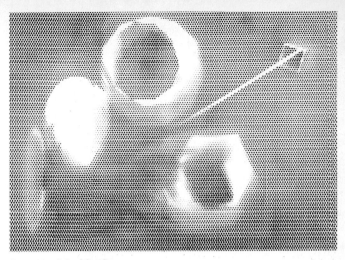

A rayograph by Man **Ray**

brought Indian film to world attention. His other work includes *Two Daughters* (1961), *Distant Thunder* (1973), and *The Middleman* (1979).

**Rayburn, Sam,** 1882–1961, US legislator. A Democratic US representative from Texas (1913–61), he helped to pass NEW DEAL legislation. Rayburn served a record 17 years (1940–61, except for two terms) as Speaker of the House. One of his protégés was Lyndon B. JOHNSON.

**Rayleigh, John William Strutt,** 3rd **baron,** 1842–1919, English physicist. He was professor (1887–1905) at the Royal Institution, London, and later head of the Cavendish Laboratory in Cambridge. For discovering the chemical element argon (with Sir William RAMSAY) he won the 1904 Nobel Prize for physics. He is known for his research in sound and light, his study of Boyle's law (see GAS LAWS) applied to low-pressure gases, and his determination of electrical units.

**rayon,** synthetic fibre made from CELLULOSE, or textiles woven from such fibre. Silklike rayon, the first SYNTHETIC TEXTILE FIBRE, was produced in 1884 by a French scientist, Hilaire de Chardonnet. In rayon manufacturing, cellulose, chiefly from wood pulp, is dissolved by chemicals and forced under pressure through minute holes in a metal spinneret, emerging as filaments. The filaments are doubled and twisted into silky yarns or cut into staple lengths and spun. Spun rayon can be treated to simulate wool, linen, or cotton.

**Rb,** chemical symbol of the element RUBIDIUM.

**Re,** chemical symbol of the element RHENIUM.

**reactance:** see IMPEDANCE.

**reactor, nuclear:** see NUCLEAR REACTOR.

**Reade, Charles,** 1814–84, English novelist and dramatist. Remembered for his historical novel *The Cloister and the Hearth* (1861), he also wrote plays, notably *Masks and Faces* (1852), and a series of novels advocating reform of criminal justice, such as *It's Never Too Late to Mend* (1856).

**Reading,** county town (1981 pop. 194,727) of Berkshire, S England, on R. Thames, 58 km (36 mi) W of London. It is a railway junction and important industrial centre, famous for the manufacture of biscuits. Light and high-tech industries have become important. There are several historic buildings including the remains of a Norman abbey. Reading Univ. was set up in 1926, having formerly been the University Extension College (founded 1892). Oscar WILDE wrote *The Ballad of Reading Gaol* while in prison here.

**reading,** process of mentally interpreting written symbols. Until Gutenberg's invention of the press (c.1450) and the Protestant Reformation's emphasis on individual interpretation of the Bible, instruction in reading was generally restricted to the clergy and certain nobility. In today's more egalitarian society, reading is considered essential for all members of society, and reading instruction is a primary purpose of elementary education. Reading is a complex skill, involving many interrelated abilities. The process is based on a succession of quick eye movements, called fixations, in which more than one word is perceived and interpreted; it takes place almost reflexively in adult readers, who can read and understand from 200 to 1000 words per minute, but must be studied and practised by the novice. Teaching methods are numerous and include the alphabetic method, memorizing names of the letters; the phonic method, learning sounds of the letters; the whole-word method, learning names of objects or actions; and the sentence method, linking sound with meaning. In the last few decades, although the need for systematic drill is recognized, reading has come to be regarded as an integrated part of language development rather than an isolated skill to be drilled out of context.

**Reagan, Ronald Wilson,** 1911–, 40th president of the US (1981–89). A film actor who was president of the Screen Actors Guild, he was an ardent supporter of the Democrats' NEW DEAL long before he joined the Republican Party in 1962 and began to champion right-wing causes. As governor of California for two terms (1967–75), he cut state welfare and medical services and education funds. After leaving office, he campaigned vigorously for the 1976 Republican presidential nomination but lost narrowly to Pres. Gerald FORD. Four years later he won the nomination and, with his running mate, George BUSH, resoundingly defeated Pres. Jimmy CARTER in the 1980 election. His presidency had barely begun when he was shot in the chest by a would-be assassin, John Hinckley, Jr, on 30 Mar. 1981; however, he recovered quickly. Advocating a balanced budget to combat inflation, Pres. Reagan reversed long-standing political trends by pursuing his programme of budget and tax cuts through Congress. He did, however, advocate increased defence spending. In 1982 Pres. Reagan sent a personal envoy to negotiate an end to the Israeli–Palestinian conflict in BEIRUT, Lebanon (see ARAB–ISRAELI WARS), and he subsequently proposed a plan for peace in the Middle East, without substantive result. His administration adopted a firm stance in its relations with the USSR and against possible Communist expansion in Central America. Reelected for a second term in 1984, Reagan sought to improve relations with the USSR and to reach a nuclear-arms control agreement, meeting Soviet leader Mikhail GORBACHEV in a series of summits (1985–88) and signing (1987) a treaty for the reduction of intermediate-range nuclear forces (INF). Increasingly disturbed by terrorist actions against US citizens and installations, Reagan in Apr. 1986 ordered an air strike on Libya, the most stridently anti-US Arab state and alleged paymaster of anti-Western international terrorism. In late 1986 the Reagan presidency suffered from disclosures that US arms had been secretly sold to Iran (in defiance of a congressional ban) and the proceeds used in part to finance the Contras seeking to overthrow the left-wing government of Nicaragua.

**realism,** in art, broadly, an unembellished rendering of natural forms. Specifically, the term refers to the mid-19th-cent. movement against French academicism. Realist painters portrayed ugly or commonplace subjects without idealization. Major realists include COURBET, J.F. MILLET, and DAUMIER. See also PHOTOREALISM.

**realism,** in literature, an attempt to describe life without idealization or romantic subjectivity. Although not limited to any one century or school, it is most often identified with the 19th-cent. French writers Gustave FLAUBERT and Honoré de BALZAC. George ELIOT introduced it in England, W.D. HOWELLS in the US Realism has been chiefly concerned with the commonplaces of middle-class life. In drama it is most often associated with Henrik IBSEN. A reaction against its emphasis on externals led to the psychological realism of Henry JAMES and others. See also NATURALISM.

**realism,** in philosophy. 1 In medieval philosophy, realism was the position that universals or general concepts have existence independent of both the human mind and individual objects. It is a position directly opposite to NOMINALISM. 2 In EPISTEMOLOGY, realism represents the theory that individual things exist independently of the mind's perception of them, as opposed to IDEALISM, which holds that reality exists only in the mind.

**real number:** see NUMBER.

**real tennis,** Fr, *jeu de paume,* racket-and-ball game, the probable ancestor of all tennis games. The court resembles a medieval courtyard with sloping galleys (penthouses) on three of the four walls, a buttress (tambour) in one corner and nets (dedans) in two of the walls. A net bisects the court. The two halves are known as the service (from which service is always taken) and the hazard. The standard court measures 29.26 by 9.75 m (96 by 32 ft), but may vary. The ball remains in play up to a height of 5.48 m (18 ft) on the side walls and 7.31 m (24 ft) on the end walls. It is a notoriously complicated game, although the basics are

similar to lawn tennis. Approximately 30 courts exist in the world; the most famous—all in London—are at Hampton Court, LORD'S cricket ground, and Queen's Club.

**Réaumur, René Antoine Ferchault de** (ˌrayəmyooə), 1683–1757, French physicist and naturalist. He invented an alcohol thermometer and the Reaumur temperature scale. He studied the composition of Chinese porcelain (which led him to develop an opaque glass), and the composition and manufacture of iron and steel, and published (1734–42) an exhaustive study of insects.

**Rebecca** or **Rebekah,** in the BIBLE, wife of ISAAC and mother of JACOB and ESAU. Jacob was his mother's favourite, and for him she devised their deception of the blind Isaac. She is one of the four Jewish MATRIARCHS. Gen. 24–27.

**recall:** see under INITIATIVE, REFERENDUM, AND RECALL.

**received pronunciation (RP),** accent of British English, historically associated with southern England, the Court, and the PUBLIC SCHOOLS. It was adopted by the BBC as an authoritative form which would be understood in all regions of the UK and English speaking world. Now no longer considered as socially prestigious, many regional varieties of RP have developed.

**recession:** see under DEPRESSION.

**Recife,** chief city (1980 pop. 1,184,215) of NE Brazil, a port on the Atlantic Ocean; also known as Pernambuco. Cut by many waterways, it lies partly on the mainland and partly on an island and is often called the Brazilian Venice. It is an important transportation centre; its economy is based on the processing and export of cotton, sugar, and coffee. Among the products of the developing industrial sector are glass, ceramics, pharmaceuticals, and synthetic rubber. Founded (1548) by the Portuguese, Recife was briefly held by the British (1595) and the Dutch (1630–54).

**reciprocity,** a key concept in anthropology, seen by M. MAUSS as the fundamental morality, and part of K. POLANYI's typology of distribution. It is essentially the return of a GIFT or action, one of the basic aspects of an exchange relationship and as such central to social relationships and the organization of social life. M. SAHLINS has characterized reciprocity as operating along a continuum from generalized reciprocity, in which there is no obligation on the receiver to return what has been given (a form characteristic of close kin), through balanced reciprocity, when exchange occurs almost immediately, and when the good or action is of an equivalent status to that which has been received, to negative reciprocity in which individuals or groups try to get something for nothing; in its most extreme form this is warfare.

**recitative,** musical declamation for solo voice, used in OPERA and ORATORIO for dialogue and narration. Its development at the end of the 16th cent., enabling words to be clearly understood and natural speech rhythms to be followed, made possible the rise of opera. In the 17th cent., the rapid patter of *recitativo secco,* punctuated by occasional accompanying chords, served only to advance the action; by the 18th cent., more strict measure and full orchestral accompaniment helped to highlight recitative passages of dramatic interest. In Wagner's operas, the melody is completely moulded to the text.

**recombinant DNA:** see GENETIC ENGINEERING.

**reconnaissance satellite,** artificial SATELLITE launched by a country to provide intelligence information on the military activities of foreign countries. There are four major types. *Early-warning satellites* detect enemy missile launchings. *Nuclear-explosion detection satellites* are designed to detect and identify nuclear explosions in space. *Photo-surveillance satellites* provide photographs of enemy military activities, e.g., the deployment of intercontinental ballistic missiles (ICBMs). There are two subtypes: close-look satellites provide high-resolution photographs that are returned to earth via a reentry capsule, whereas area-survey satellites provide lower-resolution photographs that are transmitted to earth via radio. Later satellites have combined these two functions. *Electronic-reconnaissance satellites* pick up and record radio and radar transmissions while passing over a foreign country. Both the US and the USSR have launched numerous reconnaissance satellites since 1960.

**Reconstruction,** in US history, period (1865–77) of readjustment following the AMERICAN CIVIL WAR. When the war ended the defeated South was a ruined land, and its old social and economic order had collapsed. But Reconstruction, as the victorious North defined the term, had to do not with Southern economic recovery but with two complex and interrelated problems, namely, the process and conditions under which the ex-Confederate states would be restored to the Union, and the future of the four million former slaves. Pres. Andrew JOHNSON formulated a lenient Reconstruction plan and tried to implement it without consulting Congress. He required the ex-Confederate states merely to repudiate secession and the Confederate war debt and to ratify the impending 13th Amendment (1865) abolishing slavery. The provisional governments set up by Johnson met these requirements but also enacted laws severely limiting the civil rights of blacks (the 'Black Codes') and elected Confederate leaders to state and federal offices. This outraged Northern opinion; radical Republicans in Congress, led by Thaddeus STEVENS, refused to seat Southern representatives and passed, over the president's vetoes, a series of Reconstruction acts (1867) which laid down much harsher conditions for readmission to the Union. They required the ex-Confederate states to draft, under military supervision, new state constitutions which disfranchised all who had helped the Confederacy and granted suffrage to blacks. Black civil rights were incorporated in the 14th Amendment (1868), which the Southern states were also required to ratify. This programme was fully carried out, new radical Republican state governments were formed, and by 1870 all the former Confederate states had been restored to the Union. When Johnson attempted to wreck the radicals' Reconstruction plan and defied the TENURE OF OFFICE ACT, Congress impeached him (1868); he was not convicted, but he was rendered impotent for the rest of his term. After the 15th Amendment (1870) had guaranteed blacks the right to vote, terrorist groups such as the KU KLUX KLAN tried to keep them from voting. Eventually, radical Republican governments were overthrown and white rule was restored. Reconstruction officially ended in 1877, when all federal troops were withdrawn from the South. Its legacy was the one-party 'solid South' and a lasting racial bitterness.

**Reconstruction Finance Corporation** (RFC), US government agency (1932–57) created during the GREAT DEPRESSION to stimulate the economy by lending money to financial, industrial, and agricultural institutions. During the NEW DEAL its operations were broadened to finance war plants, loan money to foreign governments, and pay for disaster damages. RFC loans totalled about $50,000 million.

**Reconstructionist Judaism:** see JUDAISM.

**recorder,** a WOODWIND instrument, much used in the RENAISSANCE and BAROQUE periods of music. The recorder was not used in classical or romantic music, having been displaced by the FLUTE, but has been revived in the 20th cent. The sound is produced by a fipple. Recorders come in eight different sizes—garklein, sopranino, descant, treble, tenor, bass, great bass, and sub-contrabass—each with a range of about two and a half octaves.

**record player** or **gramophone,** device for reproducing sound that has been recorded as a spiral, undulating groove on a disc. The disc or record is placed on the record player's motor-driven turntable, which rotates the record at a constant speed. A needle or stylus tipped with some hard material (e.g., diamond) and attached to a tracking arm is placed in the groove and vibrates in sympathy with the undulations as it moves along it. In early record players these vibrations were amplified mechanically by means of diaphragms, resonant tubes, and light horns; now the vibrations are converted into electrical signals by means of a TRANSDUCER, and the conversion to audible sound is effected by means of an AMPLIFIER and LOUDSPEAKER. The first 'phonograph' was built by Thomas EDISON in 1877. See also STEREOPHONIC SOUND.

**rectifier,** component of an ELECTRIC CIRCUIT that changes alternating current to direct current. Rectifiers operate on the principle that current passes through them freely in one direction, but only slightly or not at all in the opposite direction. See also DIODE; ELECTRON TUBE; THYRISTOR.

**recycling:** see WASTE DISPOSAL.

**Redbridge,** London borough (1981 pop. 224,731), outer NE London. It contains the towns of Ilford, Wanstead, and Woodford. It is mainly residential, with industries including the manufacture of photographic equipment and materials, and of electrical equipment.

**Red Brigades,** Ital. *Brigate Rosse,* extreme left-wing Italian urban terrorist movement formed in 1969. Its members were responsible for

many violent actions, including the kidnapping and murder (1978) of former premier Aldo MORO.

**red cedar:** see JUNIPER.

**Red Cloud,** 1822–1909, chief of the Oglala SIOUX INDIANS. He led opposition to the BOZEMAN TRAIL through Indian lands in Colorado and Montana. The Fetterman Massacre (1866) and Red Cloud's raids finally led to the trail's abandonment (1868).

**Red Cross,** international organization concerned with alleviating suffering and promoting public health. Its formation in 1863 was prompted by Jean Henry DUNANT, a Swiss citizen who had witnessed the suffering at the battle of Solferino (1859). The GENEVA CONVENTION of 1864 adopted the red cross as a symbol of neutral aid (the red crescent being added later for Muslim countries, the red lion and sun for Iran and the red star for Israel). Most governments have signed the 1864 and later treaties and conventions. There are over 100 national societies and two international bodies based in Geneva. The work of the Red Cross has grown to include aid to REFUGEES, e.g., in drought-striken African countries; exchanges of sick and wounded soldiers, initiated during the KOREAN WAR (1950–53); and disaster relief.

**Red Data Book,** a collected list of all the plants and animals in danger of extinction, published by the INTERNATIONAL UNION FOR THE CONSERVATION OF NATURE AND NATURAL RESOURCES. It is published as a loose-leaf book, with each species having a separate sheet. Replacement sheets are published as more information becomes available.

**Redford, Robert,** 1937–, American film actor and director. After playing leading roles in such films as *Butch Cassidy and the Sundance Kid* (1969), *The Sting* (1973), and *All the President's Men* (1976), he won an Academy Award as director of *Ordinary People* (1980).

**red giant:** see STELLAR EVOLUTION.

**Redgrave,** family of English actors. **Sir Michael Redgrave,** 1908–85, was the distinguished star of many plays, e.g., *Hamlet, Macbeth, Uncle Vanya,* and *The Family Reunion* (1939), and several films, e.g., *The Lady Vanishes* (1939) and *The Browning Version* (1951). His elder daughter, **Vanessa Redgrave,** 1937–, starred in the London production of *The Prime of Miss Jean Brodie* (1966) and has appeared in such films as *Blow-Up* (1967), *Isadora* (1968), *Julia* (1976), and, for television, *Playing for Time* (1980). She is also noted for her political activities with The Workers' Revolutionary Party, an interest she shares with her brother **Corin Redgrave,** 1939–. Their sister, **Lynn Redgrave,** 1944–, best known for her role in the film *Georgy Girl* (1966), has also appeared on the stage, e.g., *Saint Joan* (1977), and on television.

**Red Guards,** originally units of armed workers mobilized by the BOLSHEVIKS in the 1917 Russian revolution; in the 1960s name given to youth and student activists prominent in China's CULTURAL REVOLUTION.

**Redi, Francesco** (,raydee), 1626–97, Italian naturalist, poet, philologist, and court physician. Through controlled experiments he demonstrated that certain organisms, notably maggots in rotting meat, did not arise, as had been alleged, through spontaneous generation.

**Redmond, John Edward,** 1856–1918, Irish liberal and nationalist leader. Elected (1881) to the British Parliament as a HOME RULE member, he led the faction supporting Charles Stewart PARNELL and became chairman of the unified Irish Party in 1900. Having supported the third Home Rule bill (1912), he was stunned by the Easter Rebellion of 1916. His influence later declined, and he was opposed by the revolutionary SINN FEIN.

**Redon, Odilon** (rə,dawnh), 1840–1916, French painter and lithographer, a leading Symbolist (see SYMBOLISM). *In the World of Dreams* (1879) was the first of a series of lithographic volumes of fantastic subjects, as winged heads, strangely grinning spiders, eyes floating in space. From about 1892 Redon began to work in pastel and painted many brilliantly coloured flower pieces.

**red pepper:** see PEPPER.

**Red River Settlement,** pioneer colony, largely in MANITOBA, Canada, founded by the HUDSON'S BAY COMPANY, settled (1812–15) by impoverished Scottish and Irish immigrants, and violently opposed by the rival NORTH WEST COMPANY until the union of the two companies (1821).

**Red Sea,** narrow sea, c.2330 km (1450 mi) long and between 190 and 400 km (120 and 250 mi) wide, separating NE Africa and the Arabian

Odilon **Redon**, *Lumière*, 1893. Lithograph, 39 × 27.3 cm.

Peninsula. It connects with the Gulf of ADEN (S) through the narrow BAB EL MANDEB and divides in the north to form the Gulfs of Suez and Aqaba. The sea, which is dotted with small islands and dangerous coral reefs near the shores, forms an important link in the MEDITERRANEAN SEA–SUEZ CANAL–INDIAN OCEAN sea lane.

**red shift,** decrease in the frequency of light received as compared to frequency of emission, measured as a shift of spectral lines towards the red (low frequency) end of the spectrum. Light emitted low in a strong gravitational field shows a red shift, but in most cases the red shift results from the recession of the source (DOPPLER EFFECT). The most famous and largest red shifts are observed in the spectra of QUASARS and of distant GALAXIES due to the universal recession of widely separated objects in COSMOLOGY. See also HUBBLE'S LAW.

**reduction,** in chemistry: see OXIDATION AND REDUCTION.

**redwood:** see SEQUOIA.

**reed,** name for several plants of the GRASS family. The common reed (*Phragmites communis*) is a tall perennial widely distributed in wet places. It has tough flowering stems up to 2 m (6½ ft) high used for thatching, and has been cropped economically for cellulose production. The giant reed (*Arundo donax*), which is similar in appearance, has long been used to make fishing rods, walking sticks, and musical instruments, e.g., pan pipes.

**Reed, Sir Carol,** 1906–76, English film director. He enjoyed a working relationship on many films with Graham GREENE as his scriptwriter. Among his films are *The Stars Look Down* (1939), *Odd Man Out* (1946), *The Fallen Idol* (1948), *The Third Man* (1949), *Outcast of the Islands* (1941), *Our Man in Havana* (1960), and *Oliver!* (1968; Academy Award).

**reef:** see CORAL REEFS.

**referendum:** see under INITIATIVE, REFERENDUM, AND RECALL.

**reflection,** return of a wave, such as light, from a surface it strikes, into the medium through which it has travelled. The law of reflection states that the angle of reflection (the angle between the reflected ray and the normal, or line perpendicular to the surface at the point of reflection) is equal to the angle of incidence (the angle between the incident ray and the normal). See ECHO; MIRROR; REFRACTION.

**reflex,** automatic involuntary response to a stimulus, made without conscious effort. Examples of reflexes are the instinctive withdrawal from a painful stimulus, such as a hot object, and the patellar reflex (which can disappear in disease), a jerk of the leg caused by tapping the tendon below the knee. The nerve pathway involved in a reflex action is called a reflex arc and involves reception of the stimulus, conduction of nerve impulses to a nerve centre outside the BRAIN, and from there conduction outwards to an effector—a muscle, gland, or organ that produces the response.

**Reformation,** religious revolution in Western Europe in the 16th cent. Beginning as a reform movement within the Roman Catholic Church, the Reformation ultimately led to freedom of dissent. The preparation for the movement was long and there had been earlier calls for reform, e.g., by John WYCLIF and John HUSS. Desire for change within the church was increased by the RENAISSANCE, with its study of ancient texts and emphasis on the individual. Other factors that aided the movement were the invention of printing, the rise of commerce and a middle class, and political conflicts between German princes and the Holy Roman emperor. The Reformation began suddenly when Martin LUTHER posted 95 theses on the church door at Wittenberg on 31 Oct. 1517. Open attack on the doctrines and authority of the church followed and led to Luther's breach with the church (1520), which the Diet of Worms (1521) failed to heal. His doctrine was of justification by faith alone instead of by sacraments, good works, and meditation, and it placed man in direct communication with God. Luther's insistence on reading the Bible placed on the individual a greater responsibility for his own salvation. The new church spread in Germany and Scandinavia, especially among princes and people who hoped for a greater degree of freedom. The conflict between the Lutherans and the Catholic Emperor CHARLES V was long and bitter. A temporary settlement was reached at the Peace of Augsburg (1555), but continued discord contributed later to the THIRTY YEARS' WAR. Outside Germany, a different type of dissent developed under Huldreich ZWINGLI in Zürich, and within Protestantism differences arose, such as doctrinal arguments on the Lord's Supper. These were debated, inconclusively, at the Colloquy of Marburg (1529) by Luther and Philip MELANCHTHON on one side and Zwingli and Johannes Oecolampadius on the other. More radical ideas were spread, particularly among the lower classes, by such leaders as CARLSTADT, Thomas MÜNZER, and JOHN OF LEIDEN. In 1536 Geneva became the centre for the teachings of John CALVIN, perhaps the greatest theologian of Protestantism. In France the HUGUENOTS, fired by Calvin's doctrine, resisted the Catholic majority in the Wars of RELIGION (1562–98). Calvinism superseded Lutheranism in the Netherlands, and it spread to Scotland through the efforts of John KNOX. In England the Reformation took its own course. HENRY VIII issued the Act of Supremacy (1534), which rejected papal control and created a national church (see ENGLAND, CHURCH OF). Calvinistic thought was, however, strong in England, and it influenced later reforms. On the Continent, divisions within the Protestant churches served to forward the COUNTER-REFORMATION, which rewon some territory for Catholicism. The end (1648) of the Thirty Years' War brought some stabilization, but the force of the Reformation did not end. The movement, and its fruit, Protestantism, has continued to exert influence to the present day, with its emphasis on personal responsibility and individual freedom, its refusal to take authority for granted, and its influence in breaking the hold of the church upon life and the consequent secularization of life and attitudes.

**Reform Bills,** in British history, name given to measures in the 19th cent. that set out to extend the franchise and representation in Parliament, which despite population shifts and the rise of new social classes during the INDUSTRIAL REVOLUTION, had not altered significantly since the 17th cent. The **Reform Bill of 1832,** passed by Earl GREY's Whig ministry, redistributed seats in the interest of larger cities and gave the vote to middle-class men. Subsequent bills introduced during the 1850s and 60s failed until Benjamin DISRAELI and the Conservatives, with radical support, passed the **Reform Bill of 1867,** enfranchising working men in the towns and more than doubling the electorate. The **Reform Bill of 1884,** under William GLADSTONE, reduced rural qualifications and added 2 million voters. It was not, however, until the passage of the

REPRESENTATION OF THE PEOPLE ACTS in the 20th cent. that Britain adopted universal male and female suffrage, the latter in two stages, 1918 and 1928.

**Reformed Church in America,** Protestant denomination founded in colonial times by Dutch settlers and formerly known as the Dutch Reformed Church. In America a congregation was formed in New Amsterdam in 1628. In 1754 an assembly declared itself independent of the classis (i.e., governing body) of Amsterdam, and in 1792 a constitution was adopted. The present name became official in 1867. In 1980 the church reported a membership of 345,532.

**Reform Judaism:** see JUDAISM.

**refraction,** the deflection of a wave on passing obliquely from one transparent medium into a second medium in which its speed is different, as the passage of a light ray from air into glass. The index of refraction of a transparent medium is equal to the ratio of the speed of light in a vacuum to the speed of light in the medium. Snell's law states that the ratio of the sine of the angle $i$ of incidence (angle between the incident ray and the normal, or line perpendicular to the boundary between the two mediums at the point of refraction) to the sine of the angle $r$ of refraction (angle between the refracted ray and the normal) is equal to the ratio of the refracting medium's index of refraction $n_r$ to the original medium's index of refraction $n_i$.

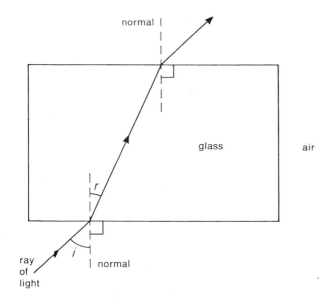

Refraction

**refrigeration,** process for drawing heat from substances to lower their temperature, often for purposes of preservation. Mechanical refrigeration systems (first patented in 1834) are based on the principle that absorption of heat by a fluid (refrigerant) as it changes from a liquid to a gas lowers the temperature of the objects around it. In the compression system, employed in electric home refrigerators, a COMPRESSOR, controlled by a thermostat, exerts pressure on a refrigerant gas (usually FREON or AMMONIA), forcing it to pass through a condenser, where it loses heat and liquefies. When the liquid is circulated through refrigeration coils, it vaporizes, drawing heat from the air surrounding the coils. The refrigerant gas then returns to the compressor and the cycle is repeated. In the absorption system, widely used in commercial installations, ammonia is used to cool brine, which is then piped into the refrigerated space. See also AIR CONDITIONING.

**refugee,** one who leaves a native land because of expulsion or persecution for political or religious reasons. Systematic, international aid to refugees began in the 20th cent., mainly under the auspices of the LEAGUE OF NATIONS, which helped repatriate or resettle refugees. After WORLD WAR II the UN was responsible for resettling and caring for 8 million displaced persons (people removed from their native countries as prisoners or slave labourers). The refugee problem has remained acute

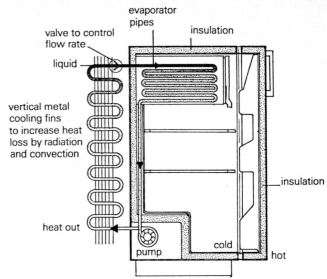

Refrigeration

worldwide, and, according to the UN High Commissioner for Refugees, by the early 1980s there were 14 to 18 million refugees, among them people fleeing from Cuba and other Caribbean nations, Vietnam, Kampuchea, South Africa, the Horn of Africa, and the Middle East, where the Palestinian refugee problem has persisted since 1948.

**Regency style,** in English architecture, flourished during the regency and reign of GEORGE IV (1811–30). The major architect was John NASH, who built the Royal Pavilion, Brighton (1815–22), an example of diversity of style with its Indian exterior and exotic Oriental furnishings. The main trend, however, was neoclassical, as seen in the work of Sir John SOANE and in Nash's Regent's Park, London. Bay windows, balconies, and eclectic furniture design were characteristic.

**Regensburg,** city (1984 pop. 128,100), Bavaria, SE West Germany, a port at the confluence of the Danube and Regen rivers. It is an industrial centre with such manufactures as machines and precision instruments. Founded by the Romans, it was a medieval trade centre, a free imperial city, and the home (16th–19th cent.) of the imperial diet. In 1810 it passed to BAVARIA. An aircraft-manufacturing centre during WORLD WAR II, it was heavily bombed. Its historic buildings include a Gothic cathedral (13th–16th cent.).

**Reger, Max** (ˌraygə), 1873–1916, German composer, pianist, and conductor. He was highly esteemed for such complex organ music as *Fantasy and Fugue in C Minor* (1898) and *Fantasy and Fugue on B-A-C-H* (1900). His many other works include compositions for orchestra and for piano and over 300 songs.

**reggae** (ˌregay), Jamaican popular music that developed in the 1960s among Kingston's poor blacks, drawing on American 'soul' music. Many of its highly political songs proclaim the tenets of the Rastafarian religious movement. Springy, offbeat rhythm characterizes its sound. Bob MARLEY and his group, the Wailers, and Toots and the Maytals are among the best-known performers.

**Reggio di Calabria,** largest city (1984 pop. 177,237), Calabria, S Italy, on the Strait of Messina. It is principally a commercial and administrative centre. It is the ancient town of Rhegion, but has experienced severe damage from earthquakes; most recently in 1908.

**Regina,** city (1981 pop. 164,313), provincial capital, S Saskatchewan, W Canada, on Wascana Creek and Lake. Oil refining is the major industry. Regina (named in honour of Queen Victoria) was founded in 1882 and was the capital (1883–1905) of the Northwest Territories before becoming (1905) the capital of newly created Saskatchewan.

**regression,** used in STATISTICS to describe the relationship between one variable and one or more other variables. The simplest relationships are linear and between only two variables, but the theory of statistics also deals with relationships which are nonlinear and multivariate. Regression equations can be used, for example, to estimate the growth of trees or agricultural crops from records of rainfall, temperature, and hours of sunshine, without necessarily knowing the causal relationships between these variables.

**Regulator movement,** organized efforts by settlers in rural parts of North and South Carolina in the 1760s to protest against political underrepresentation, the absence of law courts, and the extortion of local officials. In SOUTH CAROLINA planters and small farmers created an association to try criminals and resolve legal disputes. In NORTH CAROLINA the Regulators protested against actions of corrupt officials with acts of violence. When law and order was restored by 1771, the Regulators disbanded. Tensions persisted, however, between the 'backcountry' settlers and the 'tidewater' aristocracy living near the coast.

**Rehoboam** ('reeə,bohəm) Hebrew king, son of SOLOMON. After Solomon's death (c.922 BC) the northern tribes revolted against Rehoboam and set up the kingdom of Israel with JEROBOAM I as their king. Rehoboam continued to rule the southern kingdom of Judah. 1 Kings 11.43; 12; 14.

**Reich, Steve (Stephen Michael),** 1936–, American composer, whose fascination for the musics of West Africa and Bali influenced the 'minimalist' style of composition that he developed in the late 1960s. This is based on perpetual rhythmic and melodic transformations in a stable harmonic field. It is not, in fact, structurally like either AFRICAN or BALINESE music, but is Reich's own concoction. His music has attracted enthusiastic and varied audiences.

**Reich, Wilhelm** (reikh), 1897–1957, Austrian psychoanalyst, social theorist, and prophet of sexual revolution. Reich modified Freudian psychoanalytic theory in the 1920s and 30s, emphasizing the orgasm as the goal of therapy, and viewing sexual repression as a consequence of capitalism and 'authoritarian patriarchism'. Reich's attempts to wed Freudianism and Marxism, both in theory, and in practice through the establishment of 'sex-hygiene clinics' for workers in Vienna and Berlin, were eventually repudiated both by the psychoanalytic movement and the Communist Party, from both of which he was expelled (1933). Abandoning in his turn both Marxist and Freudian theory, Reich emigrated first to Scandinavia, then to America, where he elaborated his theory of 'orgonology', widely regarded as a bizarre product of a deranged mind. Reich's books include *The Function of the Orgasm* (1927), *The Mass Psychology of Fascism* (1932) and *The Sexual Revolution* (1936).

**Reichstadt, Napoleon, duke of:** see NAPOLEON II.

**Reichstag** (,riekhstahk), German imperial parliament; name for the Diet of the Holy Roman Empire, for the lower chamber of the federal parliament of the North German Confederation, and for the lower chamber of the federal parliament of Germany (1871–1945). Under the German empire, the Reichstag had little real power and was mainly a deliberative body. In the republic established in 1919, it became the supreme legislative body; it represented the people directly, and the upper chamber, the Reichsrat, represented the various German states. Shortly after HITLER took power (1933), he dissolved the Reichstag and called for new elections. A violent campaign ensued, and on 27 Feb. 1933, a fire destroyed part of the Reichstag building. Hitler used the fire, which was later shown to have been set by a lone arsonist, to blame the communists and whip up public furor. As a result, the Nazis won a slight majority in the elections. In March the Reichstag voted Hitler dictatorial powers. Thereafter, it was summoned to meet only sporadically and to approve important government measures. After WORLD WAR II, the Reichstag and Reichsrat were replaced by other legislative bodies.

**Reid, Thomas,** 1710–96, Scottish philosopher. He founded the Scottish 'common-sense' school of philosophy and attacked HUME's theory of ideas over its tendency to IDEALISM and SCEPTICISM, arguing instead that minds have direct contact with reality. His major works are the *Enquiry into the Human Mind* (1764) and *Essays on the Intellectual Powers of Man* (1785).

**Reid, Victor Stafford,** 1913–87, Jamaican novelist. He sought to make dialect an acceptable medium for use in his fiction. He is best known for *New Day* (1949), an attempt to link the 1865 Morant Bay Rebellion to the 1944 Jamaica Independence celebrations, and for *The Lepoard* (1968), about the Kenya independence struggle.

**Reign of Terror,** 1793–94, period of the FRENCH REVOLUTION. It was essentially a war dictatorship to preserve the republic during the FRENCH REVOLUTIONARY WARS. The Committee of Public Safety was created (6 Apr.

1793) to rule the nation and included Maximilien ROBESPIERRE, the dominant member, and Lazare CARNOT. It aimed to root out counterrevolutionaries, raise new armies, and regulate the economy. The Law of Suspects (Sept. 1793) defined those who could be arrested for treason and was enforced by the Committee of General Security and the Revolutionary Tribunal; several thousand were guillotined. The government was centralized, and the nation was mobilized militarily. Price and wage ceilings were set. In June 1794 the Revolutionary Tribunal was strengthened, and executions increased. However, popular discontent grew, and the Reign of Terror was ended by the overthrow (July 1794) of Robespierre.

**reincarnation, doctrine of,** a religious belief in rebirth, widespread in India. Ordinarily it is believed that due to its KARMA, a soul transmigrates from one life to another. Even in BUDDHISM (where there is no permanent soul) there is a belief in the cycle of birth and rebirth, which is said to be never-ending and is also believed to be causally conditioned. The cycle can be broken in NIRVĀNA. The belief is found in Tibet and Japan, and in some form or other it was present in the doctrine of PYTHAGORAS, EMPEDOCLES and PLOTINUS (and the Neo-Platonists).

**reindeer,** ruminant MAMMAL (genus *Rangifer*) of the DEER family, found in arctic and subarctic regions of Eurasia and North America. The Eurasian reindeer (*R. tarandus*) stands about 120 cm (4 ft) at the shoulder and weighs about 110 kg (250 lb); its long fur is light brown in summer and whitish in winter. Domesticated for centuries in Lapland and S Siberia, they provide meat, milk, clothing, and transport. The domestic stocks were seriously polluted by eating radioactive plants after the CHERNOBYL accident in 1986. A reindeer can travel 65 km (40 mi) a day, pulling twice its own weight. The wild reindeer of North America are called CARIBOU.

**reinforcement,** in LEARNING theories, the process by which a learned association between a STIMULUS and a RESPONSE is strengthened; or the pleasurable event (or reward) which brings about the strengthening of the learned association; or any stimulus which makes a preceding response more likely or more frequent, when contingent upon that response. 'Negative reinforcement', a stimulus which is contingent upon a response and whose removal makes that response more likely or frequent, is distinguished from 'punishment', a contingent response which makes the response less frequent or likely. Used more loosely, the term refers simply to processes which strengthen learning or performance.

**Reinhardt, Django,** (Jean Baptiste Reinhardt), 1910–53, Belgian jazz guitarist and violinist, of gypsy descent. Despite losing two fingers from his left hand in his teens, he developed an original guitar style and became the first European jazz player to influence American musicians. From his work in the 1930s with the Quintet of the Hot Club of France to later collaborations with Coleman HAWKINS and Duke ELLINGTON, he consistently produced imaginative and melodically sophisticated acoustic guitar-playing.

**Reinhardt, Max,** 1873–1943, Austrian theatrical director; b. Max Goldmann. A great innovator and a master of spectacle, he staged gigantic productions, full of pageantry and colour, at his theatres in Berlin. His world-famous productions included *The Lower Depths, Oedipus Rex,* and *The Miracle.* He founded the Salzburg Festival in 1920. He fled NAZI Germany in 1933, becoming a US citizen in 1940.

**relative density,** ratio of the DENSITY of a substance to the density of a reference substance. The reference substance is usually pure water at 4°C for liquids and solids, and hydrogen for gases. In the former case the measurement is sometimes known as *specific gravity*, and in the latter as *vapour density*.

**relativity,** name of two important theories of 20th cent. physics. Albert Einstein's special theory of relativity (1905) was essential to avoid inconsistency between the dynamics of Galileo and Newton, in which velocity is purely relative (though acceleration is absolute) and Maxwell's electromagnetism in which a particular velocity, the velocity of LIGHT, plays a crucial role. Einstein's resolution of this problem fully maintained Newton's equivalence between all observers moving with constant velocity and extending it from dynamics to all of physics, so that each of them sees the same speed of light. This reconciliation is made possible by the realization that there is no one correct universal time, but that time is relative. This means that each uniformly moving observer measures his own time with his own clock. Each such observer's time is as good for his own observations as another observer's time is good for that observer's observation, but the two times are not the same. Thus time becomes a dimension united with space in a four dimensional SPACE–TIME. Just as what we call length and what we call width depends on the way we face, so what is time and what is space depends on the speed with which we are moving. The special theory of relativity is central to all of physics, and has been tested successfully in thousands of ways. The results of the theory become especially noticeable and significant when high speeds, comparable with that of light are involved. One of the most important consequences is the equivalence of energy and mass, which implies in particular that, because of its kinetic energy, a fast moving body has greater mass than that body at rest. Not only has this been tested to great precision in particle accelerators, but it is relevant to the design of every colour television tube. The theory is special only in the sense that it does not deal with that most subtle and universal force, GRAVITATION. For this purpose Einstein created (1915) his general theory of relativity. This incorporates gravitation most successfully by giving space–time a non-Euclidean geometry, with matter causing space–time to be curved. The general theory, though not of the universal significance of the special theory, has passed the relevant tests, notably the advance of the perihelion of Mercury and the deflection of light by the Sun.

**relay**, electromechanical SWITCH in which the variation of current in one ELECTRIC CIRCUIT controls the flow of electricity in another circuit. A relay consists of a movable contact connected to an ELECTROMAGNET by a spring. When the electromagnet is energized by the controlling current, it exerts a force on the contact that overcomes the pull of the spring and moves the contact so as to either complete or break a circuit. When the electromagnet is de-energized, the contact returns to its original position.

**religion**, a system of thought, feeling, and action shared by a group that gives members an object of devotion; a code of ethics governing personal and social conduct; and a frame of reference relating individuals to their group and the universe. Usually, religion concerns itself with what transcends the known, the natural, or the expected; it is an acknowledgment of the extraordinary, the mysterious, and the supernatural. The evolution of religion cannot be precisely determined. In addition to the more elementary forms of belief and practice, such as ANIMISM, ANCESTOR WORSHIP, TOTEMISM, and SPIRITUALISM, there are the commonly termed higher religions, which embody a principle of transcendence. These include POLYTHEISM, in which there are many gods; DUALISM, which posits equally powerful deities of good and evil; MONOTHEISM, in which there is a single god; supratheism, in which the devotee participates in the religion through a mystical union with the godhead; and PANTHEISM, in which the universe is identified with God. Religions are also classified as revealed (i.e., by divine agency) or nonrevealed (i.e., the result of human inquiry). JUDAISM, CHRISTIANITY, and ISLAM are revealed religions, while Buddhist sects (where BUDDHA is recognized not as a god but as an enlightened leader), BRAHMANISM, and TAOISM are considered nonrevealed religions.

**Religion, Wars of,** 1562–98, series of civil wars in France, also called the HUGUENOT Wars. The successive Protestant leaders were Louis I de CONDÉ, Gaspard de COLIGNY, and Henry of Navarre (later HENRY IV). The Catholic party was headed by the house of GUISE. CATHERINE DE' MEDICI and her sons, CHARLES IX and HENRY III, vainly tried to straddle the issue. The wars were marked by fanatical cruelty on both sides. The first three wars (1562–63, 1567–68, 1568–70) ended favourably for the Protestants. The massacre of SAINT BARTHOLOMEW'S DAY began the fourth war (1572–73). The fifth and sixth wars (1574–76, 1577) granted religious freedom; the Catholic LEAGUE was formed in retaliation. The seventh war (1580) was inconsequential. In 1585 Henry of Navarre was named heir presumptive to Henry III, and that precipitated the War of the Three Henrys (the third was Henri, 3rd duc de Guise). After Henry IV's accession (1589) he was forced to fight the League and its ally, Spain; he defeated them in 1594. The Treaty of Vervins and the Edict of NANTES restored peace and established, at least temporarily, religious toleration.

**remand**, legal term for a court's decision to commit a defendant to custody, or release on BAIL, until the next stage of criminal proceedings. In the UK, a defendant can be remanded in custody for a maximum period of eight days, though further remands can be made, so that the person, still legally assumed to be innocent, may be held for many months. Remanded prisoners are detained in PRISON or at a POLICE station. Juvenile

defendants are committed to a remand centre. If the defendant is later convicted, the period of remand in custody may be taken into account when deciding SENTENCE.

**Remarque, Erich Maria** (rə‚mahk), 1897–1970, German novelist. His first novel and masterpiece is *Im Western nichs Neues* (1929; tr. All Quiet on the Western Front), a bitter antiwar story based on his experiences in World War I. His later works deal with the postwar situation in Germany. After 1939, Remarque lived in the US.

**Rembrandt Harmenszoon van Rijn** or **Ryn,** 1606–69, Dutch painter, etcher, and draftsman. He got his most valuable training in the Amsterdam studio of Pieter Lastman, who influenced his sense of composition and frequent choice of religious and historical themes. Rembrandt's works sometimes reflected the dramatic use of light and shadow of CARAVAGGIO, e.g., *The Money Changer* (Berlin). Rembrandt returned to Leiden, his birthplace, in 1625. There he began to teach and started the series of nearly 100 self-portraits that reveal his continued stylistic growth and profound self-awareness. In 1632 he moved to Amsterdam where he became established as a portrait painter with his group portrait *Anatomy Lesson of Dr Tulp* (1632; The Hague), a traditional subject to which he gave radical treatment. His marriage to Saskia van Ulyenburgh, a burgomaster's daughter, brought him wealth and social position. During this period, his work acquired a new richness of colour and plasticity of form, best seen in *The Sacrifice of Abraham* (1635; Leningrad). In 1642 Saskia died giving birth to Titus, their only son, who was later to become a favourite subject. During that same year, he completed his most famous group portrait, *The Shooting Company of Capt. Frans Banning Cocq* (Rijks Mus., Amsterdam), called *The Night Watch* before cleaning (1946–47) revealed it to be a daytime scene. In the last 20 years of his life, after his financial ruin, he withdrew from society and created many of his masterpieces, e.g., *Aristotle Contemplating the Bust of Homer* (1653; Metropolitan Mus., New York), and *The Polish Rider* (Frick Coll., New York City). To the late 1660s belong *The Family Group* (Brunswick) and *The Jewish Bride* (Rijks Mus., Amsterdam), both loosely structured, flamelike in colour, and psychologically penetrating. *The Syndics of the Cloth Guild* (1662; Rijks Mus., Amsterdam) has been described as the culmination of Dutch portrait painting. Rembrandt's prodigious output included 600 paintings, 300 etchings, and nearly 2,000 drawings. The universal appeal of his art lies in its profound humanity.

Rembrandt, *The Night Watch*, 1642. Oil on canvas, 359 × 438 cm. Rijks Museum, Amsterdam.

**Remembrance Sunday:** see ARMISTICE DAY.

**remora**, a warmwater FISH of the family Echeneidae, with an oval sucking disc on top of the head. The remora uses this disc to attach itself to large fish, whales, sea turtles, and small boats, thus travelling without effort and eating scraps of the host's prey. The sharksucker species may reach 90 cm (3 ft) in length.

Remora (*Echeneis naucrates*)

**remote sensing**, obtaining images of features using devices placed on ground, suborbital (aerial), or orbital (satellite) platforms. The devices can be sensitive to, for example, invisible and visible light spectra, gravity, radiation, or electromagnetism. Much modern mapping is based on remote sensing rather than traditional ground survey methods.

**Remscheid** (ˌremshiet), city (1984 pop. 123,100), North Rhine–Westphalia, W West Germany. Specializing like its neighbour SOLINGEN in the manufacture of fine steelware, it is noted for its scissors and tools.

**Remus:** see ROMULUS.

**Renaissance**    [Fr., = rebirth], term used to describe the rich development of Western civilization that marked the transition from the MIDDLE AGES to modern times. In Italy the Renaissance emerged by the 14th cent. and reached its height in the 15th and 16th cent.; elsewhere in Europe it may be dated from the 15th to the mid-17th cent. In outlook the Renaissance brought new importance to individual expression, self-consciousness, and worldly experience; culturally it was a time of brilliant accomplishments in scholarship, literature, science, and the arts (see RENAISSANCE ART AND ARCHITECTURE). More generally, it was an era of emerging nation–states and exploration, and the beginning of a revolution in commerce. The Renaissance first appeared in Italy, where relative political stability, economic expansion, wide contact with other cultures, and a flourishing urban civilization provided the background for a new view of the world. Fine libraries and learned academies and universities flourished. Scholars, poets, craftsmen, and artists were supported by such great patrons as the MEDICI family of Florence, Popes JULIUS II and LEO X, the doges of Venice, and the SFORZA family of Milan. The increased interest in and knowledge of the classical age was reflected in the works of PETRARCA, and the intellectual orientation was towards a secular HUMANISM, exemplified by the works of Lorenzo VALLA. In literature, the romance of the Renaissance was expressed by BOCCACCIO; MACHIAVELLI provided its most telling political commentary. The humanist emphasis on the individual was typified in the ideal of the Renaissance man, the man of universal genius, best exemplified by LEONARDO DA VINCI. This ideal also led to the courtier, the ideal gentleman whose behaviour was codified by CASTIGLIONE. Humanism in art found expression in a more realistic view of nature, seen in the works of Leonardo, MICHELANGELO, and RAPHAEL, while Renaissance architects such as ALBERTI, BRUNELLESCHI FF., BRAMANTE, and Michelangelo utilized classical forms. In France, classicism in literature was displayed by Pierre de RONSARD and Joachim DU BELLAY; RABELAIS expressed the Renaissance's sensual vitality. In Germany, the Renaissance interacted closely with the Protestant REFORMATION and was somewhat more sombre. The Netherlands produced ERASMUS, the most notable of all the humanists, and also gave birth to Albrecht DÜRER and the younger Hans HOLBEIN. England was represented in learning and literature by Sir Thomas MORE, Francis BACON, and William SHAKESPEARE. In Spain, Cervantes wrote his masterpiece, *Don Quixote,* and in Sweden, Queen CHRISTINA, patron of DESCARTES, encouraged scholarship, literature, and the arts at court. The Renaissance intellectual outlook and its concomitant cultural manifestations were gradually replaced by those of the ENLIGHTENMENT. The term *renaissance* is now often used to designate the flowering of various civilizations and eras.

**Renaissance art and architecture.** A radical break with medieval methods of representing the visible world occurred in Italy during the second half of the 13th cent. The sculptor Nicola PISANO evoked interest in the sculptural forms of classical antiquity. In painting, GIOTTO led the way in restoring monumentality and dignity to the human figure and working towards a more realistic depiction of space. After the Black Death in 1348 artists were less interested in naturalism activity until the second decade of the 15th cent., when FLORENCE became the centre of art and art theory. Together with the early humanists (see HUMANISM), artists shared a growing esteem and enthusiasm for physical nature, the individual, and classical antiquity. The architects BRUNELLESCHI and ALBERTI, along with the sculptor DONATELLO, were the first to visit Rome to study the ancient ruins and incorporate classical principles into their work; they were also intensely preoccupied with representing the dimensions of nature on a flat surface. With MASACCIO and UCCELLO, they pioneered the system of PERSPECTIVE, and of the study of light and shade to model from while Fra ANGELICO and Fra Filippo LIPPI developed a unifying colour scheme. Antonio POLLAIUOLO, CASTAGNO, and above all LEONARDO DA VINCI devoted themselves to the study of human anatomy. During the 15th cent. artists came to be supported not only by churchmen but also by private patrons, who demanded pictures of secular subjects, including themselves, and thus the art of portraiture flourished. The Neoplatonic writers and scholars in the circle of Luvenzo de'Medici profoundly influenced BOTTICELLI and MICHELANGELO. In the early 16th cent. the artistic centre shifted from Florence to Rome. The works of Leonardo, Michelangelo, and RAPHAEL can be said to have brought to a culmination all the heroic proportions, unequalled harmony, and noble ideals for which the High Renaissance (c.1490–1520) is known. MANNERISM followed. Meanwhile, by the beginning of the 16th cent. Venetian art had come into its full glory with the great Venetian colourists Bellini (see BELLINI, family), GIORGIONE, TITIAN, VERONESE, and TINTORETTO. Their superb achievements came as the effects of the golden age of painting in the Low Countries were felt across Europe. In the 1420s, the van EYCK brothers developed oil painting and, with it, the ability to achieve subtle variations in light and colour. They did not practise geometric perspective, but created the appearance of reality with minutely detailed observations of light and shade; they were fascinated by the surface and fixture of fabric, jewels, plants, and animals: landscape, genre and portraiture interested northern renaissance painters. Robert CAMPIN, Roger van der WEYDEN, and Hugo van der GOES of the 15th cent. were followed in the 16th cent. by such masters as BOSCH and Pieter Bruegel (see BRUEGEL, family). In Germany, SCHONGAUER and DÜRER made the first and greatest contributions in woodcuts and engraving. FRANCIS I brought Italian architects and painters, such as Leonardo, to France, and in the 1530s the influence of mannerism began to be felt at Fontainebleau. The art of England and Spain was influenced by Netherlandish painting until the 16th cent., when the Italian Renaissance began to permeate Europe. The rebirth of classical architecture that took place in Italy in the 15th cent. and spread in the following century through Europe ended the supremacy of the Gothic style. The ORDERS OF ARCHITECTURE and the structural elements of Rome —the ARCH, VAULT, DOME, and decorative forms served as a treasury for 15th-cent. designers. Brunelleschi, the earliest great architect of the Renaissance, produced the churches of San Lorenzo and Santo Spirito, Florence, and the revolutionary plan for the dome of the Cathedral of Florence. Alberti, the first major theoretical architect of the Renaissance, was influenced by the Roman Vitruvius, and he in turn influenced later architects. Several architects, including Leonardo, designed such variations on the centralized structure as the polygonal and Greek-cross plans, and BRAMANTE's circular Tempietto (c.1502) in Rome. Other great Italian architects were PALLADIO and VIGNOLA. In France, Francis I built many châteaux where Renaissance details were grafted onto Gothic structures. The LOUVRE (begun 1546) usually serves as the start of the classical period in France. The move by Inigo JONES (1619) towards pure classical style decisively established Palladian design in England. In Germany in the mid-16th cent. the medieval love for picturesque forms still dominated, although transferred to classical motifs. Nuremberg and Rothenburg ob der Tauber are rich in works of the period. In Spain, Gothic and Moorish forms mingled with the new classical forms; the palace of Charles V at Granada (1527) is a superb building of the period.

**Renan, Ernest** (rəˌnahnh), 1823–92, French historian. He studied religion from a historical point of view. The first volume of his *History of the Origins of Christianity* (8 vol., 1863–83), entitled *The Life of Jesus,* became his most widely known work. He also wrote a *History of the People of Israel* (5 vol., 1887–93). In later life, he turned to creative writing.

**René,** 1409–80, titular king of Naples (r.1438–80), rival claimant of ALFONSO V of Aragón and Ferdinand I of Naples. The second son of Louis II of Naples, he inherited through marriage Bar (1430) and Lorraine (1431). On the death (1434) of his brother, Louis III of Naples, he inherited Anjou, Provence, and a claim to the throne of Naples. He was adopted as heir by Queen Joanna II of Naples (d. 1435) but was defeated (1442) by Alfonso V and retired to France. On René's death Anjou passed to the French crown. His titles to Provence and Naples passed to his nephew Charles, count of Maine (d. 1481), and then to the French crown. His daughter, MARGARET OF ANJOU, married Henry VI of England.

**Reni, Guido** (ˌrenee), 1575–1642, Italian painter. Born in Bologna, he studied briefly with the CARRACCI. In 1600 he made the first of many visits to Rome, where his CLASSICISM challenged the realism of CARAVAGGIO. Later he established his own studio at Bologna. The ideal beauty and ravishing colour of such classicizing works as *Aurora* (1613; Rospigliosi Palace, Rome), established his fame.

Guido **Reni**, *Aurora*, 1613. Rospigliosi Palace, Rome.

**Renmark,** town (1986 pop. 3489), South Australia. Located on the MURRAY R., a settlement was established here in the 1880s, and irrigation made the surrounding Riverland District an important fruit-growing area. Wine and dried fruit are important products. The pleasant climate has encouraged the growth of a tourist industry.

**Rennes** (ren), city (1982 pop. 200,390), capital of Ille-et-Vilaine dept., regional capital of BRITTANY, NW France. Lying at the centre of a fertile lowland, the city commands routeways between the peninsula and Paris and also between the north and south coasts of Brittany. Long associated with the army, the law, and with learning (university founded 1735) it has acquired motor-vehicle manufacture and electronics industries and its population has grown rapidly in the present century. Notable buildings include the 17th-cent. palace of justice and 18th-cent. cathedral.

**Renoir, Jean** (rəˌnwah), 1894–1979, French film director; son of Pierre Auguste RENOIR. Such films as *Le crime de Monsieur Lange* (1935), *La grande illusion* (1937), and *Le règle du jeu* (1939) exemplify his humanism and cinematic mastery.

**Renoir, Pierre Auguste,** 1841–1919, French Impressionist painter and sculptor; father of Jean RENOIR. At 13 he was a decorator of factory-made porcelain. Through the late 1860s and early 1870s Renoir worked closely with MONET and played a seminal role in the development of IMPRESSIONISM. He painted joyous outdoor scenes, with flickering light and shimmering colour, as the festive *Le Moulin de la Galette* (1876; Musée d'Orsay, Paris); at the same time he began to win fashionable success with his portraits, e.g., *Madame Charpentier and her Children* (1876; Metropolitan Mus., New York). Later Renoir travelled in Italy where he studied Renaissance painting; he began to lay new emphasis on drawing the human figure. After 1880 Renoir painted many voluptuous *Bathers* and sentimental portraits of children.

**reparations,** payments sought by victorious nations over their defeated enemies as compensation for material losses and suffering caused by war. After WORLD WAR I the Treaty of VERSAILLES (1919) formally asserted Germany's war guilt and ordered it to pay reparations to the Allies. (The US did not ratify the treaty and waived all reparations though it insisted on the payment of war debts, especially by France.) The economy of postwar Germany was such that the Allies found it difficult to recover their debts. In 1923, France and Belgium occupied the RUHR district

Pierre **Renoir**, *The Bathers*, 1887. Oil on canvas, 117.5 × 171 cm. Philadelphia Museum of Modern Art.

because of German defaults, an act that embittered the Germans and was a cause of the rise of HITLER. The payment of reparations was resumed under the DAWES PLAN and the YOUNG PLAN from 1924 onwards. In 1945 the Allies again assessed Germany for damages suffered during WORLD WAR II. Payments were to be effected chiefly through the removal of assets and capital goods. Collection of reparations proceeded unevenly, and the process was ended in the early 1950s. In addition, Germany agreed to pay reparations to Israel for the suffering of Jews under the NAZIS. Japan was also forced to pay reparations after World War II, but the US ended its collections in 1949.

**replication,** one of the essential requirements of the theory of STATISTICS for the DESIGN OF EXPERIMENTS, through which experimental treatments of observations must be repeated so as to provide estimates of the variability of the response of the experimental material to the treatments applied. A treatment is said to be replicated if there are two or more instances of that treatment being applied in the experiment. Replication of treatments can be difficult in medical experiments where it would be unethical to repeat unnecessarily a treatment which is believed to be harmful to the patient.

**Representation of the People Acts,** laws passed by the British Parliament to continue the franchise reform begun by the REFORM BILLS. The Representation of the People Act of 1918 gave the vote to most women over 30 and to most men over 21. The act of 1928 enfranchised women on the same terms as men. The act of 1949 abolished plural voting rights, and the act of 1969 lowered the voting age to 18.

**Representatives, United States House of:** see CONGRESS OF THE UNITED STATES.

**reprieve:** see SENTENCE.

**reproduction,** the ability of living systems to give rise to new systems similar to themselves. The term may refer to self-duplication of a single cell, of a group of cells and organs, or of a complete organism. Reproductive processes vary tremendously, but two fundamental types may be distinguished: asexual reproduction, in which a single organism separates into two or more parts, each genetically identical to the parent; and sexual reproduction, in which a pair of specialized reproductive (sex) cells fuse, creating an individual that combines two sets of genetic characteristics. Asexual reproduction is found in all plants and in some one-celled and invertebrate animals. In one-celled organisms it takes the form of MITOSIS, the division of one individual into two new, identical individuals. Primitive organisms, such as FLATWORMS and STARFISHES, can reproduce by fragmentation, in which a piece of the parent breaks off or is broken off and develops into a new individual. Many PROTOZOA and plants reproduce by means of SPORES. In budding, the means by which YEASTS and animals such as the HYDRA reproduce, a small protuberance (bud) on the parent increases in size until a wall forms to separate the new individual. Sexual reproduction occurs in many one-celled organisms and in all multicellular plants and animals; it involves the FERTILIZATION of one sex cell (gamete) by another, producing a new cell (zygote), which develops into a new organism. In higher plants and animals two clearly different kinds of sex cells (distinguished as OVUM and SPERM) fuse. Animals have REPRODUCTIVE SYSTEMS showing increasing protection for the zygote and embryo as the complexity of the organism increased. Multicellular plants alternate reproducing sexually and asexually (see GAMETOPHYTE). Although asexual reproduction ensures that beneficial combinations of characteristics will be passed on unchanged, sexual reproduction permits the offspring to inherit endlessly varied combinations of characteristics (because of the fusion of two different parental nuclei; see MEIOSIS), providing for new variations that may improve a species and further enhance its chances of survival, thus giving rise to EVOLUTION.

**reproductive system,** in animals, the organs concerned with production of offspring. In humans and other mammals the female reproductive system produces the female reproductive cells (eggs, or ova) and includes an organ (uterus) in which the foetus develops. The male reproductive system produces the male reproductive cells (sperm) and includes an organ (penis) that deposits the sperm within the female. In the female, the mature egg, or OVUM, passes from the ovary into the fallopian tube, where fertilization occurs if sperm are present. From the fallopian tube the ovum passes into the uterus, or womb. If the egg has not been fertilized, the endometrium (lining of the uterus) degenerates and sloughs off, and MENSTRUATION occurs. If the egg has been fertilized, it becomes embedded in the lining of the uterus about one week after fertilization (see PREGNANCY). The lower end of the uterus, called the cervix, is connected to the vagina, a passage joining the uterus with the external genitals. The vagina receives sperm during sexual intercourse and is the passageway through which menstrual blood is eliminated and birth takes place. In the male reproductive system, SPERM are produced in the testes, two organs contained in the scrotum, an external sac in the groin. The testes also produce the hormone TESTOSTERONE and a portion of the seminal fluid, the liquid in which the sperm are carried. From the testes the sperm move into a passage (epididymis) and then into a long duct (vas deferens); fluids from the PROSTATE gland and seminal vesicles also enter this duct. Just before ejaculation, contractions along the ducts mix the sperm with the seminal and prostatic fluids to form semen. During ejaculation semen is propelled into the urethra (the canal through the penis) and discharged. See also BIRTH CONTROL; FERTILITY DRUG; FERTILIZATION.

**reptile,** dry-skinned, usually scaly, POIKILOTHERMIC VERTEBRATE of the class Reptilia. Reptiles are found in a variety of habitats in warm and temperate zones and range in size from 5-cm (2-in) long lizards to 9-m (30-ft) long snakes. Typically they have low-slung bodies with long tails, supported by four short legs; snakes and some lizards are limbless. They are mostly terrestrial, although a few are aquatic; all breathe air through lungs and have thick, waterproof skins. Unlike AMPHIBIANS, they do not possess GILLS at any stage of their development. They lay porous, shelled eggs or are OVOVIVIPAROUS. The living orders of reptiles are the TURTLES; ALLIGATORS, caimans, CROCODILES, and gavials; LIZARDS and SNAKES; and the TUATARAS. Reptiles evolved from amphibians and were the dominant fauna in the Mesozoic era, often called the Age of Reptiles. Dinosaurs were reptiles.

**Repton, Humphry,** 1752–1818, English landscape gardener. The first person to adopt the title of landscape gardener professionally, Repton was for several years the partner of John NASH in creating picturesque compositions of architecture and landscape. His own gardens date from 1788, one of the best known being Luscombe in Devon (grounds laid out 1800–04). His *Sketches and Hints on Landscape Gardening* was published in 1795. His general policy, revealed in his 'Red Books' prepared for clients to show how their grounds could be improved, depended upon the discovery of the latent characteristics in a place, which could then be developed and reinforced.

**republic,** sovereign nation whose chief of state is not a monarch, usually governed by representatives of a widely based electorate. The US is a federal republic, while France is a centralized republic. The UK is a constitutional MONARCHY, not a republic. The USSR, in theory a group of federated and even autonomous regions, is in fact a centralized republic.

**Republican Party,** major American political party, the other being the DEMOCRATIC PARTY. It was founded (1854) by opponents of the extension of slavery into the territories. The election of the Republican presidential candidate, Abraham LINCOLN, in 1860 precipitated the secession of the Southern states and the AMERICAN CIVIL WAR. Pres. Andrew JOHNSON's RECONSTRUCTION policies were opposed by radical Republicans such as Charles SUMNER and Thaddeus STEVENS, whose candidate, Ulysses S. GRANT, was elected in 1868 and 1872. With the election of Rutherford B. HAYES (1876), Republican domination of the South ended. In the period that followed, the Republicans seemed to some observers to differ little

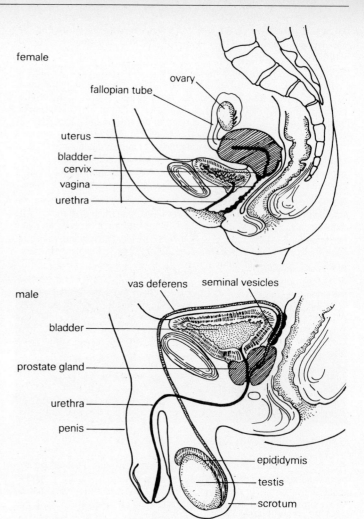

**Reproductive system**

from the Democrats in policies, but in fact they were distinguished by their support of a protective tariff and their sympathy for PROHIBITION, Sabbath observance, and immigration restriction. Theodore ROOSEVELT succeeded the assassinated William McKINLEY in 1901 and was reelected in 1904. His policies combined 'trust busting' and other domestic reforms with an imperialist foreign policy. The Republicans won the presidency three times in the 1920s but were blamed for the GREAT DEPRESSION, and lost every presidential election between 1932 and 1952, when Dwight D. EISENHOWER became president. The WATERGATE AFFAIR during the administration of Richard M. NIXON damaged the party's prestige. In 1980 a Republican, Ronald REAGAN, was elected president and reelected in 1984.

**requiem,** proper MASS for the souls of the dead, performed on All Souls Day, at funerals, and on request. Since the Second VATICAN COUNCIL, the traditional requiem has been modified: black vestments are no longer required, and the famous *Dies irae* sequence describing the Judgment and asking Jesus for mercy is now optional. Requiem music has a traditional Gregorian setting; other requiem music has been composed, e.g., by Mozart and Verdi.

**rescue archaeology,** division of archaeology concerned with removal of artifacts threatened by construction of roads, dams, buildings, pipelines, and other projects. One of the greatest feats of rescue archaeology occurred in the mid-1960s, when an international effort (funded by more than 50 countries) succeeded in preserving the temples at ABU SIMBEL, Egypt, from flooding by the ASWAN HIGH DAM. The two massive structures were moved to higher ground.

**reservoir,** storage tank or wholly or partly artificial lake for storing water. Many reservoirs are created by the erection of a DAM. Smaller municipal reservoirs, usually built of concrete, hold a supply of water sufficient to cope with an emergency. Reservoirs are also constructed to aid in flood control of rivers, maintain water levels in navigable canals, and ensure water supply for hydroelectric plants.

**residence rules,** rules which determine the place of residence of married couples, which are closely associated with forms of kinship systems and have particular significance in systems of MATRILINEAL DESCENT. Patrilocal or virilocal residence is when a couple live with the father of the husband, matrilocal or uxorilocal with the wife's kin, avunculocal with the husband's mother's brother, neolocal in a place independent of any kin.

**resin,** any of a class of amorphous solids or semisolids. Natural resins occur as plant exudations (e.g., of pines and firs), and are also obtained from certain scale insects. They are typically yellow to brown in colour, tasteless, and translucent or transparent. Oleoresins contain ESSENTIAL OILS and are often sticky or plastic; other resins are exceedingly hard, brittle, and resistant to most solvents. Resins are used in VARNISH, SHELLAC, and lacquer and in medicine. Synthetic resins, e.g., BAKELITE, are widely used in making PLASTICS. See also AMBER; TURPENTINE.

**resistance,** property of an electric conductor by which it obstructs the flow of electricity and dissipates electrical energy away from the ELECTRIC CIRCUIT, usually as heat. Resistance is basically the same for alternating- and direct-current circuits. A high-frequency alternating current, however, tends to travel near the surface of a conductor. Because such a current uses less of the available cross section of the conductor, it meets with more resistance than direct current. The unit of resistance is the OHM. See also CONDUCTION; IMPEDANCE; OHM'S LAW; SUPERCONDUCTIVITY.

**resistor,** two-terminal ELECTRIC CIRCUIT component that generates heat by offering opposition to an electric current. The most common forms of resistors are made from fine wires of special alloys wound onto cylindrical forms or from a moulded composition material containing carbon and other substances in varying amounts. Resistors are rated for the maximum amount of power that they can safely handle.

**resonance,** in physics, the phenomenon exhibited by a system (mechanical, electrical, atomic, nuclear) when an externally applied oscillation coincides in frequency with a natural frequency of oscillation of the system. This results in enhanced oscillation of the system and enhanced absorption of energy from the external oscillation. For atoms this could show itself as strong absorption of radiation at particualr frequencies, and for nuclei high probability of capture of particles at particular energies. The term resonance is also used to describe excited states of some elementary particles.

**Respighi, Ottorino** (rays,peegee), 1879–1936, Italian composer. He is best known for his romantic SYMPHONIC POEMS, *The Fountains of Rome* (1917), *The Pines of Rome* (1924), and *Roman Festivals* (1929). He also wrote other orchestral works, chamber music, piano pieces, and operas.

**respiration,** process by which an organism exchanges gases with its environment. The term commonly refers to the overall process by which oxygen is taken from air or water and transported to the cells for the OXIDATION of organic molecules, while the products of oxidation, carbon dioxide and water, are returned to the environment. In single-celled organisms, gas exchange occurs directly. The cells lose their high concentration of carbon dioxide to the environment by simple diffusion, while the environment provides its higher concentration of oxygen to the cells, also by diffusion. In complex animals, where internal cells are distant from the external environment, respiratory systems facilitate the passage of gases to and from internal tissues. In lower animals such as FLATWORMS, exchange occurs through a moist surface membrane. In FISH, blood vessels in the gills are exposed for direct exchange with the external (aquatic) environment. In plants, gas exchange occurs through the stomates, respiratory organs found mostly in leaves. In human beings and other vertebrates, gas exchange takes place in the LUNGS. In breathing —the mechanical procedure for getting air to and from the lungs— muscles enlarge the chest cavity to draw air in and reduce it to expel air. Actual gas exchange in the lungs occurs in cup-shaped air sacs called alveoli. Organisms that utilize respiration to obtain energy are aerobic, or oxygen-dependent. Organisms able to live in the absence of oxygen are called anaerobic; they obtain energy from fuel molecules solely by FERMENTATION or GLYCOLYSIS. In biochemistry, *respiration* refers to the series of biochemical oxidations in which organic molecules such as carbohydrates, amino acids, and fatty acids are converted to carbon dioxide and water. The chemical energy thus obtained is trapped and stored for later use by the cells in ADENOSINETRIPHOSPHATE (ATP).

**response,** in theories of LEARNING, a reaction of an organism to a STIMULUS. BEHAVIOURISM, or other Stimulus–Response (S–R) theories base themselves on easily measurable 'response', such as lever-presses by rats; they have therefore frequently been criticized for an impoverished view of behavioural complexity.

**rest mass:** see MASS.

**Restoration,** in English history, the reestablishment of the monarchy on the accession (1660) of CHARLES II. The term often refers to the whole period from 1660 to the fall of JAMES II in 1688. After the death of Oliver CROMWELL, reaction against Puritan and military control favoured recall of the exiled king. Upon his return to power, Charles, guided by Edward Hyde, 1st earl of CLARENDON, and others, restored militant Anglicanism and tried to assert the old Stuart absolutism. The unwillingness of both Charles and his brother and successor, James II, to accept their financial dependence on Parliament was one cause of James's deposition in the GLORIOUS REVOLUTION (1688). The period was marked by an advance in colonization and trade, the DUTCH WARS, the birth of the WHIG and TORY parties, opposition to Roman Catholicism, and the revival of drama and poetry.

**resurrection,** arising again from death to life. Belief in the physical resurrection of Jesus, as reported in the Gospels, is central to traditional Christianity, as is the conviction that it foreshadows the resurrection of all human beings (the 'general resurrection') or, according to some theologians, of those destined to eternal life. Since the early 19th cent. doubts of various kinds have been expressed about both beliefs, and while the main churches firmly adhere to them they are usually interpreted in symbolic terms in liberal circles. The orthodox belief is that on Judgment Day people's souls will be reunited with their risen (but glorified and immortal) bodies.

**retrograde motion,** in astronomy, real or apparent movement of a planet, satellite, asteroid, or comet from east to west relative to the fixed stars. The most common direction of motion in the solar system, for both orbital revolution and axial rotation, is from west to east. Bodies in the solar system with real retrograde orbits include four satellites of Jupiter, one of Saturn, one of Neptune, and some asteroids and comets. All the planets exhibit apparent retrograde motion when they are nearest the Earth (at inferior conjunction for the inferior planets and at opposition for the superior planets; see SYZYGY) because of the relative speeds of the planets in their orbits about the Sun.

**Reuben** (‚roohbən), in the BIBLE, JACOB's eldest son and ancestor of one of the 12 tribes (see ISRAEL, TRIBES OF). At the occupation of Palestine his tribe, with that of Gad, was allotted pastureland E of the Jordan.

**Réunion,** overseas French department and region in the Indian Ocean (1986 est. pop. 535,000) 2500 km² (970 sq mi). Its capital is St Denis. A French possession since 1642, it became an overseas department in 1946 and a region in 1974. It is represented in the French parliament by three deputies and two senators and has an assembly of 45 members, with a substantial majority in favour of continued French status. The island's economy is dependent on sugar cane, rum and tourism. Formerly known as Bourbon, it gave its name to the Bourbon strain of old garden roses, said to be bred from roses grown as hedges on the island.

**Reuters:** see NEWS AGENCY.

**Revelation** or **Apocalypse,** last book of the NEW TESTAMENT. It was written AD c.95 on Patmos by one John; the tradition that he was the disciple St JOHN is unlikely. This book is a mysterious prophetic work, consisting mainly of visions showing the overcoming of evil and persecution and the triumph of God and the martyrs. The careful plan depends heavily on patterns of sevens, e.g., letters to seven churches in Asia Minor and the opening of the seven seals on the scroll in the hand of God. The style is majestic, with constant allusion to OLD TESTAMENT prophecies, especially those of EZEKIEL, DANIEL, and ISAIAH. Fresh interpretations of the book have appeared in every period of Christian history.

**Revere, Paul,** 1735–1818, American Revolutionary leader. A silversmith and soldier, he joined the SONS OF LIBERTY and was a courier (1774) for the rebels. He was immortalized in LONGFELLOW's poem for his 'midnight ride' of 18 Apr. 1775, to warn the Massachusetts minutemen about British troop movements at the start of the AMERICAN REVOLUTION (see LEXINGTON AND CONCORD).

**revolutions of 1848,** series of revolutionary explosions in Europe following on an economic crisis. The most successful was the FEBRUARY REVOLUTION, in France, which overthrew LOUIS PHILIPPE and established the Third Republic. In the German states the liberal revolutions resulted in the FRANKFURT PARLIAMENT, which favoured German unification. In the HABSBURG empire METTERNICH was overturned and the revolutionists in different territories, notably Hungary, demanded more autonomy; in Italy the RISORGIMENTO sought to expel the Habsburgs. Despite their early successes, the revolutions which were led by liberals and nationalists, generally failed. They have been described as the 'revolutions of the intellectuals', and as the revolutionaries revealed that they were divided, often on social issues, the old order reestablished control. In some cases the revolutions were put down by force; in others they were taken over by middle-class 'moderates' who themselves had put down radical working-class groups.

**Reykjavik** (ˌraykyəvik), city (1984 pop. 88,745), SW Iceland, capital of Iceland. It is the country's chief port and centre of its cod fishing industry. Founded in 874 AD, it is the home of the *Althing,* or Icelandic parliament, the oldest in Europe. Its heating system uses nearby hot springs.

**Reymont, Wladyslaw Stanislaw,** 1867–1925, Polish novelist and short-story writer. His novels include *The Promised Land* (1899), attacking modern industrial society, and *The Peasants* (4 vol., 1904–09), the great prose epic of Polish village life. He was awarded the 1924 Nobel Prize for literature.

**Reynard the Fox,** hero of medieval beast epics. Mainly verse works in Latin, French, High and Low German, Dutch and Flemish, and English, beast epics were increasingly popular after c.1150. Probably originating in Alsace-Lorraine, the type passed into France, the Low Countries, and Germany. Most of the fables reflect the peasants' contempt for the upper classes and the clergy. CAXTON's *Historie of Reynart the Foxe* (1481) was translated from the Flemish.

**Reynaud, Paul** (rayˌnoh), 1878–1966, French statesman. During WORLD WAR II he replaced (Mar. 1940) Édouard DALADIER as premier. After France's military collapse, he was succeeded (16 June) by Marshal PÉTAIN, who surrendered to the Germans. Reynaud was later imprisoned by the VICHY government. After the war he was finance minister (1948) and vice premier (1953).

**Reynolds, Sir Joshua,** 1723–92, English portrait painter. The most celebrated native portrait painter of his day, he raised the artist to a position of respect in England. After studying first in London, then in Italy, Reynolds used his wit and charm to take London by storm. He was besieged with portrait commissions, ran his own gallery, and was elected president of the Royal Academy when it was founded in 1768. His annual discourses for the Academy were a significant exposition of academic style, propounding eclectic generalization over direct observation, and allusion to the classical past over the present. The Grand Style, thus propounded, greatly influenced English portraiture. Reynolds painted more than 2000 portraits and historical paintings depicting almost every notable person of his time, including Dr Johnson, Mrs Siddons, and Edmund Burke.

**Reza Shah Pahlevi,** 1877–1944, shah of IRAN (1925–41). An army officer, he led a coup in 1921 and became premier in 1923. In 1925 he deposed the last of the Kajar dynasty, proclaimed himself shah, and proceeded to modernize Iran. In 1941 he was deposed by British and Russian forces because of his German sympathies. He was succeeded by his son, MUHAMMAD REZA SHAH PAHLEVI.

**Rh,** chemical symbol of the element RHODIUM.

**Rhaeto-Romanic** (ˌreetoh rəˌmanik), generic name for several related dialects of the Romance group of the Italic subfamily of the Indo-European family of languages. They include Romansh, an official Swiss language; Ladin; and Friulian. See LANGUAGE (table).

**Rhangavis, Alexandros Rizos:** see RANGABE.

**rhea** (ˌree·ə), South American flightless BIRD (order Rheiformes), superficially resembling the OSTRICH. Weighing from 20 to 25 kg (44 to 55 lb) and standing up to 150 cm (60 in) tall, rheas lack the ostrich's plumelike tail feathers. A herbivore, the rhea inhabits the PAMPAS and SAVANNAS, often feeding with cattle.

Sir Joshua **Reynolds,** *Lady Cockburn and her three eldest sons,* 1773. Oil on canvas, 142 × 113 cm. National Gallery, London.

**Rhea,** in astronomy, natural satellite of SATURN.

**Rhea,** in Greek mythology, a TITAN; wife and sister of CRONUS; mother of ZEUS, POSEIDON, PLUTO, HESTIA, HERA, and DEMETER. She aided Zeus in the overthrow of Cronus. Associated with fertility, her worship was prominent in CRETE. In Rome Rhea was worshipped as Magna Mater and identified with Ops.

**Rhee, Syngman,** 1875–1965, 1st president (1948–60) of South KOREA. Educated in the US, he became a leader in South Korea during the US occupation following WORLD WAR II. His rule grew autocratic, and in May 1960, after riots, he was forced out of office and into exile in Hawaii.

**Rheims** (reemz), city (1982 pop. 181,985), NE France. It is a centre of the CHAMPAGNE industry. A Roman city, it has been an archiepiscopal see since the 8th cent. It is the traditional coronation place of French kings: Clovis I (496) and Charles VII (1429, with JOAN OF ARC at his side) were crowned there. Its Gothic cathedral, heavily damaged in World War I, has been restored. In 1945, at the end of World War II, Germany signed the surrender agreement in Rheims.

**rhenium** (Re), metallic element, discovered in 1925 by Walter Nodack and colleagues. It is a very dense, high-melting, silver-white metal occurring in platinum and molybdenum ores, and in many minerals. It gives improved ductility and high-temperature strength to its alloys, which are used in electrical contacts, electronic filaments, thermocouples, and photographic flash lamps. See ELEMENT (table); PERIODIC TABLE.

**Rhesus factor** or **Rh factor,** protein substance present on the surface of the red blood cells of most (85% or more) people and capable of inducing an intense antigen-antibody reaction (see IMMUNITY). People with the factor are called rhesus-positive (Rh-positive); people without it, as rhesus-negative (Rh-negative). When Rh-positive blood is given to an Rh-negative person or when foetal Rh-positive blood (inherited from the father) is mixed with maternal Rh-negative blood during pregnancy, the Rh-negative person develops antibodies to the foreign rhesus factor. A serious or even fatal reaction may occur in subsequent mixing of two blood types, as in repeat transfusions or other pregnancies involving an

*Mahony* (1930), a colonial saga based on her father's life. Her other works include *Maurice Guest* (1908), the autobiographical *The Getting of Wisom* (1910), and *The Young Cosima* (1939).

**Richardson, John,** 1796–1852, first Canadian novelist to write in English. His works include the frontier romances *Wacousta* (1832) and *The Canadian Brothers* (1840).

**Richardson, Samuel,** 1689–1761, English novelist. A prosperous printer, he was asked to compose a guide to letter writing. Working around a central theme, he wrote instead a moral NOVEL in letter form *Pamela; or, Virtue Rewarded* (1740). He later wrote two more epistolary novels, *Clarissa Harlowe* (1747–48) and *The History of Sir Charles Grandison* (1753–54). Their narrative mastery and psychological insight won them great contemporary popularity and lastingly influenced the evolution of the English novel, in spite of their prolixity and simplistic morality.

**Richelieu, Armand Jean du Plessis, cardinal** and **duc de** (ˌrishəˈlyuh), 1585–1642, chief minister of LOUIS XIII of France. He gained the favour of the king's mother, MARIE DE' MEDICI, and was made secretary of state (1616), cardinal (1622), and chief minister (1624). In 1630 Marie conspired against Richelieu, but the king had her exiled. Richelieu then enjoyed full control of the government until his death. Domestically, he centralized royal authority by destroying the political power of the HUGUENOTS with the capture of La Rochelle (1628) and the Peace of Alais (1629). Conspiracies by the nobles were rigorously suppressed. In foreign affairs, he rejected Marie de' Medici's pro-HABSBURG policy, and in 1635 France openly entered the THIRTY YEARS' WAR against the Habsburgs. In France the war led to heavy taxation and caused dissatisfaction with his rule. This expressed itself in aristocratic conspiracies and peasant uprisings. Richelieu encouraged trade and the arts; he was the founder of the learned society known as the French Academy.

**Richet, Charles Robert** (ˌreeshay), 1850–1935, French physiologist. He coined the term anaphylaxis, which refers to the violent allergic reaction experienced after injection or ingestion of a foreign substance (e.g., penicillin) to which the individual is sensitive. He received the 1913 Nobel Prize for physiology or medicine.

**Richler, Mordecai,** 1931–, Canadian novelist. His comic novels reflect his Jewish upbringing in Montreal. Best known is *The Apprenticeship of Duddy Kravitz* (1959). Others include *St. Urban's Horseman* (1969) and *Joshua Then and Now* (1980).

**Richmond,** US city (1980 pop. 219,214), state capital, East Virginia, on the James R.; settled 1637, inc. as a city 1782. A deepwater port and financial and commercial centre, it is a major tobacco market and manufacturer of tobacco products. Its industries produce chemicals, textiles, and other goods. Laid out in 1737, Richmond became capital of Virginia in 1779. During the CIVIL WAR, it was capital of the CONFEDERACY and the constant object of Union forces. Threatened in the PENINSULAR CAMPAIGN (1862) and Wilderness Campaign (1864), it fell to Gen. GRANT and was burned in April 1865. Places of interest include the capitol (1785), designed by Thomas JEFFERSON, and Hollywood Cemetery, with the graves of some 18,000 Confederate soldiers.

**Richmond upon Thames,** London borough (1981 pop. 157,304), in outer SW London. It includes the former boroughs of Barnes and Twickenham. Mainly residential, it also contains several open spaces, including Richmond Park, The Royal Botanic Gardens (at Kew), and Ham Common. Richmond Park is famous for its deer.

**Richter, Hans Werner,** 1908–85, German writer, editor, and impresario. He was active in the revival of German literature amongst a new generation of writers immediately after World War II. With Alfred Andersch he edited *Der Ruf* (1946–47). He was the initiator and organizer of the Gruppe 47, the most influential literary non-organization of the postwar decades. Also a novelist, he wrote *They Fell from God's Hand* (1951) and the satirical *Linus Fleck* (1959). Autobiographical works include the novel *Traces in the Sand* (1953) and his *Letter to a Young Socialist* (1974). Günter GRASS's *The Meeting in Telgte* (1979) is a tribute to him.

**Richter, Johann Paul Friedrich,** pseud. **Jean Paul,** 1763–1825, German novelist. Jean Paul introduced Laurence STERNE's irony and self-consciousness to the German novel. His own work ranges from the romantic–mystical and self-referential (*The Invisible Lodge, a Biography*, 2 vol., 1793) through the realistic–provincial and comic–sentimental

(*The Happy Life of the Little Schoolmaster Maria Wuz . . . A Sort of Idyll*, 1793; *The Poor-Man's Lawyer Siebenkäs*, 3 vol., 1796–97) to the *Bildungsroman* (*Titan*, 4 vol., 1800–03). Caught in the tension between idealism and realism, he produced an important theory of humour in his *Primer of Aesthetics* (3 vol., 1804).

**Richter, Sviatoslav,** 1915–, Soviet pianist. Playing in a warm, romantic style, he has a repertoire that includes works by Bach, Beethoven, Schubert, Debussy, Mozart, and Schumann.

**Richter scale:** see EARTHQUAKE.

**Ricimer,** d. 472, Roman general of the Germanic Suebi tribe. After defeating the Vandals (a Germanic tribe), he deposed (456) Avitus, Roman emperor of the West. Thereafter he ruled Italy through his puppet emperors, the most able of whom was MAJORIAN.

**rickets,** disease of children in which the bones do not harden. It is caused by inadequate absorption of calcium as a result of a deficiency of vitamin D, and often results in knock-knees, bow-legs, and deformities of the chest and pelvis. See table under VITAMINS AND MINERALS.

**Rida, Rashid,** 1865–1925, Muslim reformist. He was the most prominent pupil of Muhammad ABDUH and the foremost Muslim reformist this century. Influenced by WAHHABISM, he welded together the modernism of his master and the fundamentalism of the Wahhabis in a very potent ideological and social programme advocated in his magazine, *Al-Manar*.

**Ridley, Nicholas,** c.1500–55, English prelate, reformer, and Protestant martyr. As bishop of Rochester (1547) he strengthened the Reformed teachings at Cambridge and in 1548 under EDWARD VI took part in compiling the Book of Common Prayer. He became bishop of London in 1550. After the accession of the Roman Catholic MARY I, he was imprisoned (1553) and took part (1554) in the Oxford disputations along with Thomas CRANMER and Hugh LATIMER. Ridley refused to recant his Protestantism and was burned as a heretic with Latimer at Oxford.

**Riel, Louis** (reeˌel), 1844–85, Canadian insurgent leader in the RED RIVER SETTLEMENTS of MANITOBA (1869–70 and 1884) in SASKATCHEWAN. In an engagement (1885) at Batoche, Riel was captured, tried, and hanged.

**Riemann, (Georg Friedrich) Bernhard** (ˌreeman), 1826–66, German mathematician. His great contributions to mathematics include his work on the theory of the functions of complex variables and his method of representing such functions on coincident planes or sheets (Riemann surfaces). He laid the foundations of a NON-EUCLIDEAN GEOMETRY representing elliptic space and generalized to $n$ dimensions the work of Carl GAUSS in differential geometry, thus creating the basic tools for the mathematical expression of the general theory of relativity. Riemann was also interested in mathematical physics, particularly optics and electromagnetic theory.

**Riemenschneider, Tilman** (ˌreemənˈshniedə), c.1460–1531, German RENAISSANCE sculptor, many of whose works are altarpieces in limewood. He created slender figures with delicately carved, expressive faces in ordered compositions. His works include the stone *Adam and Eve* (Würzburg Mus., Bavaria) and the wooden altar in St Jakob, Rothenburg ob der Tauber.

**Rienzi** or **Rienzo, Cola di** (reeˌentsee), 1313?–1354, Roman popular leader. Pope CLEMENT VI made him a papal notary, and Rienzi went to Rome, where he received (May 1347) wide dictatorial powers, which he claimed to hold under the pope's sovereignty. He sought to rally other cities and dreamed of a popular Italian empire. Clement, aroused at his actions, incited the barons against him, and Rienzi was defeated (1347) and fled. Clement's successor, Innocent VI, sent him (1353) to Italy with Cardinal Albornoz, who made him a senator. Rienzi re-entered Rome in triumph, but his violent and arbitrary rule soon led to a popular uprising and his murder. Wagner's opera *Rienzi* (1842) is based loosely on his life.

**Riesener, Jean-Henri,** 1734–1806, French cabinetmaker. With J.F. OEBEN, whom he later succeeded as director of the Arsenal workshop in Paris, he created Louis XV's writing desk. His work is in the Louvre and other collections.

**Rietveld, Gerrit Thomas** (ˌreetfelt), 1888–1965, Dutch architect and designer. He created (c.1917) a chair that introduced into furniture design a light, dematerialized effect. A member of the STIJL, he designed buildings that in their weightlessness and equilibrium are related to

Mahogany commode with marquetry Jean-Henri **Riesener** (c.1775)

MONDRIAN's paintings. His best-known building is the Schröder house, Utrecht (1924).

**Rifbjerg, Klaus,** 1931–, versatile Danish poet, novelist, scriptwriter, dramatist, and director of the Gyldendal publishing house. His best-known works are *Chronic Innocence* (1958), *Amager Poems* (1965), and *Anna I Anna* (1969).

**Riga** (reegə), city (1985 pop. 883,000), capital of LATVIA, NW European USSR, on the Daugava R. near its entry into the Gulf of Riga. It is a major Baltic port, rail junction, military base, and leading industrial centre. Among its industrial products are machines, ships, and diesel engines. Long settled by Baltic tribes, Riga became (1201) the seat of the Livonian Brothers of the Sword, a German military order dedicated to Christianizing the Baltic region. Riga joined the HANSEATIC LEAGUE in 1282. After the Livonian Order was dissolved (1561) the city passed to Poland (1581), Sweden (1621), and Russia (1721). It became the capital of independent Latvia in 1920 and of the Latvian SSR in 1940. During World War II Riga was occupied (1941–44) by Germany.

**Right, Petition of:** see PETITION OF RIGHT.

**right ascension:** see ASTRONOMICAL COORDINATE SYSTEMS.

**right-handedness:** see LATERALITY.

**rigor mortis,** increasing stiffness of the muscles within eight hours after DEATH.

**Rijeka** ('reey,aykə), Ital. *Fiume*, city (1981 pop. 193,044) and leading port of Croatia, NW Yugoslavia. A major seaport, it has oil, shipbuilding, and related industries. Before World War I it was the principal port of Hungary, and it still handles trade from Hungary and Czechoslovakia. Made a free state in 1920, it was then occupied by Italy in 1922. Yugoslav possession was formally recognized in 1947.

**Rijks Museum,** or **Ryks Museum** (rieks), Dutch national museum in Amsterdam, founded in 1808 by Louis Napoleon BONAPARTE, king of Holland, as the Great Royal Museum in the Palace. The present building, designed by P.J.H. Cuypers, was opened in 1885 to house its fast-growing collection. The museum is famous for its Dutch paintings and drawings, particularly of the 17th cent. REMBRANDT, Frans HALS, VERMEER, RUISDAEL, and the Dutch primitives are well represented. The Nederlands Museum, in the same building, has sculpture, decorative arts, and historical objects.

**Riley, Bridget,** 1931–, British painter. Her OP ART images, mainly in black and white (except for the more recent stripe works) and painted on a large scale, attempt to produce visual disturbances in the viewer by the use of patterns that confuse the eye.

**Rilke, Rainer Maria** (,rilkə), 1875–1926, German poet; b. Prague. The greatest poet writing in German of this century, Rilke was essentially a homeless poet. He attached his works to the places he passed through. The fluent musical language and religious vision of *The Book of Hours* (1905) can be related to Holy Russia; the change in style to perception of the object in *The Book of Images* (1902) and *Neue Gedichte*

(1907, 1908; tr. New Poems) to his stay in Paris as RODIN's secretary. Paris is also the locale of Rilke's one novel, *The Notebooks of Malte Laurids Brigge* (1910, tr. 1930): it represents the agonized and fragmentary attempts of the potential poet of the title to exorcise in art the overwhelming multiplicity of experience in the nightmare city. In his last years, Rilke produced his greatest cycles, *Duineser Elegien* (1912–15, completed 1922; tr. 1939) and *Sonnets to Orpheus* (1922; tr. 1936).

**Rimbaud, Arthur** (ranh,boh), 1854–91, French poet whose hallucinatory and dreamlike verse anticipated the SYMBOLISTS. Works include *Le bateau ivre (The Drunken Boat); Illuminations,* prose poems; and a confessional autobiography, *Un saison en enfer (Season in Hell).* After a close and violent relationship with VERLAINE (1872–73), Rimbaud stopped writing poetry at age 19 and thereafter wandered through Europe and Africa.

**Rimini,** city (1984 pop. 130,210), Emilia-Romagna, Italy, at the point where the VIA EMILIA reaches the ADRIATIC coast. It is a popular summer holiday resort which benefits from sandy beaches and a hot, sunny climate. It suffered badly from bombardment in World War II.

**Rimsky-Korsakov, Nikolai Andreyevich,** 1844–1908, Russian composer. One of The FIVE, he used Russian folk-song history, and legend as a source for most of his operas, e.g., *The Snow Maiden* (1881), *The Maid of Pskov* (1873, rev. 1892), *The Golden Cockerel* (1909). His best-known orchestral work, *Scheherezade* (1888), exemplifies his romantic exoticism and mastery of orchestral colour. Among his students was Igor STRAVINSKY.

**rings, planetary:** see JUPITER; SATURN; URANUS.

**ringworm** or **tinea,** infection of the skin, caused by a fungus (see FUNGI). Although any area of the skin, e.g., the scalp, may be affected, the most common site is the feet, (athlete's foot). Ringworm infection causes dry, scaly, ringlike patches, which usually burn or itch. It is highly infectious and can be treated with antifungal agents applied to the skin or taken orally.

**Rio de Janeiro,** city (1980 pop. 5,093,232), SE Brazil, capital of Rio de Janeiro state, former capital of Brazil, on Guanabara Bay of the Atlantic Ocean. Brazil's second largest city and principal port, Rio (as it is popularly called) has diverse manufactures and handles much of the nation's foreign trade. It is predominantly a modern city, with a new airport and underground-railway system. A cosmopolitan city, long the cultural centre of Brazil, it is also its greatest tourist attraction. Rio is

Bridget **Riley,** *Cantus Firmus,* 1972–73. 241.3 × 215.9 cm. Tate Gallery, London.

celebrated for its pre-Lenten carnival and for its beautiful natural setting within an amphitheatre of low mountains. Noted landmarks are Sugar Loaf Mt., which dominates the harbour, and Corcovado peak, with its colossal statue of Christ. Founded by French HUGUENOTS in 1555, the city was taken by Portugal in the 1560s. It replaced Bahia (now SALVADOR) as Brazil's capital in 1763 and was supplanted by BRASILIA in 1960.

Sugar Loaf Mountain, Rio de Janeiro

**Rio Grande,** major North American river, flowing c.3000 km (1885 mi) S and SE from the San Juan Mts (SW Colorado) to the Gulf of Mexico. It forms the US–Mexico boundary between the twin cities of El Paso, Texas, and Juárez, Mexico, and Brownsville, Texas, and Matamoros, Mexico. The river, known in Mexico as the Río Bravo del Norte, is unnavigable, but is an important source of internationally regulated irrigation.

**Ripon,** town (1981 pop. 13,036), N Yorkshire, NE England, at the confluence of the rivers Laver, Skell, and Ure, 16 km (10 mi) N of Harrogate. There is some light industry here. The cathedral was started in the mid-12th cent. and completed in the early 16th cent. The ruins of the 12th-cent. Fountains Abbey are 5 km (3 mi) to the SW.

**Risorgimento** (ri'sawji,mentoh), movement of cultural nationalism and political activism in the 19th cent. that led to the unification of Italy. Italy was fragmented in the Middle Ages, and from the 16th to 18th cent. foreign influence was virtually complete. After the Napoleonic wars, revolutionary groups such as the Carbonari emerged. The literature of Alessandro MANZONI, Ugo FOSCOLO, and others stimulated nationalism. Political activity was carried on by three groups. Giuseppe MAZZINI led the radicals, who were republican and anticlerical. The conservative and clerical faction generally advocated a federation headed by the pope. The moderates favoured unification under the house of SAVOY, which ruled Sardinia. Sardinia assumed leadership of the Risorgimento in 1848 when revolts broke out across Italy. King Charles Albert of Sardinia tried to drive the Austrians out of N Italy but was defeated at Custoza (1848) and Novara (1849), and abdicated. Revolutions elsewhere were suppressed, including one at Rome, where Mazzini had formed a short-lived republic. The liberal movement, however, gradually coalesced around Charles Albert's son and successor, VICTOR EMMANUEL II, and his able minister, the Conte di CAVOUR. Cavour sought and received French aid against Austria, but the battles (1859) of Magenta and Solferino were so costly that the French signed a separate armistice. Austria retained Venetia, and Sardinia gained only Lombardy. In 1860 Tuscany, Modena, Parma, Bologna, and the Romagna voted for union with Sardinia. GARIBALDI's spectacular conquest (1860) of the kingdom of the TWO SICILIES was followed by Sardinia's annexation of Umbria and the Marches. The kingdom of Italy was proclaimed in 1861. Italy received Venetia for its role in the AUSTRO-PRUSSIAN WAR of 1866 and seized Rome from the pope in 1870. Unsatisfied Italian nationalism continued in the form of IRREDENTISM.

**rites de passage** [Fr., = rites of passage], the rituals which accompany an individual's or group's socially recognized change of status. Such rituals are most often associated with particular moments in the life cycle: birth, puberty, marriage, and death. Rites of passage, as analysed by VAN GENNEP, involve three stages, separation from the social group and the previous status, transition or liminality when the individual is part of no socially acknowledged status or group (and is, as a result, frequently seen

as both being dangerous and in a dangerous situation) and therefore cut off from regular contact with social life, and finally reincorporation into the group in a new socially recognized status.

**Ritschl, Albrecht** (,richəl), 1822–89, German Lutheran theologian. His theology, a reaction against rationalism, held that God could be known only through the revelation contained in the works and person of Jesus Christ. It stressed ethics and the human community, as opposed to metaphysics.

**Ritter, Carl,** 1779–1859, German geographer, considered to be one of the founders of modern geography. After attending Halle University, he became the tutor to the children of a Frankfurt banker from 1798 to 1814. He spent the following five years watching over his charges at university and devoted his time to travel and geography. His masterpiece, *Die Erdkunde im Verhältnis zur Natur und zur Geschichte des Menschens,* was published in 1817–18. He became professor of history at Frankfurt (1819–20) and then professor extraordinarius of history at Berlin, where he remained until his death.

**ritual,** a tightly structured performance consisting of prescribed actions which are given sacred or religious meaning and significance. Often rituals will enact MYTH. There is considerable discussion within anthropology as to what constitutes ritual. Structural functionalist anthropology, following DURKHEIM, saw rituals as reinforcing collective sentiment and social integration and was therefore not concerned to understand their content; but increasingly rituals have been analysed in terms of their meaning as structured communications and their symbolic language has been the central focus of research.

**river,** stream of water larger than a brook or creek. Runoff after precipitation flows downward by the shortest and steepest course. Runoffs of sufficient volume and velocity join to form a stream that, by the EROSION of underlying earth and rock, deepens its bed. It becomes perennial when it cuts deeply enough to be fed by groundwater or when it has an unlimited source (e.g., the SAINT LAWRENCE flowing from the Great Lakes). Sea level is the ultimate base level for a river, but the floor of a lake or basin into which a river flows may become a local and temporary base level. Rivers modify topography by both erosion and deposition (see e.g., DELTA). Young streams have steep-sided valleys, steep gradients, and irregularities in the bed. Mature rivers have valleys with wide floors and a more smoothly graded bed. Old rivers have courses graded to base level and run through broad, flat areas. See also articles on individual rivers, e.g., AMAZON; NILE.

**Rivera, Diego,** 1886–1957, one of modern Mexico's foremost painters. Inspired by native Mexican art and by his experiences in Europe (1907–09, 1912–21), he painted large murals dealing with Mexican life, history, and social problems. Like OROZCO, he was interested in the political role art could play. In his mural for the Rockefeller Center, New York (1933), his Marxist politics and his inclusion of a portrait of Lenin resulted in the Mural being destroyed before completion.

**Rivera, Primo de:** see PRIMO DE RIVERA, MIGUEL.

**Riverina,** region of New South Wales, SE Australia. Irrigated by the MURRUMBIDGEE R., it is a rich agricultural area, with food-processing industries, in an otherwise semiarid and sparsely populated part of the state. Wagga Wagga is the chief town.

**Riverside,** US city (1984 est. pop. 182,000), S California; inc. 1883. It is famous for its orange industry; the forerunner of the California Fruit Growers' Exchange was begun there in 1892. Located in a rapidly growing area, Riverside makes mobile homes, electronic and aerospace equipment, aluminium, and other products.

**Riviera,** fashionable Mediterranean resort area in SE France and N Italy, famed for its scenery, warm climate, and excellent beaches. Major resorts include NICE, Cannes, and Saint-Tropez along the French Côte d'Azur, Monte Carlo in MONACO, and Rapallo, Portofino, and San Remo in Italy.

**Riyadh** (ree,ahd), city (1981 est. pop. 1,250,000), capital of Saudi Arabia. It is situated in an oasis in the central part of the country. The nation's main commercial and transport centre, it has industries including oil refining and cement manufacturing. Its architecture formerly represented the classical Arabic style, but many large modern structures have been built recently. Important meetings of Arab leaders have been held in Riyadh.

**Rizal, José** (ree͵sahl), 1861–96, Philippine patriot, author, and physician. His novel *The Lost Eden* (1886) attacked the Spanish regime in the PHILIPPINES, and he was exiled in 1887. After his return (1893), he was arrested and executed for alleged revolutionary activities. His death sparked a revolt.

**Rizzio, David** (͵ritseeoh), 1533?–66, favourite of MARY QUEEN OF SCOTS. An Italian musician, he became Mary's secretary. Jealous nobles persuaded Lord DARNLEY, Mary's husband, that Rizzio was her lover, and with Darnley's aid they murdered him in Mary's presence in Holyrood Palace.

**Rn,** chemical symbol of the element RADON.

**RNA** or **ribonucleic acid** ('riebohnyooh͵klee·ik, -͵klayik), NUCLEIC ACID, found mostly in the cytoplasm of CELLS, that is important in the synthesis of proteins. The amount of RNA varies from cell to cell. RNA, like the structurally similar DNA, is a chain made up of subunits called nucleotides. In protein synthesis messenger RNA replicates the DNA code for a protein and moves to sites in the cell called ribosomes. There transfer RNA assembles AMINO ACIDS to form the protein specified by the messenger RNA. Most forms of RNA (including messenger and transfer RNA) consist of a single nucleotide strand, but a few forms of viral RNA that function as carriers of genetic information (instead of DNA) are double-stranded.

**Roa Bastos, Augusto** (roh͵bastos), 1917–, Paraguayan novelist and poet. His major works, *Hijo de hombre* (1960; tr. Son of Man) and *Yo el Supremo* (1974), are novelized treatments of Paraguayan history, especially the period of FRANCIA's dictatorship (1816–40).

**Roach, Max(well),** 1925–, black American jazz drummer, composer, and bandleader. One of the founding fathers of modern jazz drumming in the 1940s, he worked with the leaders of the bop revolution: Charlie PARKER, Dizzy GILLESPIE, and Thelonius MONK. He went on to lead or co-lead a number of influential small groups in the 1950s and succeeding decades. He is an immaculate time-keeper and constantly inventive soloist whose mastery of dynamics and polyrhythms has influenced countless percussionists.

**road,** a hard-surfaced, artificially built track for overland travel. The first roads probably date back to around 3500 BC, following the invention of the wheel. Between the 11th and 2nd centuries BC a network of roads was developed in China, and much later, between 1200 and 1500 AD, a road system covering 3650 km (2300 mi), stretching north from modern Ecuador, was built by the Incas of South America to whom the wheel was unknown. The first properly engineered roads were built by the Romans. Their purpose was mainly strategic, for the movement of armies, and they were straight, going over rather than circumventing hills. Roman roads consisted of a carriageway about 5 m (16 ft) wide, paved with flat stones, with a crown at the centre and ditches at the sides for drainage. Altogether the Romans built about 80,000 km (50,000 mi) of road, across an empire stretching from northern Britain to the Euphrates. Some of these roads, such as the Appian Way in Italy, are still in use today. With the decline of imperial Roman power from the 4th cent. AD the roads fell into disuse. Throughout the Middle Ages and in the centuries following their upkeep was largely neglected. From the mid 18th cent., the expansion of trade and commerce and the beginnings of the INDUSTRIAL REVOLUTION created the demand for better communications and modern roads. British engineers John MACADAM and Thomas TELFORD laid the foundation for modern road-building by developing hard self-sealing road surfaces. These consisted of layers of stone and gravel that could be packed tight by rolling and cambered for drainage. By 1820, Britain had 200,000 km (125,000 mi) of roads, which with better stagecoaches, cut some journey times by 80%. Further improvements in road engineering and expansion of the network were spurred by the appearance of the MOTOR CAR from the turn of the century. As motor vehicle speeds increased, so faster, more efficient roads were needed, leading to the development of the first MOTORWAYS in the late 1930s. Since World War II road-building efforts of the advanced countries have been largely directed towards inaugurating and expanding motorway networks. Today in Britain most freight is moved by road, seven or eight times as much as by rail.

**road runner:** see CUCKOO.

**Roanoke Island,** 19 km (12 mi) long and 4.8 km (3 mi) wide, off the NE coast of North Carolina between Albemarle and Pamlico sounds, site of the earliest English colony in North America. The first colonists, sent out by Sir Walter RALEIGH, landed in Aug. 1585 but returned to England in 1586. A second group, arriving in 1587, disappeared without trace by the time additional supplies were brought from England in 1591. Artifacts from the 'lost colony' are displayed in Fort Raleigh National Historic Site on the island.

**Robbe-Grillet, Alain** (robgree͵yay), 1922–, French novelist and film-maker. He is considered the originator of the French 'new novel' in which story is subordinated to structure and the significance of external reality is stressed above that of psychological motivation or plot development. His works include the novels *Les gommes* (1953; tr. The Erasers), *La jalousie* (1957; tr. Jealousy), *Topology of a Phantom City* (1975), and *Djinn* (tr. 1982); and screenplay, like *L'année dernière à Marienbad* (1961; tr. Last Year at Marienbad).

**robbery:** see THEFT.

**Robbia:** see DELLA ROBBIA.

**Robbins, Jerome,** 1918–, American dancer and choreographer. He danced in musical comedy, and joined the American Ballet Theatre in 1940. He is noted for exuberant ballets and musicals, e.g., *Fancy Free* (1944) and *West Side Story* (1957). At New York City Ballet since 1969, his ballets have included *Dances at a Gathering* (1969).

**Robert,** kings of France. **Robert I,** c.865–923 (r.922–23), revolted (922) against CHARLES III (the Simple) and was crowned king, but was soon killed in battle. His son-in-law, Raoul of Burgundy, succeeded him. **Robert II** (the Pious), 970–1031 (r.966–1031), was the son of HUGH CAPET. Pious and learned, he tried to strengthen royal power and acquired the duchy of BURGUNDY for the crown.

**Robert,** kings of Scotland. **Robert I** or **Robert the Bruce,** 1274–1329 (r.1306–29), was a skilful and courageous leader who freed Scotland of English control. After he defied EDWARD I of England by being crowned (1306) at Scone, Robert was defeated (1306) at Methven and fled to the island of Rathlin, off the Irish coast. Returning to Scotland in 1307, he defeated EDWARD II at Bannockburn in 1314 and captured Berwick in 1318. He was recognized as king by the English in the Treaty of Northampton (1328). **Robert II,** 1316–90 (r.1371–90), was the founder of the STUART dynasty. During most of his reign his sons directed the government, repelling English invasions and winning a great victory at Otterburn in 1388. Robert's eldest son, **Robert III,** 1337?–1406 (r.1390–1406), was crippled by a horse; thereafter, real power was held by his brother, Robert Stuart, duke of Albany, 1340?–1420.

**Robert,** dukes of Normandy. **Robert I** (the Magnificent), d. 1035, duke (r.1027–35), made his illegitimate son William (later WILLIAM I of England) his heir and died on a pilgrimage to Jerusalem. **Robert II** (Robert Curthose), c.1053–1134, duke (r.1087–1106), succeeded his father, William I of England, in Normandy. He fought against his brothers, WILLIAM II and HENRY I of England. In 1106 he was defeated and imprisoned by Henry.

**Robert Curthose** (Robert II): see under ROBERT, Dukes of Normandy.

**Robert Grosseteste:** see GROSSETESTE, ROBERT.

**Robert Guiscard** (gees͵kah), c.1015–1085, Norman conqueror of S Italy. Robert joined (c.1046) his brothers in S Italy and fought to expel the Byzantines. In 1059 Pope Nicholas II invested him with Apulia, Calabria, and Sicily. Sicily was wrested (1060–91) from the Arabs by Robert's brother Roger, and the Normans gained Calabria (by 1060), Bari (1071), Salerno (1076), and eventually most of Benevento. In 1081 Robert assaulted the Byzantine empire, conquered Corfu, and defeated (1082) Emperor ALEXIUS I. In 1084 he aided Pope GREGORY VII against Holy Roman Emperor HENRY IV. Robert then resumed his eastern wars but died of fever at Cephalonia. He was succeeded in Apulia by his youngest son, Roger.

**Robert Joffrey Ballet:** see DANCE (table).

**Robert of Courtenay,** d. 1228, Latin emperor of CONSTANTINOPLE (1219–28). He was defeated (1224) by Nicaea and Epirus, and his realm was reduced to the city of Constantinople.

**Roberts, Tom (Thomas William),** 1856–1931, Australian artist. He emigrated to Melbourne from England in 1869, and studied painting under Thomas Clark and Louis BUVELOT. He first worked as a photographer's assistant and graphic artist. After a brief visit to Europe (1891–85), where he became acquainted with the work of Bastien Lepage, Jean Léon Gerome, and James Abbot McNeill WHISTLER, he returned to Melbourne and became a leading figure of the HEIDELBERG SCHOOL. Together with Charles Conder, Arthur STREETON, and Frederick McCubbin, he encouraged the development of an Australian school of painting based on impressionist principles (see IMPRESSIONISM).

Tom **Roberts**, *Shearing the Rams*, 1890. National Gallery of Victoria.

**Roberts, William,** 1895–1980, British painter. He visited France in 1913 and was influenced by CUBISM. He signed the vorticist manifesto in 1914 with Lewis and was closely associated with the movement (see VORTICISM). From the 1920s to the 1970s Roberts painted stiff and very stylized figures, not altering his style in any significant way.

**Robert the Bruce** (Robert I): see under ROBERT, kings of Scotland.

**Robeson, Paul,** 1898–1976, black American actor and bass singer. He was noted for his roles in Eugene O'NEILL's *Emperor Jones* (1925; film, 1933) and Jerome KERN's *Show Boat* (1928; film, 1936) and for his interpretations of SPIRITUALS. His espousal of leftist causes made him a controversial figure.

**Robespierre, Maximilien Marie Isidore** (ˌrohbzpyeə), 1758–94, leader in the FRENCH REVOLUTION, called the Incorruptible. A lawyer, he became attached to the democratic and deistic theories of J.J. ROUSSEAU. He was elected to the STATES-GENERAL (1789) and the National Convention (1792), and became leader of the JACOBINS in their struggle with the GIRONDISTS. In 1793 he was elected to the Committee of Public Safety, which he dominated throughout the REIGN OF TERROR. Robespierre overthrew both the extreme left and the moderates in the Convention and also instituted a new civic religion. Robespierre's position, however, became precarious as the Convention began to feel threatened by the emergency measures of the Terror. On 27 July 1794, rightists joined the PLAIN in a rising in the Convention, and Robespierre was arrested, tried, and guillotined (July 28).

**robin** or **robin redbreast,** small bird, 14 cm (5½ in) in the THRUSH family distributed across Europe and round the Mediterranean to W Asia. The robin (*Erithacus rubecula*), is Britain's national bird, and has adapted to town life. In Britain it will tolerate humans at close quarters, feeding on the insects and other small invertebrates turned up by gardeners while they are still nearby. Over the rest of its range it is a shyer forest-dweller. Both males and females have red breasts, the male defending his territory with song and by attacking any intruder. Males will attack a bundle of red feathers with great ferocity if it is put into their territory. The American robin is an unrelated member of the thrush family (*Turdus migratorius*) 25 cm (10 in) long, and is an occasional visitor to Europe.

**Robin Hood,** legendary 12th-cent. English hero who robbed the rich to help the poor. With his band of outlaws he lived in Sherwood Forest. He figures in LANGLAND's *Piers Plowman* and many Middle English ballads.

**Robinson, Edward G.,** 1893–1973, American film actor; b. Romania as Emmanuel Goldenberg. He often played tough guys, e.g., in *Little Caesar* (1930) and *Key Largo* (1948), and character parts, e.g., in *Double Indemnity* (1944).

**Robinson, Edwin Arlington,** 1869–1935, American poet. His most lasting work is probably his early verse, mainly austere and probing portraits of residents of a small New England town, such as 'Miniver Cheevy' and 'Richard Cory'. His later poems include long psychological narratives, e.g., *Avon's Harvest* (1921), *The Man Who Died Twice* (1924), and Arthurian romances. Volumes of his collected poems were published in 1921 and 1937.

**Robinson, Ethel Florence Lindesay:** see RICHARDSON, HENRY HANDEL.

**Robinson, James Harvey,** 1863–1936, American historian. First director of the New School for Social Research (1919), his book *The New History* (1911) stressed the need to study social, scientific, and intellectual progress.

**Robinson, Joan Violet,** 1903–83, British economist. She taught at Cambridge Univ., becoming professor of economics in 1965. Robinson was an important influence in the Cambridge school of economic thought. She developed Keynesian (see KEYNES) economic theory and introduced Marxist economics into it. Many of her views were highly controversial as were her many published papers and books. She was a regular visitor to China which was the subject of some of her books, including *China: An Economic Perspective* (1958), *The Cultural Revolution in China* (1969), and *Economic Management in China* (1975). Other works were *An Essay on Marxian Economics* (1942), *Freedom and Necessity* (1970), and *Aspects of Development and Underdevelopment*.

**Robinson, Lennox,** 1886–1958, Irish dramatist, associated with the Abbey Theatre, Dublin as writer, producer, and director. An early comic success was *The White Headed Boy* (1920). His later, more sombre dramas include *The Big House* (1926) and *Drama at Inish* (1933).

**Robinson, Sugar Ray,** 1920–89, American boxer; b. Walker Smith. After winning (1946) the welterweight championship, he gained the middleweight title an unprecedented five times between 1951 (knocking out Jake La Motta) and 1958 (defeating Carmen Basilio). Of 202 professional bouts he lost only 19, most of them late in his career, and he was rated the best boxer, pound for pound, of his time.

**robotics,** the design and construction of machines (robots) that sense (by means of vision or some other type of sensor) aspects of their environment and that are capable physically (e.g., by means of a mechanical arm) of acting upon it. The Czech dramatist Karel ČAPEK coined the word *robot* (from the Czech *robota,* drudgery) in his 1921 satirical play *R.U.R.,* and robots, or automatons, have long played a role in fantasy literature. Present-day robots, which bear little resemblance to the often humanoid

**Robotics:** Robot welding at the Ford Dagenham plant

figures of SCIENCE FICTION, are essentially computer-controlled machine tools that can be programmed to perform any of a number of functions, such as welding a car chassis or assembling machine parts. Robots can perform dangerous, uncomfortable, tiring, or monotonous tasks, and do them with greater speed and accuracy than can human beings. Robots play an increasingly significant role in the movement toward industrial automation, especially in Japan, the world's leader in the production and use of robots.

**Rob Roy** [Scottish Gaelic, = red Rob], 1671–1734, Scottish outlaw; b. Robert MacGregor. Deprived of their estates, he and his highland clan lived largely by stealing cattle and selling protection against thieves. Sentenced (1727) to be transported, he was later pardoned. He is remembered chiefly as he figures in Sir Walter SCOTT's novel *Rob Roy* (1818).

**Robusti, Jacopo:** see TINTORETTO.

**Rochambeau, Jean Baptiste Donatien de Vimeur, comte de** (roshanh̦boh), 1725–1807, marshal of France. During the AMERICAN REVOLUTION he landed (1780) at Newport, Rhode Island, US, with a French army of 6000 men, and with Gen. WASHINGTON planned the victorious YORKTOWN CAMPAIGN (1781). In the FRENCH REVOLUTION he commanded the Northern Army, but resigned (1792) and was imprisoned in the REIGN OF TERROR. Napoleon restored his rank.

**Rochdale,** town (1981 pop. 97,292), Greater Manchester, NW England, on R. Roch, 16 km (10 mi) NE of Manchester. It is an important centre of the textile industry, especially famous for spinning. Other industries are woollen and rayon manufacture, and engineering. The CO-OPERATIVE movement of Great Britain was founded here in 1844.

**Rochester,** town (1981 pop. 23,840), Kent, SE England, on R. Medway. An industrial and commercial centre, it is known for the manufacture of agricultural machinery and of equipment for aircraft. It is built on the site of the ancient town of Durobrivae. There are several historic buildings including the remains of a Norman castle, and a cathedral which displays various architectural styles from many periods.

**Rochester, John Wilmot,** 2nd **earl of,** 1647–80, English poet and courtier. A notorious Restoration rake, he is best known for the witty and polished *Satyr against Mankind* (1675).

**rock,** aggregate of solid matter composed of one or more of the MINERALS forming the earth's crust. Rocks are commonly divided into three major classes depending on their origin. *Igneous rocks* (e.g., BASALT, GRANITE, OBSIDIAN, PORPHYRY, PUMICE) result from the cooling and solidification of molten matter from the earth's interior. If formed below the surface, such rock is said to be intrusive (as in a BATHOLITH). If formed at the surface, it is extrusive. *Sedimentary rocks* (e.g., CHALK, CLAY, COAL, LIMESTONE, SAND, SANDSTONE, SHALE) originate from the consolidation of sediments deposited chiefly through the action of EROSION on older rocks of all kinds. The characteristic feature of sedimentary rocks is their STRATIFICATION. *Metamorphic rocks* (e.g., GNEISS, MARBLE, QUARTZITE, SCHIST, SLATE) originate from the alteration of the texture and mineral constituents of existing rocks of any type under extreme heat and pressure within the earth (see METAMORPHISM). See also PETROLOGY.

**rock carvings and paintings,** art works pecked or incised (petroglyphs) or painted (pictographs) on natural rocks. Paintings are most commonly made from a palette of red ochre and other earth pigments. The use of cave walls and exterior rock surfaces for artistic expression is one of the most ancient and enduring forms of human communication, with the wide variety of images of humans, animals, supernatural beings, cultural objects and geometric designs reflecting daily life and the world of the spirit. Rock art is the principal surviving art form of many of the world's past cultures, extending from the great antiquity of Upper PALAEOLITHIC art in W and central Europe (see LASCAUX and ALTAMIRA), Australia, and S Africa, to the more recent, but vast distributions of rock paintings and carvings in the boreal forest regions of Canada and N Europe. Although rock painting and carving have declined with the destruction of aboriginal cultures, some contemporary groups still practise these traditions, demonstrating their continuing bond to the lands of their ancestors.

**Rockefeller,** family of American industrialists, bankers, and philanthropists. **John Davison Rockefeller,** 1839–1937, b. Richford, New York established an oil refinery with partners in 1863, and in 1870 he organized the Standard Oil Co. of Ohio. By strict economy, mergers

**Rock carvings and paintings**: Aboriginal wall paintings near Laura, Cape York, Queensland, Australia

with competitors, and ruthless elimination of opponents he soon dominated the US oil-refining industry. Rockefeller retired in 1911 with a large fortune. His philanthropies, amounting to some $500 million, included the Rockefeller Institute for Medical Research (1901; now Rockefeller Univ.) and the Rockefeller Foundation (1913); he also founded (1892) the Univ. of Chicago. Many of his descendants were also well-known in public life, among them, notably, **John D. Rockefeller,** 1874–1960, founder of the Rockefeller Center.

Rockefeller Center

**Rockefeller, Nelson Aldrich,** 1908–79, vice president of the US (1974–77). The second son of John D. Rockefeller, Junior (see ROCKEFELLER, family), he held several federal posts and was governor of New York for four terms (1966–73). A liberal Republican, he unsuccessfully sought the presidential nomination three times in the 1960s. He was named vice president under the 25th amendment of the CONSTITUTION by Gerald FORD, who had become president upon Richard NIXON's resignation.

**Rockefeller Center,** building complex in New York City, US, between 48th and 51st Streets and Fifth and Sixth Avenues, built between 1931 and 1939. Radio City Music Hall and the central fountain with Paul Manship's statue of Prometheus are well known.

**rocket,** any vehicle propelled by ejection of the gases produced by combustion of self-contained propellants. Tremendous pressure is exerted on the walls of the combustion chamber, except where the gas exits at the rear; the resulting unbalanced force, or thrust, on the front interior wall of the chamber pushes the rocket forward. The most vital component of any rocket is the propellant, which accounts for 90 to 95% of the rocket's total weight. A propellant consists of two elements, a fuel and an oxidant; engines that are based on the action–reaction principle and that use air instead of carrying their own oxidant are properly called jets (see JET PROPULSION). Liquefied gases, e.g., hydrogen as fuel and oxygen as oxidant, are more powerful propellants than solid explosives, e.g., NITROGLYCERIN as oxidant and nitrocellulose as fuel. Liquid propellants are pumped into the combustion chamber at a controlled rate, and liquid-propellant motors may be shut down and restarted. Solid-propellant rockets, once ignited, burn continuously until the propellant is consumed, and are less controllable than liquid rockets. The chemical energy of the propellants is released in the form of heat in the combustion chamber. The rocket's exit nozzle usually converges to a narrow throat, then diverges to obtain maximum energy from the exhaust gases moving through it. No currently practical single-stage rocket can reach orbital velocity (8 km/sec) or the Earth's ESCAPE VELOCITY (11 km/sec). Hence SPACE EXPLORATION requires multistage rockets; two or more rockets are assembled in tandem and ignited in turn; as their fuel is used up, each of the lower stages detaches and falls back to Earth. When extremely large thrust is required, several rockets may be clustered and operated simultaneously. Rocket navigation is usually based on inertial guidance; internal GYROSCOPES are used to detect changes in the position and direction of the rocket.

*History.* The invention of the rocket is generally ascribed to the Chinese, who as early as AD 1000 stuffed GUNPOWDER into sections of bamboo tubing to make effective weapons. The astronautical use of rockets was cogently argued in the early 20th cent. by the Russian Konstantin E. TSIOLKOVSKY; the American Robert H. GODDARD, who launched the first liquid-fuel rocket in 1926; and the German Hermann OBERTH. During World War II, a German team under Wernher VON BRAUN developed the V-2 rocket, the first long-range guided missile. After the war, rocket research in the US and the USSR intensified, leading to the development of the modern array of intercontinental ballistic MISSILES and spacecraft-launching rockets (otherwise known as launch vehicles). Important US expendable rockets have included the Agena, Atlas, Delta, Saturn, and Titan vehicles. Saturn V, the largest rocket ever assembled, during the Apollo programme delivered a payload of 44 tonnes to the Moon. The US SPACE SHUTTLE, the first reusable space vehicle, achieves orbit through a combination of several orbiter liquid-propellant engines and two expendable solid-rocket boosters. Important USSR launch vehicles have included the A-type, which launched the first artificial satellite, *Sputnik 1*, and which, with an upper stage added, launched the Vostok and Voskhod spacecrafts. A further development, A-2, currently launches the Soyuz series. More powerful is the Proton (D series) launch vehicle, and most powerful of the Soviet range is Energia, first launched in 1987. Energia is the first Soviet rocket to use liquid oxygen/liquid hydrogen propellant, and can place over 100 tonnes in low Earth orbit. In addition to the US and USSR, France, Japan, China, UK, and India have all at various times developed rockets which have successfully launched satellites. Current launch vehicles outside the USSR and US include the Chinese CZ (*Chang Zheng* [long march]) series, the European Ariane, the Indian ASLV and PSLV, and the Japanese N- and H- series. Several private enterprise launch vehicles are being developed in the US. The launching of satellites, particularly communications satellites, is now a major and lucrative business. Following the disaster in 1986, the US Space Shuttle has been withdrawn from commercial satellite launching and major commercial competitors for this business currently include Ariane, Proton, CZ-3, and by 1995 will include the H-II.

**Rockhampton,** city (1986 pop. 54,362), Queensland, NE Australia. On the Fitzroy R., the city mainly functions as a centre for the railway and as the port for Mt Morgan, significant for gold and oil speculation in the early 1900s. Beef cattle are raised in the district.

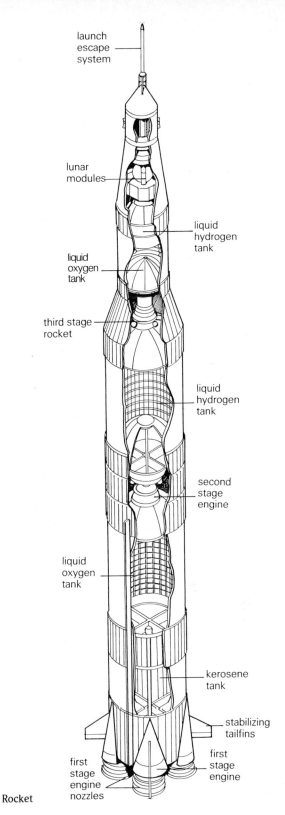

launch escape system

lunar modules

liquid hydrogen tank

liquid oxygen tank

third stage rocket

liquid hydrogen tank

second stage engine

liquid oxygen tank

kerosene tank

stabilizing tailfins

first stage engine

first stage engine nozzles

**Rocket**

**Rockingham,** city (1986 pop. 30,635), Western Australia. The state's second largest city, it has expanded to incorporate the industrial complex of Kwinana, including an oil refinery, aluminium smelter for the bauxite from Jarrahdale and Pinjarra, and steelworks.

**rock music,** hybrid of black and white American musical forms: blues (see JAZZ), rhythm and blues, GOSPEL MUSIC, COUNTRY AND WESTERN MUSIC, and harmony group music. In 1955 Bill Haley's song 'Rock Around the Clock' set off a rock 'n' roll craze because of its exciting, heavy beat and the urgent call to dance and action of its lyrics. With songs on adolescent concerns like school, cars, and young love, black artists like Chuck BERRY vied for popularity with whites like Buddy HOLLY. Most successful was Elvis PRESLEY. In the 1960s Detroit produced Motown, a black style with lead story lines sung over tight harmony by groups like the Temptations and the Supremes. Rock surged after 1962 as the BEATLES, the ROLLING STONES, and other English groups introduced a sophisticated lyricism. In 1965 the folk singer Bob DYLAN began a folk-rock synthesis. Rock also turned to social protest and rebellion as groups like the Jefferson Airplane spoke to youth seeking new experience through drugs (acid rock). A large-scale production trend brought rock MUSICALS, e.g., *Hair* (1968), and opera, e.g., *Tommy,* by the English group The Who (1969). By the end of the 1960s, rock was heard largely in concert and at festivals like that near Woodstock, New York state in Aug. 1969. In the 1970s country rock, a fusion of country and western and rock "n" roll, grew popular, as did disco, a repetitive dance music. English influence returned with punk rock, expressing the discontents of working-class youth. Punk's stripped-down form and aggressiveness were echoed in the less political and more art-conscious American new wave.

**rock temple:** see TEMPLE.

**Rockwell, Norman,** 1894–1978, American illustrator. Enormously popular, he is best known for his *Saturday Evening Post* covers. Rockwell specialized in finely drawn, richly anecdotal scenes of everyday small-town life.

**Rocky Mountains,** major mountain system of W North America, forming the CONTINENTAL DIVIDE and extending more than 4800 km (3000 mi) from New Mexico to Alaska. Mt Elbert (4399 m/14,431 ft) is the highest point. The mountains are topographically divided into the Southern, Central, and Northern Rockies (all in the US), the Canadian Rockies (Canada), and the Brooks Range (Alaska). They are rich in minerals and timber and are the site of several national parks. These include Rocky Mountain, Yellowstone, Grand Teton, and Glacier national parks in the US and Jasper, Banff, Glacier, Yoho, Kootenay, and Mt Revelstoke national parks in Canada. The Rockies were long a major barrier to transcontinental travel. The principal US pass, South Pass (SW Wyoming), was crossed by the OREGON TRAIL.

**Rocky Mountain spotted fever,** infectious disease caused by a rickettsia (bacteria-like microorganism) harboured by rodents and other small animals in the US, and carried by infected ticks that attach themselves to humans. Symptoms include chills, high fever, and a rose-coloured skin rash. The disease, which can be fatal if untreated, is treated effectively with the ANTIBIOTIC tetracycline.

**rococo,** style in architecture, especially in interiors and the decorative arts, which originated in France and spread throughout 18th-cent. Europe. In contrast with heavy BAROQUE grandiloquence, rococo was an art of exquisite refinement and linearity. The engravers J.A. MEISSONIER and Nicholas Pineau helped to spread the style through Europe. Parisian tapestry weavers, cabinetmakers, and bronze workers followed the trend. Motifs such as shells, scrolls, branches, and flowers appeared in delicate and ingenious compositions; the style also incorporated CHINOISERIE motifs. The major French exponents were the painters WATTEAU, BOUCHER, and FRAGONARD, and the architect GABRIEL. In Germany and Austria, CUVILLIÈS was the pioneer. The brilliantly decorated Italian rococo, especially important in Venice, was epitomized by TIEPOLO. In England the furniture of CHIPPENDALE was especially notable.

**Rodchenko, Aleksandr Mikhailovich,** 1891–1956, Russian painter. In 1916 he exhibited his ruler-and-compass works with TATLIN. He designed the Workers' Club exhibited in the Soviet Pavilion at the 1925 Exposition Internationale des Arts Decoratifs et Industriels Modernes, Paris (see ART DECO). In his painting he was much influenced by MALEVICH's suprematism, e.g., in *Black on Black* (1918). Rodchenko was important in the post-Revolutionary CONSTRUCTIVISM, working in all areas of industrial design.

**rodent,** member of the largest mammalian order, Rodentia, characterized by front teeth adapted for gnawing and cheek teeth adapted for chewing. The approximately 1800 species of Rodentia are worldwide in distribution and are divided into three suborders. The Sciuromorpha, or squirrel-like rodents, include SQUIRRELS, GROUND SQUIRRELS, and BEAVERS. The Myomorpha, or mouselike rodents, include a variety of MOUSE and RAT species, as well as species of HAMSTER, LEMMING, and GERBIL. The

Hystricomorpha, or porcupinelike rodents, include the PORCUPINE, GUINEA PIG, and CHINCHILLA. The CAPYBARA is the largest rodent.

**rodeo,** form of US entertainment based on the riding and roping skills of the Western cowboy. It is also an organized sport in which professional rodeo cowboys compete for millions of dollars in prizes. Staged in outdoor arenas, the modern rodeo comprises five classes: bareback bronc-riding, saddle bronc-riding, bull riding, calf roping, and steer wrestling (bulldogging). The first formal rodeo was held (1888) in Prescott, Ariz. Rodeos are now popular in many parts of the US and Canada.

**Roderick,** d. 711?, last Visigothic king in Spain (r.710–711?). Although little is known about his reign, colourful legends about this 'last of the Goths' are included in Spanish and English literature. He was overthrown in 711 by the invading Moors.

**Rodgers, Richard (Charles),** 1902–79, American composer. With Lorenz HART, he wrote such MUSICALS as *The Girl Friend* (1926), *Babes in Arms* (1937), and *Pal Joey* (1940). With Oscar HAMMERSTEIN, 2nd, he composed such musicals as *Oklahoma!* (1943), *Carousel* (1945), and *The King* and *I* (1951).

**Rodilla, Simon:** see WATTS TOWERS.

**Rodin, Auguste** (roh‚danh), 1840–1917, French sculptor. In the Salon of 1877 he exhibited a male nude, *The Age of Bronze* (1876; Paris), which was both praised and condemned. His critics unjustly accused him of casting it from life, but the furore gained him the patronage of the undersecretary of fine arts, and the government gave him a studio in Paris. From 1880 Rodin worked on studies for the *Gate of Hell,* two great bronze doors that were never finished; among the 186 figures intended for them are *Adam and Eve* (1881; Metropolitan Mus., New York) and *The Thinker* (1879–1900; Rodin Mus., Paris). These, together with his group *The Burghers of Calais* (completed in 1894) are among his most famous works. Rodin's work is realistic, but imbued with a profound, romantic poetry. He is also known for his drawings, portrait busts, and marble groups, e.g., *Ugolino* (1882), *The Kiss* (1886), and *The Hand of God* (1897–98; all Rodin Mus., Paris).

**Rodó, José Enrique** (ro‚doh), 1872–1917, Uruguayan essayist and philosopher. An exponent of MODERNISMO, he edited *La Revista Nacional de Literatura y Ciencias Sociales.* His best-known essay, *Ariel* (1900), exhorts Spanish America to hold to spiritual values unsullied by the materialism of the US.

**Rodríguez de Francia, José Gaspar:** see FRANCIA, JOSÉ GASPAR RODRÍGUEZ DE.

**Roe, Sir Alliott Verdon,** 1877–1958, English aviator. He was the first Englishman to leave the ground in an aeroplane of his own construction, in a short hop on 8 June 1908. He developed the renowned Avro series of aircraft, of which the best-known were the Lancaster, used as a bomber in World War II, and the Shackleton, still in service with the Royal Air Force in the 1980s. He was knighted in 1929.

**Roebling, John Augustus,** 1806–69, American engineer; b. Prussia. After coming to the US in 1831, he demonstrated the practicability of steel cable and began manufacturing it at Trenton, New Jersey. A pioneer in the building of suspension bridges (see BRIDGE), Roebling designed, beginning in 1844, suspension bridges of increasing size; two of the most notable are at Niagara Falls and Brooklyn.

**Roeg, Nicolas,** 1928–, British film director. A distinguished lighting cameraman before his striking directorial debut with *Performance* (1970), his films are marked by a nervy style of cross cutting and a concentration on the war between the sexes. His films include *Don't Look Now* (1973), *The Man Who Fell to Earth* (1976), and *Castaway* (1987).

**Roemer, Olaus** or **Ole,** 1644–1710, Danish astronomer. Through observations of the eclipses of Jupiter's satellites, he discovered that light travels through space at a finite, non-instantaneous velocity; his measurement of this velocity was a reasonable first approximation of the currently accepted value. Roemer made the first practical transit instrument (1690) and the earliest transit circle (1704).

**Roentgen** or **Röntgen, Wilhelm Conrad** (‚rontgən), 1845–1923, German physicist. For his discovery of a short-wave ray called the Roentgen ray or X-RAY he received (1901) the first Nobel Prize for physics.

Bureau of walnut and palisander by David **Roentgen** (c.1765)

August **Rodin**, *The Thinker*, 1879–1900. Bronze statue. Rodin Museum, Paris.

**Roentgen, David** (‚ruhnt'yen), 1743–1807, German cabinetmaker. He inherited the workshop of his father, Abraham, at Neuwied and gained commissions for furniture for the French and other foreign courts, as well as for princely houses in Germany. His MARQUETRY decoration is particularly fine, many later examples being pictorial.

**Roethke, Theodore**, 1908–63, American poet. He combined a love of the land of the Midwest with a vision of individual development, and his tone ranged from acid wit to simple feeling. His volumes include *Open House* (1941), *The Waking* (1953), and *The Far Field* (1964).

**Rogers, Carl**, 1902–87, American psychotherapist. Rogers is the originator of 'client-centred' or 'non-directive' therapy, which proposes that, by neutrally accepting the client's feelings, the therapist can create and emphatic and accepting environment in which patients determine for themselves the direction and rate of their personal change and growth. His books include *Client-Centered Therapy* (1951), *Becoming a Person* (1966), and *On Personal Power* (1977).

**Rogers, Richard**, 1933–, English architect, b.Italy. Rogers is an international figure who achieved fame by winning (with Renzo Piano) the competition for the design of the POMPIDOU CENTRE in Paris (1971–77). A structural tour-de-force, it displays its pipes and escalators on the outside, where conventional architects would have put them inside. A similar character is given to his subsequent design for Lloyds in the City of London, a controversial new building, which has a tall open space inside and services grouped in towers on the corners.

**Roger van der Weyden:** see WEYDEN, ROGER VAN DER.

**Roget, Peter Mark** (‚rozhay), 1779–1869, English physician and lexicographer. After 20 years as secretary of the Royal Society, he wrote the *Thesaurus of English Words and Phrases* (1852), later edited by his son and by his grandson, and now standard reference work.

**Rohmer, Eric**, 1920–, French film director and writer; b. Jean Marie Maurice Scherer. His thoughtful, literate studies of relationships between men and women include *My Night at Maude's* (1968), *Claire's Knee* (1970), *Chloe in the Afternoon* (1972), *The Marquise of O.* (1976), and *Le beau marriage* (1982).

**Roh Tae Woo**, 1932–, retired army general and president of South KOREA (1988–). After retiring as head of military intelligence (1981), he entered politics, becoming (1985) leader of the ruling Democratic Justice Party. Elected president of the country in 1987 amid opposition allegations of electoral fraud, he was inaugurated in Feb. 1988.

**Rojas, Fernando de** (‚rohhahs), 1465?–1541?, Spanish writer. His novel of passion in dramatic form, *La Celestina* (1499), is considered a masterpiece of Spanish literature.

**Rojas Zorrilla, Francisco de**, 1607–48, Spanish dramatist of the GOLDEN AGE. Of his many plays, the best known is *Del rey abajo, ninguno* (1650; tr. None Beneath the King), a drama of honour. His plots were borrowed by others, including CORNEILLE.

**Roland**, French hero of the medieval epic *Song of Roland* (11th or 12th cent.). Historically, Roland was one of Charlemagne's commanders, killed when the rear guard of the Frankish army, returning from Spain, was ambushed by the Basques in a pass in the Pyrenees in 778. Legend makes Roland one of Charlemagne's peers and his nephew, transforms the Basques into Saracens, and locates the pass at Roncesvalles. The poem is marked by its unified conception, its vivid and direct narrative, and its predominantly warlike spirit. Roland is also the hero of other CHANSONS DE GESTE.

**Rolfe, John**, 1585–1622, English colonist in Virginia. He immigrated (1610) to JAMESTOWN and introduced tobacco cultivation. Rolfe married (1614) POCAHONTAS, daughter of an Indian chief, who went (1616) with him to England. After her death, he returned to Virginia and remarried.

**Rolland, Romain** (ro‚lanh), 1866–1944, French author and pacifist. He wrote biographies of Beethoven (1903), Michelangelo (1908),

Tolstoy (1911), and Mahatma Gandhi (1924). His major fictional work is *Jean-Christophe* (1904–12), a 10-volume study of a German-born musician and of contemporary European civilization. His best-known play is *The Wolves* (1898). He received the 1915 Nobel Prize in literature.

**Rolle, Richard,** c.1300–49, English hermit and mystic. He was a prolific writer of religious prose in both English and Latin, and his works were widely read and much imitated.

**Rolling Stones,** English ROCK MUSIC group that rose to prominence in the mid-1960s and continues to exert great influence. Members have included singer Mick Jagger (1943–); guitarists Brian Jones (1944–69), Keith Richard (1943–), and Ron Wood (1941–); bassist Bill Wyman (1941–); and drummer Charlie Watts (1941–). The group's songs, written mostly by Jagger and Richard, include 'Satisfaction', '19th Nervous Breakdown', and 'Jumping Jack Flash'. They have appeared widely in concert and in films, e.g., *Gimme Shelter* (1970). In spite of the effectiveness of the other musicians, the group's popularity has been largely sustained by the charisma of Jagger.

**Rollins, Sonny,** (Theodore Walter Rollins), 1929–, black American jazz tenor and soprano saxophonist, composer, and bandleader. With John COLTRANE he refined and extended Charlie PARKER's imprint on saxophone improvisation and is now regarded by many as the greatest tenor player in the history of jazz. His succinctly brief solos in the 1940s were the bedrock for the later development of lengthy explorations of themes (frequently his own, but sprinkled with a number of 'standards'), with breathtaking imagination and variation.

**Rolls, Charles Stewart,** 1877–1910, British sportsman and engineer. At Cambridge Univ., where he studied engineering, he became interested in both cycling and motoring. He bought his first car, a Peugeot, in 1896, and by 1900 was winning prizes for his driving. In 1904 he met Henry ROYCE, a brilliant design engineer, who was already producing prototype cars. They went into partnership in 1906, and sold their first cars at £735 each. Rolls also took up ballooning and aeroplane flying, and became (1910) the first person to fly across the English Channel and back. He was killed later that year in an accident in a flying competition.

**Roman architecture.** Early Roman architects were inspired by post-and-lintel and more refined Greek forms, and drew on Etruscan and Asian models for the semicircular ARCH, VAULT, and DOME. To these elements they added the use of concrete, leading after the 2nd cent. BC to revolutionary structural forms. Of early Rome and the republic (c.500 BC–27 BC), the aqueducts outside the city of Rome are the most impressive remains. The principal Roman works belong to the period 100 BC–AD 300. The reign of AUGUSTUS initiated centuries of vast building enterprises. The special feature of Roman design was the combined use of arches (eventually the main structural element) and columns, which served as buttresses or decoration. Concrete replaced cut-stone construction after the 2nd cent. BC. Brick was used in all periods, especially baked brick for facing during the Empire. Stucco, porphyry, alabaster, and marble were also used to finish buildings. Brick vaults were developed fully, their buttresses integrated into the interior. Immense unencumbered vaults, e.g., those of the PANTHEON, created pure spatial effects. Splendour and utility were the Roman ideals, as opposed to the subtle refinement of the Greeks. Urban planning was extensive. Towns were laid out according to a logical plan, focusing on a forum, with colonnades and principal buildings surrounding it. In Rome itself successive forums were built by the emperors. Temples, conforming to the Etruscan type, were elevated on high bases. Facing the forum, they were without side porticos. The type is seen at the Maison Carrée, Nîmes, France. Circular temples included that of Vesta at Tivoli, Italy (1st cent. BC). The Romans themselves developed the BASILICA, baths, AMPHITHEATRE, and triumphal arch. Roman theatres combined stage and auditorium in a unified structure. Baths, probably derived from Greek gymnasia, were built on a totally unprecedented scale, in luxurious detail. Houses typically had an ATRIUM with a roof opening, and the Greek peristyle was used. Four- or five-storey urban houses suggested the modern tenement. A third house type was the luxurious country villa, which was built in all parts of the Roman empire.

**Roman art.** From the 7th to the 3rd cent. BC, ETRUSCAN ART flourished in central Italy, including Latium and Rome. After 400 BC, the imitation of Greek models, combined with a trend toward naturalism, e.g., *Mars of Todi* (Vatican), produced the establishment of Hellenistic realism by the beginning of the Roman Empire, e.g., *Orator* (Museo Archeologico, Florence). After the Roman conquest of Greece (c.146 BC), Greek artists came to Rome and found a ready market for works done in the classical manner or as copies of Greek originals. Their influence was important and indicates the eclecticism of Roman taste. Roman portraits, however, had as their origin the Roman custom of having death masks taken and preserved, along with busts copied from them. By the time of the Empire, art had become allied with the ideal of service to the state. It led to a distinctly Roman style of portrait bust, concerned with pictorial refinement and psychological penetration. The magnificent reliefs from the Arch of Titus, Rome, commemorating the conquest of Jerusalem in AD 70, mark the climax of illusionism in historical relief sculpture. From the time of TRAJAN (AD 98–117), the art of the Eastern provinces began to have greater influence. The spiral band of low reliefs on Trajan's Column (Rome) suggests the Middle Eastern or Egyptian illustrative tradition. After a brief return to the classical style under HADRIAN and the Antonines, e.g., the equestrian statue of Marcus Aurelius (Rome), the Oriental tendency towards abstraction became more apparent. It later developed into the stiff, iconographic forms of the early Christian and Byzantine eras. The last example of Roman monumental sculpture is in the reliefs of the Arch of Constantine, Rome (c.AD 315). Roman painting was also influenced by Greece; unfortunately, much of it has perished. What remains suggests that the art was mainly one of interior decoration. The largest group of paintings exists in POMPEII. Many paintings, e.g., the *Aldobrandini Wedding* and the *Odyssey Landscapes* (Vatican), are thought to be Roman copies of Greek originals. These three-dimensional techniques were duplicated in MOSAIC works, extensively produced throughout the empire. The famous pottery of Arretium (now Arezzo) was mass-produced and widely exported. Early pots had a black finish, and later examples had a red glaze with low-relief decorative figures. Roman minor arts emphasized sumptuous materials. CAMEOS and gold jewellery were extensively produced. During the 1st cent. AD, new processes were invented for making glass and imitating precious stones, which made possible the production of fine murrhine vases.

**Roman Catholic Church,** Christian church headed by the pope, the bishop of Rome. 'Roman Catholic' is a 19th-cent. British coinage, but is now in common use among English-speaking people. Roman Catholics are spread worldwide and probably number in the hundreds of millions, although no census has been made. The vast majority belong to the Roman rite. Even in the West, however, there are variant rites such as the Ambrosian, the Dominican, and the Mozarabic. In the East there are groups in communion with the pope that also have other rites— Byzantine, Antiochene, Chaldean, Alexandrian, and Armenian. All members of the church accept the gospel of Christ as handed down by the church, the teachings of the Bible, and the church's interpretations of those teachings. They also believe that God conveys His grace directly to humanity through the SACRAMENTS. The Eucharist (see MASS) is the centre of Catholic worship. The clergy, except for parish priests of the Eastern rites, may not marry, and the church structure, from the parish priests through the bishops to the pope, is administered in the papal court at Rome. Outside the secular organization of the church are the orders of regular priests, monks, and nuns (see MONASTICISM). In the early centuries of CHRISTIANITY, the pope came to command great authority in Western Europe. The contest between the PAPACY and lay rulers over ecclesiastical and lay power was very important in the Middle Ages. The pope was under French domination at Avignon (1309–78), and the church was later rocked by the Great SCHISM. The Protestant REFORMATION in the 16th cent. split the church, and the COUNTER-REFORMATION corrected many abuses. In the 19th cent. Pope PIUS IX proclaimed the doctrine of papal INFALLIBILITY. In the 20th cent. the church moved to adjust to modern political and social conditions, particularly the Second VATICAN COUNCIL (1962–65).

**romance** [O.Fr., = something written in the popular language, i.e., a Romance language]. The *roman* of the Middle Ages in Europe was a chivalric and romantic narrative (see CHIVALRY). It was lengthened into the *roman d'aventure,* or romance of love and adventure, from which the modern romance derives (see NOVEL).

**Romance languages,** group of languages belonging to the Italic subfamily of the Indo-European family of languages. See LANGUAGE (table).

**Roman Empire:** see BYZANTINE EMPIRE; HOLY ROMAN EMPIRE; ROME.

**Romanesque architecture and art** prevailed throughout Europe from the mid-11th to the mid-12th cent. ROMAN ARCHITECTURE was the main inspiration, but Byzantine and Eastern components were incorporated. Certain characteristic features of Romanesque structures, such as the massive west facades crowned by a TOWER or twin towers, the complex eastern parts housing the sanctuary, and the rhythmic alternation of piers and columns in the NAVE, represent only the advanced stages of a long evolution. The development of Romanesque architecture owes much to the primacy accorded to vaulting. Early Christian architecture had confined masonry vaulting (see VAULT) to small structures. Larger basilican buildings had wood roofs. Romanesque churches sustained massive barrel vaults, which required the reinforcement of load-bearing walls. The presence of galleries above the aisles and the few wall openings are doubtless due originally to structural considerations. They, in turn, created a sombrely impressive atmosphere. Monastic communities were centres of development: Cluniac churches at Tours and Toulouse, France, and Santiago de Compostela, Spain, connected with the great pilgrimages, featured large ambulatories with radiating CHAPELS, designed to facilitate access to the relics. Noted Romanesque buildings include: *France* the abbey church of St Madeleine Vezelay (c.1090–1130); *Germany* the cathedral of Speyer (1060; reconstructed after 1082); *Italy* the cathedral (1063–92) and baptistery (1153) in Pisa, and the church of San Miniato al Monte, Florence (c.1070). In the late 12th cent. developments in N France and in England pointed towards the Gothic (see NORMAN ARCHITECTURE). Romanesque art was marked by the revival of monumental forms, notably sculpture and fresco painting, developed in close association with architecture. An element of realism, paralleling the first flowering of vernacular literature, came to the fore in direct and naive observation of details from daily life and a heightened emphasis on emotion and fantasy. The pilgrimages and crusades contributed to a broadened formal vocabulary. Ornamental complexity, ecstatic expression, and a profusion of zoomorphic, vegetal, and abstract motifs abounded. In France, themes portrayed on the tympanums of such churches as Moissac and Autun emphasized the majesty of Christ and the terrors of hell. Metalwork was an important art, and crucifixes and other church objects were highly refined. Limoges became a major metal and enamelwork centre. The large walls of the churches encouraged fresco painting; manuscript ILLUMINATION, with a greatly expanded fund of pictorial imagery, also flourished.

**Romania** or **Rumania**, officially the Socialist Republic of Romania, republic (1985 est. pop. 23,065,000), 237,500 km² (91,699 sq mi), SE Europe; bordered by Hungary (NW), Yugoslavia (SW), Bulgaria (S), the Black Sea (SE), and the USSR (E and N). Major cities include BUCHAREST (the capital), CLUJ, Timişoara, and IAŞI. The CARPATHIAN Mts, which include the Transylvanian ALPS, cut through Romania from N to SW; the highest peak is at Moldoveanu (2543 m/ (8343 ft). The principal rivers are the DANUBE and its tributary, the Prut. The economy is almost entirely planned and controlled by the state. Traditionally an agricultural country, Romania greatly expanded its industrial base after World War II, and by 1980 industry contributed over 65% of national income. Leading manufactures include refined petroleum, iron and steel, chemicals, processed meats, furniture, textiles, and forest products. The chief farm products are wheat, maize, sugar beets, potatoes, and fruits (notably grapes for wine). Romania is a major producer of petroleum and natural gas, although the important oil reserves around Ploeşti show signs of depletion; coal, copper, and iron ore are mined. The GNP per capita (1981) is US$2540. Romanian is the official language, but sizable minorities speak German and Hungarian. By far the largest religious body is the Romanian Orthodox Church.

*History.* Present-day Romania corresponds roughly to the ancient province of DACIA, which, after Romanization (2nd–3rd cent. AD), was overrun successively by the Goths, Huns, Avars, Bulgars, Magyars, and Mongols. In the middle of the 14th cent. two Romanian principalities, MOLDAVIA and WALACHIA, emerged. They became subject to Turkish suzerainty during the 15th cent. In 1859 the election of Alexandra John CUZA as prince in both principalities marked the creation of the United Principalities of Moldavia and Walachia which were named Romania in 1862. Romania's independence was recognized in 1878 by the Treaty of Berlin and she was proclaimed a kingdom in 1881 upon the crowning of CAROL I. Romania joined (1916) the Allies in WORLD WAR I, after which it acquired BUKOVINA, TRANSYLVANIA, BESSARABIA, and part of the Banat. Romanian politics in the inter-war period were marked by an effort to

defend the European status-quo and, internally, by economic turmoil and violence. In the 1930s the anti-Semitic IRON GUARD committed acts of terror, assassinating two prime ministers and scores of other opponents. The loss of N Transylvania to Hungary and of Bessarabia and N Bukovina to the USSR forced King CAROL II to abdicate in 1940 in favour of his son MICHAEL and to hand over power to ANTONESCU. Romania joined Germany in the attack on the Soviet Union in 1941. In the face of the Red Army's advance into Romania (1944) King Michael arrested Antonescu, and the country took up arms against Germany. The Soviet occupation of Romania in 1945 led to the communist take-over in 1947: King Michael was forced to abdicate, and a people's republic proclaimed. The sovietization of the country was completed by 1950. From 1963 under GHEORGHIU-DEJ the Romanian Communist Party felt strong enough to challenge the Soviet Union's supranational pretentions and embarked upon a semi-autonomous foreign and economic policy. Nicolae CEAUSESCU became party leader in 1965 (and head of state in 1967), quickly stamping his authority on the country's public life. In the 1980s short-comings in industry, rising energy costs, and over-ambitious hard-currency borrowings produced severe economic problems, and there was increasing political criciticm of the Ceausescu regime.

Romania

**Romanian language,** member of the Romance group of the Italic subfamily of the Indo-European family of languages. See LANGUAGE (table).

**Romanic:** see ROMANCE LANGUAGES.

**Roman law,** system of law of the Romans, from the founding of ROME (753 BC) to the fall of the Eastern Empire (AD 1453); it is the basis of modern CIVIL LAW. First codified in 450 BC in the Twelve Tables (tablets on which the laws were inscribed), early Roman law was highly formalistic. Procedural knowledge was restricted to a body of patrician priests, but as a result of plebeian pressure this material was reduced to writing (c.250 BC), thus broadening the law's social base. By the late 3rd cent. BC Roman law comprised the *jus civile,* governing relations among Romans, and the *jus gentium,* governing dealings with foreigners; the latter, more flexible, eventually became universal. After c.100 BC new principles, notably the *jus honorarium,* a body of magisterial law to supplement, aid, and correct existing law, were vigorously developed. With the establishment (27 BC) of the Roman Empire, the development of law passed into the hands of the emperors, and imperial enactments were abundant. The growing complexity of the law gave birth to a class of trained jurists, most prominent of whom was PAPINIAN (d. AD 212), and by the early 4th cent. most branches of Roman law were fully developed. Codification was completed (535) during the reign of JUSTINIAN I in the *Corpus juris civilis,* the culminating work of Roman legal scholarship and the model for most of the legal systems in continental Europe. After the fall of the Western Empire, Roman law persisted as part of GERMANIC LAW and CANON LAW, and in the Eastern (Byzantine) Empire. Revival of classical studies during the Renaissance led to the resurrection of Roman law as the basis for the civil law that developed in a large part of the world. Even COMMON LAW countries, such as England, have felt the influence of Roman law, particularly in commercial law and the rules of EQUITY.

**Roman numeral:** see NUMERAL.

**Romano, Giulio :** see GIULIO ROMANO.

**Romanov** (ˌrohmənof, (Russ) rəmahnəf), ruling dynasty of Russia, 1613–1917. The first wife of Czar IVAN IV was Anastasia Romanov, whose grand-nephew Michael was chosen czar in 1613. In the following list of Michael's successors, the names of rulers not descended from him are in brackets: Alexis, 1645–76; Feodor III, 1676–82; Ivan V, 1682–89; PETER I, 1682–1725 (ruled jointly with Ivan V until 1689); [CATHERINE I, 1725–27]; Peter II, 1727–30; Anna, 1730–40; IVAN VI, 1740–41; ELIZABETH, 1741–62; PETER III, 1762; [CATHERINE II, 1762–96]; PAUL I, 1796–1801; ALEXANDER I, 1801–25; NICHOLAS I, 1825–55; ALEXANDER II, 1855–81; ALEXANDER III, 1881–94; NICHOLAS II, 1894–1917. After the murder of Nicholas II and his immediate family in 1918, the surviving Romanovs fled abroad.

**Roman religion.** The indigenous ancient Italic religion was essentially animistic, holding that spirits (numina) dwelling in natural objects controlled human destiny. The earliest unit for their worship was the family and household. When the early agricultural communities coalesced into the Roman state, the family ritual formed the basis for state ritual, ruled by the king as chief priest. The supreme triad of deities was that of JUPITER, MARS, and Quirinus. Many foreign gods were adopted from the 7th cent., and from the 3rd cent. BC the old Roman deities were equated with the Greek gods whose attributes they took on. The influence of EPICURUS and STOICISM were also felt. In the last two centuries of the republic the people, grown distant from the formalistic state religion, sought salvation and a promise of afterlife in the Greek MYSTERIES and various Middle Eastern cults, e.g., those of the GREAT MOTHER OF THE GODS, ISIS and OSIRIS, and MITHRA, creating a religious climate in which Christianity would flourish and eventually triumph.

**Roman roads,** ancient system of highways linking Rome with its most distant provinces. The roads were constructed generally in four layers of materials; the uppermost layer was a pavement of flat, hard stones, concrete, or pebbles set in mortar. These roads were remarkably durable, and many, in part, are used today. Their primary purpose was military, but they were also of great commercial importance and brought the distant provinces in touch with the capital. In Italy roads led out of Rome in every direction. The APPIAN WAY was the first of the great highways; the Flaminian Way was the most important northern route. The Romans also built and rebuilt a wide system of roads for military purposes in Britain, notably Ermine Street, FOSSE WAY, Watling Street, and the pre-Roman Icknield Street.

**Romans,** EPISTLE of the NEW TESTAMENT. It was written by St PAUL, probably in AD c.57. It is addressed by Paul to the Christian church at Rome, apparently to introduce himself and his teaching before his visit. Its subject, the achieving of salvation through faith, is central in Paul's teaching and is the theme also of GALATIANS. In Romans, Paul argues that reliance on the Mosaic Law is not enough, and that God has not broken His promise to His chosen people but is working toward universal redemption. The epistle is accepted as authoritative by theologians of different schools, e.g., by both Lutherans and Roman Catholics.

**Romansh:** see RHAETO-ROMANIC.

**romanticism,** term applied to literary and artistic movements of the late 18th and 19th cent., in revolt against CLASSICISM and against philosophical rationalism, with its emphasis on reason. Spurred in part by the libertarian and egalitarian ideals of the FRENCH REVOLUTION, the romantics are associated with belief in a return to nature and in the innate goodness of man, as expressed by Jean Jacques ROUSSEAU; admiration for the heroic and for the individuality and imagination of the artist; exaltation of the senses and emotions over reason and intellect; and interest in the medieval, exotic, primitive, and nationalistic. Critics date English literary romanticism from the publication of William WORDSWORTH and S.T. COLERIDGE's *Lyrical Ballads* (1798), though William BLAKE's mysticism foreshadowed the movement. Romantic poets like Lord BYRON, John KEATS, and P.B. SHELLEY focused on the individual's highly personal response to life, as did Thomas DE QUINCEY and William HAZLITT in prose. The GOTHIC ROMANCE and the historical novels of Sir Walter SCOTT witnessed the cult of medievalism. German romanticism flourished in the STURM UND DRANG drama of GOETHE and SCHILLER, the lyric poetry of NOVALIS and HEINE, and the philological and folk researches of HERDER and the brothers GRIMM. Romanticism was exemplified in France by CHATEAUBRIAND, Victor HUGO,

DUMAS PÈRE, LAMARTINE, Alfred de MUSSET, and George SAND. The movement's influence, however, was worldwide, as evidenced by the works of the Russian Aleksandr PUSHKIN; the Italian Giacomo LEOPARDI; and the Americans J.F. COOPER, E.A. POE, and the transcendentalists (see TRANSCENDENTALISM). In the visual arts, romantics rejected classical formalism while remaining outside the 19th-cent. realist mainstream, as with DELACROIX and J.M.W. TURNER. Romanticism in music, stressing emotion and freedom of form, reached its zenith in the work of BERLIOZ, MENDELSSOHN, SCHUMANN, CHOPIN, LISZT, and WAGNER, who attempted in his operas a synthesis of all the arts.

**Romanus,** Byzantine emperors. **Romanus I,** d. 948 (r.919–44), deposed the young CONSTANTINE VII. Romanus defended CONSTANTINOPLE against the BULGARS. His two sons overthrew him. **Romanus II,** 939–63 (r.959–63), was the profligate son of Constantine VII. Romanus's wife, Theophano, was the actual ruler. His reign saw the victories of NICEPHORUS II over the Arabs. When Romanus died, Nicephorus married Theophano and became emperor. **Romanus III,** c.968–1034 (r.1028–34), succeeded Constantine VIII by marrying his daughter, ZOË. He depleted the treasury and abolished needed taxes. His general George Meniaces took Edessa from the Arabs (1032). **Romanus IV,** d. 1072 (r.1068–71), succeeded Constantine X by marrying his widow. He was routed by the Seljuk Turks at Manzikert. His stepson deposed and blinded him, succeeding as Michael VII.

**Romany,** language belonging to the Dardic group of the Indo-Iranian subfamily of the Indo-European family of languages. Romany is the mother tongue of the GYPSIES. See LANGUAGE (table).

**Romberg, Sigmund,** 1887–1951, American composer; b. Hungary. He wrote over 70 romantic OPERETTAS, including *The Student Prince* (1924), *The Desert Song* (1926), and *The New Moon* (1928).

**Rome,** Ital. *Roma,* city (1984 pop. 2,826,733), capital of Italy and see of the pope, whose residence, VATICAN CITY, is a sovereign state within the city of Rome. Rome is also the capital of Latium, a region of central Italy, and of Rome prov. It lies on both banks of the Tiber R. Called the Eternal City, it is one of the world's richest cities in history and art, and one of its great cultural, religious, and intellectual centres. Modern Rome retains many of the great monuments of its rich past. Among them are the Forum and the COLOSSEUM, the LATERAN, SAINT PETER'S CHURCH and other great churches (e.g., St Mary Major, St Lawrence without the Walls, St Paul's without the Walls, St Peter in Chains), and graceful palaces and villas (e.g., Farnese Palace, Farnesina, Borghese Villa). The immense riches of art and its religious importance make Rome one of the most visited cities of the world. It is also a great centre of commerce with varied industries, e.g., printing, publishing, manufacturing, and motion pictures. The remainder of this article treats the history of Rome and of the **Roman Empire.**

*Rome before Augustus.* Ancient Rome was built on the east, or left, bank of the Tiber. The seven hills of the ancient city are the Palatine, Capitoline, Quirinal, Viminal, Esquiline, Caelian, and Aventine. Tradition tells of the founding of Rome by ROMULUS in 753 BC and of rule by the TARQUIN family, the Etruscan royal house (see ETRUSCAN CIVILIZATION). The young city was probably under Etruscan rule until c.500 BC, when the Romans overthrew the monarchy and established the Roman republic. The PATRICIAN class controlled the government, but the majority PLEBS in time gained much power and privilege. In 390 BC Rome was sacked by the Gauls, but during the 4th and 3rd cent. BC it extended its influence over W Latium and S Etruria, conquered the Samnites, and became master of central and S Italy. Rome also came in full contact with Greek culture, which modified Roman life tremendously. Rome's rapid conquests met the like ambitions of CARTHAGE, which ruled the W Mediterranean. In a titanic struggle called the PUNIC WARS, Rome utterly destroyed Carthage. The Roman Republic then turned its attention eastward and rapidly expanded Roman dominion. At home, however, class dissension produced slave uprisings, e.g., that of SPARTACUS, and attempts were made at reform (see GRACCHI, family). Rome was forced by the Social War (90–88 BC) to extend citizenship widely in Italy, but the republic was nevertheless doomed. The struggle between Marius and SULLA led to a civil war. POMPEY emerged as a popular champion and found an ally in Julius CAESAR, a popular democratic leader. With Marcus Licinius Crassus (see CRASSUS, family), Pompey and Caesar formed the First Triumvirate (60 BC). Caesar then left Rome and acquired fame in the GALLIC WARS. Within ten years Pompey and Caesar fell out, and by his victory at Pharsala (48 BC) Caesar became master of Rome. The rule of Caesar completed the destruction of the republic and laid the foundations of the empire.

*The Roman Empire.* After Caesar's assassination (44 BC) the Second Triumvirate was formed by Caesar's grandnephew, Octavian (later AUGUSTUS), ANTONY, and Marcus Aemilius Lepidus (see LEPIDUS, family). This alliance dissolved as well, and in 31 BC Octavian's forces defeated Antony and CLEOPATRA at Actium. Octavian emerged supreme and is usually considered the first Roman emperor. He organized provincial government and the army, rebuilt Rome, and patronized the arts and letters. His rule began a long period (200 years) of peace called the *Pax Romana* in which the empire prospered. An extensive system of ROMAN ROADS made transportation easier, and commerce and industry were developed. Literary and artistic interests were important, although they nearly always tended to imitate Greek and Eastern styles. Augustus died in AD 14 and was succeeded in turn by his stepson TIBERIUS; by CALIGULA, a cruel tyrant; and by CLAUDIUS I, who conquered half of Britain. The emperor NERO (r.AD 54–68), an unparalleled tyrant, began the persecution of CHRISTIANITY, which was spreading throughout the empire. Under TRAJAN (r.AD98–117) the empire's eastern boundaries were pushed past Armenia and Mesopotamia. Marcus Aurelius (r.161–180) ruled in what is commonly called the Golden Age of the empire, but the 3rd cent. was a time of turmoil. In 284 DIOCLETIAN was made emperor by the army. He reformed government and divided the empire into four regions, two in the East and two in the West. CONSTANTINE I (r.306–37) moved the capital from Rome to Byzantium, renamed Constantinople, and granted religious toleration to Christians. After the death (395) of THEODOSIUS I, the empire was permanently divided into E and W sections, and Rome rapidly lost its political importance. The West sank into anarchy, and Italy was ravaged by invaders. Rome was taken by ALARIC I (410) and by Gaiseric (455), and Pope LEO I is said to have kept ATTILA from sacking it. In 476 the last emperor of the West, Romulus Augustulus, was deposed by the Goths under ODOACER; this date is commonly accepted as the end of the W. Roman Empire. The Eastern or BYZANTINE EMPIRE continued until the 15th cent. The so-called Dark Ages that followed in Western Europe could not eradicate the profound imprint left by Roman civilization on thought and government, then and later.

---

## RULERS OF THE ROMAN EMPIRE *(including dates of reign)*

Augustus, grandnephew of Julius Ceasar, 27 BC–AD 14
Tiberius, stepson of Augustus, AD 14–AD 37
Caligula, grandnephew of Tiberius, 37–41
Claudius, uncle of Caligula, 41–54
Nero, stepson of Claudius, 54–68
Galba, proclaimed emperor by his soldiers, 68–69
Otho, military commander, 69
Vespasian, military commander, 69–79
Vitellius, military commander, 69
Titus, son of Vespasian, 79–81
Domitian, son of Vespasian, 81–96
Nerva, elected interim ruler, 96–98
Trajan, adopted son of Nerva, 98–117
Hadrian, ward of Trajan, 117–38
Antoninus Pius, adopted by Hadrian, 138–61
Marcus Aurelius, adopted by Antoninus Pius, 161–80
Lucius Verus, adopted by Antoninus Pius; ruled jointly with Marcus Aurelius, 161–69
Commodus, son of Marcus Aurelius, 180–92
Pertinax, proclaimed emperor by the Praetorian Guard, 193
Didius Julianus, bought office from the Praetorian Guard, 193
Severus, proclaimed emperor, 193–211
Caracalla, son of Severus, 211–17
Geta, son of Severus, ruled jointly with Caracalla, 211–12
Macrinus, proclaimed emperor by his soldiers, 217–18
Heliogabalus, cousin of Caracalla, 218–22
Alexander Severus, cousin of Heliogabalus, 222–35
Maximin, proclaimed emperor by soldiers, 235–38
Gordian I, made emperor by the senate, 238
Gordian II, son of Gordian I, ruled jointly with his father, 238
Balbinus, elected joint emperor by the senate, 238
Pupienus Maximus, elected joint emperor with Balbinus by the senate, 238
Gordian III, son of Gordian II, 238–44
Philip (the Arabian), assassin of Gordian III, 244–49
Decius, proclaimed emperor by the soldiers, 249–51
Hostilianus, son of Decius, colleague of Gallus, 251
Gallus, military commander, 251–53
Aemilianus, military commander, 253
Valerian, military commander, 253–60
Gallienus, son of Valerian, coemperor with his father and later sole emperor, 253–68
Claudius II, military commander, 268–70
Aurelian, chosen by Claudius II as successor, 270–75
Tacitus, chosen by the senate, 275–76
Florianus, half brother of Tacitus, 276
Probus, military commander, 276–82
Carus, proclaimed by the Praetorian Guard, 282–83
Carinus, son of Carus, 283–85

Numerianus, son of Carus, joint emperor with Carinus 283–84
Diocletian, military commander, divided the empire; ruled jointly with Maximian and Constantius I, 284–305
Maximian, appointed joint emperor by Diocletian, 286–305
Constantius I, joint emperor and successor of Diocletian, 305–06
Galerius, joint emperor with Constantius I, 305–10
Maximin, nephew of Galerius, 308–13
Licinius, appointed emperor in the West by Galerius; later emperor in the East, 308–24
Maxentius, son of Maximian, 306–12
Constantine I (the Great), son of Constantius I, 306–37
Constantine II, son of Constantine I, 337–40
Constans, son of Constantine I, 337–50
Constantius II, son of Constantine I, 337–61
Magnentius, usurped Constans' throne, 350–53
Julian (the Apostate), nephew of Constantine I, 361–63
Jovian, elected by the army, 363–64
Valentinian I, proclaimed by the army; ruled in the West, 364–75
Valens, brother of Valentinian I; ruled in the East, 364–78
Gratian, son of Valentinian I; coruler in the West with Valentinian II, 375–83
Maximus, usurper in the West, 383–88
Valentinian II, son of Valentinian I, ruler of the West, 375–92
Eugenius, usurper in the West, 392–94
Theodosius I (the Great), appointed ruler of the East by Gratian, later sole emperor; last ruler of united empire, 375–95

### Emperors in the East

Arcadius, son of Theodosius I, 395–408
Theodosius II, son of Arcadius, 408–50
Marcian, brother-in-law of Theodosius II, 450–57
Leo I, chosen by the senate, 457–74
Leo II, grandson of Leo I, 474

### Emperors in the West

Honorius, son of Theodosius I, 395–423
Maximus, usurper in Spain, 409–11
Constantius III, named joint emperor by Honorius, 421
Valentinian III, nephew of Honorius and son of Constantius III, 425–55
Petronius Maximus, bought office by bribery, 455
Avitus, placed in office by Goths, 455–56
Majorian, puppet emperor of Ricimer, 457–61
Libius Severus, puppet emperor of Ricimer, 461–65
Anthemius, appointed by Ricimer and Leo I, 467–72
Olybrius, appointed by Ricimer, 472
Glycerius, appointed by Leo I, 473–74
Julius Nepos, appointed by Leo I, 474–75
Romulus Augustulus, put in office by Orestes, his father, 475–76

*Later History.* The history of Rome in the Middle Ages is essentially that of two institutions, the PAPACY and the commune of Rome. Rome was ruled by the Goths in the 5th cent. and fell under Byzantine rule from the 6th to the 8th cent. With the emergence (8th cent.) of the PAPAL STATES, Rome, their capital, once again rose to importance. CHARLEMAGNE and later Holy Roman emperors visited the city to be crowned by the popes. Papal authority was challenged unsuccessfully in the 12th cent. by the communal movement led by Arnold of Brescia, and civil strife arose between GUELPHS AND GHIBELLINES. During the 'Babylonian captivity' of the popes at AVIGNON (1309–78), conditions in Rome were in constant turmoil, but in the 15th cent. the city became a centre of the RENAISSANCE. Countless artists and architects served the papal court, and Rome, as it is today, is largely a product of their work. Noble and baroque monuments were erected in the 17th and early 18th cent. In 1809 Rome and the Papal States were annexed to France by NAPOLEON I, but papal rule was restored in 1814. After a republic was declared (1849) in Rome, French troops intervened to restore the pope. When the kingdom of Italy was proclaimed (1861), it included most of the Papal States, but not Rome, which remained a virtual French protectorate under NAPOLEON III. After Napoleon III's fall, Rome became (1871) the Italian capital, but the conflict between the pope and Italy was not solved until the LATERAN TREATY (1929), which gave the pope sovereignty over Vatican City. In WORLD WAR II Rome fell to Allied forces on June 4, 1944.

**Romeril, John,** 1945–, Australian playwright. He has worked with the Australian Performing Group in Melbourne, and has been committed to community theatre and cooperatives ever since. His best-known play is *The Floating World* (1975).

**Rommel, Erwin,** 1891–1944, German field marshal, known as the 'desert fox' and regarded as one of the most brilliant generals of WORLD WAR II. He commanded the Afrika Korps in the North African campaigns (1941–43). His string of victories was broken by the British at El Alamein (1942). In 1944 he took part in the attempt on Hitler's life and was forced to take poison when the plot failed.

**Romney, George,** 1734–1802, English portrait painter. After studying in Italy, he was influenced by neo-classicism (see CLASSICISM). His portraits of women are facile and charming, e.g., his many portraits of Lady Emma HAMILTON (one is in the National Portrait Gall., London). In his last years, he turned to literary subjects such as *Milton and his Daughters*.

**Romulus,** in Roman mythology, founder of Rome. He and his twin, Remus, were sons of MARS and Rhea Silvia, daughter of Numitor, king of Alba Longa. Amulius, usurper of Numitor's throne, threw them in the Tiber, but they floated ashore. They were suckled by a she-wolf and reared by a shepherd. When grown, they slew Amulius and made Numitor king. They then founded a city (traditionally in 753 BC) on the spot where they were rescued from the Tiber. They later quarrelled, and Romulus killed Remus. Romulus populated Rome with fugitives from other countries and gave them wives abducted from the SABINE tribe. After a long reign Romulus vanished in a thunderstorm; he was thereafter worshipped as the god Quirinus.

**Romulus Augustulus,** d. after 476, last Roman emperor of the West (475–76). His father, Orestes, ruled for him. He was deposed by ODOACER and sent away with a pension.

**Ronda,** town (1981 pop. 31,383), in the southern sierras of Spain. It is remarkable for its site: the Moorish town is separated from the later Christian settlement of Mercadillo by the 125-m (400-ft) *tajo* [gorge] of the Guadalevín R. It is spanned by three bridges, one on Roman foundations, one Moorish, and one built in the 18th cent.

**Ronsard, Pierre de** (rawnh̩sah), 1524?–1585, French Renaissance poet, leader of the Pléiade (see under PLEIAD). Named poet royal, he wrote prolifically, producing poems on many themes, especially patriotism, love, and death. His best-known love poems appear in *Sonnets pour Hélène* (1578). *La Franciade* (1572), an unfinished epic, was his most ambitious effort. He was one of France's greatest poets.

**Röntgen, Wilhelm Conrad:** see ROENTGEN.

**Roosevelt, Franklin Delano,** 1882–1945, 32nd president of the US (1933–45). The scion of an old, wealthy New York family, he entered politics by winning election (1910) to the New York state senate. As leader of the New York anti-Tammany Democratic reformers, he campaigned for Woodrow WILSON in the 1912 election. He served as assistant secretary of the navy (1913–20) and ran as Democratic vice

presidential candidate with James Cox (1920) but was defeated. The next year he was stricken with poliomyelitis; though crippled for life, he eventually regained partial use of his legs. He supported Gov. Al SMITH's presidential candidacy and, at Smith's urging, ran successfully for governor in 1928. Reelected in 1930, Gov. Roosevelt adopted bold relief measures to counter the GREAT DEPRESSION. Nominated by the Democrats in 1932, he defeated Pres. HOOVER. The new president, taking office at the height of the economic crisis, acted quickly during the so-called Hundred Days (Mar.–Jan. 1933) to rush through Congress a flood of fiscal and social reform measures aimed at reviving the economy by a vast expenditure of public funds. He set up many new agencies, including the National Recovery Administration and the Public Works Administration, to reorganize industry and agriculture under government regulation. These programmes and social reforms, such as SOCIAL SECURITY, became known as the NEW DEAL. He was aided by a BRAIN TRUST of advisers, including Raymond Moley and Rex Tugwell, cabinet officers Henry WALLACE and Harold Ickes, and special counsellor Harry HOPKINS. Roosevelt was the first president to master the technique of the radio broadcast; his 'fireside chats' explained issues and policies to the people. He easily won reelection in 1936. But the US SUPREME COURT declared a number of New Deal measures unconstitutional, and he failed (1937) in an attempt to reorganize the Court. In foreign affairs his administration recognized (1933) the Soviet Union and continued a 'good neighbour' policy towards Latin America. With the outbreak (1939) of World War II, Roosevelt extended aid to Britain and began LEND–LEASE, whilst building up US armed forces by the first peacetime selective service (1940). He set a new precedent by seeking and winning (1940) a third presidential term and, later (1944), a fourth. After the Japanese attack on PEARL HARBOR, Roosevelt, as commander in chief, directed the nation's immense war effort, held conferences with Winston CHURCHILL and other Allied leaders, and worked to establish the UN. On 12 Apr. 1945, he died suddenly from a cerebral haemorrhage. His wife, **Eleanor Roosevelt,** 1884–1962, was a niece of Theodore ROOSEVELT and a distant cousin of Franklin. She worked for social betterment as a lecturer, newspaper columnist, and world traveller. A US delegate to the UN, she was made chairman of the Commission for Human Rights in 1946. In the 1950s she led the liberal wing of the Democratic party.

**Roosevelt, Theodore,** 1858–1919, 26th president of the US (1901–9). The delicate son of a distinguished family, he made determined efforts to overcome frail health. After graduating (1880) from Harvard, he served (1882–84) as a Republican New York state legislator. Bereaved by the deaths (1884) of his mother and his first wife, he retired to his ranch in the Dakota Territory. Returning to New York in 1886, he remarried and served on the Civil Service Commission, as head (1895–97) of the New York City police board, and as assistant secretary (1897–98) of the navy. In 1898 he formed, with Leonard WOOD, the ROUGH RIDERS regiment that fought in Cuba during the SPANISH-AMERICAN WAR; he came home a hero. He was elected (1900) vice president under William MCKINLEY, and upon McKinley's assassination in Sept. 1901 became president at the age of 42. An activist and an innovative leader, he set about 'trust busting' by initiating some 40 lawsuits against the big trusts (see ANTITRUST LAWS). He also fathered important conservation legislation. His energy and showmanship captured the people's imagination, and he was reelected (1904) by a landslide. His second administration secured passage of the Pure Food and Drug Act of 1906, following exposés by journalists of malpractices in the food industry. His progressive reforms (see PROGRESSIVISM) aimed at regulation, not abolition, of big business. Roosevelt decisively increased the power of the president, particularly in foreign affairs. Claiming that the US had the right to impose order in Latin America, he intervened (1903) in a civil war in Panama to foster construction of the PANAMA CANAL. He mediated (1904) the end of the RUSSO-JAPANESE WAR, for which he won the 1906 Nobel Peace Prize. Although he had hand-picked William Howard TAFT to succeed him, he became angry at Taft's apparent lack of progressive principles and split the Republican party in 1912 by running for president as the third-party PROGRESSIVE, or Bull Moose, candidate. He polled more votes than Taft but lost the election. During his busy career he found time for big-game hunting and for writing history books.

**root,** in botany, the descending axis of a plant (as contrasted with the STEM), usually growing underground but also sometimes growing in air (see EPIPHYTE) and water. Roots serve to absorb and conduct water and dissolved minerals (see SAP); to anchor the plant; and, often, to store food.

Some plants have a main root (tap root) that is larger than the branching roots; others have many slender root branches. Roots grow primarily in length, with growth occurring at the tip, which is protected by a cap of cells (root cap) that break off and are replaced as the root probes through the soil. Root hairs, tiny cellular projections from the surface of the growing portion, absorb water and minerals from the soil. Root systems help prevent soil EROSION.

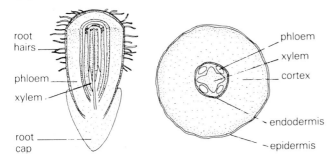

Sections through the tip of a **root**

**root,** in mathematics, the number $x$ for which an equation $f(x) = 0$ holds true, where $f$ is some FUNCTION. For example, $x = 3$ and $x = -4$ are the roots of the equation $x^2 + x - 12 = 0$. In the special case where $(fx) = x^n - a = 0$ for some number $a$, $x$ is called the $n$th root of $a$, denoted by $\sqrt[n]{a}$ or $a^{1/n}$. For example, 2 is the third, or cube, root of 8 ($\sqrt[3]{8} = 2$), because it satisfies the equation $x^3 - 8 = 0$.

**Root, Elihu,** 1845–1937, American public official. A successful corporation lawyer, he served (1899–1904) as US secretary of war and was responsible for the PLATT AMENDMENT, permitting US intervention in Cuba. As secretary of state (1905–9) under Theodore ROOSEVELT, he concluded (1908) an agreement with Japan to respect the *status quo* in the Pacific. He received the 1912 Nobel Peace Prize.

**rootstock:** see RHIZOME.

**Rorschach test:** see PROJECTIVE TEST.

**Rosa, Salvator,** 1615–73, Italian BAROQUE painter, etcher, and satiric poet of the Neapolitan school. Rosa worked in Florence and Rome. He is best known for his spirited battle pieces, his scenes of magic and witchcraft, for his marines, and especially for his tempestuous landscapes.

**Rosario,** city (1980 pop. 935,471), E central Argentina, on the Paraná R. It is a railway centre with fine port facilities and is an export centre for the central and northern provinces. Settled in the 17th cent., it grew after 1870 with the development of the PAMPA, which extends to the W.

**Rosas, Juan Manuel de,** 1793–1877, Argentine dictator, governor of Buenos Aires prov. (1829–32, 1835–52). He led his gaucho (cowboy) troops in support of the conservatives and federalism in 1820. He became governor of Buenos Aires (1829) and temporarily destroyed the unitarian cause. Returned to office in 1835, he assumed dictatorship over most of Argentina and instituted a regime of terror. In 1852, because of foreign difficulties and an economic crisis, a revolt led by URQUIZA and backed by Brazil and Uruguay succeeded, and Rosas fled to England, where he lived until his death.

**Roscommon,** inland county in W of Republic of Ireland (1986 pop. 54,551), 1779 km² (951 sq mi), bordering on Co. Galway in the SW. It is situated in the province of Connacht. The county town is ROSCOMMON. Much of the county is undulating or flat, but there are some hilly areas in the N. It is drained by the R. Suck, and the R. SHANNON forms much of the E boundary. Lough Ree is on the E boundary, and there are many other lakes, including Lough Key. Much of the county is devoted to pasture for sheep and cattle.

**Roscommon,** county town (1981 pop. 1673) of Co. Roscommon in Republic of Ireland. It is a small market town. Historic remains here include ruins of a 13th-cent. castle, and a Dominican priory.

**rose,** common name for some members of the family Rosaceae, herbs, shrubs, and trees distributed over most of the earth. Roses are often thorny, and many typically have a fleshy fruit, such as a rose hip or an apple. The largest genera are *Rubus,* including the blackberry, raspberry, loganberry, and other BRAMBLES; *Rosa,* the true roses; and *Prunus,* including the ALMOND, APRICOT, CHERRY, NECTARINE, PEACH, and PLUM. Other members of the family, also of economic importance, are the APPLE, PEAR, QUINCE, and STRAWBERRY. The true roses, the most popular ornamentals of the family, are esteemed as cultivated plants and as cut flowers for their often fragrant, showy blossoms. Attar of rose, a PERFUME oil, is obtained from the damask rose, and the rose hips of *R. rugosa* are a source of VITAMIN C. Favourite flowers in many lands since prehistoric times, roses have been used medicinally and eaten in preserves and salads.

**Roseau,** town and seaport (1978 est. pop. 20,000), capital of DOMINICA.

**rose hip:** see ROSE.

**rosemary,** evergreen, shrubby perennial herb (*Rosmarinus officinalis*) of the MINT family, native to the Mediterranean region. It has small blue flowers and aromatic leaves; the latter are used for seasoning. An extract of the flowers is used in perfumes and medicines.

**Rosenberg, Alfred,** 1893–1946, German NAZI leader. His book *The Myth of the 20th Century* (1930) supplied HITLER with the spurious philosophical and scientific basis for the Nazi racist doctrines. As minister for the occupied East European countries after 1941, he was responsible for the Nazi atrocities there. He was hanged as a war criminal.

**Rosenberg, Isaac,** 1890–1918, English poet who was killed in World War I. He joined the army as a private in 1916, and is noted for his starkly realistic war poems, written from the trenches and published posthumously in 1922.

**Rosenberg Case,** in US history, an espionage case in which Julius Rosenberg (1918–53), an electrical engineer who had worked for the army signal corps, and his wife, Ethel (1916–53), were found guilty of transmitting top-secret data on nuclear weapons to the USSR. Despite many appeals for clemency, the Rosenbergs were executed on 19 July 1953. The case aroused great controversy; many claimed that the COLD WAR political climate made a fair trial impossible and that the evidence against the Rosenbergs came from a confessed spy; others questioned the value of the material they had allegedly passed to the USSR and argued that the death penalty was too severe.

**rose of Sharon,** name for several plants, especially *Hypericum calycinum,* which does not belong to the rose family.

**Roses, Wars of the,** name given later to the struggle (1455–85) for the throne of England between the houses of LANCASTER (whose badge was a red rose) and YORK (whose badge was a white rose). In the mid-15th cent. the weak Lancastrian king HENRY VI was controlled by a faction including William de la Pole, duke of Suffolk, Edward Beaufort, duke of Somerset, and MARGARET OF ANJOU, Henry's queen. They were opposed by Richard, duke of York, who gained support from the popular unrest caused by the reverses of the HUNDRED YEARS WAR and by the corruption at court. York was appointed protector during the king's insanity (1453–54), but was excluded from the royal council when the king recovered. He then resorted to arms. The factions met at St Albans (1455), the Yorkists won, and York again became protector (1455–56). The wars, however, continued. In 1460 the Yorkists captured the king at Northampton and struck a compromise whereby Henry remained king and York was named his successor. Queen Margaret, whose son was thus disinherited, raised an army and defeated the Yorkists at Wakefield in 1460. Here York was killed, and his son Edward then assumed his claim. Margaret's army rescued the king at the second battle of St Albans (1461), but Edward meanwhile was victorious at Mortimer's Cross and assumed the throne as EDWARD IV. Henry was recaptured (1465) and the Yorkists seemed to be in command. A quarrel then developed over the king's marriage, and Richard Neville, earl of Warwick, and the king's brother George, duke of Clarence, deserted Edward. They allied (1470) with Queen Margaret, drove Edward into exile, and restored Henry VI. Edward soon returned and triumphed at Barnet and Tewkesbury in 1471. Margaret was imprisoned and Henry VI died, probably slain on Edward's orders. After 12 years of peace, Edward was succeeded (1483) by his 12-year-old son EDWARD V, but the boy's uncle Richard, duke of Gloucester, usurped the throne as RICHARD III. Opposition to Richard advanced the fortunes of Henry Tudor, now the Lancastrian claimant, and he defeated and killed Richard at Bosworth Field in 1485. Henry seized the throne as HENRY VII, and his marriage to Edward IV's daughter Elizabeth united the houses of Lancaster and York. It is generally said that the wars ended the era of feudalism in England, because the nobles who participated in them suffered a great loss of life and property, and were, as a class, unable to contest the strong Tudor monarchy.

**Rosetta Stone,** basalt slab inscribed by priests of PTOLEMY V in hieroglyphic, demotic, and Greek. Found (1799) by troops of NAPOLEON I near the city of Rosetta, N Egypt, it is now in the British Museum. The stone provided J.F. CHAMPOLLION and other scholars with the key to translating Egyptian hieroglyphic.

The Rosetta Stone

**rose window,** large, stone-traceried, circular window of medieval churches. It developed from the Romanesque wheel window. In the Gothic-style CATHEDRAL it appears over the west front or on a transept end. Early examples, e.g., at CHARTRES, were filled with plate tracery. The typical rose, as at Rheims, was filled with radiating and intermediate bars. In the final, flamboyant period, wavy curves and more intricate patterns suggest an open rose.

Rose window

**Rosh Hashanah:** see under JEWISH HOLIDAYS.

**Rosh Hodesh,** new moon. In Temple times this was observed as a semi-holyday, with feasting and special public sacrifices. In the synagogue it is marked by a special liturgy and Torah reading, but is, nowadays, in every other respect, a normal working day.

**Rosicrucianism,** philosophical movement of the 17th cent. based on the writings of Christian Rosenkreutz, allegedly a 15th-cent. German writer but probably fictional. Rosicrucians pursued spiritual enlightenment via scientific or alchemic investigations; one of the leading members in England was Francis BACON. There are still adherents today, more interested in mysticism than science.

**Ross, Sir James Clark,** 1800–62, British explorer and naval officer. He studied Eskimo life on several voyages. On an expedition with his uncle, John ROSS, he located the north magnetic pole. Studying earth magnetism in Antarctica (1839–43), he discovered Ross Sea and followed the Ross ice shelf for hundreds of miles. He also found Victoria Land and much of Graham Land.

**Ross, Sir John** (1777–1856), Scottish explorer. Searching (1818) for the NORTHWEST PASSAGE, he explored BAFFIN BAY. In 1829–33 he discovered the Gulf of Boothia (named for his patron, Sir Felix Booth) and King William Island. He wrote two books about his search for the Northwest Passage.

**Ross, Sir Ronald,** 1857–1932, English physician; b. India. He undertook research into malaria while in India and was awarded the 1902 Nobel Prize for physiology or medicine for his work on malaria and its transmission via the mosquito.

**Rosse, William Parsons,** 3rd **earl of,** 1800–67, British astronomer and maker of telescopes. Overcoming numerous casting problems, he constructed large specula for reflecting telescopes, including one that was 1.8 m (6 ft) in diameter, the largest up to that time. With this telescope, located at the family seat (Birr Castle, Ireland), he made (1848–78) numerous observations of nebulae, resolving many of them into stars and detecting for the first time the spiral nature of some of them.

**Rossellini, Roberto,** 1906–77, Italian film director. His *Open City* (1945), and *Paisan* (1946) were key neorealist films; his other works include *General Della Rovere* (1959), *The Rise of Louis XIV* (1966), and *Socrates* (1970).

**Rossetti, Christina Georgina,** 1830–94, English poet, sister of Dante Gabriel ROSSETTI. A devout Anglican, she wrote prayers and religious and allegorical poetry and love lyrics, her major works being *Goblin Market* (1862) and *The Prince's Progress* (1866). Her best-known lyrics include 'Uphill' and 'My heart is like a singing bird'.

**Rossetti, Dante Gabriel,** 1828–82, English poet and artist. In 1848, with the painters W. Holman Hunt and John Everett MILLAIS, he founded the brotherhood of PRE-RAPHAELITES. John RUSKIN championed the group and bought many of Rossetti's paintings. Rossetti's poetry, like his paintings, is noted for its pictorial effects and atmosphere of luxurious beauty. His early poem 'The Blessed Damozel' and the sonnet sequence 'The House of Life' are his finest works. The first edition of his collected poems appeared in 1870.

**Rossini, Gioacchino Antonio,** 1792–1868, Italian composer. Of his many lively operas, *The Barber of Seville* (1816) is his comic masterpiece. After composing the opera *William Tell* (1829), he retired on his fortune and wrote only songs, piano pieces, and the *Stabat Mater* (1842).

**Rosso, Il,** 1495–1540, Italian painter. A founder of MANNERISM, he was known for his distorted treatment of space, e.g., *Daughters of Jethro* (c.1523; Uffizi, Florence). As court painter to FRANCIS I of France, he worked on the palace at Fontainebleau.

**Ross Sea,** part of the Southern Ocean S of the Pacific Ocean between Victoria Land and Marie Byrd Land in ANTARCTICA, discovered in 1841 by Sir James Clark ROSS. Its southern extension is the Ross Ice Shelf, a great frozen area which is the source of huge tabular ICEBERGS. McMurdo Sound, on its W side, has been one of the most important staging points for exploration and scientific investigation of Antarctica.

**Rostand, Edmond** (ros,tahnh), 1868–1918, French poet and dramatist. He is best known for *Cyrano de Bergerac* (1897), a tour de force of dramatic poetry. Other plays include *L'Aiglon* (1900) and the barnyard fable *Chantecler* (1910).

**Rostock** or **Rostock-Warnemünde**, city (1984 pop. 241,910) N East Germany, on the Baltic Sea, capital of Rostock district. It is an industrial centre and major seaport. Manufactures include ships, machinery, and chemicals. Chartered in the 13th cent., Rostock became a leading member of the HANSEATIC LEAGUE. It was heavily damaged in WORLD WAR II.

**Rostov-na-Donu** or **Rostov-on-Don** (roștov), city (1985 pop. 986,000), S European USSR, on the Don R., 45 km (28 mi) from the Sea of Azov. It is an important route centre and port. Industries include engineering, aircraft and shipbuilding, construction of electromechanical equipment, footwear manufacturing, and tobacco and fish processing. It is a collection and assembly point for market-gardening produce from the surrounding rich agricultural region of the Kuban, and for goods from the Caucasus, the Donets coalfield, and, since the opening of the Volga–Don Canal in 1952, from the Volga Basin. The port, although closed by ice three months a year, exports wheat, petroleum, and manufactured goods. Rostov was founded in the 18th cent. as a frontier fortress against the Turks.

**Rostovtzeff, Michael Ivanovich** (roștovtsev), 1870–1952, American historian; b. Ukraine. At Yale he taught ancient history (1925–44) and was director of archaeological studies (1939–44). His *Social and Economic History of the Roman Empire* (1926) applied recent archaeological findings to a neglected aspect of Roman history.

**Rostropovitch, Mstislav Leopoldovich**, 1927–, Soviet cellist, pianist, and conductor. He made his cello debut in 1940, toured with the Moscow Philharmonic, and taught at the Moscow Conservatory until the early 1970s. He has won numerous prizes and honours in the USSR and the UK. Amongst many works written for him are Benjamin BRITTEN's Cello Sonata (1961), Cello Symphony (1963), and three unaccompanied Suites (1964, 1967, and 1971).

**rotation of crops**, agricultural practice of varying crops on a field to save or increase the soil's mineral or organic content, to maintain crop yields, and to control pests and disease. In a rotation, cultivated crops (e.g., cereals) are often alternated with LEGUMES (e.g., CLOVER), which add nitrogen to the soil. See also ORGANIC FARMING.

**Roth, Philip**, 1933–, American novelist. His witty, ironic fiction, dealing chiefly with middle-class Jewish life, includes his comic masterpiece, *Portnoy's Complaint* (1969), as well as the more sober novels *My Life as a Man* (1974) and *Zuckerman Unbound* (1981). The short stories in *Good-bye Columbus* (1959) gained Roth his initial recognition.

**Rotherham**, town (1981 pop. 122,374), S Yorkshire, N Midlands of England, at confluence of rivers Rother and Don, 10 km (6 mi) NE of Sheffield. An industrial town, it is famous for coal-mining, iron and steel, and the manufacture of glass. There is a 15th-cent. church and ancient grammar school within the town.

**Rothermere, Harold Sidney Harmsworth, 1st Viscount**, 1868–1940, English publisher. He was the financial wizard of the publishing firm headed by his brother Alfred, Viscount NORTHCLIFFE, and headed the vast newspaper empire after his brother's death.

**Rothko, Mark**, 1903–70, American painter; b. Russia; emigrated to the US in 1913. He was a leading exponent of ABSTRACT EXPRESSIONISM, and his mature works are often huge canvases with floating rectangles of luminous colour. A characteristic example is *No. 10* (1950; Mus. Mod. Art, New York City).

**Rothschild**, prominent family of European bankers. **Mayer Amschel Rothschild**, 1743–1812, son of a money-changer in the Jewish ghetto in Frankfurt, laid the foundations of the family fortune as the financial agent for the landgrave of Hesse-Kassel. Of his five sons, the oldest continued the business in Frankfurt, while the other four established branches in Vienna, London, Naples, and Paris. All five were created barons (1822) by Francis I of Austria, a title that continues in the family. The ablest of the brothers was **Nathan Meyer Rothschild**, 1777–1836, who opened the London branch in 1805. As an agent of the British government in the Napoleonic Wars, he was instrumental in the ultimate defeat of NAPOLEON I. Under his guidance and that of his son, **Baron Lionel Nathan de Rothschild**, 1808–79, the family gained immense power by floating large international loans (e.g., the Irish famine loan, 1847; the Crimean War loan, 1856), but its virtual monopoly was broken as state financing improved. Lionel became (1858) the first Jewish member of Parliament,

and many members of the family were prominent philanthropists, patrons of the arts, sportsmen, writers, or physicians.

**rotifer**, microscopic aquatic or semiterrestrial ROUNDWORM. As a rule, only female rotifers are seen; in some species the male has never been observed. Males are usually much smaller than females. Eggs usually develop parthenogenetically, i.e., without fertilization, to produce only females. Some of the eggs that are fertilized produce thick walls and can survive adverse conditions.

**rotor:** see GENERATOR; MOTOR, ELECTRIC.

**Rotterdam**, city (1985 pop. 571,081, agglomeration, 1,021,141), W Netherlands, on the Nieuwe Maas R. near the North Sea. One of the world's largest, most modern ports, it has a huge transit trade and such industries as shipyards, oil refineries, and vehicle assembly plants. The city was chartered in 1328. It grew rapidly after construction (1866–90) of the New Waterway gave ocean vessels access to the port. During World War II the city's centre was destroyed by German bombs.

**Rouault, Georges** (rooh-̦oh), 1871–1958, French artist. After a psychological crisis in 1898 he started to paint gloomy pictures of outcasts and later judges, depicting the degradation of humanity. Although associated with the circle of MATISSE he was not influenced by FAUVISM. From c.1940 he devoted himself to religious painting.

**Rouen**, city (1982 pop. 105,083, agglomeration 379,879), capital of Seine-Maritime dept., N France. Until recent years it was the lowest bridging point on the SEINE R. and the place where sea and river navigation met. To an early woollen industry based on the flocks of the surrounding chalk plateaux was added the manufacture of cotton textiles in the 18th cent. Docks were built from the late 19th cent. to handle coal, timber, and other imports. Modern industries include chemicals, paper-making (especially newsprint), and engineering. A Roman town, it became the seat of the dukes of Normandy. During the HUNDRED YEARS' WAR it was held by the English from 1419 and JOAN OF ARC was burnt to death in Rouen by the English on 30 May 1431. French control was regained in 1449. Its fine Gothic churches include the 13th–15th-cent. cathedral of Notre Dame.

**Rough Riders**, popular name for the 1st Regiment of US Cavalry Volunteers in the SPANISH–AMERICAN WAR (1898), organized largely by Theodore ROOSEVELT. Commanded by Leonard WOOD, it fought chiefly in Cuba, and its exploits were highly publicized.

**Roundheads**, derisive name for the supporters of Parliament in the ENGLISH CIVIL WAR (1642–48). The name referred to the short haircuts worn by some Puritans in contrast to the wigs worn by the king's supporters, called Cavaliers.

**roundworm**, wormlike invertebrate of the phylum Aschelminthes, having a noncellular coat, or cuticle, and a fluid-filled cavity (pseudocoelom) separating the body wall from the gut. Roundworms are widely distributed in aquatic and terrestrial habitats. The phylum includes ROTIFERS, NEMATODES, and horsehair worms.

**Rourkela Steel Township**, town (1981 pop. 214,521), Orissa state, E India, on the Sankh R. Situated in Sundargarh dist., this town was created, as its name implies, entirely to house workers and services associated with one of independent India's integrated steel-works.

**Rous, Francis Peyton**, 1879–1970, American pathologist. Working at the Rockefeller Inst., he demonstrated the viral nature of some cancers, work for which he was awarded the 1966 Nobel Prize for physiology or medicine.

**Rousseau, Henri** (rooh̦soh), 1844–1910, French naive painter. Self-taught, he is best known for his fantastic jungle landscapes, e.g., *The Snake Charmer* (1907; Musée d'Orsay, Paris), and his haunting *Sleeping Gypsy* (1897; Mus. Mod. Art, New York City).

**Rousseau, Jean Jacques**, 1712–78, French philosopher and political theorist; b. Switzerland. A member of DIDEROT's circle, he was one of the great figures of the ENLIGHTENMENT, influencing ROMANTICISM, through such figures as GOETHE; the ideas of the FRENCH REVOLUTION, notably in his impact on ROBESPIERRE; 19th-cent. idealist philosophy, via KANT and HEGEL; and literature, through TOLSTOY and others. Rousseau is widely known as a defender of the 'natural man'. In his *Discourse on Inequality* (1754) and his *Social Contract* (1762), he argued that human beings were essentially equal and without malice in the state of nature, but were corrupted by the introduction of science, commerce, and property. People had entered into a deceptive SOCIAL CONTRACT which reinforced the inequalities introduced by civilization. Freedom could only be achieved in society if the contract was reformed by all citizens, brought together as equal members of a sovereign body (implying a form of direct DEMOCRACY). The didactic novel *Émile* (1762), expounded Rousseau's theory that education should not be the imposition of knowledge, but the progressive growth of ideas, reason, and conscience through relations with things and people. The publication of *La Nouvelle Héloïse* (1761) was received with more enthusiasm than any other novel published in the 18th cent. The increasing intellectual and personal isolation of his later years produced a number of writings that founded a new, self-exploratory style of autobiography, e.g., *Confessions* (1781).

Henri **Rousseau**, *Tiger in a Storm*, 1889. Oil on canvas, 129.8 × 162 cm. National Gallery, London.

**Rousseau, Théodore**, 1812–67, French landscape painter, leader of the BARBIZON SCHOOL. His landscapes are grave and full of a deep love of solitude.

**Roussel, Albert** (rooh sel), 1869–1937, French composer. His early works are influenced by IMPRESSIONISM and 18th-cent. music; he later experimented with Asian techniques. His late works, e.g., his Second Symphony (1919–21), feature subtle melodic inflections and sharp dissonances.

**Rowbotham, Sheila**, 1943–, English feminist historian and writer. The ideas in her pamphlet 'Women's liberation and the new politics' (1969) profoundly influenced the emerging WOMEN'S MOVEMENT in Britain, and she pioneered researches into women's history. Among her books are *Women, Resistance and Revolution* (1972), *Hidden from History* (1973), and *Woman's Consciousness, Man's World* (1973).

**Rowe, Nicholas**, 1674–1718, English dramatist. His best plays, *The Fair Penitent* (1703) and *Jane Shore* (1714), stories of men's cruelty to women, prefigure later 18th-cent. domestic tragedies. His edition of SHAKESPEARE (1709) was the first to divide the plays into acts and scenes.

**rowing**, art of propelling a boat by means of oars operated by hand. In racing, each member of the rowing team (crew) uses both hands to pull one oar through the water. The boat (shell) is sometimes steered by a coxswain (or cox), who also directs the speed and rhythm of the crew's strokes. Sculling is a variant of rowing in which each oarsman controls two oars, one in each hand. Rowing crews have two, four, or eight members, with or without a cox; sculling teams consist of one, two, or four members. The most famous rowing event is the annual Oxford and Cambridge BOAT RACE.

**Rowlandson, Thomas**, 1756–1827, English caricaturist. As a humorous and critical commentator on the social scene, he quickly gained celebrity for his drawings such as *Vauxhall Gardens* (1784), and his famous *Tour of Dr. Syntax* with text by William Combe.

**Rowntree, B.S.**, 1871–1954, English empirical sociologist. He made three social surveys of poverty in the city of York and introduced the idea of the 'poverty line'.

**Roxas, Manuel**, 1894–1948, Philippine statesman. In WORLD WAR II he joined the Japanese puppet government, but secretly aided the Philippine underground. In 1946 he became the first president of the Republic of the PHILIPPINES.

**Roy, Rammohun**, 1772–1833, Indian religious and educational reformer. To rejuvenate Hinduism he sought to rid it of idolatry, discrimination against women, and the CASTE system. He founded secondary schools based on the English method and began several newspapers.

**Royal Aeronautical Society**, oldest aeronautical organization in the world, founded in 1866 in London. The Society's progressive outlook is well exemplified by the fact that at its first public meeting a lecture was given on the possibility of JET PROPULSION for aircraft. Now organized with branches in the Commonwealth, the Society is one of the UK's 15 Chartered Engineering Institutions, and some 60% of its 14,000 members are Chartered Engineers.

**Royal Air Force**, world's first autonomous military air service. It was formed in 1918 by amalgamation of the Royal Flying Corps and the Royal Naval Air Service as recommended by (then Lt-Gen.) J.C. SMUTS. By the end of World War I the RAF was the greatest air service in the world, with 290,000 men and 25,000 women, flying some 22,000 aircraft, of which 2630 were operational. In the inter-war years RAF strength declined, so that by 1934 there were only 815 operational aircraft. Expansion became urgent under the threat of WORLD WAR II, in which the RAF played a crucial role (see BATTLE OF BRITAIN: HARRIS, SIR ARTHUR). By the end of the war, the RAF had 55,000 aircraft, 9200 of them operational, and nearly 1.2 million men and women. In the 1950s almost all the piston-engined aircraft were replaced with jets, and the strategic V-bombers (Valiant, Victor, and Vulcan) were introduced. In 1968 Bomber and Fighter Commands were merged into a new Strike Command, later incorporating also Air Support Command to provide transport and other support services. In the 1980s the RAF had some 1400 aircraft, including such advanced types as the VTOL Harrier and the multi-role Tornado, and 93,000 personnel.

**Royal Albert Hall:** see ALBERT MEMORIAL.

**Royal Canadian Mounted Police**, constabulary first organized in 1873 as the Northwest Mounted Police to bring law and order to the Canadian west and to prevent Indian disorders. The present name was adopted in 1920. The corps' daring exploits in pursuit of criminals earned it a romantic reputation and the popular name 'Mounties'. It now numbers more than 19,000 and includes the police forces of all provinces except Ontario and Quebec.

**Royal Commission**, a group of eminent persons appointed by Royal Warrant to inquire into a specific area and recommend legal changes. First developed in the 19th cent., there have been over 100 Royal Commissions since then, covering a wide variety of topics. One of the first Royal Commissions was on the Poor Laws (1832-34), and the great Reform Acts of 1832 and 1867 both resulted from Royal Commission reports. They are set up on a purely ad hoc basis, and usually consist of retired judges and politicians, lawyers, and experts in the subject area. The government is under no obligation to enact their recommendations. Since World War II, they have been rarely employed.

**Royal Festival Hall**, built (1949–51) for the Festival of Britain in 1951 and designed by the Architects Dept of the London County Council headed by R.H. Matthew and J.L. Martin. It seats 3000 people attending orchestral and choral concerts. The first complete exercise in MODERN ARCHITECTURE for public buildings in the UK, it was also the first building to apply acoustical science systematically in the design, with results very close to those intended. To exclude exterior noise (a serious problem, as a busy railway runs alongside) it was planned as a box within a box, the areas for public movement and social meetings forming a magnificent sequence of flowing spaces. The building's exterior is clad in Portland stone. See also SOUTH BANK.

**Royal Institution**, one of the first scientific research centres in Britain, more properly known as the Royal Institution of Great Britain. Founded (1799) by Count RUMFORD in Albemarle Street, London, it contains a small research laboratory, and is an important centre for lectures to the general public and to schoolchildren. Former Directors include Michael FARADAY, John TYNDALL, Sir James DEWAR, Baron RAYLEIGH, and Sir William BRAGG.

**Royal National Lifeboat Institution,** body responsible for the LIFEBOAT service in Britain. It was founded by Sir William Hilary in 1824 as a volunteer force, relying on public support for its funding.

**Royal Opera House, Covent Garden,** Britain's most famous opera house, situated in Bow Street, London, the first threatre was built in 1732 and used mainly for plays, though Handel's operas *Ariodante* and *Alcina*, and his oratorio *Athalia* were performed there in 1735. This was destroyed by fire in 1808. A second theatre, opened in 1809, became the Royal Italian Opera (1847–92); during this period, the theatre was burnt down (1856) and the present building was opened in 1858. Between 1924 and 1939 the principal opera conductors were Bruno WALTER and Thomas BEECHAM. In 1946, it reopened with its own resident ballet and opera companies, which were renamed the Royal Ballet (1957) and the Royal Opera (1969). Musical directors since 1946 have include Georg SOLTI (1961–71) and Colin DAVIS (1971–86).

**Royal Shakespeare Company,** British repertory theatre with two companies, at Stratford and at the Aldwych Theatre, London; est. 1960. The mainstay of the repertory is the works of Shakespeare, but the company also presents classics and recent plays (e.g., by Tom STOPPARD).

**Royal Society** the oldest scientific society in Great Britain, more properly known as the Royal Society of London for Improving Natural Knowledge. Founded in 1660 and granted a royal charter in 1662, the Society elects annually a number of fellows, who carry the prestigious title 'Fellow of the Royal Society' (FRS); there are about 800 of them. It publishes the *Proceedings* and *Transactions*, and reports on various matters, and its officers are frequently called upon to advise the British government on science policy.

**Royal Society for the Prevention of Cruelty to Animals,** first animal welfare society in the world. Established in 1824 as a plain 'Society', the word 'Royal' was added at Queen Victoria's request in 1840. It set an example for the formation of similar societies which now exist in many countries. It has the responsibility, in cooperation with the police, for the enforcement of the statutory provisions relating to cruelty to animals. It reports to HM Government on matters relating to animal welfare, e.g., farm animal production, wildlife and countryside matters, hunting and shooting, the export of live animals, zoo licensing, and performing animals. It maintains veterinary clinics and stray-animal homes, and operates through a system involving both salaried staff, including over 400 trained inspectors, and volunteers. Education is an important aspect of its activities, through lectures and a schools educational service, and it has established its own training college for animal inspectors. During the 1980s its income has been of the order of £10m each year, but it is frequently forced to operate with a financial deficit. No support is received from the state, all income being derived from legacies (the major contribution), donations, and membership subscriptions. It is not responsible for official licensing, e.g., animal experimentation, which is strictly inspected and licensed by the Home Office.

**royalties:** see COPYRIGHT.

**Royce, Sir (Frederick) Henry,** 1863–1933, British designer and engineer. He began his career as a pioneer of electric street lighting; at the age of 19 he was chief engineer for the lighting of the streets of Liverpool. In 1884 he started his own firm of electrical and mechanical engineers, where he designed and built his first cars (1904). In 1906 he went into partnership with C.S. ROLLS; Royce designed the cars and Rolls sold them. In World War I Royce turned his attention to aero-engines, which built up the same reputation for reliability as the Rolls-Royce cars had. Royce continued to exercise personal control over all design matters at Rolls-Royce until the end of his life. He was created baronet in 1930.

**Royo Sánchez, Arístides,** 1940–, president of PANAMA (1978–82). A former minister of education, he was named president by Gen. Omar TORRIJOS HERRERA, the actual ruler of the country. After Torrijos's death (1981), Royo remained in office but encountered increasing opposition from the military, which apparently forced his resignation (1982).

**Rozvi:** see CHANGAMIRE.

**Ru,** chemical symbol of the element RUTHENIUM.

**Ruanda-Urundi,** former colonial territory in central Africa, now divided between the independent states of RWANDA and BURUNDI.

**Rub al Khali,** great sandy desert, 500,000 km² (190,000 sq mi), SE Arabia. Often called the 'Empty Quarter', it lies mostly in Saudi Arabia, but extends into Southern Yemen and the United Arab Emirates. It is extremely arid with only occasional rain showers and is virtually uninhabited, but oil is found on the eastern fringe.

**rubber,** any solid substance, usually elastic, that can be vulcanized to improve its elasticity and add strength; the term includes natural rubber, or caoutchouc, and a wide variety of synthetic rubbers, which have similar properties. Rubbers are composed chiefly of CARBON and HYDROGEN, but some synthetics also have other elements, e.g., chlorine, fluorine, nitrogen, or silicon. All are compounds of high molecular weight; each consists of a series of one kind of molecule (e.g., isoprene in natural rubber) hooked together in a long chain to form a very flexible, larger molecule, the POLYMER. Natural rubber is obtained as latex, a milky suspension of rubber globules found in a large variety of plants, chiefly tropical and subtropical. An important source is the PARÁ RUBBER TREE. Latex can be shipped for processing either as a liquid or coagulated by acid and rolled into sheets. For most purposes rubber is ground, dissolved in a solvent, and compounded with other ingredients, e.g., filler, PIGMENT, and plasticizer. Known by pre-Columbian Indians of South and Central America, rubber first attracted interest in Europe in the 18th cent. Vulcanization, a process invented (1839) by Charles GOODYEAR, revolutionized the rubber industry. It usually involves heating raw or compounded rubber with SULPHUR, causing sulphur bridges to form between molecules. The product is nonsticky, elastic, and resistant to heat and cold. Natural rubber is used chiefly to make tyres and inner tubes because it is cheaper than synthetic rubber and has greater resistance to tearing when hot. Natural rubber can be treated to make foam rubber and sponge rubber. The first synthetic rubber was made in Germany in World War I. Today, synthetics, e.g., Buna S, neoprene, butyl, and nitrile, account for most of the world's rubber production. Made from COAL, PETROLEUM, NATURAL GAS, and ACETYLENE, synthetic rubbers are resilient over a wider temperature range than natural rubber and are more resistant to aging, weathering, and attack by certain substances, notably, oil, solvents, oxygen, and ozone. SILICONE rubbers are used in insulation. POLYURETHANES are used in tyres, in shoes, and as foams. Neoprene is used for making hose and tank linings. Butyl rubber is used in inner tubes and as insulation.

**rubber plant,** name for several plants, e.g., PARÁ RUBBER TREE and Castilla tree, which are sources of the milky fluid, called latex, used to make RUBBER. The India-rubber tree (*Ficus elastica*), a common houseplant, is an Asiatic FIG.

**Rubbra, Edmund,** 1901–86, British composer and teacher, whose lyrical and richly polyphonic compositions were influenced by 16th- and 17th-cent. English composers. Amongst his compositions are church music, concertos, chamber music, and eleven symphonies.

**rubella** or **German measles,** acute, highly infectious viral disease of children and young adults, causing a rash and fever. It is mild and uncomplicated unless contracted during the first three months of pregnancy, when it can cause serious damage to the fetus (see CONGENITAL ABNORMALITIES). Natural immunity is conferred by infection. VACCINATION against rubella is advised for young women who have not had the disease. Rubella during the first months of pregnancy is an indication for abortion.

**Rubens, Peter Paul,** 1577–1640, foremost Flemish painter of the 17th cent.; b. Westphalia. He was in Italy (1600–08), and served as court painter to the duke of Mantua, who sent him on a mission to Spain where he painted the magnificent equestrian portrait of the duke of Lerma (Prado, Madrid). In 1608 he returned to Antwerp, where within five years he became known as the greatest painter of his country. He organized an enormous workshop of skilled apprentices and associates, among them VAN DYCK and JORDAENS. *Raising of the Cross* and *Descent from the Cross* (1610–11 and 1611–14; cathedral, Antwerp) date from this period. He also executed a series of large allegorical paintings of the life of Marie de' Medici (Louvre, Paris). His associates did much of the work on them, but Rubens designed them and added the finishing touches. In this way, his workshop produced numerous monumental works. In 1626 Rubens entered the diplomatic service. In Spain on a diplomatic mission (1628), he became acquainted with Velázquez, and painted the royal family. While in England, he painted *Allegory of Peace and War*

(1629–30; National Gall., London), and was knighted for his peacemaking efforts. During the last 10 years of his life, he did his most joyous and radiant pictures. *The Judgement of Paris* and *Three Graces* (both: 1639; Prado, Madrid) and *Venus and Adonis* (c.1635; Metropolitan Mus., New York) belong to this period. The volume of Rubens's work is enormous; more than 2000 paintings have been attributed to his studio, and each shows the mark of his genius. The influence of the Italians is clear in his monumental compositions, but his colour, technique, and lusty spirit are Flemish. His art unites a pagan joy of life with a passionate Catholicism. He explored all fields of painting, and some of his small works, e.g., *Peasant Dance* (Prado, Madrid) are among his masterpieces.

Peter **Rubens**, *Descent from the Cross*, 1611–14. Antwerp Cathedral.

**rubeola:** see MEASLES.

**Rubicon,** stream that in the days of early Rome divided GAUL from Italy. In 49 BC Julius CAESAR led his army across it, defying the Roman senate and commencing civil war. He reportedly said, 'The die is cast'. Thus, to cross the Rubicon is to take an irrevocable step.

**rubidium** (Rb), metallic element, discovered spectroscopically by Robert BUNSEN and Gustav KIRCHHOFF in 1861. A very soft, silver-white ALKALI METAL, it is extremely reactive, and must be kept out of contact with air and water. It has few commercial uses. See ELEMENT (table); PERIODIC TABLE.

**Rubinstein, Anton Grigoryevich,** 1829–94, Russian virtuoso pianist, composer, and educator. He founded the St Petersburg Conservatory in 1862 and was its director. His brother, **Nikolay Grigoryevich Rubinstein,** 1835–81, also a pianist and teacher, founded (1864) and headed the Moscow Conservatory.

**Rubinstein, Arthur,** 1887–1982, American pianist; b. Poland. He is particularly known for his lyric interpretations of CHOPIN and for his championing of Spanish works.

**ruby,** GEM, transparent red variety of CORUNDUM, found chiefly in Burma, Thailand, and Sri Lanka. Star rubies (showing an internal star when cut with a rounded top) are rare. Synthetic rubies are produced by fusing pure aluminium oxide.

**Rudaki, Abu Abdullah Jafar,** d.940–1, Persian poet, singer, and musician. Acknowledged as the first great Persian poet, and ranked as the master of panegyric and of the ghazal (group of rhyming couplets). He was the author of the verse form of the *Kellila and Demna*, the well-known collection of Indian Bidpai fables, and *Book of Sinbad*, a story of the king's son and the seven vizirs, which had followed, like Bidpai, a course from Indian to middle Persian, thence to Arabic and Persian; unfortunately no more than a few verses of either epic written by Rudaki have survived. According to some accounts, Radaki was blind from birth.

**Rudd, Steele,** pseud. of **Arthur Hoey Davis,** 1868–1935, Australian jounalist and novelist. His book *On Our Selection* (1899) and its sequels was a popular series of comic episodes about the struggles of a poor rural family on a Queensland farm. There have been a number of stage and film versions.

**rudder,** in aviation: see AEROPLANE.

**Rudolf,** rulers of the HOLY ROMAN EMPIRE. **Rudolf I** or **Rudolf of Habsburg,** 1218–91, German king (1273–91), first ruler of the HABSBURG dynasty, was elected king after an interregnum of 20 years in which there was no accepted German king or emperor. His defeat of Ottocar II of Bohemia greatly added to the Habsburg lands. **Rudolf II,** 1552–1612, emperor (1576–1612), was mentally unbalanced and delegated imperial power to his brother Matthias. Rudolf's reign was turbulent and a prelude to the THIRTY YEARS' WAR.

**Rudolf,** 1858–89, Austrian archduke, only son of Emperor FRANCIS JOSEPH. Rudolf's mysterious death (officially ruled a double suicide with his mistress, Baroness Mary Vetsera), at Mayerling left his cousin, FRANCIS FERDINAND, heir to the Austro-Hungarian throne. The 'Mayerling tragedy' is the subject of novels, plays, and films.

**Rudolf of Habsburg** (Rudolf I): see under RUDOLF, rulers of the HOLY ROMAN EMPIRE.

**rue,** common name for various members of the family Rutaceae, mostly woody shrubs or small trees, often evergreen and spiny, of temperate and tropical regions. They are typified by glands that produce an essential oil widely utilized for flavourings, perfume oils, and drugs; the foliage, fruits, and flowers are noticeably fragrant. Chief in importance are the CITRUS FRUITS. Several species of the family yield timber used in cabinetmaking, e.g., the ORANGE and the species called satinwood. More specifically, the name *rue* refers to the shrubby herbs of the genus *Ruta,* found from the Mediterranean to E Siberia. The common rue (*R. graveolans*) has greenish-yellow flowers, blue-green leaves, and a strong odour. Its leaves are sometimes used in flavourings, beverages, and cosmetics.

**Rufinus,** d. 395, Roman statesman, minister to THEODOSIUS I and virtual ruler for ARCADIUS. He was assassinated by Gothic mercenaries, perhaps by order of STILICHO.

**Ruga-ruga,** name given to mercenary military units used by rulers in 19th-cent. E Africa, especially TANZANIA. They comprised war captives, runaway slaves, deserters, and other groups of young men who had lost their LINEAGE ties. They were the equivalent of the Nguni age-regiments of S Africa.

**Rugby,** town (1981 pop. 59,039), Warwickshire, central England. Rugby is known chiefly as the seat of one of the great English public schools, Rugby School (est. 1567). RUGBY football originated at the school in 1823.

**rugby league,** form of RUGBY UNION played professionally, mainly in the north of England and Australia. The games differ in four main ways: in rugby league, there are 13 players not 15; a ball that leaves play is reintroduced wih a scrum, not a lineout; a try is worth three points and a goal, however scored, two points; tackled players are released and allowed to stand and heel the ball backwards to a teammate, although a scrum is formed after a number of such tackles. The Northern Rugby Football Union was formed in 1895 and allowed payment to be made to players. The name 'rugby league' dates from 1922.

**rugby union,** game that originated (1823) on the playing fields of Rugby School. The amateur version is played by two teams of 15 players on a field about 144 m (160 yd) long and 69 m (75 yd) wide, with goal lines 100 m (110 yd) apart and two H-shaped goalposts. The ball may be kicked, carried, or passed (to the sides or rear); tackling is permitted.

Scoring is by carrying the ball over the goal line (a try) or by kicking it between the goal posts and over the crossbar. Rugby Union is played internationally by Australia, Fiji, France, England, Ireland, Wales, Scotland, and New Zealand. Professional rugby, known as RUGBY LEAGUE, is played under somewhat different rules. See also BARBARIANS and TRIPLE CROWN.

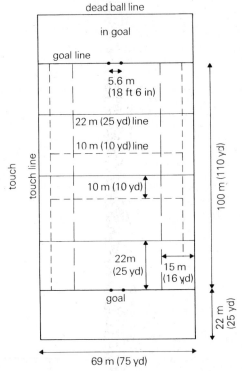

Rugby union pitch dimensions

**Ruhr** (rooə), major coal-mining and industrial region, NW West Germany, located along and N of the Ruhr R. and E of the Rhine R. Its concentration of industries, begun in the 19th cent. when the KRUPP and Thyssen concerns built large coal and steel empires, is the greatest in Germany. Among the principal cities are ESSEN, DUISBURG, Bottrop, GELSENKIRCHEN, BOCHUM, and DORTMUND.

**Ruisdael** or **Ruysdael, Jacob van** (,roysdahl), 1628/9–1682, Dutch painter and etcher, the most celebrated of the Dutch landscape painters. His work shows northern nature in a sombre mood. Overcast skies throw restless light on gnarled oak and beech trees. His later work emphasizes humanity's insignificance amid the splendour of nature. Important works include *Jewish Cemetery* (c.1660; Gemäldegalerie, Dresden) and *Windmill at Wijk* (c.1665; Rijksmuseum, Amsterdam). He also produced some very fine etchings. He influenced French and English landscapists for 200 years.

**Ruiz, Juan** (rooh,eeth), 1283?–1350?, Spanish poet and archpriest of Hita. For his *Libro de buen amor* (1330, 1343; tr. Book of Good Love), a satirical panorama of medieval society, he has been called the Spanish CHAUCER.

**rule of law**, the principle that all government and law enforcers shall operate according to and within the law, and adhere to the idea of fairness and natural justice. Of vital importance in western society, it implies limits on legislative and EXECUTIVE power and equal access to and equality before the law. In the UK, the principle was first outlined in the mid 19th cent. by A.V. DICEY, for whom the rule of law meant a limited government operating only in accordance with strict legal requirements; and trial only before the courts of the land. In the 20th cent., however, with the growth of the WELFARE STATE, the traditional concept of the rule of law has been questioned, as a result of the increasing number of citizen's rights depending on the exercise of discretion, not strict law (e.g., social security payments), and the growth of the TRIBUNAL system as an alternative to the courts. However, the rule of law is still important in helping to restrain the arbitrary power of government.

**Rulfo, Juan,** 1918–, Mexican novelist and short-story writer. His best-known work is *Pedro Páramo* (1955), an evocative novel about loneliness and obsession with the past.

**rum,** fermented, distilled, and aged alcoholic spirit made from the molasses and foam that rise to the top of boiled sugarcane juice. Naturally colourless, it becomes brown when caramel is added and the liquor is stored in casks. The best-known producer is Jamaica, but rum is also made in such places as Cuba, Brazil, Trinidad, Puerto Rico, and the US.

**Rumelia** or **Roumelia** (rooh,meeleeə), region of S Bulgaria, between the Balkan and Rhodope mountains. Historically, Rumelia denoted the Ottoman Empire's Balkan possessions (much of present-day Yugoslavia, Bulgaria, European Turkey, N Greece, and part of Albania). **Eastern Rumelia,** in present-day S Bulgaria, was created in 1878 (see BERLIN, CONGRESS OF) and was annexed by Bulgaria in 1885.

**Rumford, Benjamin Thompson, Count,** 1753–1814, British scientist and administrator; b. US. After leaving America (1776), he served as the British undersecretary of the colonies (1780–81). In contrast to the prevalent belief that HEAT was a substance, he stated that it was produced by the motion of particles. Rumford conducted valuable experiments with gunpowder, introduced improved methods of heating and cooking, and founded the ROYAL INSTITUTION in England.

**Rumi, Jalal ed-Din** or **Jalal ud-Din** (,roomee), 1207–73, Persian poet, one of the greatest Sufi poets. Rumi's lyrics express mystic thought in finely wrought symbols. His main work is *Mathnawi,* a poetic exposition of SUFISM in eight books.

**ruminant,** any of a group of even-toed mammals that chew their cud, i.e., regurgitate and rechew already swallowed food. Ruminants have three- or four-chambered stomachs. In the first chamber (the rumen), food is mixed with fluid to form a soft mass (the cud or bolus), which, after regurgitation and rechewing, passes through the rumen into the other stomach chambers for digestion. Goats, sheep, cows, camels, and antelope are ruminants.

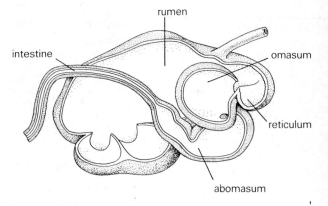

The four-chambered stomach of a ruminant

**rummy,** card game played by two to six players with a standard pack. Seven cards are dealt to each player; remaining cards are left in a stock pile. Drawing and discarding, a player's objective is to meld (put down three or four cards of the same rank or sequence in the same suit); the first player to meld all their cards wins. Variants are gin rummy and canasta.

**Rumor, Mariano,** 1915–, Italian politician. A Christian Democrat, he was premier (1968–69, 1969–70, 1973–74) and foreign minister (1974–76). He was mentioned (1976) in the Lockheed Corp. bribery scandal and narrowly avoided prosecution.

**Runcie, Robert Alexander Kennedy,** 1921–, archbishop of Canterbury (1980–). Bishop of St Albans since 1970, he was enthroned as the 102nd archbishop of Canterbury in 1980, succeeding Donald Coggan. Runcie was educated at Oxford and Cambridge. As a member (1939–45) of the Scots Guards during World War II he was a decorated tank commander. He developed links with the Eastern Orthodox Church, and in 1982 received Pope JOHN PAUL II in Canterbury Cathedral and with him published a joint declaration commending increased dialogue between their two communions. In 1983 he visited churches in China. At home he presided over critical debates on such issues as nuclear warfare, the doubts of bishops concerning articles of the creed, the deprivation of inner cities, and the ordination of women as priests.

**Runeberg, Johan Ludvig,** 1804–77, Finnish poet of the national-romantic school, writing in Swedish, who used hexameters for his epic poems. His major works are *The Elk Shooters* (1832), *King Fjalar* (1844), and his acknowledged masterpiece *The Tales of Ensign Stål* (I–II, 1848–60), about Finland's war of 1808–09. It begins with 'Our Land', which has become the Finnish national anthem.

**runes,** ancient characters used in Teutonic, Anglo-Saxon, and Scandinavian inscriptions, probably first used c.300 by the OSTROGOTHS, who may have derived them from Hellenic-Italian writing. Adapted to carving, they consisted of perpendicular, oblique, and a few curved lines. They were used extensively in N Europe, Iceland, and the British Isles before Christianity, persisting in Scandinavia into the Middle Ages.

Germanic runes

Nordic runes

Examples of runes

**Runnymede** or **Runnimede,** historic meadow, near Egham, Surrey, S England, on the south bank of the Thames R., W of London. Either on this meadow or on nearby Magna Carta Island, King JOHN accepted MAGNA CARTA (1215).

**Runyon, (Alfred) Damon,** 1884–1946, American writer and journalist. He is best known for his humorous stories, written in the slangy idiom of New York City's Broadway and underworld characters, e.g., *Guys and Dolls* (1931).

**Rupert, Prince,** 1619–82, count palatine of the Rhine; b. Prague. He was the son of FREDERICK THE WINTER KING and grandson of James I of England. He served the Dutch in the THIRTY YEARS' WAR and was an outstanding royalist general during the ENGLISH CIVIL WAR. After the English RESTORATION he was a privy councillor to Charles II and, as an admiral, played an important part in the Dutch Wars. He was one of the founders of the HUDSON'S BAY COMPANY.

**Rupert's Land,** Canadian territory held (1670–1870) by the HUDSON'S BAY COMPANY. The area, named for Prince RUPERT, the first governor of the company, comprised the drainage basin of HUDSON BAY. In 1869–70 the company transferred Rupert's Land to Canada for £300,000 but retained certain blocks of land for trading and other purposes.

**rural dean,** in the Church of England a priest who is appointed by the bishop to be chairman and representative of a section (known as the rural deanery) of his diocese. Since 1970 he also presides over a deanery synod which includes lay delegates as well as clergy.

**Rus':** see KIEVAN RUSSIA; RUSSIA; RUTHENIA.

**Ruse,** city (1983 pop. 181,185), NE Bulgaria, on the DANUBE R. It is a river port and a major route centre for international traffic. Industries include oil-refining and machine-making. Notable buildings include mosques and the ruins of its medieval castle.

**rush,** any plant of the family Juncaceae; more loosely, a tall, grasslike, often hollow-stemmed plant of various families. The common, or soft rush (*Juncus effusus*) and the hard rush (*J. inflexus*) are widely distributed in swamps and moist places of the Northern Hemisphere. The wood rushes (genus *Luzula*) grow on dry ground in hills and mountains and are relished by livestock. Rushes are used for basketwork, mats, chair seats, and as wicks. The scouring rush is a HORSETAIL.

**Rushdie, Salman,** 1947–, British author; b. India. In February 1989 Ayatollah KHOMEINI arranged for his assassination prior to the publication of Rushdie's novel *The Satanic Verses*, which had been labelled as blasphemous by some Moslems. Shortly afterwards, Iran announced the withdrawal of all diplomatic personnel from the European Community.

**Rusk, (David) Dean,** 1909–, US secretary of state (1961–69). After serving in the State Department (1946–51) and as president of the Rockefeller Foundation (1952–61), he became secretary of state in Pres. John F. KENNEDY's cabinet and continued to hold the post under Pres. Lyndon B. JOHNSON. A firm believer in the use of military force to prevent Communist expansion, he strongly defended the VIETNAM WAR.

**Ruskin, John,** 1819–1900, English critic and social theorist. His first work, *Modern Painters* (5 vol., 1843–60), begun as a defence of J.M.W. TURNER, held that art is a 'universal language' based on national and individual integrity and morality. *The Seven Lamps of Architecture* (1849) and *The Stones of Venice* (1851–53) applied this idea to architecture. Ruskin began to address social and political questions c.1857; in *Unto This Last* (1860) and *Munera Pulveris* (1862–63) he attacked the ugliness and waste of modern industrial England, and made proposals for social and educational reform which have had great influence. In 1870 Ruskin was appointed Slade Professor at Oxford, the first professor of art in England. His marriage to Euphemia Gray was disastrous, and in later life he was intermittently insane. His autobiography, *Praeterita*, was left unfinished.

**Russell, Bertrand Arthur William Russell,** 3rd **Earl,** 1872–1970, English philosopher, mathematician, and social reformer. The grandson of Lord John Russell, the 1st Earl Russell, he succeeded to the earldom in 1931. While teaching at Cambridge Univ. Russell produced his most important works, *Principles of Mathematics* (1903) and, with WHITEHEAD, *Principia mathematica* (3 vol., 1910–13), in which he attempted to show how the laws of mathematics could be deduced from the basic axioms of logic. His work had great influence on 20th-cent. symbolic logic (see LOGIC), on the SET theory of mathematics, and in LOGICAL POSITIVISM, especially in the work of his student WITTGENSTEIN. An undogmatic but zealous rationalist, Russell was deeply convinced of the logical independence of individual facts and the dependence of knowledge on the data of original experience. Well known for his social views, he was an active pacifist during World War I, and was imprisoned for his activities. In 1927 he and his wife founded the experimental Beacon Hill School, based on the principle that a love for children results in their emergence into the world of knowledge. His liberal views on marriage, sex, adultery, and homosexuality made him controversial during most of the 1930s. He abandoned pacifism during World War II but reverted to it, becoming, in the 1950s and 60s, a leader in the movement to halt the manufacture of nuclear weapons; he was again imprisoned. Along with SARTRE he organized European opposition to US involvement in the Vietnam War. Russell supported himself chiefly by his writings, many of them widely read, e.g., *On Education* (1926), *Marriage and Morals* (1929), *A History of Western Philosophy* (1945), *Unpopular Essays* (1950), and his autobiography (3 vol., 1967–69). In 1950 he was awarded the Nobel Prize for literature.

**Russell, Dora (Black),** 1894–1985, English feminist and pacifist. Campaigning for birth control and maternity leave, she worked with Margaret SANGER and Marie STOPES and founded the Worker's Birth Control Group (1924). In the 1950s and 60s she was active in the CAMPAIGN FOR NUCLEAR DISARMAMENT while married to the philosopher Bertrand RUSSELL. She wrote with him *The Prospects of Industrial Civilisation* (1923). Her other books include *Hypatia: or Women and Knowledge* (1925) and her autobiography *The Tamarisk Tree* (3 vol., 1974–85).

**Russell, George William,** pseud. **A.E.,** 1867–1935, Irish author. An Irish nationalist, editor, reformer, and painter, he was also a major figure in the IRISH LITERARY RENAISSANCE. His poems and plays, mystical and melodious, include *Homeward: Songs by the Way* (1894) and *The Candle of Vision* (1918).

**Russell, Henry Norris,** 1877–1957, American astronomer. At Princeton Univ. he taught (1905–47) astronomy and directed (1912–47) its observatory. Russell showed that a study of the motion of the periastron of the orbit of eclipsing variable stars could provide information on the internal structure of the component stars. He developed a theory of STELLAR EVOLUTION that led him to construct, independently of Ejnar

Hertzsprung, the HERTZSPRUNG–RUSSELL DIAGRAM, and he determined the abundance of various chemical elements in the solar atmosphere. He also analysed the spectra of several chemical elements.

**Russell, Lord John,** 1st **Earl,** 1792–1878, British Whig politician. He helped draft the REFORM BILL of 1832 and, as prime minster (1846–52, 1865–66), supported further unsuccessful measures of parliamentary reform.

**Russell, Rosalind,** 1911–76, American film actress. Her films include *The Women* (1939), *His Girl Friday* (1940), *Picnic* (1956), and *Auntie Mame* (1958); she also starred in the Broadway stage version of *Auntie Mame.*

**Russia,** Rus. *Rossiya.* The name of 'Russia' is properly used to designate the homeland of the Great Russians, as distinct from the other East SLAVS (see RUTHENIA). In the political sense, it has been commonly applied to a succession of states centred on Great Russia, namely the grand duchy of MOSCOW or Muscovy (1326–1721). the Czarist 'Empire of all the Russias' (1721–1917) and Soviet Russia (1917–). It is also frequently applied to the early state KIEVAN RUS' (before 1237) and quite erroneously to the whole Soviet Union (since 1922). (see UNION OF SOVIET SOCIALIST REPUBLICS). Geographically, the territorial limits of Russia have greatly expanded over the centuries far beyond the Muscovite heartland to encompass much of northern Eurasia. The RUSSIAN SOVIET FEDERATED SOCIALIST REPUBLIC (RSFSR) is the largest of the 15 constituent republics of the USSR. Russian history is usually traced back to Kievan Rus', the common progenitor of both Russia and Ruthenia, although human habitation began in the Palaeolithic Era. Throughout prehistory, the forests and steppes of Russia were settled by a great variety of nomadic peoples. By the 7th cent. BC the Scythians (see SCYTHIA) controlled the north shore of the BLACK SEA and the CRIMEA. The KHAZARS built (7th–10th cent. AD) a powerful state in the same area, and by the 9th cent. the East Slavs had settled in the N UKRAINE and nearby regions. The Kievan state is said to have been established by Rurik, leader of a band of Scandinavian traders and warriors (the Varangians), who first founded (862) a dynasty at NOVGOROD. His successor, Oleg, made (882) KIEV the capital of Kievan Rus', and Christianity became the official religion under VLADIMIR I, who adopted (988–89) the Orthodox rite. The Kievan state broke up into principalities in 1054 and was destroyed (1237–40) by invading Mongols (see TATARS) who established the empire of the GOLDEN HORDE. In the 15th cent. IVAN III, grand duke of Moscow, ceased to pay tribute to the Tatars and expanded his territory of conquest. IVAN IV further extended Russian rule and took the title 'Czar of All Russia' in 1547. The death of Czar Boris GODUNOV in 1605 was followed by the 'Time of Troubles', a period marked by the appearance of pretenders (see DMITRI) and an invasion (1610) by SIGISMUND III of Poland. The Poles were expelled in 1612 and in 1613 Michael ROMANOV was made czar, thus beginning a dynasty that ruled until 1917. PETER I (r.1689–1725) undertook the Westernization of Russia and enacted many administrative reforms, but he also increased autocracy and enserfment (see SERF). In 1703 Peter founded St Petersburg (now LENINGRAD), the new capital, on land won in the NORTHERN WAR. He also began the RUSSO-TURKISH WARS. Under CATHERINE II (r. 1762–96), Russia became a great power, expanding its borders in the west and south (see POLAND, PARTITIONS OF). The suppression of the PUGACHEV revolt (1773–75) strengthened the privileged classes. During the reign of ALEXANDER I, the French under NAPOLEON I took (1812) Moscow; but after Napoleon's defeat and the peace arranged at the Congress of VIENNA, Russia and Austria emerged as the chief powers on the Continent (see HOLY ALLIANCE). Liberalism in the Russian upper classes led to an unsuccessful revolt (1825) by the DECEMBRISTS. Under the reactionary rule of NICHOLAS I, Russia crushed an uprising (1830–31) in Poland and helped Austria subdue a revolt (1848–49) in Hungary. Its attempts to dominate the Turks led to the CRIMEAN WAR (1854–56). ALEXANDER II freed the serfs in 1861 (see EMANCIPATION, EDICT OF), but grew increasingly conservative. Meanwhile, Russia's expansion continued into the CAUCASUS, Turkestan, and the Far East (see SOVIET FAR EAST). Alexander II's assassination (1881) was followed by a period of reaction under ALEXANDER III and NICHOLAS II, the last Russian czar. The disastrous RUSSO-JAPANESE WAR (1904–5) led to the Revolution of 1905; Nicholas was forced to grant a constitution and a parliament (see DUMA). Repression continued, however, under Nicholas's premier, P.A. STOLYPIN. Leftist militancy (see BOLSHEVISM AND MENSHEVISM) and WORLD WAR I completed Russia's collapse. During the RUSSIAN REVOLUTIONS of 1917. Nicholas II was

forced to abdicate; the Bolsheviks, led by LENIN, took power. Russia withdrew from the war by the Treaty of BREST-LITOVSK, but civil war ensued and lasted until the Soviet regime emerged victorious in 1920. In 1917 Russia had been proclaimed the RSFSR and in 1922 it became part of the USSR.

**Russia Company:** see MUSCOVY COMPANY.

**Russian language,** member of the East Slavic group of the Slavic subfamily of the Indo-European family of languages. See LANGUAGE (table).

**Russian Revolution,** a series of upheavals in Russia foreshadowed by the events of 1905–6 and coming to a head with the February and October revolutions of 1917. The Revolution of 1905 began on 'Bloody Sunday' in January when troops fired on a crowd of workers, led by a priest, marching on the Winter Palace in St Petersburg. Months of disorder led to the formation of a short-lived SOVIET or workers' council, and in Poland to strikes that persisted into the following year. In October, the czar made a number of concessions, including an advisory legislature or DUMA. The two Revolutions of 1917 were precipitated by the catastrophes of World War I. Strikes and riots in the Russian capital (renamed Petrograd) proved uncontrollable, and the overthrow of the czar in mid March (February by the Old Style Calendar) was supported both by the court circle and by the growing adherents of democratic rule. The Provisional Government under Prince LVOV was devoted to constitutional principals, but sought to continue the war against Germany in conjunction with its western allies. However, military defeat at the front persisted with turmoil in the rear. The workers' Soviet in Petrograd, strengthened by LENIN's return from exile (Apr. 1917), began to demand peace and further political change. The failure of the summer campaign provoked mass desertions from the army, and the emergence of KERENSKY as premier. In September, Gen. Kornilov attempted to restore order in Petrograd, but only succeeded in sowing the confusion which gave the Bolsheviks their chance. On the night of 6 Nov. (24 Oct. OS), the

| **RUSSIAN RULERS FROM 1462 TO 1917**<br>*(including dates of reign)* |
|---|
| **House of Rurik**<br>Ivan III (the Great), 1462–1505<br>Vasily III, 1505–33<br>Ivan IV (the Terrible), 1533–84<br>Feodor I, 1584–98 |
| **House of Godunov**<br>Boris Godunov, 1598–1605<br>Feodor II, 1605 |
| **Usurpers**<br>Dmitri, 1605–06<br>Vasily IV, 1606–10 |
| **Interregnum,** 1610–13 |
| **House of Romanov**<br>Michael, 1613–45<br>Alexis, 1645–76<br>Feodor III, 1676–82<br>Ivan V and Peter I (the Great), 1682–96<br>Peter I (the Great), 1696–1725<br>Catherine I, 1725–27<br>Peter II, 1727–30<br>Anna, 1730–40<br>Ivan VI, 1740–41<br>Elizabeth, 1741–62<br>Peter III, 1762<br>Catherine II (the Great), 1762–96<br>Paul I, 1796–1801<br>Alexander I, 1801–25<br>Nicholas I, 1825–55<br>Alexander II, 1855–81<br>Alexander III, 1881–94<br>Nicholas II, 1894–1917 |

government buildings and the provisional government's headquarters in the Winter Palace were stormed by an assortment of the armed workers of the Red Guard, mutinous troops, and sailors of the Baltic fleet, and a council of people's commissars took power, with Lenin as chairman. The Bolsheviks tightened their grip by eliminating their Menshevik and Social Revolutionary partners from the 2nd congress of Soviets, which approved the coup, and in January by abolishing the constituent assembly which the provisional government had earlier summoned in preparation for democratic reforms, and by ordering the murder of the former Czar. Lenin's early decrees for 'Land and Peace' had urged the peasants to seize ownership of the countryside and undermined the remnants of the army, which was now in full flight. With the Germans advancing from the West, and the disorders spreading throughout Russia, the Bolsheviks were forced to sign the treaty of BREST-LITOVSK, and whilst withdrawing from the international conflict, to face the Russian CIVIL WAR. Inevitably perhaps, in their ruthless drive to keep power at all costs, they were obliged to postpone their plans for social and economic reconstruction. Lenin succeeded in establishing the Bolshevik Party's political dictatorship (see MARXISM-LENINISM); but the most radical revolutionary changes in Soviet society were not attempted until Stalin's further 'Revolution' was launched in 1929 (see STALINISM). Interpretations of the Russian Revolution differ widely. Soviet apologists stress the role of the masses in overturning the old order and building the first socialist state, the harbinger of worldwide revolution. Critics, whilst fully admitting the genius of Lenin, cite the Bolsheviks as the classic example of a tiny, dedicated, and disciplined revolutionary sect which succeeded in seizing and manipulating power irrespective of popular support.

**Russian Soviet Federated Socialist Republic** (RSFSR), constituent republic (1981 pop. 139,149,000), 17,070,949 km² (6,591,100 sq mi), USSR. It comprises 76% of the total area and 54% of the total population of the USSR, and is economically the most important of the USSR's 15 union republics. The RSFSR occupies most of E Europe and N Asia, extending c. 8000 km (5000 mi) from the Baltic Sea to the Pacific Ocean. It borders Norway and Finland (NW); seven other Soviet republics (W, SW, S); and Mongolia and China (S). There is a small enclave of the RSFSR in former East Prussia, centred on KALININGRAD (Koenigsberg). Russians make up 83% of its population; there are Ukrainian and non-Slavic minorities. Administratively, the predominantly Russian areas are constituted as krays or oblasts, and non-Russian areas as autonomous republics, autonomous oblasts, or okrugs. The RSFSR has nine physioeconomic regions. In the central European region MOSCOW and GORKY are among the major cities. Industrial products include motor vehicles and ships. In the N and NW European region LENINGRAD is the industrial centre. Among the region's resources are coal, oil, and timber. In the VOLGA region KAZAN, KUYBYSHEV, and VOLGOGRAD are the major cities. The region's economic activities include manufacturing, oil refining, farming, and fishing. In the N CAUCASUS region Rostov-na-Donu and Krasnodar are among the chief cities. Important products include farm machinery, coal, petroleum, and wheat. The southern half of the URALS region is a centre of iron, steel, and petroleum production. The other regions of the RSFSR are W, E, and NNE SIBERIA and the SOVIET FAR EAST.

**Russo-Japanese War,** 1904–05, imperialistic conflict growing out of rival designs on MANCHURIA and Korea. Russia had penetrated those territories and refused (1904) to negotiate with Japan over spheres of influence there. Japan then bottled up the Russian fleet at Port Arthur (now Lüshun, China), defeated a Russian army at Mukden (now Shenyang), and destroyed the Russian fleet off the Tsushima islands. US Pres. Theodore ROOSEVELT mediated between the two sides to bring an end to the war. Japan's victory marked its emergence as a world power.

**Russolo, Luigi,** 1885–1947, Italian painter. He was one of the painters who signed the manifesto of futurist painters in 1910 (see FUTURISM). He was influenced by the philosopher BERGSON and became interested in the problem of painting non-visual sensations and feelings and of the way in which memory images are used in our perception of the real world. His works of 1912–14, like those of other futurists, were preoccupied with the representation of movement.

**Russo-Turkish Wars**, 1697–1878, series of campaigns in which Russia expanded at the expense of the OTTOMAN EMPIRE (Turkey). In 1696 PETER I won the first Russian victory by capturing the fortress at Azov; it was recaptured (1711) by AHMED III. In 1736 war broke out again, with Austria as a Russian ally. The Russians recaptured Azov and won a spectacular

battle at Jassy, MOLDAVIA (1739), but the treaty forced on Russia by Austria erased most of Russia's gains. The first major Russo-Turkish War (1768–74) began when Sultan Mustafa III, encouraged by France, declared war on CATHERINE II of Russia. The Russians conquered the Crimea, installed a pro-Russian khan there, and overran Moldavia and Walachia. The treaty ending the war solidified Russia's Crimea gains (Catherine annexed it outright in 1783), gave Russia a voice in Turkish domestic matters, and allowed it navigation rights on the Black Sea. These developments alarmed the Western powers, exacerbating what became known as the EASTERN QUESTION. Catherine's second war (1787–92) gave Russia the SW UKRAINE, with Odessa. The war of 1806–12 gave it BESSARABIA. The war of 1828–29, linked with the Greek War of Independence, completed the conquest of the Caucasus and brought Russian power to its zenith. But in 1853 Turkey had the backing of Great Britain and France in the CRIMEAN WAR; the Congress of PARIS (1856) ending that war was a significant setback for Russian influence in the Middle East. The last Russo-Turkish War resulted from an anti-Turkish uprising (1875) in Bosnia and Hercegovina. Serbia and Montenegro joined in, and Russia openly entered the war in 1877. The Treaty of San Stefano (1878) ended the war on terms so beneficial to Russia that the Western powers, in alarm, revised the terms at the Congress of BERLIN.

**rust,** in botany, name for parasitic FUNGI of the order Uredinales and for the plant diseases they cause. Rusts form reddish patches of spores on their hosts. Some species grow entirely on one host, e.g., the hollyhock and snapdragon rusts; others need host plants of two separate species to complete their life cycles, e.g., *Puccinia graminis*, the black, or stem rust of wheat, which alternates in its life cycle between the wheat plant and the barberry bush, and is capable of causing great economic losses. Rusts attack GRAIN crops and many fruits, vegetables, ornamentals and trees.

**Ruth,** book of the OLD TESTAMENT. It tells the story of the fidelity of a Moabite widow (Ruth) to her widowed mother-in-law (Naomi). Ruth returns with Naomi from Moab to Bethlehem and there marries Naomi's kinsman Boaz. Ruth and Boaz were ancestors of DAVID. The story probably dates in final form from 450 to 250 BC.

**Ruth, Babe** (George Herman Ruth), 1895–1948, American baseball player. He is the most famous player in the game's history. Signed at 19 by the minor-league Baltimore Orioles, he was sold to the Boston Red Sox, for whom he became an outstanding pitcher (1914–19), winning 87 games and losing 44. After being moved to the outfield because of his hitting prowess, he was sold (1920) to the New York Yankees, where he became a baseball legend. As a Yankee he led the league in home runs for 10 seasons, setting (1927) the record of 60 home runs in one season. 'The Bambino' hit 714 home runs in his career. He led the Yankees to seven pennants, and Yankee Stadium, built in 1923, came to be known as 'the house that Ruth built'.

**Ruthenia,** the land of the Ruthenes, otherwise the western and southern parts of ancient Rus' (see KIEVAN RUSSIA). Western or 'White Ruthenia', which developed after the 14th century within the grand duchy of Lithuania, is now known as BELORUSSIA. The southern districts of Ruthenia, which developed largely within the kingdom of Poland before being divided in the 18th century between the Austrian and Russian empires, is now known as UKRAINE. The Ruthenes comprised one of the two main branches of the East SLAVS as distinct from the Great Russians; but in the 20th century they have preferred to be designated as Belorussians or Ukrainians. Since the Muscovite state, and later the Russian Empire, laid claim to all the lands of Kievan Rus', it has been standard practice among Russians to blur the distinction between Russia and Ruthenia, and to talk instead of 'all the Russias'. In Muscovite parlance, therefore, White Ruthenia became 'White Russia', and Ukraine was renamed 'Little Russia'. Undiscerning western scholars have frequently followed the Russian terminology. But Ukrainians in particular, who adopted their present name precisely for the purpose of stressing their separate non-Russian identity, strongly resent the idea that Ruthenia/Ukraine is simply part of Russia. In modern times, the only part of historic Ruthenia to retain its former name was 'Sub-Carpathian Ruthenia', a small province of ancient Rus' (capital Ushgorod), which after centuries of Hungarian rule passed in 1918 to Czechoslovakia. In 1945, it was incorporated into the Soviet Ukraine.

**ruthenium** (Ru), metallic element, discovered in 1827 by G.W. Osann in crude platinum ore. It is a hard, lustrous, silver-grey metal that is usually alloyed with other metals to provide hardness and corrosion resistance. Its compounds are used to colour ceramics and glass. See ELEMENT (table); PERIODIC TABLE.

**Rutherford, Ernest Rutherford, Lord,** 1871–1937, English physicist; b. New Zealand. He taught at McGill Univ., Montreal (1898–1907) and the Univ. of Manchester (1907–37) and was director from 1919 of the Cavendish Laboratory, Cambridge. Rutherford discovered and named alpha and beta radiation (see RADIOACTIVITY) and proposed a theory of radioactive transformation of atoms for which he received the 1908 Nobel Prize in chemistry. On the basis of experiments carried out under his direction in Manchester, he concluded (1911) that the ATOM is a small, heavy nucleus surrounded by orbital electrons. Rutherford's group in Cambridge was the first to split atomic nuclei artificially.

**rutile,** mineral, one of three forms of titanium dioxide ($TiO_2$). It occurs in crystals, often in twins or rosettes, and is typically brownish-red, although there are black varieties. Rutile is found in igneous and metamorphic rocks, chiefly in Switzerland, Norway, Brazil, and parts of the US.

**Ruysdael, Jacob van:** see RUISDAEL, JACOB VAN.

**Rwanda** (rooh͵andə), officially Republic of Rwanda, republic (1987 est. pop. 6,070,000), 26,338 km² (10,169 sq mi), E central Africa, bordered by Zäire (W), Uganda (N), Tanzania (E), and Burundi (S). KIGALI is the capital. Most of the country, consisting of steep mountains and deep valleys, is situated at 1520 m (5000 ft) or higher. The Virunga mountain range N of Lake Kivu rises to 4507 m (14,787 ft) at Mt Karisimbi. The economy is overwhelmingly agricultural, largely of the subsistence type. The major cash crops are coffee, tea, and pyrethrum; plantains, cassava, pulses, and rice are among the food crops. Tin ore, wolframite, beryl, and colombo-tantalite are mined in large quantities. Manufacturing is limited to basic consumer goods, textiles, and chemicals. Economic development is impeded by a large population and lack of easy access to the sea. The GNP is US$1612 million, and the GNP per capita is US$280 (1985). About 90% of the population are Hutu agriculturalists, 9% are Tutsi, and 1% are Twa (PYGMIES). About half follow traditional beliefs; most of the rest are Roman Catholics and there are some Muslims. Kinyarwanda and French are the official languages.

*History.* The early history of Rwanda is similar to that of BURUNDI. By the late 18th cent. a single Tutsi-ruled state, headed by a *mwami* [king], occupied most of present-day Rwanda and dominated the Hutu, the vast majority of the population. In 1890 Rwanda accepted German overrule without resistance and became part of German East Africa. Belgian forces occupied the country in WORLD WAR I, and in 1919 it became part of the Belgian mandate of RUANDA-URUNDI (a UN trust territory in 1946). In 1957 the Hutu demanded a greater voice in the country's affairs, and on the accession (1959) of Kigari V fighting erupted between them and the Tutsi. The victorious Hutu gained control of the country, and some 100,000 Tutsi fled to nearby states. Rwanda became independent in 1962, with Grégoire Kayibanda as president. In 1973 a coup installed Maj. Gen. Juvénal Habyarimana as head of a military regime. Civilian rule was restored under a new constitution in 1978, but Habyarimana remained president and was reelected in 1983 as candidate of the National Revolutionary Movement for Development, the only legal party.

**Rydberg, Abraham Viktor** (͵rydberyə), 1828–95, Swedish philosopher and writer. His *Teaching of the Bible About Christ* (1862) opposed Christian fundamentalism. He also wrote historical novels and poetry of majestic lyricism.

**Ryder, Albert Pinkham,** 1847–1917, American painter. He produced only about 160 canvases, amongst the most individual in American art. Small in size, they are grand in design and feeling, luminous and subtle in colour. Moonlight and the sea predominate in paintings that evoke a lonely, poetic mood.

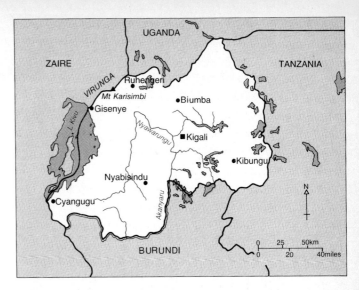

Rwanda

**Ryder Cup:** see GOLF.

**rye,** cereal plant (*Secale cereale*) of the GRASS family, important chiefly in central and N Europe. The GRAIN, or seed, is used for so-called 'black' bread, and the lighter-coloured rye bread (made from a mixture of rye and wheat flour), as a stock feed, and in the distillation of spirits. The plant, which grows well in areas where the soil is too poor and the climate too cool for wheat, is also grown for hay and pasturage and as green manure and a COVER CROP. The USSR leads in world production. ERGOT, a fungus infection, is poisonous and can make rye unsafe for use.

**Rye House Plot,** conspiracy (1683) to assassinate CHARLES II of England and his brother (later JAMES II) at Rumbold's Rye House, in Hertfordshire. The plot miscarried, and its discovery led to the executions of the Whig leaders Lord John Russell and Algernon Sidney on flimsy evidence.

**Ryks Museum:** see RIJKS MUSEUM.

**Ryle, Gilbert,** 1900–76, English philosopher. His *Concept of Mind* (1949), a paradigm of Oxford linguistic philosophy, is a sustained attack on DESCARTES' DUALISM, lampooned by Ryle as the doctrine of 'the ghost in the machine'.

**Ryle, Sir Martin,** 1918–84, English radio astronomer. He was responsible for major advances in the design of radio telescope systems. His most important work was the development of the technique of aperture synthesis. All his observations supported the big bang theory (see COSMOLOGY). He was made Astronomer Royal in 1972, and two years later shared the Nobel Prize for Physics with Antony HEWISH.

**Ryukyu Islands,** archipelago (1986 est. pop. 1,351,009), SW Japan, c.4790 km² (1850 sq mi), extending c.1050 km (650 mi) SW from Kyushu, between the E China and Philippine seas. The principal island groups are the Osumi, Tokara, and Amami Islands (N); Okinawa Islands, including OKINAWA; and Sakishima Islands (S). The climate is subtropical, with heavy rains and frequent typhoons. The entire archipelago was incorporated into the Japanese empire in 1879 and passed to the US in 1945. The Amami group was returned to Japan in 1953, the rest of the archipelago in 1972.

# S

**S**, chemical symbol of the element SULPHUR.

**Sá, Mem de**, d. 1572, Portuguese governor general of Brazil (1557?–1572). He founded the city of RIO DE JANEIRO.

**Saadi:** see SADI.

**Saadia ben Joseph al-Fayumi**, 882–942, Jewish scholar, known as Saadia Gaon; b. Egypt. Under his leadership the great Jewish Academy at Sura, Babylonia, became the highest seat of Jewish learning. He compiled a prayer book, or *siddur,* translated the Bible into Arabic; and wrote on Hebrew grammar, on philosophy, and on religion.

**Saar**, river, 240 km (510 mi) long, rising in the VOSGES Mts. of E France and flowing northwards through the SAARLAND state of West Germany to join the MOSEL R. above TRIER.

**Saarbrücken**, city (1984 pop. 189,600), capital of SAARLAND, West Germany, on the Saar R. Situated on the edge of the Saar coalfield, it is the centre of an industrial area dominated by iron and steel and engineering industries. A university has been established in the city since World War II.

**Saarinen, Eero** (‚ayroh ‚sahrinən), 1910–61, American architect; b. Finland. He established a reputation with the General Motors Technical Centre, Warren, Michigan (1951–55). An innovator, he is famous for the circular chapel and concrete-dome auditorium (1955) at the Massachusetts Institute of Technology, and for the Trans World Airlines terminal, New York City. His Dulles International Airport, Chantilly, Virginia, was finished posthumously.

Eero **Saarinen's** circular chapel at the Massachusetts Institute of Technology

**Saarland**, state (1984 est. pop. 1,050,837), 2567 km² (991 sq mi), SW West Germany. The area was formerly called the Saar or the Saar Territory. Saarland is highly industrialized, with iron and steel manufacturing based on rich coalfields. SAARBRÜCKEN is the capital. The autonomous Saar Territory was created by the Treaty of VERSAILLES. In 1935 a plebiscite reunited it with Germany. After WORLD WAR II it was again made autonomous, but French economic influence there caused friction between France and Germany. In 1957 Saarland became a state in West Germany.

**Saavedra Lamas, Carlos** (sah‚vaydhrah ‚lahmahs), 1880–1959, Argentine statesman, foreign minister (1932–38). He was a supporter of the LEAGUE OF NATIONS. He drafted an influential antiwar pact in 1932 and later helped to end the war over the Chaco (see GRAN CHACO). He received the 1936 Nobel Peace Prize.

**Saba, Umberto**, 1883–1957, Italian poet. Born Umberto Poli, the son of a Jewish mother and a Christian father, he was a native of Austrian Trieste, where he ran a second-hand bookshop for most of his life and was a friend of SVEVO. Influenced by FREUD, LEOPARDI, and UNGARETTI, his verse, collected as his *Songbook* (definitive edition 1961), constitutes a poetic autobiography and is systematically analysed in his *History and Chronicle of the Songbook* (1948).

**Sabah**, E Malaysian state (1980 pop. 1,002,608), 76,552 km² (29,545 sq mi), on the South China and Sulu seas, bordered on the south by Kalimantan (Indonesian Borneo). Mountainous and densely forested, it exports timber, rubber, and copra. It constituted the British protectorate of North Borneo from 1882 until it joined the Federation of Malaysia in 1963.

**Sabbatai Zevi**, 1626–76, Jewish mystic and pseudo-Messiah; b. Turkey. A student of the KABBALAH, in 1648 he proclaimed himself the Messiah, named 1666 as the millennium, and gathered a host of followers. He attempted to land in Constantinople in 1666, was captured, and, to escape death, embraced Islam. The Sabbatean movement was revived in the 18th cent. by Jacob FRANK.

**Sabbath** [Heb., = repose], last day of the week (Saturday), observed as a holy day of rest by the Jews. Early Christians observed the first day of the week in commemoration of the Resurrection; hence Sunday became the Christian Sabbath.

**Sabeans**, a religious community that flourished in northern Mesopotamia until the 11th cent. Members of this community reached prominence in the ABBASID court, and their religious lore of astral worship and divination was vital in the formation of Muslim esoteric and other doctrines encountered in philosophy, ALCHEMY, MAGIC, and SUFISM.

**Sabines**, ancient people of central Italy, in the Sabine Hills, NE of Rome. From the earliest days there was a Sabine element in Rome. The Sabines warred with Rome, but by the 3rd cent. BC, they were completely amalgamated with the Romans.

**Sabin vaccine**, live-virus vaccine for immunization against POLIOMYELITIS. It is named after Albert Bruce Sabin, b.1906, US physician, who developed it (c.1959).

**Sacajawea, Sacagawea** or **Sakakawea**, sometimes called **Bird Woman**, 1784–1884?, Shoshone Indian, sole woman and guide on the LEWIS AND CLARK EXPEDITION. She had been captured and sold to a Mandan Indian, then traded to Toussaint Charbonneau, interpreter for the expedition. When the expedition reached her native upper Missouri R. region, she proved invaluable as a guide and interpreter.

**Sac and Fox Indians:** see NORTH AMERICAN INDIANS.

**Sá Carneiro, Francisco,** 1934–80, prime minister of PORTUGAL (1980). A liberal reformer, he founded the Social Democratic Party in 1974, following the coup that ended repression in Portugal, and in 1979 formed the Democratic Alliance, a centre-right coalition. After becoming premier in 1980, he excluded military officers from the cabinet and introduced major democratic reforms. He died in a plane crash.

**Sacco–Vanzetti Case.** In Apr. 1920, Nicola Sacco and Bartolomeo Vanzetti were arrested for the murder of a paymaster and his guard in South Braintree, Massachusetts. Both men were anarchists (see ANARCHISM) and feared deportation; they gave false statements and were armed. Despite contradictory evidence, both were found guilty in July 1921 and sentenced to death. Many believed that the trial had been unfair and that the two men's political beliefs had convicted them. By 1927, when the Massachusetts supreme court and a governor's commission upheld the proceedings, the case had become a *cause célèbre.* The execution of Sacco and Vanzetti on 22 Aug. 1927 was preceded by worldwide sympathy demonstrations.

**Sachs, Hans** (hans zaks), 1494–1576, comic playwright of the Nuremberg school. A shoemaker, he wrote many songs, tales in verse (*Schwänke*), and Shrovetide plays. 'The Nightingale of Wittenberg' is a poem in LUTHER's honour. Sachs is a key figure in Richard WAGNER's *Die Meistersinger.*

**Sachs, Nelly** (saks), 1891–1970, German poet and dramatist. After harmless early romantic lyrics, Sachs's poetic breakthrough came late, only after her escape to Sweden, at Selma LAGERLÖF's intervention, in 1940. She developed a visionary style drawing on Expressionism and Jewish mysticism, both avant-garde and archaic, in which to lament the persecution of her people. Her lyric collections include *In the Abodes of Death* (1947), *Eclipse of the Stars* (1949), and *Flight to where No Dust Is* (1961); her best-known poetic drama is *Eli, a Mystery Play of the Suffering of Israel* (1951; tr. *O the Chimneys* 1967). She also translated Swedish poetry. In 1966 she shared the Nobel Prize for Literature with S.Y. AGNON.

**sacrament,** an outward sign of something sacred. Christians generally believe sacraments were instituted by Christ and are visible signs of invisible GRACE. Traditionally, the Orthodox, Roman Catholics, and certain Anglicans believe in seven sacraments—Eucharist (see COMMUNION), BAPTISM, CONFIRMATION, PENANCE, ANOINTING OF THE SICK, matrimony (see MARRIAGE), and HOLY ORDERS—which, they hold, actually bestow grace. Most Protestant denominations recognize two sacraments, baptism and communion, and hold that faith, rather than the sacraments, provides grace.

**Sacramento,** US city (1984 est. pop. 304,000), state capital of California, on the Sacramento R. at its confluence with the American R.; settled 1839, inc. 1850. A deepwater port, it is the shipping and processing centre for a rich fruit-growing and market-gardening area, and is important in electronics and missile manufacture. The city grew after gold was discovered (1848) at nearby Sutter's Mill, and it became state capital in 1854. Government and military bases are major employers.

**Sadat, Anwar al-,** 1918–81, president of EGYPT (1970–81). He succeeded NASSER as president. In 1973 he led Egypt into war with Israel (see ARAB–ISRAELI WARS), but later he joined (1978) with Israeli premier Menachem BEGIN in negotiating the CAMP DAVID ACCORDS. He and Begin shared the 1978 Nobel Peace Prize. He was assassinated by Muslim zealots.

**Sade, Donatien Alphonse François, comte de** (sahd), 1740–1814, French author, known as the marquis de Sade. Charged with numerous sexual offenses, he spent 27 years in prisons or asylums, writing romances, including *Justine* (1791). His theory that since sexual deviation and criminal acts exist in nature, they are natural, foreshadowed modern psychological thought. He was revered by the surrealists for his militant atheism and his worship of the sexual urge as a sign of total freedom. *Sadism,* the infliction of pain to attain sexual pleasure, is named for him.

**Sadi, Abu Abdallah Musharif al Din ibn Muslih,** 1184–1292, Persian poet, one of the finest Sufi writers (see SUFISM). His first dated composition is *The Fruit Garden* (1257), which contains within its 10 sections of facile and beautiful verse, dissertations on justice, good government, beneficence, earthly and mystic love, and other

excellences. His masterpiece is *Garden of Roses* (1258), a miscellany of prose and poetry suffused with warmth of feeling and lofty religious thought.

**Šafařík, Pavel Josef** (ˌshahfahzheek), 1795–1861, Czech philologist and archaeologist. He advanced the theory that the Slavs were originally a composite people with a common language that had split into dialects. In *Slavonic Antiquities* (1836–37) he held that the Slavs had been indigenous to Europe since the 5th cent. BC. Although now obsolete, his theories advanced Slavic studies and Pan-Slavism.

**safflower,** Eurasian thistlelike herb (*Carthamus tinctorius*) of the COMPOSITE family; also called false saffron. It has long been cultivated in S Asia and Egypt for food and medicine, and as a substitute for true SAFFRON dye; in the West it is more important as the source of safflower oil, used in cooking (see FATS AND OILS).

**saffron,** autumn-flowering plant (*Crocus sativus*) of the IRIS family, and the yellow dye obtained from it. Native to Asia Minor, it has long been cultivated for the orange-yellow stigmas of its pistils (see FLOWER), which yield saffron powder, the source of the dye. The powder is also used in perfumes, to colour medicines, and for flavouring. One ounce (28 g) of saffron powder requires stigmas from about 4000 flowers.

**Safid Rud,** river, NW Iran, 650 km (400 mi) long. With its major tributary, the Qizil Uzum, it drains much of the western part of the central Iranian plateau before flowing north to the CASPIAN SEA, through a deep gorge in the ELBURZ MOUNTAINS. It has the largest flow of any Iranian river, and a dam at the gorge entrance stores water for the irrigation of the Caspian lowlands around Rasht.

**saga,** Old Icelandic literature in prose, composed in the 13th and 14th cent., based on both oral and narrative sources. Sagas are often described as medieval 'historical novels'. There are four genres: *sagas of Icelanders,* describing the lives and feuds of Icelandic chieftains of the 10th cent.; *sagas of kings,* about the kings of Norway, of which the most celebrated is the series of sagas in *Heimskringla* by Snorri STURLUSON; *legendary sagas,* describing the adventures of semi-mythical heroic figures of the Nordic past; and *contemporary sagas,* describing events in Iceland in the 12th and 13th cent. (see STURLUNGA SAGA).

**sage,** aromatic herb or shrub (genus *Salvia*) of the MINT family. The common sage of herb gardens (*S. officinalis*), native from S Europe to Asia Minor, is a strongly-scented shrubby perennial; its dried leaves are used as a seasoning and in a tea. Ornamental sages, popularly called salvia, include the scarlet sage (*S. solendens*), noted for its neat spikes of usually red flowers.

**sage:** see SALVIA.

**sagebrush,** American name for several species of the genus *Artemesia* (see WORMWOOD), deciduous shrubs of the COMPOSITE family, especially abundant in arid regions of W North America. The common sagebrush (*A. tridentata*) is a silvery-grey, low shrub with a pungent odour of sage, although it is unrelated to true sage (see SALVIA). Sagebrush is an important forage plant.

**Sahara,** world's largest desert, c.9,065,000 km² (3,500,000 sq mi), extending c.4830 km (3000 mi) east to west and c.1930 km² (1200 mi) north to south across N Africa. Rainfall ranges from less than 12.7 cm (5 in) to 25 cm (10 in), with dry periods occasionally lasting for years. Nighttime temperatures often drop below freezing, and daytime temperatures have been recorded at over 57°C (135°F) in the shade. The surface of the desert ranges from sand dunes (erg), covering about 15%, to stone plateaus (hammada) and gravel surfaces (reg), covering about 70%, to several deeply dissected mountain massifs (Ahagger, Tibesti, and Aïr), infamous in the past for the shelter they provided to marauders preying on desert travellers. Vast underground aquifers, filled with water thought to date from the Pleistocene epoch, when the Sahara was wetter, underlie much of the region, and there are important deposits of iron ore, phosphates, oil, and natural gas.

**Saharan Arab Democratic Republic:** see WESTERN SAHARA.

**Saharanpur,** town (1981 pop. 295,355), Uttar Pradesh state, N India, on a tributary of the Hindan R. It is a district administrative, communications, and trading centre. It has food-processing industries, paper mills, and saw mills. In the British period it grew as an administrative centre and railway junction.

Salt pans in the **Sahara** at Tessuidan, Tessoum, Niger

**Sahel,** semiarid region extending across N central Africa from Senegal (W) to Ethiopia (E). It has more rainfall (20–40 cm/8–16 in) and better grazing lands than the SAHARA desert, to the north, but it is periodically afflicted by droughts that reduce its normally meagre water supply and shatter its grazing and agricultural economy. Droughts during 1967–74 and again in 1984–85 have been particularly devastating, causing mass migration and contributing to the starvation of hundreds of thousands of people.

**Sahlins, Marshall,** 1930–, American anthropologist. After early work of the evolution of kingdoms in Hawaii (see EVOLUTION, SOCIOCULTURAL), Sahlins became interested in RECIPROCITY. His book *Stone Age Economics* (1972) has been influential.

**Saida:** see SIDON.

**Saigon:** see HO CHI MINH CITY.

**sailing,** as a sport, the art of navigating a sailing boat for recreational or competitive purposes. In racing, competition is generally restricted to boats of the same class. Boats are classified according to their sails and masts. The most common types are the sloop (one mast, two sails), schooner (usually two masts and five sails), yawl (two masts, four sails), and ketch (two masts, five sails). Sloops, from 3.05 to 21.34 m (10–70 ft), are generally used for racing, and the other types, usually more than 6.1 m (20 ft) long, for recreational cruising. Especially popular today are the 4.88 to 7.01 m (16–23 ft) one-design boats, such as the Star (designed 1911), Snipe, Comet, Mercury, and Lightning. Although sailing is popular throughout the world, international competition since World War II has been dominated by the US, Great Britain, Australia, and the USSR. The oldest and most prestigious event in international racing is the AMERICA'S CUP series for large sloops, begun in 1851. Sailing competition has been on the Olympic programme since 1900.

**sailplane:** see GLIDER.

**Saint.** For canonized and uncanonized saints, see under the proper name, e.g., THOMAS AQUINAS, SAINT. For surnames and place names beginning thus, see in alphabetical position here: thus, SAINT EXUPÉRY, ANTOINE DE; SAINT LOUIS.

**saint,** in Christian theology, a person who shares in the holiness of God. To New Testament authors, the church was the community of saints, but the word came to be used for those who live in heaven. The Virgin Mary is the chief saint, and the ANGELS are counted as saints. The Roman Catholic, Anglican, and Orthodox LITURGIES commemorate the saints with special feast days. In East and West criteria for recognition of sainthood are martyrdom, holiness of life, miracles in life and after death, and a popular cult. The addition of a name to the official list of saints is called canonization. In 1969 the Roman Catholic Church carried out a radical revision of its liturgical calendar, and since that date the Church of England and other churches of the ANGLICAN COMMUNION have revised their calendars.

**Saint Albans,** cathedral city (1981 pop. 76,709), Hertfordshire, S England, 31 km (19 mi) NW of London. It is a market town with various industries, including printing. It extends eastward from the remains of the

Roman town of Verulamium. A Benedictine Abbey was founded here in 793 and became the cathedral in 1877.

**Saint Andrews,** town (1981 pop. 10,525), in Fife region, E Scotland, on promontory on St Andrews bay. A market and resort town, it has many historic buildings. The town church was originally founded in the 12th cent., and there are the ruins of a 13th-cent. castle. The university was founded in 1411, and is the oldest in Scotland. Also in the town is the Royal and Ancient Golf Club (founded 1754) which is the headquarters of the game.

**Saint Augustine,** US city (1980 pop. 11,985), NE Florida; founded 1565, inc. 1824. The oldest city in the US, it is a tourist centre and a port with some light industry. Famous sights include two Spanish structures that are now national monuments, the Castillo de San Marcos (1672–96) and Fort Matanzas (1742). The city's strategic importance made it the object of fighting on many occasions from 1586, when it was attacked by Sir Francis DRAKE, up to the CIVIL WAR, when it was occupied by Union forces.

**Saint Bartholomew's Day, massacre of,** murder of French Protestants, or HUGUENOTS, by Roman Catholics, beginning on 24 Aug. 1572. The presence of many Huguenots in Paris for the wedding of Henry of Navarre (later HENRY IV) gave CATHERINE DE' MEDICI and the reluctant King CHARLES IX a chance to plan a general massacre. Admiral COLIGNY was the first victim. The massacre spread to other parts of France and caused the resumption of the Wars of Religion (1562–98) (see RELIGION, WARS OF).

**Saint Catharines,** city (1980 est. pop. 123,956), SE Ontario, Canada, part of the regional municipality of Niagara (1980 est. pop. 367,665). It is an industrial city located on the WELLAND SHIP CANAL. Manufactures include canned fruit, wine, automobile parts, and electrical equipment. The city was founded in 1790. Port Dalhousie, site of the annual Royal Henley Regatta, became part of St Catharines in 1961.

**St Clair, Arthur,** 1743–1818, American general; b. Scotland. During the AMERICAN REVOLUTION, he abandoned Fort Ticonderoga without a fight (1777) but was exonerated by a court-martial (1778). He was the first governor of the NORTHWEST TERRITORY (1787–1802), and was defeated by Indian forces there in 1792.

**Saint Croix,** largest of the US VIRGIN ISLANDS.

**Saint David's,** village and cathedral city (1981 pop. 1428), Dyfed, SW Wales, just inland from St David's Head. The cathedral was built from the 12th cent. onwards, and was an important destination of pilgrims in medieval times.

**St Denis, Ruth,** 1877–1968, American dancer, teacher, and choreographer. She gave spectacular recitals, with oriental themes, from 1906. With her husband Ted Shawn she founded Denishawn schools in Los Angeles (1915) and New York (1920), influencing the development of MODERN DANCE. She also ran a performing company which toured extensively.

**Sainte-Beuve, Charles Augustin** (sanht-'bøv), 1804–69, French literary critic and historian. Much of his vast critical output was collected as *Les causeries du Lundi* (1851–62; tr. Monday Chats). His great work was *Port-Royal* (1840–59), a six-volume history of 17th-cent. French culture. Though his work reveals his taste, learning, and passion for truth, his biographical approach to literature has been largely abandoned.

**Sainte-Chapelle** (sanht-sha,pel), former chapel in Paris. Forming part of the buildings of the Palais-de-Justice, on the Île-de-la-Cité, it was built (1243–46) by Pierre de Montreuil for LOUIS IX and restored in the 19th cent. It consists of two chapels, one above the other, and a spire. Fifteen magnificent stained-glass windows create a blaze of colour and light. Sainte-Chapelle is one of the finest examples of medieval art.

**Saint-Etienne** (,son ,etee·en), city (1982 pop. 206,688, agglomeration 317,228), capital of Loire dept., S central France. Its growth was based on coal-mining, steel, and the manufacture of cycles, machine tools, and ribbons. The earliest railway in France was built in 1828 to carry coal from Saint-Etienne to Andrézieux on the LOIRE R.

**Saint Exupéry, Antoine de** (sanhtegzypay,ree), 1900–44, French author and aviator, lost in action in World War II. His writings, e.g., *Vol de nuit* (1931; tr. Night Flight), reflect his feeling for the open skies and his love of freedom of action. His fable *Le petit prince* (1943; tr. The Little Prince) is beloved by adults and children alike.

**Saint Gall,** Ger. *Sankt Gallen,* city (1984 pop. 74,453), capital of Saint Gall canton, NE Switzerland, near the Lake of Constance. It is the textile centre of E Switzerland. Saint Gall grew around the hermitage of St Gall. It joined the Swiss Confederation in 1454. Its library of medieval manuscripts is world famous.

**Saint-Gaudens, Augustus** (saynt-ˌgawdənz), 1848–1907, foremost American sculptor of his time and an influence in the development of US sculpture; b. Ireland. He is best known for his heroic public monuments, such as the figures of Abraham Lincoln (Lincoln Park, Chicago) and Gen. Sherman (Central Park, New York City.). He also did portrait tablets, plaques, and low reliefs.

**Saint George's,** city (1979 est. pop. 7500), capital of GRENADA.

**Saint Gotthard,** mountain massif in the Swiss ALPS, rising to 3192 m (10,472 ft). It is crossed by the Saint Gotthard Pass 2114 m (6935 ft) and by the Saint Gotthard Tunnel 15-km (9¼-mi) long, one of the world's longest rail tunnels.

**Saint Helena,** island (1976 pop. 5147), 122 km² (47 sq mi) in the S Atlantic, 1931 km (1200 mi) W of Africa. With ASCENSION and TRISTAN DA CUNHA, it comprises the British dependency of St Helena. Discovered uninhabited by the Portuguese in 1502, it became a crown colony in 1834. It is best known as the place of exile (1815–21) of NAPOLEON I.

**Saint Helens,** town (1981 pop. 114,397), Merseyside, NW England, 18 km (11 mi) E of Liverpool. An industrial town, it is famous for the manufacture of glass. Coal-mining, light engineering, and textile manufacture are other important industries. It is the birthplace of Sir Thomas BEECHAM.

**Saint Helens, Mount,** active volcano, 2950 m (9677 ft), SW Washington, US, in the Cascade Range. Dormant for 120 years, it erupted violently on 18 May, 1980, following a series of earth tremors beginning on 20 Mar. The eruption killed some 65 persons, sent a volcanic plume over 18,000 m (60,000 ft) into the air, triggered fires and mudslides, and blanketed a large area with volcanic ash. Less violent eruptions followed, notably in Apr. 1982.

**Saint John:** see VIRGIN ISLANDS.

**St John Ambulance,** organization of volunteers trained to provide instant first-aid and emergency treatment at public events. Based on the Knights Hospitaller, the St John Ambulance Association was established in 1877 to train the public in life-saving measures. It also assumed responsibility for training the police, the fire brigade, and the industrial sector. The St John Ambulance Brigade was formed 10 years later and played an important role during World War II in supporting the Army Medical Services and in Civil Defence. The Association and the Brigade amalgamated in 1968 to become known simply as the St John Ambulance, which has branches in Britain and throughout the Commonwealth.

**Saint John's,** city (1979 est. pop. 25,000), capital of ANTIGUA AND BARBUDA.

**Saint John's,** city (1980 est. pop. 86,576), provincial capital, SE Newfoundland, E Canada, overlooking a fine harbour. Its major industries, chiefly related to fishing, include fish processing and the manufacture and repair of fishing equipment, boats, and marine engines. One of the oldest settlements in North America, it is at a site discovered and named by John CABOT in 1497 and thought to have been settled shortly thereafter, the exact date being unknown. It was formally occupied by England in 1583 and taken several times by the French before coming under permanent English rule in 1762.

**Saint John the Divine, Cathedral of,** New York City, US. Chartered by the Episcopal diocese in 1873 and begun in 1892, it is still unfinished. In 1911 the original Romanesque design was altered to the Gothic style design of Ralph Adams Cram. Construction on the cathedral resumed in 1982, the work to be completed by local residents hired by the Episcopal diocese and trained in the ancient art of stonecutting.

**St Kitts–Nevis,** officially St Christopher–Nevis, federated island state (1987 est. pop. 50,000), 262 km² (101 sq mi), British West Indies, in the Leeward Islands. The capital is Basseterre, on St Kitts. The GDP is US$619 million and the GDP per capita is US$1358. The islands were discovered (1493) by Columbus and, after Anglo-French strife, were awarded (1783) to Britain. In 1967, together with ANGUILLA, which returned to British rule in 1971, they became a self-governing associated

state, which in 1983 achieved full independence as a member of the COMMONWEALTH. The first post-independence elections in 1984 were won by the People's Action Movement led by Kennedy A. Simmonds.

**St Laurent, Louis Stephen,** 1882–1973, prime minister of CANADA (1948–57). He was minister of internal affairs (1946–48) in Mackenzie KING's government, and succeeded him as Liberal Party leader and prime minister.

**Saint-Laurent, Yves,** 1936–, French FASHION designer. He took over as chief designer from Christian DIOR. Not an innovative designer, he is important because he was the first couturier to develop ready-to-wear clothes on a large scale. He has been successful with men's clothes and with perfumes for both sexes.

**Saint Lawrence,** major North American river, flowing 1197 km (744 mi) NE from Lake Ontario to the Gulf of St Lawrence and forming 193 km (120 mi) of the US–Canada border. Although closed by ice from mid-December to mid-April, the river is the chief outlet for shipping on the Great Lakes, having been canalized as part of the SAINT LAWRENCE SEAWAY.

**Saint Lawrence Seaway,** international waterway, E North America, built by the US and Canada and opened in 1959, which allows oceangoing vessels access to Lake Ontario through a 8-m (27-ft) channel on the SAINT LAWRENCE R. Principal locks on the seaway are St Lambert (5.5 m/18 ft lift); Côte Ste Catherine (9.1 m/30 ft), bypassing Lachine Rapids; Lower and Upper Beauharnois (25 m/82 ft, including the Beauharnois Canal, built 1932); Bertrand H. Snell (13.7 m/45 ft); Dwight D. Eisenhower (11.6 m/38 ft); and the Iroquois Guard Lock (91 cm/3 ft). Hydroelectric facilities are operated along the seaway, which, together with improved channels between the GREAT LAKES, forms the **St Lawrence & Great Lakes Waterway,** linking all of the lakes with the Atlantic Ocean.

**Saint Louis,** US city (1984 est. pop. 429,000), E Missouri, on the Mississippi R., below the mouth of the Missouri; settled 1764, inc. 1822. The largest city in the state, it is a major river port, railway interchange, and market. Its manufactures include basic metals, beer, chemicals, machinery, and transport equipment. Originally a fur-trading post, it was held by the French and the Spanish and passed to the US by the LOUISIANA PURCHASE. The gateway to the Missouri R. and the West, St Louis grew rapidly after the War of 1812. Eero SAARINEN's Gateway Arch, 192 m (630 ft) high, is its best-known landmark.

**St Lucia** (saynt ˌloohshə), island nation (1987 est. pop. 140,000), 616 km² (238 sq mi), West Indies, one of the Windward Islands. The capital is Castries. A lush volcanic island with mountains rising abruptly from the sea, St Lucia is much favoured by tourists. It also earns foreign exchange from traditional exports of bananas, citrus fruit, coconuts, and sugar. Industrialization has been undertaken, and oil transshipment facilities and a free-trade zone were developed in the early 1980s. The GDP is US$151 million and the GDP per capita is US$1127. The population is largely of black African descent; although English is the official language, a French patois is widely spoken. COLUMBUS probably discovered St Lucia in 1502, but hostile Carib Indians prevented early colonization attempts. The first successful settlement was by the French in the late 1600s, but Britain gained control in the late 1700s. A member of the short-lived WEST INDIES Federation (1958–62), St Lucia gained self-government as a British associated state in 1967 and independence in 1979 as a member of the COMMONWEALTH. A parliamentary government was formed after a 1982 election victory by the (conservative) United Workers' Party led by John Compton. St Lucia participated in the US-led invasion of Grenada in 1983.

**Saint Mark's Church,** Venice, named after the city's tutelary saint. The reconstruction of the original Romanesque basilical church was completed c.1071. From the 12th cent. on, it became through alterations and adornments a splendid Byzantine monument, reflecting Venice's prominence in trade with the East. In the 14th cent. the facade received Gothic additions. The plan is a Greek cross, with a central dome and a dome over each arm. The west front's five portals open on the Piazza San Marco. The facade is encrusted with marble and mosaics; the lower interior walls are sheathed in marble; and the vaults and domes are covered with mosaics set against a gold background. The bronze Four Horses of Saint Mark's, probably from a Roman triumphal arch, stand on the gallery over the main entrance.

Saint Mark's Church

burned in 1087 and was replaced by a Norman structure (13th cent.). In 1561 St Paul's burned again. Inigo JONES appended a classical facade after 1628, but the Great Fire of London (1666) almost destroyed the church. In 1668 Wren was given permission to demolish the church and build a new one. His Greek cross design was modified to include a long nave and choir. Construction of the cathedral took place between 1675 and 1710. The three-aisled NAVE and choir extend east and west from a central crossing, over which rises a huge DOME, pierced at the crown to allow a view of the lantern. The exterior dome rises above a colonnaded drum and supports the lantern and cross. St Paul's was damaged by bombs in World War II and was not completely reconstructed until 1962.

Saint Paul's Cathedral

**Saint Martin,** island, 96 km² (37 sq mi), in the Leeward Islands, West Indies. Since occupation (1648) by the Dutch and French, it has been divided. The northern part (1981 pop. 10,000; capital, Marigot) is a dependency of GUADELOUPE. The southern part (1981 pop. 13,000; chief town, Philipsburg) is in the NETHERLANDS ANTILLES. It is a tourist resort.

**Saint Moritz,** Ger. *Sankt Moritz,* town (1984 pop. 5900), Grisons canton, SE Switzerland, in the Upper Engadine. It is a famous winter sports centre and year-round resort with mineral springs. The Olympic winter games were held there in 1928 and 1948.

**Saint-Nazaire** ('so·na,zeə), city (1982 pop. of agglomeration 130,271), NW France, on the LOIRE R. estuary. Shipbuilding began in 1861 and this industry has dominated the life of Saint-Nazaire which was largely destroyed during World War II when it was a German submarine base. Rebuilt since, the shipyards have merged to create the largest shipbuilding company in France, capable of building the biggest vessels afloat. Electrical engineering and petrochemicals provide other employment.

**Saint Patrick's Cathedral,** New York City, US, largest Roman Catholic cathedral in the US, on Fifth Avenue between 50th and 51st Streets. Planned by James Renwick, the cathedral was built between 1858 and 1879. The Lady Chapel behind the high altar was added later. The cathedral has 12 side chapels.

**Saint Paul,** US city (1984 est. pop. 266,000), state capital of Minnesota, a port at the head of navigation on the Mississippi R., next to MINNEAPOLIS, with which it forms the Twin Cities; inc. 1854. The industrial, commercial, and cultural centre of a vast fertile region, it is also the focus of a railway system. Tapes and abrasives, computers, aerospace and electronic equipment, petroleum products, and vehicles are major manufactures. The area was settled in the early 1800s, and the site was an important river landing by 1823. St Paul, mapped out along the river in 1846, became territorial capital in 1849 and state capital in 1858. The railway arrived in 1862 and the city subsequently became the centre of a railway empire.

**Saint Paul's Cathedral,** London, masterpiece of Sir Christopher WREN and of the English BAROQUE, on Ludgate Hill. A Saxon cathedral there

**Saint Petersburg:** see LENINGRAD.

**Saint Peter's Church,** Rome, principal and largest church of the Christian world, built mainly between 1506 and 1626 on the site of earlier churches. Appointed by Pope Julius II in 1506, BRAMANTE, the first architect, seems to have planned a Greek cross. He was succeeded by RAPHAEL (1514), Antonio da San Gallo (1520), and MICHELANGELO (1547), who completed the structure up to the drum of the great DOME. Giocamo della Porta modified the design and finished the dome. Throughout the 16th cent. there was controversy over whether the church would be built in the form of a Greek or a Latin cross. The problem was resolved in favour of the Latin cross when Carlo Maderno added the nave and facade (1607–14). Urban VIII dedicated the church in 1626. BERNINI completed (1629–62) the great design, creating a forecourt with an elliptical piazza bounded by quadruple colonnades. The Dome of St Peter's stands 123 m (404 ft) from the pavement and has an interior diameter of 42 m (137 ft).

**Saint Pierre and Miquelon,** French overseas territory (1977 est. pop. 5900), 241 km² (93 sq mi), nine islands in the Gulf of St Lawrence. Fishing is the main occupation. The islands were colonized (1604) by France, taken by the British three times, and restored to France in 1814. They became a department in 1976, but reverted to special territorial status in 1985.

**Saint-Saëns, (Charles) Camille** (sanh sahnhs), 1835–1921, French composer. His many works are brilliantly crafted and orchestrated, but often lack imaginative force. Best known for the opera *Samson et Dalila*

(1877), he also wrote symphonies, concertos, and SYMPHONIC POEMS, notably *Danse macabre* (1874).

**Saint-Simon, Claude Henri de Rouvroy, comte de** (sanh see͵mawnh), 1760–1825, French social philosopher. He advocated a society led by scientists and industrialists and based on a scientific division of labour resulting in spontaneous social harmony. His works, among them *The New Christianity* (1825), influenced later socialist thought.

**Saint-Simon, Louis de Rouvroy, duc de**, 1675–1755, French courtier, author of voluminous memoirs (pub. 1788) of the court of LOUIS XIV. Remarkable for their psychological observation and brilliant sketches, the memoirs, despite a disregard for literary technique, are a monument of French literature. Based on his own notes and on contemporary journals covering the years 1691–1751, Saint-Simon's account is intensely personal and emotional, reflecting his inability to accept the rise of the bourgeoisie and his resentment against Louis XIV. Though full of errors, the memoirs are an indispensable historical source.

**Saint Thomas:** see VIRGIN ISLANDS.

**Saint Valentine's Day** (14 Feb.). Originally the Roman feast of Lupercalia, it was Christianized in memory of the martyr St Valentine (d. AD 270). In the Middle Ages, Valentine became associated with the union of lovers under conditions of duress. Today the holiday is celebrated with the sending, often anonymously, of romantic or comic messages called 'valentines'.

**St Vincent and the Grenadines**, nation (1987 est. pop. 135,000), 388 km² (150 sq mi), West Indies, in the Windward Islands, comprising the island of St Vincent (363 km²/140 sq mi) and the northern islets of the Grenadines, an archipelago that extends southwards from the main island. The capital is Kingstown. St Vincent is mountainous and forested, with a mild climate. Exports include bananas, arrowroot, and copra, and tourism is important, but per capita income remains very low. The GDP is US$100 million and the GDP per capita is US$860. The people are mainly descendants of African slaves brought in during the colonial period; English is spoken. St Vincent was discovered by COLUMBUS in 1498 and colonized by the British in the late 1700s. Attempts to subdue the hostile Carib Indians failed, and the British deported the Black Caribs (miscegenated Caribs) in 1797. Self-government as an associated state was granted in 1969, full independence within the COMMONWEALTH in 1979. Eruptions of the SOUFRIÈRE volcano have been very destructive, killing 2000 people in 1902 and causing the evacuation of 20,000 in 1979. The (conservative) St Vincent Labour Party held office, alone or in coalition, for most of the period to 1984, when it was defeated by the (centrist) New Democratic Party led by James Mitchell. In 1983 St Vincent and the Grenadines participated in the US-led invasion of Grenada.

**St Vitus's dance:** see under CHOREA.

**Saipan**, island (1973 pop. 12,366), capital of the NORTHERN MARIANA ISLANDS and administrative center for the U.S. Trust Territory of the PACIFIC ISLANDS.

Saint Peter's Church

**Sakai,** city (1986 est. pop. 809,734), Osaka prefecture, S Honshu, Japan, on Osaka Bay. Chief industrial products include chemicals, bicycle parts, iron and steel goods, and textiles. During the mid 15th to 16th cent. Sakai flourished as a leading port, trading with China, Asia, Portugal, Spain, and Holland. Its enormous wealth enabled it to be the establishment of self-governing, but its prosperity declined with the rise of OSAKA as a commercial centre. In 1962, the port was renamed Sakai-Senboku and in 1966 the construction of Senboku New Town, one of the largest new towns in Japan (1985 pop. 162,352), started to the southeast. The poet Senno-Rikyu (1520–91), famous as the founder of the tea ceremony and the art of flower-arranging, lived in Sakai. Between the old and new towns, there are the tombs of three emperors, including that of Emperor Nintoku—the largest mausoleum in Japan.

**Sakakawea:** see SACAJAWEA.

**sake,** Japanese fermented liquor, from 12% to 16% alcohol. Made from rice, it is yellowish and sherrylike in flavour and is usually taken hot.

**Sakhalin,** formerly Saghalien, island, c.76,400 km² (29,500 sq mi), E USSR, off the Soviet mainland in the Sea of Okhotsk, N of Hokkaido, Japan. With the KURIL ISLANDS to the E, it forms Sakhalin oblast. Cold and damp, with heavily forested mountain ranges, Sakhalin is important to the economy of the SOVIET FAR EAST for its coal and iron deposits. Japan ceded Sakhalin to Russia in 1875 in exchange for the Kuril Islands, regained control (1905) of areas south of lat. 50°N (called Karafuto), and, in 1951, renounced all claims to Sakhalin, though not to the Kuril Islands, which Soviet forces had occupied in 1945.

**Sakharov, Andrei Dmitriyevich**, 1921–, Soviet nuclear physicist and human-rights advocate; first Soviet citizen to win the Nobel Peace Prize (1975). From 1948 to 1956 he helped to develop the USSR's hydrogen bomb. In the late 1960s he emerged as an outspoken critic of the arms race and of Soviet repression. Banished to Gorky in 1980 and released in 1987, he is now a member of the Congress of the People's Deputies.

**Saki:** see MUNRO, HECTOR HUGH.

**Saladin**, 1137?–1193, Muslim warrior and sultan of Egypt, the great opponent of the Crusaders; b. Mesopotamia, of Kurdish descent. He used his position as vizier to overthrow the Fatimid dynasty and establish himself (1171) as the first Ayyubid sultan. He greatly expanded his territories, thereby clashing with the Crusaders (see CRUSADES). With a large force of Muslims (called Saracens by the Christians) he won the battle of Hattin (1187), which led to his capture of Jerusalem. The Third Crusade (1189) was gathered to regain Jerusalem. It was during this Crusade that Saladin and King RICHARD I of England fought in the conflict celebrated in chivalric romance. Saladin triumphed over the Crusaders and left the Latin Kingdom of Jerusalem with only a thin strip of coastline. Saladin was a learned man and a great patron of the arts.

**Salamanca**, city (1981 pop. 167,131), capital of Salamanca prov., W central Spain, in León, on the Tormes R. Among its industries is food processing. Taken by Hannibal (220 BC), the city was held by the Romans, Visigoths, and Moors (8th–11th cent.). Its university (founded early 13th cent.) was world famous. Among the city's landmarks are the colonnaded Plaza Mayor, a Roman bridge, and a 12th-cent. cathedral.

**salamander**, AMPHIBIAN (order Urodela) having a tail and small, weak limbs that can regenerate. Found in damp regions of the northern temperate zone, they are abundant in North America. Most are under 15 cm (6 in) long, although the giant salamander of Japan may reach 1.5 m (5 ft). Usually nocturnal and feeding on small animals such as insects and worms, salamanders are mostly terrestrial as adults, although some are aquatic and a few arboreal. Salamanders sheltering in rotten logs would run out when these went on the fire, giving rise to legends of salamanders being created in fir.

**Salamis**, island, E Greece, in the Saronic Gulf. Disputed between Athens (under SOLON) and neighbouring Megara, it was awarded to the former after arbitration by Sparta (c.596 BC). Off its shore, during the PERSIAN WARS, the Greek fleet, led by THEMISTOCLES, decisively defeated the Persians (480 BC).

**Salazar, António de Oliveira** (səlͻ͵zah), 1889–1970, dictator of PORTUGAL (1932–68). A professor of political economy, he became finance minister (1926, 1928) and stabilized the nation's finances. As premier he established (1933) a corporate state and suppressed political opposition. Although he supported the Spanish dictator, FRANCO, he allowed the Allies to use the Azores as a military base in World War II. Later he encouraged Portugal's economic development and tried to suppress revolts in its African colonies. After suffering a stroke in 1968, he was replaced as premier by Marcello CAETANO.

**Salem, 1** US city (1980 pop. 38,220), NE Massachusetts, on an inlet of Massachusetts Bay; inc. 1629. Once a world-famous port and a centre of the China trade, it is now a tourist centre with light industries. Salem was the scene (1692) of infamous witchcraft trials. The birthplace of Nathaniel HAWTHORNE is preserved, and Pioneer Village is a reproduction of a 1630 settlement. **2** US city (1980 pop. 89,233), state capital of Oregon, on the Willamette R.; inc. 1857. It is a major food-processing centre, and has wood product and electronic industries, in addition to state government. Founded 1840–41 by Methodist missionaries, it became capital of Oregon Territory in 1851 and remained the capital after statehood (1859).

**Salem,** town (1981 pop. 361,394), Tamil Nadu state, S India. It is a district administrative, railway, and commercial centre which has important textile industries, using hydroelectric power. It has grown very rapidly in population since the 1920s. It has an ancient temple that formed its original nucleus, and was a British district headquarters.

**Salerno,** city (1984 pop. 156,291) S Italy, on the Gulf of Salerno. The modern town has port and industrial activities. Originating as a Roman colony, it acquired a school of medicine in the 9th cent. which became famous throughout Europe in the Middle Ages. Salerno was the site of a fierce battle in Sept. 1943, during the Allied landings. The 11th-cent. cathedral has notable features.

**sales tax:** see TAXATION.

**Salford,** town (1981 pop. 96,525), Greater Manchester, NW England, situated immediately to the E of Manchester. The major docks on the MANCHESTER SHIP CANAL are located here. Industries found within the town include engineering and the manufacture of pharmaceutical goods and textiles. The Roman Catholic cathedral was completed in 1848, and the university was established in 1967. Salford is the birthplace of the physicist, James JOULE.

**Salic law,** rule of succession in some noble families of Europe forbidding the succession by females or those descended in the female line to titles or offices. It was mistakenly thought to be part of the *Lex Salica* (see GERMANIC LAWS), whereas those concerned only succession to property. The VALOIS and BOURBON families in France maintained it, notably in the successions of PHILIP V and PHILIP VI. In Spain the Salic law was rescinded in favor of ISABELLA II. It prevented the succession in Hanover of Queen VICTORIA of England.

**Salieri, Antonio,** 1750–1825, Italian opera composer. He settled in Vienna in 1766 and became its most popular opera composer in the late 1770s, thus making it difficult for MOZART to obtain commissions. In spite of rivalry with Mozart, Salieri praised his work, and there is no evidence that Salieri poisoned him, as legend and subsequent dramas have suggested.

**Salinas de Gortari, Carlos,** 1948–, Mexican political leader and president (1988–). Having served as planning and budget minister, he was elected president (1988) as candidate of the ruling Institutional Revolutionary Party (PRI), although opposition formations made major inroads into the PRI's traditional dominance.

**Salinger, J(erome) D(avid),** 1919–, American author. With pathos and humour he depicts the individual caught in a banal, restricting world. His only novel, *The Catcher in the Rye* (1951), quickly became a classic; also popular are his short stories, e.g., *Nine Stories* (1953), *Franny and Zooey* (1961).

**Salisbury,** city (1981 pop. 36,890), Wiltshire, S England. It was founded in 1220, when the bishopric was moved there from Old Sarum. Its great cathedral (1220–60) is a splendid example of Early English architecture and has the highest spire (123 m/404 ft) in England.

**Salisbury, Robert Arthur Talbot Gascoyne-Cecil,** 3rd **marquess of,** 1830–1903, British statesman. Conservative foreign minister under Benjamin DISRAELI, he attended the Congress of Berlin (1878). As prime minister (1885–86, 1886–92, 1895–1902), he avoided alignments in European affairs and dealt with the SOUTH AFRICAN WAR. His governments provided for free public education (1891) and workmen's compensation (1897).

Salisbury Cathedral

**Salisbury, Robert Cecil, 1st earl of,** 1563–1612, English statesman, son of William Cecil, Baron BURGHLEY. He succeeded his father as principal secretary to ELIZABETH I in 1598 and arranged the peaceful accession (1603) of JAMES I. Under James, he directed virtually the entire government, reduced the king's debts, and tried to curb James's extravagance.

**Salkey, Andrew,** 1928–, Jamaican writer; b. Panama. Now resident in the US after many years in England. He is a skilful prose stylist who has also written books for children. His chief concern is with the lives of the Jamaican peasantry and workers, e.g., in the cycle, *Hurricane* (1964), *Earthquake* (1965), *Drought* (1966), and *Riot* (1967).

**Salk vaccine,** killed-virus vaccine for immunization against POLIOMYELITIS. It is named after Jonas Edward Salk, a US physician.

**Sallust** (Caius Sallustius Crispus), 86 BC–c.34 BC, Roman historian. His major surviving work is *Bellum Catilina,* or *Catilina,* an account of the conspiracy of CATILINE.

**salmon,** marine FISH of the family Salmonidae that spawn in fresh water, including salmon, TROUT, and char. The herringlike Salmonidae are characterized by soft, rayless, adipose fins and live in cold, oxygen-rich waters. They are generally a uniform silver in colour. The Atlantic salmon (*Salmo salar*) once abundant, is threatened by pollution, damming, and overfishing but conservation is beginning to show results. The Thames R. has been cleaned so well that the salmon have now returned to it to spawn. It feeds on CRUSTACEANS at sea and small fish while spawning and reaches 7 kg (15 lb). There are six species of Pacific salmon ranging from Japan and Siberia to W North America. Like the Atlantic salmon these migrate from the sea to the rivers in which they were hatched to spawn. These species are the commercial food-fishes, protected by the International Pacific Salmon Fisheries Commission.

**salmonellosis,** infection caused by intestinal bacteria of the genus *Salmonella*. The most common form is gastroenteritis, an intestinal disease usually resulting from contaminated food. Symptoms of food poisoning include nausea, abdominal pains, diarrhoea, and fever. Treatment includes rest and replacement of lost body fluids. Salmonellosis created a political crisis in 1989 and led to the resignation of the Under-Secretary of State (Health), Edwina Currie.

**Salome** (sə͵lohmee), daughter of Herod Philip and Herodias. She is generally supposed to be the daughter who danced to obtain the head of JOHN THE BAPTIST.

**Salonica:** see THESSALONIKI.

**salsa,** American popular music, developed largely in New York City in the 1970s. It blends the rhumba and other dance forms; Cuban, Puerto Rican, Dominican, and other Latin American strains; ROCK MUSIC; and JAZZ. Salsa is chiefly performed, and often danced simultaneously, by singers; percussionists; and brass, guitar, and keyboard players. Noted artists include Machito, Eddie Palmieri, and Tito Puente.

**salt,** chemical compound (other than water) formed by neutralization reactions between ACIDS AND BASES; by direct combination of metal with nonmetal, e.g., sodium chloride (common table salt); by reaction of a metal with a dilute acid; by reaction of a metal oxide with acid; by reaction of a nonmetallic oxide with a base; or by reaction of two salts with each other to form two new salts. Most salts are ionic compounds. The chemical formula indicates the proportion of atoms of the elements making up the salt. A salt is classified as acidic, basic, or normal if it has, respectively, hydrogen (H), hydroxyl (OH), or neither in its formula. A salt undergoes dissociation when dissolved in a polar solvent, e.g., water (see HYDROLYSIS).

**SALT** (Strategic Arms Limitation Talks): see DISARMAMENT, NUCLEAR.

**salt, common:** see SODIUM CHLORIDE.

**Salt Lake City,** US city (1984 est. pop. 165,000), state capital of Utah, on the Jordan R., near the GREAT SALT LAKE, at the foot of the Wasatch Range; inc. 1851. Food-processing, oil-refining, smelting, and electronic industries are important. Founded (1847) by Brigham YOUNG as the capital of the MORMON community, it is still its economic hub. The gigantic Temple (1853–93) is at the city's heart.

**saltpetre** or **potassium nitrate,** chemical compound ($KNO_3$), occurring as colourless prismatic crystals or as a white powder. When heated, it decomposes to release oxygen. Saltpetre has been used in gunpowder manufacture since about the 12th cent.; it is also used in explosives, fireworks, matches, and fertilizers, and as a food preservative.

**Saltykov-Shchedrin, Mikhail Evgrafovich** (͵sahltikof-͵shchedreen), 1826–89, Russian novelist and satirist. His masterpiece is his only novel, *The Golovlyov Family* (1876), a study of decaying gentry. Among his other works are the satirical *History of a Town* (1869–70) and the Aesopian *Fables* (1885).

**Salvador** or **Bahia,** city (1980 pop. 1,496,276), capital of Bahia state, E Brazil. An Atlantic port, it exports cacao, tobacco, sugar, and other products of a fertile crescent, the Recôncavo. The city was found in 1549, flourished with the rise of sugar plantations, and was the leading centre of colonial Brazil and the capital of Portugal's possessions in America until 1763. An influx of plantation slaves was the source of its African heritage. It is now a tourist centre noted for its 16th-cent. cathedral.

**Salvation Army,** Protestant nonsectarian Christian organization for evangelical and philanthropic work. Begun (1865) in England as the East London Revival Society by William BOOTH, with his wife, Catherine, it was designated the Salvation Army in 1878. It was organized along military lines and sought to minister to physical as well as spiritual needs. It rapidly expanded overseas, and is now to be found in over 80 countries. The beliefs of the group generally agree with those of most Protestant evangelicals, but SACRAMENTS are not practised. The Salvation Army is distinguished by its bands, its work with the armed services, and by its aid to the victims of disasters all over the world.

**salvia,** common and generic name for a large group of over 500 plant species, mostly herbs and shrubs of temperate regions. The name means 'to heal' and refers to the medicinal properties of many of the species. The group contains many garden ornamentals, and also the widely-used potherb known as sage (*Salvia officinalis*).

**Salween,** river, c.2820 km (1750 mi) long, Southeast Asia. It rises in Tibet and flows through SW China and Burma to enter the Gulf of Martaban, in E Burma, near Moulmein. Flowing through gorges for much of its length, the river is navigable for only c.120 km (75 mi). It varies up to 20 m (65 ft) in depth between wet and dry seasons.

**Salzburg,** city (1981 pop. 139, 426), capital of Salzburg prov., W central Austria. It is an industrial, tourist, and transportation centre.

Settled by the Celts and later a Roman trading centre, it was long the residence of powerful archbishops. The city was secularized in 1802 and passed to Bavaria (1809), but was returned (1815) to Austria by the Congress of VIENNA. Salzburg's superb landmarks include a 7th-cent. Benedictine abbey and a monument to PARACELSUS. MOZART was born in Salzburg and is honoured with an annual music festival; HOFMANNSTHAL's morality play *Everyman* is performed annually in the cathedral square.

**Samaria,** ancient city, central Palestine, NW of Nablus (Shechem), Israeli-occupied Jordan. Samaria was built by King Omri as the capital of the northern kingdom of Israel in the early 9th cent. BC. It fell in 721 BC to Assyria. Destroyed in 120 BC by John Hyrcanus (see MACCABEES), it was rebuilt by HEROD the Great. It is the traditional burial place of JOHN THE BAPTIST. The city gave its name to the **Samaritans,** a sect recognizing only the PENTATEUCH of the Bible. In Jesus's time a great enmity existed between them and the Jews since each claimed to be the only true inheritors of Abraham and Moses. A small group of Samaritans still live at Nablus. They use Hebrew for prayer, but Arabic as their vernacular.

**Samaritans,** voluntary organization providing a telephone service for suicidal and despairing people. Founded in 1953 by Rev. Chad Varah, it offers anonymous and confidential help at all times around Britain. Samaritans will listen for as long as the caller needs, a process called befriending.

**Samarkand,** city (1984 pop. 515,000), Soviet Central Asia, in the UZBEK SOVIET SOCIALIST REPUBLIC, on the Trans-Caspian railway. A major cotton and silk centre, it also produces wine and tea, and such industrial goods as motor-vehicle parts. The oldest central Asian city and one of the world's oldest cities, Samarkand was situated on the ancient trade route between the Middle East and China. It was conquered (329 BC) by ALEXANDER THE GREAT, fell (8th cent. AD) to the Arabs, and became (9th cent.) a centre of Islamic culture. Sacked (1220) by JENGHIZ KHAN, it revived as the capital of TAMERLANE's empire (14th–15th cent.). Samarkand fell to the Uzbeks c.1500 and to Russia in 1868. The city's old quarter contains Tamerlane's mausoleum and many ancient mosques.

**Samba, Paul,** 1870–1914, Cameroon chief and anticolonial resistance leader. He was educated in Germany and returned to CAMEROON in 1895 where he became chief among the Bulu. Though he took no part in the popular rising of the Bulu against German rule (1899–1901), he did become a focus of resistance in subsequent years and in 1914 was executed for treason.

**Samoa** see AMERICAN SAMOA; WESTERN SAMOA.

**Sámos,** island (1981 pop. 40,519), c.469 km² (181 sq mi), SE Greece, in the Aegean Sea, near Turkey; one of the Sporades island group. Its economy is based on agriculture, wine-making, tobacco processing, and shipbuilding. A cultural and maritime centre in ancient times, it was the home of AESOP and the birthplace of PYTHAGORAS.

**Samothrace,** Gr. *Samothráki*, Greek island, 286 km² (112 sq mi), of the N AEGEAN, which has a strategic location close to the Gallipoli peninsula and the DARDANELLES. In ancient times it was a centre of worship of the Cabiri, gods of the underworld. The *Winged Victory of Samothrace* (306 BC) was unearthed in excavations in 1863 and is now in the Louvre, Paris. Turkey ceded the island to Greece in 1913.

**sample,** used in STATISTICS to indicate some smaller part of a total POPULATION which can be counted or measured in an investigation usually in order to estimate values for the population as a whole. A subjectively chosen sample, i.e., one taken by picking individuals which look typical, is often biased and frequently underestimates the variability of the population. Objective sampling therefore requires that the sample individuals are chosen at random or systematically. The sample of oranges displayed by a greengrocer outside his shop may not be entirely representative of the whole population of oranges that he has for sale.

**Samrin, Heng:** see HENG SAMRIN.

**Samson,** in the BIBLE, judge of Israel whose exceptional strength lay in his long hair. The Philistines accomplished his destruction through the woman Delilah, who cut off his hair. Captured and blinded, Samson regained his strength as his hair grew long again. He then pulled down the Philistine temple, killing both himself and his captors. Judges 13–16.

**Samson, Émile,** 1837–1913, French pottery and porcelain manufacturer. From 1864, his firm made extremely accomplished imitations of earlier Continental, English and Chinese PORCELAIN, but used hard-paste for models originally made in soft-paste. It also reproduced MAIOLICA, PALISSY ware, French faience, Delft and Isnik pottery. Although Samson's products were marked with an S in various forms, they have often deceived the unwary.

**Samsun,** city (1980 pop. 198,749), capital of Samsun prov., N Turkey, on the BLACK SEA coast. It serves as commercial centre of a rich agricultural lowland and is noted for its manufacture of tobacco. It was founded in the 6th cent. BC, and was known formerly as Amisus.

**Samuel,** two books of the OLD TESTAMENT. The narrative covers Hebrew history during the careers of Samuel, SAUL, and DAVID (roughly the 11th cent. BC). Scholars detect at least two main strands, based on divergent attitudes toward the establishment of the monarchy. One section (2 Sam. 9–20) has a claim to be the oldest piece of narrative in the Bible. The prophet Samuel (fl. 1050 BC) was the last judge of Israel.

**Samuelson, Paul A.,** 1915–, American economist. Winner of the 1970 Nobel Prize for economics, he has been on the faculty of the Massachusetts Inst. of Technology since 1941 and has held a variety of government posts. As adviser to Presidents John KENNEDY and Lyndon JOHNSON, he helped shape the tax legislation and antipoverty efforts of the 1960s. A supporter of Keynesian economics (see KEYNES), he is known for his work *Economics* (1948; 11th ed. 1980), a standard textbook for many years.

**samurai,** Japanese warriors. The samurai class came into being in the 12th cent. and provided the support on which the Kamakura (see KAMAKURA PERIOD), Muromachi and TOKUGAWA shogunates depended. After the MEIJI restoration the samurai lost their rights and privileges.

**Sana** or **San'a,** city (1981 pop. 277,817), capital of the Yemen Arab Republic. The largest city in S ARABIA, it lies inland on a high plain and is linked to the Red Sea port of Hodeida by road. An Islamic cultural centre with institutions of learning and many mosques, it is also a trade centre for cotton, coffee, grapes, and other crops grown nearby. A pre-Islamic settlement, it was held by Ethiopia in the 6th cent. and by the Ottoman Turks in the 17th cent. and from 1872 to 1918, when Yemen became independent.

**San Andreas fault,** the principal FAULT in a network of faults extending nearly 1000 km (over 600 mi) from NW California to the Gulf of California, US. It marks the boundary of two crustal plates (see PLATE TECTONICS) moving in relation to each other, causing horizontal displacement along the fault. Total displacement has been estimated at c.560 km (350 mi) since the fault's formation over 30 million years ago. Such movement causes EARTHQUAKES, thousands of which, mostly of low magnitude, occur annually.

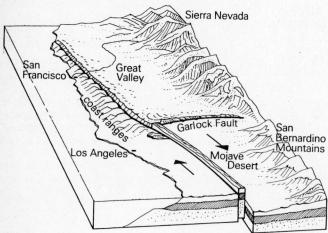

San Andreas fault

**San Antonio,** US city (1984 est. pop. 843,000), Texas, at the source of the San Antonio R.; inc. 1837. It is the site of a military training and medical complex, and the industrial, trade, and financial centre of an agricultural region. Manufactures include processed foods, clothing, and chemicals. The Spanish visited the area long before they established (1718–31) a series of missions. San Antonio was the leading Texas

settlement in the Spanish and Mexican days. In the Texas Revolution, Texans captured it (1835) and Mexicans attacked its ALAMO. The Mexican flavour remains today, and the city has a large Spanish-speaking population. In 1982 Henry Cisneros became the first Mexican-American to be elected mayor of a major city. It is known for its artists' colonies and museums, its many educational institutions, and numerous historical sites.

**San Bernardino,** US city (1984 est. pop. 130,000), S California, at the foot of the San Bernardino Mts; inc. 1854. Its manufactures include steel, cement, and aerospace products. The adjacent Norton Air Force Base is a major employer. San Bernardino is in a growing metropolitan area that includes the cities of Ontario and Riverside. Explored (1772) and settled by the Spanish, the city was laid out by MORMONS in the 1850s.

**Sánchez Ferlosio, Rafael** (ˌsahncheth feəˌlohsyoh), 1927–, Spanish novelist; b. Italy. A master of the Spanish language, he has written such novels as *Industrias y andancas de Alfanhuí* (1951; tr. The Labours and Fortunes of Alfanhuí), *El Jarama* (1956; tr. *The One Day of the Week*), and *El testimonio de Yarfoz* (1986; tr. Yarfoz's Testimony).

**San Cristóbal,** city (1980 est. pop. 272,000), capital of Táchira state in the central highlands of W Venezuela close to the Colombian border. Founded in 1561 the city is constructed on three levels with most of the buildings modern but built in the colonial style. It is an important communications centre and a reception area for the surrounding coffee districts.

**sand,** rock material occurring in the form of loose, rounded or angular grains, varying in size from 0.06 to 2 mm in diameter. It is formed by the WEATHERING and decomposition of all types of ROCK, its most abundant mineral constituent being QUARTZ. Sand has numerous uses, particularly in the manufacture of bricks, cement, glass, concrete, explosives, and abrasives. See also DESERT; QUARTZITE; SANDSTONE.

**Sand, George,** pseud. of **Amandine Aurore Lucie Dupin, baronne Dudevant** (sanhn), 1804–76, French novelist. Her unconventional life was symbolized by the male attire she adopted to protest the unequal treatment accorded to women, and by her open and notorious liaisons with the writer Jules Sandeau, with Alfred de MUSSET, and with CHOPIN. After her divorce from Baron Dudevant (1836), she supported herself and her two children chiefly by her writing. Of her 80-odd novels, *The Haunted Pool* (1846) and *Fanchon the Cricket* (1850) are masterpieces. Notable also are *Indiana* (1832) and *Lélia* (1833), expressing her feminist beliefs. All her works are distinguished by a romantic love of nature and an extravagant moral idealism. Much of her work was autobiographical, notably *She and He* (1859), which concerns her life with Musset, and *A Winter on Majorca* (1841), about her life with Chopin.

**sandalwood,** name for several fragrant tropical woods, especially that of *Santalum album,* a partially parasitic evergreen tree native to India. Oil distilled from the wood is much used as a perfume and in medicine.

**Sandburg, Carl,** 1878–1967, American poet. His experiences as a day labourer, soldier, socialist political worker, and journalist gave him the view of American life that informed his poetry. Drawing his inspiration from America's past and present, influenced by Walt WHITMAN, Sandburg wrote vigorous, impressionistic free verse that celebrated ordinary people and things. Collections of his poems include *Chicago Poems* (1916), *Cornhuskers* (1918), *The People, Yes* (1936), *Complete Poems* (1950) and *Harvest Poems, 1910–1960* (1960). Sandburg also collected folk ballads and songs in *The American Songbag* (1927) and wrote an epic biography of Lincoln (6 vol., 1926–39); children's books, e.g., *Rootabaga Stories* (1922); and the autobiographical *Always the Young Strangers* (1953).

**sand dollar:** see SEA URCHIN.

**sand eel,** FISH of the family Ammodytidae with eel-like body and small scales or none. They live in cold and temperate seas in the northern hemisphere. Sand eels are only about 20 cm (9 in) long, but they are important commercially because of their large numbers and because of their role in the food webs of the seas. Sand eels feed on tiny CRUSTACEANS, ANNELID WORMS, and the eggs and larvae of other fishes; they themselves are a favourite food of COD, haddock, halibut and HERRING. Sand eels dig themselves into sand to escape notice and to lay eggs. Humans catch sand eels both for bait and to eat.

**San Diego,** US city (1984 est. pop. 960,000), S California, on San Diego Bay. Its excellent natural harbour has made it a fishing and shipping port, and a major naval centre. Aerospace, electronics, shipbuilding, and other industries are important. Tourism and convention business are large factors in the economy. Explored and claimed by Spain in 1542, it was the site of the first of Fr. Junípero SERRA's missions and a historic fort, the Presidio (both 1769). The area has many other historic sites, including the Cabrillo National Monument. San Diego is also a cultural, medical, oceanographic, and research centre. Its aquatic park and enormous ZOO are well known.

**Sandinistas,** members of a left-wing Nicaraguan political group, the Sandinist National Liberation Front. The group, named after a former insurgent leader, was formed in 1962 to oppose the regime of Anastasio SOMOZA-DEBAYLE. In 1979 they launched an offensive from Costa Rica and Honduras that toppled Somoza. The Sandinistas established a ruling junta that nationalized such industries as banking and mining, postponed elections, and moved steadily to the left.

**sandpiper,** name for some shore BIRDS of the family Scolopacidae, including the SNIPE and CURLEW. Sandpipers are small wading birds with long, slender bills for probing in sand or mud for small invertebrates. Their plumage is usually brown or gray streaked above and buff with streaks or spots below. Most are found in flocks on seacoasts throughout the Northern Hemisphere.

**sandstone,** sedimentary ROCK formed by the cementing together of SAND grains. The hardness varies depending on the cementing material. Sandstone is widely used in construction and industry. It can also be crushed and used like sand.

**Sandwich, John Montagu, 4th earl of,** 1718–92, British politician. He was secretary of state (1763–65, 1770–71) and first lord of the admiralty (1748–51, 1763, 1771–82). He earned (1763) great unpopularity for his charges of obscenity against John WILKES and was later blamed unfairly for British defeats in the American Revolution. He supposedly invented the sandwich.

**San Francisco,** US city (1984 est. pop. 713,000; metropolitan area 3.2 million), W California, on a peninsula between the Pacific and San Francisco Bay, which are connected by the strait called the Golden Gate; inc. 1850. It is an industrial nucleus, a market for mine and farm products, centre of a transport system, and the West Coast's financial and insurance centre. With the Bay area it forms the largest West Coast port and a major focus of trade with Asia, Hawaii, and Alaska. Its industries are increasingly white-collar but include shipbuilding and oil refining. The city is also one of the nation's cultural centres. Founded by the Spanish (1776) as Yerba Buena, it was taken and renamed by the Americans in 1846. The California gold rush (1848) led to great growth; with the arrival of newcomers from all over the world in the late 19th cent. the city took on a cosmopolitan air. The earthquake and fire of 18–20 April 1906, devastated the city, but it was quickly rebuilt. The opening of the Panama Canal and San Francisco's role as a supply and embarkation point in World War II increased the city's importance. A gracious, picturesque city with a mild climate, it is famous for its individuality. Points of interest include its cable cars, which carry passengers on its steep hills; the San Francisco–Oakland Bay Bridge (opened 1936) and Golden Gate Bridge (opened 1937); Chinatown; the Castro St gay community; Fisherman's Wharf; Telegraph Hill; the mansions of Nob Hill; the opera house; symphony hall (1980); and numerous institutions of learning.

**Sanger, Frederick,** 1918– , British biochemist. One of the few recipients of two Nobel prizes, he won the chemistry award in 1958 for identifying the amino-acid sequence of INSULIN and shared the 1980 award for chemistry for developing a method, important in recombinant DNA research, for rapidly determining the chemical structure of pieces of DNA.

**Sanger, Margaret (Higgins),** 1883–1966, American leader in the BIRTH-CONTROL movement. Personal experience and work as a nurse convinced her that family limitation, especially where poverty was a factor, was a necessary step in social progress. Her promotion of birth control brought indictment and arrests, but public and court support gradually grew. She organized the first American (1923) and international (1925) birth-control conferences, formed (1923) a committee to lobby for birth-control laws, and helped establish clinics around the world.

**San Gimignano** (san'jimin,yahnoh), town, (1984 pop. 7500), Tuscany, N central Italy. A hill-top town, its thirteen tall towers are a reminder of the rivalry that existed between families in the Middle Ages. Towers were built for prestige as well as for protection and no other Italian town has so many surviving examples.

**Sanhedrin,** ancient Jewish legal and religious institution in Jerusalem. There probably were two Sanhedrins: one, like a legal court, political and civil; the other, the Great Sanhedrin, purely religious. The political Sanhedrin perished after the destruction of the Temple in AD 70, but the religious Sanhedrin continued as the rabbinic patriarchate until about AD 425. The MISHNAH refers to two Sanhedrins: one, a supreme court, comprising 71 judges; the other of 23 judges (see also BET DIN).

**San José,** city (1984 pop. 245,370), central Costa Rica, capital of Costa Rica. San José is Costa Rica's largest city and its economic, political, and social centre, dominating the central plateau. It is also the national distribution point for imports and has a busy international airport. A modern city with many parks, it has a mixture of Spanish and North American architecture. The city was founded c.1738 and has a university (est. 1844).

**San Jose,** US city (1984 est. pop. 686,000), W California; founded 1777, inc. 1850. In a rich wine- and fruit-producing area, San Jose is a fast-growing industrial city, part of the so-called Silicon Valley. Manufactures include aerospace, computer, and other high-technology products. At the southern end of San Francisco Bay, San Jose was the capital of California from 1849 to 1851.

**San Juan,** city (1980 pop. 424,600), capital, chief port, and commercial centre of PUERTO RICO, on the NE coast. Sugar, tobacco, coffee, fruit, and other agricultural products are exported. Tourism is a major industry. Sugar refining, rum distilling, metalworking, textiles, publishing, and various light manufactures are also important. Its bay was named Puerto Rico [rich port] by PONCE DE LEÓN, who began a settlement at nearby Caparra in 1508. It has one of the finest harbours in the WEST INDIES. The old city (founded 1521) is noted for its colonial atmosphere; El Morro fort (begun 1539) is the most famous of its buildings. It also has fine beaches.

**San Luis Potosí** (san looh,ees po,tohsee), city (1979 est. pop. 327,333), capital of the state of the same name NW of Mexico City in central Mexico. Founded in 1586 it was the centre of a principal silver-mining district in the colonial period and retains many notable churches and public buildings from that time. Its university was founded in 1804. In 1863 it was temporarily the seat of government of Mexican President Benito JUÁREZ. It is an important agricultural market for its region and has metal-smelting and textile industries.

**San Marino,** republic (1985 pop. 22,418), 62 km² (24 sq mi), in the APENNINES, SW of Rimini, Italy. San Marino is the capital. Farming is the main occupation, and tourism and the sale of postage stamps are the chief sources of income. San Marino claims to be Europe's oldest existing state. According to tradition, in the 4th cent. AD Marino, a Christian stonecutter, took refuge on Mt Titano, the chief geographical feature of San Marino. A community was formed by the mid-5th cent. and its independence recognized by the papacy in 1631. San Marino volunteers served with the Italians in both world wars, and Allied aircraft bombed the tiny republic in 1944. Following a period (1947–57) of Communist–Socialist rule, a series of coalitions headed by the Christian Democrats held sway until 1978, when a further Communist-led left-wing coalition took power. This collapsed in 1986, however, and was replaced by the country's first Communist–Christian Democratic coalition.

**San Martín, José de** (san mah,teen), 1778–1850, South American revolutionary leader. A professional soldier, he joined (1812) the revolution against Spain in his native ARGENTINA and commanded patriot forces in Upper Peru. In 1817 he invaded CHILE by a daring march across the Andes and defeated the Spanish at Chacabuco with the aid of Bernardo O'HIGGINS; they soon completed (1818) the liberation of Chile. San Martín seized (1821) Lima and became protector of Peru, but he resigned (1822) the post and permitted Simón BOLÍVAR to liberate the country.

**San Miguel de Tucumán,** city (1980 pop. 392,888), NW Argentina, capital of Tucumán prov. Originally founded in 1565 at the confluence of the Salí and Monteros rivers, it was moved to its present site on the Dulce R. in 1585 and retains many buildings from the colonial period. It is the principal centre of the nation's most important region of tropical agriculture and has sugar and cotton processing industries. On 9 July 1816 the convention of delegates of the former vice royalty of La Plata met in the city to sign the act of independence of Argentina.

**San Pedro Sula,** city (1983 est. pop. 323,500), NW Honduras. Increasingly industrialized, it is a Caribbean port serving the banana and sugar plantations of the north.

**San Salvador,** city (1983 pop. 445,054), central El Salvador, the country's capital and largest city. Situated on a volcanic slope, it is subject to severe earthquakes and has been rebuilt often. Most recently large areas of the southern section of the city were destroyed by earthquake in 1986. It was founded in the early 1600s and was (1831–38) the capital of the CENTRAL AMERICAN FEDERATION. It is a modern city with broad avenues and many parks.

**San Sebastián,** city (1981 pop. 175,576), capital of Guipúzcoa prov., in the Basque country of N Spain. The old fortress town was badly damaged in the Napoleonic Wars. Following the arrival of the railway (1864), it entered a new phase of growth as a fashionable resort and summer residence of the Spanish court.

**Sanskrit,** language belonging to the Indic group of the Indo-Iranian subfamily of the Indo-European family of languages. Sanskrit was the classical standard language of ancient India, and some of the oldest surviving Indo-European documents are written in Sanskrit. The oldest known stage of Sanskrit is Vedic or Vedic Sanskrit, so called because it was the language of the VEDA, the most ancient extant scriptures of HINDUISM. See LANGUAGE (table).

**Sanskrit literature,** main body of the classical literature of India. The literature is divided into two main groups and periods the Vedic (c.1500–c.200 BC), when the Vedic form of Sanskrit prevailed, and the Sanskrit (c.200 BC–AD c.1100), when classical Sanskrit (a development of Vedic) predominated. Early Sanskrit literature, however, overlapped the Vedic. The early Vedic period (c.1500–c.800 BC), that of the VEDA, was a poetic and creative age. Subsequently (c.800–c.500 BC), the priestly class concerned itself more with ritual and wrote the *Brahmanas,* prose commentaries explaining the Vedas' relation to ritual. Later portions of the *Brahmanas* are theosophical treatises; these include the philosophical *Upanishads* (see VEDANTA). In the final stage of the Vedic period (c.500–c.200 BC) the *Sutras,* which deal with Vedic ritual and customary law, were written. A sutra well known in the West is the *Kamasutra* of Vatsyayana, concerning the art and practice of love. In the middle of the sutra period, the grammar of Panini (c.350 BC) formalized classical Sanskrit. Nearly all Sanskrit literature, except for works on grammar and philososphy, is in verse. The early Sanskrit period (c.500–c.50 BC) is one of epics; the greatest of these are the MAHABHARATA, which includes the BHAGAVAD-GITA, and the RAMAYANA. Sanskrit lyric poetry is artificial in technique and mainly stanzaic. Many lyrics are gemlike miniatures, portraying emotion and nature, and most are erotic. Nonetheless, there are many lyrics that are ethical in tone. Sanskrit drama probably derived from dance and religious ritual (see ORIENTAL DRAMA). In its fables and fairy tales (AD c.400–1100) the didactic quality of Sanskrit literature is most pronounced, and often the characters in a tale themselves tell stories until there are many levels to the narrative. The PANCHATANTRA is the most important work in this style. Sanskrit today is chiefly used in academic exercises. Modern INDIAN LITERATURE is mostly written in vernacular languages and English.

**Santa Ana,** US city (1984 est. pop. 225,000), S California, in the fertile Santa Ana valley; inc. 1886. The government and business centre of a large area, it produces such manufactures as aerospace and electronic equipment, sporting goods, and electrical connectors. Marketing of local farm produce is also important.

**Santa Anna, Antonio López de,** 1794–1876, Mexican general and dictator. A clever opportunist, he ruled MEXICO during most of the period from 1824 to 1855, his fortunes rising and falling rapidly as he shifted his allegiance from party to party. His victory (1829) over the Spanish at Tampico gained him popularity and the presidency (1833). He was defeated and captured (1836) by the Texas rebels at San Jacinto, but he quickly regained his political power. He commanded the Mexican troops in the MEXICAN WAR, where his defeats forced him into exile. He returned to power (1853–55) until exiled again.

**Santa Claus:** see NICHOLAS, SAINT.

**Santa Cruz, Andrés** (ˌsantah kroohs), 1792?–1865, Bolivian president (1829–39). After serving as BOLÍVAR's revolutionary chief of staff, he succeeded Pres. SUCRE. Attempting to achieve a Bolivian–Peruvian confederation, he invaded (1835) Peru and became its protector. But his forces lost the battle of Yungay (1839), and he fled to exile in Europe.

**Santa Cruz de la Sierra,** city (1982 est. pop. 376,912), E Bolivia, capital of Santa Cruz dept. It was originally sited in the Andean foothills at the time of the Spanish conquest, being moved to its present site in the mountains in 1590. Until it was linked to central Bolivia by road and rail in the 1950s it remained an insignificant frontier town. Since then it has grown rapidly as the centre of the nation's most important area of agricultural colonization, including the production of cotton, sugar, rice, cocoa, and cattle. The recent discoveries of oil and natural gas fields within a 50-km (31-mi) radius of the city and the establishment of an international airport have added to its expansion and growth.

**Santa Fe,** US city (1980 pop. 48,899), state capital of New Mexico, at the foot of the Sangre de Cristo Mts. It is an administrative and tourist centre. Founded c.1609 by the Spanish, it was a Spanish–Indian trade centre for over 200 years. It was taken by the US in 1846. A seat of government since its founding, it is the oldest capital city in the US. It has many historic churches and an outstanding opera company.

**Santa Fé,** city (1980 pop. 374,834), NE Argentina, capital of Santa Fé prov. Founded by Spanish settlers from Paraguay in 1573 it was moved to its present site on the Paraná R. in 1651. The federal Argentine Constitution of 1853 was adopted in the city's town hall. The city contains many fine colonial churches dating from the 17th cent. and, together with the city of Rosario, retains current importance as the commercial centre of the cattle and grain region in which it is located.

**Santa Fe Trail,** caravan route of the W US, extending c.1260 km (780 mi) from Independence, Missouri, to SANTA FE, New Mexico. Following the first party of traders, led by William Becknell in 1822, annual wagon caravans made the 40- to 60-day trip over the trail to Santa Fe, returning after a 4- to 5-week stay. In 1880 the Santa Fe RR reached Santa Fe, marking the death of the trail.

**Santander,** city (1981 pop. 180,328), capital of Santander prov., N Spain. As a port it has a wide range of activities, including the processing of fish and dairy products, metallurgical, engineering and chemical industries.

**Santander, Francisco de Paula** (santanˌdeə), 1792–1840, Colombian revolutionary. He helped to liberate COLOMBIA from Spanish rule and served (1821–28) as vice president under BOLÍVAR, who later accused him of complicity in a plot (1828) to assassinate Bolívar and banished him. Later, he returned and was president of New Granada (Colombia and Panama).

**Santa Sophia:** see HAGIA SOPHIA.

**Santayana, George,** 1863–1952, American philosopher; b. Spain. He emigrated to the US in 1872, graduated from Harvard Univ., and was (1889–1912) a noted teacher there. In 1912 he retired from teaching and thereafter lived in Europe. Santayana viewed the mind as being placed in and responsive to a physical, biological context; at the same time he emphasized the mind's rational and imaginative vision of physical beauty. He considered religion an imaginative creation of real value but without absolute significance. His philosophical works include *The Sense of Beauty* (1896), *The Life of Reason* (1905–6), *The Realms of Being* (4 vol., 1927–40), and *Dominations and Powers* (1951). His only novel, *The Last Puritan* (1935), had great success.

**Santiago,** city (1984 pop. 4,225,299), central Chile, capital of Chile and of Santiago prov., on the Mapocho R. Chile's largest city, housing nearly one-third of the nation's population, it is the commercial and political heart of the republic and an active manufacturing centre with iron and steel foundries. The city is predominantly modern in appearance, but its ground plan is colonial, with broad avenues and spacious plazas. Since its founding in 1541, Santiago has survived numerous floods, earthquakes, and Indian attacks. In the early 1970s it was the scene of mass political demonstrations.

**Santiago de Compostela** or **Santiago,** city (1981 pop. 93,695), La Coruña prov., NW Spain. In the early 9th cent. the supposed tomb of the apostle St JAMES (James the Greater) was discovered in Santiago de Compostela. A shrine was built on the site and the city became one of the most famous places of medieval Christian pilgrimage. It still thrives as a pilgrimage and tourist centre. The city has a cathedral (originally built 11th–13th cent.) and is the seat of a university (founded 1501).

**Santiago de Cuba,** city (1981 pop. 345,289), SE Cuba, capital of Oriente prov. It is Cuba's second-largest city and a major port, with some industrial plants. A former capital of Cuba founded by the Spanish in the 16th cent., it was the scene of heavy fighting (1898) during the SPANISH-AMERICAN WAR. Fidel CASTRO's attack on an army garrison here (26 July 1953) launched the Cuban Revolution.

**Santiago de los Caballeros,** city (1981 pop. 278,600), N Dominican Republic. The second-largest city in the country, it is the hub of its most densely populated area, the fertile Čibao lowland. It was founded c. 1495 and is one of the oldest cities in the Americas.

**Santillana, Íñigo López de Mendoza, marqués de** (santee͵lyahnah), 1398–1458, Spanish poet, critic, and literary patron. The chief literary figure of his day, he wrote the first literary criticism and the first SONNETS in Spanish, and commissioned translations of works by VIRGIL, PETRARCA, and DANTE. He is best known, however, for his popular songs, or *serranillas.*

**Santo Domingo,** former colony of Spain, on the island of HISPANIOLA. It included what is now the DOMINICAN REPUBLIC and, in early days, the western third of the island, now the republic of HAITI. COLUMBUS discovered the island and founded the first settlement in 1492. Spanish colonists established an agricultural economy in the east. The west was undeveloped until settled by French planters in the 1600s; it was ceded to France in 1697. In 1805 Spain ceded the rest of the island to France, but the settlers in the east rebelled and attempted (1809) to restore Spanish rule. They declared independence in 1821, only to be ousted by the Haitians. The Dominican Republic was proclaimed in 1844, when the Haitians were expelled, but independence was not finally and firmly achieved until 1865.

**Santo Domingo,** city (1981 pop. 1,313,000), S Dominican Republic, capital and largest city and port of the Dominican Republic, on the Caribbean Sea. Founded 4 Aug. 1496, by Bartholomew Columbus, it may be the oldest continuously inhabited settlement in the Western Hemisphere. It was the first seat of Spanish colonial administration in the New World and was the capital of the colony of SANTO DOMINGO. Almost entirely destroyed by a hurricane in 1930, it was rebuilt and called Ciudad Trujillo (after Rafael TRUJILLO) until 1961. Now a city of wide avenues and modern buildings, it has the oldest cathedral in the Americas (begun 1514).

**Santorini:** see THERA.

**Santos,** city and port (1980 pop. 410,933), on the Atlantic coast in central Brazil. Good road, rail and sea communications link Santos with the cities of São Paulo and Rio de Janeiro and the city serves as Brazil's most important port. Half of Brazil's total exports and 40% by value of all the country's imports move through Santos. An important industrial area has developed around the steelworks, oil refineries and hydroelectric plant at Cubatão outside the city.

**Sanussi,** SUFI Muslim mystical order founded by a N African, Sayyid Mohammed bin Ali al Sanussi, during the early 19th cent. After 1840 the brotherhood became well established in W Libya from which it spread throughout much of the Sahel region. During the 20th cent. the order became a focus for resistance to the Italian colonial state. The last Sanussi leader, Sayyid Idris, served as king of Libya (r.1951–1969).

**Sanzio, Raphael:** see RAPHAEL.

**São Paulo,** city (1980 pop. 7,033,529), SE Brazil, capital of São Paulo state, on the Tietê R. The largest city of South America, it is an ultramodern metropolis dominating a vast, agriculturally rich hinterland. It is Brazil's commercial, financial, and industrial centre, manufacturing motor vehicles, heavy machinery, and other products, and is the nation's major transport centre, with (since 1975) its first underground-railway system. It is also a cultural and educational centre, with several symphony orchestras and art museums, and four universities. The city is the site of the Bienal, an important international art exposition. Founded by Jesuits in 1554, São Paulo was the site at which Emperor Dom PEDRO I declared Brazil's independence from Portugal in 1822. It was a minor commercial city until the start of coffee cultivation in the state in the 1880s. More recent growth owes much to hydroelectric power development.

**São Tomé** (sownh tooh͵me ͵preenseepə), city (1984 est. pop. 25,000), capital of SÃO TOMÉ AND PRINCIPE.

**São Tomé and Príncipe,** officially Democratic Republic of São Tomé and Principe, island republic (1982 est. pop. 100,000), 964 km² (372 sq mi), W Africa, in the Gulf of Guinea, c.240 km (150 mi) W of Gabon. São Tomé is the capital and chief town. The country consists of the volcanic islands of São Tomé, Príncipe, Pedras, Tinhosas, and Rolas, which rise to 2024 m (6640 ft) on São Tomé. Lying just north of the equator, the islands are covered with thick vegetation. The economy is based entirely on the export of tropical produce, notably cocoa (about 90% of export earnings), palm oil, coffee, copra, and bananas. Small processing factories are the only industry. The GNP is US$32 million, and the GNP per capita is US$320 (1985). The native inhabitants are mainly descendents of black slaves brought from the mainland.

*History.* The islands were discovered in 1471 by the Portuguese explorers Pedro Escobar and Jaõa Gomes; the São Tomé settlement was founded in 1483. Except for a century of Dutch rule (1641–1740), the islands were held by the Portuguese until independence was granted in 1975. The plantation economy was established in the 18th cent. Upon independence, Manuel Pinto da Costa, leader of the Movement for the Liberation of São Tomé and Príncipe, became president. The first years of independence were marked by economic hardship caused by the departure of the Portuguese and of a large number of contract and migrant workers. The government has sought to strengthen the economy through agrarian reforms and by seeking foreign investment in industry and tourism.

**sap,** plant fluid consisting of water and dissolved substances. The term is generally applied to all the fluid that moves through the xylem (see WOOD) and phloem (see BARK) of the STEMS of higher plants. Water with dissolved minerals ascends to the leaves via the xylem vessels; the solution with food produced by the leaves descends to other parts via the phloem.

**Sapir, Edward** (sə͵peeə), 1884–1939, American linguist and anthropologist; b. Germany. His studies on the ethnology and linguistics of certain US Indian groups contributed greatly to the development of descriptive linguistics.

**sapphire,** GEM, transparent blue variety of CORUNDUM, found chiefly in Thailand, India, Sri Lanka, and Burma. Like rubies, some sapphires show an internal star when cut with a round top. Synthetic stones are made by fusing aluminium oxide, with titanium oxide added for colour.

**Sappho,** fl. early 6th cent. BC, greatest of the early Greek LYRIC poets; b. Lesbos. Facts on her life are scarce and only fragments of her poetry survive, the longest seven stanzas. She wrote in Aeolic dialect, in many metres, one of which (the Sapphic) is named after her. Her love lyrics, characterized by passion and simplicity, greatly influenced CATULLUS, OVID, and SWINBURNE.

**Sapporo,** city (1986 est. pop. 1,528,878), capital of Hokkaido prefecture, SW Hokkaido, Japan. Established by the Colonization Commission in 1869, it is now one of Japan's most rapidly growing urban centres. Sapporo is a tourist mecca famous for its annual snow festival, first held in 1950. It was the site of the 1972 winter Olympics.

**saprophyte,** any plant that relies on dead organic matter for its food; most do not have CHLOROPHYLL and therefore cannot photosynthesize. Saprophytes include most FUNGI and a few flowering plants, e.g., *Monotropa,* a genus of nongreen plants, including Yellow Bird's Nest (*M. hypopitis*). They aid in the breakdown of dead plants and animals.

**Saracens,** medieval European designation of Arabs and Muslims. Originally from the Greek word for 'the Children of SARAH', the Saracens were regarded as a universal manifestation of evil, Muslim, VIKING, and otherwise. From the time of the CRUSADES the word took on the specific designation of Muslim and Arab; in Spain the equivalent word was Moor.

**Sarah** or **Sara,** wife of ABRAHAM and mother of ISAAC. She was one of the four Jewish MATRIARCHS. After she gave birth to Isaac in her old age, she became jealous of her handmaid Hagar, Abraham's concubine, whom she drove (with Hagar's son ISHMAEL) into the desert. Gen. 11–23.

**Sarajevo** ('sarə͵yayvoh), city (1981 pop. 448,500), capital of BOSNIA-HERCEGOVINA, S central Yugoslavia, on the Bosnia R. Its manufactures include metal products and textiles. Lignite and other metals are mined nearby. Founded in 1263, it was held by the Turks as a cosmopolitan trading centre from 1429, becoming Bosnia's capital in 1850 and remaining such when Austria–Hungary occupied the province in 1878. The assassination (1914) of Archduke Franz Ferdinand in Sarajevo precipitated World War I. The city became part of the Yugoslav state in 1918. Sarajevo is noted for its beautiful setting and its mosques and other fine Ottoman buildings. It was host to the 1984 Winter Olympics.

**Saratoga campaign,** in the AMERICAN REVOLUTION, a series of engagements fought (June–Oct. 1777) in NEW YORK state. To split the colonies along the Hudson, the British planned a three-pronged advance on Albany S from Canada, N from New York City, and E along the Mohawk R. The northbound force never arrived. The eastbound force, under Barry St Leger, besieged Fort Stanwix (3 Aug.) but, frightened by a rumour (22 Aug.), retreated to Canada. Coming south, John BURGOYNE captured Ticonderoga (6 July), but was later defeated in a raid on Bennington (14–16 Aug.). Burgoyne halted near Saratoga Springs, where American forces prevented him from breaking through at Freeman's Farm (19 Sept.) and Bemis Heights (7 Oct.). Outnumbered and surrounded, Burgoyne surrendered (17 Oct.). This was the first great American victory, and probably the decisive battle, of the Revolution.

**Saratov,** city (1985 pop. 899,000), S European USSR, on the Volga R. It is an important rail junction and had traditional distribution functions for grain, timber, salt, tobacco, fish, tallow, and skins. It is also an industrial centre with petroleum-refining, agricultural machinery production, food-processing, flour-milling, aircraft manufacturing, and ball-bearing industries. The city also produces natural gas and is linked by pipeline to Moscow. Founded in 1590 on the left bank of the Volga R., it moved to its present site on the right bank in the 17th cent.

**Sarawak,** state (1980 pop. 1,294,753), 125,206 km² (48,342 sq mi), Malaysia, in NW Borneo and on the South China Sea, bordered by Brunei (NE) and Kalimantan or Indonesian Borneo (S, W). Its chief products are petroleum, rice, sago, and rubber. Sarawak was ceded (1841) by the sultan of BRUNEI to James BROOKE, an Englishman, who became rajah of the independent state. A British protectorate from 1888, it remained under the rule of the Brookes until they ceded it to Britain in 1946. In 1963 it joined the Federation of Malaysia.

**sardine** or **pilchard,** FISH of the HERRING family. Sardines are 20–23 cm (8–9 in) long and live in large shoals in the eastern Atlantic, round Japan, on the west coast of the Americas, and southern Australia and New Zealand, where water temperatures are between 12°C and 20°C. The European sardine (*Sardina pilchardus*) was the basis of the Cornish pilchard industry until overfishing reduced the stocks. The sardines used for canning are caught off the coasts of France, Spain, and Portugal. In the past only the small, young fishes were used, but the minimum size caught has been increased in recent years to protect future stocks.

**Sardinia,** island (1984 est. pop. 1,628,690), 24,092 km (9,032 sq mi), W Italy, in the Mediterranean Sea. It is mainly mountainous, rising to 1,834 m (6,016 ft) in Mt Gennargentu, with sheep and goat pastures inland and some agriculture in upland valleys and southwest coastal regions. Mining (lead, zinc, antimony) and fishing are important industries. Sardinia, a source of grain and salt for ancient Rome, was for many centuries under the nominal authority of various outside overlords. After it was granted (1720) to VICTOR AMADEUS II of SAVOY, he and his successors, as kings of Sardinia, exercised feudal privileges there until 1835. Part of the kingdom of Italy from 1861, Sardinia was granted limited regional autonomy in 1947. The capital, CAGLIARI, is on the south coast.

**Sardinia, Kingdom of,** name given to the holdings of the house of SAVOY in 1720, when the Treaty of London awarded the island of Sardinia to Savoy to compensate for its loss of Sicily to Austria. The kingdom included Sardinia, Savoy, Piedmont, and Nice. The Congress of VIENNA (1815) added Liguria. It grew during the RISORGIMENTO, and in 1861 VICTOR EMMANUEL II of Sardinia became king of Italy.

**sardonyx:** see ONYX.

**Sardou, Victorien** (sah,dooh), 1831–1908, French dramatist. He wrote some 70 plays, ranging from light comedy to historical melodrama. His best farce is *Divorçons!* (1880). Other works include such BERNHARDT vehicles as *Fédora* (1882) and *La Tosca* (1887, the basis of Puccini's opera).

**Sargasso Sea,** part of the north Atlantic Ocean between the West Indies and the Azores, at about 30°N lat. This relatively still sea is the centre of a great swirl of ocean currents and is noted for the abundance of seaweed on its surface. Bermuda is in the northwestern part of the sea.

**Sargent, John Singer,** 1856–1925, American painter; b. Italy. In 1884 he moved to London, where he spent most of his life, painting the dashing, flattering portraits of social celebrities for which he is famous. A prolific painter of great facility, he was brilliant in his treatment of textures and a virtuoso in his handling of brush stroke. Sargent also painted many impressionistic watercolour landscapes early and late in his career. Notable portraits are Isabella Stewart GARDNER (Gardner Mus., Boston) and Mme X (Metropolitan Mus., New York).

**Sargodha,** town (1981 pop. 294,000), Punjab prov., Pakistan. It is a divisional and district administrative centre, set in a prosperous canal-irrigated area for which it provides marketing and services. It has grown of recent years, and has sugar and cotton textile industries and military establishments.

**sari,** a garment worn by Indian Hindu women. It consists of a strip of material about six metres long, one end of which is wound round the lower part of the body like a skirt, and tucked in at the waist, and the other brought up and across the body to cover the shoulders, and possibly the head. It is often made of rich materials with a distinctive border, but for mourning it is of plain white cotton.

**Sarmatia,** ancient district about the Don R. occupied by the Sarmatians, 3rd–2nd cent. AD. They spoke an Indo-Iranian language, and were nomadic relatives of the Scythians. The term Sarmatia is also used for the land along the Danube and over the Carpathians, where the Sarmatians were later driven by the HUNS. The Sarmatians allied with Rome against the GERMANS, who had scattered them by the 3rd cent. AD.

**Sarmiento, Domingo Faustino** (sah,myayntoh), 1811–88, Argentine educator and writer, president of the republic (1868–74). Exiled as an opponent of ROSAS, he was impressed in his travels with the educational system of the US; as president he effected educational reforms based on the US system. His best-known work is *Life in the Argentine Republic in the Days of the Tyrants* (1845), a biography of Juan Facundo QUIROGA.

**Sarnath,** archaeological site 6.4 km (4 mi) N of Varanasi (Benares), India. It is the site of the deer park where, legend has it, BUDDHA first preached.

**Saroyan, William,** 1908–81, American author. A prolific writer, he combined optimism, sentimentality, and love of country in plays, e.g., *The Time of Your Life* (1939); novels, e.g., *The Human Comedy* (1942); short stories, e.g., *My Name Is Aram* (1940); and autobiographical works.

**Sarpi, Paolo,** 1552–1623, Italian historian and polemicist. As 'theologian' to the Venetian senate, from 1606 he directed a pamphlet war against the Papacy and achieved European celebrity as a leading opponent of Rome's secular ambitions. His *History of the Council of Trent*, first published in London (1619) in an unauthorized edition dedicated to King JAMES I, seeks to show how Rome exploited the Council to strengthen Papal control and so perverted its primary purpose of ecclesiastical reform.

**Sarraute, Nathalie** (sah,roht), 1902–, French novelist; b. Russia. Her experimental 'anti-novels' focus upon the psychological preoccupations and passing sensations of individuals. They include *Tropismes* (1939), *Portrait d'un inconnu* (1949; tr. Portrait of a Man Unknown), *Le planétarium* (1959), and *Fools Say* (1976).

**sarsaparilla,** name for various plants and for an extract from their roots, used in medicine and beverages. True sarsaparilla is obtained from tropical American species of the genus *Smilax* of the LILY family; these have thick rootstalks and thin roots over 1m (3 ft) long. Wild sarsaparilla (*Aralia nudicaulis*), related to GINSENG, is used as a substitute source for the extract.

**Sarto, Andrea del,** 1486–1530, Florentine High RENAISSANCE painter. His main works were altarpieces and FRESCO cycles; among them the grisaille (shades of grey) scenes in the Chiostro degli Scalzi, Florence. His harmonious colour and graceful, balanced compositions reached maturity with the *Madonna of the Harpies* (1517; Uffizi, Florence).

**Sartre, Jean-Paul,** 1905–80, French philosopher and author, a leading exponent of EXISTENTIALISM. His writings examine the individual as a responsible but lonely being, adrift in a meaningless universe with a terrifying freedom to choose. His existentialist works include the monumental treatise *Being and Nothingness* (1943); the plays *The Flies* (1943), *No Exit* (1944), and *The Respectful Prostitute* (1947); and the novels *Nausea* (1938) and *The Age of Reason* (1945) (first of a trilogy). *The Critique of Dialectical Reason* (1960) combined MARXISM and existentialism whereas *The Family Idiot* (1982) explored FLAUBERT from a Freudian viewpoint. He was a close associate of Simone de BEAUVOIR. Sartre declined the 1964 Nobel Prize for literature.

**SAS:** see SPECIAL AIR SERVICE.

**Saskatchewan,** province of Canada (1984 est. pop. 1,008,000), area 651,900 km² (251,699 sq mi), in the W, bordered by Northwest Territories (N), Manitoba (E), North Dakota and Montana, US (S), Alberta (W). REGINA, the capital, and SASKATOON are the chief cities; 60% of the population is urban. Northern Saskatchewan is part of the desolate, mineral-rich Canadian Shield, which is covered in many lakes and drains into Hudson Bay via the Churchill and other rivers. The southern part consists of the second of the three steps of the prairie, which contains deep fertile soils and rises to the third step and Cypress Hills in the SW. This area contains large stretches of mixed forest and is drained by the Saskatchewan R. Agriculture leads the economy and Saskatchewan is a great world producer of grain, mainly hard wheat; there is some livestock farming. Mines produce uranium, copper, zinc, gold, and fossil fuels; the province is a major world producer of potash. Most industries process these raw materials. Settlement is concentrated in the S of Saskatchewan. The French establishd the first trading posts (c.1750) but the Hudson's Bay Company made the first permanent settlement (1774). In 1870 the area was ceded to the Canadian government, the local Indians were defeated, and thereafter the railway opened the area up for trade and settlement. Becoming a province in 1905, prosperity has been solidly based on wheat and potash.

**Saskatoon,** city (1981 pop. 154,210), Saskatchewan, W Canada, on the South Saskatchewan R. It is the chief centre of central and N Saskatchewan, with oil refineries, grain elevators, flour mills, stockyards, and meat- and potash-processing plants. Saskatoon was settled in 1883 and grew rapidly after the coming of the railway (1890).

**sassafras:** see LAUREL.

**Sassanid** or **Sassanian,** last dynasty of native rulers to reign (AD c.224–c.640) in Persia before the Arab conquest. ARDASHIR I was the first of the dynasty. The Sassanids were much occupied with wars, and their enemies included the Romans, White Huns, and Armenians. They restored the ancient religion of ZOROASTRIANISM, which virtually disappeared again after the fall of the dynasty. The last Sassanid ruler, Yazdagird III, fled the country when it was overrun by Arab invaders.

**Sassetta,** 1392–1450, Italian painter; b. Stefano di Giovanni. The leading painter of the Sienese school in the 15th cent., Sassetta preserved the clear, decorative colours, graceful line, and poetic feeling of the Sienese Gothic style; his best known work is the scenes from the *Life of St Francis* (1436–44, National Gall., London), part of a polyptych painted for the church of St Francis at Borgo San Sepolcro.

**Sassoon, Siegfried,** 1886–1967, English poet and novelist. An officer in World War I, he wrote of war's brutality and wastefulness in grim, forceful verse in *Counter-Attack* (1918), and other collections. His novels include the semiautobiographical trilogy collected as *The Complete Memoirs of George Sherston* (1937).

**Sassou-Nguesso, Denis,** 1943?–, Congolese army officer and president of the People's Republic of the CONGO (1979–). He served (1977–79) as the minister of national defence. As president he won approval for a new Marxist constitution and signed (1981) a friendship treaty with the USSR. He has maintained the Congo's strong economic ties with France and was (1986–87) chairman of the ORGANIZATION OF AFRICAN UNITY.

**Sastre, Alfonso,** 1926–, Spanish dramatist. His controversial plays, including *Escuadra hacia la muerte* (1953; tr. Condemned Squad), *La cornada* (1959; tr. Death Thrust), and *El camarada oscure* (1972; tr. The Gloomy Comrade), deal with injustice, alienation, and violence from a Marxist and existentialist point of view.

**Satan** [Heb., = adversary], in Judaism, Christianity, and Islam, the principle of evil conceived as a person; also called the Devil. In Christian

Sassetta, *Life of St Francis*, 1436. National Gallery, London.

tradition Satan was the leader of the angels who rebelled against God and who were cast out of heaven. He and his followers are seen as tempters of man and the source of evil in the world. He has numerous other names, such as Lucifer, Beelzebub, Evil One, and Prince of Darkness.

**satellite, artificial,** object launched by a ROCKET into orbit around the Earth or, occasionally, another solar-system body (see SPACE PROBE). A satellite in circular orbit at an altitude of 35,880 km (22,300 mi) has a period of exactly 24 hr, the time it takes the Earth to rotate once on its axis; such an orbit is called synchronous. If such an orbit also lies in the equatorial plane, it is called geostationary, because the satellite will remain stationary over one point on the earth's surface. The first artificial satellite, *Sputnik 1,* was launched by the USSR on 4 Oct. 1957. *Explorer 1,* the first American satellite, was launched on 31 Jan. 1958. Artificial satellites fulfil many roles, but may broadly be grouped into applications satellites, which are used for practical, commercial, or military purposes, and scientific research satellites which study the Earth and its space environment, and carry out astronomical observations. Astronomical satellites observe radiation from cosmic sources at wavelengths (e.g., gamma-ray, X-ray, ultraviolet, and a large fraction of the infrared) which cannot be detected at ground level because it is absorbed in the atmosphere (see RADIO ASTRONOMY). Ordinary optical (visible light) telescopes also perform much more effectively when clear of the turbulence and obscuration produced by the atmosphere. The principal types of applications satellites are the COMMUNICATIONS SATELLITE, NAVIGATION SATELLITE, RECONNAISSANCE SATELLITE, and WEATHER SATELLITE. Major US scientific research satellites include the Orbiting Astronomical Observatories (OAO), the Orbiting Geophysical Observatories (OGO), the Orbiting Solar Observatories (OSO), the High Energy Astronomical Observatories (HEAO) which observed at X-ray and gamma-ray wavelengths, many Explorer satellites, the Solar Maximum Mission (SMM), and the forthcoming Hubble Space Telescope. Important joint US–European ventures include the International Ultraviolet Explorer

(IUE) and the Infrared Astronomical Satellite (IRAS). Recent X-ray or gamma-ray satellites include the European Exosat and the Japanese Ginga. A major improvement in the accuracy with which the positions, distances, and motions of stars are known should be achieved by the European Space Agency's forthcoming Hipparcos satellite. Major Soviet space-science satellite [Bogrammes include Elektron, Proton, Prognoz, and many COSMOS satellites. Satellites are also used to survey the Earth's resources by means of special television cameras operating at a range of wavebands, and radiometric scanners. The US series of Earth resources satellites are known as EOSAT (formerly Landsat). Similar satellites have been launched by the USSR, France (Spot), India (IRS), and Japan (Momo). Ocean survey satellites include Seasat (US), ERSI (ESA), and the forthcoming Topex/Poseidon (France/US).

US and Dutch technicians preparing the Infrared Astronomical **Satellite** (IRAS) before its launch in Jan. 1983.

**satellite, natural,** celestial body orbiting a planet. The earth's only satellite is the MOON; thus satellites of other planets are often referred to as moons. The largest in the solar system is Jupiter's Ganymede, whose radius of 2638 km (1639 mi) is larger than that of the planet Mercury. See also PLANET, table; articles on individual planets.

**satellite television,** a system of broadcasting television over a very wide distance by means of an orbiting space satellite. Satellites can be used to receive and transmit signals from a geostationary orbit, an orbit which maintains a fixed position relative to the rotation of the earth. Such satellites are powered by a bank of solar cells with power back-up for when it is in shade (approximately 70 minutes per day). Signals transmitted to a satellite are known as uplink signals. Signals from a satellite are called downlink signals. In order to make use of the communication potential, signals have to be transmitted at a high frequency. An uplink signal is transmitted at between 5.925 and 6.425 GHz and downlink signals at between 3.7 and 4.2 GHz. Television signals transmitted from a satellite (LNA), the amplifier signal is sent to a downconverter, which reduces the frequency from 4 GHz to around 70 MHz. This signal is sent to the satellite receiver, which in turn feeds the composite video signal to either a monitor or, through a remodulator, to a domestic television set. The consequences of satellite television broadcasting are considerable. It is possible to broadcast over vast distances and to broadcast to several countries simultaneously. Events happening on one side of the world may simultaneously be seen on TV the other side of the world. Transmissions cannot be restricted within national borders. Television pictures were first transmitted by means of satellite on 10th July 1962 when *Telstar* was launched at Cape Canaveral and in 1964 the Olympic Games were relayed from Tokyo. The British Telecommunications Act 1981 marked the end of monopoly rights in telecommunications transmission in the UK. The commercial, political, and ideological consequences of the cable and satellite communications revolution are immense.

**Satie, Erik** (sah͵tee), 1866–1925, French composer. He rejected ROMANTICISM and IMPRESSIONISM and developed an abstract, often witty, and deceptively simple style. Satie's harmonic innovations are evident in such early piano pieces as *Sarabandes* (1887) and *Gymnopédies* (1888), while some of his later works, e.g., *Socrate* (1918), foreshadowed the neoclassicism of STRAVINSKY.

**satin spar:** see GYPSUM.

**satire,** a work of literature or art that, by inspiring laughter, contempt, or horror, seeks to correct the follies and abuses it uncovers. The Roman poets HORACE and JUVENAL became models for the two leading types of satire: Horatian satire is mild, amused, and sophisticated; Juvenalian is vitriolic and indignant. Noted satirists include VOLTAIRE, Alexander POPE, William HOGARTH, Jonathan SWIFT, Oscar WILDE, Mark TWAIN, Evelyn WAUGH, and James THURBER.

**Satō Eisaku,** 1901–75, Japanese prime minister (1964–72). A Liberal-Democrat, he signed (1969) a treaty with the US that reestablished (1972) Japanese sovereignty in Okinawa. Satō was awarded the 1974 Nobel Peace Prize for his efforts to halt the spread of nuclear weapons.

**Saturday:** see WEEK; SABBATH.

**Saturn,** in astronomy, 6th PLANET from the Sun, at a mean distance of 1427.0 million km (886.7 million mi). It has an equatorial diameter of 120,6600 km (74,980 mi) and an atmosphere of hydrogen, helium, and traces of methane and ammonia. Like Jupiter, Saturn has counterflowing easterly and westerly winds. Saturn's most remarkable feature is its ring system, composed of thousands of millions of water-ice particles orbiting around the planet. The main rings are at distances ranging from 6670 to 80,270 km (4140 to 49,880 mi) above the cloud tops, and two other tenuous rings orbit much more distantly. Saturn also has at least 17 natural satellites. The largest is **Titan** (diameter: 5150 km/3200 mi); discovered by Christiaan HUYGENS in 1655, it is the only natural satellite in the solar system with a substantial atmosphere. Saturn has six major icy satellites. The most prominent feature of heavily cratered **Mimas,** the innermost, is a large impact crater about one-third the diameter of the satellite. Certain broad regions of **Enceladus** are uncratered, indicating geological activity that has somehow resurfaced the satellite within the last 100 million years. **Tethys** also has a very large impact crater, as well as an extensive series of valleys and troughs that stretches three-quarters of the way around the satellite. Both **Dione** and **Rhea** have bright, heavily cratered leading hemispheres and darker trailing hemispheres with wispy streaks thought to be produced by deposits of ice inside various surface troughs or cracks. **Iapetus,** the outermost of the large icy satellites, has a dark leading hemisphere and a bright trailing hemisphere. The remaining 10 satellites, some sharing orbits with others, are smaller in size. The two largest of these, dark-surfaced **Phoebe** and irregularly shaped **Hyperion,** orbit far from the planet. Saturn has been encountered by three SPACE PROBES: *Pioneer 11* (1979), *Voyager 1* (1980), and *Voyager 2* (1981). Photos and other data from *Voyager 2* indicate the possibility of at least six more small satellites.

**Saturn,** in Roman mythology, god of harvests; husband of Ops; father of JUPITER, JUNO, CERES, PLUTO, and NEPTUNE; identified with CRONUS. After the TITANS' fall, he was said to have fled to Italy, settled on the CAPITOLINE HILL, civilized the people, and taught them agriculture. On his festival, the Saturnalia (17 Dec.), work ceased, gifts were exchanged, and war was outlawed; the tradition became absorbed into the celebration of Christmas.

**satyr,** in Greek mythology, forest and mountain creature. Part human, with horses' tails and ears, and goats' horns and legs, they were merry, drunken, lustful devotees of DIONYSUS.

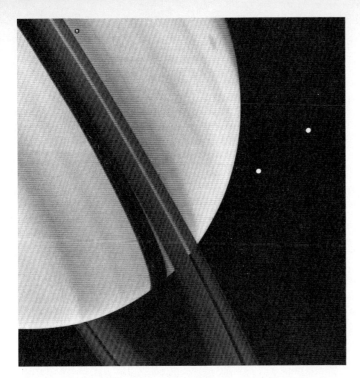

**Saturn** and two of its moons, Tethys and Dione, taken from *Voyager I*. The rings are seen as dark against the body of the planet, as light against the blackness of space.

**satyr play,** in ancient Greek drama, a play with a chorus of satyrs (men with bestial characteristics, perhaps originally representing fertility spirits), which burlesqued the language, structure, and mythological subject-matter of tragedy. In the 5th cent. BC, it was performed as an after-piece to each set of three tragedies. Only the *Cyclops* of EURIPIDES survives complete.

**sauces,** liquid used as an accompaniment to food, usually to enhance its flavour, appearance, and palatability. It is made in a number of different ways. A Béchamel sauce is made by the roux method—melted butter with flour and then milk stirred into it and allowed to cook. The addition of cheese makes this a mornay sauce. Mayonnaise and hollandaise sauces rely for their flavour and consistency on the property of egg yolks to create an emulsion with oil or fat. Fruit sauces such as tomato, cranberry, and apple are made by adding flavourings and then cooking until most of the liquid has evaporated. Soy sauce (made from SOYA beans) is the hallmark of Cantonese cooking, as satay sauce made of peanuts is of Indonesian. Mint sauce, an infusion of chopped mint leaves in vinegar, is one of the few items in British cooking not found elsewhere.

**Saudi Arabia,** officially the Kingdom of Saudi Arabia, kingdom (1985 est. pop. 12,400,000), 2,149,690 km² (829,995 sq mi), SW Asia, occupying most of the Arabian peninsula, bounded by Jordan, Iraq, and Kuwait (N), the Persian Gulf, Qatar, and the United Arab Emirates (E), Yemen, Southern Yemen, and Oman (S), and the Red Sea (W). RIYADH is the capital, JIDDA the principal port. Saudi Arabia has five major physical regions: the great RUB AL KHALI, a sand desert occupying the entire south and southeast; the Nejd, a vast, barren plateau in the centre; the Hejaz and Asir, along the RED SEA, with mountains rising from a narrow coastal plain; and the Eastern Province, along the PERSIAN GULF, site of the country's rich oil resources. The climate is usually hot and dry, although the humidity along the coasts is high. The oil industry dominates the economy. Saudi Arabia has at least one quarter of the world's oil reserves and is using its huge revenues from oil exports to diversify its industrial base. Recent irrigation projects have reclaimed many acres of desert, and dates, grains, and vegetables are produced. Nomadic BEDOUINS, who make up about 20% of the population, raise camels, sheep, goats, and horses. Income is also derived from religious pilgrims who travel from all parts of the Muslim world to the holy cities of MECCA and MEDINA. The GNP is US$108,283 million and the GNP per capita is US$10,030 (1984). The

overwhelming majority of the population are Sunni Muslim Arabs. Arabic is the official language.

*History.* ARABIA has been inhabited for thousands of years by nomadic Semitic tribes. With the birth (AD 570) of MUHAMMAD, in Mecca, Arabia was briefly the centre of Islam, but by the end of the 7th cent. the area was disunited. Modern Saudi Arabia owes its existence to IBN SAUD, an adherent of the puritanical WAHHABI Muslim sect. Beginning in 1902 he conquered the Nejd, Al Hasa, and Hejaz regions, and in 1932 he proclaimed himself king of a united Saudi Arabia. Oil was discovered in 1936; commercial production by a consortium of US oil companies began in 1938. Ibn Saud died in 1953 and was succeeded by his eldest son, Saud. In 1964 Saud was deposed by FAISAL, who secured (1974) an agreement giving the Saudis a 60% majority ownership of foreign oil concessions in their country. Under both monarchs, Saudi Arabia aided (1962–67) royalist forces against Egyptian-backed republican rebels in YEMEN. In 1975 Faisal was assassinated; he was replaced by KHALID, who inaugurated a programme of industrialization and social welfare. In the conflict with Israel, Saudi Arabia has generally supported the Arab states, although as a friend of the US it is a somewhat moderating force. Its moderating influence has also been felt in the ORGANIZATION OF THE PETROLEUM EXPORTING COUNTRIES (OPEC), in which it has acted to stabilize petroleum prices. Khalid died in 1982 and was succeeded as king by FAHD. In the early 1980s Saudi Arabia established closer ties with neighbouring states within the framework of the GULF COOPERATION COUNCIL.

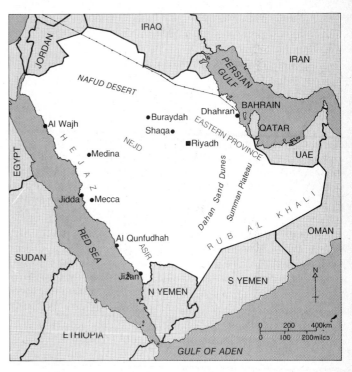

**Saudi Arabia**

**Saul,** fl. 11th cent. BC, first king of the ancient Hebrews. DAVID was first the protégé, then the rival, finally the successor, of Saul. Defeated in battle with the Philistines on Mt Gilboa, Saul committed suicide rather than be captured. Though he was unsuccessful in defeating the Philistines, Saul paved the way for national unity under David. 1 Sam. 10–31.

**Saul of Tarsus:** see PAUL, SAINT.

**Sault Sainte Marie Canals** (ˌsooh saynt məˌree), popularly called the **Soo Canals,** two toll-free ship canals on the US–Canada border. Bypassing rapids in the St Marys R. between Lakes Huron and Superior, they are a vital link in the St Lawrence & Great Lakes Waterway. The deeper US canal (2.6 km/1.6 mi long and 24 m/80 ft wide) accommodates larger vessels than the Canadian canal (2.3 km/1.4 mi long and 18 m/60 ft wide).

**Saura, Carlos,** 1932–, Spanish film director. His films often deal with the consequences of the *Spanish Civil War*, although, since the death of

Franco, they have been taking on a more personal note. His films include *The Hunt* (1966), *Peppermint Frappé* (1967), and *Cría Cuervos* (1976).

**Saussure, Ferdinand de** (soh,syooə), 1857–1913, Swiss linguist. One of the founders of modern LINGUISTICS, he established the structural study of language, emphasizing the arbitrary relationship of the linguistic sign to that which it signifies. Saussure distinguished synchronic linguistics (studying language at a given moment) from diachronic linguistics (studying the changing state of a language over time); he further opposed what he named *langue* (the state of a language at a certain time) to *parole* (the speech of an individual). Saussure's most influential work is the *Course in General Linguistics* (1916), a compilation of notes on his lectures.

**savanna** or **savannah,** tropical or subtropical grassland lying on the margin of the trade-wind belts. Its climate is characterized by a rainy period in summer and a dry winter when the grass withers. The largest savannas are in Africa.

**Savannah,** US city (1984 est. pop. 145,000), SE Georgia, near the mouth of the Savannah R.; inc. 1789. The city is a busy commercial port, and the site of a huge paper mill and chemical and other industries. The oldest city in Georgia, founded in 1733 by James OGLETHORPE, Savannah was the commercial rival of CHARLESTON. It was the object of fighting in the American Revolution and in the Civil War. In its historic district are fine old homes, churches, and shady streets.

**savings bank:** see BANKING.

**Savonarola, Girolamo,** 1452–98, Italian religious reformer. A DOMINICAN, he became popular in Florence for his eloquent attacks on moral laxity and for his predictions, some of them accurate. After the MEDICI were exiled (1494), he became spiritual ruler of Florence and imposed a severe regime. He supported the invasion of Italy by CHARLES VIII of France, hoping that Charles would help in forming a democratic government in Florence and reforming the scandalously corrupt court of Pope ALEXANDER VI. Excommunicated (1497) after ignoring the pope's order to stop preaching, Savonarola was finally hanged as a false prophet.

**Savoy,** region, E France. Chambéry, the former capital, and ANNECY are the principal urban centres. Savoy includes the area of the high ALPS south of Lake GENEVA. The seasonal movement of cattle to the high pastures (transhumance) is less common than in former times. Skiing has become a major source of winter employment and locally-generated hydroelectric power supports metallurgical and chemical industries in the valleys. The region's history is associated with that of the house of Savoy. French-speaking Savoy was annexed by France in 1792, then lost to Sardinia in 1815 who ceded it in 1860.

**Savoy, house of,** dynasty that ruled Savoy and Piedmont from the 11th cent., Sicily (1713–20), Sardinia (1720–1861), and Italy (1861–1946). Its first historical member was an 11th-cent. count who held lands in Savoy and Piedmont. Through marriage and diplomacy his successors expanded their holdings in France, Switzerland, and Italy. AMADEUS VIII acquired the ducal title in 1416. By 1536 Savoy had lost its Swiss possessions, and FRANCIS I of France occupied the rest of the duchy. In 1559 EMMANUEL PHILIBERT obtained the restoration of his duchy and made Turin his capital. His grandson VICTOR AMADEUS II became (1713) king of Sicily for his role in the War of the SPANISH SUCCESSION. Sicily was exchanged (1720) with Spain for Sardinia, and the state became known as the kingdom of Sardinia. In 1831 Charles Albert, of the cadet line of Savoy-Carignano, became king. He involved Sardinia in the RISORGIMENTO, by which his son, VICTOR EMMANUEL II, became (1861) king of Italy. Victor Emmanuel II's son, Humbert I (r.1878–1900), was assassinated. Humbert's son and successor, VICTOR EMMANUEL III, abdicated after World War II. His son, Humbert II, reigned briefly (1946) before Italy became a republic.

**Saxe, Maurice, comte de** (saks), 1696–1750, marshal of France, an illegitimate son of AUGUSTUS II of Poland. A brilliant commander, he led the French to victory at Fontenoy (1745) and Raucoux (1746) in the War of the AUSTRIAN SUCCESSION. His *Mes Rêveries* (1757) is a remarkable work on the art of war.

**saxifrage** (,saksi'frayj), name for some members of the Saxifragaceae, a diverse family of herbs, shrubs, and small trees of cosmopolitan distribution. The true saxifrages (primarily the genus *Saxifraga*) comprise a group of low rock plants often cultivated as rock-garden and border plants, e.g., the strawberry geranium (*S. sarmentosa*). The arctic and alpine *S. oppositifolia* is one of the northernmost of flowering plants. The genus *Ribes,* a group of berry-bearing shrubs including the gooseberry and CURRANT, is of minor economic importance. The mock orange, or syringa (genus *Philadelphus*), has white, sometimes fragrant flowers similar to orange blossoms, and the hydrangea (genus *Hydrangea*), another member of the family, has flat-topped clusters of white, pink, or blue flowers.

**Saxons,** Germanic people living in S JUTLAND in the 2nd cent. In the 3rd and 4th cent. they raided the coasts of the North Sea, and by the 5th cent. they had settled in N Gaul. Raiding Saxons began (c.450) to settle in Britain. By the 6th cent. they and the Angles were founding ANGLO-SAXON kingdoms, with WESSEX dominant. Continental or 'Old Saxons' in 566 became tributaries of the FRANKS, and were finally conquered (804) by CHARLEMAGNE. The treaty of Verdun (843) included Saxon lands in the area that is modern Germany.

**Saxony,** originally the land of the SAXONS, which in Frankish times was in NW Germany. In the 9th cent. the first duchy of Saxony, one of the five stem duchies of medieval Germany, was created. The duchy was broken up after the Emperor FREDERICK I ousted (1180) HENRY THE LION from the fief. In 1356 the duke of Saxe-Wittenburg was made a permanent elector of the Empire. His territory, called **Electoral Saxony,** lay east of the original stem duchy. In 1423 it passed to the WETTIN family. It was a centre of the German REFORMATION in the 16th cent. In 1697 the elector of Saxony became king of Poland as AUGUSTUS II. The death (1763) of his son, AUGUSTUS III, ended the union with Poland. The period 1697 to 1763 was one of cultural and artistic flowering in Saxony and in its capital, DRESDEN. Saxony had retained the Polish crown in the War of the POLISH SUCCESSION (1733–35) but suffered in the War of the AUSTRIAN SUCCESSION (1740–48) and the SEVEN YEARS WAR (1756–63) as a result of the rise of PRUSSIA. Saxony was raised (1806) to a kingdom by NAPOLEON I in return for changing sides (1806) in the FRENCH REVOLUTIONARY WARS, but after his defeat it lost nearly half of its land to Prussia. The remaining **kingdom of Saxony** was defeated by Prussia in the AUSTRO-PRUSSIAN WAR (1866) and joined the German Empire in 1871. Under the Weimar Republic it became (1918) the state of Saxony. In 1949 it became part of East Germany. It was abolished as an administrative unit in 1952 and divided among several districts.

**saxophone,** a WOODWIND instrument with a single reed and a brass body. It was invented by Adolphe Sax (1814–94) in the 1840s. The saxophone comes in seven sizes of which only four are found regularly. It is used mainly in JAZZ but occasionally plays in the orchestra.

**Sayers, Dorothy Leigh,** 1893–1957, English writer. Her erudite detective stories feature the nobleman-detective Lord Peter Wimsey and include *Strong Poison* (1930), *Murder Must Advertise* (1933), and *The Nine Tailors* (1934).

**Sayyab, Badr Shakir al-,** 1929–64, Iraqi poet. He was one of the best-loved exponents of 'free verse' in modern Arabic poetry. In the early stages of his career he was an enthusiastic communist and supporter of Arab nationalism, but his best poetry is of a spiritual and artistic depth which transcends ideologies. He was much influenced by modern English poetry as well as his own literary tradition.

**Sayyid Barghash ibn Said,** c.1837–1888, sultan of ZANZIBAR, E Africa (r.1870–88). He attempted to extend Zanzibari control over the mainland of TANZANIA but was thwarted by British and German imperialism. At the end of his reign his authority was recognized only on the island of Zanzibar.

**Sayyid Said,** 1791–1856, sultan of OMAN and ZANZIBAR (r.1840–56). The hereditary overlord of Arab settlements on the E African coast, he built up an extensive commercial empire, by conquest and dipomacy, based upon these dominions during the 1820s and 30s. He moved his capital from Oman to Zanzibar in 1840 and occupied the island, meeting little resistance. Zanzibar became the central market for ivory and slaves in E Africa and by the 1850s Sayyid Said from there controlled most ports between Mogadisho and Cape Delgado. He willed the Asian and African halves of his empire separately to his two sons.

**Sb,** chemical symbol of the element ANTIMONY.

**Sc,** chemical symbol of the element SCANDIUM.

**scabies,** skin infection characterized by severe itching. Caused by infestation by the parasitic mite *Sarcoptes scabiei*, the condition is easily passed on by personal contact. The female mite tunnels under the skin to lay eggs, commonly in the groin, causing red papules. Hexachlorophane kills the mites, and clothes and bedding must also be disinfested.

**Scafell Pike**, mountain, in Lake District, Cumbria, NW England. It is the highest peak in England, reaching 977 m (3162 ft).

**scalar**, quantity defined by its magnitude only. Typical physical quantities which are scalars are energy, mass, and temperature.

**Scalawags**, derogatory term used in the South after the AMERICAN CIVIL WAR to describe native white Southerners who joined the Republican Party and aided the congressional RECONSTRUCTION programme.

**scale**, in music, any series of TONES arranged in a step-by-step rising or falling of PITCH. The scale most used in Western musical composition until the end of the 19th cent. was the diatonic scale, a series of seven tones. (The addition of a final top note, with a frequency twice that of the lowest note, defines this sequence as an *octave*.) The intervals of the diatonic scale were defined by PYTHAGORAS in the 6th cent. BC as five whole tones (t) and two semitones (s) in the order ttsttts. By the time of J.S. BACH, the chromatic scale of 12 equal semitones (as in the white and black keys of a keyboard scale) had become established, and the scales beginning on these notes remained the basis of Western TONALITY until the innovations of such modern composers as SCHOENBERG. DEBUSSY used a scale of six equal whole tones in his works. Numerous different scales have been and are used in African and Asian musical systems, including equal-stepped five-, six-, and seven-tone scales.

Chromatic **scale**

**scale**, in zoology, a flattened bony or horny outgrowth of the skin of an animal, particularly in FISHES and REPTILES, that serves primarily as protection. Fish scales, composed mostly of bone, form directly in the skin membrane; the type and number of scales figure in the identification of a species. Most reptiles have horny scales, or scutes, which are also aids to identity, but some (e.g., the CROCODILE) have both horny and bony scales. In SNAKES, scales aid in movement. Birds have scales on the feet and sometimes the legs. Some mammals (e.g., the rat and the mouse) have tail scales.

**scale insect**, very small to small (0.7–8 mm/$\frac{1}{40}$–$\frac{1}{3}$ in), sexually dimorphic, sap-sucking, homopteran BUG (superfamily Coccoidea). Many species are major pests of crops grown in the tropics and subtropics, as well as under glass in temperate countries, often through accidental introduction. Wherever citrus fruits are grown there are problems from numerous scale insects, e.g., mussel scale (*Lepidosaphes ulmi*) and cottony-cushion scale (*Icerya purchasi*). For at least 2000 years before aniline dyes became available in the late 1870s, three species were of considerable importance as a source of crimson dye. One was the Mexican cochineal insect *Dactylopius coccus*, found on the prickly-pear cactus, which is still cultivated to a limited extent as a source of red dye for cosmetics, food colouring and some fabric dyeing. The Indian lac scale (*Laccifer lac*) is still cultivated for its lac, from which SHELLAC is refined, though this has now been largely replaced by synthetic resins.

**Scaliger, Julius Caesar**, 1484–1558, Italian philologist and physician in France. In his *De causis linguae Latinae* (1540) he analysed CICERO's style, criticizing the earlier studies of his humanist predecessors. He wrote commentaries on the medical and botanical works of HIPPOCRATES, Theophrastus, and ARISTOTLE, and urged an improved classification of plants. In his *Poetics* (1561), he extolled VIRGIL and SENECA.

**scallion**: see ONION.

**scallop** or **pecten**, marine BIVALVE mollusc distinguished by rounded, ridged shells with radiating ribs and flared 'wings' at the hinge. Scallops swim by flapping their shells with a powerful adductor muscle. Small scallops are known as queens.

**Scanderbeg** or **Skanderbeg**, c.1404–68, Albanian national hero. The son of an Albanian prince, he was born George Castriota. He abjured Islam in 1443, styled himself prince of Albania, and devoted the rest of his life to defending Albania against Turkish invasion, on occasion allying

Scale insects (*Saissetia oleae*)

himself with Venice, Naples, Hungary, and the pope. After his death Albania fell to the Turks.

**Scandinavia**, region of N Europe, consisting of NORWAY and SWEDEN (on the Scandinavian Peninsula), DENMARK, and usually also including FINLAND, ICELAND, and the FAEROE ISLANDS. Its people share similar histories and cultures, and most, except for the Finns and Lapps (see LAPLAND), speak closely related Germanic languages.

**scandium** (Sc), metallic element, discovered in 1879 by L.F. Nilson. Soft and silver-white, it is sometimes included in the RARE-EARTH METALS. It is in relatively greater abundance in the sun and certain stars than on earth. It is used in nickel alkaline storage batteries and as a radioactive tracer. See ELEMENT (table); PERIODIC TABLE.

**scarab beetle**, fairly large (20–30 mm/$\frac{3}{4}$–1$\frac{1}{4}$ in), black, oval and somewhat convex, dung-rolling BEETLE, *Scarabaeus*. A male, on finding a pile of cattle or similar dung, shapes some of it into a ball, of much the same size as that used in tennis. He then rolls it to where it can be conveniently buried, which can be well over 100 m (110 yd) away. The female is buried with the ball, in which she lays a single egg and then burrows her way to the surface. When the egg hatches the larva feeds on the dung, then pupates, and after emerging as an adult burrows up to the surface. Apparently the ancient Egyptians saw, in the life-cycle of this beetle, a simile of the daily rebirth of the sun: the newly-emerged beetles were thought to be self-creating and in their hieroglyphic script the scarab came to represent the verb 'to be created' or 'to exist'. By the time of the Middle Kingdom, c.2040–1786 BC, scarab amulets as good luck charms and scarab seals, with inscribed bases, were common, and scarabs continued to be an essential aspect of Egyptian culture right up to the conquest of that country in 332 BC, by Alexander the Great, and were also

Scarab beetle rolling a ball of dung

popular charms in classical Greece and Rome. The term scarab is often used today as a description for any of the 2000 or so known species of dung-feeding beetles in the family Scarabaeidae. See also BEETLE.

**Scarlatti, Alessandro,** 1660–1725, Italian composer. A leader of the Neapolitan school, he helped establish the conventions of *opera seria,* perfecting the *aria da capo* and the three-part OVERTURE. He wrote over 100 operas, church music, songs, and over 600 chamber CANTATAS. His son, **Domenico Scarlatti,** 1685–1757, a harpsichord virtuoso known chiefly for his over 500 harpsichord SONATAS, is considered the founder of modern keyboard technique. He moved to Portugal in 1719, and in 1728 to Spain, where he stayed for the rest of his life. His music often shows the influence of those countries' music.

**scarlet fever,** acute, contagious respiratory disease caused by streptococci bacteria. Symptoms include a sore throat, fever, headache, white-coated tongue with red spots (strawberry tongue), and a scarlet skin rash. The disease usually occurs in childhood and is treated by ANTIBIOTIC drugs to reduce the possibility of complications. An infection usually confers immunity.

**Scarman, Leslie George, Lord,** 1911–, British barrister and judge. He became a HIGH COURT judge (1961), and was later Chairman of the LAW COMMISSION (1965–73). He became a LAW LORD in 1977. A liberal judge, he has written on law and law reform, and has headed many judicial inquiries (including that into the disorders in Brixton, London in 1981).

**scepticism,** philosophic position holding that the possibility of knowledge is limited, because of either the limitations of the mind or the inaccessibility of its object. The term is used more loosely to denote any questioning attitude. The earliest sceptics included the Greek Sophists (5th cent. BC) and PROTAGORAS. HUME is famous for his theoretical scepticism, but more closely linked to scepticism was the AGNOSTICISM of KANT, who demonstrated that certain problems are insoluble by reason. DESCARTES used scepticism as a methodology. The scientific method, which demands that all assumptions be questioned, is sceptical to a degree, although the POSITIVISM of scientists assumes that material effect is impossible without material cause.

**Schacht, Hjalmar Horace Greeley,** 1877–1970, German financier. He conceived the plan that stabilized the German currency in the 1920s and was president of the Reichsbank (1923–30, 1933–39). Although he supported the NAZIS, he was placed in a concentration camp for his alleged part in the plot against HITLER (1944). He was acquitted (1946) of war crimes by the Nuremberg tribunal.

**Schaffner, Jacob,** 1875–1944, Swiss novelist. Rebellion against Swiss bourgeois conventions is the primary theme of his novels, including *Konrad Pilater* (1910) and *Johannes* (1922).

**Schafřík, Pavel Josef:** see ŠAFAŘÍK, PAVEL JOSEF.

**Schechter, Solomon,** 1847–1915, Hebrew scholar; b. Romania. He discovered a great treasury (genizah) of medieval manuscripts in the Ben-Ezra Synagogue in Cairo. This he purchased on behalf of Cambridge Univ. It has revolutionized knowledge of Jewish literary, social, and religious history. Schechter's identification of the hitherto missing Hebrew version of Ecclesiasticus won him an international reputation. As president of the Jewish Theological Seminary, in New York City, he brought together a faculty of scholars whose work defined the Conservative movement (see JUDAISM).

**Scheele, Karl Wilhelm** (ˌsháylə), 1742–86, Swedish chemist. A pharmacist, he prepared and studied OXYGEN (c.1773), but his published account (1777) appeared after Joseph PRIESTLEY's. He discovered NITROGEN independently of Daniel Rutherford and showed it to be a constituent of air. His treatise (1774) on MANGANESE aided in the discovery of that element and also of barium and chlorine. He isolated glycerin and many acids.

**Scheherazade:** see THOUSAND AND ONE NIGHTS.

**Scheldt,** Fr. *Escaut,* river, 430 km (270 mi) long, which rises in the chalk plateau of Artois in NE France. It flows through the cities of Cambrai and VALENCIENNES and, after being joined by the Scarpe R., enters Belgium where it is known (in Flemish) as the Schelde. Here it collects the drainage of the Lys and the Sambre before it flows into the North Sea below the city of ANTWERP, forming part of the great delta to which the RHINE and the MAAS also contribute.

**Schelling, Friedrich Wilhelm Joseph von,** 1775–1854, German philosopher. First influenced by the IDEALISM of J.G. FICHTE, he held the concept of the Absolute to represent the ultimate unity of mind and matter. Later Schelling saw history as a series of stages progressing toward that unity, and (unlike Fichte) held that nature itself progressed toward the Absolute. His concept of art as the unity of the natural and the spiritual, a bridge between German idealism and ROMANTICISM, influenced COLERIDGE.

**schema,** a term in philosophy and psychology, originating with KANT, which refers to the organization by the subject of perceptual and cognitive information or content. The term was introduced into psychology by the German philosopher Johann Herbart (1776–1851), and was used by the English psychologist Sir Frederick Bartlett (1886–1969) to refer to the organization and re-organization of perceived material in memory. In PIAGET's theory, the schema is derived from the actions (literal or mental) which the subject directs towards the object.

**scherzo** [It., = joke], term denoting various types of musical compositions, primarily lively and surprising in rhythm or melody. It replaced the minuet in the late 18th cent. as the third movement of the SYMPHONY, SONATA, and STRING QUARTET. It was usually in ternary form, with a contrasting middle section, or trio.

**Schiaparelli, Elsa** (skyahpahˌrel-lee), 1896–1973, Italian FASHION designer working in Paris and New York. Always an innovative designer, she was known for her bold outlines (e.g., padded shoulders) and flamboyant colours (e.g., the bright pink named after her). She was the first couturier to use the ZIP FASTENER.

**Schiaparelli, Giovanni Virginio,** 1835–1910, Italian astronomer. He discovered (1861) the asteroid Hesperia. While director (1862–1900) of the Brera Observatory, Milan, he observed what he called canals on the surface of the planet Mars and showed that meteor swarms move through space in cometary orbits.

**Schick test,** a diagnostic test to determine susceptibility to DIPHTHERIA. A small amount of dilute diphtheria TOXIN is injected into the skin. Redness and swelling at the site of injection within a week indicates no IMMUNITY against the toxin and the advisability of immunization if at risk.

**Schiele, Egon** (ˌsheelə), 1890–1918, Austrian expressionist painter and draftsman. His taut, linear style emphasizes anatomical structure. He used his interest in Freudian psychology in his portraits, especially his erotic works that look closely at aspects of sexuality. With KOKOSCHKA, he led the Austrian expressionist movement until his death aged 28.

**Schiller, Friedrich von,** 1759–1805, German dramatist, poet, and historian. Originally educated at the duke of Württemberg's military academy, where he was forced by the duke to study medicine, Schiller soon turned to writing. His attack on political tyranny in his first play *The Robbers* (1781) brought him fame, and Schiller fled his training as an army surgeon to become a dramatist for the Mannheim theatre, writing strident STURM UND DRANG dramas in the realist mode: *Fiesko* (1783) and *Intrigue and Love* (1784). *Don Carlos* (1787) marked a departure from prose realism to verse stylization and ended an epoch in Schiller's life. He had always swung between the imagination and the intellect, and for the next decade, philosophy (KANT), history, and aesthetic theory almost ousted poetry entirely. In 1787 he settled in Weimar, where he was appointed a professor at the Univ. of Jena (1789), married (1790) Charlotte von Lengefeld, and became close to GOETHE, who, for all the temperamental differences between the realist and the idealist, shared his ambition to make a new German classical literature, as their correspondence witnesses. Together they wrote a series of ballads and satirical distichs, while Schiller edited the literary periodicals *Die Horen* (1795–97), and *Der Musenalmanach* (1796–1800) which became their forum. He wrote several important treatises on aesthetics, among them his seminal analysis of modern self-consciousness, *On Naive and Sentimental Poetry* (1795) and his theory of play *On the Aesthetic Education of Man* (1795). He returned to drama with the great historical drama *Wallenstein* (1798–1800); *Mary Stuart* (1800); *Joan of Arc* (1801); the highly formalized experiment in alienation, *The Bride of Messina* (1803); and *Wilhelm Tell* (1804). His poetry is predominantly idealist and intellectual, abstract and musical: 'Ode to Joy' (1785) was used by BEETHOVEN for the finale of the 9th Symphony, while his high theatricality has made him a rich mine for opera composers in search of a strong text, from VERDI's *Luisa Miller* and *Don Carlos* to DONIZETTI's *Maria Stuarda*.

**Schism, Great,** or **Schism of the West** (ˌsiz(ə)m, ˌskiz(ə)m), division (1378–1417) within the Roman Catholic Church. Shortly after GREGORY XI returned the PAPACY from Avignon to Rome, he died (1378). URBAN VI was elected pope, but soon alienated those in the church. The cardinals declared Urban's election null and elected Robert of Geneva (Antipope Clement VII). Clement set up court in Avignon, but Urban continued to reign at Rome. They and their successors thus formed two lines of popes. The Council of Pisa (1409) tried unsuccessfully to depose GREGORY XII of the Roman line and Benedict XIII of the Avignon line, and elected a second antipope, Alexander V, who was soon succeeded by the energetic Baldassare COSSA as John XXIII. The schism was ended by the Council of Constance (1414–18), which accepted Gregory's resignation, deposed Benedict and John, and elected MARTIN V as pope.

**schist,** metamorphic ROCK (see METAMORPHISM) having a foliated (plated) structure in which the component flaky minerals are visible to the naked eye. Schists' mineral crystals are larger than those of SLATES and smaller than those of GNEISSES (the other two foliated metamorphic rocks).

**schistosomiasis** (ˈshistəoˌmieˈəsis): see BILHARZIASIS.

**schizophrenia** (ˈskitsəˌfreenyə), a severe mental disturbance, or PSYCHOSIS, characterized by disordered thought processes, bizarre actions, unrealistic behaviour dominated by fantasy, and incapacity to maintain normal interpersonal relationships. The term, which means 'splitting of the mind', was coined by the Swiss psychiatrist Eugen Bleuler (1857–1939) in order to emphasize the disjunction between AFFECT and COGNITION frequently experienced by patients. Schizophrenia should, however, be distinguished from MULTIPLE PERSONALITY. Schizophrenia occurs most often, though not always, in late adolescence. The variety of schizophrenia termed 'paranoid schizophrenia' is characterized by delusions of persecution or grandeur. The causes of schizophrenia are not firmly identified, but it is known frequently to be associated with neurochemical imbalances, and there may be hereditary factors predisposing some individuals to schizophrenia. Stressful environmental situations and events, and disordered patterns of family and interpersonal relationships, have also been advanced as causes or precipitating factors. In particular, the theory of 'double-bind situations', involving contradictory injunctions upon an individual, has been advanced by Gregory BATESON and R.D. LAING as a hypothesis to account for both causative and experiential aspects of schizophrenic illness. Contemporary treatment of schizophrenia is commonly in the first instance by means of tranquillizing drugs (see PSYCHOTROPIC), though PSYCHOTHERAPY is also employed.

**Schizophyta** (ˈskitsoˌfeetə), in some systems of classification, a division of the plant kingdom consisting of the BACTERIA and blue-green ALGAE. It refers to the mode of reproduction by simple splitting.

**Schlegel, Friedrich von** (ˌshləygəl), 1772–1829, German philosopher, critic, and writer, the most prominent founder of German ROMANTICISM. Educated in law, he turned to writing. With his brother, August Wilhelm, at Jena, he published the *Athenaeum,* the principal organ of the romantic school. His lectures in Jena (1800) and in Paris (1802) on history, language, and literature had a widespread influence. His study of Sanskrit and of Indian civilization, *On the Language and Wisdom of India* (1808), was outstanding. In his early period, Schlegel held that wisdom depends on the recognition of what he called 'romantic irony' that truth changes from experience to experience. Later he joined (1808) the Roman Catholic Church, and his views became more conservative. His brother, **August Wilhelm von Schlegel,** 1767–1845, was a scholar and poet. With his brother, Friedrich, he founded and edited the periodical *Athenaeum* (1798–1800). He is most noted for his extraordinary translations of SHAKESPEARE (1797–1810).

**Schleiden, Matthias Jakob** (ˌshliedən), 1804–81, German botanist. With Theodor SCHWANN, he is credited with establishing the foundations of the CELL theory. An 1838 paper, though mistaken in some aspects, recognized the significance of the nucleus in cell propagation.

**Schleiermacher, Friedrich Daniel Ernst** (ˌshlieəˈmahkhə), 1768–1834, German Protestant theologian. Originally a Moravian, he became (1794) a Reformed preacher and was a professor at Halle (1804–07) and Berlin (from 1810). His *Religion: Speeches to Its Cultured Despisers* (1799) defined religion as an absolute dependence on a monotheistic God, reached through intuition and independent of dogma, and showed both his closeness to the Romantics and his Pietist background. *The Christian Faith* (1821–22), his major work, developed systematically his earlier ideas and viewed Christianity as the highest manifestation of religion. His influence on Protestant thinking was pervasive until a reaction set in with the work of K. BARTH and E. Brunner.

**Schlemmer, Oskar,** 1888–1943, German artist. He taught at the BAUHAUS (1920–29) where he was head of the department of theatrical designs. His figure style treated the human form in geometrical shapes, and was derived from CONSTRUCTIVISM.

**Schlesinger, Arthur M(eier),** 1888–1965, American historian. He taught at Harvard (1924–54). His well-known works on colonial history include *The Colonial Merchants and the American Revolution* (1918). He is also known for his interest in social history, as in *The Rise of the City* (1933). His son, **Arthur M(eier) Schlesinger, Jr.,** 1917–, is also a distinguished historian. His *Age of Jackson* (1945) stimulated a reconsideration of the Jacksonian period. Schlesinger was an aide to Pres. KENNEDY and wrote a study of Kennedy's White House years, *A Thousand Days* (1965); he also wrote a biography of the president's brother, *Robert Kennedy and His Times* (1978).

**Schleswig-Holstein,** state (1984 est. pop. 2,613,796), c.15,670 km (6,050 sq mi), N West Germany. Kiel is the capital and chief port. Flanked on the W by the North Sea and on the E by the Baltic, Schleswig-Holstein occupies the base of the Jutland Peninsula and extends from the Elbe R. north to the Danish border. Farming, fishing, and manufacturing are important occupations. The duchy of Schleswig, created in 1115, was a hereditary fief held from the kings of Denmark. The duchy of Holstein was part of the HOLY ROMAN EMPIRE after 1111. Both were inherited (1460) by CHRISTIAN I of Denmark. Disputes over their status led in the 19th cent. to conflict between Denmark and the GERMAN CONFEDERATION. In 1864 Austria and Prussia declared war on Denmark, which was easily defeated. In 1866, after the AUSTRO-PRUSSIAN WAR, Schleswig and Holstein were annexed by Prussia. Schleswig-Holstein became a West German state in 1946.

**Schliemann, Heinrich,** 1822–90, German archaeologist who discovered the ruins of TROY. A student of HOMER from childhood, he amassed a fortune in business and retired at 41 to search for Homeric sites. Relying on details from Homer's poems, he began (1871) excavations at Hissarlik, now accepted as the site of Troy, and uncovered four superimposed towns. His other notable discoveries, described in his vast writings, were at Mycenae (1876–78), ITHÁKI (1878), and Tiryns (1884–85).

**Schmidt, Helmut,** 1918–, German political leader, chancellor of West GERMANY (1974–82). A member of the Social Democratic Party, he was minister of defence (1969–72) and of finance (1972–74) in the cabinet of Willy BRANDT. He became chancellor upon Brandt's resignation. Schmidt's chief aims as chancellor were to improve relations with East Germany and the USSR and to maintain the prosperous West German economy. In 1982 he lost a confidence vote in the lower house of the German parliament and was replaced as chancellor by Helmut KOHL of the Christian Democratic Union.

**Schmidt-Rottluff, Karl,** 1884–1976, German painter and woodcut artist. In 1905 he cofounded the BRÜCKE group, and is known for his WOODCUTS.

**Schneider Trophy Air Races,** contests for seaplanes, held between 1913 and 1931. The prestige of the race contributed substantially to the development of high-speed aircraft and high-power aero-engines (see FLIGHT, POWERED). The trophy was won outright for Britain in 1931 at 547 kph (340 mph).

**Schnitzler, Arthur** (ˌshnitslə), 1862–1931, Austrian dramatist and novelist. A medical man by profession and a contemporary, with a great affinity, to FREUD, Schnitzler represents the empty social values and neuroses of the bourgeoisie of a declining empire. His characteristic manner is detached and ironical, stylish, and non-judgmental. Among his dramas are the sequences *Anatol* (1893) and the once-scandalous *Merry-go-Round* (1897; first perf. 1920; tr. 1953), *Liebelei* (1896; tr. *Dalliance* 1914 and 1986), and *Professor Bernhardi* (1912). He is happiest in the shorter forms of prose fiction: *Leutnant Gustl* (1901) is a revealing experiment in inner monologue. His longer novels are *The Road to the Open* (1908) and *Therese* (1928).

**Schoenberg, Arnold** (ˌshuhnbeǝk), 1874–1951, Austrian composer. He became a US citizen in 1941. Schoenberg revolutionized modern music by establishing the 12-tone technique of SERIAL MUSIC as an important organizational device. His early works, e.g., *Verklärte Nacht* (1899), expanded WAGNER's and MAHLER's use of the chromatic scale. His later works are highly contrapuntal (see COUNTERPOINT). In 1908 he completely abandoned TONALITY (see ATONALITY) in a set of piano pieces and a song cycle. He first employed the 12-tone technique throughout a work in his Suite for Piano (1923). Schoenberg's other compositions include two chamber SYMPHONIES (1906; 1906–40), four string quartets, CONCERTOS for violin (1936) and piano (1942), various chamber works, and an unfinished opera, *Moses und Aron* (1932–51), considered his masterpiece. He was also a teacher; his notable students included Alban BERG and Anton von WEBERN.

**scholasticism,** philosophy and theology of Western Christendom in the Middle Ages. Basic to scholastic thought is the use of reason to deepen the understanding of what is believed on faith, and ultimately to give a rational content to faith. The formal beginnings of scholasticism are identified with St ANSELM (late 11th cent.), who attempted to prove the existence of God by purely rational means. ABELARD emphasized the rational approach in considering the most important philosophical question of the 12th cent., the question of universals (see NOMINALISM; REALISM). The early church fathers, notably St AUGUSTINE, incorporated PLATO's doctrines and NEOPLATONIC thought into Christian theology. The 13th cent., the golden age of medieval philosophy, was marked by two important developments: the growth of universities (especially at Paris and Oxford); and the availability in Latin translation of the works of ARISTOTLE and the commentaries of AVICENNA and AVERROËS. The closely wrought, rational system of St THOMAS AQUINAS is regarded as the greatest achievement of the scholastic age and the ultimate triumph of the effort to 'Christianize Aristotle'. Later opponents of Aquinas, e.g., St BONAVENTURE, DUNS SCOTUS, and WILLIAM OF OCCAM, broke the synthesis of faith and reason. The secular currents of the Renaissance and the growth of the natural sciences brought on the decline of scholastic metaphysics, although its approach continued to be followed in politics and law. In 1879 Pope LEO XIII proclaimed the system of Aquinas to be the official Catholic philosophy.

**Scholem, Gershom Gerhard,** 1897–1982, Jewish scholar; b. Berlin. His work made the study of the history of KABBALAH and Jewish mysticism an important scholarly discipline. A professor at the Hebrew Univ., Jerusalem, he wrote over 500 articles and books, including *Major Trends in Jewish Mysticism* (1941), *Sabbatai Zevi* (1973) and *Kabbalah* (1974).

**Schongauer, Martin** (ˌshohngowǝ), 1430–91, German engraver and painter. He is best known for his engravings of religious subjects, e.g., *The Wise and Foolish Virgins.* He was one of the earliest engravers to use copper plates, and his 115 engravings, signed M + S and executed with amazing virtuosity, were important to the development of German art.

**school of Paris.** The centre of international art until after World War II, Paris was a mecca for artists. The school of Paris includes many styles and movements. The practitioners and adherents of FAUVISM, CUBISM, ORPHISM, PURISM, and SURREALISM all belonged to the school of Paris, as did many others whose styles fit no one category. After the war, New York City challenged Paris's preeminence, though the school of Paris continued to produce major figures, e.g., Jean DUBUFFET.

**schools:** see MIDDLE SCHOOLS; NURSERY SCHOOLS; PREPARATORY SCHOOLS; PRIMARY SCHOOLS; PUBLIC SCHOOLS; SECONDARY SCHOOLS; SPECIAL EDUCATION.

**Schopenhauer, Arthur,** 1788–1860, German philosopher. A solitary figure who failed in attempts to rival HEGEL as a lecturer in Berlin, he considered himself the successor of KANT but equated Kant's 'thing-in-itself' with a blind impelling force manifesting itself in individuals as the will to live. Schopenhauer saw the world as a constant conflict of individual wills resulting in frustration and pain, and argued that it is only in contemplating beauty that we are freed from domination by the will. In particular, pleasure can be achieved only through the renunciation of desire (a concept that reflects Schopenhauer's studies of Hindu scripture). His most important work is *The World as Will and Representation* (1818). His doctrine of the primacy of the will influenced NIETZSCHE and FREUD, and his collection of essays and aphorisms, *Parerga and Paralipomena* (1851) influenced TOLSTOY, CONRAD, and PROUST.

**Schrader, Paul** (ˌshrahdǝ), 1946–, American film director and screenwriter. His portrayals of spiritual transcendance are often set in a violent and sleazy milieu. His films include *Blue Collar* (1978), *Hardcore* (1979), and *American Gigolo* (1979). He wrote the scripts for such films as *Taxi Driver* (1976) and *Rolling Thunder* (1977).

**Schreiner, Olive Emilie Albertina,** 1855–1920, white South African novelist and feminist. She is best known for her study of spiritual alienation, *The Story of an African Farm* (1883), under the pseudonym Ralph Iron. Other works include novels and the influential feminist tract *Women and Labour* (1911) which argued for women's equal participation in the workforce. Her pro-Boer, anti-Christian and pacifist sentiments appear in *Thoughts on South Africa* (1923) and in her letters.

**Schröder, Friedrich Ludwig** (shruhdǝ), 1744–1816, German actor, manager, and dramatist. The most celebrated German actor of his day, he introduced SHAKESPEARE to Germany, raised theatrical standards, and furthered the STURM UND DRANG movement.

**Schrödinger, Erwin,** 1887–1961, Austrian theoretical physicist. For his mathematical development (1926) of wave mechanics, a form of quantum mechanics (see QUANTUM THEORY), and his formulation of the wave equation that bears his name, he shared with Paul DIRAC the 1933 Nobel Prize for physics.

**Schubert, Franz (Peter),** 1797–1828, Austrian composer, one of the foremost exponents of ROMANTICISM. German LIEDER reached their finest expression in his lyrical songs, especially in the great cycles *Die schöne Müllerin* [the fair maid of the mill] (1823) and *Die Winterreise* [winter journey] (1827). His SYMPHONIES are the final extension of the classical SONATA forms, and the Fifth (1816), Eighth (the *Unfinished,* 1822), and Ninth (1828) rank with the finest orchestral music. Between 1820 and 1823 he tried unsuccessfully to establish himself as an operatic composer. From 1824 to his untimely death, he concentrated on writing works for piano and piano duet, three great string quartets, two piano trios, the song cycles, and the Ninth Symphony. Well known for such chamber works as the Quartet in D Minor (*Death and the Maiden,* 1824) and the Quintet in A Major (*The Trout,* 1819), Schubert also wrote stage music, choral music, MASSES, and much piano music.

**Schultz, Theodore W.,** 1902–, American economist. A specialist in agricultural economics and the economic problems of underdeveloped countries, he shared the 1979 Nobel Prize for economics. His books include *Economic Growth and Agriculture* (1968).

**Schuman, Robert,** 1886–1963, French statesman. He was finance minister (1946, 1947), premier (1947–48), and foreign minister (1948–53) in the Fourth Republic. His so-called Schuman Plan led to the formation (1952) of the European Coal and Steel Community, the first step in the creation of the EUROPEAN COMMUNITY.

**Schumann, Robert (Alexander),** 1810–56, German composer, a leader of the romantic movement. His brilliant piano music (e.g., *Carnaval, Kinderscenen*) occupied him until 1840, when he began to write orchestral music and SONGS, in which he achieved a superb fusion of vocal melody and piano accompaniment. His orchestral works (e.g., Piano Concerto in A Minor, 1841–45; *Rhenish* Symphony, 1850), infuse classical forms with an emotional intensity that foreshadowed his later nervous breakdown. An articulate critic, he championed younger composers such as CHOPIN and BRAHMS. His wife, **Clara Josephine (Wieck) Schumann,** 1819–96, was an outstanding concert pianist.

**Schumpeter, Joseph Alois** (ˌshoom'paytǝ), 1883–1950, American economist; b. Austria. After practising law and teaching at the Univ. of Graz and at Bonn, he emigrated (1932) to the US and later became a professor at Harvard. His major contributions to economics were the theory of the entrepreneur as the dynamic factor in the business cycle and the theory of the economic development of CAPITALISM.

**Schurz, Carl** (shooǝts), 1829–1906, American political leader; b. Germany. As US senator from Missouri (1869–75), he helped form the LIBERAL REPUBLICAN PARTY (1872). Later he was secretary of the interior (1877–81). In 1884 he led the MUGWUMPS against James G. BLAINE (1884). Schurz supported William MCKINLEY for president in 1896 (for his currency views) and William J. BRYAN in 1900 (for his anti-imperialism). An active editor and writer, he gained broad influence through honesty and fearlessness.

**Schuschnigg, Kurt von** (ˌshooshnik), 1897–1977, Austrian chancellor. He became chancellor after the assassination (1934) of Engelbert DOLLFUSS. In 1936 he forced E.R. von STARHEMBERG to resign as vice chancellor and became sole head of the semi-Fascist Austrian government. He prevented Austria's annexation to Germany until he lost (1937) the support of MUSSOLINI. German troops occupied Austria in 1938, and Schuschnigg was held prisoner until 1945. He later settled in the US.

**Schütz, Heinrich** (shytz), 1585–1672, German composer. His *Dafne* (1627; now lost) has been called the first German OPERA. The leading German musician of his time and the outstanding master of 17th-cent. church music, he wrote ORATORIOS and settings of the Passion that combined the Venetian style of alternating CHOIRS and the dramatic declamation of Florentine monody with German POLYPHONY. This choral style influenced German music through the time of HANDEL and BACH. Amongst his masterpieces are *The Christmas History* (1664), *Seven Last Words from the Cross* (1645), and three Passions.

**Schwann, Theodor**, 1810–82, German physiologist and histologist. Originator with Matthias SCHLEIDEN of the cell theory, he demonstrated that the cell is the basis of animal as well as plant tissue. He also demonstrated the living nature of yeasts and described the nerve sheath known by his name.

**Schwarzkopf, Elizabeth**, 1915–, German lyric soprano. She gained an international reputation for subtlety and versatility in recitals, ORATORIOS, and opera. She is particularly renowned for her LIEDER interpretations.

**Schweitzer, Albert**, 1875–1965, French theologian, b. Alsace; musician, physician, and philosopher. He established (1913) a hospital at Lambaréné, Gabon, French Equatorial Africa, which received broad international support and at which he lived for most of his life. An organist and expert on the music of Bach, Schweitzer wrote a biography of the composer (1905) and coedited his music (1912–14). Schweitzer's ethical philosophy, developed in his *Philosophy of Civilization* (1923), rests on his concept of 'reverence for life'. As a theologian, in works such as *The Quest of the Historical Jesus* (1906), he rejected the historical infallibility of Jesus while following him spiritually. Widely honoured for his many accomplishments, Schweitzer was awarded the 1952 Nobel Peace Prize.

**Schwenckfeld, Kaspar von** (ˌshvengkfelt), 1490–1561, German religious reformer. After meeting Thomas MÜNZER and CARLSTADT at Wittenberg, he devoted himself to the reform movement in Silesia. Martin LUTHER opposed his supposed Anabaptist leanings, and after Lutheranism became dominant in Silesia, Schwenckfeld was forced to move to Strasbourg and then to Ulm. An anathema was proclaimed against him by the Lutherans, and his books were banned. He offered (1540) a full statement of faith, which enunciated the distinction between the outward and transitory word of God as given in the Scriptures and an inward spirit, which was divine, eternal, and necessary for salvation. His followers, known as **Schwenckfeldians** or **Schwenckfelders,** were persecuted and fled in the 18th cent. to other parts of Europe and America. The sect still exists in Pennsylvania.

**Schwerin,** city (1984 pop. 126,390), Mecklenburg, northern East Germany. Situated on the shore of Schwerin Lake, it is regional centre for agricultural and livestock production. There are food-processing, electrical, and engineering industries. It was capital of Mecklenburg–Schwerin from 1701 to 1934.

**Schwitters, Kurt** (ˌshvitəs), 1887–1948, German artist. He invented *Merz* (trash) constructions. His COLLAGES are among the outstanding creations in this medium.

**Sciascia, Leonardo** (ˌshahshah), 1921–, Italian novelist and short-story writer. Sicily's foremost living author, his work has centred on Sicilian settings and themes, typically exploring the links between crime and power, as in *Mafia Vendetta* (1961).

**sciatica** (sieˌatikə), severe pain in the leg along the sciatic nerve and its branches. It may be caused by injury or pressure to the base of the nerve in the lower back, or by metabolic, toxic, or infectious disease. Measures for relief of pain include bed rest, immobilization of the leg, and heat.

**science fiction,** literary genre to which a background of science or pseudoscience is integral. Although fantastic, it contains elements within the realm of future possibility. Science fiction began with the late-19th-cent. work of Jules VERNE and H.G. WELLS. The appearance of the magazines *Amazing Stories* (1926) and *Astounding Science Fiction* (1937) encouraged good writing in the field, which was further spurred by post–World War II technological developments. Contemporary writers of science fiction include Robert Heinlein, Isaac ASIMOV, A.E. van Voght, Alfred Bester, Arthur C. Clarke, Frederik Pohl, Stanislaw LEM, and Ursula K. LeGuin. The genre's effectiveness as an instrument for social criticism is seen in Aldous HUXLEY's *Brave New World* (1932), Ray Bradbury's *Fahrenheit 451* (1953), and Kurt VONNEGUT's *Cat's Cradle* (1963).

**scientific notation,** means of expressing very large or very small numbers in a compact form, sometimes simplifying computation. In this notation any number is expressed as a number between 1 and 10 multiplied by the appropriate power of 10 (see DECIMAL SYSTEM; EXPONENT). For example, 32,000,000 in scientific notation is $3.2 \times 10^7$, and 0.00526 is $5.26 \times 10^{-3}$.

**scientology,** the doctrine of the Church of Scientology, founded in California in 1953 by L. Ron Hubbard, a science-fiction writer, to promote the bogus science of 'dianetics'. The church moved to East Grinstead, England, in 1959, since when it has attracted not only criticism of its spiritual methods but also litigation regarding its business affairs.

**Scilly Isles,** group of islands off LAND'S END, Cornwall, SW England (1984 est. pop. 1900). There are about 140 islands, situated c.45 km (28 mi) SW of Land's End, of which five are inhabited: Bryher, St Agnes, St Martin's, St Mary's, and Tresco. The islands have a mild climate, and are popular tourist resorts. The main economic activity, apart from tourism, is in cultivation of early flowers and vegetables.

**scintillation counter:** see PARTICLE DETECTOR.

**scion,** in horticulture: see GRAFTING.

**Scipio,** ancient Roman family of the Cornelian gens. They were patricians. During the 3rd and 2nd cent. BC they were distinguished by their love of Greek culture and learning. Their wealth and extravagance were detested by the family of CATO the Elder, who worked hard to ruin them. **Scipio Africanus Major** (Publius Cornelius Scipio Africanus) 234?–183 BC, a Roman general, was the conqueror of HANNIBAL in the PUNIC WARS. In the Second Punic War, Scipio conquered Spain and ended the war by defeating Hannibal at Zama (202 BC) in Africa. He returned home in triumph and later retired from public life; he was named Africanus after the country he conquered. **Scipio Africanus Minor,** c.185–129 BC, Roman general, was the destroyer of CARTHAGE. He was adopted by the eldest son of Scipio Africanus Major and earned a great reputation as a patron of Greek literature and of Roman writers, notably TERENCE and Laelius, and he was the lifelong friend of POLYBIUS, his protégé. As consul (147 BC) he went to Africa and terminated the Third Punic War with the capture and destruction of Carthage. On his return to Rome he attempted to destroy the Gracchan reforms (see GRACCHI). A great public quarrel arose, and Scipio was found dead in his bed. No inquiry was made, and it was generally said that he was murdered by someone of the Gracchan party.

**Scofield, Paul,** 1922–, English actor. In 1955 he played Hamlet, directed by Peter Brook at the Moscow Arts Theatre with the first English company to appear in Russia since the Revolution. He gained international renown for his portrayal of Sir Thomas MORE in *A Man for All Seasons* (stage, 1961; film, 1966) and for his Lear (1962), with the Royal Shakespeare Company, which toured in Europe and America. He has also starred in *King Lear* (film, 1971) and *Volpone* (1977).

**Scopas,** Greek sculptor, fl. 4th cent. BC. He was the first to express violent feeling in marble faces. His style is seen in fragments from the Temple of Athena Alea, Tegea, and in Roman copies of his work, e.g., *Ludovisi Ares* (Rome).

**Scoresby, William,** 1789–1857, English explorer. On yearly voyages (1803–22) to Greenland, he mapped, made soundings, and noted the flora and fauna. He studied terrestrial magnetism there and in Australia (1856). His books helped to lay the foundations of Arctic geography.

**scorpion,** invertebrate animal (order Scorpiones) with a pair of powerful, pincerlike claws and a hollow, poisonous stinger at the tip of

Roman copy of *Pothos* (350 BC) by **Scopas**, Uffizi, Florence.

the tail; an ARACHNID. Most are 2.5–7.5 cm (1–3 in) long, but some measure as much as 20 cm (8 in). They are able to live in extreme heat and are usually found in deserts. They seize and crush prey with their large claws, immobilizing it by stinging if necessary. With the exception of the fatal stings of *Androctonus australis* of the Sahara and several Mexican species, scorpion stings, although painful, are not usually dangerous to humans.

**Scorsese, Martin** ('skawr,sayzay), 1942–, American film director. His studies of violent, often deranged men are characterized by a restless, nervy style. His films include *Mean Streets* (1973), *Taxi Driver* (1976), and *Raging Bull* (1979).

**Scotland,** political division of the United Kingdom of Great Britain and Ireland (1985 est. pop. 5,136,509) 78,772 km² (30,414 sq mi), comprising the northern portion of the island of Great Britain and many surrounding islands, including the ORKNEY and SHETLAND ISLANDS and the HEBRIDES. It is bounded by England (S), Atlantic Ocean (N and W), and the North Sea (E). It has 3,700 km (2,300 mi) of deeply indented coastline. Scotland may be divided into three main geographical regions: the southern uplands, the central lowlands, and the HIGHLANDS of the north, location of Great Britain's highest peak, BEN NEVIS (1344 m/4408 ft). EDINBURGH is the capital and GLASGOW the chief port. Principal rivers are the CLYDE, FORTH, DEE, TAY, and TWEED. In 1707 Scotland was united with ENGLAND and WALES as the United Kingdom of GREAT BRITAIN. They share one PARLIAMENT, but Scotland retains its own systems of law (based on Roman law) and education. The Church of Scotland, which is Presbyterian, is legally established.

*History.* The Picts, in Scotland from prehistoric times, along with Gaels or Celts from Ireland, prevented the Romans from penetrating far into Scotland, although the Romans did succeed in introducing Christianity before they left in the 5th cent. After the Roman evacuation, four Scottish

kingdoms emerged. In the mid-9th cent. KENNETH I united and established the nucleus of the kingdom of Scotland, and by the 11th cent. his descendants ruled most of present-day Scotland. The centuries that followed were marked by dissension and turbulence among the nobles and struggle for independence from England, especially under Robert the Bruce (later ROBERT I). A brief respite of internal peace during the reign of James IV was followed by the turmoil of the REFORMATION, brought to Scotland primarily by John KNOX. By the time MARY QUEEN OF SCOTS arrived (1561) in Scotland, Catholicism had almost disappeared from the Lowlands. Mary's struggle against Protestantism ended in her loss (1567) of the throne and her subsequent execution (1587). Mary's son, James VI of Scotland, succeeded (1603)ELIZABETH I on the English throne as James I, thus uniting the two crowns. In 1707 the Act of Union formally united the governments of the two kingdoms. Union eventually proved economically favourable for Scotland, and its textile and metallurgical industries flourished in the 18th and 19th cent. The concentration of heavy industry made Scotland an important arsenal in both world wars, and in the 1970s Aberdeen became the centre of North Sea oil development. There remains a persistent nationalist movement for greater autonomy for Scotland.

**Scotland, Church of,** the established national church of Scotland. Under John KNOX Scotland came under the influence of Calvinism. Parliament abolished the jurisdiction of the Roman Catholic Church in 1560 and established (1592) PRESBYTERIANISM. However, James VI (JAMES I of England) and later Stuart monarchs attempted to restore episcopacy, and much confusion and unrest resulted (see COVENANTERS). A Presbyterian church was finally ensured by the Act of Settlement (1690) and the union (1707) of England and Scotland. In a dispute over patronage and state interference, Thomas Chalmers led a secession (1843) and formed the Free Church of Scotland. This church merged (1900) with the United Presbyterian Church to form the United Free Church of Scotland. In 1929 most of this body rejoined the Church of Scotland.

**Scotland, legal system in,** law and legal system relating to and applicable in Scotland. Though part of the UK, for historical reasons Scotland has a separate legal system guaranteed by the Act of Union (1707). Scottish law has a separate court system (see Table) and judges, though it has the House of Lords as its ultimate appeal court for civil cases. Unlike English and Welsh COMMON LAW, Scottish law is a systemized body of principles along CIVIL LAW lines. As early as 1681 Stair's *Institutions*, based on JUSTINIAN ideas, set out clearly the whole of Scottish law. Scottish judges determine cases according to codified principles rather than adhere rigidly to PRECEDENT. The Scottish LEGAL PROFESSION is divided along similar lines to the legal profession in England and Wales with solicitors undertaking general legal work, and advocates exclusively representing clients in court. In the Sheriff Courts all prosecutions are carried out by a procurator, a trained solicitor or advocate appointed by the court. Each Sheriff's Court district has a procurator-fiscal who investigates whether to bring cases to trial, and conducts important prosecutions in the public interest. The head of the Scottish legal system is the Lord Advocate. See also COURT SYSTEM IN ENGLAND AND WALES.

**Scotland Yard,** headquarters of the CRIMINAL INVESTIGATION DEPARTMENT (CID) of the London Metropolitan Police. Named after a street in London, it became police headquarters in 1829. Other CID headquarters, New Scotland Yard, were built along the Thames embankment in 1890. Scotland Yard moved to new premises in 1967 but retains its name.

**Scott, George C(ampbell),** 1926–, American actor. He has performed on the stage in *Plaza Suite* (1968), *Uncle Vanya* (1973), *Death of a Salesman* (1975), and *Present Laughter* (1982) and in such films as *The Hustler* (1961), *Dr Strangelove* (1964), *Patton* (1969; Academy Award), and *The Hospital* (1971).

**Scott, Sir George Gilbert,** 1811–78, English architect. He was prominent in the GOTHIC REVIVAL as a designer and as a restorer of Gothic edifices, notably Ely cathedral (1847) and WESTMINSTER ABBEY. He also designed (1860–70) the buildings for the home office and foreign office, the ALBERT MEMORIAL, and St Pancras Station, London. His grandson, **Sir Giles Gilbert Scott,** 1880–1960, also an architect, designed ecclesiastical buildings, including the Anglican cathedral in Liverpool (1904–27).

**Scott, Sir Peter,** 1909–, British ornithologist and artist, son of Capt. Robert SCOTT (Scott of the Antarctic). He founded the WILDFOWL TRUST in

1946 and was one of the founders and chairman of the WORLD WIDE FUND FOR NATURE. He drew the giant panda logo for the fund. Sir Peter has led ornithological expeditions to Iceland, and has been on expeditions to Australasia, Galapagos Islands, Seychelles Islands, and Antarctica. He has written and illustrated many books about birds.

**Scott, Robert Falcon,** 1868–1912, British naval officer who commanded two Antarctic expeditions. On the first (1901–04), in the *Discovery,* he discovered Edward VII Peninsula, surveyed the coast of Victoria Land, and explored the continent itself. On a second voyage, launched in 1910, he left his base on the Ross Sea and headed for the SOUTH POLE. Pulling sledges by hand, the party of five arrived there on 18 Jan. 1912, only to find that Roald AMUNDSEN had preceded them by a month. On their return, beset by illness, hunger, and blizzards, they all died.

**Scott, Ronnie,** 1927–, English jazz tenor and soprano saxophonist. Inspired by the bop pioneers in the late 1940s, his tenor partnership with Tubby Hayes in the Jazz Couriers (1957–59) was particularly fruitful. He now runs the most famous jazz club in Britain, 'Ronnie Scott's', in Soho, London.

**Scott, Sir Walter,** 1771–1832, Scottish novelist and poet. Trained as a barrister, he held a legal post in Selkirkshire for much of his life. After his collection of old ballads, *Minstrelsy of the Scottish Border* (2 vol., 1802; enl. ed., 3 vol., 1803) he began publishing his own narrative poems, *The Lay of the Last Minstrel* (1805), *Marmion* (1808) and *The Lady of the Lake* (1810), immensely popular in the 19th cent., though now largely unread. *Waverley* (1814), published anonymously, was a great success, becoming the first of the 'Waverley Novels', romances of Scottish life that reveal Scott's gift for storytelling and vivid characterization. The series included *Guy Mannering* (1815), *The Antiquary* (1816), *Old Mortality* (1816), *Rob Roy* (1817), *The Heart of Midlothian* (1818), and *The Bride of Lammermoor* (1819). In 1820, at the height of his fame, Scott was made a baronet. *Ivanhoe* (1819) was his first historical romance in prose. Most of the novels that followed were in the historical style; they include *Kenilworth* (1821), *Quentin Durward* (1823), and *The Talisman* (1825). In 1825 Scott faced financial catastrophe. He had assumed responsibility for a printing firm, Ballantyne's, in 1813 and had been meeting its expenses out of advances from his publishers, Constable and Co. When a depression ruined both firms in 1826, Scott, instead of declaring bankruptcy, set out to pay both his debt and much of Constable's; in the process his health was destroyed. After his death the rest of the debt was paid from the earnings of his books.

**Scott, Winfield,** 1786–1866, American general. A hero of the WAR OF 1812, he was appointed supreme commander of the US army (1841–61). In the MEXICAN WAR he led the southern expedition in a triumphant campaign from Veracruz to Mexico City (1847), which confirmed him as a daring strategist and bold fighter. Now very much a national hero, he ran (1852) for president as the Whig candidate but was defeated by Franklin PIERCE. Scott was vain and pompous (his nickname was 'Old Fuss and Feathers') but he is generally considered the greatest American general between George WASHINGTON and Robert E. LEE.

**Scottish education,** historically different from education in England and Wales in various respects. A system of parochial schooling was developed in Scotland in the 16–17th cent. Three universities (St Andrews, Glasgow, and Aberdeen) were founded in the 15th cent., followed by Edinburgh in 1582. These, with a wider curriculum and no religious barriers, attracted students from England where, until the early 19th cent., only the more restrictive Oxford and Cambridge were available. The present eight universities (now including Strathclyde, Heriot-Watt, Dundee, and Stirling) have some 50,000 students, and offer three-year Ordinary or four-year Honours courses of study. Fourteen Central Institutions roughly parallel the English and Welsh POLYTECHNICS. In Scotland today transfer to secondary school is at 12. The Scottish Certificate of Education Standard Grade is taken in the fourth year, and the higher Grade in the fifth or sixth year. Scottish education is administered by the Scottish Education Department, under the Secretary of State for Scotland, responsible to Parliament.

**Scottish National Party,** (SNP), nationalist formation (est. 1934) seeking full independence for SCOTLAND within the COMMONWEALTH and the EUROPEAN COMMUNITY. After holding occasional single seats in the House of Commons, the SNP achieved a breakthrough in 1974, winning 11 seats and 30% of the Scottish vote in the October elections. However, after an abortive attempt to set up a devolved Scottish assembly, SNP strength declined; in 1987 the party won three seats and 14% of the Scottish vote.

**Scotus:** see DUNS SCOTUS.

**scouring rush:** see HORSETAIL.

**screw:** see MACHINE.

**Scriabin** ('skree‚yahbin): see SKRYABIN.

**Scribe, Augustin Eugène** (skreeb), 1791–1861, French dramatist. He wrote over 300 plays and many librettos for composers such as MEYERBEER and VERDI. Among the best of his well-structured comedies is *The Ladies' Battle* (1851).

**Scriblerus Club,** English literary group (c.1713–14), formed to satirize 'false tastes in learning'. ARBUTHNOT, GAY, POPE, and SWIFT were members. *Memoirs of . . . Martinus Scriblerus* (1741) was primarily Arbuthnot's work.

**scuba:** see DIVING, DEEP-SEA.

**sculling.** see ROWING.

**Sculthorpe, Peter,** 1929–, Australian composer and teacher. His music has been influenced by the sounds and techniques of east Asian musics. He has written many orchestral and chamber works and has developed an individual style which many regard as an authentic Australian voice.

**scurvy,** condition resulting from a lack of vitamin C (ascorbic acid) in the diet. Vitamin C is found in fruit and vegetables and full-blown scurvy is rare except in groups at special risk (e.g., mentally handicapped people). See table under VITAMINS AND MINERALS.

**scutage,** feudal payment, usually cash, by a vassal to his lord, especially to a king, instead of military service. Its incidence increased in the 12th cent. with the rise of professional military knights. Kings of England financed wars for their French lands by scutage. In MAGNA CARTA (1215), King JOHN of England pledged not to impose scutage without the consent of his barons. The growth of taxes after the reign of EDWARD III displaced scutage in England.

**Scylla and Charybdis** (‚silə, kə‚ribdis), in Greek mythology, sea monsters. They lived on either side of the Straits of Messina. Scylla seized sailors and devoured them, and Charybdis, the whirlpool, caused shipwrecks. ODYSSEUS passed safely between them, as did JASON and the Argonauts.

**Scythia,** ancient region from the Danube to the borders of China, occupied by the Scythians, warlike mounted nomads who came from Russia in the 1st millennium BC. Before the 9th cent. BC they formed a kingdom in the E Crimea. In the 7th cent. BC they invaded Mesopotamia, Syria, and the Balkans. Surviving attacks by DARIUS I of Persia (512 BC) and ALEXANDER THE GREAT (c.325 BC), after 300 BC they were driven back to S Russia but were displaced there (2nd or 1st cent. BC) by the related Sarmatians (see SARMATIA).

**Se,** chemical symbol of the element SELENIUM.

**sea, law of the,** international agreement regulating the use and exploitation of the world's oceans. The UN-sponsored Law of the Sea Treaty (1982) calls for limited, and strictly controlled, mining of the seabed; establishes in general the 19.3-km (12-mi) limit for territorial waters; gives all nations' ships the right of 'innocent passage' through crucial straits; and sets up internationa antipollution regulations. Most of the industrial nations opposed the restrictions on seabed mining; but Third World nations, the chief beneficiaries of the agreement, favoured the treaty and created the majority that passed it.

**sea anemone,** predominantly solitary marine polyp (see POLYP AND MEDUSA), usually attached to submerged objects. Many of these animals are beautifully coloured and look like flowers when their tentacle-encircled feeding end is open. They are mostly 2.5–10 cm (1–4 in), long; a few are 90 cm (3 ft) in diameter. Most sea anemones are predators, immobilizing their prey with stings located in the tentacles.

**Seabury, Samuel,** 1729–96, American clergyman, first bishop of the Protestant EPISCOPAL CHURCH. Although a Loyalist during the American Revolution, he was chosen (1783) to be bishop of Connecticut and, since no bishop of the CHURCH OF ENGLAND could consecrate him owing to his inability to take the oath of allegiance, had to be consecrated (1784) by bishops of the Scottish Episcopal Church at Aberdeen.

**sea cow:** see MANATEE.

**sea cucumber,** flexible, elongated invertebrate animal with a cucumber-shaped, leathery body; an ECHINODERM. Most are under 30 cm (1 ft) long. Many sea cucumbers eject most of their internal organs when sufficiently irritated, later regenerating a new set.

Sea cucumber (*Cucumaria frondosa*) showing tube feet

**seafloor spreading:** see OCEAN.

**sea gooseberry:** see COMB JELLY.

**seahorse,** small, bony-plated FISH of the family Syngnathidae, usually found in warm waters. Its elongated head and snout, flexed at right angles to its body, suggest those of a horse. Members of different species range from 5 to 20 cm (2 to 8 in). Weak swimmers, they anchor themselves by curling their thin, prehensile tails around seaweed. While mating, the female seahorse injects eggs into a pouch on the underside of the male, where they are fertilized and then develop until the young are expelled. The related pipefish look more fishlike.

**Sea Islands,** chain of more than 100 low, sandy barrier islands, off the Atlantic coast of South Carolina, Georgia, and N Florida, US. First settled by the Spanish in the 16th cent., they became the earliest important cotton-growing area in the US, specializing in the production of long-staple (or sea island) cotton. Now a popular resort area, they include unspoiled Cumberland Island National Seashore (Georgia); Forts Sumter and Moultrie (South Carolina); and the ruins of Fort Frederica, on St Simons Island (Georgia), built (1736–48) by James OGLETHORPE to secure the region against the Spanish. Beaufort, on Port Royal Island, is the principal city.

**seal,** fin-footed MAMMAL (pinniped) of the family Phocidae, usually marine, with front and hind feet modified as flippers. Seals have streamlined bodies with a thick, subcutaneous layer of fat, and most inhabit cold or temperate regions. All species leave the water at least once a year to breed; some species migrate. Seals live on fish and shellfish; many dive deep to feed, navigating by means of echo location. True seals lack external ears. They are polygamous and gregarious, and most live in one of three geographical regions: northern, antarctic, and the warm waters of the Mediterranean, Caribbean, and Hawaiian seas. Seals are extensively hunted for food, fur, hides, and oil.

**sea lily:** see CRINOID.

**sea lion,** fin-footed marine MAMMAL (pinniped) of the eared seal family. The sea lion has external ears (unlike the true SEAL), a long, flexible neck, supple forelimbs, and hind flippers. Males may reach 2.5 m (8 ft) in length. Sea lions live close to shore in the oceans of the Southern Hemisphere and in the N Pacific, feeding on fish and SQUID. To breed they gather in colonies, where the males assemble harems. Most species are protected.

**Sea Peoples,** warlike seafaring tribes of unknown origin who raided along the coasts of the E Mediterranean in the 13th and 12th cent. BC. They caused great damage to the HITTITE empire, but later the Egyptians under RAMSES III successfully repelled them.

Seahorse

**seaplane,** aeroplane designed to take off from and alight on water. The two most common types are the floatplane, whose fuselage is supported by struts attached to two or more pontoon floats, and the flying boat, whose boat-hull fuselage is constructed with the buoyancy and strength necessary to alight and float on water. First built and flown in 1911 by Glenn CURTISS, the seaplane developed rapidly in the 1920s and 30s and for a time was the largest and fastest aircraft in the world.

**Sears Tower,** Chicago, US, the world's tallest building. Constructed (1970–74) for Sears, Roebuck and Co., it rises 110 storeys to a height of 443 m (1454 ft), 32 m (104 ft) taller than New York City's WORLD TRADE CENTER. Designed by the firm of Skidmore, Owings and Merrill, the Sears Tower is supported structurally by square tubes of welded steel. It has an exterior of black aluminium and bronze-toned glass cut by black bands and topped by a 20-storey tower.

Sears Tower

**sea slug,** usually brightly coloured and decorated marine GASTROPOD mollusc that lacks a shell as an adult. Most sea slugs, or nudibranchs, creep along the sea bottom or cling to vegetation below the tide line; a few swim in the open ocean. Most are under 2.5 cm ( 1 in) long. One of the commonest European sea slugs, the sea lemon (*Archidoris pseudoargus*), feeds on sponges growing in coastal waters.

**sea snake,** a type of REPTILE belonging to the family Hydrophidae. Sea snakes have become totally aquatic, even mating and producing their young at sea. They live in tropical waters round the Indian Ocean, Indonesia, and Australia and on the Pacific coast of Central America. Most sea snakes are between 120 and 150 cm (4 to 5 ft) long, although 3 m (10 ft) snakes have been reported. Sea snakes are easy to recognize by their laterally flattened tails. All are very venomous, the venom being injected into prey through rigid fangs at the front of the jaw, like those of the COBRA. They eat eels and other fishes. The yellow-bellied sea snake (*Pelamis platurus*) is one of the most striking, with its black back separated from its yellow ventral surface by a sharply demarcated waving line along the entire length.

**sea spider,** long-legged, spiderlike marine invertebrate animal with at least four pairs of walking legs; an ARTHROPOD. Most sea spiders are tiny and live near the shore, crawling around on the surface of animal colonies or seaweeds.

**sea squirt:** see TUNICATE.

**sea star:** see STARFISH.

**Seattle,** US city (1984 est. pop. 488,000), W Washington, built on hills between Puget Sound and Lake Washington; settled 1851–52, inc. 1869. The largest city in the Pacific Northwest, it is the region's cultural, financial, commercial, transport, and industrial centre. Aircraft, forest products, and transport equipment are the most important of its many manufactures. Seattle prospered with the coming of the railroad in 1884 and became a boom town with the 1897 Alaska gold rush. Long a centre of radical labour activity, it was the scene of a major general strike in 1919. Seattle's enormous port is the main link with oil-rich Alaska and is important in trade with Asia. The city is close to scenic mountain and coastal recreational areas. It is also an educational and cultural centre, with many museums, theatres, and musical groups. Seattle's distinctive skyline landmark is the 183-m (600-ft) Space Needle, built for the 1962 World's Fair.

**sea urchin,** ECHINODERM in the class Echinoidea. Sea urchins may be roughly spherical, flattened, or heart-shaped and are usually covered in spines and with rows of tube feet, like those of STARFISH. Heart urchins and sand dollars are sea urchins. They are found worldwide in shallow waters, living in the BENTHOS. Sea urchins feed on seaweeds, which they scrape with five teeth supported on a skeletal 'cage' called the Aristotle's lantern. Some plough through the sand in search of food and shelter, and all urchins can bury themselves quickly if alarmed. They cannot move very quickly if caught on a hard surface, but are protected by their sharp, hollow spines which break off easily and make a nasty wound. Spines are venomous in some species. The roes of the Mediterranean sea urchin (*Echinus esculenta*) are eaten as a delicacy and sea urchins are fished commercially in Japan, Malaya, South America, and the Caribbean.

**seaweed,** multicellular marine ALGAE. Most have a stemlike basal disc (holdfast) and a leaflike frond of varying length and shape. The simplest seaweeds are blue-green and green algae and occur in shallow waters as threadlike filaments, irregular sheets, or branching fronds. Brown algae, which are the largest and most numerous of the seaweeds, grow at depths of 15–23 m (50–75 ft), and include the large kelps, sources of iodine and potassium salts, potash, fertilizer, and medicines. Red algae, some of which are fernlike, are found at the greatest depths (30–61m/100–200 ft); commercial AGAR is obtained from a red alga. Some seaweeds provide food for marine animals; all provide oxygen through PHOTOSYNTHESIS. Seaweed, especially species of red algae, is an important part of the human diet in some regions.

**Sebastian,** 1554–78, king of Portugal (r.1557–78). A headstrong religious fanatic, he determined to win glory by fighting the Muslims in N Africa. In 1578 he invaded MOROCCO with a large force of mercenaries, but his lack of military experience contributed to his crushing defeat at Alcazarquivir, where he was killed.

**Sebastiano del Piombo** (‚pyomboh), c.1485–1547, Italian painter; b. Sebastiano Luciani. A pupil of GIORGIONE, he moved to Rome in 1511, where he became a friend of MICHELANGELO. His major altarpieces, e.g., *The Raising of Lazarus* (1517–19; National Gall., London) were influenced by Michelangelo and unite Roman grandeur with Venetian colour. He was an outstanding portrait painter, whose works include the *Ferry Carondolet* (Thyssen Coll., Lugano).

**Sebele I,** c.1845–1911, king of the Bakwena (r.1863–1911), one of the eight principal ethnic groups of BOTSWANA. Together with two other Tswana kings, KHAMA III and BATHOENG I, he visited England in 1895 to protest the annexation of their territories, nominally under British protection since 1885, by Cecil RHODES's British South Africa Company.

**Secession, War of:** see CIVIL WAR.

**second** (sec or s), fundamental unit of time in all systems of measurement. In practical terms, the second is $\frac{1}{60}$ of a minute and 1/3600 of an hour. Since 1967 it has been calculated by atomic standards to be 9,192,631,770 periods of vibration of the radiation emitted at a specific wavelength by a caesium-133 atom.

**secondary schools,** in Britain, the form of educational provision for all pupils beyond the primary stage up to age 16, and voluntarily for those wishing to stay to 18. The earliest form of secondary school was the grammar school, which, until the Education Act 1944 was implemented, was a selective, fee-paying form of secondary education (free only for those pupils winning scholarships to gain entry). These schools took approximately 10–20% of the age group. The 1944 Act made secondary education free and available to all, and in most areas this was initally implemented by providing *secondary grammar* and *secondary modern* schools, and in some cases *secondary technical* schools also. An examination at 11-plus allocated children to different schools, until this was virtually ended in 1965. By this time the *comprehensive* school, open to all children in the neighbourhood, had become more established, and the Labour government of 1964 was committed to a policy of fully comprehensive school provision; Conservatives have generally been doubtful about comprehensive schooling, but it is now widespread. Secondary schools prepare pupils for public EXAMINATIONS at 16 and 18, in the latter case in the 'sixth form'. The schools generally provide a wide range of extracurricular activities and careers guidance, and each school is under the general supervision of a governing body, consisting of representatives of the LOCAL EDUCATION AUTHORITY, teachers, and parents.

**Second International,** world coordinating body of Socialist parties founded in Paris in 1889 as successor to the **International Workingmen's Association,** or First International, (1864–76). The outbreak of WORLD WAR I led to an irrevocable split in the Second International with the formation of the Communist, or Third, International (COMINTERN) in 1919. Socialist parties which rejected the Soviet revolutionary model reestablished the Second International as the Labour and Socialist International (1923–40). After WORLD WAR II, cooperation between democratic socialist parties was revived within the framework of the **Socialist International** (est. 1951), which by 1986 had over 70 member parties around the world.

**Secretariat :** see UNITED NATIONS (table 2).

**secret police,** secret, often terrorist, police agency operating for its government's political purposes. In democratic societies secret or quasi-secret police are limited to investigation, and suspects have the right to an open trial. Elsewhere, where they are accountable only to the executive branch of government, secret police often investigate, apprehend, judge, and punish in secrecy. The USSR's security army, variously known as the Cheka, GPU, NKVD and now the KGB, contains both uniformed and secret police divisions, as well as intelligence, prison-camp, and military formations. It is charged with enforcing political conformity throughout state, party, armed services, and society in general, and answers directly to the party leadership. It was first founded by the Bolsheviks during the Russian CIVIL WAR, and assumed virtually unlimited powers of terror during the Stalinist era, since reduced. It operates the GULAG. In Nazi Germany (see NATIONAL SOCIALISM), the state police (Gestapo) and the Nazi Party's guard, the SS, headed by Heinrich HIMMLER, exercised widespread arbitrary powers of arrest, detention and execution. They ran the Nazi CONCENTRATION CAMPS. Technological advances in surveillance and computing have increased the capacity of modern police forces to collect information.

**secret society,** organization whose members, aims, and rites are kept secret. In some CULTURES secret societies are the sole means by which

MYSTERIES and folkways are transmitted, generally in coming-of-age rituals. They are usually limited to men, but in China the secret Hung Society for women lasted over 1500 years, and in West Africa secret societies for both sexes thrive (e.g., among the Mende). Modern secret societies (e.g., fraternal orders, FREEMASONRY) offer members various kinds of mutual aid. Some governments and churches oppose them as fostering subversion and violence (see MAFIA).

**Section d'Or** [Fr., = golden section], title of an exhibition and a magazine in Paris in 1912. It emphasized the interest of the Cubist movement (see CUBISM) not only in theories of colour and ORPHISM, but also in the mathematical system of proportion which goes back to Pythagoreans, which was considered to have innate properties of beauty.

**section system,** the division of society into different, equal groups recruited according to kinship principles. These basic social divisions are extended to include the natural world. Marriages are invariably symmetrically prescribed between specified sections. This system is characteristic in particular of Australian Aboriginal societies.

**Security Council:** see UNITED NATIONS (table 2).

**sedative:** see under HYPNOTIC.

**seder** [Heb., = order], name given to the home ritual for the first two evenings of the festival of Passover, with its special service. It conforms to a detailed order of Heb. readings, songs, and eating of symbolic foods, as prescribed in the handbook for the seder, the *Haggadah*. The main features of the seder, besides the festive meal, are the drinking of four cups of wine (corresponding to four expressions of redemption contained in the book of Exodus), the eating of *matzah*, unleavened bread (to symbolize the haste with which the Israelites left Egypt, to the extent that could not wait until their dough had risen into leavened bread), *maror*, bitter herbs (to recall the bitterness of the oppression) and a dipping of vegetables into salt-water (symbolic of the tears shed) and *haroset* (a paste, containing apples, nuts, wine, and cinnamon, which has the consistency, and is suggestive, of the mortar used by the Israelites while building store-cities and pyramids for the Pharaoh). (See also JEWISH HOLIDAYS.)

**sedimentary rock:** see ROCK.

**sedition,** in law, acts or words tending to excite disaffection against governmental authority. The scope of the offence was broad in early COMMON LAW, even permitting prosecution for insults to the king. In the UK, the offence can be committed using any words, with intent to incite hostility towards the monarch, government or Parliament. Despite its broad character, in recent years prosecutions for sedition have been rare.

**seed,** ripened ovule of the pistil of a FLOWER, consisting of the plant embryo, stored food material (endosperm), and a protective coat. True seeds vary in size from dustlike (as in some orchids) to very large (the coconut seed). Seeds of most wild, and many cultivated plants undergo a period of DORMANCY before GERMINATION. Many seeds are frequently confused with the FRUIT enclosing them, as in the GRAINS and NUTS. The seed-bearing plants (ANGIOSPERMS and GYMNOSPERMS) are the highest plants in the evolutionary scale; lower plants (MOSSES and FERNS) propagate by means of SPORES.

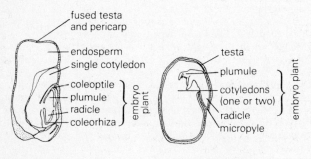

**Monocotyledonous seed**    **Dicotyledonous seed**

Seed

**Seferis, George** pseud. of **Giorgos Seferiadis** (se ferees), 1900–1971, Greek poet, critic, and diplomat. His surrealistic, highly symbolic poetry invokes classical themes and the theme of exile. Volumes include *Turning Point* (1931), *The Cistern* (1932), and *Collected Poems, 1924–1955* (tr. 1969). He was awarded the 1963 Nobel Prize in literature.

**Sefer Torah,** hand-written parchment scroll of the Law, containing the Pentateuch (see under TORAH). These are housed in a specially designated Ark (see ARON KODESH), from which they are ceremoniously removed at special times for the Reading of the Law, primarily at Monday and Thursday morning services, Sabbaths, and festivals. They are written, unvowelled, in Hebrew characters, according to an ancient scribal tradition. The scrolls are generally adorned with a velvet mantle, and a silver breastplate and pointer.

**Segal, George,** 1924–, American sculptor. Connected with the POP ART movement, he is known for his life-sized white plaster human figures in everyday situations.

**segmentary system,** lineage system identified by M. FORTES. A group of kin, defined by their descent from a common apical ancestor, e.g., FFF, are for particular events or circumstances identified with a wider group recruited again in terms of the relationship to a more remote ancestor, e.g., FFFFF, and for yet other situations become part of an even wider group recruited in terms of a yet more remote apical ancestor. The structure therefore is tree-like in form and has different levels of unity and opposition.

**segmented worm:** see ANNELID WORM.

**Segovia,** town (1981 pop. 53,237), capital of Segovia prov., central Spain. It has a 14th-cent. Moorish palace, a Gothic cathedral (1526–1616), and the Roman aqueduct of 148 arches which is c.800 m (2624 ft long).

The Roman aqueduct at **Segovia**

**Segovia, Andrés,** 1893–1987, Spanish guitarist. Famous for his transcriptions, concerts, and recordings, he is largely responsible for contemporary interest in the guitar. Such composers as FALLA, ROUSSEL, and VILLA-LOBOS wrote music for him.

**seignorial system:** see MANORIAL SYSTEM.

**Seine,** river, N France flowing generally NW c.770 km (480 mi) into an estuary on the English Channel near Le Havre. Chief cities on its route are PARIS, where many bridges span the river, and ROUEN, which is accessible to oceangoing vessels.

**Sei Shōnagon,** c.965–c.1020, Japanese writer. She was a court lady and contemporary of MURASAKI SHIKIBU. Her *Makura no Sōshi* [The pillow book of Sei Shōnagon], (tr. 1928 by Arthur Waley; tr. 1967 by Ivan Morris) consists of witty and haphazard jottings on court life.

**seismology** (seiz͵moləji), study of EARTHQUAKES and related phenomena using instruments called seismographs. In general, a recording device is connected to a heavy mass that, when earth tremors occur, remains still due to inertia. The relative motion between the EARTH and the instrument is magnified and recorded on a rotating drum by a stylus. Through the use of three such instruments the location and severity of earthquakes can be detected. Seismology is also used to locate oil (by analysing waves from detonated explosions), to detect underground nuclear tests, and to determine the configuration and depth of the ocean floor.

**Sekondi-Takoradi,** city (1987 est. pop. 123,600), S Ghana. With ACCRA and KUMASI it forms a triangle of three major cities linked by rail, in the densely populated southern half of the country. One of the two principal Ghanaian ports on the Gulf of Guinea, in 1983 with Tema it handled 3,694,000 tonnes of cargo.

**Selden, John,** 1584–1654, English jurist and scholar. From 1623 Selden was active in Parliament's struggle to assert its rights against the CROWN. A man of great erudition, he was a legal antiquarian (*England's Epinomus,* 1610), an Orientalist (*De Diis Syris,* 1617), and a student of the origins of English law. He is popularly known through *Table Talk* (1689), a record of his conversations kept by his secretary.

**Selebi-Pikwe,** town (1987 pop. 29,469), Central District, Botswana. It has large nickel-copper deposits. Mining began in 1974, but depressed world market prices for these metals have affected the town.

**Selenga,** river, c.1200 km (750 mi) long, flowing generally NE from the Hangay Mts in Outer Mongolia to Lake Baikal in Siberia. From the USSR frontier it flows N and passes through Ulan Ude; this section is navigable in summer.

**selenium** (sɪ͵leeni·əm), (Se), nonmetallic element, discovered by Jöns Jakob BERZELIUS in 1817. Selenium is used in pigments, photographic exposure meters, electronics, and xerography. See ELEMENT (table); PERIODIC TABLE.

**self-help,** notion that people find a moral and spiritual—not to mention economic—advantage in providing for their own needs, rather than relying on services provided by the state (e.g., private health care). The historical antecedents for this idea (fashionable in the 1980s in the West) are those of the 19th cent., and in particular the notion that 'captains of industry' achieved their position through diligence and hard work, rather than luck or assistance from others. This version of the rise to fortune of 19th-cent. capitalists was enshrined in Samuel Smiles's *Self-Help* (1859), open to criticism with its unproblematic representation of individual careers.

**self-help group,** non-professional organization formed by people with a common problem or situation, for the purpose of pooling resources, gathering information, and offering mutual support, services, or care. Self-help groups began to spread following World War II and proliferated rapidly in the 1960s and 70s. Among those groups addressing common problems are Alcoholics Anonymous, Body Positive (for victims of AIDS), and those for the victims and families of child abuse, suicide, and crime. Groups concerned with a shared situation include those for the elderly, single parents, and homosexuals. The definition of such groups sometimes includes social-advocacy organizations (e.g., the Claimants' Union) and halfway services (e.g., drug rehabilitation centres). Although self-help groups may draw on, or offer a bridge to, professional assistance, services (often free) are usually provided by the members themselves through meetings, publications, and individual contacts.

**Selim,** sultans of the OTTOMAN EMPIRE (Turkey). **Selim I** (the Grim), 1467–1520 (r.1512–20), deposed his father and killed his brothers. His defeat (1514) of the Persians added territory to the empire but began the

long rivalry between Persia and Turkey. By assuming the CALIPHATE, he made himself and his successors spiritual as well as temporal rulers. Although bloodthirsty and inflexible, he was an able organizer and reformer. **Selim II** (the Drunkard), c.1524–1574 (r.1566–74), suffered the Turkish naval defeat at Lepanto (1571), the first severe setback at the hands of the Christians. **Selim III,** 1761–1808 (r.1789–1807), suffered defeats (but no great loss of territory) in the second of the RUSSO-TURKISH WARS. He forced Napoleon's army out of Egypt (1801), which was restored to him. However, Egypt, Albania, and Serbia all became virtually independent during his reign. He was strangled at the order of Mustafa IV, who succeeded him.

**Seljuks:** see TURKS.

**Selkirk, Alexander,** 1676–1721, Scottish sailor whose adventures suggested to DEFOE the story of *Robinson Crusoe.* Put ashore at his own request in the Juan Fernández Islands, Selkirk remained there for over four years before his rescue (Feb. 1709).

**Selkirk, Thomas Douglas,** 5th earl of, 1771–1820, Scottish philanthropist. Emigration to America seemed to him the best solution for the poverty of his countrymen, so he acquired and successfully settled (1803) a large tract on Prince Edward Island. A later attempt, the RED RIVER SETTLEMENT (1812–16), in what is now S Manitoba and N North Dakota and Minnesota led to violence between rival settlers and litigation that cost Selkirk most of his fortune.

**Selvon, Samuel Dickson,** 1923–, Trinidadian writer. He combines superb comic vision and aspects of local dialect to explore lives of ordinary folk in the Caribbean, e.g., *A Brighter Sun* (1952), as well as the consequence of emigration to England, e.g., in *The Lonely Londoners* (1956) and *Moses Migrating* (1984).

**semantics** [Gr., = significant], in general, the study of the relationships between words and meanings. The empirical study of word meanings in existing languages is a branch of linguistics; the abstract study of meaning in relation to language or symbolic logic systems is a branch of philosophy. Both are called semantics. The field has three basic concerns: the relations of words to the objects denoted by them; the relations of words to the interpreters of them; and, in symbolic logic, the formal relations of signs to one another (syntax). Among the major linguistic semanticists is Noam CHOMSKY. A related theoretical orientation has been developed by such anthropologists as LÉVI-STRAUSS. Philosophical semanticists have included FREGE, Bertrand RUSSELL, and WITTGENSTEIN. A related field, general semantics, studies the ways in which the meanings of words influence human behaviour.

**semaphore,** method of signalling with flags or pointers, either hand-held or mechanically operated. Invented in the late 18th cent., it originally consisted of a small number of symbols, but it was extended in 1890 to provide the whole alphabet plus numerals. Its main use was for signalling between ships at sea, but it has been displaced by radio.

**Semarang,** city (1980 pop. 1,024,000), capital of Central Java prov., N Java, Indonesia, at the mouth of the Semarang R. An important port, it is one of Java's major commercial centres. There are textile and shipbuilding industries, and tobacco, sugar, rubber, coffee, and kapok are exported.

**Seme, Pixley ka Izaka,** c.1880–1951, South African nationalist leader and journalist. After studying law at Oxford he became one of the first black South African barristers. He returned to South Africa and in 1912 co-founded the South African Native National Congress (renamed the AFRICAN NATIONAL CONGRESS in 1923), serving as its first treasurer and its first president-general. The decline in popularity of the ANC in the early 1930s was attributed to Seme's conservatism.

**semicolon:** see PUNCTUATION.

**semiconductor,** solid material (see SOLID-STATE PHYSICS) whose electrical conductivity at room temperature lies between that of a metallic conductor and that of an insulator (see CONDUCTION; INSULATION). At high temperatures its conductivity approaches that of a metal, and at low temperatures it acts as an insulator. In a semiconductor there is a limited movement of electrons, depending upon the crystal structure of the material used. Incorporation of certain impurities in a semiconductor enhances its conductive properties. The impurities either add free electrons or create holes (electron deficiencies) in the crystal structures of the host substances by attracting electrons. Thus there are two semiconductor types: the n-type (negative), in which the current carriers (electrons) are negative, and the p-type (positive), in which the positively charged holes move and carry the current. Substances such as silicon, indium antimonide, gallium arsenide, and aluminium phosphide are semiconductors. Semiconductors are used in various electronic devices (see, e.g., COMPUTER; RECTIFIER; TRANSISTOR; PHOTOELECTRIC CELL).

**Seminole Indians,** NORTH AMERICAN INDIANS of the Eastern Woodlands, speaking a Muskogean language (see AMERICAN INDIAN LANGUAGES). They separated from the CREEK INDIANS in the 18th cent. To escape white encroachment they fled to Florida, where they absorbed remnants of the Apalachee tribe and runaway black slaves. They fought Andrew JACKSON (1817–18) and, led by OSCEOLA, again fought US forces in the Seminole War (1835–42), after which most of them moved to Oklahoma, becoming one of the FIVE CIVILIZED TRIBES. In the early 1980s there were some 3700 Seminole in Oklahoma; a small number were still living in Florida.

**semiotics** or **semiology,** philosophical theory deriving from the American logician C.S. PEIRCE and the French linguist Ferdinand de SAUSSURE; now it means generally the study of any cultural product (e.g., a text) as a formal system of linguistic signs. Saussure's key notion of the arbitrary nature of the sign means that the relation of words to things is not natural but conventional; thus a language is essentially a self-contained system of signs, wherein each element is meaningless by itself and meaningful only by its differentiation from the other elements. This linguistic model has influenced recent literary criticism, leading away from the study of an author's biography or a work's social setting and towards the internal structure of the text itself. See STRUCTURALISM.

**semiprecious stone:** see GEM.

**Semiramis,** mythical Assyrian queen, said to have founded BABYLON. After a long reign she vanished in the form of a dove; she was thereafter worshipped as a deity. Her legend is probably based on Sammuramat, regent of ASSYRIA (810–805 BC). She is the heroine of ROSSINI's opera *Semiramide* (1823).

**Semites,** term originally designating the descendants of Shem, son of NOAH; later applied to ARABS and other speakers of Semitic languages. By 2500 BC the pastoral nomadic Semites, who had originated in the Arabian peninsula, began migrating north and west to MESOPOTAMIA, the Mediterranean coast, and the Nile R. delta. In Mesopotamia they became dominant (see ASSYRIA; BABYLONIA). In Phoenicia they were the first great seafaring people. The Hebrews, who, with other Semites, settled in Palestine, became leaders of a new nation and religion (see JEWS; JUDAISM).

**Semitic languages,** subfamily of the Hamito-Semitic family of languages. See ALPHABET (illustration); LANGUAGE (table).

**senate, Roman,** governing council of the Roman republic. An outgrowth of the royal privy council, it gained immense power as Rome expanded in the 3rd and 2nd cent. BC, sending out armies, making treaties, and organizing the new domain. Membership in the senate was limited to ex-magistrates, who belonged almost entirely to old families. Its tone tended to be reactionary, yet there was no real challenge to its authority until the agitation of the GRACCHI. This failed, but a popular party grew up to oppose the conservatives. Although it was thoroughly defeated by SULLA, the struggle was resumed later, with Julius CAESAR heading the popular group and POMPEY heading the senatorial party. Caesar triumphed (48 BC), and though he was assassinated, the senate was proscribed (43 BC) and did not regain power. Docile under AUGUSTUS, it became a mere cipher in the later empire.

**Senate, United States:** see CONGRESS OF THE UNITED STATES.

**Sendai,** city (1986 est. pop. 678,983), capital of Miyagi prefecture, NE Honshu, Japan. A major commercial and administrative centre, its manufacturing industries have, in the past, produced chiefly consumer goods. In recent years, the city has developed an industrial area and grown rapidly, particularly since the introduction of the bullet train (SHIN KAN-SEN) in 1982. Tohoku university, sited here, is famed for its scientific research which has greatly influenced Japanese industry. Sendai was established as a castle town and seat of the Date clan in 1601. The ruins of Aoba castle stand on the hills to the west of the city.

**Sender, Ramón José** (sayn ˌdeə), 1902–82, Spanish novelist. A Loyalist in the SPANISH CIVIL WAR, he left Spain in 1939 and became a US citizen in 1946. His many novels, dealing with social injustice, include

*Imán* (1929), *Siete domingos rojas* (1932; tr. Seven Red Sundays), *El rey y la reina* (1949; tr. The King and the Queen), *El verdugo afable* (1952; tr. The Affable Hangman), and *Réquiem por un campesino español* (1960; tr. Requiem for a Spanish Peasant). He has also written plays, stories, poetry, and literary criticism.

**Seneca** (Lucius Annaeus Seneca), c.3 BC–AD 65, Roman philosopher, dramatist, and statesman. A noted orator, he tutored NERO and was virtual ruler in the first years of the emperor's reign. His suicide after accusations of conspiracy was considered remarkably noble by the Romans. A Stoic, he wrote moral and philosophical essays, and probably also nine of the ten tragedies attributed to him, which were written apparently for recitation. These, including *Hercules Furens* and *Medea,* profoundly affected Renaissance TRAGEDY with their gloomy atmosphere, bombastic rhetoric, and STOICISM.

**Seneca Indians:** see IROQUOIS CONFEDERACY.

**Senefelder, Aloys,** 1771–1834, German lithographer; b. Bohemia. He invented LITHOGRAPHY in Munich c.1796. He published an account of the nature and history of the invention in 1818.

**Senegal,** officially Republic of Senegal, republic (1987 est. pop. 6,540,000), 197,161 km² (76,124 sq mi), W Africa, bordered by the Atlantic Ocean (W), Mauritania (N), Mali (E) and Guinea and Guinea-Bissau (S). The Republic of GAMBIA is an enclave in the southwest. Major cities include DAKAR (the capital), Thiès, and Kaolack. Most of the country is low-lying and covered with savanna, which becomes semidesert in the SAHEL region of the north. The 400-km (250-mi) coastline is sandy north of Dakar and swampy or muddy to the south. Senegal is primarily agricultural, but industry is expanding. By far the most important cash crop is groundnuts, which supplies 75% of farm exports; groundnut processing (oil and oilcake) is the largest industry. The main food crops are millet, manioc, sorghum, and rice. Large numbers of cattle, sheep, and goats are bred. Industries include the manufacture of cement, chemicals, textiles, and fertilizers, and the processing of fish taken by the sizeable coastal fleet. The principal minerals extracted are phosphate rock, limestone, and iron ore; deposits of petroleum and natural gas have been found offshore. The GNP is US$2367 million, and the GNP per capita is US$370 (1985). The population is almost entirely black African, chiefly the Wolof, Fulani, and Serer. About 85% of the people are Muslim, about 5% are Christian, and the rest follow traditional beliefs. French is the official language.

*History.* In the middle of the 1st millennium AD the region was settled by migrating Wolof and Serer peoples, followed (9th cent.) by the Tukolor, whose state of Tekrur dominated the Senegal R. valley until the 14th cent. The Portuguese arrived in 1444–45 and established trading stations; they were displaced by the Dutch and French in the 17th cent. French influence was extended into the interior after 1697, but control of bases in Senegal alternated between France and Britain from the SEVEN YEARS WAR (1756–63) until 1815, when they were finally returned to France. Senegal became a French colony in 1895, remaining part of FRENCH WEST-AFRICA until it was made an autonomous republic within the FRENCH COMMUNITY in 1958. Full independence was achieved in 1960, with Léopold SENGHOR as president. By the mid-1960s Senghor had consolidated his power by removing Prime Min. Mamadou Dia and creating a one-party state. A period of civil unrest followed, marked by major demonstrations and strikes, and a worsening economic situation resulting from the drought in the Sahel region. In 1976 Senghor restored multiparty elections, which were won by his Socialist Party. After his retirement (1980), he was succeeded (1981) by Abdou Diouf, who was reelected president in 1983. In 1981 Senegal joined Gambia in a confederation known as Senegambia.

**Senegambia:** see GAMBIA; SENEGAL.

**Senghor, Léopold Sédar** (sahnh gaw), 1906–, Senegalese poet, critic, and statesman; president of the Republic of Senegal 1960–85. A gifted scholar, he was in Paris at the same time as Aimé Césaire and Léon Damas, with whom he formulated the concept of *Négritude,* which asserted the importance of a black African heritage. He has written numerous volumes of poetry, and essays in French, e.g., *Chants d'Ombre* (1945), *Hosties noires* (1948), and *Éthiopiques* (1956). His *Selected Poems* (1964) and the prose text *On African Socialism* (1964) have been translated into English.

**Sennacherib** or **Senherib I** (se nakərib), d. 681 BC, king of Assyria (r.705–681 BC). The son of Sargon, he spent his reign trying to maintain

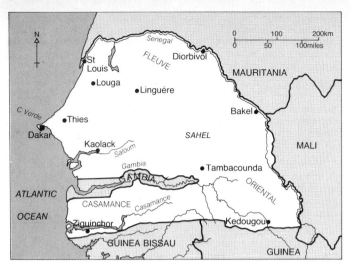

Senegal

the empire. He defeated the Egyptians (701 BC) and prepared to take Jerusalem, but instead exacted only tribute. He fought successfully in Babylonia and destroyed Babylon (c.689 BC). At NINEVEH he built a magnificent palace. He was murdered, possibly by his sons.

**Sennett, Mack,** 1880–1960, American film director and producer; b. Canada. His Keystone studios (1912–35) made thousands of short and full-length slapstick comedies. Charlie CHAPLIN, Buster KEATON, and others began their film work at Keystone.

**sense,** faculty by which external or internal stimuli are conveyed to the brain. The special senses (touch, sight, hearing, smell, and taste) convey external stimuli via receptors in the SKIN, EYE, EAR, NOSE, and taste buds (see TONGUE). Most bodily sensations, such as heat, cold, and pain, are picked up by receptors in the skin; a few, such as hunger, result from internal stimuli.

**sentence,** in law, punishment imposed on a convicted criminal. Usually prescribed by statute, it may be a fine or imprisonment (or both), or execution. If a person is convicted of more than one crime at a single trial, the sentences may be concurrent (beginning on the same date) or consecutive (one sentence beginning after the other ends). Some sentences are indeterminate, with specified maximum and minimum terms; discretionary release on parole may occur at the end of the minimum term. A sentence may be shortened (commuted) or temporarily suspended (a reprieve), but this does not nullify the conviction. A pardon terminates both the sentence and all criminal liability for a given crime.

**Seoul** or **Kyongsong,** city (1984 pop. 9,501,413), capital of South Korea, NW South Korea. The political, commercial, industrial, and cultural centre of the nation, Seoul is also a road and railway hub. It is linked by rail with its port, INCHON. Before the partition of Korea in 1945, Seoul's easy access to industrial raw materials stimulated the establishment of iron, steel, and other primary industries. With most of the raw materials now in North Korea, the city has emphasized textile manufacturing and consumer industries. Founded in 1392, Seoul served as capital of the Yi dynasty until 1910. Heavily damaged during the KOREAN WAR, the city has been extensively rebuilt along modern lines. Seoul retains three gates of its ancient wall and three imperial palaces. The 1988 Olympic Games were held in Seoul.

**separatists,** in religion, Christian groups, e.g., Pilgrims and Quakers, who withdrew from the Church of England. They desired freedom from church and civil authority, control of each congregation by its membership, and changes in ritual. They became known as Independents in the 17th cent.

**Sephardim,** Jews whose ancestors hailed from either Spanish-Portuguese stock or from Oriental countries. Spain was the leading centre of Jewish life from the 12th–15th cent., producing some of Jewry's finest poets, biblical commentators, and philosophers. In the wake of the Inquisition, many Spanish Jews were forced to become Marranos, or crypto-Jews, taking public vows of conversion to Christianity while secretly adhering to Jewish beliefs and practices.

Sephardi religious traditions, including their prayer rites and liturgical intonations, differ markedly from those of their Ashkenazi counterparts.

**sepiolite:** see MEERSCHAUM.

**Sepoy Rebellion:** see INDIAN MUTINY.

**September:** see MONTH.

**septicaemia** ('septi‚seemyə, -mi·ə), invasion of the bloodstream by bacteria (usually streptococci or staphylococci); a grave condition commonly known as blood poisoning. Primary causes include local infections that the body's defences are unable to contain and progressing tissue infections. Symptoms are fever, chills, prostration, and skin eruption. The condition is treated with massive doses of ANTIBIOTIC drugs.

**sequence,** in mathematics, ordered set of mathematical quantities, called *terms.* A sequence can be finite, like 1, 2, 3 . . . 50, which has 50 terms, or infinite, like 1, 2, 3, . . ., which has no final term. An infinite sequence may or may not have a LIMIT. Frequently there is a rule for determining the terms in the sequence, as in the FIBONACCI sequence and in various types of PROGRESSION. See also SERIES.

**sequestration,** in law, a court order for the temporary deprivation by the court of another's PROPERTY. The court will appoint certain persons (sequestrators) to take possession of all the defendant's real and personal property. It will only be returned to the owner when the reason for the sequestration has been remedied. Its origins lie in ROMAN LAW, under which disputed property was handed to a neutral third person until the dispute was settled. It has now been incorporated into both COMMON LAW and CIVIL LAW systems. In the UK, sequestration is most commonly ordered by a court in CONTEMPT OF COURT proceedings. During the 1980s it has often been used by the courts against trade unions who have refused to obey injunctions granted under anti-trade-union legislation.

**sequoia** (si‚kwoyə), name for the redwood (*Sequoia sempervirens*) and for the big tree, or giant sequoia (*Sequoiadendron giganteum*), both huge, evergreen CONIFERS, and for extinct related species. The redwood, which grows to 120 m (385 ft) in height, is probably the world's tallest tree; it is found along the central Pacific coast of the US. Its trunk is 3 to 7.5 m (10 to 25 ft) in diameter. The giant sequoia, which grows to 100 m (325 ft) in height, with a trunk of 3 to 9 m (10 to 30 ft), is found in California on the western slopes of the Sierra Nevadas; some are believed to be 3000 to 4000 years old. The reddish, decay-resistant heartwood of both species is valued for outdoor construction.

**Serbia,** constituent republic of Yugoslavia (1981 pop. 9,279,000), 88,337 km² (34,107 sq mi) E Yugoslavia. It is the largest Yugoslav republic. BELGRADE is the capital. The west and south are largely mountainous; NE Serbia, part of the Danubian plain, provides about 50% of Yugoslavia's foodstuffs. Mining is also important. The Serbs, unlike the Croats and Slovenes, belong to the EASTERN ORTHODOX CHURCH and use the Cyrillic alphabet. Slavs who became Serbs settled in the W Balkans in the 7th cent. and embraced Orthodox Christianity in the 9th cent. A Serb kingdom forged by the Nemanja dynasty emerged in the late 12th cent. which, under STEPHEN DUŠAN (r.1331–55), became the greatest Balkan empire. Defeat at Kosovo Polje (see KOSOVO) (1389) by the Ottomans ended Serb power, although small Serb states endured until 1459. Turkish rule turned the Serbs into a peasant people whose cohesion was maintained by their church. Ottoman decay led to uprisings under KARADJORDJE (1804) and MILOŠ Obrenović (1815), founders of the rival dynasties which presided in turn over Serbia's expanding autonomy before full independence was won (1878) and the quest to unite all Serbs in one state registered significant victories (BALKAN WARS, 1912–13). Serb expansion so alarmed Austria–Hungary that the assassination of Archduke Franz Ferdinand (1914) was made the pretext for what became World War I. Victory allowed the Serbs to create in 1918 the Kingdom of Serbs, Croats, and Slovenes (later Yugoslavia), effectively a greater Serbia under the KARADJORDJEVIĆ dynasty and centralized Serbian institutions. Serb resistance to AXIS dismemberment, occupation, and genocide in World War II was intense, although Serbia itself emerged territorially reduced in the new Communist-led Yugoslav federation.

**Serbo-Croatian,** language belonging to the South Slavic group of the Slavic subfamily of the Indo-European family of languages. Although it is actually one language, Serbo-Croatian is designated as Serbian when spoken by Serbs and written in a form of the Cyrillic alphabet, but as Croatian when spoken by Croats and written in a modified version of the Roman alphabet. See LANGUAGE (table).

**serf,** under FEUDALISM and the MANORIAL SYSTEM, a half-free peasant attached to the land held under the lord of the manor, for whom he performed servile labor. Serfs by custom had certain inviolable rights, and their labour service was governed by custom. In the MIDDLE AGES serfdom developed in France, Spain, and Italy, then spread to Germany and Slavic lands. In England after the Norman Conquest, most free VILLEINS became serfs. In the Hapsburg monarchy serfdom was ended (1781) by JOSEPH II, in France by the French Revolution (1789), and in Russia by ALEXANDER II (1861).

**sergeanty:** see SERJEANTY.

**serial music,** those compositions based on an arrangement (called a series or row) of patterns of pitch, rhythm, or dynamics. The term is often used synonymously with TWELVE-TONE MUSIC.

**series,** in mathematics, the indicated sum of a SEQUENCE. A series may be finite or infinite, depending on the number of terms in the sequence. As one takes sums of progressively more terms in an infinite series, these partial sums form a new sequence of values that may or may not approach a certain value, called the LIMIT of the series. If they do, the series is said to converge to that limit; if not, the series diverges. A *power series* is an infinite series whose terms contain successive integral powers of a variable and that is of the form $a_0 + a_1x + a_2x^2 + a_3x^3 + \ldots$ . Certain functions can be expressed in this form, e.g., the exponential function $e^x$ (see article on e) can be expressed as $1 + x + \dfrac{x^2}{2!} + \dfrac{x^3}{3!} + \ldots$ .

**serigraphy:** see SILK-SCREEN PRINTING.

**serjeanty** or **sergeanty,** a type of land tenure in English FEUDALISM in return for personal, often menial, service. Ceremonial relics of it survive at royal coronations.

**serotonin,** biochemical first recognized as a powerful vasoconstrictor (agent that causes constriction of blood vessels) occurring in blood serum, widely distributed in the human body, and subsequently found in wasp and scorpion venom and in various fruits and nuts. The role of the compound in humans remains obscure; its structural similarity to certain hallucinogenic drugs, such as LSD, has prompted speculation that serotonin may have a role in certain mental disorders.

**Serowe,** town (1987 pop. 23,661), capital of Central District, Botswana, 48 km (30 mi) west of the Cape Town–Bulawayo railway. Serowe is the largest of the centralized villages in which the majority of Botswana's population customarily lives. It became the tribal headquarters of the Bamangwato people in 1920 and is surrounded by arable agricultural land and cattle-grazing posts.

**serpentine,** widely distributed hydrous magnesium silicate mineral ($3MgO.2SiO_2.2H_2O$), formed by the alteration of other minerals or rocks containing magnesium. Usually green, it may also be reddish, yellowish, black, or nearly white. It is sometimes used as a gem; massive varieties are used like marble for decoration, although they are too easily damaged by exposure to be used for exteriors. Fibrous serpentine is chrysotile, a commercial ASBESTOS.

**Serra, Junípero,** 1713–84, Spanish Franciscan missionary in North America. He directed the founding of nine FRANCISCAN missions in California between 1769 and 1782.

**Sertão** [Port., = backlands], semiarid hinterland of NE Brazil where *caatinga* (thorny scrub forest) predominates. Drought-prone and the focus of regional economic development programmes, the sertão is a stock-raising region with a tradition of rugged individualism and banditry that has inspired Brazilian writers, notably Euclides da Cunha.

**Servetus, Michael** (sə‚veetəs), 1511–53, Spanish theologian and physician. He early came in contact with reformers in Germany and Switzerland, but his views, particularly about the TRINITY, were condemned by both Roman Catholics and Protestants. He fled to France, where he gained fame in medicine. After he had a work on theology secretly printed (1553), the INQUISITION moved against him. He escaped from prison, but he was seized in Geneva, on John CALVIN's order, and tried and burned there.

**Service, Robert William,** 1874–1958, Canadian poet and novelist, known for 'The Shooting of Dan McGrew,' in *Songs of a Sourdough* (1907), and other celebrations of Klondike life.

**Servile Wars,** in Roman history, three uprisings of slaves (134?–132? BC, 104?–101? BC, 73–71 BC). The first two took place in Sicily. The third was the famous uprising by SPARTACUS in S Italy that was eventually put down with great cruelty by Marcus Licinius Crassus (see CRASSUS, family) and POMPEY.

**sesame,** plant (*Sesamum indicum*) of the family Pedaliaceae cultivated for its seeds since ancient times, found chiefly in the Old World tropics. Sesame seeds, or bennes, are black or white and yield an oil that resists turning rancid. The oil is used extensively in India for cooking, soap manufacture, food, and medicine, and as an adulterant for OLIVE oil. The seeds are used in baking and confectionery.

**Sessions, Roger,** 1896–1985, American composer and teacher. His early music is romantic and harmonic; later it became austere and complex. His works include music for ANDREYEV's *Black Maskers* (1923), eight SYMPHONIES (1927–68), and string quartets (1936, 1951, 1958).

**set,** in mathematics, collection of entities, called the elements or members of the set, that may be material objects or conceptual entities. Braces, { }, are commonly used to enclose the listed elements of a set, e.g., if $A$ is the set of even numbers between 1 and 9, then $A = \{2,4,6,8\}$. The elements may also be described within braces, e.g., the set $B$ of real numbers that are solutions to the equation $x^2 = 9$ can be written as $B = \{x:x^2 = 9\}$, which is read 'the set of all $x$ such that $x^2 = 9$'. In fact, $B = \{3, -3\}$. There are three basic set operations: intersection, union, and complementation. The intersection of two sets, denoted by the symbol $\cap$, is the set containing the elements common to both. The union of two sets, denoted by $\cup$, is the set of all elements belonging to at least one of the original sets. Thus, if $C = \{1,2,3,4\}$ and $D = \{3,4,5\}$, then $C \cap D = \{3,4\}$ and $C \cup D = \{1,2,3,4,5\}$. In any discussion the set of all elements under consideration is the universal set $\mathscr{E}$; the complement of $A$, written $A_{,}$, is the set of all elements of the universal set that are not in $A$; if $\mathscr{E} = \{1,2,3,4,5\}$ and $A = \{1,2,3\}$, then $A_{,} = \{4,5\}$. A set with no elements, e.g., the set of all black polar bears, is called the null, or empty, set and is symbolized by $\varnothing$. Membership of a set is indicated by the symbol $\in$; thus, $x \in A$ means that $x$ is a member of the set $A$. If the set $B$ contains at least all the elements of the set $A$, then $A$ is a subset of $B$, written $A \subset B$. Set theory is involved in many areas of mathematics and has important applications in such other fields as computer technology and atomic and nuclear physics.

**Sete Quedas** or **Guaira,** waterfall on the Paraná R. on the boundary between Brazil and Paraguay. It is the largest waterfall by volume of water ($8260 \text{ m}^3/\text{sec}$, or nearly 2 million gallons per sec) in Latin America.

**Seton, Saint Elizabeth Ann,** 1774–1821, American Roman Catholic leader, also called Mother Seton; b. Elizabeth Ann Bayley. Soon after she was widowed, she became (1805) a Roman Catholic. In 1808 she opened a school in Baltimore at the invitation of Bishop Carroll and later moved to Emmitsburg in Maryland, where she opened the first Catholic free school. She formed the first American congregation of the Daughters of Charity (Sisters of Charity) and served as its superior. Canonized in 1975, she was the first native-born American saint. Feast: 4 Jan.

**Settlement, Act of,** 1701, passed by the English Parliament to provide that if WILLIAM III and Princess (later Queen) ANNE died without heirs, succession should pass to Sophia, electress of Hanover, granddaughter of JAMES I, and to her Protestant heirs. Fear of the JACOBITES partially prompted the measure, which also limited the power of the crown. The House of HANOVER, which became the British royal house in 1714, owed its claim to this act.

**Seurat, Georges** (sø‚rah), 1859–91, French Neo-Impressionist painter. Seurat was a brilliant draughtsman; his first works were a series of tonal drawings and small oil panels of modern scenes in Paris and its suburbs. *A Bathing Scene at Asnières* (1883–84; National Gall., London) was the first of a series of major canvases which react against Impressionist (see IMPRESSIONISM) spontaneity and emphasize monumentality and balanced, carefully structured compositions. He developed the pointillist technique of painting with tiny dots of pure colour, as in *A Sunday Afternoon on the Island of La Grande Jatte* (1884–86; Art Institute, Chicago). Many of his late works are geometric seascapes painted along the Channel coast.

**Sevan** (se‚vahn), lake, c.1400 km² (540 sq mi), SE European USSR, in Armenia, at an altitude of 1914 m (6280 ft) the largest lake of the Caucasus. The Razdan R. is its only outlet. An extensive hydroelectric system has been developed in the area.

**Sevastopol**, city (1985 pop. 341,000), SE European USSR, in the UKRAINE, on the Crimean peninsula and the Bay of Sevastopol, a BLACK SEA inlet. It is a port and major naval base. Among its industries are shipbuilding and timber production. It stands near the site of Chersonesus, a Greek colony founded in 421 BC, which became part of the empire of ROME (1st cent. BC) and of the BYZANTINE EMPIRE (4th cent. AD). A medieval trade centre, it was destroyed by the TATARS in 1399. When Russia annexed (1783) the CRIMEA, Sevastopol was refounded as the chief base of its Black Sea fleet. In the CRIMEAN WAR it was besieged for 349 days (1854–55). In World War II it was virtually destroyed during an eight-month siege (1941–42) by German and Rumanian forces, who occupied it until 1944.

**Seven against Thebes**, in Greek mythology, seven heroes. They made war on Eteocles when he refused to share the Theban throne with his brother Polynices, as agreed after the exile of their father, OEDIPUS. The brothers killed each other, and, of the seven, only Adrastus survived. Their sons, the Epigoni, conquered Thebes 10 years later and gave the kingdom to Thersander, son of Polynices. AESCHYLUS and EURIPIDES dramatized the legend.

**Seventh-Day Adventists:** see ADVENTISTS.

**Seven Wise Men of Greece**, arbitrary lists of the outstanding leaders of ancient GREECE. A usual list: Bias, Chilon, Cleobolus, Periander, Pittacus, SOLON, and THALES.

**Seven Wonders of the World**, in ancient classifications, were the Great PYRAMID of Khufu, or all the pyramids, with or without the SPHINX; the Hanging Gardens of Babylon, with or without the walls; the MAUSOLEUM at Halicarnassus; the Artemision at EPHESUS; the COLOSSUS of Rhodes; the Olympian ZEUS statue by PHIDIAS; and the Pharos lighthouse at Alexandria, or, instead, the walls of Babylon.

**Seven Years' War**, 1756–63, worldwide conflict fought in Europe, North America, and India between France, Austria, Russia, Saxony, Sweden, and (after 1762) Spain, on one side, and Great Britain, Prussia, and Hanover on the other. Two main issues were involved: French and English colonial rivalries in North America and India, and the struggle for supremacy in Europe of MARIA THERESA of Austria and FREDERICK II of Prussia. In the aftermath of the War of the AUSTRIAN SUCCESSION (1740–48) the European powers began manoeuvring for alliances preparatory to a new show of strength. Hostilities began when Prussia invaded Saxony (1756) and BOHEMIA (1757). Despite his brilliant early victories at Rossbach (1757), Leuthen (1757), and Zorndorf (1758), by 1759 Frederick's situation had become nearly hopeless. In 1760 the Russians occupied Berlin briefly, but Frederick expelled them and went on to defeat the Austrians at Torgau. His final victory came only after the accession of PETER III of Russia, who made (1762) a separate peace with him. Sweden also left the war. Now fighting alone in the east, Frederick defeated the Austrians at Burkersdorf (1762). Meanwhile, England, after an inauspicious start, won victories at Krefeld (1758) and Minden (1759), in N Germany, and soundly defeated the French at Louisburg (1758) and Quebec (1759), in North America, and at Plassey (1757) and Pondicherry (1761), in India. After protracted negotiations, peace was made at Hubertusburg and at Paris (see PARIS, TREATY OF, 1763). The war confirmed Prussia's new rank as a leading European power and made Britain the world's chief colonial power. France lost most of its overseas possessions.

**Severini, Gino**, 1883–1966, Italian painter. In 1901 he went to Rome and studied with BALLA. He went to Paris in 1906 and was influenced by divisionism; he was included in the futurist painters' group (see FUTURISM) and encouraged them to visit Paris to study CUBISM. His *Dynamic Hieroglyphic of the Bar Tabarin* (1912) shows his attempt to merge cubist formal concern with futurist imagery and ideas. In the 1920s he returned to a more naturalist style, and worked on several frescoes and mosaics.

**Severn**, river in Wales and SW England. It rises on the NE slope of Plynlimon in Cambrian Mts, and flows along a semicircular course into the Bristol Channel. It is approximately 290 km (180 mi) long. The main towns along its route are Welshpool (in Wales), SHREWSBURY, WORCESTER, Tewkesbury, and GLOUCESTER (all in England). The main tributaries are the Vyrnwy, Stour, Teme, and Avon. It is tidal up to Maisemore, to the NW of Gloucester. Because of the funnel-shaped estuary there is a tidal bore (the Severn Bore) which may reach as far upstream as Tewkesbury. The Severn Bridge, a road suspension bridge crossing the river between Avon and Gwent, was opened in 1966.

Severn Bridge

**Severus** or **Septimius Severus**, (Lucius Septimius Severus), 146–211, Roman emperor (r.193–211); b. Africa. He took the imperial throne by force, put down opponents, and reduced the empire to peace in Mesopotamia, GAUL, and Britain. He died at York. Severus left the empire to his sons, but one son, CARACALLA, took power.

**Seville**, Span. *Sevilla,* city (1981 pop. 653,833), capital of Seville prov. and chief city of Andalusia, SW Spain, on the Guadalquivir R. Seville is a major port connected with the Atlantic by a river and canal. Among its manufactures are tobacco, armaments, and perfume. Important from Phoenician times, Seville fell to the MOORS in AD 712 and was the seat (1023–1091) of an independent emirate under the Abbadids. Taken (1248) by FERDINAND III of Castile, it later was a centre for New World trade. One of the world's most beautiful cities, Seville contains many landmarks, e.g., the Moorish alcazar and the Gothic cathedral (1401–1519).

**Sèvres**, pre-eminent French porcelain factory. Founded c.1740 at Vincennes, it moved to Sèvres in 1756. Louis XV had a financial interest in the concern from its early years, and in 1759 it was named the Manufacture Royale de Porcelaine when he took complete control. In

Sèvres, soft-paste porcelain plate from the Louis XVI service (1790; Fitzwilliam Museum)

1792 it became the property of the French state. Sèvres produced luxurious soft-paste porcelain for an aristocratic market. From the 1750s until the Revolution it was renowned for superbly decorated tableware and vases. The most characteristic were painted with birds, putti, flowers or figures, in panels reserved in coloured grounds, richly embellished with gilding. It also made exquisite figures in glazed and biscuit porcelain. Hard-paste was introduced in 1769, but soft-paste remained in production until 1804. During the Empire, the patronage of Napoleon revived the factory's reputation. It has continued up to the present, but its later porcelains are not so highly regarded as those of the pre-Revolutionary era.

**sewage disposal:** see WASTE DISPOSAL.

**Seward, William Henry,** 1801–72, American statesman. As senator from New York (1849–61), he was a prominent antislavery advocate. He became secretary of state (1861) in Pres. LINCOLN's cabinet, where his efforts to dominate were overcome only by Lincoln's ingenuity. He was an able statesman, adept in handling delicate diplomatic matters such as the TRENT AFFAIR. He continued in his post under Pres. Andrew JOHNSON and supported the president's RECONSTRUCTION policy. His most notable act was the farsighted purchase of ALASKA (1867), denounced at the time as 'Seward's folly'.

**Sewell, Stephen,** 1953–, Australian playwright. He is particularly attracted to modern political themes, as in his works *Traitors* (1979) and *Welcome the Bright World* (1982).

**sewing machine,** device that stitches cloth and other materials. The machine's invention is attributed primarily to Elias HOWE (1846) and Isaac M. SINGER (1850). In the typical home sewing machine, a needle, raised and lowered at great speed, pierces cloth lying on a steel plate, casting a loop of thread on the underside of the seam. A second thread, fed from a shuttle under the plate, passes through the loop and is interlocked with the upper thread as it is drawn up by the rising needle. Modern electric-powered machines, some controlled electronically, are capable of producing many types of stitches, and specialized machines have been devised for sewing particular items.

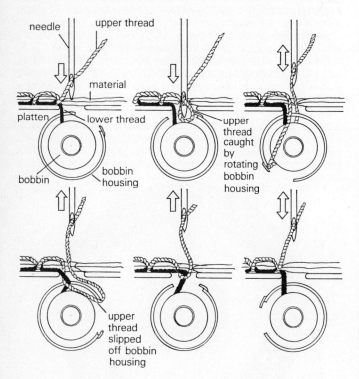

Sewing machine

**Sex Discrimination Act 1975,** in the UK, law prohibiting discrimination on the grounds of sex in the provision of goods, services, employment, education, and housing. It covers discrimination against both men and women; discrimination can be either direct, where a person is treated less favourably because of his or her sex, or indirect, where a practice though apparently neutral has a disproportionate effect on one sex. The Act (and the EQUAL PAY ACT 1970) is reviewed and enforced by the Equal Opportunities Commission, which is empowered to issue non-discrimination notices and take court action on behalf of individuals.

**sextant,** instrument (invented 1731) for measuring the altitude of a celestial body. The image of the body is reflected from the index mirror to the mirror half of the horizon glass and then into the telescope. If the movable index (or image) arm (to which the index mirror is attached) is then adjusted so that the horizon is seen through the transparent half of the horizon glass, with the reflected image of the body lined up with it, the body's altitude can be read from the index-arm position on the graduated arc.

**sex therapy,** treatment of sexual disorders and dysfunction, including IMPOTENCE, orgasmic dysfunction, premature ejaculation, and lack of sexual responsiveness. Pioneered by MASTERS AND JOHNSON in the early 1970s, sex therapy is based on the premise that sexual behaviour is learned and that problems can be alleviated through sex education, sensitization exercises, and improved communication between sexual partners. Treatment may include individual, couple, and/or group therapy.

**Sextus Empiricus,** 2nd–3rd cent. AD, philosopher and doctor, probably Greek. His surviving works, *Outlines of Pyrrhonism* and *Against the Dogmatists* comprise a summary and codification of Greek SCEPTICISM which was extremely influential on the 16th cent. Following PYRRHO, he argued that we should suspend intellectual judgment, thus avoiding the errors of dogmatism, and live in accordance with sense experience to achieve peace of mind.

**sexual orientation,** the sex or gender towards which one's adult sexuality is directed, or for which one feels sexual attraction. Orientation towards the opposite sex (heterosexuality) is more common than orientation towards the same sex (homosexuality, also termed gayness, or, in women lesbianism). Individuals having both heterosexual and homsexual orientations are bisexual. Many psychologists, including Sigmund FREUD, have postulated bisexuality as a fundamental factor both in psychosexual development in general, and in the development of NEUROSIS. Homosexuality has been viewed in many, but not all, societies as deviant, and was viewed in medicine and psychology as psychosexual 'perversion'. This view is now widely believed to be unfounded and discriminatory.

**sexual politics,** a concept originating in the WOMEN'S MOVEMENT and the GAY LIBERATION movement, which identifies hierarchies of power in cultural definitions of gender and in relationships between the sexes. The women's movement slogan 'The personal is political' expresses the need to bring political awareness to sex and gender divisions and recognizes the ways in which the attributes of male gender and the cultural norm of heterosexuality oppress women and homosexual men, with far-reaching institutional and social effects. Gender is emphasized as being distinct from biological sex, to which it has no necessary relation, but one founded on socially and culturally constructed differences.

**Seychelles** (ˌsayshelz), officially Republic of Seychelles, republic (1985 pop. 65,092), c.285 km² (110 sq mi), comprising approximately 85 islands in the Indian Ocean, c.1600 km (1000 mi) E of Kenya. The capital and only urban centre and port is Victoria, located on the largest island, Mahé (c.140 km²/55 sq mi), where about 65% of the population lives. The other principal islands are Praslin, La Digue, Silhouette, and Curieuse. Copra (accounting for 65% of export earnings in 1979) and cinnamon are the principal exports, but most crops are of the subsistence type. Fishing is being rapidly developed and is contributing to exports. In the mid-1970s tourism surpassed agriculture as the principal economic sector. The people are mainly of European and black African descent; most of them are Roman Catholic and speak a creole patois, but English and French are the official languages.

*History.* The Seychelles were discovered by Vasco da GAMA in 1502, but colonization by French planters and their slaves did not begin until 1768. Britain took possession of the islands in 1794 and administered them as part of MAURITIUS until they became a crown colony in 1903. After the first legislative elections (1948), gradual progress was made towards self-government, and Seychelles became independent in 1976 as a member of the COMMONWEALTH. The coalition government was headed by a pro-Western president, James Mancham, and a leftist prime minister, Albert René. In 1977 René assumed power in a bloodless coup and suspended the constitution. A new constitution established (1979) a one-party state headed by René as leader of the Seychelles People's Progressive Front. An unsuccessful invasion (1981) by 45 foreign mercenaries marked a third outside attempt to overthrow the regime, which accused South Africa of complicity.

**Seymour, Alan,** 1927–, Australian playwright. His *One Day of the Year* (1960), a pioneering work of contemporary realism, prefigured the generational conflict over military service which characterized Australia in the Vietnam War period.

**Seymour, Arthur,** 1914–, Guyanese poet. One of the key figures in Caribbean literary history and founder of the literary journal *Kyk-over-al* (1945), he showed an early awareness of the significance of popular culture, which he incorporated into his works, e.g., *The Guiana Book* (1948), *Selected Poems* (1965; 1983), and *Images of Majority* (1978).

**Seymour, Jane,** 1509?–37, third queen of HENRY VIII of England. Henry's resolve to marry Jane led to the trial and execution for treason of his second wife, Anne BOLEYN. Soon after, Jane and Henry were married (1536), and in 1537 their son, EDWARD VI, was born. Jane died 12 days later.

**Seymour, Thomas, Baron Seymour of Sudeley,** 1508?–49, lord high admiral of England; uncle of EDWARD VI. He married (1547) the dowager queen Catherine PARR; tried to oust his brother, the duke of Somerset, as Edward's guardian; and tried to marry the future ELIZABETH I. He was convicted of treason and executed.

**Sfax,** city (1987 est. pop. 231,911), S Tunisia, on the Mediterranean coast. It is the country's second most important city, a major port, and a leading centre of the fishing industry. It exports phosphates and olive oil.

**Sforza** (‚sfawtsah), Italian family that ruled MILAN from 1450 to 1535. The first prominent member was **Muzio Attendolo Sforza,** 1369–1424, who became a noted *condottiere* [leader of mercenary soldiers] and took the surname Sforza [the forcer]. His illegitimate son, **Francesco I Sforza,** 1401–66, was also a famous soldier. He married (1441) Bianca Maria, the illegitimate daughter of Filippo Maria Visconti (see VISCONTI, family), duke of Milan, after whose death Francesco made himself duke (1450). His eldest son, **Galeazzo Maria Sforza,** 1444–76, duke 1466–76, was a patron of the arts. He was assassinated by republicans. His son, **Gian Galeazzo Sforza,** 1469–94, became duke on his father's death. He was deprived (1480) of the duchy by his uncle, **Ludovico Sforza,** who held him prisoner until his death. Ludovico, 1452–1508, duke 1494–1500, was called *Il Moro* [the Moor] because of his swarthy complexion. His alliance with France helped to start (1494) the ITALIAN WARS, but in 1495 he turned against the French. In 1499 LOUIS XII of France expelled him from Milan. Ludovico's attempt to retake the city failed (1500) at Novara, where he was captured, and he died in prison. He is especially remembered as a patron of LEONARDO DA VINCI and BRAMANTE. His son, **Massimiliano Sforza,** 1493–1530, recovered (1512) Milan with help from the HOLY LEAGUE, but surrendered it again to the French in 1515. His brother, **Francesco II Sforza,** 1495–1535, regained the duchy with aid from the Emperor CHARLES V. He had no heirs, and Milan passed to Spain in 1559.

**Shaanxi** or **Shensi,** province (1985 est. pop. 30,020,000), 195,800 km² (75,598 sq mi); N central China. It lies W of SHANXI, with the YELLOW RIVER forming much of the border between the two provinces. Major cities include XI'AN, the capital, and Xianyang. N Shaanxi is a high loess plateau (c.1000 m/3280 ft at sea level) with a semiarid climate; irrigation has permitted some cultivation but much of the land is pasture for cattle. To the south are the fertile loess soils of the Wei river valley, which is favoured by a moister and milder climate; winter wheat, rice, and cotton are grown. Also in the south are the Qinling (Tsinling) Mts which are an important forest area. Mineral exploitation is little developed though there are important nonferrous minerals including molybdenum and mercury. Modern industrialization has only been significant since 1949, in which time Xi'an has become an important textile-manufacturing and engineering centre. The loess soils in south are central to the development of Chinese history and culture. Many of the first agricultural villages in China were here, including Banpo (Pan-P'o) near Xi'an. This was occupied from c.4500 BC to 3750 BC and has been extensively excavated. Xi'an became the effective capital in the Western Zhou dynasty (c.1066–221 BC). It was to remain as capital for much of the period until the fall of the Tang dynasty in AD 907. At that time Xi'an (or Chang'an), with a population of over 1 million, was the largest city in the world. The

splendour and the power of that culture is now manifest in the tomb of Qin Shi Huangdi with its terra-cotta army. In the 3rd cent. BC this emperor ruthlessly united and centralized China. After the Tang dynasty the area's importance declined. The province's recent history is associated with the guerrilla campaigns of civil war. In 1936 the Communist Eighth Route Army reached YAN'AN in remote N Shaanxi, at the end of their epic LONG MARCH. Yan'an became the base area where the army and Chinese Communist Party consolidated their position before moving out to win the civil war.

**Shaba,** formerly **Katanga,** region (1981 pop. 3,823,172), c.518,000 km² (200,000 sq mi), SE Zaïre. The capital is LUBUMBASHI. The eastern part of the region is an enormously rich mining area, which supplies most of the world's cobalt as well as extensive quantities of copper and other minerals. Upon Zaïrian independence in 1960, Katanga seceded and proclaimed itself a republic; a civil war ensued that was ended in 1963 with the use of UN troops. The Belgian firm that controlled the region's mining interests was nationalized in 1966.

**Shabbat,** Jewish Sabbath Day (Saturday). Orthodox tradition continues the biblical prescription of total cessation from work (see Ex. 20:10). The day is spent in prayer, festive family meals and relaxation, and is inaugurated by the lighting of candles and sanctification (see KIDDUSH) over wine.

**Shackleton, Sir Ernest Henry,** 1874–1922, English explorer. After experience gained (1901–03) in the Robert F. SCOTT expedition, he commanded a south polar expedition (1907–09) during which Mt Erebus was climbed, the south magnetic pole was located, and the plateau was crossed to within 160 km (100 mi) of the SOUTH POLE. Commanding a transantarctic expedition (1915), he led his party 290 km (180 mi) to safety on floes to Elephant Island after ice crushed his ship. From there he and a few others sailed c.1300 km (c.800 mi) on wild seas, crossed South Georgia Island to a whaling station, and rescued the Elephant Island party and others. He died on a fourth voyage and was buried on South Georgia Island in the S Atlantic.

**shadow mask tube,** a colour television CATHODE-RAY TUBE (CRT) developed by RCA for the start of the colour TELEVISION service in America. For colour receivers the CRT has to produce three separate colour pictures —red, green, and blue—which are superimposed on each other to provide a picture with a range of natural colours including pure white. In the shadow mask tube three colour phosphors are laid down in some 440,000 tried groups each containing three dots, one of each colour. Three electron guns are provided, one for each colour, and it is necessary to ensure that the red gun only hits the red phosphor, the blue gun only the blue phosphor, and the green gun only the green phosphor. This is achieved by a metal masking plate, containing one hole for each triad of phosphor dots, placed about 1 cm (½ in) behind the screen. It is lined up in relation to the guns and the phosphor dots so that the beam of electrons from each gun, after passing through the holes in the masking plate, can only hit a dot of the colour appropriate to that gun. The three colour signals are fed between the grids and cathodes of the three guns to provide three superimposed pictures that combine to form a picture of natural colour.

**Shafi'i Muhammad Ibn Idris,** 767–820, Muslim jurist and traditionist from Medina. He was the founder of the Shafi'ite school of FIQH and of the systematic study of Muslim juristic theory and methodology.

**Shaftesbury, Anthony Ashley Cooper, 7th earl of,** 1801–85, English social reformer. In the House of Commons after 1826, he was a leading advocate of government action to alleviate injustices caused by the INDUSTRIAL REVOLUTION. He introduced laws providing for care of the insane (1845) and limiting child labour (1842) and the work day (1847). He also promoted the building of model tenements.

**shag:** see CORMORANT.

**Shagari, Alhaji Shehu,** 1925–, president of NIGERIA (1979–85). A teacher, he held various government posts in the 1960s and 70s. In 1978 he helped form the National Party, and his subsequent election as president marked the end of 13 years of military rule in Nigeria. He was, however, overthrown in a bloodless coup (1985) and military rule was restored.

**Shah Jahan** or **Shah Jehan,** 1592–1666, Mughal emperor of INDIA (1628–58). During his reign MUGHAL ART AND ARCHITECTURE reached their height; the TAJ MAHAL is a leading example. He was deposed (1658) and imprisoned by his son AURANGZEB.

**Shahn, Ben,** 1898–1969, American painter and graphic artist; b. Lithuania; emigrated to the US in 1906. Shahn frequently used powerful realism or lyrical abstraction to express social and political themes, e.g., his paintings on the SACCO–VANZETTI CASE (1931–32). He was the main exponent in America of SOCIALIST REALISM. He also painted important murals, worked in photography, and created striking posters.

**Shaka,** c.1787–1828, founder of the ZULU kingdom. A military genius, he created a highly centralized state which brought under his sway most of the Nguni people, then living in small chiefdoms. His large, central standing army was a truly original institution. Existing rulers were replaced by or transformed into *indunas*, civil servants who represented the king's interests rather than acting as traditional chiefs. A system of military towns scattered throughout the kingdom kept order and acted as garrisons. The death of his mother in 1827 appears to have made Shaka mentally ill and he became more and more obsessed with the idea that his subjects were plotting against him. His cruelty and disregard for human life eventually did provoke his assassination by two of his brothers, DINGAAN and Mhlangane.

**Shakers,** popular name for members of the United Society of Believers in Christ's Second Appearing. They received their name from the trembling produced by religious emotions. Originating (1747) in England as Shaking Quakers, they grew strong under the leadership of Ann LEE (d. 1784). She and eight followers moved (1774) to New York, and by 1826 18 communities had been founded in the US. Shakers practised celibacy, lived communally, and believed in a deity with male and female natures. The movement is all but extinct. Shaker furniture and handcrafts are noted for their fine design.

**Shakespeare, William,** 1564–1616, English dramatist and poet, considered the greatest of all playwrights; b. Stratford-upon-Avon. He was the son of a Stratford businessman and probably attended the local grammar school, acquiring a grounding in the classics. In 1582 he married Anne Hathaway. They had three children. Little else in known of his life before 1592, when he appeared as a playwright in London. He may have been a member of a travelling theatre group, and some evidence in his early style suggests he may have been a schoolmaster. In 1594 he became an actor and playwright for the Lord Chamberlain's Men (the King's Men under James I). It is thought that he played supporting roles, e.g., the Ghost in *Hamlet*. In 1599 he became a part owner of the Globe Theatre, and in 1608 of the Blackfriars Theatre. He retired to Stratford in 1613.

*The Plays.* The chronology of the plays is uncertain, but style and content analysis give a reasonable approximation of their order (see chart). They fall into three rough periods. In the first are history plays, beginning with the three parts of *Henry VI*, and comedies. At this stage Shakespeare's historical tragedies (*Titus Andronicus*) lack depth of characterization and are somewhat bombastic. The comedies are essentially classical imitations, with strong elements of FARCE (*The Comedy of Errors*). The last play in this first period, *Romeo and Juliet* (c.1594), evidences Shakespeare's maturing talent. The versification is more complex, and rhythms reflect the speaker's state of mind, a technique he developed with increasing subtlety. In the second period, from *Richard II* (c.1595) through to *Twelfth Night* (c.1599), Shakespeare produced histories and tragedies in which characterization and practical elements are successfully blended. In the COMEDIES of this period he moved away from farce toward idyllic ROMANCE (*As You Like It*). The third period, from 1600, saw the appearance of Shakespeare's major TRAGEDIES, beginning with *Hamlet*, and 'problem plays'. The tragedies, after *Othello,* present clear oppositions of order to chaos, good to evil, on all levels. The style becomes increasingly compressed and symbolic. *Pericles, Cymbeline, The Winter's Tale,* and *The Tempest* are tragicomedies, with full tragic potential but a harmonious resolution through grace, a term with divine as well as artistic implications. Shakespeare has been criticized for failing to propound a philosophy, but the enduring appeal of his plays seems to lie in his human vision, which recognizes the complexity of moral questions, and in the unparalleled richness of his language.

*Sources and editions.* Eighteen of the plays appeared in print during Shakespeare's life, but the source for all except *Pericles* and *Two Noble Kinsmen* (of dubious authorship) is the First Folio of 1623. The plays were first published with act and scene divisions and stage directions by Nicholas ROWE (1709). Two major sources used by Shakespeare were Raphael HOLINSHED's *Chronicles of England, Scotland, and Ireland* (1577) for the English historical plays, and Sir Thomas North's translation (1579) of PLUTARCH's *Lives.* He altered many other source materials to suit his purposes.

*The Poetry.* Shakespeare would be well known for his poetry alone. His first published works were the narratives *Venus and Adonis* (1593) and *The Rape of Lucrece* (1594). The love poem *The Phoenix and the Turtle* appeared in 1601. But his major achievement is the *Sonnets* (1609, written in the 1590s). In them Shakespeare exercises his talent for compressing meaning, fully realized in his later work. Addressed (numbers 1–126) to the unidentified 'W.H.' and (numbers 127–152) to the mysterious 'dark lady', the SONNETS treat the themes of time, mutability, and death, and their transcendence through love and art.

**shale,** sedimentary ROCK formed by the consolidation of mud or CLAY, having the property of splitting into thin layers parallel to its bedding planes. Shales comprise an estimated 55% of all sedimentary rocks and often contain large numbers of fossils. Oil shales are widely distributed in the W US and may be a future source of petroleum.

**shallot:** see ONION.

**Shalmaneser** (shalmə‚neezə), kings of Assyria. **Shalmaneser I,** d. 1290 BC, moved the capital from Assur to Calah and established a royal residence at Nineveh. **Shalmaneser III** (r.859–824 BC) won an indecisive victory over Benhadad of Damascus and AHAB of Israel at Karkar, on the Orontes. In Calah he built an enormous ziggurat. **Shalmaneser V,** d. 722 BC, attacked Hosea of Israel, but died in the siege of SAMARIA.

**shaman** (‚shahmən, ‚shay-), a person believed to have special powers of communication with the supernatural world, who will use those powers on his own or others behalf often to heal or cure, but sometimes malevolently. Usually the shaman's means of communication involves altered states of consciousness, achieved through the taking of drugs or particular kinds of activity. It has been argued that the kinds of people who become shamans are often the most socially marginal individuals in a given society or those who in other social contexts might be classified as psychologically disturbed. Noted especially among Siberians, shamans are also found among the Eskimo, in some American Indian tribes, and in Oceania. See also WITCHCRAFT.

**Shamir, Itzhak,** 1915–, prime minister of ISRAEL (1983–84, 1986–), b. Poland. He was a leader of the terrorist Stern Gang during the British Mandate of Palestine and entered the Israeli parliament for the right-wing Likud front in 1973. He served as foreign minister under Menachem BEGIN (1980–83), whom he succeeded as prime minister in 1983. After the 1984 elections he again became foreign minister in a national unity coalition under Shimon PERES of the Labour Party and, under the coalition agreement, succeeded Peres as prime minister in 1986. He continued in this post after the 1988 elections.

**Shammai,** c.50 BC–AD c.30, Palestinian rabbi. A leader of the SANHEDRIN, Shammai adopted a stricter interpretation of HALAKAH that opposed the teachings of HILLEL.

**shamrock,** plant with leaves composed of three leaflets. According to legend, it was used by St Patrick to explain the Trinity. The identity of the true shamrock has long been debated, but the plants most often designated as shamrocks are the white CLOVER, *Trifolium repens;* the small hop clover, *T. procumbens;* and the wood sorrel, *Oxalis acetosella* (see OXALIS). The shamrock is the emblem of Ireland.

**Shandong** or **Shantung,** province (1985 est. pop. 76,900,000), 153,700 km² (59,344 sq mi), E coast of China. The major cities are JINAN the capital, and QINGDAO. The eastern part of the province forms a large peninsula between the Bohai Gulf and the Yellow Sea. Much of the land is hilly but arable. The central Shandong massif includes TAI SHAN, one of China's five sacred mountains. The YELLOW RIVER, flowing SW to NE, has been important in providing irrigation and rich silty earth. Winter wheat, soya beans, cotton, and peanuts are grown, and fishing is important along the long coastal area. The province has various agriculture-based industries and extensive mineral deposits. It produces a variety of coals and is China's fourth provincial producer. The Shengli oilfields in N Shangdong opened in 1964 and are now second in production to the Daqing oilfields in HEILONGJIANG. Since the 1970s, the Bohai Gulf has been a centre for oil exploration. Qingdao is a major port and industrial centre producing diesel locomotives and rolling stock. The frequent floods and

**SHAKESPEARE'S PLAYS** *(arranged by approximate date of composition)*

| Play | Dates* | Sources | Play | Dates* | Sources |
|---|---|---|---|---|---|
| Henry VI, Part II *(history)* | 1590/1594 | Edward Hall, *Union of the Two Noble and Illustre Families of Lancaster and York* (1548); Raphael Holinshed, *Chronicles of England, Scotland, and Ireland* (1587) | As You Like It *(comedy)* | 1599/1623 | Thomas Lodge, *Rosalynde* (1590) |
| | | | Twelfth Night *(comedy)* | 1599/1623 | Barnabe Riche, *Riche his Farewell to Militarie Profession* (1581) |
| Henry VI, Part III *(history)* | 1590/1595 | Hall; Holinshed | Hamlet *(tragedy)* | 1600/1603 | François de Belleforest, *Histoires Tragiques* (1576) |
| Henry VI, Part I *(history)* | 1590/1623 | Hall; Holinshed | The Merry Wives of Windsor *(comedy)* | 1600/1602 | Specific source not established |
| Richard III, *(history)* | 1592/1597 | Hall; Holinshed; Sir Thomas More, *History of Richard III* | Troilus and Cressida *(comedy)* | 1601/1609 | Geoffrey Chaucer, *Troilus and Criseyde* (c.1386); William Caxton, *Recuyell of the Historyes of Troye* (1474) |
| The Comedy of Errors *(comedy)* | 1592/1623 | Plautus, *Menaechmi* and *Amphitruo* | | | |
| Titus Andronicus *(tragedy)* | 1593/1594 | *History of Titus Andronicus* (chapbook); John Gower, *Appolonius of Tyre* | All's Well That Ends Well *(comedy)* | 1602/1623 | William Painter, *Palace of Pleasure* (1566–67) |
| The Taming of the Shrew *(comedy)* | 1593/1623 | George Gascoigne, *Supposes* (1566); earlier play *The Taming of a Shaw* | Measure for Measure *(comedy)* | 1604/1623 | George Whetstone, *Promos and Cassandra* (1578) |
| The Two Gentlemen of Verona *(comedy)* | 1594/1623 | Jorge de Montemayor, *Diana* (1559?) | Othello *(tragedy)* | 1604/1622 | Giovanni Battista Giraldi ("Cinthio"), *Ecatommiti* (1565) |
| | | | King Lear *(tragedy)* | 1605/1608 | Holinshed; Anon., *The True Chronicle History of King Leir* (before 1594) |
| Love's Labour's Lost *(comedy)* | 1594/1598 | Specific source not established | Macbeth *(tragedy)* | 1605/1623 | Holinshed |
| Romeo and Juliet *(tragedy)* | 1594/1597 | Arthur Brooke, *The Tragicall Historye of Romeus and Iuliet* (1562); Matteo Bandello, *Novelle* (tr. by William Painter in *Palace of Pleasure*, 1566–67) | Antony and Cleopatra *(tragedy)* | 1606/1623 | Plutarch |
| | | | Coriolanus *(tragedy)* | 1607/1623 | Plutarch |
| Richard II *(history)* | 1595/1597 | Holinshed | Timon of Athens *(tragedy)* | 1607/1623 | Plutarch; Lucian, *Misanthropos* (2nd cent. AD) |
| A Midsummer Night's Dream *(comedy)* | 1595/1600 | Specific source not established | Pericles *(tragicomedy)* | 1608/1609 | John Gower, *Confessio Amantis* (c.1390) |
| King John *(history)* | 1596/1623 | Anon. play, *The Troublesome Raigne of King John* (1591) | Cymbeline *(tragicomedy)* | 1609/1623 | Holinshed; Giovanni Boccaccio, *Decameron* (1348–53) |
| The Merchant of Venice *(comedy)* | 1596/1600 | Giovanni Fiorentino, *Il Pecarone* (1558) | The Winter's Tale *(tragicomedy)* | 1610/1623 | Robert Greene, *Pandosto* (1588) |
| Henry IV, Part I *(history)* | 1597/1598 | Holinshed | The Tempest *(tragicomedy)* | 1611/1623 | Specific source not established |
| Henry IV, Part II *(history)* | 1597/1600 | Holinshed | Henry VIII (probably written with John FLETCHER; *history*) | 1612/1623 | Holinshed; John Foxe, *Book of Martyrs* (1563) |
| Much Ado About Nothing *(comedy)* | 1598/1600 | Ariosto, *Orlando Furioso* (1516) | | | |
| Henry V *(history)* | 1598/1600 | Holinshed | Two Noble Kinsmen (of doubtful authorship; may have been written with John Fletcher; *comedy*) | 1612/1634 | Geoffrey Chaucer, "The Knight's Tale", in *Canterbury Tales* (c.1387) |
| Julius Caesar *(tragedy)* | 1599/1623 | Plutarch, *Lives* (tr. by Sir Thomas North, 1579) | | | |

***The first date is the approximate date of composition; the following date, that of first publication.**

occasional major changes in direction of the Yellow R. have, in the past, resulted in large-scale flooding and loss of life, as at the turn of the century when it changed direction from the south to the north of the peninsula. As part of the Western and Japanese aggression against China, Germany established Shandong and its sphere of interest and it was from this province that originated the antiforeign BOXER UPRISING (1900). German power did, however, aid the area's industrialization, and is reflected in the current popularity of Qingdao beer.

**Shang** or **Yin,** dynasty: see CHINA.

**Shanghai,** city (1984 pop. 12,647,800), E China, on the Yangtze and Huangpu Rs. Located in, but independent of, JIANGSU prov., Shanghai is administered directly by the central government. It is one of the world's greatest seaports, the largest city of China, and the country's most important foreign-trade centre. Despite a lack of fuel and raw materials, Shanghai is the leading industrial city of China, with steelworks, textile mills, shipyards, and oil refineries. Its factories produce various heavy and light industrial goods, such as machinery, chemicals, electronic equipment, aircraft, and precision tools. Shanghai comprises a commercial section (the former International Settlement), which is Western in appearance; an older quarter with crowded streets and wooden buildings; and industrial and residential sections ringing the city. It was a treaty port in the 19th cent. and there were extraterritorially administered British, American, and French concessions until World War II (see EXTRATERRITORIALITY). The Chinese Communist Party's first congress was held here in 1921. The city is now a key site of China's modernization programme, a centre for the new technology industries and links with the West and Japan.

**Shankar, Pandit Ravi,** 1920–, Indian composer and *sitar* virtuoso. He was musical director of All India Radio from 1949 to 1956. He has composed two Concertos for sitar and orchestra (1971 and 1981) and many Indian *rāgs*, as well as music for ballets, and for films such as *Pather Panchali* (1955), *Aparajito* (1956), and *The World of Apu* (1959). He has performed, and recordings of his sitar compositions have been popular, in many different countries; and he has also worked in concert with classical and jazz musicians, such as Yehudi MENUHIN and Bud Shank.

**Shankara:** see VEDANTA.

**Shannon,** main river in Republic of Ireland, c.384 km (240 mi) long. It rises on Cuilcagh mountain in the NW of Co. Cavan, and flows generally S through Loughs Allen, Boderg, Ree, and Derg to Limerick, where it enters a wide estuary. The estuary runs roughly W, and is c.96 km (60 mi) long, entering the Atlantic Ocean between Co. Clare in the N and Co. Kerry in the S. The major tributaries are the Suck, Brosna, Little Brosna, and Deel rivers. The main towns it passes are CARRICK-ON-SHANNON, Athlone and LIMERICK. Just N of Limerick is Ardnacrusha, an important hydroelectric power station. Shannon Airport is on the N side of the estuary, 21 km (13 mi) W of Limerick.

**Shannon Airport,** international airport in Co. Clare, Republic of Ireland, 21 km (13 mi) W of Limerick, at Rineanna, on the Shannon estuary. The airport is the starting point for transatlantic flights, and handled 1,158,270 passengers in 1985.

**Shansi,** see SHANXI.

**Shantou,** city (1984 pop. 7,895,100), E GUANGDONG prov., SE China, on the South China Sea. The East India Company established a station here in the 18th cent., and in 1860 it was forcibly opened to foreign trade by the Treaty of Tianjin. In 1980 a section near the old city was designated one of China's four special economic zones. This grants special privileges to foreign companies to encourage them to invest in these areas. It is hoped to encourage high-technology and export-based industries to develop China's economic growth and modernization.

**Shantung:** see SHANDONG.

**Shanxi** or **Shansi,** province (1985 est. pop. 26,270,000), 156,000 km² (60,232 sq mi), N China; bordered by HEBEI (E) and INNER MONGOLIA (N). To the west and south the provincial boundary largely follows the YELLOW RIVER. Major cities include TAIYUAN, the capital, and Datong. The province consists of plateaus with flanking mountain ranges. The loess soil, though reasonably fertile, requires irrigation and terracing. Winter wheat, kaoliang (a type of sorghum), and maize are important crops. The area has extensive coal reserves and is the major provincial producer.

Much coal is exported to other provinces. Iron and steel and chemicals are the major industries.

**Shapley, Harlow,** 1885–1972, American astronomer. He was a staff astronomer (1914–21) at Mt Wilson Observatory and later director (1921–52) of Harvard Observatory. He established that CEPHEID VARIABLES are pulsating stars rather than eclipsing binaries. Through his study of Cepheids in globular CLUSTERS he determined the size of the MILKY WAY galaxy as well as the position of its centre and of the Sun within the galaxy.

**sharecropping,** farm tenancy system once common in parts of the US that arose from the cotton plantation system after the CIVIL WAR. Landlords provided land, seed, and credit; croppers, initially former slaves, contributed labour and received a share of the crop's value, minus their debt to the landlord. The system's abuses included emphasis on single cash crops, high interest charges, and cropper irresponsibility. Farm mechanization and reduced cotton acreage have virtually ended sharecropping.

**Shari'a,** the system of ethical, legal, and religious principles governing the lives of pious Muslims. It is the Islamic equivalent of DHARMA, and is elaborated in the systems of Islamic law (see FIQH).

**sharif** [Arab., = honourable person], the Arab-Islamic nobility of blood. The term is used with reference to descendants of MUHAMMAD. In the Islamic middle ages, such people, the *Ashraf*, had a corporate identity entailing a number of privileges. A sharif is addressed as *sayyid*.

**Sharjah,** small state and town on the Arabian coast of the PERSIAN GULF. See UNITED ARAB EMIRATES.

**shark,** predatory cartilaginous FISH (order Selachii), found in all seas but most abundant in warm waters. About 250 species exist, ranging from the 60-cm (2-ft) pygmy shark to the 15-m (50-ft) whale shark. The whale shark (*Rhincodon typus*) is the largest living fish, a 21-m (70-ft) specimen having been recorded. Sharks have pointed snouts and crescent-shaped mouths with several rows of sharp, triangular teeth. The most feared is the white shark, or maneater (*Carcharodon carcharias*), reaching 6 m (20 ft) in length, which feeds on large fish and other animals and is known to attack swimmers and boats without provocation. Unlike other sharks, the whale shark and basking shark are harmless plankton-feeders. Shark meat is nutritious, and shark oils are used in industry. Tanned sharkskin is a durable LEATHER.

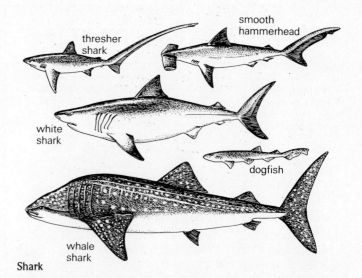

Shark

**Sharon, Ariel,** 1928–, Israeli soldier and politician. A clever military strategist, he took part in all of the ARAB–ISRAELI WARS. He served (1973–74, 1977–) in the Israeli parliament, helped to found the Likud coalition, and was minister of agriculture (1977–81) and of defence (1981–83). Gen. Sharon was the chief architect of the 1982 Israeli invasion of Lebanon. He was later severely criticized for allowing Lebanese Christian militiamen into Palestinian refugee camps in West BEIRUT, where they murdered hundreds of civilians. Forced by an official inquiry to resign the defence portfolio, he nevertheless remained in the cabinet and later became (1984) trade and industry minister.

**Sharp, Cecil (James),** 1859–1924, British collector and performer of folk music. Although it has become fashionable to criticize Sharp's efforts and to forget his genuinely socialist leanings, he was, more than any other single person, responsible for salvaging English FOLK SONG and dance, and encouraging its performance and further study at a crucial period in the transformation of rural society.

**Sharpeville,** town near Johannesburg, South Africa. On 21 Mar. 1960 police shot dead 69 black demonstrators against APARTHEID and wounded nearly 200 others. The incident attacted strong international condemnation and contributed to the withdrawal of South Africa from the COMMONWEALTH in 1961.

**Shastri, Shri Lal Bahadur,** 1904–66, Indian prime minister (1964–66). He held several governmental posts before succeeding Jawaharlal NEHRU. He was prime minister at the time of the war with Pakistan in 1965 and responsible for the subsequent agreement at Tashkent.

**Shatt al Arab,** tidal river, 193 km (120 mi) long, formed by the confluence of the TIGRIS and EUPHRATES rivers in SE Iraq and flowing southeast along part of the Iran-Iraq border to the PERSIAN GULF. The KARUN R. also enters the Shatt al Arab. Iraq and Iran have disputed navigation rights on the Shatt al Arab since 1935, when an international commission awarded the rights to Iraq, leaving Iran with control of only the approaches to its ports of Abadan and Khorramshahr. The issue contributed to the outbreak of war between the two nations in 1980 and the area has been the scene of heavy fighting since.

**Shavuot:** see under JEWISH HOLIDAYS.

**Shaw, George Bernard,** 1856–1950, Irish playwright and critic. His dramas of ideas dominated the early 20th-cent. English stage, and his criticism is considered superb. In 1925 he was awarded the Nobel Prize in literature. A Fabian socialist, Shaw was a popular speaker and wrote five novels before becoming a music critic for London newspapers in 1885. His early plays were collected in *Plays Pleasant and Unpleasant* (1898). Among the 'unpleasant' plays was *Mrs Warren's Profession* (1893), a jibe at Victorian attitudes on prostitution. The 'pleasant' plays included *Arms and the Man* (1894), satirizing romantic attitudes towards love and war, and *Candida* (1893). *The Devil's Disciple* (1897) on the American Revolution, was published along with *Caesar and Cleopatra* (1899) and *Captain Brassbound's Conversion* (1900). Shaw's major plays came in the next 15 years: *Man and Superman* (1903), on men, women, art, and marriage; *Major Barbara* (1905), arguing poverty as the root of all evil; and *Androcles and the Lion* (1912), satirizing Christianity. *Pygmalion* (1913) has been his most successful play. A satire on English class attitudes, it depicts a cockney girl's transformation into a lady by a speech professor and was the basis for the 1956 musical *My Fair Lady*. Of Shaw's later plays, *Saint Joan* (1923), a dramatic consideration of JOAN OF ARC, is best known. His most notable nonfiction work is probably *The Intelligent Woman's Guide to Socialism and Capitalism* (1928).

**shawl,** piece of fabric used as a wrap, decoratively, or for warmth. The word derives from the Indo-Persian for a finely woven woollen cloth or garment made from it. The earliest and finest shawls originated in Kashmir, in N India, where they were made from the silky inner hair of the mountain goat (see WOOL). The traditional patterns were based on plant forms or 'boteh', and these curved or cone shapes still differentiate a 'Paisley pattern', the term taken from the town, Paisley, Scotland, an important centre, in addition to Edinburgh, Norwich, Paris, Lyons, Vienna and many other places, where shawls were woven and printed for a large, international market. Shawls of this kind were most popular from the 1830s to 60s.

**Shawnee Indians** or **Shawano Indians,** NORTH AMERICAN INDIAN tribe of the Eastern Woodlands, speaking an Algonquian language (see AMERICAN INDIAN LANGUAGES). By the mid-18th cent. they were concentrated in Ohio, where they fought in most wars of the Old Northwest. In 1795 they were forced to move into Indiana. There TECUMSEH and his brother Tenskwatawa, the Shawnee Prophet, established the tribe in a village on the Tippecanoe R., which William Henry HARRISON destroyed (1811). The Shawnee were then moved farther west, eventually to Oklahoma.

**Shawqi, Ahmad,** 1868–1932, Egyptian poet. He was the greatest exponent of the neoclassical style in the modern period. Until he was exiled by the British in 1915, he had been the favourite poet of the Khedive Abbas, and was perhaps the last great court poet in the history of Arabic literature.

**shear:** see STRENGTH OF MATERIALS.

**shearwater,** oceanic BIRDS related to PETRELS and ALBATROSSES. They are migratory birds, spending most of their lives at sea, returning to coasts to nest in burrows, which in New Zealand may be shared with a TUATARA. The Australian short-tailed shearwater (*Puffinus tenuirostris*), also called the mutton bird, regularly circles the Pacific, a round trip of 32,000 km (20,000 mi), taking a surprisingly short time. This bird is killed under licence and sold as Tasmanian squab. The Manx shearwater (*Puffinus puffinus*) ranges the North Atlantic, the Mediterranean, and the Pacific. It is a remarkable homing bird, one released in Boston, US taking only 12½ days to fly the 4800 km (3000 mi) to its burrow on Skokholm, a small British island.

**Sheba,** biblical name of a region of S Arabia, including Yemen and the Hadhramaut; it was also called Saba. Its inhabitants, Sabaeans or Sabeans, established an ancient culture there, as shown by inscriptions in a Semitic language. The biblical queen of Sheba (called Balkis in the Muslim tradition) visited Solomon in the 10th cent. BC. With the rise of Islam (7th cent. AD), Sheba came under Muslim control.

**sheep,** cloven-hoofed MAMMAL, genus *Ovis*, of the family Bovidae, closely related to the goat. The sheep is one of the world's most important domesticated animals, being farmed in almost all countries, sometimes in vast numbers as on the plains of Australia, New Zealand, the Middle East, and India. The sheep was domesticated by Neolithic man, and it is commonly stated that its ancestor was probably the MOUFLON, but the fossil evidence does not support this. The sheep is a HERBIVORE, with teeth and jaws adapted for feeding on tough, short grasses, and its split upper lip allows close grazing. Many varieties have been selected for specific purposes and climates. Welsh Mountain, Suffolk, South Down, and Hampshire sheep are primarily meat animals, the Leicester and the Scottish Blackface are primarily bred for wool. However, most sheep are to some extent dual-purpose animals. The Merino, originating in Spain, and the Rambouillet of France produce the world's finest wool. The English Lincoln has been much used for cross-breeding, owing to its long, silky wool, and its large carcass size. Much of the sheep population of Australasia consists of the Corriedale, bred in New Zealand by crossing the Lincoln with the Merino. Its meat is exported as 'New Zealand lamb'. In the Mediterranean lands, sheep are bred for the production of milk. The Karakul sheep of central Asia is extremely hardy, being able to survive cold and drought, and in addition to meat and wool for its farmers, produces the 'fur' known as Persian Lamb. At the present time sheep numbers are declining in advanced countries, owing to competition from synthetic fibres, and high labour costs. There are large fluctuations in demand for fine wools due to changes in fashions for fabrics, with consequent periods of hardship for sheep farmers.

**Sheffield,** city (1981 pop. 470,685), South Yorkshire, N England. One of the leading industrial cities of England, it is famous for its cutlery, especially the fused copper and silver metalware known as Sheffield plate. Industry has, however, undergone much decline in the 1980s.

**Sheherazade:** see THOUSAND AND ONE NIGHTS.

**shehitah,** the Jewish method of slaughtering. This is performed with a razor-sharp knife, called *halaf*, which severs the oesophagus, trachea, and attendant arteries, causing an almost instantaneous drop in blood pressure and loss of consciousness. Jewish law does not permit the infliction of any pain upon animals. After the act of shehitah, a full investigation (*bedikah*) of the carcass has to be made to ensure that there are no diseases of the internal organs.

**Shehu, Mehmet** (shehooh), 1913–81, Albanian Communist leader and premier (1954–81). He was a longtime ally of Enver HOXHA, whom he succeeded as premier. Shehu died in unclear circumstances, and was later denounced by Hoxha as having been a longtime secret agent of hostile foreign powers.

**shellac,** solution of lac, a RESIN exuded by a scale insect, in alcohol or acetone. The colour ranges from light yellow to orange; the darker shellacs are the less pure. When bleached it is known as white shellac. Applied to surfaces, e.g., wood, shellac forms a hard coating when the solvent evaporates. Shellac is used as a spirit VARNISH, as a protective covering for drawings and plaster casts, for stiffening felt hats, and in electrical insulation.

**Shelley, Mary Wollstonecraft,** 1797–1851, English novelist, wife of Percy Bysshe SHELLEY. Her celebrated Gothic horror tale, *Frankenstein* (1818), about an artificially created human being, has endlessly influenced the later science fiction genre, to which her later novel, *The Last Man* (1826) also contributed. Frankenstein was the name of the monster's creator, but has passed into the language as the type of the monster himself.

**Shelley, Percy Bysshe,** 1792–1822, English poet. In 1810 he entered Oxford, where he read the radical writings of William GODWIN and others. In 1811 he and a friend published a pamphlet, *On the Necessity of Atheism,* and were expelled. Later that year he married Harriet Westbrook. His first major poem, *Queen Mab,* privately printed in 1813, advocated social and political reform through the abolition of various established institutions. In 1814 he went to France with Godwin's daughter, Mary Wollstonecraft SHELLEY. In 1816, after Harriet's suicide, he and Mary were married. *Alastor, or The Spirit of Solitude,* appeared in 1816; *The Revolt of Islam* in 1818. In that year the Shelleys settled in Italy, where his mature works were written, among them the poetic dramas *The Cenci* (1819) and *Prometheus Unbound* (1820); *Adonais* (1821), an elegy to John KEATS; and the lyrics 'Ode to the West Wind' (1819) and 'To a Skylark' (1820). In 1821 Shelley wrote 'A Defence of Poetry', his most important prose work. He was drowned while sailing in 1822. His long poems, enshrining his belief in reason and the perfectability of man, and his hatred of injustice and tyranny, are excelled by his magical lyrics.

**Shenandoah valley,** scenic depression in the APPALACHIAN MTS, c.240 km (150 mi) long, between the Blue Ridge and Allegheny mountains, in N Virginia, US. It was an important corridor in the early westward movement of pioneers and figured prominently in the 'valley campaign' of Stonewall JACKSON (1862) and other events of the Civil War.

**Shen Congwen,** 1903–, Chinese writer and art historian. Born in a remote minority area of western Hunan, Shen Congwen published many stories about his life in Hunan—collections like *Ya zi* [ducks] (1926), *Mi gan* [oranges] (1937), and his short novel *Bian cheng* [border town] (1934). After 1949, he abandoned fiction for studies of bronze mirrors and Chinese costume.

**Shensi:** see SHAANXI.

**Shenyang,** formerly Mukden, city (1984 pop. 5,261,600), capital of LIAONING prov., NE China, on the Hun R. It is one of China's leading industrial cities and the economic centre of NE China. Industries include machinery and machine tools production, steel, metals, electric power, chemicals and food processing. An important historical site, Shenyang was the capital of the Manchus in China and the site of the Japanese invasion of Manchuria in 1931 (the 'Mukden Incident').

**Shenzhen,** city (1984 pop. 337,000), S GUANGDONG prov., SE China, to the N of HONG KONG. In 1980 the Chinese government designated Shenzhen, and three other locations in S China, special economic zones. Shenzhen is the largest and most important of these zones; much of its importance (and development as a tourist centre) is because of its proximity to Hong Kong. The zones grant special privileges to attract foreign investors in order to speed up China's modernization. It is hoped that joint ventures involving Chinese and foreign capital will develop high technology industries aimed at the export market.

**Shepard, Sam,** 1943–, American playwright and actor. A product of the 1960s counterculture, Shepard combines wild humour, grotesque satire, myth, and haunting language evocative of Western films to create a subversive POP-ART vision of America. His plays include *The Tooth of Crime* (1973), *Curse of the Starving Class* (1977), *Buried Child* (1978), *True West* (1980), and *Fool for Love* (1983).

**Shepparton,** city (1986 pop. 30,238), Victoria, SE Australia. Located N of MELBOURNE on the Goulburn R. it is the major regional centre for the Goulburn Valley, an important irrigation area producing milk and fruit, with a large processing industry for these products.

**Sheraton, Thomas,** 1751–1806, English furniture designer. A Baptist preacher and writer, he published his designs in manuals such as the *Cabinet-Maker and Upholsterer's Drawing-Book* (1791–94). His style is marked by delicacy, simplicity, straight lines, classical motifs, and inlay decoration.

Design for library table from Thomas **Sheraton's** *Cabinet Maker, Upholsterer, and General Artist's Encyclopedia* (1804–07)

**Sheridan, Philip Henry,** 1831–88, Union general and outstanding cavalry officer in the AMERICAN CIVIL WAR. His charge over Missionary Ridge (Nov. 1863) in the Chattanooga campaign contributed largely to the Union victory there. In 1864, while leading the Army of the Shenandoah, he defeated the Confederates and laid waste the countryside. In April 1865 he cut off the Confederate retreat at APPOMATTOX and forced Gen. LEE to surrender.

**Sheridan, Richard Brinsley,** 1751–1816, English dramatist and politician; b. Dublin. His masterpieces, *The Rivals* (1775) and *School for Scandal* (1777), COMEDIES of manners blending RESTORATION wit and 18th-cent. sensibility, are affectionate satires on fashionable society. Other works include *The Critic* (1779), a dramatic burlesque; *The Duenna* (1775), a comic opera; and *A Trip to Scarborough* (1777). He entered Parliament in 1780 and became a public official and noted orator.

**Sherman, William Tecumseh,** 1820–91, Union general in the AMERICAN CIVIL WAR. He distinguished himself in the VICKSBURG and Chattanooga campaigns (1863). Appointed commander in the West (Mar. 1864), he embarked on the Atlanta Campaign and took the city (2 Sept.). He burned Atlanta (15 Nov.) and set off, with 60,000 men, on his famous march to the sea, devastating the country. After capturing Savannah (21 Dec.), he turned north through South Carolina, again wreaking havoc, and received the surrender of Gen. J.E. JOHNSTON (26 Apr. 1865). Sherman, whose famous statement that 'war is hell' expressed his belief in the need for ruthlessness in modern warfare, is considered one of the greatest Civil War generals. His brother, **John Sherman,** 1823–1900, was secretary of the treasury (1877–81) and secretary of state (1897–98). As a US senator from Ohio (1861–77, 1881–97), he was associated with the passage (1890) of the Sherman Antitrust Act and the SHERMAN SILVER PURCHASE ACT.

**Sherman Silver Purchase Act,** 1890, passed by the US Congress to supplant the Bland-Allison Act of 1878. It required the US government to double its purchase of silver and to increase money in circulation. When put into operation, it threatened to undermine the US Treasury's gold reserves, and it was repealed in 1893.

**Sherrington, Sir Charles Scott,** 1857–1952, English neurophysiologist. He introduced the concept of synapse (see NERVOUS SYSTEM), described the motor functions of the spinal cord, and demonstrated that when one set of muscles is stimulated, an opposing set is simultaneously inhibited. His work on reflex integration was synthesized in his classic *The Integrative Action of the Nervous System* (1906). For his isolation and functional analysis of the neurone, he shared with Edgar ADRIAN the 1932 Nobel Prize for physiology or medicine.

**sherry,** naturally dry, fortified wine containing 15% to 23% alcohol; originally made from grapes of the Jérez de la Frontera region in Spain. The term now includes wines of S Spain, the US, Latin America, and South Africa. After fermentation, sherry is fortified with BRANDY and aged. Blending and, in some cases, sweetening produce a wide variety of sherries.

**Shetland Islands,** island region off the N coast of Scotland (1985 est. pop. 26,347), 1433 km² (559 sq mi), about 81 km (50 mi) N of Orkney Island Area. The administrative centre is Lerwick. The region is composed of about 100 islands and islets, of which one-fifth are inhabited. It includes the islands of Mainland, Yell, and Unst. Fair Isle is detached from the main group and lies about 40 km (25 mi) to the S. The most northerly island of the group and of the British Isles as a whole is Muckle Flugga. The islands are bleak with few trees. Oil, produced offshore in the North Sea since the 1970s, supplements income from traditional sheep, cattle, and knitware industries. Tourism is also important. The hardy Shetland pony and the Shetland sheepdog originated there. Occupied by Norsemen by the 9th cent., the islands were annexed to Scotland in 1472.

**Shevchenko, Taras,** 1814–61, foremost poet of Ukraine, the bard of his nation. Born as serf in the region of Kiev, Shevchenko was arrested in 1847 and banished for 10 years of military penal servitude. While his early poetry was under the influence of ROMANTICISM he soon moved to Ukrainian history, especially in the long poem *The Haidamaks* (1841). In his other main poems, e.g., *The Dream* (1844) and *The Caucasus* (1845) Shevchenko is highly critical of Czar NICHOLAS I, of Russian oppression of Ukraine, and of people in the Caucasus. In later poems *NEOFITY* such as *The Neophytes* (1857) he deals with broader themes of truth, goodness, and humanity. Shevchenko contributed greatly to reawakening of Ukranian national consciousness and of sense of historical continuity. He was also a notable painter and engraver.

**Shi'ism,** one of the two major divisions of ISLAM. It arose originally around the legitimist claims to the CALIPHATE by the descendants of ALI, and developed over a period of three centuries into a theory of legitimacy based on the notion of the imamate (see IMAM), a system of Islamic law (see FIQH), and various theological and cosmological theories. The one Shi'ite sect that refused the common Shi'ite belief that the imamate was hereditary and held that it could devolve upon any capable individual in the line of ALI was the one that had the earliest viable political constitution. This was the Zaidiyya, which established a long-lived political system in the Yemen (897–1961). The largest group of Shi'ites is the so-called Twelver Shi'ites, to whom belong the vast majority of Iranians since this sect became official state religion under the Safavids; there are other Twelver communities in Iraq, Lebanon, and Pakistan, and small groups elsewhere. The Twelvers are so called because of their belief that the twelfth imam in the line of Ali disappeared in a cave at Samarra in Iraq in 873 and will come back at the end of time as the MAHDI to redeem humanity. It was only after his disappearance (Occultation, or *ghaiba*) that Shi'ism of the Twelver variety started in earnest to develop its distinctive legal and theological literature. The only other Shi'ite sects still flourishing today are the Zaidiyya, the ISMA'ILIS, DRUZE, and the NUSAYRIYYA.

**Shikoku,** island (1986 est. pop. 4,252,871), Japan. The smallest (18,770 km²/7247 sq mi) of Japan's major islands, it is located in the south and separated from HONSHU and KYUSHU by the INLAND SEA, although it will be linked with Honshu by three long bridges. The island is mostly mountainous, with little land suitable for farming, and has a subtropical climate. Population is concentrated in the industrial belt along the northern coast, where Takamatsu and Matsuyama are the largest cities.

**Shiloh** (shieloh), in the BIBLE, town, central Palestine, the modern Khirbet Seilun (Israeli-occupied Jordan), NNE of Jerusalem. It was the home of the prophets Eli and Ahijah and the place where the ARK of the Covenant rested after the conquest of Judah.

**Shiloh, battle of,** 6–7 Apr. 1862, in the AMERICAN CIVIL WAR. On 6 Apr. the Confederates routed Union troops under U.S. GRANT in a surprise attack at Shiloh Church meeting house, Tennessee. The next day Grant, with reinforcements from the Army of the Ohio, counterattacked, and the Confederates withdrew to Corinth, Mississippi. The battle, one of the war's bloodiest, with losses of over 10,000 on each side, set the stage for later Union victories in the West.

**shingles,** infection of a ganglion, or nerve centre, with severe pain and a blisterlike eruption in the area of the nerve distribution. Known also as herpes zoster (see under HERPES) and varicella zoster, it is caused by the same virus that causes CHICKEN POX. Most common in adults, especially people over the age of 50, it often involves the area of the upper abdomen and lower chest, but may appear along other nerve pathways.

**Shin Kansen,** Japanese HIGH SPEED TRAIN. The Shin Kansen or 'New Railway' between Tokyo and Osaka was opened on 1 Oct. 1964. It was the first railway to be built solely to carry high speed trains (maximum speed 210 kph/130 mph) giving a journey time of 3 h 10 min for a distance of 515 km (320 mi). Subsequently, the line has been extended to Hakata (distance from Tokyo 1069 km/663 mi) thus serving the principal population and industrial corridor of Japan. In 1975, 157 million passengers were carried, though reductions in traffic have occurred since. To date there has been no fatal accident to a passenger on the line. Three further Shin Kansen were authorized in 1970, and the Tohuku (Tokyo–Morioka) and Joetsu (Omiya–Niigata) lines are now in operation. The very high passenger volume has provided a good commercial return on the initially very large investment in the new tracks of the Tokyo–Osaka Shin Kansen.

**Shinto,** ancient native religion of Japan, practised today as a set of traditional rituals and customs involving reverence of ancestors, the celebration of popular festivals, and pilgrimages to shrines believed to house a great host of mostly beneficent supernatural beings or deities called *kami*. Shinto beliefs and rituals were transmitted orally long before the introduction (5th cent.) of Chinese writing into Japan; much of the ancient belief is gathered in three later compilations of records, rituals, and prayers: the *Kojiki* (completed AD 712), the *Nihongi* (completed AD 720), and the *Yengishiki* (10th cent.). These accounts describe the development of early Japanese religion from the worship of the forces and forms of nature to a stage of polytheism in which spiritual conceptions had only a small place. The most exalted among the deities was the sun-goddess, Amaterasu-o-mi-kami, held to be the ancestor of the line of emperors of Japan, each of whom was chief priest by divine right. In 1882 all Shinto organizations were divided into two groups, government-supervised state shrines and sectarian churches. A powerful tool in the hands of the militarists, state Shinto collapsed with the defeat of Japan in World War II and the disavowal (1946) by Emperor Hirohito of his divinity. Sectarian Shinto still thrives; there is no dogmatic system and no formulated code of morals, but some newer sects stress world peace and brotherhood. Although modifications have been introduced by the influence of BUDDHISM (since the 6th cent. AD) and CONFUCIANISM, pure Shinto (stressed after the restoration of imperial power in 1868) consists almost entirely of prayer recitation, dances by the priest, and food offerings.

**shinty,** stick-and-ball game closely related to the Irish game of HURLING. Played almost exclusively in the Scottish Highlands, the game was known as Camanachd. A modern pitch has a goal (hail) at either end and a game lasts 90 min, with 12 players on each side. The object is to hit a leather-covered ball made of cork and worsted into the opponents' goal. Like hurling, it is mostly a game of highly skilled aerial passing. Only the hail-keeper is allowed to handle the ball. Shinty was introduced to Scotland during the Middle Ages by Irish Gaels from Antrim, and not codified until 1879. The main difference between shinty and hurling is that only a narrow-bladed stick (caman) is used in shinty whereas both a narrow-bladed and a broad-bladed stick may be used in hurling.

**ship,** large craft in which persons and goods can be conveyed on water. The term *boat* properly applies only to smaller craft, but some vessels may be called by either name. Ancient ships were propelled by oars, sails, or both; the trireme used by the Greeks and the Romans was the most famous warship of ancient times. In the Middle Ages, VIKING ships, propelled by both oars and sails, carried LEIF ERICSSON to America. The introduction of the mariner's COMPASS and the transoceanic voyages of the Portuguese and of COLUMBUS and other explorers of the New World gave impetus to the building and navigation of ships. With differences in the number and positions of masts, and sails either square-rigged or fore-and-aft, a number of different types of ships appeared. Building wooden ships became an important industry, especially in Britain and the US. Later, the STEAMSHIP replaced the sailing ship and steel replaced wood, making possible the construction of much larger ships. The steam engine was followed by the steam TURBINE and, early in the 20th cent., by the DIESEL ENGINE. In the 1950s nuclear marine engines were introduced. Today, some freight ships are equipped with cargo-handling machines that rival the power of any on the docks, and the latest generation of mammoth oil-carriers includes the largest ships that ever put to sea. Although the aeroplane has led to the virtual demise of the great ocean liner, luxurious cruise ships continue to be built. The pivotal vessels of modern warfare are the AIRCRAFT CARRIER and the SUBMARINE, but any sizable NAVY still includes destroyers, cruisers, and frigates.

**shipworm** or **teredo**, is not a true worm, but a bivalve mollusc that bores into wood. Its two ridged shells act as boring drills at the front of the body, the long foot relying on its tunnel for protection. Shipworms are great pests, damaging ships and piers.

**Shirley, James**, 1596–1666, English dramatist. His plays include *The Lady of Pleasure* (1635), a comedy realistically portraying London society; *The Traitor* (1631), a tragedy; and *The Triumph of Peace* (1633), a MASQUE.

**shock**, acute failure of the circulatory system when arterial blood pressure is too low to maintain an adequate supply of blood to body tissues. It may be due to HEART FAILURE, haemorrhage, extensive third-degree burns (see BURN), severe ALLERGY, or emotional disaster. Symptoms include weakness, pallor, cold clammy skin, thirst, nausea, and, in severe cases, unconsciousness. Because shock can be fatal, emergency treatment, such as BLOOD TRANSFUSION and administration of fluids and oxygen, should be given while the underlying cause is being diagnosed.

**shock wave**, wave comprising a zone of extremely high pressure within a fluid (see FLUID MECHANICS), especially one such as the atmosphere, that propagates through the fluid at supersonic speed, i.e., faster than the speed of SOUND. Shock waves are caused by the sudden, violent disturbance of a fluid, such as that created by a powerful explosion or by the supersonic flow of a fluid over a solid object (see SONIC BOOM).

**Shoemaker, Willie** (William Lee Shoemaker), 1931–, American jockey. The most successful jockey in history, he won his first race when he was 18. In 1986, at age 54, he rode his 8000th winning mount, nearly 2000 more than any other jockey and including four Kentucky Derby winners.

**shogun**, title of the feudal military dictators who were the actual rulers of Japan from the 12th to the 19th cent. The title originally meant commander of the imperial armies against barbarians, but was established as the hereditary head of a military system of government by MINAMOTO NO YORITOMO after 1185. This first ruling shogunate based at Kamakura was followed by the the Muromachi and TOKUGAWA shogunates. The MEIJI restoration marked the end of the last of the shogunates.

**shohet**, ritual slaughterer. The licence to slaughter, called *Kabbalah*, is granted only to men of piety and learning who undergo rigorous training and regular supervision to ensure that all the laws of SHEHITAH are fully observed and that no animal is passed for consumption which is found to have any disqualifying physical defect.

**Sholapur**, town (1981 pop. 514,860), Maharashtra state, W India, on the Sina R. It is a district administrative and important commercial centre in the midst of a cotton-growing region; not surprisingly it has many textile mills. It was a notable fortress town under the Bahmini sultans in the 15th cent., and played its part in later turbulent history. British days saw its establishment as a district headquarters, the arrival of the cotton industry, and a notable riot in 1930.

**Sholokhov, Mikhail Aleksandrovich**, 1905–84, Soviet novelist. His most famous work, *And Quiet Flows the Don* (1928–40), depicts the effects of World War I, the RUSSIAN REVOLUTION (1917), and the Civil War on COSSACK life. *Virgin Soil Upturned* (1932–60) deals with agricultural collectivization. Sholokhov was awarded the 1965 Nobel Prize for literature.

**Sholom Aleichem** pseud. of **Shalom Rabinowitz** (ˌshohləm ahˌlaykham), [Heb., = peace be unto you], 1859–1916, Russian Yiddish writer. Perhaps best known for his humorous novels and stories of life among poor and oppressed Russian Jews, Sholom Aleichem was influential in establishing Yiddish as a literary language. The sketches collected in *Tevye's Daughters* (1894) formed the basis for the successful musical *Fiddler on the Roof* (1964).

**shooting**, firing with rifle, shotgun, pistol, or revolver at fixed or moving targets. In the sport of small-bore rifle shooting, the targets range in distance from 15.24 to 182.88 m (50 ft–200 yd); in pistol and revolver, from 15.24 to 45.72 m (50 ft–50 yd); and in long-range rifle, from 182.88 to 914.4 m (200–1000 yd). Competitors shoot from four positions with the rifle: prone, sitting, kneeling, and standing. The Queen's Prize is the principal contest for British and Commonwealth rifle shooting; founded by Queen Victoria in 1860, it is now held at Bisley, Surrey, headquarters of the British National Rifle Association. Shooting is an Olympic sport, and pistol shooting is an element in the PENTATHLON. See also CLAY-PIGEON SHOOTING.

**Shoreham-by-Sea**, town (1981 pop. 20,562), W Sussex, S England, on English Channel coast at mouth of R. Adur, 10 km (6 mi) W of Brighton. It is a seaport with container facilities, which handled 20.5 million tonnes in 1984. Old Shoreham (nearby to the N) was a seaport in medieval times which gradually silted up.

**Shorter, Wayne**, 1933–, black American jazz tenor and soprano saxophonist and composer. His sax-playing (inspired by John COLTRANE) and mastery of composition first came to prominence with Art BLAKEY's Jazz Messengers in the late 1950s. He matured with the Miles DAVIES band of the 1960s and contributed largely to the success of the jazz/rock fusion band 'Weather Report' in the 1970s. More recently leading his own groups, he has become one of the leading players and composers of the 1980s, crossing from jazz to rock with equal eloquence.

**shorthand**, any brief, rapid system of writing used in transcribing the spoken word. Such systems date from ancient times. Modern systems began with Timothy Bright's 500 symbols (1588). Many others followed. The phonetic system of Isaac Pitman (1837) is, with improvements, still used in English-speaking countries. Employing geometric outlines with variations in shading, slope, and position to denote variations in meaning, it is difficult to learn but permits great speed. The business shorthand system of John Robert Gregg, published in 1888, is popular. Its curved outlines resemble ordinary script; the pen is rarely lifted, and variations in length indicate variations in meaning. Some systems, such as Speedwriting, employ shortened forms of longhand. Keyboard machines are also used to write shorthand, especially in law courts.

**shortsightedness** or **myopia**, defect of vision in which distant objects cannot be distinguished but near objects can be clearly seen. Because the eyeball is too long or the refractive power of the eye too strong, the image of the object is focused in front of, rather than on, the retina (see EYE). The condition can be corrected by CONTACT LENSES or spectacles with concave lenses.

**short story**, brief prose fiction. The term embraces a variety of narratives, from stories focusing on events to character studies, from 'short short' stories to long, complex narratives (sometimes called novellas) like Thomas Mann's (see MANN, family) *Death in Venice* (1912). Most often the short story concentrates on creating a single dynamic effect, and is limited in character and situation. Precursors of the short story can be found in the BIBLE, the medieval GESTA ROMANORUM, and the works of BOCCACCIO and CHAUCER. The modern short story dates from the 19th-cent. works of Nathaniel HAWTHORNE, E.A. POE, Herman MELVILLE, Nikolai GOGOL, Guy de MAUPASSANT, and Anton CHEKHOV. Twentieth cent. masters of the form include Henry JAMES, Sherwood ANDERSON, Katherine MANSFIELD, Ernest HEMINGWAY, Katherine Anne PORTER, Flannery O'CONNOR, John CHEEVER, and Donald BARTHELME.

**short takeoff and landing aircraft** (STOL), term used for fixed-wing aircraft that can operate from short runways. They are usually relatively small, short-range aircraft of low wing and power loadings. An airport designed for STOL operations is the London 'Stolport' in the Docklands, which has a runway 1100 m (3600 ft) long. STOL aircraft include the de Havilland–Canada Dash 7 and the British Aerospace B.Ae 146.

**Shostakovich, Dmitri**, 1906–75, Russian composer. He scored his first successes with his First Symphony (1925), the opera *The Nose*

(1930), and the ballet *The Golden Age* (1930). His opera *The Lady Macbeth of the Mtsensk* (1934) was first praised as a model of socialist realism and then condemned, and many of his works were not given premières until some years after their composition. Nevertheless, Shostakovich managed to survive the changing tides of opinion. His outstanding works include a piano concerto (1933), the Piano Quintet (1940), the Second String Quartet (1944), and the Ninth (1945) and Tenth (1953) Symphonies.

**shot put,** athletics FIELD EVENT in which an iron globe like a cannon ball is propelled from shoulder level as far as possible. The shot put weighs 7.25 kg (16 lb) for men and 4 kg (8 lb 13 oz) for women.

**Shotwell, James Johnson,** 1874–1965, Canadian–American historian. He taught at Columbia (1900–1942). An internationalist, he attended the Paris Peace Conference (1918–19) and was president of the Carnegie Endowment for International Peace (1949–50). His works include *War as an Instrument of National Policy* (1929).

**showjumping,** equestrian event designed primarily to test a horse's capacity to jump high obstacles, using time as a deciding factor between contestants. The balance between jumping ability and time taken may vary from competition to competition. A competition that tests ability to jump heights alone is known as puissance; there is a small number of fences to be jumped, which become progressively higher, with a limit of four jump-offs. Originally dominated by cavalry officers, for whom it was seen as useful training, the sport is now very popular with amateurs, and is often televised. The men's world championships and the Olympic Games (in which male and female riders compete on equal terms) are the principal individual showjumping competitions, and the Nations and President's Cups the main team contests. See also EVENTING.

**Shreveport,** US city (1984 est. pop. 220,000), NW Louisiana, on the Red R. near the Arkansas and Texas borders; inc. 1839. It is an oil and natural gas centre. These resources and the area's cotton and lumber are employed in its manufactures, which include machinery, telephones, and chemicals. Oil was discovered in 1906, spurring the city's growth.

**shrew,** small, insectivorous MAMMAL of the family Soricidae, of Eurasia and the Americas. Related to MOLES, they include the smallest mammals (under 5 cm/2 in). Light-boned and fragile, with mouselike bodies, shrews are terrestrial and nocturnal and can produce a protective musky odour. They have the highest known metabolic rate of any animal and must eat incessantly to survive.

**Shrewsbury,** county town (1981 pop. 57,731), Shropshire, W Midlands of England, 63 km (39 mi) NW of Birmingham, in loop of R. Severn. A picturesque and historic market town, its industries include light and heavy engineering. The castle dates from the 11th cent. The famous boys' public school was founded in 1552. The town is the birthplace of Charles DARWIN.

**shrike** or **butcher bird,** medium-sized perching BIRD that acts like a bird of prey. Shrikes are solitary, aggressive birds which feed on small mammals, small birds, and insects. These are often impaled on thorns or spikes near the perch to form a 'larder', hence the name butcher bird. Shrikes breed from Europe across Africa and Asia to New Guinea and in North America. The great grey shrike (*Lanius excubitor*) is the most widespread and one of the largest, being 24 cm (9½ in) long. The Australian butcher bird is not a shrike.

**shrimp,** small CRUSTACEAN with 10 jointed legs and a nearly cylindrical, translucent body. Unlike the closely related LOBSTERS and CRABS, which are crawlers, shrimp and PRAWNS are primarily swimmers. Shrimp are widely distributed in temperate and tropical salt and fresh waters. The common European shrimp (*Crangon vulgaris*), the original shrimp, is about 7.5 cm (3 in) long with long antennae. Other species of shrimp throughout the world are fished, including a freshwater giant in North America, weighing 1.3 kg (3 lb).

**Shropshire,** formerly Salop, inland county in W Midlands of England (1984 est. pop. 386,600), 3490 km² (1361 sq mi), bordering on Wales in the W. The S and W of the county is hilly, including the Clee Hills and Long Mynd. The R. SEVERN crosses the county from NW to E and most of the land to the N is low-lying and flat. The county town is SHREWSBURY. Dairy farming is common in the northern lowlands, and cattle- and sheep-rearing are found in the upland areas. Coal was formerly mined around Coalbrookdale and the iron industry was once important. Now the major economic activity is farming.

**Shrove Tuesday,** the day before Ash Wednesday. It is so called because of the custom among Christians, as a preparation for LENT, of confessing their sins and being absolved (i.e., 'shriven') on it. Traditionally it was a day of merry-making before the Lenten fast; the English practice of eating pancakes, made of eggs and fat, foods discouraged during Lent, survives as a relic of this. See also MARDI GRAS.

**shrub,** any woody, PERENNIAL, bushy plant that branches into several stems or trunks at the base and is smaller than a TREE. Tree species may grow as shrubs under unfavourable conditions. In regions of extreme climatic conditions, e.g., the Arctic, where trees do not thrive, shrubs provide valuable food and wood. Common shrubs include the LILAC, mock orange, viburnum, FORSYTHIA, and AZALEA.

**shuffleboard,** sport in which players use cue sticks to push discs onto a triangular scoring diagram at either end of a concrete or terrazzo court (15.85 m/52 ft long and 1.83 m/6 ft wide). Each diagram is divided into 7-, 8-, and 10-point sections, and there is a penalty area of minus 10 points. Shuffleboard probably originated in 13th-cent. England.

**Shukshin, Vasili Makarovich,** 1929–74, Soviet writer, actor, and film director. His main theme was the Soviet countryside, and his frank portrayal of poverty and crime in the villages earned him enormous popularity with Soviet readers. His best-known short story, *Snowball Berry Red* (1973), about a criminal who tried in vain to go straight, became a successful film. An unfinished novel, *The Lyubavins* (1965), deals with the life of Urals villagers in the 1920s. He also wrote the scenario for a film on the 17th-cent. peasant rebel, Stenka Razin, *I have Come to Bring you Freedom* (1971); the film was not produced in his lifetime.

**Shulhan Arukh,** major 16th-cent. code of Jewish law, compiled by Joseph CARO. It is divided into four main sections: *Orah Hayyim*, dealing with synagogal ritual and laws of Sabbath and festivals; *Yoreh Deah*, dealing with rules of ritual slaughter and preparation of KASHER food; *Eben Ha-Ezer*, dealing with matrimonial law; and *Hoshen Mishpat*, dealing with the entire area of civil law. Being a Sephardi (see SEPHARDIM) scholar, Caro's Code reflected rather the Sephardic customs and traditions. A contemporary Polish authority, Moses ISSERLES added glosses drawing attention to variations in Ashkenazi practice. To this day it remains one of the most authoritative sources of Jewish law.

**Shultz, George Pratt,** US public official, 1920–. The dean (1962–68) of the Graduate School of Business at the Univ. of Chicago, Shultz later served under Pres. NIXON as secretary of labour (1969–70), director of the Office of Management and Budget (1970–72), and secretary of the treasury (1972–74). In 1982 he was named by Pres. REAGAN to replace Alexander HAIG as secretary of state.

**Si,** chemical symbol of the element SILICON.

**Sialkot,** town (1981 pop. 296,000), Punjab prov., Pakistan. It is a service centre, and has important craft industries, particularly metal-work. Its unusual modern industries include the manufacture of sports goods and precision equipment. It was the capital of Punjab under White Hun rule (6th cent.).

**siamang:** see GIBBON.

**Siamese language:** see THAI LANGUAGE.

**Siamese twins,** identical twins developing from a single fertilized ovum that has divided imperfectly. Siamese twins can be attached at the abdomen, chest, back, or top of the head, depending on where division of the ovum failed, and can sometimes be successfully separated surgically after birth.

**Sian:** see XI'AN.

**Sibelius, Jean (Julius Christian)** (si͵baylias), 1865–1957, Finnish composer. A highly personal, romantic composer, he represents the culmination of nationalism in Finnish music. He is best known for orchestral works such as SYMPHONIC POEMS, e.g., *Finlandia* (1900), *Valse triste* (1903), *Tapiola* (1926); a violin concerto (1903); a string quartet (1909); and seven symphonies.

**Siberia,** vast geographical region with no precise boundaries, c.7.5 million km² (2.9 million sq mi) mostly in the Russian Republic of the USSR. As generally delineated, it extends east across N Asia from the URALS to the Pacific coast region known as the SOVIET FAR EAST, and south from the TUNDRA regions along the ARCTIC OCEAN margins, through the great

TAIGA forest zone, to the STEPPES of Central Asia and Mongolia. Most of Siberia is sparsely populated, with NOVOSIBIRSK, OMSK, NOVOKUZNETSK, IRKUTSK, and Tomsk the principal cities. Russians and Ukrainians, migrating east from European Russia since the 13th cent., are now more numerous than indigenous ethnic groups. Transportation facilities are limited, the LENA, OB, and YENISEI rivers (and their tributaries) serving as the principal N–S routes and the TRANS-SIBERIAN RAILWAY (completed 1905) as the chief E–W route. Extreme cold in the north and scanty, irregular precipitation in the south limit the region's agricultural potential, and most development is based on Siberia's rich oil, natural gas, coal, iron ore, gold, timber, and other resources. Russia's conquest of Siberia was completed in 1598. From the early 17th cent. it has been notorious as the site of penal colonies and as a place of exile for political prisoners.

**Sibiu** (si‚bee·ooh), city (1983 pop. 159,599), S Transylvania, central Romania. It was founded by German colonists in the 12th cent. and retains its German medieval character. It has textile and other industries. Nearby is the 13th-cent. Cistercian monastery of Cîrta.

**sibyl,** in classical mythology, a prophetess. There were said to be as many as 10 sibyls. The most famous was the Cumaean Sibyl, who sold TARQUIN the Sibylline Books, prophecies about Rome's destiny that were burned in 83 BC.

**Sichuan** or **Szechwan,** province (1985 est. pop. 101,880,000), 570,000 km² (220,077 sq mi), SW China, between HUBEI (E) and TIBET (W). Major cities are CHENGDU, the capital, and CHONGQING. To the west, mountainous areas with a cold climate are largely unsuitable for agriculture. In the centre and east of the province lies the Sichuan Basin, whose natural fertility has been increased by irrigation. Winter temperatures are mild, humidity is high, and crops can be grown for c.11 months of the year. Sichuan is China's leading grain producer and rice and winter wheat are principal crops of the Sichuan Basin. Cash crops include sugarcane, rape seed, cotton, and silk. The mountains are important forest and pasture areas. Coal is mined in a number of locations including the Chongqing region. Oil and natural gas have been important in recent economic development, and Sichuan is China's major producer of asbestos. There is a large hydroelectric power potential. Historically, the Changjiang (Yangtze). R. flowing from W to E through the province has been a significant transport link. Since 1949 this has been supplemented by improved rail and road links binding the area more closely to the rest of China. When Japan invaded and held coastal China in the 1930s Chang Kai-Sheik's government retreated westward and transferred all government offices to Chongqing which briefly became the capital of China.

**Sicilian Vespers,** 1282, a rebellion of the Sicilians against CHARLES I of Naples that broke out at the start of VESPERS on Easter Monday. Byzantine Emperor MICHAEL VIII and PETER III of Aragón were involved in the plot, and Peter accepted the crown of SICILY. A 20-year war between Aragón and Naples ensued. Sicily remained independent of Naples until 1443, when ALFONSO V of Aragón reunited the two areas.

**Sicily,** island (1984 est. pop. 5,051,413), S Italy, in the Mediterranean Sea, separated from the mainland by the Strait of MESSINA. Mainly mountainous, it reaches a high point of 3,261 m (10,700 ft) in volcanic Mt ETNA. Though it has fertile soils and a mild climate, it has suffered chronic poverty, causing many Sicilians to emigrate. Wheat, olives, citrus, nuts, and wine are leading agricultural products, and there are oil and natural gas, textile, and chemical industries. Sicily passed from Byzantine to Arab control in the 9th cent. It was conquered by Normans (1060–91) and came under Spanish rule following the SICILIAN VESPERS revolt (1282). In 1860 GARIBALDI conquered the island, which then voted to become part of the kingdom of Sardinia and ultimately of a unified Italy. Sicily gained limited autonomy in 1947 as part of the Sicilian region 25,706 sq km (9,925 sq mi), which also includes several smaller islands. PALERMO is the regional capital.

**Sickert, Walter Richard,** 1860–1942, British artist. He worked with DEGAS in Paris in 1883. He joined the New English Art Club in 1888 and formed a rebel group in 1889 and organized 'The London Impressionist' exhibition. He was the main artist to introduce progressive French art into Britain before World War I. He was involved in forming the CAMDEN TOWN GROUP (1911), and the LONDON GROUP (1913), painting realist images of urban life.

**sickle-cell anaemia,** or **sickle-cell disease,** inherited disorder occurring mainly in Negroes, in which the red blood cells (erythrocytes) assume distorted, sickle-like shapes. Because of a genetically transmitted chemical abnormality in the HAEMOGLOBIN molecule, the deformed red blood cells tend to clump together. They are fragile and subject to rupture, and the condition causes chronic ANAEMIA, fever, abdominal and joint pains, and JAUNDICE. There is no cure, and many patients die young from circulatory complications.

**Siddons, Sarah Kemble,** 1755–1831, English actress, best-known member of the KEMBLE family. Famed for such Shakespearean roles as Desdemona in *Othello* and Volumnia in *Coriolanus,* she was unequalled as Lady Macbeth.

**siddur,** [Heb., = order], Heb. daily prayer book which follows a statutory order of prayers and blessings. It incorporates weekday and Sabbath morning, afternoon, and evening services, also services for New Moon (see under ROSH HODESH), prayers for the sick and the bereaved, marriage and burial services, Grace after Meals, as well as extracts from festival liturgy.

**sidereal period:** see SYNODIC PERIOD.

**sidereal time** (sie‚diəri·əl), time measured relative to the fixed stars. The *sidereal day* is the period during which the Earth completes one rotation on its axis, so that some chosen star reappears on the observer's celestial meridian; it is 4 min shorter than the solar day (see SOLAR TIME) because the Earth moves in its orbit about the Sun.

**sidewinder:** see RATTLESNAKE.

**Sidgwick, Henry,** 1838–1900, English moral philosopher. His *Method of Ethics* (1874), sometimes said to be the greatest work on ethics in English, attempts a unification of our moral knowledge. Although broadly utilitarian, it rejects the psychological HEDONISM of BENTHAM and J.S. MILL, and tempers the UTILITARIANISM with a basis of intuitionism. He thought that theism was a 'natural' view, but was unable to reconcile it with his philosophy. Sidgwick was an active supporter of higher education for women.

**Sidney, Sir Philip,** 1554–86, English writer. After travelling on the Continent, where he met many leading scholars and politicians, including Ramus and WILLIAM OF ORANGE, and had his portrait painted by VERONESE in Venice, Sidney became a leading courtier and poet. He wrote some of the earliest English pastoral poems, incorporated into his romance *Arcadia* (published posthumously in 1590). He also wrote the earliest English sonnet sequence, *Astrophel and Stella* (1591), and a classic defence of the value of imaginative literature, published in two editions in 1595 under alternative titles, *The Defence of Poesie* and *An Apologie for Poetry.* As a patron he gave encouragement to many writers and scholars, including SPENSER. He died while fighting against the Spanish in the Netherlands.

**Sidon** or **Saida,** city (1980 est. pop. 24,740), SW Lebanon, on the Mediterranean Sea. An ancient seaport of PHOENICIA, it remained important through Roman times and was famous for its purple dyes and glassware. Glassblowing is said to have begun at Sidon. During the 1982 Israeli invasion of S Lebanon, the city was captured from the PALESTINE LIBERATION ORGANIZATION (PLO) by Israeli forces after heavy fighting (see ARAB-ISRAELI WARS). Since 1948 there have been many Palestinian refugees in the city and neighbouring quarters.

**siege,** assault against a fortress or city with the purpose of capturing it. The history of siegecraft has been a race between the development of FORTIFICATIONS and of the weapons that could be brought to bear against them. When such medieval devices as the battering ram and catapult gave way to heavy ARTILLERY, the besiegers gained a great advantage. Nevertheless, sieges could still become prolonged struggles in which defenders were eventually overcome less by force of arms than by lack of supplies. Notable sieges include those of SYRACUSE (212 BC), LENINGRAD (1941–43), DIENBIENPHU (1954), and BEIRUT (1982).

**Siegfried** or **Sigurd** (‚seegfreed, ‚sigooəd), folk hero of early and medieval Germanic mythology. His legend, important in several epics, recounts his killing of the dragon Fafnir, his marriage to GUDRUN (or Kriemhild), his love and betrayal of BRUNHILD, and his death. See NIBELUNGEN; WAGNER.

**Siemens, Ernst Werner von,** 1816–92, German electrical engineer. He developed a seamless covering process for electric cables using gutta-percha and together with instrument-maker Johan Halske founded the firm of Siemens–Halske, one of the largest electrical engineering companies in the world. The company was responsible for the growth of the telegraph throughout Europe and, after developing underwater cables, laid the London–Calcutta line in 1870. Siemens's most important discovery was the self-exciting dynamo in 1867, which immediately went into commercial production for lighting and generation of electricity in general. He also developed electric traction and demonstrated it in 1879. With his brother, **Sir (Charles) William Siemens**, 1823–83, he invented and developed electro-gold plating. William, b. Karl Wilhelm Siemens, visited England in 1843 and started a British company manufacturing electrical apparatus, including electric trams. It also designed the steamship *Faraday* as an ocean-going cable-laying ship, and in 1867 amalgamated with his brother Ernst's German firm. William, who became a British citizen in 1859, was made a fellow of the ROYAL SOCIETY in 1862 and was knighted in 1883. With his brother Frederick, he developed a regenerative furnace that was the prototype for the open-hearth steelmaking process.

**Siena**, city (1983 pop. 61,337), in TUSCANY, central Italy. It is a tourist centre and is known for its wine and marble. Of ancient origin, it was a free commune by the 12th cent. and grew into a wealthy republic. It fell to Emperor CHARLES V in 1555 and then passed to the MEDICI. Siena's artistic fame is tied to the work of the Sienese school (13th–14th cent.), represented by such painters as DUCCIO, Simone MARTINI, and the LORENZETTI brothers. Siena is noted for its medieval town square, the Piazza del Campo, and such buildings as the Gothic Palazzo Pubblico, the Mangia tower, and the Gothic cathedral.

**Sienkiewicz, Henryk** (shen,kyeveech), 1846–1916, Polish novelist and short-story writer. His best-known historical novel, *Quo Vadis?*, concerns Christianity in NERO's time. His trilogy *With Fire and Sword* (1883), *The Deluge* (1886), and *Pan Michael* (1887–88) deals with the fight for Polish independence. He was awarded the 1905 Nobel Prize for literature.

**Sierra Leone**, officially Republic of Sierra Leone, republic (1985 est. pop. 3,517,530), 71,740 km² (27,699 sq mi), W Africa, bordered by the Atlantic Ocean (W), Guinea (N and E), and Liberia (S). FREETOWN is the capital. The 560-km (350-mi) Atlantic coastline is made up of a belt of low-lying mangrove swamps, except for the mountainous Sierra Leone Peninsula (site of Freetown), and has some wide, sandy beaches. The eastern half of the country is mostly mountainous, rising to 1948 m (6390 ft). Sierra Leone's economy is predominantly agricultural; two thirds of the people are engaged in mostly subsistence farming. Cocoa, coffee, and palm kernels are the leading cash crops, and large numbers of livestock and poultry are raised. Minerals are the main source of income; diamonds (which account for more than half of export revenue), bauxite, iron ore, and rutile (titanium mineral) are the most important. Diamond production fell sharply during the 1970s, and iron-ore mining was halted in 1975 for five years. The tourist industry is growing rapidly, and new hotels are being built in the Freetown area. Fishing is also becoming more important. Manufacturing is limited mainly to agricultural processsing and consumer goods. The GNP is US$1231 million, and the GNP per capita is US$350 (1985). The great majority of the people are black Africans, mainly the Mende and the Temne, who follow traditional beliefs; there are Muslim and Christian minorities. English is the official language, but indigenous tongues are also spoken.

*History.* The Temne were living along the coast when the Portuguese landed in 1460 on the Sierra Leone Peninsula, which, after c.1500, was the scene of European trading in ivory, timber, and small numbers of slaves. Mande-speaking people from present-day Liberia moved into the region in the mid–16th cent. and later established four Mende states. An attempt to resettle freed slaves on the peninsula failed in 1787, but in 1792 about 1100 freed slaves from Nova Scotia founded Freetown. The new colony was controlled by a private company and had little contact with the interior. Britain took over Freetown in 1808, and during the next half century about 50,000 liberated slaves were settled there. In order to forestall French ambitions in the region, the British established a protectorate over the interior in 1896. After World War II, black Africans were given some political power, but the Creoles, who were descendants of freed slaves living in Freetown, were largely excluded from the government. Independence came in 1961 (when Sierra Leone became a member of the COMMONWEALTH), with Milton Margai (a Mende) as prime minister. Siaka Stevens, leader of a Temne-based party, took office in

1967 but was immediately ousted in a military coup. He returned to power in 1968, after another army revolt. In 1971 Sierra Leone became a republic, with Stevens as president. The early 1970s were marked by considerable unrest, and troops from Guinea were brought in to support the regime. Stevens succeeded in creating a one-party state under a new 1978 constitution, his All-People's Congress becoming the sole legal party; however, student and workers' protests continued into the 1980s. In presidential elections in 1985 Maj.-Gen. Joseph Saidu Momoh, the sole candidate, was returned as Stevens's favoured sucessor.

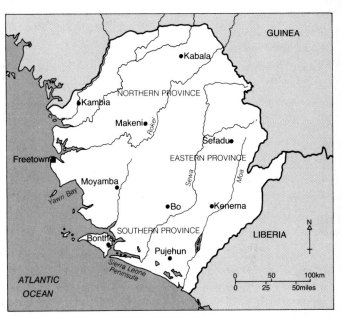

Sierra Leone

**Sierra Madre**, rugged mountain system of Mexico, mostly between 1800 and 3600 m (6000 and 12,000 ft) and rising to a high point of 5700 m (18,700 ft) at the inactive volcano ORIZABA. The system includes the Sierra Madre Oriental (E), the Sierra Madre Occidental (W), and the Sierra Madre del Sur (S), which together form the dissected edges of the central Mexican plateau. The mountains are rich in silver, gold, and other minerals.

**Sierra Nevada**, mountain range, US, c.640 km (400 mi) long and up to 130 km (80 mi) wide, mostly in E California. Known for its spectacular scenery, especially in the High Sierras. The range reaches its highest point (4418 m/14,495 ft) at Mt WHITNEY.

**Sieyès, Emmanuel Joseph** (syah,yes), 1748–1836, French statesman. Before the FRENCH REVOLUTION he was a clergyman known as Abbé Sieyès. Elected (1789) to the STATES-GENERAL, he helped to write the Declaration of the Rights of Man and Citizen and the constitution of 1791. By prudent silence, he lived through the REIGN OF TERROR, and in 1799 he entered the DIRECTORY, which he helped NAPOLEON to topple later that year. After the Bourbon restoration, he lived in exile (1816–30) in Brussels.

**Sigismund**, 1368–1437, Holy Roman emperor (1433–37), German king (1411–37), king of Hungary (1387–1437) and of Bohemia (1419–37). His election as German king was initially contested by his half brother, the former German king, WENCESLAUS. Sigismund backed Baldassarre COSSA (John XXIII), the strongest of the schismatic popes, in the Council of Constance that ended (1417) the Great SCHISM. After the conference, Sigismund secured the condemnation and burning of John HUSS, despite his promise to Huss of a safe conduct. As a result, his assuming the Bohemian crown in 1419 set off the HUSSITE Wars. His reign was one of constant turmoil, including recurring attacks by the Turks in Hungary. He was the last emperor of the LUXEMBOURG dynasty.

**Sigismund**, Polish kings. **Sigismund I**, 1467–1548, king of POLAND (1506–48), was the son of CASIMIR IV. He established a regular army and allied himself with Holy Roman Emperor MAXIMILIAN I as protection against Russia. By the double marriage of the children of his brother, Ladislaus II of Bohemia and Hungary, with the grandchildren of Maximilian, Bohemia and Hungary later passed (1526) to the Habsburgs. His son, **Sigismund II** or **Sigismund Augustus**, 1520–72, king of Poland (1548–72), created (1569) a unified commonwealth out of the Polish and Lithuanian states, and acquired Courland and parts of Livonia. He halted the spread of Protestantism by peaceful means and by encouraging Catholic reform. **Sigismund III**, 1566–1632, king of Poland (1587–1632) and king of Sweden (1592–99), was the son of John III of Sweden and Catherine, sister of Sigismund II of Poland. A Roman Catholic, he was opposed by the Protestant party in Sweden and was deposed by his uncle, who ruled as CHARLES IX. Between 1600 and 1629 Sigismund attempted to reclaim his Swedish claims. He intervened in Russia by supporting the pretender DMITRI, but his army was expelled from Russia in 1612.

**Signac, Paul** (see nyahk), 1863–1935, French painter. Signac was a follower of Seurat and painted luminous sea and harbour scenes with broader strokes. His works include *Port of St Tropez* (1916; Brooklyn Mus., New York City).

**signalling, railway,** the various systems to ensure that trains operate safely on railways. As railway traffic grew, the rather haphazard arrangements for controlling traffic such as allowing a certain time-interval between departing trains were replaced by mechanical signalling which allowed a train into a certain block of track only when the preceding train had left it. A further significant development was the invention of interlocking by John Saxby in 1856, which connected switches and signals in such a way as to prevent collisions. Such arrangements have contributed greatly to the railway's position as one of the safest modes of transport. Mechanical signalling has been supplanted by colour light signalling and the interlocking and control is increasingly being carried out by solid-state electronics and computers. In the future, traffic will be managed by centralized computer control in which there is direct and continuous communication between train and control centre.

**significance, test of,** used in STATISTICS to distinguish between events which occur according to some prescribed hypothesis and those which are due to chance. The theory of statistics provides tests which are appropriate to the kind of hypothesis being tested and the ways in which the data have been collected. As a result of such a test, a statistician will often describe a result as 'statistically significant' meaning that there is only a small probability (often 5%) that such a result could have occurred by chance.

**sign language,** a method of communication for the deaf. It was developed in France in the 18th cent. and has since been expanded and refined, especially in the US and UK. More generally, sign language can mean a substitute for, or addition to, the spoken language often used when communicating emotions or managing an immediate social situation. Where speech is impossible, systems of gestures are often developed, e.g., on racecourses, between divers, among Trappist monks. Some Australian aboriginal tribes have developed a gesture language which enables rapid communication in certain ritual situations.

**Signorelli, Luca,** fl. 1470?–1523, Italian painter of the Umbrian school. MICHELANGELO was influenced by his powerful treatment of anatomy and his vivid, dramatic realism. His apocalyptic series decorating the Cappella Nuova in the Orvieto Cathedral (1499–1502) includes *Story of the Anti-Christ, End of the World, Paradise,* and *Inferno.* The infernal scenes are remarkable for their evocation of fiends and the tortures of Hell.

**Sigurd:** see SIEGFRIED.

**Sigurjónsson Jóhann,** 1880–1919, Icelandic playwright and poet. He was the first Iclandic writer in modern times to gain international recognition. He wrote simultaneously in Danish and Icelandic, and used Icelandic folk tales for his most famous plays: *Eyvind of the Hills* (1911) and *Galdra-Loftur* (1915, tr. as *Loftur* in 1939 and again as *The Wish* in 1967). As a lyric poet he brought symbolism and modernism to Iceland.

**Sikhs,** a theistic sect established by Guru Nanak in the 15th cent. The Sikhs developed as a flourishing community in the Punjab and clashed with the Mughal emperors. Successive gurus, spiritual-cum-political leaders, led the struggle and the 10th guru, Govind Singh, organized the community's fighting militia, the Khalsa. In the 19th cent., Ranjit Singh established a Sikh kingdom which was annexed by the British after his death. The Sikhs are a thriving community in independent India. A section of Sikhs began a campaign of terror in support of their demand for an autonomous state, 'Khalistan', leading to an Indian army attack (1984) on the Golden Temple, Amritsar, used by the terrorists as a haven. Later the same year the Indian prime minister Indira GANDHI was assassinated by a Sikh. The unresolved problem of Sikh terrorism remains a major threat to the stability of India.

**Sikh Wars** (1845–49), two conflicts preceding the British annexation of the PUNJAB. In 1845, fearing British intentions, the SIKHS crossed the Sutlej R. and attacked British troops S of the Punjab. They were defeated by the British and forced to cede KASHMIR, pay a large indemnity, and accept a British protectorate. In 1848, a Sikh uprising resulted in another full-scale war; at its end the victorious British annexed all Sikh territory.

**Sikkim,** state (1981 pop. 316,385), 7096 km² (2740 sq mi), NE India, bordered by Nepal (W), the Tibet region of China (N), and Bhutan (E). The capital is Gangtok. Located in the E HIMALAYAS, most of Sikkim is mountainous. Rice, maize, and millets are the principal crops. The people are predominantly of Nepalese extraction; Buddhism is the state religion, but the majority of the population is Hindu. In 1642 a Tibetan king started a hereditary line of Sikkimese rulers that lasted until 1975. Sikkim had a 'special protected relationship' with the British from 1890 to 1947, a relationship taken over by India after its independence. In 1975 the Sikkimese voted to abolish the monarchy and to become the 22nd state of India.

**Sikorski, Wladyslaw,** 1881–1943, Polish, soldier and statesman. After fighting in the POLISH LEGIONS in WORLD WAR I, Sikorski became prime minister of the newly restored state (1922). His uneasy relations with Marshal PILSUDSKI led to the interruption of his career following the *coup d'état* in 1926; he went to France. In 1939, following the German and Soviet attacks on Poland and the internment of the Polish Government in Romania, Sikorski became prime minister and commander-in-chief once again, this time of the exiled Polish government, first in France and then in London (from June 1940). He died in an air crash at Gibraltar in July 1943.

**Sikorsky, Igor Ivan,** 1889–1972, American aeronautical engineer; b. Russia. He built and flew the first four-engined aeroplane (1913), and bombers of his design were used by the Russian Army in World War I. Sikorsky left Russia after the Revolution and arrived in the US in 1919, where he established an aircraft factory and produced successful amphibians and flying boats. He built the first practical HELICOPTER, which he flew himself on 14 Sept. 1939. His helicopters were the only ones used by the US in World War II, and have continued to be very successful.

**Silbury Hill,** a late NEOLITHIC mound near AVEBURY in S England, the largest in Europe. The hill was built in several stages, resulting in a mound 40 m (130 ft) high covering about 2 hectares (5 acres). No evidence of burial or other use for the site has been discovered, but it may be associated with ritual activities similar to those of the large MEGALITHIC MONUMENTS of the same period.

**silenus,** in Greek mythology, part bestial, part human creature of forests and mountains. Followers of DIONYSUS, the sileni are usually represented as aged SATYRS. In some legends Silenus is the oldest satyr, the son of HERMES or PAN, and the companion, adviser, or tutor of Dionysus.

**Silesia,** region of E central Europe, extending along both banks of the Oder R. and bounded in the south by the Sudetes Mts. Most of Silesia is in Poland, a much smaller part in Czechoslovakia, and a tiny area in East Germany. WROCLAW is among the chief cities. Silesia is largely agricultural and forested. The most important part is Upper Silesia, in Poland, one of the largest industrial concentrations in Europe, with extensive deposits of coal, lignite, and other resources. Austria ceded (1742) most of Silesia to Prussia during the war of the AUSTRIAN SUCCESSION. After WORLD WAR I the region was partitioned among Germany, Poland, and Czechoslovakia. The MUNICH PACT (1938) divided most of Czechoslovak Silesia between Germany and Poland, and during WORLD WAR II Germany occupied (1939–45) Polish Silesia. After the war Poland annexed most of German Silesia and expelled the German residents.

**silhouette,** outline image, especially a solidly filled-in profile drawing or cutout pasted against a lighter background. Silhouette drawings were very popular in late-18th-cent. Europe, replacing miniatures at French and German courts. Profile portraits and silhouette illustrations abounded in 19th-cent. England and America. Silhouette drawings decreased in popularity after the invention of the daguerreotype (see DAGUERRE).

**silica** or **silicon dioxide,** chemical compound ($SiO_2$). It is widely and abundantly distributed throughout the earth, both in the pure state (colourless to white) and in silicates (e.g., QUARTZ, OPAL, SAND, SANDSTONE, CLAY, GRANITE); in skeletal parts of various plants and animals, such as certain protozoa and DIATOMS; and in the stems and other tissue of higher plants. Because silica has a low thermal coefficient of expansion, it is used in objects subjected to wide ranges of heat and cold. Unlike ordinary glass, it does not absorb infrared and ultraviolet light.

**silicon** (Si), nonmetallic element, discovered by Jöns Jakob BERZELIUS in 1824. Silicon has brown amorphous and dark crystalline allotropic forms. The second most abundant element (28% by weight) of the earth's crust, it occurs in compound form as SILICA, SILICON CARBIDE, and silicates. Silicon adds strength to alloys, and is used in transistors and other semiconductor devices. It is found in many plants and animals. See ELEMENT (table); PERIODIC TABLE.

**silicon carbide,** chemical compound (SiC) occurring as hard, dark iridescent crystals that are heat resistant, and insoluble in water and other common solvents. It is used as an ABRASIVE, in refractory materials, and in special parts for nuclear reactors. Silicon carbide fibres impart increased strength and stiffness to plastics and light metals.

**silicon dioxide:** see SILICA.

**silicone,** POLYMER in which atoms of SILICON and OXYGEN alternate in a chain; bound to the silicon atoms are various organic groups, e.g., the methyl group ($CH_3$). Silicones may be liquid, RUBBER, RESIN, or grease. Water repellent, chemically inert, and stable at extreme temperatures, silicones are used as protective coatings and electrical insulators.

**Silius Italicus** (Tiberius Catius Asconius Silius Italicus), AD 26–101, Latin EPIC poet. His PUNIC WARS in 17 books is the longest extant Latin epic. It was written after his retirement from public life, and is not, on the whole, an inspired work, but it shows the influence of VIRGIL.

**silk,** fibre produced by the SILKWORM in making its cocoon, or textiles woven from such fibre. Legend has it that sericulture (the raising of silkworms) began in China in 2640 BC. Raw silk was exported, but the export of silkworm eggs was punishable by death. Silkworm eggs and seeds of the mulberry tree, on which the worm feeds, were supposedly smuggled to Istanbul (Constantinople) in AD c.550; thereafter the city was famed for its silk textiles. In the 8th cent. the Moors brought sericulture and silk weaving to Spain and Sicily, where exquisite silk fabrics were being woven by the 12th cent. Italy developed great silk-weaving centres in Lucca, Florence, and Venice in the 13th and 14th cent. The French city of Lyons became a weaving centre in the 15th cent. In 1685 HUGUENOTS fleeing France after the revocation of the Edict of Nantes brought the art to England, where it became centred at Spitalfields, in London. In the American colonies, attempts to establish sericulture ultimately failed. The Asian *Bombyx mori,* which feeds on mulberry leaves, produces the finest silk and is thus the most widely raised silkworm. Wild silk is made by the tussah worm of India and China, which feeds on oak leaves. Silk manufacture begins with the reeling (unwinding) of the silk from the cocoons. In throwing, the raw silk is twisted and doubled to achieve various strengths and thicknesses. The silk is boiled in soap to remove the natural gum, then bleached or dyed. It is woven on delicate specialized looms to produce a wide variety of fabrics, e.g., taffeta, faille, velvet, crepe. Modern silk production is highly mechanized, but the finest fabrics are still handwoven.

**silkmoth** large to very large (wingspan 50–250 mm/2–10 in) MOTH whose larva spins a cocoon of SILK in which to pupate. The most important group of silkmoths are the Bombycidae to which *Bombyx mori* the SILKWORM moth belongs. There is only one British silkmoth, the Emperor *Saturnia pavonia,* which has conspicuous eyespots on fore and hindwings to deter predators.

**silk-screen printing,** multiple PRINTING technique, also called serigraphy, involving the use of stencils. Paint is applied to a fabric mesh screen, penetrating areas not blocked by a stencil. Several stencils are used to produce a multicoloured print. As a commercial medium, silk-screen printing has been used by such modern artists as Andy WARHOL.

**silkworm,** the principal producer of natural SILK, a pale grey, hairless caterpillar with a characteristic posterior horn, the larva of the MOTH *Bombyx mori.* This originally Chinese species was domesticated over 4000 years ago and a wild form no longer exists. Silkworms are fed on mulberry leaves, and complete their growth in about 45 days, by which

time they are some 75 mm (3 in) long. Before pupating they spin a cocoon of white or yellow silk using a fine double filament some 900 m (980 yd) long. The term silkworm is occasionally used for the larvae of semidomesticated species that produce coarser silks such as shantung (e.g., oak silkmoths, *Antheraea pernyi* and *A. yamamai*).

Silkworm larvae

**Sillanpää, Frans Eemil** (ˌsillampah), 1888–1964, Finnish novelist, the foremost Finnish writer of his time. His works include *Meek Heritage* (1919), about the Finnish civil war, and *The Maid Silja* (1931), about the collapse of old values. He received the 1939 Nobel Prize for literature.

**Silone, Ignazio** (seeˌlohnay), 1900–78, Italian novelist and political activist; b. Secondo Tranquilli. An anti-Fascist, he broke with the Communist Party in 1931 and lived in exile until 1944. His writings, which typically highlight oppression in the Italian South, are directed to promoting socialism as an integral Christianity. They include the novels *Fontamara* (1933), *Pane e vino* (1937; tr. Bread and Wine), and *A Handful of Blackberries* (1952).

**silt,** mostly QUARTZ mineral particles that are between SAND and CLAY in size and are formed by WEATHERING and decomposition of preexisting rock. Hardened silt becomes a sedimentary rock called siltstone.

**Silurian period:** see GEOLOGICAL ERAS (table).

**Silva, Antonio José da,** (ˌseelva), 1705–39, Portuguese dramatist; b. Brazil. Of his vigorous satirical plays, *Wars of Rosemary and Marjoram* (1737) is considered the best. He and his family, Jews converted by force, were convicted by the INQUISITION of secretly practicing Judaism and burned at the stake.

**Silva, José Asunción** (ˌsilvah), 1865–96, Colombian poet. One of the creators of MODERNISMO, he committed suicide at 31, despondent over his debts, the death of a sister, and the loss of a manuscript at sea just before its publication. His poems, collected after his death, include 'Nocturno III', an elegy for his sister, and 'Crespúsculo'.

**silver** (Ag), metallic element, one of the first metals used by humans. Pure silver is nearly white, lustrous, soft, very ductile, malleable, and an excellent conductor of heat and electricity. It is used in mirrors, coins, utensils, antiseptics, jewellery, and for electrolytic plating of tableware (see SILVERWORK). Silver nitrate is the most importance compound. Silver reacts with hydrogen sulphide in air to form silver sulphide (tarnish). Photographic emulsions contain silver halides, because of their sensitivity to light. Silver alloys are used in dentistry and electrical contacts. Sterling silver contains 92.5% silver and 7.5% copper. Silver is obtained from the ores argentite, cerarygrite, pyrargyrite, stephanite, and proustite. See ELEMENT (table); PERIODIC TABLE.

**Silver, Arthur,** 1853–96, British textile designer. His design studio (est. 1880) produced almost 30,000 designs, mostly for furnishing textiles and wallpaper but also for dress fabrics, metal work, furniture, book jackets, interiors, and advertisements. He worked very closely with LIBERTY's and other major British firms, as well as exporting designs to France and the US.

**silverfish,** primitive wingless INSECT, *Lepisma saccharina* (order Thysanura), whose spindle-shaped body, some 12 mm (½ in) long, is covered with silvery scales. This and several related species (e.g., firebrat)

Example of a Liberty print designed by Arthur **Silver**

occur indoors in many countries and destroy bookbindings and wallpaper through eating the starch content.

Silverfish

**silversides:** see WHITEBAIT.

**silverwork,** articles made of silver or silver-plated metal, for religious, martial, mint, domestic, utilitarian, or decorative purposes. Silver is a precious metal, highly reflective, malleable, ductile, a good conductor with a low melting point, and as such is ideal for hand and machine production. Pure silver, too soft for most purposes, is alloyed with copper, and may be given a HALLMARK if to the legal standard. The metal may be cast, rolled, drawn, cut, and soldered, hammered into form, stamped, chased, pierced, inlaid, engraved, and enamelled, and these techniques were highly developed in antiquity. Minted silver coins have been in circulation since the time of the Phoenicians. Modern technology includes electrolytic plating processes, and use in electronics and research. Due to oxidization, silver is not as durable as gold, but artifacts have survived in tombs of the ancient Chaldean and Egyptian civilizations, and from the Classical periods of Greece and Rome, giving insight into religious and domestic life, while recent finds in Bulgaria show exquisite work from archaic Thrace. Synonymous with wealth and privilege, silver could be traded widely, as by the Phoenicians, or reserved exclusively, as by the Incas, for ritual and high rank. Techniques were held secret by craft communities throughout the world, and continue in India, where the ancient designs are still chiselled, pierced, and filigreed, in near-pure metal. In the Americas, the indigenous peoples formed similar communities, and are noted for inlay and advanced casting techniques. Comparable skills developed in the Far East and in China. In

Northern Europe, the Celtic and Germanic tribes held the silversmith in high esteem; through the purity of their coinage, the Sterlings have given their name to the legal standard, while Anglo-Saxon skill is seen in the treasure of Sutton Hoo. In the following periods of war and unrest, much early work was melted down for revenue, and ecclesiastical silver was destroyed during the Reformation. However, throughout Europe, between the 15th and 18th cent., silverware became highly ornate, and in the High Renaissance, artists such as CELLINI created fine pieces. In England, the 17th cent. saw a return to more refined, simple forms which developed into the later elegance of the Georgian period. By the late 18th cent., a flourishing industry produced handsome pieces in Sheffield plate, at much less cost, using a layered copper core technique, but the later products of the Industrial Revolution, meeting demand from the new middle class, were often of a more elaborate, striking design and there was an increasing use of cheaper silver plate. Some British silversmiths in the late 19th cent. pointed the way to a revival of British silverwork, particularly after World War II.

**Silvester:** see SYLVESTER.

**Sima Qian,** 145?–90? BC, Chinese historian of the Han dynasty, called the Father of Chinese history. He wrote *Shi ji* [records of the historian], a history in 130 chapters of China and all regions and peoples known at that time. It became a model for later dynastic histories.

**Simcoe, John Graves,** 1752–1806, first British governor (1792–96) of Upper Canada (ONTARIO). To make the province a strong colony, he encouraged immigration of American Loyalists and fostered agricultural development.

**Simeon:** see ISRAEL, TRIBES OF.

**Simeon I,** c.863–927, ruler (r.893–927) and first czar (925) of Bulgaria. During his rule the first Bulgarian empire attained its greatest power. He ravaged the Byzantine Empire and conquered most of Serbia. He was a patron of culture.

**Simnel, Lambert,** c.1475–1534?, impostor and pretender to the English throne. In 1486, claiming to be Edward, earl of Warwick (who was then imprisoned in the TOWER OF LONDON), he rallied Yorkist support in Ireland and invaded England. He was defeated and captured at the battle of Stoke (1487) by the forces of HENRY VII. Simnel was later pardoned.

**Simon,** in the BIBLE. **1** One of the MACCABEES. **2** Or Simon Peter: see PETER, SAINT. **3** Saint Simon, one of the Twelve Disciples of JESUS. Feast (with St Jude): Oct. 28. **4** Simon of Cyrene, bystander made to carry Jesus' cross (Mark 15.21). He was probably an African Jew. **5** Simon Magus, Samaritan sorcerer who attempted to buy spiritual power from the apostles. From this comes the term SIMONY. Acts 8.

**Simon, Herbert Alexander,** 1916–, American social scientist. A professor at Carnegie-Mellon Univ., Simon was an early authority on uses of computers in business management. For his theories on decision making he won the 1978 Nobel Prize for economics.

**Simon, (Marvin) Neil,** 1927–, American playwright. His popular comedies of middle-class life include *Barefoot in the Park* (1963), *The Odd Couple* (1965), *Plaza Suite* (1968), and *Chapter Two* (1977). His later work includes *I Ought to be in Pictures* (1980) and *Biloxi Blues* (1984). He has also written screenplays.

**Simon, Saint,** one of the Twelve Disciples. In the Gospel he is called the Canaanite or Cananean or Zelotes, terms that may refer to an association with the fanatical sect of zealots.

**Simone Martini:** see MARTINI, SIMONE.

**Simonides of Ceos,** c.556–468? BC, Greek LYRIC poet. After the PERSIAN WARS he was a rival of PINDAR at the court of Syracuse. He wrote epigrammatic verse of many kinds. Two of his finest epitaphs are on the fallen at MARATHON and THERMOPYLAE.

**Simons, Menno:** see MENNO SIMONS.

**simony** (ˌsimǝni, ˌsie-), in CANON LAW, buying or selling of any spiritual benefit for a temporal consideration. Because of the frequency of simony in earlier ages, the traditional churches have strict laws against it; e.g., in the Roman Catholic Church simony in a papal election invalidates the election, while in the Church of England the recipient of a benefice makes a formal declaration against simony.

**simple harmonic motion:** see HARMONIC MOTION.

**Simplon,** pass, 2009 m (6590 ft) high, in the Swiss Alps near Brig, at the Swiss–Italian border. Its 19.8-km (12.3-mi) railway tunnel system is Europe's longest.

**Simpson, George Gaylord,** 1902–, American palaeontologist and zoologist. His deductions, from studies of fossil material, that species reach adaptive peaks and suffer accidental dispersion contributed greatly to the study of evolution. He held several palaeontology positions at the American Museum of Natural History (1927–59) and also taught at Columbia (1945–59) and Harvard (1959–70).

**simulation,** used in STATISTICS to indicate the use of a mathematical description of an economic, physical, chemical, social, or ecological system. Whereas MODELLING of such systems includes as little detail as possible, a good simulation should include as much detail as possible. Simulations also usually have a practical purpose as opposed to the more theoretical value of models. Simulation is now widely used in business, industry, ecology, and aeronautics to predict the behaviour of large and complicated systems. The behaviour of the equipment which took human beings to the Moon was tested by simulation and appropriate procedures for a wide variety of possible emergencies were worked out within the simulation in advance of the actual voyage.

**sin,** in religion, wrongful action in disobedience to a personal God. In ancient Israel, there were personal sin and national sin—usually idolatry. Some Christians hold that all acts are good, indifferent, or sinful, others that there are no indifferent acts. Roman Catholics are required to confess mortal sins, i.e., those committed with knowing and deliberate intent in a serious matter (see PENANCE); other sins are venial. The seven deadly sins are pride, covetousness, lust, anger, gluttony, envy, and sloth.

**Sinai,** triangular peninsula, c.59,570 km² (23,000 sq mi), NE Egypt, between the SUEZ CANAL and Gulf of Suez (W) and the Gulf of AQABA and Strait of Tiran (E). The peninsula, which has a very hot and dry climate, rises to over 2590 m (8500 ft) in the south, where Moses is said to have received the Ten Commandments, and is level and sandy in the north. Some oil is produced adjacent to the Gulf of Suez. Israeli troops occupied the Sinai briefly in 1956 and again from 1967 to 1980–82, when they effected a phased, two-year withdrawal under the terms of the CAMP DAVID ACCORDS (1978) and the Egyptian-Israeli peace treaty (1979).

**Sinanthropus:** see HOMO ERECTUS.

**Sinatra, Frank** (Francis Albert Sinatra), 1915–, American singer and actor. He gained great popularity in the late 1930s with his romantic, casual renditions of songs such as 'I'll Never Smile Again'. He has appeared in many films, e.g., *From Here to Eternity* (1953).

**Sinclair, Upton,** 1878–1968, American novelist. An ardent socialist, he was deeply involved in politics, and his interest in social and industrial reform underlies most of his over 80 books. Sinclair's novels include *The Jungle* (1906), a brutally graphic account of the Chicago stockyards; *King Coal* (1917); *Oil!* (1927); and *Little Steel* (1938). He also wrote a cycle of 11 novels dealing with world events from 1914 that feature Lanny Budd as hero.

**Sindhi** (ˌsindee), language belonging to the Indic group of the Indo-Iranian subfamily of the Indo-European family of languages. See LANGUAGE (table).

**Singapore,** officially the Republic of Singapore, republic (1985 est. pop. 2,558,000), 620 km² (239 sq mi), SE Asia, S of the Malay Peninsula, comprising Singapore Island and 57 islets. The capital, Singapore city, is one of the world's largest and busiest ports. Singapore island is largely low-lying and fringed by mangrove swamps; it has a tropical rain-forest climate. Singapore is one of the world's great commercial centres; the economy is supported primarily by manufacturing, service industries, and trade; shipbuilding is also important. Agriculture plays a minor role, and the country imports most of its food. The GNP is US$18,390 million (1984), and the GNP per capita is US$6842 (1984). The predominantly urban population is mainly Chinese; Malays and Indians constitute large minorities. Buddhism, Islam, Hinduism, and Christianity are the major religions. Malay, Chinese, Tamil, and English are the official languages. *History.* Singapore was a sparsely populated island when it was purchased by the British East India Company in 1819 through the efforts of Sir Thomas Stamford RAFFLES. Ceded to Britain in 1824, it became (1826) part of the STRAITS SETTLEMENTS colony. After occupation by the Japanese in

WORLD WAR II, Singapore became a British crown colony in 1946 and a self-governing state in 1959. Under Lee Kuan Yew, the first prime minister, Singapore underwent economic development and modernization. It joined Malaya, SARAWAK, and SABAH in the Federation of MALAYSIA in 1963 but withdrew in 1965. Lee Kuan Yew's People's Action Party (PAP) has continued in power, despite growing opposition and charges of government repression. In the 1988 general elections the opposition won only one seat against 80 for the PAP.

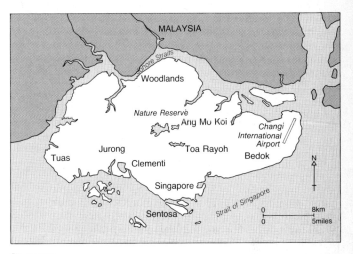

Singapore

**Singapore,** city (1974 pop. 1,327,500), capital of SINGAPORE.

**Singer, Isaac Bashevis,** 1904–, American Yiddish author; b. Poland. He went to the US in 1935. Perhaps the greatest of the Yiddish writers based in New York City, he frequently treats the loneliness of old age and the Jewish sense of alienation. His characters are often tormented by demons, as in the novel *Satan in Goray* (1955). Singer has written many novels, short stories, e.g., *The Collected Stories of Isaac Bashevis Singer* (1981), plays and children's books. He was awarded the 1978 Nobel Prize in literature. His brother, **Israel Joshua Singer,** 1893–1944, b. Poland, emigrated to the US in 1934. He also wrote in Yiddish. His epic novel, *The Brothers Ashkenazi* (1936), is about Jewish industrialism.

**Singer, Isaac Merritt,** 1811–75, American inventor. He patented a practical SEWING MACHINE (1851) that could do continuous stitching, and made 20 subsequent improvements (1851–65). Although he lost a patent infringement suit to Elias HOWE in 1854, his company was so well established that it was able to continue manufacturing machines and took the lead in a subsequent combination of products and pooling of patents.

**Sinhalese** (ˌsingəˈleez), language belonging to the Indic group of the Indo-Iranian subfamily of the Indo-European family of languages. See LANGUAGE (table).

**Sinkiang:** see XINJIANG.

**Sinn Fein** (shin fayn), [Irish, = we ourselves], Irish nationalistic movement that triumphed in the establishment of the Irish Free State (see IRELAND). Organized (1905) by Arthur GRIFFITH, an advocate of an economically and politically self-sufficient Ireland, it adopted passive resistance to the British, but gained little support before World War I. The British suppression of the Easter Rebellion (1916) greatly stimulated Sinn Fein's growth, and it was reorganized in 1917 under the leadership of Eamon DE VALERA. It set up an Irish assembly called the Dáil Éireann that declared Irish independence. The resulting disorders were countered violently by British military irregulars known as Black and Tans, but continued resistance led ultimately to the establishment (1922) of the Irish Free State. Sinn Fein virtually came to an end after De Valera withdrew (1927) and entered the Irish Dáil with the new FIANNA FÁIL party. A few intransigents merged with the IRISH REPUBLICAN ARMY, whose political arm is still known as the Sinn Fein.

**Sino-Japanese War, Second,** 1937–45. Japan used the Manchurian Incident—the bombing (1931) of a Japanese railway in Manchuria—as a pretext for occupying Manchuria and establishing the puppet state of Manchukuo. In 1933 and 1935 the Japanese won further concessions, and full war erupted after a clash (July 1937) between Japanese and Chinese forces in Beijing. The Japanese soon occupied Beijing and Tientsin and, after a protracted struggle, took Shanghai and the national capital, Nanking. In late 1938 Hankou and Guangzhou fell. The Nationalist government was driven back to a temporary capital at Chongqing, and despite vast and bloody fighting its cause continued to decline. The Japanese attack (1941) on PEARL HARBOR merged the Sino-Japanese War with WORLD WAR II. Allied aid and advisers provided some relief, but China's military position deteriorated until Apr. 1945. After Japan's capitulation, Japanese troops in China formally surrendered (9 Sept. 1945). Manchuria was restored to China, as were Taiwan and the Pescadores, which Japan had received after the First Sino-Japanese War (1894–95).

**Sino-Tibetan languages,** family of languages spoken in central and SE Asia. See LANGUAGE (table).

**sintering,** process of forming objects by heating a metal powder. When the metal powder is chemically or mechanically produced, compacted into the desired shape, and heated, the powder particles join together to form a solid object.

**sinus,** cavity or hollow space in the body, usually filled with air or blood. In humans, the paranasal sinuses, mucous-lined cavities in the bones of the face, are connected by passageways to the nose and probably help to warm and moisten inhaled air. Sinusitis is often caused by infection spreading from the nose and may require surgical treatment.

**Sion:** see ZION.

**Sioux Indians** or **Dakota Indians,** confederation of seven NORTH AMERICAN INDIAN tribes, the dominant group of the Hokan-Siouan stock (see AMERICAN INDIAN LANGUAGES). They had a typical Plains culture, including buffalo hunts and the SUN DANCE. In the mid-18th cent. the 30,000 Sioux inhabited the N Great Plains and the western prairies. The Sioux sided with the British in the AMERICAN REVOLUTION and the WAR OF 1812. They later made treaties with the US, but some Sioux revolted (1862) and massacred 800 whites. By a treaty of 1867 the Sioux agreed to retire to a Dakota reservation. When gold was found in the BLACK HILLS, an influx of prospectors precipitated Sioux resistance under such chiefs as SITTING BULL, RED CLOUD, and CRAZY HORSE. Gen. George CUSTER was defeated (1876) and his troops massacred at the Battle of the Little Bighorn. In 1890, 200 Sioux were killed at WOUNDED KNEE. Sioux and other supporters of the AMERICAN INDIAN MOVEMENT in 1973 besieged Wounded Knee to protest US neglect of Indian civil rights. The Sioux today are mostly farmers and ranchers. In 1979 they were awarded $105 million for the taking of their lands, resolving a legal action begun in 1923.

**Siqueiros, David Alfaro** (see ˌkayrohs), 1896–1974, Mexican painter. His art was generally related to his socialist revolutionary activities. Siqueiros's paintings convey violent social protest through dynamic brushwork, dramatic contrasts in light and shade, and heroic themes. Among his best-known works are murals at the National Preparatory School (1922–24) and at the Polytechnic Institute (1952), both in Mexico City.

**Siren,** in Greek mythology, one of three sea nymphs, whose song lured men to shipwreck on the rocky coast where they lived. ODYSSEUS escaped them by tying himself to a mast and stopping his men's ears; the Argonauts were saved by ORPHEUS's music.

**sirenian:** see SEA COW.

**sisal hemp,** important cordage fibre obtained from the leaves of several species of agave, of the AMARYLLIS family, and from related genera. The fibre, used especially for twine and considered second in strength to MANILA HEMP, is obtained chiefly from the true sisal (*Agave sisalana*) and henequen (*A. fourcroydes*).

**Sisley, Alfred,** 1839–99, French painter. Sisley, an IMPRESSIONIST landscape painter, was influenced by MONET; but his pictures, many of the quiet villages beside the Seine, are less brilliantly coloured than Monet's and depend on the subtlety and delicacy of his response to changing light. His best-known works are a series of pictures of the floods at Port Marly.

**Sistine Chapel** [for Sixtus IV], private chapel of the VATICAN. Built (1473) for Pope SIXTUS IV, it is world famous for its decorations. Frescoes by PERUGINO, BOTTICELLI, GHIRLANDAIO, and others are on the side walls. The best known, however, are MICHELANGELO's paintings on the ceiling of scenes from the Bible. Below these are his figures of the prophets and

Alfred **Sisley,** *Flood at Port Marly.* Musée d'Orsay, Paris.

sibyls, all prefiguring the salvation of Christianity. His awesome *Last Judgment* is on the altar wall. The chapel also has a notable collection of illuminated music manuscripts.

**Sisyphus** (ˌsisifəs), in Greek mythology, founder and king of CORINTH. Angered by his disrespect, ZEUS condemned him to push a heavy rock up a steep hill eternally.

**Sitka,** US city (1980 pop. 7,803), SE Alaska, in the Alexander Archipelago, on Baranof Island; inc. 1971. Fishing, canning, timber, and pulp-processing are its industries. Sitka was founded (1799) by Aleksander Baranof; after 1802 it became the capital of Russian America. A decisive battle between the Russians and the TLINGIT INDIANS occurred there in 1804, commemorated in the Sitka National Historical Park. In the city in 1867 the US officially took possession of Alaska, and it remained the Alaskan capital until 1900.

**Sitting Bull,** c.1831–90, SIOUX INDIAN chief and victor in the battle of the Little Bighorn (1876) against George Armstrong CUSTER. He and his followers fled to Canada, were promised a pardon, and returned (1881) to the reservation. He appeared (1885) in BUFFALO BILL's Wild West Show but encouraged the Sioux to refuse to sell their land and advocated the Ghost Dance religion (see PAIUTE INDIANS). He was killed by Indian police for allegedly resisting arrest.

**Sitwell, Dame Edith,** (1887–1964), English poet and critic. A member of a well-known literary family and a noted eccentric and wit, she wrote critical essays, biographies, and poetry influenced by the French SYMBOLISTS, which appeared in many volumes, including *Collected Poems* (1954). Her *Façade,* an entertainment in abstract, rhythmic verse, with music by William WALTON, was first performed in 1922. Her two brothers were the author **Sir Osbert Sitwell** (1892–1969), and the art critic **Sacheverell Sitwell** (1897–).

**SI units:** METRIC SYSTEM.

**Śiva** or **Shiva,** one of the major gods of HINDUISM; in the Hindu trinity he represents the force of destruction and cosmic dissolution (see also BRAHMĀ; VIṢṆU). In TANTRA, he is regarded as the Supreme Lord, and his creative energy is represented by Śakti (often a female divinity). Śiva-ism or Saivism is one of the two main components of sectarian HINDUISM.

**Sivaji,** 1627–80, Indian ruler, leader of the MAHRATTAS. He succeeded in carving out a considerable domain at the cost of the Mughal empire and the Bijapur sultanate. In 1674 he crowned himself king of the Mahratta empire.

**Sivas,** city (1980 pop. 172,864), capital of Sivas prov., central Anatolia, Turkey. It is an important route centre and has food-processing industries related to its regional agriculture. Known originally as Sebaste, it flourished under Seljuk rule and has inherited fine relics of medieval Moslem art.

**six, les,** a group of young French composers HONEGGER, MILHAUD, POULENC, Georges Auric, Louis Durey, and Germaine Tailleferre who in 1918–19 joined Eric SATIE in reacting against the impressionism of DEBUSSY and RAVEL. Their literary prophet was Jean COCTEAU.

**Six-Day War:** see ARAB–ISRAELI WARS.

**Six Nations:** see IROQUOIS CONFEDERACY.

**sixth-generation computers:** see COMPUTER GENERATIONS.

**Sixtus IV**, 1414–84, pope (1471–84), an Italian named Francesco della Rovere, a Franciscan. He struggled with LOUIS XI of France over control of the French church and Louis's attempt to interfere in Naples. A quarrel with the MEDICI family of Florence became critical after Sixtus's nephew conspired to overthrow the Medici in the so-called Pazzi Conspiracy (1478). Sixtus waged war on Florence thereafter. Although a nepotist, he was a good administrator. He consented to the Spanish INQUISITION but welcomed Jews expelled from Spain. He founded the Sistine Chapel.

**Sixtus V**, 1521–90, pope (1585–90), an Italian named Felice Peretti, a Franciscan. Sent (1565) to Spain to look into the alleged heresy of the Archbishop of Toledo, he fell out with his companion, the future GREGORY XIII, and they became lifelong enemies. As pope he lavished money on rebuilding Rome and left a huge surplus in the treasury, but in so doing he nearly ruined commerce in the Papal States. He set the maximum number of cardinals at 70 and authorized Philip II of Spain to send the Spanish ARMADA against England.

**Sjostrom, Victor**, 1879–1960, Swedish film director. After making many silent films in Sweden, he went to Hollywood in 1923, and enjoyed considerable success before returning home in 1928. His films include *The Scarlet Letter* (1926) and *The Wind* (1928). He closed his long career acting in BERGMAN's *Wild Strawberries* (1957).

**Skaggerak**, strait, c.240 km (150 mi) long and 140 km (85 mi) wide, separating Denmark and Norway. It is one of the straits linking the North Sea and the Baltic Sea.

**Skanderbeg:** see SCANDERBEG.

**Skåne**, province constituting the southernmost part of Sweden. A fertile region, it has the most prosperous agriculture and the densest rural population in Sweden. Cereals and sugar-beet are grown, together with fodder crops for dairy herds and pigs. Urban settlements include the port and industrial centres of MALMÖ and Hälsingborg, and the university town of Lund. Skåne was part of Denmark until 1658.

**skate:** see RAY.

**skating**, gliding along an ice surface on keellike runners called ice skates. Originally a means of travel, skating became a well-established sport by the 17th cent. and has since developed along two lines: speed skating and figure skating. Competition in both types, for women and men, has become an important part of the Olympic winter games. Figure skating, one of the most beautiful and graceful events in all sport, was invented by an American, Jackson Haines, in the 1860s. In the Olympics it is divided into compulsory and free skating sections; competitors skate in circular patterns based on the figure 8. The first world championships were held in St Petersburg in 1896. **Roller skating** involves gliding over a smooth surface on skates with rollers or wheels.

**Skeat, Walter William** (1835–1912), English philologist. A professor of Anglo-Saxon at Cambridge (1878–1912), he translated many early English works and wrote *An Etymological Dictionary of the English Language* (1882), a standard reference work.

**skeleton**, rigid structure which supports an animal's soft tissues. Many invertebrates have exoskeletons which encase the outside of their bodies. They are made of CHITIN and may be reinforced with calcium carbonate. INSECTS and CRUSTACEANS have exoskeletons, which they lose periodically by moulting in order to increase in size. MOLLUSC exoskeletons, which do not enclose the animal completely, grow with it. Vertebrates have endoskeletons made of cartilage or bone, which grow with the animal. The general arrangement of skeletal parts into skull, spinal column, and ribs is the same in all vertebrates. The human skeleton consists of 206 bones, held together by CONNECTIVE TISSUE (cartilage and ligaments). In addition to its supportive function, the skeleton provides sites for the attachment of MUSCLES and protects vital organs, such as the brain, spinal cord, heart, and lungs.

**Skelton, John**, c.1460–1529, English poet. He was tutor to Prince Henry (later King Henry VIII), had a European reputation as a scholar, and violently opposed Cardinal Wolsey's ambition and his educational

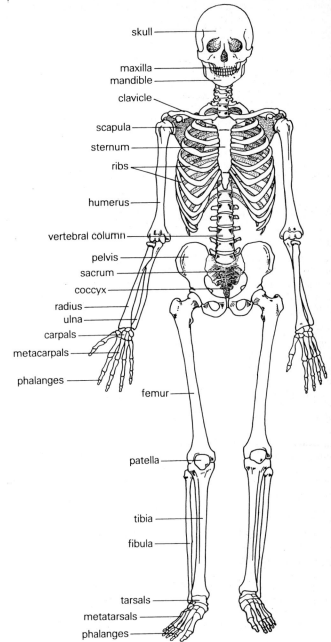

Human **skeleton**

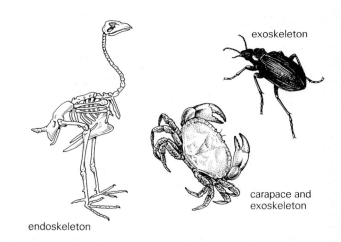

Three types of animal **skeleton**

reforms. His works include daring satires on court life, often cloaked in ingenious allegory (e.g., *The Bowge of Court*, *Speke Parott*).

**skiing,** sport of sliding over snow on skis: long, narrow, flexible runners made of highly polished wood, metal, or plastic. Other equipment includes heavy boots, attached to the skis with safety-release bindings, and a pair of poles to aid in accelerating, turning, and balancing. Competitive skiing comprises five events: (1) slalom, raced on a sharply twisting course marked off by gates against time; (2) giant slalom, on a faster and less twisting course than slalom, also timed; (3) downhill, a steep descent to achieve maximum speed in a race, also timed; (4) the ski jump, from specially prepared slopes and scored on distance and form; and (5) cross-country, a stamina test over a long course, ranging from 10 to 50 km (6–31 mi) in Olympic games. The first three are known as Alpine events, the last two as Nordic events. Originally a vital means of travel, skiing began as an organized sport in Norway in the 19th cent. Since the 1930s the sport has enjoyed a tremendous boom, spurred by the development of ski tows and ski lifts, and the use of artificial snow and of artificial ski slopes for training in non-mountain areas.

**skin,** outer covering of the body of a VERTEBRATE. In mammals, the skin is a complex organ of numerous structures serving vital protective and metabolic functions. It consists of two main cell layers: a thin outer layer (epidermis) and a thicker inner layer (dermis). The epidermis contains melanin, the pigment that gives the skin colour. Evolutionary adaptations of the epidermis include horns, hooves, HAIR, FEATHERS, and SCALES. The dermis consists of CONNECTIVE TISSUE containing blood vessels, lymph channels, nerve endings, sweat glands, sebaceous glands, fat cells, hair follicles, and muscles. The nerve endings, called receptors, perform an important sensory function, responding to various stimuli, including light touch, pressure, pain, heat, and cold. The skin provides a barrier against invasion from outside organisms and protects underlying tissues and organs from abrasion and other injury. Its pigment shields the body from the dangerous ultraviolet rays in sunlight. Skin prevents excessive loss of bodily moisture and in humans regulates body temperature.

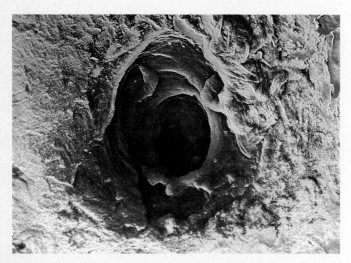

Scanning electron micrograph of a sweat pore in human **skin** ( × 130 magnification)

**skin diving:** see DIVING, DEEP-SEA.

**skink,** LIZARD of the family Scincidae, found in warm regions worldwide, and very common in parts of Africa. Some skinks are burrowers, and have reduced limbs or have lost them altogether. Most have smooth bodies and shiny scales, like the largest, the 60-cm (2-ft) giant skink (*Corucia zebrata*) of the Solomon Islands. Some have keeled scales, like the rough skink (*Tiliqua rugosa*), which also has a short fat tail that looks like a head, so that predators are confused. Skinks are carnivorous, eating insects, small mammals, and earthworms. Although many of the brightly coloured African skinks are thought to be venomous, in fact all are quite harmless.

**Skinner, B(urrhus) F(rederic),** 1904–, American psychologist, most famous proponent of BEHAVIOURISM in 20th-cent. psychology. Skinner advocates the rigorous exclusion of all 'mentalistic' terms from the psychological vocabulary. He is best known for his experimental work on

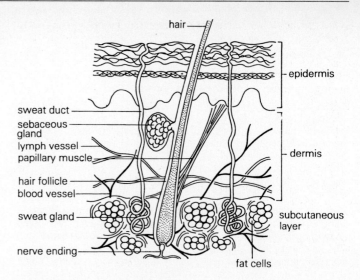

Cross section through human **skin**

the 'shaping' of animal behaviour through the technique of operant conditioning. This differs from classical conditioning (see PAVLOV) through the use of REINFORCEMENT to bring RESPONSES under the control of a STIMULUS. Skinner is also associated with the educational technique known as 'programmed learning', and with his expositions of the socio-political implications of an extreme environmentalism as, for example, in his book *Walden Two* (1961). Skinner's influence on psychology has waned with the rise of COGNITIVE SCIENCE and allied approaches.

**skittles,** a target game and variant of BOWLING in which the player tries to knock down as many skittles (pins) as possible with a ball or round disc (cheese). Nine skittles are arranged in a diamond formation at the end of an alley 0.91 m (3 ft) wide and 6.4 m (21 ft) long. Each player has three throws (a chalk) in which to knock the skittles over.

**Skopje** or **Skoplje** (ˌskawpyə, ˌskawplyə), city (1981 pop. 506,547), capital of Yugoslav MACEDONIA, S Yugoslavia, on the Vardar R. It produces metal, textiles, and glass. Dating from Roman times, it was included in both the Byzantine and Bulgar empires before becoming, for a time, the capital of the medieval Serb state, after which it fell to the Turks (1392). It was reacquired by Serbia in the first BALKAN WAR (1912), but occupied by Bulgaria in both World Wars. The city, which contains a Turkish citadel and two 15th-cent. mosques, was badly damaged (1963) by an earthquake and rebuilt in a characterless modern style.

**Skryabin Aleksandr Nikolayevich** (skreeˌahbin), 1872–1915, Russian composer and pianist. He used chords built in fourths in his piano pieces, e.g., nine SONATAS and *Satanic Poem,* to produce an exotic, mystical effect. He aspired to a fusion of arts; *Divine Poem* (1903) attempts to unite music and philosophy, and *Prometheus* (1909–10) employs coloured lights playing on a screen during the performance.

**skunk,** several related New World MAMMALS of the WEASEL family, characterized by their striking black-and-white-striped fur and the strong, offensive odour they spray for defence. When severely provoked, the skunk squirts a mist from glands under the tail that causes choking and watering of the eyes. Skunks are generally avoided by predators. They feed on rodents, insects, eggs, carrion, and vegetation, and live in one or more families in rock piles and abandoned burrows. Hunted for their fur, skunks range in size from 23 to 75 cm (9 to 30 in).

**sky diving:** see PARACHUTE.

**Skye,** island, 1735 km² (670 sq mi), largest of the Inner HEBRIDES, off W Scotland. Tourism, fishing, farming, and crofting are important; cattle and sheep are raised. 'Bonny Prince Charlie' (see Charles Edward Stuart, under STUART, JAMES FRANCIS EDWARD) took refuge there in 1746.

**skylark:** see LARK.

**skyscraper,** modern building of great height, constructed on a steel skeleton. The form originated in the US, and many late-19th-cent. technological developments contributed to its evolution. In 1887 the first lift was installed, and with the eventual perfecting of high-speed electric lifts skyscrapers were free to attain any height. The early tall masonry buildings required very thick walls in the lower storeys, which limited floor space. The use of cast iron to permit thinner walls was followed by cage construction, in which iron frames supported the floors, while the walls were self-supporting. The first fully steel-frame building was the Home Insurance Building in Chicago (1883), designed by William Jenney. Chicago subsequently became the centre of skyscraper development. Early New York City examples include the Flatiron Building (1902) and Cass GILBERT's Woolworth Building (1913), which epitomized, with its Gothic ornamentation, the adaptation of earlier styles to modern construction. Louis SULLIVAN gave impetus to a new aesthetic, emphasizing underlying structure and fenestration, e.g., the Carson Pirie Scott Building (1899–1904), in Chicago. In 1916, New York established legal control over the height and plan of buildings; regulations regarding setting back walls above a determined height gave rise to the characteristic stepped profile. Skyscraper placement and design are a major concern of city planning. In 1982 the tallest skyscraper was the Sears Tower, Chicago, 110 storeys, 473 m (1454 ft). Major New York City skyscrapers are the twin towers of the World Trade Centre, 110 storeys, 442 m (1350 ft); the Empire State Building, 102 storeys, 412 m (1250 ft); and the Chrysler Building, 77 storeys, 349 m (1046 ft).

**slander:** see LIBEL AND SLANDER.

**slang,** vernacular vocabulary not generally acceptable in formal usage. It is notable for its liveliness, humour, emphasis, brevity, novelty, and exaggeration. Most slang is faddish and ephemeral, but some words are retained for long periods and eventually become part of the standard language, e.g., blazer, bus, tout.

**slate,** fine-grained, characteristically grey-blue ROCK formed by the METAMORPHISM of SHALE. It splits into perfectly cleaved, broad, thin layers; this property is known as slaty cleavage. Better grades of slate are used for roofing.

**Slater, Samuel,** 1768-1835, American pioneer in the cotton textile industry, b. England. After serving an apprenticeship in cotton machinery manufacturing he emigrated to the United States in 1789, despite a British ban on the emigration of skilled artisans. Having memorized the complicated details of making cotton textile machines, whose exportation from England was then forbidden, he succeeded in reproducing one for the Rhode Island firm of Almy and Brown, of which Slater later become a partner.

**slavery,** institution whereby one person owns another and can exact from that person labour or other services, found among both primitive and advanced peoples. Greek slaves had some legal protection, but in the Roman Empire agricultural (estate) slavery gave landowners nearly absolute power over slaves, though manumission (emancipation) gave freedmen status in Rome's social system. Early Christians did not oppose slavery, but economic changes replaced the agricultural slave with the semifree SERF in the Middle Ages. Islam also accepted slavery: eunuch slaves guarded the harem. In the 15th and 16th cent., European exploration of the African coasts led to a lucrative, brutal slave trade carried out by the British, French, Dutch, Spanish, and Portuguese. African slaves, in demand in the Americas, were brought to Virginia, US in 1619. The slave trade developed a triangular pattern: goods were transported from British ports to the west coast of Africa, where they were exchanged for slaves, who were taken to the New World and traded for agricultural staples for the return to England. The movement to abolish slavery for economic and humanitarian reasons began in the 18th cent. Britain outlawed (1807) the slave trade and abolished (1833) slavery in the British Empire. In the US, slavery had disappeared in the North by the early 19th cent. but had become integral to the South's plantation system; the ABOLITIONISTS regarded it as an unmitigated evil. The formation of the Republican Party with its antislavery platform and the election of Abraham LINCOLN (1860) led to the secession of Southern states and the CIVIL WAR. Northern victory ended US slavery, and Lincoln's EMANCIPATION PROCLAMATION (1863) freeing the slaves in secessionist states was followed by the 13th amendment to the CONSTITUTION. In the late 19th cent. international action against the remaining slave trade (especially that of Muslim powers) began. The LEAGUE OF NATIONS and later the UNITED NATIONS have continued efforts to abolish slavery and similar systems of forced labour.

**Slavic languages,** also called Slavonic, a subfamily of the Indo-European family of languages. See LANGUAGE (table).

**Slavic religion,** pre-Christian religious practices among the Slavs of Eastern Europe. Earliest rites were based on the principle that the natural world is inhabited and directed by beneficial and harmful spirits of nature; these were later anthropomorphized into individual deities. Byelobog [the White God] and Chernobog [the Black God], representing the forces of good and evil, reflected the Slavic belief in the dualistic nature of the universe. With the coming of Christianity, the great divinities of the Slavs vanished in name, but many elements of pagan belief survived in popular tradition and in Christian Slavic religious ceremonies.

**Slavonic:** see SLAVIC LANGUAGES.

**Slavophiles and Westernizers,** mid-19th-cent. Russian intellectuals with opposing views of Russian culture. Many Slavophiles held that the Orthodox Church, the MIR, and other aspects of Russian culture made it unique and superior. They supported autocracy but favoured free speech and press, and an end to serfdom. BELINSKY, HERZEN, and other Westernizers believed Russia's progress to be dependent on adoption of Western technology and liberal government.

**Slavs,** Europe's largest ethnic and linguistic group, speakers of related Indo-European languages. They are divided into West Slavs (Poles, Czechs, Slovaks), South Slavs (Serbs, Croats, Slovenes, Macedonians, Bulgars), and East Slavs (Russians, Ukrainians, Belorussians). Some Slavs are of the Eastern Orthodox faith, and use the cyrillic alphabet; others are Catholics and use the Roman alphabet. Slavs are believed to be descendants of Neolithic tribes of GALICIA; over the centuries they have intermixed with Turko-Tatars, Germans, Mongols, Finns, Greeks, and Illyrians. A sedentary agricultural people, they were probably dominated by the conquering Scythians, Sarmatians, Goths, Huns, and Avars. By the 6th cent. Slavs were in E Germany, and in 576 and 746 they invaded the BYZANTINE EMPIRE. The westernmost tribes adopted Christianity in the 9th cent. In the 12th cent. German expansion eastward pushed the Slavs east of the Elbe R. Most powerful of the early Slavic states was KIEVAN RUSSIA, which was destroyed by the MONGOLS in the 13th cent. From the 18th cent. through WORLD WAR I the West and South Slavs struggled for liberation from Turkish, German, Russian, and Magyar domination. Pan-Slavism was continually hampered by conflicting national aspirations, e.g., Polish vs. Russian, Croatian vs. Serbian.

**sleep,** resting state in which an individual becomes relatively quiescent and unaware of the environment. During sleep, most physiological functions, such as body temperature, blood pressure, and breathing rate, decrease. It is also a time of repair and growth, when some tissues proliferate more rapidly. Sleep occurs in cycles: so-called S sleep, characterized by large, slow brain waves, fills about three-quarters of each short cycle. During the second stage, D sleep, parts of the nervous system are very active, and rapid eye movements (REM) occur; dreams take place during REM sleep. Dream or sleep deprivation results in changes in human personality and in perceptual and intellectual processes. See also DREAM.

**sleeping sickness. 1** Disease of tropical Africa caused by infection with TRYPANOSOME parasites; also called trypanosomiasis. The trypanosomes, which live more or less harmlessly in insects and most vertebrates, are transmitted by tsetse flies. In humans, infection causes fever and weakness, followed by profound lethargy, loss of consciousness, and death as the parasites invade the nervous system. The disease can be successfully treated in the early stages by various drugs. **2** See ENCEPHALITIS.

**sleepy sickness:** see ENCEPHALITIS.

**sleet,** precipitation of small, partially melted grains of ice. As raindrops or melted snowflakes fall, they pass through layers of air having different temperatures. If they pass through a layer with a temperature below the freezing point, they become sleet. Sleet occurs only during the winter, whereas HAIL may fall at any time of the year.

**Slessor, Kenneth,** 1901–71, Australian poet. Noted for a superb pictorial ability, he published a number of volumes between 1924 and 1944. The best-known, *Five Bells* (1939), contains his greatest poem, the elegy 'Five Bells'.

**Slick, Sam :** see HALIBURTON, THOMAS CHANDLER.

**slide rule,** mechanical calculating instrument consisting of scales that can slide relative to one another. The scales are logarithmic rather than linear, allowing multiplication and division to be easily performed. The use of slide rules has now been superseded by the electronic calculator.

**Sligo,** county in NW of Republic of Ireland (1986 pop. 55,474), 1779 km² (694 sq mi), bordering on the Atlantic Ocean in the N. It is situated in the province of Connacht. The county town is SLIGO. Much of the county is hilly or mountainous, with a low-lying coastal plain. In the W are the Slieve Gamph (Ox Mts). In the lowland areas cattle are raised and potatoes grown.

**Sligo,** county town (1986 pop. 17,286) of Co. Sligo, Republic of Ireland, at mouth of R. Garavogue, on Donegal Bay. An industrial town and seaport, its main industries are various forms of food processing. There are the ruins of an abbey which dates from the 13th cent., and a 19th-cent. Roman Catholic cathedral. On the hill of Carrowmore nearby is a stone circle and other ancient remains.

**slime mould** or **slime fungus,** organism usually classified with the FUNGI, but showing equal affinity to the PROTOZOA. Slime moulds have complex life cycles with an animallike motile phase, in which feeding and growth occur, and a plantlike immotile reproductive phase. The motile phase, commonly found under rotting logs and damp leaves, consists of either solitary amoebalike cells or a brightly coloured multinucleate mass of protoplasm called a plasmodium, which creeps about and feeds by amoeboid movement (see AMOEBA). In the reproductive phase, slime moulds are transformed into one or more reproductive structures, each consisting of a stalk topped by a spore-producing capsule. When the spores germinate they release amoebalike cells; in the plasmodium-forming plants, the cells grow and the nucleus subdivides to form a plasmodium.

**Slipher, Vesto Melvin,** 1875–1969, American astronomer. A leading stellar spectroscopist, he obtained from his observations of the radial velocities of spiral galaxies the first evidence suggesting the expanding universe. In 1926 he became director of Lowell Univ., where he organized the search for Pluto.

**Sloan, John,** 1871–1951, American painter and member of the New York Realists who promoted the Social Realist ideas of the ASH CAN SCHOOL. He was a member of the EIGHT, and is known for his nudes and city scenes painted with a directness that sometimes verges on satire. Sloan was also a gifted illustrator and etcher.

**sloth,** tailless, toothless, arboreal MAMMAL found in tropical forests of Central and South America. The three-toed sloth (genus *Bradypus*), with three-toed front feet and five-toed hind feet, has a dense, grey-brown furry coat and is about the size of a house cat. Clinging to branches with powerful, curved claws, sloths eat, sleep, and travel upside down. Although sluggish, they can strike swiftly with their hooked claws if attacked.

**Slough,** town (1981 pop. 106,341), Bekshire, S England, on N side of the Thames valley, 33 km (21 mi) W of London. It is a modern industrial town with a range of industries, including the manufacture of paint, plastics, and food products. The town grew rapidly from the 1920s when the first industrial estate was established.

**Slovakia,** constituent land 48,995 km² (18,917 sq mi) of Czechoslovakia, bordered by Moravia (W), Austria (SW), Hungary (S), the Ukraine (E), and Poland (N). The capital, BRATISLAVA, is a port on the Danube R. Most of Slovakia is traversed by the Carpathian Mts, with vast forests, sheep pastures, and rich mineral resources. Much industrialization has occurred since 1945, including shipbuilding and metal-processing. S Slovakia is chiefly agricultural. The area, part of the 9th-cent. empire of MORAVIA, was primarily under Hungarian rule from the 10th cent. until the end of WORLD WAR I, when Slovakia became (1918) part of the new republic of Czechoslovakia. It declared its independence in Mar. 1939 and was (1939–45) a German satellite. After 1948 the government of Czechoslovakia began to curtail Slovak autonomy, but in 1969 Slovakia was granted autonomy over local affairs.

**Slovenia,** constituent republic of Yugoslavia (1981 pop. 1,889,000), 20,246 km² (7817 sq mi), NW Yugoslavia. LJUBLJANA is the capital. It is the wealthiest and most industrialized Yugoslav republic. Manufactures include iron and steel. Farming and stock-raising are important occupations. Ruled by Rome from the 1st cent. BC, the region was settled by South Slavs (6th cent. AD) who became Roman Catholic Slovenes and passed under the rule of the FRANKS (788), the dukes of BAVARIA (843), and the Habsburgs (1335). The extent of Slovene habitation was eroded by

Two-toed **Sloth**

German and Italian pressure before and during the 19th cent., but economic development was greater than in any other South Slav land. In 1918 most Slovenes were joined in the new Yugoslav state, where their separate language spared them the more irksome effects of Serb domination. AXIS partition in World War II led to resistance under Communist leadership which had as one of its aims the reacquisition of lost Slovene territories from Italy and Austria. Most of the desired territory in Venezia Giulia was won (excepting TRIESTE), but not that in Austrian Carinthia.

**Slowacki, Juliusz** (slaw vatskee), 1809–49, Polish poet and dramatist. A leading Polish romantic, he wrote Shakespearean tragedies such as *Lilla Weneda* (1839) and *Horsztynski* (1840). His poems include *Beniowski* (1841), on the Don Juan theme. After the 1830 uprising he exiled himself to W Europe.

**slow-worm,** legless LIZARD of the family Anguidae. It is found in Europe south of the line 65°N, across to Asia Minor and south to North Africa. The slow-worm (*Anguis fragilis*) grows to about 30 cm (1 ft) and feeds on slugs, spiders, worms, and small insects and is eaten by hedgehogs, vipers, foxes, badgers, rats, and many birds. It is POIKILOTHERMIC and HIBERNATES through the winter in cold areas. Young slow-worms are golden or silver coloured with a thin black stripe down their backs, quite unlike the brownish adults. Although they are quite harmless, slow-worms are often killed, being mistaken for snakes.

**slug,** terrestrial GASTROPOD mollusc, a form of SNAIL, with a rudimentary shell and a lung for breathing air. Feeding at night, slugs devour both the roots and aerial portions of plants; some species are serious garden pests.

**Sluter, Claus,** d. c.1406, Flemish sculptor, active in Burgundy; his work, with its strongly individualized figures, introduced a new realism, dignity, and power. For the Chartreuse of Champmol, near Dijon, he produced the outstanding work of northern monumental sculpture in the Renaissance—the portal to the Ducal chapel, with five majestic statues (1391–97), and the wellhead, known as the *Well of Moses* (1395–1403), decorated with figures of prophets.

**Sm,** chemical symbol of the element samarium.

**small arms,** firearms designed primarily to be carried and fired by one person, as distinguished from heavy arms, or ARTILLERY, from which such weapons developed in the late 1300s. At first, small arms were nothing more than small, hand-held cannon fired by placing a small flame at the touchhole. In the matchlock the first real handgun a trigger moved the flame to the touchhole; in its successors, the wheel lock and flintlock, a spark-producing mechanism ignited the GUNPOWDER. Among early weapons of this kind were the musket, fired from the shoulder, and the pistol, held and fired with one hand. The rifle, invented in the 15th cent., is a firearm with a rifled bore (that is, with spiral grooves that impart a spinning motion to the bullet, giving it greater accuracy). Rifles first came into widespread use in the American colonies. Two major innovations of the early 19th cent. were the percussion cap, a small capsule filled with fulminate of mercury that exploded when struck and fired the gun instantly; and the gas-expanding bullet, which, after being dropped down the barrel of a rifle, would expand when fired to fit the barrel's rifling. Thereafter, all guns became rifled with the exception of the shotgun, a smooth-bored, short-range gun firing a single slug or several small shot. Practical breech-loading, or rear-loading, firearms came into general use about 1870; by the 1880s magazine loading, smokeless powder, and bolt action had been introduced. Although a crude 'revolving pistol' existed in the late 16th cent., the modern revolver was introduced c.1835 by Samuel COLT. Colt's revolving cylinder permitted his gun to be fired six times without reloading. The revolver and the magazine-loading rifle were the standard small arms of the later 19th cent., but around 1900 a host of new automatic weapons were developed. The heavy Gatling gun, used in the American Civil War, was the forerunner of the modern, rapid-firing machine gun, which achieved its full potential during the trench warfare of World War I and remains an important military firearm. The 1920s saw the development of submachine guns, notably the Thompson submachine gun (or 'tommy gun'), an easily portable automatic weapon that fired 450 to 600 cartridges per minute. During World War II the bolt-action rifle was supplanted by semiautomatic, lightweight, self-loading, clip-fed shoulder rifles.

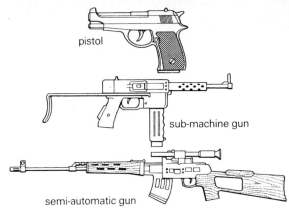

pistol

sub-machine gun

semi-automatic gun

Small arms

**smallpox** or **variola,** acute, highly contagious, sometimes fatal, disease causing a high fever and successive stages of severe skin eruptions. Caused by a virus that may be airborne or spread by direct contact, smallpox has occurred in epidemics throughout history. Edward JENNER, at the end of the 18th cent., demonstrated that cowpox virus was an effective vaccine against the disease. By the end of the 1970s, VACCINATION programmes, such as those conducted by the WORLD HEALTH ORGANIZATION, had eliminated the virus worldwide.

**Smart, Christopher** 1722–71, English poet, writer of densely allusive and imagistic visionary verse. His best-known writing is *Jubilate Agno* [Rejoice in the Lamb] the antiphonally structured hymn of praise which he began when confined for madness in 1759; it has been set to music (1943) by Benjamin BRITTEN. Also well known is his *Song to David* (1763) published on his release from confinement.

**Smeaton, John,** 1724–92, English civil engineer. Initially a maker of navigational instruments, he subsequently turned his interests to engineering. Smeaton rebuilt (1756–59) the Eddystone lighthouse and worked on the Forth and Clyde Canal, Ramsgate Harbour, and many important bridges. He was recognized as the first fully professional engineer of his time.

**smell:** see NOSE.

**smelt** or **sparling,** small, slender FISH of the family Osmeridae, allied to the grayling of the SALMON family. Most species are marine, but some spawn in fresh water and some are landlocked in lakes. The European smelt (*Osmerus eperlanus*) grows to 20 cm (8 in). Like all smelts, it is an important member of food chains. It is also eaten by humans.

**smelting,** any process of melting or fusion, especially to extract a metal from its ORE. Processes vary depending on the ore and metal involved, but they are typified by the use of the BLAST FURNACE and the reverberatory furnace.

**Smetana, Bedřich** (ˌsmetahnah), 1824–84, Czech composer. The creator of a national style in Czech music, he is best known for the opera *The Bartered Bride* (1866). In his own country, his work is more highly regarded than that of DVOŘAK. Almost all his music is programmatic, including the SYMPHONIC POEM *My Fatherland* (1879) with its famous section *The Moldau,* and his two string quartets, *From My Life* (1876, 1882).

**Smith, Adam,** 1723–90, Scottish economist, founder of the classical school of ECONOMICS. While professor of moral philosophy at the Univ. of Glasgow, he wrote his *Theory of Moral Sentiments* (1759), which attracted international interest. In the 1760s he travelled in France, met some of the PHYSIOCRATS, and started to write his masterpiece, *An Inquiry into the Nature and Causes of the Wealth of Nations,* published in 1776. Smith postulated the theory of the division of labour and emphasized that value arises from the labour used in production. He believed that in a LAISSEZ-FAIRE economy the impulse of self-interest would bring about the public welfare. Although opposed to MONOPOLY and the concepts of MERCANTILISM, he admitted that restrictions on free trade (such as the NAVIGATION ACTS) were sometimes necessary. Although some of Smith's theories were voided by the experience of the INDUSTRIAL REVOLUTION, his influence on later economists has never been surpassed.

Claus **Sluter,** the portal to the Ducal chapel, Dijon, 1391.

**Smith, Alfred Emanuel**, 1873–1944, American politician. As four-time governor of New York (1919–20, 1923–28), he achieved many reforms. A Democrat, in 1928 he ran as the first Roman Catholic candidate for president, but was defeated by Herbert HOOVER.

**Smith, Bessie**, 1898?–1937, black American singer. In the 1920s she became the favourite singer of the JAZZ public. The power and beauty of her voice earned her the title 'Empress of the Blues'.

**Smith, David**, 1906–65, American sculptor. His mature works, in wrought iron and cut steel, exhibit totemlike forms and a use of space that recalls CONSTRUCTIVISM.

**Smith, Ian Douglas**, 1919–, Rhodesian politician. As a member of the white supremacist Rhodesian Front party, he became (1964) prime minister and in 1965 unilaterally declared Rhodesia independent from Britain. Despite international pressure, Smith maintained minority white rule until an 'internal settlement' (1978) led to the installation of a black prime minister, Bishop Abel Muzorewa. Smith participated in the Lancaster House agreement (1979) and continued to lead the white minority in parliament for several years after the achievement of black majority rule and the proclamation of the republic of ZIMBABWE in 1980.

**Smith, Jedediah Strong**, 1799–1831, American explorer and one of the greatest MOUNTAIN MEN. His western travels opened the rich fur-trapping country of the Rocky Mountains and showed the way for pioneers who came later. In 1824 he helped lead a party through South Pass, in Wyoming, beginning use of that route. In 1826–27 he travelled southwest from Great Salt Lake, across the Mojave Desert to California and then with two men became the first whites to cross the Sierra Nevada and the Great Salt Desert from west to east. Smith later travelled from California up the entire Pacific coast to Ft Vancouver, surviving Indian attacks but he was killed by Comanches while en route west on the Santa Fe trail.

**Smith, John**, c.1580–1631, English colonist in America. A member of the JAMESTOWN council, the resourceful and tactful Smith carried the colony through periods of hardship (1607–9). The celebrated story of his capture by the Indian chief POWHATAN and rescue by POCAHONTAS is probably true.

**Smith, Joseph**, 1805–44, American MORMON leader, founder of the Church of Jesus Christ of Latter-Day Saints. He claimed that visions revealed (1823) to him the existence of secret records, which he said he had unearthed in 1827 in the form of golden tablets and translated as the Book of Mormon. As prophet and seer, he founded (1830) a church in Fayette, in the state of New York. The hostility of neighbours led him to move to Ohio, Missouri, and finally to Illinois. Disaffection grew within the sect, and more trouble with non-Mormons led to his arrest, along with that of his brother Hyrum, on charges of treason. On 27 June, 1844, both brothers were murdered by a mob at Carthage, Illinois. Smith's revelations, including one on plural marriage (made public eight years after his death), were accepted as doctrine by the Mormons, who increased greatly after his death.

**Smith, Pauline**, 1882–1959, white South African novelist. She wrote with considerable skill about the primitive and deprived horizons of her society. Her works, e.g., *The Little Karoo* (1924) and *The Beadle* (1926), were highly influential for the post-war generation of white South African fiction writers.

**Smith, Stevie (Florence Margaret)**, 1902–71, English poet and novelist. She is remembered for her first novel, *Novel on Yellow Paper* (1936), and for the wryly humorous and highly individual verse style of such volumes as *Not Waving but Drowning* (1957).

**Smith, Sydney**, 1771–1845, English clergyman and writer. A founder of the *Edinburgh Review* (1802). Famous for his wit, he was also a humane man who campaigned on behalf of prisoners and slaves, and for CATHOLIC EMANCIPATION in his *Letters of Peter Plymley* (1807).

**Smith, William Henry**, 1825–91, English pioneer in the distribution of books and newspapers. Representative of the third generation in a family business, Smith acquired the nickname 'Old Morality'. He entered the House of Commons in 1868, as a liberal, defeating John Stuart MILL, but ended as a conservative. He held ministerial office under DISRAELI in 1874 and became war minister, and later leader of the house, in the SALISBURY ministry (1886–91).

**smock**, a long shirt which was used as an undergarment. It was worn by both sexes and usually made from linen. It was also known as a shift, and in the 18th and 19th cent. as a chemise. By the end of the 18th cent., an overall, of similar form, worn by rural labourers, was also known as a smock. The fullness at the shoulders was often held with decorative stitching (in distinctive patterns according to the district or the labourer's trade) over the regular gathering, hence the embroidery term 'smocking'.

**smog**, dense, visible air POLLUTION, commonly of two types. The grey smog of older industrial cities like London and New York comes from the massive combustion of coal and fuel oil in or near the city, releasing ashes, soot, and sulphur compounds into the air. The brown smog characteristic of Los Angeles and Denver is caused by vehicle emissions. Smog, which usually results in reduced visibility and can irritate the eyes and respiratory system, may be dangerous to people with respiratory ailments. It can also damage metal, rubber, and other materials.

**smoking**, inhalation of the smoke from burning tobacco or other plant material; the major preventable cause of ill health all over the world. The smoking of cigarettes, in particular, is a cause of lung CANCER and contributes to the development of CORONARY HEART DISEASE (the biggest cause of death in the West), peripheral vascular disease, cervical cancer, cancers of the mouth, and diminished foetal growth. One in four people who smoke will die of a smoking-related disease. The inhalation of other people's tobacco smoke (passive smoking) is now also known to be a hazard to health. Adults are slowly stopping smoking in Europe and the US but school children are still taking up the habit in much the same numbers (smokers almost always take up the habit before the age of 21). Health promotion activists have sought to curb the advertising activities of tobacco companies. They still advertise freely in the developing world, however, where there is a rising toll of smoking-related deaths on top of conditions of extreme poverty. See also TOBACCO; NICOTINE.

**Smollett, Tobias George**, 1721–71, Scottish novelist. A ship's surgeon and later an editor, he wrote *Roderick Random* (1748), *Peregrine Pickle* (1751), *Ferdinand Count Fathom* (1753), and *Humphry Clinker* (1771), his major success, all adventure novels partly based on his own experience at sea, and strongly flavoured with satire, violence, and indignation against injustice.

**smut**, name for plant diseases caused by FUNGI of the order Ustilaginales. Smut produces sootlike masses of spores on the host, lowers its vitality, and often causes deformities. Serious threats to grain crops, smuts do not alternate hosts as do the RUSTS. Severe annual crop losses are caused by the corn smut, oat smut, and loose smut of wheat. Bunt, the most serious smut, attacks young wheat seedlings and destroys the GRAIN.

**Smuts, Jan Christiaan**, 1870–1950, South African statesman and soldier. Of Boer stock, he fought against the British in the SOUTH AFRICAN WAR. After concluding that British–Boer cooperation was essential in SOUTH AFRICA, he was instrumental in the creation (1910) of the Union of South Africa. Smuts held office continuously (1910–19) in Louis BOTHA's cabinet and was a signer of the treaty of VERSAILLES. He was prime minister (1919–24; 1939–48). During WORLD WAR II Smuts was made a field marshal and held a high place on British war councils. He was active in promoting the foundation of the UN.

**Smyrna**, Turkey: see İZMIR.

**Smyth, Dame Ethel (Mary)**, 1858–1944, British composer, conductor, and suffragette. She studied in Leipzig, and even though her Mass in D was performed with success in London in 1893, she had to turn to the continent for performances of her operas, *Fantasio* (1898), *Der Wald* (1902), and *The Wreckers* (1906), which Thomas BEECHAM conducted at Covent Garden in 1909. After joining Mrs Pankhurst's campaign for women's suffrage, she wrote *March of the Women* (1911) and spent a short time in Holloway prison. She continued to write a variety of works until about 1930, when she concentrated on writing another four volumes of her autobiography.

**Sn**, chemical symbol of the element TIN.

**snail**, GASTROPOD mollusc with a spirally coiled shell; there are thousands of species on land and in water. In aquatic species, respiration is carried on by gills; terrestrial forms often have lungs. Snails secrete a slimy substance over which they move by contractions of their muscular foot. Many species are eaten.

**Snake,** river, NW US, flowing c.1670 km (1038 mi) from Yellowstone National Park (NW Wyoming) to become the chief tributary of the Columbia R., which it joins near Pasco, Washington. A scenic river with spectacular gorges, notably Hell's Canyon (c.200 km/125 mi long and up to 2400 m/7900 ft deep), it is also an important source of hydroelectricity and irrigation.

**snake,** limbless REPTILE of the order Squamata, which also includes the LIZARDS. The snake's extremely long, narrow body has many vertebrae, and paired internal organs are arranged linearly rather than side by side. Some snakes—constrictors—suffocate their prey by wrapping their bodies around it and squeezing; others—venomous snakes—inject a toxic substance into their victims. The approximately 2700 snake species, of which about four fifths are nonvenomous, are distributed throughout most temperate and tropical zones of the world. About two-thirds of all species, most of them nonvenomous, belong to the family Colubridae, including garter and grass snakes. Most poisonous New World snakes belong to the PIT VIPER family, while venomous Old World snakes are the true VIPERS and members of the cobra family. The family Boidea includes the largest snakes, e.g., BOAS and PYTHONS. A high proportion of Australian snakes like the TIGER SNAKE are venomous, belonging to the family Elapidae which in Africa and Asia includes the COBRA, and are related closely to the SEA SNAKES, the Hydrophidae.

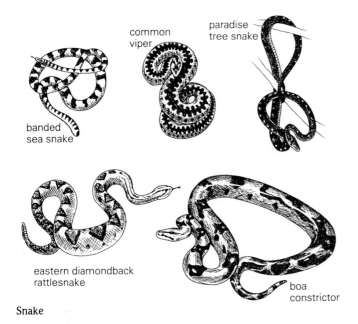

common viper

paradise tree snake

banded sea snake

eastern diamondback rattlesnake

boa constrictor

Snake

**snapdragon,** cultivated garden and greenhouse plant (*Antirrhinum majus*) of the figwort family, native to the Mediterranean area. Its showy blossoms, resembling a dragon's snout, display a wide range of colours and varieties.

**snare drum:** see DRUM.

**Snead, Sam(uel Jackson),** 1912–, American golfer. He won his first major title, the Professional Golfers' Association (PGA) championship, in 1942 and again in 1949 and 1951. He also captured the Masters three times (1949, 1952, 1954) and the British Open once (1946). A master of long-iron play, 'Slamming Sammy' won over 80 PGA tournaments, far more than any other golfer in history.

**Snell's law:** see REFRACTION.

**snipe,** shore BIRD of the SANDPIPER family, native to the Old and New World. The common snipe (*Gallinago gallinago*) is a game bird of marshes and meadows. The woodcock (*Scolopax rusticola*), is a nocturnal woodland bird. Most snipe nest on the ground, the exception being the New Zealand snipe *Coehorypha auklandica* which nests in burrows deserted by other birds.

**SNOBOL:** see PROGRAMMING LANGUAGE.

**snooker,** a recent development of BILLIARDS. It is played with 22 balls; 15 reds (one point), one black (seven), one pink (six), one blue (five), one brown (four), one green (three), and one yellow (two), and a white cue ball. Using the cue ball, players must pot red and higher-valued balls (the colours) alternately; after being potted the colours are replaced on their designated spot on the table. When all the reds have been potted, the colours must be potted in reverse order of their value, and are not then re-spotted. A player's turn continues until a shot with no score is made, when the opponent takes over; the player with the highest score wins. Penalties are incurred for potting the wrong ball or failing to hit the required ball. Players are 'snookered' if other balls obstruct their clear path. The maximum break (score) in a single turn is 147. The game was codified in 1919; world championships date from 1927.

**snow,** precipitation formed by the sublimation of water vapour into solid crystals at temperatures below freezing. A snowflake, like a raindrop (see RAIN), forms around a dust particle. Snowflakes form symmetrical (hexagonal) crystals, sometimes matted together if they fall through air warmer than that of the cloud in which they originated. Apparently, no two snow crystals are alike; they differ from each other in size, lacy structure, and surface markings. Snowfall has been produced artificially by introducing dry-ice pellets into clouds that contain unfrozen water droplets at temperatures below the freezing point. Melted, 25 cm (10 in) of snow is approximately equal to 2.5 cm (1 in) of rainfall. See also AVALANCHE; GLACIER.

**Snow, C(harles) P(ercy)** (Baron Snow of Leicester), 1905–80, English author. A physicist, he also held important positions in British administration and government. His 11-volume novel series, *Strangers and Brothers* (1940–70), which analyzes power and the relation between science and the community, also delineates the changes in English life, particularly in Cambridge Univ., in the 20th cent.

**Snow, John,** 1813–58, English physician. He introduced the use of ether in anaesthesia to the UK, and he administered chloroform to Queen Victoria during childbirth. He demonstrated that CHOLERA is transmitted by faecally contaminated water; he removed the handle of the pump in Broad Street, Soho, London, in 1855, and so ended a cholera epidemic.

**Snowdon,** highest mountain in England and Wales, situated in Gwynedd, NW Wales. It is 1085 m (3560 ft) high, and gives its name to the mountain range which it is in, and to the region of Snowdonia surrounding it. The area is now a national park, popular with climbers and walkers. There is a mountain railway running from Llanberis in the N to the summit of the mountain.

**Snowy Mountains,** highest range of the AUSTRALIAN ALPS, in New South Wales, SE Australia. It is a popular winter sports area and the site of the Snowy Mountains hydroelectric scheme, involving the transfer of water westward via dams and tunnels to irrigate the MURRAY R. basin.

**Snyder, Gary,** 1930–, American poet. Associated with the BEAT GENERATION of the 1950s, he lived in Japan from 1956 to 1968. His poetry, influenced by ZEN BUDDHISM and American Indian culture, celebrates the peace found in nature and decries its destruction; volumes include *Myths and Texts* (1960) and *Turtle Island* (1974).

**Snyders, Frans,** 1579–1657, most celebrated Flemish still-life and animal painter. Influenced by RUBENS, he often collaborated with Rubens and JORDAENS, sometimes painting the animals in their pictures. He is best known for his spirited scenes of the hunt and of animal struggles, e.g., *Stag Hunt* (c.1624; Musées Royaux des Beaux Arts, Brussels).

**Soane, Sir John,** 1753–1837, English architect. The most original architect of the CLASSIC REVIVAL period in England, Soane introduced a number of personal mannerisms into his buildings and became the leading advocate of the picturesque in architecture. After travels in Italy he achieved fame with his new buildings for the Bank of England (1788–1833) with its blank facade and ingenious spacious vaults. Just as original and more picturesque were the Dulwich Art Gallery and Mausoleum, London (1811–14). His own house, 13 Lincoln's Inn Fields, London, started 1812–13, is now the most idiosyncratic museum in England, stuffed with drawings, antiquities, and works of art. His style, using grooved strips of diagrammatic ornament to create linear flat patterns on blank walls, has proved inspiring to modern architects, as has his mastery of contrast of light and shade. His influence abroad was mainly in late 18th- to early 19th-cent. postcolonial architecture.

**soap,** any of a group of organic compounds that are metallic salts of fatty acids. A soap of tallow and wood ashes was used as early as the 1st cent. AD by Germanic tribes. In the American colonies it was made from waste fats and lye, which is a strong alkali leached from wood ashes. The

The Sir John **Soane** Museum, Lincoln's Inn Fields (1812–13)

resulting chemical reaction, called saponification, remains the basis of soap manufacture today. FATS AND OILS are heated with an alkali, e.g., sodium hydroxide (which gives hard soaps) or potassium hydroxide (which gives soft soaps). Sodium or potassium may be replaced in the alkali by other metals, e.g., aluminium, calcium, or magnesium, to make soaps used in industry as paint driers, ointments, and lubricating greases, and in waterproofing. After the alkali and fats have reacted, salt is added to form a curd of the soap. Glycerol (glycerin), a valuable by-product used as a solvent and sweetener, can then be removed by DISTILLATION. Varying the composition or method of processing affects the lathering, cleansing, and water-softening properties. Soap can be formed as bars, chips, flakes, beads, or powders and may contain perfumes, dyes, or germicides. Like modern soapless detergents (usually sulphonated alcohols), soaps cleanse by lowering the surface tension of water, by emulsifying grease, and by absorbing dirt into the foam. Soap is less effective than detergent in hard water because the salts that make the water hard react with the soap to form insoluble curds (e.g., the 'ring' left in bathtubs).

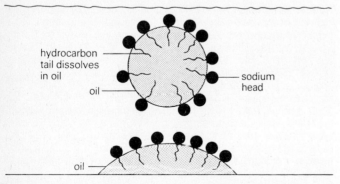

hydrocarbon tail dissolves in oil

oil

sodium head

oil

**Soap** molecules surround a grease particle making it soluble in water

**soap opera,** drama serial on RADIO or TELEVISION following the fortunes of a group of people purporting to be drawn from real life. The longest

running is the BBC radio serial *The Archers*, first broadcast in 1950 and still going. The earliest true soap opera on television was NBC's *One Man's Family* screened by US stations (1949–55). It was sponsored by Sweetheart Soap—hence the term 'soap opera'. The first British example was *Meet the Groves* (1955). The genre tends not to travel well if treated reaslistically, but a fantastical series such as *Dallas*, set among oil millionaires in Texas, appeals to consumerism around the world and had leading viewing figures in every continent in the early 1980s.

**soapstone** or **steatite,** metamorphic ROCK (see METAMORPHISM) in which the characteristic mineral is TALC. It is grey to green, has a soapy feel, and resists acids and heat. Soft and easily carved, it is a popular sculpture medium. Soapstone is also used to make sinks and laundry tubs. The chief deposits are in the US, Canada, and Norway.

**Soares, Mário** (soh͵ahresh), 1924–, prime minister (1973–76, 1983–86) and president of Portugal (1986–). Frequently exiled under the pre-1974 right-wing dictatorship, he returned to Portugal after the 1974 revolution and, as leader of the powerful Socialist Party, became a pivotal political figure. After his party's defeat in the 1985 elections, he was elected to the presidency by popular vote early the following year.

**soaring:** see FLIGHT.

**Sobhuza II,** 1899–1982, king of the Swazi from 1921 and of the kingdom of SWAZILAND. He fought successfully to preserve his country from South African incorporation and presided over an independent Swaziland from 1968, as constitutional monarch.

**soccer,** ball and goal game usually played outdoors, also called association football or simply football. Played in more than 140 countries, it is by far the most popular international sport. Two opposing teams of 11 players each compete on a field preferably measuring 100 m by 73 m (110 yd by 73 yd). A goal 7.3 m (8 yd) wide and 2.4 m (8 ft) high, backed with netting, is centred on each end line. The object of the game is to advance an inflated leather ball into the opponent's goal. The ball is kicked (often dribbled with short kicks) or advanced by the head or other parts of the body, but only the goalkeeper may use the hands. Rule infractions result in free kicks for the opposing team. Football for the first time appeared as one of Britain's main sports in the 14th cent. Association football rules were first drawn up in 1863. The Football Association was founded in 1867, and the FA Cup established in 1871. The Football League, in which teams play one another regularly in accordance with a fixed programme, originated in 1888. The highlight of international play is the WORLD CUP competition, held every four years.

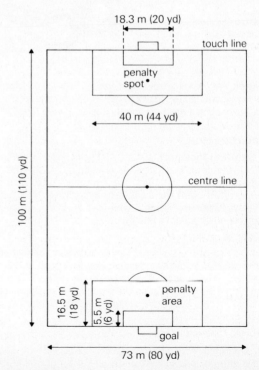

**Soccer** pitch dimensions

**Social and Liberal Democrats,** centrist British political party founded in 1988, known as the 'Democrats' for short. The party was formed as a merger of the LIBERAL PARTY and part of the SOCIAL DEMOCRATIC PARTY; the former Liberal, Paddy ASHDOWN, was elected its first leader.

**social contract,** agreement by which human beings are said to have abandoned the 'state of nature' in order to form the society in which they now live. HOBBES, LOCKE, and J.J. ROUSSEAU each developed differing versions of the social contract, but all agreed that certain freedoms had been surrendered in exchange for society's protection and that the government has definite responsibilities to its citizens. Similar ideas were used in the 18th cent. as justification for both the American and the French revolutions. The concept has generally been discarded as a theoretical basis of political life but was revived in the 20th cent. by the US philosopher John RAWLS.

**Social Credit,** economic plan in Canada. It was based on the theories of Clifford Hugh Douglas, who held that the basic cause of economic depression was unequal distribution resulting from lack of purchasing power, and proposed issuing 'social dividends' to every citizen. This scheme proved unworkable, and other measures were blocked by the federal government and the courts. The Social Credit party ruled the province of ALBERTA from 1935 to 1971.

**Social Darwinism,** belief that societies and individual human beings develop in a manner consistent with the principles of biological EVOLUTION proposed by Charles DARWIN, in such a way that only superior people are able to gain wealth and power, and that their superiority is hereditary. Social Darwinism has been used to justify IMPERIALISM, and although popular in the late 19th cent., it has been widely attacked in modern times.

**social democracy,** that form of socialist or labour thinking and political practice which pursues social reform within the constraints of parliamentary democracy. Since the success of the RUSSIAN REVOLUTION (1917), it has been customary to distinguish such reformist social democracy from revolutionary SOCIALISM and COMMUNISM. Western European social democratic parties, e.g., the SPD in Germany and the British Labour Party, usually closely associated with their national TRADE UNION organizations, have been a major force in 20th-cent. politics. They have formed many governments committed to a conception of social justice involving the erosion of traditional inequalities of wealth and privilege. Characteristically, they have attempted to achieve full employment and improved living standards by increasing the degree of social and economic planning, the extent of State control over industry, and the range and quality of welfare provision. Their commitment to 'parliamentary gradualism' has amounted in practice to the humane management of CAPITALISM, and not its transformation. This moderation or compromise has sometimes led to dissent from their own left wing and criticism from other socialist and communist parties. In Eastern Europe the social democratic parties were suppressed after World War II and *social democrat* is a term of abuse.

**Social Democratic Party** (SDP), British political party founded (1981) to offer a centrist alternative to the perceived extreme positions of the ruling CONSERVATIVE PARTY on the right and LABOUR on the left; to this end it formed a close alliance with the small LIBERAL PARTY. The SDP began with the defection of 12 Labour members of Parliament who opposed their party's leftward drift and by early 1982 held 24 parliamentary seats (including one former Conservative member). Led by David OWEN (since June 1983), the SDP contested the 1983 elections in alliance with the Liberals, but although the two parties won 25% of the popular vote they obtained only 23 seats (the SDP's representation falling to six seats). In the 1987 elections the SDP slipped to five seats (and the alliance to 22), whereupon a majority of the party opted for a full merger with the Liberals in the SOCIAL AND LIBERAL DEMOCRATS. However, Owen and an anti-merger faction maintained the SDP in being under his leadership with increasing financial difficulties.

**Social Gospel,** liberal movement within American Protestantism that attempted to apply biblical teachings to problems associated with industrialization. It grew in the late 19th cent. under the leadership of Washington Gladden and Walter RAUSCHENBUSCH, who believed in social progress and the essential goodness of man.

**socialism,** term with a range of meanings historically, centred on the idea of a community in which the means of production—land, factories, capital—are socially or collectively owned and in which production is democratically planned and controlled for the benefit of all. Such a community need not be large, and social ownership need not be state ownership. Socialist ideas arose in the early 19th cent. as a response to the misery and inequality associated with the uncontrolled capitalism of the INDUSTRIAL REVOLUTION. The utopian socialists (see UTOPIA), e.g., Charles FOURIER, Robert OWEN, P.J. PROUDHON, and Claude, duc de SAINT-SIMON, sought a substitute for competition and exploitation in various model communities based on cooperation and the social control of economic activity. In mid-19th cent., MARX and ENGELS sought to make socialism scientific, with an analysis of the laws of history and class struggle which predicted the inevitable overthrow of CAPITALISM and the arrival of socialism as an evolutionary stage on the road to final communism. In 1863 LASSALLE founded the first worker's party in Germany, and by the 1870s there were socialist parties in most European countries, pressing for universal suffrage and social reforms to improve the condition of the working class. The next 40 years produced a ferment of socialist ideas. There were those, such as Rosa LUXEMBURG, who believed that capitalism would have to be overthrown by revolution. Others, e.g., Eduard BERNSTEIN, felt that the extension of the vote to all workers and the growth of trade unions had introduced a new era in which socialism could be pursued by means of successive reforms under parliamentary democracy. The English guild socialists (see GUILD SOCIALISM) and the Italian and French syndicalists (see SYNDICALISM) rejected parliamentary activity, and in particular any notion of state control, in favour of systems based on workers' control of industry. Since the 1917 RUSSIAN REVOLUTION world socialism has effectively been split between revolutionary COMMUNISM (whose leaders continue to describe themselves as socialist), and evolutionary SOCIAL DEMOCRACY, in the shape of the reformist socialist parties which have played a major part in modern Western European politics. Since World War II social democratic governments have brought about a marked increase in economic planning and government control over industry, and an extension of the WELFARE STATE which has improved the security and the living standards of the majority. But experience of the state-dominated character of both the communist and the social-democratic models of contemporary socialism has led to disillusion on the part of the Left, and renewed advocacy of a decentralized system giving greater autonomy and more democratic control to local associations. The continuing debate on the character of socialism, and on the best means of bringing it about, indicates the continuing vitality and moral force of the idea. Socialism in the Third World tends to take the form of a struggle against COLONIALISM, followed by one-party rule and the implementation of centralized economic planning and land reform, owing more to the communist than to the social-democratic model.

**Socialist International:** see under SECOND INTERNATIONAL.

**socialist realism,** Soviet artistic and literary doctrine prescribing the optimistic depiction of socialist society in conventionally realistic terms. Proclaimed by the Union of Soviet Writers as compulsory practice in 1932, the doctrine has been less stringently enforced since STALIN's death, although it remains official policy throughout the Soviet bloc.

**Socialist Revolutionary Party,** Russian Populist party founded 1901. It called for an end to autocracy, a classless society, distribution of land to peasants, and self-determination of minorities. The party carried out political assassinations. It participated in the 1917 RUSSIAN REVOLUTION but by 1922 was suppressed by the Soviet government.

**social mobility,** the degree to which individuals or households are free to move (up or down) from one social class, or status group, to another. In 'open' societies (e.g., in the US and Britain) people are formally free to move, socially; though actual mobility is limited by other factors and rates differ widely. Upward mobility is viewed as a reward (in income, lifestyle, or status) for some quality (e.g., skill, hard work, scarce resources). In 'closed' societies (e.g., the CASTE system in India) people are fixed in the social stratum to which they are born. Intergenerational mobility compares the present position of individuals with that of their parents. Intragenerational mobility compares the position attained by individuals in the course of their own lifetime. Some groups have lost social status over time (e.g., teachers). J.H. GOLDTHORPE, in *Social Mobility and Class Structure in Britain* (1980), has argued that the apparent openness of the British occupational system has been caused by movement between different areas of the economy (expansion of white-collar and the contraction of blue-collar occupations), a pattern typical of most industrialized European nations; when abstracted from the changing occupational figures, the class structure of Britain has changed little since World War II. See also STRATIFICATION.

**social security,** public programme providing for economic security and welfare. While programmes vary from one country to another, all provide some cash payment to defray income loss or deficiency due to sickness, old age, or unemployment. (In socialist nations the insured person makes no direct contribution toward the coverage.) Germany adopted a social security programme in the 1880s and Great Britain's programme, begun in 1911, was expanded after World War II. The US Social Security Act (1935) established unemployment compensation, retirement insurance, and federal assistance for state welfare programmes. The HEALTH INSURANCE plans Medicare and Medicaid and supplemental security income (SSI) for the disabled were added later. Administered principally by the Social Security Administration of the Dept. of Health and Human Services, the US system, as constituted, appeared threatened in the 1980s by economic factors and by changing patterns in DEMOGRAPHY, most significantly, the percentage increase in the number of aged receiving benefits as compared to those persons still working and contributing to the programme through taxes.

**social welfare,** organized assistance to the needy. England's poor law (1601) was the first extensive state effort to aid the needy; it required work of the able-bodied and provided apprenticeships for children. Modern SOCIAL SECURITY programmes for broad groups of people, not just the poor, began in Germany in the 1880s with health insurance for workers; they were instituted in Britain in 1911 and the US in 1935. Great Britain and the Scandinavian countries, often termed 'welfare states,' have wide-ranging social welfare programmes, including comprehensive HEALTH INSURANCE providing free or low-cost medical services for all. Private charities, international relief bodies (e.g., the RED CROSS), and UNITED NATIONS agencies (e.g., UNICEF) also provide services.

**social work,** organized efforts to help individuals and families adjust to the community and to adapt the community to their needs. Early charitable activities were aimed at alleviating maladjustments piecemeal. The French sociologist and economist P.G.F. Le Play was the first to apply (1850s) scientific methods to the solution of the problem of poverty. Later in the 1800s, the English investigator Charles Booth developed the social survey method, providing a basis for determining the extent of social maladjustment. In the 1930s, to deal with economic DEPRESSION, the US government joined private, state, and local social work efforts. Modern methods of social work include casework (helping individuals and families with physical, mental, and such social problems as child neglect, alcoholism, drug abuse), group work (e.g., social settlement), and community organization (coordinating community efforts and funding).

**Society of Friends:** see FRIENDS, RELIGIOUS SOCIETY OF.

**Socinus, Faustus,** or **Fausto Sozzini** (soh͵sienəs), 1539–1604, Italian religious reformer, founder of Socinianism. Influenced by the writings of his uncle **Laelius Socinus,** 1525–62, Faustus left the Roman Catholic Church and came to deny the Trinity. His uncle had never actually denied this doctrine, but his works were the basis for Faustus's movement, Socinianism, which he organized in Poland after 1579. The movement died out (c.1638) because of severe Roman Catholic persecution.

**sociobiology,** application of the theory of EVOLUTION to the study of animal and human social behaviour. Sociobiologists hold that behaviour patterns are genetically determined and are governed by the process of natural selection. The theories have been used successfully to explain animal altruism and reproductive and foraging behaviour, but they are controversial when applied to human behaviour in such areas as aggressiveness, sex differences, mate selection, and parenting behaviour. Edward O. WILSON's *Sociobiology* (1975) and Richard Dawson's *The Selfish Gene* (1976) were instrumental in defining the field.

**sociology,** the scientific study of collective human behaviour. The term was coined (1838) by Auguste COMTE, who attempted to identify the unifying principles of society at different stages of human social development. Major contributions to 19th-cent. sociology were made by Karl MARX, who emphasized the economic basis of the organization of society and saw in class struggle the main agent of social progress, and by Herbert SPENCER, who applied Darwinian principles to the study of human society. The founders of modern sociology are Émile DURKHEIM, who

pioneered the scientific use of comparative empirical evidence and statistical data, and Max WEBER, who developed historical and theoretical models as a tool of sociological analysis. Theorists in the 20th cent. have focused on conflict (drawing on Marx's work), structural-functionalism (associated with Talcott PARSONS), and symbolic interaction (developed by George Herbert Mead and Herbert Blumer).

**sociology of knowledge,** the area of intellectual inquiry which argues that our ideas and perceptions of the world are, in large measure, a social product. MARX, was the first modern social theorist to address the relationship between social structure and knowledge, and gave prominence to the way material and economic factors determine cognitive and intellectual perceptions. In *Ideology and Utopia* (1936), Karl Mannheim (1893–1947) argued that knowledge of the world was a social product, hence always relative, though intellectuals could to some extent stand outside normal social structures and offer objective social criticism. Sociology of knowledge research has explored, *inter alia,* literary themes in relation to an author's social milieu, the historical or social basis of artistic styles, and scientific claims in terms of the community of scientists. The main criticism is that it depends on a relationist conception of knowledge.

**Socotra,** mountainous island (3582 km²/1383 sq mi) of Southern Yemen, at the mouth of the Gulf of ADEN, c.250 km (150 mi) E of the African mainland. The islanders fish, farm, and herd; the main exports are dried fish and pearls. Under British control from 1834, Socotra was a refuelling station before being ceded (1967) to Southern Yemen.

**Socrates,** 469–399 BC, Greek philosopher. He lived in Athens; it is not known who his teachers were, but he seems to have been acquainted with the doctrines of PARMENIDES, HERACLITUS, and ANAXAGORAS. Socrates himself left no writings, and most of our knowledge of him and his teachings comes from the dialogues of his most famous pupil, PLATO, and from the memoirs of XENOPHON. Socrates is described as having neglected his own affairs, instead spending his time discussing virtue, justice, and piety wherever his fellow citizens congregated, seeking wisdom about right conduct so that he might guide the moral and intellectual improvement of Athens. Using a method now known as the Socratic dialogue, or dialectic, he drew forth knowledge from his students by pursuing a series of questions and examining the implications of their answers. Socrates equated virtue with knowledge, holding that no one knowingly does wrong. He looked upon the soul as the seat of both waking consciousness and moral character, and held the universe to be purposively mind-ordered. His criticism of the Sophists and of Athenian political and religious institutions made him many enemies, and his position was burlesqued by ARISTOPHANES. In 399 BC Socrates was tried for corrupting the morals of Athenian youth and for religious heresies; it is now believed that his arrest stemmed in particular from his influence on ALCIBIADES and Critias, who had betrayed Athens. He was convicted and, resisting all efforts to save his life, willingly drank the cup of poison hemlock given him. The trial and death of Socrates are described by Plato in the *Apology, Crito,* and *Phaedo.*

**Söderberg, Hjalmar** (ˈsøːdə͵beryə), 1869–1941, Swedish writer. He is noted for his witty short stories and for novels, e.g., *Doctor Glas* (1905), which evoke upper-middle-class Stockholm life at the turn of the century.

**Södergran, Edith,** 1892–1923, Finnish poet writing in Swedish, considered the most important of the Swedish-language modernist writers. She lived in great isolation in a house in the Karelian Isthmus (now in Soviet territory). Her best-known work is *The Non-Existent Country* (1925).

**sodium** (Na), metallic element, discovered in 1807 by Sir Humphrey DAVY; its compounds have been known since antiquity. One of the ALKALI METALS, it is silver-white and very reactive and must be stored out of contact with air and water. The metal is used in arc-lamp lighting, as a heat-transfer liquid in nuclear reactors, and in the manufacture of tetraethyl lead. Widely used compounds include SODIUM CHLORIDE (common salt), SODIUM BICARBONATE (baking soda), SODIUM CARBONATE (soda ash), the hydroxide (lye), nitrate, phosphates, and BORAX. SOAP is made with sodium hydroxide. Sodium compounds are widely distributed in rocks, soil, oceans, salt lakes, mineral waters, and salt deposits, and are found in the tissues of plants and animals. Sodium is an essential element of the diet. See ELEMENT (table); PERIODIC TABLE.

**sodium bicarbonate,** or **sodium hydrogen carbonate,** chemical compound ($NaHCO_3$), a white crystalline or granular powder, commonly known as bicarbonate of soda or baking soda. It is soluble in water and very slightly soluble in alcohol. Because it produces carbon dioxide gas when heated above 50°C (122° F), it is used in baking powder. It is sometimes used medically to correct excess stomach acidity.

**sodium carbonate,** chemical compound ($Na_2CO_3$) soluble in water and very slightly soluble in alcohol. Pure sodium carbonate is a white, odourless powder that absorbs moisture from the air and forms a strongly alkaline water solution. One of the most basic industrial chemicals, it is usually produced by the Solvay process. The chief uses of sodium carbonate are in glassmaking and the production of chemicals.

**sodium chloride** (NaCl), common salt. It is a chemical compound containing equal numbers of positively charged sodium and negatively charged chlorine IONS. The colourless-to-white crystals have no odour but a characteristic taste. When dissolved in water, the ions move about freely and conduct electricity (see ELECTROLYSIS). Salt is essential in the diet of humans and animals, and is a part of blood, sweat, and tears. Salt is widely used for the seasoning, curing, and preserving of foods. Its major use is in the production of CHLORINE, SODIUM, and sodium hydroxide. Salt makes up nearly 80% of the dissolved material in seawater and is also widely distributed in solid deposits. Manufacture and use of salt is one of the oldest chemical industries.

**Sodom and Gomorrah,** in the BIBLE, two of the Cities of the Plain (the others being Admah, Zeboiim, and Zoar, which was spared) destroyed by fire from heaven because of their unnatural carnal wickedness. They probably now lie submerged in the southern Dead Sea.

**Sofala,** city (1987 est. pop. 140,000), N Mozambique, on the coast of the Indian Ocean. It is the port for the provinces of Sofala, Manica, and Tete. It also handles import and export trade for Zimbabwe, Zambia, Malawi, and Zaïre. Rail links to Zimbabwe and Malawi have been improved but their performance is hindered by sabotage.

**Sofia** (ˌsohfiə), city (1983 pop. 1,093,752), capital of Bulgaria, W central Bulgaria, on a high plain surrounded by the Balkan Mts. It is Bulgaria's chief industrial centre with such manufactures as machinery, metal products, and textiles. Settled by the Thracians, it was held (1st–14th cent.) by Rome, Byzantium, and the first and second Bulgarian kingdoms. It passed to Turkey in 1382 and to Russia in 1878. After 1879 it was the capital of independent Bulgaria. During World War II the Germans occupied Sofia until 1944, when it fell to Soviet forces and a Communist government was established. Landmarks include many old churches, mosques, and synagogues, the parliament building, and the former royal palace.

**softball,** a variant of baseball, played with a larger ball on a smaller field. The ball is about 30 cm (12 in) in circumference, about 8 cm (3 in) larger than a baseball; the infield is 5.6 m² (60 sq ft), about 2.8 m² (30 sq ft) smaller than a baseball infield. Two teams of nine players each compete (until 1946, 10 players). Major differences from baseball are that the ball must be pitched underhand and a regulation game is seven innings. The game was invented in Chicago in 1888.

**software:** see COMPUTER PROGRAM.

**soil,** surface layer of earth containing organic matter and capable of supporting vegetation. A few centimetres to a metre or more thick, soil consists of fine rock material, HUMUS, air, and water. The arrangement of soil particles—soil structure together with organic matter (including microorganisms and living roots)—determines the soil's capacity to retain gases, water, and plant nutrients. Soil varies with the type of vegetation, climate, and parent rock material. Soil fertility—determined in part by texture, chemical composition, water supply, and temperature—can be maintained or improved by FERTILIZERS or by cultivation practices (see COVER CROP; ROTATION OF CROPS).

**Soka Gakkai** (ˌsohkahˌgahkkie), [Value Creation Society], Japan–based lay Buddhist group, founded (1937) by Makiguchi Tsunesaburo. A militantly evangelistic movement, it teaches simple doctrines of absolute faith and immediate worldly benefits. In Japan it first ran candidates for public office in 1955, and by 1964 it had organized its own political party, Komeito, or Clean Government party. Since 1960 Soka Gakkai has been led by Daisuku Ikeda, who has pursued a program of international conversion.

**Sokolow, Anna** (ˌsokəlov), 1912–, American dancer and choreographer. A member of the Graham company (1930–39), she became assistant to Louis Horst. Her works tend to portray the less attractive side of the human condition. She has choreographed for many international companies.

**Sokoto,** city (1971 pop. 108,565), capital of Sokoto state, NW Nigeria. Industries include cement, tanneries, and agriculture. Modern Sokoto is the urban focus of a government-initiated large-scale agricultural development project, the Sokoto-Rima Valley Development, designed to produce crops like rice, wheat, and cotton. A small village in the early 19th cent., it was selected as the capital of the Fulani empire in 1809 when a walled town was constructed.

**sol:** see COLLOID.

**solar cell:** see PHOTOVOLTAIC CELL.

**solar energy,** any form of ENERGY radiated by the SUN, including light, radio waves, and X-rays. Solar energy is needed by green plants for the process of PHOTOSYNTHESIS, which is the ultimate source of all food. The energy in fossil fuels (e.g., COAL and PETROLEUM) and other organic fuels (e.g., WOOD) is derived from solar energy. Difficulties with these fuels have led to the invention of devices that directly convert solar energy into usable forms of energy, such as electricity. Solar batteries, which operate on the principle that light falling on photosensitive substances causes a flow of electricity, play an important part in astronautics but are at present too expensive to be in common use on the Earth (see PHOTOVOLTAIC CELL). Thermoelectric generators convert the heat generated by solar energy directly into electricity. Heat from the Sun is used in air-drying a variety of materials and in producing salt by the evaporation of sea water (see DESALINATION). Experimental solar heating systems can supply heat and hot water for domestic use; heat collected in special plates on the roof of a house is stored in rocks or water held in a large container. Such systems, however, usually require a conventional heater to supplement them. Solar stoves, which focus the Sun's heat directly, are employed in regions where there is much perennial sunlight.

Solar energy: The Odeillo solar oven in the French Pyrenees generates intensive heat for industrial and scientific purposes.

**solar system,** the SUN and the family of PLANETS, natural SATELLITES, ASTEROIDS, METEORS, and COMETS that are its captives. The principal members of the Sun's retinue are the nine major planets; in order of increasing distance from the Sun, they are MERCURY, VENUS, EARTH, MARS, JUPITER, SATURN, URANUS, NEPTUNE, and PLUTO. All the planets orbit the Sun in approximately the same plane (that of the ECLIPTIC) and move in the same direction (from west to east). Current theories suggest that the solar system was formed from a NEBULA consisting of a dense nucleus, or protosun, surrounded by a thin shell of a gaseous matter extending to the present edges of the solar system. Through various processes much of the material of the nebula gradually accumulated in distinct dense objects which then formed the planets and their satellites.

**solar time,** time defined by the position of the Sun. The observer's **local solar time** is 0 hr (noon) when the centre of the Sun is on the observer's meridian. The *solar day* is the time it takes for the Sun to return to the same meridian in the sky. The length of the solar day varies throughout the year because the Earth moves with varying speed in its orbit and

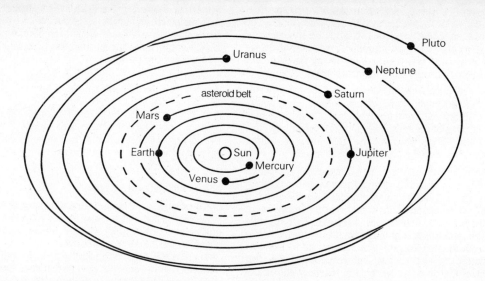

Solar system

because the equatorial plane is inclined to the orbital plane. It is thus more convenient to define time in terms of the **mean solar time,** or average of local solar time; hence every mean solar day is of equal length. The *equation of time* is the difference between the local solar time and the mean solar time at a given location. **Civil time** is mean solar time plus 12 hr; the civil day begins at midnight, whereas the mean solar day begins at noon. **Greenwich mean time** (GMT) is the local civil time at the former site of the Royal Observatory in Greenwich, UK, which is located on the PRIME MERIDIAN (0° longitude). **Standard time** is the civil time within one of the 24 time zones into which the earth's surface is divided. Within a zone all locations keep the same time, namely, the mean solar time of the central meridian (except when DAYLIGHT SAVING TIME is in effect). Zone times generally differ by a whole number of hours from GMT. See also SIDEREAL TIME.

**solar wind,** stream of ionized hydrogen and helium that radiates outward from the Sun, carrying away about 1 million tons of gas per sec. Near the Earth the solar wind normally has a velocity of 700 km/sec (450 mi/sec). The wind is believed to extend to between 100 and 200 ASTRONOMICAL UNITS from the Sun. COMET tails always point away from the Sun because of the pressure exerted by the solar wind. The interaction of the solar wind with the Earth's magnetic field is also responsible in part for such phenomena as the AURORAS and geomagnetic storms.

**solder,** metal ALLOY used in the molten state as a metallic binder. The type of solder to be used is determined by the metals to be united. Soft solders are commonly composed of lead and tin and have low melting points. Hard solders (i.e., silver solders) have high melting points. When brass is used in the solder or when brass surfaces are to be joined, the process is known as brazing, although the name is sometimes applied also to other hard soldering.

**sole,** FLATFISH of the family Soleidae. Sole live in the BENTHOS on sand or mud in shallow seas with warm or temperate waters. There are a few exceptions, e.g., *Bathysolea profunicola* which descends to the abyssal plains. The common or Dover sole (*Solea solea*) is about 30 cm (1 ft) long. It lies on the bottom on its left side, the darker right side changing colour to match the substrate. Sole is a much prized food fish, gourmets believing that its flavour is best two to three days after it has been caught.

**solenoid,** device made of a long wire wound many times into a tightly packed cylindrical coil. If current is sent through a solenoid made of insulated wire and having a length much greater than its diameter, a uniform magnetic field will be created inside the solenoid. The magnetic field can be intensified by inserting a ferromagnetic core into the solenoid.

**solfeggio** (sol,feji·oh), in music, systems of vocal exercises employing a series of syllables originally devised by the Benedictine monk Guido d'Arezzo (c.990–1080) for the purpose of vocalization and for practice in sightsinging. These 'solmization' syllables are now commonly known in the form *do, re, mi, fa, sol, la, si* (or *ti*), *do.*

**solicitor:** see LEGAL PROFESSION.

**solid:** see STATES OF MATTER.

**Solidarity,** Polish independent trade union federation formed in Sept. 1980. Led by Lech WALESA, it sponsored strikes and other forms of public protest to back demands for political and economic reform. Rural Solidarity, a Polish farmers' union, was officially recognized in May 1981. The Solidarity movement's popularity and growing support soon posed a serious threat to Poland's Communist rulers. On 13 Dec. 1981, the Polish government launched a crackdown by declaring martial law, suspending Solidarity, and imprisoning most of its leaders. Despite the formal abolishment of the union in 1982, demonstrations in support of Solidarity continued in Poland. In 1989 Solidarity was once again formally recognized and free to present candidates in elections.

**solid-state physics,** the study of properties exhibited by solids (e.g., glasses) whether crystalline or noncrystalline. Besides mechanical and thermal properties, electrical conductivity (see CONDUCTION) is one of the most important properties of solids. METALS are highly conductive and offer little resistance to electric currents. Most solid nonmetals are insulators; they offer virtually infinite resistance to electric currents. SEMICONDUCTOR materials, which possess electrical conductivity that is neither very high nor very low, are used as the basis of the TRANSISTOR and many other electronic devices.

**solid waste:** see WASTE DISPOSAL.

**solifluction,** the downslope movement of water-saturated surface deposits under the influence of gravitational force. The rate of solifluction is slow, in the region of 0.5–5.0 cm (⅕–2 in) per year. Solifluction is frequently active in the seasonally thawed layer of material overlying PERMAFROST.

**Soliman.** For Ottoman sultans thus named, see SULAYMAN.

**Solingen,** city (1984 pop. 159,200), North Rhine–Westphalia, W West Germany. Noted in the 18th cent. for its fine swords, it is still famous for its cutting tools, particularly cutlery.

**Solomon,** d. c. 922 BC, king of the ancient Hebrews, son and successor of DAVID. His mother was BATH-SHEBA. The reign of Solomon was eminently peaceful, marked by foreign alliances, notably with Egypt and with Phoenicia (he was on especially good terms with Hiram of Tyre). He developed trade and commerce. As he grew older, his despotism became worse and finally led to the revolt of JEROBOAM I. Solomon's wisdom is proverbial. He built the first Hebrew temple at Jerusalem. PROVERBS and ECCLESIASTES were ascribed to him, and the SONG OF SOLOMON bears his name.

**Solomon Islands,** independent nation (1987 est. pop. 270,000), land area c.29,785 km² (11,600 sq mi), comprising GUADALCANAL and other islands and atolls stretching in a 1450-km (900-mi) chain across the SW Pacific Ocean E of New Guinea. The capital is Honiara, on Guadalcanal. The Solomons are sparsely populated and largely covered with rain forest. Subsistence farming and fishing are mainstays of the economy, with small exports of timber, fish, copra, cocoa, and palm oil. The islands were discovered by Spain in 1568 and colonized by Europeans and missionaries in the 18th and 19th cent. Germany took possession of the N Solomons in 1885 but relinquished (1900) all except Buka and Bougainville (see PAPUA NEW GUINEA) to Britain, which had created (1893) a proctectorate in the S Solomons. During WORLD WAR II the islands were invaded (1942) by Japan and liberated (1943–44) by US forces after heavy fighting. They became self-governing in 1976 and independent in 1978 as a member of the COMMONWEALTH. The government is parliamentary, with a governor-general representing the British crown, a prime minister and cabinet, and an elected unicameral parliament. The 1984 general elections resulted in the formation of a government under Sir Peter Kenilorea, leader of the Solomon Islands United Party, but he was replaced in 1986 by Ezekiel Alebua.

**Solomon R. Guggenheim Museum**, New York; founded 1939. A major gallery of modern art, it is known for its circular building designed by Frank Lloyd WRIGHT (completed 1959). Its collection includes outstanding works by BRANCUSI and KANDINSKY.

**Solon** (ˌsohlən), c.639–c.559 BC, Athenian statesman. Elected leader (*archon*) in 594, he instituted sweeping economic and social reforms, and made important constitutional changes. Although bitterly opposed at first, Solon's reforms became the basis of the Athenian state. He also introduced a more humane law code to replace the code of DRACO.

**Soloveitchik, Joseph**, 1903–, Jewish philosopher; b. Poland. He is widely regarded as the principal Jewish thinker and authority of the age. In his lectures and writings he brings to bear a unique mastery of rabbinic literature, combined with a deep knowledge of logic and philosophy, to a wide range of modern problems and existential issues. He was awarded his PhD in 1931 from the University of Berlin; he settled in the US in 1932, and in 1941 he succeeded his father as Professor of Talmud at Yeshivah Univ.

**Soloviev, Vladimir Sergeyevich** (sələˌvyof), 1853–1900, Russian philosopher and writer. His concept of divine wisdom, expressed in such poems as *Three Meetings* (1898), influenced BLOK and other symbolists. He also wrote books such as *Russia and the Universal Church* (1899), plays, light verse, and essays on literature, politics, and philosophy.

**solstice**, either of two points on the ECLIPTIC where the Sun's apparent position on the celestial sphere (see ASTRONOMICAL COORDINATE SYSTEMS) reaches the greatest angular distance (about 23½°) above or below the celestial equator. One solstice occurs about 22 June when the Sun reaches directly overhead on the TROPIC OF CANCER, giving the longest daylight in the northern and the shortest in the sourthern hemisphere; while at about 22 Dec. The Sun reaches zenith on the TROPIC OF CAPRICORN, giving most daylight in the southern and least in the northern hemisphere.

**Solti, Sir Georg** (ˌsholtee), 1912–, British conductor; b. Hungary. He led orchestras in Switzerland, Germany, and France. In 1969 Solti became director of the Chicago Symphony Orchestra, after being musical director at the ROYAL OPERA HOUSE, Covent Garden (1961–71).

**solution**, in chemistry, homogeneous mixture of two or more substances. The dissolving medium is called the solvent, and the dissolved material is called the solute. In most common solutions, the solvent is a liquid, often water, and the solute may be a solid, gas, or liquid. Syrups are solutions of sugar, a solid, dissolved in water. Household AMMONIA is a solution of ammonia gas in water, and VINEGAR is a solution of acetic acid, a liquid, in water. Some ALLOYS, such as SOLDER or brass, are solutions of one solid in another. A solution is said to be saturated when it contains the maximum amount of solute that can be dissolved. See also COLLOID; COMPOUND; CONCENTRATION; ELECTROLYSIS; SUSPENSION.

**solvent abuse**, inhalation of vapours emitted by a variety of industrial and household products containing heavy organic compounds such as toluene. Short-term symptoms include euphoria, drowsiness, and the general appearance of drunkeness, all of which may precipitate accidents. Long-term abuse can cause damage to the liver and to other organs including the lungs and the brain.

**Solyman.** For Ottoman sultans thus named, see SULAYMAN.

**Solzhenitsyn, Aleksandr Isayevich** ('solzhəˌnitsin), 1918–, Russian émigré writer. The novel *One Day in the Life of Ivan Denisovich* (1962), based on his labour-camp experiences, was published with KHRUSHCHEV'S help, but a 1966 story was his last work published in the USSR. His novels *The First Circle* and *Cancer Ward,* both highly critical studies of life under STALIN, were published abroad in 1968. Under attack by the press, he responded in 1967 with an open letter to the Union of Soviet Writers. He was expelled from the union and from Moscow in 1969. In 1970 he was awarded the Nobel Prize for literature. *August 1914* (1971), a novel, and *The Gulag Archipelago* (1973–75), a documentary study, were also published abroad. In 1974 Solzhenitsyn was arrested and deported to West Germany. He settled in Switzerland and later accepted the Nobel Prize. *The Oak and the Calf,* a literary memoir, and *Lenin in Zurich,* a fictionalized portrait, appeared in 1975. Since 1976 he has lived in the US. His work, which shows a growing religious orientation, may be seen as retracing the path leading to present Soviet society.

**Somalia,** officially Somali Democratic Republic, republic (1987 est. pop. 5,000,000), 637,657 km² (246,200 sq mi), E Africa, directly S of the Arabian Peninsula across the Gulf of Aden, also bordered by Ethiopia and Kenya (W), Djibouti (NW), and the Indian Ocean (E). MOGADISHU is the capital. The country is arid and semidesert, with a barren coastal lowland rising to the great interior plateau (generally c.910 m/3000 ft high), which stretches to the northern and western highlands. Pastoralism is the dominant mode of life, and herding (both nomadic and sedentary) of camel, sheep, goats, and cattle is the principal occupation. Live animals, hides, skins, and clarified butter (ghee) make up the majority of exports. The major cash crops are bananas and sugarcane; subsistence crops include sorghum and maize. Processing of raw materials constitutes the bulk of the small but growing industry. The most valuable mineral resource is uranium; many other minerals are largely unexploited. Petroleum deposits have been found, and a refinery was built in 1979. The GNP is US$1271 million, and the GNP per capita is US$280 (1985). Somali, who make up more than 80% of the population, are Sunni Muslims. Islam is the state religion. There are Italian, Indian, and Pakistani minorities. Somali and Arabic are the official languages, but English and Italian are in wide use.

*History.* Muslim Arabs and Persians established trading posts along Somalia's coasts from the 7th to 10th cent., and Somali warriors joined Muslim sultanates in their battles with Christian Ethiopia in the 15th and 16th cent. Britain, France, and Italy began to dominate the region in the 19th cent. Britain established a protectorate in 1887 and concluded an agreement with France in 1888 defining their Somali possessions. Italy created a small protectorate in 1889, added territory in the south, and in 1925 detached Jubaland from KENYA. Somali-speaking districts of ETHIOPIA were combined with Italian Somaliland in 1936 to form ITALIAN EAST AFRICA. Britain conquered Italian Somaliland in WORLD WAR II, and the former colony, renamed Somalia, gained internal autonomy in 1956 and independence in 1960. The presence of some 350,000 Somalis in neighbouring countries stirred demands for a 'Greater Somalia', and fighting erupted with Ethiopia in 1964 over the OGADEN region, which Somalia claims. The Somali army invaded the Ogaden region in 1978–79 but was defeated by Ethiopian forces. Many thousands of Somali refugees fled to safety in Somalia, severely taxing its resources, and bloody border skirmishes continued into the early 1980s. An army coup led by Maj.-Gen. Muhammad Siyad Barre in 1969 resulted in the creation of a socialist state, and in 1976 the Somali Revolutionary Socialist Party was established as the country's sole political organization. In 1977 the regime ended its close ties with the USSR and expelled 6000 Soviet advisors. In 1980 Somalia granted the US permission to establish military bases. In 1988 Somalia and Ethiopia reached a ceasefire agreement on the Ogaden.

**Somerset,** county in SW England (1984 est. pop. 440,900), 3451 km² (1346 sq mi), bordering on the Bristol Channel in the NW. The county town is TAUNTON. Much of the S and W is hilly, including the Brendon Hills, the Quantock Hills, and the Blackdown Hills. In the NW there is a low-lying and formerly marshy area known as the Somerset Levels. The limestone hills of the Mendips occupy much of the NE part of the county, containing CHEDDAR GORGE. Agriculture is the main economic activity, with a concentration upon dairy farming. The county is famous for Cheddar cheese, foremost of the British hard cheeses. Wells and Glastonbury are historic and picturesque towns. Various minerals were once mined in the Mendip Hills, and building stone is quarried there today.

**Somerset, Edward Seymour, duke of,** 1506?–52, protector of England; brother of Jane SEYMOUR. He gained custody of his nephew, the young EDWARD VI, after the death (1547) of HENRY VIII, and was named protector. He wielded almost royal authority in effecting Protestant

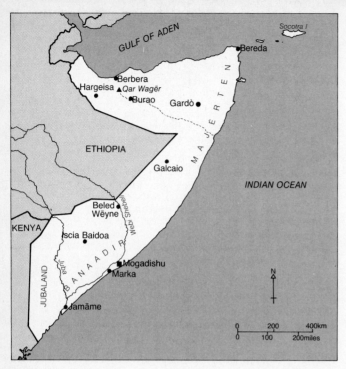

Somalia

reforms and with Thomas CRANMER introduced (1549) the first Book of Common Prayer. Somerset defeated the Scots at Pinkie (1547), but his failure to halt ENCLOSURE caused unrest. After the execution of his brother Thomas SEYMOUR, Somerset was deprived of the protectorate (1549) by John Dudley (later duke of Northumberland) and was beheaded.

**Somoza, Anastasio** (soh͵mohsah), 1896–1956, president of NICARAGUA (1937–47, 1950–56). As head of the national guard, he seized power by a coup (1937) and ruled as dictator for nearly 20 years. He was assassinated. His older son, **Luis Somoza Debayle**, 1922–67, succeeded him as president (1957–63) and liberalized the regime somewhat. His younger brother, **Anastasio Somoza Debayle**, 1925–80, also ruled as dictator and president (1967–72, 1974–79) until his regime was overthrown (1979) by leftist Sandinist rebels. He fled to Paraguay, where he was assassinated.

**sonar:** see ECHO SOUNDER.

**sonata,** in music, type of instrumental composition that arose in Italy in the 17th cent., at first merely designating an instrumental piece as contrasted to a piece with voice, called a CANTATA. The BAROQUE sonata, later called trio sonata, most commonly featured two melody instruments, usually violins or flutes, with a bass instrument and a keyboard instrument playing the thorough bass (see FIGURED BASS). In the later 18th cent. sonatas for groups of instruments were designated as string quartets or SYMPHONIES, and the term *sonata* was limited to pieces for one keyboard instrument or for one solo instrument (e.g., violin) with keyboard accompaniment. The keyboard sonata, developed by such composers as G.B. Sammartini and featuring one outstanding melodic line with harmony provided by a bass instrument, influenced the classical sonata perfected by HAYDN, MOZART, and BEETHOVEN. The first movement of the classical sonata (and sometimes other movements as well) observes a pattern called *sonata form*, consisting of two parts, a musical statement of several contrasting themes, followed by the development of those themes and a recapitulation of the original statement. This form is employed in string quartets, symphonies, and concertos as well. After the classical era LISZT developed the use of one thematic idea in all movements.

**Sonderbund,** 1845–47, defensive league of seven Roman Catholic cantons of SWITZERLAND. It was formed to protect Catholic interests and to prevent a centralized Swiss government controlled by the anti-Catholic Radical party. In 1847 the Radical majority in the federal diet dissolved the Sonderbund and dispatched an army to defeat it. The adoption of a federal constitution (1848) ended the sovereignty of the cantons and severely limited Catholic activity in the country.

**Sondheim, Stephen,** 1930–, American composer and lyricist. He wrote lyrics for Leonard BERNSTEIN's *West Side Story* (1957) and to his own music in such MUSICALS as *Gypsy* (1959), *Company* (1970), *A Little Night Music* (1973), and *Sweeney Todd* (1979). He is noted for his sophisticated, cynical lyrics and his ability to make his songs further plot development. His songs include 'Send in the Clowns'.

**song,** a musical form common to all human societies and most usually associated with a single line of melody for accompanied or unaccompanied voice. Frequently it is a setting of a poetic text. Songs in Western music can be classified into FOLK SONG (music of anonymous composition that is transmitted orally); art song, which includes the songs of the TROUBADOURS, minnesingers and MEISTERSINGERS, the 17th-cent. English ayre (or air), the German romantic LIEDER, and the Italian MADRIGAL and OPERA; and popular song, often derived from MUSICALS. Outstanding modern song compositions include those by WOLF, Richard STRAUSS, MAHLER, HINDEMITH and SCHOENBERG; DEBUSSY and POULENC; RACHMANINOFF, WARLOCK, BRITTEN, TIPPETT and Maxwell DAVIES. Notable popular songs have been written by Stephen FOSTER, Irving BERLIN, George GERSHWIN, Cole PORTER, and the BEATLES. See also CAROL; CHANTY; HYMN; PLAINSONG; ROCK MUSIC; SPIRITUAL.

**Song,** dynasty: see CHINA.

**Songhai** or **Songhay,** largest ancient empire of W Africa, in the region that is now MALI. It was founded c.700 by Berbers, and its rulers accepted Islam c.1000. Gao was its capital. Its greatest rulers were Sonni Ali (1464–92), who took TIMBUKTU, the former capital of the MALI empire; and Askia Muhammad I (c.1493–1528) whose death began the empire's decline, accelerated by a Moroccan invasion (1590).

**Songhua** or **Sungari,** chief river of NE China, c.1850 km (1150 mi) long, flowing generally N to join the AMUR R. on the China–USSR border. The river, which passes the industrial cities of Jilin (Kirin) and Harbin, is navigable for most of its length and is an important trade artery. Fengman Dam, begun under the Japanese occupation during World War II and completed in 1946, provides hydroelectricity for Jilin.

**Song of Solomon, Song of Songs,** or **Canticles,** book of the OLD TESTAMENT. It is traditionally ascribed to King SOLOMON, but may possibly be as late as the 3rd cent. BC. It is a collection of love poems, generally accepted by Jewish exegetes as an ALLEGORY or PARABLE of God's love for Israel, by Christian exegetes of his relations with either the Church or the individual soul.

**Song Qingling:** see under SOONG, family.

**sonic boom,** SHOCK WAVE produced by an object moving through the air at supersonic speed, i.e., faster than the speed of sound. An object, such as an aeroplane, moving through the air generates sound. When the speed of the object exceeds the speed of sound, there are points which are reached simultaneously by the sound created by the aeroplane over a period. The piled-up sound takes the form of a violent shock wave propagating behind the object.

**sonnet,** poem of 14 lines, usually in iambic PENTAMETER, restricted to a definite rhyme scheme. There are two prominent types: the Petrarchan, composed of an octave and a sestet (rhyming *abbaabba cdecde*); and the Shakespearean, consisting of three quatrains and a couplet (rhyming *abab cdcd efef gg*). Sonnets were highly popular in RENAISSANCE Italy, and thereafter in Spain, Portugal, France, and England. German and English romantics (see ROMANTICISM) revived the form, which remains popular. Notable sonneteers include, besides PETRARCA and SHAKESPEARE, DANTE, Edmund SPENSER, Philip SIDNEY, John KEATS, Elizabeth Barrett BROWNING, George MEREDITH, Edna St. Vincent MILLAY, and W.H. AUDEN.

**Sons of Liberty,** secret organizations formed in the American colonies to protest against the STAMP ACT (1765). They were organized by merchants, businessmen, lawyers, journalists, and others most affected by the act.

**Sontag, Susan,** 1933–, American writer. A brilliant and original thinker, she is known for her analyses of contemporary culture. Her essay collections include *Against Interpretation* (1966), *About Photography* (1977), *Illness as Metaphor* (1978), and *Under the Sign of Saturn* (1980). Sontag is also a novelist and a film-maker.

**Soong,** Chinese family, prominent in public affairs. **Soong Yao-ju,** or **Charles Jones Soong,** 1866–1918, graduated from Vanderbilt Univ. and was a Methodist missionary in Shanghai. His son **T.V. Soong,** 1894–1971, served in the KUOMINTANG government as finance minister (1928–31, 1932–33), foreign minister (1942–45), and president of the Executive Yuan (1945–47). After 1949 he lived in the US. Among his sisters, **Song Qingling,** or **Soong Ch'ing-ling,** 1892–1981, married (1914) SUN YAT-SEN. Following his death (1925) she broke with the Kuomintang after its expulsion (1927) of the Communists. She was reconciled (1937) with the Kuomintang but again left in 1946 and after 1949 served as vice chairman of the government of the People's Republic of China. Another sister, **Soong Mei-ling,** c.1897–, married (1927) Chiang Kai-Shek and campaigned to enlist US support for the Nationalist Chinese struggle against the Communists. After the Nationalists lost, she joined (1950) her husband in Taiwan. In 1978 their son, Chiang Ching-Kuo, (see under CHIANG KAI-SHEK) became president of Nationalist China (Taiwan).

**Sophia,** 1630–1714, electress of Hanover, daughter of FREDERICK THE WINTER KING and granddaughter of JAMES I of England. In 1701 the British Parliament settled the succession to the British crown on Sophia, a Protestant, and her issue. Thus her son GEORGE I became (1714) the first English king of the Hanoverian dynasty.

**Sophists** (ˌsofists), originally, itinerant teachers in 5th-cent. BC Greece who received fees for their lectures. PROTAGORAS was an early, respected Sophist. Others who followed him, less interested in the pursuit of truth than in the political use of rhetoric, were burlesqued by ARISTOPHANES and criticized by PLATO and ARISTOTLE, judgments that gave the term its present, derogatory meaning.

**Sophocles,** c.496–406 BC, Greek tragic poet, younger contemporary of AESCHYLUS and older contemporary of EURIPIDES. A respected public figure, a general and a priest, he won many dramatic prizes from 468 on, composing in all about 123 dramas. An innovator, he added a third actor, increased the size of the CHORUS, abandoned the trilogy for the self-contained tragedy, and introduced scene painting. Seven complete plays and over 1000 fragments survive. His best-known works are *Antigone* (c.441); *Oedipus Rex* or *Oedipus Tyrannus* (c.429), the apex of Greek dramatic irony; *Electra; Trachiniae; Philoctetes* (409); and *Oedipus at Colonus* (401)—a posthumous production by his grandson). Sophocles' characters are dramatically interesting in that their fates are determined more by their own characters and circumstances than by the Aeschylean gods; as such they have profoundly influenced Western TRAGEDY.

**soprano:** see VOICE.

**Sopwith, Sir Thomas Octave Murdoch,** 1888–1989, British aviator. Trained as an engineer, he took to flying for sport and won thousands of dollars in prizes as a pilot. He invested his winnings in founding (1912) the Sopwith Aviation Co., which during World War I designed 32 different types and built over 16,000 aircraft, but went into liquidation in 1920. Sopwith then joined H. Hawker and Sydney CAMM at Hawker Aircraft. He was knighted in 1953.

**Sorbonne;** see PARIS, UNIVERSITY OF.

**Sorel, Agnès** (sawˌrel), c.1422–50, mistress (1444–50) of CHARLES VII of France. She was the first officially recognized royal mistress in France and wielded much influence. The financier Jacques COEUR was rumoured to have had her poisoned.

**Sörensen, Villy,** 1929–, Danish philosopher and writer, and editor of the literary magazine *Vindrose* from 1959–63. His modern fairy stories and fantastic tales are amongst the most significant contributions to Danish prose in the 1950s and 1960s, especially *Strange Tales* (1953), *Harmless Tales* (1955), and *Guardian Tales* (1964).

**sorghum,** tall, coarse annual (*Sorghum vulgare*) of the GRASS family, similar in appearance to CORN and probably indigenous to Africa. Valued for its drought resistance, its varieties include the sweet sorghums, which yield molasses from the cane juice; the broomcorns, which yield a fibre used for brooms; the grass sorghums, used for pasture and hay; and the grain sorghums, used primarily for stock and poultry feed and, in the Old World, for human food.

**Sorocaba,** city (1980 pop. 254,672), 1000 km (160 mi) W of the city of São Paulo in SE Brazil. It is a rapidly growing industrial centre with cotton textile industries, a variety of food-processing industries and railway workshops.

**Sorokin, Pitirim Alexandrovitch,** 1889–1968, Russian-American sociologist. Banished from the Soviet Union for anti-Bolshevism, he emigrated (1923) to the US, where he taught at the Univ. of Minnesota (1924–30) and Harvard Univ. (1930–55). His controversial theories of the social process and his historical typology of cultures appear in *Social and Cultural Dynamics* (4 vol., 1937–41) and other works.

**sorority:** see FRATERNITY AND SORORITY.

**sorrel,** name for several plants, particularly species of dock (see BUCKWHEAT) and OXALIS.

**Sorrento,** rocky limestone peninsula forming the southern flank of the Bay of Naples, S Italy. The curious shapes of the rocks and caves and the remains of classical ruins have given rise to many legends relating to Greek and Roman history. The town of Sorrento is perched above cliffs on the N coast. It has long been a favoured resort and is the birthplace of the poet TASSO.

**Soshangane,** c.1790 1859, founder of the Gaza empire in present-day Mozambique. Originally the ruler of a small Nguni chiefdom swallowed up by the Zulu kingdom of SHAKA, Soshangane fled north to Delgoa Bay where he copied Shaka's methods of conquest to establish a rival state. The Gaza empire, named after Soshangane's grandfather, survived repeated attacks by the Zulu and the Portuguese and on Soshangane's death was the most powerful state between the Limpopo and the Zambezi rivers.

**Sosnowiec** ('sosnohˌvyets), city (1984 pop. 252,000), Upper Silesia, S Poland. It is a part of the KATOWICE mining and manufacturing region. The city was within Russian territory before World War I.

**Soto, Hernando de:** see DE SOTO, HERNANDO.

**Soufrière,** volcano, 1234 m (4048 ft) high, on the island of St Vincent, West Indies. Its great eruption of 1902 killed more than 1000 people and devastated a third of the island. A 1979 eruption, predicted by seismologists, was preceded by an evacuation of many islanders.

**soul,** the vital, immaterial life principle, generally conceived as existing within human beings and sometimes within all living things, inanimate objects, and the universe as a whole. In more primitive religions (forms of ANIMISM and SPIRITUALISM), the soul is thought to control both motor and mental processes; death, the cessation of these processes, is thus viewed as caused by the departure of the soul. PANTHEISM denies the individuation of human souls, and MATERIALISM declares the soul nonexistent. A widespread concept in religion is that of immortality, which usually postulates the existence of a soul that lives apart from the body after death. Dualistic concepts posit a God-given soul distinct from, and antagonistic to, an inferior, earth-bound body. For many Western philosophers the term *soul* is indefinable. Others consider *soul* synonymous with *mind*.

**sound,** pressure waves that propagate through air or other media. Sounds are generally audible to the human ear if their frequency lies between 20 and 20,000 hertz, or vibrations per second. Sound waves with frequencies below the audible range are called subsonic, and those with frequencies higher than the audible range are called ultrasonic (see ULTRASONICS). When a body, such as a violin string, vibrates, or moves back and forth, its movement in one direction pushes the molecules of the air before it, crowding them together. When it moves back again past its original position and on to the other side, it leaves behind it a nearly empty space. The body thus causes alternately, in a given space, a crowding together of the air molecules (a condensation) and a thinning out of the molecules (a rarefaction). The condensation and rarefaction make up a sound WAVE; such a wave is called longitudinal, or compressional, because the vibratory motion is forward and backward along the direction that the wave is following. Because such a wave consists of a disturbance of particles of a material medium, sound waves cannot travel through a vacuum. The velocity of sound in air at 0°C (32°F) is 331.9 m/sec (1089 ft/sec) but at 20°C (68°F) it is increased to about 344.4 m/sec (1130 ft/sec). Sound travels more slowly in gases than in liquids, and more slowly in liquids than in solids. The pitch of a sound depends upon the frequency of vibration; the higher the frequency, the higher the pitch. The DECIBEL is the unit of loudness, or intensity of sound. See also ACOUSTICS; DOPPLER EFFECT; ECHO; INTERFERENCE.

**sound barrier:** see AERODYNAMICS.

**sounding rocket,** a rocket capable of relatively cheaply placing a payload of scientific instruments above the atmosphere for some minutes. Either the results are radioed down, or the instruments with their recordings descend to the ground by parachute.

**Sousa, John Philip** (ˌsoohzə), 1854–1932, American bandmaster and composer. He improved the instrumentation and quality of band music. From 1880 to 1892 he led the US Marine Band and in 1892 formed his own band and successfully toured the world. He wrote more than 130 marches, many immensely popular, e.g., 'Semper fidelis' (1888) and 'The Stars and Stripes Forever' (1897).

**Sousa, Martim Afonso de,** 1500?–64, Portuguese soldier and administrator (1530–64) in BRAZIL. He drove French corsairs from the coast and founded colonies, initiating the settlement and colonization of Brazil.

**sousaphone,** a BRASS INSTRUMENT of the tuba family, which encircles the player's body. It was invented by J.P. SOUSA and is used in bands, particularly MILITARY BANDS, as a similarly pitched tuba would be impossible to march with.

**South, the,** region of the US, variously defined but including at most 14 states—MARYLAND, VIRGINIA, NORTH CAROLINA, SOUTH CAROLINA, GEORGIA, FLORIDA, KENTUCKY, TENNESSEE, ALABAMA, MISSISSIPPI, ARKANSAS, LOUISIANA, OKLAHOMA, and TEXAS. The basic agricultural economy of the Old South, determined by the warm climate and fertile soil, led to the development of twin institutions—the plantation system and SLAVERY—that made the South a section apart. Its doctrine of STATES' RIGHTS brought on secession, the CIVIL WAR, and, ultimately, the death of the Old South during RECONSTRUCTION. After World War II the South experienced profound economic, social, and political changes including the development of diversified industry, the emergence of a genuine two-party system, and INTEGRATION that brought the region closer to the rest of the nation. Parts of the South are now included in the dynamic SUN BELT.

**South Africa,** officially Republic of South Africa, republic (1987 est. pop. 32,400,000), 1,221,037 km² (471,442 sq mi), S Africa, bordered by the Atlantic Ocean (W), Namibia (NW), Botswana and Zimbabwe (N), Mozambique and Swaziland (NE), and the Indian Ocean (E and S). NAMIBIA (South West Africa) has been administered as an integral part of the country. LESOTHO is an independent enclave in the east. PRETORIA is the administrative capital, CAPE TOWN the legislative capital, and BLOEMFONTEIN the judicial capital. Other major cities include JOHANNESBURG and DURBAN. WALVIS BAY is an exclave in Namibia. The republic is divided into four provinces: Cape Province, Natal, Orange Free State, and Transvaal. About 14% of the land has been set aside for black Africans in ultimately independent territories (see BANTUSTAN). By 1981 four territories (TRANSKEI, BOPHUTHATSWANA, VENDA, and CISKEI) had been declared independent, but no foreign government has recognized these tribal homelands, whose so-called independence serves to strip blacks of their South African citizenship. The economy of South Africa, which is controlled by whites although nonwhites make up more than 75% of the workforce, is highly advanced and diversified. Mining, the foundation of the country's wealth, has been surpassed by industry as the chief economic sector. Manufactures include processed food, such beverages as wine, textiles, clothing, forest products, chemicals, iron and steel, machinery, and motor vehicles. Gold, the chief mineral extracted, accounts for two-thirds of mining revenue, but South Africa also ranks as a leading producer of platinum, chrome, vanadium, manganese, fluorspar, and diamonds. There are also vast deposits of copper, uranium, antimony, iron ore, and other minerals. Agriculture, stock-raising, forestry, fishing, and tourism are important. Crops include maize and other grains, vegetables, sugarcane, deciduous and citrus fruit, and tobacco. The GNP is US$63,487 million, and the GNP per capita is US$2010 (1985). The population consists of blacks (about 70% of the total); whites, mostly Afrikaners (Boers) and those of English descent (17%); coloureds, of mixed descent (9%); and Asians (3%). English and Afrikaans are the official languages, but there are 10 main black African languages, including Zulu and Xhosa. Most whites belong to the influential Dutch Reformed Church; other religious groups include independent black African Christians, Anglicans, Methodists, Roman Catholics, Lutherans, Hindus, and Jews.

*History.* Bantu-speaking black Africans moved into the region from E central Africa about 1500. The first permanent European settlement, a Dutch EAST INDIA COMPANY station, was set up in 1652. By 1707 there were about 1780 freeholders of European descent in South Africa, with about 1100 slaves. The first of a long series of wars broke out (1779) between the Xhosa people and white farmers, known as Boers, who had moved inland. Britain replaced the Dutch at the Cape in 1795 and was awarded the territory by the Congress of VIENNA in 1814. Disturbed by British rule, which accorded legal rights to free blacks and Coloureds and abolished slavery, some 12,000 Boers left the Cape in what is known as the Great TREK (1835–43) into the interior and Natal. Britain annexed Natal (1843), but the Boer republics of Orange Free State and the Transvaal were established (1850s). The discovery of diamonds (1867) and especially of gold (1886) spurred great economic development. Following increasing tension between the non-Afrikaner whites (Uitlanders) and the dominant Afrikaners, the two Boer republics declared war on Britain. The SOUTH AFRICAN WAR (Boer War; 1899–1902) was won by the British, who established (1910) the Union of South Africa, with dominion status. South Africa joined the Allies in WORLD WAR I and afterwards received a mandate over South West Africa (Namibia). Under Prime Minister J.B.M. HERTZOG South Africa gained final British recognition of independence (1931), prospered economically, and further suppressed nonwhites. J.C. SMUTS brought South Africa into WORLD WAR II on the Allied side. Through the policy of APARTHEID (complete segregation), white supremacy was strengthened during the regimes of H.F. VERWOERD, B.J. VORSTER, and P.W. BOTHA. The Afrikaner-based National Party (NP) has been in power since 1948. In 1961 South Africa became a republic and left the COMMONWEALTH. The government's refusal to yield control over Namibia, its creation of bantustans, and its rigid support of apartheid has led to growing international ostracism of the country. A new constitution adopted in 1983 created separate parliamentary chambers for whites, coloureds, and Indians (with blacks remaining outside the political structure), but elections to the coloured and Indian chambers in 1984 were boycotted by most of both the electorates. The NP government's policies have met with continuous resistance from the African population and the illegal AFRICAN NATIONAL CONGRESS, headed by imprisoned black leader Nelson MANDELA. Although the National Party won an increasing majority in the 1987 white election, the Government's partial relaxation of apartheid and pursuit of a political accommodation with the black population resulted in a rise in support for the hardline pro-apartheid Conservative Party. In Dec. 1988 South Africa signed a US-mediated agreement in New York providing for the eventual independence of Namibia, on the basis of phased withdrawal of South African troops from Namibia and Cuban forces from Angola.

### Post-war South African prime ministers
Jan Smuts (United Party), 1939–48
D.F. Malan (Nationalist), 1948–54
J.G. Strijdom (Nationalist), 1954–58
H.F. Verwoerd (Nationalist), 1958–66
B.J. Vorster (Nationalist), 1966–78
P.W. Botha (Nationalist), 1978–84

### South African presidents
C.R. Swart (Nationalist), 1961–67
J.J. Fouche (Nationalist), 1968–75
N. Diederichs (Nationalist), 1975–78
B.J. Vorster (Nationalist), 1978–79
Marais Viljoen (Nationalist), 1979–84
P.W. Botha (Nationalist), 1984–

**South African War** or **Boer War,** 1899–1902, war of the South African Republic (Transvaal) and the Orange Free State against Great Britain. Beginning with the acquisition (1814) of the Cape of Good Hope, the British had gradually increased their territorial possessions in South Africa. The Boers (Dutch) already settled in some of these areas resented the British advance; their hostility was inflamed after the discovery (1886) of gold brought an influx of British prospectors into the Transvaal. The Boers denied these newcomers citizenship and taxed them heavily, despite British protests. The situation was aggravated in 1895 by the Jameson raid (see JAMESON, SIR LEANDER STARR), which was interpreted as a British plot to seize the Transvaal. A military alliance (1896) of the TRANSVAAL and the Orange Free State followed. The British dispatched troops to defend what they considered their commercial rights, and the Boer states declared war (12 Oct. 1899). The large and well-equipped Boer forces won early victories, capturing Mafeking (now Mafikeng) and besieging Kimberley and Ladysmith. But the tide turned in 1900 with the landing of heavy British reinforcements. Under the leadership of F. S. Roberts and Lord KITCHENER, the British occupied all the major cities and formally annexed the Boer states; Kitchener remained only for mopping

**South Africa**

up. The Boers, however, began guerrilla attacks, led by such men as Louis BOTHA and J.C. SMUTS. Kitchener gained victory by interning Boer women and children and by building blockhouses to cut off large areas. His troops then combed the country, section by section. The Treaty of Vereeniging (31 May 1902) ended hostilities. The Boers accepted the British sovereign in return for a promise of responsible government in the near future; amnesty was granted to all who had not broken the rules of war. Bitterness caused by the war continued to affect political life in South Africa.

**South America,** fourth largest continent, c.17,819,000 km² (6,880,000 sq mi), extending c.7650 km (4750 mi) N to S and up to 5300 km (3000 mi) E to W. It is connected with North America by the Isthmus of Panama. The great chain of the ANDES Mts, running nearly the length of the continent and reaching a high point of 6960 m (22,835 ft) in Mt ACONCAGUA (in Argentina), is the dominant landform. Major lowlands include the LLANOS, along the ORINOCO R.; the basin of the AMAZON R., containing the world's largest rainforest; the GRAN CHACO; and the PAMPAS. South America is rich in iron ore, copper, tin, and hydroelectric potential, and has significant oil deposits. The countries of South America are Argentina, Bolivia, Brazil, Chile, Colombia, Ecuador, Guyana, Paraguay, Peru, Suriname, Uruguay, and Venezuela; the French overseas department of French Guiana is also on the continent (see separate articles). The fast-growing population, approaching 250 million in the early 1980s, is becoming increasingly urbanized. Half of it is concentrated in the nation of Brazil, which occupies more than one-third of the continental landmass. See map of South America in separate section.

**South American Indians,** aboriginal peoples of South America, from the Isthmus of Panama to Tierra del Fuego. An estimated 30 million Indians were living there when Europeans arrived. In the Andean region extensive remains show developed cultures at Chavín de Huántar and among the Paracas in Peru. The Mochica, Chimu, and NAZCA in Peru, the Chibcha and AYMARA of the Andes, and the ARAUCANIAN INDIANS of Chile had socially complex pre-Columbian cultures (see PRE-COLUMBIAN ART AND ARCHITECTURE), surpassed only by the INCA. Descendants of these peoples live in Ecuador, Peru, Bolivia, NW Argentina, and Chile. Quechua, the Inca language, is the most widespread linguistic stock (see AMERICAN INDIAN LANGUAGES). Since the Spanish conquest Indians have been used as labourers, poorly paid and lacking political representation; these conditions of semiservitude are changing slowly. Some Indians, notably the Inca, play a significant role in the national culture; but many live in small, peripheral groups. A few descendants of the Arawak and Carib Indians live in Venezuela, the Guianas, and N Brazil. The GUARANÍ INDIANS in Brazil are few and scattered, but in Paraguay their language is widely spoken and they form a significant element. Among tropical forest groups are the JÍVARO of Ecuador. The Colorado Indians of W Ecuador and the Puelches and Tehuelches, hunters of Patagonia, are virtually extinct. A dwindling number of Fuegians, so called for their campsites at Tierra del Fuego, live by hunting and fishing. In general the Indians of South America continue to be assimilated into white-dominated national cultures as their traditional ways of life and homelands are encroached on by population growth and industrial development.

**Southampton,** city (1981 pop. 211,321), Hampshire, S England, at confluence of rivers Test and Itchen at head of Southampton Water. It is the principal port in England for oceangoing liners, and is also a fast-growing container port. In 1984 it handled 24.4 million tonnes. There is a large oil refinery nearby at Fawley. Remains of the medieval town walls are still to be seen. University College, founded in 1850, received its charter as a university in 1952.

**Southampton, Henry Wriothesley,** 3rd **earl of,** 1573–1624, English nobleman and patron of letters. Best known as a patron of SHAKESPEARE, he is thought by some to be the man to whom the sonnets are dedicated. He took part in the rebellion (1601) of the earl of Essex and was sentenced to life imprisonment. JAMES I restored him to favour and he became (1619) a privy councilor. Southampton died of fever while leading an expedition against the Spanish in the Netherlands.

**South Asian Association for Regional Economic Cooperation** (SAARC), intergovernmental organization (est. 1985) to promote economic, scientific and cultural cooperation between Bangladesh, Bhutan, India, Maldives, Nepal, Pakistan, and Sri Lanka.

**South Australia,** state (1986 pop. 1,382,600), 984,381 km² (380,070 sq mi), south central Australia. Most people live in metropolitan ADELAIDE, the capital. Much of the land is semidesert or desert. Grains, meat, wool and wine grapes are important agricultural products, with farming largely confined to the wetter coastal belt and irrigated MURRAY R. valley. Iron ore, mined near WHYALLA, is the chief mineral. Steel, motor vehicles, food-processing, textiles, and electrical equipment are among the manufactures. South Australia was settled in 1836 as a free (i.e., non-penal) colony. It became a federated state of the Commonwealth of Australia in 1901 and transferred its northern areas, now as the NORTHERN TERRITORY, to the federal government in 1911.

**South Bank,** postwar cultural centre in London, on the S bank of the Thames R. First developed as part of the Festival of Britain (1951), the South Bank has some of the country's most important cultural venues. The main concert hall is the ROYAL FESTIVAL HALL. The National Theatre was built here (1967–77) after nearly half a century of unsuccessful attempts to find it a suitable site. Designed by Sir Denys Lasdun, its gloomy concrete exterior conceals superbly organized interiors; there are three auditoria, with seats for 1100, 890, and 200–400. The *National Film Theatre* (1956–58), under one of the arches of Waterloo Bridge, has 500 seats. The *Queen Elizabeth Hall,* with 1100 seats, used for concerts by chamber orchestras, etc, the *Purcell Room,* with 370 seats, used for recitals, and the *Hayward Gallery,* with no permanent collection but staging a succession of touring exhibitions, are components of a single group (built 1965–68) designed by the Architect's Dept of the Greater London Council. There are various sculptures in the open spaces around the halls.

**South Carolina,** state of the US (1984 est. pop. 3,300,000), area 80,432 km² (31,055 sq mi), situated in the SE bordered by North Carolina (N), the Atlantic Ocean (E), and Georgia (SW). COLUMBIA is the capital and largest city, followed by CHARLESTON and Greenville. The partly marshy coast gives way to a plain, separated from the rolling hills of the Piedmont plateau by the Fall Line. The BLUE RIDGE Mts are in the extreme NW. A predominantly manufacturing economy produces textiles, chemicals, nonelectrical machinery, and paper and pulp products, made from raw materials provided locally. The major agricultural products are soybeans, tobacco, cattle, eggs, corn, peaches, and cotton (which formerly dominated the economy). Forestry and fishing are significant sources of revenue, and tourists are attracted to the SEA ISLANDS and the state's historic sites. In 1980 68% of the population was non-Hispanic white and 30% was black; about 48% lived in metropolitan areas. The original inhabitants of the region were Cherokee, Catawba, and Yamasee Indians. In 1760 the British established a colony to produce rice and indigo using slave labour, the only one in which slaves outnumbered Europeans. South Carolina was one of the thirteen colonies to declare independence from Great Britain, and after the American Revolution cotton dominated the economy. It was the first state to secede from the Union (1860), and the Civil War began after confederate troops fired on Fort Sumter near Charleston (1861). Even after the war blacks were effectively disenfranchised by the so-called 'Jim Crow' laws. In the 1920s cotton farming declined because of the destruction of the crop by the boll weevil and land erosion, causing much poverty. In recent years South Carolina has successfully attracted new jobs from Europe, Japan, and elsewhere in the US.

**South China Sea,** western arm of the Pacific Ocean, (c.2,590,000 km²/1,000,000 sq mi), bordering S China, Vietnam, Malaysia, the Philippines, and Taiwan. It covers the shallow Sunda Platform (less than 61 m/200 ft deep) in the southwest and depths of up to (c.5490 m/18,000 ft) in the northeast. The Gulf of Tonkin (N) and Siam (S) are its chief embayments. Many islands dot the sea, which is subject to violent typhoons.

**South Dakota,** state of the US (1984 est. pop. 706,000), area 199,552 km² (77,047 sq mi), located in the north–central region, bordered by North Dakota (N), Minnesota and Iowa (E), Nebraska (S), and Montana and Wyoming (W). PIERRE is the capital, and Sioux Falls, Rapid City, and Aberdeen are the largest cities. The state is divided by the MISSOURI R. flowing N to S, separating broad prairies of fertile chernozem soils in the E from higher terrain in the W. This includes the mineral-rich BLACK HILLS, (which contain the country's largest gold mine), and the eroded sand and clay formations of the Badlands. Agricultural activities include cattle and sheep ranches in the arid west, and grain crops grown mostly on irrigated land in the east. The leading manufactures are processed foods, nonelectrical machinery, and timber. The giant sculptures of US presidents on MOUNT RUSHMORE and the Badlands are attractions in a growing tourist industry. Only 28% of the population lives in metropolitan areas; in 1980 92% was non-Hispanic white and 7% was native American. French explorers in the 18th cent. found sedentary Arikara Indians and nomadic, buffalo-hunting Sioux. Though the territory was acquired by the US in the LOUISIANA PURCHASE (1803), settlement did not start until gold was discovered in the Black Hills (1874) and the Sioux were defeated at the massacre of Wounded Knee (1890). Despite periodic droughts ranchers and farmers moved in. In the 20th cent. the Missouri R. was dammed to control flood waters. Many Indians on South Dakota's reservations have been leaders of the native American movement in recent years.

**Southeast Asia,** region (1980 est. pop. 357,532,000), c.4,506,600 km² (1,740,000 sq mi), bounded roughly by India (W), China (N), and the Pacific Ocean (E). As usually defined, it includes the independent nations of BRUNEI, BURMA, INDONESIA, KAMPUCHEA, LAOS, MALAYSIA, the PHILIPPINES, SINGAPORE, THAILAND, and VIETNAM. A tropical rainy climate with seasonal monsoon winds predominates over most of the area. The chief crop is rice. Population is unevenly distributed, with very high densities in many lowland areas, and there is great diversity of culture, history, ethnic composition, language, and religion. Southeast Asia was once the site of several great Eastern civilizations, notably that of the KHMER EMPIRE, in what is now Kampuchea and Laos. In the 16th cent. Europeans began to colonize the entire area, with the exception of Thailand (Siam). Southeast Asia was the scene of heavy fighting during WORLD WAR II. After the war most of the countries achieved independence. Since then, ethnic strife, generally weak economies, and political turmoil, including violent conflict (see VIETNAM WAR) between Communist and non-Communist factions (especially in Vietnam, Laos, Kampuchea, and Indonesia), have plagued the region.

**Southeast Asian languages** family of languages, sometimes called Austroasiatic, spoken in SE Asia. According to one school of thought, it has three subfamilies: the MON–KHMER LANGUAGES, the MUNDA LANGUAGES, and the Annamese–Muong subfamily. There is considerable evidence, but no definite proof, that all these groups are derived from a single ancestor. See LANGUAGE (table).

**Southeast Asia Treaty Organization** (SEATO), formed (1954) under a collective defence treaty signed in Manila (Philippines) by Australia, France, New Zealand, Pakistan, the Philippines, Thailand, the UK, and the US in response to the French defeat in INDOCHINA and the perceived threat of communist aggression. Following the withdrawal of France and Pakistan in the early 1970s, the SEATO structure was dissolved in 1977;

however, the Manila treaty remains in force, particularly in respect of the US commitment to Thailand's security.

**Southend-on-Sea,** town (1981 pop. 155,720), Essex, SE England, on N side of Thames estuary, 57 km (35 mi) E of London. It is a commercial centre, whose industries include the manufacture of electrical goods. It has a famous pier which is over 1.5 km (1 mi) long.

**Southern African Development Cooperation Conference** (SADCC), intergovernmental initiative launched in 1979 to promote the 'economic liberation' of the southern African states, particularly in relation to the economic power of South Africa. The participating countries (1986) are Angola, Botswana, Lesotho, Malawi, Mozambique, Swaziland, Tanzania, Zambia, and Zimbabwe.

**Southern Alps,** mountain range, South Island, New Zealand, paralleling the west coast. It rises to 12,349 ft (3,764 m) at Mt. Cook, New Zealand's highest point. It has numerous glaciers, e.g., Tasman and Franz Josef, and many deep gorges.

**Southern Christian Leadership Conference** (SCLC), civil rights organization founded in 1957 by Martin Luther KING, Jr., and headed by him until his assassination in 1968. Composed largely of Southern black clergymen, it advocated nonviolent passive resistance as the means of securing equality for blacks. It sponsored the massive march on Washington in 1963. Ralph Abernathy headed (1968–77) the SCLC after King's death, but its influence has declined.

**southern lights:** see AURORA.

**Southey, Robert,** 1774–1843, English writer. The third, with his friends COLERIDGE and WORDSWORTH, of the Lake Poets, he was also a historian, biographer and translator; his long narrative poems such as *Madoc* (1805) and *The Curse of Kehama* (1810) were highly regarded by his contemporaries, and he became poet laureate in 1813, but he is now remembered chiefly for his *Life of Nelson* (1813) and for short poems such as 'The Battle of Blenheim'.

**South Georgia,** island in the Southern Ocean, S of the Atlantic; Area 3755 km² (1450 sq mi) and very mountainous (Mt Paget, 2934 m/9626 ft, highest peak); British dependency in dispute with Argentina. It was discovered in 1675 by Antoine de la Roche, but the first landing was by Captain Cook in 1775 who claimed it for George III of Britain. The centre of the shore-based Antarctic whaling industry from 1904 to 1966, its only population after that was on scientific stations. It was invaded by Argentina for three weeks in 1982 as part of the Falkland Islands war, and a permanent British garrison has been in place since then.

**South Glamorgan,** county in SE Wales (1984 est. pop. 394,400), 416 km² (162 sq mi). It was formed in the local government reorganization of 1974 out of the country of Glamorganshire. It is mainly composed of the Vale of Glamorgan, which faces the Bristol Channel. Dairy farming and mixed agriculture are important. The city of CARDIFF is situated in the E of the county. Other towns are Barry and Penarth, both on the coast.

**South India, Church of,** merger of six major Protestant denominations in India. It was formed (1947) from Anglican, Methodist, Presbyterian, Reformed, Congregational, and Lutheran bodies. The union, especially in its reconciliation of the Anglican view of apostolic succession with the views of the other groups, is cited as a landmark in the ECUMENICAL MOVEMENT.

**South Orkney Islands,** small island group in the Southern Ocean N of the Weddell Sea; British dependency disputed by Argentina but covered by the ANTARCTIC TREATY. They were discovered in 1821 by British and US sealers. A Scottish National Antarctic Expedition established a meteorological station there in 1903, which still operates and is the oldest continuous one in Antarctica.

**South Pacific Forum** (SPF), intergovernmental consultative body (est. 1971) linking Australia, Cook Islands, Fiji, Kiribati, Nauru, New Zealand, Niue, Papua New Guinea, Solomon Islands, Tonga, Tuvalu, Vanuatu, and Western Samoa. In 1985 SPF members signed a treaty declaring the S Pacific a nuclear-free zone.

**South Pole,** southern end of the earth's axis, lat. 90°S and long. 0°, distinguished from the south MAGNETIC POLE. It was first reached by Roald AMUNDSEN in 1911. See also Robert Falcon SCOTT.

**South Sandwich Islands,** 11 volcanic islands in the Southern Ocean, S of the Atlantic Ocean; total area about 550 km² (212 sq mi); British dependency disputed by Argentina. The group was discovered by Captain Cook in 1775. It is uninhabited apart from temporary scientific stations.

**South Sea Bubble,** popular name in England for speculation in the South Sea Co. formed (1711) by Robert Harley. The Company assumed the national debt in return for an annual payment by the government plus a monopoly of British trade with the islands of the South Seas and South America. Fraudulent schemes resulted and the bubble burst (1720). Robert WALPOLE was made first lord of the treasury and chancellor of the exchequer and took action to restore the company's credit.

**South Seas,** name given by early explorers to the whole of the Pacific Ocean. It is now more usually applied only to the islands of the central and South Pacific and is considered synonomous with the term OCEANIA.

**South Shetland Islands,** island chain off the W coast of the Antarctic peninsula. It was discovered by the Briton William Smith in 1819 and became a major site of the sealing and whaling industries. It was claimed by Britain (1819), Argentina (1943), and Chile (1940), but is covered by the ANTARCTIC TREATY. Deception Island, at the S end of the chain, is a volcanic crater, which erupted in 1967, 1969, and 1971. Research stations of eight countries operate there.

**South Suburban,** town (1981 pop. 394,916), West Bengal state, E India. It is, as its name implies, a southern suburb of CALCUTTA, which has shown rapid growth in population. It is primarily an area of diverse industry.

**Southwark,** London borough (1981 pop. 209,735), on S side of R. Thames, in inner London. The Thames is crossed here by Blackfriars, London, Southwark, and Tower bridges. The borough contains the districts of Bermondsey, Camberwell, and Southwark. It contains the 13th-cent. Southwark cathedral, located at the S end of London bridge. The Imperial War Museum is in Lambeth Road.

**Southwell, Saint Robert,** 1561?–95, English Jesuit poet and martyr, imprisoned and hanged on admitting his priesthood. His *St Peter's Complaint* (1595) and devotional poems like 'The Burning Babe' soon became popular with Protestants as well as Catholics. He was canonized in 1970. Feast: 25 Oct.

**Southwestern Indians:** see NORTH AMERICAN INDIANS.

**South Yorkshire,** former metropolitan county in N Midlands of England (1984 est. pop. 1,305,400), 1560 km² (608 sq mi), bordering on W and N Yorkshire in the N and Derbyshire in the S. It was formed in the 1974 reorganization of local government. It is situated E of the PEAK DISTRICT at the S end of the PENNINES. The main river is the Don. Most of the county is occupied by industrial areas, especially in the Don valley. The prosperity of the area is based upon coal-mining and iron and steel manufacture. SHEFFIELD, ROTHERHAM, BARNSLEY, and DONCASTER are the main industrial and residential towns. The county council was abolished in April 1986 and the area is now administered by the borough and city councils.

**Soutine, Chaïm,** 1894–1943, French expressionist painter; b. Lithuania. In 1913 he went to Paris, meeting CHAGALL and MODIGLIANI. During the 1920s he painted a series of distorted figures, expressing the psychological abnormalities in an Expressionist style with a thick impastoed paint layer.

**sovereignty,** supreme law-making power. Modern conceptions of sovereignty may be traced back to Jean BODIN's *Les Six Livres de la République* (1576) and to the absolute authority described in Thomas HOBBES's *Leviathan* (1651). For any NATION-STATE, sovereignty has both an internal and an external dimension. Internally, the sovereign power, whether it be a monarch, or, as in Britain today 'the queen in parliament', represents the highest law-giving and law-enforcing authority within a defined territory. All other institutions are legally subordinate to it and there is no appeal against its edicts. In modern democracies of all forms the ultimate source of sovereignty is held to be the people, though of necessity it is exercised on their behalf by the state. In principle, a sovereign state cannot allow other states or organizations to make laws or use force in its territory. The external dimension of sovereignty consists in the fact that states do not recognize any power or authority as superior to themselves. A distinction is often made between de jure or formal legal sovereignty and de facto or effective, practical sovereignty.

**soviet** [Rus., = council], primary unit in the political organization of the Soviet Union. The first soviets were revolutionary committees organized by socialists among striking workers during the 1905 RUSSIAN REVOLUTION. When the 1917 Revolution broke out, workers', peasants', and soldiers' soviets sprang up all over Russia. Their central executive committees included adherents of BOLSHEVISM AND MENSHEVISM, and members of the SOCIALIST REVOLUTIONARY PARTY. When the Bolsheviks under V.I. LENIN took control of the soviets in Petrograd (later Leningrad) and other cities, their success was assured. Soviets (1918–20) in Bavaria, Hungary (see KUN, BÉLA), and the Baltic republics, however, were short-lived. The soviets, elected by universal suffrage, remain the basic political unit in the USSR, forming a hierarchy culminating in the Supreme Soviet. In practice, they are dominated by the Communist Party and the POLITBURO.

**Post-war Soviet Communist Party leaders**
Joseph Stalin, 1924–53
Georgi Malenkov, 1953
Nikita Khrushchev, 1953–64
Leonid Brezhnev, 1964–82
Yuri Andropov, 1982–84
Konstantin Chernenko, 1984–85
Mikhail Gorbachev, 1985–

**Post-war Soviet presidents**
Nikolai Shvernik, 1946–53
Klimenti Voroshilov, 1953–60
Leonid Brezhnev, 1960–64
Anastas Mikoyan, 1964–65
Nikolai Podgorny, 1965–77
Leonid Brezhnev, 1977–82
Vasily Kuznetsov (acting), 1982–83
Yuri Andropov, 1983–84
Konstantin Chernenko, 1984–85
Andrei Gromyko, 1985–1988
Mikhail Gorbachev, 1988–

**Post-war Soviet prime ministers**
Joseph Stalin, 1941–53
Georgi Malenkov, 1953–55
Nikolai Bulganin, 1955–58
Nikita Khrushchev, 1958–64
Alexei Kosygin, 1964–80
Nikolai Tikhonov, 1980–85
Nikolai Ryzhkov, 1985–

**Soviet bloc,** popular name for the allies of the USSR, (see UNION OF SOVIET SOCIALIST REPUBLICS, principally in Eastern Europe, which belong to COMECON and the WARSAW TREATY ORGANISATION. The communist regimes of the Soviet bloc prefer to call themselves the 'socialist countries'. they would include the USSR, POLAND, CZECHOSLOVAKIA, East GERMANY, HUNGARY, ROMANIA, BULGARIA, YUGOSLAVIA (to 1948), and ALBANIA (to 1968). In the more general sense, the Block is sometimes taken to include other pro-Soviet regimes such as MONGOLIA, CHINA (to 1960), North KOREA, VIETNAM, KAMPUCHEA, CUBA, MOZAMBIQUE, ETHIOPIA, and ANGOLA.

**Soviet Far East,** region (1980 pop. 6,173,000), c.6,216,000 km² (2,400,000 sq mi) comprising the entire NE coast of Asia. Often considered part of SIBERIA, the Soviet Far East is treated separately in USSR regional schemes. It borders the Yakut Autonomous SSR (NW); E Siberian Sea (N); Bering Sea (NE); Sea of Japan (SE); China (S); and Yablonovy Mts. (SW). The region includes mountains, TAIGA, and TUNDRA. It is virtually self-sufficient economically. VLADIVOSTOK and other cities produce iron, steel, petroleum, timber and other products. Resources include coal, oil, and gold. Farming, fishing, and hunting are major occupations. Over 25 ethnic groups inhabit the region. Russian colonization began in the late 16th cent. From the mid 19th to early 20th cent. various parts of the region were acquired from China and Japan, and it was incorporated into the USSR in 1922. In 1969, Sino-Soviet border clashes began along the AMUR and USSURI rivers. A navigation treaty was signed in 1978, but general border negotiations broke down in 1980.

**Soviet Russia,** the state founded in Oct. 1917 during the takeover of the Russian empire by LENIN's Bolsheviks, and superseded in 1922 by the Soviet Union (USSR). Owing to the secession of the borderlands of the former empire, including Finland, the Baltic States, Poland, Ukraine, and Georgia, Soviet Russia was confined at first to its Muscovite heartland; but in the course of the Russian Civil War (1918–21 (see CIVIL WAR, RUSSIAN) the Red Army reconquered many of the lost territories. It was the Bolsheviks' original intention to export the Revolution from Russia to Germany, but defeat of the Red Army's western campaigns in the POLISH–SOVIET WAR (1919–20) together with the Kronstadt mutiny forced an ideological retreat. Lenin's NEW ECONOMIC POLICY (Mar. 1921) marked the end of revolutionary policy. Lenin's successor, STALIN, moved away from international concerns, and under the slogan of 'Socialism in one country' concentrated on the consolidation of power in the new federal state, the Soviet Union (see UNION OF SOVIET SOCIALIST REPUBLICS).

**Soviet Union:** see UNION OF SOVIET SOCIALIST REPUBLICS.

**Soweto,** collective name for a group of segregated townships inhabited by black Africans, located 16 km (10 mi) SW of JOHANNESBURG, South Africa. In 1976 Soweto was the scene of severe racial violence that began as a black student protest against the use of the Afrikaans language instead of English in schools. The rioting spread to other black urban centres, and more than 600 lives were lost before army troops restored order.

**soya bean,** plant (*Glycine max*) of the PULSE family, native to tropical and warm temperate regions of the Orient, where it has been a principal crop for at least 5000 years. There are over 2500 varieties in cultivation, producing high-PROTEIN beans of many sizes, shapes, and colours. Soya beans are used in many forms, e.g., oil, meal, soy sauce, soy milk, and bean curd, and as a COFFEE substitute. Soya bean oil is also valuable for its use in the manufacture of other products, e.g., glycerin, soaps, and plastics. The green crop is used for forage and hay.

**Soyinka, Wole,** 1934–, Nigerian playwright, poet, and novelist. Written in English, his works fuse Western and Yoruba traditions. His play *The Invention* (1955) brought him notice in London. Other works include the plays *A Dance of the Forests* (1962), *Kongi's Harvest* (1966), and *Death and the King's Horseman* (1975); the novel *The Interpreters* (1965); and the autobiography *Aké: Years of Childhood* (1982). In 1986 Soyinka won the Nobel Prize for literature.

**Spaak, Paul Henri** (1899–1972), Belgian statesman and Socialist leader. He was Belgium's foreign minister almost continuously from 1938 to 1966, premier (1938–39, 1946, 1947–49), first president of the UNITED NATIONS General Assembly (1946), chairman of the Council for Economic Recovery (1948–49), secretary general of NATO (1957–61), and a founder of the EUROPEAN COMMUNITY.

**space astronomy,** the study of celestial bodies by means of instruments in space. The ability to place instruments in space, above the Earth's atmosphere and thus avoiding its opacity to many forms of radiation and its perturbation of the light used in optical astronomy, has materially assisted the study of celestial objects. SOUNDING ROCKETS and later SATELLITES have given us knowledge of gamma- and X-ray emissions and of ultraviolet and infrared radiation, thereby greatly aiding understanding. In optical wavelengths, a telescope placed in orbit, as is planned, will have a sharpness of vision unobtainable on the ground. Moreover, within the solar system space probes to the planets, to HALLEY'S COMET, and towards the Sun, have given us a wholly new understanding of the bodies in orbit round the Sun.

**space exploration,** the investigation of physical conditions in space and on stars, planets, and natural satellites through the use of artificial satellites, space probes (see SATELLITE, ARTIFICIAL; SPACE PROBE), and manned spacecraft. Although studies from Earth using optical and radio TELESCOPES had accumulated much data on the nature of celestial bodies, it was not until after World War II that the development of powerful rockets made direct space exploration a technological possibility. Manned spaceflight progressed from the simple to the complex, starting with suborbital and orbital flights by a single ASTRONAUT or cosmonaut (Mercury and Vostok); subsequent highlights include the launching of several crew members in a single capsule (beginning with Gemini and Voskhod), rendezvous and docking of two spacecraft (beginning with Gemini and performed internationally in the Apollo–Soyuz Test Program), lunar orbit and landing (Apollo), the launching of space stations (Salyut, MIR, and Skylab), and the launching of a reusable space vehicle, the SPACE SHUTTLE. Space exploration is motivated by curiosity, the desire to know as much as possible about the universe, and, in the case of manned spaceflight, by the physical challenge provided by new frontiers of human endeavour. The exploitation of near-Earth space has already begun, with applications satellites used for commercial and military purposes, and experiments in manned SPACE STATIONS aimed at utilizing the space environment (microgravity, high vacuum, and radiation) for specialized industrial and medical processes. In the longer term, the utilization of the mineral resources of other SOLAR SYSTEM bodies, or even the 'colonization' of other planets may become possible.

**space law,** principles of law governing the exploration and use of outer space. The 1967 Outer Space Treaty, signed by most nations, states that INTERNATIONAL LAW applies to outer space and that while all states may freely explore and use outer space, territorial claims in space are prohibited. Other treaties dealing with rescue and return of astronauts, liability for damage caused by space objects, and registration of space objects became effective, respectively, in 1968, 1972, and 1976. A treaty on the potential use of the Moon's resources, drafted by the UN in 1979, has been signed by several nations; as of 1987, the US and the UK had not signed it.

**space medicine,** study of the medical and biological effects of space travel on living organisms. The principal aim is to discover how well and for how long humans can withstand conditions encountered in space and to study their ability to readapt to the earth's environment after travel in space. Medically significant aspects of space travel include weightlessness, inertial forces experienced during liftoff, radiation exposure, absence of day-night cycle, and heat produced within the spacecraft. Participants in SPACE EXPLORATION initially suffered from symptoms such as nausea, sensory disorientation, and poor muscular coordination, but astronauts and animals living in space are now able to adapt to long periods of space travel without significant disability. Shielding and protective clothing prevent exposure to radiation from space and from nuclear reactors on board.

**spaceplane,** a popular term used to describe a reusable winged spacecraft. The first craft of this kind was the US SPACE SHUTTLE. The USSR is believed to be developing both a small (15-tonne) spaceplane, Kosmolyot, and a large space shuttle, Buran [snowstorm], similar to the US Shuttle. Although scale models of Kosmolyot were first flown in 1982, the large shuttle is expected to become operational first. The EUROPEAN SPACE AGENCY is planning a small, 21-tonne, shuttle vehicle, Hermes, for launching by the Ariane 5 ROCKET in the 1990s, and Japan is considering a similar development, Hope, for use with its H-II rocket. The next logical step is the development of single-stage-to-orbit spaceplanes which would take off from and land on a runway rather like a conventional aircraft, and would be more economical to operate than a vertically-launched shuttle. A British proposal, HOTOL, would use engines which breathe in air at low altitude and use liquid oxygen carried on board for the final boost to orbit. Similar proposals include the X-30 National-Aero-Spaceplane (US) and Sanger (West Germany).

**space probe,** unmanned space vehicle, usually carrying sophisticated instrumentation, designed to explore various aspects of the SOLAR SYSTEM. Unlike an artificial SATELLITE, which is placed in more or less permanent

Space probe: Mission control at NASA's Jet Propulsion Laboratory during the encounter of *Voyager I* unmanned spacecraft with Saturn in Oct. 1980.

## MANNED SPACEFLIGHT PROGRAMMES

| Programme | Country | Years of Launchings | Number of Crew | Missions and Major Accomplishments |
|---|---|---|---|---|
| Apollo: Command and Service Modules | US | 1968–73 | 3 | First manned circumlunar flight (Frank Borman, James Lovell, and William Anders in *Apollo 8;* 21–27 Dec. 1968); used to take Lunar Excursion Module to lunar orbit (*Apollos 10–17;* 1969–72); used to ferry astronauts to *Skylab* and return them to Earth (1973–74). |
| Apollo: Lunar Excursion Module (LEM) | US | 1969–72 | 2 | First manned lunar landing (Neil Armstrong and Buzz Aldrin in *Apollo 11,* 20 July 1969); five other successful manned lunar landings (*Apollos 12* and *14–17;* 1969–72). |
| Apollo: Lunar Rover | US | 1971–72 | 2 | Motorized lunar surface rover used on *Apollos 15–17.* |
| Apollo-Soyuz Test Project (ASTP) | US–USSR | 1975 | 3 (Apollo) 2 (Soyuz) | First international docking in space (Thomas Stafford, Deke Slayton, and Vance Brand in *Apollo 18;* Aleksei Leonov and Valery Kubasov in *Soyuz 19;* 16–18 July 1975). |
| Gemini | US | 1965–66 | 2 | First US extravehicular activity (Edward White in *Gemini 4;* 3 June 1965); first close rendezvous of two spacecraft (Walter Schirra and Thomas Stafford in *Gemini 6* with *Gemini 7;* 15 Dec. 1965); first manned docking of two spacecraft in orbit (Neil Armstrong and David Scott in *Gemini 8* with unmanned Agena rocket stage; 16 Mar. 1966). |
| Mercury | US | 1961–63 | 1 | First US manned (suborbital) flight (Alan Shepard in *Mercury-Redstone 3* or *Liberty Bell 7;* 5 May 1961); first US manned orbital flight (John Glenn in *Mercury-Atlas 6* or *Friendship 7;* 20 Feb. 1962). |
| Mir | USSR | 1986 | up to 6 | Earth-orbit space station developed from Salyut (see article). |
| Progress | USSR | 1978– | 0 | Unmanned Soyuz-type spacecraft used to ferry supplies to Salyut space station. |
| Salyut | USSR | 1971–82 | 2 + | Earth-orbit space stations (seven launched 1971–82); first manned space station; first linking of two similar-sized modules (*Cosmos 1267* to *Salyut 6,* 1981; Dr. Oleg Y. Atkov, Leonid D. Kizim, and Vladimir A. Solovyez (ferried to *Salyut 7* by *Soyuz T-10;* return to Earth of *Soyuz T-11*) set space endurance record of 237 days 8 Feb.–20 Oct. 1984). |
| Skylab | US | 1973–74 | 3 | Earth-orbit space station; three 3-man crews visited for 28, 59, and 84 days, the last setting a US space-endurance record. |
| Soyuz | USSR | 1967–81 | 1, 2, or 3 | First extravehicular transfer of crew members from one spacecraft to another (Yevgeny Khrunov and Aleksei Yeliseyev from *Soyuz 5* to *Soyuz 4;* 16 Jan. 1969); extensively used to ferry cosmonauts to Salyut space stations and return them to Earth. |
| Soyuz T | USSR | 1979–86 | 2 or 3 | Improved version of Soyuz spacecraft. |
| Soyuz TM | USSR | 1986– | 2 or 3 | Further improved version of Soyuz spacecraft. |
| Spacelab | European Space Agency | 1983– | 2 payload specialists | Orbital workshop (with open pallets for scientific instruments) carried into space by space shuttle; first mission, 1983, carried first W. German astronaut; 3 missions in 1985. |
| Space Shuttle | US | 1981–86 1988– | 2 to 8 | First reusable space vehicle (see article); first flight crewed by John Young and Robert Crippen (12–14 Apr. 1981). Grounded until 1988 after destruction of Shuttle *Challenger* in Jan. 1986. |
| Voskhod | USSR | 1964–65 | 2 or 3 | First extravehicular activity (Aleksei Leonov in *Voskhod 2;* 18 Mar. 1965). |
| Vostok | USSR | 1961–63 | 1 | First manned spaceflight (Yuri Gagarin in *Vostok 1;* 12 Apr. 1961); first simultaneous spaceflights (Andrian Nikolayev in *Vostok 3* and Pavel Popovich in *Vostok 4;* Aug. 1962); first woman in space (Valentina Tereshkova in *Vostok 6;* 16–19 June 1963). |

orbit around the Earth, a space probe is launched with enough energy to escape the gravitational field of the Earth (see ESCAPE VELOCITY) and navigate between planets. Radio contact between the control station on Earth and the space probe provides a channel for transmitting data recorded by on-board instruments back to Earth. A probe may be directed to orbit a planet, to soft-land instrument packages on a planetary surface, or to fly by one or more planets and/or natural satellites, approaching within a few thousand kilometres. So far space probes have investigated the Moon, the planets Mercury, Venus, Mars, Jupiter, Saturn, Uranus, and their satellite and ring systems, two comets, and conditions in interplanetary space. The *Voyager 2* spacecraft is expected to fly-by Neptune in August 1989 (see SPACE EXPLORATION, table).

## SPACE PROBE PROGRAMMES

| Programme | Country | Years of Launchings | Missions and Major Accomplishments |
|---|---|---|---|
| CRAF | US | Scheduled for 1993 | Comet Rendezvous, Asteroid Fly-by probe; to fly-by asteroid Hestia and match orbit with comet Tempel 2: first Mariner Mk II spacecraft. |
| Explorer | US | 1966–67, 1973 | *Explorer 35* and *49* were placed in lunar orbit and returned particles-and-fields and radio-astronomy data, respectively. |
| Galileo | US | Scheduled for 1989 | Orbiter/probe mission to Jupiter. |
| Giotto | European Space Agency | 1985 | By-passed nucleus of Halley's comet in 1986 at range of 500 km; first high-resolution images of a cometary nucleus. |
| Helios | US and West Germany | 1974, 1976 | Two interplanetary probes that passed within 48 million km (30 million mi) of Sun; studied solar wind, solar surface conditions, interplanetary magnetic field, cosmic rays, and zodiacal light. |
| ISEE | US and European Space Agency | 1977, 1978 | Three International Sun-Earth Explorers; studied solar wind; ISEE-3 diverted to fly through tail of comet Giacobini-Zinner (1985) and renamed International Cometary Explorer (ICE). |
| Luna | USSR | 1959, 1963–66, 1968–76 | First probes to enter solar orbit, impact the Moon, and photograph far side of Moon (*Lunas 1, 2* and *3;* all 1959); first probes to achieve soft lunar landing and lunar orbit (*Lunas 9* and *10;* both 1966); first automatic lunar-soil sample return and first automatic lunar-surface rover (*Lunas 16* and *17;* both 1970). |
| Lunar Orbiter | US | 1966–67 | Five spacecraft inserted into lunar orbit photographed 95% of lunar surface, focusing particularly on potential Apollo landing sites. |
| Magellan | US | Scheduled for 1989 | High-resolution radar mapping mission to Venus. |
| Mariner | US | 1962, 1964, 1967, 1969, 1971, 1973 | First successful flybys of Venus (*Mariner 2;* 1962) and Mars (*Mariner 4;* 1964), first probe (*Mariner 9;* 1971) to orbit another planet (Mars), first television pictures of Venus, first flyby (three encounters) of Mercury, and first dual-planet probe (all by *Mariner 10;* 1973). |
| Mars | USSR | 1960, 1962, 1969, 1971, 1973 | First probe to enter Martian atmosphere (*Mars 6;* 1973). |
| Phobos | USSR | 1988 | Mars orbiters intended to pass within 50 m of Martian satellite Phobos and to drop lander probes on it. |
| Pioneer | US | 1958–60, 1965–69, 1972–73, 1978 | First deep-space probe (*Pioneer 5;* 1960); first successful flybys of Jupiter (*Pioneer 10;* 1973) and Saturn (*Pioneer 11;* 1979); first radar probe of cloud-covered surface of Venus (*Pioneer-Venus 1;* 1978). Early missions (*Pioneers 1* to *4;* 1958–59) were unsuccessful lunar-orbit or -flyby attempts. *Pioneer 10* passed beyond the orbit of Neptune in 1983. |
| Ranger | US | 1961–62, 1964–65 | First probe to return thousands of high-resolution pictures before lunar impact (*Ranger 7;* 1964). |
| Sakigake, Suisei | Japan | 1985 | Two long-range fly-by missions to Halley's comet; registered cometary dust impacts at greater distances than expected. |
| Surveyor | US | 1966–68 | First probe to return thousands of pictures from lunar surface (*Surveyor 1;* 1966); first chemical analysis of lunar soil (*Surveyor 5;* 1967). |
| Ulysses | US and European Space Agency | Scheduled for 1990 | Mission to fly over the pole of the Sun after a Jupiter encounter. |
| Vega | USSR | 1984 | Two fly-by missions to Halley's comet via Venus encounters; closest approach to nucleus was 13,000 km (8000 mi); first image of a cometary nucleus. |
| Venera | USSR | 1961–62, 1965, 1967, 1969–70, 1972, 1975, 1978, 1981, 1983 | First successful Venus atmospheric entry (*Venera 4,* 1967); first probe to survive to Venusian surface (*Venera 7,* 1970); first probe to return television pictures from Venusian surface (*Venera 9,* 1975). |

| SPACE PROBE PROGRAMMES *(Continued)* | | | |
|---|---|---|---|
| *Programme* | *Country* | *Years of Launchings* | *Missions and Major Accomplishments* |
| Viking | US | 1975 | First successful Mars landers (*Vikings 1* and *2*, 1976), which conducted search-for-life experiments and returned first television pictures from Martian surface; surface also photographed extensively by orbiters in same missions. |
| Voyager | US | 1977 | Jupiter and Saturn flybys discovered Jupiter's ring, volcanoes on Jovian satellite Io, new satellites of Jupiter and Saturn, and complex structure of Saturn's ring system (*Voyagers 1* and *2*, 1979–81); *Voyager 2* reached Uranus in 1986 and will encounter Neptune in 1989. |
| Zond | USSR | 1964–65, 1967–70 | First probe to achieve circumlunar flyby and return to Earth (*Zond 5*, 1968); early missions (*Zonds 1* and *2*, 1964) were unsuccessful Venus and Mars probes. |

**Space Shuttle,** reusable US space vehicle. It consists of a winged orbiter, two solid-rocket boosters, and an external tank. Lift-off thrust is derived from the orbiter's three main liquid-propellant engines and the boosters. After 2 min the latter use up their fuel, are separated from the spacecraft, and after deployment of parachutes are recovered following splashdown. After about 8 min of flight, the orbiter main engines shut down; the external tank is then jettisoned and burns up as it reenters the atmosphere. The orbiter meanwhile enters orbit after a short burn of its two small Orbiting Maneuvering System (OMS) engines. To return to Earth, the orbiter turns around, fires its OMS engines to reduce speed, and, after descending through the atmosphere, lands like an aeroplane. The orbiter can reach altitudes of only a few hundred km; to place satellites into higher orbits, or to launch interplanetary spacecraft requires the use of an additional rocket (the small Payload Assist Module or the two-stage Inertial Upper Stage) attached to the payload and fired after deployment from the orbiter's cargo bay. Following four orbital test flights (1981–82) of the space shuttle *Columbia*, operational flights began in Nov. 1982. Between 1982 and 1986, *Columbia*, together with three later additions to the orbiter fleet, *Challenger*, *Discovery*, and *Atlantis*, launched a wide variety of communications, weather, scientific, and defence-related satellites, and carried into orbit, and returned to Earth several missions of the Spacelab scientific laboratory (see SPACE EXPLORATION, table). Highlights of these missions included the first untethered flights of astronauts outside a spacecraft using personal 'backpack' propulsion units, and retrieval, repair, and redeployment operations on several satellites. However, the 25th Shuttle mission, on 28 Jan. 1986, ended in disaster 73 sec into the flight when a faulty seal in one of the solid boosters allowed flame to ignite fuel in the external tank. The resulting explosion destroyed *Challenger*, killing all seven crew members. Following detailed investigations and improvements, the next Shuttle flight will take place no earlier than late 1988. A replacement orbiter, to bring the fleet up to four, has been commissioned. Future payloads include the *Galileo* spacecraft and the Hubble Space Telescope. See also SPACEPLANE.

**space station** or **space platform,** artificial Earth satellite, usually manned, that can serve as a base for astronomical observations, microgravity (virtually zero-gravity) materials processing, biological and medical research, satellite repair and servicing, or (possibly) weapons, or as a staging area for constructing large satellites to be placed in geosynchronous orbit. In the future, space stations may also be used as bases from which manned or unmanned planetary exploration missions may be despatched and to which they may return. Early examples of space stations were the American *Skylab*, and the series of Soviet Salyut spacecraft (see SPACE EXPLORATION, table). The most recent space station to be launched is the Soviet MIR, which is capable of being extended by linking on additional modules. It has been suggested that the new Soviet launch vehicle Energia (see ROCKET) may be used to assemble in space a 300–400 tonne station capable of housing some 30 people. The US intends to assemble a space station capable of housing 6–8 people in low earth orbit during the 1990s. Subject to the resumption of SPACE SHUTTLE flights, the assembly work should commence by 1994, and the basic station should be habitable by 1996. Initially, the station will consist of a long lattice boom, with solar panels at its ends, and four habitable modules at its centre, together with an array of free-flying platforms. The structure will be capable of further extension. One of the habitable modules will be contributed by Japan, and another, *Columbus*, will be supplied by the European Space Agency. Canada is to contribute a mobile servicing centre. Because non-US participation has been invited, the project has been named the International Space Station. The Columbus project, which also includes a free-flying polar-orbiting platform, may provide a basis for an independent European space station in the future. The American physicist Gerard O'Neill has proposed the construction of space colonies, very large space stations built from lunar or asteroidal material and inhabited by several thousand people.

Arrival of **space shuttle** *Columbia* on the launch pad at Kennedy Space Center (1982).

**space–time,** central concept in the theory of RELATIVITY that replaces the earlier concepts of space and time as separate absolute entities. In space–time, events in the universe are described in terms of a four-dimensional continuum in which each observer locates an event by three spacelike coordinates and a timelike coordinate. Time measurements differ if taken by observers moving relative to each other, hence time is relative and not absolute.

**Spain,** Span. *España*, officially the Kingdom of Spain, country (1987 est. pop. 40,000,000), 504,750 km² (194,884 sq mi), including the BALEARIC ISLANDS and CANARY ISLANDS, SW Europe, on the IBERIAN PENINSULA. Spain is bordered by the Bay of Biscay and France (N), the Mediterranean Sea (E and SE), and Portugal and the Atlantic Ocean (W). The small principality of ANDORRA is wedged between Spain and France in the PYRENEES. The Strait of Gibraltar separates Spain from N Africa. (GIBRALTAR itself is a British possession.) Spain has 15 geographic and historic regions that generally correspond to the old Christian and Moorish kingdoms. MADRID is the capital; other major cities include BARCELONA, VALENCIA, and SEVILLE. The centre of Spain forms a vast plateau extending from the CANTABRIAN Mts in the N to the Sierra Morena in the S, and from the Portuguese border in the W to low ranges in the E. The plateau is generally arid and thinly populated. It is cut from W to E by mountain chains and the valleys of the Douro (Duero), TAGUS, and GUADIANA rivers. To the NE of the plateau is the broad valley of the EBRO R. The southernmost section, ANDALUSIA, is crossed by the fertile valley of the GUADALQUIVIR R. The highest peak in continental Spain is Mulhacén 3478 m (11,411 ft), in the Sierra Nevada.

*People.* The Spanish people display great regional diversity; a desire for political independence remains particularly strong among the Catalans and the BASQUES. The Castilian dialect is the standard language, but Catalan, Galician, and Basque are spoken. Roman Catholicism is the established religion.

*Economy.* Spain is primarily an agricultural country, with wheat, olive oil, potatoes, sugar beets, and citrus fruits among the leading crops. It is also a leading producer of cork. Spanish industry produces textiles, iron and steel products, ships, motor vehicles, processed foods, and chemicals. Rich deposits of iron, coal, and zinc are mined in the Cantabrian Mts; petroleum and copper are also produced. Tourism and fishing are important sources of income. The GNP is $182,760 million and the GNP per capita is $4800 (1983).

*Government.* Spain is a constitutional monarchy. Since 1975 the reigning monarch has been King JUAN CARLOS I. Parliament consists of a lower house of 350 elected members, and an upper house of 208 elected members and 42 regional representatives appointed by the king. The leading political groups are the centrist Democratic Centre (a multi-party coalition), the Socialist Workers' Party, and the Communists. A new constitution was approved by national referendum in 1978.

*Early History.* Spain was known to early Mediterranean peoples as far back as the Stone Age. The Phoenicians established colonies c. 1100 BC and were followed by the Carthaginians and the Greeks. The Romans conquered Spain in the 2nd cent. BC and made the region a colony. Christianity was introduced in the 1st cent. AD. In 409 Spain was overrun by Germanic invaders, and in 419 a Visigothic kingdom was set up. After Spain was invaded (711) from N Africa by Muslim BERBERS, the last Visigothic kingdom collapsed. The MOORS, as the Muslim invaders were known, soon conquered the entire peninsula except for ASTURIAS and the Basque country. Under the Moors, Spanish cities, industry, and agriculture prospered and a distinctive architecture (exemplified by the Alhambra in GRANADA) flourished. But the Moors never controlled N Spain, and over the centuries the Christian kingdoms there expanded (see ARAGÓN and CASTILE) while the Moors became divided. The fall of Granada (1492) made the Spanish monarchs FERDINAND V and ISABELLA I rulers of all Spain. Catholic leaders expelled the Jews in 1492 and attempted to convert the Muslims by force. America was discovered (1492) by Columbus, and the beginnings of a huge colonial empire in the New World were established.

*The Golden Age and Decline.* Gold and silver from the Americas flowed into Spain in great quantities, and by the 16th cent. Spain was the most powerful country in the world. Under its first HABSBURG king, Charles I (r. 1516–56; Holy Roman emperor after 1519 as CHARLES V), Spain entered its Golden Age, when a brilliant artistic, cultural, and intellectual life flourished. During this period the church's dominance grew, reaching its peak in the INQUISITION. But Spanish power in Europe began its long decline during the reign of Charles's son, PHILIP II (r. 1556–98). The Spanish ARMADA was defeated (1588) by England, and continuous wars in Europe sapped the country's strength. The accession (1700) of the BOURBON dynasty in Spain provoked the War of the SPANISH SUCCESSION. Drawn into the Napoleonic Wars, Spain was occupied by French troops and given (1808) a French king, Joseph Bonaparte (see BONAPARTE, family), but by 1814 Spanish resistance forces and the British had expelled the French (see PENINSULAR WAR). In the mid-19th cent. Spain was torn by internal struggles (see CARLISTS). On the abdication (1868) of ISABELLA II, a constitutional monarchy was established, followed by a shortlived republic (1873–74). The last remnant of Spain's colonial empire in America was lost (1898) during the SPANISH–AMERICAN WAR.

*Modern Spain.* In 1923 a military dictatorship was established under PRIMO DE RIVERA. King ALFONSO XIII was deposed (1931) and a second republic was created. But opposition from both the left and the right, as well as from Catalan separatists, eventually undermined the republic. The election of a leftist coalition in 1936 precipitated the SPANISH CIVIL WAR

(1936–39). The Insurgents, under Francisco FRANCO, embraced most conservative groups, notably monarchists, the army, the church, and the fascists. After a savage conflict the pro-republican forces (Loyalists) were defeated and a dictatorship under Franco was set up. During WORLD WAR II Spain aided the AXIS but did not enter the war. The 1950s and 60s were marked by growing prosperity and by agitation for political freedom. In 1969 Franco appointed Prince Juan Carlos, grandson of Alfonso XIII, as his successor. Following Franco's death in 1975, King JUAN CARLOS and his premier, Adolfo SUÁREZ GONZÁLES, steered Spain toward parliamentary democracy. With all political parties, including the Communists, legalized by 1977, parliamentary elections in that year and in 1979 both resulted in victories for the conservative Union of the Democratic Centre (UCD). In the 1982 elections, however, the Spanish Socialist Workers' Party (PSOE) led by Felipe GONZÁLEZ won an absolute majority and formed Spain's first left-wing government since before the civil war. González and the PSOE were returned to power in the 1986 elections with a slightly reduced majority. Having joined the NORTH ATLANTIC TREATY ORGANIZATION in 1982, Spain also became a member of the EUROPEAN COMMUNITY in 1986. Despite the granting of substantial autonomy to Spain's regions in the post-Franco era, violence associated with Basque and Catalan separatism remained a serious problem in the 1980s, the Basque extremist ETA movement posing a particular threat.

**Post-war Spanish prime ministers**
Francisco Franco (Nationalist), 1939–73
Luis Carrero Blanco (Nationalist), 1973
Carlos Arias Navarro (Nationalist), 1974–76
Adolfo Suárez González (UCD), 1976–81
Leopoldo Calvo Sotelo (UCD), 1981–82
Felipe González (Socialist), 1982–

Spain

**Spallanzani, Lazzaro,** 1729–99, Italian priest and physiologist. He disproved the then prevalent theory of spontaneous generation, by showing that micro-organisms did not develop in broths that had been well boiled and properly sealed. He also proved that spermatozoa are necessary for fertilization, and carried out (on a bitch) the first artificial insemination.

**Spanish–American War,** 1898, conflict between Spain and the US. Demands by Cuban patriots for independence from Spain were supported by large numbers of Americans. Pro-rebel sentiment was inflamed by the biased reporting of the US 'yellow press', the ruthless methods Spain adopted to suppress the rebellion, heavy losses of American investment caused by guerrilla warfare, and an appreciation of Cuba's strategic importance to a projected Central American canal. The publication of a Spanish official letter disparaging Pres. MCKINLEY, and the sinking (15 Feb.) of the US battleship MAINE in Havana harbour, intensified US feeling against Spain. The US demanded Spanish withdrawal from Cuba. On 24 Apr. Spain declared war on the US. On 1 May a US naval squadron under George DEWEY thoroughly defeated the Spanish fleet in Manila harbour, in

## RULERS OF SPAIN SINCE 1474 *(including dates of reign)*

**Union of Castile and Aragon**

Isabella I (of Castile), ruled jointly with Ferdinand II (of Aragón), 1474–1504

Ferdinand II, ruled jointly with Isabella I as Ferdinand V of Castile, 1474–1504; ruled Aragón only, 1504–16; ruled Castile as regent, 1506–16

**Habsburg Dynasty**

Joanna (the Mad), daughter of Ferdinand and Isabella; ruled Castile only (jointly with Philip I in 1506), 1504–06

Philip I (the Handsome), son of Holy Roman Emperor Maximilian I; ruled Castile jointly with Joanna, 1506

Charles I (Holy Roman Emperor Charles V), son of Joanna and Philip, 1516–56

Philip II, son of Charles I, 1556–98

Philip III, son of Philip II, 1598–1621

Philip IV, son of Philip III, 1621–65

Charles II, son of Philip IV, 1665–1700

**Bourbon Dynasty**

Philip V, great-grandson of Philip IV, 1700–46

Ferdinand VI, son of Philip V, 1746–59

Charles III, younger son of Philip V, 1759–88

Charles IV, second son of Charles III, 1788–1808

Ferdinand VII, son of Charles IV, 1808

**French Intrusion**

Joseph Bonaparte, 1808–13

**Bourbon Restoration**

Ferdinand VII, restored, 1813–33

Isabella II, daughter of Ferdinand VII, 1833–68

**Elective Monarchy**

Francisco Serrano y Dominguez, regent, 1869–70

Amadeus, elected by a constituent assembly, 1870–73

**First Republic**

Estanislao Figueras, president, 1873

Francisco Pi y Margall, president, 1873

Nicolás Salmerón y Alonso, president, 1873

Emilio Castelar y Ripoll, prime minister, 1873–74

**Bourbon Restoration**

Alfonso XII, son of Isabella II, 1874–85

Alfonso XIII, son of Alfonso XII, 1886–1931

**Second Republic**

Niceta Alcalá Zamora, president, 1931–36

Manuel Azaña, president, 1936–39

**Nationalist Government**

Francisco Franco, chief of state, 1939–75

**Constitutional Monarchy**

Juan Carlos I, grandson of Alfonso XIII, 1975–

---

the Philippines. On 28 May the US established a blockade of Santiago de Cuba; when the Spanish fleet attempted to escape (1 June), it was destroyed. Meanwhile, US troops, including the famed ROUGH RIDERS, engaged in some heavy fighting (1 July) at El Canay and San Juan Hill. On 17 July Santiago was captured, effectively ending the war. An armistice was signed (12 Aug.) and peace was arranged by the Treaty of Paris (10 Dec.). The Spanish empire was practically dissolved; Cuba was freed, but under US supervisory control; Puerto Rico and Guam were ceded to the US; and the Philippines were surrendered to the US for $20 million. The US emerged from the war with new international power.

**Spanish Civil War**, 1936–39, conflict in which conservative forces in Spain overthrew the second Spanish republic. The war pitted the Nationalists, led by the landed aristocracy, Roman Catholic Church, military leaders, and the fascist FALANGE party, against the Loyalists, consisting of liberals, anarchists, socialists, and Communists. Following the election in 1936 of a left-wing coalition government, in July 1936 Gen. FRANCO led an army revolt in Morocco and invaded Spain to support right-wing rebels. The Nationalist army overran conservative areas in N Spain, while the Loyalists remained strong in CATALONIA and the BASQUE PROVINCES. Volunteers abroad formed International Brigades to fight for the Loyalists, who received supplies from the Soviet Union. Fascist Italy and Nazi Germany aided the Nationalists with modern arms and some 60,000 men. The Loyalist side was riven by factional strife that was exacerbated by the Communists' suppression of anarchists and Trotskyites. Nationalist forces, unified under Franco, gradually wore down republican strength, conquering Barcelona and Madrid in early 1939. For Italy and Germany the war was a testing ground for modern armaments and techniques to be used in WORLD WAR II. For the youth of the 1930s, saving the Spanish republic was the idealistic cause of the era. But the civil war's huge death toll, human suffering, and material devastation were unparalleled in Spanish history. The war also ushered in a long era of right-wing dictatorship, that ended only with Franco's death in 1975.

**Spanish colonial art and architecture**, fl. 16th–early 19th cent. The art of the Spanish colonies followed the development of styles in Spain, but with regional variations reflecting the culture of local populations and the influence of particular missionary groups. In 16th-cent. Spain Byzantine or Gothic themes are found merged with those of the Moorish invaders, only recently expelled. Renaissance trends were slow to catch on. In the New World all these styles combined with indigenous arts to produce a distinct Baroque form. Churches, at first only

temporary shelters, were later replaced by durable monumental structures. The earliest surviving cathedral (1512–41) is in Santo Domingo, Dominican Republic and has impressive PLATERESQUE decorations. Architecture in the New World is greatly varied. The Franciscan missions of California are introverted and defensive and contrast with those of New Mexico, which conform to the open-plan style of traditional Indian structures. In Mexico the Augustinian and Dominican missions are built on a grand scale. Plateresque decorations of the homeland are enlarged and elaborated and made to contrast with flat surfaces. The Churriguesque (see CHURRIGUERA, JOSÉ) brings this ideal to a climax, most visible in Mexico City's cathedral. Rich carvings and alternating angles emphasize the contrasts of light and dark. Central American colonial architecture–often termed earthquake baroque— exhibits a heavy stability, with surfaces embellished with stucco or stone carving. By comparison Columbian facades are more austere. A common feature of Columbian churches is the 'Camarin' behind the altar, where the Virgin's image is housed. Many New World monasteries also

**Spanish colonial art and architecture:** Mexico City's cathedral, first built 1525 and finished in 1813.

incorporate open chapels for excess congregation. In Peru the massive architectural style is heavily ornamented, sometimes with indigenous motifs. Depictions from the New Testament in such mediums as polychrome wood, terra-cotta, and architectural bas-relief are often Indian in style and express intense emotion. In the 18th cent. art and architecture enter the neo-classic era. The political message is often extant and the plight of the native is stressed. Examples include the folk lithographs of Mexico and Venezuela of the 18th and 19th cent.

**Spanish language,** member of the Romance group of the Italic subfamily of the Indo-European family of languages. See LANGUAGE (table).

**Spanish Main,** the coast of NW South America, particularly the section between Panama and the ORINOCO R., from which Spanish treasure fleets carried gold back to Spain in colonial times. Buccaneers preying on the vessels as they passed through the CARIBBEAN SEA made the term a symbol of piratical romance.

**Spanish moss,** fibrous greyish-green EPIPHYTE (*Tillandsia usneoides*) of the BROMELIAD family, found in tropical America and the Southern US. Spanish moss grows hanging from trees and has inconspicuous flowers. It is not a true MOSS.

**Spanish Succession, War of the,** 1701–14, general European war fought for the succession to the Spanish empire. CHARLES II, the Habsburg king of Spain, was childless, and negotiations over his eventual successor began long before his death. The chief claimants were Philip, Duke of Anjou, second grandson of Louis XIV of France; Archduke Charles (later Holy Roman Emperor CHARLES VI), second son of Emperor Leopold I; and Joseph Ferdinand, electoral prince of Bavaria. England and Holland, opposed to the extension of either French Bourbon or Austrian Habsburg power into Spain, favoured Joseph Ferdinand. In 1698 all the powers agreed to the complicated First Partition Treaty. By its terms, Joseph Ferdinand was to get the crown; in return, Spanish territories were to go to Austria and France. However, Joseph Ferdinand died before Charles. In 1700 the duke of Anjou, named by the dying Charles as his successor, ascended the throne as PHILIP V. England, Holland, Austria, and most of the German states then went to war against France. Bavaria sided with France, so did Portugal and Savoy until 1703, when they switched sides. Military operations began in Italy (1701) and became general in 1702. The great allied commanders, the English duke of MARLBOROUGH and the imperial general Prince EUGENE OF SAVOY, won such major victories as Blenheim and Gibraltar (1704), Ramillies (1706), Oudenarde (1708), and Malplaquet (1709). The campaigns in Spain were indecisive, however, and in 1711 England abandoned the war. Charles VI had become emperor, and the war-weary English Tory ministry was opposed to the dynastic union of Austria and Spain. In 1713 England, Holland, and France signed the Peace of Utrecht. Charles continued the war until 1714. Although Philip remained on the Spanish throne, the principle of BALANCE OF POWER had been established in European dynastic affairs.

**Spark, Muriel,** 1918–, Scottish novelist. Her witty novels expose both the petty foibles of her characters and the dark side of human experience. They include *Memento Mori* (1959), *The Girls of Slender Means* (1963), and *Loitering with Intent* (1981). *The Prime of Miss Jean Brodie* (1961) became an acclaimed stage, film, and television production.

**spark chamber:** see PARTICLE DETECTOR.

**sparrow,** name given to a number of small brown BIRDS. Strictly it applies to the genus *Passer*, gregarious seed-eaters with conical, seed-cracking bills. The birds are originally European. The HOUSE SPARROW, tree sparrow, rock sparrow and Spanish and Italian sparrows are true sparrows, related to snow finches and weavers. The HEDGE SPARROW is not a true sparrow.

**sparrow hawk:** see HAWK.

**Sparta,** city of ancient Greece, capital of Laconia, on the Eurotas R. in the S PELOPONNESUS. The CITY-STATE of Sparta was founded by Dorian Greeks who conquered Laconia (c.735–715 BC) and Messinia. It was a centre of wealth and culture. However, increasingly Sparta cultivated only the military arts, and the city became an armed camp. The ruling class, the Spartiates, gave themselves wholly to war. Only Spartiates were citizens with legal and civil rights. Below this warrior class were the perioeci (freemen permitted to carry on commerce and handicrafts) and helots (serfs bound to the land). The Spartan government was headed by two hereditary kings, and there were a council of elders and a general assembly of citizens. But the real rulers were the board of five ephors (overseers), elected annually, who conducted the business of the state secretly. By the 6th cent. BC Sparta was the strongest city in Greece. In the PERSIAN WARS Sparta fought beside Athens at THERMOPYLAE and SALAMIS (480), and at Plataea (479). Afterward, Sparta's rivalry with Athens intensified, leading to the PELOPONNESIAN WAR (431–404), which wrecked the Athenian empire. Sparta emerged triumphant but was decisively defeated by THEBES at Leuktra (371). Sparta subsequently fell an easy prey to Macedon and declined. It prospered under the Romans but was devastated by the Goths in AD 395.

**Spartacus,** d. 71 BC, Roman gladiator, leader of a slave revolt that was the last and most important of the SERVILE WARS. He escaped from the gladiators' school at Capua, gathered an army of 90,000 runaway slaves about him, and in 72 BC dominated much of S Italy. He was killed in battle when Marcus Licinius Crassus (see CRASSUS, family) and POMPEY put down the revolt. They crucified some 6000 captured slaves.

**Spartacus League,** German revolutionary group founded c.1916 Rosa LUXEMBURG and Karl Liebknecht (1871–1919), and named after the leader of a slave revolt in ancient Rome. After the Spartacus rising in Berlin in Jan. 1919, during which Luxemburg and Liebknecht were murdered by right-wing troops, the League was dissolved by the government headed by Friedrich EBERT, but it had inspired the founding of the German Communist Party in Dec. 1918.

**spearmint:** see MINT.

**Special Air Service,** a specialist unit of the British Army, formed in 1942. It specializes in secret operations and antiterrorist work, and was used in the siege of the Iranian embassy in London in 1980 and for numerous operations in Northern Ireland.

**Special Drawing Rights** (SDRs), type of international monetary reserves established (1968) by the International Monetary Fund (IMF). Created in response to concern over the limitations of gold and dollars as the sole means of settling international accounts, SDRs were designed to augment international liquidity. Also known as 'paper gold', SDRs are assigned to the accounts of IMF members in proportion to their contributions to the fund. Each member agrees to accept them as exchangeable for gold or reserve currencies, and deficit countries can use them to purchase stronger currencies. In 1976 the IMF increased the share of the less-developed countries and made SDRs the primary reserve asset of the INTERNATIONAL MONETARY SYSTEM, supplanting gold and dollars.

**special education,** an education provided for children with special needs in special schools or in ordinary schools. Day or boarding special schools have been established for certain categories of children (e.g., blind, deaf, maladjusted) in the 19th and 20th cent. In Britain, educational provision for the severely handicapped, mentally and physically, has been gradually extended, including the Education (Handicapped Children) Act 1970 which transferred authority for them from the health to the education service. The Warnock report on *Special Educational Needs* (1978) estimated that one child in six would require special educational provision of some kind at some point in their school career, and recommended greater integration of children with special needs into ordinary schools where possible (see MAINSTREAMING). There are over 1500 special schools maintained by LOCAL EDUCATION AUTHORITIES and voluntary bodies. Training centres are provided for the needs of the handicapped over the statutory school-leaving age.

**species:** see CLASSIFICATION.

**specific gravity:** see RELATIVE DENSITY.

**specific heat capacity** or **specific heat,** HEAT energy required to raise the temperature of unit mass of a substance by unit temperature. The specific heat capacity is a characteristic of a substance; it is usually measured in joules per kilogram per kelvin.

**Spectator,** English daily periodical published (1 Mar. 1711–6 Dec. 1712) by Joseph ADDISON and Richard STEELE. Supposedly written by members of a small club, and dated from London coffeehouses, it commented on manners, morals, and literature. It and its predecessor, the *Tatler,* influenced public opinion, the growth of journalism, and the development of the informal ESSAY. It was destroyed by the Stamps Act 1712 under which all publications were liable to pay government duty.

**Spector, Phil,** 1940–, American producer, composer, singer. One of pop music's most eccentric and innovative producers. He introduced the famous 'wall of sound' effect as a backcloth to a string of hits by The

Crystals, The Ronettes, The Righteous Brothers, Ike and Tina Turner, etc., in the 1960s. He also worked with the BEATLES and separately with John Lennon in the 1970s on 'Imagine' and 'Rock 'n Roll' albums.

**spectral class,** a classification of the stars by their SPECTRUM and LUMINOSITY. The stars were originally divided into seven main classes designated by the letters O, B, A, F, G, K, and M; since 1924 four other classes (R, N, S, and W) have been added. Each of the letter classes has subdivisions indicated by the numerals 0 through 9. A Roman numeral ranging from I (supergiant) to V (normal dwarf or main sequence) is added to the spectral class to specify the luminosity, or intrinsic intensity, of a star.

### SPECTRAL CLASSES: CHARACTERISTICS

| Type | Colour | Temperature | Strong Lines |
| --- | --- | --- | --- |
| O | blue-white | 35,000°C | ionized helium |
| B | blue-white | 21,000°C | helium |
| A | white | 10,000°C | hydrogen |
| F | creamy | 7000°C | ionized calcium |
| G | yellow | 6000°C | calcium |
| K | orange | 4500°C | titanium oxide |
| M | red | 3000°C | titanium oxide |

**spectroscope,** optical instrument for producing spectral lines and measuring their wavelengths and intensities, used in spectral analysis (see SPECTRUM). In the simple prism spectroscope, a collimator, with a slit at the outer end and a lens at the inner end, transforms the light entering the slit into a beam of parallel rays. A prism or DIFFRACTION grating disperses the light coming from the collimator, and the spectrum formed is observed with a small telescope. If a photographic plate is used to record the spectrum, the instrument is called a spectrograph.

**spectrum,** arrangement or display of LIGHT or other forms of ELECTROMAGNETIC RADIATION separated according to wavelength, frequency, energy, or some other property. Dispersion, the separation of visible light into a spectrum, may be accomplished by means of a PRISM or a DIFFRACTION grating. Each different wavelength or frequency of visible light corresponds to a different COLOUR, so that the spectrum appears as a band of colours ranging from violet at the short-wavelength (high-frequency) end of the spectrum through indigo, blue, green, yellow, and orange, to red at the long-wavelength (low-frequency) end of the spectrum. A continuous spectrum containing all colours is produced by all incandescent solids and liquids and by gases under high pressure. A low-pressure gas made incandescent by heat or by an electric discharge emits a spectrum of bright emission lines. A dark-line absorption spectrum is produced by white light passing through a cool gas and consists of a continuous spectrum with superimposed dark lines; each line corresponds to a frequency where a bright line would appear if the gas were incandescent. The absorption lines correspond to transitions of electrons from a lower energy level to a higher energy level when a PHOTON is absorbed by the atom, and the emission lines correspond to transitions from a higher to a lower energy level in the atom, accompanied by the emission of a photon. The frequency of each emission or absorption line is proportional to the difference in energy between the two energy levels involved (see QUANTUM THEORY). Both absorption and line spectra are useful in chemical analysis, because they reveal the presence of particular elements.

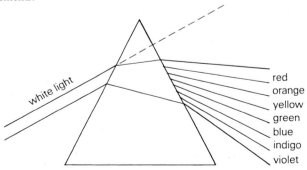

Spectrum: Dispersion of white light by a triangular prism

**speech:** see LANGUAGE.

**speed:** see MOTION.

**Speer, Albert** (shpeǝ), 1905–81, German architect and NAZI leader. He was HITLER's official architect and was Nazi minister of armaments (1942–45). He served 20 years in prison after being sentenced as a war criminal (1946) by the Nuremberg tribunal. His memoirs, *Inside the Third Reich* (tr. 1972), were widely read.

**Speke, John Hanning** (speek), 1827–64, English explorer in Africa. In 1858 he and Sir Richard BURTON discovered Lake TANGANYIKA. Speke also discovered VICTORIA NYANZA. In 1862 he proved that the Victoria NILE R. issues from the north end over Ripon Falls.

**speleology,** systematic exploration of CAVES, sometimes popularly called spelunking. It includes the measuring and mapping of caves and reporting on the flora and fauna found in them.

**Spence, Sir Basil,** 1907–1976, Scottish architect; b. India. He is best known as the architect of Coventry cathedral (1951–62). The original medieval cathedral, formerly a large parish church, was bombed during World War II. Spence preserved the surviving walls and tower and added a new cathedral at right angles to the ruins, the colourful interior of the new building being visible through a decorated glass screen uniting old and new. It contains works by leading British artists, including Jacob EPSTEIN, John PIPER, and Graham SUTHERLAND. Coventry cathedral became a symbol of recovery from the war, recognized by participants from both sides. Spence subsequently designed other churches, university buildings, offices, barracks, and public buildings including the British embassy in Rome. He was knighted in 1960 and awarded the Order of Merit in 1962.

**Spence, Catherine Helen,** 1825–1910, Australian writer and reformer; b. Scotland. She migrated with her parents to Adelaide, South Australia, in 1839 and wrote extensively on political, social, and family reform.

**Spencer, Herbert,** 1820–1903, English philosopher. Together with Charles DARWIN and Thomas Henry HUXLEY he was responsible for the acceptance of the theory of evolution, and he coined the phrase 'survival of the fittest', later attributed to Darwin. Spencer attempted to combine the contemporary ideas of LAISSEZ-FAIRE individualism and evolutionary theory; societies, he argued, were like organisms, evolving from simple, homogeneous, to complex, heterogeneous, structures (see EVOLUTION, SOCIOCULTURAL). He projected a vast work, *Synthetic Philosophy,* that would apply the principle of evolutionary progress to all branches of knowledge; the numerous volumes published between 1855 and 1893 covered such subjects as biology, psychology, sociology, and ethics. Spencer is also credited with the establishment of sociology as a discipline in the US.

**Spencer, Sir Stanley,** 1891–1959, British painter. A member (1919–27) of the New English Art Club, he produced a series of quasi-visionary transformations of his experiences of World War I, culminating in the large *Resurrection, Cookham* (1922–27; Tate Gall., London). He painted religious murals for the Oratory of All Souls, Burghclere, Berkshire (1927–32). As a war artist in World War II he painted scenes of shipyards in Port Glasgow. His later works also depict unusual sexual experiences between the sick and aged.

**Spender, Sir Stephen,** 1909–85, English poet and critic. In the 1930s he was an associate of AUDEN, MacNEICE, and DAY LEWIS. His autobiography, *World Within World* (1951), records the period. His poems are collected in many volumes, e.g., *The Still Centre* (1939) and *The Generous Days* (1971), and he has written social and literary criticism, stories, and fiction.

**Spener, Philipe Jakob** (ˌspaynǝ), 1635–1705, German theologian, founder of the devotional movement in LUTHERANISM known as Pietism. As a Lutheran pastor in Frankfurt, he instituted (1670) meetings for fellowship and Bible study to counteract the barren intellectualism in the church. These *Collegia pietatis* led to a religious revival in Germany and in other parts of Europe despite the opposition of the orthodox clergy. He helped found (1694) the Univ. of Halle.

**Spengler, Oswald,** 1880–1936, German historian and philosopher. His major work, *The Decline of the West* (2 vol., 1918–22), reflects his view that every culture passes through a life cycle from youth through maturity and old age to death, and that Western culture has entered the period of decline.

**Spenser, Edmund,** 1552?–1599, English poet. A friend of many eminent court and literary figures, such as RALEIGH and SIDNEY, he was appointed to a secretaryship in Ireland in 1580, and lived in County Cork thereafter. Patterning his literary career on VIRGIL, he first published 12 pastoral eclogues of *The Shepheardes Calendar* (1579). *Complaints* and the elegy *Daphnaida* appeared in 1591. In 1595 *Colin Clouts Come Home Againe,* a PASTORAL allegory dealing with a journey to London and the vices of court life, appeared, as did the ELEGY *Astrophel,* the SONNET sequence *Amoretti,* and the complex wedding poem *Epithalamion* in honour of his marriage. *Fowre Hymnes,* explaining his Platonic and Christian views on love and beauty, and *Prothalamion* came in 1596. In the same year the second three books of his unfinished masterpiece, *The Faerie Queene,* were published (the first three had been published in 1590). The poem is an EPIC that treats moral virtues allegorically. Its excellence lies in the interwoven layers of allegorical meaning and ambiguity, and in simultaneously innovative and archaic use of language. Spenser was recognized by contemporaries as the foremost poet of the time.

**sperm** or **spermatozoon,** specialized male sex cell. It is smaller than the female sex cell (OVUM) and has a tail (flagellum), which provides motility. The formation of sperm, like that of the ovum, by MEIOSIS, reduces the chromosome number by half. An ovum fertilized by a sperm (called a zygote) has the full number of chromosomes restored to it. See also REPRODUCTION; REPRODUCTIVE SYSTEM.

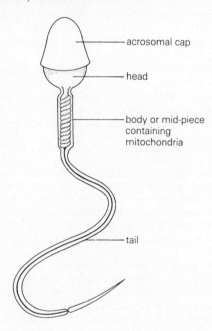

acrosomal cap

head

body or mid-piece containing mitochondria

tail

Sperm

**Spermatophyta,** plants having true stems, leaves, and roots. True VASCULAR TISSUE is present. POLLEN grains and the embryo sac are formed; the embryo sac developing into the SEED, with integuments as the seed coat. They comprise the GYMNOSPERMS and ANGIOSPERMS.

**Sperry, Elmer Ambrose,** 1860–1930, American inventor. Best known for his work on the gyroscope, he also invented a gyrocompass (1910), a high-intensity searchlight, a street-lighting system, and many electrical devices. He founded the American Inst. of Electrical Engineers.

**Spey,** river in NE Scotland, c.170 km (107 mi) long. It rises in Corrieyairack Forest in Highland region and flows generally NE through Strathspey, past Kingussie, Aviemore, and Fochabers, entering the Moray Firth at Spey Bay, Grampian region. It is fast-flowing, and famous for salmon fishing.

**sphagnum** or **peat moss** (ˌsfagnəm, ˌspagnəm), economically valuable MOSS (genus *Sphagnum*) typically growing as a mat in freshwater bogs. Sphagnums are the principal constituent of PEAT. They are highly absorbent and are commercially important as packing material and absorbent dressings.

**sphalerite** (ˌsfalərıət), zinc sulphide mineral (ZnS), occurring worldwide, sometimes in crystals but more often in massive form, in a variety of colours. Often found in association with GALENA, it is the most important source of ZINC.

**Sphenopsida,** division of the PTERIDOPHYTA consisting of the HORSETAIL plants.

**sphere,** in geometry, a solid whose surface consists of points all at the same distance $r$ (the radius) from a certain fixed point (the centre). The term *sphere* refers both to the surface and to the space it encloses. The area of the surface of a sphere is given by the formula $S = 4\pi r^2$ and the volume of a sphere is given by $V = {}^4/_3 \pi r^3$.

**sphinx,** mythical beast of ancient Egypt, usually represented in art as having a human head and the body of a lion. It frequently symbolized the pharaoh as an incarnation of the sun god RA. The most famous one is the Great Sphinx, a colossal stone figure at Al Jizah. Sphinxes were also depicted throughout the ancient Middle East and Greece.

**spice,** aromatic vegetable product, usually the dried seed, berry, stem, or root, used as a flavouring or condiment. The term was formerly also applied to pungent or aromatic foods, incense and perfume ingredients, and embalming agents. Spices include stimulating condiments (e.g., pepper and mustard), aromatic spices (e.g., cloves, nutmeg, and mace), and sweet herbs (e.g., thyme and mint). They are used whole, as powders, and as tinctures. Spices have been an important commercial item since ancient times. They are much needed in cultures that do not have modern FOOD PRESERVATION techniques, both for their preservative qualities and for their strong flavours to mask the unpleasant taste of deteriorated food.

**spider,** mostly terrestrial ARACHNID, with a two-part body, four pairs of legs, and four pairs of eyes. Spinnerets (specialized organs under the abdomen) produce silk thread for binding prey or making webs, cocoons, and lines for floating. Spiders live chiefly on insects and other arthropods; some large species prey on small snakes, mammals, and birds. All spiders paralyse their prey with venom produced in poison glands under the head; several species, such as the BLACK WIDOW, have bites that are painful or even dangerous to humans. See also BIRD-EATING SPIDER.

**Spielberg, Steven,** 1946–, American film director. His highly popular films betray a love of childhood and its fantasies. His films include *Jaws* (1975), *Close Encounters of the Third Kind* (1977), *Raiders of the Lost Ark* (1981), *Poltergeist* (1982), and *ET: The Extra-Terrestrial* (1982).

**spin,** in aeronautics: see STALL.

**spin,** the angular momentum possessed by a body (see momentum). Many ELEMENTARY PARTICLES have an intrinsic spin which is restricted by QUANTUM THEORY to be an integer or half-integer multiple of $h/2$ where $h$ is PLANCK's quantum constant. It is conventional to refer to the amplifier of $h$ as the spin of the particle; thus the ELECTRON and PROTON each have spin½, the PION has spin 0.

**spina bifida:** see NEURAL TUBE DEFECT.

**spinach,** annual plant (*Spinacia oleracea*) of the goosefoot family, probably Persian in origin. The leaves are high in VITAMINS and iron, and numerous varieties are cultivated.

**spinal column, vertebral column** or **backbone,** bony column that forms the main structural support of the SKELETON. It consists of 26 segments (vertebrae) in humans, linked by flexible joints and held together by gelatinous disks of cartilage and by LIGAMENTS. Each vertebra has a roughly cylindrical body, winglike projections, and a bony arch. The arches, positioned next to one another, create the tunnellike space that houses the SPINAL CORD.

**spinal cord,** length of nerve cells and bundles of nerves enclosed in the SPINAL COLUMN. It carries information (electrical and chemical signals) through the NERVOUS SYSTEM, including sensory impulses from the trunk and limbs to the BRAIN and commands from the brain to the muscles and glands. The spinal cord runs nearly the length of the trunk and merges with the brainstem. It is enveloped in three layers of membrane.

**spindle:** see SPINNING.

**spinet:** see PIANO.

**spinning,** the drawing out, twisting, and winding of a FIBRE into a continuous thread or yarn. From antiquity until the INDUSTRIAL REVOLUTION, spinning was a household industry. The earliest tools were the distaff, a hand-held stick on which the cotton, flax, or wool fibre was wrapped; and the spindle, a shorter stick, held in the other hand, notched at one end and weighted at the other. The twirling of the spindle twisted the fibre into thread. In Europe from the 14th to 16th cent. the distaff and spindle were replaced by the spinning wheel, a spindle set in a frame and turned by a belt passing over a wheel. The great wheel, also called the wool or walking wheel, was turned by hand; the more elaborate flax, or Saxony, wheel was operated by a foot treadle. In 18th-cent. England, improvements in the LOOM, increasing the demand for yarn, stimulated such inventions as James HARGREAVES's spinning jenny (c.1765), which spun 8 to 11 threads at once; Richard ARKWRIGHT's spinning frame (1769), which made more tightly twisted, stronger threads; and Samuel CROMPTON's mule spinning frame (1779), which combined the best features of the two earlier machines. Using water power and, later, steam, spinning became a factory enterprise.

**Spinoza, Baruch** or **Benedict,** 1632–77, Dutch philosopher. A member of the Sephardic Jewish community of Amsterdam, Spinoza received a thorough education in the tradition of medieval philosophical texts as well as in the works of DESCARTES, HOBBES, and other writers of the period. After charges of heretical thought and practice led to his excommunication from the Jewish community in Amsterdam in 1656, he Latinized his name to Benedict. He was by trade a lens-grinder, modestly rejecting offers of an academic career, but he nevertheless became celebrated in his own day and was regularly visited by other philosophers. Spinoza's system is monist, deductive, and rationalistic. Politically he posited the idea of the SOCIAL CONTRACT, but unlike Hobbes he visualized a community in which human beings derive most advantage from the rational renunciation of personal desire. He rejected the concept of FREE WILL, holding human action to be motivated by one's conception of self-preservation. A powerful, or virtuous, person acts out of understanding; thus freedom consists in being guided by the law of one's own nature, and evil is the result of inadequate understanding. He saw the supreme ambition of the virtuous person as the 'intellectual love of God'. Spinoza shared with Descartes an intensely mathematical appreciation of the universe: truth, like geometry, follows from first principles, and is accessible to the logical mind. Unlike Descartes, however, he regarded mind and body (or ideas and the physical universe) as merely different aspects of a single substance, which he called alternately God and Nature, God being Nature in its fullness. This pantheism was considered blasphemous by the religious and political authorities of his day. Of his works, only *A Treatise on Religious and Political Philosophy* (1670) was published during his lifetime. His *Ethics, Political Treatise,* and *Hebrew Grammar* are included in his posthumous works (1677).

**spire,** high, tapering, generally pyramidal structure crowning a tower. The simplest spires were the steeply pitched timber roofs of Romanesque towers. Later Romanesque spires were commonly octagonal. Gothic spires were more elaborate. In France, spires (*flèches*) were placed over the two western towers of cathedrals, e.g., those at CHARTRES, one Romanesque, one Gothic. In England a cathedral's central tower often had a spire e.g., at Salisbury. Gothic elaboration culminated in openwork tracery, as in the Tour de Beurre, Rouen. The Georgian spire of St Martin's-in-the-Fields, London (1722–26) by James GIBBS inspired many later church steeples.

**spiritual,** a religious FOLK SONG of the blacks of the southern states of the US, characterized by syncopation, polyrhythmic structure, and frequent use of a pentatonic scale of five tones. The texts are often biblical and refer to suffering and deliverance. Spirituals are generally considered to be an amalgamation of African musical traditions and religious songs of the 19th-cent. white South, which produced a form of folk music distinctly black in character. Spirituals are related to the sorrow songs that are the source of the blues (see JAZZ). Their modern counterpart is the gospel song.

**spiritualism** or **spiritism,** belief that the human personality survives death and can communicate with the living through a medium sensitive to its vibrations. The communication may be psychic, as in clairvoyance or trance speaking, or physical, as in automatic writing or ectoplasmic materializations. Spiritualistic phenomena have been under scientific investigation in the UK by the Society for Psychical Research since 1882 (see PARAPSYCHOLOGY).

**Spitsbergen,** formerly **Vestspitsbergen,** largest island (39,044 km²/15,075 sq mi) of SVALBARD, a Norwegian possession in the Arctic Ocean. The principal settlement is Longyearbyen. Coal-mining is the major industry.

**Spitz, Mark,** 1950–, American Olympic swimmer. In the 1972 Olympic Games at Munich, he won seven gold medals, a unique achievement. He won the 100-m and 200-m freestyle and butterfly, and was in the winning team in the 4 × 100-m and 4 × 200-m freestyle and 4 × 100-m medley relays. In each event he established or helped to establish a world record. Four years earlier, in Mexico, Spitz had won two Olympic gold medals.

**spleen,** large, soft, purplish-red organ that lies on the left side of the abdominal cavity, under the diaphragm. The spleen filters foreign organisms and old red BLOOD cells from the bloodstream by means of phagocytic cells that engulf and destroy them. Certain white blood cells are formed in the spleen. The spleen also manufactures red blood cells in the fetus towards the end of pregnancy and takes over again after birth if the bone marrow fails to perform that function. None of these functions appear to be vital and the spleen is often surgically removed in some diseases.

**splice,** a method of joining two pieces of rope, string, etc. together by unravelling the ends and working them together. A splice may also be used to form an eye at the end of a rope, by unravelling the end of the rope and working the strands in the opposite direction some distance along the rope's length. A backsplice, in which a short distance of rope is unravelled and worked back upon itself, is a good way of preventing an end fraying.

**Split,** city (1981 pop. 235,922), Croatia, Yugoslavia, on the Adriatic Sea. A seaport, it has shipbuilding, cement, and chemical industries. Roman interest is evident in the impressive palace of Diocletian, begun on his abdication in AD 305, which became a place of refuge from the Avars in the 7th cent.; the present-day city has been built among its walls. The city was under Venetian rule (1420–1797) and belonged to Austria until 1918. Notable buildings date from the Roman and Venetian periods.

**Spock, Benjamin McLane,** 1903–, American paediatrician. His *Common Sense Book of Baby and Child Care* (1946; later *Baby and Child Care*) has sold more copies than almost any other book published in the US. He has written widely on child-rearing.

**Spode,** English family of potters. **Josiah Spode I,** 1733–97, founded a pottery firm in 1764 at Stoke-on-Trent. He developed a translucent but durable bone china which is still made. After 1797, under his son **Josiah Spode II,** 1754–1827, the firm was known for blue-and-white transfer-printed ware with novel designs, such as Indian sporting scenes.

Spode pierced basket and stand, based on an original Chinese design

**Spohr, Louis,** 1784–1859, German composer, virtuoso violinist, and conductor. His music was placed on the same level as that of Handel and Beethoven in England during the latter part of the 19th cent. His works include 17 violin concertos and music for violin and harp (his wife was a harpist); 9 symphonies, 33 string quartets, 8 quintets, 10 operas and 4 oratorios, including the once popular *The Last Judgement* (1825–26); and an attractive Nonet, which is probably one of his most frequently performed works. He wrote an entertaining and informative autobiography.

**Spokane**, US city (1980 pop. 171,300), E Washington, at the falls of the Spokane R.; inc. 1881. It is a port of entry, and the commercial, transport, and industrial centre of the 'Inland Empire', a productive grain and livestock region. Its manufactures are diversified. Spokane's business and cultural life were reinvigorated by development for the fair 'Expo 74'. A cultural and educational centre, the city has a noted American Indian museum.

**sponge**, aquatic invertebrate animal of the phylum Porifera. All but one family are marine. Colonies of adult sponges, often brilliantly coloured, live attached to rocks, corals, or shells, exhibiting so little movement that 18th-cent. naturalists considered them plants. The sponge's body is like a sac. Water is drawn into a central cavity through many tiny holes in the body wall and expelled through a large opening at the top. Hard materials embedded in the body wall form a skeleton. The dried skeletons of colonial sponges have been used to hold liquid since ancient times. Natural sponges are light grey or brown when dried and irregular in shape.

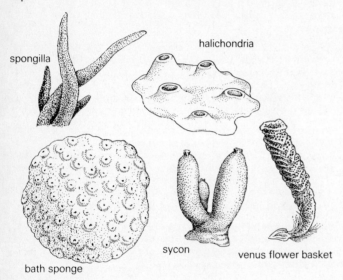

spongilla

halichondria

bath sponge

sycon

venus flower basket

Sponge

**spontaneous combustion,** phenomenon in which a substance unexpectedly bursts into flame without apparent cause. Spontaneous combustion occurs when a substance undergoes a slow oxidation that releases heat in such a way that it cannot escape the substance; the temperature of the substance consequently rises until ignition takes place.

**spore**, term applied both to a resistant or resting stage occurring among unicellular organisms such as bacteria and to an asexual reproductive cell of multicellular plants that gives rise to a new organism without FERTILIZATION. A spore is typically a mass of protoplasm containing a nucleus and surrounded by a cell wall that may be tough and waterproof, permitting the cell to survive unfavourable circumstances.

**sporophyte:** see ALTERNATION OF GENERATIONS.

**sports medicine,** branch of medicine concerned with prevention, treatment, and study of injuries received during participation in sports. 'Tennis elbow'; shoulder, knee, back, and leg injuries; stiffness and pain in joints; and tendinitis are some of the conditions involved. Treatment includes mechanical supports, specific exercise programmes, physical therapy, and in severe cases surgery. Sports medicine was initially practised primarily by physicians associated with professional sports teams, but with increased interest in amateur sports and physical fitness programmes in the 1970s and 80s, it grew rapidly.

**Sprague, Frank Julian,** 1857–1934, American electrical engineer. He improved electric-energy and wheel-suspension systems from which he developed (1887) the first electric street railway, in Richmond, Virginia. Sprague invented other railway devices (including the control system for multiple-unit trains in which each vehicle has motors controlled from the leading vehicle), created a superior electric motor adaptable to industrial machinery, and developed the electric lift.

**spring,** in geology, natural flow of water from the ground or from rocks, representing an outlet for the water that has accumulated in permeable rock strata underground. Mineral springs have a high mineral content. See also ARTESIAN WELL; GEYSER; HOT SPRING.

**Springfield. 1** US city (1984 est. pop. 102,000), state capital of Illinois, on the Sangamon R.; settled 1818, inc. as a city 1840. In a rich coal and farm area, it is a governmental, commercial, medical, insurance, and business centre, with varied industries. Abraham LINCOLN, a longtime resident, is buried nearby, and there are numerous sites associated with him. **2** US industrial city (1980 pop. 152,319), SW Massachusetts, a port on the Connecticut R.; inc. 1641. It has insurance, chemical, plastic, metallurgical, paper, and printing industries. Settled (1636) by Puritans, Springfield was a scene of Shays's Rebellion (1786–87; see under SHAYS, DANIEL), and a station on the UNDERGROUND RAILROAD. A US armoury there (1794–1966) developed the Springfield army rifles. Dr James Naismith invented (1891) basketball at Springfield College, which houses a hall of fame for the sport.

**spruce,** evergreen tree or shrub (genus *Picea*) of the PINE family, widely distributed in the Northern Hemisphere. The needles are angular in cross section, not flattened as in the related HEMLOCKS and FIRS. Spruces are a major source of pulpwood for PAPER manufacture; the light, straight-grained wood, known as whitewood, is also used in construction. The common, or Norway, spruce (*P. abies*) is one of the most widely planted conifers in British and N European forests. It is also grown in large numbers as a Christmas tree. In the west of Britain, the Sitka spruce (*P. sitchensis*) is grown for its resistance to gales and sea winds, and its high productivity. The Siberian spruce (*P. obovata*) grows in the huge coniferous forests (see TAIGA) of the USSR.

**spurge,** common name for the family Euphorbiaceae, herbs, shrubs, and trees of greatly varied structure and almost cosmopolitan distribution, although most species are tropical. The spurges are of great economic importance; the sap of most species is a milky latex, and that of the PARÁ RUBBER TREE is the source of much of the world's natural RUBBER. The genus *Manihot* includes CASSAVA, the source of tapioca and the most important tropical root crop after the SWEET POTATO. The cactuslike euphorbias (genus *Euphorbia*) are among the most common Old World desert SUCCULENTS and comprise most of the species commonly called spurge. Many are cultivated for their often colourful foliage and the showy bracts enclosing their 'naked flowers' (i.e., FLOWERS lacking petals and sometimes sepals). The poinsettia, native to Central America, is a popular Christmas plant with large rosettes of usually bright-red bracts.

**Spyri, Johanna** (ˌshpeeree), 1827–1901, Swiss author. She is best known for *Heidi* (1880) and other popular children's stories set in the Swiss Alps.

**squash:** see GOURD; PUMPKIN.

**squash,** game played on four-walled court with a small, hollow hard-rubber ball and a round-headed, gut-strung racket. A serve must hit the front wall above a service line 1.83 m (6 ft) high, with subsequent cannons off the side walls permitted. The ball may be returned before it hits the floor, and a point is scored when either player fails to return the ball before it touches the floor twice. The game may be played by partners.

**squatter sovereignty,** in US history, doctrine under which the question of whether slavery should be permitted in the territories was left to the territorial settlers themselves rather than being decided by Congress. First proposed in 1847, it was incorporated into the COMPROMISE OF 1850 and the KANSAS-NEBRASKA ACT. Its chief exponent, Stephen A. DOUGLAS, called it 'popular sovereignty', but antislavery men contemptuously called it 'squatter sovereignty'.

**squid,** carnivorous marine mollusc with 10 sucker-bearing arms; a CEPHALOPOD. Among the most highly developed invertebrates, the squid has eyes similar to those of humans, relatively sophisticated nervous and circulatory systems, and no external shell. Squids prey on fish, which they seize in their tentacles; when in danger, they emit a cloud of ink from a special sac. Squids range in size from 5 cm (2 in) to the 15-m (50-ft) giant squid, the largest of all invertebrates. Squid is a favourite food in the Mediterranean region and the Far East.

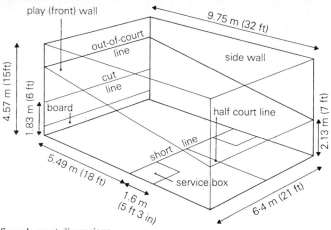

Squash court dimensions

**squill,** low, usually spring-blooming bulbous herb (genus *Scilla*) of the LILY family. The flowers, commonly deep blue but also white, rose, or purplish, are borne along a leafless stem; the leaves are usually narrow. Species of *Scilla* are used in rock gardens and borders.

**squirrel,** small or medium-sized RODENT of the family Sciuridae, found worldwide except in Australia, Madagascar, and polar regions. Typical tree squirrels (genus *Sciurus*), including the Eurasian red squirrel (*S. vulgaris*) and the North American grey squirrels, are day-active animals with slender bodies, thick fur, and bushy tails. In addition to tree squirrels the family includes GROUND SQUIRRELS (such as the chipmunk) and FLYING SQUIRREL.

**Sr,** chemical symbol of the element STRONTIUM.

**Sri Lanka,** officially the Democratic Socialist Republic of Sri Lanka, formerly Ceylon, island republic (1987 est. pop. 16,117,000), 65,610 km² (25,332 sq mi), S Asia, in the Indian Ocean, SE of India. The capital is COLOMBO. The north is mainly flat or gently rolling but hilly or mountainous in the south centre and southwest; among the mountains in the south central area is Adam's Peak (2243 m/7360 ft), sacred to Buddhists. The economy is largely agricultural. Rice is the principal food grain; its production has increased notably in recent years. The principal export crops are tea, rubber, and coconut. Sri Lanka is a leading producer of graphite and gems. Industries include the processing of agricultural products, the production of consumer goods, and the manufacture of cement. Tourism is important. The GNP is $5724 million and the GNP per capita is $360 (1984). The population is composed mainly of Sinhalese, who are Hinayana Buddhists; Hindu Tamils make up a large minority. The official language is Sinhala; Tamil and English are also spoken.

*History.* The aboriginal inhabitants were conquered in the 6th cent. BC by the Sinhalese, from N India, who established their capital at Anuradhapura. With the introduction of Buddhism in the 3rd cent. BC the island became one of the world centres of that religion. Europeans were drawn by the spice trade, and the island came under the Portuguese (16th cent.), the Dutch (17th cent.), and the British, who made it the crown colony of Ceylon in 1798. A nationalist movement arose during World War I, and the island was granted independence in 1948, becoming a member of the COMMONWEALTH. The new nation was challenged by rapid population growth, economic difficulties, and separatist demands by the Tamil minority. After the assassination of Prime Minister S.W.R.D. Bandaranaike in 1959 his widow, Sirimavo BANDARANAIKE, served as prime minister (1960–65, 1970–77), implementing such policies as nationalization of Western-owned businesses. A new constitution in 1972 adopted the Sinhalese name Sri Lanka and declared the country a republic. Economic crises and social unrest continued to plague the nation, and Mrs Bandaranaike was overwhelmingly defeated by the conservative United National Party in 1977. Western-style capitalism was promoted by Pres. J.R. JAYAWARDENE, who was reelected in 1982. Hostility among Sri Lanka's ethnic groups continued to be a serious problem in the 1980s, particularly violence associated with the aspirations of the TAMIL community. Against this background, the life of the parliament elected for a six-year term in 1977 was extended for a further six years, until 1989.

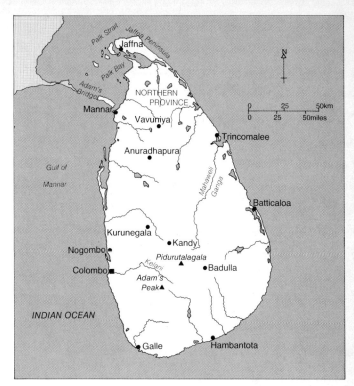

Sri Lanka

Presidential elections in 1988 were won by Ranasinghe Premadasa of the United National Party.

**Srinagar,** city (1981 pop. 594,775), Jammu and Kashmir state, N India (Pakistan disputes sovereignty), on Jhelum R. It is a district and state administrative centre commanding important routes across the HIMALAYAS and their foothills. It has notable craft industries (for example, woodwork, carpet-weaving and leather-work) that have benefited from tourists attracted by the beautiful city and its spectacular surrounding mountains. It also has an industrial estate and a large joinery mill. Srinagar is an ancient site for cities of various ages, one dating as far back as the time of ASOKA.

**Ssu-ma Ch'ien,** (ˌsoohmah chyen), 145?–90? BC, Chinese historian of the Han dynasty, called the Father of Chinese history. He wrote *Shih chi* [records of the historian], a history in 130 chapters of China and all regions and peoples known at that time. It became a model for later dynastic histories.

**Ssu-ma Kuang** 1018–86, Chinese historian and statesman. He edited *The Comprehensive Mirror for Aid in Government,* a gigantic history of China from 403 BC to AD 959. He was a conservative opponent of government reform.

**stability,** in mathematics, condition that may or may not obtain in the solution of a problem or in a simplified form of solution when the original form has proved intractable. If the solution to an oscillatory system is of the form $y = e^{-t} \sin 2t$, the oscillations die away as $t$ increases and the system is stable. If, however, it is of the form $y = t \sin 2t$, the amplitude of the oscillations increases indefinitely and the system is unstable. Sometimes a continuous system is approximated to by a discrete formulation, and a numerical approach adopted. This introduces small errors which may build up to such an extent that they eventually mask the true solution. In such a case the numerical solution has become unstable.

**stability of equilibrium,** mechanical system in which all the forces balance is said to be in equilibrium. Since perfect conditions only rarely occur it is important to know whether a slightly disturbed system returns to the equilibrium situation (in which case the equilibrium is said to be stable) or whether it deviates even further from it (unstable equilibrium). A pendulum at rest with the bob below the point of suspension is in stable equilibrium, while if the bob is balanced above the point of suspension the equilibrium is unstable.

**Staël, Germaine de** (stahl), 1766–1817, French-Swiss woman of letters; daughter of Suzanne and Jacques NECKER. Her Paris salon was a powerful political and cultural centre until 1803, when her spirited opposition to NAPOLEON I caused her exile. She retired to her estate at Coppet, on Lake Geneva, where she again attracted a brilliant circle. Her principal work, *De l'Allemagne* (1810; tr. On Germany), with its enthusiasm for German ROMANTICISM, tremendously influenced European thought and letters. Her other works include a sociological study of literature (1800); the novels *Delphine* (1802) and *Corinne* (1807); and a memoir, *Dix années d'exil* (1818; tr. Ten Years of Exile).

**Staffordshire**, inland county in W Midlands of England (1984 est. pop. 1,019,400), 2716 km² (1059 sq mi), bordering on West Midlands in the S and Cheshire in the N. The county town is STAFFORD. It is hilly in the N, but most of the county is relatively flat or gently undulating. Much of the county is industrial and urbanized, with the POTTERIES in the N. and Cannock Chase in the S.

**stagflation,** in economics, a word created in the 1970s to describe the combination of a stagnant economy and severe INFLATION. Previously, these two conditions did not exist at the same time because lowered demand, brought about by a recession (see DEPRESSION), usually produced lower, or at least stable, prices.

**stained glass,** windows made of coloured glass. An art form of great antiquity in the Far East, used by Muslim designers in their intricate windows, it became one of the most beautiful achievements of medieval art. Christian churches had coloured glass windows as early as the 5th cent., but the art of stained glass reached its height in the Middle Ages, particularly 1150–1250. As the massive Romanesque wall was eliminated, the use of glass expanded. Integrated with the lofty verticals of Gothic architecture (see GOTHIC ARCHITECTURE AND ART), large windows provided greater illumination that was regarded as symbolic of divine light. Early glaziers followed a CARTOON to cut the glass and fired the painted pieces in a kiln. Metallic oxides fused with the glass in the melting pot to produce the jewel-like colours of small pieces whose irregular surfaces created scintillating refractions of light. The pieces were fitted into channelled lead strips, the leads were soldered together, and the glass was installed in an iron framework. Outstanding examples of 12th-cent. stained glass can be found in the windows of such churches as Saint-Denis, in Paris, and CANTERBURY, in England. Among the finest 13th-cent. works are the windows at CHARTRES and the SAINTE-CHAPELLE in Paris. With improved glassmaking many medieval qualities vanished, and by the 16th cent. a lesser art was produced with larger, smoother pieces and sophisticated painting techniques. In the 19th cent., ROMANTICISM and the GOTHIC REVIVAL caused renewed interest in stained glass. Important contributions to the art were made by William MORRIS, in England, and John LA FARGE and Louis Comfort TIFFANY, in the US. In modern art the medium has been used by ROUAULT, MATISSE, and CHAGALL.

**Stainer, Sir John** 1840–1901, British composer and scholar. He did much for the standard of English music as organist of St Paul's (1872–88), writer of textbooks, and Inspector of Schools. He produced editions of early music and composed hymns and church music, of which the best known is the oratorio *The Crucifixion* (1887). He became Professor of Music at Oxford.

**stainless steel:** see STEEL.

**stalactite and stalagmite,** mineral forms found in CAVES; sometimes collectively called dripstone. A stalactite is an icicle-shaped mass of CALCITE that hangs from the roof of a cave, formed by the precipitation of calcite from ground water. A stalagmite is a cone of calcite rising from the floor of a cave, formed by the same process. Stalactites and stalagmites often meet to form solid pillars. The many colours often seen in these formations are caused by impurities.

**Stalin, Joseph Vissarionovich,** 1879–1953, Russian revolutionary, head of the USSR (1924–53). A Georgian cobbler's son named Dzhugashvili, he joined the Social-Democratic party while a seminarian and soon became a professional revolutionary. In the 1903 party split (see BOLSHEVISM AND MENSHEVISM) he sided with LENIN. Stalin attended party congresses abroad and worked in the Georgian party press. In 1912 he went to St Petersburg, where he was elected to the party's central committee. About this time he took the name Stalin ('man of steel'). His sixth arrest (1913) led to four years of Siberian exile. After the RUSSIAN REVOLUTION of March 1917, he joined the editorial board of the party paper

*Pravda.* When the Bolsheviks took power (Nov. 1917) he became people's commissar of nationalities. He also played an important administrative role in the Russian CIVIL WAR (1918–20). In 1922 Stalin was made general secretary of the party. Lenin, before he died in 1924, wrote a 'testament' urging Stalin's removal from the post because of his arbitrary conduct; but in the struggle to succeed Lenin, Stalin was victorious. By 1927 he had discarded his erstwhile allies BUKHARIN, KAMENEV, and ZINOVIEV; in 1929 TROTSKY, his major rival for the succession, was exiled from the USSR. Forcible agricultural collectivization and breakneck industrialization began in 1928. The state, instead of 'withering away', as Marx had foreseen, was glorified. Nationalism was revived as 'socialism in one country'. The military was reorganized along czarist lines. Conservatism permeated official policy on art, education, and the family. Political repression and terror reached a height in the 1930s. In a public trial Bukharin, Kamenev, Zinoviev, and others were charged with conspiring to overthrow the regime; they confessed and were executed. Stalin's terror also affected the daily lives of millions of ordinary citizens. Stalin's foreign policy in the 1930s focused on efforts to form alliances with Britain and France against NAZI Germany; the 1939 Russo-German nonaggression pact marked the failure of these efforts. In 1941 Stalin took over the premiership from MOLOTOV. The German invasion (June 22) found him unprepared; at war's end (1945) 20 million soviet citizens were dead, some of them killed by Stalin's own agents. At the TEHERAN CONFERENCE and the YALTA CONFERENCE Stalin gained Western recognition of a Soviet sphere of influence in Eastern Europe. The paranoia of his last years led to a period of terror reminiscent of the 1930s. On his death (1953) his body was placed next to Lenin's. In 1956, at the 20th Party Congress, KHRUSHCHEV, and later GORBACHEV, denounced Stalin's tyranny, but 'destalinization' has never been thoroughgoing. See UNION OF SOVIET SOCIALIST REPUBLICS.

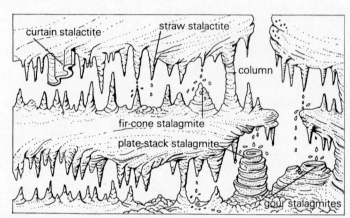

Stalactite and stalagmite

**Stalingrad:** see VOLGOGRAD.

**Stalinism,** the particular brand of COMMUNISM developed in the Soviet Union under Joseph STALIN (1922–53). It added political terror and the personality cult to the existing dictatorial practices of MARXISM–LENINISM. It also introduced collectivized agriculture, centralized economic planning, including the Five Year Plans, extensive militarization, and SOCIALIST REALISM in cultural life. Denounced by KHRUSHCHEV, it nonetheless remains as the foundation of most Soviet and Soviet-style institutions.

**stall,** in aeronautics, what happens to an aeroplane when flying speed is reduced to the point at which the airflow over the wings (see AEROFOIL) will no longer develop sufficient lift to sustain flight. The wings then stall and the nose drops; provided there is sufficient air space below, the speed through the air increases until adequate lift for level flight is regained. When the aeroplane is stalled control may be lost so that one wing drops to cause the aeroplane to go into an uncontrolled nose-down rotation, known as a *spin*. Such spins were responsible for many of the crashes in the early days of flying, until it was realized (1912) that the only way to recover control is to push the stick forward (i.e., to increase air speed) and to centralize the rudder, actions which seemed counter to the pilot's commonsense.

**Stamboliiski, Alexandŭr,** 1879–1932, Bulgarian peasant leader and statesman. An ideologue of the peasant movement, he remade the Bulgarian Agrarian National Union into a political party and assumed power in the aftermath of Bulgaria's defeat in World War I. Seeking both to transform society in the interest of its peasant majority and to reconcile Bulgaria with its neighbours, he incurred the fierce enmity of the crown, the military, the Macedonian exiles, and the traditional politicians. They combined to overthrow Stamboliiski's regime and murder him in 1923.

**Stambolov, Stefan**, 1855-95, Bulgarian politician. Leader of the Liberal Party upon Bulgaria's liberation (1878), he served as regent after the abdication of Alexander BATTENBERG (1886) and arranged for FERDINAND of Saxe-Coburg-Gotha to assume the vacant throne (1887). As premier until 1894, he established a repressive regime ultimately inherited by Prince Ferdinand. He was murdered in a Macedonian vendetta.

**stamen:** see FLOWER.

**Stamp Act**, 1765, revenue law passed by the British Parliament requiring publications and legal documents in the American colonies to bear a tax stamp. The act was vehemently denounced, and organizations formed to resist it (see SONS OF LIBERTY). The **Stamp Act Congress**, Oct. 1765, adopted the Declaration of Rights and Grievances, which declared the tax unconstitutional because the colonists were not represented in Parliament. The Stamp Act was repealed in 1766.

**standard deviation,** a measure derived from the VARIANCE and used in STATISTICS to indicate how closely data are clustered about some AVERAGE value, usually the ARITHMETIC MEAN. In a NORMAL DISTRIBUTION, three standard deviations on either side of the arithmetic mean contain approximately 99% of all the values. See also STANDARD ERROR.

**standard error,** the STANDARD DEVIATION of an AVERAGE or some other statistical parameter, and is used in STATISTICS to indicate how closely averages derived from repeated samples will cluster around some population value.

**standard of living,** level of consumption of goods and services to which an individual or group is accustomed, usually thought of in national terms. Although an evaluation of a standard of living is relative, the use of GROSS NATIONAL PRODUCT or per-capita income provides a more objective yardstick for comparing the living standards of two or more countries. The elements that make up a standard of living include not only the goods consumed but also the number of dependents in a family, educational opportunities, and the amount spent for health and recreation. In the UK the standard of living has been climbing steadily. In periods when prices rise faster than does per-capita income, the living standard may actually decline.

**standard time:** see SOLAR TIME.

**Stanford, Sir Charles Villiers** 1852–1924, Irish composer and teacher, who settled in England and became professor of composition at the Royal College of Music (1883–1924), where he taught more than a generation of English composers. He achieved great success as a composer of operas, such as *Shamus O'Brien* (1896), of church music, and of songs such as 'Songs of the Fleet'. He was appointed professor of music at Cambridge in 1887.

**Stanhope, Philip Dormer :** see CHESTERFIELD, PHILIP DORMER STANHOPE, 4th EARL OF.

**Stanislaus,** Polish kings. **Stanislaus I**, 1677–1766, king of POLAND (r.1704–09, 1733–35) and duke of Lorraine (1735–66), was born Stanislaus Leszczyński. Early in the NORTHERN WAR, CHARLES XII of Sweden deposed AUGUSTUS II of Poland and installed Leszczynski, a Polish nobleman. In 1709, however, following CHARLES XII's defeat by PETER I at Poltava, Stanislaus was forced to yield the crown to Augustus and retire to France. There his daughter, Marie Leszczyńska, married LOUIS XV, with whose help Stanislaus attempted (1733) to gain the crown when Augustus died. Stanislaus was elected, but a Russian invasion in favour of the other claimant AUGUSTUS III led to the War of the POLISH SUCCESSION. At its conclusion, he retained his royal title but renounced his actual rights in return for the duchy of Lorraine. **Stanislaus II**, 1732–98, was the last king of Poland (1764–95). With the support of Frederick II of Prussia and Catherine II of Russia (his former mistress), he was elected (1764) to succeed AUGUSTUS III. He was a virtual puppet of Russia, and during his reign Poland was dismembered (see POLAND, PARTITIONS OF).

**Stanislavsky, Constantin**, 1863–1938, Russian theatrical director, teacher, and actor, co-founder of the Moscow Art Theatre (see THEATRE, table); b. Constantin Sergeyevich Alekseyev. His innovative technique for actors, emphasizing emotional truth and inner motivation and known

today as the Stanislavsky Method, revolutionized modern acting. He was the first to produce many of CHEKHOV's plays.

**Stanley, Sir Henry Morton,** 1841–1904, English explorer and journalist. In 1871 he was sent by the New York *Herald* to find David LIVINGSTONE in Africa, where he delivered his famous greeting, 'Dr. Livingstone, I presume?' On another expedition (1874–79) he explored the length of the Congo R., and on a third journey (1879–84), under Belgian auspices, he helped to organize the future Independent State of the Congo (see ZAÏRE).

**Stanton, Elizabeth Cady,** 1815–1902, American reformer and feminist. With Lucretia MOTT she organized (1848) the first US women's rights convention, and from 1852 she led the women's movement with Susan B. ANTHONY. An able journalist, gifted orator, and persuasive promoter of FEMINISM, Stanton was president (1869–90) of the National Woman Suffrage Association and editor (1868–70) of *Revolution*, a militant women's rights magazine.

**Stapledon, William Olaf**, 1886–1950, English novelist and philosopher. A follower of H.G. WELLS, he wrote visionary science-fiction novels evoking the uttermost reaches of space and time. *Last and First Men* (1930) and *Star Maker* (1937) are his best-known works.

**star,** hot, incandescent sphere of gas (usually more than 90% hydrogen) that is held together by its own gravitation and emits light and other forms of electromagnetic radiation whose ultimate source is nuclear energy. The universe contains thousands of millions of galaxies, and each GALAXY contains thousands of millions of stars, which are frequently bunched together in star CLUSTERS of as many as 100,000. The stars visible to the unaided eye are all in our own galaxy, the MILKY WAY. The visible stars are divided into six classes according to their apparent MAGNITUDE. Stars differ widely in mass, size, temperature, age (see POPULATION, STELLAR), and LUMINOSITY. About 90% of all stars have masses between one tenth and 50 times that of the Sun. The most luminous stars (excluding supernovas) are about a million times more powerful than the Sun, while the least luminous are only a hundredth as powerful. VARIABLE STARS fluctuate in luminosity. Red giants, the largest stars, are hundreds of times greater in size than the Sun. At the opposite extreme, WHITE DWARFS are no larger than the Earth, and NEUTRON STARS are only a few kilometers in radius. The central region, or core, of an ordinary star has a temperature of millions of degrees. At this temperature nuclear energy is released by the fusion of hydrogen to form helium. By the time the energy reaches the surface of the star, it has been largely converted into visible light with a spectrum characteristic of a hot body (see SUN). The theory of STELLAR EVOLUTION studies how a star changes as it consumes its hydrogen in the nuclear reactions that power it. When all its nuclear fuel is exhausted, the star dies, possibly in a SUPERNOVA explosion.

**starch,** white, odourless, tasteless CARBOHYDRATE. It plays a vital role in the BIOCHEMISTRY of both plants and animals. Made in green plants by PHOTOSYNTHESIS, it is one of the main forms in which plants store food. Animals obtain starch from plants and store it as GLYCOGEN. Both plants and animals convert starch to GLUCOSE when energy is needed. Commercially, starch is made chiefly from CORN and POTATOES. Corn syrup and corn sugar made from cornstarch are widely used to sweeten food products. Starch is also used to stiffen laundered fabrics and to size paper and textiles.

**Star Chamber,** ancient meeting place of the king's councilors in WESTMINSTER PALACE, London, named for the stars painted on the ceiling. From the 15th cent. the role of the council as an equity and prerogative court increased and it extended its jurisdiction over criminal matters, especially under the TUDORS. Abuses of its power under JAMES I and CHARLES I led to its abolition in 1641.

**star cluster:** see CLUSTER, STAR.

**starfish** or **sea star,** star-shaped carnivorous marine invertebrate animal (an ECHINODERM), found worldwide in shallow waters. The spiny body has five or more tapering arms radiating from a central area. Usually dull yellow or orange but occasionally brightly coloured, starfish vary in size from about 1.25 cm (½ in) to over 90 cm (3 ft).

**Starhemberg, Ernst Rüdiger, Graf von** (ˌshtahrəmˈbeək), 1638–1701, Austrian field marshal. From July to Sept. 1683 he successfully held Vienna with a small garrison against a large Turkish army. His descendant, **Ernst Rüdiger von Starhemberg**, 1899–1956, took part in HITLER's 'beer-hall putsch' of 1923 but later opposed Hitler.

Starhemberg became (1930) leader of the Austrian Fascist militia and supported DOLLFUSS in 1932. He became vice chancellor (1934) but was forced to resign (1936) by SCHUSCHNIGG. In WORLD WAR II he served in the British and Free French air forces.

**starling,** member of a highly successful family of gregarious, glossy-feathered BIRDS, the family Sturnidae, found from the S Pacific north to northern Europe and Asia. The European common starling (*Sturnus vulgaris*) has spread over North America since 1890 and also flourishes in Australia and New Zealand. These noisy, energetic birds will drive other species away from nesting sites. They are accurate mimics, particularly the MYNAH bird. The group are useful agricultural allies, feeding on insects and larvae, but are a nuisance in towns, where their droppings foul buildings and people alike.

**Star of Bethlehem,** name of the luminous celestial object in the eastern sky that, as related in the New Testament, led the Wise Men to Bethlehem. Naturalistic explanations of the phenomenon, e.g., that it was caused by a conjunction of planets or by the appearance of a comet, are highly speculative.

**START,** (STrategic Arms Reduction Talks): see DISARMAMENT, NUCLEAR.

**state,** in the international context, the term usually means NATION–STATE. In the context of a single country, it may be distinguished from society, to mean that body of institutions which has the constitutional power to make and enforce laws for a given population; which has a monopoly of the legitimate use of coercion; and which, if it has legitimacy, is also regarded by its citizens as having the moral authority to rule. The exact form of the state with its powers and institutions can vary from country to country and change over time. In Britain, state institutions include both Houses of Parliament, the monarchy, the armed forces, the police, the judiciary, and the civil service of both central and local government. But the state is not simply a set of institutions; it is also a legal and political idea involving the concept of supreme power or SOVEREIGNTY. It can not be simply equated with government, for whilst a government can lose office, the 'apparatus of rule' remains in being; in principle, a constitutionally created government has control over the state for its term of office. Since the 18th cent. the history of the state in modern industrialized societies has been one of continuous growth, both in the size and range of its institutions, and in terms of its penetration into ever greater areas of social life. In Western democracies the state is involved in regulating the mixed economy and in providing a large range of welfare services; in Communist countries the state, run by a single party, directs virtually every aspect of economic, social, and intellectual life. Generally speaking, the state has been viewed positively by the political left, with the exception of anarchist and syndicalist groups, as the only agent capable of bringing about large-scale transformations of society, such as the implementation of social justice or rapid industrialization. On the political right, although there is no hesitation about the use of the state to maintain order, the expansion of the state bureaucracy and the intervention of the state in the free market are attacked as expensive and inefficient, and the state's claims to regulate the lives and property of its citizens are presented as an infringement of individual liberty, leading to the threat of TOTALITARIANISM.

**State, United States Department of,** federal executive department responsible for the implementation of American foreign policy. Created in 1789, it is the oldest federal department, and its head, the secretary of state, is the ranking member of the cabinet. While some of its original functions (such as supervision of the US Mint) have been transferred to other departments, it has expanded with the growth of the US as a world power. The Dept of State is in charge of the Foreign Service and maintains delegations (embassies, consulates, and special missions) in other countries. Such secretaries of state as John Quincy ADAMS (1817–25), Hamilton FISH (1869–77), George C. MARSHALL (1947–49), John Foster DULLES (1953–59), and Henry KISSINGER (1973–76) have played important roles in making US foreign policy.

**States-General** or **Estates-General,** French national assembly in which the three chief states (clergy, nobles, and commons) were represented as separate bodies. Like the English PARLIAMENT, it originated in the king's council, but it never gained the financial control that made the English Parliament powerful. The first States-General was summoned (1302) by PHILIP IV to obtain national approval for his anticlerical policy. Later meetings often opposed the king or even won temporary concessions, but the continuous consolidation of royal power prevented its growth. After the States-General of 1614, the estates were not convoked again until 1789. In that year LOUIS XVI assembled the estates as a last resort to solve France's financial crisis. In June 1789 the third estate (commons), joined by some of the clergy, declared itself the National Assembly, an act that began the FRENCH REVOLUTION.

**states of matter,** forms of matter differing in several properties because of differences in the motions of the molecules (or atoms or ions) of which they are composed and the forces between them. There are three common states of matter: solid, liquid, and gas. The molecules of a solid are limited to vibrations about a fixed position, giving a solid both a definite volume and a definite shape. When heat is applied to a solid, its molecules begin to vibrate more rapidly until, at a temperature called the MELTING POINT, they break out of their fixed positions and the solid becomes a liquid. Because the molecules of a liquid are free to move throughout the liquid but are held from escaping by intermolecular forces (see ADHESION AND COHESION), a liquid has a definite volume but no definite shape. As more heat is added to the liquid, some molecules near the surface gain enough energy to evaporate, or break away completely from the liquid, and change to a gaseous state. Finally, at a temperature called the BOILING POINT, molecules throughout the liquid become energetic enough to escape, forming bubbles of vapour that rise to the surface; the liquid thus changes completely to a gas. Because its molecules are free to move in every possible way, a gas has neither a definite shape nor a definite volume but expands to fill any container in which it is placed. The reverse processes of melting and evaporation are, respectively, freezing (the temperature at freezing point being the same as that for melting point), and condensation. See also CRYSTAL; GAS LAWS; KINETIC–MOLECULAR THEORY OF GASES; PLASMA.

**states' rights,** in US history, a doctrine based on the 10th amendment to the CONSTITUTION, which states: 'The powers not delegated to the United States by the Constitution, nor prohibited by it to the States, are reserved to the States respectively, or to the people.' Controversy over interpretation of this clause arose immediately. The Federalists, led by Alexander HAMILTON, favoured a broad interpretation of federal powers. Thomas JEFFERSON and the 'strict constructionists' insisted that all powers not specifically granted to the federal government be reserved to the states; the KENTUCKY AND VIRGINIA RESOLUTIONS were the first formulations of this doctrine. The issue was central to the HARTFORD CONVENTION (1814–15), called by New Englanders to express hostility to the policies of the federal government's declaration of war on Britain. The fight over the constitutionality of the second Bank of the US provided a major setback for states' rights; the Supreme Court's decision in McCulloch v. Maryland (1819) greatly expanded the scope of federal power. An extreme expression of states' rights was the ordinance of NULLIFICATION, inspired by Sen. John C. CALHOUN and passed (1832) by South Carolina in response to the tariff acts of 1828 and 1832. Ultimately, states' rights was used by the slave states to justify secession. In the 20th cent., states' rights was revived by Southern opponents of the federal civil rights programme.

**statics,** branch of MECHANICS concerned with the maintenance of equilibrium in bodies by the interaction of FORCES upon them. In a state of equilibrium the resultant of all outside forces acting on a body is zero, thus keeping the body at rest.

**station, railway,** building for train passengers. With the advent of the first timetabled RAILWAY passenger service on the Liverpool and Manchester railway, the level of traffic required not only platforms giving access to the trains for passengers, but waiting rooms and enquiry and ticket offices. All these features are provided at Manchester (Liverpool Road) station which is the oldest (1830) railway station in the world which is preserved. Expansion of traffic with the growth of railways led to larger stations with more extensive facilities, such as restaurants, shops, and hotels. Railway companies sought to impress the public with fine buildings and so often engaged leading architects. Even modest stations on branch lines were often given superior architectural treatment.

**Stations of the Cross,** pictures or carvings of 14 key incidents in Christ's progress from Pilate's house to Calvary before his crucifixion. Generally placed in churches, devout Christians visit them mainly, but not exclusively, in LENT, making them the focus of meditation on the Lord's passion. The devotions developed from the ancient practice of pilgrims to Jerusalem retracing, to the accompaniment of prayers, the several stages of Christ's last journey.

**statistics,** word with two meanings: (1) the collection, collation, and presentation of numerical information, often for political, social, and economic purposes; (2) a branch of applied mathematics dealing with the collection, analysis, and interpretation of numerical information and the use of such data to make inferences or test hypotheses in uncertain situations. In its second sense, the theory of statistics has developed rapidly during the last 50 years and now forms the basis of almost all branches of the applied sciences. The earliest uses of mathematical statistics were in the application of the theory of PROBABILITY by PASCAL and his gambling friends to games of chance. In the 1920s and 30s, R.A. FISHER and his colleagues at the Rothamsted Experimental Station developed many new techniques, originally for the design of agricultural field experiments, which have since become widely used across almost all areas of industrial and scientific research. During and since World War II, new applications of statistical theory to problems of operational research, process control, and the management of biological systems have resulted in further striking developments. At the heart of all these developments lies the problem of making predictions from a small SAMPLE of observations or experiments drawn from some larger POPULATION, as in compiling television ratings or election polls. The efficient DESIGN OF EXPERIMENTS on highly variable material such as biological populations is also one of the principal advantages gained from the development of statistical theory. Mathematical statistics has also contributed to the SIMULATION or MODELLING of complex interrelationships and processes, for example of ecological systems or space flights, often with the use of STOCHASTIC methods to imitate the uncertainty encountered in such applications. When combined with COMPUTER GRAPHICS, such simulations may be sufficiently realistic to aid in the training of resource managers and decision-makers.

**Statius, Publius Papinius,** AD c.45–c.96, Latin poet, who had the patronage of the Emperor DOMITIAN. Two of his EPICS in the manner of VIRGIL the *Thebaid* and the *Achilleid* survive, as do the *Silvae,* pleasing shorter poems.

**stator:** see GENERATOR; MOTOR, ELECTRIC.

**Stavanger,** city (1985 pop. 94,193), SW Norway. It is the principal centre of the Norwegian fish-canning industry. There is some shipbuilding and alloy steels are smelted in the vicinity using hydroelectric power. It has an 11th-cent. Gothic cathedral.

**Stead, Christina,** 1902–83, Australian novelist. She lived in England, France, and America before returning to her birthplace in 1974. Her intriguing, stylistically daring, and verbally brilliant novels include *Seven Poor Men in Sydney* (1934), *House of All Nations* (1938), her acknowledged masterpiece, the unsentimentally autobiographical *The Man Who Loved Children* (1944), as well as the posthumous *I'm Dying Laughing* (1986).

**steady-state theory:** see COSMOLOGY.

**steam engine,** machine for converting heat energy into mechanical energy, using steam as the conversion medium. When water is boiled into steam its volume increases about 1600 times, producing a force that can be used to move a piston back and forth in a cylinder. The piston is attached to a crankshaft that converts the piston's back-and-forth motion into rotary motion for driving machinery. From the Greek inventor HERO OF ALEXANDRIA to the Englishman Thomas NEWCOMEN, many people contributed to the work of harnessing steam. However, James WATT's steam engine (patented 1769) offered the first practical solution by providing a separate chamber for condensing the steam and by using steam pressure to move the piston in both directions. These and other improvements by Watt prepared the steam engine for a major role in manufacturing and transportation during the INDUSTRIAL REVOLUTION. Today steam engines have been replaced in most applications by more economical and efficient devices, e.g., the steam TURBINE, the electric MOTOR, the INTERNAL-COMBUSTION ENGINE, and the DIESEL ENGINE.

**steamship,** ocean-going passenger or cargo vessel driven by steam. The steamship developed from the paddle-steamer, which first appeared at the end of the 18th cent. in the US. However, paddle wheels were inefficient, particularly over long distance, and such vessels were often sail-assisted. In 1838 I. K. BRUNEL built the *Great Western*, which, with the advantage of a huge fuel capacity, became the first regular transatlantic steamship. The invention of the screw propeller in 1836, by the Englishman John Petit Smith, and independently by the Swedish–American John Ericsson, was a breakthrough; Brunel's *Great*

*Britain* (1845) was the first ship to incorporate this improvement and the first to be constructed of iron. In the quest for greater speed, further technological improvement followed rapidly. Hull designs became more streamlined, steel replaced iron, and in 1897 a more fuel-efficient engine, the steam-turbine, was unveiled by its English inventor Charles Parsons. The British CRUISE LINER *Mauretania*, holder of the BLUE RIBAND of the Atlantic with a speed of 27 knots, exemplified the latest in steamship technology of the first decade of the 20th cent. With the passing of the age of the ocean liner, and the quest for speed, the cheaper diesel engine came to replace the steam-turbine in most sea-going vessels.

Great Britain

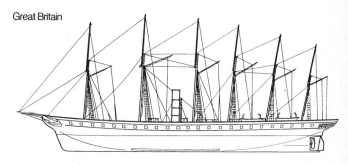

Mauretania

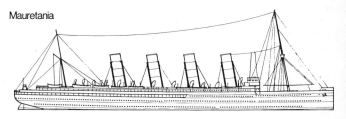

Steamship

**steatite** (ˌstee·ətiet): see SOAPSTONE.

**steel,** ALLOY of IRON, CARBON, and small proportions of other elements. Steelmaking involves the removal of iron's impurities and the addition of desirable alloying elements. Steel was first made by cementation, a process of heating bars of iron with charcoal so that the surface of the iron acquired a high carbon content. The bars were then fused together, yielding a metal harder and stronger than the individual bars but lacking uniformity in these properties. The crucible method, consisting of melting iron together with other substances in a crucible, is one of the costlier steelmaking processes, employed only for making special steels (e.g., the famous blades of Damascus). The BESSEMER PROCESS, the open-hearth process, and the basic oxygen process are more widely used. Steel is often classified by its carbon content: a high-carbon steel is hard and brittle; low- or medium-carbon steel can be welded and shaped with tools. Alloy steels, now the most widely used, contain one or more elements that give them special properties. Aluminium steel is smooth and has a high tensile strength. Chromium steel is used in car and aeroplane parts because of its hardness, strength, and elasticity. Nickel steel is the most widely used of the alloys; it is nonmagnetic and has the tensile properties of high-carbon steel without the brittleness. Stainless steel has a high tensile strength and resists abrasion and corrosion because of its high chromium content; it is used in kitchen utensils and plumbing fixtures. See also CASEHARDENING; GALVANIZING.

**Steel, David,** 1938–, British politician, leader of the LIBERAL PARTY (1976–88). Having entered parliament for a Scottish constituency in 1965, Steel succeeded Jeremy Thorpe as Liberal Party leader in 1976. He then sought to bring his small party into the political mainstream by entering into an agreement (the 'Lib–Lab pact') in 1977 to support the minority Labour government. Under the post-1979 Conservative government he pursued a new strategy, forming an alliance with the new SOCIAL DEMOCRATIC PARTY (1983) with the aim of providing a centrist alternative to both of the major British parties. After the alliance had lost ground in the 1987 elections, Steel proposed a full merger of the two parties, this leading to the formation of the SOCIAL AND LIBERAL DEMOCRATS (1988), of which he was briefly joint interim leader.

**Steele, Sir Richard,** 1672–1729, English essayist and playwright; b. Dublin. His first play, *The Funeral,* appeared in 1701 and was followed by three more comedies: *The Lying Lover* (1703), *The Tender Husband* (1705), and *The Conscious Lovers* (1722). Steele held various minor governmental posts before starting his periodical the *Tatler* (1709–11), on which he was soon joined by Joseph ADDISON. Their partnership led to the founding of the SPECTATOR (1711–12), *Guardian* (1713), and lesser periodicals, all graced by Steele's spontaneous, witty ESSAYS. A Whig partisan and member of Parliament from 1713, Steele wrote the pamphlet *Crisis* (1713) in opposition to SWIFT. He also founded (1720) the first theatrical paper.

**Steen, Jan** (stayn), 1625/6–79, Dutch GENRE and history painter. His humorous and moralistic works offer a picture of life in his day. He was extremely productive, but is best remembered for his multi-figure themes of revelry and feasting, e.g., *As the Old Ones Sing, So the Young Ones Pipe* (Mauritshuis, The Hague).

**Steer, Philip Wilson,** 1890–1942, British painter. He trained in Paris, returning to London in 1884. His work of the late 1880s was influenced by IMPRESSIONISM, and he was a friend of SICKERT and worked with him until c. 1910. His main output was from 1907 to 1910, his work being popular at the time due to its distance from more radical art of the period.

**Stefansson, Vilhjalmur,** 1879–1962, Arctic explorer; b. Canada, of Icelandic parents. Educated in the US, he led several explorations of Arctic regions, adopting and demonstrating the efficacy of Eskimo ways. He explored the MACKENZIE R. delta and remained north of the ARCTIC CIRCLE for more than five years (1913–18) without a break. He was curator of the Stefansson collection of polar material at Dartmouth College.

**Steffens, (Joseph) Lincoln,** 1866–1936, American author. A magazine editor (1902–11) and a MUCKRAKER, he wrote articles exposing municipal corruption, collected in such volumes as *The Shame of the Cities* (1904) and *Upbuilders* (1909). His famous autobiography (1931) casts light on his era.

**Steichen, Edward** (ˌstiekən), 1879–1973, American photographer; b. Luxembourg. In Paris Steichen was renowned for his painterly photographs. With Alfred STIEGLITZ he established photography as an art. He helped develop aerial photography in World War I and directed US naval combat photography in World War II. As head of the Museum of Modern Art's photography department (1947–62) he organized the *Family of Man* exhibition (1955).

**Stein, Gertrude,** 1874–1946, American author. She went abroad in 1902 and from 1903 until her death lived mainly in Paris. During the 1920s she led a cultural salon, acting as a patron for such artists as PICASSO and MATISSE and influencing such writers as HEMINGWAY, Sherwood ANDERSON, and F. Scott FITZGERALD. Stein's own innovative writing emphasized the sounds and rhythms rather than the sense of words. Her works include short stories, e.g., *Three Lives* (1909); a long narrative, *The Making of Americans* (1925); autobiographical works, notably the *Autobiography of Alice B. Toklas* (1933); critical essays, e.g., *How to Write* (1931) and *Lectures in America* (1935); 'cubist' poetry, e.g., *Tender Buttons* (1914); and operas, notably *Four Saints in Three Acts* (1934), with music by Virgil THOMSON.

**Stein, Karl, Freiherr vom und zum,** 1757–1831, Prussian statesman and reformer. He was minister of commerce (1804–7) and premier (1807–8), but was dismissed under pressure from NAPOLEON I. As premier, he abolished serfdom and all feudal class privileges or restrictions, began Jewish emancipation, abolished internal customs, and instituted local self-government. His reforms, continued by his successors, turned Prussia into a modern state and enabled it to play a leading role in the unification of Germany.

**Stein, Sir Mark Aurel,** 1862–1943, British archaeologist. He spent his early life in Europe before moving to India in 1888; from 1899 he was appointed to the Indian Education Service and carried out archaeological exploration in central Asia and western China. In 1910 Stein was made superintendent of the Indian Archaeological Survey and carried out exploration in Iran and central Asia from 1913 to 1916. He continued exploration in Iran, Iraq, and Trans-Jordan from 1926 until his death.

**Stein, Peter,** 1937–, German theatre director. Stein was producer at the Schaubühne am Hallischen Ufer in Berlin (1970–75), where, influenced by student radicalization, he introduced co-operative practices among artists and technicians which resulted in ensemble playing of great

subtlety, intensity, and intelligence. Large-scale productions included *As You Like It* and the historical study-production *Shakespeare's World*; more interiorized works were his presentations of GOETHE's *Tasso*, KLEIST's *The Prince of Homburg*, and Gorki's *Summer Guests*. Subsequently freelancing, he has produced VERDI's *Otello* in Cardiff (1986) and O'NEILL's *The Hairy Ape* in Berlin and London (1987).

Marion Moorhouse in a portrait from *Vogue* taken by Edward **Steichen**

**Steinbeck, John,** 1902–68, American writer. His works are marked by a compassionate understanding of the world's disinherited. His best-known novel, *The Grapes of Wrath* (1939), treats the plight of 1930s Dust Bowl farmers turned migrant labourers while presenting a universal picture of victims of disaster. Among Steinbeck's other novels are *Tortilla Flat* (1935), *Cannery Row* (1945), *East of Eden* (1952), and *The Winter of Our Discontent* (1961). His other books include the novella *Of Mice and Men* (1937; later made into a play); short stories, notably the exquisite 'The Red Pony' in *The Long Valley* (1938); nonfiction works, e.g., *A Russian Journal* (1948), *America and Americans* (1966); and screenplays. Steinbeck was awarded the 1962 Nobel Prize in literature.

**Steiner, Rudolf,** 1861–1925, German occultist and social philosopher. Originally an adherent of THEOSOPHY, he left that group and founded (1912) his own system, which he called anthroposophy. It attempted to explain the world in terms of human spiritual nature, or a level of thinking independent of the senses. More than 170 private schools throughout the world are based on his pedagogical and philosophic teachings.

**Steinmetz, Charles Proteus,** 1865–1923, American electrical engineer; b. Germany; went to US, 1889. He joined the General Electric Co. in 1892. His discovery of the law of hysteresis made it possible to reduce the loss of efficiency in electrical apparatus resulting from alternating magnetism. His method for calculating alternating current revolutionized electrical engineering.

**stele** (ˌsteeli, steel), [Gk., = block of stone], stone or terra-cotta slab, usually oblong, set upright. Stelae were commonly carved with inscriptions and designs and were widely used as votives, memorials, and boundary markers, e.g., in IRON AGE Europe, ancient Egypt, China, and

Mesoamerica. Greek marble funerary stelae, with painted reliefs of the dead, are notable monuments of classical art. Tombstones are modern forms of stele.

Egyptian **stele** of the XIIth Dynasty (1955 BC) from Abydos

**Stella, Frank,** 1936–, American painter. In the 1960s he was one of the main artists in the new school of Post-painterly abstraction. His precise paintings are generally large, often with concentric angular stripes or curved motifs that emphasize the frequently irregular shape of his canvases.

**stellar evolution,** life history of a STAR. The initial phase of stellar evolution is contraction of the protostar from the interstellar gas (see INTERSTELLAR MATTER). In this stage, which typically lasts millions of years, half the gravitational potential energy released by the collapsing protostar is radiated away and half goes into increasing the temperature of the forming star. Eventually the central temperature becomes high enough for the nuclear fusion of hydrogen to form helium. The star then enters its longest period in stellar evolution. Because most stars are in this stage and fall along a diagonal line in the HERTZSPRUNG–RUSSELL DIAGRAM, they are called main-sequence stars. As the star's helium content builds up, the core contracts and releases gravitational energy, which heats up the core and increases the rate of hydrogen consumption. The increased reaction rates cause the stellar envelope to expand and cool, and the star becomes a red giant. Eventually, the contracting stellar core will reach temperatures in excess of 100,000,000°K. At this point, helium burning sets in, and the star starts shrinking in size. In the further course of evolution, the star may become unstable, possibly ejecting some of its mass and becoming an exploding nova or SUPERNOVA or a pulsating VARIABLE STAR. The end phase of a star depends on its mass. A low-mass star may become a WHITE DWARF; an intermediate-mass star may become a NEUTRON STAR; and a high-mass star may undergo complete GRAVITATIONAL COLLAPSE and become a black hole.

**stem,** supporting structure of a plant, serving also to conduct and store food materials. Stems of herbaceous (see HERB) and woody plants differ: herbaceous plants usually have pliant, green stems with relatively more pith and an almost inactive CAMBIUM; woody stems are covered by BARK and increase in height and diameter because of an active cambium. Tendrils, thorns (but not the prickles of the rose, which are surface modifications of the epidermis), and runners (stolons) are specialized aerial stems; BULBS, corms, RHIZOMES, and TUBERS are specialized underground stems, although the bulk of a bulb consists of swollen leaf bases. The stems of dicotyledons (see ANGIOSPERM) and GYMNOSPERMS consist of upward-conducting xylem (see WOOD) on the inside and downward-conducting phloem, arranged on either side of the cambium. In monocotyledons, which generally lack cambium, bundles of xylem and phloem are scattered throughout the stem.

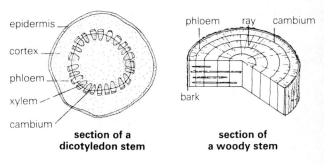

**section of a
dicotyledon stem**

**section of
a woody stem**

Sections through a **stem**

**Stendhal** pseud. of **Marie Henri Beyle** (stahnh͵dahl), 1783–1842, French author. He was an officer in Napoleon's army and later served as consul in Italy. His amorous involvements are reflected in *On Love* (1822), a psychological analysis of love that predates FREUD. Although largely unappreciated during his lifetime, his *Le rouge et le noir*(1831; tr. The Red and the Black) and *La Chartreuse de Parme* (1839), noted for their acute character analysis, rank among the world's great novels. The Stendhalian hero possesses an egoism that derives its energy from passion, has its own moral code, and unswervingly pursues happiness in the form of love or power. His *Souvenirs d'egotisme* (1892; tr. Memoirs of Egotism) was posthumously published.

**stenography:** see SHORTHAND.

**Stephanus,** family of printers: see ESTIENNE.

**Stephen,** 1100–54, king of England (r.1135–54); grandson of WILLIAM I. He swore fealty to HENRY I's daughter, MATILDA, but on Henry's death was proclaimed king. His reign was a constant struggle to maintain his throne, and he quarrelled repeatedly with the English clergy. Matilda, aided by her half-brother Robert, earl of Gloucester, captured Stephen in 1141 and reigned briefly before Stephen was released. The civil war was inconclusive and in 1153 Stephen named Matilda's son Henry, later HENRY II, as heir.

**Stephen, Sir Leslie,** 1832–1904, English writer and critic. He edited the *Cornhill Magazine* (1871–82) and was the first editor of *The Dictionary of National Biography*(1882–91). His books include *History of English Thought in the Eighteenth Century* (1876) and biographies of Samuel JOHNSON, POPE, SWIFT, George ELIOT, and HOBBES. Virginia WOOLF was his youngest daughter.

**Stephen, Saint** or **Stephen I,** 975?–1038, duke (r.977–1001) and first king (r.1001–38) of Hungary. Because of his Christianizing and pro-German policy he had to put down revolts by pagan nobles. His crown remains a sacred symbol of Hungarian national identity. Feast: 16 Aug. (in Hungary, 20 Aug.).

**Stephen I,** king of Hungary: see STEPHEN, SAINT.

**Stephen Báthory,** 1533–86, king of POLAND (r.1576–86), prince of Transylvania (1571–75). A reformer of military, legal, and financial affairs, he brought strong government after a period of chaos, and conducted a successful war against Russia over Livonia.

**Stephen Dušan,** c.1306–55, king (r.1331–46) and czar (r.1346–55) of SERBIA. After usurping his father's crown, he conquered Bulgaria, Macedonia, Thessaly, and Epirus. He brought Serbia to its greatest power and aspired to the throne of Byzantium, but his empire disintegrated after his death.

**Stephens, Alexander Hamilton,** 1812–83, American politician. He was US congressman from Georgia from 1843 to 1859. Opposed to secession, he nonetheless remained loyal to Georgia when the state seceded. Elected vice president (1861–65) of the CONFEDERACY, he consistently opposed the policies of Pres. DAVIS. After the war he was interned for several months but was again US congressman from Georgia (1873–82).

**Stephens, James,** 1882–1950, Irish poet and fiction writer. A leading figure in the IRISH LITERARY RENAISSANCE, he is best known for his fanciful prose, e.g., in *The Crock of Gold* (1912), *The Demi-Gods* (1914), and *Deirdre* (1923).

**Stephenson, George,** 1781–1848, English engineer and locomotive builder. He developed a travelling engine to haul coal (1814) and the first LOCOMOTIVE using the steam blast (1815). Together with his son **Robert Stephenson,** 1803–59, he was responsible for many innovations which led to the practical RAILWAY steam locomotive, as exemplified by his locomotive *Rocket* which won the Rainhill trials in 1829, and which was used on the Liverpool and Manchester railway. He was engineer for several of the new railways.

**steppe,** temperate grassland of Eurasia, consisting of level, generally treeless plains. The term is sometimes applied to the PRAIRIES of the US, the PAMPAS of South America, and the high VELD of South Africa. There are three vegetation zones: the wooded steppe (having deciduous trees and the highest rainfall), the tillable steppe (consisting of productive agricultural lands), and the nontillable steppe (a semidesert).

**stereochemistry,** study of the three-dimensional configuration of the atoms that make up a MOLECULE and of the ways in which this arrangement affects the physical and chemical properties of the molecule. Central to stereochemistry is the concept of isomerism. Isomers are sets of chemical compounds having identical atomic composition but different structural properties. Stereochemistry is particularly important in BIOCHEMISTRY and molecular biology. The biological influences of stereoisomers (see under ISOMER) can be quite profound. One isomer of ascorbic acid (vitamin C) is very active, the other has no activity.

**stereophonic sound,** a method of reproducing the physical separation of the various voices or instruments in recorded music. The sound is recorded simultaneously by two or more MICROPHONES placed in different positions relative to the sound source. The transmission system enables the two sound sources to be separated at the receiver, and these two signals are played back through LOUDSPEAKERS placed more or less as the recording microphones were placed. The voices or instruments composing the sound thus seem to be spread out naturally as they would be in the recording hall. In quadrophonic reproduction, which utilizes four microphones and four loudspeakers, the effect is further enhanced.

**sterilization:** see BIRTH CONTROL.

**Sterkfontein,** small valley near Krugersdorp, Transvaal, South Africa, with caverns containing fossils of the early hominid AUSTRALOPITHECUS. Sterkfontein itself provides the largest sample of *A. africanus*; Swartkrans and Kromdraai nearby are later and contain *A. robustus*. Other important hominid sites in the Transvaal are Taung and Makapansgat (both *A. africanus*). See also HUMAN EVOLUTION.

**Sterne, Laurence,** 1713–68, English writer; b. Ireland. A country churchman, he went to London in 1760 and published the first volume of his masterpiece *Tristram Shandy*. Although Dr JOHNSON and others denounced it on moral and literary grounds, it was a great success. Eight more volumes followed (1761–67). A mixture of character sketches, digressions, and dramatic action into which the author constantly obtrudes himself, *Tristram Shandy* is based on LOCKE's association of ideas. By recording internal impressions, Sterne greatly expanded the scope of the NOVEL. His other books are *Journal to Eliza* (1767) and *A Sentimental Journey* (1768).

**steroid,** any of a class of organic compounds having a particular molecular structure based on four joined hydrocarbon rings. Steroids differ from one another only in the additional atoms attached to the central structure. Naturally occurring steroids include the male and female sex hormones, adrenal hormones (see CORTICOSTEROID), bile acids,

and CHOLESTEROL. Synthetic steroids are used therapeutically. Steroids are found in plants and invertebrates as well as in higher animals.

**Stesichorus,** fl. c.600 BC, Greek LYRIC poet. He is said to have invented the choral 'heroic hymn' and to have added the epode to the strophe and antistrophe, much used thereafter, e.g., by the tragedians and PINDAR.

**Stettin:** see SZCZECIN.

**Steuben, Friedrich Wilhelm, Baron von** (ˌstoohbən), 1730–94, Prussian army officer, general in the AMERICAN REVOLUTION. He helped to train the Continental army and to mould it into a powerful striking force.

**Stevens, Thaddeus,** 1792–1868, US member of the House of Representatives from Pennsylvania (1849–53, 1859–68). A leader of the radical Republicans' RECONSTRUCTION programme after the Civil War, he viewed the defeated Southern states as 'conquered provinces'. Sincerely desiring black betterment but eager to maintain the Republican party in power, he proposed the 14th Amendment, guaranteeing civil rights. He was a leader in the impeachment of Andrew JOHNSON.

**Stevens, Wallace,** 1879–1955, American poet. While pursuing a career as an insurance executive, Stevens wrote elegant, philosophic verse often concerned with creating order from chaos. His books of poetry include *Harmonium* (1923), *The Man with the Blue Guitar* (1937), *Transport to Summer* (1947), and *Collected Poems* (1954). His ideas are elaborated in the essays of *The Necessary Angel* (1951), and the poems, plays, essays, and epigrams of *Opus Posthumous* (1957).

**Stevenson, Adlai Ewing,** 1835–1914, US vice president (1893–97). His grandson, **Adlai Ewing Stevenson,** 1900–65, was governor of Illinois (1949–53). The unsuccessful Democratic presidential candidate in 1952 and 1956, he nonetheless gained enormous respect as the spokesman for liberal reform and internationalism. His son, **Adlai Ewing Stevenson, 3rd,** 1930–, served as US senator from Illinois (1970–81). He twice ran unsuccessfully for governor of Illinois, as a Democrat in 1982 and in 1986 as an Independent.

**Stevenson, Robert Louis,** 1850–94, Scottish novelist, poet, and essayist. His first books, *An Inland Voyage* (1878) and *Travels with a Donkey in the Cevennes* (1879), were accounts of his wanderings on the Continent. In 1880 he went to the US, where he married Frances Osbourne. Four plays written with W.E. Henley had little success, but the adventure novel *Treasure Island* (1883) and *A Child's Garden of Verses* (1885) were very popular. In 1886 came three of his best-known works, *Kidnapped,* an adventure tale set in Scotland, *The Strange Case of Dr Jekyll and Mr Hyde,* a pioneering allegory of schizophrenia, and *The Master of Ballantrae* (1889). In that year he settled for health reasons (he was a lifelong sufferer from tuberculosis) in Samoa, where he wrote *The Wrong Box* (1889), *The Wrecker* (1892) and *The Ebb-Tide* (1894). He died there, leaving *Weir of Hermiston* (1896) unfinished.

**Stewart, James,** 1908–, American film actor. Famous for his slow drawl and homespun charm, he starred in such films as *Mr Smith Goes to Washington* (1939), *The Philadelphia Story* (1940), *Harvey* (1950), and *Vertigo* (1958).

**stibnite,** antimony sulphide mineral ($Sb_2S_3$), the most important ore of ANTIMONY. It is found in many parts of the world, often in association with arsenic, calcite, gold, quartz, and silver. Silvery-grey in colour, stibnite was used in ancient times by women to darken eyebrows and eyelashes. It is now used in alloys, in explosives, in vulcanizing rubber, and as an emetic.

**stick insect,** long to very long (30–330 mm/1–12 in), cylindrical-bodied, slow-moving, herbivorous INSECT (order Phasmida). Most stick insects are tropical in distribution and have legs and bodies of an appropriate colour, often with ridges and spines, to closely resemble the twigs of bushes and trees on which they live. Many adults are wingless but some of those with wings have a brightly-coloured hind pair, to startle potential predators. The majority of species reproduce sexually but PARTHENOGENESIS is quite common and in the Indian stick insect *Carausius morosus* males are very rare and apparently sexually functionless.

**Stieglitz, Alfred** (ˌsteeglits), 1864–1946, American photographer, editor, and art exhibitor. In his magazines, e.g., the seminal *Camera Work* (1902–17), and his galleries, including '291' and 'An American Place', he sought to establish photography as an art while promoting modern French and American painting. Chief among his photographs are

Stick insect (*Carausius morosus*)

Winter in New York, 1898, a photogravure taken by Alfred **Stieglitz**

the series of portraits of Georgia O'KEEFFE, his wife; and studies of New York City.

**Stiernhalm, George**, 1598–1672, Swedish linguist, antiquarian, and man of letters. Known as the 'father of Swedish verse', he wrote the first Swedish poetry in hexameters. He helped to reform the Swedish language by studying Old Norse literature and reviving the old vocabulary in modern Swedish. His most important work is *Hercules* (1658), an epic allegorical poem about a young man at the crossroads of life.

**Stifter, Adalbert** (ˌshtiftə), 1805–68, Austrian novelist. He made his reputation with six volumes of novellas, *Studies* (1842–50), which include *Abdias* and *My Great-Grandfather's Satchel*, and the collection *Coloured Stones* (2 vol., 1853). After the failed revolution of 1848, Stifter the liberal conservative turned to educational writing, and was

appointed school inspector in the Linz area. Two major novels followed, *Indian Summer* (3 vol., 1857), the *Bildungsroman* of measure and serenity to heal the torn times, and the historical novel of Bohemia's medieval past, *Witiko* (3 vol., 1865–67). Stifter died by his own hand. Too long regarded only as representative of provincial Biedermeier, Stifter is now read as a great stylist, and for the sense of precariousness hidden behind his moral and artistic achievement.

**Stijl, de** (də stiel), [Dutch, = the style], a Dutch art magazine (1917–32). It was edited by Theo van DOESBURG and was used as a mouthpiece for the ideas of MONDRIAN and Neo-Plasticism. It was also the name used by the group which included van Doesburg, Mondrian, Huszár, the poet KOK and the architect OUD. They advocated purifying art, eliminating subject matter in favour of abstract elements and primary colours. Their ideas had a great influence on architecture and design.

**stilboestrol:** see DIETHYLSTILBOESTROL.

**Stilicho, Flavius**, d. 408, Roman statesman and general. He was the chief general of THEODOSIUS I and regent for HONORIUS in the West (395–408). His rival RUFINUS influenced ARCADIUS against him. Honorius had him arrested for high treason; although there was no evidence to support the charge, Stilicho did not resist execution.

**still life**, pictorial representation of inanimate objects. Still-life elements have appeared in Western art since classical times, e.g., Hellenistic frescoes and mosaics, and Flemish artists in the 15th and 16th cent. delighted in exactly rendered still-life details, often with symbolic value. Yet still life first flourished as a separate genre in the 17th cent. CARAVAGGIO painted a *Basket of Fruit* (c.1596; Ambrosiana, Milan) and flower and fish pictures became popular in Naples; a solemn type of still life was painted in Spain. In Flanders and above all Holland, many artists, among them Willem Kalf, W.C. Heda, and Pieter Claesz, specialized in different types of still life, including, flower pieces, breakfast pieces, and banquet pictures. In France, in the 18th cent., CHARDIN's geometric arrangements of simple objects introduced a new kind of still life. French 19th-cent. masters, including such diverse figures as COURBET and CEZANNE, elevated still life as subject matter. In the 20th cent. it has been developed by Cubist artists and by Giorgio Morandi; Pop art painters also used still-life elements, choosing such objects of popular culture as soup cans and items from comic strips. In the Far East, still-life subjects were depicted as early as the 11th cent. and were often given symbolic meaning (see CHINESE ART; JAPANESE ART).

**Stimson, Henry Lewis**, 1867–1950, American statesman. He was twice secretary of war (1911–13, 1940–45). As secretary of state (1929–33) he denounced the Japanese invasion of MANCHURIA in a declaration of policy that came to be known as the Stimson Doctrine.

**stimulant,** agent that produces a temporary increase in physiological activity. The most widely used central nervous system stimulant is CAFFEINE, present in coffee, tea, and cola drinks. AMPHETAMINE and COCAINE are powerful and addictive central stimulants. See DRUGS; DRUG ADDICTION AND DRUG ABUSE.

**stimulus,** any event, in the external world or internal to an organism, which evokes a reaction or RESPONSE. This broad definition conceals a multitude of theoretical problems in psychology regarding whether the stimulus should be conceived of as a physical event, or in terms of the 'meaning' it has for the organism, or both.

**Stirling, James**, 1926–, British architect. He has designed major works in both Europe and America. His Leicester Univ. Engineering building (1959–63) was composed of the contrasting shapes of funtional elements expressed in glass and brick. After controversial buildings in the universities of Oxford, Cambridge, and St Andrews, Stirling has designed in a more formal and eclectic manner, always emphasizing the three-dimensional character of building elements. Most celebrated are his extensions to the Staatsgalerie in Stuttgart, Germany (1977–84) and the Clore Gallery at the Tate Gallery, London.

**stoat** or **ermine**, a PREDATOR, member of the family Mustelidae, related to WEASELS, polecats, and martens. The stoat (*Mustela erminea*) is found across cold and temperate Europe and Asia and in North America, where it is called the short-tailed weasel. They grow to about 45 cm (17 in) in length and feed on rabbits, rats, moles, mice, and voles, but will also take game birds and poultry and so are regarded as pests. Stoats are brown in the summer, but in cold regions they lose their summer coats by MOULTING

Staatsgalerie extension, Stuttgart by James **Stirling**

to leave a white winter coat, only the tip of the tail remaining dark. In this form they are called ermine, and are trapped for their pelts.

**stochastic** (stoh¸kastik), term used in STATISTICS to indicate a process or relationship that has some element of probability or uncertainty in it.

**stock exchange,** a market where stocks and shares, also known as securities, are bought and sold. Such markets perform an important economic function in channelling savings and investment, which are put to productive use. Most of the world's major cities have stockmarkets. In Europe they are often known as *bourses* while that in New York is known as WALL STREET. In the UK the London Stock Exchange was formed in 1773 and was the first in the world although it was not formally constituted until 1802. Other local exchanges were set up in Manchester, Birmingham, Bristol, Liverpool, Glasgow, Belfast and Dublin and in 1973 were amalgamated to form the Stock Exchange of Great Britain and Ireland. Many small companies were not quoted on the stock exchange because of the high cost of registration. Because of this, in 1980 the Unlisted Securities Market was established so that small companies could trade in shares without having to conform to the requirements of the main market. The deregulation of the stock exchange in Oct. 1986 (see 'BIG BANG') had far-reaching implications for the financial institutions in general and has increased the status of London as an international financial centre. Electronic information technology was being adopted widely after the mid-1980s giving banks, in particular, a much greater role in securities trading.

**Stockhausen, Karlheinz,** 1928–, German composer and music theorist. He often uses TWELVE-TONE MUSIC techniques and is a major proponent of ELECTRONIC MUSIC. His compositions, e.g., *Gruppen* (1959), are characterized by complex COUNTERPOINT, free RHYTHMS, dissonance, percussive effects, and the use of improvisation by performers. Throughout his career he has had a great influence on other musicians and composers.

**Stockholm,** city (1984 pop. 653,455, Greater Stockholm 1,409,048), capital of Sweden, E Sweden. It is the nation's largest city and its economic and administrative hub, with an important shipbuilding industry. A cultural centre, the city has a noted opera house (1898), the Royal Dramatic Theatre (1908), and many museums. Founded in the mid-13th cent., it became the official capital (1634) under Queen CHRISTINA. Built on several peninsulas and islands, modern Stockholm is famed for its striking design, e.g., the new city hall (1911–1923) and the residential districts. The Great Square was the site of a massacre (1520) instigated by CHRISTIAN II of Denmark. Most of the NOBEL PRIZES are awarded in Stockholm.

**Stockton,** US city (1984 est. pop. 172,000), central California, on the San Joaquin R.; inc. 1850. Located at the head of the river's delta, its harbour can accommodate seagoing trade. Processing, canning, and distribution of the San Joaquin Valley's farm products is important. Glass, paper and wood products, and ships are among its manufactures.

**Stoicism,** school of philosophy founded by Zeno of Citium c.300 BC. Influenced by Socratic ideals and by the thought of HERACLITUS, ARISTOTLE, and PLATO, the Stoics held that all reality is material but is shaped by a universal working force (God) that pervades everything. Only by putting aside passion, unjust thoughts, and indulgence, and by performing one's duty with the right disposition can a person live consistently with nature and thus achieve true freedom. The school was especially well received in the Roman world; CICERO, SENECA, EPICTETUS, and MARCUS AURELIUS were all Stoics.

**Stoke-on-Trent,** city (1981 pop. 272,446), Staffordshire, W Midlands of England, on R Trent 217 km (135 mi) NW of London. It was formed in 1910 from the amalgamation of Stoke with Burslem, Fenton, Hanley, Longton, and Tunstall. It is the centre of the POTTERIES, an area famous for the manufacture of pottery. Other industries here include coal-mining, engineering, and the manufacture of bricks. Josaiah WEDGWOOD was born in Burslem, and Arnold BENNETT in Hanley.

**Stoker, Bram,** 1847–1912, English novelist. He is best known for *Dracula* (1897), a horror novel about the vampire Count Dracula. He was manager to the actor Sir Henry IRVING.

**STOL aircraft:** see SHORT TAKEOFF AND LANDING AIRCRAFT.

**Stolypin, Piotr Arkadevich** (stə¸lipin), 1862–1911, Russian premier and interior minister (1906–11) for NICHOLAS II. His regime of courts-martial executed hundreds for revolutionary activities (1906–07). By reforming the land distribution system created in 1861 (see EMANCIPATION, EDICT OF), which gave land to the community (MIR) rather than to individuals, he tried to create a loyal class of peasant landowners. His secret police carried out repression, but he allowed reactionary groups to go on committing anti-Jewish outrages. He was assassinated by a revolutionary who was also a police agent.

**stomach,** saclike organ of the DIGESTIVE SYSTEM located between the oesophagus and the INTESTINE. The human stomach is a muscular, elastic, pear-shaped bag lying crosswise in the abdominal cavity, beneath the diaphragm. Food enters the stomach from the oesophagus, through a ring of muscles known as the cardiac sphincter, and is converted into a semiliquid state by muscular action and by the digestive enzymes in the gastric juice secreted by the glands. The pyloric sphincter, which separates the stomach from the small intestine, remains closed until the food has been appropriately modified and is ready to be emptied into the first section of the small intestine.

**Stone, Edward Durell,** 1902–78, American architect. With Philip L. Goodwin, he designed the Museum of Modern Art, New York City (1937–39). He won renown for his US Embassy, New Delhi (1958), in which he used Muslim motifs including lacy grillwork. His later buildings include the Kennedy Centre for the Performing Arts (1971), Washington, District of Columbia.

**Stone, Lucy,** 1818–93, American reformer and leader in the WOMEN'S MOVEMENT. In 1870 she founded the *Woman's Journal,* the official organ of the National American Woman Suffrage Association for nearly 50 years. After her marriage to **Henry Brown Blackwell** (1825–1909) in 1855, she called herself Mrs Stone as a matter of principle. *Woman's Journal* was edited by Stone and Blackwell. On Stone's death, their daughter, **Alice Stone Blackwell** (1857–1950), became coeditor. The Lucy Stone League was formed in 1921 to work for women's rights.

**Stone Age,** the earliest age of the THREE-AGE SYSTEM for charting human cultural development. It is divided into three periods, the PALAEOLITHIC period, or Old Stone Age, roughly coextensive with the Pleistocene GEOLOGIC ERAS (see table), the MESOLITHIC period, or Middle Stone Age, beginning at the end of the last glacial era, over 10,000 years ago, and the NEOLITHIC period, or New Stone Age, generally identified as beginning with the appearance of various technologies, such as stone grinding and polishing, pottery making, and agriculture and extending to the use of metal. The Stone Age was succeeded by the BRONZE AGE.

**Stonehenge,** group of massive standing stones on Salisbury Plain, Wiltshire, S England. Stonehenge underwent several transformations to reach its final form as the preeminent megalithic structure of the British Isles. It began in the 3rd millennium BC as a HENGE, probably with a ring of wooden posts, and single standing stone; successive stages included the

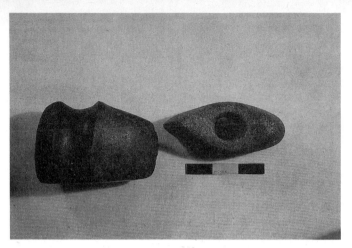

Stone Age miner's tool and battle axe

Stone Mountain Memorial

erection of 82 bluestones (transported, possibly for this construction, from S Wales) in a double circle within the enclosure; their dismantling, and the erection of enormous sarsen stones weighing up to 50 tonnes, brought from the downs more than 30 km (19 mi) distant or from the Avon valley nearby and shaped before being raised as standing stones and lintels. Its sheer size made Stonehenge an object of public speculation; it has long been connected, fancifully, to DRUIDS, or linked with distant peoples who used monumental architecture extensively. Considering the long sequence of MEGALITHIC MONUMENTS in western Europe that developed in the NEOLITHIC and BRONZE AGE, however, Stonehenge can be safely regarded as a local development. In 1963 the British astonomer Gerald Hawkins theorized that Stonehenge had been used as a huge astronomical instrument. The controversial idea gave great impetus to the study of ARCHAEOASTRONOMY, and similar interpretations have been made at CARNAC and NEW GRANGE.

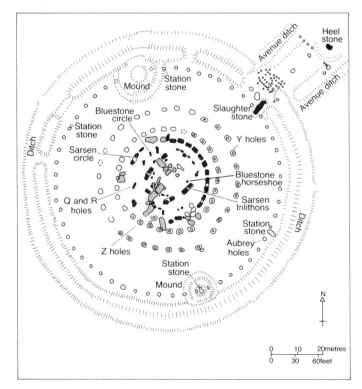

Stonehenge

**Stone Mountain Memorial,** memorial to the CONFEDERACY carved on Stone Mt, NW Georgia, near Atlanta, US. It represents, in bas-relief, the equestrian figures of Robert E. Lee, Stonewall Jackson, and Jefferson Davis. Commissioned in 1916, it was begun by Gutzon BORGLUM, the

sculptor of Mt Rushmore, but was not completed until 1969, by Walter K. Hancock.

**stoneware,** hard POTTERY made of clay fired at a high temperature of c.1200–1400°C to make it glassy (vitrified). Stoneware is heavier and more opaque than PORCELAIN, and differs from terra-cotta, or earthenware, in being non-porous. It has been produced in China since the late 3rd cent. AD, and was the forerunner of Chinese porcelain. It was being made in Germany by the 13th cent., and from the late 15th cent. was glazed by throwing salt into the kiln during firing. In the late 17th cent., salt-glazed and red dry-bodied (unglazed) stonewares were made in England by John DWIGHT, and other potters. In the late 18th cent. Josiah WEDGWOOD developed two important types: black basaltes and jasper. Today stoneware remains one of the most common types of pottery.

**stop:** see PUNCTUATION.

**Stopes, Marie Charlotte Carmichael,** 1880–1958, English birth-control campaigner and palaeontologist. She was the first woman to join the science faculty at Manchester Univ. (1904). Her commitment to birth control and sex education was to some extent informed by eugenicist ideas of racial purity. Her pioneering books, *Married Love* and *Wise Parenthood* (both: 1918) caused a furore and sold millions of copies worldwide. In the face of attacks from the medical establishment and the Catholic Church she opened Britain's first birth-control clinic in London (1921). Her many published writings include poetry and plays.

**Stoppard, Tom,** 1937–, English playwright; b. Czechoslovakia. He came to prominence with the comic and pathetic play *Rosencrantz and Guildenstern Are Dead* (1966), about characters in Shakespeare's *Hamlet.* In later works, e.g., *The Real Inspector Hound* (1968), *Travesties* (1974), and *The Real Thing* (1982), he continued to find significance in wordplay and bizarre juxtapositions of language and character.

**Storey, David (Malcolm),** 1933–, English novelist and playwright. His northern working-class upbringing and professional rugby career contributed to his novel *This Sporting Life* (1960; film, 1963). Later novels include *Flight into Camden* (1961), *Radcliffe* (1963), and *Saville* (1976). Storey is the author of many successful plays, e.g., *The Restoration of Arnold Middleton* (1967), *Home* (1970), and *The Changing Room* (1971).

**stork,** mute, long-legged wading BIRD of the family Ciconiidae. Found in most of the warmer parts of the world, it has long, broad, powerful wings. The white stork (*Ciconia ciconia*) is about 90 cm (3 ft) high, and is a frequent inclusion in European legends. Storks feed on aquatic life and on small vertebrates and insects. They will halt a migratory flight to feed on a plague of locusts when migrating to Africa for the winter. In many European towns special platforms are built on to roofs to encourage storks to nest there, as they are regarded as lucky.

**storm,** disturbance of the ordinary atmospheric conditions marked by strong winds and (usually) precipitation. Types of storms include the extratropical CYCLONE, the tropical cyclone (HURRICANE), the TORNADO, and

White stork (*Ciconia ciconia*)

the THUNDERSTORM. The term is also applied to blizzards, dust storms, and sandstorms in which high wind is the dominant meteorological element.

**Storm, Theodor** (shtawm), 1817–88, German poet and novelist. Nostalgic lyricism marks his early works, such as the story *Immensee* (1852). He is best known for his powerful novella *The Rider of the White Horse* (1888).

**Storm and Stress:** see STURM UND DRANG.

**stout,** alcoholic beverage: see BEER.

**Stowe, Harriet Beecher,** 1811–96, American writer; daughter of Lyman BEECHER; sister of Henry Ward BEECHER. Her anti-slavery novel *Uncle Tom's Cabin* (1852) was very influential in spreading abolitionist sentiment, as was the dramatization of the book that followed. Notable among the 16 volumes she wrote are a second novel of slavery, *Dred* (1856), and novels of New England life, e.g., *The Minister's Wooing* (1859), *Old Town Folks* (1869). Stowe was also dedicated to such other reform movements as temperance and woman suffrage.

**Strabo** (ˌstrayboh), b. c.63 BC, d. after AD 21, Greek geographer, historian, and philosopher. He studied and travelled widely and wrote historical sketches (47 books), quoted by later authorities but almost all lost. His *Geographia,* based on his observations and on works of predecessors, contains historical data and descriptions of people and places; it is a rich source of ancient knowledge. Almost all extant, its 17 books include two defining the scope of geography, eight on Europe, six on Asia, and one on Africa.

**Strachey, (Giles) Lytton** (ˌstraychee), 1880–1932, English biographer and critic. A member of the BLOOMSBURY GROUP, he revolutionized the art of biography, writing astringent, witty works, e.g., *Eminent Victorians* (1918) and *Queen Victoria* (1921).

**Stradivari, Antonio** or **Antonius Stradivarius** (stradeeˌvahree), 1644–1737, Italian violinmaker of Cremona. Recognized in his time, Stradivari produced over 1000 instruments, violas, cellos, and even guitars as well as violins; his workmanship brought the violin to perfection. Two of his sons worked with him and continued the craft after his death.

**Strafford, Thomas Wentworth,** 1st earl of, 1593–1641, English statesman. As lord deputy of Ireland (1632–40), he enforced the rule of CHARLES I. After the English humiliation by the Scots in the first BISHOPS' WAR, he was recalled (1639) to become the king's adviser. Strafford led the English to disaster in the second Bishops' War, and was beheaded after Parliament accused him of plotting to use Irish troops against England.

**strain:** see STRENGTH OF MATERIALS.

**Straits Settlements,** collective name for certain former British colonies in Southeast Asia. They originally consisted (1826–58) of the British EAST INDIA COMPANY territories of Pinang, SINGAPORE, and Malacca. In 1867 they became a crown colony, to which several dependencies of Singapore were later added. The Straits Settlements crown colony was dissolved in 1946. Singapore became a separate crown colony; Labuan became part of British N Borneo (see SABAH); Pinang and Malacca were incorporated into the Malayan Union (see MALAYSIA, FEDERATION OF).

**Stralsund,** city (1984 pop. c.72,000), Mecklenburg, northern East Germany, on the BALTIC SEA. It is situated on the channel between the mainland and the island of Rügen to which it is linked by road and rail. There is some shipbuilding and engineering. Founded in 1209, Stralsund became a leading Hanseatic port (see HANSEATIC LEAGUE) in the later Middle Ages and preserves many fine buildings of that period. Swedish after 1648, it became Prussian in 1815.

**Strasberg, Lee,** 1901–82, American acting teacher and director; b. Austria. He was cofounder (1931) of the Group Theatre. An initiator of the STANISLAVSKY acting method in the US, he headed New York City's Actors' Studio from 1948. His only film appearance was in *The Godfather, Part* II (1974).

**Strasbourg,** city (1982 pop. 252,264, agglomeration 373,470), capital of Bas-Rhin dept., NE France. Many products pass through its great port on the RHINE. It is heavily industrialized (e.g., metal casting, machinery, oil refining), and its goose-liver pâté is famous. It became an important city in Roman times. Destroyed (5th cent.) by the HUNS and rebuilt, it became (923) part of the HOLY ROMAN EMPIRE. It emerged as a free imperial city in the 13th cent. The city and its university were Protestant centres in the 16th cent. Seized (1681) by Louis XIV, Strasbourg increasingly adopted French customs and speech. Ceded to Germany (1871), it was regained by France in 1919. Its cathedral (1015–1439) is a masterpiece of Rhenish architecture.

**Strategic Arms Limitation Talks** and **Strategic Arms Reduction Talks:** see DISARMAMENT, NUCLEAR.

**strategy and tactics:** see MILITARY SCIENCE.

**Stratford-upon-Avon,** town (1981 pop. 20,941), Warwickshire, central England, on the Avon R. A market town with light industries, it is famous as the birthplace of William SHAKESPEARE. Annual Shakespeare festivals are held here.

**Strathclyde,** one of the early Celtic or Welsh kingdoms of Britain. It was in SW Scotland, and Dumbarton was the principal town. Little is known of its history. In 945 King Edmund of Wessex defeated Strathclyde and awarded it to King Malcolm of Scotland. It was permanently absorbed by Scotland in the 11th cent.

**Strathclyde,** region in E Scotland (1985 est. pop. 2,414,813), 18,537 km² (7229 sq mi), bordering on the Atlantic in the W and separated from Northern Ireland by North Channel. The administrative centre is GLASGOW. It was formed in 1975 from Dunbartonshire, Lanarkshire, Ayrshire, Renfrewshire, most of Argyllshire, and part of Stirlingshire. It contains the southern half of the Inner HEBRIDES. Much of the region is mountainous, apart from low-lying areas in the centre around the Firth of CLYDE. The coastline is picturesque and indented by several sea lochs. In the upland areas sheep raising and fishing are common, whereas mixed agriculture is practised in the more fertile lowland areas. The area around Glasgow is industrialized, with coalmining and heavy industry, including a recently declining ship-building industry.

**stratification,** in geology, layered structure formed by the deposition of sedimentary ROCKS. Changes between layers result from fluctuations in the intensity and persistence of the depositional agent (e.g., currents, wind, or waves) or from changes of the source of the sediment. Initially, most sediments are deposited with essentially horizontal stratification, but the layers may later be tilted or folded by internal earth forces.

**stratification,** in sociology, the process by which individuals or groups are ranked hierarchically, using some sort of objective criteria (e.g., religion, colour of skin, political belief, income, occupation, power, age, etc). Sociologists recognize three basic forms of social stratification: CASTE, estate, and social class. In a caste system, fixed rules prevent any social movement between the various caste groups. Feudal Europe was an example of an estate system, where society was ranked from the monarch and nobility at the top, to the serfs at the bottom. Social CLASS is a product of CAPITALISM, with its insistence on the freedom of the individual. In liberal and pluralist accounts, the statification system is much more open and fluid, indicating the relative value that society places on certain qualities (e.g., some occupations are highly rewarded in economic and status terms because society places high value on them). Empirical studies indicate that the high degree of SOCIAL MOBILITY between the classes in Britain is largely a product of the war and post war economic growth: the number of individuals moving from the upper working class to the lower middle class has grown but, in percentage terms, it has stayed roughly the same.

**stratigraphy:** see GEOLOGY.

**stratosphere:** see ATMOSPHERE.

**Strauss,** family of Viennese musicians. **Johann Strauss,** 1804–49, formed an orchestra (1826), toured Europe, and won fame with his waltzes. His son, **Johann Strauss,** 1825–99, also organized an orchestra (1844) and, after his father's death, merged the two groups. He wrote over 400 waltzes, including the enormously popular *Blue Danube* (1866) and *Tales from the Vienna Woods* (1868), bringing the Viennese waltz to a height of musical artistry. Among his operettas are *Die Fledermaus* (1873) and *The Gypsy Baron* (1885). Two of his brothers, **Josef Strauss,** 1827–70, and **Eduard Strauss,** 1835–1916, were also successful composers and conductors.

**Strauss, Richard,** 1864–1949, German composer and conductor. His romantic SYMPHONIC POEMS, e.g., *Death and Transfiguration* (1889), *Till Eulenspiegel's Merry Pranks* (1895), *Thus Spake Zarathustra* (1895), are evocative and richly orchestrated. His highly dramatic operas, which develop Richard WAGNER's leitmotif concept, include *Salomé* (1905) and, with librettos by HOFMANNSTHAL, *Elektra* (1909), *Der Rosenkavalier* (1911), and *Ariadne auf Naxos* (1912).

**Stravinsky, Igor (Fedorovich),** 1882–1971, American composer; b. Russia. In Russia he was a student of RIMSKY-KORSAKOV. His first strikingly original compositions, *The Firebird* (1910) and *Petrouchka* (1911), were written for DIAGHILEV's Ballets Russes. In the ballet *The Rite of Spring* (1913), a masterpiece of modern music, Stravinsky used radically irregular RHYTHMS and harsh dissonances. He later employed an austere, neoclassical style, as in *The Soldier's Tale* (1918), *Oedipus Rex* (1927), and the Violin Concerto in D (1931). After moving from Paris to Los Angeles in 1940 and becoming a US citizen (1945), he experimented with TWELVE-TONE MUSIC, e.g., *Cantata* (1952), *Septuor* (1953), and the ballet *Agon* (1957). Stravinsky's fresh, meticulously crafted, innovative music revitalized European musical expression and achieved new sonorities and orchestral colours.

**strawberry,** low, herbaceous perennial (genus *Fragaria*) of the ROSE family, native to temperate regions. It is grown for its edible red fruits, which are used fresh, frozen, in preserves and confectionery, and for flavouring. The common strawberry (*F. chiloensis*) is believed native to Chile and W North America. Most species propagate by runners, or stolons, slender horizontal stems.

**Strawson, Sir Peter Frederick,** 1919–, English philosopher. Originally a practitioner of 'ordinary-language' philosophy, working on reference, meaning, and truth, he became Britain's leading metaphysician. *Individuals* (1959) describes the structure of thoughts about the self, the world, and others, arguing that physical objects are the basis of our conceptual scheme. Similar themes are pursued in *The Bounds of Sense* (1966), an extended discussion of KANT's *Critique of Pure Reason*. His papers on language are collected in *Logico-Linguistic Papers* (1971).

**stream of consciousness,** literary technique for recording the thoughts and feelings of a character without regard to their logical association or narrative sequence. The writer attempts to reflect all the forces affecting the psychology of a character at a single moment. Introduced by the French writer Edouard Dujardin in *We'll to the Woods No More* (1888), the technique was used notably by James JOYCE, Virginia WOOLF, and William FAULKNER.

**Streeton, Sir Arthur Ernest,** 1867–1943, Australian artist. He studied at the Melbourne National Gallery School (1882–88), before joining Tom ROBERTS, Frederick McCubbin, and Charles Conder as a member of the HEIDELBERG SCHOOL. Not particularly adept at painting the human figure, he is known mainly for his landscapes which are characterized by a high-keyed palette and broad brushstrokes. Between 1899 and 1919, he was based in London, occasionally exhibiting at the Royal Academy. In the early 1920s he returned to Australia, where he became part of the art establishment; he was knighted in 1937.

**Streicher, Julius,** 1885–1946, German NAZI leader. An early member of the Nazi Party, he published *Der Stürmer,* a periodical known for its sadistic and anti-Semitic mania. He was convicted of WAR CRIMES at the Nuremberg trials and hanged.

**Streisand, Barbra,** 1942–, American singer and actress. She gained prominence playing Fanny Brice in the Broadway show (1964) and film (1968) *Funny Girl.* The first of her many best-selling records appeared in 1963. Streisand's later films include *Hello Dolly* (1969) and her own production *A Star is Born* (1976).

**strength of materials,** the capacity of materials to withstand stress (the internal force exerted by one part of an elastic body upon an adjoining part) and strain (the deformation or change in dimension occasioned by stress). When a body is subjected to a pull, it is said to be under tension, or tensional stress; when it is compressed, it is under compression, or compressive stress. Shear, or shearing stress, results when a force tends to make part of a body slide past the other part. Torsion, or torsional stress, occurs when external forces tend to twist a body around an axis. The elastic limit is the maximum stress that a material can sustain and still return to its original form. The ratio of tensile stress to strain for a given material is called its Young's modulus. Hooke's law states that, within the elastic limit, strain is proportional to stress.

**streptomycin:** see ANTIBIOTIC.

**Stresemann, Gustav** (ˌshtrayzəman), 1878–1929, German statesman. A founder (1918) of the conservative German People's Party, he served briefly (1923) as chancellor and then as foreign minister (1923–29). His primary aim was to reestablish Germany as a respected nation following World War I. He accepted the DAWES PLAN (1924) and the YOUNG PLAN (1924) for Germany's reparations payments. He also was a principal architect of the LOCARNO PACT (1925) and signed the KELLOGG–BRIAND PACT (1928). He shared the 1926 Nobel Peace Prize with Aristide BRIAND.

**stress:** see STRENGTH OF MATERIALS.

**Streuvels, Stijn** pseud. of **Frank Lateur** (strø:vəls), 1871–1969, Flemish novelist and short-story writer. Streuvels wrote moving portraits of everyday life, of which *The Flax Field* (1907) is his masterpiece.

**strike,** concerted withdrawal of labour by a group of employees. The right to strike is recognized in virtually all industrialized nations, but in some cases only after agreed conciliation and arbitration procedures have been implemented without success. In some countries there are laws against political strikes and strikes by public employees, e.g., the police. Generally the strike, which is the ultimate weapon of organized labour, is designed to inflict a cost on an employer for failing to satisfy demands over pay, conditions, or working practices. But a strike may be called in sympathy with that of another group of workers, usually in the same section of industry, or a very widespread GENERAL STRIKE may occur for political reasons, usually in a situation of national crisis affecting the interests of the working class. A wildcat strike is a local or spontaneous strike which has not been authorised by the trade union leadership, and indeed may represent a protest against it by more radical shop-floor workers. A tactical suspension of work by the employer is called a lockout. In communist countries, where there are no private employers, strikes may be directed at local conditions, or importantly, against the national government and its policies.

**Strindberg, (Johan) August,** 1849–1912, Swedish writer. His impressive production of novels, plays, stories, histories, and poems reveal him as the greatest master of the Swedish language and an influential innovator in dramatic and literary form. Strindberg's personal life was tumultuous, marked by three disastrous marriages and periods of persecution mania. Among his 70-odd plays are the naturalistic free-verse dramas *The Father* (1887), which vividly expresses his derogatory view of women, and the psychological *Miss Julie* (1888). Later plays, e.g., *A Dream Play* (1902) and *The Ghost Sonata* (1907), reflect his adoption of Swedenborgian mysticism (see SWEDENBORG) and employ experimental, expressionistic techniques that have greatly influenced modern theatre. Other works include the novels *The Red Room* (1879) and *Inferno* (1897), the stories in *Getting Married* (1884–85), and his 4-vol. autobiography, *The Son of a Servant* (1886–1909).

**stringed instrument,** musical instrument whose tone is produced by vibrating strings. Those instruments played with a bow are principally of the VIOL and VIOLIN families. Those whose strings are plucked, either by finger or with a pick (plectrum), include the lyre, any of various ancient instruments with arms projecting from the sound box and having from 3 to 12 strings; the HARP; and a number of fretted instruments, in which narrow strips of wood or metal, called frets, mark the places on the keyboard where the player's fingertips should be applied to stop the strings and produce various notes. Fretted instruments include the BALALAIKA, the BANJO, the lute, popular in the Middle Ages and Renaissance, and the mandolin, both of which have a pear-shaped body and rounded back. Related to the lute is the GUITAR, and the smaller ukulele, which has four strings. The dulcimer, psaltery, and zither are stringed instruments constructed of a variable number of strings stretched over a flat sound box. The dulcimer is struck with small mallets; the psaltery and zither are plucked. The psaltery flourished in Europe from the 12th cent. until the late Middle Ages. The dulcimer, which originated in the Middle East, was adopted in Europe in the Middle Ages. The zither is derived from the psaltery and dulcimer. Stringed instruments operated by a keyboard include the PIANO and its predecessor, the clavichord, whose strings are struck by mallets or hammers. Keyboard instruments whose strings are plucked by means of quills or jacks include the spinet and virginal, small, legless instruments similar to the clavichord, and the harpsichord. See also ORCHESTRA.

**string quartet**, a composition for two VIOLINS, VIOLA, and VIOLONCELLO, or this group of instruments. An important classical form, it is designed to be played at home by friends or family. The form was developed by Joseph HAYDN who wrote 77 string quartets; he used to play them with his brother Michael and their friend MOZART. Mozart himself wrote string quartets, as did BEETHOVEN, and the tradition has continued without a break up till the present day. 20th-cent. composers of string quartets include BARTOK, BRITTEN, and SCHOENBERG. The addition of a fifth instrument (usually viola or violoncello but sometimes DOUBLE BASS) makes a string quintet.

**strip mining:** see OPEN-CAST MINING.

**Stroessner, Alfredo** (ˌshtrø:snə), 1912–, president of PARAGUAY (1954–). He commanded the armed forces and took power in a 1954 military coup. His long totalitarian rule brought order and monetary stability. He was reelected to his eighth successive term as president in 1988, but was overthrown by a military coup in 1989.

**stroke** or **cerebrovascular accident**, sudden impairment of brain function due to an interruption in the supply of blood to the brain caused by haemorrhage, THROMBOSIS (clotting), or embolism (obstruction caused by clotted blood or other foreign matter circulating in the bloodstream). It is a leading cause of death worldwide. Stroke (sometimes called apoplexy) is most common in the elderly, but may occur at any age; predisposing conditions include atherosclerosis (see ARTERIOSCLEROSIS), DIABETES, and HYPERTENSION. Symptoms develop suddenly and can range from almost unnoticed clumsiness or headache to severe paralysis, speech and mental disturbances, and coma. Treatment depends on the cause of the stroke and may include ANTICOAGULANT drugs, surgery, or physiotherapy.

**strong interaction:** see ELEMENTARY PARTICLES.

**strontium** (Sr), metallic element, first recognized as distinct from barium by A. Crawford in 1790. A soft, silver-yellow member of the ALKALINE-EARTH METALS, it is stored away from air and water. Strontium-90 from nuclear fallout is absorbed in plants and animals, where it mimics calcium and is stored in the bones. With a half-life of 28.1 years, it is one of the most dangerous fallout isotopes since most of its radioactivity is spent over a single human lifetime. See ELEMENT (table); PERIODIC TABLE.

**Strozzi** (ˌstrot-tsee), noble Florentine family that opposed the MEDICI. Filippo Strozzi, 1426–91, began to build the famed Strozzi palace in Florence. His grandsons, Leone (1515–54) and Piero (d. 1558), were soldiers for France.

**structural functionalism**, a school of analysis dominant in pre- and postwar British anthropology. Although there are considerable differences between the individuals who are identified with this perspective the general position is that attributable to RADCLIFFE-BROWN. Structure refers in this definition to social structure—the network of social relationships and institutions which provide the framework for society; function to the way in which each of these contributes to the overall stability and harmony of the society in question. This view sees societies as essentially autonomous and static, and emphasizes the processes of conformity and consensus rather than conflict and coercion.

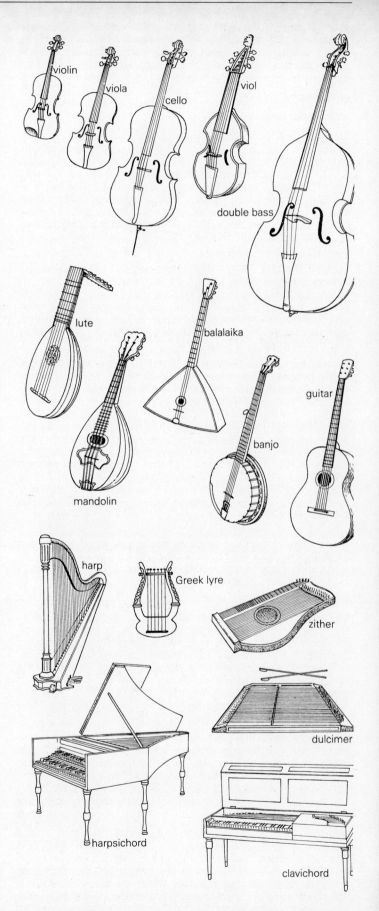

Stringed instruments

**structuralism,** an approach to the analysis of culture and language which pays particular attention to the linguistic structures and the systems within which they operate. First formulated by Ferdinand de SAUSSURE, it was greatly developed by the French anthropologist Claude LÉVI-STRAUSS, who believed that any human behaviour or institution can only be analysed through reference to an underlying network of relationships, and that these *structures* must be referrable to an underlying mode of thought. Culture is the surface structure which reveals the basic propensity of the human mind to order and classify, primarily in terms of binary oppositions (e.g., male vs. female, raw vs. cooked, left vs. right), the social and natural world into all kinds of cultural systems (KINSHIP patterns, MYTH, etc.). The elements of a network are held to have no validity except the relations which hold between them, and so these *structures* constitute the network of the system. In France after 1968, the search for the networks and their relationship with the underlying mode of thought was criticized by 'post-structuralists', who abandoned the goal of reconstructing reality quasi-scientifically in favour of 'deconstructing' the illusions of METAPHYSICS (see also SEMIOTICS.) The term *structuralism* is also used in a more restricted sense in linguistics to describe the American Structuralists (e.g., Leonard BLOOMFIELD) who emphasized the techniques of classifying and segmenting the physical features of a language.

**structural linguistics:** see LINGUISTICS.

**Strutt, John William:** see RAYLEIGH.

**Struve** (ˌshtroohvə), family of astronomers. **Friedrich Georg Wilhelm von Struve,** 1793–1864, b. Germany, directed the Dorpat Observatory (1817–34) and later the Pulkovo Observatory (1834–64) near St Petersburg (now Leningrad). He discovered numerous previously undetected double stars and was, with Friedrich BESSEL and Thomas Henderson, one of the first to make a reliable determination of stellar parallax. His son, **Otto Wilhelm von Struve,** 1819–1905, succeeded him as director of the Pulkovo Observatory. He discovered about 500 double stars and a satellite of Uranus, and he estimated the Sun's velocity. Otto Wilhelm's grandson, **Otto Struve,** 1897–1963, b. Russia, emigrated to the US in 1921. He was director of the Yerkes and McDonald observatories (1932–47), the Leuschner Observatory (1950–59) of the Univ. of California, Berkeley, and the National Radio Astronomy Observatory (1959–62). He made notable studies in stellar spectroscopy and of stellar rotation, interstellar matter, and stellar evolution.

**strychnine** (ˌstrikneen), highly poisonous bitter ALKALOID drug derived from the seeds of a tree (*Strychnos nux-vomica*) native to Sri Lanka, Australia, and India. A potent stimulant (in small doses it was formerly used as a tonic), the drug has been used as a rat poison for five centuries. Strychnine poisoning is characterized by violent convulsions and is fatal unless promptly treated with barbiturate sedatives and ARTIFICIAL RESPIRATION.

**Stuart** or **Stewart,** royal family that ruled Scotland and England. It began (c.1160) as a family of hereditary stewards of Scotland, and gained the Scottish crown with the accession of ROBERT II in 1371. The marriage of James IV of Scotland to MARGARET TUDOR, daughter of Henry VII of England, eventually made Henry's granddaughter MARY QUEEN OF SCOTS a claimant to the English throne. This claim was recognized when her son, James VI of Scotland, became JAMES I of England in 1603. After the execution of CHARLES I and the period of the Commonwealth and the Protectorate, CHARLES II was restored to the throne. With the deposition of JAMES II, the crown passed to his daughter MARY II and her husband, WILLIAM III. ANNE, the last Stuart to rule England, saw the crowns of Scotland and England permanently joined by the Act of UNION (1707). On Anne's death (1714) the crown passed to the Hanoverian GEORGE I by the Act of Settlement. The Hanoverian claim was through a granddaughter of James I. Parliamentary rule of succession was adopted to thwart the claim (upheld by the JACOBITES) to the throne by the Roman Catholic James II and his descendants. After 1807 this claim ceased to be politically important.

**Stuart** or **Stewart, Alexander, duke of Albany,** 1454?–85?, second son of JAMES II of Scotland. Imprisoned (1479) by his brother JAMES III, who suspected him of plotting against the throne, he escaped to England. To gain English support, Albany agreed to rule Scotland as England's vassal. He returned (1482) to Scotland with an English army, but was reconciled briefly with his brother. Sentenced (1483) to death by the Scots, he again fled and died in exile.

**Stuart** or **Stewart, Arabella,** 1575–1615, cousin of JAMES I of England. Her descent from MARGARET TUDOR had placed her next after James in the succession to ELIZABETH I, and many thought her title preferable. Her marriage (1610) to William Seymour (later marquess of Hertford), who was also of royal descent, was viewed as threatening by James, who imprisoned them. They escaped, but Arabella was recaptured and died in prison.

**Stuart** or **Stewart, James Francis Edward,** 1688–1766, claimant to the English throne; son of JAMES II and Mary of Modena; called the Old Pretender. After the GLORIOUS REVOLUTION (1688), he was taken to France, where he was recognized as James III of England after the death (1701) of his father. In England the Act of SETTLEMENT excluded the male STUART line from succession, and James's hopes of succeeding Queen ANNE were dashed by the peaceful succession of GEORGE I in 1714. James's supporters, called JACOBITES, made many unsuccessful plans to restore him as king, including the rising of the earl of Mar (1715), which brought James to Scotland. He later retired to Rome. His son **Charles Edward Stuart,** 1720–88, was known as Bonnie Prince Charlie and as the Young Pretender. He led the rising of 1745, which ended in defeat at Culloden Moor in Scotland (1746). Charles escaped, finally settling in Rome. He is the subject of much romantic literature. His brother **Henry Benedict Maria Clement Stuart,** known as **Cardinal York,** 1725–1807, was the last of the direct male Stuart line to claim the English throne (as Henry IX). He became (1747) a Roman Catholic cardinal and at his death bequeathed to GEORGE IV (then prince of Wales) the Stuart crown jewels.

**Stuart, Gilbert,** 1755–1828, foremost American portrait painter of his day. He worked in England and settled permanently in America in 1792, where he introduced a brilliant, elegant style of portraiture. His most celebrated portraits are those of George Washington, which established three standard images; the 'Athenaeum Head' (Mus. Fine Arts, Boston) was immortalized on the US $1 banknote. There are many replicas of these works.

**Stuart, Henry:** see DARNLEY, HENRY STUART, LORD.

**Stuart, James Ewell Brown,** (Jeb Stuart), 1833–64, Confederate cavalry commander in the AMERICAN CIVIL WAR. He was known for bold raids of reconnaissance; his circuit of Gen. MCCLELLAN's Union army (June 1862) and his foray to the rear of John POPE's forces (Aug. 1862) provided Gen. LEE with invaluable information. His failure to do so in the GETTYSBURG CAMPAIGN may have cost Lee the battle.

**Stuart, John McDouall,** 1815–66, Australian explorer. He went with Charles STURT on an expedition to the interior in 1844 and then in 1862 succeeded in crossing the centre of Australia from Adelaide to Arnhem Land..

**Stuart, Mary:** see MARY QUEEN OF SCOTS.

**Stubbs, William,** 1825–1901, English historian, the bishop of Chester (from 1884). His critical studies of source materials transformed the study of medieval history and strongly influenced ways of teaching it. He wrote *The Constitutional History of England* (3 vol., 1874–78). In politics he was a Conservative.

**stupa** [Sanskrit, = mound], Buddhist monument of tumulus, or mound, form, containing relics. The stupa is probably derived from pre-Buddhist burial mounds. The oldest known prototypes are enormous earth mounds (c.700 BC) at Lauriya Nandangarh, NE India. They were the burial places of royalty. At Sanchi and Bharnut are the earliest proper stupas, hemispherical earth masses faced with brick or stone. Processional paths surrounded the structures, the whole enclosed with a stone railing and topped by a balcony. Stupas are found in all countries where BUDDHISM was practised.

**sturgeon,** primitive marine and freshwater FISH of N Eurasia and North America. It has reduced scalation, a mostly cartilaginous skeleton, upturned tail fins, and a toothless mouth set far back under its jaw. It sucks up its food—CRAYFISH, SNAILS, larvae, and small fish—from the bottom. The largest is the Russian sturgeon, or beluga (*Acipenser huso*), reaching a length of 396 cm (13 ft) and a weight of 908 kg (1 ton). The eggs of the sturgeon are called caviar. Smoked sturgeon and caviar are valued as food.

**Sturlunga Saga,** compilation of contemporary SAGAS illustrating historical events in Iceland in the 12th and 13th cent. Most of them were written soon after the events they describe and are considered reliable historical sources, made vivid by the skill of the authors. The so-called *Islendinga Saga* by Sturla Thórðarson (1214–84), nephew of Snorri STURLUSON, is the largest of the works and forms the backbone of the *Sturlunga* compilation.

**Sturluson, Snorri,** 1179–1241, Icelandic chieftain and historian, the leading figure in medieval Norse literature. He was the author of the *Prose Edda* (see EDDA) and of the *Heimskringla*, a series of historical SAGAS about the kings of Norway down to 1177. He is also thought to have been the author of EGIL'S SAGA. One of the most influential men of his day, he became involved in political intrigues involving the king of Norway and was assassinated.

**Sturm und Drang** or **Storm and Stress,** movement in German literature, fl. c.1770–84. The name derives from a play (1776) by Friedrich von Klinger. Under the influence of J.J. ROUSSEAU and HERDER, German authors stressed with great intensity both subjectivity and the revolt of youthful genius against accepted standards. Neo-classical models were rejected in favour of Shakespeare, the natural genius. GOETHE's *Götz von Berlichingen* (1773) and *Die Leiden des jungen Werther* (1774; tr. *Sorrows of Young Werther*) and SCHILLER's *Die Räuber* (1781; tr. *Robbers*) are representative works.

**Sturt, Charles,** 1795–1869, Australian explorer. In 1827, with Hamilton Hume, he discovered the R. Darling, and in 1828 he sailed down the Murrumbidgee to the estuary of the Murray. In 1844 he set out for the continental interior, crossing the Sturt Desert.

**Stuttgart,** city (1984 pop. 563,200), capital of Baden-Württemberg, SW West Germany, on the Neckar R. It is an industrial centre with such manufactures as electrical and photographic equipment, textiles, and pianos, and is the home of the renowned Stuttgart Ballet. Chartered in the 13th cent., it became (15th cent.) the capital of Württemberg. The city's historic centre was almost entirely destroyed during WORLD WAR II and has since been restored. Historic buildings include the 12th-cent. Stiftskirche and the rococo Solitude Palace (1763–67). The city also contains such striking modern structures as the city hall and the concert hall.

**Stuttgart Ballet:** see DANCE (table).

**Stuyvesant, Peter,** c.1610–72, Dutch director-general of the North American colony of NEW NETHERLAND (1647–64). The one-legged Stuyvesant was a harsh, autocratic ruler, intolerant of religious dissenters. He expanded the colony by conquering NEW SWEDEN (1655). Overwhelmed by a surprise English attack, he surrendered (1664) New Netherland to England.

**Styron, William,** 1925–, American novelist. His powerful, deeply felt, and often poetic novels include *Lie Down in Darkness* (1951), *The Confessions of Nat Turner* (1967; Pulitzer), and *Sophie's Choice* (1979).

**Styx,** in Greek mythology, sacred river in HADES crossed by the souls of the dead, who were ferried by Charon.

**Suárez Gonzáles, Adolfo,** 1932–, Spanish political leader. He became secretary general of the reformed FALANGE movement after FRANCO's death (1975). In 1976 King JUAN CARLOS appointed him premier, and in 1977 he led his Democratic Centre Union to victory in SPAIN's first free elections in 41 years. His centrist government instituted democratic procedures, and his coalition again won the 1979 elections under the new constitution. He resigned the premiership in 1981 and the following year founded the opposition Democratic and Social Centre Party.

**subduction zone:** see PLATE TECTONICS.

**subjunctive:** see MOOD.

**submarine,** naval craft capable of operating underwater for an extended period of time. Cornelis DREBBEL built (c.1620) a leather-covered rowboat that could remain under water for as long as 15 hrs. The first submarine used in combat was invented by the American David Bushnell in 1776; many of its principles were adopted by Robert FULTON in his *Nautilus,* a submarine successfully operated (1800–01) on the Seine R., in France. Although the Confederates used several submersible craft in the Civil War, it was the work of John Holland and Simon Lake that advanced considerably the development of the modern submarine in the US. A Holland submarine became the first for the US navy in 1900; Lake's *Argonaut* (1898) was the first submarine to navigate extensively in the open sea. E-boats, the first US diesel-engine submarines, appeared in 1912 and were the first to cross the Atlantic Ocean. Both sides used submarines extensively in WORLD WAR I, especially Germany, whose

200-tonne U-boats inflicted heavy damage on Allied shipping. Larger and improved submarines played a major role in WORLD WAR II, in which the Allies and neutrals lost some 4770 ships to these raiders. The advent of nuclear energy brought about major changes in submarine propulsion and striking power. The first nuclear submarine, the USS *Nautilus,* was completed in 1954. Nuclear submarines can remain submerged for almost unlimited periods of time and can fire long-range missiles from a submerged position. Such a submarine's primary mission is to strike at enemy land targets. Some nuclear attack submarines, for deployment against shipping, have also been built.

**Subotica,** city (1981 pop. 154,611), Serbia, NE Yugoslavia. It is a commercial and communications centre of a predominantly agricultural region and has food-processing, fertilizer and other industries. It was part of Hungary until 1920 and its population is mainly Hungarian-speaking.

**subsistence,** the products necessary for survival and reproduction. A subsistence economy is defined as a system in which all goods that are needed for subsistence are produced and consumed within the society itself, with the implication that there is no SURPLUS produced, that there are no powerful or dominant unproductive groups in the society which are supported by the labour of others, and that there is no economic exchange with a wider society.

**succession theory,** a theory developed from the concept of plant communities involving a gradual directional change in the vegetation of a particular area. The initial colonizing plants give way to more productive forms until a 'climax' vegetation type is reached, usually accompanied by maximum productivity from the available resources. The processes involved include those of soil formation and animal succession and therefore the concept may be extended to biotic communities and whole ecosystems.

**succory:** see CHICORY.

**succulent,** any fleshy plant, typically with reduced leaves and an outer surface covered with a waxy substance (cutin) that reduces evaporation from the inner, water-storing tissue. Many are indigenous to dry regions. Species of CACTUS, ALOE, and YUCCA are succulents.

**Suckling, Sir John,** 1609–41, English Cavalier poet, gallant at the court of CHARLES I, wit, and gamester, said by John AUBREY to have invented cribbage. *Fragmenta Aurea* (1646) collected his poems, plays, letters, and tracts. He is best known for the lyric 'Why so pale and wan, fond lover?'

**Sucre,** city (1982 est, pop. 79,400), S central Bolivia, capital of Chuquisaca dept. and constitutional capital of Bolivia. (The administrative capital is LA PAZ.) It was founded as La Plata in 1538 and was also called Chuquisaca and Carcas before being renamed after Antonio José de SUCRE in 1839. A major agricultural centre, it supplies the mining towns of the barren ALTIPLANO. It is also the seat of the national university, San Francisco Xavier (est. c.1625), and of the Bolivian Supreme Court.

**Sucre, Antonio José de** (ˌsoohkray), 1795–1830, South American revolutionary leader. He joined (1811) the revolution against Spain and became the chief lieutenant of Simón BOLÍVAR. A military genius, Sucre won brilliant victories at Pichincha (in ECUADOR; 1822) and at Junín and AYACUCHO (in PERU; 1824); the latter battle assured South America's independence. He served (1825–28) as president of the new state of BOLIVIA and repelled (1828) a Peruvian invasion of Ecuador.

**sucrose** ($C_{12}H_{22}O_{11}$), common table sugar, a white, crystalline solid with a sweet taste. Common names, which indicate the natural source, include cane sugar, beet sugar, and maple sugar. A disaccharide (see CARBOHYDRATE), sucrose can be hydrolized to yield invert sugar, a mixture of unequal amounts of FRUCTOSE and GLUCOSE. Sucrose is obtained from the 'juice' of sugar cane or sugar beets and from the sap of the sugar maple. It is evaporated to give a brownish liquid, called molasses, and brownish raw sugar. The impurities which give the brownish colour are removed by charcoal used in the refining process.

**Sudan,** officially Republic of Sudan, republic (1986 est. pop. 21,550,000), 2,505,813 km² (967,494 sq mi), the largest country in Africa, bordered by Egypt (N), the Red Sea (NE), Ethiopia (E), Kenya, Uganda, and Zaïre (S), the Central African Republic and Chad (W), and Libya (NW). The principal cities are KHARTOUM (the capital) and OMDURMAN. The most notable geographical feature is the NILE R., which, with its tributaries, flows through eastern Sudan from south to north.

Rainfall in Sudan, plentiful in the north, diminishes as one moves south; thus the southern part of the country is characterized by swampland and rainforest, the central region by savanna and grassland, and the north by desert and semidesert. There are mountains in the northeast, south, centre, and west; the highest point is Kinyetti (3187 m/10,456 ft), in the southeast. Agriculture, mostly of a subsistence nature, dominates the economy. Long-staple cotton, the principal cash crop, is raised in the irrigated GEZIRA region, which also produces durra and other millets, groundnuts, wheat, and rice; cotton, gum arabic (about 80% of world production), sesame, and groundnuts are exported. The small mining industry extracts chromite; copper, manganese, and iron ores; and gold. A promising petroleum industry began production in 1979. The GNP is US$6169 million, and the GNP per capita is US$300 (1985). The population is divided into three main groups: northerners, who are Muslim and speak Arabic; westerners, from W Africa; and southerners, who follow traditional beliefs and speak Nilotic languages. There is a small Christian minority in the south.

*History.* Northeast Sudan, called NUBIA in ancient times, was colonized by Egypt about 2000 BC and was ruled by the CUSH kingdom from the 8th cent. BC to the 4th cent AD. Most of Nubia was converted to Coptic Christianity in the 6th cent., but by the 15th cent. Islam prevailed. In 1821 the north was conquered by Egypt, but a revolt by the nationalist MAHDI in 1881, during which the British Gen. GORDON was killed, forced an Egyptian withdrawal. In the 1890s an Anglo-Egyptian force under Herbert KITCHENER destroyed the theocratic Mahdist state, and in 1899 most of Sudan came under the joint rule of Egypt and Britain (with Britain exercising actual control). Independence was achieved in 1956. In 1955 the animist southerners, fearing that the new nation would be dominated by the Muslim north, had begun a bloody civil war; fighting, which lasted 17 years, resulted in the death of 1.5 million southerners and subsided in 1972, with the southern Sudan receiving considerable autonomy. The independent nation alternated between civil and military regimes, until 1969, when Col. Jaafur al-NEMERY led a coup that established a leftist government, with the Sudanese Socialist Union as the sole legal party. In 1982 Sudan signed a 'charter of integration' with Egypt, but in the early 1980s experienced a revival of major disaffection in the non-Moslem south. Amid anti-government demonstrations, Nemery was deposed in 1985 and replaced by a transitional military council headed by Gen. Abdel Rahman Swar el Dahab. Multi-party elections in 1986 resulted in the restoration of civilian government under the premiership of Sadiq el-MAHDI (People's Party), with a five-member Supreme Council acting collectively as head of state.

Sudan

**Sudbury,** city (1979 est. pop. 92,350), central Ontario, Canada, part of the regional municipality of Sudbury (1979 est. pop. 160,116). Located in the CANADIAN SHIELD, it is an important mining centre, producing much of the Western world's nickel and large quantities of copper and other metals. Settlement began in 1887, after mineral deposits were discovered there.

**sudden infant death syndrome (SIDS)** or **cot death,** sudden, unexpected, and unexplained death of an apparently well infant under one year. Parents are normally devastated by the tragedy and may experience a strong sense of guilt. The risk is higher in males, in low-birth-weight infants, in lower socioeconomic levels, and during cold months. Current theories suggest that the infant may have immature lungs or problems with brain-stem control of breathing and/or temperature regulation; SIDS victims are thought to have brief episodes of apnoea (breathing stoppage) before the fatal one. There is no satisfactory explanation to cover all cases as yet. An alarm system that detects breathing abnormalities is sometimes used with infants suspected of being prone to SIDS.

**Sudetenland,** region, N Czechoslovakia, named after the Sudetes, a mountain range running along the Polish-Czech border. Traditionally part of BOHEMIA, the Sudetenland had been for centuries the home of a largely German-speaking population. The area was annexed to Germany by the MUNICH PACT (1938). It was restored to Czechoslovakia in 1945, and most of the German population was expelled.

**Su Dongpo,** see SU SHI.

**Sue, Eugène** (sy), 1804–57, French novelist; b. Marie Joseph Sue. His sensational tales of Parisian slum life include *Les mystères de Paris* (1842–43) and *Le juif errant* (1844–45; tr. The Wandering Jew).

**Suetonius** (Caius Suetonius Tranquillus), AD c.69–c.140, Roman biographer. His *De vita Caesarum* (Lives of the Caesars) survives almost in full. Filled with anecdote, Suetonius' lively work was taken as a model by later biographers.

**Suez,** city and port (1987 pop. 193,965), NE Egypt, at the head of the Gulf of Suez and at the southern end of the SUEZ CANAL. Before the ARAB–ISRAELI WAR in June 1967 it was a major population centre but was evacuated during the war. It is now being repopulated.

**Suez Canal,** canal, Egypt. The chief man-made waterway in the Eastern Hemisphere, it is c.160 km (100 mi) long, connecting the Mediterranean Sea (N) with the Gulf of Suez and the Red Sea (S), and greatly reducing the distance by sea between Europe and S and E Asia. Built (1859–69) by the French engineer Ferdinand de LESSEPS, it was acquired by Great Britain in 1875 and nationalized by Egypt in 1956. The canal, which has no locks, was closed to Israeli shipping and cargoes from 1948 to 1975 and to all shipping from 1967 to 1975, following the ARAB–ISRAELI WAR of 1967. Cleared of mines and wreckage, it was reopened in 1975 and enlarged (1976–80) to accommodate oil supertankers.

THE MEETING OF THE WATERS.

Suez Canal: illustration from *Judy*, 1869

**Suffolk,** county in E England (1984 est. pop. 615,900), 3797 km² (1480 sq mi), bordering on North Sea in E and Norfolk in N. IPSWICH and Bury St Edmunds are the chief towns. It is generally low and undulating with low hills in the SW. The Little Ouse and Waveney rivers form the N border with Norfolk, and the R. Stour forms the border with Essex in the S. It is primarily an agricultural county producing cereals and root crops. There is some industry developed in the main towns, often related to agriculture. FELIXSTOWE and Lowestoft are port towns.

**suffragettes:** see WOMEN'S SOCIAL AND POLITICAL UNION; WOMEN'S SUFFRAGE.

**Sufism** (‚soohfizam), Islamic MYSTICISM. It grew out of the confluence of two currents, one of asceticism and the other of THEOSOPHY. From the 12th cent. onwards, sufism developed into a number of orders based on cults of saints with well-endowed lodges, international contacts, and connections with political authority. Some of these orders emphasized ascetic and ecstatic practice, others stressed pantheistic metaphysics of great complexity, and yet others were given to antinomianism or to extreme forms of self-mortification. Perhaps the best known outside islamic lands are the Mevlevis or 'whirling dervishes'. By the 17th cent. the great orders were so enmeshed with the social fabric of islamic societies that virtually every Muslim was the member of an order. Though still in existence, the sufi orders are now marginal to social and religious life.

**sugar,** compound of CARBON, HYDROGEN, and OXYGEN, belonging to a class of substances called CARBOHYDRATES. Sugars fall into three groups. Monosaccharides are the simple sugars, e.g., FRUCTOSE and GLUCOSE. Disaccharides, made up of two monosaccharide units, include LACTOSE, MALTOSE, and SUCROSE. The less familiar trisaccharides, made up of three monosaccharide units, include raffinose, found in sugar BEETS. Modern dieticians advise people to eat little sugar (see DIET).

**Sugar, Alan Michael,** 1947–, British entrepreneur. After leaving school at the age of 16, he started his own business, and quickly developed the skill of identifying gaps in the mass market. In 1968 he formed his own electronics company Amstrad and developed new and innovative products. He was best known for his introduction onto the popular market (1985) of a complete word-processing system for which within weeks sales reached multi-millions of pounds. His success in the international computer market persisted, with new models being introduced at prices which threatened the world's giant computer companies.

**sugarcane,** tall tropical perennial (genus *Saccharum*) of the GRASS family, native to Asia. Sugarcane somewhat resembles CORN and SORGHUM, with a large terminal panicle and a noded stalk. It and the sugar BEET are the major sources of SUGAR. The cane is harvested by cutting down the stalks and pressing them to extract the juice, which is concentrated by evaporation. Refined sugar is produced by precipitating out nonsugar components; it is almost pure SUCROSE. Cuba and India together produce over one-third of the world's cane sugar. Sugarcane by-products include molasses, RUM, ALCOHOL, fuel, and livestock feed.

**Suharto,** 1921–, president of INDONESIA (1968–). In 1965 he led the army in crushing a Communist coup and replaced Pres. SUKARNO as effective ruler. Gen. Suharto became acting president in 1967 and was elected president in 1968.

**Sui,** dynasty: see CHINA.

**suicide,** the deliberate taking of one's own life. It may be dictated by social convention, as with HARA-KIRI, in Japan, or by custom, as in those primitive societies in which nonproductive elderly individuals were expected to end their own lives for the welfare of the group. Long condemned by Judaism, Christianity, and Islam, suicide remains a crime in some countries. Britain abolished punishment for attempted suicide in 1961; in the US attempted suicide and the act of helping someone to commit suicide remain illegal in some states. Suicide and attempted suicide are now more often considered the result of psychological factors, such as severe DEPRESSION, guilt, and aggression, or of chronic illness. Suicidal behaviour is also viewed as a form of communication, a cry for help. Statistics reveal patterns that defy easy explanation. Suicide is more common among men than women, and although severe depression exists among the very young and very old, suicide among these groups is rare; it has, however, increased among adolescents in Western countries in recent years. Émile DURKHEIM, Sigmund FREUD, and Karl Menninger have studied and proposed theories of suicide.

**Suir,** river in S of Republic of Ireland, c.136 km (85 mi) long. It rises in the northern part of Co. Tipperary and flows S then E past CLONMEL to Waterford Harbour, where it joins the R. BARROW.

**suite,** in music, an instrumental form derived from dance and consisting of a series of movements usually in the same key but contrasting in rhythm and mood. As the connection with actual dancing disappeared, the BAROQUE suite evolved, establishing the basic movements as allemande, courante, sarabande, and gigue. Suites for orchestra (including the partitas of J.S. BACH) were sometimes called OVERTURES. The 19th-cent. suite became a collection of pieces from the incidental music for plays or from ballet scores (as GRIEG's *Peer Gynt Suite*).

**Sukarno,** 1901–70, Indonesian statesman. With Mohammad HATTA, Sukarno played a crucial role in establishing (1945) the republic of INDONESIA and became its first president. In 1959 he assumed dictatorial powers and in 1963 proclaimed himself president for life. He increased Indonesian ties with Communist China, and in 1965 a Communist coup attempt was put down by the military under Gen. SUHARTO, who stripped Sukarno of power. In 1966 he was removed from the presidency and remained under house arrest until his death.

**Sukkoth:** see under JEWISH HOLIDAYS.

**Sulaija:** see ABUJA.

**Sulayman,** sultans of the OTTOMAN EMPIRE (Turkey). **Sulayman I** or **Sulayman the Magnificent,** 1494–1566 (r.1520–66), son and successor of SELIM I, ruled the Ottoman Empire at its height of power and prestige. He continued his father's conquests in the Balkans and the Mediterranean, conquering (1521) Belgrade and expelling (1522) the Knights Hospitalers from Rhodes. He annexed most of Hungary and entered into an alliance with FRANCIS I of France against the Habsburgs. His vassal BARBAROSSA made the Turkish fleet the terror of the Mediterranean. On the whole, however, Sulayman was unsuccessful in his naval warfare against Holy Roman Emperor CHARLES V and Venice. He lost (1535) Tunis to Charles and failed to take Vienna (1529) and Malta (1565). He undertook several successful campaigns against Persia and conquered the Arabian coastlines. Sulayman was distinguished for his justice; his legal, military, and educational reforms were outstanding. He lived in great pomp and splendour and was a generous patron of the arts, architecture, and literature. He had two of his sons executed for conspiracy and was succeeded by another son, SELIM II. **Sulayman II,** 1642–91 (r.1687–91), was occupied during his brief reign with the war against Austria. Mustafa KÖPRÜLÜ was his grand vizier.

**Sulla, Lucius Cornelius,** 138–78 BC, Roman general, leader of the conservative senatorial party. He and MARIUS both wanted the appointment as commander against MITHRIDATES VI of Pontus; Sulla got it by marching (88 BC) against Rome. He conquered Mithridates, sacked (86 BC) Athens, and returned triumphantly to Rome. In the civil war that followed, he defeated the Marians. He captured and massacred 8000 prisoners and declared himself dictator (82 BC). Sulla retired (79 BC) after a reign notorious for cruelty and illegality.

**Sullivan, Sir Arthur (Seymour),** 1842–1900, English composer and conductor. He is famous for a series of brilliant comic operas (or OPERETTAS) written with the librettist W.S. GILBERT, e.g., *Trial by Jury* (1875), *H.M.S. Pinafore* (1878), *The Mikado* (1885), and *Ruddigore* (1887). He wrote other familiar music, including 'The Lost Chord' and 'Onward Christian Soldiers'.

**Sullivan, Louis Henry,** 1856–1924, American architect. He was of great importance in the evolution of MODERN ARCHITECTURE in the US. His dominating principle, that outward form should express function, countered the late-19th-cent. revival of traditional classicism, and gained few adherents. Associated after 1880 with Dankmar Adler, he became prominent with functionally straightforward designs like the Wainwright Building, St Louis (1890), and the Transportation Building at the World's Columbian Exposition, Chicago (1893). Sullivan's views were published as *Kindergarten Chats* (1918) and *The Autobiography of an Idea* (1924). Few of his buildings survive, but he influenced a generation of American architects.

**Sully, Thomas,** 1783–1872, American painter; b. England. Influenced by Benjamin WEST and Thomas LAWRENCE during a stay in London, he returned to America and settled in Philadelphia in 1810. An elegant and romantic portraitist, he recorded such notable subjects as Queen Victoria (Metropolitan Mus., New York) and Presidents Jefferson and Monroe (US Military Acad., West Point, New York.). Sully also painted noteworthy historical compositions, e.g., *Washington's Passage of the Delaware* (1819; Mus. Fine Arts, Boston).

**Sully-Prudhomme, René François Armond** (sy,lee-pry,dom), 1839–1907, French poet, one of the PARNASSIANS. His works include *La justice* (1878) and *Le bonheur* (1888; tr. Happiness), long philosophical poems. In 1901 he received the first Nobel Prize in literature.

**sulphonamide** or **sulpha drug,** any of a class of synthetic chemical substances derived from sulphanilamide (a red dye) and used to treat bacterial infections. These drugs inhibit the action of para-aminobenzoic acid, essential for the growth of bacteria. They were first introduced by Gerhard DOMAGK and commenced the modern age of chemotherapy. Sulphonamides are now used primarily in the treatment of urinary tract and gastrointestinal infections. Side-effects can include nausea and headaches. ANTIBIOTIC drugs have largely replaced them in the treatment of other bacterial infections.

**sulphur,** nonmetallic element, known to antiquity as the biblical brimstone and recognized as an element by Antoine LAVOISIER in 1777. Solid sulphur is yellow, brittle, odourless, tasteless, and insoluble in water. Sulphur is widely distributed in minerals and ores, some volcanic regions, and large underground deposits, and often occurs with coal, natural gas, and petroleum. It is found in most proteins and the protoplasm of plants and animals. Sulphur is used in GUNPOWDER, matches, and insecticides, and in RUBBER vulcanization and the treatment of certain skin diseases. SULPHURIC ACID is its most important compound; others are used as disinfectants, refrigerants, organic solvents, and sulpha drugs. See ELEMENT (table); PERIODIC TABLE.

**sulphuric acid,** chemical compound ($H_2SO_4$), colourless, odourless, extremely corrosive, oily liquid. It is sometimes called oil of vitriol. Concentrated sulphuric acid is a weak acid (see ACIDS AND BASES) and a poor ELECTROLYTE because relatively little is dissociated into ions at room temperature. When cold it does not react readily with such common metals as iron or copper. When hot it is an oxidizing agent. Hot concentrated sulphuric acid reacts with most metals and with several nonmetals, e.g., sulphur and carbon. When concentrated sulphuric acid is mixed with water, large amounts of heat are released. Sulphuric acid is a strong acid and a good electrolyte when diluted. A very important industrial chemical, it is produced by the oxidation and dissolution in water of sulphur dioxide ($SO_2$) over a catalyst of VANADIUM pentoxide.

**Suluku, Almany,** 1820–1906, king of the Biriwa Limba of SIERRA LEONE. His kingdom was attacked and occupied by Samourey TOURE between 1884 and 1888. He appealed for help from the British who incorporated his territory into the British protectorate of Sierra Leone in 1896.

**sumac** or **sumach,** common name for the family Anacardiaceae, trees and shrubs native chiefly to the tropics but ranging into north temperate regions and typified by resinous, often acrid sap, a source of tannin. The sap of some plants in the family, e.g., POISON IVY, also contains an ESSENTIAL OIL that is a toxic skin irritant. PISTACHIO, MANGO, and CASHEW are members of the family that provide food. The true sumacs belong to the genus *Rhus*. Most *Rhus* species contain tannin, and some are cultivated for it. Several species have brilliant autumn foliage, e.g., the common staghorn sumac (*R. typhina*).

**Sumatra,** island (1971 pop. 20,812,682), westernmost and second largest island of Indonesia, c.473,970 km² (183,000 sq mi). Hot and rainy, it is c.1790 km (1110 mi) long and up to 435 km (270 mi) wide, with swamps in the east and a densely forested, mountainous interior. Mt Kerintji (3800 m/12,467 ft), in the volcanic Barisan range, is the highest point. Sumatra is sparsely settled but of great economic importance for its rich deposits of oil, coal, gold, silver, tin, and bauxite (some on offshore islands) and its productive rubber, coffee, tea, and sugarcane plantations. MEDAN and PALEMBANG are the chief population centres.

**Sumer** and **Sumerian civilization.** A notable non-Semitic culture appeared in S Mesopotamia (Sumer) at least as early as the 5th millennium BC By 3000 BC. Sumerian city-states, e.g., Erech, Kish, Lagash, and UR, developed considerable power based on irrigated agriculture. Pottery and metalwork were made into fine arts, and the Sumerians probably invented CUNEIFORM writing. The Sumerians were the rivals of Semitic cities such as AKKAD and ultimately were conquered by them. A Sumerian revival under the third dynasty of Ur (c.2060 BC) lasted until that dynasty fell to ELAM, and the growth of BABYLONIA ended the Sumerians as a nation.

**Sumerian and Babylonian art.** The artistic tradition of MESOPOTAMIA was remarkable for its antiquity, variety, and richness. The art of the Sumerian civilization (found in excavations at UR, BABYLON, Erech, Mari, Kish, and Lagash) influenced all the major cultures of ancient Asia. Sumerian techniques and motifs were widely available because of the invention of CUNEIFORM writing before 3000 BC. Clay was the Sumerians' most abundant material; stone, wood, and metal had to be imported. From very early times, their workmanship was of the highest quality, e.g., an alabaster vase from Erech (c.3500 BC; Iraq Mus., Baghdad). A major peak of artistic achievement is represented by a marble head, *Lady of Warka,* from Erech (c.3200 BC; Iraq Mus.). Ur yielded much outstanding Sumerian work, e.g., a wooden harp with the head of a bull on top, showing mythological scenes in gold and mosaic inlay on the sound box (c.2650 BC, Univ. of Pennsylvania, Philadelphia). The famous votive stone sculptures from Tell Asmar represent tall, bearded figures with huge, staring eyes and long, pleated skirts. The ZIGGURAT temple was the most striking architectural achievement of the Sumerians; a ziggurat

Sumerian wooden harp, c.2650 BC. University of Pennsylvania, Philadelphia.

at Erech extended over 46,500 m² (more than half a million sq ft). Among other Sumerian arts, the cylinder seals, used to mark documents or property, were highly sophisticated. Sculpture reached new heights under Sargon, king of Akkad, and a bronze head from Nineveh (c.2300 BC; Iraq Mus.) is thought to be his portrait. Invasions from the east destroyed Sargon's empire, but the city of Lagash survived. It was beautified with many statues of its governor Gudea, and other works of art. The glory of Sumer was revived from 2200 to 2100BC. During this period the great ziggurat of the moon god at Ur was constructed. Invasions of Semitic peoples from what are now Iran and Syria ended the last Sumerian golden age. The palace at Mari reveals the brilliance of a vanished world. In the 18th cent. BC, BABYLONIA under HAMMURABI dominated Mesopotamia. A carved diorite head showing the marks of age on a sensitive face (1792–1750 BC; Louvre, Paris) is thought to be his portrait. A sculpture from Mari of a fertility goddess (Aleppo Mus.), holding a vase from which water flows down her skirt, attests to the genius of Babylonian sculptors. After Hammurabi's death, Mesopotamia was torn for centuries by invasions. It was not until the reign of NEBUCHADNEZZAR (c.605–562 BC) that the Babylonians developed to perfection one of their most striking arts: the polychrome-glazed brick walls modelled in relief, of which the foremost example is the Ishtar gates of Babylon. These contain 575 reliefs of lions, dragons, and bulls (6th cent. BC; one lion is in the Metropolitan Mus., New York) of superb workmanship. The king's palace, its hanging (balconied) gardens, the Ishtar gates, and the processional road made Babylon the most magnificent city of its time. Less than a century later, Babylonia fell to further invasions, with the Persians, Greeks, and Romans ruling in succession. It was not until excavations in the 19th cent.AD that archaeologists brought to light its history, artwork, and influence.

**summer solstice:** see SOLSTICE.

**Sumner, Charles,** 1811–74, US senator from Massachusetts (1851–74). An aggressive ABOLITIONIST he was physically assaulted by Rep. Preston S. Brooks after making a strong antislavery speech (19–20 May 1856). He was a leader of the radical Republicans' RECONSTRUCTION programme and was active in the impeachment of Andrew JOHNSON.

**Sun,** intensely hot, self-luminous body of gases (mainly hydrogen and helium) at the centre of the SOLAR SYSTEM. The Sun is a medium-size main-sequence STAR. Its mean distance from the Earth is defined as one ASTRONOMICAL UNIT. The Sun is c.1,392,000 km (865,400 mi) in diameter; its volume is about 1,300,000 times, and its mass 332,000 times, that of the Earth, giving it a mean density about 1.4 times that of water. At its centre, the Sun has a density over 100 times that of water, a pressure of over 1000 million atmospheres, and a temperature of about 15,000,000°K. This temperature is high enough for the occurrence of nuclear reactions, which are assumed to be the source of the Sun's energy. Hans Bethe proposed a cycle of nuclear reactions known as the carbon cycle, in which carbon acts much as a catalyst, while hydrogen is transformed by a series of reactions into helium and large amounts of high-energy gamma radiation are released. The so-called proton–proton process is now thought to be a more important energy source: the collision of two protons initiates a process that ends with the production of helium atoms and the release throughout of gamma radiation. The bright surface of the Sun is called the photosphere; its temperature is about 6000°K. During an ECLIPSE of the Sun, the chromosphere (a layer of rarified gases above the photosphere) and the corona (a luminous envelope of extremely fine particles surrounding the Sun, outside the chromosphere) are observed. See also SOLAR WIND; SUNSPOTS.

**Sun Belt,** popular name for a region of the southern US—a term that gained wide acceptance in the energy-conscious 1970s. The Sun Belt is generally considered to focus on Texas and California and to extend north and east as far as North Carolina. It thus embraces a diverse area that because of rapid economic growth, high federal spending levels, and climatic advantages has experienced rapid gains in population and political importance as a result of interregional migration from the so-called Frost Belt, Snow Belt or Rust Belt states of the N and NE US.

**sun dance,** a summer ceremony among NORTH AMERICAN INDIANS of the Plains, consisting of usually eight days of ritual smoking, fasting, and penance through self-torture. The rites were discouraged by missionaries and the US government to such an extent that they are now almost forgotten and their true meaning has been lost.

**Sunday:** see SABBATH; WEEK.

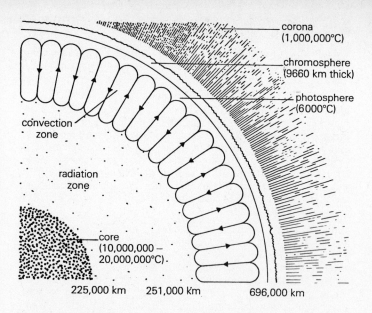

Structure of the Sun

**Sunday school,** institution for instruction in religion and morals, usually as a part of a church organization. It originated (1780) in England under Robert Raikes. The plan originally emphasized simple lessons in reading and spelling in preparation for reading the Bible, but since the growth of general education in the 19th cent. Sunday Schools have been concerned exclusively with religious instruction. The World Council of Christian Education (established 1947) aids the movement in leadership training and curriculum throughout the world.

**Sunderland,** town (1981 pop. 195,064), Tyne and Wear, at the mouth of R. Tyne, NE England. It is an industrial town and seaport which has exported coal since the 14th cent. The main industries of the town include ship-building (now in decline) and the manufacture of glass and paper. There are the remains of a Benedictine monastery in the suburb of Monkwearmouth.

**sundial,** instrument that indicates the time of day by the shadow, cast on a surface marked to show hours or fractions of hours, of an object on which the Sun's rays fall. The shadow-casting object is called a gnomon. Corrections must be made for the difference (which varies daily) between solar (or apparent) time and clock (or mean) time and for the difference in longitude between the position of a sundial and the standard-time meridian of a given locality.

**sunflower,** any annual or perennial herb (genus *Helianthus*) of the COMPOSITE family, native to the New World. The flower heads are commonly bright yellow and may reach 30 cm (1 ft) in diameter. Different parts of the common sunflower (*H. annuus*) are used in many ways: the seeds as a snack, or as an animal, or a poultry food, bread grain, and a source of oil; the flowers for the production of nectar; and the leaves for fodder. Other species are used for food (see JERUSALEM ARTICHOKE) and as garden flowers.

**Sungaria:** see DZUNGARIA.

**Sunnism** [Arab., = adherence to *sunna*, salutary precedent], the larger of the two great branches of ISLAM, the second being SHI'ISM. One way in which this distinction is maintained is by reference to legal schools (see FIQH). The other is the Sunnite acceptance of the legitimacy of MUHAMMAD's first three successors and of the consensus of previous generations of Muslims. Hence Sunnism is the more catholic branch of Islam, and has been the historical ally of Islamic states.

**sunspots,** dark, usually irregularly-shaped spots on the SUN's surface that are actually solar magnetic storms. The temperature of the spots is lower than that of the surrounding photosphere; thus the spots are, by contrast, darker. All but the smallest show a dark central portion (the umbra) with a lighter outer area (the penumbra). Sunspot activity reaches a maximum once every 11 years.

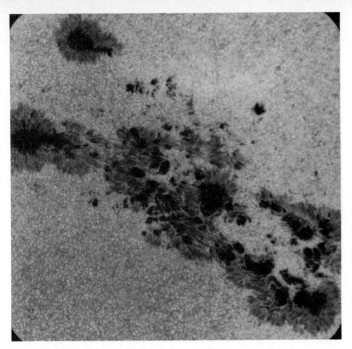

A complex group of **sunspots**

**Sun Yat-sen**, 1866–1925, Chinese revolutionary leader. Born near Guangzhou, he received (1892) a medical degree in Hong Kong and practiced in that city. Thereafter he plotted to overthrow the Ch'ing dynasty of China and to establish a republic. Influenced by Karl MARX, Sun organized (1905) in Japan a revolutionary league, the Tong Meng Hui (Revolutionary Alliance), and developed a political theory based on the Three People's Principles: nationalism, democracy, and the people's livelihood. After revolution erupted in China, Sun was elected (1911) provisional president of the Chinese republic. He soon resigned in favour of YUAN SHIKAI, who became increasingly dictatorial. Sun became director of the KUOMINTANG Party, revolted against Yüan, and became (1921) president of a self-proclaimed national government at Guangzhou. In 1924, to hasten the conquest of N China, he began cooperating with Chinese Communists and accepted aid from the USSR. After the Kuomintang–Communist split (1927), each group claimed to be his heirs. Sun's wife was Song Qingling (see under SOONG, family).

**superconductivity**, the absence of electrical RESISTANCE in certain substances when they are cooled to temperatures, in most cases, near absolute zero (see LOW-TEMPERATURE PHYSICS). The phenomenon, discovered by Kamerlingh Onnes in 1911, is displayed by some metals, including zinc, magnesium, and lead; in some alloys; and in certain compounds, such as tungsten carbide and lead sulphide. Current in a superconducting circuit will continue to flow after the source of current has been shut off. Powerful ELECTROMAGNETS, which, once energized, retain their magnetic field, have been developed, using coils of superconducting metal. Since 1986 it has been shown that certain oxides show superconductivity at much higher temperatures.

**superego** in PSYCHOANALYSIS, one of the components of FREUD's model of the psychic apparatus, together with the EGO and the ID. The superego is a part of the ego which 'splits off' in development, and represents the internalized prohibitions and codes of society, and more immediately of the parents.

**superfluidity**, the capability of liquid helium cooled below a temperature of 2.19 K (the lambda point) to flow freely, even upwards, with no measurable friction and viscosity. Superfluid helium flows easily through capillary tubes (see CAPILLARITY) that resist the flow of ordinary fluids, and a DEWAR FLASK filled with superfluid helium from a larger container will empty itself back into the original container because the liquid helium flows spontaneously in an invisible film over the surface of the flask.

**Superior, Lake,** largest (82,414 km²/31,820 sq mi) freshwater lake in the world and the largest, highest (surface elevation 183 m/602 ft), and deepest (up to 397 m/1302 ft) of the GREAT LAKES, on the US–Canada

border. Part of the St Lawrence & Great Lakes Waterway, it is connected with Lake Huron by the St Marys R. and the SAULT SAINTE MARIE CANALS.

**supernova**, exploding star (see VARIABLE STAR) that suddenly increases its energy output as much as a billionfold and then slowly fades to less than its original brightness. At peak intensity, it can outshine the entire galaxy in which it occurs. Supernovas represent a catastrophic stage of STELLAR EVOLUTION; a sudden implosion of the core of certain massive stars (see GRAVITATIONAL COLLAPSE) produces a rapidly rotating collapsed stellar remnant (see PULSAR), the explosive ejection of the stellar envelope at great velocity, and the release of enormous quantities of energy. Over 120 extended galactic radio sources have been identified as supernova remnants. Of these, only four have been positively associated with explosions that were optically observed in recorded history; they occurred in 1006, 1054 (the remnant of which is now visible as the CRAB NEBULA), 1572, and 1604.

**supersonic speed:** see SHOCK WAVE; SONIC BOOM.

**superstrings**, in ELEMENTARY PARTICLE physics, an approach in which the elementary particles are treated theoretically as multi-dimensional strings instead of infinitessimal points. This approach promises to help with the formulation of all-embracing UNIFIED THEORIES.

**supperrealism:** see PHOTOREALISM.

**Supplementary Benefit,** in Britain, payments made to people who have not suffficient income to support themselves (and their families). It is called supplementary because it may be paid to people already receiving a state benefit or pension, if their circumstances are such that the first does not cover their needs; it is subject to means-testing. By the late 1980s some £7 billion per year was being spent on supplementary benefit for over 4½ million recipients, most of whom were unemployed but including 1½ million old-age pensioners and 700,000 single-parent families.

**supply and demand,** in classical economics, factors that are said to determine price and that may be thought of as the guiding forces in an economy based on private property. Supply refers to the varying amounts of a good or service that producers will supply at different prices; in general, a higher price yields a greater supply. Demand refers to the quantity of a good or service that consumers want (and are able to buy) at any given price. According to the law of demand, demand decreases as the price rises. In a perfectly competitive market, the upward-sloping supply curve and the downward-sloping demand curve yield a supply-and-demand schedule that, where the curves intersect, reveals the equilibrium, or market, price of an item. In reality, however, monopolies, government regulation, and other factors combine to limit the effect of supply and demand.

**supply-side economics,** school of economic thought based on the belief that economic expansion will result from lower tax rates. The theory holds that a reduction in taxes will increase supply (see SUPPLY AND DEMAND) by encouraging production, providing greater incentives to work, and stimulating the savings and investment needed to support business growth. Greater supply would also mean a slowdown in inflation. A tax cut, according to supply-side economics, would not reduce overall tax revenues, because increased prosperity will offset the effects of lower tax rates. Grounded in the historic economic doctrine of LAISSEZ-FAIRE, the philosophy found modern champions in such US economists as Milton FRIEDMAN and Arthur Laffer and provided much of the rationale for Pres. REAGAN's tax-cut programme (1981). Critics of supply-side theory, including Keynesian economists (see ECONOMICS), question some of its most basic assumptions.

**suprematism,** Russian nonobjective art movement founded (1913 but more probably 1915) by Casimir MALEVICH in Moscow. Suprematism sought 'to liberate art from the ballast of the representational world'. Major works consisted of geometrical shapes flatly painted on a pure canvas surface. Malevich's *White on White* (Mus. Mod. Art, New York City) embodies the movement's principles. Its dissemination through the BAUHAUS deeply influenced modern art and design.

**Supreme Court, United States,** highest court of the US, established by Article III of the CONSTITUTION. It has ultimate jurisdiction over all cases arising under the Constitution. Since 1869, it has comprised nine members; the Chief Justice, and eight associate justices, named by the President, subject to Senate confirmation. As the court of last resort, it has two functions: interpreting acts of Congress, and determining whether federal and state laws conform to the Constitution. In MARBURY V. MADISON (1803) it established the doctrine of JUDICIAL REVIEW of congressional acts. The political complexion of the Supreme Court changes over time. During the 1950s and 1960s the 'liberal' court of Chief Justice WARREN moved to protect the rights of minorities, e.g., see BROWN V. BOARD OF EDUCATION OF TOPEKA, KANSAS (1959). This liberalism receded in the 1970s with the appointment of conservative justices by Pres. NIXON. This conservatism was illustrated in UNIVERSITY OF CALIFORNIA RECENTS V. BAKKE (1978), though in 1981 the first woman associate justice (Sandra Day O'Connor) was appointed by Pres. Reagan.

**Supreme Soviet:** see SOVIET.

**Sur:** see TYRE.

**Surabaja** or **Soerabaja** (soorə͵bieə), city (1980 pop. 2,017,000), capital of East Java prov., NE Java, Indonesia, on the Kali Mas R. Surabaja is the country's second largest city and its major naval base. A commercial and industrial centre, it has railway engineering, car assembly and oil processing plants, and manufactures textiles, glass, and fertilizer. Damaged during the Indonesian independence struggle, it has been extensively rebuilt.

**Surat** (sway͵rah), city (1981 pop. 776,876), Gujarat state, W India, at the lowest bridging point on the Tapti R. A district administrative centre, its internal trade is important, though its trade by sea has long ago yielded to BOMBAY. While still retaining its ancient handicrafts (especially cotton textiles involving gold and silver threads, and silk weaving), it has seen a remarkable growth of modern factory industry, including cotton spinning and weaving, and engineering. It shows something of a balance between small-scale and factory industry. It has of recent years grown markedly in population. Although it originated much earlier, Surat has a firm claim to fame as the site of the first factory in India of the British EAST INDIA COMPANY (1608–13) and of prolonged conflict with the rival Portuguese and Dutch, and with the Mahrattas.

**surface tension,** the cohesion forces (see ADHESION AND COHESION) at the surface of a liquid. The molecules within a liquid are attracted equally from all sides, but those near the surface experience unequal attractions and thus are drawn towards the centre of the liquid mass by this net force. A result of surface tension is the tendency of a liquid to reduce its exposed surface to the smallest possible area and to form drops.

**surfing,** sport of gliding towards the shore on a breaking wave, done on a board from 122 to 366 cm (4–12 ft) long. The larger surfboards have a stabilizing fin in the rear. The surfer paddles towards the beach until an incoming wave catches the board, then stands up and glides along or just under the crest of the wave. Developed in Hawaii, surfing spread to California in the 1920s and, by the 1960s, had become popular with youth in the US, Australia, and other countries.

**surgery,** branch of medicine concerned with the diagnosis and treatment of injuries and pathological conditions requiring manual or instrumental operative procedures. Surgery has been performed since prehistoric times (bloodletting, opening of abscesses) and was practised with great skill and cleanliness by the ancient Greeks and Romans. During the Middle Ages in Europe it fell into the hands of unskilled barber-surgeons, and postoperative infection and GANGRENE were common. Surgery became more professional in the 18th cent. and entered its modern phase in the 19th cent. with the introduction of antiseptic techniques, sterilization, and ANAESTHESIA. 20th-cent. advances include BLOOD TRANSFUSION techniques, new diagnostic tools (RADIOGRAPHY, COMPUTERIZED AXIAL TOMOGRAPHY, ULTRASOUND), microsurgery, and organ TRANSPLANTATION.

**Suriname** (soori͵nahm, ͵nam), officially Republic of Suriname, formerly **Dutch Guiana**, republic (1987 est. pop. 400,000), 163,266 km² (63,037 sq mi), NE South America, bordered by the Atlantic Ocean (N), French Guiana (E), Brazil (S), and Guyana (W). PARAMARIBO is the capital. It is part of the Guiana region. Suriname is one of the world's great producers of bauxite, which accounts for about 75% of export earnings. Rice is the chief crop, and sugarcane, citrus fruits, and coffee are also grown. In 1983 GDP was US$1285 million or US$3463 per capita. The population is mixed, and Asian Indians, Creoles, and Indonesians are the largest groups. Dutch is the official language, but most of the people speak Sranang Tongo, a native patois. The Dutch established a colony here in 1616, and Dutch possession was confirmed by the Congress of Vienna in 1815. Suriname became autonomous in 1954 and independent in 1975. Just prior to independence, some 100,000 Surinamese, mainly of Asian

descent, migrated to the Netherlands. In 1980 a bloodless military coup overthrew the democratic government. Under the leadership of Sgt. (later Lt-Col.) Desi Bouterse, the military regime pursued an uncertain course. After arresting his left-wing colleagues in 1980, he released them the following year and established closer relations with the Marxist governments of Cuba, Nicaragua, and Grenada. Under pressure from Brazil and the US, however, he expelled the Cuban ambassador in 1983 and early the following year appointed a relatively conservative civilian government. In 1985 Bouterse's position was formalized as being that of head of government. Under a new constitution approved in 1987, elections to a National Assembly were held in that year and were won by the opposition parties; early in 1988, a civilian president was elected. However, real power remained with Bouterse and the military.

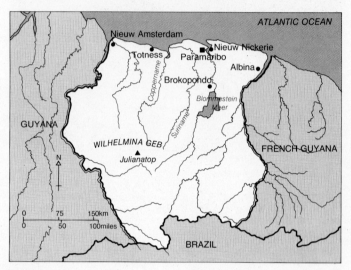

Suriname

**surplus,** products which are produced in excess of the needs of SUBSISTENCE. These goods are usually used to support a nonproductive sector of the population. The existence of surplus is seen as closely connected to the existence of stratification and social classes. It is argued by some anthropologists that the surplus generates stratification but it is also, more convincingly, argued that it is the existence of a group or groups able to exercise power over others and ensure their own supply of goods without the necessity of producing them that leads to the production of surplus.

**surplus value,** the amount of profit that the capitalist extracts from the circle of production after having paid the wage of the workforce and the fixed costs, such as rent, rates, heating, etc. For example, if a worker works an 8-hour day and in 6 hours produces enough to pay his/her wages for the day, the value he/she produces for the next two hours becomes the property of the capitalist. Heuristic device explained by MARX, the concept has had little success in locating the actual generative mechanism of profit in capitalist economies.

**surrealism,** a term first used by APOLLINAIRE in 1917 and later reused by André BRETON in the first surrealist manifesto (1924). It was defined as 'pure psychic AUTOMATISM, by which it is intended to express verbally, in writing or in any other way, the true process of thought. It is the dictation of thought, free from the exercise of reason, and every aesthetic or moral preoccupation'. Breton developed these ideas to form a movement that was defined more by a Marxist political philosophy than merely by a style. Although started in Paris it rapidly became an international movement. In literature, surrealism was confined almost exclusively to France, and was based on the associations and implications of words. Its adherents included Paul Éluard and Jean COCTEAU, famous for his surrealist films. In art the movement was dominant in the 1920s and 30s. Salvador DALI and Yves TANGUY used dream-inspired symbols such as melting clocks. Max ERNST and René MAGRITTE used incongruous elements realistically painted. These 'verists' differed from 'absolute' surrealists, such as Joan MIRÓ, who used images from the subconscious.

**Surrey,** inland county in S England (1984 est. pop. 1,019,400), 1679 km² (655 sq mi), bordering on Greater London in the NE. The county town is GUILDFORD. The North Downs run E to W across the county, with Leith Hill the highest point at 289 m (965 ft). The major rivers are the Mole and the Wey. Market gardening and dairy farming are common, especially in the S. Much of the N part of the county is urbanized and forms part of the London commuter belt.

**Surrey, Henry Howard, earl of,** 1517?–1547, English poet and translator. Surrey's version of the first two books of VIRGIL's *Aeneid* was the first extended use of English blank verse. His sonnets, like some of his mentor Sir Thomas WYATT, based on PETRARCA, were predominantly in the 'English' form (rhyming abab cdcd efef gg), which seems to have been his invention.

**surrogacy,** the carrying and delivery of an infant on behalf of another woman who is unable to bear children. Surrogate motherhood is a new development in the treatment of infertility, arising from IN VITRO FERTILIZATION. The surrogate mother, who is able to bear and deliver a child, allows an egg from the commissioning woman, fertilized by the sperm of the latter's partner (or, if he is infertile, from another donor) to be placed in her uterus. If the commissioning mother produces no eggs, then either an egg from the surrogate mother may be fertilized by sperm from the partner in vitro (outside the body) or conception takes place through normal sexual intercourse. When it is born the baby is returned to the commissioning woman. The procedure is causing difficult legal problems relating to motherhood. Surrogate mothers become attached to the offspring they have borne and may refuse to hand them over to the commissioning couples, despite the exchange of money which may also be entailed.

**survey,** in sociology, a systematic study of the whole, or a percentage of the population of a country. The survey will normally be in the form of a questionnaire which may be self-completed, or completed by a social researcher. Surveys are carried out for one or two reasons: either for a demographic description of the population surveyed, or to investigate the causal interplay of variables within the population surveyed. The former typifies the kind of social research undertaken by governments (e.g., in Britain, the FAMILY EXPENDITURE SURVEY, the GENERAL HOUSEHOLD SURVEY, and the LABOUR FORCE SURVEY). The latter is more typical of the research work undertaken by sociologists, in which statistical analysis is applied to the data-set to investigate potential relationships. A recent development has been the secondary analysis of data in which a data-set generated for one purpose is subjected to later reanalysis focusing on interpretations and conclusions not presented in the original survey report; an early example of this mode of research would be Durkheim's study of suicide.

**surveying,** accurate measurement of points and lines of direction on the earth's surface for the purpose of preparing maps or locating boundary lines. *Hydrographic surveying* records such features as bottom contours, buoys, channels, and shoals in bodies of water and along coastlines. *Land surveying* includes both *geodetic surveying,* used for large areas and taking into account the curvature of the earth's surface (see GEODESY); and *plane surveying,* which deals with areas sufficiently small that the earth's curvature is negligible and can be disregarded.

**susceptibility, electric and magnetic,** measure of the response of a substance to an applied electric or magnetic field. In MAGNETISM, for example, it is the constant of proportionality between the applied magnetic field and the resultant magnetization of the substance.

**Su Shi** or **Su Dongpo,** 1036–1101, Chinese poet and official, considered the greatest poet of the Song dynasty. His satiric verses and opposition to official policy often cost him his position. Regret for the evanescence of beauty and the short span of life are frequent themes in his work.

**suspension,** in chemistry, mixture of two substances, one of which is finely divided and dispersed in the other. Particles in a suspension are larger than those in a COLLOID or SOLUTION, and they precipitate (see PRECIPITATE) if the suspension is allowed to stand undisturbed. Common suspensions include sand in water, dust in air, and droplets of oil in air.

**Sussex, kingdom of,** one of the Anglo-Saxon kingdoms of England, located south of the Weald. It was settled (late 5th cent.) by the Saxons and converted (681–86) to Christianity. Conquered (685–88) by WESSEX, Sussex later fell (by 771) to King OFFA of MERCIA. In 825 Sussex submitted to King Egbert of WESSEX.

**Sutherland, Dame Joan,** 1926–, Australian operatic soprano. She became internationally famous after appearing in *Lucia di Lammermoor* at Covent Garden (1959). Under the tutelage of her husband, the conductor Richard Bonynge, she has successfully revived many florid Italian roles of the early 19th cent.

**Sutherland, Earl Wilbur,** 1915–74, American biochemist. He gave up clinical medicine in favour of biochemical research, concentrating on CARBOHYDRATE metabolism and then on the mechanism of hormone action, for which he received the 1971 Nobel Prize for physiology or medicine.

**Sutherland, Efua,** 1924–, Ghanaian dramatist. She founded the Experimental Theatre and the Ghana Drama Studio, and helped with the development of village theatre. Her interest in changes in her society is shown in *Edufa* (1969), *Foriwa* (1967), and *The Marriage of Anansewa* (1980).

**Sutherland, Graham,** 1903–80, English painter. In 1926 he became a Roman Catholic and his landscapes with thorns and thistles are seen as symbols of Christ's Passion. He was an official war artist (1941–45) and produced a series of work of the devastation of bombed Britain. After World War II he gained several commissions for religious works including his large tapestry design for Coventry Cathedral (1962). He also painted portraits, the best-known is that of Sir Winston Churchill (1954).

**sutra:** see SANSKRIT LITERATURE.

**Sutter, John Augustus,** 1803–80, American pioneer; b. Germany as Johann August Suter. He established a colony in California. Gold was discovered at his mill in 1848, and the activities of the fortune-seekers who swarmed over his land ruined him.

**Sutton,** London borough (1981 pop. 167,547), S England, in S London. It is made up of the districts of Beddington and Wallington, and Sutton and Cheam, and the town of Carshalton. It is mainly residential.

**Sutton Coldfield,** town (1981 pop. 102,572), West Midlands, England, 11 km (7 mi) NE of Birmingham. It is a mainly residential town.

**Sutton Hoo,** the site of a Saxon ship burial in Suffolk, S England. When the barrow was constructed, c. AD 625–30, the ship was fortuitously set in a trench in moist sand, which retained the imprint of the ship's timbers and positioned it low enough for it to escape detection by looters. The grave goods are a veritable treasure, including silver bowls and dishes of

Gilded bronze helmet (c. AD 655) from the site of the Saxon ship burial at **Sutton Hoo**, Suffolk

Roman origin, gold jewellery, a gilded bronze helmet, and Christian artifacts. Although no trace of a body was found, the burial has been believed to be that of Raedwald, an East Anglian king of the 7th cent. AD.

**Suva,** city (1976 pop. 63,628), capital of FIJI, on Viti Levu.

**Suvorov, Aleksandr Vasilyevich** (sooh,vorəf), 1729–1800, Russian field marshal. He fought in the RUSSO-TURKISH WARS of 1768–74 and 1787–92, and put down the PUGACHEV revolt and the 1794 Polish uprising. In the FRENCH REVOLUTIONARY WARS of 1798–99 he drove the French from N Italy and planned to march on Paris, but was ordered to join General Korsakov and Austrian Archduke Charles in Switzerland. While Suvorov's men were struggling through the St Gotthard Pass, Charles was ordered back to the Rhine and Korsakov was defeated. Suvorov led his troops to Lindau and refused to undertake further action with the Austrians. Russia soon withdrew from the war.

**Suwon,** city (1984 pop. 402,319), capital of Kyonggi prov., NW South Korea. Situated on the main Seoul–Pusan rail line, it has factories making textiles, chemicals, tobacco, detergent, and paper, and it is the headquarters of the South Korean Air Force. Suwon is the national centre for agricultural research and education and the surrounding area is well known for strawberries. The city was moved to its present site, some 16 km (10 mi) N of its historic location, in the 1790s by King Chongjo who fortified the town as a refuge; parts of the old fortress are preserved.

**Suzuki, Zenko,** 1911–, Japanese political leader. Elected to 12 terms in the house of representatives, he served (1960–68, 1976–77) in a number of cabinet posts. Suzuki was a founder (1955) of the Liberal–Democratic Party. In 1980 he became prime minister after the death of Masayoshi OHIRA. Unable to reinvigorate Japan's economy from its relative sluggishness, he resigned in 1982.

**Suzuki Harunobu:** see HARUNOBU.

**Svalbard,** island group, 62,051 km² (23,958 sq mi), in the Arctic Ocean, located 640 km (c.400 mi) north of and belonging to Norway. The main islands are SPITSBERGEN, the largest, and Nordaustlandet, Edgeøya, Barensøya, and Prins Karls Forland. Ice fields and glaciers cover more than 60% of the area. Coalmining is the chief industry and is done by Norway and the USSR. Whaling and fur trapping were important in the past. The islands were awarded to Norway by the Spitsbergen Treaty in 1920; currently 41 countries are signatories of this Treaty and their nationals have equal rights to Norwegians in Svalbard. The principal settlement and seat of government is Longyearbyen (pop. c.2000) on Spitsbergen; it is connected by air several times a week to Tromsø (Norway) and monthly to Murmansk (USSR).

**Sverdlovsk,** formerly Ekaterinburg, city (1985 pop. 1,300,000), E European USSR, in the eastern foothills of the central URALS, on the Iset R. It is among the region's largest cities, a western terminus of the TRANS-SIBERIAN RAILWAY, and a major producer of heavy machinery. Nearby are gold and copper mines. The city was founded in 1721 and named after CATHERINE I. In 1918, NICHOLAS II and his family were shot in Ekaterinburg. It was renamed in 1924. During World War II much industry was moved to the region from the European USSR.

**Sverdrup, Otto,** 1855–1930, Norwegian explorer. After participating in two Arctic trips, he led an expedition (1898–1902) that sought to reach the NORTH POLE by Smith Sound but failed because of ice in Kennedy Channel. However, valuable topographical observations were made and unknown lands were found and explored.

**Svevo, Italo** (,zvayvoh), pseud. of **Ettore Schmitz,** 1861–1928, Italian novelist. Born at Trieste in an Italo-German Jewish environment, he was practically unknown until discovered by James JOYCE, who helped him to publish, in Paris, his subtly ironic psychologial masterpiece *La coscienza di Zeno* (1923; tr. The Confessions of Zeno).

**Swabia,** historic region in SW West Germany. In the 9th cent. Swabia became one of the five stem duchies of medieval Germany; it included Alsace and E Switzerland. The duchy was bestowed on the Hohenstauffen dynasty in 1079 and broke up into many feudal and ecclesiastical holdings when the dynasty died out (1268). From the 14th to 16th cent. cities, nobles, knights, and prelates in the region formed Swabian leagues to protect trade and regional peace.

**Swabian League,** 1488–1534, association of Swabian cities and other powers in SW Germany for the protection of trade and for regional peace. It was supported by the Holy Roman emperors and comprised 26 cities.

The league backed the election (1519) of Emperor CHARLES V and helped to defeat the peasants in the Peasants' War. Its dissolution was brought about through internal stresses, partly caused by the religious split brought on by the REFORMATION.

**Swahili language,** member of the Bantu group of African languages. See AFRICAN LANGUAGES (table); BANTU LANGUAGES.

**swallow,** common name for small perching BIRDS of the family Hirundinidae, of almost worldwide distribution. Swallows have long, narrow wings, forked tails, and weak feet. They are extremely graceful in flight, able to make abrupt changes in speed and direction. Their plumage is blue or black with a metallic sheen. They are migratory birds; the end of European and Asian summers is marked by flocks of swallows (*Hirundo rustica*) lining up to fly south to Africa, India, or even northern Australia.

**Swammerdam, Jan,** 1637–80, Dutch naturalist. He was a pioneer in the use of the microscope and was probably the first to detect (1658) red blood cells. Before he turned to religious contemplation, his chief interest was the study of invertebrates; his descriptions of them, together with accurate and exquisitely executed drawings, were published posthumously in 1737–38.

**swamp,** shallow body of water in a low-lying, poorly drained depression, usually containing abundant plant growth. Because the bottom of a swamp is at or below the water table, swamps serve to channel runoff into the groundwater supply, thus helping to stabilize the water table. During periods of very heavy rains, a swamp can act as a natural flood-control device. The increased use of drained swampland for urban development results in greater runoff and probability of flooding as well as the destruction of wildlife habitats.

**swamp cypress,** common name for *Taxodium distichum*, a graceful coniferous tree planted for waterside ornament in Europe, but occurring in dense forests in the SE US, especially in the EVERGLADES. It is able to survive even in standing water by sending up aerial 'knee roots' above water level, thought to aid in the aeration of the root system. It is unusual among conifers in being deciduous (but see also LARCH), and for this reason is called the 'bald cypress' in the US.

**swan,** large aquatic BIRD, related to the DUCK and GOOSE, with a long, gracefully curved neck. The 150 cm (5 ft) mute swan (*Cygnus olor*) was originally a European and Asian species, but it has been domesticated and taken all over the world as an ornamental bird. In the Middle Ages in England all mute swans were the property of the Crown, and Thames and Abbotsbury swans are still marked, the Thames swans in an annual 'swan-upping'.

**Swansea** or **Abertawe,** town (1981 pop. 172,433), West Glamorgan, S Wales, at mouth of R. Tawe, on Swansea Bay. It is a seaport and large industrial town. In 1984 the port handled 5.5 million tonnes. Industries within the town include iron, steel, and tinplate manufacture. There is coal-mining and oil-refining in the district. The seaside resort of The Mumbles is nearby. The town is the seat of the Univ. College of Swansea, a constituent college of the Univ. of Wales. There are the remains of a 14th-cent. castle. Swansea is the birthplace of Beau NASH.

**Swaziland,** officially Kingdom of Swaziland, kingdom (1987 est. pop. 706,000), 17,366 km² (6705 sq mi), SE Africa, bordered by the Republic of South Africa (S, W, and N) and Mozambique (E). The administrative capital is MBABANE. The country is mountainous, with steplike plateaus descending from the Highveld in the west and then rising to the plateau of the Lebombo Mts. The four major river systems have vast hydroelectric potential and are used for irrigation. Agriculture, including forestry and ranching, is the principal sector of the economy, and sugar, wood pulp, and cattle are the leading exports. There are large mineral deposits, the most important of which are asbestos and coal. Swaziland has close economic ties with South Africa. The GNP is US$435 million, and the GNP per capita is US$670 (1985). The Swazi (a Bantu people) constitute 90% of the population; the rest are South Africans and Europeans. English and SiSwati, a Zulu dialect, are the official languages. About 60% of the people are Christians; the remainder are animists.

*History.* Fleeing Zulu attacks, the Swazi arrived in present-day Swaziland from Mozambique in the early 19th cent. Europeans seeking concessions soon moved in, and Swaziland became a British High Commission Territory in 1903. It received limited self-government in 1963 and gained full independence within the COMMONWEALTH in 1968, under King

Sobhuza II, who reigned for 61 years until his death in 1982. There followed a power struggle from which junior royal wife Ntombi emerged as Regent in 1983, and in 1986 her son was installed as King Mswati III at a ceremony attended by Pres. Botha of South Africa.

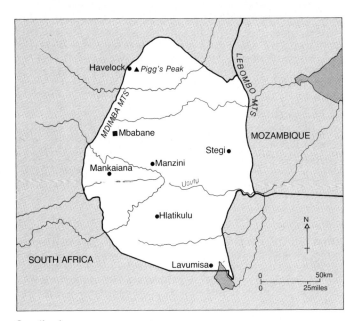

Swaziland

**Sweden,** Swed. *Sverige,* officially the Kingdom of Sweden, constitutional monarchy (1986 pop. 8,381,941), 449,750 km² (173,648 sq mi), N Europe, on the E Scandinavian peninsula; bordered by Norway (W), Finland (NE), the Gulf of Bothnia (E), the Baltic Sea (SE), and the Skagerrak and Kattegat (SW). Major cities include STOCKHOLM (the capital), GÖTEBURG, and UPPSALA. The two main geographical regions are the mountainous N, including LAPLAND, and the low-lying S, where most of the population lives. Rivers and over 100,000 lakes make up nearly one-third of the area. Sweden is a highly industrialized nation with one of the highest living standards in the world. It is a producer of iron ore, and manufactures include high-grade steel, metal goods, machinery, forest products, motor vehicles, and ships; more than half the industrial output is exported. Farming produces dairy products, grain, sugar beets, potatoes, livestock, and poultry. The GNP is $103,240 million and the GNP per capita is $12,400 (1983). Swedish is the common language, but there are small Finnish- and Lapp-speaking minorities. Virtually all Swedes belong to the Lutheran church. The 349-member parliament (*Riksdag*) is elected for a three-year term.

*History.* Most Swedes are descendants of Germanic tribes that were probably settled in Scandinavia by the Neolithic period. By the 10th cent. AD the Swedes had extended their influence to the Black Sea. Christianity, introduced c.829, became fully established in the 12th cent. under Eric IX. Sweden and Norway were united (1319) under MAGNUS VII, and in 1397 the KALMAR UNION united Denmark, Norway, and Sweden. The Danes dominated the union, however, and in 1523, stirred to resistance by a massacre (1520) of Swedish nobles at Stockholm, the Swedes rose against the Danes and established a separate state with GUSTAVUS I as king. Under GUSTAVUS II (r.1611–32), who successfully opposed the Habsburgs in the THIRTY YEARS WAR, and CHARLES X (r.1654–60), who led successful wars against Poland and Denmark, Sweden became one of the great powers of Europe, controlling Finland, Latvia, Estonia, and other parts of the Baltic coast by the end of the 17th cent. The great period of empire came to an end, however, with the rise of a unified Russia and the defeat of Sweden in the NORTHERN WAR (1700–1721). In the Napoleonic Wars, in which Sweden fought against France, Sweden lost (1809) Finland to Russia but was awarded (1814) Norway, which remained in union with Sweden until 1905. The 19th cent. was marked by industrial progress, liberalization of government, and, because of poor economic conditions, large-scale emigration to the US. In the following century Sweden avoided involvement in both world wars (and later refused to compromise its neutrality by joining NATO or the European Community) and initiated

a sweeping programme of economic expansion and social welfare legislation that made it one of the most prosperous and progressive nations in the world. From the mid-1960s, however, Swedish economic growth slowed, and the 1970s and 80s saw sizable increases in unemployment and the rate of inflation. Charles XVI Gustavus succeeded his grandfather, Gustavus VI, as king in 1973. Except for a short period (1936 and 1976–82) of conservative control, the Social Democrats have governed Sweden for over half a century. In 1986 Social Democratic prime minster Olof PALME was assassinated in Stockholm and succeeded by Ingvar CARLSSON.

**Post-war Swedish prime ministers**
Per Albin Hansson (Social Democrat), 1936–46
Tage Erlander (Social Democrat), 1946–69
Olof Palme (Social Democrat), 1969–76
Thorbjörn Fälldin (Centre), 1976–78
Ola Ullsten (Liberal), 1978–79
Thorbjörn Fälldin (Centre), 1979–82
Olof Palme (Social Democrat), 1982–86
Ingvar Carlsson (Social Democrat), 1986–

Sweden

**Swedenborg, Emanuel,** 1688–1772, Swedish scientist, religious teacher, and mystic. His religious system is sometimes called Swedenborgianism. Appointed (1716) assessor of the Royal Board of Mines, his engineering skill made him widely known; he also published many works on philosophy, natural science, the animal kingdom, the brain, and psychology before resigning in 1747. He then gave himself wholly to the contemplation of spiritual matters, believing that God had revealed the true inner doctrines of the divine word to him alone. The teachings of his New Church were set forth in 1757, when he believed the second coming of the Lord had taken place. He had not planned to found a new sect, but his disciples organized the Church of the NEW JERUSALEM after his death.

**Swedish language,** member of the North Germanic, or Scandinavian, group of the Germanic subfamily of the Indo-European family of languages. See LANGUAGE (table).

**Sweelinck, Jan Pieterszoon,** 1562–1621, Dutch organist and composer. The line of his pupils descends directly to J.S. BACH and HANDEL. His organ FUGUES give separate parts to the pedals.

**Sweet, Henry,** 1845–1912, English philologist and phonetician. An authority on Anglo-Saxon and the history of the English language, he was a pioneer in modern phonetics. His *History of English Sounds* (1874) is a landmark in that field.

**sweet gum:** see WITCH HAZEL.

**sweet pea,** annual climbing plant (*Lathyrus odoratus*) of the PULSE family, native to S Europe but now widely cultivated for its fragrant flowers. There are three main types: dwarf, summer flowering (garden sweet peas), and winter flowering (florists' sweet peas). The flowers may be various colours; the vines climb by tendrils and require support.

**sweet potato,** trailing perennial plant (*Ipomoea batatas*) of the MORNING GLORY family, native to the New World tropics. Raised mainly for human consumption, sweet potatoes are the most important tropical root crop and are grown in many varieties. Rich in VITAMIN A, they yield starch, flour, glucose, and alcohol. The sweet potato, which is unrelated to the POTATO, is often confused with the YAM, which belongs to another family.

**sweet William:** see PINK.

**swift,** name for small, swallowlike BIRDS of the family Apodidae, found worldwide, chiefly in the tropics. Swifts are the most rapid flying animals known. They feed and can even sleep on the wing, being the best adapted of all birds to an aerial life. The common swift (*Apus apus*) ranges across Europe and Asia. Nests of Oriental swiftlets (*Collocalia esculenta*), made entirely of a salivary secretion, are used in bird's-nest soup.

**Swift, Jonathan,** 1667–1745, English writer and master of SATIRE; b. Ireland. His early works were *The Battle of the Books,* upholding the superiority of the ancients to the moderns, and *Tale of a Tub,* a satire on religious excesses (both publ. 1704). Swift was active in Whig politics with ADDISON and STEELE, but turned against the party over its unfriendliness to the Anglican church. Pamphlets on ecclesiastical and political issues, in which he usually supported the Tories, engaged him from 1708 to 1714. In 1713 he joined the SCRIBLERUS CLUB and in 1714 was made dean of St Patrick's Cathedral, Dublin. He became a hero to the Irish with his *Drapier's Letters* (1724) and the savage *Modest Proposal* (1729), in which he ironically advocated the breeding of Irish babies to be fed to the rich as a means of reducing Ireland's poverty. His masterpiece, *Gulliver's Travels* (1726), a ruthless satire on human folly and 18th-cent. England, is unequalled in the intensity of its moralism. Ironically, it was later turned into an expurgated children's story.

**swimming,** self-propulsion through water, usually as a competitive sport or recreation. The principal swimming strokes are the crawl, backstroke, sidestroke, breaststroke, and butterfly. The crawl, or Australian crawl, is considered the speediest. In executing it, the body is prone and alternating overarm strokes are used. The backstroke is done in a supine position with alternate over-the-head strokes. The sidestroke entails a forward underwater stroke with the body on one side. The breaststroke is accomplished in a prone position using a frog kick and movement of the arms from a point in front of the head to shoulder level. The butterfly, the most difficult and exhausting stroke, is done in a prone position with a dolphin kick and a flail-like double arm movement. In freestyle swimming any stroke may be used, but the crawl is usually favoured. Swimming became organized as an amateur sport in the late 19th cent. It is a major Olympic event for both men and women. See also DIVING, SPRINGBOARD AND PLATFORM.

**Swinburne, Algernon Charles,** 1837–1909, English poet and critic. His first success, the poetic drama *Atalanta in Calydon* (1865), exhibited his talent for musical, sensuous language. The poems in *Poems and Ballads* (first series, 1866) were attacked by some for their sensuality and pagan and sadistic sentiments but lauded by others for their metrical skills. Swinburne's enthusiasm for Italian unification found expression in *A Song of Italy* (1867) and *Songs before Sunrise* (1871). His other poetic

works include a dramatic trilogy about Mary Queen of Scots (1865–81); the second series of *Poems and Ballads* (1878); and the long poem *Tristram of Lyonesse* (1882). His literary criticism was extensive, ranging from Marlowe to Blake. Because of his poor health, which had been weakened by epilepsy and alcoholism, he was cared for during the last 30 years of his life by Theodore Watts-Dunton.

**Swindon,** town (1981 pop. 127,348), Wiltshire, SW England, 113 km (70 mi) W of London. It is an important railway junction and market town. Industries found within the town include railway engineering and the manufacture of electronic equipment. Many new industries have been established in recent years. There is a railway museum in the town (est. 1962).

**swine:** see PIG.

**swine fever,** highly contagious viral disease of pigs, also called hog cholera. It is a notifiable disease, characterized by listlessness, high temperature, and convulsions. It causes high mortality, and is spread through contact and the use of infected swill. In the UK, import control regulations concerning the transport of pigs, boiling of swill, and a policy of slaughter of infected animals controls the disease. Some countries, e.g., the US, operate programmes of vaccination.

**swing music:** see JAZZ.

**Swiss Guards,** Swiss mercenaries who fought in various European armies from the 15th to the 19th cent. They were put at the disposal of foreign armies by the Swiss government in diplomatic treaties known as capitulations. They were especially important in the French army of LOUIS XIV and on the side of the royalists in the BOURBON Restoration. The Swiss banned all capitulations in 1874. Today the Swiss Guard exists only as the personal guard of the pope.

**switch,** electrical device having two states, on (or closed), and off (or open), and, ideally, having the property that when closed it offers a zero IMPEDANCE to a current and when open it offers infinite impedance to a current. For many operations, as in digital computers, the operation of mechanical switches, which move contacts together and apart, is too slow. When faster switching is required, a TRANSISTOR or vacuum tube is used, operated in such a way as to conduct either heavily or very little. See CIRCUIT BREAKER; RELAY.

**Switzerland,** Fr. *Suisse,* Ger. *Schweiz,* Ital. *Svizzera,* officially the **Swiss Confederation,** republic (1987 est. pop. 6,500,000), 41,287 km² (15,941 sq mi), central Europe; bordered by France (W), West Germany (N), Austria and Liechtenstein (E), and Italy (S). Major cities include BERN (the capital), ZÜRICH, BASEL, and GENEVA. The JURA Mts, in the NW, and the spectacular ALPS, in the S, occupy about 70% of the country's area. The Swiss Plateau, a narrow, hilly region between the two mountain ranges, has most of the country's population. The RHINE and RHÔNE rivers have their sources in Switzerland, and there are many lakes, among them GENEVA and CONSTANCE. With few natural resources (water power is a notable exception) and a largely barren soil, Switzerland has attained prosperity through technological skill and export manufacturing. Principal products are chemicals, pharmaceuticals, machinery, instruments, watches, jewellery, textiles, and foodstuffs (notably cheese and chocolate). Tourism and international banking are important sources of income. The GNP is $105,060 million and the GNP per capita is $16,390 (1983). German, French, Italian, and Romansh (a Rhaeto-Roman dialect) are the national languages. The population is about evenly divided between Roman Catholics and Protestants.

*History.* Conquered by Rome in 58 BC, the region that is modern Switzerland fell successively to Germanic tribes (5th cent. AD), Swabia and Burgundy (9th cent.), and the Holy Roman Empire (1033). By the 13th cent. the HABSBURGS controlled much of the region, and their encroachment on local privileges led to the formation of a defence league (1291), the basis of the Swiss confederation, by the cantons, or states, of Uri, Schwyz, and Unterwalden. Later, other cantons joined the league, and wars against the Habsburgs resulted in virtual independence in 1499. The loose Swiss confederation was seriously split in the 16th cent. by the REFORMATION (see CALVIN, JOHN; ZWINGLI), and religious civil wars racked the country for almost two centuries. However, Switzerland remained neutral in the Thirty Years War, and its independence was recognized in the Peace of Westphalia in 1648. In 1798, during the French Revolution, French armies swept into Switzerland and established the Helvetic Republic. The confederation was substantially restored in 1815 by the

Congress of VIENNA, which also guaranteed Switzerland's perpetual neutrality. In 1847 a brief and almost bloodless civil war resulted in the transformation of Switzerland into a more centralized federal state. Armed neutrality was maintained throughout both world wars. In 1981 the Swiss government took the first steps toward seeking UN membership, but in 1986 the electorate voted heavily against in a national referendum. Since 1959 Switzerland has been ruled by a coalition of the Social Democratic, Radical Democratic, Christian Democratic, and Swiss People's parties.

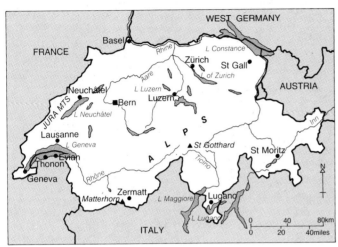

Switzerland

**sword,** weapon used in personal combat; it consists of a blade with a sharp point and one or two cutting edges, set in a hilt (handle) and usually protected by a metal case or cross guard. It developed from the dagger early in the Bronze Age. Blade materials evolved from iron to steel to finely tempered steel. Short swords with two cutting edges were used by the Greeks and Romans; very large, two-handed ones were favoured by medieval knights. Well-known swords have included the curved scimitar of the Persians and Arabs and the long, single-edge Japanese SAMURAI sword set in a long hilt. Other types are the curved sabre, favoured by European CAVALRY, and the épée, or duelling sword, a straight, narrow, and stiff thrusting weapon without cutting edges. Obsolete as a military weapon, the sword still plays a part in military ceremonies. See FENCING.

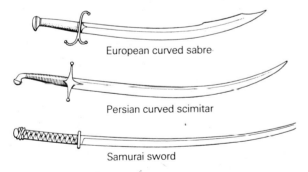

European curved sabre

Persian curved scimitar

Samurai sword

Sword

**swordfish,** large food and game FISH (*Xiphias gladius*) of warmer Atlantic and Pacific waters, related to the sailfish and MARLIN.

**sycamore:** see MAPLE.

**Sydenham, Thomas,** 1624–89, English physician. A founder of modern clinical medicine and epidemiology, he conceptualized the causes and treatments of epidemics and provided classic descriptions of gout, smallpox, malaria, scarlet fever, hysteria, and chorea. He advocated observation instead of the theories of GALEN to determine the nature of disease and introduced the use of cinchona bark (containing quinine) to treat malaria and of laudanum to treat other diseases.

**Sydenham's chorea:** see under CHOREA.

Swordfish

**Sydney,** city (1986 pop. 2,989,070), capital of New South Wales, E Australia, surounding Port Jackson inlet, on the Pacific Ocean. It is Australia's largest city, chief port, and main cultural and industrial centre. Manufactures include ships, refined petroleum, chemicals, textiles, and motor vehicles. Sydney Harbour and Port Botany are the main ports. Founded as a penal colony in 1788, Sydney is Australia's oldest settlement. Its population surged during the Australian gold rushes of the 1850s. Sydney replaced MELBOURNE as the nation's largest population centre after World War II. Landmarks include the Sydney Harbour Bridge (1932); the Gladesville Bridge (1964); the modernistic Sydney Opera House complex (1973); and the Centrepoint Tower (1981), Australia's tallest building. The city has three universities, Univ. of Sydney, Univ. of New South Wales, and Macquarie Univ., and several museums, including the National Gallery of Art and the Australia Museum.

**Sydney, Sir Philip:** see SIDNEY, SIR PHILIP.

**Syed Ahmad Khan, Sir,** 1817–98, major Indian Muslim modernist and educationist of the 19th cent. He tried to assimilate natural scientific knowledge into the framework of Islamic notions, and was very close to Muhammad ABDUH in his modernist style, but was bitterly attacked by Jamaluddin AFGHANI for his cooperation with the British.

**Sylla, Lucius Cornelius:** see SULLA, LUCIUS CORNELIUS.

**syllogism** (ˌsiləjizəm), in LOGIC, a mode of argument that forms the core of the body of Western logical thought, consisting of a sequence of three propositions such that the first two imply the conclusion. ARISTOTLE's formulations of syllogistic logic held sway in the Western world for over 2000 years. The categorical syllogism comprises three categorical propositions, statements of the form *all A are B, no A are B, some A are B* or *some A are not B*. A categorical syllogism contains precisely three terms: the major term, which is the predicate of the conclusion; the minor term, which is the subject of the conclusion; and the middle term, which appears in both premises but not in the conclusion.

**Sylvester, James Joseph,** 1814–97, English mathematician. He taught in both England and the US, and founded the *American Journal of Mathematics.* Sylvester is known for his work on algebraic invariants, matrices, determinants, and number theory, much of it in collaboration with Arthur CAYLEY.

**Sylvester II,** d. 1003, pope (999–1003), a Frenchman named Gerbert. Widely celebrated for his learning, he taught the Holy Roman Emperor OTTO III, who aided his election to the papacy. Sylvester energetically supported the Christianization of Poland and Hungary. He was the first French pope.

**symbiosis,** habitual cohabitation of organisms of different species. The term usually applies to a dependent relationship that is beneficial to both members (also called mutualism). Symbiosis includes parasitism, a relationship in which the PARASITE depends on and may injure its host; COMMENSALISM, an independent and mutually beneficial relationship; and helotism, a master–slave relationship found among social animals. Symbiosis may occur between two kinds of plants (e.g., LICHEN-forming alga and fungus), two kinds of animals (e.g., herbivores and cellulose-digesting gut microorganisms), or a plant and an animal (e.g., FIG and fig wasp).

**symbol,** a sign which is taken to represent some other phenomenon, the connection being culturally specific and meaningful. Symbols play an extremely important part in RITUAL and religious practices. Anthropologists have been particularly concerned with the social meaning underlying symbols and the ways in which these are communicated. Symbols can be considered as texts constructed from social phenomena, which have to be understood in relation to natural and emotional meanings, or they may be seen as formal closed structures whose meaning comes from their relations with each other. Psychologists (e.g., FREUD, JUNG) have been concerned to elucidate the meaning of symbols within the individual's subconscious and conscious mind.

**symbolic logic:** see LOGIC.

**symbolists,** in literature, school that originated in late-19th-cent. France in opposition to the NATURALISM and REALISM of the period. Symbolism sought to convey impressions by suggestion rather than by direct statement, and it spread from poetry to the other arts. Experiments with FREE VERSE outlived symbolism itself. BAUDELAIRE was the greatest precursor of the movement, which included the poets MALLARMÉ, RIMBAUD, VERLAINE, and, later, CLAUDEL and VALÉRY; MAETERLINCK in drama; and DEBUSSY in music. Symbolism influenced the decadents and IMAGISTS, as well as major 20th-cent. British and American poets like T.S. ELIOT and Wallace STEVENS.

**sympathetic nervous system:** see NERVOUS SYSTEM.

**symphonic poem,** type of one-movement orchestral composition created by Franz LISZT; also called **tone poem.** Based on an idea or theme from a poetic, dramatic, or other nonmusical artistic source, it often 'tells a story', as in Liszt's *Les Préludes;* Richard STRAUSS's *Don Juan;* or RESPIGHI's *Pines of Rome;* or may simply be the impressionistic portrayal of the theme, as in DEBUSSY's *Afternoon of a Faun.*

**symphony,** a major work for orchestra with one or more movements in sonata form (see under SONATA). The Italian operatic overture, called sinfonia, was standardized by Alessandro SCARLATTI at the end of the 17th cent. into three sections (fast, slow, fast). In the 18th cent. HAYDN and MOZART synthesized all preceding techniques into the Viennese classical symphony, consisting of four movements (fast; slow; a dance, e.g., minuet; fast finale, e.g., rondo). BEETHOVEN expanded the dimensions of this form, bringing in ROMANTICISM and intensifying the element of personal expression; he pioneered the use of a CHORUS in the symphony. The classical ideal continued in the symphonies of SCHUBERT, MENDELSSOHN, and SCHUMANN, but interpreted with varying degrees of romanticism. Reacting against the romantic orchestral style, BRAHMS revived the classical model as defined by Beethoven. BRUCKNER combined classical form with Wagnerian harmonies and melodic structure (see WAGNER, RICHARD). Other important composers were DVOŘÁK and TCHAIKOVSKY, in the 19th cent., and MAHLER and SIBELIUS in the 20th cent. Composers such as STRAVINSKY and HINDEMITH have treated the symphony form with much freedom, whilst VAUGHAN WILLIAMS, Carl NIELSEN and Dmitry SHOSTAKOVICH have composed in a more traditional form but modern style.

**synagogue** [from Gr., = assembly], place of assembly for Jewish worship. The institution probably dates from the Babylonian exile (6th cent. BC). By the 1st cent. AD it had become the centre of Jewish religious, intellectual, and communal life. The destruction of the Temple in AD 70 and the dispersion of the Jews increased the synagogue's importance. In modern times, in the West, its central role has shifted to purely religious activities, although recently that trend has been somewhat reversed. In the US, the Orthodox, Conservative, and Reform synagogue associations are organized in the Synagogue Council of America. See also JUDAISM.

**synchrocyclotron:** see PARTICLE ACCELERATOR.

**synchronous motor:** see MOTOR, ELECTRIC.

**synchrotron:** see PARTICLE ACCELERATOR.

**syncline:** see FOLD.

**syndicalism,** economic and political doctrine that advocates decentralized control of the means of production by organized bodies of workers. Syndicalists view any form of state as an instrument of oppression and believe that the trade union should be the basic organization unit of society. They advocate direct action such as the general STRIKE and industrial sabotage. Syndicalism, especially strong in France and Italy, declined after World War I because of competition from Communist unions, government suppression, and political splits.

**Synge, (Edmund) John Millington** (sing), 1871–1909, Irish playwright. Winning accolades for his musicianship and command of languages as a student, Synge did not begin his first play until 1900. At that time he suffered from Hodgkin's disease of which he was to die only nine years later. His many annual visits to Wicklow and his sojourn, at W.B. YEATS's advice, on the Aran Isles produced the material and language for *Riders To The Sea* (1902). His other works include *Shadow of the Glen* (1902), *The Tinker's Wedding* (1902), and *The Playboy of the Western World* (1907), this last being greeted by a week of riots in Dublin.

**synodic period,** length of time it takes a solar-system body to return to an identical alignment (e.g., conjunction or opposition; see SYZYGY) with another body as seen from the Earth. Because the Earth moves in its orbit around the Sun, the synodic period differs from the **sidereal period,** the length of time a body takes to complete an orbit relative to background stars.

**synonym** [Gr., = having the same name], word having a meaning that is the same as or very similar to the meaning of another word in the same language. Some are alike in certain meanings only, as *live* and *dwell.*

**Synoptic Gospels:** see GOSPEL.

**syntax:** see GRAMMAR.

**synthesizer:** see ELECTRONIC MUSIC.

**synthetic elements,** radioactive chemical elements discovered not in nature but as artificially produced isotopes. They are TECHNETIUM, PROMETHIUM, ASTATINE, FRANCIUM, and the TRANSURANIC ELEMENTS. Some have since been found to exist in small amounts in nature as short-lived members of natural radioactive decay series (see RADIOACTIVITY).

**synthetic textile fibres,** artificial fibres (see FIBRE) produced industrially by either synthesizing POLYMERS or altering natural fibres (see RAYON). Polyesters, e.g., Dacron, produced by the polymerization of the product of an alcohol and organic-acid reaction, are strong and wrinkle-resistant. Nylon, a synthetic thermoplastic material introduced in 1938, is strong, elastic, resistant to abrasion and chemicals, and low in moisture absorbency. It was produced in large quantities during World War II for parachutes, when silk could not be obtained. Orlon, the trade name for a polyacrylonitrile fibre made from natural gas, oxygen, and nitrogen, combines bulk, light weight, and resistance to acids and sun. Vinyl fibres are also widely used. See also FIBRE GLASS.

**syphilis,** formerly the most serious VENEREAL DISEASE, caused by the spirochaete bacterium *Treponema pallidum.* It is most commonly transmitted by sexual contact, although transmission can occur through infected blood or an open wound, or from mother to fetus. The primary stage of syphilis is characterized by a chancre, a superficial skin ULCER (which is often overlooked), at the site of infection; secondary syphilis (weeks or months later), by generalized eruption of the skin and mucous membranes and inflammation of eyes, bones, and central nervous system; tertiary (which may occur after many years), by chronic skin lesions, damage to the heart and aorta, and central nervous system degeneration. The patient is infectious during the first two stages. Syphilis is treated with PENICILLIN, usually successfully unless extensive nervous system damage has occurred.

**Syracuse,** city (1984 pop. 119,242), SE Sicily, Italy, on the Ionian Sea. Founded (734 BC) by Corinthian Greeks, it became the leading city of ancient Sicily under the tyrant Gelon, who defeated CARTHAGE in 480 BC. It was a centre of Greek culture (AESCHYLUS, PINDAR, THEOCRITUS, and ARCHIMEDES lived there) under several tyrants, e.g., Hiero I and II, DIONYSUS THE ELDER, DIONYSUS THE YOUNGER, and DION OF SYRACUSE, whose reigns alternated with periods of democracy. Syracuse defeated Athens (414 BC), reached its height, then fell to Rome (212 BC) and declined. It was later conquered by Arabs (9th cent.) and Normans (1085). Numerous ruins testify to its past greatness.

**Syr Darya,** one of the principal rivers of arid Soviet Central Asia, c.2220 km (1380 mi) long, used extensively for irrigation. It is formed in the FERGANA VALLEY, E Uzbek SSR, by the confluence of the Naryn and Kara Darya rivers (which rise in the snowy Tien Shan Mts) and flows generally NW along the edge of the KYZYL-KUM desert to the N end of the ARAL SEA. Additional water was to be diverted to it from the IRTYSH R. through a canal planned in the early 1980s.

**Syria**, officially the Syrian Arab Republic, republic (1986 est. pop. 10,300,000), 185,100 km² (71,467 sq mi), SW Asia, bordered by Israel, Lebanon, and the Mediterranean Sea (W), Turkey (N), Iraq (E), and Jordan (S). Principal cities include DAMASCUS (the capital) and ALEPPO. Most of Syria is occupied by the Syrian Desert, which is crossed by the EUPHRATES R. In the west are the Anti-Lebanon Mts, including Mt Hermon (2814 m/9232 ft), Syria's highest point; in the southwest the fertile plain of Hawran extends from the Jabal ad Duruz Mts to the Sea of GALILEE. The climate of Syria grades from a Mediterranean type with winter rain in the west (with snow on the mountains) to hot desert in the east. In the northeast, the Jazira, or land between the Euphrates and Tigris rivers has sufficient winter rain for the growth of cereals. Despite a large-scale industrialization programme begun after World War II, Syria is still predominantly agricultural; major crops are wheat, cotton, vegetables, fruits, and tobacco. Textiles, processed foods, and cement are the chief manufactures. Petroleum production in the Jezira is small compared to that of other Middle Eastern countries but provides the leading export. The state plays a major role in the economy. The Euphrates Dam at Tabqa, completed in 1976 with Soviet aid, supplies 95% of the nation's electric power. The GNP is US$19,140 million and the GNP per capita is US$1930 (1984). Most Syrians are Arabic-speaking Muslims, mainly Sunnites, including Shia and Alawites, but there are Kurdish, Turkoman, Armenian, and Circassian minorities. Christian Orthodox churches claim nearly a million members, and there are 120,000 DRUZE in the south.

*History.* Situated on trade and military routes between the Mediterranean and Mesopotamia, Syria (which historically included all of modern Syria and Lebanon, and parts of Israel, Jordan, Iraq, and Saudi Arabia) has always been an object of foreign conquest. Settled (c.2100 BC) by the Amorites, a Semitic people from the Arabian peninsula, it fell to the HITTITES (15th–13th cent BC), the Assyrians and Babylonians (11th–6th cent. BC), the Persians (6th–4th cent. BC), and the Greeks (333 BC). Syria was Hellenized by the Seleucids and had fallen to Rome by 63 BC After a period of Byzantine rule (5th–7th cent. AD) Syria was conquered (633–40) by Muslim Arabs. Most Syrians converted to Islam, and Damascus, as the usual capital of the Umayyad caliph (661–750), became the centre of the Islamic world. The area was later ruled by the Seljuk Turks, SALADIN, the MONGOLS, and the MAMELUKES. Christians also came to Syria on the CRUSADES (11th–14th cent.). It was part of the OTTOMAN EMPIRE from 1516 until the end of WORLD WAR I, and in 1920 France received a League of Nations mandate over the Levant States (roughly modern Syria and Lebanon). During WORLD WAR II Free French forces granted (1941) independence to Syria, but French troops did not leave until 1946. Syria joined with Egypt in the UNITED ARAB REPUBLIC in 1958, but withdrew in 1961. Independent Syria has been characterized by economic growth, political instability, and uncompromising hostility toward Israel (see ARAB-ISRAELI WARS). In 1981 Israel exacerbated the situation by annexing the GOLAN HEIGHTS, captured from Syria in the Six-Day War (1967). Syrian troops entered Lebanon in 1976, ostensibly to quell civil strife there, and during the 1982 Israeli invasion of Lebanon they suffered severe losses in combat with Israeli forces. The ruling Baath Arab Socialist Party (Syrian section), which came to power in a 1963 coup, maintains a policy combining socialism and Arab nationalism. In the early 1980s Syria experienced much internal unrest, moved closer to the USSR, and espoused hard-line radical Arab positions. In office since 1971, Pres. Hafez al-ASSAD is also president of the four-party National Progressive Front dominated by the Baath.

**Syriac** (ˌsiriˈak), late dialect of ARAMAIC, which is a Hamito-Semitic language. See LANGUAGE (table).

**syzygy** (ˌsiziji), alignment of three celestial bodies along a straight or nearly straight line. Viewed from one of these bodies, the other two will be either in conjunction (aligned in the same direction) or in opposition (aligned on opposite sides of the sky). An inferior planet, whose orbit lies inside the Earth's, can, in reference to the Sun as seen from the Earth, be either in inferior conjunction (lying directly between the Earth and the Sun) or in superior conjunction (on the opposite side of the Sun from the Earth); unlike a superior planet, whose orbit lies outside the Earth's, and unlike the Moon, it can never be in opposition to the Sun as seen from the Earth. See also ELONGATION.

**Szatmar, Peace of:** see RÁKÓCZY, FRANCIS II.

**Szczecin** (ˌshchetseen), Ger. *Stettin*, city (1984 pop. 384,000), NW Poland, on the Oder R., former capital of the Prussian province of

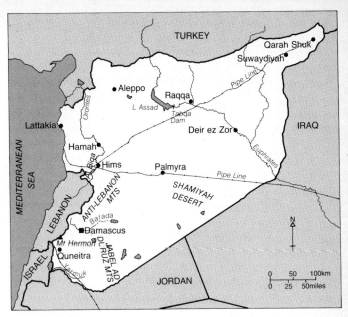

Syria

POMERANIA. It is a major Baltic port and an industrial centre with shipyards, ironworks, and chemical plants. A member of the HANSEATIC LEAGUE from the 13th cent., the city was ruled (1648–1720) by Sweden and then passed to Prussia. In 1945 it was transferred to Poland, and its German population was expelled and replaced by Poles.

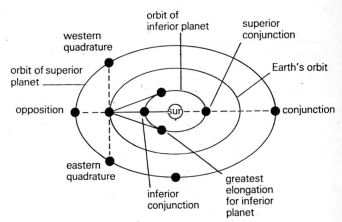

Alignments of celestial bodies necessary to produce **syzygy** (opposition, inferior conjunction, and superior conjunction) and quadrature conditions

**Szechwan:** see SICHUAN.

**Szeged** (ˌseged), city (1985 pop. 181,000), SE Hungary, on the Tisza R. Its industries include food-processing and textiles. The city, once a defensive stronghold, was rebuilt after destructive floods in 1879.

**Székely,** ethnic minority of Romania, concentrated in Transylvania. The Székely, who had adopted the MAGYAR language by the 11th cent., today number c.400,000 and differ little from the Hungarians. In TRANSYLVANIA they were regarded by the Hungarian crown as noble and were exempted from taxation. In the 16th cent. most converted from the ROMAN CATHOLIC CHURCH to CALVINISM. When the Austrians tried to impress them into service as a border militia their resistance resulted (1763) in a massacre. Székely autonomy ended after the REVOLUTIONS OF 1848.

**Székesfehérvár,** city (1985 pop. 110,000), central Hungary. It has an aluminium-rolling industry. Of Roman foundation, it was an early capital of the Hungarian nation, Hungarian kings being crowned here between 1027 and 1527.

**Szent-Györgyi, Albert von** (ˈsent-dyøːədyi), 1893–, American biochemist; b. Hungary. For his studies of biological oxidations and his discovery of ascorbic acid in adrenal glands, he received the 1937 Nobel Prize for physiology or medicine. He studied muscle chemistry, discovered the protein actin in MUSCLE, and was the first to isolate vitamin C.

**Szilard, Leo** (‚silahnd), 1898–1964, Hungarian nuclear physicist and biophysicist; emigrated to US in 1937. Working with Enrico FERMI at the Univ. of Chicago, he developed the first self-sustained nuclear reactor based on uranium fission. One of the first to realize that nuclear chain reactions could be used in bombs, and instrumental in urging the US government to create the first atomic bomb, he later actively opposed nuclear confrontation.

**Szymanowski, Karol (Maciej)** (shimə‚novskee), 1882–1937, Polish composer. His early works were influenced by BRAHMS and STRAUSS, but in compositions such as *Songs of a Fairy-Tale Princess* (1915) and the opera *King Roger* (1924), he used exotic themes and an ornate chromatic style. In the newly independent Poland of the 1920s, however, he began to draw on folk sources for works such as his *Stabat Mater* (1925–26). His later works built on these Polish foundations, but in large, abstract forms: the Second Quartet (1927) and the Second Violin Concerto (1932-33).

**Ta,** chemical symbol of the element TANTALUM.

**Taaffe, Eduard, Graf von** (ˌtahfə), 1833–95, Austrian premier (1868–70, 1879–93), of Irish descent. His efforts to reconcile the many nationalities within the Austro-Hungarian empire brought 14 years of relative calm and prosperity.

**Tabari, Muhammad Ibn Jarir,** 839?–923, Muslim scholar and jurist. He was the author of a monumental Universal History, from Creation up to his own day, which embodies, in its account of the CALIPHATE, the richest collection of reports according to the manner of the traditionists. He was also the author of the foremost philological and historical study of the KORAN.

**tablature,** in music, name for various systems of musical notation in use in Europe from the 15th to 17th cent. for keyboard and lute music and in Chinese, Japanese, and Korean musics for a much longer period. These systems used letters, numbers, or symbols to indicate PITCH and duration of tone. Lute tablatures have lines representing the strings of the lute, with numbers or letters to indicate the position for stopping the string. Tablatures are used today to notate music for guitar and ukelele. These have vertical lines representing strings of the instrument, horizontal lines for the frets, and dots to show the position of the fingers. See also STRINGED INSTRUMENTS.

**table tennis,** ball and racket game, basically a miniature form of TENNIS. It is also called ping-pong, a trade name. The game is played on a table that measures 2.74 by 1.52 m (9 by 5 ft). A transverse net 15.24 cm (6 in) high divides the surface. Players use a round-bladed bat to hit the small celluloid ball. A point is scored when a service is foul or a player fails to return a ball properly. The game originated in the late 19th cent. and was first popularized by Cambridge undergraduates. It is a major competitive sport in China and other countries in the Far East.

**taboo** or **tabu,** a prohibition (usually sacred) against contact with particular persons, things, or places. Things which have been categorized as taboo have been seen as those which do not fit neatly into any culturally acceptable classificatory system, and therefore are anomalous and potentially dangerous. See also POLLUTION.

**Tábor,** town (1984 pop. c.20,000), Bohemia, Czechoslovakia. Founded in 1420 by John Žižk (Zizka), it took its name from Mt Tabor in Palestine. Its narrow streets testify to its defensive role as a Hussite stronghold. Relics of the Hussite period are kept in the 16th-cent. town hall.

**Tabora,** town (1987 est. pop. 29,000), capital of the administrative region of W Tanzania. Founded by the Arabs in 1820, it is a trading centre on the railway line 692 km (430 mi) west-northwest of DAR-ES-SALAAM.

**Tabriz,** city (1982 est. pop. 853,300), NW Iran, on the Aji Chai (Talkheh) R. It is Iran's third city and the capital of AZERBAIJAN prov., and is an important commercial, industrial, and transport centre. Tabriz, then known as Tauris, was (3rd cent. AD) the capital of Armenia under King Tiridates III. It was sacked (c.1029) by the Oghuz Turks and captured (1054) by the Seljuk Turks. The city prospered under the Mongols (13th–14th cent.), and in 1514 it was taken by the Ottoman Turks. Owing to frequent earthquakes, Tabriz has only a few historic sites, e.g., the Blue Mosque (15th cent.).

**tachism** (ˌtashiz(ə)m) [Fr. tache = spot], a term used in 1954 by a French critic to define European lyrical abstraction in which the spontaneous formation of blots and dashes of colour stood as signs or gestures of the artist's creative impulse. Its American equivalent is the abstract expressionism of J. POLLOCK.

**Tacitus** (ˌtasi'tus), (Cornelius Tacitus), AD c.55–c.117, Roman historian. His minor works—a *Dialogue on Oratory*, a biography of his father-in-law *Agricola*, and a monograph on the land and tribes of *Germania* (Germany)—already show an interest in moral issues and the decline of standards since the old Republic. Of the *Histories*, four books and a fragment survive, covering AD 69, the disastrous Year of the Four Emperors (Galba, Otho, Vitellius, and VESPASIAN) and the beginning of 70. The 12 (wholly or partly) surviving books of the *Annals* cover most of the reigns of TIBERIUS, CLAUDIUS, and NERO. He presents, in striking literary style, a very individual study of the power of emperors, and its effect on those who wield it and those who suffer it.

**Tacoma,** US city (1984 est. pop. 159,000), W Washington, on Commencement Bay and the Puget Sound; inc. 1884. It is a seaport and rail terminus, and one of the Northwest's leading industrial cities. Wood and paper products, boats, and chemicals are important manufactures. Beautifully situated between bay and mountains, with Mt Rainier in sight, Tacoma has a mild climate and draws many tourists.

**tadpole,** larval, aquatic stage of AMPHIBIANS. Hatching from the egg, the tadpole is gill-breathing and legless and propels itself by means of a tail. During METAMORPHOSIS it develops lungs, legs, and other adult organs and, in the FROG and TOAD, loses the tail.

**Tadzhik Soviet Socialist Republic** or **Tadzhikistan** (tah,jik, tah'jiki,stahn), constituent republic (1985 pop. 4,500,000), 143,100 km² (55,251 sq mi), Soviet Central Asia. It borders China (E); Afghanistan (S); the Kirghiz SSR (N); and the Uzbek SSR (W, NW). The capital is DUSHANBE. This largely mountainous region in the Pamir–Altai System has the USSR's highest peak, Mt Communism (7495 m/24,590ft). Relatively flat plains, but still over 3000 m (9800 ft) above sea level, are on the Syr Darya R. in the N, and the Amu Darya R. in the S. Agriculture is important in the economy, with cotton-growing and stock-raising being the chief activities. Mining, engineering, food-processing, textiles, clothing manufacture, and silk production are among the main industries. Hydroelectricity and irrigation are important. The majority of the population are Tadzhiks, a Sunni Muslim Iranian people; Uzbeks are the leading minority. The Tadzhiks were successful in farming, crafts, and trade by the 9th cent. Between the 13th and 19th cent. they were ruled by the Mongols, Uzbeks, and Russians. Their territory became part of the USSR in 1924.

**Taegu** (ˌtiegooh), city (1984 pop. 2,012,039), S South Korea. A railway junction and marketplace for an extensive agricultural and mining region, Taegu also has important textile industries. It was a major bastion for UN forces during the KOREAN WAR and served as the temporary capital of Korea.

**Taejon,** city (1984 pop. 842,429), capital of Chungchong Namdo prov., W central South Korea. It is an important transport centre on the railway running S from Seoul, and a growing industrial area with cotton thread and cloth factories and a large government printing plant. Taejon, also known as Daejeon, is a relatively new city as it was almost totally destroyed during the KOREAN WAR.

**Taft, William Howard,** 1857–1930, 27th president of the US (1909–13) and 10th chief justice of the US Supreme Court (1921–30).

He was secretary of war (1904–08) and a close adviser to Pres. Theodore ROOSEVELT. Running as Roosevelt's successor in 1908, he defeated William Jennings BRYAN. He continued Roosevelt's policies, e.g., 'trust busting', railway regulation, and conservation, and, in Latin America, 'dollar diplomacy', but he was more conservative than Roosevelt and antagonized the progressive elements in his party (see PROGRESSIVISM). His relations with Roosevelt deteriorated, and in 1912 he found himself running for reelection against his former mentor, who had formed the PROGRESSIVE (Bull Moose) PARTY. The Republican vote was split, and the Democratic candidate, Woodrow WILSON, won. Taft was appointed (1921) chief justice by Pres. HARDING; his chief contribution to the court was his administrative efficiency. His son, **Robert Alphonso Taft,** 1889–1953, was a US senator from Ohio (1938–53) and the leader of conservative Republicans. An opponent of Pres. F.D. ROOSEVELT's New Deal, he was a leading advocate of isolationism before World War II. He helped write the Taft–Hartley Labor Act (1947). He strongly opposed postwar Democratic policies, voting against ratification of the North Atlantic Treaty Organization (NATO) and condemning the Korean and China policies of the Truman administration.

**Tagalog language.** see MALAYO-POLYNESIAN LANGUAGES.

**Taglioni, Maria,** 1804–84, Swedish/Italian ballet dancer. She had great success in *La Sylphide* (1832) at the Paris Opera. With her ethereal style and high elevations, she was considered the major ballerina of the Romantic period.

**Tagore, Rabindranath** (ta͵gawr), 1861–1941, Indian poet, novelist, playwright, essayist, composer, and painter. Tagore is the most famous literary figure of modern India. He was awarded the Nobel Prize for literature in 1913 for a collection of his poems, *Gitanjali.* The national anthems of India, Bangladesh, and Sri Lanka were written by him. He was one of the ideologues of Indian nationalism in the early years of the century and renounced the knighthood conferred by the British after the Jallianwalabagh massacre. *Viswabharati* at Santiniketan (W Bengal) was established by the poet as a centre for universal learning.

**Tagus,** river, 900 km (565 mi) in length, the longest in the Iberian Peninsula. Rising in the Montes Universales, it flows W through central Spain, along a portion of the Spanish–Portuguese border, and across Portugal to enter the Atlantic Ocean at LISBON.

**Tahiti,** island (1977 pop. 95,604), 1041 km² (402 sq mi), S Pacific, in the Society Islands, FRENCH POLYNESIA. The capital is Papeete. It relies on tourism and produces vanilla, fruits, and copra. Settled by Polynesians (14th cent.), it was visited in the 18th cent. by Capt. James COOK and Lt William BLIGH. It became French in 1843. GAUGUIN painted his best-known works there.

**taiga** (͵tiegə), northern coniferous-forest belt of Eurasia, bordered on the north by the treeless TUNDRA and on the south by the STEPPE, comprising about one-third of the world's forest land. The climate is characterized by long, severe winters and short summers. The principal species of trees are cedar, pine, spruce, larch, birch, and aspen.

**Taine, Hippolyte Adolphe** (ten), 1828–93, French critic and historian. His deterministic theories, viewing the individual as the product of heredity and environment, became the theoretical basis of NATURALISM. His sociohistorical method of analysis influenced philosophy, aesthetics, literary criticism, and the social sciences. Works include *On Intelligence* (1870) and *The Origins of Contemporary France* (1876–93).

**Taipei,** city (1985 pop. 2,663,683), N Taiwan, capital of TAIWAN and provisional capital of the Republic of China. Taiwan's largest city, it is the political, cultural, and industrial centre of the island. Important manufactures include motor vehicles, fertilizer, cement, and paper. Developed under Japanese rule (1895–1945), Taipei became the headquarters of Chiang Kai-Shek's Nationalists when they fled the mainland of China in 1949.

**Taiping Rebellion,** 1850–64, revolt against the Qing dynasty of China. It was led by Hong Xiuquan, a visionary who evolved a political creed including derived elements of Protestantism. His object was to found a new dynasty, the Taiping [great peace]. In 1853 the rebels captured Nanking and made it their capital. They were finally defeated by new provincial armies and aid from the Western powers. An army led by C.G. GORDON successfully defended Shanghai.

**Tai Shan,** Taoist sacred mountain in China, near JI'NAN in Shandong prov. In ancient Chinese cosmology, the Sun began its westward journey from Tai Shan. Chinese emperors periodically ascended the peak to offer sacrifices to Heaven and Earth. It has long been a place of pilgrimage and is now a major tourist site.

**Taiwan** or **Formosa,** island (1985 pop. 19,313,825), 35,961 km² (13,885 sq mi), in the Pacific Ocean, separated from the mainland of S China by the 161 km (100 mi) wide Taiwan (or Formosa) Strait. Together with the PENGHU DAO and MAZU DAO AND JINMEN DAO, it is officially known as the Republic of China. The capital is TAIPEI. Other major cities include KAOHSIUNG Tainan, Taichung, and Chilung. About a quarter of Taiwan's land area is cultivated; rice, wheat, sugarcane, and sweet potatoes are the most important crops. In the 1970s industry replaced agriculture as the major export earner. Light industry is the major manufacturing sector, with electronics and textiles predominating and providing a major market for the world. The majority of Taiwanese are ethnic (Han) Chinese who began to emigrate to Taiwan in the 15th cent. A small number (about 265,000) are Kiaoshan aborigines. First settled by the Chinese in the 7th cent., the island was reached by the Portuguese in 1590. It was held by the Dutch by the 1640s, and by China's Ch'ing dynasty in 1683. Occupied by Japan after the First Sino-Japanese War (1894–95), Taiwan remained in Japanese hands until 1945. When Chiang Kai-Shek and the Nationalists were ousted (1949) from mainland CHINA by the Communists, they shifted the seat of their government to Taiwan. The US long supported and aided the Nationalists, but in the 1970s Taiwan's international position was eroded. In 1971 it lost China's seat in the UN to the People's Republic of China, and in 1979 the US broke diplomatic relations with the Nationalists to establish relations with the People's Republic of China. Although Taiwan has regained some US support in the 1980s, Beijing has achieved international acceptance of its 'one China' policy and vigorously defends it. The People's Republic of China now offers Taiwan a settlement similar to that agreed on for Hong Kong. On his death in 1975 Chiang Kai-shek was succeeded by his eldest son Chiang Ching-kuo as chairman of the ruling Kuomintang Party and, in 1977, as president of Taiwan. He instituted a partial democratization of the political system, but himself died in 1988, being succeeded as president and Kuomintang chairman by Lee Teng-hui.

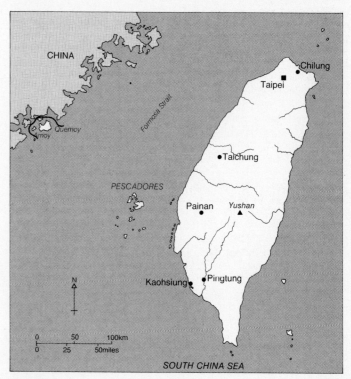

Taiwan

**Taiyuan** (͵tie-yooh͵ahn), city (1984 pop. 2,296,800), capital of SHANXI prov., N China. One of the world's richest coal and iron areas, its major industries are coal mining and steel production, with growing textile and chemicals sectors. Now a major communications centre, in the past Taiyuan has been a strategic garrison between Chinese culture and the nomadic peoples to the west.

**Taj Mahal,** MAUSOLEUM, Agra, N India, the finest example of late Indian Muslim architecture. The Mughal emperor Shah Jahan ordered it after the death (1629) of his wife, Mumtaz Mahal. Designed by a Turkish architect, it was built (1630–48) in a walled garden with an oblong reflecting pool. The white marble exterior is inlaid with semiprecious stones, floral designs, and arabesques. The dome, 24.4 m (80 ft) high and more than 15 m (50 ft) in diameter inside, forms a bulb outside, tapering to a spire topped by a crescent. The octagonal tomb chamber is lit by light passing through intricately carved screens.

Taj Mahal

**takahe:** see COOT.

**Takeshita, Noboru,** 1924–, Japanese politician and prime minister (1987–89). He entered the Diet in 1948 representing the (conservative) Liberal-Democratic Party, holding various government posts, including that of finance minister (1979–86). He succeeded Yasuhiro NAKASONE as prime minister but resigned in 1989 amidst allegations of financial corruption.

**Talbot, William Henry Fox,** 1800–77, English inventor of photographic processes. From 1839 on he patented methods of making negatives and prints, known as calotypes. His book *The Pencil of Nature* (1844) is illustrated with photographs.

**talc,** hydrous magnesium silicate mineral [$Mg_3Si_4O_{10}(OH)_2$], translucent to opaque, occurring in a range of colours and having a greasy, soapy feel. It is found in thin layers and in granular and fine-grained masses. SOAPSTONE is a granular form of talc. Important sources include Austria, Canada, India, the US, and the USSR. Talc is used in making paper (as a filler), paints, powders, soap, lubricants, linoleum, electrical insulation, and pottery.

**Talien:** see DALIAN.

**tallage,** under FEUDALISM, a tax much like AID. In Norman England it partly replaced the DANEGELD. Kings and lords levied it on the towns within their demesne lands, but it was resisted and disappeared (c.1340) under Edward III. In France the upper classes were exempt from tallage, called the *taille,* and the burden of it fell mainly on peasants.

**Tallahassee,** US city (1980 pop. 81,548), state capital of Florida, inc. 1825. State government and state universities are the major employers; wood products and processed food are manufactured. Tallahassee, in a hilly, picturesque area, is noted for its old homes and antebellum charm.

'The Open Door', a calotype from *The Pencil of Nature* (1844) by Fox Talbot

**Talleyrand** or **Talleyrand-Périgord, Charles Maurice de** (ˌtaleeˈrand), 1754–1838, French statesman and diplomat. Despite his notorious impiety, he was made (1789) bishop of Autun and was a representive of the clergy at the STATES-GENERAL of 1789. He supported the FRENCH REVOLUTION at first, but after the fall of the monarchy fled to England (1792) and then to the US (1794). Returning to France (1796), he was foreign minister under the DIRECTORY (1797–99) and NAPOLEON I (1799–1807). After Napoleon's defeat Talleyrand persuaded the allies to restore (1814) the Bourbon monarchy and represented France at the Congress of VIENNA (1815), where he scored his greatest diplomatic triumphs. He later served LOUIS PHILIPPE as ambassador to London. Often labelled an opportunist, Talleyrand consistently aimed at peace and stability for Europe as a whole.

**Tallinn,** formerly Reval, city (1985 pop. 464,000), capital of ESTONIA, NW European USSR, on the Gulf of Finland, opposite HELSINKI. It is a major Baltic port, a military base, and a centre of such industries as shipbuilding and metallurgy. Known to geographers by 1154, Tallinn was destroyed in 1219 by the Danes, who built a fortress on the site. A member of the HANSEATIC LEAGUE from 1285, it passed (1346–1710) to the Livonian Knights, Sweden, and Russia. It became the capital of independent Estonia in 1919 and of the Estonian SSR in 1940.

**Tallis, Thomas,** c.1510–85, English composer. Best known for his HYMN tunes, services, and ANTHEMS, he also wrote MOTETS, MADRIGALS, and instrumental music.

**Talma, François Joseph,** 1763–1826, French actor. The greatest tragedian of his time, he broke with past traditions and foreshadowed the great romanticists. He continued LEKAIN's reforms in costuming and diction.

**Talmud** [Aramaic from Heb., = learning], compilation of Jewish Oral Law, with rabbinical commentaries, as distinguished from the Scriptures, or Written Law. Its two divisions are the MISHNAH (in Hebrew), the text of the Oral Law, and the Gemara (in Aramaic), a commentary on the Mishnah, which it supplements. The Gemara developed out of the interpretations of the Mishnah by the Amoraim (Jewish scholars of AD c.200–c.500), whose penetrating insights and arguments made the work a treasury of information and comment. The legal sections of the Talmud are known as the HALAKAH; the poetical and exegetical digressions, legends, and anecdotes constitute the Aggada. Both the Palestinian and Babylonian schools produced Talmuds: the Talmud Yerushalmi (Jerusalem Talmud, compiled c.5th cent.) and the Talmud Babli (Babylonian Talmud, c.6th cent.); the latter became the authoritative work. A vast literature of commentaries on the Gemara, including those of Rashi and Tosaphot, interpreted the older rulings in the light of the new experience of life in Christian Europe in the Middle Ages. A similar process has helped to keep the tradition alive in modern times. See also JUDAISM.

**talus,** deposit of rock fragments detached from cliffs or mountain slopes by WEATHERING and piled up at their bases.

**Tamar:** see AMNON.

**tamarack:** see LARCH.

**tambourine:** see DRUM.

**Tamerlane** or **Timur,** c.1336–1405, Mongol conqueror, first of the TIMURIDS; b. Kesh, near Samarkand. From Samarkand, his capital, he invaded Persia, S Russia, India (where he took Delhi), and the Levant. In Asia Minor he defeated (1402) the Ottoman Turks and captured their sultan, Beyazid I. He died while planning an invasion of China. Though notorious for his acts of cruelty (he may have slaughtered 80,000 in Delhi) he was a patron of the arts.

**Tamil** (ˌtamil), Dravidian language of India. See LANGUAGE (table).

**Tammany,** popular name for the Democratic political machine in New York City. The Tammany Society was incorporated in 1789, and by the mid-1830s was a dominant political force, fighting for reforms for the common man but increasingly controlled by the privileged classes. With the added support of newly arrived immigrants willing to exchange votes for badly needed assistance, corrupt Tammany bosses, e.g., William M. TWEED, ruled the city for almost a century. Following state investigations in 1930–31, Tammany suffered a telling defeat in the election of 1932 and did not regain its strength in succeeding elections. It had a brief revival after World War II but passed out of existence as a political machine during the mayoralty of John V. Lindsay (1966–74).

**Tampa,** US city (1984 est. pop. 275,000), W Florida, a port on Tampa Bay; inc. 1855. It is a resort, a processing and shipping centre for the area's products, and a phosphate-mining centre. It has a shrimp fleet, breweries, and a famous cigar industry, centred in its colourful Ybor City section. Other products of the highly industrialized city include fertilizer, cement, steel, and electronic equipment. The Spanish explored the area in 1528, but European settlement began only in 1823. Tampa was an important military base in the SPANISH–AMERICAN WAR.

**Tampere,** city (1984 pop. 168,150, metropolitan area 251,833), and largest centre of population in interior Finland. The country's main industrial centre, it is served by local hydroelectric power. A wide range of textiles are manufactured and there are engineering, rubber, and leather-working industries.

**Tampico,** city (1979 est. pop. 248,369), E Mexico, on the Pánuco R. a few kilometres inland from the Gulf of Mexico. It is a major port and industrial centre that has burgeoned in the 20th cent. since the discovery of oil. It has fisheries, refineries, shipyards, and varied manufactures. Once a Huastec Indian site, it was settled by the Spaniards after 1530.

**Tamworth,** city (1986 pop. 30,729), New South Wales, SE Australia. Situated on the Peel R., to the W of the Liverpool Plains, this area was opened for settlement after Allan CUNNINGHAM found a route through the Liverpool Ranges, Pandora's Pass, in 1823. The centre of educational and professional services for the region, the city has industrial development based on the local agriculture, and is headquarters for a major soil conservation programme for the upper Namoi Valley.

**Tanaka, Kakuei,** 1918–, Japanese prime minister (1972–74). A Liberal–Democrat, he arranged (1972) to establish diplomatic ties with the People's Republic of China. Tanaka was forced to resign (1974) because of alleged financial malfeasance, and he went on trial (1977) for accepting over US$2 million in bribes from Lockheed Corp. He remained a powerful figure in Japanese politics.

**Tananarive:** see ANTANANARIVO.

**Tancred,** 1076–1112, a Crusader from 1096 (see CRUSADES). He took part in the captures of Antioch (1098), Jerusalem (1099), and Haifa (1100), and was regent for his uncle, BOHEMOND I. He took Edessa (1104) and was briefly ruler of Antioch. He refused to yield his conquests to Byzantine Emperor ALEXIUS I.

**Taney, Roger Brooke** (ˌtawnee), 1777–1864, 5th chief justice of the US SUPREME COURT (1836–64). As US attorney general (1831–33) and secretary of the treasury (1833–34) under Pres. JACKSON, he helped crush the second Bank of the United States. As chief justice, one of his most notable opinions was in the Charles River Bridge Case (1837), in which he reversed the Court's nationalist trend and curbed the growth of monopolies. Under his guidance, the Court also recognized the doctrine of STATES' RIGHTS. Taney's most controversial decision was in the DRED SCOTT CASE (1857); his ruling that slaves and their descendants had no rights as citizens and that Congress could not forbid slavery in the territories helped precipitate the CIVIL WAR, tarnished the image of the Court, and, until a recent rehabilitation, destroyed Taney's reputation as a jurist.

**Tang,** dynasty: see CHINA.

**Tanga,** city (1987 est. pop. 143,000), NE Tanzania, on the shores of the Indian Ocean. It is a port and distribution centre. At the terminus of the Tanga Line railway, it serves an important sisal-growing area and also the northern highlands round the mountains of Kilimanjaro and Meru, including the towns of Moshi and Arusha. This area is important for its agricultural crops including coffee, wheat, and seed beans.

**Tanganyika, Lake,** freshwater lake in the GREAT RIFT VALLEY of E Africa, c.680 km (420 mi) long and up to 72 km (45 mi) wide. Considered the second-deepest lake in the world, it has a maximum depth of c.1400 m (4700 ft).

**tangerine:** see ORANGE.

**Tangier** or **Tanger,** city and port (1982 pop. 312,227), N Morocco, on the Strait of Gibraltar. The chief town of Tangier prov., it trades in citrus fruit. An important strategic location, it was occupied in succession by Vandals, Byzantines, Arabs, English, Portuguese, and Spanish. In 1923, a treaty signed by France, England, and Spain assured the city's neutrality as an international zone. Tangier became part of Morocco in 1959 and its freeport status was restored in 1962.

**Tangshan,** city (1984 pop. 6,033,000), NE HEBEI prov., N China. It is a coal-mining and major industrial centre, with iron and steel works. Machinery, motor vehicles, chemicals, textiles, glass, and petroleum products are also manufactured. On 28 July 1976 the town was devastated by a major earthquake, registering 8 on the Richter scale. The official death toll in Tangshan was stated at 148,000 (other estimates place it higher). Since 1976 there has been a major rebuilding programme.

**Tanguy, Yves** (tahnhˌgee), 1900–55, French surrealist painter. A merchant seaman, he took up painting after seeing a work by CHIRICO. His imaginary dream landscapes are filled with amorphous floating objects and personages (see SURREALISM).

**Tanizaki Junichiro,** 1886–1965, Japanese novelist. His taste for the macabre was much influenced by European decadence, e.g., BAUDELAIRE, WILDE. Fascinated by the West, and also by traditional Japanese literature, he moved from Tokyo to Kyoto in 1923. His works include *The Makioka Sisters* (1948; tr. 1957), a detailed account of the daughters of a middle-class family in pre-war Osaka, *The Key* (1956; tr. 1961), *Some Prefer Nettles* (1929; tr. 1955), and *The Diary of a Mad Old Man* (1962; tr. 1965).

**tank, military,** armoured vehicle that has caterpillar traction and is armed with machine guns, cannon, rockets, or flame throwers. It was developed by the British and first used (Sept. 1916) in WORLD WAR I. In WORLD WAR II tanks and tank tactics were greatly improved. The German army, using large numbers of tanks, overran Poland in less than a month. In mass tank battles on the plains of Europe and N Africa the tide often swung towards the side with the best tanks. Since World War II the basic features of tanks and tank tactics have remained unchanged, although there have been refinements. Tanks are vulnerable to recoilless weapons and various antitank missiles, but they remain indispensable, because of their mobility and versatile weaponry, wherever the terrain is suitable to their operation.

**tannin, tannic acid** or **gallotannic acid** (approximate empirical formula: $C_{76}H_{52}O_{46}$), colourless to pale yellow, astringent, organic substance found in a wide variety of plants. Tannin can be extracted with hot water from the bark of oak, hemlock, chestnut, and mangrove; certain sumac leaves; plant gall; coffee; tea; and walnuts. In leather-making, animal skin is treated with tannin to make it resist decomposition. Tannin is also used to make INKS, as a mordant for DYES, and in medicine as an astringent and for treating burns.

Prototype of fighting **tanks** on trial in 1916 (above) and Challenger in the 1987 main battle tank exercise (below).

**tanning,** process by which skins and hides are made into LEATHER. Vegetable tanning (shown in Egyptian tomb paintings dating from 3000 BC) uses tannin, is usually employed for heavy leathers, and requires more than a month to complete. Mineral tanning includes alum tanning and chrome tanning, the process most common today, requiring only a few hours. In oil tanning, or chamoising, a method used by North American Indians, the pelt is treated with fats and hung to dry; the leather is usually napped on both sides. A modern tanning process employs artificial agents (syntans).

**Tanta,** city (1987 pop. 283,240), N Egypt, in the Nile delta. A transportation centre, its economy is based on cotton and sugar.

**tantalum** (Ta), metallic element, discovered in 1802 by A.G. Ekeberg. A rare, hard, malleable, blue-grey metal, it is extremely ductile and highly corrosion-resistant. Uses include electrolytic capacitors, chemical equipment, wires, abrasives, and dental and surgical instruments. See ELEMENT (table); PERIODIC TABLE.

**Tantalus,** in Greek mythology, king of Sipylos; son of ZEUS; father of PELOPS. Angered by his abominable behaviour, Zeus condemned him to TARTARUS. There he suffered thirst and hunger in the presence of water and fruit he could not reach.

**Tantra,** in HINDUISM and BUDDHISM, esoteric tradition of ritual and YOGA. It is known for the use of MANTRA (mystical words); *mandala* (sacred diagrams); worship of Śakti (female deities); and ritual use of wine, meat, and sexual intercourse, in order to awaken the force called *kundalini* and merge with the Godhead. In Hindu Tantra the practices are now interpreted as being symbolic. In Buddhist Tantra those rituals opposing the moral precepts of Buddhism have been dropped, but the complex MEDITATION practices have been retained. The goal is to obtain a blissful state (and ultimately NIRVĀNA) through these esoteric and 'contrary' practices.

**Tanzania,** officially United Republic of Tanzania, republic (1987 est. pop. 21,783,000), 945,087 km² (364,898 sq mi), E Africa, consisting of the former Tanganyika and the island of ZANZIBAR, in the Indian Ocean. Mainland Tanzania is bordered by Mozambique, Malawi, and Zambia

(S), Zaïre, Burundi, and Rwanda (W), Uganda and Kenya (N), and the Indian Ocean (E). Part of the country's boundaries are formed by three major lakes: MALAWI (Nyasa) in the south, TANGANYIKA in the west, and VICTORIA NYANZA in the north. Principal cities are DODOMA (the capital) and DAR-ES-SALAAM (the former capital). Tanzania has three geographic zones: a fertile, coastal lowland; a vast interior plateau; and several mountain regions, with the famed Mt KILIMANJARO (5895 m/19,340 ft), the highest point in Africa, in the northeast. Serengeti, in the Kilimanjaro region, is one of several national parks and wildlife reserves. The economy is overwhelmingly agricultural, with most of the work force employed in subsistence farming, raising cassava and maize. Sisal, cotton, coffee, and cashew nuts are the major cash crops and supply the bulk of exports from the mainland. Manufactures are limited largely to processed farm goods, textiles, and consumer items. Tanzania ranks among the world's leading producers of diamonds, and tin is also mined. Large iron-ore and coal reserves are mostly unexploited. The tourist industry is growing in importance. The GNP is US$6108 million, and the GNP per capita is US$290 (1985). Virtually all the people are Bantu-speaking black Africans, but there are Arab and Indian minorities. About half the people adhere to traditional beliefs; the rest are about equally divided between Muslim and Christian religions. Swahili and English are the official languages.

*History.* A fossil found in OLDUVAI GORGE in NE Tanzania has been identified as the remains of a direct ancestor of modern man, about 1.75 million years old. The area was later the site of Palaeolithic cultures. By about AD 900 traders from SW Asia and India had settled on the coast, and there were commercial contacts with China. A century later the migration of Bantu-speaking black Africans into the interior of Tanzania was well under way. Kilwa Kisiwani (situated on an island) became a major trade centre by about 1200, dealing in gold, ivory, and other goods. In 1498 the Portuguese explorer Vasco da GAMA became the first European visitor to the area; he made Kilwa tributary in 1502, and within a few years Portugal controlled most of the coast. Following incursions by the Zimba, a warlike black African group, the Portuguese were expelled in 1698. In the 18th cent. Arabs from Oman established commercial control over the region, and in 1841 the Omani capital was moved from Muscat to Zanzibar. At the same time new caravan routes, trafficking in slaves and ivory, were opened into the interior. German influence in Tanganyika grew in the 1880s, and the territory became a German protectorate in 1891. Following occupation by British and South African troops in WORLD WAR I, Tanganyika was made a British mandate. It gained independence as a COMMONWEALTH member in 1961, becoming a republic, with Julius NYERERE as president, in 1962. In 1964 it merged with newly independent Zanzibar to form the United Republic of Tanzania. The new nation

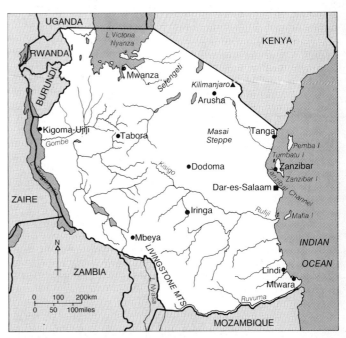

Tanzania

supported the struggle against white-minority rule in South Africa, and in 1979 its troops assisted in the overthrow of Idi AMIN in neighbouring Uganda. Nyerere retired in 1985 and was succeeded by Ali Hassan Mwinyi, who was elected president as candidate of the Chama Cha Mapinduzi (Revolutionary Party), the sole legal formation under the 1977 constitution.

**Taoism,** philosophy and religion of China. The philosophical system derives chiefly from the *Dao de jing*, a book traditionally ascribed to LAO ZI but probably written in the 4th cent. BC. It describes man's ideal state of freedom from desire and of effortless simplicity, achieved by following the *Dao* [Chin., = path], the spontaneous, creative functioning of the universe. Quietistic in outlook, the Taoists condemned as symptoms of excessive government the social virtues expounded by CONFUCIUS. Philosophical Taoism was later expounded in the brilliant writings of Zhuang Zi (c.369–c.286 BC). Later Taoism stressed the search for effects, such as immortality, supposed to flow from the *Dao*, and encouraged the study of ALCHEMY. By the 5th cent. AD Taoism had adopted many features of Mahayana BUDDHISM and offered a fully developed religious system for those who found the largely ethical system of CONFUCIANISM inadequate. In the 1950s, after the establishment of the Communist regime, Taoism was officially proscribed in China, and since the Cultural Revolution (1966–69) the religion has flourished mainly in Taiwan.

**tape recorder,** device for recording information on strips of electromagnetic tape. In an audio tape recorder, sound is picked up by a MICROPHONE and transformed into an electric current. The current is fed to a TRANSDUCER (in the recording head of the tape recorder), which converts the current into corresponding magnetic flux variations that magnetize the fine particles of iron, cobalt, or chromium oxides on the tape. Tape recorders can also be used in conjunction with a COMPUTER to store DIGITAL pulses which are coded into ALPHANUMERIC symbols.

**tapestry,** pictorial fabric used for hanging on walls, woven in plain weave, with the weft threads completely covering the warp. The warps are usually made of LINEN or COTTON, wefts of WOOL and SILK. The weft threads are discontinuous, woven in blocks manipulated by the fingers or by innumerable different-coloured bobbins. Slits occur at the junction of two adjacent areas of woven colours which run parallel to the warp; these areas may be sewn together later or left as gaps which appear on the surface of the tapestry. Other characteristics are latching or shading, pin-heads, grids, and mottled effects. The two main weaving methods are (1) high-warp weaving (Gobelin), in which the warp threads are stretched vertically between upper and lower beams, and leashes (loops of thread) are used to raise alternative warp threads to form a shed; (2) low-warp weaving (Aubusson), in which the warp threads are stretched horizontally between two beams and foot treadles make the shed. A CARTOON is placed on the underside of the warp and the tapestry is woven wrong side up. Tapestries have been woven from early times, being known in ancient Peru, China, and Egypt. Famous artists have produced cartoons for tapestries. The first important French tapestries (14th cent.) are *The Apocalypse Tapestries* now in Angers. In the late 15th cent. tapestries were woven in Arras; other important centres were Beauvais, Aubusson, Paris (see GOBELINS, MANUFACTURE NATIONALE DES), and Brussels. In the 1880s William MORRIS attempted to revive tapestry weaving using designs by Sir Edward BURNE-JONES and other artists. Jean LURÇAT helped revive the art in the 20th cent. Contemporary tapestries may be based on the designs of artists or on the weaver's original concept, and some abandon the traditional two-dimensional textile for sculptural forms.

**tapeworm,** name for parasitic flatworms in the class Cestoda, segmented worms sometimes reaching 4.5–6.0 m (15–20 ft) in length. Tapeworms attach themselves to the intestinal wall of the host, which may be a VERTEBRATE or ARTHROPOD. Humans become infected with tapeworms from eating infected meat or fish. Infestation may produce no symptoms or may produce abdominal distress and weight loss. Drug treatment destroys the parasite.

**Tapi** (formerly **Tapti**), river flowing c.370 km (230 mi) from C India W to the Arabian Sea, which it enters through an estuary at whose head stands the historic port of SURAT.

**Tapies, Antoni,** 1923–, Spanish painter. His early influences were from SURREALISM but by c.1954 he had developed a COLLAGE technique, using common materials, giving the appearance of ruined walls, which were then scrawled over with graffiti.

**tapir,** nocturnal, herbivorous MAMMAL (genus *Tapirus*) of the jungles of Central and South America and SE Asia. Related to the HORSE and RHINOCEROS, it is about the size of a donkey and piglike in appearance, with a long, flexible snout and short legs. Tapirs live in forests, browsing on twigs; they swim well and can run fast when in danger. The Central American species (*T. bairdi*) is threatened by the destruction of its rain-forest habitat.

Tapir (*Tapirus terrestris*)

**tar and pitch,** viscous, dark-brown to black substances, obtained by the destructive DISTILLATION of certain organic materials, e.g., COAL, WOOD, and PETROLEUM. Although the terms *tar* and *pitch* are sometimes used interchangeably, pitch is actually a component of tar that can be isolated by heating. Tar, more or less fluid, is now used to produce BENZENE and various other substances. Tar from pine wood is used to make SOAP and medicines. Coal tar derivatives are used to make DYES, cosmetics, and synthetic flavouring extracts. Pitch tends to be more solid than tar and is used to make roofing paper, in VARNISH, as a coal-dust binder in making fuel briquettes, and as a lubricant. ASPHALT is a naturally occurring pitch.

**Taranto,** city (1984 pop. 244,434), S Italy, on the Gulf of Taranto. It is a busy port and naval base. New industries have been sited here as part of the regional policy for the Mezzogiorno: iron and steel, cement, oil, and chemicals. Founded by Spartans as early as the 8th cent. BC, it was a wealthy city in the Greek world until it fell to Rome in 272 BC. The castle and 11th-cent. cathedral have both undergone restoration.

**tarantula,** name originally given to a small spider (*Tarentula narbonensis*) found in S Italy, now applied to other European wolf spiders, to S American BIRD-EATING SPIDERS, and scientifically to a family of harmless whip-scorpions, which are not even spiders. The Italian tarantula is a poisonous spider, named after the town of Taranto, where the legend that the poisonous bite would be fatal unless the victim danced until exhausted gave rise to the vigorous folk dance, the tarantella. Tarantulas are ground-dwelling, living in short burrows from which they leap out to hunt their food, usually insects. They do not build webs, but kill their prey instantly with a poisonous injection. The poison can kill small birds and mammals after a period of time. Male tarantulas have an elaborate courtship dance to allow them to approach the female safely.

Females carry their eggs in a cocoon attached to the body, also carrying the spiderlings when they have hatched.

**Tarascan,** MIDDLE AMERICAN INDIANS of S Mexico, speaking a language with no known relation to other languages. Tarascan settlements date from 500 BC They had a well-developed civilization by the time the Spanish arrived and were subjugated by the Spanish only with difficulty. Traditionally known for weaving and hummingbird-feather mosaics, the Tarascans are still noted for their weaving, as well as for music and lacquerware. They are chiefly an agricultural people, with some 60,000 inhabiting highly organized villages today in the state of Michoacan. Many Tarascans work as migrant labourers in the US.

**Tarawa,** most populous atoll (1973 pop. 16,000) of KIRIBATI, in the Pacific Ocean near the equator, site of the national capital, Bairiki. Formerly the administrative centre of the British Gilbert and Ellice Islands colony, Tarawa was occupied during WORLD WAR II by Japan and fell (1943) to US marines after a bloody battle.

**tariff,** tax on imported and, more rarely, exported goods. It is also called a customs duty. Tariffs, unlike other taxes, often have a broadly economic rather than narrowly financial goal, and are opposed by advocates of free trade. They may be imposed to: (1) restore the price of *dumped* goods to an economic level; (2) curb the flow of cheap imports by making them more costly than domestically produced goods in order to either conserve foreign exchange to alleviate BALANCE OF PAYMENTS problems, or to protect infant industries until they are ready to compete; (3) retaliate against certain industries without which a country would be vulnerable during war (e.g., agriculture and defence). In ancient times customs duties were assessed for the use of trade and transportation facilities, but by the 17th cent. they came to be levied only at the boundary of a country and usually only on imports. European powers established special low tariff rates for their colonies (see MERCANTILISM and NAVIGATION ACTS). The UK and France, in particular, used preferential tariffs to regulate the flow of raw materials from, and domestic manufactured goods to, their colonies. Other European nations retaliated by raising their tariffs, ushering in a period of high protective tariffs that lasted through the GREAT DEPRESSION. Since World War II the trend has been toward freer trade. Customs unions such as the COMMON MARKET have lowered or even eliminated tariffs among large groups of nations. Finally, the General Agreement on Tariffs and Trade (GATT) has, since the 1950s, been responsible for generally lower tariffs around the world. See also TRADE.

**Tarkovsky, Andrei,** 1932–86, Russian émigré film director. Memory and the search for spiritual meaning are at the heart of his poetic films, which include *Andrei Rublev* (1966), *Solaris* (1972), and *Mirror* (1975–78). He became a voluntary exile in the West, where he made *Nostalgia* (1983) and *The Sacrifice* (1986).

**taro:** see ARUM.

**tarots,** playing cards used mainly for fortune-telling, generally believed to have been introduced into Europe by gypsies in the mid-15th cent. In addition to 56 pictorial cards in four suits much like a modern 52-card deck, there are 22 additional pictorial cards, numbered 0 to 21. The pictures on the 78 cards are allegorical, representing forces of nature and the virtues and vices of man. Systems of interpretation vary greatly.

**Tarquin,** legendary Etruscan family ruling in early Rome. **Lucius Tarquinius Priscus** is said to have come to Rome on the advice of his prophetess wife, Tanaquil. There he was made king (616 BC). His son, **Lucius Tarqinius Superbus** (Tarquin the Proud), murdered his father-in-law, Servius Tullius, to get the throne. He ruled with despotism and cruelty. His son, **Sextus Tarquinius,** ravaged Lucrece, the wife of his kinsman, **Tarquinius Collatinus.** The Romans drove Tarquin the Proud from the throne (510 BC). Lars Porsena tried to restore the family; failing, he made peace with Rome.

**tarragon,** perennial aromatic Old World herb (*Artemisia dracunculus*) of the COMPOSITE family. It has long been cultivated for its leaves, used for flavouring vinegar, salads, sauces, soups, and pickles.

**Tarragona,** city (1981 pop. 111,689), capital of Tarragona prov., Catalonia, NE Spain, on the Mediterranean coast. It is a market for the olives, wine, market garden produce, and nuts from the surrounding lowland. A pre-Roman settlement, it fell to the Romans in 218 BC and became capital of their province of Tarraconensis. Its Roman remains include walls and an aqueduct. The Romanesque–Gothic cathedral has a very fine 13th-cent. cloister.

**Tarski, Alfred,** 1902–, American mathematician, b. Poland. He made invaluable contributions to mathematics and metamathematics, but his most important work is on SEMANTICS. 'The Concept of Truth in Formalized Languages' in *Logic, Semantics and Metamathematics* (1956) gives a definition of truth for formal languages. It is now generally held that this does not, as many have supposed, solve the problem of truth in natural languages, but some philosophers, inspired by Donald DAVIDSON, think that a Tarski theory of truth is the appropriate base for a theory of meaning.

**Tarsus,** city (1980 pop. 121,074), S Turkey. It was a port in classical times but later became silted up. It is a market centre and has food-processing industries. Of great antiquity, Tarsus became the capital of the region of Cilicia, guarding the route inland through the TAURUS MTS (Cilician Gates). St PAUL was born here.

**tartan:** see PLAID.

**Tartarus,** in Greek mythology, lowest region of HADES, where the wicked, e.g., SISYPHUS, TANTALUS, were punished.

**Tashkent,** city (1985 pop. 2,030,000), capital of the UZBEK SOVIET SOCIALIST REPUBLIC, Soviet Central Asia, in the foothills of the Tien Shan Mts. It is the fourth-largest city in the USSR. The largest Central Asian city and among the oldest, it is the economic heart of the region, with such products as textiles, machinery, and chemicals. The Tashkent oasis produces cotton, fruits, and grain. First mentioned in the 1st cent. BC, Tashkent came under Arabic rule (7th cent. AD) and passed to KHOREZM (12th cent.). It fell (13th–15th cent.) to JENGHIZ KHAN, TAMERLANE, and the Uzbeks. Under Russian rule after 1865, it was the capital of the Turkistan Autonomous SSR (1918–24) and replaced (1930) SAMARKAND as the capital of the Uzbek SSR. A major earthquake in 1966 heavily damaged the city.

**Tasman, Abel Janszoon,** 1603?–59, Dutch navigator. In 1642 he discovered TASMANIA, which he named Van Diemen's Land, and NEW ZEALAND. He was the first explorer to circumnavigate AUSTRALIA, proving it to be an island continent.

**Tasmania,** island state (1986 pop. 446,500), 68,332 km² (26,383 sq mi), SE Australia. It is separated from the mainland by BASS STRAIT and lies 240 km (150 mi) S of the state of Victoria. It is the smallest, wettest, and most mountainous of the Australian states. HOBART is the capital and largest city. Manufactures include metal products, textiles, and wood pulp. Copper, tin, lead, zinc, and iron ore are mined. Lamb, beef, veal, wool, fruits, and hops are important agricultural products. The Dutch navigator Abel TASMAN discovered the island and named it Van Diemen's Land in 1642. Capt. James COOK visited it in 1777, and in 1803 Great Britain took possession and established a penal colony at Hobart. The indigenous population was wiped out in the 19th cent. Tasmania became a separate colony in 1825 and was federated as a state of the Commonwealth of Australia in 1901.

**Tasmanian devil,** voracious MARSUPIAL (*Sarcophilus harrisi*) of the Dasyure family, now found only on Tasmania. Its body is about 60 cm (2 ft) long with a large head and weak hindquarters. Very strong for its size, it preys on animals larger than itself; it has been relentlessly hunted for its destruction of livestock and poultry.

**Tasman Sea,** arm of the South Pacific Ocean, between Australia and New Zealand. It was named after the Dutch explorer Abel TASMAN.

**Tasso, Torquato,** 1544–95, major Italian poet of the late (or post-) RENAISSANCE. He gained fame at 18 with the verse romance *Rinaldo,* and in 1565 was invited to the court of the ESTE at Ferrara. There he wrote the PASTORAL play *Aminta* (1573) and the first version of his masterpiece, *Jerusalem Delivered* (1575), a religious EPIC about the First CRUSADE. His last 20 years were a chapter of misfortunes, and from 1579 to 1586 he was confined as a madman. His works greatly influenced MILTON, and the legend of his doomed love for Leonora d'Este was immortalized by BYRON, GOETHE, and others.

**taste:** see TONGUE.

**Tatars** or **Tartars,** Turkic-speaking peoples living in the Soviet Union. They are largely SUNNI Muslims. Originally a nomadic tribe from E Central Asia, the Tatars intermixed with MONGOLS in the hordes of JENGHIZ KHAN, and the term Tatars came to mean invaders under Mongol leadership. When the Mongols receded eastward, the Tatars continued to dominate Russia, the Ukraine, and Siberia. They adopted ISLAM in the 14th cent. In the late 15th cent. the Tatar empire (see GOLDEN HORDE, EMPIRE OF THE) broke up into separate states that fell under Russian or Ottoman Turkish rule. By the 16th cent. most Tatars were settled agriculturists. Tatar leaders, traders, and institutions had great influence on Russian history. In 1783 the last Tatar state, the Crimea, was annexed to Russia. Most Tatars live in the Volga region and the Urals, and some live in small groups in W Siberia. The Crimean Tatars were exiled to Kazakhstan and Uzbekistan in 1945 for alleged collaboration with the Germans in WORLD WAR II; in 1956 they regained their civil rights.

Tasmanian devil (*Sarcophilus harrisi*)

**Tate, (John Orley) Allen,** 1899–1979, American poet and critic. A professor at several colleges, he edited the magazines *Fugitive* (1922–25) and *Sewanee Review* (1944–46). His perceptive critical writings include *On the Limits of Poetry* (1948) and *The Man of Letters in the Modern World* (1955). His skilful poetry, filled with bitter imagery, can be found in several volumes, notably *Collected Poems* (1977).

**Tate Gallery,** London, originally the National Gallery of British Art. The building was given by Sir Henry Tate and opened in 1897 with 65 British paintings. It was extended by the Turner Wing (1910), three galleries for modern foreign art (1916), and the John Singer Sargent Wing (1926). Its collections of works by William BLAKE and the PRE-RAPHAELITES are particularly notable. As well as British art, it also houses foreign art of the last 100 years. In 1987 the Clore Gallery, designed by James Stirling, was opened to house the Turner Bequest, those paintings, drawings, and watercolours in J.M.W. TURNER's studio at the artist's death, which he left to the nation.

**Tatlin, Vladimir,** 1885–1953, Russian painter. He visited PICASSO in Paris in 1913, which inspired his relief construction of 1913 onwards, in which he needed a variety of materials. His concept of the 'culture of materials' was the main element of the productivist movement (later called CONSTRUCTIVISM) which opposed the suprematism of MALEVICH. He produced (1920) a model for a monument to the THIRD INTERNATIONAL, an iron spiral structure enclosing revolving glass geometric forms, that was to be twice the height of the Empire State Building. Never built, it nonetheless became a symbol of Soviet constructivism.

**Tatra,** mountain range, forming the highest part of the Carpathian Mts (2663 m/8740 ft), on the border between Czechoslovakia and Poland. The serrated peaks show widespread evidence of glaciation. The High Tatra have been designated a national park and they attract mountaineers and winter-sports enthusiasts. Resorts include Zakopane (Poland).

**Tatum, Edward Lawrie,** 1909–75, American geneticist. Working with the bread mould *Neurospora crassa,* he and George BEADLE showed (1941) that particular genes control biochemical reactions in cells. Tatum and Joshua LEDERBERG later discovered (1947) the phenomenon of genetic recombination in the bacterium *Escherichia coli.* For their work, Tatum, Beadle, and Lederberg shared the 1958 Nobel Prize for physiology or medicine.

Vladimir **Tatlin,** *Monument to the Third International,* 1920. Iron and glass sculpture.

**Taunton,** county town (1981 pop. 47,793), Somerset, SW England, on R. Tone, in picturesque and fertile Vale of Taunton Deane. It is a market town, whose industries include the manufacture of agricultural machinery, cider-making, and food-processing. There are the remains of a 12th-cent. castle. Judge JEFFREYS held the 'Bloody Assizes' here in 1685.

**Taurus Mountains,** mountain chain, extending parallel to the Mediterranean coast of S Turkey. It reaches 3734 m (12,251 ft) at Ala Dag. Metallic ores are mined, and it is crossed by a historic routeway, the Cilician Gates, north of Tarsus.

**Tawney, Richard Henry,** 1880–1962, English historian; b. Calcutta. After leaving Oxford he was a tutor with the recently founded Workers' Educational Association of which he later became president. From 1931 to 1949 he was a professor at the London School of Economics. He was prominent in Labour Party politics and wrote influential books like *The Acquisitive Society* (1920) and *Equality* (1931), in a rich and highly distinctive style. His best remembered historical study is *Religion and the Rise of Capitalism* (1926).

**taxation,** system used by governments to obtain money from people and organizations. The revenue collected is used by the government to support itself and to provide public services. Although taxation is compulsory, it does not guarantee a direct relationship between the amount contributed by a citizen and the extent of services received. An enforced levy to meet an emergency is distinguished from taxation as not being part of a long-term system (e.g., capital levy, a high, one-time tax on a subject's total capital, usually imposed after a war). Fees for special services, such as postage, are not considered taxes. A government may secure its revenue without taxation, as from natural resources, manufactured products, or services, but nearly all nations today rely on taxation as their principal source of income. Ease of collection is considered a merit in a tax, and ability to pay is one test of the amount that an individual should contribute. Taxes are classified as proportional, progressive, or regressive, depending on how they relate to the ability to pay. A *proportional* tax takes the same percentage of each person's income, whether rich or poor. A *progressive* tax has a higher rate for persons with higher incomes. A general sales tax (a levy on the sale of goods and services, usually as a percentage of the selling price) is considered *regressive,* for in disregarding a person's ability to pay, it, in effect, taxes the poor more heavily than the wealthy by requiring the poor to spend a larger proportion of income on basic needs. Increases or decreases in taxes, or changes in the types of taxes levied, are often used to regulate a nation's economy. See also specific types of taxes, e.g., EXCESS PROFITS TAX; INHERITANCE TAX.

**taxidermy,** process of preserving vertebrate animals in lifelike form by mounting the cleaned skins on a man-made skeleton. Once employed chiefly to preserve hunting trophies and souvenirs, taxidermy is now used mainly by science museums.

**taxonomy,** the study of the CLASSIFICATION of plants and animals and the principles which bring about that classification. It includes the study of variations within one species that are worked on by evolution, if part of the species is isolated, to produce a new species, and of the mechanisms by which isolation is brought about.

**Tay,** longest river in Scotland, in Central and Tayside regions, c.193 km (120 mi) long. It rises on the N side of Ben Lui in Central region, and flows generally E through Strath Fillan and Glen Dochart to Loch Tay. In this upper section it is known first as the R. Fillan, and then as R. Dochart. On leaving Loch Tay it becomes known as the R. Tay and flows generally E past Aberfeldy, Dunkeld, and PERTH into its tidal estuary, the Firth of Tay. It enters the North Sea at Buddon Ness, E of DUNDEE. The Firth of Tay itself is c.37 km (23 mi) long, and is crossed at Dundee by railway and road bridges.

**Taylor, A(lan) J(ohn) P(ercivale),** 1906–, English historian. Educated at Oxford, where he taught from 1953 to 1963, he established a reputation as a brilliant lecturer and a controversial writer mainly on modern European history. Before Oxford he had worked at Manchester with L.B. NAMIER. His many works, among them well written and provocative essays, include *The Struggle for Mastery in Europe* (1954) and *English History, 1914–1945* (1965). During the 1950s he became even more well known as a broadcaster on radio and television than as a writer.

**Taylor, Cecil,** 1933–, black American pianist and composer. After a formal musical education, he turned to improvisation initially with some orthodoxy but, by the late 1950s, with a strikingly original style, synthesizing free-form jazz with modern classical overtones. He is an exhilarating solo performer who has influenced many post-bop pianists.

**Taylor, Edward,** c.1642–1729, considered America's foremost colonial poet; b. England. He came to America in 1668. A Congregational minister and ardent Puritan, he wrote verse similar to that of England's METAPHYSICAL POETS. His poetry was first published in 1939.

**Taylor, Elizabeth,** 1932–, American film actress; b. England. Noted for her beauty, she is effective in dramatic roles. Her films include *A Place in the Sun* (1951), *Cleopatra* (1962), *Who's Afraid of Virginia Woolf?* (1966; Academy Award), and *A Little Night Music* (1977).

**Taylor, Frederick Winslow,** 1856–1915, American industrial engineer. Taylor, called the father of scientific management, developed management methods that were successfully introduced into many industries. See also TIME AND MOTION STUDY.

**Taylor, Jeremy,** 1613–67, English Anglican bishop, theologian, and devotional writer. He was chaplain to Archbishop LAUD and a chaplain in ordinary to Charles I. After the Restoration (1660) he became bishop of Down and Connor in Ireland. Called the Shakespeare and the Spenser of the pulpit, he was known for his mastery of powerful imagery. His most famous works, *Holy Living* (1650) and *Holy Dying* (1651), are classic expressions of Anglican spirituality.

**Taylor, John,** 1753–1824, American political philosopher. As a member of the Virginia house of delegates and the US Senate, he was among the first to formulate the STATES' RIGHTS doctrine (see KENTUCKY AND VIRGINIA RESOLUTIONS). A Jeffersonian Democrat, he warned of the harmful effects of finance capitalism in his greatest work, *An Inquiry into the Principles and Policy of the Government of the United States* (1814).

**Taylor, Paul,** 1930–, American dancer. His early career was with Martha GRAHAM, Doris HUMPHREY, José LIMON, Antony TUDOR, and Craske, and with various modern companies including those of CUNNINGHAM and

Graham. He has had his own company since 1954, which has toured extensively. Taylor is well known for his musicality and sense of humour.

**Taylor, Zachary,** 1785–1850, 12th president of the US (1849–50). He joined the army in 1808, winning the nickname 'Old Rough and Ready' in the Black Hawk War (1832) and in campaigns against the SEMINOLE INDIANS in Florida. He won important victories in the MEXICAN WAR, concluding with the decisive battle of Buena Vista (1847) against great odds. A popular hero, he was elected Whig president in 1848. As president, he supported the WILMOT PROVISO and favoured the rapid admission of California and New Mexico to the Union as a means of ending the controversy over slavery in the territories acquired from Mexico. His free-soil views, opposing slavery, put him in opposition to the measures that were to become the COMPROMISE OF 1850. Taylor's death on 9 July 1850 removed a major obstacle to the enactment of the Compromise.

**Taylorism and Fordism,** modes of organization of the labour process in early 20th-cent. large-scale industry. *Fordism* (named after Henry FORD) characterizes the new, mass-production factory methods (continuous flow production) including attempts to increase the volume and pace of work on a production line by increasing the speed at which work moves from one worker to another. *Taylorism* (named after F.W. Taylor, 1856–1915) involves increasing output by increasing the speed at which each worker carries out his/her task; this necessitates breaking down each stage of the production process into its component parts, and giving management sole control over the production process so that they can specify the amount of time needed to perform each task. The consequent deskilling and 'mechanization' of labour is viewed as useful to management because (1) it increases output, (2) unskilled labour is cheaper to employ, and (3) once split into myriad tasks, the production process could only be coordinated by management, thus effectively removing all control from the worker. Each of these strategies of control represents a further development of the DIVISION OF LABOUR instigated by industrial CAPITALISM.

**Tay-Sachs disease,** rare hereditary disease of infants, characterized by progressive mental deterioration, blindness, paralysis, epileptic seizures, and death by the age of four. Caused by an abnormality of fat metabolism in nerve cells, producing central NERVOUS SYSTEM degeneration, the disease occurs almost exclusively among Ashkenazi Jews (of middle and N European descent). It can be detected in a fetus by AMNIOCENTESIS. There is no treatment.

**Tayside,** region in E Scotland (1985 est. pop. 397,055), 7493 km² (2922 sq mi), bordering on the North Sea in the E. The administrative centre is DUNDEE. It was formed in 1975 from the former county of Angus and most of Perthshire. The Firth of Tay forms part of the southern border. Much of the region is mountainous, but there is a large fertile area of lowlands called Strathmore where mixed agriculture is important. The R. TAY is the main river. Dundee and PERTH are the main towns.

**Tb,** chemical symbol of the element TERBIUM.

**TB:** see TUBERCULOSIS.

**Tbilisi** or **Tiflis** (təbi‚leesee), city (1985 pop. 1,158,000), capital of GEORGIA, SE European USSR, on the Kura R. and the Transcaucasian railway. Its industries produce machinery, woven silk, and processed foods. Nearby are vineyards and health resorts with mineral springs. Among the USSR's oldest cities, Tbilisi was built on a site settled in the 4th cent. BC. It was ruled (4th–11th cent AD) by the Persians, Arabs, Khazars, and Turks; was the capital of an independent Georgian state (1096–1225); and was held (13th–18th cent.) by the Mongols, Iranians, and Turks. It passed to Russia in 1801, was the capital of independent Georgia (1918–20), of the Transcaucasian Socialist Federated Soviet Republic (1922–36), and of the Georgian SSR (1936). It was a centre of nationalist disturbances in 1989.

**Tc,** chemical symbol of the element TECHNETIUM.

**Tchaikovsky, Peter Ilyich** (chie‚kofskee), 1840–93, Russian composer. He studied at the St Petersburg Conservatory and later taught at the Moscow Conservatory (1865–78). An annuity from a wealthy patroness, Mme von Meck, allowed him for years to devote himself to music. Richly orchestrated, his music is melodious, intensely emotional, and often melancholy; it has always been both popular and influential. Among the most successful of his compositions are his orchestral works, notably the last three of his six symphonies; the fantasy *Romeo and Juliet* (1869, rev. 1870, 1879); the ballets *Swan Lake* (1876), *The Sleeping*

*Beauty* (1889), and *The Nutcracker* (1892), which had a profound influence on the development of dance as an art form; the Piano Concerto in B Flat Minor (1875); and the Violin Concerto in D (1878). His operas include *Eugene Onegin* (1879) and *The Queen of Spades* (1890).

**Te,** chemical symbol of the element TELLURIUM.

**tea,** tree or bush, its leaves, and the beverage made from the leaves. The plant (*Thea sinensis, Camellia thea,* or *C. sinensis*) is an evergreen related to the CAMELLIA and native to India and probably parts of China and Japan. In the wild it grows to about 10 m (33 ft) in height, but in cultivation it is pruned to 1 to 1.5 m (3 to 5ft). Tea plants require a well-drained habitat in a warm climate with ample rainfall; the leaves are prepared by drying, rolling, and firing (heating). Black teas (e.g., pekoes), unlike green teas, are fermented before firing; oolong teas are partially fermented. Tea's stimulating properties are due to CAFFEINE, and its astringency to tannin. Grown in China since prehistoric times, tea was produced on a commercial scale there by the 8th cent. It was introduced (17th cent.) into Europe by the Dutch EAST INDIA COMPANY, and its popularity helped spur the opening of the Orient to Western commerce. In colonial America a tax on tea led to the BOSTON TEA PARTY (1773). Today tea is used by more people and in greater quantity than any beverage except water.

**teak,** tall deciduous tree (*Tectona grandis*) of the VERVAIN family, native to India and Malaysia but now widely cultivated in tropical areas. Teakwood is moderately hard, easily worked, and very durable. The wood contains an ESSENTIAL OIL that resists the action of water and prevents the rusting of iron, and the heartwood is resistant to termites. Superior to all other woods for shipbuilding, teak is also used in furniture, flooring, and general construction.

**Teapot Dome,** in US history, scandal that began during the administration of Pres. HARDING. In 1921, Secy of the Interior Albert B. Fall secretly leased the naval oil reserves at Teapot Dome, Wyoming, and Elk Hills, California, without competitive bidding. A Senate investigation (1922–23) revealed that Edward L. Doheny, who had leased the Elk Hills oil field, had 'loaned' Fall large sums of money without interest, as had Harry F. Sinclair, recipient of the Teapot Dome lease. Fall was subsequently fined and sentenced to prison. Both Doheny and Sinclair were acquitted of bribery on legal technicalities, but Sinclair was later imprisoned for contempt of the Senate and attempted jury-rigging.

**tear gas:** see POISON GAS.

**technetium** (tek,neesh(y)əm) (Tc), artificially produced radioactive element, discovered in a sample of dueteron-bombarded molybdenum in 1937 by C. Perrier and E.G. Segrè. The silver-grey metal is used in radioactive tracer studies. Spectra of some stars indicate the presence of the element; the naturally occurring element has not been found on Earth. See ELEMENT (table); PERIODIC TABLE.

**Tecumseh,** 1768?–1813, chief of the SHAWNEE INDIANS. A noted military leader, he planned a confederacy of tribes to resist US encroachment, but the defeat of his brother, the Shawnee Prophet, at Tippecanoe (1811) ended the Indian military movement. Tecumseh then fought alongside the British against the Americans in the WAR OF 1812. He died in the battle of the THAMES.

**Tees,** river in N England, approximately 112 km (70 mi) long. It rises on E slopes of Cross Fell, Cumbria, and flows SE to Barnard Castle, then E to Stockton-on-Tees and MIDDLESBROUGH, then finally NE into the North Sea at Tees Mouth, Cleveland. It is navigable up to Stockton, and tidal up to Newsham.

**teeth,** hard, calcified structures embedded in the bone of the jaw that perform the function of chewing food. In humans, deciduous or milk teeth (20) erupt at the age of about six months and begin to be replaced by permanent teeth from the age of six years onwards. An adult mouth contains 32 permanent teeth (two incisors, one canine, two premolars, and three molars in each quadrant of the jaw; the third molar, or wisdom tooth, appears late and sometimes not at all). A tooth consists of the crown, the portion visible in the mouth, and one or more roots embedded in a gum socket. The gums cushion the teeth, while the jawbone firmly anchors the roots. The centre of each tooth is filled with soft pulpy tissue containing blood vessels and nerves. Hard, bony dentine (ivory) surrounds the pulp and makes up the bulk of the tooth. The root portion has a thin, bony, overlayer of cementum, and the crown has a layer of enamel, the hardest substance in the body.

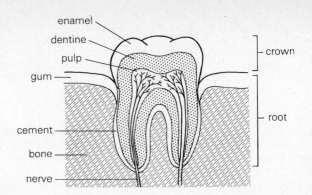

Tooth

**Teflon,** trade name for a solid, chemically inert POLYMER of tetrafluoroethylene, $F_2C = CF_2$, discovered by accident in the du Pont de Nemours experimental station, Delaware, US. Stable up to temperatures around 300°C (572°F), Teflon is used in electrical insulation, gaskets, and in making nonstick surfaces, e.g., in cooking utensils.

**Tegucigalpa** (taygoohsee,gahlpah), city (1983 est. pop. 509,000), S central Honduras, capital and largest city of Honduras. Founded in 1579 in a mountain valley, it was a Spanish colonial gold- and silver-mining centre. It vied with Comayagua, its twin city across the Choluteca R., as the republic's capital until 1880. Its older section, built on a steep slope with narrow, stair-stepped streets, is unusually picturesque.

**Teheran** or **Tehran,** city (1982 est. pop. 5,734,000), capital of Iran, N Iran, near Mt Damavand, the highest point in the ELBURZ Mts. It is Iran's largest city and its administrative, industrial, and commercial hub. It is also a leading centre for the sale and export of carpets. Teheran rose to importance after the nearby city of Rhagae (Mod. Rey) was destroyed (13th cent.) by the Mongols, and in 1786 it became the capital of Persia. Under REZA SHAH PAHLEVI (r.1925–41), the city was modernized. During World War II it was the site of the TEHERAN CONFERENCE (1943). In 1979 Iranian militants seized the US embassy in Teheran and held 52 Americans hostage for 444 days (until 20 Jan. 1981).

**Teheran Conference,** 28 Nov.–1 Dec. 1943, meeting in Iran during WORLD WAR II of US Pres. F.D. ROOSEVELT, British Prime Min. Winston CHURCHILL, and Soviet Premier Joseph STALIN. Agreement was reached on Allied plans for the war against Germany and for postwar cooperation in the UNITED NATIONS.

**Teifi,** river in SW Wales, in county of Dyfed. It rises in Llyn Teifi and flows S then W past Tregaron, Lampeter, Newcastle Emlyn, and CARDIGAN where it widens out before reaching Cardigan Bay.

**Teilhard de Chardin, Pierre** (tie,ah de ,shah'dan), 1881–1955, French palaeontologist and philosopher. A Jesuit, Teilhard was forced to abandon teaching in 1926 because of his attempts to reconcile original sin with his concept of evolution. Thereafter he worked (1926–46) in China as a palaeontologist and was involved in the discovery of Peking Man (see HOMO ERECTUS). He also wrote *The Phenomenon of Man* (published posthumously, 1955), in which he outlined his concept of cosmic evolution and his conviction that belief in evolution does not entail rejection of Christianity. He saw mankind as the axis of the cosmic flow and the key to the universe, and evolution as leading ultimately to the 'Omega Point', variously interpreted as the integration of all individual consciousness and as the second coming of Christ. His works received unusually wide popular response after their posthumous publication, but also major professional criticism.

**Te Kanawa, Dame Kiri** ('teka,nowə), 1944–, New Zealand opera singer, she made her London debut in 1971 as the Countess in *The Marriage of Figaro* at Covent Garden. She has made many recordings and has sung major roles at the Metropolitan Opera, New York, La Scala, Milan, and in Paris, San Francisco, Sydney, and elsewhere. She sang an aria at the wedding of Prince Charles and Lady Diana Spencer.

**Tel Aviv-Jaffa,** city (1983 est. pop. 327,300), W central Israel, on the Mediterranean Sea. It is Israel's second largest city and its commercial centre. The city is also a tourist resort with wide, attractive beaches. Tel Aviv was founded (1909) by Jews from JAFFA and its population grew dramatically after 1920. It was Israel's first capital (1948–49) and most foreign embassies are still located in the city. A cultural centre, it is the site of many theatres, leading museums, a university, and several musical organizations, including the Israel Philharmonic. Tel Aviv and Jaffa were merged in 1950.

**telegraph**, an electrically operated device or system for distant communication. The method used throughout most of the world, based in large part on the mid-19th-cent. work of Samuel F.B. MORSE, utilizes an ELECTRIC CIRCUIT set up customarily by using a single overhead wire and employing the earth as the other conductor to complete the circuit. In the telegraph's simplest form, an electromagnet in the receiver is activated by alternately making and breaking the circuit. Reception by sound, with the MORSE CODE signals received as audible clicks, is the basis for a low-cost, reliable method of signalling.

**Teleki, Count Paul** (ˌteleki), 1879–1941, Hungarian premier (1920–21, 1939–41). He signed (1940) the Berlin Pact (see AXIS). When it became evident that Germany would force Hungary to invade Yugoslavia, Teleki committed suicide.

**Telemachus**, in Greek mythology, son of ODYSSEUS and PENELOPE.

**Telemann, Georg Philipp**, 1681–1767, German composer. Extremely prolific, and in his day more popular than J.S. BACH, he wrote over 600 overtures, 40 operas, 12 services for the year, and other works in almost every form. His style combines COUNTERPOINT and airs from Italian opera. He made important contributions to musical life by establishing musical societies in several cities, catering for amateur musicians, and promoting the idea of concerts.

**teleology**, in philosophy, term applied to any system attempting to explain a series of events in terms of ends, goals, or purposes. It is opposed to mechanism, which holds that all events are explained by the mechanical principles of causation. Teleologists have frequently identified purpose in the universe as God's will. The teleological proof of the existence of God argues that since there is design in the world, there must be a designer (God). A more recent, evolutionary view finds purpose in the higher levels of organic life but holds that it is not necessarily based on any transcendent being.

**telephone**, device for transmitting and receiving sound, especially speech, by means of wires in ELECTRIC CIRCUITS. The telephones now in general use are developments of the device invented by Alexander Graham BELL and patented by him in 1876 and 1877. A modern telephone transmitter, which is essentially a carbon MICROPHONE, generates a signal that can be transmitted either in analogue or DIGITAL mode. Modern telephone systems are nearly all digital so that they can carry high-speed data transfers as well as voice traffic. Telephone lines used include ordinary open-wire lines; lead-sheathed CABLES consisting of many lines; coaxial cables; and, most recently, glass fibres (see FIBRE OPTICS). Coaxial cables and fibre-optic lines are placed underground, but other cables may be either overhead or underground. Long-distance transmission of telephone messages is often accomplished by means of RADIO and MICROWAVE transmissions. In some cases microwaves are sent to an orbiting COMMUNICATIONS SATELLITE, from which they are relayed back to a distant point on the earth. Sophisticated services, including automatic switching systems, automatic dialling, call forwarding, and conference calling, have been developed in recent years alongside the expansion of the use of the telephone system for data traffic. See also CELLULAR RADIO.

**telescope**, system of lenses, mirrors, or both used to gather light from a distant object and form a real (produced by the intersection of light rays) optical image of it. In the refracting telescope, or refractor (invented early 17th cent.), light is bent, or refracted, as it passes through a convex objective LENS so that it converges to a point (the focus) behind the lens forming a real image; this is then viewed through an eyepiece which is essentially a converging lens. In a reflecting telescope, or reflector (invented 1672), light is reflected by a concave paraboloidal MIRROR and brought to a focus in front of the mirror. The image is diverted to a more convenient location by one of several means (see diagrams of the Newtonian, Cassegrain, and Coudé foci) for viewing by the eyepiece. A third type of telescope, the catadioptric system, focuses light by a combination of lenses and mirrors; two examples are the Schmidt camera telescope (invented 1930), used primarily for wide-angle photography of

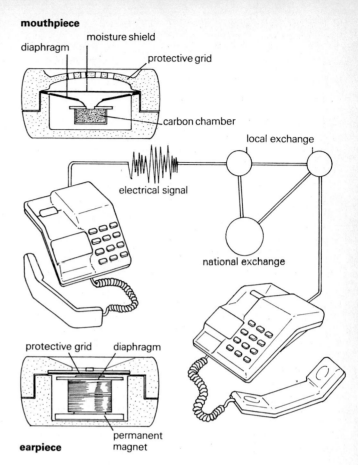

Telephone

star fields and consisting of a spherical mirror and a special correction lens used in front of the tube, and the Maksutov telescope (invented 1941), which has a spherical meniscus in place of the Schmidt's correcting plate. The size of the object's image is the product of its angular size in radians (1 radian $\approx$ 57°) as seen from the telescope and the focal length (the distance from the focus to the lens or mirror). The brightness of the image depends on the telescope's total light-gathering power and hence is proportional to the area of the objective lens or primary mirror, or to the square of its diameter. A telescope's resolving power, or smallest angular separation between two light points that can be unambiguously distinguished, is proportional to the ratio of the wavelength of light being observed to the diameter of the telescope. The magnification, or magnifying power, of a telescope is the ratio of the angular sizes of the virtual image seen by the observer and the actual angular size, or, equivalently, to the ratio of the focal lengths of the objective and the ocular, or eyepiece. The mounting of a telescope must be massive, to minimize mechanical vibration that would blur the image, and must provide rotation about two perpendicular axes, to allow the telescope to be pointed in any direction. In the altazimuth mounting, used primarily for terrestrial telescopes, one axis points to the zenith and allows rotation along the horizon, and the other allows changes in altitude. Most astronomical telescopes use the equatorial mounting, in which one axis points at the celestial pole. Rotation about this polar axis allows changes in right ascension or celestial longitude; rotation about the declination axis, at right angles to it, allows changes in declination or celestial latitude. To compensate for the Earth's rotation, a clock-drive mechanism is generally provided to turn the polar axis east to west at the rate of one rotation per sidereal day. See also BINOCULARS; LENS; OBSERVATORY, ASTRONOMICAL; RADIO ASTRONOMY.

**teletext**, system of broadcasting data utilizing a redundant portion of the television waveform by adding pulses that, when detected by appropriate circuits in the receiver, can produce words or figures on a television screen. The part of the television waveform that carries the data pulses occurs as a number of blank lines above the top of the picture. Pulses

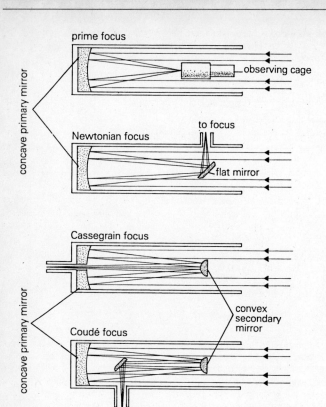

Mirror arrangements for a reflecting **telescope**

carried here are not visible when the TV is operating normally. Using up to eight of the spare lines some hundreds of pages of information are carried, any one of which can be selected by keying the appropriate number at the receiver. The pages are transmitted in rotation and after identifying the page required it usually takes a few seconds before the next transmission of that page when it can be captured and displayed. The pages are editorially arranged to cover a variety of information and entertainment magazines. Included is up-to-the-minute news, sport, weather, travel problems, flight arrival times at airports, radio and TV programme guides, financial information, and information about holidays. An important use of Teletext is subtitles for the deaf and hard of hearing. Within the UK the BBC teletext system is called Ceefax and that used by the IBA Oracle, and they are technically identical. Although a number of European countries use the UK teletext standard a different noncompatible system called Antiope is used in France.

**television,** transmission of visual images by radio waves. For a monochrome system the scene to be televised is focused onto the face of a television pickup tube which is scanned from left to right and from top to bottom by an electron beam that generates an electrical video signal varying with the brightness of the picture, point by point (see TELEVISION CAMERA). The received replica of the original video signal is applied between the grid and cathode of a CATHODE-RAY TUBE to vary the intensity of the electron beam which determines the brightness level of the light spot where the beam hits the phosphor coat backing the screen. The varying brightness at different points on the screen results in the original monochrome picture being reproduced. In the US the video signal is formed by 525 horizontal lines for each picture and there are 30 pictures transmitted each second. In Europe the standard is different with 625 lines for each picture and 25 pictures each second. For colour television the same basic principles apply but it is necessary to identify the three colours in the pictures—red, green, and blue—separately at the source and transmit them through the system to the receiver. Three pickup tubes are required, one for each colour, and the televised scene is focused onto each through an appropriate colour filter so that each tube produces an electrical video signal relating to one of the three colours. After transmission these three signals are applied to the appropriate colour terminals of the display tube. (see SHADOW MASK TUBE; TRINITRON). Viewing or taking part in television has become the major populist innovation of

the 20th cent. In Western countries it is unusual now for a household not to have a set (86% of households in Britain in 1985 had a colour set, plus 11% with black-and-white). The influence of what is broadcast is therefore immense: in many countries television is the main source of news, with coverage through either edited extracts or (increasingly) live reporting. Great events are watched worldwide by huge numbers of people, e.g., the estimated 560 million who watched the live coverage of the wedding of Prince Charles and Lady Diana Spencer. The typical pattern of broadcasting in the UK in the 1980s consisted of over 35% news and current affairs programmes, 10% films, with sport as the third most frequent category (7%); documentaries, usually hailed as television's finest area of achievement, were fifth (5%) behind SOAP OPERAS (6%). Despite repeated investigations no link has ever been proved between violent behaviour and the viewing of violence on television. The hours of such viewing, an average in the UK of 20 hours per week, constitute a problem in themselves. Television ADVERTISING, on the other hand, is extremely effective in shaping adult viewers' behaviour, as can be shown by before-and-after analysis of sales when a product is advertised on television.

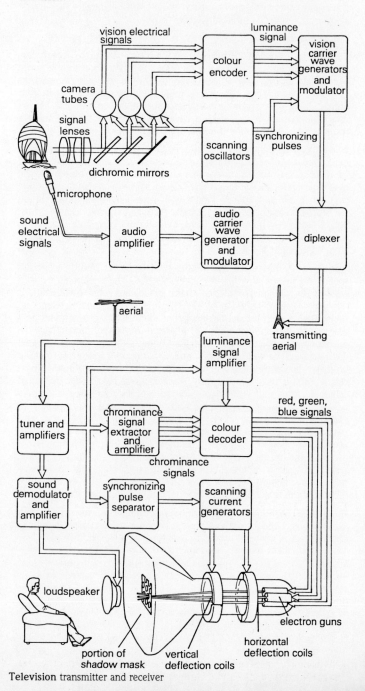

**Television** transmitter and receiver

**television camera tube,** device in a TELEVISION camera that converts the image of a scene into an electrical signal. The first of these image pickup tubes was the iconoscope, invented in 1923 by Vladimir Zworykin in America. The heart of this tube is the 'target'—a thin sheet of mica on one side of which is deposited a mosaic of tiny caesium–silver photoelectric cells. The scene being televised is focused onto these and the differing amounts of light falling upon different components of the mosaic leave the cells with charges proportional to the light falling upon them. A scanning beam discharges each component of the mosaic in turn and as it does so a discharge current proportional to the amount of charge released is produced. These currents, suitably amplified, can provide a signal for producing pictures in a television display. From the early 1950s alternative types of tube based on the photoconductive principle started to become available, in which the photoemissive mosaic is replaced by a layer of photoconductive material, e.g., selenium and lead oxides, the conductance of which varies with the intensity of the light falling on it. Apart from the improved performance the new tubes have the considerable advantage of a small and convenient size—2.5 cm (1 in) in diameter and 15 cm (6 in) long compared with the 10 cm (4 in) diameter and 30 cm (12 in) length of the earlier tubes. This is a great advantage when three tubes have to be fitted into a colour camera. As an alternative to pickup tubes a solid-state charge-coupled device (CCD) sensitive to light can be used to give an output corresponding to each picture point of the image focused onto them. The quality obtained is not yet good enough to meet broadcast standards but is good enough to be used in VIDEO cameras for home use.

**telex,** worldwide telegraph communication system. Each key on the typewriter keyboard of a telex machine is allocated a standardized electrical code, and when it is pressed this code is transmitted to cause the same letter to be printed on a similar telex machine at the other end of the communication link, typically a dedicated telex line. As the transmission of the message over the link is quicker than it can be typed, it is normal for telex machines to be equipped with a memory store so that complete messages of several pages can be stored before the transmission takes place. A multi-paged document can then be transmitted in a few minutes with a significant saving in transmission costs. All major companies are equipped with telex machines connected to an international telex communications network. The big advantage of the system is that it provides a typed copy of a message to the recipient in any part of the world within minutes of it having been prepared. Because a link must be established between sender and receiver before the message can be sent, the fact that a telex has been successfully sent means that it must also have been received at the other end. For this reason telexes containing contractual provisions can be made legally binding. Access to the telex network is now possible from personal computers and word processing systems. Telex is increasingly coming under threat from FAX which uses ordinary telephone lines and numbers and does not require typing at a dedicated keyboard.

**Telford, Thomas,** 1757–1834, Scottish architect and civil engineer. After an apprenticeship to a stonemason he went to London and was employed on the building of Somerset House. In 1793 he began to build canals, first in Shropshire where he was responsible for the aqueducts at Chirk and Pontcysyllte and then in Scotland where he built the Caledonian Canal. Turning his attention to roads and bridges, he designed the famous suspension bridges over the Menai Straits and the Conway R. He was the first president of the Institution of Civil Engineers.

**Tell, William,** legendary Swiss hero. A native of Uri, he refused obeisance to Gessler, the Austrian bailiff. As punishment he was forced to shoot an apple off his young son's head. In revenge, Tell killed Gessler, setting off the revolt that ousted the bailiffs on 1 Jan. 1308. The legend is a distortion of actual events that led in 1291 to the formation of the Everlasting League among the forest cantons of Uri, Schwyz, and Unterwalden. The best-known treatments of the story are SCHILLER's drama (1804) and ROSSINI's opera (1829).

**Teller, Edward,** 1908–, American physicist; b. Hungary. During World War II he did atom-bomb research at Columbia Univ. and at Los Alamos. Against the opposition of J. Robert OPPENHEIMER, Teller was instrumental in making possible the first successful US HYDROGEN BOMB explosion (1952).

**tellurium** (Te), semimetallic element, discovered in 1782 by Franz von Reichenstein. A silver-white, lustrous, brittle metalloid, it occurs in the minerals calaverite (a compound of gold and tellurium) and sylvanite. It is used as an additive in steel to increase ductility and as a catalyst for petroleum cracking. See ELEMENT (table); PERIODIC TABLE.

**Telugu** (ˌtelə'gooh), Dravidian language of India. See LANGUAGE (table).

**Tema,** city and port (1982 pop. 323,909), Greater Accra prov., S Ghana, on the Atlantic coast. Its economy is based on engineering, metal smelting, oil refining, and fishing.

**tempera,** painting method in which finely ground pigment is mixed with a base such as albumen, egg yolk, or thin glue. When used on wood panels, as it was for altarpieces and easel paintings, it was applied on a smooth, white gesso underpainting. Tempera produces clear, pure colours that resist oxidation. Known from antiquity, it was the exclusive panel medium in the Middle Ages. It was not supplanted by the more subtle oil paint until c.1400 in N Europe and c.1500 in Italy. A modern revival of tempera included the 19th-cent. Swiss artist Arnold Böcklin and the 20th-cent. Americans SHAHN and WYETH.

**temperament,** the adjustment in the tuning of intervals within the octave, which is particularly necessary for keyboard instruments and for harmonic music. If, for example, E is arrived at by tuning up four pure fifths from C and then transposing down two octaves, the result will be an E with the ratio 81:64, instead of the pure major third of 5:4. The difference between the two can be detected with the ear. This is not a problem for voices or for stringed and other instruments of movable pitch, where an A sharp is not the same as B flat, although they are represented by one note on the piano. But since the pure third was necessary for proper harmony, some adjustments had to be made. The first solution was that of mean-tone temperament, in which the intervals between semitones on instruments of fixed pitch were adjusted to give as nearly natural tuning as possible for C major. This meant that music in the remote keys (i.e., with more than three sharps or flats) would sound out of tune. The second solution was that of equal temperament, in which the octave was divided logarithmically into twelve parts, with equal intervals between successive semitones. J.S. BACH demonstrated the efficiency of this innovation when he wrote two sets of *24 Preludes and Fugues* for all possible keys on the 'Well-Tempered Clavichord'. Systems of equal temperament have also been used for xylophones, metallophones, and instruments of fixed pitch in Africa and Asia, dividing the octave into five, six, or seven equal intervals.

**temperance movements,** organized efforts to induce people to abstain from alcoholic beverages. In response to increasing alcoholism, local and, later, international temperance societies (e.g., the Woman's Christian Temperance Union) developed in the 19th cent. in the US, Great Britain, and N Europe. In the US they worked for liquor laws and in 1919 secured federal PROHIBITION. Outstanding temperance workers included Susan B. ANTHONY and Carry NATION.

**temperature,** the measure of the relative warmth or coolness of an object. The temperature of a substance measures not its heat content but rather the average kinetic energy of its molecules. Temperature is measured by means of a THERMOMETER or other instrument having a scale calibrated in units called degrees. A temperature scale is determined by choosing two reference temperatures and dividing the temperature difference between these points into a certain number of degrees. The most common reference temperatures are the MELTING POINT of ice and the BOILING POINT of water. On the CELSIUS scale these two reference temperatures are chosen to be 0°C and 100°C, whilst on the Farenheit scale they are 32°F and 212°F, respectively. Clearly the size of the degree depends on the particular temperature scale being used. An absolute temperature scale for which zero degree (absolute zero) corresponds to all molecules having zero average kinetic energy can be defined (see KINETIC THEORY). The Kelvin temperature scale is the absolute scale in general use and has degrees the same size as those on the Celsius scale (see diagram). On this scale the melting point of ice is 273.16°K or, conversely, absolute zero is −273.16°C. See also ENERGY; GAS LAWS; HEAT; THERMODYNAMICS.

**temple,** edifice or enclosed area dedicated to the worship of a deity or the enshrinement of holy objects. Temples have been common to most religions. Well-defined temples exist from c.2000 BC in Egypt, and there is evidence of earlier temples carved from rock in Egypt, India, China, and the Mediterranean. In Egypt in the New Kingdom, ABU SIMBEL was the finest of many cliff temples. The Egyptian temple usually had a doorway flanked by huge towers or pylons, leading to an unroofed, colonnaded

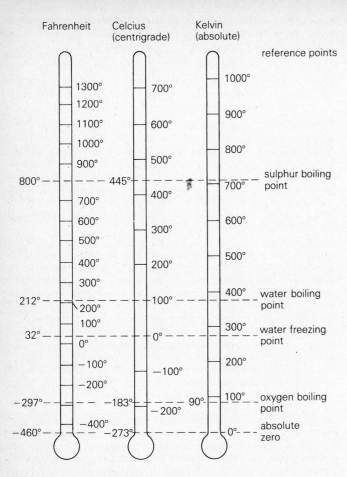

| Fahrenheit | Celcius (centigrade) | Kelvin (absolute) | |
|---|---|---|---|
| | | | reference points |
| 1300° | 700° | 1000° | |
| 1200° | | | |
| 1100° | 600° | 900° | |
| 1000° | 500° | 800° | |
| 900° | | | |
| 800° — — — 445° | | 700° | sulphur boiling point |
| 700° | 400° | | |
| 600° | 300° | 600° | |
| 500° | | 500° | |
| 400° | 200° | | |
| 300° | | 400° | water boiling point |
| 212° — — 200° | 100° | | |
| 100° | | 300° | water freezing point |
| 32° — — 0° | 0° | | |
| −100° | | 200° | |
| −200° | −100° | | |
| −297° — — −183° | | 100° — oxygen boiling point | |
| | −200° | 90° | |
| −400° | | | |
| −460° — — −273° | | 0° — absolute zero | |

Temperature scales

court; beyond were a hypostyle hall and chambers limited to priestly or royal use. The ancient Babylonian or Assyrian ZIGGURAT served as both a shrine and an astronomical observatory. The temple of Solomon in Jerusalem, the only ancient Hebrew monumental structure known, housed the Ark of the Covenant. Successive destructions and reconstructions have left no trace of the original. Greek temples were built after the Dorian immigration (before 1000 BC). The superb stone and marble central-plan buildings date from the 6th cent. BC, the best examples, e.g., the PARTHENON, from the 5th cent. The Greek temple customarily stood in a *temenos*, or sacred enclosure, with accessory buildings. It was not a place for assembled worship but a dwelling for the deity, whose colossal sculptural representation was placed in a large *naos*, or rectangular chamber. Roman temples drew on the Greek style, but also on Etruscan design, being elevated on a high base, with a deep front portico. The Roman cella, unlike the *naos*, was square in plan. Of polygonal or circular temples, the PANTHEON at Rome is the most remarkable. Many temples in Rome's Asian colonies had magnificent colonnaded entrance courts. Early Indian temples (before AD c.300) were hewn from rock walls, with lavish sculptural ornamentation. Chinese temples, on the other hand, differed from dwellings only in size and richness. In Japan, harmony with the surrounding landscape was essential to the grouping of shrines and PAGODAS.

**Temple,** in Judaism: see BET HA-MIKDASH.

**Temple, Frederick,** 1821–1902, Anglican prelate, archbishop of Canterbury (1896–1902). An advocate of educational reform, he was considered a radical before being made (1869) bishop of Exeter. He became (1885) bishop of London and in his later years was often in conflict with the High Church party. His son **William Temple,** 1881–1944, archbishop of York (1929–42) and archbishop of Canterbury (1942–44), was a philosophical theologian of distinction, but was also leader of the movement demanding greater freedom from the state for the CHURCH OF ENGLAND. He became increasingly concerned with social, economic, and international questions, was first president of the

Workers' Educational Association (1908–24), and worked successfully for the foundation of the WORLD COUNCIL OF CHURCHES.

**tempo,** in music, the speed at which a composition is played. The composer's intentions as to tempo are conventionally indicated by a set of Italian terms such as *presto* (very fast), *allegro* (fast), *andante* (moderate, literally 'walking'), *adagio* (slow), and *largo* (very slow); *accelerando* and *ritardando* are used to indicate a momentary increase or decrease of tempo. Although composers since Beethoven's time have given indications of speed by means of metronome marks, tempo has always remained a point of subjective interpretation.

**Ten Commandments** or **Decalogue,** in the Bible, the summary of divine law given by God to MOSES on Mt Sinai. In the Authorized Version they appear in Ex. 20.2–17 and in Deut. 5.6–21. They are paramount in the ethical systems of Judaism, Christianity, and Islam. The order and division of the commandments differ somewhat in different Christian churches.

**tendon,** tough cord of dense white CONNECTIVE TISSUE that attaches muscle to bone. If the muscle is thin and wide, the tendon may be a thin sheet. Tendons transfer muscle power over a distance, e.g., forearm muscles contract and pull on tendons that pull on finger bones to produce finger movements. Tendon sheaths enclose tendons at the wrist and ankle to minimize friction.

**Teneriffe** or **Tenerife:** see CANARY ISLANDS.

**Teng Hsiao-p'ing:** see DENG XIAOPING.

**Tennant Creek,** town (1986 pop. 3503), Northern Territory, northern Australia. Located 100 km (65 mi) S of Darwin, the town was important originally, in 1932, as a repeater station for the overland telegraph between Adelaide and Darwin. Rich gold discoveries were made in the area in the 1930s. In the 1950s more rich gold and copper deposits were discovered and developed.

**Tennent, Gilbert,** 1703–64, Presbyterian clergyman in colonial America, leading preacher of the GREAT AWAKENING; b. Ireland. As pastor at New Brunswick, in New Jersey, he became (1726) a leader of a revival movement among the Presbyterians and was a friend of George WHITEFIELD.

**Tennessee,** state of the US (1984 est. pop. 4,717,000), area 109,412 km² (42,244 sq mi), located in the south–central region, bordered by Kentucky and Virginia (N), North Carolina (E), Georgia, Alabama, and Mississippi (S), and, across the Mississippi R., Arkansas and Missouri (W). The capital is NASHVILLE and the largest city is MEMPHIS; Knoxville is also important. The GREAT SMOKY MTS and the Cumberland Plateau (parts of the APPALACHIAN MTS) dominate the E, leading to the rolling hills of bluegrass country in the centre, and the Mississippi R. floodplains in the W. A diversified industrial sector leads the economy, led by chemicals, processed foods, and nonelectrical machinery. Farming produces soybeans, cattle, dairy goods, pigs, tobacco, corn and hay. Tennessee is the leading producer of pyrites and zinc, and extracts coal. Tourism is attracted by the natural scenery and country music of The Grand Ole Opry in Nashville. In 1980 83% of the population was non-Hispanic white and 16% black; more than 62% lived in metropolitan areas. Although Mound Builders lived in the area, the residents were Cherokee, Chickasaw, and Shawnee Indians when the French and British explorers arrived. After the American Revolution the Indians were forcibly removed to present-day Oklahoma and the plantation economy expanded. Tennessee sided with the confederacy in the Civil War, and was its second bloodiest battlefield. After the war plantations were replaced by tenant farms, coal-mining, and textiles. In 1933 the Tennessee Valley Authority was established by the federal government to provide cheap and abundant hydroelectric power which helped diversify the state's economy.

**Tennessee,** US river, c.1050 km (650 mi) long, principal tributary of the Ohio R., which it joins at Paducah, Kentucky, after flowing N from the vicinity of Knoxville, Tennessee. The once flood-prone river has been converted by the Tennessee Valley Authority since the 1930s into a series of lakes impounded by nine major dams. Construction of a controversial canal as part of a direct water route to the Gulf of Mexico (the Tennessee–Tombigbee Waterway) began in 1971.

**Tenniel, Sir John** (ˌtenyəl), 1820–1914, English caricaturist and illustrator. Well known for his original, good-humoured political cartoons in *Punch* (1851–1901), he is also famous for his illustrations of Lewis CARROLL's *Alice in Wonderland* and *Through the Looking Glass*.

**tennis**, indoor or outdoor game for two players (singles) or four players (doubles). Although originally lawn tennis was played only on grass courts, today the surfaces are more often of clay, asphalt, or synthetics. The court measures 23.77 by 8.23 m (78 by 27 ft) for singles play; it is 1.37 m (4.5 ft) wider for doubles. A net 91 cm (3 ft) high in the middle divides the court laterally. Play is directed towards hitting the inflated, felt-covered ball with an oval-headed, fibre-strung racket into the opposite court so that the opponent cannot make a proper return. Points are scored in the progression 15, 30, 40, and game, with six games required to take a set. Usually, three set victories decide a match in men's play, two set victories in women's play. Modern tennis was developed in 1873 by an Englishman, Major Walter C. Wingfield, who borrowed from older forms of the game. The first 'world championship', was held (1877) at WIMBLEDON. In the US, where tennis was introduced in 1874, the national men's championship has been contested since 1881, the women's since 1887. The Davis Cup international team competition (begun in 1900) focused world attention on the sport. Major tournaments, originally restricted to amateurs, have been open to professionals since 1968.

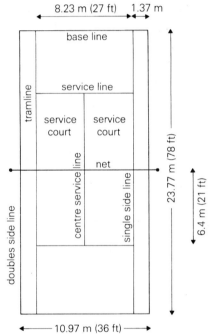

Tennis court dimensions

**Tennyson, Alfred**, 1st **Baron**, 1809–92, English poet. His first book, *Poems, Chiefly Lyrical* (1830), was followed by *Poems* (1832), which included 'The Lotos-Eaters' and 'The Lady of Shalott'. *Poems* (1842) included 'Lockesley Hall', 'Ulysses', and 'Morte d'Arthur', the first of his Arthurian cycle completed in *Idylls of the King* (1849–1885). *The Princess* (1847) was followed by *In Memoriam* (1850), an elegy sequence prompted by the death in 1833 of the poet's friend Arthur Henry Hallam. Tennyson became poet laureate in 1850. The most celebrated of his later works were *Maud* (1855), 'Ode on the Death of the Duke of Wellington' (1852), and 'The Charge of the Light Brigade' (1854). In 1883 he was made a peer. A commentator on the changing Victorian scenes and England's most famous poet, Tennyson is today valued chiefly for his verbal and metrical felicity, sensuous love of beauty, and occasional doubting melancholy.

**tenor:** see VOICE.

**tenpins:** see BOWLING.

**tense** [O.Fr., from Lat., = time], in the GRAMMAR of many languages, the category of verb forms referring to the time of action. In Latin INFLECTION the tenses are usually sets of personal verb forms and are themselves members of MOODS. English tenses are classified as simple (e.g., *look*, *looked*) or compound (e.g., *have looked*, *am looking*, *will look*).

**tenure**, in education, a guarantee of the permanence of a school, college, or university teacher's position, awarded upon successful completion of a probationary period. Tenure provides job security and tends to reinforce ACADEMIC FREEDOM. Critics argue that it lessens diligence, protects incompetent teachers, and limits opportunities for young teachers.

**Tenure of Office Act**, in US history, measure passed by Congress in 1867 over the veto of Pres. Andrew JOHNSON. The act prohibited the president from dismissing any cabinet officer or other federal officeholder whose appointment had required the consent of the Senate unless the Senate agreed to the dismissal. With this measure radical Republicans hoped to assure the tenure of the secretary of war, Edwin M. Stanton, and thus prevent any interference with their RECONSTRUCTION plan. Johnson, regarding the act as unconstitutional, dismissed Stanton anyway. His alleged violation of the act in dismissing Stanton was the principal charge in the impeachment proceedings instituted against him in 1868. Most of the act was repealed in 1887, and in 1926 the Supreme Court declared it unconstitutional.

**Ten Years' War**, 1868–78, guerrilla war fought by Cuban revolutionaries against Spanish domination of CUBA. Spanish forces carried out bloody reprisals against the patriots, who retaliated by attacking all Spanish supporters. The war dragged on until Gen. Arsino Martinez de Campos of Spain negotiated the Treaty of Zanjón, granting reforms and governmental representation to Cubans (promises that were not kept). The war foreshadowed the Cuban war of independence (1895–98) and the SPANISH-AMERICAN WAR.

**Tenzing Norgay**, 1914–86, Sherpa climber. He was a high-altitude Sherpa with the British Himalayan mountaineering expeditions in 1935, 1936, and 1938. He took part in expeditions to Karakoram in 1950 and to Nanda Devi in 1951, climbing to the east peak. In May 1953, he and Sir Edmund HILLARY became the first climbers to reach the summit of Mt Everest. He also served as chief adviser of the Himalayan Mountaineering Institute, Darjeeling.

**Teotihuacán**, archaeological site 45 km (28 mi) E of Mexico city which is one of the world's most remarkable and well-preserved ruins of the city of an ancient civilization. Evidence of the city is traceable over an area of 3.5 by 6.5 km (2.1 by 4 mi). In the central area a 'Pyramid of the Sun' (64 m (210 ft) high and 213 m (698 ft) square at the base) and a smaller 'Pyramid of the Moon' dominate a range of temples, palaces, courts, and residential areas. The people of Teotihuacán brought sculpture, ceramics, the carving of stylized stone masks, and mural painting to a high degree of refinement. Their designs indicate a complex religious system. At its peak the city's population was over 100,000.

Pyramid of the Sun (AD 300) at **Teotihuacán**

**tepee, wickiup,** and **wigwam,** types of dwelling used by NORTH AMERICAN INDIANS of various culture areas. The tepee, or tipi, used by nomadic Plains tribes, usually consisted of buffalo hides stretched over a cone formed of tent poles; it was strong and easy to move. Tribes to the south and west used the wickiup, made of brush or mats stretched over arched poles. The wigwam of the Eastern Woodlands, a domed or conical frame covered with bark or mats, might be either a single-family or a communal dwelling.

**Tepe Gawra** [Kurdish, = great mound], important settlement site in MESOPOTAMIA, N Iraq. Excavations (from 1927) unearthed 24 levels, dating from the 5th to 2nd millennium BC, with more advanced civilizations at the oldest levels (5000–3000 BC).

**terbium** (Tb), metallic element, discovered in 1843 by C.G. Mosander. Silver-grey, soft, ductile, and malleable, it is one of the RARE-EARTH METALS in the LANTHANIDE SERIES. Terbium is used in lasers, semiconductor devices, and phosphors for colour-television picture tubes. See ELEMENT (table); PERIODIC TABLE.

**Ter Borch** or **Terborch, Gerard** (teə‚bawkh), 1617–81, Dutch GENRE and portrait painter. He portrayed the life of the wealthy Dutch burgher class in technically refined paintings of great elegance and psychological subtlety. His most famous pictures include *The Guitar Lesson* (National Gall., London) and the *Parental Admonition* (c.1654/55; Berlin).

**Terbrugghen, Hendrick** (teə‚brooghən), 1588–1629, Dutch painter. Specializing in GENRE and religious subjects, he was influenced by CARAVAGGIO. His favourite genre subject was the half-length, single figure of a musician or drinker set against a light ground. *The Flute Player* (1621; Staatliche Gemaldegalerie, Kassel) is a celebrated example.

**Terence,** (Publius Terentius Afer), c.195 or 185–c.159 BC, Roman writer of COMEDY; b. Carthage. Six of his comedies survive, freely adapted from the Greek plays of MENANDER and Apollodorus of Carystus. Polished and urbane, they are characterized by gentle humour and realistic characterization.

**Teresa, Mother,** 1910–, Roman Catholic missionary in India, winner of the 1979 Nobel Peace Prize; b. Skopje (now in Yugoslavia) as Agnes Gonxha Bojaxhiu. Of Albanian parentage, she went to India at 17, becoming a nun and teaching school in Calcutta. In 1948 she left the convent and founded the Missionaries of Charity, which now operates schools, hospitals, orphanages, and food centres in more than 25 countries.

**Teresa, Saint,** 1515–82, Spanish CARMELITE nun, Doctor of the Church, one of the great mystics, and a leading figure in the COUNTER-REFORMATION. In 1562 she founded, at Ávila, the first of many convents of the Discalced Carmelites. St Teresa combined intense practicality with the most rarefied spirituality. An excellent and tireless manager, she was endowed with great personal charm, tact, and boundless good nature. With her associate, St JOHN OF THE CROSS, she produced a remarkable awakening of religious fervour that spread far beyond Spain. Her writings, notably her *Life* and the *Way of Perfection,* are among the greatest in mystical literature. Feast: 15 Oct.

**Tereshkova, Valentina Vladimirovna,** 1937–, Soviet cosmonaut. She was the first woman to orbit the Earth, in *Vostok 6* on 16–19 June 1963.

**Teresina,** city (1980 pop. 339,042), N Brazil, capital of Piauí state. Situated on the Parnaíba R. the city is the centre of a predominantly agricultural region.

**terminal:** see COMPUTER TERMINAL.

**termite** or **white ant,** social INSECT (order Isoptera), called white ant because of the usually pale-coloured body. Termites live in colonies numbering hundreds to hundreds of thousands of wingless individuals. Most of these are nonreproductive 'workers' which, unlike those of true ANTS (which are female), are of both sexes, and most termite colonies contain 'soldiers' of various forms, comprising about 5% of the total population. Another vital difference between these insects and ants is that termite colonies are not matriarchal but have a 'king' as well as a 'queen'. When founding a colony, after deliberately breaking off their wings, following a short nuptial flight, these primary reproductives are much the same size. Later, with the development of the ovaries the female's abdomen becomes greatly elongated and distended. Queens in some species (e.g., *Macrotermes*) that have large colonies can periodically produce as many as 36,000 eggs per day. These species are collected by trapping in many African countries, forming an important and tasty element in people's diet. All termites are plant-eaters, and the wood-boring species are notorious for the damage they cause to buildings and timber structures. Many species feed on living plants and through damage caused to crop plants, by feeding on roots or tunnelling into stems, can be major agricultural pests. Eucalyptus trees are prone to termite attacks, at all stages from seedling to mature tree, and this has retarded afforestation both in Australia and elsewhere in the tropics. Termite mounds built by *Macrotermes* in Africa can be up to 6 m (20 ft) high and 30 m (98 ft) in diameter, and those of *Armitermes meridionalis* in Australia are interesting because they are built with their long axes running almost exactly north–south.

Termites (order Isoptera)

**tern,** sea BIRD of the Old and New World, smaller than the related GULL, with long, pointed wings and forked tails. Also called sea swallows because of their graceful flight, they plunge headlong into the water to catch small fish. They are migratory birds, some travelling great distances. The Arctic tern (*Sterna paradisaea*) regularly follows summer from the Arctic to the Antarctic; flying over 35,000 km (22,000 mi).

**Terpsichore:** see MUSES.

**terra-cotta** [Ital. = baked earth], form of hard-baked clay widely used in the decorative arts, especially as an architectural material, either in its natural red-brown colour, painted, or with a baked glaze. Its early prevalence as a medium of artistic expression is indicated by vases, figurines, and tiles from predynastic Egypt; ancient Assyria, Persia, and China; and pre-Columbian Central America. Terra-cotta first gained architectural importance in Greece, where from c.7th cent. BC it was used for roof tiles and ornamental details. Its golden age was the RENAISSANCE, when it was widely used in the architecture of N Italy and N Germany. It was later established in Italy as a sculptural material, and reached great distinction as a decorative material in the polychrome enamelled reliefs of the DELLA ROBBIA family. Terra-cotta work in building and decoration spread from Italy in the 16th cent., often through migrant Italian artisans, to such countries as France and England. In the 18th cent. sculptors such as HOUDON used the material for sketches. Widely used in the US in modern times as an exterior covering for steel structural skeletons, terra-cotta was employed with particular skill by Louis SULLIVAN. Notable modern sculptures in terra-cotta include those by MAILLOL, EPSTEIN, and PICASSO.

**terrapin,** name used in Europe for any small freshwater members of the TORTOISE order, but strictly confined to members of the family Emydidae. Terrapins are found throughout the warmer regions of Asia, Europe, and the Americas. The European pond terrapin (*Emys orbicularis*) has a carapace, or shell, of about 20 cm (8 in). It is found in still or slow-moving waters where it feeds on fishes, amphibians, and aquatic insects. In North America the diamondback terrapin (*Malaclemys terrapin*) is a food animal, a gourmet dish.

**terrier,** class of DOG originally bred to dig from their burrows and kill small game and vermin. There are many regional variations, and breeds include the Airedale (the largest of the class), cairn, Scottish, Yorkshire, the schnauzer, and the fox terrier. Today they are mostly bred as companion dogs.

**Territorial Army,** a volunteer force trained to support the British army in time of emergency. Dating from 1908, it now has some 80,000 men and women who train regularly to maintain useful skills.

**territorial waters:** see SEA, LAW OF THE.

**territory,** in US history, a portion of the national domain that is given limited self-government, usually in preparation for statehood. The ORDINANCE OF 1787, which created the NORTHWEST TERRITORY, formed the basis upon which later territorial governments were organized. Except for the THIRTEEN COLONIES and California, Kentucky, Maine, Texas, Vermont, and West Virginia, all the states went through the territorial stage. Territorial governments have usually consisted of a governor, a bicameral legislature, a secretary, and a court system. Presently, the VIRGIN ISLANDS, GUAM, and AMERICAN SAMOA have territorial status. Canada and Australia also call their unincorporated domains territories.

**Terror, Reign of:** see REIGN OF TERROR.

**terrorism,** term usually applied to organized acts or threats of violence designed to intimidate opponents or to publicize grievances. It frequently involves bombing, kidnapping, aeroplane hijacking, the taking of hostages, and assassination. The term dates from the REIGN OF TERROR (1793–94) in the French Revolution but has taken on additional meaning in the 20th cent. Political terrorism may be part of a government campaign to eliminate the opposition, as under HITLER, MUSSOLINI, and STALIN, or it may be part of a revolutionary effort to overthrow a regime, as in guerrilla warfare. Terrorism by radicals (of both the left and right) and by nationalists became widespread after World War II. Groups that have engaged in terrorist activity include the 'provisional' wing of the IRISH REPUBLICAN ARMY; the PALESTINE LIBERATION ORGANIZATION; the RED BRIGADES in Italy; and the BAADER–MEINHOF GANG in W Germany. Present-day governments which have engaged in terrorist activity include those of Libya and South Africa, and of France, whose sinking of the Greenpeace ship *Rainbow Warrior* in New Zealand in 1985 caused an international outcry.

**Terry, Dame Ellen Alicia,** 1847–1928, English actress; mother of Edy and Edward Gordon CRAIG. As leading lady (1878–1902) to Sir Henry IRVING she was admired for her charm and grace in Shakespearean roles, especially Beatrice in *Much Ado about Nothing.*

**Tertullian,** c.160–c.230, N African Christian theologian. Converted (c.197) to Christianity, he became a formidable writer in defence of the faith. Some of his views, however, especially his moral rigorism, differed from Catholic thought, and he left the church (213) to join the schismatic Montanists. Eventually he formed his own sect, the Tertullianists.

**Tesla, Nikola,** 1856–1943, American electrician and inventor. A Serb born in Croatia, he went to the US in 1884. A pioneer in high-tension electricity, he made many discoveries and inventions of great value to the development of radio transmission and to the field of electricity, including an arc-lighting system, the Tesla induction motor, the Tesla coil, and various generators and transformers.

**Test Act,** 1673, passed by the British Parliament to exclude from public office (military and civil) all those who refused to take oaths of allegiance and supremacy, to receive communion according to the Church of England, and to renounce belief in transubstantiation. It was directed mainly against Catholics. In 1678 it was extended to members of Parliament. The act was repealed (1828) at the time of CATHOLIC EMANCIPATION.

**testes:** see REPRODUCTIVE SYSTEM.

**testosterone,** principal male sex HORMONE secreted by the testes. It is necessary for the development of the external genitals in the male fetus, and at puberty its increased levels are responsible for male secondary sex characteristics (e.g., facial hair).

**test-tube baby:** see IN VITRO FERTILIZATION.

**tetanus** or **lockjaw,** acute infectious disease of the nervous system caused by a TOXIN produced by the *Clostridium tetani* bacillus. Tetanus may follow any type of injury, including puncture wounds, animal bites,

gunshot wounds, lacerations, and fractures. The toxin acts on the motor nerves and causes muscle spasms, most frequently in the jaw (lockjaw) and facial muscles. The disease is treated with an antitoxin; preventive immunization is also available.

**Tethys,** in astronomy, natural satellite of SATURN.

**Tetley, Glen,** 1926–, American choreographer. He studied with Martha GRAHAM, and Hanya HOLM. He has worked with the Netherlands Dance Theatre (1962–65), artistic director (1969), and the Stuttgart Ballet (1974–76). His works are performed by many major companies, and he is an important influence in both Europe and the US.

**Tetouan,** city (1982 pop. 364,725), N Morocco, on the Mediterranean coast. The chief town of the Tetouan prov., its industries include the manufacture of soap, leather, textiles, and tiles. Founded in the 14th cent., the city became an important trade centre after being rebuilt in 1492 by Jewish refugees from Portugal. It was occupied by the Spanish between 1860 and 1959.

**tetracycline:** see ANTIBIOTIC.

**Teutonic Knights** or **Teutonic Order,** German military religious order founded (1190–91) in the Holy Land during the Third CRUSADE. It was made up of nobles, and its knights took monastic vows. It moved to E Europe in the early 13th cent. and in 1226 began a crusade against the pagan Prussians. Within 50 years the order established itself as the ruling government of PRUSSIA, which it Christianized by virtually exterminating the native population and repopulating it with Germans. Its governments in East Prussia, West Prussia, and (after 1309) Pomerelia were under the protection of both pope and emperor. Despite that, Poland seized (1466) West Prussia and Pomerelia. The order's own grand master, Albert of Brandenberg, accepted (1525) the Reformation and declared Prussia a secular fief with himself as duke.

**Tewodros II,** c.1818–68, emperor of ETHIOPIA (r.1855–68). He was born with the name Kassa, the son of the governor of a small frontier province. Initially little more than a brigand, he defeated one by one the contenders for the vacant imperial crown and took *Tewodros* [Theodore] as his imperial name. His reign was marked by a succession of rebellions as he attempted to reunify and centralize the country after decades of political disintegration. When a British expeditionary force invaded Ethiopia in 1867 his army deserted him and he shot himself rather than be captured.

**Texas,** state of the US, third largest in pop. (1984 est. pop. 15,989,000), second largest in area (692,405 km²/267,338 sq mi), situated in the SW, bordered by Oklahoma (N), Arkansas and Louisiana (E), the Gulf of Mexico (SE), and the Mexican states of Tamaulipas, Nuevo Leon, Coahuila, and Chihuahua (S). The capital is AUSTIN, and the largest cities are HOUSTON, DALLAS, SAN ANTONIO, EL PASO, and Fort Worth. The topography rises gradually from the wet coastal plains in the SE to the southern extension of the GREAT PLAINS, and the semiarid tableland in the NW. Texas is the leading US source of petroleum, natural gas, asphalt, sulphur, and other minerals, which dominate the economy. It is the chief manufacturer of chemicals and the main refiner of oil; nonelectrical machinery and processed foods are also important. Texas is the leading producer of cattle, which, together with cotton, wheat, and other farm products, gives it the second largest agricultural output of any state. Fishing and tourism add to the economy. The state's Spanish-origin population is second only to California's in size (c.3m, 21%), and there is also a large black population (c.1.7m, 12%); almost 80% lives in metropolitan areas. The Apache, Comanche, and other Indian tribes inhabited the area when the Spanish arrived and settled (1682). The Mexican government allowed US colonists to settle in 1821, but in 1835 they rebelled and declared independence (1836). Following a short period as a separate republic, Texas was annexed by the US, precipitating the MEXICAN WAR (1845); this began a long period of hostility towards the large Mexican population. Texas fought with the confederacy in the Civil War. In 1901 oil was discovered and the state's economy was transformed. Mexican migrants provided farm labour, some under contract, others as undocumented workers. In the 1980s the economy faltered and the collapse in oil prices (1985–86) was a serious blow to an economy accustomed to affluence, causing difficulties for some hitherto rich individuals and local governments, which had levied low taxes.

**textile design,** although never a major art-form, has attracted important talents. Raoul DUFY, the French post-impressionist painter, was the most prolific and influential textile designer; he worked in close collaboration with French couturier Paul Poiret designing dress fabrics, and with the famous Lyon silk producer Maison Bianchini-Fernier for whom he produced over 3000 designs. Other painters of the period occasionally designed fabric, e.g., PICASSO, MATISSE, and GAUDIER-BRZESKA. In England two or three adventurous companies (Heals, Edinburgh Weavers, Ascher) commissioned work from such artists as Paul NASH, Barbara HEPWORTH, Henry MOORE, and Graham SUTHERLAND. In the late 1950s and 60s styles of painting, particularly Abstract Expressionism and Pop Art, have influenced fabric, but few artists have been directly commissioned to produce textile designs.

**textiles,** fabrics made from FIBRES by WEAVING, KNITTING, CROCHET, LACE-making, knotting (e.g., MACRAMÉ), braiding, netting, or felting. Textiles are classified according to their component fibres, e.g., SILK, WOOL, LINEN, COTTON, synthetics such as RAYON and nylon, and some inorganic substances, e.g., FIBREGLASS and ASBESTOS cloth. They are also classified according to their structure or weave. Yarn, fabrics, and tools for SPINNING and weaving have been found among the earliest relics of human habitations, with various textiles typical of the remains of many ancient cultures, e.g., linens in Egypt c.5000 BC, woollens in Bronze Age Scandinavia and Switzerland, cotton in India c.3000 BC, and silk in China c.1000 BC. By the 14th cent. AD splendid fabrics were being woven on European handlooms, and TAPESTRY weaving and EMBROIDERY was highly developed. England and Flanders were particularly noted for their woollen textiles. The weaving of cotton textiles became important in Britain and the US in the 18th and 19th cent. Since the INDUSTRIAL REVOLUTION, most textiles have been produced in factories, with highly specialized machinery, but hand techniques are still widely used. **Textile printing,** the processes by which coloured designs are printed on textiles, is an ancient art. Early forms are stencil and block printing, with cylinder or roller printing developing c.1785. More recent processes include screen printing, spray painting, and electrocoating.

**TGV (Train Grand Vitesse),** French HIGH SPEED TRAIN in operation (at 260–300 kph/160–185 mph) since 1981 between Paris, Lyon, and SE France. On most of the distance between Paris and Lyon TGV operates on a new line which is exclusively used by high speed trains. Construction costs were reduced by accepting gradients of up to 3.5%, which can be negotiated by a high speed train with only modest drops in speed. By using existing railways in the approaches to cities the construction of new lines is confined to open countryside where construction costs are less, and by using the existing rail network south of Lyon, improved journey times to the whole of SE France have been achieved. As a result of the technical and commercial success of this service, a new line to the SW of Paris is being constructed and is due to open in 1990.

**Th,** chemical symbol of the element THORIUM.

**Thackeray, William Makepeace,** 1811–63, English novelist and satirist. He briefly edited a magazine before going to Paris to study art in 1834. On returning to England in 1837 he did literary hack work and illustration. In 1840 his wife became insane; to pay for her care and that of their two daughters he worked continually, contributing to magazines such brilliantly satirical writings as *The Yellowplush Correspondence* (1837–38), in which a footman comments on literary and social trends; parodies of sentimental fiction; and illustrations. His long association with *Punch* from 1842 culminated in his *Book of Snobs* (1948). His first major novel, *Vanity Fair* (1848), a satirical panorama of upper-middle-class life, was his masterpiece. It was followed by the autobiographical novel *Pendennis* (1850) and the historical romance *Henry Esmond* (1852). After an American tour, *The Newcomes* appeared (1853–55). On his second visit to the US (1855–56) he gave lectures, published in 1860 as *The Four Georges*. The Esmond story continued in *The Virginians* (1857–59). In 1860 Thackeray became editor of the new *Cornhill* magazine, in which his last novels appeared.

**Thaddaeus,** apostle: see JUDE, SAINT.

**Thailand,** officially the Kingdom of Thailand, Thai *Prathet Thai* [land of the free], formerly Siam, constitutional monarchy (1987 est. pop 53,000,000), 514,000 km² (198,455 sq mi) SE Asia, bordered by Burma (W, NW), Laos (N, E), Cambodia (SE), and Malaysia and the Gulf of Siam (S). BANGKOK is the capital. A fertile, thickly populated plain, the core of the country, rises to mountains and forests in the north and the Korat plateau in the northeast and east; a narrow, mountainous peninsula extends southwards into the Gulf of Siam. The climate is tropical monsoonal. Thailand's economy is heavily agricultural. Rice is the main

crop and the major factor in a normally favourable trade balance; rubber, teak, and tin are also valuable commodities. Industry is minor, and handicraft production exceeds factory output. Tourism is an important source of foreign exchange. The GNP is US$42,760 million (1984), and GNP per capita is US$850 (1984). Thais, ethnically related to the Shan of Burma and the Lao of Laos, constitute 75% of the population; there are large Chinese, Malay, Khmer, and Vietnamese minorities. Hinayana Buddhism is the state religion. Thai is the official language.

*History.* The Thais migrated to the area from China in the 13th cent., establishing kingdoms at Sukhothai (1238) and Ayutthaya (c.1350) and extending their power into neighbouring states. The arrival of Portuguese traders in the 16th cent. marked the beginning of Siam's relations with the West. The kingdom was threatened with colonization by the French and British in the 19th cent., but although it lost its claims to Cambodia, Laos, and other territories, adroit diplomacy enabled it to retain its independence. Although modernized under Kings Mongkut (r.1851–68) and Chulalongkorn (r.1868–1910), Siam remained an absolute monarchy until a bloodless coup in 1932 forced Prajadhikop (r.1925–35) to grant a constitution. The country was renamed Thailand in 1939. After occupation by the Japanese during WORLD WAR II, Thailand experienced internal unrest, several military coups, and periods of martial law. In the VIETNAM WAR Thailand strongly supported the US and was a site of US air bases. A bloodless coup in 1976 led to the establishment of a military government headed by Kriangsak Chamanan. Increasing political tensions led to Kriangsak's resignation and the appointment of Gen. Prem Tinsulanond as prime minister in 1980. The influx of thousands of Vietnamese and Cambodian refugees in the 1970s and 80s severely strained the Thai economy, while relations with neighbouring Laos deteriorated in the mid-1980s over a border dispute. Following multi-party elections in 1986, Gen. Prem continued as prime minister, heading a coalition government dominated by the Democratic Party. He stood down after the 1988 elections, which resulted in Maj.-Gen. Chatichae Choonhaven becoming Prime Minister.

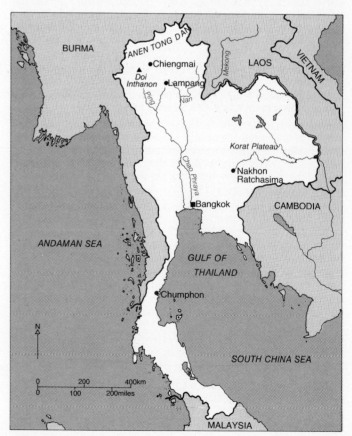

Thailand

**Thai language,** formerly Siamese, member of the Tai or Thai subfamily of the Sino-Tibetan family of languages. See LANGUAGE (table).

**Thales,** c.636–c.546 BC, pre-Socratic Greek philosopher of Miletus, reputed founder of the Milesian or Ionian school of philosophy. The first recorded Western philosopher, Thales explained the physical world as deriving not from a mythological creation but from a single underlying substance, which he believed to be water. He is said to have introduced geometry into Greece and to have predicted a solar eclipse in 585 BC. His pupils included ANAXAGORAS, ANAXIMANDER, and DIOGENES.

**thalidomide,** sleep-inducing drug found to be associated with serious CONGENITAL ABNORMALITIES in children born of women who had taken it in pregnancy. It was sold without prescription in Europe from 1957 to 1961, when its use was correlated with a high incidence of babies born with shortened, malformed limbs (c.8000 worldwide). This discovery stimulated the adoption of stricter regulations in the testing of new drugs in the US and elsewhere.

**thallium** (Tl), metallic element, discovered by William Crookes in 1861. A soft, malleable, lustrous, silver-grey metal, it resembles aluminium chemically and lead physically. The metal is used in certain electronic components, and its sulphate is used as an insecticide. See ELEMENT (table); PERIODIC TABLE.

**Thames,** principal river of England, flowing generally east c.340 km (210 mi) from the Cotswold Hills through Oxford, Reading, and the centre of London to a long estuary on the North Sea. In its upper course (near Oxford) it is often called the Isis. The Thames is spanned by more than two dozen bridges at London. The river is tidal to Teddington. A barrage at Woolwich (completed 1982) controls abnormally high tides to protect London from floods.

The **Thames** flood barrier

**Thane** (formerly **Thana**), town (1981 pop. 309,897), Maharashtra state, W India, at the head of the estuary of the Kalu R. flowing down to BOMBAY. It is a district administrative and communications centre. It is essentially a suburb and satellite of Bombay.

**Thanksgiving Day,** national holiday in the US commemorating the harvest reaped by the Plymouth Colony in 1621. The first national Thanksgiving Day was proclaimed by Pres. Washington for 26 Nov. 1789. Pres. Lincoln revived the custom in 1863. In 1941 Congress decreed that Thanksgiving should fall on the fourth Thursday of November. The customary turkey dinner is a reminder of the four wild turkeys served at the PILGRIMS' first thanksgiving feast.

**Thant, U** (thant ooh), 1909–74, Burmese diplomat, secretary general (1962–72) of the UNITED NATIONS. He became acting secretary general in 1961, on the death of Dag HAMMARSKJÖLD. Influential in settling disputes in West New Guinea (1962) and the Congo (now ZAÏRE; 1963), U Thant played a mediating role in the CUBAN MISSILE CRISIS (1962), but was less successful in efforts to resolve the VIETNAM WAR.

**Tharp, Twyla,** 1941–, American dancer and choreographer. An eclectic, innovative dancer, she danced with Paul TAYLOR and the Judson Dance Theatre before founding her own company. Her dynamic, virtuosic choreography, meticulously crafted, is performed by modern and ballet companies alike. See CHOREOGRAPHY; MODERN DANCE.

**Thatcher, Margaret,** 1925–, British political leader, the first woman prime minister of the UK (1979–). Elected (1959) to parliament, she replaced (1975) Edward HEATH as CONSERVATIVE PARTY leader and became

prime minister after the Conservative election victory in May 1979. She announced a monetarist policy designed to curtail inflation by reducing the money supply and cutting social programmes. By the early 1980s she faced a worsening economy, urban riots, and increased terrorist activity by the IRISH REPUBLICAN ARMY. In 1982 Thatcher responded forcefully to the Argentine seizure of the FALKLAND ISLANDS by dispatching troops who, after a brief war, regained the islands for Britain. The Conservative election victory of 1983 gave her a further term in office with a larger parliamentary majority, albeit with a lower proportion of the popular vote. In 1987 she won a third successive election victory (with a reduced parliamentary majority), by which time the UK economy was showing an upward turn. In 1988 she became the longest-serving British premier of the 20th cent. and in 1989 celebrated 10 years of Thatcherism.

**Thayendanegea:** see BRANT, JOSEPH.

**theatre,** building in which dramatic performances take place. Theatre in ancient Greece developed from the worship of the god DIONYSUS, when religious rituals were performed in a natural AMPHITHEATRE at the foot of a hill. The *orchestra*, a level, circular space where the drama was performed, mainly by the CHORUS, was surrounded by a large, semicircular, open-air auditorium. The original religious nature of Greek drama made audiences receptive to the cosmic themes of TRAGEDY. As the religious and choral elements of drama diminished, the orchestra was reduced in size and importance, and by the Hellenistic period (2nd–1st cent. BC) the focus of the action had shifted to a raised stage known as the *proskenion*. Roman theatres were based on Greek models but were built on a grandiose scale, being enclosed within exterior walls (although the interior was open to the air) and having elaborate stages. Roman audiences never evinced an interest in serious drama, but they accepted romantic COMEDY as long as it had elements of FARCE. Banned by the Christian church for several centuries after the fall of Rome, drama returned to the Western world in the 9th cent. in the form of liturgical plays, performed first in churches and later (by the 13th cent.) outdoors on both fixed and mobile stages, in churchyards and market squares (see MYSTERY PLAY). The development of the modern theatre dates from 1618, when Gian-Battista Aleotti built the Teatro Farnese at Parma, Italy, utilizing the proscenium arch to create a picture-frame stage and a U-shaped seating area for the audience. The separation of audience from stage was further intensified in the 19th cent. by the introduction of a curtain and the use of gas lighting, which made it possible to darken the auditorium. Today, while the proscenium arch stage continues to dominate in the commercial theatre, there has been much work to restore a vital relationship between audience and stage, and popular alternatives to the traditional designs include both the thrust stage, a platform surrounded by the audience on three sides, and the arena (theatre-in-the-round), which is completely surrounded by the audience.

**Thebes** (theebz), city of ancient S Egypt, on the NILE. In the XI dynasty (beginning c.2134 BC) it was a royal residence and a centre of worship of the god AMON. Kings and nobles were buried in the Valley of the Tombs. Thebes declined with the empire: it was sacked by the Assyrians (661 BC). The surviving temples and tombs, including that of TUTANKHAMEN, are among the most splendid in the world.

**Thebes,** ancient city of BOEOTIA, Greece. At the end of the 6th cent. BC rivalry developed with ATHENS, and Thebes sided with Persia in the PERSIAN WARS. Later, Thebes joined the confederation against SPARTA in the PELOPONNESIAN WAR and ended Spartan domination with a decisive victory at Leuktra (371 BC). Thebes joined Athens against PHILIP II of Macedon, who defeated them at Chaeronea (338). A Theban revolt caused ALEXANDER THE GREAT to destroy the city (336). It was rebuilt by CASSANDER (c.315) but never regained its former greatness. The modern Thivai occupies the site of the Theban ACROPOLIS, part of which survives.

**theft,** unlawful taking or carrying away of another's PROPERTY with intent to deprive the owner of its use, or to appropriate it to one's own or someone else's use. In England and Wales, it is governed by statute (Theft Act 1968), whilst in Scotland it is a COMMON LAW offence. In both systems the item stolen must be capable of being owned and removed by another. If the theft is accompanied by force or threat of force, it is called robbery. In both the UK and US during the 1970s a particular form of robbery, street robbery with violence (popularly called 'mugging'), attracted much public concern, even though in the UK it only amounted to 1% of all reported CRIME. See also BLACKMAIL, BURGLARY, FRAUD.

**Theiler, Max,** 1899–1972, American virologist; b. South Africa. His greatest achievement was the development of a vaccine for yellow fever, work for which he was awarded the 1951 Nobel prize for physiology or medicine.

**Themistocles** (thə͵mistəkleez), c.525–c.460 BC, Athenian statesman. He was elected an *archon* (leader) in 493 BC. In the PERSIAN WARS he persuaded the Athenians to build up their navy, and it was his strategy that brought about the decisive Athenian victory over the Persians at SALAMIS (480). He was exiled (c.471) and lived in Persia until his death.

**Theocritus,** fl. c.270 BC, Hellenistic Greek poet. Inventor of the PASTORAL, he raised that form to its height. His style is finished and sometimes artificial, but the bucolic characters in his idylls seem alive. VIRGIL, SPENSER, and others drew heavily on Theocritus.

**theodolite,** optical instrument used for a number of purposes in surveying, navigation, and meteorology. It consists of a telescope fitted with a spirit level and mounted on a tripod so that it is free to rotate about its vertical and horizontal axes. Theodolite measurements of the altitude and azimuth of a WEATHER BALLOON at precise intervals are used to compute the estimated wind velocity and direction of the portion of the atmosphere through which the balloon is passing.

**Theodora,** d. 548, Byzantine empress. She is alleged in the unreliable *Secret History* of PROCOPIUS to have been an actress and prostitute before her marriage (525) to JUSTINIAN I, who made her joint ruler. She helped to suppress the Nika rebellion caused by internal political strife, and she influenced Justinian's favourable policies toward MONOPHYSITISM.

**Theodoric the Great,** c.454–526, king of the OSTROGOTHS and conqueror of Italy. Under Byzantine emperor ZENO he was made (484) consul and sent (488) to Italy to defeat ODOACER. He took RAVENNA in 493, and shortly after Odoacer's surrender Theodoric murdered him. His great power in Italy freed him of Byzantine supervision, and his long rule was beneficent. He respected Roman institutions and improved public works. The end of his reign was clouded by a quarrel with the pope over his ARIANISM and by his hasty execution of BOETHIUS. His tomb is one of Ravenna's finest monuments.

**Theodosius,** Byzantine rulers. **Theodosius I** (the Great), 346?–95, Roman emperor of the East (379–95) and emperor of the West (392-95), was the son of Theodosius, a general of Emperor Gratian, who chose him as joint ruler. He made an advantageous peace (381) with the marauding VISIGOTHS, securing Goths for his army. He overthrew the usurper Maximus, Gratian's assassin, and restored the legal successor, VALENTINIAN II. After Valentinian was killed (392) Theodosius defeated and killed (394) the usurper Arbogast and his puppet emperor, Eugenius. Baptized in 380, Theodosius rooted out ARIANISM and paganism, and called the First Council of CONSTANTINOPLE. To reverse his excommunication for massacring rebellious citizens, he did penance before AMBROSE, bishop of Milan. He divided the empire, leaving the East to his son ARCADIUS and the West to his son HONORIUS, thus making a permanent partition. **Theodosius II,** 401–50, Roman emperor of the East (408–50), was the son and successor of Arcadius. A scholar and theologian, Theodosius called the Council of Ephesus (431), which condemned NESTORIANISM, and he upheld the Robber Synod (449; see EUTYCHES). He founded (425) the Univ. of Constantinople and published (438) the Theodosian Code. During his reign ATTILA raided the empire.

**Theognis,** fl. 6th cent. BC, Greek elegiac poet. His passionate elegies to his young friend Cyrnus counsel moderation, faithfulness, and duty.

**theology,** the systematic study of the nature of GOD and His relationship with mankind and with the world. In a broad sense the term is relevant to any religion which accepts the existence of God, but it is generally restricted to CHRISTIANITY. In this the great theological problems of ancient times were the relation of JESUS to God and the relations of Jesus and God to humanity. The struggle over ARIANISM (on the nature of Jesus) is probably the most serious theological quarrel Christianity has known, and the problem of GRACE still arouses theologians. In the Middle Ages SCHOLASTICISM systematized study of revealed truths, examining and clarifying an entire theological scheme; while scholasticism attempted to combine faith and reason, it forbade rational investigation of the bases of revealed truth. In the 19th cent. a new rational theology associated with biblical 'higher criticism' arose; it accepted the adequacy of reason to criticize every truth. There are several traditional subdivisions of theology, e.g., into natural and revealed theology, or again into dogmatic, historical, and practical (or moral) theology.

**theorem,** in MATHEMATICS and LOGIC, statement in words or symbols that can be established by means of deductive logic; it differs from an AXIOM in that a proof is required for its acceptance. A *lemma* is a theorem that is demonstrated as an intermediate step in the proof of another, more basic theorem. A *corollary* is a theorem that follows as a direct consequence of another theorem or an axiom.

**theosophy** [Gr., = divine wisdom], philosophical system with affinities to MYSTICISM that claims insight into the nature of God and the world through direct knowledge, philosophical speculation, or a physical process. Theosophy deduces the essentially spiritual nature of the universe from an assumption of the absolute reality of the essence of God. Theosophists generally believe that evil exists as a product of finite human desires; individuals can overcome it by arousing their latent spiritual powers. Emphasis is given to allegorical interpretation of sacred writings and doctrines. The Renaissance philosopher PARACELSUS combined scientific ideas with theosophical speculation. More recent theosophists include Jakob BOEHME, F.W.J. SCHELLING, and Emanuel SWEDENBORG. The philosophy and theology of the Orient, especially of India, contain a vast body of theosophical doctrine and modern theosophy draws much of its vocabulary from Indian sources. The Theosophical Society, with which theosophy is now generally identified, was founded in 1875 by Helena Petrovna BLAVATSKY. See also CABALA; GNOSTICISM; NEOPLATONISM.

**Theotocopoulos, Domenicos:** see GRECO, EL.

**Thera** or **Santorini,** volcanic island (1981 pop. 7328), c.80 km² (30 sq mi), SE Greece, in the Aegean Sea; one of the Cyclades. It is noted for its wine. In the Bronze Age Thera came under the influence of Crete (see MINOAN CIVILIZATION), but a devastating volcanic eruption (c.1500 BC) buried the island's settlements. It was resettled and later occupied (9th cent. BC) by the DORIANS. Excavations at a Minoan site have uncovered many well-preserved frescoes. Some controversial theories have equated ancient Thera with ATLANTIS.

**Theresa** or **Teresa, Saint** (Theresa of Lisieux), 1873–97, French CARMELITE nun, one of the most widely loved saints of the Roman Catholic Church, also known as the Little Flower of Jesus. Born Thérèse Martin, she entered an obscure convent at Lisieux at age 15 and died of tuberculosis nine years later. She exemplified the 'little way'—achieving goodness by performing the humblest tasks. Her spiritual autobiography became one of the most widely read religious autobiographies. She was canonized in 1925. Feast: 1 Oct.

**thermal capacity:** see HEAT CAPACITY.

**thermal equilibrium,** state finally achieved in any closed isolated system when all macroscopic mechanical movement has ceased through the effects of friction and when the flow of energy from hotter to colder parts has equalized all temperatures. No further development is then possible.

**Thermidor:** see FRENCH REVOLUTIONARY CALENDAR.

**thermochemistry:** see CHEMISTRY.

**thermocouple,** a temperature-measuring device formed by joining the ends of two strips of dissimilar metals in a closed loop, with the two junctions at different temperatures. Because the voltage that arises in this circuit is proportional to the temperature difference between the junctions, the temperature at one junction can be determined if the other junction is maintained at a known temperature.

**thermodynamics,** branch of science concerned with the nature of HEAT and its conversion into other forms of ENERGY. Heat is a form of energy associated with the positions and motion of the molecules of a body (see KINETIC–MOLECULAR THEORY OF GASES). The total energy that a body contains as a result of the positions and the motions of its molecules is called its internal energy. The first law of thermodynamics states that in any process the change in a system's internal energy is equal to the heat absorbed from the environment minus the WORK done on the environment. This law is a general form of the law of conservation of energy (see CONSERVATION LAWS). The second law of thermodynamics states that in a system the ENTROPY cannot decrease for any spontaneous process. A consequence of this law is that an engine can deliver work only when heat is transferred from a hot reservoir to a cold reservoir or heat sink. The third law of thermodynamics states that all bodies at absolute zero would have the same entropy; this state is defined as having zero entropy.

**thermoluminescence,** method for dating pottery and other fired clay material. When crystalline solids are heated, charged particles emitted by radioactive impurities but trapped in the crystal lattice are released as light, or thermoluminescence. The fact that the number of trapped particles will increase with time provides the dating application, for the crystals in a clay pot will have been trapping charged particles since its manufacture. The process has a useful application in detecting forgeries.

**thermometer,** instrument for measuring TEMPERATURE based on the variation of some physical property of a body or system with temperature. Many thermometers use the fact that most substances expand when heated and contract when cooled. A typical household or clinical thermometer consists of a small vacuum tube of uniform bore, with a temperature scale etched on its front. The tube is closed at one end and connected at the other with a chamber containing mercury or another liquid. When the chamber is heated, the fluid expands and rises into the tube. A variant of this uses a bimetallic strip consisting of two metals with different expansion coefficients soldered together into a spiral which unwinds and moves a pointer as the temperature is raised. RESISTANCE thermometers depend on the variation of electrical resistance with temperature of metals (e.g., platinum); measuring a current passing through the resistance enables the temperature to be determined. Thermometers based on THERMOCOUPLES involve measurement of the small voltage which arises when the two ends of the thermocouple are at different temperatures.

**thermonuclear energy:** see NUCLEAR ENERGY.

**Thermopylae,** pass, E central Greece, between the cliffs of Mt Oeta and the Malic Gulf. In ancient times it was an entrance into Greece from the north. There in 480 BC a small force of Spartans fought to the last man in an unsuccessful attempt to halt the invading army of Xerxes (see PERSIAN WARS).

**Theseus,** in Greek mythology, Athenian hero; son of King Aegeus. Of his many adventures the most famous was the slaying of the MINOTAUR, which he accomplished with the help of ARIADNE, daughter of King MINOS of Crete. As king of Athens he instituted several reforms, notably the federalization of the Attic communities. In the land of the AMAZONS he abducted Antiope, who bore him Hippolytus. When a vengeful Amazon army invaded Athens Theseus defeated it. Antiope was killed, and Theseus later married PHAEDRA. When he and his friend Pirithoüs attempted to take PERSEPHONE from HADES, they were imprisoned there until HERCULES rescued Theseus. When Theseus returned to Athens he found it corrupt and rebellious. He sailed to Skyros, where he was murdered by King Lycomedes.

**Thespis,** fl. 534 BC, Attic Greek dramatist, traditionally the inventor of TRAGEDY. He is said to have modified the DITHYRAMB by introducing an actor separate from the chorus, enabling spoken dialogue to develop.

**Thessalonians,** two epistles of the NEW TESTAMENT written by St PAUL (AD c.50). First Thessalonians, after recalling the founding of the Christian church at THESSALONIKI, gives advice on moral behaviour and seeks to allay fears about the fate of brethren who have died before Christ's Second Coming. Second Thessalonians, a shorter letter, strongly condemns notions that the Second Coming is at hand.

**Thessaloníki** or **Salonica,** city (1981 pop. 406,413), N Greece, in Macedonia. It is a major port and industrial centre, exporting grain, tobacco, and ores. Founded in 315 BC by Cassander, king of Macedon, it linked BYZANTIUM with the Adriatic region in Roman times and was the Roman provincial capital of Macedon after 146 BC. The kingdom of Thessaloníki (1204), comprising most of N and central Greece, was the largest fief of the Latin Empire of CONSTANTINOPLE. It was variously held by the Greeks, Byzantines, and Ottoman Turks before being conquered (1912) by Greece in the BALKAN WARS. Although the city was devasted by a fire in 1917 and damaged severely in World War II, it retains many ancient ruins and fine churches.

**Thessaly** (ˌthesəlee), ancient region of N Greece. It was settled before 1000 BC. Its chief cities were Larissa, Crannon, and Pherae. It was powerful in the 6th cent. BC, but internal conflicts caused its decline. United briefly (374) by Jason, the tyrant of Pherae, it again became a force in Greece, but it was subjugated (344) by PHILIP II of Macedon. A province

in the late Roman Empire, it passed to the Turks (1355) and then to modern Greece (1881).

**Thetis,** in Greek mythology, a nymph; mother of ACHILLES.

**thiamine:** see VITAMINS AND MINERALS (table).

**thiazide** (ˌthie·ə'zied): see DIURETIC.

**Thiers, Adolphe** (tyeə), 1797–1877, French statesman and historian. As a journalist, Thiers attacked the government of CHARLES X and helped bring about the JULY REVOLUTION of 1830. He held ministerial posts under LOUIS PHILIPPE and was premier (1836, 1840, 1848). After the FEBRUARY REVOLUTION of 1848, he opposed the Second Empire of NAPOLEON III, and after France's defeat in the FRANCO-PRUSSIAN WAR, crushed the COMMUNE OF PARIS, and became president (1871–73) of the new republic. His historical works on the French Revolution and Napoleon are today considered eloquent but superficial.

**Thimbu,** town (1977 est. pop. 8922), capital of BHUTAN.

**Third International:** see COMINTERN.

**Third World,** name applied to the technologically less-advanced countries of Asia, Africa, and Latin America. Known as developing countries, they are generally distinguished from the Western nations and the Eastern bloc. The term usually excludes China.

**Thirteen Colonies,** in US history, the British North American colonies that joined together in the AMERICAN REVOLUTION and became the original states of the US. They were: NEW HAMPSHIRE, MASSACHUSETTS, RHODE ISLAND, CONNECTICUT, NEW YORK, NEW JERSEY, PENNSYLVANIA, DELAWARE, MARYLAND, VIRGINIA, NORTH CAROLINA, SOUTH CAROLINA, and GEORGIA.

**Thirty-nine Articles,** a set of 39 doctrinal propositions adopted by the CHURCH OF ENGLAND, first in 1563 and in their final form in 1571, as a statement of its position both in general and in relation to the theological controversies of the 16th-cent. REFORMATION. Protestant in orientation, they are often deliberately ambiguous because of the Elizabethan government's desire that the national church should be as inclusive as possible. Clergy of the Church of England were formerly required to subscribe to them in detail, but since 1865 only an affirmation that the doctrine contained in them is agreeable to the Word of God has been demanded. The Articles are not authoritative in other branches of the ANGLICAN COMMUNION.

**Thirty Tyrants,** 404–403 BC, oligarchy installed in ancient Athens by the Spartan commander LYSANDER after Sparta had won the PELOPONNESIAN WAR. It was overthrown at Piraeus by THRASYBULUS.

**Thirty Years' War,** 1618–48, general European war, fought mainly in Germany. Although the war had many issues, it may be considered mainly a struggle of German Protestant princes and foreign powers (France, Sweden, Denmark, England, the United Provinces) against the unity and power of the HOLY ROMAN EMPIRE (represented by the HABSBURGS) allied with the Catholic princes of Germany. The Habsburg world then included Austria, Spain, Bohemia, most of Italy, and the S Netherlands. The war began in Prague, when the Protestant Bohemian nobles deposed the Catholic King Ferdinand (later Emperor FERDINAND II) and elected the Protestant FREDERICK THE WINTER KING. The imperialist forces under TILLY and the Catholic League under Duke Maximilian I of Bavaria quickly defeated the Bohemians (1620) and other Protestant forces in the PALATINATE (1622–23). Thus ended the war's first phase. The second phase began in 1625 when CHRISTIAN IV of Denmark invaded Germany on the side of the Protestant princes, although his chief purpose was to halt Habsburg expansion into N Germany. Defeats by WALLENSTEIN in 1626 and Tilly in 1627 forced him to withdraw. Imperialist forces promptly overran Schleswig, Holstein, and Jutland. In 1629 Christian signed a peace with the emperor, surrendering the N German bishoprics. That and the emperor's attempt to declare void Protestant titles to lands in N Germany represented a further threat to the Protestant forces. GUSTAVUS II of Sweden now entered the war. Like Christian of Denmark, he feared imperial designs in the north. He invaded Germany and defeated Tilly at Breitenfeld (1631). Gustavus was killed at Lützen (1632), although his troops were victorious. The anti-imperialist forces, including the Swedes, continued to fight, though they were defeated at Nördlingen in 1634. A general German desire for peace led to the Peace of Prague (1635). It was accepted by all participants and helped to reconcile Protestants and Catholics. A general peace seemed to be forthcoming, but Cardinal RICHELIEU of France was unwilling to see the Habsburgs retain power. He brought France openly into the war in 1635, beginning the last and bloodiest phase of the struggle. It now spread to the Low Countries, Italy, and the Iberian Peninsula. The anti-imperialist commanders Bernard of Saxe–Weimar; the Swedes Baner, Wrangel, and TORSTENSSON; and Louis II de CONDÉ and Turenne of France were victorious. Peace talks began in 1640 but proceeded slowly, not being completed until 1648 (see WESTPHALIA, PEACE OF), though the Franco-Spanish conflict continued until 1659. The war caused widespread destruction in the Empire and weakened the Habsburg position.

**thistle,** spiny, usually weedy plant, most commonly members of the COMPOSITE family that have spiny leaves and often showy heads of purple, rose, white, or yellow flowers. The Scotch thistle, usually identified as *Onopordum acanthium* and actually rare in Scotland, is the national emblem of Scotland. The Russian thistle is a member of the goosefoot family.

**Thomas, Ambroise,** 1811–96, French composer. His works include CANTATAS, ballets, and 20 operas, notably *Le Caïd* (1849), *Mignon* (1866), and *Hamlet* (1868).

**Thomas, Dylan,** 1914–53, Welsh poet. His *Eighteen Poems* (1934) brought fame and controversy, which grew with *The Map of Love* (1939), *Deaths and Entrances* (1946), and *Collected Poems 1934–1952* (1952). His largely autobiographical prose, touched with fantasy, includes *A Portrait of the Artist as a Young Dog* (1940) and *Adventures in the Skin Trade* (1955). Thomas's mastery of sound, perhaps related to his fine voice, is evident in his well-known radio drama *Under Milk Wood* (1954). His imagery is complex and sometimes difficult, but his humour and his robust love of life attract immediately.

**Thomas, Edward,** 1878–1917, English poet. A prolific prose-writer before World War I, he joined the army in 1915 and was later killed in action. He turned to poetry in 1914 under the influence of Robert FROST. His *Poems* (1917) are intense and subtle evocations of rural life.

**Thomas, Norman Mattoon,** 1884–1968, American socialist leader. Originally a Presbyterian minister, Thomas became leader of the Socialist party in 1926 and was repeatedly (1928, 1932, 1936, 1940, 1944, and 1948) its candidate for the presidency.

**Thomas, R(onald) S(tuart),** 1913–, Welsh poet. A clergyman and Welsh nationalist, his austere lyrics reflect his experience of rural life and his own spiritual self-questioning. His books include *Song at the Year's Turning* (1955) and *Laboratories of the Spirit* (1975). He writes in both English and Welsh.

**Thomas, Saint,** one of the Twelve Disciples, called Didymus (i.e., 'twin'). He refused to believe in the Resurrection until he saw Jesus's wounds; hence the expression 'doubting Thomas'. Feast: 21 Dec.

**Thomas à Kempis,** b. 1379 or 1380, d. 1471, German monk. In the Netherlands, he became (c.1413) an Augustinian priest. The great devotional work *The Imitation of Christ* has been traditionally ascribed to him, although some scholars doubt his authorship.

**Thomas Aquinas, Saint,** 1225?–74, Italian Dominican, philosopher, and theologian, Doctor of the Church; known as the Angelic Doctor. He is the greatest figure of SCHOLASTICISM, one of the principal saints of the Roman Catholic Church, and the founder of the system which Pope Leo XIII singled out (1879) for special endorsement. His major work, the monumental *Summa theologica* (1267–73), is a systematic exposition of Christian theology on philosophical principles. His shorter treatise, *On Being and Essence* (1256), contains his metaphysics. St Thomas's system embraces the moderate REALISM of Aristotle and is in opposition to the Platonism and Neo-Platonism that had prevailed in Catholic theology since the time of St AUGUSTINE. Unlike the Platonists, to whom truth was a matter of faith, St Thomas held that faith and reason constitute two harmonious realms; theology and science cannot contradict each other. Likewise, there can be no conflict between philosophy and theology. In his universe, everything is arranged in ascending order to God, the only necessary, self-sufficient being. St Thomas succeeded in synthesizing the naturalistic philosophy of Aristotle and Christian belief, the greatest achievement of medieval philosophy. Feast: 28 Jan.

**Thomas Becket, Saint** 1118–70, assassinated archbishop of Canterbury. Of good family and well educated, he attracted the attention of HENRY II, who made him chancellor (1155). Then, in an attempt to curb the growing power of the church, the king nominated his friend as archbishop of Canterbury. Foreseeing trouble, Thomas was reluctant to accept, but in 1162 he was ordained priest and consecrated archbishop. Henry and Thomas were soon opposed, particularly over the king's efforts to gain jurisdiction over 'criminous clerks', clergymen accused of crime. Thomas, refusing to accept the Constitutions of CLARENDON and opposing the growing royal power, fled to the Continent (1164). In 1170 a kind of peace was arranged, and Thomas returned to England. Meanwhile, Henry had his son crowned by the archbishop of York; the bishops who took part in this ceremony were suspended by the pope. Antipathy between the king and archbishop grew strong, and in Dec. 1170 the king issued his fateful plea to be rid of the archbishop. On 29 Dec. 1170, Thomas was murdered in Canterbury cathedral by Henry's partisans. The Christian world was shocked by Thomas's death; in 1173 he was canonized by Pope Alexander III and in 1174 the king was forced to do penance at the saint's tomb in Canterbury, which became the greatest of English shrines. Feast: 29 Dec.

**Thompson, Daley,** 1958–, English athlete. He was only 16 when he won the Welsh Amateur Athletics Association decathlon championships, and in 1976 he was the youngest member of the British team at the Montreal Olympics, when he came 18th in the DECATHLON. He took the Olympic title at the Moscow Olympics in 1980; won every major decathlon contest in the world between 1980 and 1984, and in 1984 won another Olympic gold medal in Los Angeles. The long jump is possibly his best event.

**Thomson, James,** 1700–48, Scottish poet. His most famous poem, *The Seasons* (1726–30), contains descriptions of nature that challenged the urban, artificial school of POPE and influenced forerunners of ROMANTICISM like Thomas GRAY.

**Thomson, James,** 1834–82, Scottish poet and essayist, best known for his sombre poem, *The City of Dreadful Night* (1880). His pessimism, influential on fin-de-siècle writers, was enhanced by his alcoholism.

**Thomson, Sir Joseph John,** 1856–1940, English physicist. He was head of the Cavendish Laboratory, Cambridge (1884–1919), his long tenure helping to make it a leading centre for atomic research. In 1906 he was awarded the Nobel Prize for physics for his work on the conduction of electricity through gases, which led to the discovery of the ELECTRON. His son, **Sir George Paget Thomson,** 1892–1975, was joint recipient of the 1937 Nobel Prize for physics for his work on the diffraction of electrons by crystals.

**Thomson, Virgil,** 1896–, American composer and music critic. Until c.1926 he wrote in a dissonant, neoclassic style; later he used a simplified style influenced by SATIE. His works include the operas *Four Saints in Three Acts* (1928) and *The Mother of Us All* (1947), with LIBRETTOS by Gertrude STEIN; music for films, e.g., *The River* (1937); a CANTATA on the poems of Edward LEAR (1973); and many organ, piano, and chamber works.

**Thomson, William:** see KELVIN, WILLIAM THOMSON, 1st BARON.

**Thon Buri:** see BANGKOK, Thailand.

**Thor,** Germanic **Donar,** Norse god of thunder, might, and war; also associated with marriage, the hearth, and agriculture. He was armed with a magical hammer that returned to him, iron gloves, and a belt of strength. He was identified with the Roman JUPITER, whose day became Thor's day (Thursday).

**Thoreau, Henry David,** 1817–62, one of the most influential figures in American thought and literature. An advocate of TRANSCENDENTALISM, he was a close friend of EMERSON, with whom he edited the transcendentalist magazine *The Dial*. Thoreau built a cabin at Walden Pond, near Concord, in 1845 and remained there for more than two years. There he lived out his philosophy of individualism, observing nature, reading, and expanding on his ideas and activities in a journal that he later distilled into his most famous work, *Walden* (1854). The journal was also the source of his first book, *A Week on the Concord and Merrimack Rivers* (1849), as well as of several posthumously published works, e.g., *Excursions* (1863), *Cape Cod* (1865). Thoreau was also a significant naturalist and a powerful social critic. His essay 'Civil Disobedience' (1849) has had far-reaching influence on various movements and on such leaders as GANDHI and Martin Luther KING.

**Thorfinn Karlsefni,** fl. 1002–15, Icelandic leader of an attempt to settle NORTH AMERICA. According to Norse SAGAS, he set out c.1010 to settle in

Vinland, a section of North America discovered earlier by LEIF ERICSSON. Thorfinn returned to GREENLAND after three years. There is much disagreement on the dates of his expedition and the sites visited.

**thorium** (Th), radioactive element, discovered in 1828 by Jöns Jakob BERZELIUS. A soft, ductile, lustrous, silver-white metal in the ACTINIDE SERIES, it has 12 known isotopes. It is important for its potential conversion into the fissionable fuel uranium-233 for use in NUCLEAR REACTORS. See ELEMENT (table); PERIODIC TABLE.

**Thorndike, Dame Sybil**, 1882–1976, English actress. She performed many Shakespearean and classical roles, and was particularly acclaimed in *Medea* and *The Trojan Women*. She created (1924) the title role in G.B. SHAW's *Saint Joan*.

**Thorpe, Jim** (James Thorpe), 1888–1953, American athlete. He is considered by many the greatest all-round male athlete the US has ever produced. Part Indian, he played football at the Carlisle (Pennsylvania) Indian School and led (1911–12) his team to unexpected wins over several highly rated colleges. In the 1912 Olympics he won events in both the PENTATHLON and DECATHLON. He surrendered his medals after it was revealed that he had played semiprofessional baseball, but they were restored posthumously in 1982.

**Thorvaldsen** or **Thorwaldsen, Albert Bertel** (ˌtawvahlsən), 1770–1844, Danish sculptor. He was a leader of the neo-classicists, and his adherence to Greek art is seen in his *Jason* (1802–03; Thorvaldsen Mus., Copenhagen), rendered with respect for antique prototypes. He designed (1819) the famous *Lion of Lucerne* (1819–21; Gletscherpark, Lucerne), a memorial to the SWISS GUARD, and his portrait sculptures include a monument to *Byron* (1829; Trinity College, Cambridge) and a *Self-Portrait* marble statue (1839; Thorvaldsen Mus., Copenhagen). The Thorvaldsen Museum, Copenhagen, has a large collection of his work.

**Thothmes:** see THUTMOSE.

**Thousand and One Nights** or **Arabian Nights**, a series of anonymous stories in Arabic, a classic of world literature. The cohesive plot device concerns the efforts of Scheherezade, or Sheherazade, to keep her husband, Shahriyar, legendary king of Samarkand, from killing her by entertaining him with a tale a night for 1001 nights. The best-known stories are those of Ali Baba, Sinbad, and Aladdin. Many of the stories are set in India, but their individual origins are unknown. The present form of the collection is Muslim in spirit and is thought to be from Persia or an Arabic-speaking country.

**Thrace**, region of SE Europe comprising NE Greece, S Bulgaria, and European Turkey, bordered by the Black Sea in the northeast, and the Sea of Marmara and the Aegean Sea in the south. Its major cities are ISTANBUL, Edirne, and SOFIA. Mainly an agricultural region, it produces wheat, fruit, silk, and olive oil. The ancient Thracians had a developed culture in the BRONZE AGE but were considered barbarians by the Greeks, who established colonies there by 600 BC to exploit the gold and silver mines. The region benefited from Roman rule (1st cent. BC), but from the 3rd cent AD it was a battleground for competing empires, e.g., Byzantine, Bulgarian, Ottoman. Thrace's present boundaries were established in 1923.

**Thrasybulus** ('thrasəˌbyoohləs), d. c.389 BC, Athenian statesman. Banished by the THIRTY TYRANTS installed in Athens by Sparta after the Peloponnesian War, he gathered a force of exiles in Thebes and overthrew (403) the Tyrants.

**Three-Age System**, system of charting human cultural development through technology, incorporating the STONE AGE, BRONZE AGE, and IRON AGE. It was formulated in the 19th cent. by Christian Thomsen to classify the prehistoric collections of the Danish National Museum and refined by his successor, J.J. Worsaae, and others into a global scheme. The system developed at a time when evolutionary theory had begun to transform the concept of history; technology, and the Three-Age System, became equated with a degree of cultural sophistication (see EVOLUTION, SOCIOCULTURAL). This interpretation is now outmoded, in view of the social complexity of all human societies evident from the upper PALAEOLITHIC period. The Three-Age system remains a convenient way of describing generalized cultural periods, but it is now inadequate as a form of classification in archaeological research (see ARCHAEOLOGY).

**three-day event:** see EVENTING.

**Three Emperors' League,** *Dreikaiserbund,* informal alliance formed in 1872 by the emperors of Austria–Hungary, Germany, and Russia. Its aims were to preserve the social order of the conservative powers of Europe and to keep the peace between Austria–Hungary and Russia, which were traditional rivals. The league was eventually superceded by the TRIPLE ALLIANCE AND TRIPLE ENTENTE.

**Three Kings:** see WISE MEN OF THE EAST.

**Three Mile Island**, site of a nuclear power plant 16 km (10 mi) S of Harrisburg, Pennsylvania, US. On 28 Mar. 1979, failure of the cooling system of the No. 2 NUCLEAR REACTOR led to overheating and partial melting of its uranium core and production of hydrogen gas, which raised fears of an explosion and dispersal of radioactivity. Thousands living near the plant left the area before the 12-day crisis ended, during which time some radioactive water and gases were released. A federal investigation, assigning blame to human, mechanical, and design errors, recommended changes in reactor licensing and personnel training, as well as in the structure and function of the Nuclear Regulatory Commission. The accident also increased public concern over the dangers of nuclear power and stopped construction of other reactors in the US. See also NUCLEAR ENERGY.

**thrombosis**, obstruction of an artery or vein by a blood clot, or thrombus. An arterial thrombosis is usually more serious, blocking the supply of oxygen and nutrients to some area of the body: a thrombus in one of the arteries leading to the heart (causing a heart attack) or to the brain (causing a STROKE) can result in death. A thrombus in the vein is known as phlebothrombosis or thrombophlebitis (see PHLEBITIS). Thrombosis is treated with an ANTICOAGULANT. See also CORONARY HEART DISEASE.

**throne**, chair of state or the seat of a high dignitary. The throne was at first a stool or bench and later became an ornate armchair, usually raised on a dais and surmounted by a canopy. Often lavishly decorated, thrones have been made of a variety of materials, including wood, stone, ivory, and precious metals. NAPOLEON I's throne was a gilded chair displaying eagles, lions, and other symbols. The throne of Great Britain is an oak chair in the House of Lords.

**thrush** or **song thrush, missel thrush**, name given to members of the family Turdidae, which includes the BLACKBIRD and the ROBIN. Thrush is an Old English word, originally applied to *Turdus philomelos*, the 23-cm (9-in) song thrush, found across Europe to Asia, alongside the larger 27-cm (10½-in) missel (sometimes spelt mistle) thrush (*T. viscivorus*). Both birds feed on snails, worms, and insects, as well as on fruits. Thrushes use a stone as an anvil to break open snail shells. Like all the rest of the family, thrushes sing beautifully.

**Thucydides** (thyoohˌsidideez), c.460–c.400 BC, Greek historian of Athens, one of the greatest of ancient historians. His one work, a history of the PELOPONNESIAN WAR to 411 BC, is a military record, devoid of social and political references apart from those pertaining to the war. It is studiously impartial and is noted for its eloquent speeches, particularly the funeral oration of PERICLES.

**Thugs,** Indian religious sect of murderers and thieves suppressed by the British in the 19th cent. Members of the sect worshipped the goddess Bhavani and committed their murders in sacrifice to her. They were also known as the *Phansigars* [stranglers] because they strangled their victims, usually wealthy travellers.

**Thule,** name the ancients gave to the northernmost land of Europe, an island found c.310 BC by the Greek Pytheas and since then identified with various northern lands. 'Ultima Thule' figuratively means the farthest goal of human effort.

**thulium** (Tm), metallic element, discovered in 1879 by P.T. Cleve. One of the RARE-EARTH METALS in the LANTHANIDE SERIES, it is a lustrous silver-white, soft, malleable, and ductile. It forms compounds with oxygen and the halogens, most of which are light green. Thulium-170 emits X-rays and is used in portable X-ray units. See ELEMENT (table); PERIODIC TABLE.

**thunder,** sound produced when a flash of LIGHTNING passes through air, heating the adjacent air and causing it to expand rapidly. A short flash of lightning creates a relatively short crash of thunder. Rolling thunder occurs either when there is a long flash of lightning, generating thunder over a great distance, or when obstructions such as clouds, mountains, or differing layers of air cause echoes and reverberations. See also THUNDERSTORM.

**Thunder Bay,** city (1981 pop. 121,379), W Ontario, on the Thunder Bay Inlet of Lake SUPERIOR. It is Canada's principal lakehead port on the GREAT LAKES and handles much of the grain shipped from Canada's Prairie Provinces. Other industries include oil refining and the manufacture of steel, chemicals, and transport equipment. Thunder Bay, formed in 1970 by the amalgamation of the former twin cities of Fort William and Port Arthur, is at the former site of a 17th-cent. fur trading post and of a fort built (1801) by the NORTH WEST COMPANY as its western headquarters.

**thunderstorm,** violent local atmospheric disturbance accompanied by LIGHTNING, THUNDER, and heavy RAIN, often by strong gusts of WIND, and sometimes by HAIL. The typical thunderstorm caused by convection occurs on a hot summer afternoon when the sun's warmth has heated a large body of moist air near the ground. This air rises and is cooled by expansion. The cooling condenses the water vapour in the air, forming a cumulus CLOUD. If the process continues violently, the cloud becomes immense; the summit often attains a height of 6.5 km (4 mi) above the base, and the top spreads out in the shape of an anvil as the transition to a cumulonimbus cloud occurs. The turbulent air currents within the cloud cause a continual breaking up and reuniting of the raindrops, building up strong electrical charges that result in lightning.

**Thurber, James,** 1894–1961, American humourist. He was a staff member (1927–33) of and principal contributor to the *New Yorker* magazine. A deep psychological insight underlies Thurber's wistful, ironic cartoons and stories. Collections of his works include *The Owl in the Attic* (1931), *My Life and Hard Times* (1933), *The Thurber Carnival* (1945), and *Thurber Country* (1953). He collaborated with E.B. White on the satire *Is Sex Necessary?* (1929) and with Elliott Nugent on the play *The Male Animal* (1940).

**Thuringia** (thoo͵rinjiə), historic region and former state, c.15,540 km² (6000 sq mi), SW East Germany. The area's first occupants, the ancient Germanic tribe of Thuringians, fell to the Franks in the 6th cent. AD and were converted to Christianity in the 8th cent. By the 11th cent. Thuringia's rulers, dominated after 1247 by the WETTIN dynasty of Saxony, had emerged as princes of the Holy Roman Empire. The division of the Wettin lands in 1485 gave the major share to the Ernestines, who split Thuringia into several duchies (e.g., Saxe-Coburg, Saxe-Gotha, Saxe-Weimar). A centre of the Lutheran Reformation (16th cent.), Thuringia joined the German Confederation (1815) and the German Empire (1871). After expulsion of their rulers in 1918, the duchies merged under the Weimar Republic as the state of Thuringia, with its capital at WEIMAR. The state was reconstituted as part of East Germany in 1946 but abolished as an administrative unit in 1952.

**Thursday:** see WEEK.

**Thutmose** or **Thothmes** (͵thutmohz, ͵tut-, ͵thothmeez), the name of several Egyptian pharaohs. The most notable of these was **Thutmose III** (c.1504–1450 BC XVIII dynasty) under whom Egypt attained its greatest territorial dominion. After a power struggle against his step-mother Queen Hatshepsut, he ruled unopposed from her death in c.1480. He defeated a coalition of Syrian and Palestinian peoples at Megiddo and campaigned as far as the upper Euphrates; Egyptian control now extended all the way from there to the Fourth Cataract of the Nile, and tribute flowed in from a yet wider area.

**Thyestes:** see ATREUS.

**thyme,** aromatic, shrubby herb (genus *Thymus*) of the MINT family. Common thyme, used as a seasoning, is the Old World *T. vulgaris,* an erect plant with greyish branches. It is cultivated mainly in Spain and France.

**thymus gland,** mass of glandular tissue located in the neck or chest of most vertebrates (see ENDOCRINE SYSTEM). Found in the upper chest under the breastbone in humans, the thymus is thought to be necessary for the development of the body's system of IMMUNITY. The thymus processes white blood cells known as lymphocytes, which kill foreign cells and stimulate other immune cells to produce antibodies. The gland grows throughout childhood until puberty and then gradually decreases in size. Its function in the adult is unclear.

**thyristor,** semiconductor device that can be triggered so that it passes only a portion of the cycle of an alternating current. It is used for high power rectification where large numbers of components may be connected in parallel and in machines for controlling their speed.

**thyroid gland,** important endocrine gland (see ENDOCRINE SYSTEM), situated in the neck, that regulates the body's metabolic rate (see METABOLISM). It consists of two lobes connected by a narrow isthmus. Thyroid tissue is made up of millions of tiny, saclike follicles that store thyroid hormone, production of which is stimulated by thyroid-stimulating hormone from the PITUITARY GLAND and which also requires sufficient dietary iodine. Metabolic disorders result from oversecretion or undersecretion of the thyroid.

**Ti,** chemical symbol of the element TITANIUM.

**Tiahuanaco,** archaeological site containing the impressive remains of pre-Incan ruins on the S edge of L. Titicaca in central Bolivia. Estimated to date from AD 800 the civilization which they represent was ended abruptly by some unexplained calamity around AD 900. The Aymará Indians who continue to inhabit the region have maintained their own language and social structures despite the subsequent Incan and Spanish conquests.

**Tianjin** or **Tientsin,** city (1984 pop. 7,988,900), NE China, on the Haihe R and at one end of the GRAND CANAL. Located in E central HEBEI prov., but administered directly by the central government, Tianjin is one of China's largest cities, a leading international port (serving BEIJING), and a transport centre for N China. It is also an important manufacturing centre specializing in steel, machinery, chemicals, textiles, and food processing. A 19th-cent. treaty port, it was occupied by Western powers during the BOXER UPRISING (1900) and was the site of foreign concessions until 1946.

**Tiber,** chief river of peninsular Italy, c.400 km (250 mi) long. Rising in the Apennines, it crosses the Agro Romana and Campagna, flowing through Rome to the Tyrrhenian Sea.

**Tiberias:** see GALILEE, SEA OF.

**Tiberius** (Tiberius Julius Caesar Augustus), 42 BC–AD 37, Roman emperor (r.AD 14–37); son of Tiberius Claudius Nero and Livia Drusilla, later wife of AUGUSTUS. He was governor of Transalpine Gaul and campaigned in Germany and Illyricum. In AD 14 he succeeded Augustus as emperor and continued his policies, except that he cut luxury expenses. By doing so and by reforming taxes, he improved the government's financial state but made himself extremely unpopular. In later years he grew suspicious, executing many on charges of treason, and ruled from Capri for the last ten years of his life. He was succeeded by his great nephew CALIGULA.

**Tibet,** Chin. *Xizong Zizhiqu,* autonomous region (1985 est. pop. 1,990,000), c.1,221,700 km² (471,700 sq mi), SW China; bordered by Burma (SE); India, and Nepal (S); India, Bhutan, and Kashmir (W); and Chinese provinces (N,E). Major cities include LHASA, the capital, Xigaze, and Gyangze. Tibet is largely a high arid plateau surrounded by mountain ranges, including the Himalayas in the south and the Kunlun in the north. The Yangtze, Mekong, and Brahmaputra rivers rise in Tibet. The economy is predominantly pastoral, based on the raising of livestock, particularly yaks; the leading crop is barley. Since 1949 there has been Han Chinese migration to the area. The native inhabitants are of Mongolian stock and speak a Tibeto-Burman language. They follow a form of Buddhism known as Lamaism (see TIBETAN BUDDHISM), the chief figures of which are the Dalai Lama and the Panchen Lama; until the Chinese suppressed religion in the 1960s, as many as one-sixth of the male population were Lamaist monks. An independent kingdom flourished in Tibet by the 7th cent. AD. It was under Mongol influence from the 13th to the 18th cent., when it came under nominal Chinese control. With the overthrow of the Qing (Ch'ing) dynasty in China in 1911, Tibet reasserted its independence, which it maintained until 1950. In that year China invaded Tibet, and it became an autonomous region of China in 1951. An anti-Chinese uprising in 1959 was crushed and repressive measures introduced. The Dalai Lama and many priests fled to India, but by the 1980s some Buddhist temples had resumed operation and a degree of economic liberalization had been introduced. In 1988 and 1989 there were demonstrations in Lhasa and elsewhere against Chinese control of Tibet.

**Tibetan art and architecture,** is generally known in the West from its religious works (see TIBETAN BUDDHISM). Early Tibetan art grew up strongly influenced by eastern India on the one hand and Kashmir on the other.

This contact was mainly through the spread of Mahayana Buddhism. Later in its development Tibetan culture was also considerably influenced by China. In architecture, the *chorten*, or Tibetan STUPA, was derived from Indian prototypes. Tibet was famed for its large monasteries, such as Tashi Lhunpo (founded 1445); these often housed many hundreds of monks. In Lhasa the great monastic palace of the Dalai Lama, the *Potala* (begun by the Fifth Dalai Lama in 1645) is the most impressive accomplishment of Tibetan architecture, with its steeply battered and contrastingly coloured walls, and its gilded rooftops. Tibetan sculpture, usually in bronze though also well-known in terra-cotta, owes much iconographically and, to a lesser extent stylistically, to Kashmir and later to China; the influence of Nepal was always noted. Decoration with semiprecious stones (typically turquoise and coral) is very common both in the religious and secular spheres. Tibetan painting is known from wall-paintings and *thangka* (paintings on cloth, hung in temples and shrines). Colours were traditionally prepared from vegetable and mineral sources. The iconography of the figures shown—sometimes those invoked in meditation—usually goes back to Indian prescriptive prescriptive texts. Specifically Tibetan subjects, however, include paintings showing the lineages of important religious figures, such as the great reformer Tsong-kha-pa. Stylistically, distinctive regional schools grew up, some of which borrowed heavily from China, especially in the repertoire of ornament. The dating of *thangka* is extremely difficult because of the use made by painters of canonical texts for the exact reproduction of the sacred figures; this precluded stylistic development except over a long time-span. Artists producing *thangka* and also bronzes are still to be found in parts of South Asia following the Tibetan diaspora of 1959; the position of such artists in Tibet today is difficult to assess.

The Postala, an example of **Tibetan architecture**.

**Tibetan Buddhism**, religion derived from the Indian Mahāyāna form of BUDDHISM and prevailing in Tibet, Bhutan, Sikkim, Mongolia, and parts of Siberia and SW China. Much of its ritual is based on TANTRA and on Bon shamanism, a primitive Tibetan religion. Tradition has it that Buddhism was introduced into Tibet in the 7th–8th cent. AD. Buddhist texts and commentaries were later translated from the Sanskrit. Suppressed at first by the Bon shamans, the new faith was reformed in the 11th cent. by an Indian monk, Atīśa, founder of the Kadampa sect. Ensuing corruption led to the much-needed reforms of the Yellow Hat sect (14th-15th cent.). In 1641 a ruling Mongol prince granted temporal and spiritual control over all Tibet to the fifth grand LAMA [Tibetan, = superior one], the Dalai Lama. The Dalai Lama soon became the temporal leader of Tibet, and spiritual supremacy resided with the chief abbot of the Zhaxilhünbo monastery near Xigazê, known as the Panchen Lama. Succession to either position is said to depend on direct reincarnation. Dedicated Tibetan Buddhists seek NIRVĀNA, but the popular religion retains shamanistic elements and includes hymns and prayers and the worship of many spirits. In 1959, following the Tibetan revolt against the Chinese, the 14th Dalai Lama went into exile in India. Tibetan Buddhism is a popular subject for study and research among Orientalists today, since many Sanskrit Buddhist (philosophical) texts are lost in original but retained in their Tibetan translations.

**Tibetan language**, member of the Tibeto-Burman subfamily of the Sino-Tibetan family of languages. See LANGUAGE (table).

**Tibullus** (Albius Tibullus), c.55–c.19 BC, Roman elegiac poet. A master of the Latin love ELEGY, he wrote two books, concerned with 'Delia' and 'Nemesis'.

**Ticino**, canton of S Switzerland, on the southern slope of the Alps. It takes its name from the Ticino R. The population is largely Catholic and Italian-speaking. The S is almost Mediterranean in aspect and there are numerous resorts on Lakes Maggiore and Lugano. A part of Lombardy until the 15th–16th cent., the region was conquered by the Swiss and treated as a colony until it became a canton in 1814.

**tick**, parasitic ARACHNID with worldwide distribution, excluding Antarctica. Ticks cling to skin, hair, or feathers while they sink a mouthpart, called a hypostome, into their host and suck out its blood. When they are full, they withdraw the hypostome and drop off. The three most common ticks are the dog tick (*Dermacentor reticulatus*) which infests dogs and cats, the hedgehog tick (*Ixodes hexagonus*), which will also infest humans, and the sheep tick (*I. ricinus*) which infests sheep, cattle, deer, and badgers. These unpleasant parasites are dangerous as disease carriers. The best way to remove a tick is to paint it with oil or alcohol or touch it with a lighted cigarette so that it withdraws its hypostome before dropping off. If the tick is pulled out, the hypostome may break in the skin and fester.

**tidal wave:** see TSUNAMI.

**tide**, alternate rise and fall of sea level in oceans and other large bodies of water. These changes are caused by the gravitational attraction of the Moon and, to a lesser extent, of the Sun for the Earth. At any one time there are two high tides on the Earth, the direct tide on the side facing the Moon, and the indirect tide on the opposite side. The phenomenon of the tides was first fully explained by NEWTON. The average interval between high tides is about 12 hr 25 min. The typical tidal range, or difference in sea level between high and low tides, in the open ocean is about 0.6 m (2 ft), but it is much greater near the coasts. The world's widest tidal range occurs in the Bay of FUNDY in E Canada. Tides are also raised in the Earth's solid crust and atmosphere.

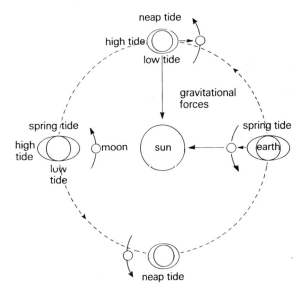

Spring **tide**, having the maximum range, occurs during the full and new phases of the Moon. At these times in the lunar cycle, the Moon, Earth, and Sun form a straight line, a condition known as syzygy. Neap tide, having the minimum range, occurs during the Moon's first and last quarters, when the Moon, Earth, and Sun form a right angle.

**Tieck, Ludwig** (teek), 1773–1853, German writer. He led the transition from STURM UND DRANG to ROMANTICISM. His fairy tales, e.g., *The Blond Eckbert* (1796); poetic drama, e.g., *Kaiser Octavianus* (1804); and fiction exemplify the romantic approach to these genres. Tieck translated *Don Quixote* and supervised the completion by his daughter Dorothea and

Wolf, Graf Baudissin, of the translations of SHAKESPEARE begun by A.W. von Schlegel (see under SCHLEGEL, FRIEDRICH VON).

**tie-dyeing,** method of textile dyeing used in Africa, India, and other parts of the world. Cotton or, sometimes, silk fabric is pleated, twisted, or folded at carefully selected points; tied or sewn in place; and dyed. The tied or sewn areas remain undyed, creating sunburst, circle, square, or other patterns. After dyeing, the thread or raffia used to tie or sew the fabric is removed, although pleats may be retained.

**Tientsin:** see TIANJIN.

**Tiepolo, Giovanni Battista** (,tyepohloh), 1696–1770, Italian painter. He was the most important Venetian painter and decorator of the 18th cent. Having won fame for his FRESCOes in the Labia Palace, he was summoned (1750) to Würzburg (Bavaria) to do frescoes illustrating the life of Emperor Frederick I. In 1762 he went to Madrid to decorate the royal palace with such frescoes as the *Apotheosis of Spain*. As pure virtuosity, Tiepolo's scintillating brushwork, superb draftsmanship, and clarity of colour are unsurpassed.

A fresco from the ceiling of the Palacio Real, Madrid, by Giovanni **Tiepolo**

**Tierra del Fuego** [Span., = land of fire], archipelago, 73,753 km² (28,476 sq mi), separated from the southern tip of mainland South America by the Strait of MAGELLAN and divided between Chile and Argentina. The region is sparsely populated and subject to high winds and heavy rainfall. The economy is based on petroleum and sheep.

**Tiffany, Louis Comfort,** 1848–1933, American artist and designer. After studying painting, he founded the interior-decorating firm of Tiffany Studios in New York City. It specialized in *favrile* glasswork, ranging from lamps and vases to stained-glass windows, characterized by iridescent colours and natural forms in the ART NOUVEAU style.

**Tiflis:** see TBILISI.

**tiger,** large carnivore (*Panthera tigris*) of the CAT family, found in the forests of Asia. Its yellow–orange coat features numerous prominent black stripes although rare white tigers are found. Males average 2.8 m (9 ft) in length and 200 kg (450 lb) in weight but the Manchurian tiger may reach 3.6 m (12 ft). Tigers are solitary, mainly nocturnal hunters and are good swimmers but poor climbers. They have been extensively hunted for their pelts. The Bengal tiger was almost extinct, but is now carefully preserved.

**tiger snake,** small venomous SNAKE of the family Elapidae, found only in Australia. The tiger snake is about 1 m (3½ ft) long and is the most dangerous of Australia's large population of poisonous snakes, being responsible for most of the deaths by snake bite in that country. They are good swimmers, usually living in swampy areas, where they feed on frogs and lizards. The tiger snake, with the black snake, brown snake, copperhead, and bandy bandy, all of Australia, are all related to the COBRA, but are not all dangerous to humans.

**Tigris,** major river of SW Asia, flowing c.1850 km (1150 mi) generally southeast from the Taurus Mts, E Turkey. In N IRAQ it is joined by important left bank tributaries: the Greater and Lesser Zab and the Diyala.

**Tiffany** opal glass vase overlaid with translucent pink (c.1895)

S of BAGHDAD it flows across a wide floodplain to join the EUPHRATES and to form the SHATT AL ARAB N of BASRA. It has a maximum flow between March and May when melting snow and spring rains occur in its headwater region. It is widely used for irrigation in Iraq and is navigable by shallow draft vessels upstream of Basra. Some of the great cities of ancient MESOPOTAMIA, including NINEVEH, Ctesiphon, and Seleucia, stood on the banks of the river, called the Hiddekil in the Bible (Gen. 2.14; Dan. 10.4).

**Tijuana** (teeh,wahnah), city (1979 est. pop. 566,344), NW Mexico, just south of the US border. A growing centre of light industry, it has prospered mainly as a border resort noted for its racetracks and bullfights. The border at Tijuana is crossed by some 14 million tourists a year.

**Tilak, Bal Gangadhar,** 1856–1920, Indian nationalist leader. When the INDIAN NATIONAL CONGRESS was founded (1885), he led the faction that stood for greater militancy and was therefore known as the 'Extremists'. He was imprisoned for long periods by the British.

**Tilburg,** city (1985 pop. 153,812), Noord Brabant prov., S Netherlands. The leading centre of Dutch wool textile manufacture, its other industries include shoemaking and the construction of railway rolling stock.

**Tilden, Samuel Jones,** 1814–86, American political leader. A successful lawyer who played a prominent part in breaking the notorious Tweed Ring (see TWEED, W.M.), Tilden was elected governor of New York in 1874 and was the Democratic candidate for president in 1876. He polled more popular votes than the Republican, Rutherford B. HAYES. There were disputed electoral votes in several states, however, and a Congressional commission of eight Republicans and seven Democrats, voting on strict party lines, awarded all the disputed states to Hayes, making him the winner by one electoral vote.

**till:** see DRIFT.

**Till Eulenspiegel:** see EULENSPIEGEL, TILL.

**Tillich, Paul Johannes** (ˌtilik), 1886–1965, American philosopher and theologian; b. Germany. He taught theology in Germany until his opposition to the Nazi regime caused his dismissal (1933). He then taught at Union Theological Seminary, New York City (1933–55), Harvard Univ. (1955–62), and the Univ. of Chicago (1962–65). His thought embraced the concept of the 'Protestant Principle' and aimed at a correlation of the questions arising out of the human condition and the divine answers drawn from the symbolism of Christian revelation.

**Tilly, Johannes Tserklaes, count of,** 1559–1632, imperial general in the THIRTY YEARS' WAR; b. Belgium. He commanded the army of the Catholic League and won victories in Bavaria and the Palatinate. He assumed command of the imperial army (1630) and stormed Magdeburg (1631), where his troops massacred the populace and sacked the city. He was defeated by the Swedish army of GUSTAVUS II at Breitenfeld (1631) and on the Lech (1632), where he was mortally wounded.

**tilting train,** advanced type of HIGH SPEED TRAIN. On curves, railway track is canted so that the centrifugal force experienced by passengers is counteracted by a component of their weight. Typically track is canted up to an angle of 6°. Higher speeds can be achieved on existing railway tracks by canting the vehicle body automatically on curves, and tilting trains exploiting this have been used on a number of railways. The speed increase in curves for the same level of human comfort, is typically between 20–40%.

**timberline,** elevation above which trees cannot grow. Its location is influenced by latitude, prevailing wind directions, and exposure to sunlight. The timberline is roughly marked by the 10°C (50°F) isotherm. In general, it is highest in the tropics and descends in elevation towards the poles.

**Timbuktu,** city (1976 est. pop. 20,483), central Mali, connected to the Niger R. by a canal system. Its salt trade and handicraft industries make it an important meeting-place for the nomads of the SAHARA. Founded (11th cent.) by the Tuareg, it became by the 14th cent. a major commercial and cultural centre in the MALI empire and was famous for its gold trade. Under the SONGHAI empire (15th and 16th cent.) the city was a centre of Muslim learning, but it declined after being sacked by the Moroccans in 1593. It fell to the French in 1894.

**time and motion study,** analysis of the operations required to produce a manufactured article in a factory, with the aim of increasing efficiency. Each operation is studied minutely and analysed in order to eliminate unnecessary motions and thus reduce production time and raise output. The first effort at time study was made by F.W. TAYLOR in the 1880s. Early in the 20th cent., a more systematic and sophisticated method of time and motion study for industry was developed, taking into account the limits of human physical and mental capacity and the importance of a good physical environment.

**time dilation:** see RELATIVITY.

**time reversal,** mathematical process of changing the sign of the time coordinate in equations describing the behaviour of ELEMENTARY PARTICLES. The laws of physics were believed to be invariant (time reversal invariance) under this process until in 1964, the American physicists J.H. Christenson, J.W. Cronin, V.L. Fitch, and R. Turlay showed in an experiment that this invariance was very weakly violated in the decay of one elementary particle (the $K°$). The effect is very small and has not yet been observed for any other process.

**Times Square:** see BROADWAY.

**Timişoara** (teemeeˌshwahrah), Hung. *Temesvár,* city (1983 pop. 261,950), W Romania, on the Beja Canal. Its manufactures include textiles and machinery. Annexed to Hungary in 1010, it fell to the Turks (1552) and to the HABSBURGS (1718). In 1920 it passed to Romania. Its Roman Catholic and Orthodox cathedrals date from the 18th cent.

**Timor,** island (34,200 km²/13,200 sq mi), largest and easternmost of the Lesser Sundas. It is long, narrow, and almost wholly mountainous. Rice, coconuts, and coffee are grown; stretches of grassland support cattle. Divided between the Portuguese and the Dutch by treaties in 1859 and 1914, the island became part of Indonesia in two stages. With the creation of the Republic of Indonesia in 1950, Dutch Timor became Indonesian. In 1975 Indonesian troops took the eastern (Portuguese) half.

**Timothy,** two epistles of the NEW TESTAMENT. With TITUS they make up the Pastoral Epistles, giving advice on governing a church. First Timothy discusses public prayer and the qualifications of the clergy. Second Timothy is more personal, emphasizing courage and fidelity and warning of trials to come.

**Timurids,** dynasty founded by TAMERLANE, or Timur. At his death (1405), his empire extended from the Euphrates to the Jaxartes and Indus rivers. By 1410 the Western empire, including Baghdad, had been lost to the so-called Black-Sheep Turkoman horde. But the Eastern empire, ruled by Shah Rukh, Tamerlane's son, flourished. His great cities, Samarkand and Herat, became the centre of Persian culture and commerce. His son, Ulagh Beg (r. 1447–49), made Samarkand a centre of Muslim civilization. After him, the Timurid empire fell to the White-Sheep Turkoman horde and the Uzbeks. BABUR is regarded as the last of the Timurids.

**tin** (Sn), metallic element, known and used by humans at least as early as the BRONZE AGE. It is a lustrous, silver-white, very soft, and malleable metal that can be rolled, pressed, or hammered into extremely thin sheets (tin foil). A tin coating, applied by dipping or electroplating, protects iron, steel, copper, and other metals from rust. Compounds of tin are used for mordants in dyeing, for weighting silk, and as reducing agents. Stannous fluoride is added to toothpastes and water supplies to prevent tooth decay. Toxic organic compounds are used as fungicides and catalysts. Cassiterite, or tinstone, is the chief ore. See ELEMENT (table); PERIODIC TABLE.

**Tinbergen, Jan** (ˌtinˈbeəgən), 1903–, Dutch economist. Professor at the Netherlands School of Economics (1933–73), he shared, with Ragnar FRISCH, the first Nobel Prize for economics (1969), for work in ECONOMETRICS. His best known works include *Econometrics* (1942) and *Income Distribution* (1975).

**Tinbergen, Nikolaas,** 1907–, British zoologist, b. Netherlands. For his work in reviving and developing the science of animal behaviour, he shared the 1973 Nobel Prize in physiology or medicine with Karl von FRISCH and Konrad LORENZ. His studies of the display behaviour of certain species revealed that such displays result from a state of conflict between opposing motivations ('fight or flee'). He also clarified the evolutionary origins of many social signals and their subsequent ritualization.

**Tindal** or **Tindale, William** see TYNDALE, WILLIAM.

**tinea:** see RINGWORM.

**Tinguely, Jean,** 1925–, Swiss sculptor. In his work of the 1940s he was interested in movement and unconventional artistic media and after the war in Paris developed these ideas producing sculptures operated by crank-handles and motors, and incorporating chance movement. His 'meta-matics' produced continuous abstract drawing patterns as well as sound effects caused by striking objects. He combined ideas on KINETIC ART and performance art in his autodestructive work, *Homage to New York* (1960), which when demonstrated in New York failed to destroy itself as planned and caused a fire.

**Tintoretto,** 1518–94, Venetian painter; b. Jacopo Robusti. He was called Il Tintoretto [little dyer] from his father's trade. He probably trained with Paris Bordone or Bonifazio Veronese. His *St Mark Rescuing a Slave* (1548; Academy, Venice) shows MICHELANGELO's influence but has startling lighting effects and a dramatic rendering of the narrative. In the next decade, his work tended toward MANNERISM, with flickering light, distorted figures, and irrational spatial elements, e.g., in his *Last Judgment* (Madonna dell'Orto, Venice). His cycle of paintings for the Scuola di San Rocco (begun 1564) includes an enormous *Crucifixion* and is remarkable for startling changes in viewpoint, frenetic movement, and mystic conception. The last phase of his art was highly visionary, with almost phosphorescent lighting effects, e.g., in his *Last Supper* and *Entombment* (San Giorgio Maggiore, Venice).

**tipi:** see TEPEE.

**Tipperary,** county in S of Republic of Ireland (1986 pop. 136,504), 4213 km² (1643 sq mi), bordering on Co. Waterford in the S. It is situated in the province of Munster. The county town is CLONMEL. It is mountainous in places, rising to 905 m (3015 ft) in Galtymore in the Galty Mts in the SW, and 783 m (2609 ft) in the Knockmealdown Mts in the S. The main river is the SUIR, which crosses the county from N to S. Lough Derg and the R. SHANNON form much of the NW border. The SW of the county is fertile lowlands where agriculture predominates, especially dairy farming.

Tintoretto, *Last Judgement*. Madonna dell'Orto, Venice.

**Tippett, Sir Michael,** 1905–, British composer. He developed a highly individual, complex style of writing, much influenced by the sprung rhythms and polyphony of the Elizabethan MADRIGAL and the harmonic style of HINDEMITH. He has been a committed pacifist and thoughtful commentator on matters of current interest, and has written his own texts for his operas and choral works. His works include the ORATORIO *A Child of Our Time* (1946); the operas *The Midsummer Marriage* (1955), *King Priam* (1962), and *The Knot Garden* (1970); and four symphonies (1945, 1958, 1973, 1977).

**Tippu, Sahib,** 1745–99, sultan of Mysor, India. He was besieged and killed at Srirangapatna.

**Tippu Tip,** c.1830–1905, Afro-Arab ruler of trade-based empire in late 19th-cent. E ZAÏRE; b. Zanzibar. A very successful caravan trader dealing mainly in ivory and slaves, in the 1870s he established a political base by becoming a chief among the Tetala of E Zaïre. From his capital at Kasonga he gradually extended his control over the entire region. His empire crumbled, however, before the advance of European imperialism in the shape of King Leopold of Belgium, and in 1890 he left Zaïre to retire to Zanzibar.

**Tiradentes** (teerə‚thentəs), 1748–92, Brazilian revolutionary patriot; b. José Joaquim da Silva Xavier. In the late 1780s he led an independence movement against Portuguese rule and for democratic government; the movement was betrayed and Tiradentes was executed.

**Tiranë** or **Tirana** (tee‚rahnə), city (1984 pop. 194,000), capital of Albania, central Albania, on the Ishm R. The country's largest city, it is located on a fertile plain and produces textiles, metal products, and other manufactures. Lignite is mined nearby. The city, founded in the early 17th cent. by the Turks, was enlarged (1920) when it became the capital. Tiranë was held (1939–43) by Italy during World War II. Government buildings and an 18th-cent. mosque are located in Scanderbeg Square, the city's centre.

**Tiresias** (tie‚reesee-as), in Greek mythology, blind soothsayer who experienced life as both man and woman. He appears in many ancient legends, e.g., OEDIPUS, and in modern works, e.g., T.S. ELIOT's *The Waste Land* (1922) and POULENC's opera *Les Mamelles de Tirésias* (1944).

**Tirso de Molina** (‚tiəsoh day moh‚leenah), pseud. of **Fray Gabriel Téllez,** 1584?–1648, Spanish dramatist and friar. A major figure of the Spanish GOLDEN AGE, he wrote *El burlador de Sevilla* (1630; tr. The Trickster of Seville), the first literary treatment of the Don Juan legend, as well as several hundred other plays.

**Tiruchirapalli** (formerly **Trichinopoly**), town (1981 pop. 362,045), Tamil Nadu state, S India, at the head of the KAVERI delta. It is a district administrative, communications, and commercial centre which dominates its region. Industry came later than in other southern towns; now, however, the town has textile and engineering works, and important railway shops. The great temple at Srirangam, a few kilometres up the Kaveri, attracts pilgrims and tourists. Tiruchirapalli is an ancient town with a remarkable hilltop fort.

**tissue,** in biology, aggregation of similar cells. In animals, the epithelial, nerve, connective, and muscle tissues are fundamental; blood and lymph are commonly classed separately as vascular tissues. Organs usually consist of several tissues. Higher plants contain meristem tissue (cells that grow, divide, and differentiate), protective tissue like cork, storage and support tissues, and vascular tissues.

**tissue culture,** in botany, the culture of plant tissues or organs growing upon a sterile medium such as AGAR, and containing nutrients and usually also HORMONES. Of great importance in modern plant breeding and rapid plant production.

**tissue fluid:** see LYMPHATIC SYSTEM.

**Tisza** (‚tiso), river c.1200 km (800 mi) long, rising in the CARPATHIAN MTS and collecting the drainage of the eastern Hungarian plain before joining the DANUBE above BELGRADE in Yugoslavia. The largest city on the river is SZEGED.

**Tisza, Count Stephen,** 1861–1918, Hungarian premier (1903–05, 1913–17). Tisza sought to make Hungary a forceful partner in the AUSTRO-HUNGARIAN MONARCHY. He first opposed war with SERBIA in 1914 but later approved it. After taking a military command in World War I he was assassinated.

**tit** or **titmouse,** name given to members of the BIRD family Paridae. These small, mainly insect-eating birds share with PARROTS and CROWS the distinction of being intelligent birds. They are able to work out ways of obtaining food from unusual places. British tits learnt how to remove bottle-tops to drink cream from milk bottles. They breed across Europe, Africa, and Asia to North America, where they are called chickadees. The 11-cm (4½-in) blue tit (*Parus caerulus*) has adapted to town life and is common in European towns along with the 14-cm (5½-in) great tit (*P major*). Both species will readily use nesting boxes.

**Titan,** in astronomy, natural satellite of SATURN.

**Titan,** in Greek mythology, one of 12 primeval deities; children of URANUS and GAIA. They were CRONUS, Iapetus, Hyperion, Oceanus, Coeus, Creus, Theia, RHEA, Mnemosyne, Phoebe, Tethys, and Themis. Their descendants, e.g., PROMETHEUS, ATLAS, HECATE, HELIOS, were also called Titans. Led by Cronus, they deposed Uranus and ruled the universe. They were in turn overthrown by the OLYMPIANS, led by ZEUS, in a battle called the Titanomachy. Afterward Cronus ruled the Isle of the Blessed and Atlas held up the sky. The others, except Prometheus, who had helped Zeus, were condemned to TARTARUS.

**Titania,** in astronomy, natural satellite of URANUS.

**Titanic,** British liner that sank on the night of 14–15 Apr. 1912, after striking an iceberg in the North Atlantic. The disaster, which occurred on the ship's maiden voyage, claimed the lives of more than 1500 of the 2200 people aboard. Many perished because of a shortage of lifeboats. More stringent safety rules for ships and an iceberg patrol were later instituted.

**titanium** (Ti), metallic element, discovered in 1791 by William Gregor. It is a lustrous, silver-white, and very corrosion-resistant metal that is ductile when pure and malleable when heated. The metal and its alloys, which are light in weight and have very high tensile strength, are used in aircraft, spacecraft, naval ships, guided missiles, and armour plate for tanks. Titanium dioxide is used as a gemstone (titania) and paint pigment. Widely distributed in compounds (e.g. RUTILE) in nature, titanium is present in the sun and certain other stars, in meteorites, and on the moon. See ELEMENT (table); PERIODIC TABLE.

**Titchener, Edward Bradford**, 1867–1927, American psychologist; b. England. He studied under WUNDT at Leipzig, and subsequently brought the new German experimental psychology to the US. Titchener's espousal of the method of INTROSPECTION led to the misunderstanding by psychologists influenced by BEHAVIOURISM that this was the method that Wundt himself employed exclusively.

**Titian** (ˌtishən), c.1490–1576, Venetian painter; b. Tiziano Vecellio. One of the most celebrated artists of the RENAISSANCE, Titian had immense influence on succeeding generations of painters, especially in his use of colour. He studied painting in the shop of Gentile and Giovanni Bellini (see BELLINI, family) and worked with GIORGIONE. After their deaths, he was considered the finest painter in Venice. In 1518 he completed the famous altarpiece of the *Assumption of the Virgin* (Church of Santa Maria Gloriosa dei Frari, Venice), and for the rest of his career he was showered with honours and commissions from the rulers of Europe. Emperor CHARLES V made him a Count Palatine, and Philip II of Spain was one of his patrons. In 1538 he painted the celebrated *Venus of Urbino* (Uffizi, Florence). In 1545, Titian went to Rome, where he met MICHELANGELO and did the striking (unfinished) portrait of Pope Paul III and his grandsons Ottavio (the second duke of Parma) and Cardinal Alessandro Farnese (Pinacoteca, Naples). For Cardinal Farnese he did a *Danaë* (Naples), of which he later made several versions. He painted the magnificent *La Gloria* (1554; Prado, Madrid) for Charles V, and in 1553 he started a cycle of mythological paintings for Philip II, which included *Diana and Callisto* and *Diana Surprised by Acteon* (both 1559; National Gall. Edinburgh), and the *Rape of Europa* (1559; Gardner Mus., Boston). Titian's work can be divided into three phases. The first shows the influence of Bellini and Giorgione, e.g., in *Sacred and Profane Love* (c.1513; Borghese Gall., Rome); the Bacchanalian scenes for Alfonso I d'Este, e.g., *Bacchus and Ariadne* (1524; National Gall., London) are richer and more sensual. Full dramatic monumentality and great sumptuousness of colour characterize the second phase, e.g., in *Christ Crowned with Thorns* (c.1542; Louvre, Paris). In his last phase, an intense mystical spirit and a new looseness of brush stroke and subtlety of colour can be seen, e.g., in *Pietà* (Academy, Venice), which was intended for his own tomb and finished by Palma Giovane.

Titian, *Pietà*. Oil on canvas, 351 × 389 cm. Academy, Venice.

**Titicaca**, largest freshwater lake in South America, c.8290 km² (3200 sq mi), located high in the ANDES between Bolivia and Peru, at an elevation of c.3810 m (12500 ft). It is by far the highest large lake in the world. The densely populated shores have been a centre of Indian life on the ALTIPLANO since before the time of the INCAS.

**Titius–Bode law**, empirical relationship between the mean distances of the planets from the Sun. If each number in the series 0, 3, 6, 12, 24, . . . (where, after 0, a new number is twice the previous number) is increased by 4 and then divided by 10 to form the series 0.4, 0.7, 1.0, 1.6, 2.8, 5.2, 10.0, 19.6, 38.8, 77.2, . . . , the law holds that this series gives the mean distances of the planets from the Sun, expressed in ASTRONOMICAL UNITS. This relationship was discovered (1766) by Johann Titius and published (1772) by Johann Bode. It agreed well with the actual mean distances of the planets then known (and of Uranus and the asteroid belt, both discovered later), but not with those of the later-discovered planets Neptune and Pluto.

**titles**, terms of sovereignty, nobility, and honour. The highest title, emperor, was originally a military title. Emperor was used by Augustus Caesar and, later, heads of the Roman and Byzantine empires, and by Charlemagne and Napoleon. Queen Victoria was called Empress of India. In the Holy Roman Empire, titles below emperor or king were *Herzog*, *Pfalzgraf*, *Markgraf*, *Landgraf*, on down to *Ritter*; when prefixed by *Reich-*, the title was held directly from the emperor. French titles below king are *duc*, *prince*, *marquis*, on down to *chevalier*; in Italy, *duca*, *principe*, *marchese*, on down to *barone*; in England, prince, duke, marquess, on down to knight; and in Spain, *duque*, *príncipe*, *marqués*, on down to *barón*.

**titmouse:** see TIT.

**Tito, Josip Broz**, 1892–1980, leader of the Yugoslav Communist Party (1937–80), marshal (1943–80), premier (1945–53), and president (1953–80) of Yugoslavia; b. Josip Broz in Jumrovec, Croatia. Wounded and taken prisoner on the Eastern front in 1915 as an NCO in the Austrian army, he joined the Bolsheviks and fought in the Russian civil war. Returning to the new Yugoslav kingdom in 1920, he became a metal-worker, union organizer, and official of the illegal Communist Party (CPY). Jailed for five years in 1928, he subsequently worked for the COMINTERN in Moscow, W Europe, and at home, before taking over the weak and faction-ridden CPY. He returned its leadership to Yugoslavia, freed it of financial dependence on Moscow and reorganized its activities. Aided by the Comintern's united-front strategy against fascism, he and the politburo he created sought to put the Party at the forefront of national and social discontent in Yugoslavia. When Germany attacked the USSR in 1941, Tito and the CPY proclaimed an all-Yugoslav national liberation war, through which they intended to win power. Leading the Partisan forces in what was simultaneously an anti-Axis resistance struggle, a civil war, a revolutionary seizure of power, and a bid for Allied support and recognition, Tito and the CPY were masters of a recreated Yugoslav state by war's end (1945). Proceeding to sovietize Yugoslavia, Tito fell foul of STALIN's determination to control his new satellites and was expelled from the COMINFORM in 1948, so initiating the breakup of the monolithic world Communist movement. Although a political operator rather than an ideologue, Tito presided over the transformation of Yugoslav Communism, based on the practical decentralization of power and the theory of workers' self-management, while maintaining the authority of the CPY. From the 1960s Tito devoted as much attention to leading the NONALIGNED MOVEMENT as to serving as arbiter of Yugoslavia's affairs and embodiment of its state and socialist legitimacy.

**Titograd**, city (1981 pop. 132,290), capital of Montenegro, SW Yugoslavia. An administrative and manufacturing centre, it has aluminium and tobacco industries. Formerly known as Podgorica, it was largely destroyed in World War II, and a modern city has been built. Its new name (in honour of Pres. TITO) was adopted in 1946.

**titration**, the determination of the CONCENTRATION of acids or bases (see ACIDS AND BASES) in SOLUTION by the gradual addition of an acidic solution of known volume and concentration to a basic solution of known volume, or vice versa, until complete neutralization (observable by the colour change in an added indicator, such as phenolphthalein) has occurred. See INDICATORS.

**Titus** (Titus Flavius Sabinus Vespasianus), AD 39–81, Roman emperor (AD 79–81). Son of Emperor VESPASIAN, he acted as co-ruler with his father after AD 71. He captured and destroyed Jerusalem in AD 70. On succeeding his father, he pursued a policy of conciliation, sought popular favour, and became known as a benevolent ruler. His brother DOMITIAN succeeded him. The **Arch of Titus** in the Forum at Rome was erected by Domitian to commemorate Titus's conquest of Jerusalem. He is the hero of operas by Gluck and by Mozart (both: *La Clemenza di Tito* [the mercy of Titus]).

**Titus,** EPISTLE of the NEW TESTAMENT. With First and Second TIMOTHY it makes up the Pastoral Epistles, purportedly by St PAUL. They deal with matters of church government.

**Tiy** (tee), fl. 1385 BC, queen of Egypt; wife of Amenhotep III, mother of IKHNATON. She was unusually influential in state affairs. **Tiy,** fl. 1167 BC, wife of RAMSES III, plotted against him but failed to gain the throne for her son.

**Tl,** chemical symbol of the element THALLIUM.

**Tlatelolco Treaty,** international agreement signed in Mexico in 1967 by South American and Caribbean states, providing for the prohibition of nuclear weapons in Latin America. Although Cuba and Guyana remained (end-1988) non-signatories, the treaty is regarded as operative for the other full adherents in the treaty zone.

**Tm,** chemical symbol of the element THULIUM.

**TNT** or **trinitrotoluene** ('trie'nietroh,tolyoo'een), $[CH_3C_6H_2(NO_2)_3]$, crystalline AROMATIC COMPOUND. Trinitrotoluene is a high EXPLOSIVE, but, unlike NITROGLYCERINE, it is unaffected by ordinary shocks and must be set off by a detonator. Because it does not react with metals, it can be used in filling metal shells. It is often mixed with other explosives, e.g., with ammonium nitrate to form amatol.

**toad,** certain insect-eating AMPHIBIANS of the order Anura, similar to the FROG but often more terrestrial as adults. Commonly referring to species with shorter legs, a stouter body, and thicker skin than the frog, the term *toad* is properly restricted to the so-called true toads (family Bufonidae) like the NATTERJACK. These are characterized by warty skins, prominent parotid glands behind the eyes, and a white, poisonous fluid exuded through the skin and from the parotid glands. Ranging from 2.5 to 18 cm (1 to 7 in) in size, toads inhabit cool, moist places and lay their eggs in water.

Male midwife **toad** (*Alytes obstetricans*) carrying eggs

**toadstool:** see MUSHROOM.

**tobacco,** plant (genus *Nicotiana*) of the NIGHTSHADE family, and the product manufactured from its leaf and used in cigars and cigarettes, snuff, and pipe and chewing tobacco. The chief commercial species, *N. tabacum,* is believed native to tropical America. The tobacco plant is a coarse, large-leaved perennial, but it is usually cultivated as an annual. Tobacco requires a warm climate and rich, well-drained soil. After being picked, the leaves are cured, fermented, and aged to develop aroma. The amount of nicotine (the ALKALOID responsible for tobacco's narcotic and soothing effect) varies, depending on tobacco strain, growing conditions, and processing. The use of tobacco originated among natives of the New World in pre-Columbian times. Introduced into Spain and Portugal in the mid-16th cent., initially as a panacea, it spread to other European countries, and by 1619 tobacco had become a leading export crop of Virginia. In recent years there has been concern over the harmful effects of nicotine, the tarry compounds, and CARBON MONOXIDE in tobacco smoke.

**Tobago:** see TRINIDAD AND TOBAGO.

**Tobey, Mark,** 1890–1976, American painter. From 1925 to 1927 he travelled in Europe and the Near East, then settled in England. Having studied Chinese calligraphy in Shanghai, he used calligraphic forms in 'white writing' pictures. He was an important influence on French TACHISM in the 1950s.

**Tobin, James,** 1918–, American economist. Sterling Professor of Economics at Yale, Tobin won the 1981 Nobel Prize for economics for his analyses of the impact of financial markets on spending and investment. He also served (1961–62) on the President's Council of Economic Advisers.

**Tobit,** biblical book included in the Western canon but not in the Hebrew Bible, and placed in the APOCRYPHA in the Authorized Version. It tells of Tobit, a devout, blind Jew in exile, and of his son Tobias. Tobias and his dog are led by the archangel Raphael to the house of Sarah, who is afflicted by the demon Asmodeus. Tobias marries Sarah, exorcises the demon, and cures his father's blindness. The book probably should be dated in the 2nd cent. BC.

**Tobruk,** city (1973 pop. 28,061), NE Libya, a port on the Mediterranean Sea. During WORLD WAR II it was an objective fiercely contested (1941–42) by the British and Germans. First seized by Allied forces, Tobruk was briefly held by the Germans and then retaken by the British.

**Toc H,** an interdenominational Christian fellowship of men and women of every social background, with branches throughout the world, which seeks to promote an understanding of the meaning and purpose of life through unreserved involvement in the community. Founded in 1915, it started its work in a soldiers' club at Talbot House (Toc H was the army signallers' designation of the initials TH) at Poperinghe, Flanders. Incorporated by royal charter in 1922, it is organized in groups and maintains residential houses called 'marks'.

**Tocqueville, Alexis de,** 1805–59, French social philosopher and historian. Prominent in French politics, he was briefly foreign minister after the REVOLUTIONS OF 1848. *Democracy in America* (2 vol., 1835), based on observations made during a trip to the US is a classic. So, too, is his study of France's Ancien Régime. A liberal, he believed that political democracy and social equality would eventually replace Europe's aristocratic institutions.

**toga,** a mantle worn by male citizens of the classical Roman empire. It was made from an elliptical length of cloth, 5.9 by 2.2 m (18 by 7 ft), doubled lengthwise and draped around the body, with the loose end flung over the shoulder. The *toga virilis* was worn after maturity, at the age of 14, and the *toga praetexta* had a purple border as a sign or rank.

**Togliatti** (toh,lyahttee), formerly Stavropol, city (1985 pop. 594,000), S European USSR, on the Volga R. It is an important river port near the Lenin Dam hydroelectric station. It is the site of the USSR's largest motor-car plant, designed by Fiat and completed in 1970 (1980 production 720,000 cars, more than half of the total Soviet production). Other industries produce nitrogenous and phosphorous fertilizers, synthetic rubber, and industrial equipment. It was renamed in 1964 after the Italian communist leader Palmiro TOGLIATTI.

**Togliatti, Palmiro,** 1893–1964, Italian Communist leader. A founder of the Italian Communist Party, he lived in exile for many years in Moscow. He returned (1944) to Italy, became party leader, and served (1944–45) in the government.

**Togo,** officially Republic of Togo, republic (1987 est. pop. 3,030,000), 56,000 km² (21,622 sq mi), W Africa, bordered by the Gulf of Guinea (S), Ghana (W), Burkina Faso (N), and Benin (E). LOMÉ is the capital. Beyond a sandy strip along the coast are, successively, a region of fertile clay soils, the Mono Tableland, a mountainous area rising to c.1200 m (3940 ft), and, in the extreme north, the rolling sandstone Oti Plateau. The standard of living in Togo is among the highest in W Africa. Most of the labour force is engaged in agriculture, but mining is of growing importance. The principal food crops are manioc, millet, yams, and maize; the leading cash crops are coffee, cocoa, palm kernels, cotton, and groundnuts. Major deposits of high-quality phosphates have been worked on a large scale since 1963, and by the early 1980s Togo ranked as the world's fourth largest phosphate producer. An oil refinery processes crude oil imported from Nigeria. The GNP is US$644 million, and the GNP per capita is US$230 (1985). The people are black Africans, principally the Ewe in the south and Voltaic-speaking peoples in the north. Most adhere to traditional beliefs, but there is a large Christian, and a smaller Muslim, minority. French is the official language.

*History.* Formerly part of the German protectorate of TOGOLAND (1886–1914), the area that is now Togo was administered by France after World War I (1922–1960). It gained independence, as the Republic of Togo, in 1960, resisting attempts by Kwame Nkrumah of Ghana (formerly the Gold Coast) to merge the two nations. The early years of the republic were characterized by political instability. Since 1967 Togo has been ruled by Lt-Col. Gnassingbé Eyadéma, who came to power in a bloodless coup. Voters approved a new constitution in 1979, reelected Eyadéma, who has assumed the role of regional mediator and senior statesman in W Africa, and selected a national assembly composed of members of the Rally of the Togolese People, the sole legal political party. The 1985 assembly elections featured a degree of democratization in that voters could chose between more than one candidate of the ruling party.

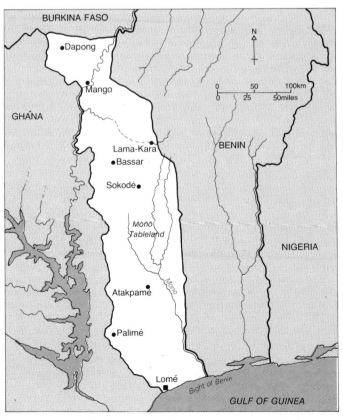

Togo

**Togo Heihachiro,** 1846–1934, Japanese admiral, Japan's greatest naval hero. In the RUSSO-JAPANESE WAR he defeated Russian fleets at Port Arthur (1904) and in the battle of Tsushima (1905), thus establishing Japanese naval superiority.

**Togoland,** historic region (c.86,800 km²/33,500 sq mi) in W Africa. Its western part is now in GHANA, and its eastern part is the Republic of TOGO.

**Tōjō Hideki,** 1884–1948, Japanese general and prime minister (1941–44). He led Japan during the war with the US and Britain until a succession of reverses led to his removal from office. He favoured fighting the war to a finish. After Japan's defeat he was tried by the Allies as a war criminal, convicted, and executed.

**Tokelau,** formerly Union Islands, dependency of New Zealand (1977 est. pop. 1625), c.16 km² (6 sq mi), South Pacific Ocean, consisting of three small atolls: Atafu, Nukunonu (the largest), and Fakaofa. The Polynesian inhabitants have a subsistence economy; copra is the chief export. Tokelau was discovered in 1765 and was a British possession from 1889 to 1925, when it was mandated to New Zealand. In 1948 New Zealand acquired formal sovereignty.

**Tokugawa** ('tohkooh,gahwah), family that held the shogunate (see SHOGUN) and controlled Japan from 1603 to 1867. Founded by TOKUGAWA IEYASU, the Tokugawa shogunate presided over a period of economic and cultural growth. Although the Tokugawa exercised a measure of centralized control, the DAIMYO were allowed some autonomy, and it was only after the fall of the Tokugawa shogunate and the MEIJI restoration that a truly centralized state emerged in Japan.

**Tokugawa Ieyasu,** 1542–1616, Japanese military leader and founder of the TOKUGAWA shogunate. He participated in the campaigns of Oda Nobunaga and TOYOTOMI HIDEYOSHI as they sought to reunify Japan, and following the latter's death (1598) he took on his rivals at the battle of Sekigahara in 1600. He became SHOGUN in 1603 and laid the foundations for the third and last of Japan's three hereditary shogunates. Amongst his advisers was the Englishman Will ADAMS. He resigned the shogunate to allow for the succession of one of his sons, but retained political control until his death.

**Tokutomi Sohō,** 1863–1957, Japanese journalist and thinker. A firm believer in the value of a democratic and Westernized Japan, he founded the Min'yūsha publishing house in 1887 to carry his views to a wide audience. This published several influential magazines and newspapers, including *Kokumin-no-tomo* [nation's friend]. Following the intervention of the European powers after Japan's success in the first Sino-Japanese war of 1894–95, he concluded that Westernization was not enough and that Japan needed to be militarily stronger in order to safeguard its independence. In 1945 he was arrested as a suspected war criminal but he was not brought to trial.

**Tokyo,** city (1986 est. pop. 8,216,250), capital and largest city of Japan, E central Honshu, at the head of Tokyo Bay. Greater Tokyo consists of an urban area, farms, and mountain villages, and the Izu Islands. It is the administrative, financial, and cultural centre of Japan. It is also a major industrial and transportation centre, with the world's first public monorail line and a high-speed 'bullet train' (SHIN-KAN-SEN) service, opened in 1964, that links it with other cities. Industrial products include electronic apparatus, cars, and a wide variety of consumer goods. Founded as Edo in 1457 by the local lord, Dokan Ota, it was the capital of the shogunate from 1603 to 1868, when the emperor was restored to power and made Edo the nation's capital, renaming it Tokyo. In 1923 an earthquake and fire destroyed nearly half the city. Heavy Allied bombing in World War II devastated much of Tokyo, including nearly all of its industrial plants. Left intact were the imperial palace and surrounding embassies, the diet (government) building, and many office buildings. The city's famed landmarks include the Meiji shrine (built 1920), ancient temples, and the Korakuen landscape garden. The Ginza is Tokyo's shopping and entertainment centre. One of the world's foremost educational cities, Tokyo has about 100 colleges and universities. Frequent rebuilding in the wake of disasters has made it one of the world's most modern cities. It was host to the Olympic Games in 1964.

**Tolbert, William Richard, Junior,** 1913–80, president of LIBERIA (1971–80). A protegé of William TUBMAN, Tolbert succeeded him as president in 1971. He was killed (1980) in a coup led by Samuel K. Doe, an army sergeant.

**Tolbukhin,** city (1983 pop. 102,292), NE Bulgaria. Market centre of Dobruja, it was under Romanian rule from 1913 to 40. Formerly known as Dobrich, it was renamed after Marshall Tolbukhin of the USSR in 1949.

**Toledo** (toh₁laydhoh), city (1981 pop. 57,769), capital of Toledo prov., central Spain, in New Castile, on the Tagus R. Pre-dating Rome, to which it fell in 193 BC, it was later (6th cent.) the capital of the Visigothic kingdom. Its archbishops have long been Spain's primates. Under the MOORS (712–1085) and the kings of CASTILE it was a centre of Moorish, Spanish, and Jewish culture and was noted for its sword blades and textiles. In the 16th cent. it was the seat of the Spanish INQUISITION. Many works by El Greco (see GRECO, EL), who lived in Toledo, hang in the cathedral (begun 1226), the Hospital of San Juan Bautista (15th–16th cent.), and the Church of Santo Tomé.

**Toledo**, US city (1984 est. pop. 344,000), NW Ohio, on the Maumee R. and Lake Erie; inc. 1837. It is one of the major GREAT LAKES shipping, commercial, and industrial cities. Glass, oil products, machines, tools, and motor vehicle parts are leading manufactures. Gen. Anthony WAYNE built Fort Industry there (1794) after the Battle of Fallen Timbers; the city was settled in 1817. The area was the object of an Ohio–Michigan border dispute (1835–36). Toledo's Museum of Art and the Univ. of Toledo are notable institutions.

**Toledo, Francisco de**, 1515?–84, Spanish viceroy of PERU (1569–81). He consolidated the Spanish conquest of Peru by breaking the power of the great landowners. He unjustly had the Inca leader Tupac Amaru executed (1571).

**Tolkien, J(ohn) R(onald) R(eul)**, 1892–1973, English novelist and scholar. A medievalist at Oxford Univ., he became famous as the author of *The Hobbit* (1937) and the epic trilogy *Lord of the Rings* (1954–55), all fantasy novels about the mythological kingdom of Middle Earth; the posthumous *Silmarillion* (1977) continues the saga.

**Tolstoy, Aleksandr Nilolayevich**, 1883–1945, Russian writer, a distant descendant of Count Leo TOLSTOY. A prolific writer of short stories and historical novels, he emigrated to France in 1918, but returned to the USSR in 1923 and became an apologist for the Stalin regime. His best-known works include the novels *Peter I* (1929–45), *Ivan the Terrible* (1942–43), and *Road to Calvary* (1920–41).

**Tolstoy, Leo, Count** (təlstoi₁), Rus. *Lev Nikolayevich Tolstoi*, 1828–1910, Russian novelist and philosopher. Of a noble family, he was orphaned at nine and brought up by aunts. He left the university without a degree and returned to his family estate, Yasnaya Polyana, where he tried to aid and educate the serfs. After a profligate period in Moscow and St Petersburg, he joined his brother, an officer, in the Caucasus (1851). In 1852 he enlisted. *Childhood* (1852), part of an autobiographical trilogy that includes *Boyhood* (1854) and *Youth* (1857), was his first published work. Leaving the army in 1855, he lived alternately on his estate and in St Petersburg. In 1862 he married Sophia Andreyevna Bers, a young, well-educated girl, who bore him 13 children. *War and Peace,* his first masterpiece, appeared in 1863–69. An epic of the Napoleonic invasion, it illustrates Tolstoy's view that history proceeds inexorably to its own ends. *Anna Karenina* (1875–77), his second masterpiece, is a tragedy of adultery with profound social and spiritual dimensions. Around 1876 Tolstoy underwent a crisis culminating in his conversion to a doctrine of Christian love, nonviolent acceptance of evil, and renunciation of wealth. He devoted the rest of his life to practising and propagating his faith, expounded in such works as *What I Believe* (1884). He considered wrong such institutions as the government and church; he was excommunicated in 1901, but his fame protected him from serious state interference. Moral issues are central to his later works, notably 'The Death of Ivan Ilyich' (1886), a story; *The Power of Darkness* (1886), a drama; and the novel *Resurrection* (1899). In the essay *What Is Art?* (1898) he argued that the artist is morally bound to create works understandable to most people, and denounced his own earlier works. In 1910 a breach with his family caused Tolstoy to leave home; he died a few days later.

**Toltec** [Nahuatl, = master builders], MIDDLE AMERICAN INDIAN civilization of Mexico, probably with ancient links to the MIXTEC and Zapotec. The Toltec warrior aristocracy gained ascendancy in the valley of Mexico after the fall (900) of TEOTIHUACÁN, making their own capital at Tollán (Tula). Masters of architecture and the arts, they were advanced workers of stone and smelters of metals, had a calendric system, and are said to have discovered the intoxicant pulque. Their religion, centring on the god QUETZALCOATL, incorporated human sacrifice, sun worship, and a sacred ball game. The Toltec dominated the MAYA (11th–13th cent.) until nomadic Chichimec peoples destroyed their empire, opening the way for the AZTEC.

**tomato**, plant (*Lycopersicon esculentum*) of the NIGHTSHADE family, and its fruit (commonly considered a vegetable because of its uses). Numerous varieties are cultivated, e.g., the small cherry tomato, the yellow pear tomato, the Italian plum tomato, and the large, red beefsteak tomato. Popular in salads and processed into juice, ketchup, and canned goods, the tomato was recognized as a valuable food only within the last century. It contains useful amounts of vitamins A and C.

**Tombstone**, US city (1980 pop. 1,632), SE Arizona; inc. 1881. During a silver boom (1877–90) it had a reputation as one of the West's richest and most lawless towns. That and its climate made it a popular tourist attraction. It was named a national historic landmark in 1962. Famous sights include Boot Hill cemetery; the Bird Cage Theater; and the O.K. Corral, scene of a famous 1881 gun battle.

**tom-tom:** see DRUM.

**tonality**, in music, quality by which all TONES of a composition are heard in relation to a central tone called the keynote, or tonic. Some relationship to a tonic is characteristic of much music and many musical systems, though in some it is not considered necessary and in others it is deliberately avoided (see ATONALITY and TWELVE-TONE MUSIC). The term *tonality* is also used in contrast to *modality* (see MODE).

**tonal languages**, languages in which the meaning or grammatical category of a word is changed by the TONE. Different types of linguistically meaningful tonal organization are employed in African and Southeast Asian languages, including Chinese.

**Ton Duc Thang**, 1888–1980, Vietnamese politician. He was an early supporter of HO CHI MINH and was imprisoned (1929–45) by the French colonial regime. After Vietnamese independence, he rose quickly in the North Vietnamese Communist Party. He was vice president (1960–69) and became president of North Vietnam, a largely ceremonial position, upon Ho's death in 1969. After 1976 Ton was president of the newly reunited Socialist Republic of Vietnam.

**tone.** In music, a tone is distinguished from noise by its definite PITCH, caused by the regularity of the vibrations that produce it. Any tone possesses the attributes of pitch, intensity, and quality. Pitch is determined by the frequency of the vibration, measured by cycles per second. Intensity, or loudness, is determined by the amplitude, measured in decibels. Quality is determined by the overtones (subsidiary tones), the distinctive timbre of any instrument being the result of the number and relative prominence of the overtones it produces. The term *whole tone* or *whole step* refers to the interval of a major second, or 200 CENTS in the tempered scale, as in moving from one white key to the adjoining white key on the piano. *Half tone, semitone,* or *half step* refers to the interval of a minor second, or 100 CENTS in the tempered scale, as in moving from a white key to the adjoining black key on the piano.

**tone poem:** see SYMPHONIC POEM.

**Tonga**, officially the Kingdom of Tonga, independent constitutional monarchy (1986 est. pop. 102,000), 699 km² (270 sq mi), in the S Pacific Ocean. It comprises c.170 islands, of which the three main groups are Tongatapu, Haapai, and Vavau. Nukualofa is the capital. Tonga has a tropical climate and a mainly subsistence farming economy. Copra and bananas are the chief exports. The islands were discovered between 1616 and 1643 and renamed the Friendly Islands by Capt. James COOK, who visited them in 1773 and 1777. English missionaries arrived (1797) and helped to strengthen British political influence. In 1900, Tonga became a British protectorate but remained internally self-governing. A new treaty in 1968 reduced British control, and Tonga became fully independent in 1970 as a member of the COMMONWEALTH. The present ruler is King Taufaahau Tupou IV, son of former queen Salote Tupou III (r.1918–65).

**tongue**, muscular organ attached to the floor of the mouth in higher animals. In humans it is important in chewing and swallowing, and in producing articulate speech. It is also the main organ of taste. The human tongue is covered by a mucous membrane containing small projections, or papillae, which give it a rough surface. Tiny taste organs, or buds, are found on the papillae. These taste buds respond to one of four stimuli (sweet, salt, sour, and bitter flavours) and are correspondingly arranged on the tongue from tip to root. Cells in the buds send impulses along associated nerves to the brain.

**Tonkin**, historic region, c.103,600 km² (40,000 sq mi), Southeast Asia, bordered by China (N), the Gulf of Tonkin (E), Annam (S), and Laos (S,

W); now part of Vietnam. The capital was HANOI. Tonkin was conquered by the Chinese in 111 BC and became independent in AD 939. Governed by native dynasties until French expeditions arrived in 1873 and 1882, Tonkin was the scene of a colonial war (complicated by Chinese intervention) that ended with a French protectorate. The Japanese occupied the region during WORLD WAR II. In 1954, after an independence struggle against the French, Tonkin became part of North Vietnam. It was incorporated into united Vietnam after the VIETNAM WAR.

**Tonkin Gulf resolution,** in US history, Congressional resolution passed in 1964 authorizing military action in Southeast Asia. After US destroyers allegedly were attacked in the Gulf of Tonkin in 1964 by North Vietnamese gunboats, Pres. Lyndon B. JOHNSON asked Congress for authority to retaliate and for a mandate for future military action. The resolution was passed overwhelmingly and Johnson and his successor, Richard NIXON, regarded it as authorization to pursue the VIETNAM WAR in Southeast Asia. Congress repealed it in 1970. In 1974 it was established that the original alleged North Vietnamese attack on the US destroyers had not in fact occurred.

**Tonks, Henry,** 1862–1937, British painter. Trained as a doctor, he started to draw in 1888 and was offered a teaching post at the Slade School in 1892, becoming Slade Professor in 1918. As a teacher Tonks had considerable influence and introduced ideas of the New English Art Club to the students. He was academic in his outlook and did not accept the ideas of Roger FRY's exhibitions of POST-IMPRESSIONISM and by the 1920s was considered conservative by more progressive artists and students.

**tonsils,** name commonly referring to the **palatine tonsils,** two ovoid masses of lymphoid tissue on either side of the throat, at the back of the tongue. The **pharyngeal tonsils, or adenoids,** are similar masses located in the space between the back of the nose and the throat. The **lingual tonsils** are situated on the back of the tongue. The tonsils act as filters against disease organisms.

**Toowoomba,** city (1986 pop. 71,362), Queensland, NE Australia. Quensland's third largest city and Australia's second largest inland city, Toowoomba is the regional capital for the Darling Downs. Originally known as the Swamp, it was given its Aboriginal name in 1858. The mild climate has encouraged the development of retirement homes and boarding schools. Agricultural activities are centred on wheat and dairying, with food-processing and agricultural machinery manufacture as local industry.

**topaz,** aluminium silicate mineral $[Al_2SiO_4(F,OH)_2]$, used as a GEM. Commonly colourless or some shade of yellow, the stone is transparent with a vitreous lustre. Topaz crystals occur in highly acidic igneous rocks and in metamorphic rocks. Important sources include Brazil, Siberia, Burma, and Sri Lanka.

**Topeka,** US city (1984 est. pop. 119,000), state capital of Kansas, on the Kansas R.; inc. 1857. It was laid out (1854) by Free Staters, and became state capital in 1861. The noted Menninger Clinic is one of its several psychiatric research and therapy institutions. Agricultural marketing and shipping are major economic activities.

**topology,** branch of MATHEMATICS concerned with those properties of geometric figures that are invariant under continuous transformations. A continuous transformation is a one-to-one correspondence between the points of one figure and the points of another figure such that points that are arbitrarily close on one figure are transformed into points that are also arbitrarily close on the other figure. Two figures are topologically equivalent if one can be deformed into the other by bending, stretching, twisting, or the like, but not by tearing, cutting, or folding; thus topology is sometimes popularly called 'rubber-sheet geometry'. A circle and a square are topologically equivalent, as are a cylinder and a sphere, but a torus (doughnut shape) is not equivalent to a sphere, because no amount of bending or twisting will change it into a sphere. Topology may be roughly divided into *point-set topology,* which considers figures as sets of points (see SET) having such properties as being open, closed, compact, connected, and so forth; *combinatorial topology,* which considers figures as combinations (complexes) of simple figures (simplexes) joined together in a regular manner; and *algebraic topology,* which makes extensive use of algebraic methods, particularly those of GROUP theory. There is considerable overlap among these branches.

**Torah** [Heb., = teachings or learning], Hebrew name for the PENTATEUCH, the first five books of the Bible. The Torah, or Written Law, which

Orthodox Jews believe was revealed directly by God to MOSES on Mt Sinai, laid down the fundamental laws of moral and physical conduct, theology and ritual. In a wider sense the Torah comprises all the teachings of JUDAISM, including the entire Hebrew Scripture, the TALMUD, and any generally accepted rabbinical interpretation. (See also under BIBLE).

**Torcello** (taw‚cheloh), village on an island north of VENICE, Italy. A lost town, possibly the forerunner of Venice itself, Torcello retains two ancient churches, Santa Fosca and the cathedral. The latter was founded in AD 639 and is a three-nave basilica with marble columns and mosaics.

**tornado,** dark, funnel-shaped cloud containing violently rotating air that develops below a heavy cumulonimbus cloud mass and extends toward the earth. The diameter of a tornado varies from a few metres to c.1.5 km (1 mi); the rotating winds reach velocities of 350 to 450 kph or more (200 to 300 mph), and the updraught at the centre may exceed 300 kph (200 mph). In comparison with a CYCLONE, a tornado covers a much smaller area but is much more violent and destructive. The atmospheric conditions required for the formation of a tornado include great thermal instability, high humidity, and the convergence of warm, moist air at low levels with cooler, drier air above. Tornadoes occurring over water are called waterspouts.

**Toronto,** city (1982 est. pop. 614,763), provincial capital, S Ontario, part of the municipality of metropolitan Toronto, on Lake Ontario. Ringed by fast-growing suburbs, it is Canada's second largest city and its largest municipality, a major commercial and financial hub, and Ontario's principal GREAT LAKES port and industrial centre. The skyline of the city, which changed dramatically beginning in the 1960s, is marked by such landmarks as the CN (Canadian National) Tower, one of the world's tallest free-standing structures; the golden towers of Royal Bank Plaza; and the avant-garde architecture of Eaton Square and the O'Keefe Centre. The city occupies the site of a French fort (1749–59), in an area purchased by the British from the Indians in 1787. Proclaimed (1793) the capital of Upper Canada (now Ontario), it was settled in part by UNITED EMPIRE LOYALISTS. It was twice raided by Americans and partly destroyed during the WAR OF 1812. Then known as York, it was renamed Toronto in 1834. Growing rapidly through immigration after 1960, it now vies with MONTREAL as the nation's most important city.

**torque** or **moment of force,** a quantity expressing the effectiveness of a force to change the net rate of rotation of a body. It is equal to the product of the force acting on the body and the distance from its point of application to the axis around which the body is free to rotate. The unit of torque is the newton-metre; older units include the foot-pound and the dyne-centimetre.

**Torquemada, Tomás de** (tawkay‚mahdhah), 1420–98, Spanish churchman. A DOMINICAN, he became (1483) inquisitor general of Castile and Aragón. His reputation for cruelty derives from the harsh procedures that he devised for the Spanish INQUISITION. He was largely responsible for the expulsion (1492) of Jews who refused baptism.

**Torrens, Sir Robert Richard,** 1814–84, Australian statesman; b. Ireland. He devised the landholding reform which substituted public registration of title for the old conveyance system; the Torrens system was first adopted in South Australia in 1858.

**Torrente Ballester, Gonzalo** (taw‚rentaybie·es‚teə), 1910–, Spanish critic, novelist, and dramatist. His thought-provoking novels include *El golpe de estado de Guadalupe Limón* (1946), *Ifigenia* (1950), *Offside* (1969), and *Fragmentos de apocalipsis* (1977).

**Torricelli, Evangelista,** 1608–47, Italian physicist and mathematician. Galileo's secretary and successor as professor of philosophy and mathematics at Florence, he invented the BAROMETER (Torricelli tube) and improved the telescope.

**Torrijos Herrera, Omar** (toh‚reehos ayrayrah), 1929–81, Panamanian military ruler. After seizing power in a military coup (1968), he curtailed civil liberties and instituted economic and social reforms. He signed (1978) the Panama–US treaties that transferred the PANAMA CANAL ZONE to PANAMA. He died in an aeroplane crash.

**torsion:** see STRENGTH OF MATERIALS.

**Torstensson, Lennart,** 1603–51, Swedish general in the THIRTY YEARS' WAR. Trained by GUSTAVUS II in the use of the new mobile field artillery, he led (1641–46) the Swedish troops to many victories. He was the military teacher of CHARLES X.

**tort,** in law, a civil wrong against a person or PROPERTY for which damages may be claimed as compensation. A tort violates duties imposed by law on all persons, as distinguished from the duties a CONTRACT imposes on the parties making it. CRIMINAL LAW involves state action against wrongdoers, while torts give the injured parties the right to sue. A wrongful act may be both a tort and a crime; thus, the crime of BURGLARY may be actionable as the tort of trespass. Torts are classified primarily as intentional, e.g., LIBEL, ASSAULT, FRAUD, or as injury arising from NEGLIGENCE. Damages are usually awarded in tort cases. They may be nominal, symbolic recognition of the wrong done, even though substantial harm did not occur; or compensatory, to redress the plaintiff's loss or injury. Where there was fraud or intentional wrongdoing, the court may award punitive or exemplary damages to punish the defendant. In some circumstances, e.g., NUISANCE, the court may issue an INJUNCTION.

**tortoise,** terrestrial chelonian, especially one of the family Testudinidae. Tortoises inhabit warm regions worldwide except in Australia. Most famous is the giant tortoise of the Galapagos islands (*Testudo elephantopus*), which can be over 120 cm (4 ft) long and weigh over 225 kg (500 lb). Tortoises are extremely long-lived; some are known to have survived for more than 150 years. They are related to TURTLES.

**Toruń,** Ger. *Thorn*, city (1984 pop. 182,000), N Poland, on the Vistula R. It has wool textile and synthetic-fibre industries, developed since World War II. First fortified in 1231 by TEUTONIC KNIGHTS who held the city to the 15th cent., it joined the HANSEATIC LEAGUE, and became Prussian (1793–1919). A university was established in 1945. The distinctive brick castle and sections of the old fortifications remain and restoration has been undertaken.

**Tory,** English political party. The name was used derogatorily for supporters of the duke of York (later JAMES II). After 1688 the Tories comprised mainly country gentry who were closely identified with the Church of ENGLAND. Reaching their zenith under Queen ANNE, with Robert Harley and Henry St John as leaders, they were discredited for JACOBITE leanings under GEORGE I. Power passed for the next 50 years to their rivals, the WHIGS. The name was later applied to the younger William PITT and his successors, but after the REFORM BILL of 1832, the name preferred by PEEL, the CONSERVATIVE PARTY, prevailed. Tory still survives in popular speech.

**Tory, Geofroy,** c.1480–1533, Parisian printer, typographer, and author. He was editor to the printer Henri ESTIENNE, and GROLIER was one of his BOOKBINDING clients. His *Book of Hours* (1525) introduced type design free from dependence on handwriting. He was printer to FRANCIS I of France.

**Toscanini, Arturo** (toskə‚neenee), 1867–1957, Italian conductor. He began his career as conductor of the Rio de Janeiro opera (1886). Returning to Italy, he conducted the premieres of LEONCAVALLO's *I Pagliacci* (1892) and PUCCINI's *La Bohème* (1896), and was later musical director at La Scala, Milan. In the US, he conducted at the METROPOLITAN OPERA (1908–14), the New York Philharmonic (1926–36), and the NBC Symphony, which was formed for him (1937–54).

**tossing the caber,** most spectacular of the HIGHLAND GAMES. The caber is a tree trunk about 3.65 m (12 ft) in length and 50 kg (90 lb) in weight. Competitors receive the caber in clasped hands stretched in front of them, and attempt to toss the upright wood so that it revolves longitudinally and lands with its base pointing in a straight line away from the competitor. 'The twelve o'clock' is the best toss. The celebrated Braemar caber weighs 54.5 kg (120 lb) and is 5.79 m (19 ft) long. It was first tossed in 1951 by George Clark, aged 51.

**totalitarianism,** term used to describe a political system in which the state, typically directed by a single party, has a complete monopoly of power, extending its control into every area of political, economic, and social life. It suppresses all opposition and freedom of discussion, by means of terror if necessary, and imposes its own IDEOLOGY by the systematic use of PROPAGANDA. The concept was developed by Carl FRIEDRICH and others in an attempt to encompass the new political forms presented in the 20th cent. by FASCISM, in particular Nazi Germany, and Soviet COMMUNISM under STALIN. The increasing power of the state under both CAPITALISM and Communism, its tendency to encroach on areas which had always been regarded as private, such as the family, and the tremendous capacity for social control introduced by technological advances in the means of communication and surveillance led some to believe that a tendency towards totalitarianism was inherent in all modern states. George ORWELL's *1984* (1949) is perhaps the best-known anti-utopian novel depicting life under a totalitarian system. But historical experience has shown the inability of allegedly totalitarian states to suppress all dissidence, and the power of individuals, especially those with strong religious or political beliefs, to resist indoctrination by propaganda.

**totem,** a mystical symbolic connection made and relationship established between a human social group, such as a group of kin, most often a clan, and an animal or plant from the natural world. It is particularly characteristic of the classificatory and symbolic systems of the Australian aborigines and the American Indians of the northwest coast. LÉVI-STRAUSS denied that the term had any real significance in itself since it was part of a much more generalized system of classification and needed to be understood as the way in which human societies tend to use plants and animals to symbolize relations between social groups.

**Totila** or **Baduila,** d. 552, last king of the OSTROGOTHS (r.541–52). By taking Naples (543) and Rome (546) he became master of central and S Italy. JUSTINIAN I spurned his peace offers and sent (552) an army under NARSES against him. Totila was routed and killed, leaving Italy under Byzantine control.

**Tottel, Richard,** 1530?–94?, English publisher. His best-known publication was *Songes and Sonnettes* (1557), popularly known as *Tottel's Miscellany*, which included a large number of poems by the Earl of SURREY and Sir Thomas WYATT.

**toucan,** perching BIRD of the New World tropics, related to the WOODPECKERS. Toucans vary in size from the jay-sized toucanets to the 60-cm (24-in) tocos of the Amazon basin. Their enormous, often brightly coloured, canoe-shaped bills are adapted to cutting up fruits and berries.

**Toulon,** city (1982 pop. 181,985, agglomeration 410,393), capital of Var dept., SE France, on the Mediterranean coast. It is a major naval base with associated arsenals and naval construction industries. In Nov. 1942 the French fleet was scuttled here to avoid German capture.

**Toulouse,** city (1982 pop. 354,289, agglomeration 541,271), capital of Haute-Garonne dept., S France, on the Garonne R. A cultural and commercial centre, it is also the centre of the French aerospace industry. A part of Roman Gaul, it was (419–508) the capital of the Visigoths and (781–843) of the Carolingian kingdom of Aquitaine. Under the counts of Toulouse, who ruled most of the region of Languedoc, it was the artistic and literary centre of medieval Europe. It passed to the French crown in 1271. An old quarter and many buildings are preserved, e.g., a Romanesque basilica and Gothic cathedral.

**Toulouse-Lautrec, Henri de** (tooh‚loohz-loh‚trek), 1864–1901, French painter and lithographer. His growth was permanently stunted, the result of a childhood accident. Influenced by DEGAS, and Japanese prints, he was inspired by Parisian low life, the life of brothels and of music halls, cabarets, and circuses. He was a brilliant draughtsman. Using garish and artificial colours, he brought new immediacy to his POSTERS, particularly those of the Moulin Rouge. His works include *At the Moulin de la Galette* (1892; Art Inst., Chicago). There is a museum of his work at Albi, his birthplace, which includes *Le salon de la rue des moulins* (1894).

**Toure, Samourey (Samori Ture),** 1830–1900, ruler of an empire in 19th-cent. W Africa; b. Guinea. A highly successful commander in the army of the king of Bisandugu, he broke away to found his own state which he gradually expanded by force and diplomacy. By 1879 he controlled most of the upper Niger region. After 1882 expansion ceased when his armies came into contact with the French. He was captured and deported by the French to Gabon in 1898.

**tourmaline,** complex aluminium and boron silicate mineral $[(Na,Ca)(Al,Fe,Li,Mg)_3Al_6(BO_3)_3Si_6O_{18}(OH)_4]$, used as a GEM. Colours are red, pink, blue, green, yellow, violet, and black; sometimes it is colourless. Two or more colours, arranged in zones or bands with sharp boundaries, may occur in the same stone. Tourmalines are found in pegmatite veins in granites, gneisses, schists, and crystalline limestone. Important sources include Elba, Brazil, the USSR, Sri Lanka, and parts of the US.

Toulouse-Lautrec, *Le salon de la rue des moulins*, 1894. Pastel, 111.5 × 132.5 cm. Musée Toulouse Lautrec, Paris.

**Tournachon, Gaspard Félix,** or **'Nadar'** ('tawrnaˌshon), 1820–1910, French photographer. Originally a journalist, he took up photography in 1853, taking portraits in his Paris studio of most of the famous men and women of the day, like Sarah BERNHARDT and Charles BAUDELAIRE. A friend of the French IMPRESSIONIST painters, 'Nadar' was a colourful and radical figure constantly experimenting with new techniques; he took the first aerial photographs from a balloon in 1858, and equipped his studio with electric light in 1860.

The first aerial photograph taken from an altitude of 520 m by **Tournachon** in 1858

**tournament** or **tourney,** in the Middle Ages, public contest between armed horsemen in simulation of real battle. Based on the ideas of chivalry and accompanied by much pageantry, the tourney probably originated in France in the 11th cent. The field, or lists, was enclosed by barriers and flanked by pavilions for notables. Because many knights were killed or injured, a less dangerous version known as tilting was devised.

**Tours,** city (1982 pop. 136,483, agglomeration 262,786), capital of Indre-et-Loire dept., W central France. It is a wine market and tourist centre. A Gallo-Roman town, it was a centre of medieval Christian learning, notably under GREGORY OF TOURS and ALCUIN. There CHARLES MARTEL halted (732) the Moorish conquest of Europe. It has produced many great artists.

**Toussaint L'Ouverture, François Dominique** (tooˌsanh loovea ̯tyooə), c.1774–1803, Haitian patriot. A self-educated, freed slave, he joined the black rebellion (1791) to liberate the slaves. With Generals DESSALINES and CHRISTOPHE, he forced (1798) the British to withdraw from HAITI, quelled (1799) a mulatto uprising, and resisted a French invasion (1802). But he was treacherously seized by the French and died in a dungeon in France. His valiant life and tragic death made him a symbol of the fight for liberty.

**tower,** structure, the greatest dimension of which is its height. Towers have belonged to two general types. The first embodies practical use, such as medieval defensive structures, bell and beacon towers, and the SKYSCRAPER. The second type is used to symbolize the authority and power of religious and civic bodies, such as the church and town-hall towers of Europe. The earliest ritual and symbolic tower is probably either the Babylonian ZIGGURAT or the Indian masonry tower. Medieval European defensive towers were massive refuges and lookouts. The TOWER OF LONDON is a noted example of the castle donjon, or keep. Italian nobles built fortified towers even for their town dwellings. In the late Middle Ages, the growth of centralized government gradually removed the need for defensive towers. The earliest European church towers are those of the 5th and 6th cent. in Ravenna, Italy, including the CAMPANILE. In Romanesque churches towers generally rose over the central crossing and the west end. In Gothic architecture, the tower grew higher and more elaborate. Renaissance towers incorporated the classical ORDERS OF ARCHITECTURE and other Roman elements. Notable modern towers, in addition to skyscrapers, include the Einstein Tower, Potsdam, Germany by Erich Mendelsohn (1919–21) and the WATTS TOWERS, Los Angeles. See also (GOTHIC ARCHITECTURE AND ART; PAGODA; MINARET; SPIRE).

**Tower Hamlets,** London borough (1981 pop. 139,996), S England, on N side of R. Thames. It extends from Blackwall in the E to the Tower of London in the W. Within the borough are the districts of Bethnal Green and Stepney, and docklands at Blackwall, Millwall, and Wapping. The dockland area has experienced much redevelopment over recent years, owing to its proximity to the City of London.

**Tower of London,** ancient fortress, east of the City of London, on the N bank of the Thames. Formerly a royal residence and jail for illustrious prisoners, it is now an arsenal and museum. A dry moat and castellated walls surround the White Tower, built c.1078. Subsequent towers include the Wakefield Tower, which houses the crown jewels. The Traitors' Gate and Bloody Tower are associated with notables including Sir Thomas MORE and Anne BOLEYN. Many persons beheaded there or on neighbouring Tower Hill are buried in the chapel. Yeomen of the Guard (Beefeaters) still guard the Tower.

**town planning,** planning for the improvement of urban centres in order to provide healthy and safe living conditions, efficient transport and communication, adequate public facilities, and aesthetic surroundings. Renaissance Italian piazzas, Pierre L'Enfant's design (1791) for Washington, DC, Baron HAUSSMANN's 19th-cent. remodelling of Paris, Frederick Law Olmsted's park systems, and 20th-cent. BRASÍLIA are all examples. Modern town planners, particularly those involved in slum clearance and construction of housing projects, must take into account such social and economic factors as zoning regulations; traffic patterns; employment opportunities; proximity to transport, schools, shops, hospitals, and parks; the availability of police, fire, and sanitation services; and the preferences of prospective residents.

**Townshend, Charles Townshend,** 2nd **Viscount,** 1674–1738, English statesman. A WHIG, he strongly supported the Hanoverian succession and was a secretary of state (1714–16, 1721–30). In the latter

The White Tower, **Tower of London**

term he shared power in the ministry with his brother-in-law, Robert WALPOLE; a disagreement over foreign policy led to Townshend's resignation. His agricultural experiments earned him the nickname Turnip Townshend. His grandson, **Charles Townshend**, 1725–67, was also an English statesman. He held relatively minor positions until William PITT made him chancellor of the exchequer in 1766. Because of Pitt's illness he became the leading figure in the ministry. He originated the hated TOWNSHEND ACTS.

**Townshend Acts,** 1767, revenue acts passed by the British Parliament to replace the repealed STAMP ACT. They placed duties on various items imported into the American colonies. The colonists reacted strongly, but the economic boycott they organized proved ineffective. However, in 1770 Lord NORTH held out an olive branch by repealing all the Townshend duties save that on tea, which was retained 'as a mark of the Supremacy of Parliament'.

**Townsville,** city (1986 pop. 96,230), Queensland, NE Australia. The capital of North Queensland, the city has administrative and educational facilities including the Institute of Tropical Medicine and the James Cook University. It is linked by rail with Mt Isa, and the port exports minerals, wool, and beef. Sugar cane is grown in the surrounding district. Offshore Magnetic Island is a popular tourist resort.

**toxaemia,** disease state caused by the presence in the blood of a bacterial TOXIN or other harmful substance. The term now usually applies to toxaemia late in pregnancy, or preeclampsia, a condition once believed to be caused by toxins, but now associated with high blood pressure, protein in the urine, and oedema (fluid retention). Toxaemia can lead to eclampsia (maternal convulsions) and death of mother and infant if untreated. Delivery resolves the condition.

**toxic shock syndrome,** acute, sometimes fatal, disease characterized by high fever, nausea, diarrhoea, lethargy, blotchy rash, and sudden drop in blood pressure. Caused by a toxin-producing strain of the *Staphylococcus aureus* bacterium, the disease is most prevalent among menstruating women using high-absorbency tampons, but can also affect men and nonmenstruating women.

**toxic waste:** see POLLUTION; WASTE DISPOSAL.

**toxin,** a poison produced by a living organism. Some toxins affect specific tissue in the host; e.g., the toxin associated with DIPHTHERIA affects mucous membranes, and that associated with BOTULISM destroys nerve tissue. Other toxins may produce fever, internal haemorrhage, and SHOCK. The presence of toxins stimulates the production of antibodies, one of the body's defence mechanisms against disease (see IMMUNITY).

**toy dog,** class containing small breeds of DOG, usually kept as companion dogs. Some have been selectively bred as miniatures of larger breeds, e.g., the toy poodle and the toy Yorkshire terrier, whereas others are distinct small breeds, e.g., the chihuahua, the Pekingese, and the Pomeranian.

**Toynbee, Arnold Joseph,** 1889–1975, English historian. In his major work, *A Study of History* (12 vol., 1934–61), he propounded the problems of history in terms of civilizations rather than of nationalities. The main thesis of the work is that the well-being of a civilization depends on its ability to respond successfully to challenges, human and environmental. Of 26 civilizations in history, he saw only Western Latin Christendom as still alive.

**Toyota,** city (1986 est. pop. 305,810), Aichi prefecture, Honshu, Japan. One of the most profitable industrial cities in Japan, Toyota has grown around a single company (Toyota Motor Company) which established its head office and a new factory in the small castle town of Koroma in 1937. The city was renamed in 1959 when the company built the largest car assembly plant in Asia. In Matsudaira, the northeastern part of the city and the old residential area of members of the Tokugawa family, there remain traditional Japanese spinning mills.

**Toyotomi Hideyoshi,** 1537–98, Japanese warrior and dictator. He was a general in the service of the dictator Oda Nobunaga and after Nobunaga's death in 1582 he took over the task of reunifying Japan. By 1591 he had achieved this by force of arms and in 1592 he turned his attention to the mainland, in the hope of conquering Korea and China with similar ease. He failed to develop any machinery of government or to make adequate arrangements for the succession of his son, and his position was filled by TOKUGAWA IEYASU.

**Trabzon,** city (1980 pop. 108,403), capital of Trabzon prov., NE Turkey, on the Black Sea coast. Formerly known as TREBIZOND, it lies at the seaward end of an historic route over the mountains to Persia and beyond. It was founded as a Greek colony in the 8th cent. BC, flourishing under Roman and Byzantine control (see BYZANTINE EMPIRE). It reached its apogee during the Empire of Trebizond (1204–1461), when it was a major trade and cultural centre. It retains city walls and fine medieval buildings.

**track events,** sports of running and hurdling, staged on an oval track. The principal events are the 100-, 200-, and 400-m sprints; the 800-, 1500-, and 5000-m races, and the 110- and 400-m hurdles.

**Tracy, Spencer,** 1900–67, American film actor. He won Academy Awards for his character portrayals in *Captains Courageous* (1937) and *Boys' Town* (1938). Other films include *Adam's Rib* (1949) and *The Last Hurrah* (1958).

**trade,** the buying of goods and services either on the domestic or the international market. Domestic trade is normally wholesale or retail. In the Western world a number of peoples, including the Egyptians, Phoenicians, Greeks, Romans, Spanish, Dutch, and English, have at one time or another dominated world trade. Today the world's major trading powers are the US, Canada, the countries of Western Europe, and Japan, which together account for about 65% of total world exports; the Communist countries make up about 10%. Trade policies imposed by national governments have varied, ranging from the MERCANTILISM of the 17th and 18th cent. and the protective TARIFF of the 19th and 20th cent. to the free trade philosophy that Britain long upheld. Free trade, which does not permit such restrictions as tariffs, trade quotas, and import licenses, was championed by Adam SMITH in his *Wealth of Nations* (1776). The opposite policy, known as protectionist, is aimed at shielding domestic industries from foreign competition. The UK is committed to free trade but as a member of the COMMON MARKET must adopt a commercial policy in common with the other members, and a number of import restrictions are in force. They particularly affect clothing and textiles under the Multi-fibre Arrangement and agricultural goods because of the COMMON AGRICULTURAL POLICY. The US followed high-tariff policies until the mid-1930s, when it signed reciprocal trade agreements with many nations that provided for selective tariff reductions. Today the US is a relatively low-tariff nation, although it still maintains a fairly restrictive system of import quotas. Japan is frequently criticised for restrictive import quotas, as well as high tariffs and other curbs on imports. After World War II, strong sentiment developed throughout the world for freer trade. The results were such new agreements as the General Agreement on Tariffs and Trade (GATT; 1948) and such regional trading blocs, or customs unions, as the Common Market (1957) and the EUROPEAN FREE TRADE ASSOCIATION (1959). International trade also plays an important political role e.g., the expansion in trade between China and the Western counties in the 1970s and 80s is taken as a sign of decreased tension between the Western and Communist powers.

**trademark,** distinctive mark placed on merchandise to indicate its origin. Its use is the exclusive legal right of its owner. In the UK trademarks are registered in the Patent Office; infringements of trademarks, e.g., imitations, are punishable as crimes and can be made the basis of civil suits.

**Trades Union Congress** (TUC), voluntary association of British trade unions (est. 1868), with 90 affiliated organizations representing some 9 million individual members (1988). The organization is non-political although many individual unions have a political fund financed by their members which is used to support the Labour Party. The TUC provides a forum for discussion and formulation of policy on a broad front, and may also mediate between unions, e.g., in demarcation disputes. In the promotion of trade-union interests, the TUC wielded considerable power in the 1960s and early 1970s, particularly under governments of the LABOUR PARTY, to which the major unions are affiliated. Under the post-1979 CONSERVATIVE government, however, its influence waned, in a period of unemployment, as new laws were enacted establishing constraints on trade-union powers and practices. The TUC is headed by a general secretary responsible to a general council and decides its policies at an annual conference. In 1988 there were breakaways.

**trade union** or **labour union,** association of workers for the purpose of improving their economic status and working conditions through COLLECTIVE BARGAINING. Historically there have been two major types of trade unions: the horizontal, or craft, union, in which all the members are skilled in a certain craft (e.g., carpenters); and the vertical, or industrial, union, composed of workers in the same industry, whatever their particular skills (e.g., car workers). A company union is an employee-controlled union having no affiliation with other labour organizations. The term *closed shop* refers to a company that employs only union members. In a union shop, employees are required to join a union within a specified time after being employed. Trade unions are essentially the product of the INDUSTRIAL REVOLUTION of the 19th cent. In Great Britain miners and textile workers were organized in the 1860s. Most European trade unions support or are affiliated with left wing political parties, especially those which support SOCIAL DEMOCRACY. In the US unions are associated with the Democratic Party. With the exception of those unions associated with syndicalist movements in France and Italy, the history of European trade unions has borne out the fear of LENIN that 'trade-union consciousness' on the part of the working class (i.e., settling for higher wages and better conditions within the system, rather than seeking to overthrow CAPITALISM) would be a formidable obstacle to revolution. TROTSKY attacked trade-union leaders for using their authority to assist capitalism in controlling the workers, and it is a general view that trade unions in effect make capitalism safe by institutionalizing conflict. The worldwide economic boom after World War II produced high levels of employment, and coincided with a high rate of unionization amongst workers in modern Western democracies. The great bargaining power that this gave to trade-union leaders was reflected in their consultation by many governments, not simply on the resolution of strikes, but on the planning of economic, industrial, and incomes policies. This phenomenon, often taking the form of tripartite talks between government, big business, and the trade unions, has been considered a form of CORPORATISM. With economic recession in the 1970s, a decline in both employment levels and union membership, and the rise of the New Right, the influence of the trade unions, in Britain at least, has much diminished. In the USSR the trade unions, though not formally a part of the state apparatus, and hence legally free, are supervised by the Communist Party and do not engage in wage bargaining, though they have social and welfare functions. In the Third World, the influence of trade unions has varied. In some areas they have enhanced the incomes of an employed urban elite at the expense of the rural peasantry; in others they have been prominent in anticolonial campaigns towards political independence. Internationally, world trade unionism was split after 1949 between two rival organizations: the World Federation of Trade Unions (founded 1945) and the International Confederation of Free Trade Unions (founded 1949). The International Labour Organization is a specialized agency of the UNITED NATIONS.

**Trading Standards Officers,** in the UK, persons concerned with checking the standard of products on sale to the public. They ensure that articles are safe, accurately described and correctly measured, e.g., petrol pumps and scales in shops and on market stalls. They investigate consumer complaints about inaccurately labelled foods and they are also responsible for checking the licences of traders offering credit. The Trading Standards Department is part of the local government structure.

**Trafalgar, battle of,** 21 Oct. 1805, naval encounter of the Napoleonic Wars, fought off Cape Trafalgar, on the SW coast of Spain. The British fleet, under NELSON, won a brilliant victory over the French and Spanish navies under Pierre de Villeneuve. Nelson was fatally wounded in the encounter.

**tragedy,** form of drama, central to Western literature, in which a person of superior intelligence and character, a leader of the community, is overcome by the very obstacles he is struggling to remove. The earliest tragedies were part of the Attic religious festival held in honour of the god DIONYSUS (5th cent. BC). The most famous ancient tragedies are probably the *Oresteia* of AESCHYLUS, SOPHOCLES' *Oedipus Rex,* and EURIPIDES' *Trojan Women.* ARISTOTLE pointed out tragedy's ritual function: The spectators are purged of their own emotions of pity and fear through their vicarious participation in the drama. The dramas of the Roman tragedian SENECA were based on certain conventions; unity of time and place, violence, bombast, revenge, and the appearance of ghosts. Seneca's plays served as models for such RENAISSANCE tragedies as Christopher MARLOWE's *Tamburlaine* (1587) and Thomas KYD's *Spanish Tragedy* (1594). These in turn prefigured the towering tragedies of the period: Marlowe's *Dr Faustus* (1588); SHAKESPEARE's *Othello, Macbeth, Hamlet,* and *King Lear* (1600–07), and John WEBSTER's *Duchess of Malfi* (1614). All of these plays dramatize the conflicts of kings, conquerors, or, at the very least, geniuses. The tradition of the tragic hero continued for the next 300 years in the work of the Spaniards LOPE DE VEGA and CALDERÓN DE LA BARCA; the Frenchmen Pierre CORNEILLE and Jean RACINE; and the Germans G.E. LESSING, GOETHE, and SCHILLER. Tragedy can reflect another vision of life, again rooted in religious drama; the mystery plays and morality plays of medieval France and England. These plays, of which EVERYMAN is the best known, emphasize the accountability and suffering of ordinary people. The tragic lot of the common man is explored in such later dramas as George Lillo's domestic tragedy *The London Merchant* (1731) and Georg BÜCHNER's political tragedy *Danton's Death* (1835). In Henrik IBSEN's *A Doll's House* (1879) and *An Enemy of the People* (1882), ordinary people behave heroically, acknowledging their faith in the validity of the tragic vision. The cataclysmic events of the 20th cent. have produced a radical diminution of that vision. In such plays as Eugene O'NEILL's *Mourning Becomes Electra* (1931), Bertolt BRECHT's *Mother Courage* (1941), Arthur MILLER's *Death of a Salesman* (1949), and Samuel BECKETT's *Waiting for Godot* (1953), life is depicted as so horrible and absurd that heroic behaviour is not only impossible, it is irrelevant.

**Traherne, Thomas,** 1637–74, English METAPHYSICAL POET. His finest work, revealing ecstatic religious experience and joy in nature and pioneering in English literature the depiction of childhood emotions, appeared in the 1670s but was lost until rediscovered and published as *Poems* (1903) and *Centuries of Meditations* (1908).

**Trajan** (Marcus Ulpius Trajanus), AD c.53–117, Roman emperor (r.AD 98–117); b. Spain. The adopted son and successor of Emperor Nerva, he brought DACIA under Roman control and conquered much of PARTHIA. He did much building in Rome including the Forum of Trajan and Trajan's Column which with its spiral series of reliefs showing his campaign successes is an important source of archaeological information. HADRIAN succeeded him.

**Tralee,** county town (1986 pop. 16,988), of Co. Kerry, Republic of Ireland, on R. Lee near Tralee bay. A small market town, it is connected to the Bay of Tralee by a ship canal. St Brendan was born at the nearby port of Fenit.

**tram,** or streetcar, a vehicle designed to run on tramway, i.e., a railway which shares the right of way with other road users. This uses a grooved rail with running surface flush with road. Introduced in 1832 in New York City, with horse-haulage, it provided transport in cities where growing size had made access by walking no longer satisfactory. Cable haulage was introduced in 1873 and was mainly used in the US. Practical systems of electric traction were developed by Werner SIEMENS (1879) and F.J. SPRAGUE (1888) and this led to widespread use of trams, which stimulated and contributed to the development of large cities. The advent of road transport led to discontinuation of tram systems in some countries, but they are still being developed in continental Europe and the US, where they are referred to as light rapid transit.

**tranquillizer,** drug which acts on the central nervous system to relieve emotional agitation. Antipsychotic drugs, or major tranquillizers, moderate the symptoms of psychotic states (e.g., SCHIZOPHRENIA), including agitation, delusions, and anxiety. These drugs include the phenothiazines (e.g., chlorpromazine) and haloperidol. Minor tranquillizers, such as the benzodiazepines (e.g. diazepam), relieve anxiety and tension. With prolonged use, dependency on minor tranquillizers can occur. See also LITHIUM.

**transactinide elements,** chemical elements with atomic numbers greater than 103, that of lawrencium, the last member of the ACTINIDE SERIES. See TRANSURANIC ELEMENTS.

**Transamazonica,** paved highway, 5000 km (3100 mi) in length, linking the most eastern and western points of Brazil. Officially opened in 1973 the highway runs approximately parallel to the Amazon R. linking Brazil's NE Atlantic coast with the state of Acre in W Brazil.

**transcendentalism** ('transen‚dentl'izəm, 'trahn-), in literature, movement that flourished in New England c.1836–60. A reaction against Calvinist orthodoxy and Unitarian rationalism, it was influenced by the German idealist philosophers, notably KANT, and by such English authors as CARLYLE, COLERIDGE, and WORDSWORTH. Its tenets included belief in God's immanence in man and nature, and in individual intuition as the highest source of knowledge. An optimistic philosophy, it emphasized individualism, self-reliance, and rejection of traditional authority. Its ideas were most eloquently expressed in the essays of EMERSON and in *Walden* (1854) by THOREAU. Other important transcendentalists included George Ripley, Bronson ALCOTT, and Margaret FULLER. Their journal was *The Dial* (1840–44); BROOK FARM stemmed from the movement.

**transcendentalism,** in philosophy, term describing systems holding that there are modes of being beyond the reach of mundane experience. It is closely associated with KANT, who states that transcendental elements of thought (such as concepts of space and time and categories of judgment) cannot be perceived directly through experience; nevertheless, they add to empirical knowledge. He called these elements *noumena* (as opposed to *phenomena*).

**Transcendental Meditation:** see MEDITATION.

**transducer,** device that accepts an input of energy in one form and produces an output of energy in some other form, with a known, fixed relationship between the input and output. One class of transducers consists of devices that produce an electrical output signal, e.g., MICROPHONE, RECORD-PLAYER cartridge, and PHOTOELECTRIC CELL. Other transducers accept an electrical input, e.g., LOUDSPEAKER, light bulb, and SOLENOID. Transducers may be either active or passive. Active transducers require a source of energy in addition to the input signal to produce the output signal, whereas passive transducers require only an input signal.

**transformational–generative grammar,** linguistic theory associated with Noam CHOMSKY, particularly with his *Syntactic Structures* (1957). It is a model of language which attempts, at the level of the sentence, to state rules by which *all* and only *all* grammatically correct sentences of the language can be generated, and to show how what is actually said or written in a language, the surface structure, is linked to the intended meaning or deep structure. The implication is that deep structure is universal, and that the rules or *transformations* give rise to the language-specific surface structure. Transformational–generative grammar has been the starting-point for a tremendous growth in the study of LINGUISTICS since the 1950s.

**transformer,** electrical device that transfers an alternating current or voltage (see POTENTIAL, ELECTRIC) from one ELECTRIC CIRCUIT to another using electromagnetic INDUCTION. A simple transformer consists of two coils of wire electrically insulated from each other and arranged so that a change in the current through the primary coil will produce a change in voltage across the secondary coil. The ratio of the alternating-current (AC) output voltage to the AC input voltage is approximately equal to the ratio of the number of turns in the secondary coil to the number of turns in the primary coil. This capability for transforming voltages is the basis for a great many applications. Transformers are classified according to their use; power transformers (see POWER, ELECTRIC) are used to transmit power at a constant frequency, audio transformers are designed to operate over a wide range of frequencies with a nearly constant ratio of input to output voltage, and radio-frequency transformers operate efficiently within a narrow range of high frequencies.

**transform fault:** see FAULT; PLATE TECTONICS.

**transform method,** in mathematics, method whereby a problem is solved by transforming it into an easier one. Some well-known transforms have been produced by LAPLACE and FOURIER. One of the simplest examples of a transform method, although not usually thought of as such, occurs in the use of logarithms, where multiplication and division are replaced, respectively, by the simpler processes of addition and subtraction. The ideas of operational calculus, where differentiation and integration operators are treated algebraically, are similar.

**transistor,** electronic device used as a voltage and current AMPLIFIER, consisting of SEMICONDUCTOR materials that share common physical boundaries. The material most commonly used is silicon into which impurities have been introduced. In $n$-type semiconductors there is an excess of free electrons, or negative charges, whereas in $p$-type semiconductors there is a deficiency of electrons and therefore an excess of positive charges. Transistors are used in many applications, including RADIO receivers, electronic computers, and automatic control instrumentation (e.g., in spaceflight and guided missiles). Since the invention (announced in 1948) of the transistor by the American physicists John BARDEEN, Walter H. Brattain, and William Shockley, many types have been designed. The $n$–$p$–$n$ junction transistor consists of two $n$-type semiconductors separated by a thin layer of $p$-type semiconductor; the three segments are called emitter, base, and collector, respectively, and are usually sealed in glass, with a wire extending from each segment to the outside, where it is connected to an electric circuit. The transistor action is such that if the electric potentials (see POTENTIAL, ELECTRIC) on the segments are properly determined, a small current between the emitter and base connections results in a large current between the emitter and collector connections, thus producing current amplification. The $p$–$n$–$p$ junction transistor, consisting of a thin layer of $n$-type semiconductor lying between two $p$-type semiconductors, works in the same manner, except that all polarities are reversed. See also INTEGRATED CIRCUIT; MICROELECTRONICS.

**transit instrument** or **transit,** telescope devised to observe stars as they cross the meridian of LONGITUDE and used for determining time. Its viewing tube swings on a rigid horizontal axis restricting its movements to the arc of the meridian. The meridian circle (a modern transit) is equipped with precisely graduated circles mounted on the horizontal axis and with stationary verniers, or reading microscopes, mounted on the fixed supports of the telescope that enable the observer to read the circles. By giving both the altitude and transit time, this instrument yields the right ascension and declination—the position on the celestial sphere—of the star (see ASTRONOMICAL COORDINATE SYSTEMS).

**transition elements** or **transition metals,** elements of group VIII and the b groups (I to VII) of the PERIODIC TABLE, characterized by the filling of an inner $d$ or $f$ electron orbital as atomic number increases. Many chemical and physical properties of these elements are due to their incompletely filled $d$ or $f$ orbitals. Transition elements generally have high densities and melting points, magnetic properties, and variable valency arising from the electrons in the $d$ or $f$ orbitals. These metals form stable coordination complexes, or complexions, many of which are highly coloured and exhibit paramagnetism (see MAGNETISM).

**Transkei,** black African homeland or BANTUSTAN (1983 est. pop. 2,500,000), 41,002 km² (15,831 sq mi), SE South Africa, declared independent by South Africa in 1976, but not recognized internationally. The first bantustan to be granted independence, it borders on Lesotho (N) and the Indian Ocean (SE); most of its inhabitants are Xhosa-speaking black Africans. The capital is Umtata. Transkei severed diplomatic relations with South Africa from 1978 to 1980 over territorial disputes.

**transmission,** in motor vehicles, system for transmitting power from the engine to the wheels. The system is designed to change the high rotational speed and low torque (turning force) of the engine's crankshaft into the higher-torque rotation needed to turn the wheels over a range of speeds. A **manual transmission** consists of a system of interlocking GEAR wheels arranged so that by operating a lever the driver can choose one of several ratios of speed between an input shaft turned by the engine and an output shaft that turns the wheels. For a standing start the driver selects the first, or lowest, gear, which produces high turning power at a low output shaft speed. Higher gears produce less torque at higher output shaft speeds. To allow smooth shifting from one gear to another, a clutch mechanism disengages the engine from the transmission during gear changes. The **automatic transmission** (introduced in 1939), in which gear changes are made without driver intervention, uses a fluid device called a torque converter to connect the engine with the gearbox and to control gear changes.

**Trans-Mongolian Railway,** opened in 1956, linking Beijing with the Trans-Baikal railway at Naushki and hence the TRANS-SIBERIAN RAILWAY at Saudinski. Built by Mongolia with help from the USSR and China, it provides a vital economic link with the outside world.

**transpiration,** in terrestrial plants, loss of water by evaporation mainly through the pores (stomata) of the LEAF but also through the plant's surface cells. The pull of transpiration on the fluid in the plant is one cause of the ascent of SAP from the ROOTS, and thus helps provide the necessary soil minerals and moisture for cell functions (see PHOTOSYNTHESIS). Desert plants are modified in ways that decrease transpiration (see SUCCULENT).

**transplantation, medical,** process by which a tissue or organ is removed and replaced by a corresponding part. Transplants usually range from those employing tissue (such as skin, bone, or cartilage) from the patient's own body (called an **autograft** transplant) to those involving the replacement of vital organs (such as the heart or kidney) from the body of another individual (**allograft**). Transplantation of complex organs calls for the surgical connection of the larger blood vessels of the donor organ to those of the recipient; connective tissue cells gradually link the graft and host tissues. Replacements for diseased or defective tissue (e.g., a cornea or the heart) are generally obtained from donors who have died; large or regenerating organs or tissues such as kidney, skin, bowel, or blood can be donated by living individuals (see BLOOD TRANSFUSION). Organs such as the heart must be transplanted as soon after the death of the donor as possible; skin, corneas, bone, and some blood fractions, however, can be stored. Transplanted tissue from another individual stimulates an immune response in the host (see IMMUNITY); therefore the main obstacle to successful transplantation is the rejection of foreign tissue by the host. To minimize rejection, a typing system (called the HLA system and similar to blood typing) is used to determine the degree of tissue compatibility between donor and recipient. IMMUNOSUPPRESSIVE DRUGS are also used to interfere with the production of antibodies (the body's usual response to foreign substances) in the recipient. In 1902 the French surgeon Alexis CARREL demonstrated a method of joining blood vessels that made the transplantation of organs feasible and stimulated the use of transplantation in experimental biology. A successful transplant of a human KIDNEY was made in Chicago in 1950; and the first human HEART transplant was performed by the South African surgeon Christiaan BARNARD in 1967. Since then, advances in biomedical engineering have also made possible the implantation of artificial body parts, such as artificial joints, and in 1982 resulted in the implantation of the first permanent artificial heart.

**Trans-Siberian railway,** railway connecting Moscow and Vladivostok, a distance of about 9000 km (5600 mi) and serving Omsk, Novosibirsk, Irkutsk, and Khabarovsk. Constructed between 1891 and 1905, it provides a route to the Pacific Ocean entirely on Russian territory. The Eastern USSR will also be served by the new Baikal–Amur line, sections of which are now open, which leaves the Trans-Siberian railway at Tayshet and follows a more northern route through Bratsk, Ust-Kut, Tynda, and Chekunda to Sovietskaya Gavan on the Pacific Coast. This railway was started in 1938 and traverses very difficult conditions such as frozen ground, high earthquake activity, and bogs, making its construction a great feat of engineering.

**transubstantiation,** the doctrine that in the EUCHARIST, as a result of the consecration, the substances (i.e., the inner realities) of the bread and the wine are converted into the substances of Christ's body and blood, while the accidents (i.e., the sensible data) of bread and wine remain unchanged. Defined as binding by the Fourth LATERAN Council in 1215, rejected by Protestants at the REFORMATION, but endorsed by the Council of TRENT, the doctrine is accepted as orthodox by the ROMAN CATHOLIC CHURCH and many other Christians, although some Roman Catholic theologians since the mid 20th cent. have been pressing for its restatement in terms more congenial to contemporary philosophy.

**transuranic elements,** radioactive chemical elements with atomic numbers greater than 92 (URANIUM). Only NEPTUNIUM (at. no. 93) and PLUTONIUM (at. no. 94) occur in nature; they are produced in minute amounts in the radioactive decay of uranium. The transuranic elements of the ACTINIDE SERIES were discovered as synthetic radioactive isotopes. Both American and Soviet scientists claim to have discovered independently the unstable transactinide elements 104, 105, and 106, and West German scientists reported discovering the unstable transactinide elements 107 and 109. See ELEMENT, table; PERIODIC TABLE.

**Transvaal,** province (1980 pop. 7,884,223), 286,065 km² (110,450 sq mi), NE South Africa, situated at an elevation of 910–1830 m (3000–6000 ft) in the VELD. It has produced much of the world's gold since deposits were discovered in the WITWATERSRAND (or Rand) in 1886. The province also mines most of the nation's vast store of diamonds and produces coal, uranium, platinum, and chromium. Much of South Africa's industry is concentrated along the Rand and around PRETORIA, JOHANNESBURG, and other Transvaal cities. First settled (mid-1830s) by Boer farmers, it became the heartland of the Afrikaner culture and of the struggle for independence from British colonial rule.

**Transylvania,** historic region and province 55,146 km² (21,292 sq mi), W Romania, separated in the S from Walachia by the Transylvanian Alps and in the E from Moldavia and Bukovina by the Carpathian Mts. CLUJ is the chief city. Transylvania has deposits of lignite, iron, and other resources, and produces steel, chemicals, and other manufactures. Agriculture, stock raising, and wine-making are also important. Part of the Roman province of Dacia, Transylvania was ruled (11th–16th cent.) by Hungary. Magyars, Germans, Romanians, and other peoples settled the area. From the 15th cent. Turkey and Austria vied for control of the region; Austrian control was established in 1711. Transylvania was part of Hungary in the Austro-Hungarian Empire (1867–1918). After WORLD WAR I the region was ceded to Romania. Hungary annexed N Transylvania in 1940; after WORLD WAR II it was returned to Romania.

**travel sickness:** see MOTION SICKNESS.

**Traven, B.,** pseud. of **Berick Traven Torsvan,** 1890?–1969, American novelist. Often set in exotic locations, his novels, e.g., *The Death Ship* (1926), *The Treasure of the Sierra Madre* (1927), *The Night Visitors* (1966), usually treat of exploiters and the exploited.

**treason,** in UK law, the CRIME of breach of duty of allegiance to the CROWN. Treasonable acts include plotting to kill the sovereign, levying war against the government, or giving aid to the country's enemies. Prosecutions for treason are rare, being largely confined to times of war except for a small number of spy cases. See also SEDITION.

**treasure trove,** in law, term applied to any money, gold, silver plate or bullion, hidden in the earth or in a private place, the owner being unknown. In the UK, all rights in such items belong to the CROWN, by virtue of the Royal Prerogative, though such rights may be granted to a private person (e.g., the finder). All finds of treasure trove must by law be declared to the CORONER for an inquiry.

**Treaty of Paris:** see PARIS, TREATY OF.

**Treaty of Versailles:** see VERSAILLES, TREATY OF.

**treaty port,** port opened to foreign trade by a treaty. The term is used especially in reference to China and Japan, which after the 15th cent. cut off most trade with the West. The Treaty of Nanking (1842), which ended the Sino-British OPIUM WAR, provided for five treaty ports. Their total in China later reached 69, and resident foreigners were granted EXTRATERRITORIALITY. Japanese ports were similarly reopened to Western trade after 1854. Treaty ports disappeared from Japan in 1899 and from China in 1946.

**Trebizond, empire of,** 1204–1461, one of the Greek states that sprang up after the overthrow (1204) of the Byzantine Empire by the army of the Fourth CRUSADE. Founded by the Comnenus brothers, David and ALEXIUS I of Trebizond, Trebizond remained independent when the Byzantine Empire was restored (1261). Although at times subject to Turks or

Mongols, Trebizond grew prosperous as the trade route through Asia Minor to the Far East, and from Russia and the Middle East to Europe. In 1461 this last refuge of Hellenistic culture fell to the Ottoman Turks under MEHMED II.

**tree,** woody PERENNIAL plant with a single main STEM (the trunk or bole) from which branches and twigs extend to form a characteristic crown. Trees are either deciduous, i.e., usually having broad leaves that are shed at the end of the growing season, or evergreen (see CONIFER), having needle- or scale-like leaves that are shed at intervals of 2 to 10 years. Some broad-leafed shrubs follow the conifer pattern, and the LARCH sheds its needle-like leaves deciduously. Trees are of great ecological, economic, and aesthetic importance.

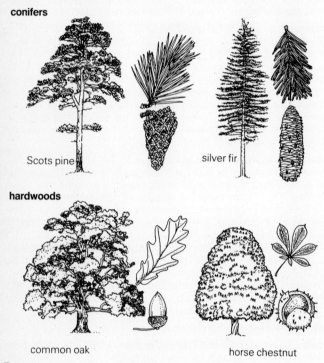

conifers

Scots pine      silver fir

hardwoods

common oak      horse chestnut

Tree

**Tree, Ellen:** see under KEAN, EDMUND.

**Tree, Sir Herbert Beerbohm,** 1853–1917, English actor-manager; b. Herbert Draper Beerbohm; half brother of Max BEERBOHM. As a manager he was noted for his Shakespearean productions, in which he stressed visual elements with elaborate effects. His wife and leading lady, **Helen Maud Holt,** 1863–1937, was especially adept at comedy.

**tree frog,** small FROG of the family Hylidae which spends its life in trees. Some tree frogs even lay their eggs in pools in tree forks or in foam up in the tree. They are found worldwide except in Antarctica, and they look very similar, with discs on their toes and green colouring. They eat insects. The Cuban tree frog is the largest, being 14 cm (5½ in) long, and the smallest tree frog is 3 cm (1¼ in) long. The European tree frog is about 5 cm (2 in) long and is found over most of Europe, and east to Asia Minor. There was a small introduced colony in England. In Australia and Brazil tree frogs have moved into humans' homes and are called house frogs.

**tree shrew,** small, arboreal prosimian, or lower PRIMATE, of the family Tupaiidae, found in S Asia. Tree shrews superficially resemble squirrels and are usually brown, reddish, or olive in colour, with large eyes, good vision, and flexible hands with sharp claws. They are territorial, omnivorous, and extremely active and quarrelsome.

**Treitschke, Heinrich von** (ˌtriechkə), 1834–96, German historian, professor, and Prussian state historiographer. Anti-Semitism and a fanatic nationalism distort the excellent scholarship of his works, notably his *History of Germany in the Nineteenth Century* (5 vol., 1879–94).

**trek,** in South African history, the great migration inland (1835–36) of Dutch farmers (Boers); called the Great Trek. Escaping British domination of the Cape of Good Hope, they founded the Orange Free State, the Transvaal, and Natal.

**trench:** see OCEAN; PLATE TECTONICS.

**Trenchard, Hugh Montague,** 1st **Viscount,** 1873–1956, first Marshal of the ROYAL AIR FORCE. He began his career as an army officer, serving in India, South Africa, and Nigeria. Invalided back to England in 1911 he learnt to fly and joined the Royal Flying Corps in 1912. On active service from the beginning of World War I, he was General Officer Commanding the Royal Flying Corps from 1915. After the war he was Chief of the Air Staff, and was largely responsible for survival of the Royal Air Force as an independent entity. He was created a viscount in 1929 on his retirement from the RAF. As Commissioner of the Metropolitan Police (1931–35) he founded the Police College at Hendon. Although by then an elderly man, he worked tirelessly in World War II, encouraging RAF units with the cheerful manner and loud voice that had earned him the nickname 'Boom'.

**Trent,** major river in Midlands of England. It rises near Biddulph Moor, Staffordshire, and flows by STOKE-ON-TRENT, Stone, Rugeley, Burton upon Trent, NOTTINGHAM, Newark-on-Trent, and Gainsborough, to join the R. Ouse and form the R. HUMBER, which flows into the North Sea in Humberside. The main tributaries are the Sow, Tame, Soar, Devon, Blyth, Dove, Derwent, and Idle. It is tidal to Cromwell Lock in Nottinghamshire. Several large coal-fired power stations are located on the banks of the R. Trent, using water from the river for cooling purposes. It is approximately 274 km (170 mi) long.

**Trent, Council of,** 1545–47, 1551–52, 1562–63, 19th ecumenical council of the Roman Catholic Church. Convoked by Pope PAUL III to meet the crisis of the Protestant REFORMATION, it was the chief expounder of the Catholic reform (see COUNTER-REFORMATION). Its definitions and reform decrees treated Scripture, the sacraments, education, the Mass, the clergy, relics, feasts, and other topics. The reforms touched all aspects of religious life and set the pattern of modern Catholicism. The official *Catechism of the Council of Trent* was published in 1566.

**Trent Affair,** a diplomatic incident between the US and Great Britain during the AMERICAN CIVIL WAR. In Nov. 1861 Capt. Charles Wilkes halted the British mail packet *Trent* and removed two Confederate commissioners, J.M. Mason (see under MASON, GEORGE) and John Slidell, and had them interned in Boston. The British reacted sharply, and for a time it appeared they might declare war on the US. The US secretary of state, W.H. SEWARD, sent a note disavowing the action and released the men, thereby ending the crisis.

**Trenton,** US city (1980 pop. 92,124), state capital (since 1790) of New Jersey, at the head of navigation on the Delaware R.; settled by Friends 1679, inc. 1792. Situated between New York and Philadelphia, it is a transport centre and an important industrial city. Its pottery industry dates from colonial times. Steel cables, rubber goods, plastics, pumps, and a variety of metal products are manufactured. On 26 Dec. 1776, having crossed the Delaware unexpectedly, George WASHINGTON defeated a Hessian force at Trenton.

**Trevelyan, Sir George Otto,** 1838–1928, English historian and politician. A Whig member of the House of Commons (1865–97), he wrote the pro-American *American Revolution* (4 vol., 1899–1907) and *George the Third and Charles Fox* (1912). His works were popular in the US. His son, **George Macaulay Trevelyan,** 1876–1962, taught history at Cambridge and was master of Trinity College (1940–51). He was a master too of the 'literary' school of historical writing, reacting against the 'scientific' school of historians. His best-known works include *British History in the Nineteenth Century* (1922), *England under Queen Anne* (3 vol., 1930–34), and *English Social History* (1941).

**Trevithick, Richard,** 1771–1833, English engineer. He pioneered high-pressure steam which he used in a steam road locomotive in 1801 and in the first railway steam locomotive in 1804.

**triangle,** in music: see PERCUSSION INSTRUMENT.

**triangulation:** see GEODESY.

**Triassic period:** see GEOLOGICAL ERA (table).

**tribe,** a non-state society. In the system of evolutionary stages elaborated in the US the term refers to a culturally united community which shares some overall political and jural authority structures and comes between a CHIEFDOM and a STATE system. See EVOLUTION, SOCIOCULTURAL.

**tribunal,** in law, a body of persons summoned to adjudicate in a dispute involving others. In the UK, the term is most commonly applied to administrative tribunals. They were largely established after World War II, as an alternative to the courts, to deal with legal disputes arising out of the provisions of the WELFARE STATE. Prominent examples include the Industrial Tribunal (dealing with unfair dismissal, redundancy, equal pay, etc.), the Rent Tribunal (dealing with LANDLORD AND TENANT disputes), and the Social Security Appeal Tribunal (dealing with claims for welfare benefits). They generally consist of a legally qualified chairperson and lay persons with specialist knowledge of the subject area. They differ from the courts in that they are more informal (having flexible rules of EVIDENCE) and inquisitorial, in that the tribunal attempts to discover the facts, rather than just listening to evidence. They aim to provide cheap and speedy justice. There is generally no APPEAL from tribunals, but their decisions are subject to JUDICIAL REVIEW by the high court. Domestic tribunals are either bodies established to regulate certain trades, e.g., the Milk Marketing Board, or disciplinary committees of the professions, e.g., the Professional Purposes Committee of the Law Society. See also COURT SYSTEM IN ENGLAND AND WALES.

**tribune,** in ancient Rome, one of various officers. There were military tribunes, senior officers of the legions, elected by the people from c.508 BC to 367 BC. The office of tribune of the PLEBS, designed to protect plebeian rights, especially against abuse by magistrates, was formed in 493 BC. By 449 BC there were ten tribunes who were plebeians elected by an assembly of plebs. The tribune's person was inviolable. He had the right to veto a decision of a magistrate and the right to prosecute corrupt magistrates before a public body. See also ROME.

**tricarboxylic acid cycle:** see KREBS CYCLE.

**trichinosis** or **trichiniasis,** parasitic disease caused by the roundworm *Trichinella spiralis,* acquired by eating raw or inadequately cooked meat, especially pork. The larvae mature in the intestines and are carried by the bloodstream to muscles, where they become embedded and remain. The host experiences irregular fever, profuse sweating, and muscular soreness; these symptoms usually subside soon after infestation, although vague muscle pain and fatigue may persist. The larvae eventually are bound in cysts in the muscle and calcify.

**Trier** (trïə), Fr. *Trèves,* city (1984 pop. 95,300), Rhineland-Palatinate, W West Germany, on the Moselle R. It is a port, an industrial centre with such manufactures as textiles and rolled steel, and the hub of the Moselle wine region. Founded c.15 BC by AUGUSTUS, it was a commercial and cultural centre under the Romans and as part of the HOLY ROMAN EMPIRE. The city was held (19th–20th cent.) by France and by Prussia. Its historic structures include an amphitheatre (c.100) and a Romanesque cathedral (11th–12th cent.). Karl MARX was born in Trier.

**Trieste,** city (1984 pop. 243,654), capital of Friuli-Venezia Giulia, NE Italy, at the head of the Adriatic. A major seaport, it is a commercial and industrial centre. A medieval free commune menaced by Venice, it placed itself (1382) under the Austrian dukes. It became a free port in 1719. A centre of IRREDENTISM, Trieste and its province were annexed (1919) by Italy. After World War II they were claimed by Yugoslavia, made (1947) a free territory under UN protection, and divided (1954) between the two countries, with Italy receiving the city. Landmarks include the Cathedral of San Giusto and Miramar castle.

**Trifonov, Yuri Valentinovich** ('tree,fohnof), 1925–81, Soviet writer. He described with great insight the moral choices confronting his heroes, who were mostly urban, middle-aged, disillusioned intellectuals (as in *The Exchange,* 1969). He was himself the son of a Party official executed in the 1937 purges, and wrote with feeling about the guilt of survivors who had denounced their colleagues (*The House on the Embankment,* 1976) or had committed atrocities during the civil war period (*The Old Man,* 1978). His last novels, published posthumously, were the unrelievedly pessimistic *Time and Place* (1981) and the partly autobiographical *Disappearance* (1987).

**trigonometry,** the study of certain mathematical relations, originally defined in terms of the angles and sides of a right-angled triangle. Six basic relations, or trigonometric functions, are defined. If *A, B,* and *C* are the angles of a right-angled triangle ($C = 90°$) and *a, b,* and *c* are the lengths of the respective sides opposite these angles, then six functions can be expressed for one of the acute angles, say *A,* as various ratios of the opposite side (*a*), the adjacent side (*b*), and the hypotenuse (*c*). Although

the actual lengths of the sides of a right-angled triangle may have any values, the ratios of the lengths will be the same for all similar right-angled triangles, large or small. It may be seen that $\sin B = \cos A, \cos B = \sin A, \tan B = \cot A,$ and so forth. When defined in this way, the values of the sine and the cosine always lie in the range 0 to 1, the values of the secant and the cosecant are always equal to or greater than 1, and the values of the tangent and the cotangent are unbounded, increasing from 0 without limit. The values of the trigonometric functions can be found in a set of tables or on a calculator. The notion of the trigonometric functions is extended beyond 90° (the largest angle size in a right triangle) by defining the functions with respect to CARTESIAN COORDINATES; the functions then take on negative as well as positive values in a pattern that repeats every 360°, or 180° in the cases of the tangent and cotangent. This repeating, or periodic, nature of the trigonometric functions leads to important applications in the study of such periodic phenomena as light and electricity. A general triangle, not necessarily containing a right angle, can also be analysed by means of trigonometry. Spherical trigonometry, the study of triangles on the surface of a sphere, is important in surveying, navigation, and astronomy.

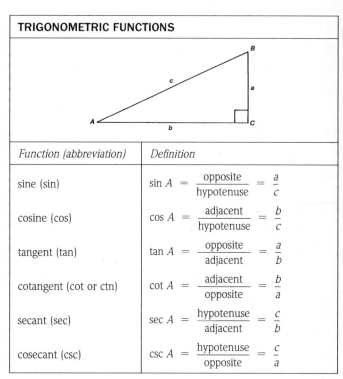

**TRIGONOMETRIC FUNCTIONS**

| Function (abbreviation) | Definition |
|---|---|
| sine (sin) | $\sin A = \dfrac{\text{opposite}}{\text{hypotenuse}} = \dfrac{a}{c}$ |
| cosine (cos) | $\cos A = \dfrac{\text{adjacent}}{\text{hypotenuse}} = \dfrac{b}{c}$ |
| tangent (tan) | $\tan A = \dfrac{\text{opposite}}{\text{adjacent}} = \dfrac{a}{b}$ |
| cotangent (cot or ctn) | $\cot A = \dfrac{\text{adjacent}}{\text{opposite}} = \dfrac{b}{a}$ |
| secant (sec) | $\sec A = \dfrac{\text{hypotenuse}}{\text{adjacent}} = \dfrac{c}{b}$ |
| cosecant (csc) | $\csc A = \dfrac{\text{hypotenuse}}{\text{opposite}} = \dfrac{c}{a}$ |

**Trigonometry:** Trigonometric functions

**trillium** attractive spring wildflower commonly called wood lily (genus *Trillium*) of the LILY family, native to N America and E Asia but grown elsewhere in cool regions as a border plant or naturalized in open woodland. The single flower may be white, pink, dark red, yellow, or green, and the leaves, petals, and sepals are typically in threes.

**trilobite,** extinct marine invertebrate animal (an ARTHROPOD) with a flat, oval body covered by a horny shell; the name refers to a pair of furrows that divide the body lengthwise into three sections. Trilobites were abundant in Cambrian and Ordovician seas; they became extinct in the Permian period (see GEOLOGICAL ERAS, table).

**Trim,** county town (1986 pop. 1968) of Co. Meath, Republic of Ireland, situated on R. Boyne, 42 km (26 mi) NW of Dublin. It is a small market town. There are several historic remains, including those of a 12th-cent. castle, and gates from the old town wall.

**Trinidad and Tobago,** officially Republic of Trinidad and Tobago, republic (1987 est. pop. 1,250,000), West Indies, N of Venezuela, comprising the islands of Trinidad (4828 km²/1864 sq mi) and Tobago (300 km²/116 sq mi). The capital is PORT OF SPAIN (on Trinidad). Trinidad is predominantly flat, with low mountains in the north; Tobago is mountainous and forested. The climate of both islands is warm and humid. More industrialized than most West Indian nations, the country exports chemicals, petroleum products, bananas, cocoa, and sugar; has natural gas resources under development; and derives some income from tourism. The GDP is US$8066 million and the GDP per capita is US$6962. More than half the people are black, and two-fifths are East Indian. English and some French patois are spoken. Trinidad was discovered by COLUMBUS in 1498 and formally ceded to Britain in 1815. Tobago, which had been held by the Dutch and French, became British in the late 1700s, and the islands were joined politically in 1888. After a brief period in the WEST INDIES Federation, they became an independent state in 1962 within the COMMONWEALTH and a republic with a parliamentary system of government in 1976. The post-independence political scene was dominated by the moderate People's National Movement, led by Eric Williams until his death in 1981 and subsequently by George Chambers. In 1980 the island of Tobago was granted internal self-government. The 1986 elections, however, resulted in a landslide victory for the reformist National Alliance for Reconstruction led by A.N.R. Robinson.

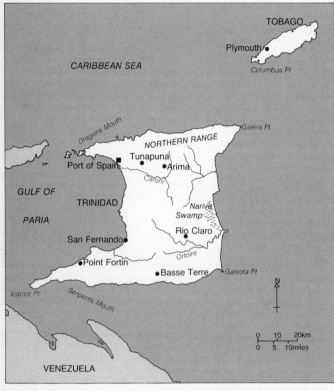

Trinidad and Tobago

**trinitron,** colour television CATHODE-RAY TUBE developed by the Sony Corporation. The phosphors are arranged in several hundred narrow vertical strips in three-colour triads. Instead of a masking plate, as in the SHADOW MASK TUBE, there is a metal grill with one vertical slot for each triad. A single gun has its electron beam split into three separate beams each with grids so that they can be independently controlled by the colour components of the video signal. The three electron beams of this gun are lined up with the vertical slots in the metal grill and the appropriate colour phosphor strip to ensure that each colour strip can only be hit by the electron beam appropriate to that colour. With the colour components applied to the grids controlling the three electron beams a natural replica of the original picture is obtained. With the greater electron transparency of the grill slots compared with the holes in the mask of the shadow mask tube, and with the greater beam density of this type of electron gun, the trinitron achieves a greater brightness than is possible with the shadow mask tube for similar sized screens. See also TELEVISION.

**trinitrotoluene** ('trie'nietroh,tolyoo'een): see TNT.

**Trinity,** fundamental doctrine of Christianity by which God is considered as existing in three persons—the Father, the Son (who became incarnate as JESUS), and the HOLY GHOST. The doctrine is foreshadowed in the NEW TESTAMENT, but received sharper definition at the first ecumenical councils.

**Trinity House,** London headquarters and name of British authority responsible for LIGHTHOUSES and LIGHTSHIPS. It was established by charter under Henry VII in 1514. The other major UK authority is the Commissioners for Northern Lights.

**Triple Alliance, War of the,** 1865–70, fought by PARAGUAY against the alliance of ARGENTINA, BRAZIL, and URUGUAY. Paraguayan dictator Francisco Solano LÓPEZ imprudently declared war (1865) to revenge Brazil's military reprisals following Uruguay's civil war. Paraguay heroically defended itself against its larger, more powerful neighbours, but a large part of its male population was killed, and the country was devastated.

**Triple Alliance and Triple Entente,** two opposing international combinations of states that dominated Europe's history from 1882 until, substantially armed, they moved inexorably into conflict as the Central Powers and the Allies, respectively, in WORLD WAR I. Although there were numerous areas of contention between the two groups, the two principal problems that finally brought them to war involved rival claims in the Balkans. The **Triple Alliance** was formed when the secret Dual Alliance of Germany and Austria–Hungary (1879) was joined by Italy in 1882. Serbia also joined in 1882, and Romania in 1883. Italy and Romania were never entirely comfortable within the alliance, however, and in fact both fought on the side of the Allies in the war. The **Triple Entente** followed the rapprochement (1890) between France and Russia and their Dual Alliance openly acknowledged in 1895. In 1904, France and Britain, despite their traditional rivalry, agreed on an ENTENTE CORDIALE, which was brought about mainly because of their disquiet over German commercial and colonial imperialism. In 1907, Britain also agreed on an Entente with Russia, thereby associating itself with Europe's second great power bloc.

**Triple Crown,** a sporting title. In horse racing, it applies to a horse which wins in the same season the St Leger, the DERBY, and the Two Thousand Guineas. In the US, the three Triple Crown races are the Kentucky Derby, the Preakness Stakes, and the Belmont Stakes. In RUGBY UNION the title goes to the country which beats all three other home countries in the same season and is thus confined to the UK.

**triple jump,** FIELD EVENT included in all major athletics programmes. After a running start the competitor hops, skips, and then jumps in three successive leaps, and tries to cover as much ground as possible. It has been an Olympic sport since 1896.

**Tripoli,** Arab. *Tarabulus al-Gharb*, city (1985 est. pop. 980,000) capital of Libya, NW Libya, a port on the Mediterranean coast of N Africa. It is Libya's largest city and a commercial and industrial centre. Manufactures include processed food and textiles. The city was founded (probably 7th cent. BC) by Phoenicians. It was captured by the Romans (1st cent. BC), the Vandals (5th cent. AD), and the Arabs (7th cent.). The Spanish took it in 1510, the Ottoman Turks in 1551. Tripoli became a major base of the Barbary pirates, whom the US fought (1801–05) in the TRIPOLITAN WAR. It passed to Italy in 1911 and was taken (1943) by the British during WORLD WAR II. Some Roman monuments remain.

**Tripoli,** city and port (1980 est. pop. 175,000), N Lebanon, on the Mediterranean coast. It is the terminus of an oil pipeline from Iraq and has a refinery, but the flow of oil has ceased since 1975. The population is predominantly Muslim of the Shia sect, but it has been afflicted with local factional fighting since the outbreak of the Lebanese civil war (1975); both its trade and industry have suffered.

**Tripolitan War,** 1800–15, intermittent conflict between the US and the BARBARY STATES. The US adopted the practice, common to European nations, of paying tribute to the N African Barbary states to buy immunity from pirate raids. When the pasha of Tripoli demanded (1800) more tribute, the US refused payment and hostilities broke out. A settlement of sorts was effected in 1805, but tribute demands continued until 1815, when a squadron under DECATUR forced the dey of Algiers to sign a treaty renouncing the practice.

**trisomy 21** (,tricsoh'mee): see DOWN'S SYNDROME.

**Tristan:** see TRISTRAM AND ISOLDE.

**Tristan, Flora,** 1803–44, French socialist and feminist, influenced by the ideas of Charles FOURIER, Robert OWEN and Mary WOLLSTONECRAFT. A stay in England produced her *London Journals* (1840) which describes British working life and early CHARTISM. She championed women's rights to education and employment and the equality of the sexes is stressed in her book *Union ouvrière* (1843), which proposes a single international trade union.

**Tristan da Cunha** (ˌtristan də ˌkoohnə), group of volcanic islands (1985 pop. 313), S Atlantic, about midway between South Africa and South America. They were discovered by the Portuguese in 1506, annexed by Great Britain in 1816, and made a dependency of the British colony of SAINT HELENA in 1938. All inhabitants were evacuated to Britain following a volcanic eruption in 1961 and returned in 1963.

**Tristram and Isolde,** medieval romance. An Anglo-Norman version of c.1185 is the oldest extant. GOTTFRIED VON STRASSBURG wrote a German version c.1200. The story, originally independent, was later incorporated into ARTHURIAN LEGEND. The basic plot in all versions involves Tristram's journey to Ireland to bring Isolde back to Cornwall to be the bride of his uncle, King Mark. A potion the couple unknowingly swallow makes them fall in love. Modern treatments of the tale include those by SWINBURNE and Richard WAGNER.

**triticale,** artificial hybrid between rye and wheat. It is a new crop, produced by genetic manipulation, which combines the high protein content and weather-resistance of RYE with the high productivity of WHEAT.

**tritium:** see HYDROGEN.

**Triton,** in astronomy, natural satellite of NEPTUNE.

**Triumvirate,** in ancient Rome, ruling board or commission of three men. The **First Triumvirate** was the alliance of Julius CAESAR, POMPEY, and Marcus Licinius Crassus (see CRASSUS, family), formed in 60 BC, but the alliance had no official sanction. The **Second Triumvirate** was legally established by the senate in 43 BC and was renewed in 37 BC. The members were Octavian (AUGUSTUS), Mark ANTONY, and Marcus Aemilius Lepidus (see LEPIDUS, family).

**Trivandrum,** city (1981 pop. 499,531), Kerala state, S India, on the SE coast of India. It is a district administrative centre and the capital of Kerala state. It has grown very rapidly since its selection as the state capital in 1956 (its 1961 pop. 239,815). It has titanium, metal, rubber, and other industries, but its main significance is administrative. It had been the capital of the princely state of Travancore since the 18th cent.

**Trois Rivières** or **Three Rivers,** city (1980 est. pop. 51,200), S Quebec, E Canada, at the junction of the St Maurice and St Lawrence Rs. It is one of Quebec's principal ports and industrial centres, with the manufacture of pulp and paper dominating the economy. Trois Rivières was founded in 1634 by CHAMPLAIN. It was a fortified port and a base for French exploration and missionary work in the interior during the 17th and 18th cent.

**Trojan War,** in Greek mythology, war between Greeks and Trojans. It began when PARIS abducted HELEN, wife of MENELAUS. Under AGAMEMNON, the Greeks besieged Troy for nine years. They finally won when, pretending to depart, they left a wooden horse, which the Trojans, ignoring the warnings of CASSANDRA and LAOCOÖN, took into the city. Warriors hidden in the horse opened the city gates to the Greek army, which sacked Troy. Among the Greek heroes were ACHILLES, Patroclus, ODYSSEUS, and Nestor; the Trojan heroes, led by HECTOR, included AENEAS, Memnon, and Penthesilea. The gods took a great interest in the war. HERA, POSEIDON, and ATHENA aided the Greeks, while APHRODITE and ARES favoured the Trojans. The war's final year forms the main part of HOMER's *Iliad*. The Trojan War probably reflected a real war c.1200 BC over control of trade in the DARDANELLES.

**Trollope, Anthony,** 1815–82, English novelist. Although he did not publish his first novel until he was 32, he produced some 50 books, many written while he was working as a civil servant in the Post Office. His Barsetshire novels, among them *The Warden* (1855), *Barchester Towers* (1857), *The Small House at Allington* (1864), and *The Last Chronicle of Barset* (1867), are a series of six books depicting, sometimes satirically, the day-to-day lives of county and professional (especially clerical) people in an imaginary agricultural area. A later novel sequence on political themes, centred on the statesman Plantagenet Palliser, included *Phineas Finn* (1869), *The Eustace Diamonds* (1873) and *The Prime Minister* (1876). The revelation in his *Autobiography* (1883) of his business-like approach to literary creation shocked some critics, and his fame diminished in the next half-century, but he is now rated only just below

the greatest 19th cent. novelists for his truthful and affectionate portrayal of ordinary humanity and the scenes of daily life.

**trombone,** a BRASS INSTRUMENT with a cup-shaped mouthpiece and a cylindrical bore. The length of the tube is varied with a U-shaped slide. Trombones are normally either tenor or bass; the tenor has a range of about three octaves upwards from E below the bass stave, and the bass trombone is pitched a fourth lower. Trombones started to appear in the orchestra in the late 18th cent. There is a small solo and chamber repertoire.

**Trondheim,** city (1985 pop. 134,075), W Norway, on the Trondheim Fjord. A seaport with important fishing and timber-working industries, it serves as a regional centre. Founded towards the end of the 10th cent., the city was the capital until 1380, and is still the ecclesiastical capital. The kings of Norway were crowned in its 12th to 13th-cent. cathedral.

**Tropic of Cancer,** parallel of LATITUDE at 23°27′ north of the EQUATOR. It is the northern boundary of the TROPICS and marks the farthest point north at which the sun can be seen directly overhead at noon. The sun reaches its vertical position over the Tropic of Cancer at about 22 June, the summer SOLSTICE in the Northern Hemisphere.

**Tropic of Capricorn,** parallel of LATITUDE at 23°27′ south of the EQUATOR. It is the southern boundary of the TROPICS and marks the farthest point south that the sun can be seen directly overhead at noon. The sun reaches its vertical position over the Tropic of Capricorn at about 22 December, the summer SOLSTICE in the Southern Hemisphere.

**tropics,** all the land and water of the earth between the TROPIC OF CANCER and the TROPIC OF CAPRICORN. The entire zone receives the sun's rays more directly than areas in higher latitudes, and therefore the average annual temperature is higher and seasonal changes in temperature are less. However, because of factors other than latitude (e.g., distance from the ocean, prevailing winds, elevation), several different climatic types are found, including rain forest, STEPPE, SAVANNA, and DESERT.

**tropism** (ˌtrohpiz(ə)m), response of a plant or one of its parts, involving orientation toward (positive tropism) or away from (negative tropism) one or more external stimuli. For example, plant roots grow toward gravity and moisture and away from light. Other tropistic stimuli are heat, electricity, and chemical agents. The term *taxis* is applied to similar involuntary movements in animals and motile unicellular plants.

**Trotsky, Leon,** 1879–1940, Russian revolutionary, a leader in the founding of the USSR; b. Lev Davidovich Bronstein. The son of a prosperous farmer, he became a Marxist in 1896. Exiled to Siberia in 1900, he escaped in 1902 with a passport bearing the name of one of his jailers, Trotsky. In London, with LENIN, he edited the Social-Democratic journal *Iskra* [the spark]. After the 1905 RUSSIAN REVOLUTION he led the St Petersburg (later Leningrad) SOVIET, or workers' council, but was soon arrested. In prison he formulated his theory of permanent revolution, predicting that in Russia a socialist revolution would succeed a bourgeois revolution, as if in a chain reaction, and that worldwide proletarian revolution would follow. Escaping from Siberia again, he worked as a journalist in Vienna, Paris, and New York. He returned to Russia in May 1917, and was a leading organizer of the Bolshevik seizure of power in Nov. 1917. In the new cabinet he was people's commissar for foreign affairs, but differences with Lenin over the Treaty of BREST-LITOVSK (1918) led him to resign. As people's commissar of war he organized the victorious Red Army in the civil war (1918–20). On Lenin's death (1924), Trotsky and STALIN were the chief rivals for succession. Stalin, general secretary of the party and a skilled infighter, opposed Trotsky's advocacy of world revolution with his plan for 'socialism in one country'. Trotsky was ousted as commissar of war (1925), expelled from the party (1927), and deported from the USSR (1929). Turkey granted him asylum. In 1933 he moved to France and in 1935 to Norway, which under Soviet pressure expelled him in 1936. In the notorious Moscow treason trials (1936–38) he was accused in his absence of heading an anti-Soviet plot. Other defendants made grotesque 'confessions' of anti-Soviet activities and were executed as Stalin sought to eliminate all opposition to his dictatorship. Trotsky settled in Mexico City and continued to oppose Stalinism in his writings, until his assassination by a Soviet agent, Ramon Merader, to whom Stalin subsequently awarded the order of the Hero of the Soviet Union.

**troubadours,** aristocratic poet-musicians (fl. late 11th–13th cent.) of S France (Provence). Their poems were sung in a dialect called *langue d'oc* and favourite subjects were courtly love, war, and nature. Many troubadours were noblemen and crusader knights; famous ones included Peire Vidal and Bertrand de Born. They declined after many were caught up in the Albigensian Crusade (see ALBIGENSES). Their counterparts in N France were called TROUVÈRES.

**trout,** FISH in the SALMON family. Trout are found in Europe and North America and have been introduced into New Zealand, living in cool waters. The European trout (*Salmo trutta*) is very variable in colour and adaptable in habitat. The brown race does not migrate and lives in smaller lakes and rivers. The silvery sea trout does migrate to the sea, returning to rivers to spawn, and grows much larger than the brown trout, 13 kg (30 lb) against 7 kg (17 lb). All trout are carnivorous, some cannibalistic, their habit of rising to take flies from the surface of the water providing the sport of fly fishing. The rainbow trout (*S. gairdneri*) is farmed for the freezer market.

**trouvères,** medieval poet-musicians (fl. late 12th–13th cent.) of N and central France. The trouvères imitated the TROUBADOURS of the south. Their songs, written in a dialect called *langue d'oïl,* include love lyrics, romances, and the heroic CHANSONS DE GESTE.

**Troy,** ancient city of Asia Minor, also called Ilion or, in Latin, Ilium; known from Homer's account of the TROJAN WAR in the *Iliad.* Excavations by Heinrich SCHLIEMANN and others identified the site of the ancient city as the mound called Hissarlik, in Asian Turkey. It was established as a Phrygian city, with a culture dating from the BRONZE AGE. The place was reoccupied in historical times, but was never again important.

**Troyes,** city (1982 pop. of agglomeration 125,240), capital of Aube dept., NE France, on the SEINE R. Light engineering has been added to the traditional industry of hosiery and knitwear manufacture. Its nodality made it an important centre of fairs, and the term 'troy weight' derives from the importance of Troyes as a trading centre from medieval times. The older quarters have 13th-cent. churches and many houses of the 16th cent. or earlier.

**troy weights:** see ENGLISH UNITS OF MEASUREMENT; WEIGHTS AND MEASURES, table.

**Trubetzkoy, Nikolaj Sergejevich** ('trooh,betskoy), 1890–1938, Russian linguist and member of the PRAGUE LINGUISTIC CIRCLE. Primarily a phonologist, his major work *Grundzüge der Phonologie* (1939) established principles for dealing with the sound systems of language and the relationships which hold between the units of that system.

**Trucial States:** see UNITED ARAB EMIRATES.

**Trudeau, Pierre Elliott** (trooh,doh), 1919–, prime minister of CANADA (1968–79, 1980–84). He served (1967–68) in Lester PEARSON's ministry and succeeded him as Liberal Party leader and prime minister. His government pursued a policy of independence of US influence and promoted Canada's control of its economy. Trudeau sought to redefine federal–provincial relations and to contain the QUEBEC separatist movement. Briefly out of office (1979–80) after the Conservatives won the 1979 election, he returned to power with the Liberals' 1980 victory. That year he proposed a new constitution for Canada, independent of the British parliament, and on 17 Apr. 1982, Queen Elizabeth II signed the CONSTITUTION ACT, 1982, which gave Canada complete independence. He resigned the premiership and party leadership in 1984.

**Truffaut, François,** 1932–84, French film director. His engrossing, often charming, films have great humane power. They include *The 400 Blows* (1959), *Jules and Jim* (1961), *Day for Night* (1973), and *The Last Métro* (1980).

**truffle,** edible, subterranean fungus (division FUNGI) found chiefly in W Europe. Truffles are small, solid, fleshy SAPROPHYTES that usually grow close to the roots of trees in woodlands. The several species range in colour from grey or brown to nearly black and have a piquant, aromatic flavour. The truffles of the forests of Périgord, France, have long been regarded as a delicacy, and their collection is an important industry. They are hunted with dogs and pigs, which are able to scent them out underground. Thus far, truffles have not been successfully cultivated.

**Trujillo,** city (1981 pop. 354,557), N Peru, capital of La Libertad dept. It serves the agricultural districts of the valleys of the rivers Moche and Chicama and previously its importance was associated with the local mining of gold, silver and copper. It is Peru's second oldest colonial city, having been founded by Francisco PIZARRO in 1537. Near the city is Chan-Chan, the ruins of the pre-Incan city and capital of the Chimu or Moche civilization.

**Trujillo Molina, Rafael Leonidas** (trooh,heeyoh moh,leenah), 1891–1961, president of the DOMINICAN REPUBLIC (1930–38, 1942–52). After seizing power by an army coup (1930), he ran an efficient but ruthless dictatorship for 31 years until his assassination. He accomplished considerable material progress, but his terroristic methods led to unprecedented repression.

**Truman, Harry S.,** 1884–1972, 33rd president of the US. He grew up on a farm near Independence, Missouri, and served in World War I. After a decade in local Democratic politics, he was elected US senator in 1934 and reelected in 1940. During World War II, he achieved national prominence as chairman of a committee investigating government spending. He was nominated for vice president in 1944 and elected along with Pres. Franklin D. ROOSEVELT. Roosevelt's death on 12 Apr. 1945, thrust Truman into the presidency at a crucial time, the closing days of World War II. After the war in Europe ended on 8 May, Truman authorized the use of the ATOMIC BOMB against Japan at HIROSHIMA (6 Aug.) and NAGASAKI (9 Aug.). On 14 Aug. Japan surrendered. Truman's domestic social reform programme, the Fair Deal, which went beyond Roosevelt's NEW DEAL by including civil rights and health insurance proposals, was frustrated by a coalition of Republicans, who won control of Congress in 1946, and conservative southern Democrats. In foreign affairs, increasing tensions with the USSR resulted in the COLD WAR. Truman took increasingly tough stands. The Truman Doctrine (1947) was aimed at protecting Greece and Turkey from Communist domination. The MARSHALL PLAN (1947) was designed to effect the economic recovery of Western Europe. NATO (1949) was a multinational defence plan. In the 1948 presidential election Truman won a stunning (and unexpected) victory over Thomas E. DEWEY. Popular fear of Communist subversion, an issue unscrupulously exploited by US senator Joseph R. MCCARTHY, dominated Truman's second term, particularly after American involvement in the KOREAN WAR. Truman chose not to run for reelection in 1952 and retired to Independence. His term of office was marked by controversy from beginning to end. Among his controversial acts were his decision to use the atomic bomb, the 'loss' of China to the Communists, and his firing of Gen. Douglas MACARTHUR during the Korean War. He was appreciated, however, outside as well as inside the US, for his plain speaking and for his ability to make hard decisions.

**trumpet,** a BRASS instrument with a cup-shaped mouthpiece and a cylindrical bore. The modern trumpet, which is usually in B♭, has three valves which alter the overall length of the tubing allowing a full range of notes to be played. The B♭ trumpet has a range of two and a half octaves upwards from the E below middle C. The trumpet has played in the orchestra since the 18th cent. but has the oldest individual solo repertoire of any wind instrument (except the organ), going back to the 17th cent.

**trust,** in law, arrangement whereby control of PROPERTY is vested by its owner (the settlor) in a trustee, who administers it for the benefit of a third party (the beneficiary). The trustee, who receives no advantage other than a fee fixed by law, may be an individual or a corporate body, e.g., a bank. In the UK it is normal to appoint trustees to administer a person's estate after his or her death in accordance with his or her wishes.

**trusteeship, territorial,** system (est. 1946) whereby nations administer dependent territories under the supervision of the UN Trusteeship Council. (See UNITED NATIONS, table). Its aim is to bring all territories to self-governing status. It succeeded the MANDATES system of the LEAGUE OF NATIONS. After World War II there were 11 trust territories; of these, all except the Pacific Islands trust territory (administered by the US) have now gained self-governing status.

**trypanosome** (tri,panə'sohm, ,tripanə'sohm, trie-), microscopic one-celled organism (see PROTOZOA) that usually lives as a parasite in the bloodstream of a vertebrate. Most undergo part of their development in the digestive tracts of insects that transmit the parasite with their bite. Some cause serious diseases in humans and animals, e.g., African sleeping sickness, caused by *Trypanosoma gambiense* and transmitted by the TSETSE FLY.

**trypanosomiasis** ('tripənəsə,mie·əsis): see SLEEPING SICKNESS.

**tsetse fly,** a blood-sucking African FLY, (family Glossinidae). Males as well as females feed only on blood, and several species (e.g., *Glossina*

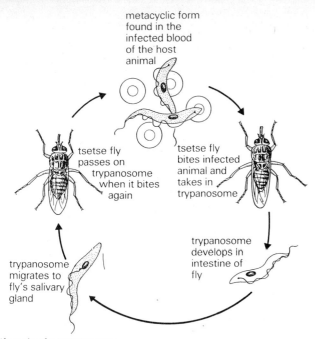

metacyclic form
found in the
infected blood
of the host
animal

tsetse fly
passes on
trypanosome
when it bites
again

tsetse fly
bites infected
animal and
takes in
trypanosome

trypanosome
migrates to
fly's salivary
gland

trypanosome
develops in
intestine of
fly

Life cycle of a **trypanosome**

*morsitans, G. pallidipes,* and *G. palpalis*) are of great socioeconomic significance as vectors of TRYPANOSOMES which cause the often fatal disease trypanosomiasis in cattle and man (sleeping sickness). Tsetse are difficult to eradicate because they do not have a free-living larval stage, which in many other insect pests is the one most susceptible to control measures. Instead, females give birth to a single fully-grown larva, at intervals of about 10 days, which immediately burrows into the soil and pupates.

Tsetse fly: (genus *Glossino*) feeding on blood

**Tshombe, Moise Kapenda** (ˌchohmbay), 1919–69, political leader in the Republic of the Congo (now ZAÏRE). When the Belgian Congo became independent in 1960, he became provisional president of the rich Katanga (now SHABA) province, which he proclaimed in secession from the rest of the Congo. He had strong Belgian backing, but eventually he was forced (1963) to capitulate. In 1964 he became premier of the Congo in a coalition government, but he was ousted in 1965 and went into exile. In 1967 he was kidnapped and taken to Algeria, where he died incommunicado.

**Tsimshian Indians:** see NORTH AMERICAN INDIANS.

**Tsin,** dynasty: see CHINA.

**Tsinan:** see JI'NAN.

**Tsinghai:** see QINGHAI.

**Tsingtao:** see QINGDAO.

**Tsiolkovsky, Konstantin Eduardovich** (tseeohlˌkohvskee), 1857–1935, Russian inventor and rocket expert. His most important theoretical work was concerned with the possibility of rocket flight into outer space. His *Investigation of Outer Space by Means of Reaction Apparatus* appeared in 1903. In 1929 he presented a design for a multistage rocket. He also conceived of artificial Earth satellites, including manned space platforms.

**Tsitsihar:** see QIQIHAR.

**tsunami, seismic sea wave** or **tidal wave** (tsoonahmi), series of catastrophic ocean waves generated by earthquakes, volcanic eruptions, or landslides beneath the sea. In the open ocean tsunamis may have wavelengths of up to several hundred kilometres but heights of less than one metre (3 ft). Because this ratio is so large, tsunamis can go undetected until they approach shallow waters along a coast. Their height as they crash upon the shore mostly depends on the geometry of the submarine topography offshore, but they can be as high as 30 m (100 ft) and cause severe damage and loss of life.

**Tsvetayeva, Marina Ivanovna** (ˈtsvetaˌyayrə), 1892–1941, Russian poet. She spent much of her life in W Europe, having left Russia in 1921 to join her husband, a former White Russian officer, in Paris. In 1939 she returned to Russia, to discover that her husband, who had become a double agent while in France, had been shot: after a period of hopeless misery, she committed suicide. Her early poems were written in praise of the White armies in their fight against Bolshevism; her mature work, written abroad and published under the titles *Craft* (1923) and *After Russia* (1928), combined elements from Futurism, Russian folklore, and the Bible.

**tuatara** or **sphenodon,** lizardlike REPTILE (*Sphenodon punctatus*), last survivor of the order Rhynchocephalia, which flourished in the early Mesozoic era before the rise of DINOSAURS. It lives on a few islands off New Zealand, where it is protected. The olive-coloured, yellow-speckled tuatara reaches 60 cm (2 ft) or more in length and has a spiny crest down its neck and back. The animal nests in a burrow and it often shares its burrow with a PETREL. It feeds on insects, and may take petrel's eggs and chicks.

**tuba,** a low-pitched BRASS INSTRUMENT with a cup-shaped mouthpiece and a conical bore, and three valves. Tubas come in several sizes, the most common being the bass tuba with a range of over three octaves upwards from C three octaves below middle C. Tubas first appeared in the 1820s.

**tuber,** enlarged tip of a RHIZOME or a swollen underground STEM that stores food. Tubers, although modified, contain all the usual stem parts BARK, WOOD, pith, and buds. The term is also applied to some swollen ROOTS, e.g., the root tubers of DAHLIA.

**tuberculosis** or **TB,** contagious disease caused by the bacterium *Mycobacterium tuberculosis,* identified by Robert KOCH in 1882. Formerly known as consumption, the disease primarily affects the lungs, although the intestines, joints, and other parts of the body may also become infected. It is spread mainly by inhalation, occasionally by ingestion through contaminated foods (e.g., unpasteurized milk) and utensils. Symptoms as the disease progresses include fever, weakness, loss of weight, and, in the pulmonary form, the spitting of blood. The incidence of tuberculosis, which once affected millions, has greatly decreased with improved sanitation, early detection through X-rays and skin tests, VACCINATION, and ANTIBIOTIC drugs, particularly streptomycin.

**Tübingen** (ˌtooh'binən), city (1984 pop. 73,600), Baden–Württemberg, on the NECKAR R., West Germany. Its famous university was founded in 1477 and contributes much to the city's character.

**Tubman, Harriet,** c.1820–1913, black American ABOLITIONIST. A slave, she escaped in 1849 and became one of the most successful 'conductors' on the UNDERGROUND RAILROAD, leading more than 300 slaves to freedom. She was a friend of leading abolitionists and worked for Union forces during the Civil War as a laundress, nurse, and spy.

**Tubman, William Vacanarat Shadrach,** 1895–1971, president of LIBERIA (1944–71). He greatly modernized the country and gave the vote to women and tribe members. He maintained a close alliance with the US.

**Tuchman, Barbara W(ertheim),** 1912–, American historian. She has won the Pulitzer Prize for history twice, for *The Guns of August* (1962), about the onset of WORLD WAR I, and for *Stilwell and the American Experience in China* (1971). Her other works include *A Distant Mirror* (1978), a panoramic study of the 14th cent.

**Tucson,** US city (1984 est. pop. 365,000), SE Arizona.; inc. 1877. Located in a desert valley surrounded by mountains, it has a dry, sunny climate and is a tourist centre. It also has electronic, optic, and research industries, and processes and distributes the area's cotton, fruits, and livestock. Copper mining is important in the area. The city (est. 1776) was transferred to the US by the Gadsden Purchase (1853). Points of interest include the nearby San Xavier mission (present building 1783–97), the Arizona-Sonora Desert Museum, and the Univ. of Arizona.

**Tudor,** royal family that ruled England (1485–1603). Its founder was a Welshman named Owen Tudor who married CATHERINE OF VALOIS, the widow of HENRY V. Their son Edmund married Margaret Beaufort (a descendant of JOHN OF GAUNT) and had a son Henry, who assumed the Lancastrian claims to the throne. Henry defeated RICHARD III at Bosworth Field and became (1485) king as HENRY VII. By his marriage to Elizabeth of York, Henry united the Lancastrian and Yorkist claims. Of his children, MARGARET TUDOR married JAMES IV of Scotland, Mary of England married LOUIS XII of France, and Henry succeeded him as HENRY VIII. Three of Henry VIII's children, EDWARD VI, MARY I, and ELIZABETH I, ruled England. The Tudors strengthened the English monarchy and witnessed a flowering of culture. The accession (1603) of JAMES I, a descendant of Margaret Tudor, began the STUART dynasty.

**Tudor, Antony,** 1909–87, English choreographer. Trained by Dame Marie RAMBERT, he went to the US (1940) and became director of the Metropolitan Opera Ballet School (1950). He choreographed for major companies including American Ballet Theatre; his works are influenced by expressionism and MODERN DANCE idioms.

**Tudor style,** phase of English architecture and decoration in the reigns (1485–1558) of Henry VII, Henry VIII, and Mary I, a transitional style between Gothic Perpendicular (see GOTHIC ARCHITECTURE AND ART) and Palladian (see PALLADIO). Manor houses, built for the new trading families, exhibit the style's characteristics of greater domesticity and privacy: rooms multiplied as the great hall's importance diminished; oak-panelled interiors had plaster relief ornament; furniture increased. Exteriors showed modified perpendicular features, e.g., square-headed, mullioned windows. Brickwork combined with half-timber, high pinnacled gables, and numerous chimneys to create a distinctive look. Principal Tudor examples are parts of Hampton Court Palace near London (begun 1515) and St John's College, Cambridge.

**Tuesday:** see WEEK.

**Tuileries** (ˌtweeləreez), former palace in Paris. Planned by Catherine de' MEDICI and begun (1564) by Philibert DELORME, it occupied part of the present Tuileries gardens. It was rarely used until 1789, when Louis XVI was forced to move there from Versailles (see FRENCH REVOLUTION). Napoleon I made it his chief residence, and it continued to function as such until destroyed by fire during the COMMUNE OF PARIS (1871). The formal gardens, by LENÔTRE, remain, affiliated with the LOUVRE.

**Tula,** city (1985 pop. 532,000), central European USSR, on the Upa R. The most important of the industrial centres S of Moscow, Tula produces armaments, machine tools, sewing machines, and agricultural and metal-working machinery. Other industries include electrical engineering, tanning, flour milling, and sugar refining. Iron ore from the Kursk Magnetic Anomaly, and natural gas from the Caucasus and W Siberia provide a wide resource base for the integrated iron and steel works. Yasnaya Polyana, the memorial estate of Leo TOLSTOY, is near Tula.

**tulip,** hardy plant (genus *Tulipa*) of the LILY family, native from the Mediterranean to Japan and widely cultivated by the Dutch. Tulips, which are grown from BULBS, have deep, cup-shaped flowers of many rich colours. Said to have been introduced into Europe from Turkey in 1554, they were objects of wild financial speculation in 17th-cent. Holland.

**tulip tree:** see MAGNOLIA.

**Tull, Jethro,** 1674–1741, English agriculturist and inventor. He advocated the use of manures, pulverizing the soil, planting with drills, and thorough tilling of the soil during the growing period. He invented (c.1701) a mechanical drill for sowing.

**Tullamore,** county town (1986 pop. 8443) of Co. Offaly, Republic of Ireland, situated on Grand Canal, 80 km (50 mi) W of Dublin. It is a small market town, whose industries include distilling and brewing. Durrow Abbey nearby was founded by St Columba in the 6th cent.

**Tulsa,** US city (1984 est. pop. 375,000), NE Oklahoma, on the Arkansas R.; inc. 1898. It is a major centre of the US oil industry, with refineries and business and research offices; aerospace and metal-fabrication industries are also important. Tulsa grew after the coming of the railway in 1882 and boomed when oil was discovered nearby in 1901. A waterway connecting the city with the Gulf of MEXICO was opened in 1971, making the city an inland port.

**tumbleweed,** plant that breaks from its roots at maturity, dries into a rounded tangle of branches, and rolls long distances with the wind, scattering seeds as it goes. Tumbleweeds are especially abundant in PRAIRIE and STEPPE regions. One of the most common is the Russian thistle (*Salsola pestifer*), not a THISTLE but a member of the goosefoot family and related to saltwort. Native to Asia, it is a pest on the prairies of the W US.

**tumour** or **neoplasm,** new growth of tissue composed of cells that grow in an abnormal way; it may be benign or malignant. Normal tissue contains feedback controls that allow for tissue repair but do not permit expansion once a certain number of cells have developed. Tumour cells, lacking such controls, proliferate and monopolize body nutrients. Benign tumours, which differ from normal tissue in structure, grow excessively and, although rarely fatal, may grow large enough to interfere with normal functioning and require surgical removal. Malignant tumours (see CANCER) also grow excessively, but their cells lack the biological controls that normally keep cells specialized; these cells can infiltrate surrounding normal tissue and may later spread (metastasize) via the BLOOD and the LYMPHATIC SYSTEM to other sites. Surgery, CHEMOTHERAPY, and RADIOTHERAPY are primary treatments for malignant tumours.

**tuna:** see MACKEREL.

**tundra,** treeless plains to the north of the coniferous forest belt in N North America and N Eurasia. For most of the year the mean monthly temperature is below the freezing point. Winters are long and severe, and mean monthly summer temperatures rarely exceed 10°C (50°F). Precipitation is slight and evenly distributed throughout the year. The underlying subsoil (PERMAFROST) is always frozen. Mosses, lichen, and some flowering plants grow during the brief summer, and the few large animal species include the caribou, arctic fox, and snowshoe rabbit. The tundra is a fragile, easily disturbed ecosystem.

**tungsten,** (W), metallic element, also known, especially formerly, as wolfram, first isolated in 1783 by the de Elhuyar brothers. Silver-white to steel-grey, very hard, and ductile, it is one of the most dense of metals and has a higher melting point than any other metal. Tungsten is used for wires and for filaments for light bulbs and electronic tubes. Tungsten STEEL is hard and strong at high temperatures. Tungsten carbide is used in place of diamond for dies and as an abrasive. See ELEMENT (table); PERIODIC TABLE.

**tunicate,** marine CHORDATE with a resemblance in the larval stage to VERTEBRATES. Familiar tunicates are the sea squirts, or ascidians, sedentary filter-feeders with cylindrical bodies, usually found attached to rocks. The tunic after which they are named is transparent or translucent and composed of CELLULOSE, a material extremely rare in the animal kingdom. Some tunicates have gelatinous containers called houses instead of tunics.

Tunicate: Star sea squirt (*Botryllus schlosseri*)

**Tunis,** city and port (1984 pop. 596,654), capital of Tunisia, NE Tunisia, on the Lake of Tunis. Its economy is based on tourism, fishing, and trade in phosphates, iron ore, and olive oil. The city has notable mosques, the Univ. of Tunis (1960), and a national museum. The ruins of CARTHAGE are nearby. Originally a Phoenician settlement it developed under the Aglabite dynasty in the 13th cent. when it became an important trade centre with Europe and the Levant. After the Turks took the city in 1534, Tunis prospered as a centre of piracy and trade. French occupation lasted from 1881 to 1956. Tunis was an important base during World War II. In 1979 it became the headquarters of the ARAB LEAGUE.

**Tunisia,** Fr. *Tunisie,* officially Republic of Tunisia, republic (1987 est. pop. 7,260,000), 164,150 km² (63,378 sq mi), NW Africa, bordered by Algeria (W), the Mediterranean Sea (N and E), and Libya (SE). TUNIS is the capital. The ATLAS MOUNTAINS in the north form a dry plateau that merges with fertile plains near the coast; in the south, below the Chott Djerid and other salt lakes, stretches the SAHARA desert. The irregular coastline has several fine harbours. Agriculture is the mainstay of the economy, but mining and tourism are important. Wheat, barley, grapes, olives, citrus fruits, and dates are the leading crops, and phosphates and petroleum are the principal minerals. Remittances from Tunisians working abroad are an important source of foreign currency. The GNP is US$8300 million, and the GNP per capita is US$1190 (1985). The population is largely Berber and Arab; Islam is the dominant religion, and Arabic the official language, although French is widely used.

*History.* Settled in the 12th cent. BC by Phoenicians, Tunisia became (6th cent. BC) the centre of the powerful city-state of CARTHAGE, which was destroyed by Rome in 146 BC. Taken by the Vandals (5th cent. AD) and the Byzantines (6th cent.), Tunisia was conquered by the Arabs in the 7th cent., and the Berber population was converted to Islam. The area came under a succession of Muslim rulers, reaching its peak of power and prosperity under the Berber Hafsid dynasty (c.1230–1574). In the late 16th cent. Tunisia was seized by the Ottoman Turks, and as one of the BARBARY STATES it became a stronghold of pirates, on whom the treasury depended for several centuries. European intervention began in the 19th cent., and in 1881 Tunisia became a French protectorate. Nationalist agitation, which had first surfaced in the 1920s, became intense after World War II, and independence was achieved in 1956. In 1957 the country became a republic, with Habib BOURGUIBA as president. Under Bourguiba, who was elected president-for-life in 1975, Tunisia has been a moderate Arab state, following a generally pro-Western foreign policy; however, support for a negotiated settlement with Israel strained the country's relations with its Arab neighbours, especially with Libya. Domestically, Bourguiba emphasized modernization and planned economic growth. In 1981 Bourguiba authorized the legal formation of opposition political parties, indicating that the authoritarian, if benign, political system established and managed by him might be shifting in the direction of liberal democracy. In both the 1981 and the 1986 assembly elections the ruling Destour Socialist Party won all the seats. Bourguiba was removed from office in late 1987, on the grounds of his senility, and replaced by Col. Zine el-Abidine Ben Ali, who changed the name of the ruling party to Destour Democratic Rally.

**tunnel,** underground passage, approximately horizontal, usually made without removing the overlying rock or soil. Methods of tunnelling vary with the nature of the material to be cut through. In soft earth, the excavation is supported by timbers as the work advances, the timbers sometimes being left as a permanent lining for the tunnel. Often two parallel excavations that will hold the side walls are constructed first, and arches connecting them are built as the material between them is extracted. Rock tunnelling is accomplished with explosives and high-speed drilling machinery. Underwater tunnelling through mud, quicksand, or permeable earth requires the use of a shield (devised and first used in 1825; see BRUNEL), a steel cylinder closed at its forward end, which holds rotating cutting blades. The cutting end is pushed ahead by hydraulic jacks, and excavated material is removed through openings in the shield face. River-crossing tunnels are also constructed by dredging a trench in the riverbed; then lowering prefabricated tunnel sections through the water into the trench, where divers connect them; and, finally, covering the trench and tunnel.

**Tunney, Gene** (James Joseph Tunney), 1898–1978, American boxer. He won (1922) the light-heavyweight title over Battling Levinsky, but lost it that same year (to Harry Greb) in his only defeat as a professional. In

Tunisia

1926 he defeated Jack DEMPSEY for the heavyweight championship and repeated his victory in 1927. He retired as champion in 1928.

**Tunsele, Mukengea** (tun͵saylay), 1830–98, king of the Lulua in the Kasai region of ZAÏRE. He subdued and incorporated many of the surrounding chiefdoms by 1875 and then gave permission to the Belgians to establish a trading post at Katanga (SHABA). Though initial contacts were profitable to both parties, Tunsele asserted his independence in 1891 and ordered the Belgians out of his country. In 1896 at the battle of Makabua, they defeated Tunsele and forced him into exile.

**Tupac Amaru** (tooh͵pak ah͵mahrooh), 1742?–81, Indian leader in PERU. He led an unsuccessful revolt (1780) against Spanish suppression of the Indians and was captured and executed.

**Tupí Indians:** see GUARANÍ INDIANS.

**Tuplolev, Andrei Nikolaevich,** 1888–1972, Russian aeronautical engineer. Designer of the first Russian jet airliner, the TU-104, for which he was awarded the Lenin Prize in 1957. In 1969 he designed the unsuccessful TU-144 supersonic transport aircraft which was withdrawn from non-communal operation after a series of accidents during development flying.

**turbine,** rotary engine that uses a continuous stream of fluid (gas or liquid) to turn a shaft that can drive machinery. In the **hydraulic turbines** used in hydroelectric power stations, falling water strikes a series of blades or buckets attached around a shaft, causing the shaft to rotate, this motion in turn being used to drive the rotor of an electric GENERATOR. In a **steam turbine,** high-pressure steam forces the rotation of discs attached to a shaft. Steam turbines are used to drive most large electric generators and ship propellers. The term **gas turbine** is usually applied to a unit whose essential components are a COMPRESSOR, a combustion chamber, and a turbine. The turbine drives the compressor, which feeds high-pressure air into the combustion chamber; there it is mixed with a fuel and burned, providing high-pressure gases to drive the turbine. In a turboprop engine, the turbine is used to turn a propeller as well as the compressor. In a turbojet engine, the gases first drive the turbine and then are expelled from the engine to provide propulsion. Gas turbines are used mainly as aircraft engines (see JET PROPULSION).

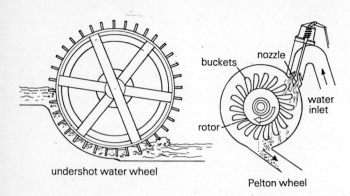

undershot water wheel

Pelton wheel

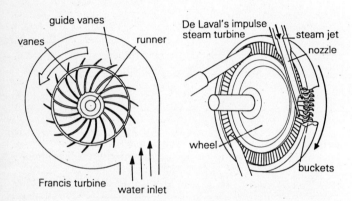

Francis turbine

De Laval's impulse steam turbine

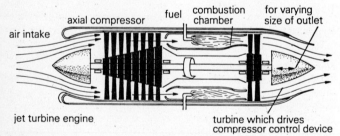

jet turbine engine

turbine which drives compressor control device

Turbine drives

**turbot:** see FLATFISH.

**Turgenev, Ivan Sergeyevich** (tooəgaynyif), 1818–83, Russian novelist, short-story writer, and dramatist. Born to a landowning family, he first achieved literary success with 'Khor and Kalinich' (1847), a story of peasant life included in *A Sportsman's Sketches* (1852); the book may have influenced ALEXANDER II's abolition of serfdom. In 1850 Turgenev wrote his best-known play, *A Month in the Country;* it was to influence CHEKHOV. The novels *Rudin* (1855), *A Nest of Gentlefolk* (1859), and *On the Eve* (1860) were followed by his masterpiece, *Fathers and Sons* (1861); like his other novels, it is a study of the intelligentsia. His later works include the novels *Smoke* (1867) and *Virgin Soil* (1877), and such stories as 'First Love' (1870) and 'Torrents of Spring' (1871).

**Turgot, Anne Robert Jacques** (tyooə‚goh), 1727–81, French economist and statesman. As intendant of Limoges (1761–74) he won acclaim for his policies of encouraging new agricultural methods, free trade, and industry. In 1774 he became controller general of finances under LOUIS XVI and tried thereafter to enact stringent reforms. His six edicts (1776), which included the abolition of guilds and the proposed taxation of all landowners, aroused the opposition of vested interests and forced his resignation (1776). Turgot was also a contributor to the ENCYCLOPÉDIE.

**Turin,** city (1984 pop. 1,049,997), capital of PIEDMONT, NW Italy. An industrial centre and transport hub, it produces motor vehicles, textiles,

and machinery. Rome, the Lombards, and the Franks held it, and it became (12th–13th cent.) a free commune. It passed to the house of SAVOY c.1280, and became, in turn, capital of Savoy (after 1562), of the kingdom of Sardinia (1720–1861), and of the new Italian kingdom (1861–64). It suffered heavy damage in World War II; most of the important buildings that remain date from the 17th–19th cent.

**Turing, Alan Mathison,** 1912–54, English mathematician. He read mathematics at Cambridge and did research at Princeton, US and the National Physical Laboratory, London. He wrote many papers on the philosophy of computability and on the potential capability of computers (as yet not invented) to solve problems beyond that of humans. During World War II he devoted his time to decoding ciphers. In 1945 he supervised the design and building of ACE, a large electronic digital computer at the National Physical Laboratory. He became a reader in mathematics at Manchester Univ. in 1948 and worked with the computer laboratory 'Mercury' development, using the prototype machine in operation there to test some of his theories. He was prosecuted for homosexuality and died from poisoning, apparently self-administered, at the age of 42 and at the height of his work.

**Turkana, Lake,** formerly Rudolf, rift valley, N Kenya. The region, which is semiarid and sparsely populated, is well known for its important evidence of HUMAN EVOLUTION recovered by Richard LEAKEY and associates. Sites are known from both sides of the lake, covering the period 1.2 to 3 million years ago, and with remains of AUSTRALOPITHECUS, HOMO HABILIS, and HOMO ERECTUS as well as other, unassigned, hominid fossils. The area has also yielded archaeological finds, geological and environmental data, and details of the evolution of many other animal species, making it one of the most important Pliocene/Lower Pleistocene sources in the world.

**Turkey,** Turk. *Türkiye,* officially the Republic of Turkey, republic (1987 est. pop. 51,500,000), 780,570 km² (301,280 sq mi), SW Asia and SE Europe, bordered by Iraq, Syria, and the Mediterranean Sea (S), the Aegean Sea (W), Greece and Bulgaria (NW), the Black Sea (N), and the USSR and Iran (E). Major cities include ANKARA (the capital), ISTANBUL, IZMIR, and ADANA. Asian Turkey, which constitutes 97% of the country, is separated from European Turkey by the BOSPORUS, the Sea of Marmara, and the DARDANELLES. European Turkey is largely rolling agricultural land, while Asian Turkey is mostly highland and mountains, with narrow lowland strips along the coasts. The Turks, a highly composite ethnic mixture, mostly speak Turkish; a very small minority speaks Kurdish. The country is almost entirely Muslim, with a small group of Orthodox Christians. The economy is basically agricultural, but industrialization has been emphasized since the late 1940s. Chief crops include wheat and other cereals, cotton, tobacco, and fruit; livestock-raising is important. Leading manufactures are iron and steel, cement, chemicals, textiles, forest products, and processed foods. Coal, copper, chromite, bauxite, and borax are mined; some petroleum is produced. Turkey is also noted for its carpets, Meerschaum pipes, and pottery. The GNP is $58,260 million and the GNP per capita is $1230 (1983).

*History.* Anatolia, the western portion of Asian Turkey, is one of the oldest inhabited regions in the world. Turkey was part of the Hittite, Persian, Roman, Byzantine, Seljuk, and Ottoman empires. However, Turkey's history as a national state does not begin until after WORLD WAR I, when the Treaty of Sèvres (1920) reduced the once mighty OTTOMAN EMPIRE to insignificance. In 1923 the present boundaries of Turkey (except for Alexandrette, acquired in 1939) were established and Turkey was formally proclaimed a republic, with Kemal ATATÜRK as its first president. During the 15 years of his authoritarian rule, the country's political and economic structure as well as its religious and social bases were transformed. Islam ceased to be the state religion; the Latin alphabet replaced Arabic script; new industries were developed under state ownership; and women were fully emancipated. Upon Kemal's death in 1938, Turkey was well on its way to becoming a Western-style state. Ismet Inönü, who succeeded Atatürk, kept Turkey neutral during most of WORLD WAR II; it joined the Allies only in Feb. 1945. From the creation of the republic until 1950 the ruling party was the Republican People's Party (RPP), founded by Kemal. Turkey became a member of the NORTH ATLANTIC TREATY ORGANIZATION in 1952 and permitted the establishment of US military bases. Political turmoil in the 1950s resulted in a military coup (1960), and a new constitution in 1961 created the second Turkish republic. Turmoil continued, however, and in 1980 the armed forces, led by Gen. Kenan Evren, once again seized power. A new constitution, approved by Turkish voters in 1982, provided for the election of Gen. Evren to a seven-year term as president. In 1983, after elections in which only officially approved parties were allowed to stand, a civilian government was formed under the premiership of Turgut Özal (Motherland Party), who continued in office after the freer 1987 elections. Tension with Greece has been a chronic problem. In 1974 a Greek-oriented coup in CYPRUS prompted Turkey to invade and occupy part of that island; war between Greece and Turkey was averted only by US, British, and UN intervention.

**Post-war Turkish presidents**
Ismet Inönü (RPP), 1938–50
Celal Bayar (Democratic Party), 1950–60
Cemal Gürsel (military), 1961–66
Cevdet Sunay (independent), 1966–73
Fahri Korutürk (independent), 1973–80
Kenan Evren (military), 1980–

**Post-war Turkish prime ministers**
Sükru Saracoglu (RPP), 1942–46
Recep Peker (RPP), 1946–47
Hasan Saka (RPP), 1947–49
Semsettin Günaltay (RPP), 1949–50
Adnan Menderes (Democratic Party), 1950–60
Cemal Gürsel (military), 1960–61
Ismet Inönü (RPP), 1961–65
Suat Hayri Ürgüplü (independent), 1965
Süleyman Demirel (Justice Party), 1965–71
Nihat Erim (independent), 1971–72
Ferit Melen (National Reliance), 1972–73
Naim Alu (independent), 1973–74
Bülent Ecevit (RPP), 1974
Sadi Irmak (non-party), 1974–75
Süleyman Demirel (Justice Party), 1975–77
Bülent Ecevit (RPP), 1977
Süleyman Demirel (Justice Party), 1977–78
Bülent Ecevit (RPP), 1978–79
Süleyman Demirel (Justice Party), 1979–80
Bülent Ulusu (military), 1980–83
Turgut Özal (Motherland Party), 1983–

**turkey**, large, nonmigratory, game and POULTRY bird of the family Meleagrididae, related to the GROUSE and PHEASANT. Turkeys are indigenous to the New World, where fossils date back to the Oligocene era. The wild turkey (*Meleagris gallopavo*) is 120 cm (4 ft) long and can weigh as much as 10 kg (22 lbs). The domestic turkey is descended from the Mexican turkey, taken to Europe by Conquistadors in the 16th cent., and is now intensively farmed. The wild turkey is a woodland bird, gregarious except at breeding time, and a good flier.

**Turkic** (ˌtuhkik), group of languages forming a subdivision of the Altaic subfamily of the URALIC AND ALTAIC family of languages. See LANGUAGE (table).

**Turkish language**, member of the Turkic subdivision of the Altaic subfamily of the URALIC AND ALTAIC family of languages. See LANGUAGE (table).

**Turkish music**, the music of the court of the Ottoman Empire and of present-day Turkey. In its theory, related to Persian and Arabian music of the Middle Ages, Turkish music developed distinct characteristics of its own from the 16th cent. onwards. A tradition of vocal composition of great refinement was created under the patronage of the sultans. As is true of Persian and Arabian musics, Turkish music utilizes diverse intervals and a large number of melodic modes (*makams*). It is particularly rich in rhythmic variety and the use of complex rhythmic modes. The principal instruments are the *ud* (lute), *kanun* (psaltery), and *ney* (flute).

**Turkish Republic of Northern Cyprus,** (TRNC), independent state declared in 1983 by representatives of the Turkish population of Cyprus, but recognized internationally only by Turkey. Covering about 40% of the land area of Cyprus, the TRNC resulted from Turkey's military occupation of the northern, Turkish-populated part of Cyprus in 1974 and the subsequent de facto partition of the island into Greek and Turkish administrations. Its predominant political leader has been Rauf Denktash.

**Turkmen Soviet Socialist Republic** or **Turkmenistan**, constituent republic (1985 pop. 3,197,000), 488,100 km² (188,455 sq mi), Soviet Central Asia. It borders Afghanistan and Iran (S); the Uzbek and Kazakh republics (E, NE); and the Caspian Sea (W). The capital is Ashkhabad. The KARA-KUM desert occupies 90% of the republic. The Kara-Kum canal (see under KARA-KUM), running E–W along the southern region, provides water for irrigation and hydroelectricity. Agriculture is the main economic activity, and cotton the most important irrigated crop. Silk and astrakhan fur are also produced; the region is famous for its karakul sheep, whose fleece is made into carpets. The terrain is rich in minerals such as ozocerite, oil, coal, sulphur, and salt; the republic produces about one-sixth of the USSR's natural gas supplies. Manufacturing industries include chemicals, textiles, tailoring, and food-processing. The Turkomans, a Sunni Muslim Turkic-speaking people, comprise 68% of the population; other groups include Russians and Uzbeks. Turkmenistan was part of the kingdom of ancient Persia and was later (8th–19th cent.) ruled by the Arabs, Turks (see KHOREZM), JENGHIZ KHAN, TAMERLANE, and Uzbeks. Under Russian rule from 1881, it became part of the USSR in 1920 and a constituent republic in 1925.

**Turks,** Turkic-speaking peoples found today in Turkey, the Soviet Union, Chinese Turkistan, Iran, and Afghanistan, totaling 73 million. Of widely varying histories and ethnic intermixtures, the different groups vary greatly in appearance and culture, being unified chiefly by linguistic

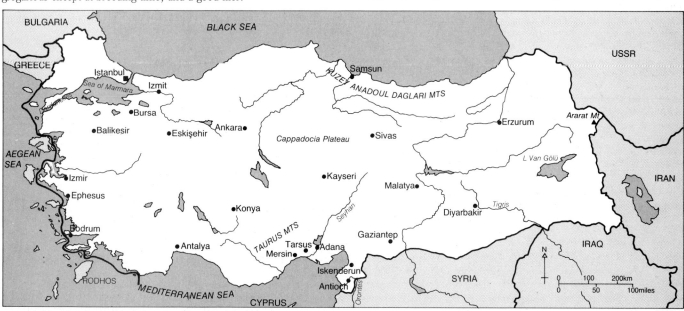

Turkey

affinity and social organization. The name Turk was first used in the 6th cent. by the Chinese for a nomadic people whose empire stretched from Mongolia to the Black Sea. Turkic peoples controlled this vast area until 924. The most important Turkic groups in the history of W Asia and Europe were the Seljuks and the Ottoman Turks. After the Turks adopted ISLAM, they began migrating in great numbers to the Middle East. By 1055 the Seljuks had conquered Iran; by 1071 they controlled Armenia, Syria, and much of Asia Minor. In the 12th cent. the Seljuk empire broke up into independent states that were overrun in the next century by JENGHIZ KHAN. After the Mongol wave receded, the Osmanli Turks completed the overthrow of the BYZANTINE EMPIRE, and in the 14th and 15th cent. they created the vast OTTOMAN EMPIRE. See also BULGARS, EASTERN; CUMANS; GOLDEN HORDE, EMPIRE OF THE; KHAZAR; TATARS; UIGURS.

**Turks and Caicos Islands,** British dependency in the Caribbean (1986 est. pop. 8000), group of 30 islands (seven inhabited) totalling 430 km (166 sq mi). Cockburn Town (on Grand Turk) is its capital. A British possession since 1766, the islands obtained internal self-government in 1976, with a 15-member legislative council. The economy is dependent on seafood exports and the islands' growing status as a tax haven.

**Turku,** Swed. *Åbo*, city (1984 pop. 162,282, metropolitan area 258,050), SW Finland. It has shipbuilding and engineering industries and acts as market centre to the richest agricultural lowland in Finland. Passenger links with STOCKHOLM are maintained throughout the year by icebreaker. The old capital of Finland under Swedish domination, it lost this position to Helsinki after the Grand Duchy passed to Russian control in 1809. Its castle, 13th-cent. cathedral, and ancient university bear witness to the city's historical role.

**turmeric:** see GINGER.

**Turner, Dame Eva,** 1892–, British opera singer, who sang with the Carla Rosa company (1915–24), and was then recruited by TOSCANINI for La Scala, Milan. She has appeared in all the major opera houses of the world and is noted for her Wagnerian roles and for singing leading parts in the operas of Verdi and Puccini, especially the title role of *Turandot*. After retiring she became a distinguished teacher.

**Turner, Frederick Jackson,** 1861–1932, American historian. He taught at the Univ. of Wisconsin (1885–1910) and Harvard (1910–24). His address 'The Significance of the Frontier in American History', delivered before the American Historical Association in 1893, was an epoch-making work that opened up new and important fields for historical study.

**Turner, Joseph Mallord William,** 1775–1851, English landscape painter, the foremost English romantic painter and the most original of English landscape artists. He began exhibiting at the Royal Academy at the age of 16. He had a remarkable ability to distill the best from the tradition of landscape (see LANDSCAPE PAINTING), and he travelled constantly, making inspirational sketches. His *Sun Rising through Vapour* (National Gall., London) shows Dutch influence, whereas *Crossing the Brook* (Tate Gall., London) shows the influence of CLAUDE LORRAIN. Despite his success, Turner lived the life of a recluse, maintaining a large gallery for exhibiting his works. His painting became increasingly abstract as he strove to portray light, space, and the elemental forces of nature. Characteristic of his later period is *Rain, Steam, and Speed* (National Gall., London). His late Venetian works, which present atmospheric effects with brighter colours, include *The Grand Canal* (Metropolitan Mus.) and *Approach to Venice* (National Gall., Washington, DC). He encountered criticism as his style became increasingly free, but was defended by Sir Thomas LAWRENCE and the youthful RUSKIN. He left more than 19,000 watercolours, drawings, and oils to the nation.

**Turner, Nat,** 1800–1831, black American slave and revolutionary. Believing himself divinely appointed to lead his fellow slaves to freedom, he commanded about 60 followers in a revolt (1831) that killed 55 whites. Although the so-called Southampton Insurrection was quickly crushed and Turner was caught and hanged six weeks later, it was the most serious uprising in the history of US slavery.

**turnip,** vegetable of the same genus (*Brassica*) of the MUSTARD family as the CABBAGE, native to Europe. Grown for its edible green leaves (greens) and its nutritious rounded primary root, it is also used as stock feed. The two principal kinds are the white (*B. rapa*) and the yellow (*B. napobrassica*), also known as swede or Swedish turnip.

**turpentine,** yellow to brown semifluid oleoresin (see RESIN) exuded from the sapwood of pines, firs, and other CONIFERS. It consists of an ESSENTIAL OIL (oil of turpentine) and a type of resin called rosin. Commercial turpentine is oil of turpentine with the rosin removed. When pure, it is a colourless, transparent, oily liquid with a penetrating odour and characteristic taste. Turpentine is used chiefly as a solvent and drying agent in paints and VARNISHES.

**turquoise,** hydrous aluminium and copper phosphate mineral $[Al_2(OH)_3PO_4.H_2O + Cu]$. Usually found in microscopic crystals, it is opaque with a waxy lustre, varying in colour from greenish-grey to (GEM-quality) sky blue. Because of their porosity, the gem varieties absorb dirt and grease, changing the colour to an unattractive green; exposure to heat or sunlight can also harm the colour. The finest specimens are from Iran; other sources are the Sinai peninsula and the SW US. Turquoise was extensively employed in the decorative arts of the ancient Egyptians and other civilizations.

**turtle,** large marine reptile in the order Chelonia. The name strictly applies to the five marine turtles, but it is also used for TORTOISES and terrapins in North America. The five true turtles are the leathery turtle, the loggerhead, Kemp's ridley, the green turtle, and the hawksbill turtle. The latter two are endangered, having been exploited for food and for tortoiseshell. The leathery turtle is the largest, with a 180-cm (6-ft) carapace and weighing 350 kg (770 lb). They all return to land to lay their eggs, burying them in the sand. The eggs are often dug up for food by humans and other animals.

**Tuscany,** region (1984 est. pop. 3,580,589), 22,989 km² (8876 sq mi), N central Italy, bordering on the Tyrrhenian Sea in the W. FLORENCE is the capital. The region is mostly hilly and mountainous. There is much industry, but farming is the chief occupation. Tuscany's Chianti wine is world famous. The region was the home of the ETRUSCAN CIVILIZATION and was conquered (mid 4th cent. BC) by the Romans. In the 11th and 12th cent. many cities became free communes, and some (PISA, Lucca, SIENA, and FLORENCE) developed into strong republics. Under the MEDICI, the ruling family of Florence, Tuscany became (1569) a grand duchy. In 1860 it voted to unite with Sardinia and became (1861) part of the new kingdom of Italy. The area was a leading cultural centre in the Renaissance.

**Tussaud, Marie Gresholtz** (too‚soh), 1760–1850, Swiss modeller in wax. While imprisoned in France during the REIGN OF TERROR, she modelled heads of famous persons, using heads from decapitated bodies. In 1802 she inherited her uncle J.C. Curtius's wax museum and emigrated to London, where she established Madame Tussaud's Exhibition, a museum that remains a major tourist attraction and now includes the celebrated Chamber of Horrors and an effective PLANETARIUM.

**Tusser, Thomas,** 1524–80, English poet. His *Hundredth good points of husbandrie* (1557) is a rich source of practical information and detail about farming and society in the Tudor period.

**Tutankhamen** or **Tutenkhamon** ('toohtən‚kahmən), fl. c.1350 BC, Egyptian king of the XVIII dynasty; son-in-law of IKHNATON. Ikhnaton had replaced the god AMON with Aton; under Tutankhamen this movement ended, and the capital was moved back to THEBES, sacred to Amon. Tutankhamen's tomb was found (1922) almost intact by Howard CARTER and the earl of CARNARVON, providing great impetus to Egyptology.

**Tutsi** or **Watutsi,** cattle-raising people of central Africa; they are also known as Watusi or Batusi. An aristocratic people, they are a minority in both RWANDA and BURUNDI, countries that are former Tutsi kingdoms. The Tutsi, who probably originated in Ethiopia, long held the peasant Hutu in feudal subjugation. In the 1970s, despite much integration of Tutsi and Hutu culture, many members of both tribes died in bloody fighting in Burundi. The Tutsi are spectacularly tall, often over 2.1 m (6 ft 11 in) in height.

**Tutu, Desmond Mpilo,** 1931–, Anglican archbishop of Johannesburg. An outspoken opponent of South Africa's APARTHEID policies and advocate of peaceful change, he received the Nobel Peace Prize in 1984.

**Tutuola, Amos,** 1920–, Nigerian novelist. He is noted for his idiosyncratic use of English style allied to magic and improbability, but is now (after initial condemnation by some African critics) recognized as a sophisticated and skilled writer. He is best known for *The Palm-Wine*

*Drinkard and His Dead Palm-Wine Tapster in the Dead's Room* (1952) and *Pauper, Brawler, and Slanderer (1987).*

**Tuuri, Antti,** 1944–, Finnish novelist and humorist, winner of the 1985 Nordic Literature Prize. His best-known works are *The People from Österbotten* (1982) and *Winter War* (1984).

**Tuvalu,** independent nation (1987 est. pop. 8500), 26 km² (10 sq mi), composed of nine low coral atolls, formerly known as the Ellice (or Lagoon) Islands, scattered over the W Pacific Ocean. The population is Polynesian. The capital is Fongafale, on Funafuti. Subsistence farming and fishing are the mainstays of the economy, with copra the chief cash crop and export. The islands were discovered by Capt. John Byron in 1764 and were administered by Britain as part of a protectorate (1892–1916) and as part of the Gilbert and Ellice Islands colony (1916–74). The colony became self-governing in 1971, and in 1974 the Ellice Islanders voted for separate British dependency status as Tuvalu. They became fully independent in 1978 as a special member of the COMMONWEALTH. In 1979 Tuvalu signed a treaty of friendship with the US, which recognized Tuvalu's possession of four small islands formerly claimed by the US. The government consists of a governor general representing the British crown, a prime minister and cabinet, and a unicameral elected parliament. Following general elections in 1985, Tomasi Papua was reelected prime minister.

**Tvardovsky, Aleksandr Trifonovich,** 1910–71, Soviet lyrical poet and literary editor. His long poem *Vasili Tyorkin* (1941–45), whose hero was a brave peasant soldier, was the most memorable work of Soviet wartime literature. The sequel to this poem, *Tyorkin in the Next World* (1953), contained criticism of Stalinism and was not published until 1963. As editor of the leading journal *Novy Mir* (1950–54 and 1958–70), he published works with outspoken criticism of the Soviet regime by SOLZHENITSYN and others.

**Twain, Mark,** pseud. of **Samuel Langhorne Clemens,** 1835–1910, one of the masters of American literature. After a boyhood in Hannibal, Mo., and work as a printer, he became a Mississippi River pilot (1857). In 1862 he moved west and began writing for newspapers, first in Virginia City, Nevada, then in San Francisco, taking as a pseudonym a term from his river pilot days, 'Mark Twain'. He first won fame with his comic tale 'The Celebrated Jumping Frog of Calaveras County' (1865). After a trip to Hawaii (1866), he became a successful humourous lecturer and, after a journey to the Holy Land, he published *The Innocents Abroad* (1869). In 1870 he married and settled in Hartford, Connecticut, where he wrote some of his best work: *The Gilded Age* (1873), a satirical novel written with Charles Dudley Warner; *The Prince and the Pauper* (1882), a children's novel; the nonfictional *Life on the Mississippi* (1883); the satire *A Connecticut Yankee in King Arthur's Court* (1889); and the two famous evocations of his youth, *The Adventures of Tom Sawyer* (1876) and *The Adventures of Huckleberry Finn* (1884). In *Huckleberry Finn,* Twain created one of the most memorable characters in American fiction, painted a realistic picture of 19th-cent. life, and revolutionized the language of fiction through his use of vernacular speech. In 1893, plunged into debt, he lectured his way around the world, recording his experiences in *Following the Equator* (1897). His later years were saddened by the deaths of two daughters and his wife, and his later works, e.g., *The Man Who Corrupted Hadleyburg* (1899), *What Is Man?* (1905), *The Mysterious Stranger* (1916), are sombre, pessimistic, and misanthropic.

**Tweed,** river, in S Scotland and NE England, approximately 155 km (97 mi) long. It rises in Borders region of Scotland at Tweed's Well and flows generally N and E past Peebles, Melrose, Kelso, and Coldstream to the North Sea at Berwick-upon-Tweed, Northumberland, England. The main tributaries are the Ettrick Water, and rivers Teviot and Till.

**Tweed, William Marcy,** 1823–78, American politician and Tammany leader. 'Boss Tweed' controlled nominations and patronage in New York City Democratic politics after 1857 through his control of the TAMMANY organization. He and the notorious **Tweed Ring,** sold political favours and defrauded the city of at least $30 million, largely through fraudulently augmented construction contracts. Jay GOULD and James Fisk were business cronies, and after 1868 Tweed extended his influence to Albany, New York State. Reformers, notably S.J. TILDEN and Thomas NAST, effected his downfall, and he died in prison.

**Tweed Ring:** see under TWEED, WILLIAM MARCY.

**Twelfth Night,** 5 Jan., the vigil or eve of EPIPHANY, so called because it is the 12th night after Christmas.

**Twelve Tables:** see ROMAN LAW.

**twelve-tone music,** those compositions based on a particular ordering (called a series or row) of the twelve pitches that constitute the diatonic SCALE divided into equal semitones. Thus it is one type of SERIAL MUSIC. Abandoning the melodic and harmonic interweaving of lines featured in works of traditional TONALITY, the twelve-tone system evolved in the 1920s in the works of A. SCHOENBERG and his pupils A. BERG and A. von WEBERN. It has been used by such contemporary composers as Milton BABBITT and Pierre BOULEZ. See also ATONALITY.

**Twenty-one Demands,** 1915, ultimatum secretly presented to China by Japan during WORLD WAR I. They included control of the German leasehold in Shandong prov., rights to exploit Manchuria and Mongolia, and control of Chinese coal deposits. Other powers were to be excluded from further territorial concessions. The Japanese also sought control of China's military, commercial, and financial affairs, but this provision was dropped, partly at US insistence. Chinese President YUAN SHIKAI was forced to accept the remaining demands.

**twilight,** period between sunset and total darkness or between total darkness and sunrise. Civil, nautical, and astronomical twilight occurs when the Sun's centre is between 0° and, respectively, 6°, 12°, and 18° below the horizon.

**Twombly, Cy,** 1928–, American painter. His early work was a kind of 'written image', an all-over scribbling composition influenced by J. POLLOCK. Later works using written text treat classical and mythological subjects. Between 1967 and 1976 he worked in New York and in Florida with RAUSCHENBERG.

**Two Sicilies, kingdom of the,** name adopted (1816) by the kingdoms of NAPLES and Sicily when they were officially merged under King FERDINAND I. The kingdom was conquered (1860) by GARIBALDI and became part of the kingdom of Italy. See RISORGIMENTO.

**Tycho Brahe:** see BRAHE, TYCHO.

**Tyler, John,** 1790–1862, 10th president of the US. The son of John Tyler (1747–1813), governor of Virginia from 1808 to 1811, the younger Tyler was also governor (1825–27) of VIRGINIA and US senator (1827–36). A moderate STATES' RIGHTS Democrat, he eventually broke with the Jacksonians and joined the new WHIG PARTY. In 1840 he was running mate to the Whig presidential candidate, William Henry HARRISON, and they waged the victorious 'Tippecanoe and Tyler too' campaign. Harrison died on 4 Apr. 1841, after only one month as president, and Tyler became the first vice president to succeed to the presidency. Tyler was never close to the Whig leaders, particularly Henry CLAY, and after he vetoed Whig measures and his cabinet had resigned, he quickly alienated most of them and found himself a president without a party. The Whigs rejected him in 1844 and nominated Clay. Tyler's chief accomplishments as president were the WEBSTER–ASHBURTON Treaty (1843) with Great Britain and the annexation of Texas as a state.

**Tyler, Wat,** d. 1381, English rebel, leader of the Peasants' Revolt of 1381. After the Black Death of 1348–49 had killed much of England's population, labour was scarce and wages rose. Parliament passed (1351) the Statute of Labourers to restrict wages, and nobles sought to hold their labour by enforcing old manorial rights. This bred discontent; rebellion broke out in 1381 after the poll tax was increased (1380). Tyler and the rebels seized Canterbury, then marched to London, burning and plundering houses. RICHARD II came to meet Tyler and promised to abolish serfdom, feudal service, and market monopolies. A second meeting ended in a brawl in which Tyler was mortally wounded. The king's promises were forgotten, and the revolt was harshly suppressed.

**Tyndale, Tindal,** or **Tindale, William,** c.1494–1536, English biblical translator and Protestant martyr. Sympathetic with the new learning, he decided to translate the New Testament into English. Opposed in England, he went to the Continent, where he met Martin LUTHER and began (1525) printing his New Testament. In England it was suppressed (1526), but he continued translating the Scriptures and writing tracts defending the English REFORMATION. He was seized (1535) in Antwerp, condemned for heresy, and executed. His work was the basis for the AUTHORIZED VERSION of the BIBLE.

**Tyndall, John,** 1820–93, English physicist, science lecturer, and writer; b. Ireland. He was professor (1853–87) and superintendent (1867–87) at the ROYAL INSTITUTION, London. He investigated light, sound, and radiant heat and studied Alpine glaciers. The scattering of light by colloidal substances on systems (see COLLOID), known as the Tyndall effect, is named after him.

**Tyne,** river in NE England, formed by the confluence of the rivers N and S Tyne, NW of Hexham, Northumberland. It flows eastwards through an increasingly industrial landscape past NEWCASTLE UPON TYNE, Felling, Wallsend, Jarrow, and South Shields and enters the North Sea near Tynemouth, Tyne and Wear. It is navigable as far as Newcastle, and tidal up to Wylam.

**Tyne and Wear,** former metropolitan county in NW England (1984 est. pop. 1,142,400), 540 km² (211 sq mi), bordering on the North Sea in the E. It was formed in 1974 around the lower R. TYNE and R. Wear, centred on NEWCASTLE UPON TYNE. It is mainly an industrial area, whose prosperity is based upon the Durham coalfield. There is much heavy industry, including a declining ship-building industry. It includes the urban areas of Tynemouth, Gateshead, South Shields, and SUNDERLAND. The county council was abolished in April 1986, and the area is now administered by the borough and city authorities.

**type,** for PRINTING, was invented in China. Related devices like seals and stamps for making impressions on clay were used in Babylon and elsewhere. Movable type made from metal moulds were used in Korea half a century before the European invention of movable type attributed to Johann GUTENBERG. There is no evidence, however, that the European invention was not independent. The first dated European printing from movable type is a papal indulgence printed at Mainz, Germany (1454). Johann FUST, using Gutenberg's press, printed the first dated European book, a psalter (1457). The MAZARIN BIBLE, completed on the press no later than 1455, however, is thought to be the first book printed in Europe. The type used in these beginnings was of the kind known as BLACK LETTER or Gothic (e.g., modern Old English or German), derived from popular handwriting styles. Roman type was used by several printers before Nicolas JENSON improved it so as to establish it as standard. Italic was first used by ALDUS MANUTIUS, who also introduced small capitals. Type characters are usually made by pouring metal into previously cut matrices, by photomechanic techniques, and, less frequently, by using plastic and other synthetic materials. Type may be handset or cast by machine. Famous type designers in addition to those named above include John BASKERVILLE, Giambattista BODONI, William CASLON, François Ambroise DIDOT, Claude GARAMOND, Frederic William Goudy, Robert Granjon, William MORRIS, Bruce Rogers, and Geofroy TORY.

**typewriter,** instrument for producing printed letters by manual operation. The first practical commercial typewriter was invented in the US in 1867 by Christopher Sholes and his colleagues, and was manufactured by the gunsmith Philo Remington in 1874. This early model had only capital letters; a shift-key model appeared in 1878. Even the earliest Remingtons had the QWERTY keyboard layout later adopted as the universal standard. Typewriters with the letters carried on a drum instead of levers were produced in the US in the 1880s. The electric typewriter came into use c.1935. In the 1960s some machine designs replaced type levers with a type-surfaced metal ball that moves rapidly across a stationary paper holder. Computer-controlled typewriters can store the data to be typed and reproduce it automatically.

**typhoid fever,** acute generalized infection caused by *Salmonella typhi.* The main sources of infection are water or food contaminated by the urine and faeces of patients or symptomless carriers. Symptoms include high fever, rose-coloured spots on the abdomen and chest, and diarrohea or constipation. Complications, especially in untreated patients (about one in four of whom may die), may be numerous. The disease is treated with the ANTIBIOTIC chloramphenicol; typhoid VACCINATION is a valuable temporary preventive measure.

**typhoon:** see HURRICANE.

**typhus,** any of a group of infectious diseases caused by rickettsias (microorganisms classified between bacteria and viruses and carried by ticks, mites, fleas, and the human louse). Epidemics occur in dirty overcrowded conditions, where mortality can be high. Symptoms include

fever and the early onset of a spotted rash and headache. Typhus is treated with ANTIBIOTIC drugs and can be prevented by VACCINATION.

**tyrant,** in ancient history, ruler who gained power by usurping the legal authority. Greek tyranny was an outgrowth of the struggle of the rising popular classes against the aristocracy. Usually, a leader won popular support, overthrew the existing government, and seized power. Many tyrants ruled well and with benefit to their subjects. The word had no connotation of moral censure until the rise of constitutional, democratic government in Athens in the 5th cent. BC. Greek tyrants included Periander of Corinth and PISISTRATUS of Athens.

**Tyre or Sur,** town (1980 est. pop. 14,000), SW Lebanon, on the Mediterranean Sea. Built on an island, it was an ancient seaport of PHOENICIA and had far-flung colonies by 1100 BC. The Tyrians founded CARTHAGE in the 9th cent. BC. Tyre was famous for its commerce and its purple Tyrian dye. Although taken by the Assyrians, Babylonians, and Persians, the city survived. It also recovered from a siege and sack by Alexander the Great, who built a mole that has since made the island a peninsula. In AD 64 the city became part of the Roman Empire. Later a Crusader stronghold, it was destroyed by Muslims in 1291. In 1982 Tyre, a stronghold of the PALESTINE LIBERATION ORGANIZATION, fell to Israeli forces after heavy fighting during the Israeli invasion of S Lebanon (see ARAB-ISRAELI WARS). There are Graeco-Roman remains.

**tyre,** rubber and fabric cover surrounding a wheel making contact with the ground on a wheeled vehicle. Today's pneumatic (air-filled) tyre developed from John Dunlop's bicycle tyre (1888), an improved version of one invented by fellow Scot Robert Thomas. By 1900, the beginning of the motoring age, tyres were already manufactured with a separate inflated inner tube and casing, made from rubber and natural fibres, but no treads. Treads were introduced some 10 years later, followed in the 1930s by improved designs incorporating stronger, synthetic fabrics. The tubeless tyre, upon which most modern tyre designs are based, was introduced in 1948. Tubeless tyres are sealed against the wheel rim, the casing having been made airtight by an inner liner. Such a tyre can support up to 50 times its own weight.

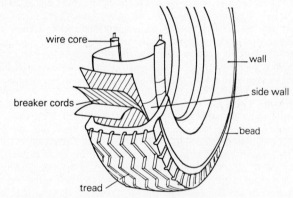

wire core — wall — side wall — breaker cords — bead — tread

Section through a radial *tyre:* Internal cords are laid at right angles to the centre line of the tread.

**Tyrol,** prov. (1984 pop. 597,928), W Austria, in the Alps. The region attracts many tourists. Farming, forestry, and salt production are important occupations. Conquered by Rome in 15 BC, Tyrol was later part of the Frankish empire. It passed to Bavaria in 1805 but was returned to Austria in 1815. S Tyrol was ceded to Italy in 1919.

**Tyrone,** former county in the W of N Ireland, 3123 km² (1218 sq mi), bordering on Co. Donegal in the W. The county town is Omagh; other main towns are Dungannon, Cookstown, and Strabane. It is mainly hilly, with the Sperrin Mts in the N. Mixed agriculture is common, and a range of manufacturing industries are found.

**Tyrrhenian Sea,** part of the Mediterranean Sea, lying between the W coast of peninsular Italy and the islands of Sardinia, Corsica, and Sicily. NAPLES and PALERMO are major ports.

**Tyumen** (tyooh‚menyǝ), city (1985 est. pop. 425,000), SW Siberian USSR, on the Tura R. On the TRANS-SIBERIAN RAILWAY, Tyumen is a major transfer point for river and rail freight. It also has shipyards, and the surrounding area is rich in oil and natural gas. Founded in 1585, Tyumen is the oldest city in Siberia.

**Tz'u Hsi** (tooh shee), see CI XI.

# U

**U,** chemical symbol of the element URANIUM.

**U2 incident,** the shooting down in May 1960 of a US photographic reconnaissance plane over the USSR and the diplomatic aftermath. Pres. EISENHOWER's refusal to apologize for the incursion provoked Soviet leader Nikita KHRUSHCHEV to break off a four-power summit conference in Paris later in the month. The captured U2 pilot, Francis Gary Powers, was exchanged in 1962 for a Soviet spy in US custody.

**Uccello, Paolo** (ooht·chelooh), c.1396–1475, Florentine painter and mosaicist; he trained with GHIBERTI and worked as a mosaicist in Venice. Uccello was fascinated by the new science of linear perspective and used it to heighten the violence of his frescoes of the *Deluge* (1450) in the Chiostro Verde in Santa Maria Novella, Florence. His most famous works are the three panels illustrating the 1432 *Battle of San Romano* (c.1452; Louvre, Paris; Uffizi, Florence; and National Gall., London) where perspective skill is combined with brilliantly decorative colour and detail.

Paolo **Uccello,** *Battle of San Romano,* c.1452. National Gallery, London.

**Udall, Nicholas,** 1505–56, English dramatist and schoolmaster. His one extant play, *Ralph Roister Doister* (c.1553), is regarded as the first complete English COMEDY. It blends influences of TERENCE and PLAUTUS with native English humour.

**Udaypur,** town (1981 pop. 232,588), Rajasthan state, NW India. It is a district administrative and commercial centre and its good railway communications have attracted some modern industry, including a cement works. Udaypur was founded by Maharana Udai (or Uday) Singh, a Rajput ruler, and continued to be the capital of a princely state of the same name, though sometimes known as Mewar, until after Indian Independence. It is an extraordinarily picturesque city, a considerable attraction to tourists. Its lake palace has become an hotel.

**Udine** (oohdinay), city (1984 pop. 100,957), archbishopric, and capital of Friuli, NE Italy. It commands a convergence of routeways including the main road to E Austria via the Val Canale. It is a service and administrative centre with chemical, textile and other industries.

**Ueda Akinari,** 1734–1809, Japanese writer. He practised medicine and literary scholarship in Osaka and Kyoto. His *Ugetsu Monogatari* [Tales of rain and moon] (1776, tr. 1971, 1974) is the most important prose-work of 18th-cent. Japan. He has a densely allusive style, nourished on Chinese and Japanese classics, and infused with a sense of the macabre, a world of demons, ghostly apparitions and strange metamorphoses.

**Ufa,** city (1985 pop. 1,064,000), Ukraino-Russian wooded steppe region, on the Belaya R. It is an important river port, a focus of rail communications, and is sited on the pipelines from the W Siberian and Volga–Urals oilfields. Petrochemicals dominate the industry. Other industries include the manufacture of aircraft and motor engines, and furniture veneers and prefabricated houses from a major timber combine. Founded in 1586, it largely escaped devastation by the Germans in World War II and received many refugee industries during that period.

**Uffizi** (oof feetee), palace in Florence, Italy, built in the 16th cent. by VASARI for Cosimo I De' MEDICI as public offices. It houses the state archives of Tuscany and the **Uffizi Gallery,** one of the richest art collections in the world. The Florentine, Italian, Dutch, and Flemish schools are all well represented. Among its Greek, Roman, and Renaissance sculptures is the *Venus* of the Medici (Greek, 3rd cent. BC).

**UFO:** see UNIDENTIFIED FLYING OBJECT.

**Uganda,** officially Republic of Uganda, republic (1987 est. pop. 15,480,000), 236,036 km² (91,133 sq mi), E central Africa, bordered by Tanzania and Rwanda (S), Zaïre (W), Sudan (N), and Kenya (E). KAMPALA is the capital. Uganda lies astride the equator. Most of the country is a fertile plateau, in the centre of which is Lake Kyoga. Around the perimeter are lakes Mobuto (Albert), Edward, and Victoria Nyanza; the Albert (Mobuto) Nile R.; and several mountain ranges, with Margherita Peak (5119 m/16,794 ft), the country's highest point, in the southwest. The economy is overwhelmingly agricultural, with cassava, plantains, millet, and sorghum the chief subsistence crops, and coffee (up to 90% of export earnings), cotton, tea, and tobacco the principal cash crops. Stock-raising, fishing, and hardwood production are also significant. Copper ore is by far the leading mineral. Uganda's economy, especially the vital farming sector, was devastated during the Idi AMIN regime of the 1970s. Virtually all the population are black Africans, two thirds of whom speak a Bantu language. English is the official language, but Swahili is widely spoken. More than half the people are Christians; most of the rest are animists, and a small minority are Muslims.

*History.* Around AD 1100 Bantu-speaking people migrated into the area that is now Uganda, and by the 14th cent. they were organized into several independent kingdoms. The most powerful of these were Bunyoro (16th–17th cent.) and later Buganda (18th–19th cent.). Visits by J.H. SPEKE (1862) and H.M. STANLEY (1875) opened the area to British influence, and Buganda became a British protectorate in 1894. The protectorate was subsequently extended to the rest of Uganda, but the independence of Buganda's rulers hampered the development of national unity. In 1962 Uganda gained independence under a federal constitution that gave Buganda a large measure of autonomy. However, under the leadership of A. Milton OBOTE, a new constitution was adopted in 1966, abolishing the traditional kingdoms and concentrating power in the hands of Obote, who became president. Obote was overthrown in 1971 by Maj.-Gen. Idi AMIN, who inaugurated a period of dictatorial rule that plunged the nation into chaos. He purged the Lango and Acholi tribes, moved against the army, and in 1972 expelled 60,000 noncitizen Asians. By 1977, it is estimated, 300,000 Ugandans had been killed in Amin's reign of terror. Finally, in 1979, an invasion by Tanzanian troops and Ugandan exiles drove out Amin's forces, and Amin fled the country.

Elections in 1980 returned Obote to the presidency, but serious civil disorders and guerrilla fighting continued. In 1985 Obote was again overthrown by a military coup and replaced as head of state by Gen. Tito Okello, who was himself deposed early in 1986 by the National Resistance Army led by Yoweri Museveni, who was installed as president.

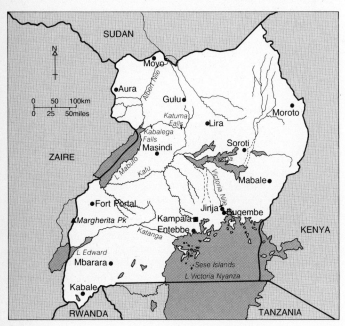

Uganda

**Ugarit** (oohgə‚reet), ancient city, capital of the Ugarit kingdom, W Syria. Excavations (begun in the 1920s) have uncovered remains of the city dating from the 5th millenium BC. Its greatest period was the 15th and 14th cent. BC, and the city declined in the 12th cent. BC. Ugaritic is a Semitic language related to classical Hebrew.

**Ugrian** or **Ugric** (‚yoohgreeən, ‚ooh-, ‚yoohgrik, ‚ooh), subgroup of the Finno-Ugric group of languages, which is, in turn, a subdivision of the Uralic subfamily of the URALIC AND ALTAIC family of languages. See LANGUAGE (table).

**Uhland, Ludwig** (‚oohlant), 1787–1862, German poet, leader of the Swabian group. His early lyrics and ballads, including 'The Minstrel's Curse' and 'The Good Comrade,' made him one of the most popular German poets of the romantic period. His biography of WALTHER VON DER VOGELWEIDE (1822) was a landmark in the rediscovery of medieval German literature.

**Uigurs** or **Uighurs,** Turkic-speaking people, numbering 4 million, living mainly in W China. They became prominent in the 7th cent. when they supported the T'ang dynasty (see CHINA). In 744 they took Mongolia. When ousted (840) by the Turkic Kirghiz, they founded an empire in XINJIANG, China, that lasted until the MONGOL invasion (13th cent.). The Uigurs were nomads with some agriculture and trade. First converted to MANICHAEISM, they later became SUNNI Muslims. Today most people in the Xinjiang Uygur are of Uigur descent.

**Ujjain,** town (1981 pop. 282,203), Madhya Pradesh state, C India, on the Sipra R. It is a district administrative, cultural, and commercial centre. It has grown quite rapidly, and has cotton mills. It is one of the most sacred cities of India, rivalling VARANASI (Benares). Cities on this site go back to the ancient past, as early as the 7th cent. BC, when the capital of the kingdom of Avanti (later Malwa) lay here. Through Ujjain, too, ran trade routes from Delhi and the northern plains to the Arabian Sea; also the prime meridian of Indian astronomers. Ujjain was in GWALIOR state before independence.

**Ukraine** or **Ukrainian Soviet Socialist Republic,** constituent republic (1985 pop. 50,843,000), 601,000 km² (232,046 sq mi), SW European USSR. It borders Poland (NW); Czechoslovakia, Hungary, Romania, and the Moldavian SSR (SW); the Black Sea and Sea of Azov

(S); the Russian Soviet Federated Socialist Republic (E, NE); and Belorussia (N). Its capital is KIEV; the chief BLACK SEA port is ODESSA. The larger part of the Ukraine is a gently undulating plain, while in the SW lie the Carpathian Mts. The main river is the DNEPR. The Ukraine is the second most important constituent republic of the USSR (after the RSFSR); it supplies 25% of the nation's foodstuffs, including wheat and other grains on some of the USSR's most fertile land, and 30% of its heavy industrial output. DNEPROPETROVSK, DONETSK, and KHARKOV are major industrial centres. Resources include petroleum, natural gas, iron, salt, and coal. The population (20% of the USSR's total) is largely Ukrainian; there are also Russian and other minorities.

*History.* The Ukrainians are descended from Neolithic pastoral tribes of the Dniepr and Dniestr valleys. In the first millennium BC much of Ukraine was inhabited by a mixture of sedentary agricultural populations ruled by a variety of nomadic people and civilizations from Central Asia. Then Ukraine experienced a long cycle of invasions: by GOTHS from the Baltic region about AD 150, and from the east first by the HUNS (c.375), then the Avars Khazars (c.600), who established their preponderance in the Black Sea steppe region for almost three centuries. During the 5–6th cent. several of the east Slavonic tribes established themselves in the western part of Ukrainian territory; one of these, the Polanians created the first major and long-lasting political entity among the eastern Slavs, the Kievan Rus (9th–13th cent.), which by accepting Christianity from Byzantium in 988, opened a new era in eastern European history. The Kievan Rus situated on the main trade route between the Baltic and the Black Sea reached the height of its power in the 11th cent.; its capital Kiev became eastern Europe's major religious, cultural, and political centre. With the Mongol conquest in the mid 13th cent. Kievan Rus ceased to be the great power of the region. In 16th–17th cent. the Ukrainian lands with the Polish–Lithuanian Commonwealth experienced a long period of military conflict, religious dissent, and social strife resulting in precarious political emancipation, e.g., that of the Ukrainian hetmanate, a rule based on the strength of the ZAPOROZHIAN COSSACKS (see also Iuan MAZEPA). The Russian conquest of the CRIMEA (1783), the 18th-cent. partition of Poland–Lithuania, and the emergence of Russia as a dominating power in eastern Europe led to the abolition of the last remnants of the Ukrainian autonomy. In the 19th cent. both parts of Ukraine witnessed a considerable national and literary revival in spite of Russian repressive measures and restrictions (see Taras SHEVCHENKO), before declaring independence in 1918 when both empires disintegrated (see Simon PETLYURA). A prolonged and bitter struggle for control of Ukraine during 1917–21 ended in Soviet victory and annexation of Galicia by Poland, which remained under Polish rule until 1939. In the interwar period the part of Ukraine under the Soviet domination derived some benefits from extensive industrialization but also suffered terribly as a result of the forcible collectivization of agriculture which resulted in the **Ukrainian famine** of 1932–33. There is no doubt that STALIN deliberately caused the famine by raising grain quotas impossibly high and by sending secret police to remove other sources of food and to prevent peasants moving elsewhere in search of bread. The Soviet regime refused offers of help from international relief organizations, so that over 6 million people died in the biggest ever man-made FAMINE. This was followed by decimation of Ukrainian cultural elite and a ruthless purge of the Ukrainian communist party. During WORLD WAR II Ukraine was devastated by the German occupation. Nearly 7 million people were killed, and over 700 towns and 28,000 villages destroyed or devastated. Of the 2.8 million *Ostarbeiter* [eastern conscript labourers] carried off to Germany 2.3 million were from Ukraine, and in 1941 alone an estimated 1.3 million Ukrainians became prisoners of war. Substantial resistance was offered by the Ukrainian Insurgent Army, which by 1944 had 40,000 men under arms; it continued its activities against Soviet security forces after the war. After the defeat of Nazi Germany nearly all ethnically Ukrainian lands became part of the USSR, and the Ukrainian Soviet Republic is today separately represented in the UNITED NATIONS. In the postwar years discriminatory policies of Russification and Sovietization and religious persecution have given rise to a vigorous dissident 'national self-defence' movement, which has led to imprisonment of a large number of Ukrainians.

*Churches.* The **Ukrainian Catholic Church** is the largest of the Eastern Catholic churches in communion with Rome, affiliated with the Roman Catholic church since the Union of Brest-Litovsk (1596) but preserving its traditional rites and its Byzantine form of worship and spirituality. It grew in stature and importance in Galicia under Austria–Hungary and between

1918–39 in Poland, Czechoslovakia, Hungary, Romania, and in America; by 1939 it had over 4 million adherents. With the incorporation of Galicia into the Soviet Union in 1944 it was subjected to severe persecution and continues to function clandestinely. The **Ukrainian Antorephalous Orthodox Church** considers itself the natural successor to the church which accepted Byzantine Christianity in 988; it was established shortly after the RUSSIAN REVOLUTION (1917), and by 1926 had some 6 million adherents, but is now heavily repressed by the Soviet authorities.

**Ukrainian language,** also called Little Russian, member of the East Slavic group of the Slavic subfamily of the Indo-European family of languages. See LANGUAGE (table).

**ukulele:** see STRINGED INSTRUMENT.

**Uladislaus** ('ooh͵lahdislows), Hungarian kings. **Uladislaus I:** see LADISLAUS III, king of Poland. **Uladislaus II,** c.1456–1516, king of Hungary (r.1492–1516) and, as Ladislaus II, king of Bohemia (r.1471–1516), was the son of CASIMIR IV of Poland. In 1478 MATTHIAS CORVINUS, king of Hungary, acquired Moravia, Silesia, and Lusatia from him. On Matthias's death (1492) Uladislaus was elected king of Hungary, but he proved a weak ruler. In 1515 he concluded a treaty with the Emperor MAXIMILIAN I by which Hungary and Bohemia eventually passed to the HABSBURG dynasty.

**ulama** [Arab., = learned men], persons of expertise in Islamic legal and religious sciences. From their ranks were recruited QADIS and MUFTIS, as well as some of the administrative personnel of Islamic lands. Their ranks also supplied members of the Muslim devotional institutions, such as prayer leaders (*imams*) and preachers (*khatibs*). The ulama became professionalized and placed under secular control with the advent of the MADRASA institution. In 19th-cent. Iran, however, the Shi'ite (see SHI'ISM) ulama hierarchy became highly centralized and secured control over resources that sustained scholarly and religious functions, paving the way for the independent political role they played in the late 19th and early 20th cent., not to speak of the Iranian Revolution.

**Ulan Bator,** formerly **Urga** (ooh͵lan ͵bataw), city (1986 pop. 500,200), capital of the Mongolian People's Republic, E central Outer Mongolia. The political, cultural, economic, and transport centre of the country, it lies on a railway linking (since 1956) the USSR and Beijing. Manufactures include woollen textiles, soap, paper, and cast iron. Founded in 1649 as a monastery town, Ulan Bator now preserves just one working monastery and is the seat of the nation's only university. It became the Mongolian republic's capital in 1924.

**Ulbricht, Walter,** 1893–1973, Communist leader (1950–71) in the German Democratic Republic (East Germany). He exiled himself (1933) to the Soviet Union and returned to Germany with the Soviet Army in 1945. A hard-line party leader, he was responsible for building (1961) the Berlin Wall.

**ulcer,** open, sometimes inflamed, sore, usually slow to heal, on the skin or mucous membranes. It may develop as a result of injury, prolonged bed rest (bedsore), vascular disease (varicose ulcer), cancerous growth (rodent ulcer), or for unknown reasons; therapy is directed at the underlying cause. Ulcers of the intestinal tract occur in areas where digestive acids erode the mucous surface (duodenal, gastric, and peptic ulcers). Their exact cause is unknown, but increased acid secretion, tissue vulnerability to acids, and emotional disturbance are believed to play a part. Antacids and drugs reducing the secretion of digestive acids are effective treatments.

**Ullmann, Liv,** 1939–, Norwegian stage and film actress; b. Japan. She is perhaps best known for her roles in films directed by Ingmar BERGMAN, e.g., *Persona* (1966), *Shame* (1968), *Cries and Whispers* (1972), and *Autumn Sonata* (1978).

**Ullswater,** lake in the Lake District, Cumbria, NW England. It is the second largest lake in England, after Lake WINDERMERE. It runs from Patterdale in the SW to Pooley Bridge in the NE.

**Ulm,** city (1984 pop. 100,400), Baden–Württemberg, S West Germany, on the DANUBE R. Its principal industry is the manufacture of commercial vehicles. Once a free Imperial city, its historic buildings include a 14th-cent. Gothic minster. It is the birthplace of Albert EINSTEIN.

**Ulsan,** city (1984 pop. 535,186), SE South Korea. It is a fast-growing industrial city and the nation's second largest port. Designated an

industrial area in 1962, Ulsan grew from a rural town to a city of large-scale sophisticated industry in less than a decade, with much investment from multinational companies. Industry includes an oil refinery and petrochemical works, aluminium refining, fertilizers, cement, shipyards, and car-assembly plants.

**Ulster,** northernmost of the historic provinces of Ireland. The area is now divided between Northern Ireland, often referred to as Ulster, and the Republic of Ireland.

**Ulster Defence Association** (UDA), regarded as the strongest of the extreme Protestant paramilitary organizations set up in Northern Ireland (see IRELAND, NORTHERN) to take violent action in response to the new wave of violence by the IRISH REPUBLICAN ARMY and other extremist Catholic groups dating from the late 1960s.

**Ulster Defence Regiment** (UDR), locally-recruited paramilitary force set up by the British government (1969) to take over internal security responsibilities from the Royal Ulster Constabulary and the discredited Ulster Special Constabulary. As the force has gradually assumed part of the security function of the British Army, its members have frequently been targets for the IRISH REPUBLICAN ARMY and other extremist Catholic groups. See also IRELAND, NORTHERN.

**Ulster Unionist parties,** Protestant loyalist formations in Northern Ireland (see IRELAND, NORTHERN) seeking to maintain the province's status as an integral part of the UK. Originally a single party called the Ulster Unionist Council (UUC, est. 1905), which dominated Northern Irish politics for 50 years, Unionist forces underwent scissions from the late 1960s. The Democratic Unionist Party (est. 1969), led by Ian PAISLEY, attracts ultra-loyalist support, while the Official Unionist Party (as the UUC became known following a split in 1974) is regarded as somewhat more moderate, and is organizationally linked with the CONSERVATIVE PARTY of Great Britain. Also active is the Ulster Popular Unionist Party (est. 1980). In the 1987 general election Unionist parties won 13 of the 17 Northern Irish seats in the House of Commons.

**ultrasonics,** the study and application of SOUND waves with frequencies greater than 20 kilohertz, i.e., beyond the range of human hearing. Ultrasound—vibrations having ultrasonic frequencies—is commonly produced by piezoelectric transducers. They are used for nondestructive testing (e.g., for flaws in metals), and for cleaning fine machine parts and surgical instruments. In medicine, ULTRASOUND devices are used to examine internal organs without surgery. Ultrasonic whistles are audible to dogs and are used to summon them.

**ultrasound,** in medicine, a technique that uses sound waves to study hard-to-reach body areas. In scanning with ultrasound, high-frequency sound waves are transmitted to the area of interest and the returning echoes recorded. First developed in World War II to locate submarines, the technique is now widely used in virtually every branch of medicine, e.g., in obstetrics to study the fetus, in cardiology to detect heart damage, in ophthalmology to detect retinal problems. It is noninvasive, involves no electromagnetic radiation, and avoids hazards such as bleeding, infection, or reactions to chemicals that are possible with other diagnostic methods. Ultrasound is also used in the treatment of some conditions, such as stones in the kidney which are broken up by the ultrasonic vibrations.

**ultraviolet radiation,** invisible ELECTROMAGNETIC RADIATION with frequencies (about $10^{15}$ to $10^{18}$ Hz) between that of visible violet light and X-rays; it ranges in wave length from about 400 to 4 nanometres. Ultraviolet (UV) radiation can be detected by the FLUORESCENCE it induces in certain substances and by its blackening of photographic film. Most of the UV component of sunlight is absorbed by the OZONE layer of the atmosphere. UV radiation can also be produced artificially in arc lamps. Vitamin D in humans is produced by the action of UV radiation on ergosterol, a substance present in the human skin.

**Ulyanovsk** ('oohlyan͵ovsk), formerly Simbirsk, city (1985 pop. 544,000), S central European USSR, on the Volga R. It serves as a port and crossing point on the Volga as well as an industrial centre in a largely agricultural region. Industrial products include machinery and motor vehicles. Founded as a military establishment in the 16th cent., it was the birthplace of Vladimir Ilyich Ulyanov or LENIN, and was renamed after him in 1924.

**Ulysses:** see ODYSSEUS.

**'Umar ibn al-Khattab**, c.592–644, 2nd caliph, designated by ABU BAKR as his successor (634). His rule inaugurated a period of phenomenal growth for the nascent Islamic community, particularly in terms of lands acquired by conquest. This highlighted the administrative inadequacy of his own role as a leader with limited powers based in Medina. His assassination may be described as a product of that growth.

**umbra:** see ECLIPSE; SUNSPOTS.

**umbrella,** a portable covering giving protection from rain or sunshine. Of great antiquity and independently invented a number of times, it was in use in China by the 10th cent. BC, and in ancient Assyria and Egypt, where it was a symbol of the Pharaoh's power. The ancient Greeks and Romans also used umbrellas, the latter being probably the first to use them as protection against rain rather than sun. Medieval Europe lost the idea of umbrellas, but they reappeared in Italy in the 16th cent. as a symbol of papal and clerical power, then spread to the rest of Europe by the 18th cent. British officers in the Peninsular War carried umbrellas, then fashionable, until forbidden to do so by the Duke of Wellington.

**Umbrian,** extinct language belonging to the Italic subfamily of the Indo-European family of languages. See LANGUAGE (table).

**Umbriel,** in astronomy, natural satellite of URANUS.

**umlaut** (‚oomlowt, ‚um), a change in the quality of a vowel within a word, caused by the influence of a vowel type sound in the following syllable of that word. The vowels of such pairs of English words as *man*, *men* are related by umlaut; in this case the vowel which caused the change has now disappeared. Umlaut is also used to denote the diacritic sign because this symbol is used in German to distinguish mutated vowels in such words as *Mann* (man) *Männer* (men).

**umma** [Arab., = group, community], technical Muslim juristic term for Muslims organized as a political community. In contemporary usage, it designates Muslims as a religious group, and is also the modern Arabic equivalent of the word nation.

**Umm al Qaiwan,** small state on Arabian coast of the PERSIAN GULF. See UNITED ARAB EMIRATES.

**Unamuno, Miguel de,** 1864–1936, Spanish philosophical writer; of Basque descent. His major work, *The Tragic Sense of Life in Men and Nations* (1913), expresses his highly individualistic EXISTENTIALISM, a philosophy based on faith in faith itself. He also wrote poetry, essays, and novels, all expressing his impassioned concern with life and death.

**uncertainty principle:** see QUANTUM THEORY.

**Uncle Sam,** name used to designate the US government. The origin of the term is uncertain, but some sources attribute it to Samuel Wilson (1766–1854) of Troy, New York. Wilson, whose nickname was 'Uncle Sam,' was an inspector of army supplies in the WAR OF 1812.

**unconscious,** a state of lacking consciousness, or an aspect of mind outside and unavailable to consciousness. In PSYCHOANALYSIS, the unconscious is that aspect or 'region' of the mind (psyche) which is the origin and repository of wishes, memories, and fantasies which are inadmissible to consciousness, and which are therefore repressed or censored; the unconscious is therefore both the seat of primitive or regressive drives and impulses, and the store of once-conscious but repressed material. For 'collective unconscious', see JUNG.

**Underground Railroad,** in US history, loosely organized system for helping fugitive slaves escape to Canada or to areas of safety in free states. Although legend has it as a highly organized group with 'passengers', 'conductors', and 'stations', in fact it seldom operated in an organized manner, and most help to fugitives was given by individual people, chiefly black.

**underground railway,** urban railway system running wholly or partly below ground. The first underground railway was the Metropolitan Railway which ran from Paddington to Farringdon Street in London, opened on 10 Jan. 1863. This was operated at first by steam but the development of electric traction made underground railways much more practical. There are two principal methods of construction. Cut-and-cover, as is implied, involves excavation of a right of way, usually following the line of a street, and then roofing over the track and restoring the original conditions at street level. 'Tube' railways are constructed by tunnelling techniques and tend to be at much deeper levels. Many large cities have extensive systems of underground railways, and there are about 30 systems in operation today, with new systems being continually opened. The most extensive system is in London with 272 stations, nine lines, and a route length of 404 km (250 mi), of which 159 km (99 mi) is underground. Whilst about 700 million journeys are undertaken on the London Underground in a year, greater ridership occurs in Moscow (about 2500 million), Tokyo (about 2300 million), New York (about 2200 million), Paris (about 1500 million) and Mexico City (about 1200 million).

**underwater archaeology,** the study of sunken ships and submerged archaeological sites. As diving technology has developed, so has the study of shipwrecks and other underwater remains. Attracting early attention were vessels such as the MARY ROSE, located by diving pioneers John and Charles Deane in 1836. The emergence in dry seasons of lake villages of the Neolithic period in Europe and the recovery of artifacts from the CENOTE at CHICHEN ITZA revealed the potential for underwater exploration. In recent years, advances in underwater equipment and recording methods have enabled sophisticated excavations to be carried out, as typified by the raising of the Mary Rose in 1982 after 13 years of effort.

**underwear,** a washable layer of clothing between body and outer garments, in Western COSTUME. Originally often made from linen (hence its name lingerie from Fr. *linge* = linen), it was sometimes of silk or wool (for warmth); later cotton was used, and now most underwear is partly or wholly made from synthetic fibres. Traditionally underwear was white and plain in shape; it became more colourful and more decoratively styled from the late 19th cent. The basic undergarment for both sexes in medieval Europe was the SMOCK or *shift*. Women also wore *petticoats* or underskirts for warmth and to give shape to their skirts as decreed by fashion: in the 16th cent. the FARTHINGALE was worn, in the 18th side-hoops or panniers, and in the 19th the CRINOLINE. Drawers covering the legs were worn by men from the 17th cent., but were not generally adopted by women until the mid 19th cent; they were approximately knee-length and were open at the crotch. Women's drawers were known informally as *bloomers*; they were replaced in the late 19th cent. by the less voluminous closed-crotch *knickers*. At that time *combinations* were also introduced: worn by both sexes, they are a one-piece garment that covers the body from neck to knees or ankles and has an opening at the crotch. Both sexes have at times been required by fashion to shape their bodies by wearing a CORSET. This reached extremes for women in the mid 19th cent., prompting dress reformers such as the German biologist Gustave Jaeger to introduce healthier and more comfortable undergarments. The *Liberty bodice*, a close-fitting buttoned woollen vest, was one such. The modern form of the *brassiere* dates from 1913. The flexible *girdle* or belt, to streamline hips, buttocks, and waist, was made of rubberized or (later) synthetic fibres. Modern underwear has tended to get progressively reduced: many men no longer wear a vest, and young women do not invariably wear a bra. Knickers (known as briefs for men) can be very small, scarcely covering genitals. Disposable paper knickers, introduced in the 1960s, were not a success.

**Undset, Sigrid** (‚oonset), 1882–1949, Norwegian novelist. In her early years she wrote many novels about women, including *Jenny* (1911). Her masterpiece, the trilogy *Kristin Lavransdatter* (1920–22), tells of love and religion in medieval Norway. Always strongly ethical, her writing deepened in religious intensity after her conversion (1924) to Roman Catholicism. She was awarded the 1928 Nobel Prize for literature.

**unemployment,** inability of members of the labour force to get jobs, for seasonal, technological, economic, or educational reasons. In the GREAT DEPRESSION (1930s) 25% of the workforce was unemployed in the US, Britain, and Germany. Unemployment in Western counties was relatively low in the 1950s and 60s, but the depression associated with the oil crisis of the 1970s had doubled this figure to 6% in Europe (9% in the US) by 1980, and other factors such as the 'shake-out' of labour as industry became more automated contributed to a further doubling in Europe to over 12% in early 1987. In all these countries, social groups already disadvantaged—blacks, disabled, inner-city dwellers—were the most severely affected. Countries with high rates of population growth, e.g., in Latin America, experience chronic high unemployment. In communist countries, full employment is maintained by appropriate public expenditure. Owing to *frictional employment* (people changing jobs) and *structural unemployment* (vacancies unfilled because people have not the right skills or live in the wrong place), zero unemployment is not possible.

**UNESCO,** abbreviation for United Nations Educational, Scientific, and Cultural Organization. See UNITED NATIONS (table 4).

**Ungaretti, Giuseppe,** 1888–1970, Italian poet; b. Alexandria. The founder of Italian 'hermeticism', his quest for the essential by condensation and pure evocation is in the tradition of the French SYMBOLISTS. His works are collected in the 12 volumes of *Vita d'un Uomo* (1942–69; tr. Life of a Man).

**unicameral system:** see LEGISLATURE.

**UNICEF,** abbreviation for United Nations International Children's Emergency Fund. See UNITED NATIONS (table 4).

**unicorn,** fabulous equine beast with a horn in the middle of its forehead. It was once considered native to India and was reportedly seen throughout the world. Pure white, it has been used as a symbol of virginity and, in ICONOGRAPHY, is associated with the Virgin Mary and with Christ. Hunting the unicorn was a TAPESTRY subject in the late Middle Ages and Renaissance.

**unidentified flying object** (UFO) or **flying saucer,** an object or light phenomenon reportedly seen in the sky whose appearance, trajectory, and general dynamic and luminescent behaviour do not suggest a logical, conventional explanation. Although many alleged sightings have been interpreted as reflections of the sun's rays from airplanes, as weather balloons, or as various meteorological phenomena, some sightings remain unexplained by investigators in terms of known phenomena.

**unified theories,** in ELEMENTARY PARTICLE physics, name given to those theories which attempt to treat two or more of the basic interactions— gravitational, weak, electromagnetic, and strong—as manifestations of a single interaction. The weak and electromagnetic interactions have been very successfully combined (electroweak theory) by S.L. Glashow, A. Salam, and S. Weinberg, and for this work they shared the 1979 Nobel prize for physics. Theories combining the electroweak and strong interactions have also been developed, and some progress has been made towards the incorporation of all four basic interactions ito an all embracing 'theory of everything'.

**uniform,** [Lat., = one form], type of dress worn to identify and differentiate members of a group sharing a similar occupation. The wearing of a uniform implies that the person is under some system of discipline. The uniform clothing itself is sometimes but not always provided by the responsible authority. A uniform often indicates status and incorporates badges of rank such as stripes or stars; individuals are sometimes identified by letters or numbers. Military uniforms were the first to develop, and began to be codified in the 17th cent. Red, an easily distinguished colour, was worn by the British army until the mid 19th cent. when it began to be replaced with brown or khaki for better camouflage. Prisons began to have uniforms for the inmates in the mid 19th cent. The uniform worn by nurses is based on the working dress of ordinary manual workers in the middle of the 19th cent., when the occupation began to be professionalized; the cap evolved differently at each hospital, and rank was signified by badges and the colour of the belt or dress. Many workers now wear a uniform consisting simply of a synthetic overall on top of their own clothes; retail workers are an example. The British school-child at the more old-fashioned sort of school still wears a uniform, popular with rich parents because of the visible prestige, unpopular with poor parents because of the expense. The wearing of uniforms by members of a sports team goes back at least 100 years; nowadays the 'strip' may include the name of the team's commercial sponsor as well as distinctive colours or patterns. Uniforms may also be worn to display political allegiance; the black shirts of the fascist party of Mussolini are an example. In Communist China during the regime of Mao Zedong clothing to uniform design was worn by both sexes as an egalitarian device.

**uniformitarianism,** the doctrine that past geological changes in the earth were brought about by the same causes as those now taking place. As first advanced in 1785 by James HUTTON, it stressed the slowness and gradualness of rates of change. It was initially overshadowed by the doctrine of CATASTROPHISM and was opposed because it seemed contrary to religious beliefs. In the 19th cent. it gained support through the efforts of Sir Charles LYELL.

**Union, Act of.** For the union of England and Scotland (1707), see GREAT BRITAIN; for the union of Ireland with Great Britain (1800), see IRELAND.

**Union of Soviet Socialist Republics** (USSR), Russian *Soyuz Sovetskikh Sotsialisticheskikh Respublik,* republic (1987 est. pop. 280,000,000), 22,402,200 km² (8,649,489 sq mi), E Europe and N Asia. The USSR, also called the Soviet Union, is the successor to the Russian Empire (see RUSSIA). It borders on Romania, Hungary, Czechoslovakia, and Poland (W); the Baltic Sea, Finland, and Norway (NW); the Barents, Kara, Laptev, East Siberian, and Chukchi seas arms of the Arctic Ocean (N); the Bering Sea, Sea of Okhotsk, and Sea of Japan arms of the Pacific Ocean (E); China, Mongolia, and Afghanistan (S); and Iran, the Caspian Sea, Turkey, and the Black Sea (SW). The capital and largest city is MOSCOW; other major cities include BAKU, GORKY, KHARKOV, KIEV, KUYBYSHEV, LENINGRAD, NOVOSIBIRSK, SVERDLOVSK, TASHKENT, and VOLGOGRAD.

*Geography.* Covering about 14% of the earth's land area, the USSR is the world's largest nation and ranks third in population. At its maximum extent from N to S the USSR is c.4000 km (2485 mi), while from E to W the distance exceeds 9000 km (5600 mi) and crosses 11 time zones. Its four regions comprise 15 constituent or union republics. European USSR includes ESTONIA, LATVIA, LITHUANIA, BELORUSSIA, the UKRAINE, the MOLDAVIAN SOVIET SOCIALIST REPUBLIC, GEORGIA, the ARMENIAN SOVIET SOCIALIST REPUBLIC, the AZERBAIJAN SOVIET SOCIALIST REPUBLIC, and part of the RUSSIAN SOVIET FEDERATED SOCIALIST REPUBLIC (RSFSR). Soviet Central Asia includes the TURKMEN SOVIET SOCIALIST REPUBLIC, KAZAKH SOVIET SOCIALIST REPUBLIC, UZBEK SOVIET SOCIALIST REPUBLIC, TADZHIK SOVIET SOCIALIST REPUBLIC, and KIRGHIZ SOVIET SOCIALIST REPUBLIC. Siberian USSR (see SIBERIA) comprises a vast region of the RSFSR, and the SOVIET FAR EAST is its extreme eastern part. Much of the USSR is low-lying. From western border to the Yenisei R., three great plains, the E European Plain, the W Siberian Lowland, and the Caspian–Turanian Lowland, are separated by the relatively small-scale relief features of the URALS and the Kazakh Upland. Both of these features are largely below 1000 m (3280 ft). On the southern borders are the higher mountains of the CAUCASUS, and the Pamirs. The Caucasus comprises three main divisions and lies between the Black Sea and the Caspian Sea; its highest point Mt ELBRUS, is the highest peak in Europe. The Pamirs, on the border with Afghanistan and China, contain the USSR's highest peak, MOUNT COMMUNISM. E of the Yenisei R., the Central Siberian Plateau is separated by the basin of the LENA R. from the mountain ranges of the SOVIET FAR EAST. The lands around Lake BAYKAL are very mountainous, created by massive block faulting, with intervening deep rift valleys. Lake Baykal, the world's deepest lake, with a floor 1300 m (4265 ft) below sea level, is situated in one such valley. Among the mountains of the Far East are those of the Kamchatka Peninsula, which includes several active volcanoes. Rivers from the Far East, including the AMUR, drain into the Pacific Ocean. The Lena, YENISEI, and OB flow into the Arctic Ocean. Further west the VOLGA, Ural, AMU DARYA, and SYR DARYA are part of an inland drainage system that flows into the Caspian Sea and Aral Sea. The European USSR is largely drained by the DON and DNEPR which flow into the Black Sea, while parts of the E European plain drain into the Baltic Sea. The country's climate and vegetation vary greatly. In the north, the Arctic Circle's dry cold climate supports TUNDRA, the larger part of the USSR is TAIGA and STEPPE land, while the Central Asian states are largely desert and semi desert.

*Economy.* Soviet industry is owned and managed by the state. Land is divided into state farms, COLLECTIVE FARMS, and small, privately held plots (3% of cropland). Agricultural land of all types covers about one-quarter of the USSR's land area, of which about 40% is used for crop production. Major crops include cereals, particularly wheat, barley, and oats, tea, cotton, and tobacco. Sugar beet, dairy products, and meat are also produced. The USSR is the world's major producer of timber and a leading fishing nation. The country also contains significant deposits of virtually all the minerals used in modern industry. It produces over 25% of the total world production of asbestos, chromium ore, gold, iron ore, manganese ore, mercury, potash, and sulphur. Among its energy resources are coal, petroleum, natural gas, hydroelectric and nuclear energy. The USSR is a great industrial nation producing a wide range of both capital and consumer goods. Its ports include ODESSA, KALININGRAD, and Leningrad.

*Peoples.* Among the over 100 ethnic groups in the USSR are the Slavic-speaking Russians, Ukrainians, and Belorussians; the Turkic-speaking Uzbeks, Tatars, Kazakhs, and Azerbaijani; and the Armenians, Georgians, Lithuanians, and Moldavians. About 75% of the population lives in European USSR. Russian is the official language of the

USSR. Although religious practice is discouraged, many people worship in the Russian Orthodox Church (see EASTERN ORTHODOX CHURCH); the Armenian and Georgian Orthodox churches are independent bodies. Other religions are Roman Catholicism, Protestantism, Islam, Judaism, and Buddhism.

*Government.* The USSR was the first state based on Marxist socialism (see also MARXISM; COMMUNISM). The Communist Party of the Soviet Union controls all levels of government, although reforms were introduced in 1988 and 1989 which strengthened citizens' choice through elections for a newly formed Congress of the People's Deputies. The party's general secretary remains the key figure in the system. The USSR is divided administratively into 15 constituent republics, which in turn include 20 autonomous republics and various smaller divisions.

*History.* For earlier history see RUSSIA; RUSSIAN REVOLUTION; SOVIET RUSSIA; CIVIL WAR, RUSSIAN. The Soviet Union was created in Dec. 1922 following the Bolsheviks' victory in the Russian Civil War, and the termination of the POLISH–SOVIET WAR (Mar. 1921). It initially consisted of just four republics—the RSFSR, Belorussia, Ukraine, and Transcaucasia, but was subsequently enlarged to include most of the former Czarist empire. In the struggle for succession after LENIN's death (1924), STALIN eliminated all his rivals, including TROTSKY. The NEW ECONOMIC POLICY (1921–28) gave way to full state ownership of agriculture and industry under the first FIVE-YEAR PLAN (1928–32). By the late 1930s agriculture had been forcibly collectivized and industrialization accelerated at immense human cost. All resistance was systematically repressed. State and party power over all aspects of life was enforced by the SECRET POLICE and bureaucracy; the COMINTERN guided Communist parties abroad. Stalin's purges of the 1930s claimed as victims such Soviet leaders as BUKHARIN, KAMENEV, and ZINOVIEV, and many millions of ordinary citizens. The USSR signed (1939) a nonaggression pact with Germany and, at the start of WORLD WAR II, invaded E Poland and gained a hard-earned victory in the Russo-Finnish War (1939–40). Following their surprise attack (1941) on the USSR, the Germans overran much of the eastern part of the country. However, after the Soviet triumph (1943) at Stalingrad (now VOLGOGRAD), the USSR began a counteroffensive that ended in Soviet victory. The wartime period, which saw Soviet and Nazi occupations alternate throughout the Baltic states, Belorussia and Ukraine, left about 20 million Soviet citizens dead. As the USSR extended its domination over much of Eastern Europe, external relations soon deteriorated into the COLD WAR. After Stalin's death (1953) Soviet domestic and foreign policy became more flexible under Nikita KHRUSHCHEV. In the field of technology the USSR developed (1949) atomic weapons, orbited (1957) the first artificial earth satellite, and launched (1961) the first manned orbital flight. In 1956 a revolt against Soviet influence was suppressed in HUNGARY. The USSR took part in talks on nuclear DISARMAMENT, but provoked (1962) the CUBAN MISSILE CRISIS. Relations with China soured in the late 1950s, and the Sino-Soviet split of 1960 has never been repaired. In 1968, Soviet troops crushed a reform movement in CZECHOSLOVAKIA. The removal of Khrushchev in 1964 had signalled the emergence of Leonid BREZHNEV as Soviet leader, and a long period of internal stagnation when dissidents seeking change in Soviet society were arrested and were forced into psychiatric treatment or exile. During the 1970s, the USSR entered an era of détente with the West, and signed the Helsinki Agreements (1975). For a time, large numbers of Soviet Jews were allowed to emigrate. Later, foreign relations with the West were threatened by the Soviet invasion of AFGHANISTAN (1979) and the Soviet-supported imposition of martial law in POLAND (1981). Brezhnev's illness and death (1982) was followed by a succession of crises, during which two further general secretaries, Yuri ANDROPOV and Konstantin CHERNENKO, died. Mikhail GORBACHEV emerged in 1985 as an advocate of change, demanding disarmament and, within the USSR, GLASNOST and PERESTROIKA. Through his travels and meetings with world leaders he has exerted a strong influence on opinion outside the USSR and on international diplomacy.

**Post-war Soviet Communist Party leaders**
Joseph Stalin, 1924–53
Georgi Malenkov, 1953
Nikita Khrushchev, 1953–64
Leonid Brezhnev, 1964–82
Yuri Andropov, 1982–84
Konstantin Chernenko, 1984–85
Mikhail Gorbachev, 1985–

**Post-war Soviet presidents**
Nikolai Shvernik, 1946–53
Klimenti Voroshilov, 1953–60
Leonid Brezhnev, 1960–64
Anastas Mikoyan, 1964–65
Nikolai Podgorny, 1965–77
Leonid Brezhnev, 1977–82
Vasily Kuznetsov (acting), 1982–83
Yuri Andropov, 1983–84

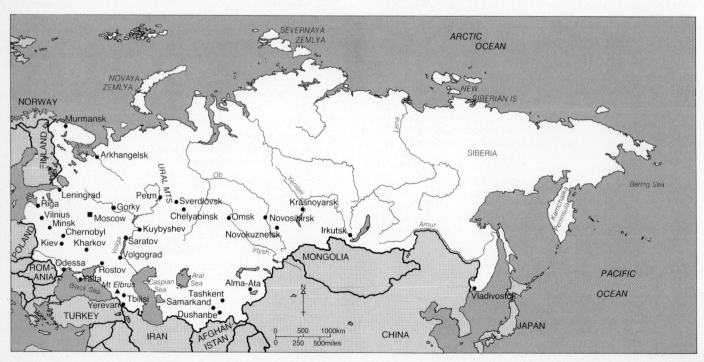

Union of Soviet Socialist Republics

Konstantin Chernenko, 1984–85
Andrei Gromyko, 1985–

Post-war Soviet prime ministers
Joseph Stalin, 1941–53
Georgi Malenkov, 1953–55
Nikolai Bulganin, 1955-58
Nikita Khrushchev, 1958–64
Alexei Kosygin, 1964–80
Nikolai Tikhonov, 1980–85
Nikolai Ryzhkov, 1985–

**Unitarianism,** in general, the form of Christianity that denies the doctrine of the TRINITY, believing that God exists only in one person. Modern Unitarianism originated in the Reformation period under such leaders as Michael SERVETUS and Faustus SOCINUS. The latter's views took root in England under John BIDDLE. In America the movement took hold in the liberal wing of Congregationalism as early as 1785, and adherents gradually formed a new denomination called the American Unitarian Association. Unitarians hold no particular profession of faith, nor has a creed been adopted. Congregational polity prevails.

**United Arab Emirates,** federation of emirates (1987 est. pop. 1,622,000), c.83,700 km² (32,300 sq mi), SW Asia, on the E Arabian Peninsula, bordered by the Persian Gulf (N), the Gulf of Oman (E), Oman (S), Saudi Arabia (S, W), and Qatar (NW). It comprises Abu Dhabi (with 80% of the area), Ajman, Dubai, Fujairah, Ras al-Khaimah, Sharjah, and Umm al-Qaiwain. The city of Abu Dhabi is the federal capital. The land is largely hot, dry desert; in the east is a portion of the JEBEL AKHDAR Mts. The economy is dominated by oil, first exploited in the 1960s; oil exports rank among the world's largest, and oil revenues have made the per capita income one of the world's highest. There are also rich natural-gas deposits. Fishing and pearling are traditional occupations. The GNP is US$27,542 million and the GNP per capita is US$22,030 (1983). The indigenous population, Sunni Muslim Arabs, is outnumbered by foreign-born workers, mostly from Asia, attracted by the petroleum boom. The official language is Arabic, but English is widely used. Formerly known as the Trucial States, Trucial Coast, or Trucial Oman, the seven constituent emirates were bound to Great Britain by truce (1820) and agreement (1892). After WORLD WAR II Britain granted autonomy to the emirates, and in 1971 the independent federation was formed; neighbouring QATAR and BAHRAIN opted for separate statehood. Following a period of severe internal tensions in the late 1970s, there seemed to be progress towards real political unity in the 1980s, under the presidency of Sheikh Zaid bin Sultan al-Nahayan, ruler of Abu Dhabi. At the same time, the United Arab Emirates established closer ties with neighbouring states within the framework of the GULF COOPERATION COUNCIL.

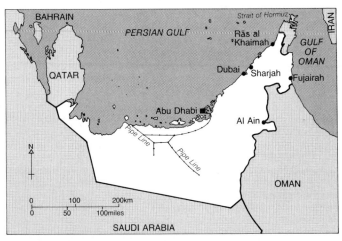

United Arab Emirates

**United Arab Republic,** political union (1958–61) of EGYPT and SYRIA. Gamal Abdal NASSER was president; the capital was CAIRO. With Yemen, the United Arab Republic formed (1958) a federation called the United Arab States. In 1961 Syria withdrew from the union, Yemen soon followed, and the union ended.

**United Colonies of New England:** see NEW ENGLAND CONFEDERATION.

**United Empire Loyalists,** Canadian settlers who remained loyal to the British crown and emigrated from the Thirteen Colonies during and immediately after the AMERICAN REVOLUTION. Numbering up to 50,000, they settled principally in NOVA SCOTIA and QUEBEC.

**United Kingdom,** officially the United Kingdom of Great Britain and Northern Ireland, constitutional monarchy (1987 est. pop. 56,618,000), 244,044 km² (94,226 sq mi), on the British Isles, off the W European continent. It comprises England, Wales, and Scotland on the island of Great Britain, and Northern Ireland on the island of Ireland. The capital is LONDON. Great Britain is one of the world's leading industrial nations. However, it lacks most of the raw materials needed for industry and must also import about half of its food supplies. Thus its prosperity is heavily dependent on the export of manufactured goods in exchange for raw materials and foodstuffs, and it is the third most active trading nation in the world. Manufacturing industries now employ just under one-third of the total workforce. Major industries include food processing, iron and steel, engineering, motor vehicles, chemicals, textiles, and aircraft. Light and service industries are increasing in importance. Production of oil from NORTH SEA wells began in 1975, and by 1979 the country was self-sufficient in petroleum. Coal is also mined. About half the land is devoted to agriculture, with dairy products, cereals, and beef cattle important commodities. Large numbers of sheep are raised for meat and wool. The coal, electricity, railway, and nuclear energy industries are publicly owned. Great Britain is the fourth most densely populated nation in Europe, and the greatest population concentration is in England. English is the universal language, but Welsh is widely spoken in Wales and some Gaelic in Scotland. The Church of England is the established church in England; the Presbyterian Church is legally established in Scotland. There are large numbers of Roman Catholics and Methodists. The hereditary monarch plays a largely ceremonial role in the government. Sovereignty rests in Parliament, which consists of a 650-member House of Commons and a House of Lords. Effective power resides in the Commons, where the leading party usually provides the executive—the cabinet, headed by the prime minister. For physical geography, see ENGLAND; IRELAND, NORTHERN; SCOTLAND; WALES; for the early history of Scotland (to 1707) and Wales (to 1536), prior to incorporation in Great Britain, see separate articles.

*Early English History.* Little is known of the earliest inhabitants of Britain, but the great structure at STONEHENGE is evidence of their advanced BRONZE AGE culture. The first Celtic invaders arrived in Britain in the early 5th cent. BC. In AD 43 the emperor CLAUDIUS I began the Roman conquest of Britain, which prospered and grew under four centuries of Roman rule. With the disintegration of the empire by the early 5th cent., Germanic peoples—the ANGLO-SAXONS and the Jutes—initiated waves of invasion and settlement that gradually coalesced into a group of small kingdoms. Raids by VIKINGS (Danes), begun in the late 8th cent., turned into full-scale invasion in 865, and by 1016 the Dane CANUTE ruled all of England. The conquest of England in 1066 by the Norman WILLIAM I (see NORMAN CONQUEST) ushered in a new era in English history with the introduction of FEUDALISM. Conflict between the kings and the nobles over abuse of royal power came to a head under King JOHN, whose unprecedented financial demands and unpopular church and foreign policies resulted in the MAGNA CARTA (1215), a landmark in English constitutional history. The HUNDRED YEARS WAR with France, which began in 1337, and the Black Death (see PLAGUE), which first arrived in Britain in 1348, hastened the breakdown of the feudal system. Dynastic wars (see ROSES, WARS OF THE) weakened both the nobility and the monarchy and ended with the accession (1485) of the TUDOR family. Under the Tudors, England flourished and was introduced to RENAISSANCE learning. HENRY VIII (r.1509–47) began the English Reformation by breaking with the papacy and establishing the Church of England. He also brought about the union (1536) of England and Wales. The English Renaissance reached its peak during the reign of ELIZABETH I, a time of great artistic achievement and overseas expansion. At her death (1603) the crowns of England and Scotland were united by the accession to the English throne of the Stuart JAMES I (James VI of Scotland). Under the STUARTS a bitter power struggle between the monarchy and Parliament culminated in the ENGLISH CIVIL WAR (1642–48). The victory of the parliamentarians led to the execution

(1649) of CHARLES I, abolition of the monarchy, and establishment of the Commonwealth and the Protectorate under Oliver CROMWELL. Following Cromwell's death, CHARLES II was invited (1660) to become king (see RESTORATION). The old issues of religion, money, and royal prerogative were not laid to rest, however, until the GLORIOUS REVOLUTION (1688) ousted JAMES II and placed (1689) WILLIAM III and MARY II on the throne. The BILL OF RIGHTS confirmed that sovereignty resided in Parliament. In 1707 the Act of Union legally united the kingdoms of Scotland and England.

*The Empire.* In the 18th cent. Britain began to play a more active role in world affairs, emerging from the SEVEN YEARS WAR (1756–63) as possessor of the world's greatest empire (see BRITISH EMPIRE). It suffered a serious loss in the AMERICAN REVOLUTION (1775–83), but it was preeminent in INDIA, settled AUSTRALIA, and acquired still more territories in the wars against NAPOLEON I. A vain attempt to solve the long-standing Irish problem (see IRELAND) brought about the union (1801) of Great Britain and Ireland. The INDUSTRIAL REVOLUTION, in the late 18th and early 19th cent., transformed social and economic life. Under Queen VICTORIA (r.1837–1901) Britain

reached the height of its commercial, political, and economic leadership. The country's aggressive diplomacy in Europe culminated in the CRIMEAN WAR, and social and political reforms were also begun. The dominant figures on the political scene were the prime ministers Benjamin DISRAELI and William GLADSTONE.

*The 20th Century.* In the early 20th cent., growing military and economic rivalry with Germany led Britain to ally itself with France and Russia (see TRIPLE ALLIANCE) and in 1914 Britain entered WORLD WAR I. Despite British victory, the war drained the nation of wealth and manpower, and in the postwar years Britain faced severe economic problems. In an effort to settle the thorny Irish problem, Northern Ireland was created in 1920 and the Irish Free State in 1921–22. Prime Min. Neville CHAMBERLAIN pursued a policy of appeasement toward the rising tide of German and Italian aggression, but this failed. In 1939 the Germans invaded Poland, and Britain entered WORLD WAR II by declaring war on Germany. The nation sustained intensive bombardment in the Battle of Britain, but the British people, inspired by Prime Min. Winston

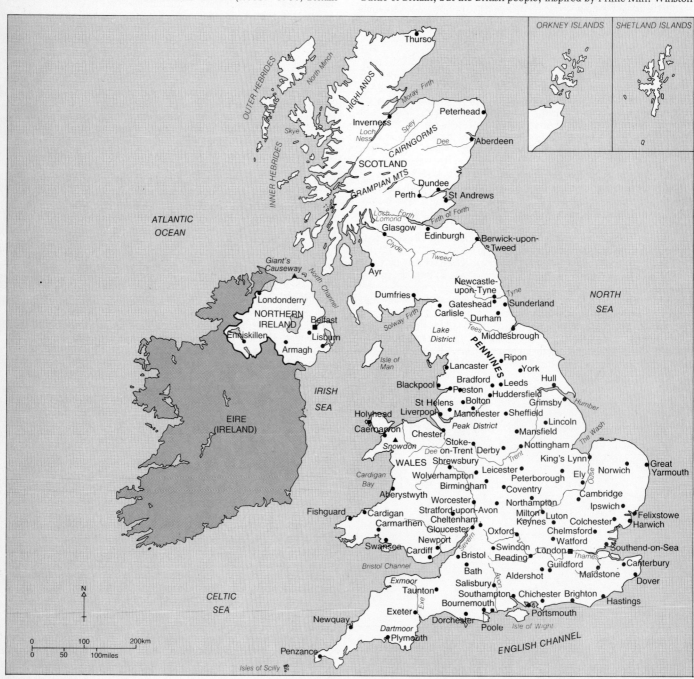

United Kingdom

CHURCHILL, rose to a supreme war effort. Following the defeat (1945) of Germany, the LABOUR PARTY, led by Clement ATTLEE, gained power and launched a programme, including nationalization of industry, to revive the war-damaged economy; it also began the dismantling of the Empire by granting independence to the Indian subcontinent and took the UK into the NORTH ATLANTIC TREATY ORGANIZATION. There followed 13 years of Conservative government, during which the country experienced rapid economic growth. However, the UK's status as a world military and economic power gradually declined, as was demonstrated by the abortive SUEZ CANAL operation in 1956. The subsequent Labour governments of Harold WILSON and James CALLAGHAN as well as the 1970–74 Conservative administration of Edward HEATH were marked by frequent economic crises and relative decline, despite the UK's entry into the EUROPEAN COMMUNITY in 1973. The situation eased somewhat with the discovery of North Sea oil, and the Conservative government which took office in 1979 under Margaret THATCHER succeeded in reducing inflation; but unemployment rose sharply, industrial decline accelerated and social problems intensified. In 1982 British forces fought a successful undeclared war with Argentina over the disputed FALKLAND ISLANDS. The following year Thatcher was returned to power, with an increased parliamentary majority, and she led the Conservatives to a third successive election victory in 1987,

albeit with a slightly reduced majority. By then signs of economic recovery were apparent.

*Population.* Great Britain is the fourth most densely populated country in Europe, the greatest population concentration being in England. The total population size has remained fairly stable over the last decade or so, with the number of births per year declining since the mid-1960s. The average number of children per family in 1984 was 1.77, which is below the level of 2.1 necessary to ensure replacement of the population. In 1984 there were 729,000 births, of which 17% were illegitimate. Despite the overall stability of population numbers, there have been changes in the composition of the population, as well as regional differences. Today 18% of the population is over the normal retirement age. Many peripheral areas of the country have recently experienced depopulation, while the SE of England becomes more crowded. The 1981 census revealed that 6.3% of the population was born outside Britain; immigration has occurred from many nations, both from within the Commonwealth and from elsewhere. In 1984 50,950 immigrants were accepted for settlement in Britain, including 14,840 from the South Asian subcontinent (i.e., India, Bangladesh, and Pakistan), and 22,570 from the rest of Asia. This immigration has made Great Britain a multiracial society, leading to an increase in the number of languages spoken within

---

## RULERS OF ENGLAND AND GREAT BRITAIN *(including dates of reign)*

### Saxons and Danes

Egbert, 802–39
Æthelwulf, son of Egbert, 839–58
Æthelbald, son of Æthelwulf, 858–60
Æthelbert, 2nd son of Æthelwulf, 860–65
Æthelred, 3rd son of Æthelwulf, 865–71
Alfred, 4th son of Æthelwulf, 871–99
Edward (the Elder), son of Alfred, 899–924
Athelstan, son of Edward, 924–39
Edmund, 3rd son of Edward, 939–46
Edred, 4th son of Edward, 946–55
Edwy, son of Edmund, 955–59
Edgar, younger son of Edmund, 959–75
Edward (the Martyr), son of Edgar, 975–78
Æthelred (the Unready), younger son of Edgar, 978–1016
Edmund (Ironside), son of Æthelred, 1016
Canute, by conquest, 1016–35
Harold I (Harefoot), illegitimate son of Canute, 1037–40
Harthacanute, son of Canute, 1040–42
Edward (the Confessor), younger son of Æthelred, 1042–66
Harold II, brother-in-law of Edward the Confessor, 1066

### House of Normandy

William I (the Conqueror), by conquest, 1066–87
William II (Rufus), 3rd son of William I, 1087–1100
Henry I, youngest son of William I, 1100–1135

### House of Blois

Stephen, grandson of William I, 1135–54

### House of Plantagenet

Henry II, grandson of Henry I, 1154–89
Richard I (Coeur de Lion), 3rd son of Henry II, 1189–99
John, youngest son of Henry II, 1199–1216
Henry III, son of John, 1216–72
Edward I, son of Henry III, 1272–1307
Edward II, son of Edward I, 1307–27
Edward III, son of Edward II, 1327–77
Richard II, grandson of Edward III, 1377–99

### House of Lancaster

Henry IV, grandson of Edward III, 1399–1413
Henry V, son of Henry IV, 1413–22
Henry VI, son of Henry V, 1422–61, 1470–71

### House of York

Edward IV, great-grandson of Edward III, 1461–70, 1471–83
Edward V, son of Edward IV, 1483
Richard III, brother of Edward IV, 1483–85

### House of Tudor

Henry VII, descendant of Edward III, 1485–1509
Henry VIII, son of Henry VII, 1509–47
Edward VI, son of Henry VIII, 1547–53
Mary I, daughter of Henry VIII, 1553–58
Elizabeth I, younger daughter of Henry VIII, 1558–1603

### House of Stuart

James I (James VI of Scotland), descendant of Henry VII, 1603–25
Charles I, son of James I, 1625–49

### Commonwealth and Protectorate

Council of State, 1649–53
Oliver Cromwell, lord protector, 1653–58
Richard Cromwell, lord protector, 1658–59

### House of Stuart *(restored)*

Charles II, son of Charles I, 1660–85
James II, younger son of Charles I, 1685–88
William III, grandson of Charles I;
    ruled jointly with Mary II, 1689–94;
    ruled alone, 1694–1702
Mary II, daughter of James II;
    ruled jointly with William III; 1689–94
Anne, younger daughter of James II, 1702–14

### House of Hanover

George I, great-grandson of James I, 1714–27
George II, son of George I, 1727–60
George III, grandson of George II, 1760–1820
George IV, son of George III, 1820–30
William IV, 3rd son of George III, 1830–37
Victoria, granddaughter of George III, 1837–1901

### House of Saxe-Coburg

Edward VII, son of Victoria, 1901–10

### House of Windsor *(family name changed during World War I)*

George V, son of Edward VII, 1910–36
Edward VIII, son of George V, 1936
George VI, 2nd son of George V, 1936–52
Elizabeth II, daughter of George VI, 1952–

the country, and changes in the religious structure. Nevertheless, English remains the universal language, although Welsh is spoken in parts of Wales. The Church of England is the established church in England, and the Presbyterian Church is legally established in Scotland; other important Christian groups include Roman Catholics and Methodists. There are substantial Jewish, Muslim and Hindu communities especially in urban areas.

*Economy.* Great Britain is one of the worlds's leading industrial nations. However, it lacks most of the raw materials needed for industry, and must also import much of its food supplies. Thus its prosperity is heavily dependent upon the export of manufactured goods in exchange for raw materials and foodstuffs, and it is the third most active trading nation in the world. Agriculture, fishing, and forestry together now employ less than 2% of the workforce. Britain produces over half its food requirements, with notable production of cereals, potatoes, sugar-beet, vegetables, fruit, livestock, and dairy produce. The fishing industry in Britain is now in decline, owing to disputes over the extent of fishing grounds, and overfishing. Forestry is a limited industry within Britain, and 90% of timber requirements are imported. Manufacturing industries, for a long time the most important industries in Britain, now employ just under a third of the workforce. The major manufacturing industries in Britain include various types of mechanical, chemical, and electrical engineering (which produce iron and steel, vehicles, aircraft, chemicals, and electronic goods, among other things), textiles and clothing manufacture, and food-processing. There is a growing trend away from heavy manufacturing industry toward lighter industries (especially those connected with computer technology), and the service industries (e.g., banking, insurance, civil service, education), which now employ approximately half the workforce. This shift has been reflected in a change in the geographical distribution of industry. Many of the most prosperous high-technology industries are now located within a triangle extending from Bristol to London to Birmingham, as opposed to the location of many heavy industries in clusters around coalfields and other resources. Coal has declined as a fuel in Britain since the 1950s, as oil and natural gas became more important. Production of oil from NORTH SEA oil wells began in 1975, and by 1979 the country was self-sufficient in petroleum. Changes in the industrial structure of Britain and its economic health have resulted in an increase in the number of unemployed within the country. In the mid-1980s over 13% of the population, i.e., over 3 million people, were unemployed. GNP in 1984 was £277,877 million and GNP per capita c.£4962. The coal, gas, electricity, railway, ship-building, nuclear energy, and telecommunications industries are (or were) publicly owned, but in the mid-1980s the government has begun privatization schemes. So far, gas and telecommunications have been denationalized.

### Post-war British prime ministers

Clement Attlee (Labour), 1945–51
Winston Churchill (Conservative), 1951–55
Anthony Eden (Conservative), 1955–57
Harold Macmillan (Conservative), 1957–63
Alec Douglas-Home (Conservative), 1963–64
Harold Wilson (Labour), 1964–70
Edward Heath (Conservative), 1970–74
Harold Wilson (Labour), 1974–76
James Callaghan (Labour), 1976–79
Margaret Thatcher (Conservative), 1979–

**United Nations** (UN), international organization formally established immediately after WORLD WAR II to maintain international peace and security and to achieve cooperation in solving international economic, social, cultural, and humanitarian problems. It replaced the LEAGUE OF NATIONS. The name was coined by Pres. F.D. ROOSEVELT in 1941 to describe the countries fighting against the Axis in World War II. It was first used officially on 1 Jan. 1942, when 26 states joined in the Declaration by the United Nations, pledging to continue their joint war effort and not to make peace separately. The UN Charter, the organization's governing treaty, was drawn up in 1945 at a conference held in San Francisco. The principal organs, as specified in the Charter, are the General Assembly, the Security Council, the Economic and Social Council, the Trusteeship Council, the International Court of Justice, and the Secretariat (see table 2). The Secretariat, with the secretary general at its head, handles all administrative functions. Trygve LIE, the UN's first

secretary general, was succeeded by Dag HAMMARSKJÖLD, U THANT, Kurt WALDHEIM, and Javier PÉREZ DE CUÉLLAR. In 1945 there were 51 member nations; in 1988 the number had reached 159 (see table 1). At the outset, close cooperation among the members was expected, but hopes for essential accord were soon dashed by the COLD WAR, which hampered the functioning of many UN organs. UN peacekeeping efforts have included the establishment of armed forces to repel (1950) the N Korean attack on South Korea (see KOREAN WAR) and the mobilization of troops and peace-keeping forces for the Congo (see SHABA), CYPRUS, and the Middle East (see ARAB-ISRAELI WARS). Although in recent years its role in peace-keeping has been less effective than in the past, the UN has remained a forum for debate intended to defuse international conflict and has continued to expand its efforts to aid economic and technological development in developing nations.

**United Nations Conference on Trade and Development:** see UNITED NATIONS (table 4).

**United Nations Development Programme:** see UNITED NATIONS (table 4).

**United Nations Educational, Scientific, and Cultural** see UNITED NATIONS (table 3).

**United Nations Environment Programme:** see UNITED NATIONS (table 4).

**United Nations High Commissioner for Refugees:** see UNITED NATIONS (table 4).

**United Nations International Children's Emergency Fund:** see UNITED NATIONS (table 4).

**United Nations Relief and Works Agency for Palestinian** see UNITED NATIONS (table 4).

**United States,** officially the United States of America, republic (1987 est. pop. 245,000,000), 9,372,143 km² (3,618,770 sq mi), North America. It is the world's fourth largest country in both area and population. The US consists of 50 states and a federal district, the site of the capital, WASHINGTON, DC. It also has numerous outlying island territories and areas. The coterminous (48-state) US extends across central North America from the Atlantic Ocean (E) to the Pacific Ocean (W) and from Canada (N) to Mexico and the Gulf of Mexico (S). The state of ALASKA occupies the northwestern part of the continent between the Arctic and Pacific Oceans, bounded by Canada (E). The state of HAWAII, an island chain, is situated in the central Pacific, c.3400 km (2100 mi) SW of San Francisco. Outlying islands include, in the WEST INDIES, PUERTO RICO (since 1952 a commonwealth associated with the US) and the US VIRGIN ISLANDS (purchased from Denmark in 1917), and, in the Pacific, AMERICAN SAMOA, GUAM, the Trust Territory of the PACIFIC ISLANDS, and WAKE ISLAND and other possessions. The largest state (1,518,807 sq km/586,412 sq mi) is Alaska, and the smallest (3144 km² (1214 sq mi) is RHODE ISLAND. The most populous is CALIFORNIA (1980 pop. 23,668,562). NEW YORK, LOS ANGELES, and CHICAGO are the largest US cities.

*Land.* The coterminous US is dominated by eastern and western mountain complexes, the five GREAT LAKES in the north, and a vast central plains region, nearly all of which is drained by one of the world's major river systems, the MISSISSIPPI, with its great tributaries, the MISSOURI and the OHIO. In the east the ancient, eroded APPALACHIAN MOUNTAINS, with many differentiated ranges, extend SW from Canada to Alabama. East and south of these mountains is the Atlantic–Gulf Coastal Plain. The Atlantic and Gulf coasts are essentially coastlines of submergence, with numerous estuaries, islands, and barrier beaches backed by lagoons. The Northeast has many fine natural harbours. Stretching over 1600 km (1000 mi) between the eastern and western mountain systems are the Interior Plains, once covered by a great inland sea. Forming the eastern portion are the fertile central lowlands, the nation's agricultural heartland; to the west are the GREAT PLAINS, a treeless, undulating plateau area that rises gradually to the foothills of the ROCKY MOUNTAINS. The lofty, geologically young Rockies extend NW from New Mexico into Canada and Alaska. Farther west are the CASCADE RANGE, with its many volcanic peaks; the SIERRA NEVADA, which includes Mt WHITNEY (4418 m/14,495 ft), the highest point in the coterminous US; and the COAST RANGES, abutting on the narrow Pacific Coastal Plain. Between the Rockies and the ranges of the far west is the Intermontane Region, an expanse of plateaus, basins, and lower ranges through which great rivers such as the COLUMBIA and the COLORADO have cut deep gorges (see GRAND CANYON). There are several

## 1. UNITED NATIONS MEMBERS *(including year of entry)*

| | | | |
|---|---|---|---|
| Afghanistan, 1946 | Denmark, 1945 | Laos, 1955 | São Tomé and Príncipe, 1975 |
| Albania, 1955 | Djibouti, 1977 | Lebanon, 1945 | Saudi Arabia, 1945 |
| Algeria, 1962 | Dominica, 1978 | Lesotho, 1966 | Senegal, 1960 |
| Angola, 1976 | Dominican Republic, 1945 | Liberia, 1945 | Seychelles, 1976 |
| Antigua and Barbuda, 1981 | Ecuador, 1945 | Libya, 1955 | Sierra Leone, 1961 |
| Argentina, 1945 | Egypt, 1945 | Luxembourg, 1945 | Singapore, 1965 |
| Australia, 1945 | El Salvador, 1945 | Madagascar, 1960 | Solomon Islands, 1978 |
| Austria, 1955 | Equatorial Guinea, 1968 | Malawi, 1964 | Somalia, 1960 |
| Bahamas, 1973 | Ethiopia, 1945 | Malaysia, 1957 | South Africa, 1945 |
| Bahrain, 1971 | Fiji, 1970 | Maldives, 1965 | Spain, 1955 |
| Bangladesh, 1974 | Finland, 1955 | Mali, 1960 | Sri Lanka, 1955 |
| Barbados, 1966 | France, 1945 | Malta, 1964 | Sudan, 1956 |
| Belgium, 1945 | Gabon, 1960 | Mauritania, 1961 | Suriname, 1975 |
| Belize, 1981 | Gambia, 1965 | Mauritius, 1968 | Swaziland, 1968 |
| Benin, 1960 | Germany, East, 1973 | Mexico, 1945 | Sweden, 1946 |
| Byelorussia, 1945 | Germany, West, 1973 | Mongolia, 1961 | Syria, 1945 |
| Bhutan, 1971 | Ghana, 1957 | Morocco, 1956 | Tanzania, 1961 |
| Bolivia, 1945 | Greece, 1945 | Mozambique, 1975 | Thailand, 1946 |
| Botswana, 1966 | Grenada, 1974 | Nepal, 1955 | Togo, 1960 |
| Brazil, 1945 | Guatemala, 1945 | Netherlands, 1945 | Trinidad and Tobago, 1962 |
| Brunei, 1984 | Guinea, 1958 | New Zealand, 1945 | Tunisia, 1956 |
| Bulgaria, 1955 | Guinea-Bissau, 1974 | Nicaragua, 1945 | Turkey, 1945 |
| Burkina Faso, 1960 | Guyana, 1966 | Niger, 1960 | Uganda, 1962 |
| Burma, 1948 | Haiti, 1945 | Nigeria, 1960 | Ukraine, 1945 |
| Burundi, 1962 | Honduras, 1945 | Norway, 1945 | USSR, 1945 |
| Cameroon, 1960 | Hungary, 1955 | Oman, 1971 | United Arab Emirates, 1971 |
| Canada, 1945 | Iceland, 1946 | Pakistan, 1947 | United Kingdom, 1945 |
| Cape Verde, 1975 | India, 1945 | Panama, 1945 | United States, 1945 |
| Central African Republic, 1960 | Indonesia, 1950 | Papua New Guinea, 1975 | Uruguay, 1945 |
| Chad, 1960 | Iran, 1945 | Paraguay, 1945 | Vanuatu, 1981 |
| Chile, 1945 | Iraq, 1945 | Peru, 1945 | Venezuela, 1945 |
| China, 1945 | Ireland, 1955 | Philippines, 1945 | Vietnam, 1977 |
| Colombia, 1945 | Israel, 1949 | Poland, 1945 | Western Samoa, 1976 |
| Comoros, 1975 | Italy, 1955 | Portugal, 1955 | Yemen, North, 1947 |
| Congo, 1960 | Jamaica, 1962 | Qatar, 1971 | Yemen, South, 1967 |
| Costa Rica, 1945 | Japan, 1956 | Romania, 1955 | Yugoslavia, 1945 |
| Côte d'Ivoire, 1960 | Jordan, 1955 | Rwanda, 1962 | Zaïre, 1960 |
| Cuba, 1945 | Kampuchea, 1955 | St Christopher and Nevis, 1983 | Zambia, 1964 |
| Cyprus, 1960 | Kenya, 1963 | St Lucia, 1979 | Zimbabwe, 1980 |
| Czechoslovakia, 1945 | Kuwait, 1963 | St Vincent and the Grenadines, 1980 | |

deserts in the Southwest, in one of which (DEATH VALLEY, California) is found the lowest point in the US (86 m/282 ft below sea level). Alaska is largely mountainous, rising to 6194 m (20,320 ft) at Mt MCKINLEY, the highest point in North America. Hawaii's islands are the tops of volcanoes rising from the ocean floor. The country has a wide variety of climates, ranging from the tropical (in Florida and Hawaii) to the subarctic tundra (in Alaska), and from the moderate Mediterranean (in S California) to the humid continental (in the northeastern states). Rainfall is heaviest in the Pacific Northwest, lightest in parts of the Southwest.

*People.* Almost three-quarters of the US population is urban, and the great majority is of European descent. Until the IMMIGRATION law of 1924, the country was a 'melting pot' of nations. The original settlers of the Atlantic colonies were chiefly from the British Isles. In addition, numerous black African slaves were imported to work the plantations in the South. By the mid-19th cent., as settlement of the West was accelerating, Irish and German immigrants came in great numbers, soon to be followed by Scandinavians. After the Civil War the new arrivals were mainly from E and S Europe (notably Italy, Greece, Poland, Russia, and the Balkans), and immigration from the Far East began. Despite early resentments and conflicts, the people of European origin have coalesced into a somewhat homogeneous group. This has been less true of arrivals from Africa, Asia, and Latin America and their descendants. Black Americans are the principal non-European group; they constitute almost 12% of the population and they are a substantial minority throughout the southern states and a majority in many southern and some northern cities. Japanese and Chinese are numerous in Hawaii, and there are large Chinese communities in eastern and West Coast cities. Immigration from E Asia has risen sharply in the 1980s. Since World War II there has been an influx of primarily Spanish-speaking peoples from the West Indies and Latin America (especially Mexico), who have tended to congregate in urban areas. There are also unassimilated groups of native Americans, many of whom live on reservations (see NORTH AMERICAN INDIANS). The people of the US enjoy religious freedom. The great majority are Christian, with Protestants outnumbering Roman Catholics and the Orthodox Eastern Church having many adherents. Judaism is the faith of another substantial group of Americans.

*Economy.* The US is the principal industrial nation in the world and has tremendous agricultural and mineral resources. Although it has been virtually self-sufficient in the past, an enormous increase in consumption (especially of energy) in the late 20th cent. is making it increasingly dependent on certain imports. Nevertheless, it is the world's foremost producer of electrical power from all sources, as it is of natural gas, lead, copper, aluminium and several other minerals, and it is among the leaders in the production of crude oil, iron ore, silver, and zinc. In total value of manufactures, the US leads all other nations by a substantial margin, being the principal producer of motor vehicles, synthetic rubber, petrochemicals, and many other products. Long considered the 'breadbasket' of the world, it has an agricultural sector of unparalleled efficiency. Although its relatively small farm population has been increasingly threatened by a cost-price squeeze, it has consistently produced surpluses of many crops (notably grains) for export. Major exports other than food products include motor vehicles and parts, aircraft and parts, chemicals, and computers and parts. Imports include ores, petroleum, machinery, transport equipment (especially vehicles), and paper. Canada, Japan, West Germany, and the United Kingdom are the leading trade partners. Since the 1970s the US balance of trade has

## 2 BODIES DESIGNATED BY THE CHARTER OF THE UNITED NATIONS

| Name | Location | Purpose and Function |
|---|---|---|
| General Assembly | New York | Chief deliberative body of UN. All member states entitled to be represented (although South Africa has been excluded since 1974). Annual session begins Sept. Studies political, social, economic issues; makes recommendations but no advisements on issues under Security Council consideration, unless the Council so requests. Passes UN budget; sets assessments. Work conducted in part through seven main committees (on specified issues); also procedural, and ad hoc standing, committees. |
| Security Council | New York | Primary responsibility to preserve peace. Compact executive organ; in theory, functions continuously. Fifteen members: five permanent "big powers" (US, USSR, China, France, UK); ten chosen (five each year) for two-year terms by General Assembly. On substantive issues a vote against by any permanent member represents a veto. Security Council acts after complaint by member or notification by General Assembly or Secretary General, or on own volition. Makes recommendations on "disputes", takes action (economic sanctions or military action) on "threats to peace", "acts of aggression". Council not limited by bar on UN "domestic" intervention. |
| Economic and Social Council | New York | Members (54) elected (18 each year) for three-year terms by General Assembly. Meets at least twice yearly; investigates economic, social questions; reports to Assembly and to other organs. Coordinates specialized agencies; arranges international consultations. Functional (e.g., on the status of women; on population) and regional commissions carry out much of the work. |
| Secretariat | New York | Performs all UN administrative functions. Headed by Secretary General, who is elected for five years. Authorized to bring situations to attention of various UN organs. Impartial party in effecting conciliation. Empowered to perform functions entrusted by other UN organs. Aided by large staff. |
| International Court of Justice | The Hague | Superseded WORLD COURT. Fifteen judges chosen by General Assembly and Security Council for nine-year terms; five reelected every three years. Nine-judge quorum. Hears disputes between member states, issues advisory opinions on matters presented by UN organs. Limited jurisdiction in disputes between states: questions of INTERNATIONAL LAW, breaches of international obligations, reparations for breaches, judgments not appealable, binding only for case and parties (no system of precedent). |
| Trusteeship Council | New York | Established for UN control of non-self-governing territories, replacing League of Nations MANDATES (see TRUSTEESHIP, TERRITORIAL). Power to administer in territory essentially complete. Consists of the administering power, other permanent Security Council members, and elected members. Only territory remaining within jurisdiction is US-administered Pacific Islands territory (Micronesia). |

## 3 SPECIALIZED AGENCIES OF THE UNITED NATIONS

| Agency | Date Affiliated with UN;[1] Headquarters | Number of Members[2] | Purpose and Function |
|---|---|---|---|
| Food and Agriculture Organization (FAO) | 1945; Rome | 158 | Improve rural conditions, agricultural production and distribution; raise nutritional levels. |
| General Agreement on Tariffs and Trade (GATT)[3] | 1958; Geneva | 92 | Work to reduce tariffs and eliminate other barriers to international trade, e.g., through MOST-FAVOURED-NATION CLAUSE. |
| International Atomic Energy Agency (IAEA)[3/] | 1957; Vienna | 112 | Promote peaceful uses of atomic energy. Buy and sell fuels and materials; assist in peaceful applications. |
| International Bank for Reconstruction and Development (IBRD) | 1945; Washington | 148 | Further economic development through guaranteed loans, technical advice. Train member-state officials. Also called World Bank; IFC and IDA (below) affiliated. |
| International Civil Aviation Organization (ICAO) | 1947; Montreal | 156 | Encourage orderly aviation growth. Improve standards for aircraft navigation, airworthiness, pilot licensing. |
| International Development Association (IDA) | 1960; Washington | 127 | Extend credit on easier terms to nations, mainly developing, that do not qualify for IBRD loans. |
| International Finance Corporation (IFC) | 1957; Washington | 127 | Aid less-developed members by promoting private enterprise in their economies. Provide risk capital. |
| International Fund for Agricultural Development (IFAD) | 1977; Rome | 139 | Finance agricultural projects to introduce, expand, improve food production, raise nutritional levels. |
| International Labour Organization (ILO) | 1946 (1919); Geneva | 150 | Improve labour conditions, living standards; promote social justice; protect foreign workers. |
| International Maritime Organization (IMO) | 1982 (1948); London | 129 | Promote cooperation on technical matters, maritime safety, navigation; encourage antipollution measures. |

## 3  SPECIALIZED AGENCIES OF THE UNITED NATIONS *(Continued)*

| | | | |
|---|---|---|---|
| International Monetary Fund (IMF) | 1945; Washington | 151 | Promote monetary cooperation, currency stabilization, trade expansion; meet balance-of-payments difficulties. |
| International Telecommunications Union (ITU) | 1947 (1865); Geneva | 160 | Regulate, standardize, plan, coordinate international telecommunications; allot radio frequencies. |
| United Nations Educational, Scientific, and Cultural Organization (UNESCO) | 1946; Paris | 158 | Reduce social tensions by encouraging interchange of ideas, cultural achievements; improve education. |
| United Nations Industrial Development Organization (UNIDO) | 1967; Vienna | 144 | Assist developing countries with financial, design, technological, market, research advice. Help formulate industrial-development policies. |
| Universal Postal Union (UPU) | 1947 (1875); Bern | 168 | Unite countries for reciprocal exchange of correspondence; aid and advise on improving postal services. |
| World Health Organization (WHO) | 1948; Geneva | 166 | Promote highest health standards; set drug and vaccine standards, health and research guidelines. |
| World Intellectual Property Organization (WIPO) | 1974 (1883); Geneva | 114 | Promote protection of intellectual property, inventions, copyrights, access to patented technology. |
| World Meteorological Organization (WMO) | 1950 (1878); Geneva | 159 | Promote cooperation between world meteorological stations; standardize observations; encourage research. |

*Key* (1) Date in parentheses is date that predecessor organization began operation.
(2) In almost all cases, agencies have member states that are not members of the UN General Assembly.
(3) Not technically specialized agencies but customarily listed as such.

## 4  SELECTED OTHER UNITED NATIONS BODIES

| *Name* | *Purpose and Function* |
|---|---|
| United Nations Development Programme (UNDP) | Promote development planning, agricultural and industrial productivity, education, health and social services in developing countries. |
| United Nations Environment Programme (UNEP) | Promote international cooperation on environmental and conservation issues. |
| United Nations International Children's Emergency Fund (UNICEF) | Assist children and adolescents worldwide, particularly in devastated areas and developing countries, with educational services, health care. Nobel Peace Prize, 1965. |
| United Nations Conference on Trade and Development (UNCTAD) | Accelerate economic growth in developing countries. Review policies of these and industrialized countries influencing trade and development. |
| United Nations High Commissioner for Refugees (UNHCR) | Seek permanent solution to refugee problem; protect refugees under its mandate; coordinate voluntary agency efforts; assist most-needy groups. Nobel Peace Prize, 1954, 1981. |
| United Nations Relief and Works Agency for Palestinian Refugees in the Near East (UNRWA) | Provide food, health services, education, vocational training for approximately 1.8 million Palestinians displaced by ARAB-ISRAELI WARS. |

been generally unfavourable, but the trade deficits have been negligible in comparison to a rising GROSS NATIONAL PRODUCT (GNP) that passed the $2.6 million million mark in 1980. Development of the US economy has been spurred by the growth of a complex network of transport (rail, highway, air, and inland waterway) and communications (telegraph, telephone, radio, and television) that has made possible the creation of the world's most sophisticated marketing mechanism.

*Government.* The US is a federal republic in which power is divided between a central governing authority and the individual states. The principal framework of government is the CONSTITUTION OF THE UNITED STATES, drawn up in 1787. The federal government consists of three branches: executive, legislative, and judicial. Executive power is vested in the PRESIDENT, who conducts the administrative business of the nation with the aid of a CABINET consisting mainly of the secretaries (heads) of the various federal departments, e.g., the departments of State, Treasury, Defence, and Agriculture. The CONGRESS OF THE UNITED STATES, the legislative branch, is bicameral, consisting of a Senate and a House of

Representatives. The judicial branch is formed by the federal courts, the highest of which is the nine-member US SUPREME COURT, which also functions as the court of last resort for the 50 state judiciary systems. Members of Congress and members of the Electoral College, which formally chooses the president and vice president, are elected by universal suffrage.

*History.* England, Spain, and France were the chief nations to establish colonies in what is now the US. The first permanent European settlement in the present US was St Augustine, Florida, founded by the Spanish in 1565, and the first permanent English settlement was established at JAMESTOWN, Virginia, in 1607. The British eventually extended their rule over most of the Atlantic coast, and in the FRENCH AND INDIAN WARS they ousted the French from Canada and the West. Increasing conflict between Britain and the American colonies led to the AMERICAN REVOLUTION, the DECLARATION OF INDEPENDENCE (1776), and the creation of the US. Governed from 1781 under the Articles of CONFEDERATION, the US opted for a stronger national government in the

Constitution, drawn up at the FEDERAL CONSTITUTIONAL CONVENTION (1787). George WASHINGTON served as the first president. Controversy over the division of power between the states and the federal government gave rise to the first political parties (see FEDERALIST PARTY; DEMOCRATIC PARTY). Settlement of the frontier added new states to the Union, and the LOUISIANA PURCHASE (1803) secured a vast new territory in the West. The violation of US shipping by the British led ultimately to the WAR OF 1812. Andrew JACKSON, the seventh president, sometimes considered the incarnation of frontier democracy, was elected in 1828 and provided a strong executive attuned to popular support. The annexation (1845) of TEXAS precipitated the MEXICAN WAR, in which the US defeated Mexico, acquiring California and most of the present Southwest. The Pacific Northwest was added by a peaceful settlement (1846) with Britain (see OREGON). Meanwhile, the South, with its doctrine of STATES' RIGHTS, was becoming estranged from the North over the issue of slavery. After the election (1860) of Abraham LINCOLN to the presidency, the South seceded from the Union and formed the CONFEDERACY. The CIVIL WAR that ensued ended in complete victory for the North. The RECONSTRUCTION period that followed was marked by bitter struggles, including the impeachment (1868) of Pres. Andrew JOHNSON. The remainder of the 19th cent. was marked by railway building, the disappearance of the American frontier, and massive industrialization. The US gained additional territory with the purchase of Alaska (1867); the annexation of Hawaii (1898); and the conquest of Spanish possessions, e.g., Puerto Rico, Guam, and the PHILIPPINES, in the SPANISH–AMERICAN WAR (1898). Despite the efforts of Pres. WILSON to keep the US neutral, the nation entered WORLD WAR I on the Allied side in 1917, but after the war it settled into an isolationist policy.

The GREAT DEPRESSION began in 1929 and reached worldwide proportions. To combat it, Pres. F.D. ROOSEVELT launched a sweeping reform programme called the NEW DEAL. The US entered WORLD WAR II on the Allied side after the Japanese attack (1941) on PEARL HARBOR. After the war the US emerged as a world power, but relations with the USSR deteriorated into the COLD WAR and the US took the lead in establishing (1949) the NORTH ATLANTIC TREATY ORGANIZATION. In the KOREAN WAR, during the administration of Harry S. TRUMAN, the US took the leading role in combating the Communist invasion of South Korea. The US economy boomed after World War II, and, spurred by Soviet advances in technology, the US embarked on a large SPACE EXPLORATION programme. The nation suffered a major trauma with the assassination of Pres. John F. KENNEDY in 1963; moreover, in the 1960s domestic turmoil and violence erupted as black Americans became dissatisfied with the slow progress of INTEGRATION and protesters demonstrated against US involvement in the VIETNAM WAR, which had escalated during the presidencies of Lyndon B. JOHNSON and Richard M. NIXON. In 1974 Nixon was forced to resign following the WATERGATE AFFAIR, and Gerald R. FORD became president. High inflation and mounting unemployment plagued the US economy in the 1970s and early 80s. Ronald REAGAN, who became president in 1981, initiated an economic plan that included large cuts in nondefence spending. In his second term there were signs of economic recovery, and although the federal budget deficit grew substantially the US Congress passed major tax reform legislation. Reelected in 1984, Reagan continued to pursue vigorous external policies in defence or pursuit of US interests, notably in CENTRAL AMERICA and the Mediterranean region. He also instituted a major enhancement of US nuclear strike

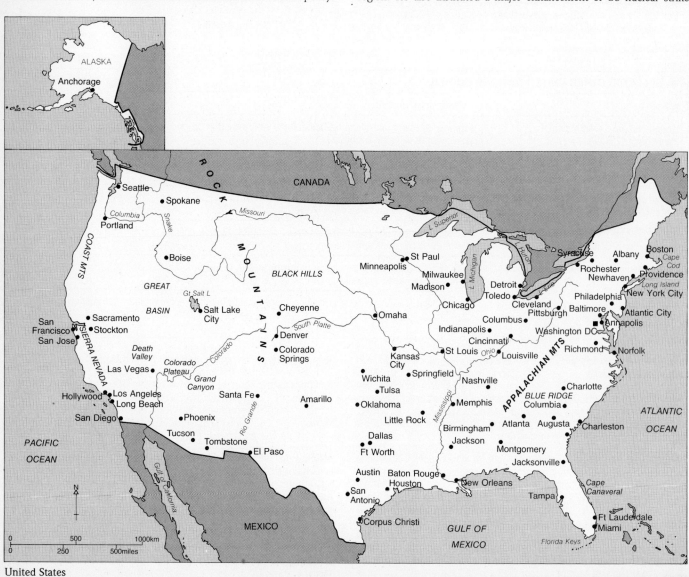

United States

## PRESIDENTS OF THE UNITED STATES *(with vice presidents, political parties, and dates in office)*

George Washington, 1789–97
*John Adams*

John Adams [Federalist] 1797–1801
*Thomas Jefferson*

Thomas Jefferson [Democratic-Republican] 1801–09
*Aaron Burr, 1801–05*
*George Clinton, 1805–09*

James Madison [Democratic-Republican] 1809–17
*George Clinton, 1809–12*
*(no Vice President, Apr. 1812–Mar. 1813)*
*Elbridge Gerry, 1813–14*
*(no Vice President, Nov. 1814–Mar. 1817)*

James Monroe [Democratic-Republican] 1817–25
*Daniel D. Tompkins*

John Quincy Adams [Democratic-Republican] 1825–29
*John C. Calhoun*

Andrew Jackson [Democratic] 1829–37
*John C. Calhoun, 1829–32*
*(no Vice President, Dec. 1832–Mar. 1833)*
*Martin Van Buren, 1833–37*

Martin Van Buren [Democratic] 1837–41
*Richard M. Johnson*

William Henry Harrison [Whig] 1841
*John Tyler*

John Tyler [Whig] 1841–45
*(no Vice President)*

James Knox Polk [Democratic] 1845–49
*George M. Dallas*

Zachary Taylor [Whig] 1849–50
*Millard Fillmore*

Millard Fillmore [Whig] 1850–53
*(no Vice President)*

Franklin Pierce [Democratic] 1853–57
*William R. King, 1853*
*(no Vice President, Apr. 1853–Mar. 1857)*

James Buchanan [Democratic] 1857–61
*John C. Breckinridge*

Abraham Lincoln [Republican] 1861–65
*Hannibal Hamlin, 1861–65*
*Andrew Johnson, 1865*

Andrew Johnson [Democratic/National Union] 1865–69
*(no Vice President)*

Ulysses Simpson Grant [Republican] 1869–77
*Schuyler Colfax, 1869–73*
*Henry Wilson, 1873–75*
*(no Vice President, Nov. 1875–Mar. 1877)*

Rutherford Birchard Hayes [Republican] 1877–81
*William A. Wheeler*

James Abram Garfield [Republican] 1881
*Chester A. Arthur*

Chester Alan Arthur [Republican] 1881–85
*(no Vice President)*

Grover Cleveland [Democratic] 1885–89
*Thomas A. Hendricks, 1885*
*(no Vice President, Nov. 1885–Mar. 1889)*

Benjamin Harrison [Republican] 1889–93
*Levi P. Morton*

Grover Cleveland [Democratic] 1893–97
*Adlai E. Stevenson*

William McKinley [Republican] 1897–1901
*Garret A. Hobart, 1897–99*
*(no Vice President, Nov. 1899–Mar. 1901)*
*Theodore Roosevelt, 1901*

Theodore Roosevelt [Republican] 1901–09
*(no Vice President, Sept. 1901–Mar. 1905)*
*Charles W. Fairbanks, 1905–09*

William Howard Taft [Republican] 1909–13
*James S. Sherman, 1909–12*
*(no Vice President, Oct. 1912–Mar. 1913)*

Woodrow Wilson [Democratic] 1913–21
*Thomas R. Marshall*

Warren Gamaliel Harding [Republican] 1921–23
*Calvin Coolidge*

Calvin Coolidge [Republican] 1923–29
*(no Vice President, 1923–25)*
*Charles G. Dawes, 1925–29*

Herbert Clark Hoover [Republican] 1929–33
*Charles Curtis*

Franklin Delano Roosevelt [Democratic] 1933–45
*John N. Garner, 1933–41*
*Henry A. Wallace, 1941–45*
*Harry S. Truman, 1945*

Harry S. Truman [Democratic] 1945–53
*(no Vice President, 1945–49)*
*Alben W. Barkley, 1949–53)*

Dwight David Eisenhower [Republican] 1953–61
*Richard M. Nixon*

John Fitzgerald Kennedy [Democratic] 1961–1963
*Lyndon B. Johnson*

Lyndon Baines Johnson [Democratic] 1963–69
*(no Vice President, 1963–65)*
*Hubert H. Humphrey, 1965–69*

Richard Milhous Nixon [Republican] 1969–74
*Spiro T. Agnew, 1969–73*
*(no Vice President, 10 Oct. 1973–6 Dec. 1973)*
*Gerald R. Ford, 1973–74*

Gerald Rudolph Ford [Republican] 1974–77
*(no Vice President, 9 Aug. 1974–19 Dec. 1974)*
*Nelson A. Rockefeller, 1974–77*

Jimmy Carter [Democratic] 1977–81
*Walter F. Mondale*

Ronald Wilson Reagan [Republican] 1981–89
*George H.W. Bush*

George H.W. Bush [Republican] 1989–
*J. Danforth Quayle*

---

capability and, in 1983, launched the Strategic Defence Initiative ('Star Wars') despite Soviet objections that the programme jeopardized prospects of East–West agreement on arms control. Eventually, in 1987, a US-Soviet agreement for the reduction of intermediate-range nuclear forces (INF) was signed. In the 1988 presidential elections Vice-Pres. George BUSH (Republican) defeated the Democrat nominee, Michael DUKAKIS.

**unit trust,** a company which invests in a wide range of other companies. The units which it issues represent holdings of shares, and the cost of managing these is taken out of the shareholders' income. Unit trusts have traditionally appealed to the small investor because of the wide spread of risk which they provide. The number in the UK burgeoned in the 1980s as popular interest in the stockmarket increased. In mid-1987 there were 128,000 unit-holder accounts in the UK and managed funds were at a peak £44,200 million. Many unit trusts specialize in their share investment by region and type of business. Prices of units are set daily and reflect the movement of the shares in which the unit trust has its holding.

**univalve:** see GASTROPOD.

**universal gas constant:** see GAS LAWS.

**universal language:** see INTERNATIONAL LANGUAGE.

**Universal Postal Union:** see UNITED NATIONS (table 3).

**universities,** institutions of higher education, providing undergraduate and postgraduate courses engaged in research. Universities arose in the Middle Ages to train young men in law, theology, and medicine. Most were established by royal or ecclesiastical initiative, but some were founded by students. The medieval university often had thousands of students and played an important role in contemporary affairs. The most famous European universities include those at Oxford, Cambridge, and Paris (all founded in the 12th cent.), Salamanca (c. 1230), Prague (1348), Vienna (1365), Uppsala (1477), Leiden (1575), and Moscow (1755). Scotland had four universities while England still only had two (see SCOTTISH EDUCATION). The early-19th-cent. English foundations were Durham Univ. (1832) and LONDON UNIVERSITY (1836), and a number of 'university colleges' founded in the second half of the century included Owens' College, Manchester (1851) and Mason Science College, Birmingham (1880). The former, joined by colleges at Leeds and Liverpool, became the federal Victoria University from 1880 to 1904, when they each became independent universities. Other university colleges gained university status at different times, e.g., Bristol (1909), Reading (1926), and Southampton (1952). The Welsh university colleges founded in the 1870s and 80s were granted a charter as a federal university in 1893. Queen's College, Belfast, became a university in 1908. In the 1960s new universities were created in England, Scotland and Northern Ireland, and the Colleges of Advanced Technology were made universities. The 47 universities in the UK have over 250,000 full-time British students, and over 25,000 overseas students. Admissions are administered by the UNIVERSITIES' CENTRAL COUNCIL ON ADMISSIONS. Universities on the European pattern are found all over the world. Some Commonwealth countries began their university systems with colleges affiliated to London Univ., later granted independent status. The earliest university in the New World is the Univ. of Mexico (1551); the oldest in the US is Harvard (1636).

**Universities Central Council on Admissions (UCCA),** body est. 1961 by the universities of the UK to provide a machinery for student applications. Candidates list up to five institutions in order of preference, and UCCA circulates the application forms as appropriate. There is a similar body for POLYTECHNICS, the Polytechnics Central Admission System (est. 1984). UCCA also provides a statistical service on the basis of its annual operations. Its headquarters are in Cheltenham, Gloucestershire.

**University of California Regents v. Bakke,** case decided in 1978 by the US SUPREME COURT, which held in a closely divided decision that race could be a factor considered in choosing a diverse student body in university admissions decisions. The Court also held, however, that the use of quotas in such AFFIRMATIVE-ACTION programmes was not permissible; thus, the Univ. of California, Davis, medical school had, by maintaining a 16% minority quota, discriminated against Bakke, a white applicant. The legal implications of the decision were clouded by the Court's division.

**university press,** publishing house associated with a university, usually bearing the university's name in its imprint. It is generally a specialized house emphasizing scholarly books, monographs, and PERIODICALS. The first English-language university presses were those of Oxford and Cambridge, both established by the end of the 16th cent. They have enjoyed since the 17th cent. a monopoly on printing the Bible and BOOK OF COMMON PRAYER in England. Universities all over the world now have their own presses, mostly subsidized. In the US, 10% of all books published come from university presses.

**unnilhexium,** (Unh), artificial radioactive TRANSURANIC ELEMENT. Claims for its production have been made by a Soviet group at Dubna, who in 1974 bombarded lead with chromium ions to obtan the $Unh^{259}$ and $Unh^{260}$ isotopes, and groups in California at the Lawrence Berkeley and Lawrence Livermore Laboratories, who, also in 1974, bombarded californium with oxygen ions to obtain the $Unh^{263}$ isotope. See ELEMENT (table); PERIODIC TABLE.

**unnilpentium,** (Unp), artificial radioactive TRANSURANIC ELEMENT. Claims for its production have been made by a Soviet group at Dubna, who in 1967 bombarded americium with neon to obtain, apparently, the $Unp^{260}$ and $Unp^{261}$ isotopes, and by an American group at the Univ. of California, Berkeley, who in 1970 bombarded californium with nitrogen nuclei to obtain the $Unp^{260}$ isotope. The names *nielsbohrium* and *hahnium* were originally proposed, respectively, by the Dubna and Berkeley groups. See ELEMENT (table); PERIODIC TABLE.

**unnilquadium,** (Unq), artificial radioactive TRANSURANIC ELEMENT. Claims for its production have been made by a Soviet group in Dubna, who in 1964, bombarded plutonium with neon ions to obtain, apparently, the $Unq^{260}$ isotope, and by an American group at the Univ. of California, Berkeley, who in 1969 bombarded californium with carbon nuclei to obtain the $Unq^{257}$ and $Unq^{259}$, and possibly the $Unq^{258}$, isotopes. The names *kurchatovium* and *rutherfordium* were originally proposed, respectively, by the Dubna and Berkeley groups. See ELEMENT (table); PERIODIC TABLE.

**Upaniṣads** or **Upanishads,** speculative and mystical scriptures of HINDUISM, composed beginning c.900 BC, forming the final section of the VEDA. A heterogeneous compilation of material from various sources that together are regarded as the wellspring of Hindu religion and philosophy, the Upaniṣads form the basis for the later philosophical schools of VEDĀNTA. The principal early Upaniṣads expound the doctrine of BRAHMAN, the universal self or soul, and its identity with the *ātman,* or individual self or soul. The early ones also contain information on Vedic sacrifice and the practice of YOGA. There are 112 Upaniṣads extant, but some of them were written much later and coincided with the sectarian movement in HINDUISM. Except for the earliest 10 or 18, none are universally accepted by scholars.

**Updike, John,** 1932–, American author. His elegantly written fiction usually deals with the tensions and tragedies of contemporary middle-class life. His novels include *Rabbit, Run* (1961), *Couples* (1978), *The Coup* (1978), and *Rabbit Is Rich* (1981).

**Upper Volta:** see BURKINA FASO.

**Uppsala,** city (1984 pop. 152,579), capital of Uppsala co., E Sweden. Once the coronation place of Swedish kings, it is now a cultural and industrial centre producing metal goods, clothing, and other manufactures. Its 13th-cent. Gothic cathedral is the burial place of GUSTAVUS I, LINNAEUS, and SWEDENBORG. Its university (est. 1477) is the oldest in Sweden.

**Ur,** ancient city of SUMER, S Mesopotamia, on the Euphrates. Also called Ur of the Chaldees, it was flourishing by 3500 BC. In the Bible it is identified as the home of ABRAHAM. Captured (c.2340 BC) by Sargon of Akkad, it later became independent. Ur, however, declined after the 6th cent. BC and never recovered. C. Leonard WOOLLEY led the excavation of the city in the 1920s.

**Urabi, Ahmed Pasha:** see ARABI, AHMED PASHA.

**Uralic and Altaic languages** (yoo͵ralik, al͵tayik), two groups of related languages thought by many scholars to form a single Uralic and Altaic linguistic family. However, other authorities hold that the Uralic and Altaic groups constitute two unconnected and separate language families. Uralic includes Finnish and Hungarian; Altaic includes Turkish and Mongolian. See LANGUAGE (table, as Ural and Altaic family).

**Urals** or **Ural Mountains,** mountain system extending N–S c.2400 km (1500 mi) across the W USSR, part of the traditional border between Europe and Asia. Narodnaya (1893 m/6212 ft), in the N, is the highest point. Except in the polar and northern sections, the mountains are densely forested, with timber production an important industry. They are also enormously rich in minerals, including coal, iron ore, aluminum, copper, manganese, potash, and oil. Huge industrial centres, part of the Urals industrial area (c.751,500 km²/290,000 sq mi), are located at SVERDLOVSK, Magnitogorsk, CHELYABINSK, Nizhni Tagil, and PERM. During World War II entire industries were transferred to the Urals from the W USSR.

**Urania:** see MUSES.

**uraninite:** see PITCHBLENDE.

**uranium** (U), radioactive metallic element, discovered in oxide form in PITCHBLENDE by M.H. Klaproth in 1789. A silver-white, hard, dense, malleable, ductile, highly reactive metal in the ACTINIDE SERIES, it occurs naturally as a mixture of three ISOTOPES. The rare uranium-235 isotope is the only naturally occurring fission fuel for NUCLEAR ENERGY. Breeder reactors convert the abundant but nonfissionable uranium-238 into fissionable plutonium-239. Uranium-235 and plutonium-239 are also practicable fissionable nuclei for ATOMIC BOMB. Because of its very long half-life of 4.5 billion years, uranium-238 is useful for dating geological samples (see radioactiveDATING). See ELEMENT (table); NUCLEAR REACTOR; PERIODIC TABLE; RADIOACTIVITY.

**Uranus** (yoo(ə),raynəs, ,yooərənəs), in astronomy, 7th PLANET from the Sun, at a mean distance of 2869.6 million km (1783.2 million mi). It has a diameter of 52,290 km (32,490 mi) and is a gaseous planet with an atmosphere composed mostly of hydrogen, helium, methane, and ammonia. Detected on 13 Mar. 1781, by William HERSCHEL, it was the first planet discovered in modern times with the aid of a telescope. The extreme (98°) inclination of Uranus's equatorial plane with respect to its orbital plane gives the planet a retrograde rotation, i.e., a rotation opposite to the direction of revolution. Uranus has five known natural satellites: **Titania,** the largest, with a diameter of 1040 km (650 mi), and **Oberon** were discovered by Herschel in 1787; **Ariel** and **Umbriel,** by William Lassell in 1851; and **Miranda,** by Gerard Kuiper in 1948. On 10 Mar. 1977, astronomers detected a system of narrow rings (now estimated to be nine in number) of small, dark particles orbiting around the planet. The *Voyager 2* SPACE PROBE flew by Uranus in 1986.

**Uranus,** in Greek mythology, the heaven, first ruler of the universe; son and husband of GAIA; father of TITANS, CYCLOPS, and Hundred-handed Ones. Uranus was castrated and dethroned by CRONUS. His blood, falling onto Earth, produced the vengeful FURIES; from his discarded flesh and the sea APHRODITE arose.

**Urban II,** c.1042–99, pope (1088–99), a Frenchman named Odo (or Eudes) of Lagery. A Cluniac monk, he worked closely with GREGORY VII and as pope furthered Gregory's reforms. His sermon at Clermont (1095) brought about the First CRUSADE.

**urbanization,** 1 The demographic processes whereby an increasing percentage of a nation's population lives in urban as opposed to rural areas. 2 The qualitative sociological changes in human behaviour that is a product of this transition. These may include less rigid, more relationistic moral standards, acquisition of cosmopolitan cultured tastes, greater ease of social mobility and contact, increase in secular social activity, greater secondary-group relationships. Some see the city as the location and focus of progressive cultural change, and urbanization as essential to modernity. Others see the city as the locus and cause of moral and social decay undermining the institutions of social stability (e.g., the FAMILY) and giving rise to crime and licence. These contradictory attitudes have been present in English culture since at least the time of the INDUSTRIAL REVOLUTION (e.g., the English Romantic movement's defence of rural virtue).

**Urban VI,** 1318?–89, pope (1378–89), a Neapolitan named Bartolomeo Prignano. Chosen as successor to Gregory XI, he proved violent and unruly, whereupon the cardinals went to Anagni and elected Robert of Geneva as antipope, thus beginning the Great SCHISM. Urban probably murdered five cardinals who opposed him; many believe he was insane.

**Urbino,** town (1984 est. pop. 16,000), Marche, E central Italy. The birthplace of RAPHAEL, it was prominent in the art world of the 15th and 16th cent., when it had ducal patrons. The 15th-cent. ducal palace has many art treasures.

**Urdu** (,ooədooh, ,uhdooh), language belonging to the Indic group of the Indo-Iranian subfamily of the Indo-European family of languages. It is the official tongue of Pakistan. See LANGUAGE (table).

**urea,** organic compound ($NH_2CONH_2$), that is the principal end product of nitrogen metabolism in most mammals. Most of the nitrogen in protein eventually appears in urea, which is concentrated in the KIDNEY and excreted in URINE.

**ureter:** see URINARY SYSTEM.

**urethra:** see URINARY SYSTEM.

**Urey, Harold Clayton** (,yooree), 1893–1981, American chemist. He taught at Johns Hopkins Univ., Maryland, Columbia Univ., New York, the Univ. of Chicago, and the Univ. of California. For his isolation of deuterium (heavy hydrogen) he won the 1934 Nobel Prize for chemistry; he later isolated heavy isotopes of oxygen, nitrogen, carbon, and sulphur.

During World War II, in connection with the atomic bomb project, he worked on methods of separating uranium isotopes and on the production of heavy water.

**urinary system,** group of organs concerned with excretion of urine from the body. In humans, the urinary system includes the kidneys, ureters, bladder, and urethra. Blood containing waste products enters each KIDNEY through the renal artery. The kidneys purify the blood by filtering out waste products, which, together with water, form URINE. From the kidneys, urine passes through thick-walled tubes called ureters into the bladder, a muscular sac that temporarily stores the urine and contracts to expel it. Urine released from the bladder flows into the urethra, the canal carrying it to the outside of the body.

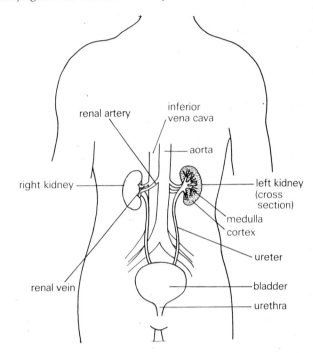

Urinary system

**urine,** clear, amber-colored fluid formed by the KIDNEY and carrying waste products of nitrogen metabolism out of the body. Urine is 95% water, in which urea, uric acid, mineral salts, toxins, and other waste products are dissolved. It may also contain ordinary substances used by the body but excreted by the kidneys when excessive amounts are present in the bloodstream. Analysis of urine is important in detecting diseases. See also URINARY SYSTEM.

**Urquiza, Justo José de** (ooə,keesah), 1801–70, Argentine general and president of the confederation (1854–60). As leader of the Entre Ríos prov. he helped sustain the power of ROSAS until 1851, when he led a revolt and defeated Rosas at the battle of Monte Caseros. He was then ruler of Argentina but was opposed by Buenos Aires prov. The battle at Pavón (1861) was indecisive, but he surrendered power to Bartolomé Mitre. Urquiza was later assassinated.

**Ursa Major** and **Ursa Minor,** [Lat., = the great bear; the little bear], two conspicuous northern CONSTELLATIONS. Part of Ursa Major is called the Plough. POLARIS, the Pole Star, is at the extreme end of Ursa Minor.

**Uruguay,** officially Eastern Republic of Uruguay, republic (1987 est. pop. 3,050,000), 177,508 km² (68,536 sq mi), SE South America, bordered by Argentina (W), Brazil (N), the Atlantic Ocean (E), and the Río de la Plata (S). The capital is MONTEVIDEO, where over one-third of the people live. An alluvial plain, known as the Banda Oriental, occupies the S, while to the N is a region of grasslands and low hills. Uruguay's economy is based on sheep and cattle. Grains for cattle and human consumption make up the bulk of the crops, and manufacturing is led by the processing of animal products; meat, wool, hides, and skins are the leading exports. In 1983 GDP was US$6100 million or US$2033 per capita. The country has abundant fisheries. Most of the population is of

Spanish and Italian descent; about 10% is mestizo. Spanish is the principal language, and Roman Catholicism the chief religion.

*History.* The first permanent European settlement in present-day Uruguay was established in 1624 by the Spanish, who controlled the Banda Oriental until the 1800s. Uruguay declared for independence with its neighbour Argentina in 1810, but in 1814, led by José ARTIGAS, determined to fight for a separate existence. In 1820 Uruguay's other neighbour, Brazil, occupied Montevideo, and it was not until 1828, after Brazil had been defeated at Ituzaingó, that an independent Uruguay was achieved. Immediately thereafter, a civil war broke out, which, becoming entwined with an uprising in Argentina, resulted in a long siege of Montevideo and did not end until 1851. In 1864 Uruguay again became involved with her neighbours, this time in a war with Brazil and Argentina against Paraguay (see TRIPLE ALLIANCE, WAR OF THE). Revolutions and counterrevolutions followed, and it was not until the regime of José Battle y Ordóñez in the early 20th cent. that Uruguay began the social and material progress that made it one of the more stable and prosperous nations of South America. However, economic problems and social unrest in the 1960s and 1970s, heightened by the terrorism of the Tupamaros, a Marxist guerrilla group, led to the installation of a repressive military regime in 1973. The ruling generals initiated moves toward a gradual return of representative democracy and political liberties, culminating in the holding of elections in 1984. These were won by the Colorados, whose leader, Julio Sanguinetti, took office in 1985, pledged to a consensus approach to economic and political issues.

Uruguay

**Ushuaia,** world's most southerly town. This settlement of 55,000 inhabitants is situated on the Argentine part of the island of Tierra del Fuego at the extreme south of the South American continent. The town overlooks the Beagle Channel named after the ship in which Darwin sailed through this channel in 1832.

**Usk** or **Wysg,** river in SE Wales, c.91 km (57 mi) long. It rises on the border of Powys and Dyfed, near Llandoverry, and flows N to Usk reservoir, then generally E and S past Brecon, Abergavenny, Usk, and NEWPORT, entering the Severn estuary just S of Newport in Gwent. It is famous for its salmon fishing.

**Ussher** or **Usher, James** (ˌushə), 1581–1656, Irish Protestant prelate and scholar. By 1606 he was chancellor of St Patrick's Cathedral, Dublin, and later became bishop of Meath (1620 or 1621) and archbishop of Armagh (1625). He was greatly admired for his learning and established a chronology that set the date of creation at 4004 BC and was long used in some editions of the AUTHORIZED VERSION of the Bible.

**Ussuri** (oohˌsoohree), river, c.590 km (365 mi) long, Soviet Far East. It flows N to the AMUR R. at Khabarovsk, forming part of the China–USSR border. Armed border clashes between Chinese and Soviet forces occurred along the river in 1972.

**Ustaše,** [Serbo-Croat = rebels], Croatian separatist and fascist movement founded in 1929 by Ante Pavelić to win CROATIA's independence from Yugoslavia. Backed by Italy and Hungary, the Ustaše engaged in terrorism, including the assassination (1934) of King ALEXANDER and French foreign minster Louis Barthou in Marseilles. When Yugoslavia was invaded and dismembered by the AXIS in 1941, Pavelić and the Ustaše were installed in power in the 'Independent State of Croatia' which they sought to rid of its Serb, Jewish, and Gypsy minorities. The massacres, deportations, and forced conversions to Roman Catholicism provoked resistance which came to be directed by the Communist-led Partisans of TITO. The defeat of Nazi Germany brought down the Ustaše regime as well, but many of its leaders fled abroad to continue anti-Yugoslav conspiracies.

**usury:** see INTEREST.

**Utah,** state of the US (1984 est. pop. 1,652,000), area 219,932 km² (84,916 sq mi), located in the W, bordered by Idaho and Wyoming (N), Colorado (E), Arizona (S), and Nevada (W). SALT LAKE CITY is the capital and largest city. The Wasatch Range of the ROCKY MTS divides this arid state from N to S, separating the COLORADO PLATEAU in the E from the Great Salt Lake desert of the GREAT BASIN in the W. GREAT SALT LAKE and the Bonneville Salt Flats are the remnants of Pleistocene-era Lake Bonneville. Mining is the main economic activity, producing copper, petroleum, coal, asphalt, potash, salt, and vanadium. Utah is a centre of the aerospace and military-related industries; nonelectrical machinery, processed foods, and transport equipment are also important. Major agricultural crops (mainly grains), depend on irrigation. The spectacular scenery of several national parks attracts tourists. Over two-thirds of the population belong to the Mormon religion; over 75% lives in metropolitan areas. Cliff-dwelling peoples preceded the Ute, Paiute, and Navaho Indians who were inhabiting the region when the Spanish arrived (1776). In 1847 Brigham YOUNG led the Mormons to the area but statehood was withheld until they renounced the practice of polygamy (1896). In the early 20th cent. the discovery of minerals and the harnessing of the Colorado R. enabled the economy to develop. In recent years defence-related industries have moved to Utah, and the population growth rate has been rapid.

**Utamaro** (Kitagawa Utamaro), 1753–1806, Japanese colour-print artist, the first of the great masters of the *ukiyo-e* school (see JAPANESE ART). His were the first Japanese prints to become familiar in the West. His idealized, sensuous women and his book of *Insects* (1788) reveal a keen observation of nature.

**Ute Indians,** NORTH AMERICAN INDIANS speaking a Shoshonean language (see AMERICAN INDIAN LANGUAGES) and having a culture typical of the western Plains. They were nomadic people who celebrated the SUN DANCE. Fierce warriors, they ranged southward from their homeland in W Colorado and E Utah to menace the villages of the PUEBLO INDIANS, selling captives into slavery. Some Ute fought with Kit CARSON against the NAVAHO in the CIVIL WAR. In 1868 they were placed on a Colorado reservation, but in 1880 were moved to less desirable land. In the early 1980s several thousand Ute still lived in Utah and Colorado, with those on reservations deriving income from oil and gas leases, farming, cattle-raising, and tourism.

**uterus:** see REPRODUCTIVE SYSTEM.

**Utica** (ˌyoohtikə), ancient N African city, NW of Carthage. Supposedly founded by Phoenicians from TYRE (c.1100 BC), it joined Rome against CARTHAGE in the Third PUNIC WAR. Later it was the capital of the Roman province of Africa. It was destroyed by the Arabs AD c.700.

**utilitarianism,** in ethics, the theory that the rightness or wrongness of an action is determined by whether its consequences are conducive to general utility. Jeremy BENTHAM, founder of the theory, held that the greatest happiness of the greatest number is the fundamental and self-evident principle of morality. His student John Stuart MILL used the principles of utilitarianism to advocate political and social reform, increased democracy, and the emancipation of women. Henry SIDGWICK systematized utilitarian thought and Herbert SPENCER developed a utilitarian ethics based on evolutionary changes.

**utility, public,** industry that is involved in meeting a vital public need and that is required by law to provide adequate service at reasonable prices to

*Woman in Bath* by **Utamaro**

all who apply for it. Important utilities include water, gas, and electric companies, and transport and communications facilities. In Europe such industries are usually owned by the state, but in the US most utilities are privately owned. By its nature, a public utility is often a MONOPOLY and thus not subject to competition.

**utility dog,** class devised for show purposes for those breeds of DOG which cannot easily be defined as HOUND, GUN DOG, TERRIER, WORKING DOG, or TOY DOG. The class includes e.g., the Dalmatian, bulldog, chow chow, akita, shah-pei, and standard-size poodle.

**Utopia** [Gr., = no place], influential book by Sir Thomas MORE (1516) depicting an ideal state that has given its name to all such visions. Utopian writers criticize present conditions and outline vast revolutionary schemes without, however, describing the concrete steps necessary to realize them. The term is applied retrospectively to PLATO's *Republic* and St AUGUSTINE's *City of God,* as well as to the more worldly Renaissance Utopias of RABELAIS and Francis BACON. ROUSSEAU's promotion of the idea of a primitive Golden Age and of man's innate goodness in turn influenced the Utopian socialist communities envisioned by Claude, duc de SAINT-SIMON, Charles FOURIER, P.J. PROUDHON, and others. Utopian experiments, however, generally proved short-lived. The Utopian romance became a popular form of literature in the 19th cent., e.g., Samuel BUTLER's *Erewhon* (1872) and Edward Bellamy's *Looking Backward* (1888), as did the satiric anti-Utopian novel in the 20th cent.,

e.g., Aldous HUXLEY's *Brave New World* (1932) and George ORWELL's *1984* (1949).

**Utrecht,** city (1985 pop. 229,969, agglomeration 504, 310), capital of Utrecht prov., central Netherlands. It is an industrial centre, with such manufactures as machinery, cement, and food. Founded by Rome, it became (7th cent.) an episcopal see. It was a major medieval centre of commerce and was ruled by bishops until ceded (1527) to Emperor Charles V. In 1713 it was the site of the signing of the Peace of Utrecht ending the war of the SPANISH SUCCESSION. It is noted for its 14th-cent. cathedral and its university (est. 1636).

**Utrillo, Maurice,** 1883–1955, French painter; son of the painter Suzanne Valadon. Utrillo's favourite theme was the street scenes of Paris. His personal style was based on a modified CUBISM and a fine sense of atmosphere and composition.

**Utzon, Jorn,** 1918–, Danish architect. He is famous for the original and spectacular Sydney Opera House; his design won first prize in international competition in 1956. Its shell roofs, actually constructed with prefabricated units, were developed in collaboration with Ove Arup as engineer. Utzon resigned from the project in 1966 and the opera house, mainly a concert hall, was finished by Australian architects. Among other distinctive and original works by Utzon are the church at Bagsvaerd near Copenhagen (1976) and the parliament building in Kuwait.

The Sydney Opera House by Jorn **Utzon**

**Uzbek Soviet Socialist Republic** or **Uzbekistan,** constituent republic (1985 pop. 17,989,000), 449,500 km² (173,552 sq mi), Soviet Central Asia. It borders Afghanistan (S); the Turkmen SSR (SW); the Kazakh SSR (W, N); the Aral Sea (N); and the Kirghiz SSR and Tadzhik SSR (E). TASHKENT, the capital, and SAMARKAND are the chief cities. Large parts of the W and NW are desert, with several major oases that are the main population centres. To the E and SE rise the mountains of the Tien Shan and Pamirs. Agricultural land is irrigated, and the extensive irrigation network totals over 150,000 km (93,000 mi) in length. Cotton (65% of the USSR's total), rice (50% of the total), and lucerne (60% of the total) are produced. Stock-raising is also important. Oil, natural gas, and coal are the major mineral resources. There are plants producing agricultural machinery, cement, textiles, and a number of chemicals. The Uzbek, a Turkic-speaking Sunni Muslim people, make up the majority of the population; other groups include Russians and Tatars. An ancient Persian province, the region was ruled (4th–19th cent.) by ALEXANDER THE GREAT, the Arabs, the Seljuk Turks of KHOREZM, JENGHIZ KHAN, TAMERLANE, the TIMURIDS, and the Uzbek, a remnant of the empire of the GOLDEN HORDE. It was largely under Russian control by 1873. In 1918 it became part of the USSR, and in 1925 became a constituent republic.

**V,** chemical symbol of the element VANADIUM.

**Vaca, Cabeza de:** see CABEZA DE VACA, Álvar Núñez.

**vaccination,** inoculation of a substance (vaccine) into the body for the purpose of producing active IMMUNITY against an infectious disease. The vaccine is usually a weakened culture of the agent causing the disease. Vaccination was used in ancient times in China, India, and Persia, and was introduced to the West in the late 18th cent. by E. JENNER. Vaccination is used today to prevent such diseases as SMALLPOX, DIPHTHERIA, POLIOMYELITIS, RABIES, and TYPHOID. It is often carried out in two or three stages to avoid unpleasant side-effects. Oral vaccines are available for some diseases.

**vacuum,** theoretically, space devoid of matter. A perfect vacuum has never been obtained; the best man-made vacuums contain less than $10^5$ gas molecules per cubic centimetre, compared with about $30 \times 10^{18}$ molecules per cubic centimetre for air at sea level. In intergalactic space, the regions with the highest vacuum are estimated to contain less than one molecule per cubic centimetre. Several kinds of **vacuum pump** have been devised, e.g., the ion pump, which ionizes gas molecules and draws them to a charged collector, and the cryogenic pump, which condenses gas molecules on an extremely cold surface of a container.

**vacuum cleaner:** see BOOTH, HERBERT CECIL.

**Vadodara** (formerly **Baroda**), city (1981 pop. 734,473), Gujarat state, W India. It is an important district administrative, commercial, and railway centre. Standing in the middle of fertile cotton-growing plains, it has developed textile industries, also chemicals, pottery, and engineering. It is a notable educational and cultural centre, with a famous university. It was the capital of a former extraordinarily fragmented princely state whose ruler, the Gaekwad, was descended from an 18th-cent. Mahratta chief.

**vagina:** see REPRODUCTIVE SYSTEM.

**Valais** (val,ay), canton of SW Switzerland, in the valley of the upper RHONE R. Largely French-speaking and Catholic, except in the east, its economy is based on pastoralism, vine-growing, hydroelectric power, and tourism. Its mountain peaks (see MATTERHORN) and resorts (see ZERMATT) attract many visitors. Valais became a Swiss canton in 1815.

**Valdivia, Pedro de** (vahl,deevyah), c.1500–54, Spanish CONQUISTADOR, conqueror of CHILE. With Francisco PIZARRO in the conquest of PERU, he received Pizarro's permission to subdue Chile in 1540. The capital, SANTIAGO, was founded in 1541, but the colony did not prosper because of the scarcity of gold and the ferocity of the ARAUCANIAN INDIANS. Valdivia returned to Peru for further aid in 1547 and helped quell the rebellion of Gonzalo PIZARRO. Governor of Chile from 1549, he founded CONCEPCIÓN (1550) and Valdivia (1552). He was killed in the Indian rebellion of 1553.

**Valence,** city (1982 pop. of agglomeration 106,041), capital of Drôme dept., SE France, on the RHÔNE R. It is the market centre for cereals, market-garden, and orchard crops. Vines and mulberries are also grown in the vicinity. The town is a centre of jewellery manufacture and has a Romanesque cathedral.

**Valencia,** region and former kingdom, E Spain, on the Mediterranean Sea. Largely mountainous, with a fertile coastal plain, Valencia is the 'garden of Spain'. Citrus and other fruits, rice, and wine grapes are among its crops. Manufactures include ceramics and textiles. The area was conquered (8th cent.) by the MOORS, became (1022) an independent emirate, and was ruled (1094–99) by the CID. It was conquered (1238) by ARAGÓN but preserved its political identity within Aragón and, later, in the Spanish state.

**Valencia,** city (1981 pop. 751,734), capital of Valencia prov., E Spain. A picturesque winter resort, it lies in a fertile region near its Mediterranean port, El Grao. It has shipyards and produces textiles and chemicals. A Roman colony, it was held (8th–13th cent.) by the MOORS. Conquered by James I of Aragón (1238), it gained commercial and cultural importance; intellectual eminence followed. Landmarks include the cathedral (13th–15 cent.), 14th-cent. fortified towers built on Roman foundations, and the Gothic silk exchange.

**Valencia,** city (1980 est. pop. 506,000), central N Venezuela, capital of Carabobo state. It was founded in the early colonial period near Lake Valencia and today is Venezuela's most industrialized city and the centre of its most important agricultural state.

**Valenciennes** (va,lonsee·en), city (1982 pop. of agglomeration 349,505), NE France, on the Escaut (SCHELDT) R. Once famous for its hand-made lace, it owed its growth in the 19th cent. to its position on the largest coalfield in France. The city is a centre of steel-making and engineering industries, some of which are now in decline. Part of Hainault, it passed to France in 1678.

**valency** or **oxidation state,** combining capacity of an ATOM expressed as the number of single bonds the atom can form or the number of electrons an ELEMENT gives up or accepts when reacting to form a compound. The valency of an atom is determined by the number of electrons in the outermost, or valency, electron shell. An atom exists in its most stable configuration when its outermost shell is completely filled; in combining with other atoms, it thus tends to gain or lose valency electrons in order to attain a stable configuration. The valency of many elements is determined from their ability to combine with hydrogen or to replace it in compounds.

**Valens,** c.328–378, Roman emperor of the East (r.364–78). Unlike his brother and co-ruler of the West, VALENTINIAN I, he embraced ARIANISM. He was killed in a disastrous defeat by the VISIGOTHS at Adrianople. THEODOSIUS I succeeded him.

**Valentine, Saint,** d. c.270, Roman martyr–priest. Possibly because his feast, 14 Feb., was close to a pagan love festival, Valentine became known as a patron of lovers. The lovers' greeting cards sent on this day are called valentines. His feast was dropped from the liturgical calendar in 1969.

**Valentine's Day:** see SAINT VALENTINE'S DAY.

**Valentinian,** Roman emperors of the West. **Valentinian I,** 321–75 (r.364–75), was co-ruler of the East with his brother VALENS. He reduced taxes and allowed religious freedom. His son, **Valentinian II,** 371?–92 (r.375–92), ruled jointly until 383 with his brother Gratian, who made THEODOSIUS I emperor of the East. He was expelled (387) from Italy by Maximus but restored (388) by Theodosius. Later he was murdered, probably by the Frankish general Arbogast. **Valentinian III,** 419–55 (r.425–55), was at first under the regency of his mother, Galla Placidia. The Vandals and HUNS invaded the empire during his reign. An ineffectual monarch, he allowed the general Aetius to rule (433–54). Valentinian murdered Aetius (454) and was himself murdered soon afterwards.

**Valentino, Rudolph,** 1895–1926, American film actor; b. Italy. He became one of the screen's first sex symbols in such silent films as *The Sheik* (1921) and *Blood and Sand* (1922).

**Valera, Eamon de:** see DE VALERA, EAMON.

**Valerius Flaccus, Gaius,** d. AD c.92, Latin EPIC poet. His *Argonautica*, in eight books and unfinished, shows the influence of APOLLONIUS RHODIUS and VIRGIL, and has some genuine poetic merit.

**Valéry, Paul** (valay ree), 1871–1945, French poet and critic. A follower of the SYMBOLISTS, he was one of the greatest French poets of the 20th cent. His masterpiece, *La jeune Parque* (1917; The Young Fate), long and somewhat obscure, and *Le cimetièce marin* (1920; tr. Graveyard by the Sea) offer the best examples of Valéry's poetics. His prose works include five collections of essays, all called *Variété* (1924–44), and four dialogues on subjects ranging from the arts to mathematics. He received many honours.

**Valkyries** (val keereez), in Germanic myth, Odin's warrior maidens. They presided over battles, chose those who were to die, and bore heroes' souls to Valhalla, hall of heroes in ASGARD. Chief among them was BRUNHILD. They are prominent in Richard WAGNER's *Die Walküre* (1854–56).

**Valla, Lorenzo,** c.1407–1457, Italian humanist. In 1430 he published *On Pleasure,* an enquiry into the true good for man, and a humanistic condemnation of SCHOLASTICISM. His treatise *De elegantia linguae latinae* (1435–44; tr. On the Elegance of the Latin Language), set out to re-establish classical usage after centuries of corruption and was long used as a textbook.

**Valladolid** ('vie·ɔdo leeth), city (1981 pop. 330,242), capital of Valladolid prov., N central Spain. Occupying a central position in Old CASTILE, it is a major route node. It serves as a market centre for a grain-growing region and has important milling and food industries. Other industries include vehicle-building and aluminium-smelting. It grew as a royal residence from the 14th cent. and was, very briefly, the Spanish capital (1600–06). The university was founded in 1346. Notable buildings include the cathedral and royal palace, the Colegio de San José and the Colegio de San Gregorio.

**Valle-Inclán, Ramón del** ( valvay een klahn), 1866–1936, Spanish writer. His most notorious works, the erotic tales in *Femeninas* (1895) and the semiautobiographical *Sonata* novels (1902–05; tr. *The Pleasant Memoirs of the Marquis de Bradomín*), show the influence of MODERNISMO, while such poetic works as *The Aroma of Legends* (1907) express a symbolist aesthetic. His originality is most marked in his *esperpentos,* grotesque caricatures of Spanish life, particularly of aristocratic and military brutality, reminiscent of the nightmare etchings of GOYA; they include the play *Luces de Bohemia* (1920; tr. Bohemian Lights) and the novel *Tirano Banderas* (1926; tr. The Tyrant Banderas)

**Vallejo, César** (vah yayhoh), 1895–1938, Peruvian poet. Of Indian and European ancestry, he dedicated himself to social justice. After 1923 he lived in Europe, where he became a Marxist and supported the Republicans in the SPANISH CIVIL WAR. His poetry includes *Los heraldos negros* (1918; tr. Black Heralds), *Trilce* (1922), *Poema humanos* (1939), and *España, aparta de mi este cáliz* (1940; tr. Spain, Let This Cup Pass from Me).

**Valley Forge,** on the Schuylkill R., NE Pennsylvania. During the AMERICAN REVOLUTION it was the encampment of the Continental Army (see CONTINENTAL CONGRESS), Dec. 1777–June 1778. The winter was severe and the suffering troops talked of mutiny, but they were held together by loyalty to Gen. WASHINGTON and the patriotic cause.

**Valois** (val wah), royal house of France that ruled from 1328 to 1589. It succeeded the CAPETIANS when PHILIP VI, son of Charles of Valois and grandson of PHILIP III, became king. The direct Valois line ended (1498) with CHARLES VIII; the dynasty was continued by LOUIS XII (Valois-Orléans) and by FRANCIS I (Valois-Angoulême). At the death of HENRY III (1589), HENRY IV of the house of BOURBON succeeded to the throne.

**Valois, Dame Ninette de** ( valwah), 1898–, Irish ballet dancer and choreographer; b. Edri Stannus. She danced in DIAGHILEV's Ballets Russes in the 1920s, and was choreographic director of the Abbey (Dublin) and Old Vic (London) theatres. In 1931 she founded the Sadlers Wells ballet school, later becoming director of the Sadlers Wells Ballet (now Royal Ballet).

**Valparaiso,** city (1984 pop. 266,876), central Chile, capital of Valparaiso dept., on a bay of the Pacific Ocean. Chile's chief port, it is a major industrial centre and the terminus of a trans-Andean railway. Its setting is a natural amphitheatre. The business district, crowded onto a narrow waterfront terrace, is connected by cable railways to residential areas on the surrounding slopes. Founded in 1536, Valparaiso grew rapidly in the late 19th cent.

**value-added tax,** levy imposed on business at all levels of production of a good or service, and based on the increase in price, or value, provided by each level. Because all stages of a value-added tax are ultimately passed on to the consumer in the form of higher prices, it has been described as a hidden sales tax. Originally introduced in France in 1954, and in the UK in 1973, it has been widely adopted throughout Europe. All countries of the COMMON MARKET have introduced a form of VAT and it is planned to make the rates uniform eventually. See also CUSTOMS AND EXCISE; TAXATION.

**vampire,** in folklore, animated corpse that sucks the blood of humans, usually enslaving its victims and making them vampires. Vampires could be warded off with charms and killed by a stake driven through the heart. Literature's most famous vampire is Count Dracula, in Bram STOKER's *Dracula* (1897).

**vanadium** (V), metallic element, discovered in 1801 by A.M. del Rio. It is a soft, silver-grey metal that adds strength, toughness, and heat-resistance to STEEL alloys. Vanadium compounds, especially the pentoxide, are used in ceramics, glass, and dyes and are important as catalysts in the chemical industry. See ELEMENT (table); PERIODIC TABLE.

**Van Allen radiation belts,** two belts of RADIATION outside the Earth's atmosphere, extending from c.650 to c.65,000 km (c.400 to c.40,000 mi). The region of the belts is called the magnetosphere. The high-energy protons and electrons, of which the belts are composed, circulate along the Earth's magnetic lines of force. These particles are probably emitted by the Sun in its periodic solar flares and, after travelling across space, are captured by the Earth's magnetic field. They are responsible for the AURORA seen about both polar regions, where the belts dip into the upper regions of the atmosphere. The belts were discovered by detectors (developed by American physicist James Van Allen and colleagues) aboard *Explorer 1,* the first US artificial satellite.

**Vanbrugh, Sir John,** 1664–1726, English dramatist and architect. His best-known plays, *The Relapse* (1696) and *The Provoked Wife* (1697), are imbued with Restoration wit and cynicism. As his repute as an architect grew, he turned away from the stage, becoming WREN's principal colleague. He is especially noted for Blenheim Palace (the culmination of English BAROQUE) and Castle Howard.

**Van Buren, Martin,** 1782–1862, 8th president of the US (1837–41). A lawyer, he became active in New York State Democratic politics and one of the leaders of the ALBANY REGENCY. He served (1821–28) in the US Senate. Elected governor of NEW YORK in 1828, he became one of Andrew Jackson's supporters and resigned (1829) to become Jackson's secretary of state (1829–31). He was elected vice president in the 1832 election and largely through Jackson's influence, he was the Democratic candidate for president in 1836 and was swept into office. To meet the economic crisis that followed the Panic of 1837, he proposed (1837) the Independent Treasury System, a statesmanlike measure which nonetheless alienated many conservative Democrats. The persistence of hard times made him very unpopular and he was defeated for reelection in 1840 by William Henry HARRISON, the WHIG PARTY candidate. He continued to be a power in Democratic politics, but in 1848 he ran for president as the candidate of the FREE-SOIL PARTY and polled enough votes to give the election to Zachary TAYLOR.

**Vancouver,** city (1980 est. pop. 410,188; 1981 metropolitan area 1,268,183), SW British Columbia, W Canada, on Burrard Inlet of the Strait of Georgia. The city, known for its mild climate and spectacular backdrop of mountains (part of the COAST RANGE), is Canada's largest western city, its principal Pacific port, and the chief western terminus of the trans-Canadian railways, highways, and airways. Oil refining, fish processing, and the manufacture of textiles dominate a diversified industrial economy. Originally called Granville, it was settled before 1875 and renamed after Capt. George VANCOUVER in 1886.

**Vancouver, George,** 1757–98, English navigator and explorer. He commanded an expedition (1791–94) to take over the Nootka Sound, assigned to England by the Nootka Convention, and thoroughly explored the NW coast of America. He also circumnavigated the island now called VANCOUVER ISLAND.

**Vancouver Island,** (1981 pop. 495,125), 32,137 km² (12,408 sq mi), SW British Columbia, Canada, separated from the mainland by Juan de Fuca, Georgia, and Queen Charlotte Straits. It is c.460 km (285 mi) long and c.50–130 km (30–80 mi) wide, and reaches a high point of 2200 m (7219 ft) at Golden Hinde Mt. Victoria is the largest city. The island was first sighted (1774) by Juan Pérez, explored (1778) by Capt. James COOK, and circumnavigated (1792) by Capt. George VANCOUVER. It was a separate colony (1849–66) before becoming part of British Columbia.

**Vandals,** Germanic group which, during much of the 5th cent., dominated the W Mediterranean from their base in N Africa. In AD 429, after battling with the Visigoths for control of Iberia, the Vandals under King Gaiseric migrated to N Africa where they established a powerful empire which is credited by some with bringing an effective end to the western half of the Roman empire. In 533 the Vandal state was conquered by the eastern Roman, Byzantine, state of JUSTINIAN.

**van der Goes, Hugo:** see GOES, HUGO VAN DER.

**Van der Post, Sir Laurens Jan,** 1906–, white South African novelist, explorer, and mystic. After early association with William PLOMER and Roy CAMPBELL, and later travels in the Far East, he served as an officer in the British Army in World War II. More recently he has been an advisor to both the Prince of Wales and Margaret THATCHER. A prolific but indifferent writer of fiction, e.g., *In a Province* (1934), he is mildly critical of white racism, but still portrays black people paternalistically. He is best known for the travel writing which comes out of his political missions, e.g., *Venture to the Interior* (1952), *The Lost World of the Kalahari* (1953), and *Journey into Russia* (1964). The three linked tales, *The Seed and the Sower* (1963) came out of his experiences as a prisoner-of-war in the Far East, while *Jung and the Story of Our Time* (1975) perhaps best characterizes the confused nature of his outlook.

**van der Waals, Johannes Diderik** ('van də ˌvahls), 1837–1923, Dutch physicist. His theory of corresponding states (1880) contained an equation of state (now named after him) for homogeneous substances in terms of pressure, volume, and temperature (see GAS LAWS); unlike the ideal gas law, his equation contains constants (different for each real substance) to account for the fact that molecules are of finite size and experience weak forces of mutual attraction (van der Waals forces). For this work and for the discovery of the law of binary mixtures he received the 1910 Nobel Prize for physics.

**van der Weyden, Roger:** see WEYDEN, ROGER VAN DER.

**Van Diemen's Land:** see TASMANIA.

**Van Dyck** or **Vandyke, Sir Anthony,** 1599–1641, Flemish portrait and religious painter and etcher. Born in Antwerp, Belgium, he was the assistant and collaborator of RUBENS. In 1620 he travelled to England and then to Italy, where he painted a series of portraits of the Genoese nobility. An outstanding example is the portrait of Marchesa Elena Grimaldi (National Gall., Washington, DC). When he returned to Antwerp in 1627, where he rivalled Rubens in popularity, he painted a famous series of religious pictures. In his portraits, Van Dyck conferred upon his sitters elegance, dignity, and refinement, qualities pleasing to royalty and aristocracy. In 1632 he was invited to England by CHARLES I, and his portraits of Charles are in the Louvre and Buckingham Palace. He became court painter and was overwhelmed with commissions. Although similar in technique to that of Rubens, his work has more restrained colour and refined form. The patrician image of English aristocrats that he created greatly influenced the direction of English portraiture. Examples of his portraits include those of Lord John and Lord Bernard Stuart (1636–40; National Gallery, London) and three children of Charles I (1635; Windsor Castle).

**Vane, Sir Henry,** 1613–62, English statesman. A Puritan, he emigrated to America in 1635 and was elected (1636) governor of Massachusetts. His support of Anne HUTCHINSON cost him reelection in 1637, and he returned to England. He sat in the Short and Long Parliaments and secured (1643) the Solemn League and Covenant with Scotland. He was influential under Oliver CROMWELL until the two quarrelled in 1653. After the RESTORATION, Vane was executed for treason.

**van Eyck** (van iek): see EYCK, HUBERT VAN.

Sir Anthony **Van Dyck**, *Lord John and Lord Bernard Stuart.* National Gallery, London.

**Van Gennep, Arnold,** 1873–1957, French anthropologist of Dutch parentage. Van Gennep was a prolific writer but is remembered above all for his book *Rites of Passage* (1909; tr. 1960), one of the most influential of anthropological texts. See RITES DE PASSAGE.

**Van Gogh, Vincent** (van ˌgokh), 1853–90, Dutch Postimpressionist painter. His works are perhaps better known generally than those of any other painter. The great majority were produced in 29 months of frenzied activity interspersed with epileptoid seizures and despair that finally ended in suicide. His early work, the Dutch period (1880–85), consists of dark, greenish-brown, heavily painted studies of peasants and miners, e.g., *The Potato Eaters* (1885; National Museum Vincent Van Gogh, Amsterdam). After moving from the Netherlands to Paris, he met PISSARRO, who encouraged him to adopt a colourful palette, e.g., *Père Tanguy* (1887; Niarchos Coll., Paris). His work from his last months at Arles and Auvers-sur-Oise is characterized by the heavy impasto and rhythmic linear style so identified with him; it includes the incomparable series of sunflowers (1888). His last works include the swirling, climactic *Starry Night* (Mus. Mod. Art, New York City) and the ominously distressed *Wheatfield with Crows* (National Museum Vincent Van Gogh, Amsterdam).

**vanilla,** vine (genus *Vanilla*) of the ORCHID family, native to hot damp climates of Central America but now cultivated in other tropical regions. The fruits yield vanilla, a popular flavouring usually marketed as an alcoholic extract. The commercial plant is usually *V. fragrans;* the source of the flavour is an aromatic essence, vanillin. Vanilla flavouring, now

Van Gogh, *Self Portrait with Bandaged Ear*, 1889. Oil on canvas, 61 × 51 cm. Musée d'Orsay, Paris.

usually artificially synthesized, is also obtained from the tonka bean, which contains coumarin, a substance with a vanillalike aroma.

**Vannucci, Pietro:** see PERUGINO.

**Van Ostade, Adriaen:** see OSTADE, ADRIAEN VAN.

**Van Riebeeck, Jan,** 1618–77, first Dutch commander of the Cape of Good Hope and founder of a permanent European settlement in South Africa. He landed at Table Bay in 1652 and established a station to supply the ships of the Dutch East India Company. He became governor of Dutch Malacca in 1622.

**Vantongerloo, Georges,** 1886–1965, Belgian sculptor and painter. During World War I he became a member of the de STIJL group. He settled in Paris in 1927, and was a pioneer of mathematical abstraction. Abandoning the restrictions of MONDRIAN's neo-plasticism after c.1930, he used mathematically defined curves and spirals.

**Vanuatu,** officially the Republic of Vanuatu, independent republic (1987 est. pop. 134,000), 14,426 km² (5570 sq mi), comprising a 724-km (450-mi) chain of islands in the South Pacific Ocean E of Australia, formerly called the New Hebrides. Espiritu Santo and Efâte, site of Vila (the capital), are the two largest islands. The population is predominantly Melanesian, and a form of Pidgin English has become the national language. Manganese, copra, beef, and frozen fish are produced for export. Additional revenues are derived from a growing tourist industry and the development of Vila as a corporate tax haven. The islands were discovered in 1606 by the Portuguese and were systematically explored in 1774 by Capt. James COOK. In 1887 they were placed under an Anglo-French naval commission, which was replaced (1906) by a condominium. In 1980 they became independent as Vanuatu, and a secession movement on Espiritu Santo was put down with aid from Papua New Guinea. A member of the COMMONWEALTH, Vanuatu has a government consisting of a president, a prime minister and council, and a unicameral parliament. The dominant political formation since independence has been the Party of Our Land.

**Van Zeeland, Paul** (ˌzəylant), 1893–1973, Belgian economist and statesman. As premier (1936–37) he suppressed the fascist Rexists and abandoned an alliance with France in favour of neutrality. He became

head (1939) of a London-based committee on refugees and high commissioner (1944) for repatriation of displaced Belgians. Later he was foreign minister in several cabinets and financial adviser to the Belgian government.

**vaporization,** change of state from a liquid or solid to a vapour. See BOILING POINT; STATES OF MATTER.

**Varanasi,** formerly Benares, city (1981 pop. 720,755), Uttar Pradesh state, N central India, on the Ganges (Ganga) R. The holiest Hindu city, it has c.1500 temples, palaces, and shrines. Steps lead to the sacred GANGES, where Hindus bathe. About 1 million pilgrims visit the city annually. BUDDHA is said to have begun preaching nearby. The mosque of AURANGZEB, on the city's highest ground, is the most notable building of India's MOGUL period. The city is also known for its silk brocades and brassware.

**Varèse, Edgard** (vaˌrez), 1885–1965, French-American composer. A bold innovator, he achieved dissonant effects by using extreme registers of orchestral instruments combined with ELECTRONIC MUSIC. His works include *Hyperprism* (1923), *Intégrales* (1924–25), *Ionisation* (1930–33), and *Poème Electronique* (1958).

**Vargas, Getúlio Dornelles** (ˌvahgas), 1883–1954, president of BRAZIL (1930–45, 1951–54). He led a revolt and established a dictatorship (1930), and introduced (1937) a corporate state. Ousted (1945) by an army coup, he was again elected president (1950); he resigned (1954) under army pressure and committed suicide.

**Vargas Llosa, Mario** (ˌvahgas ˌyohsah), 1936–, Peruvian novelist. Technically innovative, his novels are penetrating studies of Peruvian life. They include *La ciudad y los perros* [the city and the dogs] (1962; tr. *The Time of the Hero*), *La casa verde* (1966; tr. The Green House), *Conversación en 'La Catedral'* (1969), *La Tía Julia y el escribidor* (1977; tr. Aunt Julia and the Scriptwriter), *La guerra del fin del mundo* (1981; tr. The War of the End of the World), and *Historia de Mayta* (1984).

**variable star,** star that varies, either periodically or irregularly, in the intensity of its light. Variable stars are grouped into three broad classes: the pulsating variables, the eruptive variables, and the eclipsing variables. In **pulsating variables,** which account for more than half of the known variable stars, slight instabilities cause the star alternatively to expand and to contract, resulting in changes in absolute luminosity and temperature. The pulsating variables can be subdivided into short-term, long-term, semi-regular, and irregular variables. *Short-term variables* have periods ranging from less than one day to more than 50 days; among them are the important but rare CEPHEID VARIABLES. Commoner short-term variables are the RR Lyrae stars; about 2500 of this type are known in our galaxy. They have periods of less than one day, and all have roughly the same intrinsic brightness, which makes them another useful distance indicator. The *long-term variables* are the most numerous of the pulsating stars. They are red giant and supergiant stars with periods ranging from 80 to 300 days. *Semi-regular variables* are stars whose periodic variations are occasionally interrupted by sudden bursts of light. *Irregular variables* show no periodicity in their variations in brightness. The **eruptive variables** are highly unstable stars that suddenly and unpredictably increase in brightness. *T Tauri stars* are the least violent of these explosive stars. *Novas* are small, very hot stars that suddenly increase thousands of times in luminosity; their decline in luminosity is much slower, taking months or years. SUPERNOVAS, upon exploding, increase millions of times in brightness and are totally destroyed. **Eclipsing variables** are not true (intrinsic) variables but rather are BINARY STAR systems in which during the orbital motion one star gets between the other star and the direction to the Earth.

**variance,** a measure of variability used in STATISTICS. It is calculated as the average squared deviation of each individual value from the ARITHMETIC MEAN and the ANALYSIS OF VARIANCE plays a key role in many forms of statistical analysis. The STANDARD DEVIATION is the square root of the variance.

**varicella** (variˌsela): see CHICKEN POX.

**varicose vein,** blood vessel in the skin that is abnormally twisted, lengthened, or dilated, seen most often on the legs and thighs and usually attributed to inefficient valves within the vein and genetic factors. Other sites include the rectum (HAEMORRHOIDS) and scrotum (varicocele). Conditions such as pregnancy or obesity, or increased pressure from prolonged standing, reduce the support of tissues surrounding the veins, causing them to dilate. Varicose veins can be unsightly and cause aching of the legs. Treatment includes use of support hosiery and, if necessary, sclerotherapy (injection to obliterate the veins) or surgical removal.

**variola:** see SMALLPOX.

**Varna,** city (1983 pop. 295,218), E Bulgaria, on the Black Sea. A major port, it has shipyards, produces cotton textiles and other manufactures, and is a summer resort. Founded by the Greeks (580 BC), it was held (1st–14th cent.) by Rome, Byzantium, and the second Bulgarian kingdom. After 1391 it was ruled by the Turks. It was ceded to independent Bulgaria in 1878.

**varnish,** solution of gum or of natural or synthetic RESIN that dries to a thin, hard, usually glossy film; it may be transparent, translucent, or tinted. Oil varnishes are made from hard gum or resin dissolved in oil. Spirit varnishes, e.g., SHELLAC, are usually made of soft gums or resins dissolved in a volatile solvent. Enamel is varnish with added PIGMENT. Lacquer may be either a synthetic or natural varnish. As a decorative or protective coating, varnish has been used for oil paintings, for string instruments, and, by the ancient Egyptians, for mummy cases.

**Varro, Marcus Terentius,** 116 BC–27 BC, Roman writer. A legate and soldier, he was also known as one of the most erudite men of his day. He wrote an estimated 620 volumes in almost every field of knowledge. The only work to survive intact is *De re rustica libri III* [three books on farming], an important source for VIRGIL's *Georgics.*

**varve,** in geology, pair of thin sedimentary layers formed annually by seasonal climatic changes. Usually found in glacial lake deposits, varves consist of a coarse-grained, light-coloured summer layer and a finer-grained, dark-coloured winter layer. Varves, and the pollen they contain, are useful for interpreting recent climatic history. See also DATING.

**Vasa** (,vahzə), Pol. *Waza,* royal dynasty of Sweden (1523–1654) and Poland (1587–1668). GUSTAVUS I founded the dynasty in Sweden. His grandson, the Catholic SIGISMUND III of Poland, lost the Swedish throne (1599) to his uncle CHARLES IX, and thereafter the Protestant and Catholic lines warred with each other. CHRISTINA, daughter of GUSTAVUS II, was the last of the Swedish Vasa line. Sigismund's son LADISLAUS IV was succeeded by his brother JOHN II, the last of the Polish line.

**Vasarely, Victor,** 1908–, Hungarian–French painter. Taught in Budapest by MOHOLY-NAGY, he was introduced to the ideas of CONSTRUCTIVISM. It was not until c.1947 that he developed his method of geometrical abstraction that exploited visual ambiguities of perception. He was one of the main originators and practitioners of OP ART.

**Vasari, Giorgio,** 1511–74, Italian architect, writer, and painter. He is best known for his entertaining biographies of artists, *Lives of the Artists* (1550), the basic source of knowledge of Renaissance and mannerist artists. He painted portraits of the Medici and designed the UFFIZI as well as churches and palaces in Arezzo and in Pisa.

**Vasco da Gama:** see GAMA, VASCO DA.

**vascular tissue,** strands of elongated cells specially modified for the conduction of water (xylem) and food (phloem). This system is found in FERNS and the flowering plants. The tissue often contains FIBRES of economic importance.

**vasectomy,** minor surgical procedure for sterilization of the male, involving interruption of the vas deferens, the thin duct that carries sperm cells from the testicles (see REPRODUCTIVE SYSTEM). It is performed as a permanent method of CONTRACEPTION.

**vassal:** see FEUDALISM.

**Västerås,** city (1984 pop. 117,658), E central Sweden, on the northern shore of Lake Mälaren. The country's principal centre of heavy engineering, it manufactures generators for power stations, cables, and other forms of transmission equipment.

**Vatican City,** independent state, (1981 est. pop. 1000), 44 hectares/108.7 acres, in Rome, Italy. It is the seat of the central government of the ROMAN CATHOLIC CHURCH and the pope is its absolute ruler. It includes the papal palace, SAINT PETER'S CHURCH, the SISTINE CHAPEL, many museums housing some of the world's finest art treasures, the Vatican Library, the Vatican Gardens, and Belvedere Park. The state, which issues its own currency and postage stamps, has its own citizenship, flag, diplomatic corps, newspaper (*L'Osservatore Romano*), railway station, and broadcasting facility. The SWISS GUARD is the pope's personal bodyguard. Vatican City has been the residence of the pope since the late 14th cent., when the papal court was restored from AVIGNON, France, to Rome. The sovereignty of Vatican City was officially established in 1929 by the LATERAN TREATY between the PAPACY and the Italian government.

**Vatican Councils,** two ecumenical councils of the Roman Catholic Church. The first council (1869–70) was convened by Pope PIUS IX and enunciated the dogma of papal infallibility. It ended when Italian troops seized Rome for the new kingdom of Italy. The second council (1962–65), popularly called Vatican II, was convened by Pope JOHN XXIII and continued by PAUL VI. It sought to renew the church spiritually and to reconsider its place in the modern world. The council made wide-ranging changes in the liturgy (including vernacularization), moved toward greater lay participation, and encouraged the ECUMENICAL MOVEMENT.

**vaudeville,** stage entertainment consisting of unrelated songs, dances, acrobatic and magic acts, and humorous skits and sketches. From its humble beginnings in barrooms, vaudeville in the 1880s became the attraction in hundreds of theatres in the US. The rise of radio and cinema brought its decline, but the vaudeville revue was revived on television. Such entertainers as Harry HOUDINI, Eddie CANTOR, and W.C. FIELDS began their careers in vaudeville.

**Vaudreuil-Cavagnal, Pierre de Rigaud, marquis de** (voh,drøyə-kahvahn,yahl), 1698–1765, last French governor of New France (1755–60). Although devoted to the interests of native-born Canadians, he failed to check government corruption and hampered Gen. MONTCALM's conduct of military operations, thus contributing to France's loss (1760) of Canada to the British.

**Vaughan, Henry,** 1622–95, Welsh METAPHYSICAL POET. He signed himself Silurist after the ancient inhabitants of Wales. His greatest poems, in *Silex Scintillans* (1650, 1655), focus on mystical communion with God through nature and include 'Ascension Hymn', 'The World', and 'The Retreat'.

**Vaughan Williams, Ralph,** 1872–1958, English composer and a leading figure in the renaissance of English music which began in the final years of the 19th cent. He is noted for his use of English FOLK SONG, as in *Norfolk Rhapsodies* (1905–7) and arrangements of 'Greensleeves'. Among his compositions are nine symphonies, e.g., *A London Symphony* (1914, rev. 1920); the *Fantasia on a Theme by Thomas Tallis* (1910); operas; choral music; CONCERTOS; and songs, e.g., *Five Mystical Songs* (1911).

**vault,** curved ceiling over a room. It is generally composed of separate units of a material such as bricks, tiles, or blocks, so shaped that when assembled their weight can be concentrated on the proper supports. (Vaults may also be formed of homogeneous material, e.g., concrete.) The separate units exert not only the downward pressure of their weight, but also side thrusts that must be met with resistance in the form of a thickened wall or of a BUTTRESS, as in Romanesque and Gothic architecture. Vaults may also be designed so that their thrusts oppose or counteract. The Egyptians used brick vaulting for drains. The Chaldeans and Assyrians appear to have made use of high domes and barrel vaults. The Greeks used no vaults. Etruscan technique was absorbed by the Romans, who, using concrete (see ROMAN ARCHITECTURE), developed a more advanced system. Roman vaults were perfectly rigid, devoid of external thrust, and required no buttresses. Thus they could be placed over vast spaces. Medieval systems developed from Roman vaulting. The tunnel, or barrel vault, spans two walls like a continuous arch. The cross, or groined vault, at the intersection of two barrel vaults, forms four arched openings. Ribs to strengthen the groins and sides of a vault appeared in the 11th cent., and became gradually the organic supporting skeleton of Gothic architecture. The pointed ARCH was used in vaulting oblong compartments. In England these developments culminated in the 15th cent. in the Perpendicular style. Renaissance architects returned to the basic Roman forms. Modern vaulting is largely accomplished with reinforced concrete. See also GOTHIC ARCHITECTURE AND ART.

**Vavilov, Nikolai Ivanovich,** 1887–1943?, Russian botanist and geneticist. Trying to trace the origins of various crops by locating areas with the greatest number and diversity of their species, he reported (1936) Ethiopia and Afghanistan as the birthplaces of agriculture and hence of civilization. He divided cultivated plants into those domesticated from wild forms, e.g., oats and rye, and those known only in cultivation, e.g., wheat. He reportedly died in a Soviet concentration camp after losing favour to Trofim LYSENKO, whose theories he opposed.

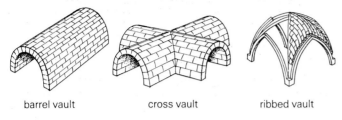

barrel vault      cross vault      ribbed vault

Vault

**Vazov, Ivan** (ˌvahzof), 1850–1921, Bulgarian writer. His work, inspired by Bulgarian political events, includes the nationalistic novel *Under the Yoke* (1893), the play *Vagabonds* (1894), and such poetry as *Songs of Macedonia* (1914).

**Vecellio:** see TITIAN.

**vector**, quantity having both magnitude and direction. Many physical quantities are vectors, e.g., force, velocity, and momentum. The simplest representation of a vector is an arrow connecting two points: $\vec{AB}$ designates the vector represented by an arrow from point $A$ to point $B$, whereas $\vec{BA}$ designates the vector of equal magnitude from $B$ to $A$. In order to compare vectors and to perform mathematical operations on them, it is necessary to have some reference system that determines scale and direction, such as CARTESIAN COORDINATES. A vector is frequently symbolized by its components with respect to the coordinate axes. Suppose, for example, that the point $A$ has coordinates (2,3) and the point $B$ has coordinates (5,7). The $x$-component of $\vec{AB}$, i.e., its size with respect to the $x$-axis, is the difference between the $x$-coordinates of the points $A$ and $B$, or $5 - 2 = 3$; the $y$-component is $7 - 3 = 4$. Thus $\vec{AB}$ becomes [3,4]. Knowledge of the components of a vector enables one to compute its magnitude (in this case, 5) by the Pythagorean theorem $[(3^2 + 4^2)^{1/2} = 5]$, and its direction (from TRIGONOMETRY). There are an infinite number of vectors with the components [3,4], all of which have the same magnitude and direction; they are considered equal. The concept of a vector can be extended to three or more dimensions. To add two vectors $\mathbf{U}$ and $\mathbf{V}$, one can add their corresponding components to find the resultant vector $\mathbf{R}$, or one can plot $\mathbf{U}$ and $\mathbf{V}$ on a set of coordinate axes and complete the parallelogram formed with $\mathbf{U}$ and $\mathbf{V}$ as adjacent sides to obtain $\mathbf{R}$ as the diagonal from the common vertex of $\mathbf{U}$ and $\mathbf{V}$. The scalar, or dot, product of two vectors $\mathbf{A}$ and $\mathbf{B}$, $\mathbf{A.B}$, is a nondirectional (scalar) quantity with a magnitude of $|\mathbf{A}|\,|\mathbf{B}|\cos\theta$, where $\theta$ is the angle between $\mathbf{A}$ and $\mathbf{B}$. The vector, or cross, product of $\mathbf{A}$ and $\mathbf{B}$, $\mathbf{A} \times \mathbf{B}$, is a vector whose magnitude is $|\mathbf{A}|\,|\mathbf{B}|\sin\theta$ and whose direction is perpendicular to both $\mathbf{A}$ and $\mathbf{B}$ and pointing in the direction in which a right-handed screw would advance if turned from $\mathbf{A}$ to $\mathbf{B}$ through the angle $\theta$. A *vector space* is a collection of vectors satisfying the laws of vector addition and scalar multiplication.

**Veda** [Skt., = knowledge], oldest scriptures of HINDUISM and the most ancient religious texts in an Indo-European language, still accepted to some extent by all Hindus as the authoritative statement of the essential truths of Hinduism. It is the literature of the Aryans who invaded NW India c.1500 BC. Influenced by indigenous religious ideas, it was compiled from c.1000 to c.500 BC. The Veda consists of four types of literature. The *Saṃhitā*, the basic compilation of prayers and hymns, ascribed to inspired seer–poets, includes a threefold canonical body of hymns—the *Ṛg-Veda, Sāma-Veda,* and *Yajur-Veda*—and the *Atharva-Veda,* a collection of magic spells. The BRĀHMANA are prose explanations of the sacrifice. The *Āraṇyakas* contain instructions for meditation as the mental performance of sacrifice. The UPANIṢADS are works of mysticism and speculation. The later part of Vedic writings expressed the idea of a single underlying reality embodied in Brahman, the absolute Self. The Vedic sacrifice, with its invocation of Vedic gods through MANTRAS or hymns, became increasingly elaborate with the passage of time, and the sacrifice came to be regarded as the fundamental agency of creation. Besides the usual prayer, etc., there are several cosmological and cosmogonical hymns. Even *Atharva-Veda* has some philosophical hymns.

**Vedānta** [Skt., = the end of the Veda], one of the six classical systems of INDIAN PHILOSOPHY. The term refers to the teaching of the UPANIṢADS (the last section of the VEDA) and also to the knowledge of its ultimate meaning. By extension the term refers to schools based on the Brahma Sūtras of Bādarāyana (early centuries AD), which summarize Upaniṣadic doctrine. Most important is the nondualist (*advaita*) Vedānta of Śaṅkara (AD 788–820), who taught that spiritual liberation is achieved not by ritual action but by eradication of ignorance, e.g., the belief that the illusory multiplicity of the world is real, and by attainment of the knowledge of BRAHMAN, the absolute Self. The qualified nondualist Rāmānuja (1017–1137) advocated devotion as the means of salvation, and held that the world and souls are real but depend on God. The dualist Vedānta of Madhva (1197–1276) asserted the permanently separate reality of the world, souls, and God. Vedānta is still a living tradition, with profound influence on the intellectual and religious life of India. Prominent modern Vedantists include Swami Vivekananda, Aurobindo GHOSE, and Sarvepalli Radhakrishnan.

**vegetable,** popular name for many food plants and for their edible parts. No clear distinction exists between a vegetable and a FRUIT. Vegetables are valuable sources of vitamins, minerals, starches, and proteins.

**vegetarianism,** theory and practice of eating only fruits, vegetables, cereal grains, nuts, and seeds, and excluding meat, fish, or fowl. Vegans also exclude eggs and dairy products. The basis of the practise may be religious, ethical, economic, nutritional, or sentimental, and its followers differ in strictness of observance. Practised since ancient times by religious groups, vegetarianism as a separate movement developed in the mid-19th cent., particularly in the UK and the US.

**Vehmgericht, Vehme** or **vehmic court** (ˌfaymgərikht), extra-legal criminal courts in medieval Germany. First established to curb lawlessness in an era of weak governments, the courts performed a useful function, but they finally became a menace because of their secrecy and terrorism. They largely disappeared in the 16th cent. as central governments grew stronger. They are also spelt Fehmgericht or Femgericht.

**Veil, Simone,** 1927–, French centrist political figure. A lawyer, she served (1974–79) as minister of health under GISCARD D'ESTAING, sponsoring (1974) a controversial abortion law. In 1979–81 she was president of the first popularly elected parliament of the EUROPEAN COMMUNITY.

**Velasco, Luís de,** d. 1564, Spanish viceroy (1550–64) of New Spain, now MEXICO. A humanitarian ruler, he helped the Indians and fostered exploration. The Univ. of Mexico was founded during his administration. His son, **Luís de Velasco,** 1534–1617, was also viceroy of New Spain (1590–95, 1607–11) and of Peru (1595–1604).

**Velasco Alvarado, Juan** (vayˌlaskoh ahlvahˌrahdhoh), 1910–, president of PERU (1968–75). As army commander in chief, he led the junta that deposed (1968) Pres. Belaúnde Terry. He expropriated US-owned oil companies, instigated land reform, and nationalized large industries. He was deposed (1975) in a bloodless coup.

**Velasco Ibarra, José María** (vayˌlaskoh eeˌbahrah), 1893–, president of ECUADOR. He served five times as president between 1934 and 1972, but was deposed by the military four times. In his last term (1968–72), he established a dictatorship to cope with political chaos and terrorism.

**Velázquez, Diego de** (vayˌlathkayth), 1460–1524?, Spanish CONQUISTADOR, first governor of CUBA. He sailed on Christopher Columbus's second voyage to Hispaniola (1493) and was sent to conquer Cuba by Diego Columbus in 1511. By 1514, with the aid of Pánfilo de NARVÁEZ, the conquest was complete. Velázquez disassociated himself from Diego Columbus and declared himself governor of Cuba. In 1519 he sent Hernán CORTÉS to conquer MEXICO. Distrusting him, Velázquez sent Narváez to compel Cortés's return to Cuba, but was defeated.

**Velázquez, Diego Rodríguez de Silva y,** 1599–1660, the most celebrated painter of the Spanish school. Born in Seville, he was apprenticed at 11 to Francisco de HERRERA and then to Francisco Pacheco. His earliest paintings, e.g., *Christ and the Pilgrims of Emmaus* (Metropolitan Mus., New York), show a strong naturalistic tendency. He was introduced to the court, and his equestrian portrait of PHILIP IV won him recognition. At 25 he was made court painter. During his first years there he painted the celebrated *Borrachos* [the drunkards] (Prado, Madrid). During a trip to Italy (1629–31) Velázquez painted two large figure compositions, *The Forge of Vulcan* (Prado, Madrid) and *Joseph's Coat* (Escorial). To his second period (1631–49) belong *Christ on the Cross,* the series of dwarfs and buffoons of the court, and the *Menippus* (all: Prado, Madrid). His only surviving nude, *Venus and Cupid,* also called the *Rokeby Venus* (1650; National Gall., London), emphasizes the vanity of the goddess. To his last period (1651–60) belong the *Coronation of the Virgin,* the famous full-length portraits of Mariana of Austria and the Infanta Margarita, and *The Maids of Honor* (all: Prado, Madrid). Velázquez's development as an artist was extraordinarily steady. His first forms were monumental, and enveloped in strong chiaroscuro (high-contrast effects). He slowly evolved a subtle, intellectual art based on exquisite colour values, with a consummate use of silver tones reminiscent of EL GRECO. However, in his worldliness and compassion he is far removed from El Greco. His paintings of every subject, from dwarf to king, suggest their dignity and individual worth.

Diego **Velazquez**, *Las Meninas*, 1656. Oil on canvas, 318 × 276 cm. Museo del Prado, Madrid.

**veld** or **veldt,** grassy, undulating PLATEAUS of South Africa and Zimbabwe, ranging in elevation from c.150 to c.1830 m (500 to 6000 ft). Abundant crops of potatoes and maize are grown, and large cattle herds are grazed; the area also has industrial and mining centres.

**velocity:** see MOTION.

**Venda,** black African homeland or BANTUSTAN (1980 est. pop. 513,890), 7410 km² (2861 sq mi), proclaimed independent (1979) by the Republic of South Africa, but not recognized internationally. It comprises two connected areas in NE TRANSVAAL, near the Zimbabwe border. The capital is Thohoyandou.

**Vendémiaire:** see FRENCH REVOLUTIONARY CALENDAR.

**veneer,** a thin layer of wood, generally with a decorative grain, laid over the surface of the structural wood of a piece of furniture and secured with glue. In this technique, which has been widely used since the 17th cent., particularly striking effects can be achieved with irregular growths, such as burrs, while MARQUETRY designs serve to give added enrichment.

**venereal disease,** any of several infectious diseases almost always transmitted through sexual contact. These diseases include GONORRHOEA, SYPHILIS, nonspecific urethritis, AIDS, and genital HERPES. Changes in sexual behaviour over the past two decades have contributed to an increased incidence in some venereal diseases worldwide. Public health programmes and use of ANTIBIOTIC drugs have reduced the severity of the diseases, but epidemics, particularly of gonorrhoea and AIDS are a major global health problem.

**Veneziano, Domenico:** see DOMENICO VENEZIANO.

**Venezuela,** officially Republic of Venezuela, republic (1987 est. pop. 18,500,000), 912,050 km² (352,143 sq mi), N South America, bordered by Brazil (S), Colombia (W and SW), Guyana (E), and the Caribbean Sea (N). Principal cities include CARACAS (the capital) and MARACAIBO. A land of vivid contrasts, Venezuela has four major geographical regions: the oil-rich coastal lowlands; the ORINOCO R. basin, whose vast plains (LLANOS) support a great cattle industry; the Guiana Highlands, a largely unexplored wilderness occupying more than half the nation's territory and noted for scenic wonders such as ANGEL FALLS; and the densely populated Venezuelan highlands, a spur of the ANDES that rises to 5007 m (16,427 ft) in the Sierra Nevada de Mérida and that is the nation's political and commercial hub. Venezuela enjoys the highest per capita income in Latin America because of its astonishing oil wealth, first exploited in 1918, which accounts for over 90% of its export earnings. More recently aluminium and iron ore have contributed an increasing share of exports. Coffee, the mainstay of the economy before the oil boom, is still produced; other leading crops are cocoa, sugar, bananas, maize, and rice. Manufactures include food products, iron and steel, aluminium, textiles, chemicals, and automobiles. In 1984 GDP was US$50,900 million or US$2947 per capita. The population is 65% mestizo, 20% white, 8% black, and 7% Indian. The principal language is Spanish; the main religion is Roman Catholicism.

*History.* COLUMBUS discovered the mouths of the Orinoco in 1498, and Spanish settlements were established on the coast in the 1520s, but the major task of conquest was accomplished by German adventurers, notably Nikolaus Federmann. For a time an adjunct of NEW GRANADA, from the 16th to 18th cent. Venezuela was frequently raided by British buccaneers. The war for independence from Spain, begun in 1810 under Francisco de MIRANDA, was completed in 1821 by Simón BOLÍVAR (born in Venezuela), who made the area part of the federal republic of Greater Colombia. A separatist movement led by José Antonio PÁEZ succeeded (1830) in making Venezuela an independent state. During much of its history the nation has been dominated by *caudillos* (military dictators) from the landholding class, notably Juan Vicente GÓMEZ, who came to power in 1908 and ruled for 27 years as an absolute tyrant until his death in 1935; he did, however, force the state (with the help of foreign oil concessions) into national solvency and material prosperity. A revolutionary junta, headed by Rómulo BETANCOURT and committed to democracy and social reform, gained power in 1945, but a coup three years later once again established a repressive military dictatorship. A popular revolt in 1958 restored democratic rule, and since that time free elections have been held. In 1976, the oil industry was nationalized. In recent years political power has alternated between the Christian Social Party and Democratic Action.

**Post-war Venezuelan presidents**
Rómulo Betancourt (AD), 1945–47
Rómulo Gallegos (AD), 1947–48
Carlos Delgardo Chalbaud (military), 1948–50
Germán Suárez Flamerich (military), 1950–52
Marcos Pérez Jimenez (military), 1952–58
Wolfgang Larrazábal (military), 1958
Rómulo Betancourt (AD), 1959–64
Raúl Leoni (AD), 1964–69
Rafael Caldera Rodríguez (COPEI), 1969–74
Carlos Andrés Pérez (AD), 1974–79
Luis Herrera Campíns (COPEI), 1979–84
Jaime Lusinchi (AD), 1984–89
Carlos Andrés Pérez (AD), 1989–

**Venezuela Boundary Dispute,** over the demarcation between VENEZUELA and British Guiana (now GUYANA), which caused tension between Great Britain and the US in the 19th cent. The dispute was intensified in 1841, when gold was discovered in the border area, but the British refused arbitration. In 1887, Venezuela cut diplomatic ties with Great Britain. In 1895, Pres. CLEVELAND declared that the US had a duty to determine the boundary and would resist British aggression beyond

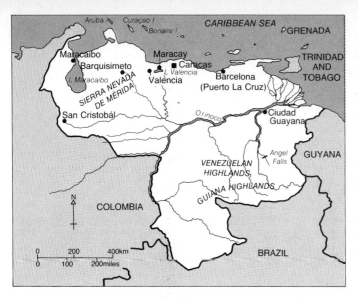

Venezuela

that line. The British recognized this broad interpretation of the MONROE DOCTRINE, and the boundary, generally favourable to Britain, was finally drawn in 1899.

**Venezuela Claims**, 1902–04, demands for unpaid loans to VENEZUELA made by Britain, Germany, and Italy, which together sent (1902) a naval force that blockaded and shelled Venezuelan seaports. The US refused to act as arbitrator but worked for an amicable settlement (1904). Britain's acceptance of the role of the US really marked the latter's emergence as a major power.

**Venice**, Ital. *Venezia,* city (1984 pop. 337,670), capital of Venetia, NE Italy. Built on 118 alluvial islets within a lagoon in the Gulf of Venice, it is joined to the mainland by bridges. Canals and bridges give access among islands; gondolas and other boats are the only conveyances. There are many lanes, squares, and a few streets, and the houses are built on piles. Tourism is important. Manufactures include ships, lace, and glass. Refugees fleeing the Lombards settled (5th cent.) the islands and organized (687) under a doge. The communities formed (9th cent.) a city that came to dominate the Adriatic and became Europe's leading sea power. Marco POLO symbolized its spirit of enterprise in the 13th cent. Serving as the main link between Europe and Asia, Venice reached the height of its power in the 15th cent. and began to decline at the century's end. It fell (1797) without resistance to NAPOLEON I, who delivered it to Austrian rule. It became part of Italy in 1866. Venice reached artistic glory during the Renaissance, with TITIAN and TINTORETTO the giants of the Venetian school. It was also the most original artistic city of 18th-cent. Italy, as represented by such painters as TIEPOLO and CANALETTO. Architecturally, Venice is marked by Byzantine influences, felt most strongly in the famous SAINT MARK'S CHURCH. Later architecture is a graceful baroque style, e.g., the churches of San Giorgio Maggiore and Santa Maria della Salute. Other landmarks include the Gothic Doges' Palaces, the Grand Canal, and the Bridge of Sighs.

**Venizelos, Eleutherios,** 1864–1936, Greek statesman and premier (1910–15, 1915, 1917–20, 1924, 1928–32, 1933); b. Crete. A leader of the republican liberals, he secured (1913) the union of Crete with Greece, led (1912–13) Greece victoriously through the BALKAN WARS and brought Greece into World War I on the side of the Allies. He attained the establishment of the Greek republic in 1924 but fought a losing battle against the restoration of the monarchy in 1935. He died in France.

**Venturi, Robert,** 1925–, American architect. A prominent figure in POSTMODERNISM, he advocated an unorthodox, mannered, eclectic, and humorous architecture and emphasized the validity and vitality of American roadside strip buildings and advertising. His influential books include *Complexities and Contradictions in Modern Architecture* (1966) and *Learning from Las Vegas* (1972).

**Venus,** in astronomy, 2nd PLANET from the Sun, at a mean distance of 108.2 million km (67.2 million mi). It has a diameter of 12,100 km (7519 mi); terrains that can be subdivided into lowland plains (20%), rolling uplands (70%), and highlands (10%); and an atmosphere whose chief gas is carbon dioxide. The entire surface of Venus is opaquely covered by a dense cloud layer. The atmospheric pressure at the surface of the planet is 90 times that of earth. Because its greatest ELONGATION is 47°, Venus can never be seen much longer than 3 hr after sunset or 3 hr before sunrise. It has no known satellites. SPACE PROBES that have encountered Venus include *Mariners 2, 5,* and *10* (1962, 1967, and 1974); *Pioneer-Venus 1* and *2* (1978); and numerous Soviet Venera spacecraft.

Venus

**Venus,** in Roman mythology, goddess of vegetation; identified from the 3rd cent. BC with the Greek APHRODITE. In imperial times she was worshipped as Venus Genetrix, mother of AENEAS; Venus Felix, bringer of good fortune; Venus Victrix, bringer of victory; and Venus Verticordia, protector of feminine chastity. Among the famous sculptures of the goddess are the *Venus of Milo* (LOUVRE) and the *Venus of Medici* (UFFIZI, Florence). She also features prominently in RENAISSANCE painting, e.g., BOTTICELLI, *Birth of Venus* (Uffizi, Florence).

**Venus figurines,** distinctive female figurines produced during the Upper PALAEOLITHIC. The most common feature of these figurines is their obesity. They were produced in a variety of materials: bas-relief carvings, stone, mammoth ivory, and clay; and their distribution extends from the Pyrenees to Russia. Their striking form has suggested to many that they were objects used in fertility cults, but the lack of any supporting evidence has limited the value of this hypothesis. One recent interpretation points to the wide distribution of the figurines as evidence of regionally-based social interaction and the possible existence of networks of communication.

**Venus' flytrap,** insectivorous or carnivorous bog plant (*Dionaea muscipula*) native to the Carolina savannas of the US, now widely cultivated as a novelty. The leaves, borne in a low rosette, resemble mechanical animal traps. They are hinged at the midrib, each half bearing sensitive bristles; when a bristle is touched by an insect, the halves snap shut and the marginal teeth interlock to imprison the insect until it is digested.

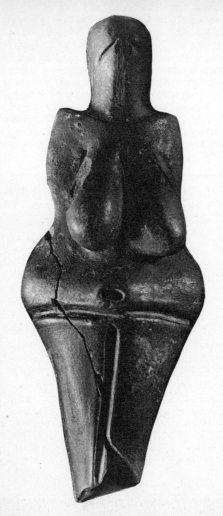

Venus figurine

Venus' fly trap (*Dionaea muscipula*) with open traps showing trigger hairs

**Veracruz**, city (1979 est. pop. 319,257), E central Mexico, on the Gulf of Mexico. Rivalling TAMPICO as the nation's main port, it is the industrial centre of a major oil region and is popular with tourists because of its scenery and beaches. Founded c.1600, throughout the colonial period it was the major port for the export of Mexican silver to Spain. It has been a frequent landing site for foreign invasions, notably by the US (1847) and France (1862). A 17th–18th-cent. fortress guards the harbour.

**verb:** see PART OF SPEECH.

**verbena:** see VERVAIN.

**Vercingetorix** ('vuhsin,jetəriks), d. 46 BC, leader of the Gauls in a revolt against Rome that was put down by Julius CAESAR. He was captured when Caesar besieged and took the fort of Alesia (52 BC). After appearing in Caesar's triumph, Vercingetorix was put to death.

**Verdaguer, Jacinto** (veə,dhahgeə), 1845–1902, Catalan national poet (see CATALONIA). His masterpiece, the epic *La Atlàntida* (1877), dealing with Iberian myths, was set to music by FALLA.

**Verdi, Giuseppe** (,veədee), 1813–1901, foremost Italian operatic composer. He is famous for such dramatic and superbly melodic operas as *Rigoletto* (1851), *Il Trovatore* (1853), *La Traviata* (1853), *La forza del destino* (1862), and *Aïda* (1871), in which the elements of his earlier style reach maturity. Three operas are based on plays by Shakespeare: *Macbeth* (1847, rev. 1865) and the two masterpieces of his old age, *Otello* (1887) and *Falstaff* (1893). Verdi is also known for his magnificent *Requiem* (1874).

**Verdun**, town (1982 pop. 240,120), NE France. A transportation centre with varied industry, it was a commercial centre under Rome and the CAROLINGIANS (9th cent.) and a free city of the HOLY ROMAN EMPIRE until seized (1552) by HENRY II. Almost destroyed in a famous WORLD WAR I battle (Feb.–Dec. 1916), it was rebuilt. The battlefield and cemeteries form a national shrine.

**Vereeniging**, city (1985 pop. 540,142), Transvaal prov., NE South Africa, on the Vaal R. Coal mining and the production of iron and steel are the town's principal industries. Founded in 1892, it was the scene of the signing of the Treaty of Vereeniging in May 1902, terminating the SOUTH AFRICAN WAR.

**Verga, Giovanni**, 1840–1922, Italian writer; b. Sicily. He began with novels of passion in the fashionable French mould, before turning to short stories (*Life in the Fields*, 1880) and a novel (*I Malavoglia* tr. The House by the Medlar Tree, 1881) realistically portraying the hardships of Sicilian life, which made him the leading representative of *verismo* (Italian Naturalism). One of the stories, *Cavalleria rusticana* (1880), was the basis for MASCAGNI's 1890 opera. That and a later collection, *Little Novels of Sicily* (1883), and *Mastro-Don Gesualdo* (1889), a second realist novel, were translated by D.H. LAWRENCE in the 1920s.

**Vergennes, Charles Gravier, comte de** (veə,zhen), 1717–87, French statesman. As foreign minister of LOUIS XVI, he signed (1778) France's alliance with the Americans in the AMERICAN REVOLUTION and helped negotiate the Treaty of PARIS (1783).

**Vergil:** see VIRGIL.

**Verhaeren, Émile** (veərah,ren), 1855–1916, Belgian poet and critic who wrote in French. His passion for social reform found expression successively in works that display a disgust with mankind, pessimism over industrialization, and finally an optimistic glorification of human energy. These include *Flemish Women* (1883), *The Hallucinated Countrysides* (1893), and *The Manifold Splendour* (1906).

**verification principle**, the criterion of meaning of LOGICAL POSITIVISM, according to which a proposition is meaningful only if it can in principle be verified. The principle was used by logical positivists to eliminate METAPHYSICS as meaningless.

**Veríssimo, Érico Lopes**, 1905–75, Brazilian writer. His novels include *Caminhos cruzadoa* (1935; tr. Crossroads), *The Rest Is Silence* (1943), and the trilogy *Time and the Wind* (1949–62). His lectures in the US were published as *Brazilian Literature* (1945). From 1953 to 1956 he was director of the Dept of Cultural Affairs of the Pan American Union.

**Verlaine, Paul** (veə,len), 1844–96, French poet. While still a young man, Verlaine formed a tempestuous liaison with a young poet, Arthur RIMBAUD. The relationship ended tragically when Verlaine shot and wounded Rimbaud. Imprisoned for two years, he returned to the Catholic faith, but his later life was marked by drunkenness and debauchery. His poetry, possessing a rare musicality, includes such early PARNASSIAN works as *Poèmes saturniens* (1866); some noble religious verse from his prison years (in *Sagesse* 1881; tr. Wisdom); and *Romances sans paroles* (1874; tr. Romances without Words), establishing him as an early SYMBOLIST. His only important prose work is *Les poètes maudits* (1884; tr. The Accursed Poets), about his fellow symbolists.

**Vermeer, Jan** or **Johannes**, 1632–75, Dutch GENRE painter. He spent his entire life in Delft. Although four times leader of the painter's guild, and admired by his contemporaries, Vermeer's reputation ebbed until his rediscovery in the late 19th cent. Today he is ranked among the greatest Dutch masters and the foremost of all colourists. His most frequent subjects were intimate interiors, often with the solitary figure of a woman, exquisitely depicted with luminous blues and yellows, pearly highlights, and subtle gradations of reflected light. Only 34 paintings can be attributed to him with certainty; they include *The Letter* (c.1655; Rijks Mus., Amsterdam), *View of Delft* (c.1662; Mauritshuis, The Hague), *Soldier and Laughing Girl* (c.1657; Frick Coll., New York City), and *Young Woman with a Water Jug* (c.1665; Metropolitan Mus., New York City).

Jan **Vermeer**, *Lady Reading at an Open Window*, c.1658. Oil on canvas, 85.7 × 72.3 cm. Gemaldegalerie, Dresden.

**vermiform appendix:** see APPENDIX.

**Vermont**, state of the US (1984 est. pop. 530,000), area 24,887 km² (9609 sq mi), located in New England, bordered by New Hampshire (E), Massachusetts (S), New York (W), and the Canadian province of Quebec (N). The capital is MONTPELIER and the largest city is Burlington. The state is dominated by the Green Mts which run N–S; the northeastern border with New York is formed by Lake CHAMPLAIN, which also crosses into Quebec. Manufacturing is the main economic sector, producing nonelectrical machinery, fabricated metals, computer components, processed foods, and pulp and paper. Milk production for New York and Boston dominates agriculture, but hay, apples, and maple syrup are also important. Stone and building materials are extracted; year-round tourism is vital to the economy. Only one-third of the population lives in urban areas; most reside in small rural villages. The original inhabitants were Iroquois and Algonquin Indians, and in the 18th cent. both New Hampshire and New York claimed the area. For ten years before joining the Union in 1791 Vermont functioned as a sovereign state. During the 19th cent. manufacturing became more prevalent, and the rural population declined as farmers migrated west to more fertile lands. In the 20th cent. the southern part of the state began to grow rapidly, as a result of new industries, such as computers.

**vermouth**, blended, fortified white wine flavoured with herbs and spices. Containing up to 19% alcohol, it is used as an aperitif and in cocktails.

**vernal equinox:** see EQUINOX.

**Verne, Jules**, 1828–1905, French novelist, father of modern SCIENCE FICTION. His enormously popular romances include the prophetic *Voyage au centre de la terre* (1864; tr. Journey to the Centre of the Earth), *Vingt mille lieues sous les mers* (1870; tr. Twenty Thousand Leagues Under the Sea), and *Le tour du monde en quatre-vingt jours* (1873; tr. Around the World in Eighty Days).

**Verner, Karl Adolf**, 1846–96, Danish philologist. His fame rests on **Verner's law**, a linguistic formulation showing that certain consonantal alternations in Germanic languages are the result of patterns of alternation in the position of word accent in the parent language.

**Verona**, city (1984 pop. 260,594), in Venetia, NE Italy. On a road to central Europe, it is the centre of an important fruit-producing region. It has had commercial and strategic importance from Roman times. A barbarian base (5th–6th cent.), it became a free commune (12th cent.) and the site (13th–14th cent.) of GUELPHS AND GHIBELLINES strife. It was ruled by Venice (1404–1797) and Austria (1797–1805, 1814–66) until union with Italy. Many monuments survived damage in World War II, e.g., a large Roman amphitheatre and the Gothic Scaligeri tombs.

**Veronese, Paolo** (veəroh͵nayzay), 1528–88, Italian painter; b. Paolo Caliari. Veronese was amongst the most celebrated Venetian decorative painters and a brilliant colourist. He was immensely prolific and painted portraits, mythological scenes, frescoes, altarpieces, and ceiling paintings. His best known works are his landscape frescoes in the Villa Maser near Treviso, and a series of vast canvases of religious feast scenes. These works, e.g., the *Marriage at Cana* (1562; Louvre, Paris) and *The Feast in the House of Levi* (1573; Accademia, Venice) are crowded with fashionable courtiers in gorgeous costumes against stately Palladian architecture; the secular character of the latter won the displeasure of the Inquisition.

Paolo **Veronese**, *The Feast in the House of Levi*, 1573. Accademia, Venice.

**Verrazano-Narrows Bridge**, New York City, US, the longest vehicular suspension bridge in the US, spanning the Narrows at the entrance to New York harbour. Designed by O.H. Ammann and completed in 1964, it has a main span of 1298 m (4260 ft).

**verre églomisé**, the technique of painting a design on the underside of a sheet of glass and backing it with gold or silver leaf. Introduced from France, it was particularly fashionable in England around 1700 for the frames of looking-glasses.

**Verrocchio, Andrea del** (və͵rohkee'oh), 1435–88, Florentine sculptor and painter. He was the leading sculptor in Florence in the second half of the 15th cent. Many of his paintings are lost; in his *Baptism of Christ* (c.1472; Uffizi, Florence) one of the angels is by his pupil, LEONARDO DA VINCI. His work is characterized by its grace and refined detail, e.g., his *Boy with Dolphin* (Palazzo Vecchio, Florence) and his lithe *David* (c.1475; Bargello, Florence). His masterpiece is his awesome equestrian statue of *Bartolommeo Colleoni* (1481–90; Piazza Santi Giovanni e Paolo, Venice) which was cast after his death.

Gilt wood wall sconce with **verre églomisé** decoration (1780)

**Versailles,** city (1982 pop. 95,240), capital of Yvelines dept., N central France. It is the site of the elaborate palace and gardens built (mid–17th cent.) for LOUIS XIV, which represent the height of the French classical style. The FRENCH REVOLUTION forced Louis XVI to move (1790) from there to Paris. Under Louis Philippe, Versailles became a national monument.

**Versailles, Treaty of,** any of several treaties signed at Versailles, France. For the treaty of 1783: see PARIS, TREATY OF. The Treaty of 1871 was signed at the end of the Franco-Prussian War by BISMARCK for Germany and THIERS for France and ratified in the Treaty of Frankfurt (1871). France was forced to give up most of Alsace and Lorraine, pay a large indemnity, and accept a German army of occupation. The Versailles Treaty of June 1919 between the Allied and Associated Powers and Germany was the chief achievement of the Paris Peace Conference, ending World War I. The 'Big Four' negotiating it were Pres. WILSON (US), Premier CLEMENCEAU

Andrea del **Verrocchio**, *Bartolommeo Colleoni*, 1481–90. Piazza Santi Giovanni e Paolo, Venice.

(France), Prime Min. LLOYD GEORGE (Britain), and Premier ORLANDO (Italy). The treaty called for the creation of the LEAGUE OF NATIONS. It forced on Germany the burden of REPARATIONS and placed limits on German armed forces. It restored Alsace and Lorraine to France, gave Prussian Poland and most of West Prussia to Poland, made Danzig a free city, put Germany's colonies under the League of Nations, placed the Saar under French administration, called for plebiscites in various territories newly

The Hall of Mirrors in the palace at **Versailles**

freed from the Central Powers, and called for the demilitarization of the RHINELAND. American opposition to the League of Nations resulted in the refusal of the U.S. Senate to ratify the treaty. In 1935, HITLER unilaterally abrogated most of the terms of the Treaty of Versailles. The Allied and Associated Powers also signed the Treaties of Saint-Germain (1920) with Austria, of Neuilly (1919) with Bulgaria, of Trianon (1920) with Hungary, and of Sèvres (1920) with Turkey. Taken together, these treaties are often referred to as the Versailles Settlement.

**versification,** principles of metrical practice in poetry. Poetic form is achieved in various ways in different literatures. Usually definite, predictable patterns are evident in the language. Greek and Roman verse was patterned on the quantity of syllables (time required to express them). The terminology developed to describe the patterns is still used, although poetry in modern languages is stress- rather than quantity-based. The fundamental unit, the line, divides into feet according to major and minor stresses. The types of feet retain their Greek names: iambus u-; trochee -u; spondee - -; pyrrhic uu; anapest uu-; and dactyl -uu. The number and type of feet determine the name of the meter, e.g., iambic PENTAMETER. A patterned arrangement of lines is called a stanza. RHYME is an important element in stanza structure. The poetry of Germanic peoples, developed independently of the Romance tradition, had strong accents or stresses, often four to a line, and a pattern of alliteration. Much Middle English verse is alliterative. CHAUCER is credited with inventing the first English stanza form, the rhyme royal. Modern poets, e.g., G.M. HOPKINS, have employed both time and stress, and have experimented with alliteration and assonance. See ALEXANDRINE; FREE VERSE; SONNET.

**vertebral column:** see SPINAL COLUMN.

**vertebrate,** any animal having a backbone or spinal column. All vertebrates belong to the subphylum Vertebrata of the phylum CHORDATA. The five classes of vertebrates are FISHES, AMPHIBIANS, REPTILES, BIRDS, and MAMMALS. Vertebrates are comparatively large, have a high degree of specialization of their parts, and are bilaterally symmetrical. All have an interior skeleton, a brain enclosed in a cranium, a closed circulatory system, and a heart divided into two, three, or four chambers; most have two pairs of appendages modified as fins, limbs, or wings in the different classes. Animals without backbones are called INVERTEBRATES.

**vertical circle,** the great circle on the celestial sphere that passes from the observer's zenith through a given celestial body or a specified celestial point. See also ASTRONOMICAL COORDINATE SYSTEMS.

**vertical takeoff and landing aircraft** (VTOL), term used for fixed-wing aircraft which are able to take off and land without forward run. They are especially suitable for use on AIRCRAFT CARRIERS. The classical, and first, VTOL aircraft to go into production is the British Aerospace Harrier, designed by Sir Sydney CAMM, and powered with a Rolls-Royce Pegasus jet engine of which the maximum jet thrust is capable of exceeding the weight of the aircraft.

**Vertov, Dziga,** 1896–1954, Polish director and film theoretician. Resident in Russia after the Russian Revolution, he proposed a documentary aesthetic which he labelled Kino-Eye, and which is often thought of as the father to *cinéma vérité*. His films include *Man with a Movie Camera* (1929), *Enthusiasm* (1931), and *Three Songs about Lenin* (1934).

**vervain,** common name for some members of the family Verbenaceae, herbs, shrubs, and trees of warmer regions of the world. Well-known wild and cultivated members of the family include species of *Lantana* and *Verbena.* Many cultivated verbenas (e.g., *V. officinalis*, much used in folk medicine for nerve complaints) have fragrant blossoms and leaves that are sometimes used for distillation of oils and for tea, as are those of the similar lemon verbena (*Lippia citriodora*). Economically, the most important member of the family is TEAK (*Tectona grandis*).

**Verwey, Albert** (via vie), 1865–1937, Dutch poet. As a leader of literary progressivism he produced melodious, evocative verse; increasing complexity and dissonance mark his later poetry.

**Verwoerd, Hendrik Frensch** (fa voot), 1901–66, South African prime minister (1958–66). A harsh proponent of white supremacy, he intensified the Nationalist policy of APARTHEID. When South Africa became (1961) a republic, he severed its connections with the British Commonwealth. He was assassinated.

**very large-scale integration** (VLSI), process or technology in microelectronics chip technology of making electronic circuits involving over 100,000 transistors on a single silicon slice one centimetre square. A circuit like this now forms the basis of a high powered MICROPROCESSOR and, in combination, desktop computers. It has brought a revolution in computer design and capability and produced the fourth generation of computers (see COMPUTER GENERATIONS).

BAe Harrier GR-5 **VTOL** fighter

**Vesaas, Tarjei,** 1897–1970, Norwegian novelist and lyric poet. He was the most important novelist using Landsmaal after World War II, and also wrote modernist poetry (*The Wells*, 1946) in the same literary language. His best-known novels are *The Birds* (1957) and *The Ice Castle* (1963), which combine the epic and the lyrical in mood.

**Vesalius, Andreas,** 1514–64, Flemish anatomist. At the Univ. of Padua he produced his chief work, the illustrated *De humani corporis fabrica* (1542), based on studies made by dissecting human cadavers. His discoveries in anatomy overthrew many hitherto uncontested doctrines of GALEN and caused criticism to be directed against himself. He was physician to Emperor Charles V and his son Philip II.

**Vespasian** (Titus Flavius Vespasianus), AD 9–79, Roman emperor (r.69–79), founder of the Flavian dynasty. Vespasian was proclaimed emperor by the soldiers, and his reign was noted for its order and prosperity. He built the COLOSSEUM. The warfare he waged against the Jewish rebels was completed by his son TITUS.

**vespers,** in the Christian Church, principal evening office. In the Roman rite it consists of prayers, psalms, a lesson, the *Magnificat,* and an antiphon. The similar Anglican evening prayer, evensong, is based on vespers.

**Vespucci, Amerigo** (vays poohtchee), 1454–1512, Italian navigator in whose honour America is named. In 1499 he sailed to the WEST INDIES and discovered the mouth of the AMAZON. Later he sailed (1501) along the N coast of SOUTH AMERICA. Vespucci evolved a system for computing nearly exact longitude. His acceptance of South America as a continent altered cosmography.

**Vesta,** in Roman mythology goddess of hearth and home; identified with the Greek HESTIA. Her six priestesses, the **vestal virgins,** were chosen in childhood from prominent Roman families. Serving for 30 years, they were sworn to chastity. Their duties included preparing sacrifices and tending the sacred fire. The vestals were very influential in Roman society.

**vestments,** [from Lat., *vestire* = to clothe], ceremonial garments worn by a priest for the performance of the offices of religion. The term is usually confined to priests within the Judaeo-Christian tradition, though virtually every priesthood has its ceremonial dress. Most forms of Christian vestments can be traced back to the secular garments worn in the later Roman empire when the early church was established. In the ROMAN CATHOLIC CHURCH they are sometimes called *canonicals* because they are prescribed by CANON LAW. There are four basic vestments: (1) the *alb*, a full-length long-sleeved white robe, worn belted; (2) the *dalmatic*, a shorter, more elaborate tunic, with coloured bands hanging form the shoulders, open at the sides and worn unbelted; (3) the *chasuble*, a short cloak consisting of a cone of cloth with a hole in the middle for the head, sometimes decorated with crosses; and (4) the *cope*, a full-length semicircular hooded cape, worn when the chasuble is not used. The *cassock*, a plain long black close-fitting robe, is always worn underneath the vestments, but is not technically a liturgical garment. Other garments include the *amice*, a sort of cowl or scarf of white linen worn around the neck and shoulders; the *stole*, a strip of silk 10–20 cm (2½ to 5 in) wide and 2.5 m (8 ft) long worn round the back of the neck with the ends either crossed in front or hanging down, in various colours for specific festivals; the *maniple*, another strip of silk of the same width but 1.0–1.5 m (3 to 4½ ft) long, worn over the left forearm with the ends hanging down. The bishop's *mitre* is also a vestment. The *surplice* [Lat., *superpellicium* = over the fur coat], a very loose full-sleeved white tunic worn unbelted, originated in the 11th cent. and is the usual vestment for members of a choir. The vestments in the Eastern churches were almost the same as the Western until the 16th cent. after which the Eastern ones are more varied in colour (including the use of black) and more decorated. The *sticharion* (equivalent to the alb) is the basic garment. Over it is worn either the *phelonion* (equivalent to the chasuble) or the *sakkos*, a short half-sleeved tunic. There are elaborate differences to show the rank of the bishop or priest. At the REFORMATION, two traditions were established within Protestant churches. The Calvinist tradition did away with vestments, in the belief that worship must be as simple as possible; Luther held that vestments were not an important issue, and permitted them to be used or not as congregations wished. The CHURCH OF ENGLAND abandoned the use of the chasuble and other Roman Catholic canonical vestments in the 16th cent. There are no definite regulations, and today Anglican priests may wear anything from a simple surplice and stole to a full set of Roman-style vestments. In the Jewish tradition, the vestments for priests and high priests were as commanded by God to Moses (Ex. 28; 39); after the destruction of the Temple in AD 70 there was no priesthood. Rabbis do not have any specified vestments. Male worshippers in the synagogue (though not in the Reform tradition) wear the *yarmulke*, a skull-cap, and the *tallit*, a fringed shawl worn over the head and shoulders; at important festivals, including the SEDER, the *kittel*, a white robe, may be worn.

**Vestris, Gaetan,** 1729–1808, Italian dancer. He was dancing master to Louis XVI, and was the first to discard the mask and use the face in mime. His son *Auguste Vestris*, 1760–1842, was the leading dancer and teacher of his time. He trained Fanny Ellsler and Auguste BOURNONVILLE.

**Vestris, Lucia Elizabeth (Bartolozzi),** 1797–1856, English actress-manager. Known as Mme Vestris, she was the first woman to lease a theatre (1831). She produced Shakespearean comedy as well as BURLESQUES and FARCES, and was known for her realistic stage settings and props.

**Vesuvius,** active volcano, SE Italy, overlooking the Bay of Naples. The height of the main cone changes with each eruption, varying within a few hundred feet of the 1219-m (4000-ft) level. Often surmounted by a faint plume of smoke, the volcano erupts frequently and is occasionally destructive. The earliest recorded eruption (AD 79) buried the Roman cities of POMPEII, HERCULANEUM, and Stabiae.

**veterinary medicine,** term applied to the diagnosis of diseases in animals, and injuries to animals, including testing for diagnostic purposes, the provision of advice based upon diagnosis, and medical or surgical treatment of animals, all of which may only be carried out legally by a registered veterinary surgeon. In the UK a lay person may legally render first aid only, as an interim measure in an emergency where it appears necessary for saving the life of an animal, or relieving its pain, when no veterinary surgeon is immediately available.

**veto,** the existence or exercise of the right to prohibit an action or measure which others wish to take. In the Security Council of the UNITED NATIONS the five permanent members, the UK, China, France, the USSR, and the US, each have a power to block any action or resolution decided on by the other members. The power of veto over legislative acts is also accorded to heads of state under some presidential systems of government. In the US the president's veto can be overridden by a two-thirds vote of Congress. The president cannot veto only a portion of a bill, nor can he veto constitutional amendments. The governors of the US states also have veto power.

**Via Emilia,** road, built by the Romans in 187 BC, which extends in an almost straight line from Milan to Rimini on the Adriatic Sea of Italy. Towns have grown up along it where routeways emerge from the Apennines to the south. Like beads on a cord, they include Bologna, Modena, Parma, and Piacenza. For part of its length it is closely followed by the Autostrada del Sole.

**Viaud, Julien:** see LOTI, PIERRE.

**Vicente, Gil** (Port. vee‚sentə, Sp. vee‚dhentay), 1470?–1536?, Portuguese dramatist and poet. A major figure of the Iberian Renaissance, he is ranked second only to CAMÕES. A humanist, he created plays for court presentation varying from farcical interludes to tragicomedies. Some religious, some satirical, they attack the corrupt clergy and the superficial glory of empire belied by increasing national poverty; they also include songs of his own composition. He wrote in Portuguese, in Spanish, and in a combination of the two.

**Vicenza** (vi‚chenzə) city (1984 pop. 111,721), Venezia, NE Italy. It is surrounded by a successful agriculture and is noted for its orchard fruits. Mulberries are also grown for rearing silkworms. It is the birthplace of Andrea PALLADIO who was responsible for the Teatro Olimpico (1580-84).

**Vichy,** city (1982 pop. 30,554), central France. Hot springs have made it a foremost spa. The **Vichy government** was the regime set up (1940) by Marshal PÉTAIN during WORLD WAR II, after the Franco-German armistice. It controlled unoccupied France and its colonies. A truncated parliament replaced the Third Republic with an authoritarian state. Vichy became a German tool in the hands of LAVAL, DARLAN, and others. When the Allies invaded Africa in 1942, Hitler seized all of France. The Vichy regime fled before the Allied advance and fell at war's end.

**Vicksburg campaign,** in the AMERICAN CIVIL WAR, the fighting (Nov. 1862–4 July 1863) for control of the Mississippi R. By late 1862, the Union controlled all of the river except for the 200 miles below Vicksburg, Mississippi. Impregnable on its bluff overlooking the river, Vicksburg repulsed all efforts to storm it by troops under the overall command of Gen. Ulysses S. GRANT. In May 1863 Grant laid siege, and after six weeks the Confederates surrendered. Vicksburg's fall split the CONFEDERACY in two.

**Vico, Giovanni Battista** or **Giambattista,** 1688–1744, Italian philosopher and historian. Vico's philosophy of history, little known until the 19th cent., was far in advance of his time and is generally regarded as the precursor of modern theories of history. For Vico, history was the account of the birth, development, and decay of human societies and institutions. He urged the study of language and mythology as a means of understanding earlier societies. He thus departed from previous systems of writing history either as the biographies of great men or as the unfolding of God's will. His cyclical theory of history was an important influence on the DIALECTICAL MATERIALISM of Karl MARX. Vico's major work was *New Science* (1725), which he completely revised in 1730 and 1744.

**Victor Amadeus II,** 1666–1732, duke of Savoy (1675–1713), king of Sicily (r.1713–20), and king of Sardinia (r.1720–30). In the War of the SPANISH SUCCESSION (1701–13), he and his cousin, EUGENE OF SAVOY, defeated the French in 1706. The Peace of Utrecht gave (1713) Victor Amadeus a kingdom in Sicily, which was seized (1718) by Spain. In 1720 he ceded his claim to Sicily in exchange for Sardinia and became its king. He abdicated in 1730.

**Victor Emmanuel,** Italian kings. **Victor Emmanuel I,** 1759–1824, king of Sardinia (1802–21), recovered Sardinia's mainland territories after Napoleon's fall. His reactionary rule led to an uprising, and he abdicated. **Victor Emmanuel II,** 1820–78, king of Sardinia (1849–61), was the first king of united Italy (1861–78). Aided by his minister, the conte di CAVOUR, he continued the wars of the RISORGIMENTO, and in 1861 the kingdom of Italy was proclaimed with Victor Emmanuel as king. His grandson, **Victor Emmanuel III**, 1869–1947, king of Italy (1900–46), joined (1915) the Allies in WORLD WAR I. During MUSSOLINI's Fascist regime he was king in name only, although he gained the titles emperor of Ethiopia (1936) and king of Albania (1939). He abdicated (1946) after WORLD WAR II. See also SAVOY, HOUSE OF.

**Victoria,** 1819–1901, queen of Great Britain and Ireland (1837–1901) and from 1867 empress of India; daughter of Edward, duke of Kent (fourth son of GEORGE III), and Princess Mary Louise Victoria of Saxe-Coburg-Saalfeld. She succeeded WILLIAM IV. As a woman, she was barred from succession in Hanover, so her accession in Britain ended the connection between the British and Hanoverian thrones. In 1840 she married her first cousin Prince ALBERT, and the marriages of their nine children linked the British royal house to the royalty of Russia, Germany, Greece, Denmark, and Romania. Victoria's first prime minister, Lord MELBOURNE, became a friend, and she came to respect PEEL, but her interest in foreign affairs caused friction with Lord PALMERSTON. In 1861, Prince Albert died; the queen's extreme grief led to her seclusion for three years. She had a close relation with the tory Benjamin DISRAELI, but she never got on well with the liberal William GLADSTONE. At her two jubilees, 1887 (Golden) and 1897 (Diamond) her popularity was demonstrated. She was of high moral character and extremely conscientious and gave her name not only to an adjective but to a noun, Victorianism. Her reign, the longest in English history, saw the rise of industrialism at home and imperialism abroad.

**Victoria,** state (1986 pop. 4,160,900), 227,620 km² (87,884 sq mi), SE Australia, on the Southern Ocean and the Tasman Sea. MELBOURNE, the capital, and GEELONG are among the major cities. The second smallest and most densely populated Australian state, Victoria is highly industrialized. Manufactures include motor vehicles, pharmaceuticals, textiles, paper, and machinery. The state has about half of the country's irrigated land and produces most of its butter, three-quarters of its cheese, and more than half of its mutton and lamb. Brown coal, oil, and natural gas are important resources. The first permanent settlements were established at Portland Bay in 1834 and at Melbourne in 1835. Originally part of NEW SOUTH WALES, Victoria became a separate colony in 1851 and was federated as a state of the Commonwealth of Australia in 1901.

**Victoria,** city (1980 est. pop. 62,551), provincial capital, SW British Columbia, part of the Capital Regional District, on VANCOUVER ISLAND and Juan de Fuca Strait. Known for its mild winters (freezing temperatures are rare) and many parks, it is the largest city on the island and the second largest in the province. Victoria was founded (1843) as Fort Camosun, a HUDSON'S BAY COMPANY post. The city was laid out and settled (beginning in 1851) as the capital of the crown colony of Vancouver Island. It became the capital of all of British Columbia in 1871.

**Victoria,** city, (1977 pop. 23,334), capital of the SEYCHELLES.

**Victoria and Albert Museum,** South Kensington, London. It opened in 1852 as the Museum of Manufacturers, at Marlborough House. The name was soon changed to Museum of Ornamental Art, and the collection included objects of all styles and periods. The present building, designed by Sir Aston Webb, was given its name in 1899 by Queen Victoria. It opened in 1909 as purely an art museum, embracing the Royal College of Art, an art library, and the collections of the India Museum. Its paintings and sculptures, especially early Italian works, are celebrated. RAPHAEL's cartoons for the SISTINE CHAPEL tapestries are among its great treasures, which include glass, jewellery, and textiles.

**Victoria Falls,** famous waterfall, S central Africa, on the Zambia–Zimbabwe border. The falls are c.1.6 km (1 mi) wide, with a maximum drop of 128 m (420 ft), and are formed as the ZAMBEZI R. plummets into a narrow gorge, now partially flooded by KARIBA DAM.

**Victorian style** or **styles,** these changed from one part of VICTORIA's reign to another, but in architecture and design fashion was eclectic in the middle years of the reign and there was a revival of older styles. Before 1851 there was a conflict of style, with Gothic having its supporters and opponents. In the late part of the reign there were new styles, e.g., art nouveau. See also CRYSTAL PALACE and GOTHIC REVIVAL.

Victoria Falls

**Victoria Nyanza** or **Lake Victoria,** lake, E Africa, c.69,490 km² (26,830 sq mi), largest freshwater lake in Africa and second largest in the world. One of the chief sources of the NILE R., it occupies a shallow depression at an altitude of 1135 m (3725 ft).

**Victory of Samothrace,** see NIKE.

**Vidal, Gore,** 1925–, American novelist, playwright, and critic. An acute and acerbic observer of the American scene, he brilliantly satirized US history and life in the novels *Myra Breckinridge* (1968), *Burr* (1973), and *1876* (1976). His other works include the plays *Visit to a Small Planet* (1955) and *The Best Man* (1960); the historical novels *Julian* (1964) and *Creation* (1981); and the essay collection *The Second American Revolution* (1982).

**video,** broadly, the term for all non-film forms of visual media coverage and technique, including in particular the methods for recording TELEVISION output on magnetic media. The video camera (see TELEVISION CAMERA TUBE), lighter and less bulky than previous equipment, cheaper to buy and to operate, and allowing for immediate playback, significantly increased television producers' scope in preparing programmes. However, video has the disadvantage that editing requires expensive equipment, whereas film can be simply cut and spliced. Furthermore, there are different systems by which the colour signals from the camera are encoded (NTSC in the US and Japan, SECAM in France, and PAL in most other countries), all mutually incompatible. The first practical video recording machine available to broadcasters was made in 1958. It used 5-cm (2-in) wide magnetic tape and employed the quadruplex format. In this format four recording heads are equally spaced round the circumference of a 5-cm (2-in) diameter wheel mounted at right angles to the tape. The heads slightly protrude and each one is in contact with the tape across its width for just over a quarter of the rotation of the head wheel. For the European standard the head wheel rotates at 250 revs/sec which gives a peripheral speed across the tape of 41 m/sec (1620 in/sec). For the American standard the speed is 240 revs/sec with a peripheral speed of 39 m/sec (1560 in/sec). Additionally the tape is pulled past the head wheel at speeds of 39.7 cm/sec (15.6 in/sec) and 38.1 cm/sec (15 in/sec) respectively for the European and American standards. Space is reserved at the edge of the tape to permit the recording of sound and cue and control tracks. An alternative VTR that became available during the 1970s employs the C-format. This is currently almost universally used by broadcasters. It employs 2.5-cm (1-in) wide tape that is drawn round a rotating drum of about 15 cm (6 in) diameter at a low angle so that the recording head on the periphery of the drum describes a helical path across the tape. The first video tape recorder designed for domestic use was the U-matic introduced in 1969. It used 18-mm (¾-in) tape contained in a cassette. Unfortunately it was both expensive and bulky for the home. The U-matic with the addition of correction units, like the time-base corrector, was eventually used by broadcasters for some production operations. During the late 1970s two 12.5-mm (½-in) tape video cassette recorders (VCRs) became fully acceptable for home use. The two standards, Betamax and VHS, are noncompatible. From the consumer's point of view, time-shift viewing (recording television programmes off-air for later viewing) has developed rapidly in many countries, much expanding viewer's ability to choose when and what to watch; and the availability of prerecorded video cassettes, either for purchase or hire, has become comparable in extent with the distribution of books through libraries and shops. By the mid 1980s some 50% of households in Britain had a video cassette recorder, the proportion being higher for households with children. In the UK the Video Recording Act 1984 was designed to bring in some control over the quality of prerecorded video cassettes, which were thought to have a possibly corrupting influence, owing to their violent and/or pornographic content. Video is used widely in education at all levels, enabling students to benefit from specialist lecturers or from technical demonstrations not easily available in the classroom. Educational videos are often recorded on disc rather than cassette, this system achieves high-quality slow motion and better definition of still frames. In industry and commerce, video has enabled many companies to provide training or promotional materials both for their own personnel and for wider distribution.

**video game:** see ELECTRONIC GAME.

**videotex,** a computer-based system that allows a user to retrieve and display ALPHANUMERIC and pictorial information at home on a PERSONAL COMPUTER. By linking the personal computer to a videotex DATABASE, it is possible to provide access to information on a scale that is virtually unlimited. There are two forms of videotex systems. One-way TELETEXT systems permit the selection and display of such general information as airline schedules, traffic conditions, and traditional newspaper content. *Viewdata* systems are more specific and provide for two-way, or interactive, communication (see CABLE TELEVISION). Thus, specific questions may be researched by indexing into the appropriate data base: e.g., bank balances can be verified and bills paid, and travel and hotel reservations can be made. Current viewdata systems include PRESTEL (Britain), Teletel (France), and the more advanced Telidon (Canada). Because videotex makes the home computer part of a network containing a larger, more powerful COMPUTER, additional computing power and data-storage facilities can be made available to the user.

**Vienna,** Ger. *Wien,* city and prov. (1981 pop. 1,531,346), capital of Austria, NE Austria, on the Danube R. It is a cultural, commercial, and transportation centre; tourism is also economically important. Settled by Celts, Vienna became a Roman military centre. It was the residence of the Holy Roman emperors and, after 1806, of the emperors of Austria. In 1529 and 1683 it was besieged by the Turks. In the 18th cent. HAYDN, MOZART, BEETHOVEN, and SCHUBERT lived there, and many magnificent buildings were erected, including the Hofburg (imperial residence), the Schönbrunn palace, and St Peter's Church. In the late 19th cent., with BRAHMS, MAHLER, SCHÖNBERG, FREUD, and SCHNITZLER in residence, the city continued to flourish, raising splendid cultural and administrative edifices around the famous boulevard, the Ringstrasse. After Austria was annexed (1938) to Nazi Germany, the city's Jewish population (c.115,000) was reduced to 6000. The city itself was heavily damaged in WORLD WAR II. Captured (1945) by the Russians, it was divided into four Allied occupation zones until 1955, when Austria was reunited as a neutral state.

**Vienna, Congress of,** 1814–15, international conference called to reorder Europe after the downfall of NAPOLEON I. All the European states that had existed before the Napoleonic upheaval were represented; however, the major powers (Austria, Russia, Prussia, and Britain) made the first decisions, with France quickly winning an equal voice in the deliberations. The problems confronting the congress were thorny and complex, but the unexpected return (1815) of Napoleon from Elba shocked it into burying differences long enough to reach important agreements and to establish a balance of power. The Final Act of Vienna was issued only nine days before Napoleon's defeat at Waterloo. The many accomplishments of the Congress of Vienna include the following: the Confederation of the Rhine was created to replace the defunct Holy Roman Empire; the Netherlands and Belgium were united; Russia got Finland and effective control over the new kingdom of Poland; Prussia was given much of Saxony and important parts of Westphalia and the Rhine Province; Sweden and Norway were united; Louis XVIII of France and Ferdinand VII of Spain were restored; the Italian states went to the major powers; and Britain acquired several strategic colonial territories. The peace terms for France were contained in a separate treaty (see PARIS, TREATY OF). An auxiliary accomplishment of the Congress of Vienna, which

The Hofburg, **Vienna**

was followed by other Congresses, was the formulation of rules of diplomacy that are still in effect.

**Vienna Circle:** see LOGICAL POSITIVISM.

**Vientiane,** city (1984 est. pop. 120,000), administrative capital and largest city of Laos, N central Laos, on the Mekong R. A trading centre for forest products, lac, textiles, and hides, it is noted for its canals, its houses built on stilts, and its many pagodas. It was the capital of a Lao kingdom from 1707, was sacked by the Siamese in 1827, and passed to the French in 1899. The population is about half that of 1975, the result of the flight of many Laotians after a Communist takeover that year and of the government's relocation programme (see LAOS).

**Viet Cong,** officially *Viet Nam Cong San* [Vietnamese Communists], Communist insurgents in South Vietnam. Some 10,000 Communist troops remained in hiding in South Vietnam when the Communists withdrew to North Vietnam after the 1954 GENEVA CONFERENCE. They resorted to open warfare to overthrow the US-supported South Vietnamese regime (see VIETNAM WAR) and were later reinforced by North Vietnamese troops. The political organization of the Viet Cong, the National Liberation Front (NLF), was established in 1960. Both were integrated into North Vietnamese structures following the reunification of Vietnam in 1976.

**Viet Minh,** officially *Viet Nam Doc Lap Dong Minh* [League for the Independence of Vietnam], coalition of Communist and nationalist groups that fought the Japanese (during WORLD WAR II) and the French (see DIEN BIEN PHU). The Communists within the coalition became dominant and formed (1951) the Communist Party of North Vietnam, which became the ruling party after the partition of Vietnam by the 1954 GENEVA CONFERENCE. See also VIETNAM WAR.

**Vietnam,** officially the Socialist Republic of Vietnam, republic (1987 est. pop. 60,000,000), 332,559 km² (128,401 sq mi), Southeast Asia, bordered by Cambodia and Laos (W), China (N), and the South China Sea (E, S). Major cities are HANOI (the capital) and HO CHI MINH CITY (formerly Saigon). The terrain is generally rugged; the two principal regions, the Red R. delta in the north and the Mekong R. delta in the south, are linked by a narrow, mountainous strip. Agriculture, primarily the growing of rice, is the basis of the economy, engaging more than 80% of the work force; corn, cassava, and sweet potatoes are also grown for subsistence, while cash crops include rubber, coffee, and tea. The mining of mineral resources, particularly coal, and heavy industry are concentrated in the north. Offshore oil deposits have been found. The GNP is US$5830 million, and the GNP per capita is US$100 (1984). An estimated 84% of the population are Vietnamese, a basically Mongoloid people. Significant minorities include highland tribal peoples such as the Nungs and Meos. Large numbers of ethnic Chinese fled the country after a border clash with China in 1979. Buddhism and Roman Catholicism are practised, but religion is discouraged by the government.

*History.* The area that is now Vietnam is composed of the historic regions of TONKIN, ANNAM, and COCHIN CHINA. European traders began to arrive in the early 16th cent. The French captured Saigon in 1859, organized the colony of Cochin China in 1867, and declared protectorates over Tonkin and Annam in 1884. The three were merged with Cambodia in 1887 to form French INDOCHINA. A nationalist movement arose in the early 20th cent., gaining momentum during the Japanese occupation in WORLD WAR II. After the Japanese withdrew in 1945 the VIET MINH, a coalition of nationalists and Communists, established a republic headed by HO CHI MINH. French attempts to reassert control and establish BAO DAI as emperor resulted in the French Indochina War (1946–54), which ended with the defeat of the French at DIENBIENPHU. At the Geneva Conference of 1954 Vietnam was provisionally divided, pending nationwide free elections, into Communist North Vietnam and nationalist South Vietnam. Fearing a Communist victory, the regime of Ngo Dinh Diem refused to hold the scheduled elections and declared the south an independent republic in 1955. The VIETNAM WAR ensued, with the US aiding South Vietnam. A ceasefire was signed and US troops withdrawn in 1973, but the Communists overran the south in 1975, reunifying (1976) the country and joining the COUNCIL FOR MUTUAL ECONOMIC ASSISTANCE in 1978. The regime launched a large-scale resettlement and reeducation programme to suppress continued opposition in the south. In 1978–79 it invaded Cambodia, overthrowing the regime of POL POT and provoking a brief invasion by China. Continued political and social upheaval took its toll on the economy, which is heavily supported by the USSR, and also prompted the flight of great numbers of refugee 'boat people'. In 1981 veteran Communist Truong Chinh was elected president of Vietnam and in mid-1986, on the death of LE DUAN, he became general secretary of the Communist Party. In late 1986 he was replaced by NGUYEN VAN LINH.

Vietnam

**Vietnam War,** 1954–75, war in Southeast Asia between the government of South VIETNAM, aided by the US, and Communist insurgents, aided by North Vietnam. Following France's defeat in the French Indochina war (1946–54), Vietnam was divided into North and South Vietnam by the Geneva Conference (1954). War soon broke out in

South Vietnam as Communist-led guerrillas (the Viet Cong) tried to overthrow the South Vietnamese government. From 1961 the US supplied support troops to South Vietnam, and following the TONKIN GULF RESOLUTION (1964) the war quickly escalated (US troops numbered c.550,000 by 1969). Optimistic US military reports were discredited by the devastating Communist Tet offensive (1968), and opposition to the war grew in the US. Under Pres. NIXON the US began a policy of increased bombing and troop withdrawals. In 1973 a cease-fire agreement was signed at Paris that allowed US troops to withdraw, but it solved few problems. The war finally ended in a Communist victory in 1975, when the North Vietnamese launched their final offensive and routed the South Vietnamese army.

**viewdata:** see VIDEOTEX.

**Vigée-Lebrun, Élisabeth** (vee‚zhay-lə‚brunh), 1755–1842, French portrait painter. Painter and friend to MARIE ANTOINETTE, she is known for more than 20 elegant portraits of the Queen, amongst them *Marie Antoinette and her Children* (1787; Versailles) and for her memoirs.

**Vignola, Giacomo da** (vee‚nyohlah), 1507–73, leading late Renaissance Italian architect, papal architect (after 1550) to Julius III; also known as Giacomo Barocchio or Barozzi. He succeeded MICHELANGELO in charge of work at St Peter's, Rome (1564). His finest productions are the Villa Caprorola, near Viterbo, and the Villa Giulia, Rome, as well as the interior for the Church of the Gesù, Rome (1568), which greatly influenced ecclesiastical architecture. He wrote (1562) a universally known treatise on the ORDERS OF ARCHITECTURE.

**Vigny, Alfred Victor, comte de** (vee‚nyee), 1797–1863, French author. Stressing the lonely struggle of the individual in a hostile universe, he expressed the philosophy of ROMANTICISM. His best-known poems are in *Poèmes antiques et modernes* (1826; tr. Poems Ancient and Modern) and *Les Destinées* (1864). Prose works include the novel *Cinq-mars* (1826; tr. The Spider and the Fly) and *Chatterton* (1835), a play.

**Vigo,** city (1981 pop. 258,724), Galicia, NW Spain, on the Atlantic coast. It is home port of a large fishing fleet and has important fish-processing industries and shipbuilding. It maintains close links with South American ports.

**Vigo, Jean** (vee‚goh), 1905–34, French film director. His films *Zéro de conduite* (1933) and *L'Atalante* (1934) are a haunting blend of anarchism, lyricism, and surrealism.

**Vijayawada,** formerly **Bezwada,** town (1981 pop. 461,772), Andhra Pradesh state, E India, at the head of the GODAVARI delta. It is the administrative centre of Krishna dist. and trades extensively in rice and tobacco, the produce of the surrounding areas. It also has important educational institutions.

**Vikings,** Scandinavian warriors who raided the coasts of Europe and the British Isles from the 9th to 11th cent. The world's best shipbuilders, they were driven as far as Greenland and North America by overpopulation, internal dissension, quest for trade, and thirst for adventure. Many Vikings settled where they had raided (see NORSEMEN). The Viking Age ended with the introduction of Christianity into Scandinavia; the emergence of the kingdoms of Norway, Denmark, and Sweden; and the rise of European states strong enough to repel invasion.

**Vila,** town (1979 pop. 14,797), capital of VANUATU, on Efâte island.

**Vile, William,** d. 1767, English furniture designer and cabinetmaker. In partnership with John Cobb (d. 1778), he produced high quality furniture, much of which was strongly architectural but with carved ROCOCO ornament. He supplied many pieces to the crown.

**Villa, Pancho** (Francisco Villa) (‚veeyah), c.1877–1923, Mexican revolutionary; b. Doroteo Arango. A bandit in N Mexico, he joined (1910) the rebels and fought vigorously for Pres. MADERO and later against Gen. HUERTA and Pres. CARRANZA. He and ZAPATA occupied (1914–15) Mexico City, but he was decisively defeated (1915) by Gen. OBREGÓN. After Villa's men killed (1916) some American citizens at Columbus, N. Mexico, a US army expedition pursued Villa in Mexico for 11 months without success. At times a rebel against injustice, but always an undirected, destructive force, Villa became a national hero.

**Villa-Lobos, Heitor** (‚veelah ‚lohbos), 1887–1959, Brazilian composer. He is known for his use of Brazilian folk music, as in his series of *Chôros* (1920–29) and *Bachianas brasileiras* (1930–45). His compositions include 12 symphonies, operas, concertos, 16 string quartets, and songs.

Mahogany library table designed by William **Vile** (c.1760)

**Villehardouin, Geoffroi de** (veehah dwan), c.1160–c.1212, French historian. A leader and chronicler of the Fourth CRUSADE. His *The Conquest of Constantinople* is an early masterpiece of French prose.

**villein,** a peasant under the medieval MANORIAL SYSTEM. By the 13th cent. in England, SERFS came to be called villeins. The villein was attached to the manor and paid dues to and performed servile labour for the lord. A number of factors caused **villeinage** to disappear in England in the 14th cent. Growing towns weakened the manorial system, and money rents began to replace labour dues. Moreover, the PLAGUE of 1349, by greatly reducing the population, improved the bargaining power of labour. In parts of Europe the system survived into the 18th or 19th cent.

**Villon, François** (vee yawnh), 1431–1463?, French poet. Confessedly a vagabond and rogue from his student days, Villon was banished from Paris after killing a man in 1455. He fell in with the *coquillards,* a band of thieves, and for them he composed his ballads in thieves' jargon. Besides these, his chief works are the *Lais* or *Petit testament* (1456) and *Testament* (1461), each of which is a series of facetious bequests to family, friends, and, especially, enemies. Interspersed in the *Testament* are ballads such as 'Ballade des dames du temps jadis', with the famous refrain, 'But where are the snows of yesteryear?' Other poems include 'Ballad of the Hanged', written during the author's anticipation of that fate. Alternately compassionate, ironic, ribald, penitent, and rebellious, Villon is one of the great medieval poets, but with an intensely personal message that ranks him with the moderns.

**Villon, Jacques,** 1875–1963, French painter; brother of Marcel DUCHAMP and Raymond DUCHAMP-VILLON. An exponent of CUBISM, he is known for his refinement of the cubist style.

**Vilnius,** city (1985 pop. 544,000), capital of LITHUANIA, W European USSR, on the Neris R. Its industries include metallurgy and food processing. Lithuania's capital from 1323, it developed as a largely Polish–Jewish city within the Polish-Lithuanian Commonwealth (to 1793). After 1795 it was ruled by Russia (see POLAND, PARTITIONS OF). The city was disputed by Poland and Lithuania from 1918 to 1938; in 1939 it was restored to Lithuania, which was annexed by the USSR in 1940. During World War II Vilnius was occupied (1941–44) by the Germans, whose virtual extermination of the Jewish population ended its long tradition as a leading E European centre of Jewish learning.

**Viña del Mar,** city (1984 pop. 307,308), central Chile, on the Pacific Ocean, near VALPARAISO. Founded in 1874, it is now one of the most popular resort cities in South America, with luxurious hotels, a gambling centre, and fine beaches. There are also some industries and a naval base.

**Vincent de Paul, Saint,** 1580?–1660, French priest renowned for charitable work. His activism and holiness brought about a revival of French Catholicism. In 1625 he founded an order of secular priests (Lazarists or Vincentians); he also founded the Sisters of Charity. Feast: 27 Sept.

**Vinci, Leonardo da:** see LEONARDO DA VINCI.

**vinegar,** sour liquid consisting mainly of acetic acid and water, produced by the action of bacteria on dilute solutions of ETHANOL derived from previous yeast FERMENTATION. The alcoholic liquor used, e.g., cider or wine, determines the characteristic colour and flavour. Acetic fermentation may be impeded by an excessive growth of mother of vinegar, a slimy mass of bacteria, or of the parasitic vinegar eel, a minute, threadlike worm. Vinegar is used in salad dressings, as a preservative, as a mild disinfectant, and, in cooking, as a fibre softener in a marinade.

**Vinson Massif,** peak, 4897 m (16,066 ft), highest point in ANTARCTICA, located in the Ellsworth Mts. Named after Carl Vinson, a US politician, it was first climbed on 17 Dec. 1966 by a US expedition led by Nicholas B. Clinch.

**viol,** family of bowed STRINGED INSTRUMENTS, the most important ensemble instruments from the 15th to the 17th cent., when they lost their dominant position to the VIOLIN family and became virtually extinct until the revival of interest in early music in the 20th cent. The viol, a chamber instrument with a soft, sweet tone, differs from the dynamically more brilliant violin in several ways. It usually has sloping shoulders, a flat back, and deeper ribs than the violin, has a fretted fingerboard, is tuned in fourths rather than fifths, and usually is played upright, resting on or between the knees, the bow held with the palm upward. The viol was built in four principal sizes treble, alto, tenor, and bass which were used in ensemble, or 'consort'. The double-bass viol, or *violone,* survived all other viols to become (with some modifications) the modern DOUBLE BASS.

**viola,** the alto of the VIOLIN family. It has four strings tuned in fifths, the lowest string being the C below middle C. A useful member of the ORCHESTRA, the viola has a small solo repertoire but is one of the parts in the STRING QUARTET.

**viola da gamba** [Ital., = knee viol], term for the bass viol, originally the name of the whole VIOL family.

**violet,** common name for some members of the family Violaceae, chiefly perennial herbs (and sometimes shrubs) found on all continents. Violets (genus *Viola* and similar related species) are popular florists', garden, and wild flowers. Violets have fragrant, deep purple to yellow or white blossoms. Various species, especially the sweet, or English, violet (*V. odorata*), have been used in perfumes, dyes, and medicines (cough medicines and puragatives), and are candied in confectionery. The common pansy was derived from *V. tricolor.* Its irregularly shaped, variously coloured flowers have five velvety petals. Some unrelated plants are also called violets, e.g., the AFRICAN VIOLET of the GESNERIA family.

**violin,** family of STRINGED INSTRUMENTS having wooden bodies whose backs and fronts are slightly convex, the fronts pierced by two *??*-shaped resonance holes. There are four strings, tuned in fifths, across which the player draws a horsehair bow; a variety of sounds may be produced by different bowing techniques. The fingers of the left hand are used to stop the strings against the fingerboard, thus changing the pitch by shortening the vibrating length of the strings. With their versatility, brilliance, and wide dynamic range, the instruments of the violin family have long dominated the ORCHESTRA. The first instrument of this type appeared about 1510 as the *viola da braccio* (arm viol). The present-day violin was developed towards the end of the 16th cent., and the peak of violinmaking was reached over the following century by such master craftsmen as the AMATI, GUARNIERI, and STRADIVARI families of Cremona, Italy. The violin, the smallest and most agile member of the family, has from the beginning been a major solo instrument, the mainstay of CHAMBER MUSIC (see also STRING QUARTET) and the principal instrument of the ORCHESTRA. It is tuned in fifths, the lowest string being the G below middle C. The larger and lower-pitched members of the family are the VIOLA and CELLO; the DOUBLE BASS is really a member of the VIOL family.

**Viollet-le-Duc, Eugène Emmanuel** (vyaw lay lə dyk), 1814–79, French architect and writer. He was the most prominent exponent of the GOTHIC REVIVAL in France, celebrated for his restoration work. His efforts included restoration of the SAINTE-CHAPELLE and work on NÔTRE-DAME DE PARIS. His other restorations include the cathedrals of Amiens, Chartres, and Rheims; the château of Pierrefonds; and the city of Carcassonne. His writings, which he illustrated himself, emphasize the organic quality of Gothic structures.

**violoncello** or **cello,** lowest member of the VIOLIN family. It has four strings tuned in fifths, the lowest string being C two octaves below middle C. Developed at the same time as the violin in the 16th cent., the cello originally had no spike but was played grasped between the player's knees. It has a magnificent solo repertoire from unaccompanied pieces to concertos, and is a mainstay of the ORCHESTRA and a member of the STRING QUARTET.

**Vionnet, Madeleine:** see FASHION (table).

**viper,** poisonous SNAKE of the family Viperidae, found in Eurasia and Africa. Characterized by erectile, hypodermic fangs, vipers range in size from under 30 cm (1 ft) to nearly 2 m (6 ft) and often have zigzag or diamond markings. Best known are the European Asp (*Vipera aspis*), native to S Europe, and the common European viper, or adder (*V. berus*), found throughout Europe and N Asia; it is the only poisonous snake found in the British Isles. The PIT VIPERS of the Americas belong to a different family.

**Virchow, Rudolf** (ˌfiəkhoh), 1821–1902, German pathologist. He taught at the Univ. of Würzburg and then directed the Pathological Inst. in Berlin. The founder of the theory of disease of the cells, he contributed to nearly every branch of medicine and to anthropology, and introduced sanitary reforms in Berlin. Elected a member of the Prussian Lower House and later of the Reichstag, he was a leader of the liberal Progressive Party opposed to Bismarck.

**Virgil** or **Vergil** (Publius Vergilius Maro), 70–19 BC, greatest of Roman poets; b. near Mantua; he came to Rome c.41 BC. Early life on his father's farm was central to his education. The *Eclogues* or *Bucolics* (37 BC) treated rural life in the manner of THEOCRITUS. Virgil then turned to realistic and didactic rural poetry in the *Georgics* (29 BC), seeking, like HESIOD, to convey the charm of real life and work on the farm. He spent the rest of his life working on his national EPIC, the *Aeneid,* one of the greatest long poems in world literature. Virgil's AENEAS is a paradoxical combination of Roman virtues—familial devotion, loyalty to the state, and piety—and of human frailty, an Augustan not an Homeric hero. The 12 books follow Aeneas from TROY's fall through his affair with the Carthaginian queen, DIDO, to the founding of the Roman state. The poem, in dactylic hexameters of striking quality, is central to all Latin literature. A favourite of AUGUSTUS, Virgil's work influenced Latin poets from 1st cent. AD, and later poets from DANTE on.

**Virginia,** state of the US (1984 est. pop. 5,636,000), area 105,716 km² (40,817 sq mi), situated in the south–central region, bordered by West Virginia and Kentucky (W), Maryland (N, NE), the Atlantic Ocean (E), and North Carolina and Tennessee (S). The capital is RICHMOND and the largest city is NORFOLK; Virginia Beach, Chesapeake and Newport News are also important. The drowned valleys and low marshes of the coastal plain, or tidewater region, are separated by the Fall Line from the rolling hills of the Piedmont plateau. Farther west, the BLUE RIDGE Mts are separated by the Valley of Virginia from the Allegheny Mts. Manufacturing is the chief source of income, chemicals, processed foods, and tobacco being the leading products. The main farm commodities are dairy products, cattle, tobacco, broiler chickens, and animal feed; oysters and crabs are fished along the coast. Tourism centres on the mountain areas and historic sites, including the restored colonial town of WILLIAMSBURG. In 1980 78% of the population was non-Hispanic white and 17% was black; almost 65% lived in metropolitan areas. In 1607 JAMESTOWN, the first permanent English settlement in North America, was founded in Virginia. It thrived on tobacco cultivation and shipping, using slave labour. It was the first state to declare independence from Great Britain in 1776, and bred the first president of the US, George WASHINGTON, as well as the drafter of the Declaration of Independence, Thomas JEFFERSON. Richmond was the capital of the Confederacy during the Civil War, and another Virginian, Robert E. LEE, commanded its army; most of the fighting was in the state. After the state's readmittance to the Union the economy diversified. In the 1950s and 1960s the racial integration of schools proceeded slowly, but was generally accepted by the 1970s. Despite some prosperity resulting from the revival of coal-mining and the growth of naval bases, Virginia's economy is still modest.

**Virginia Beach,** US city (1984 est. pop. 309,000), SE Virginia, on the Atlantic coast. Formed by the merger (1963) of the town of Virginia Beach and Princess Anne co., it encompasses 782 km² (302 sq mi), reaching 45 km (28 mi) to the North Carolina border. It is a tourist centre with beautiful beaches and several large military bases.

**Virginia Company,** name of two English colonization companies chartered by King JAMES I in 1606. One founded the PLYMOUTH COLONY; the other, later known as the London Company, founded colonies in the South, notably JAMESTOWN, Virginia.

**Virginia creeper,** woody vine (*Parthenocissus quinquefolia*) of the GRAPE family, popular as a wall covering. It has five-fingered leaves, blue-black berries, and clings by disc-tipped tendrils, with some branches hanging free. *P. tricuspidata*, also called Virginia creeper, but with three-fingered leaves, is favoured for its brilliant autumn colouring and closer adhesion to walls.

**Virginia Resolutions:** see KENTUCKY AND VIRGINIA RESOLUTIONS.

**Virgin Islands,** group of about 100 small islands, WEST INDIES, E of Puerto Rico, owned by the US and Great Britain, constituting the westernmost part of the Lesser Antilles. Their tropical climate and picturesque quality, enhanced by Old World architecture, make them a popular tourist destination. However, the population, mostly black, remains poor. Columbus discovered and named the islands in 1493. The **Virgin Islands of the US** (1981 pop. 99,000), 344 km² (137 sq mi) were purchased from Denmark in 1917; the islanders became US citizens in 1927. The Dept. of the Interior administers the islands, which have a locally elected governor and senate. The capital is Charlotte Amalie on St Thomas. The group is composed of 68 islands, but only three are important: St Croix (1980 pop. 49,013), St Thomas (1980 pop. 44,218), and St John (1980 pop. 2360). St Thomas (83 km²/32 sq mi) is mountainous, heavily cultivated, and has fine harbours. St Croix (207 km²/80 sq mi) is flatter and predominantly agricultural. Christiansted is the chief town. Much of St John (52 km²/20 sq mi) is occupied by the Virgin Islands National Park (see NATIONAL PARKS, table). Cattle are raised on all three islands, and meat-packing is important. The Danish settled St Thomas in 1672, acquired St John in 1683, and bought St Croix from France in 1733. The **British Virgin Islands** (1981 est. pop. 11,800), 153 km² (59 sq mi), are to the northeast. Of more than 30 islands, the most important are Tortola, Anegada, and Virgin Gorda. Road Town, the capital, is on Tortola. Tourism, farming, and fishing are the chief economic activities. Britain acquired the islands from the Dutch in 1666.

**Viriatus,** d. 139 BC, leader of the Lusitani, group of Iberian tribes. He headed a successful rebellion (147 BC) against Roman rule, inflicted defeats on Roman armies, and maintained an independent state until some of his followers accepted Roman bribes and killed him.

**virus,** infectious microorganism composed mainly of NUCLEIC ACID within a protein coat, ranging in size from 10 to 200 nm; they can be seen only with an electron microscope. Unlike bacteria, viruses only reproduce inside host cells. When they enter a living plant, animal, or bacterial cell, they make use of the host cell's chemical energy and protein- and nucleic-acid-synthesizing ability to replicate themselves. Some, like the bacteriophages, have protein tails used for infecting the host. Viral nucleic acids are single- or double-stranded and may be DNA or RNA. After viral components are made by the infected host cell, virus particles are released; the host cell is often dissolved. Some viruses do not kill cells but transform them into a cancerous state (see CANCER); some cause illness and then seem to disappear, while remaining latent and later causing another, sometimes much more severe, form of disease (e.g., AIDS). Viruses, known to cause cancer in animals, are suspected of causing cancer in humans; they also cause measles, mumps, yellow fever, poliomyelitis, influenza, and the common cold. Viral infections are not presently treatable with drugs, but VACCINATION is a useful control.

**Vischer, Peter,** the Elder, c.1455–1529, German sculptor, foremost of the bronze founders in Germany. His masterpiece is the reliquary of St Sebald at Nuremberg (1488–1519). Of the sons who carried on his work, two are celebrated. **Hermann Vischer,** the Younger, c.1486–1517, is best known for the tomb of Elisabeth and Hermann VIII of Henneberg (Stadtkirche, Römhild). **Peter Vischer,** the Younger, 1487–1528, executed the tomb of Frederick the Wise (Schlosskirche, Wittenberg).

**Visconti,** Italian family that ruled MILAN from the 13th cent. until 1447. Ottone Visconti, 1207–95, archbishop of Milan, was recognized as lord of the city in 1277. Both he and his great-nephew **Matteo I Visconti,** 1255–1322, supported the imperial or Ghibelline faction (see GUELPHS AND GHIBELLINES) and Matteo became imperial vicar of Milan. Later Viscontis increased and consolidated Milanese territory. **Gian Galeazzo Visconti,** 1351?–1402, who became tyrant of Pavia in 1376, embarked on a systematic programme of conquest, first in Venetia, then in central Italy. He bought (1395) the hereditary title of duke of Milan from the Emperor WENCESLAUS and defeated (1401) the German king Rupert, when Rupert tried to assert his rule in Italy. Gian Galeazzo sought to establish an Italian kingdom, but he died of the plague while preparing an attack on Florence, his chief enemy. His daughter, Valentina, married Louis d'ORLÉANS; it was through her that LOUIS XII and FRANCIS I of France derived their claims to Milan in the ITALIAN WARS. The dukedom passed to Gian Galeazzo's sons, first to **Giovanni Maria Visconti,** 1389–1412, a cruel ruler who was assassinated, and then to **Filippo Maria Visconti,** 1392–1447. Filippo Maria's daughter and heir, Bianca Maria, married Francesco I SFORZA, who became duke of Milan after the fall of the short-lived Ambrosian Republic (1447–50).

**Visconti, Luchino,** 1906–76, Italian film and stage director. His neorealist *Ossessione* (1943) and *La terra trema* (1948) were followed by such films as *The Leopard* (1963), *Death in Venice* (1970), and *Conversation Piece* (1975).

**viscosity,** resistance of a fluid to shear. This resistance acts against the motion of any solid object through the fluid, and also against motion of the fluid itself past stationary obstacles. Viscosity also acts internally on the fluid between slower- and faster-moving adjacent layers. All fluids exhibit viscosity to some degree.

**Vishakapatnam,** formerly Vizagapatam, city (1981 pop. 584,166), Andhra Pradesh state, E India. It is a district administrative centre and an important modern, deep-water port, with a sheltered harbour dredged from river alluvium. It is also a naval base, and the main location for shipbuilding in India, developed since independence. More recently it acquired a steel-works. It also has an oil refinery and other industries. There is a university at nearby Waltair. All this development has meant a great growth in population and importance. Vishakapatnam is, however, an ancient city, probably dating back to the 11th cent., though its medieval history is obscure. It became a factory of the British EAST INDIA COMPANY in the 18th cent., and was bombarded by the Japanese in 1942.

**Vishinsky, Andrei Yanuarievich** (vi͵sheenskee), 1883–1954, Soviet diplomat and jurist. He fought with the Bolsheviks (see BOLSHEVISM) in the Russian CIVIL WAR (1918–20) and later was professor of law and rector at Moscow Univ. He served as chief prosecutor at the Moscow treason trials (1936–38), deputy commissioner for foreign affairs (1940–49), foreign minister (1949–53), and permanent delegate to the UN (1953–54).

**Visigoths** or **West Goths,** a division of the Goths, one of the chief groups of ancient GERMANS. Separated from the OSTROGOTHS, or East Goths, they moved (376) into Roman territory under pressure of the HUNS. They routed the East Roman emperor VALENS at Adrianople (378), and their kings, ALARIC I and Ataulf, led them across Italy, sacking Rome in 410. The Visigoths expanded N to the Loire, made Toulouse their capital, and took Vandal lands in Spain. King Euric (r.466–c.484) brought them to their peak of power. After Alaric II lost (507) lands N of the Pyrenees to the Franks under CLOVIS, the Visigoths were essentially restricted to Spain. They became Christians and merged with the Spanish population. Anarchy followed the death (672) of King Recceswinth. Their last king, Roderick, was defeated (711) by the MOORS, who thus ended the Visigothic kingdom.

**vision:** see EYE.

**Viṣṇu,** one of the great gods of HINDUISM; in the Hindu trinity he is the preserver (see also BRAHMĀ; ŚIVA). He has an intimate connection with KRṢNA as well as with the theory of avatāra. In his 10 incarnations, he is said to have saved the earth from evil and protected the good and the virtuous.

**Vistula,** Polish *Wisa*, principal river of Poland, 1070 km (667 mi) long, rising in the CARPATHIAN MOUNTAINS and flowing through KRAKÓW, WARSAW and TORUN to the BALTIC SEA. It is navigable for much of its length, although most traffic is in the section below Warsaw. There are canal links with the ODER, Dnieper and Dniester Rs.

**vitamins and minerals,** organic compounds required in small amounts in the human diet for health and life. Vitamins provide the only source of certain COENZYMES necessary for METABOLISM, the biochemical processes that support life. Since vitamins differ widely in chemical structure, there is no common chemical grouping. They were originally classified as fat-soluble or water-soluble, but as more and more were discovered, they were also classified alphabetically. The fat-soluble

vitamins are stored in body fat and may therefore accumulate in quantities that can be toxic; vitamins A, D, E, and K are fat-soluble. Most water-soluble vitamins are rapidly excreted in the urine and thus rarely cause toxicity, even when ingested in excessive amounts; the B complex vitamins and vitamin C are water-soluble. A number of trace elements or minerals have been found to be essential to healthy development. They include calcium, iron, zinc, selenium, copper, chromium, iodine, manganese, magnesium, selenium, and molybdenum. Minute amounts of these substances are required in the diet. In many cases the result of a deficiency is not yet known, but lack of iron causes ANAEMIA, lack of iodine causes goitre, lack of zinc impairs wound healing and delays sexual maturity, and insufficient calcium can result in RICKETS and OSTEOPOROSIS. See table accompanying this article. See also DEFICIENCY DISEASE.

**Vitoria,** city (1981 pop. 192,773), capital of Álava prov. in the Basque country of N Spain. It is a market and service centre, with woodworking industries based on local timber supplies. In 1813 Wellington defeated the French here in one of the major battles of the PENINSULAR WAR. Historic buildings include a Gothic cathedral.

**Vitoria a Minas railway,** a leading example of a heavy-haul freight railway which connects iron ore mines in the State of Minas Gerais with Port Tubarao, Vitoria, Brazil. In 1984 the railway carried 96.4 milllion tonnes on a double-track line 895 km (555 mi) in length. The owners of the railway, Companhia Vale do Rio Doce, are the biggest producer of iron ore in the world and in 1985 opened the Carajas railway connecting mines at Serra do Carajas with a port at San Luiz, 890 km (551 mi) to the NE.

**Vittorini, Elio,** 1908–55, Italian novelist, critic, editor, and translator. A leading left-wing intellectual, he played a major role in the development of Italian literature from the 1930s onwards, e.g., with his influential translations of American authors. His own, often lyrically charged, fiction includes *Petty Bourgeoisie* (1931), *The Red Carnation* (1933), *In Sicily* (1941), *Men and Non-Men* (1945), and *Women of Messina* (1949).

**Vivaldi, Antonio,** c.1675–1741, Italian violinist and composer, the greatest master of the Italian BAROQUE. His style is characterized by driving RHYTHM, clarity, and lyrical melody. He is known chiefly for his instrumental music SONATAS, CONCERTOS (of which he wrote 447), and concerti grossi, e.g., *The Four Seasons* (1725). He was also a distinguished opera composer. He helped standardize the three-movement concerto form and influenced J.S.BACH, who arranged 10 of his concertos.

**viviparous,** description of those animals in which the egg develops into an embryo which obtains its food from its mother's body. In marsupials the partially developed young are born and migrate into an external pouch on the mother's body where they are fed and protected until they are fully developed. In mammals the young are kept within the mother's body, connected to her blood supply through the placenta, until they are fully developed. The stage of maturity at which the young are born varies greatly.

**vivisection:** see ANIMAL EXPERIMENTATION.

**Vladimirescu, Tudor** (vla͵deemeer'eskooh), c.1780–1821, Romanian national hero. He volunteered for the Russian army in the Russo-Turkish War (1806–12) and shortly afterwards is believed to have joined the Etairia, a society with plans to raise a Greek national revolt in the Balkans. Vlandimirescu, however, led his own revolt of peasants against boyar rule in WALACHIA in 1821. Distrusted by the Etairia, which had raised a revolt in MOLDAVIA and Walachia against the Turks in the same year, Vladimirescu was murdered and his followers dispersed.

**Vladimir I** or **Saint Vladimir** (͵vladəmiə), 956–1015, first Christian grand duke of Kiev (r.980–1015). To succeed his father Svyatoslav as ruler of KIEVAN RUSSIA he defeated his two brothers. In about 988 he became a Christian and married Anna, sister of Byzantine Emperor BASIL II. Feast: 15 July.

**Vladivostok,** city. (1985 est. pop. 600,000), Soviet Far East, on a peninsula between two bays of the Sea of Japan. It is the chief Soviet port and naval base in the Pacific (kept open in winter by icebreakers), the terminus of the TRANS-SIBERIAN RAILWAY and the Northern Sea Route, and a base for fishing and whaling fleets. Its industries include shipbuilding and food processing. Founded in 1860, it was an outpost for Russian expansion in the Far East. In 1917 it was occupied by five armies; the

## VITAMINS

| Vitamin | Important Sources | Function | Result of excess or deficiency |
| --- | --- | --- | --- |
| A | Green leafy or yellow vegetables, fish-liver oils, egg yolk, milk, butter | Essential to skeletal growth, skin, epithelial tissue, visual process, and vital to body's immune response | Deficiency can cause night blindness, permanent eye damage, skin abnormalities. *Overdose* may cause skin, hair, bone abnormalities. |
| B₁ (thiamine) | Whole grains, liver, lean pork, yeast, legumes, nuts | Important in METABOLISM of CARBOHYDRATES | Beriberi (neurological, gastrointestinal disorders; heart affected in severe cases) caused by a shortage. |
| B₂ (riboflavin) | Milk, green leafy vegetables, liver and organs, eggs | Synthesis of COENZYMES; biochemical OXIDATIONS AND REDUCTIONS | Lesions of skin, mouth, eyes result from a deficiency. |
| Niacin | Liver, lean meat, yeast, fish, wheat germ, peanuts | Component of coenzymes in oxidations and reductions | Pellagra (skin disease, diarrhoea, dementia, ultimately death) caused by a deficiency. |
| B₆ (pyridoxine) | Lean meat, liver, yeast, milk, whole grains, egg yolk | Coenzyme in metabolism of AMINO ACIDS, PROTEINS | Lack lends to decreased haemoglobin production, ANAEMIA; in infants, convulsions. |
| Biotin | Synthesized by intestinal bacteria; also found in liver, egg yolk, yeast, kidney | Coenzyme in metabolism of carbohydrates, fats, amino acids | (Deficiency produced by large doses of raw egg white; symptoms include dry skin, anaemia). |
| Pantothenic acid | Liver, kidney, egg yolk, yeast | Nutritional role unclear; part of coenzyme A, major metabolic agent | (Deficiency produced only in laboratory animals). |
| Folic acid | Green leafy vegetables, liver, yeast | Involved in synthesis of nucleic acids, rapidly synthesizing (e.g., intestinal) cells; possibly important in the very early development of the embryo | Forms of anaemia caused by a deficiency. |
| B₁₂ (cyanocobalamin) | Liver, kidney, lean meat, bivalves, fish, eggs | Amino, fatty acid metabolism; production of proteins | Associated with pernicious anaemia caused by lack of 'intrinsic factor' that B₁₂ dosage can cure. |
| C (ascorbic acid) | Citrus fruits, tomatoes, peppers, cabbage, potatoes, berries | Important in collagen (connective tissue protein) synthesis; effect on common COLD disputed | Deficiency can cause scurvy (weakened capillaries, internal haemorrhaging, anaemia, general debility, ultimately death). |
| D | Exists in human skin and is activated by exposure to sunlight; also found in fish liver oils, irradiated milk, yeast, egg yolk | Regulates utilization of calcium, phosphorus in bone formation | Lack of sunlight causes rickets: in children, bowlegs, knock-knees; in adults, softening of bones (osteomalacia). *Overdose* may cause kidney damage, calcium deposits. |
| E (tocopherol) | Peanut, vegetable oils; wheat germ, green leafy vegetables, eggs | Significance in nutrition and role in human reproduction is undetermined | Human requirement assumed, but evidence inconclusive. |
| K | Liver, green leafy vegetables; also synthesized by intestinal bacteria | Essential to blood clotting; role in liver production of the protein prothrombin | Abnormally long clotting time. Deficiency not of dietary origin. K does not treat HAEMOPHILIA. |

Japanese remained until 1922. The city was a major port for World War II LEND-LEASE supplies.

**Vlaminck, Maurice de** (vlah,manhk), 1876–1958, French painter, writer, and printmaker and a friend of DERAIN and member of the Fauve group. An untrained artist, he was interested in a technique unmediated by conventions and learnt skills. He looked at children's art, African sculpture, and VAN GOGH to develop a spontaneous expressive style. This he associated with his anarchist political ideas, and he saw individuality as opposing establishment academic art.

**VLSI:** see VERY LARGE-SCALE INTEGRATION.

**vocal cords:** see LARYNX.

**vocational education,** preparation of pupils or students for a specific occupation or range of occupations. It has often been distinguished from general or liberal education. The earliest form of vocational education, before the Industrial Revolution, was apprenticeship training. In the 19th cent. vocational education became identified in Britain with manual training. Vocational training in the 20th cent. has sometimes been interpreted as the province of specialized schools (focusing, for example, on secretarial or technical subjects), and sometimes as specific routes through the later years of secondary schooling. FURTHER EDUCATION colleges have strong vocational purposes, and developments at SECONDARY SCHOOL level sponsored by the Manpower Services Comission have been particularly clearly work-related. In higher education, courses aiming at specific occupations (e.g., pharmacy, estate management, engineering, business studies) are often referred to as vocational.

**vocative:** see CASE.

**vodka,** traditional spirituous drink of Russia, the Baltic states, and Poland; now consumed internationally. Containing over 90% alcohol (usually diluted before marketing), vodka has little or no odour or taste.

It is distilled from rye and barley malt or from the cheaper maize or potatoes.

**voice,** grammatical category according to which an action is referred to as done by the subject (active, e.g., *men shoot bears*) or to the subject (passive, e.g., *bears are shot by men*). In Latin, voice is a category of INFLECTION.

**voice,** in music. Singing voices are classified by ranges as soprano and contralto (or alto), the high and low female voices, with mezzo-soprano as an intermediate classification; and as tenor and bass, the high and low male voices, with baritone as intermediate classification. The sound of the castrato (a male singer with an artificially high voice, the result of castration in boyhood), for which many 17th- and 18th-cent. soprano and alto roles were intended, is approached today by the countertenor. Choral music generally requires a range of about an octave and a half for each voice; a solo singer must have at least two octaves. Over the centuries great changes have taken place in the art of singing within Western musical culture, and modern singers can only approximate the timbre of earlier eras. Gregorian chant may have been sung with a nasal timbre resembling Asian and Islamic techniques. BEL CANTO, the virtuosic art of vocal technique that flourished from the 17th to 19th cent., has been revived in the 20th cent. Studies of folk-music in Africa, Latin America, Oceania, and Asia, and of Japanese, Chinese, Indian, and other traditions of art music, have revealed an astonishing variety of vocal techniques.

**Voice of America** (VOA), broadcasting service of the International Communications Agency, an independent US government body. Founded in 1942, the VOA produces and broadcasts English- and foreign-language radio programmes in many parts of the world in an effort to promote a favourable impression of the US. It features news reports and entertainment.

**voiceprint,** a spectrographic representation of the range of frequencies in a person's voice. It is often thought to be as individual as a fingerprint, but it has proved difficult to interpret for legal purposes.

**Vojvodina** (voy‚vawdinə), socialist autonomous province of Serbia in N central Yugoslavia (1981 pop. 2,034,772), 21,506 km² (8303 sq mi). Novi Sad is the capital. Intersected by the Sava, Danube, and Tiza rivers, Vojvodina consists of those parts of the agriculturally rich Hungarian plain incorporated in the Yugoslav state in 1918. The province contains Yugoslavia's best arable land, much of which is farmed industrially. Its population is highly multinational. Serbs constitute 54.4%; but there are large numbers of Hungarians (18.9%), declared 'Yugoslavs' (18.2%), Croats (5.4%), Slovaks (3.4%), and Romanians (2.3%), as well as numerous others. Long a contested border region between the HABSBURG and OTTOMAN empires, after 1699 the area was extensively colonized by the Austrians with both central Europeans and Serbs fleeing north from the Ottomans. In the 18th cent. Vojvodina became the centre of the Serbs' national revival, and its commercial and intellectual significance was only gradually outstripped during the 19th cent. by the expanding Serbian principality to the south. United with Serbia at the end of World War I, the region was divided by the Germans, Hungarians, and USTAŠE in World War II. It was made an autonomous province of Serbia in 1945 and its previously large German population either fled or was expelled.

**volcano,** aperture in the crust of a planet or natural satellite through which gases, LAVA, and solid fragments are discharged. The term is also applied to the conical MOUNTAIN (cone) built up around the vent by ejected matter. Volcanoes are described as active, dormant, or extinct. On earth about 500 are known to be active. Belts of volcanoes are found along the crest of the mid-ocean ridge system (see OCEAN) and at converging crustal plate boundaries (see PLATE TECTONICS). There are also isolated volcanoes not associated with crustal movements (e.g., the Hawaiian Islands; see HAWAII). Eruptions range from the quiet type (Hawaiian) to the violently explosive (e.g., PELÉE and KRAKATOA). The *Mariner 9* space probe revealed (1971) that the planet MARS has a number of volcanoes, including the largest in the solar system, Olympus Mons. The *Voyager 1* space probe photographed (1979) at least eight active volcanoes on Io, a satellite of JUPITER.

**vole,** mouselike RODENT (called field or meadow mouse in North America) related to the LEMMING and the muskrat. Found in Eurasia, N Africa, and North America, most voles are from 9 to 18 cm (3½ to 7 in) long and have grey or brown coats and short tails. They eat mainly grasses but also feed

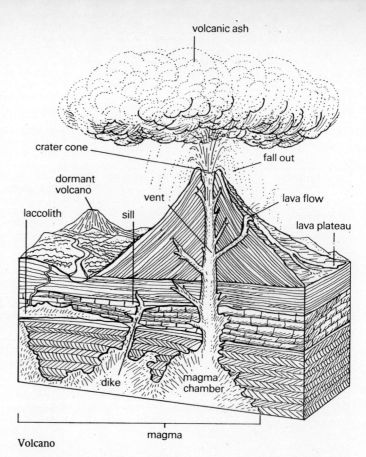

Volcano

on seeds and insects; they nest in dense growth or shallow burrows. Some are aquatic. The European water vole burrows into river banks, digging separate chambers for sleeping and food storage. It is also known as the water rat, made popular in Kenneth Graham's *The Wind in the Willows*.

**Volga,** river, c.3700 km (2300 mi) long, W USSR, longest river in Europe (as the continent is traditionally defined). It rises at an elevation of only 226 m (742 ft) in the Valday Hills near Moscow and winds E past Gorky and Kazan, then S past Kuybyshev and Volgograd to enter the CASPIAN SEA below sea level in a wide delta near Astrakhan. Canals connect the river with the Baltic Sea (N), with Moscow, and with the Don R. and the Black Sea (S). The Volga carries about half of all river freight in the USSR. Numerous dams (bypassed by locks) provide hydroelectricity along much of its course and water for irrigation of the southern STEPPES. The river, known in Russian folklore as 'Mother Volga', has played an incalculable part in the life of the Russian people.

**Volgograd** formerly **Stalingrad,** city (1985 est. pop. 974,000), SE European USSR, a port on the Volga R. and the eastern terminus of the Volga–Don Canal. Its industries include shipbuilding, oil refining, and steel production. Nearby is one of the world's largest hydroelectric power dams. Founded in 1569 as Tsaritsyn, the city fell to the Cossack rebel armies of Stenka Razin (1670) and PUGACHEV (1774). It was renamed Stalingrad in 1925. In World War II it was virtually destroyed and thousands were killed (Sept. 1942–Feb. 1943) before German forces surrendered. After the turning point at Stalingrad Soviet forces took the offensive on the eastern front. The city was renamed Volgograd in 1961.

**volleyball,** indoor or outdoor game in which opposing teams of six players hit a large, inflated ball back and forth across a net. The court, 18 m (59 ft) by 9 m (29 ft 6 in), is divided by a net 2.44 m (8 ft) high at the top. Any part of the body may be used to hit the ball. Points are scored by the serving team when its opponent allows the ball to touch the ground. Volleyball originated (1895) in Holyoke, Mass., and became an Olympic event in 1964.

**Volstead Act,** in US history, the law passed in 1919 to enforce the 18th Amendment, which prohibited the sale, manufacture, and transport of all alcoholic beverages. The law was sponsored by Rep. Andrew Volstead of Minnesota. It became void after the repeal of the amendment in 1933.

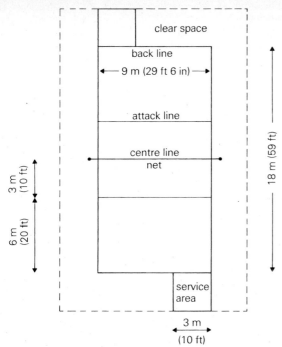

Volleyball court dimensions

**volt** (V), unit of voltage or, more technically, of electric POTENTIAL and ELECTROMOTIVE FORCE. It is defined as the difference of electric potential existing across the ends of a conductor having a resistance of 1 OHM when the conductor is carrying a current of 1 AMPERE.

**Volta,** river of Ghana, W Africa, flowing south to the Gulf of Guinea at Ada. Akosombo Dam (completed 1965), c.97 km (60 mi) from the river's mouth, impounds Lake Volta, one of the world's largest man-made lakes (c.8480 km²/3275 sq mi). The lake now extends more than 400 km (250 mi) upstream into N Ghana, beyond the point at which the Volta is formed by the confluence of the White Volta and Black Volta rivers.

**Volta, Alessandro, Conte,** 1745–1827, Italian physicist. He invented the so-called Volta's pile (or voltaic pile), the electrophorus (a device to generate static electric charges), and the voltaic CELL. The VOLT, a unit of electrical measurement, is named after him.

**voltage:** see ELECTROMOTIVE FORCE; POTENTIAL, ELECTRIC.

**voltage divider:** see POTENTIOMETER.

**Voltaire, François Marie Arouet de** (vol͵tɛə), 1694–1778, French philosopher and writer; b. François Marie Arouet. He was a leading figure of the ENLIGHTENMENT. Twice unjustly imprisoned (1717–18, 1726) and then banished to England (1726–29), he developed a hatred of judicial arbitrariness coupled with an admiration of English liberalism. Returning to France, he resided at Cirey, in Lorraine, with Mme Du Châtelet, who exerted an important intellectual influence on him. Upon her death in 1749, he went to live at the court of Prussia, but his relationship with FREDERICK II was stormy, and Voltaire left in 1753. He settled on an estate near Geneva. His triumphal return to Paris in 1778 proved too much for him, and he died soon after. Voltaire's work is immense, and his influence enormous. His *Letters concerning the English Nation* (1733) initiated the vogue for English philosophy and science (especially for Locke and Newton) that characterized the French Enlightenment. The *Philosophical Dictionary* (1764) distilled his political and religious biases. He wrote many tragedies, among them *Brutus* (1730) and *Zaïre* (1732). His great historical works *The Age of Louis XIV* (1751) and the *Essay on Manners* (1756) pioneered a new approach, emphasizing culture and commerce as much as politics and war. Most widely read today is his satirical masterpiece, *Candide* (1759), whose conclusion, 'Let us cultivate our garden', expresses succinctly Voltaire's philosophy of common sense.

**voltmeter,** instrument used to measure, in volts, differences in electric POTENTIAL, or voltage, between two points in a circuit. Most voltmeters are based on the d'Arsonval GALVANOMETER and are of the analogue type, i.e.,

they give voltage readings that can vary over a continuous range, as indicated by a scale and pointer. Digital voltmeters, which provide voltage readings represented by groups of digits, are, however, becoming increasingly common. A voltmeter is often combined with an AMMETER and an OHMMETER in a multipurpose instrument.

**Von.** For some German names beginning thus, see under the proper name; e.g., for Von Bismarck, see BISMARCK, OTTO VON.

**von Braun, Wernher** (von ͵brown), 1912–77, German-American ROCKET engineer. He was technical director (1937–45) of the German rocket research centre at Peenemünde, where the V-2 rocket and other weapons were developed. In 1945, von Braun and many members of his team were brought to the US, where he worked on guided missiles for the army and later, as director of NASA's Marshall Space Flight Center, led the development of the Saturn rockets used in the Apollo manned lunar-landing missions. He became (1970) deputy associate administrator of NASA.

**Vondel, Joost van den,** 1587–1679, Dutch poet and dramatist; b. Germany. Considered the greatest Dutch writer, he produced verse that is melodious, sonorous, and seemingly effortless. Of his highly baroque Christian dramas, the most famous are *Gysbrecht van Aemstel* (1637) and *Lucifer* (1654).

**Vonnegut, Kurt, Jr.,** 1922–, American novelist. With wry charm, dark humour, and plots that sometimes resemble science fiction he protests the horrors of the 20th cent. Vonnegut's novels include *Player Piano* (1951), *Slaughterhouse Five* (1969), and *Deadeye Dick* (1982).

**von Neumann, John** (von ͵nyoohmən), 1903–57, American mathematician; b. Hungary. Educated in Germany, he moved to the US in 1930 to Princeton Univ. During World War II he was a US Army ballistics consultant and in 1943 joined the MANHATTAN PROJECT to develop an atomic bomb. This work showed the need for automatic computers to solve large scientific problems. In 1944 he became an advisor to the ENIAC project at the Univ. of Pennsylvania, and in 1945 the group published a proposal for a new machine, in which the concept of a stored program computer was formulated. This was a fundamental breakthrough from the ideas of Charles BABBAGE and was also foreseen by Alan TURING in his 'one tape' Turing machine. Among numerous publications are books on *The Theory of Games and Economic Behaviour* (1943) and *The Computer and the Brain* (1956).

**Von Sternberg, Josef,** 1894–1969, American film director; b. Austria as Jo Sternberg. His visually atmospheric films include *The Blue Angel* (1930), *Morocco* (1930), *Shanghai Express* (1932), and *The Scarlet Empress* (1934), all of which star Marlene DIETRICH.

**voodoo,** religious beliefs and practices, W African in origin but with Roman Catholic and West Indian accretions, found in the New World, principally in Haiti. Voodooistic ritual is characterized by ecstatic trances and magical practices. Despite opposition from governments and churches, voodoo continues to flourish.

**Voronezh,** city (1985 pop. 850,000), S central European USSR, on the Voronezh R. near the confluence with the Don R. It functions as a collecting and processing centre for agricultural products of the surrounding region, and an industrial centre. Industries include the manufacture of synthetic rubber, vehicle tyres, locomotives, railway rolling stock, and agricultural and earth-moving equipment. Founded in the 11th cent. as a Khazar town, it became a Russian fortress against the Tartars in the 16th cent., and was the scene of fierce fighting and severe destruction during World War II.

**Voroshilov, Kliment Yefremovich** (vərə͵sheeləf), 1881–1969, Soviet military leader and public official. He was a Red Army commander in the Russian CIVIL WAR (1918–20), commissar for defence (1925–40), and commander in WORLD WAR II. A member of the Supreme Soviet from 1937, he became president of the USSR when STALIN died (1953). Ousted by KHRUSHCHEV in 1960, he was reelected to the party central committee in 1966.

**Vörösmarty, Mihály** (͵vørøsh'mawtee), 1800–55, Hungarian poet, the leading figure of Hungarian ROMANTICISM. He is best known for his patriotic lyrics, e.g., *The Call* (1837), and his splendid national epics, e.g., *Zolan's Flight* and *Erlan* (both: 1825).

**Vorster, Balthazar Johannes** (͵fawstə), 1915–83, South African political leader. Elected to parliament in 1953 as a member of the

Nationalist Party, he later served as minister of justice (1961–66), repressing opponents of APARTHEID. After the assassination of Hendrik VERWOERD in 1966 he became prime minister and tried to improve relations with South African blacks. He resigned for reasons of health in 1978 but served in the ceremonial position of president until a financial scandal forced his resignation in 1979.

**vorticism,** a rebel group formed by Wyndham LEWIS after his break with the Omega Workshop. Its interests were in moving away from POSTIMPRESSIONISM towards FUTURISM and abstraction. Lewis was joined by Bomberg, EPSTEIN and the poet Ezra POUND. Pound coined the term 'Vorticism' in 1913. Their ideas appeared in the two issues of *Blast*.

**Vosges,** low mountain range, extending c.190 km (120 mi), between Lorraine and ALSACE in E France. There are sharp contrasts between the low, northern, sandstone Vosges and the higher but more heavily populated, crystalline Vosges to the south. Highest point is Ballon de Guebwiller (1424 m/4672 ft). Forests of beech and conifers support wood-working industries and there is a long history of textile manufacture in small valley mills. There are vineyards on the eastern (Alsace) side.

**Voznesensky, Andrei Andreyevich** (vəznyə,syaynskee), 1933–, Russian poet. Trained as an architect, he first published his poems, e.g., 'Fire in the Architectural Institute', in 1958. He became popular and gave readings in the USSR and abroad. English translations of his work by AUDEN and other poets appear in such collections as *Antiworlds* (1967).

**Vrangelya Ostrov (Wrangel Island),** island in the Arctic Ocean, N of the eastern extremity of Siberia; area 5250 km² (2027 sq mi); mountainous and surrounded by pack-ice for much of the year. Although known to the Eskimo it was not reported until 1849 by a British expedition; it has been claimed by the US (1881), Russia (1911), and Canada (1914). At present it is administered and occupied by the Soviet Union although occasionally the US claim has been raised. The only population is a Soviet meteorological station.

**Vries, Hugo de:** see DE VRIES, HUGO.

**VTOL aircraft:** see VERTICAL TAKEOFF AND LANDING AIRCRAFT.

**Vuillard, Édouard** (vwee,yah), 1868–1940, French painter and lithographer. A member of the NABIS, he is known for his highly patterned and decorative canvases that evoke the intimacy of home life.

**Vulcan,** in Roman mythology, the god of fire. Originally a god of volcanoes, he was later identified with the Greek HEPHAESTUS.

**vulcanization** see GOODYEAR, CHARLES; RUBBER.

**Vulgate:** see BIBLE.

**vulture,** large BIRD of prey of temperate and tropical regions. Old World vultures, of the family Accipitridae, are allied to HAWKS and EAGLES; the

American vultures and CONDORS belong to the family Cathartidae. They are sometimes called buzzards. The European black vulture (*Aegypius monarchus*) is the largest bird in the Old World, being over 6½ kg (14 lb) with a wingspan of 240 cm (8 ft). It ranges from southern Europe to Japan. Vultures soar above the ground watching for dead or dying animals. If the skin of a carcase is not broken by another scavenger, vultures have to wait for decomposition to begin, as their heavy beaks cannot pierce skin.

Griffon **vulture** (*Gyps fulvus*) fending off other vultures with an aggressive display (southern Spain)

**Vygotsky, Lev Semionovich,** 1896–1934, Russian psychologist. After studying literature, Vygotsky taught and researched the psychology of art before undertaking his classic studies in developmental psychology, cognitive psychology, and psycholinguistics, in which he attempted a synthesis of psychology and historical materialism. Although Vygotsky died of tuberculosis at a comparatively young age, his 'cultural-historical' approach later formed the bedrock of Soviet psychological theory and practice. His books include *Thought and Language* (1934), published in English 1962.

**Vyrnwy, Lake,** large reservoir in Powys, mid-Wales, which was formed by damming the R. Vyrnwy. Construction took place between 1880 and 1890 and the reservoir is used to provide water for Liverpool.

**W**, chemical symbol of the element TUNGSTEN.

**Waals, Johannes Diderik van der:** see VAN DER WAALS.

**Wade, Benjamin Franklin,** 1800–78, US senator from Ohio (1851–69). One of the extreme radical Republicans, Wade was instrumental in forming the RECONSTRUCTION policies after the Civil War. As president *pro tempore* of the Senate, he would have become president had Andrew JOHNSON been convicted of impeachment charges.

**Wade–Giles system,** transliteration system for Chinese using the Roman alphabet. It was invented by Sir Thomas Wade in 1867 and developed by H.A. Giles in *A Chinese–English Dictionary* (1892). It is a complex system with TONES marked by superscripted numerals. Widely used until recent times, it is no longer used in the Peoples Republic of China, where PINYIN has replaced it, but is still popular in Taiwan and Hong Kong.

**Wadi Arabah,** Heb. *Arava,* part of the GREAT RIFT VALLEY, extending from the DEAD SEA southwards for 177 km (110 mi) to the Gulf of Aqaba, (see AQABA, GULF OF) between the hills of the NEGEV (W) and the mountains of Moab and Edom (E). The Israeli-Jordan border runs from N to S along the lowest part of the valley. The northern part of the Wadi Arabah is below sea level.

**Wafd,** Egyptian political party founded in 1919 and dominant from 1924 to 1952. It called for independence and extensive reforms, and was frequently at odds with the monarch. The party was dissolved after NASSER set up a one-party system in 1956.

**Wagadugu:** see OUAGADOUGOU.

**Wagner, Richard,** 1813–83, German composer. His OPERAS represent the fullest musical and theatrical expression of German ROMANTICISM and exerted a profound influence on later composers. He used a continuous flow of melody instead of sharply differentiated RECITATIVE and ARIA and called his operas 'music-dramas' to signify their fusion of text and music. Wagner achieved remarkable dramatic unity in his works, due in part to his development of the leitmotif, a brief passage of music used to characterize an episode or person. His LIBRETTOS, which he wrote himself, are drawn chiefly from German mythology. His operas include *Rienzi* (1838–40), *The Flying Dutchman* (1841), *Tannhäuser* (1843–45), and *Lohengrin* (1846–48), which brought the German romantic opera to its culmination. Wagner participated in the REVOLUTIONS OF 1848 and was forced to flee Dresden, where he had held a conducting post. Aided by LISZT, he escaped to Switzerland, staying there 10 years and writing essays, notably *Oper und Drama* (1851), that define his aesthetics. Wagner's *Der Ring des Nibelungen* (1853–74), a tetralogy that embodies most completely his aesthetic principles, comprises *Das Rheingold* (1853–54), *Die Walküre* (1854–56), *Siegfried* (1856–69), and *Götterdämmerung* (1874). In 1872 Wagner moved to Bayreuth, Bavaria, where he completed the Ring cycle and built a theatre, Das Festspielhaus, adequate for the performance of his works; the complete *Ring* was presented there in 1876. Wagner's other later compositions are *Tristan und Isolde* (1857–59); *Die Meistersinger von Nürnberg* (1862–67), his only comic opera; and his last work, *Parsifal* (1877–82), a sacred festival drama. His second wife, **Cosima Wagner,** 1837–1930, the daughter of Liszt, was closely involved with his work. After his death, she was largely responsible for the continuing fame of the Bayreuth festivals.

**Wagner, Robert Ferdinand,** 1877–1953, American legislator; b. Germany. A long-time Democratic senator (1927–49) from New York, Wagner was one of Pres. F.D. ROOSEVELT's most effective allies in the US Congress during the early NEW DEAL days. The National Labour Relations Act (1935) is known as the Wagner Act. His son, **Robert Ferdinand Wagner, Jr.,** 1910–, was mayor of New York City from 1954 to 1966.

**Wagner-Jauregg, Julius** (ˌvagnəˌyowreg), 1857–1941, Austrian psychiatrist. Interested in the beneficial effect of fever in psychosis, he observed improvement in a patient deliberately infected with malaria as a method of treatment, and developed the method, for which he was awarded the 1927 Nobel Prize for physiology or medicine.

**Wagram,** town, NE Austria. NAPOLEON I forced (1809) Archduke Charles of Austria to concede defeat at Wagram, under the heaviest artillery attack recorded of that time.

**wagtail,** long-tailed member of the BIRD family Motacillidae, closely related to the pipits. Wagtails breed from Europe and North Africa, across Asia to the Pacific, the grey wagtail (*Motacilla cinerea*) being the most widespread. The birds are 16–18 cm (6½–7 in) long and have the habit of wagging their tails as they stand. The related pipits do the same to a lesser degree. The birds are insect-eaters, often associated with water. The grey and white wagtails (*M. alba*) have adapted to humans and will nest in man-made structures.

**Wahhabism** (wahˌhahb·iz(ə)m), Islamic reform movement in Arabia. The founder of this movement, Muhammad Ibn Abd al-Wahhab (c.1703–91) advocated a fundamentalist HANBALISM partly inspired by IBN TAIMIYYA, and forged an ideological and political alliance with the clan of Banu Saud, after whom SAUDI ARABIA is named. On the basis of this alliance, almost the entire Arabian peninsula was overcome in the early 20th cent. by a politico-religious militia called the *Ikhwan* (Brethren) commanded by Abd al-Aziz IBN SAUD, the founder of Saudi Arabia. Wahhabism is highly puritanical in its attitude towards devotions, but the Hanbalite version of Islamic commercial law is quite liberal and appropriate for the mercantile conditions of Saudi Arabia.

**Wajda, Andrzej** (ˌviedah), 1926–, Polish film director. His films are often studies of Poland's history and contemporary politics. They include *Canal* (1956), *Ashes and Diamonds* (1958), *Everything for Sale* (1968), *Man of Marble* (1977), and *Man of Iron* (1981).

**Wakefield, Edward Gibbon,** 1796–1862, British colonial publicist. He urged that colonial land be sold at a price sufficient to compel labourers to work for landowners, and that the revenue raised from sale of land be used to finance migration. His influential ideas led to the founding (1836) of a colony of free settlers (instead of convicts) in South Australia and to the colonization of New Zealand.

**Wake Island,** atoll with three islets (Wake, Wilkes, and Peale), 7.8 km² (3 sq mi), central Pacific, between Hawaii and Guam. There is no indigenous population; it is a US military and commercial base. Wake Island, which is administered by the US Air Force, was annexed from the Spanish in 1898 and held by the Japanese, 1941–45.

**Wakley, Thomas,** 1795–1862, English physician and medical reformer. He founded *The Lancet* in 1823, a medical journal which became renowned for attacking the nepotism of the medical profession. He was a coroner and member of Parliament, and he fought vigorously for justice on a wide variety of fronts.

**Waksman, Selman Abraham,** 1888–1973, American microbiologist; b. Russia. As a microbiologist (1918–54) at the New Jersey Agricultural Experiment station, he studied the role of microorganisms in the soil and in the decomposition of organic matter. He isolated various antibiotics, including streptomycin (the first effective treatment for TUBERCULOSIS), for which he won the 1952 Nobel Prize for physiology or medicine.

**Walachia** or **Wallachia,** historic region (76,581 km²/29,568 sq mi), S Romania, separated from Transylvania and the Banat region by the Transylvanian Alps (NW); from Yugoslavia (W) and Bulgaria (S) by the Danube R.; and adjoining MOLDAVIA (NE). BUCHAREST, Romania's capital, is the chief city. Walachia contains the rich Ploeşti oil fields, and is Romania's main industrial area, producing chemicals, heavy machinery, and other manufactures. It is also a rich agricultural region. Part of the Roman province of DACIA, it emerged as a principality in 1330, but came under Turkish suzerainty at the end of the century. Prince MICHAEL THE BRAVE (r.1593–1601) ended foreign domination, but on his death Walachia again fell to the Turks. In the 19th cent. Russia occupied the area repeatedly; in 1856 Walachia and Moldavia became virtually independent. The accession (1859) of Prince Alexander John CUZA in both principalities began the history of modern ROMANIA.

**Walcott, Derek Alton,** 1930–, Jamaican poet and dramatist. He combines a profound awareness of Caribbean history with exceptional poetic skills. His best-known play is *The Dream on Monkey Mountain,* and his published verse includes *Selected Poems* (1964; 1981) and *Midsummer* (1984).

**Waldemar,** kings of Denmark. **Waldemar I** (the Great), 1131–82 (r.1157–82), gained his domain in wars with Cnut and Sweyn III. He increased his prestige by marrying his daughters to the sons of FREDERICK I, PHILIP II of France, and Eric X of Sweden. His son, Cnut IV, succeeded him. **Waldemar II,** 1170–1241 (r.1202–41), was the second son of Waldemar I. He conquered much of Estonia but lost Schwerin, in Germany. His son, Eric IV, succeeded him. **Waldemar IV** (Valdemar Atterdag), c.1320–75 (r.1340–75), by 1360 had united Denmark, which foreign rulers had dismembered. He defeated (1361) the HANSEATIC LEAGUE but was forced (1370) to grant it free trade in Denmark. He was succeeded by Olaf, son of his daughter, MARGARET I, and Haakon VI of Norway.

**Waldenses** or **Waldensians,** Protestant religious sect of medieval origin. They originated in the late 12th cent. as the Poor Men of Lyons, a band organized by Peter Valdes. As lay preachers, they stressed poverty and proclaimed the Bible as the sole rule of faith and life. The group was declared heretical in 1184 and 1215, and persecution persisted until the 18th cent. After the REFORMATION they adapted their views to those of the Reformed Church. The sect survives in Europe, mainly in Piedmont; its general synod meets at Torre Pellice, Italy.

**Waldheim, Kurt,** 1918–, Austrian politician and diplomat, secretary general (1972–81) of the UNITED NATIONS, president of Austria (1986–). When Austria entered the UN (1958), Waldheim joined its delegation and served (1965–68) as its permanent representative. After serving as foreign minister (1968–70) and failing (1971) to win the Austrian presidency, he returned to the UN and was elected secretary general. In 1986 he again contested the Austrian presidency and was elected amid controversial disclosures concerning his role as a German army officer during WORLD WAR II.

**Waldstein, Albrecht von:** see WALLENSTEIN.

**Wales,** Welsh *Cymru,* political division of the United Kingdom of Great Britain and Northern Ireland (1984 est. pop. 2,807,200), 20,761 km² (8016 sq mi), on the western peninsula of the island of Great Britain; bordered by the Irish Sea (N), the Bristol Channel (S), England (E), and Cardigan Bay and St George's Channel (W). Physically, it is dominated by the Cambrian Mts, which rise to 1085 m (3500 ft) at Mt SNOWDON. Principal cities are CARDIFF, the capital, and SWANSEA. Rivers include the SEVERN, Wye, TEIFI, and DEE. The great coalfields and major industries are concentrated in the south, as is most of the population. More than 40,000 inhabitants speak Celtic Welsh only, and 19% of the population speak Welsh and English. Wales united politically with England in 1536.

*History.* Celtic-speaking Welsh clans, in Wales since prehistory, were little affected by either the Roman or the Anglo-Saxon occupations of Great Britain, although they were converted to Christianity by Celtic monks. The disparate clans gradually coalesced, and border wars with England were constant. In the 11th cent. WILLIAM I of England set up earldoms along the Welsh border, but for 200 years Welsh soldiers resisted the English threat to their independence. Following a brief relaxation of English pressure in the 12th cent., during which Welsh medieval culture flowered, English conquest of Wales was finally accomplished in 1282 by EDWARD I, who, to placate Welsh sentiment, initiated the English custom of entitling the king's eldest son prince of Wales. Welsh antagonism toward the English overlords persisted, and in the 15th cent. OWEN GLENDOWER led a brief revolt. In 1485 a Welshman became the first Tudor king of England, Henry VII. The process of administrative assimilation of Wales begun during his reign was completed under HENRY VIII, who signed the Act of Union (1536); Welsh representatives entered the English parliament, Welsh law was abolished, and English was established as the official language of legal proceedings. Welsh political history became that of GREAT BRITAIN. The Industrial Revolution tapped the mineral wealth of Wales, and S Wales was soon the chief coal-exporting region of the world. Industrialization brought poverty and unemployment, however, especially in the 1920s and 30s. Following the boom of World War II, the government undertook a full-scale programme of industrial redevelopment, including nationalization of the mines. Political nationalism survives as an issue; in 1979 Welsh voters decisively defeated a British proposal for limited home rule.

**Walesa, Lech** (vah‚wenzə), 1943–, Polish trade-union leader. He worked as an electrician at the Lenin Shipyard in Gdánsk but was dismissed in 1976 for his antigovernment protests. In 1980 striking workers at the shipyard won his reinstatement, and he assumed leadership of the independent trade union SOLIDARITY. A moderate, he gained numerous concessions from the authorities before his arrest and internment in the military crackdown of 1981. Released in Nov. 1982, he was awarded the Nobel Peace Prize in 1983 and has remained the unofficial leader of the Polish workers' movement.

**Waley, Arthur (David),** 1889–1966, English poet and orientalist. An associate of the BLOOMSBURY GROUP, his influential translations from the Chinese and Japanese include *170 Chinese Poems* (1918), *The Tale of Genji* (1925–33) and *Monkey* (1942). He also published many scholarly works on the Far East, which, however, he never visited.

**Walker Cup:** see GOLF.

**walking,** a sport developed in the 19th cent., particularly in Britain, and included in the Olympics in 1908. It became part of the European Games in 1934, and the Commonwealth Games in 1966. The standard races are the 20-km (12.42-mi) and 50-km (31.05-mi) road walks.

**wallaby:** see KANGAROO.

**Wallace, Alfred Russel,** 1823–1913, English naturalist. From his study of comparative biology in Brazil and the East Indies, he evolved a concept of EVOLUTION similar to that of Charles DARWIN. His special contribution to the evidence for evolution was in biogeography; he systematized the science and wrote *The Geographical Distribution of Animals* (2 vol., 1876) and a supplement, *Island Life* (1881). He defined 'Wallace's Line', the boundary through the Malay archipelago that divides the Australian from the Asian fauna.

**Wallace, George Corley,** 1919–, US public official, governor of Alabama (1963–67, 1971–79, 1983–87). An avowed segregationist, he led an unsuccessful attempt to block integration of the Alabama public schools in the early 1960s. Prevented by law from succeeding himself as governor, he had his wife, Lurleen Burns Wallace (1926–68), run successfully in his place. In 1972, while campaigning for the Democratic presidential nomination, he was shot and paralysed by a would-be assassin. In 1982 he was again elected governor, this time with the support of many Alabama blacks.

**Wallace, Henry Agard,** 1888–1960, vice president of the US (1941–45). As Pres. F. D. ROOSEVELT's secretary of agriculture (1933–41) he administered the NEW DEAL agricultural programmes. He was Roosevelt's third-term vice president but in 1944 was replaced as candidate by Harry S. TRUMAN. An opponent of US COLD WAR policies, he ran against Truman in 1948 as a Progressive party candidate but won no electoral votes.

**Wallenberg, Raoul,** 1912–47?, Swedish diplomat. Assigned to Budapest during World War II, he is credited with saving as many as

20,000 Hungarian Jews from being deported to NAZI death camps, e.g., by supplying them with Swedish passports. He was arrested when the Soviet army entered Budapest, and his death in prison was reported (1947) by Soviet authorities, but has never been verified. In 1981 the US Congress declared him an honorary US citizen.

**Wallenstein** or **Waldstein, Albrecht Wenzel Eusebius von** (ˌvalənshtien, ˌvaltshtien), 1583–1634, Bohemian general in the THIRTY YEARS' WAR. The owner of vast estates in Bohemia, he raised an army (1625) for Emperor FERDINAND II and became chief imperial general. He won important victories, but the enmity of the German princes led to his dismissal in 1630. Although he was recalled in 1632, Wallenstein conducted (1634) secret peace negotiations, which led to charges of treason, and he was murdered, probably at the emperor's instigation. He is the hero of a trilogy by SCHILLER.

**Waller, Edmund,** 1606–87, English poet and member of Parliament. 'Waller's Plot' (1643) attempted to secure the city of London for CHARLES I. His polished verse, including 'Go, Lovely rose' (pub. 1645), is important for its contribution to the development of the heroic couplet.

**Waller, Fats** (Thomas Wright Waller), 1904–43, black American pianist, singer, and composer. His songs and humour made him popular, and his piano style influenced many. 'Ain't Misbehavin'' and 'Honeysuckle Rose' are among his best-known songs.

**Wallis and Futuna Islands,** French overseas territory (1976 pop. 9192), South Pacific. The two small groups of islands are volcanic. Matautu is the chief town. Timber is exported. Under French control from 1842, they became a territory in 1961, gaining substantial local autonomy under a new statute in 1984.

**Wall Street,** lower Manhattan, New York City, centre of the city's great financial district. The area is the site of major US stock exchanges and other important institutions. By extension, the term 'Wall Street' has come to designate US financial interests.

**walnut,** common name for some members of the family Juglandaceae, chiefly deciduous trees of the north temperate zone, typified by large, aromatic compound leaves. Several species are commercially important for their timber and edible nuts (usually encased in leathery or woody hulls). The family includes the HICKORY and pecan, and the true walnuts (genus *Juglans*). The dark-coloured wood of the black walnut (*J. nigra*) of E North America, and the common walnut (*J. regia*), native to W Asia, is unusually hard and durable; it is valued for furniture, panelling, musical instruments, and other uses. The nut of the common walnut is usually the walnut sold commercially.

**Walpole, Horace** or **Horatio, 4th earl of Oxford,** 1717–97, English writer; son of Sir Robert WALPOLE. An admirer of the medieval, he built a pseudo-Gothic showplace castle at Strawberry Hill, near Twickenham, and in 1757 started a press there, publishing Thomas GRAY's Pindaric odes and his own works. His reputation rests on more than 3000 letters (1732–97) that give an invaluable picture of Georgian England. His romance, *The Castle of Otranto* (1765), was the forerunner of the Gothic tale of terror.

**Walpole, Robert, 1st earl of Orford,** 1676–1745, English statesman. His successful handling of the financial wreckage of the SOUTH SEA BUBBLE led to his appointment (1721) as first lord of the treasury and chancellor of the exchequer. A WHIG, he shared power with Viscount TOWNSHEND until 1730, but thereafter his ascendancy was complete until 1742. He enjoyed the confidence of GEORGE I and GEORGE II, promoted trade, and mollified the largely Tory gentry by reducing the land tax. In foreign affairs he favoured friendship with France, but was drawn into a war with Spain. Military reverses then enabled a growing opposition to force his resignation (1742). He is usually described as the first prime minister.

**Walraff, Günter,** 1942–, German journalist. Walraff specializes in critical reportages of the work-scene and exposés of bad employment practice. He draws his material from personal experience, having worked, in disguise, in the various concerns whose conditions he exposes. In *13 Unwelcome Reports* (1969) he took on Ford and Siemens, Krupp, Henckel, and Melitta; in *The Man called Hans Esser* (1977) the news-gathering practices of the *Bildzeitung* newspaper. His most ambitious achievement was his exposé, from personal experience, of the working conditions of Turkish immigrant labourers, *The Bottom of the Heap* (1985). Walraff's revelations have led to court cases, but in some instances also to improved conditions.

**walrus,** marine MAMMAL (*Odobenus rosmarus*) found in arctic seas. Largest of the fin-footed mammals, it has long tusks, light-brown wrinkled hide, and bristly cheek pads; an adult male may weigh up to 1400 kg (3000 lb). Walruses live on beaches near shallow water in herds of about a hundred animals and eat mainly shellfish. Hunted for blubber, hides, and ivory, they are now endangered.

**Walsall,** town (1981 pop. 177,923), West Midlands, England, 13 km (8 mi) NW of Birmingham. It is an industrial town, with a variety of industries, including engineering and the manufacture of leather goods, metals, and electrical goods. There is coal-mining and limestone quarrying in the surrounding area.

**Waltari, Mika,** 1908–79, Finnish novelist writing in Finnish. He is the best-known of the pre-war 'Torch-Bearers' circle of writers on urban themes; his best novel from that period is *The Great Illusion* (1928). After the war he turned his attention to historical novels, e.g., *Sinuhe the Egyptian* (1945).

**Walter, Bruno,** 1876–1962, American conductor; b. Germany as Bruno Walter Schlesinger. He was a conductor in Germany and Austria until the NAZIS forced him to leave. In the US he led the Metropolitan Opera, NBC Symphony, and New York Philharmonic.

**Waltham Forest,** London borough (1981 pop. 214,595), lying to E of R. Lea valley. It extends from the S end of Epping forest in the N to Hackney marshes in the S. The borough includes the towns of Chingford, Leyton, and Walthamstow. It is mainly residential, with some industry including engineering, and the manufacture of various goods.

**Walther von der Vogelweide,** c.1170–c.1230, Austrian poet. The greatest of the Minnesängers, and wider in range than his lyrical peers, Walther broke with the conventional songs of unrequited courtly love to sing of 'low' love happily given and returned. His service with the Hohenstaufen Philip of Swabia involved him in dynastic dispute and produced a number of powerful anti-papal and anti-GUELPH political songs; but later, serving a different master, he sang against Philip too. His work includes a number of crusader's songs, and moral and religious poems, including a hymn to the Virgin, a lament for the poet Reinmar von Hagenau, and his last great elegy for the world. Only fragments of his melodies survive, and one item of documentation: the gift from Bishop Wolfger of Passau of five shillings to buy a fur coat.

**Walton, Izaak,** 1593–1683, English writer. His *Compleat Angler; or, the Contemplative Man's Recreation* (1653), a treatise on fishing and a picture of peace and simple virtue, is one of the most famous books in English. He also wrote biographies of his friends John DONNE (1640) and George HERBERT (1670).

**Walton, Sir William Turner,** 1902–83, British composer. His works include *Façade* (1923), settings of poems by Edith SITWELL; *Portsmouth Point* (1925), an overture; two symphonies (1935, 1961); *Belshazzar's Feast* (1931), an ORATORIO; *Troilus and Cressida* (1954), an opera; concertos for viola (1929), violin (1939), and cello (1956); chamber works; and scores for films, e.g., *Hamlet* (1947).

**waltz,** romantic dance which became popular in the 18th cent. The heavy accent on the first beat of its 3/4 metre almost certainly came from the influence of the Ländler, which was a dance common to the folk music of Austria, southern Germany, and the Alpine regions. The Viennese waltz was made famous by the two Johann STRAUSSES.

**Walvis Bay,** city (1978 est. pop. 23,000), W central Namibia, on an arm of the Atlantic Ocean. The city and surrounding area (c.1110 km²/430 sq mi) is an exclave of South Africa, administered by Namibia. The chief port of Namibia, it is a rail centre and has a fishing fleet. It was annexed by Britain and incorporated into the Cape Colony in 1878.

**wampum,** beads or discs made by NORTH AMERICAN INDIANS from mollusc shells, used for money, ornaments, or ceremonial exchange during treaties. Wampum is Algonquian for 'white string of beads', but there is also a more valuable purple variety. It was especially prized in the Eastern Woodlands and Plains areas, reaching inland tribes through trade. Wampum belts often had pictographic designs worked into them.

**Wandering Jew,** legendary Jew who mocked or mistreated Jesus on his way to the cross and who was condemned to wander on earth until Judgment Day. Common in Western European literature, the story first appeared in 13th-cent. chronicles, but the wanderer was not identified as a Jew until the 17th cent.

**Wandsworth,** London borough (1981 pop. 252,240), S of R. Thames. The Thames is crossed here by Putney, Wandsworth, Battersea, Albert, and Chelsea road bridges and by three railway bridges. It includes the districts of Putney, Balham, Tooting, and BATTERSEA. It is a residential and industrial borough, including several open spaces, e.g., Wandsworth Park.

**Wang Ching-wei** (wahng jing way), see WANG JINGWEI.

**Wang Jingwei,** 1883–1944, Chinese political leader. A disciple of SUN YAT-SEN, he led the left wing of the KUOMINTANG Party. In the Second SINO-JAPANESE WAR he left (1938) the Kuomintang and became (1940) premier of the Japanese puppet government at Nanjing.

**Wang Wei,** 699–759, Chinese poet and painter. His poetry portrays quiet, natural scenes. As a painter Wang is associated with his delicate black-ink landscapes (though no originals survive today).

**Wankel engine** (ˌvangkəl), INTERNAL-COMBUSTION ENGINE in which only rotary motion occurs, the reciprocating action of pistons in cylinders being eliminated. By a combination of a triangular cross-section rotor and epicyclic rotation inside a hollow cylinder, approximately elliptical in shape, in which the tips of the triangle always remain in contact with the cylinder, three rotating gas chambers are formed. These in turn go through the normal cycle of intake, compression, ignition, and exhaust. The complete engine has very few moving parts. It has less weight per horsepower than the conventional piston engine but has not replaced it because of the difficulty in producing a high compression ratio. It is named after its German inventor, Felix Wankel (b. 1902):

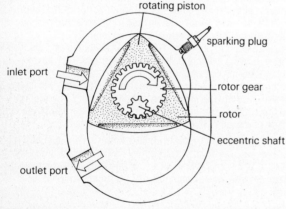

Wankel engine

**wapiti,** large North American DEER (*Cervus canadensis*), called ELK in America. Males stand up to 150 cm (5 ft) at the shoulder and weigh up to 450 kg (1000 lb). The coat is greyish brown, with a chestnut mane and a yellowish rump. Once abundant, the wapiti now lives in small numbers under protection in national parks and refuges.

**waqf** [Arab., = endowment], strictly speaking, the legal procedure in Islamic law by which one makes an inalienable endowment of the title to property, usually land, and a religious foundation while still retaining the use of it for oneself; popularly, the term has come to denote the endowment itself. Waqf legislation, which developed gradually after the death of the Prophet MUHAMMAD, has varied in its details from one school of FIQH to another.

**war, laws of,** rules of INTERNATIONAL LAW regulating the conduct of armed conflict between nations. First systematized in the work of Hugo GROTIUS in the 17th cent., the laws of war developed to minimize destruction, proscribe cruel treatment of noncombatants and prisoners of war, and establish conditions for peace negotiation. Detailed treaties governing war are mostly a product of the 19th and 20th cent., and include the Declaration of PARIS (1856), the accords of the HAGUE CONFERENCES and the GENEVA CONVENTIONS. Generally, agreements have mitigated conditions for the sick and wounded but have failed to limit weaponry. GUERRILLA WARFARE and aerial bombing today pose complex questions for theorists of the laws of war. See also WAR CRIMES.

**Warangal,** town (1981 pop. 335,150), Andhra Pradesh state, E India. It is a district administrative and marketing centre with cotton, rice, and oil mills. It is an historic town which was the capital of an Andhra kingdom as early as the 8th cent. and displays a series of fortifications built by successive rulers (notably the Kakatiyas of the 13th and 14th cent.). It eventually passed into the hands of the Nizams of Hyderabad.

**Warbeck, Perkin,** 1474?–99, pretender to the English throne. Persuaded by Yorkist adherents to impersonate the son of EDWARD IV, he landed (1497) in Cornwall and proclaimed himself Richard IV. Captured by HENRY VII, he was hanged.

**warbler,** name given to small, migratory, insect-eating BIRDS of the family Sylviidae, distributed all over the OLD WORLD from Europe to Australia. All very similar to look at, being drab olive or brown, bird-watchers find them interesting because they are a challenge to identify. The song is a characteristic of each species. The group is sometimes called the Old World warblers to distinguish them from the American warblers, or wood warblers, which belong to the family Parulidae.

**Warburg, Otto Heinrich,** 1883–1970, German biochemist. He made many important contributions to research, including the work on metabolism of cancer cells, for which he was awarded the 1931 Nobel Prize for physiology or medicine.

**war crimes,** violations of the laws of war (see WAR, LAWS OF). After WORLD WAR II three classes of offences were recognized as war crimes: crimes against peace, e.g., planning or waging a war of aggression; conventional war crimes, or violations of the accepted laws or customs of warfare; and crimes against humanity, including extermination, enslavement, deportation, and other inhumane acts. From Nov. 1945 to Oct. 1946 a tribunal at Nuremberg, Germany, established by Britain, France, USSR, and the US, tried Nazi leaders for war crimes (see CONCENTRATION CAMP; HOLOCAUST) and sentenced some of them to death. Another war tribunal, conducted (1946–47) in Tokyo by 11 nations, tried and sentenced alleged Japanese war criminals. Critics question the legal basis of some of the charges at these trials, and some view such trials as violations of SOVEREIGNTY and as acts of vengeance by the victors. See also INTERNATIONAL LAW.

**ward:** see GUARDIAN AND WARD.

**Ward, Barbara,** 1914–81, English economist and journalist. Foreign editor of *The Economist* magazine (from 1946) and governor of the British Broadcasting Corporation (1946–50), she later taught (1968–73) at Columbia Univ. In such works as *The Rich Nations and the Poor Nations* (1962) and *Nationalism and Ideology* (1966) she called for understanding and liberal policies toward developing nations.

**Ward, Mrs Humphry,** 1851–1920, English novelist and social worker; b. Mary Augusta Arnold; granddaughter of Thomas ARNOLD. *Robert Elsmere* (1888) and other novels dramatize her views on the social application of religion.

**war debts,** obligations to the US incurred by foreign nations during WORLD WAR I. Beginning in 1914 and continuing for several years after the armistice in 1918, the US extended credit to its European allies, calculated in 1922 to amount to $11.5 billion. Payments were made, mostly from German REPARATIONS, until 1931, when worldwide depression caused Pres. HOOVER to propose a one-year moratorium. After 1932 all nations defaulted except Hungary, which paid interest until 1939, and Finland, which continued to pay in full. For international obligations of World War II, see LEND-LEASE.

**Ware, Henry,** 1764–1845, American clergyman, instrumental in the founding of UNITARIANISM in the US. His appointment (1805) as Hollis professor of divinity at Harvard aroused opposition and hastened the separation of the Unitarians from the Congregationalists.

**warfare:** see AMPHIBIOUS WARFARE; FORTIFICATION; GUERRILLA WARFARE; MECHANIZED WARFARE; MILITARY SCIENCE; SIEGE.

**Warhol, Andy,** 1928–87, American artist. A leading figure in the POP ART movement, he is known for multi-image silk-screen paintings that make use of monotony and repetition. His imagery often came from commonplace objects such as dollar bills and soup cans. Warhol made a number of idiosyncratic films, e.g., *The Chelsea Girls* (1966).

**Warlock, Peter,** pseud. of Philip Arnold Heseltine, 1894–1930, British composer, critic, and author. Influenced by DELIUS from 1910, and by Bernard van Dieren from 1916, Heseltine developed an individual style which coincided with the adoption of the pseudonym Peter Warlock in 1918. He was a superb miniaturist, and his solo songs and part songs are

*Marilyn* by Andy **Warhol**, 1967

amongst the finest and most sensitive settings of the English language. His well known *Capriol Suite* (1926) expresses well the contrasts of his music and of his personality, rumbustious and meditative.

**War of 1812,** armed conflict between the US and Great Britain, 1812–15. It was partly occasioned by US insistence on neutral shipping rights during the Franco-British hostilities of the FRENCH REVOLUTIONARY WARS and the wars of NAPOLEON I. British impressment of sailors and confiscation of US ships were causes of strong anti-British sentiment. A further source of friction was that American frontiersmen suspected the British of encouraging the Indians in the NORTHWEST TERRITORY to resist American expansion—a suspicion confirmed by the battle of Tippecanoe (7 Nov. 1811) when the defeated Indians were found to have been armed with recently manufactured British rifles. The 'war hawks' in the US Congress prevailed, and war was declared on 18 June 1812. The failure of two successive American invasions of Canada and the Canadian capture of Detroit proved how ill-prepared the US forces were. The small American navy fared better; the early victories in single-ship engagements of Isaac Hull, commanding the *Constitution,* and Stephen DECATUR were notable, but they did nothing to impair British command of the seas. In 1813, however, British naval superiority on the Great Lakes was destroyed by the victory of Capt. Oliver Perry (see under PERRY, M.C.) on Lake Erie in September. The low point of the war, from the US point of view, was the British capture of Washington, District of Columbia, in Aug. 1814. But the ending of the Napoleonic Wars in Europe had made the question of maritime rights academic, and the British entered into serious negotiations to end the hostilities. The Treaty of GHENT (signed 24 Dec. 1814) brought the war to an indecisive end. But the Americans had a final triumph. On 14 Jan. 1815, after the treaty had been signed, Andrew JACKSON's troops defeated the British decisively at the battle of NEW ORLEANS. The war ushered in a period of heightened American nationalism and increasing isolation from European affairs.

**Warren, Earl,** 1891–1974, 14th chief justice of the US SUPREME COURT (1953–69); One of the most dynamic chief justices, Warren guided the Court in a number of landmark civil-rights decisions. Most notable was BROWN V. BOARD OF EDUCATION (1954), in which public school segregation was ruled unconstitutional (see INTEGRATION). While chief justice, Warren headed the commission that investigated the assassination of Pres. KENNEDY (see WARREN COMMISSION).

**Warren, Robert Penn,** 1905–, American man of letters. One of the Southern agrarian poets associated with the *Fugitive* magazine (1922–25), he won early acclaim for verse that was influenced by the METAPHYSICAL POETS. His later poems are simpler and more regional. Volumes of his poetry include *Brother to Dragons* (1953), *Promises*

(1957), and *Now and Then* (1979). Also an important novelist concerned with the moral dilemmas of the modern world, he has written *All the King's Men* (1946), about a political demagogue resembling Huey LONG; *World Enough and Time* (1950); *Band of Angels* (1955); and *Wilderness* (1961). With Cleanth Brooks he compiled the textbooks *Understanding Poetry* (1938) and *Modern Rhetoric* (1949).

**Warren Commission,** official inquiry into the assassination of US Pres. John F. KENNEDY. Established by Pres. Lyndon JOHNSON on 29 Nov. 1963, it was headed by Chief Justice Earl WARREN. After holding exhaustive private hearings and conducting its own investigations, the commission issued its report on 24 Sept. 1964. It found no evidence of a conspiracy and concluded that Lee Harvey Oswald, acting alone, had killed Kennedy; it also found that Jack Ruby, the Dallas restaurant owner who shot and killed Oswald, had also acted alone. In ensuing years, the report was subjected to close examination and widespread criticism. In 1979 a congressional committee concluded, on the basis of acoustical evidence, that two gunmen had fired at Kennedy.

**Warrington,** town (1981 pop. 81,366), Cheshire, NW England, on R. Mersey, 25 km (16 mi) SW of Manchester. It is an industrial town, whose industries include the manufacture of iron and steel, wire products, and engineering. It was an important town in Roman times, and has a grammar school which was founded in the 16th cent. It was designated a New Town in 1968.

**Warrnambool,** city (1986 pop. 22,706), Victoria, SE Australia. It functions as a port and service centre for the farming hinterland, and there are woollen textile mills and the Fletcher Jones trousers factory (est. 1919). 66 km (40 mi) along the Great Ocean Road is spectacular scenery at Port Campbell, including 'The Twelve Apostles' and 'London Bridge', carved by the sea from soft rock.

The 'Twelve Apostles', **Warrnambool**, Victoria, Australia

**Warsaw,** city (1984 pop. 1,641,000), capital of Poland, central Poland, on both banks of the Vistula R. It is an industrial centre with manufactures such as machinery and motor vehicles. Warsaw is one of Europe's great historic cities. Settled by the 11th cent., it became Poland's capital (1596); passed (1795) to Prussia; was the capital of the grand duchy of Warsaw (see POLAND); and later, under Russian rule, was the scene of nationalist uprisings (1830, 1863). In 1918 the city became the capital of the restored Polish state. During the German occupation (1939–45) in WORLD WAR II, a Jewish GHETTO was isolated that contained (1942) c.500,000 people; virtually all perished, either in CONCENTRATION CAMPS or after the armed Jewish uprising (Feb. 1943). In 1944 Polish nationalists tried unsuccessfully to oust the Germans while the Soviet army remained inactive across the Vistula. After 1945 large-scale reconstruction began that included the medieval Stare Miasto [old town], with its marketplace and 14th-cent. cathedral.

**Warsaw Treaty Organization,** known as the Warsaw Pact, mutual defence alliance established in 1955 by Albania, Bulgaria, Czechoslovakia, East Germany, Hungary, Poland, Romania and the Soviet Union. Albania formally withdrew in 1968, having not participated since its break with the Soviet Union in 1961. The Warsaw Pact is the Communist bloc's counterpart to the NORTH ATLANTIC TREATY ORGANIZATION. Its unified command has headquarters in Moscow, and its forces have been used to suppress democratic movements, e.g., in 1968 in Czechoslovakia (although Romania did not participate in that operation).

**Warton, Thomas,** 1728–90, English poet and literary historian, brother of Joseph WARTON. He was a champion of medieval and Elizabethan literature. His major work, *History of English Poetry* (1774–81), covered the 11th through to the end of the 16th cent.

**Warwick,** county town (1981 pop. 21,701), Warwickshire, W Midlands of England, on R. Avon. Engineering is one of the main industries of the town. A picturesque and historic town, it has many old buildings, including a 14th-cent. castle.

**Warwickshire,** county in W Midlands of England (1984 est. pop. 477,700), 1980 km² (772 sq mi), bordering on West Midlands in the N. The county town is WARWICK. The county was considerably reduced in size by the 1974 county-boundary changes. It is generally gently undulating rising to 226 m (741 ft) in Edgehill in the SE. The R. AVON crosses the county from NE to SW. Coal is mined in the NE, and S of the R. Avon agriculture and fruit-farming dominate. There are many historic towns in the county, including STRATFORD-UPON-AVON and RUGBY. There are many associations with William SHAKESPEARE.

**Wash, The,** a shallow, wide bay of the North Sea, extending from the coast of Lincolnshire near Boston to the coast of Norfolk at Hunstanton. The rivers Witham, GREAT OUSE, Welland, and NENE enter The Wash. The ports of Boston and KING'S LYNN are reached by navigable channels from The Wash. The Wash is fringed by large mudflats and marshy areas, although there has been much land reclamation here.

**Washington,** state of the US (1984 est. pop. 4,349,000), area 176,617 km² (68,192 sq mi), located in the Pacific Northwest, bordered by Idaho (E), Oregon (S), the Pacific Ocean (W), and the Canadian province of British Columbia (N). The capital is OLYMPIA and the largest city is SEATTLE, followed by Spokane and Tacoma. In NW Washington PUGET SOUND isolates the Olympia Peninsula (which receives the highest rainfall of any place in North America). The CASCADE RANGE forms a rain shadow to the E, and one of its volcanic peaks, Mt SAINT HELENS, erupted in a violent, destructive explosion in 1980. Winding down the centre of Washington, the COLUMBIA R. is one of the world's greatest sources of hydroelectric power. The eastern part of the state consists of the river's lowlands and the COLUMBIA PLATEAU. Washington is the leading producer of jet aircraft, especially civilian airliners manufactured by the Boeing Co. It also makes other aerospace products, timber products, processed foods, chemicals, and primary metals. The major farm products are wheat, cattle, dairy goods, and apples; salmon-fishing is important. There are deposits of bauxite, magnesium, uranium, and other minerals. Mountainous scenery attracts tourism. In 1980 90% of the population was non-Hispanic white, c.3% was black, and c.2% was Asian; over 70% lived in metropolitan areas. The Nez Percé, Yakima, and other Indians lived in the area when James Cook visited it (1778). Britain and the US contested control, finally setting the US–Canada boundary at the 49th parallel in 1846. The railway brought the first settlers in the 1880s, and during the early 20th cent. Washington was the centre of radical labour activity, with the International Workers of the World in the forefront. Aircraft manufacturing boomed during World War II and, with timber, has continued to provide the state's economic base.

**Washington, Booker T(aliaferro),** 1856–1915, black American educator. The son of a slave, he worked in salt furnaces and coal-mines after the Civil War, until he entered the Hampton Institute (Va.). He became (1879) an instructor there and developed the night school. In 1881 he was chosen to organize a normal and industrial school for blacks at Tuskegee, Alabama, and under his direction Tuskegee Institute became one of the leading black educational institutions, emphasizing industrial training as a means to self-respect and economic independence. He drew opposition from many black leaders, including W.E.B. DU BOIS, for maintaining that it was pointless for blacks to demand social equality before attaining economic independence. His many published works include his autobiography, *Up from Slavery* (1901).

**Washington, DC,** capital of the US, (1984 est. pop. 623,000; metropolitan area 3 million), coextensive with the District of Columbia, on the Potomac R.; inc. 1802. The legislative, administrative, and judicial centre of the US, it has little industry; federal employees dominate the labour force. The city is a centre of business and finance, and houses many professional and trade associations. It is also a major tourist attraction. Its location (1790) was a compromise between northern and southern interests. George WASHINGTON selected the exact site, and the 'Federal City' was designed by L'Enfant. Congress first met there in 1800. The British sacked the city during the WAR OF 1812. It developed slowly, assuming its present gracious aspect, with wide avenues and many parks, only in the 20th cent. Its many imposing government buildings are built of white or grey stone in the classical style. The CAPITOL, WHITE HOUSE, Supreme Court Building, National Archives, Constitution Hall, and Library of Congress (see LIBRARY, table) are well known. Washington has through its history been a focus of national political activity, e.g., the civil rights and antiwar demonstrations of the 1960s and 1970s. For the city's political status, see DISTRICT OF COLUMBIA.

**Washington, George,** 1732–99, 1st president of the US, commander in chief of the Continental Army in the AMERICAN REVOLUTION, called the Father of his Country; b. 22 Feb. 1732 into a wealthy family. He became a surveyor and was one of the principals of the OHIO COMPANY, whose purpose was the exploitation of Western lands. An officer in the militia, he fought in the last of the FRENCH AND INDIAN WARS and was named (1755) commander in chief of the Virginia militia with the rank of colonel. He resigned in 1759, married, and turned his attention to his plantation, MOUNT VERNON. He was a delegate (1774–75) to the CONTINENTAL CONGRESS, which named him commander of the Continental forces after the outbreak of hostilities with the British. He assumed command (3 July 1775) in Cambridge, Massachusetts, and succeeded in capturing Boston from the British (17 Mar. 1776). Unable to defend New York City, he was forced to retreat to New Jersey and then to Pennsylvania. He developed his military skill by trial and error as he went along. On Christmas night, 1776, with morale at its lowest ebb, he and his troops crossed the Delaware R. and defeated the British at Trenton and Princeton, New Jersey. Less successful in his attempts to defend Philadelphia at Brandywine and Germantown, he spent the winter of 1777–78 at VALLEY FORGE in great misery and deprivation. But he emerged with increased powers from Congress and a well-trained, totally loyal army. After the battle of Monmouth (28 June 1778), his fortunes improved and subsequent victories preceded the surrender of Gen. Cornwallis on 19 Oct. 1781 (see YORKTOWN CAMPAIGN). Washington retired to Mount Vernon, but his dissatisfaction with the new government (see CONFEDERATION, ARTICLES OF) led him back into public life. He presided over the FEDERAL CONSTITUTIONAL CONVENTION (1787), where his prestige and reputation were of immense influence in the adoption of the CONSTITUTION OF THE UNITED STATES. He was chosen unanimously as the first president and took office on 30 Apr. 1789. His efforts to remain aloof from partisan politics were unsuccessful, and the influence of Alexander HAMILTON moved him increasingly toward conservatism. His second term, openly Federalist, was bitterly criticized by the Jeffersonians. Sickened by partisan struggles, he refused a third term and retired for the last time to Mount Vernon in 1797. He died two years later, universally regarded as the man without whom the American Revolution and the new republic could not have succeeded. His wife, **Martha Washington,** 1731–1802, was born Martha Dandridge. Her first husband, by whom she had two children, was Daniel Parke Custis, who died in 1757, leaving her one of the wealthiest women in Virginia. She and Washington had no children.

**Washington, Treaty of,** May 1871, between the US and Great Britain. It settled the ALABAMA CLAIMS, which had arisen during the US CIVIL WAR, and provided for arbitration of Canadian–American boundary and fisheries disputes.

**Washington Monument,** white marble obelisk in Washington, DC, US, honouring George WASHINGTON. Completed in 1884 and opened to the public in 1888, it is 169.3 m (c.555 ft 5 in) high.

**wasp,** winged, predatory INSECT of the same order (Hymenoptera) as the ANT and BEE. Wasps have biting mouthparts and a thin stalk attaching the abdomen to the thorax, the 'wasp waist', a feature shared with ants, bees, and all related species (suborder Apocrita). Females have a sting which they can use repeatedly for paralysing prey and for nest defence. Most species are solitary, but paper wasps (*Polistes*), hornets (*Vespa*), and social wasps (*Vespula*) live in colonies consisting of one or more (in tropical areas) egg-laying queens, workers (sexually undeveloped females), and, seasonally, drones (reproductive males). They build papery nests which may be hung from a branch or overhanging rock (which includes ledges on buildings), in hollow trees, or underground. Among the solitary species are the mason (*Odynerus*) and potter (*Eumenes*) wasps that construct small nests of mud, consisting of one or more cells, each of which is stocked by the female with paralysed prey (usually caterpillars) as a larval food supply, before she lays an egg and seals the cell. A more distantly related group are the small or even minute gall wasps (family Cynipidae) whose larvae develop in galls on plants, e.g., *Andricus kollari* in marble galls on oak trees. Most numerous of all wasps are the ichneumans and their allies whose larvae are internal parasites, usually of the larvae or pupae of other insects. Some, such as the family Mymaridae are egg parasites.

**wassail** (ˌwosayl, ˌwosayl, ˌwosəl), ancient English salutation used in drinking a health, signifying 'be whole' or 'have health'; also, the liquor in which healths are drunk, especially medieval spiced drinks, and, by extension, revelries, carousals, and drinking songs.

**Wassermann, August (-Paul) von,** 1860–1925, German physician and bacteriologist. He was director of the Inst. of Experimental Therapy in Berlin and of the Inst. of Hygiene at the War Ministry (1913). He developed inoculations against cholera, typhoid, and tetanus, and devised (1906) the **Wassermann reaction** for diagnosing SYPHILIS. Positive reaction when blood or spinal fluid is tested indicates the presence of antibodies formed as a result of syphilis infection.

**waste disposal,** generally, the disposal of waste products resulting from human activity. Once a routine concern, the disposal of waste has become a pressing problem in the 20th cent. because of the growth of population and industry and the toxicity of many new industrial by-products. Traditionally, domestic and industrial waste was often dumped into nearby streams. Man-made sewers, which date back at least to the 6th cent. BC in Rome, were widely introduced in major cities in the mid-19th cent. In the absence of sewerage, waste has often been stored in underground cesspools which leach liquids into the soil but retain solids, or in simple sewage tanks, e.g., septic tanks, in which organic matter disintegrates. Raw sewage is now commonly treated before being discharged as effluent, usually by reducing solid components to a semiliquid sludge. Although sludge may be processed, e.g., as fertilizer, it has often been buried or dumped at sea, a practice denounced by many environmentalists. Sewage farming is still practised in some countries, raw sewage being used as fertilizer, and animal dung is used to manure fields. Much *solid waste*, such as municipal refuse, is deposited in open dumps. More sophisticated methods of disposal include the sanitary landfill, where waste is spread thinly and separated by layers of tamped earth, and the incineration of combustible waste which also generates steam (for heating) and/or gases (to run turbines). Special incinerators are also used to destroy some types of hazardous waste. The recycling of noncombustible products such as glass and metals, e.g., aluminium drink tins, is growing, as is the pulping of waste paper for remanufacture, offering the most satisfactory long-term solution to the accumulation of waste—next to the reuse of such materials. *Toxic wastes* include many chemicals, some generated in substantial quantities as common industrial by-products, e.g., heavy metals (notably mercury, lead, and cadmium), certain hydrocarbons, and some poisonous organic solvents. Such substances are often incinerated but when sealed in metal drums and deposited underground or in the ocean, the containers have sometimes corroded and leaked their contents, polluting the land and water supply (see POLLUTION). One of the greatest modern hazards is *radioactive waste*, produced in increasing amounts as by-products of research and nuclear power generation and particularly dangerous because many kinds of radionuclides remain lethal for thousands of years. The disposal of nuclear waste is controlled by international agreement, the London Dumping Convention. Previously (1949–82) Britain had disposed of *low* and *intermediate level wastes* in the sea. At present in the UK low-level wastes are dumped in a shallow trench, intermediate level wastes stored at temporary sites, and *high-level wastes* stored in liquid form in tanks before being turned, after a minimum of 50 years, into glass blocks. Radioactivity may leak from nuclear waste dumps into sources of drinking water. Earthquakes and deliberate or accidental human interference may also result in contamination from waste sites. In the US half of the commercial waste dumps have been closed because of radioactivity spreading outside the site. A process to solidify nuclear waste matter and reduce its potential

danger as a contaminant was being tested in the early 1980s. See also ECOLOGY; ENVIRONMENTALISM.

**water,** odourless, tasteless, transparent liquid that is colourless in small amounts but exhibits a bluish tinge in large quantities. It is the most abundant liquid on Earth. In solid form (ice) and liquid form it covers about 70% of the Earth's surface. Chemically, water is a compound of hydrogen and oxygen whose formula is $H_2O$. The two H—O bonds form an angle of about 105° an arrangement that results in a polar molecule, because there is a net negative charge towards the oxygen end (the apex) of the V-shaped molecule and a net positive charge at the hydrogen ends. Consequently, each oxygen atom is able to attract two nearby hydrogen atoms of two other water molecules. These hydrogen bondings keep water liquid at ordinary temperatures. Because water is a polar compound, it is a good solvent. Because of the hydrogen bondings between molecules, the latent heats of fusion and of evaporation, and the HEAT CAPACITY of water, are all unusually high. For these reasons water serves both as a heat-transfer medium (e.g., ice for cooling and steam for heating) and as a temperature regulator (the water in lakes and oceans helps regulate the climate). Water is chemically active, reacting with certain metals and metal oxides to form bases, and with certain oxides of nonmetals to form acids. Although completely pure water is a poor conductor of electricity, it is a much better conductor than most pure liquids because of its self-ionization, i.e., the ability of two water molecules to react to form a hydroxyl ion ($OH^-$) and a hydronium ion ($H_3O^+$). Water makes up two-thirds of the body's weight. The balance of water maintained in the body is regulated by the kidneys. Human beings can only survive a few days without water, and in temperate climates it is necessary to drink at least one litre of water per day.

**water buffalo:** see BUFFALO.

**water bug,** small to very large (4–150 mm/⅛–6 in) aquatic BUG (suborder Heteroptera), living on or below the surface, usually of quiet streams and ponds. Most prey on small fish and tadpoles as well as on other insects, and several can inflict a very painful bite when handled. Among the subaquatic species are the waterboatmen (*Corixa*), backswimmers (*Notonecta*), water scorpions (*Nepa*), saucer bugs (*Ilycoris*), and, especially in the tropics, the giant water bugs (family Belastomatidae). Pond-skaters (*Gerris*) live on the surface of still or running water, feeding on other insects which fall in, but *Halobates* is one of the very few truly marine insects, and can be found on rafts of floating seaweed, well away from land, in warm seas.

The giant **water bug** can overcome small fish, frogs, and salamanders with a needle-like bite, devouring their body fluids.

**watercolour painting,** in its wider sense, all pigments mixed with water rather than oil, including FRESCO and TEMPERA as well as aquarelle (the process now commonly called watercolour). Gouache and distemper are also watercolours, but prepared with gluey bases. The earliest existing paintings, found in Egypt, are watercolours. Gouache was used by Byzantine and Romanesque artists, and the illuminated manuscripts of the Middle Ages were produced with watercolour. The medium was used during and after the RENAISSANCE by DÜRER, VAN DYCK, and others to tint and shade drawings and woodcuts. In the 18th cent. the modern watercolour grew into a complete painting technique. Quick and easy to apply, the colours are at once brilliant, transparent, and delicate. The medium was particularly popular in England, where its greatest masters were CONSTABLE and J.M.W. TURNER. Many 19th-cent. painters used watercolour extensively, largely for landscapes. In France they included DAUMIER, DELACROIX, and GÉRICAULT, and later, CÉZANNE and DUFY.

**watercress,** hardy perennial European herb (*Nasturtium officinale*) of the MUSTARD family, found in or around water. It is cultivated commercially for its small, pungent leaflets, used as a peppery salad green or garnish. The ornamental plant whose common name is NASTURTIUM is unrelated.

**waterfall,** sudden drop in a stream or river formed where it passes over a layer of harder rock to an area of softer, more easily eroded rock. As a stream grows older, the waterfall, by undercutting and erosion, normally moves upstream and loses height until it becomes a series of rapids and finally disappears. Because of the waterpower that waterfalls can provide, many cities are located near them. Notable examples are NIAGARA FALLS and VICTORIA FALLS.

**Waterford,** county in SE of Republic of Ireland (1986 pop. 91,098), 1820 km² (710 sq mi), bordering on the Irish Sea in the S. It is situated in the province of Munster. The county town is WATERFORD. Much of the county is mountainous, including the Knockmealdown Mts and the Comeragh Mts in the N. It is drained by the R. Blackwater and the R. SUIR, which forms much of the N border. Agriculture is the main economic activity within the county. The main towns are Waterford, Lismore, and Dungarvan.

**Waterford,** county town (1981 pop. 38,473) of Co. Waterford, Republic of Ireland, on R. SUIR, near its mouth at Waterford Harbour, Irish Sea coast. It is a seaport and industrial town. In 1979 the port handled 1.2 million tonnes. The town contains several historic buildings, including Reginald's Tower which dates from 1003. There are Roman Catholic and Protestant cathedrals, which both date from the 18th cent. The town was well known for its glass manufacture in the 18th cent., but this industry died out in the 19th cent. It is the birthplace of the actor Charles KEAN.

**water gas,** colourless, poisonous gas that burns with an intensely hot, bluish flame. It is mainly a mixture of carbon monoxide and hydrogen and is almost entirely combustible. The gas is made by treating white-hot, hard coal or coke with a blast of steam, forming carbon monoxide and hydrogen. It is important in the preparation of hydrogen, as a fuel in the making of steel, and in other industrial processes, e.g., the FISCHER–TROPSCH PROCESS.

**Watergate affair,** in US history, series of scandals involving Pres. Richard NIXON. In July 1972 agents of Nixon's reelection committee were arrested in Democratic party headquarters, in the Watergate apartment building in Washington, District of Columbia, after an attempt to tap telephones there. They were tried and convicted in 1973, but District Court Judge John Sirica suspected a top-level conspiracy, and when one of the convicted burglars, James McCord, alleged a massive cover-up, the affair erupted into a national scandal. A special Senate committee, headed by Sen. Sam Ervin, held televised hearings (1973) in which John Dean, the former White House counsel, stated that members of the Nixon administration, notably Attorney General John Mitchell, had known of the Watergate burglary. The hearings also revealed that Nixon had taped conversations in the Oval Office, and when the special prosecutor appointed to investigate the affair, Archibald Cox, requested these tapes, Nixon fired him. Cox had begun to uncover widespread evidence of political espionage by the Nixon reelection committee, illegal wiretapping of citizens by the administration, and corporate contributions to the Republican party in return for political favours. His successor as special prosecutor, Leon Jaworski, succeeded in getting the tapes and subsequently obtained indictments and convictions of several high-ranking administration officials, including Mitchell and Dean. Public confidence in the president waned. In July 1974 the House Judiciary Committee adopted three articles of impeachment against him, the first for obstruction of justice. On 9 Aug. 1974, Nixon became the first US president to resign from office. One month later his successor, Gerald FORD, pardoned him.

"He says he's from the phone company . . ."

**Watergate:** Cartoon of Richard Nixon which appeared in the *Los Angeles Times* in 1972

**water lily,** common name for some members of the family Nymphaeaceae, freshwater perennials found throughout most of the world. Often having large shield-shaped leaves and showy blossoms of various colours, the family includes water lilies, lotuses, and pond lilies (genera *Nymphaea, Nelumbo,* and *Nuphar,* respectively). Well-known species include the blue or white Egyptian lotus of the genus *Nymphaea,* the national emblem of Egypt, and the Indian lotus of the genus *Nelumbo,* sacred to several Oriental religions. Many members of the family have edible seeds or TUBERS, the seeds being extremely long-lived .

**Waterloo campaign,** June 1815, last action of the Napoleonic Wars, ending with the battle of Waterloo (18 June), fought near Brussels, Belgium. NAPOLEON I, returned from exile, faced the allied armies of Britain, Prussia, Austria, and Russia. He defeated a Prussian force at Ligny, then turned his attention S to the British, under WELLINGTON. The British took up a strong position S of Waterloo; resisted successfully; and, after being joined by BLÜCHER's Prussian forces, routed the French. Napoleon abdicated on 22 June. Wellington's victory was a triumph, but the campaign itself was marked by confusion and miscalculation on both sides.

**watermelon,** plant (*Citrullis vulgaris*) of the GOURD family, native to Africa. The fleshy, juicy fruit, which can be red to pink, yellow, or white, is eaten fresh; the rind is pickled; and the seeds are also eaten. One white-fleshed variety, the citron melon, is used like citron in preserving.

**water pollution:** see POLLUTION.

**water polo,** swimming game played in a pool by teams of seven players each, including a goalkeeper. The object is to manoeuvre by head, feet, or one hand a large leather ball into goals at opposite ends of the pool. Rough defensive techniques are permitted, including ducking (holding a player under water). The game, played by club and college teams, was developed in England in the 1870s and later became popular in the US. It has been an Olympic event since 1900.

**water rat:** see VOLE.

**Waters, Muddy,** (McKinley Morganfield), 1915–83, black American blues guitarist, singer and composer. After moving to Chicago in 1943 he became one of the most famous and imitated of all blues guitarists and singers, with classic compositions and performances such as 'Hoochie Coochie Man', 'I Just Wanna Make Love to You', and 'I Got my Mojo Working'. Equally dynamic as an electric or acoustic guitarist, he had a powerfully aggressive vocal delivery.

**waters, territorial:** see SEA, LAW OF THE.

**watershed,** elevation or divide separating the CATCHMENT AREA, or drainage basin, of one river system from another. The Rocky Mts and the Andes form a watershed between westward-flowing and eastward-flowing streams. The term is also often used as synonymous with drainage basin.

**water skiing,** sport of riding on skis along the water's surface while being towed by a motorboat. Competitive water skiing consists of the slalom, in which skiers manoeuvre around a series of buoys; jumping, from an inclined ramp 1.8 m (6 ft) high; and trick riding, involving intricate routines. The sport probably originated on the French Riviera in the early 1920s.

**waterspout:** see TORNADO.

**water wheel,** ancient device for utilizing the power of flowing or falling water. The oldest known wheel, probably first used in the Middle East, was essentially a grindstone mounted on top of a vertical shaft whose vaned or paddled lower end dipped into a swift stream. In the 1st cent. BC a horizontal shaft came into use; the wheel attached to it had radial vanes around its edge. Today the water wheel has been largely replaced by the TURBINE.

**Watford,** town (1981 pop. 109,503), Hertfordshire, S England, on R. Colne, 16 km (16 mi) NW of London. It is an industrial and residential town, whose industries include brewing and the manufacture of paper.

**Watson, James Dewey,** 1928–, American biologist and educator. For their work in establishing the molecular structure of DNA, he and Francis CRICK shared the 1962 Nobel Prize for physiology or medicine with Maurice WILKINS. Watson's *Double Helix* (1968) is an account of their work.

**Watson, John Broadus,** 1878–1958, American psychologist. J.B. Watson was the founder of BEHAVIOURISM as a school and doctrine in psychology. His best-known book is *Psychology from the Standpoint of a Behaviourist* (1919).

**Watson, Thomas,** 1557?–92, English writer. He was a literary innovator: he published the earliest translation of SOPHOCLES in England, a Latin version of *Antigone*; his *Hekatompathia* (1582) was the earliest English sonnet sequence to reach print; and his *Italian Madrigalls Englished* (1590) were the earliest English versions of Italian madrigals. His friends included MARLOWE.

**Watson, Tom** (Thomas Sturges Watson), 1949–, American golfer. A graduate of Stanford Univ. (1971), he is generally considered the successor to Jack NICKLAUS as the game's foremost player. Watson won the British Open in 1975, 1977, 1980, 1982, and 1983, the Masters in 1977 and 1981, and the US Open in 1982.

**watt:** see POWER.

**Watt, James,** 1736–1819, Scottish inventor. He became an apprenticed instrument maker and optician and found work in Glasgow Univ. Whilst repairing a model of the Newcomen STEAM ENGINE he invented a separate condenser and valve system that enabled steam pressure to be applied to either side of the piston in turn, and resulted in a new improved type of engine. Watt went into partnership with Matthew Boulton in 1775, producing reciprocating machines for pumping water from mines and dry docks. The one at Londonderry in N Ireland, fitted in 1790, is still operational. He made many improvements, including, in 1782, producing rotary motion from the piston using a 'sun and planet' gearing. Steam power was subsequently harnessed to machine. The modern unit of power, the watt, is named after him.

**Watteau, Jean-Antoine** (wah,toh), 1684–1721, French painter of Flemish descent. He studied (1704–08) in the studio of Claude Gillot, a painter of theatrical life, which later became the subject of some of Watteau's finest paintings, e.g., *Love in the French Theatre* (Berlin). One of the great colourists of all time, Watteau executed gay and sensuous scenes in shimmering pastel tones, influencing fashion and garden design in the 18th cent. *The Embarkation for Cythera* (1717; Louvre, Paris) is a characteristic work; it introduced a characteristic type of ROCOCO painting, the *fête galante* (romantic figures in a park or garden setting).

Jean-Antoine **Watteau**, *Embarkation for Cythera*, 1717. Oil on canvas, 127 × 192 cm. Louvre, Paris.

**Watts Towers,** group of towers built (1921–54) by Simon Rodilla (or Rodia), 1879–1965, in Watts, Los Angeles. Unique, fanciful structures reminiscent of GAUDÍ's work, they incorporate stone, steel, cement, and discarded elements, e.g., bottle tops.

Watts Towers

**Waugh, Evelyn (Arthur St John),** 1903–66, English novelist. The foremost social satirist of his generation, he gained fame with *Decline and Fall* (1928) and *Vile Bodies* (1930). A conservative moralist who converted to Roman Catholicism, his major works are *A Handful of Dust* (1934), *Brideshead Revisited* (1945), and his World War II trilogy *Sword of Honour* (1952–61). *The Loved One* (1948) satirizes Hollywood mortuary customs. His *Diaries* (1976) and *Letters* (1980) are noted for their style, savage humour, bleak pessimism, and spectacular personal indiscretions.

**wave,** in physics, the transfer of ENERGY by some form of regular vibration, or oscillatory motion, either of some material medium (see SOUND) or by the variation of intensity of the field vectors of an electromagnetic field (see ELECTROMAGNETIC RADIATION). In longitudinal, or compressional, waves the vibration is in the same direction as the transfer of energy; in transverse waves the vibration is at right angles to the transfer of energy. The amplitude of a wave is its maximum displacement.

The distance between successive crests or successive troughs is the wavelength λ of a wave. One full wavelength of a wave represents one complete cycle, that is, one complete vibration in each direction. All waves are referenced to an imaginary synchronous motion in a circle; thus one complete cycle is divided into 360 degrees. The phase is that part of the cycle, expressed in degrees, that is completed at a certain time. The various phase relationships (see diagram) between combining waves determine the type of INTERFERENCE that takes place. The frequency $f$ or $\upsilon$ of a wave is equal to the number of crests (or troughs) that pass a given fixed point per unit of time. The period $T$ of a wave is the time lapse between the passage of successive crests (or troughs). The speed $v$, or $c$ of a wave is determined by its wavelength and its frequency according to the equation $v = f\lambda$ or $c = \upsilon\lambda$. Waves are of many kinds: sound waves, electromagnetic waves (including light and radio waves), water waves, and earthquake waves.

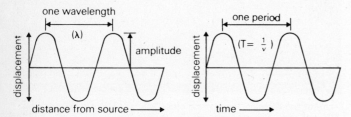

Wave diagrams showing the displacement of a wave plotted against distance from source and against time. A wave travels one wavelength during one period.

**waveguide,** in electronics, a metal tube or dielectric cylinder used for the directed propagation of electromagnetic microwaves or, in the case of optical (thin glass) fibres, light. See FIBRE OPTICS.

**Wavell, Archibald Percival Wavell,** 1st **Earl,** 1883–1950, British field marshal and viceroy of India (1943–47). In WORLD WAR II he routed (1940–41) Italian forces in N Africa, but was forced back by the Germans. He then held command in India. As viceroy, he tried to prepare India for self-rule.

**wave mechanics:** see QUANTUM THEORY.

**wax,** substance secreted by glands on the abdomen of the bee and known commonly as beeswax; also various substances resembling beeswax. Chemically, waxes are complex mixtures of esters, fatty acids, free alcohols, and higher hydrocarbons. They are usually harder and less greasy than fats, but like fats they are less dense than water and insoluble in it. Waxes can be obtained from plants (e.g., carnauba wax from palm leaves) or animals (e.g., lanolin from wool fibres and spermaceti from sperm whales). PARAFFIN and ozocerite are mineral waxes composed of hydrocarbons. Japan wax and Bayberry wax are composed chiefly of fats.

**waxplant,** common name for *Hoya carnosa*, a member of the milkweed family. A climbing plant from Australasia and S China, widely cultivated for its scented pink-and-carmine flowers borne in clusters, and giving the appearance of being fashioned in wax.

**waxwing,** any of three species (genus *Bombycilla*) of perching songbirds of the Northern Hemisphere. Waxwings have crests (raised only in alarm) and brownish-grey plumage with flecks of red pigment resembling sealing wax on the wings. The species are the cedar waxwing; the Bohemian, or greater, waxwing; and the Japanese waxwing, found only in NE Asia.

**Wayne, John,** 1906–79, American film actor; b. Marion Michael Morrison. Extremely popular, he did his best work for John FORD, playing tough, but troubled heroes. His films include *Stagecoach* (1939), *The Quiet Man* (1952), and *True Grit* (1969; Academy Award).

**weak interaction:** see ELEMENTARY PARTICLES.

**weasel,** small, lithe, carnivorous MAMMAL of the family Mustelidae, which also includes the MINK, FERRET, WOLVERINE, SKUNK, BADGER, and OTTER. All members of the family have scent glands, used chiefly for territorial marking but sometimes for defence. Found in Eurasia, N Africa, and the Americas, weasels are characterized by long bodies and necks, short legs, small ears, and dense, lustrous fur (usually brown with white underparts). They hunt small animals at night, often killing more than they can eat.

**weather,** state of the atmosphere at a given time and place with regard to temperature, air pressure, humidity, wind, cloudiness, and precipitation. The term *weather* is restricted to conditions over short periods of time; conditions over long periods are referred to as CLIMATE. The study of weather is called METEOROLOGY.

**weather balloon,** BALLOON, usually helium-inflated, used in the measurement and evaluation of atmospheric conditions. Information on atmospheric pressure and other meteorological conditions may be sent by radio from the balloon (see RADIOSONDE); monitoring of its movement (see THEODOLITE) provides information about winds at its flight level.

**weathering,** term for the processes by which ROCK at the surface of the earth is disintegrated and decomposed by the action of atmospheric agents, water, and living things. Some of the processes are mechanical, e.g., the impact of running water, or the growth of salt or ice crystals. Others are chemical, e.g., oxidation, hydration, or carbonization. Weathering aids in the formation of soil and prepares materials for EROSION.

**weather satellite,** artificial SATELLITE used to gather data on a global basis for improvement of weather forecasting. Information is provided about cloud cover, storm location, temperature, and heat balance in the earth's atmosphere. These satellites may be either polar-orbiting or geostationary.

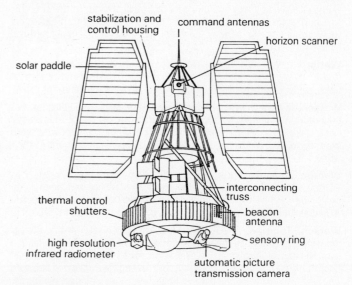

Weather satellite

**Weaver, Robert Clifton,** 1907–, US secretary of housing and urban development (1966–68). Pres. Lyndon B. JOHNSON named him to head the newly created housing department in 1966, making Weaver the first black to serve in a presidential cabinet.

**weaving,** the art of forming a fabric by interlacing threads at right angles. One of the most ancient arts, once practised chiefly by women, weaving sprang up independently in different parts of the world and is often mentioned in early literature. Archaeological remains have included textiles woven from COTTON, SILK, and WOOL. Silk weaving reached Byzantium from China in the 6th cent. AD, and cotton and silk weaving were brought to Spain by the Moors in the 8th and 9th cent. Flanders was known for its wool weaving by the 10th cent., and Flemish weavers brought to England by William the Conquerer gave impetus to the art there. In medieval France TAPESTRY weaving was highly developed. Weaving was a household industry in the American colonies. The SPINNING and weaving inventions of the 18th cent. made possible the transition to today's huge, mechanized textile industry, but fine woven textiles are still made by hand. On the LOOM, the warp threads are held under tension and are raised or lowered alternately to create a shed through which the weft (or woof) thread is inserted. Woven fabrics are classified by their structure. The basic weaves are plain, or tabby, in which the weft passes over alternate warp threads; twill, with a diagonal design made by interlacing two to four warp threads; and satin, with threads floating on the surface to reflect light, giving the fabric lustre. Pile weaves, such as those used in CARPETS, have a surface of cut or uncut loops.

**Webb, Beatrice,** 1858–1943; b. Beatrice Potter, and **Sidney James Webb,** 1859–1947, British social researchers and political activists. In 1892 they married, and thereafter they worked and wrote together as leaders of the FABIAN SOCIETY, in the building of the LABOUR PARTY, and in the creation (1895) of the London School of Economics. In 1913 they founded the *New Statesman.* Sidney Webb was elected to Parliament in 1922 and was created Baron Passfield in 1929. He served in two Labour governments. Co-authors of *The History of Trade Unionism* (1894), *Industrial Democracy* (1897), *Soviet Communism* (2 vol., 1935), and other works, the Webbs made major contributions to most of the political and social reforms of their time, and their faith in enlightened bureaucracy was decisive in shaping the character of the British welfare state.

**Webb, Mary (Meredith),** 1881–1927, English novelist. She is known for sombre, passionate novels about her native Shropshire, including *Gone to Earth* (1917) and *Precious Bane* (1924).

**Webb, Philip Speakman,** 1831–1915, English architect. He was influential in the mid-19th-cent. revival of residential architecture based on QUEEN ANNE and GEORGIAN STYLE designs. A friend and supporter of William MORRIS, he built for him (1859) the Red House, Bexley Heath, and collaborated with him afterwards. He also designed furniture, tiles, and stained glass.

**Weber, Carl Maria Friedrich Ernst von** (fən ,vaybə), 1786–1826, German composer. Considered the founder of German romantic OPERA, he wrote 10 operas, including *Abu Hassan* (1811), *Der Freischütz* [the marksman] (1821), and *Oberon* (1826). Among his instrumental works are the popular *Invitation to the Dance* (1819), the *Konzertstück* for piano and orchestra (1821), and many distinctive chamber works.

**Weber, Max,** 1864–1920, German sociologist, historian, and political economist, whose work has had a large influence on sociological theory and research. Unlike DURKHEIM, Weber believed that the aim of sociology should not be to produce predictive laws of human behaviour in a manner akin to the natural sciences, but to explain human activity in terms of the system of meanings used by the people involved in that activity. He argued that social theorizing was inevitably shaped by value judgments; but that social scientists should separate their political views from their professional task, e.g., by generating a variety of possible solutions to a problem (e.g., vandalism) without expressing a moral or political preference. In opposition to MARX's view of the dominance of the economic level in historical causation, he emphasized the role of religious values, ideologists, and charismatic leaders in shaping societies, e.g., in his *The Protestant Ethic and the Spirit of Capitalism* (1904–05) in which he related Calvinist ideals to the rise of CAPITALISM.

**Webern, Anton von** (fən ,vaybeən), 1883–1945, Austrian composer. A pupil of Arnold SCHOENBERG, he wrote TWELVE-TONE MUSIC. His music is characterized by unusual combinations of instruments, a broken melodic line, and extreme brevity. Written mainly for small orchestral groups or voice, his compositions include *Das Augenlicht* for chorus and orchestra (1935) and *Orchestral Variations* (1940).

**Webster, Ben(jamin Francis),** 1909–73, American jazz tenor saxophonist and arranger. Capable of intense and breathy lyricism and gruffly aggressive swing, he, with Coleman HAWKINS, brought the tenor saxophone to mature prominence in jazz during the 1930s. He became a key member of Duke ELLINGTON's 1940s orchestra after which he concentrated mainly on small group sessions, frequently under his own name. He lived in Europe from 1964 onwards, where his innate romanticism continued to flower.

**Webster, Daniel,** 1782–1852, American politician. A lawyer famous for his oratory, Webster won national recognition in the Dartmouth College case and McCulloch v. Maryland (both 1819). A Federalist, he represented New Hampshire in the House of Representatives (1813–17). After moving to Boston, he again served in the House (1823–27) and was senator from Massachusetts (1827–41, 1845–50). He became a leader in the new WHIG PARTY and was the presidential candidate of one of its factions in 1836. As secretary of state (1841–43) under Pres. W.H. HARRISON, he was responsible for the WEBSTER–ASHBURTON TREATY. Reelected to the Senate, he placed the issue of union above all others, even that of slavery, and his support of the COMPROMISE OF 1850 angered Northern opponents of

slavery and greatly diminished his political influence. He was again secretary of state (1850–52) in Pres. Millard FILLMORE's administration.

**Webster, John,** 1580?–1634, English dramatist. His reputation rests on two tragedies, *The White Devil* (c.1612) and *The Duchess of Malfi* (c.1614), sombre revenge dramas that reveal a profound understanding of human suffering.

**Webster, Noah,** 1758–1843, American lexicographer and philologist. His *Grammatical Institute of the English Language,* in three parts, speller, grammar, and reader (1783–85), was the first of the books that made him for many years the chief American authority on English. The first part, the *Elementary Spelling Book,* helped standardize American spelling. His *Compendious Dictionary* (1806) was followed by his greatest work, *The American Dictionary of the English Language* (1812); 12,000 of its 70,000 words had not appeared in such a work before. He completed the 1840 revision; through many revisions since then the dictionary has retained its popularity. See also DICTIONARY.

**Webster–Ashburton Treaty,** 1842, between the US, represented by Secy of State Daniel WEBSTER, and Great Britain, represented by Lord Ashburton. It settled various boundary disputes between Canada and the US, including those in the Northeast and others in the GREAT LAKES area, and served as an important precedent for future peaceful settlements of disputes between Canada and the US.

**Weddell Sea,** part of the Southern Ocean S of the Atlantic Ocean, bordered by the Antarctic Peninsula and Coats Land; named after James Weddell, who reached 74° 15′ S, 36° 14′ W in 1823. The vast Ronne and Filchner ice shelves are the southern limit of the sea.

**Wedekind, Frank** (,vaydəkint), 1864–1918, German dramatist. A forerunner of EXPRESSIONISM, he stressed man's primal instincts. *Spring Awakening, a Tragedy of Childhood* (1891, premiered 1906) is a tender, comic, angry presentation of adolescent sexuality and its vulnerability. His plays *Earth Spirit* (1895) and *Pandora's Box* (1904) representing the rise and fall of the femme fatale were the source for the libretto of Alban BERG's opera *Lulu.* He was a cabaret performer, and also acted with great power and presence in his own dramas.

**Wedgwood, Josiah,** 1730–95, English potter. Wedgwood opened a pottery at Burslem in 1759 and in 1768–69 built a factory and model village for his workers named Etruria, now in Stoke-on-Trent. He developed cream-coloured earthenware, variegated wares resembling hardstones, and a black stoneware which he called black basaltes. For his jasper, a new type of stoneware in blue or other colours, with white cameo-like relief decoration, he used designs by artists such as John FLAXMAN. Wedgwood also helped improve roads and canals, built schools, and bettered living conditions for his workers.

**Wednesday:** see WEEK.

**weed,** any wild plant, especially those competing with crop plants for soil nutrients, water, and space. Control methods include the use of various HERBICIDES and soil cultivation. Plants cultivated in one area may become weeds when introduced into another area.

**week,** period of time shorter than the month, commonly seven days (but see CALENDAR). The seven-day week is said to have originated in ancient times in W Asia, probably in Mesopotamia. It is thought to have been a planetary week predicated on the concept of the influence of the planets: the Sun, the Moon, and five bodies recognized today as PLANETS—Mars, Mercury, Jupiter, Venus, and Saturn. The Hebrew week is based chiefly on the SABBATH, which comes every seventh day. In the Roman Empire the planetary week was at first preeminent, and the use of planetary names, based on the names of pagan deities, continued even after CONSTANTINE I made (c.321) the Christian week, beginning on Sunday, official. The Roman names for the days pervaded Europe; in most languages the forms are translations from Latin or attempts to assign corresponding names of divinities. The Latin names, their translations, the English equivalents, and their derivations follow: *dies solis* [Sun's day], Sunday; *dies lunae* [Moon's day], Monday; *dies Martis* [MARS's day], Tuesday [Tiw's day]; *dies Mercurii* [MERCURY's day], Wednesday [Woden's day]; *dies Jovis* [Jove's or JUPITER's day], Thursday [THOR's day]; *dies Veneris* [VENUS's day], Friday [Frigg's day]; and *dies Saturni* [SATURN's day], Saturday.

**weevil,** very small to quite large (1.5–75 mm/¹⁄₂₀–3 in) BEETLE (superfamily Curculionoidea). This is by far the largest group of beetles, with more than 60,000 members, all of which feed on plant matter. As

**Wedgwood** vase, 'The Apotheosis of Homer', in white jasper, decorated with mid blue dip and white bas-relief ornamentation, designed by J. Flaxman (1786; British Museum)

a result many are agricultural pests, eating growing plants or harvested seeds, both as adults and as their characteristically legless larvae, which live inside their food supply. Among major and now cosmopolitan pests of stored grain are, for example, the granary and rice weevils, *Sitophilus granarius* and *S. oryzae*. Not all weevils are harmful: *Elaeidobius kamerunicus*, for example, is a principal pollinator of the oil palm. Its recent successful introduction into Malaya has eliminated the need for laborious hand pollination and, through being more efficient, has increased yields by as much as 20%. Related to the weevils are the bark beetle, some of which (*Scolytus*), are the vectors of the pathogenic fungus *Ceratocystis ulmi* which decimated elm trees in Britain in the 1970s (Dutch elm disease).

**Wegener, Alfred Lothar,** 1880–1930, German geologist, meteorologist, and Arctic explorer. He is known for his theory of CONTINENTAL DRIFT, set forth in his *The Origin of Continents and Oceans* (1915), and for his expeditions to Greenland, where he eventually lost his life.

**Weidman, Charles,** 1901–75, American dancer. He danced with Denishawn (1920–27); see ST DENIS, RUTH. He formed the company with Doris HUMPHREY in 1928. His works combined abstraction with brilliant use of mime. He is considered one of the founders of American MODERN DANCE.

**Weierstrass, Karl Wilhelm Theodor** (ˌvieəshtrahs), 1815–97, German mathematician. He developed the modern theory of functions. An advocate of the modern, rigorous approach to analysis and number theory, he did much to clarify the foundations of these subjects.

**weight,** measure, expressed in grams or pounds, of the force of gravity on a body (see GRAVITATION). Because the weights of different bodies at the same location are proportional to their masses, weight is often used as a measure of MASS. Unlike the mass, the weight of a body depends on its location in the gravitational field of the Earth or of some other astronomical body.

**weightlessness,** the absence of any observable effects of GRAVITATION. A person inside a freely-falling box accelerates at the same rate as the box itself; therefore there is no relative acceleration (and so no force) between the floor of the box and his feet, and he feels no sensation of weight. Bodies would float freely inside such a box. An orbiting satellite is in a state of 'free fall', being accelerated towards the Earth by gravity, but not getting any closer to its surface because of the transverse motion of the satellite relative to the Earth. Weightlessness is encountered by the crew of a spacecraft orbiting the Earth, or coasting through interplanetary space (with the motors switched off), for the spacecraft, crew, and spacecraft objects are all sharing the same motion ('free fall') under the action of the gravity of the Earth or Sun respectively.

**weight lifting,** competitive sport and training technique for athletes. Meets are conducted according to weight classes, ranging from flyweight to super heavyweight. The contestant raising the greatest total of weights in three standard lifts—two-hand or military press, clean-and-jerk, and snatch—is declared the winner. Weight lifting has long been popular in Europe, Egypt, Turkey, and Japan. The USSR and other E European nations have excelled in Olympic competition.

**weights and measures,** units and standards for expressing the amount of some quantity, such as length, capacity, or weight; the science of measurement standards and methods is known as metrology. Crude systems of weights and measures probably date from prehistoric times. Early units were commonly based on body measurements and on plant seeds or other agricultural objects. As civilization progressed, technological and commercial requirements led to increased standardization. Units were usually fixed by edict of local or national rulers and were subdivided and multiplied or otherwise arranged into systems of measurement. Today the chief systems in everyday use are the METRIC SYSTEM and the ENGLISH UNITS OF MEASUREMENT. The US is one of the few countries still using the latter system; in the UK both systems remain in use.

**Weil, Simone,** (way), 1909–43, French thinker. She proved an inspiration to other intellectuals before the war when she explored the condition of factory-workers by sharing it (*La Condition ouvrière*, 1951). After an intense mystical experience in 1938 she became a practising Roman Catholic, subordinating all activity to an inward spiritual attendance upon a God whose presence is absolute but not manifest. She wrote a wide range of essays on politics, philosophy, and religion (e.g., *L'enracinement*, 1949–50; tr. The Need for Roots) which were published after her death of tuberculosis and near-starvation when, as a refugee in England, she attempted to live on the rations meted out to her fellow-countrymen in occupied France.

**Weill, Kurt** (viel), 1900–50, American composer; b. Germany. In Europe he was best known for the satirical operas *The Threepenny Opera* (1928) and *The Rise and Fall of the City of Mahagonny* (1927, rev. 1930), both with librettos by BRECHT. Condemned as decadent by the NAZIS, he went to the US in 1935. There he wrote such sophisticated MUSICALS as *Knickerbocker Holiday* (1938, with Maxwell ANDERSON) and *Lady in the Dark* (1941). Among his last, more serious works was *Street Scene* (1947). He was married to Lotte LENYA.

**Weimar** (ˌviemah), city (1984 est. pop. 64,000), S East Germany, on the Ilm R. It is a cultural and industrial centre with such manufactures as textiles and chemicals. Known in the 10th cent., it became (16th cent.) the capital of the duchy of Saxe-Weimar. The presence (18th–19th cent.) of GOETHE and SCHILLER made Weimar the literary centre of Europe; later LISZT and NIETZSCHE lived there. In 1919 the city was the scene of the national assembly that established the republican government known as the 'Weimar Republic'. Landmarks include the parish church, which has an altarpiece by CRANACH, and the Goethe National Museum. The CONCENTRATION CAMP Buchenwald was located (1937–45) near the city.

**Weimar Republic** (ˌviemah), German regime which succeeded in 1919 to the empire (Reich) of the last Kaiser, WILHELM II. The republican constitution was adopted by an elected assembly convened in Weimar in summer 1919, with Friedrich EBERT as president. Beset with political and economic difficulties in the aftermath of the war, the republic was replaced by HITLER's Third Reich in 1933.

**Weir, Peter,** 1944–, Australian film director. His work, which helped to bring Australian film to world attention, includes *Picnic at Hanging Rock* (1975), *The Last Wave* (1977), *The Plumber* (1978), *Gallipoli* (1981), and *Witness* (1986).

**Weismann, August,** 1834–1914, German biologist. A professor at the Univ. of Freiburg (1866–1912), he originated the germ-plasm theory of heredity, which stresses the unbroken continuity of the germ plasm and the nonheritability of ACQUIRED CHARACTERISTICS.

**Weiss, Peter,** 1916–82, German–Swedish writer, film director, and painter. Weiss began with the subjective farewell of a young man's autobiography, *Leave-taking* (1961) and *Vanishing-Point* (1962). His philosophical drama on the nature of revolution, *The Persecution and Assassination of Jean Paul Marat as Performed by the Inmates of the Asylum of Charenton Under the Direction of the Marquis de Sade* (1964),

and his play *The Investigation* (1965) were international successes. He was a Marxist from the mid-1960s; his social and political views are expressed in the dramas *Vietnam Discourse* (1968), *Trotsky in Exile* (1970), and *Hölderlin* (1971). His last important work was the 'alternative autobiography', *Aesthetics of Resistance* (3 vol., 1975–81), prose-fiction informed by a politically-conscious lifetime.

**Weizmann, Chaim,** 1874–1952, scientist and Zionist leader, first president (1948–52) of ISRAEL; b. Russia. A British subject from 1910, he combined a life of science with efforts toward the creation of a Jewish state. During WORLD WAR I he developed a synthetic acetone for the production of explosives. In 1917 he helped procure from the British government the pro-Zionist Balfour Declaration (see BALFOUR, ARTHUR JAMES). A longtime leader of the World Zionist Organization, he was named president of Israel in 1948. He founded what is now the Weizmann Institute of Science.

## COMMON WEIGHTS AND MEASURES

| Imperial | Metric Equivalents |
|---|---|
| **Length** | |
| 1 inch (in) | = 25.4 millimetres |
| 1 foot (ft) = 12 inches | = 0.3048 metre |
| 1 yard (yd) = 3 feet | = 0.9144 metre |
| 1 (statute) mile = 1760 yards | = 1.609 kilometres |
| **Area** | |
| 1 square inch (in² or sq in) | = 6.45 sq centimetres |
| 1 square foot (ft²) = 144 sq in | = 9.29 sq decimetres |
| 1 square yard (yd²) = 9 sq ft | = 0.836 sq metre |
| 1 acre = 4840 sq yd | = 0.405 hectare |
| 1 square mile (mile²) = 640 acres | = 259 hectares |
| **Volume** | |
| 1 cubic inch (in³ or cu in) | = 16.4 cu centimetres |
| 1 cubic foot (ft³) = 1.728 cu in | = 0.0283 cu metre |
| 1 cubic yard (yd³) = 27 cu ft | = 0.765 cu metre |
| **Capacity** | |
| 1 pint (pt) = 20 fluid oz | |
| = 34.68 cu in | = 0.568 litre |
| 1 quart = 2 pints | = 1.136 litres |
| 1 gallon (gal) = 4 quarts | = 4.546 litres |
| 1 peck = 2 gallons | = 9.092 litres |
| 1 bushel = 4 pecks | = 36.4 litres |
| 1 quarter = 8 bushels | = 2.91 hectolitres |
| **American dry** | |
| 1 pint = 33.60 cu in | = 0.550 litre |
| 1 quart = 2 pints | = 1.101 litres |
| 1 peck = 8 quarts | = 8.81 litres |
| 1 bushel = 4 pecks | = 35.3 litres |
| **American liquid** | |
| 1 pint = 16 fluid oz | |
| = 28.88 cu in | = 0.473 litre |
| 1 quart = 2 pints | = 0.946 litre |
| 1 gallon = 4 quarts | = 3.785 litres |
| **Avoirdupois Weight** | |
| 1 grain | = 0.065 gram |
| 1 dram | = 1.772 grams |
| 1 ounce (oz) = 16 drams | = 28.35 grams |
| 1 pound (lb) = 16 ounces | |
| = 7000 grains | = 0.4536 kilogram |
| 1 stone (st) = 14 pounds | = 6.35 kilograms |
| 1 quarter = 2 stones | = 12.70 kilograms |
| 1 hundredweight (cwt) = 4 quarters | = 50.80 kilograms |
| 1 (long) ton = 20 hundredweight | = 1.016 tonnes |
| 1 short ton = 2000 pounds | = 0.907 tonne |

| Metric | Imperial Equivalents |
|---|---|
| **Length** | |
| 1 millimetre (mm) | = 0.039 inch |
| 1 centimetre (cm) = 10 mm | = 0.394 inch |
| 1 decimetre (dm) = 10 cm | = 3.94 inches |
| 1 metre (m) = 10 dm | = 1.094 yards |
| 1 decametre (dam) = 10 m | = 10.94 yards |
| 1 hectometre (hm) = 100 m | = 109.4 yards |
| 1 kilometre (km) = 1000 m | = 0.6214 mile |
| **Area** | |
| 1 square centimetre (cm² or sq cm) | = 0.155 sq in |
| 1 square metre (m²) | = 1.196 sq yards |
| 1 are = 100 sq metres | = 119.6 sq yards |
| 1 hectare (ha) = 100 ares | = 2.471 acres |
| 1 square kilometre (km²) | = 0.386 sq mile |
| **Volume** | |
| 1 cubic centimetre (cm³ or cu cm) | = 0.061 cu inch |
| 1 cubic metre (m³) | = 1.308 cu yards |
| **Capacity** | |
| 1 millilitre (ml) | = 0.002 pint (British) |
| 1 centilitre (cl) = 10 ml | = 0.018 pint |
| 1 decilitre (dl) = 10 cl | = 0.176 pint |
| 1 litre (l) = 10 dl | = 1.76 pints |
| 1 decalitre (dal) = 10 l | = 2.20 gallons |
| 1 hectolitre (hl) = 100 l | = 2.75 bushels |
| 1 kilolitre (kl) = 1000 l | = 3.44 quarters |
| **Weight** | |
| 1 milligram (mg) | = 0.015 grain |
| 1 centigram (cg) = 10 mg | = 0.154 grain |
| 1 decigram (dg) = 10 cg | = 1.543 grain |
| 1 gram (g) = 10 dg | = 15.43 grains |
| 1 decagram (dag) = 10 g | = 5.64 drams |
| 1 hectogram (hg) = 100 g | = 3.527 ounces |
| 1 kilogram (kg) = 1000 g | = 2.205 pounds |
| 1 tonne (metric ton) = 1000 kg | = 0.984 (long) ton |

**Weld, Theodore Dwight,** 1803–95, American abolitionist. A disciple of the evangelist Charles G. Finney, Weld trained other Finney converts at Lane Seminary in Cincinnati, and helped select (1834) the 'Seventy' agents for the American Anti-Slavery Society who successfully spread the ABOLITIONIST gospel throughout the North. Weld married (1838) the abolitionist Angelina GRIMKÉ and was an editor of the *Emancipator*. His *American Slavery as It Is* (1839) was a source for Harriet Beecher STOWE's *Uncle Tom's Cabin* and was considered second only to Stowe's book in its influence on the antislavery movement.

**welding,** process for joining separate pieces of metal in a continuous metallic bond. In cold-pressure welding, high pressure is applied at room temperature. Forge welding (or forging) is done by means of hammering, with the addition of heat. In most processes, the points to be joined are melted, additional molten metal is added as a filler, and the bond is allowed to cool. In the Thomson process, melting is caused by resistance to an applied electric current. Another process is that of the atomic hydrogen flame, in which hydrogen molecules passing through an electric arc are broken into atoms by absorbing energy. Outside the arc the molecules reunite, yielding heat to weld the material in the process.

**Welensky, Sir Roy** 1907–, prime minister of the Federation of Rhodesia and Nyasaland (1956–63). Following the secession from the federation of N Rhodesia (later Zambia) and Nyasaland (later Malawi), Welensky obtained little support for his moderate views from the white population of S Rhodesia and was eclipsed by Ian SMITH. See also ZIMBABWE.

**welfare:** see SOCIAL WELFARE.

**welfare state,** the system in which the basic provisions for the welfare of the people are the responsibility of the state and do not derive entirely from market forces. An essential part of the life of any country under SOCIALISM, the idea had many sources of inspiration in Britain. One was Liberalism, reflected in the National Insurance Act (1911). The source of the postwar British welfare state was the BEVERIDGE Report (1942) the main provisions of which were enacted by the Labour government after the war. The NATIONAL HEALTH SERVICE, though strongly opposed by the medical profession at the time, has been one of the most successful elements. Similar arrangements to those in the UK are found in European countries; the Scandinavian countries are more progressive. The US and the Republic of Ireland have never fully accepted the concept.

**Welland Ship Canal,** man-made canal, S Ontario, W of Buffalo, New York, linking lakes Erie and Ontario. It is 44.4 km (27.6 mi) long, with a minimum depth of 9 m (30 ft), and forms a vital part of the St Lawrence & Great Lakes Waterway. Eight locks (each 262 m/859 ft long, 24 m/80 ft wide, and 9 m/30 ft deep) overcome the 99-m (326-ft) difference in elevation between the lakes and bypass NIAGARA FALLS. The canal was built (1914–32) to replace a canal opened in 1829, and was modernized and enlarged in 1972.

**Wellcome, Sir Henry Solomon,** 1853–1936, English patron of medicine, b. America. Founder of the pharmaceutical company, Burroughs Wellcome & Co., in 1880 in London, he established the Wellcome Foundation in 1924. The Wellcome Trust, established after his death, is the largest charitable trust supporting medical research in the UK. In 1932 he was knighted and elected fellow of the Royal Society.

**Welles, Orson,** 1915–85, American film director and actor. *Citizen Kane* (1940), considered his masterpiece, is noted for its technical brilliance and structural complexity. His other films include *The Magnificent Ambersons* (1942), *The Lady from Shanghai* (1947), and *Touch of Evil* (1962).

**Wellesley, Richard Colley Wellesley, Marquess,** 1760–1842, British colonial administrator. As governor general of India (1797–1805), he extended British influence, wiped out French power, and, aided by his brother Arthur (later duke of WELLINGTON), checked the power of the native rulers. He was foreign secretary (1810–12), lord lieutenant of Ireland (1821–28; 1833–34), and a supporter of CATHOLIC EMANCIPATION.

**Wellington,** city (1981 pop. 342,504), capital of New Zealand, at the southern tip of North Island, on an inlet of Cook Strait. It is New Zealand's second-largest city, its chief administrative and transportation centre, and a major port. Manufactures include transportation equipment, processed food, clothing, and textiles. Founded in 1840, it became the capital in 1865. It has a symphony orchestra, ballet and opera companies, and several museums.

**Wellington, Arthur Wellesley, 1st duke of,** 1769–1852, British soldier and statesman. Stationed in India (1796–1805), he assisted his brother Richard WELLESLEY by defeating the MAHRATTA chiefs. He brilliantly directed the PENINSULAR WAR (1809–13) that drove the French out of Spain and Portugal, and defeated (1815) NAPOLEON I in the WATERLOO CAMPAIGN. As prime minister (1828–30) he secured passage of the CATHOLIC EMANCIPATION bill (which he had previously opposed), but lost office to the Whigs in 1830. Wellington later served as foreign secretary (1834–35) and minister without portfolio (1841–46) under Sir Robert PEEL. He always placed public service before party, and his funeral was a national landmark.

**Wells, H(erbert) G(eorge),** 1866–1946, English author and social thinker. Having taught biology, he made his name with scientific romances like *The Time Machine* (1895), *The Island of Doctor Moreau* (1896) and *The War of the Worlds* (1898). He is one of the founding fathers of SCIENCE FICTION. After 1900 he turned to social realism in his comic novels *Kipps* (1905), *Tono-Bungay* (1909) and *The History of Mr Polly* (1910); later he wrote a large number of novels of ideas. His works of social prophecy include *A Modern Utopia* (1905) and a forecast of atomic warfare, *The World Set Free* (1914). An influential advocate of socialism, world government, and the scientific outlook, he also wrote short stories, an autobiography, and numerous political and educational works including the famous *Outline of History* (1920) and *A Short History of the World* (1922). His private life included a much-discussed liaison with Rebecca WEST.

**Welsh language,** member of the Brythonic group of the Celtic subfamily of the Indo-European family of languages. See LANGUAGE (table).

**Wenceslas, Saint,** 907–29, duke of Bohemia. A pious Christian, he made peace with HENRY I (Henry the Fowler) of Germany. He engendered enmity among the nobles and was assassinated by his brother Boleslav I, who succeeded him. The patron saint of Bohemia, he is the 'good King Wenceslas' of the English Christmas carol. Feast: 28 Sept.

**Wenceslaus,** 1361–1419, Holy Roman emperor (uncrowned) and German king (1376–1400), king of Bohemia (1363–1419) as Wenceslaus IV, elector of Brandenburg (1373–76); son and successor of Emperor CHARLES IV. His main interest was always Bohemia, and he was ultimately deposed (1400) as German king by the ELECTORS. He never accepted his successor, Rupert, but in 1411 he agreed to the election of his half-brother, SIGISMUND, as emperor. Wenceslaus was popular with the common people of Bohemia, but quarrelled with the nobles and clergy. He supported John HUSS and tried to prevent his burning, which was carried out at the instigation of Sigismund. Wenceslaus's death and the succession of Sigismund as king of Bohemia led to the HUSSITE Wars.

**Wenceslaus IV,** king of Bohemia: see WENCESLAUS, Holy Roman emperor.

**Wenzhou,** city (1984 pop. 6,205,200), S ZHEJIANG prov., E China. It is a developing industrial city that in 1984 was designated one of the 14 coastal cities to receive increased western investment.

**Weores, Sándor** (way‚awresh), 1913–, Hungarian poet. A poet of dazzling virtuosity and versatility, Weores has for over 50 years insisted on the poet as medium and not provider of the message. His prodigious output ranges from nursery rhymes to the Hungarian RAMAYANA; *Psyche* (1972), a set of poems by an early 19th-cent. Hungarian woman, is his single greatest feat of empathy.

**werewolf:** see LYCANTHROPY.

**Werfel, Franz** (‚veəfəl), 1890–1945, Austrian writer; b. Prague. His belief in human brotherhood is expressed in his lyric verse, in expressionist and conventional plays, and in such novels as *The Forty Days of Musa Dagh* (1933), *The Song of Bernadette* (1941), and the comedy *Jacobowsky and the Colonel* (1944). In 1938, Werfel fled NAZI-occupied Austria, later settling in the US.

**Wergeland, Henrik** (‚veəgəlahn), 1808–45, Norwegian poet and patriot. Known as 'Norway's Lord Byron', he was the leading Norwegian literary figure of his era. His greatest work was the verse drama *Creation, Man, and Messiah* (1830). He worked zealously for the causes of liberty, democracy, tolerance, and international cooperation; and his *English Pilot* (1844) voiced his ultimate goal: the liberation of the human mind.

**Werner, Abraham Gottlob,** 1750–1815, German geologist. He was the first to classify minerals systematically. Although his theory of neptunism (that the Earth's lands precipitated out of an original world ocean) is now rejected, geology is indebted to him for applying chronology to rock formations and for his precise definitions.

**Wertheimer, Max:** see GESTALT PSYCHOLOGY.

**Weser** (ˌvayzə), navigable river, c.480 km (300 mi) long, in West Germany. Formed by the confluence of the Fulda and the Werra Rs. at Munden, it flows through BREMEN to the North Sea at BREMERHAVEN. At the Minden gap ('Westphalian Gate') it is crossed by the Mittelland Canal.

**Wesley, John,** 1703–91, English evangelical preacher and founder of METHODISM, was ordained (1728) a priest in the Church of England and led a group of students at Oxford, including his brother Charles and George WHITEFIELD. They were derisively called 'methodists' for their methodical devotion to study and religious duties. In 1735 the Wesleys accompanied James OGLETHORPE to Georgia, where John was deeply influenced by Moravian missionaries. On 24 May 1738, at a religious meeting in London, he experienced an assurance of salvation through faith in Christ alone, which was his message for the rest of his life. In his evangelistic work, he is said to have preached 40,000 sermons and, on the advice of Whitefield, he preached in the open air. Because of his Arminianism and belief in Christian perfection, he repudiated (c.1740) the Calvinist doctrine of election, which led to a break with Whitefield. In 1784 he established the legal status of Methodist societies, and although he did not form a separate church, he did make plans for the societies to continue after his death. His brother, **Charles Wesley,** 1707–88, was also a priest of the Church of England and a Methodist evangelical preacher. He wrote some 6500 hymns, including 'Hark! The Herald Angels Sing' and 'Jesus, Lover of My Soul'.

**Wesley, Samuel,** 1766–1837, British organist, violinist, composer, and teacher. Younger brother of the composer Charles Wesley, 1757–1834, second son of the hymn writer Charles Wesley, 1707–88, and nephew of the founder of Methodism, John Wesley, Samuel was a child prodigy who became the leading English composer of his generation, producing a large number of excellent works, including chamber music and symphonies. Few of these are performed today, apart from his organ voluntaries and some church music. His son **Samuel Sebastian Wesley** 1810–76, was also a composer. He served as organist and choirmaster in the cathedrals of Hereford (1832) and Exeter (1835), Leeds Parish Church (1842), and Winchester (1849) and Gloucester (1865) cathedrals. Apart from composing many fine anthems, church services, and pieces for organ, he played a major role in improving and developing English church music.

**Wessex,** one of the Anglo-Saxon kingdoms of England. It may have been settled as early as 495 by the Saxons. King Ceawlin (560–93) consolidated the area between the upper Thames R. valley and the lower Severn, but until the end of the 8th cent. Wessex was overshadowed successively by KENT, NORTHUMBRIA, and MERCIA. EGBERT (802–39) became overlord of all England, but the kingdom then declined in the face of Danish invasions. The Danes were halted by ALFRED (r.871–99), and thereafter the history of Wessex becomes that of England. After a period of Danish rule (1016–42), EDWARD THE CONFESSOR (1042–66), last of the Wessex line of Alfred, succeeded to the English throne.

**West, Benjamin,** 1738–1820, American painter. In 1760 he went to Europe, where he lived for the rest of his life. He settled in London, espoused neo-classicism (see CLASSICISM), and was appointed historical painter to GEORGE III in 1772. West executed more than 400 canvases, chiefly historical, mythological, and religious subjects on a heroic scale. His best-known works are *Death of General Wolfe* (1770; National Gall. of Art, Ottawa) and *Penn's Treaty with the Indians* (Pennsylvania Academy of Fine Arts, Philadelphia).

**West, Dame Rebecca,** 1892–1983, English writer; b. Ireland as Cecily Fairfield. The author of such psychological novels as *The Return of the Soldier* (1918), *The Judge* (1922), *The Birds Fall Down* (1966), and of a major historical study of Yugoslavia, *Black Lamb and Grey Falcon* (1941). She was also a journalist and literary critic, and bore a son by H.G. WELLS.

**West, Mae,** 1892–1980, American film actress. In such films as *She Done Him Wrong* (1933), *I'm No Angel* (1933), and *My Little Chickadee* (1940) she took a comic approach to sex.

**West, Nathanael,** 1903–40, American novelist; b. Nathan Weinstein. An innovative and original writer, he revealed the sterility and grotesqueness underlying the American dream. His bitter and influential novels are: *The Dream Life of Balso Snell* (1931), *Miss Lonelyhearts* (1933), *A Cool Million* (1934), and *The Day of the Locust* (1939).

**West African Economic Community,** Fr. Communauté Économique de l'Afrique de l'Ouest (CEAO), intergovernmental organization (est. 1973) of French-speaking states, successor to the West African Customs Union (est. 1966). CEAO members are Benin, Burkina Faso, Côte d'Ivoire, Mali, Mauritania, Niger, and Senegal.

**West Bank,** land between Israel and Jordan, located W of the Jordan R. and the Dead Sea, (1983 est. pop. 750,000), 5607 km² (2165 sq mi). It has been occupied by Israel since the ARAB-ISRAELI WAR of 1967. It includes the cities of HEBRON, JERICHO, and NABLUS, and the Old City of JERUSALEM. The fertile region of Samaria is in the north; largely barren Judaea is in the south. The inhabitants are mostly Muslim Arabs. After the partition of PALESTINE and the formation (1948) of Israel, the territory was annexed (1950) by Jordan. After the 1967 war, the UN Security Council called for Israel's withdrawal from the West Bank. A peaceful resolution, however, has been impeded by Israel's establishment of new Jewish settlements in the area and by the desire of most Arab inhabitants for self-determination. The recognition (1974) by Arab states (including Jordan) of the PALESTINE LIBERATION ORGANIZATION (PLO) as sole representatives of the West Bank Arabs further hindered a settlement because of continued PLO-Israeli hostility.

**West Bromwich,** town (1981 pop. 153,725), West Midlands, England, 8 km (5 mi) NW of Birmingham. It is an industrial centre famous for the manufacture of metal goods. There is coal-mining in the neighbourhood.

**Western Australia,** state (1986 pop. 1,459,000), 2,527,633 km² (975,290 sq mi). It is the largest state in Australia, comprising the entire western part of the continent. Only the SW corner is fertile. Half of the population lives in metropolitan PERTH, the capital. Wheat, wool, and meat are the chief agricultural products. The inland and northern areas are rich in minerals, notably iron ore, nickel, diamonds, and gold. Principal manufactures are industrial metals, machinery, and transportation equipment. A penal colony was established at ALBANY in 1826, and a colony of free settlers arrived in the Perth–Fremantle area in 1829. Governed at first by NEW SOUTH WALES, Western Australia received its own governor in 1831. It became a separate colony in 1890 and a federated state of the Commonwealth of Australia in 1901.

**Western European Union** (WEU), intergovernmental organization for military cooperation, formed in 1955 by Belgium, France, West Germany, Italy, Luxembourg, the Netherlands, and the UK (as successor to the five-nation Brussels Treaty Organization of 1948). Under the 1984 Rome Declaration it was decided to reactivate the WEU to increase security cooperation between the seven member states. In 1988 WEU membership increased to nine with the accession of Portugal and Spain.

**Western Isles Island Area,** island region in NW Scotland (1985 est. pop. 31,548), 2898 km² (1130 sq mi), separated from the mainland of Scotland by The Minch. The administrative centre is Stornoway, Lewis. The region was formed in 1975 and consists of the Outer Hebrides. It includes the islands of Lewis, N and S Uist, Benbecula, and Barra. The major economic activities are stock-rearing, fishing, crofting, and the weaving of tweeds. The islands have suffered a decline in population over the last century.

**western red cedar,** aromatic conifer of the genus *Thuja*, native to Asia and to N America, where it is known also as arborvitae. It has fern-like foliage in flat fronds, with scale-like leaves pressed to the stems. The young bark is red, and the cones are very small but numerous. The timber is long-lasting, and frequently used unpainted for outdoor construction work. However, even this durable timber needs occasional treatment with preservative.

**Western Reserve,** region in NE Ohio, US. Territory retained (1786) by Connecticut when that state ceded claims to other western lands, much of it was given to those of its citizens whose property was burned in the American Revolution. It became part of the NORTHWEST TERRITORY in 1800.

**Western Sahara,** formerly Spanish Sahara, region of NW Africa (1981 est. pop. 139,000), 266,000 km² (102,703 sq mi), bordered by the Atlantic Ocean (W), Morocco (N), Algeria (NE), and Mauritania (E and S). Part of the SAHARA Desert, the land is extremely arid and is covered with stones and sand. The traditional economy is based on the raising of goats, camels, and sheep and the cultivation of date palms. Rich deposits

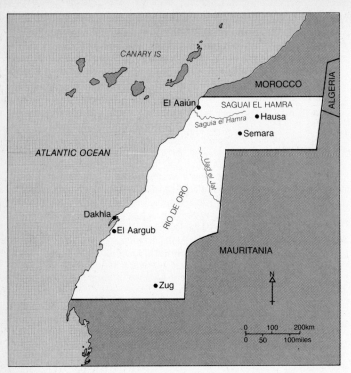

Western Sahara

of phosphates were first exploited in the 1970s; potash and iron have also been found. The people are Arabs and Berbers.

*History.* Although visited by the Portuguese in 1434, the area that is now Western Sahara had little contact with Europeans until the 19th cent. In 1884 Spain proclaimed a protectorate over the coast, and a Spanish province, known as Spanish Sahara, was established in 1958. In 1976 Spain transferred the territory to Morocco and Mauritania, but following guerrilla action by the Polisario Front, a nationalist group based in Algeria and seeking self-government for the Saharans, Mauritania withdrew in 1979. However, Morocco promptly occupied the Mauritanian portion; despite numerous peace plans, sporadic fighting has continued, with the US supporting Morocco's claim with arms shipments. The Saharan Arab Democratic Republic, proclaimed by Polisario in 1976, is recognized by the ORGANIZATION OF AFRICAN UNITY. In 1988 Polisario and the Morrocan government concluded a ceasefire agreement.

**Western Samoa,** officially the Independent State of Western Samoa, independent Commonwealth nation (1986 est. pop. 160,000), 2934 km² (1133 sq mi), comprising nine islands in the SW Pacific Ocean, of which the largest are Savai'i and Upolu. Most of the predominantly Polynesian population live on Upolu, where Apia, the capital, is located. The main islands are crossed by extinct volcanic ranges and have a tropical climate. Subsistence farming and fishing are mainstays of the economy, with tourism contributing significantly to local prosperity. Some timber is exported. Samoa was discovered by the Dutch in 1722. It granted trading privileges to the US in 1878 and to Germany and Britain in 1879. In 1899, the US annexed eastern Samoa (see AMERICAN SAMOA) and the western islands passed to German control. New Zealand occupied the German islands in 1914 during World War I and subsequently administered them as a League of Nations mandate and a UN Trust Territory. They gained independence as Western Samoa in 1962, becoming a member of the COMMONWEALTH. There is a head of state, chosen by the legislative assembly from among the royal families, but executive power is vested in the prime minister. Fluid party allegiances have produced numerous changes of government since independence.

**Western Tasmania Wilderness,** national park in western Tasmania, southern Australia, with an area of 769,355 hectares (19,244 sq mi). The conservation campaign in the 1980s to save the Franklin R. successfully halted the construction of a dam for hydroelectric power production. Dense rainforest, of economic value as a timber resource, is home of the carnivorous Tasmanian Devil, the duck-billed platypus, and other rare

species of flora and fauna. Aboriginal relics in caves indicate that the area was occupied in the Ice Age 20,000 years ago.

**West Glamorgan,** county in S Wales (1984 est. pop. 364,600), 816 km² (318 sq. mi), bordering on the Bristol Channel in the S. It was formed in the local government reorganization of 1974 from the western part of Glamorganshire. It is hilly in the N and the major rivers are the Tawe and Neath. Much of the country is industrial and urban. SWANSEA, PORT TALBOT, and Neath are the major towns. The metal industries were an important part of the economy, but have now declined. The picturesque Gower peninsula is situated in the SW.

**West Indies,** archipelago, sometimes called the Antilles, extending c.4020 km (2500 mi) in a wide arc E and S from Florida to Venezuela, and separating the Atlantic Ocean from the Gulf of Mexico and the CARIBBEAN SEA. The four main island groups are the BAHAMAS; the Greater Antilles (CUBA, JAMAICA, HISPANIOLA, PUERTO RICO); the Lesser Antilles (the Leeward and Windward islands, BARBADOS, and TRINIDAD AND TOBAGO); and the Dutch West Indies, or Netherlands Antilles (ARUBA, CURAÇAO, Bonaire). The warm climate and clear tropical seas of the islands support a large tourist industry, and there are some exports, notably bauxite and sugar. People of African descent predominate. The **West Indies Federation,** established (1958) by 10 former British possessions, broke up in 1962 because of insularity and economic disparities between its members. Jamaica and Trinidad became independent in 1962 followed by Barbados and Guyana (formerly British Guiana) in 1966. The remaining small colonies achieved internal self-government as British associated states after 1967, but they left associated status one by one as they achieved full independence during the 1970s and early 1980s.

**Westinghouse, George,** 1846–1914, American inventor and manufacturer. His railway inventions included the air BRAKE (1868) and automatic signal devices. He formed companies in 1869 and 1882 to manufacture them. He also pioneered in introducing into the US the high-tension alternating-current system for transmission of electricity. Over 400 patents were credited to Westinghouse.

**Westmeath,** county in NE of Republic of Ireland (1986 pop. 63,306), 1746 km² (681 sq mi), bordering on Co. Meath in the E. It is in the province of Leinster. The county town is MULLINGAR. Most of the county is low-lying, with a large area occupied by bog. It is drained by the R. SHANNON and crossed by the Royal Canal. There are several loughs within the county, including Loughs Ree, Sheelin, Derravaragh, and Ennell, where there is good trout fishing. The main economic activity is dairy farming. The chief towns are Mullingar and Athlone.

**West Midlands,** former metropolitan county in W Midlands of England (1984 est. pop. 2,647,000), 899 km² (351 sq mi). It was formed in the local government reorganization of 1974 from parts of Staffordshire, Warwickshire, and Worcestershire. It is a large conurbation, consisting of BIRMINGHAM, WALSALL, WOLVERHAMPTON, SUTTON COLDFIELD, Solihull, and Dudley, with COVENTRY in the extreme E corner. The county council was abolished in April 1986, and the area is now administered by the borough and city authorities.

**Westminster,** London borough (1981 pop. 163,892), in Central London. The borough contains the districts of Paddington and St Marylebone and the city of Westminster. It contains many of the major historic buildings of London, including WESTMINSTER ABBEY, the Houses of Parliament (WESTMINSTER PALACE), BUCKINGHAM PALACE, St James's Palace, and the National Gallery. Also found here are many of London's chief restaurants, theatres, and shops in the district known as the West End. Open spaces within the borough include Green Park, HYDE PARK, St James's Park and most of Regent's Park. It is situated on the N bank of the R. Thames, which is crossed here by the Vauxhall, Lambeth, Westminster, and Waterloo bridges.

**Westminster, Statute of,** 1931, an act of the British parliament that was in effect the founding charter of the COMMONWEALTH. It declared the Commonwealth to be a free association of autonomous dominions and the UK, bound only by a common allegiance to the crown. It gave legal force to the work of the IMPERIAL CONFERENCE.

**Westminster Abbey,** originally the abbey church of a Benedictine monastery in London. A major English Gothic structure, it is a national shrine. In 1245 Henry III demolished a Norman church and began a new eastern portion, inaugurating centuries of development. The chapter house was built in 1250, the cloisters and main monastic buildings in the

14th cent. The nave was completed in the 16th cent., as was Henry VIII's Lady Chapel with its noted fan vaulting. Christopher WREN and Nicholas HAWKSMOOR built (1722–40) the western towers. French influence is seen in the nave, the highest in England, and in the flying buttresses. Almost all English monarchs since William I have been crowned in the Abbey, and noted English subjects are buried there, e.g., Chaucer and Robert Browning in the Poets' Corner.

**Westminster Conference,** 1866–67, London meeting that agreed to the plan for Canadian confederation. The provisions were incorporated into the BRITISH NORTH AMERICA ACT (1867), which created the Dominion of Canada.

**Westminster Palace** or **Houses of Parliament,** in London. The present Gothic structure was built (1840–60) by Sir Charles Barry to replace ancient buildings largely destroyed by fire in 1834. Edward the Confessor built the original palace, a royal abode until the 16th cent., when it became the meeting place for Parliament. The Great Hall (late 11th cent.), the finest example of medieval open-timber work, was destroyed by fire bombs in 1941. Westminster Hall, the only original portion intact, serves as an entrance hall to the Houses.

**Weston, Edward,** 1886–1958, American photographer. Famed for stark, superbly printed images of Western landscapes, nudes, and natural formations, Weston greatly influenced photographic art.

Edward **Weston,** 'Eel River Ranch'

**Westphalia, Peace of,** 1648, general settlement of the THIRTY YEARS' WAR. It marked the end of the HOLY ROMAN EMPIRE as an effective institution and inaugurated the modern European state system. It also marked the end of the era of religious warfare, with a genuine effort being made toward religious toleration. The chief participants were France and Sweden on one side and Spain and the Holy Roman Empire on the other. Although he had died before it met, the Peace of Westphalia represents a triumph of the policies of the duc de RICHELIEU. The sovereignty of the German states was recognized, as was that of the Netherlands and the Swiss Confederation. The empire was continued in name only. Sweden and France won important territories, and the basis for France's emergence as the dominant European power was laid.

**West Point,** US military post on the Hudson R. N of New York City. An important fort during the AMERICAN REVOLUTION, since 1802 it has been the site of the United States Military Academy.

**West Sussex,** county in S England (1984 est. pop. 682,700), 1989 km² (776 sq mi), bordering in the S on the English Channel. The South Downs cross from E to W in the southern part of the county, and the highest point is at Blackdown in the NW which rises to 276 m (919 ft). The main towns are CHICHESTER and the coastal resorts of Bognor Regis and Worthing. Mixed agriculture is an important economic activity within the county. GATWICK AIRPORT is situated near Crawley in the N which is the principal industrial town.

**West Virginia,** state of the US (1984 est. pop. 1,952,000), area 62,629 km² (24,181 sq mi), situated in the east–central region, bordered by Pennsylvania and Maryland (N), Virginia (E), and Kentucky and Ohio, which lies across the Ohio R. (W). CHARLESTON is the capital and largest city, followed by Huntington and Wheeling. Almost the entire state is in the hilly and rugged Allegheny Plateau, except for the eastern panhandle, which is part of the APPALACHIAN Plateau. The state is the largest producer of coal after Kentucky, and the greatest producer of natural gas east of the MISSISSIPPI R. These mineral resources are utilized by the main industries, manufacturing chemicals, steel and other fabricated metals, and building materials. The rugged terrain is not suitable for agriculture, but cattle, dairy products, apples, and turkeys are produced; extensive hardwoods support a timber industry. Only about 36% of the population lives in metropolitan areas; 96% was non-Hispanic white in 1980. The areas's first inhabitants were Mound Builders, and Europeans began arriving in the 1670s, first fur traders and then German settlers. Expansion westward towards the Ohio R. caused conflict with the French, resulting in the last French and Indian War (1754–63). The region seceded from the state of Virginia (1863) when the latter joined the Confederacy. The economy expanded in the early 20th cent., but the coalfields were the centre of much labour conflict. In the 1960s the coal-mining region became depressed; the subsequent growth of strip-mining brought loss of income and environmental degradation.

**Wettin** (ˌvetin), Germany dynasty, the various branches of which ruled in Saxony, Thuringia, Poland, Great Britain, Belgium, and Bulgaria. The Wettins were margraves of Meissen from c.1100 and soon expanded into Saxony and Thuringia. In 1485 the dynasty split into the Albertine and Ernestine lines, various branches of which ruled until the 20th cent. From one of the Ernestine branches (Saxe-Coburg-Gotha) are descended the royal houses of Great Britain (through Prince Albert) and Belgium (through Leopold I).

**Wexford,** county in SE of Republic of Ireland (1986 pop. 102,456), 2328 km² (908 sq mi), bordering on the Irish Sea in the S and E. It is in the province of Leinster. The county town is WEXFORD. Most of the county is flat or gently undulating, but the land rises in the NW. The highest point is Mt Leinster at 796 m (2610 ft). The main rivers are the Slaney and the BARROW, which forms much of the SW border. It was the first Irish county to be colonized from England (1169).

**Wexford,** county town (1986 pop. 10,330) of Co. Wexford, Republic of Ireland, at mouth of R. Slaney, at Wexford Harbour on the Irish Sea coast. It is a fishing port and small industrial town, and host to an opera festival.

**Weyden, Roger van der** (ˌviedən), c.1400–64, Flemish artist, whose influence in the later 15th cent. was profound. He is usually believed to have studied with Robert CAMPIN and was also influenced by Jan van EYCK. A series of major works, including the *Descent from the Cross* (before 1443; Prado, Madrid) and the altarpiece of the *Last Judgment* (c.1450; Hotel Dieu, Beaune, France) show his development of a highly individual, emotionally powerful style. His portraits, mainly bust-length,

Roger van der **Weyden,** *Descent from the Cross*, pre-1443. Museo del Prado, Madrid.

are characterized by their elegance and air of aristocratic refinement, e.g., *Francesco d'Este* (Metropolitan Mus., New York).

**Weygand, Maxime** (vay,gahnh), 1867–1965, French general. He was chief of staff (1914–23) to Marshal FOCH and in WORLD WAR II became supreme Allied commander (1940), but he could not avert the fall of France. He served the VICHY government as minister of defence and delegate general to French Africa, but was arrested and held by the Germans (1942–45). Returning to France, he was accused of collaboration, but was cleared.

**whale,** aquatic MAMMAL of the order Cetacea, found in oceans worldwide. Adapted to an entirely aquatic life, they have a fishlike shape, nearly hairless skin, an insulating layer of blubber, and flipperlike forelimbs; the tail is flattened horizontally and used for propulsion. Surfacing to breathe, whales expel air through a dorsal blowhole. They have good vision and excellent hearing, and many species use echo location for underwater navigation. Most whales travel in schools, often migrating thousands of miles. There are two major groups of whales, the toothed, including the sperm whale, the beluga (or white) whale, and the narwhal; and the toothless, or baleen, including the right, humpback, and blue whales. Species vary greatly in size and include the largest animal that has ever lived, the blue whale, up to 30 m (100 ft) long and 150 tonnes. Commercial whaling has reduced all large species to endangered status. The intelligence and communication systems of the whale are subjects of scientific investigation.

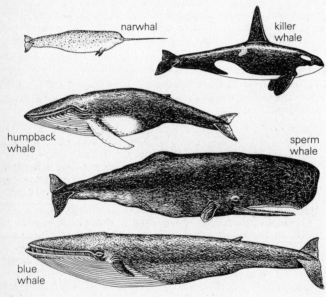

Whale

**whale shark:** see SHARK; FISH.

**whaling.** The hunting of whales is thought to have been first pursued from land by the Basques as early as the 10th cent. Whaling on a large scale was first organized at the beginning of the 17th cent., largely by the Dutch. By the mid-17th cent. it had developed greatly in America, centring first in NANTUCKET and then New Bedford, the greatest whaling port in the world until the decline (c.1850) of the industry. With the capture (1712) of a sperm whale by a Nantucket fisherman the superior qualities of SPERM OIL were discovered, and whalers went farther and farther in search of the whale into the S Atlantic and then the Pacific, sometimes on voyages of three to four years. Herman MELVILLE's *Moby Dick* is a classic account of a whaling voyage. The advent of the American Civil War, a drop in the demand for sperm oil, and a steadily decreasing number of whales caused the decline of whaling, but the development of a harpoon with an explosive head and of the factory ship that can completely process a whale inaugurated a new whaling era in the 20th cent. Japan and the USSR are the principal nations now involved in the industry. International efforts to protect the whale have made progress, but several species have been seriously depleted.

**Wharton, Edith (Newbold Jones),** 1862–1937, American author; settled in France, 1913. Her works range widely, but she is particularly known for her subtle, ironic, and superbly crafted fictional studies of turn-of-the-century New York society, as in her best and most characteristic novels, *The House of Mirth* (1905) and *The Age of Innocence* (1920). Wharton's many other novels include *The Valley of Decision* (1902), *The Custom of the Country* (1913), and *Hudson River Bracketed* (1929). Least characteristic, but most successful, of her works is the starkly tragic novella of New England, *Ethan Frome* (1911). Among Wharton's short-story collections are *Crucial Instances* (1901), *Certain People* (1930), and *Ghosts* (1937). She also wrote travel books, literary criticism, and poetry.

**wheat,** cereal plant (genus *Triticum*) of the GRASS family. Wheat is the most widely cultivated crop, estimated to occupy about one-fifth of the total crop area available in the world. Although twice the area is devoted to its culture, its total yield is slightly smaller than that of RICE. It is cultivated on a massive scale in the USSR, Canada, the US, China, India, and Argentina. Its origin and classification are contentious. Primitive wheats, such as emmer, have been found in excavations dating back to 7000 BC, and the bread wheats have been grown in the Nile valley since at least 5000 BC. Of the cultivated species, the most important is *T. aestivum*, the common, or bread wheat, which exists in two basic types: hard wheats, which have a higher protein content and are best for bread-making, and the soft wheats, which are used for cake- and pastry-making, and for animal feed. The hard wheats are able to grow in low-rainfall areas such as the prairies of N America, while the soft wheats grow in more humid areas such as the UK and much of Europe. Winter wheat varieties are sown in the autumn and mature early the following summer, whereas the spring wheats are grown where the winters are too cold for the young plants to survive. A different species, known as durum wheat (*T. durum*), makes the flour known as semolina and is used for the making of pasta. In flour-milling, after the bran and the embryo are removed, the white, starchy part of the grain is milled and bleached to produce white flour. Much of the nutritive content is lost in this process, but the modern taste for white bread probably developed because white flour was more expensive to produce, and therefore became a status symbol.

**Wheatstone, Sir Charles,** 1802–75, British physicist and inventor. He was coinventor of an early electric telegraph and also invented an automatic transmitter, an electric recording device, and an automatic telegraph. Wheatstone is credited with inventing the concertina, improving the stereoscope and dynamo, and popularizing a method for the measurement of electric resistance using a network now known as the Wheatstone bridge.

**wheel,** for vehicles, device probably invented in Neolithic Mesopotamia, inspired by the potter's wheel already in use then. These first wheels were made of three planks clamped together. The first spoked wheels appeared in the Bronze Age in N Europe, and were also known in ancient Egypt. The Romans made extensive use of wheeled vehicles, but they seem to have borrowed their technology (e.g., the use of metal linings in the hubs to resist wear) from the Celtic peoples they conquered. Wheels were also known in ancient China, possibly independently invented but possibly acquired by diffusion from the Mesopotamian origin. The ancient American civilizations did not have the wheel. See also ANIMAL TRANSPORT; ROADS.

**whelk,** large marine SNAIL having a thick-lipped spiral shell with many protuberances, found in temperate waters. Whelks are scavengers and carnivores, feeding on crabs, lobsters, and other shellfish. The largest species, the knobbed whelk, grows up to 40 cm (16 in). The common whelk (*Buccinum undatum*) lays eggs in white horny cases, often found empty on the sea shore. It is a popular food, caught in small pots, like LOBSTERS.

**Whig,** English political party, The name was probably derived from *whiggamor* [cattle driver], a 17th-cent. term of abuse for Scottish Presbyterians. The party upheld the power of Parliament against the crown and was supported by the landed gentry and merchants against the aristocratic TORY group. The accession (1714) of GEORGE I began a long period of Whig control. The dominant figure until 1742 was Sir Robert WALPOLE, who gave the party political power and shaped modern British cabinet government. After the accession (1760) of GEORGE III, the Whigs were largely in opposition, and under the leadership of Charles James FOX became identified with dissent, industry, and social and parliamentary reform. Whig ministries under the 2nd Earl GREY and Lord MELBOURNE were in power from 1830 to 1841 and passed the REFORM BILL of 1832. From the 1850s the Whigs became part of the new Liberal Party.

**Whig Party,** one of the two dominant political parties in the US in the second quarter of the 19th cent. It grew out of the NATIONAL REPUBLICAN PARTY and several smaller groups, notably the ANTI-MASONIC PARTY. Created (1834) to oppose Andrew Jackson's DEMOCRATIC PARTY it charged 'King Andrew' with executive tyranny and adopted the name of the 17th and 18th cent. English political party which had fought absolute rule. It was beset by factions from the beginning and was never able to forge a unified, positive party position. Daniel WEBSTER and Henry CLAY were its great leaders, representing, respectively, the Northern and Southern wings of the party. In 1840 they were able to unify behind a popular military hero, W.H. HARRISON, as a presidential candidate. He was elected but died after only a month in office. His successor, John TYLER, quickly alienated the Whig leaders in Congress and was read out of the party. In 1848 the Whigs elected another military hero, Zachary TAYLOR. He too died in office but his successor, Millard FILLMORE, remained a loyal party man. The party was already disintegrating, however, chiefly over the SLAVERY issue. The FREE-SOIL PARTY and its successor, the REPUBLICAN PARTY, absorbed most of the Northern Whigs. The Southern Whigs went into the Democratic Party. In 1852 Gen. Winfield SCOTT was the last Whig presidential candidate.

**Whipple, George Hoyt,** 1878–1976, American pathologist. Head of the department of pathology and dean of the school of medicine and dentistry at the Univ. of Rochester (1921–54), he studied metabolism, blood regeneration, and anaemia. For his research on using liver to treat pernicious anaemia he shared with George Minot and William Murphy the 1934 Nobel Prize for physiology or medicine.

**whippoorwill** see NIGHTJAR.

**Whipsnade Park zoo,** open-air zoological park approximately 200 hectares (500 acres) in extent established in 1932 by the Zoological Society of London in a rural environment to complement the urban zoo and research institute maintained by the Society in London. Because of the limitations imposed by climate, Whipsnade contains fewer animal species than the traditional urban zoo. It is the prototype of the modern open-range zoo, with the animals kept in large, mesh-enclosed or ditch-surrounded paddocks.

**whirlpool,** revolving current in an ocean, river, or lake. It may be caused by the configuration of the shore, irregularities in the bottom of the water body, the meeting of opposing currents or tides, or wind action on the water. There are no true whirlpools really dangerous to shipping.

**Whiskey Rebellion,** 1794, uprising by settlers W of the Allegheny Mts, E US, who opposed Alexander HAMILTON's excise tax of 1791. The settlers regarded the tax as discriminatory and rioted against the tax collectors. Pres. WASHINGTON sent troops; they put down the rebellion easily. The government's power to enforce its laws had been proved, but the FEDERALIST PARTY suffered politically for having overreacted.

**Whiskey Ring,** group of distillers and public officials who defrauded the US government of liquor taxes. Soon after the Civil War, large distillers bribed government officials in order to retain tax proceeds. Only after the ring became a public scandal did the Treasury Dept act. The distilleries were seized (May 1875), over $3 million in taxes was recovered, and eventually 110 people were convicted.

**whisky,** strong alcoholic spirit distilled from a fermented mash of grains, usually rye, barley, oats, wheat, or maize, and matured in wood casks, usually for three or more years. Inferior grades are made from potatoes, beets, or other roots. Scotch whisky, usually a blend, takes its dry, somewhat smokey flavour from the barley malt, cured with peat, used in its preparation. The somewhat similar Irish whiskey, for which no peat is used, has a full, sweet taste. American whiskeys, classified as rye or as bourbon (a maize liquor), are higher in flavour and deeper in colour than Scotch or Irish whiskies. Canadian whiskey, characteristically light, is produced from cereal grain only. First distilled in monasteries in 11th-cent. England, whisky has been manufactured commercially since the 16th cent.

**Whistler, James Abbot McNeill,** 1834–1903, American painter. In 1855 he went to Paris. His earliest works were influenced by COURBET's REALISM; he also acquired an appreciation of VELÁZQUEZ, who was to influence the colour and design of much of his work. He settled in London in 1859; in the 1860s he experimented with PRE-RAPHAELITE and classical subjects, and became interested in Japanese art. In the 1870s he painted

a series of pictures of the Thames at night which he entitled *Nocturnes*; the titles of his portraits, e.g., *Arrangement in Gray and Black* (1872; Musée d'Orsay, Paris) which is the famed portrait of his mother, similarly emphasize his belief that a painting is above all a study of form, colour, and line. Whistler was also a superb etcher, and excelled in lithography, watercolour, and pastel. A wit and dandy, he was constantly involved in polemics and lawsuits, including a particularly notorious one with RUSKIN. Whistler explained his aesthetics in critical essays, as the *Ten O'Clock* (1888).

**Whitby, Synod of:** see CELTIC CHURCH.

**White, Patrick,** 1912–, Australian novelist and experimental playwright. His ambivalent attitude to Australian society has been both a creative source in his work and the reason for his own secluded life. His complex style conveys a transcendent spiritual reality coexisting with mundane realities of Australian landscape and character. His novels include *The Tree of Man* (1955), *Voss* (1957), *Riders in the Chariot* (1961), *The Vivisector* (1970), *The Twyborn Affair* (1979), the autobiography *Flaws in the Glass* (1981), and *Memoirs of Many in One* (1987). Winner of many literary awards, White was awarded the 1973 Nobel Prize for literature.

**White, T(erence) H(anbury),** 1906–64, English author; b. India. His tetralogy *The Once and Future King* (1938–58) is a dramatic, idiosyncratic retelling of the ARTHURIAN LEGEND. He also wrote *The Goshawk* (1951) and *A Book of Beasts* (1954).

**white ant:** see TERMITE.

**White Australia policy,** the name given to Australia's restrictive immigration laws, first introduced by the colonial governments and systematized by the Commonwealth parliament in 1901. The Commonwealth legislation used the device of a dictation test in any European language. Racial restrictions were progressively dismantled in the 1960s, and finally abolished in 1973.

**whitebait,** culinary name for the fry of HERRING and sprats. Whitebait are LARVAE, of more than one species, fished commercially, frozen and sold, usually to the restaurant trade.

**white dwarf,** in astronomy, star that is abnormally faint for its white-hot temperature. It has a mass like that of the Sun, a radius like that of the Earth, and a central density about one million times that of water. White dwarfs have exhausted their nuclear fuel and represent one of the final stages of STELLAR EVOLUTION (see also GRAVITATIONAL COLLAPSE). About 500 white dwarfs have been discovered; the first of these was the companion of the bright star Sirius.

**Whitefield, George,** 1714–70, English evangelistic preacher, leader of the Calvinistic Methodist Church. At Oxford he joined the Methodist group led by John and Charles WESLEY. Beginning in 1738 he made seven trips to America, where he was influential in the GREAT AWAKENING. After becoming an Anglican priest, Whitefield adopted (c.1741) Calvinistic views, especially concerning predestination. He broke with the Wesleys and led the Calvinistic Methodists, who were numerous in Wales. Whitefield continued to draw great throngs on his evangelistic tours. He died in Newburyport, Mass.

**Whitehead, Alfred North,** 1861–1947, English mathematician and philosopher. He taught mathematics at the Univ. of London (1911–24) and philosophy at Harvard Univ. (after 1924). *Principia Mathematica* (3 vol., 1910–13), which he wrote with Bertrand Russell, is a landmark in the study of logic. Whitehead's inquiries into the structure of science provided the background for his metaphysical work. His 'philosophy of organism' (for which he developed a special vocabulary) viewed the universe as consisting of processes of becoming, and God as interdependent with the world and developing from it. His many works include *Science and the Modern World* (1925) and *Process and Reality* (1929).

**Whitehorse,** city (1980 est. pop. 15,500), territorial capital of the Yukon, NW Canada, on the Yukon R. Developed as an important supply centre during the KLONDIKE gold rush (1897–98), it is now chiefly an administrative and tourist centre for surrounding copper-mining, fur-trading, and hunting areas. Whitehorse replaced DAWSON as the territorial capital in 1952.

**White House,** official name of the mansion of the president of the US, on Pennsylvania Avenue, Washington, DC. It was designed by James

Hoban on a site chosen by George WASHINGTON and begun in 1792. John ADAMS was the first president to live there. After it was burned (1814) by the British, it was restored and painted white. It had, however, been called the 'White House' earlier. Theodore Roosevelt made the name official.

White House

**Whiteley, Brett,** 1939–, Australian artist. He studied at the Julian Ashton School of Art, Sydney (1958–59), before travelling to London where he worked and exhibited throughout the 1960s. The influence of MATISSE and BACON, in particular, were evident in his painting when he returned to Australia. He is best known for his nudes, interiors, and views of Sydney Harbour.

**White Russia:** see BELORUSSIA.

**white shark:** see SHARK.

**Whitlam, (Edward) Gough,** 1916–, Australian prime minister (1972–75). His Labour government pursued innovative reforms but was plagued by economic problems. In 1975, during a budget crisis, he was dismissed by Governor General Sir John Kerr. Defeated (1975, 1977) at the polls, he retired from politics in 1978 and became Australian ambassador to UNESCO.

**Whitman, Walt(er),** 1819–92, an outstanding American poet. Early in his life he worked as a printer, teacher, newspaper editor, and carpenter. In 1855 he published the volume that was to make his reputation, *Leaves of Grass* (containing the emblematic 'Song of Myself'), which the poet continued to enlarge and revise through a number of editions until his death. Innovative in its use of rhythmical free verse and its celebration of sexuality, the book in time proved the single most influential volume of poems in American literary history. In its own day, however, only a few, notably EMERSON, recognized its genius. Whitman worked as a Civil War nurse (1862–65), publishing war poetry in *Drum-Taps* (1865) and *Sequel to Drum-Taps* (1865–66). His later works include the prose collections *Democratic Vistas* (1871).

**Whitney, Eli,** 1765–1825, American inventor of the COTTON GIN. He completed (1793) a model gin that rapidly separated the fibre of short-staple cotton from the seed. Whitney was unable to meet the demand for the machine, and his 1794 patent received legal protection only from 1807 to 1812. Thus the invention, which created great wealth for others who copied his model, gained him little. In 1798 he began producing the first firearms with standardized, interchangeable parts.

**Whitney, Mount,** second highest peak in the US (after Mt McKinley, Alaska), in the Sierra Nevada, central California. It is 4418 m (14,494 ft) high and was named after the US geologist Josiah D. Whitney, who surveyed it in 1864.

**Whit Sunday,** the Christian festival which commemorates the descent of the Holy Spirit on the Apostles as described in Acts 2. 1–4. It is liturgically known as Pentecost and falls on the 7th Sunday and 50th day after Easter. It is reckoned the second most important feast of the Christian Church.

**Whittier, John Greenleaf,** 1807–92, American poet. A Quaker, he was a vigorous and politically powerful abolitionist editor and writer, especially from 1833 to 1840. After the Civil War he turned from politics

and devoted himself completely to poetry. Although he often celebrated the common man, as in *Songs of Labor* (1850), his best work, e.g., *Moll Pitcher* (1832), *Snow-bound* (1866), *Maud Muller* (1867), pictures the life, history, and legends of New England. Such poems as 'Barbara Frietchie', 'Marguerite', and 'The Barefoot Boy', as well as his nearly 100 hymns, made Whittier one of the most popular poets of his time.

**Whittington, Richard,** 1358–1423, English merchant and three-time lord mayor of London. He made his fortune as a mercer and supplied large loans to HENRY IV and HENRY V. A legend later arose that Whittington gained his fortune when his cat was sold to the ruler of Morocco.

**Whittle, Sir Frank,** 1907–, British aeronautical engineer. He joined the Royal Air Force in 1923 as an engineering apprentice, and became a pilot. In 1930 he filed a patent for a jet engine; in 1937 the prototype first ran, and the first flight powered by it was on 15 May 1941. Although the theory of JET PROPULSION had been discussed since antiquity, Whittle can claim credit for its practical development. Knighted in 1948, he has lived in the US since 1976.

**whooping cough** or **pertussis,** highly communicable, infectious disease, predominantly of childhood. The early stage is manifested by symptoms of an upper respiratory infection; after about two weeks, a series of paroxysmal coughs are followed by a characteristic high-pitched 'whoop' as a breath is taken. A serious disease, whooping cough may give rise to such complications as PNEUMONIA, convulsions, and brain damage; immunization reduces the incidence and severity of the disease, although an attack confers lifelong immunity.

**whortleberry:** see BILBERRY.

**Whyalla,** city (1986 pop. 26,900), S Australia. Located on the W coast of Spencer Gulf it was first established in 1902 as a port to ship local ironstone; later high-grade iron ore was discovered and exploited. During World War II a shipbuilding industry was begun, and in 1958 the steel industry was established. At nearby Port Bonython an installation processes natural gas from the Cooper Basin in the N of the state.

**Wichita,** US city (1984 est. pop. 283,000), south-central Kansas, on the Arkansas and Little Arkansas rivers; inc. 1870. The largest city in the state, it is the commercial and industrial centre of S Kansas. Besides its huge aircraft industry, it has railway shops, flour mills, meat-packing factories, and various manufactures. Founded (1868) on the site of a WICHITA INDIAN village, it boomed as a cow town in the 1870s; oil was discovered nearby in 1915.

**Wichita Indians,** NORTH AMERICAN INDIAN tribe of the Plains, speaking a Caddoan language (see AMERICAN INDIAN LANGUAGES). They once lived in Kansas, ranging into Oklahoma and Texas. Distinctive features of their culture were conical grass houses and a horn dance for land fertility. By 1765 they had been forced into Oklahoma by hostile tribes; later, reduced by smallpox to 2500, they occupied the site of Wichita, Kansas. After ceding their lands to the US (1872), they were settled on an Oklahoma reservation. In 1981 their population was estimated at 485.

**wickiup:** see TEPEE, WICKIUP, AND WIGWAM.

**Wickliffe, John:** see WYCLIF, JOHN.

**Wicklow,** county in E of Republic of Ireland (1986 pop. 94,482), 2005 km² (782 sq mi), bordering onto the Irish Channel in the E. The county town is WICKLOW. Much of the county is mountainous, apart from a narrow coastal plain. The Wicklow Mts occupy much of the county, rising to 926 m (3039 ft) in Lugnaquillia. The county is drained by the Slaney and LIFFEY rivers. There are many beautiful valleys (glens) in the mountainous area, including Glendalough and Glenmalure. There is a hydroelectric power station at Poulaphuca in the NW, with an associated reservoir. The village of Shillelagh in the S gave its name to the traditional Irish cudgel.

**Wicklow,** county town (1986 pop. 5299) of Co. Wicklow, in Republic of Ireland, at mouth of R. Vartry, 43 km (27 mi) S of Dublin, on the Irish Sea coast. It is a small port and market town. Historic remains include the ruins of a 12th-cent. castle on the cliffs nearby, and a 13th-cent. Franciscan friary.

**Wiclif, John:** see WYCLIF, JOHN.

**Wieland, Christoph Martin** (ˌveelant), 1733–1813, German poet and novelist. In an elegant rococo style, he treated themes from antiquity and fairy tales, e.g., *Oberon* (1780) which was the source for the libretto of WEBER's opera. His political satires include *The Golden Mirror* (1772) and

The Republic of Fools (1774). Wieland also edited the influential literary journal *Teutsche Merkur* (1773–1810) and translated SHAKESPEARE.

**Wiener, Norbert,** 1894–1964, American mathematician and educator. Known for his theory of CYBERNETICS and his contributions to the development of computers and calculators, Wiener also did research in probability theory and the foundations of mathematics.

**Wiesbaden** (ˌveezˈbahdən), city (1984 pop. 268,900), capital of HESSE, West Germany, on the RHINE. Its mineral springs have made it a health resort and spa since Roman times. A centre of the wine trade, it also has publishing and electrical engineering industries. It became fashionable as capital of the duchy of Nassau (1744–1866).

**Wiesel, Elie** (ˌveezəl), 1928–, Jewish writer and human rights activist. He was a survivor of several German Concentration Camps, and had devoted his life to fighting antisemitism and racism. His work received recognition in 1986 with the award of the Nobel Peace Prize. He serves as Professor of Humanities at Boston Univ. and Distinguished Professor of Judaic Studies at City Univ., New York. He has been the recipient of numerous literary awards for his writings, among whose predominant themes are the Holocaust, Soviet Jewry, contemporary faith, and mysticism.

**wig,** arrangement of artificial or human hair worn to conceal baldness or as part of a costume, either theatrical, ceremonial, or fashionable. Known from earliest times, they were fashionable in ancient Egypt, and women in the Roman empire often wore blonde wigs. In Europe from the mid 17th cent. long curled 'full-bottom' wigs were worn by men; since human hair was expensive and hard to obtain, horse's or goat's hair was often used. In the 18th cent. men's wigs were much smaller with curls over the ears and the back hair tied in a tail (or queue); these and the ladies' hair of the period were often scented and whitened with powder (flour was often used). In Britain the old styles of wig survive in the courts of law, where judges wear a version of the full-bottom wig and barristers the short style with queue. As a fashion item, a wig may be worn by a woman to vary the HAIRSTYLE of her natural hair, and by a man to conceal baldness. Modern wigs are almost all made of synthetic fibre.

**Wight, Isle of** (wiet), island county (1984 est. pop. 120,900), 381 km² (147 sq mi), S England. The island, which is a popular summer resort, is 37 km (23 mi) long and 21 km (13 mi) wide. The chief towns are Newport, the capital, and Cowes, a famous yachting centre. Conquered (AD 43) by the Romans, it was (10th cent.) the Danish headquarters, and was taken by the English crown in 1293.

**Wightman Cup,** annual lawn tennis competition between women from the US and Britain. It was founded in 1923 and named after Mrs Hazel Hotchkiss Wightman (1886–1974) who donated the trophy and was a formidable player for over 30 years. The contest consists of five singles and two doubles rubbers and is held in the US and Britain alternately.

**Wigman, Mary,** 1886–1973, German dancer and choreographer. She studied with LABAN and DALCROZE. She opened a school (1920) and toured with her company. She was a pioneer and leading influence in the central European MODERN DANCE movement well into the 1960s.

**wigwam:** see TEPEE, WICKIUP, AND WIGWAM.

**Wilberforce, William,** 1759–1833, British statesman and humanitarian. A friend of the younger William PITT and an active Evangelical, he secured passage (1807) of a bill abolishing the British slave trade, and worked to suppress slavery in the British Empire. His son, **Samuel Wilberforce,** 1805–73, was bishop of Oxford from 1845 and of Winchester from 1869. He was Church spokesman against the scientist Charles DARWIN.

**wild carrot:** see QUEEN ANNE'S LACE.

**Wilde, Oscar** (Oscar Fingall O'Flahertie Wills Wilde), 1854–1900, Irish writer. A follower of Walter PATER and Matthew ARNOLD, he glorified beauty for itself alone. His greatest and most lasting success was won by his witty society comedies, *Lady Windermere's Fan* (1892), *An Ideal Husband* (1895), and, especially, *The Importance of Being Earnest* (1895). His only novel, *The Picture of Dorian Gray* (1891) is an allegory of moral corruption. Wilde's poems *The Ballad of Reading Gaol* (1898) and his essay *De Profundis* (1905) were inspired by his two-year prison term (1895–97) for homosexual offences. He died in exile in Paris. His other writings include poems, short stories, fairy tales, essays, and

*Salomé,* a drama written in French on which Richard Strauss based his opera.

**wildebeest:** see GNU.

**Wilder, Billy,** 1906–, American film director, producer, and writer; b. Austria. Noted for his cynicism, he has won Academy Awards for *The Lost Weekend* (1945), *Sunset Boulevard* (1950), and *The Apartment* (1960). Among his other films are *Stalag 17* (1953), *Some Like It Hot* (1959), and *Fedora* (1979).

**Wilder, Thornton (Niven),** 1897–1975, American author. His plays and novels usually maintain that true meaning and beauty are found in ordinary experience. Wilder's first important literary work was the novel *The Bridge of San Luis Rey* (1927). Among his other novels are *The Cabala* (1926), *The Woman of Andros* (1930), and *Theophilus North* (1973). A serious and highly original dramatist who often employed nonrealistic theatrical techniques, Wilder achieved critical recognition with the classic play *Our Town* (1938). His other plays include *The Skin of Our Teeth* (1942) and *The Matchmaker* (1954).

**Wilderness Road,** principal route of westward US migration, c.1790–1840. Running from Virginia through the CUMBERLAND GAP to the OHIO R., it was opened by in 1775 by Daniel BOONE.

**Wildfowl Trust,** internationally known charity dedicated to the protection and conservation of wildfowl. It was founded by Sir Peter SCOTT in 1946, with its headquarters at Slimbridge in SW England, which also houses the International Waterfowl Research Bureau. The Trust has had some successes, particularly in saving the Hawaiian goose and the white-winged wood duck from extinction.

**wildlife refuge:** see NATURE RESERVE.

**wild rice,** tall aquatic grass (*Zizania aquatica*) growing up to 3.5m (12 ft) high, of a genus separate from common RICE (*Oryza*). Wild rice is a hardy annual with broad blades, reedy stems, and large terminal panicles. It grows best in shallow water along the margins of ponds and lakes in the N US and S Canada; certain varieties also grow in the South. The seed is harvested by primitive methods and has never been cultivated with success. It was an important food of certain Indian tribes, especially in the Great Lakes region and has become available as a delicacy in many countries.

**Wilhelmina,** 1880–1962, queen of the NETHERLANDS (1890–1948), daughter of WILLIAM III. Her mother, Emma of Waldeck-Pyrmont, was regent until 1898. Wilhelmina married (1901) Prince Henry of Mecklenburg-Schwerin (d. 1934). When the Germans invaded the Netherlands (1940) in World War II she and her government fled to England. She returned in 1945, later abdicating in favour of her daughter, JULIANA.

**Wilkes, John,** 1727–97, English politician and journalist. Entering Parliament in 1757, Wilkes attacked GEORGE III in his periodical the *North Briton,* and was expelled (1764) and imprisoned. Although repeatedly reelected, he was not allowed to take his seat until 1774. He then defended the liberties of the American colonies. Although a demagogue, Wilkes is usually remembered as a champion of freedom from tyranny. Towards the end of his life he became a supporter of order and stability, opposing the Gordon Riots (1780).

**Wilkins, Sir George Hubert,** 1888–1958, British explorer; b. Australia. After several Arctic expeditions, he was the first to explore the region by air (1928), travelling from ALASKA to Spitsbergen. He was knighted that same year. In 1931 he headed an Arctic submarine expedition.

**Wilkins, Maurice Hugh Frederick,** 1916–, Irish biophysicist; b. New Zealand. He successfully extracted fibres from a gel of DNA, which, when analysed by X-ray diffraction, showed a helical molecular structure. For this work he shared the 1962 Nobel Prize for physiology or medicine with James WATSON and Francis CRICK, who, on the basis of Wilkins' results and other scientific information, built a model of the DNA molecule.

**will,** in law, document expressing the wishes of a person (the testator) as to the disposition of his or her PROPERTY after death. Except in very special circumstances, it must be in writing and witnessed by two people. The testator must be of sound mind and of a specified minimum age (usually from 18 to 21). Distribution of the property of a person dying intestate (without a valid will) is determined by statute. See PROBATE.

**will**, in philosophy and psychology, term used to describe the faculty of mind that is alleged to stimulate motivation of purposeful activity. The concept has been variously interpreted by philosophers, some accepting will as a personal faculty or function (e.g., PLATO, ARISTOTLE, THOMAS AQUINAS, DESCARTES, and KANT) and others seeing it as the externalized result of the interaction of conflicting elements (e.g., SPINOZA, LEIBNIZ, and HUME). Still others describe will as the manifestation of personality (e.g., HOBBES, SCHOPENHAUER, and NIETZSCHE). The reality of individual will is denied altogether by the theological doctrine of determinism. Modern psychology considers the concept unscientific and has looked to other factors, such as unconscious motivation or physiological influence, to explain human actions.

**William**, emperors of Germany. **William I**, 1797–1888, emperor of Germany (r.1871–88) and king of Prussia (r.1861–88), was an essentially conservative ruler. Upon assuming the crown he set about reorganizing the army. When this met with opposition from parliament, he appointed (1862) Otto von BISMARCK prime minister, and was thereafter guided almost completely by Bismarck, who suppressed all opposition to the king and himself. Prussia began its series of military triumphs: the Danish war over SCHLESWIG–HOLSTEIN (1864), the Austro-Prussian War (1866), and the Franco-Prussian War (1870–71). Upon the surrender of NAPOLEON III, Bismarck had William crowned emperor of a unified Germany. William's rule was crucial in modern history, for it saw the rise of Germany as a great European power. **William II**, 1859–1941, emperor of Germany and king of Prussia (r.1888–1918), son and successor of FREDERICK III, was the grandson of William I of Germany and of Queen Victoria of England. His restless and overbearing character soon clashed with that of Bismarck, whom he dismissed in 1890. Thereafter he was the dominant force in German affairs. His naval, colonial, and commercial aspirations antagonized Great Britain, France, Russia, and the US however, and his support of Austria's Balkan policy was a direct cause of WORLD WAR I. The Allies insisted on his abdication (1918) after the defeat of Germany. He lived in exile in the Netherlands.

**William**, kings of England. **William I** or **William the Conqueror**, 1027?–87 (r.1066–87), was the illegitimate son of Robert I, duke of Normandy, and succeeded to the dukedom in 1035. At some point between 1051 and 1066 he was probably named by his cousin EDWARD THE CONFESSOR as successor to the throne, and possibly in 1064 he extracted a promise of support from HAROLD, then earl of WESSEX. In 1066, hearing that Harold had been crowned king of England, William raised an army and crossed the Channel. He defeated and slew Harold at HASTINGS and was crowned king. William immediately built castles and harshly put down the rebellions that broke out; by 1072 the military part of the NORMAN CONQUEST was virtually complete. He substituted foreign prelates for many English bishops, and land titles were redistributed on a feudal basis (see FEUDALISM) to his Norman followers. After 1075 he dealt frequently with continental quarrels. William ordered a survey (1085–87) of England, the results of which were compiled as the DOMESDAY BOOK. He was one of the greatest English monarchs and a pivotal figure in European history. His son Robert II succeeded him in Normandy, while another son, **William II** or **William Rufus**, d.1100 (r.1087–1100), succeeded him in England. William II had utter contempt for the English church and extorted large sums of money from it. He occupied Normandy when Robert II left on a CRUSADE, and gained control (1097) of the Scottish throne. He was killed while hunting, and his death may not have been an accident. His brother HENRY I succeeded him. **William III**, 1650–1702, king of England, Scotland, and Ireland (r.1689–1702), was the son of William II, prince of Orange. He became *stadtholder* of the Netherlands in 1672 and fought in the DUTCH WAR of 1672–78. In 1674 he made peace with England and married (1677) Mary, the Protestant daughter of James, duke of York (later JAMES II of England). After James's accession, William kept in close contact with the king's opponents and in 1688 was invited by them to England. He landed with an army and brought about the GLORIOUS REVOLUTION. James was allowed to escape, and William accepted (1689) the offer of Parliament and reigned jointly with his wife, MARY I. William also accepted the BILL OF RIGHTS (1689), which greatly reduced royal power. He defeated (1690) the exiled James at the battle of the Boyne in Ireland and was involved in continental wars until LOUIS XIV recognized him as king in 1697. In England he relied increasingly on WHIG ministers, who were responsible for the establishment (1694) of the Bank of England and the policy of a national debt. William's popularity was diminished after the death (1694) of his childless wife and by the war of the alliance.

He was succeeded by Queen ANNE. **William IV**, 1765–1837, king of Great Britain and Ireland (r.1830–37), was the third son of GEORGE III. Generally passive in politics, he reluctantly gave his promise to the 2nd Earl GREY to create, if necessary, enough peers to pass the REFORM BILL of 1832. Political leadership was left to the duke of WELLINGTON, Earl GREY, Viscount MELBOURNE, and Sir Robert PEEL. Good-natured but eccentric, William was only moderately popular. He was succeeded by his niece VICTORIA.

**William**, kings of the Netherlands and grand dukes of Luxembourg. **William I**, 1772–1843 (r.1815–40), was the son of Prince William V of Orange. He led the Dutch army (1793–95) in the FRENCH REVOLUTIONARY WARS. In 1815 the Congress of VIENNA made him first king of the NETHERLANDS; his domain included BELGIUM and LUXEMBOURG. Belgium rebelled in 1830 (see LONDON CONFERENCE). Forced to liberalize the Dutch constitution, he abdicated. **William II**, 1792–1849 (r.1840–49), was the son of William I. He led (1830) the Dutch army against the Belgians. As king he was compelled to grant (1848) further constitutional reforms. **William III**, 1817–90 (r.1849–90), was the son of William II. He ruled as a constitutional monarch in cooperation with the States-General. On his death his daughter, WILHELMINA, became queen of the Netherlands, and Luxembourg passed to Duke Adolf of Nassau.

**William, king of Scotland:** see WILLIAM THE LION.

**William I**, prince of Orange: see WILLIAM THE SILENT.

**William of Occam** or **Ockham**, c.1285–1349, English philosopher. An exponent of SCHOLASTICISM, he was charged (1324) with heresy by Pope John XXII and fled (1328) to the protection of the pope's great enemy, Holy Roman Emperor Louis IV; his political writings thereafter supported the temporal power of the emperor over that of the pope. Occam's teachings mark an important break with previous medieval philosophy. Adhering to the position of NOMINALISM, he rejected the Aristotelian REALISM of St Thomas Aquinas, specifically denying the existence of universals except in people's minds and language. He disputed the self-evidence of the Aristotelian final cause and of the existence of God, denying the competence of reason in matters of faith. This led him to hold that logic can be studied outside the province of metaphysics, a position that proved important in the development of scientific enquiry. In logic, Occam is remembered for his use of the principle of parsimony, formulated as 'Occam's razor', which enjoined economy in explanation with the axiom 'It is vain to do with more what can be done with less.'

**William of Orange.** For William I, prince of Orange, see WILLIAM THE SILENT; for William III, king of England, see under WILLIAM, kings of England.

**Williams, Roger,** c.1603–83, American colonial clergyman, advocate of religious freedom, founder of RHODE ISLAND; b. England. Banished by the Puritans from Massachusetts, he established PROVIDENCE in 1636 and welcomed religious dissenters there. In 1654 he became president of the combined colonies of Providence, Newport, Narragansett, and Warwick. He was a trusted friend of the Indians.

**Williams, Shirley,** 1930–, English politician. Daughter of the political scientist and philosopher Sir George Catlin and the novelist Vera Brittain, she entered Parliament in 1964 as a member of the LABOUR PARTY. She served (1976–79) as education minister in the Labour government, but in 1981 she left the party and was a founder of the SOCIAL DEMOCRATIC PARTY (SDP). In Nov. 1981 she became the first SDP member to win election to Parliament but lost her seat in the 1983 general elections and failed to reenter Parliament in the 1987 general election.

**Williams, Tennessee** (Thomas Lanier Williams), 1914–83, American playwright. His poetic dramas, filled with dramatic tension and brilliant dialogue, explore society's passions and frustrations. Williams scored his first successes with *The Glass Menagerie* (1945) and *A Streetcar Named Desire* (1947). His other plays include *Summer and Smoke* (1948), *Cat on a Hot Tin Roof* (1955), *Sweet Bird of Youth* (1959), *The Night of the Iguana* (1961), *Small Craft Warnings* (1972), and *Clothes for a Summer Hotel* (1980). Williams has also written short stories, two novels, verse, and his *Memoirs* (1975).

**Williams, William Carlos,** 1883–1963, one of the most important modern American poets. A practising doctor, Williams was an acute observer of American life. In his mature verse he developed a lucid, vital style reflecting idiomatic speech and faithful to ordinary things seen and heard. His books of poetry include *Collected Poems* (1934), *Pictures from Brueghel* (1963), and his major work, the five-volume philosophical poem *Paterson* (1946–58). Williams also wrote critical essays, e.g., *In the American Grain* (1925), short stories, plays, and novels.

**Williamsburg,** US city (1980 pop. 9870), SE Virginia, on a peninsula between the James and York rivers; settled 1632 as Middle Plantation, laid out and renamed 1699, inc. 1722. It is a great tourist attraction. Capital of Virginia from 1699 to 1779, it later declined, but in 1926 large-scale restoration began: hundreds of buildings were removed, renovated, or rebuilt, so that today Williamsburg retains its colonial appearance. William and Mary College (founded 1693) is located there.

**Williamson, David,** 1942–, Australia's most popular dramatist. He was originally associated with the PRAM FACTORY in Melbourne. With a fine ear for colloquial speech and social rituals, he wittily satirizes his own generation of middle-class Australians. His plays include *Don's Party* (1973), *The Club* (1978), *Travelling North* (1980), *The Perfectionist* (1983), and *Emerald City* (1987).

**William the Lion,** 1142?–1214, king of Scotland (r.1165–1214). William aided the rebellion in England of HENRY II's sons, but was captured by Henry and forced to sign (1174) the treaty of Falaise, which made Scotland a feudal possession of England. In 1189 he bought an annulment of the treaty from RICHARD I. His alliance (1168) with LOUIS VII of France started the long French–Scottish friendship.

**William the Silent** or **William of Orange** (William I, prince of Orange), 1533–84, principal founder of Dutch independence. A member of the house of NASSAU, he inherited (1544) the principality of Orange, in S France, and was made (1555) stadtholder of Holland, Zeeland, and Utrecht. He opposed repression of the NETHERLANDS by PHILIP II of Spain and helped form the GUEUX party (1566). The duke of ALBA was sent to put down the rebellion (1567), while William, in exile, raised an army to drive the Spanish out. In 1576 the provinces of the Netherlands united under William, but in 1580 he was forced to seek the aid of FRANCIS, duke of Alençon and Anjou. Philip put a price on William's head, and at a critical stage of the independence struggle he was assassinated.

**Willkie, Wendell Lewis,** 1892–1944, American political leader. A lawyer and head of a giant utility company, he became the unexpected Republican candidate for president in 1940. An opponent of isolationism, he supported F.D. ROOSEVELT's foreign policy but attacked NEW DEAL domestic programmes. Although defeated in the election he polled 22 million votes, the largest number received by a defeated candidate up to that time. Willkie later (1941–42) served as Roosevelt's personal emissary abroad and continued to fight isolationism within the Republican party.

**Willmott, Peter,** 1923–, British sociologist. Author (with Michael YOUNG of *Family and Kinship in East London* (1957), a classic study of post-war working-class family life in Bethnal Green, which concluded that, in these communities, the extended family unit, with its high density of interpersonal contacts, rather than the nuclear family type, was the norm. Willmott and Young also wrote *The Symmetrical Family* (1973), which argued that the rigid gender divisions of labour within the family were beginning to break down.

**willow,** common name for some members of the family Salicaceae, deciduous trees or shrubs of worldwide distribution. The family comprises the willows and poplars and is typified by male and female flowers borne in catkins on separate plants. The willows (genus *Salix*) flourish in cold, wet ground. They show a remarkable range of growth form, from dwarf, creeping stems (*S. repens*), to shrubs and tall trees (e.g., *S. alba*). Many are grown as ornamentals, especially in weeping forms, e.g., *S. Babylonica*, the weeping willow, native to China.

**Wills, Helen Newington,** 1906–, American tennis player. Generally considered to have been the foremost woman tennis player of her era, she won the US singles title seven times between 1923 and 1931 and the singles title at WIMBLEDON eight times between 1927 and 1938.

**Wilmot, John:** see ROCHESTER, JOHN WILMOT, 2ND EARL OF.

**Wilmot Proviso,** 1846, amendment to a bill put before the US House of Representatives during the MEXICAN WAR. The bill provided a $2 million appropriation for the settlement of border disputes with Mexico. The proviso, sponsored by Rep. David Wilmot of Pennsylvania, would have prohibited SLAVERY in any territory acquired in the Mexican War. The

amendment failed in the Senate and never became law, but it created bitterness and helped crystallize the conflict between North and South.

**Wilson, Sir Angus,** 1913–, English novelist; b. Frank Johnstone. His witty and entertaining novels portray a society corrupt in both its public and private aspects. They include *Anglo-Saxon Attitudes* (1956), *No Laughing Matter* (1967), and *Setting the World on Fire* (1980). Wilson has also published collections of short stories.

**Wilson, Charles Thomson Rees,** 1869–1959, Scottish physicist. He was Jacksonian professor of natural philosophy at Cambridge. Noted for his studies of atmospheric electricity, he devised a method for protecting barrage balloons from lightning during World War II. For his invention of the Wilson cloud chamber (see PARTICLE DETECTOR) for studying the activity of ionized particles, he shared with Arthur COMPTON the 1927 Nobel Prize for physics.

**Wilson, Edmund,** 1895–1972, probably the foremost American social and literary critic of the 20th cent. In the 1920s he was an editor of *Vanity Fair* and the *New Republic*. As a critic, he explored the social, psychological, and political conditions that shape literary ideas, a task facilitated by his knowledge of Marxian and Freudian theory. Among his major works are *Axel's Castle* (1931), a study of symbolism; *The Wound and the Bow* (1941); *The Shores of Light* (1952); and *Patriotic Gore* (1962). His social studies include *To the Finland Station* (1940), on the European revolutionary tradition; and *The American Earthquake* (1958), on the Great Depression.

**Wilson, Edward O(sborne),** 1929–, American biologist and leading proponent of SOCIOBIOLOGY. Educated at the Univ. of Alabama and at Harvard, he joined the Harvard faculty in 1956 and later became professor of zoology. His exhaustive study of ants and other social insects (on which he is the world's chief authority) led to publication of *Sociobiology* (1975), a controversial work on the genetic factors in human behaviour.

**Wilson, Sir (James) Harold (Baron Wilson),** 1916–, British Labour prime minister (1964–70, 1974–76). An economist, Wilson was elected to Parliament in 1945. He held office at an early age, and in alliance with BEVAN became a spokesman for the party's left wing and in 1963 was elected party leader. As prime minister Wilson worked to gain closer ties to Europe and to bolster the sagging British economy and to carry out social changes. Defeated in the 1970 elections, he returned to power in 1974, and after a referendum saw Britain join the EUROPEAN COMMUNITY, but in Mar. 1976 he unexpectedly announced his retirement. He was knighted in 1976 and received a life peerage in 1983.

**Wilson, Richard,** 1714–82, Welsh landscape painter. Wilson turned exclusively to landscape during a stay in Italy (1750–57/8) when he was inspired by Italian light and scenery and by the ideal landscapes of CLAUDE. On his return he painted Claudian Italianate scenes and country house views; his most original works were inspired by the landscape of England and his native Wales e.g., *Cader Idris, Llyn-y-Cau* (c.1765–67; Tate Gall., London).

**Wilson, (Thomas) Woodrow,** 1856–1924, 28th president of the US (1913–21). He was educated in law at Princeton Univ., the Univ. of Virginia, and Johns Hopkins Univ. (Ph.D., 1886). A noted scholar, he taught at Bryn Mawr College and Wesleyan Univ. before becoming (1890) professor of jurisprudence and political economy at Princeton. In 1902 he became president of Princeton. In 1910, as a reform Democratic candidate, he was elected governor of New Jersey. As governor (1911–13) he accomplished various important reforms. At the 1912 Democratic convention he was nominated for president on the 46th ballot, largely through the efforts of W.J. BRYAN and E.M. House. He was elected president when the Republican vote was split between W.H. TAFT and Theodore ROOSEVELT. Wilson's domestic programme, known as the 'New Freedom', was generally progressive (see PROGRESSIVISM); among its accomplishments were the FEDERAL RESERVE SYSTEM (1913), the Federal Trade Commission (1914), the Clayton Antitrust Act (1914) (see ANTITRUST LAWS), and the first federal child-labour law. In foreign affairs, the early difficulties with Mexico (see HUERTA, VICTORIANO; VILLA, PANCHO) were soon overshadowed by the outbreak of WORLD WAR I in Europe. Determined to maintain US neutrality Wilson nonetheless reacted with growing firmness to the German submarine campaign, especially after the sinking (1915) of the LUSITANIA. By threatening a diplomatic rupture (1916) he forced Germany to promise the abandonment of unrestricted submarine warfare. He ran for reelection in 1916 on the boast of having 'kept us out of war,' and narrowly defeated Charles Evans HUGHES, the Republican candidate. But after Germany announced (31 Jan. 1917) a renewal of unrestricted submarine warfare and several American vessels had been sunk, war was declared (6 Apr. 1917). Wilson viewed the war as necessary to make the world 'safe for democracy' and quickly put the nation on a war footing. Looking forward to peace, he enunciated his plans for its implementation with his FOURTEEN POINTS. When the war ended, he sailed (Dec. 1918) for Europe to take part in the peace talks. Wilson's idealism was widely admired in Europe, and he was looked upon as the best hope for a just peace. Despite his disappointment with the eventual treaty (see VERSAILLES, TREATY OF), he pinned his great hopes on the LEAGUE OF NATIONS. At home, however, isolationism had reasserted itself, particularly among the Republicans in Congress. Wilson's last efforts as president were spent in a futile attempt to win US ratification of (and thus membership in) the League. Exhausted from his labours, he suffered a stroke in Sept. 1919 and never fully recovered. He was awarded the 1919 Nobel Peace Prize.

**Wiltshire,** inland county in SW England (1984 est. pop. 536,200), 3481 km² (1358 sq mi), bordering on Avon and Somerset in the W. The county town is SALISBURY. Much of the county consists of chalk uplands, including Salisbury Plain in the S and the Marlborough Downs in the N. The county is drained by the Kennet, AVON, and Wylye rivers. Dairy farming and cereal-crop production are common. SWINDON is an important industrial and market town. STONEHENGE, AVEBURY, and SILBURY HILL are famous prehistoric monuments. Much of Salisbury Plain has been taken over by the Army for camps and exercise areas.

White Horse on Bratton Down, Westbury, **Wiltshire**

**Wimbledon,** name for the All-England Lawn Tennis Championships —the oldest and most famous of all tennis championships. They have been played annually since 1877 at the All-England Lawn Tennis and Croquet Club, Wimbledon, London, on 16 grass courts. Formerly confined to amateurs, they were opened to professionals in 1968. Winners of the men's singles four or more times are: W. Renshaw, seven times, 1881–86, 1889; H.C. Doherty, five times, 1902–06; B. Borg, five times, 1976–80; R.F. Doherty, four times, 1897–1900; A.F. Wilding, four times, 1910–13; R. Laver, four times, 1961–62, 1968–69. Winners of the women's singles four or more times are: H. WILLS Moody, eight times, 1927–30, 1932–33, 1935, 1938; M. Navratilova, eight times, 1978–79, 1982–87; D. Lambert Chambers, seven times, 1903–04, 1906, 1910–11, 1913–14; B. Hillyard, six times, 1886, 1889, 1894, 1897, 1899, 1900; S. Lenglen, six times, 1919–23, 1925; B.J. KING, six times, 1966–68, 1972–73, 1975; C. Sterry, five times, 1895–96, 1898, 1901, 1908; L. Brough, four times, 1948–50, 1955.

**Wimmera,** region in W Victoria, Southern Australia. The riverine plains extend 233,000 km² (9000 sq mi) north from the Grampian Mts to the MURRAY R. This major wheat and sheep producing area has domestic and stock water supplied by an open-channel system of reticulation from the Rocklands Reservoir on the Glenelg R. The main urban centre for the district is Horsham (1985 est. pop. 12,780).

**Winchester,** town (1981 pop. 34,127), Hampshire, S England. It was the capital of the Anglo-Saxon kingdom of WESSEX. Even after the NORMAN CONQUEST, when LONDON gained political ascendancy, Winchester remained England's centre of learning. It is the site of Winchester College (est. 1382), one of the country's great public schools. The city also exerted great ecclesiastical influence, as reflected in its magnificent cathedral (11th–14th cent.)

**wind,** flow of air parallel to the Earth's surface. The direction of wind is indicated by a weather vane. A wind is named according to the direction from which it is blowing, e.g., a wind blowing from the north is a north wind. Wind velocity is measured by means of a cup anemometer, an instrument with three or four small hollow metal hemispheres set so that they catch the wind and revolve about a vertical rod; an electrical device records the revolutions of the cups and thus the wind velocity (see BEAUFORT SCALE. Winds are caused by the unequal heating of the earth's surface by the sun. Warmer air expands, becomes lighter, and rises. Cooler air rushes in from surrounding areas to fill the empty space. This process continues, creating a steady flow of air called a convection current. This, along with the rotation of the Earth (see CORIOLIS EFFECT) and other secondary factors, causes the basic planetary wind systems that circle the Earth, bringing constant changes in the weather.

**Windaus, Adolf** (͵vindows), 1876–1959, German chemist. A professor of chemistry and director of the chemistry laboratories at the Univ. of Göttingen, he won the 1928 Nobel Prize for chemistry for his work on sterols, especially in relation to vitamins. He discovered and synthesized vitamin $D_3$, the component of vitamin D most important in preventing rickets.

**Windermere,** largest lake in England, in the Lake District, Cumbria, NW England. It extends from Waterhead, near Ambleside, southwards for approximately 16 km (10 mi) to Lakeside, near Newby Bridge. It is fed by the rivers Rothay, Brathay, and Trout Beck, and drained by the R. Leven into Morecambe Bay. It is a very popular tourist centre.

**windflower:** see ANEMONE.

**Windhoek** (͵vinthook), largest city (1981 pop. 110,644) and capital of Namibia. A communications and economic centre, it is linked with South Africa's rail network and conducts a large trade in Karakul sheep skins. In 1892 the city became the capital of the German colony of South West Africa; it was captured by South African troops in World War I. Windhoek still retains a German flavour.

**windhover:** see KESTREL.

**windmill,** mechanical device that harnesses wind power in order to pump water, grind grain, power a sawmill, or drive an electrical generator. Windmills were probably not known in Europe before the 12th cent., but thereafter they became the chief source of power until the advent of the STEAM ENGINE during the Industrial Revolution. The operational apparatus of the typical Dutch windmill is a four-to-six-armed structure that carries sails made of light wood or canvas. Revolving in the wind, the sail mechanism turns a shaft that operates the pump, millstone, or saw. Modern windmills are made of various lightweight materials. New types, such as the wind turbine used to generate electricity, are designed to turn even in light winds. Their output depending on their size and on wind speeds can vary from 1 kW to 2500 kW. Windmills are having an impact in the Third World for pumping water from artesian wells for irrigating arid land, and for generating electricity when petrol or coal is too expensive.

**Windsor,** family name of the royal house of Great Britain. The name Wettin, family name of Prince ALBERT, consort of Queen VICTORIA, was changed to Windsor by GEORGE V in 1917. ELIZABETH II decreed that she and her descendants bearing the title of prince or princess would retain the name Windsor.

**Windsor,** town (1981 pop. 30,832), Berkshire, S central England, on the Thames R. The importance of the town derives from WINDSOR CASTLE, the chief residence of English rulers since WILLIAM I. The castle was improved and rebuilt by several sovereigns.

**Windsor, Edward, duke of:** see EDWARD VIII under EDWARD, kings of England.

**Windsor, Wallis Warfield, duchess of,** 1896–1986, American-born wife of Edward, duke of Windsor, who as EDWARD VIII abdicated (1936) the British throne in order to marry her. She obtained a divorce from her second husband, E.A. Simpson, in Apr. 1937 and married Edward in June. Special letters patent denied her a share in his royal rank of duke.

**Windsor Castle,** royal castle in town of Windsor, Berkshire, S England. It was founded by William I on the site of an earlier stronghold, and has been added to since. It has been the chief royal residence since the 11th cent. The Upper Ward contains the state apartments, and the Lower Ward contains St George's Chapel (built in PERPENDICULAR style) and the Albert Memorial chapel. The Great Park to the S is open to the public, but the Home Park bordering the river is private.

**windsurfing,** form of sailing in which an individual stands on a long board to which is added a mast and a sail. It was devised in the US in the late 1960s and in two decades spread worldwide.

**wind tunnel,** enclosed, elongated chamber in which scale models and full-size aircraft, missiles, etc. can be mounted in a steady air stream (usually propelled by an electric motor driving a multi-blade airscrew) so that aerodynamic forces can be studied and measured, in particular lift and drag and control aspects at various air speeds. Vertical wind tunnels are used to establish spinning characteristics of scale models of projected new aircraft types. See AERODYNAMICS.

**Windward Islands:** see WEST INDIES.

**wine,** alcoholic beverage made by FERMENTATION of the juice of the grape. Wines are distinguished by colour, flavour, bouquet (aroma), and alcoholic content. They may be red (when the whole crushed grape is used), white (using the juice only), or rosé (when skins are removed after fermentation has begun). Wines are also classified as dry (when grape sugar ferments completely) or sweet (when some sugar remains). There are three main types of wine: natural (still), fortified, and sparkling. The alcoholic content of natural wine comes from fermentation. Fortified wine (e.g., SHERRY, port, Madeira) has brandy or other spirits added to it. Sparkling wine (CHAMPAGNE is the best known) is fermented a second time after bottling. Wine is differentiated by the variety of grape, climate, location and soil of the vineyard, and treatment of the grapes before and during wine making. Fermentation starts when wine yeasts on the skins of ripe grapes come in contact with the grape juice (called must). Run off into casks, the new wine then undergoes a series of chemical processes, including oxidation, precipitation of proteins, and fermentation of chemical compounds, that create characteristic bouquet. After periodic clarification and aging in casks, the wine is ready to be bottled. The world's leading wine producer is France, with outstanding products from Bordeaux and Burgundy, the Loire and Rhône valleys, and Alsace. Other major producers are Italy, Spain, Germany, Australia, and the US. The term *wine* is also applied to alcoholic beverages made from other plants, e.g., dandelion and elderberry. Brewer's YEAST and sugar are added to these to promote fermentation.

**Winged Victory:** see NIKE.

**Winnicott, Donald W.,** 1896–1971, English physician and psychoanalyst. He was an associate of Melanie KLEIN and exponent of the 'object relations' school of PSYCHOANALYSIS. Winnicott was important in popularizing psychoanalytic concepts in Britain during the post-war period. His work at the Tavistock clinic emphasized the importance of mother–infant relationships.

**Winnipeg,** city (1981 pop. 584,842), provincial capital, Manitoba, W Canada, at the confluence of the Red and Assiniboine rivers. Long the largest city of the Canadian prairies, it remains one of the world's great wheat-marketing centres. The city is on the site of the French-built Fort Rouge (1738) and the North West Company's Fort Gibraltar, later renamed Fort Garry, then Fort Winnipeg. It began its modern development as an outlet for produce of the prairies when it was first reached by rail in 1881.

**Winstanley, Gerrard,** 1609?–76, English visionary and political writer. During the Interregnum (1642–60) he set up a colony of diggers on St George's Hill at Cobham and wrote pamphlets on political and theological topics which have been held to anticipate later socialist and anarchist ideas. His best-known work is *The Law of Freedom* (1652).

**Winston-Salem,** US city (1984 est. pop. 143,000), central North Carolina, in the Piedmont. It is the nation's chief tobacco manufacturer, with storage and auction facilities. Brewing, textiles, and furniture manufacturing are also important. The city is the financial and shipping centre for NW North Carolina. Salem originated (1766) as a MORAVIAN

The principal **wine**-producing regions of France

settlement, and many early buildings remain. Winston was established in 1849, and the two communities merged in 1913. Wake Forest Univ. is in the city.

**wintergreen,** low evergreen plant (*Gaultheria procumbens*) of the HEATH family, native to sandy and acid woods of E North America and cultivated as an ornamental elsewhere. It has a creeping stem, erect branches, glossy, oval leaves, and small, waxy, white flowers followed by crimson fruits. The aromatic leaves are a source of wintergreen oil (now mostly obtained from the sweet birch or made synthetically), used in medicine and as a flavouring. In Europe, the name is applied to a range of low-growing plants which remain green throughout the winter.

**winter solstice:** see SOLSTICE.

**Winthrop, John,** 1588–1649, governor of the Massachusetts Bay Colony, America; b. England. A member of the MASSACHUSETTS BAY COMPANY, he led (1629) the group that founded Boston colony. As a distinguished member of the colony he was elected governor 12 times and helped shape its theocratic policies. A conservative, he opposed all efforts to liberalize religious or governmental policies. His son **John Winthrop,** 1606–76, b. England, became a lawyer and emigrated to Massachusetts Bay in 1631. In 1633 he was commissioned governor of the new colony at Saybrook (now Deep River), Connecticut, and in 1646 he founded New London. He was governor (1657, 1659–76) of Connecticut and accomplished (1664) the union of the Connecticut and New Haven colonies. A physician and an accomplished scientist and astronomer, he was elected to the ROYAL SOCIETY (1663), the first American so honoured. His son **John Winthrop** (Fitz-John Winthrop), 1638–1707, b. Massachusetts, also served as colonial governor of Connecticut. He went to England to serve in Oliver CROMWELL's army, but returned to America (1663) and fought in KING PHILIP'S WAR (1675–76). Elected governor in 1698, he served ably until his death.

**Wisconsin,** state of the US (1984 est. pop. 4,766,000), area 145,439 km² (56,154 sq mi), located in the upper Midwest bordered by Lake Superior and the Upper Peninsula of Michigan (N), Lake Michigan (E), Illinois (S), and Iowa and Minnesota (W). The capital is MADISON and the largest city is MILWAUKEE; Green Bay is also important. Wisconsin is noted for its 8500 lakes, the largest being Lake Winnebago. The northern uplands give way to prairies in the south. Manufacturing leads the economy, with machinery, processed foods, pulp and paper, and transport and farm equipment. Wisconsin is the leading state for dairy products, and cattle, corn, and pigs are also significant. About 45% of the land is forested, and there is a strong timber industry; zinc, copper, and iron are found. About 63% of the population lives in metropolitan areas; 94% was non-Hispanic white in 1980. The Winnebago, Kickapoo, and other Indian tribes living in the area in the 18th cent. were displaced by the Ottawa and Huron, forced west by European settlement further east. Great Britain controlled the area for 20 years before it became part of the US Northwest Territory (1783). Settlement began after the opening of the ERIE CANAL (1820s) and the defeat of the Indians in the Black Hawk War (1832). In the early 20th cent. Wisconsin was the centre of the Progressive movement for social legislation under Robert M. La Follette, whose family dominated politics in the middle decades. Since then the industrial sector has undergone much expansion.

**Wisdom,** biblical book included in the Western canon and the Septuagint, but not in the Hebrew Bible, and placed in the APOCRYPHA in the Authorized Version. Traditionally called the Wisdom of Solomon, the book includes an exhortation to seek wisdom and a history of God's care of the Jews. It is a supreme example of wisdom literature (pre-Christian Jewish philosophical writings).

**Wise Men of the East, Magi,** or **Three Kings,** men who came, bearing gifts of gold, frankincense, and myrrh, to adore the newborn JESUS. They were guided by the Star of Bethlehem. Christian tradition has set their number as three, called them kings, and named them Caspar or Gaspar, Melchior, and Balthasar. The EPIPHANY commemorates their visit.

**wisteria,** woody, twining vine (genus *Wisteria*) of the PULSE family, cultivated and highly esteemed for the beautiful pendant clusters of lilac, white, or pink flowers. Two species are native to North America, but the showier Asian species are commonly cultivated.

**Witbooi, Hendrik,** 1834–1905, king (r.1884–1904) of the Nama, of present-day NAMIBIA. The early years of his reign were spent in conflict with the Herero but both groups united after 1892 to face the threat posed by German colonialism. Witbooi was defeated by the Germans in 1894. In 1904 he again joined with the Herero in rebellion and died at Keetmanshoop from wounds received in battle.

**witchcraft,** malevolent power operating through individuals as an involuntary force. Witches can represent an inversion of the moral and symbolic values of society. In some societies all deaths are attributed to witchcraft, and all witches are kin of some kind; in others only non-kin are witches; in other societies those who are seen as witches are very often those who are deviant in some way (too successful, unsuccessful, nonconformist). The varying forms of witchcraft that can be identified have been analysed largely in terms of the way in which accusations of witchcraft are made, the lines along which the accusations travel then being seen as revealing the major points of stress in social relations. The last execution for witchcraft was in Scotland in 1722.

**witches' brooms,** abnormal growths on trees in the form of masses of small, erect twigs growing from one point on a tree branch, usually caused by invasion of a parasitic FUNGUS of the genus *Taphrina*.

**witch hazel,** common name for some members of the family Hamamelidaceae, trees and shrubs found mostly in Asia. The family includes the winter hazels (genus *Corylopsis*), the witch hazels (genus *Hamamelis*), the sweet gums (genus *Liquidambar*), and the witch elders (genus *Fothergilla*). The name *witch hazel* is also applied to an astringent liniment and eye lotion obtained from the leaves and bark of *H. virginiana*.

**witenagemot** ('witənəgi‚moht), [Old Eng., = meeting of counsellors], a session of counsellors (the witan) of a king in Anglo-Saxon England. Such a body existed in each Anglo-Saxon kingdom. Composed of nobles and churchmen appointed by the king, the witan advised him on important matters. It probably had the power (especially in WESSEX) to elect a king.

**Wither, George,** 1588–1667, English poet. He was imprisoned for the satire *Abuses Stript and Whipt* (1613). In prison he wrote five pastorals, *The Shepherd's Hunting* (1615). His later works include *Fidelia* (1617) and *Fair Virtue* (1622).

**Witos, Wincenty** (‚vitos), 1874–1945, Polish politician. As a self-educated peasant leader from Galicia, he was a co-founder (in 1913) and leader of the 'Piast' grouping, a moderate wing of the Polish Peasant Party. He became prime minister three times (1920–21, 1923, and 1926). His centre-right coalition government was overthrown by PILSUDSKI in May 1926. In 1932 Witos was sentenced to a term of imprisonment for purportedly preparing a coup. Following a notorious political trial other opposition leaders were arrested and confined at Brześć. Rather than face imprisonment Witos left the country and remained in exile until the outbreak of World War II. He spent the war in occupied Poland but, while imprisoned by the Germans, refused invitations to form a pro-Nazi Polish government.

**Witt, Jan de** (vit), 1625–72, Dutch statesman. As leader of the republican party he was elected (1653) grand pensionary, with control of state affairs and commerce. He negotiated an end to the first and second DUTCH WARS (1652–67) and the War of DEVOLUTION (1667–68). He sought to end the power of the house of Orange, but at the outset of the third Dutch war (1672–78) William of Orange (later WILLIAM III of England) was made stadtholder by popular acclaim, and de Witt resigned. He and his brother, Cornelius, a naval officer, although cleared of treason charges, were killed by a mob.

**Witte, Count Sergei Yulyevich** (‚vitə), 1849–1915, Russian statesman. He encouraged the development of industry with the help of foreign capital and Siberian colonization as finance minister (1892–1903) for NICHOLAS II, negotiated peace after the RUSSO-JAPANESE WAR (1904–5), and was premier from Oct. 1905 to Apr. 1906.

**Wittelsbach,** German dynasty. It ruled BAVARIA from 1182, when Count Otto of Wittelsbach was given the duchy of Bavaria by Holy Roman Emperor Frederick I and ruled as Otto I. His son, Otto II, added the Rhenish Palatinate to the family's domains. In the following centuries the two domains were sometimes ruled together and sometimes separately by different branches of the Wittelsbachs. The dynasty's high point was reached in 1742, when Elector Charles Albert became Holy Roman Emperor CHARLES VII. In 1799 all family lands were united under a single ruler, Maximilian I, who in 1806 became king of a much-enlarged Bavaria. The dynasty ended when Louis III was deposed in 1918.

**Wittenberg,** city (1979 est. pop. 53,384), Halle district, central East Germany, on the Elbe R. Today an industrial and mining centre, it was first mentioned in the 12th cent. Martin LUTHER and Philip MELANCHTHON taught at its university, which became (16th cent.) the focus of the Protestant REFORMATION. Lucas CRANACH the elder founded a school of painting there. The 15th-cent. Schlosskirche, where LUTHER nailed his 95 theses, still stands.

**Wittgenstein, Ludwig Josef Johan,** 1889–1951, Austrian philosopher. He studied (1912–13) at Cambridge Univ. under Bertrand RUSSELL. In Vienna in the 1920s he came in contact with adherents of LOGICAL POSITIVISM; they were profoundly influenced by his first major work, the *Tractatus logico-philosophicus* (1921), which expounds his version of logical atomism, positing a close, formal relationship between language, thought, and the world. Language and thought work literally like a picture of the real world, and to understand any sentence one must grasp the reference of its constituents, both to each other and to the real. Language, however, can indicate an area beyond itself; unsayable things (e.g., things not demonstrable) do exist, and sentences whose structure of meaning amounts to nonsense can result in philosophical insight. Thus Wittgenstein, unlike the logical positivists, allowed for the possibility of metaphysics. Wittgenstein returned to Cambridge in 1929, and his philosophy entered a second phase, represented by his masterpiece *Philosophical Investigations* (1953). Revising his earlier account of language he now saw it as essentially something we *use*, a facet of human practice, rather than a reflection of the world. His work greatly influenced what has come to be called ordinary-language philosophy, which maintains that all philosophical problems arise from the illusions created by the ambiguities of language.

**Witwatersrand** or the **Rand,** rich gold-mining area and chief industrial region of South Africa, in the TRANSVAAL, between the Vaal and Olifants rivers. It includes SOWETO township and the cities of JOHANNESBURG, Benoni, Boksburg, Springs, and GERMISTON. The Rand traditionally produces about one-third of the world's total gold output annually. Other major industries include steel-milling, machine-building, diamond-cutting, and the manufacture of textiles and furniture.

**Wladislaw, Wladyslaw,** and **Wladslas,** For Polish kings thus named, see LADISLAUS.

**Wobblies:** see INDUSTRIAL WORKERS OF THE WORLD.

**Wodehouse, Sir P(elham) G(renville),** 1881–1975, English novelist and humorist. He is famous for his comic stories, many of them featuring Bertie Wooster and his unflappable valet, Jeeves. His reputation has risen again since the years when his wartime record was attacked.

**Woden,** Norse **Odin,** in GERMANIC RELIGION, the supreme God. He established the laws that governed the universe, created the first man and woman, and controlled human destiny. His wife was FRIGG, and his children included Thor, Balder, and Tiw.

**Wöhler, Friedrich** (ˌvøːlə), 1800–82, German chemist. Professor at the Univ. of Göttingen, he devised a method for isolating ALUMINIUM that he also used to isolate BERYLLIUM and YTTRIUM. Wöhler's synthesis of urea opened a new era in organic chemistry and contributed to the theory of isomerism. He also contributed to the chemistry of metabolism.

**wolf,** carnivorous MAMMAL (genus *Canis*), related to the JACKAL and DOG. Three wolf species are generally recognized: the grey wolf (*C. lupus*), the red wolf (*C. niger*), and the prairie wolf, or COYOTE. The grey wolf, also called timber wolf in North America, has a shaggy coat, erect ears, and a bushy tail; the male is usually about 90 cm (3 ft) high at the shoulder and weighs about 45 kg (100 lb). Although extinct in Britain and Western Europe, the grey wolf is still wild across Eastern Europe and Asia. Recent work has shown its reputation as a ruthless killer to be exaggerated.

**Wolf, Christa** (volf), 1929–, East German novelist and essayist. After orthodox Marxist literary beginnings, Wolf's first major experimental novel, *The Quest for Christa T.* (1968) was written in the reflective–subjective mode of epistemological uncertainty, coloured by muted criticism of the East German system. This mode continued with her autobiographical *Childhood's Pattern* (1977), an exploration of her generation's implication in the NAZI past. Subsequent fictions have been located in literary history (*No Place on Earth*, 1979), or in classical mythology (*Cassandra*, 1985). She has also produced a body of essays closely linked to her fictions, collected as *The Dimension of the Author* (2 vol., 1987). Respected and suspected by the authorities, Wolf has developed into a novelist of international standing.

**Wolf, Hugo** (volf), 1860–1903, Austrian composer. One of the supreme masters of the German art song, he wrote over 300 LIEDER, in which he adapted WAGNER's musical conceptions. He also wrote an opera, choral works, and chamber music.

**Wolfe, James,** 1727–59, British soldier. He captured LOUISBURG (1758) and defeated (1759) Gen. MONTCALM on the Plains of Abraham, causing Canada to fall to the British. Both Wolfe and Montcalm were killed in the battle.

**Wolfe, Thomas (Clayton),** 1900–38, American novelist. His four huge, highly autobiographical novels, *Look Homeward, Angel* (1929), *Of Time and the River* (1935), *The Web and the Rock* (1939), and *You Can't Go Home Again* (1940), follow a young man from his boyhood in the rural South to his career as a teacher and writer in New York City. The last two books were organized by his editor, Maxwell Perkins, from the material left after Wolfe's premature death. Characterized by lyrical and dramatic intensity and by an obsessive sense of memory, time, and place, the novels present a sweeping picture of American life. Wolfe's other writings include short stories and a writer's journal.

**Wolfenbüttel,** city (1984 pop. 51,000), Lower Saxony, West Germany, on the Oker R. It was the seat of the dukes of Brunswick–Wolfenbüttel until 1753. The ducal palace was built between the 15th and 18th cent., and the famous ducal library attracts many scholars.

**Wolff, Elisabeth (Bekker)** (volf), 1738–1804, Dutch novelist. She is famous for the realistic, epistolary NOVELS she wrote with Agatha Deken (1741–1804), including *Sara Burgerhart* (1782), reminiscent of Samuel RICHARDSON's *Pamela,* and *Willem Leevend* (1784–85).

**Wölfflin, Heinrich** (vølflin), 1864–1945, Swiss art historian. His theory of form greatly influenced art criticism. His works include *Classic Art* (1899).

**wolfram:** see TUNGSTEN.

**Wolfram von Eschenbach** (ˌeshənbahkh), c.1170–c.1220, German poet. One of the greatest German Minnesängers, he led a restless, roving life. He wrote a number of lyric poems, and the great chivalric epic *Parzival.* It is the source for the libretto of Richard WAGNER's music drama *Parsifal.*

**Wolfsburg** (ˌvolfsbawg), city (1984 pop. 122,500), Lower Saxony, West Germany, on the Mittelland Canal. The origin of this modern, planned city, lies in the establishment of the Volkswagen car factories on a 'green field' site in 1938.

**Wollaston, William Hyde,** 1766–1828, English scientist. His achievements include the discovery (1802) of the dark lines (Fraunhofer lines) in the solar spectrum; the invention of the reflecting goniometer and the camera lucida; the discovery of the elements PALLADIUM and RHODIUM; and the establishment of the equivalence of galvanic and frictional electricity. He endowed the Wollaston science medal, awarded annually by the Geological Society, London.

**Wollongong,** city (1986 pop. 206,803), New South Wales, SE Australia. It is a major iron and steel centre; other manufactures include refined copper, chemicals and textiles. Port Kembla, an important port and the site of one of the world's largest integrated steelworks, was merged with Wollongong in 1947.

**Wollstonecraft, Mary,** 1759–97, English writer and feminist. After publishing *Vindication of the Rights of Woman* (1792), the first great document of FEMINISM, she lived in Paris and befriended leaders of the FRENCH REVOLUTION. She married (1797) William GODWIN, but died giving birth to a daughter who became the wife of SHELLEY and the author of *Frankenstein.*

**Wolsey, Thomas,** 1473? 1530, English statesman and prelate, cardinal of the Roman Catholic Church. He rose rapidly in the service of the young HENRY VIII and by 1514 virtually controlled English domestic and foreign policy. Becoming cardinal and lord chancellor in 1515, he tried unsuccessfully to make England the mediator between France and the Holy Roman Empire. He was twice a candidate for the papacy. His enormous wealth and lavish living caused considerable resentment, and his enemies at court used Henry's divorce from KATHARINE OF ARAGÓN as a means for his ruin. Wolsey incurred the king's anger by failing to secure from the church a quick and favourable decision on the divorce. In Oct. 1529 he lost the chancellorship and all honours except the archbishopric of York. In Nov. 1530 he was arrested on false charges of treason; he died on his way to London.

**Wolverhampton,** town (1981 pop. 263,501), West Midlands, England, 20 km (12 mi) NW of Birmingham. Industries found within the town include the manufacture of locks and various engineering products. Between the 14th and 16th cent., the town was important to the wool trade, but by the mid 18th cent. metal-working had become more important. St Peter's Church was founded in the 10th cent.

**wolverine** or **glutton,** heavy, short-legged, bearlike MAMMAL (*Gulo gulo*) related to the WEASEL, about 90 to 110 cm (3 to 3½ ft) long. It inhabits the mountains of North America and Eurasia near the timberline, feeding on many different animals. Its long, dark-brown, frost-proof fur is prized by Eskimos as trim for hoods and cuffs.

**wombat,** shy, nocturnal MARSUPIAL of Australia and Tasmania, related to the KOALA. Thick-set, with a large head, short legs, a short tail, and a shuffling gait, it is about 90 cm (3 ft) long. Wombats live in burrows in forests and grasslands and eat grass, roots, and bark.

**Women's Cooperative Guild,** social and political organization founded (1883) by women in the COOPERATIVE movement. With the Women's Trade Union League it campaigned for improved conditions for women as paid workers and in the home. From it came many of the 'radical suffragists' who fought for the vote and female equality in the industrial north of England. See WOMEN'S SUFFRAGE.

**women's education,** an area of education neglected to a greater or lesser degree in all cultures. As most of women's work has always been in traditional skills exercised and acquired at home, girls have not needed or been offered formal education. Many cultures have even perceived women's education as immoral. In medieval Europe the only access to education for girls was through the convent system. The Renaissance brought education as a luxury to the privileged classes, including their womenfolk (Lady Jane GREY was not unusual in being able to read Greek). Education for women in Britain continued to be carried out privately until the mid 19th cent., when pioneers such as Dorothea BEALE and Frances Mary BUSS promoted the cause of schools for girls. In mass elementary education in the industrializing countries girls were normally educated on an equal footing with boys. The spread of elementary schooling produced a feminization of the teaching profession, with opportunities for girls in teacher education. In secondary schooling, working-class girls in Britain and its colonial territories had to wait until the 20th cent. for equal opportunities. In the late 20th cent. there has been pressure to give girls equal access to all subjects of the curriculum, including the sciences, technical subjects, and crafts. At the levels of secondary and higher education there was resistance to girls sitting examinations; although women's colleges were opened at OXFORD UNIVERSITY and CAMBRIDGE UNIVERSITY from the 1860s, women were not admitted to their degrees until 1947 and the 1960s, respectively. Even in advanced countries the number of girls successfully completing secondary and tertiary education is often substantially lower than for boys; this is less marked in the socialist countries, but even there women tend to study the subjects that lead to lower-prestige professions.

**Women's Institutes,** organization to promote further education and a sense of community among women living in rural Britain. Founded in 1905, it is organized in local branches which hold monthly meetings of instruction in a wide variety of subjects. The equivalent for urban women are the Townswomen's Guilds.

**women's movement,** movement for women's rights and equality with men. The term was used initially to describe the 'first wave' of feminism from the 1860s to the 1920s, whose many aims coalesced around WOMEN'S SUFFRAGE. Its contemporary use refers to the Women's Liberation Movement which started in the late 1960s. In Britain, as in the US, this grew in part from the new left and its student movements, but also from a series of strikes for equal pay, starting with the Ford machinists' strike in 1968. Simone de BEAUVOIR's *The Second Sex* (1949) became a retrospective landmark for the movement's ideas. Along with Germaine GREER's *The Female Eunuch* (1970) and Betty FRIEDAN's *The Feminine Mystique* (1963), early influences on its thinking and directions were Juliet Mitchell's essay 'Women: the longest revolution' (1966) and Sheila ROWBOTHAM's pamphlet 'Women's liberation and the new politics' (1969). Their themes, connecting women's liberation with revolutionary socialism, and economic production and social inequality with women's reproductive labour—childbearing, childcare, housework and emotional nurture—were elaborated by a generation of feminist theorists. Throughout the 1970s, as the movement's activism and campaigns—for changes in legislation, in the media, the trade unions and employment practice, education, health care, access to abortion, childcare provision and lesbian and gay rights—achieved widespread social and cultural effects, different strands of feminism emerged. Socialist feminism links women's oppression with the class/economic structures of capitalism; radical feminism sees it as the root of all oppressions; liberal–bourgeois feminism demands parity within existing forms of society. These terms encompass a broad range of theories and political practices, latterly internationalized to varying degrees by the growing strength of black and Third World women's movements. See FEMINISM; SEXUAL POLITICS.

**Women's Social and Political Union,** suffrage organization founded (1903) by Emmeline PANKHURST. Its members became known as *suffragettes,* distinguishing them from members of the older and less militant NATIONAL UNION OF WOMEN'S SUFFRAGE SOCIETIES, who remained *suffragists.* Faced with the government's continued resistance to votes for women, in 1912 its militancy escalated to destruction of empty property on a huge scale, leading to the arrest and imprisonment of many suffragettes, with hunger strikes resulting in the 'CAT AND MOUSE ACT' of 1913.

**women's suffrage,** the right of women to vote. In Britain the campaign for women's suffrage began in 1866 when a group of women presented a petition to the MP John Stuart MILL, who moved an amendment on female enfranchisement to the Electoral Reform Act. In the wake of its defeat organizations were formed all over the country, uniting (1897) as the NATIONAL UNION OF WOMEN'S SUFFRAGE SOCIETIES. In the cotton towns of N England, women workers known as 'radical suffragists' campaigned for the vote and other demands through trade unions, the Labour Party and the WOMEN'S COOPERATIVE GUILD. Most effective were the militant tactics of the WOMEN'S SOCIAL AND POLITICAL UNION, which Emmeline PANKHURST founded (1903) and led with her daughter Christabel and the Pethwick-Lawrences, Emmeline (1867–1954) and her husband Frederick. World War I virtually ended the suffrage campaign. In 1928 equal voting rights for women replaced the limited woman suffrage granted in 1918. In the US suffrage was won in 1920, after a struggle led by Elizabeth Cady STANTON, Susan B. ANTHONY, Lucy STONE and others. Today women are enfranchised everywhere but in a few Muslim countries. See WOMEN'S MOVEMENT.

**Wonder, Stevie,** (Stephen Judkins), 1950–, black American singer, songwriter and instrumentalist. Blind from birth and originally inspired by Ray CHARLES, he began his career with the famous Motown label at age 10

EXCELSIOR!

SUFFRAGIST. "IT'S NO GOOD TALKING TO ME ABOUT SISYPHUS; HE WAS ONLY A MAN!"

Women's suffrage

and his third single 'Fingertips' was no. 1 in the US for several weeks when he was just 12 years old. Since then he has matured into one of the most remarkable all-round creative forces in rock music as writer, performer, and producer of his own material. Many of his compositions have become standards, attracting a multitude of cover versions.

**wood,** in botany, tissue (xylem) forming the bulk of the STEM of a woody plant. Xylem conducts the SAP upward from the ROOT system to the LEAF, stores food, and provides support. Xylem is formed in the growing season by the CAMBIUM. In temperate regions, cells formed in the spring or wet season are larger and thinner-walled than those formed in the summer or dry season; this results in conspicuous ANNUAL RINGS. Conifer wood (softwood) has a uniform, nonporous appearance; deciduous trees have a vessel-permeated xylem with a complex appearance, often called hardwood. Freshly cut wood contains much moisture and is dried (seasoned) in the sun or in kilns before use.

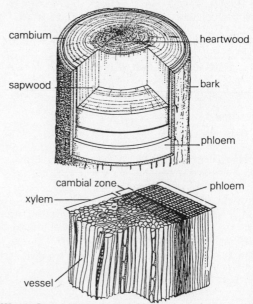

Wood: Cross section of a woody stem (above) and an enlarged view, showing xylem, phloem, and cambium (below)

**wood alcohol:** see METHANOL.

**woodchuck:** see MARMOT.

**woodcock:** see SNIPE.

**woodcut and wood engraving,** prints made from designs cut in relief (where material is cut away to leave the design that is printed) on wood, in contrast to INTAGLIO methods (where the lines that are incised are printed) such as engraving and etching. Woodcutting, the oldest form of printmaking, is done by cutting soft wood with a knife along the grain. Woodcuts appeared in Europe at the beginning of the 15th cent. At that time the same artist designed and carved the block. Later the cutting was often performed by specialists. Used for the block books that preceded printing, woodcuts were often employed as book illustrations after the invention of the printing press. During the RENAISSANCE the most eminent woodcut designers were DÜRER and Hans Holbein, the Younger (see under HOLBEIN, HANS the Elder). With the increasing popularity of engraving on metal, interest in woodcuts declined. It was not revived until the 1890s, with the prints of such artists as GAUGUIN and MUNCH. Many artists of the 20th cent. have used the woodcut; they include DERAIN, DUFY, MAILLOL, and BASKIN. The **wood engraving** is made on hard, end-grained wood carved with a graver or burin. The medium, in which lines usually print white on a black background, was popularized in 18th-cent. England by BEWICK. It was very popular in the 19th cent., in France (where its master was DORÉ), in England, and in the US.

**woodpecker,** name for some members of the family Picidae, climbing BIRDS which live in woods. Woodpeckers typically have sharp, chisel-like bills for pecking holes in trees, where they find insects. They have large claws and stiff tails which they can use to brace themselves against vertical tree trunks. There are about 200 species of woodpeckers found all over the world except for Madagascar and Australia and some oceanic islands. The European green woodpecker is 30 cm (12 in) long. It is not easily seen but can be heard drilling for food.

Great spotted **woodpecker** (*Dendrocopus major*)

**wood sorrel:** see OXALIS.

**Woodstock,** US town (1980 pop. 6804), SE New York State, in the foothills of the Catskill Mts. In the area are an artists' colony and a summer art school. In August 1969 the town gave its name to the most famous of the music festivals of the 1960s and 1970s, attended by thousands of young rock music fans in nearby Mountaindale.

**Woodville, Elizabeth,** 1437–92, queen consort of EDWARD IV. She married (1464) Edward in secret and provoked the anger of the powerful Richard Neville, earl of Warwick, but after the marriage became public she obtained many favours for her family. When Edward died (1483), their son EDWARD V became king, but was seized by his uncle, who usurped the throne as RICHARD III. Richard voided Elizabeth's marriage and Edward V and his younger brother were declared illegitimate and imprisoned. After HENRY VII seized the throne, he married (1486) Elizabeth's daughter Elizabeth.

**Woodward, Robert Burns,** 1917–79, American chemist. A professor at Harvard Univ., he was one of the first to determine the structure of such organic compounds as penicillin, strychnine, oxytetracycline, and chlortetracycline. For his synthesis of organic compounds (e.g., quinine, patulin, cholesterol, cortisone, strychnine, lysergic acid, lanosterol, reserpine, chlorophyll, and tetracycline) he won the 1965 Nobel Prize for chemistry.

**woodwind instrument,** a musical instrument whose tone is produced by a vibrating column of air. Originally made of wood, they may now also be metal or plastic. The woodwind include the instruments in the FLUTE, CLARINET, BASSOON, RECORDER, and OBOE families. The wind passage of an instrument, called its bore, may be either cylindrical (as in the clarinet and most flutes) or conical (as in the oboe). The length of the bore (the longer the bore, the lower the pitch) and the kind of mouthpiece (which affects the timbre) are more important than the material (metal or wood) and the shape (straight or round). See also ORCHESTRA.

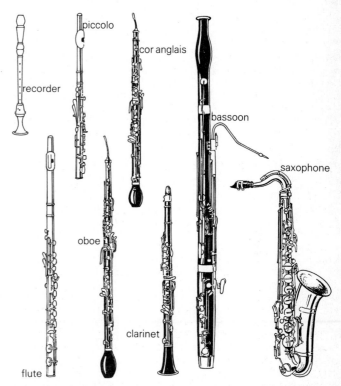

Woodwind instruments

**wool,** fibre from the fleece of the domestic SHEEP, also the hair from other livestock, e.g., the GOAT and CAMEL. Wool is an excellent heat insulator, absorbent, elastic, strong, and crease-resistant when woven. It was probably the first fibre to be made into cloth. Egyptian, Babylonian, and Peruvian archaeological remains have yielded fragments of woollen fabrics. With a heritage of sheep-raising and weaving, England became Europe's main wool-producing country, and wool was the staple of British industry until the 18th cent., until it was supplanted by COTTON. In wool-making, sheep are sheared with mechanical clippers, and the wool is sorted according to fineness, crimp, fibre length, and felting quality, and dirt and grease are removed. Wool may be bleached or dyed as fleece, yarn, or cloth. Woollen cloth is woven from short-staple fibres spun into a soft yarn. Worsted yarn, which is long-staple fibres combed into parallel arrangement and tightly twisted, produces cloth with a hard, smooth texture such as gabardine and serge. Lambswool, a fine, soft, elastic wool from lambs up to about 7 months old, is used for high-quality textiles. The non-sheep wools include: cashmere, a fine, downy wool from the undergrowth of the coat of the cashmere goat, used mainly for knitwear; mohair, a relatively coarse wool from the angora goat, used for upholstery fabrics and outer garments; camel hair, a very light wool with high heat-insulation properties, used for coats, sweaters, and good quality blankets; and alpaca, a very long, soft, silky wool from the ALPACA, a S American relative of the camel, used blended with sheep's wool for high-quality suiting materials.

**Woolf, Virginia (Stephen),** 1882–1941, English novelist. An author of experimental fiction, she was the most influential 20th-cent. woman writer in English. With her husband, Leonard Woolf, she set up the Hogarth Press in 1917. Their home was the centre for the BLOOMSBURY GROUP. In her writing she concentrated on the flow of ordinary experience through the STREAM OF CONSCIOUSNESS technique. Her prose is poetic, symbolic, and visual. Woolf's novels include *Jacob's Room* (1922), *Mrs Dalloway* (1925), *To the Lighthouse* (1927), *Orlando* (1928), *The Waves* (1931), and *Between the Acts* (1941). Her criticism is contained in *The Common Reader* (1925) and other volumes of essays, letters, and diaries. She is a writer admired and much analysed in the terms of contemporary feminist literary criticism. Certain feminist elements in her fiction one made critically and politically explicit in *A Room of One's Own* (1929) and *Three Guineas* (1938).

**Woolley, Sir Charles Leonard,** 1880–1960, British archaeologist. He directed (1922–34) an expedition at UR that greatly furthered Middle Eastern archaeology and history, then excavated several Syrian sites. His books include *The Sumerians* (1928), *Digging Up the Past* (1930), and *Excavations at Ur* (1954).

**Woolworth, Frank Winfield,** 1852–1919, American merchant. Starting (1879) with a five-and-ten-cent store in Lancaster, Pennsylvania, he extended his business throughout the US, the UK, and to other countries. In 1911 the F.W. Woolworth Co. was incorporated, with ownership of over 1000 stores in the US, and he became director of various financial firms. In 1913 he built the Woolworth Building (New York City), then the world's tallest building (241.4 m/792 ft).

**Worcester,** cathedral city (1981 pop. 75,466), Hereford and Worcester, W Midlands of England, on R. Severn. It is an industrial centre, long famous for the manufacture of glass, china, leather goods, and Worcester sauce. The cathedral was mainly built in the 14th cent., and the Three Choirs Festival is held here every third year (the other venues being HEREFORD and GLOUCESTER). Edward ELGAR was born at Broadheath, 3 km (2 mi) to the NW.

Worcester jug, engraved by Robert Hancock in 1757 (Dyson Perrins Museum, Worcester)

**Worcester,** English porcelain factory. Founded in 1751, Worcester adopted a recipe for soft-paste porcelain incorporating Cornish soapstone which gave its porcelain resistance to hot liquids and helped to make it commercially successful. Table and ornamental wares were produced with finely painted and transfer-printed decoration. The factory was in decline during the mid 19th cent. but in the second half of the century a revival took place and it produced a wide range of high-quality porcelain, some ornately decorated with piercing and jewelling.

**Wordsworth, William,** 1770–1850, English poet. After graduating from Cambridge in 1791, Wordsworth spent a year in France where a Frenchwoman, Annette Vallon, bore him a daughter, but they never married. He returned to England imbued with the spirit of the FRENCH REVOLUTION. In 1793 *An Evening Walk* and *Descriptive Sketches* were published. Prevented by the REIGN OF TERROR from returning to France, Wordsworth settled in Dorset, S England, with his sister Dorothy, 1771–1855, who throughout his life shared his poetic vision; her journals were published after her death. With his close friend Samuel Taylor COLERIDGE, Wordsworth wrote *Lyrical Ballads* (1798), an attempt to use the language of ordinary speech in poetry. This famous book, which included his 'Tintern Abbey', introduced ROMANTICISM into English poetry. A second edition (1800) contained an essay outlining Wordsworth's poetic principles. In 1798–9 Wordsworth and his sister visited Germany, and then moved to Grasmere, in the Lake District, N England where they lived thereafter. He married Mary Hutchinson in 1802. The second version of *The Prelude,* a long autobiographical poem, was completed in 1805 but not published until after his death (the other versions are 1799 and 1850). *Poems in Two Volumes* (1807) included 'Ode: Intimations of Immortality' and many of his most famous lyrics such as 'Daffodils' and 'The Rainbow''. His later work was less notable, but included *The Excursion* (1814) and *The White Doe of Rylstone* (1815). In 1843, now distanced from his early radicalism, he was named Poet Laureate. Both his innovative use of language and his celebration of the power and beauty of nature were profoundly influential on English poetry, and his lyric intensity and intellectual power have always commanded admiration even when his later political stance (castigated by BROWNING in his poem 'The Lost Leader') alienated some readers.

**work,** in physics, transfer of ENERGY by a force acting against a resistance or a body and resulting in displacement. Work $W$ has a magnitude equal to the scalar product (see VECTOR) of the force $F$ and the distance $d$ of the resulting movement; thus $W = Fd \cos \upsilon$, where $\upsilon$ is the angle between the direction of the force and the direction of movement. The SI unit (see METRIC SYSTEM) of work is the joule; 1 J is equal to the energy expended by a 1-newton force acting through a distance of 1m. The foot-pound (see ENGLISH UNITS OF MEASUREMENT) and the erg (cgs system) are the former units of work or energy expended, respectively, by a 1-lb force acting through a distance of 1 ft and by a 1-dyne force through 1 cm. One foot-pound equals 1.356 J; 1 erg equals $10^{-7}$ J.

**working dog,** class of DOG bred to perform tasks such as herding cattle, guarding persons or property, drawing sleds or light vehicles (illegal in the UK), police and rescue work, and for guiding blind persons. Many of the breeds are kept as companion dogs. The bearded collie and the rough collie are well-known herding dogs, and the corgi was specifically bred for herding cattle. The Doberman and the German shepherd are frequently used by the police and army. The boxer and the Great Dane are used as guard dogs, while the St Bernard was bred as a dual-purpose dog for herding sheep and also guarding them from wolves.

**Work Projects Administration** (WPA), 1935–43, US government agency during the NEW DEAL. It was established as the Works Progress Administration, and its name was changed in 1939. The WPA undertook extensive building and improvement projects to provide work for the unemployed. It constructed 116,000 buildings, 78,000 bridges, and (651,000 mi) 1,047,000 km of public roads. Also included under the WPA were the Federal Arts Project, Federal Theatre Project, Federal Writers' Project, and the National Youth Administration.

**World Bank,** UN agency; officially known as the International Bank for Reconstruction and Development (see UNITED NATIONS, table 3).

**World Council of Churches,** an international, interdenominational organization of Protestant and Orthodox churches, begun at Amsterdam in 1948. The council has no power over the member churches, but provides an opportunity for cooperation in matters of common concern. The headquarters are at Geneva, Switzerland. Although not a member, the Roman Catholic Church sends accredited observers to assemblies of the Council, and maintains other links with it.

**World Court,** popular name of the Permanent Court of International Justice, established in 1920 by the LEAGUE OF NATIONS. Headquartered at The HAGUE, it comprised 15 judges empowered to render judgments in international disputes brought before them. The US never joined the court, but an American jurist always sat on its bench. Dissolved in 1945, the court was supplanted by the UN International Court of Justice (see UNITED NATIONS, table).

**World Cup,** main international association football competition (see SOCCER), and one of the most prized of all sporting trophies. The gold trophy is named after Jules Rimet, honorary president of the Federation Internationale de Football Association (FIFA) from 1921–54. The competition, which takes place every four years in a different country, began in 1930.

**World Health Organization** (WHO), international body concerned with improving the health of all people of all nations, established by the United Nations in 1948. Its headquarters is in Geneva, and it is funded by contributions made by member states of the World Health Assembly, which meets annually to determine policies covering the control of epidemics, drug standards, quarantine measures, and so on. WHO sponsors national programmes of immunization, improved sanitation, and health education. It was responsible for the global eradication of SMALLPOX and its present concerns include AIDS, the prevention of smoking, and the provision of clean water around the world. 'Health for All in the Year 2000' was the policy adopted at the 1981 meeting of the World Health Assembly, and this goal means placing health on the political agenda of all governments. See also UNITED NATIONS (table 3).

**World Intellectual Property Organization:** see UNITED NATIONS (table 3).

**World Meteorological Organization:** see UNITED NATIONS (table 3).

**world-system theory.** In the 1970s, research on the causes and mechanisms of underdevelopment in the Third World led a number of writers, including Emmanuel Wallerstein, to put forward what have been called world-system theories. The essence of these is that the behaviour of states is not autonomous, but fundamentally determined by world capitalism and its patterns of trade, investment, and control. Attention is focused on the international *division of labour* between the wealthy industrialized 'core' states and the underdeveloped Third World states at the 'periphery'.

**World Trade Center,** building complex in New York City, US, consisting of 110-storey, rectangular twin towers rising to 411 m (1350 ft), second in height only to Chicago's SEARS TOWER. Located in lower Manhattan, the building was designed by Minoru Yamasaki and Emery Roth and completed in 1973 at a cost of $750 million.

World Trade Center

**World War I,** 1914–18, also called the Great War, conflict, chiefly in Europe, among most of the world's great powers. On one side were the Allied and Associated Powers (chiefly France, Britain, Russia, and the US); on the other were the Central Powers (Germany, Austria–Hungary, and Turkey). Prominent among the war's causes were the imperialist, territorial, and economic rivalries of the great powers. The German empire in particular was determined to establish itself as the preeminent power on the Continent. The Germans were also intent on challenging the naval superiority of Britain. However, the immediate cause of hostilities was to be found in the national aspirations of the subject peoples of the Austro-Hungarian empire. On 28 June 1914, Archduke FRANCIS FERDINAND, heir apparent to the Austro-Hungarian throne, was assassinated at Sarajevo by a Serbian nationalist. One month later, Austria-Hungary claimed that its humiliating demands were refused by Serbia and declared war on that country. Other declarations of war followed quickly, and soon every major power in Europe was in the war. On the Western Front, the Germans smashed through Belgium, advanced on Paris, and approached the English Channel. After the first battles of the MARNE and YPRES, however, the Germans became stalled. Gruelling trench warfare and the use of poison gas began all along the front, and for the next three years the battle lines remained virtually stationary despite huge casualties at VERDUN and in the Somme offensive during 1916. On the Eastern Front, the Central Powers were more successful. The initial Russian advance into Galicia was held near Cracow, and the Russian invasion of East Prussia was crushed at the Masurian Lakes (Aug.–Sept. 1914). In the course of 1915, the Germans captured most of central Poland, advanced into the Baltic provinces, and crossed the Carpathians into Romania. Serbia and Montenegro were also overrun. Brusilov's counter-offensive (1916) was held, and 1917 saw the Germans advancing deep into Byelorrusia and Ukraine. In the south, the Italian campaigns were inconclusive, though they benefited the Allied

cause by keeping large numbers of Austrian troops tied down there. In Turkey, the Allies' ambitious Gallipolli Campaign (1915), an attempt to force Turkey out of the war, was a costly failure. In the Middle East, T.E. LAWRENCE stirred Arab revolt against Turkey. US neutrality had been threatened since 1915, when the British ship Lusitania was sunk. By 1917 unrestricted German submarine warfare had caused the US to enter the war on the side of the Allies. An American Expeditionary Force, commanded by Gen. Pershing, landed in France and saw its first action at Château-Thierry (June 1917). In Mar. 1918 the new Soviet government signed the Treaty of BREST-LITOVSK with the Central Powers. The Germans were stopped just short of Paris in the second battle of the Marne, and an Allied counter-offensive was successful. The Turkish and Austro-Hungarian empires, disintegrating from within, surrendered to the Allies, as did Bulgaria. After revolution erupted in Germany, the emperor abdicated, and an armistice came into effect on 11 Nov. 1918. The Treaty of VERSAILLES and the other treaties that ended the war radically changed the face of Europe and the Middle East. Four great empires— Germany, Austria–Hungary, Czarist Russia, and the Ottoman empire —had disappeared by the end of the war. Replacing them were several new states, such as POLAND, CZECHOSLOVAKIA, and YUGOSLAVIA, and governments ranging from monarchies and sheikhdoms through constitutional republics to the Bolshevik dictatorship in Soviet Russia. The war itself had been one of the bloodiest in history, without a single decisive battle. A total of 65 million men had served in the armies; an estimated 10 million persons had been killed and double that number wounded. Such statistics contributed to a general revulsion against war, leading many to put their trust in multinational disarmament pacts and in the newly formed LEAGUE OF NATIONS.

**World War II,** 1939–45, conflict involving every major power in the world. On one side were the Allied Powers (chiefly Great Britain, France,

Poland, and after 1941 the US and the USSR) and on the other side the Axis powers (Germany, Japan, and Italy). The conflict resulted from the rise of totalitarian, militaristic regimes in Germany, Japan, and Italy after WORLD WAR I. Partly responsible also were the humiliating peace treaties forced on Germany after that war and the worldwide economic disorders brought on by the GREAT DEPRESSION of the 1930s. In Asia the second SINO-JAPANESE WAR (1931) was followed by continuing Japanese aggression. In 1936 Benito MUSSOLINI conquered Ethiopia for Italy, thereby dramatizing the ineffectuality of the LEAGUE OF NATIONS. French and British appeasement of Adolf HITLER's Nazi regime in Germany culminated in the MUNICH PACT (1938), which sacrificed much of Czechoslovakia to Germany. France and Britain, nevertheless, began to rearm and to offer guarantees to other potential victims of German aggression, notably Poland. In Aug. 1939 Germany and the Soviet Union, previously bitter rivals, concluded a nonaggression pact, thus freeing Hitler first to invade Poland (Sept. 1939). France and Britain declared war on Germany, but were unable to assist their Polish ally, thereby entering the so-called 'Phoney War'. Isolated Poland was overrun within the month, and partitioned between Germany and the Soviet Union. In 1939–40, the Soviets proceeded to attack FINLAND, to occupy ESTONIA, LATVIA, and LITHUANIA, and to annexe Bessarabia from Romania, whilst the Germans overran Denmark, Norway, Holland, and Belgium. In May 1940, Germans broke into France and swept to the English Channel. On June 22 France surrendered. Britain, under Prime Min. Winston CHURCHILL, was left to fight alone. The BATTLE OF BRITAIN (Aug.–Oct. 1940), Germany's attempt to bomb Britain into submission, was the only German failure of the war's early years. Axis land operations continued in N Africa and in the Balkans, where Greece and Yugoslavia were occupied. On June 22 1941, Germany invaded the Soviet Union, thereby breaking the Nazi–Soviet Pact. By December, having inflicted vast losses on the Red Army, the *Wehrmacht* stood at the gates of Moscow and Leningrad. Meanwhile, the US, under Pres. F.D. ROOSEVELT, was drawing closer to the Allies. On 7 Dec. 1941, Japan attacked PEARL HARBOR, bringing the US into the war. But Axis successes continued. By 1942 Japan had conquered the Philippines, many other Pacific islands, and all of Southeast Asia; German forces in the Soviet Union reached the Volga and the Caucasus; ROMMEL seemed about to take Cairo; and German submarines were threatening to wipe out Allied shipping. Late in 1942, however, the Allies began to rally. In N Africa, MONTGOMERY's rout of Rommel at Alamein (Oct. 1942; see NORTH AFRICA, CAMPAIGNS IN), and the landing of US troops in NW Africa, resulted in Allied victory in Africa. The Allies conquered Sicily and S Italy, and Italy surrendered (Sept. 1943). In the Pacific, US forces won (1942) the naval battles of the Coral Sea and Midway, landed on GUADALCANAL, and began the island-hopping strategy that by 1945 had won back the Philippines and brought a striking force to Japan's doorstep at IWO JIMA and OKINAWA. The German surrender at Stalingrad (1943; see VOLGOGRAD) was followed by the decisive Soviet victory at Kursk (July 1943), the largest tank battle in history. In 1944 the Soviet Army recovered most of the Baltic States, Byelorussia, and Ukraine; and Soviet troops entered Poland, Czechoslovakia, Hungary, Romania, Bulgaria, and the first piece of German territory in East Prussia. In the battle of the Atlantic, the German submarine fleet was virtually destroyed. German resistance in N Italy was stubborn, however, especially at Cassino and Anzio. On 6 June 1944 (known thereafter as D Day), the final Allied campaign began with the landing of troops in Normandy. In August a second force landed in S France. By late 1944 Belgium and France were liberated, and the war had been carried into the Netherlands and western Germany. Allied bombing, meanwhile, was destroying German industrial centres. One allied raid on Dresden in Feb. 1945 killed over 150,000 people. In Dec. 1944 the Germans' last throw on the western front came to a halt in the 'Battle of the Bulge' in the Ardennes. By Jan. 1945, however, the Allies advance into Germany had recovered. The Soviet Army had reached the Oder, threatening Berlin. On 7 Mar. the Western Allies broke through the Siegfried Line, crossed the Rhine, and overran W Germany. In Apr. 1945, after Hitler's suicide, German resistance collapsed, and on 7 May 1945, Germany surrendered unconditionally. The Allies now turned their attention to the Pacific. The Soviet Union declared war on Japan and occupied Manchuria and the northern Japanese islands. In Aug. 1945, while US troops were preparing to invade mainland Japan, Pres. TRUMAN ordered the dropping of the ATOMIC BOMB on HIROSHIMA and NAGASAKI. Japan announced its surrender on 14 Aug. 1945, thereby bringing to an end the costliest war in history.

**World Wide Fund for Nature,** formerly World Wildlife Fund, international charitable organization which raises funds for conservation projects. The World Wide Fund for Nature (WWFN) arose in 1961 from the IUCN, the INTERNATIONAL UNION FOR THE CONSERVATION OF NATURE AND NATURAL RESOURCES. The IUCN advises the WWFN and devises projects for which the WWFN raises the money. It is now represented in 23 countries and has played an important part in bringing habitats and species endangered by human activities to the public's notice. In the celebrations of its 25th anniversary in 1986, television companies throughout the world co-operated to produce a worldwide link-up programme called *World Safari,* which highlighted the achievements of the World Wide Fund for Nature.

**worm,** term for various unrelated invertebrates with soft, often long and slender bodies. The most primitive are the FLATWORMS, including the PLANARIANS, FLUKES, and TAPEWORMS. RIBBON WORMS are colourful marine carnivores, and several loosely related groups of worms (e.g., horsehair worms, NEMATODES, and ROTIFERS) are classed as ROUNDWORMS. The segmented or ANNELID WORMS include the EARTHWORMS and LEECHES. Although it has no taxonomic validity, the term *worm* is also used for the SHIPWORM (a type of CLAM), some insect larvae (e.g., the armyworm and inchworm), and the acorn worm.

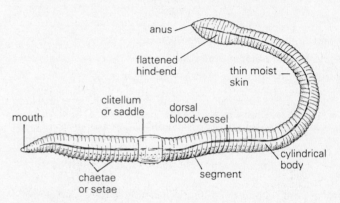

External anatomy of a **worm**

**Worms, Diet of** (wuhmz), 1521, most famous of the imperial diets held at Worms, Germany. Called by Holy Roman Emperor CHARLES V, it took up, among other business, the matter of Martin LUTHER. Luther appeared under a safe-conduct and refused to yield his position, traditionally ending his defence with 'Here I stand. I cannot do otherwise. God help me. Amen.' The Edict of Worms, issued 25 May, declared him an outlaw, thus hardening the lines of the REFORMATION.

**wormwood,** common name for plants of the genus *Artemesia* of the COMPOSITE family. *A. absinthum* has long been used to remove intestinal worms and as a flavouring for drinks (absinthe). *A. dracunculus* is the potherb tarragon, while *A. tridentata* is the common SAGEBRUSH of the western states of the US.

**Worth, Charles Frederick,** 1825–95, English FASHION designer working in Paris. With the establishment of the House of Worth, 1860, he founded modern haute couture. He was dressmaker to Empress Eugènie of France and other royal ladies, and had great prestige. Worth is credited with many of the changes in late 19th-cent. fashion, such as the shorter walking-skirt (1860s) and the bustle (early 1880s).

**Wounded Knee,** creek in South Dakota, site of the last major battle (29 Dec. 1880) of the INDIAN WARS, in which US troops killed almost 200 Sioux Indians, including women and children. In 1973, 200 members of the AMERICAN INDIAN MOVEMENT occupied Wounded Knee for 69 days, demanding a Senate investigation into the condition of American Indians.

**Wovoka,** c.1858–1932, a Paiute Indian, prophet of the messianic GHOST DANCE religion. He taught that pacifism and the sacred dance would cause the whites to disappear and would free all Indians from death, disease, and misery. After his supernatural 'bulletproof' ghost shirts failed tragically at WOUNDED KNEE, the appeal of his religion waned.

**Wrangel Island:** see VRANGELYA OSTROV.

**wren,** small, plump, perching songbird of the primarily New World family Troglodytidae. Its plumage is usually brown or reddish above and white, grey, or buff below. Wrens live and nest at low levels, feeding on insects and larvae. There is only one species living in the Old World, the European wren (*Troglodytes troglodytes*), but it is the most widespread wren, covering Europe, Asia, and North Africa. The birds known as wrens in Australia and New Zealand belong to a different family.

**Wren, Sir Christopher,** 1632–1723, English architect, astronomer, and mathematician. After the great fire of 1666, he produced a masterly plan for the rebuilding of London, which was never executed. He designed, however, many new buildings, most notably ST PAUL'S CATHEDRAL. From 1670 to 1711 he executed 52 London churches, noted for their varied and original designs and fine spires, e.g., St-Mary-le-Bow. Among his secular works were the Sheldonian Theatre, Oxford; Trinity College Library, Cambridge; and Chelsea Hospital, London. His buildings exhibit great elegance, clarity, and dignity.

Sir Christopher **Wren's** Chelsea Hospital

**wrestling,** sport in which two unarmed opponents grapple with one another. The object is to secure a fall, i.e., to pin the opponent's shoulders to the floor. Two distinctly different styles exist today. Greco-Roman wrestling, popular in continental Europe, permits no holds below the waist and takes place mostly on the ground. Freestyle wrestling, favoured in the US, Britain, and elsewhere, permits tackling, tripping, and other rough features. In amateur wrestling, contestants are classified by weight. One of the earliest sports known, wrestling was extremely popular among the ancient Greeks. Competition in both styles is part of the modern Olympic programme. Jujitsu (see MARTIAL ARTS) and sumo are forms of wrestling practised in Japan. So-called professional wrestling is less a competitive sport than a staged entertainment.

**Wright, Frank Lloyd,** 1869–1959, American architect. He worked with Louis SULLIVAN. Beginning in 1893 he built a series of homes in and around Chicago with low horizontal lines that echoed the landscape (his 'prairie style'), e.g., the Robie House, Chicago (1909). From the beginning he practised radical innovation in both structures and aesthetics. He did pioneer work in integrating machine methods and materials into a true architectural expression. Many of his innovations, e.g., open planning eliminating traditional room division to achieve fluid inner space, set standards. The Larkin Building, Buffalo, New York. (1904, destroyed 1950), and Oak Park Unity Temple, near Chicago

Exterior view of the Solomon R. Guggenheim Museum designed by Frank Lloyd **Wright**

(1906), were highly influential early designs. The Imperial Hotel, Tokyo (1916–23, demolished 1968), and Wright's home, 'Taliesin', Spring Green, Wisconsin (1911, twice rebuilt), were especially famous. Later designs included the Kaufmann house, 'Falling Water', Bear Run, Pennsylvania (1936–37), cantilevered over a waterfall; and the Guggenheim Museum, New York City (1946–59), with its spiral ramp.

**Wright, Joseph,** English painter. Wright worked mainly in Derby, where he painted leading members of the scientific, intellectual, and industrial circles in the Midlands, and subjects that reflect their interests, as *Experiment with an Air Pump* (1768; National Gall., London). His works—portraits, landscapes, and industrial GENRE scenes—are distinguished by his interest in effects of artificial light; there is a collection in the Derby Art Gallery.

**Wright, Judith,** 1915–, Australian poet. Her pioneering family origins are narrated in her book *Generations of Men* (1959). Her predominantly lyrical poetry records female experience and the use of nature to explore the universal. She is an active conservationist and prolific writer. Her poetry includes *The Moving Image* (1946). *Woman to Man* (1949), *Birds* (1962), *City Sunrise* (1964), and *The Other Half* (1966).

**Wright, Orville,** 1871–1948, and **Wilbur Wright,** 1867–1912, American aviators. Their first powered aeroplane achieved the first sustained powered and controlled flight of a heavier-than-air craft, on 17 Dec. 1903, making four short flights of which the longest was 252 m (852 ft). Turning their bicycle works into an aircraft factory, they supplied aeroplanes to the US government. Not long after Wilbur's early death from typhoid fever, Orville retired from business life a millionaire, and devoted himself to aeronautical research.

**Wright, Richard,** 1908–60, black American author. Wright wrote powerfully of the plight of blacks in America. His major works are the novel *Native Son* (1940) and the autobiography *Black Boy* (1945). He also wrote other novels, short stories, and nonfiction.

**writing,** the visible recording of LANGUAGE peculiar to the human species. Writing permits the transmission of ideas over vast distances of time and space, and is a prerequisite of complex civilization. The first known writing dates from 6000 BC. The norm of writing is phonemic: it attempts to represent all significant sounds in the language (see PHONETICS). When one letter symbolizes one phoneme the result is a complete ALPHABET. Few alphabets attain this ideal; some ancient ones (e.g., Sanskrit) and some modern ones (e.g., Finnish) approach it. The major non-alphabetic forms of writing are Chinese, in which each character represents a word or concept, and Japanese, in which each character represents a syllable. The spelling of such languages as English and French has changed so little that writing is increasingly unrelated to pronunciation, resulting in the need to teach spelling, and in 'silent' letters. Writing arose independently in Egypt (see HIEROGLYPHIC), in Mesopotamia (see CUNEIFORM), in China, and among the MAYA in Central America. Ancient writing is known from stone and clay inscriptions, but the use of perishable materials such as palm leaf, PAPER, and PAPYRUS began in ancient times. See also ACCENT; CALLIGRAPHY; PUNCTUATION.

**Wroclaw** (ˌvrotswaf), Ger. *Breslau,* city (1984 est. pop. 632,000), SW Poland, on the Oder (Odra) R. It is a port and an industrial centre with manufactures such as machines and textiles. Settled before the 11th cent., it became (1163) the capital of SILESIA and passed to BOHEMIA (1335), the HABSBURGS (1526), and PRUSSIA (1742). In 1945 it was given to Poland, and its German residents were expelled. Historic buildings include a 13th-cent. cathedral and a Gothic town hall.

**wrought iron,** commercially purified IRON. In the Aston process, pig iron is refined in a Bessemer converter (see BESSEMER PROCESS) and then poured into molten iron-silicate slag. The resulting semisolid mass is passed between rollers that squeeze out most of the slag. Wrought iron is tough, malleable, ductile, and corrosion-resistant, and melts only at high temperature. It is used to make ornamental ironwork, rivets, bolts, pipes, chains, and anchors.

**Wuhan,** city (1984 pop. 6,005,900), capital of HUBEI prov., central China, at the junction of the Han and Yangtze rivers. The great industrial, commercial, and transport hub of central China, Wuhan comprises the former cities of Hankou, Hanyang, and Wuchang. Wuhan is a centre of the Chinese iron and steel industry, which is expanding with the aid of W. German, Japanese, and American engineers. Its strategic location has given it historic importance as a military centre. Following the Treaty of Nanjing (1861), Hankou became a foreign treaty port and in 1923 it was one of the central sites of the 'February 7th' strike, the first large-scale industrial strike in China's history. In 1957 a bridge was built across the Yangtze R., N–S traffic previously having to be ferried across the river.

**Wuhsi:** see WUXI.

**Wundt, Wilhelm Max** (voont), 1832–1920, German physiologist and psychologist. He taught and conducted experiments at the universities of Heidelberg and Leipzig, and is regarded as the founder of experimental psychology. Wundt's scientific career was extraordinarily long and wide ranging, and his interests covered areas as diverse as physiological psychology, animal behaviour, the psychology of language, and cross-cultural psychology; though best known as an experimentalist, Wundt also held observational methods and independent theoretical work to be indispensable to psychology.

**Wu P'ei-fu** (wooh pay fooh), 1874–1939, Chinese general. After military service under the Ch'ing dynasty, he supported YUAN SHIKAI as president of China. After 1916 Wu warred with other leaders for control of N China. He was defeated (1926) by CHIANG KAI-SHEK's Northern Expedition.

**Wuppertal** (ˌvupəˈtahl), city (1984 pop. 381,900), North Rhine–Westphalia, W West Germany, on the Wupper R. The administrative area of Wuppertal dates from 1929, resulting from the merger of Barmen, Elberfeld and a number of smaller towns. The Wupper valley was important for bleaching cloth by the 16th cent. and textile manufacture and finishing continues, especially in Barmen, where ribbons and tapes are a speciality. Electrical engineering is also well represented. The Wuppertal Tanztheater is one of the world's leading modern dance companies.

**Württemberg** (ˌvooətəmˈbeək), former state, SW Germany. STUTTGART was the capital. It included the Swabian Jura in the S and part of the Black Forest in the W, and was divided between the medieval duchies of FRANCONIA and SWABIA. Under the HOLY ROMAN EMPIRE, the counts of Württemberg expanded (after the 11th cent.) their territory and were raised to ducal rank in 1495. Under Duke Frederick II (later King FREDERICK I), Württemberg, through its alliance with NAPOLEON I, acquired additional territory and became an electorate (1803) and a kingdom (1806). It supported Prussia in the AUSTRO-PRUSSIAN WAR (1866) and the FRANCO-PRUSSIAN WAR (1870–71) and joined (1871) the German empire. The monarchy was abolished in 1918, and in 1919 Württemberg joined the Weimar Republic. Temporarily partitioned after WORLD WAR II, it was incorporated into the new West German state of Baden-Württemberg in 1952.

**Würzburg,** city (1984 pop. 129,700), Bavaria, West Germany, on the MAIN R. A centre of the Franconian wine trade, its industries also include printing and engineering. A see was created in 741 and its prince-bishops played a dominant role until 1802. They were responsible for the medieval castle (the Marienburg), the university (1582), and the 18th-cent. Baroque palace. The Romanesque cathedral is 11th–13th cent.

**Wuxi** or **Wuhsi** (wooh shee), city (1984 pop. 3,844,800), S JIANGSU prov., E China, on the GRAND CANAL. Long famous for its silks and scenery, Wuxi remains a centre of the silk industry and an important tourist attraction, partly centred around Lake Tai. It is also well known for its high-technology and light industrial products.

**Wyatt, James,** 1746–1813, English architect. Prolific, variable, and brilliantly superficial, Wyatt was regarded as a rival to Robert ADAM, who complained, with some justification, that Wyatt imitated his work. Wyatt took over as surveyor-general from Sir William Chambers, made his reputation with the London Pantheon in Oxford Street (1770), and designed more than 130 buildings, including Heaton Hall, Manchester (1772) and Dodington, Gloucestershire (1798–1808) with its Greek portico. More celebrated were his adventures in the Gothic style, especially Lee Priory in Kent (1782) and the notorious Fonthill Abbey in Wiltshire built (1795–1807) for William Beckford who commissioned a romantic residence to be partly in ruins. The huge central tower fell down and the client's wishes were thus satisfied. Wyatt was also responsible for major restoration works, generally regarded as disastrous, on the cathedrals of Lichfield, Durham, Salisbury, and Hereford.

**Wyatt, Sir Thomas,** 1503–42, English poet, courtier, and diplomat. He travelled abroad in the service of HENRY VIII, and had a friendship (possibly adulterous) with ANNE BOLEYN before her marriage to the King. His poems include the earliest English sonnets many of them based on PETRARCA and Serafino; translations from the PSALMS; reflective satires; and other lyrics, rondeaux and lute songs.

**Wyatt, Sir Thomas,** d. 1554, English rebel. Objecting to MARY I's planned marriage to PHILIP II of Spain, he raised an army in Kent and marched (1554) on London. He failed to capture Mary or take the city, and was hanged for treason.

**Wycherley, William** (ˌwichəlee), 1640?–1716, English dramatist. His comedies include *Love in a Wood* (1671), *The Gentleman Dancing-Master* (1672), *The Country Wife* (1674), and *The Plain Dealer* (1676). Although the most vicious and licentious of RESTORATION comic dramatists, he earned a prominent place in English stage history with his brilliant wit and satire.

**Wyclif, Wycliffe, Wickliffe** or **Wiclif, John** (ˌwiklif), c.1328–1384, English reformer and philosopher who taught at Oxford. He believed that Christ is mankind's overlord and championed the people against the abuses of the church. Wyclif attacked orthodox church doctrine, especially that of transubstantiation, and held that the Scriptures are the supreme authority. Condemned (1377, 1382) as a heretic, he was left undisturbed in his retirement. His teachings were spread by 'poor priests' (see LOLLARDY) and influenced John HUSS. Wyclif began work on the first English translation of the Latin Bible.

**Wyeth, Andrew Newell** (ˌwieəth), 1917–, American painter; son of the illustrator N.C. Wyeth. One of the most popular contemporary American painters, Wyeth portrays the people and places of rural Pennsylvania and Maine in a meticulous, naturalistic style that is so intense and immediate as to appear surreal.

**Wynkyn dc Worde,** d. 1534, English printer and publisher; b. Alsace as Jan van Wynkyn. He arrived in London c.1477 and was apprenticed to William CAXTON, whose business at Westminster he carried on after Caxton's death in 1491. In 1500 he moved the business to FLEET STREET (which was subsequently to become the centre of the nation's journalism industry) and in 1509 he opened a shop in St Paul's churchyard. It is estimated that he printed approximately 800 books, including the second edition of *Mort d'Arthur* (1498) and the third edition of the *Canterbury Tales*. He published the earliest collection of *Carols* in 1521, which included the 'Boar's Head Carol'.

**Wyoming,** state of the US (1984 est. pop. 511,000), area 253,597 km² (97,914 sq mi), situated in the W, bordered by Montana (N), South Dakota and Nebraska (E), Colorado and Utah (S), and Idaho (W). CHEYENNE is the capital and Casper is the largest city. Wyoming is covered by the GREAT PLAINS in the E and by the ROCKY MTS in the W; the BLACK HILLS are located in the NE corner. Almost 50% of the land is owned by the federal government. Mining is the leading source of income for Wyoming, which is the second largest producer of coal; petroleum, natural gas, and uranium are also important. Agriculture is dominated by cattle- and sheep-ranching, while sugar beet is grown on irrigated land, and grain crops on dry land. The Yellowstone National Park, rodeos, hunting, and fishing provide a thriving tourist industry. The small manufacturing sector is dominated by petroleum refining and chemical production. Although Wyoming is the most sparsely populated state after Alaska, the population grew by over 40% in the 1970s; in 1980 92% was non-Hispanic white. The region was inhabited by Indians who hunted buffalo, including the Crow, Shoshone, Cheyenne, Arapaho, and Sioux, when fur-traders arrived in the early 19th cent. The first settlers came via the Oregon Trail in the 1840s and then with the railway (1868), subduing the Indians and starting ranching. Conflicts among settlers and cattle- and sheep-ranchers led to the war of Johnson County (1892) and other violent clashes. Wyoming's mineral wealth has led to a precarious prosperity and has also placed a serious burden on services and infrastructure.

**Wyspiański, Stanislaw** (vis‚pyanyəskee), 1869–1907, Polish dramatist, painter, and poet. With such plays as *The Legion* (1900) he founded modern Polish drama. His artistic work includes murals, stained-glass windows, and costumes.

**Wyss, Johann David** (vees), 1743–1818, Swiss author. He wrote the children's classic *The Swiss Family Robinson* (1813), based on Daniel DEFOE's *Robinson Crusoe*. His son, **Johann R. Wyss**, 1781–1830, was professor of philosophy at Berne and wrote the Swiss national anthem.

**Wyszynski, Stefan Cardinal** (vi‚zinskee), 1901–81, Roman Catholic primate of POLAND (1949–81). He was imprisoned (1953–56) by the Communist authorities. After his release, however, he achieved a degree of church autonomy unequalled in any other Communist country.

**Xe,** chemical symbol of the element XENON.

**Xenakis, Iannis** (zen‚ahkis), 1922–, French composer, architect, and civil engineer; b. Romania. Born of Greek parents, he lived in Greece from 1932 to 1947, during which time he joined the Greek resistance, and then moved to Paris. He was assistant to the architect Le Corbusier (1948–59), and in his compositions he has used models from architecture, physics, and mathematics, especially the mathematics of probability, for which he has introduced the term 'stochastic music'. His compositions include *Metastaseis* (1953–54) for orchestra, *Nomos alpha* (1965) for cello, and *Orient–Occident* (1960).

**xenon** (‚zeenon, ‚zenon), (Xe), gaseous element, discovered spectroscopically in 1898 by William RAMSAY and M.W. Travers. It is a rare, colourless, odourless, tasteless INERT GAS used in certain photographic-flash lamps, in high-intensity arc lamps for motion-picture projection, in high-pressure arc lamps to produce ultraviolet light, and in numerous radiation-detection instruments. See ELEMENT (table); PERIODIC TABLE.

**Xenophon** (‚zenəfən), c.430 BC–c.355 BC, Greek historian. A well-to-do young disciple of SOCRATES, he joined the Greek force (the Ten Thousand) that supported CYRUS THE YOUNGER of Persia. They fought well, but after the disastrous battle of Cunaxa (401 BC), they were left to fight their way home through unknown and hostile land. Xenophon told the story of this heroic retreat in his most famous work, the *Anabasis*. His other works include the *Hellenica* (a history of Greece, beginning where THUCYDIDES left off) and the *Memorabilia* [memoirs of Socrates]. After 394 BC he lived and wrote in exile in Peloponnese, though his citizen rights at Athens were restored c.369.

**xerography:** see PHOTOCOPYING.

**xerophyte,** botanical term for a plant growing in dry situations. It usually has a reduced surface area, with small leaves having protected gas exchange pores (stomata), e.g., the CONIFERS, or having succulent leaves or water-storing stems, e.g., CACTI.

**Xerxes,** d. 465 BC, king of Persia (r.485–465 BC). A member of the ACHAEMENID dynasty, he was the son of DARIUS I. Seeking to avenge his father's defeat at Marathon, Xerxes set out with vast forces to conquer Greece; at first successful, beating the Greeks at Thermopylae, he was defeated at the sea-battle of Salamis by THEMISTOCLES. He is the King Ahasuerus in the book of Esther in the Bible, and is the hero of an opera by Handel.

**Xhosa,** (‚khawsə), Bantu-speaking people of S Africa, formerly called Kaffirs by European colonialists. Farmers and cattle raisers, the Xhosa, who inhabited their lands for centuries before European settlement, lived traditionally in patrilineal clans governed by an elected chief and council. Today they live mostly in the BANTUSTAN of Transkei, but many travel to white areas of South Africa for employment.

**Xiamen** or **Amoy** (sheeah mun), city (1984 pop. 1,005,600), FUJIAN prov., SE China, facing TAIWAN across the Taiwan Strait. An important modern-day port and trading centre, it was forced open to foreign commerce and declared a treaty port in 1842. In 1984 a small special economic zone (see SHENZHEN) was established to encourage foreign investment, particularly from overseas Chinese many of whom originated from Fujian prov.

**Xi'an** or **Sian** (‚shee ‚an), city (1984 pop. 5,445,600), capital of SHAANXI prov., N central China, in the Wei river valley. Located on the main E–W railway, X'ian is the primary transport centre for central China, and one of China's industrial and commercial hubs. It produces machinery, textiles, and light industrial products and is an important cultural centre. The tomb of Qin Shi Huangdi, the Qin dynasty emperor, who unified China in 221 BC, was discovered in Xi'an in 1974. Filled with thousands of full-sized terra-cotta horses and soldiers, it is one of China's most important archaeological sites and tourist attractions.

The terra-cotta army from the tomb of Qin Shi Huangdi, **Xi'an**

**Xi Jiang,** river, S China, 2300 km (1437 mi) China's third longest river. It rises in the Yunnan plateau and flows SE receiving water from a variety of tributaries including the Lijiang which flows southwards from the karst limestone country of Guilin. The Xi Jiang carried much sediment and in its lower reaches has deposited a large flood plain and delta on which the major commercial centre of GUANGZHOU (Canton) is sited. Near its mouth the Xi Jiang is better known as the Pearl R.

**Xinjiang** or **Sinkiang** (‚shingjeeahng, ‚sinkyang), autonomous region (1985 est. pop. 12,830,000), 1,600,000 km² (617,760 sq mi), W China; bordered by the Soviet Union and the Peoples Republic of Mongolia (N), and by Afghanistan, Pakistan, and India (W). China's largest administrative unit, the total border is over 5000 km (c.3110 mi) long and includes sections bordering the provinces of QINGHAI and TIBET. Major cities include the capital, Urumqi (Urumchi), and Karamai and Kashgar. Xinjiang is part of the extensive central Asian complex of mountains, plateaus, and basins. Mountains fringe the province and the Tian Shan Mts run W to E through the centre, separating the Tarim Basin in the south from the Dzungaria Basin in the north. The central areas of these basins are extensive deserts, and settlements are mainly based at oases on the bordering gravel terraces and in the valleys of the Tarim and Ili rivers. To the east, the GANSU corridor has been the traditional overland route from China to W Asia. The province has a continental climate with low annual rainfall and very cold winters. The physical conditions largely explain the area's limited economic development and small population.

Cultivation is largely limited to the river valleys and the oases. Wheat and rice are basic crops, and cash crops include cotton and fruits, such as grapes, apples, and pears. Much of the land is best suited to (poor) pasture and Xinjiang is an important livestock area. Since 1949 the province has been more effectively linked to the rest of China—the Xinjiang railroad was completed in 1963 and links Urumqi with Lanzhou in Gansu province, and there has been increased investment in the area's vast and varied mineral deposits. A petroleum field has been developed on a small scale in the W Dzungaria Basin and there are large reserves in the Tarim Basin, though remoteness has hindered their development. Industrialization is limited; the main industry is light engineering. Other than Tibet, Xinjiang is the only province in which the minority peoples outnumber the Chinese. Minorities constitute about 60% of the total population and include Uygur, Kazak, Hui, Kirgiz, and Mongol peoples. Since 1949 there has been extensive Han migration to the area, particularly of demobilized troops. The army has been prominent in the reclamation of much of the area's farmland. Xinjiang has only recently become part of the Chinese state and cultural area. In Chinese the name means 'new territory'. Although, during the Han (202 BC–AD 220) and Tang (AD 610–906) dynasties, Chinese military and political power occasionally penentrated this far west, these largely nomadic peoples kept their political and cultural independence. But in the 18th cent. the Qing (Ch'ing) dynasty extended its power westwards to capture much of what is now Xinjiang. As the Chinese state disintegrated in the early 20th cent., the people of the area found themselves under local warlord control and Soviet influence. Since 1949 the area has been firmly integrated into the rest of China.

**Xizang:** see TIBET.

**Xochimilco,** lake S. of Mexico City to which it is connected by the man-made canal La Viga. Famous for its *chinampas* or 'floating gardens', which originated as pre-Colombian intensive irrigated cropping systems, it is now primarily a tourist attraction for boating excursions.

**X-ray,** invisible, highly penetrating ELECTROMAGNETIC RADIATION of much shorter wavelength (higher frequency) than visible light. The wavelength range for X-rays is from about $10^{-8}$ m to about $10^{-11}$ m. Discovered in 1895 by Wilhelm ROENTGEN, X-rays are produced by the impact of high-energy electrons (of several thousands of eV) on a metal anode in a highly evacuated glass bulb. Among other applications, X-rays are used in the study of crystal structure and in the diagnosis and treatment of disease (see RADIOLOGY; RADIOTHERAPY).

**xylem:** see STEM; WOOD.

**xylophone,** a pitched PERCUSSION INSTRUMENT, consisting of a set of wooden bars of varying lengths, played with hard-headed beaters. The orchestral xylophone has a range of about three octaves. A xylophone with tubular resonators is known as a marimba. Xylophones are found in many different musical traditions round the world, e.g., in the *gamelan* orchestras of Bali and Java.

**XYZ Affair,** name given to an incident (1797–98) in Franco-American diplomatic relations. In 1797 Pres. John ADAMS named a three-man commission—John MARSHALL, Elbridge GERRY, and C.C. Pinckney—to resolve Franco-American disputes. It was hinted to them that the French foreign minister, Charles Maurice de TALLEYRAND, would require bribes and loans totalling $250,000 before talks could begin. The commissioners held secret negotiations concerning the money with three of Talleyrand's agents, later designated in despatches as X, Y, and Z. When news of the talks became public and created an uproar in the US, the whole mission collapsed. Franco-American differences were finally settled by the Convention of 1800.

**Y**, chemical symbol of the element YTTRIUM.

**Yahweh:** see GOD.

**Yahya Khan, Agha Muhammad,** 1917–80, Pakistani general and president (1969–71). He was commander in chief of the army (1966–69) and succeeded Gen. AYUB KHAN as president. The defeat (1971) of Pakistan's army and the secession of Bangladesh from Pakistan forced his resignation. He was placed under house arrest for five years.

**yak,** bovine MAMMAL (*Bos grunniens*) of TIBET and adjacent regions. Oxlike in build, with humped shoulders, a long, thick coat, and large, upcurved horns, it has been hunted to near extinction. The wild yak may reach 165 cm (65 in) at the shoulder. Today yaks live in isolated herds at elevations above 4500 m (14,000 ft). Long domesticated, they are a source of milk, meat, and leather, and are used as draught animals.

**Yalta Conference,** 1945, meeting at Yalta (Crimea, USSR), of British Prime Min. CHURCHILL, US Pres. F.D. ROOSEVELT, and Soviet Premier STALIN. Among the chief decisions agreed upon by the 'Big Three' were these: (1) a four-power occupation of Germany (with France being the fourth power); (2) a founding conference for the UN to be held later that year; (3) the Soviet Union's agreement to enter the war against Japan after Germany's defeat; receiving occupation areas in the East in return; and (4) a guarantee of representative government in Poland. Because of the secrecy of its agreements and what were considered by some to be undue concessions to the Soviet Union, the Yalta Conference has long been the subject of heated controversy.

**Yalu,** river, c.800 km (500 mi) long, flowing generally southwest to the Bay of Korea at Dandong and forming part of the China–North Korea border. The river generates hydroelectricity at the Supung Dam above Sinuiju, North Korea, and is also used for floating timber to sawmills. China's involvement in•the KOREAN WAR began (1950) when its troops crossed the Yalu.

**yam,** common name for some members of the family Dioscoreaceae, tropical and subtropical climbing herbs and shrubs with starchy RHIZOMES often cultivated for food. The thick rhizomes, especially of the genus *Dioscorea,* often weigh up to 15 kg (30 lbs) and are an important food source for humans and livestock. The SWEET POTATO, often erroneously called yam, belongs to the MORNING GLORY family.

**Yamani, Sheikh Ahmed Zaki,** 1930–, Saudi Arabian petroleum and mineral resources minister (1962–86). The longest-serving and most influential oil minister within the ORGANIZATION OF THE PETROLEUM EXPORTING COUNTRIES, he masterminded the sharp rise of world oil prices in the 1970s while generally exercising a moderating influence. He was unexpectedly dismissed (1986) in an apparent switch in Saudi oil policy.

**Yan'an** or **Yenan** (ˌyenˌan), city (1984 pop. 3,853,600), N SHAANXI prov., N central China. It is a regional market centre. Famed as the terminus of the LONG MARCH (1934–35) and capital of the Chinese Communist base areas (1936–47), the city and its monuments attracted millions of visitors in the 1960s and 1970s. Since 1978 and the deemphasis of Mao Zedong's leadership, far fewer visitors have gone to Yan'an.

**Yangtze** or **Changjiang,** great river of China, c.5550 km (3450 mi) long; the longest river in Asia. It rises as the Jinsha in SW China, forms the Yangtze proper at Yibin, and continues generally E c.2410 km (1500 mi) through rich agricultural and industrial regions to enter the EAST CHINA SEA in a vast delta near SHANGHAI. The river is China's chief commercial artery and is navigable by ocean vessels for c.970 km (600 mi), to WUHAN. The great Gezhouba Dam, opened in 1981 and completed in 1986, was built across the river at Yichang, to regulate seasonally fluctuating water levels and harness the river's great hydroelectric potential (2.7 billion kW) as it leaves the spectacular Yangtze gorges. There are plans for an even more ambitious scheme upstream in the Three Gorges section of the river (see HUBEI).

**Yantai, Yentai** or **Chefoo,** city (1984 pop. 699,400), SHANDONG prov., E coast of China. A developing port and industrial centre, in 1984 it was designated one of the 14 coastal cities to welcome outside investment. In the 19th cent. it developed as a summer resort for Westerners, and as a missionary centre. It remains an important tourist area based on its beaches. It is also famous for its wines and brandy.

**Yaoundé** (yaoohnˌday), city (1984 est. pop. 552,000), capital of the United Republic of Cameroon. It is the country's administrative, financial, and communications centre, and a regional trade centre for coffee, cocoa, copra, sugarcane, and rubber. Established as a military outpost by the Germans in 1899, the town flourished as a centre of administration after 1907. It was (1919–40, 1946–60) the capital of the French CAMEROONS and became (1960) the capital of the United Republic of Cameroon.

**yard:** see ENGLISH UNITS OF MEASUREMENT; WEIGHTS AND MEASURES, table.

**Yarmuk,** river, 90 km (50 mi) long, major tributary of the JORDAN R. Rising in S Syria and N Jordan, it forms the boundary between these countries for some miles. It also borders the GOLAN HEIGHTS on the south before entering the Jordan R. S of the sea of Galilee (see GALILEE, SEA OF). It flows in a deep and spectacular gorge and provides almost half the total flow of the Jordan R.

**Yaroslav,** 978–1054, grand duke of Kiev (r.1019–54); son of VLADIMIR I. Designated by his father to rule Novgorod, he wrested Kiev from his brother. He consolidated Kiev's power, but civil war among his sons followed his death.

**Yaroslaval,** city (1985 pop. 626,000), central European USSR, on the Volga R. 260 km (162 mi) NE of Moscow. It is an industrial and oil-refining centre, and river port where the railway line from Moscow to Arkhangelsk crosses the Volga R. It produces textiles, petrochemicals, ships, synthetic rubber, and tyres, and was founded in 1024.

**yaws,** tropical infectious disease, mainly of early childhood, caused by a spirochaete bacterium, *Treponema pertenue,* and transmitted by contact with infected persons or their clothing, and by insects. An ulcerating lesion appears at the site of contact followed by fever and pains, with similar lesions later appearing all over the body. If untreated, the lesions deteriorate into deep ulcers affecting the bones. The disease can be treated with PENICILLIN. Infection with the disease confers considerable natural immunity.

**Yb,** chemical symbol of the element YTTERBIUM.

**year,** time required for the Earth to complete one orbit about the Sun. The **tropical,** or **solar, year** measured relative to the Sun is the time (365 days, 5 hr, 48 min, 46 sec of mean SOLAR TIME) between successive vernal EQUINOXES. The **sidereal year** is the time (365 days, 6 hr, 9 min, 9.5 sec of mean solar time) required for the Earth to complete an orbit of the Sun relative to the stars; it is longer than the tropical year because of the

PRECESSION OF THE EQUINOXES. The **anomalistic year** is the time (365 days, 6 hr, 13 min, 53.0 sec of mean solar time) required for the Earth to go from its perihelion point once around the Sun and back to this point; its greater length is due to the slow rotation of the Earth's orbit as a whole.

**yeast,** name for certain microscopic, unicellular FUNGI, and for commercial products consisting of masses of yeast cells. Yeasts consist of oval or round cells that reproduce mainly by budding (a small outgrowth on the cell's surface increases in size until a wall forms to separate the new individual, or bud) but also by means of SPORES. They are used in alcoholic FERMENTATION and to leaven BREAD. Brewer's yeast is high in B-complex vitamins and is used as a dietary supplement. It is also used to make yeast-extract spreads which are used in sandwiches and hot drinks. Certain other fungi are also sometimes called yeasts.

**Yeats, William Butler,** 1865–1939, Irish poet and playwright. The son of an artist, he studied painting and lived in London and in Sligo, where many of his poems are set. Fascinated by Irish legend and the occult, he soon became a leader of the IRISH LITERARY RENAISSANCE. *The Wanderings of Oisin* (1889), a narrative poem, and the lyric collections *The Rose* (1893) and *The Wind Among the Reeds* (1899) combine an interest in SYMBOLISM with an intense nationalism, a feeling strengthened by his hopeless passion for the Irish patriot Maud Gonne. Verses from this period include 'The Lake Isle of Innisfree' and 'When You Are Old'. In 1898 he helped found the Irish Literary Theatre, where his *The Countess Cathleen* (1899) and *Cathleen ni Houlihan* (1902) were performed. *The Hour Glass* (1904), *The Land of Heart's Desire* (1904), and *Deirdre* (1907) appeared at the ABBEY THEATRE. His prose tales were collected in *The Celtic Twilight* (1893) and the symbolic *Secret Rose* (1897). As he grew older, Yeats's poetry moved from transcendentalism to a more physical realism. Polarities between the physical and the spiritual were central in poems like 'Sailing to Byzantium' and 'The Second Coming'. His later volumes such as *Michael Robartes and the Dancer* (1921), *The Tower* (1928) and *Last Poems* (1939) contain some of the greatest 20th-cent. verse in English. The prose *A Vision,* an occult view of history written after 1917 with his wife, Georgie Hyde-Lees, was a source for much of his later work. Yeats received the Nobel Prize in literature in 1923.

**yellow fever,** acute infectious disease caused by a virus transmitted by the bite of the female *Aëdes aegypti* mosquito. It causes fever, chills, prostration, JAUNDICE, and, in severe cases, internal haemorrhage, renal failure, and death. Endemic to many tropical and subtropical areas, the disease is one of six notifiable to the WORLD HEALTH ORGANIZATION and now usually occurs only in sporadic outbreaks. Immunization is an effective preventive measure and is essential for visitors to endemic areas.

**Yellowknife,** town (1980 est. pop. 9,981), capital of the Northwest Territories, NW Canada, on Great Slave Lake and the Yellowknife R. It was founded in 1935, moved to a new site in 1945, and became the territorial capital in 1967. Gold mining is the principal industry.

**Yellow River,** Chinese *Huang He,* great river of N China, c.4830 km (c.3000 mi) long; sometimes called 'China's Sorrow' for the devastating floods once common along its lower course. From the Qinghai Mountains, its source in Qinghai prov., W China, it flows generally E, with a 'great northern bend' (around the Ordos Desert), to the mouth on the Gulf of Bohai, an arm of the YELLOW SEA N of the Shandong Peninsula. The river is named after the great quantities of yellow silt that it carries from China's fertile loess land region and has deposited seawards over the millennia to form a great, now densely populated delta called the North China Plain. In its lower course the silt-filled river has raised its bed higher than the surrounding countryside. For centuries dykes have been built to contain the floodwaters, but when the dykes have broken devasting floods have occurred. Many died when, in the late 19th cent., the river changed its outlets from S of the Shandong Peninsula to its present outlet. In 1938 the dykes were deliberately broken to try to stem the Japanese advance. Since 1949 a major construction programme has been developed, designed to control future flooding and harness the river for increased irrigation and hydroelectric power. The Sanmen Gorge, E of XI'AN, is one of the major dams built for that purpose.

**Yellow Sea** or **Huang Hai,** western arm of the Pacific Ocean, between China's east coast and Korea. The shallow sea, which has a maximum depth of c.150 m (500 ft), is underlaid by potentially rich oil deposits. Bo Hai, in the northwest, is the largest inlet. South of Korea it becomes the EAST CHINA SEA.

**Yeltsin, Boris,** 1931–, Soviet politician and Communist reformer. His outspoken criticism of conservatism provoked his dismissal as first secretary of the Moscow City Communist Party (1987) and as a candidate politburo member (1988). In 1989, however, he won overwhelming popular election to the restyled Congress of People's Deputies, from which he secured a seat on the Supreme Soviet.

**Yemen, North,** officially the Yemen Arab Republic, republic (1987 est. pop. 7,200,000), 195,000 km² (75,290 sq mi), SW Asia, on the SW Arabian peninsula, bordered by Saudi Arabia (N, NE), South Yemen (SE), and the Red Sea (W). SANA is the capital and HODEIDA the main port. The country consists of a narrow, coastal plain, highlands rising to more than 3660 m (12,000 ft) in the interior, and a portion of the great Rub al Khali desert in the east. The highlands are the wettest part of ARABIA; the rainy season is from April to September. Yemen is very poor, with a per capita income that is among the lowest in the world (US$443 in 1981). Most of the population is engaged in growing grains, vegetables, fruits, cotton, coffee, and qat (a narcotic shrub), and raising sheep, goats, and camels. Manufacturing, largely based on agricultural products, provides little revenue, and salt is the only commercially exploitable mineral. Handicrafts play an important role in the economy, as do remittances sent home by the 1,400,000 Yemenis working abroad, mainly in Saudi Arabia. The great majority of the inhabitants are Arabs, about equally divided between Zaidi Shiite and Shafai Sunnite Muslims. Arabic is the official and universal language.

*History.* Once part of the ancient Sabaean kingdom (fl. c.750 BC–115 BC), Yemen was later ruled by the Himyarites, Romans, Ethiopians, and Persians. In the 7th cent. AD the area became a province of the Muslim caliphate, and after the caliphate's fall it was ruled by the Rassite dynasty, imams of the Zaidi sect of Islam, until 1962. Yemen was nominally part of the OTTOMAN EMPIRE from the 16th cent. until 1918. In 1962 an army coup led to the proclamation of a republic. Civil war followed, with Egypt supporting the republicans and Saudi Arabia and Jordan backing the royalists; it ended in 1970 with the republic in place. In 1972 war erupted with South Yemen; following a ceasefire, an agreement to merge the two states was signed but not implemented. Fighting broke out again in 1979, and despite reaffirmation of unification plans, progress toward unity remained elusive. Meanwhile, Pres. Ahmed Hussein el Ghashmi had been assassinated in 1978 and succeeded by Ali Abdullah Saleh, who was reelected for a five-year term in 1983.

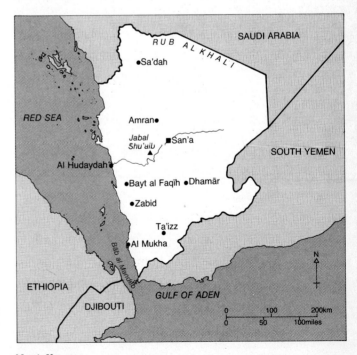

North Yemen

**Yemen, South,** officially the People's Democratic Republic of Yemen, republic (1987 est. pop. 2,500,000), 287,683 km² (111,074 sq mi), SW Asia, on the S Arabian peninsula, bordered by Saudi Arabia (N), Oman

(E), the Gulf of Aden (S), and North Yemen (NW). Southern Yemen also includes several islands, e.g., Perim and SOCOTRA. The capital is ADEN. A narrow coastal plain rises to a highland plateau fringed in the northeast by the sandy wastes of the Rub al Khali desert. In the centre of the country is Wadi Hadhramaut, a fertile valley, with South Yemen's best farmland. South Yemen is one of the world's poorest nations. Agriculture, mostly of a subsistence nature, is the mainstay of the economy; coffee, cotton, dates, tobacco, and grain are grown, and livestock is raised. Fishing is a major activity along the coast. The refining of imported petroleum is the most important industry. The GNP is US$900 million and the GNP per capita US$457 (1982). Most of the people are Sunni Muslim Arabs, and Arabic is the official language.

*History.* Once part of a larger region called Al-Yaman, where the Minaean, Sabaean, and Himyarite empires flourished in ancient times, the area that is now South Yemen was conquered by Muslim Arabs in the 7th cent. AD. In the 16th cent. it became part of the OTTOMAN EMPIRE. The British entered the area in 1839, and between 1886 and 1914 they signed a number of protectorate treaties with local rulers. Under British rule the area was known as Aden Colony and Protectorate. In the 1960s nationalist groups demanding independence began a terrorist campaign against the British, and independence was granted in 1967. The Marxist National Liberation Front (NLF) gained control of the government and established a left-wing regime with close ties to the USSR, with whom it signed a 20-year treaty of friendship in 1979. After a brief war with its more moderate neighbour, North Yemen, in 1972, an agreement for unification of the two countries was signed but has never been implemented. Sporadic fighting broke out again in 1979, and despite cordial meetings there has been no real progress toward unity. In the 1980s a power struggle within the ruling Yemen Socialist Party (successor to the NLF) culminated in open warfare in Aden in early 1986 from which the pro-Soviet hardliners emerged victorious. Haider Abu Bakr al Attas was subsequently elected for a five-year term as president.

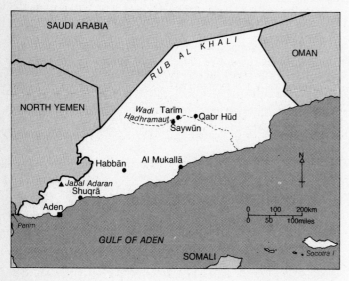

South Yemen

**Yenan:** see YAN'AN.

**Yenisei,** one of the great rivers of Siberia, c.4020 km (2500 mi) long. It is formed by the confluence of the Bolshoi Yenisei and Maly Yenisei rivers near the Mongolian border and flows W, then generally N, to enter the Arctic Ocean through the Kara Sea. The river is frozen during the winter; the ice of its upper course melts earlier in the spring than that of its lower course, causing extensive flooding. Part of the Yenisei's great hydroelectric potential is harnessed at KRASNOYARSK.

**Yentai:** see YANTAI.

**yeoman,** class in English society. It generally means a free landowner of a rank lower than the gentry. Certain retainers in noble and royal households were also called yeomen. The Yeomen of the Guard, often called Beefeaters, became the bodyguard of the English monarch. The more modern military use of the term dates from the 18th cent., when volunteer calvary units called yeomanry were used to suppress riots.

**yerba maté:** see MATÉ.

**Yerevan,** city (1985 pop. 1,133,000), capital of the ARMENIAN SOVIET SOCIALIST REPUBLIC, SE European USSR, on the Razdan R. Its industries include metallurgy, toolmaking, and food processing. Known in the 7th cent. AD, it was the capital of ARMENIA under Persian rule and later (14th–19th cent.) part of the empires of TAMERLANE, Persia, Turkey, and Russia. In 1920 it became the capital of the Armenian SSR.

**Yesenin, Sergei Aleksandrovich** (yi syaynin), 1895–1925, Russian poet. His simple lyrics of peasant life and of nature gave way to such IMAGIST works as *Pugachev* (1922). Disillusionment with the RUSSIAN REVOLUTION (1917), his failed marriages (to the American dancer Isadora DUNCAN, 1922, and to Sophia Tolstoy, 1925), and alcoholism contributed to his suicide.

**Yeshibah,** male college for talmudic study. Study of TORAH is the most important duty for a Jew; and study for a number of years in a Yeshibah is a pre-requisite for mastering the primary Hebrew and Aramaic sources. The Yeshibah also strives to raise its students to a high level of personal piety.

**yeti** or **abominable snowman,** manlike creature associated with the Himalayas. Known only through tracks ascribed to it and alleged encounters, it is supposedly 1.8–2.1 m (6–7 ft) tall and covered with long hair. While many scholars dismiss it as a myth, others claim that it may be a kind of ape. There are reports of a similar creature in North America, with 43-cm (17-in) footprints, called Bigfoot, or Sasquatch.

**Yevtushenko, Yevgeny Aleksandrovich** ('yevtooh shengkoh), 1933–, Soviet poet. With VOZNESENSKY and others he helped revive Russian lyric poetry. In works such as *Babi Yar* (1961) and *The Heirs of Stalin* (1962) he exposed serious defects in Soviet society. His long poems include *The Bratsk Station* (1964–65) and *Kazan University* (1970). Later works such as *A Dove in Santiago* (1978) and *The Mother and the Neutron Bomb* (1982) were more ideologically conformist and critical of the West, but he strongly supported GLASNOST in 1988/89.

**yew,** slow-growing, evergreen tree (*Taxus baccata*), up to 9m (30 ft), related to the CONIFERS, but in the separate order Taxales. Single SEEDS are produced, with hard, stony coats surrounded by a fleshy, red aril.

**Yiddish language,** member of the West Germanic group of the Germanic subfamily of the Indo-European family of languages. Although it is not a national language, Yiddish is spoken by about 4 million Jews all over the world, especially in Argentina, Canada, France, Israel, Mexico, Romania, the US, and the USSR. Before the annihilation of 6 million Jews by the Nazis, Yiddish was the tongue of more than 11 million people. See LANGUAGE (table).

**YMCA:** see YOUNG MEN'S CHRISTIAN ASSOCIATION.

**yoga** [Skt., = union], general term for spiritual disciplines, followed for centuries by devotees of both HINDUISM and BUDDHISM, to attain higher consciousness and liberation from ignorance, suffering, and rebirth. It is also the name of one of the six orthodox systems of INDIAN PHILOSOPHY. *Raja yoga* [royal yoga] was expounded by Patanjali (2nd cent. BC), who divided the practice into eight stages, the highest of which is Samadhi, or identification of the individual consciousness with the Godhead. Hindu tradition in general recognizes three main types of yoga: *jnana yoga,* the path of wisdom and discrimination; *bhakti yoga,* the path of love and devotion to a personal God; and *karma yoga,* the path of selfless action. *Hatha yoga,* widely practiced in the West, emphasizes physical control and postures. The concentration on breathing and the alternative stretching and relaxing designed to affect all parts of the body have been found to have beneficial effects on health, most clearly in lowering raised blood pressure. *Kundalini yoga,* associated with TANTRA, is based on the physiology of the 'subtle body.' It attempts to open centres of psychic energy called *chakras,* said to be located along the spinal column, and to activate the *kundalini,* a force located at the base of the spine. Yoga is usually practised under the guidance of a guru, or spiritual teacher. Contemporary systems of yoga stress attaining spiritual realization without withdrawing from the world, as the older traditions taught.

**yogurt,** a semisolid milk product made by introducing bacteria (usually *Streptococcus* or *Lactobacillus*) into warm milk. It seems to be of Asian origin. There is now in Western countries a large consumer market for fancy yogurts made from skimmed milk and with added flavourings, e.g., chocolate or fruit.

**Yohannes IV,** c.1849–89, emperor of ETHIOPIA (r.1872–89). The ruler of the province of Tigre in N Ethiopia, he won the battle for the imperial title following the suicide of TEWODROS II. His reign was spent desperately defending his empire against a succession of foreign aggressors. During the 1870s he repelled two invasion attempts by Egypt and in 1887 his forces defeated the Italians at Dogali. In 1889 Yohannes lost his life at the hands of the Mahdists (see MAHDI) of Sudan at Metemma.

**Yokohama,** city (1986 est. pop. 3,012,884), capital of Kanagawa prefecture, SE Honshu, Japan. The second largest city and the largest international trade port (opened 1859) in Japan, it is part of the extensive urban-industrial belt around Tokyo. When US Commodore Matthew C. PERRY first visited Yokohama in 1854, it was a small fishing village. Among its present industries are shipyards, steel mills, oil refineries, chemical plants, and many types of factory. Yokohama has the largest China town in Japan, and is currently (1987) undergoing a large urban renewal project.

**Yom Kippur:** see under JEWISH HOLIDAYS.

**York,** city (1981 pop. 123,126), N Yorkshire, N England. Its manufactures include chocolate and precision instruments, and it is a great rail centre. A major Roman military post, it was later important in the Kingdom of NORTHUMBRIA. An archbishopric since the 7th cent., it is the ecclesiastical centre of N England and the site of the Norman cathedral of St Peter (York Minster). ROWNTREE surveyed poverty in the city three times.

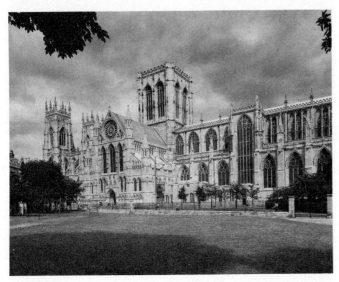

York Minster

**York, house of,** royal house of England, dating from the creation (1385) of Edmund of Langley, fifth son of EDWARD III, as duke of York. The claims to the throne of his grandson, Richard, duke of York, in opposition to HENRY VI, head of the house of LANCASTER, resulted in the Wars of the ROSES. The royal members of the house of York were EDWARD IV, EDWARD V, and RICHARD III. The houses of York and Lancaster were united by the marriage (1486) of the Lancastrian HENRY VII to Elizabeth, daughter of Edward IV.

**Yorktown campaign,** 1781, the closing military operations of the AMERICAN REVOLUTION. After his unsuccessful Carolina campaign (1780–81), Gen. CORNWALLIS retreated into Virginia, fortified Yorktown, and awaited reinforcements from Sir Henry CLINTON in New York. Clinton delayed, however, and the French fleet under Adm. de GRASSE blockaded Chesapeake Bay. Generals Washington and ROCHAMBEAU rushed south with French troops, while STEUBEN and LAFAYETTE maintained a brilliant holding action. Unable to escape, Cornwallis surrendered on 17 Oct. 1781, thereby bringing victory to the rebellious Colonies.

**Yoruba,** people of SW Nigeria, numbering about 13 million. They are unusual among Africans in their tendency to form urban communities. Today many of the largest cities of Nigeria, e.g., LAGOS and IBADAN, are in Yorubaland. The old Yoruba kingdom of Oyo dominated both BENIN and Dahomey, but after 1700 its power slowly waned. In the early 19th cent. the Yoruba were divided among several smaller states.

**Yoshida Shigeru** (‚yohsheedǝh), 1878–1967, Japanese statesman. He led the Liberal Party after 1945 and was prime minister five times between 1946 and 1954. During his administration a new constitution was promulgated, land reforms instituted, and the postwar US occupation ended.

**Young, Brigham,** 1801–77, American MORMON, leader of the Church of Jesus Christ of Latter-Day Saints. He was perhaps a greater moulder of Mormonism than its founder, Joseph SMITH. He became prominent after the persecution of Mormons in Missouri and was a leader in the move to Nauvoo, Illinois. After Smith's assassination (1844), he was the chief figure in maintaining church unity and was henceforth the dominant man in Mormonism. Young led (1846–47) the great migration west and directed the settlement at Salt Lake City. He headed the church, and after the creation of the Utah provisional government, he became territorial governor. Trouble between the US and the Mormons over polygamy and church power led to the US military expedition of 1857–58, but Young avoided an open break with the government, although he lost his post as governor. It seems he had, in total, 27 wives, and unjustified charges of sensuality were often levelled against him. He was, in reality, a stern moralist, as well as a brilliant leader.

**Young, Edward,** 1683–1765, English poet and dramatist, famous for his long didactic poem *The Complaint, or Night Thoughts on Life, Death, and Immortality* (1742–45), an influence on the 'graveyard' aspect of ROMANTICISM. He also wrote a series of satires, *The Universal Passion* (1725–28).

**Young, Lester,** 1909–59, black American musician. Young was, with Coleman HAWKINS, a major influence on tenor saxophone style; his work greatly influenced the modern JAZZ of the 1950s. Billie HOLIDAY gave him the nickname 'President', which later became 'Pres'.

**Young, Michael,** 1915–, British sociologist. He collaborated with Peter WILLMOTT on studies of working-class family life in the 1950s and 60s. Young's *The Rise of the Meritocracy* (1958) is a satire arguing that the social system of the future will be one in which social position will not be ascribed but won, according to the formula *I.Q. + Effort = Merit*.

**Young, Thomas,** 1773–1829, English physicist, physician, and Egyptologist. He was professor of natural philosophy (1801–03) at the ROYAL INSTITUTION, where he presented the modern physical concept of energy, and was elected (1811) a staff member of St George's Hospital, London. He stated (1807) a theory of colour vision known as the Young–Helmholtz theory and described the vision defect called ASTIGMATISM. Reviving the wave theory of LIGHT, Young applied it to refraction and dispersion phenomena. He also established a coefficient of elasticity (Young's modulus; see STRENGTH OF MATERIALS) and helped to decipher the ROSETTA STONE.

**Young Men's Christian Association** (YMCA), organization concerned with the spiritual and social well-being and the physical and intellectual development of young men. Begun (1844) in London, it took root in the US in 1851 and now has branches on all continents. Membership, which is not limited to Christians, was 10 million in 1982.

**Young Plan,** agreed schedule for German REPARATIONS, devised in 1929 by an international committee including the American Owen D. Young (1874–1962), to replace the DAWES PLAN. The Young Plan was adopted in 1930, but the GREAT DEPRESSION disrupted all international payments, and the Plan was abandoned in 1932.

**Young Pretender:** see under STUART, JAMES FRANCIS EDWARD.

**Young's modulus:** see STRENGTH OF MATERIALS.

**Young Turks:** see OTTOMAN EMPIRE.

**Young Women's Christian Association** (YWCA), organization devoted to promoting the welfare of women and girls through opportunities for spiritual, social, intellectual, and physical development. The nondenominational movement grew out of mid-19th-cent. British homes and prayer unions for young women. The world organization, based in Geneva, was established in 1894. In 1982 it included over 2.4 million members.

**Yourcenar, Marguerite,** 1903–87, French novelist; b. Belgium as Marguerite de Crayencour. She has lived in the US since 1939. She is noted for her imaginative reconstructions of historical eras and people, as in *Les mémoires d'Hadrien* (1951), about the Roman emperor, and *L'oeuvre au noir* (1968; tr. The Abyss), set in N Europe in the 16th cent.

In 1980 she became the first woman to be admitted to the French Academy.

**Ypres, battles of,** three major battles of WORLD WAR I fought at Ypres, in SW Belgium. In the first (Oct.–Nov. 1914) the British, at great cost, stopped the German 'race to the sea'. In the second (Apr.–May 1915) the Germans unsuccessfully assaulted the British salient. Poison gas was used for the first time. In the third (Oct.–Nov. 1917), also known as Passchendaele, the British attacked the German line but advanced only 8 km (5 mi) at a cost of 300,000 lives.

**Ypsilanti** or **Hypsilanti,** prominent Greek family of Phanariots. **Alexander Ypsilanti,** c.1725–c.1807, was dragoman (minister) of the Ottoman emperor and *hospodar* [governor] of Walachia (1774–82, 1796–97) and of Moldavia (1768–88). He was executed by the sultan for conspiracy. His son, **Constantine Ypsilanti,** 1760–1816, was *hospodar* of Moldavia (1799–1801) and of Walachia (1802–06). He was deposed for being pro-Russian and was reinstated in 1807 by the Russians. He encouraged the Serbian revolt against Turkey. His elder son, **Alexander Ypsilanti,** 1792–1828, was a leader in the Greek War of Independence and led unsuccessful uprisings in Moldavia and Walachia. After being defeated by the Turks, he was imprisoned in Austria, where he died. His younger brother, **Demetrios Ypsilanti,** 1793–1832, also played a prominent part in the Greek revolt. In 1821 he captured Trípolis, Turkey's chief fort on the Peloponnesus. In 1828 he became commander of the Greek forces in E Greece. He resigned in 1830 after differences with other Greek leaders.

**ytterbium** (i͵tuhbiəm), (Tb), metallic element, discovered by J.C.G. de Marignac in 1878. Soft, malleable, ductile, lustrous, and silver-white, it is one of the RARE-EARTH METALS belonging to the LANTHANIDE SERIES, and forms many compounds. It is widely distributed in a number of minerals, but has no commercial uses. See ELEMENT (table); PERIODIC TABLE.

**yttrium** (͵itriəm), (Y), metallic element, first isolated by Friedrich WÖHLER in 1828. Yttrium is an iron-grey metal, usually included in the RARE-EARTH METALS. Its oxide is used in making red phosphors for colour-television picture tubes. Yttrium oxide, when fused with barium carbonate and copper oxide forms a compound which is superconducting at temperatures up to c.100K. See ELEMENT (table); PERIODIC TABLE.

**Yuan** or **Mongol,** dynasty: see CHINA.

**Yuan Shikai** (yoohan shuh kie), 1859–1916, president of China (1912–16). He was entrusted with defending the Qing empire against the revolution of 1911, but on his advice the Emperor Xuan Tong (Henry PU YI) resigned. Soon after, SUN YAT-SEN, who had been elected the first president of China, resigned in Yuan's favour. Yuan's rule proved dictatorial, and in 1916 he briefly assumed the title of emperor.

**Yucatán,** peninsula, c.181,000 km² (70,000 sq mi), extending from SE Mexico into Belize and Guatemala. It is a low, flat limestone tableland rising to c.150 m (500 ft) in the south. Its northern continuation is the oil-rich Campeche bank, under Campeche Bay and the Gulf of Mexico. The climate is hot and dry in the north, hot and humid in the south. Centuries before the Spanish arrived (early 16th cent.), Yucatán was the seat of the great civilization of the MAYA, whose descendants predominate in today's population. The developing economy is based on tourism and the production of henequen (a fibre), oil, and timber.

**yucca,** stiff-leaved, SUCCULENT shrubs and trees (genus *Yucca*) of the LILY family, native mainly to Mexico and the SW US. Yuccas produce a large stalk, growing up to 4.5m (15 ft), of white or purplish blossoms. They are pollinated by the yucca moth, and in its absence they rarely produce FRUIT. Species include the Adam's-needle (*Y. filamentosa* and others), hardy in Europe, including Britain, and the Spanish dagger or bayonet (*Y. gloriosa*). Roots of some species are used for soap.

**Yugoslavia,** Serbo-Croatian *Jugoslavija,* officially the Socialist Federal Republic of Yugoslavia, federal republic (1987 est. pop. 23,200,000), 255,804 km² (98,766 sq mi), SE Europe, on the Balkan Peninsula; bordered by Italy and the Adriatic Sea (W), Austria and Hungary (N), Romania and Bulgaria (E), and Greece and Albania (S). It is a federation of six People's Republics: SERBIA, CROATIA, BOSNIA AND HERCEGOVINA, MACEDONIA, SLOVENIA, and MONTENEGRO. Principal cities include BELGRADE (the capital), ZAGREB, SKOPJE, SARAJEVO, and LJUBLJANA. About four-fifths of Yugoslavia is mountainous. The chief mountain chain, the Dinaric ALPS, runs parallel to the ADRIATIC coast; the country's high point (2864 m/9396

Yuccas in flower

ft) is the Triglav, in the Julian Alps, in the NW. The island-studded Adriatic coast, known as DALMATIA, is dotted with numerous ports. The most heavily industrial nation in the Balkans, Yugoslavia is rich in minerals, notably lignite, bauxite, iron, and copper. The major industries are metal processing, electronics, and production of textiles, machinery, and chemicals. Crops include corn, wheat, sugar beets, and potatoes, and there are extensive vineyards. Tourism is important. The GNP is $58,520 million and the GNP per capita is $2570 (1983). The Yugoslav people consist of Croats and Slovenes, who use the Roman alphabet and constitute the vast majority of the Roman Catholics (about 30% of the population); and Serbs, Macedonians, and Montenegrins, who use the Cyrillic alphabet and belong to the EASTERN ORTHODOX CHURCH (about 40%) and to ISLAM (about 10%). The Serbs and Croats share the same language, Serbo-Croatian; other ethnic groups have their own languages.

*History.* The Yugoslav state was formed at the end of World War I (1918) when representatives of the South Slavs of the disintegrating Habsburg monarchy declared their independence and sought unification with the victorious Serbian kingdom. Montenegrins deposed their dynasty and did likewise. The movement for Yugoslav union had existed since the 1830s (see YUGOSLAVISM), but came to the fore under the threats of Italian imperialism and social revolution in the ex-Habsburg lands. The proclamation of the Kingdom of Serbs, Croats, and Slovenes under the KARADJORDJEVIĆ dynasty represented unification on Serb terms, as was confirmed by the constitution adopted in 1921. This provided for a parliamentary but unitary state in which Serb practices and institutions were extended to the entire kingdom. Croats and Macedonians (then regarded as Serbs) were especially aggrieved, and political life was chaotic. In 1929 King ALEXANDER established a personal dictatorship and renamed the state Yugoslavia, intending to stifle dissent, impose a nominally Yugoslav identity on his subjects, and secure the country against its rapacious neighbours. He was assassinated in 1934 in an USTAŠE plot backed by Italy and Hungary. No progress was made in solving the national or constitutional questions until, in 1939, Croatia was granted autonomy by Prince Regent Paul. Outraged by this innovation and the country's increasing subjugation to the AXIS powers, Serb officers overthrew Prince Paul in March 1941. Within days Germany and its allies had invaded and dismembered Yugoslavia. Resistance flared when the Axis-imposed Ustaše regime in Croatia began to murder its Serb, Jewish, and Gypsy minorities. Two rival resistance movements sought to direct the struggle: the royalist Serb Četniks of Draža MIHAILOVIĆ and the Communist-led Partisans of Josip Broz TITO. Civil war proceeded alongside anti-Axis resistance. Aided by their appeal to Serbs and non-Serbs alike, by their greater military prowess, by the Allied support that resulted, and by their promise of political and social change, Tito's forces were victorious. King PETER was deposed and Yugoslavia became a Communist-ruled federation allied to and modelling itself on the USSR. But Tito's refusal utterly to subordinate his regime to Moscow led to his expulsion from the COMINFORM (1948) and to reform in Yugoslavia. The Party (renamed League in 1952) sought new legitimacy on the basis of national independence, liberalization and economic development, and decentralization through workers' self-management. When economic difficulties and nationalism re-emerged in the 1960s, further decentralization was decreed, with the republics and provinces—and their Communist elites—gaining effective control over their own affairs. At Tito's death in 1980, Yugoslavia had become a loose confederation with a complex, collective, and ethnically balanced system of government which was better fitted to forestall domination of one people or republic by another than to cope with economic or political crises. In fact, in the 1980s ethnic conflict as well as economic and political crises intensified in Yugoslavia.

Yugoslavia

**Yugoslavism** (Serbo-Croat *Jugoslavenstvo*), a nationalist idea and movement originating in Croatia in the 19th cent. and advocating the cultural, linguistic, and, ultimately, political unification of the South Slavs (Serbs, Croats, Slovenes, and, sometimes, Bulgarians). Modern Yugoslavism was the creation of Ljudevit Gaj (1809–72), a journalist and linguistic reformer, who sought to create the linguistic basis for union by convincing Croats to adopt as their literary language the same variant of Serbo-Croat as was being urged on the Serbs by Vuk KARADŽIĆ. From the 1860s, Bishop J. J. Strossmayer of Djakovo (1815–1905) offered a less romantic version of Yugoslavism, preaching Slav reciprocity, enlightenment, toleration, and practical cooperation. He had little success, either in overcoming Serbs' suspicious of a programme emanating from the Catholic Habsburg monarchy or in rallying Croats increasingly drawn to the greater Croatian nationalism of Ante Starčević (1823–96). Collaboration between South Slav politicians in Austria–Hungary gave new life to the Yugoslav idea in the early 20th cent., and during World War I the Yugoslav Committee worked successfully abroad to promote the cause of a Yugoslav state. However, the state formed in 1918 disappointed many, being seen as a greater Serbia rather than a free and equal association of peoples. King ALEXANDER's

efforts to impose a common Yugoslav identity in the 1930s, and attempts by the Communists in the 1950s to forge a higher Yugoslav culture, both provoked resentment. Today Yugoslavism means merely the acceptance of the need for a Yugoslav state as a community of sovereign peoples.

**Yukawa, Hideki,** 1907–81, Japanese physicist. In 1935 he predicted the existence of the meson, an ELEMENTARY PARTICLE that is heavier than an electron but lighter than a proton and that generates the strong nuclear force between particles in the atomic nucleus. After particles corresponding to his prediction were discovered in 1947, Yukawa was awarded the 1949 Nobel Prize for physics.

**Yukon,** major river of NW North America, flowing c.3200 km (2000 mi) from Atlin Lake in BRITISH COLUMBIA, Canada, through the SW YUKON Territory and across central Alaska before entering the BERING SEA through a large delta near Norton Sound. Rich in hydroelectric potential and an important salmon-fishing area, it is, for three months of the year, navigable by river boats to WHITEHORSE, in the Yukon, c.2860 km (1755 mi) upstream.

**Yukon Territory,** region of Canada, (1984 est. pop. 22,100), area 482,515 km² (186,299 sq mi), situated in the NW, bordered by the Beaufort Sea (N), Northwest Territories (E), British Columbia (S), and Alaska, US (W). WHITEHORSE is the capital and residence of two-thirds of the population. Yukon Territory is almost wholly mountainous; between the Coast Mountains in the W and the McKenzie Mts in the E lies an area of rough upland. Most of the area is drained into the Bering Sea by the Yukon R., except for the N, which is part of the Mackenzie R. system. Mining is the dominant economic activity, involving the extraction of asbestos, copper, zinc, lead, and precious metals. Tourism is gaining in importance because of Yukon's great natural beauty. The northern part is uninhabited and most of the population live along valleys; a quarter of the population is Yukon Indian. Fur traders arrived in the 1840s followed by gold prospectors in the 1890s. Acquired by the Canadian government in 1870 it became a separate territory in 1898 in response to the rapid population increase associated with the great Klondike gold rush. Yukon Territory is now governed by a federally appointed commissioner and an elected legislative council. Since World War II the Alaska Highway and other all-weather roads have helped open up the region. The dependence of the economy on mining has resulted in recession in the 1980s, and the revival of gold-mining in re-opened mines.

**Yun'gang caves,** cave sculptures 16 km (10 mi) W of Datong in Shanxi prov., N China. They were carved out of the sandstone rocks, mainly during the northern Wei dynasty between 460 and 494 AD. They range in height from just a few centimetres to 17 m (55 ft) and are one of the great examples of Buddhist art, reflecting Indian, Persian, Greek, and Chinese artistic influences.

Yun'gang grotto near Jatong

**Yunnan,** province (1985 est. pop. 34,060,000), 394,000 km² (152,123 sq mi), SW China. It lies south of SICHUAN prov. and bordered by Burma (W) and Laos and Vietnam (S). Major cities are the capital, KUNMING, and Dongchuan. To the west the land is mountainous, with pasture and forestry areas; deeply dissected mountain ranges running N–S, and plateau land (c.1500 m-/4920 ft-high) lies to the east. The climate is of the highland monsoon type, with a sharp contrast between dry and wet seasons. Throughout most of the year the temperatures are springlike and there is a long frostfree period. Agriculture is concentrated on the eastern plateau areas; rice, wheat, and corn are major crops, with tea and tobacco principal export crops. Economic development has been hampered by physical barriers and distance from the rest of China. Although the province has large coal deposits and large water power reserves, there is little industry. What there is, is concentrated in Kunming which has an iron and steel works, and is the centre of the provincial rail network. Yunnan's 'frontier' character is marked by the presence of many non-Han or minority peoples who are mainly to be found in the western mountain areas.

**Yusuf Ibn al-Hasan,** c.1606–c.1638, sultan of Mombasa, SE Kenya (r.1626–c.1632). He was brought up by the Portuguese as a Christian, but converted to Islam in 1631 and subsequently massacred the Portuguese inhabitants of Fort Jesus in Mombasa. His attempts to raise a general revolt against the Portuguese failed and he ended his life in Arabia, a pirate killed by pirates.

**YWCA:** see YOUNG WOMEN'S CHRISTIAN ASSOCIATION.

**Zabaleta, Nicanor,** 1907–, Spanish harp virtuoso, lecturer, and composer. He has played with orchestras and given solo recitals all over the world, and at the leading music festivals. Several composers have written pieces specially for him, and he has arranged works for the harp as well as written his own original compositions.

**Zabrze,** Ger. *Hindenburg,* city (1984 pop. 197,000), Upper Silesia, S Poland. It is a mining and industrial centre, German before 1945. A canal link with the Oder R. was established in the early 19th cent. and improved in the 1930s.

**Zacharias** or **Zachary, Saint,** pope (741–52), a Calabrian Greek. A guardian of church authority, he persuaded the Lombards to restore some towns to the papacy and favoured the Frankish king PEPIN THE SHORT. His letters, notably to St BONIFACE, are still extant. Feast: 15 Mar.

**Zadar,** Ital. *Zara,* city (1981 pop. 116,174), Croatia, NW Yugoslavia, on the Adriatic Sea. Situated on a peninsula, it was a Roman settlement which later came under the control of Venice. It was the capital of Austrian Dalmatia from 1815 to 1918, then Italian, and Yugoslav from 1945. Zadar suffered damage in World War II but has remains of fortifications and a number of medieval churches.

**Zagazig,** city (1987 pop. 202,575), N Egypt, in the Nile delta NE of CAIRO. It trades in cotton and grain and is linked by canal to ISMĀ'ILÍA.

**Zagreb,** city (1981 pop. 1,174,512), capital of CROATIA, NW Yugoslavia, on the Sava R. It is the country's second largest city and a major financial, industrial, cultural, and communications centre. Manufactures include machinery and chemicals. Site of a Roman town, Zagreb was ruled by Hungary from the 13th cent. and, under the AUSTRO-HUNGARIAN MONARCHY, became (1868) the capital of a theoretically autonomous Croatia. After 1918 it became part of YUGOSLAVIA. A typical central European city, it contains the historic Kaptol old town, with the Catholic cathedral (begun 1093), and a 19th cent. new town on the plain below. Extensive modern suburbs extend towards and across the Sava to the south.

**Zagros Mountains,** mountain system of SW Iran between the Mesopotamian plain and the Persian Gulf (S) and the central Iranian plateau (N). It extends c 1770 km (1100 mi) from the Turkish-Soviet frontier (N) to the Strait of Hormuz (S) with an average width of c.402 km (250 mi). Numerous peaks rise over 4000 m (13,000 ft). The Zagros decrease in elevation and become increasingly arid toward the south. Kurds, Lurs, Bakhtiaris, Kashkais, and other minorities are the chief inhabitants. Iran's great oil fields lie along the western foothills around the head of the PERSIAN GULF.

**zaibatsu** [Jap., = wealthy families],the great family-controlled banking and industrial combines of modern Japan. The leading zaibatsu are Mitsui, Mitsubishi, Sumitomo, and Yasuda. Most zaibatsu developed after the MEIJI restoration, when the new government granted them a privileged position in the economic development of Japan through subsidies and favourable tax policies. They maintained close ties with political parties. After World War II the Allies tried, but failed, to break their influence. They still wield great economic power.

**Zaïre** (zie͵iə), officially Republic of Zaïre, formerly Democratic Republic of the Congo, republic (1987 est. pop. 34,670,000), c.2,344,000 km² (905,000 sq mi), central Africa, bordered by Angola (SW), the Congo Republic (W), the Central African Republic and Sudan (N), Uganda, Rwanda, Burundi, and Tanzania (E), and Zambia (SE). Principal cities

include KINSHASA (the capital), KANANGA, and LUBUMBASHI. Virtually all of Zaïre, which lies astride the equator, is part of the vast CONGO (Zaïre) R. drainage basin. North central Zaïre is a large plateau covered with rain forest. To the east, on the Uganda border, are the Ruwenzori Mts, which rise to over 4880 m (16,000 ft), and lakes Mobuto, Edward, and Tanganyika. Savanna-covered plateaus in the southeast rise to c.2070 m (6800 ft). Zaïre's mineral wealth is the mainstay of the economy, accounting for about 75% of export earnings. Most important are copper, diamonds (of which it is the world's leading producer), cobalt (65% of world reserves), zinc, manganese, and uranium; offshore petroleum production began in 1975. The leading farm exports are palm products, coffee, and rubber; large amounts of timber (notably ebony and teak) are also produced. Manufactures include processed metals, foodstuffs, textiles, clothing, iron and steel, cement, and chemicals. The GNP is US$5044 million, and the GNP per capita is US$170 (1985). The population is made up of black Africans, most of whom speak Bantu; there are also Nilotic speakers in the north, and scattered groups of PYGMIES. French is the official language, but Swahili and Lingala are widely spoken. Most of the people adhere to traditional religious beliefs, but about 25% are Roman Catholic and a large number belong to independent black African Protestant groups.

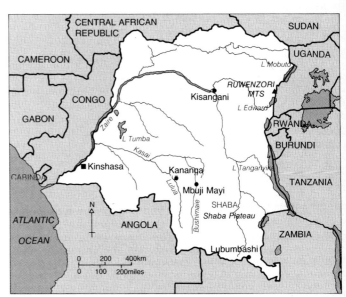

Zaïre

*History.* Pygmies were probably the earliest inhabitants of the region, but by the end of the 1st millennium BC black Africans migrated into Zaïre from the northwest. The Bantu worked the copper deposits from about 700 AD, eventually coalescing into independent, often complex, states. Following the visit of Diogo Cão in 1482, the Portuguese, who were active in trading, established a presence in the region. The territory was unified by LEOPOLD II of Belgium, who in 1885 privately founded an independent state, the Congo Free State, headed by himself, in the Congo Basin; it was annexed by Belgium in 1908, becoming the colony of the

Belgian Congo. Under Belgian rule the Congo became a rich field for European investment, especially in vast mining operations and great plantations. Nationalist sentiment, led by Joseph KASAVUBU and Patrice LUMUMBA, reached a peak in the 1950s, and Belgium was forced to grant independence in 1960. However, the new Republic of the Congo was soon torn by ethnic and personal rivalries. Within weeks the army mutinied, and Moïse TSHOMBE declared the copper-rich province of Katanga (now SHABA), of which he was provisional president, to be independent. The ensuing civil war, which involved UN forces, Belgian troops, and US and Soviet support of opposing factions, did not end until 1963, when Katanga agreed to rejoin the republic. By the end of the 1960s the country had begun to experience a degree of political stability. Col. Joseph Mobotu (later MOBUTU SESE SEKO), who had seized power in 1960 and established the Popular Movement of the Revolution as the sole legal party in 1967, has served as president since 1970. The country's name was changed to the Democratic Republic of the Congo in 1964 and to Zaïre in 1971. A drop in world copper prices in the mid-1970s created severe economic problems for Zaïre, which resulted in widespread discontent. Severe economic problems and unrest continued in the 1980s, although the Mobutu regime remained firmly in power.

**Zaïre**, river: see CONGO.

**Zama** (ˌzahmə), ancient town near the N coast of Africa, in present Tunisia. Scipio Africanus Major defeated HANNIBAL at or near Zama in the final battle of the Second PUNIC WAR (202 BC), but there were several towns named Zama.

**Zambezi**, river, flowing c.2740 km (1700 mi) through S central Africa to the Mozambique Channel. Part of its large hydroelectric potential is harnessed by KARIBA DAM (completed 1959), on the Zimbabwe–Zambia border, and Cabora Bassa Dam (completed 1975), in Mozambique. VICTORIA FALLS and many rapids restrict navigation to local traffic.

**Zambia**, officially Republic of Zambia, formerly Northern Rhodesia, republic (1986 est. pop. 6,660,000), 752,614 km² (290,584 sq mi), S central Africa, bordered by Zaïre (N), Tanzania (NE), Malawi and Mozambique (E), Zimbabwe, Botswana, and Namibia (S), and Angola (W). Major cities include LUSAKA (the capital), KITWE, and NDOLA. Zambia is on a highland plateau, which rises in the east; the country's highest point (c.2170 m/7120 ft) is on the Nyika plateau, adjacent to Malawi. VICTORIA FALLS and the huge Lake Kariba (formed by KARIBA DAM), both on the border with Zimbabwe, are part of the ZAMBEZI R., which drains the western part of the country. Zambia's economy is dependent almost entirely on its mineral wealth, notably copper, of which it is one of the world's leading producers, and cobalt; coal, zinc, lead, and manganese are also important. However, most of the population is engaged in subsistence farming, growing maize, groundnuts, and tobacco, and raising cattle. The GNP is US$2593 million, and the GNP per capita is US$390 (1985). About 98% of the inhabitants are Bantu-speaking black Africans, but English is the official language. More than half the population is Christian, equally divided between Roman Catholics and Protestants; the rest adhere to traditional religious beliefs.

*History.* Some Bantu-speaking peoples migrated into the region that is now Zambia around AD 1200, but the ancestors of most modern Zambians arrived from present-day Angola and Zaïre between the 16th and 18th cent. The British explorer David LIVINGSTONE first visited Zambia in 1851 and later discovered Victoria Falls. In 1890 Cecil RHODES's British South Africa Company began to administer the area under treaties signed with African leaders; it became the protectorate of Northern Rhodesia in 1911 and passed under British administration in 1924. Massive copper deposits were discovered in N central Zambia in the late 1920s, and European colonists began to pour into the area. However, the resulting economic prosperity was not shared with the black African labourers who worked in the mines, and who staged periodic strikes to protest their ill-treatment, finally organizing a nationalist movement in 1946. In 1953, despite the protests of the black nationalists, Southern Rhodesia (now Zimbabwe), Northern Rhodesia, and Nyasaland (now Malawi) were brought together by Britain in the Federation of Rhodesia and Nyasaland. The federation was dissolved in 1963, when Nyasaland and Northern Rhodesia withdrew, and the Republic of Zambia was proclaimed independent within the COMMONWEALTH in 1964, with Kenneth KAUNDA as president. Kaunda, who ended European economic domination and in 1972 created a one-party state, was elected for a fourth time in 1983 as candidate of the ruling United National Independence Party. In the 1970s and 1980s

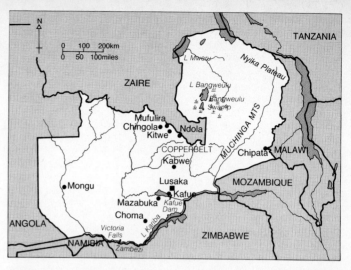

Zambia

Zambia suffered severe economic hardship as a result of its opposition to the white regime in Zimbabwe.

**Zamość**, city (1984 est. pop. 29,000), SE Poland. A planned town of the 16th cent., it was founded by Jan Zamojski in 1579. It was built according to Renaissance town-planning principles inside elaborate fortifications.

**Zampieri, Domenico**: see DOMENICHINO.

**Zanzibar**, region (1984 est. pop. 556,000), 2461 km² (950 sq mi), Tanzania, E Africa, consisting chiefly of the islands of Zanzibar and Tumbatu, in the Indian Ocean. The major city is also named Zanzibar. The economy of the region is almost entirely agricultural, and Zanzibar and the nearby island of Pemba produce the bulk of the world's cloves. In the early Muslim era, rival Arab and Persian sultanates were established on the island of Zanzibar. The Portuguese gained control in 1503, using the island as a base for territorial expansion on the African coast and for the slave trade. In 1698 Zanzibar and Pemba fell to the Oman (or Muscat) Arabs, who pushed deep into Africa in search of slaves, gold, and ivory. The islands became a British protectorate in 1890 and an independent nation in 1963. In 1964 Zanzibar deposed the sultan, and the two islands merged with Tanganyika to form TANZANIA. President Idris Abdul Wakil of Zanzibar (elected in 1985) is ex officio second vice president of Tanzania.

**Zanzibar**, city (1987 est. pop. 270,000), capital of the island and region of Zanzibar, offshore from mainland Tanzania. A commercial centre and port, it is situated on the west side of Zanzibar island behind a deep-water harbour. In the 19th cent. the city flourished as the base for Arab and European activities in E Africa.

**Zapata, Emiliano**, c.1879–1919, Mexican revolutionary. An Indian tenant farmer, he tried to recover (1908) expropriated village lands, and he led (1910–19) an army of Indians in the Mexican revolution with the goal of repossessing the land. In defence of this agrarian programme, he fought successive federal governments and largely controlled S Mexico. His army occupied Mexico City three times (1914–15), but he finally retired to Morelos, where he was treacherously killed by a government emissary. Zapata is still revered by Mexican Indians.

**Zápolya, John** (ˌzahpolyə), see under JOHN, kings of Hungary.

**Zápolya, John Sigismund**: see under JOHN, kings of Hungary.

**Zápolya, Stephen**, d. 1499, palatine (regent) of Hungary (r.1492–99). He fought (1479–81) against the Turks and conquered (1481–85) the archduchy of Austria for King MATTHIAS CORVINUS. His son became King JOHN I of Hungary.

**Zaporozhian Cossacks**, free warriors living in self-governing communities along the banks of the lower Dnieper in UKRAINE. From the 16th cent. onwards the Zaporozhian Cossacks built a fortified island stronghold called the *sich*, which although often changing location served as a military base and as a commerical and administrative centre for the whole region. The leader of the Zaporozhian Cossacks was known as the *Hetman,* and was effectively ruler of the Cossack part of Ukraine during the period 1648–1764. The last *sich* was finally abolished in 1775 when all of Zaporozhia was placed under direct Russian imperial rule.

**Zaporozhye,** formerly Aleksandrovsk, city (1985 pop. 852,000), S European USSR, in the UKRAINE. It is an industrial centre noted for its alloy steel, rolled steel, engineering, and chemical industries. The local abundance of hydroelectricity from the nearby station on the Dnepr Dam has been decisive in the development of industries producing non-ferrous metals, such as aluminium and titanium. The city was founded in 1770 as a fortress against the Crimean Tartars.

**Zaragoza** or **Saragossa** (thahrah‚gohthah, sara‚gosə), city (1987 pop. 590,750), capital of Zaragoza prov. and chief city of Aragón, NE Spain, on the Ebro R. It is the centre of a fertile agricultural region and manufactures wood products. Held by the Romans, Goths, and MOORS (from the 8th cent.), it was taken (1118) by ALFONSO I of Aragón. In the PENINSULAR WAR the city yielded to a French siege (1808–9) only after some 50,000 defenders had died. Zaragoza is rich in art and contains two cathedrals.

**Zara Yaqob,** c.1410–68, emperor of ETHIOPIA (r.1434–68). The most celebrated of the medieval Ethiopian rulers, he brought the empire to its greatest ever extent. He worked closely with the church to Christianize the people and attempted, unsuccessfully however, to take the administration of the country out of the hands of feudal chiefs.

**Zaria,** city (1987 est. pop. 224,000), Kaduna state, N Nigeria. It lies at the junction of the rail branch from Nguru to Lagos. A market town, it trades in sugar, ground nuts, and cotton. Its industries include railway engineering and tanning. Thought to have been founded in the 16th cent., the old walled town still remains. It is an educational centre for the North, with Ahmadu Bello Univ. which was established in 1962.

**zebra,** herbivorous, hoofed African MAMMAL (genus *Equus*), distinguished from other HORSES by its striking pattern of alternating white and dark brown (or black) stripes. Standing about 120 cm (4 ft) high at the shoulder, the zebra has a heavy head, a stout body, and a short, thick mane. It inhabits open plains or brush country in herds of up to 1000, often mixing with other grazing animals, e.g., ANTELOPE, and can run at speeds of up to 60 kph (40 mph).

**zebu,** domestic MAMMAL of the CATTLE family, *Bos indicus,* found in E Asia, India, and Africa. It has a large, fatty hump and is fawn, grey, black, or bay. The zebu has great endurance and is used in India for riding and draft purposes. In the US zebus are called Brahman cattle.

**Zebulun:** see ISRAEL, TRIBES OF.

**Zechariah** or **Zacharias** ('zekə‚rieə, 'zakə‚rieəs), book of the OLD TESTAMENT. The first eight chapters, dating from 520–518 BC, express in a series of nocturnal visions the prophet's concern for the rebuilding of the Temple at Jerusalem. The remaining chapters come from two different hands and are usually dated in the 4th and 3rd cent. BC.

**Zedekiah** ('zedə‚kieə), last king of Judah (r. c.597–586 BC). He was set on the throne as the puppet of NEBUCHADNEZZAR, but he allied himself with the Egyptians. The Babylonians then destroyed the kingdom of Judah and carried Zedekiah with his people into captivity in Babylonia.

**Zeeland, Paul van:** see VAN ZEELAND, PAUL.

**Zeiss, Carl,** 1816–88, German precision glass lens manufacturer. After serving his apprenticeship and becoming a master glass instrument maker, he was invited to make instruments for Ernst Abbe, professor of physics at Jena Univ., Germany. In 1846 he started his own lens factory at Jena with Abbe as his partner. He organized his factory into different departments, one for each type of instrument, and produced a range of lenses including lenses for spectacles, microscopes, field glasses, telescopes, astronomical equipment, and cameras. Labour relations were exceedingly good, working conditions first-class, and employees had generous profit-sharing participation.

**Zelaya, José Santos** (say‚lahyah), 1853–1919, president of NICARAGUA (1894–1909). Zelaya ruled as dictator and developed transport, coffee growing, and education while draining the country's resources for his own profit. His attempt to foment revolutions in neighbouring states alarmed the US, which helped rebel forces to overthrow him.

**zemstvo** (‚zemstvoh), [Rus., from *zemlya* = land], local assembly in Russia, 1864–1917. Begun under ALEXANDER II, the zemstvo handled education, health, and other district matters, and chose delegates to the provincial assembly. In 1917 (see RUSSIAN REVOLUTION) the SOVIET replaced the zemstvo.

**Zen Buddhism,** Buddhist sect of Japan and China, based on the practice of MEDITATION rather than on adherence to a particular scriptural doctrine. Its founder in China was the legendary Bodhidharma (5th cent. AD), who taught 'wall-gazing' and followed the Yogācāra or Consciousness School of BUDDHISM, which held consciousness as real, but not its objects. The characteristic Zen teaching of sudden enlightenment, or *satori,* goes back to Hui-neng, an illiterate master of the 7th cent. who defined enlightenment as the direct seeing of one's own 'original nature' (i.e., Buddha). The golden age of Zen (8th–9th cent.) developed a unique style of oral instruction, including nonrational elements such as the *koan,* a subject given for meditation, usually in the form of a paradoxical saying, to test the enlightenment of students of Zen. After the persecution of Buddhism in 845, Zen emerged as the dominant Chinese sect. Two main schools, the *Lin-Chi* (Jap. *Rinzai*), emphasizing the *koan* and *satori,* and the *Ts'ao-tung* (Jap. *Soto*), emphasizing the practice of meditation (*zazen*), were transmitted to Japan in the 14th cent. and greatly influenced politics and culture (e.g., poetry, painting, landscape gardening, the tea ceremony, and flower arranging) before declining in the 16th and 17th cent. Revised in the 18th cent., Zen thought was made known in the West by the writings of D.T. Suzuki, and after World War II it attracted interest in the US.

**Zeno,** d. 491, Roman emperor of the East (474–75, 476–91), who succeeded his son, LEO I. He made peace with the Vandal king GAISERIC and made concessions to ODOACER in Italy. He freed the East from the raids of the Ostrogoths and encouraged their king, Theodoric the Great, to invade Italy (488).

**Zeno of Elea,** c.490–c.430 BC, Greek philosopher of the Eleatic school founded by PARMENIDES. Zeno's only known work, extant in fragmented form, uses a series of paradoxes to show the error of commonsense notions of time and space, thereby demonstrating Parmenides' doctrine that motion and multiplicity are logically impossible. Contemporary thinkers have shown renewed interest in the problems Zeno raised.

**zeolites,** aluminosilicates which have the ability to liberate, and when dried, to absorb, large quantities of water. Discovered in 1756, they can now be made in the laboratory and in a variety (over 60) of different crystal structures. Their general formula is: $M_x(AEO_2)_x(SiO_2)_ymH_2O$, where M is an exchangeable cation (see ION). Zeolites are used for separating gases and liquids; as ion-exchangers, especially in softening water; and as catalysts. Almost all the petrol produced nowadays is generated from petroleum (crude oil) or natural gas using a zeolitic CATALYST.

**Zephaniah** or **Sophonias** ('zefə‚nieə, 'sofə‚nieəs), book of the OLD TESTAMENT. The prophet castigates Jerusalem for various sins, particularly the worship of false gods, and announces an imminent divine judgment from which only a godly remnant will escape. The main part of the book probably dates from the reign of King Josiah of Judah (c 640–609 BC), and antedates the religious reforms he carried out in 621 BC.

**Zeppelin, Count Ferdinand von,** 1838–1917, German inventor. After army service in the Franco-Prussian War, Zeppelin designed and built the first rigid AIRSHIP, which first flew on 2 July 1900. By 1910 he was operating three airships commercially; these were requisitioned by the German Army for use in World War I. From 1916 Zeppelin turned his attention to multi-engined aeroplanes, which were also successful.

**Zermatt,** small town (1984 pop. c. 3500), Valais canton, Switzerland, in the high Pennine Alps. Surrounded by some of the highest Alpine peaks, including the MATTERHORN, it has been a popular mountaineering resort since the 1840s.

**Zeromski, Stefan** (zhe‚romskee), 1864–1925, Polish novelist, short-story writer, and poet. In such novels as *Homeless People* (1900), *Ashes* (1904), and *Faithful River* (1912) he expressed a deep concern with freedom and social justice.

**Zerqa,** city (1984 est. pop. 265,700), central Jordan, on the Zerqa R. 20 km (12 mi) northeast of AMMAN. It has an oil refinery, chemical, metal, and fertilizer industries. Like Amman it has grown rapidly since 1948 with the influx of Palestinian refugees.

**Zeus,** in Greek mythology, supreme god; son of CRONUS, whom he succeeded, and RHEA; brother and husband of HERA. After the overthrow of the TITANS, when lots were cast to divide the universe, the underworld went to HADES, the sea to POSEIDON, and the heavens and earth to Zeus. An amorous god, he loved goddesses, nymphs, and mortals, and fathered many children. Ruling from his court on Mt Olympus, Zeus was the symbol of power, rule, and law; the rewarder of good; and the punisher of evil. Also the god of weather (his most famous weapon was the thunderbolt) and fertility, he was worshipped in connection with almost every aspect of life. The Romans equated Zeus with their own supreme god, JUPITER.

**Zhangjiakou:** or **Changkiakow** (‚jang-‚jeeah-‚kow), city (1970 est. pop. 1,000,000), NW Hebei prov., China. A major trade centre for N China and Mongolia, it has food-processing plants, machine shops, and tanneries. An important Ch'ing dynasty military centre, it declined somewhat after the opening (1905) of the Trans-Siberian RR.

**Zhanjiang,** city (1984 pop. 4,700,300), GUANGDONG prov., SE China, on the South China Sea. A developing industrial centre and port, in 1984 it was designated one of 14 coastal cities to obtain special privileges to encourage foreign investment. Future development is based on the assumed potential petroleum development in the South China Sea. It is an important military base—defending Chinese interests in the South China Sea and in the conflict with Vietnam. It was leased to France in 1898 and remained under French control until World War II.

**Zhao Ziyang,** 1919–, general secretary of the Chinese Communist Party (1987–). Zhao was purged in the CULTURAL REVOLUTION, but was later rehabilitated. In 1975 he was named governor of Sichuan prov., where he made his reputation as an administrator. He was elected to the politburo in 1979 and later succeeded HUA GUOFENG as premier. Zhao is a reformer like HU YAOBANG whom he replaced as general secretary of the Communist Party in January 1987. He stood down as premier in favour of LI PENG in 1988.

**Zhdanov,** formerly Mariupol, city (1985 pop. 522,000), S European USSR, in the UKRAINE, on the N shore of the Sea of Azov. Although ice-bound for two months a year, it is an important port exporting coal and metallurgical products. Industry includes an integrated metallurgical plant, and an integrated iron and steel plant that utilizes iron ore from the Kerch Peninsula and coal from the Donets coalfield. Other industries are fish-processing, general machine construction, shipbuilding, and graphite production. Founded in 1775 by Greek colonists, the city gained its present name in 1948, after Andrey Aleksandrovich Zhdanov, the Soviet statesman.

**Zhejiang** or **Chekiang,** province (1985 est. pop. 40,300,000), 101,800 km² (39,305 sq mi), E coast of China, S of SHANGHAI. Major cities are HANGZHOU the capital, and NINGBO. The northern section of Zhejiang is the river valley of the YANGTZE and is suitable for intensive agriculture. Most of the province is mountainous and supports various crops, including tea, grown on terraced slopes. The plain areas though limited are very productive rice lands. There are many offshore islands including the Zhoushan Archipelago, an important fishing area. Industrialization is limited; Hangzhou, since 1949, has added iron and steel manufacture to its long-established textile industry.

**Zhengzhou** or **Chengchow,** city (1984 pop. 4,800,400), capital of HENAN prov., central China. It is one of China's textile centres and has a growing industrial sector. It is also a major railway centre, linking Beijing and Guangzhou on the N–S railway and Xi'an and Shanghai on the E–W railway. 24 km (15 mi) to the north lies the YELLOW RIVER where, in 1938, Chiang Kai-Shek's troops broke the dykes in a vain attempt to check the Japanese advance. Zhengzhou was the site of major fighting during the Cultural Revolution (1966–69).

**Zhivkov, Todor,** 1911–, Bulgarian Communist leader. He was a partisan leader in World War II and became (1954) Communist Party first secretary. He also held important posts in the government, including premier (1962–71) and head of state (from 1971).

**Zhou,** dynasty: see CHINA.

**Zhou Enlai,** 1898–1976, Chinese Communist leader. He studied in Europe and there became a founder of the Chinese Communist Party. He returned (1924) to China and joined SUN YAT-SEN, who was then cooperating with the Communists. In 1927 Zhou organized a general strike in Shanghai that led to the city's capture by CHIANG KAI-SHEK and the

Nationalists in the Northern Expedition. After the break (1927) between Chiang and the Communists, Zhou held prominent Communist military and political posts. He participated in the LONG MARCH (1934–35) of the Communist army, and after the creation of the People's Republic of China (1949) he was foreign minister (1949–58) and premier (1949–76). He headed the Chinese delegation to the Geneva Conference of 1954 and to the Bandung Conference (1955). Zhou prevented the breakdown of the state and the party during the CULTURAL REVOLUTION. The high esteem in which he was held was made clear by the demonstrations in his memory in Tien An Men Square and other cities in 1976. This was subsequently declared a 'revolutionary' event.

**Zhoukoudien,** village near Beijing, China, with caves containing remains of HOMO ERECTUS—Peking Man (formerly Sinanthropus). The site was excavated from the 1920s, but earlier finds were lost or destroyed in World War II. Discoveries include stone tools (choppers and flakes), animal bones and plant remains indicating a cool temperate climate, and the first evidence of the use of fire. The deposits' depth shows prolonged occupation, probably on a seasonal basis, 0.5 million years ago. See also HUMAN EVOLUTION.

**Zhuang Zi** or **Zhuang Zhou,** c.369–c.286 BC, Chinese philosopher. His Taoist writings continued themes developed by LAO ZI in the form of poetic passages, metaphors and parables of an excellent literary style. He wrote of the spontaneity of nature which is an expression of the *Dao*, the first principle of the universe, and the need for men to follow it rather than struggle to change it.

**Zhu De,** 1886–1976, Chinese Communist soldier. In 1922 he went to Europe, where he joined the Chinese Communist Party. He returned to China and in 1927, when CHIANG KAI-SHEK broke with the Communists, Zhu joined MAO ZEDONG. Zhu led (1934–35) his section of the Red Army on the LONG MARCH to NW China and commanded Communist forces in the Second SINO-JAPANESE WAR. He left his military post to become deputy chairman of the People's Republic of China (1954) and chairman of the National People's Congress (1959).

**Zhukov, Georgi Konstantinovich,** 1896–1974, Soviet marshal. He fought in the RUSSIAN REVOLUTION (1917) and the civil war (1918–20). In WORLD WAR II he defended Moscow (1941), defeated the Germans at Stalingrad (1943), helped lift the Leningrad siege (1944), and took Berlin (1945). Defence minister after 1955, he was ousted by KHRUSHCHEV (1957); when Khrushchev fell (1964), Zhukov appeared again in public.

**Zia ul-Haq, Mohammad** (‚ziə ool ‚hak), 1924–88, president of Pakistan (1978–). An army general, he headed the junta that overthrew (1977) Prime Min. Z.A. BHUTTO and imposed martial law. Zia assumed the presidency in 1978 and proved a pertinacious ruler, negotiating a massive arms deal with the US. He was killed in an air accident in 1988.

**ziggurat,** form of TEMPLE common to the Sumerians, Babylonians, and Assyrians, built from the end of the 3rd millennium BC to the 6th cent. BC. It was a pyramidal brick structure with receding tiers, set on a rectangular, square, or oval platform, with a shrine at the summit.

A **ziggurat** at Ur, c.2100 BC

**Zimbabwe** (zim‚bahbway), officially Republic of Zimbabwe, formerly Rhodesia, republic (1987 est. pop. 8,660,000), 390,580 km² (150,803 sq mi), S central Africa, bordered by Zambia (N), Mozambique (NE and

E), and Botswana (SW and W). Principal cities include HARARE (the capital) and BULAWAYO. Most of Zimbabwe consists of a high plateau, the highveld (above 1219 m/4000 ft), that crosses the country from southwest to northeast; on either side of it are the middleveld (below 1219 m/4000 ft) and the lowveld (below 914 m/3000 ft). The Eastern Highlands, a narrow belt along the Mozambique border, is the site of Mt Inyangani (2592 m/8503 ft), the country's highest point. The economy is supported mainly by agriculture and mining. The principal cash crops include tobacco, maize, tea, cotton, and groundnuts. The leading mineral exports are gold and nickel. Forests in the southeast yield valuable hardwoods. Most of Zimbabwe's power is generated by a hydroelectric station on the ZAMBEZI R. at Kariba Lake. The GNP is US$5559 million, and the GNP per capita is US$680 (1985). The population consists primarily of Africans, with about 180,000 whites who remained after independence, and small Asian and Coloured minorities. English is the official language, but the two major African groups, the Ndebele and Shona, speak their own languages. Most of the Africans practise traditional religions, 20% of the population is Christian, and the Asians are Muslim and Hindu.

*History.* Early Iron Age cultures in present-day Zimbabwe were supplanted by Bantu-speaking peoples who migrated into the area after the 5th cent. AD. In the early 16th cent. the Portuguese developed trade with Shona-dominated states, which in the 1830s became subject to Ndebele invaders. In 1889 Cecil RHODES's British South Africa Company obtained a charter to colonize the region, which they called Rhodesia. The company founded (1890) Fort Salisbury and in 1893 defeated the Ndebele and took control of the territory. In 1922 the settlers voted to reject incorporation into the Union of South Africa, choosing instead to make Southern Rhodesia a self-governing British colony, a status achieved in 1923. Thereafter a series of white governments developed the economy but failed to share the benefits with the African majority. Joining Northern Rhodesia (now Zambia) and Nyasaland (now Malawi), in 1953 Southern Rhodesia became a member of the Federation of Rhodesia and Nyasaland, which disbanded in 1963, when the other members moved towards independence. Ian SMITH, a staunch conservative who became prime minister in 1964, proclaimed unilateral independence from Britain in 1965, an act the British denounced as rebellion but failed to take effective action against. In 1970 Rhodesia became a republic, with complete separation of the franchise along racial lines. UN economic sanctions were applied against the Smith regime, and two African nationalist groups, led by Joshua Nkomo and Robert MUGABE, launched guerrilla attacks against the government. Smith and three moderate black leaders agreed (1978) to set up an interim biracial government, and elections were held in 1979, but Britain and the black nationalists rejected the settlement. Finally, a London conference reached an accord on legal independence under black majority rule, and the new state of Zimbabwe came into being in 1980 as a member of the COMMONWEALTH. The government of national unity, established upon independence, ended in 1982, when Prime Min. Mugabe ousted Nkomo from the cabinet. In 1988 Zimbabwe became a one-party state under Mugabe's Zimbabwe African National Union (ZANU); at the same time, Nkomo was brought back into the government to signify reconciliation between his Ndebele people and Mugabe's majority Shona people. Meanwhile, under a new constitution adopted in late 1987, Mugabe had become the country's first executive president.

**Zimbabwe, Great,** the chief centre of a powerful African IRON AGE kingdom in S Zimbabwe between AD 1000 and 1450. The site is a sprawling complex of drystone walls, dominated by a singularly massive structure called the Great Enclosure. The people of Zimbabwe traded, and probably controlled the trade, of luxury items, such as gold and ivory, and at the height of their prosperity imported cloth, glass, and porcelain.

**zinc** (Zn), metallic element. A lustrous, bluish-white, fairly reactive metal, zinc is ductile and malleable when heated. It is commercially important in GALVANIZING iron and in the preparation of certain alloys, e.g., BRASS and sometimes BRONZE. It is used for the negative plates in certain electric batteries, and for roofing and gutters. Zinc compounds are numerous and widely used. Zinc is essential for growth of plants and animals. See ELEMENT (table); PERIODIC TABLE.

**zinnia,** plant (genus *Zinnia*) of the COMPOSITE family, native chiefly to Mexico. The common garden zinnia (*Z. elegans*) is a rather coarse, easily

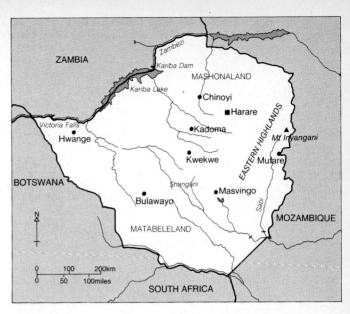

Zimbabwe

cultivated annual, popular as a cut flower for its warm colours ranging from white and yellow to red and purple and for its bold, stiff aspect.

**Zinoviev, Grigori Evseyevich** (ze,nawvee-ef), 1883–1936, Soviet leader. He sided with LENIN in the 1903 Social-Democratic party split (see BOLSHEVISM AND MENSHEVISM). After the RUSSIAN REVOLUTION of Nov. 1917, he led the COMINTERN (1919–26) and served on the Communist party politburo (1921–26). After Lenin's death (1924) Zinoviev, KAMENEV, and STALIN shared power. In 1925 Stalin turned on Zinoviev and Kamenev, and they joined the TROTSKY faction. Zinoviev was expelled from the party in 1927 but was readmitted in 1928 with little power. In 1935 he was tried for alleged involvement in the death of Stalin's aide Sergei M. Kirov. In 1936 Zinoviev, Kamenev, and others were tried for treason and executed.

**Zinzendorf, Nikolaus Ludwig, Graf von** (,tsintsəndawf), 1700–60, German churchman, patron, and bishop (from 1737) of the refounded MORAVIAN CHURCH. Reared under Pietistic influences, he established (1722) a Moravian colony called Herrnhut on his Saxony estates, but was exiled (1736) for his religious views. He founded Moravian congregations in Holland, England, the West Indies, and North America. He was allowed to return to Saxony in 1747.

**Zion** or **Sion,** part of JERUSALEM. It is defined in the BIBLE as the City of David. There is controversy about its exact location. The name is symbolic of Jerusalem, of the Promised Land, of Israel's hope of returning to Palestine (hence the term ZIONISM), and, among Christians, of heaven.

**Zionism,** movement for reconstituting a Jewish state in Palestine, taking its name from the hill in Jerusalem on which the ancient palace of King David, and later the Temple, were built. Dating from the Roman destruction of Jerusalem (AD 70) and the dispersion of the JEWS, the movement emerged in its modern form as a response to European ANTI-SEMITISM. The first World Zionist Congress was convened (1897) in Basel, Switzerland, by Theodore HERZL. The movement, under Chaim WEIZMANN, was given impetus by the British government's Balfour Declaration (see BALFOUR, ARTHUR JAMES) of 1917, which promised the Jews a national homeland in PALESTINE, then part of the OTTOMAN EMPIRE. After WORLD WAR I, increased Jewish settlement in the British mandate of Palestine led to armed conflict with the majority Arab inhabitants, which intensified after WORLD WAR II as many survivors of the European HOLOCAUST sought to enter Palestine. Zionism was divided between followers of the militant Zionist leader Vladimir Jabotinsky (including Menachem BEGIN), who demanded unrestricted immigration throughout Palestine, and those, led by David BEN-GURION, who reluctantly accepted the UN plan for partition. After the creation of the state of ISRAEL (1948), the World Zionist Congress was separated from the Israeli government. The present-day Zionist movement facilitates immigration to Israel and supports cultural and educational activities in Israel and elsewhere.

**zip-fastener,** used for clothes or luggage. It consists of two flexible strips, usually made from metal or plastic, which have interlocking projections which can be linked or undone with a sliding clip. The term was registered in 1925, but the inventor remains unknown. The first fashion designer to use zips was Elsa SCHIAPARELLI, in the 1930s.

**zirconium** (Zr), metallic element, discovered in oxide form by M.H. Klaproth in 1789. It is a very strong, malleable, ductile, lustrous, silver-grey metal that is extremely resistant to heat and corrosion. Zirconium is used in flashbulbs and to clad uranium fuel for nuclear reactors; its compounds are used as refractory material in furnaces, crucibles, and ceramic glazes. See ELEMENT (table); PERIODIC TABLE.

**zither:** see STRINGED INSTRUMENT.

**Zizka, John,** d. 1424, Bohemian general, commander of the Hussite forces in the Hussite Wars. He achieved brilliant military successes over the Catholic forces of Emperor SIGISMUND, even though he was totally blind after 1420. One of the great military innovators of all time, he anticipated modern tank warfare with his use of artillery in armoured wagons.

**Zn,** chemical symbol of the element ZINC.

**zodiac,** zone of the sky that includes about 8° on either side of the ECLIPTIC. The apparent paths of the Sun, the Moon, and the major planets all fall within this zone. The zodiac is divided into 12 equal parts of 30° each, each part being named for a CONSTELLATION and represented by a sign (see table). Because of the PRECESSION OF THE EQUINOXES, the equinox and solstice points have each moved westward about 30° in the last 2000 years; thus the zodiacal constellations, which were named in ancient times, no longer correspond to the segments of the zodiac represented by their signs. The zodiac is of importance in ASTROLOGY.

### SIGNS OF THE ZODIAC

| Constellation | Symbol | Dates |
|---|---|---|
| Aries, the Ram | ♒ | 21 Mar.–19 Apr. |
| Taurus, the Bull | ♓ | 20 Apr.–20 May |
| Gemini, the Twins | ♈ | 21 May–21 June |
| Cancer, the Crab | ♉ | 22 June–22 July |
| Leo, the Lion | ♊ | 23 July–22 Aug. |
| Virgo, the Virgin | ♋ | 23 Aug.–22 Sept. |
| Libra, the Balance | ♌ | 23 Sept.–23 Oct. |
| Scorpio, the Scorpion | ♍ | 24 Oct.–21 Nov. |
| Sagittarius, the Archer | ♎ | 22 Nov.–21 Dec. |
| Capricorn, the Goat | ♏ | 22 Dec.–19 Jan. |
| Aquarius, the Water Bearer | ♐ | 20 Jan.–18 Feb. |
| Pisces, the Fishes | ♑ | 19 Feb.–20 Mar. |

**zodiacal light,** faint band of light sometimes seen just after sunset or before sunrise, extending up from the horizon at the Sun's setting or rising point. It is caused by reflection of sunlight from tiny dust particles concentrated in the plane of the ECLIPTIC.

**Zoë,** d. 1050, Byzantine empress, daughter of Constantine VIII. She ruled jointly with her first husband, ROMANUS III, and, after his murder (1034), with her second husband, Michael IV, who perhaps was involved in the murder. Michael's successor and nephew, Michael V, briefly exiled Zoë in 1042, but she soon deposed and blinded him. She then ruled with her third husband, Constantine IX, and her sister, Theodora. Their reign was remarkable for intellectual brilliance and extraordinary corruption. Notable in this period was the final schism between the Eastern and Western churches.

**Zog,** 1896–1961, king of the Albanians (r.1928–46). Born Ahmed Bey Zogu, the son of a Muslim tribal chief, he held various government posts (1920–24) before seizing power with Yugoslav help and having himself elected president in 1925. Thereafter he sought to replace Yugoslav patronage with that of Italy. In 1928 he proclaimed himself king. Although successful for a time both in fending off MUSSOLINI's grip and in creating a rudimentary political and administrative structure for his country, he fled when Italy invaded and annexed Albania in 1939. He spent the rest of his life in exile.

**Zola, Émile** (zoh‚lah), 1840–1902, French novelist, the leading exemplar of NATURALISM. Influenced by TAINE, he wrote a vast series of novels depicting Second Empire French society in minute and often sordid detail. Best known are *L'assommoir* (1877; tr. The Dram Shop), *Nana* (1880), and *Germinal* (1885). His zeal for social reform and staunch anti-Catholicism led him to take a strong stand in the DREYFUS AFFAIR with his article 'J'accuse' (1898). Prosecuted for libel, he escaped to England, remaining there until amnestied a few months later.

**Zollverein** (‚tsolferien), customs union established in 19th-cent. Germany to eliminate tariff barriers and to promote the economic unity of Germany. It had its beginnings in 1818, and by 1854 its members included virtually all of the numerous German states. After the unification of Germany in 1871, the laws and regulations of the Zollverein passed into the legislation of the German Empire.

**zoogeography,** the study of the distribution of animals throughout the world, resulting in the division of the planet into regions. These are (1) the *Palaearctic* region, comprising Europe, the north coast of Africa, Asia Minor, the Middle East, Afghanistan, USSR, Mongolia, northern China, Korea and Japan; (2) the *Nearctic* region, which includes Greenland, Canada, USA (except Hawaii), and Mexico to the Tropic of Cancer; (3) the *Neotropical* region, made up from tropical Mexico, Central and South America, Trinidad and Tobago, and the Falkland Islands; (4) the *Ethiopian* region, comprising Africa south of the Sahara, and the SW tip of Arabia; (5) the *Oriental* region, covering tropical Asia, Ceylon, the East Indies to Borneo and Bali, the Philippines and its adjacent islands; (6) the *Australian* region, formed from Australia, Tasmania, and New Guinea. New Zealand, Madagascar, the West Indies, and the Galapagos islands are not included in regions, having unique faunas, and neither is Antarctica, which has very few animals living on it.

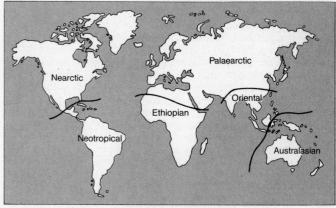

Zoogeography: The six zoogeographical regions of the world

**zoological garden** or **zoo,** place where living animals are kept in captivity for exhibition or study, or for conservation purposes. The most usual groups of animals kept are the MAMMALS, BIRDS, and REPTILES. Zoo management includes the maintenance of healthful conditions, the treatment of sick animals, the breeding of animals, and the effective display of animals for educational purposes. Zoos exchange information on nutrition and health, and publish research results on the taxonomy, anatomy, and physiology of captive animals. Most of the world's major cities maintain zoos, one of the most famous and extensive being that of the Zoological Society of London, which maintains a scientific research establishment and public parks in London and at WHIPSNADE, the latter having pioneered the technique of keeping animals as far as possible in open surroundings. Important zoos include the Giardino Zoologico in Rome, the Tiergarten in Berlin, the Jardin des Plantes in Paris, and the National Zoological Park in Washington DC, US. In the UK, zoos and other collections of animals, e.g., those maintained for ANIMAL EXPERIMENTATION, must be licensed and are subject to Home Office inspection. In the past zoos have tended to keep unusual animals as attractions, which led to the trapping in the wild of the more rare species. In recent years, however, zoos have tended to emphasize their role in scientific animal study and, as natural habitats become destroyed, in the preservation of endangered species. In some cases, breeding programmes have been initiated with the intention of returning animals to the wild. This presents problems including the high cost, the possibility of harmful inbreeding when only a few stock animals are available, the loss of genetic variability, and the loss of behavioural patterns necessary for survival in the wild. Further, there is no point in releasing animals if their natural habitat has been changed or destroyed. Collections of wild animals also include those in game farms, where some species are bred on a commercial basis, and also those kept solely for scientific and medical research in universities and research institutes. Safari parks are very extensive paddocks, based on the African nature reserves, through which visitors pass in vehicles to observe the animals roaming in a state of semi-freedom. Zoos may be state-supported, as are those of Paris, Moscow, and Washington DC. Others are maintained by scientific societies, such as the London Zoo, while many are supported by civic authorities. Almost all zoos derive a major part of their income from admission charges levied from the public. Animal-rights movements are pressing for the eventual closure of all zoos, and are especially vociferous about collections kept for research purposes. It is claimed that there is no point in studying the behaviour of animals not in their natural environments, that non-destructive experimentation is a form of mental cruelty, and that experiments causing pain, or involving the deaths of animals are inexcusable.

**zoology,** in biology, the study of animals. Early efforts to classify animals were based on physical resemblance, habitat, or economic use. The invention of the microscope and the use of experimental techniques expanded zoology as a field and established many of its branches, e.g., CYTOLOGY, histology, embryology (see EMBRYO), PHYSIOLOGY, and GENETICS. Modern zoology studies cell structure and function, as well as social and ecological aspects of animals.

**Zoroaster,** c.628 BC–c.551 BC, religious teacher and prophet of ancient Persia, founder of ZOROASTRIANISM. Zoroaster is derived from the Greek form of Zarathushtra (or Zarathustra), his Persian name. During his lifetime the new religion he founded spread rapidly. The circumstances of Zoroaster's death are not known.

**Zoroastrianism** ('zoroh,astrianizəm), religion founded by ZOROASTER, but with many later accretions. Its scriptures are the *Avesta* or the *Zend Avesta*. According to Zoroaster, there are good spirits, or *ahuras,* headed by Ahura Mazdah (also Ormazd or Ormuzd), opposed by evil spirits, the *daevas* or *divs,* led by Ahriman. The war between these two supernatural hosts will result in the ultimate triumph of Ahura Mazdah. The first period of Zoroastrianism was under the ACHAEMENIDS. Alexander's conquest of Persia sent Zoroastrianism into a decline. It reemerged (AD c.226) under Ardashir I, who established the Sassanian dynasty and tried to revive Achaemenian culture. In the mid 7th cent. Persia fell to Islam, and Zoroastrianism virtually disappeared. Apart from the PARSIS of India, and same 20,000 persons practising the religion in Iran, Zoroastrianism today flourishes in diaspora. Followers of this religion are now settled in the US, Canada, and some parts of Europe and Asia (including Pakistan).

**Zorrilla y Moral, José** (thaw,reelyah ee moh,rahl), 1817–93, Spanish romantic dramatist and poet. His works include the popular play *Don Juan Tenorio* (1844); *Granada* (1852), a retelling of legends in verse; and an autobiography.

**Zr,** chemical symbol of the element ZIRCONIUM.

**Zuccaro, Zuccari** or **Zucchero** (,tsoohk-kahroh), Italian painters, two brothers who were leading late mannerists in Rome (see MANNERISM). **Taddeo Zuccaro,** 1529–66, was painter to Pope Julius III and Pope Paul IV. He and his brother painted historical and mythological scenes for Caprarola Palace, as well as frescoes in the Vatican. Taddeo's other works in Rome include the *Dead Christ* (Borghese Gall.). **Federigo Zuccaro,** c.1540–1609, was associated with his brother, but travelled extensively in Europe. He painted portraits of Queen Elizabeth and Mary Stuart and did work for Philip II in the ESCORIAL in Spain. He constructed and decorated the Zuccari Palace, Rome, and was one of the first to develop lectures and theoretical discussions on art.

**Zuckmayer, Carl** (,tsookmieə), 1896–1977, German dramatist. His successful comedies include *The Merry Vineyard* (1925), *The Captain of Köpenick* (1931), and *The Devil's General* (1946); the last two were

adapted as films. During World War II Zuckmayer lived in the US. His best-known screenplay is for Heinrich MANN's *The Blue Angel* (1930). He published his autobiography, *A Part of Myself,* in 1966.

**Zuider Zee** (,ziedə zay), former North Sea inlet, N Netherlands. Most of it was enclosed by a dam (1932) to form the IJSSELMEER.

**Zulu,** black African tribe whose historic home is ZULULAND, in South Africa. Most Zulu live as members of an extended family in a fenced compound (kraal), headed by the oldest man. Their economy depends mainly on cattle raising. The prolonged absence of a majority of the men, many employed in distant cities and mines, has, however, weakened tribal society. The Zulu became historically important with the conquests of their chief Chaka (d. 1828), and they later resisted Boer settlers. In 1878, under CETSWAYO, they defeated several British forces, but they were subdued in 1879. Their lands were annexed by Britain in 1887.

**Zululand,** historic region and home of the ZULU, c.25,900 km² (10,000 sq mi), NE Natal prov., Republic of SOUTH AFRICA. Parts of it are now in the BANTUSTAN (African homeland) of KwaZulu.

**Zungaria:** see DZUNGARIA.

**Zuñi,** pueblo (1981 est. pop. 6,999), W New Mexico, United States, in the Zuñi Indian reservation. Built c.1695, it is on the site of one of the seven original Zuñi villages attacked in 1540 by CORONADO, who was seeking the mythical gold-rich cities of Cibola. The inhabitants are PUEBLO INDIANS (see NORTH AMERICAN INDIANS) of the Zuñian linguistic family (see AMERICAN INDIAN LANGUAGES). Sedentary farming people, they are noted for basketry, pottery, turquoise jewellery, and weaving, and for ceremonial dances of the traditional religion most still practise.

**Zurbarán, Francisco de,** 1598–1664, Spanish BAROQUE painter. Working mainly in Seville and Madrid, he painted altarpieces and pictures of saints for the monasteries and churches of Spain and the Spanish colonies; their combination of austere realism and intense spirituality perfectly conveys the monastic attitude. His work was influenced both by the severe simplicity of wood sculpture and by the dramatic lighting of CARAVAGGIO. An important series of saints painted for the Carthusian monastery at Jerez is now in the Museo de Bellas Artes, Cadiz.

**Zürich,** city (1984 pop. 354,500), capital of Zürich canton and the largest Swiss city, N Switzerland, on the Lake of Zürich. It is the commercial and intellectual centre of German-speaking Switzerland. Among its manufactures are machine tools, clothes, and paper. Built on a site occupied since Neolithic times, the city was conquered (58 BC) by the Romans and, after the 5th cent., passed to the Alemanni, the Franks, and Swabia. It was an imperial free city after 1218 and joined the Swiss Confederation in 1351. Under the influence of ZWINGLI (16th cent.) it became the leading power of the Swiss Reformation. It has the largest Swiss university and a world-famous polytechnic school (both est. 19th cent.).

**Zweig, Arnold** (tsviek), 1887–1968, German novelist and dramatist. Among his best-known works is the trilogy of novels including *Education Before Verdun* (1935), *The Case of Sergeant Grischa* (1927), and *The Crowning of a King* (1937), and *The Axe of Wandsbek* (1947), a powerful study of life in Germany in 1937. A Zionist, Zweig went to Palestine during the NAZI era. After 1948 he lived in East Germany.

**Zweig, Stefan** (tsviek), 1881–1942, Austrian biographer, novelist and MS collector. Now mainly known for his autobiography *The World of Yesterday* (1942), Zweig was a perceptive psychological biographer (*Mary Stuart,* 1935), best-selling novelist (*Letter from an Unknown Woman,* 1922; *Beware of Pity,* 1939; both filmed) and conserver of past culture. He died by his own hand in Brazil. He bequeathed his remarkable collection of musical autographs to the British Library.

**Zwickau,** city (1984 pop. 120,063), Saxony, southern East Germany. On the southern edge of the Erz-Gebirge (Ore Mts), it has a long connection with the mining of metalliferous ores. Coal is also mined in the vicinity and there are motor-vehicle works. Notable buildings include the castle and clothiers' hall.

**Zwingli, Huldreich** or **Ulrich** (,tsvinglee), 1484–1531, Swiss Protestant reformer. A Roman Catholic priest, he was considerably influenced by the humanist precepts of ERASMUS. He later accepted Martin LUTHER's doctrine of justification by faith alone, but his independent study of the Scriptures had led him after 1516 to question and finally to renounce the teaching of the Roman church. He became (1518) a vicar in Zürich and began preaching against many church practices. The beginning of the REFORMATION in Switzerland dates from his lectures (1519) on the New Testament, in which he proclaimed the Scriptures to have sole authority. In 1523, Zwingli presented his doctrines in 67 theses, which were approved by a general council in Zürich and instituted in the local churches. In 1525 the Catholic Mass was replaced by a reformed service in his church. He became embroiled in an argument with the Lutherans about the nature of the Eucharist, and Zwingli and Luther could reach no agreement at the Marburg Colloquy (1529). Zwingli was killed at Kappel in a war with the Catholic Swiss Cantons. The Reformation in Switzerland passed to John CALVIN, who built his theological system on the groundwork laid by Zwingli, but he resisted Zwingli's more radical teaching on baptism and the Lord's Supper.

# PICTURE ACKNOWLEDGMENTS

We are grateful to the following for permission to reproduce copyright photographs:

Aldus Archive
Alinari/Mansell Collection
Heather Angel
Anglo-Chinese Educational Institute
Aquilla Architectural Press
Art and Architecture Collection
Art Gallery of Ontario
Art Institute of Chicago
James Austin
Australian Information Service

Barnabys
Belmont Galleries, London
Birmingham City Airport
British Museum
British Railways Board

Camera Press
J. Allan Cash
Rupert Cavendish Antiques, London
Martin Charles
Conway Library
Courtauld Institute of Art

Douglas Dickins
Dyson Perrins Museum

E.T. Archive
European Parliament

Fitzwilliam Museum
Ford
Werner Forman Archive

Sally and Richard Greenhill
Guggenheim Museum

Sonia Halliday
Harry Hammond
Tom Hanley
Clive Hicks
David Horwell
Eric Hosking
Hulton Deutsch Collection
Hutchison Library

Imperial College
Imperial War Museum

Japanese National Tourist Office
Jefferson Medical College, Thomas Jefferson University

A.F. Kersting
David King
Kunsthistorisches Museum, Vienna/JCK Collection
Kunstsammlung Nordrhein-Westfalen

Frank Lane Agency
London Express News and Features

Magnum
Mansell Collection
Foto Marburg/JCK Collection
Mary Rose Trust
Mas, Barcelona
Metropolitan Museum of Art/JCK Collection
Tony Morrison
Mountain Camera
Musée d'Albi
Museum of Modern Art/ JCK Collection

NASA/Mitchell Beazley
National Gallery
National Gallery of Scotland
Novosti Press Agency

Percival David Foundation of Chinese Art
Philadelphia Museum of Art
Phillips Collection/JCK Collection
Photobank
Planet Earth
Popperfoto
Prado/JCK Collection
Premaphotos

Quadrant Picture Library

Réunion des Musées Nationaux
Rijksmuseum, Amsterdam
Noel Riley
Royal Botanic Gardens, Kew
Royal Photographic Society

Science Museum
Dr Ghopal Murti/Science Photo Library
Nick Silver
David Simson
Harry Smith Horticultural Collection
Société Française de Photographie
Sothebys
Suomen Rakennustaiteen Museum

The Tank Museum
Tate Gallery
John Topham Picture Library

Unilever

Victoria and Albert Museum
Virgin Records

Wallace Collection
Wedgwood